Congressional Quarterly's

POLITICS IN AMERICA 1998

THE 105th CONGRESS

By Philip D. Duncan & Christine C. Lawrence

With CQ's Political Staff

A DIVISION OF
CONGRESSIONAL QUARTERLY INC.
1414 22ND STREET N.W.
WASHINGTON, D.C. 20037

Congressional Quarterly Inc.

Printed in the United States of America

ISBN 0 87187-909-3 (hard)   ISBN 0 87187-917-4 (paper)

The Library of Congress catalogued an earlier edition of this title as follows:

Congressional Quarterly's Politics in America: 1994, the 103rd Congress / by CQ's political staff: Phil Duncan, editor.

p.   cm.

Includes index.

1. United States. Congress — Biography. 2. United States. Congress — Committees. 3. United States. Congress — Election districts —Handbooks, manuals, etc. I. Duncan, Phil. II. Congressional Quarterly Inc. III. Title: Politics in America.

JK1010.C67 1993   328.73'073'45'0202

ISSN 1064-6809

POLITICS IN AMERICA 1998
THE 105TH CONGRESS

EDITOR
Philip D. Duncan

ASSISTANT EDITOR
Christine C. Lawrence

MANAGING EDITOR
Jeffrey L. Katz

CONTRIBUTING EDITORS
Ronald D. Elving   Colette Fraley

PRINCIPAL WRITERS
Alan Greenblatt   Jonathan D. Salant   Greg Giroux

CONTRIBUTING WRITERS
Geoff Earle, Danny Glover, Chuck McCutcheon, Elizabeth A. Palmer, Carol Ritchie, Bob Benenson, David Hosansky, Stuart J. Robinson, Maureen Groppe, Will Heyniger, Juliana Gruenwald, Jeff Plungis, Lisa Caruso, Philip Marwill, John Diamond, Josh Rolnick, Kristen Lonergan, Lori Nitschke, Marc R. Birtel, Rose Krebs, Julie Granof, David Hawkings

EDITING & PRODUCTION ASSISTANT
Yolanda A. Dawson

MEMBERS' STATISTICS
Kevin M. Shanley (Manager), Tobias S. Ball (manager), Jessica A. Olson, David Segnovich, Jamie Peterson, Joe Emerson, Emily Rosado, Vanita Gowda, Anthony L. Porretta, Philip Marwill, Norberto Santana Jr., Marc R. Birtel, Graham L. Barron

COMMITTEE REPORTING/RESEARCH
Christina L. Lyons (Editor), Anthony L. Porretta, Eileen Simpson, Norberto Santana Jr., Russell Tisinger

BOOK RESEARCHERS
Myra Engers Weinberg (Senior Researcher), Melissa W. Kaye, Elana Mintz, Christopher Swope, Sarah Widoff, Donna Hemans, Peter King, Elizabeth Boehmler, Jennifer Chen, Alexis M. DeVane, David Reinstein, Rose Krebs

COPY EDITORS
Marileen C. Maher (Chief), Ron Brodmann, Patricia Joy, Maura Mahoney, Jody Rupprecht, Kelli L. Rush, Charles Southwell, Eve O. Stone

DAVID S. KAPLAN INTERNS
Suzanne E. Dougherty, Evan Morris

PHOTOGRAPHERS
Scott J. Ferrell, Douglas Graham

COVER DESIGN
Ben Santora
Paula Anderson

MAPS
InContext Of Washington D.C.,Inc.
Election Data Services

PRODUCTION
Paul Pressau, Jessica Forman, Sothear Menh, Stuart J. Robinson, Lisa Stanford

COMPUTER SERVICES
Adriaan Bouten, Scott Hall, Donna Robinson, Cindy Smith

CD ROM
Tom Moore

Phil Duncan came to Congressional Quarterly in 1979 and joined the politics staff of CQ's *Weekly Report* magazine in 1980. He has been involved in all nine editions of "Politics in America" dating to 1982, writing for the first four editions and serving since 1989 as the book's editor. Born in 1957 in Knoxville, Tenn., Duncan graduated from Davidson College in 1979 and worked for *The Charlotte Observer* and *The Knoxville News-Sentinel* before joining CQ. He lives in Falls Church, Va., with his wife, Leslie; daughter, Meredyth; and son, Tyler.

Christine Lawrence came to CQ in 1987 as editor of the *CQ Almanac.* In 1989, she moved to the *Congressional Monitor* as an editor and later was a senior reporter. In 1994, she became assistant editor of "Politics in America." Born in 1952 in Buffalo, N.Y., and raised on Long Island, she earned a master's degree in English literature from Georgetown University and a master's in journalism and public affairs from American University. She lives in Bethesda, Md., with her husband, Andy; and two sons, Reid and Matthew.

Jeffrey L. Katz came to CQ in 1990. He wrote for CQ's *Governing* magazine for two years before joining the *Weekly Report,* where he has reported on welfare and other social policy issues. Born in 1956 in Philadelphia, and raised there and in suburban Chicago, Katz has a bachelor's degree in journalism from the University of Illinois. He worked for *The Commercial Appeal* of Memphis and *The Milwaukee Journal,* and received a congressional fellowship from The American Political Science Association, before joining CQ. He lives in Bethesda, Md., with his wife, Mollie; daughter, Emily; and son, Benjamin.

The chief editorial contributors to "Politics in America" were members of its news staff. Alan Greenblatt and Jonathan D. Salant covered the 1996 elections for the *Weekly Report.* Greg Giroux is an editorial assistant at the magazine. Ronald D. Elving is political editor for the *Weekly Report.*

Dedicated to our friend and colleague David S. Kaplan (1960-1995), whose work graced the previous six editions of Politics in America. During 11 years at Congressional Quarterly, Dave made an indelible mark with his boundless enthusiasm for reporting on Congress and politics, his dedication to fair and balanced analysis, and his strict insistence on accuracy in every detail. He set a standard of excellence that we all strive to meet.

PREFACE

With the Republican Congress and the Democratic White House now agreed on a broadly drawn proposal to balance the federal budget by 2002, the curtain rises on what should be a revealing exhibition of democracy in action: watching conservatives, moderates and liberals work their way line by line through the budget to decide exactly how much to spend and tax to meet their common goal of making the red ink turn black.

In the House as well as the Senate, a majority in each party voted in late May for the budget agreement, creating a sense of shared responsibility that is new in recent congressional history. After Republicans took control of both chambers in 1995, the party's conservative leaders drafted a budget to their liking, passed it and essentially gave it to President Clinton with a take-it-or-leave-it ultimatum, expecting him to capitulate. He did not, and the ensuing partial shutdowns of the federal government proved to be a public relations disaster for the GOP. That put Clinton in the driver's seat on the budget during 1996. By the fall, Republicans were so eager to have done with the 104th Congress that they agreed to a short-term budget with billions in extra spending sought by Clinton. That acquiescence freed Republicans from Washington so they could return home to focus on the November election.

That election produced a historic split decision, with a Democratic president winning a second term for the first time in 52 years and Republicans successfully defending their control of Congress for the first time in 68 years. Even House Speaker Newt Gingrich, architect of 1995's confrontational conservatism, saw that a page of history had turned. "And so we find ourselves here with a Democratic president and a Republican Congress," he said as members assembled for the 105th. "And we have an absolute moral obligation to make this system work. This Congress will be the 'Implementation Congress.'"

We hope that the profiles of senators and House members in "Politics in America" will help the reader follow and understand the "implementation" to come, on the budget and on an array of other issues. Although the Congress is under Republican control, the institution today is much more "little d" democratic than it was in the 104th, when so much of the agenda was driven by Gingrich and his small band of loyalists in the House.

With Gingrich's clout diminished by an ethics scandal that led him to be reprimanded by his colleagues, numerous Republican chairmen of House committees and subcommittees are asserting more authority in policy matters. On issues such as the environment, the voice of Republican moderates grows stronger. Even the House Democratic minority is finding ways to influence legislation.

Senate Majority Leader Trent Lott has eclipsed Gingrich as the GOP's premier legislative force. But Democrats are a potent minority in the Senate, with leader Tom Daschle emerging as a shrewder tactician than even many of his own colleagues anticipated he would be when he took his post in 1995. On any given day, a young conservative such as Rick Santorum or a veteran liberal like Edward M. Kennedy can capture the spotlight.

There may be no drama in the 105th Congress to match the 100-days march of the House GOP's "Contract With America" in early 1995, but on a range of issues, there will be plenty of action with great meaning for American society.

In this biennial edition of "Politics in America," as in the eight preceding it, we have made our assessments of the senators and representatives primarily by watching them in action in Congress and by researching the public record. We have drawn on the vast collective expertise of Congressional Quarterly's reporters and editors. We also asked each member of the House and Senate to provide written information about his or her work, and many were kind enough to do so.

Although there is considerable legislative information in these pages, this is primarily a book about people; legislative detail is often truncated. Evaluating politicians is a necessarily subjective business, but we try our best to write in a fair and balanced manner, hewing to CQ's half-century tradition of impartiality and nonpartisanship in covering the legislative and electoral process.

This edition of "Politics in America" is the second to be issued in CD-ROM format, for the benefit of readers with properly equipped computers. On the Internet, information from PIA is available at http://www.cq.com/pia/

As legislative and political events unfold, we will periodically update members' profiles where appropriate. Those updated profiles will appear on Congressional Quarterly's proprietary online information service, Washington Alert.

Phil Duncan
May 30, 1997

BUDGET

Passage of concurrent resolutions to adopt a five-year plan to balance the budget by 2002 by cutting projected spending, as well as taxes, for a net deficit reduction of $204.3 billion. Senate vote 92 on 5/23/97; House vote 148 on 5/21/97..

ALABAMA
- Shelby R (R) Y
- Sessions J (R) Y
- 1 Callahan S (R) Y
- 2 Everett T (R) Y
- 3 Riley B (R) Y
- 4 Aderholt R (R) Y
- 5 Cramer R (D) Y
- 6 Bachus S (R) Y
- 7 Hilliard E (D) N

ALASKA
- Stevens T (R) Y
- Murkowski F (R) Y
- AL Young D (R) Y

ARIZONA
- McCain J (R) Y
- Kyl J (R) N
- 1 Salmon M (R) N
- 2 Pastor E (D) Y
- 3 Stump B (R) Y
- 4 Shadegg J (R) N
- 5 Kolbe J (R) Y
- 6 Hayworth J (R) Y

ARKANSAS
- Bumpers D (D) N
- Hutchinson T (R) Y
- 1 Berry M (D) Y
- 2 Snyder V (D) Y
- 3 Hutchinson A (R) Y
- 4 Dickey J (R) Y

CALIFORNIA
- Feinstein D (D) Y
- Boxer B (D) Y
- 1 Riggs F (R) Y
- 2 Herger W (R) Y
- 3 Fazio V (D) Y
- 4 Doolittle J (R) Y
- 5 Matsui R (D) Y
- 6 Woolsey L (D) Y
- 7 Miller G (D) N
- 8 Pelosi N (D) N
- 9 Dellums R (D) N
- 10 Tauscher E (D) Y
- 11 Pombo R (R) N
- 12 Lantos T (D) Y
- 13 Stark P (D) N
- 14 Eshoo A (D) Y
- 15 Campbell T (R) Y
- 16 Lofgren Z (D) Y
- 17 Farr S (D) Y
- 18 Condit G (D) Y
- 19 Radanovich G (R) Y
- 20 Dooley C (D) Y
- 21 Thomas B (R) Y
- 22 Capps W (D) Y
- 23 Gallegly E (R) Y
- 24 Sherman B (D) Y
- 25 McKeon H (R) Y
- 26 Berman H (D) Y
- 27 Rogan J (R) Y
- 28 Dreier D (R) Y
- 29 Waxman H (D) N
- 30 Becerra X (D) N
- 31 Martinez M (D) Y
- 32 Dixon J (D) N
- 33 Roybal-Allard L (D) N
- 34 Torres E (D) Y
- 35 Waters M (D) N
- 36 Harman J (D) Y
- 37 Millender-McD. J (D) N
- 38 Horn S (R) Y
- 39 Royce E (R) Y
- 40 Lewis J (R) Y
- 41 Kim J (R) Y
- 42 Brown G (D) N
- 43 Calvert K (R) Y
- 44 Bono S (R) Y
- 45 Rohrabacher D (R) N
- 46 Sanchez L (D) Y
- 47 Cox C (R) N
- 48 Packard R (R) Y
- 49 Bilbray B (R) Y
- 50 Filner B (D) N
- 51 Cunningham R (R) Y
- 52 Hunter D (R) N

COLORADO
- Campbell B (R) Y
- Allard W (R) N
- 1 DeGette D (D) N
- 2 Skaggs D (D) Y
- 3 McInnis S (R) Y
- 4 Schaffer B (R) Y
- 5 Hefley J (R) Y
- 6 Schaefer D (R) Y

CONNECTICUT
- Dodd C (D) Y
- Lieberman J (D) Y
- 1 Kennelly B (D) Y
- 2 Gejdenson S (D) Y
- 3 DeLauro R (D) Y
- 4 Shays C (R) Y
- 5 Maloney J (D) Y
- 6 Johnson N (R) Y

DELAWARE
- Roth W (R) Y
- Biden J (D) Y
- AL Castle M (R) Y

FLORIDA
- Graham B (D) Y
- Mack C (R) Y
- 1 Scarborough J (R) N
- 2 Boyd A (D) Y
- 3 Brown C (D) N
- 4 Fowler T (R) Y
- 5 Thurman K (D) Y
- 6 Stearns C (R) Y
- 7 Mica J (R) Y
- 8 McCollum B (R) N
- 9 Bilirakis M (R) Y
- 10 Young C (R) Y
- 11 Davis J (D) Y
- 12 Canady C (R) Y
- 13 Miller D (R) Y
- 14 Goss P (R) Y
- 15 Weldon D (R) N
- 16 Foley M (R) Y
- 17 Meek C (D) N
- 18 Ros-Lehtinen I (R) Y
- 19 Wexler R (D) Y
- 20 Deutsch P (D) Y
- 21 Diaz-Balart L (R) Y
- 22 Shaw E (R) Y
- 23 Hastings A (D) N

GEORGIA
- Coverdell P (R) Y
- Cleland M (D) Y
- 1 Kingston J (R) Y
- 2 Bishop S (D) Y
- 3 Collins M (R) Y
- 4 McKinney C (D) Y
- 5 Lewis J (D) N
- 6 Gingrich N (R) Y
- 7 Barr B (R) Y
- 8 Chambliss S (R) Y
- 9 Deal N (R) Y
- 10 Norwood C (R) Y
- 11 Linder J (R) Y

HAWAII
- Inouye D (D) Y
- Akaka D (D) Y
- 1 Abercrombie N (D) Y
- 2 Mink P (D) N

IDAHO
- Craig L (R) Y
- Kempthorne D (R) Y
- 1 Chenoweth H (R) N
- 2 Crapo M (R) N

ILLINOIS
- Moseley-Braun C (D) Y
- Durbin R (D) Y
- 1 Rush B (D) N
- 2 Jackson J (D) N
- 3 Lipinski W (D) N
- 4 Gutierrez L (D) N
- 5 Blagojevich R (D) Y
- 6 Hyde H (R) N
- 7 Davis D (D) N
- 8 Crane P (R) N
- 9 Yates S (D) X
- 10 Porter J (R) Y
- 11 Weller J (R) Y
- 12 Costello J (D) Y
- 13 Fawell H (R) Y
- 14 Hastert D (R) Y
- 15 Ewing T (R) Y
- 16 Manzullo D (R) Y
- 17 Evans L (D) N
- 18 LaHood R (R) Y
- 19 Poshard G (D) Y
- 20 Shimkus J (R) Y

INDIANA
- Lugar R (R) Y
- Coats D (R) N
- 1 Visclosky P (D) Y
- 2 McIntosh D (R) N
- 3 Roemer T (D) Y
- 4 Souder M (R) Y
- 5 Buyer S (R) Y
- 6 Burton D (R) Y
- 7 Pease E (R) Y
- 8 Hostettler J (R) Y
- 9 Hamilton L (D) Y
- 10 Carson J (D) Y

IOWA
- Grassley C (R) Y
- Harkin T (D) Y
- 1 Leach J (R) Y
- 2 Nussle J (R) Y
- 3 Boswell L (D) Y
- 4 Ganske G (R) N
- 5 Latham T (R) Y

KANSAS
- Brownback S (R) Y
- Roberts P (R) Y
- 1 Moran J (R) Y
- 2 Ryun J (R) Y
- 3 Snowbarger V (R) Y
- 4 Tiahrt T (R) Y

KENTUCKY
- Ford W (D) Y
- McConnell M (R) Y
- 1 Whitfield E (R) Y
- 2 Lewis R (R) Y
- 3 Northup A (R) Y
- 4 Bunning J (R) Y
- 5 Rogers H (R) Y
- 6 Baesler S (D) Y

LOUISIANA
- Breaux J (D) Y
- Landrieu M (D) Y
- 1 Livingston R (R) Y
- 2 Jefferson W (D) ?
- 3 Tauzin W (R) Y
- 4 McCrery J (R) Y
- 5 Cooksey J (R) Y
- 6 Baker R (R) Y
- 7 John C (D) Y

MAINE
- Snowe O (R) Y
- Collins S (R) Y
- 1 Allen T (D) Y
- 2 Baldacci J (D) Y

MARYLAND
- Sarbanes P (D) N
- Mikulski B (D) Y
- 1 Gilchrest W (R) Y
- 2 Ehrlich R (R) Y
- 3 Cardin B (D) Y
- 4 Wynn A (D) Y
- 5 Hoyer S (D) Y
- 6 Bartlett R (R) Y
- 7 Cummings E (D) Y
- 8 Morella C (R) Y

MASSACHUSETTS
- Kennedy E (D) N
- Kerry J (D) N
- 1 Olver J (D) N
- 2 Neal R (D) N
- 3 McGovern J (D) N
- 4 Frank B (D) N
- 5 Meehan M (D) N
- 6 Tierney J (D) N
- 7 Markey E (D) N
- 8 Kennedy J (D) N
- 9 Moakley J (D) N
- 10 Delahunt B (D) N

MICHIGAN
- Levin C (D) Y
- Abraham S (R) Y
- 1 Stupak B (D) Y
- 2 Hoekstra P (R) Y
- 3 Ehlers V (R) Y
- 4 Camp D (R) Y
- 5 Barcia J (D) Y
- 6 Upton F (R) Y
- 7 Smith N (R) Y
- 8 Stabenow D (D) Y
- 9 Kildee D (D) Y
- 10 Bonior D (D) Y
- 11 Knollenberg J (R) Y
- 12 Levin S (D) Y
- 13 Rivers L (D) Y
- 14 Conyers J (D) N
- 15 Kilpatrick C (D) N
- 16 Dingell J (D) Y

MINNESOTA
- Wellstone P (D) N
- Grams R (R) N
- 1 Gutknecht G (R) Y
- 2 Minge D (D) Y
- 3 Ramstad J (R) Y
- 4 Vento B (D) Y
- 5 Sabo M (D) Y
- 6 Luther W (D) Y
- 7 Peterson C (D) Y
- 8 Oberstar J (D) N

MISSISSIPPI
- Cochran T (R) Y
- Lott T (R) Y
- 1 Wicker R (R) Y
- 2 Thompson B (D) N
- 3 Pickering C (R) Y
- 4 Parker M (R) Y
- 5 Taylor G (D) Y

MISSOURI
- Bond C (R) Y
- Ashcroft J (R) N
- 1 Clay W (D) N
- 2 Talent J (R) Y
- 3 Gephardt R (D) N
- 4 Skelton I (D) Y
- 5 McCarthy K (D) Y
- 6 Danner P (D) Y
- 7 Blunt R (R) Y
- 8 Emerson J (R) Y
- 9 Hulshof K (R) Y

MONTANA
- Baucus M (D) Y
- Burns C (R) Y
- AL Hill R (R) N

NEBRASKA
- Kerrey B (D) Y
- Hagel C (R) Y
- 1 Bereuter D (R) Y
- 2 Christensen J (R) Y
- 3 Barrett B (R) Y

NEVADA
- Reid H (D) Y
- Bryan R (D) Y
- 1 Ensign J (R) Y
- 2 Gibbons J (R) Y

NEW HAMPSHIRE
- Smith R (R) N
- Gregg J (R) Y
- 1 Sununu J (R) Y
- 2 Bass C (R) Y

NEW JERSEY
- Lautenberg F (D) Y
- Torricelli R (D) Y
- 1 Andrews R (D) Y
- 2 LoBiondo F (R) Y
- 3 Saxton J (R) Y
- 4 Smith C (R) Y
- 5 Roukema M (R) Y
- 6 Pallone F (D) Y
- 7 Franks B (R) Y
- 8 Pascrell B (D) Y
- 9 Rothman S (D) Y
- 10 Payne D (D) N
- 11 Frelinghuysen R (R) Y
- 12 Pappas M (R) Y
- 13 Menendez R (D) Y

NEW MEXICO
- Domenici P (R) Y
- Bingaman J (D) Y
- 1 Schiff S (R) #
- 2 Skeen J (R) Y
- 3 Redmond B (R) Y

NEW YORK
- Moynihan D (D) N
- D'Amato A (R) Y
- 1 Forbes M (R) Y
- 2 Lazio R (R) Y
- 3 King P (R) N
- 4 McCarthy C (D) Y
- 5 Ackerman G (D) Y
- 6 Flake F (D) Y
- 7 Manton T (D) Y
- 8 Nadler J (D) N
- 9 Schumer C (D) Y
- 10 Towns E (D) N
- 11 Owens M (D) N
- 12 Velazquez N (D) N
- 13 Molinari S (R) Y
- 14 Maloney C (D) Y
- 15 Rangel C (D) N
- 16 Serrano J (D) N
- 17 Engel E (D) N
- 18 Lowey N (D) Y
- 19 Kelly S (R) Y
- 20 Gilman B (R) Y
- 21 McNulty M (D) N
- 22 Solomon G (R) Y
- 23 Boehlert S (R) Y
- 24 McHugh J (R) Y
- 25 Walsh J (R) Y
- 26 Hinchey M (D) N
- 27 Paxon B (R) Y
- 28 Slaughter L (D) N
- 29 LaFalce J (D) Y
- 30 Quinn J (R) Y
- 31 Houghton A (R) Y

NORTH CAROLINA
- Helms J (R) N
- Faircloth L (R) N
- 1 Clayton E (D) Y
- 2 Etheridge B (D) Y
- 3 Jones W (R) Y
- 4 Price D (D) Y
- 5 Burr R (R) Y
- 6 Coble H (R) Y
- 7 McIntyre M (D) Y
- 8 Hefner W (D) Y
- 9 Myrick S (R) Y
- 10 Ballenger C (R) Y
- 11 Taylor C (R) Y
- 12 Watt M (D) N

NORTH DAKOTA
- Conrad K (D) Y
- Dorgan B (D) Y
- AL Pomeroy E (D) Y

OHIO
- Glenn J (D) Y
- DeWine M (R) Y
- 1 Chabot S (R) Y
- 2 Portman R (R) Y
- 3 Hall T (D) Y
- 4 Oxley M (R) Y
- 5 Gillmor P (R) Y
- 6 Strickland T (D) Y
- 7 Hobson D (R) Y
- 8 Boehner J (R) Y
- 9 Kaptur M (D) N
- 10 Kucinich D (D) N
- 11 Stokes L (D) N
- 12 Kasich J (R) Y
- 13 Brown S (D) N
- 14 Sawyer T (D) Y
- 15 Pryce D (R) Y
- 16 Regula R (R) Y
- 17 Traficant J (D) N
- 18 Ney B (R) Y
- 19 LaTourette S (R) Y

OKLAHOMA
- Nickles D (R) Y
- Inhofe J (R) N
- 1 Largent S (R) N
- 2 Coburn T (R) N
- 3 Watkins W (R) Y
- 4 Watts J (R) Y
- 5 Istook E (R) N
- 6 Lucas F (R) Y

OREGON
- Wyden R (D) Y
- Smith G (R) Y
- 1 Furse E (D) Y
- 2 Smith B (R) Y
- 3 Blumenauer E (D) N
- 4 DeFazio P (D) N
- 5 Hooley D (D) Y

PENNSYLVANIA
- Specter A (R) N
- Santorum R (R) Y
- 1 Foglietta T (D) Y
- 2 Fattah C (D) Y
- 3 Borski R (D) N
- 4 Klink R (D) Y
- 5 Peterson J (R) Y
- 6 Holden T (D) Y
- 7 Weldon C (R) Y
- 8 Greenwood J (R) Y
- 9 Shuster B (R) N
- 10 McDade J (R) Y
- 11 Kanjorski P (D) N
- 12 Murtha J (D) Y
- 13 Fox J (R) Y
- 14 Coyne W (D) N
- 15 McHale P (D) Y
- 16 Pitts J (R) Y
- 17 Gekas G (R) Y
- 18 Doyle M (D) Y
- 19 Goodling B (R) Y
- 20 Mascara F (D) Y
- 21 English P (R) Y

RHODE ISLAND
- Chafee J (R) Y
- Reed J (D) N
- 1 Kennedy P (D) N
- 2 Weygand B (D) N

SOUTH CAROLINA
- Thurmond S (R) Y
- Hollings E (D) N
- 1 Sanford M (R) N
- 2 Spence F (R) Y
- 3 Graham L (R) Y
- 4 Inglis B (R) Y
- 5 Spratt J (D) Y
- 6 Clyburn J (D) N

SOUTH DAKOTA
- Daschle T (D) Y
- Johnson T (D) Y
- AL Thune J (R) Y

TENNESSEE
- Thompson F (R) N
- Frist B (R) Y
- 1 Jenkins B (R) Y
- 2 Duncan J (R) Y
- 3 Wamp Z (R) Y
- 4 Hilleary V (R) Y
- 5 Clement B (D) Y
- 6 Gordon B (D) Y
- 7 Bryant E (R) Y
- 8 Tanner J (D) Y
- 9 Ford H (D) Y

TEXAS
- Gramm P (R) N
- Hutchison K (R) Y
- 1 Sandlin M (D) Y
- 2 Turner J (D) Y
- 3 Johnson S (R) Y
- 4 Hall R (D) Y
- 5 Sessions P (R) Y
- 6 Barton J (R) N
- 7 Archer B (R) Y
- 8 Brady K (R) Y
- 9 Lampson N (D) Y
- 10 Doggett L (D) Y
- 11 Edwards C (D) Y
- 12 Granger K (R) Y
- 13 Thornberry W (R) Y
- 14 Paul R (R) N
- 15 Hinojosa R (D) Y
- 16 Reyes S (D) Y
- 17 Stenholm C (D) Y
- 18 Jackson-Lee S (D) N
- 19 Combest L (R) Y
- 20 Gonzalez H (D) Y
- 21 Smith L (R) Y
- 22 DeLay T (R) Y
- 23 Bonilla H (R) Y
- 24 Frost M (D) Y
- 25 Bentsen K (D) Y
- 26 Armey D (R) Y
- 27 Ortiz S (D) Y
- 28 Rodriguez C (D) Y
- 29 Green G (D) Y
- 30 Johnson E B (D) N

UTAH
- Hatch O (R) Y
- Bennett R (R) Y
- 1 Hansen J (R) Y
- 2 Cook M (R) Y
- 3 Cannon C (R) Y

VERMONT
- Leahy P (D) Y
- Jeffords J (R) Y
- AL Sanders B (I) N

VIRGINIA
- Warner J (R) Y
- Robb C (D) Y
- 1 Bateman H (R) Y
- 2 Pickett O (D) Y
- 3 Scott R (D) N
- 4 Sisisky N (D) Y
- 5 Goode V (D) Y
- 6 Goodlatte R (R) Y
- 7 Bliley T (R) Y
- 8 Moran J (D) Y
- 9 Boucher R (D) N
- 10 Wolf F (R) Y
- 11 Davis T (R) Y

WASHINGTON
- Gorton S (R) Y
- Murray P (D) Y
- 1 White R (R) Y
- 2 Metcalf J (R) Y
- 3 Smith L (R) Y
- 4 Hastings R (R) Y
- 5 Nethercutt G (R) Y
- 6 Dicks N (D) Y
- 7 McDermott J (D) N
- 8 Dunn J (R) Y
- 9 Smith A (D) Y

WEST VIRGINIA
- Byrd R (D) Y
- Rockefeller J (D) Y
- 1 Mollohan A (D) N
- 2 Wise B (D) Y
- 3 Rahall N (D) N

WISCONSIN
- Kohl H (D) Y
- Feingold R (D) Y
- 1 Neumann M (R) Y
- 2 Klug S (R) N
- 3 Kind R (D) Y
- 4 Kleczka J (D) Y
- 5 Barrett T (D) Y
- 6 Petri T (R) Y
- 7 Obey D (D) N
- 8 Johnson J (D) Y
- 9 Sensenbrenner F (R) Y

WYOMING
- Thomas C (R) N
- Enzi M (R) N
- AL Cubin B (R) N

TABLE OF CONTENTS

TABLE OF CONTENTS

TABLE OF CONTENTS

TABLE OF CONTENTS

TABLE OF CONTENTS

EXPLANATION OF STATISTICS

COMMITTEES

Standing and select committees and subcommittees are listed for Senate and House members, as are major joint committees. Committee assignments listed with member profiles are preliminary; the most complete listings available at press time start on page 1607.

ELECTIONS

House

General-election returns are given for House members for 1996 and 1994. Returns do not include candidates receiving less than 1 percent of the vote. Primary returns are given for House members for 1996. No primary results are listed if a candidate ran unopposed or was nominated by caucus or convention. Because percentages have been rounded to the nearest whole number, election totals do not always add up to 100 percent.

Senate

Primary and general-election returns are given for each senator's most recent election. No primary results are given if a candidate ran unopposed or was nominated by caucus or convention.

PREVIOUS WINNING PERCENTAGES

Winning election percentages are given for each member's entire congressional career. If no percentage is given, the member either did not run or lost the election that year. Percentages are included for both general elections and special elections. For senators with previous service in the House, elections to the House are indicated with a footnote.

DISTRICT VOTE FOR PRESIDENT

The vote presidential candidates received in the congressional district is given for 1996 and 1992. The tabulations are for the area within each current district, as it existed at the time of the Nov. 5, 1996, elections.

Data for the district vote for president were compiled by Polidata of Lake Ridge, Va., with the assistance of Congressional Quarterly. The data are estimates of the 1996 and 1992 election results based on the best information available at the local level as allocated, aggregated and analyzed by Polidata.

In the statistics that accompany each profile, the 1992 district vote for president was calculated using data only for the major candidates. Percentages for the 1996 district vote for president are calculated using all votes cast for president. For states with at-large House seats, 1992 percentages may not coincide with 1992 presidential vote percentages on the state data pages because state page percentages were calculated based on the vote for all candidates.

For more information on the district vote for president statistics, contact Polidata at polidata@aol.com

CAMPAIGN FINANCE

Figures are given for all members of Congress and their general-election opponents as reported by the Federal Election Commission (FEC) in its printed year-end summary report published on April 14, 1997. If no figures are listed, the candidate either did not file a report (reports are not required if receipts and expenditures are less than $5,000) or the reports listed receipts and expenditures of zero.

For House members, figures are given for the 1996 and 1994 elections. For senators, figures are given for their most recent election.

Except where noted, campaign finance data cover the receipts and expenditures of each candidate during the two-year election cycle. Data for 1996 cover the period Jan. 1, 1995 - Dec. 31, 1996. Data for 1994 cover the period Jan. 1, 1993 - Dec. 31, 1994.

Other candidate transactions, such as contributions to other campaigns, loan repayments, pur-

KEY TO PARTY ABBREVIATIONS

ACP — A Connecticut Party
ADEP — A Delaware Party
AKI — Alaskan Independence
AM — American
AMI — American Independent
BP — Best Party
C — Conservative
CAP — Capitalist
CC — Concerned Citizens
CIL — Conservative Party of Ill.
CPL — Christian Pro-life
D — Democratic
GR — Grassroots
GREEN — Green
I — Independent
IA — Independent American
IF — Independence Fusion
IFP — Independents for Perot
IG — Independent Grassroots
INDC — Independence
IP— Independent Party
KTAX — Taxpayers Party of Ky.
L — Liberal
LAWR — LaRouche Was Right
LIBERT — Libertarian
LU — Liberty Union
MSTAX — Mississippi Taxpayers
NA — New Alliance
NJC — N. J. Conservative Party
NL — Natural Law
P — Prohibition
PACIFIC — Pacific Party
PAT — Patriot Party
PFP — Peace and Freedom
POP — Populist
R — Republican
REF — Reform
RPI — Ross Perot Independent
RTL — Right to Life
SW — Socialist Workers
TAX — Taxpayers
TLC — Term Limits Candidate
UNI — United Independents
USTAX — U.S. Taxpayers
UWS — United We Serve
VG — Vermont Grassroots
VREF — Virginia Reform
WW — Workers World

chase and redemption of certificates of deposit, and debts owed to or by the campaign committees at the end of the election year, were not subtracted from the receipts and expenditures totals.

The figures for political action committee (PAC) receipts are based on the FEC summary report for each candidate. Amounts designated include contributions from both PACs and candidate committees. PAC contributions received by a candidate but returned within 20 days are not reflected in the FEC compilation. In cases where CQ was able to determine that a member does not accept PAC contributions, a zero appears in the column for PAC contributions.

The FEC updates its information from time to time. For further information, see the FEC web page at www.fec.gov.

KEY VOTES

A series of key votes has been selected from the roll-call votes taken during the 104th and 105th congresses. The following captions give the bill number, the major sponsor, a brief description of the bill, a breakdown of the vote, the date the vote was taken and the president's position on the issue (if he took one). The following symbols are used:

Y — voted for (yea)
N — voted against (nay)
— paired for
+ — announced for
X — paired against
– — announced against
P — voted "present"
C — voted "present" to avoid possible conflict of interest
? — did not vote or otherwise make a position known.
I — ineligible

SENATE KEY VOTES

1997

S J RES 1. Balanced-Budget Constitutional Amendment — Passage. Passage of the joint resolution to propose a constitutional amendment to balance the budget by the year 2002 or two years after ratification by three-fourths of the states, whichever is later. Three-fifths of the entire House and Senate would be required to approve deficit spending or an increase in the public debt limit. A simple majority could waive the requirement in times of war or when the United States is engaged in a military conflict that causes an imminent national security threat. Rejected 66-34: R 55-0; D 11-34 (ND 6-31, SD 5-3), March 4, 1997. (A two-thirds majority vote of those present and voting (67 in this case) is required to pass a joint resolution proposing an amendment to the Constitution.) A "nay" was a vote in support of the president's position.

S RES 75. Chemical Weapons Treaty — Adoption. Adoption of the resolution of ratification of the treaty to prohibit production, acquisition, stockpiling, transfer or use of chemical weapons. The treaty mandates that the 162 signatory nations destroy all chemical weapons they possess. The resolution includes 28 conditions clarifying U.S. interpretation of the treaty, including one specifying that the United States can use tear gas in certain military operations. Adopted 74-26: R 29-26; D 45-0 (ND 37-0, SD 8-0), April 24, 1997. A two-thirds majority of those present and voting (67 in this case) is required for adoption of resolutions of ratification. A "yea" was a vote in support of the president's position.

1996

S 1541. Farm Bill — Passage. Passage of the bill to reauthorize for seven years, through 2002, all major federal farm programs, overhauling certain programs to give farmers a fixed, declining payment regardless of market conditions rather than traditional subsidies and to give farmers more flexibility in deciding what to plant. The bill reauthorizes the food stamp program for seven years and expands conservation and rural development programs. Passed 64-32: R 44-6; D 20-26 (ND 13-23, SD 7-3), Feb. 7, 1996.

HR 956. Product Liability — Conference Report. Adoption of the conference report to limit punitive damages in product liability cases to two times compensatory damages or $250,000, whichever is greater, with lower limits for small businesses. Under the bill, a plaintiff could bring a lawsuit up to two years after discovering both the cause and the injury itself. The bill would limit the time to file a suit to 15 years after the delivery of a product, but the limit would apply only to some types of products. The bill also would abolish joint and several liability for non-economic damages. Adopted (thus sent to the House) 59-40: R 47-6; D 12-34 (ND 9-27, SD 3-7), March 21, 1996. A "nay" was a vote in support of the president's position.

HR 3448. Small Business Tax Package - Minimum Wage Increase — Wage Delay and Exemptions. Bond, R-Mo., amendment to delay by six months a 90-cent increase in the minimum wage; to exempt employees of businesses with annual gross sales under $500,000 from the minimum wage increase; and to deny any new employees the minimum wage increase for the first six months of employment. Rejected 46-52: R 46-5; D 0-47 (ND 0-37, SD 0-10), July 9, 1996. A "nay" was a vote in support of the president's position.

HR 3734. Budget Reconciliation-Welfare Overhaul — Conference Report. Adoption of the conference report on the bill to reduce spending over six years by about $54.1 billion, mostly by cutting aid to legal immigrants and scaling back food stamp and Supplemental Security Income (SSI) spending. The bill ends the federal guarantee of welfare benefits, gives states broad discretion over their own programs through block grants, generally requires welfare recipients to work within two years of receiving benefits and limits recipients to five years of welfare benefits. The bill also imposes tighter eligibility standards on low-income children seeking SSI benefits due to disability and denies most legal immigrants SSI and food stamp benefits. Adopted (thus cleared for the president) 78-21: R 53-0; D 25-21 (ND 17-20, SD 8-1), Aug. 1, 1996. A "yea" was a vote in support of the president's position.

S 2056. Sexual Orientation Non-Discrimination — Passage. Passage of the bill to prohibit job discrimination based on sexual orientation by extending the remedies of the 1964 Civil Rights Act to sexual orientation. Rejected 49-50: R 8-45; D 41-5 (ND 35-2, SD 6-3), Sept. 10, 1996. A "yea" was a vote in support of the president's position.

HR 1833. Abortion Procedure Ban — Veto Override. Passage, over President Clinton's April 10 veto, of the bill banning an abortion procedure where the physician partially delivers the fetus before completing the abortion. Anyone convicted of performing such an abortion would be subject to a fine and up to two years in prison. An exception would be granted when the procedure is necessary to save the life of a woman, provided no other medical procedure can be used. Rejected 57-41: R 45-6; D 12-35 (ND 7-30, SD 5-5), Sept. 26, 1996. A two-thirds majority of those present and voting (66 in this case) of both houses is required to override a veto. A "nay" was a vote in support of the president's position.

1995

HR 2491. Fiscal 1996 Budget Reconciliation — Passage. Passage of the bill to cut spending by about $900 billion and taxes by $245 billion in order to balance the budget by 2002. The bill would reduce spending on Medicare by $270 billion, Medicaid by $182 billion, Welfare by $65 billion, the earned-income tax credit by $43.2 billion and agriculture programs by $13.6 billion. The bill allows for oil drilling in the Arctic National Wildlife Refuge, scales back the capital gains tax and expands Individual Retirement Accounts. Passed 52-47: R 52-1; D 0-46 (ND 0-36, SD 0-10), Oct. 28, 1995. (in the legislative day and the Congressional Record dated Oct. 27). Before passage the Senate struck all after the enacting clause and inserted the text of the S1357 as amended. A "nay" was a vote in support of the president's position.

S J Res 31. Flag Desecration — Passage. Passage of the joint resolution to propose a constitutional amendment to grant Congress the power to prohibit the physical desecration of the U.S. flag. Rejected 63-36: R 49-4; D 14-32 (ND 7-29, SD 7-3), Dec. 12, 1995. (A two-thirds majority vote of those present and voting, 66 in this case, is required to pass a joint resolution proposing an amendment to the Constitution.) A "nay" was a vote in support of the president's position.

HOUSE KEY VOTES

1997

HR 1122. Abortion Procedure Ban — Passage. Passage of the bill to impose penalties on doctors who perform certain abortion procedures, in which the person performing the abortion partially delivers the fetus before completing the abortion. An exception would be granted where the procedure was necessary to save the life of the woman. Passed 295-136: R 218-8; D 77-127 (ND 51-99, SD 26-28); I 0-1, March 20, 1997. A "nay" was a vote in support of the president's position.

1996

HR 2854. Farm Bill — Passage. Passage of the bill to reauthorize through 2002 all major federal farm programs, replacing current price-support programs with a system of fixed annual payments to farmers that would decline over the next seven years. The bill gives farmers more flexibility in deciding what to plant, extends the sugar and peanut support programs with some modifications and phases out price supports for butter and dry milk. Passed 270-155: R 216-19; D 54-135 (ND 21-112, SD 33-23); I 0-1, Feb. 29, 1996.

HR 2202. Immigration Restrictions — Public Education. Gallegly, R-Calif., amendment to give states the option to deny public education to illegal aliens. The amendment allows parents to challenge the state's decision by proving that they are citizens or lawfully present in the U.S. Adopted 257-163: R 213-20; D 44-142 (ND 25-104, SD 19-38); I 0-1, March 20, 1996. A "nay" was a vote in support of the president's position.

HR 125. Assault Weapons Ban Repeal — Passage. Passage of the bill to repeal the current ban on certain semiautomatic assault-style weapons and eliminate the prohibition on selling or manufacturing such guns. The bill also repeals the ban on large-capacity ammunition feeding devices and any combination of parts that could be assembled into a large-capacity ammunition feeding device; requires mandatory minimum prison sentences for committing violent crimes with certain firearms and increases penalties for subsequent offenses; and directs the Justice Department to set up a program enhancing prosecution of violent criminals who use firearms. Passed 239-173: R 183-42; D 56-130 (ND 26-103, SD 30-27); I 0-1, March 22, 1996. A "nay" was a vote in support of the president's position.

HR 1227. Employee Commuting Act/Minimum Wage Increase. Riggs, R-Calif., amendment to increase the minimum wage by 90 cents per hour over two years, thereby raising the minimum wage from its current level of $4.25 per hour to $4.75 per hour on July 1, 1996 and to $5.15 per hour on July 1, 1997. Adopted 266-162: R 77-156; D 188-6 (ND 136-0, SD 52-6); I 1-0, May 23, 1996. A "yea" was a vote in support of the president's position.

HR 3610. Fiscal 1997 Defense Appropriations — Spending Freeze. Shays, R-Conn., amendment to reduce the bill's total appropriation to the amount provided by the fiscal 1996

Defense Appropriations Act, approximately $243 billion. Rejected 194-219: R 60-161; D 133-58 (ND 113-23, SD 20-35); I 1-0, June 13, 1996.

HR 3734. Budget Reconciliation — Welfare Overhaul — Conference Report. Adoption of the conference report on the bill to reduce spending over six years by about $54.1 billion, mostly by cutting aid to legal immigrants and scaling back food stamp and Supplemental Security Income (SSI) spending. The bill would end the federal guarantee of welfare benefits, give states broad discretion over their own programs through block grants, generally require welfare recipients to work within two years of receiving benefits and limit recipients to five years of welfare benefits. The bill also would impose tighter eligibility standards on low-income children seeking SSI benefits due to disability and deny most legal immigrants SSI and food stamp benefits. Adopted 328-101: R 230-2; D 98-98 (ND 62-76, SD 36-22); I 0-1, July 31, 1996. A "yea" was a vote in support of the president's position.

1995

HJ Res 1. Balanced-Budget Amendment — Passage. Passage of the joint resolution to propose a constitutional amendment to balance the budget by the year 2002 or two years after ratification by three-fourths of the states, whichever is later. Under the proposal three-fifths of the entire House and Senate would be required to approve deficit spending or an increase in the public debt limit. A simple majority could waive the requirement in times of war or in the face of a serious military threat. Passed 300-132: R 228-2; D 72-129 (ND 34-105, SD 38-24); I 0-1, Jan. 26, 1995. (A two-thirds majority vote of those present and voting (288 in this case) is required to pass a joint resolution proposing an amendment to the Constitution.) A "nay" was a vote in support of the president's position.

HR 961. Clean Water Act Revisions — Passage. Passage of the bill to authorize $2.3 billion a year for five years for state revolving loan funds that provide money for clean water projects under the Federal Water Pollution Control Act of 1972; ease or waive numerous federal water pollution control regulations and subject them to cost-benefit analysis; allow states to continue to rely on voluntary measures to deal with unmet water pollution problems; restrict the ability of federal agencies to declare wetlands off-limits to development; require the federal government to reimburse landowners if wetlands regulations cause a 20 percent decrease in land value; and for other purposes. Passed 240-185: R 195-34; D 45-150 (ND 19-114, SD 26-36); I 0-1, May 16, 1995. A "nay" was a vote in support of the president's position.

HR 2099. Fiscal 1996 VA, HUD Appropriations — Environmental Enforcement Stokes, D-Ohio, amendment to strike the bill's provisions prohibiting the Environmental Protection Agency from enforcing environmental laws, including sections of the clean water act and the Clean Air Act and the Delaney Clause of the Federal Food, Drug and Cosmetic Act regarding pesticides on food. Adopted 212-206: R 51-175; D 160-31 (ND 122-10, SD 38-21); I 1-0, July 28, 1995. A "yea" was a vote in support of the president's position.

HR 2425. Medicare Revisions — Passage. Passage of the bill to cut $270 billion over seven years from Medicare, the federal health insurance program for the elderly. The bill would make all health care fraud federal crimes, limit increases in payments to hospitals and other providers to keep solvent the Medicare Part A trust fund until fiscal 2010, and freeze the Part B Medicare premium at 31.5 percent of program costs. Passed 231-201: R 227-6; D 4-194 (ND 0-137, SD 4-57); I 0-1, Oct. 19, 1995. A "nay" was a vote in support of the president's position.

HR 2491. 1995 Budget-Reconciliation — Passage. Passage of the bill to cut spending by about $900 billion and taxes by $245 billion over the next seven years in order to provide for a balanced budget by fiscal 2002. Over seven years the bill would reduce spending on Medicare by $270 billion, Medicaid by $170 billion, welfare programs by $102 billion, the earned-income tax credit by $23.2 billion, agriculture programs by $13.4 billion, student loans by $10.2 billion and federal employee retirement programs by $9.9 billion. The bill abolishes the Commerce Department; allows oil drilling in the Arctic National Wildlife Refuge in Alaska; and increases the debt limit from $4.9 trillion to $5.5 trillion. Passed 227-203: R 223-10; D 4-192 (ND 0-137, SD 4-55); I 0-1, Oct. 26, 1995. A "nay" was a vote in support of the president's position.

VOTING STUDIES

Each year, Congressional Quarterly prepares voting studies that represent the percentage of the time a member of Congress has supported or opposed a given position. The votes are listed under two columns — S for support and O for opposition. For example, a score of 25 under the S column in the presidential support study would indicate that the member supported the president on 25 percent of the votes that were used in the study. An explanation of each of the voting studies follows.

Presidential Support

CQ tries to determine what the president personally, as distinct from other administration officials, does and does not want in the way of legislative action. This is done by analyzing his messages to Congress, news conference remarks and other public statements and documents.

Occasionally, important measures are so extensively amended that it is impossible to characterize final passage as a victory or defeat for the president. These votes have been excluded from the study.

Presidential support is determined by the position of the president at the time of a vote, even though that position may be different from an earlier one or may have been reversed after the vote was taken.

Votes on motions to recommit, to reconsider or to table often are key tests that govern the legislative outcome. Such votes are included in the presidential support tabulations. Failure to vote lowers both support and opposition scores equally. All presidential-issue votes have equal statistical weight in the analysis.

Party Unity

Party unity votes are defined as votes in the Senate and House that split the parties, a majority of voting Democrats opposing a majority of voting Republicans. Votes on which either party divides evenly are excluded.

Party unity scores represent the percentage of party unity votes on which a member voted "yea" or "nay" in agreement with a majority of the member's party. Failure to vote, even if a member announced a stand, lowers the member's score.

Opposition-to-party scores represent the percentage of party unity votes on which a member voted "yea" or "nay" in disagreement with a majority of the member's party. A member's party unity and opposition-to-party scores add up to 100 percent only if he participated on all party unity votes.

Conservative Coalition

As used in this study, the term "conservative coalition" means a voting alliance of Republicans and Southern Democrats against the non-Southern Democrats in Congress. This meaning, rather than any philosophical definition of the "conservative" position, provides the basis for CQ's selection of votes.

A conservative coalition vote is any vote in the Senate or House on which a majority of voting Southern Democrats and a majority of voting Republicans oppose the stand taken by a majority of voting non-Southern Democrats. Votes on which there is an even division within the ranks of voting non-Southern Democrats, Southern Democrats or Republicans are not included.

The Southern states are defined as Alabama, Arkansas, Florida, Georgia, Kentucky, Louisiana, Mississippi, North Carolina, Oklahoma, South Carolina, Tennessee, Texas and Virginia.

The conservative coalition support score represents the percentage of conservative coalition votes on which a member voted "yea" or "nay" in agreement with the position of the conservative coalition. Failure to vote, even if a member announced a stand, lowers the member's score.

The conservative coalition opposition score represents the percentage of conservative coalition votes on which a member voted "yea" or "nay" in opposition to the position of the conservative coalition. Failure to vote, even if a member announced a stand, lowers the member's score.

INTEREST GROUP RATINGS

Ratings for members of Congress by four interested groups are given for the years since 1989 (102nd Congress). The groups were chosen to represent liberal, conservative, business and labor viewpoints. Following is a description of each group, along with notes regarding their ratings for particular years.

Americans for Democratic Action (ADA)

Americans for Democratic Action was founded in 1947 by a group of liberal Democrats that included Sen. Hubert H. Humphrey and Eleanor Roosevelt. In 1997, the president was Jack Sheinkman.

American Federation of Labor-Congress of Industrial Organizations (AFL-CIO)

The AFL-CIO was formed when the American Federation of Labor and the Congress of Industrial Organizations merged in 1955. With affiliates claiming more than 13 million members, the AFL-CIO accounts for approximately three-quarters of national union membership. In 1997, the president was John J. Sweeney. 1996 ratings were not available at press time.

Chamber of Commerce of the United States (CCUS)

The Chamber of Commerce of the United States represents local, regional and state chambers of commerce as well as trade and professional organizations. It was founded in 1912 to be "a voice for organized business." In 1997, the president was Richard L. Lesher.

American Conservative Union (ACU)

The American Conservative Union was founded in 1964 "to mobilize resources of responsible conservative thought across the country and further the general cause of conservatism." The organization intends to provide education in political activity, "prejudice in the press," foreign and military policy, domestic economic policy, the arts, professions and sciences. In 1997, the chairman was David A. Keene.

OTHER STATISTICS AND MAPS

Each state profile contains figures on the population, area, presidential election vote and composition of the legislature. Also included is gubernatorial information (the "first elected" category indicates current string of service; when followed by an asterisk, previous service is noted under "political career"). The U.S. congressional delegations reflect status as of May 1997 and the membership of the state legislatures indicates status as of January 1997. These numbers do not reflect later changes. Information on the makeup of the state legislatures was obtained from the National Conference of State Legislatures and state officials.

The references to term limits for state offices generally applies to state legislative offices.

Information on urban statistics was obtained from 1990 census materials and from the U.S. Conference of Mayors. Party affiliation is given where possible. N-P indicates a nonpartisan position.

Data on presidential vote were calculated

based on the vote for all the presidential candidates. Due to rounding and the exclusion of some minor candidates, percentages may not add to 100.

The demographic breakdowns on population, ethnic and racial makeup, settlement patterns, birth, ages, income and area were obtained from U.S. Department of Commerce information. Some people are classified as both black and Hispanic, and some Hispanics are not classified by the Census Bureau as either black or white. Numbers are not intended to add to 100 percent.

Each House district description contains statistics about the population, background and age of residents. Statistics are given for white, black and Hispanic origin, and for other groups if they equal 1 percent or more of the total district population. Some persons are classified as both black and Hispanic, and some Hispanics are not classified by the Census Bureau as either black or white.

As of May 19, the Census Bureau had not recalculated demographics for districts newly drawn for the 1996 election.

Maps for all states and selected urban areas were prepared by Election Data Services of Washington, D.C., Inc., using Census Bureau maps as a base. County names appear in capital letters. City names appear in upper and lower case.

REDISTRICTING

Several court challenges to districts that were designed to elect minorities to Congress remained alive years after the 1990 census they were based on. These challenges could still prompt changes to maps in a handful of states.

So-called "majority minority" districts in several states were challenged on the grounds that they violate the Constitution's right to equal protection under the law. The challenges already have forced map changes in five states, adding new elements to what is usually a once-a-decade ritual of redistricting after reapportionment after the decennial census.

Five U.S. Supreme Court justices — enough to make a majority — have expressed little tolerance for using race as the central criteria in drawing district lines, even though such districts were drawn to comply with the Voting Rights Act.

The justices first called into question the constitutionality of drawing districts with bizarre shapes to ensure the election of a minority in their 1993 *Shaw v. Reno* ruling, which involved North Carolina's congressional map.

The Supreme Court went further in its skepticism of minority-majority districts in its 1995 ruling in *Miller v. Johnson*. The case involved a challenge to one of Georgia's three black-majority districts, which the high court struck down. It said districts were probably unconstitutional whenever race was the "predominant factor" in crafting electoral lines, unless the state proved there was a compelling state interest to do so.

The court again cast serious doubt on using race as the main element in crafting district lines in June 1996. It re-examined the North Carolina case after a panel of federal judges upheld the state's lines, and also addressed a challenge to three minority-majority districts in Texas. The Supreme Court found the three Texas districts and one in North Carolina to be unconstitutional racial gerrymanders. At the same time, the court stopped short of ruling out race-conscious redistricting altogether, leaving state legislators uncertain about how much of a factor race could play in drawing district lines.

Still, the high court's rulings have resulted in additional challenges to minority-majority districts, most of which remained in play.

A challenge was filed in December 1996 against South Carolina's black-majority 6th congressional District (now held by Democrat James E. Clyburn). A federal three-judge panel had yet to rule on the case as of mid-1997.

In Virginia, a federal three-judge panel struck down the black-majority 3rd District in February 1997, using the criteria set forth in *Miller v. Johnson*. Virginia's attorney general filed an appeal, but there were indications the state Legislature might address the issue itself first. The seat is held by Democrat Robert C. Scott.

Also in February 1997, a separate three-judge panel in New York invalidated the state's Hispanic-majority 12th District (represented by Democrat Nydia M. Velázquez). The judges gave the state Legislature until the end of July 1997 to re-draw the state's map.

Meanwhile, the fate of Illinois' Hispanic-majority 4th District, represented by Democrat Luis V. Gutierrez, remained in doubt. The Supreme Court in late 1996 ordered a federal three-judge panel to re-examine its March 1996 decision upholding the district's lines in light of the high court's rulings in the Texas and North Carolina cases. The parties in the case were awaiting a ruling as of May 1997.

Several challenges required changes to congressional maps in the affected states. After a series of rulings that went against minority-majority districts, candidates in Georgia, Louisiana, Florida and Texas were forced to run under new lines for the 1996 election.

Georgia's map was redrawn by a three-judge federal panel to include only one black-majority district. That prompted a group of black voters to sue, arguing that the judges should have drawn two districts favored to elect an African-American. The Supreme Court heard arguments in the case in December 1996 and was expected to rule on the case before July 1997.

Widespread changes occurred in Texas. A federal three-judge panel redrew the state's congressional map in 1996 and threw out the results of the state's March congressional primary and April runoff in 13 districts affected by the line changes. Candidates in the 13 districts were ordered to run in a special election on Election Day. The top two finishers in three races were forced into a December runoff where no candidate received a majority of the vote on Election Day.

Federal judges in North Carolina put off making changes to that state's map until after the 1996 election. The state Legislature approved a new map in March 1997. The biggest changes would be made to the 12th District (represented by Democrat Melvin Watt), which was struck down by the Supreme Court, and to the 1st, the state's other black-majority district (represented by Democrat Eva Clayton). In mid-1997, lawmakers were awaiting approval of the new map by the Justice Department and a federal three-judge panel. Even if the map is approved, opponents of the new plan might still appeal to the Supreme Court.

All but one member whose districts were struck down as unconstitutional and redrawn as a result were re-elected in 1996, despite predictions by civil rights activists to the contrary. The exception was Louisiana Rep. Cleo Fields, a black Democrat, whose black-majority 4th District was ruled unconstitutional. He chose not to run for re-election after his district was dismantled when a federal three-judge panel redrew the state's map.

In June 1995, the Supreme Court upheld California's congressional map against a voting rights challenge.

Meanwhile in a non-race related case, the Supreme Court in December 1996 upheld Ohio's current congressional map, rejecting a lawsuit by former Rep. Clarence E. Miller, R-Ohio, and others, who argued that electoral districts should be drawn to be politically neutral.

Kentucky's Legislature altered the state's congressional lines in 1994 but the changes did not go into effect until the 1996 election. The changes to five of the state's six congressional districts were minor and aimed at moving some counties that were split into single congressional districts.

CONGRESS BY THE NUMBERS

Throughout this book, CQ frequently refers to a congressional session by its number. Following is a list of what years are covered within a session.

	YEARS COVERED	ELECTION YEAR		YEARS COVERED	ELECTION YEAR
98th Congress	1983-85	1982	102nd Congress	1991-93	1990
99th Congress	1985-87	1984	103rd Congress	1993-95	1992
100th Congress	1987-89	1986	104th Congress	1995-97	1994
101st Congress	1989-91	1988	105th Congress	1997-99	1996

SENATORS' NEXT ELECTION YEARS

Senators marked with an asterisk had announced by press time that they would retire at the end of the 105th Congress. Republican senators are in roman, Democratic senators in *italic*.

1998

34 Senators: 16 Republicans, 18 Democrats

Bennett, Robert F., R-Utah
Bond, Christopher S., R-Mo.
Boxer, Barbara, D-Calif.
Breaux, John B., D-La.
Brownback, Sam, R-Kan.
Bumpers, Dale, D-Ark.
Campbell, Ben Nighthorse, R-Colo.
Coats, Daniel R., R-Ind.*
Coverdell, Paul, R-Ga.
D'Amato, Alfonse M., R-N.Y.
Daschle, Tom, D-S.D.
Dodd, Christopher J., D-Conn.
Dorgan, Byron L., D-N.D.
Faircloth, Lauch, R-N.C.
Feingold, Russell D., D-Wis.
*Ford, Wendell H., D-Ky.**
*Glenn, John, D-Ohio**
Graham, Bob, D-Fla.
Grassley, Charles E., R-Iowa
Gregg, Judd, R-N.H.
Hollings, Ernest F., D-S.C.
Inouye, Daniel K., D-Hawaii
Kempthorne, Dirk, R-Idaho
Leahy, Patrick J., D-Vt.
McCain, John, R-Ariz.
Mikulski, Barbara A., D-Md.
Moseley-Braun, Carol, D-Ill.
Murkowski, Frank H., R-Alaska
Murray, Patty, D-Wash.
Nickles, Don, R-Okla.
Reid, Harry, D-Nev.
Shelby, Richard C., R-Ala.
Specter, Arlen, R-Pa.
Wyden, Ron, D-Ore.

2000

33 Senators: 19 Republicans, 14 Democrats

Abraham, Spencer, R-Mich.
Akaka, Daniel K., D-Hawaii
Ashcroft, John, R-Mo.
Bingaman, Jeff, D-N.M.
Bryan, Richard H., D-Nev.
Burns, Conrad, R-Mont.
Byrd, Robert C., D-W.Va.
Chafee, John H., R-R.I.
Conrad, Kent, D-N.D.
DeWine, Mike, R-Ohio
Feinstein, Dianne, D-Calif.
Frist, Bill, R-Tenn.
Gorton, Slade, R-Wash.
Grams, Rod, R-Minn.
Hatch, Orrin G., R-Utah
Hutchison, Kay Bailey, R-Texas
Jeffords, James M., R-Vt.
Kennedy, Edward M., D-Mass.
Kerrey, Bob, D-Neb.
Kohl, Herb, D-Wis.
Kyl, Jon, R-Ariz.
Lautenberg, Frank R., D-N.J.
Lieberman, Joseph I., D-Conn.
Lott, Trent, R-Miss.
Lugar, Richard G., R-Ind.
Mack, Connie, R-Fla.
Moynihan, Daniel Patrick, D-N.Y.
Robb, Charles S., D-Va.
Roth, William V. Jr., R-Del.
Santorum, Rick, R-Pa.
Sarbanes, Paul S., D-Md.
Snowe, Olympia J., R-Maine
Thomas, Craig, R-Wyo.

2002

33 Senators: 20 Republicans, 13 Democrats

Allard, Wayne, R-Colo.
Baucus, Max, D-Mont.
Biden, Joseph R. Jr., D-Del.
Cleland, Max, D-Ga.
Cochran, Thad, R-Miss.
Collins, Susan, R-Maine
Craig, Larry E., R-Idaho
Domenici, Pete V., R-N.M.
Durbin, Richard J., D-Ill.
Enzi, Michael B., R-Wyo.
Gramm, Phil, R-Texas
Hagel, Chuck, R-Neb.
Harkin, Tom, D-Iowa
Helms, Jesse, R-N.C.
Hutchinson, Tim, R-Ark.
Inhofe, James M., R-Okla.
Johnson, Tim, D-S.D.
Kerry, John, D-Mass.
Landrieu, Mary L., D-La.
Levin, Carl, D-Mich.
McConnell, Mitch, R-Ky.
Reed, Jack, D-R.I.
Roberts, Pat, R-Kan.
Rockefeller, John D. IV, D-W.Va.
Sessions, Jeff, R-Ala.
Smith, Gordon H., R-Ore.
Smith, Robert C., R-N.H.
Stevens, Ted, R-Alaska
Thompson, Fred, R-Tenn.
Thurmond, Strom, R-S.C.
Torricelli, Robert G., D-N.J.
Warner, John W., R-Va.
Wellstone, Paul, D-Minn.

ALABAMA

Governor: Fob James, Jr. (R)
Elected: 1994*
Length of term: 4 years
Term expires: 1/99
Salary: $81,151.20
Term limit: 2 terms
Phone: (334) 242-7100
Born: September 15, 1934; Lanett, Ala.
Education: Auburn U., B.S. 1955.
Military Service: Army.
Occupation: Solid waste disposal company executive; erosion prevention company executive; manufacturer of consumer and industrial products.
Family: Wife, Bobbie Mooney; three children.
Religion: Episcopal.
Political Career: Governor, 1979-83 (as a Democrat)*

Lt. Gov.: Don Siegelman (D)
First Elected: 1994
Length of Term: 4 years
Term Expires: 1/99
Salary: $45,360
Term Limit: 2 terms
Phone: (334) 242-7100
State election official: (334) 242-7200
Democratic headquarters: (334) 326-3366
Republican headquarters: (334) 324-1990

REDISTRICTING

Alabama retained its seven House seats in reapportionment. Map issued by federal court Jan. 27, 1992, became law March 27, after a map passed by the Legislature was rejected by the Justice Department.

STATE LEGISLATURE

Bicameral legislature. Meets annually; limited to 30 legislative days within 105 calendar days; special sessions common.

Senate: 35 members, 4-year terms
1996 breakdown: 22D, 12R, 1 vacancy; 33 men, 1 woman
Salary: $10/day plus $50/day expenses while Legislature in session; $2,280 per month living expenses.
Phone: (334) 242-7800

House of Representatives: 105 members, 4-year terms
1996 breakdown: 72 D; 33 R; 101 men, 4 women
Salary: $10/day plus $50/day expenses while Legislature in session; $2,280 per month living expenses.
Phone: (334) 242-7600

URBAN STATISTICS

City	Population
Birmingham Mayor Richard Arrington Jr., D	265,965
Mobile Mayor Michael C. Dow, I	196,278
Montgomery Mayor Emory Folmar, R	187,543
Huntsville Mayor Loretta Spencer, N-P	159,789
Tuscaloosa Mayor Alvin DuPont, N-P	77,759

U.S. CONGRESS

Senate: 0 D, 2 R
House: 2 D, 5 R

TERM LIMITS

For state offices: No

ELECTIONS

1996 Presidential Vote

Bob Dole	50%
Bill Clinton	43%
Ross Perot	6%

1992 Presidential Vote

George Bush	48%
Bill Clinton	41%
Ross Perot	11%

1988 Presidential Vote

George Bush	59%
Michael S. Dukakis	40%

POPULATION

1990 population		4,040,587
1980 population		3,893,888
Percent change		+38%
Rank among states:		22
White		73%
Black		25%
Hispanic		1%
Asian or Pacific islander		1%
Urban		60%
Rural		40%
Born in state		76%
Foreign-born		1%
Under age 18	1,058,788	26%
Ages 18-64	2,458,810	61%
65 and older	522,289	13%
Median age		33

MISCELLANEOUS

Capital: Montgomery
Number of counties: 67
Per capita income: $15,569 (1991)
Rank among states: 41
Total area: 51,705 sq. miles
Rank among states: 29

ALABAMA

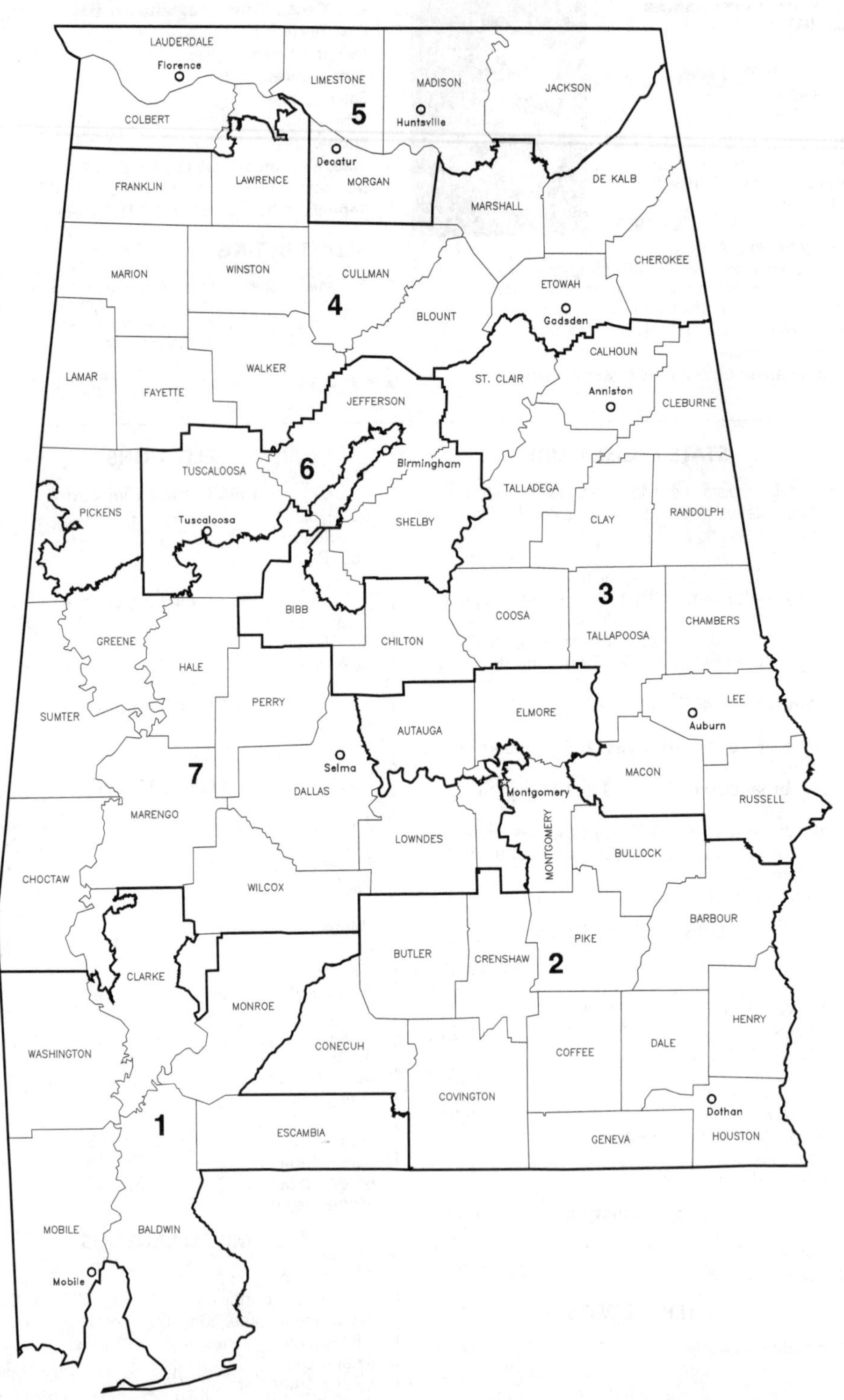
LAUDERDALE
Florence
COLBERT
LIMESTONE
MADISON
Huntsville
JACKSON
5
Decatur
FRANKLIN
LAWRENCE
MORGAN
MARSHALL
DE KALB
MARION
WINSTON
CULLMAN
CHEROKEE
ETOWAH
Gadsden
4
BLOUNT
CALHOUN
LAMAR
FAYETTE
WALKER
ST. CLAIR
JEFFERSON
Anniston
CLEBURNE
TUSCALOOSA
6
Birmingham
PICKENS
Tuscaloosa
TALLADEGA
CLAY
RANDOLPH
SHELBY
BIBB
COOSA
3
TALLAPOOSA
CHAMBERS
GREENE
HALE
CHILTON
PERRY
LEE
Auburn
SUMTER
AUTAUGA
ELMORE
7
Selma
DALLAS
Montgomery
MACON
RUSSELL
MARENGO
LOWNDES
MONTGOMERY
BULLOCK
CHOCTAW
WILCOX
BARBOUR
BUTLER
CRENSHAW
PIKE
2
CLARKE
MONROE
HENRY
WASHINGTON
CONECUH
COFFEE
DALE
COVINGTON
Dothan
1
ESCAMBIA
GENEVA
HOUSTON
MOBILE
BALDWIN
Mobile

Richard C. Shelby (R)

Of Tuscaloosa — Elected 1986, 2nd term

Biographical Information
Born: May 6, 1934, Birmingham, Ala.
Education: U. of Alabama, A.B. 1957, LL.B. 1963.
Occupation: Lawyer.
Family: Wife, Annette Nevin; two children.
Religion: Presbyterian.
Political Career: Ala. Senate, 1971-79; U.S. House, 1979-87.
Capitol Office: 110 Hart Bldg. 20510; 224-5744.

Committees
Special Aging
Appropriations
Defense; Foreign Operations; Transportation (chairman); Treasury & General Government; VA, HUD & Independent Agencies
Banking, Housing & Urban Affairs
Financial Institutions & Regulatory Relief; Housing Opportunity & Community Development; Securities
Select Intelligence (chairman)

In Washington: In his new role as Intelligence Committee chairman, Shelby was at the center of one of the most contentious partisan fights in the early months of the 105th Congress.

Shelby presided over confirmation hearings for Anthony Lake, whom President Clinton nominated to succeed John M. Deutch as director of Central Intelligence. Lake's nomination was controversial from start to finish; after three days of testimony before the intelligence panel, he abruptly withdrew his name from consideration and accused Republicans of treating him unfairly. Democrats complained that Shelby and the GOP had politicized the confirmation process, dragging it out to air baseless doubts about Lake's fitness for the CIA job.

The Lake episode just served to deepen the grudge that many Senate Democrats already held against Shelby. He earned their enmity when he switched to the GOP one day after the November 1994 election that gave Republicans control of Congress. The timing of the jump added insult to an already injured Democratic Party.

The switch itself, though, was hardly surprising. Rumors had circulated for more than a year that he was threatening to defect if the Republicans gained a Senate majority or if they needed his vote to take the lead.

Shelby's heart had long been more with conservative Republicans than with most of his Democratic colleagues. He had never been shy about expressing his differences with his own party in Congress or with the Clinton administration.

In the Democratic-controlled 103rd Congress, Shelby's opposition to Clinton's fiscal policies became embarrassingly visible for the White House. As a network television crew filmed Vice President Al Gore visiting Shelby in 1995 to seek his support for Clinton's budget plan, Shelby launched into a critical attack on it. He called Clinton's plan light on spending cuts and heavy on taxes. Later, he cosponsored a Republican substitute.

And Shelby's 1997 ascent to the Intelligence chair spelled big trouble for Clinton's nomination of Lake — who had been his national security adviser — to head the CIA. Shelby questioned whether Lake was the right man for the job and said Clinton should have chosen a less controversial nominee.

Specifically, Shelby and other Republicans said they were troubled about Lake's involvement in the Clinton administration's decision to give tacit approval of the shipment of arms from Iran to the Muslim-dominated Bosnian government. He also expressed concern about the administration's subsequent decision not to inform Congress about the Iran-Bosnia situation. Lake was questioned repeatedly about the matter during his confirmation hearings.

Shelby also repeatedly asked why two staffers on the National Security Council, which Lake headed, did not inform him about a briefing they were given by the FBI detailing an alleged plot by the Chinese government to influence U.S. elections. He asked Lake why he did not have a system in place to ensure such "dynamite" information would reach the agency's top official. Shelby said the issue was important because it was illustrative of Lake's management abilities.

Shelby infuriated Democrats by twice postponing the start of the Lake hearings. After the second postponement, the panel's vice chairman, Democrat Bob Kerrey of Nebraska, said he was concerned Lake's nomination was turning into a "political football" and that the process Shelby was using to examine Lake was threatening the committee's tradition of bipartisanship.

Shelby also raised Kerrey's ire by insisting that senators be given access to a more detailed FBI file on Lake than the summaries that were initially supplied to Shelby and Kerrey. After threatening a third delay over the issue, Shelby agreed to move forward with the hearings as he continued to negotiate the issue with the White House.

After Lake's withdrawal, Kerrey complained that his nomination had been badly handled by the committee, citing in particular Shelby's demand for the more detailed FBI file on Lake.

But an unflappable Shelby said he was only

concerned with conducting a "vigorous" examination of the nominee. "Whether you have a fair hearing is in the eyes of the beholder," he said in response to Kerrey's criticism. Shelby dismissed accusations that his actions on the Lake affair were driven by partisan politics. And he reacted much more favorably to Clinton's nomination in March 1997 of acting CIA director George J. Tenet to head the agency.

It was not the first time since becoming a Republican that Shelby had heard himself called a partisan "attack dog."

Shelby and fellow Republican Lauch Faircloth of North Carolina were the most aggressive GOP questioners during Senate hearings into the Whitewater controversy, which surrounded a failed land deal involving President and Hillary Rodham Clinton.

On several occasions, Shelby compared the Whitewater affair to the Watergate scandal, which brought down the Nixon administration. For example, he made the comparison when the White House refused to provide the notes former White House associate counsel William Kennedy III made during a meeting of Clinton's attorneys and other administration officials. Citing this and the inability of senior White House staff to recall details about their activities, Shelby said, "Sound's strangely familiar, doesn't it?"

He also compared former White House counsel Bernard Nussbaum's refusal to give Justice Department officials full access to deputy counsel Vincent W. Foster Jr.'s papers with President Richard M. Nixon's assertions of executive privilege during Watergate.

Even as a Democrat, Shelby had spoken out on the Whitewater matter. He was the first senator to call for the resignation of Deputy Treasury Secretary Roger C. Altman, who was accused of misleading the Banking Committee in early 1994 when he said he had had "only one substantive contact" with the White House on the Whitewater case. Altman later resigned.

In switching parties, Shelby was not only rewarded with a seat on the Appropriations Committee, something Democrats had denied him, but also he was given the chairmanship of the panel's Treasury, Postal Service and General Government Subcommittee. Shelby's clout was boosted for the 105th Congress when he took over the helm of the Appropriations Transportation Subcommittee, a post that will allow him to wield influence over the multibillion-dollar highway reauthorization bill that is on the agenda for the 105th.

In his role as the treasury-postal panel chairman, Shelby had his first experience with working in a leadership position with Kerrey, who served as the ranking Democrat. As with the Lake controversy, their relationship got off to a rocky start.

Kerrey and Shelby got into a tiff during floor debate on a spending rescissions bill in 1995. It began when Kerrey offered an amendment to retract $325 million previously appropriated for construction projects. Republicans complained that Kerrey had targeted too many GOP-sponsored projects and tried but failed to kill his amendment. Shelby angrily upped the ante and proposed to slash $1.8 billion from approved projects. He won approval of his amendment but House and Senate conferees eventually agreed to reduce the cut to $580 million from 39 projects.

The two lawmakers, however, did find areas of agreement. Shelby and Kerrey tried in 1995 to kill the drug czar's office, saying the idea was a failure. The Appropriations Committee voted in 1995 to eliminate the office and shift funding to drug interdiction efforts. Their effort eventually failed and money was included for the drug czar's office.

Shelby also set his sights on the Internal Revenue Service. In crafting the fiscal 1997 treasury-postal spending bill, Shelby did not include funding for the IRS' much criticized multibillion-dollar computer upgrade program. "For years, the IRS creatively padded programs in its tax systems modernization budget that had long since ceased to be related to modernization," Shelby said.

Shelby also found himself in a position to help some Democrats who had aided him in steering funding for federal projects to Alabama during his days as a Democrat. During consideration of the fiscal 1996 treasury-postal spending bill, Shelby spoke in favor of home-state projects being sought by Sens. Robert C. Byrd of West Virginia and Daniel K. Inouye of Hawaii.

NASA and its contractors are important to the Alabama economy, and Shelby strongly supports continued funding for NASA's space station. Faulting those trying to strike funding for the project during floor consideration of the fiscal 1997 VA-HUD and independent agencies spending bill, Shelby said, "It's an American destiny to take steps in space. We must not stop now."

Since moving into the GOP, Shelby has emerged as a stalwart on the party's right flank. He has sponsored legislation to make English the nation's official language and to abolish the current tax system and replace it with a flat tax rate. In 1997, he was one of 26 Republicans voting against ratification of a treaty to outlaw chemical and biological weapons worldwide.

But Shelby has opposed a majority of his Republican colleagues on issues of special concern to trial lawyers. He does not back legislation that would place limits on damage awards in product liability cases, a top priority for the leadership in the 105th Congress. In 1996, he was one of only five Republicans to vote against ending debate on product liability legislation.

During consideration of a 1995 bill to make it more difficult for investors to win securities fraud lawsuits, Shelby offered an amendment to make it easier for plaintiffs to collect damages against company officials. The amendment, however, failed.

In 1991, Shelby was one of 11 Democrats to vote to seat Clarence Thomas on the Supreme Court after Anita F. Hill went public with allegations that Thomas had sexually harassed her.

At Home: Shelby was the icing on the cake for

Senate Republicans in 1994 as he switched parties the day after the GOP won a majority. The appeal of the switch to voters will be tested in 1998 when he runs for election for the first time as a Republican.

His party switch aside, Shelby has spent most of the last quarter century steadily climbing Alabama's political ladder. He first ran for Congress in 1978, when his former Tuscaloosa law partner, Democratic Rep. Walter Flowers, gave up his seat for what turned out to be an unsuccessful Senate primary campaign. Shelby, whose support for such issues as the Equal Rights Amendment had typed him as a progressive Democrat during eight years in the state Legislature, went for Flowers' open seat.

Shelby's strong base in Tuscaloosa, where he had served as a prosecutor, helped him win 48 percent in the primary. In the runoff, he defeated Chris McNair — a black state representative — by a 3-2 margin, in a campaign free of racial tensions. He easily won that November and never faced significant GOP opposition until he challenged Republican Sen. Jeremiah Denton in 1986.

Denton led in public opinion polls throughout the campaign. The Republican had a following among advocates of his staunchly conservative, pro-Reagan politics and those who viewed the former naval officer and longtime Vietnam prisoner of war as a national hero.

But in the Senate, Denton spent much time pursuing goals such as promoting chastity among teenagers — an agenda without strong appeal to many voters in 1986, a time of great concern about economic issues. He was frequently ridiculed for being loose with his words (about spousal rape, for instance, he said, "Damn it, when you get married, you kind of expect you're going to get a little sex"). Denton, not skilled at personal politicking, was criticized for not keeping in touch with his constituency.

But Shelby had problems of his own, caused by his cool relationship with Democratic liberals. He won just 51 percent in the primary, barely avoiding a runoff. He bested Denton in the fall by just 1 percentage point, with the help of a large black turnout.

Shelby had little trouble winning re-election in 1992. McNair — then a Jefferson County commissioner — filed at the last minute to oppose him in the Democratic primary.

But McNair was not widely known across the state, and he could not compete with Shelby's huge campaign treasury. Nor could McNair rely on the backing of Alabama's two influential black political organizations. The New South Coalition and the Alabama Democratic Conference endorsed both Shelby and McNair. McNair carried Jefferson County by a wide margin, but he only won one other county in the state.

Alabama Republicans failed to recruit a major candidate to take on Shelby. Businessman Richard Sellers was the only Republican to file. Largely ignored by state and national party figures and with a campaign treasury a fraction of Shelby's, Sellers lost by a margin of nearly 2-to-1.

SENATE ELECTIONS

1992 General*

Richard C. Shelby (D)	1,022,698	(65%)
Richard Sellers (R)	522,015	(33%)
Jerome Shockley (LIBERT)	31,811	(2%)

Previous Winning Percentages: 1986 (50%) **1984*** (97%) **1982*** (97%) **1980*** (73%) **1978*** (94%)

** Shelby was elected to the House as a Democrat in 1978-84. He was elected to the Senate as a Democrat in 1986-92.*

CAMPAIGN FINANCE

	Receipts	Receipts from PACs		Expend-itures
1992				
Shelby (D)	$2,816,778	$1,258,166	(45%)	$2,451,191
Sellers (R)	$149,603	0		$149,578

KEY VOTES

1997	
Approve balanced-budget constitutional amendment	Y
Approve chemical weapons treaty	N
1996	
Approve farm bill	Y
Limit punitive damages in product liability cases	N
Exempt small businesses from higher minimum wage	Y
Approve welfare overhaul	Y
Bar job discrimination based on sexual orientation	N
Override veto of ban on "partial birth" abortions	Y
1995	
Approve GOP budget with tax and spending cuts	Y
Approve constitutional amendment barring flag desecration	Y

VOTING STUDIES

	Presidential Support		Party Unity		Conservative Coalition	
Year	**S**	**O**	**S**	**O**	**S**	**O**
1996	32	64	92	6	87	8
1995	29	68	88	10	91	5
1994†	53	26	41	41	78	3
1993	45	53	36	61	93	5
1992	65	35	45	55	89	11
1991	69	31	54	46	83	18

† Shelby switched to the Republican Party on Nov. 9, 1994. As a Democrat, he was eligible for 60 presidential support votes in 1994; as a Republican he was eligible for two presidential support votes in 1994. His presidential support score includes votes he cast both as a Democrat and as a Republican. His 1994 party unity and conservative coalition scores include only votes he cast as a Democrat.

INTEREST GROUP RATINGS

Year	ADA	AFL-CIO	CCUS	ACU
1996	5	n/a	77	90
1995	5	0	89	91
1994	30	83	50	55
1993	35	73	82	64
1992	30	58	60	63
1991	35	67	40	76

Jeff Sessions (R)

Of Mobile — Elected 1996, 1st term

Biographical Information

Born: Dec. 24, 1946, Hybart, Ala.
Education: Huntingdon College, B.A. 1969; U. of Alabama, J.D. 1973.
Military Service: Army, 1973; Army Reserve.
Occupation: Lawyer.
Family: Wife, Mary Blackshear; three children.
Religion: Methodist.
Political Career: U.S. Attorney, 1981-93; Ala. attorney general, 1995-97.
Capitol Office: 495 Russell Bldg. 20510; 224-4124.

Committees

Environment & Public Works
Clean Air, Wetlands, Private Property & Nuclear Safety; Superfund, Waste Control & Risk Assessment
Select Ethics
Judiciary
Administrative Oversight & the Courts; Youth Violence (chairman)
Joint Economic

The Path to Washington: In a twist of political fate, Sessions in 1996 captured the Senate seat vacated by the man who a decade earlier had denied him a federal judgeship.

In June 1986, Democratic Sen. Howell Heflin of Alabama cast the pivotal vote in the Senate Judiciary Committee against Sessions, because of racially tinged remarks that he allegedly made. Sessions' nomination never reached the Senate floor.

In the 105th Congress, Sessions not only succeeds Heflin (who retired), but also takes his seat on Judiciary — a "great irony," Sessions allows. He is chairman of Judiciary's Youth Violence Subcommittee.

Sessions holds a seat on the Environment and Public Works Committee, which has primary Senate jurisdiction over an omnibus transportation bill that is a top agenda item in the 105th. And he serves on the Ethics Committee and the Joint Economic Committee.

Sessions hews to a pro-business line, and he campaigned as a supporter of cutting taxes and adding a balanced-budget amendment to the Constitution. He said of his home state, "There's still a strong feeling here that money sent to Washington doesn't come back in effective ways." He scored a 6-point victory over Democratic state Sen. Roger Bedford, who argued that Sessions would cut federal services crucial to the state.

Sessions castigated Bedford, chairman of the state Senate Judiciary Committee, as being "very much in the lapdog of the trial lawyers." (Bedford had blocked overhaul of state tort law, an effort led by Republicans unhappy with Alabama juries' penchant for high awards to plaintiffs in liability cases.) Session also criticized Bedford for his dependence on labor money to fuel his campaign.

But as was the case with other Alabama GOP candidates in 1996, Sessions gave more prominence to social issues than to fiscal ones. "Without personal discipline and moral and religious faith, our nation's future is jeopardized," he said. He appealed to Alabama's conservative Christian activists with his advocacy of a constitutional amendment permitting school prayer. Sessions opposes abortion in most cases, and he is a firm advocate of gunowners' rights.

When the Judiciary Committee in 1986 blocked his nomination to a federal judgeship, Sessions was serving as the chief federal prosecutor for the Southern District of Alabama, building a reputation through his prosecution of drug dealers.

In 1994, Sessions ran for state attorney general, and with a corruption scandal raging in Montgomery, he rode a vow to clean up the ethics mess to an overwhelming victory. Sessions unseated Democrat James H. Evans, who had been targeted by the GOP after putting Republican Gov. Guy Hunt (1987-93) in jail on corruption charges.

Two years after that victory, Sessions was on the move again, lured into the Senate race by Heflin's retirement after 18 years in Washington.

Six other Republicans joined Sessions in the party primary. He led the pack with 38 percent, landing in a runoff with Sid McDonald, a former state legislator who headed the state's largest long-distance carrier. McDonald poured about $1 million of his own money into the race, and he accused Sessions of accepting campaign contributions from tobacco interests while his office was investigating a tobacco company. But Sessions successfully defended himself against a state ethics charge that he had shared information with the company while it was under investigation. He won nomination with 59 percent of the vote.

In the general election, Bedford had trouble getting the more conservative elements of his party behind him; state House Speaker Jimmy Clark was a notable Democratic defector to the Sessions camp. Bedford accused Sessions of cronyism in his use of outside counsel in the attorney general's office. And he complained that Sessions had issued an opinion as attorney general that allowed GOP Gov. Fob James Jr. to seat a political contributor on the Auburn University board of trustees.

Sessions sought to tarnish Bedford's image by accusing him of earmarking state funds for a water line that raised the value of property he co-owned. Also, he disputed Bedford's characterization of himself as a "Reagan Democrat," running ads to note that in each of the years Ronald Reagan won the presidency, Bedford was a convention delegate for Democratic candidates.

In the end, Sessions prevailed with 52 percent of the vote to 46 percent for Bedford. Sessions' victory gave Alabama two Republican senators for the first time since Reconstruction.

An Eagle Scout and the son of a country store owner in Camden, Sessions was an attorney for a firm in Russellville before becoming assistant U.S. attorney in 1975. His work in that job won him the recognition of the White House, and in 1986, President Reagan nominated Sessions to be a federal judge. But Sessions' words doomed his nomination.

According to sworn statements by Justice Department lawyers, Sessions called the NAACP and the American Civil Liberties Union "un-American" and "communist-inspired" and said they "force civil rights down the throats of people." He also reportedly said of the Ku Klux Klan, "I used to think they're OK," until learning that some Klan members were "pot smokers."

Sessions said the remarks were in jest or had been misinterpreted. Coming to Sessions' defense was Sen. Jeremiah Denton, R-Ala., (1981-87) who said the nominee's comments were "distorted" or taken out of context. Denton also said Sessions was a victim of a political conspiracy stemming from his effort to prosecute blacks for voter fraud.

But Heflin opposed the nomination, saying he was unsure whether Sessions could be fair and impartial in the lifelong position of federal judge. On June 5, 1986, Heflin announced a last-minute decision to vote against Sessions in the Judiciary Committee. "The question is, 'Will Jeff Sessions be a fair and impartial judge?' " Heflin asked. "The answer is, 'I don't know.' . . . I regret that I cannot vote for confirmation." Following his words, a 9-9 tie vote kept Sessions' nomination from going to the floor.

The defeat of the Sessions nomination was only the second time in 48 years that the Judiciary Committee had declined to send a president's judicial nominee to the full Senate for consideration.

During the 1996 campaign, Bedford accused Sessions of "playing the race card" for advertising the endorsement of the Democrat by prominent black political leaders such as Birmingham Mayor Richard Arrington Jr.

SENATE ELECTIONS

1996 General		
Jeff Sessions (R)	786,436	(52%)
Roger Bedford (D)	681,651	(46%)
Mark Thornton (LIBERT)	21,550	(2%)
1996 Primary Runoff		
Jeff Sessions (R)	81,622	(59%)
Sid McDonald (R)	56,131	(41%)
1996 Primary		
Jeff Sessions (R)	80,694	(38%)
Sid McDonald (R)	47,320	(22%)
Charles Woods (R)	23,796	(11%)
Frank McRight (R)	21,818	(10%)
Walter D. Clark (R)	18,513	(9%)
Jimmy Blake (R)	15,305	(7%)
Albert Lipscomb (R)	7,600	(4%)

CAMPAIGN FINANCE

	Receipts	Receipts from PACs	Expend-itures
1996			
Sessions (R)	$3,905,870	$936,673 (24%)	$3,862,359
Bedford (D)	$3,216,772	$447,820 (14%)	$3,088,324

KEY VOTES

1997	
Approve balanced-budget constitutional amendment	Y
Approve chemical weapons treaty	N

1 Sonny Callahan (R)

Of Mobile — Elected 1984, 7th term

Biographical Information
Born: Sept. 11, 1932, Mobile, Ala.
Education: McGill H.S., graduated 1950; U. of Alabama,.
Military Service: Navy, 1952-54.
Occupation: Moving and storage company executive.
Family: Wife, Karen Reed; six children.
Religion: Roman Catholic.
Political Career: Ala. House, 1971-79, served as a Democrat; Ala. Senate, 1979-83, served as a Democrat; sought Democratic nomination for lieutenant governor, 1982.

Capitol Office: 2418 Rayburn Bldg. 20515; 225-4931.

Committees
Appropriations
Energy & Water Development; Foreign Operations, Export Financing & Related Programs (chairman); Transportation

In Washington: The Republican electoral sweep of 1994 vaulted a number of previously little-known Republicans into positions of influence in Congress, but few sights on Capitol Hill are as remarkable as that of Callahan presiding as chairman of the Appropriations Subcommittee on Foreign Operations. During a decade in the House minority, Callahan persistently questioned the rationale for foreign aid; now he chairs the subcommittee that dispenses it.

Callahan is a loyal Republican soldier, firmly committed to his party's goal of balancing the federal budget. In the 104th when he brought the foreign operations spending bill to the floor, Callahan insisted that it not exceed the $12.1 billion cap predetermined by GOP leaders. And when the White House requested additional foreign aid funding in its fiscal 1998 budget, Callahan called it "a hard sell."

Though Callahan's chairmanship affords him ample opportunity to influence debates on international affairs, he forgoes grand strategizing on policy and focuses on holding his subcommittee's bill within budget boundaries, taking cues from Appropriations Chairman Robert L. Livingston of Louisiana, who was hand-picked by Speaker Newt Gingrich to refocus appropriators on finding ways to save money rather than spend it.

"I have long believed if we are going to ask the American people to make sacrifices in domestic spending and programs here at home, then it would be difficult, if not impossible, to ask the American taxpayer to continue spending more money in foreign assistance programs," Callahan once wrote in his column for hometown papers.

Chairing the foreign operations subcommittee is not a job Callahan particularly relishes, as was clear when Republicans organized for the 105th Congress: He sought to trade his position for a chair on an Appropriations subcommittee with more impact in his home state. Callahan said he hoped to trade places with Frank R. Wolf of Virginia, chairman of the Transportation Subcommittee (on which Callahan sits), but Wolf kept his job. The chair of the Energy and Water Subcommittee was open at the start of the 105th, but it went to Joseph M. McDade of Pennsylvania, who has far more seniority than Callahan.

So Callahan returned to the Foreign Operations chair for the 105th, faced again with the challenge of negotiating around the bill's perennial fights over funding for international family planning activities. The topic almost derailed both bills Callahan managed in the 104th.

During House consideration of the fiscal 1997 foreign operations measure, abortion foes in the House added a provision cutting aid to overseas groups that spend their own money on abortions. The Senate opposed the restriction and the White House pledged a veto if it stayed. The provision held up negotiations on the foreign operations bill, and ultimately it was one of six measures folded into an omnibus spending bill at the session's end.

Callahan's prescription for getting around the impasse had been a proposal to limit aid for international groups that use their own money to perform or promote abortions. Funding for such organizations would be capped at 50 percent of the level they received in fiscal 1995.

But the Senate Appropriations Subcommittee on Foreign Operations boosted overall funding for population control and knocked out the abortion language.

Although conferees ultimately abandoned the House language, Republicans succeeded in imposing tight funding limits on the program. The final version provided $385 million for family planning activities, but none of the money could be spent until July 1, 1997, unless both chambers voted to release the aid by Feb. 28, 1997. In one of the key early votes of the 105th, the House did just that, handing the Clinton administration a victory. Callahan, who opposes abortion, voted against releasing the funds early.

Conferees on the fiscal 1997 bill also stripped House-passed restrictions on economic aid for Turkey. When the House considered the bill in June 1996, it had easily adopted amendments

ALABAMA 1
Southwest — Mobile

The proud, history-steeped city of Mobile dominates the 1st. Since Mobile was founded in 1702, the French, British, Spanish and Confederate flags have flown over the city, lending it a cosmopolitan heritage distinct from other Alabama cities. Mobile compares itself with New Orleans; indeed, it claims to celebrate the oldest Mardi Gras festival in the United States.

The city's Church Street East is the most diverse of Mobile's historic districts. The original structures in the area were destroyed by great fires in 1827 and 1839. Rebuilt in the late 19th century, the buildings, set among old oaks and gaslights, span a wide architectural range, including Federal, Greek Revival, Queen Anne and Victorian.

The 1st backs Republicans for most statewide and federal races, but it is not a GOP monolith. Democratic strength lies in the rural counties in the northern part of the district, which have sizable black populations, and in Prichard, a suburb of Mobile with a 79 percent black population. George Bush carried the 1st in 1992, and Bob Dole easily defeated Bill Clinton by 14 percentage points here in 1996. However, Alabama's Republican governor, Fob James Jr., carried the district by fewer than 5,000 votes in 1994.

The city of Mobile, with just under 200,000 people, lost population during the 1980s. But Mobile County as a whole grew by a modest 4 percent, while Baldwin County, to the east across Mobile Bay, grew by 25 percent, second-fastest in the state. The small Baldwin County city of Daphne more than tripled in size, growing from 3,400 to 11,300.

Mobile is Alabama's only port city. While the commercial shipbuilding industry has been stagnant for several years, the ship repair business has thrived, keeping Mobile's shipyards busy. The 1985 completion of the Tennessee-Tombigbee Waterway, which connects Mobile Bay and the Tennessee River, was promoted as a tool to allow Mobile's port to compete with New Orleans in trade volume, but trade on the massive waterway has yet to live up to expectations.

Timber and textiles also fuel the 1st's economy. Paper companies dot the district, farming trees from the forests that cover much of the district's rural counties. Alabama River Pulp's $1.1 billion pulp mill near Claiborne (Monroe County), which opened seven years ago, was one of the largest industrial expansion in the history of Alabama. The racial climate in Monroeville, the county seat, inspired the 1960 novel "To Kill a Mockingbird," but tensions have eased since then. Now, there are several blacks in city and county government.

Wedged between Mississippi and Florida, the 1st contains all of Alabama's tiny coastline. Along the Gulf of Mexico, fishermen trawl for shrimp. Each October, the National Shrimp Festival at Gulf Shores draws more than 200,000 visitors.

1990 Population: 577,226. White 403,193 (70%), Black 164,448 (28%), Other 9,585 (2%). Hispanic origin 4,585 (<1%). 18 and over 414,476 (72%), 62 and over 88,450 (15%). Median age: 33.

restricting $25 million in economic aid to Turkey unless it lifted its blockade of assistance to Armenia and acknowledged that genocide was committed against Armenians between 1915 and 1923. The proposals, strongly backed by Armenian-American groups, triggered protest from Ankara. Callahan, backing Turkey's views, expressed displeasure with the amendments. "I think that the Congress made a mistake in the language that we inserted in the bill," he said.

During consideration of the fiscal 1997 bill, there was little discussion of the level of U.S. aid to Russia, although that program had in the past been controversial. Debate over the aid was effectively put on hold pending the outcome of Russia's presidential elections in June 1996. In the past, Callahan had been a dogged critic of U.S. aid to Russia, a crusade that sometimes put him in a face-off with Livingston, who supported the Clinton administration's policy of sending aid to Russia and the former Soviet republics.

In 1995, the first year Callahan managed the foreign operations bill, the measure was stalled four months over abortion-related language. Conferees in October 1995 remained at loggerheads over a House-passed provision to reinstate Reagan-era restrictions on U.S. aid to international family planning groups. The provision would have banned funding for any organization providing abortions overseas, and for the United Nations Population Fund unless it withdrew from China, which has been criticized for using coercive family planning techniques. House negotiators demanded that a slightly modified version of the provision remain in the bill, a stance rejected by Senate conferees.

On that bill, Callahan consented to modest funding increases, including $25 million for the International Development Association (IDA), which pushed the bill's price tag close to his original $12 billion ceiling. After some prodding, he agreed to go up another $125 million — $100 million for the IDA and $25 million for U.N. programs. That boosted overall funding to $12.1 billion. Callahan's concessions won the backing of Clinton, who had made a late-night call to the

House chairman to request more funding.

The fiscal 1996 foreign operations bill finally passed in January 1996 when an agreement was reached that funds for family planning programs would be reduced by 35 percent from the fiscal 1995 level of $548 million unless a separate bill authorizing those programs became law by July 1. No authorization bill was enacted, however.

Normally easygoing and genial, Callahan is comfortable with the personal give-and-take of the political process. He is the GOP version of a character type once abundant in his region: the Democratic courthouse politician. That is not surprising because Callahan himself was once a Democrat. Today, though, he is a reliable pro-business Republican.

In Washington, Callahan soon showed a knack for cultivating key friendships, and his contacts propelled him into important positions. He got a seat on Public Works as a freshman, then moved onto Energy and Commerce, and finally in the 103rd landed a seat on Appropriations.

Callahan is not averse to using his appropriations seat to help the people of Mobile. When the House took up a transportation spending bill in September 1996, Callahan offered an amendment to bar Amtrak, the national passenger railroad, from shutting down a route from Mobile to New Orleans for six months, costing the railroad an estimated $3 million. Callahan withdrew the amendment after other lawmakers said it would be unfair to protect a single route.

At Home: Callahan had a tough first campaign for Congress in 1984, but his re-election margins have ranged from comfortable to unanimous.

When GOP Rep. Jack Edwards announced his retirement in late 1983, his endorsement went to Callahan. The only suspense in the race was over which party Callahan would choose. Elected to the state Legislature as a Democrat, Callahan moved right. He formally joined the GOP in February 1984, and, confident of victory, waged a lackadaisical House campaign. Callahan's primary foe, Mobile lawyer Billy Stoudenmire, attacked him as a Democratic interloper. Callahan drew enough conservative Democrats across party lines to win with 60 percent of the vote.

Democrats nominated Frank McRight, a Mobile trial lawyer who won his primary by attacking local government corruption. Then in the November campaign it was reported that Callahan had received an illegal campaign contribution two years earlier from a city official later indicted on other charges.

Changing the subject, Callahan reminded voters that McRight had twice been the Carter-Mondale campaign chairman in Mobile, and he repeatedly asked how McRight would vote for president in 1984. In the end, Callahan owed much of his 51 percent victory to Ronald Reagan's smashing triumph in the 1st.

Since then, Callahan's lowest tally was 59 percent in 1988 against John M. Tyson Jr., a high-profile member of the state school board and part of a well-known political family who ran a poorly organized, underfunded campaign.

HOUSE ELECTIONS

1996 General		
Sonny Callahan (R)	132,206	(64%)
Don Womack (D)	69,470	(34%)
Bob Burns (LIBERT)	3,311	(2%)
1994 General		
Sonny Callahan (R)	103,431	(67%)
Don Womack (D)	50,227	(33%)

Previous Winning Percentages: 1992 (60%) **1990** (100%) **1988** (59%) **1986** (100%) **1984** (51%)

CAMPAIGN FINANCE

	Receipts	Receipts from PACs		Expend-itures
1996				
Callahan (R)	$337,917	$174,970	(52%)	$402,128
Womack (D)	$92,342	$56,600	(61%)	$39,826
1994				
Callahan (R)	$339,576	$145,620	(43%)	$416,080
Womack (D)	$69,917	$23,600	(34%)	$55,721

DISTRICT VOTE FOR PRESIDENT

1996		1992	
D	84,184 (39%)	**D**	84,202 (37%)
R	113,202 (53%)	**R**	118,421 (52%)
I	14,671 (7%)	**I**	26,797 (12%)

KEY VOTES

1997	
Ban "partial birth" abortions	Y
1996	
Approve farm bill	Y
Deny public education to illegal immigrants	Y
Repeal ban on certain assault-style weapons	Y
Increase minimum wage	N
Freeze defense spending	N
Approve welfare overhaul	Y
1995	
Approve balanced-budget constitutional amendment	Y
Relax Clean Water Act regulations	Y
Oppose limits on environmental regulations	N
Reduce projected Medicare spending	Y
Approve GOP budget with tax and spending cuts	Y

VOTING STUDIES

	Presidential Support		Party Unity		Conservative Coalition	
Year	**S**	**O**	**S**	**O**	**S**	**O**
1996	37	59	91	5	100	0
1995	20	78	93	4	97	1
1994	38	55	82	11	94	0
1993	28	69	92	5	93	0
1992	82	16	83	12	96	0
1991	65	25	72	15	70	3

INTEREST GROUP RATINGS

Year	ADA	AFL-CIO	CCUS	ACU
1996	0	n/a	100	100
1995	5	0	100	88
1994	5	13	92	100
1993	0	0	90	96
1992	5	27	75	96
1991	0	17	90	100

2 Terry Everett (R)

Of Enterprise — Elected 1992, 3rd term

Biographical Information
Born: Feb. 15, 1937, Dothan, Ala.
Education: Enterprise State Junior College,.
Military Service: Air Force, 1955-59.
Occupation: Newspaper executive; construction company owner; farm owner; real estate developer.
Family: Wife, Barbara Pitts.
Religion: Baptist.
Political Career: No previous office.
Capitol Office: 208 Cannon Bldg. 20515; 225-2901.

Committees
Agriculture
Forestry, Resource Conservation & Research; Risk Management & Specialty Crops
National Security
Military Installations and Facilities; Military Procurement
Veterans' Affairs
Oversight & Investigations (chairman)

In Washington: Farm policy and military matters have been the main legislative fare for Everett, and in both those areas he keeps close watch on the interests of his constituency.

In the 104th, as Congress rewrote federal farm policy, Everett went to bat for the peanut farmers in his south Alabama district, complaining that their interests were being subjugated to those of large-scale manufacturers who use peanuts and want a cheap and abundant supply of the legume. Everett knows a thing or two about the profit motive, having made himself wealthy through farming, land development and other business ventures. He also brings some relevant personal experience to his work on the National Security and the Veterans' Affairs Committees, having served in the Air Force in the late 1950s.

A member of the Agriculture Committee, Everett skirmished in the 104th with those who sought to kill the government price support system available to peanut farmers. The decades-old program boosts peanut prices through a combination of government loans and production limits.

Everett dismissed claims that killing the price support system would save consumers money. He said that peanut program foes were "motivated primarily by big candy manufacturers and peanut butter manufacturers would lead us to believe that a candy bar or a jar of peanut butter would cost less if the peanut program was eliminated. What they do not tell us is that American consumers pay less for peanut products than they do in Canada."

Other Southern lawmakers rallied to the program's defense, warning that killing price supports would devastate small farmers and hard-scrabble rural areas. Everett and his allies said the farm bill already included provisions reforming the program by reducing the loan rate and easing the system of domestic quotas on peanuts.

"The reforms and modifications made in the peanut program should satisfy even the peanut manufacturers except for their need to add to their bottom line," Everett told the House in February 1996. "This is corporate greed, pure and simple." The amendment to kill the peanut program was turned back narrowly, 209-212.

That battle won, Everett voted for the GOP-backed "Freedom to Farm" bill, which phased out most New Deal-era crop subsidies and gave farmers greater flexibility in deciding what to plant.

Even after the House passed the farm bill, Everett and other peanut program defenders remained on alert. When the House took up the fiscal 1997 agriculture spending bill, an attempt was made to cap the price of peanuts at $640 per ton. Everett reacted angrily to the amendment, calling it "price fixing without question." He said: "It is kind of odd that these folks want to fix the price to a farmer . . . who sweats and earns his living by his brow, but they do not want to fix the price to the sheller or the manufacturer. They can charge as much as they want to."

On the National Security Committee, Everett has backed the larger defense budgets promulgated by the GOP. He said the committee's fiscal 1997 defense bill would "help shore up the inadequacies of Clinton's defense budget."

From the committee, Everett also is able to attend to his district's numerous military bases and defense contractors. The 2nd is home to Maxwell and Gunter Air Force bases and to Fort Rucker, where Army and Air Force helicopter crews train. To help save local jobs, Everett would also like to consolidate all the Navy's helicopter training at Fort Rucker, which employs about 12,000 people.

A local interest prompted Everett to complain about one facet of the fiscal 1997 defense spending bill. He was unhappy that it did not allow more private companies to undertake defense repair work at the nation's large military maintenance depots. Under existing law, 60 percent of each year's depot-maintenance workload must be performed by federal employees, while 40 percent can be bid on by private contractors. The Pentagon expressed interest in changing the "60/40" law to allow for more work by private

Defense and agriculture fuel the economy of the 2nd. The substantial defense presence stands as testament to the influence of Bill Dickinson, who represented the 2nd from 1965 to 1993 and rose to ranking Republican on the House Armed Services Committee.

Maxwell and Gunter Air Force bases, on the edge of Montgomery, employ about 8,500 people; Gunter was annexed by Maxwell in March 1992. Fort Rucker, northwest of Dothan, is where many Army and Air Force helicopter pilots and crews train. More than 10,000 military and civilian personnel work at Fort Rucker. Lockheed-Martin has a missile factory in Troy (Pike County).

Southeastern Alabama is known as the Wiregrass region for the wiry roots of its native grass. The soil was first tilled for cotton, but in the early part of the century, the boll weevil wiped out more than two-thirds of the cotton crop. Now the sparsely populated area grows more peanuts than almost any other part of the country. The Coffee County town of Enterprise (Everett's hometown) erected a monument to the boll weevil as a tribute to the insect whose destruction of the cotton crop persuaded farmers to switch to peanuts.

Although redistricting for the 1990s split the city of Montgomery between the 2nd and the new black-majority 7th District, it is still the 2nd's largest city. Montgomery has long been a stronghold for the national GOP, voting for Republican presidential candidates as far back as 1956. The other sizable city in the 2nd is Dothan (population 54,000), at the southeastern corner of the district in Houston County, near the Florida and Georgia borders.

In 1996, Bob Dole beat Bill Clinton in the district by 56 percent to 37 percent. Dole ran stronger in Houston County and the parts of

ALABAMA 2
Southeast — Part of Montgomery; Dothan

Montgomery County in the district, where he got 62 percent, than elsewhere in the 2nd, where he garnered 52 percent.

Everett won every county but three (Barbour, Bullock and Conecuh) in 1996. In his first election in 1992, the margins Everett ran up in Montgomery (by 19 percentage points) and Houston (by 20 points) enabled him to withstand losses in 10 of the district's 13 other counties to win election over George C. Wallace Jr.

Originally a cotton and peanut market town, Dothan has grown and diversified by attracting new industries, including large plants run by Michelin and Sony. Sony manufactures and exports audio and video tapes and computer disks here. Largely non-union, Dothan's plants represent most of the 2nd's large industry, although Elmore County has some textile plants.

Rural Barbour and Bullock counties were the original home base for former governor and presidential candidate George C. Wallace. They have large black populations (Bullock is majority-black) and are loyally Democratic. Clinton won Bullock County with 70 percent in 1996; Republican Everett managed only 33 percent.

Elmore and Autauga counties grew during the 1980s as people who work in Montgomery moved out of the city. Elmore grew by 13 percent, Autauga by 6 percent. They both vote Republican.

1990 Population: 577,227. White 431,639 (75%), Black 139,265 (24%), Other 6,323 (1%). Hispanic origin 4,765 (<1%). 18 and over 423,324 (73%), 62 and over 90,554 (16%). Median age: 33.

companies, but House and Senate negotiators agreed not to change existing law.

Everett told the House that a private helicopter remanufacturing company in his district has tried repeatedly to bid on depot-level maintenance for Army Blackhawk helicopters. "But the 40 percent share set aside for the private sector is nearly fully consumed by fixed-wing work [as opposed to rotary-wing work needed for helicopters] comprised of emptying ashtrays and changing windshield wiper blades," Everett said. "The 60/40 depot-level maintenance policy is archaic and based on a public/private work-sharing arrangement that has no relevance to readiness or military capability. . . . This is not a cogent industrial base policy for our national defense."

As chairman of the Veterans' Affairs Subcommittee on Compensation, Pension Insurance and Memorial Affairs in the 104th, Everett sponsored a bill, passed by the House in July 1996, to make an estimated 2.8 percent cost of living adjustment (COLA) in benefits for 2.2 million veterans with injuries connected to their military service and for 300,000 survivors of veterans who died from service-connected injuries. A typical payment to a moderately disabled veteran, $266 per month, increased about $7 per month, under the bill. In the 105th, Everett chairs the committee's new Oversight and Investigations Subcommittee.

Everett also has been a persistent critic of the computer modernization program at the Department of Veterans Affairs. He said he worried that the VA's program would ultimately cost taxpayers $1.5 billion without offering faster or better service. "We are looking at Veterans Benefits Administration (VBA) waste, which borders on scandal, and the sad thing is our nation's veterans will suffer for this waste and abuse through increasingly lengthy claims processing time and growing VBA inefficiency," Everett said.

Everett is a close follower of the Republicans' anti-tax, pro-spending cuts script, and he consistently votes a conservative line — opposing abortion, supporting a repeal of the ban on certain semiautomatic assault-style weapons and voting to deny public education to illegal immigrants.

He blasted the Democratic Party for criticizing the GOP effort to hold down the rate of spending growth on Medicare, saying, "I believe that there is nothing more abhorrent than using the power of this institution to terrify the elderly, the disabled, and the poor. But the House Democrats are doing just that. While they are well aware that the Medicare program is in a state of crisis, they continue to spout fear and rhetoric."

At Home: Everett began his 1992 House race a virtual unknown and ended it by defeating a man with arguably the most famous name in Alabama politics — state Treasurer George C. Wallace Jr., son of the former governor and presidential candidate. An insurgent within his own party, Everett claimed the GOP nomination by defeating a state senator who was the choice of the party establishment.

Everett proved to have a winning combination of message and means. Starting out poor, he made a fortune in business, and in his House campaign he spent hundreds of thousands of dollars of his own money blanketing the district in billboards and radio and TV ads blaring: "Send a message, not a politician." Everett refused contributions from PACs in his 1992 campaign and said he would work to do away with PACs if elected.

In rhetoric that echoed that of independent presidential candidate Ross Perot, Everett denounced gridlock in Washington, pointed to his success building businesses and appealed to voters to back him "for the sake of your children."

Everett denounced Wallace as a representative of the Old Guard who was weaned in the corridors of power. To distinguish himself further, he said that instead of accepting a recent congressional pay raise, he would donate the money to local high school seniors to help them pay for college.

In the end, Everett won with a bare plurality of 49 percent. Wallace won his home county of Barbour and made a strong showing in rural areas, but he lost in two more populous urban centers at opposite ends of the district, Houston County (Dothan) and the city of Montgomery.

With that tough campaign behind him, Everett has had no trouble winning re-election.

HOUSE ELECTIONS

1996 General		
Terry Everett (R)	132,563	(63%)
Bob E. Gaines (D)	74,317	(35%)
Michael Probst (LIBERT)	2,653	(1%)
1994 General		
Terry Everett (R)	124,465	(74%)
Brian Dowling (D)	44,694	(26%)

Previous Winning Percentages: 1992 (49%)

CAMPAIGN FINANCE

	Receipts	Receipts from PACs		Expend-itures
1996				
Everett (R)	$818,229	$173,741	(21%)	$983,814
Gaines (D)	$171,212	$45,500	(27%)	$171,208
1994				
Everett (R)	$371,419	$121,269	(33%)	$224,606
Dowling (D)	$22,789	$2,000	(9%)	$22,742

DISTRICT VOTE FOR PRESIDENT

	1996		1992
D	81,520 (37%)	**D**	82,550 (35%)
R	122,099 (56%)	**R**	124,272 (53%)
I	12,727 (6%)	**I**	27,377 (12%)

KEY VOTES

1997	
Ban "partial birth" abortions	Y
1996	
Approve farm bill	Y
Deny public education to illegal immigrants	Y
Repeal ban on certain assault-style weapons	Y
Increase minimum wage	N
Freeze defense spending	N
Approve welfare overhaul	Y
1995	
Approve balanced-budget constitutional amendment	Y
Relax Clean Water Act regulations	Y
Oppose limits on environmental regulations	N
Reduce projected Medicare spending	Y
Approve GOP budget with tax and spending cuts	Y

VOTING STUDIES

	Presidential Support		Party Unity		Conservative Coalition	
Year	**S**	**O**	**S**	**O**	**S**	**O**
1996	34	66	94	5	100	0
1995	19	81	96	3	99	1
1994	44	55	79	20	97	3
1993	32	68	95	4	86	14

INTEREST GROUP RATINGS

Year	ADA	AFL-CIO	CCUS	ACU
1996	5	n/a	94	100
1995	0	8	100	92
1994	0	33	75	100
1993	10	25	91	96

3 Bob Riley (R)

Of Ashland — Elected 1996, 1st term

Biographical Information
Born: Oct. 3, 1944, Ashland, Ala.
Education: U. of Alabama, B.A. 1965.
Occupation: Auto dealer; trucking company executive; farmer.
Family: Wife, Patsy Adams; four children.
Religion: Baptist.
Political Career: Ashland city council, 1972-76; candidate for mayor of Ashland, 1976.
Capitol Office: 510 Cannon Bldg. 20515; 225-3261.

Committees
Banking & Financial Services
Capital Markets, Securities & Government Sponsored Enterprises; General Oversight & Investigations
National Security
Military Readiness; Military Research & Development

The Path to Washington: With the GOP compass now pointing "true South," in certain respects Riley is a prototypical modern Republican. He hails from the South, shies from the label of "career politician" and is deeply conservative on both social and fiscal issues.

Repeating a pattern seen throughout the South in recent years, Riley in 1996 won a historically Democratic seat vacated by Glen Browder, who ran unsuccessfully for the Democratic Senate nomination.

Like many traditional conservatives, Riley says that providing for the national defense should be the central concern of the federal government. He will be able to ply that philosophy from a seat on the National Security Committee. He also serves on the Banking Committee.

The military has been a major source of jobs in the district, but Fort McClellan, which appeared on the base closure list in 1995, is slated to be shut down by 1999. The district's other facility, the Anniston Army Depot, traditionally has to fight for its workload.

A number of district jobs have also been lost in recent years due to plant closings, and concern about job flight abroad has led Riley to criticize NAFTA. He lists a balanced federal budget as his top priority, and he also favors an across-the-board cut in tax rates. He favors eliminating the Department of Education and supports most efforts to give states more power.

Riley has no military experience himself, but he has performed numerous other types of work. He owns a car dealership and a trucking company; he has also raised cattle and sold commercial and residential real estate.

Riley got entangled with one of his six primary opponents, businessman B.B. Comer, over the question of whether he had ever previously sought office. Comer ran a television ad taking issue with Riley's claims to political purity, because Riley had served on the Ashland City Council during the 1970s and lost a mayoral race as well. Riley explained that he meant he had never run for an office equivalent to Congress.

Since all the candidates hewed to a uniformly conservative line, they sought to draw attention to themselves using gimmickry, including nicknames and a campaigning 9,300-pound elephant.

But Riley separated himself from the other contenders — including Comer, who forced Riley into a runoff — through old-fashioned means: raising money and stumping the district tirelessly. A devout Christian, he refused to campaign on Sundays.

Riley drew much of his grass-roots support during the 1996 campaign from conservative Christian activists who liked his strong positions on social and cultural issues. He opposes abortion and supports voluntary prayer in schools. Riley opposes homosexuals serving in the military and a law granting unpaid family and medical leave to workers.

He is right in line with Republican thinking on certain other prominent issues, such as term limits, which he supports. Riley, who agreed with the GOP wisdom in the 104th Congress that sought to achieve balance in the federal budget by slowing the growth of many domestic programs, felt no need to distance himself from Speaker Newt Gingrich and the House GOP agenda. Gingrich and former Vice President Dan Quayle both stumped for Riley.

Riley's Democratic opponent, state Sen. Ted Little, tried to tie Riley to the less popular aspects of that agenda, particularly the notion of slowing Medicare's growth. But Little did not fully embrace the national Democratic platform himself, referring to himself as an "independent Democrat."

Riley was able to pin Little down by mocking his efforts to fashion himself as a fiscal conservative. Riley also tied Little to the issue of high-profile jury decisions in tort trials, blaming Little for the failure of a GOP tort overhaul bill to pass the Alabama Senate. In the end, Riley won the seat by 4 percentage points — 51 percent to 47 percent.

ALABAMA 3
East — Anniston; Auburn

The 3rd District is a 14-county amalgam of defense facilities, high-tech businesses, universities, textile mills and poor rural communities. But it lacks a single defining characteristic. Politically, it is conservative Democratic territory that is prone to support Republicans for governor and president.

Anniston, the Calhoun County seat and one of the largest cities in the district with a population of 26,600, is home to two huge military facilities: Anniston Army Depot, the district's largest employer, and Fort McClellan.

Fort McClellan, which houses the Chemical Decontamination Training Facility, was on the 1991 and 1993 lists of defense bases recommended for closure. It was reprieved both times when its supporters convinced the base-closing commission that it was the only place where the United States and its allies can train soldiers using active but non-lethal chemical weapons. But McClellan again appeared on the Pentagon's 1995 list, and it is scheduled to close by October 1999.

Calhoun County has not staked its future on the perpetual presence of Fort McClellan. Area business and civic leaders in 1982 joined to form Forward Calhoun County, an economic development program aimed at promoting diversification by attracting new industry to help the area mitigate the loss of Fort McClellan.

More than half the 3rd's population is contained in its four most populous counties: Calhoun, Lee, Talladega and St. Clair. Bob Dole won all four counties in the 1996 presidential election. Auburn (Lee County) is home to Auburn University, the state's largest, with about 21,000 students. The first Sunday in May, racing fans flock to the Talladega Superspeedway for the Winston 500.

St. Clair grew by 21 percent during the 1980s, swelled by people who work in Birmingham and Calhoun County. St. Clair is Republican terrain. Riley received 64 percent of the vote in St. Clair, and his 6,223-vote margin there exceeded his winning overall margin of 6,028 votes. Dole received 62 percent in St. Clair in 1996.

The 3rd still contains a thriving textile industry. The Russell Corp., with headquarters in Alexander City (Tallapoosa County), makes uniforms for professional football teams. The cotton and dairy industries have waned as farmers have turned to growing pine trees on their farmland and supplementing their income by raising poultry and catfish.

Macon is the only county in the 3rd with a black majority (86 percent) and it has the second-highest black percentage of any county in the country. (Jefferson County, Miss., is first.) Macon has had a long history of racial and economic troubles. The county seat, Tuskegee, was at the center of a 1960 landmark Supreme Court ruling striking down a racial gerrymander (*Gomillion v. Lightfoot*). Tuskegee University, founded in 1881 through the efforts of Booker T. Washington, was one of the nation's first black colleges. Macon traditionally ranks among the most Democratic counties in the country. Bill Clinton won 86 percent of the Macon County vote in 1996.

1990 Population: 577,227. White 422,187 (73%), Black 149,922 (26%), Other 5,118 (1%). Hispanic origin 3,442 (<1%). 18 and over 429,511 (74%), 62 and over 89,951 (16%). Median age: 32.

HOUSE ELECTIONS

1996 General		
Bob Riley (R)	98,353	(51%)
T.D. "Ted" Little (D)	92,325	(47%)
Lucy Lawrence (NL)	2,335	(1%)
1996 Primary Runoff		
Bob Riley (R)	9,124	(64%)
B.B. Comer (R)	5,163	(36%)
1996 Primary		
Bob Riley (R)	7,978	(39%)
B.B. Comer (R)	4,069	(20%)
Ben Hand (R)	2,360	(12%)
Jack Sexton (R)	2,202	(11%)
Rick Hagans (R)	1,643	(8%)
Don Sledge (R)	1,275	(6%)
Joe "Nobody" Magee (R)	692	(3%)

CAMPAIGN FINANCE

	Receipts	Receipts from PACs		Expend-itures
1996				
Riley (R)	$861,425	$247,899	(29%)	$868,833
Little (D)	$804,886	$288,226	(36%)	$799,043

DISTRICT VOTE FOR PRESIDENT

	1996		1992
D	88,511 (44%)	**D**	92,142 (42%)
R	98,289 (49%)	**R**	105,034 (48%)
I	13,184 (7%)	**I**	23,772 (11%)

KEY VOTES

1997

Ban "partial birth" abortions Y

4 Robert B. Aderholt (R)

Of Haleyville — Elected 1996, 1st term

Biographical Information

Born: July 22, 1965, Haleyville, Ala.

Education: Birmingham Southern U., B.A. 1987; Samford U., J.D. 1990.

Occupation: Municipal judge; lawyer; gubernatorial aide.

Family: Wife, Caroline.

Religion: Protestant.

Political Career: Republican nominee for Ala. House, 1990.

Capitol Office: 1007 Longworth Bldg. 20515; 225-4876.

Committees

Appropriations

District of Columbia; Transportation; Treasury, Postal Service & General Government

The Path to Washington: Hesitant of manner and soft-spoken, Aderholt holds to certain dominant Republican ideals with an unshakable grip. During his 1996 campaign, he acknowledged that he was not fully up to speed on all the issues awaiting him in Washington — but he made a proud point of saying that he knew where he stood on those that mattered to him.

Aderholt, the youngest Republican freshman, is in line with his party's program of fiscal austerity. But as much as he desires a balanced budget, promoting conservative social-issue policies is paramount in Aderholt's scheme of things.

He favors a constitutional ban on abortions, except to save the life of the woman. His campaign biography boasted of his fight to preserve the GOP platform's anti-abortion plank as a delegate to the 1992 convention.

He is also an unstinting supporter of the rights of gun owners, and he would like to see a law specifically protecting voluntary school prayer. Aderholt says that Alabamians overcome their political differences in the act of bowing their heads at the dinner table.

In March 1997, the House passed by a 295-125 vote an Aderholt-sponsored resolution that said "public display, including display in government offices and courthouses, of the Ten Commandments should be permitted." A judge in Aderholt's district had been ordered to remove a copy of the Ten Commandments from his courtroom.

His conservative views on social issues earned him campaign appearances by former Vice President Dan Quayle and Speaker Newt Gingrich, along with most of the other Republican House leaders.

Democrat Tom Bevill had represented the district for 15 terms, after two years of Republican reign after the "Goldwater sweep" of 1964.

Aderholt said he was drawn to the race by a belief that the district shared certain demographic characteristics with the neighboring 1st District of Mississippi, which also had long been held by a Democrat but which proved fertile for a GOP takeover when the seat opened up in 1994.

In the general election, Aderholt narrowly defeated former state Sen. Bob Wilson Jr., who embraced a similarly conservative platform on social issues, although Wilson was not as ardent as Aderholt in his opposition to gay rights.

Voters rejected Wilson's thesis that the district needed a Democrat with a spending philosophy in line with that of Bevill, who guided federal dollars to the rural and largely poor district during 25 years on the Appropriations Committee, much of that time as chairman of the Energy and Water Development subcommittee.

Aderholt is one of just two Republican freshmen serving on Appropriations (the other is Anne M. Northup of Kentucky). But he insists that his constituents would rather keep their money through a tax cut than have the government spend more on projects in the district. During his campaign, he even floated the idea that the federal government take a five-year break from building or acquiring new property. Aderholt makes an exception for Corridor X, a highway project that has linked the district to Memphis and is scheduled to extend south to Birmingham.

"I'm going to fight for what we ought to get for this district," Aderholt told The New York Times in July 1996.

Appointed to serve his hometown of Haleyville as a municipal court judge, Aderholt took a leave from his job on Republican Gov. Fob James Jr.'s legal staff to make his congressional run. He lost a bid for the state House in 1990, for which he was nominated just a month after graduating from law school.

Aderholt comes from a political family. He recalls being taken as an 11-year-old to meet Kansas Republican Sen. Bob Dole, who was then running for vice president, at a fundraiser. His father is a circuit court judge and his father-in-law is a former state agriculture commissioner who ran unsuccessfully for Congress in 1990.

ALABAMA 4
North Central — Gadsden

With fewer blacks and more unionized workers, the 4th has a different character from districts farther south. The 14-county stripe across northern Alabama has mine workers in the west, light and heavy industry in the east, and poultry farms throughout.

The 4th has a long populist Democratic heritage; the only district with a more reliably Democratic vote is the majority-black 7th. The "common man" rhetoric of former Gov. James E. Folsom Sr. (who grew up in the 4th's Cullman County) always played well in this region. And Folsom's son, James Jr., swept all but one county in the district in his unsuccessful gubernatorial run in 1994.

There is a GOP presence in the 4th dating back to the Civil War. Winston County actually seceded briefly from Alabama when the state seceded from the Union and became the "free state of Winston." Bob Dole received 55 percent of Winston's vote in 1996, as did George Bush in 1992.

The district's only sizable city is Gadsden, an industrial center of 42,500 people in Etowah County. Gadsden's economic base is still dependent on textiles and heavy industries, but it has diversified a bit in recent years. Goodyear Tire and Rubber Co. and Gulf States Steel remain local mainstays. Tyson Foods employs 1,300 in the area, and Delphi Packard Electric, a maker of automotive electrical parts, opened a facility in 1995. Gadsden's other major industrial employers, Mid-South Industries and its subsidiary, Emco, turn out a diverse range of products, including toasters, fryers and handguns as well as components for mines, bombs and torpedoes.

The district's largest concentration of Democrats are in the Gadsden area; the city has a 28 percent black population.Bill Clinton carried Etowah with 48 percent of the vote in 1996.

The textile and apparel industries have been in decline for several years throughout the South, afflicted by cheap imports and financially weak companies. The effect has been felt across the 4th. Counties dependent on textile jobs, such as Marion in the western part of the district, saw their unemployment levels hit double digits in the late 1980s and early 1990s before declining.

The 4th has one of the biggest concentrations of poultry farms and processors in the country. Cullman is one of the top counties in the nation in sales of broilers. De Kalb, Marshall and Blount counties are also major chicken-producing counties.

De Kalb also has a large textile presence. The county seat, Fort Payne, calls itself the "Sock Capital of the World." Ten million dozen pairs of socks are made per week in Fort Payne's hosiery mills. Fort Payne is also home to the popular country music group Alabama.

Coal has been mined in the western part of the 4th for generations, and the United Mine Workers exerts a strong influence for Democratic candidates. In 1996, Clinton carried five of the district's seven westernmost counties. But Dole's and Aderholt's decisive margins in the central counties of Cullman and Marshall propelled the Republicans to narrow victories.

1990 Population: 577,227. White 534,038 (93%), Black 38,020 (7%), Other 5,169 (1%). Hispanic origin 2,188 (<1%). 18 and over 432,149 (75%) 62 and over 102,196 (18%). Median age: 35.

HOUSE ELECTIONS

1996 General		
Robert B. Aderholt (R)	102,741	(50%)
Robert T. "Bob" Wilson (D)	99,250	(48%)
Alan Barksdale (LIBERT)	3,718	(2%)
1996 Primary		
Robert B. Aderholt (R)	10,410	(49%)
Kerry Rich (R)	5,860	(27%)
Barry Guess (R)	2,434	(11%)
Mickey Moseley (R)	1,596	(7%)
Ronny Branham (R)	1,021	(5%)

CAMPAIGN FINANCE

	Receipts	Receipts from PACs		Expend-itures
1996				
Aderholt (R)	$779,046	$182,472	(23%)	$763,117
Wilson (D)	$1,023,914	$190,950	(19%)	$1,023,515

DISTRICT VOTE FOR PRESIDENT

	1996		1992
D	92,031 (43%)	D	104,557 (44%)
R	101,876 (48%)	R	107,087 (45%)
I	17,743 (8%)	I	28,565 (12%)

KEY VOTES

1997

Ban "partial birth" abortions Y

5 Robert E. 'Bud' Cramer (D)

Of Huntsville — Elected 1990, 4th term

Biographical Information
Born: Aug. 22, 1947, Huntsville, Ala.
Education: U. of Alabama, B.A. 1969, J.D. 1972.
Military Service: Army, 1972; Army Reserve, 1976-78.
Occupation: Lawyer.
Family: Widowed; one child.
Religion: Methodist.
Political Career: Madison County district attorney, 1981-91.
Capitol Office: 2416 Rayburn Bldg. 20515; 225-4801.

Committees
Science
Space & Aeronautics (ranking)
Transportation & Infrastructure
Aviation; Surface Transportation

In Washington: Cramer's stout and successful defense of NASA's space station combined with a centrist voting record helped him withstand hard Republican charges in 1994 and 1996. His opponent both times was well-funded and well-connected Wayne Parker, son-in-law of Ways and Means Committee Chairman Bill Archer of Texas. Cramer managed just 50 percent of the vote in 1994, and Republicans felt sure they could capture the 5th in 1996, just as they have taken numerous other traditionally Democratic Southern districts in recent years.

But Cramer's carefully balanced voting record in the 104th Congress made it hard for Parker to peg him as a liberal, and with space-station work progressing and the overall economy humming along, Parker found it difficult to stir voters to anger. Cramer won the rematch with 56 percent.

Cramer is the ranking Democrat on the Science Committee's Space and Aeronautics Subcommittee, and from there he watches out for America's space program, an economic pillar in the 5th District, home to the Marshall Space Flight Center. Marshall builds the pressurized modules that space station astronauts would live in while conducting experiments. Cramer vigorously defends the space station against critics who say it is a waste of money.

The critics were flying high in 1993: The House by just one vote (215-216) rejected an amendment to kill it. Heading into the 1994 funding battle, even some prominent space station supporters, such as then-Science Committee Chairman George E. Brown Jr., D-Calif., seemed less than confident. This troubled Cramer, who said, "We're going to lead this charge, and I still think we can win the battle." After NASA downsized the project and enlisted more international cooperation (and funding), Congress gave it a go-ahead.

When Republicans took control in the 104th, space station supporters wondered how the big new crop of deficit-conscious GOP freshmen would feel about the big-ticket project. Cramer girded for battle, and, citing previous failed attempts to kill the station, said, "It's time for us to get off NASA's back."

As it turned out, the GOP leadership was foursquare behind the project. Attempts to eliminate space station funding failed 132-287 in 1995 and 127-286 in 1996, and in April 1997, a 112-305 House vote seemed to indicate that the station's toughest battles were behind it.

Cramer got a scare in July 1995, when an Appropriations subcommittee recommended cutting NASA funding by eliminating three space centers — including Marshall, along with centers in Maryland and Virginia. Cramer said the proposal threatened the space station's coalition of support, and warned that he would reconsider voting for the station if Marshall were eliminated. Speaker Newt Gingrich and other top GOP leaders weighed in, and the Appropriations Committee restored funding for the space centers, instead cutting NASA programs not popular with Republicans, like global warming research.

Cramer's voting record is a blend of conservative stands and more moderate ones. In the 103rd Congress, he supported a balanced-budget constitutional amendment and opposed two gun control measures strongly backed by President Clinton. But he backed Clinton on some high-profile votes — notably the crime bill in 1994 and Clinton's 1993 budget, which raised taxes.

In 1995, he said he favored welfare overhaul proposals put forward by moderate "blue dog" Democrats, which fused some of the stricter elements of Republican proposals with Democratic calls for more funding for child care. But Cramer was one of just nine Democrats to vote for the Republicans' first (and most hard-line) attempt to redo the welfare system. (Several of those nine Democrats subsequently switched parties.)

In the debate on immigration law overhaul, he supported a proposal pushed by Republicans to deny public education to illegal immigrants. Also in the 105th, he voted to repeal the ban on certain semiautomatic assault-style weapons, and he supported banning a particular abortion technique that opponents call "partial birth" abortion.

ALABAMA 5
North — Huntsville

Space- and defense-related growth radiating from Huntsville has spurred the boom that made the 5th the fastest-growing district in the state during the 1980s, with a nearly 10 percent population gain. The Defense Department, NASA and the Tennessee Valley Authority (TVA) have helped cushion the 5th's economy from recession. The federal government is the district's largest employer.

With just under 160,000 people, Huntsville, the seat of Madison County, is the state's fourth-largest city. It went from cotton town to boom town during World War II when the Army built the Redstone Arsenal to produce chemical-warfare material. After the Soviet Union launched Sputnik in October 1957, Wernher von Braun headed the Marshall Space Flight Center to perform the principal research for the fledgling NASA.

Companies that built plants here — Boeing, IBM and General Electric among them — stayed and diversified when the high-tech government contracts dwindled; other industries moved in. Computer giant Intergraph Corp. has its headquarters here. Chrysler employs about 3,000 at an assembly plant.

As Huntsville has grown, businesses and people have moved out of the city and into surrounding Madison County; Intergraph has built a facility in Madison. SCI Systems employs about 5,000. The city of Madison's population more than tripled during the 1980s (it is now 22,000). Madison County grew by 21 percent, fourth-fastest in the state, in the 1980s.

Huntsville's federal installations and active labor unions in the metals, automobile and chemical plants along the Tennessee River provide a Democratic base.

Led by recent Republican gains in Madison County, the 5th was one of 14 southern congressional districts that voted for Bob Dole for president in 1996 while sending a Democrat to the House. Cramer improved on his razor-thin 1994 victory to win by a more comfortable 56 percent to 42 percent over his GOP opponent. But like many districts in the Deep South, the 5th is becoming more Republican; it has voted for the GOP in the last four presidential elections.

Downstream from Huntsville along the Tennessee, blue-collar jobs begin to predominate. Towns such as Decatur, a chemical manufacturing center, and the Quad Cities of Florence, Sheffield, Tuscumbia and Muscle Shoals came into being as a result of the TVA. Tuscumbia is the birthplace of Helen Keller. Blues pioneer W. C. Handy was born in Florence; an annual jazz and blues festival celebrates Florence's native son. Logging dominates in the rural eastern part of the district.

The TVA has two huge nuclear complexes in the 5th — Browns Ferry at Athens and Bellefonte at Scottsboro. Before Three Mile Island, a 1975 fire at Browns Ferry had been considered the nation's worst nuclear accident. The plant was closed from 1975 to 1977, and again in 1985. After a six-year shutdown, one of Browns Ferry's three reactors began operation again in 1991.

1990 Population: 577,227. White 481,509 (83%), Black 85,945 (15%), Other 9,773 (2%). Hispanic origin 4,549 (<1%). 18 and over 433,310 (75%), 62 and over 79,672 (14%). Median age: 33.

However, Cramer sided with abortion-rights activists on several issues in the 104th, voting to permit abortions at overseas military hospitals, to allow federal employees' health care plans to cover abortions and to maintain a requirement that states fund Medicaid abortions for poor women in cases of rape, incest or to save the life of the woman. He also voted with the majority of Democrats to raise the minimum wage and to block a GOP effort to allow companies to offer workers comp time in lieu of overtime pay,

As his support for the space station indicates, Cramer is willing to look to the federal government to provide an economic boost to his district. He also keeps an eye out for the 5th from the Transportation and Infrastructure Committee, where he has the No. 3 Democratic seat on the Surface Transportation Subcommittee, which in the 105th is working on a reauthorization bill funding road, public transit and other transportation projects.

Since the New Deal era, federal programs have helped dramatically improve living standards in North Alabama. Two federal agencies of particular importance in the region — the Tennessee Valley Authority (TVA) and the Appalachian Regional Commission — were both targeted for elimination in 1995 by an amendment to the spending bill funding energy and water programs. Cramer said they had already sustained significant cuts at the committee level, making further reductions excessive.

Of the TVA, he said, "This amendment does not speak to other alternate ways for us to run those almost 50 dams. This amendment does not talk about the flood control issues that our region of the country would be saddled with. . . . This amendment ensures that rural communities in the Tennessee Valley will lose access to a variety of information sources, including education, health care, and business opportunities."

Cramer also expressed concern in the 104th when a science authorization bill proposed eliminating many facilities operated by the National

Weather Service, including the one in Cramer's district. Cramer said the closings could delay the issuing of warnings about tornadoes or other dangers, and he offered an amendment to require the weather service to certify that an area's safety would not be degraded by closing a center.

"Do not use our citizens as guinea pigs," he pleaded on the House floor. "Do not, just for the sake of balancing the budget . . . risk our citizens' lives. I have had people sitting in church who were blown away by tornadoes, and I cannot stand here and let the gentleman say this is simply a budget issue."

Cramer came to Congress with a strong interest in working to protect abused children. He supports federal grants to fund creation of programs modeled on the Children's Advocacy Center in Huntsville, which he established during his tenure as a prosecutor in Madison County. The center offers shelter and counseling to abused children.

At Home: After Cramer's narrow 1994 victory over Parker, the Democrat was considered one of the nation's most vulnerable incumbents in 1996. Parker's confidence was reflected in one of his ads, in which an elderly woman held up a piece of toast and said, "Bud Cramer, you're toast."

But Cramer's voting record provided cover from many of Parker's attacks, and the generally good state of the economy took tempered the anti-Clinton sentiment that had aided Parker in 1994. Republican presidential nominee Bob Dole carried the 5th, but with an unremarkable 49 percent, just six points ahead of Clinton. Cramer's solid victory left him the only white Democrat in the Alabama House delegation, due to the departures of colleagues Glen Browder and Tom Bevill.

In 1994, Parker sought to tie Cramer as closely as possible to Clinton by highlighting his support for the president's 1993 budget and 1994 crime bill.

Cramer reminded voters of his efforts to save the space station and to promote job creation. He recounted his diverse resume, which included a decade as Madison County (Huntsville) district attorney. And he mounted a blistering personal attack against Parker, intimating that if elected, Parker might be a pawn of his powerful father-in-law, especially in the battle for federal space dollars between Huntsville and the Houston area that Archer represents.

In the end, Cramer's margin of victory was the narrowest of any House winner in the Deep South. It stood in sharp contrast to his first two House races, both of which he won easily.

When seven-term Democratic Rep. Ronnie G. Flippo ran for governor in 1990, Cramer was well-positioned to seek the open 5th. Coupled with his strong base in the district's most populous county and an ample campaign treasury, Cramer ran far ahead of the crowded Democratic primary field, taking 44 percent of the vote. In the runoff, state Public Service Commissioner Lynn Greer tried to paint Cramer as an upscale city slicker and liberal "national Democrat," but Cramer won handily. He took 67 percent that November, and 66 percent in 1992.

HOUSE ELECTIONS

1996 General		
Robert E. "Bud" Cramer (D)	114,442	(56%)
Wayne Parker (R)	86,727	(42%)
Shirley Madison (NL)	2,484	(1%)
1994 General		
Robert E. "Bud" Cramer (D)	88,693	(50%)
Wayne Parker (R)	86,923	(49%)

Previous Winning Percentages: 1992 (66%) **1990** (67%)

CAMPAIGN FINANCE

	Receipts	Receipts from PACs	Expend-itures
1996			
Cramer (D)	$983,293	$428,051 (44%)	$1,006,341
Parker (R)	$882,970	$0 (0%)	$886,648
1994			
Cramer (D)	$549,632	$291,550 (53%)	$565,457
Parker (R)	$436,787	$914 (0%)	$430,822

DISTRICT VOTE FOR PRESIDENT

1996	1992
D 98,006 (43%)	**D** 102,124 (41%)
R 111,416 (49%)	**R** 110,256 (44%)
I 18,348 (8%)	**I** 36,918 (15%)

INTEREST GROUP RATINGS

Year	ADA	AFL-CIO	CCUS	ACU
1996	40	n/a	63	55
1995	45	67	71	52
1994	40	78	58	38
1993	45	83	18	38
1992	55	58	50	44
1991	40	83	40	40

KEY VOTES

1997	
Ban "partial-birth" abortions	Y
1996	
Approve farm bill	Y
Deny public education to illegal immigrants	Y
Repeal ban on certain assault-style weapons	Y
Increase minimum wage	Y
Freeze defense spending	N
Approve welfare overhaul	Y
1995	
Approve balanced-budget constitutional amendment	Y
Relax Clean Water Act regulations	Y
Oppose limits on environmental regulations	N
Reduce projected Medicare spending	N
Approve GOP budget with tax and spending cuts	N

VOTING STUDIES

	Presidential Support		Party Unity		Conservative Coalition	
Year	S	O	S	O	S	O
1996	65	35	59	41	98	2
1995	55	44	54	44	95	5
1994	85	14	78	19	94	3
1993	82	17	79	21	91	9
1992	39	58	75	23	81	15
1991	38	61	77	22	89	11

6 Spencer Bachus (R)

Of Birmingham — Elected 1992, 3rd term

Biographical Information

Born: Dec. 28, 1947, Birmingham, Ala.

Education: Auburn U., B.A. 1969; U. of Alabama, J.D. 1972.

Military Service: National Guard, 1969-71.

Occupation: Lawyer; manufacturer.

Family: Wife, Linda Hinson; three children, two stepchildren.

Religion: Baptist.

Political Career: Ala. Senate, 1983; Ala. House, 1983-87; Ala. Board of Education, 1987-91; candidate for Ala. attorney general, 1990; Ala. Republican Party chairman, 1991-92.

Capitol Office: 442 Cannon Bldg. 20515; 225-4921.

Committees

Banking & Financial Services
Capital Markets, Securities & Government Sponsored Enterprises; General Oversight & Investigations (chairman)

Transportation & Infrastructure
Railroads; Surface Transportation

Veterans' Affairs
Health

In Washington: Bachus' conservative voting record is in step with his constituency, which is one of the most Republican in the country. On the Banking Committee in the 103rd Congress, he was one of the earliest GOP freshmen to gain attention for demanding a congressional inquiry into the Whitewater real estate dealings of Bill and Hillary Rodham Clinton. When Republicans won control of the House in 1994, Bachus benefited handsomely, assuming the chairman's gavel on the Banking Subcommittee on General Oversight and Investigations.

With that responsibility as a major focus of his efforts in the 104th, Bachus was more active investigating agencies than he was in introducing legislation. He was a persistent critic of President Clinton's policies toward Mexico, and he won a fair amount of attention with a resolution offered at the very end of the 104th that called on Clinton to pledge that he would not pardon former associates convicted in Whitewater-related trials.

Bachus claimed Democrats were so fearful of his resolution that they were willing to block a last-minute spending bill, and so partially shut down the government, if his pardon measure was brought to a floor vote. Republican leaders eventually withdrew the resolution, pointing to a letter signed by more than 200 members that carried Bachus' message. Republicans said that had the same effect as a resolution.

Bachus defied GOP leaders in his opposition to a Clinton administration package that shored up the weakening Mexican peso. He accused the administration of "playing games" in refusing to hand over its records relating to the $20 billion plan; he threatened to subpoena the records, arguing that the administration was not providing them as swiftly as required by a House resolution.

Bachus especially was angered by Treasury Secretary Robert E. Rubin's active role in the process, saying that the former Goldman, Sachs head should have recused himself since the brokerage house had a direct financial stake in keeping Mexican securities solvent.

"You can't forget who you are or where you came from," Bachus said. "Obviously, it was a serious misjudgment and conflict of interest for [Rubin] to be given the keys to the U.S. Treasury" in assisting Mexico.

Bachus' subcommittee in the 104th earned the distinction of being the first Republican-controlled House panel to issue a subpoena in 40 years. Bachus called on 10 current or former Resolution Trust Corporation (RTC) employees, who had been balking at his inquiry, to testify as to why the agency had such a poor record recovering funds from failed Texas thrifts.

As a freshman, Bachus had been a persistent critic of the RTC, complaining about "excessive compensation" to employees of the federal agency, which handles the savings and loan cleanup. The RTC said it had to offer higher pay than other government agencies to attract the experienced hands required for the complex task of closing out insolvent thrifts. When the House in 1993 debated appropriating an additional $18.6 billion for the RTC, Bachus said that, given budget pressures, there was "no justification" for higher pay and bonuses. "The RTC has been arrogant, loud, pushy and unapologetic in its pursuit of compensation and benefits greater than other government and private-sector employers," he complained.

Bachus also conducted hearings on the question of contracting with companies associated with the Nation of Islam to provide security in some public housing projects, and his subcommittee looked into the counterfeiting of U.S. currency in Iran. "Every time we have witnessed a terrorist act throughout this world, we can know that they have probably used counterfeit currency to fund their operations," he surmised.

He investigated claims that National Credit Union Administration examiners were used to promote a conference the agency was holding and to solicit funds from institutions that they audited. "This is like a state trooper stopping a motorist on the highway and asking for a contribution to the policemen's ball," Bachus quipped.

Alabama Republicans were elated with 1992 redistricting, and the 6th was a major reason they were so happy. The map adopted by a three-judge federal panel was a slightly modified version of a plan that had been drawn by a GOP state senator.

Redistricting placed most of Birmingham's black voters in a new, majority-black 7th, a move that helped produce a 6th District that is 90 percent white and heavily Republican. Its voters in 1992 traded in Democratic Rep. Ben Erdreich for GOP challenger Bachus.

The intensity of the district's GOP vote is striking. In 1988, George Bush won the areas that make up the 6th with 76 percent, a mark topped by only one other district in the country: Bush's home in Houston. In 1992, Bush won here with more than 60 percent. Four years later, Bob Dole beat Bill Clinton here by 67 percent to 28 percent — his best district nationwide.

The largest portion of the 6th's population is in Jefferson County, where Birmingham is moving away from its image as a declining steel town toward one as a financial center. AmSouth, Central Bank of the South and Southtrust are among the large banks with headquarters in Birmingham.

Most of the city was placed in the 7th, although Birmingham's symbol, a cast-iron statue of Vulcan, the Roman god of fire and metalworking, is in the 6th, on the summit of Red Mountain. The 55-foot-tall statue, one of the world's largest iron figures, is a monument to the city's iron industry.

Jefferson County's well-to-do, almost exclusively white, bedroom communities such as Homewood, Mountain Brook and Hoover are home to people who work in Birmingham's business district.

ALABAMA 6
Part of Birmingham and suburbs

According to the 1990 census, Mountain Brook, a city of 19,810, had 38 blacks. Nearly all the Jefferson County suburbs in the 6th are at least 90 percent white. Hoover (95 percent white) and Trussville (99 percent) were the fastest-growing cities in the Birmingham metropolitan area during the 1980s; both more than doubled in population.

South of Jefferson is Shelby County, the most Republican county in the state — and the fastest-growing. Shelby's population increased by 50 percent in the 1980s as Birmingham commuters moved into cities such as Alabaster (which grew by 108 percent during the 1980s) and Pelham (39 percent growth). Shelby was Bush's best Alabama county in 1988 (79 percent) and 1992 (68 percent). Shelby gave 73 percent of its votes to Dole, easily his best showing in the state.

Democratic votes can be tilled from the portion of Tuscaloosa County in the 6th. The city of Tuscaloosa (population 77,800) is split between the 6th and 7th districts. It has an industrial base that includes manufacturers of chemicals, fertilizer and rubber products, but it is more often identified as the home of the University of Alabama (18,500 students). Clinton garnered 35 percent of the votes in the 6th's portion of Tuscaloosa County.

1990 Population: 577,226. White 517,777 (90%), Black 53,309 (9%), Other 6,140 (1%). Hispanic origin 3,211 (<1%). 18 and over 441,662 (77%), 62 and over 85,223 (15%). Median age: 34.

During his 1992 campaign, Bachus made an issue of Democratic Rep. Ben Erdreich's support for the National Endowment for the Arts' (NEA) funding of controversial projects, and in Congress he has kept on beating that drum, seeing many others join in the anti-NEA march after voters in 1994 sent dozens of new conservatives to the House. In 1993, Bachus proposed a measure to prohibit the NEA from funding projects or programs "that depict or describe in a patently offensive way sexual or excretory activities or organs; or depict or describe in a patently offensive way religion or religious symbols."

In 1994, Bachus proposed that the NEA eliminate grants to individual artists and cultural programs — the grants that typically have generated controversy. But that would have entailed a huge NEA funding cut — $92.7 million — and Bachus lost, 132-297. The House later approved a modest trim in NEA funding.

Most of Bachus' positions are consistent with the conservative GOP script. He said the "motor voter" bill Democrats pushed through in the 103rd would result in the registration of "millions of welfare recipients, illegal aliens and taxpayer-funded entitlement program recipients." A skeptic of health reform, he once said he had heard "not one complaint about quality" in talking with constituents about health care.

He wrote a provision in a fiscal 1996 spending bill that blocked the Environmental Protection Agency (EPA) from spending any funds to enforce permit limits or compliance schedules for sewer overflows unless Congress revised the clean water act. His move prevented a court settlement that would have required Jefferson County, Ala., to improve its sewage treatment system; Bachus said he favored cleaning up the affected area, but said his provision provided "a departure from the insane legislation now on the books."

But Bachus sometimes takes stands not normally associated with the right flank of the GOP. He has defended foreign aid, saying it is not a give-away of money that could be used domestically, but a "wise investment" that helps "stabilize the economies of other countries and, therefore, opens up new avenues for exports."

At a hearing in early 1996, when budget tensions between Congress and the Clinton administration were particularly high, Bachus took to task fellow Banking Committee members who lit into Rubin, reminding them of a civility pledge they had signed the week before.

Bachus has seats on a couple of other committees where members typically work in a bipartisan fashion: Transportation and Infrastructure and Veterans' Affairs. Bachus serves on the Surface Transportation Subcommittee, which gives him a ringside seat as members in the 105th work on a massive reauthorization bill funding highways and mass transit systems.

At Home: Bachus benefited handsomely from a 1992 remap that eviscerated Rep. Erdreich's district, transforming his old 6th into a solidly Republican bastion. Erdreich, a five-term moderate with close ties to Birmingham's banking and business communities, waged a million-dollar campaign to keep his job, but he could not overcome the new lines; Bachus won with 52 percent of the vote, and has been easily re-elected since.

At the time of his first House bid, Bachus had been in politics for almost a decade, serving in the state Legislature, on the state Board of Education and then as chairman of the Alabama GOP. Bachus had to fight for his party's nomination, barely finishing first in a four-way primary and then winning a runoff against former state GOP Executive Director Marty Connors.

The cost of that battle left Bachus' campaign at a financial disadvantage in the general election, but the local banking community did not remain entirely in Erdreich's camp, and Bachus was boosted by an endorsement from The Birmingham News, the largest-circulation newspaper in the 6th. Bachus staked out conservative positions on most issues, including a pledge to support term limits that included a personal promise not to serve more than eight years in the House.

HOUSE ELECTIONS

1996 General		
Spencer Bachus (R)	180,781	(71%)
Mary Lynn Bates (D)	69,592	(27%)
1994 General		
Spencer Bachus (R)	155,047	(79%)
Larry Fortenberry (D)	41,030	(21%)

Previous Winning Percentages: 1992 (52%)

CAMPAIGN FINANCE

	Receipts	Receipts from PACs		Expend-itures
1996				
Bachus (R)	$466,986	$172,385	(37%)	$511,226
Bates (D)	$37,978	$6,950	(18%)	$36,522
1994				
Bachus (R)	$453,345	$184,670	(41%)	$332,233

DISTRICT VOTE FOR PRESIDENT

1996		1992	
D	72,062 (28%)	**D**	77,506 (27%)
R	174,869 (67%)	**R**	180,798 (64%)
I	10,736 (4%)	**I**	26,235 (9%)

KEY VOTES

1997	
Ban "partial birth" abortions	Y
1996	
Approve farm bill	Y
Deny public education to illegal immigrants	Y
Repeal ban on certain assault-style weapons	Y
Increase minimum wage	Y
Freeze defense spending	N
Approve welfare overhaul	Y
1995	
Approve balanced-budget constitutional amendment	Y
Relax Clean Water Act regulations	Y
Oppose limits on environmental regulations	N
Reduce projected Medicare spending	Y
Approve GOP budget with tax and spending cuts	Y

VOTING STUDIES

	Presidential Support		Party Unity		Conservative Coalition	
Year	**S**	**O**	**S**	**O**	**S**	**O**
1996	37	61	92	7	90	2
1995	17	80	95	3	97	2
1994	44	56	91	6	94	3
1993	33	67	96	3	93	5

INTEREST GROUP RATINGS

Year	ADA	AFL-CIO	CCUS	ACU
1996	5	n/a	94	95
1995	0	0	100	92
1994	15	22	82	95
1993	0	0	100	100

7 Earl F. Hilliard (D)

Of Birmingham — Elected 1992, 3rd term

Biographical Information
Born: April 9, 1942, Birmingham, Ala.
Education: Morehouse College, B.A. 1964; Howard U., J.D. 1967; Atlanta U., M.B.A. 1970.
Occupation: Lawyer; insurance broker.
Family: Wife, Mary Franklin; two children.
Religion: Baptist.
Political Career: Ala. House, 1975-81; Ala. Senate, 1981-93.
Capitol Office: 1314 Longworth Bldg. 20515; 225-2665.

Committees
Agriculture
Forestry, Resource Conservation & Research; Livestock, Dairy & Poultry
International Relations
International Economic Policy & Trade; International Operations & Human Rights

In Washington: The first black to serve in Congress from Alabama since Reconstruction, Hilliard busied himself in the 104th with rhetorical flamethrowing at the Republican majority, deriding what he said were GOP assaults on Medicare, education and affirmative action. For the 105th, his colleagues in the Congressional Black Caucus elected him first vice chairman.

In June 1995, Hilliard compared House Speaker Newt Gingrich to Adolf Hitler. "There is a similarity between Newt and Hitler," he told the New York Times. "Hitler started out getting rid of the poor and those he said were a drag on a society, and Newt is starting out the same way. I want to see how far Americans will let him and his young Republican cohorts take them up that ladder." When the House in January 1997 adopted a resolution to reprimand Gingrich for violations of House ethics rules and to fine him $300,000, Hilliard was one of two Democrats to vote against the reprimand. He felt it was not severe enough.

Commenting on Republican efforts to restrain the rate of growth in Medicare spending, Hilliard told the House in November 1995 that "just like the wolf that hid in a sheepskin to kill his prey, so have the Republicans attempted to act as though they were trying to save Medicare." Hilliard said the GOP was willing to strangle the government-backed health care program for the elderly in order to make room in the budget to deliver "to the rich of America the obscene and bloated Republican-sponsored tax break."

He portrayed Republicans as a threat to a variety of education programs, from Head Start to loans and grants to college students. "We know the Republicans do not care about the nation's children, and we also know they do not care about public education," Hilliard said. "After all, most of their kids are in private schools anyway." Defending federal affirmative action programs against attack by conservatives, Hilliard said, "We must not let the Republican angry-white-male syndrome keep others from full participation in the American dream."

Hilliard had a personal run-in with the Republican majority in June 1995, when he complained that he was denied the opportunity to participate in a House floor vote on a GOP proposal to eliminate the Office of Technology Assessment (OTA). As Hilliard and Pennsylvania Democrat Thomas M. Foglietta approached the rostrum intending to vote to preserve the office, the Republican in the chair ended the tally before they could weigh in, and the proposal to kill the office narrowly prevailed.

Furious Democrats threatened to protest by disrupting House floor action. "Yesterday on the floor of this House the voice of freedom was stilled by the forces of repression," Hilliard railed. "The strong arms of the Republican army flexed their mighty parliamentary weight and refused two duly elected members of this body the opportunity to vote before this Congress. In doing so, the Republicans crushed the very voice of democracy," he said. Republican leaders agreed to allow a second vote on the OTA, and that second roll call produced a 220-204 verdict to salvage the office. (Eventually, though, OTA critics succeeded in shutting it down.)

Hilliard's verbal bombardment of the GOP made him a more visible figure in the 104th and played well in his solidly Democratic, black-majority district. But he also earned a dose of unflattering attention when media reports highlighted the number of overseas trips he took at taxpayer expense. Hilliard was declared the No. 1 congressional traveler in a 1995 NBC News report, part of a series titled, "The Fleecing of America." The television program found that he spent 38 days overseas in a single year on six government trips.

Hilliard, who won a seat on the International Relations Committee during the 104th, made no apologies. Campaigning for re-election in his district in 1996, he told The New York Times that his constituents were more anxious about federal budget cuts promised by the Republicans than about his overseas trips. "Honest to goodness, I haven't been apologetic about any of those trips," he said. "Leaders got to be strong. They got to be able to

ALABAMA 7
West Central — Parts of Birmingham, Montgomery and Tuscaloosa

The majority-black 7th is the product of the Voting Rights Act's mandate to increase minority-group representation in the House. In Hilliard, Alabama has its first black member of Congress since Reconstruction.

The district sprawls over all or part of 14 counties, but it is anchored by two population centers: Birmingham and Montgomery. In between are the rural counties of the Black Belt, one of the most economically deprived regions in the nation.

While the term Black Belt is said to refer not to the racial composition but to the rich, cotton-growing soil in rural, west-central Alabama, all but one of the rural counties in the Black Belt portion of the district have black-majority populations. This area is in a perpetual state of poverty; it has not known prosperity since before the Civil War, when cotton plantation owners made fortunes from slave labor.

Seven of the eight counties with the highest poverty rates in Alabama are in the Black Belt portion of the 7th. The poverty rate in Greene, Wilcox and Perry counties was more than 40 percent, according to the 1990 census; the others had rates above 30 percent.

The 7th extends a finger into southwestern Jefferson County (Birmingham), scooping out downtown Birmingham and the majority-black cities of Bessemer and Fairfield. Half the district's black population — and 45 percent of its total population — is in Jefferson County. Reminders of the civil rights struggle that led to the 7th's creation dot the district; it is chronicled at Birmingham's Civil Rights Institute, which opened in 1992.

Four black girls died on Sept. 15, 1963, when the Sixteenth Street Baptist Church in downtown Birmingham was bombed. In March 1965, Selma (Dallas County) was the site of a bloody confrontation between civil rights demonstrators and police when the Rev. Dr. Martin Luther King Jr. led marchers across the Edmund Pettus Bridge. The Civil Rights Memorial in Montgomery commemorates the 40 Americans who died while fighting for civil rights in the 1950s and 1960s.

In an ironic twist, the portion of Montgomery within the black-majority 7th contains the state Capitol, which doubled as the Confederate Capitol from February 1861 to July 1861.

Politically, the 7th is every bit as Democratic as the 6th is Republican. It is far and away the most solidly Democratic district in Alabama, routinely running up two-thirds of the vote or better for the Democratic presidential candidate. In 1996, Bill Clinton won the district by 49 percentage points and carried every county. Hilliard did almost as well, winning by 44 percentage points and losing only one county, Tuscaloosa.

1990 Population: 577,227. White 185,454 (32%), Black 389,796 (68%), Other 1,977 (<1%). Hispanic origin 1,909 (<1%). 18 and over 407,367 (71%), 62 and over 96,220 (17%). Median age: 32.

justify the positions they take."

The 7th District includes some of the poorest rural counties in the country, and Hilliard has used his seat on the Agriculture Committee to speak for struggling farmers. In October 1995 he lashed out at Republican attempts to overhaul federal farm policy when the House considered a budget-reconciliation bill. "The Republicans are treating our farmers like a bunch of ruined chickens, throwing them into the equivalent of the legislative compost heap, to slowly decompose, to rot, to wither and then to simply waste away," he said. In the end, however, he was one of 54 Democrats who voted in February 1996 for the GOP-backed Freedom to Farm bill, which brought federal farm policy more in line with free-market principles. He also voted for a failed Democratic alternative that would have authorized $3.5 billion for rural development, conservation, research, education and extension services and retained existing agriculture supports.

Hilliard is a reliable vote for his party's line on most economic and social issues. But he did buck President Clinton on NAFTA and GATT, and he was one of 56 Democrats voting in March 1996 to repeal the ban on certain semiautomatic assault-style weapons.

A staunch defender of earlier judicial rulings aimed at increasing minority-group representation in the House through redistricting, Hilliard spoke out strongly against the Supreme Court's July 1993 decision in *Shaw v. Reno*, which deemed race-conscious redistricting constitutionally suspect if the districts created had no common interest other than race. Calling into question the majority opinion in the case, Hilliard said, "It is ridiculous, but Justice [Sandra Day] O'Connor wrote, 'Our political system today is a system in which race no longer matters.' She is wrong. Racial problems still confront many of us."

At Home: Years of steady political maneuvering preceded Hilliard's 1993 arrival in Washington. Before running for the House, he served 18 years in the Alabama Legislature, earning a reputation as a player of political hardball willing to try tactics such as seeking a vote on a bill when its opponents were absent from the chamber.

Hilliard won a hard-fought 1992 Democratic contest in the 7th, overcoming accusations of unethical conduct. The Birmingham News endorsed black activist and lawyer Hank Sanders in the Democratic primary and runoff and Republican Kervin Jones in the general election. The paper faulted Hilliard for what it termed ethical lapses, including his use of more than $50,000 in state Senate campaign funds for his business in 1990.

Hilliard had the backing of longtime Birmingham Mayor Richard Arrington, one of the state's most powerful black politicians. Arrington's support was crucial in the fight against Sanders, who through his long work as a civil rights activist had built up a large following of his own in the black community. Arrington's organization, the Jefferson County Citizens' Coalition, helped Hilliard carry the 7th's most populous county by nearly 9,800 votes in the runoff. With that advantage, Hilliard withstood Sanders' near sweep of the district's other counties, and he won nomination by 670 votes. From there, Hilliard fairly breezed into office, trouncing Jones in November with 69 percent of the vote. Hilliard won even more resoundingly in 1994.

In 1996, there was some speculation that superstar Charles Barkley of the NBA's Phoenix Suns might run against Hilliard, but Barkley told Alabama Republicans that he was more interested in running for governor. Hilliard won a third term with more than 70 percent of the vote.

HOUSE ELECTIONS

1996 General		
Earl F. Hilliard (D)	136,651	(71%)
Joe Powell (R)	52,142	(27%)
Ken Hager (LIBERT)	3,157	(2%)
1994 General		
Earl F. Hilliard (D)	116,150	(77%)
Alfred J. Middleton Sr. (R)	34,814	(23%)

Previous Winning Percentages: **1992** (69%)

CAMPAIGN FINANCE

	Receipts	Receipts from PACs		Expend- itures
1996				
Hilliard (D)	$218,582	$170,350	(78%)	$223,582
Powell (R)	$224,413	$6,152	(3%)	$224,029
1994				
Hilliard (D)	$334,130	$257,424	(77%)	$337,772

DISTRICT VOTE FOR PRESIDENT

	1996		1992
D	145,845 (73%)	**D**	137,518 (72%)
R	47,269 (24%)	**R**	46,205 (24%)
I	4,738 (2%)	**I**	8,691 (5%)

KEY VOTES

1997	
Ban "partial birth" abortions	N
1996	
Approve farm bill	Y
Deny public education to illegal immigrants	N
Repeal ban on certain assault-style weapons	Y
Increase minimum wage	Y
Freeze defense spending	Y
Approve welfare overhaul	N
1995	
Approve balanced-budget constitutional amendment	N
Relax Clean Water Act regulations	Y
Oppose limits on environmental regulations	N
Reduce projected Medicare spending	N
Approve GOP budget with tax and spending cuts	-

VOTING STUDIES

	Presidential Support		Party Unity		Conservative Coalition	
Year	S	O	S	O	S	O
1996	80	20	93	7	39	61
1995	77	15	86	9	33	59
1994	69	23	81	6	33	53
1993	75	21	90	6	30	68

INTEREST GROUP RATINGS

Year	ADA	AFL-CIO	CCUS	ACU
1996	85	n/a	31	15
1995	80	100	23	12
1994	80	100	25	29
1993	90	100	9	4

ALASKA

Governor: Tony Knowles (D)
First elected: 1994
Length of term: 4 years
Term expires: 12/98
Salary: $81,648
Term limit: 2 consecutive terms
Phone: (907) 465-3500
Born: January 1, 1943; Tulsa, Okla.
Education: Yale U., B.A. 1968.
Military Service: Army, 1962-65.
Occupation: Restaurateur.
Family: Wife, Susan Morris; three children.
Religion: Roman Catholic.
Political Career: Alaska House, 1975-79; Anchorage mayor, 1982-87; Democratic nominee for Alaska governor, 1990.

Lt. Gov.: Fran Ulmer (D)
First elected: 1994
Length of term: 4 years
Term expires: 12/98
Salary: $76,188
Phone: (907) 465-3520

State election official: (907) 465-4611
Democratic headquarters: (907) 258-3050
Republican headquarters: (907) 276-4467

LEGISLATURE

Bicameral Legislature. Meets January-mid-May, with a limit of 120 calendar days.

Senate: 20 members, 4-year terms
1996 breakdown: 13R, 7D; 17 men, 3 women
Salary: $24,012 per year
Phone: (907) 465-3701

House of Representatives: 40 members, 2-year terms
1996 breakdown: 24R, 16 D, 1 I; 35 men, 5 women
Salary: $24,012 per year
Phone: (907) 465-3725

URBAN STATISTICS

City	Population
Anchorage	226,338
Mayor Rick Mystrom, R	
Fairbanks	30,843
Mayor James Hayes, D	
Juneau	26,751
Mayor Dennis Egan, N-P	

U.S. CONGRESS

Senate: 0 D, 2 R
House: 0 D, 1 R

TERM LIMITS

For state offices: No

ELECTIONS

1996 Presidential Vote

Bob Dole	51%
Bill Clinton	33%
Ross Perot	11%

1992 Presidential Vote

George Bush	39%
Bill Clinton	30%
Ross Perot	28%

1988 Presidential Vote

George Bush	60%
Michael S. Dukakis	36%

POPULATION

1990 population		550,043
1980 population		401,851
Percent change		+37%
Rank among states:		49
White		76%
Black		4%
Hispanic		3%
Asian or Pacific islander		4%
Urban		67%
Rural		33%
Born in state		34%
Foreign-born		5%
Under age 18	172,344	31%
Ages 18-64	335,330	65%
65 and older	22,369	4%
Median age		29.4

MISCELLANEOUS

Capital: Juneau
Number of counties: 25 divisions
Per capita income: $21,932 (1991)
Rank among states: 6
Total area: 591,000 sq. miles
Rank among states: 1

ALASKA

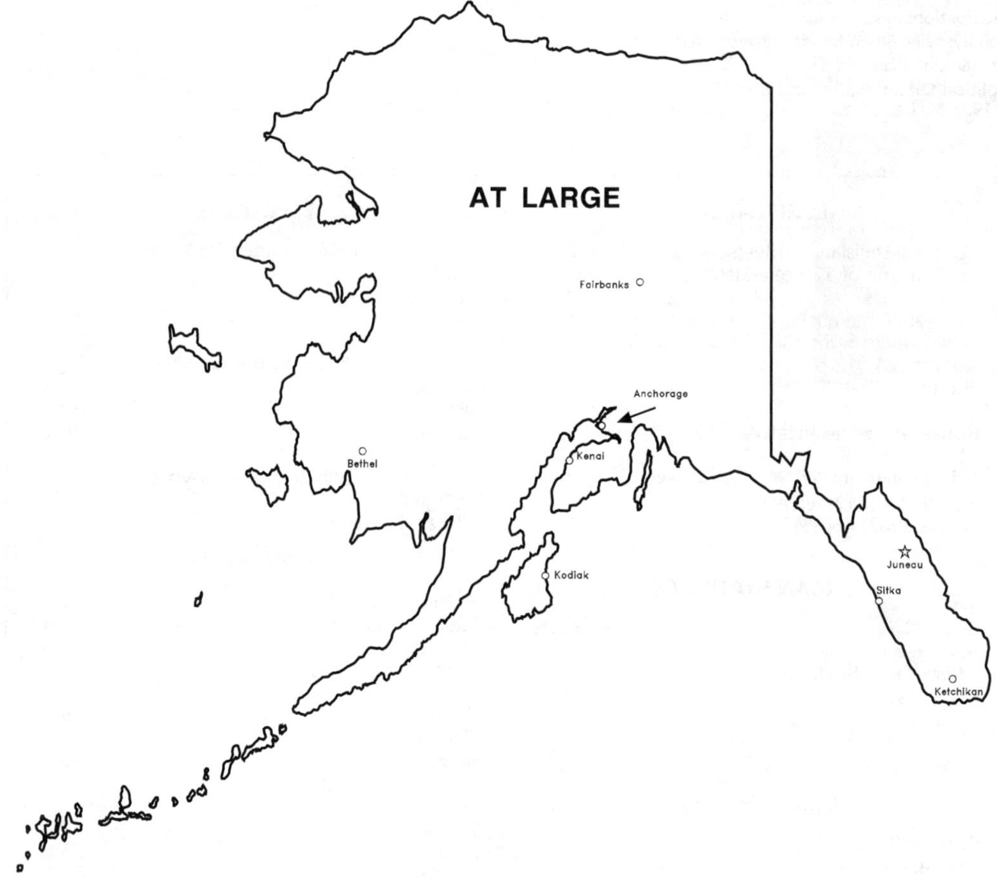
AT LARGE
Fairbanks
Anchorage
Kenai
Bethel
Kodiak
Juneau
Sitka
Ketchikan

Ted Stevens (R)

Of Girdwood — Elected 1970; 5th full term

Appointed to the Senate 1968.

Biographical Information

Born: Nov. 18, 1923, Indianapolis, Ind.

Education: U. of California, Los Angeles, B.A. 1947; Harvard U., LL.B. 1950.

Military Service: Army Air Corps, 1943-46.

Occupation: Lawyer.

Family: Wife, Catherine Ann Bittner; six children.

Religion: Episcopalian.

Political Career: U.S. attorney for Alaska, 1953-56; Republican nominee for U.S. Senate, 1962; Alaska House, 1965-68, majority leader and speaker pro tempore, 1967-68; sought Republican nomination for U.S. Senate, 1968.

Capitol Office: 522 Hart Bldg. 20510; 224-3004.

Committees

Appropriations (chairman)
Commerce, Justice, State & Judiciary; Defense (chairman); Foreign Operations; Interior; Legislative Branch; VA, HUD & Independent Agencies

Commerce, Science & Transportation
Aviation; Communications; Oceans & Fisheries; Science, Technology & Space; Surface Transportation & Merchant Marine

Rules & Administration

Joint Library

In Washington: Stevens has served a long time in the Senate, so long that he is now the chamber's second-most senior Republican, with 28 years' service. And his patience paid off in a big way at the start of the 105th Congress, as he became chairman of the Appropriations Committee, a job that came open with the retirement of Oregon's Mark O. Hatfield.

Two years before, in 1995, the story had been different for Stevens. Although his party was then taking control of Congress after eight years in the minority, the only full committee chair available to Stevens was on Rules and Administration — perhaps the lowest-profile gavel in the Senate.

Also in the 104th, Stevens returned to the chair of Appropriations' Defense Subcommittee (he was chairman of that panel when Republicans last held the Senate majority in the 1980s). In that role he helped boost Pentagon spending while preserving its allocations from a White House hungry for more domestic funds. Stevens also continued his longstanding efforts to funnel domestic dollars home to Alaska.

Stevens' committee assignments in recent years have resembled the child's game of "Chutes and Ladders." In the summer of 1994, he was lobbying colleagues to support his bid to leapfrog over South Dakota Sen. Larry Pressler for the top GOP spot on the Commerce Committee. Pressler had more seniority on the committee, but Stevens had been in the Senate a decade longer and enjoyed a reputation as more of a legislative heavyweight than Pressler. But with Stevens' sharp mind comes a hot temper, and he could not overcome the simple fact that too many colleagues considered him difficult to work with at times. Pressler became Commerce chairman, and Stevens had to be satisfied with chairing Rules, the Defense Appropriations Subcommittee and two other lower-profile subcommittees. (Pressler was turned out of the Senate in the 1996 election.)

When Finance Committee Chairman Bob Packwood, R-Ore., resigned in disgrace in October 1995, his gavel fell to William V. Roth Jr., R-Del. Roth gave up the helm at Governmental Affairs, and Stevens got that chairmanship.

Stevens gave administration officials a preview of what his tenure as Appropriations chairman might be like during endgame negotiations over the fiscal 1997 Interior spending bill. Minutes after negotiators called Stevens into the chairman's office in September 1996, the Alaskan was shouting, red-faced, at Leon E. Panetta, President Clinton's chief of staff. Stevens was determined to force the White House to drop restrictions that limited use of a special fund for out-of work Alaskan timber workers. Stevens told Panetta that he had just told a roomful of Senate Republicans that they could not trust Panetta because his word was no good.

But after Panetta produced documents that bolstered his case, Stevens immediately shook hands as though nothing unusual had happened and left. Longtime Stevens watchers say they have often watched Stevens throw a fit and then exit the room with a wink. "I believe in using my emotions, not losing my emotions," Stevens said in a 1996 interview. "Once you've done that, you walk out the door and go over and have a drink with the opposing [party]."

Stevens publicly bragged on his combative style at the first Appropriations Committee markup over which he presided. "Sen. Hatfield had the patience of Job and the disposition of a saint. I don't," Stevens announced. "The watch has changed. I'm a mean, miserable SOB."

But for all his bluster, Stevens remains a throwback to the clubby pragmatism that once permeated the Senate and its spending committee; he generally gets along well with ranking Appropriations Democrat Robert C. Byrd of West Virginia. Stevens takes a different tack on a number of issues, from abortion to arts spending, than the younger generation of Republicans now regnant in the Senate. But he has swallowed his reservations on a number of votes since the GOP took power, and he actively campaigned for lots of Senate candidates in 1996 to help shore up support for his bid to chair Appropriations.

Stevens has been a steadfast defender of congressional perks and privileges and of federal workers' pay and pensions generally. Nevertheless, on assuming the Governmental Affairs chairmanship, Stevens pledged that he would continue GOP efforts to reform the civil service system.

In 1995, he switched his vote from the year before to support passage of a balanced-budget constitutional amendment. (He had also voted for the amendment in 1986.) When Hatfield came under attack within the Republican Conference for being the lone Republican to oppose the move (at the cost of its passage), Stevens rushed to his defense, saying it wasn't a "healthy concept to think everyone has to fit into the same keyhole to belong to the Republican Party."

He has opposed efforts to change the campaign finance system, and in the 103rd he opposed legislation to impose more restrictions on lobbying. He said that blocking lobbyists from spending money on members and staff "is going to harm this town. The Kennedy Center will fold up if they don't buy these tickets," he said. "You are going to close 90 percent of the restaurants in Washington." The lobby reform bill died at the end of the session, but similar measures, which Stevens supported, passed the Senate unanimously in July 1995.

Stevens' work for increased congressional salaries and benefits helped make him popular enough in the 1970s and early 1980s to hold the post of party whip for eight years, and in December 1984, he ran a strong race for majority leader, losing to Bob Dole of Kansas by only three votes, 28-25. For years afterward, he harbored ambitions to be party leader, but time seems to have precluded that possibility.

He voted in 1995 for passage of the Congressional Compliance Act, which was designed to end Congress' exemption from prominent labor laws, but he questioned the Congressional Budget Office's estimates of its expense. "If it costs so little to apply to Congress, why are private businesses complaining so loudly [about regulations]?" he asked.

The bill's progress was held up for several months near the end of the 103rd Congress as Stevens, who was then the ranking member on Rules, underwent and recovered from back surgery. Stevens had surgery for prostate cancer in August 1991, an experience that played a part in him helping push through legislation establishing a prostate cancer research center within the National Cancer Institute.

Stevens is a vociferous defender of Alaska's needs, and in 1995 he cosponsored fellow Alaskan Sen. Frank H. Murkowski's legislation to lift the ban on exporting Alaskan oil. They had less success with proposals to spur timber harvesting in the Tongass National Forest and to open the Arctic National Wildlife Refuge to oil drilling because of the firm opposition of the Clinton White House. Accusing the Clinton administration of conducting a "war on the West," Stevens said, "We insist we're going to stop these dictatorial actions."

In February 1995, Stevens was granted the dubious honor of the "Alaskan Pipeline Award" by Citizens Against Government Waste, which claimed he had funneled some $30 million in pork to his state over the past year.

He breaks with some conservatives on another issue important to Alaska, funding for public broadcasting. Because of the state's sparse population, public radio is an important community bulletin board, and for Stevens that supersedes any ideological concerns about the liberal leanings of public radio. He has criticized public broadcasting for "testing the limits of public acceptance," but he remains a supporter. "The people who need this system are not extreme," he said. Stevens fought behind the scenes to preserve public broadcasting funding in 1995, but admitted he won less than he had hoped for.

As ranking member and now chairman of Defense Appropriations, Stevens has been determined to establish the panel as an independent voice on military programs, rather than merely a bursar for the programs authorized by the Armed Services Committee. In doing so, he has faced opposition both from Armed Services and from the subcommittee's traditionally more powerful House counterpart.

In 1995, he praised Defense Secretary William J. Perry's efforts to reshape the U.S. military, but complained that the rest of Clinton's team regarded U.S. forces more as an international relief corps than as a combat force. He also expressed concern that in the absence of the Soviet threat, the public is too eager for defense moneys to shift to domestic programs. "There are so many areas out there that members of the public put ahead of maintaining our defenses," he complained.

At Home: Stevens' careful defense of Alaska's interests has made him invulnerable at the polls. Although he has not had his way on every issue, he always seems to have the right political approach — stubborn but pragmatic.

He easily turned back a primary challenge in 1996 by former state Rep. Dave W. Cuddy, a banking millionaire who hoped to find a weak incumbent underbelly. But conservatives who did not love Stevens were willing to stick with him because of his clout, and Cuddy's late-season attacks accusing Stevens of misusing campaign funds for personal trips were disproved by the Senate Ethics Committee and backfired. Democrats had a large but weak field of political unknowns, and the eventual nominee, Theresa Nangle Obermeyer, spent part of the campaign year in jail for charges that grew out of her "stalking" of Stevens. Even the state's Democratic governor announced for Stevens, and Obermeyer finished third behind the Green Party nominee.

Until he hit Alaska at age 29, Stevens had been something of a nomad. Born in Indianapolis in 1923 to parents who divorced at the start of the Great Depression, he eventually moved to live with an aunt in California, where he went to high school and learned to surf. After flying C-46 transports throughout China during World War II and earning the Distinguished Flying Cross, he graduated from the University of California, Los Angeles, and worked his way through law school, in part by selling his blood and tending bar, according to a revealing profile in the Anchorage Daily News.

Stevens, who had been majority leader in the Alaska House, got to Washington by appointment when Democratic Sen. E.L. Bartlett died in 1968. The appointment came from GOP Gov. Walter J. Hickel. Stevens would soon be in the Senate arguing for Hickel's confirmation as secretary of the Interior under President Richard M. Nixon.

Stevens had begun his pursuit of a Senate seat not long after Alaska became a state in 1959. He got the party's nomination for the job in 1962 but managed just 41 percent against Democrat Ernest J. Gruening that fall. He tried for the nomination again in 1968 but was defeated in the primary. The party's nominee, however, lost that November to Democrat Mike Gravel, and when Bartlett died in December, Hickel turned to Stevens.

Once in Washington, Stevens began digging in politically. In the 1970 contest to fill the final two years of Bartlett's term, he won with 60 percent (even as the GOP was losing the governorship). In that campaign, against liberal Democrat Wendell P. Kay, Stevens favored greater oil and mineral development; Kay was a firm conservationist.

Despite his record as a GOP loyalist, Stevens' focus on the economy and defense policy and lack of zeal on social issues has alienated some of the staunch conservatives — including a number of religious fundamentalists — in the Alaska Republican Party. He was denied the chairmanship of the Alaska delegation to the 1980 Republican National Convention. After compiling a strongly pro-Reagan voting record before the 1984 convention, he was named delegation chairman, but he has not held that title since.

Stevens' electoral strength daunted prominent Democrats from challenging him in 1990. But the fact that he was practically unchallenged did not stop the minority of Alaskans who had a gripe with Stevens from voting for his obscure challengers. In the primary, Robert M. Bird, a teacher and anti-abortion activist, took 25 percent of the Republican vote against Stevens. And in the general election, Stevens' 66 percent share of the vote was actually smaller than it had been in 1984. This was notable mainly because his Democratic opponent was Michael Beasley, a political gadfly who had run in statewide primaries without ever receiving more than 9 percent of the vote.

SENATE ELECTIONS

1996 General		
Ted Stevens (R)	177,893	(77%)
Jed Whittaker (GREEN)	29,037	(13%)
Theresa Nangle Obermeyer (D)	23,977	(10%)
1996 Primary *		
Ted Stevens (R)	71,043	(59%)
Dave W. Cuddy (R)	32,994	(28%)
Theresa Nangle Obermeyer (D)	4,072	(3%)
Jed Whittaker (GREEN)	3,751	(3%)
Joseph A. "Joe" Sonneman (D)	2,643	(2%)
Michael J. Beasley (D)	1,968	(2%)

Previous Winning Percentages: 1990 (66%) **1984** (71%) **1978** (76%) **1972** (77%) **1970†** (60%)

† Special election

** In Alaska, all primary candidates are listed on one ballot and the winners from each party meet in the general election.*

KEY VOTES

1997	
Approve balanced-budget constitutional amendment	Y
Approve chemical weapons treaty	Y
1996	
Approve farm bill	Y
Limit punitive damages in product liability cases	Y
Exempt small businesses from higher minimum wage	Y
Approve welfare overhaul	Y
Bar job discrimination based on sexual orientation	N
Override veto of ban on "partial birth" abortions	Y
1995	
Approve GOP budget with tax and spending cuts	Y
Approve constitutional amendment barring flag desecration	Y

CAMPAIGN FINANCE

	Receipts	Receipts from PACs		Expend-itures
1996				
Stevens (R)	$3,271,582	$1,203,797	(37%)	$2,711,710

VOTING STUDIES

	Presidential Support		Party Unity		Conservative Coalition	
Year	**S**	**O**	**S**	**O**	**S**	**O**
1996	44	54	89	9	87	8
1995	30	66	86	10	88	5
1994	45	42	69	25	84	13
1993	31	65	80	18	88	7
1992	78	20	80	18	84	11
1991	83	14	78	20	85	10

INTEREST GROUP RATINGS

Year	ADA	AFL-CIO	CCUS	ACU
1996	20	n/a	85	80
1995	5	8	94	73
1994	25	43	67	77
1993	25	55	91	80
1992	20	33	80	74
1991	10	42	60	76

Frank H. Murkowski (R)

Of Fairbanks — Elected 1980, 3rd term

Biographical Information
Born: March 28, 1933, Seattle, Wash.
Education: U. of Santa Clara, 1951-53; Seattle U., B.A. 1955.
Military Service: Coast Guard, 1955-56.
Occupation: Banker.
Family: Wife, Nancy Gore; six children.
Religion: Roman Catholic.
Political Career: Alaska commissioner of economic development, 1966-70; Republican nominee for U.S. House, 1970.

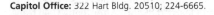

Capitol Office: 322 Hart Bldg. 20510; 224-6665.

Committees
Energy & Natural Resources (chairman)
Finance
International Trade; Long-Term Growth, Debt & Deficit Reduction; Taxation & IRS Oversight
Indian Affairs
Veterans' Affairs

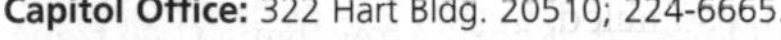

In Washington: Highly combative in style, Murkowski appears to relish knocking heads with the White House at every opportunity. The 104th Congress gave the senator plenty of opportunities: As chairman of the Senate Energy and Natural Resources Committee, Murkowski managed the issues that put President Clinton and the environmental community most directly in conflict with the conservative, pro-development policies of the Republican Party.

Not long after the 105th Congress began, Murkowski found opportunity to renew the confrontation by delaying for months the confirmation of Frederico F. Peña's nomination as secretary of energy. At issue for Murkowski was Clinton's reluctance to open a temporary nuclear waste storage site at Yucca Mountain in Nevada. Eventually, the storage site plan went forward and Peña was confirmed, but not until well after the blossoms of spring had arrived in the capital.

Ironically, Murkowski may find himself in league with Clinton on what promises to be the biggest issue before his committee in the 105th Congress: deregulating the multibillion-dollar electric utility industry. Murkowski sounds uncharacteristically like Clinton when he urges caution on the issue, and, like Clinton, he supports allowing states to decide when and whether to open their markets.

As an advocate of slow privatization, Murkowski will find himself in hot debate with a rapid-pace faction that features House Majority Whip Tom DeLay of Texas and Dale Bumpers of Arkansas, the ranking Democrat on Murkowski's committee. Many believe that despite bills being filed and hearings lining up, the issue is too complex and too contentious to be resolved this Congress.

"We all support competition," Murkowski told utility lobbyists in January. "The challenge is making sure we get from the current fully regulated market to a more deregulated, competitive one without littering the path with unhappy consumers, bankrupt electric utilities and poorer service."

But any alliance with the White House on energy deregulation seemed far away as the 105th Congress began: Murkowksi, teed off in characteristic style, getting into a shouting match with Energy Undersecretary Thomas Grumbly at a hearing on Murkowski's bill opening temporary nuclear waste storage at Yucca Mountain.

Senate supporters of the waste site — who passed a identical bill in the 104th — say the waste is endangering communities across the country as it piles up at nuclear plants that weren't designed to handle it. The administration says that building an interim site would complicate scientific efforts to determine the Nevada site's suitability as a permanent high-level waste repository. Clinton has promised he would veto the Murkowski-backed bill, but he agreed to administration negotiations with Murkowski in order to free up the Peña nomination.

Democrats angrily accused Murkowski of holding Peña hostage to the issue, and the senator admitted to using the nomination to pressure the White House to bargain over the waste bill. "I've been accused of holding Secretary Peña hostage," Murkowski said. "That isn't the issue. The issue here is the administration holding this nuclear waste issue hostage."

Murkowski's pugnacious style provided high drama during hearings by the Senate Special Committee on Whitewater. On the opening day of hearings, he waved aloft a briefcase owned by the late deputy White House Counsel Vincent W. Foster Jr. Murkowski, arguing that White House officials should have spotted 27 pieces of a shredded suicide note in it immediately (instead of four days after Foster's suicide, as they had claimed).

Democrat John Kerry of Massachusetts countered with his own briefcase demonstration showing how the notes could have been missed, and accused Murkowski of using surprise theatrics. "It was calculated to attract every camera in this room," Kerry said.

Murkowski's contentiousness failed more than once during the 104th Congress, and the experience may temper his partisanship in pursuit of his home state interests. A popular federal parks bill was near death more than once in the 104th Congress because of Murkowski's insistence on certain provisions. At one point, the massive legislation affecting more than 100 parks, lands and rivers provisions, teetered on the brink of collapse over the fate of a single timber company in southeast Alaska. Murkowski also failed, in the face of a Clinton veto threat, in his efforts to open more of the Arctic wilderness on Alaska's North Slope to oil drilling.

The battle over North Slope drilling has sizzled for as long as Murkowski has been in the Senate. Murkowski and his home-state GOP colleagues, Ted Stevens and House Resources Committee Chairman Don Young, argue that opening a 30-mile-by-75-mile swath of the Arctic National Wildlife Refuge (ANWR) would spur domestic oil production and cut reliance in imports. But Democrats and some Republicans say the drilling would harm the fragile ecosystem.

In the 104th, drilling proponents won a crucial vote, 56-44, to kill an amendment to the budget that would have prohibited oil exploration in the plain. But they could not garner the numbers to overcome a veto of their own plans.

Overall, the parks bill was a study in missed opportunities. The legislation was popular at the start, including improvements to parks and public lands in many states and congressional districts. But Murkowski's added a controversial provision that would have opened 20 million acres of federal land in Utah for potential development, in hopes that Democrats would not risk scuttling the rest of the bill just to kill the Utah provision. The tactic backfired as Democrats sank the bill in a skirmish over the minimum wage.

Murkowski regrouped, rewrote the bill without the Utah provisions, and the bill sailed into conference. At that point, the GOP leadership wanted to seek consensus, but Murkowski and Young opted to include controversial environmental provisions, including language that critics said would allow overcutting in Alaska's Tongass National Forest. The conference report was met by a bipartisan chorus of catcalls and a veto threat from the White House.

Republican leaders, eager to salvage some key items from the stalled conference report, considered folding them into the omnibus appropriations bill. That spurred Murkowski and Young to give up the Tongass logging and some other objectional provisions in order to keep control over the legislation. It was not enough, however, for Democrats and some Republicans, who put a procedural hold on the report in the Senate.

Meanwhile, Murkowski's problems continued in the House. An Alaska land exchange provision forced House leaders to pull the report from the floor because it contained a tax provision that originated in the Senate, rather than in the House as required by the Constitution. Young and George Miller, D-Calif., dumped the conference report, created yet another version of the bill minus the Tongass logging provisions, and got it through the House in the waning hours of the 104th Congress.

With no time for conferees to meet and the House finished with major business, the Senate either had to swallow the House bill whole or amend it and get the House to agree to it by unanimous consent, a risky venture.

Murkowski still didn't have what he wanted for an Alaska pulp mill, which would have to shut down and lay off employees under Tongass logging policy. The senator met with White House officials with only hours left to the session, and finally agreed on a plan to allow it to log for another 24 months. Murkowski still wanted to negotiate smaller details in the bill, but with leaders threatening to gavel down the Congress, he strode to the floor to announce the agreement, and the bill was cleared by voice vote.

"It's been kind of a torture chamber around here," he said after the final vote. "I've never given birth, but now I have some idea of how painful the process can be."

But the 104th wasn't all failure for Murkowski. The senator scored a major victory with the success of a bill lifting the ban on exporting oil from Alaska's North Slope. The Senate's final passage of the bill, in a 69-29 vote, capped the senator's longtime effort to allow Alaska to enter the lucrative world oil market. The ban had been enacted in 1973 after an embargo by petroleum-exporting countries led to sharp hikes in gasoline prices, oil shortages and long lines at gasoline pumps. But the relative glut on the international oil market in recent years has led to lower prices and greater use of foreign oil.

The measure was opposed by Northwestern senators, who feared the loss of jobs at refineries in their states when Alaskan oil went elsewhere. It was also opposed by environmentalists, who said it was a first step toward opening the ANWR.

On the Foreign Relations Committee (where Murkowski served through the 103rd), he was an exponent of expanding trade with the Far East, particularly as it benefits Alaska. That was perhaps his main pursuit on the Subcommittee on East Asian and Pacific Affairs, a panel he chaired in the 1980s and again in the 104th Congress. He leads frequent trade missions to the region, including a trip to Japan and Hong Kong in December 1996 to push sales of Alaskan natural gas. He urged permanent most-favored-nation status for China, and proposed a program to permit South Koreans to visit the United States — particularly Alaska — without having to go through the lengthy process of obtaining U.S. visas. He was also one of the sponsors of a congressional resolution urging Clinton to approve a visit by Taiwanese President Lee Teng-hui over sharp objections from the government of China.

He has been a critic, however, of North Korea's communist regime. When the Clinton administration reached an agreement it said would bring an end to North Korea's nuclear weapons program, Murkowski balked at the U.S. Contribution of fuel oil and other benefits worth hundreds of millions of dollars, saying it carried the "scent of appeasement."

At Home: Murkowski has never given Alaskans much reason to love or hate him. But his attention to home-state concerns has helped dissuade big-name Democrats who might otherwise have taken him on. The net result has been a remarkably consistent share of the vote for candidate Murkowski: 54 percent in both 1980 and 1986 and 53 percent in 1992.

Murkowski's latest re-election was a testament to the virtue of advance preparation. Expecting a tough race, Murkowski raised and spent nearly twice what his Democratic opponent did. His challenger, former state commerce commissioner Tony Smith, all but disappeared beneath the weight of Murkowski's advertising.

The Democrats had been at a loss for an opponent to Murkowski in 1986, finally settling on a political unknown, Glenn Olds, president of Alaska Pacific University.

Olds sought to overcome his political anonymity by arguing that Murkowski had done little to stem the precipitous slide of Alaska's energy-based economy. But if voters were angry over the oil price slump, most did not vent their frustrations on Murkowski. The incumbent, aided by his connections to the local banking industry, amassed a substantial treasury, touted his efforts to remove a ban on exports of North Slope oil — and stayed 10 percentage points ahead of Olds.

Except for four years in state government and one failed campaign for the House, Murkowski had spent his entire adult life in banking before he announced for the Senate in June 1980.

His status as a relative newcomer to politics hardly seemed an advantage against Democrat Clark S. Gruening, a popular two-term state legislator and grandson of the legendary Ernest Gruening, a former Alaska senator and governor. But Democratic disunity and the Reagan tide enabled Murkowski to win with unexpected ease.

To win the Democratic nomination, Gruening had to get past two-term incumbent Sen. Mike Gravel. It was a matter of revenge for Gruening; Gravel had ousted Gruening's grandfather from the Senate 12 years before.

In the general election, Murkowski accused Gruening of being too liberal for the state's electorate, claiming the Democrat had supported the legalization of marijuana. He also tied Gruening to the environmentalist Sierra Club, anathema to pro- development Alaskans.

A Seattle native who moved to Alaska while in high school, Murkowski got his first taste of elective politics in 1970. That year he defeated a member of the John Birch Society in a Republican primary for Alaska's at-large House seat. He lost the general election to Democratic state Sen. Nick Begich, but the experience whetted his appetite. After nine years as a bank president in Fairbanks, he announced for the Senate.

SENATE ELECTIONS

1992 General		
Frank H. Murkowski (R)	127,163	(53%)
Tony Smith (D)	92,065	(38%)
Mary E. Jordan (GREEN)	20,019	(8%)
1992 Primary		
Frank H. Murkowski (R)	37,486	(81%)
Jed Whittaker (R)	9,065	(19%)

Previous Winning Percentages: 1986 (54%) **1980** (54%)

CAMPAIGN FINANCE

	Receipts	Receipts from PACs	Expend- itures
1992			
Murkowski (R)	$1,657,932	$680,013 (41%)	$1,663,865
Smith (D)	$913,975	$246,996 (27%)	$910,138
Jordan (GREEN)	$4,092	0	$4,091

KEY VOTES

1997	
Approve balanced-budget constitutional amendment	Y
Approve chemical weapons treaty	Y
1996	
Approve farm bill	Y
Limit punitive damages in product liability cases	Y
Exempt small businesses from higher minimum wage	Y
Approve welfare overhaul	Y
Bar job discrimination based on sexual orientation	N
Override veto of ban on "partial birth" abortions	Y
1995	
Approve GOP budget with tax and spending cuts	Y
Approve constitutional amendment barring flag desecration	Y

VOTING STUDIES

	Presidential Support		Party Unity		Conservative Coalition	
Year	S	O	S	O	S	O
1996	36	63	93	4	92	3
1995	25	67	94	4	91	2
1994	32	61	89	8	84	9
1993	24	70	82	7	80	5
1992	72	27	82	11	82	13
1991	89	11	88	10	90	10

INTEREST GROUP RATINGS

Year	ADA	AFL-CIO	CCUS	ACU
1996	15	n/a	92	95
1995	0	0	100	91
1994	10	0	90	96
1993	20	20	100	86
1992	25	30	100	70
1991	5	42	60	86

AL Don Young (R)

Of Fort Yukon — Elected 1973; 12th full term

Biographical Information

Born: June 9, 1933, Meridian, Calif.

Education: Yuba Junior College, A.A. 1952; California State U., Chico, B.A. 1958.

Military Service: Army, 1955-57.

Occupation: Elementary school teacher; riverboat captain.

Family: Wife, Lula Fredson; two children.

Religion: Episcopalian.

Political Career: Fort Yukon City Council, 1960-64; mayor of Fort Yukon, 1964-68; Alaska House, 1967-71; Alaska Senate, 1971-73; Republican nominee for U.S. House, 1972.

Capitol Office: 2111 Rayburn Bldg. 20515; 225-5765.

Committees

Resources (chairman)

Transportation & Infrastructure
Coast Guard & Maritime Transportation; Water Resources & Environment

In Washington: Taking over as chairman the Resources Committee in the 104th Congress, Young eagerly mapped out plans to remake the federal land management system and revisit a host of environmental regulations laid down over a quarter-century by Democratic congresses. And the conservative GOP troops on his committee, which he had helped stack with like-minded Westerners and Southerners, seemed eager to help shift policy toward "wise use" of natural resources.

But as the 104th Congress unfolded, Young and his fellow pro-development Republicans were demonized as "anti-environment" by Democrats, and even by some environmentally minded GOP moderates. Eyeing public opinion polls as the November 1996 election approached, the House Republican leadership waved a caution flag at Young and his allies, and instead looked for ways to convince environmentally-minded voters that the "G" in GOP stood for "green." Young, who in the early days of the 104th had pledged House passage of bills protecting property rights, reining in enforcement of the Endangered Species Act and revamping wetlands classification standards, set out a less ambitious course for the 105th.

Young said he wanted the White House to take the lead on endangered-species legislation, while he focused on oversight of agencies under his committee's jurisdiction. "There is going to be a wait-and-see period," Young said in late 1996. "I am not going to stick my head out there and get it beat off."

And when President Clinton in late 1996 proposed stringent new rules for wetlands development, ending Reagan-era regulations that gave speedy approval to property owners to drain wetlands of up to 10 acres, Young held back. He said he was being careful not to get too far out in front of public opinion. "Why should we respond to it?" Young said of the Clinton policy. "When the public gets fed up with the policy, then Congress will respond."

Young, who had served as ranking member on Resources since 1985 (it used to be called Interior, then Natural Resources), has had a tumultuous relationship with California Democrat George Miller, the former panel chairman and now ranking member. The ideological outlooks of Young and Miller could not be more different. Miller's support for environmental laws seems to equal Young's passion for taking on federal bureaucrats. While Miller and Young did work together on some issues in the 104th — a fisheries measure and a big parks and lands bill were cooperative ventures — they clashed mightily on endangered species and other environmental issues.

Young is well-known for berating colleagues on the floor, and he has shown impatience at times with consulting some of his more moderate colleagues. Yet he also has a pragmatic streak, and despite his temperamental nature, he remains on decent terms even with some colleagues who are the targets of his ire.

A former riverboat captain, Young is an individualist who regularly demands — often in angry outbursts — that Washington stay out of his state's way. But throughout his House career, Young's colleagues have done anything but respect his wishes for his gargantuan district, the state of Alaska.

After the 1990 enactment of yet another bill that restricted Alaskan land use — in this case, curbing logging in the Tongass National Forest — Young offered a warning. "They had better not come back at me again," he said. "I may be only one, but they had better not come back at me again. They had better leave my people alone and leave my state alone."

Young was able in the 104th to chalk up some notable achievements for oil and gas interests in his state, including lifting the 22-year ban on the export of oil from Alaska's North Slope, a move intended to spur domestic oil production. Young also helped secure a provision in the 1996 safe drinking water law that authorized millions of dollars in grants for Alaska communities.

He also joined with Miller in pushing through a major rewrite of the 1976 Magnuson Fishery Conservation and Management Act, which both environmentalists and those in the fishing industry praised as helping to bolster domestic fishing, an important source of Alaskan jobs. President Clinton

Alaska's longstanding loyalty to the Republican Party paid off in 1995, when all three of its members of Congress became chairmen of key committees. Pro-development forces in the state looked forward to flexing this newfound power. But while House Resources Chairman Don Young helped successfully end the export ban on Alaskan oil, he was stymied in his push for increased logging in the Tongass National Forest. And even before the 104th Congress began, Senate Energy Chairman Frank H. Murkowski won concessions from Interior Secretary Bruce Babbitt on allowing cruise ship visits to Glacier Bay National Park.

In few, if any, states does the federal government play as prominent a part as it does in Alaska. It is a love-hate relationship. In the minds of many Alaskans, the federal government and its ownership of 68 percent of the state's land poses the greatest barrier to economic prosperity from the development of oil, gas and other natural resources. For example, because the oil — and the state tax revenue — generated from the massive Prudhoe Bay site is declining, state officials face intense pressure to open new fields.

But oil exploration in the federally owned Arctic National Wildlife Refuge (ANWR) has been repeatedly blocked by Congress. National environmental groups strongly believe that it would disrupt a pristine wilderness. Resentment of the federal government is equaled only by the state's dependence on it and the role Washington plays in providing federal jobs, military installations, and the most basic social services.

The March 1989 crash of the Exxon Valdez supertanker focused attention on the environmental risks of oil development. The pro-oil majority that controlled the state Legislature during the 1980s — associated with the GOP majority — saw its influence threatened; within months of the wreck, the Legislature passed a spate of environmental protection measures.

Environmental activists used publicity about the spill to dampen congressional interest in allowing oil to be drilled on ANWR's coastal plain. The state is heavily dependent on the oil industry to provide jobs and 80 percent of state revenues. The potential for state revenue shortfalls and other economic trouble is rekindling resentment toward the federal government.

From this longstanding sentiment springs the state's maverick political tradition, characterized by iconoclasm with a decidedly conservative bent. Alaska has voted Democratic for president only once since statehood, in 1964. The GOP has held all three of the state's seats in Congress since 1981.

In 1992, independent presidential candidate

ALASKA
At large

Ross Perot won 29 percent of the vote in Alaska, his second-best showing among the states and almost enough to pull him into second place ahead of Bill Clinton. George Bush carried the state with 40. Bob Dole fared better in 1996, winning the state with 51 percent of the vote; Clinton came in second with 33 percent. Perot dropped to 11 percent.

The nation's largest state in land area, Alaska ranks 49th in population, with just over 550,000 residents. Despite Alaska's permafrost reputation, residents enjoy the state's breathtaking natural beauty and warm summers. Still, it takes a hardy type to live this far north in the winter.

The state's population nexus is Anchorage, with slightly more than 226,000 residents. Its international airport is a key trade crossroads. Thanks to its equidistance from Tokyo, Frankfurt and New York City, Anchorage International leads the country in terms of landed cargo weight. Four of Anchorage's top ten non-government employers are oil-related; the top private employer is a huge grocery store chain with more than 3,000 employees.

In the wake of Pentagon plans to scale back defense spending, Anchorage closely monitors the status of Elmendorf Air Force Base and the Army's Fort Richardson, but so far both have escaped base-closure lists.

With revenues from the oil industry uncertain, efforts have intensified to diversify the economy. A promising alternative is tourism, which recently has been growing rapidly.

Fishing is already big business. Alaska fishing accounted for more than 50 percent of U.S. production in 1990 and employs about a quarter of the state's work force. Bristol Bay, off the southwest coast, is the world's largest producer of red salmon.

About 350 miles north of Anchorage is Fairbanks (population 31,000), the traditional trading center for the villages of inland Alaska. The city grew as the supply center for the Alaska oil pipeline (which runs north to Prudhoe Bay).

Southeast Alaska is separated from the rest of the state by the St. Elias Mountains and the Gulf of Alaska. Juneau, the state capital, is inaccessible by land. Alaska's vast "bush" region is dotted with mostly tiny towns. Native Indians and Eskimos predominate in remote Alaska.

1990 Population: 550,043. White 415,492 (76%), Black 22,451 (4%), Other 112,100 (20%). Hispanic origin 17,803 (3%). 18 and over 377,699 (69%), 62 and over 29,577 (5%). Median age: 29.

signed the bill in October 1996.

Young, who sponsored the bill, said he is no fan of regulation in general and environmental regulation in particular. But he agreed that the measure would result in "better fishing than what we have today."

But Young fell far short in the 104th on many of his other goals, such as allowing oil exploration in the Arctic National Wildlife Refuge, spurring timber harvesting in the Tongass, and rewriting the species act. Conservatives also failed to make headway on rewriting laws governing grazing and mining on public lands.

Young's most visible retreat was from the effort to overhaul the 1973 Endangered Species Act (ESA). Property-rights activists, like Young, contend that federal regulators often have implemented the law in an extreme fashion, barring individuals and businesses from reasonable economic uses of their private property in order to protect a variety of lesser-known birds, rodents and insects.

Young and California Republican Richard W. Pombo got a bill through the Resources Committee in October 1995 that greatly restricted the government's ability to bar development within animal and plant habitats. But critics argued that the bill would gut the ESA at the behest not of small landowners, but of corporate developers. In the end, the measure went nowhere as Speaker Newt Gingrich hesitated to bring it to the floor while Republicans were searching for ways to improve their image on the environment.

An omnibus parks and lands bill eventually cleared Congress on the final day of the 104th, although it underwent numerous transformations before leaving the Capitol. Young's plan of attack was to include numerous lands bills in the measure, hoping to attract enough support to ease the conference report through both chambers. But in seeking to broaden the bill, the House negotiators loaded it with provisions that almost killed it; particularly controversial were provisions aimed at overturning Clinton administration rules on grazing on public lands and allowing timber harvesting in Alaska.

Proponents of the all-inclusive strategy reckoned that House members would vote for a bill that contained favored provisions, even in the face of some objectionable items. But the strategy failed as Clinton threatened to veto the bill over the grazing language. GOP leaders eventually dumped the conference report and created a new bill without the controversial provisions, which earned the praise of environmentalists. The House passed that bill easily in September 1996.

No friend of the National Park Service, Young backed a committee bill that would have provided for a comprehensive review of the national park system. He joins with other conservatives who argue that Congress in the past has focused more on adding coveted sites to the park system than on properly maintaining what is already within the system. Young says that the park service is a model of mismanagement, that it needs to be more accountable to the public and is staffed with arrogant bureaucrats "that run around in their little uniforms acting like God."

"The Park Service is probably the least well-run agency of all the Interior agencies," said Young. "It has been the sacred cow of the environmentalists, with no oversight. Why is the infrastructure falling apart? No one has asked the right questions. All you hear is, 'Give me more money, you suckers.'" Although the park-review plan was attached by the committee to the GOP's broad deficit-reducing measure, it was later dropped.

Young is aggressively partisan, even though he is a product of Alaska's free-for-all, weak-party politics. As a member of the panel that makes House Republicans' committee assignments, Young has been known to grill applicants on party loyalty before supporting them for a seat. Young was also one of 26 Republicans to vote in 1997 against reprimanding Gingrich for violating House ethics rules.

Since he came to the House in 1973 as an advocate of the trans-Alaska oil pipeline, Young has fought many a losing battle against "outsiders" from the Lower 48 who want to preserve much of Alaska's unspoiled wilds from the miners, loggers, drillers and developers whose interests Young tenaciously promotes.

Young may never stop seething about passage of a 1980 Alaska lands bill that reserved large portions of the state as federal wilderness. In his three-year fight against that bill, Young whittled down its wilderness acreage considerably and won provisions for development. But when the bill was passed in the House in 1979, he complained, "People can sit on this floor and say it is all right to take what is already the people's of Alaska. That is immoral. . . . None of you has to go home to unemployment created by national legislation." Then he broke down in tears.

At Home: Whatever the national issues at stake, each of Young's House campaigns ends up in a debate over his personality. The contests seem to turn on whether Alaskans accept Young's portrayal of himself as a rough-hewn defender of home-state interests or see him instead as an obnoxious obstructionist who does more harm than good for Alaska.

Young thought he provided a definitive answer in 1988, when he defeated a highly touted Democratic challenger, former state prosecutor Peter Gruenstein, with 62 percent of the vote. But in 1990, Young barely held off college president and former Valdez Mayor John E. Devens, winning with 52 percent. Two years later, Devens returned for a rematch, better financed and better known. He held Young below the 50 percent mark in a four-candidate field, but could not oust the cantankerous Republican.

A co-founder of Prince William Sound Community College, Devens made his name during the Exxon Valdez disaster in 1989. As Valdez mayor, Devens coordinated the city's response to the oil spill, appeared on national news shows and testified before congressional committees. He also set the stage for his first House campaign, faulting Young for not quickly returning home to oversee the cleanup.

Throughout the 1990 race, Devens struggled to raise money to campaign in the enormous state. He saved his sparse dollars for a late TV ad blitz. Devens' closing rush narrowed the gap, but Young prevailed.

Saddled with 57 overdrafts at the House bank, Young seemed even more vulnerable in 1992. His low tally in a new closed GOP primary — drawing fewer votes than the top two Democrats — fueled speculation he would not survive.

But late in the fall, Young was praised at home for putting business interests ahead of "liberal East Coast" environmentalists, as one editorial put it. He also picked up the endorsement of his primary opponent, a female state senator who supported abortion rights. Perhaps most significant, Young conceded in his advertising that voters found him "abrasive" and "arrogant." He apologized but promised to continue fighting for Alaskan interests.

In 1994, Young won 57 percent over former state Commerce Commissioner Tony Smith, who ran a largely negative campaign.

In 1996, he faced state Sen. Georgianna Lincoln, a former Republican. She hoped to build on the sizable bloc of voters who are forever disenchanted with the irascible incumbent. Young can be coarse — in 1995, he had lectured a group of high school students about the meaning of an obscene term for sodomy. But benefiting from his stature as a committee chairman, he defeated Lincoln with 59 percent of the vote, his best showing of the decade.

Born in California, Young moved to Alaska to teach, then became a licensed riverboat captain and a member of the Dog Mushers Association.

Young has lost only one election in his political career: his first, in 1972. His opponent, freshman Democratic Rep. Nick Begich, disappeared without a trace along with House Majority Leader Hale Boggs, D-La., during an October airplane flight from Anchorage to Juneau. However, the missing Begich was re-elected over Young by almost 12,000 votes.

With his strong base in the Alaska "bush," Young rebounded quickly from his 1972 setback. He had hardly ended campaigning when Begich's seat was declared vacant in December. In the 1973 special election, Young edged out Emil Notti, the former state Democratic chairman. In 1974, Young weathered a vigorous challenge from state Sen. William L. Hensley. He won by comfortable margins in the next several elections.

Young then twice faced Pegge Begich, a former Democratic national committeewoman for Alaska and Nick Begich's widow. Begich criticized Young's attendance record, but Young brushed off the attacks, winning with 55 percent in 1984 and 57 percent in 1986.

HOUSE ELECTIONS

1996 General		
Don Young (R)	138,834	(59%)
Georgianna Lincoln (D)	85,114	(36%)
William J. Nemec II (AKI)	5,017	(2%)
John J.G. "Johnny" Grames (GREEN)	4,513	(2%)
1996 Primary *		
Don Young (R)	70,002	(58%)
Georgianna Lincoln (D)	38,105	(32%)
John J.G. "Johnny" Grames (GREEN)	2,096	(2%)
William J. Nemec II (AKI)	1,980	(2%)
Jim Dore (R)	5,936	(5%)
Sybil Skelton (R)	2,482	(2%)
1994 General		
Don Young (R)	118,537	(57%)
Tony Smith (D)	68,172	(33%)
Jonni Whitmore (GREEN)	21,277	(10%)

Previous Winning Percentages: **1992** (47%) **1990** (52%) **1988** (62%) **1986** (57%) **1984** (55%) **1982** (71%) **1980** (74%) **1978** (55%) **1976** (71%) **1974** (54%) **1973**† (51%)

† Special election

** In Alaska, all primary candidates are listed on one ballot and the winners from each party meet in the general election.*

CAMPAIGN FINANCE

	Receipts	Receipts from PACs		Expend-itures
1996				
Young (R)	$1,171,389	$591,043	(50%)	$1,176,954
Lincoln (D)	$251,074	$20,550	(8%)	$245,941
Nemec (AKI)	$0	0		$50
1994				
Young (R)	$963,387	$387,217	(40%)	$930,513
Whitmore (GREEN)	$24,377	$1,000	(4%)	$24,033

DISTRICT VOTE FOR PRESIDENT

	1996		1992
D	80,380 (33%)	**D**	78,294 (31%)
R	122,746 (51%)	**R**	102,000 (40%)
I	26,333 (11%)	**I**	73,481 (29%)

KEY VOTES

1997	
Ban "partial birth" abortions	Y
1996	
Approve farm bill	Y
Deny public education to illegal immigrants	Y
Repeal ban on certain assault-style weapons	Y
Increase minimum wage	Y
Freeze defense spending	N
Approve welfare overhaul	Y
1995	
Approve balanced-budget constitutional amendment	Y
Relax Clean Water Act regulations	Y
Oppose limits on environmental regulations	N
Reduce projected Medicare spending	Y
Approve GOP budget with tax and spending cuts	Y

VOTING STUDIES

	Presidential Support		Party Unity		Conservative Coalition	
Year	**S**	**O**	**S**	**O**	**S**	**O**
1996	38	57	86	9	92	0
1995	22	65	85	5	89	1
1994	44	54	80	17	97	3
1993	42	44	73	15	82	2
1992	75	22	73	19	85	10
1991	66	26	66	24	86	11

INTEREST GROUP RATINGS

Year	ADA	AFL-CIO	CCUS	ACU
1996	0	n/a	81	89
1995	5	36	91	91
1994	10	33	92	100
1993	15	67	73	85
1992	25	67	88	84
1991	10	55	67	67

ARIZONA

Governor: Fife Symington (R)
First elected: 1991
Length of term: 4 years
Term expires: 1/99
Salary: $75,000
Term limit: 2 consecutive terms*
Phone: (602) 542-4331
Born: Aug. 12, 1945; New York, N.Y.
Education: Harvard U., B.A. 1968.
Military Service: Air Force, 1968-71.
Occupation: Real estate developer.
Family: Wife, Ann Pritzlaff; five children.
Religion: Episcopalian.
Political Career: No previous office.
**Symington is eligible for one more four-year term; when he leaves office a new two-term limit will take effect.*

No lieutenant governor

Secretary of State: Jane Dee Hull (R)
First elected: 1994
Length of term: 4 years
Term expires: 1/99
Salary: $54,600
Phone: (602) 542-4285

State election official: (602) 542-8683
Democratic headquarters: (602) 257-9136
Republican headquarters: (602) 957-7770

REDISTRICTING

Arizona gained one House seat in reapportionment, increasing from five districts to six. Map issued by federal court May 6, 1992.

STATE LEGISLATURE

Bicameral legislature. Meets January to April, with a limit of 107 calendar days.

Senate: 30 members, 2-year terms
1996 breakdown: 18R, 12D; 22 men, 8 women
Salary: $15,000
Phone: (602) 542-3559

House of Representatives: 60 members, 2-year terms
1996 breakdown: 38R, 22D; 35 men, 25 women
Salary: $15,000
Phone: (602) 542-4221

URBAN STATISTICS

City	Population
Phoenix	983,403
Mayor Skip Rimsza, N-P	
Tucson	405,390
Mayor George Miller, D	
Mesa	288,091
Mayor Wayne Brown, N-P	
Glendale	148,134
Mayor Elaine Scruggs, N-P	
Tempe	141,865
Mayor Neil Giuliano, D	

U.S. CONGRESS

Senate: 0 D, 2 R
House: 1 D, 5 R

TERM LIMITS

For state offices: Yes
Senate: 4 consecutive terms
House: 4 consecutive terms

ELECTIONS

1996 Presidential Vote

Bill Clinton	47%
George Bush	44%
Ross Perot	8%

1992 Presidential Vote

George Bush	38%
Bill Clinton	37%
Ross Perot	24%

1988 Presidential Vote

George Bush	60%
Michael S. Dukakis	39%

POPULATION

1990 population		3,665,228
1980 population		2,718,215
Percent change		+35%
Rank among states:		24
White		81%
Black		3%
Hispanic		19%
Asian or Pacific islander		2%
Urban		88%
Rural		12%
Born in state		34%
Foreign-born		8%
Under age 18	981,119	27%
Ages 18-64	2,205,335	60%
65 and older	478,774	13%
Median age		32.2

MISCELLANEOUS

Capital: Phoenix
Number of counties: 15
Per capita income: $16,401 (1991)
Rank among states: 35
Total area: 114,000 sq. miles
Rank among states: 6

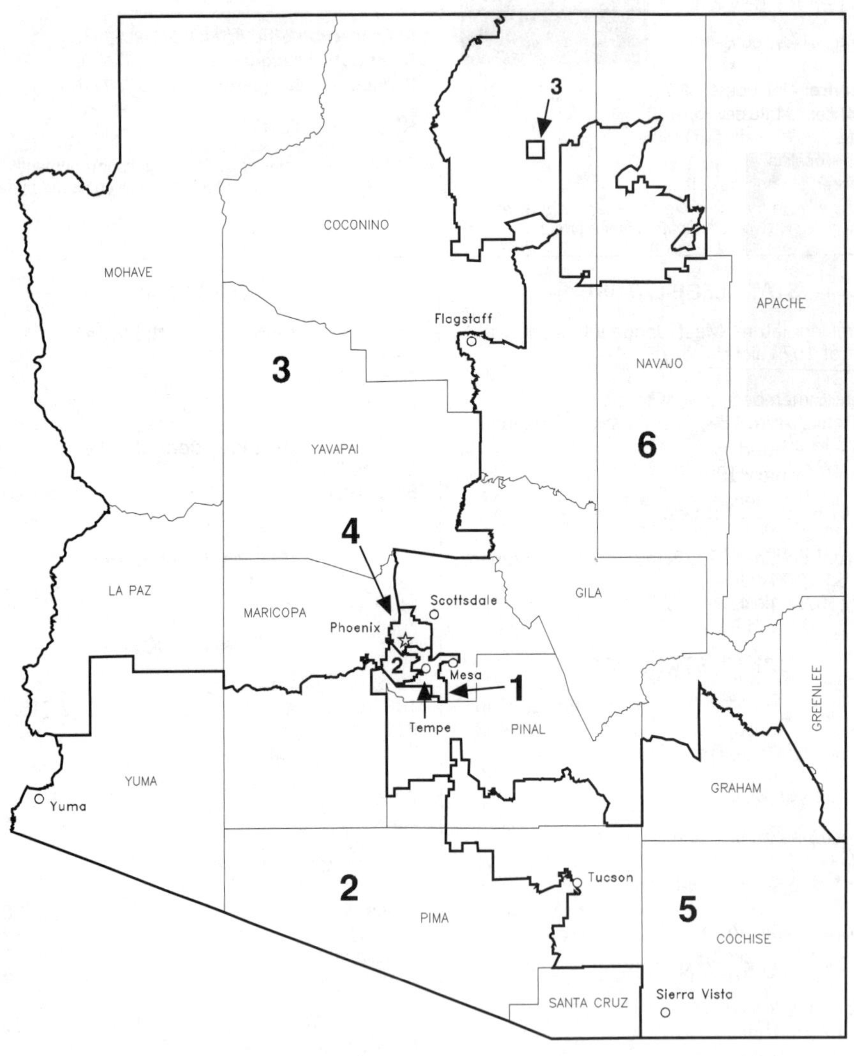

3
COCONINO
MOHAVE
Flagstaff
APACHE
3
NAVAJO
YAVAPAI
6
4
Scottsdale
GILA
LA PAZ
MARICOPA
Phoenix
2
Mesa
1
Tempe
PINAL
GREENLEE
YUMA
Yuma
GRAHAM
Tucson
2
5
PIMA
COCHISE
Sierra Vista
SANTA CRUZ

John McCain (R)

Of Phoenix — Elected 1986, 2nd term

Biographical Information
Born: Aug. 29, 1936, Panama Canal Zone, Panama.
Education: U.S. Naval Academy, B.S. 1958; National War College, 1973-74.
Military Service: Navy, 1958-81.
Occupation: Navy officer; Senate Navy liaison; beer distributor.
Family: Wife, Cindy Lou Hensley; six children.
Religion: Baptist.
Political Career: U.S. House, 1983-87.
Capitol Office: 241 Russell Bldg. 20510; 224-2235.

Committees
Armed Services
Personnel; Readiness; Seapower
Commerce, Science & Transportation (chairman)
Indian Affairs

In Washington: At the dawn of the 1990s, McCain was being dragged through the headlines as one of the Keating Five, the five senators accused of interceding with federal regulators in behalf of savings and loan operator Charles H. Keating Jr., who was ultimately jailed. A protracted ethics investigation ended with McCain getting a mild rebuke in February 1991.

Now in the decade's twilight years, he has emerged as one of the Senate's leading proponents of reforms that he feels will give the business of politics a better name. In 1995, he brokered a compromise that led to passage of Senate rules restricting gifts and meals paid for by lobbyists. McCain's resolution limited senators to accepting meals, gifts and tickets under $50 and eliminated lobbyist-financed vacations for legislators. "If a constituent is having a barbecue, it is appropriate for a senator to have a hamburger," McCain said. "But we do not need tickets to lavish balls to do our jobs. We do not need $100 gift baskets to do our jobs. And we do not need unlimited, expensive free meals to do our job."

In 1997, he renewed his push for legislation to change the way congressional campaigns are financed.

Indeed, some Republicans have wondered whether McCain's zeal for reform is his attempt to permanently erase the stain of the Keating Five scandal. McCain says his 1992 re-election was a referendum on that matter (he won with 56 percent), and he explains that his campaign finance efforts stem from a dislike of fundraising. "I don't know a politician who enjoys fundraising," he said. "The system is such that the American people have lost faith."

Whatever its origins, McCain's interest in changing the way Congress operates has helped catapult him onto the national scene. He was on the short list of potential running mates for GOP presidential nominee Bob Dole in 1996, even though he had initially endorsed Sen. Phil Gramm, R-Texas, over Dole in the primaries. In the fall, McCain became a mainstay of the Dole campaign, stumping across the country and becoming a fixture at rallies for Dole and running mate Jack F. Kemp. "Every time you looked up you saw Dole, Kemp and McCain," said Tom Slade, chairman of the Florida GOP.

A member of the Senate Republicans' campaign finance reform task force, McCain has nonetheless devoted most of his attention to a bipartisan effort on that issue: a bill he cosponsored with Democrat Russell D. Feingold of Wisconsin. Their measure would ban so-called soft money, the unregulated contributions used for party-building activities such as "get out the vote" operations — but increasingly used for issue-oriented campaign commercials as well. McCain's bill also would ban political action committee contributions; and it would provide free or low-cost television time and discounted postage rates to candidates who agree to abide by voluntary spending limits.

McCain-Feingold did not quite make it to the Senate floor in the 104th, blocked by a Republican-led filibuster in June 1996. Proponents fell six votes short of the 60 needed to cut off debate and take up the bill.

In January 1997, McCain and Feingold joined the House sponsors of the legislation, Republican Christopher Shays of Connecticut and Democrat Martin T. Meehan of Massachusetts, in a White House meeting with President Clinton. The president, tainted by revelations of fundraising abuses in behalf of his own re-election, told the lawmakers he would personally campaign for their bill. The meeting focused mainly on how to bring the issue home to people living outside the Beltway. "I am deeply appreciative of the president's commitment," McCain said. "Pressure is building to make this happen."

McCain hit the road to try to increase that pressure in March 1997, making a campaign-style swing to Boston and Philadelphia. The trip was designed to kick off a nationwide petition drive to force Congress to take up reform legislation. "We have a system awash in money dominated by special interests, a system that cries out for repairs," McCain said at a sparsely attended rally in Boston. "Change will not come from within the Beltway. We need your help."

McCain acknowledges that his support for campaign finance legislation has not enhanced his popularity within the Senate GOP Conference. "The majority of them view it as an honest position," McCain said. "Does it make me eligible to be voted Homecoming Queen or Miss Congeniality? I don't think so."

McCain did win one intraparty skirmish early in 1997, as the Senate prepared to authorize a committee investigation into campaign finance abuses in the last presidential campaign. Senate Majority Leader Trent Lott had signed off on a plan by which the committee would probe only the practices of the White House. But when the issue came up at a Republican Conference luncheon, McCain insisted the probe also look at congressional fundraising. "Appearances are important," McCain said. When nine other Republican senators signaled their agreement with McCain, it was enough to force Lott to reverse course (or risk losing a floor showdown with a united bloc of Democrats). Senate Minority Leader Tom Daschle called it "one of the biggest turnabouts" of its kind he had seen.

As McCain pushes for his legislation, including the low-cost or free television time provision, he has a unique opportunity to urge broadcasters' acquiescence. He is the newly installed chairman of the Senate Commerce, Science and Transportation Committee, which has jurisdiction over telecommunications.

McCain is no fan of regulation. He was the lone Republican to vote against final passage of the huge 1996 bill deregulating the telecommunications industry — saying it did not go far enough. But he also wants broadcasters to pay for their new high-definition television channels. The Federal Communications Commission believes selling the digital spectrum could raise anywhere from $11 billion to $70 billion. "Billions of dollars of a very important commodity owned by the American public should not be given away," McCain said.

That amount of revenue would go a long way toward helping deficit hawks, McCain among them, balance the budget. McCain already swings the budget-cutting axe freely. Although he voted for a bill to overhaul federal farm policy when it passed the Senate in February 1996, he was the only Republican senator to oppose the conference report in March 1996, saying the legislation would spend too much money. Unlike most of his military-minded colleagues in his conference, he opposes the B-2 bomber.

In August 1996, he tried unsuccessfully to amend the fiscal 1997 energy and water development appropriations bill by stripping $22 million for the Advanced Light Water Reactor. The amendment was killed, 53-45. "This kind of thing is so symbolic of the failure of Congress to reform in the face of special interests," said McCain, who added that he was more frustrated than angry. "I've lost my ability to become enraged."

He has called for a commission to target federal subsidies for businesses. It would be modeled after the successful panel that targeted military bases for closure, submitting its list of closings to Congress as one recommendation to be accepted or rejected as a whole.

In order to take the gavel at Commerce, McCain gave up his chairmanship of Indian Affairs, where he worked on several issues in the 104th, including regulation of Indian gaming (he proposed that a federal commission do the job), making it easier to adopt Indian children (he advised setting strict deadlines throughout the adoption process to afford all parties — including the child's tribe — a chance to participate), and overhauling the Bureau of Indian Affairs to give tribes greater influence over its operations. "The BIA must be changed into an agency that truly assists the efforts of tribal governments to determine their own future and govern themselves," said McCain, who called the bureau "one of the worst-managed and inefficient agencies of the federal government."

A feisty, energetic partisan, son and grandson of renowned Navy admirals, McCain came of age as a Navy fighter pilot and, from 1967 to 1973, as a prisoner of war in Vietnam. Clearly a hawk, he is now in a position to shape defense and foreign policy as a member of the Armed Services Committee.

He does not disguise his disdain for the fact that as a young man, President Clinton bypassed military service while McCain went to Vietnam. He has said Clinton lacks credibility leading the nation into battle. "I think his lack of military service emphasizes his need to consult on matters he knows nothing about."

Nevertheless, McCain remains one of the stoutest defenders of the president's prerogatives to guide foreign and military policy. "We cannot have 535 commanders-in-chief," McCain said midway through the 103rd Congress when lawmakers were pressing to end the U.S. mission in Somalia.

While reluctant to make policy from Capitol Hill, McCain has accused Clinton of abandoning a tenet of U.S. military policy: never put troops in harm's way unless vital national interests are at stake.

Still, in December 1995, he opposed efforts to cut off funding for American troops in Bosnia, helping instead to craft a resolution allowing the president to fulfill his commitment to send troops, provided he also promised to begin beefing up the armed forces of Bosnia's Muslim-led government. The resolution passed, 69-30.

McCain said his stand was informed by his experience as a prisoner of war in Vietnam during a time of antiwar protest in the United States and congressional debate on cutting off funds for the war. "We were definitely kept informed of protests and whatever was happening here in Congress," he recalled. McCain said cutting off funding for the Bosnia mission was wrong "because troops are already being deployed as we speak. And we need to be behind the troops completely now."

In July 1995, McCain backed Clinton's decision to resume full diplomatic relations with Vietnam. He called the move "in the national interest."

McCain and then-Rep. Robert K. Dornan, R-Calif., got into a tussle in September 1995 over the defense authorization bill, which sought to create an office at the Pentagon to centralize handling of cases of servicemen missing in action. In a closed session involving the House and Senate military personnel subcommittees, Dornan said in front of stunned staffers that McCain had abandoned families of servicemen missing in Vietnam, and he told the senator he had worked with McCain's family to get him out of a North Vietnamese prison. McCain questioned why Dornan had made the issue so personal. "He made some strong statements about me abandoning the families, and I just walked out of the room," McCain said. "My only option was to walk out."

At Home: From the time Sen. Barry Goldwater announced plans not to run again in 1986, McCain was seen as his likely successor.

McCain started with a strong pool of political capital. He had impressed Republican activists by winning election to the House in 1982, soon after his 1981 arrival in the state. Subsequent trips around Arizona as a member of Ronald Reagan's 1984 steering committee boosted his visibility. He became such a hot property that potential intraparty rivals backed away.

Democrats, too, were wary of his stature. Gov. Bruce Babbitt decided he would rather risk a run at the presidency than tangle with McCain for the Senate. After a host of other Democrats also passed up the race, party leaders were relieved when ex-state Sen. Richard Kimball, then a member of the Corporation Commission, declared.

But Kimball never hit stride as a Senate candidate. He spent months holed up to research his stands on issues, which did not enhance his visibility. McCain won with 61 percent of the vote.

McCain was not in the Senate long before he found himself embroiled in the Keating Five scandal. Although he was given only a mild rebuke by the Senate Ethics Committee, the scandal appeared to leave him vulnerable in 1992.

But Arizona Democrats failed to recruit any big-name contenders, in part because McCain's approval ratings remained at or near the 50 percent level in 1991. Neither of the two Democrats who joined the race — retired Air Force Lt. Gen. Truman Spangrud and community activist Claire Sargent — had any political experience.

Sargent handily won the Democratic primary, but she lacked the money and name recognition to present a serious threat to McCain in the fall. Even the entrance of impeached former GOP Gov. Evan Mecham into the race as an independent did little to help her cause. McCain's 56 percent was 24 points ahead of Sargent's tally.

McCain's initial opening to Congress came in 1982, when GOP Rep. John J. Rhodes decided to give up his 1st District seat. McCain won nomination by convincing voters that his experience as Navy liaison to the Senate gave him a knowledge of "how Washington works."

When rivals charged that he was a carpetbagger who would forget Arizona once in Washington, McCain said, "I went to Hanoi, and I didn't forget about the United States of America." He won two House terms by huge margins.

There was never much question McCain would be a Navy man; his father commanded U.S. forces in the Pacific during the Vietnam War, and his grandfather was a Pacific aircraft carrier commander in World War II. In a Hanoi prison camp, McCain's captors sarcastically called him the U.S. Navy's "crown prince." The roots of McCain's political successes lie in his long ordeal in Vietnam, the years he spent tortured and in solitary confinement in Hanoi-area camps after his plane was shot down in 1967.

SENATE ELECTIONS

1992 General		
John McCain (R)	771,395	(56%)
Claire Sargent (D)	436,321	(32%)
Evan Mecham (I)	145,361	(11%)
Kiana Delamare (LIBERT)	22,613	(2%)

Previous Winning Percentages: 1986 (61%) **1984*** (78%) **1982*** (66%)

** House election*

KEY VOTES

1997	
Approve balanced-budget constitutional amendment	Y
Approve chemical weapons treaty	Y
1996	
Approve farm bill	Y
Limit punitive damages in product liability cases	Y
Exempt small businesses from higher minimum wage	Y
Approve welfare overhaul	Y
Bar job discrimination based on sexual orientation	N
Override veto of ban on "partial birth" abortions	Y
1995	
Approve GOP budget with tax and spending cuts	Y
Approve constitutional amendment barring flag desecration	Y

CAMPAIGN FINANCE

	Receipts	Receipts from PACs	Expend-itures
1992			
McCain (R)	$3,344,311	$1,196,056 (36%)	$3,481,915
Sargent (D)	$288,413	$40,770 (14%)	$287,682
Mecham (I)	$89,910	0	$86,433

VOTING STUDIES

Year	Presidential Support S	O	Party Unity S	O	Conservative Coalition S	O
1996	31	66	93	5	89	11
1995	35	63	86	10	79	16
1994	42	53	88	8	69	25
1993	27	70	88	8	78	12
1992	75	25	84	13	82	13
1991	86	14	87	11	90	8

INTEREST GROUP RATINGS

Year	ADA	AFL-CIO	CCUS	ACU
1996	0	n/a	100	95
1995	0	8	100	91
1994	10	0	80	96
1993	15	18	82	83
1992	20	33	90	85
1991	5	17	70	86

Jon Kyl (R)

Of Phoenix — Elected 1994, 1st term

Biographical Information
Born: April 25, 1942, Oakland, Neb.
Education: U. of Arizona, B.A. 1964, LL.B. 1966.
Occupation: Lawyer.
Family: Wife, Caryll Collins; two children.
Religion: Presbyterian.
Political Career: U.S. House, 1987-95.
Capitol Office: 724 Hart Bldg. 20510; 224-4521.

Committees
Energy & Natural Resources
Forests & Public Land Management; Water & Power (chairman)
Select Intelligence
Judiciary
Administrative Oversight & the Courts; Immigration; Technology, Terrorism & Government Information (chairman)

In Washington: Even among the conservative, activist senators who have come over from the House in recent years, Kyl stands out for his unblinking devotion to reducing spending on the federal government's domestic functions while pouring dollars into defense. But Kyl, whose Republican father, John H. Kyl, represented Iowa in the House for a dozen years, has an appreciation of institutional process that leads him to join occasionally with Democrats to offer legislation and affords him the patience to pursue "revolutionary" principles over several years.

One battle that continued from the 104th Congress is ratification of the Chemical Weapons Convention. Kyl, who voted against the pact in April 1997, led opposition to the pact, which was negotiated by Republican administrations. Kyl contends that the treaty cannot be verified, is subject to cheating by Russian and non-signatory nations such as Iran and Libya, and will lead to intrusion of U.S. private sector plants. The treaty was approved by the Senate 74-26 in April 1997.

Kyl in the 105th serves as chairman of the Judiciary Technology, Terrorism and Government Information Subcommittee. Kyl chairs the Water and Power panel of the Energy and Natural Resources Committee, which has jurisdiction over areas of crucial importance to his fast-growing desert state and will have a role in any major utility deregulation efforts.

He passed on a chance to chair Judiciary's Immigration Subcommittee, but he takes a hard line on the issue and favors a reduction of legal immigration levels. Crime is a major concern of Kyl's, and he sponsored a constitutional amendment to ensure the rights of victims. Another bill of his would force federal prisoners to pay a share of their in-prison health care costs to combat overutilization of prison health services and control costs; the funds raised would go into a victims' fund.

Outside the area of crime, the bulk of Kyl's characteristically diligent work in the Senate has come in the defense and foreign policy areas. During his four terms in the House he was its leading advocate of anti-missile defenses, and he now has that role in the Senate. The Clinton administration plans to implement a missile defense system that conservatives such as Kyl find unacceptable; Kyl wants to spend as much as $20 billion to create a more powerful system.

Other senators crafted a bipartisan compromise on the issue during consideration of the fiscal 1996 defense authorization bill, but Kyl complained that his side had given away the store. He pooh-poohed administration worries that bumping up against strictures in the Anti-Ballistic Missile Treaty would undercut relations with Russia. "I think it is a very important first step in abrogating or totally renegotiating the ABM Treaty," he said. He did not fear Clinton's veto threats, telling a Washington Times editorial board meeting that "the president probably wants to veto the bill for any number or reasons. . . . We ought to be on record for what we believe in, send the bill, and if he wants to make a political issue out of it, let him veto it. Then we can consider at that point whether to make any changes to satisfy him or not."

Despite his ideological differences with Clinton — he was the No. 2 opponent of the president's positions on 1996 Senate floor votes — Kyl on occasion will reach across the aisle to work with Democratic colleagues. He teamed with Democrat Patrick J. Leahy of Vermont to crack down on "cybercrimes" committed by computer hackers, and joined with Ron Wyden, an Oregon Democrat, to offer legislation to prevent health maintenance organizations from stopping doctors from discussing possible treatments with their patients.

Kyl, who was a close ally of Republican Newt Gingrich of Georgia while serving in the House, has at times chafed at the comparatively slow pace of life in the Senate. "Finally, there's a revolution, and I'm over in the Senate," he complained in April 1995. Kyl was a leader of the Conservative Opportunity Society (COS), a caucus of House GOP activists that Gingrich founded at the beginning of his climb to the Speakership. In 1989, the year Gingrich became House GOP whip, Kyl became chairman of the COS.

Kyl is wise to the ways of the legislative process; he was unconcerned that his proposed constitutional amendment to require a two-thirds supermajority to raise taxes had no immediate chance of passing, saying, "It takes seven or eight years to pass a constitutional amendment."

Among Kyl's other fiscally conservative measures are another amendment to the Constitution that would require a balanced budget and limit spending to 19 percent of the previous year's gross domestic project, and a bid to repeal the estate tax.

Kyl has shown a willingness to vote against Arizona interests in favor of the bigger picture. He argued against an amendment to reimburse states for costs associated with illegal immigrants because it came on a bill to limit federal demands on state governments, saying it had no business on the underlying bill. And he let appropriators have $13.4 million that had been earmarked for the Central Arizona project, saying the work was unnecessary or already completed.

At Home: Long touted as a rising GOP star, Kyl made off with the Senate seat of retiring Democrat Dennis DeConcini in 1994 without intraparty opposition and without the tough November test he had prepared to meet.

Kyl is a natural for Arizona's electorate: He is an articulate conservative, though his earnest manner can come across as slightly wooden. Running for the Senate after eight years in the House, he raised $4.3 million and had no trouble dispatching his Democratic competition, first-term Rep. Sam Coppersmith, whom he successfully saddled with Clinton's unpopularity in the Southwest at that time.

When DeConcini announced his retirement, Kyl had already entered the Senate campaign of 1994 with no visible seam in his political armor. And as Kyl breezed through to the GOP nomination, Coppersmith struggled through a three-way battle to secure the Democratic line. Coppersmith finished first in the Sept. 13 primary, but his campaign against Kyl was delayed for more than two weeks beyond that because Secretary of State Richard D. Mahoney was so close that a recount was required. The desperate primary fight left Coppersmith with a depleted purse, and if the financial playing field was uneven, the issue mix proved even more clearly favorable to Kyl. Voters in Arizona were in a mood to hear the themes Kyl always had stressed —too much government, too much taxation and too much regulation.

In the end, Coppersmith was able to carry only a few counties, the most populous being Pima (which includes Tucson, where the University of Arizona is located). But even there, Coppersmith led by only about 4,000 votes. In Maricopa County, the home of both candidates as well as most of the state's population, Kyl won by a commanding 134,000 votes.

SENATE ELECTIONS

1994 General		
Jon Kyl (R)	600,999	(54%)
Sam Coppersmith (D)	442,510	(40%)
Scott Grainger (LIBERT)	75,493	(7%)

Previous Winning Percentages: **1992*** (59%) **1990*** (61%) **1988*** (87%) **1986*** (65%)

** House election*

CAMPAIGN FINANCE

1994	Receipts	Receipts from PACs		Expend-itures
Kyl (R)	$4,314,138	$1,074,778	(25%)	$4,138,203
Coppersmith (D)	$1,578,595	$261,988	(17%)	$1,577,556
Grainger (LIBERT)	$43,767	$1,200	(3%)	$37,740

KEY VOTES

1997	
Approve balanced-budget constitutional amendment	Y
Approve chemical weapons treaty	N
1996	
Approve farm bill	Y
Limit punitive damages in product liability cases	Y
Exempt small businesses from higher minimum wage	Y
Approve welfare overhaul	Y
Bar job discrimination based on sexual orientation	N
Override veto of ban on "partial birth" abortions	Y
1995	
Approve GOP budget with tax and spending cuts	Y
Approve constitutional amendment barring flag desecration	Y

VOTING STUDIES

	Presidential Support		Party Unity		Conservative Coalition	
Year	S	O	S	O	S	O
1996	22	75	96	2	95	3
1995	21	78	97	2	93	7
House Service:						
1994	41	53	93	4	94	6
1993	30	67	95	3	93	5
1992	90	10	95	4	96	4
1991	81	19	95	5	97	3

INTEREST GROUP RATINGS

Year	ADA	AFL-CIO	CCUS	ACU
1996	5	n/a	100	100
1995	0	0	100	100
House Service:				
1994	5	0	0	90
1993	5	0	100	96
1992	5	33	75	92
1991	5	8	90	100

1 Matt Salmon (R)

Of Mesa — Elected 1994, 2nd term

Biographical Information
Born: Jan. 21, 1958, Salt Lake City, Utah.
Education: Arizona State U., B.A. 1981; Brigham Young U., M.A. 1986.
Occupation: Communications company executive.
Family: Wife, Nancy Huish; four children.
Religion: Mormon.
Political Career: Ariz. Senate, 1991-95.
Capitol Office: 115 Cannon Bldg. 20515; 225-2635.

Committees
International Relations
Asia & the Pacific; International Operations & Human Rights
Science
Energy & Environment; Space & Aeronautics

In Washington: Salmon got a splash of media attention early in his second term, when he made the suggestion — a provocative one, considering Salmon's conservatism — that House Speaker Newt Gingrich step aside temporarily until the ethics charges brought against him were resolved. Gingrich had admitted in December 1996 that he violated House rules by failing to seek proper legal advice on his use of tax-exempt funds for political purposes and by providing "inaccurate, incomplete and unreliable statements" to the House ethics committee.

"At the very least, it may be prudent for the Speaker to step aside at least temporarily, until these issues are resolved," Salmon said in an early January 1997 statement. Later on an ABC news program, he said it would "strengthen Newt Gingrich if he would step aside for a time until his good name is cleared. Our agenda is too important to let any one man, or any one person, get in the way." For good measure, Salmon also suggested that President Clinton step aside, pending resolution of questions about irregularities in the financing of his 1996 campaign.

But Gingrich (and Clinton) stayed put, and when it came time on Jan. 7 for House members to cast ballots for Speaker, Salmon voted to re-elect Gingrich. Nine House Republicans expressed their concern over Gingrich's ethics troubles by voting for other Republicans for Speaker or by simply answering "present" to the roll call.

Prior to his weighing in on the issue of Gingrich's suitability for the Speakership, Salmon had mainly specialized in international affairs. His interest in foreign policy is a bit unusual for a member of the GOP Class of 1994, a group largely preoccupied in the 104th Congress with domestic policy concerns.

As a Mormon missionary in Taiwan, Salmon got a taste of life in Asia, and he claims fluency in Mandarin. Upon entering the House, he got a seat on the International Relations Committee, where in the 105th Congress he sits on the Asia and the Pacific Subcommittee and on the International Operations and Human Rights Subcommittee. In these posts, he faces one of the vexing dilemmas in modern American foreign policy: how to press China on its human rights record without resorting to trade sanctions that could spoil U.S. relations with a nation sure to be an economic powerhouse in the next century.

In July 1995, expressing concern about China's commitment to human rights. Salmon said, "As China engaged the Western world, I was heartened, I was encouraged by her desire to become more open politically, economically and socially. But as with many Americans, much of that optimism was extinguished by Tiananmen Square, and part of me died that day. Since that day China has steadily marched backward, stifling freedom, flouting human rights, and demonstrating disregard."

And in March 1996, when Chinese military forces took actions that appeared to be aimed at intimidating Taiwan, Salmon demanded that Congress send an unambiguous signal that the United States would respond forcefully if China launched a military strike on Taiwan. "It's time we draw a line in the sand," he said.

Yet in June 1996, when members advocating a hard line against China sought to block Clinton from renewing China's most favored nation trading status, they were thwarted by a House coalition of liberals and conservatives, including Salmon. The effort to deny China MFN standing was rejected 141-286. Proponents of extending MFN argued that they were not overlooking China's behavior, but rather were attempting to keep the Chinese government engaged and not undermine the market reforms that were slowly improving the standard of living in that nation.

Although Democrats have enjoyed some recent success in the 1st District (Sam Coppersmith held it for a term before leaving to run for the Senate in 1994), Salmon seems confident that the district's electorate stands well to the right of center, judging from the fact that he votes a staunchly conservative line in the House. In some instances his fiscal frugality has outdone even

ARIZONA 1
Southeastern Phoenix — Tempe; Mesa

After 1992 redistricting, voters here elected Democrat Sam Coppersmith, but when he ran unsuccessfully for the Senate in 1994, Salmon returned the district to Republican hands. More than half of its voters are registered Republicans.

The 1992 remap removed some Democratic areas from the 1st: Hispanic neighborhoods surrounding Sky Harbor Airport and the Gila River Indian reservation just south of Phoenix. Mapmakers put East Mesa in the 6th, a step that gives the 1st a more centrist electorate.

Remaining in the district are more moderate Republican voters in West Mesa, Tempe, Chandler and parts of Phoenix. Under certain circumstances they will consider voting for a Democrat. In 1992, the business-oriented Coppersmith added enough of them to the district's Democratic minority to win with 51 percent of the vote and become the first Demo-crat to capture the district since 1950.

The district has become competitive in presidential elections. George Bush won the 1st by 29 percentage points in 1988. But four years later his margin was only 6 points; Bob Dole's lead was less than 1 percentage point. Ross Perot, who got a quarter of the district's votes in 1992, fell to 7 percent in 1996.

The 1st encompasses most of Mesa, where population exploded by almost 90 percent during the 1980s, exceeding 288,000. The district's other suburban pillars are Tempe (population 142,000) and Chandler (population 90,500). Electronics and high-technology companies have thrived here in recent years, spawning a sizable class of well-to-do managers and technicians. They generally have conservative political instincts, as do the thousands of retirees who have settled in the area.

Mesa was founded by Mormons in 1878; it still has a politically active Mormon community and is the site of Arizona's Mormon temple. Mesa is home to eight manufacturing companies on the Fortune 500 list.

Tempe, just to the west, was developed around a flour mill in 1871; today it is primarily a manufacturing city, with more than 200 businesses producing a range of goods, from clothing to electronics. The city usually votes Republican in state and local elections, but Arizona State University's 42,463 students and 1,600 faculty members provide Tempe with a significant Democratic presence. The Fiesta Bowl provides an annual economic shot in the arm for the university.

The district also takes in a politically diverse portion of southeastern Phoenix, a tabletop-flat area of the "Valley of the Sun" that includes some upper middle-class neighborhoods with a distinctly Republican bent.

Another new addition to the 1st in redistricting — a small, southern portion of Scottsdale — adds to Republican strength in the district.

1990 Population: 610,872. White 530,941 (87%), Black 19,280 (3%), Other 60,651 (10%). Hispanic origin 80,350 (13%). 18 and over 457,975 (75%), 62 and over 67,266 (11%). Median age: 30.

that of the GOP leadership. In June 1996, he was one just 19 Republicans voting against his party's fiscal 1997 budget plan. The defectors complained that the budget allowed for a short-term increase in the deficit and included, at the Senate's insistence, $4 billion extra in domestic spending.

Also, early in the 104th Congress Salmon supported a version of the balanced-budget constitutional amendment that would have required three-fifths majorities in each chamber to pass tax increases.

"The people who . . . elected me, elected me to come here and fight hard for them, not for government," Salmon said during debate on the balanced-budget amendment. "They elected me to come here to stop spending and fight taxes at the same time, and I intend to do that."

But Salmon has supported federal spending on a couple of big-ticket items that some other tight-fisted Republicans oppose. A member of the Science Committee, he has voted to continue funding for NASA's space station. The investment in the space station, he says, "finds practical applications for daily life on Earth, and it is money well spent. . . . Unlike other government programs, every dollar spent on space programs returns at least $2 in direct and indirect benefits."

Salmon also has favored building more B-2 bombers beyond the 20 planes the Pentagon has said are sufficient. Salmon said in 1995 that the additional planes were needed because they could help save the lives of servicemen and women. "With stealth and precision-guided munitions, one B-2 with a crew of two is as effective as 75 conventional aircraft which place 132 air crew at risk."

Salmon was a stalwart supporter of "Contract with America" initiatives to rein in federal regulation, and his conservative views extend to social policy issues as well. He opposes abortion and voted in March 1996 to repeal the ban on certain semiautomatic assault-style weapons.

Salmon supports term limits, but in March 1995 he rejected as too timid the GOP leadership's version of a term limits constitutional amendment; it would have imposed a 12-year limit on members of each chamber. Salmon voted for two other, stricter versions of a term limit amendment: one would have imposed a six-year lifetime limit on House members and a 12-year limit on senators; the second called for a 12-year cap on congressional terms and also allowed states to impose shorter terms.

"Let me tell you one compelling reason, one big, large, fat reason why we should vote for term limits," Salmon told the House. "It is the number 5 trillion, because this Congress, over the last few decades, has plunged this country $5 trillion in debt. Maybe, just maybe, if we know we are going to be here for a time certain, 6 years, we will have some guts and make the proper decisions to make the cuts where they need to be cut." In 1995 and again in 1997, the term-limits movement ran aground in the House.

At Home: Salmon has gone places fast in a political career that began only in 1990 with his election to the state Senate. In a pair of two-year terms there, he rose to become assistant majority leader and served as chairman of the Rules Committee. Before entering the legislature, Salmon had worked for the communications company U.S. West.

In winning the affluent, urban-suburban 1st in 1992, Democrat Coppersmith broke a 42-year GOP hold on the district. When he gambled (and ultimately lost) on a Senate bid in 1994, Salmon and four other Republicans jumped in to compete for the opening. Unlike his main rivals, former Scottsdale City Council member Susan Bitter Smith and Mesa lawyer Linda Rawles, Salmon did not air a single ad. But he built a first-class grass roots organization, made effective use of direct mail and earned an endorsement from Republican Sen. John McCain, as well as backing from the National Rifle Association and the American Medical Association. He won nomination with 39 percent of the vote, 17 points ahead of his nearest rival.

Democrats also nominated a state senator, Chuck Blanchard, and he offered voters a profile similar to Coppersmith: a fiscally conservative, socially moderate, pro-business centrist. Blanchard had graduated first in his class from Harvard Law School and clerked for Supreme Court Justice Sandra Day O'Connor, a fellow Arizonan. He also was the state co-chairman of Bill Clinton's 1992 presidential campaign.

Blanchard thought he could isolate Salmon as an extremist, and he faulted the Republican's stands on issues such as gun control, abortion and the environment. He also attacked Salmon for signing the House GOP's "Contract With America."

Given voters' mood in 1994, though, Blanchard found that his party label and his past support for Clinton were a bigger liability than Salmon's image as a strong conservative.

Boosted by a surge in GOP voting that enabled the party to retain Arizona's governor's office, capture an open Democratic Senate seat and win another Democratic-held House seat (the 6th), Salmon prevailed by 17 points, 56 percent to 39 percent. In 1996, he moved up to 60 percent of the vote.

HOUSE ELECTIONS

1996 General		
Matt Salmon (R)	135,634	(60%)
John Cox (D)	89,738	(40%)
1994 General		
Matt Salmon (R)	101,350	(56%)
Chuck Blanchard (D)	70,627	(39%)
Bob Howarth (LIBERT)	8,890	(5%)

CAMPAIGN FINANCE

	Receipts	Receipts from PACs	Expend-itures
1996			
Salmon (R)	$494,855	$219,536 (44%)	$456,089
1994			
Salmon (R)	$539,023	$200,440 (37%)	$508,421
Blanchard (D)	$464,005	$148,698 (32%)	$440,372

DISTRICT VOTE FOR PRESIDENT

1996		1992	
D	108,063 (46%)	D	88,247 (34%)
R	109,426 (46%)	R	105,784 (40%)
I	17,091 (7%)	I	68,143 (26%)

KEY VOTES

1997	
Ban "partial-birth" abortions	Y
1996	
Approve farm bill	Y
Deny public education to illegal immigrants	Y
Repeal ban on certain assault-style weapons	Y
Increase minimum wage	N
Freeze defense spending	N
Approve welfare overhaul	Y
1995	
Approve balanced-budget constitutional amendment	Y
Relax Clean Water Act regulations	Y
Oppose limits on environmental regulations	N
Reduce projected Medicare spending	Y
Approve GOP budget with tax and spending cuts	Y

VOTING STUDIES

	Presidential Support		Party Unity		Conservative Coalition	
Year	S	O	S	O	S	O
1996	33	67	91	8	90	8
1995	17	82	96	3	93	6

INTEREST GROUP RATINGS

Year	ADA	AFL-CIO	CCUS	ACU
1996	10	n/a	88	100
1995	0	0	96	92

2 Ed Pastor (D)

Of Phoenix — Elected 1991; 3rd full term

Biographical Information
Born: June 28, 1943, Claypool, Ariz.
Education: Arizona State U., B.S. 1966, J.D. 1974.
Occupation: Teacher; gubernatorial aide; public policy consultant.
Family: Wife, Verma Mendez; two children.
Religion: Roman Catholic.
Political Career: Maricopa County Board of Supervisors, 1977-91.
Capitol Office: 2465 Rayburn Bldg. 20515; 225-4065.

Committees
Appropriations
Energy & Water Development; Transportation

In Washington: The electoral fortunes of the Democratic Party have bounced Pastor around a good bit since he came to Congress in 1991, but in the the 105th Congress he is happy to be back where he started in the 103rd: on the Appropriations Committee.

His subcommittee assignments there are Energy and Water Development, whose work is important in the arid West; and Transportation, which in the 105th is working on the massive reauthorization bill funding road, public transit and other transportation projects.

Pastor was first appointed to Appropriations after the 1992 election. The large group of Democrats first elected that November insisted that they get a share of the openings on top committees. Democratic leaders tapped Pastor for Appropriations; although not a true freshman, he was considered part of the class of 1992 for organizational purposes because he had won a 1991 special election to replace veteran Democratic Rep. Morris K. Udall.

But after just one term, Pastor got booted off Appropriations. The 1994 elections turned the House over to the GOP, and party ratios on committees shifted in favor of the new majority. With the "last on, first off" rule applying, Pastor was among the junior members who did not make the cut for the diminished number of Democratic seats on Appropriations.

Although the 1996 election kept the GOP in control, enough Democrats on Appropriations retired or sought higher office to make room in 1997 for Pastor and several others to return to the panel for the 105th.

The Republican surge to power in 1994 complicated Pastor's life in another regard. An active member of the Congressional Hispanic Caucus, he was elected chairman of the group in November 1994, just as the new GOP leadership announced it was taking away the budgets, staffs and offices of 28 House legislative service organizations (LSOs), including the Hispanic caucus. Although the group still could meet, any staff work would have to be done from members' personal offices. Pastor defended the caucus after his election as chairman, saying, "It is important to have some means to augment or increase the visibility of those groups in Congress which are in the minority."

Republicans did not budge on the LSO ban, but there was some good news for the Hispanic Caucus at the end of Pastor's two-year term as chairman: Its ranks increased by two with the election in 1996 of Democrat Silvestre Reyes of Texas, who replaced retiring Democratic Rep. Ronald D. Coleman, and California Democrat Loretta Sanchez, who knocked out GOP Rep. Robert K. Dornan.

During his tenure leading the caucus, Pastor and his Hispanic colleagues put up a fight against Republican efforts to clamp down on illegal immigration and on government services and benefits provided to immigrants.

In the House, Republicans first pushed a bill combining legal and illegal immigration issues. It proposed further limits on the number of immigrants admitted to the country legally each year and barred legal immigrants from receiving certain government benefits, and it sought to prevent illegal immigration by beefing up the Border Patrol, establishing new methods for conducting background checks, and denying illegal immigrants certain federal benefits.

Pastor and other Democrats targeted the provisions dealing with legal immigration for special criticism, making the case that the bill was punishing people who had played by the rules. Their efforts bore some fruit, as the House voted to strike most of the language on legal immigration from the broader immigration conference report. The House did, however pass a controversial amendment to deny public education to illegal immigrants, a proposal Pastor and his allies strongly opposed.

The Senate passed a bill dealing exclusively with illegal immigration, and controversy over the public schooling amendment hindered the two chambers from reaching agreement. The schooling provision ultimately was dropped in the inter-

ARIZONA 2
Southwest — Southwestern Tucson; southern Phoenix; Yuma

The 2nd is Arizona's most Hispanic and most Democratic district. Redistricting in 1992 gave the 2nd a bare Hispanic-majority population: 50 percent, up from 36 percent in the 1980s. Hispanics make up 45 percent of the voting-age population.

Some Hispanic activists lobbied mapmakers for a heavier minority concentration, but Pastor had no trouble winning here. He won his first reelection in 1992 with two-thirds of the vote as Bill Clinton's 51 percent tally in the 2nd was easily his best showing in any Arizona district. After experiencing only a slight drop-off in his 1994 victory margin, Pastor won again in 1996 with two-thirds of the vote.

Pima County (Tucson), located in the southwest, surpassed Maricopa County (Phoenix) in 1996 to account for the largest share of the district's votes (36 percent). Democrats are strong in Hispanic neighborhoods here, and also in the community surrounding the University of Arizona.

Just south of Tucson, the copper-mining town of Ajo and the San Xavier and Papago Indian reservations also favor Democrats. Tucson has begun to see the same influx of retirees and people attracted by high-tech companies that has transformed politics in other parts of Arizona. But Tucson's long Democratic tradition is still strong; Bill Clinton won 70 percent in the Pima County part of the 2nd in 1996.

Though the bulk of Pima County's land area lies within the boundaries of the 2nd, most of the county's residents live in eastern Tucson in the 5th District.

Most of the Maricopa vote also comes out of Hispanic areas. The south side of Phoenix, included in the 2nd, traditionally has been the city's poorest economically and most faithfully Democratic. Remapping strengthened the Democratic slant by including the minority neighborhoods near Sky Harbor Airport, which had been in the 1st District.

The most Republican part of the 2nd is on the district's western edge, in Yuma County. It casts about one-fifth of the total district vote, and it went for George Bush in 1992 and Bob Dole in 1996. Yuma also has backed Pastor's GOP challengers in 1992, 1994 and 1996, even though they lost overwhelmingly districtwide.

Incorporated as Arizona City in 1871 and renamed two years later, Yuma, the county seat, lies south of California on the Colorado River; it continues in its traditional role as a regional commercial crossroads. Interstate 8 running through the city heads west to San Diego. Yuma County's economic base is agricultural, but two military bases — the Yuma Marine Corps Air Station and Yuma Proving Grounds — contribute significantly to the economy.

Rounding out the 2nd is Santa Cruz County, where the heavily Hispanic border town of Nogales and its Mexican sister city of the same name are a major crossing point between the two countries. Clinton won Santa Cruz in 1992 but ran several percentage points below his district average. In 1996, he ran as well in Santa Cruz as he did throughout the district.

1990 Population: 610,871. White 367,125 (60%), Black 41,578 (7%), Other 202,168 (33%). Hispanic origin 308,256 (50%). 18 and over 414,281 (68%), 62 and over 72,554 (12%). Median age: 28.

est of reaching a compromise, but if that gave Pastor some cause for satisfaction, he still voted in September 1996 against the final immigration conference report. It was largely hammered out by House and Senate Republicans and the Clinton White House, without much input from congressional Democrats. The final bill included items that were in neither the House nor the Senate bill, including new restrictions on legal immigrants.

Also in the 104th, immigration issues were a component of the debate on overhauling the welfare system. Republicans argued that the nation's generous welfare benefits offered an incentive for people to enter the country, and they proposed denying various welfare benefits to legal immigrants.

Pastor objected vigorously to that proposal. "The United States is a nation of immigrants," he said in a Hispanic Caucus news release. "Immigrants are hardworking, taxpaying Americans who make substantial contributions to the U.S. economy. Legal immigrants do not come to the United States just to get welfare. In fact, 95 percent of immigrants support themselves without welfare."

Over the course of the 104th, liberal Democrats had persuaded President Clinton to twice veto Republican welfare proposals. But with the 1996 election approaching, Clinton wanted to undercut a Republican campaign theme by coming to terms with congressional Republicans on welfare. The overhaul legislation enacted in August 1996 included language barring legal immigrants from receiving Supplemental Security Income benefits.

In the summer of 1996, Republicans brought forward a bill to make English the official language of the U.S. government. Proponents said the measure would save money, citing as one example the extra expense of having to print ballots in multiple languages in some areas. And they said that encouraging all U.S. residents to speak English would be a unifying force in society.

Pastor, unmoved, said the bill was unconstitutional, and that it would not have the unifying impact Republicans intended. "Language minorities want to learn English and participate in American institutions," he said. "But this legislation will further isolate non-native speakers of English and discourage them from fully integrating themselves into society."

The Hispanic Caucus introduced its own measure, "English Plus," which expressed the value of multilingualism to the nation, to counter the Republican initiative. Although the GOP measure passed in the House, it got no further.

At Home: Hispanics began making preparations to contend for the 2nd not long after the 1990 election; Udall had said he would retire at the end of the 102nd, but the transition came sooner than expected, after Udall, weakened by Parkinson's disease, resigned in May 1991.

The Democratic primary preceding the September special election was Pastor's biggest hurdle. (Democrats have a wide voter-registration advantage in the 2nd.) Tom Volgy, mayor of Tucson (Pima County), the 2nd's largest city, was his main opponent.

The five-candidate primary turned into a turf battle between Pastor and Volgy. Pima County residents long had considered the 2nd theirs; Pastor's base was Maricopa County (Phoenix), where he had served four terms on the Board of Supervisors. Pastor emphasized his 15 years of public service: He was an aide to former Democratic Gov. Raul Castro before being elected to the board.

Pastor was the establishment's choice, winning endorsements of both leading Hispanic and Anglo officeholders. Volgy ran well in Pima but finished a distant third in Maricopa. Pastor won with 37 percent of the vote, 5 points ahead of Volgy.

In the September special election, Pastor faced Republican Pat Conner, a Yuma County supervisor. He criticized Pastor for taking $2,800 in campaign contributions from thrift executive Charles H. Keating Jr. in 1988 and a $1,000 set of golf clubs from a lobbyist later indicted in a state corruption probe.

The charges did not faze voters: Pastor had given the money from Keating to the IRS in 1988, and he had returned the clubs. Pastor won with a comfortable 56 percent of the vote, moved up to 66 percent in 1992 and has coasted since.

HOUSE ELECTIONS

1996 General		
Ed Pastor (D)	81,982	(65%)
Jim Buster (R)	38,786	(31%)
Alice Bangle (LIBERT)	5,333	(4%)
1994 General		
Ed Pastor (D)	62,589	(62%)
Robert MacDonald (R)	32,797	(33%)
James Bertrand (LIBERT)	5,060	(5%)

Previous Winning Percentages: 1992 (66%) **1991**† (56%)

† Special election

CAMPAIGN FINANCE

	Receipts	Receipts from PACs	Expend-itures
1996			
Pastor (D)	$486,368	$242,835 (50%)	$405,526
Buster (R)	$103,398	$18,066 (17%)	$101,730
1994			
Pastor (D)	$368,594	$206,804 (56%)	$349,627

KEY VOTES

1997	
Ban "partial birth" abortions	N
1996	
Approve farm bill	N
Deny public education to illegal immigrants	N
Repeal ban on certain assault-style weapons	N
Increase minimum wage	Y
Freeze defense spending	Y
Approve welfare overhaul	N
1995	
Approve balanced-budget constitutional amendment	N
Relax Clean Water Act regulations	N
Oppose limits on environmental regulations	Y
Reduce projected Medicare spending	N
Approve GOP budget with tax and spending cuts	N

DISTRICT VOTE FOR PRESIDENT

	1996		1992
D	81,502 (64%)	**D**	74,588 (51%)
R	35,843 (28%)	**R**	41,757 (29%)
I	9,256 (7%)	**I**	28,767 (20%)

VOTING STUDIES

	Presidential Support		Party Unity		Conservative Coalition	
Year	**S**	**O**	**S**	**O**	**S**	**O**
1996	75	20	89	10	43	55
1995	83	16	91	8	27	69
1994	83	15	95	5	42	58
1993	86	14	95	4	27	73
1992	20	75	89	9	25	73
1991	33†	67†	92†	7†	24†	76†

† Not eligible for all recorded votes.

INTEREST GROUP RATINGS

Year	ADA	AFL-CIO	CCUS	ACU
1996	85	n/a	38	5
1995	95	100	21	4
1994	80	78	42	14
1993	90	92	27	4
1992	85	83	13	12
1991	83†	100†	25†	0†

† Not eligible for all recorded votes.

3 Bob Stump (R)

Of Tolleson — Elected 1976, 11th term

Biographical Information
Born: April 4, 1927, Phoenix, Ariz.
Education: Arizona State U., B.S. 1951.
Military Service: Navy, 1943-46.
Occupation: Cotton farmer.
Family: Divorced; three children.
Religion: Seventh-Day Adventist.
Political Career: Ariz. House, 1959-67; Ariz. Senate, 1967-77, president, 1975-77.
Capitol Office: 211 Cannon Bldg. 20515; 225-4576.

Committees
National Security
Military Installations and Facilities; Military Procurement
Veterans' Affairs (chairman)
Oversight & Investigations

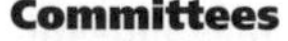

In Washington: Stump has rarely sought the spotlight during his two decades in Congress, but now that he is a full committee chair — of the Veterans' Affairs panel — a measure of attention comes his way automatically. Congress' current focus on deficit reduction makes it a challenge for any chairman seeking resources for programs he oversees, but Stump is fortunate that many in the GOP majority believe veterans should get special preference when funds for domestic programs are divvied up.

Stump has served in both parties — first elected as a Democrat in 1976, he switched to the GOP in 1981 — and he has risen to the No. 2 spot on the National Security Committee, right behind committee Chairman Floyd D. Spence, R-S.C. His first priority, though, has never been partisan politics or grand strategizing on defense policy, but tending to the work of the Veterans' Affairs Committee.

As the panel's ranking Republican for three terms, Stump developed a close working relationship with the Democratic chairman, G.V. "Sonny" Montgomery of Mississippi, one of the most conservative House Democrats. On almost every issue that came before the committee, the two men forged a bipartisan consensus. Stump and Montgomery changed places in the GOP-led 104th Congress, and their working relationship stayed much the same.

But Montgomery retired at the end of the 104th, and now the ranking Democrat is Lane Evans of Illinois. He is one of the House's more liberal members, and it will be interesting to see how he and Stump work together. Whereas both Montgomery and Stump served in the military during World War II, Evans is a Vietnam-era veteran who has sought expanded medical benefits for younger-generation soldiers, such as those who served in the Vietnam and Persian Gulf wars.

For four years, Stump helped Montgomery block an Evans led effort to provide compensation for Vietnam veterans who said their exposure to the herbicide Agent Orange had caused them to develop cancer. Stump argued that studies showed no definitive link between certain cancers and Agent Orange. But Evans persisted and eventually succeeded in getting a compromise bill enacted in January 1991; Stump supported it.

Stump and Evans crossed swords in the 104th over an effort by Evans to provide health and vocational benefits to children of Vietnam veterans exposed to Agent Orange who were born with spina bifida, a crippling birth defect. Supported by many Senate Democrats, the provision was included in the fiscal 1997 spending bill funding the Department of Veterans' Affairs (VA). Critics worried about the precedent of granting children medical benefits linked to alleged service injuries of their parents. "I don't believe there's any scientific proof of a link between a parent's exposure to Agent Orange and a child's spina bifida," Stump said. In a compromise, conferees on the VA spending bill agreed to include the benefits but delay the effective date until Oct. 1, 1997, to give the Veterans' Affairs committees time to weigh the issue further.

Another medical matter is likely to occupy a good share of the committee's time during the 105th: Persian Gulf Syndrome, the name given to a range of medical symptoms reported by Gulf War veterans, many of whom believe their illnesses are connected to exposure to Iraqi chemical weapons. Evans has already pressed for increased treatment and compensation for veterans with the syndrome.

Stump's first term as chairman was spent finding ways to keep government funding for veterans' programs at a steady level. In March 1995, when the House considered a measure rescinding $17.3 billion in previously appropriated funds for fiscal 1995, members voted, 382-23, to restore $206 million in spending on veterans programs that the Appropriations committee had sought to cut. The $206 million was to be taken from President Clinton's National Service program, which gives young adults federal stipends for community work. Stump said the service program was a waste that "pays so-called volunteers to perform services that millions of Americans already do without seeking one dollar."

During the 104th, Stump won House approval of

ARIZONA 3
North and West — Glendale; part of Phoenix; Hopi reservation

The most eye-catching feature of the 3rd is the oddly shaped appendage on its northeastern edge. That cartographic flight stems from a decision by federal judges who drew Arizona's House lines to put the reservations of the Hopi and Navajo Indians — two tribes whose land disputes reach back generations — into separate congressional districts. Redistricting, however, did little to change the fundamental political personality of the 3rd.

Once dominated by "pinto Democrats" — ranchers and other conservative rural landowners — the 3rd has become prime GOP turf over the years. And remapping in 1992 only hastened the Republican shift by moving Flagstaff and its Democratic loyalties into the 6th.

Voter registration in the 3rd is now majority Republican. Bob Dole carried the 3rd with 48 percent of the vote in 1996.

More than 55 percent of the district's vote is cast in the Maricopa County suburbs west of Phoenix. In Glendale, which produces wide GOP margins, the population grew by more than 50 percent in the 1980s. Glendale's economy, once grounded in agriculture, has diversified to include manufacturing jobs in the aerospace, electronics, communications and chemical industries.

In nearby Sun City, an affluent and largely GOP retirement community, the politically active residents typically turn out for elections at an 80 percent or better rate.

The district moves west out of Phoenix, following I-10 into La Paz County, which was created in 1982 by a ballot initiative that split Yuma County, to La Paz's south. The La Paz community of Quartzsite swells during the winter, as travelers flock to take advantage of its warm climate and see its rock and mineral shows.

Mohave County, in Arizona's northwest corner, is home to three groups in constant political tension: Indians, pinto Democrats in Kingman and Republican retirees in Lake Havasu City. Dole won the county in 1996, but with only 43 percent, 1,368 votes more than Bill Clinton.

Coconino County, where partisan sentiments are mixed, is now split between the 3rd and 6th districts. Most of "the Arizona strip," which includes a heavily Mormon region with strong GOP ties, remains in the 3rd. Sedona, a Republican bastion in the southern part of the county, also remains in the 3rd.

Just north of Flagstaff, the 3rd includes a narrow arm that reaches east to pick up the Hopi reservation, which lies in Coconino and Navajo counties. The federal court went to great lengths to separate the Navajo from the Hopi, who bitterly complain that the Navajo have long been encroaching on land designated by the federal government as Hopi. The mapmakers even went so far as to include in the 3rd the tiny Hopi village of Moenkopi, which is completely surrounded by Navajo lands that are in the 6th. Moenkopi is connected to the 3rd by an uninhabited stretch of state Route 264.

1990 Population: 610,871. White 534,991 (88%), Black 11,849 (2%), Other 64,031 (10%). Hispanic origin 72,113 (12%). 18 and over 457,293 (75%), 62 and over 140,889 (23%). Median age: 36.

much of his committee's legislative agenda, including a measure to overhaul the veterans' health care system. Passed 416-0 in August 1996, the bill would allow the VA to move more veterans out of hospitals and into less expensive outpatient clinics, by directing the department away from its current emphasis on hospital care. Supporters, including the VA and veterans' groups, said the changes would allow the VA to cut costs and use the savings to treat additional veterans.

The existing VA rules required veterans in many cases to check into a VA hospital to receive treatment. Outpatient care was largely limited to severely disabled veterans whose injuries were connected to their military service or to patients who had already been treated in a VA hospital.

In May 1996, Stump did something he hadn't done in 15 years: He held a news conference. The event, at which Stump criticized Clinton's legal defense in a sexual harassment suit, was only his second news conference ever. The first was in his district in 1981, when he announced he was switching parties. Stump also doesn't issue press releases. "I just don't like this self-promotion crap," he once said. "It's phony."

Clinton stirred up a tempest when his lawyer asserted in a court filing that as commander in chief he is in the military and so a sexual-harassment lawsuit against him brought by Paula Corbin Jones must be postponed until his active duty is completed. Conservatives and veterans' advocates howled in protest. "You are not a person in military service, nor have you ever been," Stump wrote in a letter to Clinton.

In his early House years, Stump was known as one of the Democratic Party's most conservative members. When he announced he was leaving the party, he said he had concluded he would be more comfortable — both politically and personally — in conservative Republican ranks than on the liberal-dominated Democratic side. Like many of his rural constituents, Stump, a cotton farmer, was raised as a "pinto Democrat," a distinctive group of rural Arizonans who trace their roots to the South and hold to the conservative philosophy dominant in that region.

Stump had served on the Armed Services Committee as a Democrat, and after he switched parties, the GOP gave him a seat on their side of the panel with no loss in seniority. On the committee (now named National Security), Stump is a strong supporter of the military and has backed Republican efforts to spend more money on defense than the Clinton administration requests.

Stump also made some news in early 1997, when he was one of 26 Republicans to vote "no" as the House reprimanded Speaker Newt Gingrich and assessed him a $300,000 penalty for violating ethics rules. Stump said Gingrich deserved the reprimand but not the "ridiculous" monetary penalty.

At Home: Stump served 18 years in the state Legislature and rose to the presidency of the state Senate during the 1975-76 session. When GOP Rep. Sam Steiger tried for the U.S. Senate in 1976, Stump ran for his House seat.

In the 1976 Democratic primary, he defeated a more liberal, free-spending opponent, Sid Rosen, a former state assistant attorney general. Stump drew 31 percent to Rosen's 25 percent, with the rest scattered among three others. In the fall campaign, Stump's GOP opponent was fellow state Sen. Fred Koory, the Senate minority leader. Stump wooed conservative Democrats by criticizing his party's vice presidential nominee, Walter F. Mondale. He also was helped by the candidacy of state Sen. Bill McCune, a Republican who ran as an independent and drained GOP votes from Koory.

Secure in the seat after his first election, Stump had plenty of time to contemplate his party switch. When he declared he would seek re-election as a Republican in 1982, it caused barely a ripple at home.

Stump said his decision would not cost him any significant support in either party. He was right, at least initially. Conservative rural Democrats proved willing to move with him, and the district's Republican voters — many of them retirees who had brought GOP voting habits with them — were glad to have him in their camp. Stump coasted to victory in 1982 with 63 percent of the vote. His subsequent re-elections were uneventful until 1990, when a virtual unknown, Roger Hartstone, garnered 43 percent of the vote. A commercial photographer and self-described environmentalist, the Democrat launched a write-in effort after Stump successfully challenged his nomination petitions.

Hartstone ran an effective grass-roots campaign, searing Stump as "the phantom of Congress" who rarely returned to the district. Hartstone attacked Stump's record on environmental and fiscal matters. Stump also was criticized for missing four important budget votes on a weekend when he attended an Arizona State University football game; Stump said the House leadership had assured him no crucial votes would occur.

In 1992, Hartstone won the Democratic nomination to oppose Stump. He rehashed his themes from 1990, but voters were less impressed the second time around. Stump climbed above 60 percent and has stayed there ever since.

HOUSE ELECTIONS

1996 General		
Bob Stump (R)	175,231	(67%)
Alexander "Big Al" Schneider (D)	88,214	(33%)
1994 General		
Bob Stump (R)	145,396	(70%)
Howard Lee Sprague (D)	61,939	(30%)

Previous Winning Percentages: **1992** (61%) **1990** (57%) **1988** (69%) **1986** (100%) **1984** (72%) **1982** (63%) **1980*** (64%) **1978*** (85%) **1976*** (48%)

** Stump was elected as a Democrat in 1976-80.*

KEY VOTES

1997	
Ban "partial birth" abortions	Y
1996	
Approve farm bill	Y
Deny public education to illegal immigrants	Y
Repeal ban on certain assault-style weapons	Y
Increase minimum wage	N
Freeze defense spending	N
Approve welfare overhaul	Y
1995	
Approve balanced-budget constitutional amendment	Y
Relax Clean Water Act regulations	Y
Oppose limits on environmental regulations	N
Reduce projected Medicare spending	Y
Approve GOP budget with tax and spending cuts	Y

CAMPAIGN FINANCE

	Receipts	Receipts from PACs		Expend-itures
1996				
Stump (R)	$244,389	$122,366	(50%)	$233,997
Schneider (D)	$31,287	$6,500	(21%)	$23,567
1994				
Stump (R)	$189,792	$107,478	(57%)	$152,718
Sprague (D)	$4,353	$500	(11%)	$5,851

DISTRICT VOTE FOR PRESIDENT

1996			1992		
D	113,614	(41%)	D	86,060	(32%)
R	131,364	(48%)	R	109,840	(41%)
I	27,043	(10%)	I	73,356	(27%)

VOTING STUDIES

	Presidential Support		Party Unity		Conservative Coalition	
Year	S	O	S	O	S	O
1996	34	66	97	3	98	2
1995	20	80	97	3	98	2
1994	27	73	99	1	94	6
1993	27	73	99	1	98	2
1992	85	15	98	1	94	6
1991	78	22	97	3	97	3

INTEREST GROUP RATINGS

Year	ADA	AFL-CIO	CCUS	ACU
1996	0	n/a	94	100
1995	0	0	100	92
1994	0	11	75	100
1993	0	0	91	100
1992	0	8	75	100
1991	0	0	90	100

4 John Shadegg (R)

Of Phoenix — Elected 1994, 2nd term

Biographical Information
Born: Oct. 22, 1949, Phoenix, Ariz.
Education: U. of Arizona, B.A. 1972, J.D. 1975.
Military Service: National Guard, 1969-75.
Occupation: Lawyer.
Family: Wife, Shirley Lueck; two children.
Religion: Episcopalian.
Political Career: No previous office.
Capitol Office: 430 Cannon Bldg. 20515; 225-3361.

Committees
Budget
Government Reform & Oversight
National Economic Growth, Natural Resources & Regulatory Affairs; National Security, International Affairs & Criminal Justice
Resources
National Parks & Public Lands; Water & Power

In Washington: It is testimony to Shadegg's staunchly conservative views that he was asked to succeed House Speaker Newt Gingrich as chairman of GOPAC, a Republican political action committee that Gingrich helped found. Shadegg took the reins of the group in September 1995, as it was facing scrutiny because of allegations it had violated federal election laws.

Shadegg was one of those in the Republican Class of 1994 who benefited from Gingrich's effort to give freshmen a quick chance to exercise influence in the 104th Congress. The Arizonan got a seat on the Budget Committee, was named an assistant party whip and was appointed to the House GOP Policy Committee.

Shadegg was looking forward to even greater things in the 105th Congress — specifically, a seat on the Ways and Means Committee. But when the GOP leadership filled four openings on that prestigious panel, Shadegg was left out, a big disappointment. "The language I was given was, 'John's got the next seat,'" he told The Wall Street Journal in early 1997. One of the four seats went to Shadegg's Arizona colleague, J.D. Hayworth.

In light of Shadegg's missing out on Ways and Means, it is worth noting that, like a number of his classmates on the GOP right, he had rocked the party boat at times in the 104th by advocating an even harder conservative line than the leadership preferred.

Shadegg voted "no" in January 1996 when Gingrich asked his troops to vote to end a partial government shutdown that had resulted from a breakdown in budget negotiations between Congress and the Clinton White House. On that vote, Shadegg was one of 15 Republicans — 12 of them from the class of 1994 — who bucked the leadership.

Many Republicans worried that the public was laying blame for the shutdown on the GOP, but Shadegg criticized then-Senate Majority Leader Bob Dole for seeking compromise with the White House to put federal employees back to work. "Bob Dole made a huge miscalculation," Shadegg told the Los Angeles Times. "It is an act of betrayal. . . . This guy has been in Washington so long and made so many deals, he thinks the way to solve the problem is to do a deal."

In June 1996, Shadegg again stiffed the GOP leadership by opposing the fiscal 1997 budget blueprint drafted by top House and Senate Republicans. Shadegg joined 18 other Republicans in voting against the agreement because it projected a short-term increase in the budget deficit and included an additional $4 billion for domestic programs.

Early in the 104th, Shadegg backed a version of a balanced-budget constitutional amendment requiring a three-fifths majority vote in each chamber to raise taxes, an alternative that most GOP leaders thought too stringent to win approval. Shadegg said the three-fifths requirement would provide "the kind of discipline we desperately need in this body."

"The power of taxation," Shadegg once told the House, "is the power to put a gun at the heads of the American people and take money from them." In 1992, he led a successful campaign in Arizona for a statewide referendum amending the state constitution to require a two-thirds majority vote of the Legislature to raise taxes.

One of his favorite anti-tax lectures goes like this: "In 1950, the year after I was born, the average American family with children paid $1 out of $50 to the federal government in income taxes. Today, that family with children pays $1 out of $4. That is a 1,200-percent increase. . . . The answer is that American people are not taxed too little. They are taxed too much."

On social-policy issues, Shadegg is a similarly stalwart conservative. He opposes abortion, disapproves of same-sex marriages and voted in March 1996 to repeal the ban on certain semiautomatic assault-style weapons.

He has favored phasing out funding for the National Endowment for the Arts (NEA) and the National Endowment for the Humanities (NEH). In July 1995, he opposed a GOP leadership plan to preserve NEA funding for at least three years, and

ARIZONA 4
Northern Phoenix; Scottsdale

Because of rapid growth in northern Phoenix and its suburbs during the 1980s, the 4th's size is only a fraction of its former self. The sparsely populated northeastern part of the state that made up most of the old 4th was shifted to the 6th in 1992 redistricting.

But the electorate of the 4th remains virtually unchanged. This is Arizona's least minority-influenced district — 92 percent of its residents are white — and arguably its most conservative.

Previously in the 4th, most of the vote was cast in the comfortable confines of northern Phoenix and its Maricopa County suburbs. Now, the district is entirely within Maricopa, making it one of Arizona's two all-urban districts.

The 4th is one of four Arizona districts centered in Phoenix, incorporated in 1881 and the ninth-largest city in the nation. As both the state capital and Maricopa County seat, Phoenix is understandably the hub of activity in the state, although it is constantly battling Tucson to retain its pre-eminence in the eyes of employers relocating to Arizona. More than 4,000 manufacturing companies, employing nearly 200,000 people, are in the Phoenix metropolitan area.

Northern Phoenix's white-collar population provides generous support for Republican candidates, as do similarly upscale residents in Scottsdale and other Maricopa County suburbs. In the 1996 presidential election, the 4th was Bob Dole's best district in Arizona, giving him 48 percent of the vote to Bill Clinton's 44 percent.

Redistricting extended the district farther west into Maricopa County, picking up bedroom communities, including part of Glendale, that add to Republican strength in the 4th. Several high-technology firms have made their home in the 4th District. Honeywell has two plants in the district, and a number of residents work in Motorola's Government Tactical Electronics and Communications Division in Scottsdale.

The tourism industry adds to the economic base in the district. Scottsdale is an affluent resort community that attracts visitors with its warm, sunny climate, myriad golf courses and fashionable shops. Scottsdale grew by more than 46 percent during the 1980s and has continued its expansion into the 1990s to a current population of about 168,000 people.

Many here are retirees; others commute to work at the management level in Phoenix corporations. In addition to Motorola Inc. and Honeywell, aerospace manufacturer Allied-Signal Co., American Express Travel Related Services Co., US West Communications, Viad Corp. and Arizona Public Service are among the largest employers in Phoenix. Community names such as Paradise Valley and Carefree bespeak the lifestyle ideal.

Democrats have a base of support in the southern part of the 4th, where the district stretches into downtown Phoenix. But only about one-third of the voters in the 4th are registered Democrats, compared with more than 50 percent who call themselves Republicans.

1990 Population: 610,871. White 562,888 (92%), Black 11,434 (2%), Other 36,549 (6%). Hispanic origin 47,468 (8%). 18 and over 464,379 (76%), 62 and over 83,823 (14%). Median age: 34.

he successfully negotiated with House leaders to phase out the agency's funding in two years.

When the annual spending bill funding the two agencies came to the House floor in June 1996, Shadegg offered an amendment to cut $13 million in funding for the NEH, saying, "We simply can no longer afford to continue to subsidize the humanities." The House rejected his amendment, 168-254.

A member of the Resources Committee, he holds to the conservative Western creed that the federal government often interferes unduly with private property owners' rights.

Shadegg's district is home to many retirees, and he was particularly eager in the 104th to dispel Democratic charges that the GOP intended to cut Medicare, the federal health insurance program for the elderly.

Shadegg called the Democrats' attack "bunk and garbage," saying it is "just flat a lie, it ain't true. You don't raise spending from $4,800 per individual to $6,700 per individual and define that as a cut anywhere but inside the beltway that surrounds this city." The GOP balanced-budget measure, passed by the House in October 1995, reduced the projected spending growth for Medicare by $270 billion over seven years.

At Home: When GOP Rep. Jon Kyl left the 4th in 1994 for a successful Senate bid, Shadegg had the right stuff to muscle through a competitive Republican primary and win election comfortably in November.

His family name is well known in Arizona GOP circles: His late father, Stephen Shadegg, was a longtime political adviser to Barry Goldwater, the former five-term Arizona senator and 1964 GOP presidential nominee. Goldwater endorsed Shadegg at the beginning of his House campaign. Shadegg had his own political connections, having worked in the state attorney general's office and served as counsel to the House Republican caucus in the Arizona legislature.

For much of the GOP primary campaign,

Shadegg was thought to be trailing two other candidates: former Maricopa County Supervisor Jim Bruner and former state Rep. Trent Franks.

Bruner was the best-known entrant in the race, although that prominence stemmed partly from his casting the deciding vote on the county board to authorize a tax to raise $238 million to build a baseball stadium if Phoenix was awarded a major-league franchise. Polls indicated that voters opposed the tax. Franks, who had worked for former GOP Gov. Evan Mecham, drew strong support from conservative religious activists.

But a large percentage of primary voters remained undecided until late in the campaign, and Shadegg closed strong, combining TV ads with effective direct-mail pieces. He surged to victory with 43 percent to 30 percent for Franks and 21 percent for Bruner.

In the general election, Democrat Carol Cure gamely sought to portray herself as a centrist and Shadegg as a fringe conservative. But in the 4th, Arizona's most Republican district by registration, her effort was futile, and she polled just 36 percent as Shadegg ran up a victory tally of 60 percent. In 1996, he won a second term with two-thirds of the vote.

HOUSE ELECTIONS

1996 General		
John Shadegg (R)	150,486	(67%)
Maria Elena Milton (D)	74,857	(33%)
1996 Primary		
John Shadegg (R)	34,306	(74%)
Robin Silver (R)	11,944	(26%)
1994 General		
John Shadegg (R)	116,714	(60%)
Carol Cure (D)	69,760	(36%)
Mark J. Yannone (LIBERT)	7,428	(4%)

CAMPAIGN FINANCE

	Receipts	Receipts from PACs	Expend-itures
1996			
Shadegg (R)	$504,330	$183,033 (36%)	$512,249
Milton (D)	$116,920	$3,100 (3%)	$116,003
1994			
Shadegg (R)	$603,311	$143,977 (24%)	$590,725
Cure (D)	$282,024	$44,100 (16%)	$281,562

DISTRICT VOTE FOR PRESIDENT

1996		1992	
D	103,916 (44%)	**D**	86,922 (31%)
R	115,043 (48%)	**R**	118,927 (43%)
I	16,531 (7%)	**I**	70,682 (26%)

KEY VOTES

1997	
Ban "partial birth" abortions	Y
1996	
Approve farm bill	Y
Deny public education to illegal immigrants	Y
Repeal ban on certain assault-style weapons	Y
Increase minimum wage	N
Freeze defense spending	N
Approve welfare overhaul	Y
1995	
Approve balanced-budget constitutional amendment	Y
Relax Clean Water Act regulations	Y
Oppose limits on environmental regulations	N
Reduce projected Medicare spending	Y
Approve GOP budget with tax and spending cuts	Y

VOTING STUDIES

	Presidential Support		Party Unity		Conservative Coalition	
Year	S	O	S	O	S	O
1996	30	70	96	4	90	10
1995	19	81	96	3	90	10

INTEREST GROUP RATINGS

Year	ADA	AFL-CIO	CCUS	ACU
1996	5	n/a	88	100
1995	0	0	100	92

5 Jim Kolbe (R)

Of Tucson — Elected 1984, 7th term

Biographical Information
Born: June 28, 1942, Evanston, Ill.
Education: Northwestern U., B.A. 1965; Stanford U., M.B.A. 1967.
Military Service: Navy, 1968-69.
Occupation: Real estate consultant.
Family: Divorced.
Religion: Methodist.
Political Career: Ariz. Senate, 1977-83; Republican nominee for U.S. House, 1982.
Capitol Office: 205 Cannon Bldg. 20515; 225-2542.

Committees
Appropriations
Commerce, Justice, State & Judiciary; Interior; Treasury, Postal Service & General Government (chairman)

In Washington: Kolbe encountered some turbulence in the 104th Congress, losing a bid for a spot in the GOP leadership and enduring unwelcome attention to his personal life. But the 105th began with brighter prospects for the energetic Arizonan, as he was elevated to the "college of cardinals" — the 13 House Appropriations subcommittee chairmen who hold sway on spending bills. Kolbe took over the Treasury and Postal Service panel, formerly chaired by Iowa's Jim Ross Lightfoot, who waged an unsuccessful 1996 Senate campaign.

In the latter part of 1996, the biggest news about Kolbe had to do with his sexual orientation. In August 1996, under fire from gay rights activists unhappy that he backed legislation opposing same-sex marriages, Kolbe acknowledged his homosexuality. He made the declaration after learning that a gay-oriented magazine was about to break the news.

"The fact that I am this way has never, nor will it ever, change my commitment to represent all the people of Arizona's 5th District," Kolbe said at the time. "I am the same person." He said he supported the same-sex marriage bill because it allowed states to establish their own definition of marriage and did not require them to accept a definition adopted by others.

Not long after his first House election in 1984, Kolbe began to be discussed as someone with higher ambitions, either for a leadership role in the House or for a statewide office. But he passed on a gubernatorial opportunity in 1990 and on a Senate shot in 1994, and other Republicans won those offices instead. After the GOP's House takeover in the 1994 election, Kolbe sought the chairmanship of the House Republican Conference's Policy Committee, but he lost roughly on a margin of 2-to-1 to Christopher Cox of California. His defeat was partly attributed to a late starting campaign: Until late in the year, Kolbe had expected to accede to the chairmanship of the Republican Research Committee in the 104th Congress, but the new majority party wound up eliminating that post. Cox also benefited from being a Californian (no other member of the House's largest delegation had found a spot in the Republican leadership) and a more conservative voter than Kolbe.

Kolbe supports abortion rights and voted against the effort in the 104th Congress to ban a particular abortion technique that opponents call a "partial birth" abortion. He also tried unsuccessfully in the fiscal 1996 Labor-Health and Human Services spending bill to maintain provisions requiring states to provide Medicaid funding for abortions in case of rape, incest or danger to the life of the woman. The House instead dropped the provisions for rape and incest.

Kolbe's best-known area of legislative endeavor is his advocacy of free trade. In the 103rd Congress, he was a front-line vote hunter for his party leadership (and the White House) on both NAFTA in 1993 and, the following year, on renewal of the GATT treaty.

He has long been among Congress' most vocal advocates for the *maquiladora* assembly plant arrangement, by which U.S. companies manufacture components, then ship the items to Mexico, where they are assembled.

In the fiscal 1997 VA-HUD spending bill, Kolbe unsuccessfully tried to strike language designed to prevent the "dumping" of supercomputers in the U.S. market. The language would restrict the National Science Foundation from buying a foreign-made supercomputer if the Commerce Department determines the computer is being sold at a below market rate. Kolbe argued that the language would violate GATT, procurement laws and the spirit of promoting free trade.

Each year, Kolbe files a steady stream of bills aimed at protecting, preserving or opening a variety of Arizona parks, canyons, forests or ancient ruins. He also often speaks out for funds aimed at flood control solutions, and for the Central Arizona Project, a massive system that brings water to Phoenix and other areas of the state. But in the fiscal 1997 Energy and Water appropriations bill, he agreed to cut $20.6 million for the Central Arizona Project to help free up money for solar and renewable energy research.

ARIZONA 5
Southeast — Tucson

Registered Democrats barely outnumber Republicans in the 5th, but the numerical advantage is insignificant, especially considering that many of those who call themselves Democrats are of the rural, conservative, "pinto" variety. Thirteen percent of the district's voters are registered as independents.

At election time, this mix of swing voters and independents tends to yield an advantage for Republican candidates in elections for higher office. The district regularly had backed Republican nominees in past presidential elections, until Bill Clinton appeared on the ballot. In 1992, Clinton finished first in the 5th, taking 42 percent of the vote. Four years later, Clinton's percentage improved to 47 percent. Meanwhile, GOP Rep. Jim Kolbe was re-elected with 69 percent of the vote.

The 5th takes in the northeastern corner of Pima County, which includes most of Tucson. The only part of the city that is not in the 5th — its Hispanic neighborhoods — is strongly Democratic. Redistricting by federal judges in 1992 put that southern part of the city into the 2nd District to help ensure the election of a Hispanic there.

In 1996, Clinton defeated Dole by 10,000 votes in the portion of Pima located in the 5th. That more than made up for his losing the other three counties located fully or partly in the district.

Tucson, once Arizona's territorial capital, was the state's most populous city until it was surpassed by Phoenix in 1920. Largely a college town and resort center in the 1950s, Tucson today hosts an impressive number of high-technology companies.

Tucson and Prescott, in the northern part of the state, battled for the claim to be the territorial capital in the 1860s and 1870s. The dispute was settled in 1889 by making Phoenix, located about halfway between the two cities, the permanent capital.

Wealthy residents of the Santa Catalina foothills and retirees who worked at Davis-Monthan Air Force Base add to the Republican strength in the district. Green Valley, an outlying Pima County town that rivals Sun City among Arizona's largest retirement communities, also has become a major GOP force.

Democratic candidates get some help in the Tucson part of the 5th from voters in the residential area around the University of Arizona. (The campus itself is in the 2nd.) Although the university's student body of 35,700 leans conservative, the faculty and staff retain a Democratic allegiance, and they are more likely to vote than are students.

Outside Pima County, the 5th is largely desert.

The Old West county of Cochise, anchoring southeastern Arizona, is the home of Tombstone, "the town too tough to die." Notorious for its boomtown lawlessness in the late 1800s, Tombstone still mines some silver, but now its economy relies mainly on the tourist trade.

1990 Population: 610,871. White 537,525 (88%), Black 18,172 (3%), Other 55,174 (9%). Hispanic origin 100,874 (17%). 18 and over 465,370 (76%), 62 and over 107,977 (18%). Median age: 34.

He has been a strong supporter of plans to build the world's largest land-based telescope on Forest Service land on Mount Graham in Arizona. Construction has bogged down over concerns that the project would harm the habitat of the threatened red squirrel, but Kolbe argued that plans already had been altered to protect the squirrel.

Like most Western-state Republicans, Kolbe is an advocate of the gunowners' rights agenda. He voted against the ban on semiautomatic assault-style weapons and against a five-day waiting period for handgun purchases.

At Home: Though it provoked brow-knitting among some Arizona conservatives, Kolbe's declaration of his homosexuality did not diminish his political standing in the solidly Republican 5th, at least in 1996. He had little trouble turning back a challenge in the September primary and rolled up more than two-thirds of the vote in November.

Kolbe's initial House victory in 1984 did more than just avenge his narrow loss to Democrat James F. McNulty Jr. in the 1982 House election. It proved that Kolbe had won over some rural residents of the 5th who had regarded him as a city slicker. Articulate and brimming with nervous energy, Kolbe does not evoke the laid-back image associated with the rural Southwest. He seems more comfortable with the bustle of high-growth Tucson than with the slower pace of the district's desert and mountain towns.

In the 1982 GOP primary, he devoted much attention to Republican-rich Tucson and surrounding Pima County to win a tight three-way nomination contest. For rural residents, that linked him firmly with the city. Democrat McNulty, a plain-spoken man with a folksy air, pulled enough support from them for a 2,407-vote edge in November.

In gearing up for the rematch, Kolbe was determined not to fall into the same trap. Free of any primary opposition, he canvassed the 5th's desert and mountain counties. He aired TV advertisements showing him traversing the state on a horse. Kolbe reminded voters that he had spent much of his boyhood on a cattle ranch near the town of Sonoita — while McNulty was born and bred in Boston.

Kolbe's strategy paid off. Aided by a much better showing in the counties outside Pima, Kolbe ended up with a 6,204-vote victory.

Kolbe's comeback also owed much to a change in the prevailing political conditions in the 5th. In 1982, McNulty had the advantage of running with two popular statewide Democrats at the top of the ticket. In 1984, Ronald Reagan's popularity helped Kolbe.

McNulty decided against a 1986 rematch, and local Democrats could not find a nominee of stature. Kolbe won with 65 percent, and he has not had a close general-election contest since.

In January 1988, Kolbe opened the door to a conservative primary challenge when he became the first Republican in Arizona's congressional delegation to call on embattled GOP Gov. Evan Mecham to resign. Mecham ultimately was removed from office by the GOP-controlled Legislature, but his conservative backers vowed revenge against Kolbe. Two Mecham supporters ran in the 5th's GOP primary; but most of the former governor's activists were bent on defeating state legislators — seven veterans were upset. Kolbe easily won both the primary and general election.

Before setting his sights on Congress, Kolbe served six years in the Arizona Senate, where as a member of the state GOP's moderate-to-liberal wing he clashed with more conservative colleagues on social service issues.

HOUSE ELECTIONS

1996 General		
Jim Kolbe (R)	179,349	(69%)
Mort Nelson (D)	67,597	(26%)
John C. Zajac (LIBERT)	7,322	(3%)
Ed Finkelstein (REF)	6,630	(3%)
1996 Primary		
Jim Kolbe (R)	34,190	(70%)
Joe Sweeney (R)	14,704	(30%)
1994 General		
Jim Kolbe (R)	149,514	(68%)
Gary Auerbach (D)	63,436	(29%)
Phillip W. Murphy (LIBERT)	7,821	(4%)

Previous Winning Percentages: **1992** (67%) **1990** (65%) **1988** (68%) **1986** (65%) **1984** (51%)

CAMPAIGN FINANCE

	Receipts	Receipts from PACs	Expend-itures
1996			
Kolbe (R)	$420,771	$165,194 (39%)	$415,550
1994			
Kolbe (R)	$496,848	$152,484 (31%)	$478,730
Auerbach (D)	$111,571	$25,500 (23%)	$113,889

DISTRICT VOTE FOR PRESIDENT

	1996		1992
D	126,192 (47%)	**D**	115,986 (42%)
R	116,917 (44%)	**R**	104,301 (38%)
I	20,724 (8%)	**I**	56,425 (20%)

KEY VOTES

1997	
Ban "partial birth" abortions	N
1996	
Approve farm bill	Y
Deny public education to illegal immigrants	N
Repeal ban on certain assault-style weapons	Y
Increase minimum wage	N
Freeze defense spending	N
Approve welfare overhaul	Y
1995	
Approve balanced-budget constitutional amendment	Y
Relax Clean Water Act regulations	Y
Oppose limits on environmental regulations	N
Reduce projected Medicare spending	Y
Approve GOP budget with tax and spending cuts	Y

VOTING STUDIES

	Presidential Support		Party Unity		Conservative Coalition	
Year	**S**	**O**	**S**	**O**	**S**	**O**
1996	49	51	86	12	86	14
1995	29	70	89	10	90	10
1994	50	47	81	17	75	17
1993	44	56	83	15	80	16
1992	77	21	84	13	81	19
1991	76	21	83	15	89	11

INTEREST GROUP RATINGS

Year	ADA	AFL-CIO	CCUS	ACU
1996	5	n/a	94	90
1995	15	0	100	60
1994	15	11	100	80
1993	5	8	100	88
1992	25	25	88	76
1991	10	17	100	80

6 J.D. Hayworth (R)

Of Scottsdale — Elected 1994, 2nd term

Biographical Information
Born: July 12, 1958, High Point, N.C.
Education: North Carolina State U., B.A. 1980.
Occupation: Sports broadcaster; public relations consultant; insurance agent.
Family: Wife, Mary Yancey; three children.
Religion: Baptist.
Political Career: No previous office.
Capitol Office: 1023 Longworth Bldg. 20515; 225-2190.

Committees
Veterans' Affairs
Benefits
Ways & Means
Human Resources; Social Security

In Washington: A big man with a booming voice and outsized personality, Hayworth is unswervingly devoted to the conservative Republican agenda, and his biting criticism of liberal views has irritated more than a few House Democrats.

At the start of his second term in 1997, Hayworth landed a job that puts him in an even better position to irritate the minority: a post on the powerful Ways and Means Committee.

By putting Hayworth there, the GOP leadership ensured itself a loyal vote. Unlike some other House Republicans who got jittery about the popularity of their party's strongly conservative image as the 1996 election approached, Hayworth stayed the course.

"I've done everything I said I would do," Hayworth said. "I have not deviated from that one iota. What you see is what you get."

Hayworth as a freshman was often known to sit in the front row of the House chamber as members delivered their floor speeches, and from that perch he sometimes could be seen nodding vigorously in agreement with conservative speakers and scowling disdainfully at liberals.

As the House in 1996 debated a resolution to allow it to adjourn for the July 4 recess, Wisconsin Democratic Rep. David R. Obey complained that the GOP majority refused to compromise with the Democrats on appropriation bills and had resorted to sophomoric tactics to hold things up. He set his sights on Hayworth.

"To the gentleman from Arizona, every time somebody says something you don't like, you open your mouth and you start shouting from your seat," Obey said. "You are one of the most impolite members I have ever seen in my service in this house."

Hayworth's "body language" once drew a rebuke from Democratic Sen. Robert C. Byrd of West Virginia, when Hayworth and several of his conservative House colleagues crossed the Capitol to lobby the Senate in November 1995. Hayworth and his allies wanted senators to approve an amendment to cut off federal grants to organizations that lobby the federal government.

Noting Hayworth and the other House members lining the wall of the Senate chamber, Byrd said, "I do not mean to be discourteous to our colleagues from the House. But it is a little disconcerting to see them buttonholing members of the Senate."

Hayworth seems to take such criticism in stride. He says he was prepared for people to have lower expectations of him when he entered politics because of his reputation as a "somewhat irreverent, gregarious" sports broadcaster on TV.

In the House, Hayworth's smooth script-reading and broadcasting voice have earned him a kind of "master of ceremonies" niche: The GOP leadership frequently calls on him to announce routine House business such as reciting for the record the names of members who plan to give "special order" speeches after the House completes legislative business for the day.

Hayworth also enjoys sharing his thoughts with the House. In 1995 alone, he went to the floor nearly 200 times, often emphasizing the GOP's commitment to balance the budget. His speeches have titles such as: "Stand Firm: Balance the Budget;" "House Republicans Favor Fiscal Sanity;" "The American People Want a Balanced Budget, Not Excuses;" and "Liberal Democrats Should Either Put Up or Shut Up."

Hayworth may not become an influential legislative strategist, but he does have some particular interests, one of which is the health of the mining industry (copper mining is an important business in the 6th). In 1995, he spoke in favor of ending a freeze on low-cost sales of federal lands to miners prospecting for hard-rock minerals.

Supporters of the freeze are critical of the "patenting" system in the 1872 Mining Law, which allows miners to purchase federal land for as little as $2.50 an acre. In the Interior Department spending bill for fiscal 1995, Congress placed a one-year moratorium on most such claims. But Hayworth and many other Westerners stress the benefits of encouraging mining activity. "The nation as a whole prospers when the mining industry and those working in it can earn a

ARIZONA 6
Northeast — Flagstaff; Navajo reservation

The 6th rivals the western 3rd in size, with American Indian reservations occupying much of its territory. However, only 22 percent of the district's population comes from this expansive area. The great majority of the people and the political weight are located in the growing metropolitan cities in the southwestern section of the district.

From the Navajo reservation, which occupies all of the northeastern corner of the state except for the Hopi reservation, the district runs southward through the San Carlos and Fort Apache reservations, then takes in Greenlee County and parts of Graham and Pinal counties. The eastern border of the 6th is the Arizona-New Mexico line; the western side of the district includes the cities of Gilbert and part of Mesa, in the Phoenix suburbs, as well as the Gila reservation south of Phoenix and the Salt River and Fort McDowell reservations north of the city.

Rural voters, while occupying much of the land in the 6th, do not carry a huge voice in this district. Most of the people located in rural areas do not have the propensity to vote or register. The federal court that drew the new map included the city of Flagstaff "to balance out the interests of Maricopa County."

With about 50,000 people, Flagstaff, the seat of Coconino County, is the district's largest city. Two interstate highways — I-40 and I-17 — intersect in Flagstaff, making it the commercial center of northern Arizona. Thanks to its proximity to the Grand Canyon, Flagstaff sees a lot of tourist traffic; other leading industries in the area are lumbering and mining. Flagstaff also is home to the Lowell Observatory, where astronomers in 1930 discovered the planet Pluto.

Voters in East Mesa and Gilbert add a conservative flavor to the district.

The 6th is one of the most competitive districts in the state, as the congressional election results demonstrate. In three elections since its creation, it has been won by a Democrat, by a Republican, and, in 1996, by a Republican again, albeit narrowly, even as Bill Clinton was carrying the district by less than 7,000 votes.

Approximately 67 percent of the district's voting population is located in Maricopa County, which is one of the smallest areas geographically. Maricopa County, much of which contains various retirement communities, is overwhelmingly Republican.

Hayworth won big in Maricopa in 1996, taking 55 percent and beating Democrat Steve Owens there by about 23,500 votes. That made up for Hayworth's losing in the other seven counties or parts of counties that constitute the 6th District. His Maricopa showing enabled Hayworth to win re-election by less than 2,500 votes overall.

Democrats dominate in the northern part of the 6th, where the population is concentrated in mining towns and reservations and they have had a history of being strongest in Flagstaff, where more than 15 percent of the residents are Hispanic. This is slowly changing, though, as more people migrate to Flagstaff from Orange County, a primarily Republican area.

The Navajos show a particular affinity for the Democratic Party. In Apache County, where the Navajo influence is most pronounced, Democrats outnumber Republicans by almost 4-to-1. Clinton carried the county by more than 7,000 votes — his entire margin of victory in the district — while Owens won by more than 6,000 votes.

1990 Population: 610,872. White 429,716 (64%), Black 8,211 (1%), Other 172,945 (28%). Hispanic origin 79,277 (13%). 18 and over 424,811 (70%), 62 and over 99,143 (16%). Median age: 31.

decent, living wage," Hayworth told the House.

The freeze was lifted in the conference agreement on the fiscal 1996 interior bill, but that action did not stand: The House voted 277-147 in September 1995 to retain the mining freeze.

Hayworth would also give Congress more control over the federal bureaucracy. He introduced a bill in December 1995 that would require both congressional and presidential approval of all future regulations issued by government agencies.

The measure, Hayworth said, is aimed at promoting "compliance with Article I of the U.S. Constitution, which grants legislative powers solely to Congress," according to its preamble. "In practice, however, Congress routinely delegates its lawmaking duties to politically unaccountable bureaucrats who craft regulations with the full force of law," he wrote in a letter to members.

Under Hayworth's bill, any regulation other than those pertaining to an agency's employees or its general statement of policy would require congressional approval and the president's signature.

At Home: Democrats had high hopes in 1996 of making Hayworth a one-term congressman. Their nominee, former state party chairman Steve Owens, was a former aide to Vice President Al Gore and had strong support from the national Democratic Party. The importance of his candidacy was on display in the summer when he was invited to address the Democratic National Convention in Chicago.

Owens portrayed Hayworth as a slavish follower of Speaker Newt Gingrich and hammered at his support of the Republicans' balanced-budget bill, which sought to reduce spending growth on Medicaid and Medicare, not a popular position in a haven for retirees. He was helped by the support of the AFL-CIO, which spent more than $1 million on TV ads criticizing Hayworth's votes.

But the incumbent proved to be as feisty on the campaign trail as he was in the House. He characterized Owens as a liberal lawyer and went after the labor unions. The National Republican Congressional Committee ran its own ads in behalf of Hayworth, criticizing the unions' campaign. Hayworth cited some of the local projects to which he gave attention, such as extending the boundaries of the Walnut Canyon National Monument and preserving a 701-acre undeveloped tract in Scottsdale. And Hayworth raised money early and often; he spent about three times as much in winning re-election as he did in his first campaign. Even though President Clinton carried the 6th over Bob Dole, Hayworth held on by one percentage point.

A North Carolina native who attended North Carolina State University on a football scholarship, Hayworth held sports broadcasting jobs in Cincinnati and Greenville, S.C., before landing in Phoenix. He moved into political commentary, an outgrowth of his longstanding interest in government. An aficionado of the presidency of Dwight D. Eisenhower and a political history buff, Hayworth can readily recount anecdotes from Arizona's colorful past.

Though Hayworth's 1994 House bid was his first political campaign, he was already a familiar figure thanks to his seven years doing reporting and commentary on Phoenix's CBS affiliate. A jovial presence on TV and a prominent participant in area charitable events off the air, he entered the campaign with a reservoir of good will. At campaign appearances, he exuded a boisterous bonhomie that invited people to come over and chat.

Combining congeniality with conservatism, Hayworth easily topped a five-candidate primary field to capture the GOP nomination. He received 45 percent of the vote, outpolling his nearest foe, state House Majority Whip David Schweikert, by 24 points. Then in November he defeated freshman Rep. Karan English by tying her to Clinton and the House Democratic leadership.

Even during the primary campaign, Hayworth aimed most of his attacks at English, who, he liked to say, "was sent to Washington to represent the 6th District but ended up representing a guy from Arkansas." He said her August 1993 support for Clinton's budget (which passed on a 218-216 vote) spurred him to leave "the sidelines," as he referred to his media-commentary position, and enter the political game.

Hayworth also faulted English for supporting a bill to overhaul the 1872 Mining Law. Many in the 6th's copper mining communities saw no reason to change the pro-industry bias of the law.

English, a former state legislator and Coconino County (Flagstaff) supervisor, won the 6th in 1992 espousing fairly conservative economic ideas, including support for a balanced-budget amendment. But in office she was slow to gain her footing — taking months, for instance, to open a district office in the vote-rich "East Valley" of Maricopa County. She never got her head above water and lost to Hayworth by 14 points.

HOUSE ELECTIONS

1996 General		
J.D. Hayworth (R)	121,431	(48%)
Steve Owens (D)	118,957	(47%)
Robert Anderson (LIBERT)	14,899	(6%)
1994 General		
J.D. Hayworth (R)	107,060	(55%)
Karan English (D)	81,321	(41%)
Sequoia R. Fuller (LIBERT)	7,687	(4%)

CAMPAIGN FINANCE

	Receipts	Receipts from PACs	Expend-itures
1996			
Hayworth (R)	$1,511,069	$544,197 (36%)	1,499,443
Owens (D)	$801,552	$259,874 (32%)	$762,046
1994			
Hayworth (R)	$544,756	$155,181 (28%)	$538,650
English (D)	$797,220	$366,114 (46%)	$785,765

DISTRICT VOTE FOR PRESIDENT

	1996		1992
D	120,000 (47%)	**D**	91,247 (38%)
R	113,477 (44%)	**R**	91,477 (38%)
I	21,428 (8%)	**I**	56,368 (24%)

KEY VOTES

1997	
Ban "partial birth" abortions	Y
1996	
Approve farm bill	Y
Deny public education to illegal immigrants	Y
Repeal ban on certain assault-style weapons	Y
Increase minimum wage	N
Freeze defense spending	N
Approve welfare overhaul	Y
1995	
Approve balanced-budget constitutional amendment	Y
Relax Clean Water Act regulations	Y
Oppose limits on environmental regulations	N
Reduce projected Medicare spending	Y
Approve GOP budget with tax and spending cuts	Y

VOTING STUDIES

	Presidential Support		Party Unity		Conservative Coalition	
Year	S	O	S	O	S	O
1996	37	63	96	4	94	6
1995	19	81	98	2	95	5

INTEREST GROUP RATINGS

Year	ADA	AFL-CIO	CCUS	ACU
1996	0	n/a	94	100
1995	0	0	100	100

ARKANSAS

Governor: Mike Huckabee (D)
First elected. 1996 (Assumed office 7/96)
Length of term: 4 years
Term expires: 1/99
Salary: $60,000
Term limit: 2 terms
Phone: (501) 682-2345
Born: August 24, 1955; Hope, Ark.
Education: Ouachita Baptist U., B.A. 1975; S.W. Theological Seminary, 1977; John Brown U., Ph.D. 1994.
Occupation: Television station president; pastor; communications company president.
Family: Wife, Janet McCain; three children
Religion: Baptist.
Political Career: Lieutenant governor, 1993-96.

Lt. Gov.: Winthrop P. Rockefeller (R)
First Elected: 1993
Length of Term: 4 years
Term Expires: 1/99
Salary: $29,000
Term Limit: 2 terms
Phone: (501) 682-2144

State election official: (501) 682-5070
Democratic headquarters: (501) 374-2361
Republican headquarters: (501) 372-7301

REDISTRICTING

Arkansas retained its four House seats in reapportionment. The legislature passed the new map March 26, 1991; the governor signed it April 10. Federal court upheld map Nov. 15; Supreme Court upheld map June 1,1992.

STATE LEGISLATURE

General Assembly. Meets 60 calendar days, January-March, in odd-numbered years.

Senate: 35 members, 4-year terms
1996 breakdown: 28D, 6R, 1 vacancy; 33 men, 1 woman.
Salary: $12,500
Phone: (501) 682-6107

House of Representatives: 100 members, 2-year terms
1996 breakdown: 86D, 13R, 1 vacancy; 77 men, 22 women
Salary: $12,500
Phone: (501) 375-7771

URBAN STATISTICS

City	Population
Little Rock	175,727
Mayor Jim Dailey, N-P	
Fort Smith	72,798
Mayor C. Raymond Baker, N-P	
North Little Rock	61,829
Mayor Patrick Henry Hays, D	
Pine Bluff	57,140
Mayor Jerry Taylor, I	
Jonesboro	46,535
Mayor Hubert A. Brodell, I	

U.S. CONGRESS

Senate: 1 D, 1 R
House: 2 D, 2 R

TERM LIMITS

For state offices: Yes
Senate: 2 terms
House: 3 terms

ELECTIONS

1996 Presidential Vote

Bill Clinton	54%
Bob Dole	37%
Ross Perot	8%

1992 Presidential Vote

Bill Clinton	53%
George Bush	35%
Ross Perot	10%

1988 Presidential Vote

George Bush	56%
Michael S. Dukakis	42%

POPULATION

1990 population		2,350,725
1980 population		2,286,435
Percent change		+3%
Rank among states:		33
White		83%
Black		16%
Hispanic		1%
Asian or Pacific islander		1%
Urban		54%
Rural		46%
Born in state		67%
Foreign-born		1%
Under age 18	621,131	26%
Ages 18-64	1,379,536	59%
65 and older	350,058	15%
Median age		33.8

MISCELLANEOUS

Capital: Little Rock
Number of counties: 75
Per capita income: $14,753 (1991)
Rank among states: 47
Total area: 53,187 sq. miles
Rank among states: 27

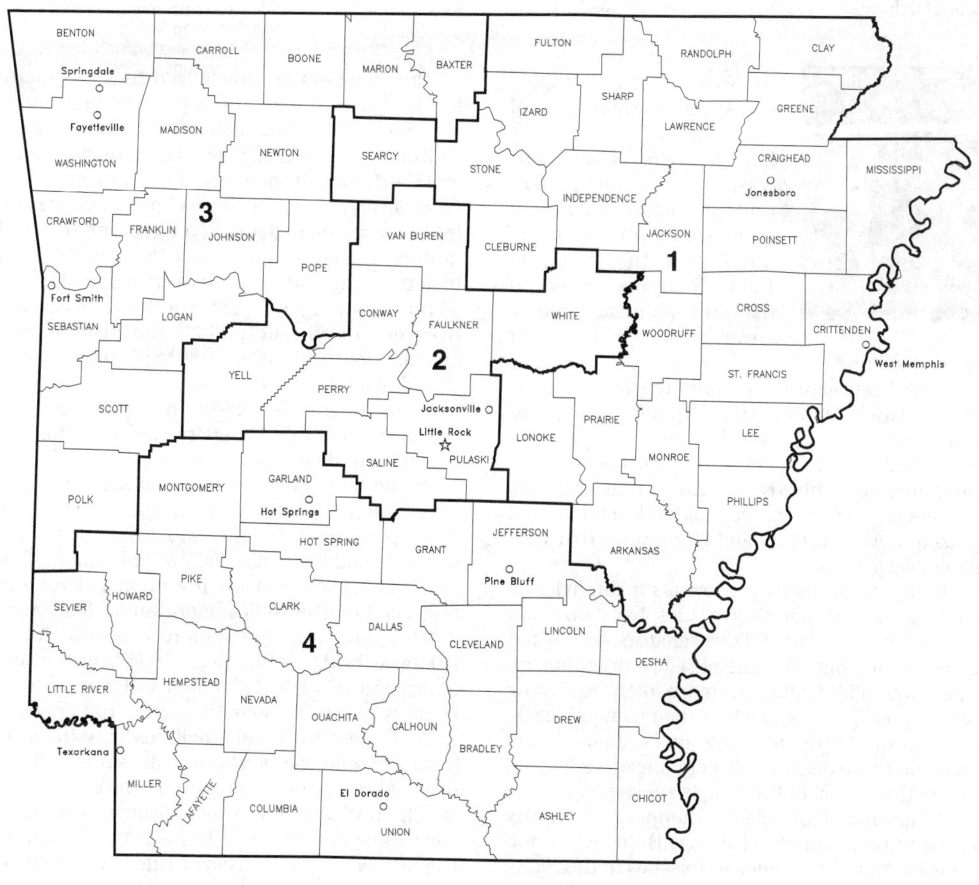
BENTON
CARROLL
BOONE
MARION
BAXTER
FULTON
RANDOLPH
CLAY
Springdale
Fayetteville
MADISON
IZARD
SHARP
GREENE
LAWRENCE
NEWTON
SEARCY
STONE
CRAIGHEAD
Jonesboro
MISSISSIPPI
WASHINGTON
INDEPENDENCE
CRAWFORD
FRANKLIN
3
JOHNSON
VAN BUREN
CLEBURNE
JACKSON
POINSETT
1
POPE
Fort Smith
LOGAN
CONWAY
FAULKNER
WHITE
CROSS
SEBASTIAN
WOODRUFF
CRITTENDEN
2
West Memphis
YELL
ST. FRANCIS
PERRY
SCOTT
Jacksonville
Little Rock
PRAIRIE
LONOKE
LEE
PULASKI
SALINE
MONROE
GARLAND
MONTGOMERY
POLK
Hot Springs
PHILLIPS
JEFFERSON
HOT SPRING
GRANT
ARKANSAS
PIKE
Pine Bluff
HOWARD
SEVIER
CLARK
LINCOLN
DALLAS
4
CLEVELAND
DESHA
HEMPSTEAD
LITTLE RIVER
NEVADA
OUACHITA
CALHOUN
DREW
BRADLEY
Texarkana
MILLER
LAFAYETTE
El Dorado
CHICOT
COLUMBIA
ASHLEY
UNION

Dale Bumpers (D)

Of Charleston — Elected 1974, 4th term

Biographical Information

Born: Aug. 12, 1925, Charleston, Ark.

Education: U. of Arkansas, 1946-48; Northwestern U., J.D. 1951.

Military Service: Marine Corps, 1943-46.

Occupation: Lawyer; farmer; hardware company executive.

Family: Wife, Betty Flanagan; three children.

Religion: Methodist.

Political Career: Governor, 1971-75.

Capitol Office: 229 Dirksen Bldg. 20510; 224-4843.

Committees

Appropriations
Agriculture, Rural Development & Related Agencies (ranking); Commerce, Justice, State & Judiciary; Defense; Interior; Labor, Health & Human Services & Education

Energy & Natural Resources (ranking)

Small Business

In Washington: Bumpers has spent no small part of his Senate career criticizing federal programs he sees as wasteful. His budget-cutting proposals have met with some strong resistance over the years; in 1993, Bumpers observed that "the political clout is always with spending, not spending cuts."

That frustration is one now felt by the many "deficit hawks" in Congress' Republican majority. But their rise to power has not brought new momentum to Bumpers' crusades, because the programs he criticizes — NASA's space station, high-technology weapons, federal mining and grazing fees — are, by and large, ones that conservatives embrace.

Bumpers' distinctive style suits the individualist Senate and its permissive rules, but it does not always sit well with fellow senators. He is not quarrelsome, but he takes pleasure in argument. The fewer allies he has, the more likely he is to be on his feet at his back-of-the-chamber desk, extemporaneously weaving facts, figures and anecdotes to explain to absent colleagues why an action they are about to take is senseless.

A natural iconoclast, Bumpers is rarely deterred by an empty chamber. He delivers orations on topics from nuclear missiles to the rights of satellite-dish owners that can be dazzling to hear, if wearying to those who work with him regularly. Calm, patient and engaging in private, Bumpers can seem downright obstreperous when he gets going in public.

One subject that always gets him going is the space station. Thwarted in previous attempts to kill the multibillion-dollar project, Bumpers held out hope in the 104th that it would be an irresistible target, particularly with Republicans hearing criticism that they were cutting only "people programs" in their quest to balance the budget. "To continue [the space station] in light of the draconian cuts everyone is talking about, I think would just be bizarre," he said in 1995.

But Bumpers acknowledged that contractors for the space station project provide thousands of jobs across 36 states, with much of the work concentrated in politically powerful Texas, Florida and California. Proponents of the project reiterated their claims about the technological and biological research benefits of the orbiting space laboratory. Bumpers argued that the space station's high price tag and expense overruns made it cost 25 times its weight in gold. For the sixth consecutive year, the Senate in 1996 rejected Bumpers' amendment to appropriate only enough money to shut down the project.

"This thing is like Rasputin — you cannot kill it," an exasperated Bumpers said after his 1995 amendment died.

While he leads the charge on some spending cuts, Bumpers is not above using his seat on the Appropriations Committee to help out his constituents and the causes he prefers. Among those are health programs for the poor, aid for rural areas and rice subsidies important to his state.

He placed a $4 million earmark for an Arkansas bridge in the fiscal 1996 transportation appropriations bill. An alumnus of Northwestern University, he boosted the agriculture research dollars going to Illinois facilities in 1997 so the school would get a share. The same bill also directed research funding to Arkansas.

The previous year's agriculture spending bill gave Bumpers a chance to keep the Agriculture Department from enforcing a rule banning "fresh" labels on chickens that have been frozen for transport, then thawed for sale. Bumpers and other Southeastern lawmakers formed a coalition from the top chicken-raising states that went up against West Coast members, whose producers compete with the frozen chickens from Southeastern processors.

In the same bill, Bumpers aimed his budget-cutting ax at a favorite target, the Market Promotion Program, which subsidizes advertising of American agricultural products overseas. Conferees on the 1996 spending bill put back in $40 million he had managed to cut from the program, but they retained his language targeting the program to small producers and barring foreign corporations from receiving subsidies.

Bumpers has looked out for small business in other arenas. A sponsor of a 1991 bill to exempt small businesses from the minimum wage, he sought the same exemption from the 1996 wage increase. However, he voted against an amendment that would have exempted small businesses, in part because the amendment included "training wage" provisions that Bumpers found objectionable.

He also teamed up with Small Business Committee Chairman Christopher S. Bond, R-Mo., on a bill to reduce the impact of regulations on small businesses. Attached to 1996 legislation increasing the federal debt ceiling, the Small Business Regulatory Enforcement Fairness Act allows small business to sue federal agencies if they did not comply with a 1980 law requiring them to consider the impact on small businesses when writing regulations. Bumpers said the 1980 law was not working.

On the Energy and Natural Resources Committee, Bumpers has a long history of disputes with oil and mining interests. He joined efforts in the late 1970s to fight deregulation of oil and natural gas prices, and he favored a stiff windfall-profits tax on the oil companies.

In the 105th, Bumpers is the committee's top Democrat, and he seems likely to bring his populist perspective to the debate on deregulating the electric utilities industry. In early 1997 Bumpers introduced a deregulation plan that delays full competition until 2003, mandates huge increases in the use of renewable energy resources and tries to protect individual consumers from bearing the cost of unwise utility investments.

A critic of nuclear power, Bumpers has failed in past efforts to bar utilities from passing on to consumers the costs of closing nuclear power plants. Bumpers was the most vociferous Senate opponent of the Clinch River breeder reactor in Tennessee. He came within one vote of killing the expensive project in 1982 and finally won in 1984.

In the 100th Congress, Bumpers finally won an eight-year struggle to change the system of leasing oil and gas drilling rights on federal lands — a campaign that began when he found that land in Arkansas near hundreds of producing wells was leased for $1 an acre.

Bumpers has been frustrated, however, in his efforts to change laws governing mining and grazing on federal lands. As he has done since 1988, Bumpers argued in the 104th Congress that the 1872 mining law — which allows the "patenting," or sale, of federal land containing gold, silver, copper or other "hard rock" minerals for as little as $2.50 an acre — is a "scandalous anachronism." But Western GOP senators (and some Democrats from the region) stoutly resist proposals that would charge more for the use of public lands.

In September 1996, Bumpers managed to get the Senate to agree to his amendment to the fiscal 1997 Interior Appropriations bill that proposed fee increases only for large-scale grazing-rights users such as corporations. But after Bumpers' amendment was approved, the spending bill was pulled from the floor and sent to an omnibus spending package that did not include Bumpers' language.

Bumpers' most notable recent "kill" of a big-ticket federal project came in 1993, when Congress finally gave in to efforts to end work on the multibillion-dollar superconducting super collider in Texas.

Bumpers followed up on that victory in 1995 with a successful amendment terminating the gas turbine modular helium reactor. The Senate voted 62-38 to stop trying to turn spent plutonium into energy. "Just like the super collider and a host of other technologies we have undertaken," Bumpers said, "there always comes a time to shut these things down."

In the 1980s, Bumpers was perhaps best known as one of the Senate's most outspoken supporters of arms control. With the Cold War over, he has tried to combine his zeal for budget cutting with his desire to limit the military. But he had little success in the 104th.

The Senate rejected his attempts in 1996 to cut funds for FA-18 Hornet combat jets not requested by the Clinton administration. Bumpers also challenged in vain the Senate's 15 percent increase in nuclear defense spending for fiscal 1997.

In 1993, he sponsored an amendment to the defense appropriations bill to cut $400 million for national intelligence programs; it lost, 64-35. Another amendment to the same bill that would have ended production of the Trident II missile at a savings of $1.14 billion was defeated 63-34. A similar attempt in 1995 also failed.

For Bumpers, who once accused President Ronald Reagan of not wanting "to spend money on anything that does not explode," the MX missile was a special target. He offered repeated amendments in the 1980s to kill the MX, which finally was capped at 50 in a 1985 compromise.

In 1990, Bumpers unsuccessfully targeted Navy battleships and military base closings. His amendment to retire one of the two remaining Iowa-class battleships equipped with cruise missiles fell by 11 votes. His amendment to nullify the secretary of Defense's list of bases to be closed suffered the same fate; among the bases slated for closure was Eaker Air Force Base in Blytheville, Ark., which was shut down in 1991.

In 1996, Bumpers and his Texas colleagues congratulated the Army for reconsidering a planned transfer of 600 jobs from the Red River Army Depot in Texarkana.

As liberal as Bumpers can seem at times, his iconoclasm makes him difficult to label. In 1978 he was the only senator to vote against popular "sunset" legislation for periodic reviews of all federal agencies. In 1987, as Small Business chairman, he allied with then-Sen. Dan Quayle of Indiana to oppose Labor Committee Chairman Edward M. Kennedy's bill requiring all employers to provide health insurance. In 1988, he clashed with liberal House members over revamping the scandal-plagued program that reserves federal contracts for minority-owned firms. House negotiators felt Bumpers' bill was too tough on minority firms. And in 1994, Bumpers and fellow Arkansas Democrat David Pryor were among the six Southern Democrats who joined Republicans in blocking Senate action on legislation to bar the permanent replacement of striking workers.

In many ways Bumpers — who preceded both Pryor and Bill Clinton as governor of Arkansas — paved the way for Clinton. He modernized the state's government and moved its politics to the left on issues such as education and race relations. Both as governor and as senator, Bumpers has had no trouble winning voter acceptance, despite his state's conservative tendencies. His eloquent oratory and amiable manner have overcome whatever reservations the voters might harbor about his liberalism.

At Home: "A smile and a shoeshine" was the phrase Winthrop Rockefeller used to describe the political phenomenon that removed him from the Arkansas governorship in 1970. It was a slur on Bumpers' intellectual substance, but it was not a bad description of the campaign that lifted him from a small-town law practice to the state Capitol in a remarkably short time.

After four years of Republican rule under Rockefeller, the state was ready to go Democratic again under a modern leader. Bumpers was so clearly the right man that a smile, a shoeshine and a sophisticated set of TV ads were more than enough to give him a victory over the legendary race-baiter Orval E. Faubus in a Democratic primary runoff and an easy win over Rockefeller.

Bumpers' gubernatorial campaign was so vague that the state had little reason to know what it was getting when he took office in January 1971. In fact, it was getting a man with a fair degree of liberal Yankee influence, a graduate of Northwestern University law school and an admirer of Adlai E. Stevenson, who was governor of Illinois when Bumpers got his law degree.

Bumpers came to the governorship without any political experience beyond the School Board in Charleston, Ark., but during four years in office, he presided over a streamlining of state government. He closed many of the bureaucratic fiefdoms that old-guard Democrats had controlled, and, by early 1974, he was ready for a bigger stage. State Democrats braced for a titanic struggle between the governor and Sen. J. William Fulbright, who had helped raise money for Bumpers in 1970.

As it turned out, the struggle failed to live up to its advance billing. Bumpers defeated Fulbright by nearly 2-to-1 in the Democratic primary without offering a critical word or a divisive issue.

Bumpers' 1980 re-election was nothing to worry about either. He won a second term with 59 percent of the vote, then improved to 62 percent in his 1986 contest against Republican Asa Hutchinson, a former U.S. Attorney who now holds Arkansas' 3rd District House seat. In 1992, Republicans put forward Mike Huckabee, a Baptist minister who is now governor. But making his political debut against Bumpers in a year when favorite-son Clinton was on the presidential ballot, Huckabee managed just 40 percent of the vote.

SENATE ELECTIONS

1992 General		
Dale Bumpers (D)	553,635	(60%)
Mike Huckabee (R)	366,373	(40%)
1992 Primary		
Dale Bumpers (D)	322,458	(65%)
Julia Hughes Jones (D)	177,273	(35%)

Previous Winning Percentages: **1986** (62%) **1980** (59%) **1974** (85%)

CAMPAIGN FINANCE

	Receipts	Receipts from PACs		Expend-itures
1992				
Bumpers (D)	$1,940,691	$652,385	(34%)	$1,878,472
Huckabee (R)	$905,215	$13,119	(1%)	$910,212

KEY VOTES

1997	
Approve balanced-budget constitutional amendment	N
Approve chemical weapons treaty	Y
1996	
Approve farm bill	N
Limit punitive damages in product liability cases	N
Exempt small businesses from higher minimum wage	N
Approve welfare overhaul	N
Bar job discrimination based on sexual orientation	Y
Override veto of ban on "partial birth" abortions	N
1995	
Approve GOP budget with tax and spending cuts	N
Approve constitutional amendment barring flag desecration	N

VOTING STUDIES

	Presidential Support		Party Unity		Conservative Coalition	
Year	**S**	**O**	**S**	**O**	**S**	**O**
1996	71	10	83	8	18	68
1995	87	11	90	7	33	61
1994	95	5	85	14	63	38
1993	91	8	89	10	44	54
1992	28	72	69	29	71	29
1991	40	59	82	16	70	30

INTEREST GROUP RATINGS

Year	ADA	AFL-CIO	CCUS	ACU
1996	85	n/a	17	0
1995	85	92	32	4
1994	80	63	40	4
1993	80	73	18	8
1992	90	75	10	15
1991	70	67	20	24

Tim Hutchinson (R)

Of Bentonville — Elected 1996, 1st term

Biographical Information

Born: Aug. 11, 1949, Bentonville, Ark.

Education: Bob Jones U., B.A. 1971; U. of Arkansas, M.A. 1990.

Occupation: Minister; college instructor; radio station executive.

Family: Wife, Donna Jean King; three children.

Religion: Baptist.

Political Career: Ark. House, 1985-93; U.S. House, 1993-97.

Capitol Office: 245 Dirksen Bldg. 20510; 224-2353.

Committees

Environment & Public Works
Clean Air, Wetlands, Private Property & Nuclear Safety; Drinking Water, Fisheries & Wildlife

Labor & Human Resources
Aging; Children & Families

Veterans' Affairs

The Path to Washington: Call him the reluctant senator.

When Arkansas Republicans came calling for a Senate candidate in 1996, Hutchinson turned them down. He was not interested, he said, in trying to become the first Republican elected to the Senate by Arkansas voters. (Several Republican senators were selected by the legislature during Reconstruction.)

The state GOP persisted. Arkansas' other House Republican, Jay Dickey, threw his support to Hutchinson. Party officials kept the pressure on and Hutchinson finally relented.

The draft-Hutchinson effort stemmed from a chain reaction launched by the Whitewater scandal. In May 1996, Democratic Gov. Jim Guy Tucker announced that he would resign after being convicted of two felonies in a case related to Whitewater. Tucker's conviction prompted Lt. Gov. Mike Huckabee to drop his unopposed bid for the GOP Senate nomination and ascend instead to the governor's office. That created the opening for Hutchinson.

In his voting record and ideological outlook, Hutchinson — a Baptist minister and member of the Arkansas House for eight years before his election to the U.S. House in 1992 — reflects the views of the conservative religious community.

Though Hutchinson's political career shifted from Little Rock to Washington at the same time as President Clinton's, familiarity has not bred consent with Clinton's legislative agenda. The new senator comes from the one part of Arkansas that is historically Republican. He warns that Clinton "believes in a very activist government. ... He believes that big government and new government programs will solve the problems that face our society."

During two terms in the House, Hutchinson was most vocal on three issues: the federal deficit, welfare reform and abortion. On the latter, Hutchinson sees no middle ground. He refers to the Supreme Court's landmark *Roe v. Wade* abortion rights ruling as "tragic" and calls abortion "an issue on which we, who believe in the sanctity of human life, cannot bend, buckle or bow."

He has carried that zeal to the Senate, where he introduced legislation to deny funds to international family-planning and population-control groups that use their own money to perform abortions or lobby against anti-abortion laws overseas.

Hutchinson can speak on social issues from his place on the Labor and Human Resources Committee.

Hutchinson also sits on the Environment and Public Works Committee, where, at a February 1997 hearing with Environmental Protection Agency Administrator Carol M. Browner, he was among Republicans openly critical of two stringent clean air standards proposed by the EPA. When committee Chairman John H. Chafee of Rhode Island expressed doubts about the standards, Hutchinson called his skepticism "well-justified."

In moving to the Senate, Hutchinson traded the chairmanship of the House Veterans' Affairs Subcommittee on Hospitals and Health Care for a seat on the Senate Veterans' Affairs Committee. He has remained cautious regarding what has come to be known as Gulf War syndrome, questioning the budget implications of a liberalized policy toward compensating veterans of the Persian Gulf conflict who report health problems related to their service in the war.

Hutchinson backed a balanced-budget constitutional amendment in a March 1997 Senate vote, he supports a presidential line-item veto and he says he wants the federal government to be "dramatically cut," though he admitted early in the 105th Congress that the elimination of Cabinet agencies is not going to happen as long as Clinton does not want it to. "It's just an exercise in futility to move legislation he's going to veto," Hutchinson said.

Hutchinson has been known to temper his budget-cutting zeal when the ax falls too close to home. In 1993, when then-House colleague Dan Burton of Indiana proposed cutting

$462,000 for the National Center for Agricultural Law Research and Information at the University of Arkansas School of Law, Hutchinson protested: "I normally about 99 percent of the time agree with the [budget-cutting] efforts the gentleman makes. . . . However, this agricultural law research center is in my district, and I do know that it is doing an outstanding job in an area that is very important." Funding for the center was preserved.

When House Republicans were drafting their "Contract With America" in the fall of 1994, Hutchinson urged that it include a welfare reform plan with tough restrictions on eligibility for unwed mothers. More moderate Republicans objected, and the final contract language represented a compromise between the two sides.

Hutchinson started from behind in his 1996 Senate campaign. But Democrat Winston Bryant, Arkansas' attorney general, was weakened by a surprisingly strong primary challenge from state Sen. Lu Hardin, who forced Bryant into a runoff.

During the general-election campaign, Bryant repeatedly branded Hutchinson a lackey for House Speaker Newt Gingrich. That message was amplified by an advertising campaign by the Arkansas Democratic Party. One ad featured a federal worker laid off during the partial federal government shutdown. The worker said on camera: "Tim Hutchinson had the gall to shut down the government with Newt Gingrich and then announce he needed his paycheck, leaving the rest of Arkansas holding the bag."

Hutchinson tried to counter by playing up his independence. In the most prominent example, he was one of only four Republicans to break party ranks and vote against killing a resolution requiring the House ethics committee to release the report of the outside counsel brought in to investigate alleged improprieties in Gingrich's political fundraising activities. The day before, Bryant had held a news conference challenging Hutchinson to support the resolution.

Hutchinson also challenged Bryant's characterization of the House GOP record. Hutchinson's advertisements claimed that the Republicans had cut taxes, increased student loans and added funding for Medicaid, limiting only the size of future increases. "Shame on you, Winston Bryant," the ad said. "Arkansas deserves better."

What had been a close race all along broke in Hutchinson's favor during the closing weeks of the campaign, despite the large plurality given favorite son Clinton in the presidential race.

Bryant was forced on the defensive by disclosures that his office did not meet filing deadlines in criminal cases, which resulted in some charges being dismissed. Hutchinson seized on the missteps, criticizing what he characterized as Bryant's "pattern of mismanagement."

Ultimately, Hutchinson prevailed with 53 percent of the vote. His old 3rd District seat was taken over by his younger brother, Asa. They are one of two brother combinations in the 105th, the other being Sen. Carl Levin and Rep. Sander M. Levin, both Michigan Democrats.

SENATE ELECTIONS

1996 General

Tim Hutchinson (R)	445,942	(53%)
Winston Bryant (D)	400,241	(47%)

Previous Winning Percentages: 1994* (68%) **1992*** (50%)

** House election*

CAMPAIGN FINANCE

	Receipts	Receipts from PACs	Expend-itures
1996			
Hutchinson (R)	$1,691,276	$482,175 (29%)	$1,604,014
Bryant (D)	$1,606,053	$474,056 (30%)	$1,577,838

KEY VOTES

1997

Approve balanced-budget constitutional amendment	Y
Approve chemical weapons treaty	N

House Service:

1996	
Approve farm bill	Y
Deny public education to illegal immigrants	Y
Increase minimum wage	N
Freeze defense spending	N
Approve welfare overhaul	Y
1995	
Approve balanced-budget constitutional amendment	Y
Relax Clean Water Act regulations	Y
Oppose limits on environmental regulations	N
Reduce projected Medicare spending	Y
Approve GOP budget with tax and spending cuts	Y

VOTING STUDIES

	Presidential Support		Party Unity		Conservative Coalition	
Year	**S**	**O**	**S**	**O**	**S**	**O**
House Service:						
1996	30	67	93	5	88	12
1995	17	81	95	4	91	6
1994	38	62	93	5	86	14
1993	31	69	91	8	91	9

INTEREST GROUP RATINGS

Year	ADA	AFL-CIO	CCUS	ACU
House Service:				
1996	5	0	94	100
1995	0	0	96	92
1994	5	22	75	95
1993	5	0	100	100

1 Marion Berry (D)

Of Gillett — Elected 1996, 1st term

Biographical Information
Born: Aug. 27, 1942, Stuttgart, Ark.
Education: U. of Arkansas, 1960-62; U. of Arkansas, Little Rock, B.S. 1965.
Occupation: Farmer; White House aide.
Family: Wife, Carolyn Lowe; two children.
Religion: Methodist.
Political Career: Ark. Soil and Water Conservation commissioner, 1986-94, chairman, 1992-94; Gillett City Council, 1976-80.
Capitol Office: 1407 Longworth Bldg. 20515; 225-4076.

Committees
Agriculture
Department Operations, Nutrition & Foreign Agriculture; Forestry, Resource Conservation & Research
Small Business

The Path to Washington: Berry likely will follow the same moderate path as the Democrat he succeeded, Blanche Lambert Lincoln, who decided not to seek re-election in 1996 after learning she was pregnant with twins. Soon after winning the seat, in fact, Berry joined the Coalition, a group of center-right House Democrats better known as the "blue dogs."

Berry supports a constitutional amendment requiring a balanced budget, supports gun owners' rights, opposes parole for violent criminals and wants to review government regulations on business with an eye toward eliminating those that are unnecessary. He supports the welfare overhaul bill signed by President Clinton, which limits welfare recipients to five years' worth of benefits.

During his campaign, Berry drew a sharp distinction between his positions and some actions of the Republican-led 104th Congress. He opposed GOP efforts to amend the 1994 crime bill and create state block grants rather than specifically designating funding for more police officers.

He criticized GOP attempts to balance the federal budget largely by slowing the growth of Medicare and Medicaid spending, and he took issue with their plan to reduce taxes. He said tax cuts should wait until after the budget is balanced and then be targeted toward the middle class.

General manager and part-owner of a family farm since 1968, Berry says he will be a voice for agriculture, industry and small-business owners in the 105th Congress. As befits his farming background, Berry sought and obtained a seat on the Agriculture Committee.

Berry began his political career in 1976, when he was elected to the Gillett City Council. In 1982, he became Bill Clinton's gubernatorial campaign coordinator in Arkansas County, a task he also performed in 1986 and 1990. Berry spent two years, 1993-94, as chairman of the Arkansas County Democratic Committee.

In 1986, then-Gov. Clinton named him to the Arkansas Soil and Water Conservation Commission. He chaired the panel in 1992.

Following Clinton's election to the White House, the president named Berry as his liaison to the U.S. Agriculture Department. Officially, Berry served as special assistant to the president for agricultural trade and food assistance. He also served as a staff member of the White House Domestic Policy Council.

When Lincoln unexpectedly announced her retirement, Berry was one of three Democrats who jumped into the race to succeed her. He nearly won a majority against two primary opponents, but found much tougher going in the runoff against Tom Donaldson, deputy prosecutor of Crittenden County.

Donaldson forced Berry on the defensive over Clinton's decision to sign the Republican farm bill, which moved the nation's agriculture program to a more market-based approach; Berry won by fewer than 3,000 votes out of more than 58,000 cast.

The 1st District is Democratic in its outlook, and Clinton's presence on the November ballot, where the hometown boy was expected to do well despite his support for the farm bill, boded well for the party on the congressional level.

The Republicans had renominated Warren Dupwe, a former Jonesboro city attorney who two years before had polled 47 percent of the vote against Lincoln, the highest percentage recorded by a GOP candidate in the district in more than 100 years. Dupwe had continued to campaign for the seat since that loss.

Berry tried to link Dupwe to the House Republicans' plans to scale back the growth of Medicare and Medicaid, a chief concern in the 1st, the state's poorest district and where people over age 65 represent more than 15 percent of the population.

In the end, the district's Democratic heritage was too much for Dupwe to overcome, and the Republican tide that carried him to a strong showing in 1994 had ebbed in 1996. Berry won with 53 percent of the vote, nine points ahead of Dupwe.

ARKANSAS 1
Northeast — Jonesboro; West Memphis

Covering most of the eastern third of the state, the 1st divides into three geographic regions: the hilly northwest, the Mississippi River Delta and, between them, the alluvial plain. Though soybeans flourish on the fertile bottomland along the river, and rice thrives on the plain, the 1st is the state's poorest district and the one with the strongest Old South flavor. In keeping with a tradition that goes back to the Civil War, most of the white voters here support Democratic candidates, particularly in local races.

The large corporate farms in this area, like the cotton plantations that preceded them, sprawl over tens of thousands of acres and coexist with poor, largely black communities. Farm employment has declined annually since the 1940s. Until the 1980s, there was some work in small mills along the river, but many of those jobs went overseas, exacerbating generations-old poverty.

The Delta counties along the Mississippi River have large black populations and are solidly Democratic. Though all the counties lost population during the 1980s, the Delta still accounts for about one-quarter of the district vote.

The largest city in the Delta is West Memphis (Crittenden County), with just over 28,000 people; it is a trucking center and bedroom community for Memphis, Tenn. North of there is the somewhat smaller city of Blytheville (Mississippi County). In 1988, Blytheville attracted 500 new jobs with the opening of Nucor-Yamato Steel Co., a U.S.-Japan venture, and in 1992 Nucor opened another plant on its own. But the city suffered a blow in 1992 when Blytheville Air Force Base closed, eliminating 3,000 military and 600 civilian jobs.

The Ozark Mountain counties in the northwestern part of the 1st are culturally distant from the Delta. Home to annual fiddle contests and outhouse races, most of these counties grew during the 1980s with an influx of retirees, many of them from the North. These newcomers diluted the area's traditional Democratic vote and helped put the 1st in the Republican column for president in 1984 and 1988. Searcy County, at the western edge of the 1st, did not even support Bill Clinton for president in 1992 and 1996; it was the only county in the district he failed to carry.

The other pocket of growth in the 1st, Lonoke County, also is becoming more Republican. The growth is concentrated in Cabot, a suburban town on the highway to Little Rock. Outside Cabot, Lonoke County is like the rest of the alluvial plain, with its conservative Democratic tradition and huge rice farms. The lakes and rivers in and around Arkansas County lure fishermen and duck hunters.

Jonesboro is the district's largest city, with 46,500 people. It has a fairly stable economy built around Arkansas State University (9,800 students) and industrial enterprises engaged in die casting, toolmaking, printing and conveyor-belt production. Jonesboro and outlying communities in Craighead County cast about 12 percent of the vote in the 1st; the area is reliably, though not overwhelmingly, Democratic. Berry garnered only 41 percent in Craighead, though he made up for it by winning 20 of the other 24 counties.

1990 Population: 588,588. White 478,761 (81%), Black 105,199 (18%), Other 4,628 (1%). Hispanic origin 3,652 (1%). 18 and over 425,369 (72%), 62 and over 106,287 (18%). Median age: 34.

HOUSE ELECTIONS

1996 General		
Marion Berry (D)	105,280	(53%)
Warren Dupwe (R)	88,436	(44%)
Keith Carle (REF)	5,734	(3%)
1996 Primary Runoff		
Marion Berry (D)	30,592	(52%)
Tom Donaldson (D)	27,717	(48%)
1996 Primary		
Marion Berry (D)	39,011	(47%)
Tom Donaldson (D)	25,402	(31%)
Kirby J. Smith (D)	17,780	(22%)

CAMPAIGN FINANCE

	Receipts	Receipts from PACs		Expend-itures
1996				
Berry (D)	$873,821	$253,672	(29%)	$871,389
Dupwe (R)	$574,667	$115,263	(20%)	$574,846

DISTRICT VOTE FOR PRESIDENT

	1996		1992
D	116,634 (58%)	D	131,585 (59%)
R	65,707 (33%)	R	71,160 (32%)
I	16,259 (8%)	I	20,116 (9%)

KEY VOTES

1997

Ban "partial birth" abortions Y

2 Vic Snyder (D)

Of Little Rock — Elected 1996, 1st term

Biographical Information
Born: Sept. 27, 1947, Medford, Ore.
Education: Willamette U., B.A.; U. of Oregon, M.D.; U. of Arkansas, Little Rock, J.D..
Military Service: Marine Corps, 1967-69.
Occupation: Physician; lawyer.
Family: Single.
Religion: Presbyterian.
Political Career: Ark. Senate, 1991-97.
Capitol Office: 1319 Longworth Bldg. 20515; 225-2506.

Committees
National Security
Military Installations and Facilities; Military Procurement
Veterans' Affairs
Oversight & Investigations

The Path To Washington: Snyder burst onto the political scene in spectacular fashion in 1990 when, in his first run for public office, he blindsided state Sen. Doug Brandon in the Democratic primary.

In 1996, he narrowly defeated the front-runner in the Democratic primary runoff for the open 2nd District, then went on to claim the seat vacated by retiring Democratic Rep. Ray Thornton, who was elected to the Arkansas Supreme Court that year.

Snyder possesses medical and law degrees; he spent a year in Vietnam with the Marines and served on medical missions in Thailand, Sudan, Sierra Leone and Honduras.

He has a reputation as both a liberal and a maverick. He supports the ban on certain semiautomatic assault-style weapons, wants to repeal Arkansas' sodomy law, and fought legislation requiring young people to be fingerprinted when they got their driver's licenses, calling it an infringement on liberty and privacy.

Snyder cites his credentials as an environmentalist, noting his efforts to stop gravel mining in some environmentally sensitive areas. He is a member of the Arkansas Wildlife Federation, the Arkansas Audubon Society and Ducks Unlimited.

Snyder opposes a balanced-budget constitutional amendment but favors balancing the budget. He wants the Pentagon to shoulder substantial spending cuts, mentioning the B-2 stealth bomber as a program that should be trimmed. He is in a position to work toward trimming the defense budget from his seat on the House National Security Committee.

Snyder favors some targeted tax cuts, including a break for college tuition and for health insurance for the self-employed.

After Thornton announced his retirement, prosecuting attorney Mark Stodola entered the 2nd District Democratic race to front-runner status. Snyder and John Edwards, a former aide to retiring Sen. David Pryor, also sought the seat.

Stodola cemented his front-runner position in the primary, receiving 48 percent of the vote. Snyder was 16 points behind. But in the runoff, Snyder edged Stodola by 2 percentage points.

Snyder ran an unconventional campaign, limiting his campaigning and fundraising to the 90 days before the primary. He talked about how he refused to participate in the state legislative pension plan, and he pledged not to take a congressional pension unless that system was changed.

Stodola had tried to position himself to the right of Snyder, talking about his efforts to fight crime, but Snyder resisted his opponent's efforts to push him too far from the center. Snyder cited his support for small business, his efforts in the state legislature to pass legislation keeping violent criminals in jail, and his work to enact underage drinking laws and to repeal the state sales tax on food.

The Republican nominee was Bud Cummins, a businessman and lawyer. Cummins won the nomination by defeating Bill Powell, who was the Republican standard-bearer in 1994 and hoped for a second chance in 1996. Powell had polled 43 percent of the vote against Thornton in that 1994 contest, giving Republicans hope that they could capture the open seat.

Snyder embraced the general Democratic themes in the fall campaign, pledging to oppose efforts to cut Medicare, education and environmental protection.

Cummins tried to portray Snyder as too liberal, citing his efforts to repeal the sodomy laws. He said it was an indication that Snyder embraced the homosexual rights agenda. Snyder said that he opposed the sodomy laws because he considered them an invasion of privacy, not because he was fighting for gay rights. He said his effort to repeal the sodomy laws was not a top priority but just one of more than 100 legislative initiatives he had been involved in during his tenure in the state legislature.

Snyder accused Cummins of going negative because he was trailing in opinion polls. The race tightened at the end, but Snyder prevailed by 4 points, 52 percent to 48 percent.

ARKANSAS 2
Central — Little Rock

The political and commercial capital of Arkansas, Little Rock dominates the 2nd. The city and surrounding Pulaski County have a combined population of almost 350,000 — nearly 60 percent of the district's total — and their political weight is usually enough to determine the outcome of the 2nd's elections.

With a population one-third black and a well-organized labor community, Little Rock is a Democratic stronghold. The suburbs along the Arkansas River bluffs are home to a large managerial and professional community that prefers to vote Republican, but it will support moderate, business-minded Democrats. Bill Clinton got 59 percent of Pulaski County's 1996 presidential vote. And Snyder took 57 percent there in the House race, compiling a 16,647 vote margin that enabled him to withstand his losses elsewhere.

Little Rock did not experience anything like the boom felt by other Sun Belt cities during the 1980s, but the city's 10 percent growth was more than triple that of the state as a whole. Together with North Little Rock — a much smaller, separately incorporated city just across the Arkansas River — Little Rock is more insulated from economic downturns than other parts of Arkansas because of the state government presence, and the legal and service industries that support it.

Little Rock is also home to a large branch of the University of Arkansas (11,000 students) and to five major hospitals that serve the metropolitan area and outlying rural communities. There is also a military presence: Little Rock Air Force Base, in northeastern Pulaski County near the town of Jacksonville, has more than 6,600 active-duty personnel.

Once a symbol of the resistance to desegregating public schools in the South, Little Rock today has shed much of its racial tension, and in 1990 the city electorate approved a local tax increase to boost funding for the school system.

Downtown Little Rock has a spruced-up business corridor and convention center. But the retail trade has moved to the western suburbs, home to the more affluent residents. Poor and working-class blacks live in east Little Rock.

Many whites have left the city for the once-rural counties that surround Pulaski. While the 20 percent growth in Saline and Faulkner counties during the 1980s weakened their Democratic traditions, the GOP lacks organization there. And Democrats still find a hospitable union movement in the aluminum industry in Saline, the nation's prime domestic source of bauxite.

Republicans have a longer tradition in rural White County, to the east. The GOP has perhaps its strongest organization in the state here, bolstered by the firmly conservative intellectual direction from the academic community at Harding University (about 3,500 students), an institution affiliated with the Church of Christ. Rural Conway, Yell and Perry counties are more Democratic.

1990 Population: 587,412. White 476,858 (81%), Black 103,436 (18%), Other 7,118 (1%). Hispanic origin 4,731 (1%). 18 and over 434,184 (74%), 62 and over 87,011 (15%). Median age: 33.

HOUSE ELECTIONS

1996 General		
Vic Snyder (D)	114,841	(52%)
Bud Cummins (R)	104,548	(48%)
1996 Primary Runoff		
Victor F. Snyder (D)	31,435	(51%)
Mark Stodola (D)	29,821	(49%)
1996 Primary		
Mark Stodola (D)	36,314	(48%)
Victor F. Snyder (D)	24,730	(32%)
John Edwards (D)	15,262	(20%)

CAMPAIGN FINANCE

	Receipts	Receipts from PACs	Expend-itures
1996			
Snyder (D)	$799,317	$217,948 (27%)	$798,145
Cummins (R)	$731,094	$107,915 (15%)	$730,699

DISTRICT VOTE FOR PRESIDENT

1996		1992	
D	124,545 (55%)	D	130,435 (56%)
R	83,218 (37%)	R	84,922 (36%)
I	14,667 (7%)	I	19,348 (8%)

KEY VOTES

1997

Ban "partial birth" abortions N

3 Asa Hutchinson (R)

Of Fort Smith — Elected 1996, 1st term

Biographical Information

Born: Dec. 3, 1950, Bentonville, Ark.

Education: Bob Jones U., B.S. 1972; U. of Arkansas, J.D. 1975.

Occupation: Lawyer.

Family: Wife, Susan Burrell; four children.

Religion: Baptist.

Political Career: City attorney of Bentonville, 1977-78; U.S. attorney, 1982-85; Republican nominee for U.S. Senate, 1986; Republican nominee for Ark. attorney general, 1990; Ark. Republican party chairman, 1990-95.

Capitol Office: 1535 Longworth Bldg. 20515; 225-4301.

Committees

Judiciary
Constitution; Crime

Transportation & Infrastructure
Aviation; Surface Transportation

Veterans' Affairs
Health

The Path to Washington: Hutchinson, who twice mulled over a run for the Senate in 1996, went to the House instead.

A former state GOP chairman who unsuccessfully challenged Democratic Sen. Dale Bumpers in 1986, Hutchinson considered trying for the seat being vacated by retiring Democratic Sen. David Pryor. But he decided against challenging then-Lt. Gov. Mike Huckabee for the GOP nomination.

When Huckabee dropped out of the race in order to succeed Gov. Jim Guy Tucker, who resigned after being convicted in a Whitewater-related case, Hutchinson again pondered whether to run. He demurred as Republican leaders persuaded his older brother, Rep. Tim Hutchinson, to give up his safe House seat to run for the Senate.

Asa Hutchinson then was tapped to replace his brother as the GOP nominee in the 3rd District, the most Republican of Arkansas' four congressional districts. (The GOP had held the seat for 30 years; longtime Rep. John Paul Hammerschmidt invariably breezed to re-election, except in 1974, when a 28-year-old law professor and political newcomer named Bill Clinton held the incumbent to 52 percent of the vote.)

Hutchinson got a big break when the original Democratic nominee, lawyer and publisher Boyce Davis, withdrew, saying he could not raise enough money to make the race competitive. The Democrats then turned to University of Arkansas business professor Ann Henry, who ran a spirited campaign but ended up losing to Hutchinson by 14 points.

The brothers campaigned together, sharing fried chicken, potato salad, baked beans and iced tea with 400 of the party faithful at a rally and dinner in the final weeks of the campaign.

With both Hutchinsons winning their respective races, Arkansas becomes the second state with a brother-brother combination in the Senate and House. The other is Michigan, with Sen. Carl Levin and Rep. Sander Levin.

The election also provided a measure of revenge for the Hutchinsons. Democrat Winston Bryant, who defeated Asa in the 1990 state attorney general's race, lost to Tim in the 1996 U.S. Senate contest.

Not only did Hutchinson succeed his brother in the House, he also succeeded him on the House Transportation and Infrastructure Committee. Applying former Speaker Thomas P. "Tip" O'Neill's dictum that all politics is local, Hutchinson said he would seek help for a new airport in northwest Arkansas, home base of Wal-Mart and Tyson Foods. He also got seats on the Judiciary and Veterans' Affairs committees.

The former U.S. attorney, who once prosecuted members of a militia-style group, said reducing crime would be one of his top priorities. In particular, he said he would push federal agencies to boost their interdiction efforts in an attempt to reduce the flow of illegal drugs into the country.

Hutchinson got his start in government right after graduating from the University of Arkansas law school when he became Bentonville city attorney. He was named by President Ronald Reagan as the U.S. attorney for the Western District of Arkansas in 1982, leaving before his unsuccessful 1986 Senate campaign.

The younger Hutchinson, like his older brother, leans to the right on issues. He supports term limits, opposes a five-day waiting period on handgun purchases and backs the move to overhaul the welfare system by shifting more responsibilities to the states.

He is a strong supporter of efforts to balance the federal budget. He wants to shrink the deficit through spending cuts rather than tax increases. He said he would have supported the Republicans' efforts in the 104th Congress to balance the budget by 2002, including the GOP proposal to reduce the rate of growth in spending on Medicare, the federally backed health insurance program for the elderly.

At the same time, he backs a per-child tax credit for working families and supports efforts to simplify the tax code and flatten rates.

ARKANSAS 3
Northwest — Fort Smith; Fayetteville

The hilly 3rd, Arkansas' most reliably Republican constituency, has roots of GOP allegiance dating back to the Civil War. That conflict struck many of the small-scale farmers here as one fought mostly in behalf of the wealthy, slave-holding planters in the flatter parts of Arkansas.

In 1988, George Bush won two-thirds of the district's presidential vote; even in 1996, Arkansan Bill Clinton lost eight of the district's 16 counties. Crawford and Sebastian counties voted against Clinton in seven of his last eight elections (two presidential and six gubernatorial campaigns); Clinton's only loss in this span occurred in 1980, when he was unseated by Republican Frank D. White.

Back in 1974, this is where Clinton cut his teeth in electoral politics. As a 28-year-old law professor at the University of Arkansas in Fayetteville, Clinton held GOP Rep. John Paul Hammerschmidt to 52 percent; it was the only time Hammerschmidt won re-election with less than two-thirds of the vote.

Carroll County (once home to temperance advocate Carry Nation) conveys the conservative, Bible Belt character of the nearly all-white 3rd its tourist attractions. The area hosts year-round performances of The Great Passion Play, depicting Christ's last days on Earth. It also has the Bible Museum; the huge Christ of the Ozarks statue; and the Inspirational Wood Carvings Gallery. The warm baths at Eureka Springs are a more earthly attraction.

For generations, the rough terrain here made for a struggling economy dependent on relatively unproductive farmland. Vast pine forests in the Ouachita Mountains provide jobs in sawmills scattered through the rural counties. The large livestock business in the western portion of the 3rd gives a distinctly Western feel to the area around Fort Smith, on the Oklahoma border.

In recent years, the economy has been boosted by retirees and two home-grown national corporations, Tyson Foods Inc. and Wal-Mart. Arkansas is the nation's leading broiler producer, and Tyson is the state's poultry industry leader. The company also has moved into hogs, a growth industry along Arkansas' western border. In the 1980s, Tyson's headquarters city, Springdale (Washington County), grew about 20 percent, to almost 30,000.

Bentonville (Benton County) hosts the headquarters of Wal-Mart, as well as a distribution center for the discount chain. Concentrating on small-town markets, founder Sam Walton built Wal-Mart into a retailing behemoth (2,301 stores); he died in 1992 as one of the nation's wealthiest men.

The Ozark economy also has benefited from an influx of retirees. The area's mild climate and natural assets — Beaver Lake and Bull Shoals Lake, the Buffalo River and two national forests — have drawn people to newly developed planned communities.

The district's population centers are the manufacturing and livestock city of Fort Smith (Sebastian County), the state's second-largest city with 72,800 residents, and the university city of Fayetteville (Washington County), with just over 42,000 residents. The last Democratic presidential candidate to win Sebastian County was Harry S Truman, in 1948.

1990 Population: 589,523. White 565,293 (96%), Black 9,675 (2%), Other 14,555 (2%). Hispanic origin 6,753 (1%). 18 and over 440,403 (75%), 62 and over 109,410 (19%). Median age: 35.

HOUSE ELECTIONS

1996 General		
Asa Hutchinson (R)	137,093	(56%)
Ann Henry (D)	102,994	(42%)
Tony Joe Huffman (REF)	5,974	(2%)

CAMPAIGN FINANCE

	Receipts	Receipts from PACs		Expend-itures
1996				
Hutchinson (R)	$373,369	$101,025	(27%)	$366,628
Henry (D)	$466,533	$62,250	(13%)	$441,734
Huffman (REF)	$7,176	$3,000	(42%)	$6,992

DISTRICT VOTE FOR PRESIDENT

	1996		1992
D	107,096 (44%)	D	109,111 (43%)
R	110,457 (45%)	R	107,351 (43%)
I	22,986 (9%)	I	35,991 (14%)

KEY VOTES

1997

Ban "partial birth" abortions Y

4 Jay Dickey (R)

Of Pine Bluff — Elected 1992, 3rd term

Biographical Information
Born: Dec. 14, 1939, Pine Bluff, Ark.
Education: U. of Arkansas, B.A. 1961, J.D. 1963.
Occupation: Lawyer; restaurateur.
Family: Divorced; four children.
Religion: Methodist.
Political Career: Pine Bluff city attorney, 1968-70.
Capitol Office: 2453 Rayburn Bldg. 20515; 225-3772.

Committees
Appropriations
Agriculture, Rural Development, FDA & Related Agencies; Energy & Water Development; Labor, Health & Human Services, Education & Related Agencies

In Washington: The first Republican to represent southern Arkansas in the House since Reconstruction, Dickey captured the 4th from Democrats in 1992 and by 1996 was popular enough to win a third term with more than 60 percent of the vote. After Republicans took control of the House in 1994, GOP leaders awarded him a seat on the Appropriations Committee — a fair prize for a man who was registered Democratic before he launched his first House bid. Dickey switched to the GOP before starting his campaign, because, he said, "I didn't want to go up there [to Washington] and have two battles — one against the bureaucracy and one against my own party."

Before Dickey, the 4th was held for 14 years by Democrat Beryl Anthony Jr., but 109 overdrafts at the House bank and a relatively liberal voting record felled him in the 1992 Democratic primary.

In switching to the GOP, Dickey did not make a long ideological journey. Many of his positions are in line with the views of the conservative Democrats who have long been influential in southern Arkansas politics. This voting bloc has been suspicious of the Republican Party since Civil War days, but Dickey is making inroads in the district's traditional voting patterns.

In the 105th Congress, he serves on two Appropriations subcommittees that could be helpful to the 4th's economy — Agriculture and Rural Development, and Energy and Water Development. He also sits on the Labor-HHS subcommittee.

The fiscal 1997 spending bill overseen by the Labor-HHS panel drew the attention of Dickey, a staunch opponent of abortion. He successfully amended the measure to ban federally funded research using human embryos. "It's lethally experimenting with a life," Dickey said of research on human embryos. "It is an attack on our conscience."

Also in the 104th, Dickey's concern about abortion prompted him to join 14 other Republicans in voting against the GOP leadership on the rule bringing the party's welfare reform bill to a floor vote. Dickey worried that provisions in the welfare bill aimed at reducing out-of- wedlock births might prompt more poor women to seek abortions. He and other anti-abortion members wanted the House to consider two amendments addressing their concerns. But the rule did not provide for votes on those amendments.

In the 103rd, Dickey took on the White House over the issue of state funding of abortions. Dickey introduced a bill to reverse a policy of the Clinton administration's Department of Health and Human Services requiring that states use Medicaid funds to pay for poor women's abortions in cases of rape or incest. Dickey argued that while states should be allowed to fund such abortions under Medicaid, the federal government should not require that states do so.

On the House version of the fiscal 1997 Labor-HHS bill, Dickey also won approval of an amendment cutting $2.6 million from Centers for Disease Control program researching firearms injury prevention. Dickey said the research was primarily used by gun control advocates. But he failed in trying to attach an amendment to the District of Columbia appropriations bill that would have prohibited unmarried couples from adopting children.

Dickey was an early agitator for congressional reform, testifying in the 103rd before the Joint Committee on the Organization of Congress as part of a bipartisan group that expressed concern about Congress exempting itself from laws that all other Americans must obey. Dickey told the reform committee, "Voters are fed up with us being treated like some type of royalty up here."

He joined the bipartisan team in proposing a number of changes in the rules affecting lawmakers' activities, including cutting back on official mailings to a member's district during an election year; overhauling the nation's campaign finance system, including limits on contributions from political action committees; reducing lawmakers' pensions; prohibiting the use of frequent flier miles for anything but official use by the member; and applying any unused money from lawmakers'

ARKANSAS 4
South — Pine Bluff; Hot Springs

Though now in Republican hands, the 4th traditionally has been staunchly Democratic; in the three decades before the 1990s, the GOP offered a House candidate here only six times.

A recent convert to the GOP, Dickey first won in 1992 by capturing the votes of the many Democrats disaffected with their nominee. He also maximized his vote in the parts of the 4th where Republicans have some presence: around the urban centers of Pine Bluff and Hot Springs and along southern Arkansas' "El Dorado fringe."

The 4th stretches from the Texas border on the west to the Mississippi River on the east. It has more blacks (27 percent of the population) of any Arkansas district, and most of its white voters retain a Civil War-era allegiance to the Democratic Party in elections for local office. In presidential voting, Jimmy Carter in 1976 and Bill Clinton in 1992 and 1996 carried the district.

The 4th's economy depends on agriculture. Scores of paper and plywood mills, most owned by Georgia Pacific and International Paper, dot the district. Rice and soybeans are grown in the Delta counties, and hogs have become an important industry on the western fringe.

With 57,000 people, Pine Bluff (Jefferson County) is the district's largest city and Dickey's hometown. It has a 53 percent black population and casts the highest minority vote of any city in Arkansas. Like the rest of the 4th, Pine Bluff is heavily dependent on the timber industry. International Paper employs about 1,400 people here.

The Pine Bluff Arsenal, which once produced the nation's entire supply of biological weapons, no longer manufactures them. Instead, the arsenal, with about 1,000 military and civilian personnel, tests and refurbishes gas masks, including many used in Operation Desert Storm in early 1991.

The district's second-largest city, with 32,000 people, is Hot Springs (Garland County), a popular resort for more than a century. Clinton grew up here after leaving his birthplace in the southwestern Arkansas town of Hope (Hempstead County). The bathhouses and spas of Hot Springs National Park are the center of a tourist economy and a haven for retirees. Garland County's population grew by 5 percent in the 1980s, helping make Hot Springs more Republican.

Farther south is the El Dorado fringe, Arkansas' narrow "oil band" running along the bottom of the state from Texarkana, on the Texas border, through El Dorado.

Surrounding Union County is the site of several oil refineries and chemical plants; politically active, conservative oil operators make the area a pocket of Republican strength. In 1994, Dickey won Union County and three other southern-border counties, Ashley, Miller and Columbia.

1990 Population: 585,202. White 423,832 (72%), Black 155,602 (27%), Other 5,768 (1%). Hispanic origin 4,740 (1%). 18 and over 429,638 (73%), 62 and over 113,139 (19%). Median age: 35.

office accounts directly toward deficit reduction. He also has sponsored legislation denying pension benefits to members of Congress convicted of felonies in the future.

Dickey initially refused to go along with Republican efforts to reopen the federal government in January 1996 after its shutdown. In retaliation, Speaker Newt Gingrich, R-Ga., canceled a scheduled fundraising appearance. "In essence, I've been spanked," Dickey said. "But I'm not going to repent. [Gingrich] asked us to be in perfect lock step. But my commitment is to the constituents of my district, and that supersedes teamwork. When [Sen. Bob] Dole collapsed and said, 'Enough's enough, let's put them back to work,' Gingrich caved in."

Prior to running for Congress, Dickey was a successful lawyer and businessman, owner of two Taco Bell franchises, a commercial sign company and a travel agency, all in the Pine Bluff area. He won in 1992 with the financial support of the district business community, and in the 103rd followed the pro-business line on family and medical leave (voting against it) and NAFTA (supporting it). In the 104th, he initially opposed raising the minimum wage but ultimately did support a conference report that combined the wage hike with some business tax breaks. On the fiscal 1996 Labor-HHS spending bill, he pushed through an amendment transferring $26.4 million from the National Labor Relations Board to Head Start.

He also backed the efforts of Rep. James T. Walsh, R-N.Y., to temporarily cut off funding for tougher standards for meat and poultry inspection so that federal officials could get input from meat packers. The amendment was bitterly opposed by the Clinton administration and some congressional Democrats, who claimed it could risk exposing thousands of people to deadly levels of the E. coli bacteria and other food-borne pathogens.

But Dickey cited his experience with Taco Bell in claiming that the new standards were convoluted and would put many meat packers out of business. He and his allies argued that the judgment of government bureaucrats should not replace that of professionals who deal with meat every day. "It is an insult to those of us who care about our customers," Dickey said. "When we hand food to that person over the counter, we do it as a matter of trust."

At Home: With native son Clinton heading the 1996 ballot, Arkansas Democrats had high hopes of taking back the 4th from Dickey. They came up with an attractive candidate in Methodist minister Steve Copley. But Dickey raised campaign funds for his re-election early and often. By mid-1996, he had taken in more than a half-million dollars. That was too much for Copley, who withdrew from the race, apparently because he felt he could not raise enough money to be competitive with Dickey. In Copley's place, a political unknown, writer Vincent Tolliver, carried the Democratic banner. He was not much of a factor in the fall election, and Dickey won with little trouble.

Dickey initially won the seat in 1992 thanks to a split in the Democratic ranks. Business interests in the 4th had always been cozy with Anthony, a businessman himself and a member of the influential Ways and Means Committee. But in the 1992 Democratic primary, Secretary of State W.J. "Bill" McCuen went after Anthony guns ablaze, calling him a liberal and an out-of-touch incumbent.

A product of the Garland County (Hot Springs) courthouse, McCuen earned notoriety for taking a 1990 motorcycle trip on state business with two female assistants. He also was criticized for accepting a $324,000 no-bid contract for computers that turned out to be worthless.

These and other controversies might have kept McCuen from winning the Democratic line were it not for a big, last-minute infusion of anti-Anthony advertising by the National Rifle Association.

With McCuen as the Democratic standard-bearer, Dickey and the GOP knew their chances of November victory were dramatically higher. Business leaders, including a cousin of Anthony's, came out for Dickey and saw to it that his campaign was financially competitive, even though he did not accept PAC money.

McCuen ran a viciously negative campaign — he hinted that incest was a cause of Dickey's divorce, something Dickey, his wife and his children denied — that further helped Dickey attract mainstream Democratic support. He won with 52 percent, even as Clinton carried the district handily in presidential voting.

In 1994, Dickey survived another negative campaign, launched by state Sen. Jay Bradford, winning by the narrowest margin of any GOP incumbent in the South. Five Clinton Cabinet officials stumped for the well-funded challenger, but Bradford's support of the assault weapons ban hurt him among gun-rights voters. Dickey again took 52 percent of the vote.

HOUSE ELECTIONS

1996 General		
Jay Dickey (R)	125,956	(64%)
Vincent Tolliver (D)	72,391	(36%)
1994 General		
Jay Dickey (R)	87,469	(52%)
Jay Bradford (D)	81,370	(48%)

Previous Winning Percentages: 1992 (52%)

CAMPAIGN FINANCE

	Receipts	Receipts from PACs		Expend-itures
1996				
Dickey (R)	$656,708	$0	(0%)	$452,572
1994				
Dickey (R)	$821,053	$0	(0%)	$832,117
Bradford (D)	$799,791	$154,835	(19%)	$797,708

DISTRICT VOTE FOR PRESIDENT

1996		1992	
D	126,896 (60%)	**D**	134,692 (58%)
R	66,034 (31%)	**R**	73,891 (32%)
I	15,972 (8%)	**I**	23,677 (10%)

KEY VOTES

1997	
Ban "partial birth" abortions	Y
1996	
Approve farm bill	Y
Deny public education to illegal immigrants	Y
Repeal ban on certain assault-style weapons	Y
Increase minimum wage	N
Freeze defense spending	N
Approve welfare overhaul	Y
1995	
Approve balanced-budget constitutional amendment	Y
Relax Clean Water Act regulations	Y
Oppose limits on environmental regulations	N
Reduce projected Medicare spending	Y
Approve GOP budget with tax and spending cuts	Y

VOTING STUDIES

	Presidential Support		Party Unity		Conservative Coalition	
Year	**S**	**O**	**S**	**O**	**S**	**O**
1996	23	68	90	4	88	8
1995	17	80	94	3	95	3
1994	42	58	90	7	89	8
1993	37	60	88	9	93	7

INTEREST GROUP RATINGS

Year	ADA	AFL-CIO	CCUS	ACU
1996	0	n/a	100	100
1995	0	0	100	88
1994	0	22	75	95
1993	10	8	91	100

CALIFORNIA

Governor: Pete Wilson (R)
First elected: 1990
Length of term: 4 years
Term expires: 1/99
Salary: $120,000 (accepts $114,000)
Term limit: 2 terms
Phone: (916) 445-2841
Born: Aug. 23, 1933; Lake Forest, Ill.
Education: Yale U., B.A. 1955; U. of California, Berkeley, J.D. 1962.
Military Service: Marine Corps, 1955-58.
Occupation: Lawyer.
Family: Wife, Gayle Edlund.
Religion: Presbyterian.
Political Career: Calif. Assembly, 1967-71; mayor of San Diego, 1971-83; U.S. Senate, 1983-91.

Lt. Gov.: Gray Davis (D)
First elected: 1994
Length of term: 4 years
Term expires: 1/99
Salary: $94,500
Phone: (916) 445-8994

State election official: (916) 445-0820
Democratic headquarters: (916) 442-5707
Republican headquarters: (818) 841-5210

REDISTRICTING

California gained 7 House seats in reapportionment, increasing from 45 districts to 52. Map drawn by special panel was approved by state Supreme Court Jan. 27, 1992; federal court Jan. 28 rejected effort to block use of map in 1992 pending appeal. Federal appeals court March 3 dismissed challenge to the map.

STATE LEGISLATURE

Bicameral Legislature. Two-year session meets year-round, with recess.

Senate: 40 members, 4-year terms
1996 breakdown: 24D, 15R,1I; 33 men, 7 women
Salary: $75,600
Phone: (916) 445-4251

Assembly: 80 members, 2-year terms
1996 breakdown: 44D, 36R; 61 men, 19 women
Salary: $75,600
Phone: (916) 445-3614

URBAN STATISTICS

City	Population
Los Angeles	3,458,398
Mayor Richard Riordan, R	
San Diego	1,110,554
Mayor Susan Golding, R	
San Jose	782,248
Mayor Susan Hammer, N-P	
San Francisco	723,549
Mayor Willie Brown, D	
Oakland	372,242
Mayor Elihu Mason Harris, D	

U.S. CONGRESS

Senate: 2 D, 0 R
House: 29 D, 23 R

TERM LIMITS

For state offices: Yes
Senate: 2 terms
Assembly: 3 terms

ELECTIONS

1996 Presidential Vote

Bill Clinton	51%
Bob Dole	38%
Ross Perot	7%

1992 Presidential Vote

Bill Clinton	46%
George Bush	33%
Ross Perot	21%

1988 Presidential Vote

George Bush	51%
Michael S. Dukakis	48%

POPULATION

1990 population		29,760,021
1980 population		23,667,902
Percent change		+26%
Rank among states:		1
White		69%
Black		7%
Hispanic		26%
Asian or Pacific islander		10%
Urban		93%
Rural		7%
Born in state		46%
Foreign-born		22%
Under age 18	7,750,725	26%
Ages 18-64	18,873,744	63%
65 and older	3,135,552	11%
Median age		31.5

MISCELLANEOUS

Capital: Sacramento
Number of counties: 58
Per capita income: $20,952 (1991)
Rank among states: 8
Total area: 158,706 sq. miles
Rank among states: 3

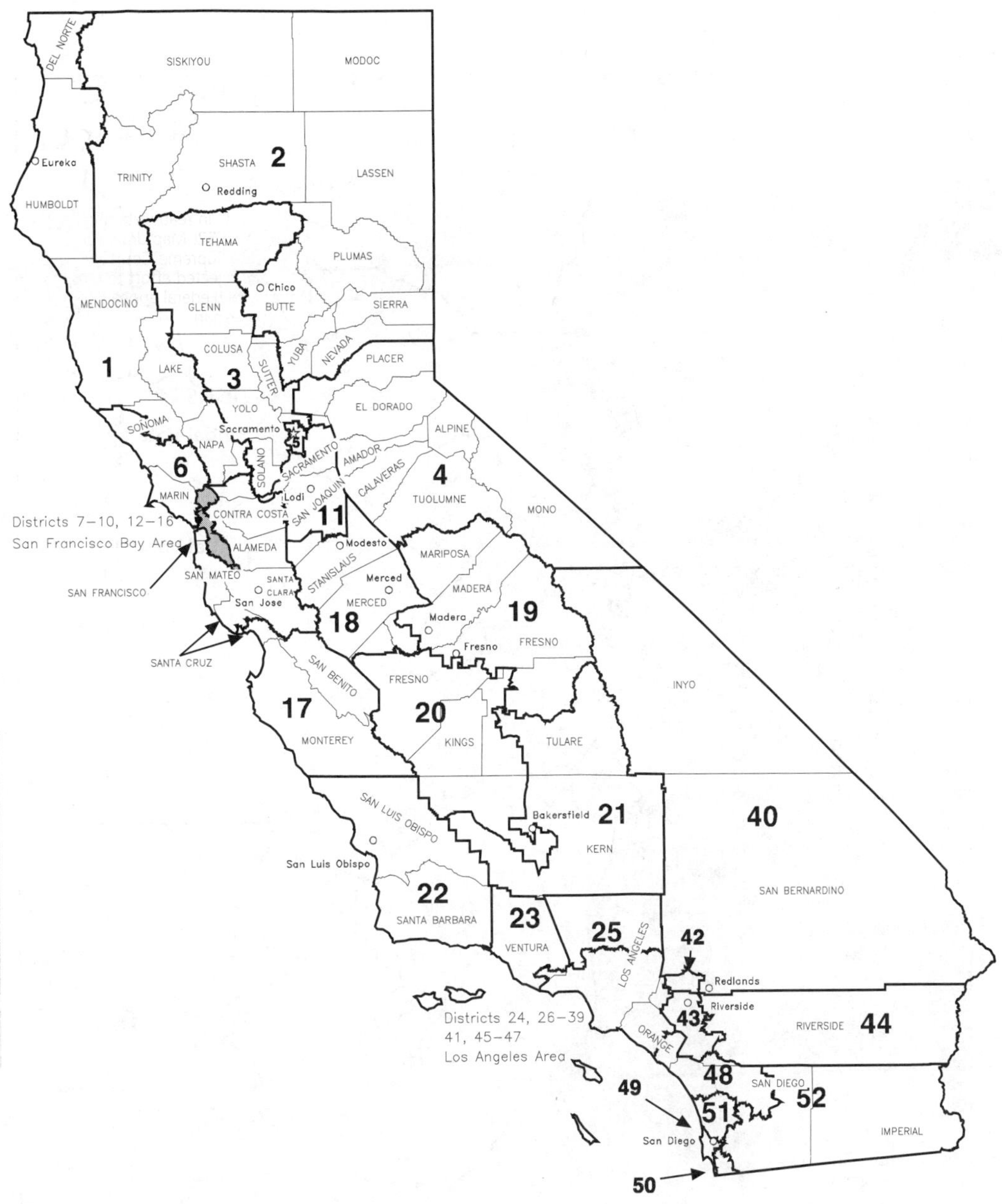
DEL NORTE
SISKIYOU
MODOC
SHASTA
2
LASSEN
Eureka
TRINITY
Redding
HUMBOLDT
TEHAMA
PLUMAS
Chico
MENDOCINO
GLENN
BUTTE
SIERRA
COLUSA
YUBA
NEVADA
PLACER
1
LAKE
3
SUTTER
YOLO
EL DORADO
SONOMA
Sacramento
5
ALPINE
NAPA
SACRAMENTO
AMADOR
6
SOLANO
CALAVERAS
4
MARIN
Lodi
SAN JOAQUIN
TUOLUMNE
MONO
Districts 7–10, 12–16
San Francisco Bay Area
CONTRA COSTA
11
ALAMEDA
Modesto
MARIPOSA
SAN FRANCISCO
SAN MATEO
SANTA CLARA
STANISLAUS
Merced
MADERA
San Jose
MERCED
19
18
Madera
FRESNO
Fresno
SANTA CRUZ
SAN BENITO
FRESNO
INYO
17
20
MONTEREY
KINGS
TULARE
SAN LUIS OBISPO
Bakersfield
21
40
KERN
San Luis Obispo
22
SAN BERNARDINO
SANTA BARBARA
23
25
VENTURA
LOS ANGELES
42
Redlands
Riverside
43
RIVERSIDE
44
Districts 24, 26–39
41, 45–47
Los Angeles Area
ORANGE
48
SAN DIEGO
49
52
51
IMPERIAL
San Diego
50

CALIFORNIA
SAN FRANCISCO AREA DISTRICTS

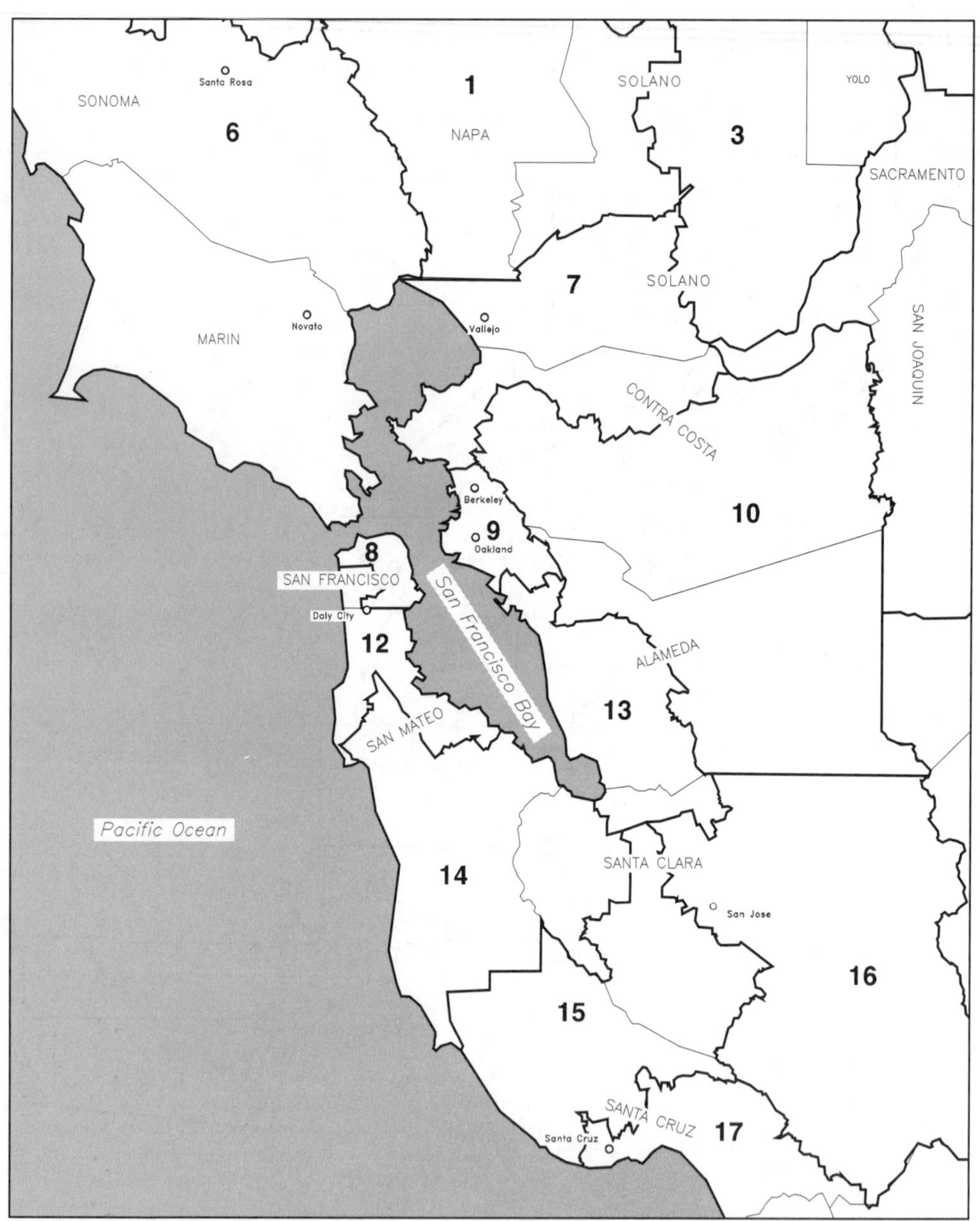

CALIFORNIA
LOS ANGELES AREA DISTRICTS

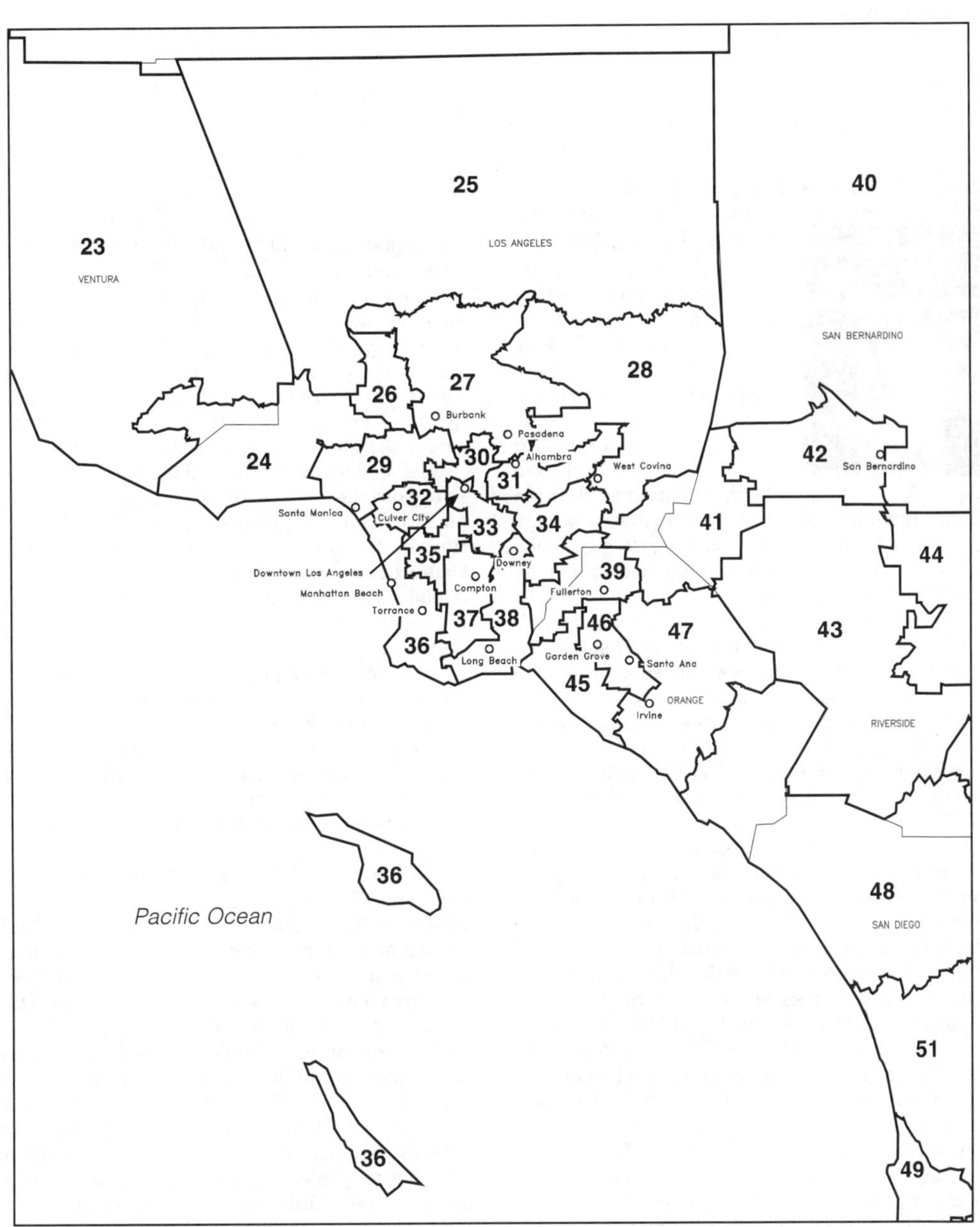

Dianne Feinstein (D)

Of San Francisco — Elected 1992; 1st full term

Biographical Information

Born: June 22, 1933, San Francisco, Calif.

Education: Stanford U., A.B. 1955.

Occupation: Public official.

Family: Husband, Richard Blum; one child; three stepchildren.

Religion: Jewish.

Political Career: San Francisco Board of Supervisors, 1970-78, president, 1970-71, 1974-75, 1978; mayor of San Francisco, 1978-89; Democratic nominee for governor, 1990.

Capitol Office: 331 Hart Bldg. 20510; 224-3841.

Committees

Foreign Relations
East Asian & Pacific Affairs; International Operations (ranking); Near Eastern & South Asian Affairs

Judiciary
Immigration; Technology, Terrorism & Government Information (ranking); Youth Violence

Rules & Administration

Joint Library

In Washington: Although she has been the city's mayor, the stereotype of liberalism associated with the term "San Francisco Democrat" has never fit Feinstein, whom some political wags have dubbed a "double-death Democrat" for her support of both the death penalty and abortion rights. But mixing liberal and conservative punches has been a Feinstein trademark, especially since her constituency has broadened to include the whole of California.

Feinstein straddles the state's ideological gulf without appearing indecisive. In the Democratic-controlled 103rd Congress, she sponsored two landmark bills pleasing to liberals. Now under the GOP majority, she is known as a Democrat whom Republicans can work with on certain issues: From her seat on the Judiciary Committee in the 104th, she was a key Democratic backer of the GOP's efforts to toughen immigration standards.

She goes her own way, though, as Republicans learned bitterly when she switched her position on the balanced-budget constitutional amendment in the 104th. Feinstein had supported the amendment in 1994, but when its chances of enactment improved with the Republican takeover of Congress, she was one of six former supporters to come out against it in 1995.

In shifting, Feinstein expressed concern for the solvency of Social Security and said she hoped to take that program "off budget," or, remove it from budget-balancing calculations. But her proposal to do that failed, as did the budget amendment itself. She offered a similar Social Security provision in 1997, with identical results.

Feinstein was a key ally of Republicans who wanted to restrict the flow of illegal immigrants into the country, although that matter was left out of legislation enacted in 1996. She helped fend off efforts to weaken employee verification pilot projects and birth certificate standards, supported the idea of a border crossing fee, and offered language to tighten protections against students who use invitations to attend private schools as a ruse to get into the country.

She voiced support for some other GOP ideas, such as overhauling product liability law and expanding private property rights, but she voted against the actual bills on those subjects — calling them "extreme." She opposed the welfare overhaul enacted in 1996, in part because she found its funding formula unfair to her state.

Her concern for California's interests led her to oppose the 1995 list of defense bases slated for closure, which included a major air force installation in Sacramento. She joined several other Californians in winning a duties exemption on chemicals used against AIDS, and also defended the interests of California poultry processors in a fight with southeastern producers.

Feinstein has a heterodox record on civil liberties issues, supporting a bill to ban employment discrimination based on sexual preference but also supporting a proposed constitutional amendment to allow laws banning desecration of the flag. She contends that the flag should be viewed as "a revered national object, not simply as one of many vehicles for free speech."

Feinstein voted during the 104th against a ban on a specific abortion procedure that its opponents call "partial birth" abortion, which President Clinton vetoed. In the 105th, she sponsored an amendment to the measure to ban post-viability abortions except to save the woman's life or protect her health, but it failed, 28-72.

She fought with California GOP Rep. Jerry Lewis over his ultimately unsuccessful move to take the 1.4 million acre Mojave National Preserve out of the National Park System. The preserve had been created as part of a 7.5 million-acre desert protection law that Feinstein sponsored in the 103rd Congress, the largest federal land protection measure in 14 years.

Feinstein negotiated more than 50 changes to her desert bill to win over leery senators and special interest groups. During final consideration of the bill in October 1994, Republicans threw up an obstacle course of filibusters, hoping to deny Feinstein a victory and dent her re-election campaign against GOP Rep. Michael Huffington. But

Senate Majority Leader George J. Mitchell shepherded colleagues back from the campaign trail for a rare Saturday session.

Feinstein scored a clear victory in November 1993 with her legislation banning 19 semiautomatic assault-style weapons. "It really comes down to a question of blood or guts — the blood of innocent people or the Senate of the United States having the guts to do what we should do when we take that oath to protect the welfare of our citizens," she said.

Feinstein and others made the case for the ban with gory accounts of gun-related deaths. When GOP Sen. Larry E. Craig of Idaho, a board member of the National Rifle Association, hinted that Feinstein didn't have much weapons knowledge, she recounted how she had tried to find the pulse of fellow San Francisco Supervisor Harvey Milk after he was gunned down at City Hall in 1978. The assault weapons ban passed, 56-43.

At Home: Feinstein's 1994 campaign was one of the nation's most closely watched Senate contests. Huffington had secured a seat in Congress in 1992 by spending more than anyone had ever spent before on a House race ($5.4 million), and while still a freshman he embarked on another record-setting bid to unseat Feinstein. Lavishing nearly $30 million (nearly all from his own pocket) on his broadcast campaign, Huffington dominated the airwaves.

He came on strong in the polls throughout the spring, leaping from a percentage in the teens to one near 40 percent in head-to-head matchups. Not until Feinstein and other Democrats turned attack ads on Huffington did his climb come to a halt.

In the fall, the contest was overshadowed by the immigration issue. Huffington made support for Proposition 187 (denying public services to illegal aliens) the centerpiece of his campaign. Feinstein opposed the measure and labeled Huffington a hypocrite when it was revealed he had employed an illegal immigrant in his household. Huffington's campaign then discovered an illegal immigrant had worked for Feinstein in the early 1980s.

On Election Day, Feinstein ran strongly in Northern California, easily carrying the nine Bay Area counties. One anomaly in the general regional split was that Huffington's home county of Santa Barbara toward the south of the state went for Feinstein. Overall, she won with 47 percent.

Until her election to the Senate, Feinstein was best known as the former mayor of San Francisco, although she had been a leading contender for the Democratic Party's vice presidential nomination in 1984. Her victory in the 1992 special Senate election was made all the sweeter because the seat she won had belonged to Republican Pete Wilson, to whom she lost the 1990 gubernatorial election. After beating Feinstein, Wilson resigned from the Senate and appointed John Seymour in his place. By ousting Seymour, who never managed to gain much notice back home, Feinstein won the right to serve the remaining two years of Wilson's term.

SENATE ELECTIONS

1994 General		
Diane Feinstein (D)	3,977,063	(47%)
Michael Huffington (R)	3,811,501	(45%)
Elizabeth Cervantes Barron (PFP)	255,036	(3%)
Richard Benjamin Boddie (LIBERT)	178,951	(2%)
Paul Meeuwenberg (AMI)	142,630	(2%)
Barbara Blong (GREEN)	137,710	(2%)
1994 Primary		
Diane Feinstein (D)	1,635,837	(74%)
Ted J. Andromidas (D)	297,128	(13%)
Daniel Davy O'Dowd (D)	271,615	(12%)

Previous Winning Percentages: 1992† (54%)

† *Special election*

CAMPAIGN FINANCE

	Receipts	Receipts from PACs		Expend-itures
1994				
Feinstein (D)	$14,597,791	$1,570,773	(11%)	$14,407,179
Huffington (R)	$29,992,884	$0	(0%)	$29,969,695
Blong (GREEN)	$3,568	0		$3,568
Barron (PFP)	$50	0		$50
Carroll (X)	$165	0		$160

KEY VOTES

1997	
Approve balanced-budget constitutional amendment	N
Approve chemical weapons treaty	Y
1996	
Approve farm bill	Y
Limit punitive damages in product liability cases	N
Exempt small businesses from higher minimum wage	N
Approve welfare overhaul	N
Bar job discrimination based on sexual orientation	Y
Override veto of ban on "partial birth" abortions	N
1995	
Approve GOP budget with tax and spending cuts	N
Approve constitutional amendment barring flag desecration	Y

VOTING STUDIES

	Presidential Support		Party Unity		Conservative Coalition	
Year	S	O	S	O	S	O
1996	88	10	81	19	53	47
1995	83	16	79	20	39	56
1994	92	8	89	11	44	56
1993	89	8	88	10	37	59

INTEREST GROUP RATINGS

Year	ADA	AFL-CIO	CCUS	ACU
1996	95	n/a	38	20
1995	95	100	37	13
1994	70	63	40	8
1993	85	100	9	13

Barbara Boxer (D)

Of Greenbrae — Elected 1992, 1st term

Biographical Information

Born: Nov. 11, 1940, Brooklyn, N.Y.

Education: Brooklyn College, B.A. 1962.

Occupation: Congressional aide; journalist; stockbroker.

Family: Husband, Stewart Boxer; two children.

Religion: Jewish.

Political Career: Candidate for Marin County Board of Supervisors, 1972; Marin County Board of Supervisors, 1977-83; U.S. House, 1983-93.

Capitol Office: 112 Hart Bldg. 20510; 224-3553.

Committees

Appropriations
District of Columbia (ranking); Interior; Legislative Branch; VA, HUD & Independent Agencies

Banking, Housing & Urban Affairs
Financial Institutions & Regulatory Relief; Financial Services & Technology (ranking); International Finance

Budget

Environment & Public Works
Clean Air, Wetlands, Private Property & Nuclear Safety; Superfund, Waste Control & Risk Assessment; Transportation & Infrastructure

In Washington: Boxer's determined style causes her to operate most often as an unremitting activist, rather than as a go-along, get-along player within the legislative arena. Some politicians will horse-trade and compromise in pursuit of their goals, but that seems not to be Boxer's first instinct. She is not reluctant to offer amendments that obviously have no chance of adoption, just to make a point about how she feels things ought to be.

Boxer was the only senator whose voting record in the 104th got a perfect 100 rating from Americans for Democratic Action, a liberal advocacy group. But it's not her unfashionable adherence to liberal tenets that works against her in the clubby, and currently Republican and conservative, Senate so much as her insistent manner. She will filibuster at times, but more often she will simply persist in offering amendments and resolutions with little hope of enactment; even when her amendments pass, she often votes against the bills that underlie them.

Boxer has fought hard against a ban on a specific abortion procedure its opponents call "partial birth" abortion. In the 104th, she offered an amendment to the ban aimed at shielding from prosecution doctors who act to preserve "the life and health" of a woman, but her amendment was killed, 51-47. In the 105th, she joined with fellow California Democrat Dianne Feinstein on a proposal to prohibit post-viability abortions except to save the woman's life or protect her health. "It is the height of ego, to me, to decide we're going to be not only lawmakers but doctors," Boxer said, but the amendment failed, 28-72.

On another women's health issue, Boxer lent credence to her stubborn streak in arguing for a proposal to exempt mammograms from a regulatory overhaul bill. Noting that 46,000 women die each year of breast cancer, she threatened to filibuster the bill unless her provision was included, warning, "I will stand on my feet for 46,000 minutes or 46,000 hours or whatever it takes." Although her amendment passed unanimously, Boxer still opposed the bill.

Most of Boxer's many amendments — to strengthen child abuse laws, offer more drinking water contaminant information, protect consumers in cable TV pricing, and the like — have come to grief. Her move to waive the proposed balanced-budget constitutional amendment for federal relief for natural disasters was killed, 70-28. Boxer opposes the balanced-budget amendment, and of the GOP's overall fiscal policy blueprint, she once said, "The big winners in this budget, I think, will be America's millionaires and billionaires and the Pentagon."

An early critic of Oregon Republican Sen. Bob Packwood for his sexual peccadilloes, Boxer was a steady voice through the summer of 1995 in calling for public hearings on the matter. Over the objections of Ethics Committee Chairman Mitch McConnell, R-Ky., who threatened to call for public hearings about Democratic senators' indiscretions, Boxer finally succeeded in winning a vote on the issue, but her resolution lost, 48-52. Despite that setback to her cause, Packwood's troubles worsened and after the Ethics Committee released its damning report he resigned in disgrace in 1995.

Up for re-election in 1998, Boxer seeks to broaden her appeal beyond liberal voters by securing help where she can for California. Toward that end, for the 105th she won a seat on the Appropriations Committee. She also sits on the Transportation and Infrastructure Subcommittee on the Environment and Public Works Committee, which will help redirect transportation funds over the next several years and so can be a voice for such major projects as the Alameda Corridor in Los Angeles and expanding Highway 101 through Northern California.

California lost thousands of defense jobs in the 1995 round of base closures, and Boxer derided the closure commission for inflicting economic pain on the state. "The commission went bonkers," she stated. She helped steer through environmental protection for the Presidio, a former military base at San Francisco's Golden Gate. Boxer also supported the GOP's toughened immigration standards and sought to force the federal government to reimburse states and localities for costs associated with illegal immigration.

She displayed a lighter side in her move to protect a regulation concerning the freshness of chickens, which would have helped California processors protect their market against southeastern poultry processors. To illustrate the point about relative freshness, Boxer displayed a picture of a frozen chicken, labeled fresh, that was used as a bowling ball. "Do we believe for a minute that a chicken that is frozen like this should be marked 'fresh' if it can knock down bowling pins?" she asked. But, again, she failed to convince and her motion died, 38-61.

At Home: If Boxer puts some people off with her assertiveness, her nature was crucial to her come-from-behind victory in the 1992 Democratic senatorial primary and to her survival that November, when she held off a late charge by the GOP nominee, conservative TV commentator Bruce Herschensohn.

Boxer was not an early favorite in her race. Fellow House Democrat Mel Levine was thought better capable of raising money and organizing Southern California; Lt. Gov. Leo T. McCarthy was also in the chase and well-known statewide. Moreover, as the campaign unreeled, Boxer had to defend her 143 overdrafts at the House bank and other stories of shoddy office practices and missed votes in the House.

But Boxer was missing votes because she was raising money and campaigning furiously from one end of the state to the other. Levine meanwhile relied almost entirely on TV ads that proved disappointing; and McCarthy failed to ignite enthusiasm beyond his base among labor and traditional liberals. Boxer's numbers kept rising up to the June primary, and she won it going away.

Herschensohn overcame a shaky summer to run an effective fall campaign that almost overtook Boxer, whose organization sputtered after the primary. But in the end, she won by five percentage points. She benefited from a late barrage of ads depicting Herschensohn as a right-wing extremist and from a late story about him visiting a nightclub featuring adult entertainment.

She also got a boost from the national Democratic ticket and from the dynamism of her pairing with Feinstein, who was seeking California's other Senate seat, also up that year. The two women often campaigned together, an ironic rebuke to all the political pros who had said California would never elect one liberal Jewish woman from the Bay Area — let alone two. In fact, Boxer and Feinstein had not been close politically or personally before 1992. But with Feinstein running well ahead of GOP Sen. John Seymour, the alliance was clearly a plus for Boxer.

Boxer had entered the House as the beneficiary of one of the decade's more creative acts of district line-drawing. In 1982, she won overwhelmingly in the San Francisco portion of the 6th and ran up comfortable margins in outlying blue-collar communities, countering Republican Dennis McQuaid's majority in Marin County. Within days of her 1990 re-election (which she won with 68 percent), she announced her Senate candidacy.

SENATE ELECTIONS

1992 General		
Barbara Boxer (D)	5,173,443	(48%)
Bruce Herschensohn (R)	4,644,139	(43%)
Genevieve Torres (PFP)	372,816	(3%)
Jerome McCready (AMI)	372,780	(3%)
June R. Genis (LIBERT)	235,918	(2%)
1992 Primary		
Barbara Boxer (D)	1,339,126	(44%)
Leo T. McCarthy (D)	935,209	(31%)
Mel Levine (D)	667,359	(22%)
Charles Greene (D)	122,954	(4%)

Previous Winning Percentages: **1990*** (68%) **1988*** (73%) **1986*** (74%) **1984*** (68%) **1982*** (52%)

* *House elections*

KEY VOTES

1997	
Approve balanced-budget constitutional amendment	N
Approve chemical weapons treaty	Y
1996	
Approve farm bill	Y
Limit punitive damages in product liability cases	N
Exempt small businesses from higher minimum wage	N
Approve welfare overhaul	N
Bar job discrimination based on sexual orientation	Y
Override veto of ban on "partial birth" abortions	N
1995	
Approve GOP budget with tax and spending cuts	N
Approve constitutional amendment barring flag desecration	N

CAMPAIGN FINANCE

	Receipts	Receipts from PACs	Expend-itures
1992			
Boxer (D)	$10,349,048	$896,683 (9%)	$10,368,600
Herschensohn (R)	$7,915,259	$627,158 (8%)	$7,859,072
Genis (LIBERT)	$9,302	0	$9,301

VOTING STUDIES

	Presidential Support		Party Unity		Conservative Coalition	
Year	**S**	**O**	**S**	**O**	**S**	**O**
1996	88	10	94	6	18	82
1995	85	10	93	5	5	93
1994	85	13	91	8	19	78
1993	91	9	95	5	10	90
House Service:						
1992	5	51	50	4	8	50
1991	21	66	76	1	8	73

INTEREST GROUP RATINGS

Year	ADA	AFL-CIO	CCUS	ACU
1996	100	n/a	23	5
1995	100	100	26	0
1994	95	88	20	0
1993	90	91	9	8
House Service:				
1992	60	100	0	0
1991	80	100	25	0

1 Frank Riggs (R)

Of Windsor — Elected 1994, 3rd term
Did not serve 1993-95.

Biographical Information

Born: Sept. 5, 1950, Louisville, Ky.

Education: St. Mary's College; U. of Maryland; Golden Gate U., B.A. 1980.

Military Service: Army, 1972-75.

Occupation: Police officer; real estate developer; educational software executive.

Family: Wife, Cathy Anne Maillard; three children.

Religion: Episcopalian.

Political Career: Windsor School Board, 1984-88; U.S. House, 1991-93; defeated for re-election to U.S. House, 1992.

Capitol Office: 1714 Longworth Bldg. 20515; 225-3311.

Committees

Education & Workforce
Early Childhood, Youth & Families (chairman); Postsecondary Education, Training & Life-Long Learning

Transportation & Infrastructure
Surface Transportation; Water Resources & Environment

In Washington: A loyal soldier of the Republican revolution at the start of the 104th Congress — voting for the "Contract With America" 100 percent of the time in 1995 — Riggs leavened his conservatism as Election Day drew near, most conspicuously in May 1996, when he sponsored the amendment on the House floor to increase the minimum wage. His careful positioning helped him stave off an energetic Democratic challenge and retain the seat he won in 1990, lost in 1992 and won back in 1994.

Though as a candidate for re-election he extolled the funding he obtained for his district from his perch on the Appropriations Committee, at the start of the 105th Riggs did something highly unconventional, if not unprecedented: He left the powerful money panel in order to become chairman of the Early Childhood, Youth and Families Subcommittee of the Education and the Workforce Committee. The committee has jurisdiction over all elementary and secondary school programs, including Head Start, special education, school lunches and child nutrition. The subcommittee could be a political plus for Riggs, enabling him to work on education and child-related issues that are a special concern of many women, a voting constituency that of late has weakly supported GOP candidates.

In February 1997, the subcommittee began hearings into reauthorizing the Individuals with Disabilities Education Act (IDEA), the main special education program. A similar attempt died in 1996 in the Senate. Democrats complained that they were not being consulted on the matter, and they objected to a provision that would enable school districts to deny all services to disabled children in extreme disciplinary cases.

After President Clinton's 1997 State of the Union speech, Riggs joined Education and the Workforce Chairman Bill Goodling, R-Pa., in giving a cool reception to Clinton's 10-point plan to improve the country's education system. He argued that leaders ought to fix the 760 existing federal education programs before starting more.

Riggs also returned in the 105th to the Transportation and Infrastructure Committee, where he had served in his first term (when it was called Public Works and Transportation). The committee is writing the new surface transportation authorization bill. He is already looking at obtaining federal help to alleviate the congestion along U.S. 101, a major commuter route.

Still, neither position gives Riggs as much money-funneling clout as Appropriations afforded him. While he believed that overall federal spending should be restrained, he did use his Appropriations seat to try to direct the moneys that are spent toward programs that he and his constituents favor.

For example, the fiscal 1997 energy-water development appropriations bill included a $2.5 million channel dredging project for Humboldt Harbor in Eureka — where Riggs and local officials envision major new commercial shipping — after House GOP leaders insisted that Energy and Water Development Appropriations Subcommittee Chairman John T. Myers, R-Ind., lift his ban on new or unauthorized projects in the bill.

Riggs, indeed, boasted of his prowess in obtaining federal largess for the district. "I am certainly not bashful about fighting for my district," he said. From agricultural research in fighting pest infestation in Napa Valley vineyards to aquaculture projects to help restore dwindling salmon fisheries in the coastal Pacific, Riggs fought unabashedly for projects for Northern California. Bringing home projects is "absolutely critical in terms of demonstrating to my constituents that I'm working to improve their lives," he said. "I'm actually getting things done."

The 1st, which follows California's rugged northern coast from Oregon to San Francisco Bay, has wide swaths of timberland, and conflicts between loggers and environmentalists are ever-present. Riggs was at the center of a heated environmental controversy during House floor debate on the fiscal 1997 Interior spending bill. The fight stemmed from a May 1996 decision by the U.S.

CALIFORNIA 1
Northern Coast — Eureka

The 1st stretches along the Pacific Coast from the Oregon line almost to metropolitan San Francisco. It includes the big coastal counties of Mendocino, Humboldt and Del Norte, with their breathtaking forests and ocean waves crashing on boulders and beaches. But while these counties dominate the 1st's image, they have less than one-third of its people. Practically their only population center is the port city of Eureka in Humboldt County, the lone port for hundreds of miles, which earns its feast-or-famine living by shipping the region's world-class logs.

Just east of Mendocino is Lake County, where the economy is a mix of ranching, farming and tourism. South of Mendocino, 1992 redistricting altered the 1st. Most of Sonoma County was transferred to the 6th, including Santa Rosa, which had grown by 37 percent in the 1980s to become the largest city in the old 1st. Sonoma as a whole cast about half the total district vote in 1990. In 1992, after redistricting, the part of the county remaining in the 1st accounted for less than 10 percent of the district vote.

The 1st still includes much of Sonoma County's prime wine-producing country. And the district gained even more distinction in this arena by annexing all of neighboring Napa County. Wineries, large and small, line Highway 29 throughout the scenic Napa Valley, the source for much of the most prestigious wine in the Western Hemisphere.

Farther east, the 1st also expanded what had been a toehold in the southwestern corner of Solano County, where its holdings now spread north and east to enfold the cities of Fairfield and Vacaville. In the 1980s, the combined population of these two communities rose by roughly 50 percent to more than 150,000. In the 1992 elections, about 40 percent of the 1st's total vote came from Napa and Solano counties.

The politics of coastal Northern California have long required balancing the union sentiments of lumberjacks and other laborers with the Republican stands of timber owners, ranchers and retirees. Travis Air Force Base, at the district's southeastern extreme, has been a counterweight to the waves of "ecotopian" immigrants arriving in search of lifestyle nirvana in the coastal highlands to the north.

In partisan terms, losing so much of Sonoma County was expected to hurt Democratic candidates in the 1st, especially because the compensating territory in Napa and Solano counties had been relatively more Republican. But 1992 was an unusually ripe year for Democrats in California. Bill Clinton and Democratic Senate nominees Dianne Feinstein and Barbara Boxer almost achieved a triple sweep of all seven counties in the 1st (Boxer lost one: Del Norte). The Democrats' little-known House candidate, Dan Hamburg, also held on to win, carrying Humboldt, Mendocino and Solano with just enough margin to survive losing the other four counties. In 1994, all counties in the district but Mendocino and Sonoma went for Republican Riggs; GOP Gov. Pete Wilson carried all but Sonoma.

1990 Population: 573,082. White 487,230 (85%), Black 22,602 (4%), Other 63,250 (11%). Hispanic origin 64,233 (11%). 18 and over 423,418 (74%), 62 and over 87,396 (15%). Median age: 34.

Fish and Wildlife Service, which oversees the Endangered Species Act, to designate about 700,000 acres of federal, state and county land in California as a critical habitat for the marbled murrelet, a threatened seabird. About 40,000 acres was on private land controlled mostly by the Pacific Lumber Co., with the balance of the acreage in the hands of private landowners. Under a Riggs amendment approved by the Appropriations Committee, the bill would have lifted the critical habitat designation for most of the private acreage while leaving protections in place for the 3,000-acre Headwaters Grove, home to numerous ancient redwoods.

Riggs argued that the critical-habitat designation would put undue restrictions on the land and lead to job losses. Because of the federal designation, California regulators could prevent timber harvesting in the name of habitat protection, he said.

But Democratic opponents hammered away at Riggs' plan as a bailout for special interests that would undermine the Fish and Wildlife Service's enforcement of the Endangered Species Act. They repeatedly focused their attacks on the floor on Pacific Lumber Co. and Texas financier Charles Hurwitz, the chief executive of Houston-based Maxxam Inc., which acquired Pacific Lumber Co. in a 1986 takeover. George Miller of California, the ranking Democrat on the Resources Committee, decried the Riggs amendment as befouling "the aisles of this Congress." The House approved, 257-164, an amendment by Norm Dicks, D-Wash., to strike the Riggs language. Backers of the Riggs language conceded that charges of special-interest politics helped defeat the measure.

Although Riggs is philosophically in step with timber companies, ranchers and other district business interests, he also is cognizant that many voters in the 1st were drawn to the area by its breathtaking coastal views and other natural attributes. He links arms with environmentalists who oppose offshore oil drilling. Riggs joined a bipartisan effort to extend through fiscal 1996 the moratorium on offshore oil drilling first enacted in 1982. Backers of the drilling ban fear that offshore rigs will degrade scenic vistas and devalue coastal property.

Riggs' return to the House in 1995 reunited the Gang of Seven, a group of Republicans first elected in 1990 who forced the Democratic leadership to fully disclose the financial mismanagement of the House bank. Six of the Gang now are serving in the House; the seventh, Rick Santorum of Pennsylvania, was elected to the Senate in 1994.

At Home: Riggs was high on the Democrats' hit list in 1996, and their candidate carried a famous last name in Northern California politics: Michela Alioto. A paraplegic since a ski-lift accident, Alioto was showcased at the Democratic National Convention in Chicago, seconding the nomination of her former boss, Vice President Al Gore. She followed the textbook Democratic strategy of trying to link Riggs to House Speaker Newt Gingrich.

But Riggs made an issue of Alioto's lack of political experience and called her a carpetbagger; she moved to the district shortly before the filing deadline and had not voted in some recent elections. He criticized Alioto for opposing the death penalty and touted his success using the Appropriations Committee to secure federal funds for local projects. Riggs was held to 50 percent but managed to win re-election, the first time the district had returned an incumbent to the House since 1988.

Riggs began his comeback in 1994 quietly, lying low until the filing deadline and letting the media attention focus on the Democratic primary, in which incumbent Dan Hamburg (who beat Riggs in 1992) faced a challenge from former Rep. Douglas H. Bosco, whom Riggs had defeated in 1990.

Bosco ran hard against Hamburg's environmentalism and highlighted statements Hamburg had made favoring legalization of possessing marijuana in small amounts. Hamburg won renomination fairly easily, but the struggle weakened him both financially and politically.

When Hamburg had won in 1992, the statewide political climate was favorable for Democrats. But the reverse was true in 1994. Riggs carried six of the seven counties in the 1st and took 53 percent of the vote overall. His best county by far was Humboldt, which includes the north coastal lumbering-shipping city of Eureka — an indication that traditionally Democratic blue-collar voters deserted Hamburg.

Riggs' 1994 victory was far more impressive than his win in 1990, when he beat Bosco with only a 43 percent plurality. Riggs benefited that year from the unexpectedly strong showing of a Peace and Freedom candidate who got 15 percent of the vote and split Bosco's base.

Before his first campaign for the House, Riggs served four years on the Windsor School Board, and he ran the district campaign for President Ronald Reagan in 1984 and for two GOP gubernatorial efforts.

HOUSE ELECTIONS

1996 General		
Frank Riggs (R)	110,242	(50%)
Michela Alioto (D)	96,522	(43%)
Emil Rossi (LIBERT)	15,354	(7%)
1994 General		
Frank Riggs (R)	106,870	(53%)
Dan Hamburg (D)	93,717	(47%)

Previous Winning Percentage: 1990 (43%)

CAMPAIGN FINANCE

	Receipts	Receipts from PACs	Expend-itures
1996			
Riggs (R)	$1,388,458	$508,727 (37%)	$1,390,399
Alioto (D)	$1,268,872	$269,206 (21%)	$1,228,870
1994			
Riggs (R)	$594,860	$142,887 (24%)	$605,185
Hamburg (D)	$834,455	$399,459 (48%)	$834,611

DISTRICT VOTE FOR PRESIDENT

1996		1992	
D	113,861 (48%)	**D**	119,491 (47%)
R	83,669 (35%)	**R**	74,597 (29%)
I	23,024 (10%)	**I**	61,160 (24%)

KEY VOTES

1997	
Ban "partial birth" abortions	Y
1996	
Approve farm bill	Y
Deny public education to illegal immigrants	Y
Repeal ban on certain assault-style weapons	Y
Increase minimum wage	Y
Freeze defense spending	Y
Approve welfare overhaul	Y
1995	
Approve balanced-budget constitutional amendment	Y
Relax Clean Water Act regulations	Y
Oppose limits on environmental regulations	N
Reduce projected Medicare spending	Y
Approve GOP budget with tax and spending cuts	Y

VOTING STUDIES

	Presidential Support		Party Unity		Conservative Coalition	
Year	S	O	S	O	S	O
1996	39	58	82	13	78	20
1995	20	76	90	7	91	7
1992	62	31	71	17	79	17
1991	72	28	81	14	78	19

INTEREST GROUP RATINGS

Year	ADA	AFL-CIO	CCUS	ACU
1996	10	n/a	81	85
1995	10	8	100	83
1992	25	36	88	75
1991	30	25	90	65

2 Wally Herger (R)

Of Marysville — Elected 1986, 6th term

Biographical Information
Born: May 20, 1945, Sutter County, Calif.
Education: American River College, A.A. 1967; California State U., 1968-69.
Occupation: Rancher; gas company executive.
Family: Wife, Pamela Sargent; eight children.
Religion: Mormon.
Political Career: Calif. Assembly, 1981-87.
Capitol Office: 2433 Rayburn Bldg. 20515; 225-3076.

Committees
Budget
Ways & Means
Trade

In Washington: A conservative Northern California rancher, Herger stands guard to prevent environmentalists from encroaching on the rights of loggers, ranchers and private property owners in his district.

He is a fixture in floor debates centered on the burdens he finds inherent in federally mandated environmental protections. Typically, he leaves his listeners with little doubt about where he stands; during discussion in the 104th Congress of a bill that would ease regulations under the Clean Water Act, Herger said the old law had "evolved into an impenetrable maze of conflicting and confusing rules, restrictions and enforcement measures that are wreaking havoc throughout the country, and particularly in my Northern California district."

He and fellow California Republican Richard W. Pombo introduced legislation in the 105th to make sure the Endangered Species Act would not block levee repairs. Herger's district suffered mammoth flooding in the winter of 1996-97, and he pointed to a major January 1997 levee break on the Feather River north of Sacramento as proof of the need for their language.

Herger claimed that necessary repairs recommended by a 1990 study had been deferred because of requirements that efforts be made to protect the habitat of the threatened elderberry beetle. "We're literally wasting millions of dollars in terms of environmental hoops we're jumping through," Herger said.

Herger and Pombo watched in satisfaction as their legislation won approval early in the 105th from the Resources Committee. But the language prompted a Clinton veto threat, because some environmentalists said the Herger-Pombo provision provided an opening in the Endangered Species Act that would permit any project related to flood control, including massive dam projects. And GOP leaders pulled the bill after it was gutted on the floor in May 1997 by an amendment offered by supporters of the environmental regulation.

Herger has long been an outspoken critic of the law, which he says has cost his district jobs and must be changed, an opinion Pombo shares.

Herger expressed that view strongly enough that a teacher criticized him in May 1995 for heaping "verbal abuse" on her at a Stockton, Calif., field hearing of the Resources Committee task force on endangered species. In a letter addressed to task force Chairman Pombo, Laurette Rogers complained that Herger "yelled at me repeatedly, whipped up the crowd, and did not even allow me a fair chance to respond."

The San Anselmo teacher was invited by Democratic aides to testify at an April field hearing about a project she heads in which grade school students work with local ranchers to protect the endangered California freshwater shrimp. She said that when her fourth- and fifth-graders described their project to the task force, they were "booed and heckled" by the audience at the hearing.

When she testified, Rogers said, Herger grilled her not about her project but about whether it was right that a real estate developer on the witness panel, who came from Herger's district, should be prevented by the law from building houses on his property.

Herger said later in an interview that he did not berate Rogers, but he did note that many people in his district are "out of work because of the extremism of the Endangered Species Act."

Herger sits on the Budget and Ways and Means committees. On the latter, he has joined a new generation of Republican members who have brought more bare-knuckled rhetoric to a committee that traditionally tried to make deals without an abundance of partisanship. Herger has used his position on the powerful committee to oppose the Clinton administration on a range of policy fronts.

With other House Westerners, Herger has fought administration proposals to raise the fees that ranchers pay to graze their livestock on federal lands. Critics of current fees say they are unreasonably low, but Herger argued in 1995 that what the Clinton administration "counts as reform is nothing more than a thinly veiled

Redistricting can end a politician's career by shifting a single square mile of political turf. But it can also switch broad swatches of territory and leave an incumbent unscathed. The 2nd demonstrates the latter. The 1992 map tore away enough of the 2nd to encompass several New England states, while adding enough new real estate to make the district even bigger. It became California's least densely populated district and its least racially diverse.

The 2nd combines the northern portions of the old 2nd and the old 14th, consolidating much of the state's northern, rural Mormon population.

The changes, however, scarcely alter the 2nd's political coloration. It is a Republican-voting district; Rep. Herger's re-election tallies in the 1990s have been above 60 percent.

Its asphalt spine is Interstate 5 (which runs from Canada to Mexico), with its central feature the mighty Mount Shasta. The population is widely dispersed through the mountainous forests and rangelands, except for population centers in Redding (a 120-year-old mining and timber town on I-5) and Chico (home to a campus of California State University with 14,000 students).

The district has suffered from fires and flood in recent years. Flooding in the Pacific Northwest was widespread during the winter of 1997, and the 2nd was particularly hard hit where the Feather and Yuba rivers meet. All 10 counties in the district were declared disaster areas.

CALIFORNIA 2
North and East — Chico; Redding

California suffered its worst fire season in modern history in 1996, and the northern timber counties of Siskiyou, Trinity and Shasta saw millions of acres burn. The timber industry has been depressed, with 32 mills in the district shut down since 1990.

Running eastward to Nevada, the 2nd embraces the three vast and remote counties of California's far northeastern corner (Modoc, Lassen and Plumas). These three lean to the GOP in most statewide elections, but with a combined registration of about 31,000 voters, they have little electoral impact.

The 2nd also includes all of Sierra and Nevada counties, named for the mountain range that marches through them.

Sierra County is sparsely populated, but just north and west of I-80 lie Nevada City and Grass Valley, which help make Nevada County the third-richest cache of votes in the 2nd (and the most decidedly Republican by registration). A few miles over the Yuba County line is Beale Air Force Base.

1990 Population: 573,322. White 525,091 (92%), Black 8,716 (2%), Other 39,515 (7%). Hispanic origin 34,425 (6%). 18 and over 424,975 (74%), 62 and over 105,763 (18%). Median age: 35.

attempt to stop grazing on public lands."

In 1993, Herger opposed a proposal that the government conduct a National Biological Survey, an inventory of all plant and animal species in the country. He said the survey would do "nothing more than further restrict private property rights and diminish the value of lands for families that depend on natural resources for their existence."

Herger and other conservatives won a victory when they gained approval of an amendment requiring the government to obtain written permission before entering private property to conduct a survey. In the 104th Congress, Herger cheered on efforts by the new House GOP majority to gut the biological survey.

Herger's district includes eight national forests, and he often is out front when forest issues are considered. Generally protective of the timber industry, he has opposed efforts to convert private lands into national parks.

He played a leading role early in the 104th when the GOP succeeded in allowing more aggressive clearing of dead and dying trees from federal lands over the objections of the Clinton administration. Herger argued the move would provide jobs and leave forests less vulnerable to fire and took issue with the Forest Service's implementation of the plan. He also sponsored a bill to ban the agency from hiring based on race or gender preferences.

There is not much suspense when Herger approaches the electronic voting device on the House floor; he votes with a majority of Republicans against Democrats nearly all the time.

He did buck his party leaders prominently on one occasion during the 104th, sponsoring a successful amendment that eliminated $14 million earmarked to buy property for a military museum. Herger said he supported the idea of the museum but argued that the military already owned sufficient land on which to build one. His amendment was adopted, 261-137.

Herger sponsored a provision of the 1996 welfare overhaul law to provide state and local prisons up to $400 when they report inmates who are fraudulently receiving Supplemental Security Income (SSI) payments. Herger said he was alerted to the problem by a sheriff in his district who noted prisoners had extra money around the first of the month to spend at the prison commissary — particularly on Snickers bars.

Herger surprised some of his colleagues in the 1993 debate on NAFTA. He announced he would oppose the trade pact a week before the House voted, but in the end, he voted for it. Minority Whip Newt Gingrich reportedly was displeased that a member holding a relatively safe seat would oppose NAFTA. But Herger is not a cheerleader for unrestricted free trade. He also had political grounds to be ambivalent. In 1992, more than one-fourth of the presidential vote in Herger's district went to Ross Perot, a staunch foe of NAFTA.

Herger has been active on one foreign policy matter: alleged human rights abuses committed by the government of India against the Sikh minority in Punjab state. Members of the small Sikh community in Yuba City told him of their concern for relatives in Punjab, prompting him to try, unsuccessfully, to cut off foreign aid and trading privileges for India.

At Home: Expected to face tough Democratic competition for the open 2nd in 1986, Herger won by a wide margin. He has had little difficulty since.

The north-central California district had been Democrat Harold T. Johnson's for 22 years before Republican Gene Chappie upset him in 1980. When Chappie decided to retire in 1986, a GOP succession was in doubt. But Herger, who was in his third state Assembly term, came in with a voter base that constituted nearly half the 2nd District and had an easy primary.

He spent most of the fall campaign on the offensive, linking himself to President Ronald Reagan and Gov. George Deukmejian and calling his opponent, Shasta County Supervisor Stephen C. Swendiman, a "tax-and-spend Democrat." When Swendiman portrayed him as a "backbencher" in the legislature, Herger highlighted his support of popular measures such as workfare and tougher sentencing for criminals. Herger took 58 percent of the vote.

In 1992, redistricting replaced all or part of five counties in the 2nd. The new area is even more sparsely populated and mountainous than Herger's old district. It contains much of the state's rural Mormon population and has a history of electing conservative Mormon representatives like Herger.

HOUSE ELECTIONS

1996 General		
Wally Herger (R)	144,913	(61%)
Roberts A. Braden (D)	80,401	(34%)
Patrice Thiessen (NL)	7,253	(3%)
William Brunner (LIBERT)	5,759	(2%)
1996 Primary		
Wally Herger (R)	71,452	(84%)
Devvy Kidd (R)	13,107	(16%)
1994 General		
Wally Herger (R)	137,863	(64%)
Mary Jacobs (D)	55,958	(26%)
Devvy Kidd (AMI)	15,569	(7%)
Harry H. "Doc" Pendery (LIBERT)	5,417	(3%)

Previous Winning Percentages: 1992 (65%) **1990** (64%) **1988** (59%) **1986** (58%)

CAMPAIGN FINANCE

	Receipts	Receipts from PACs		Expend-itures
1996				
Herger (R)	$743,383	$343,167	(46%)	$536,724
Braden (D)	$166,438	$9,100	(5%)	$161,918
1994				
Herger (R)	$617,958	$258,159	(42%)	$572,629
Jacobs (D)	$168,931	$38,000	(22%)	$167,907
Kidd (AMI)	$0	0		$0

DISTRICT VOTE FOR PRESIDENT

1996		1992	
D	89,736 (36%)	**D**	93,823 (36%)
R	126,430 (51%)	**R**	101,505 (39%)
I	22,161 (9%)	**I**	67,298 (26%)

KEY VOTES

1997	
Ban "partial birth" abortions	Y
1996	
Approve farm bill	Y
Deny public education to illegal immigrants	Y
Repeal ban on certain assault-style weapons	Y
Increase minimum wage	N
Freeze defense spending	N
Approve welfare overhaul	Y
1995	
Approve balanced-budget constitutional amendment	Y
Relax Clean Water Act regulations	Y
Oppose limits on environmental regulations	N
Reduce projected Medicare spending	Y
Approve GOP budget with tax and spending cuts	Y

VOTING STUDIES

	Presidential Support		Party Unity		Conservative Coalition	
Year	**S**	**O**	**S**	**O**	**S**	**O**
1996	32	65	95	4	92	6
1995	15	85	97	2	93	5
1994	36	56	90	3	86	6
1993	20	77	94	4	91	7
1992	73	16	90	4	81	8
1991	68	30	86	8	95	3

INTEREST GROUP RATINGS

Year	ADA	AFL-CIO	CCUS	ACU
1996	0	n/a	100	100
1995	0	0	100	92
1994	5	0	91	100
1993	5	0	91	100
1992	5	25	75	95
1991	5	18	89	100

3 Vic Fazio (D)

Of West Sacramento — Elected 1978, 10th term

Biographical Information
Born: Oct. 11, 1942, Winchester, Mass.
Education: Union College, B.A. 1965.
Occupation: Journalist; congressional and legislative consultant.
Family: Wife, Judy Kern; four children.
Religion: Episcopalian.
Political Career: Calif. Assembly, 1975-79.
Capitol Office: 2113 Rayburn Bldg. 20515; 225-5716.

Committees
Appropriations
Agriculture, Rural Development, FDA & Related Agencies; Energy & Water Development (ranking); Legislative

Caucus Chairman

In Washington: Having decided against a challenge to David E. Bonior of Michigan for minority whip in the 105th Congress, Fazio remains the No. 3 House Democratic leader as chairman of the party caucus. The big change in his portfolio for the 105th came on the legislative side, where he took the Democratic seat on Appropriations' Energy and Water Development Subcommittee, leaving the ranking post on the Legislative Branch subcommittee.

During his first two years in the House minority, Fazio was part of a group of Democrats who did not shy away from lobbing bombs at the new Republican majority — repaying Newt Gingrich and his supporters for the brickbats they threw at Democrats when they ruled the House.

For example, Fazio in 1997 was quick to call for Gingrich to leave the Speakership after the ethics committee found him guilty of violating House rules. "The Speaker of the House must put the institution of Congress ahead of his personal or party ambitions and step aside," he said.

And he tried to step up pressure on the Republican-led House to overhaul campaign finance law when he introduced legislation on that subject early in the 105th with fellow California Democrat Sam Farr. Their bill called for a voluntary spending limit of $600,000 on House campaigns, and it set limits on what candidates could spend on their own races. As an incentive to abide by the limits, the bill would give complying candidates discounts on broadcast time and postal rates. "It's common-sense legislation that curtails the influence-peddling of special interest groups," Fazio said.

Despite their obviously deep philosophical differences on a range of issues, Fazio and Gingrich found something to agree on in 1996: supporting efforts to authorize a controversial $949 million dam 40 miles upstream from Sacramento. The Auburn Dam promised to be one of the costliest flood-control, navigation and dredging projects in history. Environmental and taxpayer groups painted it as an enormous, destructive boondoggle. But Gingrich, Fazio and other members of the California delegation portrayed the project as a matter of life and death for the 400,000 people in the Sacramento flood plain and the only hope of preventing a disaster far costlier than the dam itself.

The Clinton administration said the area would be adequately protected by fortifying existing dams and levees at a cost of $57.3 million, a fraction of the Auburn Dam's price tag. But Fazio was unmoved. "It's the lowest common denominator approach that doesn't count for much," he said.

When the House Transportation and Infrastructure Committee took up the measure authorizing the dam, a bipartisan coalition defeated it, 28-35. The panel then accepted, 36-16, an amendment by James L. Oberstar of Minnesota, the committee's ranking Democrat, to authorize the $57.3 million project fortifying existing levees on the American and Sacramento rivers and modifying the Folsom Dam, about 10 miles below the spot designated for the Auburn Dam.

Fazio has always kept a sharp lookout for ways that his district and state can tap into the flow of federal dollars. On Appropriations in the 104th, he pushed through an amendment to the fiscal 1997 energy and water development spending bill to increase funding for solar and renewable energy research by $10 million. Of that, $6 million would go to wind energy research (a favorite in California), the only funding that program would get in fiscal 1997 in the bill.

But he was unable to block the closure of McClellan Air Force Base in his district. The facility was one of those targeted by the Pentagon's base closing commission. When the House took up the commission's recommendations in toto in July 1995, he voted "no," but was on the short side of a 75-343 tally.

In June 1995, Fazio clashed with the GOP majority over its ultimately successful attempt to eliminate the Office of Technology Assessment (OTA), a congressional agency that advised lawmakers on technological issues. Fazio voted

CALIFORNIA 3
North Central Valley

The 3rd bears little resemblance to the district so designated before 1992. The old 3rd had included much of Sacramento and some of its suburbs to the east, but now the 3rd scalps only the northwestern corner of Sacramento County before running far away to the north, west and south to incorporate tracts from the old 2nd and 4th districts.

The 3rd includes all of Yolo County and the eastern portion of Solano County, which were in the old 4th. This accounts for the 3rd's ready-made incumbent, Fazio, who had represented Yolo and eastern Solano counties as well as that portion of Sacramento's suburbs now included in the 3rd.

Now, however, Fazio has far fewer Solano County residents than he did in the 1980s. After a decade of intense growth, Solano was casting 30 percent of the vote in Fazio's old district. In 1996, the Solano precincts cast less than 10 percent of the total vote in the new 3rd.

Remapping gave the 3rd the spacious northern county of Tehama, which serves as a bridge between the flat agricultural lands of the upper Sacramento River Valley and the timber-rich highlands of the Trinity-Shasta region to the north. The 3rd also picked up the farm-oriented counties of Glenn, Colusa and Sutter, the northern terminus of the state's richly productive Central Valley region.

Despite its vast new lands, however, the 3rd's most populous county is still Sacramento. Even though only the northwestern corner of the county remains, it accounted for more than a third of the total district vote in 1996. This corner includes McClellan Air Force Base (just outside the city limits of Sacramento) — which was slated to shut down under the 1995 round of base closings. President Clinton said he would try to find private employers to help keep 8,700 jobs there. Residents here work in aerospace and other high-tech industry as well as in Sacramento's main business — state government. In this vote-rich enclave, both George Bush and Bob Dole prevailed narrowly over Bill Clinton; but Fazio came up a winner in the county in 1992, 1994 and 1996, winning by about 9,600 votes the last time out.

In 1992, Fazio padded his winning vote overall by running up a score in Yolo County, outpolling his challenger by 20,000 votes. Two years later, Yolo saved his seat for him, though Fazio's margin was cut to 12,000 votes. In 1996, Fazio again won Yolo by more than 20,000 votes. Yolo is one of five California counties that voted for Walter F. Mondale for president in 1984, and it includes the college community of Davis, home of a sprawling University of California campus, which has a student population of 23,300.

In winning re-election in 1996, Fazio lost five of the district's eight counties: the Republican-leaning Colusa, Glenn and Tehama and the solidly Republican Sutter County and the tiny corner of Butte County included in the district.

1990 Population: 571,374. White 469,595 (82%), Black 18,339 (3%), Other 83,440 (15%). Hispanic origin 81,213 (14%). 18 and over 417,336 (73%), 62 and over 76,236 (13%). Median age: 31.

against the bill's conference report because it did away with OTA. "It made the bill unacceptable to me," he said. And in July 1996, he objected to a House rule barring minority Democrats from setting up separate home pages on the World Wide Web to distribute committee information. He said the new House policy "perverts the whole idea of the free flow of information on the Web."

In the 103rd Congress, when Democrats ran the House and reformers were pushing lobby-regulation legislation restricting the gifts and meals lawmakers could accept, Fazio depicted the measure as frivolous. "I don't think, other than on a level of political inevitability, anybody has made the case that something needs to be done," he said.

But after the Democrats' debacle of 1994 — Fazio himself won just 50 percent of the vote — he moved more in line with the public's desire for change. After President Clinton in his 1995 State of the Union address called on lawmakers to voluntarily forgo gifts from lobbyists, Fazio kept the ball rolling at a meeting of the Democratic Caucus. "I brought it up knowing members were interested in it," Fazio explained. "We discussed how members might individually respond to the president's request."

Later in 1995, Fazio sided with an effort — driven largely by reform-minded GOP freshmen — to impose a strict ban on gifts to House members. The House passed the gift ban by a vote of 422-8.

Fazio led the Democratic Congressional Campaign Committee (DCCC) for the 1992 and 1994 campaign cycles. He could have pushed for the job earlier, but deferred in order to spend more time with his family. Fazio in 1990 acknowledged that his youngest daughter, then a teenager, had leukemia. In January 1996, Anne Fazio, who was 22, died from complications related to pneumonia. She had graduated from the University of California at Davis the previous June.

With Fazio leading the DCCC, Democrats weathered some bad redistricting breaks and held their comfortable House majority in 1992. As late as the end of 1993, few were predicting anything more than modest House losses for the party in 1994. But as 1994 progressed, the party's prospects grew dimmer as Clinton stumbled and Republicans adroitly transformed the public's anti-Congress sentiment into a conviction that things might be better if the 40-year Democratic House majority was ended.

Hoping to energize the Democrats' political base, Fazio tried to draw attention to elements of the "religious right" that he said were exerting control over the GOP. He spoke of "intolerance" and "subterranean tactics" by religious conservatives. But the strategy did not hold back the GOP tide: Democrats lost a net of 53 seats in the House.

At Home: Redistricting has weakened Fazio's hold on his seat. In 1992, he raised nearly $2 million and spent almost all of it to garner just a bare majority of the vote. Things were supposed to get easier in 1994, when no well-known Republican came forward, but so anti-Democratic was the voters' mood that an underfunded real estate broker Tim Lefever, pushed Fazio to the brink again.

Hence, Fazio was high on the Republican target list in 1996, with Lefever back for a second try. He put up billboards that read, "Vic Fazio: Extreme Liberal" and ran a television ad that morphed convicted murderer Richard Allen Davis into Fazio's face. For his part, Fazio touted his clout as a member of the Appropriations Committee and his own anti-crime initiatives. And he attacked Lefever for opposing abortion rights. Aided by Clinton's California victory, Fazio took 54 percent.

Fazio was up and running early for 1992, heeding the alarm he heard in his lowered vote share in 1990 (55 percent). Voters then had seemed to be punishing him for his reputation as a House insider, as well as for his defense of higher pay for members in the 101st Congress.

That situation scarcely eased for Fazio in the 102nd Congress, with the House bank scandal and other institutional embarrassments. And 1992 redistricting reconfigured Fazio's turf radically. That helped attract a well-known challenger, former state Sen. H. L. Richardson, who had represented an Orange County district for 22 years ending in 1988. He was a founder of Gun Owners of America and a champion of the religious conservatives with ready access to campaign cash. But he also gave Fazio a target for counterattack. Fazio accused Richardson of missing thousands of votes as a legislator and painted him as a carpetbagger and extremist. Richardson had lived in the state capital region for many years but remained widely identified with Southern California. Fazio held on with 51 percent.

Fazio was raised and educated in the East and came to California as a journalist who covered and then worked for the state Assembly. He won a seat in that body in a 1975 special election and was re-elected easily in 1976. In 1978, he was the only Democrat ready to run for Congress when his area's embattled Democratic incumbent, Robert Leggett, suddenly retired. His Republican foe was a former Ronald Reagan aide who ran well in rural areas, but Fazio claimed the seat with 55 percent and won re-election comfortably through the 1980s.

HOUSE ELECTIONS

1996 General		
Vic Fazio (D)	118,663	(54%)
Tim Lefever (R)	91,134	(41%)
Timothy R. Erich (REF)	7,701	(3%)
Erin D. Donelle (LIBERT)	4,239	(2%)
1996 Primary		
Vic Fazio (D)	51,575	(82%)
Rodger McAfee (D)	11,419	(18%)
1994 General		
Vic Fazio (D)	97,093	(50%)
Tim Lefever (R)	89,964	(46%)
Ross Crain (LIBERT)	8,100	(4%)

Previous Winning Percentages: 1992 (51%) **1990** (55%) **1988** (99%) **1986** (70%) **1984** (61%) **1982** (64%) **1980** (65%) **1978** (55%)

CAMPAIGN FINANCE

	Receipts	Receipts from PACs	Expend-itures
1996			
Fazio (D)	$2,412,373	$1,348,260 (56%)	$2,320,330
Lefever (R)	$663,127	$94,765 (14%)	$645,209
1994			
Fazio (D)	$1,757,508	$1,069,170 (61%)	$1,972,033
Lefever (R)	$253,321	$19,064 (8%)	$251,369

DISTRICT VOTE FOR PRESIDENT

1996		1992	
D	103,507 (45%)	**D**	99,781 (41%)
R	101,651 (44%)	**R**	90,799 (37%)
I	15,921 (7%)	**I**	53,323 (22%)

KEY VOTES

1997	
Ban "partial birth" abortions	N
1996	
Approve farm bill	N
Deny public education to illegal immigrants	N
Repeal ban on certain assault-style weapons	N
Increase minimum wage	Y
Freeze defense spending	Y
Approve welfare overhaul	Y
1995	
Approve balanced-budget constitutional amendment	N
Relax Clean Water Act regulations	N
Oppose limits on environmental regulations	Y
Reduce projected Medicare spending	N
Approve GOP budget with tax and spending cuts	N

VOTING STUDIES

	Presidential Support		Party Unity		Conservative Coalition	
Year	S	O	S	O	S	O
1996	78	15	85	10	57	43
1995	77	18	84	12	52	43
1994	87	13	93	5	50	50
1993	93	7	94	6	41	59
1992	28	68	88	9	44	48
1991	34	61	87	9	24	68

INTEREST GROUP RATINGS

Year	ADA	AFL-CIO	CCUS	ACU
1996	80	n/a	25	0
1995	85	100	38	8
1994	75	78	42	14
1993	85	92	27	8
1992	90	75	50	8
1991	75	83	30	0

4 John T. Doolittle (R)

Of Rocklin — Elected 1990, 4th term

Biographical Information
Born: Oct. 30, 1950, Glendale, Calif.
Education: U. of California, Santa Cruz, B.A. 1972; U. of the Pacific, J.D. 1978.
Occupation: Lawyer.
Family: Wife, Julie Harlow; two children.
Religion: Mormon.
Political Career: Calif. Senate, 1981-91.
Capitol Office: 1526 Longworth Bldg. 20515; 225-2511.

Committees
Agriculture
Forestry, Resource Conservation & Research; Risk Management & Specialty Crops
Resources
Forests & Forest Health; Water & Power (chairman)
Joint Economic

In Washington: Although the House majority and the public policy debate has shifted to the right, Doolittle, an anchor of the conservative wing, has yet to achieve many of his legislative aims.

Although he is now a subcommittee chairman — heading Resources' Water and Power panel — he was unable to get the support of his GOP colleagues for a costly dam project in his district and to revise the laws governing water use in the vast Sacramento Valley.

Doolittle's panel took the lead in 1995 in pushing a proposal to sell off some federal agencies that provide low-cost, government-generated hydroelectric power. Doolittle, like many other conservative Republicans, believes that the central economic mission of the federal power administrations has been achieved.

Doolittle said the agencies should be auctioned to the highest bidder to maximize the return to taxpayers. "I don't think the federal government is a good steward," he said. "You ought to get these facilities into the hands of people who have a direct stake in what they've got."

He was able to persuade the full committee in September 1995 to include the sale of the Southeastern Power Administration and the Alaska Power Administration in a draft deficit-reducing reconciliation bill, explaining that the sale would save $2.3 billion over seven years. But Doolittle found later that garnering support for the sale was difficult because those Republicans and Democrats whose constituents were served by the power agencies were concerned that a sale would lead to high power prices or that recreational uses might be curtailed.

And the sale of Southeastern became a major issue in that year's Kentucky gubernatorial election. Under Doolittle's proposal, Southeastern would be auctioned to the highest qualified bidder, and the terms of the proposed sale would include the federal dams that produce the power. Kentuckians worried that transferring the dams to private utilities would lead to restrictions on fishing and other recreation in the now federally managed reservoirs.

Kentucky Democrats began using the proposed sale to raise questions about the Republican leadership in Congress and ran radio and television ads to tie Kentucky GOP gubernatorial nominee Larry Forgy to Washington. Forgy called House Speaker Newt Gingrich of Georgia to make the case against the sale. Before the House voted on the reconciliation bill in October 1995, GOP leaders dropped the idea of selling Southeastern. It wasn't enough to help Forgy, who lost the governor's race to Democrat Paul E. Patton.

Doolittle also had little luck trying to get the House to back his effort to complete the huge Auburn Dam that lies in his district. The Transportation and Infrastructure Committee in June 1996 backed the wishes of moderate New York Republican Sherwood Boehlert, the conservationist chairman of the Subcommittee on Water Resources and Environment, and beat back an attempt to gain federal funds to finish the $949 million dam.

The giant flood-control project on the American River, about 40 miles upstream from Sacramento had become a target for national environment and taxpayer groups, which painted it as an enormous, destructive boondoggle. The dam's construction started in the 1970s, then stopped because of earthquake concerns. Opposing Doolit-tle's effort to resurrect it, the Sierra Club mounted a campaign to kill the dam for good. Unflatter-ing articles and editorials began to appear in major newspapers.

Advocates, led by Doolittle and a bipartisan central California delegation, portrayed the project as critical for the 400,000 people in the Sacramento flood plain. But the appeals to Sacramento's safety could not compete with fiscal and environmental concerns, especially since dam opponents proposed alternative flood-control projects that they said would cost less and provide almost as much protection. Republicans and Democrats teamed up to defeat an amendment that would have authorized federal funds for the dam.

"While we lost the battle, the war is not over," Doolittle told the San Francisco Chronicle after

CALIFORNIA 4
Northeast Central

The number is new, and six of its counties were removed in 1992 redistricting, but the 4th is still at heart the district that elected Doolittle in 1990 (when it was designated the 14th).

The 4th is one of just two districts in Northern California that voted for George Bush in 1992, and it was one of two in the area that voted for Bob Dole four years later. Dole won every county in the 4th in 1996, as did Doolittle. The 4th is also one of just three districts in all of California where racial minorities constitute less than 15 percent of the population.

This is not to say the district has not changed with redistricting. Gone are the Republican-leaning northern counties of Modoc, Lassen, Plumas and Sierra. Republicans may also miss Nevada County. Democrats in the district were sorry to see San Joaquin County become part of the 11th District. San Joaquin included Democratic-voting Lodi and a portion of Stockton.

Left intact at the center of the district were the old core counties of Placer, El Dorado, Amador and tiny Alpine (where 614 people voted in the 1996 election). Placer and El Dorado were the second- and third-largest contributors to the old 14th District vote (after San Joaquin). Now they rank No. 1 and No. 3, respectively. Both gave Dole a barely higher percentage than he received districtwide. Amador was more closely contested, with Dole receiving 48 percent.

Amador and El Dorado counties triggered the great California gold rush of the mid-19th century (Placerville, the El Dorado county seat, was once among the state's largest cities). Far more recently, the natural beauty of the area, which includes Lake Tahoe, has spawned a more sustainable boom: Amador, Placer and El Dorado were among the eight fastest-growing counties in the state in the 1980s.

Immediately to the south, redistricting brought in three highland counties (Calaveras, Tuolumne and Mono) that, taken as a whole, provide about one-seventh of the 4th's vote and offer a rough balance between the parties. Tuolumne County, which includes most of Yosemite National Park, was carried by Dole in 1996.

Remapping also gave the 4th the northeastern corner of Sacramento County, where the immediate suburbs of the state capital have grown out to meet the town of Folsom. Once known only for its prison (immortalized in song by Johnny Cash), Folsom is now home to Aerojet, a source of space shuttle technology. Folsom grew by a stunning 171 percent in the 1980s before being hit hard by layoffs at Aerojet, which later started hiring again.

Sacramento County as a whole votes Democratic, but the portions bordering Placer and El Dorado counties behave more like their upland neighbors.

1990 Population: 571,033. White 529,202 (93%), Black 10,059 (2%), Other 31,772 (6%). Hispanic origin 42,424 (7%). 18 and over 426,723 (75%), 62 and over 84,051 (15%). Median age: 35.

the vote. At the same time, he acknowledged that the "odds are not good" that the dam will win majority support in the full House.

Doolittle then tried to get back at Boehlert when, at the start of the 105th, he proposed a change in House GOP rules making subcommittee chairmanships subject to the approval of the entire Republican Conference. The measure was seen as a way of gaining leverage over moderate subcommittee chairmen like Boehlert. But the proposal was defeated by a 2-1 margin.

Doolittle was able to get the Resources Committee to sign off on a bill he introduced that would revise a 1992 law regulating the way water in California's Central Valley is used by agricultural interests. The bill, approved in December 1995, would have revised the Central Valley Project Improvement Act by allowing water from the project for fish and wildlife conservation to be reused by agricultural and urban interests. The Central Valley Project controls one-fifth of the usable water in California and has long been dominated by agricultural interests. The existing law limited the benefits to farmers in favor of the preservation of fish and wildlife. California Republicans bitterly fought the 1992 act and hoped to revise it.

Doolittle said his measure seeks to "correct" provisions of the law that do not work or are ambiguous. It would allow the Interior Department's Bureau of Reclamation to enter into new contracts with Central Valley interests for non-environmental purposes, provided they participate in a state fish recovery program. Opponents, including California environmentalists, said the bill would allow for the perpetual renewal of subsidized water contracts to the irrigators whose wastewater contaminates wildlife refuges and rivers. Six months after gaining his committee's approval, Doolittle said he would shelve the bill until California's deputy interior secretary tries to mediate the differences between the various users.

Doolittle also sits on the Agriculture Committee, where he supported GOP efforts to rewrite existing farm policy to bring it more in line with free market principles. The "Freedom to Farm" bill passed the House in February 1996.

Doolittle came to prominence in the House as one of the "Gang of Seven," which made headlines in 1991 and 1992 by helping force disclosure of the names of all members with overdrafts at the House bank. True to his conservative roots, Doolittle, in the 104th Congress, joined the Conservative Action Team (CAT), a group of about 40 Republicans that created its own whip organization to promote its legislative agenda. The CATs said their priorities included re-establishing school prayer, ending abortion funding, abolishing the Education Department, increasing funding for the Strategic Defense Initiative, and reaffirming the right of parents to make decisions regarding the education, religious training, medical care and discipline of their children.

The group weighed in on the 1997 budget debate by offering their own balanced-budget plan, which would have proposed greater non-defense discretionary spending cuts and greater tax cuts than the agreement worked out between the White House and congressional Republicans. But the House rejected it, 119-313. Doolittle then voted for the Budget Committee's proposal.

But Doolittle is also a firm supporter of his party's leaders. He refused to denounce Gingrich for House ethics violations. When the House voted in January 1997 to reprimand Gingrich and assess a $300,000 penalty, Doolittle was one of 26 Republicans to vote "no."

At Home: In 1990, Doolittle inherited what had been a safe district for his six-term predecessor, Republican Norman D. Shumway, another Mormon who defined the delegation's right flank. Doolittle also inherited Shumway's 1988 Democratic challenger, Patricia Malberg, a former junior college teacher. Malberg had run a spunky if quixotic campaign against Shumway and managed 37 percent.

She kept right on running against Doolittle in 1990, strongly opposing his agenda of the death penalty, nuclear power, the Human Life Amendment, offshore oil drilling and the big-dam option at Auburn. The clash seemed to favor the Republican in a district inclined to social as well as economic conservatism. But Malberg also stressed her outsider status to advantage, contrasting her old-fashioned campaign with Doolittle's big-dollar, high-power, PAC-financed effort.

In the end, Doolittle had just enough in his base to win the seat with 51 percent. That encouraged Malberg to stretch her political career out another two years and hope for help in 1992 from the redistricting process. What happened instead was that Doolittle shed some of his more Democratic precincts in San Joaquin County, giving him an outright Republican registration plurality for the first time. Doolittle won again, if barely.

In 1994, the Democrats nominated a Roseville businesswoman, Katie Hirning, who was willing to take political action committee money and got some from computer people. But it was a big GOP year and Doolittle won his third term with his first showing over 60 percent. He faced Hirning again in 1996, and won with 60 percent.

HOUSE ELECTIONS

1996 General		
John T. Doolittle (R)	164,048	(60%)
Katie Hirning (D)	97,948	(36%)
Patrick Lee McHargue (LIBERT)	9,319	(3%)
1994 General		
John T. Doolittle (R)	144,936	(61%)
Katie Hirning (D)	82,505	(35%)
Damon C. Falconi (LIBERT)	8,882	(4%)

Previous Winning Percentages: 1992 (50%) **1990** (51%)

CAMPAIGN FINANCE

	Receipts	Receipts from PACs		Expend-itures
1996				
Doolittle (R)	$717,259	$225,134	(31%)	$604,778
Hirning (D)	$199,656	$60,308	(30%)	$199,179
1994				
Doolittle (R)	$680,288	$211,125	(31%)	$664,109
Hirning (D)	$357,191	$129,337	(36%)	$354,786

DISTRICT VOTE FOR PRESIDENT

	1996		1992
D	107,076 (38%)	**D**	97,501 (34%)
R	145,223 (51%)	**R**	117,155 (41%)
I	21,233 (8%)	**I**	73,060 (25%)

KEY VOTES

1997	
Ban "partial birth" abortions	Y
1996	
Approve farm bill	Y
Deny public education to illegal immigrants	Y
Repeal ban on certain assault-style weapons	Y
Increase minimum wage	N
Freeze defense spending	N
Approve welfare overhaul	Y
1995	
Approve balanced-budget constitutional amendment	Y
Relax Clean Water Act regulations	Y
Oppose limits on environmental regulations	N
Reduce projected Medicare spending	Y
Approve GOP budget with tax and spending cuts	Y

VOTING STUDIES

	Presidential Support		Party Unity		Conservative Coalition	
Year	S	O	S	O	S	O
1996	27	70	94	5	98	0
1995	14	86	97	2	98	1
1994	35	60	96	1	94	3
1993	21	79	94	2	91	9
1992	81	19	97	3	96	4
1991	73	22	89	5	95	0

INTEREST GROUP RATINGS

Year	ADA	AFL-CIO	CCUS	ACU
1996	5	n/a	94	100
1995	0	0	96	100
1994	5	13	82	100
1993	10	8	91	100
1992	5	17	75	100
1991	5	9	78	100

5 Robert T. Matsui (D)

Of Sacramento — Elected 1978, 10th term

Biographical Information
Born: Sept. 17, 1941, Sacramento, Calif.
Education: U. of California, Berkeley, A.B. 1963, J.D. 1966.
Occupation: Lawyer.
Family: Wife, Doris Okada; one child.
Religion: Methodist.
Political Career: Sacramento City Council, 1971-78.
Capitol Office: 2308 Rayburn Bldg. 20515; 225-7163.

Committees
Ways & Means
Human Resources; Trade (ranking)

In Washington: Now his party's No. 3 man on the Ways and Means Committee, Matsui is a pro-business Democrat with the intellect and political smarts to lobby effectively for his causes. Through ten terms in the House — nine of them on the influential tax-writing panel — Matsui has managed to combine a generally liberal approach to tax policy with an intense interest in serving California business. While liberals can count on him voting with them on social policy issues, such as welfare and health reform, Matsui most consistently applies his capacity for hard work to the business side of the committee's ledger, especially where West Coast industries are concerned.

During the 104th Congress there was speculation that Matsui might challenge Charles B. Rangel of New York for the top Democratic spot on Ways and Means in the 105th. But after the GOP retained its House majority in the 1996 election, Matsui made no effort to dislodge Rangel, and while the two differ on some issues, they appear to have cordial relations.

Matsui held the liberal banner high on a couple of contentious measures debated in the 104th, opposing Republican packages that overhauled the welfare system and national immigration policy. Expressing concern for the poorest of the poor, Matsui called the welfare bill "weak on work and tough on America's children." Also, he was one of just 67 House members to oppose a bill banning federal recognition of homosexuals' marriages.

But while the GOP's social conservatism holds no appeal for Matsui, he finds common ground with Republican supporters of free trade. In fact, Matsui expressed concern in early 1996 when presidential candidate Patrick J. Buchanan's "fair trade" rhetoric fanned protectionist fires in the GOP. "The Democrats have not, generally speaking, been the leading party on free trade," Matsui told the Washington Times. "If the Republicans become a protectionist party, the free-trade cause is in real trouble."

In 1993, Matsui was head of the NAFTA Liaison Group, a House task force that worked with the Clinton administration to assemble enough votes in the House to enact the broad free trade agreement between the United States, Canada and Mexico. Matsui's was a challenging task, given the deep divisions among congressional Democrats (and in the country) over NAFTA. The trade pact had a relentless House foe in Majority Whip David E. Bonior, and Majority Leader Richard A. Gephardt also opposed it. The Reagan and Bush administrations had done most of the negotiating on NAFTA, which automatically made many congressional Democrats doubt the wisdom of approving it. Organized labor waged a fierce campaign against NAFTA, warning that it would promote the flight of U.S. jobs to low-wage workers in Mexico.

President Clinton's prospects for winning House passage hinged on combining a substantial majority of GOP members with a significant minority of Democrats. Working mostly behind the scenes, Matsui drew on his expertise as a member of the Ways and Means Trade subcommittee in trying to convince colleagues that a "yes" vote on NAFTA was economically sensible and politically defensible. Initially, House GOP leaders seemed somewhat ambivalent about helping Clinton score a big legislative victory, but eventually, Minority Whip Newt Gingrich and Republican Conference Chairman Dick Armey emerged to help assemble the Republican votes.

NAFTA passed the House on Nov. 17, 234-200, giving Clinton an opportunity to claim that his administration was promoting economic growth by encouraging expanded international trade. Although a majority of Democrats voted against NAFTA, fully 40 percent of Matsui's party colleagues voted with him for the pact. Republicans supported the agreement overwhelmingly, 132-43.

As 1994 progressed and Clinton's popularity slipped, a number of Democrats began to put some distance between themselves and the administration. Matsui, though, remained a consistent backer of the president. "Bill Clinton's suc-

CALIFORNIA 5
Sacramento

No incumbent likes to see his district renumbered, a happenstance that confuses constituents, supporters and journalists alike. But for Matsui, the incumbent from Sacramento whose 3rd District was redesignated the 5th in the 1992 redistricting, there was little else to regret in the new map.

Matsui's geographical base continues to shrink as the Sacramento metropolitan area grows. Population in the city of Sacramento grew 34 percent during the 1980s, to 369,000. So even though the map drawn in 1992 was generally Republican-friendly, Matsui got a district more concentrated in Sacramento and more Democratic in party registration.

Despite the big Democratic numbers, the old 3rd had been a swing district in statewide elections. Republicans George Bush and Ronald Reagan carried it in the presidential elections of the 1980s, and GOP Sen. Pete Wilson won it in the 1990 gubernatorial contest. But in 1992 and 1996, with some of its more affluent suburban territory pared away, the district went for Democrat Bill Clinton, giving him 57 percent in the latter election. The 5th also gave generous victory margins to the campaigns of Democratic Senate nominees Dianne Feinstein and Barbara Boxer.

On paper, the city of Sacramento has several reasons to be reliably Democratic. Labor is better organized here than in all but a few other counties in California. The dominant newspaper is The Sacramento Bee, the flagship of the McClatchy chain and a decidedly liberal voice. The city also has a strong mixture of blacks and Hispanics, who constitute more than one-fourth of the district population. There are more than 72,000 Asian-Americans in the 5th, placing it 11th in that category (although three-fourths of those old enough to vote were not registered in 1992).

But the bedrock of Sacramento politics is the presence of the state government, the source of about 50,000 jobs and a natural pro-government attitude. Years of recession have drained the state treasury and Republican governors have sought to limit government spending, but the wellspring of well-being in Sacramento is unlikely to change any time soon.

There is another Sacramento, of course, that makes its living in financial services, agribusiness or in the high-tech industries that have sprung up in Sacramento County in recent years. Stimulated by high defense budgets in the 1980s, this sector has suffered from the recent downturn in military spending.

East of the city in Rancho Cordova, Mather Air Force Base has been closed, and the Sacramento Army Depot has been turned over to Packard Bell, a computer company. Although the depot facility is an example of successful defense conversion, the overall impact of defense cutbacks has hurt the area's economy. In any event, most of the political impact of this other Sacramento is felt in the county's suburbs and exurban areas, most of which have now been apportioned among three adjoining districts and do not affect Matsui's re-election campaigns.

1990 Population: 573,684. White 376,389 (66%), Black 73,567 (13%), Other 123,728 (22%). Hispanic origin 84,426 (15%). 18 and over 421,787 (74%), 62 and over 78,443 (14%). Median age: 32.

cess is our success; his failure is our failure," he said of the Democratic Party in 1993.

Matsui has a personal connection to the White House: Doris Matsui, his wife, serves as deputy assistant to the president. She drew some unwanted attention during a fundraising scandal that marred the closing days of Clinton's successful re-election bid in 1996. One of her duties for Clinton was heading a working group meant to "manage and oversee all campaign activities" of the Asian-Pacific American community. Revelations about illegal or improper campaign contributions prompted the Democratic National Committee to return more than $1 million in contributions from Asian-Americans, but Doris Matsui and the White House said she played no direct role in fundraising.

In the 100th Congress, working with Democratic Rep. Norman Y. Mineta of California, Matsui was an important force behind passage of legislation to provide federal redress to the surviving Japanese-Americans who were interned during World War II.

In 1942, when he was 6 months old, Matsui and his family were ousted from their Sacramento home and sent to a detention camp, where they lived for more than three years. In a tribute to Mineta, who resigned during the 104th Congress, Matsui called the bill of redress "one of the most monumental legislative feats that has occurred" in recent decades. "It is not often when a government is willing to say to its own citizens, 'We made a mistake, and we want to provide an apology and some minor token redress to you.' "

At Home: Matsui weighed running for statewide office in 1988 and 1990, but when he looks back on what might have been, he may rue most the 1992 Senate race he had to abandon after learning that his father was dying of cancer. Such a year of political opportunity may not be duplicated soon: Two Senate seats were open, and both were won by Democrats. Had he run, Matsui could have looked to a solid base in Sacramento, the state capital and one of California's booming growth areas. His business contacts and proven fundraising ability also would have benefited him in a year in which the sources of political money were stretched thin.

Matsui's political career began on the local level. His experience in a World War II internment camp helped him establish a bond with Sacramento's large Asian community, and he won two elections for the City Council. In 1972, the year after Matsui joined the council, he chaired U.S. Rep. John E. Moss' re-election campaign. His fundraising skills helped Moss win easily that year, and again in 1974 and 1976.

In 1978 Matsui was preparing to run for the county Board of Supervisors when Moss announced his retirement after 26 years. Matsui filed for Congress, as did two other prominent Sacramento Democrats, but his $225,000 primary campaign budget gave him a clear advantage. He ran television commercials identifying himself as "Citizen Matsui," setting himself apart from his rivals, both of whom had been heavily involved in state politics.

Matsui won the primary and then took the general election comfortably against Republican Sandy Smoley, considered the Sacramento GOP's strongest candidate to run for the House in many years. Republicans have made no similar effort to capture the district since.

HOUSE ELECTIONS

1996 General		
Robert T. Matsui (D)	142,618	(70%)
Robert S. Dinsmore (R)	52,940	(26%)
Joseph B. Miller (LIBERT)	2,548	(1%)
Gordon Mors (AMI)	2,231	(1%)
Charles Kersey (NL)	2,123	(1%)
1994 General		
Robert T. Matsui (D)	125,042	(68%)
Robert S. Dinsmore (R)	52,905	(29%)
Gordon Mors (AMI)	4,649	(3%)

Previous Winning Percentages: **1992** (69%) **1990** (60%) **1988** (71%) **1986** (76%) **1984** (100%) **1982** (90%) **1980** (71%) **1978** (53%)

CAMPAIGN FINANCE

	Receipts	Receipts from PACs		Expend-itures
1996				
Matsui (D)	$663,586	$414,781	(63%)	$814,857
Dinsmore (R)	$18,320	$16	(0%)	$18,792
1994				
Matsui (D)	$841,836	$582,794	(69%)	$929,895
Dinsmore (R)	$73,033	$14	(0%)	$74,212

DISTRICT VOTE FOR PRESIDENT

	1996		1992
D	119,678 (57%)	**D**	120,577 (51%)
R	70,925 (34%)	**R**	73,562 (31%)
I	10,863 (5%)	**I**	42,566 (18%)

KEY VOTES

1997	
Ban "partial birth" abortions	N
1996	
Approve farm bill	N
Deny public education to illegal immigrants	N
Repeal ban on certain assault-style weapons	N
Increase minimum wage	Y
Freeze defense spending	N
Approve welfare overhaul	N
1995	
Approve balanced-budget constitutional amendment	N
Relax Clean Water Act regulations	N
Oppose limits on environmental regulations	Y
Reduce projected Medicare spending	N
Approve GOP budget with tax and spending cuts	N

VOTING STUDIES

	Presidential Support		Party Unity		Conservative Coalition	
Year	**S**	**O**	**S**	**O**	**S**	**O**
1996	86	13	90	7	41	57
1995	83	14	89	8	36	62
1994	86	6	92	2	28	58
1993	88	8	92	4	34	66
1992	26	71	88	6	29	67
1991	28	60	78	5	16	62

INTEREST GROUP RATINGS

Year	ADA	AFL-CIO	CCUS	ACU
1996	85	n/a	19	0
1995	90	100	22	8
1994	75	67	42	11
1993	80	92	27	8
1992	80	55	29	8
1991	70	80	25	0

6 Lynn Woolsey (D)

Of Petaluma — Elected 1992, 3rd term

Biographical Information
Born: Nov. 3, 1937, Seattle, Wash.
Education: U. of Washington, 1955-57; U. of San Francisco, B.S. 1980.
Occupation: Personnel service owner.
Family: Divorced; four children.
Religion: Presbyterian.
Political Career: Petaluma City Council, 1985-93.
Capitol Office: 439 Cannon Bldg. 20515; 225-5161.

Committees
Budget
Education & Workforce
Postsecondary Education, Training & Life-Long Learning; Workforce Protections

In Washington: During the welfare overhaul debates of the 104th Congress, Woolsey came with a singular experience: When she was in her late 20s, with three children, she was temporarily on welfare.

Divorced from her stockbroker husband, she had no house and no job skills. After lying about her circumstances to land her first job and surviving three years on various forms of government aid that supplemented her wages, Woolsey remarried and left the assistance rolls.

Woolsey often relied on her insider's view of the welfare system to make debating points when the House Republican majority came forward with plans to change welfare fundamentally by instituting work requirements and setting limits on benefits. She tried to amend Republican proposals to provide parents on welfare with child care services, arguing that such assistance is essential to moving people from welfare to work.

In 1995, Republicans attached their first welfare overhaul plan to a large budget proposal. The measure ended the entitlement status of most welfare programs, converting them into block grants to the states. Democrats portrayed the bill as an attack on the poor, and, since it was included in the overall GOP spending plan, they claimed that it cut spending on welfare in order to offset tax cuts for the wealthy.

President Clinton vetoed that measure. Republicans responded by bringing up a similar bill in late December. Woolsey was one of many Democrats to attack the measure, comparing it with the Dr. Seuss book, "The Grinch who Stole Christmas."

"This Grinchlike welfare bill is not just stealing Christmas from poor children," she said. "It's stealing their basic safety net."

Clinton vetoed that measure as well. Having failed twice, and with the looming 1996 elections whetting appetites for a legislative success to please voters, Republicans made some concessions they hoped would satisfy the White House. Woolsey fought this measure as well, warning colleagues that their vote on the bill was "a matter of life and death for millions and millions of children." Clinton said the measure had flaws, but over the objections of Democratic liberals, he decided in August to sign it anyway, depriving GOP presidential nominee Bob Dole of an issue in the fall campaign.

While Woolsey was disappointed that Clinton accepted the welfare bill, she showed her pragmatic side during the 1996 Democratic National Convention. There was some talk by liberals about waging a fight over platform language on welfare, but Woolsey said Democrats shouldn't "fall on their swords" over the issue. She urged party unity, saying that would help attract support from undecided voters in November.

As in the welfare debate, Woolsey also relied on her life experiences when she joined Republican Henry J. Hyde of Illinois in proposing legislation to enlist the Internal Revenue Service in helping track down parents who who fail to make child-support payments. In many cases (including her own), Woolsey said, single women go on welfare because they do not receive the required support from former husbands. She and Hyde tried unsuccessfully to attach the proposal to the welfare legislation.

Notwithstanding her cooperation with Hyde on that issue, Woolsey is a strong liberal and harsh critic of the GOP. She sits on the Budget Committee, where the minority's role is usually limited to "speechifying" against the majority's proposals. She took a dig at Speaker Newt Gingrich during the late 1995 budget standoff after he complained that Clinton had slighted him by forcing him to leave Air Force One by the rear exit following an overseas trip. "Why doesn't the cry baby speaker cry about real babies?" she asked.

When a conservative Republican chaplain prominent in the anti-abortion movement was invited to offer the House's morning prayer, Woolsey protested to Gingrich the selection of someone she called anti-gay and anti-choice.

Woolsey has been an outspoken opponent of

CALIFORNIA 6
Northern Bay Area; Sonoma and Marin counties

Once a seriocomic example of partisan gerrymandering, the 6th is now a model of compactness and community of interest. It includes all of high-profile Marin County, but instead of reaching in multiple directions for additional votes as it once did, the 6th now weds Marin to the most populous portions of neighboring Sonoma County.

The Marin identity notwithstanding, most of the district's votes are now cast in Sonoma County, where the 6th hugs the Pacific Coast from scenic Bodega Bay north to the Mendocino County line and reaches inland for fast-growing population centers such as Santa Rosa.

Once a service town for farmers, Santa Rosa has attracted corporate as well as individual refugees from the congestion of metropolitan San Francisco. It grew by more than one-third in the 1980s, and it is the largest city in the 6th. A few miles down state Highway 12 is Sonoma, a rustic town enlivened by a campus of the California State University system. Fifteen miles to the west on the Sonoma-Marin county line sits the unpretentious city of Petaluma, which once proclaimed itself the "chicken-plucking capital of the world."

To the south, Marin County is home to the city of San Rafael, the famed prison at San Quentin and a group of commuter suburbs such as Kentfield, Ross, San Anselmo and Fairfax. It has marvelous scenery: Mount Tamalpais, Stinson Beach and the Point Reyes National Seashore. But it is best-known for its onetime artist colonies and more affluent suburbs that cling to the San Francisco Bay (Sausalito, Tiburon) or nestle deep in the hills between the ocean and the bay (Larkspur, Mill Valley).

To mention some of these names is to evoke wistful sighs from former residents, visitors and "California dreamers," who know the area only through song lyrics and other myths of the counterculture. In the past decade, the politics of this social and cultural matrix have supplanted Marin's older GOP pattern. Marin had voted for Republican Gerald R. Ford for president in 1976 and for Ronald Reagan in 1980. When former San Francisco Rep. Phillip Burton masterminded the state's redistricting in 1981, he borrowed Democratic wards from three counties to overpower Marin's old GOP vote (in behalf of his brother, John, who was elected to represent the area in Congress).

But the county's partisan preferences changed during the 1980s. In 1984, Marin was one of just five California counties that voted for Walter F. Mondale. By 1992, GOP registration in the county (as well as in the 6th generally) was down to 30 percent. That figure is remarkably low, considering that the 6th is overwhelmingly white (only two of the state's 52 congressional districts have fewer minorities).

In 1992 and 1996, Bill Clinton won Marin by more than 2-to-1. Marin's liberal activists in 1992 also elevated one of their own, five-term Rep. Barbara Boxer, into the Senate and delivered her House seat to another Democratic woman, Woolsey. But Woolsey is a graduate of the City Council in Petaluma, signaling the ascendance of Sonoma County in the 6th.

1990 Population: 571,227. White 513,914 (90%), Black 13,280 (2%), Other 43,783 (8%). Hispanic origin 51,030 (9%). 18 and over 443,956 (78%), 62 and over 88,219 (15%). Median age: 36.

most of the GOP's legislative priorities. When the House considered a proposal to ban a particular abortion technique that opponents call "partial birth" abortion, Woolsey called the bill a "frontal attack" on abortion rights.

The Republican majority usually sided with management concerns in legislative disputes involving business and organized labor during the 104th Congress, and Woolsey almost always disagreed. She opposed a Republican plan to allow companies to replace striking workers, and she voted against a Republican proposal to allow employers to offer employees comp time instead of overtime pay.

When Republicans for the 104th renamed the old Education and Labor Committee (where Woolsey sat) the Economic and Educational Opportunities Committee, Woolsey joked that she had been assigned to the "Economic and Educational Opportunity to Cut Everything Committee." She is still on the panel in the 105th, but it has been renamed again, to Education and the Workforce.

Woolsey was an early backer of a single-payer health care reform plan that would cover all Americans regardless of income. She also has called for cutting the defense budget 50 percent over five years. She has voted against defense authorization bills for failing to make enough cuts in defense programs she sees as wasteful, and she has criticized a "shameful, discriminatory policy toward gays in the military."

Woolsey's firm liberal views fit her district, which includes all of Marin and much of Sonoma County. She is outspoken on environmental concerns, opposing offshore oil and gas drilling as well as energy exploration in the Arctic National Wildlife Refuge. She supports a Clinton administration proposal to expand the Point Reyes National Seashore in her district by 38,000 acres.

Woolsey's concern for the environment helped persuade her to vote against NAFTA in 1993; she argued that Mexico had lax environmental regulations, and she also said Mexico treated its workers undemocratically by not allowing them to organize and bargain for wages. She has opposed expanding the free trade pact by admitting Chile, because she says California's wine-growers need tariff protection from cheaper Chilean imports.

In addition to looking out for the concerns of vintners, Woolsey organized most of the California congressional delegation to help save the Two Rock Coast Guard Training Station near Petaluma from closure. The delegation convinced the administration to preserve the base and its 650 jobs, arguing that California had taken more than its share of hits in other defense cutbacks and base closures.

At Home: The 6th opened in 1992 when incumbent Democrat Barbara Boxer filed for the Senate seat being vacated by Democrat Alan Cranston. Woolsey, who had served eight years on the Petaluma City Council, overcame a field of eight other Democrats using geography and gender as assets.

Woolsey, one of only two candidates from Sonoma, led the balloting there over former county Supervisor Eric J. Koenigshofer. She finished second in Marin, close behind former county Supervisor Denis Rice. Sonoma voters cast more than half the ballots, so Woolsey won nomination.

The general election was expected to be a real test for Woolsey. Republican nominee Bill Filante, a 14-year veteran of the state Legislature, was the favorite. Known in the Legislature as "the last liberal Republican," he repeatedly had won in a Democratic district. By June, he had raised almost twice as much money as Woolsey. Then tragedy struck.

In early August, Filante underwent emergency brain surgery, and later it was disclosed that only part of a cancerous tumor had been removed. Filante became so ill that he was forced to suspend his campaign in mid-September, but it was too late under California law to replace him on the ballot.

Republicans urged Filante's supporters to vote for him anyway and force a special election. But Woolsey swept to a 65 percent to 34 percent victory. Filante died a month after the election.

In 1994, Woolsey's vote share dipped to 58 percent, but in 1996 she moved back up into the comfort zone, winning with 62 percent of the vote.

HOUSE ELECTIONS

1996 General		
Lynn Woolsey (D)	156,958	(62%)
Duane C. Hughes (R)	86,278	(34%)
Ernest K. Jones Jr. (PFP)	6,459	(3%)
Bruce B. Kendall (NL)	4,141	(2%)
1994 General		
Lynn Woolsey (D)	137,642	(58%)
Michael J. Nugent (R)	88,940	(38%)
Louis Beary (LIBERT)	6,203	(3%)
Ernest K. Jones Jr. (PFP)	4,055	(2%)

Previous Winning Percentages: 1992 (65%)

CAMPAIGN FINANCE

	Receipts	Receipts from PACs	Expend-itures
1996			
Woolsey (D)	$632,305	$274,357 (43%)	$542,131
Hughes (R)	$294,169	$8,166 (3%)	$292,181
1994			
Woolsey (D)	$655,259	$330,644 (50%)	$649,388
Nugent (R)	$459,430	$37,608 (8%)	$456,901

DISTRICT VOTE FOR PRESIDENT

1996		1992	
D	155,513 (57%)	**D**	169,301 (56%)
R	78,166 (29%)	**R**	71,564 (24%)
I	18,431 (7%)	**I**	60,920 (20%)

KEY VOTES

1997	
Ban "partial birth" abortions	N
1996	
Approve farm bill	N
Deny public education to illegal immigrants	N
Repeal ban on certain assault-style weapons	N
Increase minimum wage	Y
Freeze defense spending	Y
Approve welfare overhaul	N
1995	
Approve balanced-budget constitutional amendment	N
Relax Clean Water Act regulations	-
Oppose limits on environmental regulations	Y
Reduce projected Medicare spending	N
Approve GOP budget with tax and spending cuts	N

VOTING STUDIES

	Presidential Support		Party Unity		Conservative Coalition	
Year	**S**	**O**	**S**	**O**	**S**	**O**
1996	84	16	98	2	4	96
1995	86	11	97	2	10	90
1994	77	23	98	1	8	92
1993	78	20	96	2	9	91

INTEREST GROUP RATINGS

Year	ADA	AFL-CIO	CCUS	ACU
1996	95	n/a	19	0
1995	100	100	17	4
1994	100	100	25	0
1993	100	100	9	4

7 George Miller (D)

Of Martinez — Elected 1974, 12th term

Biographical Information
Born: May 17, 1945, Richmond, Calif.
Education: San Francisco State U., B.A. 1968; U. of California, Davis, J.D. 1972.
Occupation: Lawyer; legislative aide.
Family: Wife, Cynthia Caccavo; two children.
Religion: Roman Catholic.
Political Career: Democratic nominee for Calif. Senate, 1969.
Capitol Office: 2205 Rayburn Bldg. 20515; 225-2095.

Committees
Education & Workforce
Early Childhood, Youth & Families; Workforce Protections
Resources (ranking)
Water & Power

In Washington: Miller has always been energetic and outspoken, but with Republicans in control of the House, he seems to have stepped up his level of intensity, doing battle with conservatives' designs on environmental, labor and social policy. Miller is more than willing to confront Republicans verbally — and sometimes physically — over their proposals.

Miller is the ranking Democrat on the Resources Committee, and he and committee Chairman Don Young of Alaska provide one of the livelier shows in town as they butt heads across the spectrum of issues involving property owners' rights and environmental regulations. Miller, who chaired the committee in the 103rd Congress (when it was called Natural Resources), has some personality traits similar to Young's. Both are rough-edged, adamant about environmental and resource development issues, and sometimes surly in the heat of debate.

Philosophically, the two are worlds apart. Miller has vigorously advocated environmentalist-backed efforts. Young leads the GOP conservatives who want to establish what they see as a proper balance between environmental preservation and prudent use of natural resources.

Despite Miller's brusque, hard-charging persona, he knows that compromise is part of the legislative game, and behind closed doors he can shuck the rhetoric and cut a deal. Some issues in the 104th were too controversial to submit to compromise — revision of the Endangered Species Act, for instance — but Miller did work with Young and other Republicans to pass some fisheries measures, and also a major parks and lands bill that cleared at the end of the session.

Republican members pushed a bill through Resources in October 1995 that overhauled the Endangered Species Act (ESA), greatly restricting the government's ability to bar development within animal and plant habitats. Property-rights activists, like Young and California Republican Richard W. Pombo, the bill's co-sponsors, contend that federal regulators often implement the ESA in an extreme fashion, barring individuals and businesses from lawful economic uses of their private property in the name of protecting a variety of lesser-known birds, rodents and insects.

Miller said the GOP bill reflected its sponsors' desire to gut the ESA. "Repealing habitat protection is the backdoor way of condemning these species to extinction," he said. The measure never went further than the committee.

Miller also balked at a measure sponsored by Young, which cleared in the 104th, to lift the 22-year ban on exporting oil from Alaska's North Slope. Enactment of the legislation was a major victory for Young, who said that lifting the export ban would encourage production and thus potentially help the nation withstand future shortages of oil from foreign sources. Miller countered that allowing Alaskan crude to be shipped overseas would deplete domestic oil reserves and cost jobs in West Coast refineries that use Alaskan oil.

But Miller and Young came together to push through Congress a major rewrite of the 1976 Magnuson Fishery Conservation and Management Act. Environmentalists and the fishing industry praised the legislation as a reasonable approach toward bolstering domestic fishing. President Clinton signed the bill in October 1996.

On another fishing matter, however, Miller is unhappy with a GOP proposal that he says would allow needless dolphin deaths at the hands of tuna fisherman. At issue is legislation implementing a 1995 international agreement, known as the Declaration of Panama, that would lift the ongoing U.S. embargo on Latin American tuna. Latin American countries have been barred from the U.S. market because they catch tuna with encircling nets, which can also trap dolphins.

Miller and his allies on the issue say that implementing the Panama agreement would set a poor precedent for future trade agreements by compromising domestic environmental laws to satisfy trading partners. Miller said the implementing bill would "weaken the meaning of the

CALIFORNIA 7
Northeastern Bay Area

California Republicans were generally pleased with the court-fashioned redistricting plan for 1992, which seemed to level the state's political playing field. But there were exceptions. Some in the GOP had hoped that the new map would enable them to go after House veteran Miller, the senior Democrat on what was then the House Natural Resources Committee (since renamed the Resources Committee) and the scourge of Western Republicans on water and environmental issues. But the new map raised Democratic registration in the 7th, making Miller safer than ever.

The 7th has long been based in Contra Costa County, which begins at San Pablo Bay, heads south over the San Pablo Mountains and spreads inland well to the east of Berkeley and Oakland. Since World War II, the county has seen its population swell from 100,000 to 800,000. In response, the map for the 1990s confines the 7th to those northernmost portions of the county where the growth is oldest.

The new 7th still includes the shore of San Pablo Bay, studded with industrial cities such as Richmond, San Pablo, Pinole and Martinez. Here, oil terminals, factories and warehouses stretch for miles, belying the region's reputation for natural beauty. In 1988, sensitive wetlands in Martinez were soiled by an oil spill. Less than two years later, an explosion at the Shell Oil refinery rattled windows seven miles away. This part of the 7th is multiracial (Richmond is nearly one-half black), predominantly blue collar and heavily Democratic.

Historically, this Democratic vote was diluted by Republican influence in the suburbs to the south and east — on the sunny side of the San Pablo ridge. Concord became the county's biggest city and passed the 100,000 mark in the 1970s. Suburban expansion began altering the political balance. Jimmy Carter had carried the 7th easily in 1976, but it went for Ronald Reagan in 1980 and 1984. Slowly, Miller too was feeling the center of gravity shift. His vote share in 1990 was his lowest since 1974.

But the trend was reversed in 1992. The court-appointed "special masters" decided that the bayside residents of the 7th had more in common with their neighbors to the west (in El Cerrito, on the Alameda County line) and to the north (across San Pablo Bay and Suisun Bay in Solano County). So they drew into the 7th the cities of Vallejo, Benicia (site of an early state capital), Cordelia and Suisun City. These communities, home to farm support services and industry, are traditionally Democratic. So, though they were new to Miller in 1992, they helped increase his vote throughout the district.

At its new southern limit, the 7th still includes Concord. But nearly all the other suburban territory has been relocated to the 10th District, dropping the GOP share of registered voters. Bill Clinton won the district easily in 1996, beating Bob Dole by 40 percentage points.

1990 Population: 572,773. White 358,843 (63%), Black 95,091 (17%), Other 118,839 (21%). Hispanic origin 76,154 (13%). 18 and over 421,122 (74%), 62 and over 71,416 (12%). Median age: 32.

be seriously injured and harassed without limits...and still have the tuna called safe for dolphins." The House easily approved the bill in April 1997, however.

Miller also carries his liberal views into his work on the Education and the Workforce Committee (formerly called Economic and Educational Opportunities), where he is the No. 2 Democrat. A strong backer of labor protections, Miller fiercely objected to GOP efforts to pass a measure that would allow companies to offer their employers comp time in lieu of pay for overtime work. The measure passed the House in March 1997 and came before the Senate in May, although Clinton threatened a veto.

Republican proponents of the bill contend that it would give working families more flexibility, but Miller and other allies of organized labor argue that unscrupulous companies could coerce employees to choose the form of compensation management preferred. Miller offered a substitute amendment that included numerous protections for workers; it was rejected, 193-237.

Before the Democrats' defeat in the 1994 elections, Miller was eyeing a top leadership position in the House. Not long after assuming the Natural Resources chairmanship in 1991, he began positioning himself to succeed Missouri Democrat Richard A. Gephardt as majority leader if Gephardt ran for president in 1992. He did not, but at times in 1993 and 1994, Miller called for House Democrats to keep the GOP minority on a tighter leash, and speculation arose that he might try for the Speaker's post, then held by Thomas S. Foley.

But once Democrats lost House control, Miller drew back. He did not challenge Gephardt for minority leader after the 1994 elections, and has contented himself with harassing the GOP majority in committee and on the floor.

When the House passed a measure in May 1996 to temporarily repeal the 4.3 cents per gallon gasoline tax, a proposal pushed by GOP presidential candidate Bob Dole, Miller scoffed, calling it political gamesmanship. "This bill that is before us to cut the gas tax is not about putting more gasoline in the tanks of the American consumer's automobile," he said. "This is about putting fuel in Bob Dole's campaign for the presidency that was stalled and out of gas on the side of the road."

Miller is not shy about throwing himself into the partisan fray — literally. In November 1995, when the House debated a bill to bar the use of funds for deploying troops to Bosnia without prior congressional approval, feelings ran high. Democrats charged that Republicans were trying to limit the president's powers. After Virginia Democrat James P. Moran blasted the bill as a politically motivated GOP attack on Clinton, Moran and Miller engaged in a shoving match with conservative California Republicans Robert K. Dornan and Randy "Duke" Cunningham; the tussle spilled off the House floor into a hallway.

In November 1995, Miller went after GOP Speaker Newt Gingrich by filing a complaint with the ethics committee charging that Gingrich violated House rules when he allowed Donald Jones, a private businessman with interests in telecommunications companies, to volunteer in the Speaker's office and work on telecommunications legislation. The ethics panel in March 1996 scolded Gingrich for allowing Jones to volunteer in the Speaker's office, but suggested no punishment.

Miller also joined Democratic whip David E. Bonior of Michigan and three other Democrats in filing a set of complaints in December 1995 against Gingrich that included charges that the Speaker violated tax, federal election and bribery laws as well as House rules by using a network of organizations, some of them tax-exempt, to fuel the drive for a Republican takeover of Congress. In January 1997, Gingrich was found guilty of violating some House ethics rules. The House voted to reprimand Gingrich and assessed him a $300,000 penalty.

At Home: Not only is Miller a third-generation resident of Northern California — a rare distinction in the mobile local culture — he also is the third George Miller in his family to earn a living in government. Miller's grandfather, George Miller Sr., was the assistant civil engineer in Richmond. His father, George Jr., represented the area in the state Senate for 20 years. George Miller III was a first-year law student in 1969 when his father died. Only 23, Miller won the Democratic nomination to succeed his father but lost the election to Republican John Nejedly.

Miller went to work as a legislative aide to state Sen. George Moscone, the Democratic floor leader. In 1974, when Democratic Rep. Jerome Waldie decided to run for governor, Miller sought Waldie's seat in Congress, challenging a local labor leader and the mayor of Concord, the largest city in the district.

Miller was reinforced by the strong support of Assemblyman John T. Knox in Richmond, the district's second-largest city. Miller won the primary with 38 percent. In the general election, against moderate Republican Gary Fernandez, Miller exploited Watergate, disclosing his campaign finances twice a month and chiding his opponent for not doing likewise. He won 56 percent of the vote and has been a safe re-election bet since.

HOUSE ELECTIONS

1996 General		
George Miller (D)	137,089	(72%)
Norman H. Reece (R)	42,542	(22%)
William C. Thompson (REF)	6,866	(4%)
Bob Liatunick (NL)	4,420	(2%)
1994 General		
George Miller (D)	116,105	(70%)
Charles V. Hughes (R)	45,698	(27%)
William A. "Bill" Callison (PFP)	4,798	(3%)

Previous Winning Percentages: **1992** (70%) **1990** (61%) **1988** (68%) **1986** (67%) **1984** (66%) **1982** (67%) **1980** (63%) **1978** (63%) **1976** (75%) **1974** (56%)

CAMPAIGN FINANCE

	Receipts	Receipts from PACs	Expend- itures
1996			
Miller (D)	$332,333	$150,750 (45%)	$434,745
Reece (R)	$42,576	$16 (0%)	$41,147
1994			
Miller (D)	$432,904	$221,475 (51%)	$442,581
Hughes (R)	$2,805	$0 (0%)	$2,432

DISTRICT VOTE FOR PRESIDENT

	1996		1992
D	131,707 (65%)	**D**	140,159 (61%)
R	50,140 (25%)	**R**	51,356 (22%)
I	12,178 (6%)	**I**	39,038 (17%)

KEY VOTES

1997	
Ban "partial birth" abortions	N
1996	
Approve farm bill	N
Deny public education to illegal immigrants	N
Repeal ban on certain assault-style weapons	N
Increase minimum wage	Y
Freeze defense spending	Y
Approve welfare overhaul	N
1995	
Approve balanced-budget constitutional amendment	N
Relax Clean Water Act regulations	N
Oppose limits on environmental regulations	Y
Reduce projected Medicare spending	N
Approve GOP budget with tax and spending cuts	N

VOTING STUDIES

	Presidential Support		Party Unity		Conservative Coalition	
Year	S	O	S	O	S	O
1996	77	18	90	4	4	96
1995	84	12	93	3	5	87
1994	72	19	92	2	3	83
1993	74	23	90	2	7	91
1992	14	77	88	6	13	77
1991	23	73	92	3	3	89

INTEREST GROUP RATINGS

Year	ADA	AFL-CIO	CCUS	ACU
1996	90	n/a	13	0
1995	95	100	17	8
1994	90	100	25	0
1993	100	100	0	8
1992	85	92	25	0
1991	95	100	20	0

8 Nancy Pelosi (D)

Of San Francisco — Elected 1987; 5th full term

Biographical Information
Born: March 26, 1940, Baltimore, Md.
Education: Trinity College, A.B. 1962.
Occupation: Public relations consultant.
Family: Husband, Paul Pelosi; five children.
Religion: Roman Catholic.
Political Career: Calif. Democratic Party chairman, 1981-83.
Capitol Office: 2457 Rayburn Bldg. 20515; 225-4965.

Committees
Appropriations
Foreign Operations, Export Financing & Related Programs (ranking); Labor, Health & Human Services, Education & Related Agencies
Select Intelligence
Human Intelligence, Analysis & Counterintelligence

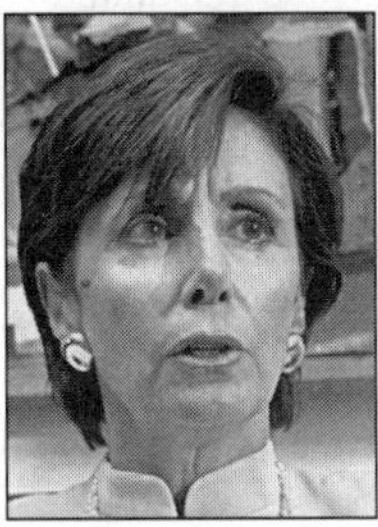

In Washington: Pelosi was one of two Democrats on the House ethics subcommittee who looked in depth at the political fundraising practices of House Speaker Newt Gingrich in the 104th Congress. Traditionally, ethics work is hush-hush, behind-the-scenes stuff, and that is how Pelosi tried to go about it. Others seemed less circumspect. At times during the Gingrich investigation, the membership of the committee was a veritable fount of media pronouncements and news leaks aimed at saving or skewering the Speaker.

But once the verdict was official — a reprimand and a $300,000 penalty for Gingrich — and Pelosi left the ethics committee after a six-year stint, she let fly with her feelings about the case.

"It's clear the Republicans will do anything — anything — to protect Newt Gingrich," Pelosi told the San Francisco Chronicle in January 1997. "He [Gingrich] is such a hypocrite. I think if a person loved the House of Representatives, if he loved his party, he would step aside."

Pelosi said she believed Gingrich should have been censured by the House, which would have cost him the speakership. But she told her local paper that she went along with the lighter punishment out of concern that an extended battle would have torn apart the House.

At one tense moment during the Gingrich inquiry in early 1997, Pelosi and her Democratic colleague on the ethics subcommittee, Maryland's Benjamin L. Cardin, were angry enough to take public exception to ethics Chairwoman Nancy L. Johnson of Connecticut when she unilaterally canceled a week-long series of public hearings on the Gingrich case.

Pelosi and Cardin sent a letter urging Johnson to reverse her decision. House Parliamentarian Charles W. Johnson informed them and Johnson that House rules did not allow Johnson to cancel the public hearings without agreement from the full ethics committee, which has an equal number of Republicans and Democrats. "The ethics process is being turned upside down," Pelosi said. "I think this is a major departure from the regular order. I see it as an abuse of power."

Pelosi has all the self-assurance one would expect from a woman born into the political business, and it has not gone unnoticed by the Democratic leadership as evidenced by her committee assignments — Appropriations and Select Intelligence — and her high-profile party responsibilities.

Pelosi did not hold public office before coming to Congress in 1987. But her father, Thomas J. D'Alesandro Jr., was a House member during the New Deal and then mayor of Baltimore. She made her own way in politics, however, moving to the West Coast and serving as California Democratic Party chairman and finance chairman of the Democratic Senatorial Campaign Committee before running for the House.

Pelosi won a seat on Appropriations at the start of the 102nd Congress in 1991. In the 105th, she serves as ranking member on the Foreign Operations Subcommittee, where she tries to block GOP efforts to reduce foreign aid, particularly for international family planning programs. She has been on the Intelligence Committee since the start of the 103rd.

Pelosi is a liberal Democrat from one of the nation's most liberal districts, so she is part of a distinct minority in the conservative-dominated Republican House. On top of that, she is meeting stiff resistance from the Clinton administration in her efforts to punish China for what she calls its "continued disregard for basic human rights."

Pelosi is a chief proponent of linking most-favored-nation (MFN) trade status for China with improvements in its human rights record; she and her allies in this cause believe that economic threats with bite can best get the attention of China's leaders. Pelosi — whose San Francisco district includes thousands of Chinese-Americans — has sought to condition continued MFN status for China on "significant progress" in human rights there, such as releasing political prisoners and halting the use of prison laborers to make goods for export to the United States.

This line of argument was rejected by the Bush administration, but Pelosi expected a more sympathetic ear in Bill Clinton, who campaigned in 1992 on linking China MFN to human rights improve-

CALIFORNIA 8
San Francisco

San Francisco retains a bohemian air most cities never tried to cultivate in the first place. "The City," as natives call it, is one of the few places where you can still find society columns in the daily papers. But most of the town's high and mighty natives first made their family fortunes in merchandising to the torrent of newcomers attracted during the mid-19th Century gold rush.

The City remains a beacon for newcomers of all stripes. Tourism is the city's largest industry, bolstered by internationally famous sights such as the Golden Gate Bridge, Fisherman's Wharf and Lombard Street, "the world's crookedest street." Many visitors also find time to dine in North Beach or other neighborhoods chock-ablock with restaurants. Chinese cuisine in particular has enjoyed a renaissance in the 1990s, as famous chefs flee Hong Kong before the British cede control to China.

Like most areas of California, San Francisco is seeing its first outward migration since the gold rush era as inhabitants seek fortune in new industries in other western states. But it more than makes up for that population loss with immigrants from Asia and Latin America.

Its traditional openness and vigor has attracted waves of countercultural types, including the beatniks of the 1950s and the hippies of the 1960s. The town is the cultural capital of the nation's homosexuals; the gay vote is about 15 percent of the electorate. Although the predominantly gay Castro District has toned down some in response to the AIDS crisis, it is still home to large numbers of runaways and its mostly upscale denizens march in colorful parades celebrating gay pride and Halloween.

San Franciscans have little trouble choosing sides in federal elections. In 1996, San Francisco County (which is conterminous with the city) gave 74 percent of its vote to Bill Clinton. Pelosi won with 84 percent.

The 8th resembles the old 5th, except that it comes even closer to encompassing all of San Francisco within a single congressional district.

The old 5th had to give up the city's far northwest (including the bridgehead of the Golden Gate Bridge) to the 6th (centered in Marin County at the other end of the bridge). This constituted roughly one-fifth of the city's population. But the map adopted in 1992 reclaimed these sections of the city (including Seacliff, Park Presidio and environs north of Golden Gate Park). Sacrificed instead (this time to the 12th District that adjoins to the south) were the neighborhoods south of Golden Gate Park and west of Twin Peaks.

The shift added nearly 50,000 more city residents to the newly renumbered San Francisco district. The removal of the southwestern neighborhoods did affect the district's racial mix. Whites had accounted for 59 percent of the old 5th; they constitute 52 percent in the 8th. Among the minority communities, the largest is the Asian-American, which is nearing 30 percent. The Chinese and Japanese are joined by increasing numbers of Koreans, Filipinos and Southeast Asians.

1990 Population: 573,247. White 298,038 (52%), Black 73,310 (13%), Other 201,899 (35%). Hispanic origin 89,908 (16%). 18 and over 481,160 (84%), 62 and over 92,882 (16%). Median age: 35.

ments. But she has been sorely disappointed: Clinton now preaches U.S. engagement with China and its vast market, and he supports continuing the nation's MFN trade status.

While MFN supporters point to tremendous growth in U.S. exports to China over the last seven years, Pelosi notes that the U.S. trade deficit with China has grown from $10 million in 1985 to $34 billion in 1995. She adds that illegal Chinese copying of U.S. music CDs amounts to "piracy of intellectual property rights," and she says workers domestically lose jobs as companies move plants into China's cheap-labor market.

In the 104th Congress, opponents of MFN for China took a new tack, realizing the House was unlikely to disapprove Clinton's designation of the trade status for China. In addition to offering resolutions killing the trade status (which were rejected in 1995 and 1996), Pelosi and others sought approval of symbolic resolutions expressing congressional frustration with some of China's actions, including its threats against Taiwan, its weapons sales and its repression of political dissidents. These resolutions passed overwhelmingly.

Pelosi criticized Clinton when it came to light in early 1996 that China was reportedly shipping nuclear components to Pakistan. If true, Pelosi said, the administration should cut off China from Export-Import Bank loans and credits, as stipulated by nuclear non-proliferation laws. But Clinton also had the option of waiving the sanctions if doing so was in "the national interest." Reports that Clinton was considering a waiver struck Pelosi as further evidence that the administration places commercial interests over human rights. "This administration's policy is no policy," she said. "If you look to see who's in charge, it's Motorola and Boeing." Both companies have large operations in China.

Pelosi in the 104th did have the satisfaction of seeing her work in another area come to closure. Congress cleared a measure providing for conversion of the Presidio, an historic military base in her district. The Presidio measure, included in an omnibus parks and lands bill, set up a public-private trust to help manage the hundreds of buildings that cover more than 1,400 scenic acres at the foot of the Golden Gate Bridge.

To move the ball through the Republican House, Pelosi modified the Presidio measure she had sponsored in 1994, coming up with new language intended to "increase revenues to the maximum extent possible." Unlike the original bill, which gave the Interior Department control over the trust, the new measure called for the trust to be an independent government corporation outside the department's jurisdiction. It also included a 12-year time limit for the park to reach economic self-sufficiency, or the property would revert to the General Services Administration.

The redrafted version touched off grumbling from some San Francisco civic activists who felt it went too far in promoting commercial uses of the Presidio. But many supporters praised Pelosi for drafting a workable compromise that overcame previous resistance to the measure in the GOP.

Satisfied with the changes, House Republicans helped carry the bill to victory by a 317-101 margin in September 1995. But the measure got tied in with an omnibus parks bill, which languished for months in a House-Senate conference committee, tied up by disputes over unrelated wilderness bills. Eventually committee leaders dumped the bill's controversial provisions, and it cleared with the Presidio language on the last day of the session.

At Home: When she began her first House campaign, Pelosi was more familiar to national Democratic activists than to San Francisco voters. But the financial and political contacts she had developed over years of party service provided Pelosi with a critical edge in the special Democratic primary to succeed Democratic Rep. Sala Burton, who died in February 1987.

Pelosi entered the contest backed by much of the city and state party establishment. She also had powerful friends in the national Democratic hierarchy. While chairing the state party, she helped attract the 1984 Democratic National Convention to San Francisco.

Her most important support was delivered in dramatic fashion just before the seat became vacant. Burton indicated several days prior to her death from cancer that she wanted Pelosi to be her successor. That backing was crucial because the 5th had long been dominated by the organization loyal to Sala Burton and her late husband, Rep. Phillip Burton.

Pelosi's last real hurdle was a vigorous challenge from San Francisco Supervisor Harry Britt, a Democrat and a leading homosexual politician. In a district where the gay vote was roughly 15 percent of the electorate, Britt started with a large base. He also aimed his campaign at a wider audience, citing his efforts on rent control and his opposition to new real estate development.

But Pelosi was energetic and cool under fire. She fell short of 50 percent of the vote in the April ballot but took her GOP foe easily in a June runoff.

Pelosi then established the district as her own. In 1992, redistricting altered her turf slightly but still left it with a heavy Democratic registration advantage. She has topped 80 percent throughout the decade.

HOUSE ELECTIONS

1996 General		
Nancy Pelosi (D)	175,216	(84%)
Justin Raimondo (R)	25,739	(12%)
David Smithstein (NL)	6,783	(3%)
1994 General		
Nancy Pelosi (D)	137,642	(82%)
Elsa C. Cheung (R)	30,528	(18%)

Previous Winning Percentages: 1992 (82%) **1990** (77%) **1988** (76%) **1987†** (63%)

† Special election

CAMPAIGN FINANCE

	Receipts	Receipts from PACs	Expend-itures
1996			
Pelosi (D)	$458,456	$153,153 (33%)	$465,863
1994			
Pelosi (D)	$375,158	$167,200 (45%)	$370,000
Cheung (R)	$20,088	$0 (0%)	$19,882

DISTRICT VOTE FOR PRESIDENT

	1996		1992
D	165,795 (74%)	**D**	187,201 (76%)
R	31,282 (14%)	**R**	39,396 (16%)
I	7,104 (3%)	**I**	21,180 (9%)

KEY VOTES

1997	
Ban "partial birth" abortions	N
1996	
Approve farm bill	N
Deny public education to illegal immigrants	N
Repeal ban on certain assault-style weapons	N
Increase minimum wage	Y
Freeze defense spending	Y
Approve welfare overhaul	N
1995	
Approve balanced-budget constitutional amendment	N
Relax Clean Water Act regulations	N
Oppose limits on environmental regulations	Y
Reduce projected Medicare spending	N
Approve GOP budget with tax and spending cuts	N

VOTING STUDIES

	Presidential Support		Party Unity		Conservative Coalition	
Year	**S**	**O**	**S**	**O**	**S**	**O**
1996	80	16	91	2	2	98
1995	80	14	92	3	11	85
1994	74	19	93	1	0	97
1993	77	19	93	2	7	93
1992	12	80	91	1	2	90
1991	24	69	89	4	3	86

INTEREST GROUP RATINGS

Year	ADA	AFL-CIO	CCUS	ACU
1996	95	n/a	13	0
1995	85	100	22	0
1994	90	89	25	0
1993	95	92	18	0
1992	90	92	25	0
1991	90	92	20	0

9 Ronald V. Dellums (D)

Of Oakland — Elected 1970, 14th term

Biographical Information

Born: Nov. 24, 1935, Oakland, Calif.
Education: San Francisco State U., B.A. 1960; U. of California, Berkeley, M.S.W. 1962.
Military Service: Marine Corps, 1954-56.
Occupation: Psychiatric social worker.
Family: Wife, Leola "Roscoe" Higgs; three children.
Religion: Protestant.
Political Career: Berkeley City Council, 1967-71.
Capitol Office: 2108 Rayburn Bldg. 20515; 225-2661.

Committees

National Security (ranking)
Military Procurement

In Washington: During more than a quarter-century in the House, Dellums has held an unwavering opinion of U.S. spending on the military: He thinks there is too much of it. That was his view when he entered Congress in 1971 as a critic of the Vietnam War, and he still preferred plowshares to swords in 1993, when seniority lifted him to the chairmanship of the Armed Services Committee for the 103rd Congress.

To hawks who call for higher defense budgets, Dellums answers with pleas to cut, and to divert the money saved to domestic programs for the poor. "I did not join the Armed Services Committee to learn about missiles, planes and ships," he once said. "I joined because I knew I would need to become an expert in this field in order to argue successfully for military spending reductions that would free up resources for the desperate human needs that I see every day in my community."

Dellums served only one term as chairman of Armed Services. The Republican takeover of the House in 1995 elevated Floyd D. Spence of South Carolina to the chair, and Dellums dropped down to ranking minority member on the panel, which the GOP renamed National Security.

When Dellums took up the chairman's gavel in 1993, many noted the irony that he would be presiding over the crafting of defense budgets that offended his moral and fiscal sensibilities.

But from the outset, Dellums stressed his commitment to the deliberative process and the democratic principle of majority rule. Even Dellums' ideological opponents noted his even-handed manner during committee meetings.

Dellums places great importance on collegiality and courtesy, holding them up as ideals when other members veer toward vitriol.

During one heated debate in early 1995 on the defense and foreign policy plank of the GOP's "Contract With America," Dellums exhorted his colleagues to treat one another with respect. But then Spence spoke disparagingly of Democratic "liberals . . . people who have dedicated their lives to tearing down our national security."

Dellums listened to the comments with no visible reaction, his bowed head between his hands. Finally he said this: "The beauty and the brilliance of this system is that we have different points of view. . . . This debate should not go forward with that kind of rancor."

As committee chairman, Dellums tried to make the case that in the post-Cold War world, the U.S. military should be leaner — an agile force, to be sure, but a less costly one. Now, with Republicans running Congress, Dellums is back in a role he played in the early 1980s: trying to prevent the defense budget from growing larger. Defense hawks on National Security — a number of them Dellums' own Democratic colleagues — want to allocate more money to the Pentagon than the Clinton administration requests.

But in one of his cost-cutting efforts, Dellums has found a prominent Republican ally who is a "deficit hawk": Budget Committee Chairman John R. Kasich of Ohio, also the fourth-ranking Republican on National Security. The two want to kill funding for production of more B-2 "stealth" bombers beyond the 20 the Pentagon says it needs. Kasich joined Dellums in offering an amendment to the fiscal 1996 defense authorization bill to strike an extra $553 million for building future B-2s. But their proposal was rejected, 203-219.

Decisive in the outcome were 73 Democrats who voted for the added money, many of them from states such as California, Florida and Louisiana where jobs depend either on the B-2 program or on other projects by contractor Northrop-Grumman. Two days after the vote, Dellums said he was dumbfounded that many fellow Black Caucus members voted for the B-2 money while federal social programs faced cuts. But other B-2 opponents grumbled that Dellums was slow off the mark in soliciting support from minority members, some of whom are a tough sell anyway because they have constituents doing defense-related work.

Dellums and Kasich tried again to kill the B-2

CALIFORNIA 9
Alameda County — Oakland; Berkeley

The 1992 court-ordered district map in California made the old 8th District far more compact, compressing it into Alameda County and renumbering it the 9th. Gone are the old district lines reaching clear across Contra Costa County and the eastern reaches of Alameda County to the Central Valley.

The 9th consists of Oakland and Berkeley, and a few subsidiaries: the bayside industrial sites of Emeryville and Alameda and the bedroom suburbs of Albany (north of Berkeley) and Piedmont (an independent enclave in the Oakland hills).

Emeryville, which lies between Berkeley and Oakland, has grown more commercial in recent years. It is home to a large office/shopping mall complex that includes Kimball's East, a nationally known jazz club.

Removing the old district's inland suburbs left Dellums safer than ever in an Oakland-Berkeley-based constituency. Dellums won his last election in the old district with 61 percent — roughly his career average. Since then he has won with more than 70 percent in the new 9th.

The politics of the 9th are more complex than these numbers suggest, but Dellums has long since mastered the complexities. Despite his credentials as a liberal and a dove, he has defended the presence of the military, especially the Navy, and opposed the closing of the Alameda air station, the Naval Aviation Depot in Alameda and the Oakland Naval Supply Center (all slated to be closed in 1997).

Dellums is a native of Oakland, which dominates the district, and a product of the deep-rooted African-American community that dominates Oakland. Nearly 45 percent of the city is black, and Oakland's historic tensions between blacks and police gave birth in the 1960s to the Black Panther Party. Overall, the 9th is about one-third black; Asians and Hispanics together account for more than one-fourth of the people.

The city also has always had wealthy, mostly white neighborhoods in the hills overlooking the bay (made famous in 1991 by wildfires that obliterated scores of homes).

Berkeley, Oakland's northern neighbor, was founded at about the same time in the mid-1800s. But while Oakland has always been a port, Berkeley (population 103,000) has always been a college town. As the home of the first and foremost campus of the world-renowned University of California, Berkeley is one of those places people think they know about whether they have been there or not. Although best known for its 1960s student protests, the campus is also renowned for its Nobel Prize winners, peaceful brooks and Bay views.

The 9th is a reliable cache of support for Democrats. Bill Clinton pulled down 75 percent in 1996, while Bob Dole garnered only 13 percent.

1990 Population: 573,458. White 260,128 (45%), Black 182,159 (32%), Other 131,171 (23%). Hispanic origin 68,775 (12%). 18 and over 446,911 (78%), 62 and over 80,221 (14%). Median age: 33.

production funds when the defense appropriations bill reached the floor in September 1995. They fell barely short, losing 210-213. On this vote, Dellums fared better with the Black Caucus: Four members switched sides to kill the funding. Dellums contended that the B-2 vote had "very little to do with national security." The issue, rather, was "who builds it, where it's built, where it takes off and where it lands."

Dellums unfailingly has opposed GOP efforts to add funding for an anti-missile defense system. He chided Republicans in the 104th for overdrawing the missile threat and understating the scope of President Clinton's missile defense program. Republicans had added a provision in the fiscal 1996 defense bill to establish a goal of deploying by 2003 a missile defense system that would cover U.S. territory. Clinton cited the provision as a major reason for his veto of the bill; Dellums backed that veto.

Dellums did find common ground with Spence in July 1996 on a bill reorganizing U.S. intelligence operations. The National Security Committee approved the measure after eliminating nearly all provisions to increase the authority of the director of the CIA over military-related intelligence.

From Vietnam through the Persian Gulf conflict with Iraq, Dellums has generally opposed using U.S. military force abroad. But in recent years, he has shown a willingness to support sending troops overseas on peacekeeping missions.

President Clinton, during his first term, sent a military force to Rwanda with relief aid, continued for a time President George Bush's humanitarian mission to Somalia and dispatched troops to Haiti to help restore democracy after the nation's military rulers fled the scene. Dellums supported the Rwanda and Somalia efforts, and he backed U.S. military involvement in Haiti.

And when the House in November 1995 considered a GOP resolution to prohibit funding for deployment of U.S. troops in Bosnia, Dellums voted "no," citing the fact that the warring parties in the former Yugoslavia were negotiating a peace agreement. "I think we have a moral obligation to stand on the threshold of peace," he said.

At Home: When the House bank scandal

unfolded in the 102nd Congress, Dellums was cited as having written 851 overdrafts, one of the highest totals in the chamber. But this news did him no political harm in 1992: He pushed his share of the vote over the 70 percent threshold for the first time.

In the 103rd Congress, despite his elevated status as chairman of Armed Services, Dellums could not prevent the proposed closing or downsizing of several large military bases in his district — with the attendant loss of thousands of jobs. Yet in 1994, a poor year for Democrats generally, Dellums was comfortably re-elected, taking more than two-thirds of the vote.

Year-in and year-out, Dellums enjoys strong support from his mainly liberal constituency. He is revered in the black precincts of Oakland and in the liberal university community in Berkeley, both in the district's dominant Alameda County portion.

Redistricting for the 1990s gave Dellums a boost, extending his turf slightly to the south in Alameda County while excising its Contra Costa portion, where he had struggled for support among suburban, white, largely affluent and conservative voters.

Dellums once wanted to be a professional baseball pitcher, but he has said that encounters with racial prejudice spoiled that dream, leaving him with little ambition after high school. After two years in the Marines, he went to college with the help of the GI Bill and six years later took a degree in psychiatric social work.

He was a social worker in San Francisco, managing federally assisted poverty programs, when friends persuaded him to pursue his ideas about poverty and discrimination by running for the Berkeley City Council in 1967. He has since won every time he has run for office.

In 1970, Dellums launched a primary challenge to six-term Democratic Rep. Jeffery Cohelan. At the time, the East Bay region was in a state of turmoil. Student protest over the war in Vietnam was becoming increasingly intense, and the Black Panther movement was gaining strength in Oakland's ghettos.

Dellums put together a coalition of blacks, students and left-leaning intellectuals that has been the core of his support ever since. His major issue was Cohelan's tardiness in opposing the Vietnam War. Dellums registered nearly 15,000 new voters in the district and easily ousted Cohelan with 55 percent in a primary that was tantamount to election.

For most of the next two decades, sporadic forays against Dellums in the primary and general election proved futile. He did slip to 61 percent in 1990 as his share of the vote in Contra Costa County dropped to 34 percent. But since redistricting, his electoral skies have been all blue.

HOUSE ELECTIONS

1996 General		
Ronald V. Dellums (D)	154,806	(77%)
Deborah Wright (R)	37,126	(18%)
Tom Condit (PFP)	5,561	(3%)
Jack Forem (NL)	3,475	(2%)
1996 Primary		
Ronald V. Dellums (D)	73,353	(85%)
Randal Stewart (D)	12,876	(15%)
1994 General		
Ronald V. Dellums (D)	129,233	(72%)
Deborah Wright (R)	40,448	(23%)
Emma Wong Mar (PFP)	9,194	(5%)

Previous Winning Percentages: **1992** (72%) **1990** (61%) **1988** (67%) **1986** (60%) **1984** (60%) **1982** (56%) **1980** (55%) **1978** (57%) **1976** (62%) **1974** (57%) **1972** (56%) **1970** (57%)

CAMPAIGN FINANCE

	Receipts	Receipts from PACs	Expend-itures
1996			
Dellums (D)	$428,339	$118,325 (28%)	$415,090
Wright (R)	$34,775	$16 (0%)	$34,491
1994			
Dellums (D)	$478,283	$176,591 (37%)	$482,877
Wright (R)	$18,588	$14 (0%)	$18,453

DISTRICT VOTE FOR PRESIDENT

1996	1992
D 156,998 (75%)	**D** 186,714 (79%)
R 26,321 (13%)	**R** 29,394 (12%)
I 6,277 (3%)	**I** 21,207 (9%)

KEY VOTES

1997	
Ban "partial birth" abortions	N
1996	
Approve farm bill	N
Deny public education to illegal immigrants	N
Repeal ban on certain assault-style weapons	N
Increase minimum wage	Y
Freeze defense spending	Y
Approve welfare overhaul	N
1995	
Approve balanced-budget constitutional amendment	N
Relax Clean Water Act regulations	N
Oppose limits on environmental regulations	Y
Reduce projected Medicare spending	N
Approve GOP budget with tax and spending cuts	N

VOTING STUDIES

	Presidential Support		Party Unity		Conservative Coalition	
Year	S	O	S	O	S	O
1996	72	23	95	3	2	96
1995	90	9	97	1	2	97
1994	74	26	92	1	0	100
1993	75	24	91	1	5	93
1992	12	86	89	4	4	94
1991	25	69	90	3	3	92

INTEREST GROUP RATINGS

Year	ADA	AFL-CIO	CCUS	ACU
1996	100	n/a	0	0
1995	100	100	0	8
1994	100	100	17	5
1993	100	100	0	4
1992	95	92	25	0
1991	90	100	20	0

10 Ellen O. Tauscher (D)

Of Pleasanton — Elected 1996, 1st term

Biographical Information
Born: Nov. 15, 1951, Newark, N.J.
Education: Seton Hall U., B.A. 1974.
Occupation: Child care screening executive.
Family: Husband, William Y. Tauscher, one child.
Religion: Roman Catholic.
Political Career: No previous office.
Capitol Office: 1440 Longworth Bldg. 20515; 225-1880.

Committees
Transportation & Infrastructure
Surface Transportation; Water Resources & Environment
Science

The Path to Washington: Tauscher arrived for her first day of orientation on Capitol Hill in a chauffeured car, but this multimillionaire businesswoman can hardly be described as a "limousine liberal." She sounds Republican notes as she talks about creating a leaner government with a balanced budget, although she won her seat running on typical Democratic Class of 1996 themes.

Tauscher said she supports deficit reduction, but not at the expense of student loans, Head Start, environmental protection or programs that provide benefits to senior citizens.

Such a stance, she said, fits the interests of her affluent commuter district. "They want their cake and eat it, too," she said shortly after winning the election. "And they can have it with me."

Tauscher narrowly unseated Bill Baker, a combative two-term Republican for whom this district had been drawn. (Baker had previously served in the state Assembly.) Some of the issues Tauscher ran on had been test-marketed unsuccessfully by Baker's 1994 opponent — the main difference in the outcomes being Tauscher's willingness to spend more than $1.5 million of her own money to spread the message. She won by just over 4,000 votes, taking 49 percent.

Baker himself conceded that his stance on gun control was a political Achilles' heel. He supported the law to require a five-day waiting period to buy handguns but voted against a ban on certain semiautomatic assault-style weapons. The East Bay district is home to several residents who lost family members in a 1993 massacre in San Francisco's 101 California building, and one of the victim's relatives appeared in a Tauscher ad.

Tauscher is a physically imposing but approachable woman who supports abortion rights. She does not want the federal government to have significant involvement in schooling, saying decisions are best made at the local level. But she would like to see the government offer financial incentives to states that perform well.

One area in which Tauscher will be able to look out for the specific interests of her district is transportation. As Baker did, she serves on the Transportation and Infrastructure Committee, where she will look out for the East Bay's matrix of highways as well as Bay Area Rapid Transit (BART), the mass transit system that fueled her district's population growth. Tauscher also sits on the Science Committee.

One way Tauscher will be able to burnish her credentials as a pro-business Democrat is in her advocacy of a targeted reduction in capital gains taxation. Tauscher supports offering a 50 percent reduction to venture capitalists who hold their investments for at least five years in companies worth $100 million or less (raising the present ceiling from $25 million).

Tauscher founded three companies that register and screen child care providers, and in 1996 she published a child care reference guide. She was one of the first women to hold a seat on the New York Stock Exchange, working as an investment banker for Prudential-Bache Securities (now Prudential Securities), Bear Stearns and then Drexel Burnham Lambert.

Much of her family's wealth is derived from stock her husband holds in Vanstar Corp., the $2 billion-a-year computer company he runs.

Tauscher's father served as a local officeholder in New Jersey. Tauscher got her start in politics helping others campaign, serving as a co-chair of California Democrat Dianne Feinstein's successful 1992 and 1994 Senate runs.

Bay Area Democratic Reps. George Miller and Anna G. Eshoo helped persuade Tauscher to challenge Baker, her first bid for public office. Her one primary opponent dropped out of the race to give Tauscher a clear shot against the incumbent, although his name remained on the ballot.

Baker tried to make Tauscher's wealth an issue against her. He aired radio ads that likened her to a lottery winner or Monopoly player who could find better uses for her money than to "buy a seat in Congress."

Although Baker dismissed Tauscher's ads linking him to Speaker Newt Gingrich, as "cute," in the end they proved a more successful campaign.

CALIFORNIA 10
Eastern Contra Costa and Alameda counties

The 10th stands as a monument to the objectives and methods of California's redistricting in 1992.

The product is a district that straddles two counties but unites the affected portions of both in a community of interest. The residents of the 10th are primarily suburbanites living on the sunrise (and sunny) side of the inland ridge east of San Francisco Bay. The landscape features hills and hidden valleys, and the long dry months leave the slopes golden brown.

More than two-thirds of the district's residents live in Contra Costa County, and the rest in Alameda County.

For decades, in election after election, thousands of GOP votes from the Bay ridges and eastward were swamped in the tide of Democratic ballots cast in the cities that hug the East Bay shoreline: Oakland and Berkeley in Alameda County, Richmond and Martinez and others in Contra Costa.

But after the Bay Area Rapid Transit (BART) system took hold in the 1970s, the growth in once-sleepy towns such as Orinda, Pleasant Hill, Walnut Creek and Antioch was so great that its political ramifications could no longer be denied when new district lines were drawn for the 1990s.

Most of this growth has been in Contra Costa County, but Alameda communities such as Castro Valley, Dublin, Pleasanton and Livermore have been on the move as well. Livermore is the site of the Lawrence Livermore National Laboratory, one of the nation's leading facilities for experimental physics. But high-tech growth has been generalized through the area: Pleasanton's population grew by 44 percent in the 1980s.

By cutting a new district for these voters, the court-appointed cartographers created something that suggests a harp in shape and looks like a solid Republican district in demographics. The proportion of racial minorities in the 10th (less than 18 percent) is the fourth lowest in the state. But in the process of creating this community of interest, the mappers also confirmed the partisan character of surrounding districts.

All six districts that border the 10th opted for Bill Clinton in 1996. And five of them are represented in the House by Democrats, all of whom won re-election in 1996 with at least 65 percent of the vote.

At the same time, it would be a mistake to view the 10th as a Northern California version of Orange County. Tauscher's victory over two-term Republican Bill Baker in 1996 attests to this. Some of the residents here represent white flight from Oakland that is now generations old. But many of the newer commuters are younger and may still identify with San Francisco or Berkeley. While concerned with taxes, crime, schools and drugs, many hold more liberal views on other social and economic questions.

In the 1996 presidential and congressional elections, the 10th cast more votes than any other California congressional district. Both Tauscher and Clinton carried the Alameda and Contra Costa portions of the district.

1990 Population: 572,008. White 502,626 (88%), Black 13,220 (2%), Other 56,162 (10%). Hispanic origin 49,985 (9%). 18 and over 431,405 (75%), 62 and over 72,800 (13%). Median age: 35.

HOUSE ELECTIONS

1996 General		
Ellen O. Tauscher (D)	137,726	(49%)
Bill Baker (R)	133,633	(47%)
John Place (REF)	6,354	(2%)
Valerie Janlois (NL)	3,047	(1%)
1996 Primary		
Ellen O. Tauscher (D)	44,106	(75%)
Daniel P. White (D)	15,045	(25%)

CAMPAIGN FINANCE

	Receipts	Receipts from PACs		Expend-itures
1996				
Tauscher (D)	$2,573,780	$187,876	(7%)	$2,571,595
Baker (R)	$1,454,337	$368,260	(25%)	$1,398,556
Place (REF)	$94,119	0		$91,607
Janlois (NL)	$5,588	0		$5,531

DISTRICT VOTE FOR PRESIDENT

1996			1992		
D	138,386	(48%)	D	127,450	(42%)
R	122,296	(43%)	R	107,191	(36%)
I	17,930	(6%)	I	66,180	(22%)

KEY VOTES

1997

Ban "partial birth" abortions N

11 Richard W. Pombo (R)

Of Tracy — Elected 1992, 3rd term

Biographical Information
Born: Jan. 8, 1961, Tracy, Calif.
Education: California State Polytechnic U., Pomona, 1979-81.
Occupation: Rancher.
Family: Wife, Annette Cole; three children.
Religion: Roman Catholic.
Political Career: Tracy City Council, 1990-93.
Capitol Office: 1519 Longworth Bldg. 20515; 225-1947.

Committees
Agriculture
Forestry, Resource Conservation & Research; Livestock, Dairy & Poultry (chairman); Risk Management & Specialty Crops
Resources
National Parks & Public Lands; Water & Power

In Washington: A fourth-generation rancher with a deep-seated suspicion of the federal government, Pombo was regularly at war with the House Democratic majority in the 103rd Congress on land-use and environmental issues and fiscal policies.

When Republicans took control in the 104th, Pombo and his Western allies on the Resources Committee set out to drastically change federal environmental regulations, which in their view often impinge on the rights of private property owners. Pombo particularly aimed to rewrite the 1973 Endangered Species Act (ESA), because he contends that it emphasizes preserving plants and animals over the well-being of people.

But after conservative Republicans pushed bills through the House to overhaul the federal clean water act and ease other environmental regulations, public opinion polls began to show that the GOP was gaining an image as anti-environment. Democrats milked that sentiment for all it was worth, GOP leaders pulled back, and the drive to overhaul the species act was stymied.

The law has become a focal point of complaints from congressional property-rights activists, who say federal regulators often have carried it out in an extreme fashion, barring individuals and businesses from otherwise lawful economic uses of their private property in order to protect a variety of lesser-known birds, rodents and insects.

The act requires federal wildlife agencies to list species that are facing possible extinction as endangered or threatened, and it makes it a criminal offense to capture, harm or kill a member of a listed species. "Over 20 years, the law has lost its purpose," Pombo said. "It is being used for things other than saving endangered species, such as growth control, gaining control of mining, timber, agriculture, private property."

Pombo and Resources Committee Chairman Don Young of Alaska introduced a measure to overhaul the Endangered Species Act. The bill, which Resources approved in October 1995, would have greatly restricted the government's ability to bar development within animal and plant habitats. Pombo said he supports species protections but that federal regulators have used the law to trample the rights of private property owners.

"The law punishes private property owners for having endangered species on their property, which, in turn, has caused people to fear the Endangered Species Act, not embrace it," Pombo said.

But opponents of Pombo's effort argued that the bill would gut the law at the behest not of small landowners, but of corporate developers. Action on the measure stalled as GOP leaders focused on buffing up the party's image for the 1996 election.

As part of that public-relations effort, House Speaker Newt Gingrich in March 1996 appointed an environmental task force, charged with bridging intraparty ideological and regional differences on environmental issues. Pombo and New York Republican Sherwood Boehlert, a leader of the GOP moderates, were tapped to head the task force.

But disagreements continued as task force meetings got under way. Boehlert said the party took a wrong turn on environmental policy in 1995 by pushing an overly broad agenda. Pombo disagreed, contending that promises to tame the federal bureaucracy were instrumental in the GOP's gaining a House majority in 1994.

Denied a broad overhaul of the Endangered Species Act in the 104th, Pombo in the 105th came at the issue from a more incrementalist, angle — one inspired by flooding in Northern California. Pombo and fellow conservative California Republican Wally Herger said the law had contributed to flooding in their districts because it inhibits routine maintenance of levees.

They introduced a bill, which Resources approved in April 1997, that would allow local reclamation districts and others responsible for maintaining the nation's levee system to conduct basic maintenance without first submitting to

CALIFORNIA 11
Parts of San Joaquin and Sacramento counties; Stockton; Lodi

Although many of the 11th District's residents still look to the state's capital city for their income, activities and media, the city of Sacramento itself is entirely outside the district, which wraps around the city to the east and south. Even the sizable suburb of Elk Grove (population 17,500) sits on the district line but votes in the 5th.

Most of the voters in the county live in the 5th District. But most of the county's square mileage is in the 11th, which incorporates the eastern and southern two-thirds of Sacramento County and aggregates them with nearly all of San Joaquin County to the south.

So the biggest single source of votes in the 11th is the city of Stockton, 45 miles to the south on Interstate 5. Fifteen minutes north of Stockton on the same road is Lodi (population 51,900).

The farms, orchards and ranches in this part of the vast Central Valley grow asparagus, avocados, walnuts, artichokes, peaches and apricots, much of which is processed through Lodi. But the small city remains best known for the Credence Clearwater Revival song "Lodi," in which the refrain repeats: "Oh Lord, stuck in Lodi, again."

The 11th has regular borders on the west and east, following the county lines for Sacramento and San Joaquin counties in both cases. On the south end, the district takes in the towns of Tracy, Lathrop and Manteca and extends at some points to the Stanislaus County line (excepting the town of Ripon). The district's southern limit is defined west of Lathrop by the tracks of the old Union Pacific Railroad — a reminder of that entity's historic role throughout the state.

Stockton, however, is the district's center, not just because it is the county seat of San Joaquin (where three-fourths of the district vote is cast) but because it has stood on its own economically for more than a century. The inland waterways that snake into the Central Valley from San Francisco Bay have their southern terminus here, making Stockton an important port. In the 1980s, the city grew by more than one-third and now approaches 211,000 residents.

On paper, the farmworkers of the valley and the laborers of Lodi and Stockton make the 11th a Democratic district. But there are enough suburban voters in Sacramento County, and enough conservative Democrats in both counties, to make the district politically competitive.

In 1996, Bill Clinton won the district by just 814 votes over Bob Dole. Clinton held a narrow edge in the San Joaquin County part of the district while Dole barely led in the Sacramento County portion. In the House race, Pombo did about equally well in both counties.

1990 Population: 571,772. White 428,076 (75%), Black 33,137 (6%), Other 110,559 (19%). Hispanic origin 120,755 (21%). 18 and over 404,673 (71%), 62 and over 74,685 (13%). Median age: 31.

what proponents of the bill say is a lengthy review process under the act.

The law requires a review of flood projects aimed at ensuring that they do not hurt threatened plants or animals. Pombo said the review is so cumbersome that it delays upkeep and encourages those responsible for the levees to put off basic maintenance, placing human lives and property at risk. But the House disagreed with him. When the bill reached the floor in May 1997, the House approved an amendment by Boehlert that all but gutted the bill, prompting Pombo to pull it from the floor, conceding defeat. Fifty-four Republicans voted for Boehlert's amendment.

In a January 1997 letter to his constituents, Pombo took aim at the "extremist environmental movement who will do anything to save bugs and rodents.... Holes in the levees due to rodents and bugs have created a catastrophe all in the name of preserving habitat." In the letter, Pombo blamed a lack of levee maintenance on the threatened "Elderberry Beatle" [sic], which lives in bushes sometimes found on levees. The misspelling prompted Washington Post columnist Al Kamen to joke that Pombo aimed to rewrite the Endangered Species Act "just in case the surviving Beatles come together."

Pombo also sits on the Agriculture Committee, an important spot for his heavily agricultural Central Valley district. In the 105th, he serves as chairman of the Livestock, Dairy and Poultry Subcommittee.

In the 104th, he backed the Republican effort to overhaul federal farm policy, voting for the sweeping "Freedom to Farm" bill, which phased out most New Deal-era crop subsidies and instituted a system of fixed but declining payments that farmers would receive over seven years regardless of their planting decisions.

Pombo also weighed in on the immigration law debate in the 104th, seeking to ensure that Central Valley farmers would have enough workers to help them harvest their crops. He pushed to create a new migrant worker program permitting the admission of up to 250,000 foreigners per year to harvest U.S. crops.

Pombo offered his guest-worker plan in March 1996 during the House consideration of the broad immigration bill; he said that without his proposed change, growers might lack the necessary labor at harvest time.

Although existing immigration law allows farmers to petition for migrant workers, Pombo and his allies said the process is too cumbersome for growers. Unless Congress creates an adequate legal migrant program, he said, illegal immigrants will continue to be drawn to and hired for these jobs, or the jobs will go unfilled. Pombo called his plan "an insurance policy against unharvested food, closed farms and higher food costs."

But critics said such a program would boost rather than deter illegal immigration, with many of the temporary workers staying on as illegal immigrants. And they said agribusinesses were simply trying to ensure a supply of cheap labor. The House rejected the amendment, 180-242.

Pombo was more successful with a measure requiring growers and shippers to pay more for a federal program that resolves disputes in the trading of perishable produce. The measure, which Congress cleared in November 1995, phased out over three years the fees paid by retailers and grocery wholesalers who buy fruits and vegetables. It increased licensing fees for growers and shippers from $400 to $550 to offset the reduction.

At Home: The 1992 GOP primary in the 11th was supposed to be dominated by Sacramento County Supervisor Sandra Smoley. A nurse with 20 years on the county board, she had the backing of Republican Gov. Pete Wilson. Pombo was fairly new to campaigning, having been elected to the Tracy City Council in 1990. But he came from nowhere to upset Smoley by 4,000 votes in a five-way race. Pombo branded her a liberal for her abortion rights stand and her support for a bill banning discrimination against homosexuals. He won with a 36 percent plurality.

The Democratic nominee was Patricia Garamendi, half of a power couple that included state Insurance Commissioner John Garamendi. She had a well-known name, though not a stellar electoral record, having lost two hard-fought special elections for the state Legislature. Still, Pombo's conservatism made him the underdog. Garamendi, well-connected in national Democratic circles, was much better financed and had strong support from women's groups and organized labor.

Both candidates relied on TV attack ads. She called Pombo an extremist tool of the Christian right. He said she was just an ambitious politician, while he was a rancher out to defend his neighbors. The cumulative effect of Garamendi's three consecutive negative campaigns soured voters on her, and Pombo won by 2 percentage points. Since then, Pombo has won re-election comfortably.

HOUSE ELECTIONS

1996 General		
Richard W. Pombo (R)	107,477	(59%)
Jason Silva (D)	65,536	(36%)
Kelly Rego (LIBERT)	5,077	(3%)
Selene L. Bush (NL)	3,006	(2%)
1994 General		
Richard W. Pombo (R)	99,302	(62%)
Randy A. Perry (D)	55,794	(35%)
Joseph B. Miller (LIBERT)	4,718	(3%)

Previous Winning Percentages: 1992 (48%)

CAMPAIGN FINANCE

	Receipts	Receipts from PACs		Expend-itures
1996				
Pombo (R)	$576,957	$214,441	(37%)	$470,749
Silva (D)	$17,921	$7,500	(42%)	$17,862
1994				
Pombo (R)	$803,626	$252,600	(31%)	$657,627
Perry (D)	$147,285	$101,349	(69%)	$146,682

DISTRICT VOTE FOR PRESIDENT

	1996		1992
D	85,117 (46%)	**D**	79,432 (41%)
R	84,303 (45%)	**R**	75,319 (39%)
I	12,373 (7%)	**I**	41,006 (21%)

KEY VOTES

1997	
Ban "partial birth" abortions	Y
1996	
Approve farm bill	Y
Deny public education to illegal immigrants	Y
Repeal ban on certain assault-style weapons	Y
Increase minimum wage	N
Freeze defense spending	N
Approve welfare overhaul	Y
1995	
Approve balanced-budget constitutional amendment	Y
Relax Clean Water Act regulations	Y
Oppose limits on environmental regulations	N
Reduce projected Medicare spending	Y
Approve GOP budget with tax and spending cuts	Y

VOTING STUDIES

	Presidential Support		Party Unity		Conservative Coalition	
Year	S	O	S	O	S	O
1996	29	71	95	5	98	2
1995	14	86	97	2	99	1
1994	38	58	82	13	94	0
1993	25	73	86	13	89	11

INTEREST GROUP RATINGS

Year	ADA	AFL-CIO	CCUS	ACU
1996	5	n/a	94	100
1995	0	0	96	100
1994	5	25	92	100
1993	10	8	91	100

12 Tom Lantos (D)

Of San Mateo — Elected 1980, 9th term

Biographical Information
Born: Feb. 1, 1928, Budapest, Hungary.
Education: U. of Washington, B.A. 1949, M.A. 1950; U. of California, Berkeley, Ph.D. 1953.
Occupation: Professor.
Family: Wife, Annette Tillemann; two children.
Religion: Jewish.
Political Career: Millbrae Board of Education, 1958-66.
Capitol Office: 2217 Rayburn Bldg. 20515; 225-3531.

Committees
Government Reform & Oversight
Human Resources; National Security, International Affairs & Criminal Justice
International Relations
International Economic Policy & Trade; International Operations & Human Rights (ranking)

In Washington: The traits Lantos exhibits in the House are derived from a lifetime of varied experience. Born in Hungary, Lantos has the civilized air of a man bred in a prewar Central European culture — and the stubbornness of a fighter in the anti-Nazi resistance in Budapest. He retains the intellectual self-assurance — some say arrogance — of the professor he once was.

Despite his courtly manner, Lantos has brought an assertive and sometimes confrontational approach to his roles on the Government Reform and Oversight and International Relations committees. Lantos is the ranking member on International Relations' International Operations and Human Rights Subcommittee.

Lantos' confrontational side was evident early in the 104th when he condemned the Republicans for their partisan legislative push during the 100 days of the "Contract With America."

"The climate, in terms of partisanship, has deteriorated enormously," Lantos told the San Francisco Chronicle in April 1995. "The mood is surly, the attitude of people is very negative and there is a degree of confrontation I haven't seen in years." Lantos described the Republican majority as "goose-stepping" along on its agenda, the newspaper reported. The comment prompted an immediate and furious reply from GOP members, who objected that Lantos was labeling them Nazis.

Lantos said his intent was not to label them Nazis but to characterize the manner in which the Republicans were proceeding, without dissent or debate. "It was a new adjective and upon reflection I'm glad I used it," Lantos told the newspaper. "A parliamentary body in a political democracy must be a rational and deliberative body and, in many ways, this has not been that in the last 100 days."

Lantos was outraged when Oklahoma Republican Tom Coburn made remarks about the February 1997 broadcast of a widely acclaimed dramatic film about the Holocaust, "Schindler's List," on NBC. Coburn maintained that the broadcast took network television "to an all-time low with full frontal nudity, violence and profanity being shown in our homes." His comments earned him the ire even of prominent Republicans, who castigated him for failing to recognize the film's historical accuracy.

Lantos, who was incarcerated in a Hungarian Nazi work camp in 1944 and escaped, led a group of members in a news conference condemning Coburn's remarks. "I find it far less discouraging that some child may have learned a four-letter word. . . . I am more concerned about the 1.5 million children killed in the Holocaust," he said.

Coburn took to the House floor the next day and said, "I feel terrible that my criticism of NBC . . . has been misinterpreted as a criticism of 'Schindler's List' or the millions of Jews who died senselessly during the Holocaust."

Lantos, who is Jewish, is an enthusiastic supporter of Israel and a critic of its Arab adversaries. As a Holocaust survivor, Lantos also says devotion to human rights should drive U.S. foreign policy.

He was one of the first members to call for a tough U.S. response to what he called Serbia's aggression against the other former Yugoslavian republics of Croatia and Bosnia-Herzegovina. Frustrated by the early failure of multilateral efforts to resolve the conflict, Lantos called on the Clinton administration to act alone if necessary to arm Bosnia's Muslim-led government forces, despite a U.N. embargo that barred weapons shipments to any of the warring parties. Lantos was one of 93 Democrats supporting an August 1995 GOP measure requiring the president to end the Bosnian arms embargo. President Clinton vetoed the bill.

But once the warring parties agreed to sit down in Dayton, Ohio, in November 1995 to try to reach a U.S.-brokered peace agreement, Lantos backed Clinton's pledge to police the peace with 20,000 U.S. ground troops as part of a NATO force. He spoke strongly against an October 1995 House resolution urging Clinton to seek congressional approval before sending the troops to Bosnia. Lantos called the resolution "an irresponsible and reckless effort to raise doubts in the minds of the participants in the peace negotiations." Although the resolution passed, 315-103, U.S. troops were sent to Bosnia once the peace agreement was final.

CALIFORNIA 12
Most of San Mateo County; southwest San Francisco

Not too long ago, San Francisco supplied the vote for two congressional districts that often were split between the city's eastern and western halves. But because it now takes more than 570,000 inhabitants to make a district in California, San Francisco musters just one whole district and about one-fourth of another. The whole one is now the 8th, while the remaining city population is in the 12th.

The city portion of the 12th consists of the Twin Peaks area and the Sunset District south of Golden Gate Park. The nearby presence of the Pacific is palpable here, as clouds and fog often enshroud the area. The district's city portion also includes Lake Merced, the city zoo and a California State University campus (locally still called San Francisco State). The Sunset District is increasingly Chinese, and the 12th is 16 percent Asian.

The city portion of the district is Democratic: Bill Clinton beat Bob Dole there by 67 percent to 22 percent in 1996.

More than 70 percent of the 12th District residents live south of the San Francisco city limits in San Mateo County, and many of them live just over the city limits. The first suburb is Daly City, where spines of close-set homes appeared atop the rocky hillsides after World War II and inspired folk singer Pete Seeger's song "Little Boxes." Hard by the sea itself is Pacifica, harder to reach and blessed in good weather with magnificent views. Across the peninsula on the bay side lies South San Francisco, proclaimed "The Industrial City" by a Hollywood-style sign inscribed in a hillside. "South City," as locals call it, lies between the San Francisco International Airport and Candlestick Park, home of football's 49ers and baseball's Giants.

The center portion of the northern peninsula is occupied by a huge state fish and game refuge. To the west are steep coastal mountains, to the east are heavily populated suburbs. Two freeways carry commuters south along the eastern portion of the peninsula: The Junipero Serra Freeway (I-280) glides along the less populated western route, while the Bayshore Freeway (U.S. 101) plows through the often smoggy, always crowded bayside suburbs. Halfway between the two freeways is another north-south artery, El Camino Real. This one-time route of Spanish soldiers and Roman Catholic priests is now an endless procession of overnight lodgings, restaurants and video stores, punctuated by some offices and upscale shopping.

Principal among the Bayshore communities are South San Francisco, San Bruno, Millbrae and Burlingame (which passes by before reaching the southbound commuter reaches the county seat of Redwood City) and Foster City to the east. Farther into the peninsula's highlands lies Hillsborough, one of the most exclusive estate communities on the West Coast.

San Mateo County has been somewhat less reliably Democratic than other counties around the bay. Lantos' district voted for Ronald Reagan in 1980 and 1984 before switching to support Michael S. Dukakis in 1988. San Mateo portions of the 12th gave 62 percent to Clinton in 1996.

1990 Population: 571,535. White 372,572 (65%), Black 23,649 (4%), Other 175,314 (31%). Hispanic origin 81,606 (14%). 18 and over 455,454 (80%), 62 and over 95,211 (17%). Median age: 36.

Lantos has been critical of China since its government's crackdown on pro-democracy demonstrators in Tiananmen Square in June 1989, and he has consistently urged an end to most-favored-nation (MFN) trading status for the Chinese, which allows Chinese goods to enter the United States with low, non-discriminatory tariffs. He has been critical of Clinton's refusal to deny the trading status to the Chinese, in light of their human rights abuses and threats of military action against Taiwan.

He was particularly angry in May 1995 that the White House at first refused to issue a visa to Taiwanese President Lee Teng-hui so he could privately visit the United States to receive an honorary degree from his alma mater, Cornell University. The White House resisted issuing the visa because of concerns it would strain relations with China, but the adminstration later relented.

Lantos introduced a resolution, that passed the International Relations Committee and the House unanimously, urging the president to issue the visa. "I think it is long overdue that we stop kowtowing to the Communist butchers in Beijing and to stand on our own principles," Lantos told the House.

Although Lantos was critical of Clinton's China policy, he supported the president's effort in early 1997 to accept Mexico as a full partner in the battle against drugs. Under a 1986 law, the president must annually identify major producers and conduits for illegal narcotics. He must also determine whether those nations are cooperating with U.S. anti-drug efforts. Clinton certified that Mexico was cooperating, even though in 1996 there had been a spate of embarrassments highlighting Mexico's failure in the drug war.

The House in March 1997 approved, 251-175, a resolution reversing Clinton's decision to certify Mexico. "The president clearly understands that Mexico's record is far from perfect," Lantos told the House. "But it is better than it has been, and it is critical that this Mexican government work with us in fighting against illegal drugs."

Lantos opposed efforts by the GOP-led International Relations Committee to abolish three foreign policy agencies and to reduce the foreign aid budget by $1 billion less than the previous year. In fact, when the bill was first considered in May 1995, Lantos and other Democrats boycotted the markup, saying they had not had enough time to review the legislation.

Lantos' sense of righteous anger was also on national display during the 101st Congress, when Lantos — then the chairman of the Government Operations Subcommittee on Employment and Housing — held hearings on alleged corruption at the Department of Housing and Urban Development. One witness was former Reagan administration Interior Secretary James G. Watt, who defended efforts by well-connected Republican consultants to obtain HUD subsidies for housing developers. Lantos laced into Watt, one of the most conservative members of the Reagan "movement."

"What I find most obnoxious so far is the unmitigated hypocrisy of people like James Watt who exude unction, piety and noble motives, who carry on a crusade to destroy these programs and at the same time shamelessly milk them," Lantos said. The hearings helped persuade Congress to pass legislation placing new restrictions on HUD operating procedures.

At Home: It took Lantos two difficult and expensive elections before he could settle securely into his district. But his efforts since have given him an enviable comfort level.

He was working on Capitol Hill as a consultant to the Senate Foreign Relations Committee when Republican Bill Royer won a 1979 special election to replace Democrat Leo J. Ryan, who had been assassinated the year before in Jonestown, Guyana. Ryan's assassination brought out a host of Democrats who claimed to be his logical political heir, and by the time the primary was finished, the party was badly splintered. Royer picked his way through the Democratic debris to win the seat for the GOP.

But Lantos, well-known within local Democratic circles, left his job right after Royer's victory and began preparing a challenge for 1980. The one-time economics professor at San Francisco State University had held elective office only as a school board president in suburban Millbrae. But he had been active in party efforts and had built up name recognition as a foreign affairs commentator for a Bay Area TV station. Royer, who had been a city councilman and county supervisor for 23 years before moving on to Congress, went into the contest with a solid political foundation.

Yet Lantos, who had held himself apart from the 1979 Democratic feuding, was able to unite his party around him for 1980. Although Lantos was less well-known than Royer and was short of campaign funds, he was politically astute and took advantage of the incumbent's overconfidence. Lantos filled the airwaves with advertising, while Royer, believing the election was his, yanked his own ads as an economy move. Lantos won by 3 percentage points.

Royer made it clear that he would be back two years later, and Lantos began raising money early. He pursued it not only at home, but within Jewish communities in the districts of other members — a habit that led initially to some hard feelings among his colleagues. By 1982, he was among the best-funded House candidates in the country. He dismissed Royer's comeback attempt and has won re-election handily ever since.

HOUSE ELECTIONS

1996 General		
Tom Lantos (D)	149,052	(72%)
Storm Jenkins (R)	49,278	(24%)
Christopher V.A. Schmidt (LIBERT)	6,111	(3%)
Richard Borg (NL)	3,472	(2%)
1994 General		
Tom Lantos (D)	118,408	(67%)
Deborah Wilder (R)	57,228	(33%)

Previous Winning Percentages: 1992 (69%) **1990** (66%) **1988** (71%) **1986** (74%) **1984** (70%) **1982** (57%) **1980** (46%)

KEY VOTES

1997	
Ban "partial birth" abortions	N
1996	
Approve farm bill	N
Deny public education to illegal immigrants	N
Repeal ban on certain assault-style weapons	N
Increase minimum wage	Y
Freeze defense spending	Y
Approve welfare overhaul	N
1995	
Approve balanced-budget constitutional amendment	N
Relax Clean Water Act regulations	N
Oppose limits on environmental regulations	Y
Reduce projected Medicare spending	N
Approve GOP budget with tax and spending cuts	N

CAMPAIGN FINANCE

	Receipts	Receipts from PACs	Expend-itures
1996			
Lantos (D)	$246,333	$33,825 (14%)	$591,305
Jenkins (R)	$4,536	$2,016 (44%)	$4,016
1994			
Lantos (D)	$314,688	$94,300 (30%)	$322,016
Wilder (R)	$148,058	$13,082 (9%)	$146,133

DISTRICT VOTE FOR PRESIDENT

1996		1992	
D	141,084 (64%)	**D**	139,244 (58%)
R	58,260 (26%)	**R**	64,967 (27%)
I	11,994 (5%)	**I**	38,125 (16%)

VOTING STUDIES

	Presidential Support		Party Unity		Conservative Coalition	
Year	S	O	S	O	S	O
1996	82	13	91	3	14	78
1995	77	11	87	4	16	78
1994	79	15	85	5	44	53
1993	79	16	91	5	39	61
1992	19	81	90	6	31	69
1991	30	65	89	6	35	62

INTEREST GROUP RATINGS

Year	ADA	AFL-CIO	CCUS	ACU
1996	95	n/a	13	0
1995	90	100	25	22
1994	70	88	50	24
1993	90	100	18	9
1992	95	92	25	8
1991	75	100	11	11

13 Pete Stark (D)

Of Hayward — Elected 1972, 13th term

Biographical Information
Born: Nov. 11, 1931, Milwaukee, Wis.
Education: Massachusetts Institute of Technology, B.S. 1953; U. of California, Berkeley, M.B.A. 1960.
Military Service: Air Force, 1955-57.
Occupation: Banker.
Family: Wife, Deborah Roderick; five children.
Religion: Unitarian.
Political Career: Sought Democratic nomination for Calif. Senate, 1969.
Capitol Office: 239 Cannon Bldg. 20515; 225-5065.

Committees
Ways & Means
Health (ranking); Human Resources
Joint Economic (ranking)
Joint Taxation

In Washington: Throughout a long House career, Stark has shown an aptitude for translating his liberal goals into pragmatic legislation. But this trait contrasts with another side of his persona: the confrontational, outraged liberal whose mouth seems disengaged from discretion.

As chairman of the Ways and Means Health Subcommittee for 10 years (he is now its ranking Democrat), Stark built a reputation as one of Congress' premier experts on health care issues. Although his sometimes barbed tongue can make him a less than charming committee-mate, his knowledge and persistence gave him the distinction of crafting a health care reform bill that in large part won approval from Ways and Means in mid-1994, when Democrats were trying furiously to rescue the Clinton administration's top legislative priority.

Stark had less success laboring in the minority during the 104th Congress, when he was relegated to the role of lead complainant against GOP efforts to stunt the growth of Medicare costs. Powerless to make any changes to Republican bills, Stark complained that "there are not words to describe the despicable behavior of the Speaker" — although he found some with which to vent.

The specific action of Speaker Newt Gingrich that Stark deemed "despicable" was a change to the GOP's Medicare overhaul plan that guaranteed that payments to health care providers would not be reduced. Stark called the provision, which helped win the bill backing from the American Medical Association, "a $3 billion bribe."

The plan was never enacted. Stark also opposed the one major health bill that did become law during the 104th, guaranteeing "portability" of health insurance for individuals who lose or leave their jobs. The House adopted the conference report, 421-2, with Stark casting half the vote in opposition. Actually, Stark liked the overall bill, but he opposed a provision it contained to allow a pilot program testing medical savings accounts.

Stark's complaints veered to the personal in February 1995, when he called Republican Nancy L. Johnson of Connecticut a "whore for the insurance industry." The insult created an uproar, with a group of 32 women House members demanding that Stark apologize, which he did in a letter to Johnson. A year earlier, as the Health Subcommittee under Stark's gavel marked up an amendment to strip price limits on prescription drugs, Stark interrupted Johnson to observe, "The gentle lady got her degree from pillow talk," a reference to her physician husband.

Stark's frustration with GOP moves to overhaul the welfare system became especially evident during Ways and Means consideration of the plan in August 1995. Chairman Bill Archer, R-Texas, broke his gavel as he sought order, but Stark continued to taunt him, saying, "You can bang that gavel all you want, but I am not going to stop talking." When Health Subcommittee Chairman Bill Thomas, R-Calif., leaped to his feet and shouted for the sergeant at arms, Stark replied, "Oh great, just like Nazi Germany."

Stark did not limit his invective to Republicans. Like a number of House Democrats, Stark was angered when President Clinton agreed with the Republican call for a balanced budget, complaining that he had been blindsided.

"I was decrying reductions in Medicare to pay for tax cuts as my leadership told me," Stark said. "Now, I'm disloyal for believing it," because Clinton's budget plan also slowed the growth of Medicare.

Seeing the agenda being so thoroughly controlled by conservatives was a rude turnaround for Stark, who in the 103rd Congress had sponsored legislation that guaranteed universal health care coverage. Stark's health overhaul bill had a simpler framework than Clinton's. He particularly disagreed with the administration proposal to create regional health care alliances, which were to take over the role of insurance companies and employee benefits managers. But like the president's bill, Stark's ensured health care coverage

CALIFORNIA 13
East Bay — Oakland; Hayward; Santa Clara

The 13th is a renumbered version of the old 9th, which had been sending Pete Stark to the House for 20 years. Although somewhat altered in 1992 redistricting, the new constituency remains Democratic by registration.

The old 9th began at Hayward, a city of 111,000 on the eastern shore of San Francisco Bay. The district then ran inland over the San Leandro Hills to take in the agricultural southeastern portions of Alameda County. The 1980s transformed these environs, as high-tech industry accelerated population growth. So great was the growth that remapping moved eastern Alameda County into a newly drawn 10th District with suburban Contra Costa County.

Now Stark's district begins in Oakland, on the bay side of the Bay Area Rapid Transit (BART) tracks just south of San Leandro Bay. Here the 13th takes in the Oakland Coliseum, home of the baseball Athletics and again home of the football Raiders, and Oakland International Airport. Despite the landmarks, there is relatively little of Oakland's residential population here. The bayshore is dominated by the freeway, miles of warehouses and older factories — many of which no longer function.

The first suburb south of Oakland proper is San Leandro, an old Portuguese enclave with a strong blue-collar vote. Once attracted to Ronald Reagan, the area has returned to the Democratic fold — one of many such venues that account for the turnaround in California's presidential preferences.

Hayward has a large campus of the California State University system and mixes business and professionals' office complexes with the usual East Bay commerce. Farther south along the multilane traffic crunch of Interstate 880 is Newark, followed by Fremont — the East Bay southern terminus for BART and site of the last operating auto plant in California, a joint venture of General Motors and Toyota. The district line coincides with the eastern limits of these cities, as it does those of San Leandro and Hayward. In each case, the limit is reached in the highlands. The district no longer reaches into the suburb-dotted interior.

At its southern extreme, the 13th crosses the county line into Santa Clara County and takes in the alluvial mud flats at the southern end of San Francisco Bay. This is home to a little less than 10 percent of the 13th's residents. At the southwestern extreme, the district takes in a slice of the old Moffett Field Air Station, once home to government-operated dirigibles (the hangars are still visible from the Bayshore Freeway). The southeastern extreme reaches through the industrial city of Milpitas and appropriates a section of San Jose.

By shedding the eastern reaches of Alameda County, Stark's district lowered the non-Latino white share of population from 64 percent in 1990 to 55 percent in 1992. The black community remains small and mostly concentrated in Oakland. But in 1992, nearly two residents in five were either Latino or Asian-American.

1990 Population: 572,441. White 367,553 (64%), Black 42,228 (7%), Other 162,660 (28%). Hispanic origin 105,225 (18%). 18 and over 426,316 (74%), 62 and over 66,786 (12%). Median age: 32.

for all Americans by creating vast new federal responsibilities.

Even during the days of Democratic control, Stark sometimes seemed more intent on shocking his listeners and lobbing grenades than reaching a consensus on legislation. At an August 1990 news conference, he erupted at the mention of Bush administration Health and Human Services Secretary Louis W. Sullivan. Stark said Sullivan, who is black, "comes about as close to being a disgrace to his profession and his race as anyone I've ever seen."

After House Republicans rose to Sullivan's defense and denounced Stark for his remarks, Stark apologized -- sort of. "To the secretary, I have to say I blew it," Stark told the House. "I should not have brought into the discussion his race, because it obscures the fact that he is carrying a bankrupt policy for an administration which has been impacting the poor and the minorities of this country And I apologize for obscuring that." A few days later, though, Stark sent Sullivan a formal letter of apology.

In the 103rd, Stark became chairman of the District of Columbia Committee, and he pushed another item on his eclectic liberal agenda -- statehood for the District. Stark had long been a member of the backwater D.C. panel, and he wanted to see Congress drop its role as overseer of the internal affairs of the federal city. But a statehood vote in the 103rd failed.

When Republicans took control of the House in 1995, they abolished the D.C. Committee, entrusting its responsibilities to subcommittees on Appropriations and on Government Reform and Oversight. As a parting gift Stark authorized one-time payments totalling more than $25,000 to eight Democratic D.C. Committee staffers.

At Home: The flap over Stark's rash criticism of Sullivan may have cost Stark some votes in 1990, when he carried the district easily against Republican real estate agent Victor Romero but saw his share of the vote drop by 15 percentage points.

In 1992, remapping changed Stark's district dramatically but left the Democratic registration percentage unchanged at 58 percent. Stark was opposed by foster-care home operator Verne Teyler and prevailed easily with 60 percent; in 1994 and 1996 he pushed his vote share back toward its previous levels with 65 percent showings.

Stark grew up in Wisconsin, went to college in Massachusetts and then served in the Air Force before going West for business school and a career in banking. At age 31 he had already founded two banks, but he really made a name for himself by raising an 8-foot neon peace symbol over one of them in suburban Walnut Creek in the 1960s.

In 1969 he made his first try for public office, losing a primary for a state legislative seat to George Miller, a young law school student with whom he now serves in the House. Three years later, Stark decided to take on another George Miller -- this one a crusty old-school conservative who had represented Oakland in Congress as a Democrat for 28 years. Stark spent his money generously and made the Vietnam War a major issue on his way to an 11,000-vote win. The November election was competitive, as Republicans were dominating most of the races that fall. But Stark managed 53 percent.

Only once since then has Stark had a close call. Lulled by years of easy re-election, he prepared only a token effort in 1980. But conservative Republican William J. Kennedy, a tireless campaigner, galvanized a host of volunteers in the midst of Ronald Reagan's first presidential landslide and held Stark to 55 percent.

Stark's 1996 Republican opponent, James S. Fay, attempted to make Stark's hot-headedness an issue, distributing a flyer depicting a prostitute and headlined "meet Pete Stark's whore." Fay also distributed videotapes to news agencies of Stark yelling profanely at a reporter in his congressional office. But Stark turned Fay aside easily.

HOUSE ELECTIONS

1996 General		
Pete Stark (D)	114,408	(65%)
James S. Fay (R)	53,385	(30%)
Terry C. Savage (LIBERT)	7,746	(4%)
1994 General		
Pete Stark (D)	97,344	(65%)
Larry Molton (R)	45,555	(30%)
Robert "Bob" Gough (LIBERT)	7,743	(5%)

Previous Winning Percentages: **1992** (60%) **1990** (58%) **1988** (73%) **1986** (70%) **1984** (70%) **1982** (61%) **1980** (55%) **1978** (65%) **1976** (71%) **1974** (71%) **1972** (53%)

CAMPAIGN FINANCE

	Receipts	Receipts from PACs	Expend-itures
1996			
Stark (D)	$334,985	$155,333 (46%)	$630,357
Fay (R)	$61,949	$8,016 (13%)	$60,106
Savage (LIBERT)	$3,970	0	$3,532
1994			
Stark (D)	$710,201	$439,425 (62%)	$391,319
Molton (R)	$26,680	$14 (0%)	$26,249

DISTRICT VOTE FOR PRESIDENT

1996		1992	
D	115,633 (62%)	**D**	116,829 (54%)
R	51,084 (28%)	**R**	55,100 (26%)
I	13,085 (7%)	**I**	43,026 (20%)

KEY VOTES

1997	
Ban "partial birth" abortions	N
1996	
Approve farm bill	N
Deny public education to illegal immigrants	?
Repeal ban on certain assault-style weapons	?
Increase minimum wage	Y
Freeze defense spending	Y
Approve welfare overhaul	N
1995	
Approve balanced-budget constitutional amendment	N
Relax Clean Water Act regulations	N
Oppose limits on environmental regulations	Y
Reduce projected Medicare spending	N
Approve GOP budget with tax and spending cuts	N

VOTING STUDIES

	Presidential Support		Party Unity		Conservative Coalition	
Year	**S**	**O**	**S**	**O**	**S**	**O**
1996	65	23	82	4	0	94
1995	81	11	89	3	3	84
1994	72	21	92	2	0	94
1993	71	25	91	3	9	89
1992	14	80	81	6	4	83
1991	24	71	87	3	8	86

INTEREST GROUP RATINGS

Year	ADA	AFL-CIO	CCUS	ACU
1996	80	n/a	6	0
1995	100	100	13	8
1994	95	100	27	0
1993	100	100	0	4
1992	95	83	13	4
1991	100	100	20	0

14 Anna G. Eshoo (D)

Of Atherton — Elected 1992, 3rd term

Biographical Information
Born: Dec. 13, 1942, New Britain, Conn.
Education: Canada College, A.A. 1975.
Occupation: Legislative aide.
Family: Divorced; two children.
Religion: Roman Catholic.
Political Career: Democratic National Committee, 1980-92; San Mateo County Board of Supervisors, 1982-92; Democratic nominee for U.S. House, 1988.
Capitol Office: 308 Cannon Bldg. 20515; 225-8104.

Committees
Commerce
Health & Environment; Telecommunications, Trade & Consumer Protection

In Washington: Eshoo is a "New Democrat," liberal on many issues but a firm believer in free trade and business development. By touting Silicon Valley's highly skilled, high-paying jobs as the future of the U.S. economy, she has coopted much of the high-tech business support that helped elect Republicans in this district for many years.

Even though the 1994 election cast her into the House minority, Eshoo at the start of the 104th got a plum committee assignment — on Commerce — that puts her in a good position to look out for Silicon Valley employers and other business interests.

Eshoo fought hard in the 104th for legislation to overhaul laws governing investor lawsuits, a topic she said was "the No. 1 legislative issue in Silicon Valley."

Supporters said the bill was aimed at closing loopholes in the existing system that lead to the filing of frivolous lawsuits. Among other things, the overhaul bill required plaintiffs to provide more evidence of fraud before filing lawsuits, and the bill restricted fees for attorneys who file class-action shareholder lawsuits.

"Meritless lawsuits are crippling our high-technology industry," Eshoo said, noting that top Silicon Valley technology companies have paid more than $600 million to settle such lawsuits, a third of which went to legal fees.

Both the House and Senate approved the bill, and proponents were fairly confident Clinton would sign it. Instead, he vetoed it.

Eshoo then got involved in the House effort to override Clinton's veto. She and nearly half of the chamber's Democrats deserted the president, marking the first time a Clinton veto was overridden by the House. The Senate also overrode Clinton's veto, enacting the bill.

The 104th offered Eshoo several other opportunities to exert influence on high-technology issues. From her Commerce seat, she sponsored an amendment to the telecommunications bill limiting the involvement of the Federal Communications Commission in implementing standards for compatibility between cable boxes, televisions, VCRs and other home automation systems. The legislation allows companies to develop products and software to run home automation systems with little interference from the government.

Eshoo also introduced legislation to strengthen parental control over material available online to children. The bill aimed to replace the "indecency" standard of the telecommunications overhaul with a "harmful to minors" standard. Eshoo argued that the indecency standard was so broad it violated freedom of speech — a position later sustained under judicial appeal.

Eshoo also fought to lessen restrictions on computer exports.

Eshoo's disagreement with Clinton on securities litigation was a rarity, as she votes with the president on most issues. Eshoo loudly opposed Republican efforts to slow the growth of Medicare during the 104th, and she sponsored a bill that sought to raise the individual cap on lifetime insurance payments from $1 million to $10 million.

Eshoo has become a major proponent of ensuring that children have access to health care. She criticized Republican attempts to eliminate Medicaid's guarantee of health coverage for poor children. Eshoo also opposed GOP efforts to rein in environmental regulations and cut back student loan funding.

She opposed repealing a ban on certain semiautomatic assault-style weapons. And when a Clinton vs. Congress impasse on the budget led to partial government shutdowns in late 1995 and early 1996, Eshoo suggested that members donate the paychecks to charity until the issue was resolved.

Eshoo shares with her conservative adversaries a support for congressional term limits. She would allow up to three 4-year terms for House members.

In the 104th, Eshoo fought hard to stop job-killing military base closings in California, partic-

CALIFORNIA 14
Southern San Mateo and northern Santa Clara counties

Sustained population growth in the San Francisco Peninsula enabled mapmakers in 1992 to fashion a full district from suburbs south of the San Mateo Bridge and north of San Jose. The 14th generally resembles the old 12th District. But on the north it has annexed more of San Mateo County, including Belmont, San Carlos and Redwood City, whose 66,000 residents make it the district's second-largest city. About 40 percent of the district population is now in San Mateo County, the rest in Santa Clara County.

At its southern end, the district has lost the long tail that had dangled all the way to rural Gilroy and taken in some remote Santa Cruz County turf along the way. The 14th is more compact, with its center in the affluent suburbs on either side of the San Mateo and Santa Clara county line. Some of these communities have existed for more than a century, preserving their individual character despite waves of population growth. Working hardest to do so are the exclusive enclaves of Atherton, Woodside and Portola Valley. But Palo Alto, too, has stabilized its growth and sustained much of its leafy, small-town charm. Its population of 56,000 does not include the students, faculty and staff who live on the sprawling, adjacent campus of Stanford University.

Farther south, change has been more overwhelming in Mountain View, Sunnyvale, Los Altos and Cupertino. Miles of fruit groves have given way to high-tech factories: Hewlett-Packard and Apple Computer are in the area; Lockheed Martin is nearby. With the rise of microprocessing, this corridor has come to be known worldwide as Silicon Valley. Sunnyvale, its informal capital, grew slowly in the 1980s; but with 117,000 residents (most of them in the 14th) it is easily the district's most populous city.

The lure of comfy suburbs so close to jobs has kept peninsula land values climbing for decades. Million-dollar homes are common, and even ramshackle units come with high price tags in East Palo Alto and other low-income communities along the Bayshore Freeway.

With its wealth, old and new, this was the Bay Area's one Republican district in past years, consistently favoring GOP presidential candidates.

It also sent a succession of Republicans to Congress, although it preferred the moderate-to-liberal models such as Paul N. McCloskey Jr., Ed Zschau and Tom Campbell. But the 14th is different enough, and the House elections of the 1990s were lopsided enough, that no one is likely to call this district Republican again soon.

Population shifts and redistricting lowered the percentage of whites from 86 percent to 78 percent. Bill Clinton won the 14th by a 2-1 margin in 1992. He nearly equaled the margin four years later, defeating Dole with 58 percent of the vote, while Eshoo was re-elected with 65 percent.

1990 Population: 571,131. White 445,884 (78%), Black 28,237 (5%), Other 97,010 (17%). Hispanic origin 77,305 (14%). 18 and over 456,226 (80%), 62 and over 78,985 (14%). Median age: 34.

ularly lobbying for her district's Onizuka Air Force Base. Eshoo also asked NASA and Clinton to locate the Stratospheric Observatory for Infrared Astronomy (SOFIA) project in California. The project could bring more than $800 million to the state over 20 years. Eshoo strongly opposed cutting funds for the U.S. Geological Survey, whose studies are valuable to her earthquake prone district.

One of the tough calls Eshoo faced as a freshman in the 103rd was NAFTA. The trade pact was fiercely opposed by many of the 14th's core Democratic constituencies — organized labor, environmentalists and human rights activists. Despite her business-minded views on trade, Eshoo did not come easily to her final conclusion to endorse NAFTA. "I could lose my seat, regardless of the way I vote," she said on a fact-finding trip to Mexico.

The AFL-CIO organized that trip, hoping to turn members against the treaty by showing them teeming slums occupied by workers in the dozens of low-paying foreign-owned factories in Tijuana.

But after a day listening to Mexicans recount stories of exploitative treatment by U.S. and other foreign-owned companies, Eshoo observed, "If we vote against NAFTA, we just validate the status quo."

In announcing her decision to back the trade pact, Eshoo noted that it would eliminate Mexican tariffs and other barriers imposed on computers and related goods, promising higher exports. There were cries of betrayal from organized labor and some other Democrats who had worked hard to elect Eshoo when the 14th was open in 1992 — a race in which most Silicon Valley executives backed Eshoo's GOP foe.

But a grateful Clinton administration weighed in for Eshoo, eager to hold her up as a symbol of the White House's desire for good relations with the high-tech industry. In early 1994, Vice President Al Gore was the featured attraction at two district fundraisers for Eshoo.

Although her district includes a number of

high-income taxpayers who feel the pinch of Clinton's 1993 tax increase, Eshoo has faithfully supported his economic initiatives. On social policy matters she is reliably liberal, standing on much the same ground as her three Republican predecessors in the district, Paul N. McCloskey Jr., Ed Zschau and Tom Campbell (who now represents the neighboring 15th); they defined the left of the House GOP spectrum on social issues.

At Home: A San Mateo County supervisor since 1983, Eshoo ran unsuccessfully for the House in 1988 against Campbell, taking a solid 46 percent.

After Campbell decided to run for the Senate in 1992, Eshoo parlayed her campaign experience, an aggressive style and heightened voter interest in female candidates into victory.

Eshoo also was aided by redistricting, which had increased the number of registered Democrats in the 14th.

Eshoo was joined in the Democratic primary by six male candidates. Recognizing Eshoo's built-in advantage from having run before, they attacked her record and credibility, and her strategy of making her gender an issue. Eshoo campaigned like a front-runner, refusing to attack and distributing a 58-page book called "First Things First" outlining her issue positions. She won nomination with 40 percent.

Republicans nominated Tom Huening, another San Mateo County supervisor. He called for congressional reform and attempted to organize a post-election meeting of all House freshmen in Omaha, Neb.

He cast himself in the mold of Campbell and Zschau, supported deeper spending cuts than did Eshoo — except for defense — and took a firm stand against tax increases. But with Clinton doubling George Bush's tally in the district's presidential balloting, Eshoo won with 57 percent of the vote. His winning tally has kept climbing in the two elections since then.

HOUSE ELECTIONS

1996 General		
Anna G. Eshoo (D)	149,313	(65%)
Ben Brink (R)	71,573	(31%)
Timothy Thompson (PFP)	3,653	(2%)
Joseph W. Dehn III (LIBERT)	3,492	(2%)
1994 General		
Anna G. Eshoo (D)	120,713	(61%)
Ben Brink (R)	78,475	(39%)

Previous Winning Percentages: 1992 (57%)

CAMPAIGN FINANCE

	Receipts	Receipts from PACs	Expend-itures
1996			
Eshoo (D)	$575,018	$242,790 (42%)	$544,566
Brink (R)	$453,937	$2,236 (0%)	$432,849
1994			
Eshoo (D)	$605,439	$203,995 (34%)	$487,660
Brink (R)	$226,710	$19,496 (9%)	$223,118

DISTRICT VOTE FOR PRESIDENT

1996	1992
D 137,561 (58%)	**D** 143,727 (54%)
R 73,302 (31%)	**R** 71,736 (27%)
I 13,939 (6%)	**I** 53,042 (20%)

KEY VOTES

1997	
Ban "partial birth" abortions	N
1996	
Approve farm bill	N
Deny public education to illegal immigrants	N
Repeal ban on certain assault-style weapons	N
Increase minimum wage	Y
Freeze defense spending	Y
Approve welfare overhaul	N
1995	
Approve balanced-budget constitutional amendment	N
Relax Clean Water Act regulations	N
Oppose limits on environmental regulations	Y
Reduce projected Medicare spending	N
Approve GOP budget with tax and spending cuts	N

VOTING STUDIES

	Presidential Support		Party Unity		Conservative Coalition	
Year	**S**	**O**	**S**	**O**	**S**	**O**
1996	82	16	90	7	12	86
1995	86	14	93	7	24	75
1994	81	19	98	2	11	89
1993	84	16	96	3	14	86

INTEREST GROUP RATINGS

Year	ADA	AFL-CIO	CCUS	ACU
1996	85	n/a	29	0
1995	85	100	33	16
1994	95	89	33	0
1993	95	92	27	4

15 Tom Campbell (R)

Of Stanford — Elected 1988; 3rd full term
Did not serve 1993-95.

Biographical Information

Born: Aug. 14, 1952, Chicago, Ill.

Education: U. of Chicago, B.A. 1973, M.A. 1973; Harvard U., J.D. 1976; U. of Chicago, Ph.D. 1980.

Occupation: Professor; federal official; lawyer.

Family: Wife, Susanne Martin.

Religion: Roman Catholic.

Political Career: U.S. House, 1989-93; sought Republican nomination for U.S. Senate, 1992; Calif. Senate, 1993-95.

Capitol Office: 2442 Rayburn Bldg. 20515; 225-2631.

Committees

Banking and Financial Services
Capital Markets, Securities & Government Sponsored Enterprises; Financial Institutions & Consumer Credit

International Relations
Africa; International Economic Policy & Trade

In Washington: Campbell's career is a rejoinder to F. Scott Fitzgerald's edict that there are no second acts in American lives. After giving up a secure House seat in 1992 to run unsuccessfully for the Senate, Campbell scored an impressive comeback in a 1995 special election to return to the House from a new district. A moderate who was frequently at odds with his party during his initial tour of duty in Congress, Campbell rejoined a Republican Conference grown considerably more conservative during his three-year absence.

Ironically, Campbell's opponent in the special election to succeed retired Democrat Norman Y. Mineta test-marketed the Democratic strategy of beating up GOP House candidates for association with Speaker Newt Gingrich, R-Ga., who was proving unpopular in many swing districts. "Tom Campbell: One More Vote For Newt," declared one Democratic slogan in 1995.

That characterization proved too loose a fit on Campbell, who was already well-known for his independence within the GOP ranks. "You have to have some appreciation for the humor — and I would if I weren't caught in the middle of it — of being called a hopeless liberal by Bruce Herschensohn and Sonny Bono [his GOP rivals for the Senate nod] in 1992, and being called a hopeless right-winger in this race," Campbell said during the 1995 campaign.

And it ultimately proved to be a false characterization, as Campbell at the start of the 105th Congress ended up as one of nine Republicans who refused to give their assent to Gingrich's re-election as Speaker. According to participants, Campbell directly challenged Gingrich's veracity at a conference peacemaking session the day before the 105th convened. Gingrich was under fire for ethical violations, including giving false information to the ethics committee; although Gingrich blamed his lawyer for the latter, Campbell held the Speaker himself culpable.

Campbell recognized his move would win him no brownie points. Just prior to the vote he said, "If the Speaker stays the Speaker and I vote against him, it certainly diminishes my ability to influence my colleagues." Campbell cast his vote for Banking and Financial Services Committee Chairman Jim Leach of Iowa, the most prominent Republican to oppose Gingrich. Campbell serves on the Banking Committee, as well as the International Relations panel.

Instead of glad-handing and other buddy-buddy means of political suasion, Campbell, who earned doctorates in both law and economics before his 28th birthday, attempts to hold sway by means of floor speeches that are like little constitutional law lectures or macroeconomic theory pronouncements. He rarely misses an opportunity to propound the constitutional grounding for his stances on issues as diverse as same-gender marriages, aid to children, or immigration policy. Explaining his opposition to a ban on so-called partial-birth abortions, he stated, "This bill is unconstitutional. Our highest obligation is to uphold and defend the Constitution because that is the oath that we take. Hence, we should vote no."

Campbell breaks with the majority of his party not only in support of abortion rights but also in allegiance to gun control and environmental protection, and a belief that a balanced budget must take precedence over any tax cuts. He was one of three Republicans who signed a letter to Gingrich in January 1996 arguing that tax cuts should be considered separately from budget negotiations.

He also takes a softer line on immigration that many of his GOP colleagues, opposing a bill by fellow California Republican Elton Gallegly that would have blocked illegal immigrants from receiving public education; he argued that since resources weren't being provided to deport all illegal immigrant children, it was better to educate them "than that they be on a street corner or in a gang." Campbell offered an amendment to the fiscal 1997 spending bill covering the departments of Labor, Health and Human Services, and Education that softened prohibitions against illegal immigrants receiving health aid. He sponsored a bill early in the 105th to try to restore to legal

CALIFORNIA 15
Santa Clara County — San Jose

In the two decades Democrat Norman Y. Mineta represented the district, San Jose grew to be the third-largest city in the state, showing up its better-known neighbor 40 miles to the north, San Francisco. By the time he retired in 1995, the district took in half of seaside Santa Cruz County — a completely refigured district in which heavily trafficked state Highway 17 is the spinal column.

The 15th has its northern extreme at the Great America theme park between the Bayshore Freeway (Highway 101) and the southern tip of the San Francisco Bay. The park is in the city of Santa Clara, which lies at the south end of Silicon Valley but retains some of the character of an old college town in the midst of high-tech plants and proliferating subdivisions. (The University of Santa Clara was founded here by Jesuits in 1851.)

With 94,000 people, Santa Clara is the largest city wholly within the 15th. It has usually been Democratic — although not as decidedly so as San Jose — and it helps keep Democratic registration in the 15th close to half. Campbell, who represented a neighboring district from 1989 to 1993, overcame those numbers with solid wins in the 1995 special election and his bid for a full term in 1996.

At the southeastern end of Santa Clara is an imposing interchange where Interstates 880 and 280 cross. Southeast of this landmark, the 15th has San Jose's western neighborhoods, including developments that spread out along the Almaden Expressway. Also proceeding south from the intersection of the interstates is Highway 17, which runs all the way to the Pacific Ocean — with the district following it nearly all the way.

Some of the exit ramps from 17 lead to growing middle-class suburbs such as Campbell and Monte Sereno.

Other off-ramps lead to more affluent communities in the hills — Los Gatos and Saratoga — where some of the better-paid professionals of Silicon Valley live. All of these Santa Clara County suburbs can be good ground for statewide Republican candidates.

Continuing south on Highway 17 is the epicenter of the 1989 Loma Prieta earthquake, the area's worst since 1906. Not far away, the road and the district cross into Santa Cruz County, a demarcation surrounded by hillsides heavy with redwoods. Heading down the slope, the 15th takes in Scotts Valley and Felton.

Racing toward the sea, the district even reaches into the city of Santa Cruz. All told, Santa Cruz County contributes only about 10 percent of the district population. It usually helps Democrats. Voters from the University of California campus and the computer companies that surround it were strong Mineta supporters.

Bill Clinton carried the 15th in both 1992 and 1996, the latter with a majority. Campbell has altered the equation, and both counties in the district supported his re-election bid in 1996.

1990 Population: 572,485. White 470,821 (82%), Black 12,957 (2%), Other 88,707 (15%). Hispanic origin 61,884 (11%). 18 and over 444,446 (78%), 62 and over 67,179 (12%). Median age: 34.

immigrants some of the benefits they lost under the 1996 welfare law also.

But Campbell is far from a liberal and does vote with the GOP most of the time. He offered a successful amendment to make it easier for congressional money panels to use dynamic economic modeling, a theory that calculates the positive effect of tax cuts on budget revenues. And he opposed a 90-cent-per-hour boost in the minimum wage, contending that an increase in the salaries of some workers would cost other workers, particularly teenagers, their jobs.

Campbell proudly voted against certain earmarks for his old district, but he found other ways of plumping for high-tech businesses and has paid close attention to the concerns of his new home. He joined Congress too late to have much impact on the 1996 telecommunications law, but he has spoken out in favor of encryption protections important to Silicon Valley computer companies. The 15th features many flower farms and he has pressured the Clinton administration to raise tariffs on cut flowers from Columbia.

Campbell's concern about the health of NAFTA led him to organize an International Relations subcommittee hearing on the impact of the possible secession of Quebec from Canada. Although the hearing drew little attention at home, it was broadcast in Canada and was covered extensively by the Canadian media.

Campbell was a leading backer of a March 1996 ballot initiative that opened up the California primary ballot system to allow voters to choose which party's primary they preferred to vote in. Campbell donated $50,000 from his campaign treasury to the cause, which was thought to make it more likely that a moderate member of a party might call on a broader slice of the electorate and seize a nomination. But Campbell denied any suggestion that the initiative was meant to pave the way for a second Senate run in 1998.

At Home: Campbell had represented the neighboring 14th District, now held by Democrat

Anna G. Eshoo, for four years before entering the 1992 Senate contest. When the 15th opened up with Mineta's resignation to work for a defense contractor, Campbell hardly hesitated to file his papers.

Still boyish looking upon returning to the House at age 43, Campbell has always been an overachiever. The son of a federal judge, Campbell has been a Supreme Court law clerk and a White House fellow. At the time of the special House election, Campbell was teaching at Stanford University and living on its campus, well outside the 15th. He suggested it would be presumptuous to move into the district prior to winning the congressional race.

But the Senate race, and a subsequent stint in the California Senate, made the mediagenic Campbell well-known to his neighbors in the 15th, who didn't buy the idea that he would be a "Gingrich clone." The attacks may have backfired, as they helped Campbell win the strong financial backing of national and California Republicans who have sometimes found him less than a perfect ideological match. The chance to take this nominally Democratic district covered over any intraparty divisions, and Campbell ran unopposed on the GOP side.

And he proved lucky in drawing Jerry Estruth, a former San Jose City Council member who was not the first choice of Democratic recruiters and had some exposure due to questions about the city's financial management during his tenure. Estruth had difficulty sticking to the anti-Gingrich script; Estruth's press secretary admitted, "We'd rather run against a more conservative candidate."

In 1996, Campbell won easily, taking 59 percent of the vote, as Bill Clinton carried the district 53 percent to 35 percent over Republican nominee Bob Dole.

In the 1988 14th District GOP primary, Campbell knocked off first-term Rep. Ernie Konnyu, who had quickly earned a reputation for boorish personal behavior and extremely conservative views. Campbell then prevailed over Eshoo in the November general election.

HOUSE ELECTIONS

1996 General		
Tom Campbell (R)	132,737	(59%)
Dick Lane (D)	79,048	(35%)
Valli Sharpe-Geisler (REF)	6,230	(3%)
Ed Wimmers (LIBERT)	5,481	(2%)
Bruce Currivan (NL)	3,372	(1%)
1995 Election †		
Tom Campbell (R)	54,372	(59%)
Jerry Estruth (D)	33,051	(36%)
Linh Keiu Dao (I)	4,922	(5%)

Previous Winning Percentages: 1990 (61%) **1988** (52%)

† Special election

CAMPAIGN FINANCE

	Receipts	Receipts from PACs	Expend-itures
1996			
Campbell (R)	$2,529,996	$533,436 (21%)	$2,177,865
Lane (D)	$64,997	$6,500 (10%)	$64,732
Sharpe-Geisler (REF)	$23,735	0	$21,472
1995 Special			
Campbell (R)	$874,032	$214,170 (25%)	$555,731
Estruth (D)	$449,689	$198,950 (44%)	$418,536

DISTRICT VOTE FOR PRESIDENT

1996		1992	
D	125,438 (53%)	**D**	127,060 (46%)
R	83,846 (35%)	**R**	83,301 (30%)
I	17,506 (7%)	**I**	64,192 (23%)

KEY VOTES

1997	
Ban "partial-birth" abortions	N
1996	
Approve farm bill	Y
Deny public education to illegal immigrants	N
Repeal ban on certain assault-style weapons	N
Increase minimum wage	N
Freeze defense spending	Y
Approve welfare overhaul	Y

VOTING STUDIES

	Presidential Support		Party Unity		Conservative Coalition	
Year	**S**	**O**	**S**	**O**	**S**	**O**
1996	54	46	73	27	43	57
1995	33+	67+	94+	6+	100+	0+
1992	57	16	70	13	63	17
1991	61	28	69	19	62	30

+ Not eligible for all recorded votes.

INTEREST GROUP RATINGS

Year	ADA	AFL-CIO	CCUS	ACU
1996	40	n/a	88	60
1995	0	0	0	0
1992	30	27	71	68
1991	25	25	70	70

16 Zoe Lofgren (D)

Of San Jose — Elected 1994, 2nd term

Biographical Information
Born: Dec. 21, 1947, Palo Alto, Calif.
Education: Stanford U., B.A. 1970; U. of Santa Clara, J.D. 1975.
Occupation: Lawyer; professor; congressional aide.
Family: Husband, John Marshall Collins; two children.
Religion: Unspecified.
Political Career: Santa Clara County Board of Supervisors, 1981-95.
Capitol Office: 318 Cannon Bldg. 20515; 225-3072.

Committees
Judiciary
Courts & Intellectual Property; Immigration & Claims
Science
Energy & Environment; Space & Aeronautics

In Washington: Lofgren was one of only 13 Democrats in the Republican-dominated Class of 1994, and she was the only freshman Democrat from a district west of the Rocky Mountains. But if nearly all the news media attention during the 104th Congress was focused on the large and rambunctious Republican freshman class, Lofgren sometimes was able to influence the shape of legislation, to a degree noteworthy for a first-term member of the House minority.

Rhetorically, Lofgren is typically a strong — sometimes biting — supporter of the Democratic line. Assessing the House's work at one point in 1995, she said, "I'm frustrated by the sheer volume of the stupid things we've done."

But this outlook does not prevent Lofgren from working in a quieter way to influence the content of bills that Republicans are pushing. From her seat on the Judiciary Committee, she has made targeted attempts to revise GOP proposals, and met with some success.

"I haven't introduced a lot of bills," she told the Los Angeles Times, "because they're not going anywhere. But when there's an apparent willingness on the majority side to work with me to improve something in a rational way, then I try to do that."

A case in point was her response to a GOP bill on prisons that the House debated in February 1995. "I have made no secret that I have philosophical problems with this bill overall," she said. But, speaking for an amendment she cosponsored, she said, "To the extent that this bill passes, I think it is very important that this be a workable bill."

In working with Republicans, Lofgren sometimes distances herself from fellow liberals on Judiciary. She was, for example, the only committee Democrat to support a requirement that the loser in a civil lawsuit pay both sides' legal fees. Trial lawyers and legal aid advocates object to "loser pays," arguing that it discriminates against the poor.

On a bill intended to prevent crimes against children and the elderly, Lofgren won adoption of an amendment to expand protection to more victims (including children up to age 14). Some Judiciary Democrats objected, with one grousing about federal chest-thumping to appear "tough on crime."

When Judiciary considered anti-terrorism legislation in the wake of the April 1995 bombing of a federal office building in Oklahoma City, Lofgren shared the concern of some civil libertarians that the measure would allow excessive government intrusion into individuals' rights. She won approval of an amendment to curb the bill's extension of law enforcement powers by requiring authorities to obtain a court order before searching certain suspected terrorists' credit records.

Lofgren often scrutinizes legislation with an eye toward its impact on women and families. During Judiciary consideration of an immigration bill in the 104th, she won approval of four amendments that restored protections for battered spouses and children. On the telecommunications bill that set new ground rules for the communications technology industry, she was able to attach a provision regarding affordable access to the Internet for public schools.

And on a Republican bill aimed at limiting federal regulatory powers, she won exemption for emergency actions to remove unsafe airplanes from service and respond to oil spills.

Still, many of Lofgren's proposals have been brushed aside the by the GOP majority. She was not allowed to offer an amendment to shift funding away from missile-defense systems so schools nationwide could extend school hours to 5 p.m., a setback that made her bristle. "I can attest that there is not a single 'A' student in the juvenile hall. The more we put into education, the more we put into achievement for our young people, the more we will see problems resolved and a country that is full of excellence and hope instead of despair."

She also failed in an effort to alter a bill limiting Congress' ability to impose mandates on states without providing funds to help them com-

CALIFORNIA 16
Santa Clara County

Fast-growing Santa Clara County, at the southern end of San Francisco Bay, gained 200,000 residents in the 1980s and now sprawls across four congressional districts.

The 16th, however, is now the main San Jose district, containing about two-thirds of the county's land and more than one-third of its 1.5 million residents. Much of the district consists of most of San Jose, which, with 782,000 residents in 1990, ranked as the nation's 11th-largest city. Only Los Angeles and San Diego are larger in California.

The 16th takes in the heart of San Jose, including the recently renovated downtown civic center and a large urban campus of California State University that is still known locally as San Jose State.

San Jose dates to 1777, when the Spanish founded it as a way station between the missions of San Francisco and Monterey. It also served briefly as the capital in the early days after California's annexation by the United States. However, it languished in the shadow of San Francisco and Oakland. But the migration of industry southward from Oakland (45 miles to the north) and from the San Francisco peninsula has gradually reoriented San Jose to the north and away from the agricultural valleys to the south, east and west.

Now, even as growth has leveled off in other parts of the Bay Area, San Jose has continued to grow, expanding by nearly one-fourth just in the 1980s. Some of the new residents were drawn by jobs in the high-tech sector. Per capita income in the city itself nearly doubled in the 1980s and was about $4,000 higher than the statewide average in 1991.

A combination of this growth, the success of such Silicon Valley companies as Hewlett-Packard and Intel, and the lack of physical space in the Santa Clara Valley, have led to a housing crunch in the San Jose area. To help make the area more accessible, Congress in 1996 approved money to extend the Tasman Light Rail system through the 16th district from the city of Santa Clara to Mountain View. With the growth have come strain and some resistance. In 1992, local voters defeated a bond issue for a baseball stadium that was supposed to lure the Giants from San Francisco.

Leaving the city from the south, Highway 101 winds through the scenic countryside, vineyards and wineries of the Santa Clara Valley, with tasting rooms lining the road around Morgan Hill and San Martin. At the district's southern edge lies Gilroy, a farm town famous for its annual garlic festival.

The 16th is Northern California's most Hispanic district; Hispanics making up 37 percent of the population. Twenty percent of its residents are Asian. The presence of recent immigrants is reflected in the low number of votes cast relative to the population.

When 32-year veteran Democratic Rep. Don Edwards announced his retirement in 1994, the nomination went to Lofgren, a former aide and community activist.

Both Lofgren and Bill Clinton got more than 60 percent of the votes cast in 1996.

1990 Population: 571,551. White 315,049 (55%), Black 29,659 (5%), Other 226,843 (40%). Hispanic origin 210,463 (37%). 18 and over 409,054 (72%), 62 and over 49,967 (9%). Median age: 29.

ply. Lofgren proposed barring states from passing unfunded mandates on to local governments. Her amendment lost by a wide margin.

Lofgren supports abortion rights, and during 1995 debate on a bill to ban a particular abortion technique that opponents call "partial birth" abortion, she countered those portraying the procedure as grisly and cruel. Lofgren told a story of a couple who chose that method of abortion after learning that the brain of the fetus had developed outside the skull. "Privately, many members might agree that if it was their wife or daughter, they might make the same decision," she said.

And although Lofgren will sometimes credit Republicans for identifying problems that merit attention, she can be unstinting in criticizing their legislative tactics. Arguing her point of view, Lofgren likes to cite her experiences in local government, as she did when opposing the GOP's effort to effect speedy passage of a balanced-budget constitutional amendment early in the 104th. "You know, as a member of the Board of Supervisors in Santa Clara County, I am mindful we spend more time analyzing the impact of a use permit for a golf course than this body has spent analyzing the impact of this amendment," she said.

Lofgren also felt Republicans were going too far too fast when they pushed for a constitutional amendment to prevent flag desecration. "Real conservatives do not try to amend the Constitution three times in six months," she said, citing GOP efforts to pass a term limits constitutional amendment as well as the balanced-budget and flag-desecration proposals.

Lofgren also serves on the Science Committee, where partisan flare-ups were common in the 104th. She generally supported White House efforts to promote government support of businesses developing new technologies, and she favored funding for research on global warming, not a popular endeavor in the GOP.

At Home: If 1992 was the Year of the Woman, then 1994 was the Year of the Mom, at least for Lofgren.

She easily defeated Republican Lyle J. Smith after an upset victory in the Democratic primary over former San Jose Mayor Tom McEnery. Lofgren succeeded veteran liberal Democrat Don Edwards, who retired after 32 years in the House.

In the primary, Lofgren benefited from an uproar that ensued when state election officials barred her from describing herself as "County Supervisor/mother" on the ballot.

Acting Secretary of State Tony Miller said that California law forbids candidate descriptions based on a status, such as motherhood or fatherhood, rather than an occupation. Lofgren declared the law emblematic of the way unpaid work by women is not properly appreciated by society. The ensuing flap drew national attention to Lofgren's candidacy, helping create momentum that propelled her past McEnery.

It also provided Lofgren with the perfect framework for discussing some of her key issues: reducing violent crime in neighborhoods and increasing federal support for programs that help families and children.

Lofgren, who launched her campaign while standing on a kitchen breadbox in the living room of her house in San Jose, stressed her middle-class roots as the daughter of a truck driver and a secretary and her concerns as a mother about violence in the schools and streets. She also successfully cast McEnery as a millionaire politician rooted in the downtown business community.

It was a strategy that helped dramatize the relatively undramatic issue differences between Lofgren and McEnery, both of whom were fairly moderate Democrats, not liberals in the Edwards mold. Lofgren benefited from a high turnout among women, who were drawn to the polls on primary day by the statewide candidacies of Kathleen Brown for governor and Dianne Feinstein for senator.

Lofgren's first job after graduating from Stanford University was in Edwards' Washington office. She returned to California to attend law school, continuing to work for Edwards in his district office, and later served as executive director of Community Housing Developers, a nonprofit organization involved in creating low-income housing. In her private law practice, she specialized in immigration law.

First elected to the Santa Clara County Board of Supervisors in 1980, Lofgren worked to maintain mental health services and health care for poor residents during a time of stress on the county budget. Often her efforts placed her in conflict with McEnery, who as mayor was responsible for the redevelopment of downtown San Jose, including the construction of the McEnery Convention Center. Lofgren frequently argued that the downtown redevelopment funds would have been better spent on education and human services, a theme that carried over into her House campaign. Lofgren's prescription for dealing with violent crime was to emphasize prevention rather than punishment, through programs aimed at helping children and their families.

In 1984, Lofgren was a key supporter of Measure A, which established a half-cent sales tax to finance highway improvements in Santa Clara County. She also held seats on numerous transportation boards and chaired a committee studying the expansion of the Bay Area Rapid Transit system to the South Bay.

In 1996, Lofgren's first House re-election campaign was a breeze, as she took two-thirds of the vote

HOUSE ELECTIONS

1996 General		
Zoe Lofgren (D)	94,020	(66%)
Chuck Wojslaw (R)	43,197	(30%)
David R. Bonino (LIBERT)	4,124	(3%)
Abaan Abu-Shumays (NL)	1,866	(1%)
1994 General		
Zoe Lofgren (D)	74,935	(65%)
Lyle J. Smith (R)	40,409	(35%)

CAMPAIGN FINANCE

	Receipts	Receipts from PACs	Expend-itures
1996			
Lofgren (D)	$256,457	$111,253 (43%)	$191,393
Wojslaw (R)	$86,332	$516 (1%)	$77,796
1994			
Lofgren (D)	$683,670	$161,044 (24%)	$646,764

DISTRICT VOTE FOR PRESIDENT

	1996		1992
D	91,786 (61%)	**D**	86,418 (52%)
R	43,257 (29%)	**R**	44,693 (27%)
I	9,659 (6%)	**I**	33,882 (21%)

KEY VOTES

1997	
Ban "partial-birth" abortions	N
1996	
Approve farm bill	N
Deny public education to illegal immigrants	N
Repeal ban on certain assault-style weapons	N
Increase minimum wage	Y
Freeze defense spending	Y
Approve welfare overhaul	N
1995	
Approve balanced-budget constitutional amendment	N
Relax Clean Water Act regulations	N
Oppose limits on environmental regulations	Y
Reduce projected Medicare spending	N
Approve GOP budget with tax and spending cuts	N

VOTING STUDIES

	Presidential Support		Party Unity		Conservative Coalition	
Year	**S**	**O**	**S**	**O**	**S**	**O**
1996	77	23	91	9	16	84
1995	82	14	89	7	19	77

INTEREST GROUP RATINGS

Year	ADA	AFL-CIO	CCUS	ACU
1996	85	n/a	31	5
1995	95	100	21	8

17 Sam Farr (D)

Of Carmel — Elected 1993; 2nd full term

Biographical Information
Born: July 4, 1941, San Francisco, Calif.
Education: Willamette U., B.S. 1963.
Occupation: State legislative aide.
Family: Wife, Shary Baldwin; one child.
Religion: Episcopalian.
Political Career: Monterey County Board of Supervisors, 1975-81; Calif. Assembly, 1981-93.
Capitol Office: 1117 Longworth Bldg. 20515; 225-2861.

Committees
Agriculture
Forestry, Resource Conservation & Research; Livestock, Dairy & Poultry
Resources
Fisheries Conservation, Wildlife & Oceans; Water & Power

In Washington: Farr was a solid vote for the Clinton administration during the 104th Congress, when much of the White House's legislative strategy was being shaped by the man Farr succeeded in the 17th, Leon E. Panetta.

Panetta left Congress in 1993 to become director of the Office of Management and Budget for President Clinton and then moved into the post of White House Chief of Staff.

Joining the 103rd Congress after winning a 1993 special election, Farr got just a taste of life in the majority before voters in 1994 put Republicans in charge on the Hill. Farr took issue with much of the new majority's agenda, opposing GOP efforts to ease environmental regulations, to deny certain federal benefits to immigrants and to restrict access to abortions.

Farr had some time in the spotlight in the 104th as sponsor of the measure that House Democrats pushed to overhaul the campaign finance system. His measure would have established a voluntary spending limit on House candidates of $600,000 per two-year election cycle. In return for agreeing to the limit, candidates would get deep discounts on broadcast advertising and postage rates. His measure also would have banned so-called soft money — contributions that can be made in any amount to political parties as long as the money is not designated to any certain campaign. "The trend is for more money to be spent, not less," Farr said. "If we end the money chase, our elections will focus more on issues and on policy debates and less on the issue of collecting dollars."

Although both parties professed that the campaign finance system should be changed, neither Farr's bill nor a Republican measure could muster a majority when the House considered them in July 1996. The Democratic bill lost, 177-243, garnering slightly more support than the Republican alternative, which was defeated 162-259.

Farr complained that the Republican bill required candidates to raise a majority of their campaign funds from within their district (a disadvantage for the many Democrats who come from poorer districts). And he criticized Republicans for not proposing to limit the amount of money candidates could spend on their campaigns. "There was not reform in their reform bill," Farr said of the GOP plan. "Democrats realized it, and more importantly, Republicans realized it."

The 17th includes the scenic coastal Monterey Peninsula as well as the town of Salinas, a marketing center for local crops, which include such truck-farm commodities as avocados and artichokes. Farr looks out for farming interests in the 17th from his seat on the Agriculture Committee.

On that panel in the 104th, Farr cast a critical eye on the GOP's "Freedom to Farm" bill, which aimed to phase out most New Deal-era crop subsidies, replacing them with a system of fixed, but declining, payments that farmers would receive over seven years regardless of market prices or their planting decisions.

Farr said he embraced the concept of bringing farm policy more in line with free-market principles and giving farmers greater flexibility in deciding what to plant. He told the House that farmers in his district produce over $2.5 billion worth of fresh fruits, vegetables and horticultural crops without any federal price supports. "They have succeeded by embracing the full benefits, and potential risks, of the market. They are the models for American agriculture."

But when the House voted on the measure in February 1996, Farr called the bill "broken" because it failed adequately to address issues of "conservation, research, rural development and market promotion," which he said "are all crucial to future success and sustainability of market driven agriculture."

Farr did not feel that the House version of "Freedom to Farm" addressed a problem that he sees in his district: the loss of farmland to urban sprawl. He was one of only two House Democrats to vote against an amendment to the farm bill that would have authorized funding for the Conservation Reserve Program, which pays farmers to idle environmentally sensitive land, and for wetland protection.

CALIFORNIA 17
Monterey and San Benito counties

The 17th was redrawn and renumbered in 1992. But the district changed little under the new map, which removed the less-populated half of Santa Cruz County at the northern end and snipped off the district's old appendix (a coastal section of San Luis Obispo County) at the Southern end. In Santa Cruz County, the 17th keeps all the significant population centers, including the namesake city (population 50,000), the University of California at Santa Cruz and several sizable seaside communities such as Soquel, Aptos and Capitola.

Also intact within the new district are Monterey and San Benito counties. San Benito, with about 37,000 people, is ranching country and swings little weight in district elections. Santa Cruz and Monterey counties had cast about 80 percent of the vote in the old 16th; they cast about 93 percent in the 17th in 1996.

The district includes Monterey Peninsula with its fabulous 17-mile drive along Highway 1, legendary golf courses and chic colonies such as Carmel, where Clint Eastwood was mayor for a time. The city of Monterey itself (population 32,000) remains a charming place with a fishing fleet and a small canning industry. Another dominant element on the map is the vast military preserve at Fort Ord, which was ordered closed in 1994.

Congress agreed to transfer the base from the Army to the state's university system. The California State University at Monterey Bay opened in 1995 and has about 1,400 students. It includes a program that makes use of the new Monterey Bay National Marine Sanctuary to study the marine environment of California's central coast. Farther down coastal Highway 1 is Big Sur, yet another retreat for artists and the affluent.

Despite these magnets for tourists and retirees, the central enterprise in the 17th remains agriculture, which has sustained the area for centuries. The inland area's capital is Salinas (population 109,000), the county seat of Monterey County and a marketing center for the avocados, artichokes and other trademark truck-farm crops. This is also the focal point for Hispanics, who constitute nearly one-third of the district's population. Other farming centers in the district include Watsonville, Hollister and King City.

Democratic Rep. Leon E. Panetta, who resigned in 1993 to join the Clinton administration, had swept all the counties in fair political weather and foul. But with Panetta gone, the district was more competitive in the June 1993 special election that chose Farr as his successor. And though Democrats are a majority among the registered voters, the district has been a question mark in statewide voting.

In 1992, Democratic Senate nominee Barbara Boxer lost in San Benito County and had only a plurality in Monterey County; she carried the 17th by piling up a big vote in Santa Cruz County. Bill Clinton managed a majority districtwide in both of his presidential elections, mainly by dominating in Santa Cruz County.

1990 Population: 570,981. White 396,687 (69%), Black 25,342 (4%), Other 148,952 (26%). Hispanic origin 180,572 (32%).18 and over 419,952 (74%), 62 and over 71,674 (13%). Median age: 31.

He cast that lonely dissenting vote because the Conservation Reserve amendment did not include a program to help states protect farmland from urbanization pressures — a provision that was part of the Senate version of the farm bill. "One of my biggest concerns in America is the erosion of good, prime, agriculture land," Farr told the House. "America seems to be doing urban sprawl better than it can do agriculture policy."

But during conference negotiations on the farm bill, conferees adopted the Senate's $35 million initiative to buy easements on farmland threatened by development. Farr then voted in March 1996 for the final version of the farm bill.

Farr is a consistent supporter of environmental protections, voting against Republican efforts to ease clean water regulations and to limit the regulatory authority of the Environmental Protection Agency (EPA). He has a seat on the Resources Committee, where he sits on the Water and Power Subcommittee and on the Fisheries Conservation, Wildlife and Oceans Subcommittee.

His district boasts spectacular Pacific Ocean views, and in 1995, he pushed to retain a moratorium on offshore oil drilling along the California coast. He received a 100 percent rating from the League of Conservation Voters in 1996.

When the House in November 1995 considered the final version of a GOP-backed appropriations bill that included funding for the EPA, Farr objected, saying it would hurt the environment by cutting EPA's budget by more than $1.5 billion. "In my coastal district, less money will be given to help local communities keep the Monterey Bay clean and healthy," Farr said.

The 17th District was dealt a blow in 1994 when the Army's Fort Ord was ordered to be closed. Farr worked hard in the 104th to make the transition of the military base to civilian a smooth one, by helping secure $51 million in defense spending to be used to open the California State University Monterey Bay campus at the old base. The base is slated to house a new Defense Department Finance Center, a veterans clinic, and an environmental research center for the University of California.

Farr said that the new campus and research center would stimulate economic growth and enable the Monterey Bay region to become a center for a marine and environmental science.

A former Peace Corps volunteer, Farr protested Republican efforts to cut or scale back funding for Clinton's national service program, called AmeriCorps. "The AmeriCorps is a great value to this country," Farr told the House. "AmeriCorps workers are involved in every aspect of our communities, teaching in schools, feeding the homeless and counseling troubled youth."

Farr did take issue with one aspect of Clinton's record, however: the president's ultimate support of a compromise welfare overhaul measure, worked out with congressional Republicans who had pushed the issue throughout the 104th. Farr opposed the final welfare bill, joining 97 other liberal Democrats in doing so.

Farr is a strong supporter of abortion rights. In the 104th, he voted to allow federal employees' health care plans to cover abortion and to permit military personnel to have abortions at overseas hospitals, if they pay for the procedure themselves. He also backed a requirement that states fund Medicaid abortions for poor women in cases of rape or incest or to save the life of the woman. He has opposed conservatives' efforts to ban a particular abortion technique that opponents call "partial birth" abortion.

At Home: Farr first won the 17th in a 1993 special election to replace Panetta, a contest in which he got strong assistance from the Clinton White House.

In the initial round of voting in the April 1993 special election, Farr got 26 percent in a field of more than two dozen candidates. In the June runoff, he beat back his Republican opponent — along with three minor-party candidates and two independents — with 54 percent of the vote.

Farr left 10 other Democrats behind in the initial balloting by mastering a turnout technique increasingly important in California House elections: voting by mail. Farr trailed by about 1,600 votes at the polls on Election Day, but he pulled well ahead when officials tallied up 10,600 absentee ballots cast for him.

In the runoff, Farr's Republican opponent was Pebble Beach lawyer Bill McCampbell, who had lost badly to Panetta in 1992. McCampbell had not been the GOP's first choice to contest the vacant seat, but he defeated nine rivals in the initial GOP balloting to win a shot at Farr.

Farr, a 12-year veteran of the California Assembly, was a strong candidate in a district already heavily Democratic. Moreover, the area Farr represented in the California Assembly included more than half the territory within the 17th.

Farr hammered McCampbell for working as a lobbyist for Transkei, a black South African homeland — labeling him "pro-apartheid" in campaign literature. McCampbell slapped Farr with a $10 million defamation and libel suit. In the end, Farr's 54 percent tally put him 13 points ahead of McCampbell.

McCampbell was back in 1994, and the year's strong Republican tide was felt even in the 17th, as Farr slipped to 52 percent and McCampbell improved to 44 percent; a Green Party candidate took 3 percent.

In 1996, though, Farr moved up into the comfort zone, running more than 20 percentage points ahead of his GOP challenger.

HOUSE ELECTIONS

1996 General		
Sam Farr (D)	115,116	(59%)
Jess Brown (R)	73,856	(38%)
John H. Black (NL)	6,573	(3%)
1996 Primary		
Sam Farr (D)	52,481	(88%)
Art Dunn (D)	6,032	(10%)
Robert Wigod (D)	1,304	(2%)
1994 General		
Sam Farr (D)	87,222	(52%)
Bill McCampbell (R)	74,380	(44%)
E. Craig Coffin (GREEN)	5,591	(3%)

Previous Winning Percentages: **1993**† (54%)

† Special election

CAMPAIGN FINANCE

	Receipts	Receipts from PACs	Expend-itures
1996			
Farr (D)	$619,270	$298,266 (48%)	$563,235
Brown (R)	$450,424	$62,345 (14%)	$455,239
1994			
Farr (D)	$424,071	$242,204 (57%)	$387,872
McCampbell (R)	$443,704	$14 (0%)	$451,490

DISTRICT VOTE FOR PRESIDENT

1996	1992
D 109,941 (55%)	**D** 111,937 (53%)
R 64,178 (32%)	**R** 57,990 (27%)
I 12,795 (6%)	**I** 42,317 (20%)

KEY VOTES

1997	
Ban "partial birth" abortions	N
1996	
Approve farm bill	N
Deny public education to illegal immigrants	N
Repeal ban on certain assault-style weapons	N
Increase minimum wage	Y
Freeze defense spending	Y
Approve welfare overhaul	N
1995	
Approve balanced-budget constitutional amendment	N
Relax Clean Water Act regulations	N
Oppose limits on environmental regulations	Y
Reduce projected Medicare spending	N
Approve GOP budget with tax and spending cuts	N

VOTING STUDIES

	Presidential Support		Party Unity		Conservative Coalition	
Year	**S**	**O**	**S**	**O**	**S**	**O**
1996	84	16	92	5	27	73
1995	84	13	93	6	20	79
1994	81	15	94	1	11	78
1993	76††	22††	91††	3††	15††	83††

INTEREST GROUP RATINGS

Year	ADA	AFL-CIO	CCUS	ACU
1996	90	n/a	31	0
1995	90	100	17	4
1994	90	88	45	0
1993	93††	83††	29††	7††

†† Not eligible for all recorded votes.

18 Gary A. Condit (D)

Of Ceres — Elected 1989; 4th full term

Biographical Information

Born: April 21, 1948, Salina, Okla.

Education: California State U., Stanislaus, B.A. 1972.

Occupation: Public official.

Family: Wife, Carolyn Berry; two children.

Religion: Baptist.

Political Career: Ceres City Council, 1972-76, mayor, 1974-76; Stanislaus County Board of Supervisors, 1976-82, chairman, 1980; Calif. Assembly, 1983-89.

Capitol Office: 2245 Rayburn Bldg. 20515; 225-6131.

Committees

Agriculture

Livestock, Dairy & Poultry; Risk Management & Specialty Crops (ranking)

Government Reform & Oversight

National Economic Growth, Natural Resources & Regulatory Affairs; National Security, International Affairs & Criminal Justice

In Washington: Condit took a lead role during the 104th Congress in organizing and positioning the "blue dog" coalition on a range of high-profile issues. A group of two dozen or so center-right House Democrats, the Blue Dogs have staked out a middle ground on such thorny matters as balancing the budget, overhauling welfare and restraining Medicare costs. They say their middle-of-the-road approach is what most American voters want, and that voters are weary of partisan bickering.

"Members of the Coalition and others who share our political point of view are going to do very well [in the general election] throughout the country," Condit said in the summer of 1996. "We are probably right on point in terms of the issues the American public"cares about.

Condit himself is well to the right of his party on fiscal, regulatory reform and environmental issues; he was one of five Democrats to vote with Republicans on 94 percent of the "Contract with America" agenda in 1995.

But he moves back in the Democratic direction on several other issues: He backs abortion rights in most cases and voted in 1996 for a minimum wage increase and against a GOP effort to repeal the ban on semiautomatic assault-style weapons.

Still, Condit's relationship with his party has seen some turbulence. Early in the 104th, when House and Senate conferees met to negotiate final changes on a bill prohibiting unfunded federal mandates — legislation Condit had helped write — Minority Leader Richard A. Gephardt did not put him on the conference committee. Condit got a seat at the table anyway — a Republican seat — compliments of Speaker Newt Gingrich.

"I would have preferred for Mr. Gephardt to let me on," said Condit, adding that while most Democrats supported the bill when it passed the House, Gephardt named only bill opponents to the conference. Gephardt aides said he followed the usual practice, based on seniority, for appointing conferees, which in this case meant the two senior Democrats on the Government Reform and Oversight panel got the minority seats on the conference — even though both had opposed the bill.

Condit was most visible in the 104th working with the blue dogs to craft a seven-year balanced budget proposal. Their plan shunned the GOP's call for tax cuts, imposed more modest restraints on anticipated spending for Medicare and Medicaid and spared other programs the GOP had targeted for big cuts or outright elimination.

In October 1995, the blue dogs' plan was rejected, 72-356. The group tried again in April 1996 and fared somewhat better, losing 130-295 and drawing commendation from many quarters for putting forward a sensible compromise between the Republicans and the White House.

At the start of the 105th, the Blue Dogs were back, offering a five-year budget blueprint similar to their earlier proposals. It called for delaying tax cuts until federal outlays balance with revenues and it included a downward adjustment in the Consumer Price Index (CPI). Some analysts say the CPI overstates the inflation rate; and it is clear that a downward adjustment would save the government billions of dollars in cost-of-living-adjustment payouts to recipients of Social Security and other entitlements. But because a CPI adjustment would mean smaller increases in Social Security checks, it is a highly controversial, politically dangerous proposal.

Yet in May 1997 when the White House and congressional Republicans reached a budget agreement that balanced tax cuts with spending reductions, it proved satisfactory to most House members, including Condit.

In working on budget issues, Condit has developed a friendship with GOP Budget Committee Chairman John Kasich of Ohio. Condit asked Kasich to appear at a California fundraiser for him in March 1997, and Kasich agreed. But objections from GOP partisans squelched the event, prompting Condit to complain to the San Francisco Chronicle that Kasich was being "vilified by narrow-minded zealots . . . [who] believe the sun rises and sets according to partisan affiliation."

Given the attention paid to budget issues, it surprises some to learn that Condit's major com-

CALIFORNIA 18
Central Valley — Modesto; Merced

Founded in 1870, Modesto took nine decades to reach a population of about 37,000. In the decade that followed, its population nearly doubled. In the 1970s, its population rose by more than one-half to exceed 100,000. By 1990, it had risen by more than one-half again, nearing 165,000 — a total growth of more than 300 percent in 30 years.

Part of this expansion was spurred by businesses fleeing the congestion and land prices of California's coastal cities. Modesto, the Stanislaus County seat, lies near the midpoint of the state on the north bank of the Tuolumne River. Highway 99 passes through, and Interstate 5, the only other major artery through the Central Valley, passes a few miles to the west.

But most of the growth came from growing things — the Valley's phenomenally successful agricultural industry. Modesto bottles, cans, packs and processes the extraordinary variety of fruits, vegetables, grains, fibers and wines produced in the Valley. The Gallo winery here is responsible for about one-fourth of the domestic wine market.

Booming Modesto helped drive the Stanislaus County population from 266,000 to 370,000 in the 1980s, surpassing the population of better-known counties such as Monterey and Santa Barbara. In essence, the 18th consists of Stanislaus and Merced counties, where the city of Merced (56,000) has attracted large numbers of Southeast Asian immigrants and grew by 20,000 in the 1980s. Stanislaus and Merced counties cast roughly 70 percent and 25 percent of the 18th District vote, respectively.

The 18th also takes in the southwest corners of San Joaquin County (the city of Ripon) and Madera County (stopping short of Chowchilla). It also slices off the northeastern tip of Fresno County. But these are sparsely populated areas; all three together cast less than 5 percent of the district vote for president.

Farmers prosper or fail on the weather, the cost of water and the market price. The government is responsible for two out of three, although under the 1996 farm bill, the government will increasingly be less involved in setting the market price. Even so, farm districts need a member's attention, and this one has been accustomed to getting it from savvy insider Democrats.

Politically, the 18th resembles the district that elected Tony Coelho to six terms beginning in 1978 and turned to Condit when Coelho resigned in 1989. Coelho's wider ambitions were often a distraction; Condit seems a closer fit.

In statewide and national elections, the 18th is highly competitive. It voted Republican for president throughout the 1980s. Bill Clinton struggled here, barely winning the district in 1996, as he beat Bob Dole by just over 1,300 votes.

Though many Valley residents are Hispanic and growing numbers are Asian (26 and 6 percent, respectively, in the 18th), they have yet to exercise commensurate influence in the voting booths.

1990 Population: 571,393. White 432,658 (76%), Black 16,206 (3%), Other 122,529 (21%). Hispanic origin 148,329 (26%). 18 and over 391,176 (68%), 62 and over 70,670 (12%). Median age: 30.

mittee focus in Congress is actually on the Agriculture Committee, where he serves in the 105th as ranking member on the Risk Management and Specialty Crops Subcommittee. Agribusiness is the economic focus of the 18th, and for all his focus on restraining government spending to balance the budget, Condit is not averse to seeing Uncle Sam help district farmers.

When the GOP's "Freedom to Farm" bill overhauling federal agriculture programs was in conference negotiations in early 1996, Condit offered an amendment to cap annual funding for the Market Promotion Program (MPP) at the House's $100 million level, rather than the Senate's $70 million; the final figure was set at $90 million. The program, which helps promote U.S. agricultural products overseas, is a favorite target of "deficit hawks," who call it a boondoggle for large corporations and trade associations that subsidizes overseas television and print advertising campaigns they should pay for themselves. But program supporters such as Condit say it has helped boost sales of U.S. food products overseas.

Condit opposed an amendment to the fiscal 1996 agriculture spending bill that would have eliminated $110 million for the MPP. "By eliminating the Market Promotion Program, Congress will be sending a message to Americans and American business that we can do without $1.4 billion in exports generated by this important program," Condit told the House.

After some hesitation, Condit wound up voting for the farm bill, the comprehensive overhaul legislation that phased out most New Deal-era crop subsidies, replacing them with a system of fixed, but declining, payments that farmers would receive over seven years regardless of market prices or their planting decisions.

Condit's perspective on environmental issues is shaped by his strong belief in property owners' rights. He backed a Republican measure, which passed the House in March 1995, that would have greatly expanded the Constitution's guarantee of "just compensation" for landowners. The measure would have allowed landowners to demand compensation when federal enforcement of certain environmental laws restricted property owners' use of their land, thus diminishing its value.

"Through its ability to regulate, the government has increasingly tended to 'take' the uses and benefits of a property rather than condemn it and pay its owner fair market value as is required by the Fifth Amendment," Condit said.

As a member of the Government Reform and Oversight Committee, Condit in early 1997 joined with his Democratic colleagues in criticizing the scope of Chairman Dan Burton's investigation into questionable campaign fundraising practices during the 1996 elections. The Democrats complained that Burton, an Indiana Republican, was only probing President Clinton's fundraising, and they called on him to widen the inquiry to include congressional fundraising practices, which would mirror a similar investigation in the Senate.

During a March 1997 debate on funding the committee's investigation, Condit played up the fact that Burton was seeking access to more than three times the funding of the Senate investigation to cover less ground.

"This is confusing to the American people," Condit said. "They [Senate investigators] are spending [just] $4 million to do a bigger and broader, more encompassing investigation than what we are considering here in the House."

At Home: After the previous occupant of this district, Democratic Whip Tony Coelho, resigned from the House amid questions about his personal finances, Condit, a popular state legislator, was a logical choice for district Democrats and an easy winner in a September 1989 special election.

Candidates rarely have the best wishes of their political adversaries when they seek higher office. However, Democratic state Assembly Speaker Willie L. Brown Jr. was glad to see Condit go. Condit was a member of the "Gang of Five," a group of moderate-to-conservative Assembly Democrats who bridled at the liberal Brown's ironhanded rule. In May 1988, the five launched an effort to remove Brown as Speaker, but the move failed.

Brown's retaliation — Condit lost his leadership position and choice committee assignments — appeared to short-circuit Condit's political rise. An Oklahoma native and the son of a Baptist preacher, Condit was first elected to local office in his conservative, farm-oriented home base at age 24, and he served six years on the Stanislaus County Board of Supervisors before his 1982 election to the Assembly. By the end of his first term, Condit was named assistant Assembly majority leader; two years later, he became chairman of the Government Organization Committee.

There were seven other contenders in the open-ballot, all-party special election when Coelho's seat opened up in 1989. But Condit's hold on Democrats was strengthened by support from Coelho, who remained locally popular despite his ethics problems. Condit's main rival was Clare Berryhill, one of three Republicans on the ballot. A district farmer, former state legislator and a one-time director of the state Food and Agriculture Department, Berryhill tried to appeal to the district's farm constituency. But Condit had little to worry about. He defeated Berryhill by 57 percent to 35 percent, and since then has won re-election with ease.

HOUSE ELECTIONS

1996 General		
Gary A. Condit (D)	108,827	(66%)
Bill Conrad (R)	52,695	(32%)
James B. Morzella (LIBERT)	2,233	(1%)
Page Roth Riskin (NL)	1,831	(1%)
1994 General		
Gary A. Condit (D)	91,105	(66%)
Tom Carter (R)	44,046	(32%)
James B. Morzella (LIBERT)	3,901	(3%)

Previous Winning Percentages: 1992 (85%) **1990** (66%) **1989**† (57%)

† Special election

CAMPAIGN FINANCE

	Receipts	Receipts from PACs	Expend-itures
1996			
Condit (D)	$639,682	$334,338 (52%)	$678,001
Conrad (R)	$75,462	$7,466 (*%)	$75,271
1994			
Condit (D)	$413,208	$166,840 (40%)	$387,494

DISTRICT VOTE FOR PRESIDENT

	1996		1992
D	77,560 (46%)	**D**	74,357 (41%)
R	76,217 (45%)	**R**	67,898 (37%)
I	12,161 (7%)	**I**	39,645 (22%)

KEY VOTES

1997	
Ban "partial birth" abortions	Y
1996	
Approve farm bill	Y
Deny public education to illegal immigrants	Y
Repeal ban on certain assault-style weapons	N
Increase minimum wage	Y
Freeze defense spending	Y
Approve welfare overhaul	Y
1995	
Approve balanced-budget constitutional amendment	Y
Relax Clean Water Act regulations	Y
Oppose limits on environmental regulations	N
Reduce projected Medicare spending	N
Approve GOP budget with tax and spending cuts	N

VOTING STUDIES

	Presidential Support		Party Unity		Conservative Coalition	
Year	S	O	S	O	S	O
1996	53	47	52	48	82	18
1995	49	51	45	52	77	20
1994	63	32	58	39	64	33
1993	50	49	61	36	57	43
1992	38	62	61	36	58	42
1991	36	61	62	33	73	27

INTEREST GROUP RATINGS

Year	ADA	AFL-CIO	CCUS	ACU
1996	35	n/a	63	70
1995	40	67	79	60
1994	45	67	92	38
1993	60	67	55	50
1992	55	83	75	48
1991	60	92	40	58

19 George P. Radanovich (R)

Of Mariposa — Elected 1994, 2nd term

Biographical Information
Born: June 20, 1955, Mariposa, Calif.
Education: California State Polytechnic U., B.S. 1978.
Occupation: Vintner; bank manager; carpenter.
Family: Wife, Ethie Weaver.
Religion: Roman Catholic.
Political Career: Mariposa County Board of Supervisors, 1989-92, chairman, 1991; sought Republican nomination for U.S. House, 1992.
Capitol Office: 213 Cannon Bldg. 20515; 225-4540.

Committees
Budget
Resources
Forests & Forest Health; National Parks & Public Lands; Water & Power

In Washington: A small-business entrepreneur and local officeholder when he launched his first House bid, Radanovich told voters he wanted to reduce regulations and shift authority to the state and local levels. In Congress, he preaches that gospel from his seats on two committees dealing with issues at the heart of the "Republican Revolution" — Budget and Resources.

Radanovich was elected president of the Class of 1994 for the second session of the 104th Congress. In that capacity, he was a high-profile defender of his party's conservative platform, arguing strenuously for a balanced budget. Radanovich took to holding up a misshapen chair as a symbol of how he saw society as having gone out of whack. According to his model, one leg, representing government, had grown too large, threatening the balance of the family, business and religious/civic "legs."

One of Radanovich's aphorisms is that "bureaucracies have little respect for private property." Environmental laws such as the Endangered Species Act are a special Radanovich target; he argues that they hamper farmers and ranchers in California from making a living. In a speech on the House floor in March 1995, Radanovich painted this mocking picture: "There is a million dollars spent on discussing the eating disorders of pigeons. I will tell you, if . . . I was a pigeon, and had an endangered species person following me around day to day, watching everything I did, I would have an eating disorder, too." Radanovich added that he was not opposed to scientific research, but he feels the central government is too removed from the everyday needs of people to spend their tax dollars wisely.

This belief makes Radanovich a big booster of block grants, which are funds transferred from Washington to states and localities without tight strictures as to how the money should be spent. "What I hope what we are doing by block granting is getting those funds into the district and placing them into the proper hands for people to take care of the problem locally." He has been an ardent supporter of GOP-led efforts to attack "unfunded mandates" — federal requirements imposed on states without provision for funds to implement them.

Radanovich failed in a 1996 attempt to end funding for the Legal Services Corp., which provides legal counsel to the poor. He offered an amendment that would have transferred $109 million in funds from the agency to drug enforcement — a move that opponent Alan B. Mollohan, D-W.Va., termed "clever," but which failed nonetheless, 169-254.

A reliable Republican vote, Radanovich also chafes at what he sees as federal encroachment on personal liberties. "There is no better example of federal mandates being inconsistent with the Constitution than that of federal statutes which require that states pass laws requiring the use of motorcycle helmets or face reduced highway funding," Radanovich said in September 1995, shortly before those "mandates" were abolished.

On the Budget Committee, Radanovich has espoused "supply-side" theories for promoting economic growth. "If you want to raise revenue, you have got to cut taxes. You cannot raise revenue by raising taxes. . . . That is the big lesson we have learned over the last four years, and . . . that is what this new majority is trying to implement in their tax cuts." He said in 1995 that "the resolve for a balanced budget would not be there without the freshman class," and he argued against raising the federal debt ceiling until a budget-balancing plan was in place. His home county of Mariposa was the only one in the country to become an official economic disaster area because of the government shutdowns of 1995-96, which closed Yosemite National Park. But Radanovich stuck to his guns on the underlying fiscal arguments that had led to the shutdown.

On the Resources Committee, he monitors water-supply issues of concern to his district's agricultural interests. He has supported selling the Central Valley Project, a vital source of water, to the state's farmers. He has also backed stricter regulation of poultry producers who label frozen

CALIFORNIA 19
Central Valley — Fresno; Madera

At its core, the 19th District resembles the old 18th. They have in common all of Madera County (including the cities of Madera and Chowchilla) and most of the city of Fresno.

The district now includes Mariposa County, the eastern half of rural Fresno County and the northern third of Tulare County. Missing is downtown Fresno but included is all of the city north of Belmont Avenue and all parts east of Chestnut Avenue. It includes the California State University campus and its 17,000 students.

The old 18th did not include much more of Fresno County than the city itself, which forms the knot in what resembles a bow tie. The rest of the county unfurls in either direction, approaching San Benito Mountain on the west and embracing Kings Canyon National Park on the east. In between lie thousands of square miles of San Joaquin Valley desert, crisscrossed by irrigation canals and patterned with farms, groves, vineyards and ranches.

Fresno County produces about $3.1 billion in agricultural products a year, more than any other county in the United States.

Fresno is an older agribusiness center, saddled with fearsome summer heat and a workaday image. Despite its civic center, symphony orchestra and 10-block downtown mall, one mid-1980s survey called Fresno the least desirable place to live in America (and a satirical TV miniseries named for the city added insult to injury).

Yet Fresno continues to grow impressively. Its population (354,000) increased by 63 percent in the 1980s. Many of the newest arrivals are Central Americans and Southeast Asians who have enlivened and diversified the culture, which had already included a sizable Armenian contingent.

With the addition of Mariposa County, the 19th gained at least a portion of three of the area's major national parks, including Yosemite National Park, contributing to tourism.

Redistricting in 1992 gave the district a more rural tilt. Democratic registration dropped by about 12 percentage points, so that they accounted for about half of all registered voters. The two old districts were different enough to explain why the Democratic incumbent from the old 18th, Richard H. Lehman, lasted only one term after the lines were redrawn. Lehman struggled in 1992 against a political neophyte and then lost by 17 percentage points to Republican Radanovich in 1994.

The 19th gave Bob Dole 52 percent of its votes in 1996, one of his best showings in the state. He carried all four counties that had portions in the district with an outright majority.

1990 Population: 573,043. White 421,138 (73%), Black 18,859 (3%), Other 133,046 (23%). Hispanic origin 135,408 (24%). 18 and over 404,642 (71%), 62 and over 77,591 (14%). Median age: 31.

chicken as fresh.

Armenian-Americans make up one of Radanovich's key constituencies, and he offered an amendment to the fiscal 1997 foreign operations spending bill to trim $3 million in aid to Turkey until Ankara formally acknowledged the Armenian genocide between 1915 and 1923. That proposal was adopted by a vote of 268-153, over the objection of the Clinton administration.

Radanovich drew some notice in June 1995, when he began sending form letters in response to constituent mail, contending that personalized responses were a waste of resources.

At Home: The wines for which California is famous are produced primarily in the valleys of Napa, Sonoma and Santa Clara, but Radanovich's dream was to establish a winery in his native Mariposa County, in the foothills of the Sierra Nevada, where livestock grazing generally takes precedence over farming. He persisted, and Radanovich Winery now ships about 4,000 cases annually of sauvignon blanc, merlot and other wines.

In building his business, the vintner gained first-hand familiarity with the issues of water allocation, farm labor, taxes and regulation. That led him to a seat on the Mariposa County board of supervisors in 1989 and to his first bid for Congress in 1992. He acquitted himself well that year, finishing a close second in the GOP primary to Fresno paper executive Tal L. Cloud, who held Democratic Rep. Richard H. Lehman to 47 percent of the vote in November.

The 19th had become shaky ground for Lehman after the 1992 redistricting, which transferred out the city of Stockton and added largely Republican rural areas. Overall Democratic registration dropped from 59 percent to 47 percent. The district showed its new colors in 1992 by voting for President George Bush and only narrowly giving Lehman a sixth term. Two years later the numbers and Radanovich caught up with him.

In his first campaign, Radanovich was an unknown in Fresno County, the source of nearly three-fourths of the district vote; his base was in Mariposa County, newly added to the 19th and home to only one in 40 district residents.

But in 1994, Cloud chose not to run again, and the recognition Radanovich had built up helped him place first in a three-way GOP primary. Radanovich began the fall campaign as an underdog to Lehman, but the GOP challenger showed a flair for personal campaigning, and he raised enough money (more than $460,000) to be competitive with the well-financed Democratic incumbent (who spent more than $1 million).

Radanovich gained ground in step with the national GOP's upward momentum, and on Election Day he rolled up 57 percent of the vote, sweeping all four counties in the district. Even in Democratic-leaning Fresno County, with its large concentrations of minorities and government employees, he won by more than 16,000 votes.

Like many other GOP candidates in 1994, Radanovich sought to tie the incumbent to President Clinton, citing Lehman's record of backing the White House position on roughly seven votes out of 10 in 1993. Although Lehman's presidential support score was actually slightly below the House Democratic average of 77 percent for that year, Radanovich drove the point home successfully, sometimes holding up a cardboard Clinton figure that he carried with him as a prop.

In campaigning for the class presidency in 1995, Radanovich noted that he would have a safe seat and could spend time helping other Republicans. His confidence proved in 1996 to be well-founded, as he won re-election by the highest margin of any California Republican.

HOUSE ELECTIONS

1996 General		
George P. Radanovich (R)	137,402	(67%)
Paul Barile (D)	58,452	(28%)
Pamela J. Pescosolido (LIBERT)	6,083	(3%)
David P. Adalian Sr. (NL)	4,442	(2%)
1994 General		
George P. Radanovich (R)	104,435	(57%)
Richard H. Lehman (D)	72,912	(40%)
Dolores Comstock (LIBERT)	6,579	(4%)

CAMPAIGN FINANCE

	Receipts	Receipts from PACs	Expend-itures
1996			
Radanovich (R)	$755,455	$250,201 (33%)	$618,220
Barile (D)	$6,511	$1,000 (15%)	$6,509
Pescosolido (LIBERT)	$6,031	0	$5,973
1994			
Radanovich (R)	$469,544	$122,209 (26%)	$468,818
Lehman (D)	$1,079,809	$627,959 (58%)	$1,079,999
Comstock (LIBERT)	$146	0	$47

DISTRICT VOTE FOR PRESIDENT

	1996		1992
D	85,744 (40%)	**D**	85,049 (38%)
R	111,666 (52%)	**R**	97,124 (44%)
I	12,495 (6%)	**I**	41,052 (18%)

KEY VOTES

1997	
Ban "partial birth" abortions	Y
1996	
Approve farm bill	Y
Deny public education to illegal immigrants	?
Repeal ban on certain assault-style weapons	#
Increase minimum wage	N
Freeze defense spending	N
Approve welfare overhaul	Y
1995	
Approve balanced-budget constitutional amendment	Y
Relax Clean Water Act regulations	Y
Oppose limits on environmental regulations	N
Reduce projected Medicare spending	Y
Approve GOP budget with tax and spending cuts	Y

VOTING STUDIES

	Presidential Support		Party Unity		Conservative Coalition	
Year	**S**	**O**	**S**	**O**	**S**	**O**
1996	32	62	87	4	90	2
1995	16	84	95	3	94	3

INTEREST GROUP RATINGS

Year	ADA	AFL-CIO	CCUS	ACU
1996	0	n/a	94	100
1995	0	0	100	96

20 Cal Dooley (D)

Of Visalia — Elected 1990, 4th term

Biographical Information
Born: Jan. 11, 1954, Visalia, Calif.
Education: U. of California, Davis, B.S. 1977; Stanford U., M.A. 1987.
Occupation: Farmer.
Family: Wife, Linda Phillips; two children.
Religion: Protestant.
Political Career: No previous office.
Capitol Office: 1201 Longworth Bldg. 20515; 225-3341.

Committees
Agriculture
Forestry, Resource Conservation & Research (ranking); Livestock, Dairy & Poultry
Resources
Energy & Mineral Resources; Water & Power

In Washington: Dooley's family has farmed in California's Central Valley for four generations, growing everything from alfalfa to cotton to walnuts. Although he is working in Washington, Dooley's eyes remain fixed on his ancestral land from his perches on the Agriculture Committee and the Resources Committee.

On Agriculture during the 104th, Dooley joined the debate on the GOP's attempt to enact a sweeping rewrite of federal farm policy to bring it more in line with free-market principles. Dooley gave rhetorical support to changing the status quo. "The time has come to break our addiction to a farm policy that seduces us with income supports but leads us down a path of reduced opportunities," he said.

Dooley placed a lot of emphasis on helping American farmers expand sales abroad, by funding government-backed export assistance programs and research into international markets, and by supporting NAFTA, GATT and other initiatives to lower trade barriers around the world. "The future success of American agriculture lies in our ability to compete in international markets," he said.

He also sought to ensure that growers would have a sufficient supply of labor, a big concern at harvest time when many hands are needed in a hurry. He supported a measure aimed at providing agricultural companies enough temporary foreign workers to harvest crops.

But when the GOP's "Freedom to Farm" bill came to the House floor in February 1996, Dooley was a "no" vote. The bill phased out most New Deal-era crop subsidies, replacing them with a system of fixed, but declining, payments that farmers would receive over seven years regardless of market prices or their planting decisions.

Dooley objected to that approach, arguing that farmers would need a safety net of price supports to help see them through occasional years of low prices. And he argued that the fixed-payment approach amounted to a kind of welfare that could pay more than farmers deserve in some years and less than they need in others.

Nonetheless, the farm bill passed the House 270-155, with 54 Democrats voting to support it. The Senate also approved the legislation, and President Clinton signed it into law.

For the 105th, Dooley is ranking Democrat on the Agriculture Subcommittee on Forestry, Resource Conservation and Research.

On the Resources Committee, Dooley typically sympathizes with agricultural interests in their disputes with proponents of aggressive federal environmental protection efforts. In the 104th, he and Republican Sen. Hank Brown of Colorado formed the Western Water Caucus to combat what they saw as overly restrictive control of water flow on federal lands in the West.

Dooley also argued for amending the omnibus water bill of 1992, which included environmental controls that in his view make it too difficult for large farming operations to qualify for water subsidies.

Dooley's views on water issues often put him in conflict with the top Democrat on Resources, California colleague George Miller. Miller's urbanized Bay Area constituency does not share the rural Central Valley's passion for spreading millions of acre-feet of water over farmland.

Dooley in the 104th voted for a GOP initiative barring the Environmental Protection Agency from enforcing certain regulations governing air and water pollution, toxic waste cleanup and pesticide use. He said he saw the vote as the best chance to stop the EPA from requiring that Fresno and other cities in the 20th spend what he sees as unreasonable sums of money on water treatment programs to comply with regulations.

"EPA has got to give more attention to risk assessment, to a cost-benefit analysis of their regulatory actions," he said. "When people do a risk assessment, it's pretty difficult to justify forcing Fresno to spend almost $200 million."

Dooley often is in sync with conservative Southern Democrats on fiscal policy matters. He supports a balanced-budget constitutional amendment and in the 103rd he voted against

CALIFORNIA 20
Parts of Kern, Kings and Fresno counties

Many Democrats complained after the California Supreme Court handed down the 1992 congressional district map, but not Dooley, who got a good deal. His district is derived from the old 17th, which Dooley seized from a troubled Republican incumbent in 1990. But that district was generally Republican; the 1992 map trimmed away much of the GOP vote.

The 20th reaches from Fresno to Bakersfield (in Kern County). But it has far less of the latter than the old 17th had; moreover, its share of Fresno comes from that city's southeastern neighborhoods, which are home to many blacks and Hispanics who reliably support Democratic candidates.

The new district shifted west, away from the upland portions of Fresno and Tulare counties and toward the the portions of Fresno, Kings and Kern counties known as the Westlands. Here, federal water projects have spawned vast farms with battalions of workers. Motorists on Interstate 5 see nary a town while they pass fields filled with virtually every fruit, nut, vegetable, fiber and livestock animal known in the Temperate Zone. Fresno County's annual agricultural output, in excess of $3 billion, ranks first in the nation.

The 20th also bears much of the burden of the Valley's urban and rural poor. The rates of unemployment, crime, teen pregnancy and disease far outstrip statewide averages.

East of the city of Fresno, the 20th takes in the towns of Sanger, Reedley, Parlier, Dinuba, Orange Cove and Kingsburg — each with its own ethnic flavor and history. Kingsburg, where Sun-Maid Growers raisins and Del Monte Foods peaches are processed, still adorns its main street with icons of Swedish Dala Horses. The Scandinavians who came here a century ago have largely turned Republican, as have waves of Armenians, Japanese and migrants from the Dust Bowl, who first were farmworkers.

But where crops must be picked by hand, there will always be new immigrants. In recent generations, the new arrivals have been from Mexico and Central America. Delano, site of the famous farmworker strike in the 1960s, is in the Kern County portion of the 20th.

Hispanics constitute a 55 percent majority in the 20th; blacks and Asians together are 12 percent. But these groups, restrained by low rates of voter registration and turnout, have yet to play a significant role in primaries or general elections.

The 20th has consistently voted Democratic for both the House and White House, in the 1990s. In 1996, Bill Clinton won with 52 percent of the votes, while Dooley garnered 57 percent.

1990 Population: 573,282. White 279,140 (49%), Black 36,933 (6%), Other 257,209 (45%). Hispanic origin 317,372 (55%). 18 and over 373,560 (65%), 62 and over 61,308 (11%). Median age: 27.

Clinton's landmark 1993 budget, which raised taxes and reduced the deficit.

On most social-policy issues, however, he hews to the liberal national Democratic Party line. In 1993 he supported a five-day waiting period for handgun purchases. In 1994, he voted for a ban on certain semiautomatic assault-style weapons, and in 1996, he opposed GOP-led efforts to repeal that ban.

Dooley consistently sides with abortion-rights advocates. In the 104th, he voted to maintain a requirement that states fund Medicaid abortions for poor women in certain cases, he voted to allow privately funded abortions at overseas military hospitals, and he supported allowing federal employees' health care plans to cover abortions. In 1997, Dooley voted for the early release of $385 million for international family planning programs, a Clinton administration request that was opposed by anti-abortion forces. Also, he has opposed conservatives' efforts to ban a particular abortion technique that its critics call "partial birth" abortion.

In March 1997, Dooley joined with Tim Roemer, D-Ind., and James P. Moran, D-Va., to unveil the "New Democrat Coalition" (NDC). Claiming 32 charter members in the House, the group promised to respond "to the public's demand for non-bureaucratic but activist government." On the House Democratic ideological spectrum, the NDC falls somewhere between the right-of-center "blue dogs" and the chamber's 100-some reliably liberal members.

At Home: In 1996, Dooley benefited from the legal troubles of two Republican opponents. Paul Young, who had taken 43 percent of the vote against Dooley in 1994, was back for another try, but his bid was hampered because he was serving time in jail on a contempt of court charge in a tax dispute. The GOP nomination went instead to state Rep. Trice Harvey.

But Harvey had to overcome negative attention he received after he was charged with sexual harassment by a former employee in late 1995. The case was settled when the accuser reached a financial settlement with the state. Dooley prevailed, 57 percent to 39 percent.

Although he sometimes suggests a flatland version of the cinematic Mr. Smith, Dooley is far from a rube. He earned an agribusiness degree from Stanford University, and his family has connections in state and local politics. Dooley's brother and sister-in-law were senior aides to former Gov. Edmund G. "Jerry" Brown Jr.

Dooley was an aide to state Sen. Rose Ann Vuich, a Fresno Democrat legendary for her constituent service. The Vuich persona helped him overcome the more liberal flavor of his relatives' politics.

In his 1990 House bid, he sidestepped not only his associations with party liberals but also the issue at the heart of the coastal liberals' agenda: the "Big Green" environmental initiative. He preferred a farmers' alternative permitting wider pesticide use. Still, no one would have confused his campaign with a Republican's. He put forward the sociological sorrows of rural Tulare and Fresno counties, where the rates of unemployment, crime, pregnancy and disease run ahead of statewide averages.

His opponent, six-term GOP Rep. Charles "Chip" Pashayan Jr., overestimated his strength after an easy 1988 victory and was tainted by the 1989 savings and loan scandal. Dooley prevailed with 55 percent of the vote.

After an easy victory in 1992, Dooley slipped a bit in the Republican high-water election of 1994, but his 57 percent tally was still comfortable.

HOUSE ELECTIONS

1996 General		
Cal Dooley (D)	65,381	(57%)
Trice Harvey (R)	45,276	(39%)
Jonathan Richter (LIBERT)	5,048	(4%)
1994 General		
Cal Dooley (D)	57,394	(57%)
Paul Young (R)	43,836	(43%)

Previous Winning Percentages: **1992** (65%) **1990** (55%)

CAMPAIGN FINANCE

	Receipts	Receipts from PACs		Expend-itures
1996				
Dooley (D)	$625,231	$327,906	(52%)	$662,818
Harvey (R)	$505,055	$51,117	(10%)	$505,054
1994				
Dooley (D)	$312,806	$219,475	(70%)	$275,544
Young (R)	$10,504	$764	(7%)	$10,346

DISTRICT VOTE FOR PRESIDENT

	1996		1992
D	62,164 (52%)	**D**	55,942 (47%)
R	48,446 (41%)	**R**	44,674 (38%)
I	6,617 (6%)	**I**	18,568 (16%)

KEY VOTES

1997	
Ban "partial birth" abortions	N
1996	
Approve farm bill	N
Deny public education to illegal immigrants	N
Repeal ban on certain assault-style weapons	N
Increase minimum wage	Y
Freeze defense spending	Y
Approve welfare overhaul	Y
1995	
Approve balanced-budget constitutional amendment	Y
Relax Clean Water Act regulations	Y
Oppose limits on environmental regulations	Y
Reduce projected Medicare spending	N
Approve GOP budget with tax and spending cuts	N

VOTING STUDIES

	Presidential Support		Party Unity		Conservative Coalition	
Year	S	O	S	O	S	O
1996	81	19	73	25	67	33
1995	63	35	60†	37†	83†	14†
1994	69	24	78	18	69	28
1993	66	27	83	13	36	61
1992	30	65	77	18	56	42
1991	38	62	84	16	62	38

† Not eligible for all recorded votes.

INTEREST GROUP RATINGS

Year	ADA	AFL-CIO	CCUS	ACU
1996	55	n/a	44	15
1995	55	67	71	17
1994	55	22	92	22
1993	75	67	64	25
1992	75	75	50	20
1991	60	75	50	10

21 Bill Thomas (R)

Of Bakersfield — Elected 1978, 10th term

Biographical Information
Born: Dec. 6, 1941, Wallace, Idaho.
Education: San Francisco State U., B.A. 1963, M.A. 1965.
Occupation: Professor.
Family: Wife, Sharon Lynn Hamilton; two children.
Religion: Baptist.
Political Career: Calif. Assembly, 1975-79.
Capitol Office: 2208 Rayburn Bldg. 20515; 225-2915.

Committees
House Oversight (chairman)
Ways & Means
Health (chairman); Trade
Joint Library
Joint Printing
Joint Taxation

In Washington: Knowledgeable and belligerent, Thomas helps lead the Republican charge on two completely different fronts. As chairman of the Ways and Means Subcommittee on Health, Thomas has helped rewrite insurance law and been a point man on the Medicare issue. As the head of the House Oversight Committee, he deals with the majority's housekeeping tasks, from privatizing parking lots to investigating contested elections.

Thomas has earned a place in Speaker Newt Gingrich's inner circle. The two were roommates during their early days in Washington in the late 1970s. But Gingrich had lost some faith in Thomas as the 1990s rolled around, and when Republicans were getting organized in late 1994 to take over the House, the Speaker-to-be gave others many of the transitional duties that looked to be Thomas' as chairman of House Oversight.

But Thomas has been a faithful vote for the leadership and a team player on such issues as health care. And he has stood out for engaging in more than a few partisan spats with Democrats. In one incident during the 104th Congress, Florida Democrat Sam M. Gibbons grabbed Thomas' tie in anger over the GOP's Medicare overhaul plans and their means of legislating them, until the Californian insisted he let go.

Thomas has most often butted heads with fellow Californian Pete Stark, the Health Subcommittee's top Democrat and its former chairman. When Stark accused Republicans of "bribing" doctors by protecting their fees to win support for the 1995 Medicare package, Thomas said Stark's contention was "absolutely false. . . . Unless you have one shred of evidence to prove it, you owe everyone of us that you have slandered an abject apology."

When Stark wouldn't shut up at a Ways and Means meeting on welfare, Thomas leapt to his feet and shouted for the sergeant at arms. Stark said, "Oh great, just like Nazi Germany." Thomas also sought to cut off Democrats who were complaining on the House floor about a Republican move to recess when the government was partially shut down. "Turn that mike off!" Thomas screamed to a staffer as Democrats continued to make speeches. "Off now! And keep it off!"

Thomas, a supporter of GOP efforts to restrain Medicare costs in part by encouraging increased use of managed care plans, sponsored a bill in the 104th to make health insurance more affordable and accessible. His legislation sought to increase the portability of health insurance and restrict the use of exclusions because of pre-existing conditions. It also would have capped non-economic damages for medical malpractice systems. It shaped the House's offer in negotiations with the Senate, which had produced a more generous package, and helped ensure that provisions essential to conservatives were kept in part if not intact in the enacted version.

From his House Oversight chair in the 104th, Thomas oversaw the privatization of several House services and slashed committee staffing by about a third. (He favors narrowing the gap in pay between top committee staff and their counterparts on members' personal staff.) He commissioned the first-ever outside audit of House finances, which offered Republican leaders hard evidence of what they had long contended: That under the Democrats, the House was in financial shambles, funds were poorly accounted for and frequently overspent, and members were sometimes the culprits. But the GOP soon found that running the House was no picnic. They ran into big difficulties with a new computer system and with some of their newly installed officers.

Thomas earned the enmity of Democrats by cutting off funding for the outside counselor investigating Gingrich's ethics violations just two weeks after the 105th convened, but Thomas countered that the work of the investigation was done. And the partisan nature of reviewing contested elections remains an open wound in Thomas' relations with the minority party.

Thomas said in March 1997 that a complaint brought by ousted California Republican Robert K. Dornan, alleging that massive voter fraud had

CALIFORNIA 21
Kern and Tulare counties — Bakersfield

One aim of the court-ordered California redistricting of 1992 was to create more districts in which both parties could be competitive. But where that goal conflicted with other priorities, such as compactness and community of interest, it was shelved.

A case in point is the 21st, which is a model of compactness and community of interest. It is especially so in contrast to its predecessor, the old Bakersfield-based 20th District, which Thomas also represented. It shared a border with Nevada and still offered beachfront on the Pacific. Beginning high in the Sierras, it took in all of Inyo County, most of Kern County, a swath of Los Angeles County and most of San Luis Obispo County on the coast.

By comparison, the new 21st looks sensible enough to be an Iowa district. About three-fourths of its vote is in Kern County (overall population 543,000). The rest comes from new territory pulled in from Tulare County (overall population 312,000) to the north.

Tulare County brings into the district the magnificence of the Sequoia National Forest and the western slope of Mount Whitney, which at 14,494 feet is the tallest peak in the United States outside of Alaska. The county also brings in many small towns. The county seat is Visalia, a farming city of 76,000 on Highway 99, straddling the line with the 20th. Running south through Tulare County just east of Highway 99, the district's lines are drawn to include the towns of Tulare, Farmersville, Porterville and Lindsay. This was one of America's fastest-growing metropolitan areas in the 1980s; population expanded 27 percent.

South of Shafter, the southern appendage of the 20th District cuts into the Bakersfield metro area along Interstate 5. Farther west, the 21st picks up the towns of Maricopa and Taft.

But the district's heart beats in Bakersfield, a city the size of Little Rock, Ark. (about 175,000). Bakersfield was brought to life by a gold rush in 1885 and again by an oil strike in 1899. Farmers from the Southwest came in force during the 1930s Dust Bowl years, and the city boomed yet again in the 1980s — when its growth rate of nearly 66 percent ranked ninth among U.S. cities.

The predominance of cotton, other crops, country music and oil hereabouts can still make a Texan feel at home, even if the Texan came to work in the defense-related industries tied to nearby China Lake Naval Air Weapons Station or Edwards Air Force Base (in Kern's southeast corner). Edwards is a frequent landing site for space shuttles because of its seven-mile landing strip in Rogers Dry Lake.

The 21st is actually slightly less white than the old 20th, but after a dip in 1992 the GOP registration returned to virtually the same level, almost half. When Republicans have this large a registration plurality, they nearly always win big at the polls. Bob Dole and Thomas carried both the Tulare and Kern sections of the 21st in 1996.

1990 Population: 571,300. White 443,958 (78%), Black 23,106 (4%), Other 104,236 (18%). Hispanic origin 115,954 (20%). 18 and over 398,248 (70%), 62 and over 74,387 (13%). Median age: 31.

cost him the election against Democrat Loretta Sanchez in 1996, was unique. The "scope of the charges," Thomas said, made "the circumstances surrounding this disputed election . . . fundamentally different." Worried that high numbers of non-citizens had participated in the Orange County contest, Thomas asked the Immigration and Naturalization Service for help in checking the names of those who voted in the district against computerized immigration records.

House Oversight investigated several contested 1994 elections, finding insufficient evidence in each case to seriously challenge the state-certified results. "Their real fear is that we're going to operate the way they have," Thomas said of the Democrats in 1995. "We will not duplicate the Democrats' way of stealing seats." Back in the 99th Congress, Thomas was the lone GOP member of a Democratic-dominated task force that decided an extremely close 1984 election in Indiana's 8th District in favor of Democrat Frank McCloskey. He was declared the winner by four votes even though state officials had certified his GOP challenger as the victor. Thomas furiously opposed the task force report, calling it a "rape" and "an arrogant use of raw power."

Thomas in the 104th offered a plan for overhauling campaign finance laws. His legislation lowered the amount candidates may receive from PACs from $5,000 to $2,500. At the same time, his bill raised the individual contribution limit from $1,000 to $2,500. It required candidates to receive at least 50 percent of their contributions from residents of the district where they run, and it greatly increased the amount political parties could spend on general election efforts. Thomas called his bill "the most serious anti-incumbent legislation that anyone has introduced."

At Home: Thomas has often described himself as a pragmatic conservative, a label that has worked for him at the polls. Some Republican hard-liners have viewed Thomas as more committed to pragmatism than to conservatism. He faced a 1990 primary challenge from the right. Thomas won easily, but he gave up 27 percent to swimming-pool repairman Rod Gregory. In the 1990 general election, Thomas' 60 percent was his lowest since his first House election in 1978.

In 1992, Thomas again faced an opponent in the primary: Financial consultant Carlos Murillo got more than one-third of the Republican vote. Once nominated, however, Thomas was more secure than ever in his newly drawn district, and he won with 65 percent.

In 1994 and 1996, Thomas swatted down primary opponents and cruised again to easy November victories.

Thomas began his political career in 1974, leaving academia to run, successfully, for the state Assembly as a staunch conservative (support for the death penalty was his central issue). But in 1978, when GOP Rep. William Ketchum died after the June primary and left the nomination open, Thomas positioned himself as the moderate Republican candidate. He was the ranking GOP legislator in the area, but it took him seven ballots at a party nominating convention to defeat two, more conservative, opponents.

Thomas and Ketchum had had some differences (Thomas had backed Gerald R. Ford in the California primary in 1976 and Ketchum had supported Ronald Reagan), but Thomas got a general-election endorsement from Ketchum's widow and easily defeated Democrat Bob Sogge, a former state Senate aide.

HOUSE ELECTIONS

1996 General		
Bill Thomas (R)	125,916	(66%)
Deborah A. Vollmer (D)	50,694	(26%)
John Evans (REF)	8,113	(4%)
Jane Bialosky (NL)	3,380	(2%)
Mike Hodges (LIBERT)	3,049	(2%)
1996 Primary		
Bill Thomas (R)	53,564	(79%)
Karen Gentry (R)	14,030	(21%)
1994 General		
Bill Thomas (R)	116,874	(68%)
John L. Evans (D)	47,517	(28%)
Mike Hodges (LIBERT)	6,899	(4%)

Previous Winning Percentages: **1992** (65%) **1990** (60%) **1988** (71%) **1986** (73%) **1984** (71%) **1982** (68%) **1980** (71%) **1978** (59%)

CAMPAIGN FINANCE

	Receipts	Receipts from PACs	Expend-itures
1996			
Thomas (R)	$1,080,395	$650,824 (60%)	$768,689
Vollmer (D)	$33,752	$3,100 (9%)	$33,295
Evans (REF)	$5,420	$1,000 (18%)	$5,505
1994			
Thomas (R)	$607,652	$380,227 (63%)	$434,146
Evans (D)	$31,214	$2,000 (6%)	$31,101

DISTRICT VOTE FOR PRESIDENT

	1996		1992
D	66,492 (34%)	**D**	66,284 (33%)
R	109,344 (56%)	**R**	94,727 (46%)
I	15,000 (8%)	**I**	43,016 (21%)

KEY VOTES

1997	
Ban "partial birth" abortions	Y
1996	
Approve farm bill	Y
Deny public education to illegal immigrants	Y
Repeal ban on certain assault-style weapons	Y
Increase minimum wage	N
Freeze defense spending	N
Approve welfare overhaul	Y
1995	
Approve balanced-budget constitutional amendment	Y
Relax Clean Water Act regulations	Y
Oppose limits on environmental regulations	N
Reduce projected Medicare spending	Y
Approve GOP budget with tax and spending cuts	Y

VOTING STUDIES

	Presidential Support		Party Unity		Conservative Coalition	
Year	**S**	**O**	**S**	**O**	**S**	**O**
1996	41	56	88	10	98	0
1995	23	75	92	7	96	4
1994	47	46	84	10	86	6
1993	52	47	86	11	91	7
1992	66	17	77	8	79	8
1991	72	22	80	12	95	3

INTEREST GROUP RATINGS

Year	ADA	AFL-CIO	CCUS	ACU
1996	5	n/a	94	90
1995	10	0	100	72
1994	10	29	100	84
1993	5	17	100	78
1992	15	10	88	90
1991	10	18	100	79

22 Walter Capps (D)

Of Santa Barbara — Elected 1996, 1st term

Biographical Information

Born: May 5, 1934, Omaha, Neb.

Education: Portland State U., B.S. 1958; Augustana Theological Seminary, M.A. 1960; Yale U., S.T.M. 1961, Ph.D 1965.

Occupation: Professor.

Family: Wife, Lois Grimsrud; three children.

Religion: Lutheran.

Political Career: Democratic nominee for U.S. House, 1994.

Capitol Office: 1118 Longworth Bldg. 20515; 225-3601.

Committees

International Relations
Asia & the Pacific; Western Hemisphere

Science
Basic Research; Space & Aeronautics

The Path to Washington: Capps, a religion professor who once wrote a book warning about the dangers he saw in an increased religious presence in politics, survived a life-threatening car accident in 1996 to succeed in his repeat effort to cast Republican Andrea Seastrand as too conservative for this mainline, coastal district.

Capps' liberal views may at times leave him out of step with his constituents. He favors increased protection of the environment, opposed the new law designed to discourage same-sex marriages, and has opposed a state ballot proposition to deny illegal immigrants access to most government services.

Critiquing the welfare overhaul law enacted by the 104th Congress, Capps declared during the campaign, "Changes have to be made, but I wouldn't eliminate programs that are the reason we have government — to help those families and individuals that can't help themselves."

The district has been held by Republicans since World War II; the burden Capps will operate under in seeking re-election was not made any lighter by his committee assignments. Making a splash on the International Relations and Science committees is no mean feat for any freshman. Capps is an expert on the Vietnam War, though, and the district's Vandenberg Air Force Base is a leading site of space research.

Capps lost to Seastrand by fewer than 1,600 votes when the 22nd was open in 1994 and was encouraged to make an encore run by Democratic Sen. Bob Kerrey of Nebraska (Capps' home state). Kerrey, a wounded veteran, shared teaching duties one semester for Capps' class on the Vietnam War — a course that became famous as the subject of a profile by CBS' "60 Minutes."

Before coming to Congress, Capps had taught philosophy at the University of California's Santa Barbara campus since 1964. He was a pioneer not only in the academic study of the Vietnam conflict, but in conflict resolution as well.

He said during the campaign that he would like to see Congress run more like a forum, with more close consultation with experts on given issues.

Two months after winning the 1996 Democratic nomination without opposition, Capps and his wife were injured when a drunk driver crossed over into their lane and hit them head on. Capps recovered from head, arm and leg injuries.

"I never want to forget what it's like to go through the world in a wheelchair," said Capps at a news conference at his rehabilitation center in July 1996. "I would never wish for a car accident like this. But I have learned from it. . . . Love and caring for one another is what is at the core of what links us."

He conceded that the accident, which was the center of much media attention locally, was a boon for him politically.

Capps said the experience made him even more ardent in his opposition to GOP attempts to slow the growth of Medicare. Contending that Democrats have "been properly chastened about the role of government" since their attempts to boldly remake the nation's health care infrastructure during the 103rd Congress, Capps sees efforts to increase general access to health insurance as his top first-term priority.

He can be counted on to resist pressures to cut domestic programs such as Head Start and student loans.

Although Seastrand received some support from business groups, their efforts were not as visible as high-level independent expenditure campaigns from labor unions, environmental organizations and supporters of abortion rights who rushed to Capps' aid. Their combined efforts were worth an estimated $1 million to Capps' cause.

A Seastrand campaign ad that criticized Capps' opposition to capital punishment appeared to backfire. The ad stated that Capps was the only person aside from Richard Allen Davis to be "disappointed" when Davis was sentenced to death in a Northern California courtroom during the campaign. Davis had gained nationwide notoriety when he was convicted of murdering a 12-year-old girl.

CALIFORNIA 22
Santa Barbara; Santa Maria; San Luis Obispo

Santa Barbara County, with about 370,000 residents, was the mainstay of the old 19th District. It was connected to the Los Angeles metro area to the south via Ventura County, which had most of its land (though not most of its people) in the 19th. The two neighboring counties shared the calm waters of the Santa Barbara Channel and the rugged grandeur of Los Padres National Forest, a 1.7 million-acre preserve spread over several small mountain ranges running parallel to the coast.

But in 1992, redistricting separated these two counties, pulling Santa Barbara away to the north and combining it with San Luis Obispo. The two newly joined coastal counties are topographically similar, separated only by the Cuyama River that runs down from the Sierra Madre Mountains to the Pacific.

The 22nd takes in all of both counties, except for the coastal town of Carpinteria, just south of Santa Barbara, and adjacent acreage on the Ventura County line. Included for good measure are four islands offshore in the Santa Barbara Channel.

San Luis Obispo includes its namesake city (home to California Polytechnic State University and about one-fifth of the county's 217,000 residents) and the northern end of the Los Padres forest. North of the city, Highway 101 angles inland to Atascadero, Paso Robles and San Miguel. Alternatively, tourists can take the breathtaking Highway 1, which continues to hug the coast on its way to memorable Morro Bay and then to San Simeon — the fabled mansion of media magnate William Randolph Hearst.

About 60 percent of the district's vote is still cast in Santa Barbara County, whose population centers include Vandenberg Air Force Base and the small cities of Lompoc and Santa Maria. The city of Santa Barbara was founded 200 years ago by the Spanish on a natural harbor discovered 250 years before that by the Portuguese.

More than most of contemporary California, Santa Barbara has striven to maintain some of its Iberian charm — in part with a measured pace of life. A major campus (18,500 students) of the University of California is just outside of town. Many of the city's nearly 86,000 residents are retirees; others have settled here less to make money than to make the most of the money they have.

The old 19th had a slight Democratic tilt in registration, but it generally voted Republican. In the 22nd, the two parties are about even in registration. In 1992, both counties preferred Bill Clinton for president. Four years later, Bob Dole eked out a victory in the 22nd. In the House race, Capps beat incumbent Republican Andrea Seastrand when his winning margin in Santa Barbara County exceeded her lead in San Luis Obispo County.

1990 Population: 572,891. White 467,841 (82%), Black 16,024 (3%), Other 89,026 (16%). Hispanic origin 122,020 (21%). 18 and over 442,869 (77%), 62 and over 88,765 (15%). Median age: 32.

HOUSE ELECTIONS

1996 General

Walter Holden Capps (D)	118,299	(48%)
Andrea Seastrand (R)	107,987	(44%)
Steven Wheeler (I)	9,845	(4%)
Richard D. "Dick" Porter (REF)	3,975	(2%)

CAMPAIGN FINANCE

	Receipts	Receipts from PACs	Expend-itures
1996			
Capps (D)	$968,864	$256,810 (27%)	$904,831
Seastrand (R)	$1,223,561	$401,614 (33%)	$1,232,118
Porter (REF)	$103,320	0	$103,320

DISTRICT VOTE FOR PRESIDENT

1996		1992	
D	108,208 (44%)	**D**	106,815 (41%)
R	108,722 (44%)	**R**	92,045 (35%)
I	17,311 (7%)	**I**	61,030 (24%)

KEY VOTES

1997

Ban "partial birth" abortions	N

23 Elton Gallegly (R)

Of Simi Valley — Elected 1986, 6th term

Biographical Information
Born: March 7, 1944, Huntington Park, Calif.
Education: California State U., Los Angeles, 1962-63.
Occupation: Real estate broker.
Family: Wife, Janice Shrader; four children.
Religion: Protestant.
Political Career: Simi Valley City Council, 1979-80; mayor of Simi Valley, 1980-86.
Capitol Office: 2427 Rayburn Bldg. 20515; 225-5811.

Committees
International Relations
Western Hemisphere (chairman)
Judiciary
Courts & Intellectual Property; Immigration & Claims
Resources
National Parks & Public Lands

In Washington: Soon after he entered Congress in 1987, Gallegly emerged as the House's most aggressive Republican voice on immigration and illegal aliens. Most of his early proposals were considered too hard-line to have any real chance of passage; but, as time wore on and public opinion evolved, Gallegly's ideas looked more and more mainstream.

Still, even with his party in the House majority during the 104th Congress, Gallegly was stymied in his attempt to amend the major immigration bill under discussion — the most significant rewrite of the relevant laws in a decade.

A college dropout and one of the few nonlawyers to serve on the Judiciary Committee, Gallegly was disappointed in his hopes of chairing the panel's Immigration and Claims Subcommittee at the start of the 104th. But Speaker Newt Gingrich did reward Gallegly's stalwart past efforts by naming him chairman of a bipartisan congressional task force on immigration. This post helped Gallegly attract attention for his signature amendment to the immigration bill, a proposal to bar illegal immigrants' children from public schools.

Gallegly argued that border states such as California could no longer afford to foot the bill for educating children who were in the United States illegally, and he further contended that free schooling acted as a magnet attracting illegal immigrants.

In effect, the amendment sought to overturn the Supreme Court's 1982 *Plyler v. Doe* decision, in which the court ruled, on a 5-4 vote, that school-aged illegal aliens may not be denied public education. Gallegly thought a more conservative court might yield a different ruling, and he also noted that the court in Plyler had cited the "absence" of any expressed congressional intent on the matter in its decision.

"We're not penalizing children," Gallegly said. "We're merely not rewarding them."

Gallegly's amendment passed the House, 257-163, in March 1996, but that was just the beginning of the measure's odyssey.

The provision delayed for several months a House-Senate conference on the underlying immigration bill, which restricted illegal immigration by beefing up the border patrol and making it easier for illegal immigrants to be detained at the border or deported after arrival. The Senate's version of the bill contained no provision akin to the Gallegly language, which was opposed even by some conservative Republican senators.

The amendment also became an issue in the presidential campaign, with President Clinton threatening to veto the bill if it contained the Gallegly amendment. Republican presidential nominee Bob Dole tried to convince his former Senate colleagues to pass the bill with the Gallegly provisions intact, so as to call Clinton's bluff and blame him for the legislation's death.

But the bill's GOP sponsors wanted something to show for their efforts, and even Gallegly eventually went along with the idea of dropping his schools proposal, which passed the House again as a stand-alone bill in September 1996 but was never taken up by the Senate.

Gallegly had been angered earlier in the process when a provision to require employers to verify the legal status of new employees by calling the federal government was converted into a voluntary pilot program.

In the end, however, Gallegly said the larger immigration bill, which was cleared at the very end of the 104th Congress as part of an omnibus spending package, was "still the best bill we've had in modern history to deal with illegal immigration."

Because of a series of natural disasters that have beset California in recent years, disaster relief has been another item high on Gallegly's agenda. Early in the 103rd, when severe flooding along the Mississippi River destroyed many homes and ruined crops, Gallegly joined a group of fiscal conservatives who argued that any federal flood relief must be paid for by making cuts elsewhere in the budget. But when parts of Simi Valley were damaged by a California quake in

CALIFORNIA 23

Most of Ventura County; Oxnard; Ventura; Simi Valley

Ventura County came into its own with the redistricting of 1992. Another decade of rapid growth (26 percent in the 1980s) had lifted its population to 669,000 — more than enough for a full district. The lines of the 23rd District are nearly identical to those of Ventura County.

There are two small exceptions, at the southwest and northeast corners, and one large exception in the southeast near the Los Angeles County line. Here, the city of Thousand Oaks (with 104,000 people the second-largest in the county) was drawn into the Los Angeles-based 24th District.

The 23rd still comprises more than 80 percent of Ventura County, including the cities of Ventura, Oxnard, Simi Valley, Camarillo and Santa Paula. About 97 percent of the district vote was cast by county residents in 1996 (the rest was cast in Carpinteria and neighboring precincts just across the Santa Barbara County line).

Gallegly began his political career as a local officeholder in Simi Valley, a burgeoning Ventura County suburb of about 100,000 residents. Until recently, those who had heard of Simi Valley probably associated it with a winery. But here in 1992, a jury with no blacks acquitted four white police officers from Los Angeles in the beating of a black motorist named Rodney King, who had been apprehended after a high-speed chase. The verdict ignited the worst rioting in Los Angeles in nearly 30 years.

Simi Valley accounts for little more than one-sixth of the 23rd District, but it is not atypical of the district (blacks constitute only a minuscule 3 percent of the 23rd's population).

Ventura County absorbed much of the destruction in the 1994 Northridge earthquake. Part of Highway 126 collapsed about 10 miles northwest of the quake's epicenter, and 6,000 residences were damaged in surrounding communities.

The district's Republican registration in 1994 was just 41 percent, a few percentage points lower than Democratic registration. But any California district where the GOP registers more than 40 percent of the voters (and the Democrats fewer than 50 percent) usually elects Republicans, and the 23rd is a case in point. In 1992, Gallegly won by 13 percentage points over a spirited Democratic woman, and both Republican candidates for the Senate carried the district (while losing statewide).

The one big Republican disappointment in 1992 was George Bush, whose 35 percent of the district vote was 3 percentage points behind Bill Clinton's. Ross Perot got 27 percent, well above his statewide average.

When the California GOP made a comeback in 1994, Gallegly was a big beneficiary, widening his margin of victory to 39 percentage points. He also won comfortably in 1996, while Clinton eked out a 4 point plurality.

1990 Population: 571,483. White 439,346 (77%), Black 14,432 (3%), Other 117,705 (21%). Hispanic origin 171,722 (30%). 18 and over 412,637 (72%), 62 and over 66,068 (12%). Median age: 31.

1994, Gallegly supported Clinton's earthquake relief bill, even though it added to the deficit.

Gallegly calls himself a free trader, but he was evidently not convinced by arguments that passing NAFTA would help stem illegal immigration by raising Mexico's standard of living. Gallegly offered a terse one-sentence House speech explaining his "no" vote on the trade pact: "Mr. Chairman, I rise in opposition to this 3,755-page, 800-pound document referred to as NAFTA." He also opposed GATT.

Gallegly has supported most Republican budget-cutting initiatives, such as a balanced-budget amendment to the Constitution. And Simi Valley is close enough to Los Angeles that many of its residents are concerned about the spread of urban crime. Gallegly has put forth a series of crime proposals, including one to make drive-by shootings a federal offense and one instituting mandatory minimum sentences for drug crimes involving children.

He will sometimes back anti-crime measures not associated with conservatives. In the 103rd, Gallegly supported a five-day waiting period requirement for handgun purchases. He was one of 42 Republicans who voted for the Clinton-backed crime bill in August 1994, even though it included a ban on certain semiautomatic assault-style weapons that he had opposed on a stand-alone vote in May 1994.

Although he failed to get the chair of the Immigration subcommittee, Gallegly does hold a gavel in the 105th, chairing the International Relations Subcommittee on the Western Hemisphere.

At Home: Having weathered the Democratic storm that swept across his state and his district in 1992, Gallegly was around to enjoy the ride when the GOP made its comeback in 1994: He won a place in the new Republican House with 66 percent of the vote in 1994 (and held it in 1996 with 60 percent).

Early in 1992, redistricting put Gallegly in a district with another incumbent, Robert J. Lagomarsino, who was six terms more senior and considered one of the delegation's toughest survivors. But Lagomarsino, who hailed from Ventura, was persuaded to move north up the coast to the new 22nd District, where he subsequently lost in the Republican primary to multimillionaire Michael Huffington.

Gallegly, meanwhile, had little trouble in the primary before facing what was widely considered a tough challenge from Anita Perez Ferguson, a former teacher who had run respectably well against Lagomarsino in 1990.

Racial issues were especially sensitive locally in 1992. Gallegly comes from Simi Valley, where a jury acquitted the Los Angeles police officers accused of beating Rodney King (touching off the worst riots seen in the United States in more than two decades). But Gallegly dug at Ferguson for not always using her Hispanic middle name in her campaign, and feelings were often raw in both camps. In the end, the matchup may have been oversold. Gallegly was held to 54 percent, his lowest vote share ever, but that was still 13 points ahead of Ferguson.

Gallegly first won his seat in 1986, when Republican Rep. Bobbi Fiedler ran for the Senate. He had to fend off a primary opponent with some celebrity — Tony Hope, son of comedian Bob Hope.

Hope had returned to the area after a 10-year stay in Washington, and Gallegly cast him as an interloper. He touted his own record as mayor of Simi Valley, where he was well known for having boosted economic development.

Gallegly did face the issue of heavy financial backing from local real estate developers. Some of their projects needed approval by the City Council on which he sat. But Hope was squeamish about deploying his substantial financial resources in the race. And while Gallegly was not a familiar figure to voters outside Simi Valley when the race began, he used direct mail to spread his name and message across the populous San Fernando Valley portion of the district. He won easily over Hope and had no trouble in November, taking two-thirds of the vote.

HOUSE ELECTIONS

1996 General		
Elton Gallegly (R)	118,880	(60%)
Robert R. Unruhe (D)	70,035	(35%)
Gail Lightfoot (LIBERT)	8,346	(4%)
Stephen Hospodar (NL)	2,246	(1%)
1994 General		
Elton Gallegly (R)	114,043	(66%)
Kevin Ready (D)	47,345	(27%)
Bill Brown (LIBERT)	6,481	(4%)
Robert T. Marston (GREEN)	4,457	(3%)

Previous Winning Percentages: **1992** (54%) **1990** (58%) **1988** (69%) **1986** (68%)

CAMPAIGN FINANCE

	Receipts	Receipts from PACs	Expend-itures
1996			
Gallegly (R)	$486,919	$122,513 (25%)	$294,940
Unruhe (D)	$25,140	$2,521 (10%)	$24,642
1994			
Gallegly (R)	$397,806	$89,369 (22%)	$300,846
Ready (D)	$24,876	$8,500 (34%)	$24,813

DISTRICT VOTE FOR PRESIDENT

	1996		1992
D	93,046 (46%)	**D**	82,613 (38%)
R	85,508 (42%)	**R**	74,106 (35%)
I	19,237 (9%)	**I**	58,177 (27%)

KEY VOTES

1997	
Ban "partial birth" abortions	Y
1996	
Approve farm bill	Y
Deny public education to illegal immigrants	Y
Repeal ban on certain assault-style weapons	Y
Increase minimum wage	N
Freeze defense spending	N
Approve welfare overhaul	Y
1995	
Approve balanced-budget constitutional amendment	Y
Relax Clean Water Act regulations	Y
Oppose limits on environmental regulations	N
Reduce projected Medicare spending	Y
Approve GOP budget with tax and spending cuts	Y

VOTING STUDIES

	Presidential Support		Party Unity		Conservative Coalition	
Year	**S**	**O**	**S**	**O**	**S**	**O**
1996	34	57	88	5	90	6
1995	16	82	92	2	95	1
1994	49	42	86	6	94	0
1993	41	59	92	5	95	5
1992	80	19	91	7	96	4
1991	81	18	94	3	95	3

INTEREST GROUP RATINGS

Year	ADA	AFL-CIO	CCUS	ACU
1996	0	n/a	100	100
1995	0	0	100	84
1994	10	25	92	95
1993	10	8	73	96
1992	15	50	75	84
1991	10	8	90	85

24 Brad Sherman (D)

Of Sherman Oaks — Elected 1996, 1st term

Biographical Information
Born: Oct. 24, 1954, Los Angeles, Calif.
Education: U. of California, Los Angeles, B.A. 1974; Harvard U., J.D. 1979.
Occupation: Accountant; lawyer.
Family: Single.
Religion: Jewish.
Political Career: Calif. State Board of Equilization, 1991-97.
Capitol Office: 1524 Longworth Bldg. 20515; 225-5911.

Committees
Budget
International Relations
International Economic Policy & Trade; Western Hemisphere

The Path to Washington: Sherman, a self-described "recovering nerd," loves to delve into the minutiae of policy questions. But he has a keen enough sense of humor to be able to pull back and see the big picture. After spending six years on the California Board of Equalization, which implements sections of the state's tax code, Sherman joked in 1996 that he was running for Congress because it was the only job held in lower public esteem than tax collector.

He intends to hew closely to district interests, from helping to resolve a ZIP Code dispute, to steering the Santa Monica Mountain National Recreational Area to completion.

His district is home to many Jews and Armenians. Sherman, who got a seat on the House International Relations Committee, favors moving the American Embassy in Israel to Jerusalem from Tel Aviv, and he would like more pressure put on Turkey to acknowledge its historic crimes against Armenians. He would have China clean up its human rights record in return for most-favored-nation trading status.

On domestic trade, Sherman believes that the federal government has for too long ignored tax barriers to trade between states. He wants Congress to try to persuade or require the states to harmonize their tax laws.

He was not against tweaking out-of-state companies when it served California interests, however. To assist manufacturers in 1993, he helped rewrite the state tax code so that companies from other states selling products in California were dunned more heavily than companies that employed Californians to make their products.

Sherman will support tough measures on immigration, advocating a tamper-proof worker identification card. He disagrees with the approach taken by neighboring Republican Rep. Elton Gallegly, who offered an amendment during the 104th Congress to deny public schooling to illegal immigrant children. But Sherman would like to see improved efforts to seal the U.S.-Mexico border and wants the federal government to reimburse Los Angeles County for expenditures on immigrant services.

On most domestic issues, Sherman, who also serves on the Budget Committee, is likely to vote in line with his Democratic brethren. He favors balancing the budget, but will resist attempts to cut the Environmental Protection Agency, student loans or Medicare.

Sherman leans to the liberal side of certain social questions, supporting abortion rights and Medicaid funding of the procedure. Besides favoring gun control measures such as the ban on certain semiautomatic assault-style weapons, Sherman wants a ban on sales of the cheap handguns known as Saturday night specials. He also favors increased federal regulation of tobacco.

Sherman got his start in politics stuffing envelopes as a child for Democratic Rep. George E. Brown Jr., a longtime family friend. In 1996, Sherman sewed up the backing of most area Democrats before the primary — including the endorsement of retiring 10-term Rep. Anthony C. Beilenson. Sherman's willingness to finance his own campaign — he eventually spent nearly $400,000 — helped him easily outpace six challengers in the primary.

He faced a tougher battle against Republican Rich Sybert, a toy company executive and former gubernatorial aide who had held Beilenson below 50 percent in 1994. Sybert also opened his own pocketbook widely and, like Sherman, fashioned himself as a moderate.

But Sybert handed Sherman a good deal of ammunition with conservative opinion columns he had written for the Pasadena Star. He also got into trouble by claiming the endorsement of retired Gen. Colin L. Powell before he had it.

Sherman accused Sybert of illegally coordinating an attack campaign in which an independent group published leaflets characterizing Sherman as running at the behest of "East Coast Labor Bosses." In the end, Sherman's lengthy direct mail pieces lent him an air of substance. He also benefitted from the voting trend in the district, which went heavily for President Clinton. Sherman tallied 50 percent, 8 percentage points up on Sybert.

CALIFORNIA 24
Northwest Los Angeles County suburbs

The 24th exemplifies the intent of the California Supreme Court's 1992 redistricting plan, which was to foster greater competition. This was not good news for Democratic Rep. Anthony C. Beilenson, who had consistently and comfortably been re-elected in the old 23rd.

Most of the current 24th comes from the far northwestern reaches of Los Angeles County along the Ventura County line, where Democrats are less prevalent than in Bel Air and Beverly Hills, which were removed in redistricting. Republicans run well in Thousand Oaks, a well-established Ventura County bedroom community added in redistricting.

So it came as no surprise that Beilenson experienced career-low victory margins in 1992 and 1994, and that the 24th featured a close House race in 1996 when he retired. Sherman's nearly 22,500-vote margin in the Los Angeles County portion of the district offset his having lost in Ventura by nearly 10,000 votes. In presidential voting, Bill Clinton's huge margins in Los Angeles County also offset his losses in Ventura (which casts only a quarter of the 24th's vote).

The eastern end of the 24th begins in the San Fernando Valley, in Van Nuys and Encino. Its main artery, the Ventura Freeway, splits the valley and heads west. This area is thoroughly suburban. Its industries tend to be service-oriented; traditional heavy industry is limited to a few struggling aerospace contractors.

A few miles west of Encino is Tarzana, envisioned by "Tarzan" author Edgar Rice Burroughs as 550 acres of sanctuary from civilization. But just six years after he bought the land in 1919, Burroughs divvied it up into tracts; the resulting community is just another subdivision along the Ventura Freeway.

The 24th's commercial districts are found about a mile south of Route 101 along Ventura Boulevard. There are miles of suburban fast-food outlets and strip mall stores, and while there are some high-rise office towers, they tend to house branch offices of banks, not their headquarters. Transportation issues, especially the traffic congestion, dominate in the valley.

As Route 101 heads west toward Thousand Oaks, development thins. The valley narrows, with the Santa Monica Mountains National Recreation Area to the south and the Santa Susana Mountains to the north.

Industries out here tend to be biotechnology companies and others of the "clean" variety. South of the recreation area lie coastal Malibu and the Santa Monica Bay.

Malibu is reached most easily by the Pacific Coast Highway, with canyon roads wandering off to connect smaller communities in the hills. Malibu tends to be less Democratic than other towns this side of the mountains.

Development is sparse by design; Malibu has seen the fate of its built-up southeastern neighbor, Santa Monica, and opted instead for controlled residential construction on its beaches and hillsides. While many in the San Fernando Valley are tearing their hair out over traffic, many in Malibu are free to focus instead on the environment.

1990 Population: 572,563. White 484,496 (85%), Black 11,845 (2%), Other 76,222 (13%). Hispanic origin 72,221 (13%). 18 and over 450,849 (79%), 62 and over 78,094 (14%). Median age: 35.

HOUSE ELECTIONS

1996 General		
Brad Sherman (D)	106,193	(50%)
Rich Sybert (R)	93,629	(42%)
Ralph Shroyer (PFP)	6,267	(3%)
Erich Miller (LIBERT)	5,691	(3%)
Ron Lawrence (NL)	3,068	(1%)
1996 Primary		
Brad Sherman (D)	27,513	(54%)
Elizabeth "Liz" Knipe (D)	7,580	(15%)
Jeffrey A. Lipow (D)	5,360	(10%)
Michael Jordan (D)	4,786	(9%)
Craig "Tax Freeze" Freis (D)	2,540	(5%)
Mark S. Pash (D)	1,774	(3%)
Elisa J. Charouhas (D)	1,650	(3%)

CAMPAIGN FINANCE

	Receipts	Receipts from PACs	Expend-itures
1996			
Sherman (D)	$1,380,322	$221,755 (16%)	$1,364,516
Sybert (R)	$899,820	$272,823 (30%)	$898,786

DISTRICT VOTE FOR PRESIDENT

1996		1992	
D	117,724 (52%)	**D**	128,572 (48%)
R	83,412 (37%)	**R**	79,728 (30%)
I	16,165 (7%)	**I**	57,625 (22%)

KEY VOTES

1997

Ban "partial birth" abortions — N

25 Howard P. 'Buck' McKeon (R)

Of Santa Clarita — Elected 1992, 3rd term

Biographical Information
Born: Sept. 9, 1939, Los Angeles, Calif.
Education: Brigham Young U., B.S. 1985.
Occupation: Clothing store owner.
Family: Wife, Patricia Kunz; six children.
Religion: Mormon.
Political Career: William S. Hart School Board, 1978-87; Santa Clarita City Council, 1987-92, mayor, 1987-88.
Capitol Office: 307 Cannon Bldg. 20515; 225-1956.

Committees
Education & Workforce
Oversight & Investigations; Postsecondary Education, Training & Life-Long Learning (chairman)
National Security
Military Procurement; Military Readiness

In Washington: McKeon once observed that in his constituency, "most people would just as soon the government went away." But even in this conservative-dominated district, there are some federal functions the locals embrace, such as funding for continued production of the B-2 bomber and for earthquake disaster relief.

The 25th includes the epicenter of California's January 1994 earthquake, and the resulting damage prompted McKeon to plead that Washington play an activist role in rejuvenating the local economy and infrastructure. He implored colleagues to support President Clinton's multibillion-dollar disaster relief package, which was only partly financed by offsetting spending cuts elsewhere in the budget. "We can now help to alleviate the human suffering by funding the necessary disaster assistance to rebuild people's homes, businesses and lives," McKeon said.

And with the GOP House takeover in 1995, McKeon gained responsibility for overseeing one of the federal government's larger endeavors: job training. At the start of the 104th, McKeon became chairman of the Postsecondary Education, Training and Life-Long Learning Subcommittee on the Economic and Educational Opportunities Committee. (The full committee's title was changed in 1997 to Education and the Workforce.)

From his subcommittee chair, McKeon took the lead on a bill to overhaul the government's job-training activities — a complex network of more than 100 programs that cost about $20 billion a year. Each chamber passed a bill to eliminate many of the job programs and consolidate others, and a conference committee also reached agreement. But the legislation fell prey to partisan bickering and died at the end of the session.

The measure the House passed in 1995 would have created three block grants to the states, with an annual authorization of up to $5.6 billion. But the conference report that emerged in July 1996 consolidated the 100 disparate programs into a single block grant for state and local governments. But it snubbed Democratic concerns by repealing President Clinton's 1994 school-to-work law and failing to earmark $1.3 billion for workers laid off because of international competition. It did not have the support of a single Democratic conferee.

Conservative groups, such as the Eagle Forum, headed by Republican activist Phyllis Schlafly, also balked at the legislation, arguing that it would give the federal government "Big-Brother-like" control over education and the labor market.

But in May 1997 McKeon was successful in gaining House passage of a job training overhaul bill that consolidated more than 60 federal job training and adult education programs into three state block grants. The measure had strong bipartisan support as both Democrats and Republicans agreed that existing programs often leave potential recipients confused and unserved.

In 1995, McKeon was also busy lobbying for continued production of the B-2 bomber. The radar-evading stealth plane is built by thousands of his constituents at a Northrop-Grumman plant in Palmdale. McKeon used his National Security Committee seat to join with other B-2 proponents in laying the groundwork for buying more planes than the 20 previously funded. They were successful in adding $493 million to the fiscal 1996 Pentagon request for B-2 procurement.

They also foiled an effort to strike B-2 funds from the House version of the defense appropriations bill. Opponents of continued B-2 funding argue that the plane was designed to conduct nuclear attacks against the Soviets in the 1970s and 1980s. The collapse of the Soviet Union, coupled with the emphasis on reducing the U.S. deficit, makes the plane a juicy target for budget cutters.

But B-2 supporters contend that once the plane is equipped with highly accurate "smart" bombs, it will be just the kind of weapon to give U.S. forces an edge in non-nuclear combat. "We have 15 years invested in this and over $40 billion, and now when they can build the planes cheaper,

CALIFORNIA 25
Northern Los Angeles County; Lancaster; Palmdale

The 25th encompasses northern Los Angeles County, running to the borders of Ventura County to the west, Kern County to the north and San Bernardino County to the east. Much of the land area is consumed by the San Gabriel Mountains in the Angeles National Forest and other lands controlled by the federal Bureau of Land Management. The district's southwestern end reaches down into the city of Los Angeles.

This district is a mix of rural and suburban areas, with three roughly equally sized pockets of population separated by the federal lands: the Antelope Valley in the northeast, the Santa Clarita Valley in the west, and L.A.'s upper San Fernando Valley in the far southwest.

This boot-heel corner of the 25th includes the Northridge section of Los Angeles, the epicenter of a major earthquake (6.6 on the Richter scale) that hit on Jan. 17, 1994. Damage in the district included the collapse of the Northridge Meadows apartment complex, where 16 people died.

The northwestern part of the San Fernando Valley in the 25th is primarily residential, as is most of the valley, with electronics and aerospace manufacturing to the west side.

The Santa Clarita Valley, just north of the San Fernando Valley, also is primarily composed of Los Angeles suburbs, but along with its vast tracts of new homes it is attracting new manufacturing that cannot afford to locate in Los Angeles proper. Santa Clarita — a city of 111,000 created in 1987 when the communities of Valencia, Canyon Country, Saugus and Newhall merged — has attracted industry, office and retail centers, and even two amusement parks. ITT Aerospace Controls transferred about 400 workers to the area, and the U.S. Postal Service has opened a 1,800-employee processing center. McKeon was the new city's first mayor.

Up in the high desert past the national forest is the Antelope Valley, the fastest-growing area of the three. It consists of a lot of desert, a little of Edwards Air Force Base and two cities, Lancaster and Palmdale. This area's economy revolves around aerospace; it is home to about 80 percent of Edwards' 11,000 workers.

Palmdale is where a consortium of high-tech companies, including Northrop Grumman, has been building the B-2 bomber. Also, Lockheed Martin was preparing to begin research and production on the joint strike fighter and a reusable launch vehicle.

Palmdale also is the home of Plant 42, known as the Flight Test Center, which runs a range of aircraft through their paces, including the space shuttle and the SR-71.

The Antelope Valley is not nearly as dependent on Los Angeles as are the Santa Clarita and San Fernando valleys, but over the past decade it has attracted some residents who are willing to commute the 50 or so miles it takes to get to jobs in Los Angeles.

Registered Republicans are a near majority of voters in the 25th. All three of the district's population centers are considered quite conservative, with Antelope Valley residents the most conservative.

1990 Population: 573,105. White 458,364 (80%), Black 25,724 (4%), Other 89,017 (16%). Hispanic origin 94,172 (16%). 18 and over 414,953 (72%), 62 and over 54,250 (9%). Median age: 31.

when the production line is there, we are talking about cutting it. That just does not make sense," McKeon told the House. "The real issue is, if B-2 production is capped, our ability to produce modern bomber aircraft will vanish quickly."

McKeon also has been an advocate of the higher defense budgets put forth by the GOP-run committee, complaining that "the decline in defense spending that began in the aftermath of the Cold War has drastically accelerated under the Clinton administration."

The millionaire owner of a chain of Western-wear stores, McKeon normally backs his party's efforts to reduce federal spending, voting for measures providing tax and spending cuts and reducing the rate of spending growth on Medicare. In 1997, he gave his unqualified support to Speaker Newt Gingrich, who was reprimanded and assessed a penalty of $300,000 by the House for violating ethics rules in his political fundraising activities. McKeon was one of 26 Republicans to vote against the reprimand, telling The Washington Times that the "whole process was politicized." McKeon also called the $300,000 fine "outrageous," the newspaper reported.

McKeon demonstrated some legislative savvy in the 104th by slipping a provision into an omnibus parks and lands bill prohibiting the Agriculture Secretary, who oversees the Forest Service, from transferring land within the Angeles National Forest in McKeon's district. The provision was important to district residents because land in the Elsmere Canyon section of the forest was under consideration for transfer to a company planning to build a solid waste landfill.

The 190-million-ton landfill was designed to be a major repository for trash from Los Angeles County. McKeon told his House colleagues that "the tract proposed for the landfill is on the western edge of the Angeles National Forest, it is an integral part of the forest's ecosystem and provides unique and spectacular educational and recreational opportunities for visitors to the forest." Then he added, "to sacrifice a prime area of National Forest land for a questionable landfill project is clearly not in the public's interest." McKeon's provision blocking the transfer passed the House in 1995 and the Senate in 1996.

At Home: In 1992, the real race for the newly created 25th was in the GOP primary, which McKeon won by a slim 705 votes out of nearly 62,000 ballots cast. McKeon finished just ahead of Phillip D. Wyman, a 14-year state Assembly veteran.

Each tried to outdo the other with endorsements to prove his conservative bona fides, in particular his aversion to taxes. Stressing that his business skills would make government more efficient, McKeon pointed to his family's successful chain of stores that thrived even in the midst of the 1990 recession and its aftermath.

McKeon got the support of GOP Rep. Bill Thomas, whose previous district included much of what is now the 25th. In the end, Wyman held most of his north county base in the Antelope Valley around Palmdale. But McKeon prevailed by scoring well in Santa Clarita, where he had served as a city councilman for five years.

The general election was something of an anticlimax. The Democrat, James H. "Gil" Gilmartin, a lawyer and rancher, and independent Rick Pamplin, a screenwriter who tied his campaign to Ross Perot, tried to make a race of it. But McKeon had a sizable spending advantage, and then as now, voter registration in the district favored the GOP. McKeon took 52 percent, finishing 19 points ahead of Gilmartin. Since then he has won re-election with ease.

HOUSE ELECTIONS

1996 General		
Howard P. "Buck" McKeon (R)	122,428	(62%)
Diane Trautman (D)	65,089	(33%)
Bruce Acker (LIBERT)	6,173	(3%)
Justin Charles Gerber (PFP)	2,513	(1%)
1996 Primary		
Howard P. "Buck" McKeon (R)	49,883	(85%)
David B. Starr (R)	9,076	(15%)
1994 General		
Howard P. "Buck" McKeon (R)	110,301	(65%)
James H. Gilmartin (D)	53,445	(31%)
Devin Cutler (LIBERT)	6,205	(4%)

Previous Winning Percentages: 1992 (52%)

CAMPAIGN FINANCE

	Receipts	Receipts from PACs		Expend-itures
1996				
McKeon (R)	$458,140	$168,576	(37%)	$384,011
Trautman (D)	$16,831	0		$16,434
1994				
McKeon (R)	$483,320	$138,670	(29%)	$474,945
Gilmartin (D)	$34,858	0		$34,857

DISTRICT VOTE FOR PRESIDENT

	1996		1992
D	84,212 (41%)	**D**	83,305 (36%)
R	97,002 (47%)	**R**	89,987 (39%)
I	18,320 (9%)	**I**	57,398 (25%)

KEY VOTES

1997	
Ban "partial birth" abortions	Y
1996	
Approve farm bill	Y
Deny public education to illegal immigrants	Y
Repeal ban on certain assault-style weapons	+
Increase minimum wage	N
Freeze defense spending	N
Approve welfare overhaul	Y
1995	
Approve balanced-budget constitutional amendment	Y
Relax Clean Water Act regulations	Y
Oppose limits on environmental regulations	N
Reduce projected Medicare spending	Y
Approve GOP budget with tax and spending cuts	Y

VOTING STUDIES

	Presidential Support		Party Unity		Conservative Coalition	
Year	S	O	S	O	S	O
1996	33	66	94	5	92	4
1995	15	83	97	2	98	2
1994	47	51	94	4	100	0
1993	30	67	94	4	93	5

INTEREST GROUP RATINGS

Year	ADA	AFL-CIO	CCUS	ACU
1996	0	n/a	100	100
1995	0	0	100	88
1994	5	11	100	95
1993	5	8	100	100

26 Howard L. Berman (D)

Of North Hollywood — Elected 1982, 8th term

Biographical Information
Born: April 15, 1941, Los Angeles, Calif.
Education: U. of California, Los Angeles, B.A. 1962, LL.B. 1965.
Occupation: Lawyer.
Family: Wife, Janis Schwartz; one child, one stepchild.
Religion: Jewish.
Political Career: Calif. Assembly, 1973-83.
Capitol Office: 2330 Rayburn Bldg. 20515; 225-4695.

Committees
International Relations
Asia & the Pacific (ranking)
Judiciary
Courts & Intellectual Property; Immigration & Claims
Standards of Official Conduct (ranking)

In Washington: During a dozen years in the House, Berman has earned a reputation as a serious-minded legislator who prefers hearing rooms to TV studios. Early in 1997 he was called on to take one of the least desirable jobs in the House — ranking member on the House ethics committee.

After his selection by the House Democratic leadership, Berman said "having agreed to accept this assignment . . . these are the standards that will guide me: The ethics committee is neither a member protection agency nor a forum for deciding partisan and ideological battles. Those battles should be carried out at the polls." He will serve with Utah Republican James V. Hansen, who will be committee chairman.

Members of both parties had expressed dismay over how extensively partisan politics seeped into the investigation of Speaker Newt Gingrich over alleged violations of House ethics rules, and both parties wanted to restore the bipartisan accord that once dominated the panel. The choice of Hansen and Berman to lead the committee was an attempt by both parties to give the ethics committee a clean start after the controversial reign of Connecticut Republican Nancy L. Johnson, who had publicly sparred with ranking Democrat Jim McDermott of Washington over the Gingrich investigation.

As a member of the Judiciary and International Relations panels, where he is the ranking member on the Asia and the Pacific Subcommittee, Berman sparred with Republicans on a range of issues, particularly their attempts to overhaul immigration policy and to cut back foreign aid.

Berman spent much of his energy in the 104th Congress trying to kill provisions in a broad immigration bill that would have curtailed federal benefits for legal immigrants and cut back the number who can enter the country. The struggle pointed up the complexity in Berman's position on immigration. Although he objected to GOP efforts to drop the number of visas for legal immigrants, he is not opposed to making it more difficult for illegal immigrants to enter — a position backed by many southern Californians, since their state has been hard-pressed financially by an influx of illegals. Yet Berman will not go so far as to deny a public school education to illegal immigrant children. When the House passed such a measure in September 1996, Berman voted "no."

Berman steadfastly opposed provisions Republicans included in the broad immigration bill that targeted family reunification visas, which were to be curbed and restricted to immediate relatives. After the first five years — when extra visas would be provided to help clear out waiting lists — the bill would have cut family visas from about 480,000 per year to 330,000. The bill also would have eliminated current visa slots for the siblings and most adult children of U.S. citizens, including tens of thousands already on waiting lists. Berman had led the fight in Judiciary against the cuts, saying they would unfairly separate new arrivals from family members. As the bill moved to the floor in March 1996, however, his effort picked up significant conservative support.

Republicans Dick Chrysler of Michigan and Sam Brownback of Kansas joined Berman in offering the amendment to strike most of the legal immigration restrictions. "Legal immigration has been good for this country," Berman said in asking for support. "Don't tear it apart; don't tear family unification apart." The amendment passed, 238-183, with 75 Republicans voting for it.

Before the bill passed, Berman worked to kill an amendment pushed by farm-state lawmakers that would have created a new migrant worker program, admitting up to 250,000 foreigners per year to harvest the nation's crops. Supporters said that without the program, growers may be caught without enough help at harvest time.

But Berman and other opponents said agriculture businesses were simply trying to ensure a supply of cheap, pliant labor. And he added that in the middle of the fight against illegal immigration, it doesn't make sense to replace illegal aliens with legalized foreign guest workers. "This is the most audacious amendment I can imagine to this bill," Berman told the House. "You're opening up the

CALIFORNIA 26
San Fernando Valley

The 26th is the heart of the San Fernando Valley. The district begins at the Angeles National Forest and drops south through the valley down to the Ventura Freeway.

The Northridge earthquake of Jan. 17, 1994 (6.6 on the Richter scale), had its epicenter just west of the 26th and spread its damage across the district. A section of Interstate 405 within the 26th collapsed, gas leaks started fires that consumed 70 homes in Sylmar, and an oil line exploded in San Fernando, where the quake flattened 63 homes and damaged another 835.

This part of the valley has undergone striking demographic changes. Areas such as Pacomia and Van Nuys that had only a small minority presence 20 years ago are now heavily Hispanic.

Also new are the small clusters of black families that have appeared throughout this district. While the number of blacks in downtown Los Angeles has dropped over the past 10 or so years, it has risen in the county overall.

A variety of manufacturing facilities are spread throughout the 26th, but the biggest concentration of the heaviest industry is toward the north, in Pacomia and Sylmar.

The area is desperately searching for a replacement for its lucrative but dying aerospace industry. Defense conversion issues are a primary concern, with an eye toward getting the area's aerospace contractors into advanced transportation such as magnetic-levitation trains.

General Motors, which had been the district's largest employer, closed up shop in Van Nuys in August 1992, putting a squeeze on a city already reeling from the loss of the Lockheed plant in neighboring Burbank in the 27th District.

Van Nuys is trying to avoid having the GM plant site cut up into shopping malls and is struggling to attract another large manufacturer to the area. The city has tried to sell itself as a site to build electric cars; California's stringent clean air rules soon will demand some kind of alternatively fueled vehicles.

The 26th is a good district for a Democrat, though it is much less affluent, much less Jewish and has fewer voters than the district Berman represented before 1992 redistricting. Voter registration levels in the area's Hispanic communities are dramatically lower than in Berman's old district.

The open spaces of Sylmar, rare for the Los Angeles area, have made this community at the district's northern edge one of the fastest-growing areas in the city.

Just south of Sylmar is San Fernando, an independent city embedded within Los Angeles; 83 percent of its 22,600 middle-class residents classify themselves as Hispanic.

On the 26th's eastern edge is Sun Valley, distinctive within the district in that it is made up primarily of an Anglo working class with relatively few Hispanics. North Hollywood, along the Ventura Freeway, is a mix, its east side heavily Hispanic and its west side much less so. Much of the district's Jewish population lives toward the west.

1990 Population: 571,523. White 305,795 (54%), Black 35,611 (6%), Other 230,117 (40%). Hispanic origin 301,153 (53%). 18 and over 410,112 (72%), 62 and over 55,596 (10%). Median age: 29.

most blatant, massive loophole in illegal immigration." The amendment was defeated, 180-242.

Despite all his work on the bill in the House, Berman was disappointed with its final outcome. Democrats had been virtually shut out of the conference committee, and the final bill included items that were in neither the House nor the Senate bill, including new restrictions on legal immigrants. Berman ended up voting against the conference report in September 1996.

Berman had some success early in the 104th with an effort to secure federal reimbursement to states for the costs of incarcerating illegal aliens. He attached the language to a GOP crime bill that would speed the deportation of illegal aliens who commit crimes. The Congressional Budget Office estimated the annual cost of his proposal at about $650 million, with the lion's share going to California. While Rules and Judiciary committee leaders opposed the amendment because it would create a new entitlement program, other GOP leaders and Sun Belt members expressed strong support. Meanwhile, Berman warned that insufficient support would send a clear message: "Republican leadership to California: Drop Dead."

After considerable behind-the-scenes scrambling, Berman agreed to a compromise that would guarantee a federal payment of $650 million annually from fiscal 1996 to 2000 to affected states.

From his International Relations seat, Berman opposed the committee's wide-ranging bill to consolidate the foreign affairs bureaucracy and reduce funding for overseas programs. Although the committee approved an amendment to earmark $280 million in each of the next two years for programs benefiting children, many Democrats opposed the earmark, charging that Republicans were trying to mask overall cuts of foreign aid. "You're trying to have it both ways," said Berman in May 1995, "emasculate development assistance and say 'we're working for the kids.' "

In May 1996, Berman was chosen for an eight-member select subcommittee to investigate President Clinton's tacit acceptance of Iran arming the Bosnian Muslims during the civil war in the former Yugoslavia, even as the administration was arguing publicly for continuation of an arms embargo in the region. The select panel released its 200-plus page report in October and the GOP majority accused senior Clinton administration officials of making false statements to Congress concerning the administration's knowledge of the arms shipments. But administration officials joined congressional Democrats in denouncing the report as an election-eve attempt to tarnish the president.

"It is our belief that no laws were broken, no wrongdoing occurred, no covert actions took place, no false statements given, no U.S. interests harmed," said a statement by the subcommittee's Democrats — Berman, Lee H. Hamilton of Indiana and Alcee L. Hastings of Florida.

Berman also keeps a hand in partisan affairs back home. Berman and fellow Rep. Henry A. Waxman co-founded a highly successful political organization in western Los Angeles County.

At Home: The "Berman-Waxman" organization dominates the West Los Angeles political scene. It is less a machine than a network of like-minded politicians who pool resources to back candidates — expected to be legislative allies — with money, organization, computer technology and the skills of Berman's brother, Michael, a consultant. Howard Berman's influence in Democratic politics stretches to the late 1960s, when he and Waxman, students at UCLA, were involved in the Federation of Young Democrats. Berman succeeded Waxman in the federation's presidency in 1967 and helped him win a seat in the state Assembly the following year.

In 1972, it was Berman's turn to run. He challenged a veteran GOP member of the Assembly in a traditionally Republican district that had grown more Democratic. Pulling in funds from his contacts and mobilizing Young Democrats, students and recent migrants from the inner city, Berman won. In Sacramento he built up a cadre of followers in the Legislature and allied himself with Speaker Leo T. McCarthy and Gov. Edmund G. "Jerry" Brown Jr. He was a consummate facilitator and tactician with a relaxed style.

In 1980, Berman bet his career chips on a challenge to McCarthy, who had been his ally. The clash ended badly for both men: Their rivalry opened the door for a third candidate, Willie L. Brown Jr., to become Speaker (a job he would hold into the 1990s). Soon thereafter, Brown helped pass a congressional redistricting plan that included a perfect district for Berman. Still, Berman had to work for it when the GOP nominated a wealthy auto dealer who had strong financial backing. Berman walked precincts and, with his brother's help, ran an extensive direct-mail campaign. He won with 60 percent of the vote and has had little trouble since.

In early 1996, Berman expressed some interest in challenging GOP Los Angeles Mayor Richard Riordan, when his term ended the following year. But by the fall, Berman had backed away.

HOUSE ELECTIONS

1996 General		
Howard L. Berman (D)	67,525	(66%)
Bill Glass (R)	29,332	(29%)
Scott K. Fritschler (LIBERT)	3,539	(3%)
Gary Hearne (NL)	2,119	(2%)
1996 Primary		
Howard L. Berman (D)	26,745	(84%)
Steven E. Gibson (D)	5,177	(16%)
1994 General		
Howard L. Berman (D)	55,145	(63%)
Gary E. Forsch (R)	28,423	(32%)
Erich D. Miller (LIBERT)	4,570	(5%)

Previous Winning Percentages: **1992** (61%) **1990** (61%) **1988** (70%) **1986** (65%) **1984** (63%) **1982** (60%)

CAMPAIGN FINANCE

	Receipts	Receipts from PACs	Expend-itures
1996			
Berman (D)	$436,348	$157,300 (36%)	$408,096
Glass (R)	$83,133	0	$78,469
1994			
Berman (D)	$468,464	$190,295 (41%)	$432,535
Forsch (R)	$38,939	$984 (3%)	$38,922

DISTRICT VOTE FOR PRESIDENT

	1996		1992
D	71,416 (65%)	**D**	72,673 (57%)
R	27,129 (25%)	**R**	31,013 (24%)
I	7,930 (7%)	**I**	24,167 (19%)

KEY VOTES

1997	
Ban "partial birth" abortions	N
1996	
Approve farm bill	N
Deny public education to illegal immigrants	N
Repeal ban on certain assault-style weapons	N
Increase minimum wage	Y
Freeze defense spending	Y
Approve welfare overhaul	N
1995	
Approve balanced-budget constitutional amendment	N
Relax Clean Water Act regulations	?
Oppose limits on environmental regulations	?
Reduce projected Medicare spending	N
Approve GOP budget with tax and spending cuts	N

VOTING STUDIES

	Presidential Support		Party Unity		Conservative Coalition	
Year	**S**	**O**	**S**	**O**	**S**	**O**
1996	82	11	87	5	20	73
1995	83	8	86	6	21	76
1994	83	15	91	2	14	78
1993	78	10	86	3	20	73
1992	21	78	89	5	17	79
1991	32	63	83	7	14	81

INTEREST GROUP RATINGS

Year	ADA	AFL-CIO	CCUS	ACU
1996	90	n/a	19	0
1995	80	100	27	5
1994	90	88	30	0
1993	95	92	20	5
1992	85	73	25	8
1991	85	82	22	11

27 James E. Rogan (R)

Of Glendale — Elected 1996, 1st term

Biographical Information
Born: Aug. 21, 1957, San Francisco, Calif.
Education: U. of California, Berkeley, B.A. 1979; U. of California, Los Angeles, J.D. 1983.
Occupation: Lawyer.
Family: Wife, Christine Apffel; two children.
Religion: Christian.
Political Career: Glendale Municipal Court judge, 1990-94; Calif. Assembly, 1994-97, majority leader, 1995-97.
Capitol Office: 502 Cannon Bldg. 20515; 225-4176.

Committees
Commerce
Energy & Power; Telecommunications, Trade & Consumer Protection

The Path to Washington: Rogan is the product of a childhood riddled with difficulty, but the stars have shined on his political career since its infancy.

The former judge and state legislator was the immediate choice of area Republicans to succeed retiring 12-term Rep. Carlos J. Moorhead. The national party touted his candidacy as one of their best hopes throughout the campaign year of 1996, and House Republicans, recognizing a potential star in their midst, rewarded him with a seat on the Commerce Committee in the 105th.

Moorhead had served as Republican ranking member on Commerce in the 103rd Congress but was denied its chairmanship at the start of the 104th because he was seen as having been too conciliatory toward Democrats in the past. Rogan reached across the aisle to make deals in Sacramento; he may be more conservative than Moorhead, but he is certainly equally amiable.

Rogan, a born-again Christian, draws praise across party lines as articulate, calm and willing to compromise. He wins respect even from those who disagree violently with his opposition to affirmative action and abortion rights in most cases, or his support of gunowners' rights and school vouchers. In a 1996 survey of the Legislature by the independent California Journal, Rogan was rated the best overall member of the Assembly.

Rogan's Democratic opponent, Doug Kahn, attempted to link him to unpopular spending cuts proposed by House Republicans. But Rogan, like many Republicans running in tight races in 1996, likened his own positions on some issues to those held by President Clinton.

Clinton carried the district in 1996 with a greater margin than he had in 1992. Kahn, an heir to the Annenberg publishing fortune, vastly outspent Rogan and drew closer than he had in his two attempts to unseat Moorhead, losing by just 7 percentage points.

The closeness of the race came as some surprise to Rogan, who had previously enjoyed a flawless ascent up the political ladder. His switch from the Democratic Party helped him as a Los Angeles County prosecutor draw the attention of Republican Gov. George Deukmejian, who appointed him a municipal judge in 1990. At age 33, he was the state's youngest sitting judge.

Rogan's House campaign's World Wide Web home page depicted him wearing judicial robes, but he had since traded them in for a seat in the state Assembly. He easily won an eight-way special primary in 1994 for the nomination to succeed a legislator convicted of racketeering.

Shortly after winning a full term, Rogan was approached by GOP colleagues who envisioned him as their first Assembly Speaker in a quarter-century. Republicans held a volatile one-seat majority in the chamber, and Rogan played a key role in reconciling the leadership struggle.

Republicans hoped that Assembly Democrats, some of whom had worked with Rogan on issues from strengthening domestic violence laws to legalizing the medical use of marijuana, would find him a compromise choice. But because Rogan had already decided to run for Congress, he opted for the slightly less taxing role of majority leader.

It was a swift rise for the high school dropout. Rogan never knew his biological father; his stepfather was an alcoholic. His mother was a convicted felon and welfare recipient, and he was raised mostly by his grandparents. He attended a community college and received a law degree from the University of California at Los Angeles.

After working briefly as a corporate lawyer, Rogan became a deputy district attorney. He once won a drunken driving case by making a point visually, pouring out 10 beers in front of jurors.

In the Assembly, Rogan voted against a bill to outlaw certain cheap handguns. He won a reputation as a strong supporter of gun rights, but nevertheless broke a logjam on another gun control measure. His amendment made it a felony for gang members and convicted criminals to carry concealed weapons and added a provision to allow citizens who were otherwise law-abiding to be charged only with a misdemeanor.

CALIFORNIA 27
Northeastern Los Angeles County; Pasadena; Burbank

Set in the rolling San Gabriel Mountains, the 27th is dominated on the north by the Angeles National Forest and spread evenly with suburbs through the south.

The district is a mirror of the demographic changes that California has seen in the past decade. Immigration has transformed WASP neighborhoods into rainbows of ethnicity. This development, along with new areas the 27th gained in redistricting, has made this once reliably Republican seat much more competitive.

After years of easy re-election victories, GOP Rep. Carlos J. Moorhead drew only 50 percent of the vote in 1992 and 53 percent in the Republican landslide of 1994. Republican Rogan won with 50 percent in 1996, as Bill Clinton carried the district again in presidential voting.

The major cities of the 27th — Burbank, Glendale and Pasadena — suffered extensive property damage but no loss of life in the 1994 Northridge earthquake. Burbank took a big hit in 1990 when Lockheed began closing its 64-year-old plant and moving or laying off the 12,000 workers there. The area is still heavily blue-collar, but it now relies more on its entertainment industry, including the NBC and Disney studios. Economic pain has moderated the city's traditional bias against growth.

Once a sleepy bedroom community, Glendale now has 180,000 residents, making it the largest city in the district and the third largest in Los Angeles County (after L.A. proper and Long Beach). About 35,000 Soviet Armenians have settled here since 1985, followed by large numbers of Filipinos, Koreans and Hispanics; now, less than half of Glendale's public school students speak English as their first language. The Soviet Armenians are joining a small, much wealthier, Iranian Armenian community that has lived in Glendale since the shah was overthrown in the late 1970s.

These changes have taken their toll on the city's Republican voting habits. Clinton won the city in 1992 by about 100 votes — unthinkable just a few years ago.

While Burbank and Glendale are less than 2 percent black, 19 percent of Pasadena's 132,000 residents are black. It is the heavily black and Hispanic half of Pasadena that the district gained in 1992 redistricting. The only part of Pasadena outside the 27th District is a heavily Republican sliver to the east, in the 28th. The city includes many engineering firms that have flocked to CalTech and its Jet Propulsion Laboratory, which is in nearby La Cañada.

Pasadena is flanked by the working-class suburbs of Altadena on the north and South Pasadena to the southwest, and by the wealthy community of San Marino to the southeast. Altadena is 39 percent black and overwhelmingly Democratic, while South Pasadena is only 3 percent black and favors Republicans.

1990 Population: 572,594. White 406,235 (71%), Black 47,493 (8%), Other 118,866 (21%). Hispanic origin 56,154 (10%). 18 and over 445,260 (78%), 62 and over 88,053 (15%). Median age: 34.

HOUSE ELECTIONS

1996 General		
James E. Rogan (R)	95,310	(50%)
Doug Kahn (D)	82,014	(43%)
Elizabeth Michael (LIBERT)	6,645	(4%)
Walt Contreras Sheasby (GREEN)	4,195	(2%)
1996 Primary		
James E. Rogan (R)	46,020	(88%)
Joe Paul (R)	6,521	(12%)

CAMPAIGN FINANCE

	Receipts	Receipts from PACs	Expend-itures
1996			
Rogan (R)	$805,884	$291,283 (36%)	$763,574
Kahn (D)	$1,057,536	$127,762 (12%)	$1,052,335
Michael (LIBERT)	$9,666	0	$3,300

DISTRICT VOTE FOR PRESIDENT

	1996		1992
D	98,348 (49%)	D	98,057 (44%)
R	81,282 (41%)	R	80,986 (37%)
I	13,324 (7%)	I	42,071 (19%)

KEY VOTES

1997

Ban "partial birth" abortions Y

28 David Dreier (R)

Of San Dimas — Elected 1980, 9th term

Biographical Information

Born: July 5, 1952, Kansas City, Mo.
Education: Claremont McKenna College, B.A. 1975; The Claremont Graduate School, M.A. 1976.
Occupation: Real estate developer and property manager.
Family: Single.
Religion: Christian Scientist.
Political Career: Republican nominee for U.S. House, 1978.
Capitol Office: 237 Cannon Bldg. 20515; 225-2305.

Committees

Rules
Rules & Organization of the House (chairman)

In Washington: Just now in his mid-40s, the fit and dapper Dreier is well into his second decade of congressional service. He was on hand for his party's earlier political "revolution" — the one that elected Ronald Reagan to the White House in 1980 and sent Dreier (at age 28) and a bevy of other young conservatives to the House.

Dreier shares the unblinking social and economic conservativism of the latter-day Republican revolutionaries — the ones whose election in 1994 helped deliver the House into GOP hands.

But in a House chamber where ideological warring and rhetorical rancor is common, Dreier retains a friendly air — identifying colleagues on the floor, for instance, not only by their home state but also by their hometown. Unlike a number of less-senior conservatives who promise not to tarry long in the House, Dreier — the No 2 Republican on the Rules Committee — has an abiding interest in the institution and has devoted much of his career toward its reorganization.

In April 1997, Dreier hosted a hearing on civility in Congress as chairman of the Subcommittee on Rules and Organization of the House. In an irony lost on no one, Dreier had to shut down the meeting as verbal hostilities erupted on the House floor between Democrats who were accusing Speaker Newt Gingrich of lying and Republicans who had demanded a vote to strike that attack from the official record.

The contretemps stemmed from Gingrich's ethics case, in which he was found to have offered misleading information to a congressional investigation. Dreier was one of Gingrich's leading public defenders, appearing frequently on television to acknowledge the Speaker's errors but to try to put them in perspective as fairly minor. Still, despite the brouhaha, Dreier believes the GOP Congress has raised the level of esteem in which the institution is held by the public — if only slightly. "I think people have shifted from corrosive cynicism to healthy skepticism," he said.

Despite his chumminess with Gingrich — Dreier serves as an adviser and member of the Speaker's unofficial kitchen Cabinet — and his lofty position on Rules, Dreier made no showy presence during the first term of GOP rule. When Republicans took the House in 1994, there was talk that Dreier might get the Rules chair, leapfrogging New York Republican Gerald B.H. Solomon, who in the 103rd had briefly campaigned against Gingrich for party leader. But Solomon's conservative credentials were solid and Gingrich decided to let seniority prevail.

In behalf of the banking industry, which had a dispute in the 104th with insurers about the shape of banking and securities legislation, Dreier let his feelings be known. But, in general, Dreier has been pleased to support the broader Republican agenda without pursuing much of one of his own.

One area of particular interest of Dreier's is free trade; he is one of the House's leading voices for it. He works with Democrats as part of the bipartisan rump group that forms itself each spring to defend China's favorable trading status with the United States. He was a tireless crusader for NAFTA in 1993 and considered passage of that trade agreement and GATT nothing less than what any self-respecting Republican should do: open up trade across borders and expand markets worldwide. "I do not consider myself to be a Pat Buchanan Republican," he declared.

Dreier acknowledged the relatively isolationist stance adopted by many of his newer House colleagues and said he was "trying my darndest" to help them focus on freeing and growing markets. Although Dreier is now in his ninth term, he is still younger than many members even of the Class of 1996. He pursues a heavy, steady exercise regimen and maintains a youthful air, despite slightly thinning locks.

Dreier is a longtime proponent of lowering the capital gains tax rate, which he calls "a drag on the economy," and in 1996 he opposed raising the minimum wage. "Increasing a federally mandated minimum wage is a job-killer," he declared.

As it is for many members from Southern California, illegal immigration is a top concern of Dreier's, and he supported GOP efforts during the

CALIFORNIA 28
Northeastern Los Angeles suburbs

The Angeles National Forest and its mountains run through the northern half of the 28th District. The 210 Freeway, also known as the Foothill Freeway, runs through the lower half, an area spread evenly with Los Angeles bedroom communities.

From west to east along the 210, the district takes in a sliver of eastern Pasadena and the cities of Sierra Madre, Arcadia, Monrovia, Covina and San Dimas. La Verne and Claremont lie farther east. Temple City is south of Arcadia, and West Covina and Walnut are to the south of Covina. These are comfortable suburban neighborhoods typical of Southern California.

Much of the development here arrived right after World War II, and many of the people who arrived then are still here. In large part, these are people whose parents grew up nearby and whose children and grandchildren are now populating Orange County and San Bernardino.

Arcadia, a city of 48,000, boasts of its "beautiful homes, tree-lined streets, magnificent gardens and its more than 3,489 private swimming pools."

Driving through the district, it is hard to tell when one city has been left behind and another entered. The district just misses some much less wealthy areas, such as El Monte, southeast of Temple City. The industry that does exist here is confined to small defense subcontractors and service industries.

The city of Duarte, south of Monrovia, is known for its City of Hope National Medical Center, a nonprofit treatment and research hospital specializing in rare medical problems that treats its patients for free. Bradbury is an exclusive town of about 800 residents set in the hills just north of Duarte.

While the residents of the 28th primarily identify themselves as citizens of the separate towns in which they live, they also identify as residents of the San Gabriel Valley. Although many of them commute to downtown Los Angeles for work, they do not consider themselves part of that city, to the extent that residents have agitated unsuccessfully for years to declare the San Gabriel Valley a county of its own.

The cities within the valley work closely together on such issues as transportation and water. A light rail line stops in Covina and continues west into Los Angeles.

Like in many of Los Angeles' suburbs, residents here tend to be socially moderate and economically conservative. Politically, the district is spread as evenly as its buildings. Dreier, who has gotten at least 58 percent of the vote in every re-election, drew 61 percent in 1996. But Bill Clinton narrowly carried the district in the presidential election with 45 percent of the vote.

1990 Population: 572,927. White 406,342 (71%), Black 32,778 (6 %), Other 133,807 (23%). Hispanic origin 56,398 (10%). 18 and over 423,910 (74%), 62 and over 77,009 (13%). Median age: 33.

104th to tighten the nation's borders. He voted in favor of a proposal by neighboring Republican Elton Gallegly that would have denied public schooling to illegal immigrants. Dreier termed this a natural outgrowth in Congress of the popular will in his state, which in 1994 passed an initiative to cut illegal immigrants off from all public services save for emergency medical care.

Gingrich appointed Dreier head of a California task force meant to look out for the interest of the largest state, which otherwise enjoyed no representation among top-level GOP leaders. (California Republican Christopher Cox holds the highest position among Golden Staters as chairman of the party's Policy Committee.) He also named Dreier to head a task force to see whether further changes should be wrought to the committee system for the 105th.

Dreier's task force returned a tepid report, and in contrast to the first Republican term, no major changes to committee structures were made in 1997. Dreier testified along with Indiana Democrat Lee H. Hamilton in 1997 before a task force seeking to revise the House's ethics system in the wake of the Gingrich case, arguing in favor of allowing outsiders, including former members, to take part in investigations.

The proposal grew from the work of the Joint Committee on the Organization of Congress, a panel Hamilton co-chaired in the 103rd; Dreier was co-vice chair. Few of the Joint Committee's recommendations were embraced in the Democratic-controlled 103rd, but when the 104th convened, the House GOP majority put in place a number of changes: The number of standing committees was reduced by three, and the number of subcommittees was cut; about half the committees were renamed to reflect new Republican legislative priorities; and the number of congressional employees was reduced, mostly by cutting committee staff and personnel working for member-backed legislative support organizations. Also, one of the first measures the House GOP brought to a vote was a bill that eliminated Congress' exemption from a host of regulatory laws.

The committee proposed legislation that would institute two-year budgeting, require Congress to comply with labor laws and other employment regulations, and broaden lobbying and ethics reform, among other things. Dreier considered the committee's final recommendations too timid — he wanted a much more sweeping reorganization of the committee structures in both the House and Senate.

But he gave his support to the committee's final product when the House leadership guaranteed him an open rule that would allow for Republican amendments when the legislation reached the House floor.

Prior to joining Rules, Dreier used his positions on the Banking and Small Business committees to promote the privatization of government services and elimination of federal agencies he deems unnecessary — the Small Business Administration, for instance. Dreier brought his distaste for bureaucracy to the 1988 debate over aid for the homeless. "We are creating a permanent homeless infrastructure in this country," he said. "What we essentially created is another grassroots lobby that Congress will be unable to say 'no' to in the future."

Although Dreier supports his party's call to cut off funding for the Corporation for Public Broadcasting in an age of budget austerity, he is a huge fan of public radio. Dreier's calls for private donations and personal offerings of challenge grants are a fixture of the fund drives of Washington station WAMU-FM as well as for fund drives for public radio stations in California.

At Home: Dreier frequently is listed among the possible GOP candidates for a Senate run, but as yet, despite amassing a massive campaign treasury, he has shown little movement toward abandoning his safe House seat.

After a narrow victory over a Democratic incumbent in 1980, Dreier was made secure by redistricting. A decade later, a new redistricting plan left Dreier to run in a different but almost equally compatible district. Despite a general weakening of the Republican vote in the state in 1992, Dreier won with 58 percent, and he has been above 60 percent since then.

Dreier first came to Congress after waging a four-year campaign against Democratic Rep. Jim Lloyd. Using the influential GOP establishment linked to the Claremont colleges as his springboard, Dreier started in 1978. Underfinanced and only 26 years old, Dreier still came within 12,000 votes of Lloyd. Dreier's 1980 bid showed greater maturity and more effort to discuss issues. He followed much of the national Republican agenda, supporting the Kemp-Roth tax cut and Reagan's presidential candidacy.

National GOP sources, rating Lloyd the most vulnerable Democratic incumbent in the state, helped Dreier outspend him by almost 2- to-1 and brought in Reagan to campaign for him. This time Dreier won with 52 percent.

Dreier ended up in another fight two years later — with a fellow Republican. Redistricting had moved his Pomona political base out of the 35th, where he had won in 1980, into the neighboring 33rd. But the 33rd was also home to GOP Rep. Wayne Grisham.

The primary pitted a sedate, casual Grisham against an aggressive, dynamic Dreier. With voters given a choice between different personalities, not different ideologies, Dreier's energy, organization and fundraising brought him a solid victory.

HOUSE ELECTIONS

1996 General		
David Dreier (R)	113,389	(61%)
David Levering (D)	69,037	(37%)
Ken Saurenman (LIBERT)	4,459	(2%)
1994 General		
David Dreier (R)	110,179	(67%)
Tommy Randle (D)	50,022	(30%)
Jorj Clayton Baker (LIBERT)	4,069	(2%)

Previous Winning Percentages: **1992** (58%) **1990** (64%) **1988** (69%) **1986** (72%) **1984** (71%) **1982** (65%) **1980** (52%)

CAMPAIGN FINANCE

	Receipts	Receipts from PACs	Expend-itures
1996			
Dreier (R)	$831,156	$308,415 (37%)	$396,104
Levering (D)	$50,262	0	$50,651
1994			
Dreier (R)	$559,455	$140,995 (25%)	$279,050
Randle (D)	$28,848	$4,500 (16%)	$28,905

DISTRICT VOTE FOR PRESIDENT

	1996		1992
D	88,709 (45%)	**D**	82,958 (38%)
R	86,358 (44%)	**R**	90,644 (41%)
I	15,215 (8%)	**I**	45,623 (21%)

KEY VOTES

1997	
Ban "partial birth" abortions	Y
1996	
Approve farm bill	Y
Deny public education to illegal immigrants	Y
Repeal ban on certain assault-style weapons	?
Increase minimum wage	N
Freeze defense spending	N
Approve welfare overhaul	Y
1995	
Approve balanced-budget constitutional amendment	Y
Relax Clean Water Act regulations	Y
Oppose limits on environmental regulations	N
Reduce projected Medicare spending	Y
Approve GOP budget with tax and spending cuts	Y

VOTING STUDIES

	Presidential Support		Party Unity		Conservative Coalition	
Year	S	O	S	O	S	O
1996	33	66	97	2	94	2
1995	17	82	97	2	97	0
1994	38	62	96	1	97	0
1993	34	64	94	3	93	7
1992	84	13	90	8	98	0
1991	84	15	89	10	100	0

INTEREST GROUP RATINGS

Year	ADA	AFL-CIO	CCUS	ACU
1996	0	n/a	100	100
1995	0	0	96	80
1994	5	0	92	100
1993	0	0	100	96
1992	0	8	75	100
1991	0	0	90	100

29 Henry A. Waxman (D)

Of Los Angeles — Elected 1974, 12th term

Biographical Information
Born: Sept. 12, 1939, Los Angeles, Calif.
Education: U. of California, Los Angeles, B.A. 1961, J.D. 1964.
Occupation: Lawyer.
Family: Wife, Janet Kessler; two children.
Religion: Jewish.
Political Career: Calif. Assembly, 1969-75.
Capitol Office: 2204 Rayburn Bldg. 20515; 225-3976.

Committees
Commerce
Health & Environment; Oversight & Investigations
Government Reform & Oversight (ranking)

In Washington: The 105th Congress gives Waxman a new arena in which to throw his partisan barbs. As ranking Democrat on the Government Reform and Oversight Committee, he is the lead thorn in the side of House Republicans attempting to investigate alleged campaign finance abuses of the Clinton White House.

As the committee in early 1997 tried to get its bearings under a new chairman, Indiana Republican Dan Burton, Waxman was a walking soundbite complaining about the investigation's "subpoena party," "unprecedented scope" and "needless waste of taxpayer dollars," deriding the process as "'Watergate wannabe . . . more concerned with scoring political points than with reform."

Waxman griped about his minority side's meager budget (a quarter of the GOP's) and about the committee's initial dozens of subpoenas going exclusively to Democratic targets, as well as about Burton's authority to issue those subpoenas without consulting the full committee. Burton relented slightly on the last point, agreeing to give Waxman 24 hours' notice before issuing new subpoenas. But should he object, Waxman was given no avenue of appeal. "In effect," he said, "I get a chance to talk to Mr. Burton and see if I can influence him."

Some Republicans worried that Waxman might influence the committee's progress all too much. Although Burton is a tenacious partisan, he has his hands full matching the wiles of Waxman, who has managed, regardless of which party holds Congress or the presidency, to cut deals right and left and advance his liberal agenda.

Waxman revealed the secret of his success during the 104th, when he commented about Republicans, "They think compromise is a dirty word even though compromise can further your ideas, and even help you improve your ideas." As Republicans sometimes did in the 104th, Waxman can set pie-in-the-sky policy goals, but more often he is maneuvering patiently and persistently to secure one small slice at a time. He has often gotten much of what he wants in the end.

"God never meant liberals to be stupid," Waxman once said, and he lives to be proof of that.

He had to watch in horror as Republicans sought during the 104th to make massive changes in programs he had nursed to full growth, such as in their efforts to make Medicaid into a block grant to states. But he did not watch in silence, and in working to define the Democratic response to GOP attempts to overhaul such entitlements, he helped doom them politically.

He also could watch with satisfaction as a cause he had pursued for years — discouraging smoking — gained new ammunition.

As chairman of the Energy and Commerce Subcommittee on Health and Environment from 1979 to 1995, Waxman was the tobacco industry's staunchest foe. At an April 1994 hearing of the health subcommittee, Waxman and other anti-smoking members subjected seven leading tobacco company executives to a six-hour grilling on the health effects of using tobacco. "The truth is that cigarettes are the single most dangerous consumer product ever sold," Waxman said.

A former smoker who has the zeal of the converted, Waxman in 1996 lit into GOP presidential nominee Bob Dole when he casually suggested that tobacco might be no more addictive than milk. And Waxman could barely suppress his glee (and certainly did not suppress his scheduler from booking him for TV appearances), as big tobacco continued to get black eyes in the courts in cases involving cigarette manufacturers' complicity in smoke-related deaths. Waxman devoted 36 pages of the Congressional Record in July 1995 to a reprinting of apparent Philip Morris research on the addictive effects of nicotine on third-graders, college students and others.

Waxman hoped his old tobacco hearings would be reopened as affidavits were released by the Food and Drug Administration that suggested early industry knowledge of the addictiveness of nicotine. He acknowledged there was little chance that would happen "because the tobacco

CALIFORNIA 29
West Los Angeles County; Santa Monica; West Hollywood

The 29th begins at the coast in Santa Monica and curves northeast to take in some of California's best-known areas: West Los Angeles, Beverly Hills, West Hollywood, most of Hollywood, the Hollywood Hills and just a bit of the San Fernando Valley.

The district avoided the worst of the 1994 Northridge earthquake, which was concentrated on the northern side of the Santa Monica Mountains. But even in Santa Monica, inspectors found that more than 500 buildings had been badly damaged.

This affluent, predominantly white district is heavily Democratic. The city of Santa Monica is strikingly more liberal than its coastal counterparts south of Los Angeles, giving 55 percent of its vote to Walter F. Mondale in 1984 and at least 63 percent to every Democratic presidential nominee since then.

Although Santa Monica's 87,000 residents are mostly affluent, the city has a large renter population; 75 percent of the city's housing units are occupied by renters, who have brought about strict rent control laws. It boasts substantially more commercial activity than Malibu, its northern neighbor, with several very successful commercial-industrial parks, shopping malls and regular street fairs.

The city and its environs grew steadily in the 1980s. Pacific Palisades, just north of Santa Monica right on the coast, has some large new developments. But because so much of the area is already fully developed, much of the new construction consists of knocking down existing structures and replacing them.

Heading out of the city on Santa Monica Boulevard, the flat land turns to the rolling foothills of the Santa Monica Mountains. Set onto the hills' southern slopes are Westwood, home to the University of California-Los Angeles (with 34,700 students), and Bel Air, the retirement home of former President Ronald Reagan.

Just past Westwood is Beverly Hills, with its fabulously elaborate homes north of Sunset Boulevard and low-rise (but high-rent) apartment buildings south of it. Another affluent community, Brentwood, gained international notoriety as the scene of a murder case involving former football star O.J. Simpson.

A key to Waxman's success in the district is the heavily Jewish area of Fairfax, just east of Beverly Hills. Its residents have supported him devotedly for many years.

Farther east along the boulevard is West Hollywood, a city of 36,000 residents that incorporated in 1984. It has a large, politically well-organized homosexual population and a high concentration of senior citizens.

Before the last round of redistricting, many of the motion-picture industry's heavyweights were packed into one district. Now they are split between two: the 29th retains the bulk of the Hollywood area and all of Universal City to the north, but the 30th District pokes up just enough to take in the Paramount Studios lot and the southeastern side of Hollywood — including the eastern half of the intersection of Hollywood Boulevard and Vine Street, the symbolic center of the movie industry.

1990 Population: 571,566. White 478,696 (84%), Black 19,931 (3%), Other 72,939 (13%). Hispanic origin 75,315 (13%). 18 and over 495,536 (87%), 62 and over 106,905 (19%). Median age: 37.

industry has given over $2 million to Newt Gingrich and the Republican majority and they're getting their money's worth because they've stopped the Congress' investigation and they bought silence."

But for all his attacks on Republicans and his votes against their policies on welfare, abortion and tax cuts, Waxman as usual found a way to work with his opponents. Commerce Chairman Thomas J. Bliley Jr. may hail from a tobacco district in Virginia, but Waxman found him to be someone he could deal with on other issues.

With the nation's hazardous waste superfund needing reauthorization, Waxman and top Commerce Democrat John D. Dingell of Michigan presented a united front. They had often split on environmental issues when Democrats were in the majority, but in the new Republican world they offered a single Democratic face. Despite negotiations in good faith on the issue, the bill died in the Senate in 1996.

But Waxman was able to work toward success on other issues. He and Bliley (among others) negotiated for five days in July 1996 and emerged with a compromise on regulation of pesticides used in food that broke an 18-year deadlock. Insisting on strict health standards, Waxman ensured that consumption of the regulated food products would cause only about a one-in-a-million risk of cancer. In addition, the compromise contained strict standards to safeguard the health of infants and children.

A safe drinking water bill that was hailed by leaders of both parties as the major environmental achievement of the 104th was largely the result of bipartisan agreement, specifically between Waxman and Bliley.

Still, Waxman is undeniably seeing his expansive vision of the federal government's role curtailed by the GOP agenda, and by President

Clinton's willingness to compromise. Waxman supported a Democratic alternative to the first Republican bill to overhaul welfare, but admitted he did so reluctantly. "I don't think I would have voted for that in another time," he said.

Waxman began the 103rd Congress poised to be one of the key players in Clinton's effort to reform the health care system. He was in the top rank of health experts in Congress, and he had long worked to achieve universal health care coverage, the key tenet of Clinton's plan. But on this front, the 103rd brought frustration. Clinton's reform proposal foundered, and efforts to develop a substitute came to nothing in Energy and Commerce; no legislation even made it to the markup stage in Waxman's subcommittee.

For most of the time Waxman was Health and Environment chairman, conservative Republicans held the White House, but that did not prevent the Californian from compiling an impressive record of legislative victories. His formula for success was to go after problems bit by bit, year after year, rather than launch a broad frontal assault, as Clinton did when he sought to overhaul the entire health care system in the 103rd.

At Home: With his own re-election campaigns mere formalities, Waxman has built political influence by helping others win elections. The Los Angeles-based organization he co-founded with Rep. Howard L. Berman has been a force in congressional and state-level politics in California.

Not only are Waxman's constituents politically involved, no small number of them also are wealthy. And that has enabled him to build an impregnable position for himself (he won 68 percent in both 1994 and 1996) and an impressive apparatus for extending his political influence far and wide. Waxman's political machinations have long been a joint venture with Berman, a college chum who joined him in the House in 1982.

The Waxman-Berman alliance was originally forged at UCLA, when the two budding politicians became active in the state's Federation of Young Democrats. Their first visible success came in 1968, when Waxman challenged Democratic Assemblyman Lester McMillan in a primary.

McMillan had been in office 26 years and was nearing retirement. Rather than waiting until the seat opened up, Waxman decided to take on the incumbent. With massive volunteer help, much of it recruited from the ranks of the Young Democrats, Waxman beat McMillan with 64 percent of the vote.

That election saw the beginning of what has since become a Waxman-Berman trademark — computerized mailings. Each voter is identified by a variety of sociopolitical characteristics and given a campaign pitch specifically tailored to his or her interests.

Although sometimes called a machine, the Waxman-Berman operation has been frustrated as often as it has been successful in the 1990s. While the name partners remain secure, they were unable to promote Democratic House colleague Mel Levine to the Senate in 1992 and were badly beaten in their campaigns against term limits for state and federal legislators.

HOUSE ELECTIONS

1996 General		
Henry A. Waxman (D)	145,278	(68%)
Paul Stepanek (R)	52,857	(25%)
John Peter Daly (PFP)	8,819	(4%)
Mike Binkley (LIBERT)	4,766	(2%)
Brian Rees (NL)	3,097	(1%)
1994 General		
Henry A. Waxman (D)	129,413	(68%)
Paul Stepanek (R)	53,801	(28%)
Michael J. Binkley (LIBERT)	7,162	(4%)

Previous Winning Percentages: **1992** (61%) **1990** (69%) **1988** (72%) **1986** (88%) **1984** (63%) **1982** (65%) **1980** (64%) **1978** (63%) **1976** (68%) **1974** (64%)

CAMPAIGN FINANCE

	Receipts	Receipts from PACs	Expend-itures
1996			
Waxman (D)	$417,504	$228,400 (55%)	$365,082
Stepanek (R)	$135,868	$17,000 (13%)	$135,677
1994			
Waxman (D)	$174,641	$126,895 (73%)	$186,127
Stepanek (R)	$70,807	$5,514 (8%)	$70,777

DISTRICT VOTE FOR PRESIDENT

1996		1992	
D	150,771 (67%)	**D**	183,233 (66%)
R	53,354 (24%)	**R**	55,924 (20%)
I	10,639 (5%)	**I**	37,217 (14%)

KEY VOTES

1997	
Ban "partial birth" abortions	N
1996	
Approve farm bill	N
Deny public education to illegal immigrants	N
Repeal ban on certain assault-style weapons	N
Increase minimum wage	Y
Freeze defense spending	Y
Approve welfare overhaul	N
1995	
Approve balanced-budget constitutional amendment	N
Relax Clean Water Act regulations	N
Oppose limits on environmental regulations	Y
Reduce projected Medicare spending	N
Approve GOP budget with tax and spending cuts	N

VOTING STUDIES

	Presidential Support		Party Unity		Conservative Coalition	
Year	S	O	S	O	S	O
1996	76	15	89	3	6	86
1995	86	7	89	4	8	86
1994	76	23	93	2	3	94
1993	82	18	90	2	18	75
1992	16	81	90	5	13	85
1991	27	63	84	6	14	70

INTEREST GROUP RATINGS

Year	ADA	AFL-CIO	CCUS	ACU
1996	90	n/a	13	0
1995	95	100	13	4
1994	90	100	25	0
1993	100	100	18	4
1992	95	82	25	0
1991	90	83	10	0

30 Xavier Becerra (D)

Of Los Angeles — Elected 1992, 3rd term

Biographical Information
Born: Jan. 26, 1958, Sacramento, Calif.
Education: Stanford U., A.B. 1980, J.D. 1984.
Occupation: Lawyer.
Family: Wife, Carolina Reyes; two children.
Religion: Roman Catholic.
Political Career: Calif. Assembly, 1990-92.
Capitol Office: 1119 Longworth Bldg. 20515; 225-6235.

Committees
Ways & Means
Health

In Washington: Becerra has willingly donned the cloak of advocate for the nation's immigrants. With Republicans in power and pursuing an agenda that includes major restrictions on immigration and services for immigrants, Becerra has been a leader in the rear-guard fight on these issues, and also on overhaul of the welfare system.

In the 105th Congress, he has a louder megaphone through which to speak on such matters in his new capacity as chairman of the Congressional Hispanic Caucus. Additionally, House Democratic leaders, who are ever eager to add diversity to the top tier committees, granted Becerra a seat on the Ways and Means Committee in 1997. He is the first Hispanic to serve on the powerful panel.

Becerra watched the Hispanic Caucus pool drain a bit in January 1997 as Cuban-American Reps. Ileana Ros-Lehtinen and Lincoln Diaz-Balart, both Florida Republicans, resigned in anger over a trip that he and fellow Southern California Democrat Esteban E. Torres took to Cuba in December 1996.

Becerra has a confident and assertive manner and supports a decidedly liberal agenda. As a member of the Judiciary Subcommittee on Immigration and Claims in the 104th, he criticized GOP efforts to enact a more restrictive immigration policy. Becerra had personal as well as political interest in the debate, since his own parents entered the United States as immigrants.

In the 104th's early deliberations on a comprehensive immigration bill, Becerra supported the concept of family-based immigration and fought hard against proposals that he felt would choke off the immigration channels for adult children of legal immigrants. Discouraging the reuniting of parents and children, he said, was "a complete contradiction of what we're trying to do to promote family values."

Becerra tried unsuccessfully to amend the immigration bill to increase funding for the Immigration and Naturalization Service so the agency could process pending applications for citizenship, some of which face long delays. He did win support for an amendment that would refund the application fees of people on the waiting list who would be rejected under new immigration law.

Becerra laid some of the responsibility for illegal immigration at the feet of businesses and agricultural operations that rely on immigrant labor. He argued that the federal government should do more to enforce labor standards, which would discourage the employment of illegal aliens.

Becerra also argued, unsuccessfully, against proposals to reduce welfare costs by disqualifying legal immigrants from receiving assistance. He reminded advocates of this approach that "legal immigrants pay every single tax that U.S. citizens pay."

The welfare overhaul legislation enacted in 1996 eliminated many benefits to legal immigrants; Becerra was one of 98 Democrats voting against the welfare bill in July 1996. Republican leaders had tempered it sufficiently to secure a promise from President Clinton that he would sign it.

Becerra also was a vocal opponent of conservatives' efforts to mandate that the federal government conduct business and print documents in English only.

When the Judiciary Committee debated a balanced-budget constitutional amendment in the 104th, Becerra took a poke at proponents' argument that because families must balance their budgets, so too should government. Becerra noted that families undertake all manner of deficit-financing schemes, including home mortgage loans, auto loans and student loans.

He sought to offer an amendment which would put each federal department's year-end surplus into a rainy day fund that the department could use the following year, instead of the surplus reverting to the general treasury. Sending surplus funds to the treasury, Becerra said, encourages a "use or lose mentality" in federal agencies. Consideration of this amendment was

CALIFORNIA 30
Central, East and Southeast Los Angeles

This densely populated district starts west of downtown Los Angeles, swings up and around, and comes down on downtown's eastern side. The western side of the 30th — East Hollywood, the mid-Wilshire area and especially Koreatown — was hit hard by rioting in May 1992.

More than 100,000 Koreans live in Koreatown in a compact corner of the 30th's southwest portion. Rioters torched more than 300 businesses, and damage was estimated at $200 million. Since that time, the City of Los Angeles has designated the western side of the 30th a redevelopment area, allowing special financing programs for rebuilding projects in addition to federal funding for streetscape improvement and low-income housing.

Voter registration is low in the 30th and even lower in Koreatown, described as a "transitional area," with many recent arrivals who are either illegal or applying for residency. Koreans are just now beginning to flex their political muscle. There was considerably higher voter participation in the district in 1996 than 1992, due partly to a California ballot initiative to end affirmative action. Koreatown tends to look inward and does not rely on tourism as heavily as do Chinatown and Little Tokyo.

Just north of Koreatown is the mid-Wilshire area, with high-rise office buildings along Wilshire Boulevard and apartment buildings everywhere else. Farther north is lower-middle-class East Hollywood, less densely populated and less affluent than the mid-Wilshire area. The homes get bigger and more expensive to the west, in the 29th District.

Dodger Stadium, north of downtown in Elysian Park, serves as the 30th's centerpiece. Elysian Park is a blue-collar neighborhood, with a moderate number of Hispanics. Directly west of Elysian Park are the communities of Silver Lake (half of which is in the 29th, half in the 30th) and Echo Park, which have strong reputations for community activism and liberal voting.

The areas are troubled by some gang activity and graffiti. An estimated one-fourth of their residents are homosexual.

On the northeastern end of the district is the bedroom community of Eagle Rock, a hilly, middle-class pocket of relative affluence that votes Democratic but is more toward the political center than other parts of the 30th. The eastern side leads to Highland Park, a heavily Hispanic, blue-collar area with a significant Mexican immigrant presence.

Across the Pasadena Freeway from Highland Park is Lincoln Heights, and on the district's southeastern tip, Boyle Heights, both of which are heavily Hispanic. Between Boyle Heights and Lincoln Heights is tiny Mount Washington, the 30th's most affluent section, with great views of the city and a reputation for social activism. The district is overwhelmingly Democratic; in 1996, Bill Clinton drew 71 percent.

1990 Population: 572,538. White 249,412 (44%), Black 20,039 (4%), Other 303,087 (53%). Hispanic origin 351,876 (61%). 18 and over 415,463 (73%), 62 and over 56,090 (10%). Median age: 29.

blocked in committee.

In the 103rd Congress, Becerra long remained undecided on NAFTA, but in the end he voted for the trade pact. What decided his vote, he said, was that California's exports to Mexico had increased nearly 200 percent since 1987 and that 100,000 jobs in the state exist solely because of trade with Mexico.

At Home: In 1990, Becerra left Sacramento, where he had been a state deputy attorney general and legislative aide, and moved into the Los Angeles community of Monterey Park to wage and win a bid for the California Assembly. He had not completed his first term there when he launched a campaign for the open 30th, though his home stood outside the district.

Becerra was recruited to serve in the newly drawn, overwhelmingly Hispanic 30th by retiring Democrat Edward R. Roybal, who represented a major part of it for 30 years.

Although drafted by Roybal, Becerra was not the outgoing incumbent's first choice. Henry Lozano, Roybal's top district aide, was deemed heir apparent. (Roybal's daughter, Lucille Roybal-Allard, was anointed for the adjoining 33rd, which includes another major portion of Roybal's old constituency.) But Lozano was not interested in a competitive race. He dropped out, and Becerra got Roybal's support.

He outran nine other candidates in the primary, including school board member Leticia Quezada, another popular rising star in the Latino community. Becerra won nomination with not quite a third of the vote. Thanks to the backing of Roybal and other Latino leaders, Becerra was able to shrug off the carpetbagger label applied by some of his opponents.

Typical for heavily Hispanic districts, and the 30th's precincts in particular, turnout was very low, with only about 33,000 ballots cast.

Becerra won the general election with 58 percent of the vote. He was re-elected in 1994 with 66 percent in 1994 and 72 percent in 1996. The 1996 election saw higher-than-usual voter turnout in the district, due in part to a California ballot initiative to end affirmative action.

HOUSE ELECTIONS

1996 General		
Xavier Becerra (D)	58,283	(72%)
Patricia Jean Parker (R)	15,078	(19%)
Pam Probst (LIBERT)	2,759	(3%)
Shirley Mandel (PFP)	2,499	(3%)
Rosemary Watson-Frith (NL)	1,971	(2%)
1994 General		
Xavier Becerra (D)	43,943	(66%)
David A. Ramirez (R)	18,741	(28%)
R. William Weilburg (LIBERT)	3,741	(6%)

Previous Winning Percentages: 1992 (58%)

CAMPAIGN FINANCE

	Receipts	Receipts from PACs	Expend-itures
1996			
Becerra (D)	$244,064	$151,474 (62%)	$223,890
1994			
Becerra (D)	$287,205	$184,970 (64%)	$234,096

DISTRICT VOTE FOR PRESIDENT

	1996		1992
D	61,114 (71%)	**D**	56,378 (63%)
R	17,053 (20%)	**R**	21,750 (24%)
I	4,165 (5%)	**I**	11,842 (13%)

KEY VOTES

1997	
Ban "partial birth" abortions	N
1996	
Approve farm bill	N
Deny public education to illegal immigrants	N
Repeal ban on certain assault-style weapons	N
Increase minimum wage	+
Freeze defense spending	Y
Approve welfare overhaul	N
1995	
Approve balanced-budget constitutional amendment	N
Relax Clean Water Act regulations	N
Oppose limits on environmental regulations	Y
Reduce projected Medicare spending	N
Approve GOP budget with tax and spending cuts	N

VOTING STUDIES

	Presidential Support		Party Unity		Conservative Coalition	
Year	**S**	**O**	**S**	**O**	**S**	**O**
1996	71	14	88	2	8	84
1995	79	8	83	2	4	84
1994	73	21	88	2	11	72
1993	71	23	91	1	9	86

INTEREST GROUP RATINGS

Year	ADA	AFL-CIO	CCUS	ACU
1996	85	n/a	23	0
1995	85	100	9	9
1994	100	78	36	0
1993	95	92	20	4

31 Matthew G. Martinez (D)

Of Monterey Park — Elected 1982; 8th full term

Biographical Information
Born: Feb. 14, 1929, Walsenburg, Colo.
Education: Los Angeles Trade-Technical College, 1959.
Military Service: Marine Corps, 1947-50.
Occupation: Upholstery company owner.
Family: Separated; five children.
Religion: Roman Catholic.
Political Career: Monterey Park City Council, 1974-80, mayor, 1974-75; Calif. Assembly, 1981-82.
Capitol Office: 2234 Rayburn Bldg. 20515; 225-5464.

Committees
Education & Workforce
Early Childhood, Youth & Families (ranking); Workforce Protections
International Relations
Asia & the Pacific; Western Hemisphere

In Washington: A number of the Democrats first elected to the House in 1982 have gone on to bigger things: Harry Reid of Nevada, Richard J. Durbin of Illinois and Robert G. Torricelli are in the Senate. Bill Richardson is United Nations representative. Several others in the class now play prominent roles on House committees.

Martinez, though, has always been one of the lower-profile members of the 1982 class, and with Republicans in control of the House, there are even fewer opportunities for him to draw the spotlight.

There is little in the conservative GOP playbook that comports with Martinez's thinking, but he generally leaves the flights of liberal oratorical rage to other, more animated Democrats. He votes a pro-labor, socially liberal line, devoting special attention to the needs of children and the elderly.

In the 105th Congress, Martinez serves as the ranking member on the Education and the Workforce Committee's Early Childhood, Youth and Families Subcommittee. He also has a seat on the International Relations Committee.

During the 104th's contentious debate on welfare overhaul, Martinez made the case that the GOP's proposals for changing the welfare system would hurt children and senior citizens. He spoke in favor of federal nutrition programs, saying they "protect the elderly, who are responsible for the greatness of our nation, [and] protect the children, who are our future." He argued that the GOP's approach to welfare reform did little to alleviate the root causes of poverty that force people onto the assistance rolls — lack of jobs, skills and child care.

He was one of 98 liberal Democrats to oppose the final version of the welfare bill that the House passed in July 1996. President Clinton signed the measure in August.

From his seat on the Education Committee in the 104th, Martinez criticized the GOP for trying to cut back federal education funding. He said the proposed cuts would hinder Americans at the bottom of the economic ladder, and he accused Republicans of "taking care of the rich and ignoring the children of today."

In the Democratic-controlled 103rd Congress, when Martinez chaired the Education and Labor Subcommittee on Human Resources, he sponsored legislation, along with Massachusetts Democratic Sen. Edward M. Kennedy, that expanded and improved the Head Start program. The bill, which reauthorized Head Start through fiscal 1998, also required new performance controls and quality standards for Head Start centers. The bill cleared Congress easily with strong bipartisan support.

An abortion rights supporter, Martinez voted in the 104th to allow privately funded abortions at overseas military hospitals; to allow federal employees' health plans to cover abortion; and to require states to fund Medicaid abortions for poor women in cases of rape, incest or threat to the life of the woman. However, he has supported conservatives' efforts to ban a particular abortion technique that opponents call "partial birth" abortion.

In 1993, Martinez voted against the Brady bill, which requires a five-day waiting period before the purchase of a handgun. And when the House in 1994 considered legislation to ban 19 types of semiautomatic assault-style weapons, Martinez at first said he would vote no, arguing that the bill would ship gun manufacturing jobs overseas while not stopping criminals from obtaining the weapons.

But Martinez was heavily lobbied by the Clinton administration, and he ended up voting for the assault weapons ban. Martinez said after the vote that although he was a member of the National Rifle Association and had supported its views in the past, "their position gets to be more militant all the time." In March 1996, he voted against a GOP-led effort to repeal the assault weapons ban.

During the 104th, Martinez served as ranking member on the Education Committee's Employer-Employee Relations Subcommittee, where he was a consistent supporter of the views of organized labor. He voted for a 90-cent

CALIFORNIA 31
Eastern Los Angeles County; El Monte; Alhambra; Azusa

The middle-income, blue-collar 31st takes in the southern San Gabriel Valley heading west from its section of East Los Angeles to Azusa, including along the way a fistful of good-size, independent cities. The influx of Hispanics to the area is turning even the district's Republican areas Democratic.

Hispanics make up 59 percent of the district's population but just 42 percent of its voters. Asians account for 23 percent of the population but just 10 percent of the voters. This pattern of low minority registration is seen throughout Los Angeles.

Like many members of newly arrived immigrant groups, the district's Hispanics and Asians identify strongly with the Democratic Party despite cultural patterns that might otherwise tag them as conservatives. In the 31st, there are about twice as many voters registered Democratic as Republican.

A number of engineers live here and work for small employers in the district or head south toward Long Beach. Many Los Angeles municipal and county employees also call the 31st home.

The East Los Angeles section of the 31st is the residential section of that lower-income community; its business neighborhoods are south, in the 34th.

Monterey Park and San Gabriel are the relatively wealthy areas of the district. Almost 60 percent of Monterey Park's 61,000 residents are Asian, and more than 30 percent are Hispanic. San Gabriel is now about one-third Asian and one-third Hispanic. Less than 1 percent of each city's residents are black. Republicans used to be able to count on San Gabriel's residents, but Martinez has won in the city.

In the middle of the district are Rosemead, South El Monte and El Monte. Half of Rosemead's 52,000 residents are Hispanic, 85 percent of South El Monte's population of 21,000 is and nearly three-fourths of El Monte's 106,000 inhabitants are.

Baldwin Park resembles the East Los Angeles part of the 31st; its residents range from the middle-income to the poverty level.

Most of the businesses in the district are small or midsize. Irwindale has a few exceptions, such as a Miller Brewing Co. facility, one of the district's largest employers. Many of the city's rock quarries have been converted into industrial parks. Heavy industry exists only outside the district, in such nearby areas as Vernon.

Farther east, Azusa is another former Republican stronghold that now supports Martinez. The city has been able to attract a concentration of high-tech companies.

The San Gabriel Valley is considered more moderate than L.A.'s east side and less likely than other parts of Los Angeles County to stick to partisan lines. But the 31st stuck close to those lines in 1996 presidential voting. Bill Clinton won the 31st with 65 percent of the vote, above his statewide average. And Martinez' winning percentage was his highest ever.

1990 Population: 572,643. White 276,310 (48%), Black 9,561 (2%), Other 286,772 (50%). Hispanic origin 335,086 (59%). 18 and over 403,689 (70%), 62 and over 62,671 (11%). Median age: 28.

increase in the minimum wage, and he has opposed a Republican effort to allow companies to offer their employees comp time in lieu of overtime pay. Labor groups and many Democrats argued that the measure would open the door to workers being coerced to take time off when they really wanted pay for their overtime work.

Martinez opposed another Republican initiative, the so-called TEAM bill, which would have allowed non-union companies to set up and control worker-management committees that could discuss pay and benefits. Martinez, echoing the opinion expressed by organized labor, said the bill could be used to discourage employees from joining unions and would potentially "foment dictatorial practices in the workplace."

In 1990, when the Education and Labor Committee considered a bill reauthorizing the Job Training Partnership Act (JTPA), Martinez, who was a former chairman of the Employment Opportunities Subcommittee that had the JTPA under its jurisdiction, was repeatedly grilled about details of the bill by one of the panel's Republicans (former Rep. Steve Bartlett). Clearly unnerved, Martinez had to rely on staff to hand him the answers to Bartlett's questions. Though the JTPA bill ultimately died, Martinez was able to push through a measure to provide job training and counseling for displaced homemakers.

At Home: Over the years, Martinez's low profile has emboldened challengers to make several forays against him. None has succeeded.

Martinez has a place of some prominence within the Hispanic population of the Los Angeles area. After winning re-election to the House in 1990, Martinez considered but declined a January 1991 run for the Los Angeles County Board of Supervisors from a district designed, under a court-ordered plan, to favor a Hispanic.

A former Republican, Martinez got his start on the Monterey Park City Council and served as mayor. He served briefly in the state Assembly after defeating veteran incumbent Jack R. Fenton in a 1980 Democratic primary.

In 1982, Democratic Rep. George E. Danielson resigned to accept a judgeship, and Martinez took a plurality in a special election to fill the vacancy. But he then barely survived a runoff with Republican business consultant Ralph Ramirez, who held him to 51 percent.

Seeking a full House term later that year, Martinez met GOP Rep. John H. Rousselot, whose vocal brand of conservatism had earned him a national following. Rousselot's district had been dismembered in redistricting, and he decided to run in the heavily Hispanic 30th rather than challenge another GOP incumbent.

Appealing to voters' conservative social instincts and to their ethnicity, Rousselot used $1,500 in campaign funds for Spanish lessons for his wife and appeared in a Mexican Independence Day parade. But the demographics were too tough; Martinez won with 54 percent.

In 1984, Martinez sank most of his campaign funding into a primary battle with Gladys C. Danielson, the wife of his Democratic predecessor. While her challenge fell far short, it did soften up Martinez for his GOP opponent, lawyer Richard Gomez, who attacked him for poor constituent service and sought a base in the district's growing Asian-American population. Martinez ended up taking 52 percent of the vote.

After this series of close calls, Martinez in 1986 drew a non-Hispanic opponent and finally topped 60 percent.

In 1988, Martinez crushed what had been seen as a tough primary challenge from former Monterey Park Mayor Lily Chen, then in Novem-ber he deflected a comeback attempt by Republican Ramirez, this time taking 60 percent of the vote.

From 1990 through 1994, Martinez's general-election tallies hovered around 60 percent, although in the 1994 Democratic primary he posted just 55 percent against several challengers. Voters in November 1996 gave Martinez his highest-ever share of the vote: 67 percent.

HOUSE ELECTIONS

1996 General		
Matthew G. Martinez (D)	69,285	(67%)
John V. Flores (R)	28,705	(28%)
Michael B. Everling (LIBERT)	4,700	(5%)
1994 General		
Matthew G. Martinez (D)	50,541	(59%)
John V. Flores (R)	34,926	(41%)

Previous Winning Percentages: 1992 (63%) **1990** (58%) **1988** (60%) **1986** (63%) **1984** (52%) **1982** (54%) **1982**† (51%)

† Special election

CAMPAIGN FINANCE

	Receipts	Receipts from PACs	Expend-itures
1996			
Martinez (D)	$110,095	$67,700 (61%)	$83,015
Flores (R)	$39,456	$11,516 (29%)	$39,439
1994			
Martinez (D)	$132,510	$104,700 (79%)	$123,767
Flores (R)	$81,385	$594 (1%)	$81,517

DISTRICT VOTE FOR PRESIDENT

	1996		1992
D	70,288 (65%)	**D**	59,616 (52%)
R	27,736 (26%)	**R**	37,250 (32%)
I	7,043 (7%)	**I**	18,449 (16%)

KEY VOTES

1997	
Ban "partial birth" abortions	Y
1996	
Approve farm bill	N
Deny public education to illegal immigrants	N
Repeal ban on certain assault-style weapons	N
Increase minimum wage	Y
Freeze defense spending	N
Approve welfare overhaul	N
1995	
Approve balanced-budget constitutional amendment	N
Relax Clean Water Act regulations	N
Oppose limits on environmental regulations	Y
Reduce projected Medicare spending	N
Approve GOP budget with tax and spending cuts	N

VOTING STUDIES

	Presidential Support		Party Unity		Conservative Coalition	
Year	S	O	S	O	S	O
1996	78	20	73	21	51	39
1995	80	13	81	9	25	66
1994	83	14	90	6	61	36
1993	77	20	86	8	43	55
1992	16	79	87	6	31	58
1991	31	52	71	10	30	43

INTEREST GROUP RATINGS

Year	ADA	AFL-CIO	CCUS	ACU
1996	80	n/a	31	10
1995	85	100	26	12
1994	70	67	58	15
1993	90	100	30	13
1992	95	91	25	4
1991	65	100	20	11

32 Julian C. Dixon (D)

Of Los Angeles — Elected 1978, 10th term

Biographical Information

Born: Aug. 8, 1934, Washington, D.C.
Education: California State U., Los Angeles, B.S. 1962; Southwestern U., LL.B. 1967.
Military Service: Army, 1957-60.
Occupation: Legislative aide; lawyer.
Family: Wife, Betty Lee; one child.
Religion: Episcopalian.
Political Career: Calif. Assembly, 1973-79.
Capitol Office: 2252 Rayburn Bldg. 20515; 225-7084.

Committees

Appropriations
Commerce, Justice, State & Judiciary; District of Columbia; National Security
Select Intelligence
Human Intelligence, Analysis & Counterintelligence (ranking)

In Washington: After years of defending the District of Columbia and championing home rule for its residents, Dixon found himself on the outs in 1995 as the new Republican majority imposed a financial control board and new budgetary restrictions on the District. Particularly galling for Dixon was that many of the District's financial difficulties developed when he was chairman of the Appropriations Committee's District of Columbia Subcommittee.

It is no wonder then that Dixon's anger at District officials and at the two accounting firms that had audited the city's books was that of a man betrayed. "I have personally come to the conclusion that the District government has not acted in good faith with the Congress," he said at the start of a February 1995 D.C. subcommittee hearing on the city's financial crisis.

Also no wonder that when Dixon's office supplied a three-page list of his accomplishments in the 104th Congress, it was silent as to his work on the D.C. subcommittee.

For the 105th Congress, Dixon has left his post as ranking Democrat of the subcommittee, but he remains a panel member.

Home rule, which Congress granted in 1973, allows the city to elect a mayor and city council and to manage its own budget, although the budget must be approved by Congress. The city receives an annual federal payment to compensate it for tax revenue lost from hosting the federal government, which pays no property taxes.

Dixon had been a loyal supporter of the District when he chaired the subcommittee. Hence, it was a mark of how desperate the city's financial situation appeared in late 1994 and early 1995 that even Dixon began to criticize city officials for shortcomings in fiscal management. During House consideration of the fiscal 1995 D.C. budget, Dixon acknowledged that the city had a financial crisis and needed spending reductions. He denounced suggestions, however, that Congress should scale back its federal payment to the city, which some Republican panel members had suggested. "To hold back funding ... is not going to help the District at this point; it's going to put it further in the hole," he said.

But when faced with the prospect that the D.C. spending bill would not be approved by the House because of concerns about the city's fiscal problems, Dixon agreed to compromise. He worked with the panel's ranking Republican, James T. Walsh of New York — who served as the panel's chairman in the 104th Congress — and with Virginia Republican Thomas J. Bliley Jr. to draft a compromise amendment aimed at reining in the District's spending. The compromise required the city to specify to Congress how it planned to make $150 million in cuts in fiscal 1995, and it required that the city incur no deficit in fiscal 1995.

"The District government is in a precarious financial situation and has lost its credibility with this Congress, so I feel it necessary, in order to get sufficient support for this bill, to enter into an agreement," said Dixon, who had resisted attempts by members to cut the city's $720 million federal payment. In the end, the federal payment was cut to $712 million, the figure ultimately agreed to by House and Senate conferees. Conferees also required the city to cut its budget by $140 million.

In the fiscal 1996 budget, Dixon fought efforts to force the District to use tax dollars to pay tuitions at private schools, and in the fiscal 1997 budget, he unsuccessfully tried to allow the city to spend local money on abortions, as the city was able to do when Democrats controlled Congress. The Republican majority voted to prohibit public funding for abortions except in cases of rape, incest or a health threat to the woman.

Dixon is a well-liked House insider, known for his hard work and diplomacy, but he generally keeps a low profile. Born and reared in a black, middle-class D.C. neighborhood, he has stuck with the D.C. Subcommittee, a job with little prestige and no benefits to his district, because he cares about his hometown.

He also cares about California. He was a key

CALIFORNIA 32
West Los Angeles; Culver City

This compact, diverse district begins about a mile inland from Venice Beach, runs east through Culver City and ends up in south-central Los Angeles. Sandwiched between these areas are dozens of distinct ethnic neighborhoods.

Economically, the 32nd runs the gamut, taking in very wealthy neighborhoods such as Rancho Park in the north, middle- and upper-middle-income suburbs in the west and very poor sections of south-central Los Angeles in the east.

This area is undergoing its second demographic sea change in 30 years. A generation ago, its Jewish population migrated toward the district's northwest end, and the center of the district became predominantly black.

Now there is a new wave of immigrants: Hispanics. Blacks are still the district's largest racial group, but their dominance is slipping as more blacks migrate toward Los Angeles' suburbs. Forty percent of the district's residents are black, 30 percent are Hispanic and 8 percent are Asian.

Despite vast differences between the district's neighborhoods — the Baldwin Hills area actually features operating oil wells — a huge majority of the people in the 32nd vote Democratic. About three-fourths of the district's registered voters are Democrats.

The district's strong Democratic outlook was evident in 1996, when both Bill Clinton and Dixon received more than 80 percent of the vote.

The eastern end of the 32nd is a black working-class area; moving north, the concentration of Hispanics increases. The northeast, near Pico Union, has considerable multifamily housing; to the southeast there are more single-family homes and higher levels of home ownership.

While south-central Los Angeles could be described as "blighted," it is not the type of blight typically found in the very poor areas of Chicago or New York. South-central's blight shows itself in its commercial districts rather than in its residential areas; its residents actually live in fairly well-maintained, older single-family homes.

South-central's commercial areas suffered some of the worst violence during the city's 1992 riots. Many of the stores targeted were owned by Koreans who had been attracted to the area's low property costs. The epicenters of the riot were elsewhere, but substantial violence traveled up Crenshaw Boulevard from Inglewood and down Western Avenue from Koreatown.

Curiously, none of this area used to be known as south-central Los Angeles. South-central traditionally has been thought of as being farther east, but post-riot media coverage has widened the term's scope.

On the issues, people living on the 32nd's eastern side tend to have crime and economic concerns uppermost in mind, while residents on the western side of the district tend to mirror the coast's high level of environmental concern.

1990 Population: 572,595. White 184,266 (32%), Black 230,872 (40%), Other 157,457 (27%). Hispanic origin 173,076 (30%). 18 and over 435,038 (76%), 62 and over 78,322 (14%). Median age: 32.

player behind a 1994 supplemental spending bill to provide federal aid to victims of the January 1994 Northridge earthquake in Southern California. In the 104th, he fought for increased spending for the Immigration and Naturalization Service in order to boost the number of border patrol agents, and he supported additional funds for states that bear the cost of jailing illegal aliens convicted of crimes.

Dixon also has served on Appropriations' Defense Subcommittee, now called National Security, where he has helped direct defense conversion funds back to his home state to compensate for defense industry cutbacks.

From his Appropriations post, Dixon has helped secure federal funds for Los Angeles' Metro Rail subway. He also has pushed for greater access to the subway system for inner-city residents. And in the fiscal 1997 omnibus appropriations bill, he helped secure a $400 million loan for the Alameda Corridor, a 20-mile route connecting the ports of Los Angeles and Long Beach with the national railroad system.

And as a member of the House Intelligence Committee, he said he would push for an investigation into published allegations that the CIA helped fuel the crack cocaine trade in Los Angeles in an attempt to raise money for the contras in Nicaragua. Dixon participated in community forums about the allegations. "It is clear that a thorough airing of the matter is essential," he said.

Dixon's reputation as a reliable, low-key Democratic loyalist earned him six years as chairman of the House ethics committee. When he joined the committee in 1983 and became its chairman in 1985, Dixon expected to serve the usual two-term rotation. However, he was asked by the Democratic leadership to stay on for a third term to handle an investigation of the Democratic leadership.

His judicious conduct of the case involving former Speaker Jim Wright's financial transactions gave no one cause to fault his impartiality. When the turning point came, Dixon voted to pursue most of the charges. Wright resigned from the House in May 1989, obviating any need for a final judgment from the ethics committee.

Dixon's handling of the Wright case made him an oft-quoted figure as the ethics committee in 1996 and 1997 feuded internally over investigating charges against Speaker Newt Gingrich, R-Ga. The committee's ability to work in a bipartisan fashion under Dixon was contrasted with its problems under chairwoman Nancy L. Johnson, R-Conn., and ranking Democrat Jim McDermott of Washington. For example, Dixon said, he used to meet daily with former Rep. John T. Myers, R-Ind., the committee's ranking minority member, to discuss the Wright case. He said the procedure was for the chairman and the ranking member to work out a deal before going to the full committee. Johnson and McDermott, by contrast, had a stormy relationship.

"The regular procedure has broken down, and the procedure of the chairman and ranking member negotiating has been . . . violated," Dixon said.

He also criticized Steven H. Schiff, R-N.M., an ethics committee member who publicly announced that he believed Gingrich should be re-elected as Speaker. "I think that it's appropriate that we can tell members how we intend to vote," Schiff said.

But Dixon said, "I'm unaware of a member of the ethics committee heretofore communicating to the leadership of either party their predisposition to vote a certain way on a sanction. . . . It's my recollection during my tenure that members were exceptionally cautious on making public utterances on issues pending before them."

At Home: Dixon followed a political path blazed by Yvonne Brathwaite Burke, a prominent black official of the 1960s and '70s. When Burke first ran for the House in 1972, Dixon resigned as an aide to state Sen. Mervyn M. Dymally (who later served in Congress) and captured Burke's open Assembly seat. In 1978, when Burke left to run what would be an unsuccessful bid for state attorney general, Dixon beat eight Democratic primary foes to win Burke's House seat.

The primary was a power struggle among political brokers in Los Angeles' black community. Dixon's closest competitor, state Sen. Nate Holden, was backed by Kenneth Hahn, a white Los Angeles County supervisor with considerable popularity in the black areas of South Los Angeles. Another rival, City Councilman David S. Cunningham, was supported by Mayor Tom Bradley. Dixon was the choice of Rep. Henry A. Waxman and then-state Rep. Howard L. Berman (now a House member).

The Waxman-Berman machine helped Dixon win the primary. Dixon ran unopposed that November and regularly collected more than three-fourths of the district vote in each re-election bid thereafter until 1990, when he "slipped" to 73 percent. Redistricting in 1992 did little to alter his situation, and he has won his last three terms with ease.

HOUSE ELECTIONS

1996 General		
Julian C. Dixon (D)	124,712	(82%)
Larry Ardito (R)	18,768	(12%)
Neal Donner (LIBERT)	6,390	(4%)
Rashied Jibri (NL)	1,557	(1%)
1994 General		
Julian C. Dixon (D)	98,017	(78%)
Ernie A. Farhat (R)	22,190	(18%)
John Honigsfeld (PFP)	6,099	(5%)

Previous Winning Percentages: 1992 (87%) **1990** (73%) **1988** (76%) **1986** (76%) **1984** (76%) **1982** (79%) **1980** (79%) **1978** (100%)

CAMPAIGN FINANCE

	Receipts	Receipts from PACs	Expend-itures
1996			
Dixon (D)	$93,520	$64,850 (69%)	$97,495
1994			
Dixon (D)	$181,245	$115,145 (64%)	$141,941
Farhat (R)	$43,914	$614 (1%)	$43,910

DISTRICT VOTE FOR PRESIDENT

	1996		1992
D	130,394 (81%)	**D**	147,623 (78%)
R	19,348 (12%)	**R**	23,956 (13%)
I	5,764 (4%)	**I**	17,561 (9%)

KEY VOTES

1997	
Ban "partial birth" abortions	N
1996	
Approve farm bill	N
Deny public education to illegal immigrants	N
Repeal ban on certain assault-style weapons	N
Increase minimum wage	Y
Freeze defense spending	Y
Approve welfare overhaul	N
1995	
Approve balanced-budget constitutional amendment	N
Relax Clean Water Act regulations	N
Oppose limits on environmental regulations	Y
Reduce projected Medicare spending	N
Approve GOP budget with tax and spending cuts	N

VOTING STUDIES

	Presidential Support		Party Unity		Conservative Coalition	
Year	**S**	**O**	**S**	**O**	**S**	**O**
1996	82	15	89	9	39	59
1995	85	13	91	6	24	74
1994	87	9	93	1	14	78
1993	94	6	93	4	36	64
1992	18	77	85	6	23	71
1991	26	66	88	4	14	84

INTEREST GROUP RATINGS

Year	ADA	AFL-CIO	CCUS	ACU
1996	90	n/a	19	0
1995	95	100	17	4
1994	75	88	33	10
1993	80	100	18	8
1992	80	75	13	4
1991	85	100	20	0

33 Lucille Roybal-Allard (D)

Of Bell Gardens — Elected 1992, 3rd term

Biographical Information
Born: June 12, 1941, Los Angeles, Calif.
Education: California State U., Los Angeles, B.A. 1965.
Occupation: Non-profit worker.
Family: Husband, Edward Allard; two children, two stepchildren.
Religion: Roman Catholic.
Political Career: Calif. Assembly, 1987-93.
Capitol Office: 2435 Rayburn Bldg. 20515; 225-1766.

Committees
Banking & Financial Services
Capital Markets, Securities & Government Sponsored Enterprises; Financial Institutions & Consumer Credit
Budget

In Washington: In the still-early stages of her congressional tenure, Roybal-Allard can only dream of gaining the legislative clout achieved by her father and House predecessor, Edward R. Roybal.

During a House career that lasted 30 years, Democrat Roybal always was a member of the majority party, and he ended his tenure as chairman of an Appropriations subcommittee. But just two years after Roybal-Allard's easy 1992 win to succeed her father in the Los Angeles-based, Hispanic-majority 33rd District, Democrats lost control of Congress, and she found herself as a junior member of the House minority party.

Nonetheless, Roybal-Allard's solid political grounding has enabled her to quickly maneuver into several lower-profile but significant leadership positions.

At the beginning of the 105th Congress, Roybal-Allard was elected to chair the delegation of California House Democrats, who held a 29-to-23 seat advantage over their home-state Republican colleagues.

The election of Roybal-Allard set a precedent, as the delegation's chairmanship traditionally had gone to its most senior member.

However, George E. Brown Jr., the dean of the state's Democratic delegation, urged the election of a more junior member, citing a need for fresh ideas and noting that more senior members often have too many responsibilities to do justice to the California delegation.

Roybal-Allard is a staunchly liberal Democrat; she sided with a majority of her party against a majority of Republicans on 95 percent or more of House votes in each of her first four years in Congress. Given that record, it would not be surprising if Roybal-Allard used the platform of the Democratic delegation chair to speak against much of the congressional Republican agenda. However, upon her election to head the Democratic group, Roybal-Allard said she would seek out California-related issues that could unite both Democrats and Republicans, and try to leverage the power of what is by far the biggest state delegation in the House.

"As I tell my colleagues from other states, I want their worst nightmare to come true — the California delegation coming together on key issues," she told the Los Angeles Times.

The Democratic leadership awarded Roybal-Allard a seat on the Budget Committee, where in May 1996 she persuaded members to adopt an amendment to the fiscal 1997 budget resolution. It required that any changes in the welfare system should not exacerbate domestic violence problems faced by low-income women. The provision, approved by voice vote, was the only Democratic amendment to the resolution adopted by the Republican-controlled panel.

That July, Roybal-Allard proposed a bill that aimed to give unemployment insurance benefits to women forced to leave jobs because of domestic violence. The bill also proposed that employers be required to allow domestic violence victims reasonable leave without penalty to seek medical assistance, counseling, safety planning and legal assistance, and to make necessary court appearances.

Allard also championed the rights of battered women in her role during the 104th as chair of Congress' Violence Against Women Task Force.

Issues of particular concern to Hispanics are a top priority for Roybal-Allard, who is the first Mexican-American woman in Congress and served in the 104th as second vice chairman of the Congressional Hispanic Caucus.

In her legislative work, she tries to balance the related but not always overlapping needs of the two chief components of her constituency: the minority "underclass," mired in chronic poverty, and a substantial Latino working class of laborers and shop owners who have grabbed a low rung on the economic ladder and aspire to buy homes and secure good educations for their children.

As a member of Budget and of the Banking and Financial Services Committee, Roybal-Allard has supported steps to stimulate investment in

CALIFORNIA 33
East-Central Los Angeles

As has been the case since it was established for the 1992 election, the 33rd had by far the worst voter turnout of any House district in the nation in 1996. Just 57,828 votes were cast in the contest that sent Roybal-Allard to a third House term.

However, there was a glimmer of optimism for those trying to get the district's overwhelming Hispanic majority, including large numbers of recent immigrants from Mexico, to get involved in the political process. The 1996 vote total, low as it was, was nearly 14 percent higher than in the House contest held in the 1992 presidential-election year.

There is no doubt about the party preferences of those residents who do vote, though. Roybal-Allard got at least 80 percent of the votes cast in her last two contests. In presidential voting, Bill Clinton also hit the 80 percent mark in 1996.

Much of the densely populated 33rd is economically deprived, though it avoided further hardship by being just east of south-central Los Angeles' worst May 1992 rioting.

Local officials are pinning some of their hopes for economic development on Los Angeles' Red Line subway, which opened in January 1993 inside the 33rd, as well as the Blue Line commuter train that runs from Long Beach to downtown through much of the district.

Bright spots for the district's economy include some new "green" industries, such as recycling companies. The district depends less on military contractors than does much of the rest of Los Angeles, so neither the defense industry's 1980s boom nor its early 1990s problems played much of a role in the economy here.

The northwest corner of the 33rd reaches into Los Angeles' downtown area and is composed primarily of office buildings.

It is laced with Los Angeles' legendary crowded expressways. Some residents live in single-room occupancy hotels and shelters for homeless families and women, but the bulk of this area's residents live just north and south of downtown in Pico Union and Chinatown. Stores in Pico Union's downtown were looted in the 1992 riots, but the wholesale destruction seen in most of south-central did not occur.

Two cities in the district's midsection, Commerce and Vernon, house much of the 33rd's industry, with facilities including food processing plants and metal-plating operations.

The southeast areas of the district, including Cudahy, Maywood, Bell and Bell Gardens, are very poor and primarily residential, tending to have more single-family homes than apartment buildings.

South Gate lies just south of Cudahy. This city has converted itself over the past several years from heavy industries to small businesses and light manufacturing. It is not as Democratic as the rest of the district; it voted Republican for president throughout the 1980s, but for Clinton in 1992 and 1996.

The 33rd tops the state in two areas: It is 84 percent Hispanic, and 92 percent of its residents are members of minority groups.

1990 Population: 570,943. White 203,891 (36%), Black 25,473 (4%), Other 341,579 (60%). Hispanic origin 477,975 (84%). 18 and over 384,158 (67%), 62 and over 44,759 (8%). Median age: 26.

small businesses, which provide most of the jobs in the 33rd.

She has worked with the Federal National Mortgage Association (Fannie Mae) to bring residents of her district into a program aimed at helping low- and moderate-income families purchase homes. The program helps first-time buyers qualify for mortgages by reducing down payments and closing costs and setting less rigid requirements for obtaining credit.

Roybal-Allard has faithfully backed President Clinton's economic and social policies. After considerable soul-searching, she went with Clinton and against her allies in organized labor in 1993 to support NAFTA, which linked the United States, Mexico and Canada in a free-trade zone.

While critics said the agreement would shift blue-collar jobs to low-wage workers in Mexico, Roybal-Allard observed that in the modern economy, "change is becoming a fact of life," and she said NAFTA could help expand export opportunities. She also voted in 1994 to implement GATT, again going against the wishes of organized labor.

Representing a huge Spanish-speaking immigrant population, Roybal-Allard defends federal spending for programs such as bilingual education in public schools, and she strongly opposes proposals to make English the official language of the United States.

At Home: With political blood flowing in her veins and a six-year tenure in the California Assembly as her seasoning, Roybal-Allard handily fulfilled expectations in 1992 that she would succeed her father upon his House retirement.

She drew insubstantial opposition in the Democratic primary and won nomination with 75 percent of the vote. That November, she ran up a 2-1 margin against Republican Robert Guzman, an education consultant. Her winning margins have increased since, to 81 percent in the 1994 general election and 82 percent in 1996.

The one blemish on her victories has been the astoundingly low voter turnout. The 33rd District is home to tens of thousands of immigrants from

Central and South America; many of them are non-citizens, and many of those non-citizens are illegal aliens. Typically, these people have been reluctant or unwilling to enter the bureaucratic maze that citizenship applications entail.

However, there was a turnout uptick in 1996, in part a reflection of efforts by Hispanic activists and the Clinton administration to get more immigrants to become citizens and then register to vote. Just more than 50,000 ballots were cast in the 1992 general election and slightly more than 41,500 in November 1994. But in 1996, the number of House voters moved up to nearly 58,000.

Roybal-Allard had jumped at the chance to run in the 33rd. Redistricting before the 1992 election had given it an 84 percent Hispanic population, even more favorable turf than the old 25th District in which her father had served. The 33rd has the largest Hispanic presence in any House district in the nation.

Before launching her House campaign, Roybal Allard had won three terms in the state House, and all her election victories were by wide margins. She also scored points for galvanizing grass-roots opposition to a toxic waste incinerator proposed for the city of Vernon, which was in her state legislative district and is in the 33rd.

That five-year battle was successful, and Roybal-Allard parlayed the experience into enactment of a bill requiring environmental impact reports for such facilities.

HOUSE ELECTIONS

1996 General		
Lucille Roybal-Allard (D)	47,478	(82%)
John P. Leonard (R)	8,147	(14%)
Howard Johnson (LIBERT)	2,203	(4%)
1994 General		
Lucille Roybal-Allard (D)	33,814	(81%)
Kermit Booker (PFP)	7,694	(19%)

Previous Winning Percentages: 1992 (63%)

CAMPAIGN FINANCE

	Receipts	Receipts from PACs	Expend-itures
1996			
Roybal-Allard (D)	$151,659	$81,450 (54%)	$144,278
Leonard (R)	$6,221	$16 (0%)	$6,208
1994			
Roybal-Allard (D)	$152,596	$102,095 (67%)	$124,271

DISTRICT VOTE FOR PRESIDENT

	1996		1992
D	48,636 (80%)	**D**	33,642 (63%)
R	8,538 (14%)	**R**	12,607 (24%)
I	2,691 (5%)	**I**	7,149 (13%)

KEY VOTES

1997	
Ban "partial birth" abortions	N
1996	
Approve farm bill	N
Deny public education to illegal immigrants	N
Repeal ban on certain assault-style weapons	N
Increase minimum wage	Y
Freeze defense spending	Y
Approve welfare overhaul	N
1995	
Approve balanced-budget constitutional amendment	N
Relax Clean Water Act regulations	N
Oppose limits on environmental regulations	Y
Reduce projected Medicare spending	N
Approve GOP budget with tax and spending cuts	N

VOTING STUDIES

	Presidential Support		Party Unity		Conservative Coalition	
Year	**S**	**O**	**S**	**O**	**S**	**O**
1996	80	16	95	3	12	84
1995	89	8	98	1	4	95
1994	87	13	99	1	14	86
1993	80	18	95	3	20	80

INTEREST GROUP RATINGS

Year	ADA	AFL-CIO	CCUS	ACU
1996	90	n/a	25	0
1995	95	100	13	4
1994	100	78	33	0
1993	95	92	20	4

34 Esteban E. Torres (D)

Of West Covina — Elected 1982, 8th term

Biographical Information

Born: Jan. 27, 1930, Miami, Ariz.

Education: East Los Angeles College, 1959-63; California State U., Los Angeles, 1963-64; U. of Maryland, 1965; American U., 1966.

Military Service: Army, 1949-53.

Occupation: International trade executive; autoworker; labor official.

Family: Wife, Arcy Sanchez; five children.

Religion: Unspecified.

Political Career: Sought Democratic nomination for U.S. House, 1974; UNESCO ambassador, 1977-79.

Capitol Office: 2269 Rayburn Bldg. 20515; 225-5256.

Committees

Appropriations
Foreign Operations, Export Financing & Related Programs; Transportation

Banking and Financial Services

In Washington: Torres' loyalty to the Democratic leadership in Congress and its key constituencies, including organized labor, helped earn him a deputy whip's post in the 102nd Congress and a seat on the Appropriations Committee in the 103rd Congress.

Given Torres' close ties to unions, his pledge in 1993 to vote for NAFTA (which most in the labor movement opposed) was a boost to the Clinton administration's efforts to line up support for the treaty. When the officials heading President Clinton's transition to a second term in 1996 went in search of a new secretary of Labor, Torres' name was in the mix.

A labor leader for the United Auto Workers before he came to Congress, Torres earned consideration for the Cabinet post when opposing forces battled over two other candidates: White House Public Liaison aide Alexis Herman and former Democratic Sen. Harris Wofford of Pennsylvania, who was named to head Clinton's National Service program after his defeat for re-election in 1994. Labor groups such as the AFL-CIO favored Wofford, who they believed would be a stronger advocate for their interests, but female and black activists backed Herman, who is black.

With his Hispanic heritage and his labor background, Torres emerged as a possible compromise pick for the Labor post. The Wall Street Journal recommended Torres for the job because of his vote for NAFTA, and his candidacy for the Labor slot gained such momentum that NBC at one point mistakenly reported that Clinton had tapped Torres for the job and asked Herman to head the Small Business Administration instead. The Los Angeles Times reported that Torres was confident enough he was going to Labor that he encouraged his son-in-law to campaign for his House seat once he left it.

Torres' name also came up in connection with the vacancy for secretary of Housing and Urban Development (HUD), but ultimately, Clinton chose Herman to head Labor and Andrew M. Cuomo to take the top job at HUD.

So Torres returned to his work on Appropriations, where in the 105th he gained a spot on the Transportation Subcommittee, putting him in a good position to defend California's interests as lawmakers on the companion Transportation and Infrastructure Committee consider reauthorization of the nation's highway and mass-transit programs.

Democratic leaders also indicated their continued affinity toward the Californian early in the 105th when they asked him to fill a temporary slot on Banking and Financial Services, where he had once served. He was appointed to the panel just before it began work on a Republican proposal for overhauling the nation's housing programs.

A former assembly line welder who sometimes shows off the tattoos on his hands from his days as a street gang member, Torres has opted for a quiet role in most of his activities. But in 1993 he was thrust into the limelight when it came time to vote on NAFTA. Torres was lobbied hard to vote against the pact and pushed by the Clinton administration to vote for it.

He voted yes — but for a price. He told Clinton he wanted the establishment of a jointly funded binational North American Development Bank (NADBank) that would help industries and workers hurt by the trade agreement. The White House agreed, and pledged $225 million for the bank. In 1996, he appeared at the opening of the NADBank U.S. Community Adjustment and Investment Office.

When announcing his vote for the trade pact, Torres told the House: "What has surprised me is that my friends in the North American labor movement, so far, have failed to grasp the enormous opportunity and potential in the NAFTA for spreading the vision and reality of industrial democracy throughout this hemisphere."

Early in 1997, Torres found himself amid controversy again. An opponent of efforts to tighten sanctions against Cuba in 1996, he traveled with fellow Democrat Xavier Becerra of California, the new chairman of the Congressional Hispanic Caucus, to the island nation in December of that year. The trip, sponsored by San Antonio-based

CALIFORNIA 34
East Los Angeles County suburbs; West Covina

The 34th is emerging as a middle-class Hispanic district that likes to vote Democratic; it is an almost ideal place for someone like Torres to run. It begins with more than one-third of East Los Angeles, runs east through Montebello and Pico Rivera, goes up north a bit for La Puente and drops down to pick up most of Whittier and all of Santa Fe Springs and Norwalk.

The section of East Los Angeles that is in the 34th is the heart of East L.A.'s business district. Stores are well-kept and generally are owned or operated by Hispanics. The area just to the north, around the 60 Freeway, is populated by what used to be called "Muppies," or Mexican yuppies, who have come in and fixed up many old homes.

Montebello is an upper middle-class Hispanic area, with a lot of home-grown residents who have never lived elsewhere. It lies to the east of the small city of East Los Angeles and is bordered by four freeways, making it a convenient for commuters. It is heavily Democratic: Torres took 68 percent of its vote in 1992, the first time he ran here.

Pico Rivera has been described as pure Middle America, Hispanic-style. This area also is very supportive of Torres. The biggest employer in the city is Northrop Grumman, which builds part of the B-2 bomber here. In 1994, the plant was downsized from about 7,800 employees to about 5,900 employees; it is scheduled to close in 1999.

Up in the district's northeastern corner, past Rose Hills Memorial Park (one of the country's largest cemeteries), is La Puente, a working-class, heavily Hispanic city with 37,000 residents and a registered-voter base that is about two-thirds Democratic.

Down south a bit, the district includes most of Whittier, the 34th's most Republican area. The city is still recovering from being the epicenter of an October 1987 earthquake. Some houses damaged in the quake have been repaired, but vacant lots are not uncommon. Multifamily homes are mixed closely with single-family homes in some areas, but not in the part of Whittier just outside the district, where half-million-dollar houses (and the GOP) dominate.

Farther south is Santa Fe Springs, an industrial area featuring light manufacturing and oil wells. Two-thirds of the city's 15,500 residents are Hispanic, but they have not flexed their political muscles here as they have elsewhere.

At the southern end of the 34th is Norwalk, the district's largest city with 94,000 residents. Though the city has close to a majority of Hispanics and a majority of Democrats, residents tend to be conservative-minded in presidential voting. However, Norwalk went heavily for Bill Clinton in 1992. The city is bounded by four freeways, including the Glenn Anderson, which was completed in 1994. Los Angeles' Green Line light rail opened in 1995, giving the area a boost.

Bill Clinton easily carried the district in the 1996 presidential race, getting 64 percent of the votes. Torres won an eighth House term just as comfortably, with 68 percent.

1990 Population: 573,047. White 325,099 (57%), Black 11,060 (2%), Other 236,888 (41%). Hispanic origin 357,143 (62%). 18 and over 402,266 (70%), 62 and over 64,984 (11%). Median age: 29.

Southwest Voter Research Institute, prompted Cuban-American Reps. Ileana Ros-Lehtinen and Lincoln Diaz-Balart, both Florida Republicans, to resign from the Hispanic Caucus in protest in January 1997.

Torres, who did not see his father again after his father was deported during the Depression when Torres was five, has been active in the debate over immigration. He was given the role of offering a Democratic leadership-backed amendment when the Appropriations Committee in February 1994 considered a bill providing emergency earthquake relief to California.

The amendment, which was adopted by the committee, modified a proposal by California GOP Rep. Ron Packard that would have cut off all disaster aid, except for emergency medical assistance, to illegal immigrants. Under Torres' amendment, illegal immigrants would remain eligible for emergency food, shelter, medical services and safety programs.

In 1996, he voted against immigration overhaul legislation the GOP pushed to crack down on illegal immigrants. It passed 305-123.

On Banking, where he served through the 102nd Congress, Torres was generally comfortable with the agenda of activist liberal Democrats who called the shots. He worked as a conciliator, smoothing the rough edges of members' personal and philosophical conflicts to help keep legislation moving. He was one of a small group of Democrats on good terms with the panel's irascible chairman, Henry B. Gonzalez of Texas.

The most contentious battle Torres took on was an attempt to strengthen federal regulation of the nation's credit reporting industry. The proposal, which gives consumers greater access to their credit histories and makes it easier for them to correct errors, died in the 102nd Congress because of opposition from credit bureaus and their congressional allies, but it gained momentum in the 103rd and became law as part of the fiscal 1997 omnibus spending bill. Torres said "the monumental change ... means peace of mind for millions of Americans."

Although his past lives as a former street-gang member and assembly line worker give Torres a "tough guy" image, he has a gentler side. In the spring of 1993, a retrospective of his artwork was shown in a Washington, D.C., gallery, and some of his artwork is featured on his World Wide Web page. He has created oil and acrylic paintings, prints, and pencil and ink sketches.

"Eventually someday I'd like to be able to retire to my art. It's a way of life, a way of experiencing life, both as an artist and activist," Torres told The Washington Post. "There's a lot of frustration and revolt in me that comes out in my work."

His fondness for the arts earned Torres the nomination of Minority Leader Richard A. Gephardt, D-Mo., to sit on the 17-member Board of Regents of the Smithsonian Institution in March 1997. The first Latino member of Congress appointed to the board, he will help set policy for and oversee the management of the Smithsonian, which he has criticized for ignoring Hispanics' contributions to American development and culture.

At Home: Torres was an assembly line welder in Los Angeles during the 1950s and became active in the United Auto Workers. In the 1960s, he was tapped by UAW President Walter Reuther to start a community action project in heavily Hispanic East Los Angeles. In 1968, Torres founded The East Los Angeles Community Union (TELACU), which grew into one of the country's largest anti-poverty agencies.

Torres developed Democratic contacts as an activist, but he lost a 1974 primary in his initial bid for the House. Soon thereafter he found his way into President Jimmy Carter's administration as an adviser on Hispanic affairs, and later he was named ambassador to the United Nations Educational, Scientific and Cultural Organization (UNESCO). When he made his second House bid in 1982, Torres billed his campaign as "Autoworker to Ambassador, the American Dream."

Torres' second try for Congress proved far easier than his first. He was running in an open 34th District created by redistricting, and he had help from the political organizations of Democrats Henry A. Waxman and Howard L. Berman. In the primary, he held off former Democratic Rep. Jim Lloyd (who had lost his seat in a neighboring district in 1980 to Republican David Dreier). In the general election Torres prevailed with 57 percent.

Since then, he has regularly won a vote share of 60 percent or better. Redistricting in 1992 changed his district little geographically and not at all politically. The 68 percent he won in 1996 was his best ever.

While cruising to re-election every two years, Torres has kept an eye on Los Angeles politics. In 1990, he hinted at a run for the Los Angeles County Board of Supervisors. But GOP incumbent Pete Schabarum, instead of announcing that he would step down, simply failed to file as a candidate by the March 1990 deadline. By that time, Torres had filed to run again for the House.

HOUSE ELECTIONS

1996 General		
Esteban E. Torres (D)	94,730	(68%)
David G. Nunez (R)	36,852	(27%)
J. Walter Scott (AMI)	4,122	(3%)
David Argall (LIBERT)	2,736	(2%)
1994 General		
Esteban E. Torres (D)	72,439	(62%)
Albert J. Nunez (R)	40,068	(34%)
Carl M. "Marty" Swinney (LIBERT)	4,921	(4%)

Previous Winning Percentages: **1992** (61%) **1990** (61%) **1988** (63%) **1986** (60%) **1984** (60%) **1982** (57%)

CAMPAIGN FINANCE

	Receipts	Receipts from PACs	Expend-itures
1996			
Torres (D)	$186,727	$66,200 (35%)	$207,398
Nunez (R)	$11,752	$266 (2%)	$11,171
1994			
Torres (D)	$236,822	$98,745 (42%)	$178,972
Nunez (R)	$5,153	$14 (0%)	$5,115

DISTRICT VOTE FOR PRESIDENT

	1996		1992
D	91,603 (64%)	**D**	78,889 (51%)
R	39,277 (27%)	**R**	48,181 (31%)
I	10,396 (7%)	**I**	27,944 (18%)

KEY VOTES

1997	
Ban "partial birth" abortions	N
1996	
Approve farm bill	N
Deny public education to illegal immigrants	N
Repeal ban on certain assault-style weapons	N
Increase minimum wage	Y
Freeze defense spending	Y
Approve welfare overhaul	N
1995	
Approve balanced-budget constitutional amendment	N
Relax Clean Water Act regulations	N
Oppose limits on environmental regulations	Y
Reduce projected Medicare spending	N
Approve GOP budget with tax and spending cuts	N

VOTING STUDIES

	Presidential Support		Party Unity		Conservative Coalition	
Year	**S**	**O**	**S**	**O**	**S**	**O**
1996	81	15	91	5	25	69
1995	86	10	85	6	20	73
1994	90	6	90	2	25	67
1993	87	11	86	3	16	77
1992	20	70	84	5	19	73
1991	25	70	94	3	14	84

INTEREST GROUP RATINGS

Year	ADA	AFL-CIO	CCUS	ACU
1996	100	n/a	14	0
1995	90	100	21	4
1994	75	75	42	10
1993	90	92	20	0
1992	85	92	29	4
1991	80	92	20	5

35 Maxine Waters (D)

Of Los Angeles — Elected 1990, 4th term

Biographical Information
Born: Aug. 15, 1938, St. Louis, Mo.
Education: California State U., Los Angeles, B.A. 1970.
Occupation: Head Start official.
Family: Husband, Sidney Williams; two children.
Religion: Christian.
Political Career: Calif. Assembly, 1977-91.
Capitol Office: 2344 Rayburn Bldg. 20515; 225-2201.

Committees
Banking & Financial Services
Capital Markets, Securities & Government Sponsored Enterprises; General Oversight & Investigations (ranking)
Judiciary
Constitution

In Washington: Waters is a forceful and provocative liberal who has made a career out of vigorously challenging her ideological opponents. With Republicans running the House, Waters has difficulty finding a sympathetic audience for her pleas for assistance to the inner cities, but she is at her rhetorical best as an insurgent. And she has a bigger megaphone in the 105th Congress as chairwoman of the Congressional Black Caucus.

From the first day of the 104th Congress, Waters made plain her displeasure with the ascension of Newt Gingrich and his conservative legion. When Gingrich was escorted down the House aisle to be sworn in as Speaker in January 1995, Waters remained seated. "From time to time I give myself permission to exercise some integrity with respect to my feelings," she reported. She told the Los Angeles Times in May 1995, "This new group and Newt kind of disgust me." At the start of the 105th, she was one of five members to vote "present" when the House reprimanded Gingrich for ethical failings, finding the punishment insufficiently severe.

Waters is not one to worry too much about the niceties of the House or heed the mournful cries for civility. When quarreling with a colleague, she has been known to tell her adversary to "shut up," and she once suggested in a news conference that a conservative member of the California delegation seek psychiatric treatment.

No one doubts the integrity of Waters' feelings, but many members of Congress — in both parties — find her unrelenting sense of the rightness of her opinions unappealing. Her in-your-face tactics led San Francisco Mayor Willie Brown to comment, "She'd cut out your heart and then do your eulogy — in tears."

When Brown was the Speaker of the California Assembly and Waters his majority whip, the two were an effective pair, and Brown gave her free rein to pursue projects of personal interest such as divesting state assets from South Africa. To say that Waters enjoys no such powerful patron in the House is an understatement. Waters proved in backroom bargaining sessions in Sacramento that she could compromise as well as the most pragmatic pol, but in Washington she has had to scratch and claw her way without a formal seat at the table.

One telling incident has been recounted in both a lengthy Waters profile contained in "War Without Bloodshed," a 1996 book about Washington politics by Eleanor Clift and Tom Brazaitis, and "Twilight," Anna Deavere Smith's play about the 1992 Los Angeles riots. Much of the worst rioting (which Waters calls a rebellion) happened in her House district, and she was miffed when the White House convened a meeting without inviting her or any other members representing inner-city districts. She showed up at the White House gate and waited until Democratic Speaker Thomas S. Foley persuaded President George Bush they would be better off inviting her in. The president's advisers reportedly agreed that her summation about disengaged youth being the root of the problem was correct.

With the help of the Democratic leadership, which often found her frustrating and uncontrollable, Waters in the 103rd Congress secured funding for a program to provide job training and pocket money to at-risk young people. It was one of the first programs axed by the new Republican majority in a 1995 rescissions bill.

She carries her advocacy for the poor into the Banking and Financial Services Committee, where she has worked to stop banks from charging transaction fees to small depositors. Waters serves as ranking member of the General Oversight and Investigations Subcommittee, and in the 105th she picked up a seat on Judiciary.

When the banking panel was marking up a plan to provide $50 million for groups that develop low-income housing, Waters objected to the reference to the Georgia-based Habitat for Humanity, the only group mentioned. When Gingrich appeared before the committee to plead for the special allocation, Waters tore into him. But Gingrich reminded Waters and the panel that she had attached her job training program to an

CALIFORNIA 35
South-central Los Angeles

This very poor, very heavily minority district contains what many consider the flash point of April 1992's rioting, the intersection of Normandie and Florence avenues. That is where a white truck driver, Reginald Denny, was dragged from his vehicle and beaten by a group of blacks.

The incident serves to emphasize the homegrown nature of the riots: All of those arrested in the beating case lived within six blocks of the intersection. The rioters tended to torch their own neighborhoods, which in the 35th includes part of south-central Los Angeles and three independent cities: Inglewood, Hawthorne and Gardena.

The eastern edge of the district is the most desperately poor. As one heads west toward Inglewood, relative affluence increases. The commercial districts in this area along Vermont and Manchester (and to a lesser extent Western) avenues were devastated by looting and burning.

To the west of south-central is Inglewood, whose police force was able to keep much of the rioting there under control. Inglewood suffered some damage but was spared the wholesale destruction found in south-central. Inglewood is a historically white city that has changed dramatically; now, more than half its 110,000 residents are black.

The city is home to the Hollywood Park racetrack and the Los Angeles Lakers, who play in the Great Western Forum. Several shipping companies have set up shop here to take advantage of the location due east of Los Angeles International Airport.

Hawthorne, with 71,000 residents, is about 10 percent Asian, with the rest split almost equally among Hispanics, whites and blacks. Its political power, however, is largely concentrated among its whites because they tend to register to vote at higher levels than the other groups.

Hawthorne was the birthplace of Northrop Corp., a major defense contractor that in 1994 merged with another company in the field, Grumman, forming the Northrop Grumman Corp. The city is alone in the district in having allowed large apartment buildings to be built.

For years, Gardena (population 50,000) received a strong revenue stream from being the only city in Los Angeles County that allowed poker parlors. Their contributions made up about 15 percent of the city's budget. The extra money allowed the city to save a substantial sum, part of which it used to start a municipal insurance company to keep its costs down.

The southern part of the city is heavily Japanese. They represent about a quarter of the city's total population and have been politically influential for some time: The city elected its first Japanese mayor in 1972. Honda has its U.S. headquarters here.

Overall, the district is 43 percent black (the highest proportion of blacks in the state), 43 percent Hispanic and 6 percent Asian — a full 90 percent minority.

Politically, the 35th is the most Democratic district in California. Bill Clinton won 84 percent here in 1996.

1990 Population: 570,882. White 121,505 (21%), Black 243,848 (43%), Other 205,529 (36%). Hispanic origin 246,201 (43%). 18 and over 389,470 (68%), 62 and over 51,632 (9%). Median age: 27.

unrelated flood relief bill, and her amendment to strike references to the group was rejected, 10-12.

In July 1994, when Republicans on the banking panel were grilling Clinton staffers on the Whitewater matter, Waters told Peter T. King, R-N.Y., to "shut up" after she objected to his pointed questioning of Margaret Williams, Hillary Rodham Clinton's chief of staff. The next day on the House floor, King said Waters' remark, "even for the gentlelady from California, went to a new low." Waters rose to respond that "the day is over when men can intimidate and badger women." Republicans objected to her use of the word badger, and then a parliamentary uproar ensued as Waters continued speaking after the chair ordered her to halt.

Waters is also willing to spar with leaders of her own party, as she demonstrated when President Clinton spent much of 1995 taking a long look at updating affirmative action. Waters was an early supporter of Clinton and served as national co-chairman of his 1992 campaign. She said she understood his need to placate centrists and conservatives on occasion, but when push came to shove on this issue Waters threatened to bolt the party. "No party is so important that we will belong to it if it undermines us on this issue," she said in a widely quoted remark. "No president is so important that we will belong to him if he undermines us on this issue." Clinton decided that he would look to "mend, not end" affirmative action programs.

Waters maintains that if she yields her stance and engages in the give and take typical to Washington politics, her constituents will feel burned, seeing her as just another politician willing to sell them out. On their behalf, she bristles with anger at the Republican notion that volunteer programs and self-reliance are suitable substitutes for massive government assistance. "Volunteers are great. But volunteers cannot be relied on. Anybody who wants to run a real business does not say: I'm going to run this business with volunteers."

Crack cocaine was the subject of perhaps Waters' most high-profile effort during the 104th, which was to determine the validity of news reports and rumors that the Central Intelligence Agency had been complicit in inner-city crack dealing, with the cash proceeds going to the Nicaraguan contras. Waters pressed for congressional hearings and when one took place under the auspices of the Senate Intelligence Committee, she was in the front row.

With the largely black audience expressing skepticism about official denials of CIA misdeeds, Intelligence Chairman Arlen Specter, R-Pa., allowed Waters — who told Specter he was not asking the "right questions" — to grill the witnesses herself. Waters joined the senators and asked a prepared list of questions, which elicited testimony from contra leaders that they had in fact met several of the drug dealers named in San Jose Mercury News articles.

At Home: The 35th, built on Watts and other black and Hispanic neighborhoods in south-central L.A., resembles at its heart the Assembly district Waters represented for 14 years in Sacramento. Waters got her chance to move up in 1990, with the retirement of 28-year Rep. Augustus F. Hawkins. For years she had been preparing for the move. During legislative debates over redistricting in 1982, Waters maneuvered to remove from Hawkins' district a blue-collar, mainly white suburb she saw as unfriendly territory.

Waters comes from modest circumstances. She was born in St. Louis as one of 13 children in a welfare family and was raised in public housing projects. As a teenager, she bused tables in a segregated restaurant. Married just after high school, Waters moved in 1961 with her first husband and two children to Los Angeles, where she worked in a clothing factory and for the telephone company.

Waters' public career began in 1966, when she volunteered as an assistant teacher in the new Head Start program while pursuing a college degree. From Head Start she got into community-organizing activities and then into politics. After working as a volunteer and a consultant to several candidates, Waters won an upset state Assembly victory in 1976.

Making her presence felt immediately, Waters pushed on her first day to have the gender-neutral term "assembly member" replace the official title of "assemblyman." Despite the derision of some male colleagues, Waters argued her case and won, although the vote was quickly overturned.

Waters sponsored much successful legislation, including measures requiring state agencies to set minimum goals for awarding contracts to minority- and women-owned businesses; barring strip searches for those accused of non-violent misdemeanors; and creating a state child abuse prevention training program. During her House campaign, Waters touted her sponsorship of the Imperial Courts Learning Center, California's first public school within a public housing project.

Waters' 1990 election to the House was never in doubt; she won 79 percent. She survived 1992 redistricting unscathed and has won handily since.

HOUSE ELECTIONS

1996 General		
Maxine Waters (D)	92,762	(86%)
Eric Carlson (R)	13,116	(12%)
Gordon Michael Mego (AMI)	2,610	(2%)
1994 General		
Maxine Waters (D)	65,688	(78%)
Nate Truman (R)	18,390	(22%)

Previous Winning Percentages: 1992 (83%) **1990** (79%)

CAMPAIGN FINANCE

	Receipts	Receipts from PACs	Expend-itures
1996			
Waters (D)	$191,620	$58,695 (31%)	$235,851
Carlson (R)	$2,440	$16 (1%)	$2,428
1994			
Waters (D)	$210,667	$100,502 (48%)	$177,791
Truman (R)	$9,142	0	$9,580

DISTRICT VOTE FOR PRESIDENT

	1996		1992
D	92,773 (84%)	**D**	100,432 (78%)
R	12,063 (11%)	**R**	16,685 (13%)
I	4,129 (4%)	**I**	11,950 (9%)

KEY VOTES

1997	
Ban "partial birth" abortions	N
1996	
Approve farm bill	N
Deny public education to illegal immigrants	-
Repeal ban on certain assault-style weapons	-
Increase minimum wage	Y
Freeze defense spending	Y
Approve welfare overhaul	N
1995	
Approve balanced-budget constitutional amendment	N
Relax Clean Water Act regulations	-
Oppose limits on environmental regulations	Y
Reduce projected Medicare spending	N
Approve GOP budget with tax and spending cuts	N

VOTING STUDIES

	Presidential Support		Party Unity		Conservative Coalition	
Year	S	O	S	O	S	O
1996	67	24	86	5	12	80
1995	82	12	91	4	11	89
1994	72	24	92	3	6	92
1993	77	22	92	4	14	86
1992	11	77	82	4	10	88
1991	23	70	85	3	5	84

INTEREST GROUP RATINGS

Year	ADA	AFL-CIO	CCUS	ACU
1996	85	n/a	19	0
1995	95	100	0	9
1994	100	89	25	10
1993	100	100	9	4
1992	95	92	13	0
1991	90	100	11	0

36 Jane Harman (D)

Of Torrance — Elected 1992, 3rd term

Biographical Information
Born: June 28, 1945, New York, N.Y.
Education: Smith College, B.A. 1966; Harvard U., J.D. 1969.
Occupation: Lawyer; White House aide; congressional aide.
Family: Husband, Sidney Harman; four children.
Religion: Jewish.
Political Career: No previous office.
Capitol Office: 325 Cannon Bldg. 20515; 225-8220.

Committees
Select Intelligence
Technical & Tactical Intelligence
National Security
Military Personnel; Military Research & Development

In Washington: A survivor of three tough elections, Harman carefully calibrates her record to appeal to the politically competitive 36th: She votes a progressive line on social-policy issues such as abortion and gun control, stands with conservatives in supporting constitutional amendments to balance the budget and impose congressional term limits, and pursues a resolutely pro-defense line from her seat on the National Security Committee. Harman calls her district "the aerospace capital of the universe"; it is home to facilities operated by Northrop-Grumman, TRW, Aerospace Corp. and other players in the aerospace field.

Tough, smart and ambitious, Harman was a key member of a group that persuaded the House in 1995 to fund the production of additional B-2 "stealth" bombers. A division of Hughes Electronics, an important employer of Harman's constituents, builds the B-2's radar. Harman's reputation as an astute legislator was reinforced late in the 104th when the Democratic leadership awarded her a seat on the Intelligence Committee.

Harman arrived in Washington in 1992 quite well-connected. She had worked in the Carter White House, as a Senate subcommittee staff director and in a high-profile Washington law firm. These experiences gave her numerous well-placed friends and an understanding of how Washington works.

Harman has employed that know-how to win some key battles for her district in the annual debate over how much money should go toward the nation's defense. In June 1995, Harman and other B-2 bomber supporters were able to turn back an amendment that would have blocked production of additional B-2s.

"We did everything that you have to do," Harman said after the House rejected, 203-219, the amendment prohibiting additional production. Harman and other bomber supporters organized a bipartisan group of members to lobby colleagues and coordinate with contractors who could underscore the B-2's economic benefit in members' districts.

For the B-2 backers, the hardest votes to win were on the Democratic side of the aisle. Most Democrats opposed the add-on to Clinton's defense budget that included the B-2 funds. And the administration's civilian Pentagon leaders as well as the senior military brass insisted that no additional B-2s were needed.

Before the vote, Harman said she knew that her side had a tough sales job making its case for expanding the stealth bomber fleet. "We have a very hard job to explain why this cut — which isn't school lunches or vaccinations — still has a human face," she said. "This is how we deter aggression and do war-fighting without putting more human faces at risk." Harman focused her lobbying efforts on fellow California Democrats, 10 of whom wound up voting with her.

While Harman often finds herself in alliance with hawkish Republicans on National Security, she has opposed certain efforts by GOP conservatives to include social-policy initiatives in the Pentagon's budget.

During committee debate on the fiscal 1996 defense authorization bill, Harman fought a provision advanced by California Republican Robert K. Dornan that called for the immediate discharge of service personnel infected with HIV, the virus that causes AIDS. Dornan cited complaints from some in the armed services that HIV-infected personnel are non-deployable. As a result, he said, healthy service members could be forced to spend an inordinate amount of time at sea or stationed overseas.

Harman argued that Pentagon officials were content with the policy status quo, which enables the military to discharge HIV-infected personnel incapable of doing their jobs. Her amendment to strike the HIV discharge provision failed, 16-37. Versions of the Dornan provision remained in the bill, which was vetoed by President Clinton in December 1995.

Harman, one of only three women on National Security, was asked to be part of a committee task force overseeing the Army's response to reports

CALIFORNIA 36
West Los Angeles County; Manhattan Beach; Torrance

The 36th hugs the Pacific coast, running south from Venice Beach to San Pedro and the port of Los Angeles. Along the way, it takes in some of California's most Democratic and most Republican areas.

The 36th's economic core is along the ocean and the Pacific Coast Highway. Its main industry, aerospace, is found in the upper third of the district in El Segundo, home of Lockheed-Martin, TRW, Allied Signal, and Aerospace Corp. plants. Shrinking spending in both the military and civilian sectors of the aerospace business has been devastating; it is not unusual to see people with doctorates collecting unemployment compensation.

The northern end of the district is anchored by Venice, a "very, very crunchy, nuts-and-berries kind of place," as one local observer put it. Venice is widely regarded as the most liberal place in California outside Berkeley. Designed by Abbot Kinney to duplicate the Italian city, Venice opened in 1904 complete with canals and gondolas. Its heyday was short; by 1958 the city had fallen into such disrepair that Orson Welles used it as the location for the seedy town in the film "Touch of Evil." The area has been revitalized by wealthy full-time residents and weekenders drawn by the town's beautiful location and funky reputation.

Just south of Venice and Marina del Rey lies Los Angeles International Airport, which stretches all the way to Interstate 405, the eastern border of the district. The airport's expansion during the 1980s is expected to meet air traffic demands until an expansion plan is approved at the end of the 1990s. The airport is not expected to receive much public works money in the meantime, although a light-rail extension of Los Angeles' new rapid transit system was brought to one of the airport parking lots by the end of 1995.

The land is fairly flat continuing down the coast, past El Segundo and through some of the wealthiest ocean suburbs in the region, including Manhattan, Hermosa and Redondo beaches.

The land and the incomes take a steep rise at the Palos Verdes Peninsula, where the bulk of the district's Republicans live. Nearly three-fourths of the peninsula's 90,000 residents are white. The area is almost uniformly upscale, and some communities qualify as havens of the truly wealthy: For instance, the average per capita income of the 1,900 residents in Rolling Hills is $85,000.

A voter registration surge in the months before the 1992 elections turned a 15,000-vote GOP margin into a slight Democratic plurality. That shift helped produce Harman's 16,000-vote victory that year and her nail-biting 812-vote victory in 1994. She won more easily in 1996, taking 52 percent of the vote.

Bill Clinton also won in the 36th in both 1992 and 1996, taking 47 percent in the most recent presidential election.

1990 Population: 573,663. White 446,003 (78%), Black 18,392 (3%), Other 109,268 (19%). Hispanic origin 85,277 (15%). 18 and over 462,022 (81%), 62 and over 74,844 (13%). Median age: 35.

in the fall of 1996 that Army drill sergeants at several training bases allegedly had pressured female recruits for sex. Harman and two committee Republicans, Tillie Fowler of Florida and Steve Buyer of Indiana, said they would try to find out why the network of Army policies intended to prevent the harassment of recruits broke down and why some victims were slow to report the incidents.

Harman, Fowler and several other women in the House said that the average female recruit might find existing Army mechanisms for reporting abuse to be intimidating. "There has to be a human face and, hopefully, a female face," for young women to complain to, Harman said.

Harman also served through the 104th on the Science Committee, where she was on the lookout to bring bring high-technology jobs to her district to replace those lost to defense cutbacks. She objected to the Republican-backed omnibus science bill that passed the House in May 1996, complaining that it lacked "vision." She said the measure did not provide enough money for environmental research programs and for the Mission to Planet Earth, a global climate-study program. "We need to be doing more, not less, research into difficult scientific questions like climate change," Harman told the House. "Good science is good business. We must be visionary, not reactionary."

Harman is the daughter of immigrants — her father fled Nazi Germany, then emigrated to the United States — and she spoke passionately of the need to split off restrictions on legal immigration from a broad immigration overhaul measure considered by the House in March 1996. The House ultimately agreed to drop the legal immigration restrictions on a vote of 238-183, deleting provisions that would have cut back on how many legal immigration slots would be available each year.

Harman, who was a member of a bipartisan House task force on immigration, told her colleagues that "legal immigration is the lifeblood of this country, enriching it both economically and culturally."

At Home: Married to the founder of Harman International, a leading audio equipment maker, Harman moved from Washington to the 36th in 1991 and the next year spent $2.3 million to win a seat in Congress (the third-highest total of all House candidates in 1992).

The 36th emerged from 1992 redistricting as a revamped version of the old 27th, with liberal Santa Monica gone and the wealthy Palos Verdes Peninsula added. It looked likely to elect a Republican until the GOP nominated Joan Milke Flores, a local official known for her strong anti-abortion views. Harman made abortion rights the centerpiece of her House campaign. Three minor-party candidates helped split the non-Democratic vote and hand Harman victory with 48 percent.

In 1994, the GOP staged another high-tension primary won by Susan Brooks, a local mayor and a moderate on abortion. But the intraparty wounds again were slow to heal, as runner-up contender Ron Florance refused to endorse Brooks. Able to once again divide and conquer, Harman also had the resources to defend her votes for Clinton's economic agenda and to advertise her heavy lifting for the district economy. Still, the GOP tide in the state was strong enough to carry Brooks to an apparent victory on Election Day, and she came to Washington to join in post-election sessions with the Class of 1994.

It was the counting of thousands of absentee ballots (an increasingly large factor in California elections) that enabled Harman to surge ahead and secure a second term by an 812-vote margin.

Brooks kept her campaign machine running and entered the 1996 cycle with a full head of steam. But where state and national trends were in her favor in 1994, such was not the case in 1996. Harman was happy to stand with Clinton, who carried the 36th with 47 percent in presidential voting, while Brooks shared the GOP ballot with Bob Dole, who never caught on in California. Although Brooks got more votes than Dole in the district, she polled 44 percent to Harman's 52 percent.

HOUSE ELECTIONS

1996 General		
Jane Harman (D)	117,752	(52%)
Susan Brooks (R)	98,538	(44%)
Bruce Dovner (LIBERT)	4,933	(2%)
Bradley McManus (NL)	3,236	(1%)
1994 General		
Jane Harman (D)	93,939	(48%)
Susan Brooks (R)	93,127	(48%)
Jack Tyler (LIBERT)	4,932	(3%)
Joseph G. "Joe" Fields (AMI)	3,810	(2%)

Previous Winning Percentages: 1992 (48%)

CAMPAIGN FINANCE

	Receipts	Receipts from PACs		Expend-itures
1996				
Harman (D)	$1,703,775	$503,319	(30%)	$1,579,938
Brooks (R)	$491,748	$103,895	(21%)	$486,564
1994				
Harman (D)	$1,291,118	$516,849	(40%)	$1,300,855
Brooks (R)	$583,078	$106,386	(18%)	$580,837

DISTRICT VOTE FOR PRESIDENT

	1996		1992
D	109,244 (47%)	**D**	111,014 (41%)
R	96,872 (41%)	**R**	95,646 (36%)
I	18,510 (8%)	**I**	62,458 (23%)

KEY VOTES

1997	
Ban "partial birth" abortions	N
1996	
Approve farm bill	N
Deny public education to illegal immigrants	N
Repeal ban on certain assault-style weapons	N
Increase minimum wage	Y
Freeze defense spending	N
Approve welfare overhaul	Y
1995	
Approve balanced-budget constitutional amendment	Y
Relax Clean Water Act regulations	N
Oppose limits on environmental regulations	Y
Reduce projected Medicare spending	N
Approve GOP budget with tax and spending cuts	N

VOTING STUDIES

	Presidential Support		Party Unity		Conservative Coalition	
Year	**S**	**O**	**S**	**O**	**S**	**O**
1996	61	30	70	23	61	31
1995	63	29	62	28	66	28
1994	86	12	79	17	72	25
1993	85	10	88	7	41	57

INTEREST GROUP RATINGS

Year	ADA	AFL-CIO	CCUS	ACU
1996	60	n/a	60	26
1995	65	80	54	25
1994	60	67	83	19
1993	85	92	18	17

37 Juanita Millender-McDonald (D)

Of Carson — Elected 1996; 1st full term

Biographical Information

Born: Sept. 7, 1938, Birmingham, Ala.

Education: U. of Redlands, B.S.; California State U., Los Angeles, M.A.; U. of Southern California,.

Occupation: Teacher.

Family: Husband, James McDonald Jr.; five children.

Religion: Baptist.

Political Career: Carson City Council, 1990-92, mayor pro tempore, 1991-92; Calif. Assembly, 1992-96.

Capitol Office: 419 Cannon Bldg. 20515; 225-7924.

Committees

Small Business
Regulatory Reform & Paperwork Reduction; Tax & Exports

Transportation & Infrastructure
Aviation; Surface Transportation

In Washington: Millender-McDonald, who first won the 37th in a March 1996 special election, has shown in her brief House career that she has no fondness for proposals by the Republican majority to rein in spending on social programs. Her district is one of the poorest in California and she argues for allocating resources to help the underprivileged.

Millender-McDonald's electoral good fortune came after the fall of Democratic Rep. Walter R. Tucker III, who resigned from Congress Dec. 15, 1995, a week after a federal jury convicted him on felony charges of extortion and tax evasion. The charges stemmed from actions he took as mayor of Compton, prior to his election to Congress.

Millender-McDonald has made a priority of large-scale infrastructure projects in and around her territory, and she is in a postion to advance them from her seat on the Transportation and Infrastructure Committee. The panel will be marking up legislation in 1997 to authorize perhaps $175 billion in new highway and mass transit spending, and Millender-McDonald is certain to continue her quest for more federal dollars supporting the Alameda Corridor project. This continuing project, which runs the length of her district, would link Los Angeles railyards with the ports of that city and Long Beach. It received $400 million in direct loans as part of the fiscal 1997 transportation spending law.

Millender-McDonald was also pleased to trumpet a $20 million authorization to bring three Veterans Administration buildings in Long Beach up to code. In her maiden floor remarks, she made it clear that one of her top priorities is to ensure her earthquake-prone district receives federal protection.

Millender-McDonald took the lead on an issue that helps illustrate the continuing racial divide in the country. Concerned by articles in the San Jose Mercury News that said the Central Intelligence Agency had been involved in cocaine trafficking in inner-city neighborhoods, she has introduced legislation to establish a select congressional committee to investigate. Millender-McDonald sponsored a hearing into the matter in her district in October 1996. A month later, she hosted CIA Director John M. Deutch as he took questions from her constituents in Watts about the allegations.

A regional whip, Millender-McDonald is a reliable vote for her party's liberal wing, consistently supporting abortion rights and other progressive causes. Since coming to Congress she has backed organized labor's point of view in voting to raise the minimum wage, block employers from offering compensatory time off in lieu of overtime pay, and voting against a successful effort to make it harder for Federal Express workers to unionize.

Millender-McDonald opposed a law that blocked federal recognition of same-sex marriages and voted to prohibit funding for certain tobacco programs. She opposed turning off the cash spigot funding the space station.

A former teacher, she is a vocal supporter of the Goals 2000 national educational standards initiative and favors more spending on bilingual education. (She voted against a bill to prohibit illegal immigrants from receiving a public education.) Millender-McDonald spoke against effectively raising the rent for public housing residents and voted against the welfare overhaul bill. "Welfare reform is not true reform unless it contains job training, child care and job location assistance," she declared.

The 37th is a majority-minority district, with Hispanics and blacks representing three-fourths of the population. Millender-McDonald sometimes takes to the floor to commemorate such events as Black History Month, and she spoke out strongly in favor of federalizing the crime of church burning after a rash of black churches in the South were torched. (Her father had been a minister in Alabama.)

At Home: At the same time Millender-McDonald won the right to complete Tucker's unexpired House term, Democratic voters also chose her to be their nominee for election to a full term in November 1996. She prevailed easily over

CALIFORNIA 37
Southern Los Angeles County; Compton; Carson

The 37th includes some of Los Angeles' poorest and most overwhelmingly Democratic communities, taking in the Carson, Compton and Lynwood areas of the city.

Residents of the 37th have quite a stake in efforts aimed at post-Cold War adjustments to the nation's defense industries. The closing of the Long Beach shipyard and planned closing of the naval station just south of the district are likely to squeeze the area anew.

Long Beach's port area draws many of its blue-collar workers from the district (the naval station alone employs more than 10,000 civilian and military personnel), and many others in the 37th work in small businesses that support the port. Military contractors concentrated in the southern end of the district also are suffering.

Carson, just north of the port, is a blue-collar city of 84,000, with its population split almost evenly among Hispanics, blacks, whites and Asians. This area was largely spared in the rioting of the spring of 1992, even though it is sandwiched between Long Beach and Compton, which both suffered fairly heavy damage.

Scores of Compton's businesses went up in the smoke of 135 separate fires. California's recession had been hurting the already-poor area, and many of the surviving jobs were lost as businesses damaged in the riot closed. The lots with burned buildings and debris have been cleared, leaving them vacant. Although there's been some renewal, it is hard to distinguish much of the land from the many vacant lots the city had before the riots.

Compton's Hispanic community has grown tremendously in the past decade. Forty-four percent of the city's 90,000 residents are Hispanic and 53 percent are black.

At the north end of the district is Lynwood, 70 percent of whose 62,000 residents are Hispanic and 21 percent of whom are black. The area sustained some damage during the riots, with more than 60 fires reported and 138 arrests.

One potential ray of light for the district is the Alameda Corridor project, an attempt to create a smooth conduit for goods to enter California through Long Beach without the traffic hassles of the Long Beach Freeway. The project runs the length of the district up Alameda Street and includes rail and road transportation improvements.

Another addition to the district is the 105 Freeway, known for years as the Century Freeway. The name gave rise to a local joke that the road, planned since the middle part of this century, would not be completed until the next. But it bears a new name — that of Democratic Rep. Glenn M. Anderson, who died in 1994. And it was recently completed. Now the area has finally been connected to the metropolitan area's freeway grid.

Bill Clinton carried the 37th in 1996 with 82 percent of the vote, his second best district in the state.

1990 Population: 572,049. White 149,689 (26%), Black 192,420 (34%), Other 229,940 (40%). Hispanic origin 258,278 (45%). 18 and over 375,216 (66%), 62 and over 49,338 (9%). Median age: 26.

Republican businessman Michael Voetee, a self-described "sacrificial lamb."

McDonald waited until Tucker's conviction to announce her candidacy for the 37th, and then she overtook fellow state Rep. Willard H. Murray Jr., who had begun campaigning nine months earlier, and a crowd of other Democrats. Among the also-rans were Compton Mayor Omar Bradley, Lynwood Mayor Paul H. Richards, Compton City Clerk Charles Davis, and Robin Tucker, the wife of the disgraced congressman, who had his endorsement.

Murray had the backing of Democratic Rep. Maxine Waters, a power in Los Angeles County politics for a generation. Millender-McDonald's campaign was handled by a consultant with ties to Willie Brown, the mayor of San Francisco and former longtime Speaker of the state Assembly.

Millender-McDonald, who held local office in Carson prior to her service in Sacramento, outpaced Murray in fund-raising, in part with the help of EMILY's List, a fundraising organization for Democratic women candidates. She weathered criticism from her foes for accepting contributions from political action committees.

She scored points against Murray by criticizing his support for the state's placement of the troubled Compton Unified School District in receivership. The state took control of the school district under the terms of a bailout deal Murray sponsored in 1993. Millender-McDonald sponsored a bill in the Assembly in 1996 to return non-fiscal control to the school district. She also gained publicity in 1995 by supporting a state move to take over Lincoln Park Cemetery in Carson amid accusations of mismanagement and embezzlement. In response to problems at the cemetery, Millender-McDonald sponsored bills to outlaw necrophilia and require annual state inspections of cemeteries.

In a sparse turnout, Millender-McDonald won the special election with nearly 14,000 (27 percent); Murray had 20 percent. Robin Tucker ran sixth with 7 percent. In the concurrent

Democratic primary voting for nomination to the 105th Congress, Millender-McDonald beat Murray by just over 1,000 votes, 24 to 21 percent.

The only sour note in Millender-McDonald's victory was the defeat of her son, Keith, in his bid to replace her in the Assembly. He lost in the Democratic primary to former state Rep. Dick Floyd. In 1992, Floyd, who is white, lost to Juanita McDonald when redistricting that year forced him into the same district with another white assemblyman. They split the white vote, sending McDonald to Sacramento.

HOUSE ELECTIONS

1996 General		
Juanita Millender-McDonald (D)	87,247	(85%)
Michael E. Voetee (R)	15,399	(15%)
1996 Special Election		
Juanita Millender-McDonald (D)	13,868	(27%)
Willard H. Murray Jr. (D)	10,396	(20%)
Omar Bradley (D)	6,975	(14%)
Paul H. Richards (D)	6,035	(12%)
Robert M. Sausedo (D)	4,495	(9%)
Robin Tucker (D)	3,661	(7%)
Charles Davis (D)	2,555	(5%)
Murry J. Carter (D)	1,574	(3%)
Joyce Harris (D)	1,322	(3%)
1996 Primary		
Juanita Millender-McDonald (D)	10,213	(24%)
Willard H. Murray Jr. (D)	8,999	(21%)
M. Susan Carrillo (D)	6,681	(15%)
Omar Bradley (D)	5,746	(13%)
Paul H. Richards (D)	5,523	(13%)
Robin Tucker (D)	2,632	(6%)
Charles Davis (D)	2,131	(5%)
Joyce Harris (D)	660	(2%)
Dale C. Tatum (D)	580	(1%)

CAMPAIGN FINANCE

	Receipts	Receipts from PACs	Expend-itures
1996			
Millender-McDonald (D)	$337,030	$94,500 (28%)	$327,257
Voetee (R)	$43,806	$16 (0%)	$42,972

DISTRICT VOTE FOR PRESIDENT

	1996		1992
D	88,877 (82%)	**D**	90,523 (74%)
R	13,874 (13%)	**R**	19,299 (16%)
I	4,798 (4%)	**I**	12,905 (11%)

KEY VOTES

1997	
Ban "partial birth" abortions	N
1996	
Increase minimum wage	Y
Freeze defense spending	Y
Approve welfare overhaul	N

VOTING STUDIES

	Presidential Support		Party Unity		Conservative Coalition	
Year	**S**	**O**	**S**	**O**	**S**	**O**
1996	84	16	92	7	27	71

INTEREST GROUP RATINGS

Year	ADA	AFL-CIO	CCUS	ACU
1996	83	n/a	20	0

38 Steve Horn (R)

Of Long Beach — Elected 1992, 3rd term

Biographical Information
Born: May 31, 1931, San Juan Bautista, Calif.
Education: Stanford U., A.B. 1953; Harvard U., M.P.A. 1955; Stanford U., Ph.D. 1958.
Military Service: Army Reserves, 1954-62.
Occupation: Professor; college president.
Family: Wife, Nini Moore; two children.
Religion: Protestant.
Political Career: U.S. Commission on Civil Rights vice chairman/member, 1969-82; sought Republican nomination for U.S. House, 1988.

Capitol Office: 438 Cannon Bldg. 20515; 225-6676.

Committees
Government Reform & Oversight
District of Columbia; Government Management, Information & Technology (chairman)
Transportation & Infrastructure
Surface Transportation; Water Resources & Environment

In Washington: Horn, a longtime student of Congress, has kept his moderate bearings and not gotten swept up in the conservative activism that rules nowadays in the House Republican Conference. To be sure, Horn concurs with the GOP's right flank on many issues, but he also has maintained a more liberal stance on enough social issues to appeal to his Democratic-leaning district.

Horn sits on two committees that have large roles to play in the 105th Congress' first session, Government Reform and Oversight, and Transportation and Infrastructure.

Horn chairs the former committee's Government Management, Information and Technology Subcommittee, where he attends to various "good government" reforms. And as the full Government Reform Committee conducts its high-profile investigation of political fundraising abuses in the 1996 campaign, Horn may find an opportunity to argue for change in the campaign finance system. He does not accept PAC contributions and has sponsored a bill to establish an independent commission to propose changes in campaign finance law.

Horn holds a seat on the Surface Transportation Subcommittee, which in the 105th gets the first crack at a massive reauthorization of highway and mass transit programs. Horn's chief concern will certainly be securing funds toward completion of the Alameda Corridor project, an intermodal link between the ports of Long Beach and Los Angeles (which are each located in his district) and the L.A. rail yards. He says he will also seek to protect funding for alternative modes such as bike paths and mass transit.

Another major parochial concern of Horn's is fending off funding threats to the C-17 transport plane, which is built in the 38th. Horn offered an amendment to the fiscal 1996 military construction bill to cut $99 million for a berthing wharf at San Diego's North Island Naval Air Station, arguing that the three nuclear-powered aircraft carriers that the Navy wanted to send to San Diego could be placed at the Long Beach Naval Shipyard. But the facility in Horn's district had been slated for closure in the 1995 round of base closings and his amendment failed, 137-294.

Horn maintains that his top legislative priority is a balanced budget and he supported a balanced-budget amendment to the Constitution, as well as the GOP's 1995 budget-balancing plan. Horn is less enthralled by GOP tax policy, though; he was one of only 11 Republicans to oppose a resolution bringing a $189 billion tax cut to the House floor, although he voted in favor of the cuts themselves.

He told a Lions Club in his district that "the flat tax seems to be everybody's popular sort of demagogic issue. . . . What you have with the flat tax are a lot of people who are bringing in numbers out of the air with no basis, and we really don't know what the implications are."

Horn supported the GOP's efforts to limit congressional terms and ease many federal regulations, and he pushed through the House a bill to offer Los Angeles partial relief from federal clean water standards.

But Horn casts some "green" votes, as when he bucked his party's leaders in support of killing provisions in a spending bill that would have blocked the Environmental Protection Agency from enforcing major portions of environmental law.

Horn most frequently breaks with his party on social policy issues. He supports the rights of gays, including their ability to serve in the military and he also supports abortion rights, including access to a particular abortion procedure its opponents call "partial birth" abortion.

Horn has voted in favor of gun control legislation: He termed a 1996 effort in the House to repeal a ban on certain semiautomatic assault-style weapons "crazy." Horn also likes the idea of federal arts funding.

In the 103rd, he voted for a bill to grant workers unpaid leave for family emergencies, and in the 104th, he sponsored a move to apply the enacted family leave law, and other workplace

CALIFORNIA 38
Long Beach; Downey; Lakewood

Though there is a working-class Democratic tradition in the 38th (and a Democratic registration advantage), blue-collar conservatism often will shift the area toward Republican candidates. Horn beat his Democratic opponent 49 percent to 43 percent in 1992, and he was comfortably re-elected in 1994 before the margin narrowed in 1996. But Bill Clinton has carried the district twice, handily beating Bob Dole 53 percent to 36 percent in 1996.

Long Beach, along the coast, is the world's busiest container port and by far the largest city in the district with 429,000 residents. All but the western end is within the 38th. About a quarter of the city's residents are Hispanic, and more than half are non-Hispanic whites. The remaining quarter are a rainbow of ethnicities, including a sizable contingent of Cambodians. Some four dozen languages are spoken in the Long Beach Unified School District's schools. Overall, the district is about one-fourth Hispanic, 9 percent Asian and 8 percent black.

The beautiful Queen Mary is docked here, but the Long Beach Naval Shipyard was slated to close in August 1997. Although important, the shipyard is just part of the 38th's industrial landscape. Aerospace plants extend along the flat, brown land, sharing space with fuel tanks and oil wells. McDonnell Douglas is among the district's largest employers, although its work force is down by about half from the 40,000 employed in 1990.

The southwestern side of Long Beach suffered in the April 1992 riots that ripped through the area. More than 400 fires were reported, more than 300 people were injured and at least one person was killed. Much of the damage was along the Pacific Coast Highway and in the city's Cambodian area along Anaheim Street.

Downey, a middle- to upper-middle-income city of 91,000 at the district's northern tip, has a Republican lean. The city houses the huge Boeing North American (formerly Rockwell International) aerospace plant (where the space shuttle is manufactured) on its south end, as well as many of the high-tech workers who are employed there. While Boeing North American is still a major employer, employment levels have dropped off dramatically from their peaks of yesteryear.

Just south of Downey is Paramount, a blue-collar city of 48,000. About 60 percent of Paramount's residents are Hispanic, far higher levels than are found elsewhere in the 38th. The city's chronic employment and crime problems have lessened some in recent years.

Directly east of Paramount is Bellflower, a quiet bedroom city of 62,000 that is similar to Downey. It has no industry that compares with Boeing North American.

More than half of Lakewood's 74,000 residents are in the 38th. This community, just south of Bellflower, was built all at once after World War II to house veterans and other workers who came to the area to work in the aerospace industry and decided to stay. One of the city's claims to fame is the Lakewood Center Mall, one of America's first shopping malls.

1990 Population: 572,657. White 396,372 (69%), Black 44,337 (8%), Other 131,948 (23%). Hispanic origin 146,899 (26%). 18 and over 435,049 (76%), 62 and over 80,792 (14%). Median age: 31.

protections, to White House employees.

When the House voted, 295-125, in March 1997 to express its support for the public display of the Ten Commandments in government buildings, Horn was disbelieving. "I have had long, long feelings that political figures should not use religion for political gain." Horn was also angry that the bill had been brought to the floor without benefit of committee hearings.

Horn was a busy chairman of his Government Reform and Oversight subcommittee during the 104th, spending months reviewing more than 40,000 documents relating to travel by senior executive branch officials. Horn complained in a hearing that some Cabinet secretaries had taken frequent official trips to their hometowns, "with an official event seemingly occurring as an afterthought to justify the trip."

The travel habits of lower-level federal employees also rankled Horn, who introduced legislation to require that all government travel be paid for with government credit cards. Too many federal employees were using their personal cards to rack up discounts and frequent flyer miles, Horn complained, at a cost he estimated at $80 million.

He also fretted that government agencies were not heeding the ticking time bomb of the year 2000, which computers may interpret as 1900 because they only read the last two digits. Horn offered mostly poor letter grades to federal agencies in judgment of how prepared they seemed to be.

It was a fitting gesture coming from a former academic. Horn is a lifelong student of Congress, with a library of books on the institution that runs into the thousands. He has observed Capitol Hill as a congressional fellow, as a Senate aide, as the vice chairman of the U.S. Commission on Civil Rights for 11 years and as a political scientist at

Cal State Long Beach (where he was president from 1970 to 1988). Horn has written books about the Senate Appropriations Committee and about ethics and campaign finance.

His roots are in the progressive wing of the Republican Party. When he worked in the Senate, the GOP, though a minority, played a crucial role in civil rights legislation. As an aide to Republican Sen. Thomas H. Kuchel of California (1953-69), Horn helped draft the Voting Rights Act of 1965 in the office of Minority Leader Everett McKinley Dirksen, R-Ill. (1951-1969).

At Home: Horn was outspent by a margin of nearly 2-to-1 by his 1996 opponent, environmental lawyer Rick Zbur. Despite Zbur's million-dollar effort to link Horn to the locally unpopular policies of House Speaker Newt Gingrich, such a characterization struck voters as too long a reach. Zbur's professed homosexuality was less of an issue than Horn's efforts in behalf of the local economy, helping Horn rack up a 10-point victory margin even as President Clinton carried the district handily.

Horn's first bid for the House was in 1988, in the old 42nd, just south of the seat he holds now. He ran third in an eight-person Republican primary won by Dana Rohrabacher.

There also were eight entrants in the 1992 GOP primary in the 38th, and Horn barely nudged into first with a 30 percent tally, 105 votes ahead of his nearest rival.

In the general election, Horn faced an uphill challenge against Long Beach City Council member Evan Anderson Braude, stepson of the late Democrat Glenn M. Anderson, who in 1992 was the retiring 12-term incumbent. Anderson Braude had a financial advantage and the district's 12-point Democratic voter-registration edge in his favor.

But Horn's progressive image appealed to voters, and his opponent fell flat with a last-minute assault that included the insinuation that Horn was somehow a foreign agent for having consulted with the University of the United Arab Emirates.

Horn prevailed, 49 percent to 43 percent. In the more Republican climate of 1994, he pushed his winning tally up to nearly 60 percent.

HOUSE ELECTIONS

1996 General		
Steve Horn (R)	88,136	(53%)
Rick Zbur (D)	71,627	(43%)
William A. Yeager (GREEN)	4,610	(3%)
Paul N. Gautreau (LIBERT)	3,272	(2%)
1994 General		
Steve Horn (R)	85,225	(58%)
Peter Mathews (D)	53,681	(37%)
Lester W. Mueller (LIBERT)	3,795	(3%)
Richard K. Green (PFP)	2,995	(2%)

Previous Winning Percentages: 1992 (49%)

CAMPAIGN FINANCE

	Receipts	Receipts from PACs	Expend-itures
1996			
Horn (R)	$454,093	$0 (0%)	$470,077
Zbur (D)	$1,009,305	$151,507(15%)	$1,011,672
1994			
Horn (R)	$486,212	$520 (0%)	$442,982
Mathews (D)	$436,048	$19,483 (4%)	$433,706

DISTRICT VOTE FOR PRESIDENT

1996		1992	
D	91,673 (53%)	**D**	88,728 (45%)
R	62,053 (36%)	**R**	66,647 (34%)
I	14,310 (8%)	**I**	43,596 (22%)

KEY VOTES

1997	
Ban "partial birth" abortions	N
1996	
Approve farm bill	Y
Deny public education to illegal immigrants	Y
Repeal ban on certain assault-style weapons	N
Increase minimum wage	+
Freeze defense spending	N
Approve welfare overhaul	Y
1995	
Approve balanced-budget constitutional amendment	Y
Relax Clean Water Act regulations	Y
Oppose limits on environmental regulations	Y
Reduce projected Medicare spending	Y
Approve GOP budget with tax and spending cuts	Y

VOTING STUDIES

	Presidential Support		Party Unity		Conservative Coalition	
Year	S	O	S	O	S	O
1996	49	49	71	28	73	27
1995	35	62	80	19	77	22
1994	65	29	65	30	81	14
1993	64	35	69	28	68	32

INTEREST GROUP RATINGS

Year	ADA	AFL-CIO	CCUS	ACU
1996	40	n/a	80	63
1995	25	17	88	58
1994	30	33	91	57
1993	40	58	91	63

39 Ed Royce (R)

Of Fullerton — Elected 1992, 3rd term

Biographical Information
Born: Oct. 12, 1951, Los Angeles, Calif.
Education: California State U., Fullerton, B.A. 1977.
Occupation: Tax manager.
Family: Wife, Marie Therese Porter.
Religion: Roman Catholic.
Political Career: Calif. Senate, 1983-93.
Capitol Office: 1133 Longworth Bldg. 20515; 225-4111.

Committees
Banking & Financial Services
Domestic & International Monetary Policy; Financial Institutions & Consumer Credit
International Relations
Africa (chairman); Asia & the Pacific

In Washington: Royce does not assume the role of conservative stemwinder like his Orange County GOP colleague Dana Rohrabacher or former GOP fire breather Robert K. Dornan, although he is every bit their equal when it comes to voting against the Clinton administration.

On questions of taxing, spending, abortion policy, gun control, foreign affairs and most other topics of import, Royce typically opposes the White House. He also has taken on other members of the House as he crusades for less federal spending, particularly in the form of funding for projects in members' districts. As co-chairman of the so-called Porkbusters Coalition, Royce has singled out projects that he says fail to meet a basic criteria — they are not requested by the administration, they are not beneficial to more than one district and they do not advance national interests.

Using that criteria, he and fellow porkbuster Minnesota Democrat David Minge targeted two projects included in the fiscal 1996 military construction bill. One, requested by Washington Democrat Norm Dicks, sought $10.4 million for a new physical fitness center at the Bremerton Puget Sound Naval Shipyard, a project that the Navy did not request but that Dicks said is part of a five-year service plan.

The second, requested by Pennsylvania Democrat Thomas M. Foglietta, was for $6 million to upgrade the foundry and propeller shop at the Philadelphia Naval Shipyard, a facility that was on the 1991 base closure list. The Navy never requested the money, but the subcommittee added the project to the bill.

Royce argued against the Philadelphia shipyard project during the June 1995 House debate, saying that providing funds for work at a base slated for closure would set a bad precedent. And he said the money Dicks wanted for the new physical fitness center would add badminton, squash, aerobics and paddleball to an existing gym when other programs face steep budget cuts.

Unfortunately for Royce, his argument was not pure. Republican Curt Weldon of Pennsylvania recalled how Royce visited his office in May 1995 to ask the chairman of the House National Security Military Research and Development Subcommittee to add $34 million for a local California project the Pentagon had not requested. Royce did not contradict Weldon. The Royce-Minge amendment ultimately failed, 158-270.

Royce, who sits on the International Relations Committee, also targeted the Overseas Private Investment Corporation (OPIC) as an example of unnecessary federal spending. He said OPIC "epitomizes corporate welfare by subsidizing wasteful private foreign investment by large corporations — to the tune of $26 million taxpayer dollars a year."

He was outraged by a bill that he said would double America's commitment to OPIC, which provides loan guarantees and risk insurance for private companies doing business overseas. Without such insurance, many companies would be reluctant to invest in developing countries, supporters say. "Increasing funding for OPIC defies logic," Royce said in September 1996. "Time and time again we have seen that government interference in the economy leads to inefficiency and delays improvement."

The House agreed with Royce, and in a surprising vote, rejected, 157-260, legislation that would have reauthorized the agency for five years. OPIC was still funded, however, under the fiscal 1997 foreign operations spending bill. In the 105th Congress, Royce will chair the Africa Subcommittee on International Relations. He also has a seat on the Banking and Financial Services Committee.

Royce plans to continue his porkbuster activities in the 105th by calling for a "lockbox" provision to House rules requiring that any spending cuts made in funding bills through an amendment on the House floor be channeled directly into deficit reduction and not spent elsewhere. He also backs an effort that would define "pork" as any unauthorized, unreviewed expenditure. If an item in a House bill meets these criteria, it would

CALIFORNIA 39
Parts of Orange and Los Angeles counties — Fullerton

This district straddles the line between Orange and Los Angeles counties. It is where the more affluent parts of Los Angeles County's suburbs meet the less affluent sections of Orange County; it is a seamless fit.

From all appearances, and spiritually speaking, this is an Orange County district. Its L.A. County portion looks like what many think of when they envision Orange County: bedroom communities, small commercial areas and regional malls. Its residents tend to vote Republican, hold conservative economic views and not identify themselves as Los Angelenos.

Residents throughout the 39th typically work at jobs inside the district's borders. About three-fifths of the people are non-Hispanic whites, but there is a sizable presence of Hispanics (almost 23 percent) and Asians (14 percent).

The economy is a top concern here, as it is throughout Southern California, but so is crime. There is not a lot of violent crime or gang activity within the borders of the 39th, though this problem exists just across the line in Anaheim and in Santa Ana, and it is creeping this way.

Most of the terrain here is flat, with some hills in Fullerton and La Habra Heights. Though the cities in the district are largely residential, many have an industrial area: Machine shops, plastic injection-molding facilities, aerospace subcontractors and food manufacturers are among the installations.

Fullerton, the 39th's largest city, is upper-middle class, a label that applies to much of the district. Fullerton is home to a variety of industries and the district's largest employers, including Hughes Aircraft's ground systems division, which was bought by the Raytheon Co. in January 1997. Division employees design and manufacture such things as radar, communications equipment and air traffic control equipment. Other major employers are Beckman Instruments, which manufactures scientific equipment, and Hunt-Wesson, whose plants make ketchup and other foodstuffs.

There is little variation among the communities inside the 39th. One of the only interruptions in the thoroughly developed area is Knott's Berry Farm, a major amusement park in Buena Park toward the south. Especially affluent areas include La Habra Heights, and the eastern, more Republican half of Whittier, both of which are in the 39th's northern region in L.A. County.

On the flip side, Hawaiian Gardens in L.A. County is more working-class and more Democratic than is the norm in the 39th. The district also picks up an industrial portion of Anaheim to the east.

Though this is a district landlocked in freeways, its southwestern corner reaches down to within four miles of the Pacific Ocean.

Republicans hold a substantial voter-registration advantage over Democrats in the 39th, and at election time that usually translates into a comfortable cushion for GOP candidates. That has narrowed in recent presidential elections, however.

1990 Population: 573,574. White 417,689 (73%), Black 15,095 (3%), Other 140,790 (25%). Hispanic origin 130,920 (23%). 18 and over 430,089 (75%), 62 and over 68,307 (12%). Median age: 32.

be eliminated. Royce also said he will continue his push for the elimination of the departments of Energy and Commerce.

In fact, Royce proposed rolling back Clinton's 1993 4.3-cent gasoline tax increase and to make large cuts in the Department of Energy (DOE) budget to offset the revenue losses. He introduced the measure in the spring of 1996 in the wake of consumer anger over rising fuel prices. "As is the case with so much of our government today, the DOE represents an outdated response to a brief period of crisis and is basically irrelevant today," Royce told the House. "We should repeal the 1993 gas tax, cut the Department of Energy budget, and give the money back to motorists." Although a measure passed the House, 301-108, in May 1996 to repeal the gas tax, it was in part a response to election-year politics. GOP presidential candidate Bob Dole had called for a suspension of the gas tax for the rest of the election year. The Senate, however, failed to follow suit.

These proposals reflect one of Royce's core tenets, which he once expressed at a party rally in California: "The problem is government is just too big and spends too much." A corollary belief: "We don't have deficits because we are not taxed enough. We have deficits because Congress spends too much."

During a decade in the California Senate, Royce made a mark on anti-crime measures. While there he won enactment of a bill making it a felony to stalk and threaten someone with injury — giving the police recourse when the stalker has not yet attacked his intended victim.

He was able to broaden this law in 1996, as he watched President Clinton sign a bill he sponsored that would make it a federal crime to cross state lines with the intent to stalk or harass someone. Royce had first introduced the measure in 1993 — his first year in the House. "There are thousands of people trying to escape stalkers by moving to another state, but there hasn't been any protection for them when they are followed. . . . Now there is," Royce told reporters after the bill was signed.

Although Royce was thrilled his measure made it into law, he was less pleased at his treatment at the September 1996 White House bill signing ceremony. He told The Orange County Register that when he arrived at the Oval Office, the spot designated for him to stand was to President Clinton's far right, well out of camera range. But that was just the start. When it came time to thank the anti-stalking bill's sponsors, the president left him out, Royce told the newspaper. Clinton instead mentioned Texas GOP Sen. Kay Bailey Hutchinson, whom Royce had recruited to sponsor the bill in the Senate.

"I think it is typical of this administration," Royce told the newspaper. "After two years of watching the president take credit for what a Republican Congress has done, I'm not surprised that he would not mention the fact that I was the Republican author for the bill."

Royce intends to introduce a bill in the 105th that he calls a "victims' Bill of Rights." The measure would ensure that victims be informed, present and heard at critical stages during the trial of their alleged assailants, would require that trials be speedy, and would demand full restitution from convicted offenders. He was able in 1990 to include certain of these victims rights proposals in a California ballot initiative known as Proposition 115, which state voters passed overwhelmingly.

Illegal immigration has been a major concern of Royce's. He supports proposals to increase Border Patrol agents, to stop payment of federal welfare and unemployment benefits to illegal immigrants and to increase penalties for immigrant smuggling. In the 104th, he backed an effort to deny public education to illegal immigrants.

In his independent bid for president in 1992, Ross Perot won a hefty 22 percent in the 39th, and Royce in 1993 played a visible role in getting Perot together with the House GOP freshmen to call for cutting the deficit and reforming congressional procedures.

At Home: With 10 years under his belt in Sacramento, Royce was ready to move up in 1992 when Republican Rep. William E. Dannemeyer decided to seek the Senate seat held by fellow Republican John Seymour.

Although remapping for the 1990s somewhat altered the borders of Dannemeyer's district (it lost Anaheim and, with it, Disneyland), the 39th is essentially the constituency that time and again re-elected Dannemeyer, one of the House GOP's most outspoken voices against abortion and homosexuality.

Royce had represented a sizable slice of the 39th's territory in the Senate, and he drew no primary opposition. His Democratic opponent, Molly McClanahan, was regarded as an effective member of the Fullerton City Council.

But she proved too liberal for this bastion of Orange County conservatism. Royce beat her by almost 20 points. He also won easily in 1994 and 1996, running each time against the same candidate.

HOUSE ELECTIONS

1996 General		
Ed Royce (R)	120,761	(63%)
R.O. "Bob" Davis (D)	61,392	(32%)
Jack Dean (LIBERT)	10,137	(5%)
1994 General		
Ed Royce (R)	113,037	(66%)
R.O. "Bob" Davis (D)	49,459	(29%)
Jack Dean (LIBERT)	7,862	(5%)

Previous Winning Percentages: 1992 (57%)

CAMPAIGN FINANCE

	Receipts	Receipts from PACs	Expend-itures
1996			
Royce (R)	$621,689	$250,675 (40%)	$489,076
1994			
Royce (R)	$401,249	$138,175 (34%)	$403,335
Davis (D)	$3,691	0	$3,755

DISTRICT VOTE FOR PRESIDENT

	1996		1992
D	83,246 (41%)	**D**	78,305 (34%)
R	97,247 (48%)	**R**	100,669 (44%)
I	15,909 (8%)	**I**	50,834 (22%)

KEY VOTES

1997	
Ban "partial birth" abortions	Y
1996	
Approve farm bill	Y
Deny public education to illegal immigrants	Y
Repeal ban on certain assault-style weapons	Y
Increase minimum wage	N
Freeze defense spending	N
Approve welfare overhaul	Y
1995	
Approve balanced-budget constitutional amendment	Y
Relax Clean Water Act regulations	Y
Oppose limits on environmental regulations	N
Reduce projected Medicare spending	Y
Approve GOP budget with tax and spending cuts	Y

VOTING STUDIES

	Presidential Support		Party Unity		Conservative Coalition	
Year	**S**	**O**	**S**	**O**	**S**	**O**
1996	34	66	89	10	73	25
1995	17	82	95	5	84	16
1994	32	63	93	3	78	17
1993	23	77	92	6	75	25

INTEREST GROUP RATINGS

Year	ADA	AFL-CIO	CCUS	ACU
1996	15	n/a	88	100
1995	0	0	96	100
1994	10	11	83	95
1993	20	8	91	96

40 Jerry Lewis (R)

Of Redlands — Elected 1978, 10th term

Biographical Information
Born: Oct. 21, 1934, Seattle, Wash.
Education: U. of California, Los Angeles, B.A. 1956.
Occupation: Insurance executive.
Family: Wife, Arlene Willis; four children, three stepchildren.
Religion: Presbyterian.
Political Career: San Bernardino School Board, 1965-68; Calif. Assembly, 1969-79; Republican nominee for Calif. Senate, 1973.
Capitol Office: 2112 Rayburn Bldg. 20515; 225-5861.

Committees
Appropriations
National Security; VA, HUD & Independent Agencies (chairman)
Select Intelligence
Technical & Tactical Intelligence (chairman)

In Washington: Lewis is the first to admit that he has not controlled events in his recent congressional career, but that events have plainly controlled him. "I'm not one who anticipated the revolution," he confessed in 1995. "Once it happened, I realized I'd be playing on a field that I did not design."

In late 1992, Lewis was denied a House leadership slot by a new generation of Republicans in a central "pre-revolutionary" skirmish. Now his task as chairman of an Appropriations subcommittee is cutting spending while trying to placate myriad interest groups and his project-thirsty colleagues.

Lewis' subcommittee — Veterans' Affairs, Housing and Urban Development and Independent Agencies — oversees the most diverse portfolio of any Appropriations panel. The fortunes of veterans seeking medical care, public housing residents, rocket scientists, homeowners near toxic waste sites and hurricane victims are all affected by the bill that goes through his subcommittee.

Lewis also serves on the Select Intelligence Committee, where he gains a second gavel for the 105th, as chairman of the Technical and Tactical Intelligence Subcommittee. On defense issues, Lewis has supported his party's efforts to raise Pentagon spending levels above President Clinton's desires, although he also backed funding of U.S. troops in Bosnia once Clinton deployed them. He is a leader of a group of lawmakers determined to spare the B-2 "stealth" bomber from the knives of the deficit hawks.

A legislator from the old school, Lewis sometimes breaks with his party to protect the perquisites of office. The only item in the House GOP's "Contract With America" he did not support was the term limits amendment, and he was one of the few members willing to state publicly his opposition to freezing congressional pay. He knocked party leaders for allowing a vote on salaries, saying, "The members need from time to time to be protected from themselves."

Still, Lewis succeeded in his broadest mandate as VA-HUD chairman during the 104th Congress, which was to cut spending. He chopped nearly $15 billion from the programs he oversees in two years — the most of any appropriator — but it didn't come easily. If some of Lewis' younger colleagues found him diffident about his budget-whacking chores, he has joined them in attempting to use the power of the purse to affect authorizations and policy. He tried, for example, to hold off funding the superfund hazardous waste program until it was reauthorized — something not accomplished during the 104th. And he succeeded in adding language to a spending bill to require study of changes he desired in federal management of the vast desert lands in and around his district.

The highest-profile scrimmage on a Lewis bill took place during floor consideration of the fiscal 1996 VA-HUD package. Lewis worked with Commerce Committee Chairman Thomas J. Bliley Jr., R-Va., in conceiving a set of 17 riders that would have effectively blocked the ability of the Environmental Protection Agency (EPA) to enforce major provisions of such laws as the Clean Air and clean water acts. The package was stripped by a narrow House vote, providing Democrats with one of their first major victories during the 104th; but that triumph was short-lived. Lewis called for a revote the following week, and the move to strip out the riders was defeated on a tie vote. The riders proved a huge political liability, and so Lewis honored a third vote of the House, instructing conferees to delete the controversial provisions.

"Next year, frankly, I'm not going to carry this kind of burden," Lewis said. The riders and a one-third cut in EPA's enforcement budget helped widen a rift between Lewis and ranking VA-HUD Democrat Louis Stokes of Ohio. When Stokes headed the panel during the 103rd, their relations were cordial, with Lewis regularly referring to Stokes as "my chairman." But Democrats like Stokes were not the only ones angered by some of the cuts Lewis sought to enforce.

CALIFORNIA 40
San Bernardino County — Redlands

The 40th is a desert district of massive proportions. It takes in most of San Bernardino County's 20,000 square miles and all of Inyo County's 10,000. San Bernardino County is the largest in the nation; between it and Inyo, the 40th covers almost one-fifth of California.

Most of the district's residents are packed into the far southwest corner in three areas: the Inland Empire, the Victor Valley region and the Morongo Basin.

The Inland Empire section of the district's south includes just a few eastern areas in the city of San Bernardino and such cities as Highland and Redlands, largely bedroom communities with many retirees from Norton Air Force Base. Yucaipa, a bit farther east, has an especially high number of retirees. Loma Linda, just west of Redlands, is a Seventh-day Adventist community and home to the Loma Linda University Medical Center, best known for its infant heart transplant program (including the 1984 "Baby Fay" case, in which an infant was given a baboon's heart).

Victor Valley, north of San Bernardino, has typified the area's explosive growth. It includes the cities of Victorville, Hesperia, Apple Valley and Adelanto and once looked to the military for support. But that presence is diminishing, with the closing of both George and Norton Air Force bases. The city of San Bernardino has leased the Norton site, however, and has opened a golf course and is developing a trade center that includes an international airport and an industrial park. City officials say they hope the project will replace many of the lost miliary jobs.

Victor Valley's growth over the past 10 years has been fueled by Los Angeles workers looking for affordable housing. From their homes here, these commuters head south on Interstate 15 through the San Bernardino Mountains' Cajon Pass — "down the hill," as they put it — and two hours later they are in downtown Los Angeles.

The Morongo Basin, east of the Inland Empire along the southern border with Riverside County, is the smallest of the three population centers, taking in cities such as Yucca Valley, Joshua Tree and Twentynine Palms. These are just north of the Joshua Tree National Monument and depend heavily on the nearby military presence, which includes the massive Twentynine Palms Marine Corps base.

The district also includes Fort Irwin, where the Army trained Desert Storm's troops for desert maneuvers, and the China Lake Naval Weapons Center. Between 60,000 and 80,000 troops a year train at Fort Irwin. The rest of the 40th is barren. It includes most of the Death Valley National Monument (some of which is in Nevada), whose tourists drive the economy of many of the area's small, scattered towns, such as Lone Pine, Independence and Bishop.

Lewis drew strong support across the district in 1992 and 1994, beating the same opponent by more than 2-to-1. In 1996, he outpaced GOP standard-bearer Bob Dole by 16 percentage points.

Dole nearly captured a majority of the three-way vote, up from the 40 percent George Bush garnered in 1992. But it was still a far cry from the 64 percent Bush captured in 1988.

1990 Population: 573,625. White 470,785 (82%), Black 31,210 (5%), Other 71,630 (12%). Hispanic origin 92,180 (16%). 18 and over 407,236 (71%), 62 and over 81,470 (14%). Median age: 31.

The GOP's outnumbered but critical moderates joined forces with Democrats to kill the EPA riders and to force Lewis to add back more than $600 million for housing and assistance programs. Lewis bucked conservatives and his party leaders to preserve funding for Clinton's prized National Service initiative to placate Democrats and those moderate Republicans: "To zero out the program would help none of us," he said. But he saw conservatives change tack and succeed with an amendment to shift the program's funding into veterans' health care accounts.

Lewis sometimes spoke of the difficulty of juggling priorities when the same pot of money might be directed toward veterans or to outer space. If his fiscal 1996 bill was spared, for the first time in five years, an up-or-down vote on killing the space station, there were plenty of Democratic amendments trying to shift that project's funds toward other priorities. And Lewis, who noted that NASA was "my favorite agency in my bill," failed in his efforts to kill other space programs and the Selective Service system, while having to fend off members who wanted to siphon funds from the Federal Emergency Management Agency, which Lewis prized for its help in rebuilding areas neighboring his district following the 1994 Northridge earthquake.

In the end, the loaded-down bill was vetoed and the programs under its purview were funded by an omnibus spending bill almost halfway into the fiscal year. In 1996, Lewis worked more closely with Stokes, spending hours on end hammering out differences in meetings in hopes of avoiding further bloodletting on the floor. "Last year was a major readjustment for everybody," he said in 1996. "We're out of the wish-list business and in the business of funding programs reasonably to meet real needs."

But Lewis' conciliatory manner provoked grumbling from the conservative wing of the GOP Conference. They felt Lewis bent back too far in allowing Clinton and House Democrats to dictate policy on the environment and National Service. He ended up one of the targets of a proposed rule change to give the conference more leverage over subcommittee chairmen, although the plan failed at the start of the 105th.

While Lewis grew willing to concede that the Contract With America had points of merit he initially had overlooked, he complained to the Los Angeles Times in 1995 that "it has encouraged an environment of working in lock step, and I'm not sure that is good for any governing body."

Lewis has grown accustomed to marching out of lock step. He had to fight a Gingrich-backed challenge to his conference chairmanship at the end of 1990, and in 1991 he was replaced as the California member on the panel in charge of making GOP committee assignments. When the big freshman class of 1992 arrived, the Republican newcomers did not know Lewis and did not relate to his old-fashioned success story. He was denied the conference chair just before the 103rd Congress, losing 88-84 to Dick Armey, the Texan who had positioned himself to be Gingrich's right-hand man.

At Home: A successful insurance broker, Lewis entered GOP politics in the 1960s and won a seat on the San Bernardino School Board. After three years there, he sought a state Assembly seat in 1968 and won the first of five terms.

With an Assembly constituency that covered more than half a congressional district (then numbered the 37th), Lewis was an obvious choice for Republicans in 1978, when GOP Rep. Shirley N. Pettis retired. Earlier in his career, Lewis had worked as a field representative for Jerry Pettis, Shirley's husband, who represented the district for eight years before his death in a plane crash in 1975. Declaring himself a candidate in the "Pettis tradition," Lewis won the five-candidate GOP primary with 55 percent of the vote, then won the general election handily.

He had his pick of two districts after the 1982 redistricting and chose the one (then numbered the 35th) that, although less Republican, included his home. He soon established dominance, winning with at least 70 percent or more three times in the 1980s.

He attracted a primary challenger in 1990, when his rise within the House GOP hierarchy raised his profile in California and led to speculation that he might aim for a Senate seat in 1992. (His name is still mentioned for the same seat, which is up again in 1998.) He dispatched the primary challenge, from lawyer and political neophyte Mark I. Blankenship. Lewis did face a backlash in 1990 after he publicly supported President George Bush's unpopular budget agreement in October. Although he won comfortably, his 61 percent tally was his lowest since his first contest in 1978.

HOUSE ELECTIONS

1996 General		
Jerry Lewis (R)	98,821	(65%)
Robert "Bob" Conaway (D)	44,102	(29%)
Hale McGee (AMI)	4,963	(3%)
Joseph T. Kelley (LIBERT)	4,375	(3%)
1996 Primary		
Jerry Lewis (R)	46,108	(77%)
George Craig (R)	13,836	(23%)
1994 General		
Jerry Lewis (R)	115,728	(71%)
Donald M. "Don" Rusk (D)	48,003	(29%)

Previous Winning Percentages: 1992 (63%) **1990** (61%) **1988** (70%) **1986** (77%) **1984** (85%) **1982** (68%) **1980** (72%) **1978** (61%)

CAMPAIGN FINANCE

	Receipts	Receipts from PACs	Expend-itures
1996			
Lewis (R)	$588,476	$403,836 (69%)	$239,448
Conaway (D)	$13,578	0	$12,085
1994			
Lewis (R)	$424,000	$305,940 (72%)	$209,763
Rusk (D)	$40,853	0	$39,544

DISTRICT VOTE FOR PRESIDENT

	1996		1992
D	73,316 (38%)	**D**	76,363 (35%)
R	94,916 (49%)	**R**	86,453 (40%)
I	20,719 (11%)	**I**	53,955 (25%)

KEY VOTES

1997	
Ban "partial-birth" abortions	Y
1996	
Approve farm bill	Y
Deny public education to illegal immigrants	Y
Repeal ban on certain assault-style weapons	?
Increase minimum wage	Y
Freeze defense spending	N
Approve welfare overhaul	Y
1995	
Approve balanced-budget constitutional amendment	Y
Relax Clean Water Act regulations	Y
Oppose limits on environmental regulations	N
Reduce projected Medicare spending	Y
Approve GOP budget with tax and spending cuts	Y

VOTING STUDIES

	Presidential Support		Party Unity		Conservative Coalition	
Year	S	O	S	O	S	O
1996	43	51	82	11	94	0
1995	21	75	92	6	98	1
1994	50	41	77	18	81	8
1993	42	56	83	15	89	11
1992	77	14	77	17	85	6
1991	81	16	78	16	84	5

INTEREST GROUP RATINGS

Year	ADA	AFL-CIO	CCUS	ACU
1996	5	n/a	94	83
1995	5	9	95	68
1994	0	13	82	88
1993	0	8	100	88
1992	10	17	86	83
1991	0	18	100	83

41 Jay C. Kim (R)

Of Diamond Bar — Elected 1992, 3rd term

Biographical Information

Born: March 27, 1939, Seoul, South Korea.

Education: U. of Southern California, B.S. 1967, M.S. 1973; California State U., Los Angeles, M.S. 1980.

Occupation: Civil engineer.

Family: Wife, June Kim; three children.

Religion: Methodist.

Political Career: Diamond Bar City Council, 1990-91; mayor of Diamond Bar, 1991-93.

Capitol Office: 227 Cannon Bldg. 20515; 225-3201.

Committees

International Relations
Asia & the Pacific; Western Hemisphere

Transportation & Infrastructure
Public Buildings & Economic Development (chairman); Water Resources & Environment

In Washington: While controversy over questionable Asian campaign contributions was dogging Democrats and the White House in 1997, Republicans suffered problems in that regard as well. Kim, the first Korean-American ever elected to Congress and a person the GOP likes to hold up as proof of its efforts to reach out to new constituencies, is at the center of a campaign probe that has resulted in huge fines and the conviction of his campaign treasurer.

A federal probe was prompted by reports in the Los Angeles Times that Kim's firm, JayKim Engineers, had illegally contributed $485,000 to his 1992 House campaign, violating a federal ban on corporate contributions to federal campaigns. The reports said Kim's company had offered free office space, staff and supplies to his campaign, paid Kim's salaries and expenses, and covered costs for airline tickets, telephone bills and other expenditures. Five South Korea-based companies have pleaded guilty to giving illegal contributions to Kim's campaign and have been fined an aggregate of $1.6 million.

Kim himself has not been charged, although he and his wife, June, have been implicated by two former Kim campaign treasurers. Kim denies any wrongdoing, and despite the legal and ethical storms gathering around him on the West Coast, in Washington he goes about his work on the International Relations Committee and the Transportation and Infrastructure Committee.

On the latter panel, where he chairs the Public Buildings and Economic Development Subcommittee, Kim has effectively snagged federal transportation dollars for his district. With perhaps $175 billion at stake as Congress undertakes a massive rewrite of surface transportation law in the 105th, Kim hopes to change spending formulas to secure more money for California. "They should be pretty happy because I represent Orange County," said Kim, who raised about $38,000 from transportation interests during the 1996 election cycle. "Since I'm a chairman, I've got a lot of influence."

Kim wants new formulas to account for truck traffic from seaports and increased road use stemming from NAFTA, so that the federal government bears the cost, rather than the states. Among the prizes Kim already has won during his first two terms are about $100 million for flood control along the Santa Ana River, more than $91 million for road improvements in and around his district, and construction of car-pool connector lanes between I-405 and I-55 in Southern California. He helped block weight restrictions on buses on Orange County highways, helped preserve federal co-signing of a $1.35 billion Orange County toll road bond sale, and arranged for states rather than the Environmental Protection Agency to implement certain regulations under the Clean Air Act.

But Kim has been shadowed by the campaign irregularities from his first House race. (Extensive local media reports on Kim's finances — particularly in the Los Angeles Times and the Orange County Register — have detailed a long pattern of slipshod business bookkeeping and weak compliance with campaign reporting requirements, including disclosure irregularities in Kim's 1990 Diamond Bar City Council bid.)

Seokuk Ma, a former Kim campaign treasurer, was convicted in April 1997 of four counts of accepting and concealing at least $23,000 in illegal contributions. (Kim has returned at least $17,000 in illegal contributions to the FEC.) Jay and June Kim said in court papers that they would have "reluctantly" taken the Fifth Amendment and not testified for fear of self-incrimination had they been called, even though they had "information that bears on his innocence," according to their attorney.

Ma told the federal jury that he accepted cash donations in violation of federal election laws because he could not question his superiors due to Korean cultural norms. Ma said he didn't ask questions when June Kim told him to sign blank election report pages. "My culture is very different," Ma said. "I respect Congressman Kim very much. If they ask me to do something like that, I

CALIFORNIA 41
Parts of Orange, Los Angeles and San Bernardino counties

One goal of California's court-ordered 1992 remapping was to create as many districts as possible that follow county and city borders. The suburban 41st was not one of the successes: It splits three counties and runs up against a fourth. Its center is the intersection of Orange, Los Angeles and San Bernardino counties, and it reaches east to the northwestern border of Riverside County.

Primarily, this district consists of bedrooms for Los Angeles and the rest of Orange County. Some people in the eastern end of the district head farther east to work in the factories in Fontana.

Nearly half the district's voters are in San Bernardino County, 20 percent in Orange County and 30 percent in Los Angeles County. In Orange County, the 41st includes Yorba Linda (birthplace and burial site of Richard M. Nixon), part of Anaheim Hills and bits of Brea and Placentia. In Los Angeles County, it takes in Diamond Bar, a little bit of Walnut and a big bit of Pomona. In San Bernardino County, it includes Chino, Chino Hills, Montclair, Upland and Ontario.

The Orange County section of the 41st is a representative slice of the county: It is white-collar, conservative and affluent. Republicans outnumber Democrats here. In 1996, Kim found his strongest support in Orange County — 68 percent. He received 51 percent in Los Angeles County, 59 percent in San Bernardino County and 59 percent overall.

The section of San Bernardino County in the 41st is called the Inland Empire's West End. Real estate prices are relatively low, and many of its residents head south down the Carbon Canyon to work in Orange County.

Chino Hills' 28,000 residents are among the 41st's most conservative and affluent. Just north is Chino, a middle-income area whose 60,000 residents are almost evenly registered in both the parties.

North of Chino is the largest city in the district, Ontario, with 133,000 residents split between the 41st and the 42nd, which has the Democratic eastern side. The city's burgeoning airport — increasingly a passenger and cargo gateway into Los Angeles — is one of the area's primary growth engines. The airport's ability to bring passengers in and send goods out has spawned hotels, restaurants and distribution facilities nearby. Upland, in the northern corner of the district, resembles its eastern neighbor, Rancho Cucamonga, in the 42nd. It is another conservative, wealthy area.

The economics begin to shift downward moving southwest to Montclair and into Los Angeles County, with the 41st's piece of Pomona. Montclair lacks the retailing and manufacturing activity that supports Ontario. Just south of Pomona is Diamond Bar, a more affluent suburb where Kim served as mayor before entering Congress.

Bob Dole won the 41st in 1996 with 47 percent of the vote. George Bush won with 43 percent in 1992, considerably below his 66 percent showing in 1988.

1990 Population: 572,663. White 389,458 (68%), Black 39,205 (7%), Other 144,000 (25%). Hispanic origin 180,331 (31%). 18 and over 400,070 (70%), 62 and over 43,038 (8%). Median age: 30.

cannot refuse. If I say no, it's kind of an insult to them."

Members of the large and growing Korean community in Los Angeles were motivated by ethnic pride to help Kim's campaign, according to some of the executives later found to have broken campaign laws — particularly because they felt politically isolated after the city's 1992 riots. On July 16, 1992, a scheme was hatched by South Korea-based corporations to funnel illegal campaign dollars to Kim at a dinner meeting of the Korea Traders Club of Los Angeles. A club letter contained in court records details a plot to make the illegal contributions. Kim was the featured speaker at the meeting but has denied any knowledge of the plan.

"They simply didn't understand election law, that's my opinion," Kim has said. "You don't do that kind of plot for a few thousand dollars — a quarter of a million, maybe. In the meantime, I got hurt. They tried to help me and hurt me badly."

The companies would illegally reimburse their employees for making contributions to Kim's campaign. In one instance, a plea agreement reached with Hyundai Motor America detailed its money funneling scheme. Six days after a check, retrieved before it could be reported to the FEC, was returned in August 1992 to Hyundai, the company's president D.O. Chung approved a $4,500 "special bonus" to Executive Vice President Myung Juhn. Juhn then wrote out checks totaling that amount to four employees (in the memo section of the checks was written Chang Joon Kim, the congressman's name before he Americanized it). By the end of the month, the employees donated the money to Kim's campaign.

Jane Chong, who was Kim's 1992 campaign treasurer and later his office manager, alleged in interviews with the FBI in April 1996 that Kim and his wife destroyed evidence and knowingly accepted illegal contributions. She claimed Jay and June Kim routinely accepted corporate contributions and crossed the word "Inc." off checks so they could be reported as non-corporate contributions. She also alleged that June Kim kept secret lists in Korean to indicate what corporations had made donations, and that Mrs. Kim had asked her to destroy computer records indicating the true source of contributions. Chong told the FBI she regularly fabricated false identifications about contributors in Federal Election Commission reports. Kim called Chong's allegations "totally unsubstantiated."

The bad publicity has tarnished the storybook tale of Kim's life since coming to America — an immigrant who rose to prominence in business and became the first Korean-American elected to Congress. Soon after taking office, he arranged to sell JayKim Engineers. But in mid-1993, the company collapsed into receivership after defaulting on a $1 million bank loan guaranteed by Kim and his wife.

Kim is a loyal vote across the board for the GOP. He said he had some doubts in the 104th about plans to prohibit welfare benefits for legal immigrants, but he supported the move at the urging of party leaders. He also supported a successful effort in 1996 to split legal immigration provisions from an overhaul of immigration law covering illegal aliens. "It is an insult to legal immigrants to lump them together with illegal aliens, who are lawbreakers," Kim said.

At Home: The political fallout of Kim's campaign finance troubles resonated in his 1994 primary. Four Republicans sought to deny him renomination; together they amassed nearly 60 percent of the vote. But the crowded field was his salvation; he was renominated with 41 percent.

Yorba Linda businessman Bob Kerns, who finished third in the 1994 primary, made another run for the GOP nomination in 1996, centering his campaign on Kim's ethical difficulties. "It's building up a pattern," Kerns said. "He can't just claim he's ignorant all the time." But Kerns was woefully underfunded and Kim enjoyed strong party support, including help from Speaker Newt Gingrich, who appeared at a district fundraiser. Kim won renomination with 58 percent and had no trouble in the fall.

Fresh out of the South Korean Army at age 22, Kim moved to California. He worked in low-wage jobs and eventually graduated from college and earned a degree in civil engineering before starting JayKim Engineers. He adopted the United States as home and legally changed his name from Chang Joon to Jay. In 1990, his profile as a prominent businessman and political outsider won him a seat on the Diamond Bar City Council.

The 41st is solidly Republican, so the district's 1992 GOP primary was the decisive electoral event. In the six-way race, Kim offered himself as an alternative to professional politicians. He outhustled his opponents, energizing both the 10 percent of the district that is Asian-American and his Diamond Bar constituency. He finished first with 30 percent of the vote, just ahead of former Pomona Mayor Charles W. Bader. The general election was a breeze.

HOUSE ELECTIONS

1996 General		
Jay C. Kim (R)	83,934	(59%)
Richard L. Waldron (D)	47,346	(33%)
Richard G. Newhouse (LIBERT)	7,135	(5%)
David F. Kramer (NL)	5,030	(4%)
1996 Primary		
Jay C. Kim (R)	24,321	(58%)
Bob Kerns (R)	17,461	(42%)
1994 General		
Jay C. Kim (R)	81,854	(62%)
Ed Tessier (D)	49,924	(38%)

Previous Winning Percentages: 1992 (60%)

CAMPAIGN FINANCE

	Receipts	Receipts from PACs	Expend-itures
1996			
Kim (R)	$579,517	$112,415 (19%)	$579,673
1994			
Kim (R)	$810,846	$93,845 (12%)	$810,211
Tessier (D)	$73,594	$5,500 (7%)	$73,244

DISTRICT VOTE FOR PRESIDENT

1996		1992	
D	71,393 (43%)	**D**	64,666 (35%)
R	76,867 (47%)	**R**	78,902 (43%)
I	13,007 (8%)	**I**	41,112 (22%)

KEY VOTES

1997	
Ban "partial birth" abortions	Y
1996	
Approve farm bill	Y
Deny public education to illegal immigrants	Y
Repeal ban on certain assault-style weapons	Y
Increase minimum wage	N
Freeze defense spending	N
Approve welfare overhaul	Y
1995	
Approve balanced-budget constitutional amendment	Y
Relax Clean Water Act regulations	Y
Oppose limits on environmental regulations	N
Reduce projected Medicare spending	Y
Approve GOP budget with tax and spending cuts	Y

VOTING STUDIES

	Presidential Support		Party Unity		Conservative Coalition	
Year	S	O	S	O	S	O
1996	34	66	98	2	98	2
1995	15	85	98	2	98	2
1994	44	56	96	4	100	0
1993	35	65	92	8	98	2

INTEREST GROUP RATINGS

Year	ADA	AFL-CIO	CCUS	ACU
1996	0	n/a	100	100
1995	0	0	100	92
1994	5	0	100	95
1993	10	0	100	92

42 George E. Brown Jr. (D)

Of Riverside — Elected 1962, 17th term
Did not serve 1971-73.

Biographical Information

Born: March 6, 1920, Holtville, Calif.
Education: El Centro Junior College, 1938; U. of California, Los Angeles, B.A. 1946.
Military Service: Army, 1942-46.
Occupation: Management consultant; physicist.
Family: Wife, Marta Macias; two children, five stepchildren.
Religion: Methodist.
Political Career: Monterey Park City Council, 1954-55; mayor of Monterey Park, 1955-58; Calif. Assembly, 1959-63; sought Democratic nomination for U.S. Senate, 1970.
Capitol Office: 2300 Rayburn Bldg. 20515; 225-6161.

Committees

Agriculture
Department Operations, Nutrition & Foreign Agriculture; Forestry, Resource Conservation & Research
Science (ranking)

In Washington: Brown is in his late seventies and the survivor of a seemingly endless string of tough re-election battles. But neither time nor the shifting political sands of his Southern California district have mellowed his manner or commitment to old-style labor-liberalism.

A former Science Committee chairman, Brown retains his ranking slot on the committee for the 105th, having passed up the chance to exercise his seniority and snag his party's top spot on Agriculture. As the fiscal 1998 science authorization bill made its way through Science and the House, it became immediately apparent that Brown was having an easier time working with Republicans, including newly installed Chairman F. James Sensenbrenner Jr. of Wisconsin, than he had with the GOP regime that led the panel during the 104th. At one point during work on the bill in April 1997, Brown, noting that he was in agreement with an amendment offered by conservative California Republican Dana Rohrabacher, said his old antagonist was at risk of "becoming a pragmatic statesman."

Brown and Sensenbrenner worked together on an amendment to the science bill that helped head off the annual attempt by "deficit hawks" to kill NASA's space station.

During the 104th, in contrast, Brown and former Chairman Robert S. Walker of Pennsylvania, who retired after one term at the Science helm, got along about as well as a couple of cats in a room with one bowl of milk. Brown, who had been deposed from his four-year chairmanship with the GOP takeover of Congress, mocked Walker's close ties to the Republican leadership, which Brown said centered on taking calls on his "bat phone."

Brown blasted Republican attempts to remake the federal government as a more lean and efficient entity, crying that they aimed to destroy vital programs. He opposed signature GOP legislation such as an overhaul of welfare, a massive 1995 tax cut package, and a balanced-budget constitutional amendment. He also voted against a farm bill produced by the Agriculture Committee to phase out commodity subsidies in favor of a more market-oriented system. But Brown, who holds a degree in physics and studied nuclear engineering at the graduate level, raised specific objection to cuts in the areas where the Science Committee had some jurisdiction.

He said that a plan to abolish the Commerce Department "borders on lunacy" and contended that Republicans were making a mockery of the science bill through their efforts to cut programs they didn't like. His many amendments to raise funding were turned aside, including a 1995 proposal to raise the science authorization level by about $1.5 billion — a substitute Brown claimed "recognizes what science really is: an investment in our future, not some ideological playground."

As the Science Committee prepared to mark up its portion of an omnibus regulatory overhaul package, Brown raised cain when Republicans introduced a major rewrite on the day the committee was to meet. He asked for a 24-hour delay so that Democrats could redraft their amendments, but Walker allowed only a two-hour delay.

Brown liked to complain that Walker was "the most autocratic, non-democratic chairman I have ever had the pleasure of working with."

Brown had long been a tepid ally of the space station, and his wariness only grew during the 104th. Complaining that Republicans were cutting too much from the program, and thus making it a project not worth pursuing, Brown voted "present" on an amendment to kill the project's authorization. He also supported a move by top Democratic appropriator David R. Obey of Wisconsin to transfer all the space station's funding into housing, veterans' and other space programs. Neither effort succeeded, and in 1997 Brown returned to his old habit of voting in support of the space station.

He disagreed in the 104th with the GOP's approach to environmental regulation and opposed much of the GOP's social policy agenda. Brown didn't care for the GOP's attempts to rewrite the 1994 crime law and voted against bills

CALIFORNIA 42
San Bernardino County — San Bernardino

This is the heart of the Inland Empire, with a small manufacturing base of its own and vast bedroom suburbs for people employed in neighboring Orange County and Los Angeles County.

Most of San Bernardino's 164,000 people live in the 42nd. It is an older community that grew about 40 percent during the 1980s. As brisk as that growth rate sounds, it was far outpaced by the population explosion in the district's other cities to the west such as Rancho Cucamonga and Ontario, each of which grew to include more than 100,000 residents. Employment in the area began to pick up in 1996 after a five-year slump, but the district still lags behind the state as a whole.

San Bernardino is one of the last havens of affordable housing within tolerable commuting distance of Los Angeles; many who live here drive 90 minutes to get to jobs in L.A. Local leaders are trying to attract more industry to spare residents this treadmill of long-distance driving.

This area was a fruit-packing center in the 1930s. Today, its citrus industry shares space with electronics and aerospace firms.

San Bernardino suffered a setback in its diversification by the closing of Norton Air Force Base in March 1994. The city since has leased the site for $1 and has converted it into a commercial airport. A Department of Defense accounting center is also on the site. The site is envisioned as an international trade center; it includes a golf course and an industrial park for small businesses. Cleanup of hazardous wastes, which had been a potential impediment, is ongoing and, city officials say, should not block development. Officials say the conversion may create 6,000 to 7,000 jobs.

Colton, a town of about 40,000 just southwest of San Bernardino, is about half Hispanic, 37 percent white, 8 percent black and 4 percent Asian. Many of its residents head a few miles west to work in Fontana's factories. Fontana (population 88,000) is the area's factory town. It has a bit of a tough reputation: The Ku Klux Klan has been active here, and it is the home of Hell's Angels.

Local industry has been suffering. Kaiser Steel's Fontana works employed 9,000 in its heyday, but the company began slipping in the late 1970s, declared bankruptcy in 1983 and closed and sold the Fontana plant. The buyer, California Steel Industries, has about 1,000 employees producing coiled steel, but the raw steel for that work has to come from elsewhere. The old Fontana blast furnace was dismantled and shipped to China. A speedway has opened on the site.

The western part of the 42nd rejects the "Inland Empire" label. Many of Rancho Cucamonga's 100,000 residents identify with Los Angeles, a half-hour west on Interstate 10. Rancho Cucamonga is almost 70 percent white, 20 percent Hispanic and about 5 percent each black and Asian.

The city of San Bernardino, with its large minority population, consistently votes Democratic in presidential elections. Much of the rest of the district, however, follows such areas as Rancho Cucamonga in voting Republican. In 1996, Clinton's vote total and winning percentage exceeded Brown's in the House race.

1990 Population: 571,844. White 377,500 (66%), Black 63,239 (11%), Other 131,105 (23%). Hispanic origin 196,418 (34%). 18 and over 381,173 (67%), 62 and over 50,749 (9%). Median age: 28.

banning federal recognition of same-gender marriages and banning an abortion procedure its opponents call "partial birth" abortion.

Brown, an affable cigar smoker and patient listener, was first elected as a spirited antiwar crusader in 1962. By the spring of 1965, he was accusing President Lyndon B. Johnson of pretending "that the peace of mankind can be won by the slaughter of peasants in Vietnam." For five years, he refused to vote for any military spending.

Throughout his House career, broken by a one-term absence after a failed Senate bid in 1970, he has consistently opposed the militarization of space and supported environmental protection.

The old peace advocate in Brown (a Quaker by upbringing) still surfaces in debates, particularly on space-based military programs. Brown's efforts to curb the military's role in space research and policy led him in 1987 to resign from the Intelligence Committee. He said he was stepping down in protest of Reagan administration policies on classifying information. But he was also under pressure from conservative Democrats who agreed with the administration's contention that Brown had divulged classified information on U.S. military satellite capabilities. Brown said he had relied only on published material.

Although Brown generally casts the liberal votes one would expect of him, creeping pragmatism has led him on occasion to cast some pro-defense votes he once might have denounced. In 1980, he began voting for the B-1 bomber, a California product. "If the B-1 was being built in some other state and I didn't have two Air Force bases and a lot of retired military people who feel strongly about the B-1, I'd probably have voted the other way," Brown explained.

At Home: Brown holds the record for most terms served from California in Congress, but his long run has not been earned easily. He has not garnered better that 60 percent of the vote since 1978. But as his longtime campaign manager likes to point out, "a win's a win."

His 1996 victory was his narrowest yet. Brown suffered badly in the 1992 redistricting and clings to a diminishing island of Democratic support in a sea of Southern California Republicanism. His 1996 GOP challenger, Superior Court Judge Linda M. Wilde, nearly matched his fundraising efforts and was an attractive and articulate spokesman for the conservative slant on issues such as crime and welfare.

Wilde was Brown's first female opponent, which led to a major gaffe on his part. In a late season debate Brown said, "I imagine Linda, because she is a lady, is afraid of math." The remarks drew groans but did little to dent Brown's beloved-crusty image as the grand old man of Inland Empire politics. Wilde was hurt by opposition in the district to an anti-affirmative action state ballot initiative and the relative lack of interest generated by the campaign (the contest drew nearly a third fewer votes in the district than the presidential race). Brown, long endangered, has held on through extraordinary attention to constituent service, and he prevailed by 996 votes.

In 1994, the Republican who rode out to meet Brown was a young and energetic conservative whose name, Rob Guzman, gave him instant appeal among the district's Hispanics. It did not give him instant appeal in the primary, however, and he had to spend much of what he had raised to secure his nomination. Thereafter, he made the most of the help he could get from the national and state GOP and ran 12 percentage points ahead of party registration in the district. He came within 2,629 votes of winning.

In 1992, the GOP candidate was Dick Rutan, one of the aviators who flew a lightweight plane around the world on one tank of fuel in 1986. Rutan seemed right for the anti-politician mood, and the race drew national press. But Rutan proved ill at ease with the public and raised only half what Brown had to spend. Brown won by seven points.

Brown had known turbulent political seas earlier in his career as well. After serving as a local official and state assemblyman from a near suburb of Los Angeles, he won a House seat in 1962 and held it until he tried for the Senate in 1970. That year's primary boiled down to Brown and Rep. John V. Tunney, son of former boxing champion Gene Tunney. Brown's opposition to the Vietnam War gave him an initial advantage in the year President Richard M. Nixon chose to invade Cambodia. But Tunney recovered by calling Brown a radical and accusing him of encouraging campus violence. Tunney won the primary and the Senate seat.

Brown bounced back quickly. In 1972 he moved to a newly created district in the San Bernardino-Riverside area and won an eight-candidate primary with 28 percent of the vote. He won easily that November and held the district without too much trouble until 1980, when his long string of sub-60 percent re-elections started. His GOP opponent that year — and in four more elections during the 1980s — was John Paul Stark, a hard-right Republican with a base among conservative Christian activists.

HOUSE ELECTIONS

1996 General		
George E. Brown Jr. (D)	52,166	(50%)
Linda M. Wilde (R)	51,170	(50%)
1996 Primary		
George E. Brown Jr. (D)	24,930	(78%)
Alfred "Al" Palazzo (D)	7,133	(22%)
1994 General		
George E. Brown Jr. (D)	58,888	(51%)
Rob Guzman (R)	56,259	(49%)

Previous Winning Percentages: **1992** (51%) **1990** (53%) **1988** (54%) **1986** (57%) **1984** (57%) **1982** (54%) **1980** (53%) **1978** (63%) **1976** (62%) **1974** (63%) **1972** (56%) **1968** (52%) **1966** (51%) **1964** (59%) **1962** (56%)

CAMPAIGN FINANCE

	Receipts	Receipts from PACs	Expend-itures
1996			
Brown (D)	$705,243	$326,214 (46%)	$722,544
Wilde (R)	$702,302	$230,244 (33%)	$685,623
1994			
Brown (D)	$517,136	$338,762 (66%)	$485,455
Guzman (R)	$295,531	$19,814 (7%)	$308,574

DISTRICT VOTE FOR PRESIDENT

	1996		1992
D	76,745 (54%)	**D**	76,964 (46%)
R	51,106 (36%)	**R**	54,978 (33%)
I	12,342 (9%)	**I**	35,828 (21%)

KEY VOTES

1997	
Ban "partial birth" abortions	N
1996	
Approve farm bill	N
Deny public education to illegal immigrants	N
Repeal ban on certain assault-style weapons	N
Increase minimum wage	Y
Freeze defense spending	Y
Approve welfare overhaul	N
1995	
Approve balanced-budget constitutional amendment	N
Relax Clean Water Act regulations	N
Oppose limits on environmental regulations	Y
Reduce projected Medicare spending	N
Approve GOP budget with tax and spending cuts	N

VOTING STUDIES

	Presidential Support		Party Unity		Conservative Coalition	
Year	**S**	**O**	**S**	**O**	**S**	**O**
1996	87	10	93	4	25	73
1995	83	9	88	4	14	72
1994	82	10	79	3	22	61
1993	84	10	82	2	20	80
1992	19	71	88	5	27	63
1991	38	59	83	7	30	65

INTEREST GROUP RATINGS

Year	ADA	AFL-CIO	CCUS	ACU
1996	90	n/a	25	0
1995	85	100	29	8
1994	80	78	33	10
1993	90	92	27	0
1992	95	91	25	5
1991	70	92	20	15

43 Ken Calvert (R)

Of Riverside — Elected 1992, 3rd term

Biographical Information

Born: June 8, 1953, Corona, Calif.

Education: Chaffey College, A.A. 1973; San Diego State U., B.A. 1975.

Occupation: Real estate executive.

Family: Divorced.

Religion: Protestant.

Political Career: Sought Republican nomination for U.S. House, 1982.

Capitol Office: 1034 Longworth Bldg. 20515; 225-1986.

Committees

Resources
Energy & Mineral Resources; Water & Power

Science
Energy & Environment (chairman); Space & Aeronautics

In Washington: Calvert has now secured his district, winning his past two elections with 55 percent, despite the negative publicity he received from a 1993 tryst with a prostitute, which seemed to attract more attention than his legislative accomplishments.

In the 104th Congress, he was given the chairmanship of a high-profile Resources Subcommittee on Energy and Mineral Resources, where he faithfully backed the party-line favoring mining and business interests. But in the 105th, he was transferred to head a Science panel on Energy and Environment.

Calvert introduced a measure in the 104th, approved by the House in July 1996, to allow states to take over the responsibility of collecting royalty payments for oil, gas and coal leases on federal lands. The bill would not alter the federal government's role in deciding what tracts of land to open for oil and gas exploration, but it would give the states the power to administer leases and collect royalties once those leases are awarded. States already get a share of the royalties for onshore oil and gas leases. By collecting the fees themselves, states believe they will be able to keep more of the money.

Calvert said the legislation would increase revenues into federal coffers by $51 million and by $33 million for states. "Our existing laws, regulations, policies and procedures related to oil and gas leasing lack clarity and consistency and impose unnecessary and unreasonable costs and burdens on lessees and the government alike," Calvert said when the House took up the bill.

He also supported GOP efforts to lift the existing moratorium on the issuance of new mining patents. Under the 1872 Mining Law, miners are allowed to establish low-cost patents — essentially ownership claims — on federal land. Many in Congress would like to update the law to charge more for the federal land. But Western members, in particular, have objected that revisions would greatly increase the royalties that miners would have to pay the government.

The one-year moratorium on the low-cost sales was lifted by conferees on the fiscal 1996 Interior spending bill. But in a bipartisan slap at Western mining interests, the House voted overwhelmingly in September 1995 to send the spending bill back to conference with instructions to reinstate the year-old freeze.

The motion was put over the top by a coalition of 91 Republicans. They included environmentalists — who opposed efforts by Western members to make it easier to extract hardrock minerals such as gold and silver from public lands — and conservative deficit hawks, mainly from the East and Midwest, who view the low-cost sales of federal lands as a taxpayer ripoff.

Calvert and other western Republicans attempted to justify the bill's provision to end the patent freeze. They noted that it would increase the price of mining land claims well above $2.50 an acre by charging miners fair market prices for the surface value of the lands they are prospecting. "This bill solves the mining claims problem," Calvert said. He backed changes to the 1872 Mining Law that are favored by the mining industry. But the bill would not include the value of the minerals under the soil in the calculation of fair market value, a factor cited by members who described even the revised patenting procedure as a giveaway of public lands.

From both of his committee seats, Calvert has expressed concern that an overemphasis on preserving endangered species unduly restricts property owners' rights. He backed an amendment to the GOP's large regulatory overhaul bill, which passed the House in February 1995 as part of the House GOP's "Contract With America," to extend the moratorium on new listings and designations under the Endangered Species Act until Dec. 31, 1996.

"In the last Congress, rats, bugs, and even weeds were more important than people," Calvert told the House. "Certain bureaucrats have become so eager to list new species as endangered, they have lost sight of the intent of the Endangered Species Act and ignored human concerns."

Calvert said the endangered Stephens kanga-

CALIFORNIA 43
Riverside County — western suburbs

California gained seven House seats in the 1990 reapportionment, and this district is part of that bounty. The old 37th District grew so much during the 1980s that by the time redistricting rolled around, there were enough people in it to fill two complete districts: the 43rd, which takes in Riverside County's western edge, and the 44th, the county's eastern expanse.

The 43rd serves as a bedroom district for three California regions. Its southern edge is just close enough to San Diego to house people who work in that city; immediately west of the 43rd lies Orange County and its aerospace industries and scattered small businesses; and beyond that — a full two- or three-hour drive for marathon commuters in the 43rd — are the office towers of downtown Los Angeles.

But in addition to its bedrooms, the district contains some of the largest avocado and citrus producers in the state, dairy ranchers to the west and March Air Force Base to the southeast of Riverside.

The largest city in the 43rd is Riverside, the county seat, which was established as a silkworm-breeding center around 1870 and soon after jumped into the business of growing navel oranges. After decades of steady growth, the city's population began to take off in the 1950s.

Since this period of explosive growth started, Riverside city has been shifted in and out of the Riverside County congressional district. In the 1960s, it was completely included; in the '70s, it was completely removed; in the '80s, it was split, but in a manner beneficial to the already dominant GOP.

With a population of 227,000, the city can now anchor a district by itself. The 43rd has all of Riverside, including the city's more Democratic northern neighborhoods, its blue-collar communities and the area around the University of California at Riverside (8,900 students).

Despite the addition of Riverside's Democratic areas, the district tends to back Republicans. Bob Dole won the district in 1996 by 3 percentage points. The GOP's edge is bolstered by such fast-growing Riverside suburbs as Corona and Norco (populations 76,000 and 23,000, respectively). About 80,000 people live in unincorporated county territory.

Parts of Riverside County were hard hit by brush fires in the dry autumn of 1993. Subsequent newspaper and TV news stories suggested more homes could have been saved had better fire breaks been dug into the arid hills separating housing developments. Calvert, among others, suggested that better fire breaks would have been there had it not been for rigorous protection of the Stephens kangaroo rat by the Endangered Species Act.

1990 Population: 571,231. White 432,614 (76%), Black 33,851 (6%), Other 104,766 (18%). Hispanic origin 142,785 (25%). 18 and over 401,020 (70%), 62 and over 59,365 (10%). Median age: 30.

roo rat was partly responsible for the destruction of 29 homes in his district. In fall 1993, Southern California was battling several wildfires. Because homeowners lived in critical habitat for the kangaroo rat they were unable to obey California law by clearing dry weeds and brush away from their homes, Calvert said, causing their homes to burn more easily.

From his Science subcommittee chair, Calvert said in early 1997 that he intends to address the scientific issues surrounding reauthorization of the Clean Air Act. His subcommittee has oversight of research and development at the Environmental Protection Agency (EPA). Although Calvert said he supports the Clean Air Act, he cautioned that new ozone and particulate matter standards proposed by the EPA should be fully "understood and supported by the public" before being implemented.

"I believe that rational regulation is essential to maintaining air quality," Calvert said at a hearing on the issue. "However, we in California have also suffered from irrational regulation — at the state level as well as the federal level."

Calvert's political troubles began in April 1994, when he was forced to admit he had engaged in sexual activity in a car with a prostitute in November 1993 in Corona, Calif., contradicting the story he had told after the incident was first reported. In the early morning hours of Nov. 28, police had spotted Calvert in his parked car, apparently engaged in sexual activity with a woman. After the first press report on the matter, Calvert said that "nothing happened," and that he and the woman in his car had been discussing parenting problems.

But the Riverside Press-Enterprise went to court to obtain the Corona police report on the incident. It said Calvert had tried to drive away when police approached, stopping only after ordered to do so three times. The newspaper printed this and other details from the report April 23, and Calvert released a statement changing his account. He said his behavior was "inappropriate" and said he had been depressed over his recent divorce and his father's suicide and had wanted companionship. He said that he did not know the woman was a prostitute and he did not pay her for sex.

Calvert also found himself in a bit of hot water in November 1995 when he invited the Rev. Lou Sheldon of the Traditional Values Coalition to deliver the morning prayer in the House. Several Democrats objected to Sheldon's appearance, saying that he is best known for his virulent anti-homosexual preaching. Sheldon's Anaheim-based organization is among the groups considered part of the Christian right political movement. Calvert told the House after the prayer that Sheldon has "been a wise counselor and good friend to me. His dedication to the Almighty and his strong moral convictions are an inspiration to us all."

At Home: A narrow 1982 House election defeat taught Calvert that absentee ballots can be crucial. In 1992, Calvert concentrated on getting ballots to potential absentees. The tactic helped him win the closest House contest in the country. It was only after 17,000 absentee ballots were counted that Calvert's apparent 1,200-vote loss to Mark A. Takano turned into a 519-vote win.

Seven Republicans and seven Democrats sought the open seat. Calvert had been active in Riverside County GOP circles, losing to Al McCandless in the 1982 House primary in the old 37th District, running the local party in the mid-1980s and helping run campaigns for Gov. Pete Wilson and former Gov. George Deukmejian. Takano, a junior high school English and history teacher, was on the elected board of trustees of Riverside Community College.

Takano had a fairly low-key primary, but Calvert drew fire from candidates to his right on abortion. Joe Khoury, a college professor and frequent candidate, waged an expensive, high-profile effort, but Calvert finished with 28 percent of the vote, 6 percentage points ahead of Khoury.

The 43rd has a tendency to vote Republican, but several factors held Calvert back. A weakened economy and 12 percent unemployment concerned many. Calvert ran a relatively lackluster campaign, stressing his business acumen, while the outgoing Takano worked tirelessly.

Takano also hurt Calvert, a commercial real estate developer, with charges that too-rapid growth had contributed to local economic woes. George Bush almost lost the district, and Takano nearly won.

Given Calvert's narrow first victory, the scandal over his liaison with the prostitute made his 1994 race look politically bleak. In the June primary, Calvert turned back another challenge from Khoury, with only 51 percent. But voters' mood in November was so strongly Republican that it compensated for Calvert's flaws. Democrats offered Takano, again, but the rematch yielded a comfortable Calvert victory; he won with 55 percent.

He earned the same percentage in November 1996, after winning a primary challenge with 74 percent of the vote.

HOUSE ELECTIONS

1996 General		
Ken Calvert (R)	97,247	(55%)
Guy C. Kimbrough (D)	67,422	(38%)
Annie Wallack (NL)	6,576	(4%)
Kevin Akin (PFP)	3,309	(2%)
Gene L. Berkman (LIBERT)	3,086	(2%)
1996 Primary		
Ken Calvert (R)	39,364	(74%)
David Davis (R)	13,517	(26%)
1994 General		
Ken Calvert (R)	84,500	(55%)
Mark A. Takano (D)	59,342	(38%)
Gene L. Berkman (LIBERT)	9,636	(6%)

Previous Winning Percentages: 1992 (47%)

CAMPAIGN FINANCE

	Receipts	Receipts from PACs	Expend-itures
1996			
Calvert (R)	$639,987	$247,335 (39%)	$594,665
Kimbrough (D)	$46,408	$8,750 (19%)	$47,371
1994			
Calvert (R)	$782,022	$264,718 (34%)	$768,290
Takano (D)	$564,995	$277,658 (49%)	$562,401

DISTRICT VOTE FOR PRESIDENT

	1996		1992
D	78,384 (43%)	**D**	76,040 (38%)
R	82,940 (46%)	**R**	76,837 (38%)
I	16,406 (9%)	**I**	48,197 (24%)

KEY VOTES

1997	
Ban "partial birth" abortions	Y
1996	
Approve farm bill	Y
Deny public education to illegal immigrants	Y
Repeal ban on certain assault-style weapons	?
Increase minimum wage	N
Freeze defense spending	N
Approve welfare overhaul	Y
1995	
Approve balanced-budget constitutional amendment	Y
Relax Clean Water Act regulations	Y
Oppose limits on environmental regulations	N
Reduce projected Medicare spending	Y
Approve GOP budget with tax and spending cuts	Y

VOTING STUDIES

	Presidential Support		Party Unity		Conservative Coalition	
Year	S	O	S	O	S	O
1996	32	63	88	7	86	2
1995	17	81	95	3	96	2
1994	55	40	86	8	92	0
1993	37	61	89	8	98	2

INTEREST GROUP RATINGS

Year	ADA	AFL-CIO	CCUS	ACU
1996	0	n/a	100	95
1995	0	0	100	84
1994	5	13	100	90
1993	0	0	100	96

44 Sonny Bono (R)

Of Palm Springs — Elected 1994, 2nd term

Biographical Information
Born: Feb. 16, 1935, Detroit, Mich.
Education: Graduated from Inglewood H.S. 1953.
Occupation: Restaurateur; entertainer.
Family: Wife, Mary Whitaker; four children.
Religion: Roman Catholic.
Political Career: Mayor of Palm Springs, 1988-92; sought Republican nomination for U.S. Senate, 1992.
Capitol Office: 324 Cannon Bldg. 20515; 225-5330.

Committees
Judiciary
Courts & Intellectual Property; Immigration & Claims
National Security
Military Personnel; Military Procurement

In Washington: Bono made a show-biz career out of being the butt of other peoples' jokes, and his political persona is not far removed from that of the earnest, good-natured, none-too-bright straight man for his wife and singing partner Cher in the 1960s and 1970s.

Ridicule does not seem to worry him, perhaps because he finds solace in the fact that he has succeeded in three careers — first making a name for himself in the entertainment field, then operating a popular restaurant, and finally, one month shy of his 60th birthday, taking a seat in Congress.

Though he could not read music or play an instrument, Bono cut 10 gold records — the most famous of which, "I Got You, Babe," he wrote himself. And it was his idea to create the Sonny and Cher TV variety show, which enlarged the duo's fame.

"If anybody really thinks for a minute I couldn't possibly have done the things I've done and be where I'm at today if I was a dope," Bono told the Los Angeles Times in 1995. "I've had three careers. . . . To think that could possibly be an accident, you would have to not be very bright."

Inevitably, though, the enduring image of Bono as Cher's straight man encourages many Congress-watchers to portray the California Republican as out of his depth in the legislative process. Bono's formal academic training ended with high school (from which he was a dropout), and he cuts a decidedly non-lawyerly figure on the Judiciary Committee, where he is one of only three panel members without a law degree. He lobbied without success at the start of the 105th to be given the gavel of the Courts and Intellectual Property Subcommittee, which is likely to rewrite copyright protections for cyberspace.

For the 105th, Bono has given up his seat on the Banking and Financial Services Committee in exchange for a slot on National Security. In the 104th, he voted a straight conservative line on defense issues, supporting efforts to beef up President Clinton's Pentagon spending requests and opposing a U.S. troop presence in Bosnia. Like many members of his class, he has little use for the United Nations, favoring its abolishment and terming it "a useless waste of billions of dollars."

Although Bono can be thoughtful about the meaning of his own celebrity, his speeches on and off the floor tend to have a dreamy, rambling cast; even his prepared remarks can seem offhand and elliptical. His celebrity has made him notable on the Hill — he attracts more attention from tourists than any non-Kennedy — and he was the second most requested guest at House GOP fundraisers in 1996, behind only Speaker Newt Gingrich.

Bono once observed that his GOP Class of 1994 was too "hard-edged" and "antagonistic" when it first entered Congress, but the generally amiable song and dance man has thrown a few bombs himself since coming to Washington.

He once said, half in jest, that rare plants and animals could be given "a designated area and then blow it up." And he turned a September 1996 fundraiser for Virginia Republican Robert W. Goodlatte into an embarrassment, calling Clinton "a criminal" and alleging that the Central Intelligence Agency maintains a "hit squad" in Haiti that is "killing people to keep that nation's U.S.-backed leader in power." Bono apologized for his characterization of the president but maintained that there is evidence of CIA-sponsored assassinations; he said the GOP had tried to subpoena relevant records, but "they won't give us the documentation. But it's there."

From time to time, Bono expresses exasperation with committee discussions that he feels are so fraught with legalese and bureaucratic jargon as to be incomprehensible. When Judiciary was working in 1995 on a bill to expand the rights of police to conduct searches, Bono complained that "it's been flying in the room like I can't believe today. We have a very simple and concise bill here. I think it would be to everyone's pleasure if we would just pass this thing." That drew a terse admonition from one committee veteran, New York Democrat Charles E. Schumer, who

CALIFORNIA 44
Eastern Riverside County

The 44th contains only Riverside County but does not include the city of Riverside itself. Serving as bedroom communities for Riverside, Los Angeles, San Bernadino Valley, and Orange County, the towns in the district have been some of the fastest growing in California.

Population growth has been especially explosive in Moreno Valley, which is just east of Riverside and has 139,000 residents. Before growth restrictions and the recession put on the brakes, it was picking up an additional 10,000 families a year. The city anchors the western side of the 44th, with cities such as Beaumont and Perris nearby.

The eastern portion of the district's population lives in the Coachella Valley, which is traversed by Interstate 10 on its way out to Blythe and beyond to the Arizona border. Contained in the Valley is Indio, a community that houses a population that is close to a third Latino and claims home to an annual date festival.

Out here, the leisure class of the oasis resorts of Rancho Mirage and Palm Springs contribute their ample wealth to the local economies. Former President Gerald R. Ford has made his home in the area, but it is better known for its Hollywood set.

Although one-quarter of Palm Springs' residents are 65 or older, the city is a bit younger than it used to be; the median age of its residents dropped 3 years during the 1980s. The city expanded from 32,000 residents in 1980 to 40,000 in 1990 — a 25 percent growth rate (which is positively sluggish by the high standards of this booming area).

A few miles southeast of Palm Springs is Palm Desert, where the population almost doubled in the 1980s, to 23,000. Here the older set became more dominant: The 65-and-over population went up almost 150 percent.

While this area is famed as a retirement destination, and while the number of older residents did grow rapidly, overall in Riverside County their influx was overshadowed by a larger immigration of younger people. The percentage of residents 65 and older in the county dropped from 15 percent to 13 percent during the 1980s.

Despite the growth of the district's suburbs and resorts, farmers continue to play a major role in the economy and politics of the 44th. Irrigation ditches knife across Riverside County, and cotton, date and livestock producers battle to keep their scarce water resources from being diverted to the urbanized areas. Riverside was originally a trade center for the citrus ranches of the Santa Ana River basin; the first domestic navel orange was grown here in the 1870s. Now farming centers around Blythe, a burg of 8,000 reached by taking Interstate 10 some 80 miles through the desert.

This has long been a reliably Republican district — the GOP's slight registration advantage understates the point.

Bill Clinton carried the district in the Democratic year of 1992, beating George Bush by 5 percentage points. But he could not repeat the feat four years later, finishing a scant half a percentage point behind Bob Dole.

1990 Population: 571,583. White 437,286 (77%), Black 29,354 (5%), Other 104,943 (18%). Hispanic origin 160,696 (28%). 18 and over 417,411 (73%), 62 and over 121,465 (21%). Median age: 34.

told Bono, "We're making laws here, not sausages."

When the panel approved a bill that defined marriage as a union between a man and a woman, Bono apologized to Massachusetts Democrat Barney Frank, who is a homosexual, for supporting it. "I'm not homophobic," Bono said, noting his love for his daughter Chastity, who is a lesbian, and his friendship with Frank, who was then one of three openly gay members of Congress. "I simply can't handle it yet, Barney," Bono told his colleague. "I wish I was ready, but I can't tell my son it's OK. . . . I can't go as far as you deserve and I'm sorry."

As a Judiciary freshman, Bono made headway with one legislative initiative: A bill stipulating that only a three-judge panel, rather than a single federal judge, can block implementation of a referendum that has triumphed at the ballot box but is challenged in court. Bono's interest in this matter stemmed from the fight in California over Proposition 187 — a state ballot initiative to disqualify illegal immigrants from receiving most public services — which was blocked by a federal judge shortly after its November 1994 passage. The House passed the measure in September 1995, but the Senate never took it up.

Although Bono votes a reliably conservative line on most issues, his endorsement of abortion rights separates him from many of his party colleagues. In 1995, he was one of 44 House Republicans who opposed an effort to prohibit abortions at overseas military hospitals unless the life of the woman was in danger. Abortion foes sought the ban to reverse a 1993 Clinton administration executive order that allowed service women to obtain such abortions if they paid for the procedure themselves. But Bono did support an effort to ban a particular abortion technique that opponents call a "partial-birth" abortion.

In 1995, Bono supported a proposal to give a $500 tax credit for each child of parents earning up to $200,000 a year, even though some in his own party wanted to restrict the credit to those earning half that, or even less. Bono said on NBC's news show "Meet The Press:" "The other side, I don't think they clearly understand the middle class; $200,000 isn't really that much. If you make $200,000, you probably get $100,000. If you've got a few kids, those are not high dollars today. They used to be, but they're not today."

At Home: After the Sonny and Cher act and marriage broke up, Bono moved to Palm Springs and opened a restaurant, and he ended up serving as the city's mayor — a remarkable feat for a man who says he never even voted until age 53. He likes to tell the story of his political awakening, which he says came when he went to the Palm Springs City Hall to get permits to remodel his home and open the restaurant. "I thought it would take a half hour," Bono recalls. "I should have set aside a year." In protest of red tape, he sought and won the mayoralty.

Bono, mayor from 1988 to 1992, glided through his first House campaign in 1994, scoring comfortable primary and general election victories in the conservative 44th. The district came open with the retirement of Republican Al McCandless.

Before winning election to the House, Bono had tried in 1992 for an even bigger prize: a Senate seat. In the GOP primary he was plainly new to many national issues and often unsteady on the stump, but in the end, he collected more than 415,000 votes, good enough for a respectable third-place tally of 17 percent. The primary winner, conservative commentator Bruce Herschensohn, lost to Democrat Barbara Boxer in the general election.

After his Senate bid, Bono soldiered on in the GOP, building relationships with influential Republicans and looking for another opening. At one point, Bono said he would challenge McCandless in the 44th, but party insiders helped dissuade him. Bono next toyed with the idea of running for lieutenant governor, but was warned off by GOP Gov. Pete Wilson's staff. When McCandless decided to retire from the House, Bono happily jumped back into that race.

With his former rival Herschensohn as his campaign chairman, Bono studied up on the basics of conservative GOP positions, wore his inexperience like a badge and took the sting out of the inevitable jokes about his show business credentials by making them himself.

In November, Bono won 56 percent against Democrat Steve Clute, a former state representative who argued that Bono was too inexperienced to be effective in Washington. Given the conservative tilt of the district, Clute needed Bono to commit some kind of massive blunder to even the odds and that did not occur.

In 1996, Democratic former telecommunications executive Anita Rufus decried Bono's remarks about Clinton and Haiti but made no headway. Bono didn't bother opening a campaign office until after Labor Day, and then was sidelined during the weeks before election day by a bleeding ulcer, yet still scored an easy 58 percent victory.

HOUSE ELECTIONS

1996 General		
Sonny Bono (R)	110,643	(58%)
Anita Rufus (D)	73,844	(39%)
Donald Cochran (AMI)	3,888	(2%)
Karen Wilkinson (NL)	3,143	(2%)
1994 General		
Sonny Bono (R)	95,521	(56%)
Steve Clute (D)	65,370	(38%)
Donald Cochran (AMI)	10,885	(6%)

CAMPAIGN FINANCE

	Receipts	Receipts from PACs	Expend-itures
1996			
Bono (R)	$474,769	$240,003 (51%)	$458,527
Rufus (D)	$116,441	$15,025 (13%)	$116,240
1994			
Bono (R)	$732,425	$124,715 (17%)	$731,238
Clute (D)	$340,635	$148,323 (44%)	$340,587

DISTRICT VOTE FOR PRESIDENT

	1996		1992
D	85,397 (44%)	**D**	87,180 (41%)
R	86,414 (45%)	**R**	76,772 (36%)
I	17,830 (9%)	**I**	50,867 (24%)

KEY VOTES

1997	
Ban "partial-birth" abortions	Y
1996	
Approve farm bill	Y
Deny public education to illegal immigrants	Y
Repeal ban on certain assault-style weapons	Y
Increase minimum wage	Y
Freeze defense spending	N
Approve welfare overhaul	Y
1995	
Approve balanced-budget constitutional amendment	Y
Relax Clean Water Act regulations	Y
Oppose limits on environmental regulations	N
Reduce projected Medicare spending	Y
Approve GOP budget with tax and spending cuts	Y

VOTING STUDIES

	Presidential Support		Party Unity		Conservative Coalition	
Year	**S**	**O**	**S**	**O**	**S**	**O**
1996	37	63	93	6	98	2
1995	21	77	91	3	87	2

INTEREST GROUP RATINGS

Year	ADA	AFL-CIO	CCUS	ACU
1996	0	n/a	94	95
1995	0	0	100	96

45 Dana Rohrabacher (R)

Of Huntington Beach — Elected 1988, 5th term

Biographical Information

Born: June 21, 1947, Coronado, Calif.

Education: Los Angeles Harbor College, 1965-67; California State U., Long Beach, B.A. 1969; U. of Southern California, M.A. 1971.

Occupation: White House speechwriter; journalist.

Family: Single.

Religion: Baptist.

Political Career: No previous office.

Capitol Office: 2338 Rayburn Bldg. 20515; 225-2415.

Committees

International Relations
Asia & the Pacific; International Economic Policy & Trade

Science
Energy & Environment; Space & Aeronautics (chairman)

In Washington: A fervent conservative, Rohrabacher is an activist on a range of issues — promoting an "America first" brand of foreign policy, arguing for stricter immigration controls, lobbying to extend patent protections to small inventors and pushing for completion of NASA's space station.

Rohrabacher, who served as assistant press secretary for Ronald Reagan's 1976 and 1980 presidential campaigns and as a White House speechwriter for Reagan, thinks there are a lot of things the federal government should not spend money on, such as the United Nations and public services for illegal aliens. But he does want the federal government to open its checkbook for the big-ticket space station, parts of which are built in the 45th District. Rohrabacher watches over the project from his post as chairman of the Science Committee's Space and Aeronautics Subcommittee.

And as if his plate isn't full enough with his congressional interests, Rohrabacher also finds time to get heavily involved in local politics. He initiated an effort to recall a GOP assemblywoman who had been elected Speaker with Democrats' support, and he also drafted the candidate who replaced her.

In the House, Rohrabacher is most vocal from his seat on the International Relations Committee. A skeptic of entanglements abroad, he opposes American involvement in the United Nations, calling the body "a collection of tin-pot dictatorships and corrupt regimes from around the world." In his view, "everything done through the United Nations can be better accomplished on a bilateral basis."

Not surprisingly, Rohrabacher supported a February 1995 GOP bill that would have reduced U.S. payments for U.N. peacekeeping operations.

Republicans touted the measure as a legislative expression of their argument that President Clinton had frittered U.S. forces on peacekeeping missions irrelevant to U.S. security interests and subordinated U.S. policy to U.N.-dominated goals. Democrats blasted the bill as an isolationist's creed that would disqualify the United States from cooperating in multilateral efforts to suppress threats to peace. Rohrabacher rejected that argument, saying: "Americans have sacrificed their lives and well-being for an ungrateful world for far too long."

Rohrabacher is quite critical of China because of the government's suppression of a student-led democracy movement and its threats against Taiwan. He introduced a resolution in June 1996 to deny the Chinese most-favored nation (MFN) trading status. Under MFN, which is granted to all but a handful of nations, Chinese goods enter the United States with low, non-discriminatory tariffs. "China has gobbled up every economic carrot we've offered and their behavior hasn't improved one bit," Rohrabacher told the Los Angeles Times. "It's time to kick this weasel out of the garden." The House rejected his resolution, 141-286.

He is equally critical of the Castro regime in Cuba and backed an International Relations measure aimed at choking off foreign investment in Cuba, which the committee approved in July 1995. The bill targets investments in Cuba by corporations from Third World countries, an increasingly important source of hard currency for Castro's government. The measure would allow U.S. nationals whose properties have been confiscated by Castro's government to file suit in this country against foreign companies that buy or lease those properties. Democrats charged the legislation would create an entirely new right to sue in U.S. courts — one available only to those who have lost property in Cuba. But Rohrabacher and other proponents said it is perfectly reasonable to subject foreign owners of expropriated properties to U.S. lawsuits. "These are really the scum of the globe who cut deals this way to make money off tyranny," Rohrabacher said.

From his Science Committee perch, Rohrabacher has steadfastly defended the space station. McDonnell Douglas, a prime project contractor, is a major employer in the 45th. In the past few years, the House has rejected several

CALIFORNIA 45
Coastal Orange County

There are two distinct flavors of communities in the 45th — coastal and interior — but they both taste Republican.

Seal Beach anchors the coastal section. A quarter of its 25,000 residents live in a seniors-only community, which makes for quite a gray city: 37 percent of Seal Beach's residents are over age 65, 22 percent are over 75, and 7 percent are over 85. Ninety percent of its residents are non-Hispanic whites.

Heading southeast down the coast is Huntington Beach, whose permanent population of 182,000 — mostly young aerospace and other high-tech workers and their families — is supplemented in the summer by those eager to "shred" some waves in surfing competitions; hence its nickname, "Surf City."

Huntington Harbor is an affluent section of the city, with such accoutrements as backyard boat slips. The rest of the city consists of huge housing tracts with a few small-business districts sprinkled in.

Huntington Beach also has a McDonnell Douglas plant that is the prime design and manufacturing facility for the space station. It employs 5,600 people, which so far has cushioned the 45th from the worst of Southern California's recession, but the district obviously has a lot of eggs in the space station basket.

Newport Beach resembles the other coastal communities — more bedrooms for aerospace white-collar workers — but looks a little different. Its terrain lifts into some rolling hills, and Newport Bay runs right up its middle.

Compared with the coast, the 45th's interior areas tend to be more blue-collar and less affluent, and they have a higher number of Democrats. But they are conservative, and they vote Republican. Many of the interior's blue-collar workers are employed by aerospace companies within the district or commute to those in Anaheim, Torrance or Long Beach.

Westminster, just inland from Huntington Beach, is heavily Republican, but with a high Democratic registration for this district. Costa Mesa, between Huntington Beach and Newport Beach, has a mix of white- and blue-collar workers and boasts a huge shopping mall, South Coast Plaza, which is placed on maps of the region.

The district reaches north between Cypress and Garden Grove to take in Stanton. Democrats are in much greater numbers here than elsewhere in the district. The city (population 30,000) is not as wealthy as others in the 45th; 15 percent of its housing units are either mobile homes or trailers. To the north, the district takes in a small residential slice of Anaheim.

George Bush won the district in 1992 with 42 percent of the vote; Bob Dole topped that in 1996, gaining 51 percent. Bill Clinton took 32 percent in 1992 and pulled up to 38 percent in 1996. Ross Perot, who had garnered 25 percent in the district in 1992, dropped to 8 percent four years later.

1990 Population: 570,874. White 468,855 (82%), Black 7,110 (1%), Other 94,909 (17%). Hispanic origin 84,684 (15%). 18 and over 450,058 (79%), 62 and over 70,820 (12%). Median age: 33.

attempts by "deficit hawks" to eliminate funding for the multi-billion dollar project.

Rohrabacher also backed efforts in the 104th to restrict aid to illegal and legal immigrants; he said that providing services to immigrants was costing California and the federal government billions of dollars. He supported a measure, which passed the House in September 1996, to deny public school education to illegal immigrants. He argued that children who come into the United States illegally were unfairly taking resources away from citizens. "Whose children do we care about?" he asked. "We care about our children first, and we make no apology for it."

Rohrabacher in recent years has been passionately pursuing efforts to maintain patent rights for the nation's small inventors. On the House floor in April 1997, he strongly opposed a measure offered by Howard Coble, R-N.C. that would provide for the publication of patents 18 months after they are filed. The House passed the measure, despite complaints by many small inventors who say it jeopardizes the rights of inventors to have their innovations kept secret until their patent is granted.

Rohrabacher offered a substitute to the patent measure that did not include the 18-month provision, which he said would allow foreign competitors to "steal" U.S. technology. He also complained that the overhaul measure was being pushed to please big corporations at the expense of small inventors. The House rejected his amendment, 178-227.

A former reporter and editorial writer for the conservative Orange County Register, Rohrabacher, an avid surfer, counts heavy-metal rocker Sammy Hagar as a friend and says John Wayne taught him how to drink tequila. He has said he patterns his life on that of Ernest Hemingway, a man's man. But Rohrabacher announced in December 1996 that he is engaged to marry his former campaign manager, so his future lifestyle may be more tame.

At Home: Rohrabacher's bulldog partisanship may not make him the most popular member of his delegation or his party. But it has sold well with the voters in his archconservative Orange County district. He emerged from a tough field of primary contenders in 1988 and since then has had little difficulty dominating his November contests. Although his vote share dipped slightly in 1992, a good year for Democrats all over California, it soared again in 1994 and 1996.

Rohrabacher has had more cause for concern regarding primary rivals, two of whom held him below 50 percent of the vote in 1992, and sporadic bouts of bad publicity (as when the New Republic in 1990 accused him of dabbling in drugs as a youth, a charge he has stoutly denied).

The 1988 race was Rohrabacher's first try for elective office. He took the plunge when 42nd District GOP Rep. Daniel E. Lungren announced he was leaving to become state treasurer.

Rohrabacher was at first regarded as an underdog in a tough GOP primary field that included an Orange County supervisor who had Lungren's support and university president Steve Horn (who would run and win in a neighboring district in 1992). Despite the competition, Rohrabacher found his way. A campaign fundraiser featuring retired Marine Lt. Col. Oliver L. North of Iran-contra fame raised Rohrabacher's standing among conservatives while adding $100,000 to his coffers. He ended up with 35 percent of the primary vote, well ahead of his nearest rival.

Republicans in Orange County are not supposed to worry about re-election or redistricting. But in 1992, Rohrabacher closely watched both. The new map may have slightly reduced the GOP majority in his redrawn base, but the percentage of Democrats did not rise, indicating some voter dissatisfaction with both parties. Rohrabacher outspent his Democratic opponent by 10 to 1. But his share of the vote dropped roughly another 4 percentage points, leaving him at the 55 percent mark. The anxiety was short-lived. In 1994, he was back up to nearly 70 percent of the vote.

His seat secure, Rohrabacher has leeway to delve into local politics. In June 1995, he helped launch a recall against Republican Assemblywoman Doris Allen, one day after she was elected Speaker with unanimous support of Democrats and her own vote. Rohrabacher then drafted political newcomer Scott Baugh, a corporate attorney, to run in the race to replace Allen. Baugh's political inexperience became evident when he and some campaign workers, who included Robin Carmony, a former Rohrabacher campaign manager who became engaged to the congressman in 1996, were indicted by an Orange County grand jury on charges ranging from lying on campaign finance reports to filing bogus petitions to put a decoy Democratic candidate on the ballot, the Orange County Register reported. In October 1996, Rohrabacher paid $2,617 in fines for failing to properly report campaign contributions he made to California candidates, including a $15,000 loan to Baugh, the Los Angeles Times reported. Rohrabacher paid the fines to the California Secretary of State's Political Reform Division in August, the newspaper reported.

HOUSE ELECTIONS

1996 General		
Dana Rohrabacher (R)	125,326	(61%)
Sally J. Alexander (D)	68,312	(33%)
Mark F. Murphy (LIBERT)	8,813	(4%)
Rand McDevitt (NL)	3,071	(1%)
1994 General		
Dana Rohrabacher (R)	124,006	(69%)
Brett Williamson (D)	55,489	(31%)

Previous Winning Percentages: **1992** (55%) **1990** (59%) **1988** (64%)

CAMPAIGN FINANCE

	Receipts	Receipts from PACs	Expend-itures
1996			
Rohrabacher (R)	$264,217	$83,709 (32%)	$272,859
Alexander (D)	$55,821	$4,300 (8%)	$51,491
1994			
Rohrabacher (R)	$179,316	$60,270 (34%)	$187,656
Williamson (D)	$85,872	$2,700 (3%)	$85,803

DISTRICT VOTE FOR PRESIDENT

1996		1992	
D	81,299 (38%)	**D**	80,646 (32%)
R	108,240 (51%)	**R**	105,893 (42%)
I	17,831 (8%)	**I**	63,609 (25%)

KEY VOTES

1997	
Ban "partial birth" abortions	Y
1996	
Approve farm bill	Y
Deny public education to illegal immigrants	Y
Repeal ban on certain assault-style weapons	Y
Increase minimum wage	N
Freeze defense spending	Y
Approve welfare overhaul	Y
1995	
Approve balanced-budget constitutional amendment	Y
Relax Clean Water Act regulations	Y
Oppose limits on environmental regulations	N
Reduce projected Medicare spending	Y
Approve GOP budget with tax and spending cuts	Y

VOTING STUDIES

	Presidential Support		Party Unity		Conservative Coalition	
Year	**S**	**O**	**S**	**O**	**S**	**O**
1996	28	71	91	8	76	22
1995	15	85	94	6	82	18
1994	28	71	96	3	69	31
1993	23	77	95	5	68	32
1992	74	26	93	5	88	13
1991	70	30	91	8	89	11

INTEREST GROUP RATINGS

Year	ADA	AFL-CIO	CCUS	ACU
1996	15	n/a	93	100
1995	0	0	96	100
1994	10	22	75	86
1993	20	0	100	92
1992	20	25	75	96
1991	15	17	90	100

46 Loretta Sanchez (D)

Of Garden Grove — Elected 1996, 1st term

Biographical Information
Born: Jan. 7, 1960, Lynwood, Calif.
Education: Chapman U., B.S. 1982; American U., M.B.A. 1984.
Occupation: Financial adviser; strategic management associate.
Family: Husband, Stephen Simmons Brixey III.
Religion: Roman Catholic.
Political Career: Candidate for Anaheim City Council, 1994.
Capitol Office: 1529 Longworth Bldg. 20515; 225-2965.

Committees
Education & Workforce
Oversight & Investigations; Postsecondary Education, Training & Life-Long Learning
National Security
Military Research & Development

The Path to Washington: Sanchez became a giant-killer with her stunning upset of Republican Rep. Robert K. Dornan. After absentee ballots indicated she would unseat Dornan by a narrow margin, Sanchez instantly turned into one of the biggest media stars of the Democratic class of 1996.

Party leaders awarded her seats on two committees: National Security, and Education and the Workforce.

Sanchez had run for office once before, finishing eighth in a field of 16 candidates competing for two spots on the Anaheim City Council in 1994. She ran under her married name of Brixey but chose her maiden name for the House race.

A businesswoman — the principal owner of AMIGA Associates, a public-sector consulting firm — Sanchez was able to exploit the shifting regional demographics that are undercutting Orange County's traditional image as a conservative bastion.

Sanchez had been a Republican herself until 1992. Her parents immigrated from Mexico and met at a Los Angeles manufacturing plant, where her father was a machinist and her mother was a secretary who helped organize plant workers into a union.

Sanchez's effort was aided by unusually high turnout among Hispanic voters angry about a ballot initiative to end most state affirmative action programs. Sanchez supports such programs and opposes efforts to require that government publications be printed in English only.

Sanchez supports the rights of homosexuals and abortion rights and would not ban a particular abortion technique opponents call "partial birth" abortion.

She also favors targeted tax cuts and gun control. She took a tough stance against crime during the campaign, and she supports the death penalty.

Sanchez opposes flat tax plans and any reductions in the student loan program. Although Sanchez shares GOP concerns about the federal government's direct role in classroom education, she does not support private-school vouchers, preferring to improve public schools.

Her victory margin in the campaign might have come from suburbanites weary of Dornan's famously combative image, his staunch support of gun owners' rights and his unremitting opposition to abortion. (Dornan's fervent support of military spending, especially for the B-1 bomber, won him the sobriquet "B-1 Bob.")

Despite Orange County's conservative image, Dornan never had an electoral lock on the district. He invariably outspent his opponents by overwhelming margins, yet only once (in 1988) in nine victories did he reach 60 percent of the vote.

Returning to the district in 1996 after his unsuccessful campaign for the Republican presidential nomination, Dornan found the political landscape changed.

Though Sanchez had been considered an underdog even to win the Democratic nomination in a four-way field, she drew increasing support as the year went on from constituencies sensing Dornan's vulnerability.

National teachers' unions and abortion rights groups contributed to Sanchez's campaign. The partners of three openly gay members of Congress, including a Republican, hosted a Washington fundraiser, and her "get out the vote" effort was coordinated by a group still angry about Dornan's support of military aid to the Nicaraguan contras in the 1980s.

Sanchez's attacks on Dornan in numerous fliers mailed to district residents took their toll.

Dornan also engaged in negative attacks, criticizing Sanchez's association with Howard O. Kieffer, a three-time felon who volunteered on her primary campaign and lent it office space, phones and postage.

After it was clear that Dornan had lost, his vitriol increased. Told during a CNN appearance that Sanchez had suggested he accept defeat, Dornan said it was "a typical pond-scum lying charge from the filthiest campaign" ever.

CALIFORNIA 46
Part of Orange County; Santa Ana; Garden Grove

The 46th is a blue-collar district, full of older suburban homes and younger families. Its defense subcontractors are the backbone of the region's large defense and aerospace companies. But as these industries flag in the post-Cold War era, so does the local economy.

Most of the Orange County 46th's population is contained within two cities, Santa Ana in the south and Garden Grove in the north.

Santa Ana, with 294,000 residents, is the area's hub and the seat of Orange County. It has the crime and gang problems typical of many California cities, and these problems are spilling into Garden Grove and adjacent districts. (Garden Grove has struggled with Asian gangs.)

Garden Grove is a more residential area than Santa Ana. It divides roughly into three sections: the western, more affluent part; the center, which is a mix of Vietnamese, Koreans and Hispanics; and the eastern, very heavily Hispanic part. Little Saigon sits just south of the district in Westminster.

Garden Grove is perhaps best known for the "positive thinking" television ministry of Robert Schuller and his Crystal Cathedral.

In recent years, there has been an influx of Indochinese refugees into Garden Grove, spurring a conservative backlash from some of its white, blue-collar workers. The city is 20 percent Asian and 23 percent Hispanic. The district at-large is half Hispanic — a percentage that is increasing — and 12 percent Asian.

The northern part of the 46th includes the southern part of Anaheim, a chunk that has the look and feel of Garden Grove, which it borders.

The 46th does not include the wealthier area of Anaheim off to the east known as Anaheim Hills, which is split between the 41st and 47th districts. The part of Anaheim that is in the 46th includes Disneyland, many of whose employees live in the district. The park employs about 9,000 in the winter and 12,000 in the summer. Thousands of jobs at a variety of hotels and other supporting businesses depend on the park.

Other than Disneyland, no one employer within the 46th drives its economy; the district is dotted with defense subcontractors and small businesses. Some residents head an hour west to the shipyard in Long Beach, but most scatter to companies all over Orange County.

Orange County's ideology generally matches that of the Republican Party. But the 46th, the least Republican of the county's congressional districts, is an exception. Though George Bush carried the 46th by a wide margin in 1988 and narrowly in 1992, the Democratic Party has a growing registration advantage.

Abysmal voter turnout continues to plague the 46th. Fewer than 105,000 ballots were cast in the 1996 presidential election, about 150,000 less than were tallied from the neighboring 47th. But Hispanics, perceiving Republicans as hostile to affirmative action and immigration (two contentious issues in California, especially in 1996), voted more solidly Democratic than before. That helped Sanchez oust conservative nine-term Republican Rep. Robert K. Dornan, and enabled Clinton to get 49 percent in the presidential race.

1990 Population: 571,380. White 380,053 (67%), Black 14,226 (2%), Other 177,101 (31%). Hispanic origin 285,529 (50%). 18 and over 405,602 (71%), 62 and over 49,393 (9%). Median age: 27.

HOUSE ELECTIONS

1996 General		
Loretta Sanchez (D)	47,964	(47%)
Robert K. Dornan (R)	46,980	(46%)
Lawrence J. Stafford (REF)	3,235	(3%)
Thomas E. Reimer (LIBERT)	2,333	(2%)
J. Carlos Aguirre (NL)	1,972	(2%)
1996 Primary		
Loretta Sanchez (D)	7,142	(35%)
Michael P. "Mike" Farber (D)	6,125	(30%)
James "Jim" Prince (D)	5,574	(27%)
Robert J. Brennan (D)	1,758	(9%)

CAMPAIGN FINANCE

	Receipts	Receipts from PACs	Expend-itures
1996			
Sanchez (D)	$823,120	$237,439 (29%)	$811,219
Dornan (R)	$748,336	$56,667 (8%)	$741,984

DISTRICT VOTE FOR PRESIDENT

	1996		1992
D	51,330 (49%)	D	44,352 (37%)
R	42,780 (41%)	R	47,689 (40%)
I	8,229 (8%)	I	27,542 (23%)

KEY VOTES

1997	
Ban "partial birth" abortions	N

47 Christopher Cox (R)

Of Newport Beach — Elected 1988, 5th term

Biographical Information

Born: Oct. 16, 1952, St. Paul, Minn.

Education: U. of Southern California, B.A. 1973; Harvard U., M.B.A. 1977, J.D. 1977.

Occupation: White House counsel; lawyer; professor.

Family: Wife, Rebecca Gernhardt; two children.

Religion: Roman Catholic.

Political Career: No previous office.

Capitol Office: 2402 Rayburn Bldg. 20515; 225-5611.

Committees

Commerce
Oversight & Investigations (vice chairman); Telecommunications, Trade & Consumer Protection

Government Reform & Oversight
Civil Service

In Washington: Cox occupies a rung on his party's leadership ladder as chairman of the Republican Policy Committee, and he has been a key negotiator on some of the more complex pieces of legislation in the House GOP agenda. His grasp of substance and his ability to work out compromises make him a valuable player, although some of the party's more gregarious conservatives cannot quite warm up to his erudite manner and his intellectualizing of issues.

Cox was part of negotiations in the 104th that led to passage of the telecommunications deregulation measure, and he led the fight on legislation to make it more difficult for shareholders to sue companies for non-performance. After President Clinton vetoed the shareholder bill, Cox helped mobilize the override effort — the only successful such effort of the 104th Congress.

Cox did not have the same success with legislation to overhaul product liability laws, which fell victim to a presidential veto.

The 104th also saw Cox win two smaller battles he has been fighting for years: enactment of a bill to end the federal helium program and passage of a measure to ease some metric requirements for business.

In the House, Cox's cool, low-key style is a marked contrast to the manner of hotter-running California conservatives such as Dana Rohrabacher and Randy "Duke" Cunningham. Cox's poise as a spokesman for Republican principles has been noticed beyond the House. He made a small splash in the national news during the 1996 presidential campaign when conservative columnist and commentator George Will urged the GOP to nominate Cox as Bob Dole's vice presidential candidate.

The qualities that drew Will's attention to Cox could make the Californian a candidate for advancing in House GOP leadership ranks, especially if the party is looking for a younger, telegenic Westerner with a ready command of facts and figures to buttress GOP policy arguments and an undisputed ideological commitment to limiting the size and reach of the federal government. Talking to the Los Angeles Times, now-Speaker Newt Gingrich once said of Cox, "He's a very solid conservative, but within a framework of always looking for a solution, not just being against things."

For a time in the 103rd Congress, Cox contemplated leaving the House to wage a 1994 campaign for the Senate. He backed out of a long-shot statewide race, and so was on hand when Republicans became the House's majority party in 1995. As the GOP was getting organized for the 104th, Cox helped Gingrich solve a problem: too little representation in the party's upper echelon for California, which sends more Republicans to the chamber than any other state. Cox won the Policy Committee chair by a 148-77 tally over the late-starting bid of Arizona Rep. Jim Kolbe. Also, Gingrich named Cox and Reps. David Dreier and Jerry Lewis to a "California task force" that the new Speaker said would advise the leadership.

Before coming to Congress, Cox worked in the White House as senior associate counsel to President Ronald Reagan. His duties included drafting reform proposals for the federal budget process, and throughout his tenure in Congress he has carried on his interest in that area, first serving as co-chairman of the GOP Task Force on Budget Process Reform and then taking a seat on the Budget Committee at the start of the 103rd Congress.

Cox crafted his proposals to reform the budget process into legislation, which he first introduced in 1990. Cox's proposal included a "truth-in-budgeting" provision that would require the government to use real-dollar figures in making spending assumptions, rather than relying on inflation-adjusted figures. On the first day of the 104th, House Republicans voted to employ this "zero-based" approach in drafting budgets.

In the era of Democratic congressional rule, Cox complained that budget procedures often did not afford members enough time to consider money bills. When the House in 1991 considered a $151 billion transportation bill, Cox said mem-

CALIFORNIA 47
Coastal — Central Orange County; Irvine

The 47th is very safe GOP territory. Registered Republicans outnumber Democrats here by about 2-to-1, helping Bob Dole beat Bill Clinton in the district in 1996 by 54 percent to 36 percent.

The 47th sports several different kinds of coast. To the north is part of Newport Beach, a wealthy enclave noted for its beautiful sandy beaches and luxurious housing. To the south, rocky Laguna Beach attracts more scuba divers than swimmers. Between them is the Crystal Cove State Park, which covers about half of the district's coastline.

Laguna Beach's 23,000 residents are considered more liberal than those in Newport Beach, and the city is renowned as "the arts colony." To the east is Laguna Hills, home to one of the country's largest senior populations at Leisure World. Further east is Lake Forrest and the El Toro Marine Corps Air Station, which is scheduled to be closed.

While much of Southern California is characterized by random suburban sprawl, Irvine's 110,000 residents live in a city whose corporate and residential areas are meticulously planned.

The University of California at Irvine (17,200 students) is trying to shed its traditional role as a commuter school. The campus had concentrated on engineering and developed an advanced center for bio-medical research. The computer manufacturers AST Research Inc., Toshiba America Info Systems and Unisys Corp. are some of the high-tech companies that located here.

Just north of Irvine on the 5 Freeway is Tustin, a city of 51,000 divided into two areas: The south has this city's business district and its lower- to middle-income residents; the north, into the hills a bit, is its high-income area.

Farther north on the freeway is Orange, one of the county's oldest cities. There are 111,000 residents here, Victorian-style homes in the downtown area, affluent suburbs to the west near Anaheim and lower-income areas off to the east. The east also includes some farms.

Villa Park is Orange County's smallest city and is likely to remain that way: It is completely surrounded by Anaheim and Orange. The city forbids more than two houses per acre within much of its borders, which has kept crowding down (only 6,300 people live here), the skyline low and housing prices high.

The district also includes suburban areas of Santa Ana and portions of Anaheim, including the Anaheim Stadium.

The 47th also has a lot of unincorporated county land to the east. Silverado Canyon was a bustling silver mining area in the early 1920s and is now a secluded farming area. Much of the district's eastern end is grassy, hilly land that large development companies, with an eye on potential future growth, have snatched up.

1990 Population: 571,518. White 477,665 (84%), Black 10,495 (2%), Other 83,358 (15%). Hispanic origin 74,700 (13%). 18 and over 441,680 (77%), 62 and over 73,898 (13%). Median age: 34.

bers had not been able to study it in detail, and he voted against it, even though it included funding for Orange County road improvements.

"Informed debate and factual exposition have been replaced by misinformation and chaos," Cox wrote in a journal article about the experience.

Cox has supported both broad- and narrow-gauged measures to reduce federal spending. In 1993, he voted for the Penny-Kasich proposal to cut $90.4 billion in spending over five years.

In 1992, Cox and fellow Republicans tried to trim money from the appropriations bill that funds the operations of the House. They were hoping to put Democrats in the position of resisting operational cuts at a time of anti-Congress fervor fanned by scandals at the House bank and the House Post Office. The effort fell short.

In 1993, Cox also unsuccessfully attempted to slash the budget for the General Accounting Office by nearly 25 percent. At a congressional oversight hearing, he questioned whether GAO was "a Democratic lap dog or a congressional watchdog."

Cox has had some experience with the budget-cutting ax falling close to home. He supported a recommendation by the base-closure commission to close the Tustin Marine Corps base in his district, but he objected in 1993 when El Toro Marine Corps Air Station in the 47th was targeted for closure. (Cox's wife, Rebecca Gernhardt Cox, sat on the base-closing commission, but she recused herself from the El Toro vote.)

Cox said he initially was willing to see El Toro close, but he changed his mind after realizing the high costs associated with closing the base. He even attempted unsuccessfully to see Defense Secretary Les Aspin to argue his case.

In the 103rd, Cox differed with California Democratic Sen. Dianne Feinstein on funding for a federal court house in Santa Ana. Feinstein voted with the Senate Appropriations Committee in 1993 to approve $84 million to build the courthouse, but Cox had wanted her to push for the full $168 million in funding recommended in President Clinton's budget proposal. The House had approved $148.2 million in funding.

In all his congressional doings, what stands out most about Cox is his intelligence. He attended a selective program at Harvard that earned him joint degrees in law and business, and in Congress he discourses easily on topics ranging from U.S. policy in Haiti to the arcana of economic theory. When Federal Reserve Chairman Alan Greenspan testified once before the Joint Economic Committee, Cox engaged him in an esoteric discussion on the Phillips curve, an economic theory that describes the inverse relationship between unemployment and inflation.

At Home: After three easy House elections, Cox set his sights on a 1994 bid for the Senate seat held by Democrat Feinstein. He raised money and actually announced his candidacy, but quickly yielded to the bottomless pockets of another Republican House member, multimillionaire Michael Huffington, who went on to lose to Feinstein in November.

Cox was working for Reagan in 1988 when 40th District GOP Rep. Robert E. Badham announced plans to retire. Cox was no stranger to the Orange County district. A University of Southern California alumnus, he had signed on as a partner with a Newport Beach law firm after his graduation from Harvard and a clerkship with the U.S. Court of Appeals in San Francisco.

The odds of Cox winning to succeed Badham initially looked long: The 40th seemed likely to go to one of the well-known state legislators in the area. But when the prime prospects declined to run, Cox resigned from his White House job and joined a field of GOP primary candidates that eventually grew to 14. The departing Badham had endorsed another Republican, Irvine city councilman Dave Baker. But Cox managed to enlist significant help from members of Orange County's prominent Irvine family.

More important to Cox's success, though, were his Washington connections. His literature pictured him with Reagan and then-Vice President George Bush in the White House. He got endorsements from 18 conservative members of Congress, and he benefited from campaign appearances by Robert H. Bork, an unsuccessful Reagan administration Supreme Court nominee, and former National Security Council aide and Iran-contra figure Oliver L. North.

Cox pulled away from the field, winning 18 of the district's 20 municipalities in the primary. In November, he took 67 percent of the vote. Cox has won with similar ease since then.

Cox may be the only person who published Pravda before coming to Congress. Cox, then working for the Newport Beach law firm, and his father (a retired publisher) produced an English-language version of the official Soviet newspaper to show how the Soviet government propagandizes its own people. Based in St. Paul, Minn., where Cox grew up, the paper folded after Cox turned his attention to running for Congress.

HOUSE ELECTIONS

1996 General		
Christopher Cox (R)	160,078	(66%)
Tina Louise Laine (D)	70,362	(29%)
Iris Adam (NL)	6,807	(3%)
Victor A. Wagner Jr. (LIBERT)	6,530	(3%)
1994 General		
Christopher Cox (R)	152,413	(72%)
Gary Kingsbury (D)	53,035	(25%)
Victor A. Wagner Jr. (LIBERT)	7,175	(3%)

Previous Winning Percentages: 1992 (65%) **1990** (68%) **1988** (67%)

CAMPAIGN FINANCE

	Receipts	Receipts from PACs	Expend-itures
1996			
Cox (R)	$829,803	$400,023 (48%)	$527,738
Laine (D)	$74,286	$5,750 (8%)	$73,980
1994			
Cox (R)	$488,705	$108,420 (22%)	$246,400
Kingsbury (D)	$60,477	0	$60,846

DISTRICT VOTE FOR PRESIDENT

1996		1992	
D	91,916 (36%)	**D**	86,279 (31%)
R	137,024 (54%)	**R**	127,700 (46%)
I	17,680 (7%)	**I**	64,227 (23%)

KEY VOTES

1997	
Ban "partial birth" abortions	Y
1996	
Approve farm bill	Y
Deny public education to illegal immigrants	Y
Repeal ban on certain assault-style weapons	#
Increase minimum wage	N
Freeze defense spending	N
Approve welfare overhaul	Y
1995	
Approve balanced-budget constitutional amendment	Y
Relax Clean Water Act regulations	Y
Oppose limits on environmental regulations	N
Reduce projected Medicare spending	Y
Approve GOP budget with tax and spending cuts	Y

VOTING STUDIES

	Presidential Support		Party Unity		Conservative Coalition	
Year	S	O	S	O	S	O
1996	30	67	91	3	84	8
1995	14	83	94	1	93	3
1994	36	60	92	2	86	11
1993	32	63	89	4	91	9
1992	78	15	85	6	94	0
1991	77	23	85	10	89	8

INTEREST GROUP RATINGS

Year	ADA	AFL-CIO	CCUS	ACU
1996	5	n/a	88	100
1995	0	0	96	100
1994	0	11	82	100
1993	0	0	100	100
1992	5	17	75	100
1991	10	8	80	100

48 Ron Packard (R)

Of Oceanside — Elected 1982, 8th term

Biographical Information

Born: Jan. 19, 1931, Meridian, Idaho.

Education: Brigham Young U., 1948-50; Portland State U., 1952-53; U. of Oregon, D.M.D. 1957.

Military Service: Navy Dental Corps, 1957-59.

Occupation: Dentist.

Family: Wife, Roma Jean Sorenson; seven children.

Religion: Mormon.

Political Career: Carlsbad School Board, 1962-74; Carlsbad City Council, 1976-78; mayor of Carlsbad, 1978-82.

Capitol Office: 2372 Rayburn Bldg. 20515; 225-3906.

Committees

Appropriations

Foreign Operations, Export Financing & Related Programs; Military Construction (chairman); Transportation

In Washington: Like many conservatives, Packard tops his list of personal priorities with the goal of balancing the government's books. He helped cut spending during the 104th Congress as an Appropriations cardinal, but he also nursed his habit of dipping into the federal cookie jar to procure goodies for his district.

For the 105th, Packard takes charge of the Appropriations Subcommittee on Military Construction, a panel with a propensity for pork-barrel politicking. Although Packard in the 104th attacked congressional perks such as ice delivery and free haircuts as chairman of the Legislative Branch Subcommittee, he also helped secure $788 million for California in the fiscal 1996 military construction bill, including $113 million for Camp Pendleton and $39 million for bachelor enlisted quarters at Miramar Marine Corps Air Station. Talking about the money he hoped to secure as Military Construction chairman, Packard noted, "Now I'm in a position to really do something about it."

Packard's two other Appropriations subcommittees are Foreign Operations, Export Financing and Related Programs, as well as Transportation; on the latter he promises to fight for highway funds for Orange County. He opposes efforts to turn the shuttered El Toro Marine Corps Air Station, which neighbors his district, into a commercial airport.

As Legislative Branch chairman during the 104th, Packard made significant cuts to congressional committee staff and eliminated a congressional support agency. "I cut 12 cents out of every dollar Congress spends on itself," he bragged. "If every other part of government cut just one cent out of every dollar it spends, our books would be in the black today."

Packard proved willing as a chairman to dispense with controversial provisions or amendments that threatened to slow down the progress of his bills. He let Senate and House GOP leaders dissuade him from eliminating any of Congress' four joint committees — Joint Economic, Taxation, Printing and Library.

In addition to cutting committee staff and resisting members' calls to maintain or resurrect perks such as a members-only car wash, Packard sought to modernize congressional computers and consolidate the Capitol Hill police force.

Packard is a longtime proponent of denying illegal immigrants any public benefits aside from emergency medical care, and he supported a measure during the 104th to block illegal immigrants from attending public schools. Packard got into a dispute with supporters of tough immigration enforcement, though, when he successfully attached language to House-passed legislation to shut down two Southern California highway checkpoints run by the Immigration and Naturalization Service. In 1991, Packard had secured $31 million to convert one of the checkpoints into a 24-hour operation. Since that hadn't been accomplished, Packard reasoned that the resources could be better allocated at the border itself. In the end, he was willing to go along with a plan to increase funding for the checkpoints to ensure their round-the-clock performance.

Packard drew some unwanted attention in 1995 when he told The Associated Press during a fact-finding tour of Bosnia: "We want peace to work. If American troops can help bring that about, then we will be very supportive." After President Clinton cited Packard as a supporter of his Bosnia policy, Packard said he had been misunderstood. He voted against funding a troop deployment to Bosnia.

When the Appropriations Subcommittee on Foreign Operations began debating cuts in family planning assistance, Packard, a former Mormon missionary and ardent opponent of abortion, declared that "many members do not support family planning, period." Asked by Nancy Pelosi, D-Calif., whether he was opposed even to family planning in the United States, Packard said, "I am."

Packard was angered by information courses and pamphlets offered to government workers that he found explicit and permissive. "Why the government is involved in teaching people how to

CALIFORNIA 48
Part of Orange, San Diego and Riverside counties

Like many of Southern California's coastal districts, the 48th is firmly in the Republican column. The party here has a nearly 2-1 registration advantage over the Democrats, a level surpassed in California only by the 47th District just up the coast.

The typical district resident has been described as conservative, upper-middle class and well-educated, with 2.5 kids and two cars.

Each of the 48th's three counties gave Bob Dole strong support in 1996. Overall, he won 56 percent of the district's presidential vote, compared with 34 percent for Bill Clinton and 8 percent for Ross Perot. Slightly more than half of the district's vote was cast in Orange County, 42 percent was from San Diego County and 7 percent was cast in Riverside County.

Heading down the Pacific Coast Highway, the 48th takes in some of Laguna Beach and all of Dana Point and San Clemente in Orange County, and Camp Pendleton Marine Corps Base and Oceanside in San Diego County.

The coastal area relies heavily on tourism. The economies of Oceanside, and to a lesser extent San Clemente, also depend on the Marine base. Camp Pendleton supplied many of the personnel for Desert Shield/Desert Storm in 1990-91; Oceanside, the 48th's largest city with 128,000 residents, suffered the loss of retail business and the loss of the soldiers' part-time labor in area businesses.

The district breaks into Riverside County to the north only to pick up Temecula, a newer, pro-business, pro-growth community whose 27,000 residents live in the wine-producing Temecula Valley. Other new cities such as Dana Point and Laguna Niguel have incorporated in the past several years. Laguna Niguel is a planned community due east from Laguna Beach.

San Marcos, in San Diego County, has burgeoned; its population more than tripled in the 1970s and grew by 123 percent in the 1980s to 39,000. Even the town of San Juan Capistrano, famous for the swallows that flock to its ancient Spanish mission each spring, is being transformed. But the town's historic nature lingers; artifacts of California's mission period were unearthed here recently.

The 48th has escaped some of the economic suffering felt throughout the rest of Southern California. Its economy relies more on service industries and on tourism, and not as much on aerospace and military contracts as does the neighboring 47th's. A steady stream of visitors to the 48th District's beach communities provides a cushion for the economy.

This area may have been considered "lily white" in the late 1970s, but there has been steady, though slow, growth in its minority populations. About 17 percent of its residents are Hispanic, 5 percent are Asian and 4 percent are black. The area also has a growing number of military retirees.

1990 Population: 572,928. White 476,994 (83%), Black 23,164 (4%), Other 72,770 (13%). Hispanic origin 98,746 (17%). 18 and over 426,279 (74%), 62 and over 71,638 (13%). Median age: 31.

use illicit drugs and how to be involved in aberrant sex techniques is beyond me," he complained. The House passed, 283-138, his amendment barring federal employee training that is unrelated to official duties, designed to change values or lifestyles, or includes content related to AIDS or HIV beyond informing employees of medical ramifications and workplace rights.

Packard exudes the smiling geniality of a neighborhood dentist — his profession before Congress — and he normally has operated in a low-key manner, working behind the scenes with Appropriations colleagues to line up support for expenditures he favors. His shopping list has included funding for: construction of a $200 million, 12,000-space parking garage in Anaheim to serve patrons of Disneyland and function as a hub for express-bus and car-pool commuters; work on the $1.5 billion Santa Ana River flood control project in Orange, San Bernardino and Riverside counties; a study of beach erosion problems along Orange County's southern coast; repair of flood damage at Camp Pendleton; development of the Gas Turbine Modular Helium Reactor by General Atomics in San Diego; and expansion of the Border Patrol presence to prevent illegal immigration from Mexico.

In February 1994, when Congress was considering an $8.6 billion emergency aid bill to help meet the costs of the California earthquake, Packard succeeded in amending the disaster-relief legislation to deny housing grants and other long-term assistance to illegal immigrants. Sensing the potential popular appeal of Packard's initiative, Esteban E. Torres and Julian C. Dixon, both California Democrats on Appropriations, negotiated with him and panel colleague Jerry Lewis, R-Calif., to secure a commitment that illegal immigrants would get basic emergency services — shelter, food and medical care.

In August 1993, Packard made a sooner-than-expected return to work after emergency heart surgery so he could be on hand to vote against final passage of Clinton's budget, a plan he predicted would be "disastrous for economic recovery." Packard had triple bypass surgery in mid-

July after going to Bethesda Naval Hospital in Maryland with chest pains.

During his first decade in Congress, Packard served on the Public Works Committee, gaining skill in the art of horse trading to win authorization for the same kind of public works projects he now touts on Appropriations.

On social issues, Packard often sides with the most conservative wing within the GOP. In his first term, when the Education and Labor Committee took up a bill granting student religious groups "equal access" to school facilities, Packard talked of giving children moral and religious values. That worried other committee Republicans, who were selling the bill as simply a device to protect free expression.

During the 1987 debate about legislation to pay Japanese-Americans interned during World War II, Packard endorsed a federal apology but opposed compensation. He said that he was one of 17 children raised on an Idaho farm, and when the family was about to lose its property, his father went to work for a government contractor in the South Pacific. Within days of the Japanese attack on Pearl Harbor, his father was taken prisoner, leaving his family destitute during the war. Giving money to the internees, Packard said, "would demean a time when our family learned to work together, pull together and pray together."

At Home: Nothing in Packard's electoral career is likely to match the tumult of the 1982 contest that made him one of the few ever elected to Congress as a write-in candidate.

When GOP Rep. Clair W. Burgener announced his retirement that year, Packard and 17 other Republicans filed for the primary. A veteran of Carlsbad city politics, Packard emerged as a front-runner. But he found himself in a pitched battle with recreational vehicle tycoon Johnnie Crean.

A political neophyte, Crean sank close to $1 million into his bid, which consisted largely of personal attacks on his rivals, some wildly inaccurate. Afterward, Crean blamed his campaign's conduct on his consultants, whom he fired the day after the primary. Crean earned the abiding scorn of many Republicans but won the nomination over Packard by 92 votes.

Many GOP partisans were unhappy with the outcome, and they helped persuade Packard to enter the general election as a write-in candidate. Crean tried to mend fences and reform his image. He argued that Republicans choosing Packard would split the GOP vote, electing the Democratic nominee, Roy Pat Archer, a professor of government. Republican officials came out for Crean, and Packard's funding dried up.

But Packard was still strong at the grass roots. While media coverage kept the Crean controversy fresh, Packard sent out 350,000 pieces of mail proclaiming himself the legitimate GOP alternative. On Election Day, his poll workers handed out pencils with Packard's name, urging their use. Packard won with a 37 percent plurality, five points ahead of Archer. Crean ran third. Since then, Packard has not been seriously challenged.

HOUSE ELECTIONS

1996 General		
Ron Packard (R)	145,814	(66%)
Dan Farrell (D)	59,558	(27%)
William Dreu (REF)	8,013	(4%)
Sharon K. Miles (NL)	8,006	(4%)
1994 General		
Ron Packard (R)	143,275	(73%)
Andrei Leschick (D)	43,446	(22%)
Donna White (PFP)	8,520	(4%)

Previous Winning Percentages: **1992** (61%) **1990** (68%) **1988** (72%) **1986** (73%) **1984** (74%) **1982** (37%)

CAMPAIGN FINANCE

	Receipts	Receipts from PACs	Expend-itures
1996			
Packard (R)	$353,383	$232,116 (66%)	$264,625
Farrell (D)	$11,000	0	$10,645
1994			
Packard (R)	$206,835	$151,074 (73%)	$210,125
Leschick (D)	$3,928	0	$3,726

DISTRICT VOTE FOR PRESIDENT

	1996		1992
D	80,646 (34%)	**D**	71,621 (29%)
R	132,545 (56%)	**R**	108,581 (44%)
I	18,731 (8%)	**I**	65,980 (27%)

KEY VOTES

1997	
Ban "partial birth" abortions	Y
1996	
Approve farm bill	Y
Deny public education to illegal immigrants	Y
Repeal ban on certain assault-style weapons	Y
Increase minimum wage	N
Freeze defense spending	N
Approve welfare overhaul	Y
1995	
Approve balanced-budget constitutional amendment	Y
Relax Clean Water Act regulations	Y
Oppose limits on environmental regulations	N
Reduce projected Medicare spending	Y
Approve GOP budget with tax and spending cuts	Y

VOTING STUDIES

	Presidential Support		Party Unity		Conservative Coalition	
Year	S	O	S	O	S	O
1996	38	57	89	6	96	4
1995	18	82	97	3	97	2
1994	45	55	90	9	97	3
1993	30	61	82	5	75	2
1992	81	13	85	10	90	2
1991	83	17	84	12	92	5

INTEREST GROUP RATINGS

Year	ADA	AFL-CIO	CCUS	ACU
1996	0	n/a	93	94
1995	0	0	100	92
1994	0	0	92	95
1993	0	0	100	96
1992	0	8	71	100
1991	5	8	90	95

49 Brian P. Bilbray (R)

Of San Diego — Elected 1994, 2nd term

Biographical Information

Born: Jan. 28, 1951, Coronado, Calif.

Education: Southwestern College, 1970-74.

Occupation: Tax firm owner.

Family: Wife, Karen Walker; two children, three stepchildren.

Religion: Roman Catholic.

Political Career: Imperial Beach City Council, 1977-79; mayor of Imperial Beach, 1979-85; San Diego County Board of Supervisors, 1985-95.

Capitol Office: 1530 Longworth Bldg. 20515; 225-2040.

Committees

Commerce

Finance & Hazardous Materials; Health & Environment; Oversight & Investigations

In Washington: First swept into the House by the GOP tide of 1994, Bilbray was rewarded for his conquest of a Democratic incumbent with a seat on the influential Commerce Committee.

There, and on the House floor, Bilbray typically has voted with the conservative faithful in his party. But he is not unwilling to deal with Democrats, particularly when cooperation may advance a San Diego cause. He once told the Los Angeles Times that he had been scolded by fellow Republicans for merely speaking with his San Diego House colleague, Bob Filner, a liberal Democrat. "The hassle with Filner isn't just that he's a Democrat," said Bilbray, "but he is perceived as being on the extreme left, and a lot of people resent my association with that aspect." Bilbray said he keeps up his association with Filner "because Bob's a human being — even if he is a pinko Commie."

Bilbray and Filner share an interest in seeking to give San Diego a permanent waiver from certain federal sewage treatment requirements. A Bilbray-sponsored bill to do that was the first measure passed by the House under its "Corrections Day" legislative calendar. Republicans instituted the Corrections Day procedure in 1995 to speed floor consideration of bills that aim to address what the GOP sees as glaring wrongs — in the San Diego case, a burdensome regulation. Bilbray sought to exempt San Diego from a rule under the 1972 Clean Water Act requiring the city to treat its sewage twice before discharging it into the ocean. Critics of Bilbray's bill said it was unnecessary, because the Environmental Protection Agency was poised to grant the city a five-year waiver from the requirement. But Bilbray's bill, which the House passed 269-156 in July 1995, provided for a permanent waiver.

Bilbray has come under fire from some California environmental and surfing groups for his stand on the sewage treatment matter and for his vote in May 1995 to relax regulatory provisions of the Clean Water Act. Bilbray and other conservatives argued that changes to the act were needed to reduce excessive regulatory costs to businesses and to give states and localities greater flexibility to meet water quality standards. Environmentalists howled that conservatives were putting forward a "polluter's bill of rights," introducing loopholes and waivers to the act that would increase pollution and ultimately clog the nation's rivers and lakes with industrial wastes and sewage.

Bilbray is a former lifeguard who sometimes still surfs the waves around San Diego. His World Wide Web page includes a photograph of him on a surfboard coasting through ocean waves. As a result, he chafes at being portrayed as anti-environment. "To have somebody come up and say Brian doesn't care about clean water is like saying Jesse Jackson doesn't care about civil rights," Bilbray told the Los Angeles Times in September 1995. "You're talking to someone who has built his political career on the environment." When he was mayor of Imperial Beach, Bilbray became so frustrated with the federal response to complaints that the Tijuana River was carrying pollution from Mexico onto U.S. beaches that he climbed aboard a bulldozer and dammed the offending stream. The highly publicized deed earned Bilbray lasting identification among area voters as a foe of unresponsive federal bureaucrats.

In June 1996, Bilbray took the environmentalists' side on a key House vote involving protection of a threatened sea bird species, the marbled murrelet. Bilbray was among 81 Republicans voting to drop a provision in the fiscal 1997 interior appropriations bill that would have lifted protections for the murrelet on 40,000 acres of private land in Northern California.

Illegal immigration is another big concern of Bilbray's constituents, and in the 105th Congress he introduced legislation to deny citizenship to U.S.-born children of illegal immigrants. The bill was identical to a measure he introduced in the 104th Congress. He said the measure would help discourage illegal immigration and save taxpayers millions of dollars in education, health and welfare expenditures that now go to children of

CALIFORNIA 49
North San Diego; Coronado; Imperial Beach

The coastal 49th is the economic engine that drives the surrounding districts. It includes San Diego's downtown, most of its military bases, most of its other large employers and most of its coast. The 51st and the 50th districts to the north and south of the 49th, respectively, are packed with the area's bedrooms.

The district begins just south of Del Mar and includes La Jolla, Point Loma and northern and downtown San Diego. It then skips through the San Diego Bay to Imperial Beach, and swings north up the slender Silver Strand Boulevard to take in Coronado, a peninsula that reaches up to the mouth of the bay. The northern and southern parts of the district are not connected by any land. Though this is an urban district, traffic is manageable here; it is possible to hop on the Interstate 5 Freeway in La Jolla and arrive in Imperial Beach in just 20 minutes.

Compared with the south side of the city, the 49th is relatively homogeneous. Only 13 percent of its residents are Hispanic, compared with 41 percent in the 50th District; only 7 percent of the 49th's residents are Asian, and 5 percent are black, compared with 15 percent and 14 percent, respectively, in the 50th.

The 49th is also a lot more Republican than southern San Diego: The GOP has a small voter-registration edge here, compared with a double-digit deficit in the 50th District. Despite the registration numbers, Bill Clinton won the 49th in 1992 with 43 percent of the vote; George Bush got 32 percent and Ross Perot 25 percent. In 1996 — a few months after Republicans gathered here to nominate Bob Dole for president — Clinton won again, with 49 percent. Dole polled 40 percent and Perot dipped to 7 percent.

Despite Clinton's strong showing, Republican Bilbray was able to win a second term, defeating professor Peter Navarro, 53 percent to 42 percent. While Clinton's share of the vote increased, so did Bilbray's; he had polled only 49 percent in ousting Democratic Rep. Lynn Schenk in 1994.

The beautiful community of Coronado is home to 27,000 residents, many of them retired Navy officers. Thirteen percent of its population is 65 or older.

Just across the bridge from Coronado on the mainland is the National Steel and Shipbuilding Co. (known as NASSCO), which employs 3,000 to 8,000 people, depending on the nature of the projects going on at the facility. It is the only shipyard in the western United States that still builds large oceangoing ships. It has been owned by its employees since 1989.

The area is heavily dependent on the military; Miramar Naval Air Station and other military facilities employ tens of thousands, and one-sixth of San Diego's gross product depends directly on military procurement, retirement benefits and salaries.

Defense cutbacks will whittle at that in coming years, but the local economy is diversifying, as exemplified by the dozens of biotechnology and biomedical firms that have set up shop in the valley just north of La Jolla.

1990 Population: 573,362. White 470,562 (82%), Black 30,408 (5%), Other 72,392 (13%). Hispanic origin 73,210 (13%). 18 and over 480,143 (84%), 62 and over 84,971 (15%). Median age: 32.

illegal aliens.

"We are penalizing those who go through the proper channels to become legal citizens of our nation, and we are also diverting resources from our citizens in order to pay for illegal immigrants," Bilbray said when introducing the original bill. Bilbray said his proposal "fine tunes" the 14th Amendment, which reads: "All persons born or naturalized in the United States and subject to the jurisdiction thereof, are citizens of the United States and of the State wherein they reside." The bill would specify that those "subject to the jurisdiction thereof" refers to children born to U.S. citizens or legal immigrants. Those born to parents who are in the country illegally would not be considered citizens.

Although Bilbray is generally supportive of the conservative tenet that less government is a good thing, he thinks the federal government should help shoulder costs that California incurs because of illegal immigration. He was unhappy with a provision in a package of Medicaid changes approved by the Commerce Committee in September 1995 that required states to pay for the emergency medical care of illegal aliens. "The federal government needs to stop being a deadbeat dad and start paying for the medical costs of illegal aliens," Bilbray said. "These people are not the residents of any states. Why should hospitals in California bear the brunt of this problem?" He said that emergency care for illegal aliens costs more than $1 billion a year in California.

Though the GOP leadership generally can count on Bilbray's support, he did not always stick to their script, as was evident on three key votes in March 1996: He was one of just 42 Republicans to vote against repealing the ban on certain semiautomatic assault-style weapons; he was one of 49 Republicans voting to maintain a requirement that states fund Medicaid abortions in cases of rape and incest and to protect the life of the woman; and he was one of 21 Republicans voting against an omnibus fiscal 1996 spending bill that the leadership barely managed to pass, 209-206.

Republican efforts to restrain the growth of spending on Medicaid and Medicare have generated much controversy, but in April 1995 Bilbray was adamant that costs had to be contained. "Spending in Medicare and Medicaid is rising 10 percent a year," he said. "The escalation in spending is just not acceptable." Bilbray was willing to accept a smaller tax cut than the $353 billion the House approved, but only if the revenue retained went toward deficit reduction, not to "continue to bloat Medicare and Medicaid."

At Home: High on the Democratic target list after his narrow 1994 victory, Bilbray caught a break when the Democratic freshman he had ousted, Lynn Schenk, declined a rematch. Instead, the Democrats wound up with Peter Navarro, an economics professor at the University of California at Irvine, whose personal style turned off even some in his own party. Bilbray won by 11 points, taking 53 percent of the vote.

Bilbray first ran for the House in 1994 as a local official frustrated in his dealings with the federal government. Despite Schenk's million-dollar-plus defense, Bilbray appealed to bedrock Republicans and to just enough of the district's numerous swing voters to eke out victory with a 49 percent plurality. Schenk had 46 percent, and 3 percent each went to the Libertarian and Peace and Freedom candidates.

Schenk's connections — she served in former Gov. Edmund G. "Jerry" Brown Jr.'s Cabinet and held a seat on the Energy and Commerce Committee — helped her amass a campaign treasury of nearly $1.4 million, almost half of it from PACs. Bilbray's resources were not meager, topping $750,000, but he worked hard to portray the incumbent as an insider and a friend of special interests. He drew support from followers of Ross Perot (the Texan had won 25 percent of the vote in the 49th in 1992), and he capitalized on the visibility and connections he had made during 18 years in local politics.

Bilbray, owner of a tax preparation service, was first elected to the Imperial Beach City Council in 1976, and he went on to serve as the city's mayor from 1979-85. The media splash surrounding the dam-building episode helped him win election in 1984 to the San Diego County Board of Supervisors, where he was serving when he tried for the House in 1994.

In the House primary, Bilbray's toughest competitor among three Republican rivals was physician John Steel. He tried to cast Bilbray as a tax-and-spend politician, but the strategy backfired when two local party leaders withdrew their Steel endorsements in reaction to his negative campaigning. Bilbray won nomination with 51 percent of the vote to Steel's 37 percent.

Against Schenk, Bilbray tied into the national Republican campaign strategy of linking House Democrats to the unpopular Clinton administration. He faulted Schenk for supporting President Clinton's budget proposals and crime bill, and his ads used the tag line, "If you like Clinton, you'll love Schenk." Immigration was a key campaign issue. Schenk opposed California's controversial Proposition 187, the anti-illegal immigrant initiative. Bilbray strongly supported it. Two months before the general election, the San Diego County Board of Supervisors, including Bilbray, declared a state of emergency due to the high cost of illegal immigration to local budgets.

HOUSE ELECTIONS

1996 General		
Brian P. Bilbray (R)	108,806	(53%)
Peter Navarro (D)	86,657	(42%)
Ernie Lippe (LIBERT)	4,218	(2%)
Kevin Philip Hambsch (REF)	3,773	(2%)
Peter Sterling (NL)	3,314	(2%)
1994 General		
Brian P. Bilbray (R)	90,283	(49%)
Lynn Schenk (D)	85,597	(46%)
Chris Hoogenboom (LIBERT)	5,288	(3%)
Renate M. Kline (PFP)	4,948	(3%)

CAMPAIGN FINANCE

	Receipts	Receipts from PACs		Expend-itures
1996				
Bilbray (R)	$1,193,729	$492,201	(41%)	$1,122,073
Navarro (D)	$450,929	$198,365	(44%)	$450,424
Hambsch (REF)	$4,595	0		$3,207
1994				
Bilbray (R)	$754,211	$148,374	(20%)	$750,654
Schenk (D)	$1,388,353	$655,566	(47%)	$1,392,948

DISTRICT VOTE FOR PRESIDENT

1996		1992	
D	110,920 (49%)	**D**	114,081 (43%)
R	91,478 (40%)	**R**	82,834 (32%)
I	15,084 (7%)	**I**	65,856 (25%)

KEY VOTES

1997	
Ban "partial-birth" abortions	Y
1996	
Approve farm bill	Y
Deny public education to illegal immigrants	Y
Repeal ban on certain assault-style weapons	N
Increase minimum wage	Y
Freeze defense spending	?
Approve welfare overhaul	Y
1995	
Approve balanced-budget constitutional amendment	Y
Relax Clean Water Act regulations	Y
Oppose limits on environmental regulations	N
Reduce projected Medicare spending	Y
Approve GOP budget with tax and spending cuts	Y

VOTING STUDIES

	Presidential Support		Party Unity		Conservative Coalition	
Year	S	O	S	O	S	O
1996	44	54	80	17	63	24
1995	24	74	88	9	85	9

INTEREST GROUP RATINGS

Year	ADA	AFL-CIO	CCUS	ACU
1996	20	n/a	94	74
1995	15	8	96	72

50 Bob Filner (D)

Of San Diego — Elected 1992, 3rd term

Biographical Information
Born: Sept. 4, 1942, Pittsburgh, Pa.
Education: Cornell U., B.A. 1963; U. of Delaware, M.A. 1969; Cornell U., Ph.D. 1973.
Occupation: Public official; college professor.
Family: Wife, Jane Merrill; two children.
Religion: Jewish.
Political Career: San Diego School Board, 1979-83, president, 1982; candidate for San Diego City Council, 1983; San Diego City Council, 1987-92, deputy mayor, 1991.

Capitol Office: 330 Cannon Bldg. 20515; 225-8045.

Committees
Transportation & Infrastructure
Railroads; Surface Transportation
Veterans' Affairs
Benefits (ranking)

In Washington: A one-time aide to Sen. Hubert H. Humphrey, Filner is a similarly irrepressible liberal who found himself with many like-minded colleagues in his first term in the 103rd Congress. But after the 1994 election, when voters booted Democrats out of the House majority for the first time in four decades, Filner had a harder time making headway with his philosophy of "practical politics defined by a true commitment to progressive ideals."

A former teacher, Filner came to Congress eager to share the lessons he learned on the San Diego School Board and the City Council. But, like many Democrats, he became disenchanted when Republicans assumed power. "My friends in San Diego . . . say they have never seen me so depressed," Filner told USA Today in June 1995.

Casting about for a role to play in the minority, Filner jumped to the defense of Filipino veterans who have been denied benefits despite their service in World War II. And he argued for a new trust fund to help workers laid off by defense contractors find new jobs.

Eventually, Filner was thrust into the center of a raging debate over the regulation of a wastewater treatment facility in his San Diego district — but, ironically, in this instance he found himself defending an argument that Speaker Newt Gingrich had made his own.

The effort to force San Diego to upgrade its wastewater treatment facility began in 1972, with enactment of tougher federal standards that would have required the city to treat its sewage twice before discharging it into the ocean. San Diego obtained extensions of the deadline for meeting the requirement for years, but the Environmental Protection Agency (EPA) sued the city in 1988 over its facility at Point Loma, which pumps nearly 200 million gallons of treated sewage into the Pacific Ocean.

City officials like Filner, who at the time served on council, and the EPA battled in court into the 1990s, and in 1994, President Clinton signed a law allowing San Diego to apply for a waiver from the rules. The EPA in June 1995 granted preliminary approval of the waiver.

But GOP lawmakers, led by freshman Brian P. Bilbray, a former San Diego County supervisor, had adopted the issue by then. Bilbray's cause piqued the interest of Gingrich, who saw the local dispute as the ideal platform for a national debate over what many Republicans perceive as unnecessary federal regulations. He chose San Diego's proposed permanent waiver for its wastewater facility as the first item on the "Corrections Day" calendar that he created to overturn such "silly" federal rules quickly.

The debate placed Filner, who later would fight other Republican efforts to alter environmental regulations, in the awkward position of defending the GOP's push to grant San Diego the waiver, which he had sought for eight years, including his first two years in the House. He urged his colleagues to support the bill because "it is the right thing to do for both the environment and the taxpayers of San Diego." The House passed the bill 269-156 in July 1995.

Filner achieved success in the 104th on another parochial matter, the proposed relocation of a fleet of giant Marine Corps helicopters to Miramar Naval Air Base in northern San Diego County. With help from California Democratic Sen. Barbara Boxer, he persuaded Clinton to delay the decision to move the 112 helicopters to Miramar because of safety and environmental concerns in densely populated areas around the base.

In June 1996, Filner discussed the issue with Clinton and Navy Secretary John Dalton. Filner, who had endured a tough primary challenge from a more conservative Democrat months earlier, then surprised his constituents at a San Diego rally for Clinton with the news that Clinton would ask the Pentagon to consider moving the helicopters to other bases, including March Air Force Base in Riverside.

Filner and Boxer vowed to continue the battle to keep the helicopters out of Miramar in the 105th Congress. The Pentagon had not scheduled

CALIFORNIA 50
Central and south San Diego; Chula Vista; National City

This ethnic, blue-collar urban-suburban district is a world apart from the districts that surround it. It is far more diverse: 41 percent of its residents are Hispanic, 15 percent are Asian and 14 percent are black. It is also as Democratic as the others are Republican.

The northern part of the district, just south of San Diego's downtown, houses the worst of San Diego's urban problems: its highest crime rates, its most serious gang activity and so on. It is built up with rows of two-story apartment complexes, and while certain parts are being gentrified by "urban pioneers," much of the area is downtrodden.

Farther south, the booming suburb of Chula Vista splits the city of San Diego in two; even more southern areas of San Diego such as San Ysidro and Otay Mesa are contiguous only by a legal line that extends through the bay. Residents of the southern region, cut off geographically from the rest of San Diego, sometimes feel cut off politically as well.

Chula Vista has a large number of military personnel and tends to be more Republican than the rest of the 50th. On Chula Vista's east end is East Lake, one of the county's largest developments. Any new housing growth the 50th experiences is likely to be here; much of the rest of the district is either stagnant or built out.

Otay Mesa is an industrial area south of Chula Vista that represents the last opportunity for expansion of San Diego's large-scale manufacturing. The area is heavily developed between the 5 and 805 freeways, but farther east is mostly empty land zoned for industry.

The San Diego-Tijuana border crossing at San Ysidro is the world's busiest. The area's problems stem not so much from the number of immigrants, but from criminals who prey on them.

But the constant traffic creates an uneasiness that contributes to anti-immigration sentiment in the state. In 1994, that sentiment found expression in a state ballot initiative (Prop. 187) denying all but emergency public benefits to illegal immigrants.

The area is reeling from the loss of General Dynamics, formerly the district's (and the county's) largest private-sector employer. The company sold its Tomahawk missile manufacturing operations in 1992 to Hughes, which closed the San Diego plant and moved manufacturing to Arizona. This signaled the beginning of the end. By 1997, the company had only about 150 employees in the area.

Bill Clinton carried the district in 1992, garnering 49 percent of the votes to 30 percent for George Bush and 21 percent for Ross Perot. Clinton did even better in 1996, capturing 60 percent of the vote to Bob Dole's 32 percent and Perot's 6 percent. In the House race, Filner won re-election with 62 percent, his best showing yet.

1990 Population: 573,463. White 266,652 (46%), Black 82,735 (14%), Other 224,076 (39%). Hispanic origin 232,660 (41%). 18 and over 398,704 (70%), 62 and over 59,801 (10%). Median age: 28.

the move to occur until 1998. "We will try to halt funding for it during the course of the year," Filner said in late 1996, noting that even if the Pentagon decided to send the helicopters to Miramar, civil suits by angry residents who live nearby could delay the transfer.

True to the voting record he amassed as a freshman — which earned him a rating of 100 from the liberal advocacy group Americans for Democratic Action — Filner in his second term consistently opposed the agenda of the Republican majority. And like many California Democrats, he battled at every turn GOP efforts to deny federal benefits to illegal immigrants.

Border crossings by illegal immigrants are a problem in Filner's district, so he has supported more funding for the Border Patrol. But he objects to what he feels is the hostile tone of many who decry illegal immigration. He opposed the 1994 ballot initiative (Prop 187) that sought to disallow illegal aliens from receiving almost all public services (it was overwhelmingly approved). "Let us recognize the basic humanity of all individuals," he said in 1993. "Let us work together to get at the economic development that is so crucial for helping all people have a better way of life."

Filner similarly defended the interests of his immigrant constituents in March 1994, when he objected to a GOP amendment targeting bilingual education.

A member of the Transportation and Infrastructure Committee, Filner is in a good position to protect his state's interests in the 105th Congress as lawmakers consider how much to authorize for federal highway programs over the next several years. He also gained a slot as ranking Democrat on the Veterans' Affairs Subcommittee on Benefits.

At Home: Filner in 1994 survived the electoral tide that swept Republicans into control of Congress, but two years later, his liberal views helped make him the target of an intraparty challenge from a moderate Democrat. Juan Vargas, a Hispanic, replaced Filner on the San Diego City Council in 1993 and later was named deputy mayor, another job Filner once held. Touted as a potential mayoral candidate, Vargas in 1996 instead set his sights on Filner's House seat.

The ethnic makeup of the predominantly minority district, which includes a Hispanic population of 41 percent, played to Vargas' favor. He had tried for the seat in 1992, after it was created in redistricting, but his 19 percent tally in the Democratic primary earned him a fourth-place finish; Filner won that primary with 26 percent.

In 1996, Vargas highlighted his lifelong ties to the district and his social conservatism. He said he decided to make the bid in part because the House, with the help of Filner, had defeated a measure that would have allowed punishment of people who desecrate the U.S. flag. He also opposes abortion, while Filner supports abortion rights.

But Filner's efforts to remind voters of his legislative contributions to the district — grants to improve schools and health clinics and his battle against stricter, and more expensive, sewage treatment standards — paid dividends. He won renomination by 10 points, taking 55 percent of the vote to Vargas' 45 percent.

Republicans targeted Filner for defeat in the general election. But their candidate, Baptist minister Jim Baize, who won the primary by less than 1 percent of the vote on the strength of absentee ballots, faced an uphill battle. Filner secured his largest margin of victory yet, winning 62 percent of the vote.

Filner won the 50th in 1992 just as he had climbed other rungs of the political ladder — with single-minded devotion to fundraising and tireless campaigning. He overcame five adversaries in the Democratic primary, upsetting presumed front-runners state Sen. Wadie P. Deddeh and ex-Rep. Jim Bates.

Bates was trying to return to Congress. Republican Randy "Duke" Cunningham ousted him in 1990 after the House ethics committee reproved him for sexually harassing staff aides. Deddeh, a real estate developer and state legislator since the 1960s, assumed the mantle of Democratic front-runner as Bates faltered. But Filner attacked him for his opposition to abortion and his apparent failure to make timely payments on property taxes.

Filner had the strong support of labor and women's groups. And he made a concerted effort to win minority voters, undeterred by the presence of a Latino and a black activist on the ballot. Filner's credentials were enhanced considerably by his history as an early civil right Freedom Rider (he was imprisoned for a time after sitting in at a Mississippi lunch counter in 1960) and his years as an activist in San Diego politics. He 26 percent tally put him 3 points ahead of Deddeh.

Filner, who moved to California from New York in 1970 to teach at San Diego State University, dispatched Republican Tony Valencia in the general election, taking 57 percent of the vote. In 1994, he easily won a second term.

HOUSE ELECTIONS

1996 General		
Bob Filner (D)	73,200	(62%)
Jim Baize (R)	38,351	(32%)
Dan Clark (REF)	3,253	(3%)
Earl M. Shepard (NL)	2,138	(2%)
Philip Zoebisch (LIBERT)	1,398	(1%)
1996 Primary		
Bob Filner (D)	18,809	(55%)
Juan Vargas (D)	15,673	(45%)
1994 General		
Bob Filner (D)	59,214	(57%)
Mary Alice Acevedo (R)	36,955	(35%)
Ricardo Duenez (LIBERT)	3,326	(3%)
Guillermo Ramirez (PFP)	3,002	(3%)
Kip Krueger (GREEN)	1,954	(2%)

Previous Winning Percentages: 1992 (57%)

CAMPAIGN FINANCE

	Receipts	Receipts from PACs	Expend-itures
1996			
Filner (D)	$1,135,190	$490,480 (43%)	$1,142,370
Baize (R)	$129,225	$13,171 (10%)	$120,562
1994			
Filner (D)	$832,812	$434,300 (52%)	$818,051
Acevedo (R)	$353,023	$83,258 (24%)	$352,091

DISTRICT VOTE FOR PRESIDENT

	1996		1992
D	78,881 (60%)	**D**	69,546 (49%)
R	42,730 (32%)	**R**	42,830 (30%)
I	7,764 (6%)	**I**	30,267 (21%)

KEY VOTES

1997	
Ban "partial birth" abortions	N
1996	
Approve farm bill	N
Deny public education to illegal immigrants	N
Repeal ban on certain assault-style weapons	N
Increase minimum wage	Y
Freeze defense spending	Y
Approve welfare overhaul	N
1995	
Approve balanced-budget constitutional amendment	N
Relax Clean Water Act regulations	N
Oppose limits on environmental regulations	#
Reduce projected Medicare spending	N
Approve GOP budget with tax and spending cuts	N

VOTING STUDIES

	Presidential Support		Party Unity		Conservative Coalition	
Year	S	O	S	O	S	O
1996	77	13	90	2	12	86
1995	86	8	92	4	14	82
1994	79	21	98	2	17	83
1993	77	23	96	4	9	91

INTEREST GROUP RATINGS

Year	ADA	AFL-CIO	CCUS	ACU
1996	90	n/a	29	0
1995	80	100	17	9
1994	100	78	50	0
1993	100	100	9	8

51 Randy 'Duke' Cunningham (R)

Of San Diego — Elected 1990, 4th term

Biographical Information

Born: Dec. 8, 1941, Los Angeles, Calif.

Education: U. of Missouri, B.A. 1964, M.A. 1967; National U., M.B.A. 1985.

Military Service: Navy, 1967-87.

Occupation: Computer software executive.

Family: Wife, Nancy Jones; three children.

Religion: Christian.

Political Career: No previous office.

Capitol Office: 2238 Rayburn Bldg. 20515; 225-5452.

Committees

Appropriations

District of Columbia; Legislative; National Security

In Washington: A "Top Gun" flight instructor during his 20-year Navy career, Cunningham in Congress is a hard-charging conservative whose blunt talk has gotten him into more than a few scrapes with Democrats. He was busy in the 104th using his chairmanship of an Economic and Educational Opportunities subcommittee to advance the GOP proposal to convert many federal nutrition and education programs into block grants for the states.

For his loyalty to the Republican leadership and his commitment to conservative causes, Cunningham in the 105th was rewarded with a seat on the Appropriations Committee, where his assignments include the National Security subcommittee — particularly important to him because defense dollars have a big impact in the 51st District, where many residents work at one or another of San Diego's numerous military installations. Cunningham had served on the National Security Committee (formerly Armed Services) since his first term; he left National Security and Economic and Educational Opportunities upon joining Appropriations in 1997.

As chairman in the 104th of the Early Childhood, Youth and Families Subcommittee, Cunningham had responsibility for overseeing child nutrition programs. He, along with Bill Goodling of Pennsylvania, chairman of the full Economic and Educational Opportunities Committee, backed the House version of a welfare overhaul bill that would have turned the school lunch and breakfast program into a block grant. That approach, they said, would give states more flexibility while restraining federal spending.

But Democrats and even some Republicans were cold to the idea; they said the school feeding program did not need overhauling because it was working well. When House members and senators met in a conference on the welfare bill, the Senate insisted on eliminating the plan to block-grant the school feeding program.

Conferees agreed to a compromise that allowed seven states to receive their school lunch and breakfast programs in the form of a block grant. But it mattered little, since Clinton vetoed that version of the welfare bill in January 1996.

Cunningham also was active in the 104th on legislation revising the main education program for children with disabilities, the Individuals with Disabilities Education Act (IDEA). Enacted in 1975, IDEA aimed to ensure that states and school districts provided equal education opportunities to disabled students. Among the changes in IDEA sought by Cunningham and his allies was permission for states to stop educational services to disabled children in extreme disciplinary cases.

When the Opportunities Committee considered the bill in May 1996, it voted along party lines to reject a Democratic amendment to scuttle the disciplinary provision. Under the GOP-backed bill, disabled students could be expelled without educational services when their misconduct was unrelated to the disability and involved the use of weapons or illegal drugs. Existing law barred states from denying an education to disabled students regardless of misconduct.

"Under the law today, there is disagreement and confusion among schools and families over how and when to discipline children with disabilities. This is particularly tough in the most difficult and violent cases," Cunningham told the House when it considered the bill in June 1996. "But we replace confusion with clarity and simplicity. We ensure safe classrooms and safe schools." The reauthorization of IDEA died in the Senate in the 104th, and Congress renewed work on it in 1997.

Cunningham's background made him a natural choice to serve on the National Security Committee and now on Appropriations' National Security Subcommittee. He is a former air combat instructor with two Silver Stars and 10 Air Medals. He has derided President Clinton for avoiding military service when he was younger, and he strongly supports GOP efforts to spend more on defense than the Clinton administration requests. Commenting on House passage of the fiscal 1997 defense bill, Cunningham said: "Unlike President Clinton's drastic defense cuts, our budget provides

CALIFORNIA 51
San Diego area — Northern county suburbs

The 51st reverses the pattern found throughout much of Southern California: In this case, as one moves inland from the coast, the political mood becomes more conservative, in part because of many coastal residents' emphasis on environmental issues.

This group of San Diego suburbs constitutes a very Republican district: Registered Republicans outnumber Democrats by about 20 points.

The Interstate 15 freeway runs north through the 51st's conservative areas like a spine, passing the Miramar Naval Air Station, Poway, Rancho Bernardo and Escondido. To the west, Interstate 5 heads north along the district's coastal communities: Del Mar, Encinitas and Carlsbad.

Del Mar is a small beach community, an overwhelming proportion of whose 5,000 residents are white non-Hispanics — 93 percent. Carlsbad, a city of 63,000 residents, grows and distributes most of the West Coast's fresh-cut flowers.

The 51st's beach communities have more permanent residents than others in the area. San Diego's primary tourist beaches are to the south, in the 49th District.

Moving inland, the Miramar Naval Air Station anchors the district's southern border. It is home to the Navy Fighter Weapons School — popularly known as the "Top Gun" pilot school — and former employer of Navy ace Rep. Cunningham (he was an instructor here). The air station employs 8,000 civilian and military personnel.

Up I-15 is Poway, an independent city of 44,000 surrounded by the city of San Diego. Poway has more of a rural, horsy feel to it than the surrounding suburban sprawl. Just north of Poway is an expanse of evenly developed suburbs that includes Rancho Bernardo, an area within San Diego's city limits that has attracted many retirees.

San Diego's relentless spread across the county has caught up to the old city of Escondido, farther north. With 109,000 residents, it is larger than some of the bedroom communities closer to San Diego, but its age gave it a head start on growth. East and north of Escondido are avocado and citrus orchards and a lot of land that speculators have bought.

The district also includes Rancho Santa Fe, where 39 members of the Heaven's Gate cult poisoned themselves to death in March 1997.

In 1996, Bob Dole took 52 percent of the district's presidential vote to Bill Clinton's 39 percent and Ross Perot's 7 percent. Perot was not much of a draw in the district after garnering 27 percent of the vote there in 1992.

Overall, Dole won San Diego County by slightly less than 13,000 votes. That paled in comparison with the nearly 200,000-vote margin George Bush enjoyed in 1988. But it was a bit of an improvement over Bush's 1992 showing, when he became the first GOP presidential candidate in four decades to lose the county.

1990 Population: 572,982. White 484,704 (85%), Black 10,225 (2%), Other 78,053 (14%). Hispanic origin 78,053 (14%). 18 and over 431,928 (75%), 62 and over 77,087 (13%). Median age: 33.

the level of spending the armed services told us they need to protect our nation."

He also praised the bill's provisions benefiting San Diego, noting that it provided $63.4 million for construction of 466 housing units for San Diego military families and $59.5 million for dredging at North Island Naval Aviation Depot to prepare for the homeporting of three nuclear aircraft carriers.

Cunningham also leaps to defend what he sees as the interests of the Navy. His passion on that score was evident during May 1995 House debate on a bill rewriting the nation's clean water laws. An amendment came up that would have stricken a provision exempting discharges from naval nuclear propulsion facilities from the definition of radioactive waste under the water pollution law.

Cunningham, who saw the amendment as a liberal Democratic attack on the military, said it was supported by "the same people that would vote to cut defense $177 billion, the same ones that would put homos in the military." When independent Rep. Bernard Sanders of Vermont demanded that Cunningham yield for a response, Cunningham said, "No, I will not. Sit down, you socialist." Cunningham half-heartedly apologized for the "homos" quote, saying, "I used the shorthand term, and it should have been homosexuals instead of homos. We do misspeak sometimes."

Cunningham was more contrite the next day, when he showed up at a news conference called by the Human Rights Campaign Fund, a homosexual rights group, at which other House members criticized his remark. "To me using that short term was not wrong, but if it is offensive then I apologize and I will not use it again," he said.

Prone to strong expressions of his views, Cunningham had a hand in earning the 104th Congress its reputation as one of the most uncivil in recent memory.

When the House debated a resolution in November 1995 blocking Clinton's plan to deploy 20,000 U.S. troops to Bosnia unless Congress approved funds for the deployment, Virginia Democrat James P. Moran blasted the bill as a politically motivated GOP attack on Clinton. Angry at Moran's statement, Cunningham and fellow California GOP Rep. Robert K. Dornan then engaged in a shoving match with Moran and California Democrat George Miller that spilled off the House floor into a hallway.

It irks Cunningham that Californians must foot a bigger tax bill for services such as health care, schools and law enforcement in part because of illegal immigration. He supported the 1994 state ballot initiative (Proposition 187) that denied nearly all public services to illegal immigrants. When the House in March 1996 passed an immigration bill that increased border patrols and denied certain federal benefits to illegal and legal immigrants, he called the bill "a victory for San Diegans."

The sponsor of a measure in the 104th that would make English the official language of the U.S. government, Cunningham called English a "unifying force" in America. Democrats decried the effort, saying the bill would prevent many people from understanding their government. Cunningham reintroduced the measure in the 105th.

At Home: Cunningham was elected to Congress on his first try for public office in 1990. His background as a career military officer, an educator and a businessman caught the eye of GOP Rep. Duncan Hunter, who represented an adjoining district and recruited Cunningham to challenge Democratic Rep. Jim Bates in 1990, when Bates was battling primary challengers and charges of sexually harassing women on his staff.

The old 44th District included most of San Diego proper, including the central city, and Cunningham did not even live in it when he decided to run. But he left his beach home in exclusive Del Mar and bought a home in the older, middle-class suburb of Chula Vista to take a shot at Bates.

Despite the appeal of his military credentials in the Navy-oriented precincts of the 44th, Cunningham appeared too conservative for a district with just 34 percent GOP registration and most of the minority voters in the San Diego area.

He targeted both evangelical Christians and older, conservative Democrats to supplement the district's base GOP vote. It worked just well enough, as he eased past the scandal-marred Bates by fewer than 2,000 votes.

In 1992, redistricting renumbered the 44th as the 50th and left it almost as Democratic as before. The new map also had three solidly Republican districts in the San Diego area, one of which, the 51st, included Cunningham's old home in Del Mar. The problem was that the new 51st also included Rep. Bill Lowery, a GOP colleague of Cunningham's.

Although he had a decade of seniority on Cunningham, Lowery also had some political liabilities. He had fallen below 50 percent of the vote in 1990, and that was before revelations that he had written 300 overdrafts at the House bank.

Once Cunningham set plans to seek a new base in his old stomping grounds, Lowery retired. Cunningham won nomination and election in his new district with little trouble, and he has soared through re-election since.

HOUSE ELECTIONS

1996 General		
Randy "Duke" Cunningham (R)	149,032	(65%)
Rita Tamerius (D)	66,250	(29%)
Miriam E. Clark (PFP)	5,407	(2%)
J.C. "Jack" Anderson (LIBERT)	5,298	(2%)
Eric Hunter Bourdette (NL)	3,037	(1%)
1996 Primary		
Randy "Duke" Cunningham (R)	65,268	(86%)
Donald J. Pando (R)	10,502	(14%)
1994 General		
Randy "Duke" Cunningham (R)	138,547	(67%)
Rita K. Tamerius (D)	57,374	(28%)
Bill Holmes (LIBERT)	6,968	(3%)
Miriam E. Clark (PFP)	4,099	(2%)

Previous Winning Percentages: 1992 (56%) **1990** (46%)

CAMPAIGN FINANCE

	Receipts	Receipts from PACs	Expend-itures
1996			
Cunningham (R)	$734,663	$327,231 (45%)	$425,525
Tamerius (D)	$20,901	$2,000 (10%)	$19,935
1994			
Cunningham (R)	$495,226	$225,028 (45%)	$395,144
Tamerius (D)	$66,960	$13,942 (21%)	$65,035

DISTRICT VOTE FOR PRESIDENT

1996		1992	
D	97,128 (39%)	**D**	86,870 (32%)
R	130,459 (52%)	**R**	108,470 (40%)
I	16,963 (7%)	**I**	73,580 (27%)

KEY VOTES

1997	
Ban "partial birth" abortions	Y
1996	
Approve farm bill	Y
Deny public education to illegal immigrants	Y
Repeal ban on certain assault-style weapons	?
Increase minimum wage	N
Freeze defense spending	?
Approve welfare overhaul	Y
1995	
Approve balanced-budget constitutional amendment	Y
Relax Clean Water Act regulations	Y
Oppose limits on environmental regulations	N
Reduce projected Medicare spending	Y
Approve GOP budget with tax and spending cuts	Y

VOTING STUDIES

	Presidential Support		Party Unity		Conservative Coalition	
Year	S	O	S	O	S	O
1996	30	67	93	5	84	8
1995	18	80	96	4	94	5
1994	55	45	90	9	94	6
1993	30	70	96	2	98	2
1992	82	13	91	4	96	2
1991	78	22	89	9	97	3

INTEREST GROUP RATINGS

Year	ADA	AFL-CIO	CCUS	ACU
1996	10	n/a	81	100
1995	0	0	100	92
1994	15	22	100	95
1993	0	0	91	100
1992	5	17	75	96
1991	5	17	90	95

52 Duncan Hunter (R)

Of El Cajon — Elected 1980, 9th term

Biographical Information
Born: May 31, 1948, Riverside, Calif.
Education: U. of Montana, 1966-67; U. of California, Santa Barbara, 1967-68; Western State U., B.S.L. 1976, J.D. 1976.
Military Service: Army, 1969-71.
Occupation: Lawyer.
Family: Wife, Lynne Layh; two children.
Religion: Baptist.
Political Career: No previous office.

Capitol Office. 2265 Rayburn Bldg. 20515; 225-5672.

Committees
National Security
Military Procurement (chairman); Military Readiness

In Washington: Defeated in his bid to move up in the Republican leadership after his party won the House majority in 1994, Hunter refocused his energy to the National Security Committee, where he chairs the Military Procurement Subcommittee.

Hunter has been on National Security (formerly Armed Services) since he joined the House in 1981, and now, at a comparatively young age (he turns 50 in 1998), he is the panel's No. 3 Republican. The two men above him, Chairman Floyd D. Spence of South Carolina and Arizona's Bob Stump, are both two decades older.

Hunter is an aggressive promoter of spending more on defense than the Clinton administration desires. This stance is good politics in the 52nd District, where defense-related work is an important part of the employment base.

When National Security began work on the fiscal 1996 defense authorization bill, Hunter led the debate over the future design of new submarines. He saw the Navy as unwilling to explore technologies that, in his view, could yield a less costly and more effective sub design than the Navy was planning to pursue in its new-generation subs beginning in fiscal 1998.

The committee turned down the Navy's plan to buy all its submarines from General Dynamics' Electric Boat Division in Groton, Conn., which only builds subs. Instead, the committee backed a plan aimed at setting the stage for long-term competition between the two U.S. commercial shipyards that build nuclear-powered ships — Electric Boat and Newport News (Va.) Shipbuilding and Dry Dock, which builds subs, aircraft carriers and non-nuclear commercial ships.

In the final version of the defense funding bill, Congress ordered the Navy to buy one new sub from Groton in fiscal 1998 and fiscal 2000 and a new sub from Newport News in 1999 and 2001, after which it should award future sub contracts on the basis of competition. And, at the insistence of Hunter, the defense bill ordered the Navy to encourage design innovations in each of the four subs. In early 1997, the shipyards announced that at the Navy's urging they would work cooperatively on the four new attack subs, rather than each shipyard building a separate ship.

When the House turned in June 1996 to the fiscal 1997 defense spending bill, Hunter squared off against the Appropriations Committee's ranking member, Wisconsin Democrat David R. Obey, who wanted to reduce the spending levels in the bill. Obey offered an amendment — in part a jab at Hunter — that would have barred the expenditure of funds for any congressional add-on for which the Pentagon had no officially defined "requirement," and for which the jobs created would cost more than $100,000 apiece. This second point was to be calculated using Pentagon data, assembled at Hunter's request, which summarized the number of jobs created in each congressional district for each added project.

Hunter, a decorated Vietnam War veteran, responded that Congress has the right and the competence to make independent judgments on military expenditures. He noted, for instance, that Congress had funded more F-117 stealth fighters than the Pentagon had requested, and those aircraft played a key role in the 1991 war with Iraq. "Sometimes, as in the case of the F-117, Congress is right," Hunter said. Obey's amendment was rejected 101-319.

Hunter also went to bat for continued production of the B-2 "stealth" bomber. He fought an amendment, backed by many House "deficit hawks," to the fiscal 1996 authorization bill that would have deleted $553 million that the committee added to buy components that could be used to build two additional B-2s, if the plane was funded in the next fiscal year. The Clinton administration and senior military brass insisted that they had other, more urgent uses for added defense funds.

But avid B-2 proponents like Hunter and Washington state Democrat Norm Dicks touted the plane as a weapon of revolutionary potential because of its combination of radar-evading design, long range and a huge payload of highly accurate bombs. The amendment killing the B-2 funds was rejected, 203-219, in June 1995.

CALIFORNIA 52
Inland San Diego and Imperial counties

The 52nd is California's far southeastern corner, including the whole of Imperial County and about half of San Diego County's land area. A vast barren area in the middle of the district divides its two main population concentrations — a suburban west and an agricultural east.

The bulk of the district's San Diego County residents are in three suburban cities on the western edge of the 52nd: El Cajon is the largest of the three with 89,000 residents, La Mesa's population is 53,000 and Spring Valley's is 56,000. Economically, La Mesa is a bit better off than the other two, and votes a bit more Democratic, but otherwise the three cities are very similar.

These suburbs have a mix of blue and white collars, with many defense workers and a lot of military personnel; the important role of the military-industrial complex in San Diego's economy contributes significantly to the conservative tenor of the area.

East along the 8 Freeway out of El Cajon are mountains, followed by a different type of mountains that consist mostly of boulders piled on boulders. This area is the Anza-Borrego Desert State Park, which looks to the casual observer less like a nature refuge than a rock refuge.

The huge Salton Sea just east of the park used to be a terrific fishing and recreational area, but agricultural runoff has increased the sea's salinity level above that of the Pacific Ocean, and that has killed most of the fish.

Beyond the park, the land flattens into desert. The district's agricultural sector begins a few miles before El Centro, Imperial County's largest city with 31,000 residents. Everything east is agriculture.

This is the Imperial Valley — known as the "salad bowl of the country" — and it lives and dies on farming. During the recession of the early 1990s, its unemployment at one point soared to 33 percent.

Like California as a whole, the Imperial Valley area has had more than its share of tough luck lately: A plague of white flies devastated crops in the early 1990s, then there were floods, followed by more flies.

The region depends on the increasingly overtaxed Colorado River for its lifeblood: water. The river defines the California-Arizona border on the district's eastern edge, and water issues dominate the farmers' political attention. The importance of irrigation is vividly evident here; along some roads, stark desert lies on one side while plush alfalfa fields flank the other.

Heavily Republican San Diego continues to make the 52nd a GOP stronghold. The district is more than one-fifth Hispanic, and about 3 percent each black and Asian.

Bob Dole won the 52nd in 1996, with 48 percent of the vote to Bill Clinton's 41 percent and Ross Perot's 8 percent. Clinton actually won Imperial County in both 1992 and 1996, but the effect was muted; San Diego County casts almost 90 percent of the district's ballots.

1990 Population: 573,203. White 479,206 (84%), Black 17,788 (3%), Other 76,209 (13%). Hispanic origin 129,771 (23%). 18 and over 415,866 (73%), 62 and over 75,381 (13%). Median age: 31.

Hunter argues for more restrictions on illegal immigration, an issue of great concern to his Southern California district. He voted for GOP measures in the 104th to curb federal services for both legal and illegal immigrants, and supported a GOP proposal to deny public education to illegal immigrants. He also has pushed for a more visible barrier to stop immigrants from coming over the Mexican border — the erection of a triple fence.

Hunter was able to get some federal funds for two more fences along the 14-mile stretch of border from the Pacific Ocean to Otay Mesa, known as "Smugglers Alley," in the final agreement on a broad immigration bill that cleared Congress in September 1996. The area currently has a 10-foot-tall steel fence built largely by the California National Guard.

The union of Border Patrol agents opposed the idea, claiming it would present safety problems to agents. "I think the triple fence would be a lot safer than having agents doing what they do now: searching the swamps of the Tijuana River at night looking for illegal aliens," Hunter told the Los Angeles Times.

It is on trade issues that Hunter veers farthest from most of his Republican colleagues. He has frequently called for tough measures to reduce the United States' trade imbalance with Japan. And, although his district takes in most of California's border with Mexico, Hunter voted against both NAFTA and GATT. In 1996, he and Ohio Democrat Marcy Kaptur coauthored the NAFTA Accountability Act, which would require a reassessment of the impact of NAFTA and pave the way for the renegotiation of certain portions of the agreement.

Hunter's shot at a leadership spot came in 1994 when he gave up his position as head of the Research Committee to run for chairman of the Republican Conference. He lost, 102-122, to Ohio Republican John A. Boehner, who came to Congress 10 years after Hunter. Boehner quickly had established himself as a leader of junior Republicans when he led an effort to force

Democrats to disclose names of members who had overdrafts at the House bank.

One of those members was Hunter, who had run up 399 overdrafts at the House bank. Hunter was not helped by having released earlier estimates that understated his involvement.

A leader of the Conservative Opportunity Society (COS), founded by Newt Gingrich of Georgia in the early 1980s, Hunter was elected chairman of the House Republican Research Committee in 1989 — the same year Gingrich became minority whip. Hunter stuck by his old friend in January 1997, casting one of 26 Republican votes against recommending that Gingrich be reprimanded and assessed a $300,000 penalty for violating ethics rules.

At Home: Hunter has an unusual background for a conservative Republican. For the three years before his initial House campaign, he lived and worked in the Hispanic section of San Diego. Running his own storefront law office, Hunter often gave free legal advice to poor people. When former President Ronald Reagan called for abolition of the Legal Services Corporation, Hunter was one of the dissenters.

Hunter's work in the usually Democratic inner city helped produce his 1980 upset victory over Democrat Lionel Van Deerlin, a nine-term House veteran. Another reason was Hunter's ceaseless campaigning. He made endless rounds of the compact district, popping up at defense plants and on street corners, shaking 1,000 hands every day while Van Deerlin remained in Washington, assuming he would score a comfortable victory.

Hunter, who won a Bronze Star for participating in 25 helicopter combat assaults in Vietnam, blasted at what he called Van Deerlin's "anti-defense" record. He promised his own pro-Pentagon stance would keep jobs in the San Diego area, which boasts the nation's largest naval base and numerous defense industries. The message helped propel Hunter to a 53 percent majority.

Before Democrats had a chance to prove that win a fluke, the redistricting plan for 1982 gave Hunter a safely Republican seat. He won re-election with 69 percent that year and did better yet through the remainder of the decade. District Democrats did not even field a candidate in 1990.

Life got more complicated in 1992. Redistricting made Hunter move his home, but it left his base relatively intact (his district lost its coastline but still starts in metropolitan San Diego and runs east all the way to Arizona). GOP registration slipped to 46 percent, but California Republicans rarely lose a district where their registration is higher than 40 percent. Hunter's real problems stemmed from his 399 overdrafts at the House bank. Janet M. Gastil, a former school board member, got the Democratic nomination unopposed. Armed with the overdrafts issue, the relatively underfunded challenger kept Hunter on the defensive and held him to 53 percent.

Gastil was back in 1994 but the timing was no longer right; Hunter outpolled her 2-1, and he had an easy ride in 1996, winning by 35 points.

HOUSE ELECTIONS

1996 General		
Duncan Hunter (R)	116,746	(65%)
Darity Wesley (D)	53,104	(30%)
Janice Jordan (PFP)	3,649	(2%)
Dante Ridley (LIBERT)	3,329	(2%)
1994 General		
Duncan Hunter (R)	109,201	(64%)
Janet M. Gastil (D)	53,024	(31%)
Joe Shea (LIBERT)	5,240	(3%)
Art Edelman (PFP)	3,221	(2%)

Previous Winning Percentages: 1992 (53%) **1990** (73%) **1988** (74%) **1986** (77%) **1984** (75%) **1982** (69%) **1980** (53%)

CAMPAIGN FINANCE

	Receipts	Receipts from PACs		Expend-itures
1996				
Hunter (R)	$605,890	$264,902	(44%)	$632,305
Wesley (D)	$40,183	$3,500	(9%)	$40,178
1994				
Hunter (R)	$579,526	$191,721	(33%)	$559,926
Gastil (D)	$181,683	$12,867	(7%)	$181,855
Edelman (PFP)	$6,892	$1,000	(15%)	$6,891

DISTRICT VOTE FOR PRESIDENT

	1996		1992
D	81,401 (41%)	**D**	74,913 (34%)
R	94,035 (48%)	**R**	81,421 (37%)
I	16,657 (8%)	**I**	63,176 (29%)

KEY VOTES

1997	
Ban "partial birth" abortions	Y
1996	
Approve farm bill	Y
Deny public education to illegal immigrants	Y
Repeal ban on certain assault-style weapons	Y
Increase minimum wage	N
Freeze defense spending	N
Approve welfare overhaul	Y
1995	
Approve balanced-budget constitutional amendment	Y
Relax Clean Water Act regulations	Y
Oppose limits on environmental regulations	N
Reduce projected Medicare spending	Y
Approve GOP budget with tax and spending cuts	Y

VOTING STUDIES

	Presidential Support		Party Unity		Conservative Coalition	
Year	S	O	S	O	S	O
1996	29	68	91	4	96	2
1995	16	81	91	4	95	2
1994	33	67	88	6	92	6
1993	25	71	91	2	86	5
1992	80	19	90	6	98	2
1991	80	16	84	6	92	5

INTEREST GROUP RATINGS

Year	ADA	AFL-CIO	CCUS	ACU
1996	10	n/a	94	100
1995	0	0	91	88
1994	0	33	73	100
1993	5	8	91	100
1992	15	27	88	100
1991	5	27	78	100

COLORADO

Governor: Roy Romer (D)
First elected: 1986
Length of term: 4 years
Term expires: 1/99
Salary: $70,000
Term limit: 2 terms
Phone: (303) 866-2471
Born: Oct. 31, 1928; Garden City, Kan.
Education: Colorado State U., B.S. 1950; U. of Colorado, LL.B. 1952; Yale U., 1954.
Military Service: Air Force, 1952-53.
Occupation: Lawyer.
Family: Wife, Bea Miller; seven children.
Religion: Presbyterian.
Political Career: Colo. House, 1959-63; Colo. Senate, 1963-67; Democratic nominee for U.S. Senate, 1966; Colo. commissioner of agriculture, 1975; chief of staff to Gov. Richard Lamm, 1975-77; Colo. treasurer, 1977-87

* *Romer is ineligible to serve a fourth term; when he leaves office in 1999, a new two-term limit takes effect.*

Lt. Gov.: Gail Schoettler (D)
First elected: 1994
Length of term: 4 years
Term expires: 1/99
Salary: $48,500
Phone: (303) 866-2087
State election official: (303) 894-2200
Democratic headquarters: (303) 830-8989
Republican headquarters: (303) 893-1776

REDISTRICTING

Colorado retained its six House seats in reapportionment. The legislature passed the new map March 19, 1992; the governor signed it March 24.

STATE LEGISLATURE

General Assembly. Meets January-May.

Senate: 35 members, 4-year terms
1996 breakdown: 20R, 15D; 25 men, 10 women
Salary: $17,500
Phone: (303) 866-2316

House of Representatives: 65 members, 2-year terms
1996 breakdown: 41R, 24D; 41 men, 24 women
Salary: $17,500
Phone: (303) 866-2904

URBAN STATISTICS

City	Population
Denver	467,610
Mayor Wellington E. Webb, D	
Colorado Springs	281,140
Mayor Robert M. Isaac, R	
Aurora	222,103
Mayor Paul E. Tauer, N-P	
Lakewood	126,481
Mayor Linda Morton, N-P	
Pueblo	98,640
Councilman Cathy Garcia	

U.S. CONGRESS

Senate: 0 D, 2 R
House: 2 D, 4 R

TERM LIMITS

For state offices: Yes
Senate: 2 consecutive terms, effective 1991
House: 4 consecutive terms, effective 1991

ELECTIONS

1996 Presidential Vote

Bob Dole	46%
Bill Clinton	44%
Ross Perot	7%

1992 Presidential Vote

Bill Clinton	40%
George Bush	36%
Ross Perot	23%

1988 Presidential Vote

George Bush	53%
Michael S. Dukakis	45%

POPULATION

1990 population		3,294,394
1980 population		2,889,964
Percent change		+14%
Rank among states:		26
White		88%
Black		4%
Hispanic		13%
Asian or Pacific islander		2%
Urban		82%
Rural		18%
Born in state		43%
Foreign-born		4%
Under age 18	861,266	26%
Ages 18-64	2,103,685	64%
65 and older	329,443	10%
Median age		32.5

MISCELLANEOUS

Capital: Denver
Number of counties: 63
Per capita income: $19,440 (1991)
Rank among states: 14
Total area: 104,091 sq. miles
Rank among states: 8

COLORADO

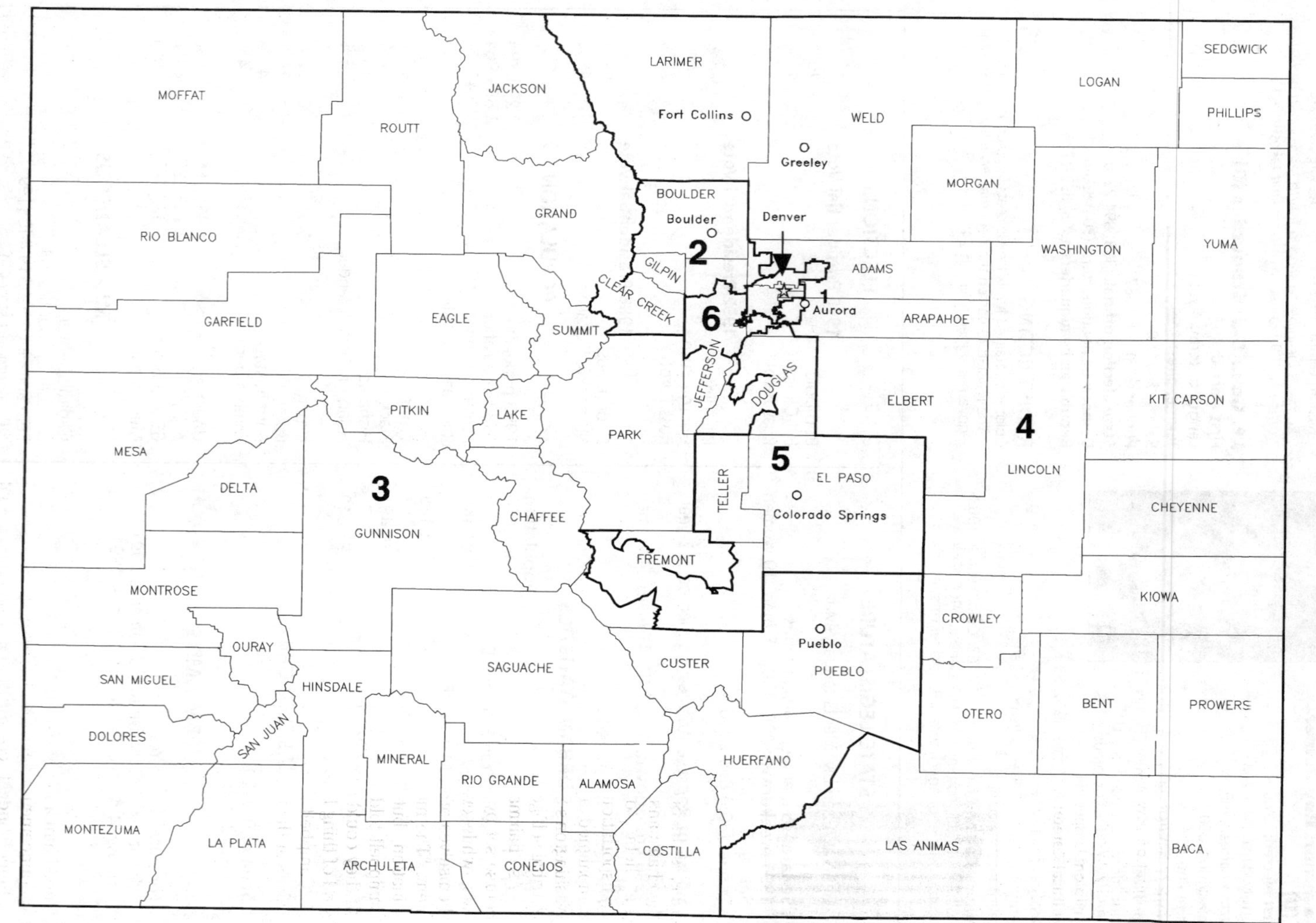

MOFFAT
ROUTT
JACKSON
LARIMER
Fort Collins
WELD
LOGAN
SEDGWICK
PHILLIPS
Greeley
RIO BLANCO
GRAND
BOULDER
Boulder
Denver
MORGAN
WASHINGTON
YUMA
2
GILPIN
CLEAR CREEK
ADAMS
1
Aurora
ARAPAHOE
GARFIELD
EAGLE
SUMMIT
6
JEFFERSON
DOUGLAS
ELBERT
KIT CARSON
PITKIN
LAKE
PARK
4
LINCOLN
MESA
DELTA
3
5
TELLER
EL PASO
Colorado Springs
CHEYENNE
GUNNISON
CHAFFEE
FREMONT
MONTROSE
KIOWA
CROWLEY
OURAY
Pueblo
SAGUACHE
CUSTER
PUEBLO
SAN MIGUEL
HINSDALE
OTERO
BENT
PROWERS
DOLORES
SAN JUAN
MINERAL
RIO GRANDE
ALAMOSA
HUERFANO
MONTEZUMA
LA PLATA
ARCHULETA
CONEJOS
COSTILLA
LAS ANIMAS
BACA

Ben Nighthorse Campbell (R)

Of Ignacio — Elected 1992, 1st term

Biographical Information

Born: April 13, 1933, Auburn, Calif.

Education: San Jose State U., B.A. 1957; Meiji U. (Tokyo, Japan), 1960-64.

Military Service: Air Force, 1951-53.

Occupation: Jewelry designer; rancher; horse trainer; teacher.

Family: Wife, Linda Price; two children.

Religion: Unspecified.

Political Career: Colo. House, 1983-87; U.S. House, 1987-93.

Capitol Office: 380 Russell Bldg. 20510; 224-5852.

Committees

Appropriations
Commerce, Justice, State & Judiciary; Foreign Operations; Interior; Treasury & General Government (chairman); VA, HUD & Independent Agencies

Energy & Natural Resources
Energy Research Development Production & Regulation; National Parks, Historic Preservation & Recreation; Water & Power

Indian Affairs (chairman)

Veterans' Affairs

In Washington: Less than two years after breaking with his Democratic colleagues and switching to the Republican Party, Campbell at the start of the 105th Congress found himself in an influential position over a subject of deep personal concern as chairman of the Senate Committee on Indian Affairs.

Campbell, a member of the Northern Cheyenne tribe, is the Senate's only American Indian. He got the chairmanship after Arizona's John McCain took the helm of the Commerce, Science and Transportation Committee, and after Indian groups campaigned against the next Republican in line, Washington's Slade Gorton, whom they see as a foe of tribal self-government.

As chairman, Campbell intends to continue the course set by McCain in championing tribal interests, while encouraging them to gradually wean themselves of their reliance on the federal government. "The movement has been toward self-determination, but it was limited self-determination," Campbell told The Washington Post in early 1997. "If they could handle it, they could do it. That's the kind of thing I support."

Campbell isn't known for bantering with journalists at the Capitol or for actively seeking the legislative spotlight. His new chairmanship affords him an opportunity to get more recognition for his Senate work. His outside interests are perhaps better known: Campbell drew attention in 1996 for posing astride his Harley-Davidson motorcycle in a Banana Republic clothing ad and for organizing a "Bikers for Dole" rally of motorcyclists at the Republican National Convention.

His decision to join the GOP in March 1995 guaranteed him a moment in the national spotlight. His announcement came the day after he voted for a balanced-budget constitutional amendment that failed to win Senate passage; he decided he no longer was comfortable calling himself a Democrat.

The switch infuriated and dismayed Democrats. But on announcing his new party affiliation, Campbell underscored that he would continue on an independent course. "I have always been considered a moderate, much to the consternation of the Democratic Party," Campbell said. "My moderacy will now be to the consternation of the right wing of the Republican Party."

In keeping with that statement, Campbell did express strong support for the successful Democratic attempt in the spring of 1996 to raise the minimum wage, a proposal many other Republicans initially resisted.

But he joined the conservative camp on some other high-profile issues. In September 1996, after being injured in a motorcycle accident that left him hospitalized, he announced his support of efforts to override President Clinton's veto of a bill banning an abortion technique that opponents call a "partial-birth" abortion. Although declaring his continued support of a woman's right to abortion, Campbell said in a statement read on the Senate floor that after talking with hospital workers he met while recuperating from his accident, he had concluded the particular procedure was "an atrocity."

Campbell has long been at odds with the Clinton administration's efforts to boost grazing fees and mining royalties on federally owned lands. Soon after starting his Senate career in 1993, Campbell was among a group of Western Democrats arguing that the plan would work a hardship on ranchers and miners and depress an already weak economy.

Campbell attracted the support of several Western senators for a bill he proposed to limit the grazing fee increase to 25 percent. The bill, which was unsuccessful, drew criticism from environmentalists and lawmakers who said it would not generate a fair return for public land use. When Interior Secretary Bruce Babbitt came out with a series of new regulations in May 1995 governing conditions for ranchers on grazing land, Campbell attacked the Interior plan as "a misconstrued proposal based on divisiveness, arrogance, emotion and politics."

Campbell's switch to the GOP was followed by an assignment to the Appropriations Committee, where he has looked after Colorado's military bases and its war veterans in his roles on the military construction and veterans' affairs subcommittees. In July 1996, he thwarted an attempt to kill the Animas-

La Plata water project in southwestern Colorado, which critics derided as an environmentally harmful boondoggle. Campbell and others framed the debate around keeping the government's word to Indian tribes who would get the project's water.

At Home: After "pretty seriously" mulling a bid for Colorado governor in 1998, Campbell decided in early 1997 to run for the Senate again. "A lot of people convinced me I ought to stay where I am," he said. "I've got seniority now and chairmanship of a committee, and I can make a little more impact here."

Campbell, a third-term House member when he ran for the Senate in 1992, won the Democratic nomination over two well-known rivals, former Gov. Richard D. Lamm and former Boulder County Commissioner Josie Heath, the unsuccessful 1990 Senate nominee.

Campbell entered the general election race with a wide lead over GOP nominee Terry Considine, a businessman and a former state senator who had championed a term-limits ballot initiative Coloradans passed in 1990. Considine narrowed the gap with ads criticizing Campbell's low-voting attendance record in congressional committees and highlighting a trip by Campbell and his wife to Alaska, paid for by Chevron Oil.

Campbell struck back with TV spots that questioned Considine's dealings with the failed Silverado Banking, Savings & Loan Association. Both candidates ran afoul of previous statements on their military service records, but Campbell's misstep seemed particularly embarrassing. He had to correct a statement in his campaign literature that said he had been trapped behind enemy lines in Korea for five weeks. Campbell acknowledged that such an incident never happened while he served in Korea with the Air Force police.

The core of Campbell's campaign was his compelling life story. His father was an alcoholic, and his mother suffered from tuberculosis. He dropped out of high school, served in the Air Force and worked his way through college driving a truck before finding success as an Olympian — he was on the U.S. judo team at the 1964 Games — a craftsman of contemporary Indian jewelry and a cattle rancher in southwest Colorado. Considine managed to run well ahead of George Bush, who lost Colorado, but Campbell prevailed by 9 percentage points.

Campbell began his political career in 1982, winning a conservative-minded state House district. During four years in the legislature, he was a dependable vote for farmers and ranchers on water rights. Though he occasionally sided with environmentalists, Campbell's views put him among conservatives in the Democratic Caucus.

That positioned Campbell well for his 1986 challenge to GOP Rep. Mike Strang. "People are sick and tired of plastic politicians — professional politicians who have done nothing else with their lives," Campbell said. He won by drawing a big vote in blue-collar Pueblo and holding his own on the conservative Western Slope.

Campbell quickly established himself and won two easy re-elections before making his move for the Senate in 1992.

SENATE ELECTIONS

1992 General*		
Ben Nighthorse Campbell (D)	803,725	(52%)
Terry Considine (R)	662,893	(43%)
Richard O. Grimes (PI)	42,455	(3%)
Matt Noah (CPL)	22,846	(1%)
Dan Winters (I)	20,347	(1%)

Previous Winning Percentages: 1990* (70%) **1988*** (78%) **1986*** (52%)

** Campbell was elected to the House and Senate as a Democrat. He switched to the Republican Party in March 1995.*

CAMPAIGN FINANCE

	Receipts	Receipts from PACs	Expend-itures
1992			
Campbell (D)	$1,594,544	$741,686 (47%)	$1,561,347
Considine (R)	$2,704,514	$428,319 (16%)	$2,645,791
Noah (CPL)	$88,174	$3,000 (3%)	$79,293

KEY VOTES

1997	
Approve balanced-budget constitutional amendment	Y
Approve chemical weapons treaty	N
1996	
Approve farm bill	Y
Limit punitive damages in product liability cases	Y
Exempt small businesses from higher minimum wage	N
Approve welfare overhaul	Y
Bar job discrimination based on sexual orientation	N
Override veto of ban on "partial birth" abortions	+
1995	
Approve GOP budget with tax and spending cuts	Y
Approve constitutional amendment barring flag desecration	Y

VOTING STUDIES

	Presidential Support		Party Unity		Conservative Coalition	
Year	**S**	**O**	**S**	**O**	**S**	**O**
1996	42	46	76	16	79	13
1995†	38	62	79	20	79	19
1994	81	16	74	21	44	47
1993	82	17	77	19	46	51
House Service:						
1992	27	45	57	15	42	17
1991	34	56	75	21	62	24

† Campbell switched to the Republican Party on March 3, 1995. As a Democrat in 1995 he was eligible for three presidential support votes, 72 party unity votes, and four conservative coalition votes. As a Republican in 1995 he was eligible for 99 presidential support votes, 350 party unity votes, and 53 conservative coalition votes. His presidential support and conservative coalition scores for 1995 include votes he cast both as a Democrat and a Republican. His 1995 party unity scores reflect votes he cast as a Republican. As a Democrat his party unity support score was 47 percent and his opposition score was 51 percent.

INTEREST GROUP RATINGS

Year	ADA	AFL-CIO	CCUS	ACU
1996	45	n/a	82	78
1995	30	22	94	59
1994	55	88	44	25
1993	75	80	18	12
House Service:				
1992	55	71	43	38
1991	55	92	40	45

Wayne Allard (R)

Of Loveland — Elected 1996, 1st term

Biographical Information

Born: Dec. 2, 1943, Fort Collins, Colo.
Education: Colorado State U., D.V.M. 1968.
Occupation: Veterinarian.
Family: Wife, Joan Malcolm; two children.
Religion: Protestant.
Political Career: Colo. Senate, 1983-91; U.S. House, 1991-97.
Capitol Office: 513 Hart Bldg. 20510; 224-5941.

Committees

Banking, Housing & Urban Affairs
Financial Institutions & Regulatory Relief; Housing Opportunity & Community Development; Securities
Environment & Public Works
Clean Air, Wetlands, Private Property & Nuclear Safety; Superfund, Waste Control & Risk Assessment
Select Intelligence

The Path to Washington: Allard is the latest in a line of recently elected Western GOP senators who combine an amiable personal manner with staunchly conservative views. Like Idaho's Dirk Kempthorne and Wyoming's Craig Thomas, he hopes to curb the federal government's spending and authority while protecting his state's rural residents and industries.

Allard entered the Senate after compiling a solidly conservative record during three terms in the House. He advocated eliminating the departments of Education, Energy and Commerce, he spoke up for gunowners' rights, and he supported a constitutional amendment banning abortion under most circumstances. He pushed for moving responsibilities from the federal government to the states, and he sought to curb "unfunded mandates" — requirements handed down by the federal government without providing states the funds to meet them.

Early in his Senate tenure, Allard got to weigh in on another cause he had backed in the House: a balanced-budget constitutional amendment. He voted for the measure in March 1997, but it fell short of the two-thirds' majority needed for passage.

Colorado-born Allard, who grew up on a ranch and went on to become a large-animal veterinarian, brings his Westerner's perspective to the Senate Environment and Public Works Committee, which grapples with numerous issues that stir controversy in the West, including the federal government's management of public lands, and the balancing of environmental protection with the rights of private property owners.

As a member of the Resources Committee when he served in the House, Allard in 1994 tried unsuccessfully to eliminate funding for the National Biological Survey, a field census intended to assist scientists in protecting threatened species by keeping tabs on their population levels. Allard feared that it would expand the scope of the Endangered Species Act and objected to letting government officials prowl on private land. He repeated his attacks on the renamed National Biological Service in 1995.

Allard also crossed swords with the Forest Service when the agency required the release of water for wetlands preservation before granting special use permits to local and private entities that control water in Colorado. Allard saw that as another infringement of property rights.

Allard was one of eight House members — four Republicans and four Democrats — elected to the Senate in 1996. His victory over Democratic nominee Tom Strickland enabled the GOP to retain the Senate seat of retiring Hank Brown.

The contest to replace Brown was a top priority for both national parties, and Democrats and Republicans staged competitive primaries.

Colorado Democrats, smarting from the 1995 defection of the state's other senator, Ben Nighthorse Campbell, to the GOP, were eager to win back a seat.

As Colorado's complex system of nominating congressional candidates — including local and state party assemblies — unfolded and other candidates dropped out, the August GOP primary became a showdown between Allard, from the mainly rural 4th District in eastern Colorado, and state Attorney General Gale Norton.

She had better statewide name recognition, although Allard drew a measure of attention in the 104th as chairman of a House Agriculture subcommittee, and he led in fundraising.

Both touted their conservative views. But Norton hoped to attract support from moderates with her support for abortion rights, contrasting her position with Allard's.

Allard portrayed himself as a down-to-earth, common-sense lawmaker who keeps his political career in perspective. He has kept his veterinary license current even though he sold his practice in the early 1990s. Allard won the nomination with a comfortable 57 percent tally, continuing a summer 1996 trend in which abortion opponents prevailed over more moderate rivals in GOP primary contests — not only in Colorado, but also in Georgia and Kansas.

Allard then headed into a contentious general-election contest against Strickland, who had survived a nasty Democratic primary.

A lawyer with a prominent Denver firm, Strickland accused Allard of having one of the most extreme voting records in Congress and of being beholden to campaign contributions from tobacco companies and gun lobbyists.

In a televised debate, Allard caused a stir when he responded affirmatively to a hypothetical question about whether he would support public hangings to deter crime.

The League of Conservation Voters targeted Allard for defeat, citing his votes on bills involving water and air pollution, the use of public lands and citizens' right to know about toxic chemical releases. Allard brushed off such criticisms, saying his interest is in promoting environmental policies based upon "sound science" instead of emotional appeals.

Allard attacked Strickland as a wealthy corporate lobbyist who made his fortune defending clients with environmental problems. And he sought to deflect the "extremism" charge by citing his ability as a House member to work with liberals such as Rep. Patricia Schroeder, D-Colo.

Allard's campaign drew strong support from conservative Christian groups. A state ballot initiative giving parents the "inalienable" right to control their children's education helped spur turnout in the Senate race; it was supported by Allard and conservative Christian activists.

But perhaps the most effective pitch Allard used was asking Colorado voters whether they wanted a veterinarian or a lawyer-lobbyist to represent them in the Senate. Allard won with 51 percent of the vote, 5 percentage points ahead of Strickland.

Allard's other Senate committee assignments are Banking, Housing and Urban Affairs, and Select Intelligence. (In April 1997, he was one of 26 Republican senators to vote against ratifying the Chemical Weapons Convention.)

The 1996 election contest was not the first time Allard succeeded in following Brown. In 1990, after eight years of dividing his time between the Colorado Senate and his Loveland veterinary practice, Allard seemed on the verge of retiring from politics. But Brown, who was then representing the 4th District, decided to run for the Senate, which opened the way for Allard.

SENATE ELECTIONS

1996 General		
Wayne Allard (R)	750,325	(51%)
Tom Strickland (D)	677,600	(46%)
Randy MacKenzie (NL)	41,620	(3%)
1996 Primary		
Wayne Allard (R)	115,064	(57%)
Gale Ann Norton (R)	87,394	(43%)

Previous Winning Percentages: 1994* (72%) **1992*** (58%) **1990*** (54%)

** House election*

KEY VOTES

1997	
Approve balanced-budget constitutional amendment	Y
Approve chemical weapons treaty	N
House Service:	
1996	
Approve farm bill	Y
Deny public education to illegal immigrants	Y
Increase minimum wage	N
Freeze defense spending	N
Approve welfare overhaul	Y
1995	
Approve balanced-budget constitutional amendment	Y
Relax Clean Water Act regulations	Y
Oppose limits on environmental regulations	N
Reduce projected Medicare spending	Y
Approve GOP budget with tax and spending cuts	Y

CAMPAIGN FINANCE

	Receipts	Receipts from PACs		Expend-itures
1996				
Allard (R)	$2,198,131	$1,061,594	(48%)	$2,233,429
Strickland (D)	$3,313,065	$395,145	(12%)	$3,294,915

VOTING STUDIES

	Presidential Support		Party Unity		Conservative Coalition	
Year	**S**	**O**	**S**	**O**	**S**	**O**
House Service:						
1996	34	61	90	6	94	4
1995	20	79	94	5	92	5
1994	40	60	96	3	94	6
1993	20	80	92	7	73	27
1992	84	14	92	4	83	17
1991	80	20	94	6	95	5

INTEREST GROUP RATINGS

Year	**ADA**	**AFL-CIO**	**CCUS**	**ACU**
House Service:				
1996	10	0	100	100
1995	0	0	96	88
1994	5	0	83	95
1993	15	0	91	96
1992	5	10	75	92
1991	0	0	100	95

1 Diana DeGette (D)

Of Denver — Elected 1996, 1st term

Biographical Information
Born: July 29, 1957, Tachikawa, Japan.
Education: Colorado College, B.A. 1979; New York U., J.D. 1982.
Occupation: Lawyer.
Family: Husband, Lino Lipinsky; two children.
Religion: Presbyterian.
Political Career: Colo. House, 1993-97.
Capitol Office: 1404 Longworth Bldg. 20515; 225-4431.

Committees
Commerce
Finance & Hazardous Materials; Health & Environment

The Path to Washington: DeGette is following in the political footsteps of a feminist icon, Democratic Rep. Patricia Schroeder, who retired in 1996 after 12 terms representing the Denver-based 1st District.

Having landed a prized spot on the Commerce Committee, DeGette is the only first-term Democrat to sit on one of the three most prestigious House committees: Commerce, Appropriations, and Ways and Means.

She sees the Commerce Committee as an avenue to address such key Denver banking concerns as balancing the needs of small independent banks with those of larger institutions engaging in interstate banking.

DeGette, who previously served in the Colorado House, expects to continue fighting for some of the same issues Schroeder championed, such as supporting abortion rights. DeGette hopes to ensure enforcement of existing laws protecting physicians who perform abortions.

She also has worked on family issues, including the problem of domestic violence, and sees education — including student loans and Head Start funding — as a key topic. She entered Congress saying she hoped that certain provisions in the welfare reform law passed in 1996 become "less onerous."

For DeGette, the environment is a top priority. She plans to press for expedited and increased funding to clean up the nation's superfund sites, including the chemical-laden Rocky Mountain Arsenal, which is slated for cleanup over 10 years.

Her strong support for affirmative action programs is derived from her background as a civil rights attorney; DeGette specialized in disability and sex and age discrimination cases.

"If we didn't need [affirmative action] any more, then why do I keep getting cases?" she said in an interview with the Denver Post during the 1996 campaign.

DeGette first entered politics because she felt she could more directly influence public policy as a legislator than as a litigator.

She spent four years in the Colorado House, eventually serving as assistant minority leader.

The 1996 contest to replace Schroeder in the diverse urban district received national attention, in part because of DeGette's Republican opponent, Joe Rogers, a black attorney and former aide to Colorado Republican Sen. Hank Brown.

But before her showdown with Rogers, DeGette, seen as the early front-runner for the Democratic nomination, overcame a tough primary challenge from former Denver City Councilman Tim Sandos.

Both the primary and general election campaigns involved some interesting voting group dynamics. DeGette picked up additional black support in the primary when a third candidate, Les Franklin, who is black and the former head of Democratic Gov. Roy Romer's job training office, gave up his primary bid and encouraged his supporters to vote for DeGette, who is white. Sandos, who is Hispanic, was also seeking support from minority voters.

DeGette won the nomination with 56 percent of the vote.

Meanwhile, Rogers, who had been planning to run against Schroeder before she made her surprise retirement announcement in 1995, hoped to tap into Denver's minority community and attract Democratic voters. In the 1st, more than 10 percent of the population is black and more than 20 percent is Hispanic.

Rogers won the endorsement of a group of black ministers who usually support Democrats, and focused his campaign on education, including merit pay for teachers, and crime issues, including his support for the death penalty.

But DeGette picked up support from Denver Mayor Wellington Webb, a black Democrat.

In addition, DeGette won the backing of EMILY's List, a powerhouse group that funds Democratic women candidates who support abortion rights.

She defeated Rogers by a solid 17-point margin, polling 57 percent of the vote, just a bit under the winning tallies Schroeder that enjoyed through the years.

COLORADO 1
Denver

With nearly 468,000 people, Colorado's capital anchors the 1st and is a Democratic bastion.

Bill Clinton swept Denver by nearly 67,000 votes in 1992; he won the rest of Colorado by just 288 votes. Clinton lost Colorado four years later, but Denver voters again displayed their resolutely Democratic colors, giving Clinton 62 percent of their votes and a 61,800-vote margin. In the 1996 Senate race, Democrat Ted Strickland amassed 64 percent of Denver's votes in his narrow loss to Republican Wayne Allard.

Denver's liberal cast is due in no small part to its large minority population — 22 percent Hispanic and 13 percent black. Denver's last two mayors have been minorities — Federico F. Peña (Clinton's Energy secretary, who previously served as his Transportation secretary) and Wellington Webb, Denver's first black mayor.

Peña put so much emphasis on major building projects — including a new airport, a new convention center and a 40,000-seat baseball stadium — that one critic accused him of having an "edifice complex." Yet Peña's building spree was the latest example of Denver's ability to roll with the punches. It was founded on the eve of the Civil War in response to rumors of gold in Cherry Creek (a stream that flows near downtown). By 1908, when Democrats assembled in Denver to nominate William Jennings Bryan a third time for president, it was a thriving cow town. By the 1970s, Denver had established itself as headquarters for large-scale energy operations in the Rockies.

Now, a boom and bust cycle later, the economy is more diversified. Among the new entries: major-league baseball's Colorado Rockies and hockey's Avalanche, which won the Stanley Cup in 1996, its first season after moving from Quebec.

Much of the recovery in recent years has been due to fixed-life construction projects. The largest, the new $4.9 billion Denver International Airport, opened in late February 1995 after several delays. The facility, about 25 miles northeast of the city, covers 53 square miles and is billed as one of the world's largest airport sites.

But local officials also got some bracing news in 1995, when Fitzsimons Army Medical Center, which employs thousands of military and civilian personnel, showed up on the Pentagon's base-closure list. The facility is expected to close by the end of the decade.

Redistricting in 1992 did little to change the 1st's political complexion. Denver lost 5 percent of its population during the 1980s, so the district has moved north and east into Adams and Arapahoe counties to pick up much of Commerce City and the northern chunk of the city of Aurora. The 1st regained several neighborhoods in the city's southwest corner that had been in the 6th and picked up one household in Jefferson County.

Yet 85 percent of the district's population still lives in Denver, and the additions are largely blue-collar neighborhoods that swell Democratic majorities.

Much of the new land the 1st takes in is part of the vast Rocky Mountain Arsenal near Commerce City, formerly a chemical weapons storage site that is being converted into a wildlife preserve.

1990 Population: 549,068. White 400,581 (73%), Black 70,961 (13%), Other 77,526 (14%). Hispanic origin 120,506 (22%). 18 and over 424,133 (77%), 62 and over 87,184 (16%). Median age: 34.

HOUSE ELECTIONS

1996 General		
Diana DeGette (D)	112,631	(57%)
Joe Rogers (R)	79,540	(40%)
Richard Combs (LIBERT)	5,668	(3%)
1996 Primary		
Diana DeGette (D)	21,523	(56%)
Tim Sandos (D)	16,952	(44%)

CAMPAIGN FINANCE

	Receipts	Receipts from PACs		Expend-itures
1996				
DeGette (D)	$898,672	$217,837	(24%)	$889,219
Rogers (R)	$442,534	$91,967	(21%)	$423,755

DISTRICT VOTE FOR PRESIDENT

1996		1992	
D	132,549 (61%)	**D**	135,372 (56%)
R	66,855 (31%)	**R**	63,207 (26%)
I	10,337 (5%)	**I**	43,243 (18%)

KEY VOTES

1997

Ban "partial birth" abortions — N

2 David E. Skaggs (D)

Of Boulder — Elected 1986, 6th term

Biographical Information

Born: Feb. 22, 1943, Cincinnati, Ohio.
Education: Wesleyan U., B.A. 1964; Yale U., LL.B. 1967.
Military Service: Marine Corps, 1968-71; Marine Corps Reserve, 1971-77.
Occupation: Lawyer; congressional aide.
Family: Wife, Laura Locher; one child, two stepchildren.
Religion: Congregationalist.
Political Career: Colo. House, 1981-87, minority leader, 1983-85.

Capitol Office: 1124 Longworth Bldg. 20515; 225-2161.

Committees

Appropriations
Commerce, Justice, State & Judiciary; Interior
Select Intelligence
Human Intelligence, Analysis & Counterintelligence; Technical & Tactical Intelligence (ranking)

In Washington: Skaggs' largely liberal approach to fighting Republican rule plays well among his left-of-center constituents in and around Boulder, and his military carriage (he fought in Vietnam with the Marines) and deliberate manner help him win over rural voters who are more conservative than he.

After carrying the 2nd narrowly in 1986, Skaggs has won five re-elections by solid, if not overwhelming, margins. Having proved his staying power in a politically competitive district, Skaggs in early 1997 was thinking about testing his appeal before a statewide audience in 1998, when Sen. Ben Nighthorse Campbell faces his first campaign since switching to the GOP in 1995. True to his deliberate manner, Skaggs said he would "take the next few months to look this up one side, down the other, talk to a lot of people, check my gut and probably make a decision in the late spring."

Skaggs' most-publicized project in the opening months of the 105th Congress was his effort to alter the tenor of the times on Capitol Hill. He joined with Illinois Republican Ray LaHood in organizing a three-day retreat where members were supposed to learn to assuage their tempers and restore a spirit of comity to policy disputes. The event, held in Hershey, Pa., in March 1997, had the blessing of top House leaders of both parties and was underwritten by a $700,000 grant from the Pew Charitable Trusts. More than 200 members participated, and for a time after the event, there was talk in the House of a desire to sustain the "spirit of Hershey."

Skaggs works comfortably with members on the other side of the aisle, but he is no fence-sitter. He is a reliable Democratic vote, and party leaders have rewarded him with seats on the Appropriations and Intelligence committees.

One of Skaggs' main jobs in Congress has been trying to construct a bulwark against the GOP's multiple efforts to amend the Constitution; the Denver Post in 1995 called him "the Democratic leadership's point man on constitutional arcana."

"This Congress is really treating the Constitution of the United States as if it were just a working document in draft form," Skaggs complained in March 1996. He opposed prospective amendments to limit congressional terms, require a balanced federal budget, and allow the banning of flag desecration.

Not satisfied with voting consistently against GOP initiatives, Skaggs has twice sued to block enacted legislation. In the first instance, he sought to overturn a House rule adopted on the 104th's opening day requiring a three-fifths supermajority to raise taxes. Undeterred by an unfavorable ruling in federal district court, Skaggs and his allies appealed. And Skaggs had fun with the Republican rush to waive the rule on several occasions during the 104th.

When a constitutional amendment requiring the same three-fifths majority was introduced, Skaggs warned, "The Constitution can't be waived for convenience's sake."

Skaggs also joined with five other members of Congress who sued to block a new law granting the president a form of line-item veto power the day after it took effect in 1997. They won a favorable ruling in April.

One notable area where the Democratic leadership can count on Skaggs is gun control — no easy issue for a member from the West, where gun rights sentiment is strong. In the 103rd, Skaggs voted to impose a five-day waiting period on handgun purchases, and he supported a ban on certain semiautomatic assault-style weapons. Skaggs consistently sides with abortion-rights advocates, even opposing efforts to ban a particular abortion technique that opponents call "partial-birth" abortion; only about one-third of House members take that stand. He was one of just 67 members who opposed a bill effectively prohibiting the federal government from giving legal standing to homosexual marriages.

On environmental issues, also sensitive ground in the West, Skaggs has a conservationist tilt. With the help of Colorado Republican Wayne Allard, Skaggs succeeded in adding a provision to

COLORADO 2
Northwest Denver suburbs; Boulder

The 2nd is almost equal parts suburbs and mountains. But it is probably defined most in the national mind by the college town of Boulder, the largest community in the 2nd, with slightly more than 83,000 people.

Lying at the base of the Front Range of the Rockies, Boulder is a sort of Berkeley East. It was best known in the 1970s as the setting for comedian Robin Williams' television series, "Mork and Mindy," and since then as the headquarters of Celestial Seasonings, the herbal tea producer.

The large academic community at the University of Colorado (25,000 students), augmented by many young professionals drawn to the area's scenery and outdoorsy lifestyle, give Boulder's politics a decidedly liberal hue.

The rest of Boulder County is less so, with the old farming center of Longmont anchoring the northern end of the county and suburbs such as Lafayette, Louisville and Broomfield clustered in the south. Boulder County pulsates with government research facilities such as the National Oceanic and Atmospheric Administration and related scientific and high-tech companies.

For years, the county was comfortable voting GOP for president. When it went for Michael S. Dukakis in 1988, it was the first time since 1964 that Boulder County had backed a Democrat for president. In 1992, it veered left with a vengeance. Former California Gov. Edmund G. "Jerry" Brown Jr. easily swept the county in the Democratic presidential primary.

In November, Bill Clinton swamped George Bush in Boulder County by 2-to-1. At the same time, the successful statewide ballot measure to gut local gay rights ordinances in cities such as Boulder was rejected by nearly 60 percent of the county's voters. Clinton fell just short of a majority win in 1996.

Slightly more than 40 percent of the district's residents live in Boulder County. Most of the rest live closer to Denver in portions of two suburban counties, Adams and Jefferson; each has nearly 30 percent of the people in the 2nd. Adams has a more blue-collar flavor; Jefferson is historically Republican. Nearly half the district's land area (but only 2 percent of its voters) is a short drive west in the mountain counties of Clear Creek and Gilpin. To help lure tourist dollars, Gilpin County's 19th century mining towns of Central City and Black Hawk have legalized gambling.

Less of a tourist draw but certainly one of the district's best-known sites is the controversial former Rocky Flats plutonium plant near the Boulder-Jefferson county line. An erstwhile manufacturer of triggers for nuclear weapons, the plant is now in a decontamination and cleanup phase that has provoked close scrutiny.

1990 Population: 549,072. White 508,752 (93%), Black 4,606 (<1%), Other 35,714 (7%). Hispanic origin 51,896 (9%). 18 and over 407,402 (74%), 62 and over 52,988 (10%). Median age: 32.

an omnibus parks bill enacted by the 104th Congress that bans future dam construction on the upper portion of North St. Vrain Creek in Colorado's Front Range. His bill to designate a quarter million acres of Rocky Mountain National Park as protected wilderness, though, has proved an unsuccessful perennial.

Skaggs has at times demonstrated his desire for governmental thrift, but not necessarily along the same avenues as GOP deficit hawks. He supported a move to freeze fiscal 1997 defense spending at the previous year's level and voted against lifting the federal debt ceiling. He opposed a 1996 law scheduled to phase out farm subsidies.

He has repeatedly sought to kill off funding for TV Marti, which broadcasts programming into Cuba. Contending that its signal was scrambled and thus useless, Skaggs moved in 1996 to shift its $11 million in funding to the hiring of more border patrol officers. Surprised that his move passed muster in the House, Skaggs saw TV Marti's funding restored by the Senate. Skaggs won with amendments to add $3.5 million to an Energy Department program that aids individuals in weatherizing their homes, and to increase energy conservation funding by $8 million.

He was the lead opponent of a policy move that played out on a series of spending bills. Oklahoma Republican Ernest Istook wanted to block nonprofit recipients of federal grants from lobbying or engaging in political advocacy, arguing that they should not be given money to lobby the hand that fed them. Skaggs' attempt to delete the Istook language from a fiscal 1996 spending bill went down to defeat, 187-232, although the provision never made it into law.

But while Skaggs usually is a Democratic loyalist, he has an independent streak that sometimes brings him into conflict with his party's line. (He accused the party of being "intellectually mushy" in the 1994 campaigns.) In the 103rd Congress, he raised constitutional objections when the Clinton administration appeared to be preparing for a U.S. invasion of Haiti without first seeking congressional approval.

On the Intelligence Committee, where he served through the 103rd Congress (he regained his seat during the 104th when Greg Laughlin of

Texas jumped to the GOP), Skaggs' work is guided by his belief in the need for increased openness within the intelligence community.

Skaggs' district includes the troubled Rocky Flats nuclear compound, the plutonium-processing facility that stopped production because of safety problems. As a member of Appropriations' Energy and Water subcommittee in 1991, he tried to force more study before the Bush administration could reopen Rocky Flats, but he was blocked by Senate appropriators. But Skaggs also pushed to keep jobs from being moved out of the complex. In 1992, he persuaded members of the subcommittee to block the Energy Department's proposed consolidation of hundreds of production jobs until the department could prove that it would save money. The move would have transferred some 800 non-nuclear jobs to Kansas City.

At Home: Since barely winning his first term in 1986, Skaggs has benefited over the years from the GOP's inability to muster strong opposition.

Skaggs got into politics after moving to Colorado in 1971, becoming a precinct committeeman and then Democratic district chairman. That led him to Washington as the chief aide to Democratic Rep. Tim Wirth after the 1974 election. After a term, he moved back to Colorado and won a seat in the state House in 1980.

Skaggs' ties to Wirth and his high profile in the Boulder area made him a logical successor when Wirth ran for the Senate in 1986. He won the Democratic nomination handily but was the underdog against Republican Mike Norton, who had held Wirth to 53 percent of the vote in 1984 and had campaigned almost non-stop since. But Skaggs tarred Norton as inconsistent while successfully positioning himself as a centrist. He won with 51 percent of the vote.

In 1988, Skaggs faced GOP state Rep. David Bath, a conservative Christian activist and former Democrat; in 1990, Jason Lewis, a self-described "William F. Buckley Republican" best known as the husband of a Denver TV anchorwoman; in 1992, Bryan Day, a conservative minister; and in 1994 and 1996, beauty school graduate and former state Rep. Patricia "Pat" Miller, who was backed by conservative Christians. In all those races, Skaggs never dropped below 57 percent.

GOP foes have sought to portray Skaggs as too liberal for the district's political mainstream. But as a Vietnam veteran, Skaggs has had considerable latitude in positioning himself.

Republicans thought they might make hay in 1992 with the disclosure that Skaggs had 57 overdrafts at the House bank, a total that exceeded the combined overdraft count of the rest of the Colorado congressional delegation. But Skaggs waged an aggressive campaign that portrayed Day as too conservative for the 2nd. Day's effort was strapped for funds, and he polled only one-third of the vote.

In 1994, Republicans in the 2nd failed to catch the year's big GOP wave when they nominated Miller, an abortion opponent, over three more moderate candidates who supported abortion rights. Skaggs took 57 percent of the vote.

Miller, better financed for a repeat run in 1996, fared no better. Skaggs pilloried her not only for her stance on abortion, but also for having spoken in front of a militia group. Again he won 57 percent.

HOUSE ELECTIONS

1996 General		
David E. Skaggs (D)	145,894	(57%)
Pat Miller (R)	97,865	(38%)
Larry E. Johnson (I)	6,304	(2%)
W. Earl Allen (LIBERT)	5,721	(2%)
1994 General		
David E. Skaggs (D)	105,938	(57%)
Patricia "Pat" Miller (R)	80,723	(43%)

Previous Winning Percentages: 1992 (61%) **1990** (61%) **1988** (63%) **1986** (51%)

KEY VOTES

1997	
Ban "partial birth" abortions	N
1996	
Approve farm bill	N
Deny public education to illegal immigrants	N
Repeal ban on certain assault-style weapons	N
Increase minimum wage	Y
Freeze defense spending	Y
Approve welfare overhaul	Y
1995	
Approve balanced-budget constitutional amendment	N
Relax Clean Water Act regulations	N
Oppose limits on environmental regulations	Y
Reduce projected Medicare spending	N
Approve GOP budget with tax and spending cuts	N

CAMPAIGN FINANCE

	Receipts	Receipts from PACs		Expend-itures
1996				
Skaggs (D)	$773,940	$307,876	(40%)	$778,880
Miller (R)	$457,243	$27,808	(6%)	$458,442
1994				
Skaggs (D)	$640,841	$297,662	(46%)	$576,719
Miller (R)	$86,589	$11,807	(14%)	$83,999

DISTRICT VOTE FOR PRESIDENT

	1996			1992	
D	128,077	(49%)	**D**	123,341	(45%)
R	103,192	(40%)	**R**	82,991	(30%)
I	16,587	(6%)	**I**	66,550	(24%)

VOTING STUDIES

	Presidential Support		Party Unity		Conservative Coalition	
Year	**S**	**O**	**S**	**O**	**S**	**O**
1996	85	15	92	7	33	67
1995	90	10	89	9	31	68
1994	90	10	96	3	19	78
1993	82	18	93	6	27	73
1992	30	70	88	10	38	63
1991	36	63	91	8	24	76

INTEREST GROUP RATINGS

Year	ADA	AFL-CIO	CCUS	ACU
1996	90	n/a	19	0
1995	85	100	21	0
1994	80	67	50	10
1993	75	92	36	13
1992	90	82	38	8
1991	85	75	40	0

3 Scott McInnis (R)

Of Grand Junction — Elected 1992, 3rd term

Biographical Information

Born: May 9, 1953, Glenwood Springs, Colo.

Education: Fort Lewis College, B.A. 1975; St. Mary's U. of San Antonio, J.D. 1980.

Occupation: Lawyer; police officer.

Family: Wife, Lori Smith; three children.

Religion: Roman Catholic.

Political Career: Colo. House, 1983-93, majority leader, 1991-93.

Capitol Office: 215 Cannon Bldg. 20515; 225-4761.

Committees

Rules

Rules & Organization of the House

In Washington: Seats on the influential House Rules Committee typically are hard to come by; it is a small panel, and assignments traditionally have gone to members with at least a few terms' seniority. That's the way McInnis saw it as he was finishing his first House term in 1994. So he was surprised after the November election when the GOP leadership called to ask him to join Rules. "I first wanted to make sure they didn't misdial the number," McInnis told The Denver Post. He had not even been lobbying for the assignment.

But Speaker-to-be Newt Gingrich, R-Ga., wanted to add several younger-generation Republicans to Rules for the 104th, and McInnis was an appealing package: He had previous experience managing legislation as majority leader of the Colorado House, and as a freshman he had compiled a conservative record with a tinge of Western libertarianism (he opposes a government ban on abortion).

McInnis was part of a well-rounded slate Gingrich picked for Rules; it included a woman and a Cuban-American man also from McInnis' class of 1992, and a woman from the class of 1994.

The Rules Committee position gave McInnis greater visibility, as he managed rules to govern House debate on the floor regularly. He also is a frequent choice of the Republican leadership to act as Speaker of the House during floor debate.

In the last two years, McInnis has become a reliable vote for his party, as befits a member of the extended leadership. His record of voting with the GOP increased to 91 percent in the 104th Congress, compared to roughly 84 percent in the preceding one.

When he joined the House, McInnis got a seat on the Natural Resources Committee (now called Resources), which deals with the federal land-use and water-rights questions of vital importance in the sprawling 3rd. He knows the issues well, having served in the state House as chairman of the Agriculture, Livestock and Natural Resources Committee.

Though he had to give up his Resource seat when he joined the Rules Committee, McInnis remained active in resource issues important to Colorado.

In 1995, he and Sen. Ben Nighthorse Campbell, R-Colo., joined together to oppose a provision in the GOP's enormous budget blueprint that called for selling off a variety of lands owned by the federal government that were used as resorts.

With a significant number of these properties in Colorado, McInnis and Campbell fought the provision, which was supported by the House and Senate chairmen with jurisdiction over the issue: Don Young, R-Alaska and Sen. Frank Murkowski, R-Alaska. The provision was withdrawn.

McInnis and Campbell also joined forces to get funds for a controversial water project known as Animas-La Plata. The House voted to strip the $9.5 million for the project included in the annual energy and water appropriations bill, but the Senate approved the money. Conferees later agreed to provide $8.5 million for the project, which is designed to create a system of canals and reservoirs in southwestern Colorado.

The close friendship between McInnis and Campbell may have ruptured early in 1997, when Campbell reportedly decided to run for re-election in 1998. McInnis had been mentioned as a statewide candidate, and had said he was not interested in running for governor, leaving him the option of a Senate race if Campbell retired, a move that McInnis reportedly had expected.

McInnis is a relatively quiet member of the House, tending to fight his battles behind closed doors as opposed to more public forums. But behind that quiet demeanor is someone who enjoys playing practical jokes on friends and other members.

McInnis has been known to place non-working telephones in meeting rooms just to watch his fellow members get frustrated when they cannot make calls. And he sometimes sends his lunch or dinner bill to colleagues in the members' dining room to see their reaction when asked to pay for it.

COLORADO 3
Western Slope; Pueblo

This expansive district captures much of the vast spectrum of Colorado: the rural poor, the resort rich, the old steel mill town of Pueblo and the isolated Hispanic counties of southern Colorado. Taken together, the 3rd is probably the state's most politically competitive district.

Most of its voters live on the Western Slope of the Rockies, an area that features two different lifestyles, two different sets of voting habits.

Upscale ski resorts anchor the "granola belt," a swath of terrain that extends west and south from Boulder to include the communities of Aspen (Pitkin County), Vail (Eagle), Breckinridge (Summit), Steamboat Springs (Routt), Crested Butte (Gunnison), Telluride (San Miguel) and Durango (La Plata).

The granola belt is about as liberal as any stretch of real estate in the country. It was integral to former California Gov. Edmund G. "Jerry" Brown Jr.'s victory in the first-ever Colorado Democratic presidential primary in March 1992 (13 of 21 counties he carried were entirely in the 3rd). It also was a cornerstone of opposition to the ballot measure to limit gay rights in November 1992 (11 of 15 counties that voted "no" were in the 3rd). While this area was firmly in Bill Clinton's corner in 1992, he narrowly won most of the counties in 1996 and lost La Plata county to Bob Dole.

Juxtaposed to it are rural counties as conservative in their politics and social attitudes as other parts of the ranching West. In 1992, they tended to support both George Bush and the measure limiting gay rights. In 1996, most of those counties went for Dole, helping him to beat Clinton in the district, 45 percent to 43 percent.

What united the two different sectors politically in 1992 was strong support for the Senate bid of the district's three-term representative, then-Democrat Ben Nighthorse Campbell, and significant interest in Ross Perot's independent presidential candidacy. Each in his own way, the American Indian jewelry maker and the Dallas billionaire reflected the frontier ethic.

Although much of the district is federally owned national forest, it is one of the most energy-rich corners of America. The Western Slope is a prime source of oil shale, uranium, zinc and a number of other minerals, as well as the source of the Colorado River, which provides water for much of the Front Range and Southern California.

Yet the boom-and-bust cycles of the extractive industries have led many towns in the 3rd to look for more stable employment from smaller businesses. This is the case in Pueblo, the district's largest city with about 100,000 people, where the decline of the local steel industry has led many members of the heavily unionized work force to accept non-union jobs from an array of smaller employers.

Pueblo County, the district's most populous, has been friendly to Clinton. He beat Dole there, 57 percent to 35 percent, four years after having beaten George Bush by 54 percent to 29 percent. Mesa County, the district's second most populous, was something of a counterweight. Dole won there by 53 percent to 37 percent.

1990 Population: 549,062. White 503,752 (92%), Black 3,613 (<1%), Other 41,697 (8%). Hispanic origin 95,372 (17%). 18 and over 403,933 (74%), 62 and over 83,990 (15%). Median age: 34.

He once even added something to a hot dog consumed by a fellow practical joker from the Colorado legislature who was visiting Washington that turned the man's urine orange for twelve hours.

In the beginning of his congressional career, McInnis was one of a number of young Republicans who decided to save their money by sleeping in their congressional offices while they were in Washington. He eventually moved into a local apartment.

During the 1995-96 federal government shutdown, McInnis was careful to support the numerous federal workers in his state. He announced that he would not take his pay until other federal workers got theirs (he put his checks in an escrow account), and he was able to persuade some Colorado banks to give loans to workers who were not getting paid.

McInnis got a plethora of media exposure in Colorado after the July 1994 forest fire on Storm King Mountain (in the 3rd) that killed 14 firefighters. Many officeholders came to the site, and McInnis had a personal interest: His parents' home was threatened. But after the media trumpeted McInnis' graphic description of the scene of destruction — "a peek inside the door of Hell" — he heard some criticism that the comment seemed inconsistent with his expressed goal of comforting the relatives of firefighters who died.

At Home: The 3rd District contest in 1992 paired two experienced politicians. McInnis, a five-term state lawmaker and House majority leader since 1991, battled Democratic Lt. Gov. Mike Callihan to succeed Campbell (then a Democrat), who ran successfully for the Senate. Neither McInnis nor Callihan had primary opposition.

Democrats had held virtually uninterrupted control of the district since 1964, but the 3rd is politically competitive. Typically, Democrats run well in Pueblo and in the San Luis Valley, while the western part of the 3rd, particularly the northwest corner, goes Republican.

As lieutenant governor, Callihan had become known to far more voters in the vast, rural district than McInnis, whose legislative district included only a small portion of the 3rd. But organizational problems plagued Callihan, and he was not the most efficient campaigner, talking at length with a few voters rather than chatting briefly and moving on to meet many more.

Questions arose that he might be "too nice a guy" to stave off the more aggressive McInnis. One of his rituals was setting up on a street corner, sometimes with his family, to shake hands with pedestrians and wave at passing motorists.

McInnis touted his legislative experience, stressing the work he had done for local agricultural interests. He mocked the lieutenant governorship as a ceremonial office and said that as majority leader he had been "the first one out of the foxhole" on controversial issues. In the end, McInnis scored a solid 11-point victory, even though Bill Clinton carried the 3rd. In 1994, McInnis easily won a second term, and, despite his party's difficulties elsewhere, he cruised to victory in 1996 with 69 percent of the vote.

HOUSE ELECTIONS

1996 General		
Scott McInnis (R)	183,523	(69%)
Al Gurule (D)	82,953	(31%)
1994 General		
Scott McInnis (R)	145,365	(70%)
Linda Powers (D)	63,427	(30%)

Previous Winning Percentages: 1992 (55%)

CAMPAIGN FINANCE

	Receipts	Receipts from PACs	Expend-itures
1996			
McInnis (R)	$734,455	$220,257 (30%)	$270,892
Gurule (D)	$80,809	$ 15,700 (19%)	$79,406
1994			
McInnis (R)	$582,403	$205,677 (35%)	$387,210
Powers (D)	$241,304	$108,676 (45%)	$241,305

DISTRICT VOTE FOR PRESIDENT

1996			1992		
D	115,665	(43%)	**D**	107,330	(40%)
R	120,627	(45%)	**R**	92,314	(35%)
I	23,498	(9%)	**I**	67,201	(25%)

KEY VOTES

1997	
Ban "partial birth" abortions	Y
1996	
Approve farm bill	Y
Deny public education to illegal immigrants	Y
Repeal ban on certain assault-style weapons	Y
Increase minimum wage	N
Freeze defense spending	Y
Approve welfare overhaul	Y
1995	
Approve balanced-budget constitutional amendment	Y
Relax Clean Water Act regulations	Y
Oppose limits on environmental regulations	N
Reduce projected Medicare spending	Y
Approve GOP budget with tax and spending cuts	Y

VOTING STUDIES

	Presidential Support		Party Unity		Conservative Coalition	
Year	S	O	S	O	S	O
1996	37	61	91	7	88	12
1995	18	77	91	5	88	8
1994	42	56	85	14	83	11
1993	36	63	83	15	89	11

INTEREST GROUP RATINGS

Year	ADA	AFL-CIO	CCUS	ACU
1996	5	n/a	88	100
1995	5	0	96	88
1994	15	11	83	81
1993	15	8	91	88

4 Bob Schaffer (R)

Of Fort Collins — Elected 1996, 1st term

Biographical Information
Born: July 24, 1962, Cincinnati, Ohio.
Education: U. of Dayton, B.A. 1984.
Occupation: Property manager; marketing executive; congressional aide.
Family: Wife, Maureen Elizabeth Menke; four children.
Religion: Roman Catholic.
Political Career: Colo. Senate, 1987-97; Republican nominee for lietenant governer, 1994.
Capitol Office: 212 Cannon Bldg. 20515; 225-4676.

Committees
Agriculture
Forestry, Resource Conservation & Research
Education & Workforce
Postsecondary Education, Training & Life-Long Learning; Workforce Protections
Resources
Forests & Forest Health

The Path to Washington: Although only 34 years old when elected to the House in 1996, Schaffer was already a veteran legislator, having been a member of the Colorado state Senate since 1987.

He was also following in the footsteps of another conservative from eastern Colorado, three-term Rep. Wayne Allard, who won a Senate bid to succeed retiring Republican Hank Brown, who represented the 4th from 1981 to 1991.

As Allard did, Schaffer serves on the Agriculture and Resources committees. These are fitting assignments for a member who finds himself representing a district known as Colorado's breadbasket.

The vast 4th District stretches over the eastern third of the state and includes farms and cattle ranches, as well as far-outlying suburbs of Denver.

Schaffer also sits on the Education and the Workforce Committee.

Allard's departure from the House resulted in a tough three-way battle for the Republican nomination in which Schaffer faced off against two other state legislators, state Sen. Don Ament and state Rep. Pat Sullivan.

Schaffer presented himself as the true conservative in the race. He emphasized social issues to appeal to Christian conservatives and supporters of gun owners' rights.

Abortion also played a role: While Schaffer opposes abortion, both Ament and Sullivan support them in some cases.

After winning the nomination, Schaffer faced Democratic nominee Guy Kelley, a University of Colorado regent. Schaffer described himself as the heir to Allard's tradition in the 4th District.

Among his major campaign themes were calls to lower taxes and shrink the size of government.

Kelley, meanwhile, highlighted education issues.

Schaffer's strong conservative bent led some Democrats to hope that centrists could be lured to Kelley's side. But the district's Republican leanings enabled Schaffer to win with an 18-point cushion, 56 percent to 38 percent.

Politics has consumed most of Schaffer's adult life.

He jokes that he got interested in politics when he was about 3 or 4 years old and his schoolteacher parents described the concept of taxation to him. "I became an activist," he says. "I decided immediately that I didn't like Democrats and I liked Republicans."

By the time he hit his mid-20s, he had been elected to the state Senate, following a stint as a speech writer after college.

On the Agriculture Committee, Schaffer wants to work to lower farmers' taxes and to open up overseas markets for U.S. goods by breaking down barriers to trade.

As a member of the Resources Committee, Schaffer supports major revisions to the 1973 Endangered Species Act; many conservatives have contended that the law infringes on the rights of private property owners.

He supports scaling back the authority of the Environmental Protections Agency.

By slowing the rate of growth in federal spending, Schaffer says, the federal budget deficit can be eliminated in 2002.

To ensure that this goal is reached, he says, he will push for a balanced-budget amendment to the Constitution.

Schaffer also advocates reducing the size of the federal bureaucracy by eliminating the departments of Commerce, Education, Energy, and Housing and Urban Development and the National Endowment for the Arts.

Schaffer, a former chairman of the Colorado Senate Finance Committee, says he will work to lower taxes on working Americans by reducing the capital gains tax by at least half and by eliminating estate taxes.

He also hopes to focus on social and cultural issues in an effort to stem what he sees as a decline in family stability and a tendency toward overdependence on government.

COLORADO 4

North and east — Fort Collins; Greeley

Cows, colleges and conservatives abound in the 4th, which covers the agricultural breadbasket of Colorado, the eastern third of the state.

Usually, the district votes Republican. But it is not a knee-jerk Republicanism; the most populous county in the 4th (Larimer) is comparatively liberal and is growing quickly, by 25 percent in the 1980s and about 19 percent from 1990 to 1996.

Larimer's politics have been leavened in recent years by some of the same forces that have made neighboring Boulder one of the Rockies' most liberal counties. The largest of nine colleges in the district (Colorado State University) is in the county seat of Fort Collins (population 99,000), and there has been a steady influx of newcomers to the area drawn by jobs in high-tech companies such as Hewlett-Packard, one of the 4th's biggest employers.

In 1992, Bill Clinton became the first Democratic presidential candidate to carry Larimer County since 1964. Earlier in the year, Larimer had voted for former California Gov. Edmund G. "Jerry" Brown Jr. in the Democratic presidential primary. (Brown carried only one other county in the district.) But Bob Dole's 5,000-vote margin in Larimer in 1996 helped him carry the district handily.

Yet it is hard to see Fort Collins and its environs ever becoming another Boulder. Colorado State (22,000 students) is a land-grant college focused on agricultural research. Ranching is still a major income producer in much of the county and across the 4th.

About one-third of the district's residents live in Larimer County; one-fourth live in neighboring Weld, where the economy is more dependent on agriculture. For years Greeley (with almost 61,000 people) has been known as the home of Montfort of Colorado, one of the largest feed lots and packing plants in the country. The facility is now operated by Omaha-based ConAgra.

Remapping in 1992 altered district boundaries slightly around the Denver suburbs, although the city's far northern and eastern suburbs in Adams and Arapahoe counties still make up roughly 15 percent of the 4th's population. The rest of the voters live on the Eastern Plains, a vast agricultural region of cattle, corn and wheat covering the terrain between Denver and the Kansas border. Some of the most Republican counties in Colorado are on the Eastern Plains. Elbert County gave Dole 61 percent of its votes in 1996. The county is close enough to Denver to be home for many "weekend cowboys," white-collar workers who own ranches they visit on weekends.

While Elbert County grew 41 percent in the 1980s, most counties on the plains have been losing population for decades. One of them, Baca County in southeast Colorado, has been a center of agrarian ferment; the American Agricultural Movement was born there in the mid-1970s.

South toward the New Mexico border the Hispanic population tends to increase, along with the residents' willingness to vote Democratic.

1990 Population: 549,070. White 501,555 (91%), Black 3,839 (<1%), Other 43,676 (8%). Hispanic origin 80,971 (15%). 18 and over 396,906 (72%), 62 and over 72,519 (13%). Median age: 32.

HOUSE ELECTIONS

1996 General		
Bob Schaffer (R)	137,012	(56%)
Guy Kelley (D)	92,837	(38%)
Wes McKinley (AM)	7,428	(3%)
Cynthia Parker (NL)	6,790	(3%)
1996 Primary		
Robert W. Schaffer (R)	15,138	(40%)
Don Ament (R)	11,474	(30%)
Pat Sullivan (R)	11,124	(29%)

CAMPAIGN FINANCE

	Receipts	Receipts from PACs		Expend-itures
1996				
Schaffer (R)	$503,952	$143,083	(28%)	$464,165
Kelley (D)	$267,662	$59,200	(22%)	$261,425
McKinley (AM)	$22,601	$0	(0%)	$22,600

DISTRICT VOTE FOR PRESIDENT

	1996		1992
D	102,620 (41%)	**D**	93,922 (37%)
R	122,530 (49%)	**R**	97,062 (38%)
I	18,631 (7%)	**I**	63,402 (25%)

KEY VOTES

1997

Ban "partial birth" abortions	Y

5 Joel Hefley (R)

Of Colorado Springs — Elected 1986, 6th term

Biographical Information

Born: April 18, 1935, Ardmore, Okla.

Education: Oklahoma Baptist U., B.A. 1957; Oklahoma State U., M.S. 1962.

Occupation: Community planner; management consultant.

Family: Wife, Lynn Christian; three children.

Religion: Presbyterian.

Political Career: Colo. House, 1977-79; Colo. Senate, 1979-87, Assistant Majority Leader, 1981-86.

Capitol Office: 2230 Rayburn Bldg. 20515; 225-4422.

Committees

National Security
Military Installations and Facilities (chairman); Military Research & Development

Resources
National Parks & Public Lands

Small Business

In Washington: Hefley has always championed a robust defense budget, and as chairman of the National Security Subcommittee on Military Installations, he works to increase expenditures on military housing and personnel programs, arguing that these investments boost troop morale and help promote readiness.

Promoting a strong defense is good politics in Hefley's 5th District, home to the U.S. Air Force Academy, the North American Air Defense Command (NORAD), Peterson Air Force Base, the Army's Fort Carson and various defense contractors.

In April 1996, his subcommittee approved a 10 percent increase in the Pentagon's funding request for military facilities and housing for military families, voting to authorize $900 million above the $9.1 billion the Pentagon had sought. The extra money included funds for better barracks, new and remodeled family housing and nine day-care centers. Explaining the panel's add-on for such quality-of-life bricks and mortar, Hefley said, "While the Pentagon says it's a high priority, we didn't see it in the budget request."

When the House approved the fiscal 1996 military construction bill in September 1995, the bill exceeded President Clinton's budget request by $479 million. Democratic critics of the added funds questioned why the House would move to restrain spending on Medicare, education and heating assistance programs while providing money for projects the Pentagon did not request.

But Hefley and other proponents of the bill said the legislation addressed a desperate shortfall in adequate family housing and barracks. "Administrations of both parties have permitted the nation's military infrastructure to deteriorate," Hefley said. "We are at a crossroads, and this bill is a milestone to begin to turn this problem around."

Hefley has also been a strong backer of increased levels of funding for ballistic missile defense (the former SDI program). He tried without success in 1993 to increase the House missile-defense figure from $3 billion to the Senate committee-approved figure of $3.46 billion.

Unhappy with Clinton's decision to send U.S. troops to war-torn Bosnia, Hefley in November 1995 introduced a resolution in the House that aimed to block Clinton's plan to deploy 20,000 U.S. troops to police a peace agreement unless Congress approved funds for the deployment. The House passed the bill, 243-171, marking a rare congressional effort to tie the president's hands in his constitutional role as commander in chief of the armed forces.

Hefley's resolution also flew in the face of administration warnings that such a vote might abort the Bosnia peace negotiations in Dayton, Ohio, which began in November. But Hefley and his allies contended that Congress had to act immediately to head off a U.S. deployment. If a peace agreement was concluded that assumed U.S. troops would be sent to Bosnia, they warned, it would be harder to block the move, since opponents would bear the stigma of torpedoing the deal. "The farther along we go down the road," warned Hefley, "the more difficult it will be to say no if we decide to say no."

The measure went nowhere in the Senate, however.

Hefley's willingness to direct more money to the Pentagon certainly does not carry over to other parts of the government. He has offered numerous budget-cutting amendments to annual appropriations bills through the years.

During House debate on the fiscal 1996 spending bill for the Department of Housing and Urban Development (HUD), Hefley offered an amendment to cut an additional $113 million in HUD funding for administrative salaries and expenses. It was rejected, 184-239. He linked up with North Carolina Republican Sen. Lauch Faircloth to introduce legislation terminating HUD outright, but no action occurred on that bill in the 104th.

Hefley went after the Economic Development Administration (EDA) in July 1995, trying to cut the agency's entire $349 million budget. But the EDA, which promotes economic development in

COLORADO 5
South Central — Colorado Springs

As Colorado's fastest-growing district in the 1980s, the 5th had to jettison nearly 100,000 residents in remapping to reach population parity with the state's five other districts.

Pared away were three counties on the mountainous western side of the 5th, its large slice of suburban Jefferson County, a sliver of neighboring Douglas County on the north and all of rural Elbert County on the east. District lines also were redrawn in suburban Arapahoe and mountainous Fremont counties.

While substantial, the changes did not alter the essence of the 5th. It is an overwhelmingly Republican district that revolves around Colorado Springs. With more than 281,000 people, the city is the second largest in the state and the southern anchor of the rapidly growing Front Range. The population of El Paso County, which Colorado Springs dominates, grew 28 percent in the 1980s, double the statewide growth rate.

With its sunny climate, nearby springs and Pikes Peak looming in the distance, Colorado Springs began as a resort. Tourism remains an economic mainstay.

But since World War II, Colorado Springs has become one of the nation's premier military centers. North of the city is the Air Force Academy, east is Peterson Air Force Base (headquarters of the U.S. Space Command) and Falcon Air Force Base, south is Fort Carson, and deep in a mountain to the west is the North American Air Defense Command, maintaining a round-the-clock alert for an enemy attack, even in this post-Cold War era.

Colorado Springs is nervous about its future, but the city so far has not been significantly affected by defense cutbacks. The economy has diversified beyond defense-related companies. Employers range from the U.S. Olympic Committee, with its training complex, to more than two dozen evangelical organizations, including Focus on the Family, which brought nearly 1,000 jobs to the area when it moved from California.

One aspect of Colorado Springs, though, has remained constant: its conservative politics. Only in the worst of GOP years does the 5th stray into the Democratic column and 1996 did not qualify as one of them. Bob Dole swept the district with 59 percent of the vote, up from the 50 percent George Bush garnered four years earlier. Bill Clinton was a distant second in his re-election bid with 33 percent, while Ross Perot earned 6 percent. El Paso County voted nearly 2-to-1 for Dole.

The Democrats have no reliable source of votes elsewhere in the 5th. The portions of suburban Arapahoe and Douglas counties in the 5th are firmly Republican, as are the mountain precincts in Teller County and the portion of Fremont County in the 5th.

Douglas County, which provides exurban housing for Denver commuters, had the highest growth rate of any county in Colorado in the 1980s, more than doubling its population. Teller County, which includes the old gold mining town of Cripple Creek (which has legal gambling), grew by 55 percent.

1990 Population: 549,066. White 487,334 (89%), Black 30,672 (6%), Other 31,060 (6%). Hispanic origin 40,459 (7%). 18 and over 394,039 (72%), 62 and over 49,724 (9%). Median age: 31.

poor communities, has strong GOP defenders, including Kentucky Republican Harold Rogers, chairman of the Commerce, Justice, State and Judiciary Appropriations Subcommittee. He defended the agency, saying he had watched it work in his Kentucky district. Hefley's amendment was defeated, 115-310.

In the fiscal 1996 foreign operations spending bill, Hefley tried to cut by half a $595 million appropriation for aid to Russia and the other former Soviet republics. Hefley called the program "a total waste of taxpayer dollars" and said there were not enough controls governing use of the money, but the House rejected his amendment, 104-320.

He also has sought to economize on the Resources Committee, where he sits on the National Parks and Public Lands Subcommittee. He has proposed creating a National Park Service review commission that would develop a list of insignificant or undesirable park sites to be turned over to local officials or private interests. The measure would also require the Interior secretary to set up criteria on how to add sites to the park system.

Hefley feels that lawmakers have focused more on adding coveted sites in their districts to the park system than on properly maintaining the facilities already in the system. Calling his bill a balanced approach that would prevent the Park Service from expanding too quickly in the future, Hefley said: "This bill does not in itself shut down any parks, but . . . it establishes a process for an honest, thoughtful review of the park system."

Hefley had some environmentalist members on board with him in the Democratic-controlled 103rd Congress, and the House passed his measure. But in the superheated partisan atmosphere of the 104th, opponents of the proposal succeeded in branding it a "park closing" bill, and the House defeated it in September 1995.

Hefley's position on term limits has been interesting to follow. He was once an outspoken advocate of statutory limits on congressional terms, and he vowed to stay in the House for no more than six terms. But after watching GOP Sen. Bill Armstrong of Colorado leave Congress in 1990, Hefley reconsidered. Strict limits on tenure were, he decided, "un-American," adding: "I came here to give Americans more freedom, not less."

When the House in March 1995 considered a constitutional amendment setting a 12-year service limit on members in each chamber, Hefley voted "no." That measure failed, and term limit supporters returned to the House in February 1997 armed with 11 versions of a term limits constitutional amendment — seven of which reflected efforts to comply with individual state initiatives. All restricted House members to six years and senators to 12. Hefley heeded the instructions from his state's voters and supported the Colorado version of the amendment. He also supported a proposal that limited members in each chamber to 12 years' service. All 11 versions failed.

At Home: A business-oriented legislator who lists calf-roping as one of his hobbies, Hefley seems a good fit for the 5th, which combines affluent white-collar suburbs with cattle-ranching areas and mountain communities. But unlike his GOP predecessor Ken Kramer, Hefley is not known as a "movement conservative," and that caused him some difficulty when he first sought this seat.

Hefley entered the 1986 contest as the front-runner. After 10 years in the state legislature, he was widely known in his Colorado Springs base. But while his legislative record satisfied his mainly conservative constituency, Hefley generally avoided lining up with the legislature's ideological right. His display of what some considered "moderate tendencies" prompted a primary challenge in 1986 from millionaire Harold A. Krause, a Republican national committeeman from the several Denver suburbs that were then part of the district.

Hefley tried to portray himself as the candidate with "proven experience" and Krause as a novice "who's trying to buy his way to the top." But he found his years of experience being used against him. Krause maintained that if legislative experience alone could solve the country's problems, "we'd already have a balanced budget and no trade deficit."

Krause had the money to wage a serious TV campaign in Colorado Springs, while the high cost of media in Denver made it difficult for Hefley to raid Krause's suburban base. In the end, though, money was not enough. Hefley hit pay dirt by appealing to the parochialism of El Paso County voters, reminding them that electing Krause would give the Denver area four House members. In November, Hefley had no trouble with Democratic businessman Bill Story.

In 1988, Kramer threatened to stage a comeback, complaining that Hefley was not a strong enough advocate of SDI. But Kramer was persuaded to drop his challenge and was offered a political appointment in the Department of the Army. Hefley was re-elected handily.

HOUSE ELECTIONS

1996 General		
Joel Hefley (R)	188,805	(72%)
Mike Robinson (D)	73,660	(28%)
1996 Primary		
Joel Hefley (R)	36,994	(77%)
Bill Hughes (R)	11,236	(23%)
1994 General		
Joel Hefley (R)	138,674	(100%)

Previous Winning Percentages: 1992 (71%) **1990** (66%) **1988** (75%) **1986** (70%)

CAMPAIGN FINANCE

	Receipts	Receipts from PACs		Expend-itures
1996				
Hefley (R)	$310,296	$135,016	(44%)	$329,794
Robinson (D)	$16,018	0		$16,017
1994				
Hefley (R)	$161,325	$81,920	(51%)	$137,960

DISTRICT VOTE FOR PRESIDENT

	1996		1992
D	89,464 (33%)	D	70,671 (28%)
R	160,364 (59%)	R	125,664 (50%)
I	16,714 (6%)	I	57,450 (23%)

KEY VOTES

1997	
Ban "partial birth" abortions	Y
1996	
Approve farm bill	Y
Deny public education to illegal immigrants	Y
Repeal ban on certain assault-style weapons	Y
Increase minimum wage	N
Freeze defense spending	N
Approve welfare overhaul	Y
1995	
Approve balanced-budget constitutional amendment	Y
Relax Clean Water Act regulations	Y
Oppose limits on environmental regulations	N
Reduce projected Medicare spending	Y
Approve GOP budget with tax and spending cuts	Y

VOTING STUDIES

	Presidential Support		Party Unity		Conservative Coalition	
Year	S	O	S	O	S	O
1996	30	70	95	5	94	6
1995	20	79	93	6	91	7
1994	32	65	95	4	89	11
1993	28	72	94	6	95	5
1992	74	25	92	5	90	8
1991	71	29	88	9	95	5

INTEREST GROUP RATINGS

Year	ADA	AFL-CIO	CCUS	ACU
1996	10	n/a	94	100
1995	5	0	92	84
1994	0	22	75	100
1993	5	0	91	100
1992	20	27	88	92
1991	10	25	90	100

6 Dan Schaefer (R)

Of Lakewood — Elected 1983; 7th full term

Biographical Information
Born: Jan. 25, 1936, Guttenberg, Iowa.
Education: Niagara U., B.A. 1961; State U. of New York, Potsdam, 1961-64.
Military Service: Marine Corps, 1955-57.
Occupation: Public relations consultant.
Family: Wife, Mary Lenney; four children.
Religion: Roman Catholic.
Political Career: Colo. House, 1977-79; Colo. Senate, 1979-83, president pro tempore, 1981-83.
Capitol Office: 2160 Rayburn Bldg. 20515; 225-7882.

Committees
Commerce
Energy & Power (chairman); Telecommunications, Trade & Consumer Protection
Veterans' Affairs
Benefits

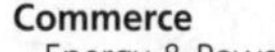

In Washington: Schaefer's lack of star quality and a thin legislative résumé once led The Denver Post to editorialize that his career was a good argument for term limits. But since then, Republican control of the House has made a big difference in Schaefer's visibility and clout: He now leads the charge for two major items on the GOP's congressional agenda.

Along with Texas Democrat Charles W. Stenholm, Schaefer is author of the template text for a balanced-budget amendment to the Constitution. Their effort did not bear fruit in the 104th Congress, and it met renewed resistance in early 1997. But Schaefer will still have plenty to do in the 105th Congress as chairman of the Commerce Subcommittee on Energy and Power, which will help pilot the course as Congress seeks to deregulate the $208 billion electrical utilities industry.

On both social- and fiscal-policy issues, Schaefer is one of the more reliable votes for the House GOP leadership. Even on congressional term limits — which Schaefer says he personally opposes — he votes with the majority of his party. Since Colorado voters expressed their preference for term limits in a 1990 state ballot initiative, Schaefer has said the clock on his congressional career began running down then, and he intends to make the 2000 House campaign his last.

Utilities deregulation proponents hail Schaefer's bill, first introduced in July 1996 and reintroduced for the 105th, as a workable vehicle for their drive to promote retail competition in the industry. Schaefer, a staunch free-enterprise conservative, said he worked closely with business interests in crafting his legislation. "We go to industry, and we ask industry, 'What can we do to make your job easier and to help you in this competitive world we have?' rather than writing legislation and having industry comment on what we write."

Schaefer is the congressional champion at raising funds from utility interests, according to a study by the Center for Responsive Politics. Schaefer told The Post in 1996, "Even if they make donations, it doesn't mean I'm going to write something they're going to like." Indeed, utility officials complained as the 105th got under way that they had not been sufficiently consulted by Schaefer and his staff as the deregulation legislation was drafted.

Schaefer's bill would require all states to open their electricity markets to competition within four years — a compromise between those pushing for alternatively slower or faster plans. The essential thrust of his bill is to give states more authority to set the terms of electrical service, but should they fail to do the job, he would have the Federal Energy Regulatory Commission step up to the plate. "Electricity monopolies are the most extreme form of government interference in the free market that exists today," he believes.

Environmentalists are concerned that deregulation will lead to increases in electricity consumption as well as pollution. The Sierra Club ran ads against Schaefer in 1995 because of his votes on some key environmental issues, but he is a surprise ally for their cause in the electricity fight. Schaefer's suburban Denver district includes the Energy Department's National Renewable Energy Laboratory, and his bill would require all electric power generators to maintain "renewable energy credits" by generating energy through renewable means or buying credits from other companies that do.

Renewable energy, Schaefer argues, is "not necessary today or tomorrow. But if anyone's got any sense at all, they'll know our grandchildren are going to need it." Schaefer offered an amendment to the fiscal 1997 energy and water development funding bill that added $42.1 million for renewable energy research; it passed, 279-135.

Unlike many of his GOP colleagues, Schaefer saw no reason during the 104th to get behind efforts to abolish the Energy Department. He has been a strong backer of the development of the Waste Isolation Pilot Plant; located in New Mexico, the project is considered vital to the clean up of Colorado's Rocky Flats plutonium superfund site.

COLORADO 6
Denver suburbs — Aurora; Lakewood

The 6th connects the eastern, southern and western suburbs of Denver. Generally white-collar and Republican-oriented, they have an added link in the 1990s — a concern about their economic future.

Like others across the country whose prosperity has been closely tied to military and aerospace spending, many residents of the 6th are unsure how they will fare during the nation's economic transition.

Denver's Lowry Air Force Base, which employed a number of workers in the Arapahoe County suburbs on the 6th's eastern side, stopped operations in September 1994. Nearby, Denver's Stapleton Airport has been replaced by the new Denver International Airport, although technical problems in the new facility delayed its opening until late February 1995.

The 6th has enough economic diversity to provide a safety net of sorts. Many of the federal government's regional facilities have headquarters in the Denver Federal Center in Lakewood, just west of Denver. The Coors brewery and the National Renewable Energy Lab are in nearby Golden. The 6th has also benefited from the growth of the telecommunications industry. Two of the nation's largest cable companies, Telecommunications Inc. and Liberty Media, merged and are headquartered there, employing about 2,400.

Golden is in a portion of western Jefferson County added to the 6th in redistricting for the 1990s. Jefferson also includes the affluent communities of Evergreen and Conifer and mountain homes hidden in the foothills of the Rockies.

But with 20 percent population growth in the state in the 1980s, the 6th in 1992 redistricting had to lose more people than it gained. Pared away were a few neighborhoods in southwest Denver as well as the northern portion of the city of Aurora on the eastern side of the district. The 6th, which in the 1980s included portions of Adams, Arapahoe, Denver and Jefferson counties, now is limited to portions of only Arapahoe and Jefferson. The district population is almost evenly divided between the two.

But the district retains other pieces of Americana. Near the affluent community of Cherry Hills Village just south of Denver is the Cherry Hills Country Club, site of a number of professional golf tournaments, including the 1960 U.S. Open, won by a young Arnold Palmer. Near Golden is the grave of the legendary frontiersman and showman William F. "Buffalo Bill" Cody. Not far from Evergreen is Troublesome Gulch, where the media staked out Gary Hart's home at the end of his quest for the Democratic presidential nomination in May 1987.

In general, GOP candidates enjoy a long head start in the 6th, thanks to the moderate to affluent bedroom communities. But the large number of registered independents will occasionally look at other options. In 1992, 25 percent of the voters pulled levers for Ross Perot. But four years later, nearly all the voters had returned to the major party fold, helping to give Bob Dole a small edge in the district.

1990 Population: 549,056. White 503,500 (92%), Black 19,455 (4%), Other 26,101 (5%). Hispanic origin 35,098 (6%). 18 and over 406,715 (74%), 62 and over 54,741 (10%). Median age: 33.

Schaefer also has supported bills to provide for the safe transportation of hazardous waste materials and to permit states to levy penalties against federal facilities like Rocky Flats when they violate solid waste disposal laws. He was not so charitable, though, toward passage of a Colorado wilderness bill, a measure that languished in Congress for a decade. Schaefer joined with the state's three other House Republicans to propose an alternative wilderness bill that lacked water-rights language deemed essential to passage by others in the state's delegation. The rest of the delegation eventually regrouped, and a compromise wilderness bill became law during the 103rd Congress.

Schaefer's district also serves as home base for several national cable operators, and he avidly looks after their interests from his seat on Commerce's Telecommunications, Trade and Consumer Protection Subcommittee. He spent several months during the 104th ensuring that a massive overhaul of telecommunications law included deregulation of cable prices, contending that cable was not as essential a service as the telephone. "In an age when TV violence is exploding, literacy is dropping, and the family is generally disintegrating, is TV really a right that the government should be creating?" Schaefer wondered at a Commerce hearing.

Schaefer's work on the balanced-budget amendment has brought him a goodly share of disappointment. The measure passed the House in 1995, only to die by a single vote in the Senate. Proponents hoped voters in 1996 would send them more allies, but early in the 105th, they found the Senate no more sympathetic, and even in the House (where Democrats gained some ground in the election), the amendment faced rough seas.

In the 104th, Schaefer's version of the amendment became the lead vehicle when not enough Democrats embraced another version, contained in the House GOP's "Contract With America," that required a three-fifths supermajority vote in Congress for any tax increase. Schaefer said he supported the tougher proposal, but offered tamer language due to the reality of the vote count. His plan passed the House with a dozen votes to spare.

Although Schaefer generally supports Republican efforts to privatize services and trim the federal government of fat, he blocked a move during the 104th by appropriators to sell off part of the Strategic Petroleum Reserve to help finance the fiscal 1997 Interior spending bill. He argued that selling made no sense economically because the oil was going to be sold for less money than it had cost to buy. The House sustained Schaefer's point of order that the sale was against rules preventing legislating on a spending bill; in 1995, his amendment to block a similar sale had been voted down, 157-267, but that provision died anyway.

Together with Rep. Timothy J. Penny, D-Minn., Schaefer in 1994 proposed more than $500 billion in budget cuts over a five-year period. Most notable was a proposed freeze on cost of living adjustments during alternate years, a move aimed at shoring up the Social Security system.

Schaefer, a former minor league catcher (and stock car racer), plays another high-profile role every year as coach of the Republican squad for the annual congressional softball game. Under his tutelage, the GOP team is 1-3.

At Home: Schaefer has been the sole representative of the 6th since it was created in 1982. Though interested in running that year, Schaefer deferred to Jack Swigert, the popular former Apollo astronaut. Swigert won but died of cancer before he was sworn in.

When Schaefer entered the special election to fill the vacancy, his biggest hurdle was the Republican nomination. Aided by national conservative GOP leaders, Schaefer won a fourth-ballot victory at a district convention in January 1983 and has won re-election comfortably ever since.

In 1988, the Democrats recruited a candidate they thought could wrest the 6th from Schaefer: former GOP state Sen. Martha Ezzard. A fiscal conservative, she was also known as an outspoken environmentalist and feminist.

Against Schaefer, Ezzard quickly proved her prowess as a fundraiser and won headlines by dubbing the incumbent "the invisible congressman." Schaefer defended his style as "quietly effective," championed his efforts to secure federal funds for local programs and said Ezzard would raise taxes. Ezzard badly underestimated the GOP loyalty of the district's voters and the draw of Schaefer's parochial focus; he won with 63 percent.

Schaefer came late to politics. The Iowa-born son of a construction worker, he was raised in North Dakota and educated in New York. After several years as a high school history teacher, he moved to Colorado and opened a public relations firm. Schaefer assisted the campaigns of other local GOP candidates and then successfully ran for the state House in 1976. Two years later he moved up to the state Senate. Personable and unflappable, he became its president pro tem in 1981. When he ran for Congress, he was assistant Senate majority leader.

HOUSE ELECTIONS

1996 General		
Dan Schaefer (R)	146,018	(62%)
Joan Fitz-Gerald (D)	88,600	(38%)
1994 General		
Dan Schaefer (R)	124,079	(70%)
John Hallen (D)	49,701	(28%)
John Heckman (COPP)	2,536	(1%)

Previous Winning Percentages: **1992** (61%) **1990** (65%) **1988** (63%) **1986** (65%) **1984** (89%) **1983**† (63%)

† Special election

CAMPAIGN FINANCE

	Receipts	Receipts from PACs		Expenditures
1996				
Schaefer (R)	$742,059	$549,239	(74%)	$760,648
Fitz-Gerald (D)	$120,960	$32,000	(26%)	$119,224
1994				
Schaefer (R)	$453,270	$305,036	(67%)	$495,506
Hallen (D)	$52,602	$2,000	(4%)	$52,171

DISTRICT VOTE FOR PRESIDENT

1996		1992	
D	102,778 (43%)	**D**	99,045 (37%)
R	118,281 (49%)	**R**	101,613 (38%)
I	13,862 (6%)	**I**	68,165 (25%)

KEY VOTES

1997	
Ban "partial birth" abortions	Y
1996	
Approve farm bill	Y
Deny public education to illegal immigrants	Y
Repeal ban on certain assault-style weapons	Y
Increase minimum wage	N
Freeze defense spending	N
Approve welfare overhaul	Y
1995	
Approve balanced-budget constitutional amendment	Y
Relax Clean Water Act regulations	Y
Oppose limits on environmental regulations	N
Reduce projected Medicare spending	Y
Approve GOP budget with tax and spending cuts	Y

VOTING STUDIES

	Presidential Support		Party Unity		Conservative Coalition	
Year	S	O	S	O	S	O
1996	33	66	97	3	98	2
1995	19	80	98	2	98	1
1994	35	65	92	4	92	8
1993	33	67	94	5	89	11
1992	82	17	95	3	96	2
1991	71	27	90	9	92	5

INTEREST GROUP RATINGS

Year	ADA	AFL-CIO	CCUS	ACU
1996	0	n/a	100	100
1995	5	9	96	92
1994	10	22	83	90
1993	5	8	91	92
1992	5	27	75	88
1991	5	17	90	95

CONNECTICUT

Governor: John G. Rowland (R)
First elected: 1994
Length of term: 4 years
Term expires: 1/99
Salary: $78,000
Term limit: 2 terms
Phone: (203) 566-4840
Born: May 24, 1957; Waterbury, Conn.
Education: Villanova U., B.S. 1979.
Occupation: Insurance broker; business consultant.
Family: Wife, Patricia; three children.
Religion: Roman Catholic.
Political Career: Conn. House, 1981-85; U.S. House, 1985-91; Republican nominee for governor, 1990.

Lt. Gov.: Jodi Rell (R)
First elected: 1994
Length of term: 4 years
Term expires: 1/99
Salary: $55,000
Phone: (203) 566-2614

State election official: (203) 566-3106
Democratic headquarters: (203) 278-6080
Republican headquarters: (203) 547-0589

REDISTRICTING

Connecticut retained its six House seats in reapportionment. Redistricting commission filed the map with secretary of state Nov. 27, 1991; governor's signature was not required.

STATE LEGISLATURE

Bicameral General Assembly. Meets January-June.

Senate: 36 members, 2-year terms
1996 breakdown: 19R, 17D; 27 men, 9 women
Salary: $16,760
Phone: (203) 240-0500

House of Representatives: 151 members, 2-year terms
1996 breakdown: 97D, 54R; 108 men, 43 women
Salary: $16,760
Phone: (203) 240-0400

URBAN STATISTICS

City	Population
Bridgeport	141,686
Mayor Joseph Ganim, D	
Hartford	139,739
Mayor Mike Peters, D	
New Haven	130,474
Mayor John DeStefano, D	
Waterbury	108,961
Mayor Philip A. Giordano, R	
Stamford	108,056
Mayor Stanley Esposito, R	

U.S. CONGRESS

Senate: 2 D, 0 R
House: 4 D, 2 R

TERM LIMITS

For state offices: No

ELECTIONS

1996 Presidential Vote

Bill Clinton	53%
Bob Dole	35%
Ross Perot	10%

1992 Presidential Vote

Bill Clinton	42%
George Bush	36%
Ross Perot	22%

1988 Presidential Vote

George Bush	52%
Michael S. Dukakis	47%

POPULATION

1990 population		3,287,116
1980 population		3,107,576
Percent change		+6%
Rank among states:		27
White		87%
Black		8%
Hispanic		6%
Asian or Pacific islander		2%
Urban		79%
Rural		21%
Born in state		57%
Foreign-born		8%
Under age 18	749,581	23%
Ages 18-64	2,091,628	64%
65 and older	445,907	14%
Median age		34.4

MISCELLANEOUS

Capital: Hartford
Number of counties: 8
Per capita income: $25,881 (1991)
Rank among states: 1
Total area: 5,018 sq. miles
Rank among states: 48

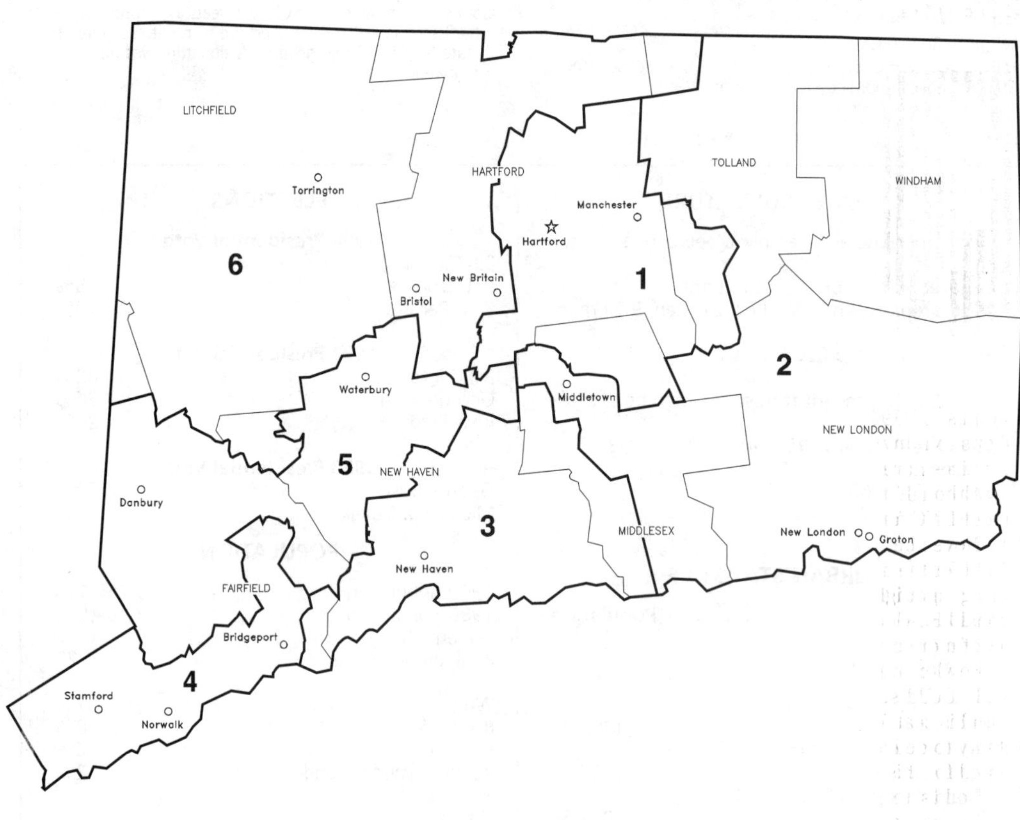
LITCHFIELD
Torrington
HARTFORD
TOLLAND
WINDHAM
Manchester
Hartford
6
New Britain
Bristol
1
2
Waterbury
Middletown
NEW LONDON
5
NEW HAVEN
Danbury
3
MIDDLESEX
New London
Groton
New Haven
FAIRFIELD
Bridgeport
4
Stamford
Norwalk

Christopher J. Dodd (D)

Of East Haddam — Elected 1980, 3rd term

Biographical Information

Born: May 27, 1944, Willimantic, Conn.
Education: Providence College, B.A. 1966; U. of Louisville, J.D. 1972.
Military Service: Army Reserve, 1969-75.
Occupation: Lawyer.
Family: Divorced.
Religion: Roman Catholic.
Political Career: U.S. House, 1975-81.
Capitol Office: 444 Russell Bldg. 20510; 224-2823.

Committees

Banking, Housing & Urban Affairs
Financial Services & Technology; Housing Opportunity & Community Development; Securities (ranking)
Foreign Relations
European Affairs; International Operations; Western Hemisphere, Peace Corps, Narcotics and Terrorism (ranking)
Labor & Human Resources
Children & Families (ranking); Employment & Training
Rules & Administration

In Washington: His two-year stint as general chairman of the Democratic National Committee (DNC) complete, Dodd headed into the 105th Congress with the satisfaction of having helped his party re-elect a president for the first time in the post-World War II era.

But Bill Clinton's 1996 victory may be overshadowed by Democrats' failure to recapture control of Congress, where in the early months of 1997 the Republican majority set its sights on investigating controversial fundraising practices during the 1995-96 election cycle.

Although there was a swirl of media reports about DNC fundraising improprieties shortly before the November 1996 election and in the months after, Dodd for the most part seemed to escape the unflattering spotlight. The DNC's former co-chairman Donald Fowler, who served with Dodd, was the target of more criticism than the Connecticut senator.

Fowler ran the party's day-to-day activities, while Dodd served as the DNC's main spokesman. With his zeal for partisan combat, sharp tongue and ability to deliver a meaty sound bite, Dodd was well suited for this role.

Dodd's response to the controversy over fundraising was to say that it highlighted the need for reforming the campaign finance system. He said that Republicans engaged in many of the same fund-raising practices that Democrats were being criticized for. He called on Congress to address the problem of "soft money" donations, which are largely unregulated funds that go to political parties rather than individual candidates. He backed a bill sponsored by Sens. John McCain, R-Ariz., and Russell D. Feingold, D-Wis., to overhaul campaign finance laws.

Days before the 1996 election, Dodd suggested that both parties agree to accept no more contributions from non-Americans and to ban "soft money" donations. "We don't have to wait to change the law," Dodd said during an appearance with Republican National Committee Chairman Haley Barbour on NBC's "Meet the Press."

If Dodd wants to change the campaign finance system, it is not because he lacks skill functioning within it. At the end of 1996, he had more than $1.2 million cash on hand for his 1998 re-election bid. Just as the Democratic Party has grown more comfortable with and adept at raising money from business interests, so has Dodd. A member of the Banking, Housing and Urban Affairs Committee, he has received more money from the banking and real estate industries than from any others.

On occasion in the 104th, Dodd's "day job" in the Senate was a useful complement to his work as party general chairman. In April 1996, Dodd led opposition in the Senate to a GOP effort to indefinitely extend the authorization for the Senate panel investigating the Whitewater affair, involving President and Hillary Rodham Clinton's investment in a failed land deal. Dodd and other Democrats argued strenuously that the GOP wanted to extend the investigation in order to bollix up the Clinton re-election effort. In the end, Republicans agreed to just a short-term extension for the Whitewater committee.

Dodd has always been an active legislator, delving into issues on most of his major committees — Banking, Labor and Human Resources, Foreign Relations, and Rules and Administration.

He has also managed to walk the tightrope between his own liberal tendencies and the needs of Connecticut's insurance and defense industries.

A recognized leader on children's issues (he founded the Senate Children's Caucus with Republican Arlen Specter of Pennsylvania in 1983), Dodd successfully pushed through a reauthorization of Head Start in 1994, as well as contributing to the renewal of the 1965 Elementary and Secondary Education Act.

During the 104th Congress, Dodd pushed to get more funding for child care added to legislation to overhaul the welfare system.

Dodd voted for welfare overhaul when the Senate first passed the measure in September 1995, after he and other Democrats wrung some concessions from Republicans, including an additional $3 billion over five years to provide care for children of parents moving from welfare to work. "In every survey I've seen, the single largest obstacle to getting people off welfare and into work is the lack of child care," Dodd said.

Despite the provisions for child care, Dodd said he was only reluctantly supporting the welfare bill, and he warned that he would later oppose it if negotiations with the House pulled the bill to the right. He carried through on that threat by voting against the conference report. Clinton vetoed the legislation. Dodd also opposed the final welfare reform measure that passed Congress in 1996 after Clinton agreed to sign it.

Dodd applied all his tenacity and his deal making skills to finally achieve enactment of the Family and Medical Leave Act in the Democratic-controlled 103rd Congress. He pushed the measure through the Senate Labor Committee four times in seven years and twice saw the bill clear Congress, only to be vetoed by President George Bush.

Clinton had pledged during the 1992 campaign to sign it if he was elected, and Dodd was among those who recommended sending Clinton the version negotiated with Republicans in earlier Congresses (granting 12 weeks of leave and exempting businesses with fewer than 50 workers) rather than refighting old battles. Clinton signed the bill into law in February 1993, the first major legislative milestone of his administration.

Foreign policy is another key interest of Dodd's. As the ranking Democrat on the Western Hemisphere, Peace Corps, Narcotics and Terrorism Subcommittee, he has paid particularly close attention to Central America.

Early in the 104th Congress, Dodd led the charge against an amendment to a 1995 spending rescissions bill that would have effectively prevented the Clinton administration from providing any further loans to Mexico without the approval of Congress. The move came in response to the administration's decision to bypass lawmakers and extend Mexico a $20 billion credit line. Dodd and other Democrats argued that the amendment, which was being pushed by Sen. Alfonse M. D'Amato, R-N.Y., would deal a potentially lethal blow to Mexico's economy and roil international financial markets. D'Amato ended up withdrawing the amendment so that the rescissions legislation could move forward.

Dodd was also a leading opponent of legislation offered by Foreign Relations Committee Chairman Jesse Helms, R-N.C., and Rep. Dan Burton, R-Ind., to tighten the U.S. economic embargo of Cuba. The bill's most controversial provision allowed U.S. citizens whose properties were expropriated by the government of Cuban leader Fidel Castro to seek legal redress in U.S. courts against foreign corporations that took over those properties. Dodd contended that U.S. courts would be choked with lawsuits brought by Cuban-Americans against foreign companies. He also objected to creating a special right for Cuban-Americans that is not extended to citizens or nationals from other countries where properties have been confiscated.

Despite these arguments, Clinton, after first opposing the legislation, decided to sign it, amid a furor that arose in February 1996 after Cuban military planes shot down two civilian aircraft being flown toward the island nation by Cuban-American opponents of Castro.

In March 1994, Dodd and four other usually loyal Democrats lashed out at the Clinton administration's handling of the Haitian situation, arguing that it was not doing enough to restore to power ousted President Jean-Bertrand Aristide. "I think it is fair to ask why this administration sends combat troops to Mogadishu or launched cruise missiles at Baghdad but does not even rattle a saber at the leaders at Port-au-Prince," Dodd complained.

In July, when it seemed the administration might be ready to intervene militarily, Dodd backed off, saying, "I don't think a military invasion is warranted." But in September, he helped fight off Republican-led efforts to set a withdrawal deadline for U.S. troops who were sent to Haiti to restore democratically elected government.

Pacifist instincts notwithstanding, Dodd can be hawkish about protecting defense-related industry in Connecticut. He has doggedly sought funding for building the *Seawolf* submarine in Groton, Conn.

During Senate consideration of the fiscal 1996 defense authorization bill, Dodd worked successfully to fend off an effort by Sen. John McCain, R-Ariz., to eliminate funding for construction of a third *Seawolf* submarine. McCain then offered an amendment to cap funding for the three submarines at $7.2 billion; Dodd won passage of a substitute amendment to increase the cap by $35 million.

In addition to helping his home-state industries, he has also been receptive to business interests on a variety of other issues as well, even when it meant taking on Clinton.

In the 104th, Dodd was a key Democratic supporter of legislation to overhaul laws governing investor lawsuits. Supporters said the bill was aimed at closing loopholes in the existing system that led to the filing of frivolous lawsuits.

Congress approved the bill, and though Dodd was fairly confident Clinton would sign it, the president instead vetoed it. Even though Dodd's role as party general chairman made it a bit awkward, Dodd rallied support to override the president's veto, an effort that succeeded. Dodd sought to downplay his differences with Clinton. "As I've said all along, there are times when I'll differ with my president, and now is clearly one of those times," Dodd said.

Dodd's support for product liability legislation approved in the 104th Congress also was at odds with the president, who vetoed the measure. Dodd had urged Clinton to sign the bill, which limited manufacturer liability for defective products. saying, "The business community cares about this a lot."

At Home: Considered vulnerable to defeat at the outset of his 1992 re-election campaign, Dodd put to rest any doubts about his vote-getting abilities with a solid victory over millionaire Republican Brook Johnson.

In early 1991, it looked like Dodd might be in trouble because of his opposition to the use of military force in the Persian Gulf and his reluctance to oppose independent Gov. Lowell P. Weicker Jr.'s state income tax. More than half the people polled in a survey that year said they wouldn't vote for him again.

But Dodd took the warning signs to heart, stocking his campaign coffers, increasing his visibility at home and stressing his efforts in behalf of the *Seawolf* submarine program and his work on family leave legislation. Johnson, although flush with his own cash, ended up losing by 21 points.

The Dodd name has been a household word in Connecticut politics for four decades.

From the day Democratic Sen. Abraham A. Ribicoff declared his retirement in 1979, Dodd was viewed as his heir apparent. He was overwhelmingly popular in his 2nd District, which he had first won in 1974. His father, the late Thomas J. Dodd — a tough-talking, two-term senator who was among his party's most virulent anti-communists — was still revered by many voters, despite his 1967 Senate censure for personal use of campaign funds.

The younger Dodd's GOP opponent was former New York Sen. James L. Buckley, who carried the standard of the state Republican Party's newly resurgent conservative wing. The millionaire brother of columnist William F. Buckley Jr., James Buckley argued that his previous experience and national reputation would make him a significant force for conservatism in the Senate.

But Buckley's patrician style did not play well, while Dodd proved an exuberant campaigner, slipping into crowds with the comfort of a born politician, conversing both in English and fluent Spanish. He attacked Buckley as a conservative ideologue who, as a senator, had neglected the needs of the poor.

Dodd easily outdistanced Buckley, earning a larger plurality than his father did in winning his first Senate term in 1958.

Dodd's reputation as a rising star was enhanced by his landslide 1986 re-election. The GOP nominee was 66-year-old Roger W. Eddy, a party national committeeman and former state representative.

Eddy, inventor of the widely used Audubon birdcall, had an image as a "gentleman farmer," but his campaign style turned out to be surprisingly hard-hitting. He attacked Dodd's Central America stands, describing him as "the senator from communist Nicaragua" and told members of the state AFL-CIO that "Japan is sucking us dry."

Dodd brushed off the attacks as "disappointing" and went on to amass the largest Senate vote percentage in state history.

Dodd grew up with Connecticut politics, and he went after public office himself at age 30. He was practicing law in New London in 1974 when Republican Rep. Robert H. Steele left his secure 2nd District seat to run for governor. Dodd attached himself to the camp of Democratic gubernatorial candidate Ella T. Grasso early in the spring and began lining up delegate support.

By the time of the convention, he was the clear favorite over John M. Bailey Jr. — son of the state party chairman — and Douglas Bennet, a one-time aide to Ribicoff. He locked up the party's endorsement on the first round of convention balloting, and won easily in the general election.

SENATE ELECTIONS

1992 General

Christopher J. Dodd (D, ACP)	882,569	(59%)
Brook Johnson (R)	572,036	(38%)
Richard D. Gregory (CC)	35,315	(2%)

Previous Winning Percentages: **1986** (65%) **1980** (56%) **1978*** (70%) **1976*** (65%) **1974*** (59%)

* *House election*

CAMPAIGN FINANCE

	Receipts	Receipts from PACs	Expend-itures
1992			
Dodd (D)	$3,827,475	$1,337,814 (35%)	$4,122,268
Johnson (R)	$2,400,715	0	$2,395,262

KEY VOTES

1997	
Approve balanced-budget constitutional amendment	N
Approve chemical weapons treaty	Y
1996	
Approve farm bill	N
Limit punitive damages in product liability cases	Y
Exempt small businesses from higher minimum wage	N
Approve welfare overhaul	N
Bar job discrimination based on sexual orientation	Y
Override veto of ban on "partial birth" abortions	N
1995	
Approve GOP budget with tax and spending cuts	N
Approve constitutional amendment barring flag desecration	N

VOTING STUDIES

	Presidential Support		Party Unity		Conservative Coalition	
Year	**S**	**O**	**S**	**O**	**S**	**O**
1996	80	19	88	11	37	61
1995	92	8	86	13	28	68
1994	90	5	84	9	22	69
1993	97	2	91	8	28	68
1992	32	68	83	17	34	66
1991	49	49	83	16	43	58

INTEREST GROUP RATINGS

Year	ADA	AFL-CIO	CCUS	ACU
1996	85	n/a	38	10
1995	95	92	32	4
1994	80	75	38	0
1993	75	82	36	12
1992	75	92	30	11
1991	75	92	20	24

Joseph I. Lieberman (D)

Of New Haven — Elected 1988, 2nd term

Biographical Information

Born: Feb. 24, 1942, Stamford, Conn.
Education: Yale U., B.A. 1964, LL.B. 1967.
Occupation: Lawyer.
Family: Wife, Hadassah Freilich; four children.
Religion: Jewish.
Political Career: Conn. Senate, 1971-81, majority leader, 1975-81; Democratic nominee for U.S. House, 1980; Conn. attorney general, 1983-89.
Capitol Office: 706 Hart Bldg. 20510; 224-4041.

Committees

Armed Services
Acquisition & Technology (ranking); Airland Forces; Seapower
Environment & Public Works
Clean Air, Wetlands, Private Property & Nuclear Safety; Drinking Water, Fisheries & Wildlife
Governmental Affairs
Oversight of Government Management & the District of Columbia (ranking); Investigations
Small Business

In Washington: On the Senate's ideological spectrum, Lieberman stands somewhere near the middle, often backing the Clinton administration, but also joining with GOP moderates to try to strike a balance in policymaking between conservative Republicans and liberal Democrats.

Lieberman's personal perspective, informed by his Orthodox Jewish faith, is fairly conservative, and during the 104th Congress, he emerged as a crusader against what he sees as the negative impact of popular culture on traditional values in American society.

Aiming at television broadcasters, Lieberman successfully pushed for the development of mechanisms to help parents screen children from inappropriate TV programming. In 1995, he teamed with North Dakota Democrat Kent Conrad to win Senate approval of a requirement that all new televisions be equipped with an electronic device — a "v-chip" — that enables parents to block out programs that have objectionable material. The legislation called on the broadcast industry to develop a rating system designed to be used with the v-chip.

The industry formally announced its self-policing system in December 1996, but Lieberman said it did not offer parents enough information. "The ratings system the networks put into effect . . . is a missed opportunity, a half-step," he said. "Parents will not be happy if they come to believe that the v-chip has become a u-chip, and the U stands for 'Useless.'"

Lieberman continues to monitor the handling of the voluntary ratings system and to lobby for easily accessible information that will help parents guide their kids' TV viewing, with legislation on the subject being "the last resort."

He wants the TV industry to develop an explicit voluntary content standard, a process he hopes will lower the amount of programming that is objectionable. He encourages broadcasters to revive and protect the traditional "family hour" of programming, between 8 p.m. and 9 p.m., and to commit to providing educational programming.

Television is not the only medium Lieberman has scrutinized. The music industry, particularly companies producing "gangsta rap," were targeted by Lieberman, conservative former Education Secretary William Bennett and liberal activist C. Delores Tucker for selling music with obscene and violent lyrics. "These lyrics explicitly and brazenly celebrate murder, rape, torture and drug use, and denigrate our most fundamental values," Lieberman said at a 1996 news conference. "It is wrong to profit from messages that poison our culture."

Lieberman has directed similar criticism at video game manufacturers, periodically issuing "report cards" with the conservative National Institute on Media and the Family to assess the implementation of that industry's voluntary rating system. Manufacturers and retailers developed that system after Lieberman and Wisconsin Democrat Herb Kohl threatened in the 103rd Congress to push legislation mandating ratings.

As the collaboration with Kohl suggests, Lieberman often teams up with less ideologically minded senators, both Democrat and Republican.

In one such venture, Lieberman worked with Rhode Island Republican John H. Chafee, chairman of the Environment and Public Works Committee (on which Lieberman sits), to strengthen oil spill prevention and response laws. The move came in the wake of a big oil spill from a barge off the Connecticut-Rhode Island coast. Going back to his tenure as Connecticut attorney general, Lieberman has been a proponent of protections for the environment and for consumers.

Also, Lieberman in the 104th participated in efforts by a bipartisan group of centrist senators to craft and sell their own balanced-budget plan. The group's final proposal included reductions in entitlement spending and in taxes, but Democratic leaders said it cut too much in those areas; GOP leaders said it cut too little. Nonetheless, the centrist plan drew 46 votes on the floor: 24 Democrats and 22 Republicans supported it.

"England has Charles and Diana," Lieberman

told his Senate colleagues. "America has the Republican and Democratic parties. And both partnerships seem to have irreconcilable differences, but we have no queen to call for a divorce. We have no choice but to bridge the gap between our parties and produce a budget we can live on."

In an era when many voters are cynical about politicians, Lieberman's commitment to other things besides politics enhances his popularity. He will not campaign during the Jewish high holy days and rarely participates in Senate sessions held on Friday night or Saturday, the Jewish Sabbath. Also, his non-ideological image is an asset in Connecticut, where the electorate in recent years has tended to swing between the two parties.

Still, Lieberman has found much to like in the Clinton agenda. In 1996, he agreed with President Clinton on 90 percent of the floor votes where Clinton took a position, the sixth-highest presidential-support score in the Senate.

In March 1995 Lieberman was named chairman of the Democratic Leadership Council (DLC), the group that has worked for years (Clinton was early activist as Arkansas governor) to give the national Democratic Party a more moderate image.

As DLC chairman, Lieberman has touted "New Democrat" causes such as welfare reform; he wrote a column for The New York Times stressing the good points of the welfare overhaul plan that Clinton signed into law in 1996 over the objections of many liberal Democrats.

But Lieberman departs from the DLC line on some issues. He supported a minimum wage increase and he backs tuition vouchers allowing parents to send their children to private schools — both policies that the DLC opposes.

As DLC chairman, Lieberman has spearheaded efforts to get like-minded Democrats elected to public office. In 1996, he and three House Democrats formed a national network designed to support "New Democrat" candidates for federal, state and local office. The network seeks out candidates with "a mainstream philosophy, a belief in working in the center and forming coalitions to get things done."

Lieberman is in the habit of helping assemble bipartisan working groups of senators to study and develop solutions to problems. Reflecting his wide-ranging interests, Lieberman uses this mechanism to explore matters such as science and technology issues, teenage pregnancy, the future of Hong Kong, and national security needs.

A member of the Armed Services Committee, Lieberman looks out for Connecticut's defense-related industries and has more enthusiasm for a robust defense budget than do many Democrats. In 1996, he and Indiana Republican Daniel R. Coats got the Senate's approval to establish a nonpartisan commission that will look at the Pentagon's national defense strategy and determine what forces will be needed to maintain that strategy into the 21st century.

With the decision of Democratic Sen. John Glenn of Ohio not to seek re-election in 1998, Glenn's top Democratic spot on the Governmental Affairs Committee will likely go to Lieberman in the 106th Congress.

At Home: Lieberman was initially not considered much of a threat to oust 18-year GOP Senate veteran Lowell P. Weicker Jr. in 1988, but he wound up scoring the only Democratic upset of that year's Senate elections.

All year long, Lieberman had argued that it was a myth that Connecticut benefited from Weicker's maverick reputation. But the electoral appeal of the Republican's go-it-alone style had seemed impenetrable.

After months of trailing in opinion polls, Lieberman launched a series of animated ads late in the campaign that portrayed Weicker as a sleeping bear, dozing through important votes but waking loud and ornery when personally piqued. The imagery of the bear ads clicked, and their appearance in the closing weeks of a yearlong campaign was perfectly timed. With Lieberman peaking late, Weicker did not have a chance to counterpunch.

The challenger began the campaign well-known from prior political service. Earlier in his career, he had ended a 10-year stint in the state Senate (and his job there as majority leader) for an unsuccessful U.S. House bid. But two years later, he bounced back, becoming the top state vote-getter in his 1982 election as attorney general.

During his nearly two terms in that office, he won many headlines for his pro-consumer lawsuits against car dealers, grocery stores and public utilities, as well as for his efforts toward stiffer enforcement of hazardous-waste disposal laws and child-support payment requirements.

His visibility on these issues did not endear him to the "Old Guard" in Connecticut's Democratic Party, but his efforts had the liberal lilt needed to woo traditionally Democratic voters, and the party chose to unite behind him in his challenge to Weicker. Lieberman also raised doubts about Weicker's commitment to Social Security, a Democratic touchstone issue.

At the same time, Lieberman's profile also enabled him to court crossover voters. His demeanor was far more restrained than Weicker's; where the Republican campaigned with his sleeves rolled up and jacket slung over his shoulder, Lieberman seemed reluctant to loosen his tie. He stressed a family-man image, and his faith-based avoidance of Saturday campaigning precluded him from attending the convention that nominated him.

Lieberman also held the conservative ground on a few select issues. He supported allowing military involvement in drug interdiction and backed the 1983 invasion of Grenada, both of which Weicker opposed. Lieberman also backed a moment of silence in schools, which could be used for prayer.

This combination won him an endorsement from noted conservative William F. Buckley Jr., who had long disdained Weicker for his social liberalism.

Some conservatives concluded that a Lieberman victory would be no great catastrophe, so they sat out the Senate race. That deprived Weicker of crucial GOP support on Election Day, while Lieberman held his Democratic base and won enough independent votes to eke out a narrow victory.

While Democrats were pleased with his success, some liberals felt a twinge of remorse over the departure of Weicker, who so often had championed their causes in the Senate and in the national GOP. Some observers credit that voter guilt with helping Weicker in his successful 1990 bid, as an independent, for governor.

Even though 1994 was a big year for Republicans in state after state, Lieberman was untouchable. Rated "safe" for re-election in all pre-election forecasts, he rolled up 67 percent of the vote against GOP former state Sen. Jerry Labriola.

SENATE ELECTIONS

1994 General

Joseph I. Lieberman (D,ACP)	723,842	(67%)
Jerry Labriola (R)	334,833	(31%)
Gary R. Garneau (CC)	20,989	(2%)

Previous Winning Percentages: 1988 (50%)

CAMPAIGN FINANCE

	Receipts	Receipts from PACs		Expend-itures
1994				
Lieberman (D)	$3,870,610	$1,122,269	(29%)	$3,238,026
Labriola (R)	$168,067	$6,950	(4%)	$166,064

KEY VOTES

1997	
Approve balanced-budget constitutional amendment	N
Approve chemical weapons treaty	Y
1996	
Approve farm bill	Y
Limit punitive damages in product liability cases	Y
Exempt small businesses from higher minimum wage	N
Approve welfare overhaul	Y
Bar job discrimination based on sexual orientation	Y
Override veto of ban on "partial birth" abortions	N
1995	
Approve GOP budget with tax and spending cuts	N
Approve constitutional amendment barring flag desecration	N

VOTING STUDIES

	Presidential Support		Party Unity		Conservative Coalition	
Year	S	O	S	O	S	O
1996	90	10	75	24	63	37
1995	81	18	71	28	46	53
1994	85	11	75	24	44	53
1993	94	4	83	17	56	44
1992	37	63	77	23	37	63
1991	49	46	80	19	38	63

INTEREST GROUP RATINGS

Year	ADA	AFL-CIO	CCUS	ACU
1996	75	n/a	54	35
1995	95	100	33	10
1994	65	71	30	8
1993	65	82	45	20
1992	70	83	50	22
1991	65	83	30	25

1 Barbara B. Kennelly (D)

Of Hartford — Elected 1982; 8th full term

Biographical Information

Born: July 10, 1936, Hartford, Conn.

Education: Trinity College (Washington, D.C.), B.A. 1958; Trinity College (Hartford, Conn.), M.A. 1973.

Occupation: Public official.

Family: Widowed; four children.

Religion: Roman Catholic.

Political Career: Hartford Court of Common Council, 1975-79; Conn. secretary of state, 1979-82.

Capitol Office: 201 Cannon Bldg. 20515; 225-2265.

Committees

Ways & Means
Social Security (ranking)

Democratic Caucus vice chairman

In Washington: Drawing on lessons she learned long ago about how to operate among a bunch of pols, Kennelly has worked methodically — and usually behind the scenes — to become a force in the House. At the start of the 104th Congress she won election as vice chair of the Democratic Caucus, an attainment that makes her the top woman in her party's House leadership. Kennelly's competitor for the vice chair post was another woman who has played the inside game well, New York's Louise M. Slaughter. The vote was 93-90 for Kennelly.

It is no surprise that Kennelly feels at ease around political operators; she grew up with them. Her father was John Bailey, the legendary Connecticut party boss and chairman of the Democratic National Committee under Presidents John F. Kennedy and Lyndon B. Johnson. And her late husband, James J. Kennelly, was a former Connecticut state House speaker. He died in 1995 at age 64.

Kennelly's knack for getting along with the leadership showed early. She had been in the chamber less than a year when she won a seat on the prestigious Ways and Means Committee. In December 1984 she was appointed to the Steering and Policy Committee. And in the June 1989 Democratic leadership shakeup that followed Texan Jim Wright's resignation as Speaker, Kennelly made a long-shot bid for the open post of caucus chairman. She lost to Steny H. Hoyer of Maryland, who had been the caucus vice chairman.

Her next chance to advance came in August 1991, when David E. Bonior of Michigan moved up to whip from the position of chief deputy. Then-Speaker Thomas S. Foley of Washington, under pressure from women, blacks and Southern conservatives, all of whom felt excluded from party decision-making, decided to make the leadership a bit more diverse. Kennelly was tapped as one of three chief deputy whips.

With infrequent exception, Kennelly votes a liberal line. One exception in the 104th was her backing of legislation banning federal recognition of same-sex marriages, a stand many other Democrats also took. Also, she switched her vote on a constitutional amendment banning desecration of the American flag. She opposed the amendment in 1990, but voted for it in 1995.

Generally, though, she has found herself in disagreement with the Republican majority. She opposed efforts to deny public education to illegal immigrants and to allow employers to offer compensatory time instead of overtime pay to their workers. She supported raising the minimum wage and voted against exempting small businesses from paying the higher minimum.

Kennelly opposed legislation banning a particular abortion technique that opponents call "partial birth" abortion, taking to the House floor to oppose the bill. "Do we know no restraint?'" she asked. "Is nothing sacred for the individual from the interference of government?"

Kennelly voted for the final welfare overhaul bill that President Clinton signed into law in 1996, after working assiduously to modify key elements of what the GOP was seeking in the way of welfare reform.

She opposed the initial House Republican welfare bill and expressed disappointment that even moderate Republicans refused to back most efforts to amend it in 1995. "They've taken a pledge to the Contract [With America], and you can see by their votes they're keeping it," she said.

Kennelly failed to win approval for an amendment requiring states to assure that child care would be available for welfare recipients who land jobs or participate in training programs. "I'm saying before you require that anyone go to work, make sure the child is in a safe place and cared for," she said. But Republicans called the provision an unfunded mandate and her amendment was defeated in a Ways and Means subcommittee.

At the urging of Kennelly and others, the GOP did agree to strengthen efforts to force parents to pay child support, including new state and federal registries to help find parents who fail to pay child support, a new system of collecting and disbursing child support payments, and tougher

CONNECTICUT 1
Central — Hartford

With Hartford as the hub and 19 surrounding communities as its spokes, the 1st is a classic example of a core urban center with interdependent suburbs. Many of the 1st's 548,000 residents work in Hartford.

Situated 100 miles southwest of Boston and 110 miles northeast of New York, Hartford is well-positioned to remain a regional commerce center. Companies such as Aetna, the Travelers and CIGNA helped earn Hartford the moniker "insurance capital of the world." But the city also is the state capital and a major financial center.

During the 1980s, banks, insurance companies and related businesses flourished, creating pockets of extreme wealth in the bedroom communities outside Hartford. But when the stock market plummeted, real estate sagged and defense contracts began to dwindle, Hartford caught the brunt of it all.

The situation appeared to stabilize in 1992 as unemployment leveled off and the aerospace industry targeted commercial customers to replace lost military contracts. Like much of Connecticut, the 1st is watching anxiously to see how defense-related companies weather the post-Cold War downsizing.

United Technologies, the state's largest private employer with headquarters in Hartford, undertook extensive layoffs in the district. The state government, Hartford's largest employer, has been in a similar belt-tightening mode.

Once the domain of the Democratic political czar John Bailey, the 1st now belongs to his daughter, Kennelly. In her past six elections, Kennelly has garnered an average of 73 percent of the vote; political security has given her latitude to become an inside player on Capitol Hill. She is vice chairman of the Democratic Caucus.

Minorities, which make up slightly more than a quarter of the 1st, play an increasingly powerful role. In 1981, Hartford became the first New England city to elect a black mayor. Hispanics were involved in shaping state legislative and congressional districts in 1992 and have put up candidates for several local offices.

Registered Democrats outnumber Republicans in the 1st by nearly two to one. In 1988, Democrat Michael S. Dukakis won the old 1st District, thanks primarily to Hartford's large black community, and Bill Clinton had little trouble winning in both 1992 and 1996. While in 1992 he was just shy of a majority in the three-way race, he polled more than 59 percent of the vote four years later, despite the presence of both Bob Dole and Ross Perot on the ballot. Voters who are unaffiliated with either party could be a key swing group in future national and statewide elections.

The district has a rich literary history. Mark Twain and Harriet Beecher Stowe both hailed from Hartford. The Hartford Courant, founded in 1764, is the nation's oldest newspaper in continuous circulation.

1990 Population: 548,016. White 429,116 (78%), Black 77,824 (14%), Other 41,076 (7%). Hispanic origin 55,179 (10%). 18 and over 423,317 (77%), 62 and over 93,458 (17%). Median age: 35.

enforcement provisions. Kennelly tried to go further, but Ways and Means rejected her proposal to allow states to suspend or restrict driver's licenses and other licenses of deadbeat parents if they refused to honor a child-support agreement. However, the provision was later added to the bill.

Republicans initially rejected Kennelly's attempt to eliminate a provision reducing cash benefits for the family of a child whose paternity had not been established. Kennelly argued that if the mother did everything she could to identify the child's father, she should get full benefits even if the state was unable to track him down. The provision was later modified to penalize only those welfare recipients who refused to cooperate with paternity establishment.

Also, she was a strong supporter of the earned-income tax credit, opposing Republican efforts to scale back the program.

"This is a tax increase on 15 million working American families," she said. "It is incomprehensible to me why families earning less than $28,000 a year are singled out for a tax increase."

She supported giving tax credits to families who adopt children, a notion popular in the GOP, but urged members to press ahead on the more difficult questions of how to promote adoption of children with special physical or emotional needs, and of siblings who do not want to be separated.

One tax issue that received considerable attention in the 103rd was the "nanny tax" — the Social Security tax that people are typically required to pay in behalf of their domestic employees. Several Clinton administration appointees were found to have run afoul of the law, including one nominee for attorney general, Zöe Baird, who ultimately withdrew because of her non-compliance with the law. In the aftermath of Baird's nomination, Kennelly introduced legislation to raise the annual earnings threshold where Social Security payments were required. However, she fought attempts to raise the limit so high that career domestic workers, many of them women, would be denied the benefits of a social safety net.

She said she was satisfied with the final law, which included a $1,000 limit. "The law," she said, "never intended you to have to pay this tax for your 12-year-old baby-sitter."

Kennelly is a latecomer to feminist issues; she says her three daughters persuaded her to become active. But she does not hold back on big issues or small ones. In 1991, hers was a loud voice expressing outrage that the Senate wanted to vote on Clarence Thomas' nomination to the Supreme Court without hearing from Professor Anita F. Hill about allegations of sexual harassment. And when invitations for congressional leaders to lunch with Clinton on Inauguration Day 1993 stopped at the level of party Whip Bonior, she argued persuasively that a president who campaigned on diversity might like to have a woman in the room.

At Home: Despite a slow start getting into politics herself, Kennelly has proved she learned well at her father's knee. Whether battling Republicans or working the angles inside her own party, Kennelly has shown real political savvy and longevity.

Her first political job came in 1975; the former social service director was appointed to the Hartford City Council and later won a full term on her own.

It took a strikingly independent move to win her next office. Gloria Schaffer, the Democratic secretary of state, decided to step down from her post in 1978. Party protocol called for replacing her with another Jewish woman to balance the ethnic makeup of the statewide ticket. Kennelly ignored precedent. At the party convention she finagled the nomination from the party favorites and won easily in November.

In 1981, two weeks after six-term Democratic Rep. William R. Cotter died of cancer, Kennelly announced her candidacy to replace him. Other Democrats dropped out, and she was nominated by acclamation.

Kennelly had little trouble in the January 1982 special election against GOP nominee Ann P. Uccello, a former mayor of Hartford. Running in a Democratic stronghold, Kennelly had a huge financial lead and won with nearly 60 percent.

Since then, Kennelly has rolled up huge tallies in each of her six re-election campaigns, never falling below 62 percent.

Even a taped television report in 1990 showing Kennelly and other members of the Ways and Means Committee romping on the beach during a taxpayer-paid trip to Barbados was not enough to hurt her seriously. She defeated Republican nominee James P. Garvey with 71 percent of the vote.

Kennelly shows no signs of tiring of the political life, although she has expressed interest in moving up a rung to statewide office. She was discussed as a possible candidate when two governors announced their retirements — Democratic incumbent William A. O'Neill in 1990 and and independent Lowell P. Weicker Jr. in 1993 — but she decided against making those races.

HOUSE ELECTIONS

1996 General		
Barbara B. Kennelly (D,ACP)	158,222	(74%)
Kent Sleath (R)	53,666	(25%)
1994 General		
Barbara B. Kennelly (D,ACP)	138,637	(73%)
Douglas T. Putnam (R)	46,865	(25%)
John F. Forry III (CC)	3,405	(2%)

Previous Winning Percentages: **1992** (67%) **1990** (71%) **1988** (77%) **1986** (74%) **1984** (62%) **1982** (68%) **1982†** (59%)

† Special election

CAMPAIGN FINANCE

	Receipts	Receipts from PACs	Expend-itures
1996			
Kennelly (D)	$580,196	$342,482 (59%)	$543,033
Sleath (R)	$8,457	0	$8,459
1994			
Kennelly (D)	$502,330	$354,325 (71%)	$579,121
Putnam (R)	$25,833	$14 (0%)	$24,693

DISTRICT VOTE FOR PRESIDENT

	1996		1992
D	136,775 (59%)	**D**	133,686 (50%)
R	68,483 (30%)	**R**	82,086 (31%)
I	20,862 (9%)	**I**	52,154 (20%)

KEY VOTES

1997	
Ban "partial birth" abortions	N
1996	
Approve farm bill	N
Deny public education to illegal immigrants	N
Repeal ban on certain assault-style weapons	N
Increase minimum wage	Y
Freeze defense spending	N
Approve welfare overhaul	Y
1995	
Approve balanced-budget constitutional amendment	N
Relax Clean Water Act regulations	N
Oppose limits on environmental regulations	Y
Reduce projected Medicare spending	N
Approve GOP budget with tax and spending cuts	N

VOTING STUDIES

	Presidential Support		Party Unity		Conservative Coalition	
Year	S	O	S	O	S	O
1996	84	16	86	13	49	49
1995	77	18	86	11	41	59
1994	90	10	94	4	42	58
1993	88	12	95	5	32	68
1992	22	77	92	6	29	71
1991	30	70	94	6	24	76

INTEREST GROUP RATINGS

Year	ADA	AFL-CIO	CCUS	ACU
1996	80	n/a	25	10
1995	85	100	33	12
1994	85	67	50	10
1993	90	100	18	8
1992	100	92	25	4
1991	80	83	20	0

2 Sam Gejdenson (D)

Of Bozrah — Elected 1980, 9th term

Biographical Information
Born: May 20, 1948, Eschwege, Germany.
Education: Mitchell College, A.S. 1968; U. of Connecticut, B.A. 1970.
Occupation: Dairy farmer.
Family: Wife Betsy Henley-Cohn; two children; two stepchildren.
Religion: Jewish.
Political Career: Conn. House, 1975-79.
Capitol Office: 1401 Longworth Bldg. 20515; 225-2076.

Committees
International Relations
International Economic Policy & Trade (ranking)
House Oversight (ranking)
Joint Library
Joint Printing

In Washington: Although Gejdenson's last three reelections have come with 52, 43 and 51 percent of the vote, his shaky standing in the 2nd has not restrained him from partisan drumbeating in Washington. As ranking Democrat on the House Oversight Committee, he job is to take on the GOP majority over institutional matters such as committee funding levels, and he does so with relish.

Starting off the 105th with his usual feistiness, Gejdenson in March 1997 led the fight against the GOP majority's proposed budget for House committee operations. The measure included a 48 percent funding increase for the Government Reform and Oversight Committee, which is investigating campaign fundraising for the 1996 election — and which, in the opinion of Gejdenson and other Democrats, seemed intent on exposing misdeeds by the Clinton campaign. The House eventually approved $20 million for Government Reform, but the committee would be allowed to go back to House Oversight to request as much as $7.9 million more set aside in a "reserve fund" for investigations. Democrats called that a "slush fund" that could be spent to fish for information potentially embarrassing to the Clinton administration.

Before approving the committee funds, the GOP leadership first had to quell a rebellion in its ranks by 11 fiscally conservative members unhappy that Congress was increasing funding for its own operations. Eventually, the rebels backed down, mollified by leadership promises that overall committee spending would be frozen, although the "reserve fund" remained in place. Gejdenson mocked the arrangement. "Now, if you want to be for an increase, vote for an increase. If you want to be for a slush fund, stand up and admit that you think you need a slush fund. But do not fool yourselves. This is not a freeze," he told the House.

Gejdenson also has had a rocky relationship with the chairman of House Oversight, conservative California Republican Bill Thomas. During the ethics investigation of Speaker Newt Gingrich in the 104th, Gejdenson and Thomas traded accusations over the release of a transcript from a committee meeting in which Republicans voted to cut off funds for James M. Cole, the independent counsel investigating Gingrich. Thomas accused Gejdenson of leaking the transcript; Gejdenson denied it.

Gejdenson is the No. 2 Democrat on the International Relations Committee, and the ranking member, Lee H. Hamilton of Indiana, is retiring at the end of the 105th. So Gejdenson, who is more liberal and partisan than Hamilton, is in line to take the panel's top Democratic seat if he returns for the 106th.

During the 104th, Gejdenson strongly favored a committee bill that penalized foreign companies that aid the oil industries of Iran or Libya. Although Clinton administration officials had expressed some concern over the measure because of objections from U.S. allies and trading partners, the House cleared the measure in July 1996, and Clinton signed it in August. The legislation was intended to punish Iran and Libya for their sponsorship of terrorism and for their efforts to acquire weapons of mass destruction. It was championed by the American Israel Public Affairs Committee and other groups that regard Iran as the main threat to Middle East stability. Gejdenson, who is Jewish, is a strong supporter of Israel.

During committee consideration, Gejdenson cited a string of terrorist bombings in Israel (in which involvement by Tehran was suspected) in defending the campaign to economically isolate Iran and Libya. "I am sorry if we offend our friends," said Gejdenson. "But the sight of arms and legs strewn over the street in Tel Aviv offends me."

Gejdenson has long been interested in overhauling the Export Administration Act. Written in 1979 and revised in 1985, the law strictly limits the export to communist nations of industrial goods and dual-use materials — items that have possible military applications such as computers and machine tools. With the Soviet Union disintegrated and many of the old Eastern bloc nations working to democratize, Gejdenson has argued that national security will not be threatened by relaxing controls on much sophisticated technology that has civilian and military uses. (A more relaxed policy also could

CONNECTICUT 2
East — New London

The fate of the nuclear attack submarine *Seawolf* had shaped the economic and political future of the 2nd more than any other factor. A region once devastated by the death of the wool industry had staked its economic future on the submarine's survival.

In the 1980s, more than half the 2nd's jobs, particularly those along the seacoast, were provided by defense-related companies. With the Pentagon budget shrinking in the post-Cold War era, the 2nd is virtually guaranteed ongoing job losses. About 8,700 people work at the region's largest employer, Groton-based Electric Boat Co., down from about 15,000 employees entering the 1990s. A division of General Dynamics, EB's well-being rested with submarine orders. Construction of Trident missile submarines was nearing an end, and hopes for building dozens of *Seawolf* attack subs were deflated when President George Bush in 1992 recommended scrapping the program.

But then the Navy came to Electric Boat's aid, intending to give the shipyard the contract to build the first two ships of a new class of smaller, cheaper subs, arguing that building submarines is the company's sole line of work. But the Virginia delegation, which represents the Newport News Shipbuilding and Dry Dock Co., EB's main competitor, argued against the Navy's plan. Ultimately, conferees on the fiscal 1996 defense authorization bill split the difference: the first sub would be built at Groton, and the second sub at Newport News. But the Navy in 1997 urged that the two shipyards cooperatively build each of the four new attack subs.

The 2nd's voters showed a predilection for voting Republican in presidential contests of the 1980s, but in 1992 and 1996 they embraced Democrat Bill Clinton. But Gejdenson met stiff GOP resistance in his bid for re-election in 1992; it took nearly a week for vote-counters to declare him winner.

Gejdenson's 1994 re-election was no easier. In spite of pro-Gejdenson appearances by Clinton and other administration officials, the election was one of the closest in congressional history. But by 1996, Gejdenson got a little more breathing room, winning the district with 52 percent.

The largest district in the state geographically and considered rural by East Coast standards, the 2nd includes some of Connecticut's poorest villages and towns.

Unlike Lowell, in neighboring Massachusetts, the communities along the Quinnebaug and Shetucket rivers never really recovered from the wool mills' departures in the 1960s. After several decades of area economic stagnation, Gejdenson coordinated an effort to designate the former mill towns as a National Heritage Corridor, with museums and recreational opportunities. The corridor plan fits in well with southeastern Connecticut's strategy to rejuvenate the economy with tourism.

Mystic, with its historic seaport, museums, aquarium and other attractions, is the biggest success story. Another lure for visitors is the Foxwoods casino in Ledyard. Run by the Mashantucket Pequot tribe, it draws tens of thousands of people a day.

1990 Population: 548,041. White 511,184 (93%), Black 20,209 (4%), Other 16,648 (3%). Hispanic origin 16,394 (3%). 18 and over 421,044 (77%), 62 and over 78,188 (14%). Median age: 33.

open overseas trading doors for Connecticut's high-tech and military related businesses.)

The House in July 1996 easily passed a major rewrite of the nation's export control law, but the Senate showed scant interest. Although the bill had significant bipartisan support, Gejdenson complained that it did not go far enough in enabling exporters to compete internationally.

Gejdenson has faced one major quandary throughout a House career in which he has mainly voted a liberal line. His state's economy relies heavily on defense contractors, including General Dynamics' Electric Boat Co., which builds nuclear submarines in the 2nd and is one of the largest employers in southern New England. He joined with other Democratic members whose districts rely on defense contracts and voted in June 1996 against freezing the defense budget at the prior year level. Deficit hawks wanted the Pentagon to share the pain of government downsizing, but the freeze lost.

Gejdenson takes a two-pronged approach to the defense issue, promoting efforts to diversify his district's economy while also lobbying hard for the Navy submarine program. When construction of the *Seawolf*-class nuclear submarine at the Groton-based Electric Boat faced extinction in 1995, the Navy proposed contracting with the shipyard to build the first two copies of a new class of smaller, cheaper subs. But the Virginia delegation, representing the Newport News Shipbuilding and Dry Dock Co., the Groton yard's main competitor, wanted a piece of the action. Conferees on the fiscal 1996 defense authorization bill agreed that Newport News Shipbuilding and Electric Boat would each build up to two of the new subs. In early 1997, the shipyards announced that at the Navy's urging they would work cooperatively on the four new subs, rather than each yard building separate subs.

At Home: The 2nd has some of Connecticut's more conservative voters, and it was not until his fourth House campaign in 1986 that Gejdenson won with more than 56 percent of the vote. He posted percentages in the 60s in the 1986, 1988 and 1990, but since then has had his hands full three times against the same GOP foe, Edward W. Munster.

In 1992, Munster, a state senator not well known in the 2nd, waged an underfunded challenge to Gejdenson that got no help from the top of the GOP ticket: George Bush won only 30 percent of the presidential vote in the 2nd, nearly losing to independent Ross Perot in the district. But Munster used Gejdenson's 51 overdrafts at the House bank as evidence that the incumbent had "gone Washington," and he polled a strong 49 percent of the vote.

Munster roared back in 1994, this time with more funding and name recognition, and with the year's strong GOP winds at his back. Gejdenson also faced a third-party challenge from physician David Bingham, who ended up with 15 percent of the vote.

On Election Night, the tally showed Gejdenson up by just two votes. The Connecticut Supreme Court ultimately certified that he prevailed by 21 votes. Munster challenged the outcome in the House (the House Oversight Committee, where Gejdenson sits, weighed the matter), but Munster dropped the challenge in April 1995.

Munster returned for round three in 1996, even though some GOP insiders quietly hoped for a fresh face to challenge Gejdenson. Munster got some negative feedback from voters who thought he had been a sore loser two years earlier. Gejdenson reminded voters of House GOP conservatives' efforts to alter such programs as college student loans, Medicare and Medicaid, and he suggested that Munster would lend support to undermining the politically popular programs. This time he finished 7 percentage points ahead of Munster, with 52 percent of the vote.

In his first bid for Congress in 1980, Gejdenson thought he would coast after defeating John N. Dempsey Jr., the son of a former governor, in the Democratic primary. But GOP nominee Tony Guglielmo benefited from Ronald Reagan's big victory in the district, and Gejdenson got just 53 percent.

Guglielmo was back in 1982, but that year's economic downturn put him on the defensive, and Gejdenson won with 56 percent.

In 1984, Gejdenson was unexpectedly pressed by lightly regarded Roberta Koontz, a botany professor. Bolstered by Reagan's landslide in the 2nd and capitalizing on voters' concerns about Gejdenson's liberalism, Koontz held Gejdenson to 54 percent.

In 1986, Francis M. "Bud" Mullen, a former director of the federal Drug Enforcement Administration, complained that Gejdenson would not take a seat on the Armed Services Committee (now National Security) and had opposed some Reagan defense programs. But Gejdenson countered with evidence that he had helped bring billions of dollars in ship- and submarine-building contracts to the 2nd. He mauled Mullen, then won comfortably until his encounters with Munster.

HOUSE ELECTIONS

1996 General		
Sam Gejdenson (D,ACP)	115,175	(52%)
Edward W. Munster (R)	100,332	(45%)
Dianne G. Ondusko (INDC)	6,477	(3%)
1994 General		
Sam Gejdenson (D)	79,188	(43%)
Edward W. Munster (R)	79,167	(43%)
David Bingham (ACP)	27,716	(15%)

Previous Winning Percentages: **1992** (51%) **1990** (60%) **1988** (64%) **1986** (67%) **1984** (54%) **1982** (56%) **1980** (53%)

CAMPAIGN FINANCE

	Receipts	Receipts from PACs		Expend-itures
1996				
Gejdenson (D)	$1,185,748	$398,558	(34%)	$1,177,255
Munster (R)	$412,714	$74,844	(18%)	$423,658
Ondusko (I)	$3,771	0		$3,637
1994				
Gejdenson (D)	$1,415,185	$501,553	(35%)	$1,422,126
Munster (R)	$442,902	$116,337	(26%)	$426,390
Bingham (ACP)	$176,029	$1,000	(1%)	$176,088

DISTRICT VOTE FOR PRESIDENT

1996		1992	
D	123,595 (53%)	**D**	113,553 (43%)
R	73,863 (32%)	**R**	79,110 (30%)
I	29,790 (13%)	**I**	72,782 (27%)

KEY VOTES

1997	
Ban "partial birth" abortions	N
1996	
Approve farm bill	N
Deny public education to illegal immigrants	N
Repeal ban on certain assault-style weapons	N
Increase minimum wage	Y
Freeze defense spending	N
Approve welfare overhaul	Y
1995	
Approve balanced-budget constitutional amendment	N
Relax Clean Water Act regulations	N
Oppose limits on environmental regulations	Y
Reduce projected Medicare spending	N
Approve GOP budget with tax and spending cuts	N

VOTING STUDIES

	Presidential Support		Party Unity		Conservative Coalition	
Year	**S**	**O**	**S**	**O**	**S**	**O**
1996	80	16	90	7	33	67
1995	83	14	93	5	27	73
1994	87	13	95	1	17	83
1993	83	17	97	2	18	82
1992	16	84	96	4	17	81
1991	23	77	96	3	11	89

INTEREST GROUP RATINGS

Year	ADA	AFL-CIO	CCUS	ACU
1996	90	n/a	20	0
1995	90	100	13	4
1994	80	89	36	10
1993	95	100	9	8
1992	90	92	38	12
1991	95	100	20	0

3 Rosa DeLauro (D)

Of New Haven — Elected 1990, 4th term

Biographical Information
Born: March 2, 1943, New Haven, Conn.
Education: London School of Economics, 1962-63; Marymount College, B.A. 1964; Columbia U., M.A. 1966.
Occupation: Political activist.
Family: Husband, Stanley Greenberg; three stepchildren.
Religion: Roman Catholic.
Political Career: No previous office.
Capitol Office: 436 Cannon Bldg. 20515; 225-3661.

Committees
Appropriations
Agriculture, Rural Development, FDA & Related Agencies; Labor, Health & Human Services, Education & Related Agencies

Chief Deputy Whip

In Washington: DeLauro has liberal views, lots of energy and political smarts that she developed growing up in an activist family and later serving as a senior Hill staff member. After winning election to the 3rd in 1990, she soon drew the eye of Democratic leaders, who put her on the Appropriations Committee in 1993.

That reward was snatched away when Republicans won a House majority in 1994 and cut the Democrats' allotment of committee seats. But with several Appropriations Democrats leaving Congress at the end of the 104th, DeLauro was able to get back onto the committee in 1997.

DeLauro has survived the transition to minority status rather well. She was appointed one of the party's four chief deputy whips; she got a seat on a new Policy Committee set up by Minority Leader Richard A. Gephardt; and she serves on the Democratic Steering Committee, which makes committee assignments.

DeLauro likes little that the Republicans propose. She voted in the 104th against welfare overhaul legislation, against tax cuts, against slowing the growth of Medicare spending, against allowing companies to offer employees comp time in lieu of overtime pay, against denying public education to illegal immigrants, against repealing the ban on certain semiautomatic assault-style weapons and against conservatives' efforts to restrict abortion. Not the least bit reticent with her opinions, DeLauro also takes to the House floor very frequently (370 times in the 104th Congress) to chastise the GOP majority.

Early in the 105th when the House was considering a measure overhauling the federal public housing system, DeLauro blasted the requirement that some residents perform community service in order to remain in public housing. She and other Democrats charged the provision was "servitude" because it imposed a requirement on public housing recipients that is not demanded of others who receive federal assistance. "The real name for this is forced labor. The residents of public housing are not criminals," DeLauro charged. "We do not require tobacco farmers to volunteer in exchange for federal crop insurance."

She was particularly critical of Republicans' euphoria when Bob Dole, the former Senate majority leader and GOP presidential nominee, announced that he would loan House Speaker Newt Gingrich the $300,000 he needs to pay the penalty assessed by the House ethics committee for violating House ethics rules.

"Republicans are celebrating the fact that the gentleman from Georgia, Newt Gingrich, is paying a $300,000 fine for lying to Congress," DeLauro told the House. "The Speaker should not be applauded for violating the ethics law of this body. . . . Let us not forget, let us not forget that the Speaker pled guilty. It is nothing to celebrate. It is, in fact, a sad day for the House of Representatives." (Gingrich later said he would pay half of the fine on his own, borrowing $150,000 from Dole and repaying all of that by 1999.)

DeLauro was one of five Democrats who filed a complaint with the ethics committee in December 1995 accusing Gingrich of using GOPAC, a political action committee he chaired until early 1995, to help finance his re-election effort and those of fellow Republicans running for the House. GOPAC claimed to be involved in helping only local and state races, allowing it to avoid registering as a federal PAC, which would have required it to disclose its finances fully. After an independent counsel found that Gingrich violated federal tax laws by creating the network of tax-exempt organizations, the ethics committee recommended that Gingrich be reprimanded by the House and assessed the $300,000 penalty.

DeLauro is also not hesitant to go after her own party's president, if her liberal sensibilities are offended. She was not happy when President Clinton announced in May 1997 that he had reached agreement with congressional Republicans on a budget including certain tax cuts. She fired off a letter to Clinton, signed by 110 House Democrats, urging him not to support the capital gains and estate tax cuts outlined in the deal.

CONNECTICUT 3
South — New Haven

To the outside world, New Haven is synonymous with Yale University. The prestigious Ivy League school with its famous theater, renowned academics and rich history is a symbol of top-drawer higher education. But while Yale has been a fixture in New Haven since the 18th century, the prosperous academic community has little in common with the poorer white ethnics and minorities who dominate the city.

New Haven is a busy port along Long Island Sound with a substantial population of blue-collar workers. One-third of its 130,000 residents are black. But sizable swaths of the community are economically impoverished; one-fifth of New Haven's people have incomes below the poverty level. Most of the national headlines the city has garnered in recent years have been about racial tensions, violent crime and the high infant mortality rate.

There has long been tension between the upscale and intellectual Yalies and the townfolk around them. Many residents believe that their tax burden is unduly heavy because the university — the city's largest landowner — is not required to pay taxes on property it uses for academic purposes. Yale often is pilloried as an enclave for the elite that cares little about the city as a whole.

The university has tried to mend fences, allocating millions for projects to improve the city and help its residents. Yale also continues to be the largest employer in the city.

New Haven, with all of its problems, still possesses its share of culture and the arts. It is home to the Shubert Theater, a historically successful off-broadway theater. The Palace Theater and the Long Wharf Theater also attract a multitude of plays and performances from New York City. The New Haven Green still serves an important presence in the city, acting as a centerpiece for the downtown activities.

One thing the Yalies and the townies agree on: They like Democratic candidates.

Districtwide, defense manufacturers and hundreds of related subcontractors employ the most people. One of the biggest is Sikorsky, located in Stratford. Workers in this sector seem likely to face continued uncertainty in the years ahead as military budgets come under ongoing scrutiny.

Italian-Americans dominated House elections in the 3rd from 1952 through 1980, and they re-emerged as a force in 1990 with the election of DeLauro, daughter of an Italian immigrant. The 3rd went Republican in 1980 but reverted to the Democrats two years later. The Democratic bent of New Haven's blacks and its white ethnics makes the district tough turf for the GOP in House elections. Still, migration from the city to the suburbs has diminished the city's clout in the 3rd, and given the GOP a chance in contests for higher office.

1990 Population: 547,765. White 460,918 (84%), Black 65,293 (12%), Other 21,554 (4%). Hispanic origin 27,023 (5%). 18 and over 426,557 (78%), 62 and over 95,287 (17%). Median age: 35.

"Administration officials have assured us that your goal is to reach a budget agreement that will have the support of a majority of the Democratic Caucus," they wrote. "A budget deal which includes these back-loaded tax cuts is a budget that will not meet that goal."

When DeLauro was forced off Appropriations at the start of the 104th, she moved to the National Security Committee, where she led the fight to lift the ban on service personnel and military dependents obtaining abortions at overseas military facilities, even if they pay for the procedure themselves. In one of his first acts as president, Clinton in 1993 signed an executive order ending an earlier version of the ban. Anti-abortion activists bitterly opposed Clinton's action.

Conservative California Republican Robert K. Dornan, chairman of the Military Personnel Subcommittee in the 104th, made it a priority to reinstate the ban. He was successful on the first defense bill considered by the Republican-led House. Since then, the House has voted to reinstate the ban on each succeeding defense authorization and spending bill. DeLauro has tried unsuccessfully each time to lift it.

She cast the issue in terms of fairness: For military personnel and their dependents stationed in countries where abortions are banned or medical services unreliable, she argued, access to U.S. military hospitals is the only practical way they can exercise their constitutional right to an abortion. Otherwise, she contended, "we would ask women who served in the military . . . to park their constitutional rights at the water's edge." But Dornan contended that the performance of abortions in federally funded facilities inevitably entailed a public subsidy of the procedure, even if a woman paid a fee.

Also from her National Security seat, DeLauro fought for the defense-related companies in her state, particularly the region's largest employer, General Dynamics' Groton-based Electric Boat Co. Electric Boat had the contract for the Navy's nuclear attack *Seawolf* submarine, but that program was winding down. To keep Electric Boat in business and ensure competition for submarine contracts in the long term, the Navy intended to give the shipyard the contract to build the first two ships of a new class of smaller, cheaper subs, arguing that building submarines is the company's sole line of work.

But Electric Boat's competitor, the Newport News Shipbuilding and Dry Dock Co., joined by members of the Virginia congressional delegation, mounted a vigorous attack on the plan. Conferees on the fiscal 1996 defense authorization bill split the difference, giving both the Groton and Newport News yards subs to build. But in early 1997, the shipyards announced that at the Navy's urging they would work cooperatively on the four new attack subs, rather than have each shipyard building separate subs.

Eschewing power suits in favor of earth-tone clothes, bright scarves and funky jewelry, DeLauro rarely is mistaken for a conformist. Although associated with many liberal causes since the 1960s, she refers to herself as a "progressive moderate."

DeLauro has long been active on women's health issues. During debate on a 1993 reauthorization bill for the National Institutes of Health, DeLauro noted her own battle with ovarian cancer, which she said was diagnosed only "by chance." She said, "For years, women's health concerns have been systematically ignored by the federal government." Early in the 105th, she introduced a bill that would require minimum hospital stays for breast cancer treatment, including two days for mastectomies and one day for lymph node dissections. Clinton had raised the issue of "drive-through mastectomies" in his February 1997 State of the Union address.

At Home: DeLauro's political instincts are rooted in her upbringing in Wooster Square, a tightknit Italian neighborhood of New Haven. Her father was an Italian immigrant and her mother, a factory worker. Both parents were aldermen in New Haven; her mother, Louisa, is the longest-serving board member. DeLauro often went to political gatherings as a child.

Her husband, Stanley Greenberg, is a prominent Democratic pollster. DeLauro spent seven years as chief of staff to Democratic Sen. Christopher J. Dodd of Connecticut and was director of EMILY's List, which raises funds for women candidates.

After her surprisingly close first election in 1990, DeLauro expected to face anti-tax activist Thomas Scott again in 1992. So while working to amass a record on taxes and jobs, she also raised an impressive amount of money for the rematch. When the showdown arrived, political circumstances nationally and locally had shifted in her favor. Anti-tax fervor in Connecticut also had subsided somewhat, depriving Scott of his best issue. DeLauro not only beat Scott again, she also easily outran Clinton in every corner of the 3rd.

In both races, Scott, a former state senator, portrayed DeLauro as a far-left radical out of sync with the 3rd's working-class, ethnic voters.

In 1994, DeLauro faced Susan E. Johnson, a college professor and attorney. Johnson had political advantages — she was a black Republican and had the endorsement of the independent A Connecticut Party — but the popular DeLauro won re-election handily, with 63 percent of the vote. She did even better in 1996, garnering 71 percent.

HOUSE ELECTIONS

1996 General		
Rosa DeLauro (D,ACP)	150,798	(71%)
John Coppola (R)	59,335	(28%)
1994 General		
Rosa L. DeLauro (D)	111,261	(63%)
Susan E. Johnson (R,ACP)	64,094	(37%)

Previous Winning Percentages: **1992** (66%) **1990** (52%)

CAMPAIGN FINANCE

	Receipts	Receipts from PACs	Expend-itures
1996			
DeLauro (D)	$603,976	$247,938 (41%)	$424,582
1994			
DeLauro (D)	$657,657	$288,250 (44%)	$655,245
Johnson (R)	$12,886	$1,614 (13%)	$8,297

VOTING STUDIES

	Presidential Support		Party Unity		Conservative Coalition	
Year	S	O	S	O	S	O
1996	84	16	93	7	29	71
1995	85	14	94	6	26	73
1994	82	13	96	3	31	69
1993	84	16	95	4	20	80
1992	17	82	94	6	25	73
1991	26	72	95	5	19	78

KEY VOTES

1997	
Ban "partial birth" abortions	N
1996	
Approve farm bill	N
Deny public education to illegal immigrants	N
Repeal ban on certain assault-style weapons	N
Increase minimum wage	Y
Freeze defense spending	N
Approve welfare overhaul	N
1995	
Approve balanced-budget constitutional amendment	N
Relax Clean Water Act regulations	N
Oppose limits on environmental regulations	Y
Reduce projected Medicare spending	N
Approve GOP budget with tax and spending cuts	N

INTEREST GROUP RATINGS

Year	ADA	AFL-CIO	CCUS	ACU
1996	85	n/a	19	0
1995	85	100	25	4
1994	90	78	42	5
1993	95	100	9	4
1992	90	92	13	4
1991	95	92	20	0

DISTRICT VOTE FOR PRESIDENT

	1996		1992
D	129,756 (57%)	**D**	121,163 (45%)
R	71,009 (31%)	**R**	96,085 (35%)
I	22,916 (10%)	**I**	54,147 (20%)

4 Christopher Shays (R)

Of Stamford — Elected 1987; 5th full term

Biographical Information

Born: Oct. 18, 1945, Stamford, Conn.

Education: Principia College, B.A. 1968; New York U., M.B.A. 1974, M.P.A. 1978.

Occupation: Real estate broker; public official.

Family: Wife, Betsi de Raismes; one child.

Religion: Christian Scientist.

Political Career: Conn. House, 1975-87; Republican candidate for mayor of Stamford, 1983.

Capitol Office: 1502 Longworth Bldg. 20515; 225-5541.

Committees

Budget

Government Reform & Oversight
Human Resources (chairman); National Security, International Affairs & Criminal Justice

In Washington: Republicans and Democrats have often been in a state of near-war since Shays joined the House in 1987, but he has rather successfully cut his own path, one that has him siding with Democrats on some high-profile issues and leading the GOP charge on others. Shays' frequent forays into alliances with the Democrats do not seem to have hurt his position with the Republican leadership, which gave him a seat on the Budget Committee and entrusted him with several important roles in the 104th Congress.

In fact, Shays was a lead sponsor of the first major piece of legislation to become law under the Republican Congress, the Congressional Accountability Act. For years, Shays had been crusading for the bill, which placed Congress under some of the labor, civil rights and health laws that apply to the private sector.

"If a law is right for the private sector, it is right for Congress," Shays liked to say. Republicans made the bill part of their "Contract With America," and it passed the House on the 104th's opening day. The accountability act applies 10 major labor laws to Congress, including statutes to prevent employer discrimination, provide worker safety protections, and guarantee family and medical leave.

Early in 1995, the Republican leadership also gave Shays the tough assignment of heading a GOP budget task force on Medicare. That group came out with a plan to reduce the projected spending increase on Medicare by $282 billion over seven years. Shays' vigorous defense of the controversial plan helped the GOP leadership sell it within the party.

Later that year, Shays also played a high-profile role in Congress' showdown with the White House over a broad budget agreement. Republicans were convinced President Clinton would blink first, and Shays was part of a group of GOP fiscal hard-liners threatening that Congress would not increase the federal debt ceiling unless Clinton came to terms with the GOP on the budget.

"I feel so strongly about this [budget-balancing reconciliation] bill that if Newt got down on his knees and asked me to vote for the debt ceiling, I would say 'no way,' " Shays said. In March 1996, Shays was one of just 30 Republicans voting "no" as the House voted 328-91 to extend the debt limit to $5.5 trillion. By then, GOP leaders had shelved their strategy of trying to force Clinton into a broad budget agreement.

Because of his stands on a number of issues — support for gun control, environmental protections and abortion rights in most instances — some conservative Republicans regard Shays as insufficiently loyal to party orthodoxy. But Shays maintains that on fiscal policy, he is a more consistent conservative than many in his party.

These so-called conservatives, says Shays, continue to support big spending on the military and on other federal functions they endorse, while failing to offer realistic proposals for funding their desires without running up the deficit. He backs elimination of NASA's multibillion-dollar space station program, and in June 1996, he joined Barney Frank, D-Mass., to propose a freeze of fiscal 1997 defense spending at the previous year's level. Their amendment was rejected, 194-219.

In May 1994, Shays and Frank teamed up to alter the defense authorization bill. The House approved, 268-144, their amendment to reduce the number of U.S. personnel stationed in Europe by up to 75,000 if European allies were not paying 75 percent of the non-salary costs of their deployment by the end of fiscal 1998.

Shays and Frank tapped into the deeply rooted belief on Capitol Hill that many wealthy allies — who are also commercial competitors of the United States — skimp on their military because they can rely on American protection. Opponents argued that U.S. interests were furthered by stationing forces overseas, closer to potential trouble spots.

Reporters on Capitol Hill often turn to Shays for analysis of internal GOP battles and questions on issues where the party's moderates play key roles. Shays is always eager to oblige, which

CONNECTICUT 4
Southwest — Stamford; Bridgeport

Few districts offer the sharp contrasts of the 4th. It includes the affluent white-collar communities of Connecticut's "Gold Coast," along Long Island Sound, where some of America's wealthiest people rub elbows at polo matches.

But it also has Bridgeport, a decaying former whaling community that earned notoriety in 1991 when the city was almost declared bankrupt. One neighborhood in the city, which is plagued by poverty, was dubbed Mount Trashmore because of its three-story garbage pile. (The eyesore finally was removed in 1992 after dominating the area for two decades.)

Taking in Bridgeport as well as better-off Stamford and Norwalk, the 4th has the largest urban population of any Connecticut district. Bridgeport produced one-quarter of all munitions used by the Allied forces in World War II; its strategic importance made it one of two Connecticut cities to be protected by Nike missile bases in the 1950s and early 1960s.

But as the missiles shielded Bridgeport from external enemies, the city deteriorated from within; population shrank in the 1970s and remained static in the 1980s, standing at 142,000 as of 1990. About 15 percent of its residents fell below the poverty line.

To revive the city's failing economy, Bridgeport residents overwhelmingly approved a proposal to bring a casino into the area. But the proposal was rejected by the state legislature. As something of a consolation, the city won $25 million a year for three years (through 1998) from the state for improvement projects, including the construction of a minor league ballpark.

In stark contrast to Bridgeport's problems are the economic conditions in towns such as Westport, Darien, Fairfield and Greenwich. The per capita income in Fairfield County is the fifth highest in the country, even with Bridgeport.

Voting and unemployment data reflect the contrasts in the 4th. Bridgeport voted overwhelmingly for Bill Clinton in 1992, though George Bush carried most of the district's other communities. Jobless rates in Stamford and Norwalk frequently have fallen below the state average. Although Bridgeport's unemployment rate had routinely led Connecticut, it was down to 5.8 percent in early 1997. Clinton narrowly carried the district in 1996 with 51 percent of the vote, though Republican Shays was re-elected with 60 percent.

The dominant political force in the district is the Republican-minded upper-crust towns along the coast. These towns, which are a short drive or train ride from New York City, attract a high number of residents who commute into the city for work. About half of the towns have GOP mayors, and together they host dozens of corporate headquarters and their officers. Stamford has one of the largest concentrations of corporate headquarters in the nation, including well-known names such as Pitney Bowes, Champion International and Xerox. Also, Swiss Bank plans to relocate its North American headquarters from Manhattan to Stamford in the fall of 1997.

1990 Population: 547,765. White 438,475 (80%), Black 71,944 (13%), Other 37,346 (7%). Hispanic origin 61,014 (11%). 18 and over 426,140 (78%), 62 and over 92,570 (17%). Median age: 35.

yields him publicity on issues that play well politically for him. He insists on informality, telling journalists to call him Chris instead of the more traditional "congressman."

Shays' liberal leanings on social and congressional reform issues put him at the forefront of two Republican rebellions in the 104th that nearly cost GOP leaders control of the House floor.

In 1995, the Republican leadership seemed in no hurry to call a vote on a pair of congressional reform measures — a bill to ban House members from accepting virtually any gifts outside of those from close personal friends and family, and a measure requiring lobbyists to increase dramatically the information they must divulge about who pays them and what issues they work on.

Shays and other pro-reform Republicans threatened to vote with Democrats against a spending bill on the House floor, unless the two reform bills were included in it. Facing a likely defeat, GOP leaders hastily pulled the spending measure from the schedule, and shortly afterward, Majority Leader Dick Armey announced that the gift and lobby bills would soon be considered by the House. The lobby bill later became law, and the gift ban became the House rule.

Shays also was one of about two dozen Republicans who sided with Democrats in 1996 on a series of procedural votes aimed at forcing a vote on a Democratic-driven measure increasing the minimum wage. Despite Armey's opposition to the wage increase, he and the rest of the GOP leadership eventually yielded to pressure to allow a vote, and the wage increase passed after it was paired with a package of GOP-backed tax cuts.

Such high-profile opposition to his party's leaders was nothing new for Shays. In September 1994, when Clinton staged a big White House ceremony to sign a broad anti-crime bill, he applauded Shays for his role in bringing together a sizable group of GOP moderates who were decisive in getting the legislation passed.

Most Republicans and some Democrats had complained that the legislation as it emerged from conference spent too much on social programs aimed at prevention. The bill also included a ban on certain semiautomatic assault-style weapons, anathema to gunowners' rights proponents. The combined forces of opposition defeated the rule that would have brought the conference report to the floor. Shays was one of just 11 Republicans to support the rule.

Shays had lobbied other pro-gun control Republicans to vote with him, and he was dismayed by the tactics he was up against: The Republican National Committee hand-delivered copies of a proposed resolution condemning Republicans who backed the assault weapons ban. Shays also got a barrage of negative calls in his district, a lobbying effort he said was orchestrated by the National Rifle Association.

Urged on by Shays and other GOP moderates, the White House ultimately trimmed enough of the social-program spending in the crime bill to broaden its appeal. On the final tally, 46 GOP votes for the bill were crucial in passing it.

Shays has a seat on the Government Reform and Oversight Committee, where he chairs the Human Resources Subcommittee. Shays served on the predecessor panel, Government Operations, where in the 101st Congress he played an active role in the probe of Reagan-era misdeeds at the Department of Housing and Urban Development.

At Home: In the 1987 special election held after veteran GOP Rep. Stewart B. McKinney died, Shays' personable style helped him overcome obstacles on his left and right. Campaigning from the center, Shays was positioned for success in the 4th, long a bastion of moderate Republicanism. He won the special election with a solid 57 percent of the vote and has not been seriously challenged since. Shays' ability to move easily between the worlds of extreme wealth and poverty present in the 4th has held him in good stead.

Shays stepped up to Congress from the state Legislature, where he had a reputation as a stubbornly principled moderate-to-liberal. In 1985, after criticizing what he said were lax ethical standards in Connecticut's judicial system, Shays attempted to make a courtroom statement criticizing a judge for reducing charges against a lawyer who was accused of tampering with a will. Shays was slapped with a contempt citation and a short jail sentence, but he received plenty of favorable publicity.

Though that episode helped Shays expand his cadre of loyalists, it made some local Republicans wary. At the GOP nominating convention for the House special election, Shays initially was denied a line on the ballot and qualified for the primary only after last-minute maneuvering. Nonetheless, with an extensive grass-roots network and tireless campaigning, Shays won nomination with a 38 percent plurality.

In the general election, Shays prevailed by a comfortable margin over Democrat Christine M. Niedermeier, who was widely known because she had run a strong 1986 campaign against McKinney.

In five re-elections since then, Shays has never dropped below 60 percent of the vote.

HOUSE ELECTIONS

1996 General		
Christopher Shays (R)	121,949	(60%)
Bill Finch (D)	75,902	(38%)
Edward H. Tonkin (LIBERT)	2,815	(1%)
1994 General		
Christopher Shays (R)	109,436	(74%)
Jonathan D. Kantrowitz (D)	34,962	(24%)
Irving Sussman (LIBERT)	1,976	(1%)

Previous Winning Percentages: 1992 (67%) **1990** (77%) **1988** (72%) **1987†** (57%)

†Special election

CAMPAIGN FINANCE

	Receipts	Receipts from PACs		Expend-itures
1996				
Shays (R)	$577,706	$17,520	(3%)	$552,597
Finch (D)	$188,194	$25,000	(13%)	$185,986
1994				
Shays (R)	$362,196	$37,020	(10%)	$438,259
Sussman (LIBERT)	$6,281	$1,518	(24%)	$6,280

DISTRICT VOTE FOR PRESIDENT

	1996			1992	
D	113,411	(51%)	**D**	109,122	(42%)
R	88,181	(40%)	**R**	110,072	(42%)
I	14,825	(7%)	**I**	40,802	(16%)

KEY VOTES

1997	
Ban "partial birth" abortions	Y
1996	
Approve farm bill	Y
Deny public education to illegal immigrants	Y
Repeal ban on certain assault-style weapons	N
Increase minimum wage	Y
Freeze defense spending	Y
Approve welfare overhaul	Y
1995	
Approve balanced-budget constitutional amendment	Y
Relax Clean Water Act regulations	N
Oppose limits on environmental regulations	Y
Reduce projected Medicare spending	Y
Approve GOP budget with tax and spending cuts	Y

VOTING STUDIES

	Presidential Support		Party Unity		Conservative Coalition	
Year	**S**	**O**	**S**	**O**	**S**	**O**
1996	53	47	69	31	33	67
1995	44	56	71	29	49	51
1994	56	44	67	33	42	58
1993	55	45	63	37	36	64
1992	40	60	62	38	42	58
1991	58	42	65	35	57	43

INTEREST GROUP RATINGS

Year	ADA	AFL-CIO	CCUS	ACU
1996	30	n/a	69	60
1995	40	8	79	40
1994	55	22	100	38
1993	60	42	64	58
1992	65	67	38	40
1991	60	42	70	50

5 Jim Maloney (D)

Of Danbury — Elected 1996, 1st term

Biographical Information
Born: Sept. 17, 1948, Quincy, Mass.
Education: Harvard U., B.A. 1972; Boston U., J.D. 1980.
Occupation: Lawyer.
Family: Wife, Mary Draper; three children.
Religion: Roman Catholic.
Political Career: Conn. Senate, 1987-95; Democratic nominee for U.S. House, 1994.
Capitol Office: 1213 Longworth Bldg. 20515; 225-3822.

Committees
Banking & Financial Services
Housing & Community Opportunity
National Security
Military Personnel; Military Procurement

The Path to Washington: A former state senator who was unsuccessful in his first bid for Congress, Maloney pulled off an upset on his second try in 1996: He defeated three-term Republican Rep. Gary A. Franks.

Maloney had served eight years in the state Senate before giving up his seat to run for Congress in 1994, when he lost to Franks by just six percentage points. A lawyer from relatively affluent Danbury, Maloney was known in the legislature for his commitment to economic development issues.

Though he is an unabashed liberal, Maloney often sounds more like a moderate Republican when calling for policies to promote commerce and create jobs. Boosting employment is a priority in the 5th district, where a number of businesses have recently laid off thousands of workers or closed their doors completely.

Before serving in the state legislature, Maloney spent four years as the executive director of Danbury's anti-poverty agency. There, he oversaw initiatives such as the Women, Infants and Children nutrition program, Meals on Wheels for the elderly and the Head Start program for preschool children from low-income families.

Maloney's expertise in financial matters helped him win a seat on the Banking and Financial Services Committee, where he hopes to push for capital and investment policies that could benefit cities in his district suffering from a decline in heavy manufacturing. The Democratic leadership also put Maloney on the National Security Committee, where he can look out for companies in Connecticut that do defense-related work.

Maloney says he will work to strengthen vocational training programs to assist workers in coping with economic dislocations and will promote research and development that could spur job growth. He vows to protect education programs from budget cuts and to make college more accessible to people who wish to attend.

In addition, Maloney says his other priorities will be protecting the nation's environment, cracking down on crime, and working to ensure the solvency of Medicare, the federal health program for the elderly, and Medicaid, the federal-state program for the poor and disabled, well into the future.

When Maloney formally announced in early 1996 that he would again challenge Franks, even fellow Democrats did not give him much of a chance.

Franks, one of only two black Republicans in Congress at the time, seemed to be at the peak of his popularity. For example, Franks made headlines when he found himself in conflict with House Speaker Newt Gingrich in 1995 over a Franks proposal that aimed to eliminate federal affirmative action programs.

Franks, who said the Republican leader was reneging on a promise to support the effort, eventually backed down. But in doing so, he publicly questioned Gingrich's veracity at a time when the Speaker and other House leaders had already determined that the proposal had the potential to be more politically damaging than helpful.

While Franks' actions clearly angered many in Congress, including a significant number of white Republicans as well as Democrats, the moves seemed to play well back in the 5th, which is predominantly white and working class.

In fact, Franks became so confident that his position was secure that he ignored his re-election campaign for several weeks during the summer to go on a national tour promoting a book he had written about his experiences as a black Republican.

In the meantime, Maloney was carefully assembling a strong grass-roots organization and solid fundraising machine that made him a more formidable candidate than he had been in the 1994 campaign. When the 1996 campaign turned serious after Labor Day, Franks tried to play it safe by making few public appearances and restricting the media's access to him.

But Maloney pounced on the opportunity, accusing Franks of being out of step with the district and afraid to defend his record. Maloney clinched the victory with 52 percent of the vote.

CONNECTICUT 5
West — Waterbury; Danbury

Three of Connecticut's 10 largest cities are in the 5th — Waterbury, Danbury and Meriden. But any Democratic tendencies in those urban areas are counterbalanced by two dozen smaller towns where Republicans usually run well among middle-class voters and by a number of Fortune 500 companies whose headquarters employ a substantial white-collar work force.

Registered Democrats outnumber Republicans almost 3-to-2 in the 5th, though many of the nominal Democrats — especially those in the working-class Naugatuck Valley — consider the national party too liberal. But in 1996 Democrats dominated the Northeast, including the 5th, which ousted Republican Rep. Gary A. Franks and voted Democratic for president for the first time since 1968.

In Connecticut's heated three-way 1990 gubernatorial election, Waterbury and Danbury voted for former 5th District Rep. John G. Rowland; Meriden split between Rowland and former Sen. Lowell P. Weicker Jr., who became the state's first independent governor. Four years later the 5th went strongly for Rowland, who won the governorship on his second try.

In Waterbury, the 5th's largest city with 109,000 people, Democrats have had some trouble retaining a dominant position even in local politics. Waterbury had a Republican mayor in the latter half of the 1980s and elected a Republican mayor in 1995. Rowland, a Waterbury native, ran well in the city in his three House campaigns. And Franks, also born in Waterbury, made enough of a dent in the city's usual Democratic margin to win three House elections.

Republicans get their strongest electoral support from a number of smaller, wealthier towns in the district, places filled with white-collar businesspeople who commute to corporate jobs in Danbury and venues closer to New York City.

Danbury, in Fairfield County, is home to some of the 5th's most affluent residents. The median family income in Danbury averages around $50,000, and its public school system is among the nation's finest. The city's unemployment rate in November 1996 was 4 percent, under the state average. Located in the media and cultural orbit of New York, the city boasts several corporate headquarters, including Union Carbide, one of the district's larger employers. The city also draws visitors to the Danbury Fair Mall, New England's largest shopping center.

But the wealth has not spread to the district's two other cities.

Downtown Waterbury was sprucing up in the mid-1980s, but when New England fell into recession in the late 1980s, renewal stalled. Waterbury once was hailed as the "brass capital of the world" and was known for the watches it made. But those industries are no more, and the city is searching for ways to fill the void. Two hospitals are the city's major employers.

To the east is Meriden, roughly equidistant from Hartford and New Haven. Once a vital commercial center that was the region's silversmithing capital, Meriden remains a mostly blue-collar community, with many residents working for defense contractors outside the district.

1990 Population: 547,764. White 499,448 (91%), Black 26,455 (5%), Other 21,861 (4%). Hispanic origin 34,132 (6%). 18 and over 416,643 (76%), 62 and over 84,175 (15%). Median age: 34.

HOUSE ELECTIONS

1996 General

Jim Maloney (D,ACP)	111,974	(52%)
Gary A. Franks (R)	98,782	(46%)
Rosita Rodriguez (CC)	2,983	(1%)

CAMPAIGN FINANCE

	Receipts	Receipts from PACs		Expend-itures
1996				
Maloney (D)	$621,220	$255,806	(41%)	$614,440
Franks (R)	$735,938	$357,978	(49%)	$644,293

DISTRICT VOTE FOR PRESIDENT

	1996		1992
D	110,596 (48%)	**D**	93,966 (35%)
R	92,570 (40%)	**R**	111,327 (42%)
I	24,265 (11%)	**I**	60,891 (23%)

KEY VOTES

1997

Ban "partial birth" abortions Y

6 Nancy L. Johnson (R)

Of New Britain — Elected 1982, 8th term

Biographical Information

Born: Jan. 5, 1935, Chicago, Ill.

Education: Radcliffe College, B.A. 1957; U. of London, 1957-58.

Occupation: Civic leader.

Family: Husband, Theodore Johnson; three children.

Religion: Unitarian.

Political Career: Republican candidate for New Britain Common Council, 1975; Conn. Senate, 1977-83.

Capitol Office: 343 Cannon Bldg. 20515; 225-4476.

Committees

Ways & Means
Health; Oversight (chairman)

In Washington: For Johnson, the 104th Congress might have been the best of times, as the Republican takeover of the House put her in the chair of a subcommittee on Ways and Means. Instead, it was more like the worst of times, as she struggled to conduct an impartial ethics inquiry of the man most responsible for the GOP's House majority, Speaker Newt Gingrich. As chairwoman of the Committee on Standards of Official Conduct, Johnson displeased lawmakers on both sides of the aisle as well as voters in the 6th, who nearly ousted her from office in November 1996.

After two years of investigating Gingrich's network of political fund raising activities and organizations and the financing of a college course he taught, the ethics committee recommended that Gingrich be reprimanded and assessed a $300,000 penalty. The House overwhelmingly approved that recommendation in January 1997.

But if Johnson could take some measure of satisfaction from the House ending up on the side of the ethics committee, the journey to that destination was tortuous for her.

In newspaper editorials across the country and in speeches by House Democratic colleagues, she was pounded with accusations that she was trying to protect Gingrich. At the same time, Johnson heard many Republicans implore her not to "cave in" to what they saw as a Democratic vendetta to take out Gingrich. "I deal with great pressure from my side," she said at one point. "Do I know it's there? Do I hear second-hand about groups that are worried? Of course I do."

Johnson, named to the ethics committee in 1991, had hoped to leave the committee after two terms. But she stayed on for the 104th after Gingrich and Democratic leader Richard A. Gephardt of Missouri decided not to make any new appointments to the panel until after the Speaker's case was heard. She finally escaped the panel in January 1997 after the vote to punish Gingrich. "This is a tough penalty," she said. "I believe it is an appropriate penalty that shows that no one is above the rules."

The days leading up to the resolution of the Gingrich matter were fraught with controversy. Johnson and the other ethics committee Republicans abruptly abandoned plans for a week-long series of public hearings at which special counsel James M. Cole was to outline his case against the Speaker. Democrats howled that Republicans were reneging on a deal to hold the hearings, but GOP members said that Democrats had carped so much about delays in receiving Cole's written report that the hearings were scrubbed so he could concentrate on writing it.

Over many months, Johnson had sparred with the top Democrat on the ethics committee, Jim McDermott of Washington. He called her "arbitrary, authoritarian and autocratic"; Johnson accused him of "angry partisanship." The committee, the only one in the House evenly split among Republicans and Democrats, had depended in the past on the top members of each party working closely together to lead the panel to bipartisan agreement. That kind of rapport did not develop between Johnson and McDermott. In September 1996, McDermott called a media briefing without Johnson present and accused Republicans of delaying release of Cole's report. Johnson shot back that McDermott was violating House rules with his outspokenness about a matter pending before the ethics committee.

Johnson had taken over the ethics chairmanship from McDermott at the start of the 104th. Through 1995 there was grousing from Democrats that the Gingrich matter was not being pursued aggressively enough, and at year's end Johnson heard a roar of disapproval following the release of Federal Election Commission documents in an unrelated case. The FEC documents showed that all five Republicans on the ethics panel had ties to GOPAC, a political action committee Gingrich once headed, and whose activities were an aspect of the committee's investigation of Gingrich.

Constituents began calling Johnson's district office demanding an outside counsel in the case. Connecticut's largest newspaper, The Hartford

CONNECTICUT 6
Northwest — New Britain

The 6th blends the pastoral and peaceful — villages and small towns, dairy farms and nurseries — with more modern influences: hundreds of defense subcontractors. The Litchfield Hills, at the foot of the Berkshires, have attracted escapees from New York.

But for many other residents of the 6th, downsizing in the defense industry may mean hard times ahead.

United Technologies Corp. made sharp reductions in its Connecticut work force with thousands of those layoffs affecting divisions spread throughout the 6th, including Hamilton Standard in Windsor Locks, Pratt & Whitney in Southington, and Otis elevators and Carrier air conditioning, both in Farmington. When Pratt & Whitney announced it was scaling back, the Shop Rite grocery store in Southington said it, too, would shut down. Similar stories of retrenchment are often heard at some 300 defense subcontractors in the 6th.

Nowhere are economic problems more evident than in New Britain, the largest city in the 6th and one hit particularly hard by industrial decline. Since the Fafnir ball-bearing plant closed in the late 1980s, the city of 75,000 people has seen a number of its businesses fold or move.

Take a walk down one of New Britain's two main thoroughfares, Arch or Broad streets, and the struggle is obvious. The sidewalks and roads are crumbling; much of the housing is archaic. A city once filled with Polish immigrants is now a melting pot of blacks, Asians, Hispanics, Italians and Poles straining to get along.

The city's largest employer, tool manufacturer Stanley Works, has enabled New Britain to retain its longtime moniker "Hardware City."

Smaller communities in the district are not immune from bigger-city problems. Many retail stores have abandoned Main Street locales in favor of shopping malls. A 4.5 percent state income tax imposed in 1991 put an extra pinch on middle-income families struggling to get through recessionary times.

In a state where most people have been accustomed to comfortable lifestyles, unemployment is bringing difficulties normally associated with inner cities, such as drug abuse and homelessness. Officials are wrestling with questions about where to build homeless shelters, how to set up community health clinics and where to find money for drug treatment centers.

Residents of the 6th supported Republican presidential candidates in the good-times 1980s, but the dramatically different economic climate of 1992 helped Bill Clinton score a comfortable victory in the district. Clinton again won easily in 1996, taking 50 percent of the vote against Bob Dole and Ross Perot.

The House seat switched from Democratic to Republican control with Johnson's narrow open-seat victory in 1982. Johnson, bruised by the ethics brouhaha with Speaker Newt Gingrich, narrowly won re-election in 1996.

1990 Population: 547,765. White 520,212 (95%), Black 12,544 (2%), Other 15,009 (3%). Hispanic origin 19,374 (4%). 18 and over 423,834 (77%), 62 and over 91,007 (17%). Median age: 35.

Courant, published an editorial titled, "The Foul Odor of Cover-up." Democrats took to the House floor to demand that the ethics committee Republicans fully disclose their ties to GOPAC. In December 1995, the panel agreed to bring in an outside counsel to look into the Gingrich matter, and his work over the next year laid the foundation for the punishment meted out to Gingrich.

In December 1996, Gingrich admitted publicly that he failed to properly manage the financing of his political activities through charitable foundations. He also conceded a more serious offense: giving the ethics committee misleading information in the course of its investigation. After Cole released his 213-page report in January, the House voted, 395-28, to reprimand Gingrich and assess the $300,000 penalty. He is the first Speaker ever to receive such a punishment, although a number of Democrats and even a few Republicans said Gingrich's transgressions should have disqualified him from continuing as Speaker.

Though accused by Democrats of playing the loyal soldier in Gingrich's army while head of the ethics panel, Johnson on other issues has been a part of a group of GOP moderates that occasionally dissents from the conservative line.

"There never was a [Republican] revolution in the Northeast," Johnson explained. "Republicans won because people are comfortable with us as independent representatives."

In July 1995, for example, she blasted a House vote against allowing federal employees to purchase health insurance that includes abortion coverage. The vote came during debate on the fiscal 1996 Treasury-Postal Service appropriations bill. "This is not about abortion," she said. "This is about equality. This is about personal responsibility."

She also criticized Republican plans to offer a $500-per-child tax break to families making up to $200,000 a year. "Give me a break. We don't need that money going to people who make $200,000 a year," Johnson said after the Ways and Means Committee approved the bill in March 1995.

In April 1996, she opposed a constitutional

amendment requiring a supermajority vote for tax increases. The vote on the measure was 243-177, short of the required two-thirds majority. "I want to leave each generation free to establish that balance between taxing and spending that they believe is in their interest," Johnson said. "Democracy is about taking responsibility . . . to appropriate and to tax."

And she opposed efforts by Republicans to eliminate the portion of President Clinton's 1994 crime bill that provided grants for municipalities to hire more police officers. The Republicans wanted to roll the program into a block grant. Johnson said the program had helped her hometown build a community policing program.

She supported her party's welfare overhaul plans, though she did win approval of an amendment in Ways and Means in June 1995 to guarantee Medicaid benefits for welfare recipients with no private health insurance coverage. She said it was necessary to "guarantee that destitute women and children have guaranteed certain amounts of financial support and medical benefits." But the committee rejected a Johnson amendment that would have given mothers with children under age 10 an exemption from the five-year time limit if they could not find child care. The bill allowed an exemption for those with children age six or younger.

At Home: Battered by the ethics investigation of Gingrich, Johnson in 1996 eked out a victory over Democratic lawyer Charlotte Koskoff, whom she had beaten by more than 2-to-1 two years earlier. Koskoff criticized Johnson's handling of the case, and she rode disenchantment to a 49 percent tally, fewer than 1,600 votes behind Johnson.

When first elected to the House in 1982, Johnson was a rarity — a Republican winning an open district dominated by blue-collar Democrats. But for her, that sort of victory was nothing new. In 1977 she had become the first Republican in 30 years to represent the industrial city of New Britain in the state Senate, and she was re-elected easily.

The wife of an obstetrician, Johnson was a longtime activist in New Britain community affairs. When the Republican town chairman asked her in 1976 to run for the state Senate, she agreed and went on to defeat Democrat Paul S. Amenta by 150 votes.

When Democratic Rep. Toby Moffett announced at the end of 1981 that he was giving up the 6th to challenge GOP Sen. Lowell P. Weicker Jr., Johnson moved eagerly to take his place. She quickly captured the backing of the party establishment and influential GOP donors, opening an early lead over her primary opponent, conservative Nicholas Schaus.

Johnson's Democratic foe was a state Senate colleague, William E. Curry Jr. A liberal in the Moffett mold, Curry had won a hard-fought primary with an impressive grass-roots organization stocked with labor, environmentalists and consumer groups. But he was badly underfunded, and concentrated much of his campaigning in New Britain. He won there, but his margins in other Democratic areas were too anemic to overcome Johnson's popularity with Republicans and many independents. She won 52 percent and never had another tough campaign until 1996.

HOUSE ELECTIONS

1996 General		
Nancy L. Johnson (R)	113,020	(50%)
Charlotte Koskoff (D,ACP)	111,433	(49%)
Timothy A. Knibbs (CC)	3,303	(1%)
1994 General		
Nancy L. Johnson (R)	123,101	(64%)
Charlotte Koskoff (D,ACP)	60,701	(31%)
Patrick J. Danford (CC)	8,915	(5%)

Previous Winning Percentages: 1992 (70%) **1990** (74%) **1988** (66%) **1986** (64%) **1984** (64%) **1982** (52%)

CAMPAIGN FINANCE

	Receipts	Receipts from PACs	Expend-itures
1996			
Johnson (R)	$825,021	$435,082 (53%)	$931,406
Koskoff (D)	$270,576	$108,307 (40%)	$273,133
Knibbs (CC)	$0	0	$430
1994			
Johnson (R)	$569,415	$330,040 (58%)	$597,703
Koskoff (D)	$109,625	$55,100 (50%)	$105,290
Danford (CC)	$16,755	0	$16,025

DISTRICT VOTE FOR PRESIDENT

1996		1992	
D	121,607 (50%)	**D**	110,828 (40%)
R	89,003 (37%)	**R**	99,633 (36%)
I	26,865 (11%)	**I**	67,995 (24%)

KEY VOTES

1997	
Ban "partial birth" abortions	N
1996	
Approve farm bill	Y
Deny public education to illegal immigrants	Y
Repeal ban on certain assault-style weapons	N
Increase minimum wage	Y
Freeze defense spending	N
Approve welfare overhaul	Y
1995	
Approve balanced-budget constitutional amendment	Y
Relax Clean Water Act regulations	N
Oppose limits on environmental regulations	Y
Reduce projected Medicare spending	Y
Approve GOP budget with tax and spending cuts	Y

VOTING STUDIES

	Presidential Support		Party Unity		Conservative Coalition	
Year	S	O	S	O	S	O
1996	57	42	73	25	75	22
1995	38	59	77	21	82	16
1994	67	31	60	37	64	33
1993	66	32	64	32	57	43
1992	62	37	66	32	75	23
1991	63	35	53	46	68	32

INTEREST GROUP RATINGS

Year	ADA	AFL-CIO	CCUS	ACU
1996	20	n/a	81	55
1995	20	8	78	56
1994	30	22	100	52
1993	40	45	91	65
1992	40	42	75	58
1991	35	42	70	55

DELAWARE

Governor: Thomas R. Carper (D)
First elected: 1992
Length of term: 4 years
Term expires: 1/01
Salary: $95,000
Term limit: 2 terms
Phone: (302) 739-4101
Born: Jan. 23, 1947; Beckley, W.Va.
Education: Ohio State U., B.A. 1968; U. of Delaware, M.B.A. 1975.
Military Service: Navy, 1968-73; Naval Reserve 1973-92.
Occupation: Public official.
Family: Wife, Martha Ann Stacy; two children.
Religion: Presbyterian.
Political Career: Del. treasurer, 1977-83; U.S. House, 1983-93.

Lt. Gov.: Ruth Ann Minner (D)
First elected: 1992
Length of term: 4 years
Term expires: 1/01
Salary: $41,500
Phone number: (302) 577-3017

State election official: (302) 739-4277
Democratic headquarters: (302) 996-9458
Republican headquarters: (302) 651-0260

STATE LEGISLATURE

General Assembly. Meets January-June.

Senate: 21 members, 4-year terms
1994 breakdown: 13D, 8R; 15 men, 6 women
Salary: $27,500
Phone: (302) 739-5086

House of Representatives: 41 members, 2-year terms
1994 breakdown: 27R, 14D; 32 men, 9 women
Salary: $27,500
Phone: (302) 739-4087

URBAN STATISTICS

City	Population
Wilmington Mayor James Sills, D	71,529
Dover Mayor James L. Hutchinson, N-P	27,630
Newark Mayor Ron Gardner, I	26,371
Brookside County Executive Dennis E. Greenhouse	15,307
Pike Creek County Executive Dennis E. Greenhouse	10,163

U.S. CONGRESS

Senate: 1 D, 1 R
House: 0 D, 1 R

TERM LIMITS

For state offices: No

ELECTIONS

1996 Presidential Vote

Bill Clinton	52%
Bob Dole	37%
Ross Perot	11%

1992 Presidential Vote

Bill Clinton	44%
George Bush	35%
Ross Perot	20%

1988 Presidential Vote

George Bush	56%
Michael S. Dukakis	43%

POPULATION

1990 population		666,168
1980 population		594,338
Percent change		+12%
Rank among states:		46
White		80%
Black		17%
Hispanic		2%
Asian or Pacific islander		1%
Urban		73%
Rural		27%
Born in state		50%
Foreign-born		3%
Under age 18	163,341	25%
Ages 18-64	422,092	63%
65 and older	80,735	12%
Median age		32.9

MISCELLANEOUS

Capital: Dover
Number of counties: 3
Per capita income: $20,349 (1991)
Rank among states: 11
Total area: 2,045 sq. miles
Rank among states: 49

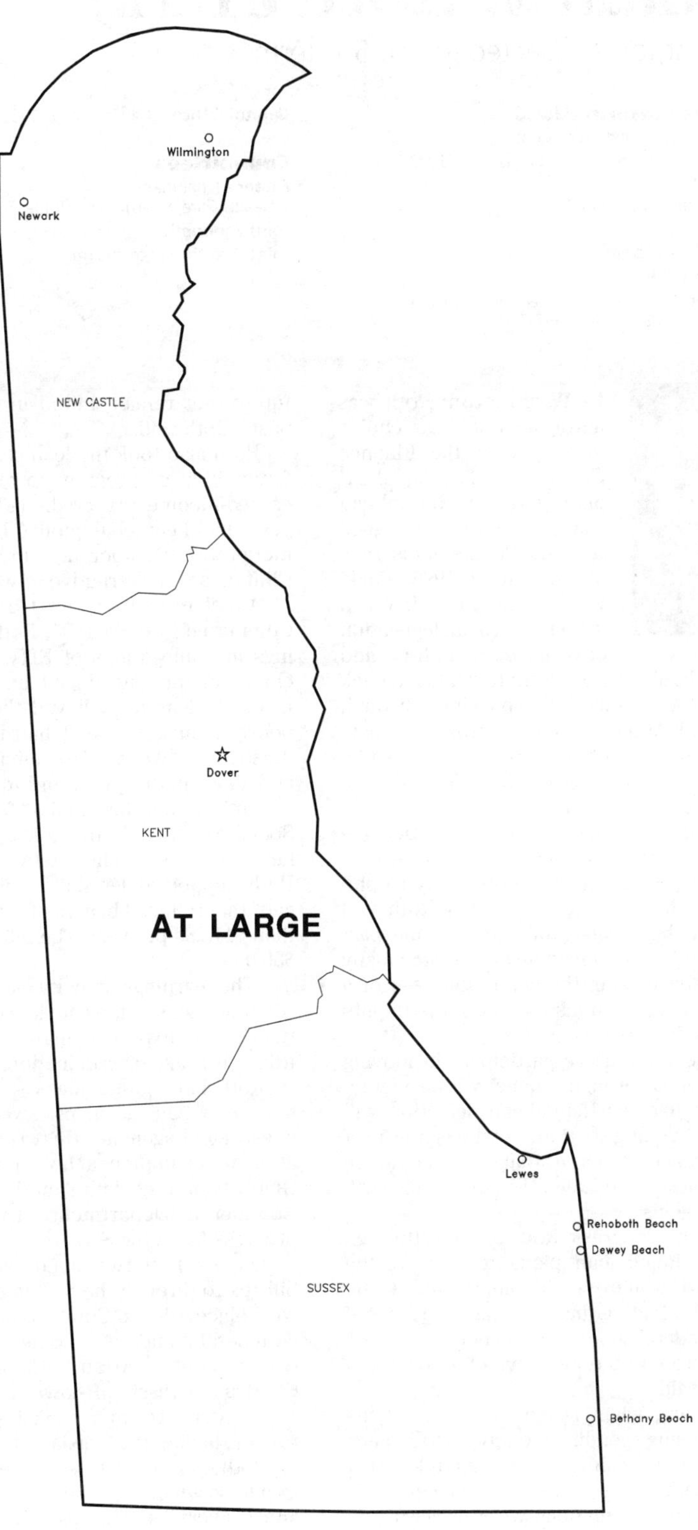
Wilmington
Newark
NEW CASTLE
Dover
KENT
AT LARGE
Lewes
Rehoboth Beach
Dewey Beach
SUSSEX
Bethany Beach

William V. Roth Jr. (R)

Of Wilmington — Elected 1970; 5th term

Biographical Information
Born: July 22, 1921, Great Falls, Mont.
Education: U. of Oregon, B.A. 1944; Harvard U., M.B.A. 1947, LL.B. 1949.
Military Service: Army, 1943-46.
Occupation: Lawyer.
Family: Wife, Jane Richards; two children.
Religion: Episcopalian.
Political Career: Republican nominee for lieutenant governor, 1960; U.S. House, 1967-71.

Capitol Office: 104 Hart Bldg. 20510; 224-2441.

Committees
Finance (chairman)
Health Care; International Trade; Taxation & IRS Oversight
Joint Economic
Joint Taxation (vice chairman)

In Washington: Roth was hardly anyone's first choice to take over the Finance Committee after its chairman, Oregon Republican Bob Packwood, resigned from the Senate in disgrace in the fall of 1995. Packwood had long been a leader on crucial legislation covering tax policy and welfare overhaul, whereas Roth had taken a back seat even on some bills passing through Governmental Affairs, where he was chairman. But Roth was next in line at Finance, and so he made the great leap forward after 25 years as a politician of middling rank.

At the helm of Finance, Roth has not become a prominent GOP strategist; other senators with stronger policy concerns are more likely to philosophize in the media arena. But if Roth will never match the swagger or ego of some past holders of the Finance chair, he has pleased many in his party by making the committee less of a fiefdom and more of an instrument of the Republican leadership.

He has been an active participant in moving the party agenda through a panel with a margin thin enough that one Republican defection will stall any bill. In doing so, Roth — who is now past 75 — has assuaged concerns that he would not be energetic enough to keep Finance on track toward GOP goals.

In the 104th Congress, Roth ushered through Finance the Republican plans to convert the Medicaid and welfare entitlements into state-administered block grants, ending decades of guaranteed federal support to the poor.

"It's time to end the incentives for staying in poverty," he said.

On Medicare, when Democrats accused the GOP of proposing spending reductions to finance tax cuts for the wealthy, Roth responded that those arguments were "pure demagoguery." He said the spending reductions were necessary to ensure the long-term financial viability of the program. "We believe Medicare must move into the future, not remain mired in the policies of the past," Roth said.

Roth also took the lead scaling back on a different kind of program to aid the poor — the earned-income tax credit (EITC) — which for years had been championed by Republicans and moderate Democrats, including President Clinton, as an alternative to welfare.

As chairman of the Governmental Affairs Committee in early 1995, Roth held public hearings into allegations of EITC fraud. As Finance chairman, he introduced an overhaul bill and made it clear he believed the program was so poorly managed that it had to be pruned back drastically. "We need to eliminate waste, fraud and abuse in this program," Roth said.

But on another major federal entitlement, Social Security, Roth took a different tack. To help seniors struggling to live on a fixed income, Roth supported legislation lifting the "earnings cap" that reduced benefits for those earning more than $11,280 per year. The bill raised that limit to $30,000.

"The earnings penalty sends a message to senior citizens that we no longer value their experience and expertise in the work force," said Roth. "It is age discrimination."

Roth likes grand ideas — massive tax cuts, huge new savings plans, sweeping revisions of government agencies. He was one of the few senators to champion a bold plank of the House GOP's "Contract With America": Eliminating the Commerce Department. That idea did not progress far in the Senate.

On the first two major government reform bills to go through the Senate in 1995 — applying workplace rules to Congress and curbing unfunded federal mandates — other members of Roth's Governmental Affairs Committee, such as Charles E. Grassley, R-Iowa, and ranking member John Glenn, D-Ohio, played a more prominent role in shaping the legislation.

Roth's clout was tested early in the 104th Congress when he fashioned a compromise regulatory overhaul bill. His bill would have taken unprecedented steps to force agencies to justify the need for a regulation. But it did not go far enough to suit some conservative Republicans, partly because Roth had crafted it in consultation with Democrats. Governmental Affairs endorsed it in March 1995, but then Majority Leader Bob Dole put forth his own broader proposal. Just before floor consideration of his bill, Dole asked J. Bennett Johnston, D-La., to help make the measure more acceptable to Democrats.

Good sport Roth quickly came on board with Dole as a co-sponsor, but he joined six other GOP moderates in amending the bill to better suit his tastes and those of the Democratic minority. Still, the measure met stiff resistance, and Dole had to pull the bill after three failed attempts to cut off debate in July 1995.

Roth did manage to carve out an active role in pushing two other proposals into law early in the 104th, including a move to make permanent a popular tax deduction for health insurance for self-employed workers. The other legislation was a paperwork reduction bill. "Paperwork burdens, like other regulatory burdens, are a hidden tax on the American people — a tax without measure — but a tax no less real," Roth said. Roth left the Governmental Affairs Committee in the 105th.

In the 103rd Congress, Roth joined a group of moderate Republicans in supporting many of the Clinton administration's initiatives. He was one of just three Republican senators who declined to sign a letter by then-Minority Leader Dole that took aim at the president's crime bill. He also supported a proposed overhaul of the superfund law, a five-day waiting period for handgun purchases and the Family and Medical Leave Act, and won praise from Sen. Dianne Feinstein, D-Calif., for his support of the California Desert Protection Act.

On the other hand, he neither supported the administration's health care reform plan, nor worked closely with moderates who tried to salvage the doomed proposal.

On a good-government issue, Roth took the lead in 1994 in an unsuccessful attempt to restructure the way the Pentagon buys big-ticket items. "We must go well beyond simply streamlining the process of awarding contracts," he said. "Instead, we must provide major cultural and structural reform across the federal buying system."

In 1993, Roth found himself on the defensive as he tried to preserve the Hatch Act, which prohibits federal workers from engaging in political activities. At odds with the administration and the Democratic majority in Congress, Roth managed to amend the bill overhauling the act to maintain existing restrictions on employees of the Justice Department's criminal division. But several other Roth amendments failed, and the bill easing some Hatch Act restrictions ultimately cleared Congress.

Indeed, Roth often found himself at odds with members of both parties in the 103rd Congress.

He offered an amendment to Clinton's deficit-reduction package in 1993 to exempt small businesses and family farms from a portion of the higher taxes in the bill. But Roth failed at first to win even the unanimous support of his fellow Republicans, many of whom objected to the complicated exemption.

Roth has always spent a healthy block of his time looking out for Delaware. In the 104th Congress, Roth concentrated on one issue with a big impact back home: preserving the fiscal health of Amtrak. The federal passenger railroad is more than a tourist vehicle in Delaware, since many state residents depend on it as a commuter line to get to jobs in Philadelphia, Baltimore and Washington.

Roth has proposed designating a small portion of the federal gasoline tax as a dedicated source of revenue for the financially troubled railway, but he has been unable to use his Finance Committee clout to get that idea off the ground in the face of stiff opposition from highway interests.

In the 102nd Congress, he worked to protect the ability of Delaware banks to sell insurance across state lines and continue to underwrite insurance. In 1992, he held up unemployment legislation until he was satisfied that the funding formula applied equally to all states.

The importance of personal savings has been a recurring theme throughout Roth's career. One of his first major bills as Finance chairman featured an expansion of tax-free savings through Individual Retirement Accounts (IRAs). The overall GOP tax package passed by the panel in October 1995 contained a provision raising the income-eligibility level for deductible IRAs from $40,000 to $100,000 for couples and from $25,000 to $85,000 for individuals.

When the Senate Finance Committee geared up in 1986 to produce a bill rewriting the federal tax code, Roth proposed a kind of value-added tax on gross business receipts to raise up to $115 billion over five years. Roth wanted to use that revenue to, among other things, pay for letting taxpayers establish tax-sheltered "Super Saver Accounts."

Roth has long been active in federal pay and procurement issues. He was a sponsor in 1990 of a federal pay overhaul proposal and also supported locality-based raises for federal workers living in cities with a higher cost of living, a provision included in the final legislation and a significant change in the General Scale pay system.

Roth had a brief season in the national spotlight as an original co-author of President Ronald Reagan's 1981 tax cut — 25 percent across the board — with Jack F. Kemp, then a GOP House member from New York.

At Home: The mild-mannered Roth has never been able to generate a great deal of emotion among Delaware voters. But he has been doggedly attentive to state interests, and he has been rewarded for that service with victories in seven statewide elections — two for the House and five for the Senate. He is the longest-serving politician in Delaware history. Born in Montana and educated at Harvard, Roth came to Delaware to work as a lawyer for a chemical firm and got involved in politics. After narrowly losing a 1960 bid for lieutenant governor, he became state GOP chairman.

In 1966, he entered the race for Delaware's at-large U.S. House seat against veteran Democrat Harris B. McDowell Jr. He talked about Vietnam — backing U.S. efforts but berating the Johnson administration for not explaining the situation more fully — and about open-housing legislation (he opposed it but was willing to endorse state GOP convention language favoring it). Riding the coattails of GOP Sen. J. Caleb Boggs and a national Republican wave that carried 47 GOP freshmen to the House in 1966, Roth pulled off an upset.

With the retirement of GOP Sen. John J. Williams in 1970, Roth became the uncontested choice of his party against the Democratic state House leader, Jacob W. Zimmerman. A Vietnam dove, Zimmerman had little money or statewide name recognition, and Roth won 59 percent.

In 1976, Roth had a strong Democratic challenger — Wilmington Mayor Thomas C. Maloney. But Roth's efforts against busing to achieve school integration had given him an excellent issue to run on, and Maloney was hurt by the coolness of organized labor. Roth was too strong in the suburbs for Maloney to beat him.

In 1982, Roth faced his most difficult Senate test. As cosponsor of the supply-side tax cut, he was a visible target for complaints about the then-flagging economy. David N. Levinson, Roth's hard-charging Democratic opponent, encouraged voters to link Roth to Reagan's economic policies and the woes he claimed they had produced.

The incumbent did not hide his tax legislation; billboards advertising his candidacy read, "Bill Roth, the Taxpayer's Best Friend." But he was also careful to demonstrate his concern for Frost Belt economic needs, voting against 1981 reductions in three programs important to Delaware. Though Levinson ran with a unified Democratic Party behind him, it was not enough.

In 1988, Roth aimed to become the first Delaware senator to win a fourth term since Williams was re-elected in 1964. Expecting a tough campaign, Roth amassed a huge treasury. But Democrats' grandest designs were deflated when Rep. Thomas R. Carper declined to challenge Roth. Then, maverick Lt. Gov. S. B. Woo spoiled their plans for a smooth nomination by beating the party-backed candidate in the primary by 71 votes. The Democratic disarray enabled Roth surpass 60 percent for the first time in his long career.

Democrats again tabbed Roth as vulnerable when he sought a fifth term in 1994, and they appeared to have a capable challenger: three-term state Attorney General Charles M. Oberly III.

Oberly promoted his crime-fighting credentials as the state's chief prosecutor and called Roth's into question. Media reports also questioned whether the 73-year-old Roth was too old to serve another six-year term. Oberly, 47, also kept pace with the incumbent in fundraising.

Some state Republicans openly expressed their hope that Roth would step aside, but he forged ahead, and according to Election Day exit polls, three out of five voters said Roth's age was not an issue in the race. He won with 56 percent.

SENATE ELECTIONS

1994 General

William V. Roth Jr. (R)	111,088	(56%)
Charles M. Oberly (D)	84,554	(42%)
John C. Dierickx (LIBERT)	3,387	(2%)

Previous Winning Percentages: **1988** (62%) **1982** (55%) **1976** (56%) **1970** (59%) **1968*** (59%) **1966*** (56%)

* *House election*

CAMPAIGN FINANCE

	Receipts	Receipts from PACs	Expend-itures
1994			
Roth (R)	$2,220,825	$899,579 (41%)	$2,233,279
Oberly (D)	$1,579,006	$451,979 (29%)	$1,561,440
Dierickx (LIBERT)	$628	0	$628

KEY VOTES

1997	
Approve balanced-budget constitutional amendment	Y
Approve chemical weapons treaty	Y
1996	
Approve farm bill	Y
Limit punitive damages in product liability cases	N
Exempt small businesses from higher minimum wage	Y
Approve welfare overhaul	Y
Bar job discrimination based on sexual orientation	N
Override veto of ban on "partial birth" abortions	Y
1995	
Approve GOP budget with tax and spending cuts	Y
Approve constitutional amendment barring flag desecration	Y

VOTING STUDIES

	Presidential Support		Party Unity		Conservative Coalition	
Year	**S**	**O**	**S**	**O**	**S**	**O**
1996	42	56	88	9	84	13
1995	42	55	84	14	88	12
1994	56	44	76	22	66	34
1993	40	60	77	22	78	22
1992	67	22	79	14	79	18
1991	83	16	78	20	68	28

INTEREST GROUP RATINGS

Year	ADA	AFL-CIO	CCUS	ACU
1996	10	n/a	85	85
1995	5	8	68	74
1994	35	38	70	68
1993	45	18	100	80
1992	25	27	100	75
1991	20	25	60	81

Joseph R. Biden Jr. (D)

Of Wilmington — Elected 1972, 5th term

Biographical Information

Born: Nov. 20, 1942, Scranton, Pa.

Education: U. of Delaware, B.A. 1965; Syracuse U., J.D. 1968.

Occupation: Lawyer.

Family: Wife, Jill Jacobs; three children.

Religion: Roman Catholic.

Political Career: New Castle County Council, 1970-72.

Capitol Office: 221 Russell Bldg. 20510; 224-5042.

Committees

Foreign Relations (ranking)
European Affairs (ranking); International Economic Policy, Export & Trade Promotion

Judiciary
Technology, Terrorism & Government Information; Youth Violence (ranking)

In Washington: At the start of the 105th Congress, Biden realized his ambition of playing a leading role on foreign policy matters, albeit as a member of the minority, when he took over as ranking Democrat on the Foreign Relations Committee, succeeding Claiborne Pell of Rhode Island, who retired.

Although he had to relinquish his post as ranking member on the Judiciary Committee to claim the top Democratic seat on Foreign Relations, Biden said he made the trade because he thought he could be more effective as the Clinton administration's chief foreign policy ally in the Senate.

Biden said his move was made easier by an agreement with Patrick J. Leahy of Vermont, the new ranking Democrat on Judiciary, that will allow him to remain the party's "point man" on crime and drug issues. On the Judiciary Committee, Biden is ranking Democrat on the Youth Violence Subcommittee.

On Foreign Relations, Biden expects to be a more vocal advocate for the Democrats than his relatively passive predecessor, particularly in dealing with fiercely partisan Chairman Jesse Helms, R-N.C., who, in the past, has bottled up nominations and treaties in an effort to wring concessions from the White House. "The difference between Pell and me is, I won't be quiet about it. I will engage it if I encounter it," Biden said.

Early in the new Congress, Biden bore the brunt of negotiations with Helms over a treaty banning chemical weapons, a high priority for President Clinton. The two men eventually worked out 28 issues Helms had raised, though five more of the chairman's demands had to be taken to the Senate floor, where they were defeated. The treaty itself was approved 74-26 on April 24, a victory for Clinton and Biden.

"The United States Senate said, 'We are going to be engaged in the world,' " Biden declared afterward. "Any other decision . . . would have said that the neo-isolationists were on the rise, that the internationalists were on the run."

Biden has been consistently liberal on foreign policy issues in the past. As a member of Foreign Relations, he has pressed for arms control agreements, opposed the use of military force in the Persian Gulf and insisted that Congress be a full partner with the White House in decisions to send U.S. forces to hostile areas.

At the start of the 103rd Congress, Biden, then-chairman of the European Affairs Subcommittee, shifted toward a more hawkish stance, urging Clinton to consider air strikes against the artillery positions of Bosnian Serbs.

Despite his criticism of the West's response to the war in Bosnia, Biden opposed an amendment in May 1994 by then-Senate Minority Leader Bob Dole, R-Kan., requiring Clinton to cease complying with the U.N. arms embargo against the Muslim-led Bosnian government. Less than two months later, Biden voted for a similar Dole amendment, which was narrowly defeated. In July 1995, Biden joined 20 other Democrats in breaking from Clinton to support another Dole measure to lift the Bosnian arms embargo, which passed the Senate 69-29.

In one of his greatest legislative accomplishments, Biden, who was chairman of the Judiciary Committee in the 103rd Congress, served as caretaker for passage of a comprehensive $30.2 billion omnibus anti-crime package. Six years in the making, the 1994 legislation included money for prison construction and crime prevention programs, as well as funds to place more police officers on the nation's streets.

It also applied the death penalty to dozens of new or existing federal crimes and imposed a ban on 19 specific types of semiautomatic assault-style weapons.

The previous crime bill Biden attempted to push through died in a partisan standoff in the 102nd Congress after passing both chambers and emerging from conference.

In the Republican-controlled 104th, as ranking Democrat on Judiciary, Biden was forced into defending many of the provisions in the 1994 crime bill from GOP threats. "Where is the logic of dismantling this crime bill other than to say it has the name Clinton on it and therefore it is bad?" Biden asked in February 1995 at the prospect of reopening the 1994 package he helped broker. He also led the floor fight to restore fiscal 1996 appropriations to fund crime bill initiatives, most notably the "cops-on-the-streets" program to help communities hire new police officers. Biden also succeeded in restoring money for programs to combat domestic violence, establish "drug courts" to handle first-time non-violent drug offenders, and help state and local law enforcement upgrade their technical resources.

Biden also was instrumental in crafting one of the major crime-fighting bills of the 104th Congress — the antiterrorism bill, which Congress passed in response to the April 1995, bombing of the Alfred P. Murrah federal building in Oklahoma City. But in many ways the final bill was more reflective of Biden's minority status than of his law enforcement priorities.

The measure gave the federal government signficant new tools to battle domestic and international terrorism, but it excluded provisions that Biden and others on both sides of the aisle fought to include that would have expanded government wiretapping authority in terrorism cases. And it contained provisions bitterly opposed by Biden and other Democrats to limit federal appeals, or habeas corpus petitions, by death row and other inmates.

Biden characterized the final measure as "a habeas corpus bill with a little terrorism thrown in."

When Biden chaired Judiciary, his performance on some high-profile issues fell short of his efforts on the 1994 crime bill.

His handling of the 1991 confirmation hearings for Supreme Court nominee Clarence Thomas disappointed many. The nationally televised hearings in which University of Oklahoma law professor Anita F. Hill accused Thomas of sexually harassing her were an acute embarrassment to Biden, whose committee had failed to conduct more than a cursory investigation of Hill's charges until after they were leaked to the news media.

Biden's chatty, deferential approach to Thomas did nothing to inspire fellow Democrats on the panel and did not begin to counter the hard-edged attack on Hill mounted by Pennsylvania Republican Arlen Specter and other GOP senators. Still, it was hardly surprising coming from a chairman who a year earlier had told President George Bush's first Supreme Court nominee, David H. Souter, "You are free to refuse to answer any questions you deem to be improper."

Early in his Senate career, Biden was known as someone whose mouth frequently outran his mind, who was impatient with the details and the sustained labor of legislating.

An Irish Catholic middle-class son of a Scranton, Pa., auto dealer, Biden has always exhibited a quick intelligence and considerable eloquence. He often speaks with a self-deprecation that is part of his charm. But he still talks too much. When members are given five minutes for opening remarks, Biden is at risk of needing 20.

Early in the 104th, Biden gave two examples of his verbal inconsistency. At first, he blasted the Clinton administration's nomination of Henry W. Foster Jr. to be surgeon general, but after meeting with the White House he issued a statement saying he would reserve judgment on Foster. He also ended up voting for the 1995 version of the balanced-budget constitutional amendment, even though he had voted against it in 1994. Early in the 105th Congress, he again voted for the amendment, which failed to muster the necessary two-thirds majority required for passage in the Senate.

Biden's tenure as chairman of the Judiciary Committee began after the Democrats regained the Senate majority in the 1986 election. He was succeeded in the 104th as chairman by Sen. Orrin G. Hatch of Utah, who served as the panel's ranking Republican in the 103rd.

Hatch and Biden sparred during the Thomas-Hill hearings but have developed cordial relations. They did, however, lock horns during the 104th over GOP moves to stall Senate confirmation of Clinton judicial nominations. And they battled over Republican-sponsored legislation to overhaul the federal regulatory process and to require the government to compensate property owners when federal regulations reduce the value of their land.

Part of what makes Biden such a compelling political figure, and what commands such attention to his personal development, are the tragedies and dramas of his public life.

Just weeks after his 1972 Senate election, Biden's wife and infant daughter were killed and his two sons seriously injured in an automobile accident. Biden said at first that he did not want to take the oath of office. Persuaded by Majority Leader Mike Mansfield to assume his seat, Biden was sworn in at his son's bedside.

After spending more than a decade rebuilding his life and career, Biden launched a long-awaited presidential campaign in June 1987. But in a season focused on candidates' character, he fell under the weight of reports that he had plagiarized passages in his speeches and a 1965 law school paper, and finally, that he had exaggerated his résumé. He withdrew from the race in September.

No sooner did the uncomfortable episode fade from public view than a brush with death put Biden back in the news. In February 1988, he had the first of two operations for a near-fatal brain aneurysm. By early 1989, Biden was back in action.

At Home: Biden was in the underdog role when, at age 29 in 1972, he made an audacious bid to unseat GOP Sen. J. Caleb Boggs. With service on the New Castle County Council his only electoral credential, Biden seemed a sure loser. But his celebrated brashness helped Biden pull off a major upset.

Biden ran hard on a dovish Vietnam platform and accused the Republican of being a do-nothing senator. He called for more spending on mass transit and health care services. Boggs awoke to the threat too late, and his "safe" seat disappeared by 3,162 votes.

Delaware Democratic leaders, certain that a challenge to Boggs was hopeless, had given Biden little support in 1972. He gave them little attention in return for most of his first term.

By 1978, Biden had made up with the state party. Of greater importance in his re-election bid that year, however, was his opposition to busing students to achieve racial integration. As he ran for re-election, a long-distance busing plan was taking effect in New Castle County, outraging voters in suburban Wilmington.

With this anti-busing position offsetting his liberalism on some other social issues, Biden seemed unbeatable in 1978, and big-name Delaware Republicans refrained from taking him on. The task fell to an obscure southern Delaware poultry farmer, James H. Baxter, who gamely tried to paint the Democrat as too far left for the state. Biden easily beat him.

In 1984, the Republican who eventually emerged to take on Biden was John M. Burris, a businessman and former Republican leader of the Delaware House who spent most of his time trying to brand Biden a fiscal profligate, echoing themes from Baxter's 1978 campaign. Burris chastised the incumbent for voting against a proposed constitutional amendment to balance the budget and he sought to remind voters of his own role in helping to enact a state balanced-budget amendment under GOP Gov. Pierre S. "Pete" du Pont IV.

Burris succeeded in keeping the focus of the campaign on economic issues; Biden dwelt heavily on his "budget freeze" proposal. But that was the Republican's sole consolation. Biden crushed him in New Castle County and carried Delaware's two downstate counties en route to a 60 percent to 40 percent win.

The collapse of Biden's 1988 presidential campaign amid allegations of plagiarism raised questions at the time about his political future — not only his hopes for the White House, but also his future in the Senate.

Biden looked potentially vulnerable to a Republican challenge in 1990. Conservatives were eager to avenge the 1987 defeat of the Supreme Court nomination of Robert H. Bork, who lost on Biden's watch as Judiciary chairman.

However, Biden's home-state downturn did not last long. His triumph over life-threatening health problems in 1988 helped revive the affections of supporters who had grown skeptical of him. His victory over deputy state attorney general M. Jane Brady with 63 percent of the vote restored him to a position of dominance in Delaware politics. He won with similar ease in 1996, taking 60 percent against Republican challenger Raymond J. Clatworthy.

SENATE ELECTIONS

1996 General

Joseph R. Biden Jr. (D)	165,465	(60%)
Raymond J. Clatworthy (R)	105,088	(38%)
Mark Jones (LIBERT)	3,340	(1%)

Previous Winning Percentages: 1990 (63%) **1984** (60%) **1978** (58%) **1972** (50%)

CAMPAIGN FINANCE

	Receipts	Receipts from PACs	Expend-itures
1996			
Biden (D)	$1,636,013	0	$1,966,313
Clatworthy (R)	$1,332,167	$71,734 (5%)	$1,326,427

KEY VOTES

1997	
Approve balanced-budget constitutional amendment	Y
Approve chemical weapons treaty	Y
1996	
Approve farm bill	Y
Limit punitive damages in product liability cases	N
Exempt small businesses from higher minimum wage	N
Approve welfare overhaul	Y
Bar job discrimination based on sexual orientation	Y
Override veto of ban on "partial birth" abortions	Y
1995	
Approve GOP budget with tax and spending cuts	N
Approve constitutional amendment barring flag desecration	N

VOTING STUDIES

	Presidential Support		Party Unity		Conservative Coalition	
Year	S	O	S	O	S	O
1996	92	8	79	20	42	58
1995	81	15	84	13	30	60
1994	82	10	86	8	31	69
1993	94	3	91	8	32	66
1992	28	70	90	8	18	79
1991	33	65	88	8	10	85

INTEREST GROUP RATINGS

Year	ADA	AFL-CIO	CCUS	ACU
1996	80	n/a	46	20
1995	95	92	37	17
1994	80	86	20	0
1993	80	91	33	21
1992	100	100	20	0
1991	90	83	20	5

AL Michael N. Castle (R)

Of Wilmington — Elected 1992, 3rd term

Biographical Information
Born: July 2, 1939, Wilmington, Del.
Education: Hamilton College, B.A. 1961; Georgetown U., LL.B. 1964.
Occupation: Lawyer.
Family: Wife, Jane DiSabatino.
Religion: Roman Catholic.
Political Career: Del. deputy attorney general, 1965-66; Del. House, 1967-69; Del. Senate, 1969-77, minority leader, 1976-77; lieutenant governor, 1981-85; governor, 1985-93.
Capitol Office: 1227 Longworth Bldg. 20515; 225-4165.

Committees
Banking & Financial Services
Domestic & International Monetary Policy (chairman); Housing & Community Opportunity
Education & Workforce
Early Childhood, Youth& Families; Postsecondary Education, Training
& Life-Long Learning
Select Intelligence
Human Intelligence, Analysis & Counterintelligence

In Washington: One of three co-chairmen of a group of moderate House Republicans known as the Tuesday Lunch Bunch, Castle has been central in several high-profile tussles between the conservative and centrist factions of the House's majority party.

Recognizing Castle's facility in working with other Republicans as well as with Democrats, the GOP leadership in 1997 made him part of a bipartisan "whip group" charged with building support for passage of a balanced-budget constitutional amendment. Castle strongly supports the amendment but disagrees with those on the GOP right who want to include a provision requiring a three-fifths majority vote of both chambers of Congress in order to raise taxes.

Castle was a key player in two major endeavors of the 104th Congress: crafting a tax-cut plan and overhauling the nation's welfare system.

After the GOP leadership proposed a $189 billion tax cut in 1995, Castle led a group of moderate Republicans who urged that tax cuts be contingent upon Congress' meeting deficit-reduction targets each year. "Everyone would like to skip the vegetables and go straight to the dessert," Castle said at a Rules Committee meeting on amendments to the tax bill. "But it's irresponsible to make tax cuts until the spending cuts are taken."

Though he was not permitted to offer the moderates' contingency amendment, GOP leaders did agree to add a weakened version of it to the bill, and Castle's group backed down.

On the welfare front, in March 1995, Castle voted for the leadership-backed welfare overhaul, even though he said Democrats were "not all wrong" in expressing concerns about the availability of child care for welfare recipients, the importance of education and job training, and the need to ensure that a job pays more than welfare. Despite his reservations, he said the welfare system "needs to be shocked — even if it leads to trial and error."

After President Clinton vetoed that bill, Castle sought the middle ground and joined conservative Democrat John Tanner of Tennessee in a welfare proposal that supporters said took some of the harsh edges off the Republican plan.

While it still ended the federal entitlement to welfare benefits, the Castle-Tanner plan would have required states to put more money into their welfare programs, and it included more federal money to assist states in moving welfare recipients into jobs within two years. It also would have required states to provide vouchers redeemable for goods and services to children whose parents did not meet the work requirement.

Clinton endorsed the Castle-Tanner measure, and it became the Democratic substitute when the welfare measure hit the floor. Although it was defeated, 168-258, when the House debated welfare reform in mid-July 1996, elements of the plan were included in the GOP bill that passed the House.

Castle grappled with the welfare issue even before coming to the House. When he arrived in Congress in 1993, Castle already was known by many members as the governor who had worked in 1988 with Arkansas Gov. Bill Clinton to forge a centrist welfare reform proposal that was the backbone of a welfare law Congress passed that year. In winning the White House in 1992, Clinton promised an overhaul of the welfare system, but that never became a priority during his first two years in office.

During the 103rd Congress, Castle worked on the welfare issue from the Education and Labor Committee and as part of a House GOP task force that drafted legislation imposing stiff penalties on welfare recipients who did not find work within two years. When the administration's own welfare proposal still had not arrived on the Hill by April 1994, Castle needled his old co-chairman, Clinton. At an Education and Labor hearing he asked an administration welfare specialist, "When will the White House bill come down? It's not that I'm complaining, I just want to know."

As a House freshman, Castle made a mark by helping rescue a major Clinton initiative — a broad anti-crime bill. He became a pivotal dealmaker in August 1994, when Clinton's $33.2 billion crime bill — painstakingly balanced between

DELAWARE
At large

Delaware is a bellwether in national elections — it has supported the winning presidential ticket 12 times in a row — and pursues ticket-splitting with rare relish in the elections within its borders.

The state's four major statewide officeholders — its governor, two senators and U.S. representative — are evenly split between the parties. Its independence was prevalent in 1992, when Delaware voted to send a Democrat to the White House, its Republican governor to the U.S. House and its Democratic House member to the governor's mansion. Four years later, it voted overwhelmingly to re-elect a Democratic president, governor and senator, but gave a huge victory to its Republican House member, too.

Delaware's split-ticket mania is sometimes attributed to the compactness of the state. Personal campaigning is more important than party identification. Voters expect to see their candidates, and over the course of a campaign, candidates are able to meet a large part of the electorate.

Despite its track record of voting for presidential winners, Delaware has had trouble producing any of its own. No president has ever been elected from Delaware, and neither of the two candidates emerging from the state in 1988, former Republican Gov. Pierre S. "Pete" du Pont IV and Democratic Sen. Joseph R. Biden Jr., traveled far on the road to the White House.

Up in the small but relatively densely populated area north of the Chesapeake and Delaware Canal, Democrats are strong in Wilmington, the state's largest city. Fifty years ago, almost half the state's residents lived in Wilmington, but the city's 72,000 residents now cast only about 10 percent of Delaware's vote. As the city has shrunk, its suburbs have grown; New Castle County, which encompasses them both, casts about 65 percent of the state's total vote.

The GOP's strength lies in Wilmington's suburbs and down south of the canal, in the poultry farms and coastal marshes of the Delmarva Peninsula, whose name is an amalgam of its ingredients: Delaware and the eastern ends of Maryland and Virginia.

Thanks to its liberal business-incorporation rules, Delaware is the on-paper home to about half the Fortune 500 and nearly 250,000 smaller corporations. Wilmington is the very real home to DuPont & Co., Delaware's largest employer. It employs 105,000 worldwide.

Dover, Delaware's capital, is set in the state's midsection, in Kent County. It, too, has a strong Democratic constituency. A few miles south of the city is Dover Air Force Base. The base employs about 8,000 military and civilian personnel who played a critical role in transporting cargo to the Middle East during the Persian Gulf War. But it has also brought something of a grim image to the city; its huge mortuary has received thousands of dead servicemen over the past three decades, including Persian Gulf casualties. Other major Dover employers include Kraft, General Foods, Playtex, Scott Paper and a variety of chemical corporations.

Down at the southern end of the state is Sussex County, Delaware at its most rural. Sussex produces more poultry than any other county in the country, along with sorghum, corn and soybeans.

Tourism also has its place in this county, at its far southeast end. A string of beach resorts from the mouth of the Delaware Bay down the peninsula to Fenwick Island draw thousands of beachgoers each year. A series of storms that have battered the coast have washed away a number of beach rebuilding projects.

Rehoboth Beach is a popular summer resort whose sizable gay population has lately become a permanent fixture.

The increasing number of retirees residing in the beach communities have made Sussex the fastest-growing county in the state; they add to the county's conservative tenor.

Ronald Reagan and George Bush won consistently in Sussex in the 1980s. But in 1992, Bush managed just 39 percent, 1,300 votes more than Bill Clinton. And in 1996 Bob Dole lost Sussex by 1,004 votes to Clinton.

A new bypass that leads to the beach may forever change the character of the southern counties. Relief Route 1 promises to cut the travel time between northern and southern Delaware and is expected to boost the local economies. But area farmers are concerned about attracting city and suburban folks from New Castle County as new residents.

1990 Population: 666,168. White 535,094 (80%), Black 112,460 (17%), Other 18,614 (3%). Hispanic origin 15,820 (2%). 18 and over 502,827 (75%), 62 and over 98,658 (15%). Median age: 33.

funds for prevention and punishment— seemed dead in the water after the House rejected a rule governing debate on the bill.

Much to the chagrin of conservatives who were ready to celebrate the bill's demise, a group of Republicans led by Castle, John R. Kasich of Ohio and Susan Molinari of New York began to negotiate directly with the administration. Castle recruited 20 from his party to sign a letter recommending changes in the bill. Ultimately, the White House agreed to cut back the bill's prevention programs and toughen penalties on sex offenders. The bill, $3 billion smaller, passed, 235-195, with 46 Republicans providing its margin of victory.

Castle serves on the Banking Committee, useful given Delaware's large corporate constituency. He chairs the Subcommittee on Domestic and International Monetary Policy. The panel's main attention-getter so far has been its study of whether changes should be made to coins and bills. Castle supports shifting from a $1 dollar bill to a $1 dollar coin, and his subcommittee also has looked at doing away with the penny.

In 1997, Castle was appointed to a bipartisan task force charged with making recommendations about how the House ethics process works. After the long, bitter fight over the ethical conduct of House Speaker Newt Gingrich, R-Ga., the creation of the task force was one thing both parties could agree to do.

In August 1994, Castle suggested a fundamental change in the way Congress pays for emergency relief when disasters strike or military crises arise. In a series of votes on budget procedures that were essentially symbolic (because the Senate was not expected to consider them, and did not), Castle offered an amendment that would have eliminated emergency spending authority. Instead, he proposed an annual reserve fund of about $5 billion to respond to disasters. His amendment was defeated, 184-235.

In 1994, Castle supported Clinton's position on 71 percent of House floor votes, putting him near the top of the list of Republicans most often in agreement with the president. His presidential support score plunged to 35 percent in 1995, then rose to 57 percent in 1996.

During the 104th, Castle bucked his party majority in opposing repeal of the ban on certain semiautomatic assault-style weapons, and previously he supported a five-day waiting period for handgun purchases. He voted in 1996 to increase the minimum wage, he sides with abortion-rights advocates on some votes, and he supported passage of the family and medical leave bill.

At Home: Although a lawyer by trade, Castle has spent most of his life in politics and government. He became Delaware's deputy attorney general in 1965 when he was 26, and began a 10-year career in the Delaware General Assembly two years later. He was lieutenant governor from 1981 to 1985 before being elected governor. He was re-elected in 1988 with 71 percent of the vote.

Under state law, Castle could not seek a third term as governor in 1992. As soon as he decided to seek the state's at-large House seat, he was rated the favorite, but victory did not come easily. In a four-way GOP primary, he got 56 percent of the vote, and in November he managed 55 percent against a vigorous challenge from the state's former lieutenant governor, Democrat S. B. Woo.

Castle switched places with the state's former representative, Democrat Thomas R. Carper, who is now governor.

Castle's re-elections have been romps, with more than two-thirds of voters backing him.

HOUSE ELECTIONS

1996 General		
Michael N. Castle (R)	185,576	(70%)
Dennis E. Williams (D)	73,253	(27%)
George A. Jurgensen (LIBERT)	4,000	(1%)
Felicia B. Johnson (P)	3,009	(1%)
1994 General		
Michael N. Castle (R)	137,960	(71%)
Carol Ann DeSantis (D)	51,803	(27%)
Danny Ray Beaver (LIBERT)	3,869	(2%)

Previous Winning Percentages: 1992 (55%)

CAMPAIGN FINANCE

	Receipts	Receipts from PACs	Expend-itures
1996			
Castle (R)	$578,078	$198,480 (34%)	$376,350
Williams (D)	$9,350	$5,750 (61%)	$6,437
Jurgensen (LIBERT)	$2,287	0	$2,287
1994			
Castle (R)	$691,261	$218,657 (32%)	$400,083
DeSantis (D)	$46,917	$3,450 (7%)	$45,863

DISTRICT VOTE FOR PRESIDENT

	1996		1992
D	140,355 (52%)	**D**	126,054 (44%)
R	99,062 (37%)	**R**	102,313 (36%)
I	28,719 (11%)	**I**	59,213 (21%)

KEY VOTES

1997	
Ban "partial birth" abortions	Y
1996	
Approve farm bill	Y
Deny public education to illegal immigrants	Y
Repeal ban on certain assault-style weapons	N
Increase minimum wage	Y
Freeze defense spending	Y
Approve welfare overhaul	Y
1995	
Approve balanced-budget constitutional amendment	Y
Relax Clean Water Act regulations	N
Oppose limits on environmental regulations	Y
Reduce projected Medicare spending	Y
Approve GOP budget with tax and spending cuts	Y

VOTING STUDIES

	Presidential Support		Party Unity		Conservative Coalition	
Year	S	O	S	O	S	O
1996	57	43	76	24	71	29
1995	35	65	83	17	85	15
1994	71	29	81	18	92	8
1993	54	43	82	17	84	16

INTEREST GROUP RATINGS

Year	ADA	AFL-CIO	CCUS	ACU
1996	25	n/a	88	60
1995	25	8	92	56
1994	20	33	100	67
1993	20	25	91	75

FLORIDA

Governor: Lawton Chiles (D)
First elected: 1990
Length of term: 4 years
Term expires: 1/99
Salary: $104,817
Term limit: 2 terms
Phone: (904) 488-4441
Born: April 3, 1930; Lakeland, Fla.
Education: U. of Florida, B.S. 1952, LL.B. 1955.
Military Service: Army, 1953-54.
Occupation: Lawyer.
Family: Wife, Rhea May Grafton; four children.
Religion: Presbyterian.
Political Career: Fla. House, 1959-67; Fla. Senate, 1967-71; U.S. Senate, 1971-89.

Lt. Gov.: Kenneth "Buddy" MacKay (D)
First elected: 1990
Length of term: 4 years
Term expires: 1/99
Salary: $100,403
Phone: (904) 488-4711

State election official: (904) 488-7690
Democratic headquarters: (904) 222-3411
Republican headquarters: (904) 222-7920

REDISTRICTING

Florida gained four House seats in reapportionment, increasing from 19 districts to 23. Federal court approved the map May 29, 1992. A three-judge federal panel ruled that the 3rd District was unconstitutional on April 17, 1996. New map approved by legislature May 2; governor signed May 21.

STATE LEGISLATURE

Legislature. Meets February-April; session often extended.

Senate: 40 members, 4-year terms
1996 breakdown: 23R, 17D; 34 men, 6 women
Salary: $24,912
Phone: (904) 487-5270

House of Representatives: 120 members, 2-year terms
1996 breakdown: 62R, 58D; 89 men, 31 women
Salary: $24,912
Phone: (904) 488-1157

URBAN STATISTICS

City	Population
Jacksonville	635,230
Mayor John Delaney, R	
Miami	358,648
Mayor Joe Carollo, R	
Tampa	280,015
Mayor Dick Greco, N-P	
St. Petersburg	240,348
Mayor David J. Fischer, N-P	
Hialeah	188,004
Mayor Raul Martinez, D	

U.S. CONGRESS

Senate: 1 D, 1 R
House: 8 D, 15 R

TERM LIMITS

For state offices: Yes
Senate: 2 terms
House: 4 terms

ELECTIONS

1996 Presidential Vote

Bill Clinton	48%
Bob Dole	42%
Ross Perot	9%

1992 Presidential Vote

George Bush	41%
Bill Clinton	39%
Ross Perot	20%

1988 Presidential Vote

George Bush	61%
Michael S. Dukakis	39%

POPULATION

1990 population		12,937,926
1980 population		9,746,324
Percent change		+33%
Rank among states:		4
White		83%
Black		14%
Hispanic		12%
Asian or Pacific islander		1%
Urban		85%
Rural		15%
Born in state		30%
Foreign-born		13%
Under age 18	2,866,237	22%
Ages 18-64	7,702,258	60%
65 and older	2,369,431	18%
Median age		36.4

MISCELLANEOUS

Capital: Tallahassee
Number of counties: 67
Per capita income: $18,880 (1991)
Rank among states: 18
Total area: 58,664 sq. miles
Rank among states: 22

FLORIDA

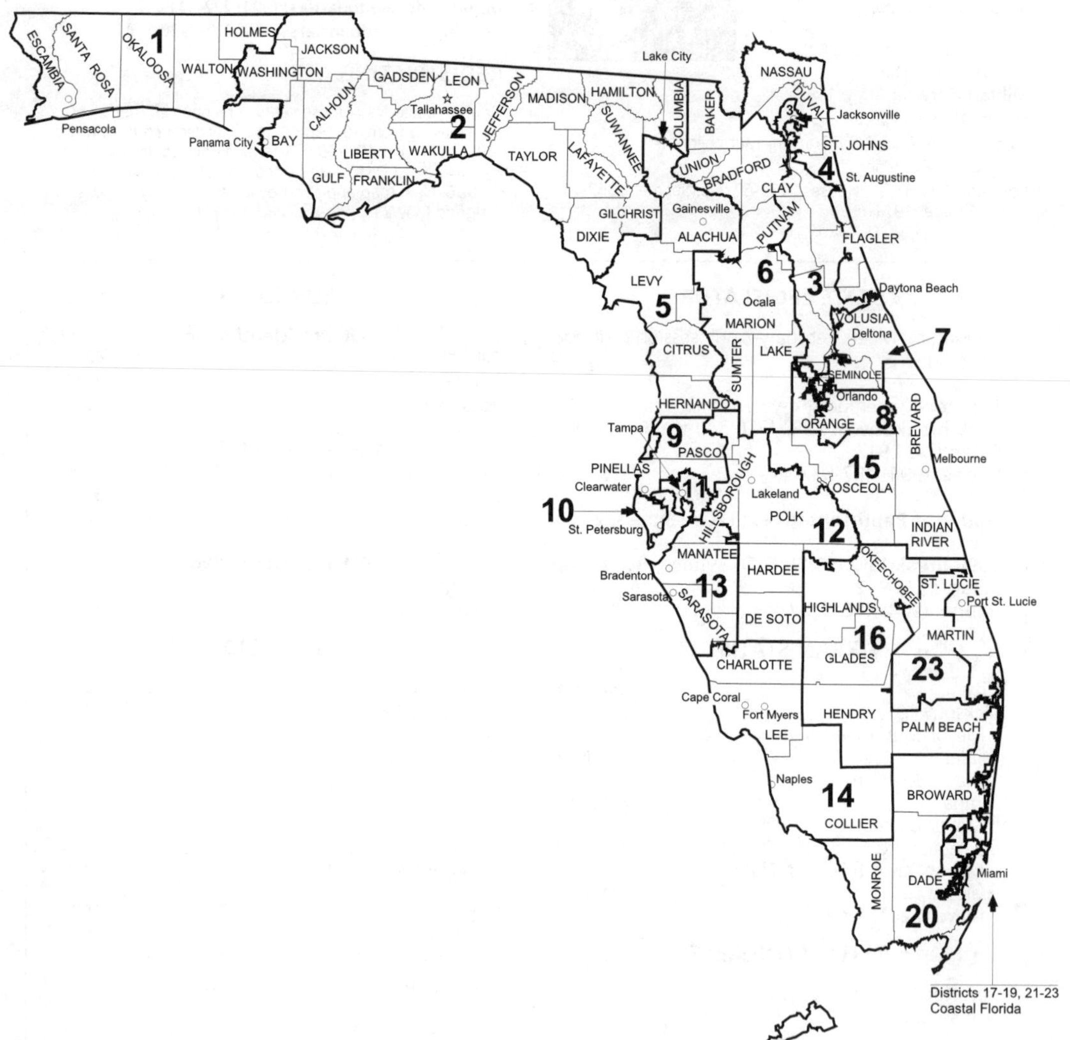

1
ESCAMBIA
SANTA ROSA
OKALOOSA
WALTON
HOLMES
WASHINGTON
JACKSON
Pensacola
Panama City
BAY
CALHOUN
GADSDEN
LEON
Tallahassee
2
LIBERTY
WAKULLA
GULF
FRANKLIN
JEFFERSON
MADISON
HAMILTON
TAYLOR
SUWANNEE
LAFAYETTE
Lake City
COLUMBIA
BAKER
NASSAU
DUVAL
Jacksonville
ST. JOHNS
St. Augustine
4
UNION
BRADFORD
CLAY
GILCHRIST
Gainesville
ALACHUA
DIXIE
PUTNAM
FLAGLER
LEVY
6
3
Daytona Beach
Ocala
5
MARION
VOLUSIA
Deltona
7
CITRUS
SUMTER
LAKE
SEMINOLE
Orlando
HERNANDO
8
ORANGE
BREVARD
Tampa
9
PASCO
Melbourne
PINELLAS
15
Clearwater
11
HILLSBOROUGH
Lakeland
OSCEOLA
10
St. Petersburg
POLK
12
INDIAN RIVER
MANATEE
HARDEE
OKEECHOBEE
Bradenton
13
ST. LUCIE
Sarasota
SARASOTA
HIGHLANDS
Port St. Lucie
DE SOTO
16
MARTIN
GLADES
CHARLOTTE
23
Cape Coral
Fort Myers
HENDRY
LEE
PALM BEACH
Naples
14
BROWARD
COLLIER
21
MONROE
DADE
Miami
20
Districts 17-19, 21-23
Coastal Florida

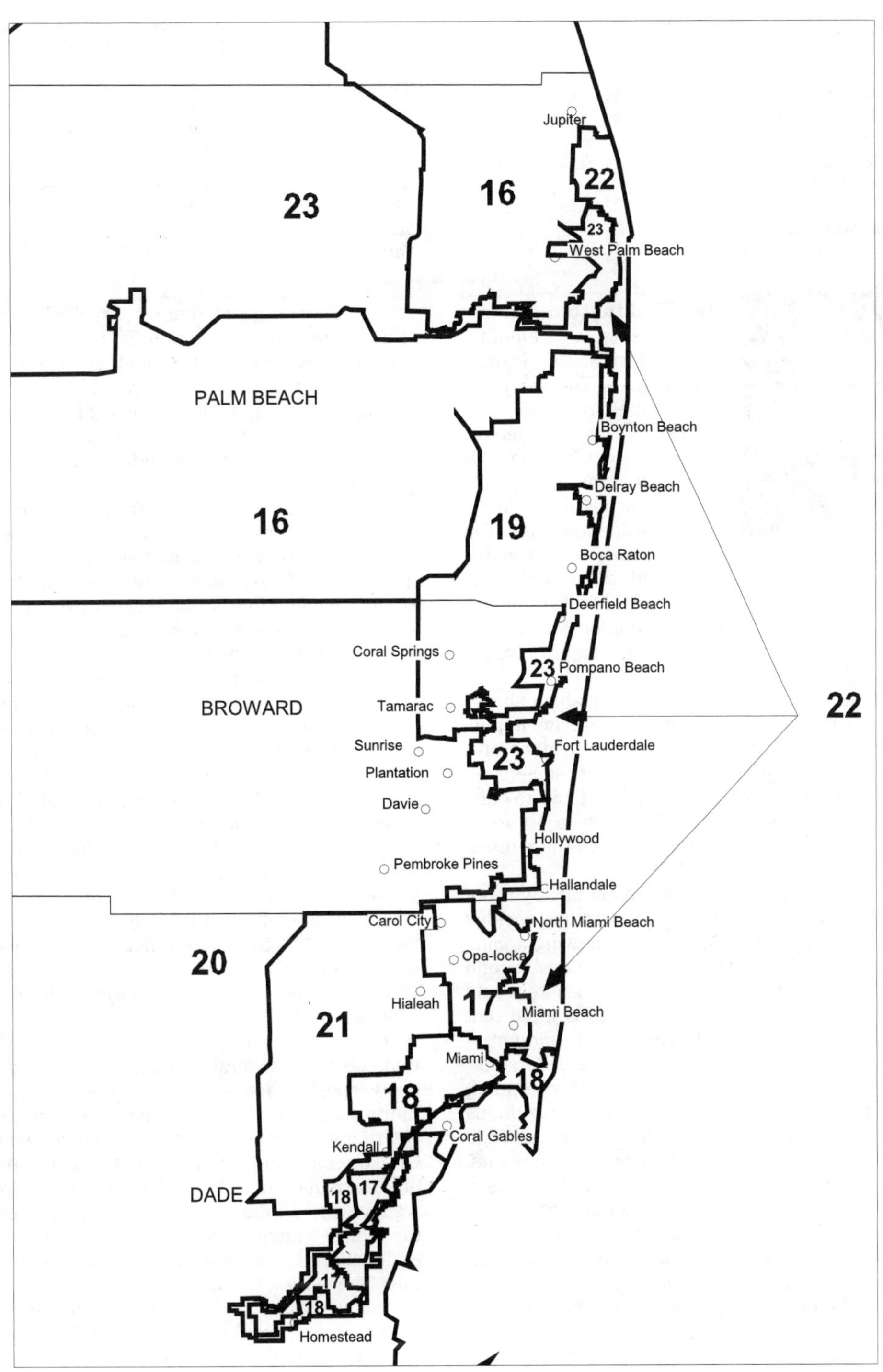
Jupiter
22
16
23
23
West Palm Beach
PALM BEACH
Boynton Beach
Delray Beach
16
19
Boca Raton
Deerfield Beach
Coral Springs
23
Pompano Beach
BROWARD
Tamarac
22
Sunrise
23
Fort Lauderdale
Plantation
Davie
Hollywood
Pembroke Pines
Hallandale
Carol City
North Miami Beach
20
Opa-locka
Hialeah
17
Miami Beach
21
Miami
18
18
Coral Gables
Kendall
DADE
18
17
17
18
Homestead

Bob Graham (D)

Of Miami Lakes — Elected 1986, 2nd term

Biographical Information
Born: Nov. 9, 1936, Dade County, Fla.
Education: U. of Florida, B.A. 1959; Harvard U., LL.B. 1962.
Occupation: Real estate developer; cattle rancher.
Family: Wife, Adele Khoury; four children.
Religion: United Church of Christ.
Political Career: Fla. House, 1967-71; Fla. Senate, 1971-79; governor, 1979-87.
Capitol Office: 524 Hart Bldg. 20510; 224-3041.

Committees
Energy & Natural Resources
Energy Research Development Production & Regulation; Forests & Public Land Management; National Parks, Historic Preservation & Recreation
Environment & Public Works
Clean Air, Wetlands, Private Property & Nuclear Safety (ranking); Superfund, Waste Control & Risk Assessment; Transportation & Infrastructure
Finance
Health Care; International Trade; Long-Term Growth, Debt & Deficit Reduction (ranking)
Select Intelligence
Veterans' Affairs

In Washington: It's not easy being a Democrat from Florida, as Graham has learned. The party has had some statewide successes of late, re-electing Gov. Lawton Chiles in 1994 and delivering a plurality for President Clinton in the 1996 presidential race. But Republican strength at the grass roots is building, and with the GOP running Congress, Graham often finds himself playing second fiddle in the media to junior Sen. Connie Mack, a fast-rising member of the majority party's leadership.

With a centrist voting record, Graham should enjoy a measure of influence as Senate Republicans court him and other Democratic moderates to help pass legislation. But many of the Senate's staunch GOP conservatives are in no rush to compromise, and it's harder for Graham to force action now than it was when he held the reins as Florida's governor from 1979-87.

Though the current environment clearly is not one he would have chosen, Graham has decided to run for re-election in 1998, eschewing a campaign for his old job as governor as Chiles' second term expires. He said staying in the Senate would strengthen the political middle. "It is important that moderate Republicans and moderate Democrats step forward and provide leadership."

No sweeping visionary, Graham has responded to the political climate through assiduous attention to Floridians' parochial concerns. While he is more conservative than many Democrats, Graham is not viewed as a maverick. He is a strong supporter of environmental safeguards and the elderly, but he also strikes a pose as pro-business (supporting a capital gains tax cut), anti-crime (backing the death penalty) and anti-communist (voting to help the contras in the 1980s and supporting tougher sanctions against Cuba).

His parochialism was on display early in the 105th Congress when he joined with GOP Sen. John W. Warner of Virginia to propose a way to distribute federal highway funds among the states. The proposal, known as STEP 21 (for "Streamlined Transportation Efficiency Program for the 21st Century"), would guarantee each state a return of at least 95 percent of the funds it remits to Washington. Fast-growing Florida pours a lot of money into Uncle Sam's coffers, and it expects a return commensurate with its status as a megastate.

In the 104th Congress, Graham cosponsored an amendment to the fiscal 1997 spending bill for veterans, housing, space and environmental programs to shift veterans' health care funding to states such as Florida that have growing populations of veterans. As a result, the Department of Veterans Affairs announced it would transfer $14 billion in health care dollars from the Northeast to the South and Southwest. New Veterans' Affairs Committee Chairman Arlen Specter, R-Pa., said he would try to change the formula in the 105th Congress. "I'm not satisfied with the reallocation of VA medical funds," Specter said. "This is a very big change, and I intend to fight it."

Graham supported the final welfare overhaul legislation in 1996, saying, "I believe that it's time to take that leap of faith." But he voted against an earlier version of the bill in July 1996, after trying unsuccessfully to strike provisions that would have denied benefits to legal immigrants, a sizable constituency in South Florida. His motion was tabled, 62-34.

He also argued against plans to give proportionately more federal funds to states that previously spent a lot on welfare benefits (which Florida did not). "We start under the banner of 'We're going to end welfare as we've known it,' " Graham said, "and yet distribute the money based on a formula which is predicated on welfare as we knew it." Graham proposed an amendment in the Senate Finance Committee to distribute federal welfare funds based on each state's poverty rate. The motion failed, 8-12.

"Should there be some recognition of high-growth states?" said Sen. Alfonse M. D'Amato, R-N.Y., who opposed the amendment. "I say yes. How do we deal with it? I don't know."

Graham was one of only three senators in the 104th to vote against legislation aimed at clamping down on illegal immigration across the nation's borders.

Professional baseball's spring training is a big tourist lure for Florida, and in February 1995, Graham embraced Clinton's intervention in the baseball strike. Clinton called an unusual White House meeting between owners, players and baseball federal mediator Bill Usery Jr. The meeting was not successful and ended with the president appealing to Congress to "step up to the plate."

Graham's voting record in the 104th displayed his centrist tendencies. He supported repeal of federal speed limits, while opposing deregulation of the telecommunications industry. He backed constitutional amendments outlawing flag burning and mandating a balanced-federal budget.

A supporter of abortion rights, he voted to confirm Clinton designee Dr. Henry W. Foster Jr. as surgeon general and voted against a technique that opponents call "partial birth" abortions. He voted to allow states to ignore same-gender marriages but also supported banning job discrimination based on sexual orientation.

In 1994, Graham was one of the few senators pushing hard to get the Clinton administration to use U.S. military force to restore ousted Haitian President Jean-Bertrand Aristide to power. Many in Congress were highly skeptical about the United States' intervening militarily in Haiti, but Graham voiced the view of many Floridians that the Haitian refugee influx would not abate until the island's military rulers were removed. In 1994, Graham asked the Clinton administration to declare a state of emergency in response to a heightened flow of refugees from Cuba. In March 1996, he voted to strengthen the Cuban trade embargo.

Graham's solid focus on bread-and-butter issues has helped him bridge Florida's conservative Southern Democratic element and its more liberal populations. This, together with the state's increasing electoral clout, has drawn some attention to Graham in recent presidential campaigns.

In 1992, Graham was on Clinton's final list of six contenders for vice president; reportedly, it came down to Graham and Tennesseean Al Gore. Clinton decided on Gore just in time to allow Graham to file for re-election to his Senate seat.

In 1988, when likely nominee Michael S. Dukakis was running high in the polls, Graham let it be known that he was available for the No. 2 spot, suggesting that his Southern roots and moderate record would be a plus. Dukakis instead picked Texas Sen. Lloyd Bentsen, another candidate with those credentials.

There is a studied quality to everything Graham does. He is well-known for methodically jotting down notes and reminders to himself in little spiral notebooks that go everywhere with him. If Graham makes a mistake, it is apt to stem from belated action rather than haste. Early in his first term as governor, the St. Petersburg Times called him "Governor Jell-O." But by his fourth year in office, he was seen as a competent manager, and he won re-election handily.

During the 1994 election cycle, Graham served as head of the Democratic Senatorial Campaign Committee. Though he presided over the catastrophic eight-seat loss that cost Democrats control of the Senate in November 1994, no special blame for the debacle attached to Graham. Some Florida Democrats grumbled that their party did not recruit a credible Senate candidate to challenge Mack.

Taking the campaign post offered Graham a chance to be a loyal party soldier, perhaps bolstering relations with Democratic colleagues who think he strays too often from the party line and is reluctant to take the lead on tough issues. Graham, for instance, was one of five Democrats to support a key Republican amendment to pare back Clinton's proposed economic stimulus bill in March 1993. But he nevertheless voted with his party in a failed effort to break a GOP filibuster that eventually killed the bill.

One issue on which Graham has been anything but wavering is the death penalty. While in the Florida Statehouse, he earned the sobriquet "the killingest governor," and he carried his pro-death penalty stand to the Senate. He authored a successful amendment to strip from a 1990 crime bill provisions that would have allowed death row inmates to appeal their sentences using claims of racial disparity in capital punishment decisions. The Senate bill also would have broadened the application of the death penalty in federal cases, but in a House-Senate conference, all the capital punishment provisions were dropped.

At Home: Graham is gearing up for re-election in 1998 after announcing that he would not try to return to the governor's mansion. "I gave serious thought to the decision I made," Graham told the St. Petersburg Times. "I made it. I feel comfortable with it. There are plenty of Democrats in Florida in the same position I was in in 1977 — not very well known, but with the potential to be a winning candidate [for governor]."

Graham inherited an interest in politics from his father, a wealthy dairy farmer who was a state senator in the 1930s and '40s and an unsuccessful candidate for governor in 1944. After graduating from the University of Florida and Harvard Law School, Graham joined his father in the real estate business. His projects, including development of the new town of Miami Lakes, helped him amass a fortune.

Graham was eased into politics by his half-brother Phil, publisher of The Washington Post. Before his suicide in 1963, Phil Graham had introduced his half-brother to many influential Democrats, including Lyndon B. Johnson, for whom Bob Graham worked at the 1960 Democratic National Convention.

Graham's victory in a 1966 state House campaign began his unbroken string of electoral successes. He moved up to the state Senate in 1970. Though Graham was popular in his own base, he was little known elsewhere when he entered the 1978 contest to succeed Democratic Gov. Reubin Askew. Regarded as rather bland, Graham was thought to have little chance in a field of bigger-name contenders.

But Graham came up with the "workdays" gimmick that became his trademark. He spent 100 days working at average, often manual labor, jobs in various regions of Florida; these efforts drew enormous publicity and gave the wealthy candidate a "common man" appeal. Graham finished a strong second in the primary, then raced past state Attorney General Robert L. Shevin in the runoff, gaining momentum for the general election. He defeated GOP drugstore magnate Jack M. Eckerd with 56 percent.

Graham was not overwhelmingly popular in his early years as governor. His support for capital punishment earned him conservative backing, but it also made him a target for anti-death penalty protesters. On other issues, Graham's caution and attention to detail gave rise to the "Governor Jell-O" nickname.

But beginning in 1982, Graham became more assertive, pushing hard for his initiatives and environmental causes, including the Save Our Rivers and Save Our Coasts projects. His high profile helped him sweep to re-election that year over GOP Rep. L. A. "Skip" Bafalis.

In his 1986 Senate challenge to Republican incumbent Paula Hawkins, Graham began the year substantially ahead, and he never lost his lead.

Graham had all the vital advantages. Though Hawkins was highly rated in voter surveys, he ranked higher. The governor maintained an image of vigor by performing muscular tasks as part of his "workdays" program, while Hawkins had to have surgery during the campaign to relieve painful back problems.

More important, Graham had an image of competence built on a record of accomplishment on environmental, economic and social issues. Hawkins was an early Senate advocate of action against drug trafficking and child abuse, but she had not played a visible role on major economic, foreign policy or defense issues. And she had committed several embarrassing and widely reported gaffes. This issue of substance was probably the decisive factor in Graham's comfortable 55 percent victory.

By the time Graham sought re-election in 1992, he was the state's most popular politician. He was also the subject of a flurry of national attention during the summer when Clinton considered him as a running mate.

Back home, the GOP exhibited little interest in attracting a top-flight opponent against Graham. Republicans settled on former Rep. Bill Grant, defeated for re-election in 1990 after he had switched parties to join the GOP. Grant had been hounded more recently by disclosures that he had 106 overdrafts at the House bank. Graham captured nearly two-thirds of the vote.

SENATE ELECTIONS

1992 General		
Bob Graham (D)	3,244,299	(65%)
Bill Grant (R)	1,715,156	(35%)
1992 Primary		
Bob Graham (D)	968,618	(84%)
Jim Mahorner (D)	180,405	(16%)

Previous Winning Percentages: 1986 (55%)

CAMPAIGN FINANCE

	Receipts	Receipts from PACs	Expend-itures
1992			
Graham (D)	$3,026,137	$905,596 (30%)	$2,979,552
Grant (R)	$248,228	$19,050 (8%)	$242,251

KEY VOTES

1997	
Approve balanced-budget constitutional amendment	Y
Approve chemical weapons treaty	Y
1996	
Approve farm bill	Y
Limit punitive damages in product liability cases	N
Exempt small businesses from higher minimum wage	N
Approve welfare overhaul	Y
Bar job discrimination based on sexual orientation	Y
Override veto of ban on "partial birth" abortions	N
1995	
Approve GOP budget with tax and spending cuts	N
Approve constitutional amendment barring flag desecration	Y

VOTING STUDIES

	Presidential Support		Party Unity		Conservative Coalition	
Year	S	O	S	O	S	O
1996	86	14	81	19	61	39
1995	84	16	80	20	49	51
1994	90	8	85	15	53	47
1993	90	10	85	15	61	39
1992	35	65	73	27	53	47
1991	47	51	80	18	60	40

INTEREST GROUP RATINGS

Year	ADA	AFL-CIO	CCUS	ACU
1996	85	n/a	46	15
1995	95	92	47	13
1994	75	75	30	8
1993	65	82	36	16
1992	75	75	20	15
1991	65	75	20	38

Connie Mack (R)

Of Cape Coral — Elected 1988, 2nd term

Biographical Information
Born: Oct. 29, 1940, Philadelphia, Pa.
Education: U. of Florida, B.S. 1966.
Occupation: Banker.
Family: Wife, Priscilla Hobbs; two children.
Religion: Roman Catholic.
Political Career: U.S. House, 1983-89.
Capitol Office: 517 Hart Bldg. 20510; 224-5274.

Committees
Banking, Housing & Urban Affairs
Financial Institutions & Regulatory Relief; Financial Services & Technology; Housing Opportunity & Community Development (chairman)
Finance
International Trade; Long-Term Growth, Debt & Deficit Reduction (chairman); Taxation & IRS Oversight
Joint Economic (vice)

Republican Conference chairman

In Washington: With the Senate under Republican control, Mack is one of the Southern conservatives playing a newly prominent role in party affairs and in the policymaking process.

Evidence of how Mack is overshadowing Florida's senior senator, Democrat Bob Graham, was on display in the summer of 1996, when Mack made the short list of potential running mates for GOP presidential nominee Bob Dole. Four years before, it had been Graham in the veepstakes spotlight, until Bill Clinton bypassed him in favor of Tennesseean Al Gore.

In the 105th Congress, Mack is the Republican Conference chairman, the party's No. 3 leadership slot. His relationship with Majority Leader Trent Lott goes back to when the two men were in the House and belonged to Newt Gingrich's Conservative Opportunity Society, a group that wanted House Republicans to be more active in confronting Democrats and breaking their grip on the House majority.

Also in the 105th, Mack moved from the Appropriations Committee, where he had chaired the Legislative Branch subcommittee, to the Finance Committee, where he will chair a Subcommittee on Long-Term Growth, Debt and Deficit Reduction. The Finance Committee has jurisdiction over Medicaid and Medicare, two programs of particular interest to Florida's large elderly population. "I will be at the table to make various points, various issues as they relate to Florida," Mack said.

Early in 1997, Mack clearly showed his conservative bent when he weighed in on another key issue for the 105th Congress: how to allocate federal highway funds into the next century. He introduced legislation to eliminate most of the federal gasoline tax and return primary responsibility for highway building to the states. This approach would save money by reducing federal administrative costs, he says, and it would give states more control over their road projects. "This is fundamental to those of us who talk about turning power back to the states," Mack said.

Also, Mack plans to renew efforts to overhaul the nation's public housing system in his role as chairman of the Housing Opportunity and Community Development Subcommittee on the Banking, Housing and Urban Affairs Committee. In the 104th Congress, both the House, led by GOP Rep. Rick A. Lazio of New York, and the Senate, led by Mack, passed measures to consolidate many housing programs into block grants. The legislation died in conference, however, when Senate negotiators refused to accept some of the more far-reaching House proposals. Mack's legislation also sought to make public housing tenants more self-sufficient and to set in place a system to restrain federal spending to meet tighter federal budget goals. "Under today's rules, the residents of public housing face disincentives to move to self sufficiency," he said.

In the 104th, Mack used his chairmanship of the Legislative Branch subcommittee to push through cuts in Congress' own budget. A strong supporter of cutting the federal bureaucracy as a means of reducing the deficit, he said Congress should go first in trimming its spending.

"It's important that this committee set an example" Mack explained. "If we're going to be a smaller government, we should reflect that and lead the way in the legislative appropriations bill."

In July 1996, the Senate adopted an amendment to the fiscal 1997 legislative branch appropriations bill to toughen lobbying restrictions for former members of Congress and top staff aides. But the measure quickly was dropped in conference.

Mack has a reputation for speaking his mind, and his outspokenness was evident early in the 104th as he led a putsch by junior Republican senators that aimed to oust Oregon's Mark O. Hatfield as Appropriations Committee chairman because Hatfield voted against the balanced-budget constitutional amendment.

In the Senate's March 1995 vote on the balanced-budget amendment, Hatfield was the only Republican to vote "no," and the measure fell just one vote short of the two-thirds majority required for passage. Shortly before the vote, Hatfield had seen that his opposition would doom the amendment, and he tendered an offer of resignation to then-Senate Majority Leader Dole. Dole declined to accept that offer, but in the days after defeat of the amendment, he did nothing to discourage Mack and freshman GOP Sen. Rick Santorum of Pennsylvania from pursuing an effort to punish Hatfield. In the end, they backed down from forcing the question to a vote of all Republican senators, and Hatfield kept his seat. "I made it pretty clear that my objective was to see that Sen. Hatfield was to step down as chairman," Mack said after a meeting of all GOP senators. "It ought to be equally clear that that's not going to occur." Hatfield later closed the book on his Senate career, declining to seek re-election in 1996.

Mack's outspokenness drew a rebuke from Sen. Robert C. Byrd, D-W.Va., in December 1995. In a speech on the Senate floor, Byrd said he had "not recalled such insolence" on the Senate floor or such "harsh and severe" speeches as those that marked the end of the session, and he called on all senators to lower their charged rhetoric and show more respect for the institution, each other and the office of the presidency.

Byrd's lecture clearly was directed at Mack and Santorum, who a week earlier had charged President Clinton with deliberately not speaking the truth and breaking his word on the budget. Mack said the president's "commitment to principle is non-existent" and that he "broke his word" on the budget.

"Those are fighting words" that would be expected in an "ale house or beer tavern" but not the Senate, Byrd said. It showed "utter disrespect for the office of the president," he said. "I was shocked to hear such strident words. Have civility and common courtesy and reasonableness taken leave of this chamber?" Recalling the "giants" of the Senate in years long past, Byrd said, "Little did I know that I would live to see pygmies."

Mack took the floor soon thereafter to say he was sorry that his comments were considered disrespectful, and he had not intended for them to be so.

As befits a politician from Florida, with its sizable Cuban-American population, Mack vented his anger in February 1996 after Cuban military planes shot down two civilian aircraft being flown toward the island nation by Cuban-American opponents of Fidel Castro's government.

Mack called on the Clinton administration to seek the indictment of all Cuban officials responsible for the aircraft shootdown. In a March 1996 letter to Clinton, Mack and Dole said that "pursuing justice is the least we can do to honor the brave young Americans killed by Castro's regime." Mack also supported the Helms-Burton law (named for its sponsors, Senate Foreign Relations Committee Chairman Jesse Helms, R-N.C., and Indiana GOP Rep. Dan Burton), which tightened the U.S. economic embargo against Cuba.

In April 1996, Mack and Graham won an amendment to legislation curbing illegal immigration. By a vote of 62-37, the Senate agreed retain a 30-year-old law that gave preferential treatment to Cuban immigrants, stripping a provision to repeal it from the bill. Current law permits Cuban immigrants, whether legal or illegal, to claim permanent residence status one year after arriving on U.S. shores. Supporters of repeal said the preference has been abused by illegal immigrants. But opponents said repealing the law would send the wrong signal to Castro.

On some health-related issues, Mack charts a course one would not necessarily expect from a conservative. He signed onto legislation in the 104th to repeal a measure aimed at discharging HIV-infected military personnel from the armed services. Defense Department officials and others note that more than half the 1,000-plus HIV-positive men and women in the military have families who would lose all health care benefits in the event of a discharge.

In October 1993, Mack surprised colleagues with an intensely personal floor speech backing a controversial attempt to earmark funds for a breast cancer study on Long Island, N.Y. Mack explained that he found it difficult to argue about earmarks when his brother had died of cancer after a 12-year battle; his mother and his wife are breast cancer survivors; his daughter has fought cervical cancer; and Mack himself was diagnosed with and treated for melanoma, the same type of cancer that killed his brother.

In early 1992, Mack broke with President George Bush over the controversial use of fetal tissue for medical research. The possibility that such research might provide new treatments or even cures for degenerative ailments such as diabetes, Parkinson's disease and Alzheimer's disease was of obvious interest to Florida's large population of retirees.

The Bush administration had imposed a ban on fetal tissue research, which Congress was moving to repeal. Mack voted against an administration-backed compromise that would have established a registry of fetal tissue from miscarriages. Scientists said the registry was unlikely to supply a sufficient quantity of usable tissue.

Still, on other social policy issues, Mack toes the conservative line. In the 104th, he supported banning a particular abortion technique that opponents call "partial birth" abortion, and he voted against prohibiting job discrimination based on sexual orientation. He also voted against the confirmation of Dr. Henry W. Foster Jr. as surgeon general; his nomination floundered over revelations that he performed abortions. And he voted for a constitutional amendment prohibiting flag burning.

At Home: It is no small feat to win a Senate seat in a state as large and diverse as Florida. But if Mack's victory in 1988 had impressive elements, it was still a little surprising that the contest was so close, considering the factors working in his favor. Despite a significant head start, a financial advantage, Democratic infighting and an extremely strong GOP tide at the presidential level, Mack's victory was so narrow that the outcome was settled only by the count of absentee ballots.

Mack, a telegenic candidate in a state where media is extremely important, seemed to be charmed for much of the Senate contest. He entered the race as an underdog against Democratic Sen. Lawton Chiles, but Chiles, who is now governor, surprised his party by announcing his retirement in late 1987. That boosted Mack, who had already nailed down enough Republican support to ward off a serious primary challenger. The Democratic nominee, Rep. Buddy MacKay, emerged bruised from a contentious primary, although with a degree of momentum.

Throughout the general-election campaign, Mack framed the voters' choice as one between a conservative and a liberal. He maintained a theme of "less taxing, less spending, less government and more freedom." Even before the October runoff was settled, he ran ads with the tag line: "Hey, Buddy, you're liberal."

But even some Republicans considered Mack's message too simplistic and narrow. MacKay was highly regarded among political insiders for his legislative work, both in the House and previously in the state Legislature, and his voting record put him closer to the center of the political spectrum than to the left. Some prominent environmentalists in the Republican Party said they could not support Mack because he had not addressed environmental issues crucial to fast-growing Florida. In his campaign, MacKay said the choice was "mainstream vs. extreme."

On election night and for a few days after, the race was too close to call, but absentee ballots ultimately put Mack over the top. MacKay considered challenging the results, suggesting that the state's computerized voting system might have failed in some key counties, but he soon abandoned that plan. Two years later, MacKay was elected lieutenant governor.

In 1994, Mack won re-election with 70 percent against Democrat Hugh Rodham, the brother of first lady Hillary Rodham Clinton. Mack's colleague, Graham, was chairman of the Democratic Senatorial Campaign Committee and was criticized for failing to recruit a stronger challenger.

Mack may have politics in his genes. His great-grandfather, John L. Sheppard, was a Democratic House member from Texas; his grandfather, Morris Sheppard, also served in the House, then moved on to a 28-year tenure in the Senate. Mack's step-grandfather, Tom Connally, also served Texas in the Senate, from 1929 to 1953.

But it was another forebear who provided Mack with enviable name recognition when he got into politics: His paternal grandfather was the original Connie Mack, the legendary owner and manager of the Philadelphia Athletics baseball team. Like his grandfather, Mack uses the familiar rather than the given version of his name: Cornelius McGillicuddy III. (Mack's baseball past and his free-market beliefs came together in early 1993, when he embraced an end to the national pastime's congressional exemption from antitrust laws.)

After Republican Rep. L.A. "Skip" Bafalis decided to run for governor in 1982, Mack's name gave him a winning edge over four GOP primary opponents for the 13th District House seat. Once nominated, he was guaranteed election and re-election in that solidly Republican constituency.

SENATE ELECTIONS

1994 General

Connie Mack (R)	2,894,726	(70%)
Hugh E. Rodham (D)	1,210,412	(29%)

Previous Winning Percentages: 1988 (50%) **1986*** (75%) **1984*** (100%) **1982*** (65%)

* *House elections*

CAMPAIGN FINANCE

	Receipts	Receipts from PACs		Expend-itures
1994				
Mack (R)	$4,364,771	$1,004,290	(23%)	$3,735,719
Rodham (D)	$634,503	$139,700	(22%)	$617,190

KEY VOTES

1997	
Approve balanced-budget constitutional amendment	Y
Approve chemical weapons treaty	N
1996	
Approve farm bill	Y
Limit punitive damages in product liability cases	Y
Exempt small businesses from higher minimum wage	Y
Approve welfare overhaul	Y
Bar job discrimination based on sexual orientation	N
Override veto of ban on "partial birth" abortions	Y
1995	
Approve GOP budget with tax and spending cuts	Y
Approve constitutional amendment barring flag desecration	Y

VOTING STUDIES

	Presidential Support		Party Unity		Conservative Coalition	
Year	**S**	**O**	**S**	**O**	**S**	**O**
1996	32	63	85	6	92	0
1995	22†	77†	93†	5†	91†	5†
1994	40	60	89	11	94	6
1993	25	75	94	5	98	2
1992	83†	16†	91†	8†	82	13
1991	86	14	88	11	90	8

† *Not eligible for all recorded votes.*

INTEREST GROUP RATINGS

Year	ADA	AFL-CIO	CCUS	ACU
1996	0	n/a	100	100
1995	0	0	100	91
1994	10	0	90	96
1993	10	0	100	92
1992	10	18	100	96
1991	15	50	70	90

1 Joe Scarborough (R)

Of Pensacola — Elected 1994, 2nd term

Biographical Information

Born: April 9, 1963, Doraville, Ga.

Education: U. of Alabama, B.A. 1985; U. of Florida, J.D. 1990.

Occupation: Lawyer.

Family: Wife, Melanie Hinton; two children.

Religion: Baptist.

Political Career: No previous office.

Capitol Office: 127 Cannon Bldg. 20515; 225-4136.

Committees

Education & Workforce
Oversight & Investigations

Government Reform & Oversight
Government Management, Information & Technology; National Economic Growth, Natural Resources & Regulatory Affairs

National Security
Military Installations and Facilities; Military Research & Development

In Washington: During the first year of the 104th Congress, Scarborough was one of the most visible and oft-quoted members in the huge Republican Class of 1994. The absolutist nature of his conservative views on fiscal policy helped earn him a reputation as unwilling to compromise with President Clinton on a deficit-reduction plan.

"I have yet to apologize for anything we've done because we were right," Scarborough said. "We're not to be loved. We're to be respected. Who loves their accountant? Who loves the person who makes them balance their checkbook? I care more about the future of this country than I do about being loved."

Scarborough felt so strongly about reducing the deficit that in October 1995 he voted against the GOP leadership's budget-reconciliation bill because he thought it did not cut spending enough — one of only 10 Republicans to take that stance. Later, when a House-Senate conference produced a final budget plan, Scarborough voted for it. After Clinton vetoed that plan, provoking a weeks-long standoff with Congress that resulted in parts of the federal government shutting down, Scarborough blamed the closure on Clinton's refusal to go along with the GOP proposal. "I don't think any of us ever expected the White House to fight a balanced budget this long," he said.

As the budget stalemate dragged into 1996, the public came to lay most of the blame for the impasse on the Republican Congress, and some party freshmen were chastised by constituents furloughed from federal jobs. In late January the GOP leadership agreed to a temporary funding measure that reopened all of the government. Scarborough went along with his party's leaders on that vote, but he was not happy about it. "A one-year revolution is not possible in Washington," he groused. "The Founding Fathers set up a process to prevent it. You take a positive step forward, and if the Senate doesn't stop you, the White House will."

He also criticized then-Senate Majority Leader Bob Dole of Kansas — who was fighting to secure the GOP presidential nomination — for being too eager to reach a budget agreement with the White House. "I think like all politicians, myself included, you listen to your constituents," Scarborough said. "For him, he listens to future constituents. There are a lot of people in New Hampshire right now who don't like the fact that subsidies on heating oil have not been paid because of the government shutdown."

Scarborough stayed sour about giving in to Clinton into April 1996, when the House GOP leadership won approval of a compromise measure funding government functions through the rest of fiscal 1996. The plan passed 399-25, with Scarborough among the dissenters who complained that it ceded too many policy issues to Clinton and allowed the president to spend too much.

"We made a commitment last fall to stare down the president, and we blinked," he said. "We turned over the agenda to the president, and that's not why we got sent up here. We were sent here to force the president to balance the budget."

Scarborough's media visibility and his unyielding fiscal views were not the ingredients for a successful effort to become the freshman GOP class president. When the freshmen voted in February 1996 to pick a leader for the rest of the year, they chose lower-profile George P. Radanovich of California.

"Our goals are the same," Scarborough said of his rival. "We agreed on so much that we want to do that [the outcome] was more a matter of style. We are coming up to the time when we need a consensus-builder like George. But on reform of Congress and balancing the budget, we're on the same page."

In the 104th, Scarborough was part of a group of freshmen who urged House GOP leaders not to back moderate Republicans who were pushing an increase in the minimum wage. "Some of us are saying we don't have to cave in on an issue when all the facts are on our side," he said. Nonetheless, the leadership eventually brought the mini-

FLORIDA 1
Panhandle — Pensacola; Fort Walton Beach

In 1994, after years of backing Republicans in statewide and national elections while steadfastly supporting conservative Democrats for local posts, the voters of the 1st finally laid that tradition aside.

In the past, many voters here felt some guilt when they deserted the Old South tradition of voting Democratic. The conservatism of Democratic Rep. Earl Hutto, who retired, seemed to suit them just fine, allowing Hutto in 1992 to overcome having lost almost all of Panama City, his home and political base, in redistricting. But the district swung Republican with Scarborough's victory in 1994, and it reaffirmed the trend two years later.

Two enterprises dominate the westernmost part of Florida's Panhandle — military bases and tourism. Tourists are attracted to the soft, white-sand beaches along the Gulf Coast. The military bases are partly an outgrowth of work by Hutto's predecessor in the House, Robert L.F. Sikes.

The huge Eglin Air Force Base primarily develops and tests weapons systems and hosts combat-ready fighter wings. Pensacola's Naval Air Station features a naval education and training center. Among the district's other bases are those involved in naval research and development, the Air Force Special Operations Command, and a Navy helicopter training center.

The strong military presence helps give the 1st a right-of-center political complexion. This image is reinforced by national attention in recent years to the presence of anti-abortion supporters who murdered two doctors who had performed abortions.

In Pensacola, the district's largest city, the military's contribution to the economy is complemented by manufacturing of chemicals, plastics, textiles and paper. Despite its large natural harbor, Pensacola's potential as a trading port is restricted somewhat because nearby Mobile and New Orleans have much of the gulf trade.

The 100-mile stretch of beach from Pensacola to Panama City, dubbed the "Miracle Strip" by boosters, has also been called the "Redneck Riviera" because it attracts visitors from Georgia, Alabama and other Southeastern states. Along the coastal strip, military and other retirees have settled in Fort Walton Beach and Destin, both in Okaloosa County, just a few miles from Eglin Air Force Base.

Inland, the sparsely settled rural area is occupied mostly by soybeans, corn, tomatoes, cantaloupes, cattle and pine trees.

The district was not particularly hard hit by the recent recession. Many of its tourists arrive by car for relatively low-cost vacations. The rounds of base closings in the 1990s did not cost the area major job reductions. The bases provide numerous civilian jobs, and many enlisted personnel remain in the area after leaving the service.

1990 Population: 562,518. White 472,474 (84%), Black 72,083 (13%), Other 17,961 (3%). Hispanic origin 11,588 (2%). 18 and over 419,490 (75%), 62 and over 78,983 (14%). Median age: 33.

mum wage legislation to the House floor. Scarborough voted against the final bill.

Scarborough, who sits on the National Security Committee, is a stout defender of Pentagon spending and a supporter of the space station, but he takes a dim view of putting taxpayers' dollars into the Education Department. As chairman of a House Education Task Force, Scarborough lobbied for eliminating the department, which he thinks has done little to improve the quality of U.S. schools.

"The great federal experiment in education is over," Scarborough said. "It failed. It is time to move on."

In the 105th Congress, he will be in a position to continue his crusade against the department as a member of the House Education and the Workforce Committee.

He is also no fan of the Commerce Department and would like to abolish that Cabinet agency as well. "We're all steadfast in believing that the Commerce Department continuation is not in the country's best interest," he said.

Scarborough also wants to save money by ending U.S. participation in the United Nations. He introduced a bill in October 1995 — on the U.N.'s 50th anniversary — that would require the United States to pull out of the world body within four years of the bill's enactment. It would also mandate withdrawal of all U.S. forces from U.N. peacekeeping operations.

Not surprisingly, Scarborough firmly opposed sending U.S. troops on a peacekeeping mission to Bosnia. "They have not been able to make their case that getting involved in a three-way civil war halfway across the world is worth the death of young American men and young American women that would be sent to Bosnia," he said on the House floor.

On social issues such as abortion policy and gun owners' rights, Scarborough hews to the conservative line. But on some key environmental votes, he has parted ways with many of his colleagues on the right. In July 1995 he joined with

Republican moderates to oppose conservatives' efforts to bar the Environmental Protection Agency from enforcing many environmental laws. And in June 1996, he took the environmentalists' side on a vote involving protection of a threatened seabird species, the marbled murrelet. Scarborough was among 81 Republicans voting to drop a provision in the fiscal 1997 Interior appropriations bill that would have removed protections for the murrelet on 40,000 acres of private land in Northern California.

In his spare time, Scarborough played bass with fellow Republicans in a rock band called "The Amendments." Other members included Scott L. Klug of Wisconsin, John M. McHugh of New York and Jim Nussle of Iowa.

At Home: When the 1st came open in 1994, Scarborough's scrappiness as a campaigner and support from anti-abortion activists helped him snatch the GOP nomination from Lois Benson, a former Pensacola city councilwoman and state legislator. In November, he coasted to election with 62 percent of the vote.

A Pensacola lawyer just past his 31st birthday in the spring of 1994, Scarborough indicated that he would seek the GOP nomination before eight-term Democrat Earl Hutto announced his decision to retire. Scarborough had already gained a reputation as a persistent fighter when he led a 1993 protest that he claimed helped reduce a tax increase proposed by the Pensacola City Council.

Still, few expected Scarborough — the former front man for a rock band named "The Establishment" — to emerge at the top of a five-person House primary field that included Benson and a well-known Escambia County commissioner.

Promoting a platform of "Retaking America" that included paeans to conservative family values, government reform and states' rights, Scarborough pushed his message on a local cable TV talk show and sought out churchgoing voters. Scarborough assailed Benson, a supporter of abortion rights and the best-funded Republican aspirant, as a liberal.

Benson ran ahead of Scarborough in the first-round voting, but just barely — both took 31 percent. In the runoff, Benson sought to sow seeds of doubt in voters minds about Scarborough, noting that he had blamed the nation's budgetary problems partly on the increasing costs of "middle class entitlements," such as Social Security. But Scarborough's more conservative profile was in step with voters' mood in 1994, and he won nomination with 54 percent of the vote.

Democrats nominated lawyer and car dealer Vince Whibbs Jr., a conservative whose father had been mayor of Pensacola. But no matter Whibbs' ideology and roots, the electorate in the 1st was not of a mind to support a Democrat, and Scarborough won going away.

He had another easy time of it in 1996, taking 73 percent of the vote.

HOUSE ELECTIONS

1996 General		
Joe Scarborough (R)	175,648	(73%)
Kevin Beck (D)	66,415	(27%)
1994 General		
Joe Scarborough (R)	112,901	(62%)
Vince Whibbs Jr. (D)	70,389	(38%)

CAMPAIGN FINANCE

	Receipts	Receipts from PACs	Expend-itures
1996			
Scarborough (R)	$510,154	$176,542 (35%)	$428,856
Beck (D)	$35,100	$13,250 (38%)	$30,613
1994			
Scarborough (R)	$346,104	$71,988 (21%)	$345,687
Whibbs (D)	$271,955	$126,700 (47%)	$271,953

DISTRICT VOTE FOR PRESIDENT

1996	1992
D 77,127 (31%)	D 59,272 (26%)
R 146,749 (59%)	R 117,699 (51%)
I 24,310 (10%)	I 53,029 (23%)

KEY VOTES

1997	
Ban "partial birth" abortions	Y
1996	
Approve farm bill	Y
Deny public education to illegal immigrants	Y
Repeal ban on certain assault-style weapons	Y
Increase minimum wage	N
Freeze defense spending	N
Approve welfare overhaul	Y
1995	
Approve balanced-budget constitutional amendment	Y
Relax Clean Water Act regulations	Y
Oppose limits on environmental regulations	Y
Reduce projected Medicare spending	Y
Approve GOP budget with tax and spending cuts	N

VOTING STUDIES

	Presidential Support		Party Unity		Conservative Coalition	
Year	S	O	S	O	S	O
1996	30	67	82	10	75	20
1995	22	74	89	7	84	11

INTEREST GROUP RATINGS

Year	ADA	AFL-CIO	CCUS	ACU
1996	10	n/a	94	95
1995	15	8	88	96

2 Allen Boyd (D)

Of Monticello — Elected 1996, 1st term

Biographical Information
Born: June 6, 1945, Valdosta, Ga.
Education: North Florida Junior College, A.A. 1966; Florida State U., B.S. 1969.
Military Service: Army, 1970-71.
Occupation: Farmer.
Family: Wife, Stephanie A. Roush; three children.
Religion: Methodist.
Political Career: Fla. House, 1989-97.
Capitol Office: 1237 Longworth Bldg. 20515; 225-5235.

Committees
National Security
Military Installations and Facilities; Military Procurement
Small Business
Government Programs & Oversight; Regulatory Reform & Paperwork Reduction

The Path to Washington: Boyd, a former state legislator with a moderate voting record, appears to be an ideological match for this ancestrally Democratic but politically competitive district in Florida's panhandle. A farmer by trade, Boyd brings an agribusiness perspective to Washington and favors fiscally conservative, pro-growth economics.

He has also been a booster of education, an area he will almost certainly continue to defend as a member of Congress.

For example, Boyd has said he will pursue policies to increase access to student loans for college students. He also favors easing the financial burden on students and their families by changing the tax code to provide targeted tax deductions for college tuition.

Boyd has been close to state and local law enforcement groups and says he will work on the federal level to expand jail space, toughen penalties imposed on violent offenders and steer more resources to public safety programs.

First elected to the state House in 1988, Boyd ascended the leadership ladder quickly, becoming the chamber's majority whip at one point, then serving as chairman of the Governmental Operations Committee before eventually becoming chairman of the Rules and Calendar Committee, the panel that determines the House's legislative agenda.

In Washington, Boyd landed a seat on the National Security Committee, from which he will be able to oversee activities at Tyndall Air Force Base, a major Panama City air defense training facility located in the western part of the district. Boyd also sits on the Small Business Committee.

As a member of National Security, Boyd will take the slot previously occupied by three-term Florida Democrat Pete Peterson, who held the 2nd District seat before retiring in 1996. (Peterson now serves as U.S. ambassador to Vietnam.)

Florida Democrats, searching for a candidate cut from the same centrist swath as Peterson, did not have to look far to find Boyd, whose conservative fiscal tendencies and moderation on social issues made him appealing to Democrats, Republicans and independents. The district's Democratic tradition in House voting has been firm: Peterson easily won all three of his contests, and Democrats maintain a strong lead in voter registration.

Boyd's appeal did not prevent two other well-known Democrats from jumping into the race to challenge him for the Democratic nomination: Anita L. Davis, an African-American county commissioner from Leon County (Tallahassee); and former judge David L. Taunton.

Boyd finished a strong first in balloting but fell just short of the clear majority mandated by state law to avoid a runoff.

In the runoff against second-place Davis, Boyd touted his moderate voting record and argued that his legislative experience made him more qualified for a congressional seat than his opponent.

Davis, decidedly outmatched in fundraising, had a difficult time expanding beyond her Tallahassee base and into the district's more rural areas. Boyd easily outpaced Davis, 64 percent to 36 percent, to claim the nomination.

In the general election, Boyd faced Republican Bill Sutton, a former bank president who had served as the state's commerce secretary in the late 1980s under GOP Gov. Bob Martinez. Sutton's campaign centered around fiscal issues and emphasized his close ties to Tallahassee's business community.

But Boyd's down-home demeanor, high name recognition, and strong support from a diverse, widespread coalition of agriculture interests, law enforcement officials, educators and prominent business leaders, proved too much for Sutton to overcome.

In what many expected might be a close race between two moderates, Boyd carried 18 of the district's 19 counties in easily defeating Sutton by a 59 percent to 41 percent margin.

FLORIDA 2
Panhandle — Tallahassee; part of Panama City

Mention of "Florida" may initially elicit thoughts of tourism and retirees. But along the Panhandle exists "the other Florida" that engenders a maxim that the farther north you go in Florida, the further South you get.

Florida's 2nd District embodies this "other Florida." It is replete with rural, working-class communities that receive sustenance from agriculture and forestry.

Remapping in 1996 did not significantly alter the geographic contours of the district, which stretches from Panama City (Bay County) east across the Panhandle almost to Gainesville. Newly added territory includes Dixie and Gilchrist counties on the southeastern end of the Panhandle. Overall, the vast district encompasses 17 counties and portions of two others.

The new 2nd remains three-quarters white and almost one-quarter black.

Leon County, which includes Tallahassee, is the district's anchor and most populous county, accounting for 34 percent of the 2nd's population. Decidedly Democratic, Leon contains the sizable academic communities of Florida State University and Florida A&M, and a large state government work force.

Bay County, with its healthy supply of bays and powdery beaches, attracts vacationers and retired military veterans. This is a strongly Republican region.

The 2nd's major military installation is Tyndall Air Force Base, located in Bay and employer of 7,200 military and civilian personnel and several hundred contractors. The Coastal Systems Station, a Navy research and development lab in Panama City, employs 1,400.

Overall, the 2nd is steadfastly Democratic. In the face of the 1994 Republican tidal wave, Democrats swept the 2nd in all seven major state-level races, including the razor-thin gubernatorial race. Many of the rural counties have Democratic registration percentages in the nineties; only 3 percent of Liberty County registered voters are Republicans.

Republicans can make inroads here in presidential elections. George Bush easily won the 2nd in 1988; Bill Clinton twice won the district, albeit by less than comfortable margins, and lost several counties to Bob Dole.

Augmenting the district's Democratic proclivities is a sizable African-American population — 24 percent, a percentage exceeded by only three other Florida districts. Gadsden County, which borders Leon County and Georgia, is majority-black.

Jackson County, which borders both Georgia and Alabama, is the hub of soybean and peanut production in the state. Tobacco is an important crop, especially in Columbia and Suwannee counties (the Suwannee River, immortalized in Stephen Foster's song, forms the western boundary of its namesake county). There are logging interests all over the forest-rich 2nd. With its proximity to oyster bed-rich Apalachicola Bay, Franklin County on the Gulf Coast has for years been Florida's prodigious supplier of seafood.

As of May 19, the census Bureau had not recalculated population data, racial and ethnic breakdowns, and age statistics for districts newly drawn for the 1996 election.

HOUSE ELECTIONS

1996 General		
Allen Boyd (D)	138,100	(59%)
Bill Sutton (R)	94,030	(41%)
1996 Primary Runoff		
Allen Boyd (D)	75,587	(64%)
Anita L. Davis (D)	41,677	(36%)
1996 Primary		
Allen Boyd (D)	68,588	(49%)
Anita L. Davis (D)	37,050	(26%)
David L. Taunton (D)	36,027	(25%)

CAMPAIGN FINANCE

	Receipts	Receipts from PACs		Expend-itures
1996				
Boyd (D)	$809,791	$389,214	(48%)	$807,103
Sutton (R)	$291,322	$63,548	(22%)	$287,292

DISTRICT VOTE FOR PRESIDENT

1996		1992	
D	114,189 (48%)	D	101,797 (42%)
R	98,857 (41%)	R	90,666 (38%)
I	25,349 (11%)	I	47,130 (20%)

KEY VOTES

1997

Ban "partial birth" abortions	Y

3 Corrine Brown (D)

Of Jacksonville — Elected 1992, 3rd term

Biographical Information
Born: Nov. 11, 1946, Jacksonville, Fla.
Education: Florida A&M U., B.S. 1969, M.A. 1971; U. of Florida, Ed.S. 1974.
Occupation: College guidance counselor; travel agency owner.
Family: One child.
Religion: Baptist.
Political Career: Fla. House, 1983-93; candidate for Fla. House, 1980.
Capitol Office: 1610 Longworth Bldg. 20515; 225-0123.

Committees
Transportation & Infrastructure
Aviation; Surface Transportation
Veterans' Affairs
Health

In Washington: Liberals like Brown had a tough enough time in the 104th adjusting to a Congress under Republican control, but she faced the added burden of fighting on a second front. The 3rd, which had been a horseshoe-shaped majority black district, was ruled unconstitutional by a U.S. district court in April 1996.

Responding to the court decision, the Florida Legislature approved a new congressional map that gave Brown a district in which blacks are 42 percent of the voting-age population. But that hurdle, at least, Brown was able to clear. In November 1996, she won a third term with more than 60 percent of the vote — her best-ever election tally.

On the legislative front, though, Brown saw House Republicans push through their ambitious conservative agenda over her strong, and occasionally voluble, opposition. She voted against efforts to lower tax rates, ban a particular abortion technique that opponents call a "partial-birth" abortion and enact a constitutional limit on congressional terms. She was a vocal defender of affirmative action, likening the educational and economic opportunities it affords to her great-grandmother's sweet potato pie and suggesting that minorities warrant a larger helping of special consideration.

"Affirmative action is a thin slice — four percent," she said. "To tell you the truth, we ought to be going after the other 96 percent."

Brown opposed the GOP's welfare-overhaul initiative through the bill's several permutations during the 104th. "Republicans are in a hurry to pay for the tax breaks for the rich at the expense of hungry children, the elderly and veterans," Brown said during consideration of the first welfare package in March 1995. "Shame, shame, shame. Republican shame."

She said the GOP was employing "reverse Robin Hood tactics," reducing social welfare spending to pay for tax cuts she deemed unnecessary. She scoffed at Republicans who complained that their efforts to slow the projected rate of growth of Medicare and Medicaid were being described as "cuts" in spending.

"I understand that the Republican leadership is unhappy about us using the word 'cut' to describe the Republicans' revolting and offensive Medicare plan," Brown said. "OK, fine, maybe cut is not quite the right word. Well, how about g-u-t?"

Brown's rhetorical bludgeons did not budge the House GOP majority, and only President Clinton's veto pen blocked the Republican plan for reining in Medicare and Medicaid costs. Brown also lost out in an effort to secure $154.7 million for a Veterans Administration (VA) facility in Brevard County, Fla., during consideration of the fiscal 1996 spending bill that funded the VA and other agencies. Her amendment, sponsored with Florida Republican Dave Weldon, was ruled out of order as an appropriation that had not been authorized, although Clinton had requested the project in his budget.

Generally a reliable liberal vote, Brown has usually supported President Clinton's legislative agenda, with two notable exceptions: She voted against lifting the ban on homosexuals in the military and she opposed passage of NAFTA. In both instances, compelling local factors induced Brown to split with the administration. There are several military installations in and around Brown's North Florida district, including the Jacksonville and Cecil Field Naval Air Stations. Cecil, located in the neighboring 6th District, is scheduled to close by August 1999, but Jacksonville is still home to many retired military personnel, and Brown's vote against lifting the ban on gays probably reflected the prevailing sentiment in her district.

Her vote against NAFTA was grounded in the economic uncertainty felt by many in the 3rd as the Pentagon cuts back spending. "Let us be clear about this bill: It is a job killer," Brown said of NAFTA. "In Florida we daily see the toll that base closures and corporate downsizing have on jobs. Now is not the time to start a program that encourages our companies to move to Mexico."

She would like to see more emphasis placed

Mention the word "wishbone" to a Jacksonville resident and you'll likely receive one of two responses.

In a city boasting an expansion football team (the Jaguars) that in its second year made the conference championship game, and whose residents can drive about an hour to Gainesville to watch the 1996 college football champion Florida Gators, a description of a football formation might be the reply.

But the word "wishbone" to a northeast Floridian meant an accurate description of the 3rd District — until 1996 remapping made it more compact.

The "wishbone" was created in the post-1990 census redistricting process that sought to increase African-American congressional representation. Starting in Ocala in north-central Florida, the district extended north and west to include predominantly black areas of Gainesville and Lake City before moving eastward to pick up a large portion of Duval County (Jacksonville). The district then shot south to Orlando, while picking up minority areas in St. Augustine and Daytona Beach. In all, the 3rd touched portions of 14 counties.

In April 1996, a federal three-judge panel ruled that this majority-minority district was an unconstitutional racial gerrymander and ordered it redrawn. The new plan broke off the wishbone's western arm — the district now spans a wider swath from Jacksonville to Orlando. The 3rd has a black voting-age population of 42 percent and contains portions of nine counties. It is a notch or two less Democratic, but Republicans still have little chance of success in the 3rd.

Just over half of the district's population resides in Duval County; the 3rd's portion of

FLORIDA 3
North — parts of Jacksonville and Orlando

Duval is heavily African-American (46 percent) and steadfastly Democratic, voting for Bill Clinton 64 percent to 31 percent even as Bob Dole was winning Duval overall.

Although the 3rd is one of the state's poorest districts, Jacksonville's military facilities, including Naval Air Station Jacksonville on the city's southside, have provided middle-class means to many people in the area.

Just over one-fifth (21 percent) of district residents are from Orange County, which includes Orlando. More than 80 percent of Orlando's blacks reside in the 3rd, and just north of the city is nearly all-black Eatonville, hometown of the late author Zora Neale Hurston.

The eastern half of Putnam County is included in the 3rd. Often referred to as the "Bass Fishing Capital of the World," Putnam is a blue-collar region that Clinton easily carried in 1992 and 1996.

The 3rd does contain some tinges of conservatism, particularly in Clay County, one of the state's most heavily Republican counties (most of which lies in the 6th District), and in the Palatka area (Putnam County) on the St. Johns River. But GOP areas are few and far between in the 3rd, which remains strongly Democratic.

As of May 19, the Census Bureau had not recalculated population data, racial and ethnic breakdowns, and age statistics for districts newly drawn for the 1996 election.

on the military's human resources, such as better training. She sees the military as a place where families, particularly poor families, can find opportunities and learn self-discipline.

Brown serves on the Transportation and Infrastructure Committee, so she is in a position to argue for sending funds North Florida's way as the 105th takes up a big surface transportation bill. She supports the effort of Transportation Committee Chairman Bud Shuster, R-Pa., to take highway trust funds off-budget. She initially opposed Shuster's move in 1995 to lift federal speed limits but voted for the final bill, which passed.

Having survived a nasty 1992 primary to get to Congress, Brown hopes to stay there by joining with other Congressional Black Caucus members in making sure that minorities have access to campaign funding sources. In the 105th, Brown serves as the organization's secretary.

In the 103rd, Brown headed a Black Caucus task force on campaign finance, which had as one of its goals the protection of PAC contributions. Minority members often defend the use of PACs; since many minorities represent poor districts where constituents cannot afford to contribute to their campaigns, PACs can be key to their fundraising.

Brown ran into some questions about her own finances when her 1992 primary opponent, former state Rep. Andrew E. Johnson, filed charges with the Florida Commission on Ethics claiming that Brown made a staff member from her state representative's office work in her private travel agency. Brown agreed in February 1994 to pay Florida $5,000 to settle the ethics probe but denied any wrongdoing. Brown sold the agency for an amount between $50,000 and $100,000, according to her 1994 financial disclosure form.

At Home: Though Brown handily won re-election in her reshaped district in 1996, her success came with only modest help from non-minority voters. Exit polls indicated that she received about one-third of the share of white votes against Republican lawyer Preston James Fields.

After the black-majority 3rd was created in 1992 redistricting, Brown was one of four candidates in the district's Democratic primary. She clearly outworked another black legislator in the race and finished on top in the first-round voting, but fell short of a majority and headed to a runoff with the only white candidate, state Rep. Johnson. He emphasized the district's unusual shape and frequently criticized Brown for having supported the creative cartography that went into drawing the 3rd. During the campaign, Johnson, who said he was "the blackest candidate in the race" because of his position on issues, attacked Brown's integrity, claimed she did not live in the district and filed the campaign finance charges.

Promising to be an advocate for the poor and underprivileged, Brown won the runoff with 64 percent of the vote. In the general election, she defeated Republican Don Weidner with 59 percent.

Controversy over Brown's ethics problems spawned a 1994 Democratic primary challenge by former Commerce Department official Alvin Brown that at first glance appeared competitive. But he was a novice fundraiser and candidate, and the incumbent swept to renomination with 67 percent. In the general election, Corrine Brown faced Marc Little, a conservative black talk-show host. Shortly before Election Day, he unleashed TV spots hitting Brown on the ethics controversy. But Brown held him off without too much difficulty, winning with 58 percent of the vote.

HOUSE ELECTIONS

1996 General		
Corrine Brown (D)	98,047	(61%)
Preston James Fields (D)	62,166	(39%)
1994 General		
Corrine Brown (D)	63,845	(58%)
Marc Little (R)	46,895	(42%)

Previous Winning Percentages: 1992 (59%)

CAMPAIGN FINANCE

	Receipts	Receipts from PACs	Expend-itures
1996			
Brown (D)	$336,015	$235,316 (70%)	$330,201
Fields (R)	$49,949	$3,250 (7%)	$38,413
1994			
Brown (D)	$389,606	$243,395 (62%)	$383,017
Little (R)	$212,599	$12,964 (6%)	$212,235

DISTRICT VOTE FOR PRESIDENT

1996		1992	
D	102,516 (60%)	**D**	91,420 (51%)
R	54,075 (32%)	**R**	63,109 (35%)
I	14,216 (8%)	**I**	24,454 (14%)

KEY VOTES

1997	
Ban "partial birth" abortions	N
1996	
Approve farm bill	Y
Deny public education to illegal immigrants	N
Repeal ban on certain assault-style weapons	N
Increase minimum wage	Y
Freeze defense spending	N
Approve welfare overhaul	N
1995	
Approve balanced-budget constitutional amendment	N
Relax Clean Water Act regulations	N
Oppose limits on environmental regulations	Y
Reduce projected Medicare spending	N
Approve GOP budget with tax and spending cuts	N

VOTING STUDIES

	Presidential Support		Party Unity		Conservative Coalition	
Year	S	O	S	O	S	O
1996	80	15	85	9	59	41
1995	83	12	90	6	32	65
1994	88	10	89	4	44	50
1993	86	9	92	5	39	52

INTEREST GROUP RATINGS

Year	ADA	AFL-CIO	CCUS	ACU
1996	90	n/a	31	0
1995	100	100	13	12
1994	85	78	50	24
1993	75	100	18	4

4 Tillie Fowler (R)

Of Jacksonville — Elected 1992, 3rd term

Biographical Information
Born: Dec. 23, 1942, Milledgeville, Ga.
Education: Emory U., A.B. 1964, J.D. 1967.
Occupation: White House aide; congressional aide; lawyer.
Family: Husband, L. Buck Fowler; two children.
Religion: Episcopalian.
Political Career: Jacksonville City Council, 1985-92, president, 1989-90.
Capitol Office: 109 Cannon Bldg. 20515; 225-2501.

Committees
National Security
Military Installations and Facilities; Military Readiness
Transportation & Infrastructure
Railroads; Surface Transportation

In Washington: Fowler is the only Republican woman on the National Security Committee and a strong supporter of the defense spending bills drafted by her party. She says they have "restored balance" to President Clinton's defense budget requests — in other words, they have given the Pentagon more to spend than the White House had sought.

When the House considered the final version of the fiscal 1997 defense authorization bill in August 1996, Fowler said: "The bill provides $10.8 billion more than the president requested for fiscal 1997. However, this is not even enough to keep pace with inflation. Given the many threats to America's interests overseas and the number of operations other than war to which this administration has committed our forces, the funding levels in this bill are not only appropriate, but necessary."

When allegations surfaced in the fall of 1996 that Army drill instructors at several training bases had pressured female recruits for sex, Fowler was asked by committee Chairman Floyd D. Spence of South Carolina to help lead the committee's investigation of the matter. Fowler, along with the Indiana Republican Steve Buyer and California Democrat Jane Harman, emphasized that they would try to find out why the network of Army policies intended to prevent the harassment of recruits broke down and why some victims were slow to report the incidents.

Some conservative House members argued that the Army training incidents highlighted the tensions imposed on the armed forces by laws and Pentagon policies aimed at broadening the role of women in the military. Fowler did not go down that road, stating simply, "It's very important that they [men and women] continue to be trained together." She said she was dismayed that some of the victims had been reluctant to report inappropriate sexual advances. "There needs to be some other way in which these 18- and 19-year-old trainees feel comfortable that they can report [harassment]," she said.

Fowler's insistence on a robust defense budget reflects the interests of her district. The 4th is home to Jacksonville's Mayport Naval Air Station and many of her constituents work at the nearby Jacksonville Naval Aviation Depot. The city has long been a Navy town. When the House debated the annual defense authorization bill in August 1996, Fowler praised the measure, saying that it not only improved the quality of life for military personnel and their dependents, but also enhanced the readiness of military forces and ensured that combat equipment would be modernized.

She told the House that she was pleased that a House-Senate conference committee which ironed out the defense bill retained current law regarding depot maintenance and repair issues. Earlier in 1996, Fowler had taken exception to a Pentagon plan aimed at shifting more of its weapons-overhaul work from government-owned depots to private companies. During a committee hearing on the plan, Fowler and other members from districts with Pentagon depots argued that administration estimates of cost savings from privatization were wildly optimistic. Moreover, they warned, reliance on private firms to support critical equipment might leave troops in the lurch during wartime. "What about strikes, bankruptcies, mergers, lawsuits over proprietary data?" Fowler asked.

In addition to disagreeing with Clinton on the level of military spending, Fowler objected to one of the president's top priorities for U.S. troops — peacekeeping in Bosnia. In the 104th, she backed a measure that would have prohibited the deployment of ground forces to Bosnia unless Congress specifically appropriated the funding. "For me, the bottom line is this: I simply could never look into the eyes of a mother or father or spouse or child of a soldier killed in Bosnia and say that American interests in Bosnia were worth their sacrifice," she told the House in November 1995.

Fowler, who serves in the leadership as a deputy whip, concurs with the more conservative elements of the GOP on issues such as term lim-

FLORIDA 4
Northeast — part of Jacksonville

Nearly half a millennium ago, Ponce de Leon was searching for the "Fountain of Youth" and arrived instead upon the northeastern coast of Florida, in present-day St. Johns County. This area, referred to as "America's First Coast," lies in the 4th.

Redistricting in 1996 did not significantly alter the district boundaries, which encompass much of eastern and northern Jacksonville and Atlantic coastal communities from the Georgia state line down to Daytona Beach.

Jacksonville, as a result of its 1968 merger with Duval County, is the nation's largest city in land area. As befits its reputation as a center of insurance, telecommunications, banking and medical industries, Jacksonville's largest employers include Blue Cross/Blue Shield, Prudential, AT&T, First Union and Barnett banks, and a branch of the Mayo Clinic. America Online, the world's most widely used Internet services provider, has a 1,400-employee service center in the city. Workers who handle cargo and build and repair ships form much of Jacksonville's blue-collar community.

The military is an important employer here. Naval Air Station (NAS) Jacksonville, specializing in antisubmarine warfare, employs more than 16,000, and its Naval Aviation Depot has increased employment as other U.S. installations downsize or shut down. Naval Air Station Mayport, located 15 miles east of downtown Jacksonville, includes more than 13,000 active-duty and 1,600 civilian personnel.

The Association of Tennis Professionals (ATP) has headquarters in northeastern St. Johns County; the PGA's long-planned World Golf Village is also being built in the county.

Flagler, most of which lies in the 4th, experienced a population increase of 163 percent in the 1980s, the fastest clip of any county in the United States, and grew an additional 42 percent in the first half of the 1990s, the nation's eighth-fastest growing county. The influx of retirees to the Palm Beach area fuels the population boom, and these newcomers are voting Republican.

Nassau is regarded as an Interstate 95 stopping point for more popular attractions like Jacksonville, Orlando and Miami. Nassau is predominantly rural, and many residents work in the paper and timber industries. But the presence of Amelia Island, a popular resort and retirement destination housing its posh Plantation and the Ritz-Carlton, and Fernandina Beach burnish the reputation of a county long viewed as a mere bedroom community to its southern neighbor, Jacksonville.

The 4th remains overwhelmingly white. Most African-Americans in the area are included in the neighboring 3rd.

Although the areas that comprise the 4th were traditionally Democratic, the district now is a Republican stronghold. Bob Dole easily carried the 4th in 1996 and George Bush's 53 percent posting in 1992 made the 4th his third-best district in the state.

As of May 19, the Census Bureau had not recalculated population data, racial and ethnic breakdowns, and age statistics for districts drawn for the 1996 election.

its, immigration and crime. She says that illegal immigration exacts a heavy toll upon her state's taxpayers and that crime will not yield to gun control initiatives. She voted in March 1996 to repeal the ban on certain semiautomatic assault-style weapons.

In the 104th, Fowler joined the chorus of conservatives calling for more restrictions on both legal and illegal immigrants. This is a sensitive issue in Florida, one of the nation's top five states of residence for illegal immigrants. She opposed an effort to strip restrictions on legal immigrants from a broad immigration bill that the House approved in March 1996. Fowler argued that "current law encourages many legal immigrants to participate in welfare programs directly or to bring elderly family members to the United States to retire at the taxpayer's expense." Most of the legal immigration restrictions were removed from the final immigration bill, however.

Fowler is a strong proponent of congressional term limits. She says she came to Congress with a clear message from the people of Florida: "They want term limits." The first bill she introduced would have limited House members to eight years and senators to 12 years, the same length of service as Florida voters approved in 1992. But in both the 104th and 105th Congresses, term limit supporters could not muster the two-thirds majority vote needed for adoption of a constitutional amendment on the subject.

On some other issues, Fowler strikes a more moderate posture. In 1996 she backed an increase in the minimum wage, and she has sided with abortion rights supporters on some votes. In the 104th she voted to allow women at overseas military bases to have an abortion, if they paid for the procedure themselves; no taxpayer funding was involved, and it was "a simple matter of fairness," she said. She also voted for an amendment requiring states to pay for Medicaid abortions in cases of rape or incest.

Fowler does not support federal funding of abortions except in cases of rape, incest or threat to the life of the woman. "But I feel very strongly about those exceptions," she once told the House. "As the mother of two daughters, it is horrifying to me to think of anyone's daughter having to suffer the consequences of rape or incest without recourse."

Fowler voted against an amendment that would have allowed federal employee health care plans to cover abortion, and support a bill banning a particular abortion technique that opponents call a "partial birth" abortion.

At Home: Before entering Congress, Fowler worked in Washington as a legislative assistant for Rep. Robert G. Stephens Jr., a Georgia Democrat who served from 1961 to 1977, and as general counsel in the White House Office of Consumer Affairs during the Nixon administration.

She was the first woman and first Republican — out of only three Republicans on the 19-member Jacksonville City Council — to be elected council president. Later she chaired the Finance Committee and worked successfully with council Democrats.

Fowler announced her House candidacy in June 1992, when the 22-term incumbent, Democrat Charles E. Bennett, had said he was going to run again. But Bennett changed his mind and retired, and Fowler found herself facing Democrat Mattox Hair, a former state legislator and judge.

Though both were experienced politicians, Fowler repeatedly tagged Hair as standing with "good old boys" in the Florida Legislature, whom she said favored tax increases and legislative pay raises. Fowler's early entry into the race gave her a fundraising jump, and she lined up bipartisan support. By the time Hair announced, 22 friends who had supported his 1984 state Senate bid already had signed on to help Fowler.

Fowler won easily, taking 57 percent of the vote. She ran unopposed in 1994 and 1996.

Before the 1996 election, Fowler saw her district lines redrawn, an outgrowth of an April 1996 judicial ruling that the neighboring 3rd District was an unconstitutional racial gerrymander. A new map enacted by the state Legislature in May 1996 made modest changes to five north Florida districts, including Fowler's, but it did not greatly alter the partisan balance in any of them.

HOUSE ELECTIONS

1996 General		
Tillie Fowler (R)	unopposed	
1996 Primary		
Tillie Fowler (R)	42,047	(89%)
Gregg Robert Trude (R)	4,957	(11%)
1994 General		
Tillie Fowler (R)	unopposed	

Previous Winning Percentage: 1992 (57%)

CAMPAIGN FINANCE

	Receipts	Receipts from PACs	Expend-itures
1996			
Fowler (R)	$474,024	$134,562 (28%)	$280,593
1994			
Fowler (R)	$255,779	$77,787 (30%)	$103,233

DISTRICT VOTE FOR PRESIDENT

1996		1992	
D	98,263 (37%)	**D**	73,725 (30%)
R	149,985 (56%)	**R**	129,063 (53%)
I	19,626 (7%)	**I**	40,218 (17%)

KEY VOTES

1997	
Ban "partial birth" abortions	Y
1996	
Approve farm bill	Y
Deny public education to illegal immigrants	Y
Repeal ban on certain assault-style weapons	Y
Increase minimum wage	N
Freeze defense spending	N
Approve welfare overhaul	Y
1995	
Approve balanced-budget constitutional amendment	Y
Relax Clean Water Act regulations	Y
Oppose limits on environmental regulations	N
Reduce projected Medicare spending	Y
Approve GOP budget with tax and spending cuts	Y

VOTING STUDIES

	Presidential Support		Party Unity		Conservative Coalition	
Year	**S**	**O**	**S**	**O**	**S**	**O**
1996	33	58	85	7	92	4
1995	25	71	90	7	94	5
1994	62	37	86	11	94	6
1993	54	44	81	17	93	7

INTEREST GROUP RATINGS

Year	ADA	AFL-CIO	CCUS	ACU
1996	10	n/a	92	95
1995	5	0	100	79
1994	15	22	92	90
1993	15	0	82	83

5 Karen L. Thurman (D)

Of Dunnellon — Elected 1992, 3rd term

Biographical Information

Born: Jan. 12, 1951, Rapid City, S.D.

Education: Santa Fe Community College, A.A. 1971; U. of Florida, B.A. 1973.

Occupation: Teacher.

Family: Husband, John Thurman; two children.

Religion: Episcopalian.

Political Career: Dunnellon City Council, 1975-83, mayor, 1979-81; Fla. Senate, 1983-93.

Capitol Office: 440 Cannon Bldg. 20515; 225-1002.

Committees

Ways & Means
Oversight

In Washington: Thurman's ideological mix is a good fit for her politically competitive northern Florida district — from typically liberal positions backing antipoverty programs and abortion rights to more conservative views on reducing regulation and protecting gun-owners' rights.

Thurman won a third House term in 1996 with 62 percent of the vote, making considerable progress since her first election in 1992 with a 49 percent plurality. And a month after her most recent contest, Thurman's rise continued, as she was named to the Ways and Means Committee.

But Thurman then stumbled into one of the fiercest partisan battles of recent years: the controversy involving House Speaker Newt Gingrich, R-Ga., who had admitted to misleading the House ethics committee concerning the financing of his political activities and a series of college lectures he conducted.

Thurman was enveloped in the fray after receiving from local Democratic activists the "Gingrich tape" — a secretly recorded conference call among Republican leaders in which the Speaker discussed public relations strategies to play down his ethics problems.

Thurman allowed the tape to be passed on to the ranking Democrat on the ethics committee, Jim McDermott of Washington, who was widely reported to have leaked it to the media just days before the House's January 1997 vote on how to punish Gingrich.

Thurman's involvement in the incident began in late December 1996, when she received the tape from activists John and Alice Martin of Fort White, Fla. The Martins said they had been listening to a police scanner that Dec. 21 when they happened upon the Gingrich conference call (which they were able to do because one of the participants, House Republican Conference Chairman John A. Boehner of Ohio, was vacationing in Florida and speaking on a cellular phone).

The Martins, who said they thought the conversation might be important, recorded and then forwarded it to Thurman, their House member.

Thurman kept the tape until early January, when the Martins visited Washington, D.C., for the swearing-in of a Democratic House freshman from northern Florida. She then advised the couple to give the tape to McDermott, allowing them to write a cover letter to him in her House office.

Two days after McDermott received the tape, The New York Times published a transcript of the conference call, reporting it had received the tape from an unnamed Democratic House member.

Some of the Democrats seeking a severe punishment for Gingrich hoped the tape would show that he was trying to manipulate public opinion in violation of an agreement he had made with James M. Cole, the ethics committee's special counsel in charge of the Gingrich investigation.

However, the ploy backfired. Republicans railed that the tape leak was part of a desperate Democratic conspiracy to bring down Gingrich, who led the Republican takeover of Congress in the 1994 elections. By arguing that the taping violated federal wiretapping laws, they managed to change the subject in the days before the climactic House vote from Gingrich's ethics to alleged Democratic illegalities.

Thurman, McDermott and the Martins were questioned by federal law enforcement authorities (McDermott also resigned from the ethics committee before it took final action on the Gingrich matter), as Republicans warned they could face charges. (The Martins pleaded guilty to a charge of illegally intercepting a cellular call.) However, the fury over the tape quickly died down after the House voted to reprimand Gingrich and slap him with a $300,000 penalty. Thurman again went about her legislative activities, which show her to be a Democratic loyalist yet moderate enough to enjoy broad appeal back home.

Thurman has been a faithful backer of President Clinton's economic policies. She took a risk as a House freshman by supporting his 1993 deficit-reduction package, which included tax increases. She said it would make businesses stronger, provide jobs and "do some things that this country has needed over the last 12 years" of

FLORIDA 5
Northern West Coast — Parts of Alachua and Pasco counties; Hernando and Alachua counties

The 5th District extends from north-central Florida along the Gulf Coast to just north of the Tampa Bay area. It includes several distinct regions: The northern portion of the 5th is predominantly rural, and the southern area is laden with retirees. One of the country's largest universities is in the district.

Remapping in 1996 removed some rural, ancestrally Democratic counties and part of GOP-leaning Marion County. It added the rest of reliably Democratic Alachua, part of which had been included in the black-majority 3rd, and parts of Levy and Columbia counties, which have a conservative Democratic tradition. Redistricting did not significantly change the district's political makeup; the 5th's political preferences remain Democratic.

Alachua is the 5th's most populous county and contains the city of Gainesville. The city is home to the University of Florida, winner of the 1996 college football championship and educator of more than 39,000 students.

Some of Alachua's largest private-sector employers are hospitals, although many technological firms are starting up in the area because of the university's presence. The progressive-minded academic community, coupled with a sizable black population, gives Alachua a Democratic lean. Bill Clinton beat Bob Dole here 54 percent to 34 percent in 1996; 1988 Democratic presidential nominee Michael S. Dukakis had one of his best showings in the state here, barely losing the county.

Citrus County is bounded on the west by the Gulf of Mexico and on the north by the Withlacoochee River; the Tsala Apopka chain of lakes and the Withlacoochee State Forest comprise much of the county's eastern region. Manatees frequent Crystal River and draw tens of thousands of tourists annually.

The eastern part of the district includes a slice of southwestern Marion County, where Republicans tend to do well even though it includes Thurman's hometown of Dunnellon. Levy, the northernmost coastal county in the 5th, is wedded to timber and fishing and includes the archipelago of Cedar Key, which served as the southern terminus for Florida's first intrastate railroad and now is a popular tourist attraction.

Hernando and Pasco, the district's two southernmost counties, have experienced tremendous growth, especially in the coastal areas.

Hernando was Florida's second fastest growing county in the 1980s; its population increased by 127 percent. The county has one of the state's highest percentages of elderly people: In 1996, Clinton won three Florida counties in which registered Republicans outnumber Democrats; Hernando was one of them.

About one-fifth of the district's residents live in Pasco, a western slice of which lies in the district. Most of the county's population growth has taken place in this western part, especially around U.S. Route 19, which passes through New Port Richey.

As of May 19, the Census Bureau had not recalculated the population data, racial and ethnic breakdowns, and age statistics for districts newly drawn for the 1996 election.

Republican presidencies.

During the 104th Congress, Thurman was an outspoken critic of certain aspects of the House Republicans' plan to overhaul the federal welfare system. She was especially disturbed by provisions to limit food stamp eligibility for low-income Americans.

"What happens when companies downsize or a recession hits?" Thurman said in a House floor speech in July 1996. "Families that worked hard, but struggled from paycheck to paycheck, will look to us to help feed their children, and we will have to turn them away." However, Thurman did support the final compromise welfare overhaul bill that was signed by Clinton.

Given Florida's large elderly population, it is not surprising that Thurman helped carry the Democratic attack on the Republican effort to reduce future growth in Medicare spending.

She assailed the Republicans' 1995 budget-reconciliation bill, which purported to eliminate the deficit by 2002, for containing what she called cuts in the Medicare program. And like many Democrats, she said the bill (later vetoed by Clinton) sought to cut taxes for the wealthy on the backs of older Americans.

On occasion, Thurman does vary from her party's economic orthodoxy. For example, she supported a bill, part of the House Republicans' "Contract With America" effort, that would have overhauled the federal regulatory process and limited the ability of agencies to impose new rules. "The American people want their government to produce necessary and meaningful regulations and not burden them with unnecessary ones," Thurman said during a February 1995 floor speech.

Thurman's district is heavily agricultural, with large citrus and peanut crops. In February 1996, she blasted a proposed amendment to an omnibus farm bill by Republican deficit hawk Christopher Shays of Connecticut that sought to eliminate federal marketing quotas that support the price of domestically grown peanuts.

Thurman rejected the contention of the amendment's supporters that removing the quotas would lower the prices consumers paid for peanut products. "Eliminating the program will not affect the price paid by consumers; only the manufacturers will benefit," Thurman said. The amendment was defeated narrowly.

In 1993, Thurman opposed NAFTA, saying it posed an economic threat to local farmers. Thurman said that although Clinton had taken steps to protect some commodities from unfair competition, "the agriculture community is not united" on the trade pact.

As in most of the South, restrictions on gun ownership are not broadly popular in the 5th. Thurman reflects that sentiment, voting against two gun control bills that Clinton pushed during the 103rd Congress and accepting campaign contributions from the National Rifle Association (NRA). In 1996, she supported repeal of the ban on certain semiautomatic assault-style weapons.

Yet Thurman publicly denounced the NRA in July 1995 while serving, as a member of the Government Reform and Oversight Committee, on a special panel reviewing the ill-fated 1993 federal siege of the Branch Davidian compound in Waco, Texas. In a letter to the House ethics committee that she co-signed with Democratic Rep. Cardiss Collins of Illinois, Thurman accused Republicans of "improper dealings" with the NRA, which had harshly portrayed the Waco siege as an extreme government effort to confiscate the Branch Davidian members' guns.

At Home: Thurman's very modest showing in 1992, after a 10-year state Senate career and in a House district she had helped design, emboldened the Florida GOP for the 1994 race. And they did their flamboyant best that year to take her out, recruiting drag-racing champion "Big Daddy" Don Garlits as her opponent. But Thurman dismissed Garlits with relative ease, taking 57 percent of the vote despite the Republicans' national triumph.

A much lower-profile Republican field in 1996 produced Dave Gentry, publisher of the Gainesville-based National Crime Monthly magazine, as the nominee. In November, Thurman easily dispatched Gentry, topping 60 percent.

First elected to the Florida Senate in 1982, Thurman chaired the Subcommittee on Congressional Reapportionment as the state began to redraw its district lines following the 1990 census.

Critics said she tried to carve out a new congressional district for herself that included much of her state Senate district and preserved her strongest bases of support.

When she did claim the 5th District nomination in 1992, Republican nominee Tom Hogan, a lawyer and former prosecutor, portrayed Thurman as a "professional, big-money politician." She prevailed, but with just 49 percent of the vote and a six-point victory margin over Hogan.

Garlits, who had a large local following, was expected to present a stiffer challenge in 1994. But as a political newcomer, he proved a maladroit campaigner, and Thurman used TV ads to highlight his foot-in-mouth syndrome.

HOUSE ELECTIONS

1996 General		
Karen L. Thurman (D)	161,027	(62%)
Dave Gentry (R)	100,023	(38%)
1994 General		
Karen L. Thurman (D)	125,780	(57%)
"Big Daddy" Don Garlits (R)	94,093	(43%)

Previous Winning Percentages: 1992 (49%)

CAMPAIGN FINANCE

	Receipts	Receipts from PACs	Expend-itures
1996			
Thurman (D)	$532,432	$398,359 (75%)	$521,859
Gentry (R)	$68,189	$451 (1%)	$62,164
1994			
Thurman (D)	$565,499	$453,210 (80%)	$564,265
Garlits (R)	$312,878	$15,476 (5%)	$308,963

DISTRICT VOTE FOR PRESIDENT

	1996		1992
D	133,426 (50%)	**D**	109,706 (42%)
R	98,641 (37%)	**R**	88,698 (34%)
I	34,772 (13%)	**I**	61,819 (24%)

KEY VOTES

1997	
Ban "partial birth" abortions	N
1996	
Approve farm bill	N
Deny public education to illegal immigrants	N
Repeal ban on certain assault-style weapons	Y
Increase minimum wage	Y
Freeze defense spending	Y
Approve welfare overhaul	Y
1995	
Approve balanced-budget constitutional amendment	N
Relax Clean Water Act regulations	N
Oppose limits on environmental regulations	Y
Reduce projected Medicare spending	N
Approve GOP budget with tax and spending cuts	N

VOTING STUDIES

	Presidential Support		Party Unity		Conservative Coalition	
Year	S	O	S	O	S	O
1996	77	23	84	16	75	25
1995	67	25	75	21	66	29
1994	73	27	80	19	69	31
1993	74	26	88	11	57	43

INTEREST GROUP RATINGS

Year	ADA	AFL-CIO	CCUS	ACU
1996	75	n/a	25	15
1995	60	82	39	23
1994	65	89	67	19
1993	80	100	18	17

6 Cliff Stearns (R)

Of Ocala — Elected 1988, 5th term

Biographical Information
Born: April 16, 1941, Washington, D.C.
Education: George Washington U., B.S. 1963.
Military Service: Air Force, 1963-67.
Occupation: Hotel executive.
Family: Wife, Joan Moore; three children.
Religion: Presbyterian.
Political Career: No previous office.
Capitol Office: 2352 Rayburn Bldg. 20515; 225-5744.

Committees
Commerce
Energy & Power; Telecommunications, Trade & Consumer Protection
Veterans' Affairs
Health (chairman)

In Washington: Stearns was among the first in his party to learn that while serving in the House majority has its advantages, it's never easy being on top. Early in the 104th Congress, he had the misfortune of being in the Speaker's chair presiding over the chamber when a bitter partisan fight broke out over a private book deal negotiated by Speaker Newt Gingrich.

The catalyst of the parliamentary chaos was Carrie P. Meek, D-Fla., who in a brief floor speech faulting the book deal said, "If anything now, how much the Speaker earns has grown much more dependent on how hard his publishing house hawks his book." Gingrich defenders objected, and Stearns ruled that Meek's comments should be stricken from the House's official record, because "innuendo and personal references to the Speaker's personal conduct are not in order" and because "a higher level of respect is due the Speaker."

Democrats howled in outrage and challenged the ruling, and a harried Stearns struggled trying to bring the chamber to order. On a 217-178 roll call, the GOP majority voted to delete Meek's words. When the official Congressional Record was published, Stearns' comments had been slightly altered, which Democrats said was a violation of a rule that Republicans had put in place at the start of the 104th.

First elected in 1988, Stearns was an active proponent of "traditional values" even before the elections of the 1990s brought wave after wave of culturally conservative Republicans to the House. When matters such as abortion, homosexuality and pornography are under discussion, Stearns can be heard arguing against liberal attitudes and policies that he says are wrong for America.

As Republicans gathered to organize for the 104th Congress, Stearns sought a place on the party leadership ladder, running as the conservative candidate for the job of Republican Conference vice chairman. But even though the November 1994 election boosted conservatives' strength within the party, he lost the post to moderate Susan Molinari of New York by a vote of 124 to 100.

When he first came to Washington, Stearns got off to a fast start, winning his freshman class spot on the GOP Committee on Committees, which made committee assignments for Republican members. At the beginning of the 103rd Congress in 1993, Stearns got a good assignment himself — a seat on Energy and Commerce, now called just the Commerce Committee.

On Commerce, Stearns has taken an interest in issues such as computer pornography and television violence. He has proposed removing sections of current law which shield Internet providers from prosecution if computer operators use the Internet to obtain pornography or if minors use it to obtain indecent materials. While he supported the development of technology to allow TV viewers to block violent or sexually explicit programming, he preferred allowing the TV industry to devise its own approach, rather than requiring the manufacture of a so-called v-chip.

Stearns supported the House's major rewrite of the nation's telecommunications laws in the 104th, and he won adoption in committee of an amendment to allow broadcast companies to own more stations within a given market. He argued that the development of new technologies made ownership restrictions outdated.

But Stearns focuses most of his attention on social issues. He voted to outlaw a particular abortion technique that opponents call a "partial birth" abortion, saying it violates the Fifth Commandment, "Thou shalt not kill." Stearns has proposed a National Pornography Victims Awareness Week, and he supports allowing schools to observe a moment of silence for prayer.

Since his early days in the House, Stearns has been involved in the debate over government funding for the National Endowment for the Arts (NEA). In 1989, lawmakers agreed to cut funding for the NEA by $45,000 — the amount of two controversial grants that went to fund projects many

FLORIDA 6
North Central — Lake and Marion counties; part of Jacksonville

A federal court's 1996 decision that the wishbone-shaped 3rd District was unconstitutionally drawn required reconfiguring the 6th District as well. Most of the 6th lay inside this "wishbone," which connected parts of Ocala, Jacksonville, Daytona Beach and Orlando.

The redrawn 6th encompasses much of north and central Florida, running from the Georgia border to southwest of Orlando. It lies to the west of and runs roughly parallel to the Jacksonville-to-Orlando 3rd and covers a greater north-south distance. The 6th includes many rural areas that are traditionally Democratic but have grown increasingly receptive to the GOP.

The district's northeast boundaries extend into southwest Duval County (Jacksonville). Located in the 6th is Cecil Field, a naval air station 14 miles west of downtown Jacksonville that will shut down operations by 1999. NAS Jacksonville, located in the 3rd District, is an employment source for many residents of the 6th.

Just south of Duval is Clay County, most of which is included in the 6th. Clay is predominantly white, young and affluent - usually a recipe for success for Florida Republicans. In 1996, Republican nominee Bob Dole garnered 65 percent of the vote in Clay, and over the past three presidential elections no other Florida county has cast as high an average percentage (66 percent) for the Republican presidential ticket.

Union County, the smallest in land area of Florida's 67 counties, is covered by forests and contains many large prison facilities. Despite having the state's lowest per capita income, Union gave Republican Jeb Bush 72 percent of its vote in the 1994 gubernatorial election, the best showing in the state for the former president's son. Strong GOP percentages also are recorded in Baker County, a culturally conservative territory on the Georgia border, just north of Union.

Nearly one-third of the 6th's residents are from Marion County, which includes Ocala. Here are about 700 horse farms; the limestone-based soil produces pasture grasses ideal for horses. Marion's chief employers include Lockheed Martin; Emergency One, which manufactures fire engine equipment; and Mark III van conversions.

Lake, the 6th's next most populous county, is dotted with about 1,400 lakes, which make up one-sixth of the county's square mileage. Fittingly, Lake is popular for bass fishing and water sports. Large employers here include medical facilities and companies associated with the citrus industry.

The GOP leanings of the district's three most populous counties (Marion, Lake and Clay) overwhelm any Democratic predilections elsewhere, making the 6th reliably Republican territory.

As of May 19, the Census Bureau had not recalculated population data, racial and ethnic breakdowns, and age statistics for districts newly drawn for the 1996 election.

found offensive. Despite the compromise, Stearns pushed for further cuts in the agency's budget. The House overwhelmingly rejected his proposal to cut its funding by 5 percent.

In 1991, he tried unsuccessfully to cut $7.4 million from the NEA. In 1992, Stearns had better luck, winning House approval of an amendment to freeze fiscal 1993 funding for the NEA at the fiscal 1992 level. In 1994, after the performance of a controversial AIDS-awareness drama in Minneapolis that had received some NEA funding, Stearns offered an amendment to reduce the NEA's total funding by 5 percent. Lawmakers instead decided on a 2 percent cut.

When Republicans took control of Congress, the agency's survival was in doubt. But moderates salvaged something of a victory when the House leadership agreed to a compromise that provided the agency with $99.5 million in funding over a two-year phase-out period. Stearns upset some moderates when he offered a floor amendment to the compromise reached on the spending bill that would cut another $10 million in agency funding.

Stearns has criticized proposals to allow immigrants infected with HIV, the AIDS virus, to settle in the United States. "Before we open up our doors to just anyone," said Stearns in 1993, "wouldn't it be sound public policy to take care of our own citizens?"

He has also fought the Clinton administration, as well as some GOP leaders, over international trade agreements. He opposed both GATT and NAFTA in the 103rd Congress. When the Mexican peso collapsed, Stearns joined conservative commentator and presidential aspirant Patrick J. Buchanan in a news conference in early 1995 to denounce the Clinton administration's proposed bailout of the depleted currency. Stearns was one of 14 Republicans "taken to the woodshed" (as one of them put it) by Speaker Gingrich for voting against their party on a procedural motion regarding the bailout. "We have to be careful we don't create a loyalty test on each and every vote," Stearns insisted. Nevertheless, he admitted after the scolding, "I think the leadership will have support on all procedural votes now."

Stearns also bucked the party when he was one of 25 Republicans who joined Democrats to block a compromise House-Senate spending bill because it did not provide what they considered adequate funding for veterans' medical care. Stearns is chairman of the Veterans' Affairs Subcommittee on Health, and he has worked to get funding for two Gainesville projects — a new psychiatric wing at a veterans hospital and a biotechnology center at the University of Florida.

At Home: As a neophyte campaigner in a district that had never sent a Republican to Congress, Stearns in 1988 looked to have an uphill fight. But his limited political background gave him a salient, populist theme, and he rode it to victory over a favored Democrat.

From the outset, Stearns cast the 1988 election in the 6th as a choice not between himself and a particular politician, but between himself and the entire concept of a politician. A heavy underdog to state House Speaker Jon Mills, the Democratic nominee, Stearns stressed that "the time has come for a citizen congressman."

Stearns had developed some valuable contacts in the process of turning an investment in a dilapidated motel into a successful local motel and restaurant management company (called the House of Stearns). He was a director of the local chamber of commerce (where he was active in tourism development), served on the board of a major local hospital and was involved in church and civic groups. With those alliances and instinctive political savvy, Stearns was able to beat two better-connected candidates for the GOP nomination, and he went on to out-hustle Mills.

While Stearns campaigned tirelessly, an overconfident Mills spent time in Washington getting to know Democratic House leaders. Some Mills supporters had last-minute premonitions that the race was tightening, but none expected the shock they got on Election Day, when Stearns won handily in a district that also gave George Bush strong support in presidential voting.

Democrats began 1990 optimistic about regaining the 6th, but they failed to recruit a strong challenger. Art Johnson, a Gainesville lawyer, won the nomination in a lightly attended primary. In his low-budget challenge, Johnson argued that Stearns' staunch conservatism was out of sync with the district. But Stearns drew on a solid record in his first term, including obtaining funds for the Gainesville veterans' psychiatric hospital and holding frequent town meetings. Stearns won with 59 percent of the vote, and his re-elections since then have been romps.

HOUSE ELECTIONS

1996 General		
Cliff Stearns (R)	161,464	(67%)
Newell O'Brien (D)	78,886	(33%)
1994 General		
Cliff Stearns (R)	148,698	(99%)

Previous Winning Percentages: 1992 (65%) **1990** (59%) **1988** (53%)

CAMPAIGN FINANCE

	Receipts	Receipts from PACs		Expend-itures
1996				
Stearns (R)	$596,914	$328,184	(55%)	$301,045
O'Brien (D)	$39,324	$12,000	(31%)	$38,183
1994				
Stearns (R)	$352,023	$223,869	(64%)	$189,905

DISTRICT VOTE FOR PRESIDENT

	1996		1992
D	96,943 (39%)	D	77,741 (33%)
R	126,012 (50%)	R	108,956 (46%)
I	27,978 (11%)	I	51,650 (22%)

VOTING STUDIES

	Presidential Support		Party Unity		Conservative Coalition	
Year	S	O	S	O	S	O
1996	33	67	93	6	90	10
1995	15	83	96	3	96	3
1994	35	64	98	1	89	11
1993	33	66	91	6	93	5
1992	79	19	92	4	94	6
1991	71	29	88	10	95	5

KEY VOTES

1997	
Ban "partial birth" abortions	Y
1996	
Approve farm bill	Y
Deny public education to illegal immigrants	Y
Repeal ban on certain assault-style weapons	Y
Increase minimum wage	N
Freeze defense spending	N
Approve welfare overhaul	Y
1995	
Approve balanced-budget constitutional amendment	Y
Relax Clean Water Act regulations	Y
Oppose limits on environmental regulations	N
Reduce projected Medicare spending	Y
Approve GOP budget with tax and spending cuts	Y

INTEREST GROUP RATINGS

Year	ADA	AFL-CIO	CCUS	ACU
1996	5	n/a	88	100
1995	0	0	96	96
1994	0	22	75	100
1993	15	17	73	96
1992	5	11	75	92
1991	25	33	70	90

7 John L. Mica (R)

Of Winter Park — Elected 1992, 3rd term

Biographical Information
Born: Jan. 27, 1943, Binghamton, N.Y.
Education: Miami-Dade Community College, A.A. 1965; U. of Florida, B.A. 1967.
Occupation: Government consultant.
Family: Wife, Pat Szymanek; two children.
Religion: Episcopalian.
Political Career: Fla. House, 1977-81; Republican nominee for Fla. Senate, 1980.
Capitol Office: 106 Cannon Bldg. 20515; 225-4035.

Committees
Government Reform & Oversight
Civil Service (chairman); National Security, International Affairs & Criminal Justice
Transportation & Infrastructure
Railroads; Surface Transportation

In Washington: "I have the inclination of Newt Gingrich," Mica once said of himself, "but I hope I have the political wisdom of Bob Michel. You want to get things done, but sometimes you need to throw bombs."

When the GOP finally seized control of the House after 40 years, Mica — who had been on hand for his party's final two years in the minority — got a chairmanship on a Government Reform and Oversight subcommittee, and he set out with a vengeance to ease regulations on business, change federal employment policies, and investigate Clinton administration foibles and perceived abuses.

As chairman of the Civil Service Subcommittee, Mica sponsored several substantial bills in the 104th, but his need to launch some rhetorical bombs was also much in evidence.

He drew the most attention with his characterization of President Clinton as a "little bugger" in a November 1995 House floor speech. His words were taken down as an inappropriately personal complaint against the president, and Mica apologized to his colleagues, who voted, 199-189, to grant him continued speaking privileges for the day.

Mica, who complained about Mexico seeking U.S. help in bolstering its currency when the country "hasn't been doing diddly squat to cooperate with us" in the war on drugs, also raised eyebrows and the hackles of many of his Democratic colleagues with his likening of welfare recipients to alligators.

When the House first took up a welfare overhaul plan in March 1995, Mica held up a sign that said, "Please don't feed the alligators." He explained that such signs are posted in Florida "because unnatural feeding and artificial care creates dependency. When dependency sets in, these otherwise able-bodied alligators can no longer survive on their own."

Although he conceded that "people are not alligators," several Democratic members, after much booing and hissing, took up his rhetorical point and used it to portray the Republicans as heartless toward children in poverty.

Mica, a multimillionaire, has a businessman's perspective, honed from his background in consulting, lobbying and real estate ventures. He is a reliable vote for GOP nose-counters, unstinting in his desire to restrict the reach of the federal government.

His chairmanship of the Civil Service Subcommittee provided one of the clearest examples of the contrast between the old Hill ways under the Democrats and the new GOP regime. Mica was perfectly willing to take on the core constituency under his purview, sponsoring a bill that would have required federal employees to pay a higher contribution rate to their pension fund.

That action, coupled with Mica's belief that half the government could be safely contracted out to the private sector, led the president of the American Federation of Government Employees to call Mica "the most dangerous man in history to chair" the panel, denouncing Mica's "Attila the Hun slash and burn attacks." (Full committee Chairman William F. Clinger, R-Pa., vouched for Mica, saying, "He's not Attila the Hun — he's not going to go out there and destroy the civil service.") Mica, for his part, threw back at various unions that were working to defeat him in 1996, bragging that they would "rue the day they ever crossed me."

Mica was equally aggressive in pursuit of a better deal for veterans seeking federal employment, sponsoring legislation to expand hiring preferences for veterans to obtain and keep jobs with agencies. Noting that the share of federal jobs held by veterans had dropped 10 percent in 10 years, Mica noted, "If snail darters or any other species were disappearing at that rate, Congress would be jumping up and down demanding to know why. We owe our veterans no less."

Mica did not see his big hopes for civil service legislation enacted into law. His other moves would have afforded employees of the Executive Office of the President greater workplace protec-

FLORIDA 7

Central — Southern Seminole and Volusia counties; Deltona; Port Orange

The 7th is an overwhelmingly suburban district created in 1992 redistricting as a result of robust growth in the Orlando area.

Although the district has been reliably Republican in presidential and congressional elections, GOP support is not uniform across the 7th. Republicans seem firmly entrenched in Seminole County, which accounts for nearly half the district's population, and in the piece of Orange County that makes up about 10 percent of the district. But Democrats at the top of the ticket are competitive in Volusia County. Bill Clinton carried the portion of Volusia within the 7th with 48 percent in 1996.

Interstate 4 traverses the district from Daytona Beach to Orlando. It is a familiar roadway to residents of Seminole County, which grew by 60 percent during the 1980s, mainly because of its location directly north of Orlando.

Many county residents hop onto I-4 to commute south to jobs in the aerospace industry and at such Orlando institutions as Walt Disney World, Sea World, the University of Central Florida and Orlando International Airport. The interstate is so clogged that Mica secured a seat on the Transportation and Infrastructure Committee to try to get funding for improved access into the city.

Altamonte Springs and Casselberry, just north of the Orange County line, are Republican, upper-middle-class bedroom communities predominated by professionals. North along the interstate is affluent Heathrow. Sanford is the southern terminus of Amtrak's Virginia-to-Florida auto train.

Heading into Volusia County, unincorporated Deltona is the district's largest community, with 50,000 residents. It has a mixture of retirees and young working couples, as well as a growing Hispanic contingent.

The district's next largest area, Port Orange, directly south of Daytona Beach, also has some light industry and business, as well as some blue-collar retirees who help give it a Democratic cast.

The 7th includes about one-third of Daytona Beach. As Florida's population began to boom in the 1950s, Daytona became the most popular resort on the state's east coast for vacationers not wanting to make a longer trip down the peninsula. The city woos winter visitors who flock to the Daytona International Speedway auto race in February.

However, the boardwalk and some of the city's motels are reaching middle age, and competition from neighboring beaches and inland attractions has increased. Daytona's success at winning new jobs has been modest compared with neighboring Orlando and Jacksonville. Leading private employers include those involved in medical supplies, electronics and transportation.

1990 Population: 562,518. White 524,479 (93%), Black 22,410 (4%), Other 15,629 (3%). Hispanic origin 31,198 (6%). 18 and over 435,985 (78%), 62 and over 106,020 (19%). Median age: 36.

tions, and offered greater assistance to employees who lost their jobs as a result of government downsizing.

Mica was highly critical of Clinton administration moves to borrow from federal pension funds to keep the government solvent during the budget crisis of 1995-96, accusing Treasury Secretary Robert E. Rubin of "stealing" from and "bastardizing" the accounts. He was equally critical of Attorney General Janet Reno when she appeared before the Government Reform panel to testify about the 1993 standoff involving the Branch Davidian cult. In the 104th, he was a tough questioner of Clinton administration officials on drug policy and hiring practices at the White House, which he has described as "the last plantation." And in the 105th, Mica was glad to be on board as the Government Reform and Oversight Committee, under new Chairman Dan Burton, R-Ind., began investigating possible irregularities in the financing of Clinton's 1996 campaign.

Mica, who has long sought cuts in administrative agencies, sponsored a bill in the 104th to fold the Commerce Department and major trade agencies into a single entity. Shortly after taking office, Mica played a high-profile role in blocking a measure to give Cabinet status to the Environmental Protection Agency (EPA).

He was a key player in the Republican Party's effort in the 104th to ease the burden of federal regulations, sponsoring a provision to require federal agencies to review or sunset all their major regulations after seven years. He was a particular target of environmentalists who opposed the efforts to overhaul regulation; this drew Mica's ire.

"No matter what the Republicans do on the environment, it will never be enough," he complained. Mica supported a move to block the EPA's ability to enforce key environmental laws, saying the agency had abused its authority.

He supported adding $200 million for Everglades protection to the 1996 farm bill. "We are trying to come up with initiatives that put our money where our mouth is, that result in real cleanup projects that are tangible, and the Everglades project is tangible," he said. "I have no problem spending money on the environment. But it's the way the money gets spent that's the problem."

On the first day of the 105th Congress, Mica resubmitted a bill to authorize construction of a $70 million visitors center beneath the Capitol's East Front Plaza. Despite bipartisan support, the measure never moved beyond the hearing stage during the 104th.

Mica also serves on the Transportation and Infrastructure Committee, with a seat on the Surface Transportation Subcommittee that gives him a role in one of the bigger undertakings of the 105th: reauthorizing the nation's highway and mass transit programs.

At Home: Mica is the brother of Daniel A. Mica, a Democrat who represented Florida from 1979 to 1989. Another Mica brother was an aide to Democratic Gov. Lawton Chiles. However, John Mica became a Republican in his high school days, when he was a member of "Youth for Nixon."

And like a number of others in the House class of 1992, including those in the Florida delegation, Mica has considerable past political experience. He served in the state Legislature in 1977-1981 and was chief of staff and administrative assistant for Sen. Paula Hawkins, R-Fla., in 1981-85.

Redistricting and a retirement gave Mica an opening to run for Congress in 1992. GOP Rep. Craig T. James decided not to seek a third House term, and the new Florida map for the 1990s gave the 7th a clear Republican tilt.

There was a hard-fought, three-way GOP primary, and Mica won it impressively, taking a majority of the vote and thus avoiding a runoff. The Democratic nominee, lawyer Dan Webster, was on the attack from the word go. He tried to use Mica's extensive lobbying activities against him, calling him "the epitome of the professional politician" and warning that he might owe more favors to business clients than to constituents.

But Mica refused to be thrown on the defensive, retorting that all members are lobbyists for their districts. He said most of his lobbying was in behalf of local clients, citing the help he had provided to Daytona Beach Airport — whose status was upgraded from regional to international a month before the election — to Orlando International Airport and to the Central Florida Research Park.

Abortion was an issue in the campaign because of the clear contrast between the candidates: Webster was an abortion-rights supporter, while Mica said he would accept abortion only in cases of rape, incest or when a woman's life was endangered.

George Bush carried the 7th by 11 points in presidential voting, and Mica won by an even more comfortable margin, polling 56 percent of the vote. Mica won re-election with nearly three-fourths of the vote in 1994.

In 1996, he took 62 percent against former state Sen. George Stuart Jr., a Democrat who had some campaign expense irregularities.

HOUSE ELECTIONS

1996 General		
John L. Mica (R)	143,637	(62%)
George Stuart Jr. (D)	87,822	(38%)
1994 General		
John L. Mica (R)	131,711	(73%)
Edward D. Goddard (D)	47,747	(27%)

Previous Winning Percentages: 1992 (56%)

CAMPAIGN FINANCE

	Receipts	Receipts from PACs		Expend-itures
1996				
Mica (R)	$541,805	$227,396	(42%)	$539,973
Stuart (D)	$169,588	$73,300	(43%)	$165,921
1994				
Mica (R)	$409,715	$195,727	(48%)	$300,058
Goddard (D)	$29,166	$4,750	(16%)	$28,075

DISTRICT VOTE FOR PRESIDENT

	1996		1992
D	101,397 (44%)	**D**	80,655 (34%)
R	108,978 (47%)	**R**	104,443 (45%)
I	19,563 (9%)	**I**	49,111 (21%)

KEY VOTES

1997	
Ban "partial birth" abortions	Y
1996	
Approve farm bill	Y
Deny public education to illegal immigrants	Y
Repeal ban on certain assault-style weapons	Y
Increase minimum wage	N
Freeze defense spending	N
Approve welfare overhaul	Y
1995	
Approve balanced-budget constitutional amendment	Y
Relax Clean Water Act regulations	Y
Oppose limits on environmental regulations	N
Reduce projected Medicare spending	Y
Approve GOP budget with tax and spending cuts	Y

VOTING STUDIES

	Presidential Support		Party Unity		Conservative Coalition	
Year	S	O	S	O	S	O
1996	33	67	95	4	94	6
1995	16	84	96	3	97	2
1994	41	58	92	6	97	3
1993	31	69	94	5	93	7

INTEREST GROUP RATINGS

Year	ADA	AFL-CIO	CCUS	ACU
1996	0	n/a	100	100
1995	0	0	100	92
1994	10	22	83	95
1993	5	8	82	96

8 Bill McCollum (R)

Of Longwood — Elected 1980, 9th term

Biographical Information
Born: July 12, 1944, Brooksville, Fla.
Education: U. of Florida, B.A. 1965, J.D. 1968.
Military Service: Navy, 1969-72; Naval Reserve, 1972-92.
Occupation: Lawyer.
Family: Wife, Ingrid Seebohm; three children.
Religion: Episcopalian.
Political Career: Seminole County Republican Executive Committee chairman, 1976-80.
Capitol Office: 2266 Rayburn Bldg. 20515; 225-2176.

Committees
Banking & Financial Services
Financial Institutions & Consumer Credit
Select Intelligence
Human Intelligence, Analysis & Counterintelligence (chairman)
Judiciary
Courts & Intellectual Property; Crime (chairman)

In Washington: Much of McCollum's latter-day career has revolved around the question of time served — by members of Congress and by convicted criminals. Now in his 17th year as a House member, he thinks that members serve too long, and he sponsors a constitutional amendment to limit terms. McCollum also believes that criminals serve too little time, in many instances, and so as chairman of the Judiciary Subcommittee on Crime he sponsors many bills to toughen sentences on perpetrators of all stripes.

Typical was a bill he offered in 1996 to toughen sentences for juveniles convicted of violent crimes. McCollum complained that juvenile courts are too lax and too often send violent offenders "back home to mama." He said they should instead "be thrown in jail, the key should be thrown away, and there should be very little or no effort to rehabilitate them."

McCollum would like to serve in the Senate one day, but he decided early in the 105th Congress against challenging Democratic Sen. Bob Graham in 1998, announcing for a 10th House term instead. McCollum's version of the term limits amendment, which would allow House members to serve 12 years, angered proponents of more restrictive limits, and groups associated with the cause threatened to run TV ads against his Senate candidacy linking him to Cuban dictator Fidel Castro.

So instead, McCollum steadily accrues seniority in the House, showing more patience for working within the legislative process than some Republicans who pine for swift enactment of their conservative agenda.

McCollum worked for years on the minority side, proffering fully baked alternatives to Democratic legislation; now that his party is in control, McCollum translates the Republicans' tough tack on crime into adoptable language. He is a senior member of the Judiciary Committee, ranking third on the GOP side there, and he is the No. 2 Republican on the Banking and Financial Services Committee.

McCollum has displayed a willingness to work around embattled Banking Chairman Jim Leach, R-Iowa, who is on the outs with party leaders for refusing to support Newt Gingrich for Speaker in 1997. McCollum participated in a bipartisan committee rump group that talked separately with banking lobbyists during the 105th as the committee sought to update regulation of the industry, and he tried to add provisions to Leach bills to alter their thrust. McCollum also serves on the Select Intelligence Committee and for the 105th will chair its Human Intelligence, Analysis and Counterintelligence Subcommittee.

But most of McCollum's legislative efforts — once the term limits amendment has gone down to its biennial defeat, that is — are spent in the area of crime. During the 104th, McCollum succeeded in toughening sentences for drug offenders, overturning a pair of recommendations from the U.S. Sentencing Commission. McCollum accepted Democratic arguments that some of the sentencing provisions had been employed in a racist manner, but he insisted that such problems were not disproportionate.

McCollum also offered legislation to get the Justice Department involved in auto-theft tracking; to lengthen sentences for transporting a child across state lines for criminal sexual activity; and to federalize intellectual property theft. He argued in support of a bill offered by Ed Bryant, R-Tenn., that would have lengthened penalties for federal prisoners who try to escape, arguing that the current additional five years they must serve "is no big deal" for convicts already serving long sentences.

McCollum was co-chairman of a joint panel that investigated the FBI's role in the Branch Davidian standoff outside Waco, Texas, in 1993. He calls himself the "grandfather of restriction" when it comes to the Legal Services Corporation and sponsored a plan with Texas Democrat Charles W. Stenholm to curb the agency's activities. But he could not go along with the sentiment of many in his party to abolish Legal Services altogether. "I think the leadership is disappointed," McCollum

FLORIDA 8
Central — Orange County; part of Orlando

In a state famous for its coastline, Orlando is the only one of Florida's four large metropolitan areas without one. But that has not hindered economic development or population growth in and around the city. In fact, metropolitan Orlando has a more diversified economic base than many of Florida's beach meccas, where the economy is skewed toward tourism, construction and real estate speculation.

This is not to underestimate the impact of tourism. Walt Disney is still Orange County's leading private employer, with Disney World and Epcot. These are joined by attractions such as Sea World and Universal Studios, which is just across the 3rd District line. Universal Studios plans to expand into Universal City in the late 1990s; attractions will include a new theme park and expanded television and film production facilities..

Disney has been a catalyst for growth in metropolitan Orlando. The tourists it helps attract provide steady traffic through Orlando's airport, which has taken on international flights and become a hub for adjacent warehousing and distribution facilities. Thanks to Disney and Universal, there is work in movie and television production.

Also in Orlando is the world headquarters of Westinghouse's power generation unit, and Minute Maid has a processing plant for oranges. The University of Central Florida (26,000 students) is growing on the city's east side. Its emphasis on high-tech fields such as lasers fits in well with the area's numerous aerospace and defense contractors working on missiles and aircraft-control systems. Orlando's Naval Training Center, which has been slated for closure by 1999, provides simulators and training for the military. The shutdown will put about 4,000 full-time employees out of work, but the site has since become a regional Defense Finance and Accounting Center hub and a U.S. Customs communication center.

When McCollum first won election to the House in 1980, his district stretched from the gulf almost to the Atlantic. Population growth has led the district to be whittled down in successive redistricting; it now includes parts of Orange County plus the Kissimmee area in Osceola County.

Growth has brought problems to the Orlando area. Demand for water has increased dramatically, and sinkholes occasionally open up as the water table drops. More frequent problems are congested highways and overcrowded schools.

The parts of Orlando in the 8th contain a mixture of residents, many of them retirees and young families. North and east of the city are the affluent Orange County communities of Winter Park and Maitland. Home to Orlando's older, established elite, they strongly support the Republican Party. To the west, near Lake Apopka, lie Ocoee and Winter Garden. Fresh vegetables grow along the lake, while the foliage industry (houseplants, shrubbery and the like) has a presence in the city of Apopka.

Hispanics, especially Puerto Ricans, account for a significant minority of residents in Buena Ventura Lakes, near Kissimmee, and in Kissimmee itself, which is promoted as a centrally situated base for tourists visiting local attractions.

1990 Population: 562,518. White 499,776 (89%), Black 29,433 (5%), Other 33,309 (6%). Hispanic origin 63,997 (11%). 18 and over 436,210 (78%), 62 and over 76,727 (14%). Median age: 32.

said. "McCollum cannot be arm-twisted."

That was not the only instance in which he parted ways with his party's most conservative members. He refused to go along with an amendment offered by Bob Barr, R-Ga., that stripped an anti-terrorism bill of many new law enforcement powers. Barr and his allies saw danger in giving the government too much power, but McCollum said Barr's amendment would gut the bill. Also, McCollum got a cool response from his GOP brethren when the party was organizing for the 104th Congress, McCollum, who was vice chairman of the Republican Conference in the 103rd, took a beating in his bid to succeed Gingrich as party whip. McCollum ran a distant third, garnering only 28 votes despite the fact that he had contributed more than $900,000 to help fund the 1994 campaigns of 160 GOP candidates.

Nevertheless, McCollum was entrusted with the job of carrying crime provisions of the House GOP's 1994 campaign platform, the "Contract With America." He pushed the GOP legislation through his Crime Subcommittee in six separate pieces, rather than as a single big and complex bill. The proposal that drew the most controversy was a McCollum bill to cut a provision in the 1994 crime law intended to help finance 100,000 new police officers in communities across the country. Republicans advocated a block-grant approach, letting localities use the federal money for whatever crime-fighting expenses they deem appropriate. President Clinton vowed to veto the measure if it became law. McCollum said, "There never were going to be 100,000 cops anyway, because most communities in this country cannot afford to pay the additional cost it takes to get that kind of police officer on the streets."

McCollum also pushed legislation to allow victims to sue criminals for restitution, and to allow prosecutors to use warrantless searches as evidence, so long as the police conducted the searches "in good faith." On that issue, the Democrats tried to replace bill language with the text of the Fourth Amendment — thereby underscoring their concerns that the bill may be unconstitutional. "Don't wipe out the bill by voting for the Constitution," McCollum pleaded.

Another of the GOP crime bills was designed to speed the deportation of criminals who are illegal immigrants. McCollum takes a hard line against illegal immigration; as a member of the 1996 GOP platform committee, he authored a plank calling for a constitutional amendment declaring that children born in the United States of parents not legally present are not automatically citizens. Although he supported the omnibus illegal immigration language enacted during the 104th, he took issue with one provision that would have imposed a $6 fee on cruise ship passengers to help offset the cost of policing the ships to ensure they do not bring in illegal aliens. Contending that the levy would "be very detrimental to the cruise ship industry," he offered a successful amendment to strip it from the bill during Immigration and Claims Subcommittee action.

At Home: As drawn for the 1990s, the 8th contains less than half of the 5th District that McCollum had previously represented, stretching south and east from Orlando instead of north and west. Redistricting placed many of the city's black neighborhoods in an adjacent district, thereby enhancing the Republican nature of the 8th.

McCollum got his start in the old 5th shortly after his predecessor, Republican Rep. Richard Kelly, nearly was defeated in 1978. McCollum was already a candidate in the 1980 primary against Kelly when the FBI snared the incumbent in its Abscam investigation.

McCollum, a former Seminole County GOP chairman, was making his first bid for public office. But his early start helped him organize a stronger campaign than either Kelly or state Sen. Vince Fechtel, who joined the field later. Few issue differences separated the men, but McCollum successfully marketed his own image as a morally upstanding family man qualified to fill a "leadership vacuum."

He won 43 percent in the primary, running first in Seminole County and in the Orange County suburbs of Orlando, and also carrying the Gulf Coast GOP strongholds of Pasco and Pinellas counties. Kelly ran third. In the runoff, McCollum again brought his organizational strength to bear against Fechtel, carrying six of the district's eight counties and winning 54 percent.

Democrats chose lawyer David Best, the same candidate who had polled 49 percent against Kelly in 1978. McCollum, clearly more conservative than Best, caught the district's prevailing mood and was elected with 56 percent.

In 1982, McCollum's Democratic opponent was Dick Batchelor, a popular Orange County state representative considered a formidable, although underfunded, campaigner. Fearful of being dragged down by voter discontent with Reaganomics or concern over Social Security, McCollum did not emphasize his party label. Instead, he reprised the family man theme from his 1980 campaign (compared with the unmarried Batchelor) and said he had "restored integrity" to the district. He won 59 percent of the vote and has never been below 60 percent since then.

HOUSE ELECTIONS

1996 General		
Bill McCollum (R)	136,473	(67%)
Al Krulick (D)	65,784	(33%)
1994 General		
Bill McCollum (R)	131,376	(100%)

Previous Winning Percentages: **1992** (69%) **1990** (60%) **1988** (100%) **1986** (100%) **1984** (100%) **1982** (59%) **1980** (56%)

CAMPAIGN FINANCE

	Receipts	Receipts from PACs		Expend-itures
1996				
McCollum (R)	$893,053	$440,373	(49%)	$421,409
Krulick (D)	$34,445	$7,750	(22%)	$34,066
1994				
McCollum (R)	$445,919	$269,314	(60%)	$448,334

VOTING STUDIES

	Presidential Support		Party Unity		Conservative Coalition	
Year	**S**	**O**	**S**	**O**	**S**	**O**
1996	33	66	93	5	96	4
1995	19	78	93	5	94	5
1994	40	51	83	8	78	6
1993	40	58	90	8	95	5
1992	73	22	89	8	92	2
1991	76	21	81	13	86	3

KEY VOTES

1997	
Ban "partial birth" abortions	Y
1996	
Approve farm bill	Y
Deny public education to illegal immigrants	Y
Repeal ban on certain assault-style weapons	Y
Increase minimum wage	N
Freeze defense spending	N
Approve welfare overhaul	Y
1995	
Approve balanced-budget constitutional amendment	Y
Relax Clean Water Act regulations	Y
Oppose limits on environmental regulations	N
Reduce projected Medicare spending	Y
Approve GOP budget with tax and spending cuts	Y

INTEREST GROUP RATINGS

Year	ADA	AFL-CIO	CCUS	ACU
1996	0	n/a	100	95
1995	5	0	100	84
1994	0	13	91	95
1993	0	0	100	96
1992	15	25	86	92
1991	10	18	89	90

DISTRICT VOTE FOR PRESIDENT

	1996		1992
D	91,121 (43%)	**D**	68,853 (33%)
R	101,006 (48%)	**R**	100,166 (47%)
I	18,068 (9%)	**I**	42,624 (20%)

9 Michael Bilirakis (R)

Of Palm Harbor — Elected 1982, 8th term

Biographical Information
Born: July 16, 1930, Tarpon Springs, Fla.
Education: U. of Pittsburgh, B.S. 1959; George Washington U., 1959-60; U. of Florida, J.D. 1963.
Military Service: Air Force, 1951-55.
Occupation: Lawyer; restaurateur; engineer.
Family: Wife, Evelyn Miaoulis; two children.
Religion: Greek Orthodox.
Political Career: No previous office.
Capitol Office: 2369 Rayburn Bldg. 20515; 225-5755.

Committees
Commerce
Energy & Power; Health & Environment (chairman)
Veterans' Affairs
Health

In Washington: Known during his dozen years in the Republican House minority as conscientious and congenial, Bilirakis in the 104th got a front-line assignment in the GOP's budget-balancing war with the Democratic minority and President Clinton.

As chairman of the Commerce Subcommittee on Health and Environment, Bilirakis wrestled with the complex issue of how to rein in the spending growth of federal health entitlement programs. The job put him in the position of trying to help his party achieve budget savings while protecting the interests of Florida's many elderly residents; it was a challenge that at times frayed his reputation for staying on good terms with colleagues.

In the end, Republican aims to revamp Medicaid and Medicare came to naught, blocked by Democratic opposition and GOP worries that voters would take revenge at the polls in November 1996. But if Bilirakis could not cite legislative accomplishments on the entitlements issue, he at least emerged from the experience with his political popularity intact: Democrats had hoped that senior citizens in Bilirakis' district would turn on him, but he won an eighth term with almost 70 percent of the vote.

Before the 104th Congress, Bilirakis' work on Capitol Hill had consisted primarily of toeing the party line on most votes while keeping up good relations with the majority Democrats so he could get their help in funneling federal dollars to his district. Bilirakis' easy-going style contrasted with the increasingly partisan posture of many in the House Republican minority.

But when the GOP took control of the House in 1995, Bilirakis was not punished for his prior outreach to Democrats. In fact, with Bilirakis in the Commerce Health subcommittee chair, GOP leaders had a useful symbol for their argument that the party's plan to rein in the cost of Medicaid and Medicare would save the programs, not hurt older people; why else, they asked, would Bilirakis — whose district has so many seniors that it has been called "the waiting room for heaven" — agree to lead the charge?

But Bilirakis and the GOP met fierce resistance. Florida's governor, Democrat Lawton Chiles, traveled across the state and to Washington several times to warn that he was "scared to death" of the impact of the GOP's plan to turn Medicaid into a block grant program. Republicans hoped to hold Medicaid spending growth to 5 percent, while Florida was anticipating an increase in its Medicaid rolls in excess of 10 percent. Bilirakis said Medicaid costs could be controlled without harm to those who needed service, but he knew he was swimming in shark-infested waters. "I guess anybody who says they're not nervous would be lying," he said in September 1995 about proposed Medicare changes.

Later that fall, House Speaker Newt Gingrich announced changes in the Medicaid funding formula to benefit Florida. More money was added to, among other things, help Florida pay for emergency care for illegal aliens. The GOP plan also included a Bilirakis amendment requiring states to address financial protection for spouses of nursing home patients.

But nothing could ease the strain on relations in the usually friendly Florida delegation. Democratic Rep. Alcee L. Hastings accused Bilirakis and fellow GOP Rep. Dan Miller of "walking in lockstep with something they know will harm the state of Florida," the St. Petersburg Times reported.

Although the GOP plan for Medicaid and Medicare died, Bilirakis did have a hand in one health care measure that passed in the 104th — the insurance "portability" legislation. In the 103rd, responding to Democrats' desires to enact an overhaul of the health care system, Bilirakis had introduced a modest insurance-reform measure. In the GOP-controlled 104th, that plan was tapped as a starting point by Gingrich, who put Bilirakis and Bill Thomas, R-Calif., in charge of drafting a bill. The core of the final product allows employees to keep their health insurance if they lose or leave their job. Bilirakis called it a

FLORIDA 9

West — Northern Pinellas and Hillsborough counties; central Pasco County; Clearwater

The 9th sits above Tampa and St. Petersburg, patching together pieces of three counties. North Pinellas County accounts for about half the district's population; the rest is split between north Hillsborough and central Pasco counties.

Although the 9th looks like a Republican district, Democrats can be competitive here.

Lawton Chiles carried the areas within the 9th in the 1990 gubernatorial race, and Buddy MacKay held a slight edge in his unsuccessful 1988 Senate race. Bilirakis got less than 60 percent of the vote in two successive re-election bids before winning handily in 1994 (when he ran unopposed) and 1996.

The parts of Pinellas County in the district are solidly Republican. Democrats running for state and federal office are lucky to win 45 percent in that portion of the Pinellas vote.

Clearwater, historically a beach resort, has benefited from the arrival of high-technology industry to metropolitan St. Petersburg. Honeywell, much of which is just south of the district in the 10th, is a significant employer in the area.

Light industry, services and a tourism trade, some of it associated with the gulf beaches, all have a role in the county's economy.

Real estate development is also important; the area has attracted middle- to upper-middle-class retirees.

North of Clearwater is Palm Harbor, the district's second-largest city, which features more boat docks than beaches. Many residents here still commute into Tampa-St. Petersburg.

Continuing north, a substantial Greek community lives in Tarpon Springs, a century after their ancestors first came to harvest the offshore sponge beds.

Democrats are more competitive in Pasco County. Many of the retirees who have settled in the county in recent years come from working-class backgrounds in the Northeast and Midwest and cling to Democratic voting habits, particularly in contests for local office.

Even so, Bilirakis was dismayed that 1992 redistricting stripped the 9th of western Pasco County, an area filled with retirees and military veterans whose interests he tried to promote.

The 9th still includes some residents in areas of west Pasco. Many of the retirees also recently relocated to the area in communities such as Zephyrhills. Some are former union members who remain conservative Democrats. The growth of development in Pasco County has generally been from west to east, moving into rolling hills containing dairy farms and some citrus. Redistricting also cost the 9th the easternmost part of Pasco County.

Hillsborough County accounts for about one-fifth of the district's population. One development of note is Carrollwood Village, a bedroom community for Tampa. Bill Clinton barely won the 9th's sections of Pasco and Pinellas in 1996, while Bob Dole held the edge in the portions of Hillsborough.

1990 Population: 562,518. White 532,324 (95%), Black 19,245 (3%), Other 10,949 (2%). Hispanic origin 22,946 (4%). 18 and over 447,843 (80%), 62 and over 142,351 (25%). Median age: 39.

"reasonable beginning for our nation's health-insurance problem."

Bilirakis' subcommittee had a piece of the bill reauthorizing the Safe Drinking Water Act, the major environmental legislation of the 104th. And Bilirakis helped launch a bill by Commerce Committee Chairman Thomas J. Bliley Jr., R-Va., to rewrite the regulations on the use of pesticides in food.

Bilirakis took over the Health and Environment Subcommittee chairmanship in 1995 from Democrat Henry A. Waxman of California, with whom he had generally worked well when the GOP was in the minority. In the 99th Congress, Bilirakis collaborated with Waxman to get Medicare demonstration projects for victims of Alzheimer's disease included in a budget-reconciliation measure. In the 100th Congress, Bilirakis was one of 61 House Republicans to vote for the Democrats' version of catastrophic health insurance. These instances of cooperation aside, however, when Bilirakis took the subcommittee gavel from Waxman, some of the Democrat's highest-priority initiatives — notably his crusade against the tobacco industry — were halted.

Despite his overall conservatism, Bilirakis sometimes breaks from the limited-government stance in favor of more activism. In the 104th, he spoke in support of protecting the Women, Infant and Children nutritional program. He broke from the GOP majority in supporting an increase in the minimum wage. And as a member of the Veterans Affairs Committee, he is frequently a booster of expanding benefits for veterans or active military personnel. In 1996, Congress appropriated money for a new spinal cord injury unit at a VA Medical Center in Florida for which he had lobbied.

Environmental issues, particularly trying to protect his state's water supply, are part of Bilirakis' agenda. In the 102nd Congress, he successfully lobbied for adding conservation standards for electric energy and plumbing fixtures to the National Energy Security Act.

Co-chairman of the congressional Hellenic Caucus, Bilirakis is a champion of Greek causes. He frequently delivers floor speeches commemorating special events in Greece, and he lets no opportunity pass to criticize the Turks, who continue to control northern Cyprus. Bilirakis has asked the Clinton administration to try to find the fate of Greeks and Americans still missing after the Turkish invasion of Cyprus in 1974. In a 1995 speech, Bilirakis asserted that the amount of U.S. aid money sent to Turkey annually is roughly equal to the amount needed to maintain the country's 30,0000-plus troops occupying Cyprus. "A coincidence?" he asked. "I think not."

At Home: When Bilirakis in 1982 announced his plans to try for the newly created 9th, local GOP leaders were bemused. But lawyer-restaurateur Bilirakis surprised the media, the party hierarchy and most supposed experts on Florida politics, turning innocence into a virtue and winning the district. Once elected, he quickly became entrenched.

A Democrat until 1970, Bilirakis had switched parties that year to back Rep. L. A. "Skip" Bafalis' bid for governor. He was intermittently involved in local GOP campaigns after that, but when he entered the 1982 GOP primary in the 9th, the strong favorite was state House Republican leader Curt Kiser. Kiser, though, took his nomination for granted, and in the meantime Bilirakis blanketed the district with signs saying that his was "a hard name to spell but an easy one to remember."

Using his own resources and contributions from the Tarpon Springs Greek community, Bilirakis flooded the airwaves with ads stressing his service to the area, as a judge in county and municipal courts, and as president of several community organizations. Bilirakis finished well ahead of Kiser and Clearwater Mayor Charles LeCher and beat Kiser in the runoff.

Bilirakis emphasized his personality in his general-election campaign against Democratic state Rep. George Sheldon. When he did speak out on issues, he espoused conservative positions — defending President Ronald Reagan's economic program and arguing for a constitutional ban on abortions — and he attacked Sheldon's more liberal voting record. Bilirakis won with 51 percent.

In 1990 and 1992, Bilirakis slipped just below 60 percent against Democrat Cheryl Davis Knapp, a liberal nurse from Safety Harbor. She ran an unheralded, unfunded campaign in 1990, accusing Bilirakis of doing too little for the environment, the homeless and women's rights. Bilirakis, who had been unopposed in 1988, got 58 percent. Two years later Knapp drew more money and attention and used some of the same campaign themes. Bilirakis won 59 percent.

Before facing Knapp that second time, Bilirakis had brushed off a 1992 GOP primary challenge from state Rep. Patricia A. "Trish" Muscarella.

She criticized him for opposing abortion rights and for seeking a sixth term despite supporting congressional term limits, but Bilirakis was renominated with two-thirds of the vote.

HOUSE ELECTIONS

1996 General		
Michael Bilirakis (R)	161,689	(69%)
Jerry Provenzano (D)	73,799	(31%)
1996 Primary		
Michael Bilirakis (R)	45,183	(80%)
Pamela Mills Corbino (R)	11,236	(20%)
1994 General		
Michael Bilirakis (R)	unopposed	

Previous Winning Percentages: **1992** (59%) **1990** (58%) **1988** (100%) **1986** (71%) **1984** (79%) **1982** (51%)

CAMPAIGN FINANCE

	Receipts	Receipts from PACs	Expend-itures
1996			
Bilirakis (R)	$740,666	$376,371 (51%)	$846,392
Provenzano (D)	$84,714	$29,150 (34%)	$84,370
1994			
Bilirakis (R)	$347,964	$185,695 (53%)	$191,717

DISTRICT VOTE FOR PRESIDENT

1996		1992	
D	121,675 (45%)	**D**	94,244 (34%)
R	122,308 (45%)	**R**	112,039 (41%)
I	27,725 (10%)	**I**	67,742 (25%)

KEY VOTES

1997	
Ban "partial birth" abortions	Y
1996	
Approve farm bill	Y
Deny public education to illegal immigrants	Y
Repeal ban on certain assault-style weapons	Y
Increase minimum wage	Y
Freeze defense spending	N
Approve welfare overhaul	Y
1995	
Approve balanced-budget constitutional amendment	Y
Relax Clean Water Act regulations	Y
Oppose limits on environmental regulations	N
Reduce projected Medicare spending	Y
Approve GOP budget with tax and spending cuts	Y

VOTING STUDIES

	Presidential Support		Party Unity		Conservative Coalition	
Year	**S**	**O**	**S**	**O**	**S**	**O**
1996	33	67	91	9	90	10
1995	19	78	92	7	95	4
1994	47	47	84	11	89	6
1993	44	54	87	10	95	5
1992	64	34	86	12	85	15
1991	78	19	81	14	78	14

INTEREST GROUP RATINGS

Year	ADA	AFL-CIO	CCUS	ACU
1996	5	n/a	94	90
1995	5	8	96	84
1994	20	56	75	86
1993	20	33	73	79
1992	20	42	75	80
1991	15	8	80	89

10 C.W. Bill Young (R)

Of Indian Rocks Beach — Elected 1970, 14th term

Biographical Information
Born: Dec. 16, 1930, Harmarville, Pa.
Education: Pennsylvania public schools.
Military Service: National Guard, 1948-57.
Occupation: Insurance executive; public official.
Family: Wife, Beverly F. Angelo; three children.
Religion: Methodist.
Political Career: Fla. Senate, 1961-71, minority leader, 1967-71.
Capitol Office: 2407 Rayburn Bldg. 20515; 225-5961.

Committees
Appropriations
Labor, Health & Human Services and Education; Legislative; National Security (chairman)
Select Intelligence
Technical & Tactical Intelligence

In Washington: In the 1960s, Young was a trail-blazing conservative Republican when Florida barely had a GOP, but now, as he moves past the quarter-century mark in his congressional career, he is surrounded in the House by younger, more confrontational party colleagues.

When GOP Speaker-to-be Newt Gingrich was putting his leadership team in place for the 104th Congress and looking for a new Appropriations Committee chairman, Young was one of the senior members of the panel skipped over in favor of Robert L. Livingston of Louisiana. Gingrich felt more comfortable entrusting Livingston with the job of steering Appropriations away from its traditional role as a dispenser of federal programs and projects and toward the task of aggressively cutting spending.

There was a consolation prize for Young: the chairmanship of Appropriations' National Security Subcommittee. In that job he oversees the one area of the federal budget that has seen significant funding increases of late, despite deficit pressures. On Appropriations and as a member of the Select Intelligence Committee, Young promotes a more robust budget for defense and intelligence functions than the Clinton administration requests.

During the November 1995 debate on the $243 billion military spending bill, Young defended the nearly $7 billion in funds the GOP was seeking on top of President Clinton's request for the Pentagon, saying the administration budget was anemic. "The people who have to fight the wars . . . say that the 10-year decline in national defense has got to stop," Young said. About two-thirds of the added funding was earmarked to buy additional arms — including B-2 "stealth" bombers and transport ships for Marine Corps assault troops — and to accelerate the development of new weapons, including anti-missile defenses.

The next year's spending bill for the Pentagon, which became law in September 1996 as part of an omnibus measure that included five other spending bills, also was higher than the president wanted. Yet while Young and other GOP defense mavens argued that Clinton was shortchanging defense, the strong countervailing demand among Republicans for deficit reduction meant that the defense appropriators could boost Clinton's $234.6 billion request for the defense bill by only 4 percent ($9.7 billion).

House and Senate negotiations on the fiscal 1997 defense spending bill were delayed for a month while Young recuperated from open heart surgery. In the meantime, the White House pressed Congress to shift at least $1 billion from defense to domestic programs.

Despite the pressure to reduce defense spending, Young was able to use the measure to direct some money home, including $6.5 million for a proposed Brain Institute at the University of Florida and $3 million for a criminal justice program at St. Petersburg Junior College. Young also added to the bill $10 million to continue research on underwater vehicles. The funds were to be awarded on a competitive basis, but the odds-on favorite for part of the money was the University of South Florida's Marine Science Center, also in St. Petersburg.

Several congressional add-ons in the bill boosted funds for research on combating certain diseases, including $14 million to research bone marrow transplants, a treatment for leukemia. Young has been the leading congressional advocate of funding a federally sponsored bone marrow donor registry through the defense budget. The endeavor now bears his name — the C.W. Bill Young Marrow Donor Recruitment and Research Program. Money for the registry initially got into a defense funding bill in 1986, when then-Sen. Paul Laxalt of Nevada slipped it in. That year, Laxalt announced his retirement, and Young came into contact with a 10-year-old girl from his district who had cancer and could not find a bone marrow donor. Since then, Young has been the program's tireless congressional advocate, and he counts it as his proudest achievement. After adopting the cause, Young learned in late 1990

FLORIDA 10
West — Southern Pinellas County; St. Petersburg

The modern era of Florida politics began in this St. Petersburg-based district four decades ago.

In 1954, the district made William C. Cramer the state's first Republican House member in the 20th century. Cramer owed his election to the influence of conservative retirees. Other GOP candidates prospered later as the retirees' influence expanded elsewhere in Florida.

The retirees are still crucial in the politics of the 10th. But candidates cannot afford to ignore the growing numbers of young people drawn by its steadily diversifying economy. The young newcomers, like many of their peers elsewhere in Florida, also tend to identify with the GOP.

Not too long ago, St. Petersburg was known almost exclusively as a retirement haven. The retirees who settled here, many of them storekeepers, office workers and civil servants from small Midwestern towns, brought their Republican preferences with them. The economy was mostly service-oriented, geared to the needs of tourists and elderly residents. Rush hour saw many younger workers from St. Petersburg driving to jobs in faster-pace Tampa, which provided employment in a greater variety of fields.

But St. Petersburg has broadened its economic base by stressing that it offers a good climate for business investment. Where the Shuffleboard Hall of Fame was once the big attraction, visitors now are drawn to the Salvador Dali Museum and Sunken Gardens. The Women's Tennis Association is here. The city's lengthy quest for a major-league baseball team — which prompted the construction of Tropicana Field — has finally paid off. The Tampa Bay Devil Rays begin playing in 1998.

St. Petersburg and Pinellas County companies such as Honeywell, AT&T Paradyne and Raytheon E-Systems are busy with research, development, production and marketing of computers, communications equipment and other high-tech items.

A number of the major employers and subcontractors are engaged in defense-related work. Defense cuts and nervousness about the economy throughout the area undercut George Bush's support in 1992 and Bob Dole's in 1996. Strong support for Ross Perot in 1992 enabled Bill Clinton to carry the 10th with only 40 percent. Perot's support subsided in 1996, when Clinton carried the district with 51 percent. But statewide GOP candidates are still more likely to campaign here than in the Tampa-based 11th, and Young was easily re-elected in 1996.

Although the median age in Pinellas County has dropped over the years as younger residents have replaced retirees, the southern part of the county is already so crowded that it is growing much more slowly than the state as a whole.

Elsewhere, Pinellas Park is generally a blue-collar, lower middle-class community, with some residents living in mobile home parks. Largo includes a large concentration of retirees. Residents of the adjacent gulf beaches are generally less affluent than those who live along the Sarasota or Miami-Fort Lauderdale coasts.

1990 Population: 562,518. White 498,333 (89%), Black 53,001 (9%), Other 11,184 (2%). Hispanic origin 13,017 (2%). 18 and over 462,536 (82%), 62 and over 167,505 (30%). Median age: 42.

that his eldest daughter had a form of leukemia treatable only through a marrow transplant. She received a transplant that restored her health.

During his first term as chairman of Appropriations' Defense Subcommittee, Young had to contend with an insurrection on his panel. A first-term Republican, conservative Mark W. Neumann, voted against the fiscal 1996 defense spending bill. He was unhappy because a conference committee had watered down a provision he had sponsored on the House floor requiring congressional approval before Clinton could send U.S. troops to Bosnia.

With the consent of Gingrich, Appropriations Committee Chairman Livingston demoted Neumann from the Defense Subcommittee to the Military Construction panel, citing his vote against the defense spending bill.

The next day, a number of Neumann's Class of 1994 colleagues met with Gingrich to protest the demotion. Neumann was then given a prized seat on the Budget Committee, and he was allowed to kept his seat on Appropriations, though not on the Defense Subcommittee.

When asked about the situation, Young took pains to underscore that the matter was handled above his pay grade. "I had nothing to do with his appointment and nothing to do with his reassignment," Young said of Neumann.

Young is one of three Republicans in the Florida House delegation whose district voted for Clinton over Bob Dole for president in 1996. Although Young easily won a 14th term, he sometimes takes a more moderate line than many of his GOP brethren.

Young voted in early 1995 with most House Republicans for a bill that eased many regulations under the Clean Water Act. But later, he was one of 51 Republicans voting to strike language to limit the regulatory authority of the Environmental Protection Agency (EPA).

In June 1995, when the Appropriations

Committee was considering the Interior appropriations bill, the committee backed an amendment by Young to preserve a moratorium on oil and gas drilling off large portions of the U.S. coastline. An end to the moratorium had been sought by Livingston.

Many of the amendment's supporters were, like Young, from coastal districts where residents worry about the impact of offshore rigs on the environment and on their property values. Young said the moratorium was necessary to protect the ocean environment. Pointing to the potentially harmful effect of oil spills on breeding grounds for fish and shrimp, he said, "The ecological system is very balanced and fragile."

Also in the 104th, Young parted from the majority of Republicans to oppose repealing the ban on certain semiautomatic assault-style weapons. In the 103rd Congress, Young had sided with the White House in supporting the assault-weapons ban, as well as a five-day waiting requirement on handgun purchases.

And Young was among 93 Republicans who supported a 90-cent increase in the minimum wage when the House first considered the Democratic-backed measure in May 1996. Young had supported a GOP leadership amendment to exempt small businesses from the wage increase, but that amendment failed.

At Home: A high school dropout from a Pennsylvania mining town, Young worked his way to success in the insurance business before going into politics in 1960. Ten years later, he inherited Florida's most dependable Republican House seat from William C. Cramer, who left it to run for the Senate in 1970.

Young had met Cramer in 1955, and he worked in his 1956 campaign and as his district aide in 1957. In 1960 the Pinellas County GOP urged Young to challenge a veteran Democratic state senator. He won, becoming the only Republican in the state Senate. By 1967, there were 20 others, and Young was minority leader.

When Cramer ran for the Senate in 1970, there was little question who would replace him. Young won 76 percent of the primary vote and 67 percent in the general election. He was one of just three Republicans in the state's 12-member House delegation.

Young's stiffest general-election challenge came in 1992. His Democratic opponent was Karen Moffitt, an associate professor in education and medicine. She had never held elected office and had just moved to the district from Tampa. But Moffitt was well-known, partly because her ex-husband, Lee Moffitt, was a former state House Speaker and a campaign supporter.

Karen Moffitt combined some of the outsider's credo — support for term limits, a line-item veto and cuts in congressional staffs — with typical Democratic positions favoring abortion rights and national health care. Young took some licks, especially for making defense contractors a major source of his campaign funding. But he responded to the threat with a stepped-up campaign that spent more than $450,000. He won 57 percent, and since then has had no re-election problems.

HOUSE ELECTIONS

1996 General		
C.W. Bill Young (R)	114,426	(67%)
Henry Green (D)	57,365	(33%)
1994 General		
C.W. Bill Young (R)	unopposed	

Previous Winning Percentages: 1992 (57%) **1990** (100%) **1988** (73%) **1986** (100%) **1984** (80%) **1982** (100%) **1980** (100%) **1978** (79%) **1976** (65%) **1974** (76%) **1972** (76%) **1970** (67%)

CAMPAIGN FINANCE

	Receipts	Receipts from PACs	Expend-itures
1996			
Young (R)	$267,516	$176,421 (66%)	$265,355
Green (D)	$37,277	$5,500 (15%)	$36,554
1994			
Young (R)	$183,053	$113,820 (62%)	$146,246

DISTRICT VOTE FOR PRESIDENT

1996		1992	
D	120,612 (51%)	**D**	107,570 (40%)
R	89,829 (38%)	**R**	98,325 (36%)
I	23,562 (10%)	**I**	64,115 (24%)

KEY VOTES

1997	
Ban "partial birth" abortions	Y
1996	
Approve farm bill	Y
Deny public education to illegal immigrants	Y
Repeal ban on certain assault-style weapons	N
Increase minimum wage	Y
Freeze defense spending	N
Approve welfare overhaul	?
1995	
Approve balanced-budget constitutional amendment	Y
Relax Clean Water Act regulations	Y
Oppose limits on environmental regulations	Y
Reduce projected Medicare spending	Y
Approve GOP budget with tax and spending cuts	Y

VOTING STUDIES

	Presidential Support		Party Unity		Conservative Coalition	
Year	S	O	S	O	S	O
1996	32	48	68	6	75	8
1995	19	74	89	7	87	2
1994	54	44	84	12	78	14
1993	34	63	82	11	91	9
1992	65	34	81	16	90	8
1991	73	23	72	22	78	16

INTEREST GROUP RATINGS

Year	ADA	AFL-CIO	CCUS	ACU
1996	5	n/a	85	88
1995	10	0	100	72
1994	25	33	83	81
1993	15	25	91	88
1992	15	42	63	76
1991	30	8	80	85

11 Jim Davis (D)

Of Tampa — Elected 1996, 1st term

Biographical Information
Born: Oct. 11, 1957, Tampa, Fla.
Education: Washington and Lee U., B.A. 1979; U. of Florida, J.D. 1982.
Occupation: Lawyer.
Family: Wife, Peggy Bessent; two children.
Religion: Episcopalian.
Political Career: Fla. House, 1988-97, majority leader, 1994-97.
Capitol Office: 327 Cannon Bldg. 20515; 225-3376.

Committees
Budget
International Relations
Africa

The Path to Washington: Davis arrived on Capitol Hill in 1997 with an impressive résumé and sharp political skills.

A lawyer, Davis took just six years to climb the leadership ladder in Florida's state House, becoming majority leader. Often described as low-key and hard-working, Davis earned a reputation in Tallahassee for doing his homework and being an effective player behind the scenes.

Davis served on the Appropriations Committee in the state House and helped write eight balanced budgets. Perhaps owing to his expertise in fiscal affairs, he landed a seat in the 105th on the Budget Committee, where he planned to defend education, crime and entitlement programs. He is also on the International Relations Committee.

Davis succeeded veteran Democrat Sam M. Gibbons, who retired from the 11th after representing the Tampa area for 34 years. Gibbons briefly served as chairman of the House Ways and Means Committee, but he got bumped to the ranking Democratic position when the GOP took control of Congress in 1995.

Davis was far from a sure thing when Gibbons surprised many in early 1996 by announcing his departure; he was the least known of four Democrats who jumped into the race. Former Tampa Mayor Sandy Warshaw Freedman was the consensus front-runner, followed by a prominent county commissioner and a popular former state senator.

The centerpieces of Davis' darkhorse campaign were education and crime. The only Democrat to air television spots during the primary, Davis put a dent in Freedman's lead by implying she bore some responsibility for the severe injuries of two police officers in a 1995 shooting incident that occurred when she was mayor.

Although Freedman finished first in the primary, she failed to win a majority and was forced into a runoff with Davis, who edged Hillsborough County Commissioner Phyllis Busansky for second place by 274 votes.

In the runoff, Davis played up his endorsements from local teacher, police and firefighter unions, exposing Freedman's unpopularity with those groups during her tenure as mayor.

Davis scored a decisive victory over Freedman, cruising to a double-digit win.

He then turned his attention to Republican nominee Mark Sharpe, who was making his third try for the seat after unsuccessful bids against Gibbons in 1992 and 1994. A former naval intelligence officer, Sharpe had held Gibbons to a career-low 52 percent in his second bid.

Sharpe attempted to paint Davis as a tax-and-spend liberal by highlighting Davis' votes in the legislature to increase taxes and fees. Davis effectively countered by pointing out that a majority of Republicans, including a state senator who co-chaired Sharpe's campaign, had also supported the increases.

Davis continued to emphasize education and crime and coasted to a 16-point victory few would have predicted at the campaign's outset.

Davis, who was elected president of the 42-member House Democratic freshman class, said his first priority in the 105th Congress was to get the country's fiscal house in order. He favored a balanced-budget constitutional amendment. Another of Davis' top priorities was protecting education programs, especially expanding access to college by boosting funding for student loans.

Another issue high on Davis' agenda was cracking down on crime. He also looked for opportunities to make adjustments to the welfare overhaul that became law in 1996.

Davis said he would have supported the welfare legislation had he been in Congress at the time it passed. But Davis vowed to push for reopening the issue, hoping to add provisions that would protect legal immigrants and children.

Davis, a Tampa native, went to college in Virginia and returned to Tampa to practice law in 1982, after finishing his degree at the University of Florida. He won election to the state legislature in 1988.

FLORIDA 11
West — Southern Hillsborough County; Tampa

Ever since a Key West cigar factory moved to Tampa in 1886, this has been a city with a blue-collar orientation. Cubans came to work in the cigar business, and they were joined later by Georgians, Alabamans and other Southerners looking for jobs in factories around the harbor.

Tampa's cigar industry is greatly diminished. But other traditional industries are still strong, among them brewing, commercial fishing, steel-making and ship construction. The city is also a major port; much of the phosphate mined from adjacent Polk County is shipped from here. That gives it an interest in international markets.

The large working-class community makes Tampa the Florida city that most closely approximates Northern industrial, Democratic-leaning cities. But the Democratic tendency that this Tampa-based district historically has shown in state and national elections has been waning. George Bush carried surrounding Hillsborough County in the 1992 presidential race, and his son Jeb won it in his unsuccessful 1994 gubernatorial campaign. But Bill Clinton brought Hillsborough back into the Democratic column in 1996.

Unlike many Northern industrial cities, Tampa has diversified to compete for the lucrative tourist trade. Busch Gardens, which started as a brewery tour, has expanded into a 335-acre amusement park that is a leading Florida tourist attraction.

Tampa also has a growing financial sector. Chase Manhattan is one of the district's largest employers and Salomon Bros. and Citicorp recently moved some operations here. Tampa International Airport and GTE Florida also are major employers. The University of South Florida, one of the state's largest colleges, with about 36,000 students, is on the city's northern end.

The university's presence, combined with MacDill Air Force Base, has helped attract some high-technology industries. However, MacDill lost its F-16 training facility in 1994. Local officials hope that the relocation of the National Oceanic and Atmospheric Administration's aircraft operations center to the base will stabilize matters.

The base also continues to serve as Special Operations Command and Central Command; Gen. H. Norman Schwarzkopf was based here before the Persian Gulf War, and he retired in the 11th after the conflict.

The district is 14 percent Hispanic. The influence of Cuban and Spanish culture is most pronounced in Ybor City, a long-established community in southeast Tampa named after the man who brought the cigar factory here from Key West. Although relatively few people still live in Ybor City, the area is undergoing a commercial resurgence. Hispanics are more prevalent in West Tampa and the community of Town and Country.

Blacks, who account for 17 percent of the district's population, live mostly in inner-city Tampa.

1990 Population: 562,519. White 442,900 (79%), Black 96,872 (17%), Other 22,747 (4%). Hispanic origin 78,295 (14%). 18 and over 430,766 (77%), 62 and over 81,578 (15%). Median age: 33.

HOUSE ELECTIONS

1996 General		
Jim Davis (D)	108,500	(58%)
Mark Sharpe (R)	78,856	(42%)
1996 Primary Runoff		
Jim Davis (D)	23,633	(56%)
Sandy Warshaw Freedman (D)	18,434	(44%)
1996 Primary		
Sandy Warshaw Freedman (D)	23,505	(35%)
Jim Davis (D)	16,753	(25%)
Phyllis Busansky (D)	16,479	(24%)
Pat Frank (D)	10,586	(16%)

CAMPAIGN FINANCE

	Receipts	Receipts from PACs		Expend-itures
1996				
Davis (D)	$935,836	$247,121	(26%)	$935,314
Sharpe (R)	$754,893	$214,163	(28%)	$755,184

DISTRICT VOTE FOR PRESIDENT

	1996		1992
D	98,154 (52%)	D	81,711 (41%)
R	75,165 (40%)	R	78,360 (39%)
I	14,860 (8%)	I	39,072 (20%)

KEY VOTES

1997

Ban "partial birth" abortions Y

12 Charles T. Canady (R)

Of Lakeland — Elected 1992, 3rd term

Biographical Information
Born: June 22, 1954, Lakeland, Fla.
Education: Haverford College, B.A. 1976; Yale U., J.D. 1979.
Occupation: Lawyer.
Family: Wife, Jennifer Houghton.
Religion: Presbyterian.
Political Career: Fla. House, 1984-90, majority whip 1986-88; Republican nominee for Fla. Senate, 1990.
Capitol Office: 2432 Rayburn Bldg. 20515; 225-1252.

Committees
Agriculture
Department Operations, Nutrition & Foreign Agriculture
Judiciary
Constitution (chairman); Courts & Intellectual Property

In Washington: When Republicans took control of the House in 1995, Canady, though just starting his second term, moved into the chair of Judiciary's Constitution Subcommittee. That put him at center stage in the Republican revolution, as Canady's panel was the factory for a number of the measures party conservatives most wanted to pass.

From the balanced-budget constitutional amendment, to legislation denying federal recognition to same-sex marriages, to a measure banning an abortion technique that opponents call "partial birth" abortion, Canady's subcommittee churned out bill after bill, including some of the most controversial initiatives on the GOP agenda.

Canady has been frequently in the spotlight as a floor leader in legislative debate, but he is perhaps most identified with the effort to outlaw the abortion technique in which a doctor partially delivers a fetus before completing the abortion. Sponsoring a bill in June 1995 to ban such abortions, Canady said the legislation would prevent an "inhuman act" and "protect those who are most in need of protection." The bill would subject doctors who perform the procedure to fines or up to two years in jail. Democrats characterized the measure as unwarranted federal involvement in medical decision-making. The subcommittee approved the bill on a party-line 7-5 vote.

The full Judiciary Committee passed the bill in July, after a rancorous debate in which even the description of the measure was disputed. Canady called it the "Partial-Birth Abortion Ban Act." But critics said there is no medical procedure called a "partial birth abortion," and they warned that the bill could be broadly interpreted to forbid a whole range of medical procedures.

Both the House and Senate passed the bill after lengthy debates. During House consideration of the measure, Canady won approval to use charts to graphically illustrate the procedure, which he then described at length.

President Clinton vetoed the bill in April 1996, arguing that it did not protect women whose lives or future fertility might be at risk unless the abortion procedure was available. The House voted to override the veto, but the Senate did not.

Early in the 105th Congress, Canady again shepherded the measure through the House; in May, Senate proponents of the measure again passed the ban, but they were again short of the two-thirds majority needed to override another promised Clinton veto.

Canady's anti-abortion stance led him into a confrontation with his own leadership on another issue: welfare overhaul. In the spring of 1995, he was one of 15 Republicans to vote against the rule governing floor debate on the GOP welfare bill.

He and some other abortion foes were concerned that provisions in the bill aimed at reducing out-of-wedlock births could prompt more poor women to seek abortions. Canady and his allies wanted the House to consider two amendments addressing their concerns. But the rule did not provide for votes on those amendments. After wrangling for much of the 104th, Republicans finally came up with a welfare plan Clinton agreed to sign; Canady supported its passage in July 1996.

The Republicans were unsuccessful in moving through the House another controversial measure important to Canady — repeal of affirmative action laws.

Early in the 104th, Canady set his sights on moving a bill to outlaw virtually all federal affirmative action programs. Canady's bill, approved by his Constitution Subcommittee in March 1996, aimed to eliminate federal programs that give special consideration to women and minorities, either by imposing hiring requirements or providing incentives for federal agencies, grant recipients and federal contractors. His bill allowed affirmative action based on economic need.

The Supreme Court ruled in June 1995 that federal affirmative action programs must meet strict standards, and the Justice Department then issued new guidelines for federal agencies.

But even with Senate Majority Leader Bob Dole of Kansas sponsoring nearly identical legislation in that body, Canady could not persuade

FLORIDA 12
Central — Polk County; Lakeland; parts of Hillsborough County

Across much of Florida, land once devoted to agriculture is being eaten away by shopping centers, motels and condominiums. But in Polk County, centerpiece of the 12th District, citrus is still a major force.

Thousands of jobs are connected with the growing, picking, packing, processing and loading of oranges, orange concentrate and grapefruit. Besides Minute Maid, there are many smaller growers whose efforts make the 12th among the nation's foremost citrus-producing districts.

However, Polk County's citrus industry has hit bumpy times in recent years, and periodic freezes have prompted some growers to move farther south. Also moving south are elements of the county's other leading industry, phosphate mining. The removal and processing of phosphate, the raw material of fertilizer, has fluctuated in recent years because of uneven demand for the product and the county's dwindling supply. IMC-Agrico Co. remains a leading private employer, however. Electric power plants, a booming industry in energy-hungry Florida, rapidly are replacing phosphate mining as a leading sector in the district.

Food processing is also important in Polk County; Pepperidge Farms and Bee Gee Shrimp are leading employers. Lakeland, the county seat, is also headquarters for Publix supermarkets, one of the largest private employers in the state. From 1993 to 1995, an additional 1,200 manufacturing jobs were created in Polk County, while the rest of the state lost manufacturing jobs.

Tourists are drawn to Cypress Gardens, a botanical and water-show attraction in Winter Haven, just east of Lakeland.

The county grew by 26 percent in the 1980s, partly because of an influx of retirees, many of them from the South and Midwest. In the main, these retirees are less affluent than immigrants to Florida who settle in condominium communities along the Gulf Coast; a number of the newcomers to the 12th have moved into mobile home parks. Large fundamentalist churches are commonplace in the district, and their members contribute to the area's conservative leanings.

In the areas that make up the 12th, George Bush took two-thirds of the presidential vote in 1988, and he carried the district with 46 percent in 1992. Bob Dole narrowly won the district in 1996, beating Bill Clinton by 46 percent to 43 percent. Ross Perot garnered 10 percent in the district.

The shaky economy held down Bush's margin in the district in 1992. It also made for the state's most competitive open-seat House race, with Canady squeezing by Democrat Tom Mims. Canady gained an 8,000-vote edge districtwide by earning 4,000-vote margins both in Polk County and in the relatively small part of Hillsborough County that is in the 12th. Canady has twice won re-election handily.

The part of eastern Hillsborough County within the district includes Plant City, noted for its annual strawberry festival. Agriculture is a key here, with citrus and winter vegetables of some importance. The 12th also has part of Brandon, a Tampa suburb. Also in the district are De Soto and Hardee counties, and parts of Highlands and Pasco counties.

1990 Population: 562,519. White 473,311 (84%), Black 71,083 (13%), Other 18,125 (3%). Hispanic origin 34,550 (6%). 18 and over 419,836 (75%), 62 and over 115,006 (20%). Median age: 35.

House GOP leaders to bring his measure to the floor. He plans to try again in the 105th.

Although his subcommittee held hearings in early 1995 on the matter of school prayer, Canady said in July that year that he was not leaning toward any of the bills circulating in the House. "We are in the process of trying to get a full understanding of the problem," he said. "I think we need to listen to everybody on this issue." Divisions emerged within GOP ranks over how to proceed, and the House did not consider a constitutional amendment on school prayer in the 104th.

Canady's panel did bring forth a constitutional amendment, by Rules Committee Chairman Gerald B.H. Solomon, R-N.Y., to ban flag burning. The measure would have allowed Congress and the states to pass laws prohibiting burning or other physical desecration of the U.S. flag. The House approved the flag-burning ban in June on a 312-120 vote, easily surpassing the two-thirds needed to pass a constitutional amendment.

Canady said the flag is "a national asset which deserves our respect and protection." Opponents maintained that such an amendment would undermine the freedom of expression guaranteed under the First Amendment.

The Senate narrowly failed to pass the amendment, but supporters plotted another try in 1997.

Canady also has been a key figure in pushing institutional reform. His subcommittee passed a bill to dramatically tighten registration requirements for lobbyists, and he was part of a group that managed to get the bill through the House despite what looked like a concerted effort by the GOP leadership to defeat or at least derail the measure.

Early in 1995, the Senate passed the bill, to close loopholes in the 1946 lobbying bill, largely by requiring most lobbyists to register and note who they work for and how much they are paid. Canady and his allies in the House knew it was extraordinary that the bill had made it through the

Senate, which had blocked similar changes in the 103rd Congress. They decided that the best way for the House to proceed was to accept the Senate bill intact. That way it would not get bogged down in a conference committee and would go straight to the president for his promised signature.

That meant the key to their strategy was to avoid amendments in the House all through the process, from subcommittee through House passage. They easily succeeded in committee, but met with difficulty getting a House floor vote.

House GOP leaders finally agreed to bring the lobbying bill to the floor after a group that included Canady and mostly moderate Republicans such as Christopher Shays of Connecticut threatened to go against the leadership on a spending bill.

Even then, supporters of the lobbying bill faced another problem: The leadership allowed the measure to be considered under an open rule, meaning that anyone could offer any amendment to the bill. But adoption of even one amendment would send the bill to conference, where it most likely would have died.

After extensive efforts by Shays, Canady and Democrat Barney Frank of Massachusetts, all amendments to the bill were defeated. The measure cleared Congress, and Clinton signed it.

At Home: The son of a former top aide to Florida Gov. Lawton Chiles, Canady grew up around politics of the Democratic Party variety. When he started his political career in the Florida House, he ran as a Democrat. But Canady always has considered himself a conservative, and one term into his state legislative career, he felt that the fit between him and his party was not a good one.

When Michael S. Dukakis became the Democrats' presidential nominee in 1988, Canady started thinking seriously about joining the GOP. In his re-election campaign that year, Canady said friends would ask how he could run on a ticket with Dukakis. "I never could give them a satisfactory answer," he said. "We had basic philosophical differences across the whole spectrum."

When the state Legislature finished its work in the summer of 1989, Canady announced he was becoming a Republican. The next year he ran for the state Senate on the GOP ticket. He lost.

In the 1992 House campaign for the open 12th, Canady and the Democratic candidate, state Rep. Tom Mims, offered voters similar backgrounds. Both had experience in the Florida House and were known in the district. Their fathers were political pros. Louie Mims was the 1992 Democratic nominee for Polk County sheriff, a job he had formerly held.

But abortion was a point of disagreement between the two candidates. Mims was generally supportive of abortion rights, while Canady opposed abortion except in cases of rape, incest or when pregnancy endangered a woman's life.

With an intensive grass-roots effort, Canady won 52 percent. He was aided by a campaign visit from President George Bush, who carried the district. In 1994, Canady sailed to re-election with 65 percent. And in 1996, he took 62 percent against his second cousin, Democrat Mike Canady.

HOUSE ELECTIONS

1996 General		
Charles T. Canady (R)	122,553	(62%)
Mike Canady (D)	76,500	(38%)
1994 General		
Charles T. Canady (R)	106,123	(65%)
Robert Connors (D)	57,203	(35%)

Previous Winning Percentages: 1992 (52%)

CAMPAIGN FINANCE

	Receipts	Receipts from PACs	Expend-itures
1996			
Canady (R)	$259,228	$116,524 (45%)	$213,131
Canady (D)	$23,343	$11,250 (48%)	$12,818
1994			
Canady (R)	$333,277	$146,505 (44%)	$333,623
Connors (D)	$200,084	$120,380 (60%)	$192,849

DISTRICT VOTE FOR PRESIDENT

	1996		1992
D	87,969 (43%)	**D**	68,586 (35%)
R	94,161 (46%)	**R**	90,351 (45%)
I	20,595 (10%)	**I**	39,714 (20%)

KEY VOTES

1997	
Ban "partial birth" abortions	Y
1996	
Approve farm bill	Y
Deny public education to illegal immigrants	Y
Repeal ban on certain assault-style weapons	Y
Increase minimum wage	Y
Freeze defense spending	N
Approve welfare overhaul	Y
1995	
Approve balanced-budget constitutional amendment	Y
Relax Clean Water Act regulations	Y
Oppose limits on environmental regulations	N
Reduce projected Medicare spending	Y
Approve GOP budget with tax and spending cuts	Y

VOTING STUDIES

	Presidential Support		Party Unity		Conservative Coalition	
Year	S	O	S	O	S	O
1996	37	63	93	7	94	6
1995	20	80	95	4	95	4
1994	54	46	94	6	100	0
1993	31	69	94	6	93	7

INTEREST GROUP RATINGS

Year	ADA	AFL-CIO	CCUS	ACU
1996	5	n/a	94	85
1995	5	0	100	76
1994	5	0	92	90
1993	10	8	82	100

13 Dan Miller (R)

Of Bradenton — Elected 1992, 3rd term

Biographical Information

Born: May 30, 1942, Highland Park, Mich.
Education: U. of Florida, B.S. 1964; Emory U., M.B.A. 1965; Louisiana State U., Ph.D. 1970.
Occupation: Businessman.
Family: Wife, Glenda Darsey; two children.
Religion: Episcopalian.
Political Career: No previous office.
Capitol Office: 102 Cannon Bldg. 20515; 225-5015.

Committees

Appropriations
Interior; Labor, Health & Human Services and Education
Budget

In Washington: A college professor and businessman before coming to Congress, Miller is carving out a reputation as a soft-spoken but uncompromising opponent of government intrusion into the marketplace.

He once told the House: "There are two questions I ask on each piece of legislation. First, how does it affect the deficit? And, second, does the federal government have to get involved?"

During the 104th Congress, Miller showed a willingness to push his beliefs even though that caused problems for an important home-state interest. As Congress worked on an omnibus farm bill, Miller repeatedly led unsuccessful attempts to scale back or eliminate sugar price supports. Sugar cane growers are a force in Florida politics, and Miller drew considerable criticism from agriculture lobbies and some Florida lawmakers.

But Miller, who supports a balanced-budget constitutional amendment, insisted that Republicans had to be willing to confront their own constituencies in the course of scaling back the scope and cost of the federal government. "I'm willing to take on a powerful interest in my home state," he said. "It's the symbolism of being willing to go after corporate welfare. . . . We have to show that we're willing to go after difficult issues."

The goal of the Republican-backed "Freedom to Farm" bill was to replace New Deal-era crop subsidies with a system of fixed, but declining, payments that farmers would receive over seven years regardless of market prices or their planting decisions.

In getting the legislation to a point where it could pass, the GOP leadership accommodated certain commodity interests by revising rather than eliminating their federal price-support programs. Balking at concessions, Miller voted for amendments to the farm bill targeting the marketing loan program for cotton and the peanut price-support program. Both survived with revisions.

After his own amendment to phase out sugar price supports failed in February 1996, he voted against "Freedom to Farm," one of only 19 Republicans to do so as the measure carried 270-155. It was passed by the Senate and signed into law by President Clinton.

Miller, who holds a seat on the Appropriations Committee, warned that he might renew his efforts to eliminate price supports in annual agriculture appropriations bills. He also has opposed the expansion of government-funded export promotion programs, which help promote U.S. agricultural products abroad and provide credits and loan guarantees to U.S. exporters. Since major agribusiness concerns are among the beneficiaries of these programs, Miller and other critics lump them into the "corporate welfare" category.

Miller waged some other uphill battles in the 104th. From his seat on Appropriations, he proposed installing a debt clock in the Capitol that would show how deeply the federal government was falling into the red. "A debt clock hanging in the U.S. Capitol will allow the thousands of visitors who pass through each year to see the progress Congress is making on behalf of future generations," he wrote in a letter to Speaker Newt Gingrich.

He also wanted to zero out $240 million in fiscal 1998 funding for the Corporation for Public Broadcasting. Neither proposal made it out of committee.

Swinging his budget-cutting ax very close to home, Miller also tried unsuccessfully to replace congressional pensions with a 401(k) plan. But he won little interest from leadership and failed to get a vote on the proposal.

From his seat on the Budget Committee, Miller trod on the turf of another important constituency in Florida: senior citizens. He played an active role in trying to scale back Medicare benefits as part of the GOP's deficit-reducing, budget-reconciliation bill in 1995. He rejected criticism from Democrats that the GOP wanted to reduce Medicare benefits by as much as $270 billion in order to free up the money to provide Americans with a $250 billion tax cut.

"The numbers being close is coincidental more than anything else," he said.

FLORIDA 13
Southwest — Sarasota and Manatee counties; Sarasota; Bradenton

When redistricting and retirements created 10 open seats in Florida in 1992, Republicans knew they had little to worry about in the newly designed 13th. The district's GOP registration was the second highest in the state, barely below that of the adjacent 14th.

Sarasota County accounts for slightly less than half the 13th's population, and Manatee County represents just under 40 percent. The rest of the 13th's residents live in parts of Charlotte and Hillsborough counties. More populous Sarasota was expected to have the upper hand in district politics, but in the 1992 GOP House runoff, Miller, who is from Manatee County, bested a foe from Sarasota County.

The political personality of the 13th is influenced most by retirees from suburbs and small towns of the Midwest. These people changed their addresses but not their party registrations, and they contribute to the burgeoning strength of the GOP in Florida.

Although they closely identify with the GOP, residents of the 13th are not necessarily conservative on social issues. The 1992 open House race, for example, was dominated by candidates who supported abortion rights. The proximity to gulf beaches, barrier islands and a large state park also makes the environment a bipartisan concern, with residents attuned to the problems of beach erosion and the effects of rapid population growth.

Sarasota County cultivates a refined image with its art museums, theaters and symphony performances. It generally draws a more highly educated and wealthier class of retirees than most other west coast communities in Florida. Leading private employers include tourism, retailing, health care and banking. The city of Sarasota includes some minorities and retirees who are not quite as affluent as those on the barrier islands of Longboat Key, Siesta Key and Casey Key.

Sarasota County grew by 37 percent in the 1980s. The area poised for the next growth spurt is immediately south of the city, down the coast along Route 41 to Venice. The residents of Venice itself tend to be a little older and of more modest means than residents on the county's northern end. Growth along I-75, which runs north and south through the district, also has been spurred by the plethora of residential and office space available.

Manatee, which grew by 43 percent in the 1980s, has some residents who commute to work over the Sunshine Skyway Bridge to Tampa Bay. Leading employers in the county include Tropicana, which grows, picks and packs citrus, and Wellcraft Marine, which builds pleasure boats.

Bradenton, the county seat and retail center, has a more noticeable mix of incomes and ethnic groups than most parts of the 13th. It is not quite as Midwestern-oriented as Sarasota.

The 13th goes south into Charlotte County to pick up parts of Port Charlotte and Murdock. Residents there are generally older, less affluent and more Democratic. It also extends north into Hillsborough County to pick up Sun City Center and Ruskin, where Republicans fare well.

1990 Population: 562,518. White 521,811 (93%), Black 30,631 (5%), Other 10,076 (2%). Hispanic origin 24,306 (4%). 18 and over 465,139 (83%), 62 and over 199,396 (35%). Median age: 47.

Despite objections from advocates for the elderly, he suggested that comparatively well-off senior citizens pay higher Medicare premiums. "Means-testing is very acceptable," he said. But the Medicare issue proved politically explosive, and Clinton vetoed the budget legislation.

Miller, who sits on Appropriations' Labor-HHS-Education Subcommittee, joined some other appropriators in criticizing the National Labor Relations Board over its practice of seeking injunctions against companies. He accused the board of being "overzealous," and, in a clear warning shot, reminded the NLRB in a letter that "all parts of the federal government are being reviewed for ways to cut spending."

As a freshman in the 103rd Congress, Miller voted fairly consistently with his party, opposing all of Clinton's budget proposals and supporting the Penny-Kasich proposal to cut $90 billion from the budget over five years.

He voted against requiring a five-day waiting period for the purchase of a handgun, but he supported Clinton-backed legislation banning 19 types of semiautomatic assault-style weapons. When the GOP majority mounted an effort in 1996 to repeal the assault weapons ban, Miller was one of 42 Republicans to vote "no."

Miller, who says he considers himself middle-of-the-road on abortion, supports "reasonable" state restrictions. He voted in 1996 to allow federal employee health care plans to cover abortions and to allow abortions at overseas military hospitals, if the woman paid for the procedure herself. But in March 1996, he voted against maintaining a requirement that states fund Medicaid abortions for poor women in cases of rape or incest or to protect the life of the woman. He also joins with conservatives who support banning a particular abortion technique that opponents call "partial birth" abortion.

He joined the majority of Republicans in helping the Clinton administration in November 1993 win passage of NAFTA, after overcoming worries that the trade pact would hurt Florida agriculture. Miller ultimately concluded that "the only decision we face today is between openly embracing new markets for American products, or burying our heads in the sand."

At Home: Among all Florida's districts, the 13th ranks near the top in terms of registered Republicans. Given the GOP advantage over Democrats, Miller's biggest hurdle in the open-seat 1992 race was the primary.

Miller was well-known because of his business endeavors and involvement in community affairs. He had been chairman of the local Chamber of Commerce, headed the hospital board and the local economic development council, and was on the boards of numerous other organizations including the Manatee County Mental Health Center, the county Council on Aging and the local symphony.

The five-candidate GOP field was paced by businessman Brad Baker and Miller. Baker had a heavy presence in the district with television ads, billboards and direct mail. And Miller could boast of an endorsement from retiring GOP Rep. Andy Ireland.

Miller prevailed in the runoff with 53 percent of the vote by clobbering Baker in Manatee County, where Miller had been strongest in the primary.

He then painted his Democratic opponent, Rand Snell, a former aide to Democratic Gov. Lawton Chiles, as a government insider — a black mark in the conservative 13th. Miller won with 58 percent of the vote. He was unopposed in 1994.

In 1996, despite having made an enemy of the sugar industry, Miller took 64 percent of the vote against Democrat Sanford Gordon, a little-known, retired economics professor.

HOUSE ELECTIONS

1996 General		
Dan Miller (R)	173,573	(64%)
Sanford Gordon (D)	96,053	(36%)
1994 General		
Dan Miller (R)	unopposed	

Previous Winning Percentages: 1992 (58%)

CAMPAIGN FINANCE

	Receipts	Receipts from PACs	Expend-itures
1996			
Miller (R)	$379,784	$83,143 (22%)	$387,149
Gordon (D)	$73,502	$13,500 (18%)	$73,500
1994			
Miller (R)	$298,893	$77,020 (26%)	$278,042

DISTRICT VOTE FOR PRESIDENT

1996		1992	
D	120,414 (43%)	**D**	100,896 (35%)
R	129,808 (46%)	**R**	124,327 (43%)
I	29,226 (10%)	**I**	65,349 (22%)

KEY VOTES

1997	
Ban "partial birth" abortions	Y
1996	
Approve farm bill	N
Deny public education to illegal immigrants	Y
Repeal ban on certain assault-style weapons	N
Increase minimum wage	N
Freeze defense spending	Y
Approve welfare overhaul	Y
1995	
Approve balanced-budget constitutional amendment	Y
Relax Clean Water Act regulations	Y
Oppose limits on environmental regulations	N
Reduce projected Medicare spending	Y
Approve GOP budget with tax and spending cuts	Y

VOTING STUDIES

	Presidential Support		Party Unity		Conservative Coalition	
Year	S	O	S	O	S	O
1996	38	59	91	8	82	18
1995	22	78	93	6	89	9
1994	41	58	94	4	78	17
1993	39	61	84	15	80	20

INTEREST GROUP RATINGS

Year	ADA	AFL-CIO	CCUS	ACU
1996	10	n/a	88	95
1995	5	0	96	80
1994	20	11	100	90
1993	10	17	91	88

14 Porter J. Goss (R)

Of Sanibel — Elected 1988, 5th term

Biographical Information
Born: Nov. 26, 1938, Waterbury, Conn.
Education: Yale U., B.A. 1960.
Military Service: Army, 1960-62.
Occupation: Businessman; newspaper founder; CIA agent.
Family: Wife, Mariel Robinson; four children.
Religion: Presbyterian.
Political Career: Sanibel City Council, 1974-80, mayor, 1975-77, 1981-82, mayor, 1982; Lee County Commission, 1983-88, chairman, 1985-86.
Capitol Office: 108 Cannon Bldg. 20515; 225-2536.

Committees
Select Intelligence (chairman)
Rules
Legislative & Budget Process (chairman)

In Washington: Goss moved from one committee shrouded in silence (House ethics) to chair another panel in the 105th Congress that also does its work out of the public spotlight (Select Intelligence). A former CIA agent, Goss is not expected to try to remake the nation's spy organizations, as was attempted in the 104th Congress, but he will have an unusual opportunity to shape the panel, which is responsible for oversight of the nation's intelligence community, from the CIA to the National Reconnaissance Office. Goss has been on Intelligence for just one term, so under House rules he can chair the panel for the next six years if the GOP keeps control of the House.

As chairman of the House Rules Subcommittee on Legislative and Budget Process, Goss has also looked at whether a joint House-Senate Intelligence panel should be created, whether the number of people with access to classified information should be reduced and whether the number of members taking part in the intelligence oversight process should be increased. The overriding question, Goss has said, is: "Do we have the right process in terms of our oversight?"

In the 104th, Goss' Intelligence and ethics responsibilities overlapped when the latter panel concluded that the ambiguity of a new House secrecy oath precluded any punishment of then-Rep. Robert G. Torricelli, D-N.J., who revealed allegations of CIA complicity in the murders of an American innkeeper and rebel leader in Guatemala. (Torricelli was elected to the Senate in 1996.)

Goss took the chair on Intelligence in 1997 just as the House ethics committee wrapped up a two-year investigation of alleged improprieties in the political fundraising activities of Speaker Newt Gingrich. Goss was chairman of an ethics subcommittee that studied the charges and worked with the special counsel, James M. Cole, in designing a punishment: a $300,000 penalty and a reprimand.

Goss called the punishment — which allowed Gingrich to keep his leadership post — "serious but fair," and added, "It was extraordinarily imprudent of Mr. Gingrich not to seek and follow a less aggressive and less risky course" in financing his political projects. "I do, however, believe Mr. Gingrich's forthright and contrite statement that there was no attempt to deceive our committee."

Before the ethics committee finished the Gingrich case, Goss and GOP Rep. Steven H. Schiff of New Mexico, who also sat on the Gingrich-inquiry subcommittee, sent a letter to Majority Whip Tom DeLay saying they would support the Speaker for re-election. They said they had no reason to believe that Gingrich would be ineligible to serve as Speaker, an early hint that any punishment handed down would probably not be severe enough to knock Gingrich from the leadership.

Still, it was the Goss-led subcommittee that in September 1996 voted to expand the investigation, including looking at whether Gingrich lied to the panel. He was generally credited for putting aside partisan politics to ferret out the truth, and he became the de facto chairman of the full committee after communications between chairwoman Nancy L. Johnson, R-Conn., and top Democrat Jim McDermott of Washington broke down.

Goss was able to work with fellow subcommittee member Benjamin L. Cardin, D-Md., who said the subcommittee remained largely above the fray by "keeping the bridges of communication open." Cardin and Goss were close neighbors in the Cannon House Office Building, and their offices were just steps from Cole's temporary office. "Porter and I have never had a strained relationship," Cardin said. "We have always been able to communicate on any day."

In January, Goss joined House Democrats in an unsuccessful floor vote seeking to lift the committee's Jan. 21 deadline for a vote on Gingrich's punishment.

Goss' work in the ethics arena is not done yet. He is part of a 10-member task force chosen by House leaders to study the ethics process.

FLORIDA 14
Southwest — Lee and Collier counties; Cape Coral; Fort Myers; Naples

The 14th is an area of steadfast Republicanism and robust population growth. Fifty-seven percent of district residents are registered Republicans, the highest percentage in the state. And in the three counties that make up the district, population grew by more than 50 percent during the 1980s.

Lee County, which accounts for more than half the district's population, grew at a 63 percent clip. The increase was pushed by Cape Coral, whose population swelled by 134 percent; it is now the district's largest city. Originally a retirement community, Cape Coral has been attracting young professionals, service industries and land developers. Located near the gulf and along the Caloosahatchee River, the city features canals, easy access to the gulf and reasonable land costs.

To the west lie the barrier islands of Captiva and Sanibel, which have tried to curb development to protect their natural beauty and preserve their images as upscale resort getaways. Across the river east of Cape Coral is Fort Myers, an older city once known for raising gladiolus. Land once devoted to cultivation has given way to development. The health care industry is also an important employer. Small pockets of blacks and blue-collar Democrats give Fort Myers a slightly less Republican cast than Cape Coral.

The region's growth spurred approval of a new state college, tentatively named Florida Gulf University, to be built in Lee County. The area also received boosts from the completion of Florida International Airport and the expansion of Interstate 75. The highway follows the gulf from Tampa, swinging east near Naples (Collier County) to cross the Everglades at Alligator Alley.

Naples, situated on the gulf, has exclusive high-rise condominiums and large homes in its midst. The upper-income retirees, many from New England and the Midwest, support wide-ranging cultural activities, including the Naples Philharmonic center. Marco Island is a planned community noted for its wealthy residents and strong GOP inclination. Elsewhere in Collier County, citrus growers are increasingly attracted to the availability of open land and low risk of freezes. Immokalee, in the county's northern interior, has a large farm area and is home to many migrant and seasonal workers.

Collier, which grew 77 percent in the 1980s, is a solid GOP base; George Bush won 53 percent in 1992 and Bob Dole polled 59 percent in 1996.

Democrats often find their best chance in the district in Charlotte County, where Bush edged Democrat Bill Clinton in 1992, 39 percent to 37 percent, and Dole beat Clinton, 46 percent to 41 percent, in 1996.

Charlotte, once known as a retirement haven, has drawn a younger crowd recently, spurring 90 percent population growth in the 1980s. Most of Charlotte County is in the 14th District, except for some areas around Port Charlotte.

1990 Population: 562,518. White 517,105 (92%), Black 31,828 (6%), Other 13,585 (2%). Hispanic origin 37,384 (7%). 18 and over 455,977 (81%), 62 and over 170,636 (30%). Median age: 43.

He has already proposed some changes of his own, as chairman of the House Rules subcommittee that oversees the ethics panel. "It is my view — and the view of many of our colleagues on both sides of the aisle — that our process does not work very well," he said in January 1996. Under his plan, a member who files a complaint deemed frivolous by the committee could be required to repay the cost of the investigation. A majority vote of the ethics committee, which has an even number of Republicans and Democrats, would be necessary to throw out a complaint. Goss also proposed that when the committee voted to begin an investigation, members would be chosen at random from the full House to serve on a panel charged with overseeing the probe.

Goss had joined the ethics committee in 1991 and probed the House bank scandal. At the time, he took the politically unpopular stand of calling for full disclosure of the members with overdrawn House bank accounts.

An anti-abortion conservative, Goss veers from GOP orthodoxy on the environment. His Florida Gulf Coast district relies heavily on tourism, and Goss strongly opposes oil drilling on the continental shelf off Florida. In the 104th, he backed an amendment to the fiscal 1996 VA-HUD appropriations bill to strike language reining in the Environmental Protection Agency. The amendment prevailed, 212-206, but the House leadership, which opposed the proposal, held a revote and won on a tie.

Goss gained notice in the foreign policy arena as an outspoken critic of the Clinton administration's policy toward Haiti. He questioned the merit of restoring Jean-Bertrand Aristide to power, equating the democratically elected leader with the military leaders who ousted him. "I think it's very clear that President Aristide is a conflict-seeker, not a consensus-maker," said Goss. "Yes, there are atrocities . . . but there are atrocities on both sides. We need to negotiate a solution, not send Marines to enforce a solution."

Critical of U.S. immigration policy toward Haiti and the United Nations-endorsed economic embargo on the nation, Goss proposed repatriating refugees to an island off the coast of Haiti and delivering Aristide there as well. When U.S. military action in Haiti appeared imminent in 1994, Goss won House approval of a non-binding amendment opposing the use of force and supporting his safe-haven plan. But the measure eventually was overturned by a succeeding vote, and, in any event, Clinton sent in U.S. troops.

In December 1995, Goss led a U.S. delegation to Haiti to monitor the island nation's presidential election. "The political process is getting better in Haiti," Goss said, noting that the government had improved voter registration and beefed up training for election officials. But, Goss added, serious difficulties remained, including violence against journalists and a "climate of fear" among many voters. "Some people are not participating in this election because they are too scared," he said.

At Home: A comfortable victor in five House elections, Goss seems well-suited for his district. He won his first bid for Congress with 71 percent of the vote in 1988 and hasn't been tested since.

Local roots are not an obvious political selling point in fast-growing southwest Florida, where so many residents are new arrivals. But in 1988 Goss emphasized his expertise in local issues to convince voters that he would do the best job of protecting the environment that lured them there in the first place. Goss moved to the district in 1971 and was drawn into politics by some of the same quality-of-life issues he stressed in the campaign. When picturesque Sanibel Island was hit by rapid development in the early 1970s, Goss played a key role in pushing for the town to incorporate and agree on growth-management laws. He became the small city's first mayor in 1975 and helped produce a development model that has been studied in public-policy schools and other localities.

Nearly a decade later, Goss was named to the Lee County Commission by then-Gov. Bob Graham, a Democrat. Goss, quickly tagged as the commission's environmentalist, got involved in controversial debates about managing growth countywide. He easily won a full term, which positioned him to compete for the House seat when GOP Rep. Connie Mack decided to run for the Senate.

Goss had stiff competition for the Republican nomination: In particular, former Rep. L.A. "Skip" Bafalis, who had left the House for an unsuccessful gubernatorial bid in 1982, reappeared; among the three other GOP contenders was retired Brig. Gen. James Dozier, who during his Army career was the victim of a well-publicized kidnapping by Italy's Red Brigades.

Bafalis tried to label Goss a closet Democrat, saying Goss had contributed to Democratic candidates. But having moved back into the district only shortly before launching his comeback bid, Bafalis no longer had much political strength. His fundraising lagged while Dozier's bid fizzled. Goss raised enough money to fund plenty of television and direct mail. He swept the October runoff and won the general election easily.

HOUSE ELECTIONS

1996 General		
Porter J. Goss (R)	176,961	(73%)
Jim Nolan (D)	63,833	(27%)
1994 General		
Porter J. Goss (R)	unopposed	

Previous Winning Percentages: 1992 (82%) **1990** (100%) **1988** (71%)

CAMPAIGN FINANCE

	Receipts	Receipts from PACs		Expend-itures
1996				
Goss (R)	$277,680	$28,750	(10%)	$372,563
Nolan (D)	$17,713	$2,500	(14%)	$19,956
1994				
Goss (R)	$182,364	$7,520	(4%)	$142,940

DISTRICT VOTE FOR PRESIDENT

	1996		1992
D	107,508 (38%)	**D**	87,901 (31%)
R	144,132 (51%)	**R**	129,400 (46%)
I	30,144 (11%)	**I**	63,086 (22%)

KEY VOTES

1997	
Ban "partial birth" abortions	Y
1996	
Approve farm bill	N
Deny public education to illegal immigrants	Y
Repeal ban on certain assault-style weapons	Y
Increase minimum wage	N
Freeze defense spending	N
Approve welfare overhaul	Y
1995	
Approve balanced-budget constitutional amendment	Y
Relax Clean Water Act regulations	N
Oppose limits on environmental regulations	Y
Reduce projected Medicare spending	Y
Approve GOP budget with tax and spending cuts	Y

VOTING STUDIES

	Presidential Support		Party Unity		Conservative Coalition	
Year	S	O	S	O	S	O
1996	39	61	90	7	84	16
1995	23	77	92	8	94	6
1994	51	49	94	6	89	11
1993	41	59	94	6	95	5
1992	75	25	91	9	85	15
1991	86	14	90	10	86	14

INTEREST GROUP RATINGS

Year	ADA	AFL-CIO	CCUS	ACU
1996	10	n/a	88	95
1995	10	0	88	80
1994	10	22	92	86
1993	10	8	91	92
1992	5	17	75	88
1991	5	8	80	90

15 Dave Weldon (R)

Of Palm Bay — Elected 1994, 2nd term

Biographical Information

Born: Aug. 31, 1953, Amityville, N.Y.

Education: State U. of New York, Stony Brook, B.S. 1978; State U. of New York, Buffalo, M.D. 1981.

Military Service: Army Medical Corps, 1981-87; Army Reserve, 1987-92.

Occupation: Physician.

Family: Wife, Nancy; one child.

Religion: Christian.

Political Career: No previous office.

Capitol Office: 216 Cannon Bldg. 20515; 225-3671.

Committees

Banking & Financial Services
Domestic & International Monetary Policy; Financial Institutions & Consumer Credit

Science
Space & Aeronautics

In Washington: In the social-policy arena, physician Weldon prescribes remedies that go down well with the culturally conservative voters whose influence is growing along central Florida's East Coast. When he rises to speak on the House floor, Weldon is often arguing against abortion, for instance, or calling for an overhaul of the welfare system.

He has been a passionate proponent of congressional efforts to ban a particular abortion technique that opponents call "partial birth" abortion. "This is a place where the government of the United States has to draw the line and say, this is beyond the pale," he once told colleagues.

Weldon describes his political philosophy as "pro-life, pro-family," and before he came to Congress he was co-founder of the Space Coast Family Forum, a group that endorses candidates opposed to abortion. He says he became a staunch abortion foe after he and his wife, unable to bear children of their own, decided to adopt. They faced a lengthy wait and were told that such a delay would not have occurred before the U.S. Supreme Court's 1973 *Roe v. Wade* decision legalizing abortion.

Religion plays an important part in Weldon's life. He says he tries to read the Bible and pray every day, and he lists among his political influences House Speaker Newt Gingrich, Majority Leader Dick Armey and his "idol . . . Jesus Christ."

Elected in 1996 to a second term with 51 percent of the vote, Weldon shifted to a new committee in the 105th, joining Banking and Financial Services and leaving Economic and Educational Opportunities (now Education and the Workforce). Considering all the business issues the Banking Committee deals with, it may be a more useful assignment for Weldon in terms of campaign fundraising than his previous panel.

Weldon favors making the federal government leaner and less costly, but that goal sometimes bumps up against the fact that many jobs in his district are linked either directly or indirectly to the operations of NASA's Kennedy Space Center in Brevard County. Also, in the 15th District and all across Florida, many retirees have concerns about politicians' efforts to rein in spending on Medicaid and Medicare.

Weldon supports continued funding of the space station and other NASA programs, disagreeing with those who portray many facets of the space program as unaffordable, given deficit-reduction pressures. Weldon has called the space station and space shuttle programs "essential to our nation's continued international leadership in space." He sits on the Science Committee's Space and Aeronautics Subcommittee.

The sizable contingent of federal workers in the 15th put Weldon in an uncomfortable spot when the federal government was partially shut down in December 1995, after the collapse of budget negotiations between the Republican Congress and the Democratic White House. With many of his federal-worker constituents not drawing a paycheck, Weldon blamed the furloughs on President Clinton. But he also expressed dismay when media reports said the impasse occurred in part because Gingrich was peeved that Clinton had snubbed him and Senate Majority Leader Bob Dole during a long flight back from Israel on Air Force One. "To a certain extent," Weldon said ruefully of his party, "our fate lives or dies on the things [Gingrich] says and does, and that's not a perfect situation."

Weldon decided not to draw his own paycheck for the duration of the government's partial shutdown. "I should not be treated any differently than the federal employees who, through no fault of their own, have been furloughed from their jobs by President Clinton," he said. Defending his party's efforts to press for a budget agreement, Weldon added, "I have got a lot of government workers in my district . . . I have got engineers who are furloughed, and guess what . . . they call me up, and they send me letters, and they say, 'Don't give in. I know I'm laid off, I know I'm not working, but you have got to balance the budget. We cannot continue to run these deficits.' "

Also during congressional wrangling on the

FLORIDA 15
Central — Brevard, Osceola and Indian River counties; Palm Bay; Melbourne

Brevard County is 72 miles long on the Atlantic Coast and only 20 miles wide. But it is less famous for its beaches than for what is launched from them. This is the self-proclaimed "Space Coast," home of NASA's Kennedy Space Center.

The county boomed during the era of the Mercury, Gemini and Apollo space flights in the 1960s, then stalled when space exploration slipped as a national priority. The high-technology industries that had been lured to the area trimmed jobs, but a core of engineers and other skilled workers remained.

In the 1980s, the shuttle program and increased military spending brought new opportunities for aerospace and defense-related work, spurring another round of population growth. The 1986 explosion of the shuttle *Challenger* cast an economic and psychological pall over Brevard that began to lift when shuttle flights resumed in late 1988.

The space program still has an enormous economic impact on the county, and some of the companies it contracts with have taken on defense contracts as well. This reliance on government spending, either through space or defense funding, has forced several companies to adjust to a peacetime economy. Among the leading private employers are the Harris Corp., Northrop Grumman, Boeing and Lockheed Martin.

Tourists are drawn to the space enterprises and to the beaches. Indian River still has some citrus, and cattle graze in southwest Brevard. Patrick Air Force Base provides support for the space program.

Brevard's population grew by 46 percent during the 1980s. Most residents live along the Indian River. Titusville, the county seat, is just north of the space center. Many of its residents are in working-class trades related to the space industry. The Cocoa Beach and Rockledge area, near the space center's entrance, tends to draw tourists. Farther south, Melbourne has more defense-related industries.

The region is trying to diversify its economic base. Among the non-defense businesses in the district are Sea Ray, a marine products company in Brevard County; and Disney, which operates a resort in Vero Beach and plans to run cruise ships out of Port Canaveral. The Florida Marlins and Los Angeles Dodgers have spring training facilities in the district.

The 15th typically will vote Republican at the top of the ticket. In 1996, Bob Dole took 46 percent of the vote to Bill Clinton's 41 percent. In the past, Brevard played a key role in electing Democrats to the House. Former Rep. Jim Bacchus garnered a 10,000-vote margin over Republican Bill Tolley in the county in 1992.

The retirees who have settled into Vero Beach and other coastal communities in Indian River County are fairly affluent and accustomed to voting Republican. Democrats have made few inroads there.

1990 Population: 562,519. White 507,476 (90%), Black 42,761 (8%), Other 12,282 (2%). Hispanic origin 19,240 (3%). 18 and over 440,627 (78%), 62 and over 124,935 (22%). Median age: 37.

budget, Weldon and other members of the Florida delegation were among those most concerned about a GOP leadership plan to let the states run the Medicaid program through block grants from the federal government. The Republican proposal gave the states greater leeway to make coverage and benefits decisions about their Medicaid recipients, but it also required that states not spend the federal money on anything except health care for the poor, that the states add some of their own money, and that a minimum amount be spent on each of the current beneficiary groups: women and children, the elderly and the disabled. Members from Florida and other Southern states with high numbers of retirees fretted that the proposal could end up costing their states more.

One priority for Weldon has been to secure funding for construction of a veterans' hospital in the 15th. His predecessor, Democrat Jim Bacchus, had successfully negotiated with Veterans Affairs' officials to build the hospital in Brevard County, instead of near Orlando as the department had planned. In July 1995, Weldon unsuccessfully proposed transferring funds designated for the Federal Emergency Management Agency to pay for construction of the VA facility. He told the House that the population of veterans in Florida had grown 25 percent in a decade, but that medical facilities to serve them had not expanded. Weldon did obtain federal funding for a VA clinic in his district. He also got federal funds for another local need — restoring Brevard County beaches.

Weldon was the freshman representative on the House Republican Policy Committee and was a member of the Speaker's Health Care Task Force, the only first-termer to serve on the panel.

At Home: In 1990 and 1992, Democrat Bacchus won the 15th narrowly over Republican nominee Bill Tolley, whose conservatism was just a shade too doctrinaire for the district's voters in those years. But Bacchus unexpectedly chose not to seek re-election in 1994, and Weldon overcame criticism in the primary and general elections that he, like Tolley, was too far right for the district.

In 1996, the Democrats nominated former Navy submarine commander John L. Byron, who again argued that Weldon was too conservative for the 15th, citing the incumbent's support for the House GOP agenda. As a sign of how seriously Republicans took the challenge, Weldon was one of the House incumbents highlighted at the Republican National Convention in San Diego. "Some people call this a Republican revolution," Weldon told the delegates. "This is a common-sense revolution."

Bryon also criticized Weldon as being inattentive to his constituents, trying to appeal to the large number of military retirees by criticizing the incumbent's failure to secure federal funding for a VA hospital. Weldon said the clinic he did obtain money for could be turned into a full-service hospital in the future. Weldon won a bare majority but finished eight points ahead of Bryon, as an independent siphoned off 6 percent of the vote.

Weldon's active role in the Space Coast Family Forum gave his initial House campaign a ready-made base of support among conservative, anti-abortion voters. He took 24 percent of the vote in a seven-way GOP primary, landing in a runoff with Carole Jean Jordan, an abortion rights supporter and president of the Florida Federation of Republican Women. She did her best to turn his backing among Christian conservative activists into a negative, while Weldon's supporters countered with fliers and mailings that assailed Jordan as a liberal party insider. Shortly before the runoff, Jordan won a ruling from the state party that Weldon's campaign had broken the "GOP code of conduct" by distributing fliers that misrepresented her position on issues such as homosexuals in the military and health care. Despite Jordan's support among party establishment figures, Weldon had more foot soldiers, and he won nomination with 54 percent of the vote.

In the general election, Weldon's Democratic opponent was Sue Munsey, a former Republican who had headed the Cocoa Beach Area Chamber of Commerce. She tried a strategy similar to Jordan's. Seeking to link Weldon to "extremists" and "fanatics," Munsey aired television ads showing a health clinic that had been bombed by abortion foes. Editorials in the largest newspapers in the district, Florida Today and The Orlando Sentinel, faulted Weldon's ideas as "narrow."

But 1994 found the district's voters in a more conservative mood than they had been in the previous two elections. The extremist label either did not stick to Weldon, or it did not matter. An intense, deliberate campaigner, he emphasized his support for mainstream GOP fare: tax cuts, welfare reform and other aspects of the House GOP's "Contract With America." Aided by an extensive get-out-the-vote effort conducted by groups such as the Christian Coalition, Weldon won with 54 percent.

Like many Floridians, Weldon is a transplant from the North. He grew up on Long Island as the son of a postal clerk and got his undergraduate and medical degrees in the New York State university system.

HOUSE ELECTIONS

1996 General		
Dave Weldon (R)	138,968	(51%)
John L. Byron (D)	115,954	(43%)
David Golding (I)	15,349	(6%)
1994 General		
Dave Weldon (R)	117,027	(54%)
Sue Munsey (D)	100,513	(46%)

CAMPAIGN FINANCE

	Receipts	Receipts from PACs		Expend-itures
1996				
Weldon (R)	$827,126	$310,131	(37%)	$774,408
Byron (D)	$333,725	$163,297	(49%)	$332,687
1994				
Weldon (R)	$481,540	$108,812	(23%)	$478,303
Munsey (D)	$494,364	$225,451	(46%)	$494,364

DISTRICT VOTE FOR PRESIDENT

1996		1992	
D	112,044 (41%)	**D**	83,407 (31%)
R	126,513 (46%)	**R**	117,195 (43%)
I	34,708 (13%)	**I**	69,536 (26%)

KEY VOTES

1997	
Ban "partial birth" abortions	Y
1996	
Approve farm bill	Y
Deny public education to illegal immigrants	Y
Repeal ban on certain assault-style weapons	Y
Increase minimum wage	N
Freeze defense spending	N
Approve welfare overhaul	Y
1995	
Approve balanced-budget constitutional amendment	Y
Relax Clean Water Act regulations	Y
Oppose limits on environmental regulations	N
Reduce projected Medicare spending	Y
Approve GOP budget with tax and spending cuts	Y

VOTING STUDIES

	Presidential Support		Party Unity		Conservative Coalition	
Year	S	O	S	O	S	O
1996	38	62	93	7	94	6
1995	17	83	96	3	93	5

INTEREST GROUP RATINGS

Year	ADA	AFL-CIO	CCUS	ACU
1996	5	n/a	100	100
1995	0	0	100	96

16 Mark Foley (R)

Of West Palm Beach — Elected 1994, 2nd term

Biographical Information

Born: Sept. 8, 1954, Newton, Mass.

Education: Palm Beach Community College, 1973-75.

Occupation: Catering company founder; real estate broker; restaurant chain owner.

Family: Single.

Religion: Roman Catholic.

Political Career: Lake Worth City Council, 1977-79; sought Democratic nomination for Fla. House, 1980; Lake Worth city commissioner, 1982-84; Republican nominee for Fla. House, 1986; Fla. House, 1991-93; Fla. Senate, 1993-95.

Capitol Office: 113 Cannon Bldg. 20515; 225-5792.

Committees

Agriculture
Department Operations, Nutrition & Foreign Agriculture; Risk Management & Specialty Crops

Banking & Financial Services
General Oversight & Investigations; Domestic & International Monetary Policy

Science

In Washington: In the GOP Class of 1994 to which Foley belongs, support for a balanced federal budget is an article of faith. But the pursuit of that priority in the 104th Congress threatened to pinch an interest dear to Foley: the federal price-support program that benefits sugar cane growers, an important constituency in the 16th.

From his seat on the Agriculture Committee, Foley summoned all his polish and persuasiveness in an effort to protect his district's cane growers as Congress overhauled federal farm programs to reduce their cost.

Republican takeover of the House and Senate in 1994 strengthened the hand of those who wanted to dramatically diminish Washington's role in agriculture. Florida's cane growers feared that without Washington-imposed price supports and import restrictions, they would be driven out of business by a flood of less-expensive sugar imported from Europe, Cuba, Brazil and elsewhere.

Eliminating price supports for sugar, Foley said, would threaten the jobs of thousands of his constituents. "This is not something that you can just discuss arbitrarily in a vacuum. There are lives that depend on it."

Rather than stonewall change, Foley and other price-support proponents decided to support modest program adjustments in the Agriculture Committee, whose members are historically sympathetic to commodities' interests. By making some concessions in committee to budget pressures, Foley and his allies hoped to enhance their credibility in arguing later on the House floor against outright elimination of price supports.

"Once people look at the reforms, they'll be pleased," Foley said of the committee product. "If status quo was the situation, this [sugar program] would be dealt a fatal blow" on the House floor, he predicted.

However, free-market purists were not impressed with the committee's changes to the sugar program, dismissing them as superficial. When the full House debated the farm bill in February 1996, leading the charge against price supports were Connecticut Republican Christopher Shays and Foley's Florida GOP colleague, Dan Miller, from the West Coast 13th District. They argued that the federal government's sugar program inflated sugar prices by about $1.4 billion a year, a cost borne largely by consumers. Foley said that having Miller as an adversary "creates a unique dynamic. It's difficult when somebody from your own state is leading the charge against you."

Miller and Shays offered an amendment to phase out sugar price supports over five years. Foley called it a "Dr. Kevorkian" proposal that would "kill the domestic sugar industry." After a tense debate, the amendment was rejected, 208-217. In the final "Freedom to Farm" agriculture bill that Congress cleared, sugar price supports survived.

In another area of the farm bill, Foley won approval of an amendment allocating $210 million for environmental restoration programs around the Florida Everglades, including the purchase of property to buffer the ecologically fragile area.

Another Florida and Foley concern is illegal immigration. In early 1995, Foley successfully sponsored an amendment to one of the six GOP crime bills that provided for speedier deportation of aliens imprisoned for committing non-violent crimes. Foley told the House, "The state of Florida has approximately 5,504 criminal aliens in state corrections facilities on any given day, annually costing Florida taxpayers on average more than $14,000 per inmate."

Weighing in on behalf of fiscal austerity, Foley in the 104th pushed for establishing a "lockbox" that would hold whatever money the House cuts from its broad appropriations bills. The money in the "lockbox" would be earmarked for reducing the deficit in order to prevent members from shifting it to other programs within the same appropriations bill. House Appropriations Committee Chairman Robert L. Livingston of Louisiana and many others on his panel opposed the lockbox idea as an unwarranted infringement

FLORIDA 16
Central — Coastal Martin, Palm Beach and St. Lucie counties

The large 16th is something of a link between Central Florida and the southeast's Gold Coast. Although most of its land mass is in four lightly populated counties along the western edge of Lake Okeechobee, most of its population lives in three Atlantic coast counties.

Republicans hold a bare registration edge in the 16th, which means GOP candidates typically run better than their statewide average in top-of-the-ticket races.

The area has attracted newcomers from more congested areas farther south along the coast. Palm Beach County, which accounts for nearly half of the district's population, grew at an overall rate of 50 percent during the 1980s. St. Lucie County, one of the fastest growing areas in the state, grew by 72 percent, and Martin County grew by 58 percent. In solidly GOP Martin County, growth management has become the most important local concern.

The 16th includes parts of north Palm Beach County. Controversies over the pace of development and its impact on the environment have been present in the community of Jupiter, which tripled in size in the 1970s and more than doubled in the 1980s. Many of the newcomers are young, middle-income families who commute south to work in an area from West Palm Beach to Boca Raton.

Transportation is a concern here — deciding where to build access roads and how to move travelers through the county. Some bedroom communities are no longer interested in attracting more residents. Jupiter, a mix of conservative Democrats and Republicans, provides a reliably Republican vote.

The region is of interest to boaters because of its access to the Atlantic as well as to the Intracoastal Waterway.

Palm Beach Gardens is headquarters for the Professional Golfers Association and features a golf resort. Wellington is a GOP stronghold. Other areas attractive to retirees are Fountains of Lake Worth, where many residents live on a fixed income and lean Democratic; Golden Lakes Village, and Sentry Village, a heavily Jewish, Democratic-inclined community that has attracted national media attention because it is gated to keep out crime.

Farming is important in less-developed areas of the county, especially sugar, cattle, vegetables and citrus. Pratt & Whitney builds jet engines at a plant northwest of Palm Beach Gardens, while golf courses and beaches draw tourists to the coast.

Some residents work at a Northrop-Grumman facility, which produces aircraft components in Stuart.

Citrus is an important industry in St. Lucie County, where Indian River Citrus is known for its sweet grapefruit. Port St. Lucie quadrupled in population in the 1980s, with Republicans cutting into the county's traditional Democratic bent, though Bill Clinton still carried the county in 1996. Fort Pierce, which grew by a relatively modest 9 percent during the 1980s, has a wider spread of incomes than the rest of the coastal communities.

The other four counties in the district — Glades, Hendry, Highlands and Okeechobee — are largely agricultural, with some predominantly fixed-income retirees. Lake Okeechobee, which is adjacent, offers plenty of recreational opportunities for fishing and boating. Clinton carried both Glades and Okeechobee in both 1992 and 1996.

1990 Population: 562,519. White 523,225 (93%), Black 22,616 (4%), Other 16,678 (3%). Hispanic origin 35,517 (6%). 18 and over 447,765 (80%), 62 and over 156,318 (28%). Median age: 40.

on their power, but many of Foley's less-senior GOP colleagues liked the concept.

"Newt [Gingrich] and Dick Armey, you all created us," Foley said, referring to the House Speaker and majority leader.

Foley found another publicity-winning way to burnish his credentials as a fiscal conservative when he moved to end the tradition of every member of Congress receiving a personalized, gold-embossed set of the U.S. Code. Each 223-volume set cost taxpayers $2,500, Foley said. "Thus, to provide every new member of the last two Congresses, they have spent over $500,000 . . . on books that are available in every House office building, in the House counsel's office and, of course, in the Library of Congress across the street," Foley said. His bill to halt the expenditure was attached to the fiscal 1996 legislative branch spending measure.

He offered to the House Rules Committee during a July 1996 hearing another way to save money: merge the Appropriations and Budget committees.

And he tried unsuccessfully to roll back increases in the fiscal 1997 defense authorization bill. Foley was blocked by a Republican rule from offering an amendment to freeze defense spending at the previous year's level.

Foley is more permissive regarding abortion than many other Republicans. For instance, in 1995 he was one of 41 Republicans who voted for a proposal to allow military personnel to have abortions at overseas U.S. military facilities as long as the woman paid for the procedure herself.

In 1996, he voted to allow federal employees' health plans to pay for abortions. He has, however, voted to ban a particular abortion technique that opponents call "partial birth" abortion (and to ban same-sex marriages.)

Foley's views on abortion rights may stem from his libertarian beliefs. He is on the board of advisers of the Republican Liberty Caucus, a national libertarian group headquartered in Florida.

Foley was one of the first Republicans to suggest publicly that ethics questions about Gingrich were damaging junior GOP members. "We're associated with him so closely, so we're going to take it on the chin," Foley said. When the House ethics committee agreed to hire an outside counsel to investigate a charge that Gingrich violated federal tax laws in raising money for a college course he had taught at Georgia's Kennesaw State and Reinhardt colleges, Foley was pleased. "It would be in his best interest, as well as everyone else's, to clear the air," Foley said.

In 1997, after attending a House GOP conference in which Gingrich discussed the ethics charges against him, Foley reported that the Speaker portrayed himself as a victim. "He said, 'I have been attacked, I have been abused, I have been sullied,'" Foley said. He voted for Gingrich's re-election as Speaker.

At Home: Born into an Irish-Catholic family on the outskirts of Boston, Foley moved to Florida as a child and says he began his political career at the age of 5, distributing fliers for a local candidate.

Before winning election to the House in 1994, Foley served two separate stints in municipal office in Lake Worth and two years each in the Florida House and Senate. In 1975, he opened a restaurant with his mother called The Lettuce Patch and later became a real estate broker.

From the moment he launched his campaign to succeed retiring GOP Rep. Tom Lewis, Foley was regarded as a strong favorite to win the 16th. But his image as a moderate did generate some acrimony from conservatives in the GOP primary. His opponents were Highlands County Commissioner Audrey Vickers and conservative John Anastasio, a Port St. Lucie lawyer who had challenged Lewis in 1992. Foley won nomination with 61 percent of the vote, then headed into a November contest against John P. Comerford, who had lost to Lewis as the Democratic nominee in 1992.

Foley, who chaired the state Senate's Agriculture Committee, greatly outpaced Comerford in fundraising, bringing in $639,000 and getting solid help from PACs run by the citrus and sugar industries. Comerford spent about one-fourth as much.

Foley's Senate constituency stretched across most of the 16th, and his West Palm Beach base gave him an advantage in Palm Beach County, the district's most affluent and socially moderate area. Adding to that the GOP's registration edge in the 16th and Lewis' endorsement, Foley won with a comfortable 58 percent. He waltzed to a second term in 1996.

HOUSE ELECTIONS

1996 General		
Mark Foley (R)	175,674	(64%)
Jim Stuber (D)	98,813	(36%)
1994 General		
Mark Foley (R)	122,734	(58%)
John Comerford (D)	88,646	(42%)

CAMPAIGN FINANCE

	Receipts	Receipts from PACs		Expend-itures
1996				
Foley (R)	$785,107	$246,390	(31%)	$613,392
Stuber (D)	$86,957	$29,000	(33%)	$84,523
1994				
Foley (R)	$639,107	$265,542	(42%)	$629,406
Comerford (D)	$163,725	$70,832	(43%)	$163,311

DISTRICT VOTE FOR PRESIDENT

	1996		1992
D	133,029 (47%)	**D**	97,860 (36%)
R	119,033 (42%)	**R**	107,538 (39%)
I	29,544 (10%)	**I**	67,700 (25%)

KEY VOTES

1997	
Ban "partial birth" abortions	Y
1996	
Approve farm bill	Y
Deny public education to illegal immigrants	Y
Repeal ban on certain assault-style weapons	Y
Increase minimum wage	Y
Freeze defense spending	Y
Approve welfare overhaul	Y
1995	
Approve balanced-budget constitutional amendment	Y
Relax Clean Water Act regulations	Y
Oppose limits on environmental regulations	N
Reduce projected Medicare spending	Y
Approve GOP budget with tax and spending cuts	Y

VOTING STUDIES

	Presidential Support		Party Unity		Conservative Coalition	
Year	**S**	**O**	**S**	**O**	**S**	**O**
1996	43	57	83	16	78	22
1995	26	74	90	9	94	5

INTEREST GROUP RATINGS

Year	ADA	AFL-CIO	CCUS	ACU
1996	10	n/a	94	90
1995	10	0	96	84

17 Carrie P. Meek (D)

Of Miami — Elected 1992, 3rd term

Biographical Information

Born: April 29, 1926, Tallahassee, Fla.
Education: Florida A&M U., B.S. 1946; U. of Michigan, M.S. 1948; Florida Atlantic U., 1979.
Occupation: Educational administrator; teacher.
Family: Divorced; three children.
Religion: Baptist.
Political Career: Fla. House, 1979-82; Fla. Senate, 1982-93.
Capitol Office: 401 Cannon Bldg. 20515; 225-4506.

Committees

Appropriations
Treasury, Postal Service & General Government; VA, HUD & Independent Agencies

In Washington: Meek returns to the Appropriations Committee for the 105th Congress after a one-term enforced absence: A junior member of the panel in the 103rd, she lost her place when the GOP's 1994 House takeover reduced the number of Democratic slots on Appropriations. With the exit of several committee Democrats in 1996, there was again room for Meek in 1997.

After her first House election in 1992, Meek landed the Appropriations assignment by painstakingly introducing herself to all the members of the Democratic leadership and the Steering and Policy Committee, which decides committee assignments, and working with Florida delegation colleagues. She succeeded in part because Democrats wanted diversity on Appropriations, traditionally a white male preserve.

The Appropriations post gives her an "insider" venue from which to challenge the GOP majority's proposed cuts in spending on social programs. In the 104th, Meek's attacks on the GOP were mainly launched from the House floor. In August 1995, she criticized Republican efforts to cut Head Start. "It is one of the few programs, federal programs, which has succeeded over the years," she said. "But now to cut it is a dangerous thing, because what we are doing on one hand is giving a big tax cut to the rich and we are cutting off at the pass these poor children who need Head Start."

In June 1995, she criticized the Republicans' proposal to scale back Medicaid's projected growth. "They show little concern about the impact of these proposals on children, the elderly, and the severely disabled," Meek said. "They are concerned about management and about how they can use this money to make their coffers stronger. They like to cut dollars, but they do not like to create alternatives. I have heard no alternatives to Medicaid since I have been here."

Meek voted against efforts to end sugar price supports — sugar is a major Florida commodity — and, with a number of her Congressional Black Caucus colleagues, she voted in June 1995 to buy more B-2 stealth bombers. Fifteen of the 36 black Democrats who are voting members of the caucus joined 58 other Democrats to support buying additional B-2s. Meek, old enough to remember World War II, said she found the argument raised by Norm Dicks, D-Wash., about military preparedness persuasive. She also noted that Dicks made his case to her early enough for her to think it over, whereas B-2 foes solicited her vote late in the game — after she had given her word. "People don't realize that personal contact makes a difference," Meek said.

Representing a district that was the scene of a major riot in 1980 and has seen more than its share of violence, Meek is a strong supporter of gun control. In April 1996, toward the end of the House floor debate on repealing the ban on certain semiautomatic assault-style weapons, Meek delivered a brief and angry speech denouncing proponents of repeal. Shouting to be heard over catcalls, Meek said that retaining the assault weapons ban was the very least Congress should do to deter gun violence. "I want to see every gun controlled because some of these people do not even need to have a gun in their hands," she said. "They are already bad enough without that."

Her district also includes large numbers of Haitian refugees — their neighborhood in Miami is known as Little Haiti — and she as been a strong supporter of efforts to bring democracy to that island nation. In June 1995, during House debate on the fiscal 1996 foreign operations appropriations bill, she strongly opposed an amendment by Porter J. Goss, R-Fla., barring aid to Haiti unless it held free presidential balloting later that year. Republicans rallied behind the amendment, charging that the recent parliamentary election in Haiti had been marred by widespread irregularities.

In response, Meek delivered an emotional speech in which she said it was "wrong morally" for Goss to imply that the government of Haitian President Jean-Bertrand Aristide was not committed to holding free elections. She argued that the amendment would only undercut the pro-democracy movement in Haiti. "Let us encourage them in the right direction," she said. "Let us not threaten them."

After five hours of debate and procedural wran-

FLORIDA 17

Southeast — Parts of North Dade County; parts of Miami, Carol City

The 17th has the state's highest percentage of black residents and is Florida's most staunchly Democratic district. Democrats account for more than 75 percent of the registered voters, and they routinely deliver the highest percentage of votes for Democrats running statewide.

It is a district that has seen widespread devastation. Starting at the Broward County line, the district runs through such northern Miami suburbs as Carol City and Opa-Locka, then picks up the impoverished Miami neighborhoods of Liberty City and Overtown. It follows U.S. 1 heading southwest to include predominantly black neighborhoods in Richmond Heights, Perrine, Homestead and Florida City. Some of these areas were leveled by Hurricane Andrew in 1992.

Unincorporated Carol City is predominantly black and Hispanic. (Hispanics account for about one-quarter of the district's population.) Most residents are blue-collar workers who commute south to Miami. The area has a mix of single-family homes, apartments and housing projects. Opa-Locka, which suffers from high unemployment and high crime rates, is overwhelmingly black. As in the rest of the district, local political organizations usually center on churches. Opa-Locka is also noted for its Arabian theme and its large private airport.

Unincorporated Rolling Oaks is an affluent black neighborhood near Pro Player Stadium (home of football's Dolphins and baseball's Marlins). The North Miami Beach area, which is partially in the 17th, has some of the largest numbers of whites in the district, many of whom are Jewish retirees on fixed incomes. They are politically well-organized, Democratic and interested in health care and crime. The west side of North Miami, in the district, is a mix of blacks, whites and Hispanics, and somewhat less Democratic.

The Miami neighborhoods in the 17th include Little Haiti, which has a growing core of recent immigrants from the Caribbean. They tend to be Democrats but are not yet a political force.

The black neighborhoods of Liberty City — where Meek lives — and Overtown have been plagued by economic despair and violence. A 1980 riot left 18 dead after an all-white jury acquitted four white Miami police officers in the beating death of a black insurance executive. Riots erupted again in 1989 after a Latino officer shot a black motorcyclist.

Some improvements have been made. There are new apartment complexes and stores in Liberty City. The Miami Arena (home of pro basketball's Miami Heat and hockey's Florida Panthers, both of whom are planning to move) and new housing developments are reinvigorating part of Overtown. But progress is slow.

The district takes in the ethnically mixed areas of South Miami, then delves into the more rural communities near U.S. 1 that Andrew pummeled. Perrine, Richmond Heights and Florida City are heavily black; Homestead is mixed. Some residents were homeless or living in trailers for months after Hurricane Andrew.

1990 Population: 562,519. White 205,611 (37%), Black 328,316 (58%), Other 28,592 (5%). Hispanic origin 129,628 (23%). 18 and over 391,015 (70%), 62 and over 67,772 (12%). Median age: 30.

gling, the House finally voted on Meek's substitute to weaken the conditions on aid for Haiti. It rejected that proposal, 189-231, and adopted Goss' amendment, 252-164.

And as befits a representative from South Florida, Meek strongly backed legislation by Sen. Jesse Helms, R-N.C., and Rep. Dan Burton, R-Ind., to tighten the U.S. economic embargo of Cuba. She talked about the refugees who have fled Cuba and settled in Miami. "The brutality of the situation in Cuba is something we live with every day," Meek said on the House floor in February 1996. "We see what happens with the Cuban people when atrocities are perpetrated against their families who are in Cuba. So many of our constituents have fled from Castro's prisons. So many of our constituents still have relatives, mothers and fathers, brothers and sisters. So many of my constituents have left everything they worked for. Whatever they had in Cuba, they do not have anymore. Just as we helped the people of South Africa and the people of Haiti, we must now help the people of Cuba in the time of their greatest need and in the hour of their greatest hope."

Early in the 104th Congress, Meek instigated a brouhaha when she took to the House floor in January 1995 to criticize Speaker Newt Gingrich's book deal with media mogul Rupert Murdoch's HarperCollins subsidiary. Meek used her one-minute address at the start of the day to question the deal. "While the Speaker may have given up the $4.5 million advance, he stands to gain that amount and much more," Meek said. "That is a whole lot of dust where I come from. If anything now, how much the Speaker earns has grown much more dependent on how hard his publishing house hawks his book."

Gingrich ally Robert S. Walker, R-Pa., moved to strike Meek's comments from the record. The presiding officer, Cliff Stearns, R-Fla., agreed. "Innuendo and personal references to the Speaker's personal conduct are not in order," Stearns said.

The Democrats howled in outrage and challenged the ruling. The Republicans voted to table the appeal, 214-169, and then deleted Meek's words by a vote of 217-178. When the Congressional Record was published, Stearns' comments had been altered. Democrats again took to the floor, this time to complain that the Republicans were changing the record despite a new rule prohibiting changes except for technical, typographical or grammatical corrections. Gingrich finally announced that Stearns' original language would be part of the permanent record.

Meek later distributed the draft of her speech, which included this final line: "Who does this Speaker really work for? Is it the American people or his New York publishing house?"

As a former domestic worker, Meek brought a unique perspective to the "nannygate" debate, which led Congress to try to raise the $50-a-quarter threshold for paying Social Security taxes for domestic workers. During the 103rd Congress, several Clinton administration nominees and appointees were faulted for failing to pay taxes for their workers.

Meek agreed the threshold was too low but did not want it raised so high that employers would not be required to pay into Social Security at all. She worried that domestics who worked for a number of families would never reach the threshold and would have nothing to draw on when they retired.

On the House floor, Meek said she, her mother, her sister and many neighbors had done domestic work. In her experience, she said, "families that employed [domestics] would express much affection and gratitude towards them, but they did nothing for their employees' future economic security."

She argued against a House provision to raise the earnings threshold to $1,800 a year, saying it was too high. She said a Senate Finance Committee bill to boost the threshold to $610 a year was "very reasonable," even though she had introduced her own bill raising it to only $300 a year. Congress ultimately cleared a bill in 1994 increasing it to $1,000 a year.

At Home: Meek grew up in a poor Tallahassee neighborhood referred to as Black Bottom when segregation was the norm. The daughter of sharecroppers and the granddaughter of slaves, Meek has been a domestic worker, a teacher and a college administrator. She served 14 years in the Florida legislature before running for the House in what is the most heavily black and reliably Democratic of Florida's 23 House districts.

In 1992, Meek heard some criticism that at age 66, she would not be able to provide the district with vigorous, long-term representation. One of her two primary opponents, Darryl Reaves, said he was challenging Meek so the new black-majority 17th would not "crown somebody queen."

But the age issue did not resonate with voters, and Meek's campaign was indeed a coronation. She won the primary with 83 percent of the vote and was unopposed in the general election. The GOP again did not field an opponent in 1994.

Republicans nominated marketing consultant Wellington Rolle in 1996, but he was never a factor. Meek won with 89 percent.

HOUSE ELECTIONS

1996 General		
Carrie P. Meek (D)	114,590	(89%)
Wellington Rolle (R)	14,502	(11%)
1994 General		
Carrie P. Meek (D)	unopposed	

Previous Winning Percentages: 1992 (100%)

CAMPAIGN FINANCE

	Receipts	Receipts from PACs	Expend-itures
1996			
Meek (D)	$400,916	$134,650 (34%)	$257,039
1994			
Meek (D)	$347,207	$155,825 (45%)	$166,452

DISTRICT VOTE FOR PRESIDENT

1996		1992	
D	115,764 (85%)	**D**	99,455 (73%)
R	16,827 (12%)	**R**	27,638 (20%)
I	3,944 (3%)	**I**	9,959 (7%)

KEY VOTES

1997	
Ban "partial birth" abortions	N
1996	
Approve farm bill	Y
Deny public education to illegal immigrants	N
Repeal ban on certain assault-style weapons	N
Increase minimum wage	Y
Freeze defense spending	N
Approve welfare overhaul	N
1995	
Approve balanced-budget constitutional amendment	N
Relax Clean Water Act regulations	N
Oppose limits on environmental regulations	Y
Reduce projected Medicare spending	N
Approve GOP budget with tax and spending cuts	N

VOTING STUDIES

	Presidential Support		Party Unity		Conservative Coalition	
Year	S	O	S	O	S	O
1996	76	18	88	9	45	53
1995	82	14	86	6	26	64
1994	83	14	92	3	31	64
1993	91	7	90	6	43	57

INTEREST GROUP RATINGS

Year	ADA	AFL-CIO	CCUS	ACU
1996	85	n/a	33	5
1995	95	100	13	8
1994	95	78	50	10
1993	75	92	18	9

18 Ileana Ros-Lehtinen (R)

Of Miami — Elected 1989; 4th full term

Biographical Information
Born: July 15, 1952, Havana, Cuba.
Education: Miami-Dade Community College, A.A. 1972; Florida International U., B.A. 1975, M.S. 1986.
Occupation: Teacher; private school administrator.
Family: Husband, Dexter Lehtinen; two children, two stepchildren.
Religion: Roman Catholic.
Political Career: Fla. House, 1983-87; Fla. Senate, 1987-89.
Capitol Office: 2440 Rayburn Bldg. 20515; 225-3931.

Committees
Government Reform & Oversight
District of Columbia; National Security, International Affairs & Criminal Justice
International Relations
International Economic Policy & Trade (chairwoman); International Operations & Human Rights; Western Hemisphere

In Washington: Republicans are happy to have minorities in their ranks in order to broaden the party's image, and as the first Cuban-American elected to Congress, Ros-Lehtinen has gained some prominence in the House. An ardent foe of Cuban President Fidel Castro, she has happily affiliated with the GOP conservatives who share her distaste for Castro.

But as many Republicans in the 104th Congress began to put forth conservative views on immigration, Ros-Lehtinen found herself voting against major GOP agenda items. She opposed measures overhauling the welfare system, curbing illegal immigration and designating English as America's official language. She is also sympathetic to gun control efforts and some labor-backed positions.

Ros-Lehtinen came to Miami from Cuba when she was seven and, like her Florida Republican colleague Lincoln Diaz-Balart, who is also a Cuban immigrant, she refused to sign the GOP's "Contract With America." They objected to provisions in its welfare reform section that proposed denying some federal benefits to legal immigrants. When the final welfare reform bill passed the House in July 1996, Ros-Lehtinen and Diaz-Balart were the only two Republicans voting against it.

When the House considered the GOP's first welfare overhaul bill in March 1995, Ros-Lehtinen addressed what she called an "anti-immigrant sentiment" that is "growing from an unreal perception that immigrants only come to the United States to take advantage of our generous society and become a burden on the state while never integrating nor becoming productive citizens." She told the House: "Nothing could be further from the truth. Immigrants have contributed greatly to all facets of American life in the economic, cultural, and political fields. I appeal to my colleagues to not be swayed by those who would place all of the problems of this nation on the backs of immigrants."

Ros-Lehtinen also argued against a Republican measure designed to curb illegal immigration through tighter border controls and easier deportation proceedings. Although the original bill had included provisions aimed at reducing the flow of legal immigrants, those provisions were later stripped out. Even so, Ros-Lehtinen opposed the final measure saying it was unnecessarily anti-immigrant. "I don't think this bill is in the American tradition," she said. "I don't think it really stems the problems of illegal immigration, and it puts new restrictions on legal immigrants and U.S. citizens."

The immigration bill was stalled most of 1996 because of a provision, authored by California conservative Republican Elton Gallegly, that would have allowed states to deny illegal immigrants public schooling. In the end, House conferees agreed to drop the provision, in exchange for a vote on it as a free-standing bill. The House passed it in September 1996, 254-175, but it went no further. Ros-Lehtinen voted against the bill, calling it a "mean-spirited attempt that will hold children responsible for their parents' actions."

Their unhappiness with the welfare and immigration bills prompted Ros-Lehtinen and Diaz-Balart in March 1996 to rejoin the Congressional Hispanic Caucus, which is dominated by House Democrats. They had dropped out at the start of the 104th to comply with the spirit of the GOP move to do away with such organizations. But they later decided it was important to show unity against anti-immigrant feelings.

However, in January 1997, Diaz-Balart and Ros-Lehtinen resigned again from the caucus, this time to protest that its chairman, Xavier Becerra, D-Calif., took a trip to Cuba in December 1996.

Ros-Lehtinen, a former teacher and owner of a bilingual private school in south Florida, also upbraided the House for passing a GOP bill declaring English the official language of the federal government. She said immigrants to the United States know they need to learn English and "no law is needed to stress this." But the bill passed, 259-169, in August 1996.

She broke ranks with her party in 1996 and voted to raise the minimum wage by 90 cents and against exempting small businesses from the wage increase. Also in 1996, Ros-Lehtinen was one of 42 Republicans to vote against repealing the ban on

FLORIDA 18
Southeast — Parts of Dade County; part of Miami

This is one of two Hispanic-majority Florida districts. Although it includes much of downtown Miami, its spiritual heart is the inner-city neighborhood known as Little Havana.

Many of Miami's Cubans came to this country in the 1960s, fleeing Castro's takeover. Many were well-educated professionals and businesspeople in Cuba, and they have achieved positions of status here. The Cubans, Puerto Ricans, Haitians, Nicaraguans and Colombians who have arrived more recently tend to be unskilled workers.

The Cuban-American community for a time was consumed with discussing and plotting to overthrow Castro; U.S. elections were not a focus. They are now. The GOP's hawkish anti-communist stance helped persuade most Cuban voters to register Republican, making this a safe GOP district. The 18th is hardly homogeneous, however. And Bill Clinton narrowed what had been a more than 2-1 margin in favor of GOP presidential candidates.

South Miami Beach, traditionally home to Jewish retirees, is attracting young professionals and some Hispanics. It features the art deco district of colorful hotels. Downtown Miami is a nerve center for international trade and finance. Brickell Avenue contains high-rise offices and residences for Hispanics and the upper middle class; it is a swing area politically.

Across a causeway is Key Biscayne, an upper middle-class suburb and one of the city's first areas to turn Republican. Richard M. Nixon used to vacation here. Back on the mainland and heading south from downtown along the coast is Coconut Grove, a trendy neighborhood that attracts young liberals. Next comes Coral Gables, home of the University of Miami. The southern end of Coral Gables is more Anglo and has expensive houses and yacht clubs.

The 18th includes the east side of Kendall, an upper middle-class suburban area that leans Republican. The district extends farther south, to include small parts of Cutler Ridge and Perrine, then loops around Homestead Air Reserve Base into South Miami Heights. (Homestead, formerly an Air Force base, slated for closure, reopened in 1994 as a partially commercialized air reserve base.) This area includes blue-collar, conservative Democrats and Cubans and was hit by Hurricane Andrew in 1992.

The west side of Kendall is somewhat more Democratic and is home to young professionals, white-collar workers, some Cubans and a Jewish community. Olympia Heights and Westchester attract middle-class Cuban-Americans from Miami who want greener spaces. Florida International University (nearly 30,000 students) is in Westchester.

Most of Miami in the 18th is south of the Miami River except for Allapattah, an older section of the city that has become more Hispanic. The Cubans who remain in Little Havana tend to be older and less affluent. Crime tends to be more of a problem with recent refugees. The west side of the city is also predominantly Hispanic but more middle-class. The Orange Bowl is in the district, as is most of Miami International Airport.

1990 Population: 562,519. White 499,210 (89%), Black 23,351 (4%), Other 39,958 (7%). Hispanic origin 375,148 (67%). 18 and over 450,048 (80%), 62 and over 116,996 (21%). Median age: 38.

certain semiautomatic assault-style weapons. In the previous Congress, she had supported the assault weapons ban as well as a bill requiring a waiting period before the purchase of a handgun.

Despite disagreements with her party on its attitude toward immigrants, Ros-Lehtinen supports other GOP doctrine, including efforts to shrink the government and rein in federal spending. As a member of the International Relations Committee, she backed committee bills that aimed to reduce foreign aid spending and to terminate certain international agencies, such as the Agency for International Development, United States Information Agency and the Arms Control and Disarmament Agency.

As chairman of the Africa Subcommittee in the 104th, she opposed an amendment in May 1995 to the foreign aid bill that would have increased aid to Africa from $629 million to $802 million. She worried that if Africa received more aid, that would likely mean less for Latin America and the Caribbean, areas she said are "of great concern to every member of the Florida delegation." In the 105th, she chairs the International Economic Policy and Trade Subcommittee.

Ros-Lehtinen's deep and abiding interest in the House has been to bring down Castro. To that end, she was a proponent of the so-called Helms-Burton bill — named for its sponsors, Senate Foreign Relations Chairman Jesse Helms of North Carolina and Indiana GOP Rep. Dan Burton — that was designed to punish foreign companies that invest in Cuba. The Clinton administration had at first opposed the measure because of sharp criticism from the European Union and Canada, who complained of U.S. meddling in their trade practices.

But Clinton ended up supporting the measure after February 1996, when Cuban military planes shot down two civilian aircraft being flown toward the island nation by Cuban-American opponents of Castro, killing four.

After intense negotiations with the administration, House and Senate conferees hammered out a final bill that was harder on Castro's government than either the original House or Senate bill. "The Helms-Burton bill will penalize those who have become Castro's new patron saviors — foreign investors who callously traffic in American confiscated properties in Cuba to profit from the misery of the Cuban worker," Ros-Lehtinen said.

She was particularly outraged when Castro made a visit to New York in the fall of 1995. She took to the House floor to bitterly denounce those members of the House who met with the "Cuban tyrant." Ros-Lehtinen said "it was quite revolting to see how this dictator" was warmly greeted in the Bronx "by three of my colleagues from the other side of the aisle who hail from New York City," who she said ignored the "the well-known repression of the Castro regime.

At Home: After entering the special election to replace the late Democrat Claude Pepper in 1989, Ros-Lehtinen was instantly the leading contender for the GOP nomination.

She has stood out politically since 1982, when she became, at age 30, the first Hispanic elected to the state Legislature. Although not a major power broker in Tallahassee, Ros-Lehtinen was an articulate campaigner and leading member of South Florida's Cuban-American community.

That community tends to vote Republican, and national GOP strategists were itching to rally that vote and snatch the 18th from Democratic hands. Ros-Lehtinen easily beat three other candidates for the GOP nomination.

Some Democratic insiders, building their own bridges to Cuban-Americans, backed Rosario Kennedy, also a Cuban-American. But Gerald Richman, a Miami Beach lawyer with limited political experience, beat Kennedy in a runoff.

While Democrats struggled to unify, Ros-Lehtinen enjoyed generous GOP support, including visits from President George Bush and Vice President Dan Quayle. To reach the 18th's Jewish voters, Ros-Lehtinen stressed her support for Israel, traveling there during the campaign.

Richman, who is Jewish, reacted to GOP suggestions that Cuban-Americans deserved a voice in Congress by saying the 18th was "an American seat." Although Ros- Lehtinen and some media criticized Richman's comment as bigoted, he did strike a chord with some voters. Ros-Lehtinen won, but by a smaller margin than anticipated.

Richman's showing led some to believe Ros-Lehtinen's re-election was uncertain. But she prepared well, and several formidable Democrats skipped the 1990 race. She won 60 percent against the Democratic nominee, industrialist Bernard Anscher, who was one of the 1989 primary losers.

Her 1992 Democratic opponent, lawyer Magda Montiel Davis, criticized Ros-Lehtinen's anti-abortion stance and called for more travel and communication with Cuba. Ros-Lehtinen responded with a TV ad that tried to link Davis, through her husband's legal work, to Castro and former Panamanian leader Gen. Manuel Antonio Noriega. The incumbent won 2-to-1 in a redrawn district that was 67 percent Hispanic (up from 51 percent within the previous district lines). In 1994 and 1996, Ros-Lehtinen was unopposed.

HOUSE ELECTIONS

1996 General
Ileana Ros-Lehtinen (R) — unopposed
1994 General
Ileana Ros-Lehtinen (R) — unopposed
Previous Winning Percentages: 1992 (67%) **1990** (60%) **1989**† (53%)

† Special election

CAMPAIGN FINANCE

	Receipts	Receipts from PACs	Expend-itures
1996			
Ros-Lehtinen (R)	$485,356	$136,591 (28%)	$163,902
1994			
Ros-Lehtinen (R)	$464,277	$99,986 (22%)	$148,381

DISTRICT VOTE FOR PRESIDENT

	1996		1992
D	71,654 (43%)	**D**	55,119 (34%)
R	85,998 (52%)	**R**	92,422 (56%)
I	7,788 (5%)	**I**	16,940 (10%)

KEY VOTES

1997	
Ban "partial birth" abortions	Y
1996	
Approve farm bill	Y
Deny public education to illegal immigrants	N
Repeal ban on certain assault-style weapons	N
Increase minimum wage	Y
Freeze defense spending	N
Approve welfare overhaul	N
1995	
Approve balanced-budget constitutional amendment	Y
Relax Clean Water Act regulations	N
Oppose limits on environmental regulations	Y
Reduce projected Medicare spending	Y
Approve GOP budget with tax and spending cuts	Y

VOTING STUDIES

	Presidential Support		Party Unity		Conservative Coalition	
Year	S	O	S	O	S	O
1996	47	51	73	22	75	24
1995	23	74	86	10	90	7
1994	58	37	74	21	64	25
1993	57	42	75	24	77	23
1992	61	36	73	24	79	19
1991	67	32	75	22	73	24

INTEREST GROUP RATINGS

Year	ADA	AFL-CIO	CCUS	ACU
1996	30	n/a	73	60
1995	15	17	88	76
1994	25	67	82	65
1993	30	75	82	79
1992	25	50	57	78
1991	40	42	50	70

19 Robert Wexler (D)

Of Boca Raton — Elected 1996, 1st term

Biographical Information
Born: Jan. 2, 1961, Queens, N.Y.
Education: Emory U., 1978-79; U. of Florida, B.A. 1982; George Washington U., J.D. 1985.
Occupation: Lawyer.
Family: Wife, Laurie; two children.
Religion: Jewish.
Political Career: Fla. Senate, 1990-97.
Capitol Office: 1609 Longworth Bldg. 20515; 225-3001.

Committees
International Relations
Asia & the Pacific; International Operations & Human Rights
Judiciary
Crime; Immigration & Claims

The Path to Washington: A seven-year member of the Florida legislature before coming to Congress in 1997, Wexler has spent much of his political career focusing on crime and safety issues, with particular emphasis on tougher sentences for rapists and child molesters.

During his tenure in state government, Wexler, a lawyer from Boca Raton, also received high marks from the state's teachers for his work to remove guns and drugs from public schools.

These legislative experiences led Wexler to a seat on the House Judiciary Committee, where he is expected to continue to focus on criminal justice initiatives, especially in the area of juvenile offenders.

Wexler, whose district includes large numbers of retirees from the Northeast, many of them Jewish, also snagged a seat on the International Relations Committee, where he is expected to become a strong and vocal advocate for Israel and peace in the Middle East.

On the issue of higher education, Wexler has said he plans to support policies to expand access to student loans. Wexler also advocates establishing tax credits to reduce the financial burden on students and their families.

With the district's high percentage of retirees clearly in mind, Wexler has pledged to protect major entitlement programs such as Social Security, Medicare and Medicaid from severe budget cuts.

Wexler says he supports balancing the budget, but contends that Congress must do a better job of setting budget priorities while also guaranteeing the long-term solvency of entitlement programs and continued investments in areas such as education and environmental protection.

When four-term Democratic Rep. Harry A. Johnston announced his retirement in late 1995, all eyes turned to Wexler as the most likely successor. The 19th, which includes parts of Palm Beach and northern Broward counties, is the most consistently Democratic-voting white-majority district in Florida.

But despite early speculation that he was the favorite, Wexler drew stiff intraparty challenges from two of his Democratic colleagues in the Legislature: state Rep. Ben Graber and state Sen. Peter Weinstein.

A fourth Democrat, Peter James Tsakanikas, also entered the race. But Tsakanikas' candidacy was viewed with suspicion by many Democrats, who quickly pointed out that he had been the Republican nominee against Johnston in 1994.

Wexler received the most votes in the September primary, with Weinstein finishing a distant second. But since Wexler fell short of a 50 percent majority threshold, he was forced into an October runoff with Weinstein.

Granted a second shot at an upset, Weinstein, a lawyer from Coral Springs in Broward County, mounted a spirited challenge in the runoff. Weinstein, who was first elected to the state Senate in 1982, pointed to his experience as the chamber's majority leader and his service on the Judiciary Committee as factors that demonstrated his ability to get things done.

A New York native, Weinstein also played up his family's connections to that state in an attempt to appeal to the district's large contingent of former New Yorkers.

But despite Weinstein's strong showing in his home territory of Broward County, Wexler's strength in populous Palm Beach County (including West Palm Beach and Boca Raton), where he won 83 percent of the vote, ensured the nomination comfortably.

In the general election, Wexler had little trouble dispensing with Republican nominee Beverly "Bev" Kennedy, a Pompano Beach financial consultant who had been the Republican nominee in the neighboring 20th District in 1992 and 1994.

Although she had no problem securing the Republican nomination, Kennedy was underfinanced and never found a way to effectively deflect charges from Wexler that she was a carpetbagger and political opportunist. Wexler cruised to victory.

FLORIDA 19

Southeast — Parts of Palm Beach and northern Broward counties; Boca Raton

The 19th is one of Florida's most compact and most Democratic districts. It lies generally west of Interstate 95, running north-south from Lake Worth in Palm Beach County to Tamarac in Broward County. The district's population is nearly evenly split between the two counties.

The large registration edge that Democrats enjoy among voters in some other Florida districts is illusory in state and federal elections because conservative Democrats often vote Republican at the top of the ticket.

But the 19th is filled with devoted, lifelong Democrats who retired here from the Northeast. It routinely rolls up some of the state's most impressive margins for Democratic candidates and it does so with the smallest percentage of black residents of any district in Florida.

In 1996 it was the only district in the country outside New England with a white population over 90 percent to give Bill Clinton at least 60 percent of the vote.

The district's retirees, many of whom are Jewish and from New York, give the area a Northeastern orientation. Delis and bagel bakeries are popular, and residents strongly support cultural offerings in nearby West Palm Beach and Fort Lauderdale. Health care and Social Security are vital concerns.

Although safely Democratic, the 19th has pockets of strong Republican support, and those areas are growing rapidly. Republicans are slightly more competitive in the district's Palm Beach County communities.

Lake Worth, Boynton Beach and Delray Beach are all less Democratic than the district as a whole. That is partly because they are somewhat less retirement-oriented and have a mix of young professionals and families in single-family homes.

Boca Raton, which has some single-family homes as well as exclusive condominium subdivisions, is among the district's most Republican communities.

Also in Boca Raton are large private employers, including IBM, Siemens Stromberg-Carlson, which produces telephone switching systems, and Sensormatic, which produces retail security devices. Motorola is in Boynton Beach.

Just south of the Palm Beach-Broward line lies Deerfield Beach. Many residents here are retired New Yorkers who live in middle-income condominium complexes; they vote Democratic in huge numbers.

To the west is fast-growing Coral Springs, the district's largest city, which grew by 113 percent in the 1980s. Friendly territory to the Republican party, the city features upper middle-class houses that attract professionals, some of whom commute to Fort Lauderdale.

Continuing east and south, the district picks up more Democratic strongholds. They include Margate, which has some blue-collar workers, Tamarac and Coconut Creek, which grew by two-thirds in the 1980s.

1990 Population: 562,519. White 533,138 (95%), Black 15,447 (3%), Other 13,934 (2%). Hispanic origin 34,985 (6%). 18 and over 461,448 (82%), 62 and over 178,485 (32%). Median age: 42.

HOUSE ELECTIONS

1996 General		
Robert Wexler (D)	188,745	(66%)
Beverly "Bev" Kennedy (R)	99,073	(34%)
1996 Primary Runoff		
Robert Wexler (D)	23,439	(65%)
Peter Weinstein (D)	12,580	(35%)
1996 Primary		
Robert Wexler (D)	21,142	(47%)
Peter Weinstein (D)	13,073	(29%)
Benjamin "Ben" Graber (D)	9,206	(21%)
Peter James Tsakanikas (D)	1,214	(3%)

CAMPAIGN FINANCE

	Receipts	Receipts from PACs		Expend-itures
1996				
Wexler (D)	$885,141	$295,824	(33%)	$872,367
Kennedy (R)	$121,186	$8,467	(7%)	$121,117

DISTRICT VOTE FOR PRESIDENT

1996			1992		
D	189,787	(65%)	D	155,436	(53%)
R	81,341	(28%)	R	88,807	(31%)
I	20,200	(7%)	I	46,888	(16%)

KEY VOTES

1997

Ban "partial birth" abortions N

20 Peter Deutsch (D)

Of Fort Lauderdale — Elected 1992, 3rd term

Biographical Information
Born: April 1, 1957, Bronx, N.Y.
Education: Swarthmore College, B.A. 1979; Yale U., J.D. 1982.
Occupation: Lawyer; nonprofit executive.
Family: Wife, Lori Ann Coffino; two children.
Religion: Jewish.
Political Career: Fla. House, 1983-93.
Capitol Office: 204 Cannon Bldg. 20515; 225-7931.

Committees
Commerce
Energy & Power; Health & Environment; Oversight & Investigations

In Washington: When he entered Congress at age 35, Deutsch already had a decade of experience in the Florida Legislature under his belt. Now is his third House term, he has shown signs of replicating the reputation that he earned in Tallahassee: hard-charging, often less than charming, and tenacious in advancing his constituents' interests as well as his own.

Deutsch has embraced two constitutional amendments that are favored by most conservatives — one mandating a balanced budget and another imposing congressional term limits — and he is a member of the New Democrat Coalition, a group of House Democrats that positions itself to the right of the party leadership (especially on fiscal policy) but to the left of the "blue dog" Democrats.

On a range of issues, though, Deutsch votes a liberal line. In disputes on abortion, he is a down the-line supporter of abortion rights. He backs gun control measures. He voted for a minimum wage increase in 1996 and generally sides with organized labor. He takes a dim view of GOP efforts to spend more on defense than the Clinton administration proposes. And he opposed Republicans seeking to limit the regulatory authority of the Environmental Protection Agency.

On the Commerce Committee, Deutsch has denounced a cause popular with many GOP conservatives: abolition of the Commerce Department. In July 1995, he scorned legislation introduced by Dick Chrysler, R-Mich., to dismantle the department and move various of its agencies such as the Census Bureau and Patent and Trademark Office to other departments. Deutsch said Chrysler "comes to this with a fundamental nonunderstanding of how policy is made."

Representing a large population of elderly residents, Deutsch was a strong opponent of Republican efforts in the 104th to rein in the growth of Medicare costs. "Seniors in this country believe that Republicans want to save Medicare probably as much as the Jewish community in this country believes that [Nation of Islam leader Louis] Farrakhan should be the head of the Jewish Federation," Deutsch said. He warned that the GOP plan for Medicare would eventually make it unaffordable for less-affluent seniors to get medical care from private-practice physicians, driving them against their will into health maintenance organizations.

Deutsch criticized the GOP for attaching to a piece of health legislation an unrelated provision benefiting Rupert Murdoch's Fox Broadcasting Co. A tax break for the sale of television stations to minority-led partnerships was being eliminated, but one such transaction was exempted from that elimination, to Fox's advantage.

In April 1995, the bill was already at the White House, where President Clinton said he would sign it, but Deutsch tried to force a House vote to strip the tax benefit from the bill. That effort failed, and Deutsch then tried to get the House to approve a resolution calling on the comptroller general to look into whether passage of a tax provision that did not originate in the House had violated House rules. Again, he failed.

"This House passed legislation that provided for a $63 million gift to Rupert Murdoch," Deutsch thundered on the House floor. "It was done in the most sleazy, offensive way to this institution. What a shame on this institution, and what a shame on the Speaker that it was done." (Speaker Newt Gingrich earlier had made a lucrative book-publishing deal with HarperCollins, a part of Murdoch's media empire.)

In debate on the fiscal 1996 agriculture appropriations bill, Deutsch successfully pushed an amendment ending a $2 million subsidy for the U.S. Mink Export Development Council, which promotes the sale of mink overseas. Deutsch said two companies, one of them a Canadian subsidiary, accounted for 98 percent of the subsidy funds. "It's corporate welfare at its absolute worse," Deutsch said.

Deutsch invests a lot of his energy in tending to district matters. "Whether it stems from a broad need or the individual constituent, service

While the two cultures that coexist in the 20th are as different as the music of Lawrence Welk and Jimmy Buffett, the retirees and suburbanites of Broward County hold the key to political success in the 20th.

The portion of Broward County in the 20th holds 75 percent of the district's residents. Though Republicans can be competitive here, voters typically support Democrats in statewide elections.

Democrats derive their pivotal backing in Broward from planned retirement villages with heavily Jewish populations, such as Sunrise Lakes. Many of the middle-income retirees who dwell in these sprawling developments hail from areas of New York where, generally speaking, everyone voted, and everyone voted Democratic.

But another important and growing voting bloc in the 20th is the young people who are moving into Broward bedroom communities such as Pembroke Pines (population 65,000), the largest city wholly within the district, and Cooper City (population 21,000). Pembroke Pines grew more than 80 percent in the 1980s, and Cooper City's population almost doubled.

While there is little industry in the district, Motorola has a radio and pager production facility in Broward County. The mainly white professionals and midlevel managers commute to jobs in Miami and Fort Lauderdale along modern highways such as I-595 and I-75.

Although the 20th takes up most of Dade County, this portion of the district is the least significant politically, with about 29,000 registered voters. Hurricane Andrew hammered the

FLORIDA 20
South — Southern and western Broward County; Hollywood; the Keys

largely agricultural community of Homestead in 1992; Homestead Air Force Base, part of which is in the 20th, was later downsized, prompting an exodus of active duty and retired military personnel. The remaining Homestead Air Reserve Base exists alongside a significant Hispanic population.

Much of the district's land area, particularly in western Dade and mainland Monroe counties, has practically no people, but it teems with life: The Florida Everglades is the largest subtropical wilderness in the United States.

Virtually all of Monroe County's 78,000 residents live on the Florida Keys, which stretch 135 miles from the mainland to Key West, the largest city on the Keys, in the Gulf of Mexico.

With its traditions of tolerance, independence and even lawlessness, Key West has a unique political culture. The significant homosexual community routinely forms alliances with Republican environmentalists who battle an entrenched Democratic power structure. Many of these Republicans will not hesitate to vote for a Democrat for statewide office if the candidate has strong environmentalist credentials.

1990 Population: 562,518. White 518,114 (92%), Black 24,913 (4%), Other 19,491 (3%). Hispanic origin 69,459 (12%). 18 and over 440,467 (78%), 62 and over 107,945 (19%). Median age: 37.

to South Florida remains my No. 1 priority," he has said.

One of the "needs" any politician in South Florida must address is the strong yearning that many voters — especially Cuban-Americans — have to see Communist leader Fidel Castro toppled.

In the 104th, Deutsch supported legislation sponsored by Sen. Jesse Helms, R-N.C., and Rep. Dan Burton, R-Ind., tightening the U.S. economic embargo of Cuba. And he joined a bipartisan chorus of politicians railing at Castro in February 1996, after Cuban military planes shot down two civilian aircraft being flown toward the island nation by Cuban-American opponents of Castro.

Deutsch called the shootdown "one of the most brazen, really cruel, vicious, evil acts in the 20th century." He continued: "What this country needs to do . . . is bring the last and only dictator, the last and only Communist ruler in our hemisphere, to an end. We have the power to do that within this building, within this hall, within this chamber, with the help of the chamber on the other side and the support of the president."

In May 1995, Deutsch criticized the Clinton administration after a Coast Guard vessel picked up 13 people who had left Cuba in a raft and returned them to a military base inside Cuba. "Our country has become a partner with Castro in repression of his people," Deutsch said. "The 13 people that have been returned to Cuba . . . were sent back to a country which this government has continuously called . . . the most repressive government in this hemisphere, a terrorist government, a government . . . that stands out as one of the worst abusers of human rights in the history of this planet."

Deutsch successfully lobbied Clinton to issue an executive order in January 1996 allowing photographs of missing children to be displayed in federal buildings. Deutsch acted after a 9-year-old in his district was killed. The boy had last been seen walking home from his Dade County school; a handyman later was arrested and confessed to raping and killing the boy. At Deutsch's urgings, the fiscal 1997 omnibus spending bill included $1.5 million to teach law enforcement officials how to handle missing children cases.

Environmental matters are another big concern in the 20th. Deutsch is an opponent of offshore oil drilling, and he backed a provision in the 1996 farm bill authorizing $200 million for restoring the Everglades. He unsuccessfully pushed legislation requiring Florida's sugar growers to pay an assessment to finance part of the Everglades restoration.

The 1996 Stanley Cup finals gave Deutsch a chance for some local boosterism. He bet on the Florida Panthers hockey team against the eventual Stanley Cup winners, the Colorado Avalanche. Making good on his bet with Patricia Schroeder, D-Colo., Deutsch in June 1996 forked over a Key lime pie. Schroeder's home-state Avalanche whipped Deutsch's Panthers in four straight games.

At Home: Deutsch emerged a comfortable victor after a bruising 1992 campaign for the Democratic nomination in the 20th. Since then he has won re-election by progressively larger margins.

Deutsch started gearing up for a congressional run in 1990 when he became chairman of the state House's congressional reapportionment subcommittee. The Florida district map eventually was drawn by a federal court, but when Deutsch learned that it placed him in the same district with Democrat Dante B. Fascell, a 38-year House veteran, Deutsch said, "He's going to have to beat me." Fascell retired, but he and retiring Reps. Lawrence J. Smith and William Lehman issued a letter of support for Deutsch's primary opponent, Broward County Commissioner Nicki Englander Grossman, saying she alone possessed the "knowledge and temperament" to represent the 20th.

Grossman, a commissioner since 1982, had the support of virtually all the 20th's Democratic leaders. Because the two candidates differed little on substantive issues — both supporting abortion rights, Israel and extending affordable health care to all Americans — their campaigns turned personal. Grossman hammered Deutsch for soliciting money from a lobbyist in front of a reporter. Deutsch, who had a big financial advantage, fought back in a late blitz of mail and TV ads. One flier depicted a bountiful table spread, with the caption "Nicki Grossman put this meal on our tab." The text charged that Grossman had entertained at Broward County taxpayers' expense. Deutsch won the nomination with surprising ease, taking 63 percent of the vote.

In November, GOP nominee Beverly "Bev" Kennedy tried to paint Deutsch as a political insider and emphasized her background as a businesswoman and political neophyte. But she took just 39 percent of the vote and fared no better when she tried a second time in 1994.

In 1996 the Republicans nominated a different candidate, engineer and marine consultant Jim Jacobs, but it made no difference; Deutsch cruised to re-election with 65 percent of the vote.

HOUSE ELECTIONS

1996 General		
Peter Deutsch (D)	159,208	(65%)
Jim Jacobs (R)	85,717	(35%)
1994 General		
Peter Deutsch (D)	114,615	(61%)
Beverly "Bev" Kennedy (R)	72,516	(39%)

Previous Winning Percentages: 1992 (55%)

CAMPAIGN FINANCE

	Receipts	Receipts from PACs		Expend-itures
1996				
Deutsch (D)	$1,139,955	$449,179	(39%)	$435,604
Jacobs (R)	$30,317	$1,100	(4%)	$29,928
1994				
Deutsch (D)	$1,010,949	$435,083	(43%)	$1,011,936
Kennedy (R)	$111,246	$6,014	(5%)	$111,869

KEY VOTES

1997	
Ban "partial birth" abortions	N
1996	
Approve farm bill	Y
Deny public education to illegal immigrants	Y
Repeal ban on certain assault-style weapons	N
Increase minimum wage	Y
Freeze defense spending	Y
Approve welfare overhaul	Y
1995	
Approve balanced-budget constitutional amendment	Y
Relax Clean Water Act regulations	N
Oppose limits on environmental regulations	Y
Reduce projected Medicare spending	N
Approve GOP budget with tax and spending cuts	N

DISTRICT VOTE FOR PRESIDENT

	1996		1992
D	148,297 (59%)	**D**	115,380 (47%)
R	78,704 (31%)	**R**	82,216 (33%)
I	23,296 (9%)	**I**	48,268 (20%)

VOTING STUDIES

	Presidential Support		Party Unity		Conservative Coalition	
Year	**S**	**O**	**S**	**O**	**S**	**O**
1996	78	15	84	13	43	51
1995	76	20	83	14	42	53
1994	83	15	91	8	47	50
1993	87	13	92	7	27	73

INTEREST GROUP RATINGS

Year	ADA	AFL-CIO	CCUS	ACU
1996	70	n/a	53	18
1995	85	92	42	28
1994	60	67	75	19
1993	90	100	18	13

21 Lincoln Diaz-Balart (R)

Of Miami — Elected 1992, 3rd term

Biographical Information

Born: Aug. 13, 1954, Havana, Cuba.

Education: U. of South Florida, B.A. 1976; Case Western Reserve U., J.D. 1979.

Occupation: Lawyer.

Family: Wife, Cristina Fernandez; two children.

Religion: Roman Catholic.

Political Career: Democratic nominee for Fla. House, 1982; Fla. House, 1987-89; Fla. Senate, 1989-92.

Capitol Office: 404 Cannon Bldg. 20515; 225-4211.

Committees

Rules

Rules & Organization of the House

In Washington: Diaz-Balart's choice committee seat — he serves on Rules — reflects the GOP's eagerness to showcase the minority members of the party. But the staunchly conservative tone of the GOP House caused Diaz-Balart to rebel against some key elements of the Republican legislative agenda in the 104th Congress, including bills overhauling the welfare system, curbing illegal immigration and designating English as the federal government's official language. He also tends to support the positions of organized labor, putting him at odds with the GOP's pro-business majority.

But Diaz-Balart's principal goal in Congress has been to keep the economic pressure on the government of Cuba, the nation where he was born, in hopes of ultimately overthrowing Cuban President Fidel Castro. His dedication to Cuban democracy resulted in his arrest outside the White House in May 1995 for protesting the Clinton administration's policy of repatriating Cuban refugees picked up at sea. Diaz-Balart called the policy a "dirty, secret and immoral deal."

An immigrant to America, like his Florida Republican colleague Ileana Ros-Lehtinen, Diaz-Balart refused to sign the House GOP's 1994 "Contract With America" campaign platform. He objected to provisions in its welfare overhaul section that called for denying federal programs to legal immigrants. He and Ros-Lehtinen continued to argue against the provisions as the welfare bill made its way through the 104th. They were the only two Republicans to vote against the bill's final version.

When the House first passed the GOP welfare bill in March 1995, Diaz-Balart said he was "very disappointed" that the bill would deny legal immigrants who have not yet become citizens access to certain government programs, such as Aid to Families with Dependent Children, food stamps and Medicaid.

"I think that ban is unfair. I think it is unnecessary," he said. "I think there is somewhat of an element of irrationality involved because a great percentage of those who may be ineligible, because they are not citizens, will become citizens, so the savings will be minimal at best from the point of view of those who say this ban will save the government money."

He also reacted strongly to a measure that aimed to curb illegal immigration, complaining that the measure was unnecessarily anti-immigrant. "It's simply targeting people because of their political vulnerability," Diaz-Balart said. Both he and Ros-Lehtinen voted against it.

The immigration bill was stalled most of 1996 because of a provision in the House bill that would have allowed states to deny illegal immigrants public schooling. In the end, House conferees agreed to drop the provision, in exchange for a vote on it as a free-standing bill. The House passed it in September 1996 , 254-175, but it went no further.

"We do not blame the children for the conduct of their parents," Diaz-Balart said, adding that it would be "a grave mistake" to adopt the schooling measure. "That, among other reasons, is why we are the moral leader of the world."

Their unhappiness with the welfare and immigration bills caused Diaz-Balart and Ros-Lehtinen in March 1996 to rejoin the Congressional Hispanic Caucus, which is dominated by House Democrats. They had dropped out at the start of the 104th Congress to comply with the spirit of the GOP move to do away with such organizations. But they later decided it was important to show unity as anti-immigrant feelings began to grow throughout the country.

However, in January 1997, Diaz-Balart and Ros-Lehtinen resigned again from the caucus, this time to protest that its chairman, Xavier Becerra, D-Calif., took a trip to Cuba in December 1996.

Diaz-Balart also took exception to a bill declaring English the official language of the federal government, which the House passed, 259-169, in August 1996.

Besides requiring that all official government business be conducted in English, the measure, which was not considered by the Senate, also

FLORIDA 21
Southeast — Part of Dade County; Hialeah

Of South Florida's two Hispanic-majority districts, the 21st is the newest both politically and in its history as a Hispanic stronghold.

The 21st is immediately west of the black-majority 17th District and Hispanic-majority 18th. While the focus of the 18th is Little Havana, where 1960s Cuban exiles settled, the 21st centers on Hialeah, where many of those exiles later relocated.

Although Rep. Ileana Ros-Lehtinen hoped to amass as many Cuban-Americans as possible into her 18th District, the 21st actually has the state's highest percentage of Hispanics, 70 percent. Republicans make impressive showings here. Bob Dole captured 50 percent of the vote here in 1996, George Bush took 58 percent in 1992. Diaz-Balart rarely has a Democratic challenger.

Much of the district's fierce Republicanism can be traced to Hialeah, which accounts for about one-third of district residents. Hialeah began growing rapidly after World War II, when many soldiers who trained in South Florida moved to the area. In the 1960s and 1970s, it became increasingly popular with middle-to-low-income Cuban-Americans looking for more space than they could find in Miami. Its location near the airport made it accessible to jobs there, and it offered a mix of midsize single-family homes and apartment complexes.

Hialeah also has a large industrial area. Much of the apparel industry there has been struggling recently with competition from imports, especially from Caribbean Basin countries that have cheaper labor costs. The package delivery company UPS has its main South Florida facility near here. Also present is the Hialeah racetrack. Politicians make a point of stopping by Chico's to eat black beans and rice, drink Cuban coffee and shake hands.

Farther south is Miami Springs, a largely Republican and Anglo bedroom suburb of Miami. An unincorporated area west of the airport, known as Doral, is growing fast thanks to industry and corporate relocations. Ryder Systems, with its truck and airplane rentals, has its world headquarters here. Carnival Cruise Lines, a district office of the Federal Reserve and IVAX, a biotechnology company, also are in the area. There is also some light industry, primarily distribution centers with economic ties to the airport. Sweetwater, another predominantly Hispanic municipality, attracts Cubans and Nicaraguans and has a high concentration of elderly residents.

The fast-growing area of Kendall in the district is generally Anglo; it also has some second-generation Cuban-Americans. It is considerably more Democratic than the district as a whole. Kendall Lakes is more compact, conservative and older. Tamiami is a generally Hispanic area, with young professionals in single-family homes and a strong Republican orientation.

1990 Population: 562,519. White 492,513 (88%), Black 23,073 (4%), Other 46,933 (8%). Hispanic origin 391,534 (70%). 18 and over 424,355 (75%), 62 and over 70,384 (13%). Median age: 33.

repealed a federal law mandating that states with large concentrations of non-English speaking voters provide bilingual ballots. That section of the bill riled Diaz-Balart.

"I say that portion, the Voting Rights Act portion of this legislation, which constitutes aggression on linguistic minorities in this country, is anti-democratic," he told the House.

Diaz-Balart is sympathetic to the concerns of labor unions. He voted for a Democratic-backed bill raising the minimum wage by 90 cents an hour and against a GOP measure that would have exempted small businesses from the wage boost. He also has opposed a measure that would have allowed companies to offer their workers compensatory time off in lieu of overtime pay. Labor groups said the bill might lead to companies coercing workers to take whatever form of compensation management preferred.

But it was his focus on ways to continue to isolate Castro that mostly occupied Diaz-Balart in the 104th. He blasted the Clinton administration for its opposition to the so-called Helms-Burton bill — named for its sponsors, Senate Foreign Relations Chairman Jesse Helms of North Carolina and Indiana Republican Rep. Dan Burton — that aimed to punish foreign companies that invest in Cuba.

Clinton ended up supporting the measure after February 1996, when Cuban military planes shot down two civilian aircraft being flown toward the island nation by Cuban-American opponents of Castro, killing four.

After intense negotiations with the administration, House and Senate conferees hammered out a final bill that was harder on Castro's government than either the original House or Senate bill.

At the administration's request, the conferees gave the president power to postpone indefinitely legal action authorized by the bill, either by delaying the effective date of the provision or by suspending the right to bring lawsuits. But they added tough new restrictions barring executives from foreign companies that "traffic " in expropriated properties claimed by a U.S. national, along with their families, from entering the United

States. The measure was sharply criticized by Canada and the European Union.

In July 1996, Clinton allowed the lawsuit provision to take effect, but exercised the option to block legal actions for at least six months, which he did again in January 1997. That effort to find the middle ground caused Diaz-Balart to argue that Clinton had caved in to pressure from foreign economic interests. "Character of Jell-O, backbone of Jell-O," said Diaz-Balart, "that's what President Clinton demonstrated today."

But administration officials contended that the threat of imminent lawsuits should be enough to persuade overseas companies and investors to pull out of Cuba and help bring down the Castro regime.

Also included in the Cuba sanctions bill was a provision pushed by Diaz-Balart designed to bolster the ability of a government-funded television station, TV Marti, to beam independent news and entertainment into Cuba. The shows are rarely seen because its single television signal is routinely blocked by Cuban jammers.

The sanctions bill would allow TV Marti to switch broadcast frequencies from VHF to UHF channels, which Diaz-Balart said would be harder to jam. He said Cuba would have to scramble to jam signals that could be received throughout the island on a variety of channels because jamming equipment in Havana is immobile and not designed to block UHF signals. But the failure of TV Marti to penetrate the wall of jamming has prompted some lawmakers to call for scrapping it entirely.

At Home: Diaz-Balart was born in Havana to a prosperous and politically active family. His grandfather, father and uncle served in Cuba's House before the family fled to the United States in 1960.

Diaz-Balart secured his 1992 election to the House by first working overtime as a state senator to ensure that Miami would have a second Hispanic-majority district after redistricting. Ultimately, it took a court-drawn plan to accomplish what a deadlocked Legislature and Diaz-Balart's efforts could not.

He then easily bested a fellow Cuban-American state senator in a two-way Republican primary that turned personal and nasty. That hurdle cleared, in November he drew no Democratic opposition.

Diaz-Balart won the primary against Javier D. Souto, a less polished fellow state senator whose anti-Castro credentials were more impeccable in the exile community than Diaz-Balart's. Souto also fled Cuba in 1960 and trained in the United States for an invasion of Cuba. He later infiltrated the country to set up organized resistance to Castro. Souto ran a less visible, less well-financed campaign, and despite his amiable style, he tried to make an issue over whose anti-Castro rhetoric was more believable. The negative campaigning seemed to backfire. He managed only 31 percent to Diaz-Balart's 69 percent, in a sparse, hurricane-delayed primary. Since then, Diaz-Balart has had no major-party challenger.

HOUSE ELECTIONS

1996 General
Lincoln Diaz-Balart (R) — unopposed

1994 General
Lincoln Diaz-Balart (R) — unopposed

Previous Winning Percentages: 1992 (100%)

CAMPAIGN FINANCE

	Receipts	Receipts from PACs	Expend-itures
1996			
Diaz-Balart (R)	$381,906	$174,316 (46%)	$130,085
1994			
Diaz-Balart (R)	$357,384	$123,103 (34%)	$125,082

DISTRICT VOTE FOR PRESIDENT

	1996		1992
D	72,892 (45%)	**D**	47,576 (32%)
R	82,413 (50%)	**R**	86,187 (58%)
I	7,903 (5%)	**I**	15,852 (11%)

KEY VOTES

1997	
Ban "partial birth" abortions	Y
1996	
Approve farm bill	Y
Deny public education to illegal immigrants	N
Repeal ban on certain assault-style weapons	Y
Increase minimum wage	Y
Freeze defense spending	N
Approve welfare overhaul	N
1995	
Approve balanced-budget constitutional amendment	Y
Relax Clean Water Act regulations	N
Oppose limits on environmental regulations	Y
Reduce projected Medicare spending	Y
Approve GOP budget with tax and spending cuts	Y

VOTING STUDIES

	Presidential Support		Party Unity		Conservative Coalition	
Year	**S**	**O**	**S**	**O**	**S**	**O**
1996	49	47	75	22	88	10
1995	26	74	87	12	96	3
1994	60	38	71	29	78	19
1993	60	38	75	23	75	23

INTEREST GROUP RATINGS

Year	ADA	AFL-CIO	CCUS	ACU
1996	30	n/a	60	60
1995	20	25	79	72
1994	25	78	83	71
1993	35	83	73	75

22 E. Clay Shaw Jr. (R)

Of Fort Lauderdale — Elected 1980, 9th term

Biographical Information
Born: April 19, 1939, Miami, Fla.
Education: Stetson U., B.S. 1961; U. of Alabama, M.B.A. 1963; Stetson U., J.D. 1966.
Occupation: Nurseryman; lawyer.
Family: Wife, Emilie Costar; four children.
Religion: Roman Catholic.
Political Career: Fort Lauderdale assistant city attorney, 1968; Fort Lauderdale chief city prosecutor, 1968-69; Fort Lauderdale associate municipal judge, 1969-71; Fort Lauderdale City Commission, 1971-73; vice mayor of Fort Lauderdale, 1973-75; mayor of Fort Lauderdale, 1975-81.
Capitol Office: 2408 Rayburn Bldg. 20515; 225-3026.

Committees
Ways & Means
Human Resources (chairman); Trade

In Washington: President Clinton promised to "end welfare as we know it," but the promise might not have been fulfilled by the 104th Congress without the efforts of pragmatic conservatives like Shaw.

As chairman of the House Ways and Means Subcommittee on Human Resources, Shaw worked sedulously through the 104th to shape a welfare overhaul plan that conservative Republicans could accept and that at least some Democrats could stomach. He helped produce three versions; Clinton vetoed legislation with the first two versions, but he signed the third into law, after it had passed the House with nearly unanimous GOP backing and consent from exactly half the Democrats (98 voted for it, 98 against).

Even after Clinton announced he would sign the bill, Shaw kept on preaching the importance of bipartisan cooperation. "Let's be patient with each other," he said. "And let's work together over the next few years to be sure this works."

The overhaul transformed a major federal entitlement program into a block grant to the states. It ended the federal guarantee to provide welfare checks to all eligible low-income mothers and children. Federal funding would be sent to states in predetermined lump-sum payments, with recipients required to work within two years and limited to five years of benefits. An array of federal benefits, including food stamps and Supplemental Security Income, were denied to most legal immigrants.

Shaw and other GOP lawmakers argued that getting the federal government out of the way would allow welfare programs to be customized to fit local needs. They also counted on motivating welfare recipients by imposing the work requirements and limits on benefits.

"What we're looking for is an attitudinal change across the entire country," Shaw said. The idea was to make welfare "not a way of life, but simply a short-term bridge over tough times."

Shaw argued in February 1997 that the new bill may actually be a boon for welfare recipients. With fewer people receiving welfare and the amount of federal funds available expected to remain about the same, those still on the rolls will benefit, Shaw said. "States are going to have more money to help the needy prepare to enter the labor force. The more we start talking about people having to go to work, the more we find they are getting off the welfare rolls. The threat of welfare reform is already having a very significant impact" on the decline of caseloads, he said.

At the same time, Shaw raised the possibility that the 1996 legislation might not be the last word on the subject of welfare; he agreed to consider new aid to states to help care for legal immigrants who stand to lose food stamps and other federal benefits under the new law. "It is something we are going to take a look at," Shaw said. Any aid would be in the form of additional block grants to the states, he said.

While Shaw said he would work with the administration to help welfare recipients find jobs in inner cities, he gave a cold shoulder to calls from Clinton and other Democrats for some substantive changes to the welfare law. "We've already crossed that bridge, and I don't want to go back," he said.

Even before the Republicans took control of the House in 1995, Shaw publicly called for a cooperative effort between Democrats and Republicans to craft a workable, bipartisan approach to overhauling welfare. He expressed concern over several of the specifics in the GOP's "Contract With America," saying they might be "unduly harsh," and signaled early in the 104th that he did not necessarily intend to use the contract as a starting point for a subcommittee bill.

In particular, he questioned a proposal to deny cash benefits to unwed mothers younger than 18. And he scoffed at suggestions by some GOP leaders, including House Speaker Newt Gingrich, that the children of these mothers possibly should be placed in orphanages.

"I would rather rehabilitate human beings," Shaw said. "I think the party that prides itself in family values will not support warehousing kids

FLORIDA 22

Southeast — Coastal Broward, Dade and Palm Beach counties; Fort Lauderdale

The 22nd is a long shoestring of a district, hugging the south Atlantic coast from Juno Beach south to Miami Beach. It is roughly 90 miles long and in some places just a few blocks wide. Its width never extends beyond three miles.

The strange shape, which enables the 22nd to pick up fragments of about 50 different municipalities, was dictated largely by the desire to place minority-oriented neighborhoods in districts to the west, notably the 23rd. Four House incumbents lived within its borders when the 22nd was drawn in 1992.

Most residents of the coastal neighborhoods are white, and their economic status ranges from comfortable to wealthy. Corporate executives abound. There are also quite a few retirees in oceanfront condominiums.

The district is less Republican than the state overall, and thus competitive politically. Although George Bush captured 57 percent of the presidential vote here in 1988, he lost the district to Bill Clinton in 1992. Clinton won again in 1996, capturing 54 percent of the vote to 38 percent for Bob Dole. Though Shaw had an easy time winning re-election in 1996, polling 62 percent of the vote, his re-election bid in 1992 was one of the state's most fiercely fought that year.

Within the borders of the 22nd are the ports of Palm Beach and Fort Lauderdale, as well as the mouth of the port of Miami. The district also contains the Miami Beach and Fort Lauderdale convention centers, the performing arts center in Miami Beach, the famous Breakers hotel in Palm Beach and Fountainbleau in Miami Beach, fashionable shopping areas such as Worth Avenue in Palm Beach and Las Olas Boulevard in Fort Lauderdale, and miles of beaches.

Partisan orientations vary considerably among the municipalities within Broward County. Hallandale is strongly Democratic, while Hollywood is more competitive.

Republicans hold the upper hand in Pompano Beach and Fort Lauderdale, which has the largest concentration of district residents. Fort Lauderdale is dominated by conservative Democrats and Republicans, an outgrowth of the conservative retirees who settled there from the Midwest three decades ago. Fort Lauderdale is still less influenced by the liberal attitudes of Northeastern Jewish émigrés than are most other major South Florida cities.

Democrats start with a solid base in the Dade County portions of the district, which have more of the Northeastern influence. They include the huge condominiums that line Biscayne Boulevard in the northeast part of the county, whose residents form a potent voting bloc. These southernmost stretches of the 22nd are heavily Jewish and more Hispanic than other parts of the district. Clinton got 71 percent of the vote in the Dade County portion of the district in 1996.

Republicans have a clear edge in the Palm Beach part. The city of Palm Beach is affluent and staunchly Republican.

1990 Population: 562,519. White 529,651 (94%), Black 16,795 (3%), Other 16,073 (3%). Hispanic origin 72,140 (13%). 18 and over 490,832 (87%), 62 and over 196,619 (35%). Median age: 48.

in orphanages." He also said that he was reluctant on welfare to "simply box it up and ship it" to the states.

But GOP leaders, including Texas Republican Bill Archer, chairman of Ways and Means, subsequently sent Shaw a message: Stick to the contract.

By March 1995, Shaw acknowledged that his views had changed. "There is an evolution of thought there," he said. "I'm not denying that at all. It's not an inconsistency." For instance, after listening to testimony on the issue of not providing cash benefits to unwed teenage mothers, Shaw said he concluded that unwed teens "are not responsible enough to raise their kids. One witness referred to it as federally funded child abuse."

When it came time to mark up the measure in subcommittee, Shaw demonstrated little desire to compromise with Democrats on the main points of the bill. In June 1996, for example, he argued against an amendment by Charles B. Rangel, D-N.Y., to provide vouchers to children of welfare recipients who exceeded the five-year time limit on benefits. Shaw noted that states could exempt up to 20 percent of their welfare recipients from the time limit. When asked whether that would be enough exemptions to meet the need, Shaw said, "Is there a point in time where people have to take responsibility for their own lives and their family's lives?" The amendment failed, 3-8.

Shaw also won a victory when Republican leaders, discounting the advice of many on the GOP right flank, decided not to combine the welfare legislation with a Medicaid overhaul that Clinton had promised to veto. "This really puts it on the president's back, whether he's for welfare reform or not," Shaw said.

When Clinton vetoed the welfare bill in January 1996, Shaw argued that the president did not really want to change the system. "President Clinton, who ran on a promise to end welfare as we know it, unfortunately listened to the extreme liberal wing of his party and left the current welfare system in place," Shaw said.

But Shaw came back with a new version of the welfare bill. He repeatedly urged members from both parties to be flexible to get a bill enacted, and eventually his persistence paid off. At a time when congressional Republicans were hungry to burnish their image as capable of governing — and thus deserving of voter support for a continued majority in the 105th Congress — enactment of welfare reform was a major image booster for the GOP.

On an issue of parochial interest, Shaw — who represents an area with a large number of elderly residents — sponsored legislation protecting senior citizen housing complexes from discrimination lawsuits. Federal law generally prohibits discrimination against families with children. Housing complexes for senior citizens were excepted, but it had been unclear which housing qualifies. Shaw's measure defined senior citizen housing complexes as those in which at least 80 percent of the units are occupied by at least one person who is 55 or older.

At Home: Shaw polled 62 percent of the vote in 1996, his second consecutive easy victory following a tough race after 1992's redistricting.

In that 1992 contest, Shaw was pitted against Democratic state Senate President Gwen Margolis in the most expensive and one of the most contentious House races in Florida. She had an edge in the portions of Dade County in the 22nd, which she represented in the Legislature and which are strongly Democratic. Shaw, whose base is in Fort Lauderdale, got early support from the north, in coastal Palm Beach County, where Republicans predominate.

Margolis had a high-profile role in the state Senate, where she was occasionally criticized for being divisive. Her attempts to draw a House district favorable to herself contributed to a remapping stalemate.

She characterized Shaw as an extreme conservative who opposed abortion, handgun control and the family leave bill. Shaw attacked Margolis as a tax-and-spend liberal whose ineffective leadership created legislative chaos. He stressed that while he opposed federal funding for abortion, he supported a woman's right to an abortion in the first trimester of pregnancy.

Shaw's edge in Palm Beach County canceled Margolis' advantage in Dade, and he swamped her by nearly 2-to-1 in the populous Broward County portions of the 22nd. He won with 52 percent of the vote, and in 1994 he jumped to 63 percent against a wealthy Palm Beach heiress.

It was Democratic squabbling that helped Shaw secure the old 15th District. In 1980, Democratic primary voters dumped 70-year-old Rep. Edward J. Stack for a younger candidate, former state Rep. Alan Becker. Shaw, who had been mayor of Fort Lauderdale since 1975, was unopposed for the GOP nomination. Shaw denounced Becker as a liberal carpetbagger; the Democrat had moved into the 15th in 1979 after four terms in the Legislature representing North Miami. Shaw won with 55 percent.

HOUSE ELECTIONS

1996 General		
E. Clay Shaw Jr. (R)	137,070	(62%)
Kenneth D. Cooper (D)	84,496	(38%)
1994 General		
E. Clay Shaw Jr. (R)	119,690	(63%)
Hermine L. Wiener (D)	69,215	(37%)

Previous Winning Percentages: **1992** (52%) **1990** (98%) **1988** (66%) **1986** (100%) **1984** (66%) **1982** (57%) **1980** (55%)

CAMPAIGN FINANCE

	Receipts	Receipts from PACs	Expend-itures
1996			
Shaw (R)	$764,768	$428,932 (56%)	$548,109
Cooper (D)	$85,078	$14,300 (17%)	$85,040
1994			
Shaw (R)	$860,784	$407,627 (47%)	$808,984
Wiener (D)	$530,400	$39,300 (7%)	$522,269

DISTRICT VOTE FOR PRESIDENT

1996	1992
D 124,685 (54%)	**D** 114,320 (45%)
R 86,653 (38%)	**R** 94,972 (37%)
I 17,409 (8%)	**I** 44,238 (17%)

VOTING STUDIES

	Presidential Support		Party Unity		Conservative Coalition	
Year	**S**	**O**	**S**	**O**	**S**	**O**
1996	39	58	87	10	88	8
1995	25	75	90	9	92	6
1994	60	35	85	11	89	6
1993	48	51	86	12	98	2
1992	75	24	76	20	92	6
1991	80	17	78	16	97	0

KEY VOTES

1997	
Ban "partial birth" abortions	Y
1996	
Approve farm bill	Y
Deny public education to illegal immigrants	Y
Repeal ban on certain assault-style weapons	?
Increase minimum wage	Y
Freeze defense spending	N
Approve welfare overhaul	Y
1995	
Approve balanced-budget constitutional amendment	Y
Relax Clean Water Act regulations	Y
Oppose limits on environmental regulations	Y
Reduce projected Medicare spending	Y
Approve GOP budget with tax and spending cuts	Y

INTEREST GROUP RATINGS

Year	ADA	AFL-CIO	CCUS	ACU
1996	10	n/a	94	95
1995	15	0	96	68
1994	15	13	92	74
1993	10	17	91	92
1992	15	25	75	84
1991	0	17	100	90

23 Alcee L. Hastings (D)

Of Miramar — Elected 1992, 3rd term

Biographical Information

Born: Sept. 5, 1936, Altamonte Springs, Fla.

Education: Fisk U., B.A. 1958; Howard U., 1958-60; Florida A&M U., J.D. 1963.

Occupation: Lawyer.

Family: Divorced; three children.

Religion: African Methodist Episcopal.

Political Career: U.S. District Court judge, 1979-89; Democratic nominee for Fla. secretary of state, 1990.

Capitol Office: 1039 Longworth Bldg. 20515; 225-1313.

Committees

International Relations
Africa; Asia & the Pacific

Science
Space & Aeronautics

In Washington: Hastings is not the first federal judge to serve in Congress, but he is the first one to serve after the House impeached him on bribery charges and sent his case to the Senate, which convicted him and removed him from office.

With such a history, it is not surprising that Hastings was greeted in Washington by skepticism that he would be able to work effectively with members who had voted in 1988 to impeach him.

But Hastings has surprised the skeptics by bearing no apparent grudges about the past and by focusing instead on building legislative influence.

"Succeeding is the best revenge," he said after nine months in office. "My goal was to get beyond people viewing me as an impeached judge. I think I've accomplished that in grand style."

He has done that, in part, through his work on the International Relations Committee, where he is a strong supporter of aid to Africa and an equally strong defender of President Clinton. In the 104th Congress, he unsuccessfully tried in committee to beat back Republican-backed legislation aimed at reducing support for United Nations' peacekeeping efforts. Hastings' proposal essentially would have allowed the administration to continuing paying its U.N. bills in the same fashion as other U.N. member states.

Hastings was a member of an International Relations select subcommittee formed to investigate Iran's arming of Bosnian Muslims. Republicans alleged that the Clinton administration knew about the arms operation, tacitly approved of it and did not inform Congress, while all the time publicly professing support of an international embargo on arming the Bosnians. Hastings and the other subcommittee Democrats portrayed Republicans as pursuing the inquiry just to score election-year political points against Clinton. "It is our belief that no laws were broken, no wrongdoing occurred, no covert actions took place, no false statements given, no U.S. interests harmed," said a statement by Hastings, Lee H. Hamilton of Indiana, and Howard L. Berman of California.

When the House took up legislation authorizing the activities of the State Department through fiscal 1997, Hastings joined his fellow Democrats in refusing to sign the conference report. "This conference report is just another example of this Congress micromanaging foreign policy and preventing the president from doing his job," he said.

And when the committee held hearings into Clinton's Haiti policy, Democrats countered Republican criticism of the administration with charges that the GOP was engaged in an election-year effort to tarnish the president's success in restoring democratic rule to Haiti. Hastings called the Republican criticisms of Clinton's Haiti policy "pure, unadulterated political posturing."

Hastings has not always been enamored of Clinton's foreign policies. Long before Clinton sent the U.S. military into Haiti in September 1994, Hastings and other black caucus members called for military intervention to restore President Jean-Bertrand Aristide. In May 1994, he was one of three lawmakers arrested for demonstrating in front of the White House against the U.S. policy of returning Haitian refugees to their country.

In July 1993, Hastings traveled to Sudan with other members of the Africa Subcommittee and saw firsthand the mass starvation there. In June 1994, he sponsored a resolution condemning the widespread killings in Rwanda and called the atrocities genocide. He said the White House had not done enough to address the problem: "This administration has been avoiding using the term genocide in connection with Rwanda for fear that if we call it genocide we will have to take steps to stop the killing," he said.

Hastings also tends to matters closer to home. He buttonholed votes on the House floor to stave off an attempt in the 1995 farm bill to phase out the sugar subsidy over five years. When the vote was announced, 208-217, and the motion was defeated, Hastings shot a thumbs-up at the galleries and the sugar lobbyists let out a cheer.

Appealing to the strong antipathy in South

One of the most unusual creatures in Florida's congressional map for the 1990s is the kitelike 23rd.

The district extends over seven counties. Most of its landmass is in western St. Lucie, Martin and Palm Beach counties, near Lake Okeechobee. But most of the people in the 23rd live inland from the Atlantic, along a narrow strip that follows Interstate 95. Half the district residents live in Broward County; one-third live in Palm Beach County.

The district is heavily Democratic and designed to help black House candidates, though the election of an African-American was not assured. Blacks account for only a bare majority of the district's total population and about 44 percent of its voting-age population.

Agriculture dominates the western part of the district. Western St. Lucie and Martin counties as well as southeast Okeechobee County are citrus territory, with vegetable and lettuce crops also attracting some migrant workers. Although the sugar industry has a strong presence near Belle Glade in western Palm Beach County, U.S. Sugar's closing of a vegetable plant in 1994 translated into a loss of 700 jobs. Although Okeechobee is mostly white, the rest of this part of the district includes a high percentage of blacks and some Hispanics. The northeastern part of the district also extends into Fort Pierce to include most of its black neighborhoods.

The long strip of the district that runs adjacent to I-95 includes many public sector workers, especially county government and public school employees. Public employee unions are strong political organizing forces, as are neighborhood associations.

The residents of Riviera Beach, an overwhelmingly black city, cast an extraordinarily high percentage of their votes for Democrats. Most residents are middle-class, and some work at the nearby Pratt & Whitney plant. The portions of West Palm Beach in the district, which are also majority-black, include some neighborhoods that attract professionals. The portions that are in the 23rd from Delray Beach and Boynton Beach are about one-half black; Lake Worth is a little less so. The part of Boca Raton included is overwhelmingly white and a GOP enclave.

FLORIDA 23
Southeast — Parts of St. Lucie, Martin, Broward and Palm Beach counties

Heading into Broward, the parts of Deerfield Beach and especially Pompano Beach in the 23rd are majority-black. Deerfield Beach is mainly lower middle-class, with some farm workers commuting west, while Pompano is more middle-class.

The district broadens somewhat in Broward County to include mainly black neighborhoods in Fort Lauderdale and, to the west, Lauderhill and Lauderdale Lakes. But it also includes predominantly white areas of Lauderdale Lakes that are middle-class and, in some cases, retirement-oriented.

Norland, a predominantly black area, accounts for most of the district's residents in Dade County. Before Hastings won the 23rd in 1992, he had a law office there.

1990 Population: 562,519. White 251,923 (45%), Black 290,519 (52%), Other 20,077 (4%). Hispanic origin 52,706 (9%). 18 and over 407,318 (72%), 62 and over 86,056 (15%). Median age: 32.

Florida toward Cuban leader Fidel Castro, Hastings took to the House floor in February 1996, after Cuban military planes shot down two civilian aircraft being flown toward the island nation by Cuban-American opponents of Castro.

"I would hate like the dickens to feel that an unarmed airplane coming into the United States with no obvious military mission would be shot down," he said. "We have forced planes down from Cuba into Florida air space without having to shoot them down and certainly had the ability to shoot them down. On that score, there is no question but that the act itself was extremely ruthless, and appropriate action and response should be undertaken."

And in a state with a large number of retirees, Hastings spoke out on the against Republican efforts to reduce projected spending increases on Medicare. "As the Republicans in Congress move toward their goal of reducing the federal deficit at any cost, they are about to approve deep, unprecedented cuts in the financing and delivery of health care to our nation's elderly and poor," Hastings said. "These cuts will be far deeper, and have far greater consequences than the proposed cuts in almost any other part of the budget, totaling $270 billion over seven years, while financing a tax break for the wealthy. I am concerned that these draconian cuts will overwhelm my district, and the nation."

He called GOP efforts to restrain Medicaid costs "equally disheartening" and said the GOP plan "is soaked in demographic denial [because] it ignores Florida's status as a growth state. Under the Republican proposal, the annual Medicaid growth rate would be capped at a percentage far below what the state would need to take care of its underserved and unserved population."

Hastings was confident enough in his legislative role to run for chairman of the Congressional Black Caucus for the 104th Congress, but the caucus picked Democrat

Donald M. Payne of New Jersey, a lower-key compromiser, over Hastings by a secret ballot vote of 23-15. "I had great ideas, and he had the numbers," said Hastings, who described Payne as "extremely capable." In the 105th Congress, he did not seek the caucus chairmanship again; it went to Maxine Waters, D-Calif.

The Senate removed Hastings from the federal bench in 1989. On Sept. 17, 1992, a federal judge in Washington ruled that the Senate improperly evicted Hastings because a committee of senators, not the full Senate, heard the case. But in January 1993, the Supreme Court ruled in another case that federal courts have no constitutional authority to review the proceedings of Senate impeachment trials.

Hastings faced another legal challenge in 1993 when a Florida law student tried to have his House election nullified on grounds that he was disqualified from federal office when the Senate removed him from the bench. The suit was dismissed.

When the House in January 1997 approved sanctions against Speaker Newt Gingrich for violating House rules, Hastings was one of only five Democrats to vote "present."

At Home: Hastings ran unsuccessfully for Florida secretary of state in 1990, but he won a majority of the votes in the areas that subsequently constituted the new 23rd District. Remappers designed the 23rd as a "minority access" district, giving it just a slight black majority — enough to offer minorities a chance, but no guarantee, of electing one of their own to the seat. Hastings tried for the seat in 1992, believing a black candidate with high name recognition could beat front-running state Rep. Lois Frankel, a progressive white Democrat.

Frankel contended that her record demonstrated a commitment to issues important to white and black constituents, but Hastings shot back that she was a white opportunist who should not run in a district that ought to be represented by a minority.

Frankel took 35 percent to Hastings' 28 percent in the primary. Hastings surged past her in the runoff to win nomination with 58 percent. In November against GOP real estate developer Ed Fielding, he won 59 percent, and his subsequent re-elections have been suspenseless.

HOUSE ELECTIONS

1996 General		
Alcee L. Hastings (D)	102,146	(73%)
Robert Paul Brown (R)	36,897	(27%)
1994 General		
Alcee L. Hastings (D)	unopposed	

CAMPAIGN FINANCE

	Receipts	Receipts from PACs		Expend-itures
1996				
Hastings (D)	$301,424	$119,150	(40%)	$276,708
Brown (R)	$13,450	$5,000	(37%)	$13,417
1994				
Hastings (D)	$236,918	$103,495	(44%)	$217,742

DISTRICT VOTE FOR PRESIDENT

	1996		1992
D	106,540 (75%)	**D**	99,156 (61%)
R	26,158 (18%)	**R**	39,299 (24%)
I	8,987 (6%)	**I**	23,756 (15%)

KEY VOTES

1997	
Ban "partial birth" abortions	N
1996	
Approve farm bill	?
Deny public education to illegal immigrants	N
Repeal ban on certain assault-style weapons	N
Increase minimum wage	Y
Freeze defense spending	N
Approve welfare overhaul	N
1995	
Approve balanced-budget constitutional amendment	N
Relax Clean Water Act regulations	N
Oppose limits on environmental regulations	Y
Reduce projected Medicare spending	N
Approve GOP budget with tax and spending cuts	N

VOTING STUDIES

	Presidential Support		Party Unity		Conservative Coalition	
Year	S	O	S	O	S	O
1996	82	14	89	7	45	51
1995	82	14	92	5	23	77
1994	64	18	77	2	17	64
1993	89	11	90	3	18	73

INTEREST GROUP RATINGS

Year	ADA	AFL-CIO	CCUS	ACU
1996	95	n/a	20	0
1995	95	100	8	4
1994	80	88	36	7
1993	90	92	18	4

GEORGIA

Governor: Zell Miller (D)
First elected: 1990
Length of term: 4 years
Term expires: 1/99
Salary: $107,197
Term limit: 2 terms
Phone: (404) 656-1776
Born: Feb. 24, 1932; Young Harris, Ga.
Education: Young Harris Junior College, 1951; U. of Georgia, A.B. 1957, M.A. 1958.
Military Service: Marine Corps, 1953-56.
Occupation: Professor.
Family: Wife, Shirley Ann Carver; two children.
Religion: Methodist.
Political Career: Mayor of Young Harris, 1959-60; Ga. Senate, 1961-65; sought Democratic nomination for U.S. House, 1964, 1966; lieutenant governor, 1975-91; sought Democratic nomination for U.S. Senate, 1980.

Lt. Gov.: Pierre Howard (D)
First elected: 1990
Length of term: 4 years
Term expires: 1/99
Salary: $70,011
Phone: (404) 656-5030

State election official: (404) 656-2871
Democratic headquarters: (404) 874-1994
Republican headquarters: (404) 365-7700

REDISTRICTING

Georgia gained one House seat in reapportionment, increasing to 11. Legislature passed map March 31, 1992; governor signed March 31. A new map with minor changes became law July 19, 1993. Federal court on Sept. 12, 1994, invalidated 11th District, halted election. Supreme Court stayed decision Sept. 23, allowing election. Supreme Court on June 29, 1995, struck the 11th District. A three-judge federal panel struck the 2nd District on Oct. 30, 1995. The panel imposed a new congressional map on Dec. 13, 1995. Supreme Court heard appeal Dec. 9, 1996.

STATE LEGISLATURE

General Assembly. Meets January to mid-March.

Senate: 56 members, 2-year terms
1996 breakdown: 34D, 22R; 49 men, 7 women
Salary: $11,347.80
Phone: (404) 656-0028

House of Representatives: 180 members, 2-year terms
1996 breakdown: 103D, 77R; 148 men, 32 women
Salary: $11,347.80
Phone: (404) 656-5082

URBAN STATISTICS

City	Population
Atlanta Mayor Bill Campbell, D	394,017
Columbus Mayor Bobby Peters, N-P	178,681
Savannah Mayor Floyd Adams Jr., N-P	137,560
Macon Mayor Jim Marshall, N-P	106,612
Albany Mayor Thomas Coleman, N-P	78,122

U.S. CONGRESS

Senate: 1 D, 1 R
House: 3 D, 8 R

TERM LIMITS

For state offices: No

ELECTIONS

1996 Presidential Vote

Bob Dole	47%
Bill Clinton	46%
Ross Perot	6%

1992 Presidential Vote

Bill Clinton	43%
George Bush	43%
Ross Perot	13%

1988 Presidential Vote

George Bush	60%
Michael S. Dukakis	40%

POPULATION

1990 population		6,478,216
1980 population		5,463,105
Percent change		+19%
Rank among states:		11
White		71%
Black		27%
Hispanic		2%
Asian or Pacific islander		1%
Urban		63%
Rural		37%
Born in state		65%
Foreign-born		3%
Under age 18	1,727,303	27%
Ages 18-64	4,096,643	63%
65 and older	654,270	10%
Median age		31.6

MISCELLANEOUS

Capital: Atlanta
Number of counties: 159
Per capita income: $17,364 (1991)
Rank among states: 29
Total area: 58,910 sq. miles
Rank among states: 21

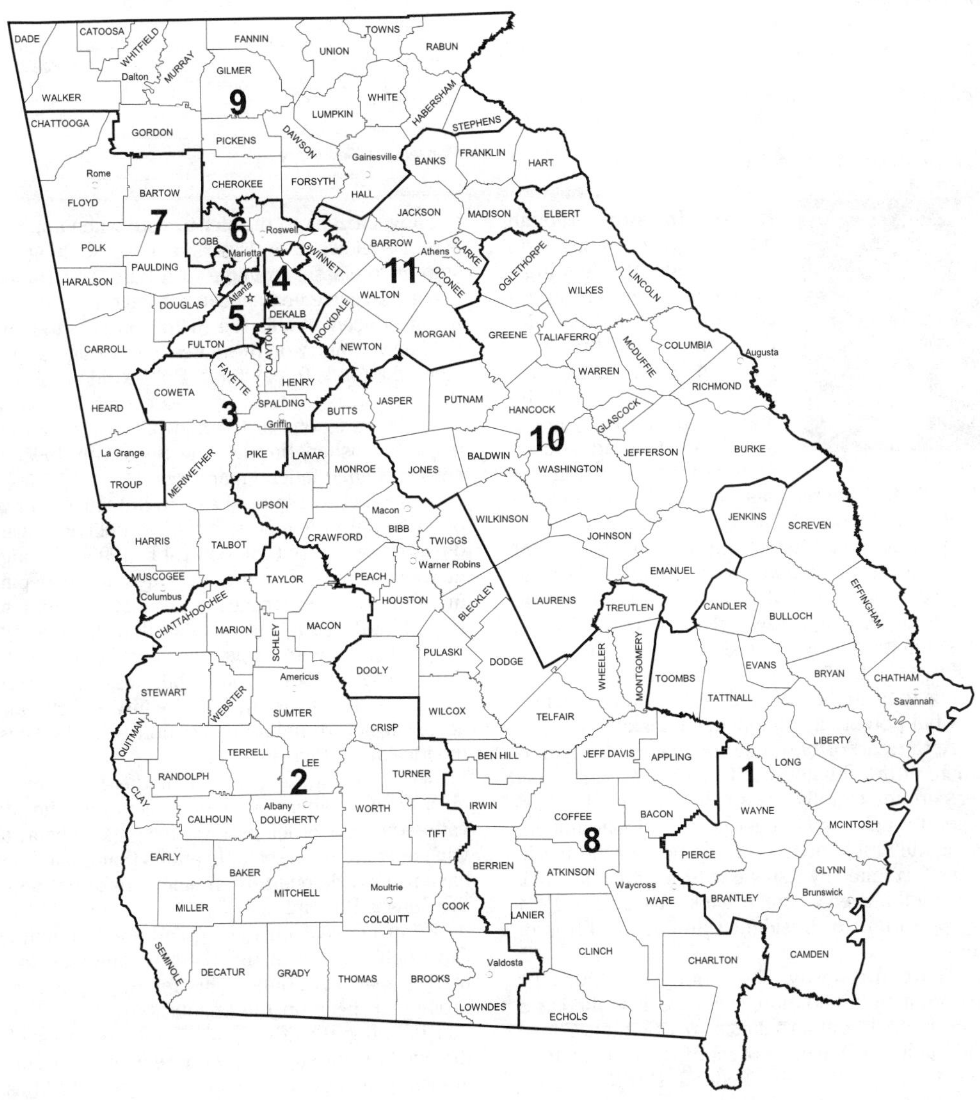
DADE
CATOOSA
WHITFIELD
Dalton
MURRAY
FANNIN
UNION
TOWNS
RABUN
GILMER
WALKER
9
WHITE
LUMPKIN
HABERSHAM
STEPHENS
CHATTOOGA
GORDON
PICKENS
DAWSON
Gainesville
BANKS
FRANKLIN
HART
Rome
BARTOW
CHEROKEE
FORSYTH
HALL
FLOYD
7
6
Roswell
JACKSON
MADISON
ELBERT
POLK
COBB
Marietta
GWINNETT
BARROW
Athens
CLARKE
PAULDING
4
11
OCONEE
OGLETHORPE
WILKES
LINCOLN
HARALSON
Atlanta
WALTON
DOUGLAS
5
DEKALB
ROCKDALE
MORGAN
GREENE
TALIAFERRO
MCDUFFIE
COLUMBIA
Augusta
CARROLL
FULTON
CLAYTON
NEWTON
WARREN
RICHMOND
COWETA
FAYETTE
HENRY
JASPER
PUTNAM
HANCOCK
GLASCOCK
HEARD
3
SPALDING
Griffin
BUTTS
10
JEFFERSON
BURKE
La Grange
PIKE
LAMAR
BALDWIN
MONROE
JONES
WASHINGTON
TROUP
MERIWETHER
UPSON
Macon
BIBB
WILKINSON
JENKINS
SCREVEN
HARRIS
TALBOT
CRAWFORD
TWIGGS
JOHNSON
EMANUEL
MUSCOGEE
Warner Robins
Columbus
TAYLOR
PEACH
HOUSTON
EFFINGHAM
LAURENS
TREUTLEN
CHATTAHOOCHEE
MARION
SCHLEY
MACON
BLECKLEY
CANDLER
BULLOCH
PULASKI
DODGE
WHEELER
MONTGOMERY
TOOMBS
EVANS
BRYAN
CHATHAM
STEWART
Americus
DOOLY
WEBSTER
TATTNALL
Savannah
SUMTER
CRISP
WILCOX
TELFAIR
QUITMAN
BEN HILL
JEFF DAVIS
APPLING
LIBERTY
TERRELL
LEE
LONG
RANDOLPH
TURNER
2
1
CLAY
Albany
IRWIN
COFFEE
BACON
WAYNE
CALHOUN
DOUGHERTY
WORTH
TIFT
MCINTOSH
8
PIERCE
EARLY
BERRIEN
ATKINSON
GLYNN
BAKER
Waycross
WARE
Brunswick
MITCHELL
Moultrie
BRANTLEY
MILLER
COOK
COLQUITT
LANIER
CLINCH
CAMDEN
SEMINOLE
DECATUR
GRADY
Valdosta
CHARLTON
THOMAS
BROOKS
LOWNDES
ECHOLS

Paul Coverdell (R)

Of Atlanta — Elected 1992, 1st term

Biographical Information

Born: Jan. 20, 1939, Des Moines, Iowa.
Education: U. of Missouri, B.A. 1961.
Military Service: Army, 1962-64.
Occupation: Financial executive; Peace Corps director.
Family: Wife, Nancy Nally.
Religion: Methodist.
Political Career: Ga. Senate, 1971-89, minority leader, 1975-89; candidate for U.S. House (special election), 1977; Ga. Republican Party chairman, 1985-87.
Capitol Office: 200 Russell Bldg. 20510; 224-3643.

Committees

Agriculture, Nutrition & Forestry
Forestry, Conservation & Rural Revitalization; Marketing, Inspection & Product Promotion (chairman)
Foreign Relations
East Asian & Pacific Affairs; International Economic Policy, Export & Trade Promotion; Western Hemisphere, Peace Corps, Narcotics and Terrorism (chairman)
Small Business

Conference Secretary

In Washington: Although his background suggests some moderate leanings, Coverdell consistently sided with conservative Republicans in his first four years in the Senate. As a result, in December 1996 he had no trouble defeating Montana's Conrad Burns, 41-14, to win election for the 105th Congress as the GOP Conference Secretary, the party's No. 4 leadership job.

Coverdell laid the groundwork for his ascent into the hierarchy two years earlier, when he backed Trent Lott of Mississippi in his successful challenge for whip. Now Lott, as majority leader, affectionately calls Coverdell "Mikey," after the child in the Life cereal advertisements who was willing to heed the call of his elders and delve into new but potentially unappetizing tasks.

At the start of 1997, one such task was to coordinate efforts by nonprofit ideological and business groups to rally grass-roots support for passage of a balanced-budget constitutional amendment, the first item on Lott's agenda for the 105th. The effort failed by a single vote, as it had in 1995. Coverdell played a similar backstage role in 1994 in opposition to President Clinton's health care initiative.

Along the way, he founded the Fair Government Foundation, which he described as a conservative counterbalance to Common Cause and Public Citizen. One of its first efforts in 1996 was to argue that the Federal Election Commission's budget was too big.

Lott tapped Coverdell to help set the GOP's education agenda as chairman of a special task force in the 105th meant to counterbalance the efforts of more moderate Labor and Human Resources Chairman James M. Jeffords, a Vermont Republican. Coverdell also assumes for the 105th the chairmanship of the Agriculture Subcommittee on Marketing, Inspection and Product Promotion.

Coverdell has been an outspoken critic of the the 1993 "motor voter" law, which requires states to allow citizens to register to vote when applying for or renewing a driver's license. Calling the statute "a classic example of a bully government placing an extreme financial burden on our states," he introduced a bill in the 104th Congress to make the law voluntary on the states until Congress provided the funds to pay for it. But he did not follow through on a threat to propose that bill as an amendment to one of the first bills the new GOP majority pushed through the Senate in 1995, to curb unfunded federal mandates.

Coverdell worked to have an influence on two other high-profile pieces of the Republicans' agenda when the party took control in 1995. Although he was one of the leading advocates of a sweeping measure to curb damages in product liability lawsuits, he offered a scaled-back bill as soon as the proposal he favored was quashed by the Senate. When an even more modest bill passed, he pressured the House to take a "reality check" and accept it before public perception turned against the idea altogether.

While pushing enactment of the 1995 law to curb federal paperwork requirements on the private sector, Coverdell used the leverage of delay to win some limits on the obligations that businesses have to provide quarterly financial information to the Census Bureau.

From his seat on the Agriculture Committee, Coverdell worked in the 104th to limit the free-market zeal that some of his fellow Republicans brought to bear on the peanut subsidy program that is integral to the rural Georgia economy. In the end, peanut supports were reduced, but more modestly than those for some other commodities.

In the 103rd Congress, he joined with conservatives on two abortion votes — upholding a ban on federal funding of abortions except under certain circumstances and voting against a bill establishing criminal and civil penalties for blocking access to an abortion clinic — even though he had expressed support for abortion rights as a Senate candidate. He also voted against giving Clinton discretion on whether to lift the ban on homosexuals in the military, and in favor of locking the pre-Clinton ban into place. Yet during his 1992 campaign, Coverdell let the gay community know of his efforts to end discrimination while he was director of the Peace Corps.

Coverdell endorsed Sen. Phil Gramm for the 1996 GOP presidential nomination and also has backed the Texan's conservative alternatives to two major legislative initiatives: the stalled medical insurance overhaul of the 103rd Congress and the welfare overhaul bill in the 104th.

At Home: Coverdell lost to Democrat Wyche Fowler Jr. in a special House election in 1977 but returned the favor in 1992 by ousting Fowler from the Senate.

The victory did not come easily. Coverdell had to persevere through a tough July primary, an August primary runoff, a second-place finish on Nov. 3 and a late November general-election runoff. His margin of victory in the primary was about 1,500 votes; in the general-election runoff, it was 2 percentage points.

Fowler did not look that beatable at the beginning of the year, after two Republicans with statewide visibility declined to run. But Coverdell had decent credentials of his own. He was an Atlanta insurance marketing executive and former state GOP chairman with nearly two decades' experience in the state Senate (14 years as GOP minority leader) before serving as Peace Corps director during George Bush's administration.

Coverdell's narrow win in the primary runoff over Bob Barr (then the chief federal prosecutor in Atlanta, now a House member) provided little momentum for the fall. But Coverdell kept up a barrage of attacks that cast Fowler as part of an entrenched network of self-serving Washington politicians. He linked the incumbent to the House bank scandal, despite Fowler's insistence that he never had any overdrafted checks during his House tenure from 1977 to 1987. Coverdell also hammered Fowler for voting against authorizing the use of military force in the Persian Gulf and for opposing the death penalty.

Still, Fowler would have won if not for Georgia law, which at the time required the winner to receive a majority of the vote. Fowler's 35,000-vote lead on Nov. 3 was short of the needed majority because of the 70,000 votes that went to the Libertarian candidate, Jim Hudson.

The unexpected result appeared to jostle Fowler into action. He worked hard to shore up votes within his liberal constituency, which some said he had taken for granted early in the race. But there was a widespread feeling that Fowler had missed his best chance for victory, as turnout among black and low-income voters for the runoff was expected to be light. President-elect Bill Clinton and Vice President-elect Al Gore campaigned during the runoff for Fowler. First lady Barbara Bush and Senate Minority Leader Bob Dole campaigned for Coverdell, who also drew support from Libertarian Hudson, the Christian Coalition and the National Rifle Association.

In the end, Coverdell won the runoff by 16,237 votes out of 1.25 million cast, 1 million votes fewer than were cast Nov. 3.

In 1994, the Democratic Georgia General Assembly changed the state's election law; now a plurality of 45 percent is sufficient to win a general election.

SENATE ELECTIONS

1992 General Runoff		
Paul Coverdell (R)	635,114	(51%)
Wyche Fowler Jr. (D)	618,877	(49%)
1992 General		
Wyche Fowler Jr. (D)	1,108,416	(49%)
Paul Coverdell (R)	1,073,282	(48%)
Jim Hudson (LIBERT)	69,878	(3%)
1992 Primary Runoff		
Paul Coverdell (R)	80,435	(50%)
Bob Barr (R)	78,887	(50%)
1992 Primary		
Paul Coverdell (R)	100,016	(37%)
Bob Barr (R)	65,471	(24%)
John Knox (R)	64,514	(24%)
Charles Tanksley (R)	32,590	(12%)
Dean Parkinson (R)	7,352	(3%)

KEY VOTES

1997	
Approve balanced-budget constitutional amendment	Y
Approve chemical weapons treaty	N
1996	
Approve farm bill	Y
Limit punitive damages in product liability cases	Y
Exempt small businesses from higher minimum wage	Y
Approve welfare overhaul	Y
Bar job discrimination based on sexual orientation	N
Override veto of ban on "partial birth" abortions	Y
1995	
Approve GOP budget with tax and spending cuts	Y
Approve constitutional amendment barring flag desecration	Y

CAMPAIGN FINANCE

	Receipts	Receipts from PACs	Expend-itures
1992			
Fowler (D)	$4,322,671	$1,592,996 (37%)	$4,894,620
Coverdell (R)	$3,281,002	$585,557 (18%)	$3,193,774
Hudson (LIBERT)	$7,726	0	$7,689

VOTING STUDIES

	Presidential Support		Party Unity		Conservative Coalition	
Year	**S**	**O**	**S**	**O**	**S**	**O**
1996	34	66	98	2	97	3
1995	21	79	98†	2†	96†	4†
1994	35	65	92	5	88	9
1993	25	74	91	6	95	2

† Not eligible for all recorded votes.

INTEREST GROUP RATINGS

Year	ADA	AFL-CIO	CCUS	ACU
1996	5	n/a	92	100
1995	0	0	100	96
1994	5	0	90	100
1993	10	0	100	92

Max Cleland (D)

Of Lithonia — Elected 1996, 1st term

Biographical Information

Born: Aug. 24, 1942, Atlanta, Ga.

Education: Stetson U., B.A. 1964; Emory U., M.A. 1968.

Military Service: Army, 1965-68.

Occupation: Veterans administration official; congressional aide.

Family: Single.

Religion: Methodist.

Political Career: Ga. Senate, 1971-75; sought Democratic nomination for lieutenant governor, 1974; Ga. secretary of state, 1983-96.

Capitol Office: 461 Dirksen Bldg. 20510; 224-3521.

Committees

Armed Services
Airland Forces; Personnel (ranking); Readiness

Governmental Affairs
International Security, Proliferation & Federal Services; Oversight of Government Management & the District of Columbia; Investigations

Small Business

The Path to Washington: Like many of his colleagues in the Senate, Cleland brings to the job a lengthy political résumé. But few of them have a personal history so compelling.

As a young Army captain in the Vietnam War, Cleland lost both legs and one arm reaching for a loose grenade that exploded. Adjusting to life in a wheelchair, it was not long — 1970 — before he embarked on a career in politics, campaigning successfully for the Georgia Senate. His tenure in that job coincided with the governorship of Jimmy Carter, and after the man from Plains won the presidency in 1976, he appointed Cleland to head the Veterans Administration. Cleland was back on the campaign trail in Georgia in 1982, when he won the first of four terms as Secretary of State.

He gave up that post in 1996 to seek the Senate seat of retiring four-term Democrat Sam Nunn. In a hard-fought contest against wealthy Republican businessman Guy Millner, Cleland prevailed by just more than 30,000 votes out of more than 2.1 million cast.

With the popular Nunn leaving office, Georgia's open Senate race was seen as a key test of whether Democrats could stem the Republican tide that seemed to be rising all across the South in the 1994 election. Cleland, a big vote-getter in races for his state office, portrayed himself as a centrist Democrat in the mold of Nunn.

With no primary opposition, Cleland had the luxury of watching as a six-man primary fight unfolded on the Republican side. The leading contenders in the July primary were Millner, a conservative businessman who had taken 49 percent of the vote as the GOP challenger to Democratic Gov. Zell Miller in 1994, and former state Sen. Johnny Isakson, a more moderate candidate who had taken 45 percent as the GOP gubernatorial nominee against Miller in 1990.

Millner and Isakson ended up in an August runoff contest that had to fight for media attention with the Atlanta-based summer Olympic Games. The runoff became something of a referendum on the abortion issue, as Isakson ran television ads highlighting his support for abortion rights, and Millner's opposition to abortion.

Millner won the runoff, and almost immediately the contest between him and Cleland turned nasty. In one episode, Millner contended that Cleland, as secretary of state, had urged parole for a convicted killer who had a politically powerful father. The parolee later committed another murder.

Cleland's campaign acknowledged that he wrote a letter in behalf of the man, but said Millner had distorted the entire matter along the lines of the Republicans' 1988 "Willie Horton" ad attacking Democratic presidential nominee Michael S. Dukakis' prison furlough policy.

Millner's campaign also had a bout of negative publicity in the fall, when news reports called attention to his membership in a club considered exclusionary toward African-Americans and Jews. Millner subsequently resigned from the club.

In an effort to woo moderate Republicans who had backed Isakson, Millner made the pitch that Cleland in the Senate would be a pal of liberal policies such as those espoused by Democratic Sen. Edward M. Kennedy of Massachusetts. Millner, who drew on his considerable personal fortune to help wage his campaign, also criticized Cleland for refusing to participate in multiple debates, sending out numerous news releases asking, "Where's Max?"

For his part, Cleland portrayed Millner as an ideological extremist who as a senator would throw in with Republican efforts to (as he put it) harm Medicare and cut student loan programs.

Cleland took a number of centrist positions — supporting welfare overhaul, a balanced-budget constitutional amendment, line-item veto authority for the president, tough standards for teachers and combining the Labor and Education departments.

He called for voluntary spending limits on the campaign, a challenge Millner refused. And he praised enactment in the 104th of a health insurance portability law, which aimed to make it easier for workers to keep their insurance if they leave or lose their jobs.

On Election Night, Bill Clinton failed to carry Georgia for president as he had in 1992, but Cleland still managed to eke out a win, one of just a few Senate-race bright spots for Democrats, who overall slipped further into minority status in the chamber.

Among the issues that have been priorities for Cleland is making public buildings accessible to disabled people. When he arrived on Capitol Hill for freshman orientation in December 1996, much attention focused on how accessible the Capitol complex — including the Senate floor — was for a lawmaker in a wheelchair.

Cleland won assignment to the Armed Services Committee, a particular request of his because of Georgia's many military bases and veterans; his predecessor Nunn and Nunn's predecessor Richard B. Russell both chaired the committee.

Cleland also has a seat on Governmental Affairs, where he hopes to pursue his interest in revising campaign finance laws. He has described himself and other victors in highly expensive Senate contests as "survivors of war."

Cleland supports the idea of a constitutional amendment that could limit campaign finance expenditures. As a fallback, he has endorsed a campaign finance overhaul proposal by Republican Sen. John McCain of Arizona and Democratic Sen. Russell D. Feingold of Wisconsin that includes voluntary limits on spending.

SENATE ELECTIONS

1996 General		
Max Cleland (D)	1,103,993	(49%)
Guy Millner (R)	1,073,969	(48%)
John Cashin (LIBERT)	81,262	(4%)

CAMPAIGN FINANCE

	Receipts	Receipts from PACs		Expend- itures
1996				
Cleland (D)	$2,944,283	$710,670	(24%)	$2,926,391
Millner (R)	$9,917,102	$563,120	(6%)	$9,858,955

KEY VOTES

1997	
Approve balanced-budget constitutional amendment	Y
Approve chemical weapons treaty	Y

1 Jack Kingston (R)

Of Savannah — Elected 1992, 3rd term

Biographical Information
Born: April 24, 1955, Bryan, Texas.
Education: U. of Georgia, A.B. 1978.
Occupation: Insurance broker.
Family: Wife, Libby Morris; four children.
Religion: Episcopalian.
Political Career: Ga. House, 1985-93.
Capitol Office: 1507 Longworth Bldg. 20515; 225-5831.

Committees
Appropriations
Agriculture, Rural Development, FDA & Related Agencies; Foreign Operations, Export Financing & Related Programs; Military Construction

In Washington: Kingston, who took the 1st out of Democratic hands in 1992, got a thank you from the GOP leadership at the start of the 104th Congress, in the form of a seat on the Appropriations Committee. In his rookie term on the panel, Kingston used his newfound "power of the purse" as readily as many veteran appropriators who push issues of concern to their constituents and sometimes try to punish lawmakers who block their agendas.

As a member of the committee's Agriculture, Rural Development, FDA and Related Agencies Subcommittee, Kingston is well-positioned to protect the interests of the farmers in his district who raise Vidalia onions, peanuts, tobacco and other crops. In the 104th, Kingston's concern for local agricultural interests put him at odds with fellow GOP conservatives pushing the party's "Freedom to Farm" legislation, a major overhaul of U.S. agriculture policy aimed at phasing out New Deal-era crop subsidies.

Kingston resisted efforts to alter the federal price-support programs for peanuts and cotton, staple crops in Georgia. "When we talk about farm subsidies . . . we need to keep in mind that the people who are being subsidized are not necessarily the farmers," he said on the House floor in June 1995. "They are the American consumers."

However, Kingston made a concerted effort to end, or at least curtail, the subsidy to farmers of one crop not big on the Georgia scene: sugar. He called sugar supports "the sweetest deal of all" and contended that they benefit only wealthy growers. Consumers, he said, lose money because of the sugar subsidy; in 1995 Kingston claimed the cost for a ton of sugar in the United States is 13 cents more than the average price in the rest of the world.

Although Kingston's chief criticism of the sugar program was that it inflates what consumers pay for sugar, he did have another interest in the debate: Savannah Foods, the nation's largest sugar refiner, is based in the 1st. He said current policy had caused sugar shortages and forced some refineries to close shop temporarily.

During conference negotiations on the fiscal 1996 agriculture spending bill, Kingston proposed, but later withdrew, an amendment to kill the sugar program. A year later, on the fiscal 1997 agriculture bill, he won the addition of language that would have capped the price of raw cane sugar at 21.15 cents per pound, but that provision was dropped in conference with the Senate.

Kingston did not take his defeats at the hands of the powerful sugar lobby lightly. After the highest profile sugar vote of the 104th — a 208-217 House floor vote in March 1996 that ended the bid to kill the price-support program — he accused sugar lobbyists of filling the Capitol "with pockets full of money." And when legislators from sugar-growing Florida lobbied against Kingston's later plan to cap the price of sugar, he persuaded the Appropriations' Agriculture Subcommittee to cut funding for a $27.7 million farm-research center planned for Fort Pierce, Fla. The full committee restored the Fort Pierce money.

Kingston ultimately voted with the vast majority of Republicans for final passage of the "Freedom to Farm" legislation. In the bill, the peanut subsidy program was modified, but it survived. Peanut program critics had proposed phasing it out by 2002, but they lost, 209-212.

Kingston is a reliable opponent of the Clinton administration, even on one Clinton priority that most Republicans back — lifting barriers to international trade. Kingston opposed NAFTA in 1993, concerned about its impact on jobs in rural areas of the 1st, and in 1994 he voted against GATT.

More than once Kingston has staked out positions on the right side of the conservative-dominated House Republican Conference. In the 104th he voted against a bill that increased the nation's debt limit, even though GOP leaders counseled a vote for the debt-limit increase so as not to provoke a showdown with the Clinton administration over funding the government. He opposed a bill increasing the minimum wage in 1996, even after the measure was sweetened with business tax

GEORGIA 1
Southeast - Savannah; Brunswick

The 1st District is a microcosm of Georgia's racial, demographic and political composition. Remapping in 1995 added predominantly black areas around Savannah that had been cordoned off in the erstwhile majority-black 11th. That boosted the black population of the 1st to nearly 31 percent, just above the state average. The district's population grew 10 percent from 1990 to 1995, just below the state clip of 11 percent.

The 1st, like Georgia, is ancestrally Democratic but increasingly receptive to the GOP. Kingston's 1992 election marked the first time since Reconstruction that southeast Georgia had not sent a Democrat to Washington.

Thirty-seven percent of the 1st's population resides in Chatham County, dominated by the city of Savannah, which James Oglethorpe founded in 1733. Many of the town squares he envisioned and designed are well-preserved, including Chippewa Square, where some of the movie "Forrest Gump" was filmed. Savannah is ethnically diverse, with a significant African-American population. There are large numbers of Jews, Greeks, French Huguenots, and Irish; descendants of the latter organize a large St. Patrick's Day parade.

Major industry in Savannah includes Gulfstream Aerospace, which designs and manufactures jet aircraft, and Union Camp, a manufacturer of paper, chemicals and wood products. Hunter Army Airfield in Savannah and Fort Stewart in Liberty County account for tens of thousands of jobs for the military and civilians.

South of Chatham is Bryan County, the 1st's fastest growing county in population from 1990 to 1995. Bob Dole captured 57 percent of Bryan's votes in 1996, his best showing in the district. Republicans also run well in Glynn County; along the county's coast are a number of upscale beach resort communities, such as St. Simons Island and Jekyll Island. The Treasury Department's Federal Law Enforcement Training Center is at a former naval air station near Brunswick that was converted in the mid-1970s.

Burgeoning Camden County in the extreme southeast corner houses the Kings Bay Naval Submarine Base, which supports the Navy's submarine-launched ballistic missile program and employs about 9,000. The county includes the Cumberland Island National Seashore, a picturesque, wildlife-laden tourist attraction.

Farming provides a substantial part of the district's economy. Cotton has long been a major crop in southeastern Georgia; Eli Whitney invented the cotton gin near Savannah, and Georgia was the first state to grow cotton commercially. Other primary crops include corn, soybeans, wheat, peanuts, tobacco, and sweet Vidalia onions, discovered in Toombs County in 1931.

No other Georgia congressional district more closely paralleled statewide voter sentiments in 1996. Dole beat Bill Clinton in the district by 48 percent to 45 percent, while Democratic Senate nominee Max Cleland edged Guy Millner 49 percent to 48 percent.

As of May 19, the Census Bureau had not recalculated population data, racial and ethnic breakdowns, and age statistics for districs newly drawn for the 1996 election.

breaks that won over many other Republicans.

Kingston quickly and repeatedly jumped to the defense of Newt Gingrich whenever Democrats attacked the Speaker's character or assailed him for alleged ethical lapses. The most notable exchange came amid the House debate on the budget-reconciliation bill in November 1995.

Democrats took to the floor to chide Gingrich for suggesting that Congress' budget standoff with President Clinton came in part because Clinton made him sit in the back of Air Force One and exit from the rear on a return trip from the funeral of assassinated Israeli Prime Minister Yitzhak Rabin. To make his point, George Miller, D-Calif., displayed a New York Daily News cover sketch of Gingrich, crying and in diapers, under the headline "CRY BABY." Kingston made a "point of order" that the display violated House rules, and the presiding officer ruled that posters should not be used to "demean" other members. Democrat Lloyd Doggett of Texas appealed their ruling. That appeal was tabled, 231-171.

As a freshman, Kingston found fault with congressional accounting methods he saw as phony. "When we say there is going to be a cut, what we mean is there is going to be a decrease in the projected increase, not a real cut the way you and I think of a cut in our households or businesses," he said. When Republicans took over the House in 1995, they changed chamber rules on accounting methods. Later in the 104th, Republicans employed Kingston's argument in responding to Democratic charges that the GOP was proposing "cuts" in Medicare and Medicaid. Republicans said they aimed to reduce the rate of projected spending growth on the programs.

Kingston is a pithy participant in the one-minute speeches that House lawmakers can make before legislative work begins each day.

In the 103rd Congress, he faulted Clinton's health care proposal, complaining that it required people to pay the same for coverage whether or not they practice healthy habits. "If you are a 55-year-old person who does not ever exercise — you may smoke a little bit too much, you may drink a little bit too much, you may eat a lot of fried foods — your premium is going to be the same as [a] 23-year-old marathon runner," Kingston said in 1993. "People who take care of themselves should pay a lower premium than those that do not."

And in a 1993 interview with the Atlanta Journal and Constitution, he had this to say about the nation's welfare program: "All these Great Society programs of Lyndon Johnson, none of them have done a doggone thing."

Kingston rose on the House floor in November 1995 to lambaste the Equal Employment Opportunity Commission for insisting that the restaurant chain Hooters, known for its shapely and scantily clad waitresses, hire male waiters and be more sensitive to men. "There's nothing that men like more than an abundance of Buffalo wings and breasts," Kingston said, angering several female lawmakers, even though Kingston clarified that he was referring to chicken breasts.

At Home: The Supreme Court's demand that Georgia alter the boundaries of its congressional districts in 1996 had little impact on the conservative bent of Kingston's district, yet he, like several of the state's House members, flirted briefly with the idea of seeking the open Senate seat of retiring Democrat Sam Nunn.

He opted not to run, explaining that the demands of a Senate campaign would keep him away from his four young children, and citing his Appropriations Committee seat as an inducement to remain in the House. Kingston won re-election with more than two-thirds of the vote.

When Democrat Lindsay Thomas retired from the 1st in 1992, Kingston was well-positioned to woo voters into the Republican column for a House election; many of them already had been voting Republican for president.

An insurance agent from Savannah, Kingston since 1985 had held a state House seat in Chatham County, the district's most populous. He drew minor primary opposition, while his eventual Democratic opponent, Barbara Christmas, a school principal in rural Camden County, struggled through a crowded primary and a runoff against former Hinesville Mayor Buddy DeLoach.

Christmas was a woman and a political "outsider," two hot qualities in 1992. She also got some mileage out of her last name, choosing "Christmas in November" as her campaign theme and dubbing her daylong visits to each of the district's 22 counties "Christmas Days."

Kingston emphasized his eight years' service in the state House and portrayed Christmas as lacking legislative know-how. He also said she would pursue a liberal agenda, citing a contribution Christmas received from the National Organization for Women — which, a Kingston brochure noted, supported homosexual rights. Conservative Phyllis Schlafly sent a mailing calling Christmas an "ultra-liberal, radical feminist."

Christmas, a mother and grandmother, protested, but to no avail. Kingston took 58 percent, and in 1994, he won re-election easily.

HOUSE ELECTIONS

1996 General		
Jack Kingston (R)	108,616	(68%)
Rosemary Kaszans (D)	50,622	(32%)
1994 General		
Jack Kingston (R)	88,788	(77%)
Raymond Beckworth (D)	27,197	(23%)

Previous Winning Percentages: 1992 (58%)

CAMPAIGN FINANCE

	Receipts	Receipts from PACs		Expend-itures
1996				
Kingston (R)	$557,574	$176,055	(32%)	$452,178
Kaszans (D)	$46,939	$2,500	(5%)	$46,023
1994				
Kingston (R)	$513,973	$203,596	(40%)	$296,202
Beckworth (D)	$0	0		$5,338

DISTRICT VOTE FOR PRESIDENT

	1996		1992
D	81,804 (45%)	**D**	76,900 (42%)
R	87,895 (48%)	**R**	81,443 (44%)
I	11,491 (6%)	**I**	26,023 (14%)

KEY VOTES

1997	
Ban "partial birth" abortions	Y
1996	
Approve farm bill	Y
Deny public education to illegal immigrants	Y
Repeal ban on certain assault-style weapons	Y
Increase minimum wage	N
Freeze defense spending	Y
Approve welfare overhaul	Y
1995	
Approve balanced-budget constitutional amendment	Y
Relax Clean Water Act regulations	Y
Oppose limits on environmental regulations	N
Reduce projected Medicare spending	Y
Approve GOP budget with tax and spending cuts	Y

VOTING STUDIES

	Presidential Support		Party Unity		Conservative Coalition	
Year	**S**	**O**	**S**	**O**	**S**	**O**
1996	29	65	89	7	84	10
1995	17	83	95	5	93	7
1994	42	56	88	11	94	3
1993	26	73	89	9	84	14

INTEREST GROUP RATINGS

Year	ADA	AFL-CIO	CCUS	ACU
1996	5	n/a	86	100
1995	0	0	100	96
1994	5	11	83	100
1993	10	8	91	100

2 Sanford D. Bishop Jr. (D)

Of Albany — Elected 1992, 3rd term

Biographical Information
Born: Feb. 4, 1947, Mobile, Ala.
Education: Morehouse College, B.A. 1968; Emory U., J.D. 1971.
Occupation: Lawyer.
Family: Divorced.
Religion: Baptist.
Political Career: Ga. House, 1977-91; Ga. Senate, 1991-93.
Capitol Office: 1433 Longworth Bldg. 20515; 225-3631.

Committees
Agriculture
Department Operations, Nutrition & Foreign Agriculture; Risk Management & Specialty Crops
Select Intelligence
Human Intelligence, Analysis & Counterintelligence

In Washington: Endangered by a mid-decade redistricting that gave him a white-majority constituency, Bishop nonetheless won a third term in 1996, underscoring his reputation as a politician skilled at broadening his base beyond the black community.

First elected in 1992 from a black-majority district with a substantial white minority. Bishop came to Washington vowing to become known not as "the black congressman" from the 2nd District, but simply "the congressman." He won handily in 1994, but the Georgia map was scrambled before the 1996 election; Bishop ended up running and winning in a reshaped 2nd where blacks made up only 35 percent of the voting-age population.

One secret to Bishop's electoral success is the assiduous attention he pays to his district's agricultural interests. The 2nd grows more peanuts than anyplace else in America, and from his seat on the Agriculture Committee during the 104th Congress, Bishop had a hand in reforming and protecting the peanut price-support program, which was part of the overhaul of federal farm programs enacted in 1996.

Also, Bishop's voting record rates him as perhaps the most conservative member of the Congressional Black Caucus. In 1996, he was one of only three in the caucus to support the final version of the welfare overhaul bill, which President Clinton signed into law. He backs a balanced-budget constitutional amendment. And he is the only black member of the "blue dog" coalition of right-leaning House Democrats.

Like most of the blue dogs, Bishop casts a skeptical eye on gun control efforts. In the 103rd Congress, he opposed a five-day waiting requirement for handgun purchases. He did support a ban on certain semiautomatic assault-style weapons in the 103rd, saying that Congress should take some step — even if only a symbolic one — to show its concern about gun violence. In 1996, however, Bishop voted with the GOP majority to repeal the assault-weapons ban.

Despite his departures from liberal dogma, Bishop still votes a loyally Democratic line on numerous issues. He supports abortion rights and has taken labor's side in its legislative disputes with the business-oriented GOP majority.

Bishop has also had some harsh words for budget cuts proposed by the Republicans, arguing they will "put a dagger in rural America. From health care to agriculture to education, the Republican budget targets rural America, where we can least afford to lessen our efforts."

On the Agriculture Committee, Bishop worked with Georgia Republican colleague Saxby Chambliss to design a new peanut price support system that limited imports and regulated production to help boost prices for farmers who participate. Critics of the price support program complain that it inflates prices for consumers and those who use peanuts in their products.

In February 1996, when an amendment was offered during House debate on the farm bill to phase out the peanut program by 2002, Bishop rose to defend the program. "To reduce the peanut loan rate to a world market price is to ask United States farmers to match heavily subsidized Chinese peanut prices that have no relationship to the actual cost of production of peanuts in China," Bishop said. He also claimed that 100 percent of recent Chinese peanuts examined by the Food and Drug Administration have failed United States' health standards. "It is clear this amendment is not going to help anyone," Bishop said. "It is going to hurt the peanut farmer in America, and it is going to hurt the American consumer." The amendment failed, 209-212.

Bishop was equally critical of an amendment to the fiscal 1996 agriculture spending bill that would have barred funds for tobacco crop insurance, arguing that passage of the amendment would devastate the economy in tobacco-growing regions of the South. "This amendment is misguided, it is punitive, it is a slap in the face to Southern states. It is a slap in the face of farmers, small family farmers, who work hard. Why shouldn't they have crop insurance if they grow a legal product?" Bishop railed. Republicans and

GEORGIA 2

Southwest — Parts of Macon, Columbus, Albany and Valdosta

Smoothing out the lines of the southwest Georgia-based 2nd district in 1995 reduced its black-voting age population from 52 percent to 35 percent. It also changed the district from being a strongly Democratic area to one in which Republicans are competitive.

The district's new boundaries are more like the 1980s version of the 2nd — which also was roughly one-third black and did not split counties — than the early 1990s version, which had arm-like appendages that enveloped black areas of Columbus, Macon, Albany and Valdosta.

Although southwest Georgia has a long-standing Democratic tradition, politics here are no longer monolithic. Pockets of GOP strength exist in Lee County in the central part of the district, and Bob Dole won a handful of counties in the southern part of the district in 1996. Overall, Bill Clinton garnered 49 percent in the 2nd to beat Dole by only 5 percentage points.

The heavily agricultural region has been struggling economically for decades. Although Georgia is known as the "Peach State" and the fruit is widely grown throughout Georgia, the state is no longer first in producing it. Georgia could well be called the "Peanut State," for it leads the nation in producing that legume and most of the state's peanuts are grown in the 2nd.

Pecans are an agricultural anchor in Georgia, which produces about 30 percent of the nation's crop. Dougherty, Mitchell and Lee counties in the central part of the 2nd are the best pecan-producing areas, and Baconton (Mitchell County) hosts the annual Pecan Harvest Festival. Corn predominates in the southwestern area of the district along the Florida border, and tobacco production is especially high in the district's southeast.

Dougherty, which includes Albany, is the district's most populous county. In the heart of plantation country and popular among quail hunters, Dougherty also is reliably Democratic: Clinton polled 56 percent there while Sen. Max Cleland topped 60 percent. Large Albany employers include Procter and Gamble, Cooper Tire Co., Miller Brewing, and Bob's Candies, the world's largest peppermint candy canes maker.

The district has a considerable military presence. Moody Air Force Base near Valdosta provide employment for 4,700 military and civilian personnel, and the Marine Corp Logistics Base in Albany, which acquires and maintains supplies for the Marines, employs 3,200. Fort Benning, the state's largest military base, lies just across the district line in the 3rd's Muscogee County.

Southwest Georgia's link to presidential history has earned it the sobriquet of "Presidential Pathways." Franklin D. Roosevelt found the therapeutic waters of Warm Springs soothing for his polio, and a few years later he built the well-preserved cottage at which he died in 1945. North of Warm Springs, in tiny Plains (Sumter County), is the hometown of Jimmy Carter.

The 2nd includes Cairo (Grady County), the birthplace of Jackie Robinson, who broke baseball's color barrier a half century ago.

As of May 19, the Census Bureau had not recalculated population data, racial and ethnic breakdowns, and age statistics for districts newly drawn for the 1996 election.

Democrats were equally divided as the amendment went down, 199-223.

An early NAFTA foe, Bishop told the House in 1993 that Georgia peanut farmers were 100 percent against the trade pact. NAFTA will eventually "put American workers and American farmers out of work," he said. In 1994, though, he voted with the Clinton administration on GATT.

Bishop served notice shortly after arriving in Washington that he was willing to stand apart from the liberal majority in the Black Caucus. A member of the Veterans' Affairs Committee, he said he would support Mississippi Democrat G.V. "Sonny" Montgomery as committee chairman, despite other black members' complaints about Montgomery's civil rights record. Bishop told the Atlanta Constitution that his decision to support Montgomery was "a statement of my independence," adding that his district included hundreds of veterans loyal to the chairman.

In the 105th Congress, the Democratic leadership — always looking to add diversity to key "insider" panels — appointed Bishop to the Intelligence Committee, where he joins California Democrat Julian C. Dixon as the second black.

At Home: After twice winning the 2nd with more than 60 percent of the vote, Bishop saw his prospects for 1996 clouded when, in December 1995, a panel of federal judges handed down a sweeping remake of Georgia's congressional district map. It put Bishop's Columbus home in the 3rd District and reduced the black voting-age population in the 2nd from 52 percent to 35 percent.

The court ruling was the latest twist in a long-running redistricting drama that had muddled Georgia's House politics since the early 1990s.

When the Georgia legislature was initially map-drawing for the decade, the Justice Department twice rejected plans that gave the 2nd a majority of white residents. On its third try, the legislature made the 2nd Georgia's third black-majority district. Bishop was on the Reapportionment Committee that helped draw that map, which won Justice Department approval and was used in 1992 and 1994 voting.

But in June 1995, the U.S. Supreme Court struck down that map, agreeing with plaintiffs who said it was a racial gerrymander that violated their constitutional guarantee of equal protection under the law. The 5-4 decision in *Miller v. Johnson* firmed up the court's 1993 ruling in a North Carolina case, *Shaw v. Reno*, also involving the issue of race-based redistricting. In that case, the court majority questioned the propriety of creating "bizarrely shaped" districts to aggregate minority voters. In the Georgia case, the court more explicitly rejected using race as the "predominant factor" in redistricting.

The Supreme Court ruling returned Georgia's map to a three-judge federal panel, which in a 2-1 ruling in December 1995 issued a new map that dismantled two of the state's three black-majority House districts, including Bishop's.

The new map put the homes of Bishop and Cynthia A. McKinney, another black Democratic incumbent, into districts where white GOP incumbents lived. Bishop's home was in the new 3rd, but rather than stay there and take on Republican Mac Collins, Bishop moved to the new 2nd District, which contained 28 of the 35 counties he had previously represented.

In the July 1996 Democratic primary, Bishop defeated two white opponents, winning renomination with 59 percent of the vote. His Republican opponent in November was businessman Darrel Ealum, who charged that Bishop was more liberal than the majority in his reshaped constituency. Ealum drew an endorsement of the state branch of Ross Perot's Reform Party, but Bishop persuasively argued that he had sought to bridge the gap between black and white voters. Bishop won by eight points, 54 percent to 46 percent.

Bishop distinguished himself as a civil rights lawyer right out of college and during 16 years in the Georgia legislature before trying for Congress. He was talked into running in 1992 by Columbus business leaders just days before the filing deadline. They helped finance his challenge to Democratic Rep. Charles Hatcher. Early in the year, Hatcher had been identified as one of the chief House bank abusers, with 819 overdrafts.

Despite his check-writing problems, Hatcher finished first in the primary, garnering 40 percent of the vote. Bishop ran second with 21 percent, qualifying for the runoff.

During the runoff, Hatcher repeatedly apologized for his overdrafts. He charged that Bishop's Columbus financial supporters were trying to buy a second seat. (Portions of Columbus also fell in the 3rd District.) But Bishop's call for a "new generation of leadership" resonated with rural voters and others disenchanted with Hatcher. Bishop won nomination 53 percent to 47 percent, and in November, he coasted past Republican physician Jim Dudley, taking 64 percent of the vote.

Two years later, Bishop won with similar ease in both the Democratic primary (defeating James C. Bush, Hatcher's former district coordinator) and in the general election.

HOUSE ELECTIONS

1996 General		
Sanford D. Bishop Jr. (D)	88,256	(54%)
Darrel Ealum (R)	75,282	(46%)
1996 Primary		
Sanford D. Bishop Jr. (D)	56,660	(59%)
W.T. Gamble (D)	31,615	(33%)
Walter H. Lewis (D)	7,116	(7%)
1994 General		
Sanford D. Bishop Jr. (D)	65,383	(66%)
John Clayton (R)	33,429	(34%)

Previous Winning Percentages: 1992 (64%)

CAMPAIGN FINANCE

	Receipts	Receipts from PACs	Expend-itures
1996			
Bishop (D)	$762,132	$338,677 (44%)	$774,474
Ealum (R)	$375,205	$37,266 10%)	$329,309
1994			
Bishop (D)	$493,190	$249,554 (51%)	$473,931
Clayton (R)	$10,168	$764 (8%)	$9,736

DISTRICT VOTE FOR PRESIDENT

	1996		1992
D	82,429 (49%)	**D**	82,220 (46%)
R	72,934 (44%)	**R**	71,749 (40%)
I	11,494 (7%)	**I**	23,278 (13%)

KEY VOTES

1997	
Ban "partial birth" abortions	N
1996	
Approve farm bill	Y
Deny public education to illegal immigrants	N
Repeal ban on certain assault-style weapons	Y
Increase minimum wage	Y
Freeze defense spending	N
Approve welfare overhaul	Y
1995	
Approve balanced-budget constitutional amendment	?
Relax Clean Water Act regulations	Y
Oppose limits on environmental regulations	Y
Reduce projected Medicare spending	N
Approve GOP budget with tax and spending cuts	N

VOTING STUDIES

	Presidential Support		Party Unity		Conservative Coalition	
Year	S	O	S	O	S	O
1996	71	27	75	25	90	10
1995	71	23	78	15	50	38
1994	88	10	87	7	58	25
1993	88	12	89	7	59	41

INTEREST GROUP RATINGS

Year	ADA	AFL-CIO	CCUS	ACU
1996	60	n/a	44	30
1995	85	90	41	13
1994	75	56	64	25
1993	75	100	18	13

3 Mac Collins (R)

Of Hampton — Elected 1992, 3rd term

Biographical Information

Born: Oct. 15, 1944, Butts County, Ga.
Education: Jackson H.S., graduated 1962.
Military Service: National Guard, 1964-70.
Occupation: Trucking company owner.
Family: Wife, Julie Watkins; four children.
Religion: Methodist.
Political Career: Butts County Commission chairman, 1977-81; candidate for Ga. Senate, 1984, 1986; Ga. Senate, 1989-93.

Capitol Office: 1131 Longworth Bldg. 20515; 225-5901.

Committees

Ways & Means
Human Resources; Social Security

In Washington: "Send a Working Man to Congress," was Collins' campaign slogan in 1992, and this high school-educated trucking company owner quickly worked himself into a good spot in the House, taking a seat on the Ways and Means Committee in 1995. As he participates in the committee's consideration of complex and controversial subjects, Collins maintains his plain-speaking, "regular guy" persona.

Despite being a newcomer to the committee in the 104th, Collins more than once had some blunt talk for senior Democrats who railed at GOP policy proposals. There were noteworthy exchanges between Collins and Florida Rep. Sam M. Gibbons, the committee's ranking Democrat and former chairman. In February 1995, Gibbons accused Republicans of crafting a welfare bill that was "radical . . . cruel . . . and mean to children." Collins' reply: "That is bull, and you know it."

Gibbons heard a similar retort the next year when he lashed out at Republicans for their proposals to restrain the cost of social-welfare programs, especially Medicare. "You're spouting bull," said Collins, a member of the unofficial congressional Cowboy Boot Caucus.

Collins likes to say that he is a "representative," not a "politician." But he has long been wise in the ways of electioneering. As a boy in Flowvilla, Ga., politics were family table talk; his mother was the first woman elected to the City Council there. Coming into his first House campaign in 1992, Collins had eight years' experience in public office — four as a Butts County Commissioner and four as a Georgia state senator.

A reliable vote for the Republican leadership, Collins posted party unity scores near the 100 percent mark in the 104th Congress. He voted with the majority of Republicans against the majority of Democrats 97 percent of the time in 1995 and 98 percent of the time the following year.

That loyalty has endeared him to Republican leaders. Collins began to lobby for a seat on Ways and Means in 1994, anticipating vacancies in the 104th Congress because three Republicans on the panel were waging bids for statewide office. The GOP takeover of the House in 1994 gave Republicans even more slots on the panel, and Collins got one of them. Since then, he has been made a deputy whip, and in October 1996 he was named to head an eight-member Ways and Means task force that began a comprehensive study of all types of transportation taxes.

The task force grew out of Collins' unsuccessful effort in the 104th to repeal the 4.3-cent federal tax on aviation jet fuel. Republicans included a two-year repeal of that tax in their balanced-budget plan, but Clinton vetoed that measure. Early in the 105th Congress, lawmakers voted a temporary renewal of the tax on airline tickets, and they are debating other transportation taxes in the context of renewing the nation's highway law.

Explaining the objective of his task force, Collins told The Associated Press in 1996: "What we're doing is looking into how those taxes are assessed, what they're assessed upon, how they affect the industry, how they affect the consumer . . . to see if it's fair and equitable. If so, you do nothing. If it's not, we'll make some recommendations that hopefully will make it more fair and equitable."

It didn't take long for Collins to have an impact on the legislative process after arriving in Congress. He made his first mark in May 1993, when the House was considering a measure to allocate $1.5 billion to help small- and medium-sized businesses compete globally. GOP efforts to trim the bill were turned back, but Collins unexpectedly scored with an amendment to bar any money in the bill from having a "direct financial benefit to any person who is not a citizen or national of the United States" or a legal alien.

When voting time on the amendment ran out, Collins was prevailing with the support of most Republicans and several Democrats. Many more Democrats, perhaps skittish about being criticized as coddling illegal aliens, then lined up to change their votes. As Republicans applauded, 37

GEORGIA 3
West Central — Columbus; Atlanta suburbs

The 3rd is an eclectic mix of urban, suburban and rural counties extending from the Alabama border to the southeast of Atlanta.

The 3rd previously included all or part of sixteen counties because of its proximity to the oddly-shaped, black-majority 2nd. But 1995 remapping smoothed out the boundaries; now the 3rd includes all of nine counties and splits only one — Clayton, an Atlanta suburban area shared with the 5th.

The district's black population increased to almost 25 percent primarily because of the addition of Columbus (Muscogee County). Just outside of Columbus is Fort Benning, the state's largest military base. Known as the "Home of the Infantry," Fort Benning employs about 20,000 active-duty personnel. During the Civil War, Columbus was one of the leading suppliers of war materials for the Confederacy, and the city's Confederate Naval Museum is a tourist draw. The city's large black population makes Muscogee favorable terrain for Democrats, although Collins won the county in 1996.

At the northern end of the district is Clayton County, home to one-fifth of the 3rd's residents. The sprawling and ever-bustling Hartsfield International Airport is a prime driver of the district's economy. Others look to military facilities for economic sustenance — Fort Gillem is in northeast Clayton and Fort McPherson is in the 5th district's southern Atlanta suburbs. Ford also makes Taurus automobiles in Clayton and adjoining Fulton County. Jonesboro, the county seat, is perhaps best known as the literary setting for Margaret Mitchell's "Gone With The Wind."

Abutting Clayton to the south are the burgeoning areas of Fayette and Henry. Fayette more than doubled its population in the 1980s, and Henry's population grew 63 percent. This is staunchly Republican territory — in 1996, Bob Dole beat Bill Clinton in both counties by more than 25 percentage points.

West of Fayette is Coweta County, where the atmosphere changes, although GOP voting habits do not. Newnan's wealth is tied less to Atlanta's recent growth than to the more distant past; a hospital zone that was spared during the Civil War, Newnan is known for its stately antebellum mansions. Dole racked up 57 percent of the county's votes in 1996.

Textiles are especially important to the Spalding County economy. Dundee Mills, a towel manufacturer, is one of the largest employers here. The county also is home to the Atlanta Motor Speedway.

The most loyal support for Democratic candidates comes from the counties at the district's ends — Muscogee and Clayton — and in some rural areas in the southern part of the district. In 1996, Clinton won Talbot and Meriwether counties; the latter was the only county Collins lost that year.

But the precarious Democratic tendencies in these areas is offset by the overwhelming Republican trend in the southern Atlanta suburbs.

As of May 19, the Çensus Bureau had not recalculated population data, racial and ethnic breakdowns, and age statistics for districts newly drawn for the 1996 election.

Democrats switched their votes from "nay" to "yea." In the end, Collins' amendment won, 263-156.

A dependable vote against the Clinton administration's budget proposals and social policy initiatives, Collins stood apart from the White House even on NAFTA, which a majority of Republicans backed. In 1994, Collins also opposed GATT.

In his role as protector of constituents' interests, Collins fought in the 104th against a proposal by budget-cutters in his own party to sell the Southeastern Power Administration and 23 Corps of Engineers dams and lakes, including some in Georgia. Collins argued that privatization could lead to steeper power costs for consumers and could restrict recreational use of the lakes in his district. His view ultimately prevailed.

Although Collins' district was altered only minimally by a court-drawn redistricting plan in 1996, he thrust himself into the debate about the new map. His argument, however, was not with the Supreme Court, which ordered the new map, or the three-judge federal panel that originally ruled Georgia's 11th District unconstitutional on the grounds of "racial gerrymandering," but with the Justice Department. He said it was to blame for the court ruling because it had written the guidelines that governed creation of the unconstitutional 1992 lines. Collins called on Congress to reimburse the Georgia Legislature for the $25,000-a-day special session it held to redraw the districts, but his proposal was never considered.

At Home: Georgia's new congressional map did not greatly alter the boundaries or the conservative tilt of Collins' district, yet he briefly flirted in 1996 with seeking the open Senate seat of retiring Democrat Sam Nunn. Rather than take that risk, though, he chose to run again for the House.

Collins' Democratic challenger, Jim Chafin, sought to make a negative out of the incumbent's fealty to the GOP line. "Mac Collins has been a loyal foot soldier in Newt Gingrich's Republican

Revolution. . . . He deserves a medal for his loyalty in going along with the radical Republican leadership 99 percent of the time," Chafin said. "But he doesn't deserve a medal for independence or leadership. And he doesn't deserve your vote."

Voters did not buy the pitch. Collins won a third term with 61 percent of the vote.

The first round of 1990s redistricting in Georgia had worked to Collins' advantage because it crippled Democratic Rep. Richard Ray, dramatically altering his 3rd District and giving it a mixture of independent voters, Reagan Democrats and GOP suburbanites who did not know him. Collins won the 1992 GOP primary in the 3rd and then set out pillorying five-termer Ray as a politician who had lost touch with the folks back home.

Collins revived a 1980s charge that Ray, a member of the Armed Services Committee, had accepted an illegal contribution from Unisys, a defense contractor. Ray denied the charge, and he waged an aggressive, $1.1 million campaign defending his moderate-to-conservative record and tearing into Collins.

Both men opposed homosexuals in the military and supported anti-abortion policies, a capital gains tax cut and a balanced-budget constitutional amendment. But on ground largely unfamiliar to him, Ray could not overcome voters' anti-Congress mood. George Bush carried the 3rd by 11 percentage points, and Collins, who often stumped in jeans and cowboy boots and spent less than $250,000, won with 55 percent of the vote.

In 1994, Collins swatted away an aggressive challenge from Democratic attorney Fred Overby, who spent more than $1 million but took only 34 percent of the vote.

HOUSE ELECTIONS

1996 General		
Mac Collins (R)	120,251	(61%)
Jim Chafin (D)	76,538	(39%)
1994 General		
Mac Collins (R)	94,717	(66%)
Fred Overby (D)	49,828	(34%)

Previous Winning Percentages: 1992 (55%)

CAMPAIGN FINANCE

	Receipts	Receipts from PACs	Expend-itures
1996			
Collins (R)	$527,416	$289,014 (55%)	$485,354
Chafin (D)	$123,915	$34,450 (28%)	$122,393
1994			
Collins (R)	$504,907	$191,807 (38%)	$503,867
Overby (D)	$1,294,536	$92,100 (7%)	$1,284,414

DISTRICT VOTE FOR PRESIDENT

	1996		1992
D	88,260 (43%)	**D**	82,790 (40%)
R	104,247 (50%)	**R**	96,444 (46%)
I	13,525 (7%)	**I**	28,381 (14%)

KEY VOTES

1997	
Ban "partial-birth" abortions	Y
1996	
Approve farm bill	Y
Deny public education to illegal immigrants	Y
Repeal ban on certain assault-style weapons	Y
Increase minimum wage	N
Freeze defense spending	N
Approve welfare overhaul	Y
1995	
Approve balanced-budget constitutional amendment	Y
Relax Clean Water Act regulations	Y
Oppose limits on environmental regulations	N
Reduce projected Medicare spending	Y
Approve GOP budget with tax and spending cuts	Y

VOTING STUDIES

	Presidential Support		Party Unity		Conservative Coalition	
Year	**S**	**O**	**S**	**O**	**S**	**O**
1996	32	68	98	2	98	2
1995	15	85	97	1	95	4
1994	36	63	90	8	86	14
1993	29	71	94	6	91	9

INTEREST GROUP RATINGS

Year	ADA	AFL-CIO	CCUS	ACU
1996	5	n/a	94	100
1995	0	0	100	92
1994	0	22	75	95
1993	10	25	82	100

4 Cynthia A. McKinney (D)

Of Lithonia — Elected 1992, 3rd term

Biographical Information
Born: March 17, 1955, Atlanta, Ga.
Education: U. of Southern California, B.A. 1978.
Occupation: Professor.
Family: Divorced; one child.
Religion: Roman Catholic.
Political Career: Democratic nominee for Ga. House, 1986; Ga. House, 1989-93.
Capitol Office: 124 Cannon Bldg. 20515; 225-1605.

Committees
Banking & Financial Services
Financial Institutions & Consumer Credit; General Oversight & Investigations
International Relations
International Operations & Human Rights; Western Hemisphere

In Washington: McKinney fought for political survival on two fronts during the 104th Congress: in the U.S. Supreme Court and on the campaign trail. She lost her battle in the Supreme Court, which in 1995 invalidated Georgia's congressional district map as a "racial gerrymander" that violated the Constitution's guarantee of equal protection under the law, citing McKinney's then-11th District as the offending black-majority seat.

But at the polls, McKinney scored a surprisingly comfortable victory in the newly drawn, white-majority 4th District. Only one-third of the district's voting-age population is black, compared with 64 percent in her old 11th, yet in both the primary and general elections, McKinney dispatched her opponents by double-digit margins. (The home of GOP Rep. John Linder also was in the new 4th, but in 1996 he ran and won re-election in the new 11th, where blacks are only 11 percent of the voting-age population.)

McKinney's House district gained national notice after the June 1995 Supreme Court ruling. The 5-4 decision in *Miller v. Johnson* firmed up the court's 1993 ruling in a North Carolina case, *Shaw v. Reno*, also involving the issue of race-based redistricting. In that case, the court majority questioned the propriety of creating "bizarrely shaped" districts to aggregate minority voters. In the Georgia case, the court more explicitly rejected the use of race as the "predominant factor" in redistricting.

McKinney called the ruling "a setback for democracy." She said, "It is a shame that we are even here arguing whether or not we have gone overboard on perfecting democracy."

Her criticism went beyond rhetorical jabs, however. When the Georgia Legislature undertook the task of drawing new lines and its Senate was considering a plan that had just one black-majority district, McKinney hinted that black Democrats might form a third party based on the Rev. Jesse Jackson's Rainbow Coalition. She said that Senate plan would have used "traditional Democratic black voters as spare parts to bolster the prospects of certain favorite sons who are white Democrats."

And nearly two months later, she introduced legislation in the U.S. House that would have allowed states to experiment with new forms of electing lawmakers. Her proposal would have allowed states to draw multimember districts and allowed voters to cast several votes and fill numerous seats. She said the existing system of winner-take-all, single-member districts works to the disadvantage of blacks and that her plan would "help heal the racial divisions created by current legal battles over districts drawn to ensure minorities comprise a majority."

The state's congressional lines ultimately were drawn by a three-judge federal panel, which in a 2-1 ruling in December 1995 issued a map that dismantled two of the state's three black-majority districts — McKinney's 11th and the 2nd, represented by black Democrat Sanford D. Bishop Jr. Under the new map, Georgia's only black-majority constituency is the Atlanta-based 5th, home of black Democratic Rep. John Lewis.

"I suppose they couldn't wait to toss us out of our districts, even before our constituents had a say in the matter," McKinney said after the judges' decision. A group of black voters, joined by the Justice Department, appealed that decision to the Supreme Court to have the lines redrawn again, and McKinney again defended the concept of majority-minority districts the day the justices heard oral arguments in December 1996. "Minority districts work," she insisted.

Because of her youthful face, trademark braids and bright stylish attire (often including gold tennis shoes), McKinney in her early days on Capitol Hill was sometimes mistaken for a staffer. "I got up here in Congress by being myself," she told The Boston Globe in 1994. "What's frustrating is that people are so accustomed to seeing white men in suits on the Hill that I still have to defend my presence here."

The first black woman elected to the House from Georgia, McKinney can be outspoken and reluctant to compromise — traits prone to inhib-

When McKinney decided to run in the DeKalb-based 4th District after a federal court ruled in 1995 that her majority-black, Atlanta-to-Savannah 11th district was an unconstitutional racial gerrymander, Republicans targeted her for defeat. She was liberal, black and a scathing critic of Speaker Newt Gingrich, who represents the adjacent 6th.

But while much of the new district's terrain was unfamiliar to McKinney, the strong Democratic tendencies were not. In the 1996 presidential race, Bill Clinton captured 64 percent of the district's votes, similar to his 65 percent showing in the 11th District four years earlier.

DeKalb County, just east of Atlanta, accounts for 87 percent of the district's population. As Atlanta blossomed into the South's financial capital during the 1960s and 1970s, De Kalb was the pacesetter of suburban growth. With more than a half-million people, De Kalb is now Georgia's second most populous county. But growth here has slowed as development has spread into outlying jurisdictions. Lately, the hot spots have been farther east, in Gwinnett and Rockdale counties. Still, DeKalb has the state's highest population density — 2,100 people per square mile.

Democratic candidates get a warm reception in the central and western parts of De Kalb. Decatur, the county seat, was a 19th century commercial hub until it lost out as a railroad center to Atlanta; it still has some industry and a Democratic complexion. Emory University is one of the district's largest employers. The university and the communities around it — many of them with substantial Jewish or black populations — give local politics a liberal slant. Chamblee, a blue-collar community in northern De Kalb, has a large

GEORGIA 4
Atlanta suburbs — Parts of De Kalb and Gwinnett counties

immigrant community of both Asians and Hispanics, and they bolster the Democratic vote. Republicans run well in northern DeKalb, home to many affluent whites, and in fast-growing Gwinnett County, but these areas are Republican dents in the district's strongly Democratic armor.

Health care is one of the district's economic linchpins. The Centers for Disease Control and Prevention is near Emory University. DeKalb Medical Center, Emory University Hospital, and the Veterans Administration Medical Center also are among the county's largest employers.

A popular attraction is Stone Mountain Park in the eastern part of the county. The park features a mammoth granite outcropping into which a sculpture of Robert E. Lee and other Confederate heroes are carved.

In the past 30 years, DeKalb has undergone a political metamorphosis. In 1968, Democratic presidential candidate Hubert Humphrey received barely one-fourth of DeKalb's votes, and Jimmy Carter in 1976 had one of his lowest percentages here. But DeKalb opted narrowly for Michael S. Dukakis in 1988, and Bill Clinton in 1996 garnered 67 percent of the county's votes, more than 20 points above his statewide showing.

As of May 19, the Census Bureau had not recalculated population data, racial and ethnic breakdowns, and age statistics for districts newly drawn for the 1996 election.

it legislative accomplishment. Her four years in the Georgia House did not produce a broad legislative record, and her legislative achievements in Congress also have been few.

In the 104th Congress, she failed in her bid to curb U.S. arms sales to dictators, human-rights abusers and other global thugs. She offered her proposal, which the Clinton administration opposed, to foreign aid legislation, but the House defeated it on a 157-262 vote. McKinney serves on the International Relations Committee, as well as the Banking and Financial Services Committee.

McKinney's views are firmly anchored on the left side of the Democratic spectrum, and she has not been hesitant about sharing her dislike for the philosophy of the GOP majority. In the 104th, she attacked Republicans for what she called their "blitzkrieg against the poor" who are on welfare, and she accused fellow Georgian Newt Gingrich of engendering hate. To bolster her case, she read on the House floor a racist letter she had received that referred to blacks as "monkeys in the jungle" and concluded by saying, "Mr. Speaker, the spirit of GOP welfare lives in these words."

In February 1995, McKinney joined Democrats Patricia Schroeder of Colorado and Harry A. Johnston of Florida in filing an ethics complaint against Gingrich, one of a number of such filings. In January 1997, she voted with an overwhelming House majority to reprimand Gingrich and assess him a $300,000 penalty for ethics violations.

McKinney also has carried her battles to partisan rivals on the other side of the Capitol building. In January 1996, she and Schroeder sent a caustic letter to Sen. Alfonse M. D'Amato, R-N.Y., berating him for his Whitewater investigation of President Clinton and first lady Hillary Rodham Clinton. They called the probe "a political witch hunt designed to distract President Clinton," and urged D'Amato to stop "tormenting the first lady" and "leave the television spectacles to daytime talk shows."

At Home: Although McKinney had the advantage of incumbency in her 1996 bid for a third term, few Georgia pols expected her to win reelection after the Supreme Court dismantled her black-majority district.

But in the four-candidate Democratic primary in July, she rolled up 67 percent of the vote, easily outdistancing her closest rival, lawyer Comer Yates. He had waged a respectable 1994 campaign in the old 4th District as the Democratic challenger to GOP Rep. Linder , taking 42 percent of the vote.

Then, in November, McKinney registered a 58 percent to 42 percent victory over Republican businessman-attorney John Mitnick.

Both contests were racially charged. McKinney lashed out at Yates for conducting what she called a racially tinged "push-poll" on her 1994 vote against a resolution that condemned a roundly criticized speech by Khalid Abdul Muhammad, then a top aide to Nation of Islam leader Louis Farrakhan. And she blasted Mitnick, a Jew, when he raised the same issue and accused McKinney of "buddying up" with Louis Farrakhan on many occasions."

McKinney forced her father and longtime campaign adviser, state Rep. Billy McKinney, to resign soon after he called Mitnick "a racist Jew" at a church forum, but neither Cynthia McKinney's ties to Farrakhan nor her own campaign's missteps lent any significant momentum to Mitnick. "I continue to be the candidate nobody wants but the people," McKinney said after her victory.

McKinney first won election to the House in 1992 by moving into the new black-majority 11th, running an aggressive, if low-budget, primary campaign and beating two better-financed, better-connected black legislators. That November, she was elected with 73 percent of the vote over Republican farmer Woodrow Lovett. She faced Lovett again in November 1994, winning a second term with 66 percent of the vote.

In the 1992 primary, McKinney went after state Sen. Eugene Walker, a De Kalb County resident and the presumptive favorite for the Democratic nomination when the campaign began, and state Rep. Michael Thurmond, the chairman of the state House black caucus and the recipient of The Atlanta Constitution's endorsement. She said both were too closely connected to the state's dominant white Democratic power structure and unresponsive to Georgia's black voters.

McKinney won the endorsement of a prominent black politician, former Atlanta Mayor and Rep. Andrew Young, whose 1990 gubernatorial bid she had actively supported. She led the primary field with 31 percent of the vote and landed in a runoff with George L. DeLoach, the only white candidate of five contenders. He was a surprise second in the primary, winning the support of white voters from a core of rural counties in the otherwise largely suburban and urban district. McKinney took 56 percent to DeLoach's 44 percent in the runoff, then coasted in November.

HOUSE ELECTIONS

1996 General		
Cynthia A. McKinney (D)	127,157	(58%)
John Mitnick (R)	92,985	(42%)
1996 Primary		
Cynthia A. McKinney (D)	42,508	(67%)
Comer Yates (D)	15,126	(24%)
Ron Slotin (D)	3,993	(6%)
David Hughes (D)	1,370	(2%)
1994 General		
Cynthia A. McKinney (D)	71,560	(66%)
Woodrow Lovett (R)	37,533	(34%)

Previous Winning Percentages: 1992 (73%)

CAMPAIGN FINANCE

	Receipts	Receipts from PACs		Expenditures
1996				
McKinney (D)	$1,063,250	$364,959	(34%)	$1,015,197
Mitnick (R)	$655,053	$119,274	(18%)	$654,287
1994				
McKinney (D)	$306,775	$189,181	(62%)	$274,232
Lovett (R)	$11,083	$1,514	(14%)	$12,019

DISTRICT VOTE FOR PRESIDENT

1996			1992		
D	141,017	(64%)	**D**	124,625	(55%)
R	69,824	(32%)	**R**	80,578	(35%)
I	8,006	(4%)	**I**	22,824	(10%)

KEY VOTES

1997	
Ban "partial birth" abortions	N
1996	
Approve farm bill	?
Deny public education to illegal immigrants	N
Repeal ban on certain assault-style weapons	N
Increase minimum wage	Y
Freeze defense spending	Y
Approve welfare overhaul	N
1995	
Approve balanced-budget constitutional amendment	N
Relax Clean Water Act regulations	N
Oppose limits on environmental regulations	?
Reduce projected Medicare spending	N
Approve GOP budget with tax and spending cuts	N

VOTING STUDIES

	Presidential Support		Party Unity		Conservative Coalition	
Year	S	O	S	O	S	O
1996	80	20	94	2	4	94
1995	79	14	90	2	8	74
1994	77	23	98	1	3	97
1993	76	23	93	2	7	91

INTEREST GROUP RATINGS

Year	ADA	AFL-CIO	CCUS	ACU
1996	100	n/a	20	0
1995	85	100	4	13
1994	100	100	33	0
1993	100	100	9	0

5 John Lewis (D)

Of Atlanta — Elected 1986, 6th term

Biographical Information

Born: Feb. 21, 1940, Troy, Ala.

Education: American Baptist Theological Seminary, B.A. 1961; Fisk U., B.A. 1963.

Occupation: Civil rights activist.

Family: Wife, Lillian Miles; one child.

Religion: Baptist.

Political Career: Sought Democratic nomination for U.S. House (special election), 1977; Atlanta City Council, 1982-86.

Capitol Office: 229 Cannon Bldg. 20515; 225-3801.

Committees

Ways & Means
Health

Chief Deputy Whip

In Washington: With his party in the House minority, Lewis has taken a higher profile on the House floor, rising to vent liberal rhetorical anger — usually at Republicans, for their spending and tax cuts, but sometimes even at the Democratic White House, as when President Clinton signed a welfare overhaul bill that the Democratic left opposed.

Lewis is one of House Democrats' four chief deputy whips, and he is widely respected by his party colleagues because of his pioneering role in the civil rights movement.

When Democrats ran the House, Lewis was known as a quiet, behind-the-scenes conciliator. But now, he and the other whips make it their business to stand up and censure the conservative policies of the GOP majority.

When the House took up the Republicans' seven year budget plan in the fall of 1995, Lewis took to the floor and said, "An ugly spirit has risen in our nation's capital. A mean spirit. A cruel spirit. A spirit that gave rise to this Republican bill. Republicans spend more on defense, but cut Head Start, school lunches and student loans. They choose bombers over babies, defense contractors over children, Star Wars over schools."

Lewis has also tried to make life hard on his home-state colleague, Speaker Newt Gingrich. Lewis was one of five House Democrats to contend early on that Gingrich had committed violations of House ethics rules. After an investigation by a special counsel brought in by the House ethics committee, the House reprimanded Gingrich and fined him $300,000.

Lewis was particularly critical of Republicans' happiness when former Senate Majority Leader Bob Dole announced in April 1997 that he would loan Gingrich the $300,000 he needed to pay the penalty. Lewis went to the floor to condemn Republicans for praising the Dole loan, and then he was banned from speaking on the floor for the rest of the day after saying the penalty was levied because Gingrich "has admitted lying to Congress." Republicans demanded that Lewis' words be "taken down" — purged from the official record of proceedings — and the GOP majority tabled, or killed, 223-199, a motion that would have permitted Lewis to speak. (Gingrich later said he would pay half of the fine from his own resources, borrowing $150,000 from Dole and repaying all of that by 1999.)

Lewis earlier had pushed hard to win public release of the special counsel's ethics report on Gingrich. He offered a resolution in September 1996 that would have required the ethics committee to make special counsel James M. Cole's report public, in response to allegations that Gingrich misused tax-exempt foundations for political purposes. But the House voted, 225-179, virtually along party lines, to kill the resolution.

When Lewis brought the resolution to the floor calling for the report's release, he was challenged by Georgia Republican John Linder, who called for Lewis to be ruled out of order because he was discussing an item before the ethics committee on the House floor. But Lewis stood his ground, telling Linder: "I will not be harassed, bullied or silenced. You know, Mr. Linder, I've learned in my life there are times when the rules must be challenged to confront or dramatize injustice. I will not sit down or keep silent until you release that report to the American people."

In December 1996, Gingrich admitted that he failed to properly manage the financing of his political activities through charitable foundations. He also conceded a more serious offense: giving the ethics committee misleading information during its investigation. After Cole released his 213-page report in January, the House voted, 395-28, to reprimand and fine Gingrich.

Lewis was equally indignant at Clinton for compromising with the GOP on welfare overhaul. Lewis called the welfare bill "mean" and "downright low down." Urging the House to vote it down, Lewis said, "This bill will put 1 million more children into poverty. How, how can any person of faith, of conscience vote for a bill that puts a million more kids into poverty? Where is the compassion, where is the sense of decency,

GEORGIA 5
Parts of Atlanta

The obvious symbol of the 5th is Atlanta's alluring skyline, with the state Capitol, the steel-and-glass office skyscrapers and the towering hotels that make the city the commercial center of the Southeast and the symbolic capital of the New South.

However, in the shadows of those buildings is another Atlanta, a mostly black city struggling with typical urban social problems — unemployment, crime and drugs. While Atlanta's business boom spurred continued suburban sprawl through the 1980s, the city's population dropped slightly, to just over 394,000.

But Atlanta underwent a major facelift in preparation for the 1996 Summer Olympics. Hundreds of millions of dollars in Olympics-related construction projects gave a boost to the local economy. The Games themselves focused international attention on Atlanta, although not all of it was favorable. A bombing at a public park marred the festive atmosphere.

The district takes in most of Atlanta and surrounding Fulton County, as well as some suburban territory in neighboring counties, including a small piece of western De Kalb and some of northwestern Clayton. Remapping in 1995 generally left the district's boundaries intact.

The district's 57 percent black voting-age population is almost identical to its predecessor's percentage. African-Americans help make the 5th a Democratic bastion: Bill Clinton defeated Bob Dole by better than three to one in 1996 in what was his best district in the state.

Fulton is reliable Democratic, though there are pockets of GOP strength in its wealthier northern suburbs. The area along West Paces Ferry Road in the Buckhead vicinity is dotted with elegant homes, including the Governor's Mansion.

The heart of the district is Atlanta itself. Its downtown has enjoyed more attention in recent years with the help of such attractions as Underground Atlanta, a tourist shopping complex, and the nearby Coca-Cola museum. Tourists also can pay homage here to the Rev. Dr. Martin Luther King Jr., the late civil rights leader. His birthplace, the church where he preached, his Center for Non-Violent Change and his gravesite are along Auburn Avenue east of Five Points. In the city's southwest is the historically black Atlanta University Center, including Morehouse and Spelman Colleges.

South of Atlanta, the district takes in East Point, a lower-middle-class community. Many of its residents work at Hartsfield Atlanta International Airport in northwest Clayton County. The 1991 closure of Eastern Airlines took a bite out of aviation employment, costing 10,000 people their jobs. But other job opportunities in the metropolitan area have generally mitigated the loss of Eastern.

Among the 5th's largest employers are Delta Airlines, the Fort McPherson Army Forces Command, Coca-Cola, Cable News Network, Bell South and timber giant Georgia Pacific.

Nearly 85 percent of the district's vote comes out of Fulton County. Of the rest, the biggest share (about 10 percent) comes from northwest Clayton County, home to many airport workers and a growing Asian population.

As of May 19, the Census Bureau had not recalculated population data, racial and ethnic breakdowns, and age statistics for districts newly drawn for the 1996 election.

where is the heart of this Congress?"

From his first day in Congress in 1987, Lewis enjoyed a special status because of his exceptional role in the front lines of the civil rights movement. Many House members vividly recall the news photo of a young Lewis being beaten by state troopers as he and other civil rights leaders crossed the Edmund Pettus bridge in Selma, Ala., during a 1965 march. Yet the violence Lewis faced did not alter his strong commitment to non-violent change. As a politician Lewis has sought — and won — biracial support.

Lewis was successful in May 1996 in getting the House to pass a bill designating the route from Selma to Montgomery as a National Historic Trail. He recounted for the House the history of the civil rights march, saying it was a turning point in the journey to the Voting Rights Act of 1965. "The history along this route is precious," Lewis said. "The trail reminds us of where we were in 1965 and how far we have come as a nation and as a people." The measure was cleared at the end of the 104th as part of a broad parks and lands bill.

From his seat on the Ways and Means Committee, Lewis has criticized the Republicans' tax-cut proposals. When the committee in March 1995 approved a measure that gave families and businesses an array of tax credits and rate reductions, Lewis charged that the programs being cut to pay for the tax reductions disproportionately affected those at the bottom of the economic ladder. "We have cut money for poor, disabled and elderly for the sake of those earning more than $100,000 a year," he complained.

In an odd alliance, Lewis joined Gingrich in August 1995 to redraw Georgia's congressional district map. The U.S. Supreme Court in June 1995 had invalidated Georgia's map as an unconstitutional racial gerrymander. Lewis and Gingrich then submitted a new district map to a federal judge that was designed to protect Georgia's 11 incumbent House members. Calling them "the unlikeliest of allies," the Atlanta Constitution reported that the Gingrich-Lewis plan proposed two "mostly black" congressional districts and a third "with a significant black population."

But a three-judge federal panel in December 1995 issued a different map that dismantled two of the state's three black-majority House districts -- the 11th and the 2nd. Lewis now represents the only black majority district in Georgia.

At Home: Lewis' 1986 victory in the 5th symbolized the rise of Southern blacks into the halls of political power. But to get to Congress, Lewis had to weather a bitter contest with a longtime ally, state Sen. Julian Bond.

The relationship between the civil rights leaders dated to the early 1960s. Lewis, the son of an Alabama sharecropper, was director of the Student Nonviolent Coordinating Committee (SNCC); Bond, from a middle-class Philadelphia background, was the group's spokesman. Lewis spoke at the 1963 March on Washington. His fearlessness in the face of arrests and beatings was legendary. But when radical elements took over SNCC, Lewis moved on to head the Atlanta-based Voter Education Project.

Lewis lost his first political bid, a 1977 House primary, to Wyche Fowler Jr. In 1981, he won the first of two terms on the Atlanta City Council; he gained a following among blacks as well as whites in north Atlanta who appreciated his attention to neighborhood matters. Bond, meanwhile, served 20 years in the Georgia legislature, where he pushed through a redistricting plan that transformed the 5th District from nearly half white to almost two-thirds black. When Fowler announced his 1986 challenge to GOP Sen. Mack Mattingly, Bond was the favorite to succeed him in the 5th.

Bond finished ahead in the primary. But Lewis, whose interracial appeal brought him a sizable white vote, forced Bond into a runoff. The campaign became nasty. Bond belittled Lewis' command of issues. But Lewis delivered sharper blows, implying that Bond had held a desk job in the civil rights revolution and calling on Bond to join him in taking drug tests. Though he never accused Bond outright of using drugs, the implication was there for those who already saw Bond as a jet-setter.

Winning more than 80 percent of the vote in majority-white precincts and cutting into Bond's margin among blacks, Lewis won the nomination with 52 percent. The Democratic rift had little effect on Lewis in the general election; he prevailed by a 3-1 margin. By his first re-election, Lewis was a settled incumbent, running without primary opposition and winning with ease in the general election. That pattern was repeated in 1990.

In 1992, redistricting deprived the 5th of some black voters, but the map kept the black majority in Lewis' turf well over 60 percent. Lewis drew both primary and general-election opponents, but neither offered a vigorous challenge, and he won both races with ease.

Lewis again won easily in 1994. Subsequent redistricting in 1995 did not change the makeup of Lewis' district, and he drew no GOP opposition in 1996.

HOUSE ELECTIONS

1996 General	
John Lewis (D)	136,555 (100%)
1994 General	
John Lewis (D)	85,094 (69%)
Dale Dixon (R)	37,999 (31%)

Previous Winning Percentages: 1992 (72%) **1990** (76%) **1988** (78%) **1986** (75%)

CAMPAIGN FINANCE

	Receipts	Receipts from PACs	Expend- itures
1996			
Lewis (D)	$262,227	$217,630 (83%)	$207,661
1994			
Lewis (D)	$549,837	$440,360 (80%)	$323,725
Dixon (R)	$49,945	$814 (2%)	$47,476

DISTRICT VOTE FOR PRESIDENT

	1996		1992
D	134,248 (74%)	D	141,728 (70%)
R	41,385 (23%)	R	46,139 (23%)
I	5,005 (3%)	I	14,436 (7%)

KEY VOTES

1997	
Ban "partial birth" abortions	N
1996	
Approve farm bill	N
Deny public education to illegal immigrants	N
Repeal ban on certain assault-style weapons	N
Increase minimum wage	Y
Freeze defense spending	Y
Approve welfare overhaul	N
1995	
Approve balanced-budget constitutional amendment	N
Relax Clean Water Act regulations	N
Oppose limits on environmental regulations	Y
Reduce projected Medicare spending	N
Approve GOP budget with tax and spending cuts	N

VOTING STUDIES

	Presidential Support		Party Unity		Conservative Coalition	
Year	S	O	S	O	S	O
1996	84	16	97	2	10	88
1995	83	13	94	2	6	91
1994	71	26	93	3	6	94
1993	79	21	98	2	9	91
1992	11	81	95	1	6	83
1991	22	71	96	2	3	89

INTEREST GROUP RATINGS

Year	ADA	AFL-CIO	CCUS	ACU
1996	100	n/a	19	0
1995	100	100	9	9
1994	100	100	25	5
1993	100	100	9	0
1992	95	92	13	0
1991	85	92	0	0

6 Newt Gingrich (R)

Of Marietta — Elected 1978, 10th term

Biographical Information

Born: June 17, 1943, Harrisburg, Pa.

Education: Emory U., B.A. 1965; Tulane U., M.A. 1968, Ph.D. 1971.

Occupation: Professor.

Family: Wife, Marianne Ginther; two children.

Religion: Baptist.

Political Career: Republican nominee for U.S. House, 1974, 1976.

Capitol Office: 2428 Rayburn Bldg. 20515; 225-4501.

Speaker of the House

In Washington: Unlike most figures of legend who lead their minions out of the desert, Gingrich actually got to see the promised land, being sworn in as Speaker when the Republicans took control of the House in 1995. But like many people whose dearest wishes come true, Gingrich has found the experience to be a mixed blessing: His leadership has been marred by scandal, unrest among his troops, and a level of personal unpopularity that is practically without rival in American politics.

Gingrich has resolved his ethics case and, if he hardly escaped the process unscathed, he appears to have lessened the ill will some members of the GOP Conference began to feel for him. Gingrich enjoyed a prominent place on the dais as jubilant Republicans announced a budget outline reached in negotiations with President Clinton in May 1997. Yet even then, his position appeared to have been eclipsed by GOP Senate Majority Leader Trent Lott of Mississippi.

Gingrich began his Speakership on a roll, wresting control of important legislation from obedient committee chairmen and drawing comparisons not only to legendary Speakers of the past but to Clinton in terms of his ability to shape the national agenda. In April 1995, when Gingrich triumphantly addressed a national television audience to trumpet House approval of nearly all the bills derived from the "Contract With America" campaign platform, Clinton feebly reminded a skeptical news conference of his constitutional "relevance."

Yet Gingrich's star, though brilliant, appeared to burn too bright to be sustained. House passage of contract items such as a balanced-budget amendment to the Constitution, a massive tax cut package and an overhaul of welfare proved to be the easy part of governance. (The one major contract failure was the defeat of a constitutional amendment to limit congressional terms.) Many Republican members held their noses and voted for bills they did not entirely agree with in confidence that the Senate would "fix" them.

The narrow Republican majority aided Gingrich's efforts toward loyalty. With a large and unyielding class of GOP freshmen elected in 1994, Gingrich could credibly argue that he was in no position to compromise, because he was driven by the anti-Washington fuel of these new members. Gingrich claimed he had no room to give, and so more moderate Republicans stuck with the agenda rather than handing victories to Democrats and undermining their newfound, long hoped for, majority status.

With media appearances and speculation about a possible presidential run, Gingrich became clearly the face of the new Congress. He was an eager and articulate spokesman for Republican ideas new and old, cheerfully offering fellow members, the foot soldiers of his revolution, reading lists and aphorisms coined off the cuff. He was not always able to put his best face forward, however. News magazines writing about Republican rewrites of social legislation rudely caricatured him as "the Gingrich who stole Christmas."

If the criticisms of Gingrich were not entirely sporting, the Georgian brought many public relations problems on himself, such as when he accepted a $4.5 million advance for writing and editing books from media mogul Rupert Murdoch's HarperCollins imprint at a time when Murdoch was lobbying on telecommunications legislation. Gingrich returned the money and accepted a $1 advance against royalties just before the 104th got under way. (There was a good deal of speculation in the media that his hints about maybe running for president were ploys to generate interest in his book "To Renew America.")

As the fiscal 1996 appropriations season began — already behind schedule because of the attention and floor time absorbed by the contract — Gingrich and other GOP leaders pursued a strategy of larding the spending bills with policy riders that would take much time and trouble to pass if they were stand-alone legislation. Since they saw the spending bills as "must pass" legislation, they

GEORGIA 6
Atlanta suburbs — Roswell; part of Marietta

Anchored in Atlanta's burgeoning northern suburbs, the 6th covers parts of four counties that are laden with Republican voters who work in high-technology and other white-collar occupations. This area is referred to as the Golden Crescent; it is sandwiched between three of the state's major interstate highways — I-75, I-85 and the I-285 perimeter highway.

Remapping in 1995 removed GOP-leaning northern De Kalb County and added more territory in fast-growing and reliably Republican Gwinnett County. The 6th remains the state's most affluent district and one of the country's most loyal Republican areas. It also is largely white: The 6th's black voting-age population is just over 6 percent, lower than in every other Georgia district except one (the 9th) and only slightly higher than the old 6th's percentage.

Cobb County, which lies northwest of Atlanta, accounts for more than 50 percent of the district's vote. About three-fourths of Cobb's residents are in the 6th; the rest of the county is in the 7th. Voters in the 6th District part of Cobb gave Bob Dole a decisive 59 percent in 1996.

Though it is well within Atlanta's orbit, Marietta (which is divided between the 6th and 7th districts) provides Cobb County with its own population and commercial center. A well-known Marietta landmark is the "big chicken," a 56-foot-tall, fowl-shaped sign with a KFC chicken outlet at its base.

Marietta has a thriving base of service-oriented small businesses. Cobb County is headquarters for a number of well-known larger concerns, including Sprint and Home Depot. Numerous corporations have office space in the "Platinum Triangle," near the intersection of I-75 and I-285.

Many workers in the district commute to jobs at the Dobbins-N.A.S. Joint Reserve Base and an adjoining facility operated by Lockheed Martin; both are in the 7th District.

Marietta has three colleges — Kennesaw State College, Southern College of Technology and Life College (one of the largest chiropractic schools in the nation). An important local tourist attraction is the Kennesaw Mountain National Battlefield.

In the central part of the 6th are solidly GOP suburbs in northern Fulton County. The Sandy Springs area just north of the Perimeter, is, like much of the 6th, replete with upwardly mobile entrepreneurs and small-business owners.

Fa rther north in Fulton are Alpharetta and Roswell. Alpharetta was once home to a number of large farms that since have been converted into suburban developments. Roswell used to be a cotton-milling center, but now is a booming bedroom community with the sort of white-collar, managerial types that seem ubiquitous in the Atlanta area. About one-fourth of the district's vote is cast in Fulton County, where Dole captured 62 percent of the vote.

The remaining share of the vote in the district — about 25 percent — comes from southern Cherokee County and northwestern Gwinnett County. Both counties are among the state's fastest growing counties and strongly Republican. Dole won the 6th's portions of these counties with 62 percent and 65 percent, respectively.

As of May 19, the Census Bureau had not recalculated population data, racial and ethnic breakdowns, and age statistics for the districts newly drawn for the 1996 election.

reckoned the Senate and the president would be forced to swallow some relatively small policy items they might not otherwise accept; among these were provisions restricting some workplace and collective bargaining protections and the Environmental Protection Agency's ability to enforce key environmental laws, as well as numerous abortion tangles. They also taunted Clinton by zeroing out certain programs he cherished, such as the National Service initiative.

The Senate refused even to bother with some of the House product, such as the bill funding the departments of Labor, Health and Human Services, and Education. And contrary to what many Republicans had expected, Clinton proved quite willing to wield his veto pen. Congress had not even finished with all its appropriations bills when the new fiscal year began. Partial funding of certain programs was provided by a series of continuing resolutions, to which the GOP leadership also added extraneous policy riders.

As Clinton criticized these, he found his thematic voice. He attacked Republicans for threatening programs such as Medicare, Medicaid, education and the environment, and scored huge political points in doing so. As budget negotiations wore on through the fall of 1995, public opinion polls showed the public largely blaming Republicans for not compromising with Clinton on the budget. Clinton derailed most of the GOP's first year's efforts and their brightest hopes by vetoing Gingrich's massive budget-balancing plan, seeming to grow in stature as he did so.

As all this unfolded, Gingrich became the incredible shrinking man. He lost some credibility within his own ranks during extensive meetings at the White House on the budget; Gingrich spoke openly about how charming he found the president to be. House Majority Leader Dick Armey, a Texas Republican, began attending the meetings to lend conservative backbone.

Then, a fit of pique toward Clinton greatly

exacerbated Gingrich's already poor national image. He revealed that a partial government shutdown came about in part because he felt Clinton had snubbed him on Air Force One during the trip to Israel to attend the funeral of slain Prime Minister Yitzhak Rabin. As his press secretary paced nervously in the back of the room, Gingrich described to reporters his anger about having to leave the plane by the rear door.

This outburst topped news broadcasts and Democrats took to the House floor to gleefully parade a mockup of the front page of the New York Daily News, which depicted a crying Gingrich in diapers.

In December 1995, the Democrat in a special congressional election in California's Silicon Valley test-marketed the idea of tarring his Republican opponent for associating with Gingrich. Although the strategy failed there, it would be adopted by dozens of Democratic candidates in 1996. A demonized Gingrich had become the poster child for opponents of the Republican revolution to limit the size and scope of government.

Also in December 1995, Gingrich got bad news about the ethics charges against him, which he always shrugged off as purely politically motivated: The House ethics committee voted to hire an independent counsel to investigate whether Gingrich violated federal tax laws in raising money for a televised college course he taught. The panel unanimously found that Gingrich violated House rules on three separate instances but called for no punishment at that point. (Gingrich in 1988 had filed the ethics complaints that led to the downfall of Speaker Jim Wright, D-Texas, and Democrats were eager to return the favor.)

Adding to Gingrich's woes was the partial government shutdown. The most staunchly conservative House Republicans thought they could use the stick of a shutdown to force Clinton to compromise on the budget. But when it became clear that Republicans were getting blamed for the shutdown, Senate Majority Leader Bob Dole of Kansas (he later resigned to devote himself to his 1996 presidential run), decided it was time for, in his words, "adult leadership." He pressured the House to reopen the government.

Gingrich eventually came around to Dole's point of view, and told an unhappy GOP Conference meeting in January 1996 that members should vote to fund the government or find themselves a new leader. All but 15 Republicans went along with the plan.

As the 1996 election season started in earnest, congressional Republicans soon grew tired of being bashed for voting in line with Gingrich. The man to whom they had given extraordinary loyalty had become a political burden. Committee chairmen began asserting their control over legislation and many members clamored for compromise legislation that they could parade to their constituents as tangible accomplishment. Gingrich and conservatives were forced in May 1996 to accede to a minimum wage increase, as moderate Republican joined with Democrats in passing the measure in the House.

Rank-and-file Republicans also pressured the leadership to bring a compromise welfare bill to the floor, rather than continuing to keep it linked to an overhaul of Medicaid, which Clinton had vowed to veto. The welfare bill, a safe-drinking water plan, a law to expand access to health insurance and the minimum wage boost all became law in a summer 1996 flurry of activity, as the parties prepared for their national conventions. But Gingrich appeared to reap no political benefit from these developments, as attention was focused on new Senate leader Lott. Although Gingrich chaired the San Diego convention, he was almost absent from the platform, making one short, uncharacteristically conciliatory speech.

By September 1996, Republicans were so eager to return home to campaign for re-election that they agreed to give Clinton virtually all the extra money he wanted for fiscal 1997. Gingrich said it was better "in this political environment" to acquiesce in a fatter spending bill and fight out the issue in the fall campaign.

Republicans held the House in November 1996 and Gingrich was renominated for Speaker by acclamation, despite the ongoing ethics investigation. In an emotional and contrite speech, he said Republicans would bury the confrontational tactics of their first two years in the majority.

"And so we find ourselves here with a Democratic president and a Republican Congress," he said. "And we have an absolute moral obligation to make this system work. This Congress will be the 'Implementation Congress.'"

Though Gingrich was renominated for Speaker, House Republicans transferred some decision-making authority from him to committees and broke up the Speaker's Advisory Group, a cadre of leaders that had been the nerve center of Gingrich's operations in the 104th.

In late December 1996, the ethics subcommittee investigating Gingrich issued a 22-page "statement of alleged violations" and released Gingrich's own admission that he violated House rules. The subcommittee's statement described how tax-exempt money was used for political purposes and said that Gingrich provided the panel in December 1994 and March 1995 information that he should have known was "inaccurate, incomplete and unreliable." Gingrich admitted that he submitted false information to the panel, although he insisted that he did so unintentionally. He also said that he failed to seek proper advice on the use of tax-exempt donations to advance partisan political causes.

In January 1997, Gingrich became the first Republican re-elected Speaker in 68 years. But there were no cheers of "Newt" from the party faithful this time around, and nine Republicans did not support him. "To the degree I was too brash, too self-confident or too pushy, I apologize," Gingrich said after taking the rostrum. "To whatever degree in any way that I have brought controversy or inappropriate attention to the House, I apologize."

Less than three weeks later, the House voted, 395-28, to reprimand Gingrich and assess him a financial penalty of $300,000. It was the first time a Speaker had been punished for violating House rules. "Mr. Gingrich ran a lot of very yellow lights," special counsel James M. Cole said. "Orange lights. There were bells and whistles going off. He was taking risks. Going right up to the edge."

Gingrich blamed his lawyer for the mistakes and a double standard for the penalty. He had clearly taken hits in the eyes of his own followers; one GOP House member described him as "road-kill." But Gingrich, still the indispensable man, began to repair his image with a successful foreign policy trip to Asia. And by May 1997, he could boast of helping bring the party closer to realizing its dream of eliminating the deficit, as the outline of a long-awaited budget agreement with Clinton won decisive approval in the House, 333-99.

At Home: Despite the 6th District's Republican edge, Gingrich has not been given a free ride. In 1996, just as Republicans targeted House Democratic leaders, so did the Democrats come up with an attractive and well-financed candidate to oppose Gingrich. He was Michael J. Coles, millionaire co-founder of the Great American Cookie Co. Inc.

It wound up being the most expensive House race of the year. Gingrich spent $6.3 million in winning the seat with 58 percent of the vote. Coles spent $3.3 million — $2.4 million from his own pocket, and polled 42 percent.

Two years earlier, former Democratic Rep. Ben Jones tried to make his comeback against Gingrich. Greatly outspent, Jones, who played Cooter on the TV series "The Dukes of Hazzard," still made plenty of noise, raising questions about Gingrich's ethics and accusing him of ignoring his district and refusing to debate. Gingrich won with 64 percent.

In 1990, in the old 6th District, a determined challenger dragged Gingrich to within 974 votes of a loss. The man who almost retired Gingrich that year was Democrat David Worley, an aggressive young lawyer. A former congressional aide, Worley announced his first House campaign in mid-1987. His main thrust was that Gingrich's proposed revamp of the U.S. retirement system was actually a plot to destroy Social Security. He accused Gingrich of hypocrisy on ethics (pointing to, among other things, his efforts to have a political associate appointed to be a federal judge).

However, Gingrich proved he could give as good as he got. He portrayed Worley, a Harvard-educated district native, as a Boston liberal and as a stooge of the ethically tarnished House Speaker Wright and won all but one of the district's 12 counties.

In 1990, Worley tried again, arguing that Gingrich had become enamored with national politics at the expense of district concerns. Budget battles kept Gingrich in Washington most of the fall, bolstering Worley's portrait of the incumbent as out of touch. Gingrich barely prevailed.

HOUSE ELECTIONS

1996 General		
Newt Gingrich (R)	174,155	(58%)
Michael Coles (D)	127,135	(42%)
1994 General		
Newt Gingrich (R)	119,432	(64%)
Ben Jones (D)	66,700	(36%)

Previous Winning Percentages: **1992** (58%) **1990** (50%) **1988** (59%) **1986** (60%) **1984** (69%) **1982** (55%) **1980** (59%) **1978** (54%)

CAMPAIGN FINANCE

	Receipts	Receipts from PACs	Expend-itures
1996			
Gingrich (R)	$6,252,069	$1,098,746 (18%)	$5,577,715
Coles (D)	$3,327,354	$101,036 (3%)	$3,325,030
1994			
Gingrich (R)	$2,012,572	$768,480 (38%)	$1,817,792
Jones (D)	$318,659	$250 (0%)	$321,774

DISTRICT VOTE FOR PRESIDENT

	1996		1992
D	100,584 (33%)	**D**	79,696 (30%)
R	184,970 (61%)	**R**	146,520 (55%)
I	15,345 (5%)	**I**	39,827 (15%)

KEY VOTES†

1997	
Ban "partial birth" abortions	Y
1996	
Deny public education to illegal immigrants	Y
Approve welfare overhaul	Y
1995	
Approve balanced-budget constitutional amendment	Y
Reduce projected Medicare spending	Y
Approve GOP budget with tax and spending cuts	Y

VOTING STUDIES

	Presidential Support		Party Unity		Conservative Coalition	
Year	**S**	**O**	**S**	**O**	**S**	**O**
1996	25†	75†	97†	3†	100†	0†
1995	10†	90†	98†	0†	100†	0†
1994	44	54	90	5	97	0
1993	42	56	87	6	95	5
1992	76	10	82	5	85	2
1991	78	19	88	7	95	5

† As Speaker of the House, Gingrich voted at his discretion.

INTEREST GROUP RATINGS

Year	ADA	AFL-CIO	CCUS	ACU
1996	0	n/a	100	100
1995	0	0	100	100
1994	5	13	91	100
1993	0	0	91	96
1992	10	22	88	100
1991	5	17	100	100

7 Bob Barr (R)

Of Smyrna — Elected 1994, 2nd term

Biographical Information

Born: Nov. 5, 1948, Iowa City, Iowa.

Education: U. of Southern California, B.A. 1970; George Washington U., M.A. 1972; Georgetown U., J.D. 1977.

Occupation: Lawyer; CIA analyst.

Family: Wife, Jerilyn Ann; four children.

Religion: Methodist.

Political Career: Sought Republican nomination for Ga. House, 1984; U.S. attorney, 1986-90; sought Republican nomination for U.S. Senate, 1992.

Capitol Office: 1130 Longworth Bldg. 20515; 225-2931.

Committees

Banking & Financial Services
Domestic & International Monetary Policy; Financial Institutions & Consumer Credit

Government Reform & Oversight
National Economic Growth, Natural Resources & Regulatory Affairs; National Security, International Affairs & Criminal Justice

Judiciary
Constitution; Crime

In Washington: A twice-divorced former U.S. attorney might seem an unlikely champion for traditional marriage and limiting the reach of federal law enforcement, but Barr took a high profile in behalf of those causes during the 104th Congress, and he earned a reputation as a hard-nosed conservative to be reckoned with.

A statement Barr made in September 1995 succinctly conveyed his concerns about the scope of federal law enforcement. "We need to ask ourselves if we have too many officers with guns out there trying to enforce too many regulations," he said. At the time he was seeking to ax the Bureau of Alcohol, Tobacco and Firearms and streamline other federal law enforcement functions.

A member of the Judiciary Committee and leader of a GOP task force on firearms that was set up by Speaker Newt Gingrich, Barr moved assertively to influence Congress' deliberations on a measure designed to combat domestic and international terrorism. The impetus for the legislation was the April 1995 bombing of a federal office building in Oklahoma City.

Barr voted against the bill when it cleared Judiciary in June 1995, on the grounds that it gave too much power to federal law enforcement authorities. Then he began working with Judiciary Chairman Henry J. Hyde, R-Ill., to craft a version that the House's more conservative Republicans would accept. Reaching agreement in late November, they offered a bill that required that plastic explosives be marked for easier detection and provided federal authorities with enhanced access to telephone records. To lure conservatives, the compromise measure included significant new restrictions on death row appeals.

The bill was scheduled for floor debate in December, but House leaders pulled it off the schedule when they found that nearly 100 Republicans were opposed to or undecided about it because of the new powers it gave to federal law enforcement officials.

Over Hyde's objections, Barr offered an amendment when the bill reached the floor in March 1996 stripping the bill of key provisions, including a provision allowing the government to use illegally obtained wiretap evidence in terrorism cases and another making it easier to prosecute those who sell or trade guns later used to commit a crime. Hyde fumed that Barr's amendment would leave only a "frail representation of what started out as a robust answer to the terrorist menace." But Barr was supported by a majority of Republicans and some liberal Democrats, all of whom were reluctant to entrust more power to the federal government. His amendment was approved, 246-171, and the bill passed, 229-191.

When the measure went to a House-Senate conference, there was some pressure to restore many of the provisions Barr's amendment had removed. But Barr, a conferee, was not budging. "I am not willing to sacrifice constitutional protections in order to give federal law enforcement officials more power they don't need," he said.

As ultimately cleared, the bill subjected convicted terrorists to the death penalty and boosted the authorization for law enforcement spending, but it did not allow the FBI to wiretap all telephones used by a suspected terrorist, as President Clinton had requested, and it required only plastic explosives to contain "taggant" tracers. Although it was less than he had hoped for, Clinton signed the bill into law in April 1996.

Later that year, three incidents gave new impetus to terrorism legislation: the bombings of Centennial Olympic Park in Atlanta during the Summer Olympics and of a U.S. military housing complex in Saudi Arabia, and the explosion of TWA Flight 800 off New York. Clinton renewed his call for expanded federal authority to counter terrorists, but Barr balked, saying "a knee-jerk legislative reaction to a criminal act, even a heinous one like the killing of civilians in Atlanta . . . is not the kind of sound basis from which important crime legislation, with important effects on civil liberties, should come."

A strong supporter of Second Amendment rights, Barr pushed hard for a vote in the House on repealing the 1994 ban on certain semiauto-

Starting in suburbs north and west of Atlanta, the 7th runs west to the Alabama border, taking in 10 full counties and part of another. But in terms of population concentration, it is bottom-heavy. Nearly half the district's voters live in just three counties that adjoin Atlanta's Fulton County — Cobb, Douglas and Carroll. The state's 1995 remapping process provided minimal changes to the 7th.

The areas that make up the 7th are ancestrally Democratic — the district is home to Thomas B. Murphy, Speaker of the Georgia House since 1974 — but recently are trending Republican. Newt Gingrich represented much of this area in the 1980s, and its Republican leanings were evident in 1996, when Bob Dole won the 7th by double digits.

The district takes in the southwestern part of Cobb County, a collection of largely white-collar, middle-income suburbs, and much of the county seat, Marietta. The Marietta area today has a diverse economic base, with numerous small businesses, several corporate headquarters and military- and aerospace-related employment at Lockheed Martin and the Dobbins-N.A.S. Atlanta Joint Reserve Base. The Lockheed facility laid off several thousand workers in the late 1980s, but a new contract to manufacture the F-22 advanced tactical fighter has provided many jobs to the area.

Cobb was the site of many Civil War battles, and the Kennesaw Mountain National Battlefield Park west of Marietta is a tourist draw. Another of the 7th's popular attractions is the amusement park Six Flags over Georgia, located in southeastern Cobb.

The 7th's portion of Cobb is not as Republican as the 6th's. Dole captured just over 50 percent of the vote there compared with the nearly 59 percent he received in the 6th's allotment of Cobb.

GEORGIA 7
Northwest — Rome; part of Marietta

Abutting Cobb to the south and west are burgeoning Paulding and Douglas counties. From 1990 to 1995, Paulding's population grew 44 percent, fastest in the state and sixth-fastest in the nation.

Carroll is the only county that touches both Fulton and the Alabama border. Carrollton, the county seat, is the headquarters of Southwire Corp., an electrical wire and cable manufacturer that employs over 3,000 in the area.

Moving beyond the metropolitan Atlanta orbit, the land is given over to agricultural pursuits, and there are a number of small towns traditionally reliant on textile trades. Many of the counties on the western edge of the 7th endured economic difficulties in the 1980s and began searching for new sources of income. Chattooga County now has a state prison, and Bartow County now houses an Anheuser-Busch brewery. The biggest city in this part of the 7th is Rome, the seat of Floyd County. Rome is a mill town that was once the district's largest city. Though eclipsed now by Marietta, it is a regional health care center.

The beef and timber industries and a few manufacturers provide jobs for residents of the counties along the Alabama border.

At the southwestern extreme of the district, Troup County lies midway between Atlanta and Columbus, with Interstate 85 slicing across its middle.

As of May 19, the Census Bureau had not recalculated population data, racial and ethnic breakdowns, and age statistics for districts newly drawn for the 1996 election.

matic assault-style weapons. The House approved the repeal measure in March 1996 on a 239-173 vote; it also increased minimum mandatory sentences for people convicted of using a firearm during the commission of a violent or drug-related federal crime. Barr said stiffer prison penalties would be a more effective deterrent to crime than a weapons ban. "The devil is the person with a gun who murders anybody," Barr told the House. "That is the person this bill addresses."

Barr also was at the center of the action on another controversial Judiciary bill — one banning federal recognition of same-sex marriages and allowing states to refuse to recognize such unions authorized by other states. The ban passed the House 342-67 in July 1996.

Barr said he introduced the bill in response to a Hawaii court case brought by two lesbians seeking to marry; the Hawaii Supreme Court had made a preliminary ruling that denying marriage to homosexual couples might violate the state Constitution's guarantees of equal protection. Were Hawaii eventually to legalize these marriages, Barr worried that other states and the federal government might be forced to recognize them also.

Barr insisted that it is Congress' responsibility to define marriage for purposes of federal law. "Enough is enough. Congress is drawing the line and saying marriage, as it's been known for thousands of years, will remain the legal union between one man and one woman: nothing more and nothing less." And he added, "The very foundations of our society are in danger of being burned. The flames of hedonism, the flames of narcissism, the flames of self-centered morality are licking at the very foundations of our society: the family unit."

Barr's opponents on this matter, though far

outnumbered, were biting in their criticism of the proposal, and not beneath making hay of his two divorces. "Divorce does more to dissolve marriage than does the marriage of two men," said Massachusetts Democratic Rep. Barney Frank, who is in a long-term homosexual relationship. Democrats said the federal government had no business writing its own definition of marriage into the federal code.

In addition to holding conservative stances on social issues, Barr sometimes has gone his party leadership one better in fiscal frugality. When budget talks between Congress and the White House broke down in January 1996, Barr was one of 12 members of the Class of 1994 to buck Speaker Gingrich's directive to vote to reopen the federal government. But he proved his loyalty to Gingrich in early 1997, when he was one of only 26 Republicans voting "no" when the House reprimanded the Speaker and assessed him a $300,000 penalty for ethics violations.

Barr also sits on the Banking and Financial Services and the Government Reform and Oversight committees.

At Home: Born in Iowa, Barr attended college at the University of Southern California, took master's and law degrees at George Washington and Georgetown universities, respectively, and, while in school in Washington, D.C., worked as an intelligence analyst at the CIA. He moved to Georgia to practice law in the late 1970s, became a U.S. attorney in 1986 and served in that position until 1990.

Two years later, he made his first try for Congress, seeking the GOP Senate nomination. He ran second in a five-candidate primary and then lost narrowly in the runoff to Paul Coverdell, who went on to win the seat. After the election, Barr kept his political apparatus in place, and soon he was preparing a 1994 challenge to 7th District Democratic Rep. George "Buddy" Darden.

Barr secured the GOP nomination with a 57 percent to 43 percent victory over gynecologist Brenda Fitzgerald. Their contest got nasty — she accused him of being an anti-Vietnam War protester in college, a charge he denied — and that tone continued during the fall campaign.

Darden had won five full House terms by convincing voters he was a nice fellow and a centrist, but Barr threw him on the defensive with charges that he was friendly with the unpopular Clinton administration and helpful to the liberal House Democratic leadership. Darden counterattacked, saying Barr did not live up to the moral standards he proclaimed. In TV ads and debates, Darden accused Barr of failing to reimburse his ex-wife for his children's medical bills and for once defending an "admitted" child molester.

Darden's attacks gained attention, but they sullied his "nice guy" image and may have negatively influenced some voters who had backed him in the past. The conservative swing evident nationwide in 1994 was especially pronounced in Georgia, and Barr captured the 7th with 52 percent of the vote.

In 1996, Barr faced Democratic state Rep. Charlie Watts. What started as a heated battle fizzled. Barr won comfortably, with 58 percent of the vote.

HOUSE ELECTIONS

1996 General		
Bob Barr (R)	112,009	(58%)
Charlie Watts (D)	81,765	(42%)
1994 General		
Bob Barr (R)	71,265	(52%)
George "Buddy" Darden (D)	65,978	(48%)

CAMPAIGN FINANCE

	Receipts	Receipts from PACs	Expend-itures
1996			
Barr (R)	$1,277,554	$383,623 (30%)	$1,272,303
Watts (D)	$308,981	$81,300 (26%)	$308,368
1994			
Barr (R)	$648,262	$88,873 (14%)	$622,336
Darden (D)	$879,928	$410,775 (47%)	$846,821

DISTRICT VOTE FOR PRESIDENT

	1996		1992
D	77,659 (40%)	**D**	80,267 (38%)
R	99,967 (51%)	**R**	99,187 (47%)
I	16,671 (9%)	**I**	31,666 (15%)

KEY VOTES

1997	
Ban "partial birth" abortions	Y
1996	
Approve farm bill	Y
Deny public education to illegal immigrants	Y
Repeal ban on certain assault-style weapons	Y
Increase minimum wage	N
Freeze defense spending	N
Approve welfare overhaul	Y
1995	
Approve balanced-budget constitutional amendment	Y
Relax Clean Water Act regulations	Y
Oppose limits on environmental regulations	N
Reduce projected Medicare spending	Y
Approve GOP budget with tax and spending cuts	Y

VOTING STUDIES

	Presidential Support		Party Unity		Conservative Coalition	
Year	**S**	**O**	**S**	**O**	**S**	**O**
1996	29	68	96	3	98	2
1995	17	83	98	2	97	1

INTEREST GROUP RATINGS

Year	ADA	AFL-CIO	CCUS	ACU
1996	5	n/a	94	100
1995	0	0	96	92

8 Saxby Chambliss (R)

Of Moultrie — Elected 1994, 2nd term

Biographical Information
Born: Nov. 10, 1943, Warrenton, N.C.
Education: Louisiana Tech U., 1961-62; U. of Georgia, B.B.A. 1966; U. of Tennessee, J.D. 1968.
Occupation: Lawyer; hotel owner.
Family: Wife, Julianne Frohbert; two children.
Religion: Episcopalian.
Political Career: Sought Republican nomination for U.S. House, 1992.
Capitol Office: 1019 Longworth Bldg. 20515; 225-6531.

Committees
Agriculture
Forestry, Resource Conservation & Research; General Farm Commodities; Risk Management & Specialty Crops
National Security
Military Readiness; Military Research & Development

In Washington: Agriculture plays an important role in the economy of Georgia's 8th District, and one of Chambliss' top priorities in the 104th was protecting farm support programs that benefit district growers, whose chief crops include peanuts and tobacco. Peanuts, for example, are a $2.5 billion industry in Georgia and a major cash crop in the 8th. Many producers in Georgia worried that GOP aims to restructure fundamentally the federal role in agriculture would eliminate the government system of quotas and price supports and devastate their farms.

Chambliss ultimately voted in February 1996 for the GOP's "Freedom to Farm" bill, which brought federal farm policy more in line with free-market principles. but only after a struggle in which he helped to save the peanut program from elimination.

On the Agriculture Committee in September 1995, he was one of four Republicans to join with a solid Democratic bloc in opposing the Freedom to Farm bill. The rebellious Republicans made no excuses for putting the interests of their districts ahead of the desires of House leadership. Chambliss sent out a press release titled: "Chambliss Holds Tight For Farmers." "I've been sent to Washington not to vote the way the leadership wants me to vote, but to vote for my constituents," Chambliss said.

And he lobbied House Speaker Newt Gingrich, R-Ga., and other House leaders to protect farm programs. "Agriculture is important to us as a party," he explained.

In one of his earlier deeds as a House freshman, Chambliss took on the majority leader of his own party, Dick Armey of Texas, over the issue of agriculture subsidies. In February 1995, Armey and Andrew Jacobs Jr., D-Ind., circulated a "Dear Colleague" letter that denounced the peanut program for artificially restricting production and raising prices by an estimated hundreds of millions a year. "We believe it's just plain wrong the federal government operates a cartel which is specifically designed to raise the price of food on the American people," the letter stated.

Chambliss replied the next day, and he did not tread softly. "It is abominable for the House majority leader to propose legislation suggesting irrational elimination of a program when it is by no means the consensus of the Republican Party," Chambliss said in a press release. "I am infuriated that this [Armey proposal] would come out when we haven't had the opportunity to consider cooperative revisions."

He followed that up with a hand-delivered letter to Armey asking the majority leader to back off from his position. Then, on March 1, Chambliss co-signed a "Dear Colleague" letter with nine other representatives that criticized the Armey-Jacobs letter as "an absolute misrepresentation of the facts."

In its final form, the Freedom to Farm bill wound up modifying, not killing, the peanut program. It froze the average loan rate at $610 per ton, compared with the current rate of $678; eliminated national quotas for subsidized peanuts; and allowed growers to transfer, sell or lease their quotas across county lines. The House passed the bill 270-155, with Chambliss and all but 19 Republicans voting "yea."

Chambliss has supported the GOP leadership on almost all other issues, backing an agenda that he says reflects his constituents' conservative views. He voted for legislation linked to the "Contract With America" 98 percent of the time in 1995. "I think the Contract With America will go down in history as one of our most important political documents," Chambliss said.

He has supported a balanced-budget constitutional amendment and in 1995 endorsed GOP efforts to balance the budget in seven years partly through restraining the rate of growth in spending on Medicaid and Medicare.

Also in the 104th, he backed efforts to limit punitive damages in product liability cases, to overhaul the federal welfare system and to ban certain late-term abortions. Chambliss voted in 1996 for the final bill raising the minimum wage, but he opposed the initial House version.

GEORGIA 8
South Central — Macon; Warner Robins

Covering a 30-county, wrench-shaped swath of central and south Georgia, the 8th is largely rural. Half of the district's counties have fewer than 10,000 residents.

Democrat J. Roy Rowland represented much of this area in the 1980s, but post-census redistricting made the 8th more Republican, and Rowland won with a career-low 56 percent. Two years later Chambliss scored an easy victory, marking the first time since Reconstruction that this area elected a Republican to Congress.

But remapping in 1995 reverted the district to a Democratic-leaning form, primarily by increasing the 8th's black voting-age population to 28 percent from 18 percent.

Bill Clinton in 1996 captured 19 of the district's counties, helping him beat Bob Dole in the 8th by a slim 47 percent to 45 percent margin. The district found Max Cleland even more appealing, giving him 55 percent and victories in all but two counties — Appling and Treutlen, in the southeastern part of the district.

The 8th's economic underpinnings lie in agribusiness. Tobacco is copiously grown throughout the 8th; the southern-area counties of Coffee, Berrien and Irwin were among the state's top 10 tobacco-producing counties in 1995. The same three counties also account for most of the 8th's ample corn production. Timber is important to the 8th, and as befits "The Peach State," that fruit is heavily grown here (with aptly named Peach County the state leader).

Warner Robins Air Force Base (Houston County) provides many paychecks for middle Georgians. The base, which employs about 4,600 military and 12,400 civilian personnel, gives Houston a more conservative tenor. Chambliss and Dole easily carried Houston in 1996, and Republican U.S. Senate candidate Guy Millner lost the county by a mere 90 votes out of more than 32,000 cast. Moody Air Force Base and the Marine Corps Logistics Center are just across the district line in Lowndes County.

In the northern part of the district is Bibb County, which accounts for one-fourth of the district's population and includes the city of Macon, an old textile and railroad town that has long been a trading and processing center for the nearby agricultural lands. Atlanta is a little more than an hour up Interstate 75, but the boom in the capital region has not percolated in Macon. The city's population dropped almost 9 percent during the 1980s, to 107,000.

Major employers in the Macon area include the Medical Center of Central Georgia and Brown and Williamson Tobacco Corp. Macon has a cherry blossom festival that draws thousands of visitors each spring, and there are redevelopment and preservation efforts, including renovation of some small pre-Civil War houses into low-cost housing. Popular Macon attractions include The Lanier Cottage, the birthplace of famed Georgia poet Sidney Lanier, and the Georgia Music Hall of Fame.

Macon is majority-black, contributing to Bibb's Democratic proclivities. Clinton captured 54 percent of the county's votes in 1996.

As of May 19, the Census Bureau had not recalculated population data, racial and ethnic breakdowns, and age statistics for districts newly drawn for the 1996 election.

A proponent of gun owners' rights and the vice chairman of the Congressional Sportsmen's Caucus, Chambliss voted in 1996 to repeal the ban on certain semiautomatic assault-style weapons.

In 1995, he supported an effort by Rep. Dan Burton, R-Ind., to weaken a proposed ban on most gifts to members from lobbyists. Burton's alternative would have allowed lawmakers to continue receiving gifts, meals and trips, but would have strengthened disclosure requirements.

Chambliss also sits on the National Security Committee, where he looks after Georgia's defense industry. He helped obtain additional funding to add ramp space for the C-130s housed at Moody Air Force Base, and fought efforts by President Clinton to privatize military repair depots in California and Texas rather than transfer the work to depots such as the one at Robins Air Force Base. Both bases are in the 8th District.

In 1995 and 1996, Chambliss toured every major military base in the state.

At Home: Fresh off his re-election to the House, Chambliss early in 1997 considered a run for governor in 1998. But in April, he decided against trying to make the move.

He had a difficult time returning to Congress. His election tally dropped from 63 percent in 1994 to 53 percent in 1996, thanks in large part to a court-ordered redistricting between the two elections that scrambled Georgia's House map.

In the remap, Chambliss' home base of Moultrie was moved to the 2nd District, and in the 8th, where he sought a second term, 10 of 30 counties were new to him.

Democrats had an appealing challenger in former U.S. Attorney Jim Wiggins, a decorated Vietnam War veteran who talked about his background fighting crime and drugs and also highlighted his concern for veterans' issues.

Thinking that the changes in the district might throw Chambliss off-balance, organized labor made him a target, running television ads attacking him on such issues as his support for the GOP budget plan that included changes in Medicare funding.

But redistricting had not altered the fundamental fact that conservatism is the dominant political philosophy in south Georgia, and Chambliss' votes as a House freshman were acceptable to a majority of voters. His high-profile advocacy of the district's agricultural interests also was well received. Chambliss saw his margin drop from more than 36,000 votes in 1994 to just over 9,200 votes in 1996, but he held off Wiggins' charge.

Chambliss, a lawyer who married his college sweetheart from the University of Georgia and coached Little League baseball and YMCA basketball for two decades, initially was attracted to run in the 8th when redistricting before the 1992 election made the district more friendly to the GOP by removing black voters. But Chambliss lost in his party's House primary that year, and the district reelected veteran Democratic Rep. J. Roy Rowland.

Chambliss continued to canvas the district after losing the primary. He listened to voters' concerns, and formulated his 1994 campaign around the problems they wanted resolved.

After Rowland announced plans to retire in 1994, Chambliss got the GOP nomination without a fight, and he was able to concentrate on fundraising and improving his name identification while the Democratic hopefuls slugged it out in a seven-way primary. After a runoff, the Democratic nomination went to Craig Mathis, a lawyer and the son of former Rep. Dawson Mathis (1971-81).

Mathis campaigned as a conservative Democrat, and he stressed the experience he gained fighting defense base closures when he worked as legislative counsel for Rep. Sonny Callahan, R-Ala. But Chambliss said Mathis did not understand the district's concerns, portraying him as a Washington insider who had returned to Georgia only to seek office.

Chambliss said Mathis, if elected, would have to fall in line with the Clinton White House, and, given Clinton's unpopularity in the 8th in 1994, that was a big drag on the Democrat, helping propel Chambliss well past 60 percent of the vote.

HOUSE ELECTIONS

1996 General		
Saxby Chambliss (R)	93,619	(53%)
Jim Wiggins (D)	84,506	(47%)
1994 General		
Saxby Chambliss (R)	89,591	(63%)
Craig Mathis (D)	53,408	(37%)

CAMPAIGN FINANCE

	Receipts	Receipts from PACs	Expend-itures
1996			
Chambliss (R)	$1,076,562	$394,492 (37%)	$1,081,914
Wiggins (D)	$282,201	$133,191 (47%)	$277,400
1994			
Chambliss (R)	$685,239	$161,825 (24%)	$680,079
Mathis (D)	$389,023	$120,100 (31%)	$352,437

DISTRICT VOTE FOR PRESIDENT

1996		1992	
D	90,662 (47%)	D	79,079 (39%)
R	85,224 (45%)	R	95,225 (47%)
I	14,643 (8%)	I	30,144 (15%)

KEY VOTES

1997	
Ban "partial birth" abortions	Y
1996	
Approve farm bill	Y
Deny public education to illegal immigrants	Y
Repeal ban on certain assault-style weapons	Y
Increase minimum wage	N
Freeze defense spending	N
Approve welfare overhaul	Y
1995	
Approve balanced-budget constitutional amendment	Y
Relax Clean Water Act regulations	Y
Oppose limits on environmental regulations	N
Reduce projected Medicare spending	Y
Approve GOP budget with tax and spending cuts	Y

VOTING STUDIES

	Presidential Support		Party Unity		Conservative Coalition	
Year	**S**	**O**	**S**	**O**	**S**	**O**
1996	35	65	96	4	100	0
1995	17	82	97	2	99	1

INTEREST GROUP RATINGS

Year	ADA	AFL-CIO	CCUS	ACU
1996	0	n/a	100	100
1995	0	0	100	96

9 Nathan Deal (R)

Of Gainesville — Elected 1992, 3rd term

Biographical Information
Born: Aug. 25, 1942, Millen, Ga.
Education: Mercer U., B.A. 1964, J.D. 1966.
Military Service: Army, 1966-68.
Occupation: Lawyer.
Family: Wife, Sandra Dunagan; four children.
Religion: Baptist.
Political Career: Assistant district attorney, 1970-71; juvenile court judge, 1971-72; Hall County attorney, 1977-79; Ga. Senate, 1981-93, president pro tempore, 1991-93.
Capitol Office: 1406 Longworth Bldg. 20515; 225-5211.

Committees
Commerce
Finance & Hazardous Materials; Health & Environment; Telecommunications, Trade & Consumer Protection
Education & Workforce
Postsecondary Education, Training & Life-Long Learning

In Washington: Deal had a fairly quiet first term in the House, settling in with other centrist Southerners in the Democratic majority who, as the 103rd Congress wore on, grew increasingly restive about what they saw as the liberal bent of the Clinton administration.

But after Republicans took control of the House, Deal was much in the news. First, he drew attention when his plan to overhaul the welfare system was embraced by House Democratic leaders as an alternative to the GOP's "Contract With America" proposal.

Then, to the chagrin of Democrats and the delight of Republicans, Deal made another big news splash with his April 1995 announcement that he was joining the GOP.

Once in Republican ranks, Deal faded into the background again, even though GOP leaders gave him a slot on the influential Commerce Committee, which addressed such high-profile topics as telecommunications and health insurance during the 104th. There is no doubt, however, about Deal's loyalty to his new party. In 1996, his first full year in the GOP, on floor votes pitting a majority of Republicans against a majority of Democrats, Deal's party unity score was 92.

In Georgia, partisan Democrats howled about Deal's party switch, noting that just three months before he jumped, he had said: "If I choose to switch [parties] during the term, I think the honest thing to do is to resign and have a special election." Deal, of course, did not follow that course, and his seat on Commerce helped him amass a sizable treasury for his first race as a Republican. Few voters seemed much bothered by the change of heart: He won re-election in 1996 with 66 percent of the vote.

The positions Deal took as a Democrat may have prepared voters in the 9th to anticipate his party switch. In the 103rd, he voted against family and medical leave legislation and the "motor voter" bill; he opposed banning certain semiautomatic assault-style weapons and opposed lifting the ban on homosexuals in the military.

In 1993, he and 20 other first-term Democrats who dubbed themselves the "Fiscal Caucus" pressured the Clinton administration to make more spending cuts. And in May 1994, Deal played a prominent role when the Mainstream Forum, a coalition of moderate and conservative Democrats, unveiled a welfare-overhaul plan that aimed to get welfare applicants working or training for work as soon as they applied for assistance.

Deal's disenchantment with Democrats became increasingly clear at the start of the 104th, when he became a leader in another group of conservative Democrats — The Coalition, also known as the "blue dogs." He voted to pass all but two of the 33 bills based on the GOP's "Contract With America." "I voted like a Republican even when I was a Democrat," Deal stated after he switched parties.

As a Republican, Deal, who had previously stated his support of a constitutional right to abortion, sided with anti-abortion lawmakers on three high-profile votes in the 104th. He voted to ban a particular abortion technique that opponents call "partial birth" abortion, to prohibit privately funded abortions at overseas military hospitals and to reinstate a prohibition on family planning assistance funds going to foreign organizations that perform abortions or offer abortion counseling. Early in the 105th Congress, he again sided with the majority of abortion opponents as they unsuccessfully sought to block President Clinton's request for an early release of funds to promote international family planning and population control programs.

Deal does part ways with most of his GOP colleagues on some issues. In May 1996, he supported an increase in the minimum wage and opposed an effort to exempt small businesses from paying it — a reflection perhaps of his working-class Democratic roots. And as the debate on welfare reform proceeded through the 104th, he worked to convince his new GOP colleagues of the merits of compromise with the

GEORGIA 9
North — Dalton; Gainesville; Toccoa

The 9th, anchored in north Georgia's mountains, runs across the state, from Alabama on the west to South Carolina on the east. At the local level, Democrats have long been dominant in most parts of the district. When the 9th was open in 1992, then-Democrat Deal held it easily for his party.

Deal racked up a career-high percentage in his first congressional race since his 1995 switch to the Republican Party, in part because the district's GOP presence is strong. The district is overwhelmingly white — remapping in 1995 kept the 9th's black voting-age population at 3.5 percent — and Republican. In 1996, both Bob Dole and unsuccessful GOP senatorial nominee Guy Millner won every county in the 9th, often by overwhelming margins.

The 9th has Republican pockets of long standing, particularly in the north-central counties of Union, Fannin, Gilmer and Towns; their allegiance to the GOP dates to the Civil War. Republicans are becoming more prevalent in the southern part of the district, where Cherokee and Forsyth counties are filling up with Atlanta suburbanites.

Cherokee (which is shared with the 6th) and Forsyth are two of the state's fastest growing counties — their populations increased by 27 percent and 41 percent, respectively, from 1990 to 1995.

In economic terms, the 9th is a blend of new and old. For many of those living in the metropolitan Atlanta orbit, white-collar and service-oriented occupations predominate. Elsewhere, apparel manufacturing, poultry processing and carpet-making are major providers, and tourism and recreation are increasingly important.

Raising and processing chickens is big business in Hall County (Gainesville) and Whitfield County (Dalton), the district's two most populous counties. Gainesville calls itself the "poultry capital of the world," and in the center of town is the Georgia Poultry Federation's monument to the industry: an obelisk with a chicken statue on top.

Dalton, in the northwestern part of the district, is one of the country's top carpet-making centers. Despite its substantial blue-collar employment base, Whitfield County generally favors Republicans in statewide and federal contests. In 1996, Dole and Millner racked up 57 percent and 65 percent, respectively.

In the district's extreme northwestern corner are Walker, Catoosa and Dade counties, conservative pillars whose economic fortunes are linked to Chattanooga, just over the border in Tennessee. Millner's 67 percent tally in Catoosa was his best showing in the state.

Millions who have never set foot in Georgia have seen its rugged northeast on film. "Deliverance" was set in Rabun County, and "Smokey and the Bandit" was made in the area.

Tourist dollars play a crucial role in the district's economy. Dotting the mountains are an array of attractions, including Cloudland Canyon (Walker County), the manmade Lake Lanier (Hall County), the wineries of Habersham County and, in White County, the hamlet of Helen, a replica of a Swiss village.

As of May 19, the Census Bureau had not recalculated population data, racial and ethnic breakdowns, and age statistics for districts newly drawn for the 1996 election.

Clinton administration, a course that some House conservatives were reluctant to follow.

As a freshman Democrat, Deal had sought federal funding for the National Park Service to help Georgia relocate a heavily traveled U.S. highway that cuts through the Chickamauga and Chattanooga National Military Park. As a Republican in the 104th, he secured that funding in the 104th Congress, snaring an additional $21.9 million.

At Home: Deal's April 1995 jump to the GOP piqued the interest of potential 9th District candidates in both parties. But two possible Republican rivals — state Rep. Steve Stancil and Robert L. Castello, whom Deal had easily defeated in the 1994 general election — chose not to challenge Deal, who had the backing of Republican leaders, including House Speaker and fellow Georgian Newt Gingrich.

The lack of a primary challenge enabled Deal to focus his campaign efforts and financial resources on the Democratic nominee, state Rep. McCracken "Ken" Poston.

Deal's move to the GOP became Poston's rallying cry. He urged voters to punish Deal for that move and for breaking the pledge to resign and seek re-election in a special election if he switched parties. "The party switch is important because it's indicative of a character trait," Poston said. "It says this guy wouldn't hold up in a strong wind."

Deal said he never offered to resign and run again but had merely suggested that as one way to change parties. He was one of the GOP incumbents who had to contend with an AFL-CIO independent-expenditure campaign calling for his defeat. The union organization spent millions in an effort to oust Republicans from control of the House.

But Deal's position on the Commerce Committee gave him entree to numerous business and industry PACs, and he used their contributions to fuel a campaign that ended up overwhelming Poston, who lost by more than 30 percentage points points.

Deal won a state Senate seat in 1980 and had put together a string of effortless re-elections by the time Democratic Rep. Ed Jenkins announced in 1992 he was leaving the 9th. Deal and two others sought the Democratic nomination; Deal ran first in the primary with 45 percent of the vote, then won a runoff by 10 points.

The GOP nomination went to Daniel Becker, who made abortion the focus of a "morality in government" campaign; he aired anti-abortion TV ads featuring graphic photos of allegedly aborted fetuses. Becker's appeal proved to be limited. Although George Bush carried the 9th District with 49 percent of the vote, Becker managed only 41 percent.

Deal's conservative first-term voting record helped protect him from the Republican electoral tide in 1994.

He won re-election by a solid margin, even as Democratic incumbents lost in the neighboring 7th and 10th districts.

HOUSE ELECTIONS

1996 General		
Nathan Deal (R)	132,532	(66%)
McCracken "Ken" Poston (D)	69,662	(34%)
1994 General*		
Nathan Deal (D)	79,145	(58%)
Robert L. Castello (R)	57,568	(42%)

Previous Winning Percentages: 1992* (59%)

** Deal was elected to the House as a Democrat 1992-1994.*

CAMPAIGN FINANCE

	Receipts	Receipts from PACs	Expend- itures
1996			
Deal (R)	$747,417	$384,842 (51%)	$865,898
Poston (D)	$508,435	$118,093 (23%)	$429,454
1994			
Deal (D)	$489,911	$215,091 (44%)	$368,648
Castello (R)	$23,740	$14 (0%)	$22,953

DISTRICT VOTE FOR PRESIDENT

1996		1992	
D	74,125 (35%)	**D**	71,216 (35%)
R	115,861 (55%)	**R**	98,713 (49%)
I	20,840 (10%)	**I**	32,981 (16%)

KEY VOTES

1997	
Ban "partial birth" abortions	Y
1996	
Approve farm bill	Y
Deny public education to illegal immigrants	Y
Repeal ban on certain assault-style weapons	Y
Increase minimum wage	Y
Freeze defense spending	Y
Approve welfare overhaul	Y
1995	
Approve balanced-budget constitutional amendment	Y
Relax Clean Water Act regulations	Y
Oppose limits on environmental regulations	N
Reduce projected Medicare spending	Y
Approve GOP budget with tax and spending cuts	Y

VOTING STUDIES

	Presidential Support		Party Unity		Conservative Coalition	
Year	**S**	**O**	**S**	**O**	**S**	**O**
1996	37	63	92	8	94	6
1995†	23	77	93	6	95	5
1994	63	36	61	36	86	8
1993	58	40	68	31	80	20

† Deal switched to the Republican Party on April 10, 1995. As a Democrat in 1995 he was eligible for 23 presidential support votes, 218 party unity votes, and 37 conservative coalition votes. As a Republican in 1995 he was eligible for 110 presidential support votes, 417 party unity votes, and 74 conservative coalition votes. His 1995 scores include votes he cast both as a Democrat and a Republican.

INTEREST GROUP RATINGS

Year	ADA	AFL-CIO	CCUS	ACU
1996	5	n/a	81	90
1995	0	0	96	80
1994	15	33	92	67
1993	15	42	73	61

10 Charlie Norwood (R)

Of Evans — Elected 1994, 2nd term

Biographical Information
Born: July 27, 1941, Valdosta, Ga.
Education: Georgia Southern U., B.S. 1965; Georgetown U., D.D.S. 1967.
Military Service: Army, 1967-69.
Occupation: Dentist.
Family: Wife, Gloria Wilkinson; two children.
Religion: Methodist.
Political Career: No previous office.
Capitol Office: 1707 Longworth Bldg. 20515; 225-4101.

Committees
Commerce
Energy & Power; Health & Environment
Education & Workforce
Oversight & Investigations (vice)

In Washington: When he was a dentist in Georgia, Norwood was irked by federal regulations that he saw as onerous to small-business owners like himself, especially mandates issued by the Occupational Safety and Health Administration (OSHA). In his 1994 challenge to a freshman Democratic incumbent, Norwood promised voters he would work to reduce the role the federal government plays in people's lives. The 10th elected Norwood by an overwhelming margin, and in Congress he has been a stalwart supporter of the House GOP leadership, helping pass the "Contract With America" agenda and sticking to a conservative line even after some Republicans began to fret in early 1996 that critics were portraying the party as too extreme.

"I've done exactly what I said I was going to do," Norwood told the Atlanta Journal-Constitution in February 1996. "I haven't fooled anybody about anything. My votes have been very predictable, and people are very appreciative of that."

Norwood's 1996 re-election situation changed dramatically when redistricting made the 10th substantially more black and Democratic. Norwood also found himself facing a conservative Democratic challenger, who saw political advantage in linking Norwood to House Speaker Newt Gingrich. In the end, Norwood managed to secure a second term, but his re-election tally dropped from 65 percent in 1994 to just over 52 percent in 1996.

While Norwood has hewed to the party line laid down by Gingrich much of the time, his campaign could cite a few breaks. For instance, he objected to the proposed privatization of the federal power marketing administrations, an issue important in the 10th.

And on at least two issues that received widespread publicity in the second half of the 104th Congress, Norwood took a step away from doctrinaire conservatism. In August 1996 he voted for legislation to help workers keep their health insurance coverage as they change jobs and to increase the deductibility of health insurance for the self-employed. He said the bill made "health care more available and affordable for millions of Americans . . . without increasing government bureaucracy or writing thousands of pages of new regulations."

In May 1996, Norwood voted against raising the minimum wage by 90 cents an hour, but in August, when the wage increase won final passage in the House, he switched and voted "yea." The final version of the wage bill included other provisions sought by Republicans, including $10 billion in business tax cuts over five years, a $5,000 tax credit to offset the cost of adoption and an expansion of Individual Retirement Accounts.

Norwood has a seat on the Commerce Committee, and as would be expected given his background, he has made OSHA a particular focus of his work. He would like to bar OSHA from enforcing many workplace protection laws and shift the agency's focus to education and assistance; he supported legislation that would curtail the agency's power to issue citations and make random inspections of businesses.

Norwood peppers his speeches with examples of small-business owners whom he feels have been improperly targeted by OSHA regulators. Once in a floor speech he told of a Maine dentist who was fined $8,000 for exposing his employees to direct contact with blood and body fluids. The dentist, Norwood explained, had only one employee, a receptionist, and that person did not work with patients' teeth.

"OSHA is one agency that has turned a reasonable and an important mission into a bureaucratic nightmare for the American economy and the American people," Norwood said. "OSHA is one agency that needs to be restructured or reinvented or just maybe plain removed."

Early in the 104th Congress, Norwood was a vocal proponent of a GOP measure requiring government regulators to use risk assessment and cost-benefit analysis when they issue new rules. Norwood said the legislation was necessary

GEORGIA 10
Northeast — Augusta

Of the 11 incumbent Georgia representatives who ran in 1996 under the redistricting plan enacted the previous year, Norwood faced the toughest challenge. He ran in a northeast Georgia district in which 17 of the 24 counties were new and in which the black voting-age population is more than twice the level of the old 10th.

Augusta is the district's largest city. It hosts the annual Master's golf tournament, and its River Walk on the western bank of the Savannah River is a popular site for watching festivals, concerts and boating competitions. Northwest of the city lies J. Strom Thurmond Lake, the largest manmade lake east of the Mississippi.

Richmond County casts about 30 percent of the 10th's votes, and its large black population — more than 40 percent of the county's residents — identify it with the Democrats. Bill Clinton captured 54 percent of Richmond's votes in 1996.

Large employers in this area include the Savannah River Site, a Department of Energy nuclear facility that lies on the Savannah River's eastern bank, in South Carolina's Aiken and Barnwell counties. Post-Cold War defense downsizing has hurt the facility; 10,000 jobs have been cut since 1993, and the facility expects to trim another 1,500 jobs by the summer.

The Medical College of Georgia (in Augusta) is a major employer in the district, as is Fort Gordon, located a few miles southwest of Augusta and home to the U.S. Army Signal Corps. About 6,500 active-duty and 4,600 civilian personnel are employed at Fort Gordon.

Most of the district's agricultural activity occurs in the counties south of Augusta. In 1995, Burke and Jefferson were the top two oat-producing counties in Georgia and ranked among state leaders in soybean production. Dairy production is a staple of the 10th, and other major crops include corn, cotton and peanuts.

Eatonton (Putnam County) is the birthplace of Joel Chandler Harris, author of the Uncle Remus stories, and Alice Walker, whose book "The Color Purple" won the 1983 Pulitzer Prize. Otis Redding made his home in Jones County in the southwest of the district, and Oliver Hardy was born in Harlem, near Augusta. Harlem hosts an annual festival honoring the late comic.

No other Georgia congressional district in 1996 featured a closer congressional or presidential race. Norwood won by 4 points, a sharp contrast to his 30-point blowout of a Democratic incumbent two years earlier.

The district's politics are prone to extremes. In Columbia County, which lies just north of Richmond and casts about one-sixth of the 10th's votes, Dole racked up 67 percent of the vote, his best percentage statewide. In the center of the district lies majority-black Hancock County, which gave Clinton 81 percent of its votes, his statewide high.

And Johnson County in the south was Georgia's only county to opt for both Clinton and Millner in 1996. Both won the county easily — Clinton by 17 percentage points, Millner by 10 points

As of May 19, the Census Bureau had not recalculated population data, racial and ethnic breakdowns, and age statistics for districts newly drawn for the 1996 election.

because of the "immense cost piled onto the American economy by federal bureaucrats." Opponents countered that the bill would saddle federal agencies with burdensome paperwork requirements and expose them to costly litigation, because the measure allowed companies to sue an agency over the cost-benefit method used.

Norwood, seeking to take the measure one step further, supported an amendment allowing citizens to petition federal agencies to review existing regulations with an economic impact of $25 million or more. "Industries should not have to come to us to save them from overzealous bureaucrats," Norwood said. "By passing this amendment, we give individual American citizens the power to fight for themselves." But the amendment lost in the House, 206-220.

In one area of concern to his constituency, however, Norwood led a fight for continued federal involvement: On the Commerce Committee he argued against budget-cutters' efforts to generate revenue by selling federal power marketing agencies, which supply low-cost electric power from federally owned dams; among the candidates for the proposed selloff was the Southeastern Power Administration, whose service area includes the 10th District. About a half-dozen other Republicans on Commerce joined with Norwood to block the proposal. Norwood said many of his constituents who buy power from Southeastern feared their rates would increase if the agency was sold to a private utility.

Norwood also has a seat on the Education and the Workforce Committee.

At Home: Norwood's planning for a 1996 re-election campaign was scrambled in June 1995, when the U.S. Supreme Court invalidated Georgia's congressional district map as an unconstitutional "racial gerrymander." The court returned Georgia's map to a three-judge federal panel, which in a 2-1 ruling in December 1995 issued a new map that dismantled two of the state's three black-majority

House districts — the 11th and the 2nd. The panel's map also substantially changed Norwood's district, adding 17 new counties as it took away 12 others, increasing the district's black population from about one-fifth to almost one-third.

Norwood's position on the Commerce Committee helped him make contacts with the business community and build a sizable bankroll for his re-election bid. He got financial help from banks, insurance companies, the telephone and cable industries, the airline and trucking industries, grocery chains, textile mills and paper companies. Norwood portrayed his challenger, attorney David Bell, as a liberal trial lawyer, but Bell said he was a conservative Democrat who supported a balanced budget and welfare reform, and at the same time he criticized the GOP's commitment to education funding, the environment, Medicare and the minimum wage.

Organized labor jumped into the picture, and blasted Norwood with negative television advertising on issues such as Medicare. Norwood countered by trying to tie Bell closely to the unions. The incumbent said he would give up his contributions from the tobacco industry, for which Bell criticized him, if the Democrat would give up his union contributions (Bell did not take him up on the offer). Norwood survived, but his 52.3 percent election tally was the lowest of any Georgia incumbent in 1996.

In 1994, the record of first-term Democratic Rep. Don Johnson motivated Norwood to make his first bid for public office. But first he had to get through a tough GOP primary that included Ralph T. Hudgens, who as the Republican nominee against Johnson in 1992 had taken 46 percent of the vote.

Hudgens ran first with 47 percent of the vote in the 1994 Republican primary, almost good enough to avoid a runoff. But Norwood's second-place showing of 38 percent earned him a place in the second-round voting, and there he scored a surprise 51 percent victory.

In the general-election contest with Johnson, Norwood benefited hugely from widespread voter antipathy toward the Clinton administration and Johnson's support for the president's 1993 budget plan, which included tax increases and deficit-reduction measures. Johnson had promised in 1992 not to vote for a tax increase, and after he backed Clinton's budget, the conservative editorial page of the Augusta Chronicle waged a campaign to defeat him that included an apology for the paper's endorsement of Johnson in 1992. The Chronicle also dubbed the incumbent "Judas Johnson" after he voted for the 1994 crime bill. Norwood told voters that Johnson could not be trusted to represent the district's views in Washington.

Johnson tried to resuscitate his foundering campaign by accusing Norwood of advocating 25 percent spending cuts in Medicare and Social Security over five years. But it was a lost cause, as Norwood trounced Johnson by 30 points, 65 percent to 35 percent.

HOUSE ELECTIONS

1996 General		
Charlie Norwood (R)	96,723	(52%)
David Bell (D)	88,054	(48%)
1994 General		
Charlie Norwood (R)	96,099	(65%)
Don Johnson (D)	51,192	(35%)

CAMPAIGN FINANCE

	Receipts	Receipts from PACs		Expend-itures
1996				
Norwood (R)	$1,681,950	$664,419	(40%)	$1,622,486
Bell (D)	$629,294	$150,671	(24%)	$604,043
1994				
Norwood (R)	$764,934	$141,873	(19%)	$787,441
Johnson (D)	$776,751	$296,807	(38%)	$773,927

DISTRICT VOTE FOR PRESIDENT

	1996		1992
D	94,968 (48%)	D	91,995 (46%)
R	90,213 (46%)	R	83,748 (42%)
I	11,669 (6%)	I	25,257 (13%)

KEY VOTES

1997	
Ban "partial birth" abortions	Y
1996	
Approve farm bill	Y
Deny public education to illegal immigrants	Y
Repeal ban on certain assault-style weapons	Y
Increase minimum wage	N
Freeze defense spending	N
Approve welfare overhaul	Y
1995	
Approve balanced-budget constitutional amendment	Y
Relax Clean Water Act regulations	Y
Oppose limits on environmental regulations	?
Reduce projected Medicare spending	Y
Approve GOP budget with tax and spending cuts	Y

VOTING STUDIES

	Presidential Support		Party Unity		Conservative Coalition	
Year	S	O	S	O	S	O
1996	29	65	94	2	98	0
1995	17	82	97	2	97	2

INTEREST GROUP RATINGS

Year	ADA	AFL-CIO	CCUS	ACU
1996	0	n/a	100	100
1995	0	0	100	100

11 John Linder (R)

Of Tucker — Elected 1992, 3rd term

Biographical Information
Born: Sept. 9, 1942, Deer River, Minn.
Education: U. of Minnesota, Duluth, B.S. 1963; U. of Minnesota, D.D.S. 1967.
Military Service: Air Force, 1967-69.
Occupation: Financial executive; dentist.
Family: Wife, Lynne Leslee Peterson; two children.
Religion: Presbyterian.
Political Career: Ga. House, 1975-81; Republican nominee for Ga. Senate, 1980; Ga. House, 1983-91; Republican nominee for U.S. House, 1990.

Capitol Office: 1005 Longworth Bldg. 20515; 225-4272.

Committees
Rules
Legislative & Budget Process
National Republican Congressional Committee
Chairman

In Washington: Linder's new district leaves him in the neighborhood of Speaker Newt Gingrich, and Linder is simpatico with Gingrich's conservative philosophy and challenge-the-Democrats style. Gingrich rewarded his friend and adviser just after the 1996 election with the chairmanship of the National Republican Congressional Committee (NRCC).

Linder will find himself appearing frequently on policy programs defending the GOP position on campaign finance as that issue barks for attention in the 105th. Linder opposed broadening the House investigation of 1996 political fundraising to include allegations of financial impropriety at the congressional as well as the presidential level, saying that any possible malfeasance on the part of his colleagues is "not as systematic as what went on at the White House."

Linder traveled to New York City in March 1997 for a private meeting with Ronald S. Lauder, a cosmetics executive who gave $200,000 in "soft money" to the Republican Party in 1996. Lauder's company, Estee Lauder Inc., lobbies Congress on a number of tax issues. Linder said of the meeting: "I told him we are engaged in a profound struggle. It's about the direction of the country. And we need people like him involved in this debate."

Although some Republican moderates began the 105th advising a more centrist legislative course, Linder contends there is no need for the party to trim its sails; he thinks the GOP can expand its slim House majority by sticking to a message of smaller government and personal responsibility. Linder, who favors replacing the income tax with a national sales tax, supports his party's position on the vast majority of floor votes, including on such issues as the balanced-budget constitutional amendment, immigration and welfare law overhaul, and putting a choke collar on the regulatory bureaucracy.

Rather than fret that the reduced House GOP majority in the 105th indicates some voter unease with conservatism, Linder says the party should draw strength and resolve from the fact that in 1996 it maintained congressional control in the face of President Clinton's re-election and independent expenditure campaigns run by groups such as the AFL-CIO. "We won," Linder said. "It's time to just say we won."

Organized labor's opposition to the GOP's agenda on workplace issues prompted some characteristically biting rhetoric from Linder. Complaining about Democrats who opposed Republican legislation to allow employers to offer compensatory time off in lieu of overtime pay, Linder said, "This is about Big Labor jerking the chain and turning their lap dogs into pit bulls."

Two years before naming him NRCC head, Gingrich helped Linder get a leg up by arranging a seat for his associate on the Rules Committee when the GOP took over the House. Linder refused an offer during the 104th to take over the chairmanship from Gingrich of GOPAC, one of many ancillary campaign organizations Gingrich was associated with that helped lead him into ethical trouble.

Linder, whose friendship with the Speaker predates their time in Congress, remains a top defender of Gingrich in the House. Linder nevertheless in January 1997 voted in support of imposing a $300,000 penalty on Gingrich for providing false information to the ethics committee and breaching tax law. Linder's attitude seemed to be one of trying to acknowledge mistakes and putting them behind. "There is no argument that Newt signed an erroneous statement," Linder acknowledged a few days before Gingrich and the ethics committee reached a kind of plea-bargain agreement.

The Gingrich soap opera was a continuing distraction for House Republicans. Linder complained that the Federal Election Commission showed its true colors as a partisan tool of Democrats as it prepared to investigate Gingrich about whether he illegally used funds from GOPAC to help federal candidates. He termed the agency part of a "large federal bureaucracy that's out to get Newt."

Redistricting contributes to the defeat of many incumbents, and officeholders today recoil at the possibility of running in unfamiliar terrain.

Although Linder's old 4th District was one of the most revamped by Georgia's 1995 remapping process, his fortunes probably improved because of it. His old 4th, which comprised all or part of four counties in the northeast Atlanta suburbs, gave George Bush just 46 percent of the presidential vote in 1992. And Linder got 51 percent and 58 percent in his 1992 and 1994 House races, respectively.

But Linder's new 11th District, which comprises 13 counties from the Atlanta suburbs to the South Carolina line, gave him 64 percent of the vote in 1996. Bob Dole amassed 54 percent in the presidential race, his third-best performance in the Peach State.

More than 40 percent of the 11th's votes are cast in Gwinnett County, the state's fourth-most populous. Gwinnett, which has nearly 500,000 residents, expanded 35 percent from 1990 to 1996.

Georgia's fastest growing areas generally vote solidly Republican, and Gwinnett (which is shared with the 4th and 6th) is no exception. Dole carried Gwinnett at-large with 59 percent; he got 62 percent in the 11th's portion of the county.

Just south of Gwinnett is another burgeoning region, Rockdale County. From 1990 to 1996, Rockdale's population swelled 21 percent. The area's largest employers include Lithonia Lighting (2,000 employees) and AT&T (1,200 employees).

Like its northern neighbor, Rockdale harbors strong Republican tendencies: Dole swept the county with 57 percent in 1996.

A popular Rockdale attraction is the $30 million Georgia International Horse Park, located in Conyers. The facility, which opened in 1995, hosted the 1996 Atlanta Summer Olympic Games' equestrian events.

GEORGIA 11
Northeast — Part of Gwinnett County; Athens

Democrats will find their strongest support in Clarke County, home to the University of Georgia. Its 29,500 students and about 2,100 faculty members have moved Clarke well to the left of the district mainstream. Bill Clinton won Clarke by 18 percentage points in 1996; he lost the overall district by a comparable margin. Clarke is a Democratic island in a sea of Republicanism — it is the only non-border Georgia county Clinton carried in 1996 that is surrounded entirely by counties Dole won.

The district's remaining territory is more rural and less heavily Republican, but is still favorable terrain for the GOP. Besides Clarke, the only other county in the 11th Dole lost that year was Hart, on the South Carolina border.

Franklin County includes the hometown of Ty Cobb, the prolific baseball player who starred for the Detroit Tigers in the early part of this century. The city hall at Royston, a small town in the county, features a memorial to Cobb, who was nicknamed "The Georgia Peach." He is buried at the town cemetery.

As of May 19, the Census Bureau had not recalculated population data, racial and ethnic breakdowns, and age statistics for districts newly drawn for the 1996 election.

At one stage, Linder offered a retaliatory resolution calling for an independent counsel to investigate Minority Leader Richard A. Gephardt, who was under investigation for a real estate investment. The House rebuffed Linder.

Linder has been a big backer of the GOP's efforts to downsize the federal government and give states more responsibility. During consideration of a plan to reduce Medicaid's projected growth by $163.4 billion and increase the role of states in the program's management, Linder commented that "My governor has said that he can do a better job for this amount of money if we give him the flexibility."

Linder was first elected in 1992 and, like many who have come to the House since the end of the Cold War, he has comparatively limited interest in foreign policy. Faced with the argument that a U.S. abstention from a mission to Bosnia would shake NATO, Linder said, "I'm not the least bit interested in the prestige of NATO." Arguing that NATO is a relic of a bygone era, Linder said, "It's time for us to give it a decent burial, with full military honors, and find a new policy and a new arrangement, because the old threats are no longer there."

Linder has opposed the Clinton administration on virtually every economic and social policy issue of note, except for NAFTA and GATT, which he backed. On the House floor, Linder is usually low-key, but never sparing. His summation of the president's first budget: "Tax now, cut never." Linder on Clinton's health care proposal: "An unworkable, unaffordable and incomprehensible bureaucratic nightmare." On Clinton's National Service legislation: A "silly bill . . . To pay people $25,000 a year to volunteer for America is not my idea of volunteer service."

As a freshman, Linder sat on the Science and Banking committees, and he was an automatic skeptic of Democratic efforts to direct federal money to private companies to encourage them to pursue "worthy" ventures, such as high-technology work. Instead, Linder advocates cutting the capital gains tax, "so that businessmen with a keen eye to profits will find these technologies that have a future and make the investments in them."

But Linder takes a more charitable view toward government funding of NASA, comparing that investment to past government-backed ventures that expanded the nation's frontiers, such as the Louisiana Purchase, the Lewis and Clark expedition and "Seward's Folly," the purchase of Alaska. "The only frontier left in the world is space, and it would indeed be a folly for us to turn our back on it," Lewis once said.

From his early days in Congress, Linder served notice he would try to shake up the status quo. In a Republican caucus meeting at the outset of the 103rd, he proposed setting a six-year limit for GOP members to occupy the top seats on committees and subcommittees. With strong support from Linder's class of 1992 peers, the proposal was adopted, despite grumbling from some more senior Republicans.

At Home: Linder's district was redrawn in December 1995, giving him far more rural territory while leaving him a chunk of the Atlanta suburbs. Linder was unhappy with the new lines, which he felt might aid Democrats, and joked that he might have to sell his house and move into a motor home to introduce himself to new constituents. But in his first general election under the new lines, he rolled up 64 percent of the vote against state House Democratic Whip Tommy Stephenson.

During 14 years in the Georgia state House, Linder earned a reputation for battling its Democratic leadership. He sought to limit the state House Speaker to three terms, reduce the number of state legislators and cap state expenditures.

Linder first ran for Congress in 1990, challenging Democratic Rep. Ben Jones. He took 48 percent of the vote, and, after 1992 redistricting forced Jones into another district where he eventually lost, the 4th, with a more Republican tilt, was open for Linder to try again.

Linder showed a willingness to go for the political jugular: When he discovered that his toughest GOP primary foe, state Rep. Emory Morsberger (a former Democrat) had written a $103 check to the Gwinnett County Democratic Party in 1990, Linder ran a TV ad criticizing the contribution. He led Morsberger in the primary, 34 percent to 28 percent, and then won the runoff with 62 percent.

The Democratic nominee, state Sen. Cathey Steinberg, labeled Linder a conservative "extremist" and "Pat Robertson with a Southern drawl." When Steinberg got money from EMILY's List, which raises funds for women candidates, Linder said it showed she was out of Georgia's political mainstream. Some conservative Democrats concurred, and they helped Linder win 51 percent.

In 1994, Democrat Comer Yates waged a well-funded challenge to Linder, reprising the theme that Linder's views were too extreme for the suburban constituency. Linder was re-elected with 58 percent of the vote.

HOUSE ELECTIONS

1996 General		
John Linder (R)	145,821	(64%)
Tommy Stephenson (D)	80,940	(36%)
1994 General		
John Linder (R)	90,063	(58%)
Comer Yates (D)	65,566	(42%)

Previous Winning Percentages: 1992 (51%)

CAMPAIGN FINANCE

	Receipts	Receipts from PACs	Expend-itures
1996			
Linder (R)	$816,043	$393,533 (48%)	$780,653
Stephenson (D)	$58,239	$10,227 (18%)	$58,200
1994			
Linder (R)	$833,464	$310,525 (37%)	$671,801
Yates (D)	$532,143	$98,275 (18%)	$521,432

DISTRICT VOTE FOR PRESIDENT

1996		1992	
D	88,092 (37%)	**D**	82,317 (36%)
R	128,320 (54%)	**R**	111,643 (49%)
I	17,668 (8%)	**I**	34,824 (15%)

KEY VOTES

1997	
Ban "partial birth" abortions	Y
1996	
Approve farm bill	Y
Deny public education to illegal immigrants	Y
Repeal ban on certain assault-style weapons	Y
Increase minimum wage	N
Freeze defense spending	N
Approve welfare overhaul	Y
1995	
Approve balanced-budget constitutional amendment	Y
Relax Clean Water Act regulations	Y
Oppose limits on environmental regulations	N
Reduce projected Medicare spending	Y
Approve GOP budget with tax and spending cuts	Y

VOTING STUDIES

	Presidential Support		Party Unity		Conservative Coalition	
Year	**S**	**O**	**S**	**O**	**S**	**O**
1996	34	65	94	4	98	2
1995	18	82	96	3	95	4
1994	46	54	95	4	100	0
1993	32	68	97	3	100	0

INTEREST GROUP RATINGS

Year	ADA	AFL-CIO	CCUS	ACU
1996	0	n/a	100	100
1995	0	0	100	88
1994	0	11	92	95
1993	5	0	100	100

HAWAII

Governor: Benjamin J. Cayetano (D)
First elected: 1994
Length of term: 4 years
Term expires: 12/98
Salary: $94,890
Term limit: 2 consecutive terms
Phone: (808) 586-0034
Born: November 14, 1939; Honolulu, Hawaii.
Education: U. of California, Los Angeles, B.A. 1968; Loyola Marymount U., J.D. 1971.
Occupation: Lawyer.
Family: Wife, Vicky Liu; three children.
Religion: Unspecified.
Political Career: Hawaii House, 1975-78; Hawaii Senate, 1979-86; lieutenant governor, 1987.

Lt. Gov.: Mazie Hirono (D)
First elected: 1994
Length of term: 4 years
Term expires: 12/98
Salary: $94,780
Phone: (808) 586-0255

State election official: (808) 453-8683
Democratic headquarters: (808) 536-2258
Republican headquarters: (808) 526-1755

REDISTRICTING

Hawaii retained its two House seats in reapportionment. The map was adopted by a commission July 19, 1991; the governor's signature was not required.

STATE LEGISLATURE

Bicameral legislature. Meets January-April.

Senate: 25 members, 4-year terms
1996 breakdown: 23D, 2R; 20 men, 5 women
Salary: $32,000
Phone: (808) 586-6720

House of Representatives: 51 members, 2-year terms
1996 breakdown: 39D, 12R; 44 men, 7 women
Salary: $32,000
Phone: (808) 586-6400

URBAN STATISTICS

City	Population
Honolulu	365,272
Mayor Jeremy Harris, D	
Hilo	37,808
Mayor Stephen Yamashiro, D	
Kailua	36,818
Mayor Jeremy Harris, D	
Kaneohe	35,448
Mayor Jeremy Harris, D	
Waipahu	31,435
Mayor Jeremy Harris, D	

U.S. CONGRESS

Senate: 2 D, 0 R
House: 2 D, 0 R

TERM LIMITS

For state offices: No

ELECTIONS

1996 Presidential Vote

Bill Clinton	57%
Bob Dole	32%
Ross Perot	8%

1992 Presidential Vote

Bill Clinton	48%
George Bush	37%
Ross Perot	14%

1988 Presidential Vote

Michael S. Dukakis	54%
George Bush	45%

POPULATION

1990 population		1,108,229
1980 population		964,691
Percent change		+15%
Rank among states:		40
White		33%
Black		2%
Hispanic		7%
Asian or Pacific islander		62%
Urban		89%
Rural		11%
Born in state		56%
Foreign-born		15%
Under age 18	280,126	25%
Ages 18-64	703,098	63%
65 and older	125,005	11%
Median age		32.6

MISCELLANEOUS

Capital: Honolulu
Number of counties: 4
Per capita income: $21,306 (1991)
Rank among states: 7
Total area: 6,471 sq. miles
Rank among states: 47

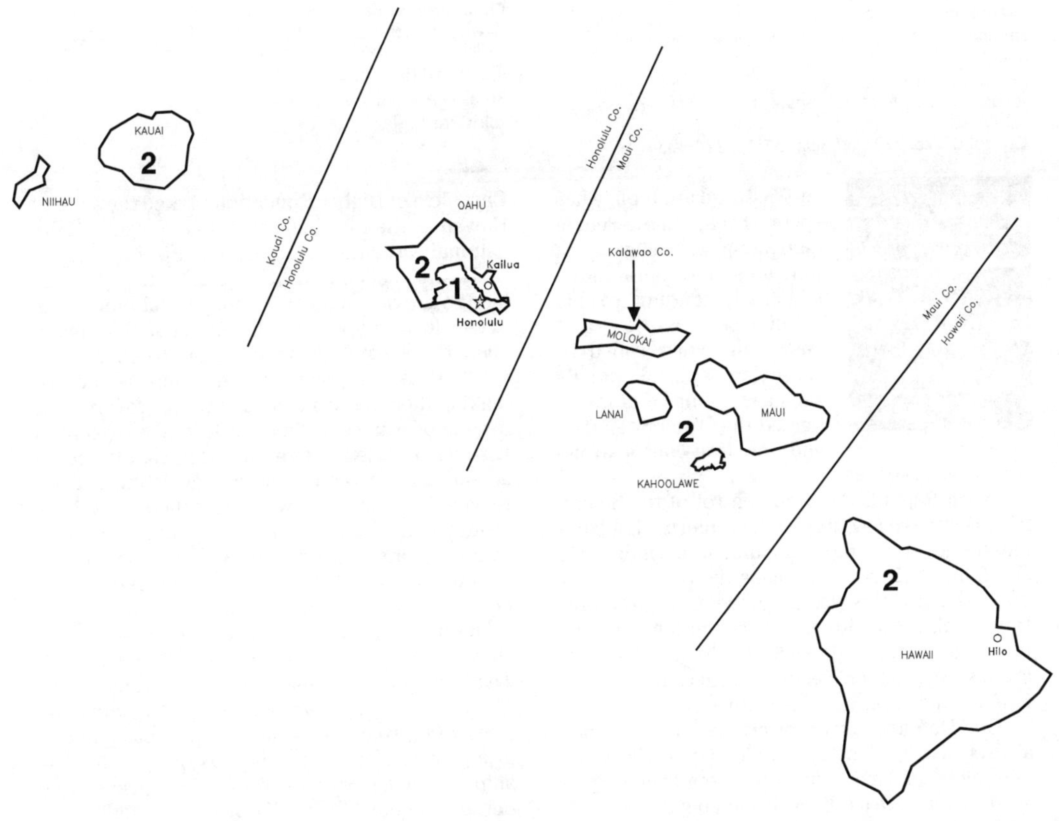
KAUAI
2
NIIHAU
Kauai Co.
Honolulu Co.
OAHU
2
1
Kailua
Honolulu
Honolulu Co.
Maui Co.
Kalawao Co.
MOLOKAI
LANAI
MAUI
2
KAHOOLAWE
Maui Co.
Hawaii Co.
2
HAWAII
Hilo

Daniel K. Inouye (D)

Of Honolulu — Elected 1962, 6th term

Biographical Information
Born: Sept. 7, 1924, Honolulu, Hawaii.
Education: U. of Hawaii, A.B. 1950; George Washington U., J.D. 1952.
Military Service: Army, 1943-47.
Occupation: Lawyer.
Family: Wife, Margaret Shinobu Awamura; one child.
Religion: Methodist.
Political Career: Hawaii Territorial House, 1954-58, majority leader; Hawaii Territorial Senate, 1958-59; U.S. House, 1959-63.
Capitol Office: 722 Hart Bldg. 20510; 224-3934.

Committees
Appropriations
Commerce, Justice, State & Judiciary; Defense (ranking); Foreign Operations; Labor, Health & Human Services & Education; Military Construction
Commerce, Science & Transportation
Aviation; Communications; Oceans & Fisheries; Surface Transportation & Merchant Marine (ranking)
Indian Affairs (ranking)
Rules & Administration
Joint Printing

In Washington: Inouye has spent 34 years in the Senate cultivating an image as a judicious and fair-minded legislator, tending to his committee work and answering when called to serve on special panels such as the ones that investigated the Watergate affair and the Iran-contra arms-for-hostages scandal.

When Republicans won control of the Senate in 1994, Inouye lost his perch as chairman of committees governing the communications industries and Indian affairs. He remains the top Democrat on those panels, as well as on the Appropriations' Defense Subcommittee, and even in the minority, Inouye manages to do what he always done during his long career: secure a generous share of federal funds for his home state.

On Defense Appropriations, Inouye has always displayed a firm command of the numbers, although he has rarely been out front on policy decisions. He has backed such big-ticket items as the Strategic Defense Initiative, and supported more funding for the B-2 bomber than the Pentagon requests.

The defense panel has afforded Inouye a number of opportunities to support projects that benefit Hawaii. He saluted passage of the fiscal 1997 defense spending bill with a news release touting some $268 million in projects for his home state. Included were $7 million for the National Defense Center of Excellence for Research in Ocean Sciences in Honolulu, which studies, among other things, how dolphins find underwater objects with echolocation, and $1 million to combat the accidental introduction to Hawaii from Guam of brown tree snakes, which threaten native birds.

Inouye has also enjoyed success in steering money to Hawaii from the bill that funds military construction. The Senate's spending bill for 1996, for instance, contained $30 million in projects for Hawaii.

Some of Inouye's efforts have benefited the University of Hawaii. A 1996 survey by the Chronicle of Higher Education ranked the state of Hawaii as the fifth highest state recipient of educational earmarks, with just under $17 million.

Hawaii depends on shipping from the mainland to provide many of its goods, and Inouye has been a loyal supporter of the Merchant Marine. In 1996, the Senate considered a bill to change the way private shipowners are compensated for making their vessels available to the government in time of war, replacing it with a new system of flat fees. Charles E. Grassley, R-Iowa, offered an amendment to reduce bonus payments that are received by mariners who are called to service. Inouye argued against the cut, pointing out that over the years he has received several benefits for his military service that are not provided to merchant mariners who served in the military.

Inouye has also tried to secure one particular ship for Hawaii — the battleship USS Missouri. The Navy offered to make the Missouri and some other vintage battleships available to states and nonprofit groups for use as museums, and a group from Honolulu hoped to bring home the ship — which hosted the formal Japanese surrendered that ended World War II — as an addition to a memorial at Pearl Harbor. But some senators wanted the Navy to keep the ships in reserve status. Inouye added an amendment to a defense spending bill to prohibit the Navy from spending any money to maintain the ships, effectively requiring it to give them away.

Another longtime focus of Inouye's energies has been the Senate Indian Affairs Committee, which he chaired from 1987 until 1995, and where he remains the ranking Democrat. "This committee has been known as the scrap heap of the Senate," he once said. "I'm going to do everything in my power to change that." In the 104th, Inouye turned over his gavel to Sen. John McCain of Arizona; in the 105th, the committee is chaired by Sen. Ben Nighthorse Campbell of Colorado, the only American Indian in the Senate.

When House Republicans in 1995 proposed a bill to rescind $17.1 billion in government spending, Inouye and McCain strongly criticized the bill for targeting Indian programs. Inouye compared it with the federal government's reneging on past treaty obligations. "We have broken too many promises already," he said. "We shouldn't continue that process."

McCain and Inouye also joined forces to put forward a bill on Indian gaming, an issue that gains in prominence as the lucrative industry prospers. Their bill would bring Indian gaming under federal regulatory authority. Many Indian tribes supported the proposal, although some states wanted more control over Indian gaming within their borders, including the authority to block new casinos.

Inouye has been a strong supporter of a planned Museum of the American Indian, to be added to the Smithsonian's array of museums on the National Mall in Washington, D.C. Federal funding for the museum came under some criticism in the 104th, especially in the House. When the Senate Appropriations Committee considered a fiscal 1996 spending bill for the Interior Department, Inouye offered an amendment to provide $19 million for the museum. The amendment caused controversy, because Inouye at first proposed offsetting the museum appropriation by reducing funding for the National Endowment for the Humanities. But a compromise was worked out for the offsetting money to come from the strategic petroleum reserve account.

Inouye's reputation for integrity and ethical deportment was dented in the 102nd Congress when his former barber accused him of making unwanted sexual advances, prompting nine other women to make similar accusations in the news media.

The Senate Ethics Committee dropped a review of the charges when the accusers declined to participate in its investigation. But the incident was clearly a factor in Inouye's 1992 re-election tally of 57 percent, his lowest ever. Damage was still evident in the month after the election, when Inouye bowed out of a scheduled address to the University of Hawaii's December commencement ceremonies, citing concern that the controversy surrounding him could detract from the occasion.

Interestingly, Inouye was the first to congratulate Sen. Robert C. Byrd, D-W.Va., for making a Senate floor speech in 1994 saying it was time for colleague Bob Packwood, R-Ore., who also was battling sexual harassment charges, to resign rather than further damage the image of the Senate. Inouye told a Honolulu TV station the next day that he agreed with Byrd.

Inouye is of an earlier political era, a time when behind-the-scenes collegiality was more important than public appearances, and when loyalty to the Senate as an institution was the norm. Bred in Hawaii's Democratic machine, Inouye has a private and personal style. He is most comfortable working quietly with colleagues he calls friends, having mastered the touch of being a party man without being regarded as partisan.

In that context, Inouye's statements about Packwood (who eventually resigned) seem out of character. Inouye has usually been all but fanatical in his loyalty to colleagues. He even taped a radio advertisement for Oregon Senator Mark O. Hatfield, a former colleague on Appropriations, when Hatfield had a tough race in 1990.

And when the image of the entire Congress was suffering because of some members' apparent complicity in problems that led to the collapse of the savings and loan industry, Inouye was the one senator to speak up publicly on behalf of the Keating Five — the senators who suffered the most for their links to the industry.

The intensely political, impersonal tactics that now dominate Senate action, and the need to communicate the party's agenda outside the chamber, are contrary to Inouye's style. This helps explain why his 1989 bid for majority leader attracted only 14 of the Senate's 55 Democratic votes. Seniority helped him little. Inouye never expanded his base beyond old hands and colleagues on the Appropriations Committee.

The victor, Maine's George J. Mitchell, named Inouye chairman of the Democratic Steering Committee, which hands out committee assignments. Inouye had been secretary of the Democratic Conference.

If Inouye has not been closely associated with many national legislative achievements, he did take center stage during two congressional investigations of executive branch misdeeds.

His 1987 appointment to chair the select Senate committee investigating the Iran-contra affair stemmed not only from his impartial manner but also from the esteem accorded him 14 years earlier during hearings on the illegal activities that led to the downfall of the Nixon administration. During the 1973 Watergate hearings, Inouye earned a reputation as a tough but judicious interrogator of President Richard M. Nixon's aides and associates.

Inouye's work and rhetoric on the Iran panel, while competent, did not measure up to expectations. And so he missed a chance to shine at a time when he was still hoping to be the next majority leader.

His leadership campaign also suffered from the storm of protest that arose from a measure he put in a 1987 appropriations bill that would have spent $8 million to build schools for North African Jews in France. Unfortunately for Inouye, the project became a symbol of the kind of special interest projects members favor.

In early 1988 the Senate rescinded the money at Inouye's request, after news accounts that he had received a $1,000 contribution from a member of the board of a New York-based group that supports Jewish refugees and had lobbied Inouye for the project. In an emotional speech Inouye conceded no impropriety, only an error in judgment, and he said he feared he had embarrassed his colleagues.

At Home: A military hero, Inouye won his first election in 1954, helped guide Hawaii to statehood in 1959 and was a founder of the Democratic organization that has dominated state politics.

His stature in Hawaii's Japanese community approached reverence. During the war, he had fought in Europe as a member of the all Japanese-American 442nd Regiment. When his loss of an arm denied Inouye his ambition to be a surgeon, he went first into law and then into politics.

He became one of Hawaii's first House members, then in 1962 became the first Japanese-American in the Senate. He went on to four more landslide wins over modest and mainly polite GOP opposition. But in 1992, Inouye's pedestal was rocked by a pair of maverick challengers: Democratic Maui County Commissioner Wayne K. Nishiki and Republican state Sen. Rick Reed.

Nishiki and Reed had been closely linked since the 1970s, when they published a local newspaper that showcased their strong environmentalist views. Nishiki and Reed then built careers out of challenging Hawaii's Democratic establishment, which they claimed had overly close ties with the state's business community, developers and even organized crime.

It was clear from the start that this would not be another deferential campaign. As Inouye prepared for the Dec. 7, 1991, ceremonies marking the 50th anniversary of Japan's attack on Pearl Harbor, Nishiki ran an ad in the Honolulu newspapers accusing the senator of being in league with Japanese real estate speculators who he said had contributed to high housing prices in Hawaii. The ad asked whether Inouye was "a traitor or simply incompetent." Inouye expressed outrage over the language and timing of the broadside.

Nishiki could not shake his image as a stalking horse for Reed, and Inouye coasted to a better than 3-to-1 margin in the primary. But Reed, an easy winner in the GOP primary, did not wait until the general election to go after the Democrat. Reed tried to link Inouye with Hawaii businessman Larry Mehau, a Democratic Party insider whom Reed accused of being involved in organized crime. Reed referred to Inouye as "the kingpin" of Hawaii's political machine.

But sex, not crime, would be the main event in Reed's assault. A Reed ally — posing as a potential Inouye employee who had heard rumors of sexual misconduct by the senator — secretly recorded a conversation with Inouye's barber, Lenore Kwock. Although Reed denied authorizing the snooping, he ran a radio ad in October featuring Kwock's claims that Inouye had forced sex on her 17 years earlier and had made unwanted advances to her since.

Inouye called the accusation "unmitigated lies." Kwock angrily rebuked Reed for publicizing her story without her permission. Reed, faced with a strong backlash from the public and the media, withdrew the ad.

Yet the allegation did smudge Inouye's reputation and likely contributed to his diminished showing at the polls (57 percent): Never before had he won less than two-thirds of the vote. Much of the vote he lost did not go to Reed (who trailed by more than 100,000 votes) but to Linda B. Martin, the nominee of Hawaii's environmentalist Green Party.

SENATE ELECTIONS

1992 General		
Daniel K. Inouye (D)	208,266	(57%)
Rick Reed (R)	97,928	(27%)
Linda B. Martin (GREEN)	49,921	(14%)
Richard O. Rowland (LIBERT)	7,547	(2%)
1992 Primary		
Daniel K. Inouye (D)	141,273	(76%)
Wayne K. Nishiki (D)	44,505	(24%)

Previous Winning Percentages: **1986** (74%) **1980** (78%) **1974** (83%) **1968** (83%) **1962** (69%) **1960*** (74%) **1959†** (68%)

** House election*
† Special House election

KEY VOTES

1997	
Approve balanced-budget constitutional amendment	N
Approve chemical weapons treaty	Y
1996	
Approve farm bill	Y
Limit punitive damages in product liability cases	N
Exempt small businesses from higher minimum wage	N
Approve welfare overhaul	N
Bar job discrimination based on sexual orientation	Y
Override veto of ban on "partial birth" abortions	N
1995	
Approve GOP budget with tax and spending cuts	N
Approve constitutional amendment barring flag desecration	N

CAMPAIGN FINANCE

	Receipts	Receipts from PACs		Expend-itures
1992				
Inouye (D)	$2,732,805	$805,465	(29%)	$2,971,128
Reed (R)	$440,852	$500	(0%)	$438,851
Martin (GREEN)	$12,783	0		$7,278

VOTING STUDIES

	Presidential Support		Party Unity		Conservative Coalition	
Year	S	O	S	O	S	O
1996	83	14	83	13	47	45
1995	83	15	80	15	53	40
1994	92	5	89	8	41	56
1993	85	4	78	6	34	59
1992	38	55	78	12	32	58
1991	51	47	77	19	50	43

INTEREST GROUP RATINGS

Year	ADA	AFL-CIO	CCUS	ACU
1996	85	n/a	33	11
1995	95	100	41	0
1994	75	88	20	0
1993	85	100	20	13
1992	65	92	10	4
1991	80	92	20	14

Daniel K. Akaka (D)

Of Honolulu — Elected 1990; 1st full term

Appointed to the Senate 1990.

Biographical Information

Born: Sept. 11, 1924, Honolulu, Hawaii.

Education: U. of Hawaii, B.Ed. 1952, M.Ed. 1966.

Military Service: Army Corps of Engineers, 1945-47.

Occupation: Elementary school teacher and principal; state official.

Family: Wife, Mary Mildred Chong; five children.

Religion: Congregationalist.

Political Career: Sought Democratic nomination for lieutenant governor, 1974; U.S. House, 1977-90.

Capitol Office: 720 Hart Bldg. 20510; 224-6361.

Committees

Energy & Natural Resources
National Parks, Historic Preservation & Recreation; Water & Power (ranking)

Governmental Affairs
International Security, Proliferation & Federal Services; Investigations

Indian Affairs

Veterans' Affairs

In Washington: In a legislative body known for oversize personalities and powerful egos, Akaka is thoroughly unassuming. He is surely the most remarkably unremarkable member of "the world's most exclusive club."

Akaka in the Senate has continued in the style he maintained during nearly 14 years in the House, keeping a low profile and a very tight focus on Hawaiian interests. Parochial matters have been his main concern on the Energy and Natural Resources, Governmental Affairs, Veterans' Affairs and Indian Affairs committees.

In the 104th Congress, Akaka and other Hawaiian lawmakers took exception to a bill designating English as the nation's official language. A defender of his state's Hawaiian-language programs, Akaka believed the bill would undermine the bilingual education programs, promote frivolous litigation and foster ethnic and racial tensions. "This bill is deeply misguided," Akaka testified before the Governmental Affairs Committee in March 1996. "Designating English the official language is about as useful as designating blue the official color of the Pacific Ocean." The House passed a version of the bill, but the Senate bill died in committee.

Akaka also spoke frequently against a proposal to store spent nuclear fuel on Palmyra Atoll, an uninhabited U.S. territory in the Pacific 1,000 miles south of Hawaii. A New York company had acquired Palmyra and circulated draft legislation to waive U.S. environmental rules and allow a repository for 200,000 tons of radioactive waste, primarily from Russian reactors.

Calling the plan "a crazy idea," in June 1996 Akaka first sponsored a bill to prohibit any such storage facilities outside the 50 states, then another bill to give Hawaii jurisdiction over Palmyra, Midway and six other Pacific islands that are U.S. territories. While the House acted on neither, Akaka won a statement from the White House in August expressing the administration's strong opposition to the Palmyra plan.

On most votes, Akaka is dependably liberal. He was one of 11 Democrats to vote against the welfare overhaul the Senate passed in September 1995, and he also opposed the balanced-budget amendment, the line-item veto law and the ban on a particular abortion technique that opponents call "partial birth" abortion. Interestingly, in May 1996 he strayed from the liberal line to support the moderate "Centrist Coalition" budget resolution, which reduced Medicare, Medicaid and domestic spending. It narrowly lost on the Senate floor.

Several pieces of legislation that Akaka sponsored in the 104th were enacted in some form, among them a measure that compensates Native Hawaiians by transferring federal land to a trust in return for lands seized by the United States during the state's territorial period. The law builds on a measure that Akaka helped push through the Senate in 1992: an apology to Hawaiians for the 1893 U.S. overthrow of the native government. Also in the 104th, Akaka had laws signed that will refinance home loans for American Indian veterans, fund research on using hydrogen as a fuel source, and further explore marine mineral resources.

None question Akaka's devotion to Hawaii's interests. In 1994, he was involved in efforts by the Interior and Transportation departments to cut aircraft noise pollution over national parks, and he sponsored another bill to that end in 1995. "Somewhere in this great land of ours there must be places where we are able to take refuge from civilization to renew our spirit," he said.

A protector of Hawaii's sugar industry, he successfully fought an effort by Judd Gregg, R-N.H., to cap sugar prices and loosen import quotas during debate on the agriculture spending bill in July 1996.

That vote echoed a similar battle on sugar subsidies that Akaka won against former Sen. Bill Bradley, D-N.J, in 1990. Of that fight with Bradley, a former basketball star, Akaka told a newspaper: "I'm only 5-feet-7, but I slam-dunked him."

The remark recalls an incident earlier in Akaka's career. In 1984, the House Democratic leadership was one vote short on a crucial roll call as it sought to block President Ronald Reagan's request for production of the MX missile. With time running out, Illinois Democrat Marty Russo located Akaka, who had been recorded as a pro-MX vote, lifted him out of a phone booth and escorted — carried, said some witnesses — him into the chamber. Akaka then changed his vote, giving the anti-MX forces a key victory.

At Home: When Democratic Sen. Spark M. Matsunaga died in April 1990, Akaka was a logical choice to fill out the remaining four years of his term. Akaka had carried Hawaii's 2nd District by huge margins in seven House contests. A Native Hawaiian — the only one ever to serve in Congress — he was on good terms with Democratic Gov. John Waihee III, who made the appointment. Akaka was close to the leadership of the state Democratic Party and had received support throughout his career from Japanese-Americans, a crucial voting bloc.

However, with Akaka facing a special election in November 1990, there was a degree of trepidation about his ability to hold the seat. Akaka had been a rather sedate figure during his House career and was not readily identifiable to many Hawaiians. Some Democrats feared that Akaka might be overwhelmed by his more aggressive opponent, 1st District GOP Rep. Patricia F. Saiki.

On paper, Akaka had major advantages over Saiki. He had won seven House elections to her two. He benefited from Hawaii's Democratic leanings and had solid backing from prominent state Democrats such as senior Sen. Daniel K. Inouye.

Yet the image persisted that Saiki, a moderate with a more assertive personality and a base in Honolulu, was the favorite in the campaign. GOP strategists touted Hawaii as their best chance for a Senate "takeaway."

As it turned out, both Akaka and the state Democratic machine that backed him were underestimated. Akaka played to his strengths: his personality and his ability to deliver federal largess to Hawaii, which he proved as a member of the House Appropriations Committee. Akaka won with a surprisingly solid 54 percent.

Akaka was up for a full term in 1994, and although potential candidates began to position themselves even before the 1992 election, a serious challenge never materialized. Saiki, who was appointed by President George Bush to head the Small Business Administration after her 1990 defeat, entered the race to succeed retiring Gov. Waihee, who also declined to challenge Akaka.

Akaka ultimately was unopposed in the Democratic primary and faced only minor opposition in the general election from Maria M. Hustace, a biennial fixture in Hawaii congressional races ever since her first campaign against Akaka in 1986. Akaka won 72 percent of the vote, the highest tally of any Senate incumbent in 1994.

Akaka rose through the Honolulu education bureaucracy before entering politics in 1971 as appointed head of the state Office of Economic Opportunity. In 1976, the 2nd District opened up with the unsuccessful Senate candidacy of Democratic Rep. Patsy T. Mink. Akaka faced formidable primary opposition from state Sen. Joe Kuroda but won with a narrow plurality; he took the general election with 80 percent and won subsequently with similar ease.

SENATE ELECTIONS

1994 General		
Daniel K. Akaka (D)	256,189	(72%)
Maria M. Hustace (R)	86,320	(24%)
Richard O. Rowland (LIBERT)	14,393	(4%)

Previous Winning Percentages: **1990** (54%) **1988*** (89%) **1986*** (76%) **1984*** (82%) **1982*** (89%) **1980*** (90%) **1978*** (86%) **1976*** (80%)

** House elections.*

CAMPAIGN FINANCE

	Receipts	Receipts from PACs	Expend-itures
1994			
Akaka (D)	$604,080	$304,368 (50%)	$418,630
Hustace (R)	$29,545	$250 (1%)	$29,293

KEY VOTES

1997	
Approve balanced-budget constitutional amendment	N
Approve chemical weapons treaty	Y
1996	
Approve farm bill	Y
Limit punitive damages in product liability cases	N
Exempt small businesses from higher minimum wage	N
Approve welfare overhaul	N
Bar job discrimination based on sexual orientation	Y
Override veto of ban on "partial birth" abortions	N
1995	
Approve GOP budget with tax and spending cuts	N
Approve constitutional amendment barring flag desecration	N

VOTING STUDIES

	Presidential Support		Party Unity		Conservative Coalition	
Year	**S**	**O**	**S**	**O**	**S**	**O**
1996	88	12	95	5	26	74
1995	83	11	93	5	21	75
1994	97	3	94	6	31	69
1993	94	6	95	5	28	71
1992	30	70	92	8	26	74
1991	35	64	91	9	25	75

INTEREST GROUP RATINGS

Year	ADA	AFL-CIO	CCUS	ACU
1996	95	n/a	31	5
1995	95	100	24	0
1994	85	88	20	0
1993	90	91	18	4
1992	90	92	20	0
1991	90	92	20	5

1 Neil Abercrombie (D)

Of Honolulu — Elected 1990; 4th full term
Also served Sept. 1986-Jan. 1987.

Biographical Information

Born: June 26, 1938, Buffalo, N.Y.

Education: Union College, B.A. 1959; U. of Hawaii, M.A. 1964, Ph.D. 1974.

Occupation: Educator.

Family: Wife, Nancie Caraway.

Religion: Unspecified.

Political Career: Sought Democratic nomination for U.S. Senate, 1970; Hawaii House, 1975-79; Hawaii Senate, 1979-86; sought Democratic nomination for U.S. House, 1986; U.S. House, 1986-87; Honolulu City Council, 1988-90.

Capitol Office: 1233 Longworth Bldg. 20515; 225-2726.

Committees

National Security
Military Installations and Facilities; Military Research & Development

Resources
Fisheries Conservation, Wildlife & Oceans (ranking)

In Washington: Even in Democratic-dominated Hawaii, Abercrombie's spirited defense of liberal causes does not suit all tastes, as was plain at the polls in November 1996, when he prevailed by fewer than 6,700 votes over staunch GOP conservative Orson Swindle.

It was Abercrombie's tightest-ever re-election — he beat Swindle by 11 percentage points in 1994 — but despite that scrape, Abercrombie seems no more likely to alter his political stripes than he does to conform to the close-clipped appearance that most members of Congress maintain. With his full beard and flowing hair, he looks as though he would be quite comfortable on the road with the Grateful Dead; in fact, he was their guest at a June 1991 Washington concert. He is an enthusiastic member of the Congressional Progressive Caucus, which vowed on the opening day of the 104th Congress to fight the new GOP majority with a series of bills proposing cuts in military spending and increases in funding for programs aimed at helping the poor.

But Abercrombie, a member of the National Security Committee, is by no means averse to all defense spending. The military has historically had a large presence in Hawaii, with Pearl Harbor and other installations contributing mightily to the state's economy. Although Abercrombie opposes some specific big-ticket defense programs — such as the B-2 stealth bomber and a space-based missile system — he does not usually vote against the overall defense spending bill. In fact, in June 1996 he was one of 58 Democrats who voted against an attempt by liberals and "deficit hawks" to freeze fiscal 1997 military spending at the prior year level.

In July 1995 he was one of an ad hoc group of Democrats trying to round up votes in their party against the B-2 on the annual defense spending bill. The main argument used by Abercrombie and the other B-2 opponents was that in a time of fiscal austerity, the bomber absorbed too large a share of the money available for the Pentagon. "This is a test of integrity in budgeting," Abercrombie told the House. "This is a glide path, not to a balanced budget; this is a glide path to balanced-budget oblivion." But the amendment against the B-2 failed, 203-219.

Abercrombie's interest in securing defense funds for his state was evident in his work on the fiscal 1997 defense bill, when he obtained $189 million for numerous military construction projects in Hawaii, including the replacement of 372 units of on-base family housing at Schofield Army Barracks and the construction of bachelor-enlisted quarters at Marine Corps Base Hawaii.

Abercrombie also is an active proponent of a strong merchant marine. In the 104th, he backed a bill that aimed to revitalize the nation's merchant marine by creating a program in which the government would pay U.S.-flagged ship operators for use of their ships during war or a call-up by the Defense secretary. "How can we be the great power on the earth in the 21st century if we don't have a merchant marine?" Abercrombie said when the committee approved the bill.

He also sits on the Resources Committee, where he is ranking Democrat on the Fisheries, Conservation, Wildlife and Oceans Subcommittee. Generally speaking, he is opposed to conservatives' views on land-use and resource-management issues. In October 1995, he blasted the GOP's balanced-budget bill, telling the House that it included a "sham mining law reform package."

As approved by Resources, the measure included an overhaul of the 1872 mining law that would allow miners to continue purchasing federal land on which they prospect for minerals — a process as known as "patenting." Existing law enables miners to patent their federal land claims at $2.50 an acre, a price that critics say is far too low. The committee bill required miners to pay fair market prices for the surface land values of their claims, but the price excluded the value of the mineral deposits presumed to be on those lands. "It makes no sense to sell our minerals for a pittance of their intrinsic value," Abercrombie told the House. "It would be like selling a bottle of Dom Perignon for the price of the cork."

HAWAII 1
Honolulu — Pearl City

The compact 1st District takes in the narrow plain between the Koolau mountain range and the Leeward (western) coast of the island of Oahu. But this small area includes the city of Honolulu, the engine that drives all of Hawaii.

Honolulu is Hawaii's capital, home to most of its businesses and about one-third of its people. In its western end are the Pearl Harbor Naval Reservation and Hickam Air Force Base, major parts of a military sector that is vital to Hawaii's economy.

East of downtown Honolulu is Waikiki, heart of the tourist trade that is Hawaii's leading industry. Waikiki, with its numerous high-rise hotels, is one of the most densely populated places anywhere during tourist season. Those who come with dreams of "grass-shack" Hawaii are disappointed. But others who visit find it the perfect mix of stunning scenery, sandy beaches and urban amenities.

Farther east are Honolulu's most affluent neighborhoods, which include a large population of whites, known as haoles in the Hawaiian language.

The middle-class neighborhoods of central Honolulu are dominated by Americans of Japanese ancestry; for many in that ethnic group, employment in state government has been the route to economic security.

Kalihi, in northwest Honolulu, is a working-class community heavily populated by Filipinos and native Hawaiians. Scattered throughout are Chinese, Koreans, Vietnamese, Samoans, Portuguese, Puerto Ricans and members of other ethnic groups.

To the west are such towns as Pearl City, Aiea, Mililani Town and part of Kapolei, expected to become Oahu's "second city" by the 21st century.

Ewa Beach is connected to the district by a band rimming Pearl Harbor; Japan's attack on the naval base in December 1941 was the catalyst for the United States' entry into World War II. Inland is Camp H. M. Smith Marine Corps Base, the headquarters for the unified military command for the Pacific.

The 1st contributes to Hawaii's strong Democratic tilt. Japanese-Americans long have dominated the state Democratic Party; they are joined in their partisan tendencies by many other "minority group" constituents who make up the majority of 1st District residents.

The large military-oriented community, a growing number of Japanese-Americans gaining corporate advancement and the Republican leanings of many white residents occasionally allow a GOP candidate to carry the district. Republican Patricia F. Saiki made history by winning the House seat in 1986 and 1988.

But in 1990, Saiki lost a Senate bid to Democrat Daniel K. Akaka. Democrat Abercrombie easily won House contests that year and in 1992, and took just under 55 percent in 1994. His race was tougher in 1996, but he managed to hold on with 50 percent. Bill Clinton soundly defeated Bob Dole by 23 percentage points in the district, while Ross Perot earned 6 percent.

1990 Population: 554,119. White 161,228 (29%), Black 13,807 (2%), Asian and Pacific Islander 368,904 (67%), Other 10,180 (2%). Hispanic origin 30,598 (6%). 18 and over 431,485 (78%), 62 and over 85,443 (15%). Median age: 34.

On social policy issues, Abercrombie's voting record lists sharply to port: He favors abortion rights and gun control, voted against overhauling the welfare system and opposed GOP efforts to limit legal and illegal immigrants' access to public benefits, including an attempt to deny public education to illegal immigrants.

Though typically a laid-back, friendly fellow, Abercrombie can nevertheless launch powerful attacks when his liberal instincts are riled, as was the case when the House in February 1995 debated a bill to provide the president with a line-item veto, an idea Abercrombie vehemently opposed. "No matter who is the executive in our contemporary world, it is the legislative against the executive power. If we turn over our responsibilities to the executive, we are undermining the basis of freedom," he told the House.

Despite his passionate plea, the House passed the line-item veto bill, 294-134.

Abercrombie was also busy in the 104th co-writing a mystery thriller called "Blood of Patriots." The novel turns on the connection between mysterious campaign donations and political extremism. The book opens with a man and woman disguised as Capitol Hill staff members walking into the House during a vote, drawing Uzi submachine guns and killing 125 members of Congress, including the Republican Speaker. Abercrombie told The Washington Post that the book grew out of a conversation he had with a friend about the campaign finance system. He said that under the current system, "someone can sink millions into a campaign and it will be almost impossible to trace."

At Home: The 1st did not seem a very promising target for the GOP when challenger Swindle launched his 1994 campaign. Abercrombie had won comfortably in 1990 and 1992, and Swindle's only political claim to fame was his role as spokesman for Ross Perot's 1992 independent presidential bid.

However, his background as a decorated fighter pilot and a prisoner of war for six years in

Vietnam helped him catch the eye of the district's many military-minded voters, and he polled a respectable 43 percent, to Abercrombie's 54 percent.

Swindle returned for a rematch in 1996, and even though it was a stronger year for Democrats nationally, Swindle found an audience for his conservative calls to downsize government. Abercrombie slipped further, taking a bare majority to Swindle's 46 percent.

Abercrombie has faced electoral adversity before. In 1986, he actually won and lost the 1st District seat on the same day. Democratic Rep. Cecil Heftel had resigned the seat to run for governor, and a special election to fill out his term was scheduled to coincide with the September 1986 primary.

Abercrombie emerged as the favorite to succeed Heftel. A veteran of protest politics — he took 13 percent of the vote in the 1970 Democratic Senate primary as an anti-Vietnam War candidate — Abercrombie had become a leading liberal activist in the state Legislature.

But Abercrombie's ideological cast and reputation for abrasiveness left him open to attacks from Republican activist Patricia F. Saiki, his main competitor in the open-ballot special election, and from Democratic businessman Mufi Hannemann, an aggressive newcomer. Hannemann scored the hardest hit: He unearthed a 17-year-old newspaper article in which Abercrombie suggested what seemed to be a favorable attitude about decriminalizing marijuana use. Although Abercrombie furiously denied that he countenanced drug use, the issue was damaging.

Abercrombie managed to win the special election with 30 percent to 29 percent for Saiki and 28 percent for Hannemann. But he narrowly lost the primary to Hannemann, making him ineligible to run for a full term that November. (GOP nominee Saiki went on to defeat Hannemann, becoming the only Hawaii Republican ever to hold a House seat.)

Abercrombie restarted his political career in 1988 by winning a seat on the Honolulu City Council. When Saiki left the 1st District open in 1990 to challenge interim Democratic Sen. Daniel K. Akaka in the special election caused by the death of Democratic Sen. Spark M. Matsunaga, Abercrombie was primed for redemption.

Using an engaging and less combative style, Abercrombie took 46 percent of the Democratic House primary vote to defeat state Sen. Norman Mizuguchi and lawyer Matt Matsunaga, the son of the late senator. He then had little trouble returning the seat to Democratic control, topping GOP state Rep. Mike Liu with 61 percent.

The Republicans failed to recruit a well-known candidate in 1992, and Abercrombie coasted.

HOUSE ELECTIONS

1996 General		
Neil Abercrombie (D)	86,732	(50%)
Orson Swindle (R)	80,053	(46%)
Mark Duering (NON)	4,126	(2%)
1996 Primary		
Neil Abercrombie (D)	65,732	(72%)
Richard Thompson (D)	25,905	(28%)
1994 General		
Neil Abercrombie (D)	94,754	(54%)
Orson Swindle (R)	76,623	(43%)
Alexandra Kaan (BP)	2,815	(2%)
Roger L. Taylor (LIBERT)	2,514	(1%)

Previous Winning Percentages: 1992 (73%) **1990** (61%) **1986*** (30%)
Special election.

CAMPAIGN FINANCE

	Receipts	Receipts from PACs	Expend-itures
1996			
Abercrombie (D)	$682,898	$437,284 (64%)	$674,404
Swindle (R)	$643,854	$62,163 (10%)	$627,839
1994			
Abercrombie (D)	$371,788	$237,950 (64%)	$391,451
Swindle (R)	$279,263	$18,064 (6%)	$276,355

DISTRICT VOTE FOR PRESIDENT

	1996		1992
D	98,410 (57%)	**D**	87,632 (48%)
R	58,432 (34%)	**R**	72,156 (39%)
I	10,631 (6%)	**I**	23,438 (13%)

KEY VOTES

1997	
Ban "partial birth" abortions	N
1996	
Approve farm bill	N
Deny public education to illegal immigrants	N
Repeal ban on certain assault-style weapons	N
Increase minimum wage	Y
Freeze defense spending	N
Approve welfare overhaul	N
1995	
Approve balanced-budget constitutional amendment	N
Relax Clean Water Act regulations	N
Oppose limits on environmental regulations	Y
Reduce projected Medicare spending	N
Approve GOP budget with tax and spending cuts	N

VOTING STUDIES

	Presidential Support		Party Unity		Conservative Coalition	
Year	**S**	**O**	**S**	**O**	**S**	**O**
1996	76	22	89	10	47	53
1995	80	16	87	8	23	73
1994	71	27	95	2	17	81
1993	69	23	90	5	14	86
1992	9	89	92	2	2	92
1991	21	78	95	2	8	92

INTEREST GROUP RATINGS

Year	ADA	AFL-CIO	CCUS	ACU
1996	90	n/a	25	0
1995	90	100	8	8
1994	100	89	25	0
1993	100	100	9	4
1992	95	91	13	0
1991	100	100	10	0

2 Patsy T. Mink (D)

Of Honolulu — Elected 1990; 10th full term
Also served 1965-77.

Biographical Information

Born: Dec. 6, 1927, Paia, Maui, Hawaii.
Education: U. of Hawaii, B.A. 1948; U. of Chicago, J.D. 1951.
Occupation: Lawyer.
Family: Husband, John Francis Mink; one child.
Religion: Protestant.
Political Career: Hawaii Territorial House, 1956-58; Hawaii Territorial Senate, 1958-60; Hawaii Senate, 1962-64; U.S. House, 1965-77; sought Democratic nomination for president, 1972; Democratic nominee for U.S. Senate, 1976; assistant U.S. secretary of State, 1977-78; Honolulu City Council, 1983-87; sought Democratic nomination for governor, 1986; sought Democratic nomination for mayor of Honolulu, 1988.
Capitol Office: 2135 Rayburn Bldg. 20515; 225-4906.

Committees

Budget
Education & Workforce
Early Childhood, Youth & Families; Oversight & Investigations (ranking)

In Washington: When Mink first came to Congress in 1965, she was a New Deal Democrat who strongly supported President Lyndon B. Johnson's "Great Society" programs. Now in her second House career — her service was interrupted by a 1976 Senate primary defeat and a host of other political posts — Mink is fighting a rear-guard action in a Republican Congress that is determined to diminish or dismantle many of the initiatives she helped create a generation ago.

Early in the 104th Congress, she protested GOP plans to turn control of the food stamp program over to the states through block grants. "I was here when it happened," Mink said in defense of the entitlement. "I think it would be a real tragic mistake."

Whether in the majority or minority, Mink, who returned to the House in a 1990 special election, is an aggressive advocate who makes her presence known. She epitomizes the subject of many a conservative Republican's bad dream — a "tax and spend" Democrat. Since her return to Congress, Mink has almost always received 100 percent ratings from the liberal interest group Americans for Democratic Action and the AFL-CIO.

But despite nearly 40 years in political life and more than 18 total years in the House, Mink lacks the senior status that can mean political clout in Washington. Although several of her fellow Great Society freshmen went on to become committee chairs, Mink's hiatus meant that she had to start over again in seniority in 1990 despite her proven abilities as a legislator.

Mink told House Democratic leaders that she was interested in the ranking slot on the Budget Committee. When the Democratic Caucus voted on the position in organizational meetings before the start of the 105th Congress, Louise M. Slaughter of New York unsuccessfully challenged John M. Spratt Jr. of South Carolina for it, and Mink stayed out of the fray.

Nevertheless, Mink's current assignments on the Education and the Workforce Committee and on Budget provide her forums to fight the Republican rollback of social welfare programs.

In the Democratic-controlled 103rd Congress, Mink said she viewed her Budget post as a platform to "redirect our budget priorities" toward education, health care and job creation, and on the old Education and Labor Committee, she supported legislation to do just that, including the Clinton administration's "Goals 2000" education bill, national service legislation and universal health care.

During the 104th, Mink sought to abate the GOP's efforts to revamp the nation's welfare system. When the House voted on a plan to end welfare's entitlement status for the first of three times in the 104th, Mink offered a substitute. Her version would have increased spending on education, child care and job training by increasing the top corporate tax rate. It was defeated, 96-336.

Throughout her career, Mink has led the charge on such issues as child care and ovarian cancer research. In 1994 testimony before the Senate Judiciary Committee, Mink spoke about having been given an experimental drug known as DES, which proved to be a carcinogen, during pregnancy. Twenty-five years later, after learning from a follow-up researcher that she had been dosed, Mink received a settlement from drug manufacturer Eli Lilly.

Mink in the 104th tangled with Republicans on the Workforce Protections Subcommittee on bills of key concern to labor, frequently finding herself voted down when she offered amendments designed to ensure labor policies remain friendly to unions.

She also derided a successful GOP plan to limit the ease with which death row inmates could file habeas corpus appeals. "Innocence is not a technicality," Mink maintained.

Mink also has strongly opposed GOP efforts to pass a balanced-budget constitutional amendment, once calling it a "straitjacket that would cripple the future of our country."

With Hawaii in the news of late as the scene of court battles over the right of homosexuals to

HAWAII 2
Suburban and Outer Oahu — "Neighbor islands"

The heavily Democratic 2nd takes in seven major "neighbor islands," plus hundreds of reefs and atolls. But more than half of the people in the 2nd live on Oahu.

Although it has a racial and ethnic patchwork similar to that of the 1st District, the 2nd has a somewhat higher proportion of white residents (more than one-third of the population is white). There are some predominantly white, conservative-leaning communities, mostly on Oahu and Maui, that regularly vote Republican.

But these areas barely dent Democrats' dominance of the 2nd. Mink has coasted to victory by overwhelming margins since redistricting, and Bill Clinton beat George Bush and Bob Dole by large margins in the 1992 and 1996 presidential contests.

Hilo, on the "Big Island" of Hawaii, is the district's largest city with nearly 38,000 people; but the Oahu cities of Kailua and Kaneohe are very close behind. Kailua, on Oahu's Windward (eastern) side, is one of the few majority-white cities in Hawaii. The Asian and Pacific Islander majority of neighboring Kaneohe is more typical of Hawaii's ethnic mix. Across the island at the edge of Pearl Harbor, working-class Waipahu is more than 80 percent Asian or Pacific Islander.

Oahu's numerous military installations are central to the life and economy of the 2nd. However, one facility, the Barber's Point Naval Air Station, is scheduled to close in July 1999, freeing prime waterfront real estate for development. Away from Honolulu, population on Oahu thins, and tourist outposts are more dispersed. Laie is a Mormon enclave that includes a campus of Brigham Young University. Oahu's north coast is famous for its surfing. The Leeward (western) side has many native Hawaiians.

The spacious island of Hawaii saw its population expand by nearly a third during the 1980s. Much of the growth was on the scenic Leeward, or Kona, coast. The city of Hilo is a commercial center on the rainy eastern part of the Big Island; its attraction to tourists is its proximity to the active Mauna Loa and Kilauea volcanoes and extinct Mauna Kea. Agricultural products — including sugar, macadamia nuts, flowers, cattle and coffee — make up a major segment of the island's economy.

After Oahu, the island of Maui has the state's most developed tourism industry. Maui County has three other islands, including relatively undeveloped Molokai and Lanai, a longtime pineapple plantation, much of which is being converted into a tourist resort. The third, Kahoolawe, is a deserted island that was only recently returned to state control after being used as a military bombing range from the late 1930s until 1990.

Although Kauai has a large sugar industry, the island makes much of its living from tourism. The coastal resorts and Kauai's populace were staggered in September 1992, when Hurricane Iniki scored a direct hit on the island. Several hotels have yet to reopen and unemployment remains high as full recovery waits.

1990 Population: 554,110. White 208,388 (38%), Black 13,388 (2%), Asian and Pacific Islander 316,332 (57%), Other 16,002 (3%). Hispanic origin 50,792 (9%). 18 and over 396,618 (72%), 62 and over 69,025 (12%). Median age: 31.

marry there, many conservatives in Congress expressed alarm that such a thing could come to pass, and they supported legislation in the 104th to block federal recognition of same-gender marriages.

Mink made clear her feelings that marriage should remain exclusively the union of a man and a woman, but she voted against the "gay marriage" ban because, she contended, it violated the "full faith and credit" clause of the Constitution, which requires states to recognize marriages conducted in other states.

With an eye toward protecting a major cash crop in her state, Mink railed against conservative lawmakers such as Jack Kingston, R-Ga., who sought to lower subsidies for sugar in the 1996 farm authorization and appropriations bills. The subsidies were scaled back but survived.

France's resumption of nuclear testing in the South Pacific prompted Mink to protest French President Jacques Chirac's appearance before a joint session of Congress in February 1996. She was not able to force a vote on her resolution bemoaning Chirac's speech as a violation of "the dignity and integrity of the proceedings of the House," but she did lead a boycott of the appearance by several dozen members, mostly Democrats.

At Home: The congressional careers of Mink and Democratic Sen. Daniel K. Akaka of Hawaii are intertwined. Akaka succeeded Mink when she ended her first House stint with a losing 1976 Senate bid. Fourteen years later, Akaka's appointment to succeed the late Democratic Sen. Spark M. Matsunaga opened the way for Mink's return to the House.

Mink is one of the hardiest figures in Hawaii politics. In 1956, she won a seat in the territorial House, then moved to the Senate two years later. Mink was out of office during the early days of statehood but won a state Senate seat in 1962.

Two years later, Mink narrowly won a primary

for a U.S. House seat and was elected along with incumbent Matsunaga. Quickly establishing herself as an outspoken activist, Mink easily won re-election in 1966 and 1968.

In her 1970 contest — her first in the new, 2nd District — Mink ran unopposed. With Richard M. Nixon scoring the first GOP presidential victory ever in Hawaii, Mink slipped to 57 percent of the vote in 1972. She rebounded to 63 percent in 1974.

However, Mink's rise was halted in 1976, when she bid for the seat of retiring Republican Sen. Hiram L. Fong. Her Democratic primary rival, House colleague Matsunaga, had backing from much of the state party leadership. Playing off his image as a conciliator against Mink's more ideological bearing, Matsunaga won with 51 percent to Mink's 41 percent and went on to serve in the Senate until his death in April 1990.

Mink then signed on with Americans for Democratic Action, serving as president from 1978 to 1981. She embarked on a bumpy return to politics, winning two terms on the Honolulu City Council but losing primary bids for governor in 1986 and Honolulu mayor in 1988.

Thus, Mink's 1990 bid to succeed Akaka took the form of a comeback. In the September 1990 special election, her toughest foe was Mufi Hannemann, who had lost a 1986 House contest to Republican Patricia F. Saiki in the 1st District. A young, business-oriented candidate, Hannemann portrayed Mink as a candidate of a more liberal past. But touting her years of experience, Mink hung on, winning the special election by 2 percentage points and the primary for a full term by a slightly larger margin.

The November campaign was much easier. Republican Andy Poepoe, a businessman and longtime state officeholder, had run a distant fourth in the special election; Mink won easily.

History was on Mink's side in 1992 and 1994 — Hawaii voters have never turned out a Senate or House incumbent since statehood was achieved in 1959 — and she breezed past her primary and general-election opponents. The only surprise came when her 1994 Republican opponent mysteriously disappeared after the September primary, a development that drew national attention.

In 1996, she had to turn aside three primary challengers, including state Sen. Robert Bunda, who said he was seeking to break "the inertia of timeworn thinking" that hindered Hawaii's growth. But voters did not buy that characterization and renominated Mink with 60 percent. She won her tenth full term easily in November.

HOUSE ELECTIONS

1996 General		
Patsy T. Mink (D)	109,178	(60%)
Tom Pico Jr. (R)	55,729	(31%)
Nolan Crabbe (NON)	7,723	(4%)
James M. Keefe (LIBERT)	4,769	(3%)
Amanda "Mandy" Toulon (NL)	3,564	(2%)
1996 Primary		
Patsy T. Mink (D)	64,371	(60%)
Robert "Bobby" Bunda (D)	33,886	(32%)
Hana Kauhi (D)	4,071	(4%)
David L. Bourgoin (D)	2,288	(2%)
Charles "Lucky" Collins (D)	2,069	(2%)
1994 General		
Patsy T. Mink (D)	124,431	(70%)
Robert H. Garner (R)	42,891	(24%)
Lawrence R. Bartley (LIBERT)	10,074	(6%)

Previous Winning Percentages: **1992** (73%) **1990** (66%) **1990**† (35%) **1974** (63%) **1972** (57%) **1970** (100%) **1964-1968***

† Special election
* One of two Hawaii House members elected at large.

CAMPAIGN FINANCE

	Receipts	Receipts from PACs	Expend-itures
1996			
Mink (D)	$280,536	$132,614 (47%)	$315,187
Pico (R)	$91,292	$5,516 (6%)	$88,935
1994			
Mink (D)	$215,369	$97,450 (45%)	$157,523

DISTRICT VOTE FOR PRESIDENT

	1996		1992
D	106,602 (57%)	**D**	91,630 (49%)
R	55,511 (30%)	**R**	64,635 (35%)
I	16,727 (9%)	**I**	29,558 (16%)

KEY VOTES

1997	
Ban "partial birth" abortions	N
1996	
Approve farm bill	Y
Deny public education to illegal immigrants	N
Repeal ban on certain assault-style weapons	N
Increase minimum wage	Y
Freeze defense spending	Y
Approve welfare overhaul	N
1995	
Approve balanced-budget constitutional amendment	N
Relax Clean Water Act regulations	N
Oppose limits on environmental regulations	Y
Reduce projected Medicare spending	N
Approve GOP budget with tax and spending cuts	N

VOTING STUDIES

	Presidential Support		Party Unity		Conservative Coalition	
Year	S	O	S	O	S	O
1996	77	22	94	5	25	75
1995	81	17	94	6	12	87
1994	74	26	97	1	3	94
1993	73	26	95	3	2	98
1992	14	81	94	3	13	79
1991	19	77	96	3	3	97

INTEREST GROUP RATINGS

Year	ADA	AFL-CIO	CCUS	ACU
1996	95	n/a	25	5
1995	95	100	8	8
1994	100	100	17	0
1993	100	100	0	4
1992	100	100	25	0
1991	100	100	20	0

IDAHO

Governor: Phil Batt (R)
First elected: 1994
Length of term: 4 years
Term expires: 1/99
Salary: $85,000
Term limit: 2 terms
Phone: (208) 334-2100
Born: March 4, 1927; Wilder, Idaho
Education: U. of Idaho, 1944-48.
Military Service: Air Force, 1945-47.
Occupation: Farmer.
Family: Wife, Jacque Sallis; three children.
Religion: Baptist.
Political Career: Idaho House, 1965-67; Idaho Senate, 1967-78; lieutenant governor, 1978-82; Republican nominee for governor, 1982; Idaho Republican party chairman, 1992.

Lt. Gov.: C. L. "Butch" Otter (R)
First elected: 1986
Length of term: 4 years
Term expires: 1/99
Salary: $22,500
Phone: (208) 334-2200

State election official: (208) 334-2300
Democratic headquarters: (208) 336-1815
Republican headquarters: (208) 343-6405

REDISTRICTING

Idaho retained its two House seats in reapportionment. Legislature passed the map Jan. 21, 1992; governor signed it Jan. 28.

STATE LEGISLATURE

Bicameral Legislature. Meets January-March.

Senate: 35 members, 2-year terms
1996 breakdown: 30R, 5D; 30 men, 5 women
Salary: $12,360
Phone: (208) 334-2000

House of Representatives: 70 members, 2-year terms
1996 breakdown: 59R, 11D; 51 men, 19 women
Salary: $12,360
Phone: (208) 334-2000

URBAN STATISTICS

City	Population
Boise	125,738
Mayor Brent Coles, R	
Pocatello	46,117
Mayor Peter Angstadt, I	
Idaho Falls	43,929
Mayor Linda Milam, N-P	
Nampa	28,365
Mayor Winston K. Goering, R	
Lewiston	28,082
Mayor Gayle McGarry, N-P	

U.S. CONGRESS

Senate: 0 D, 2 R
House: 0 D, 2 R

TERM LIMITS

For state offices: Yes
Senate: 4 Terms
House: 4 Terms

ELECTIONS

1996 Presidential Vote

Bob Dole	52%
Bill Clinton	34%
Ross Perot	13%

1992 Presidential Vote

George Bush	42%
Bill Clinton	28%
Ross Perot	27%

1988 Presidential Vote

George Bush	62%
Michael S. Dukakis	36%

POPULATION

1990 population		1,006,749
1980 population		943,935
Percent change		+7%
Rank among states:		42
White		94%
Black		<1%
Hispanic		5%
Asian or Pacific islander		1%
Urban		57%
Rural		43%
Born in state		51%
Foreign-born		3%
Under age 18	308,405	31%
Ages 18-64	577,079	57%
65 and older	121,265	12%
Median age		31.5

MISCELLANEOUS

Capital: Boise
Number of counties: 44
Per capita income: $15,401 (1991)
Rank among states: 44
Total area: 83,564 sq. miles
Rank among states: 13

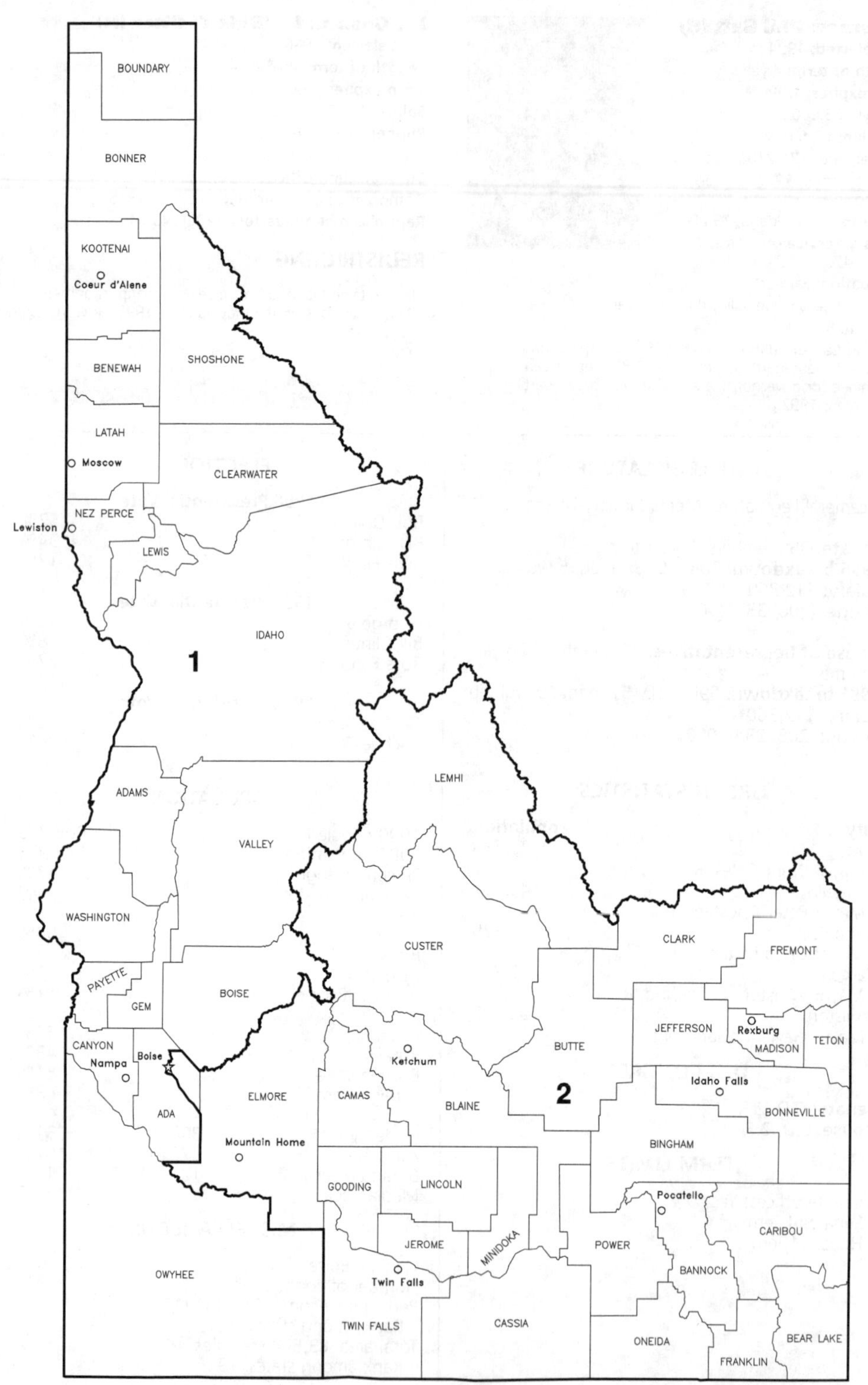
BOUNDARY
BONNER
KOOTENAI
Coeur d'Alene
SHOSHONE
BENEWAH
LATAH
Moscow
CLEARWATER
NEZ PERCE
Lewiston
LEWIS
IDAHO
1
ADAMS
VALLEY
LEMHI
WASHINGTON
CUSTER
CLARK
FREMONT
PAYETTE
GEM
BOISE
JEFFERSON
Rexburg
MADISON
TETON
CANYON
Nampa
Boise
BUTTE
Ketchum
Idaho Falls
ELMORE
CAMAS
BLAINE
2
BONNEVILLE
ADA
Mountain Home
BINGHAM
GOODING
LINCOLN
Pocatello
CARIBOU
JEROME
MINIDOKA
POWER
OWYHEE
Twin Falls
BANNOCK
TWIN FALLS
CASSIA
ONEIDA
BEAR LAKE
FRANKLIN

Larry E. Craig (R)

Of Payette — Elected 1990, 2nd term

Biographical Information
Born: July 20, 1945, Council, Idaho.
Education: U. of Idaho, B.A. 1969; George Washington U., 1969-70.
Military Service: National Guard, 1970-71.
Occupation: Farmer; rancher.
Family: Wife, Suzanne Scott; three children.
Religion: Methodist.
Political Career: Idaho Senate, 1975-81; U.S. House, 1981-91.
Capitol Office: 313 Hart Bldg. 20510; 224-2752.

Committees
Special Aging
Agriculture, Nutrition & Forestry
Forestry, Conservation & Rural Revitalization; Research, Nutrition & General Legislation
Appropriations
Energy & Water Development; Labor, Health & Human Services & Education; Legislative Branch; Military Construction; VA, HUD & Independent Agencies
Energy & Natural Resources
Energy Research Development Production & Regulation; Forests & Public Land Management (chairman); Water & Power
Veterans' Affairs

In Washington: A devout conservative who has long defended Western mining, ranching and timber interests and crusaded for a balanced-budget constitutional amendment, Craig now has a place in the leadership where he can work on those and other priorities: the chairmanship of the Senate Republican Policy Committee.

Craig won the right to head the group that develops the party's policies and agenda in the Senate in the leadership shuffle that followed Majority Leader Bob Dole's June 1996 resignation to campaign for president. With Oklahoma's Don Nickles climbing to the majority whip's spot, there was a three-way contest for the Policy Committee chair. Craig took 26 votes to 19 for Daniel R. Coats of Indiana and eight for Robert F. Bennett of Utah. In a runoff, Craig defeated Coats 30-22.

In electing Craig, Senate Republicans picked a candidate who, like most of their other newly elected leaders, started his life on Capitol Hill in the GOP House minority, doing battle with liberal Democrats. These days, he carries the conservative fight to the Clinton administration. Craig's preparation for leading the Policy Committee was chairing the Republican Steering Committee, an ad hoc caucus of 30-plus senators, most of them conservatives like Craig.

The balanced-budget amendment has been Craig's most visible challenge to Clinton. For 14 years Craig has campaigned for such an amendment, and he has carried that mission beyond the halls of Congress. Founder of CLUBB (Congressional Leaders United for a Balanced Budget), Craig has long urged state legislatures to demand that Congress enact a balanced-budget amendment or call a constitutional convention to draft one.

Craig sees the amendment as the best means to make the necessary spending cuts that, he says, Clinton has sought to avoid. "The president's budget is typical," he said in March 1997. "All the tough choices are for someone else to make. It's clear those tough choices won't be made and the deficit will continue to deepen unless we've got an amendment forcing change."

But in both the 104th and 105th Congresses, Craig and other amendment proponents came up one short of the 67 votes needed for passage, despite intense behind-the-scenes lobbying efforts aimed at converting a handful of uncommitted Democratic senators.

Craig's other recent high-profile challenge to the Clinton administration has been over the storage of nuclear waste at commercial power plants. He sponsored legislation in the 104th to build a temporary storage complex at Yucca Mountain, Nev., which is under consideration as a possible permanent burial site. Over the strenuous objections of Nevada Democratic Sens. Richard H. Bryan and Harry Reid, the Senate in July 1996 passed the bill 63-37 — a comfortable margin, but still four votes shy of the total needed to override a threatened Clinton veto.

Craig and his fellow Westerners have characterized the Clinton administration's plans to increase mining and grazing fees and to restrict logging on public lands as a "war on the West." Although Clinton has been fighting a losing battle in the Senate, where his proposals have encountered stiff opposition from Western lawmakers, Craig has had to tread carefully to counter environmentalists' charges that the GOP cares more about promoting economic development than about preserving natural resources.

As chairman of the Energy and Natural Resources Committee's panel on forests and public lands, Craig introduced a bill in the 104th to establish new management practices for dead and diseased timber on federal land. Craig and other supporters of the legislation contended that current management practices often prevent federal forest managers from offering salvage timber for sale before it decays beyond productive use. But environmentalists fought the measure, arguing that Craig was manufacturing a crisis in order to expedite logging to benefit timber companies.

In December 1996, shortly before being named to head a Senate Republican task force on environmental matters, Craig vowed to revise and streamline management policies on Forest Service and Bureau of Land Management lands. He circulated a draft bill allowing states to petition Congress for the power to manage the lands as well as make it more difficult for environmental groups to challenge federal land use decisions.

Environmental groups again cried foul; the Wilderness Society said in a statement that Craig "seems intent on turning back the forest management clock to the days when the public had little, if any, say in how our forests were managed." But Craig insisted he was willing to accommodate his critics, inviting them to attend a series of public workshops to reach a consensus on a bill. "Everybody, including those who oppose the legislation, is saying the Forest Service doesn't work any more," he said in an interview. "This is not a political expression. It's an expression on the part of the legislative branch to reconstitute an agency of the executive branch so it'll work."

Besides targeting Clinton's land-use reforms, Craig has taken aim at existing environmental laws, such as the Endangered Species Act, which he claims trample on private property rights and inhibit job growth. In August 1994, he told an Idaho audience, "Easterners should stop interfering with environmental issues.... The only endangered species in New York City is probably a free white human being." (He later apologized for a "poor choice of words" after his comments created an uproar among New York political leaders.)

Craig touched off another controversy in May 1995, when he said that Westerners were becoming increasingly frightened by the presence of "an armed federal entity" and called for thousands of federal officers who patrol national forests, parks and wildlife refuges to stop carrying guns. His comments prompted Rep. George Miller, D-Calif., to accuse Craig and other Republicans of making comments that "legitimize and incite" public fears about government.

Without exception, Craig finds that gun control proposals violate his belief that government's intrusion into citizens' lives should be limited. When Clinton used his weekly radio address to pressure Congress into passing his 1994 crime bill, Craig delivered a Republican response that criticized the inclusion of an amendment to ban 19 types of semiautomatic assault-style weapons. Passage of the bill in August was one of two major defeats for the National Rifle Association in the 103rd Congress and for Craig, who serves on the organization's board of directors.

Despite his stance on gunowners' rights, Craig showed in the 104th that he was willing to work with the Clinton administration on other law enforcement issues. In July 1996, he led a bipartisan task force of congressional leaders and administration officials that sought to develop a compromise anti-terrorism measure in the wake of a pipe-bomb explosion at the Olympic Games in Atlanta.

After a week of negotiations, Craig and then-White House Chief of Staff Leon E. Panetta announced a tentative deal. But the proposal was shot down by conservative House Republicans who were uncomfortable with proposals to give law enforcement agents expanded authority to gather evidence through wiretapping.

Earlier, Craig showed a pragmatic streak in urging Majority Leader Trent Lott to break the stalemate over a minimum-wage increase that slowed the Senate to a crawl in the spring of 1996. Although the deal Lott eventually agreed to ignored conservative demands to link the increase with labor bills opposed by Democrats, Craig contended that the deadlock was keeping the GOP from addressing its other priorities. "We just couldn't get hung up on this one issue for that long," he explained.

Craig has protected Idaho farming interests, especially sugar beet growers, as a member of the Agriculture Committee, where he has fought efforts to end price supports on sugar. He will get other opportunities to help his state in the 105th with his new seat on the Appropriations Committee.

One of 52 Republicans swept into the House in 1980, Craig proudly counted himself a leader in the "Reagan Revolution." But by the end of President Ronald Reagan's tenure in the White House, Craig was among those Republicans who seemed more ideologically consistent than Reagan himself; at times he sounded dismayed that even after eight years under a president supposedly opposed to federal largess, the deficit had multiplied.

Craig has been one of the most consistent supporters of the Republican Party line in the Senate, voting with the GOP 98 percent of the time in 1996. One notable exception to his pattern of party support is on the issue of free trade: He voted against NAFTA and GATT in the 103rd Congress.

Craig shares a close personal and ideological relationship with his conservative Idaho Senate colleague, Dirk Kempthorne. He also is close to Lott — the two are members of the "Singing Senators" vocal quartet that performs at GOP fundraisers and other functions.

At Home: Craig's 1990 ascent to the Senate was a fairly smooth affair, as he mobilized the renowned statewide organization of retiring GOP Sen. James A. McClure to roll over his Democratic opponent, Ron Twilegar, a former state legislator and Boise City Council member.

Idaho Democrats also cooperated to some extent by failing to field a well-known candidate. Rep. Richard Stallings, whose strong wins in the conservative 2nd District cast him as the party's best potential statewide candidate, opted against the race. After prolonged consideration, former Gov. John V. Evans, the 1986 nominee against GOP Sen. Steve Symms, also decided not to run.

Craig, by contrast, declared less than a week after McClure's January 1990 retirement announcement that he would vacate his 1st

District seat and enter the race. State Attorney General Jim Jones also filed for the Republican nomination but ran an underfunded campaign. He was no match for the well-funded, well-organized Craig, who won 59 percent of the vote. Twilegar won his primary with 64 percent over an obscure Idaho Falls businessman.

Craig's reputation as a stalwart opponent of abortion produced one of the more awkward moments of his campaign. In a debate with Twilegar, Craig responded to a question by saying that if his wife were impregnated by rape, it would be up to her to decide if she should seek an abortion. Twilegar, who favored abortion rights, then archly asked whether Craig's wife should be the only woman in the country to have a choice. But that was one of the few Twilegar shots that hit the mark. Mostly, his criticism of Craig's attendance record and votes on environmental issues had little effect. Craig's popularity in the 1st District, coupled with support in the more conservative 2nd, propelled him past the Democrat to a 61 percent to 39 percent victory.

In 1996, Craig's opponent was Walt Minnick, who ran as a Democrat but had strong Republican credentials. Minnick was a onetime White House aide to President Richard M. Nixon and a former executive at a Boise lumber company. Democrats saw a brief ray of hope when Minnick attacked Craig for not fighting hard enough to get nuclear waste moved out of Idaho, a longstanding sore point with residents.

One Democratic survey conducted in early October showed Craig with just a two-point lead, 41 percent to 39 percent. But Craig returned home from Washington, campaigned vigorously and ended up winning easily, capturing 57 percent to Minnick's 40 percent.

When Craig began his political career in the state Senate, he was known as something of a moderate. But in his 1980 House campaign, he allied with Symms, then campaigning for the Senate. After winning a tough primary, Craig was rated a solid favorite over underfinanced Democrat Glenn W. Nichols. Yet Nichols gave him trouble, drawing attention by walking the length of the 1st, from Canada to Nevada, criticizing Craig's "Sagebrush Rebellion" sympathies. Still, Craig won with 54 percent.

Craig had one last tough House contest in 1982; his opponent was Democrat Larry LaRocco, who succeeded Craig in 1990 and held the 1st for two terms. LaRocco drew strong support from the economically depressed Northern Panhandle, where he had worked as a field representative for former Democratic Sen. Frank Church, but Craig again won with 54 percent.

After that, Craig developed a track record of success that also was marked by an eerie streak of bad fortune for his Democratic opponents. In 1984, the Democrat who initially decided to challenge Craig was killed in an auto accident. Two years later, his original 1986 opponent died when the plane he was piloting crashed. In both races, Craig took at least 65 percent against the substitute Democratic nominee. The 1988 campaign was more conventional, but the election outcome was the same.

SENATE ELECTIONS

1996 General

Larry E. Craig (R)	283,532	(57%)
Walt Minnick (D)	198,422	(40%)
Mary J. Charbonneau (I)	10,137	(2%)
Susan Vegors (NL)	5,142	(1%)

Previous Winning Percentages: **1990** (61%) **1988*** (66%) **1986*** (65%) **1984*** (69%) **1982*** (54%) **1980*** (54%)

* *House elections*

CAMPAIGN FINANCE

	Receipts	Receipts from PACs		Expend-itures
1996				
Craig (R)	$2,695,939	$1,027,626	(38%)	$2,809,897
Minnick (D)	$2,179,155	$86,377	(4%)	$2,140,878

KEY VOTES

1997	
Approve balanced-budget constitutional amendment	Y
Approve chemical weapons treaty	N
1996	
Approve farm bill	Y
Limit punitive damages in product liability cases	Y
Exempt small businesses from higher minimum wage	Y
Approve welfare overhaul	Y
Bar job discrimination based on sexual orientation	N
Override veto of ban on "partial birth" abortions	Y
1995	
Approve GOP budget with tax and spending cuts	Y
Approve constitutional amendment barring flag desecration	Y

VOTING STUDIES

	Presidential Support		Party Unity		Conservative Coalition	
Year	**S**	**O**	**S**	**O**	**S**	**O**
1996	32	68	98	2	97	3
1995	20	80	98	2	96	4
1994	29	69	96	2	94	6
1993	15	85	96	3	93	7
1992	83	15	99	1	97	3
1991	91	9	97	3	90	8

INTEREST GROUP RATINGS

Year	ADA	AFL-CIO	CCUS	ACU
1996	0	n/a	100	95
1995	0	0	100	96
1994	0	13	80	100
1993	5	18	91	100
1992	0	17	90	100
1991	5	25	100	86

Dirk Kempthorne (R)

Of Boise — Elected 1992, 1st term

Biographical Information

Born: Oct. 29, 1951, San Diego, Calif.
Education: U. of Idaho, B.A. 1975.
Occupation: Public affairs manager; securities representative; political consultant; building association executive.
Family: Wife, Patricia Merrill; two children.
Religion: Methodist.
Political Career: Mayor of Boise, 1986-92.
Capitol Office: 304 Russell Bldg. 20510; 224-6142.

Committees

Armed Services
Airland Forces; Personnel (chairman); Strategic Forces
Environment & Public Works
Drinking Water, Fisheries & Wildlife (chairman); Transportation & Infrastructure
Small Business

In Washington: Kempthorne achieved a longtime goal in the 104th Congress. After a difficult battle that started in the 103rd Congress, the former Boise mayor won approval of a bill aimed at reining in "unfunded mandates." His success, coming in the face of heavy resistance from such powerful Senate Democrats as Robert C. Byrd of West Virginia, greatly elevated his standing among Republicans trying to move power out of Washington.

At the same time, Kempthorne drew criticism from environmental groups opposed to his efforts to revise the Endangered Species Act and the Safe Drinking Water Act to pare environmental regulations.

At the beginning of the 104th, Kempthorne's priority was curbing unfunded mandates — requirements that the federal government placed on states and local governments without providing funds to pay for them. Conservatives complained that the mandates were forcing state and local officials to divert resources from their own priorities to pay for new federal laws, such as environmental safeguards and increased Medicaid coverage. Many Democrats defended the federal requirements as necessary for public health and safety.

Kempthorne had particular empathy for local officials struggling with federal rules on everything from clean drinking water to wheelchair access to public buildings. As a former two-term mayor, he was a natural to push unfunded mandates legislation. "We should not be here to dictate to the states," he said. "Return the responsibility for local decisions back to local people and to the leaders they elect."

In the Democratic-controlled 103rd, Kempthorne introduced a plan that would have blocked unfunded mandates. But public interest groups and many Democrats balked, arguing that such an aggressive approach would undermine laws that protect the public and safeguard civil rights. Kempthorne set to work on a compromise measure with Democratic Sen. John Glenn of Ohio, then chairman of the Governmental Affairs Committee, and the Clinton administration. The compromise bill essentially would have allowed lawmakers to raise a parliamentary point of order against any bill imposing more than $50 million in unfunded mandates. In the Senate, the bill would have required 60 votes to waive the point of order, a tough procedural hurdle.

The measure failed to win approval, but after the 1994 elections changed the political landscape dramatically, Kempthorne was brimming with confidence. Introducing a similar bill on the first day of the GOP-controlled 104th Congress, he said: "I believe there is no mightier army than an idea whose time has come."

Republicans rallied behind the unfunded mandates proposal, which was part of the House GOP leadership's "Contract With America" legislative agenda. Even many Democrats, prodded by the local and state officials they represented, climbed aboard the bandwagon.

By March 1995, President Clinton had signed a somewhat diluted version of the unfunded mandates legislation. To address Democratic concerns, it allowed a simple majority in both chambers to override points of order against a bill with an unfunded mandate. But it also contained provisions long sought by conservatives, such as requiring cost-benefit analyses of various federal regulations.

Kempthorne's efforts on other issues also reflect his drive to give states and localities a greater say in decision-making. As chairman of the Drinking Water, Fisheries and Wildlife subcommittee of the Environment and Public Works Committee, he insisted on provisions in a bill revising the Safe Drinking Water Act to exempt many small water systems from federal standards. Although criticized by environmentalists, he was able to hold on to some exemptions during difficult House-Senate negotiations, and the bill was eventually signed into law.

Kempthorne had less success with other regulatory relief legislation in the 104th. A bill he sponsored to scale back federal measures to protect endangered and threatened species failed to make headway in the Senate. And he ran into a Democratic roadblock with a proposal that would set new limits on the amount that parties would have to pay in damages when rivers and streams are polluted by hazardous waste.

Also in the 104th, Kempthorne expressed some skepticism over a treaty negotiated by the Clinton administration to permanently ban the testing of all nuclear weapons, fearing that it could undercut the safety and reliability of the dwindling U.S. arsenal.

Kempthorne's conservative instincts were much in evidence as soon as he entered Congress in 1993. He argued that a Democratic-sponsored bill reauthorizing the clean water act would hinder the states' ability to develop pollution control projects. He also sought to scale back "motor voter" legislation, which required states to expand voter-registration opportunities, by seeking an exemption for any state registering 75 percent or more of its voting-age residents.

Kempthorne carries his skepticism of government bureaucracies even further than most Republicans. For instance, the two big international trade agreements approved in the 103rd left him cold: He was one of only 10 Republican senators to vote against NAFTA in 1993 and one of only 11 Republicans to vote against GATT in 1994. He voiced deep concerns about the World Trade Organization, arbiter of trade disputes among nations. "The United States should seriously reconsider any agreement which gives up sovereignty to any multinational group that will place the needs of international trade over the interests of the American people," he said.

Kempthorne is also wary of U.S. involvement in U.N. peacekeeping missions. Once at an Armed Services subcommittee hearing, he grilled a Clinton administration Pentagon appointee about U.S. participation in the U.N.'s humanitarian mission in Somalia, asking, "How many Americans are we willing to sacrifice for the nebulous goal of peacemaking and nation-building in this chaotic land?" On the defense authorization bill in 1994, he tried to nullify a $300 million payment to the U.N. for the U.S. share of peacekeeping operations. He proposed instead using the money to beef up training for U.S. forces.

At Home: Kempthorne's opponent in the 1992 Senate race was a four-term House Democrat, and the Republican loved to tell voters that he, unlike his foe, was not a Beltway-based officeholder.

But Kempthorne was hardly a political outsider. Before his Senate victory, he had served as mayor of Boise, Idaho's largest city. His Senate candidacy was strongly backed by the Idaho Republican establishment; at the top of his campaign structure was popular former GOP Sen. James A. McClure.

By capitalizing on Idaho's sizable bedrock Republican vote, Kempthorne won the race to fill the seat vacated by retiring GOP Sen. Steve Symms. Kempthorne also benefited from voter resentment toward Washington, which hampered Democratic Rep. Richard Stallings' bid.

In campaigning, Kempthorne took careful positions on natural resource issues, which are matters of wide debate in Idaho. He opposed giving federal wilderness lands a reserved water right, as happened in neighboring Nevada, although he endorsed negotiations among all interested state groups to devise a long-sought wilderness plan for Idaho.

He ran on a platform of balancing the federal budget. In one speech before a Lions Club, he said the budget should be capped at its current level and that the federal budget could be balanced in five years if spending growth was limited to 3 percent or less each year. Kempthorne early and often accused Stallings of being part of the gridlock paralyzing Capitol Hill. He also made an issue of Stallings' eight overdrawn checks at the House bank.

Stallings had secured eastern Idaho's House seat by compiling a moderate-to-conservative voting record, and he hoped to translate that success statewide. But Stallings could not close ground, and Kempthorne won with 57 percent of the vote.

Kempthorne has moved easily between the worlds of business and government. From 1978 to 1981 he served as executive director of the Idaho State Home Builders Association. His first direct involvement in statewide politics came in 1981, when he managed the unsuccessful gubernatorial campaign of then-Lt. Gov. Phil Batt. His successful run for mayor in 1985 was based on a platform of rebuilding the city's downtown. He was re-elected to a second term in 1989.

SENATE ELECTIONS

1992 General		
Dirk Kempthorne (R)	270,468	(57%)
Richard Stallings (D)	208,036	(43%)
1992 Primary		
Dirk Kempthorne (R)	67,001	(57%)
Rodney (Rod) W. Beck (R)	26,977	(23%)
Milt Erhart (R)	22,682	(19%)

CAMPAIGN FINANCE

	Receipts	Receipts from PACs	Expend-itures
1992			
Kempthorne (R)	$1,351,127	$599,151 (44%)	$1,305,338
Stallings (D)	$1,224,232	$605,068 (49%)	$1,222,222

VOTING STUDIES

	Presidential Support		Party Unity		Conservative Coalition	
Year	**S**	**O**	**S**	**O**	**S**	**O**
1996	32	68	98	2	97	3
1995	21	79	97	2	95	5
1994	31	69	98	2	94	6
1993	15	85	97	3	90	10

INTEREST GROUP RATINGS

Year	ADA	AFL-CIO	CCUS	ACU
1996	0	n/a	100	95
1995	0	0	100	96
1994	0	13	80	100
1993	5	9	91	100

KEY VOTES

1997	
Approve balanced-budget constitutional amendment	Y
Approve chemical weapons treaty	N
1996	
Approve farm bill	Y
Limit punitive damages in product liability cases	Y
Exempt small businesses from higher minimum wage	Y
Approve welfare overhaul	Y
Bar job discrimination based on sexual orientation	N
Override veto of ban on "partial birth" abortions	Y
1995	
Approve GOP budget with tax and spending cuts	Y
Approve constitutional amendment barring flag desecration	Y

1 Helen Chenoweth (R)

Of Boise — Elected 1994, 2nd term

Biographical Information
Born: Jan. 27, 1938, Topeka, Kan.
Education: Whitworth College, 1955-58.
Occupation: Public affairs and policy consultant; congressional aide.
Family: Divorced; two children.
Religion: Christian.
Political Career: No previous office.
Capitol Office: 1727 Longworth Bldg. 20515; 225-6611.

Committees
Agriculture
Forestry, Resource Conservation & Research
Resources
Forests & Forest Health (chairman); National Parks & Public Lands; Water & Power
Veterans' Affairs
Health

In Washington: Few first-term House members receive as much attention as Chenoweth did during the 104th Congress, but then few are so prone to be provocative. On a range of issues — abortion, gun ownership, states' rights and federal land use policies, to name a few — Chenoweth's views and statements warm the hearts of hard-core GOP conservatives and infuriate liberal Democrats. Reflecting in July 1995 on landing in the media spotlight as a freshman, she said, "I got in the middle of this media rush, and you think, 'Well, I [wonder] if I should just back out?' But then I thought of what my dad always said: 'You never say, "Whoa!" in a mudhole.' "

Chenoweth came to Washington eager to defend her district against the "War on the West" — the tag line many Westerners use for President Clinton's proposals to raise fees and impose new restrictions on mining, grazing and logging on federal lands. She positioned herself for battle by winning seats on both the Agriculture and the Resources committees — panels whose work affects the everyday lives of many Idahoans. At the start of the 105th Congress, she took over as chairman of the Resources Subcommittee on Forests and Forest Health.

One Idaho public official has likened Chenoweth to a mountain goat, telling the Denver Post that she is "stubborn, impulsive and unquestioningly self-confident." Chenoweth has worked to scale back environmental regulations on businesses and private landowners. She contends that conservationists must be more willing to share the West's resources with commercial interests. During her 1994 campaign she called for allowing metal mining in a state recreation area. In Washington, she has proposed "a hunting season in the [Yellowstone] National Park" as a means of thinning elk, opposing an Interior Department plan to use Canadian wolves.

One of her chief targets has been the 1973 Endangered Species Act. Chenoweth sides with private property owners who say it unfairly denies them use of their land. She has held "endangered salmon bake" fundraisers, making light of protections for Idaho's threatened salmon runs. She also once joked that "the white Anglo-Saxon male" was an endangered species.

Chenoweth has complained about the red cockaded woodpecker "altering the flight patterns from Air Force bases," and she linked efforts to preserve the habitat of the kangaroo rat to the fiery destruction of homes in a wooded area in southern California.

As conservative as she is, Chenoweth is far from a ready vote in the Republican column. She bucked the party on two key items contained in the "Contract With America" and has given the GOP leadership fits on certain budget votes. In January 1996 she was one of only 15 Republicans opposed to a GOP plan to reopen the government after a prolonged partial shutdown that occurred when Congress and Clinton could not work out their differences on the budget.

After the vote, Speaker Newt Gingrich canceled a scheduled appearance at a fundraiser in Chenoweth's district, but she said, "One vote on a loony bill is not a test of his leadership." She again ignored Gingrich's importuning during the floor vote on the fiscal 1997 budget resolution, leading him to throw up his hands when she refused to vote with him. A month later, she threw an appropriations bill into a losing, tie situation, and the leadership had to scramble to find other Republicans willing to switch their votes.

Chenoweth opposes abortion, and she was the only major political figure in Idaho to support an unsuccessful state ballot initiative that would have restricted civil rights protection for homosexuals. In the House, she pushed in 1995 for an end to federal financing of abortions in cases of rape or incest.

A member of a House task force on firearms, she has been outspoken in support of gun owners' rights. In the wake of the April 1995 bombing of a federal office building in Oklahoma City, Chenoweth drew national attention when she was identified as a favorite of certain activists in the citizens' militia movement.

IDAHO 1
West — Boise; Nampa; Panhandle

Chenoweth's win in 1994 followed partisan form, returning this mainly conservative district to the Republican fold after a four-year Democratic hiatus. From the New Deal until the Great Society, the 1st nearly always sent Democrats to Congress, but it had broken that habit by 1966.

The 1st ranges nearly 500 miles from British Columbia to Nevada. In its lower half, Boise's white-collar constituency combines with voters in agricultural communities to provide Republicans with a solid base. The strongest Democratic bloc is in blue-collar areas of the Northern Panhandle.

Despite the district's conservatism, Chenoweth barely won re-election in 1996, while Bob Dole carried all but three of the district's 19 counties in the presidential race. Though Dole garnered only 51 percent of the votes, that was good enough for a 16 percentage point margin over Bill Clinton. Ross Perot finished in double digits. The district's Sagebrush independence was especially prevalent in 1992, when Perot got a quarter of its votes.

Ada County (Boise) has about 20 percent of Idaho's population. It is the only county split between the districts; the line bisects Boise, the state's capital and its largest city. Boise has a strong Republican vote cast by white-collar employees of the lumber, paper, food processing, electronics and construction companies that have headquarters there. The 1st takes in most of Ada County's territory and about two-thirds of its population.

The 1st skips Boise's downtown and takes in its mainly residential, western portion. Chenoweth carried the 1st's portion of Boise by just a couple of hundred votes in 1996.

The Republican grip is stronger in Canyon County (Nampa), on Ada's western border. Canyon, Idaho's second most populous county, gave Dole over 59 percent. The county is the state's top producer of cattle and corn and a leader in sugar beets.

To the north is a spread of mainly rural areas, including vast Idaho County. GOP turf gives way to the Panhandle, where Democratic habits were implanted by a long period of labor activism in the timberlands, metal mining areas and the industrial city of Lewiston.

Some Democratic-leaning areas have relatively stable economies. Lewiston, in Nez Perce County, has a grain-shipping port and the Potlatch pulp and paper factory; Latah County has the University of Idaho in Moscow (about 10,000 students). But the collapse of silver prices in the early 1980s crushed mining-dependent Shoshone County, which still has a jobless rate of more than twice the state average.

In parts of this mountain and lake country, an expanding tourist industry and the arrival of many retirees have boosted the population and weakened the Democrats' position. Chenoweth garnered just under 50 percent in Kootenai County (Coeur d'Alene), the Panhandle's most populous jurisdiction, while Dole ended 5,000 votes ahead of Clinton here in 1996.

1990 Population: 503,357. White 477,807 (95%), Black 1,112 (<1%), Other 24,438 (5%). Hispanic origin 23,070 (5%). 18 and over 358,537 (71%), 62 and over 77,332 (15%). Median age: 33.

At a Resources Committee meeting in May 1995, Chenoweth suggested that "the most peaceful and responsible thing this body could do is listen to the complaints of people who have resorted to violent action."

She was cosponsor of an unsuccessful move to block the 1996 anti-terrorism bill's provisions limiting prisoners rights to habeas corpus appeals, saying that the federal government had all the law enforcement power it needed.

Chenoweth has criticized officials of both the FBI and the Bureau of Alcohol, Tobacco and Firearms (ATF). In July 1995 she sponsored an amendment to block ATF employees from receiving bonuses or merit pay increases; it lost, 111-317. She said she would seek to eliminate funding for the agency during the 1996 appropriations cycle. "It's just a matter of time before Congress does this," she said.

At a March 1995 hearing in Boise on the use of force by federal agents, Chenoweth had said she planned to introduce legislation that would require federal law enforcement officials to get written permission from local sheriffs if they intended to carry firearms into their areas of jurisdiction. She appeared on national television news programs in May to promote the bill. Gingrich did not support the legislation, but he said it "should be taken very seriously as a symptom" of anti-federal hostility.

At Home: Chenoweth was often on the defensive in both her 1994 and 1996 House campaigns, fending off negative publicity generated by some controversial statements and dealing with allegations that she circumvented federal campaign contribution limits.

Though the 1994 race marked her first bid for elective office, Chenoweth was no newcomer to state GOP politics. She served as executive director of the Idaho Republican Party from 1975 to 1977, before joining the staff of Republican Steve Symms, who served in the House and then the Senate.

Chenoweth's 1994 opponent, two-term Democratic Rep. Larry LaRocco, adopted a strategy devoted largely to characterizing her as an "extremist." Days after her victory in the GOP primary, LaRocco labeled Chenoweth a "mouthpiece for the radical right" who would "turn back the clock" in Idaho, and he aired a five-week-long series of radio ads that featured two women discussing "this Chenoweth lady" who "just seems to get crazier and crazier."

But in a state where Clinton's approval ratings in 1994 were among the lowest in the nation, LaRocco's party label (he was the only Democrat in the Idaho congressional delegation) proved a hindrance. Chenoweth linked LaRocco to the Clinton administration's land-use proposals and highlighted his votes for Clinton's 1993 economic stimulus package and the 1993 deficit-reduction bill that raised taxes.

In the end, Chenoweth returned the 1st to its Republican roots by rounding up 55 percent of the vote and handing LaRocco the worst defeat for an Idaho incumbent since 1932.

Chenoweth's remarkable finish ended a campaign that had begun with an equally surprising upset in a four-way battle for the GOP nomination. Less than a week before the primary, the Republican favorite, former Lt. Gov. David Leroy, appeared to have a comfortable double-digit lead. But polls failed to gauge the strength of Chenoweth's support among the party's social and religious conservatives. Chenoweth won nomination with 48 percent, running 20 points ahead of Leroy.

In the 1996 GOP primary, Chenoweth ran far ahead of physician William A. Levinger, but the outcome nonetheless raised questions about her prospects for re-election. Levinger received nearly a third of the GOP vote even though he expended hardly any money and spent three weeks of the campaign in a mental health unit for having disrobed during a TV appearance.

The Democratic challenger, Boise attorney and former gubernatorial aide Dan Williams, was assisted by environmental groups and other independent expenditure campaigns targeting Chenoweth. But she stumped the district hard late in the campaign, firming up her conservative base. Her winning tally dropped five points from 1994, to an even 50 percent, but that put her 6,445 votes ahead of Williams.

Chenoweth overcame reports about her campaign finances. In September 1996, Chenoweth admitted that she received an illegal $50,000 loan from a former business client, which she said she would pay back. The Federal Election Commission investigated other campaign contributions in the wake of Democratic complaints.

HOUSE ELECTIONS

1996 General		
Helen Chenoweth (R)	132,344	(50%)
Dan Williams (D)	125,899	(48%)
Marion Ellis (NL)	6,535	(2%)
1996 Primary		
Helen Chenoweth (R)	38,616	(68%)
William A. Levinger (R)	18,054	(32%)
1994 General		
Helen Chenoweth (R)	111,728	(55%)
Larry LaRocco (D)	89,826	(45%)

CAMPAIGN FINANCE

	Receipts	Receipts from PACs	Expend-itures
1996			
Chenoweth (R)	$1,131,669	$339,481 (30%)	$1,129,263
Williams (D)	$665,426	$268,317 (40%)	$659,753
1994			
Chenoweth (R)	$799,284	$115,851 (14%)	$796,149
LaRocco (D)	$848,404	$522,116 (62%)	$845,902

DISTRICT VOTE FOR PRESIDENT

	1996		1992
D	91,297 (35%)	D	75,499 (31%)
R	134,783 (51%)	R	101,787 (42%)
I	33,130 (13%)	I	67,677 (28%)

KEY VOTES

1997	
Ban "partial birth" abortions	Y
1996	
Approve farm bill	Y
Deny public education to illegal immigrants	Y
Repeal ban on certain assault-style weapons	Y
Increase minimum wage	N
Freeze defense spending	N
Approve welfare overhaul	Y
1995	
Approve balanced-budget constitutional amendment	Y
Relax Clean Water Act regulations	Y
Oppose limits on environmental regulations	N
Reduce projected Medicare spending	Y
Approve GOP budget with tax and spending cuts	Y

VOTING STUDIES

	Presidential Support		Party Unity		Conservative Coalition	
Year	S	O	S	O	S	O
1996	27	70	89	7	88	8
1995	20	76	91	4	91	5

INTEREST GROUP RATINGS

Year	ADA	AFL-CIO	CCUS	ACU
1996	10	n/a	88	95
1995	5	0	92	91

2 Michael D. Crapo (R)

Of Idaho Falls — Elected 1992, 3rd term

Biographical Information

Born: May 20, 1951, Idaho Falls, Idaho.
Education: Brigham Young U., B.A. 1973; Harvard U., J.D. 1977.
Occupation: Lawyer.
Family: Wife, Susan Diane Hasleton; five children.
Religion: Mormon.
Political Career: Idaho Senate, 1985-93, president pro tem, 1989-93.
Capitol Office: 437 Cannon Bldg. 20515; 225-5531.

Committees

Commerce
Energy & Power; Finance & Hazardous Materials; Oversight & Investigations
Resources
Fisheries Conservation, Wildlife & Oceans; Water & Power

In Washington: As president pro tem of the Idaho Senate from 1989 to 1993, Crapo was an influential insider in his state's powerful GOP establishment. He gave up that clout in 1993, coming to Washington to serve in the House minority under a Democratic president. But in just two years, Washington started looking more like Boise, as the GOP captured Congress and set out to put the federal government on a conservative course.

Consistent with his background, Crapo has played an important although generally low-profile role in the Republican revolution. His plum committee assignments testify to his good relationship with the GOP leadership: The wide-ranging jurisdiction of the Commerce Committee, on which he serves, includes consideration of utilities deregulation, which could mean higher electricity prices for Western consumers who benefit from federally owned power plants. He also sits on the Resources Committee, which grapples with the whole range of Westerners' concerns about federal policies on mining regulation, grazing fees, timber harvesting, water rights and balancing property owners' rights against legal imperatives to protect endangered species.

Crapo is the No. 2 Republican on Commerce's Energy and Power Subcommittee, which claims initial jurisdiction as the 105th Congress confronts the complex issue of introducing more free-market competition into the electric utilities business. Crapo seems likely to weigh carefully the potential impact of various deregulation approaches on ratepayers in his state. In early 1995, when budget-cutters floated the idea of selling the federally owned Bonneville Power Administration to help balance the budget, he objected.

Crapo has proposed a "deficit-reduction lockbox" that would be the designated destination for any spending cuts Congress makes. Most Americans, Crapo says, have no idea that when members cut funding for a project or program from an appropriations bill, the money is not necessarily "saved," but instead goes back into the bill's overall money pool. "It's important for us to have a system where when we make cuts, it counts," he said. Crapo's amendment was added to the 1996 Labor-HHS spending bill. But the measure fell by the wayside as Congress resorted to an omnibus appropriations package.

Crapo bucked his party's majority on trade issues in opposing both NAFTA and GATT, but on most fiscal issues and social policy concerns, he is a faithfully conservative follower of the GOP leadership. He does, however, seem to take a step or two away from the intensely anti-federal government rhetoric of some Western Republicans in the House. Crapo has defended some programs that benefit his constituents.

Mink farmers got his attention in 1996, when he unsuccessfully opposed an amendment to end federal subsidies aimed at helping develop overseas markets for U.S.-produced mink. Crapo argued that small, family-owned mink ranches were aided through the Market Promotion Program. He also defended import quotas for sugar, which protect domestic sugar producers, and advocated increased funding for nuclear energy research. His district is home to the Idaho National Engineering and Environmental Laboratory.

Ending federal support for public broadcasting is a popular cause among many conservatives, but after hearing protests from constituents — public stations are a lifeline in some sparsely settled areas — Crapo opposed an amendment to cut funding for the Corporation for Public Broadcasting, preferring instead to reduce, not end, the appropriation.

The expressed wishes of Idahoans also led Crapo to vote in early 1997 against a constitutional amendment setting a 12-year limit on congressional service. Crapo had in the past supported a 12-year limit for each chamber, and he said he wanted to do so again in the 105th. But Idaho voters in 1996 approved an initiative requiring their lawmakers to support a six-year limit in the House and 12 years in the Senate. Failure to do so would result in a notation on the ballot that the incumbent had disregarded voters' instructions.

Republican Crapo's 1992 win ended the four-term Democratic hold, established by Richard Stallings, on the 2nd District seat. The Stallings era was a rare break in GOP domination of this conservative region. Stallings' failure to carry the 2nd in his 1992 Senate race sealed his fate against Republican Dirk Kempthorne.

Bob Dole won all but one of the district's 26 counties in 1996, as had George Bush four years earlier. Although Dole improved on Bush's 1992 percentage, he fell considerably short of Bush's 1988 showing of capturing two-thirds of the votes cast. Ross Perot, who led Bill Clinton in all but six of the district's counties in 1992, finished third in all of them in 1996.

By far, most district residents are of Northern European heritage. Members of the Church of Jesus Christ of Latter-day Saints make up the largest religious group; like most Mormon areas, the district is strongly conservative.

Much of the district is farmland irrigated by the Snake River. The district's western edge has part of Boise (Ada County), including the state Capitol, major businesses and some affluent communities.

To the east, near Idaho Falls, is the Idaho National Engineering and Environmental Laboratory, a federal research complex. Idaho Falls' economy is highly dependent on contractors employed by the laboratory. (Lockheed Martin Corp., the Department of Energy and Argonne National Laboratory all have workers here.)

Boise is one of the nation's most economically vibrant small cities. Many of its businesses reflect the region's links to the land: The J. R. Simplot Co. raises potatoes and cattle, and Ore-Ida makes frozen french fries. Boise Cascade is a diversified forest products company. But some are industrial, such as the Morrison

IDAHO 2
East — Pocatello; Idaho Falls; Twin Falls

Knudsen heavy construction company, or cutting-edge, such as Micron Technology. Boise State University, with about 15,000 students, also is in the district. Dole carried the 2nd's part of Ada County by a scant 68 votes.

To the east is Elmore County, site of the Mountain Home Air Force Base. In the south-central part of the district is Twin Falls, hub of the Magic Valley region, where potatoes, sugar beets, grain, livestock and trout are raised and GOP votes are cast.

Farther east, in Bannock County, is Pocatello, where the largest employers are Idaho State University, with about 12,000 students, and the Union Pacific Railroad. There are Democratic votes in the academic and blue-collar communities; Dole edged Clinton in Bannock by 4 percentage points in 1996.

After irrigating the potato and wheat fields of Bingham County, the Snake runs through Idaho Falls. In the Upper Snake River Valley is Rexburg, home of Mormon-run Ricks College, a two-year school with about 7,500 students.

In the mountainous center of the district is Blaine County and the bucolic Ketchum-Sun Valley area. Urban exiles, artists and outdoor enthusiasts boosted Blaine's population by 38 percent in the 1980s and gave it a liberal tinge unusual for Idaho. Blaine was the only county in the 2nd that Clinton carried in 1992 and 1996.

1990 Population: 503,392. White 472,644 (94%), Black 2,258 (<1%), Other 28,490 (6%). Hispanic origin 29,857 (6%). 18 and over 339,807 (68%), 62 and over 67,196 (13%). Median age: 30.

Crapo offered the Idaho version of the term-limits amendment on the House floor, saying he was bound by his constituents to support it. It lost, as did all other term-limits proposals.

Frequently unhappy with Clinton administration policies affecting the rural West, Crapo joined the chorus of colleagues resisting the administration's ultimately unsuccessful effort in the 103rd to reform the 1872 mining law. This statute lets miners lay claims on federal land and extract minerals at very low cost. Most Western Republicans and some Democrats from the region objected strongly when the House approved an overhaul of the law in November 1993. The measure imposed royalties on hard-rock minerals extracted from federal lands, increased fees miners must pay for land claims and set up environmental safeguards to protect against mining-related damage.

Opponents said the new royalties, fees and regulations would make many mines unprofitable and force them to close. Crapo offered a motion to recommit the reform bill to the Natural Resources Committee to develop royalty schemes that would result in no net loss of jobs. He lost, 148-270, but progress on the legislation later ground to a halt.

In the 104th, the GOP majority included mining-overhaul language to conservatives' liking in the party's budget-balancing reconciliation bill, but it was vetoed by President Clinton in 1995. Lawmakers instead had to settle for extending a one-year freeze on the processing of patent applications that had been included in the fiscal 1995 Interior appropriations bill.

Crapo is ever-watchful that legislation designating wilderness areas does not include language giving the federal government more control over states' decisions on water rights. He praised the Safe Drinking Water Act, which passed through the Commerce Committee in the 104th, for not applying a "one size fits all" approach to the states. He has opposed increasing taxes on irrigated water and raising the fees paid by ranchers who use federal rangeland.

A stout defender of gunowners' rights, Crapo opposed a five-day waiting period requirement for handgun purchases, and he voted against banning certain semiautomatic assault-style weapons. "Let's get tough on criminals, and let's not make law-abiding citizens face a restriction of their constitutionally protected rights," he said. In 1995, Crapo was one of seven Republicans to oppose legislation allowing improperly collected evidence to be used in court if law enforcement agents believed they were acting properly.

Crapo supported a largely symbolic amendment by Idaho GOP colleague Helen Chenoweth to block Bureau of Alcohol, Tobacco and Firearms (ATF) employees from receiving bonuses or merit pay increases. Although the measure failed, it gave Crapo and others a chance to vent steam about the ATF, which was criticized for its handling of the Branch Davidian cult in Texas and the Ruby Ridge, Idaho, standoff, both of which ended in bloodshed and death. Arguing that other efforts to change ATF had been stymied, Crapo said a message needed to be sent.

In the 104th Congress, Crapo got a waiver allowing him to serve on the Agriculture Committee while keeping his Commerce seat. He returned the favor by backing the GOP's "Freedom to Farm" bill, which phased out most New Deal-era crop subsidies, replacing them with a system of fixed, but declining, payments that farmers would receive over seven years regardless of market prices or their planting decisions.

At Home: Democrats knew it would be tough to hold the conservative 2nd if Rep. Richard Stallings ever left it, and they were right. When the popular moderate Democrat tried in 1992 for a promotion to the Senate, Crapo won with a decisive 61 percent.

Crapo and his Democratic opponent, state Auditor J.D. Williams, both of whom easily won their parties' nominations, had earned "nice guy" reputations during their political careers, and for the most part, they avoided sharp attacks. Williams concurred with Crapo's opposition to abortion and support for gunowners' rights.

Educated at Brigham Young and Harvard, Crapo is a Mormon — a political plus in the 2nd. He was first elected to the state Senate in 1984. He campaigned for the House as an "outsider" who would fight wasteful spending and higher taxes in Washington, but Williams said Crapo as a legislator had supported higher taxes and a Senate pay raise.

Williams hoped that running with Stallings on the ballot would give him a boost, but that scenario did not develop. Idaho was one of 18 states that voted to re-elect George Bush, and Boise Mayor Dirk Kempthorne easily defeated Stallings in the Senate race. Crapo topped 60 percent and has been re-elected easily since.

HOUSE ELECTIONS

1996 General		
Michael D. Crapo (R)	157,646	(69%)
John D. Seidl (D)	67,625	(29%)
John Butler (NL)	3,977	(2%)
1996 Primary		
Michael D. Crapo (R)	51,778	(86%)
Peter Rickards (R)	8,382	(14%)
1994 General		
Michael D. Crapo (R)	143,593	(75%)
Penny Fletcher (D)	47,936	(25%)

Previous Winning Percentages: 1992 (61%)

CAMPAIGN FINANCE

	Receipts	Receipts from PACs		Expend-itures
1996				
Crapo (R)	$710,998	$415,207	(58%)	$755,679
Seidl (D)	$164,146	$15,500	(9%)	$163,532
1994				
Crapo (R)	$511,946	$315,251	(62%)	$352,461
Fletcher (D)	$29,941	$23,300	(78%)	$26,862

DISTRICT VOTE FOR PRESIDENT

	1996		1992
D	74,146 (33%)	**D**	61,514 (27%)
R	121,812 (53%)	**R**	100,858 (45%)
I	29,388 (13%)	**I**	62,718 (28%)

KEY VOTES

1997	
Ban "partial-birth" abortions	Y
1996	
Approve farm bill	Y
Deny public education to illegal immigrants	Y
Repeal ban on certain assault-style weapons	Y
Increase minimum wage	N
Freeze defense spending	N
Approve welfare overhaul	Y
1995	
Approve balanced-budget constitutional amendment	Y
Relax Clean Water Act regulations	Y
Oppose limits on environmental regulations	N
Reduce projected Medicare spending	Y
Approve GOP budget with tax and spending cuts	Y

VOTING STUDIES

	Presidential Support		Party Unity		Conservative Coalition	
Year	S	O	S	O	S	O
1996	29	68	95	5	96	4
1995	20	78	94	3	96	4
1994	40	60	95	4	97	3
1993	33	67	95	4	93	5

INTEREST GROUP RATINGS

Year	ADA	AFL-CIO	CCUS	ACU
1996	0	n/a	100	95
1995	5	0	100	92
1994	5	11	83	90
1993	5	8	91	96

ILLINOIS

Governor: Jim Edgar (R)
First elected: 1990
Length of term: 4 years
Term expires: 1/99
Salary: $123,100
Term limit: No
Phone: (217) 782-6830
Born: July 22, 1946; Vinita, Okla.
Education: Eastern Illinois U., B.S. 1968; U. of Illinois, 1969-70.
Occupation: Legislative aide.
Family: Wife, Brenda Smith; two children.
Religion: American Baptist.
Political Career: Candidate for Ill. House, 1974; Ill. House, 1977-79; Ill. secretary of state, 1981-91.

Lt. Gov.: Bob Kustra (R)
First elected: 1990
Length of term: 4 years
Term expires: 1/99
Salary: $86,839
Phone: (217) 782-7884

State election official: (217) 782-4141
Democratic headquarters: (217) 528-3471
Republican headquarters: (217) 525-0011

REDISTRICTING

Illinois lost two seats in reapportionment, dropping from 22 districts to 20. The legislature failed to act on a new map by June 30, 1991, deadline. Federal court approved a map Nov. 6.

STATE LEGISLATURE

Bicameral General Assembly. Meets January-June.

Senate: 59 members, 4-year terms
1996 breakdown: 31R, 28D; 48 men, 11 women
Salary: $45,669
Phone: (217) 782-5715

House of Representatives: 118 members, 2-year terms
1996 breakdown: 60D, 58R; 83 men, 35 women
Salary: $45,669
Phone: (217) 782-8223

URBAN STATISTICS

City	Population
Chicago	2,783,726
Mayor Richard M. Daley, D	
Rockford	139,943
Mayor Charles E. Box, D	
Peoria	113,504
Mayor James A. Maloof, N-P	
Springfield	105,227
Mayor Karen Hasara, N-P	
Aurora	99,581
Mayor David L. Pierce, I	

U.S. CONGRESS

Senate: 2 D, 0 R
House: 10 D, 10 R

TERM LIMITS

For state offices: No

ELECTIONS

1996 Presidential Vote

Bill Clinton	54%
Bob Dole	37%
Ross Perot	8%

1992 Presidential Vote

Bill Clinton	49%
George Bush	34%
Ross Perot	17%

1988 Presidential Vote

George Bush	51%
Michael S. Dukakis	49%

POPULATION

1990 population		11,430,602
1980 population		11,426,518
Percent change		+0%
Rank among states:		6
White		78%
Black		15%
Hispanic		8%
Asian or Pacific islander		2%
Urban		85%
Rural		15%
Born in state		69%
Foreign-born		8%
Under age 18	2,946,366	26%
Ages 18-64	7,047,691	62%
65 and older	1,436,545	13%
Median age		32.8

MISCELLANEOUS

Capital: Springfield
Number of counties: 102
Per capita income: $20,824 (1991)
Rank among states: 10
Total area: 56,345 sq. miles
Rank among states: 24

ILLINOIS

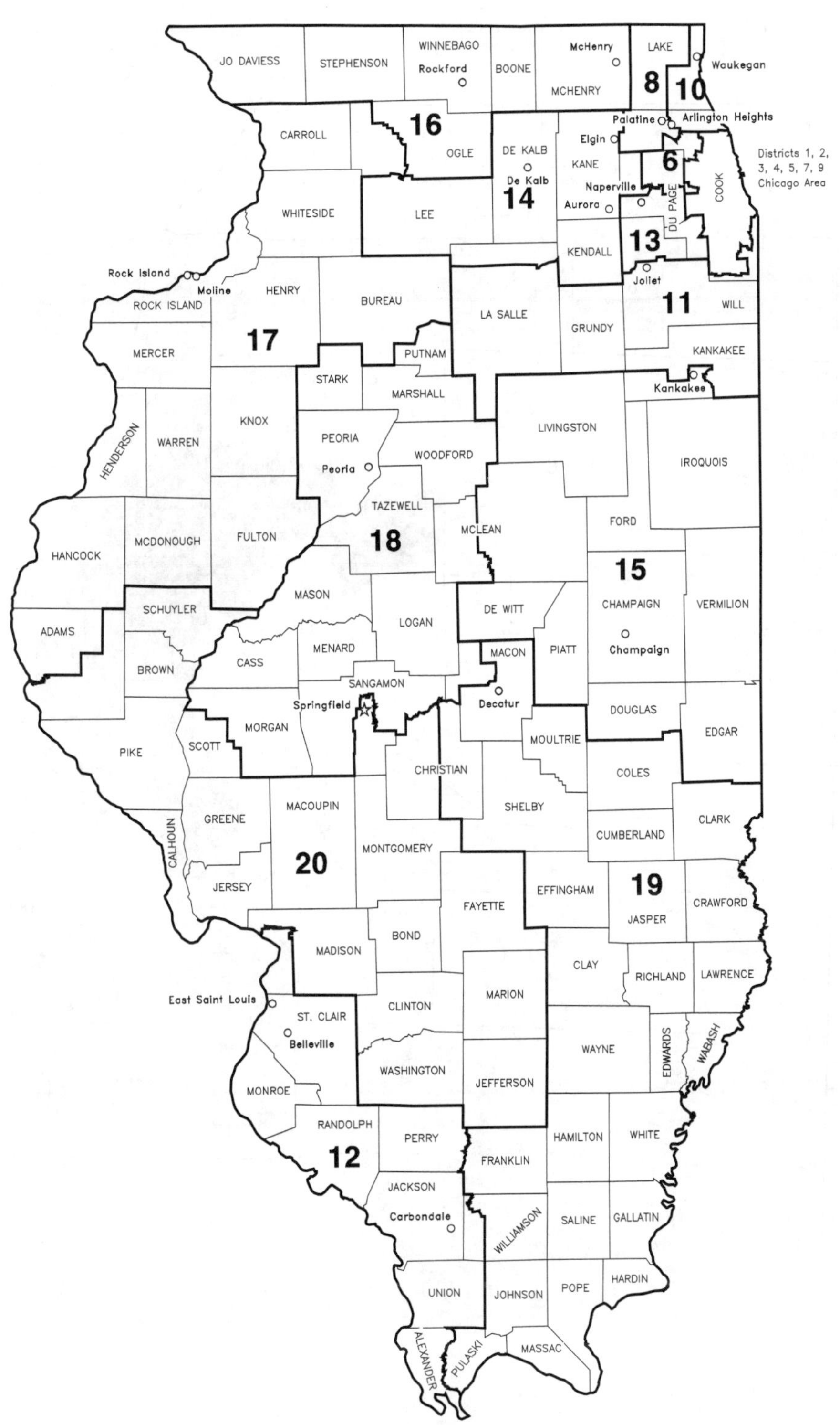

JO DAVIESS
STEPHENSON
WINNEBAGO
Rockford
BOONE
McHenry
MCHENRY
LAKE
Waukegan
8
10
16
CARROLL
OGLE
DE KALB
De Kalb
Elgin
Palatine
Arlington Heights
KANE
6
Naperville
Aurora
14
DU PAGE
COOK
Districts 1, 2, 3, 4, 5, 7, 9 Chicago Area
WHITESIDE
LEE
13
KENDALL
Joliet
Rock Island
Moline
HENRY
BUREAU
LA SALLE
ROCK ISLAND
11
WILL
GRUNDY
MERCER
17
PUTNAM
KANKAKEE
STARK
MARSHALL
Kankakee
KNOX
LIVINGSTON
HENDERSON
WARREN
PEORIA
Peoria
WOODFORD
IROQUOIS
TAZEWELL
FORD
HANCOCK
MCDONOUGH
FULTON
MCLEAN
18
15
MASON
SCHUYLER
DE WITT
CHAMPAIGN
VERMILION
ADAMS
LOGAN
Champaign
MENARD
MACON
PIATT
BROWN
CASS
SANGAMON
Springfield
Decatur
DOUGLAS
MORGAN
MOULTRIE
EDGAR
PIKE
SCOTT
CHRISTIAN
COLES
MACOUPIN
SHELBY
GREENE
CALHOUN
CLARK
CUMBERLAND
MONTGOMERY
20
EFFINGHAM
19
JERSEY
FAYETTE
JASPER
CRAWFORD
BOND
MADISON
CLAY
RICHLAND
LAWRENCE
MARION
East Saint Louis
ST. CLAIR
CLINTON
Belleville
WAYNE
EDWARDS
WABASH
WASHINGTON
JEFFERSON
MONROE
RANDOLPH
PERRY
HAMILTON
WHITE
12
FRANKLIN
JACKSON
Carbondale
WILLIAMSON
SALINE
GALLATIN
UNION
JOHNSON
POPE
HARDIN
ALEXANDER
PULASKI
MASSAC

ILLINOIS
CHICAGO AREA DISTRICTS

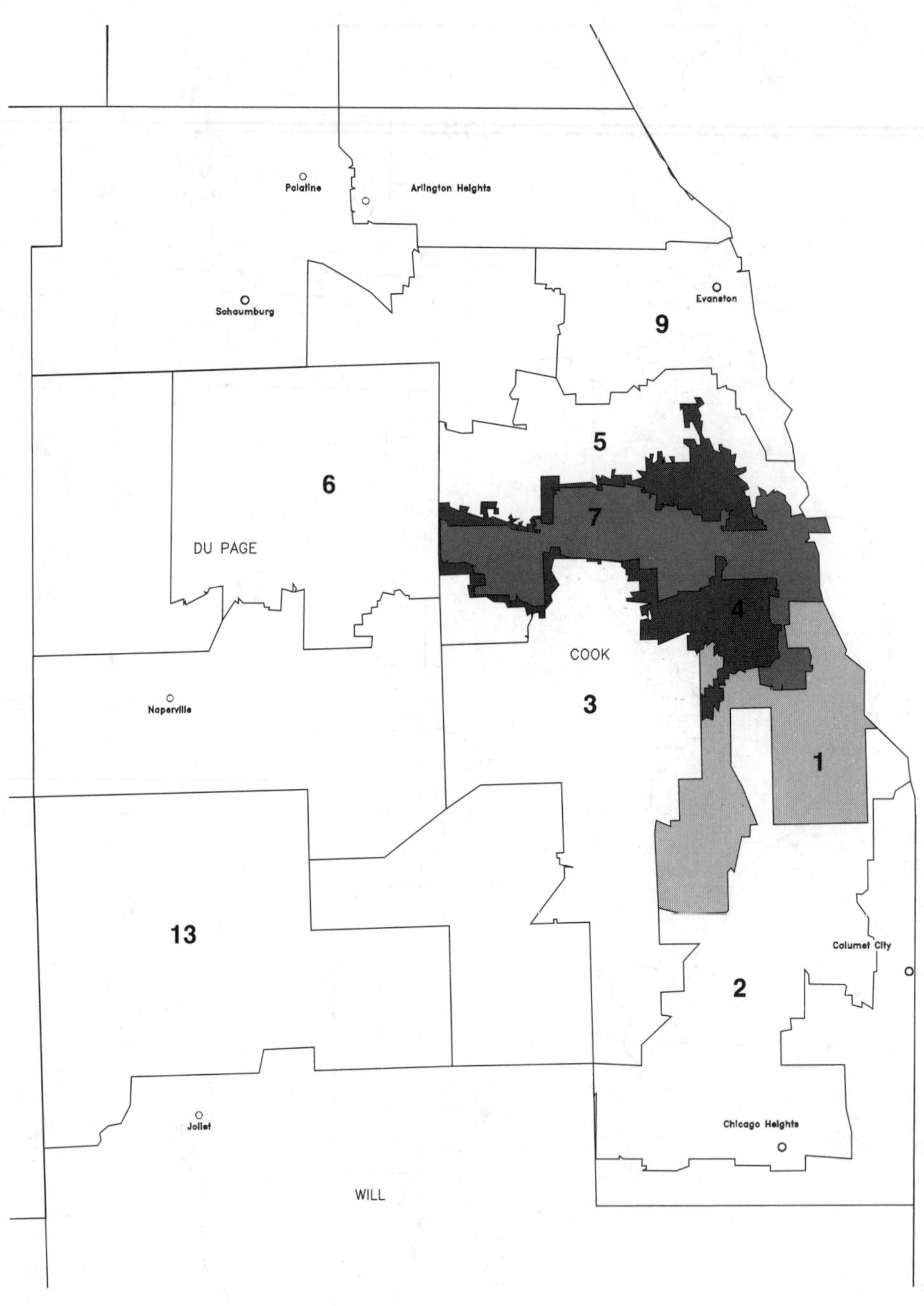

Carol Moseley-Braun (D)

Of Chicago — Elected 1992, 1st term

Biographical Information
Born: Aug. 16, 1947, Chicago, Ill.
Education: U. of Illinois, Chicago Circle, B.A. 1967; U. of Chicago, J.D. 1972.
Occupation: Lawyer.
Family: Divorced; one child.
Religion: Roman Catholic.
Political Career: Ill. House, 1979-88, assistant majority leader, 1983; Cook County recorder of deeds, 1988-92.
Capitol Office: 324 Hart Bldg. 20510; 224-2854.

Committees
Special Aging
Banking, Housing & Urban Affairs
Financial Institutions & Regulatory Relief; International Finance (ranking); Housing Opportunity & Community Development
Finance
Health Care; International Trade; Social Security & Family Policy

In Washington: Carol Moseley-Braun will go down in history as the first African American woman elected to the Senate. But still unanswered, as she finishes her first term and sets out to win a second in 1998, is the question of how well she upheld the soaring hopes of her advocates and admirers.

After four years in office, Moseley-Braun has been both an eloquent spokeswoman for minorities and women and a bitter disappointment to many of her supporters, who swept her into office in 1992 in a wave of anger over the nomination of Clarence Thomas to the Supreme Court.

Her political vulnerability was heightened after Moseley-Braun took an unscheduled "private" trip in August 1996 to Nigeria and met with its dictator, Gen. Sani Abacha.

Since Abacha seized power in a November 1993 military coup, he has jailed the country's elected president and persecuted political dissidents. Abacha drew international condemnation after his regime hanged playwright Ken Saro-Wiwa and nine environmental activists.

The State Department chided Moseley-Braun for failing to seek a briefing with the Clinton administration before taking the trip. Human rights organizations, including TransAfrica, expressed deep disappointment over her actions.

Moseley-Braun dismissed the criticisms, saying it was her responsibility as a senator to maintain contacts with world leaders.

The trip revived political problems that plagued her first term: her relationship with a former senior campaign staffer who faced allegations of sexual harassment, high turnover among her staff and charges of financial mismanagement in the handling of her campaign funds.

The senator's woes have overshadowed a legislative record in which she has pushed for pension reform for women and funds to repair crumbling schools and shepherded an amendment for home-state soybean growers onto a bill revamping the nation's agriculture policy.

In keeping with her image as a champion for women and minorities, Moseley-Braun introduced the Women's Pension Equity Act of 1996, and three of the proposal's six provisions were folded into two unrelated bills. During the Republicans' first big attempt to reduce spending in 1995, she joined with Sen. Paul Wellstone, D-Minn., to object to cuts in low income energy assistance, job training and senior citizen consumer counseling on medical insurance. The pair forced Majority Leader Bob Dole, R-Kan., to allow them two floor amendments for education and job training and energy assistance — both of which failed. They also forced the Clinton administration to find a way to restore funds to the counseling program.

Moseley-Braun was also one of five women senators in 1995 who turned up the pressure on the Ethics Committee to hold public hearings on charges of sexual misconduct against Sen. Bob Packwood, R-Ore. And for Illinois' more than 52,000 soybean farmers, Moseley-Braun has been a keen advocate. She sponsored an amendment to the omnibus farm bill overhauling a formula setting loan rates on soybean bushels from a fixed amount to a moving average, a change that benefits farmers. In addition, Moseley-Braun was one of four lawmakers who petitioned the Energy Department to declare biodiesel — a fuel made from soybean and other vegetable oils — an alternative fuel.

But a bill that extended a tax deduction for health insurance for the self-employed led Moseley-Braun into trouble in 1995. An exemption she inserted in the conference report helped a partnership of the Tribune Co., which is in her home state, and music producer Quincy Jones complete a contract to buy two television stations. One of the stations was owned by Rupert Murdoch. When it became clear that Murdoch would benefit — to the tune of tens of millions of dollars —more than 150 Democrats wrote to Clinton, urging him to veto the bill.

The Nigeria trip upset her supporters not only because of her contact with a brutal dictator, but because it highlighted her persistent staff troubles. When she went to Nigeria in August 1996, her third chief of staff, Edith Wilson, left, saying she resigned because she had not been told about the trip. The senator disputes this and says she fired Wilson.

Supporters were also dismayed to learn that Kgosie Matthews, who served as Moseley-Braun's campaign manager and is her former fiancé, joined the senator on the Nigeria trip. Matthews had worked as a lobbyist for Nigeria from May to July 1994. Matthews remains a source of controversy from the 1992 campaign, when several staff members anonymously accused him of sexual harassment. A lawyer hired by the senator investigated the harassment charges and declared them unfounded.

Moseley-Braun's political survival may come down to money. Despite serving more than two years on one of Congress' powerful money panels, the Senate Finance Committee, the senator still has a campaign debt of more than $500,000 left over from 1992. That has prompted even her friends to question in private her chances of winning a second term.

She is also still embroiled in a legal dispute with her campaign's former treasurer and chief financial officer, Earl W. Hopewell, who has filed suit seeking $196,000 he says he is owed.

At Home: The daughter of a police officer and a medical technician, Moseley-Braun grew up in Chicago's neighborhoods and had direct exposure to urban poverty. In 1978, voters elected her to the state Legislature where, for more than a decade, she worked as a legislative floor leader for the city and its first black mayor, Harold Washington. She rose to become the first woman assistant majority leader.

But it was outrage over the Senate's handling of Hill in the Thomas hearings that propelled Moseley-Braun into the Senate race in 1992 and helped her upset two-term Democratic incumbent Alan J. Dixon in a three-way primary. Then voter disgust with the economy cinched a win over GOP challenger Richard S. Williamson, despite some serious flaws in her campaign that election.

Moseley-Braun found a perfect foil in Williamson, a wealthy, conservative lawyer who had held appointive jobs in the Reagan and Bush administrations. Money poured into her campaign and summer polls placed her seemingly out of Williamson's reach. But there were missteps. Her campaign suffered from disorganization and infighting, while the candidate at times appeared ill-versed about certain national issues. Moseley-Braun's performance as recorder of deeds came under fire.

Then, in late September 1992, Moseley-Braun was stung by strong criticism of her handling of her mother's finances. Moseley-Braun accepted, with her siblings, a $28,750 inheritance from her mother even though her mother was being supported by Medicaid and state law might have required that the income be applied to her mother's expenses. After a state investigation was completed just before the election, Moseley-Braun paid the state roughly $15,000 in back medical expenses for her mother. There was no criminal investigation, and a state official described the payment as voluntary.

These problems were not enough to blunt Moseley-Braun's overall appeal as a personable and energetic politician. And in the end, she ran strongly in Chicago and the southern part of the state, offsetting Williamson's strength in the Chicago suburbs. She won with 53 percent of the vote, spending nearly $6.6 million.

SENATE ELECTIONS

1992 General		
Carol Moseley-Braun (D)	2,631,229	(53%)
Richard S. Williamson (R)	2,126,833	(43%)
Chad Koppie (CIL)	100,422	(2%)
1992 Primary		
Carol Moseley-Braun (D)	557,694	(38%)
Alan J. Dixon (D)	504,077	(35%)
Albert F. Hofeld (D)	394,497	(27%)

CAMPAIGN FINANCE

	Receipts	Receipts from PACs		Expend-itures
1992				
Moseley-Braun (D)	$6,628,567	$646,746	(10%)	$6,594,570
Williamson (R)	$2,320,713	$472,839	(20%)	$2,300,924
Koppie (CIL)	$263,470	0		$262,121

INTEREST GROUP RATINGS

Year	ADA	AFL-CIO	CCUS	ACU
1996	90	n/a	46	5
1995	100	83	32	9
1994	85	75	33	4
1993	85	73	36	0

KEY VOTES

1997	
Approve balanced-budget constitutional amendment	Y
Approve chemical weapons treaty	Y
1996	
Approve farm bill	Y
Limit punitive damages in product liability cases	Y
Exempt small businesses from higher minimum wage	N
Approve welfare overhaul	N
Bar job discrimination based on sexual orientation	Y
Override veto of ban on "partial birth" abortions	N
1995	
Approve GOP budget with tax and spending cuts	N
Approve constitutional amendment barring flag desecration	N

VOTING STUDIES

	Presidential Support		Party Unity		Conservative Coalition	
Year	S	O	S	O	S	O
1996	83	15	88	10	24	76
1995	83	15	86	13	18	81
1994	82	13	86	9	13	84
1993	99	1	95	5	17	83

Richard J. Durbin (D)

Of Springfield — Elected 1996, 1st term

Biographical Information
Born: Nov. 21, 1944, East St. Louis, Ill.
Education: Georgetown U., B.S.F.S. 1966, J.D. 1969.
Occupation: Lawyer; congressional and legislative aide.
Family: Wife, Loretta Schaefer; three children.
Religion: Roman Catholic.
Political Career: Democratic nominee for Ill. Senate, 1976; Democratic nominee for lieutenant governor, 1978; U.S. House, 1983-97.
Capitol Office: 364 Russell Bldg. 20510; 224-2152.

Committees
Budget
Governmental Affairs
International Security, Proliferation & Federal Services; Investigations
Judiciary
Administrative Oversight & the Courts (ranking); Immigration; Technology, Terrorism & Government Information

The Path to Washington: Durbin saw his share of legislative battles during 14 years in the House, where he earned prominence as a goad of the tobacco industry and rose to become chairman (and then ranking member) of an Appropriations subcommittee.

Promoted to the Senate in 1996, Durbin landed a committee assignment — on Governmental Affairs — that puts him in the thick of one of the 105th Congress' earliest big fights. The committee, under Chairman Fred Thompson, R-Tenn., is looking at allegations of misdeeds in the financing of the 1996 presidential and congressional elections, including reports of fundraising practices that seem to come right up to the edge of the law.

In April 1997, Durbin expressed concern that Thompson and the Republican majority on the panel might play politics with the investigation. "The real test will be whether the investigation will be fair and bipartisan," he said, expressing hope for something more than "mud wrestling over past campaigns."

Beyond the realm of campaign finance, Durbin's legislative skills — he was once the Illinois Senate parliamentarian — and his support for anti-poverty programs bolster Senate liberals. In addition to Governmental Affairs, Durbin sits on the Budget and Judiciary committees.

When Durbin served in the 103rd Congress as chairman of Appropriations' Agriculture Subcommittee, he showed a keen interest in Agriculture Department programs aimed at feeding low-income people and encouraging farmers to use more environmentally friendly methods of cultivation. Some farm-state lawmakers and Republican conservatives complained that Durbin was shifting agriculture spending priorities away from farm programs and toward accounts such as food stamps and the Food and Drug Administration.

He waged a successful effort to funnel more money into the Women, Infants and Children (WIC) nutrition program during a round of budget cuts in 1994. Continuing to exert influence even after Republicans took control of the House in 1995, Durbin helped shield the WIC program from budget cuts during the 104th Congress. He also played a significant role in a 1995 battle to allow the Agriculture Department to move toward more-scientific meat inspections.

Durbin's prescription for reducing the deficit includes eliminating NASA's space station project, and blocking the Republicans from approving more spending for defense than the Clinton administration says is necessary.

Durbin does not favor enshrining a balanced-budget requirement in the Constitution. While his Senate predecessor, fellow Democrat Paul Simon, was a leading Democratic proponent of a balanced-budget amendment, Durbin voted against the proposal in March 1997, just as he had in the House in 1995. The 1997 "nay" vote came after a Durbin amendment to permit Congress to waive balanced-budget requirements during a recession or serious economic emergency was killed, 35-64.

In the House, Durbin had a reputation as a sometimes acerbic debater. In the 103rd, he mocked some "deficit hawks" backing the "A-to-Z" spending-cut proposal, which sought to commit the House to at least 56 hours of floor debate on making specific spending cuts. Durbin took a poke at the idea's supporters by listing alphabetically by members' names 1,113 requests that his Appropriations subcommittee had received to allocate funds for specific agricultural projects. Some outspoken advocates of cutting federal spending, Durbin said, also were "fervent about getting their share."

Durbin's most enduring crusade in his House years was against smoking. He waged a relentless and impassioned campaign against the tobacco industry.

Durbin, who was 14 when his chain-smoking father died of lung cancer, led the successful effort in the late 1980s to ban smoking on most domestic airline flights. Later, as chairman and then ranking member on Appropriations' Agriculture panel, he tried to scale back government support for tobacco farmers, falling just two votes short on an anti-tobacco floor vote in 1996.

On another big policy issue — abortion — Durbin's position shifted while he was in the House. He opposed abortion in his early days in the chamber, then began backing federal abortion funding for poor women under certain circumstances, such as rape or incest. In the 104th Congress, he sided with abortion-rights advocates, voting to require states to fund Medicaid abortions for poor women, to allow privately financed abortions at overseas military hospitals and to allow federal employees' health care plans to cover abortions. He has opposed efforts to ban a particular abortion technique that opponents call "partial birth" abortion.

When Simon announced that he would not seek re-election in 1996, Durbin — who had been booted from his post as an Appropriations "cardinal" by the House GOP takeover — jumped at the chance to succeed him. He said moving to the Senate would give him more clout in opposing the conservative agenda of House Speaker Newt Gingrich.

With endorsements from Simon and Illinois' other Democratic senator, Carol Moseley-Braun, Durbin had little trouble winning the Democratic primary.

His chances of victory in the general election were enhanced when GOP primary voters shunned moderate Lt. Gov. Bob Kustra, the favorite of the party establishment. Instead they nominated state Rep. Al Salvi, a little-known conservative with firm anti-abortion and pro-gun-owners' rights views — not the usual formula for statewide success in Illinois.

With a throng of Democrats in Chicago in August for the party's national convention, Durbin took the opportunity to ask them to help stock his campaign treasury for the fall. He got some additional media exposure as chairman of the Illinois delegation at the convention.

Salvi battled back from a huge early deficit in the polls on the strength of his performance as a campaigner. He traveled the state with his wife and five children, including a newborn, projecting a family-man image. He also fired at Durbin's congressional pay raises, his congressional pension and his overdrafts at the now-defunct House bank. One campaign ad for Salvi called Durbin "a big-taxin', big-spendin', pay-grabbin' liberal congressman."

But Durbin responded in kind by sullying Salvi as an extreme conservative, faulting him for opposing a ban on certain semiautomatic assault-style weapons and for accepting campaign contributions from the tobacco industry. The voters' verdict was a decisive one: Durbin defeated Salvi by 15 percentage points.

SENATE ELECTIONS

1996 General		
Richard J. Durbin (D)	2,384,028	(56%)
Al Salvi (R)	1,728,824	(41%)
Steven H. Perry (REF)	61,023	(1%)
1996 Primary		
Richard J. Durbin (D)	512,520	(65%)
Pat Quinn (D)	233,138	(30%)
Ronald F. Gibbs (D)	17,681	(2%)
J. Ahmad (D)	17,211	(2%)
Paul Park (D)	9,505	(1%)

Previous Winning Percentages: **1994*** (55%) **1992*** (57%) **1990*** (66%) **1988*** (69%) **1986*** (68%) **1984*** (61%) **1982*** (50%)

** House elections*

KEY VOTES

1997	
Approve balanced-budget constitutional amendment	N
Approve chemical weapons treaty	Y
House Service:	
1996	
Approve farm bill	Y
Deny public education to illegal immigrants	N
Increase minimum wage	Y
Freeze defense spending	Y
Approve welfare overhaul	Y
1995	
Approve balanced-budget constitutional amendment	N
Relax Clean Water Act regulations	N
Oppose limits on environmental regulations	Y
Reduce projected Medicare spending	N
Approve GOP budget with tax and spending cuts	N

CAMPAIGN FINANCE

	Receipts	Receipts from PACs		Expend-itures
1996				
Durbin (D)	$4,767,940	$1,153,210	(24%)	$4,966,804
Salvi (R)	$4,754,916	$522,330	(11%)	$4,752,025
Miller (LIBERT)	$27,853	0		$27,888

VOTING STUDIES

	Presidential Support		Party Unity		Conservative Coalition	
Year	S	O	S	O	S	O
House Service:						
1996	75	16	82	8	24	67
1995	83	17	91	7	23	77
1994	78	22	97	2	22	78
1993	77	22	93	6	34	66
1992	12	86	93	5	21	77
1991	25	73	92	6	30	70

INTEREST GROUP RATINGS

Year	ADA	AFL-CIO	CCUS	ACU
House Service:				
1996	80	0	27	0
1995	85	100	25	8
1994	95	78	25	0
1993	90	92	27	13
1992	90	83	13	4
1991	95	92	30	5

1 Bobby L. Rush (D)

Of Chicago — Elected 1992, 3rd term

Biographical Information

Born: Nov. 23, 1946, Albany, Ga.

Education: Roosevelt U., B.A. 1973; U. of Illinois, Chicago Circle, 1975-77.

Military Service: Army, 1963-68.

Occupation: Insurance broker; political aide.

Family: Wife, Carolyn Thomas; five children.

Religion: Protestant.

Political Career: Candidate for Chicago City Council, 1975; sought Democratic nomination for Ill. House, 1978; Chicago City Council, 1983-93.

Capitol Office: 131 Cannon Bldg. 20515; 225-4372.

Committees

Commerce
Energy & Power; Telecommunications, Trade & Consumer Protection

In Washington: A gifted political pitchman and organizer, Rush quickly became a valued vote-counter for his party's leadership when Democrats controlled the House. Because of his past association with the radical Black Panthers, the media instantly plucked him from the freshman horde after the 1992 election; Rush was a TV celebrity before his first term even began.

But he set his sights on a behind-the-scenes role in the legislative process — a place in the party whip structure — and got it. Freshman Democrats chose Rush as one of three class whips. And in the 104th, although his party was relegated to the minority, Rush got a plum assignment on the Commerce Committee.

Rush also moved a rung up the whip structure in the 104th, becoming a whip at large. But Democrats have less need for vote-counting skills now that Republicans run the House and structure most votes so they can win them. So Rush's legislative persona has shifted: Where before he was a fairly quiet wheeler-dealer, now he devotes much energy to the oratory of frustration, lashing out at Republicans as they seek to limit funding for programs that he regards as vital to his inner-city constituents.

When Speaker Newt Gingrich announced in 1995 that Chicago would be one of the cities in which he would help sponsor a program that rewards children for reading books, Rush said that he was "offended."

"If Newt comes to Chicago, rather than bringing books, he should bring jobs," Rush said. "We don't need him to assume the duties of chief librarian of the United States."

He also attacked Gingrich personally when the Republicans unveiled their plan to slow the rate of growth in spending on Medicare. He called the bill "legislative terrorism" and said the GOP reminded him of an old horror movie about "the original bloodsuckers," adding, "the bloodsuckers in this Congress are led by Count Dracula," referring to the Speaker.

The 104th was notorious for its lack of comity, and one National Republican Congressional Committee fund raising mailing drew out the worst from both sides. The NRCC mailed a poster featuring pictures of 28 Democratic members "wanted" for voting against provisions contained in the House GOP's "Contract With America." The poster disproportionately featured black members, who complained that the mailing made them fear for their safety.

Rush said that if he or his family was harmed by anyone inspired by the poster, "I intend to deal directly in the most physical of manners with" Rep. Bill Paxon of New York, then the NRCC chairman.

It was an irony not lost on Rush that after a youth spent in the sights of law enforcement, his maiden appearance on a wanted poster occurred only after his swearing-in as a member of Congress.

For most of his life, Rush has worked within organizations — both inside and outside the mainstream: He was a Boy Scout, volunteered for the Army and became leader of the Illinois Black Panthers; in the 1970s he moved into elective politics, first working with insurgents fighting Chicago's Democratic machine, then wielding power as a Chicago alderman, state party official and national director of voter registration for Bill Clinton's 1992 presidential campaign.

Urban economic revitalization is Rush's chief priority, one he pursued in the 103rd from the Banking Committee. Rush maintains that "massive disinvestment" by establishment lenders has caused economic abandonment in many urban areas, bringing high unemployment that spawns a host of social problems. Lawlessness at the Chicago housing projects Cabrini-Green and Robert Taylor Homes has drawn national attention.

The Chicago Housing Authority fell into such sorry shape by 1995 that it was taken over by the Department of Housing and Urban Development. Still, Rush felt that Republicans who sought to alleviate inner-city conditions by cutting funding for urban programs were misguided at best. Rush argued on the House floor that nothing contained in the 1996 overhaul of welfare could have helped a young boy whose slaying in a project in his dis-

ILLINOIS 1
Chicago — South and southwest sides

As early as the 1920s, Chicago's near South Side was the center of a booming black population and the core of the nation's first urban black-majority House district.

Even as the great migration from the South between 1940 and 1970 expanded the boundaries of Chicago's black neighborhoods, the 1st retained a rather compact form in the southeast section of Chicago.

In recent years, the territory covered by the 1st has grown, largely to compensate for the deterioration and depopulation of the 1st's low-income portions. During the 1980s, the district lost one-fifth of its population.

The 1st begins on the east side at 26th Street in the historic black hub, then moves south through mainly residential neighborhoods to 103rd Street, at the edge of a once thriving industrial belt.

At its midsection, the district swings west through inner-city communities. However, it also reaches an arm into Chicago's southwest side and close-in suburbs, home to most of the 1st's white residents and much of its sparse Republican vote. The district came under challenge in 1995 as part of a pending lawsuit brought against the Hispanic-majority 4th District.

The changing geography has had little impact on the district's demographics or politics. The 1st remains a majority-black Democratic stronghold. In some recent years, low voter turnout in the district undercut the chances of statewide Democratic candidates.

But 1992 efforts by Rush, who led Clinton's national minority voter outreach program, and by Carol Moseley-Braun, who was bidding to become the first black woman senator, spurred a turnout that was above average for Illinois' House districts.

The 1st has had just eight House members since 1929, all of them black. Rush has his base in the near South Side. Much of this area is fighting to stem urban blight. East of the Dan Ryan Expressway is the crime-plagued Stateway Gardens housing project; the 1st District crosses the highway to take in Comiskey Park, home of baseball's White Sox.

To the southeast is Hyde Park, site of the University of Chicago (11,900 students) and its mainly white, largely liberal community.

Then come Woodlawn and South Shore, black areas with alternating pockets of poverty and stability. In the southeast end of the 1st are solid middle-class black communities such as Chatham and Avalon Park.

The 1st District crosses town through mainly low-income black areas such as Englewood, then banks south and crosses Western Avenue, a widely recognized boundary between white and black Chicago.

This area includes such communities as Lithuanian Village and Beverly, an enclave of affluent Irish-Americans, and suburban Evergreen Park. The 1st also takes in parts of Oak Lawn, Alsip and Blue Island.

1990 Population: 571,530. White 155,885 (27%), Black 398,318 (70%), Other 17,327 (3%). Hispanic origin 20,548 (4%). 18 and over 418,800 (73%), 62 and over 96,054 (17%). Median age: 33.

trict attracted extensive publicity.

Rush, an early supporter of Clinton's 1992 White House bid, lobbied the president to include more funding for food stamps, which were cut by the welfare law, in his fiscal 1998 budget. He took issue with a tougher public housing eviction policy that Clinton ordered, but if Rush was disappointed by the president's signature on the welfare bill, he did not air that grievance in public. He instead focused his political attacks on Republicans.

Rush opposed such high-profile GOP agenda items as term limits and a line-item veto during the 104th. When the GOP sought to loosen the exclusionary rule and allow a "good faith" exemption for illegal police searches, Rush, who said he had cried at a 1995 dramatic movie about the Panthers, claimed to be the only member of Congress "ever to have been victimized by illegal search and seizure."

Rush did support a GOP-driven initiative to update telecommunications law during the 104th. As a member of the Commerce Committee, Rush succeeded in inserting a provision that calls upon the Federal Communications Commission to identify and eliminate barriers to small and minority-owned businesses providing telecommunications and information services.

Rush's prime committee seat offers him some jurisdiction over a rival political clan. Clinton's second-term Commerce Secretary, Bill Daley, is the brother of Chicago Mayor Richard M. Daley, with whom Rush has frequently locked horns.

Secure in his own district, Rush has become an adept fundraiser for other Democrats. His support for the candidacy of fellow Rep. Richard J. Durbin in the 1996 Senate primary helped Durbin overcome his main primary opponent's complaints about his minority hiring record. Durbin went on to win the Senate seat.

At Home: Rush, a potential mayoral aspirant in 1999, is seeking to become a stronger political force at home. He wins re-election with ease, but he has made moves to expand his base by helping hand-picked candidates in pursuit of local offices. He has also made a name for himself flacking videotapes by personal performance guru Anthony Robbins on Chicago cable television.

Born in southern Georgia, Rush grew up in Chicago, where his mother moved after her marriage broke up. She worked as a GOP activist, because whites dominated the Democratic machine. Rush was in an integrated Boy Scout troop and volunteered for the Army, but, disillusioned by a racist commanding officer, joined the Student Non-Violent Coordinating Committee, then went AWOL after the assassination of the Rev. Dr. Martin Luther King Jr. (But he was soon honorably discharged.)

Rush joined the Black Panthers, eventually heading the Illinois chapter, and spent six months in prison on a weapons charge. He quit the Panthers and went to college, and in the 1970s he began running for the Chicago City Council and the state legislature, challenging the Democratic machine and losing. In 1983, Rush was elected alderman, riding the coattails of Harold Washington, who was elected in an upset as Chicago's first black mayor.

After Washington's unexpected death in 1987, Rush allied himself with mainstream Democrats, earning the enmity of some old political associates who formed a more radical party named after Washington. During nearly 10 years on the council, Rush was an activist on education, housing and community development issues. As head of the environment committee, he pushed through tough toxic waste legislation and pressured the city to remove asbestos from public housing units.

In 1992, Rush won the House Democratic primary over Rep. Charles A. Hayes, a longtime labor leader who, at 74, was not known for his legislative vigor. Rush offered his own energetic style in contrast, and just days before the primary, Hayes was named as one of the top abusers of the House bank, with 716 overdrafts. Rush took 42 percent to Hayes' 39 percent.

Rush has coasted to electoral victory ever since.

HOUSE ELECTIONS

1996 General		
Bobby L. Rush (D)	174,005	(86%)
Noel Naughton (R)	25,659	(13%)
Tim M. Griffin (LIBERT)	3,449	(2%)
1996 Primary		
Bobby L. Rush (D)	74,281	(89%)
Caleb A. Davis Jr. (D)	8,894	(11%)
1994 General		
Bobby L. Rush (D)	112,474	(76%)
William J. Kelly (R)	36,038	(24%)

Previous Winning Percentages: 1992 (83%)

CAMPAIGN FINANCE

	Receipts	Receipts from PACs	Expend-itures
1996			
Rush (D)	$174,714	$167,485 (96%)	$156,219
Naughton (R)	$21,656	$628 (3%)	$20,220
1994			
Rush (D)	$196,510	$152,936 (78%)	$195,833
Kelly (R)	$42,986	$2,639 (6%)	$37,066

DISTRICT VOTE FOR PRESIDENT

	1996		1992
D	179,744 (85%)	**D**	214,045 (81%)
R	22,912 (11%)	**R**	32,628 (12%)
I	6,378 (3%)	**I**	17,195 (7%)

KEY VOTES

1997	
Ban "partial birth" abortions	N
1996	
Approve farm bill	N
Deny public education to illegal immigrants	?
Repeal ban on certain assault-style weapons	N
Increase minimum wage	Y
Freeze defense spending	Y
Approve welfare overhaul	N
1995	
Approve balanced-budget constitutional amendment	-
Relax Clean Water Act regulations	N
Oppose limits on environmental regulations	Y
Reduce projected Medicare spending	N
Approve GOP budget with tax and spending cuts	N

VOTING STUDIES

	Presidential Support		Party Unity		Conservative Coalition	
Year	**S**	**O**	**S**	**O**	**S**	**O**
1996	78	15	90	4	10	86
1995	83	11	88	2	9	82
1994	68	24	87	2	6	86
1993	76	19	93	1	2	95

INTEREST GROUP RATINGS

Year	ADA	AFL-CIO	CCUS	ACU
1996	95	n/a	25	0
1995	85	100	15	4
1994	100	89	33	5
1993	95	100	9	0

2 Jesse L. Jackson Jr. (D)

Of Chicago — Elected 1995; 1st full term

Biographical Information
Born: March 11, 1965, Greenville, S.C.
Education: North Carolina A&T U., Greensboro, B.S. 1987; Chicago Theological Seminary, M.A. 1990; U. of Illinois, J.D. 1993.
Occupation: Lawyer.
Family: Wife, Sandra.
Religion: Baptist.
Political Career: No previous office.
Capitol Office: 313 Cannon Bldg. 20515; 225-0773.

Committees
Banking & Financial Services
Domestic & International Monetary Policy; Housing & Community Opportunity
Small Business
Empowerment; Government Programs & Oversight

In Washington: Projecting an energetic personality and benefiting from his universally known name, Jackson in December 1995 won a special House election to succeed Democratic Rep. Mel Reynolds, who had resigned from Congress after an August conviction on charges of sexual misconduct.

The name was Jackson's trump card in the short special election campaign. Chicago has been the home base for Operation PUSH (People United to Serve Humanity) and the National Rainbow Coalition, the activist organizations founded by Jesse Jackson Sr., the preacher, civil rights crusader and two-time Democratic presidential contender.

The younger Jackson followed in his father's footsteps, serving as vice president at-large of Operation PUSH and as national field director for the Rainbow Coalition. But unlike his father, Jesse Jr. parlayed those activities into an inside role in the national Democratic Party organization (he is secretary of the Democratic National Committee's Black Caucus). He introduced his father at the August 1996 Democratic National Convention in Chicago and shared the podium with him.

In the House, Jackson has a couple of committee assignments that are particularly relevant to the needs of his urban constituency. He serves on the Housing and Community Opportunity Subcommittee of the Banking and Financial Services Committee, and on the Empowerment Subcommittee at Small Business.

Jackson does not have his father's looming physical presence nor the pulpit cadences of his oratory. But he is a forceful speaker in his own right. He showed his adeptness at floor debate during House consideration in May 1997 of a sweeping bill to overhaul the public housing system. Jackson and other liberal Democrats objected to a provision in the bill that would require unemployed, able-bodied public housing tenants who are not on welfare to perform eight hours a month of community service.

Jackson argued that the provision would discriminate against the poor by mandating that public housing residents work without pay. But Republicans countered that the community service requirement was reasonable because housing is part of the compensation.

Jackson offered an amendment that sought to eliminate a provision requiring housing authorities to evict tenants who failed to meet the community service requirement, but it was rejected, 160-251. He then tried to exempt from the community service requirement single parents, grandparents or spouses who are the primary caregivers for children ages 6 or younger, senior citizens or the disabled. It was also rejected, 181-216.

Jackson's record on House floor votes is predictably liberal, showing strong support for labor unions, abortion rights and environmental protections. He voted against the GOP-backed proposal to deny public education to illegal immigrants, and he was one of 98 Democrats who refused to support the compromise welfare-overhaul bill that President Clinton signed into law in 1996. He opposed repealing the ban on certain semiautomatic assault-style weapons.

Jackson frequently takes to the House floor to talk about civil rights and other topics. In February 1997, for example, he began a series of three special orders on Black History Month. "I was born, as a matter of African-American history, on March 11, 1965," he said. "On March 7, 1965, in our history it is known as bloody Sunday. It is the Sunday that the gentleman from Georgia [Rep. John Lewis], Martin Luther King Jr., and Jesse Jackson and many others in our history walked across the Edmund Pettus Bridge [in Selma, Ala.] for the right to vote. Because of the struggle that they engaged in in 1965, I now stand here as the 91st African-American to ever have the privilege of serving in the U.S. Congress."

In September 1996, he talked about the need to improve education. "My father always says that it is a real sad day in our country when jails are becoming a step up," Jackson said. "After all, in

More than two-thirds of the residents of the 2nd are black, and Democrats dominate in contests from the presidency right down the ballot. But redistricting changed the makeup of the district, adding suburban turf. Under the map for the 1990s, only slightly more than half the district's residents live within the Chicago city limits.

The new suburbanites are slightly less Democratic than those who live in the city of Chicago. Bill Clinton took 96 percent of the vote in the portion of the district within Chicago and 74 percent of the votes from the suburban portion.

Jackson polled 99 percent of the vote within the Chicago section of the district and 88 percent from the suburbs.

Jackson had won a special election to succeed Mel Reynolds, who resigned after being convicted of charges stemming from having sexual relations with an underage campaign worker. Reynolds had benefited from the more moderate suburbanites who had been added to the district.

Reynolds' predecessor, Gus Savage, had been a polarizing figure. Savage appealed to a mainly urban constituency, using hard-edged rhetoric that blamed white racism for the problems of his district's many low-income black residents; he had increasingly targeted Jews for criticism.

Reynolds earlier had lost two primary challenges to Savage but was able to capitalize on the demographic shift in the district. He made a strong appeal to suburban voters, including Jews, conservative white ethnic groups and blacks with more moderate views. Reynolds steamrolled the incumbent in the suburbs and edged him in the city.

ILLINOIS 2

Chicago — Far South Side; south suburbs; Chicago Heights

Within the city, the 2nd is roughly U-shaped. Much of the western arm, which runs north to 63rd Street, is low-income.

There are middle-class pockets, though, in such far South Side sections as Morgan Park and Pullman. The eastern arm begins at 71st Street in the South Shore area. In neighboring South Chicago, belching factories once employed thousands.

South of the city are working-class suburbs. Several, including Harvey, Markham and Robbins, are nearly all black. Some, including Ford Heights and parts of urbanized Chicago Heights, are poor, while others, such as Country Club Hills, are more affluent.

The district's southernmost reaches have most of its white population. Jewish residents are numerous in such well-to-do suburbs as Homewood, Flossmoor and Olympia Fields. Bloom Township has a longstanding Italian-American community; this is the most Republican area in the 2nd.

Thanks to the suburban influence, the 2nd has the highest median family income of Chicago's four predominantly minority districts. It also has fewer families in poverty than either the 1st, 4th or 7th districts. Still, 15 percent of its families live below the poverty level.

1990 Population: 571,530. White 154,902 (27%), Black 391,425 (68%), Other 25,203 (4%). Hispanic origin 37,860 (7%). 18 and over 402,216 (70%), 62 and over 69,334 (12%). Median age: 31.

jails they have heat in the wintertime and they have air conditioning in the summertime. They have three square meals a day. They have organized recreation. They have health care and medical attention while they are in jail. They have library facilities. They have organized religion. . . . You can get your high school diploma while you are in jail. You can get a GED. For many people in my district, certainly in the city of Chicago and around the country, many young men are now joining their fathers for the first time in jails. This is the first time we are looking at two and three generations of young men and in many cases young women who are part of our penal system."

And he weighed in on the environment in April 1996, blasting the Republican record. "The majority leadership in this body has attempted to roll back years of environmental progress to provide favors for its special interest friends," Jackson said. "Because of budget cuts by the majority in this Congress, the Environmental Protection Agency has missed thousands of inspections and enforcement actions. This same majority has shifted costs from polluters to taxpayers, while cleanups have been slowed at 400 toxic waste sites and stopped at 60 superfund sites. Because funds to implement six administrative rules have been cut, hundreds of millions of pounds of pollution entered our water supply that could have been prevented. It is time for the majority in the 104th Congress to clean up its environmental act."

At Home: In the November 1995 Democratic special primary campaign — the decisive election in the majority-black 2nd District — state Senate Democratic leader Emil Jones Jr. tried to turn Jackson's greatest asset into a liability. Jones contended that Jackson Sr. was attempting to use his enormous clout to boost his politically inexperienced son to high office. "I'm running against both Jacksons, junior and senior," Jones said.

But the younger Jackson was able to fend off

the attack, in a manner similar to that of the scions of the Kennedy political dynasty who have won office. A lawyer who graduated from Washington's elite St. Alban's Episcopal High School, he presented himself as a vibrant member of a new generation of black leadership, yet because of his father's fame he also enjoyed a degree of name recognition that none of his rivals for the nomination could hope to match.

To counter criticism that he was too young for the job of congressman, Jackson argued that being the son of Jesse Jackson Sr. amounted to a lifetime of political experience. When he was born in 1965, his father was an associate of the Rev. King. The younger Jackson's campaign biography said that he rallied support in 1981 for striking air traffic controllers who had been fired by President Ronald Reagan; he was 16 years old at the time. He was old enough to vote in 1984, when his father staged his first presidential bid. In his House campaign, he proudly noted that he spent his 21st birthday in a Washington jail after a protest against apartheid.

In the Democratic primary, Jackson appeared charismatic next to Jones, who is twice Jackson's age, and state Sen. Alice Palmer, 56, a former Northwestern University student affairs director. Jackson won not quite half of the primary ballots, with Jones finishing under 40 percent and Palmer and two other candidates far back.

Jackson presented the contrast between himself and his opponents as one of opportunity, not age. "The only way one grows into leadership in Congress is to get elected young enough that you become Speaker of the House or chairman of the Ways and Means Committee," he said.

Jackson presented voters with a 10-point agenda, including development of economic incentives to draw businesses to the economically struggling 2nd and the creation of a "single payer" national health care plan. He also took a stand on a hot local issue, backing a plan to build a third Chicago-area airport in rural environs just south of the 2nd District line.

The general-election outcome was a foregone conclusion. Jackson rolled up more than 75 percent of the vote against Republican Thomas Joseph "T.J." Somer, a white lawyer and former police officer. The following November, he polled 94 percent of the vote to win a full term.

HOUSE ELECTIONS

1996 General		
Jesse Jackson Jr. (D)	172,648	(94%)
Frank H. Stratman (LIBERT)	10,880	(6%)
1995 Special		
Jesse Jackson Jr. (D)	48,145	(76%)
Thomas Joseph "T.J." Somer (R)	15,171	(24%)

CAMPAIGN FINANCE

	Receipts	Receipts from PACs	Expend-itures
1996			
Jackson (D)	$815,231	$225,094 (28%)	$729,699
1995 Special			
Jackson (D)	$348,997	$41,500 (12%)	$310,776
Somer (R)	$35,790	0	$30,857

DISTRICT VOTE FOR PRESIDENT

	1996		1992
D	170,821 (85%)	**D**	194,796 (80%)
R	22,204 (11%)	**R**	31,730 (13%)
I	6,395 (3%)	**I**	16,968 (7%)

KEY VOTES

1997	
Ban "partial birth" abortions	N
1996	
Approve farm bill	N
Deny public education to illegal immigrants	N
Repeal ban on certain assault-style weapons	N
Increase minimum wage	Y
Freeze defense spending	Y
Approve welfare overhaul	N
1995	
Relax Clean Water Act regulations	I
Oppose limits on environmental regulations	I
Reduce projected Medicare spending	I
Approve GOP budget with tax and spending cuts	I

VOTING STUDIES

	Presidential Support		Party Unity		Conservative Coalition	
Year	**S**	**O**	**S**	**O**	**S**	**O**
1996	85	15	96	4	12	88
1995	67†	33†	94†	6†	50†	50†

† Not eligible for all recorded votes.

INTEREST GROUP RATINGS

Year	ADA	AFL-CIO	CCUS	ACU
1996	100	n/a	19	0
1995	0	100	0	0

3 William O. Lipinski (D)

Of Chicago — Elected 1982, 8th term

Biographical Information
Born: Dec. 22, 1937, Chicago, Ill.
Education: Loras College, 1957-58.
Military Service: Army Reserve, 1961-67.
Occupation: Parks supervisor.
Family: Wife, Rose Marie Lapinski; two children.
Religion: Roman Catholic.
Political Career: Chicago City Council, 1975-83.
Capitol Office: 1501 Longworth Bldg. 20515; 225-5701.

Committees
Transportation & Infrastructure
Aviation (ranking); Railroads

In Washington: Like the middle-class white ethnics who dominate his suburban Chicago district, Lipinski holds conservative views on social issues, is wary of tax increases and remains a staunch ally of organized labor. He had a re-election scare in 1994, and afterwards found much to like in the agenda of the new Republican majority in the House; his near-defeat made him slightly more vocal in support of issues that resonate with his constituents, if not his Democratic colleagues.

Lipinski is a rare northern member of the Blue Dog Coalition, a group of conservative Democrats mainly hailing from the South or West. Like many in the coalition, Lipinski reaches across the aisle to join forces with more moderate Republicans when possible. Lipinski has employed the strategy of having Republican members sponsor some of his amendments, in hopes that a face from the majority ranks would lend them more heft.

"I'm no rubber stamp for the Democrats," he boasted during his 1996 campaign. Still, Lipinski, a senior Democrat on the Transportation and Infrastructure Committee and ranking member on its Aviation Subcommittee, used his position to fight against some of the GOP's efforts to curb labor protections during the 104th Congress.

But he has generally supported Republican attempts to revamp or privatize agencies under the panel's purview. Lipinski joins with Transportation Chairman Bud Shuster, R-Pa., in wanting to remove highway money from the general budget. And he has supported GOP signature initiatives in other areas, including toughening immigration law.

He was one of only nine Democrats who voted in 1995 for the GOP's first bill to overhaul welfare, although about half the Democratic caucus had come on board by the time Republicans offered their third bill, which was enacted. Lipinski said he had reservations about the plan but found its provisions preferable to the status quo.

Lipinski also polished his social conservative image with his sponsorship of a proposed constitutional amendment to allow Congress and the states to ban flag desecration and with strong floor statements in favor of bills to recognize English as the official U.S. language and to allow states not to recognize same-gender marriages. "There is nothing radical or racist about declaring English the official language of the United States," Lipinski argued.

He strongly opposed the 1991 civil rights bill, denouncing its "quotas," and he feels that special treatment for minorities disadvantages people of other ethnic backgrounds. "My constituents suffer discrimination," he told the Chicago Sun-Times. "They had nothing to do with slavery."

But Lipinski is not in the GOP corner during every fight. He opposed Republican efforts to repeal the ban on certain semiautomatic assault-style weapons and the party's budget-balancing package in 1995, and he fights Republicans at every turn as they seek to change the balance of power between management and labor. He opposed Republican legislation to create employer and employee bargaining teams, to allow businesses to offer compensatory time instead of overtime payments, and to end certain collective bargaining protections for federal transit workers. Lipinski led floor opposition against a provision in an aviation law that made it harder for Federal Express employees to unionize, and he voted for the 1996 increase in the minimum wage.

"I have nothing against people in this economy becoming millionaires, becoming billionaires," Lipinski said. "But I believe that it is really the duty and the responsibility of the . . . government to try to create a economy that improves the standard of living of all the citizens of this country."

A wiry, terse-talking smoker, Lipinski is the picture of an old-style urban pol. A Catholic of Polish and Irish lineage from working-class roots, he worked his way up in the Chicago Democratic machine and still leads the party's 23rd Ward organization. He is a persistent and sometimes emotional spokesman for conservative ethnic values who bristles that the label "white ethnic" has become derogatory code language. "These same political types who have made the term fashion-

ILLINOIS 3
Chicago — Southwest side; south and west suburbs

The working- and middle-class constituency on Chicago's southwest side is the foundation of Lipinski's electoral success. This is part of the city's "Bungalow Belt," with block after block of small, neatly kept brick homes mainly occupied by people with ethnic roots in Poland and other Eastern European nations, Italy and Ireland.

During the 1980s, most of Lipinski's district was within the city limits. But with the 1991 redistricting, his territory was shunted west, as a new Hispanic-majority district was created to go with the city's three black-majority districts.

The 3rd now roughly follows the pattern of white migration to the southwest suburbs. Only a quarter of its residents live within Chicago's borders.

Still, there is a similarity between the southwest side and the 3rd District's close-in suburbs, including Berwyn, Burbank, Hometown and parts of Cicero and Oak Lawn. Residents in both areas tend to think of themselves as Democrats, but on social issues they are more conservative than the national Democratic Party's line.

There is a significant Republican vote in the more affluent suburbs in western Cook County and in some of the newer subdivisions at the district's southern end. The conservative tilt of these voters makes the 3rd something of a swing district. George Bush in 1988 won 61 percent of the vote in the 3rd.

But in 1992, opposition to Bush's economic policies sent many of the district's "Reagan Democrats" back to their traditional party or to the populist campaign of Ross Perot. Bill Clinton carried the 3rd, though with his smallest plurality of any Chicago-based district. In 1996, Clinton carried the district easily with an outright majority.

Partly because of Lipinski's skill at ward-level organizing, the 3rd is a pillar of the Chicago Democratic machine that has revived during the mayoralty of Richard M. Daley.

Midway Airport, located within the city and surrounded by southwest side residential communities, is a job-provider for the 3rd District, but also a source of noise and pollution. The facility could be threatened if a proposed new airport for the south Chicago area ever gets beyond the talking stage. A few years ago, United Parcel Service opened in Willow Springs its largest central processing facility, adding 5,400 jobs to the area.

The 3rd is bisected by an industrial belt adjacent to Interstate 55 (the main route to the mostly residential suburban area) and the Chicago Sanitary and Ship Canal. Although near downtown and surrounded by suburbia, this area has few residences among its factories and railroad yards. Bedford Park, one of the district's largest communities in size, had only 566 residents in 1990.

1990 Population: 571,531. White 533,458 (93%), Black 11,015 (2%), Other 27,058 (5%). Hispanic origin 42,101 (7%). 18 and over 442,224 (77%), 62 and over 110,981 (19%). Median age: 36.

able have at the same time tried to make it unfashionable to exhibit many of [the] beliefs real ethnics hold, implying that it's immoral to oppose all abortions, racist to support capital punishment," Lipinski once said.

A generation ago, the House Democratic Caucus was replete with members like Lipinski, but times have changed. Lipinski was a member of the lonely band of Democrats seeking recognition of their opposition to abortion in the 1996 party platform.

Throughout his House career, Lipinski has worked largely on matters of parochial concern to Chicago. He is now the 4th-ranking Democrat on the Transportation Committee, which deals with a range of Chicago concerns, such as improvements at O'Hare airport, the fate of aging Midway airport (in Lipinski's district), and the replacement of revetments to prevent erosion of the city's 24-mile Lake Michigan shoreline. He supported one-term Chicago Republican Rep. Michael Patrick Flanagan's lobbying for more shoreline money in 1995, but, in defense of Midway, Lipinski opposes efforts by other Chicagoland lawmakers who are seeking funding for a third metropolitan airport.

Lipinski also works to secure funding for highway projects sought by Illinois colleagues. "Who knows better where a certain amount of federal money should be spent locally than the congressman?" he has asked.

In the 103rd Congress, Lipinski got a forum of his own as he took over the chairmanship of the Merchant Marine Subcommittee of the Merchant Marine and Fisheries Committee. That put him at the center of action as Congress worked to revitalize the faltering U.S. maritime industry. In 1994, the committee approved a subsidy bill; cruise-ship companies howled about paying higher fees to help generate revenue for the subsidy, but Lipinski said the per-passenger fee increase "amounts to less than lunch at McDonald's, a small price to pay for thousands of American jobs." When the Merchant Marine bill came to the floor, Lipinski got a rare moment in the spotlight as a spokesman for the $1 billion-plus measure.

Lipinski's tenure on Merchant Marine ended at the outset of the 104th, when the new Republican majority abolished the committee altogether.

At Home: Lipinski's support for parts of the GOP agenda proved to be a winning electoral strategy. After receiving his lowest-ever general election tally in 1994, in 1996 he beat the same GOP foe by a comfortable 33-point margin.

In 1994, Republicans hoped that infighting between Lipinski and an alderman would create an opening for their challenger in the 3rd, political newcomer Jim Nalepa. A real estate developer and former Army officer, Nalepa tried to taint Lipinski by associating him with the Clinton administration and Chicago machine politics. Lipinski was also dogged by an Illinois term limits group that sent out several mailings against him.

But Lipinski made peace with the alderman, showed the machine's muscle by taking 74 percent of the city vote (along with 45 percent of the suburban vote), and highlighted his independence by including Republican candidates on the "palm cards" he handed out to guide voters on Election Day. Lipinski held on with 54 percent.

It was Lipinski's second tough election in a row. In 1992, redistricting forced him into a primary with fellow Democratic Rep. Marty Russo. The redrawn 3rd's reach into the suburbs seemed to benefit Russo, whose former district was mainly suburban. Lipinski lost some of his Chicago base. But many of the close-in suburbs shared the ethnic characteristics and socially conservative views of his urban turf. And in his remaining base, Lipinski was hugely popular. He had an army of precinct workers and the support of key members of the city's Democratic organization.

Lipinski swamped Russo by more than 25,000 votes in Chicago and ran within 3,500 votes of Russo in the suburbs, winning overall with 58 percent. The GOP initially had designs on the conservative-leaning 3rd, but the party could not recruit a strong challenger, and Lipinski took 64 percent in November.

A lifelong Chicago resident, Lipinski developed his political contacts while working in city government. Beginning as a weekend athletic instructor, he spent 17 years in the Parks Department and rose to an administrative position. In 1975, Lipinski was elected to the City Council, where he lobbied for the establishment of the Southwest Rapid Transit Line; as chairman of the Education Committee, he opposed mandatory busing, a hot-button issue for his heavily ethnic constituency.

His 1982 primary challenge to Democratic Rep. John G. Fary in the old 5th District was the result of an intraparty split. Fary had been a loyal supporter of Mayor Richard J. Daley. But after Daley's death, Fary aligned with Mayor Jane Byrne. By the early 1980s, Fary was being pressured to retire by allies of the mayor's son, Richard M. Daley, then a prospective challenger to Byrne who became mayor in 1987. Fary resisted, and Lipinski ran as the candidate of the Daley forces, winning nomination with 60 percent.

HOUSE ELECTIONS

1996 General		
William O. Lipinski (D)	137,153	(65%)
Jim Nalepa (R)	67,214	(32%)
George Skaritka (REF)	3,643	(2%)
1994 General		
William O. Lipinski (D)	92,353	(54%)
Jim Nalepa (R)	78,163	(46%)

Previous Winning Percentages: 1992 (64%) **1990** (66%) **1988** (61%) **1986** (70%) **1984** (64%) **1982** (75%)

CAMPAIGN FINANCE

	Receipts	Receipts from PACs	Expend-itures
1996			
Lipinski (D)	$449,859	$255,490 (57%)	$455,967
Nalepa (R)	$228,012	$66,084 (29%)	$202,334
1994			
Lipinski (D)	$378,373	$237,350 (63%)	$366,804
Nalepa (R)	$279,148	$62,647 (22%)	$277,722

DISTRICT VOTE FOR PRESIDENT

1996		1992	
D	114,089 (53%)	**D**	108,211 (41%)
R	78,853 (37%)	**R**	102,626 (39%)
I	19,441 (9%)	**I**	52,892 (20%)

VOTING STUDIES

	Presidential Support		Party Unity		Conservative Coalition	
Year	**S**	**O**	**S**	**O**	**S**	**O**
1996	65	34	61	36	59	41
1995	52	46	66	28	55	42
1994	72	26	73	22	67	28
1993	67	30	73	22	66	32
1992	34	52	67	20	63	29
1991	38	59	72	22	68	30

KEY VOTES

1997	
Ban "partial birth" abortions	Y
1996	
Approve farm bill	Y
Deny public education to illegal immigrants	Y
Repeal ban on certain assault-style weapons	N
Increase minimum wage	Y
Freeze defense spending	Y
Approve welfare overhaul	Y
1995	
Approve balanced-budget constitutional amendment	Y
Relax Clean Water Act regulations	?
Oppose limits on environmental regulations	Y
Reduce projected Medicare spending	N
Approve GOP budget with tax and spending cuts	N

INTEREST GROUP RATINGS

Year	ADA	AFL-CIO	CCUS	ACU
1996	70	n/a	38	40
1995	50	82	35	36
1994	45	88	42	38
1993	45	83	27	33
1992	50	67	29	48
1991	45	75	20	30

4 Luis V. Gutierrez (D)

Of Chicago — Elected 1992, 3rd term

Biographical Information
Born: Dec. 10, 1954, Chicago, Ill.
Education: Northeastern Illinois U., B.A. 1975.
Occupation: Teacher; social worker.
Family: Wife, Soraida Arocho; two children.
Religion: Roman Catholic.
Political Career: Chicago City Council, 1986-93.
Capitol Office: 2438 Rayburn Bldg. 20515; 225-8203.

Committees
Banking & Financial Services
Capital Markets, Securities & Government Sponsored Enterprises; Housing & Community Opportunity
Veterans' Affairs
Health (ranking)

In Washington: Although Gutierrez has easily won three House contests in the overwhelmingly Democratic, Hispanic-majority 4th, questions about the constitutionality of the district's boundaries have prevented him from resting easy.

The oddly shaped 4th was created in 1991 redistricting as Illinois' first and only Hispanic-majority district. It was challenged in court as an unconstitutional racial gerrymander. In March 1996, a three-judge federal panel described the distended, C-shaped district as an "uncouth configuration" and "a Rorschach ink blot." But the judges upheld the map on grounds that it served a compelling state interest of remedying past and present discrimination against Hispanics.

However, in November 1996, the Supreme Court, which had ordered the redrawing of unusually designed black- and Hispanic-majority districts in other states, sent the 4th District case back to the Illinois panel for reconsideration.

Gutierrez has limited input in the judicial proceedings on his district, and his sway in the legislative arena is also modest, especially now that Republicans control the House. But he fashioned a role for himself as an active partisan spokesman and piquant critic of the GOP, appearing on the floor frequently to fault the conservative majority.

In November 1995, Gutierrez jumped on House Speaker Newt Gingrich's statement that suggested Gingrich had taken a tough stand in a budget showdown with President Clinton in part because of a perceived snub. The Speaker said that Clinton had not conferred with him on a long flight home from the Middle East following the funeral of assassinated Prime Minister Yitzhak Rabin of Israel. Gingrich complained that upon landing, Clinton left the plane by the front door, while Gingrich and others were shown the back exit.

After mockingly describing his own "traumatic experience" of being giving a window rather than an aisle seat on a recent flight and having to exit with the rest of the passengers, Gutierrez laid into Gingrich: "Newt, have some decency. . . . The future of our Nation is more important than where you sit on an airplane. The next time you throw a temper tantrum, leave the American public out of it."

The following September, Gutierrez called on Gingrich to live up to his rhetoric about personal responsibility by stepping down as Speaker while the House investigated ethics complaints against him.

Rhetorical barbs have long been a Gutierrez trademark, although they largely caused self-inflicted wounds in his early House tenure. His nationally televised, freshman-term criticisms of Congress — then controlled by the Democrats — drew an icy response from his party colleagues.

In February 1994, just a year into his tenure, Gutierrez denounced Congress' shortcomings on the widely watched CBS program "60 Minutes."

Gutierrez's mocking of the ways of Washington drew raves from critics of Congress: After the show, his office reported receiving more than 500 phone calls and faxes praising his integrity and candor.

But within the House, many of Gutierrez's colleagues reacted with sneers, calling him a self-serving phony who had cut his political teeth in the rough-and-tumble of the Chicago City Council, then pronounced himself a great congressional reformer. Talk spread that some Democrats were so angry at Gutierrez that they wanted to get the party caucus to reprimand him.

Though that did not develop, Gutierrez has not enjoyed an inside lane to more prestigious committee assignments. He sits where he did as a freshman: on Banking and Financial Services (formerly Banking, Finance and Urban Affairs), and on Veterans' Affairs.

When the Democratic leadership appointed the first-ever Hispanic to Ways and Means in the 105th, the seat went to Xavier Becerra of California, who like Gutierrez was first elected in 1992. Gutierrez for the 105th had to make do with the ranking Democratic seat on the Veterans' Affairs Health Subcommittee.

Gutierrez is more careful these days not to

ILLINOIS 4

Chicago — Parts of North Side, southwest side

Drawing the 4th to create a Hispanic-majority district required a creative touch. Whether it was too creative was still undecided more than five years after the district map was enacted.

The Supreme Court in November 1996 ordered a three-judge federal panel in Illinois to re-examine its rejection of a challenge that the 4th was unconstitutionally designed with race as the major factor.

The district was created as a result of a boom in Chicago's Hispanic population. The 1990 census reported that Chicago had 545,852 Hispanic residents, more than twice as many as in 1970.

However, most Chicago Hispanics live in two blocs, one northwest of downtown and the other nearby to the southwest, and a direct linkup between these areas would have bisected the black-majority 7th District. To avoid this, the 4th takes in a mostly Hispanic section of the North Side, follows a narrow, 10-mile band along the northern border of the 7th to the Cook County line, then moves south and east along the 7th to hook up with the other Hispanic concentration.

Despite its reach, 92 percent of the 4th's population is within Chicago; 5 percent is in adjacent Cicero. Most of the suburban territory is composed of railroad tracks, forest preserves, cemeteries and interstates.

Puerto Ricans hold sway in much of the northern part of the 4th. The former "Polish downtown" along lower Milwaukee Avenue is now mainly Hispanic. Parts of the West Town community are "gentrifying," but nearby Humboldt Park is mainly low-income and has one of the city's worst gang problems. To the north is Logan Square, which still has a substantial Polish community.

The southern part of the 4th is largely composed of two Mexican-American sections: Little Village, with a thriving business district and many single-family homes, and Pilsen, a poorer area that is upholding its history as a point of entry for immigrants.

In the 4th's southern reaches are ethnically mixed sections, including parts of Bridgeport and Back of the Yards. The latter area declined when the famed stockyards closed in the early 1970s, but community organizers have helped attract light industry and revive the retail trade.

The 4th lags far behind other Illinois House districts in voter participation. Many of the district's Puerto Ricans are poor and have yet to establish community roots. Many of the residents of Mexican origin are recent arrivals.

There were concerns among Hispanic activists when the district was created that a strong non-Hispanic white candidate could prevail. In fact, two white Chicago aldermen did file to run in the 1992 Democratic House primary. However, both dropped out of the race, and Gutierrez, of Puerto Rican heritage, took command of the district.

1990 Population: 571,530. White 277,739 (49%), Black 36,193 (6%), Other 257,598 (45%). Hispanic origin 371,663 (65%). 18 and over 383,497 (67%), 62 and over 53,817 (9%). Median age: 27.

offend sensibilities in his own party, but he still tries to maintain an image as a congressional reformer.

Soon after taking his House seat, Gutierrez led a group of freshmen seeking to freeze Congress members' cost of living adjustment, a sum that he said was "more money than most Americans make in two months." The Democratic leadership later agreed to suspend the pay increase.

In June 1995, the House by voice vote passed a Gutierrez amendment to the fiscal 1996 legislative branch appropriations bill barring unsolicited mass mailings by members of Congress within 90 days of an election. The amendment, which was enacted, lengthened the former 60-day ban on mass mailings.

Gutierrez is an advocate for low-income individuals and his fellow Hispanics. A member of the Banking and Financial Services Subcommittee on Housing and Community Opportunity, he joined Democrat Barney Frank of Massachusetts in 1995 on an unsuccessful amendment to a housing bill that proposed to continue limiting public housing rental rates to 30 percent of a tenants' income.

Early in the 105th Congress, Gutierrez undertook to overturn provisions in the 1996 welfare overhaul law to cut off food stamps and Medicaid benefits to legal immigrants.

Gutierrez in September 1996 had proposed a bill to restore those benefits while cutting billions of dollars in tax breaks for businesses. "Immigrants are making enormous contributions to America," he said. "Sadly, Congress' new welfare law treats them as scapegoats."

On Veterans' Affairs, Gutierrez has supported greatly expanding the VA's reproductive health care services for women veterans and backed funding for developing a program at the VA to deal with employees' sexual harassment complaints. He also has supported claims by Vietnam War veterans that they have suffered illnesses caused by exposure to the defoliant Agent Orange.

Gutierrez' ethnic background put him in the middle of an unusual Capitol Hill incident in 1996.

Returning to his office from a celebration of Puerto Rico with his daughter and niece, Gutierrez was confronted by a security officer who questioned his assertion that he was a member of Congress, then said, according to Gutierrez, "Everything would be all right if you and your people would go back to the country you come from."

At Home: As soon as the Hispanic-majority 4th was created for the 1992 election, Gutierrez was favored to win it. A Chicago alderman since 1986, he came into the campaign for the district with several advantages, not least of which was the endorsement of Chicago Mayor Richard M. Daley.

Hispanics accounted for 65 percent of the 4th's population but less than 40 percent of its voters. Whites made up 58 percent of the registered voter base, and Daley's support almost guaranteed that the crucial non-Hispanic white vote would go to Gutierrez.

Gutierrez had one primary opponent, former Alderman Juan M. Soliz, a Mexican-American. But Soliz's campaign was poorly funded; Gutierrez won with nearly 60 percent. That November, he easily became the first Hispanic elected to the House from Illinois. Soliz tried again in the 1994 Democratic primary, but Gutierrez topped 60 percent.

Running without a prominent Hispanic opponent in 1996, Gutierrez easily won his primary with 71 percent. For the first time, he had no Republican opponent, and took 94 percent against a Libertarian candidate.

Gutierrez and Daley were not always on cordial terms. In the 1983 mayor's race, Gutierrez backed Democrat Harold Washington over Daley. Gutierrez later challenged a Daley ally, veteran Rep. Dan Rostenkowski, for his 32nd Ward Democratic Committee seat and got less than a fourth of the vote. But after Washington's death in 1987, Gutierrez allied with Daley's camp.

HOUSE ELECTIONS

1996 General		
Luis V. Gutierrez (D)	85,278	(94%)
William Passmore (LIBERT)	5,857	(6%)
1996 Primary		
Luis V. Gutierrez (D)	27,140	(71%)
John Joseph Holowinski (D)	8,206	(21%)
William Garcia (D)	2,234	(6%)
Victor Amador (D)	736	(2%)
1994 General		
Luis V. Gutierrez (D)	46,695	(75%)
Steven Valtierra (R)	15,384	(25%)

Previous Winning Percentages: 1992 (78%)

CAMPAIGN FINANCE

	Receipts	Receipts from PACs	Expend-itures
1996			
Gutierrez (D)	$412,557	$161,325 (39%)	$261,252
1994			
Gutierrez (D)	$406,609	$201,824 (50%)	$367,811
Valtierra (R)	$12,995	$14 (0%)	$12,603

DISTRICT VOTE FOR PRESIDENT

	1996		1992
D	82,239 (80%)	D	82,497 (65%)
R	14,669 (14%)	R	29,091 (23%)
I	5,158 (5%)	I	15,392 (12%)

KEY VOTES

1997	
Ban "partial birth" abortions	N
1996	
Approve farm bill	N
Deny public education to illegal immigrants	N
Repeal ban on certain assault-style weapons	N
Increase minimum wage	Y
Freeze defense spending	Y
Approve welfare overhaul	N
1995	
Approve balanced-budget constitutional amendment	N
Relax Clean Water Act regulations	N
Oppose limits on environmental regulations	Y
Reduce projected Medicare spending	N
Approve GOP budget with tax and spending cuts	N

VOTING STUDIES

	Presidential Support		Party Unity		Conservative Coalition	
Year	S	O	S	O	S	O
1996	81	16	88	5	6	92
1995	83	11	90	5	10	86
1994	63	28	91	4	6	92
1993	72	24	90	4	11	82

INTEREST GROUP RATINGS

Year	ADA	AFL-CIO	CCUS	ACU
1996	100	n/a	14	0
1995	95	100	21	16
1994	90	100	33	0
1993	100	100	9	4

5 Rod R. Blagojevich (D)

Of Chicago — Elected 1996, 1st term

Biographical Information

Born: Dec. 10, 1956, Chicago, Ill.

Education: Northwestern U., B.A. 1979; Pepperdine U., J.D. 1983.

Occupation: Lawyer.

Family: Wife, Patricia Mell; one child.

Religion: Eastern Orthodox.

Political Career: Assistant Cook County state's attorney, 1986-88; Ill. House, 1993-97.

Capitol Office: 501 Cannon Bldg. 20515; 225-4061.

Committees

Government Reform & Oversight
Government Management, Information & Technology; National Security, International Affairs & Criminal Justice

National Security
Military Procurement; Military Research & Development

The Path to Washington: Blagojevich reclaimed for the Democrats a district that for 36 years was the province of Dan Rostenkowski, the former powerhouse Ways and Means Committee chairman.

"Rosty," as he was known, was indicted on 17 counts, including the misuse of personal and congressional funds, extortion of gifts and cash, and obstruction of justice.

His ethical problems paved the way for one of 1994's most shocking upsets: the election of Republican Michael Patrick Flanagan, who trounced the beleaguered Rostenkowski with 55 percent of the vote.

But Flanagan turned out to be a one-term wonder. He was a loyal soldier of the House Republican revolution, voting, for example, 100 percent of the time for the planks in the House GOP's "Contract With America." All the while, he was squarely in the sights of the Democrats, who had targeted him for defeat.

Their nominee, state Rep. Blagojevich (pronounced "bla-GOY-a-vich"), was well-connected to the Chicago Democratic organization, which, though not as powerful as it was under the late Mayor Richard J. Daley, still makes its presence felt on occasion.

It did in this race, thanks to Blagojevich's father-in-law, city Alderman Richard Mell, one of the last strong ward leaders in Chicago; and Chicago Mayor Richard M. Daley, son of the legendary mayor and a close friend of Mell's.

With the backing of the party organization, Blagojevich defeated two opponents in the primary: fellow state Rep. Nancy Kaszak, who ran as a political outsider and had the backing of EMILY's List, a fundraising group for women Democratic candidates; and Ray Romero, a lawyer and former business executive.

Blagojevich then turned his attention to Flanagan. Following the national playbook of Democrats, Blagojevich portrayed himself as a moderate and his opponent as an extremist.

He stressed his opposition to proposed GOP cuts in the projected growth of Medicare, the federal health insurance program for the elderly, and to Medicaid, the federal-state health insurance program for the poor and disabled.

Flanagan, who had moved away from the Republican Party line in the second session of the 104th Congress, contended that he served as Chicago's link to the House GOP majority. He pointed to the federal funding Congress authorized during the 104th Congress for erosion projects along Lake Michigan.

Flanagan concentrated on constituent service and held many town meetings. He contended that his conservative voting record was in line with the 5th District, which supported Republicans Ronald Reagan and George Bush for the presidency in 1984 and 1988, respectively.

But district voters in 1996 were not hospitable to voting Republican. Blagojevich crushed Flanagan with 64 percent of the vote.

Blagojevich, a former Golden Gloves boxer who served as an assistant state's attorney before winning election to the state legislature, made crime a centerpiece of his legislative career and his congressional campaign.

In Springfield, he pushed legislation revoking gun permits for people convicted of stalking or domestic violence and supported efforts to require violent criminals to spend more of their sentences behind bars.

Campaigning for Congress, he said he would work on legislation to provide assistance to cities, such as Chicago, that are fighting crime and gang violence. He has called for prohibiting people under age 21 from possessing handguns, making it a felony offense to threaten someone who refuses to join a gang, and requiring people convicted of defacing public property with graffiti to perform community service.

He angled for a seat on the Appropriations or Judiciary committees, which are tough spots for freshmen usually. He was assigned instead to the Government Reform and Oversight and National Security committees.

ILLINOIS 5
Chicago — North Side

The 5th, which spans the North Side of Chicago, can be thought of as two distinct districts. On the district's lakefront east side is a mainly liberal, partly upscale area. Across town, the northwest side is part of Chicago's "Bungalow Belt," where middle- and working-class residents from a variety of southern and eastern European backgrounds hold more conservative views.

Both groups have Democratic traditions, but their voting behavior can vary widely. "Lakefront liberals" may balk at the local Democratic organization during primary campaigns, but they regularly vote Democratic in November. Democratic voters on the northwest side usually take cues from the party's organization in primaries, but the area can swing to GOP candidates in general elections for major office.

The result of this mix is a district that usually, though not always, votes Democratic. Bill Clinton scored an overwhelming victory here in 1996, garnering 63 percent. But four years earlier he barely got a majority here (though he still won the 5th by 17 points). And George Bush and Ronald Reagan won the district in 1988 and 1984, respectively.

And Republican Michael Patrick Flanagan scored a stunning upset over Democrat Dan Rostenkowski in the House race here in 1994, though he lost to Blagojevich two years later.

The district ranges east to Lake Michigan just north of downtown, taking in some of the upscale high-rises along Lake Shore Drive's "Gold Coast." Nearby is the Lincoln Park community, home to numerous political activists, young professionals and DePaul University students.

Opponents of the city's Democratic Party machine had their heyday here in the 1970s, during the waning days of Richard J. Daley's reign as mayor. Somewhat dormant in recent years, the lakefront liberals emerged again when one of their number, activist Dick Simpson, challenged Rostenkowski in the 1992 and 1994 primaries.

The district follows Lincoln Avenue northwest past well-to-do Ravenswood and multi-ethnic Lincoln Square. To the west along Lawrence Avenue is a Korean-American community. The 5th then drops south to Jackowo, still a first stop for immigrants from Poland.

Much of the district's western end is a grid of small brick houses where families of city workers, commuters and O'Hare Airport employees live. Few blacks live here: In her 1992 bid to become the first black woman senator, Democrat Carol Moseley-Braun had trouble in parts of the northwest side. Harold Washington was anathema to many northwest voters during his tenure as Chicago's first black mayor in the mid-1980s.

The 5th also takes in two independent towns, Norridge and Harwood Heights, that are within Chicago's city limits, and such suburban Cook County communities as Franklin Park, Northlake and Melrose Park. A subsidiary of Panasonic is expanding its Franklin Park operation to design and build systems that integrate robots into factory production.

1990 Population: 571,530. White 496,212 (87%), Black 8,518 (1%), Other 66,800 (12%). Hispanic origin 75,841 (13%). 18 and over 467,584 (82%), 62 and over 103,218 (18%). Median age: 35.

HOUSE ELECTIONS

1996 General		
Rod R. Blagojevich (D)	117,544	(64%)
Michael Patrick Flanagan (R)	65,768	(36%)
1996 Primary		
Rod R. Blagojevich (D)	33,907	(50%)
Nancy Kaszak (D)	26,115	(38%)
Ray Romero (D)	8,001	(12%)

CAMPAIGN FINANCE

	Receipts	Receipts from PACs		Expend-itures
1996				
Blagojevich (D)	$1,513,249	$295,151	(20%)	$1,552,073
Flanagan (R)	$738,892	$320,115	(43%)	$724,124

DISTRICT VOTE FOR PRESIDENT

1996			1992		
D	120,097	(63%)	**D**	124,437	(51%)
R	56,519	(30%)	**R**	80,139	(33%)
I	12,913	(7%)	**I**	39,153	(16%)

KEY VOTES

1997

Ban "partial birth" abortions	N

6 Henry J. Hyde (R)

Of Bensenville — Elected 1974, 12th term

Biographical Information
Born: April 18, 1924, Chicago, Ill.
Education: Duke U., 1943-44; Georgetown U., B.S. 1947; Loyola U., J.D. 1949.
Military Service: Navy, 1942-46; Naval Reserve, 1946-68.
Occupation: Lawyer.
Family: Widowed; four children.
Religion: Roman Catholic.
Political Career: Republican nominee for U.S. House, 1962; Ill. House, 1967-75, majority leader, 1971-73.

Capitol Office: 2110 Rayburn Bldg. 20515; 225-4561.

Committees
International Relations
International Operations & Human Rights
Judiciary (chairman)
Constitution

In Washington: Hyde, rotund and orotund, has performed yeoman's service in the Republican revolution. Although he has more than two decades of seniority in the House, Hyde adapted swiftly to the new conservatives elected in the 1990s and helped them adapt to the House. As chairman of the Judiciary Committee, he steered several major elements of the "Contract With America" safely onto the floor.

There are limits, though, to Hyde's affinity with younger-generation conservatives. He is a steadfast opponent of a constitutional amendment limiting congressional terms, an idea that has faltered in the House despite strong support from "citizen legislators" on the GOP's right flank.

Hyde's Judiciary Committee has been called upon to respond to many news events and societal trends that particularly disturb Republicans, including illegal immigration, church burnings and same-gender marriages (a new federal response to each was enacted during the 104th). In addition to working on anti-crime measures spelled out in the contract, Hyde's committee in the 104th became a battleground as Republicans sorted through how to respond to domestic terrorism. Dealing with that issue exposed another rift between Hyde and less-senior conservatives.

After much delay, Hyde pushed an anti-terrorism bill through Judiciary only to have to spend months negotiating with freshman committee Republican Bob Barr of Georgia, who had concerns about granting new authority to law enforcement officers. "My party has moved away from me," complained Hyde as Barr, after being placated in negotiations, successfully sponsored a floor amendment to strip many committee-approved provisions from the anti-terrorism bill.

There has indeed been much movement in the House GOP since Hyde came to Congress in 1975 — nearly all of it to the right, and a good share of it (on the abortion issue at least) instigated by him. As a House freshman he shook up the established order by successfully sponsoring a ban on federal funding of most abortions.

That made him a conservative icon, a status he enjoys to the present, although in the minds of some Republicans, Hyde's halo is tarnished by his disdain for term limits, his support for gun control and family leave laws, and his occasional alliances with Democrats to push specific plans such as compelling parents to pay child support.

Hyde's rhetoric lofts more than it stabs and he expresses his views passionately, but usually pleasantly. These qualities have helped Hyde keep toes within conservative bounds while not alienating GOP moderates. When Republicans wonder who might succeed Speaker Newt Gingrich, Hyde's name is on some wish lists.

But Hyde is now well into his 70s and not likely to relish the day-to-day demands of running the House. And he may lack the sort of open ambition that would allow him to elbow his way past those already holding leadership positions. When Gingrich's ethics problems were a focus in early 1997, Hyde consistently resisted talk of his being drafted to fill in as an interim Speaker should Gingrich falter, loyally noting that the Georgian "brought us out of Egypt and across the Red Sea."

Hyde displayed his willingness to be a good soldier and take orders from Gingrich during the early days of the 104th, for instance allowing the term limits constitutional amendment, which he vehemently opposed, to sail through his committee to a floor vote. Hyde said it was no problem setting aside his own priorities: "There has not been time to implement items of my personal agenda, but they are small potatoes. I'm fully in accord with the priorities of this leadership."

In the 105th, Hyde is more likely to push initiatives of personal concern, such as an overhaul of forfeiture laws to make it more difficult for the government to seize private property before a suspect is convicted of a crime. Still, his ability to set the agenda is constrained: In early 1997, the GOP leadership moved to the floor a version of a bill to ban a specific abortion procedure its opponents call "partial birth" abortion after Hyde's committee had marked up a different version.

And in 1997, Hyde was once again put in the

ILLINOIS 6
Northwest and west Chicago suburbs

All the growth stages of Chicago's western suburbs are represented in the 6th. To the south are such long established suburbs as Elmhurst, Villa Park, Lombard, Glen Ellyn and Wheaton, which grew up along an early commuter rail line. To the north are suburbs that boomed in the 1960s, as nearby O'Hare established itself as one of the world's busiest airports. In between are newer suburbs that have seen much of the area's recent population growth.

The 6th is mainly white-collar and overwhelmingly Republican. Two-thirds of its population is in Du Page County, often cited by political analysts as a symbol of GOP affluence; the remainder of the district is in equally Republican parts of suburban Cook County. Hyde has long been a politically dominant figure in the area.

Failure by a statewide Republican candidate to do extremely well in the 6th, and in Du Page County as a whole, means certain defeat. In 1996, Bob Dole carried Du Page with 51 percent. Dole carried the district as a whole with less than 50 percent of the vote, on his way to losing the state by 17 percentage points.

O'Hare (an extension of the city of Chicago) is a major employer of district residents and the economic engine for much of the 6th. Rosemont, a Cook County suburb just east of the airport, has few residents, but it has business offices and thousands of hotel rooms. The Horizon arena is in Rosemont.

Des Plaines, the largest city wholly within the 6th, is pretty much built out, as is neighboring Park Ridge, a mainly Republican suburb whose best-known native is a Democrat: Hillary Rodham Clinton. On the airport's west side are newer subdivisions in Elk Grove Village (where United Airlines has headquarters) and Bensenville (Hyde's hometown), which had double-digit growth rates during the 1980s.

The Du Page suburbs at the southern end of the 6th are mainly bedroom communities whose residents commute to downtown Chicago or to such burgeoning suburban employment centers as nearby Oak Brook and Naperville.

During the 1980s, residential subdivisions, some of them quite pricey, sprung from farmland and open space in northern Du Page. The growth was fueled by the development boom that turned Schaumburg (just over the line in the 8th) into a semi-urban center. The city of Carol Stream, at the western edge of the 6th, more than doubled in population during the 1980s. Such towns as Roselle, Bloomingdale and Glendale Heights also grew at healthy, albeit more modest, rates.

Years ago, Du Page's farms drew a number of migrant workers, including some Hispanics. Today, Hispanics make up 5 percent of the 6th's population, which is overwhelmingly white; blacks account for slightly more than 1 percent.

The 6th also backs into western Cook County to take in LaGrange Park and parts of Westchester and Brookfield.

1990 Population: 571,530. White 524,739 (92%), Black 8,461 (1%), Other 38,330 (7%). Hispanic origin 30,126 (5%). 18 and over 437,195 (76%), 62 and over 84,164 (15%). Median age: 34.

position of pushing through Judiciary a term limits amendment, an idea he opposes so strongly that he filed a brief with the Supreme Court as it considered the question in its 1994-95 term. Hyde calls term limits "a terrible mistake, a kick in the stomach of democracy," and was happy when the Supreme Court ruled state term limit ballot initiatives unconstitutional. Hyde enjoyed the triumph of watching the term limits movement dissolve into factionalism, and the proposed constitutional amendment garnered fewer votes in 1997 than it had two years previous.

Hyde is a hulk of a man with a luminous white mane and enormous hands, and his imposing physical presence is paired with a rousing oratorical style. Whatever legislation Hyde supports, he is often its most impressive spokesman, pouncing on flaws in foes' arguments with all the wit and sarcasm he once used as a Chicago trial lawyer.

Hyde earned his initial fame with an amendment in 1976 that became a fixture in the annual appropriations scene. The so-called Hyde amendment banned federal funding for most abortions until 1993 when, in light of the election of President Clinton, Hyde struggled with conservatives to fashion compromise language allowing funding for abortions in cases of rape and incest.

In 1995, with the GOP flexing its new majority muscle in Congress, Hyde lent his voice as a younger Republican, Ernest Istook of Oklahoma, carried the charge to restore the original, restrictive abortion language. "Rape is horrible," Hyde said, but "the only thing worse than rape is abortion. That's killing."

Hyde and Istook have offered competing versions of a so-called religious liberties amendment to the Constitution to ensure the right to religious expression in public places.

Hyde joined with abortion foes in worrying about whether a welfare overhaul would lead to more abortions and about military personnel receiving abortions overseas. But the central abortion battle for Hyde during the 104th may have come with his selection as chairman of the party's 1996 platform committee. With the GOP nomination settled, a fight over the abortion plank drew most of the attention during the lead-up to the San Diego GOP Convention, and Hyde quickly served notice that "I am not going to be an opening wedge in a manipulation of the platform to a softer anti-abortion tone." Despite the political concerns of party moderates, Hyde maintained the party's call for a constitutional ban on abortions, declaring the platform "a victory for life."

Hyde, a member of the International Relations Committee, was also called upon to chair a special subcommittee investigating the Clinton administration's possible complicity in shipment of arms from Iran to Bosnia. As the million-dollar panel's work got under way in the spring of 1996, Hyde said it was not likely to turn up any bombshells, and in this he proved prophetic. His other major foray into foreign policy during the 104th was a move to repeal the 1973 War Powers Resolution, which requires presidents to withdraw U.S. forces from overseas military missions within 60 days unless Congress authorizes their deployment. Hyde termed the law a "useless anachronism," but as he noted himself, Republican members were wary of granting enlarged powers to Clinton.

At Home: Though he has for years symbolized the stalwart Republican tendencies of Chicago's western suburbs, Hyde grew up in the city as an Irish Catholic Democrat. He began having doubts about the Democratic Party in the late 1940s; by 1952, he had switched parties and backed Dwight D. Eisenhower for president.

In 1962, Hyde — a lawyer and Republican precinct committeeman — was the GOP choice to challenge Democratic Rep. Roman Pucinski in a northwest Chicago district. A Republican had represented the heavily ethnic district before Pucinski won it in 1958, and Hyde came within 10,000 votes of taking it back for the GOP.

Elected to the Illinois House in 1966, he was one of its most outspoken and articulate debaters. In 1971, Hyde became majority leader; he unsuccessfully ran for Speaker in 1973.

In 1974, longtime GOP Rep. Harold Collier retired from the suburban 6th District just west of Chicago. Much of the 6th was unfamiliar to Hyde, but he dominated the six-man GOP primary.

The general election was tougher. Hyde's Democratic opponent was Edward V. Hanrahan, a former Cook County state's attorney who had been indicted for allegedly attempting to obstruct a federal investigation into a 1969 incident in which Chicago police officers killed two Black Panther Party leaders. Hanrahan was acquitted but lost re-election as prosecutor in 1972.

Although Hanrahan's exploits had made him a sort of folk hero among local blue-collar workers, he could not keep pace with Hyde in fundraising, organizing or personal campaigning. Using phone banks and an army of precinct workers, Hyde's staff turned out enough voters to give him a 53 percent tally against Hanrahan while GOP districts nationwide were falling to Democrats.

Hyde since has been invincible.

HOUSE ELECTIONS

1996 General		
Henry J. Hyde (R)	132,401	(64%)
Stephen de la Rosa (D)	68,807	(33%)
George Meyers (LIBERT)	4,746	(2%)
1996 Primary		
Henry J. Hyde (R)	53,720	(84%)
Bob Bailie (R)	6,200	(10%)
Robert L. Wheat (R)	4,315	(7%)
1994 General		
Henry J. Hyde (R)	115,664	(73%)
Tom Berry (D)	37,163	(24%)
Robert L. Hogan (LIBERT)	2,633	(2%)
Robert L. Wheat (UNI)	1,918	(1%)

Previous Winning Percentages: **1992** (66%) **1990** (67%) **1988** (74%) **1986** (75%) **1984** (75%) **1982** (68%) **1980** (67%) **1978** (66%) **1976** (61%) **1974** (53%)

CAMPAIGN FINANCE

	Receipts	Receipts from PACs		Expend-itures
1996				
Hyde (R)	$546,467	$322,583	(59%)	$434,160
De La Rosa (D)	$6,991	$1,187	(17%)	$11,139
1994				
Hyde (R)	$367,184	$170,445	(46%)	$423,027
Berry (D)	$18,095	$11,750	(65%)	$14,449

DISTRICT VOTE FOR PRESIDENT

1996		1992	
D	93,359 (43%)	**D**	86,444 (33%)
R	105,797 (48%)	**R**	121,863 (47%)
I	18,796 (9%)	**I**	52,734 (20%)

KEY VOTES

1997	
Ban "partial birth" abortions	Y
1996	
Approve farm bill	Y
Deny public education to illegal immigrants	Y
Repeal ban on certain assault-style weapons	N
Increase minimum wage	N
Freeze defense spending	N
Approve welfare overhaul	Y
1995	
Approve balanced-budget constitutional amendment	Y
Relax Clean Water Act regulations	Y
Oppose limits on environmental regulations	N
Reduce projected Medicare spending	Y
Approve GOP budget with tax and spending cuts	Y

VOTING STUDIES

	Presidential Support		Party Unity		Conservative Coalition	
Year	S	O	S	O	S	O
1996	39	61	92	7	90	6
1995	21	78	94	5	97	3
1994	54	46	85†	13†	83	14
1993	38†	58†	82†	14†	82	9
1992	60	14	59	14	58	4
1991	85	14	83	13	92	8

† Not eligible for all recorded votes.

INTEREST GROUP RATINGS

Year	ADA	AFL-CIO	CCUS	ACU
1996	10	n/a	100	90
1995	0	0	96	68
1994	5	11	96	90
1993	10	17	82	87
1992	15	44	75	94
1991	10	17	70	80

7 Danny K. Davis (D)

Of Chicago — Elected 1996, 1st term

Biographical Information

Born: Sept. 6, 1941, Parkdale, Ark.

Education: Arkansas A.M.&N. College, B.A. 1961; Chicago State U., M.A. 1968; Union Institute, Ph.D. 1977.

Occupation: Health care consultant; teacher.

Family: Wife, Vera; two children.

Religion: Baptist.

Political Career: Chicago City Council, 1979-90; sought Democratic nomination for U.S. House, 1984, 1986; Cook County commissioner, 1990-97; candidate for Chicago mayor, 1991.

Capitol Office: 1218 Longworth Bldg. 20515; 225-5006.

Committees

Government Reform & Oversight
Government Management, Information & Technology; Postal Service

Small Business
Empowerment; Tax & Exports

The Path to Washington: The third time proved the charm for Davis, who twice waged unsuccessful primary challenges to incumbent Democratic Rep. Cardiss Collins in the 1980s. Davis, a close associate of the late black Chicago Mayor Harold Washington, claimed Collins was too close to the traditional Democratic power brokers.

When Collins announced her retirement after 11 full terms, Davis — a Cook County commissioner and former Chicago city alderman — jumped into the race to succeed her. The best-known of the contenders, he immediately became a front-runner, thanks to his reputation as a forceful orator and strong defender of inner-city programs.

But his opposition to the Democratic organization, including an abortive 1991 challenge to Mayor Richard M. Daley, came back to haunt him. The party hierarchy lined up behind other candidates in the 7th District primary, the winner of which would be all but assured of victory in the heavily black and Democratic district.

Many party leaders supported Chicago Alderman Percy Z. Giles, who was expected to be a top-line contender but found himself ensnared in allegations linking him to an ongoing corruption scandal. Though he was not charged, his campaign was damaged severely.

With Giles wounded by the investigation and no other candidate able to catch on, Davis easily lapped a 10-person field to win.

During the primary campaign, he touted his efforts to improve education, reduce crime, and spur economic growth. He was endorsed by retiring Democratic Sen. Paul Simon, 1st District Democratic Rep. Bobby L. Rush, and most of organized labor, including the AFL-CIO, United Auto Workers, Teamsters, and the Chicago Teachers Union.

In the fall, he had no trouble defeating Republican nominee Randy Borow, who called for tax cuts to spur economic growth in urban areas. Davis defended government-funded efforts to help inner cities and called for more federal funding for job training programs.

Davis supports increasing federal aid to education and the AmeriCorps community volunteer program. He also called for summer jobs programs for youth, funding to schools for local anti-violence programs, and efforts to fight drugs in schools. He supports abortion rights, a single-payer national health care system, and legislation to prevent discrimination against gays and lesbians in the military, housing and employment. He opposes term limits and taxpayer-financed vouchers to allow students to attend private or religious schools. He supports the Equal Rights Amendment, wants to increase job training for welfare recipients, and has proposed making federal elected officials subject to sexual harassment laws. He said he would work to protect the environment and ward off cuts to Medicare, the federal health insurance program for the elderly and disabled.

But despite his decidedly left-of-center views, Davis said he wants to work with lawmakers on the other side of the aisle. He said this year's freshman class was more interested in finding solutions than in fighting the partisan battles that characterized the start of the 104th Congress.

A native of Arkansas who first came to Chicago in 1961, Davis is a former high school teacher and college instructor. He has worked as a health planner and administrator, has hosted a weekly radio talk show, and has a long history of community involvement in civil rights and housing issues. He co-chaired President Clinton's 1992 campaign in Illinois and was named by Clinton to the board of directors of the National Housing Partnership.

Davis challenged Collins for the Democratic House nomination in 1984, one year after Collins had backed Mayor Jane Byrne for renomination over Washington, the eventual winner. Davis lost by 10 percentage points but held Collins under a majority of the vote. Davis tried again in 1986 but lost decisively.

In the 105th Congress, Davis sits on the Small Business and Government Reform and Oversight committees.

ILLINOIS 7
Chicago — Downtown; West Side

The black-majority 7th links Chicago's bustling downtown business district with the city's poorest minority neighborhoods. These economic extremes are symbolized by two stretches of apartment buildings. One lines Lake Shore Drive running north from downtown: These are the plush high-rises of the "Gold Coast." The other is in the 7th's southern end, on a barren stretch overlooking the Dan Ryan Expressway: a huge housing project, the Robert Taylor Homes. Abject poverty, crime, drugs, teenage pregnancy and other urban ills are rife here.

Poverty also is persistent on the city's West Side, home to most of the district's blacks. Parts of this area are moonscapes of abandoned factories and rubble-strewn lots.

Although the 7th fills up daily with white commuters, the permanent population is nearly two-thirds black. A reliably Democratic district across the ballot, the only genuine political contests in the 7th are the Democratic primaries.

At the eastern end of the district are downtown Chicago and the corporate headquarters, financial institutions and professional organizations that make Chicago the Midwest's leading business center. Sears Tower, the world's tallest building measured to its roof, is here.

Across the Chicago River is the upscale "Magnificent Mile" shopping area, the skyscraping John Hancock building and the Gold Coast. But even on the North Side there is anguish, in the troubled Cabrini-Green housing project. South of downtown, the 7th picks up Soldier Field (home of professional football's Bears), Chinatown and white, ethnic Bridgeport, the political base of the Daley family. The district then edges through black areas including the Robert Taylor Homes, whose buildings were once seen as exemplars of progressive social policy but today are denounced as vertical ghettos.

The near West Side is bisected by the Eisenhower Expressway. To the north is a mainly black and poor area. The United Center, where basketball's Bulls and hockey's Black Hawks play, is here. To the south of the highway is the University of Illinois at Chicago (24,600 students) and the hospitals that make up the West Side Medical Center.

The West Side neighborhoods of Garfield Park and Lawndale define Chicago ghetto life. As late as the 1950s, Lawndale was a largely Jewish area, but an influx of blacks spurred a "white flight" exacerbated by blockbusting real estate agents. Parts of Lawndale never have recovered from riots in the 1960s and a siege of arson-for-profit blazes in the 1970s.

The Austin neighborhood, at Chicago's western edge, has some better-off areas that border the largely prosperous suburbs of Oak Park and River Forest. Oak Park is the most settled of Chicago's western suburbs; most of its housing stock was built before 1940. Farther west are middle- and working-class suburbs, several of which are largely black.

1990 Population: 571,530. White 165,724 (29%), Black 375,170 (66%), Other 30,636 (5%). Hispanic origin 24,763 (4%). 18 and over 406,971 (71%), 62 and over 70,143 (12%). Median age: 30.

HOUSE ELECTIONS

1996 General		
Danny K. Davis (D)	149,568	(82%)
Randy Borow (R)	27,241	(15%)
Chauncey L. Stroud (I)	1,944	(1%)
1996 Primary		
Danny K. Davis (D)	22,188	(33%)
Dorothy J. Tillman (D)	13,433	(20%)
Ed H. Smith (D)	8,215	(12%)
Bobbie L. Steele (D)	8,148	(12%)
Percy Z. Giles (D)	7,378	(11%)
Joan Powell (D)	2,753	(4%)
Joan A. Sullivan (D)	2,751	(4%)
Samuel Mendenhall (D)	2,035	(3%)

CAMPAIGN FINANCE

	Receipts	Receipts from PACs		Expend-itures
1996				
Davis (D)	$429,921	$164,800	(38%)	$410,662
Borow (R)	$60,152	$1,072	(2%)	$33,155
Stroud (I)	$1,380	0		$10,094

DISTRICT VOTE FOR PRESIDENT

	1996		1992
D	152,647 (82%)	**D**	184,383 (78%)
R	25,764 (14%)	**R**	35,437 (15%)
I	5,041 (3%)	**I**	15,952 (7%)

KEY VOTES

1997

Ban "partial birth" abortions	N

8 Philip M. Crane (R)

Of Wauconda — Elected 1969; 14th full term

Biographical Information
Born: Nov. 3, 1930, Chicago, Ill.
Education: DePauw U., 1948-50; Hillsdale College, B.A. 1952; U. of Michigan, 1952-54; U. of Vienna (Austria), 1953, 1956; Indiana U., M.A. 1961, Ph.D. 1963.
Military Service: Army, 1954-56.
Occupation: Professor; author; advertising executive.
Family: Wife, Arlene Catherine Johnson; eight children.
Religion: Protestant.
Political Career: Sought Republican nomination for president, 1980.

Capitol Office: 233 Cannon Bldg. 20515; 225-3711.

Committees
Ways & Means
Health; Trade (chairman)
Joint Taxation

In Washington: Crane, a onetime "wunderkind" among movement conservatives who offered himself as a younger alternative to Ronald Reagan in the 1980 GOP presidential sweepstakes, has now served in the House long enough to rank second in seniority among all of the chamber's Republicans.

But Crane shares the hard-edged, uncompromising sensibility prevalent among the GOP newcomers who have thrust the party into majority control of Congress, and he can match the most ardent among the youngsters on issues from tax reduction to government funding of the arts.

Crane ranks second on the Ways and Means Committee and chairs its Trade Subcommittee. He does not share the skepticism of free trade harbored by some "America Firsters" on the GOP Right. Rather, through his subcommittee he has sought to promote American trade with countries such as China, Chile, Bulgaria and Cambodia. His panel also is overseeing a restructuring of the customs service.

Getting trade legislation through Congress usually requires building a bipartisan coalition, but Crane has provoked grumbling from some Ways and Means Democrats who say he shuts them out of the drafting process. When his subcommittee during the 104th planned to mark up legislation granting fast-track authority on trade agreements, Democrats complained that instead of consulting with them, Republicans handed down a completed version just before the markup. (Fast track authority enables the president to request expedited, no-amendments congressional passage of trade agreements.)

In light of questionable 1996 campaign donations winging President Clinton's way from an Indonesian construction company, Crane was happy to use the oversight capabilities of his subcommittee to demand documents from the U.S. trade representative's office related to trade policy toward Indonesia.

As that inquiry suggests, Crane remains a staunch partisan. He dug in his heels against Democratic-driven efforts in 1996 to increase the minimum wage. He chided fellow Republicans who broke with the party to support the politically popular increase, arguing that "Playing 'me too' with the Democrats kept us in the minority for 40 years. Only by unapologetically distinguishing our party's ideas from the Democrats' demagoguery can we keep our majority in Congress."

Crane liked the legislation's tax provisions, which offered about $10 billion worth of tax breaks to business, but he voted against the final package anyway.

Crane has long argued in favor of a flat tax, an idea which gained currency in Republican circles during the 104th. Crane said he first conceived of his version of the flat tax — which he has been plumping since the 1970s and mentioned in his abortive 1980 presidential bid — as akin to a tithe wherein taxpayers would offer 10 percent of their income to the government.

Crane's version would exempt businesses and the first $10,000 in income. Crane said he would back a flat-tax version proposed by House Majority Leader Dick Armey, R-Texas, that set its rate at 17 percent. but he contended that Armey bought into a "Marxist argument" because he would tax business. Crane also favors abolishing the estate and gift taxes.

More than once during his career, Crane's opinions on tax policy have been ahead of the curve of debate on the subject. But when the ideas he espoused began working their way through the legislative process, Crane was not known for fighting in the trenches for their passage. He was one of the earliest congressional supporters of tax indexing, introducing legislation as far back as 1974. But while he could claim victory with its passage in 1981, he was not prominent in the key negotiations on the issue.

In another area where Crane anticipated the younger Republican revolutionaries, he has long opposed federal funding for the arts and public broadcasting. His Privatization of the Arts Act, which languished when Democrats controlled Congress, looked like it would take on new life in

ILLINOIS 8
Northwest Cook County — Schaumburg; Palatine

There are House districts in the Chicago area where the major concerns are economic development and jobs. Then there are districts, such as the suburban and affluent 8th, where the main worries are overdevelopment and traffic.

The 8th is made up of the suburbs of northwest Cook County (which provide about 60 percent of the district's votes); the developing exurbia of southwestern Lake County; and the more remote (but also growing) lake-country towns near Wisconsin. These areas combine to make the 8th the most Republican district in Illinois.

Yet there are signs that recent suburban growth may have tempered the staunch conservatism that long made Crane virtually untouchable. After struggling in 1992, Crane in 1994 won a plurality against three primary opponents before easily dispatching his Democratic challenger in the fall. Crane recovered his footing in 1996.

Although George Bush carried the 8th in 1988 with a ringing 71 percent (and by a lesser margin four years later), Bob Dole was able to eke out a victory in 1996 with just under a majority. Still, it was Dole's second best performance in the state.

The district has some well-established suburbs in its southeast corner, the nearest part to Chicago, including Mount Prospect and the southern part of Arlington Heights (the rest is in the 10th District). The biggest boom has been farther west; development has been abetted by access to Interstates 90 and 290 and proximity to O'Hare Airport (in the 6th District). Just 30 years ago, Schaumburg was still mainly rural. Today, it is a satellite city of 68,000 and the largest community totally within the 8th. The Motorola electronics company is in Schaumburg, as is Delta Air Lines' regional office. Hoffman Estates has expanded nearly as fast; and retailer Sears has moved its merchandising group to the city.

Rolling Meadows, with some high-tech industry, and mainly residential Palatine lie to the north. At the west end of Cook County is a portion of Elgin that has experienced residential growth.

Some exclusive communities have sought to remain exclusive. Barrington Hills, which sprawls among Cook, Lake, McHenry and Kane counties, has slightly more than 4,000 residents. But growth is unbridled in other Lake County communities: Lake Zurich grew by 81 percent in the 1980s to 15,000 residents. The Kemper insurance company is based in nearby Long Grove.

The northern part of the district, with its "chain o' lakes," has a number of vacation homes but is far less densely populated. Residents who rely on seasonal employment are also less well-off than the district norm.

At the northeast edge of the 8th is Gurnee, across the 10th District line from Waukegan. Spurred by its location on Interstate 94, Gurnee nearly doubled in population in the 1980s, to just under 14,000. It is also home to a thriving outlet mall.

1990 Population: 571,530. White 527,051 (92%), Black 9,442 (2%), Other 35,037 (6%). Hispanic origin 31,570 (6%). 18 and over 420,358 (74%), 62 and over 53,816 (9%). Median age: 32.

the GOP-run 104th, and Crane scored points contending that the National Endowment for the Arts is "non-essential." He complained that the John F. Kennedy Center for the Performing Arts in Washington, D.C., which received $10.3 million from the government in fiscal 1995, is an example of the nation subsidizing cultural events for residents in the capital. (Defenders of the appropriation note that the Center attracts many tourists as well as locals.)

Despite Crane's protestations, the NEA survived funding fights in the 104th, and even its enemies acknowledge they may not have the votes to kill it during the 105th.

Noting that several children's programs broadcast on public television generate millions of dollars through merchandising and licensing, Crane contended that public broadcasting could easily survive without federal support. But his 1995 amendment to kill such funding over the course of three years was easily turned aside, 72-350.

Crane's minimalist attitude about the federal government's proper scope of responsibilities mirrors the beliefs of Class of 1994 Republicans who want to shutter government agencies. "There are four functions of government that we should fund: defense, state, justice and the treasury," Crane told the Chicago Sun Times in 1995. "Even the Department of Agriculture, which was created in the 1850s, is not essential."

Crane also finds common cause with the isolationist wing of his party in opposing payment of the United States' back dues to the United Nations, signing a February 1997 letter to Speaker Newt Gingrich that said, "in short, there is no United States debt."

Crane launched his 1980 presidential campaign from his base as chairman of the American Conservative Union. After Crane spent a year trying to organize support for the New Hampshire primary, William Loeb, then the acerbic Manchester Union Leader publisher and political baron, ran articles accusing Crane of heavy drinking and womanizing. By the time

New Hampshire voted, Crane was a minor candidate and received just 1.8 percent of the vote. He won five convention delegates but withdrew and endorsed Reagan.

At Home: For more than two decades, Crane thrived in the conservative environment of the affluent northwest Chicago suburbs and exurbs. It was thus a jarring change in 1992 and 1994 when he faced threatening challenges. In 1996, though, he had no such problems, winning renomination with 75 percent of the vote; Democrats had to recruit a last minute stand-in to oppose him.

In 1992, Gary Skoien, a developer and former state official, tried to wrest the GOP nomination from Crane. Skoien called himself a pragmatic conservative and portrayed Crane as an obstructionist who had let his ties to the district attenuate. Skoien won several newspaper endorsements, but Crane maintained the loyalty of local Republican organizations and hung on to win with 55 percent.

In the fall, Crane faced Democrat Sheila A. Smith, owner of an appliance and lighting fixtures factory. While pursuing such Democratic Party issues as defense spending cuts and increased funding for public works, Smith told the usually Republican constituency that she was a different kind of Democrat. But Crane's promise to continue his practice of never voting for a tax increase earned him another term, albeit with an unspectacular 56 percent.

Skoien was back in 1994, but he was joined in the GOP primary by state Sen. Peter Fitzgerald. A longtime Crane protégé, Fitzgerald spent more than $900,000 on the race, most of it his own money.

While Skoien continued his wooing of moderate Republicans, Fitzgerald went after Crane's conservative base. Crane's fiscally conservative image was damaged when he was included in a "PrimeTime Live" television show about trips that members of Congress took on the tab of special interest groups. Crane also had lost some party organization support and had to reestablish his credentials, which he did partly by appearing on the radio show of convicted Watergate conspirator G. Gordon Liddy. Crane won only 40 percent of the primary vote while Fitzgerald and Skoien split the opposition. In the strong GOP tide in the fall, Crane won with 65 percent.

Prior to 1992, Crane had fallen below 60 percent only in his first two House contests. In 1969, he entered the Republican primary in a special election that followed Rep. Donald Rumsfeld's appointment by President Richard M. Nixon to head the Office of Economic Opportunity. With the aid of fellow conservative activists, Crane topped a seven-candidate field with 22 percent of the vote.

Crane's Democratic opponent in the special election tried to paint him as an ideological extremist. But Crane's soft-spoken and articulate manner helped him win with 58 percent.

HOUSE ELECTIONS

1996 General		
Philip M. Crane (R)	127,763	(62%)
Elizabeth Ann "Betty" Hull (D)	74,068	(36%)
H. Daniel Druck (LIBERT)	3,474	(2%)
1996 Primary		
Philip M. Crane (R)	40,489	(75%)
Don Huff (R)	13,364	(25%)
1994 General		
Philip M. Crane (R)	88,225	(65%)
Robert C. Walberg (D)	47,654	(35%)

Previous Winning Percentages: **1992** (56%) **1990** (82%) **1988** (75%) **1986** (78%) **1984** (78%) **1982** (66%) **1980** (74%) **1978** (80%) **1976** (73%) **1974** (61%) **1972** (74%) **1970** (58%) **1969†** (58%)

† Special election

CAMPAIGN FINANCE

	Receipts	Receipts from PACs	Expend-itures
1996			
Crane (R)	$758,798	$456,114 (60%)	$534,151
Hull (D)	$30,394	$3,550 (12%)	$30,804
1994			
Crane (R)	$695,150	$143,895 (21%)	$722,267
Walberg (D)	$66,977	$6,818 (10%)	$66,960

DISTRICT VOTE FOR PRESIDENT

1996		1992	
D	86,907 (41%)	**D**	76,327 (31%)
R	105,742 (50%)	**R**	118,714 (48%)
I	19,482 (9%)	**I**	54,269 (22%)

KEY VOTES

1997	
Ban "partial-birth" abortions	Y
1996	
Approve farm bill	Y
Deny public education to illegal immigrants	Y
Repeal ban on certain assault-style weapons	Y
Increase minimum wage	N
Freeze defense spending	N
Approve welfare overhaul	Y
1995	
Approve balanced-budget constitutional amendment	Y
Relax Clean Water Act regulations	Y
Oppose limits on environmental regulations	N
Reduce projected Medicare spending	Y
Approve GOP budget with tax and spending cuts	Y

VOTING STUDIES

	Presidential Support		Party Unity		Conservative Coalition	
Year	S	O	S	O	S	O
1996	34	65	96	2	92	4
1995	14	79	92	2	93	1
1994	24	60	90	2	69	17
1993	18	82	93	3	82	18
1992	83	12	94	2	90	6
1991	71	20	87	5	89	5

INTEREST GROUP RATINGS

Year	ADA	AFL-CIO	CCUS	ACU
1996	0	n/a	100	100
1995	0	0	100	100
1994	5	0	83	100
1993	15	0	91	96
1992	0	8	71	100
1991	0	0	89	100

9 Sidney R. Yates (D)

Of Chicago — Elected 1948, 24th term
Did not serve 1963-65.

Biographical Information

Born: Aug. 27, 1909, Chicago, Ill.
Education: U. of Chicago, Ph.B. 1931, J.D. 1933.
Military Service: Navy, 1944-46.
Occupation: Lawyer.
Family: Wife, Adeline Holleb; one child.
Religion: Jewish.
Political Career: U.S. House of Representatives, 1948-62; Democratic nominee for U.S. Senate, 1962; Ambassador to the Trusteeship Council of the United Nations, 1962-64.
Capitol Office: 2109 Rayburn Bldg. 20515; 225-2111.

Committees

Appropriations
Foreign Operations, Export Financing & Related Programs; Interior (ranking)

In Washington: As the oldest and longest-serving House member, Yates has the distinction of being the only Democrat in the House to have served under Republican rule before 1995. The last time Republicans controlled Congress, in 1953, Yates was already in his third term.

Yates, who is six decades older than the youngest member of the House, Harold E. Ford Jr., D-Tenn., said just before the GOP took control of the Hill with the start of the 104th Congress that "It wasn't much fun to be in the minority then. We'll have to wait and see how much fun it is now."

Yates was often frustrated during the 104th Congress, and while that is likely to remain the case in the 105th, one thing may make the burden more bearable: Yates has announced that this term, his 24th, will be his last.

Yates' priorities — arts funding and environmental protection — run counter to the currents of conservative Republican desire. In his frustration, Yates grew fond of quoting turn-of-the century Speaker Thomas Brackett Reed, who said that the role of the minority is merely to make a quorum and draw its salaries.

For four decades, Yates has served on the powerful Appropriations Committee and for nearly 20 years wielded tremendous power as a member of the panel's "college of cardinals" (he claims credit for the moniker). He ends his career as the ranking member of the Interior Appropriations Subcommittee.

Yates missed a number of votes after being hospitalized with an embolism in his left lung in June 1995; but even in the winter of his long career, Yates managed to have an impact, drawing funds for his district and leading a revolt against a controversial Interior spending bill.

"My promise isn't to deliver," Yates told the Chicago Sun-Times in 1996. "My promise is to fight, and I did that." Although there are other members in the Democratic Party better known for their environmental views, Yates is considered by the "green" movement to be one of its staunchest supporters.

The House twice sent the fiscal 1996 spending bill back to conference over mining and forest issues. Yates and his allies insisted on an extension of a moratorium on mining patents, which even some Republican deficit hawks deride as a giveaway to private interests. Yates was also offended by the attempt to open up Alaska's Tongass National Forest to increased timber harvesting.

After the appropriations measure finally passed in December 1995, President Clinton vetoed the bill; Interior monies were freed with a catchall package enacted nearly midway through the fiscal year.

Republicans did not even attempt to include the mining and forest provisions in the fiscal 1997 Interior bill, but this did not please Yates much. He was upset about reduced spending levels for arts agencies such as the National Endowment for the Arts, which the Republicans had failed to kill, and offered numerous failed amendments to restore funding in markups and floor debate — including an amendment that would have restored NEA funding, offset by a large increase in mining royalty fees. He also failed in attempts to strip language from a rescission bill that allowed for increased salvage harvesting of dead and dying trees from federal land.

At the helm of the Interior subpanel, now chaired by Ralph Regula, R-Ohio, Yates earned a reputation as taskmaster. His hearings were among the most detailed in the House, and he regularly did much of his own research. On the floor, Yates would admonish members who did not have the same command of his bill's facts, and during hearings he would probe administration witnesses like a crafty lawyer and nudge his colleagues toward consensus.

Yates is the second-ranking Democrat on Appropriations. He has served longer than David R. Obey of Wisconsin, the man ahead of him on the Democratic side. But Yates, a proponent of the House's seniority system, stayed out of the

ILLINOIS 9
Chicago — North Side Lakefront and suburbs; Evanston

The political core of the 9th is a wedge that takes in the northeast corner of Chicago and the near-in suburbs of Evanston and Skokie. This district, the most ethnically and racially diverse in the Chicago area, is also one of the most liberal voting areas in Illinois. It provides a secure base for Democrats and offsets more conservative turf in the district's western end.

A bit more than two-thirds of the district's residents are non-Hispanic whites; the remaining constituency is divided nearly evenly among blacks, Hispanics and people of Asian heritage. Although the sizable minority population has an influence on its partisan direction, the 9th stands out as the most Democratic white-majority district in the state.

In 1996, Bill Clinton won comfortably here with 69 percent of the vote.

About two-thirds of the district's residents live within Chicago's boundaries. The 9th reaches a point at Diversey Street and Lake Michigan. A series of high-rises along Lake Shore Drive, many of them upscale, overlook Lincoln Park and the Lakeview community. This part of the 9th was home to some of the "lakefront liberals" who rose up to challenge the Democratic machine during the 1970s.

The community of New Town is a center for the Chicago gay population. To the north, at Addison and Clark, is venerable Wrigley Field, the Chicago Cubs' "friendly confines." The surrounding neighborhood had grown a bit seedy over the years, but an influx of young professionals has made "Wrigleyville" a hot real estate market.

The community of Uptown is mainly working-class, with some low-income areas. Much of the district's Hispanic population lives here; there is a settlement of Vietnamese immigrants as well. The largest black concentration in the Chicago part of the district is nearby.

Bordering the lake just to the north is the campus of Loyola University (15,800 students). Rogers Park, tucked in the city's northeast corner, is polyglot and mainly middle-class. Much of the district's Jewish population lives in the Chicago community of West Ridge and in Skokie, an adjacent suburb.

Evanston, with a population of more than 70,000, is the district's lakeside suburb. Blacks make up a fifth of the city's population and live mainly in the urbanized south part of the city. Northwestern University and its 14,200 students dominate northern Evanston; the surrounding residential areas anchor suburban Chicago's affluent North Shore region.

In the district's western reaches, its ethnicity and political attitudes change. Many of the residents are of Irish, Italian and East European heritage and have moved from the city's "bungalow belt" to single-family homes in comfortable Norwood Park and Niles or upscale Forest Glen. Conservative attitudes prevail in much of this area.

1990 Population: 571,530. White 417,578 (73%), Black 69,034 (12%), Other 84,918 (15%). Hispanic origin 55,719 (10%). 18 and over 467,139 (82%), 62 and over 110,132 (19%). Median age: 35.

fray as Obey vaulted over several more senior members to become committee chairman in a bitter 1994 battle to succeed the late William H. Natcher, D-Ky.

More comfortable behind the scenes, Yates can be provoked to take center stage as he did during the Reagan years. His urbane and low-key style masks a stubbornness that allows him to stick with an issue for years, if necessary, to get what he wants. His tenacity came through in 1981 when the Interior Subcommittee simply ignored Reagan's requested cuts.

As Interior Subcommittee chairman, Yates almost single-handedly blocked a proposed 50 percent funding cut for the NEA, and in 1988 he engineered a far-reaching moratorium against administration plans to lease offshore lands for drilling.

A fierce, Truman-era liberal, Yates sometimes takes too liberal a position for his own party. Yet he is a pragmatic politician: As conservatives made their perennial run at the arts endowment in 1994, Yates and fellow Democrat Rep. Norm Dicks of Washington countered deep cuts offered by GOP Reps. Cliff Stearns of Florida and Spencer Bachus of Alabama with reductions of their own until the House finally reached a compromise of merely 2 percent. That was enough to drive home a point to endowment officials about funding priorities. In 1995, Yates agreed not to make a ruckus about spending cuts in committee in return for Regula fighting to preserve at least some funding against GOP attempts to abolish the agency on the floor.

Yates also managed to secure significant funds for the Chicago area during the 104th, inserting earmarks totaling more than $65 million for Chicago-area parks, housing, shoreline and sewage projects. He also succeeded in upping the funding for the U.S. Holocaust Memorial Museum, another of his pet arts projects.

At Home: Yates entered Congress in January 1949, but a two-year hiatus that followed his gamble for the Senate in 1962 — when he challenged then-Minority Leader Everett M. Dirksen — has prevented him from enjoying the full measure of that seniority. Nonetheless, as Yates aged he could always tout his influential Appropriations position to fend off the occasional younger challenger insisting it was is time for the long-tenured incumbent to go.

In 1982, Yates won two-thirds of the vote to swat aside Republican Catherine Bertini, an articulate moderate who later held appointive positions in the Reagan and Bush administrations. Since then, the local GOP has conceded to Yates. In fact, Yates has not had a close House race since 1956, when he won with 54 percent.

Yates' long House career began with a longshot candidacy. In 1948, recently returned to his Chicago law practice after World War II, Yates was drafted at the last minute by the Chicago Democratic organization to run against Republican Rep. Robert J. Twyman, who was expected to win re-election easily. But the Democratic ticket swept Illinois that year, and Yates came in with an 18,000-vote majority. He kept his seat with narrow wins in 1950 and 1952 before settling in comfortably.

After seven terms, Yates sacrificed his electoral security for a Senate challenge to Dirksen that had the backing of Chicago Mayor Richard J. Daley and the Democratic organization. But some Democrats thought Yates was undercut by his party's leadership: They contended that President John F. Kennedy secretly favored Dirksen, considering him the friendliest GOP Senate leader he was likely to get. The Cuban missile crisis took place in the final month of the campaign, and Dirksen was consulted often and openly by the White House.

But Yates, who received 47 percent of the vote, rejected rumors of a Kennedy-Dirksen compact. In 1963, Kennedy appointed Yates U.S. representative to the U.N. Trusteeship Council, a post he held for more than a year.

In the fall of 1964, the Chicago Democratic organization suddenly found a judgeship for Rep. Edward Finnegan, whom it had chosen to replace Yates in the House. Since Finnegan already had been renominated, the local party had the right to designate a candidate for the vacancy. To no one's surprise, Yates was the choice. Spared the trouble of a primary, Yates easily won his way back to the House for the start of a second, much longer stay.

HOUSE ELECTIONS

1996 General		
Sidney R. Yates (D)	124,319	(63%)
Joseph Walsh (R)	71,763	(37%)
1996 Primary		
Sidney R. Yates (D)	44,259	(84%)
Terrence R. Gilhooly (D)	5,725	(11%)
Seth Barrett Tillman (D)	2,763	(5%)
1994 General		
Sidney R. Yates (D)	94,404	(66%)
George Edward Larney (R)	48,419	(34%)

Previous Winning Percentages: **1992** (68%) **1990** (71%) **1988** (66%) **1986** (72%) **1984** (68%) **1982** (67%) **1980** (73%) **1978** (75%) **1976** (72%) **1974** (100%) **1972** (68%) **1970** (76%) **1968** (64%) **1966** (60%) **1964** (64%) **1960** (60%) **1958** (67%) **1956** (54%) **1954** (60%) **1952** (52%) **1950** (52%) **1948** (55%)

CAMPAIGN FINANCE

	Receipts	Receipts from PACs		Expend-itures
1996				
Yates (D)	$164,273	$18,000	(11%)	$184,005
Walsh (R)	$111,378	$6,066	(5%)	$115,401
1994				
Yates (D)	$201,668	$33,550	(17%)	$217,952
Larney (R)	$48,166	$1,514	(3%)	$48,121

DISTRICT VOTE FOR PRESIDENT

	1996		1992
D	139,166 (69%)	**D**	155,503 (61%)
R	52,263 (26%)	**R**	68,485 (27%)
I	9,732 (5%)	**I**	29,314 (12%)

KEY VOTES

1997	
Ban "partial birth" abortions	N
1996	
Approve farm bill	N
Deny public education to illegal immigrants	N
Repeal ban on certain assault-style weapons	N
Increase minimum wage	Y
Freeze defense spending	Y
Approve welfare overhaul	N
1995	
Approve balanced-budget constitutional amendment	N
Relax Clean Water Act regulations	N
Oppose limits on environmental regulations	Y
Reduce projected Medicare spending	N
Approve GOP budget with tax and spending cuts	N

VOTING STUDIES

	Presidential Support		Party Unity		Conservative Coalition	
Year	S	O	S	O	S	O
1996	72	19	84	4	8	82
1995	76	7	80	2	1	81
1994	72	28	94	2	0	94
1993	75	17	91	2	2	86
1992	14	77	88	2	4	90
1991	23	68	90	3	5	92

INTEREST GROUP RATINGS

Year	ADA	AFL-CIO	CCUS	ACU
1996	85	n/a	7	0
1995	85	100	17	4
1994	100	89	25	0
1993	85	100	0	0
1992	95	100	29	0
1991	95	100	22	6

10 John Edward Porter (R)

Of Wilmette — Elected 1980; 9th full term

Biographical Information

Born: June 1, 1935, Evanston, Ill.

Education: Massachusetts Institute of Technology, 1953-54; Northwestern U., B.S., B.A. 1957; U. of Michigan, J.D. 1961.

Military Service: Army Reserve, 1958-64.

Occupation: Lawyer.

Family: Wife, Kathryn Cameron; five children.

Religion: Presbyterian.

Political Career: Republican nominee for Cook County Circuit Court judge, 1970; Ill. House, 1973-79; Republican nominee for U.S. House, 1978.

Capitol Office: 2373 Rayburn Bldg. 20515; 225-4835.

Committees

Appropriations

Foreign Operations, Export Financing & Related Programs; Labor, Health & Human Services, Education & Related Agencies (chairman); Military Construction

In Washington: Porter stands athwart the major fault lines running through the contemporary Republican Party. The spending bill he oversees as an Appropriations Committee cardinal is the biggest single pot of domestic money; it funds many government programs that he and other GOP pragmatists see as worthwhile initiatives. But typically he operates under orders from the House Republican leadership to reduce spending on these programs, and in some cases he faces pressure from the right to eliminate them altogether.

Porter has more than his share of differences with prevailing Republican orthodoxy. He breaks with most of his party colleagues in supporting gun control and robust environmental protections, and he thinks abortion should remain a legal option (though he did vote in the 105th Congress to ban a particular abortion technique that opponents call a "partial-birth" abortion). His commitment to deficit reduction led him during the 104th to oppose tax cut plans proffered by the GOP leadership and to cast a wary eye on increases in Pentagon spending.

As chairman of the Appropriations Subcommittee on Labor-HHS-Education, Porter dishes out funds for international family planning programs and Medicaid funding, two arenas for annual fights over abortion. In the 104th, Porter's bill was the staging ground for fights over a range of other issues, including worker protections, AIDS and education. In particular, the battle over the fiscal 1996 Labor-HHS bill fed numerous Democratic campaign ads that pilloried the GOP for seeking to cut federal spending on student loans, summer jobs programs, Goals 2000 education grants and assistance for low-income citizens in paying heating bills. The Labor-HHS bill funds an alphabet soup of agencies doing work that many on the GOP right see as no business of the federal government, including the Corporation for Public Broadcasting (CPB) and the National Endowments for the Arts and Humanities (NEA and NEH).

Recoiling at portrayals of the GOP as uncaring budget slashers, Porter in the 104th declared himself and his party "fans" of such programs as Head Start and Job Corps. But he contended that any program, no matter how worthwhile, could contribute to the larger goal of deficit reduction.

Some think Porter's blend of fiscal conservatism and social-issue moderation would make him an appealing candidate statewide, but he took a pass on the open 1996 Illinois Senate race. Porter received early encouragement to run in 1998 from Senate Majority Leader Trent Lott of Mississippi, but he opted against making that race, too.

More than once as chairman, Porter has played the role of loyal party man and gamely defended cuts in programs he supports in principle. Parrying Democratic criticism of a GOP proposal to cut more than $3 billion for the Department of Education, Porter said, "The sky is not falling," noting that most schools receive their funds from state and local governments.

Still, Porter's evident lack of fervor for cutting many programs backed by Democrats has caused him some problems within the House Republican Conference. Porter was one target of a party rules change proposed by John T. Doolittle, R-Calif., just before the 105th Congress that would have required Conference approval of subcommittee chairmen; it was voted down.

One area where Porter was able to increase spending during the 104th was in health, proposing a boost of $642 million for the National Institutes of Health in fiscal 1996. "Dollar for dollar, it's the best investment of taxpayer dollars you can make," he said. Porter's district is home to two major drug companies, Abbott Laboratories and Baxter Health Care, and to the headquarters of the Walgreen Drug Store chain.

Porter was one of just 11 House Republicans to oppose a $189 billion package of tax cuts approved by the House early in the 104th, citing what for him was the higher priority of reducing the deficit. That plan fell short of enactment, as did a 1996 move to repeal the 4.3 cents per gallon

ILLINOIS 10
North and Northwest Chicago suburbs — Waukegan

Drivers following lake-hugging Sheridan Road north from Evanston reach some of Chicago's oldest and wealthiest suburbs. Affluent North Shore communities here such as Wilmette, Kenilworth, Winnetka and Glencoe have long set a Republican tone in Illinois' northeastern section.

GOP candidates rarely sweat the outcome in the 10th, which includes northern Cook County suburbia and a swath of Lake County that reaches to Wisconsin. Bill Clinton carried the district in 1996, but that was not typical; George Bush won in both 1992 and 1988.

When there is competition in district elections, it is almost always within the GOP. In the 1992 House primary, Porter — who combines a conservative stance on fiscal policy with more liberal positions on social issues — got 62 percent against an anti-abortion challenger. Porter won easily that November and in both general elections since.

Most of the residences in the wealthy near-in suburbs were built before 1940; although these communities are hardly in decline, their growth days may be past. Highland Park, site of the summertime Ravinia music festival, won a national award for downtown revitalization.

Nearby is the Army's Fort Sheridan, which was closed under the 1989 base-closing law and has been converted partly to Navy housing. However, the Great Lakes Naval Training Center a few miles north remains one of the 10th's largest employers. Under the 1993 closure round, it became the nation's only Naval training center; the resulting expansion is expected to add millions to the economy.

In between the facilities are two affluent suburbs, Lake Forest and Lake Bluff, that have been gaining residents. The district's boom has been in newer subdivisions near its western border. Arlington Heights (partially in the 8th District) and surrounding communities expanded rapidly in the 1980s. Buffalo Grove's population grew 64 percent; Wheeling and Prospect Heights were up 29 percent. At the outer edge of Chicago's commuting zone, Lake County communities such as Mundelein, Vernon Hills and Libertyville also attracted numerous new residents.

Although most of the 10th's communities are known as bedroom suburbs, several major employers are scattered here. The Walgreen drug store chain (Deerfield), Zenith Electronics Corp. (Glenview), Allstate Insurance Co. (Northbrook) and Underwriters Laboratories (Northbrook) have headquarters here.

The Cook County portion of the 10th generally provides slightly more of the votes than the Lake County part. The Cook vote is solidly Republican, the Lake vote slightly less so.

Lake County has the 10th's largest blocs of Democratic voters in the industrial cities of Waukegan and North Chicago. Just over half of Waukegan's residents are white, and the city has slightly more than half the entire district's minority-group residents. The Outboard Marine Corp., which makes boat motors, is based in Waukegan; Abbott Laboratories' home is in North Chicago.

1990 Population: 571,530. White 494,355 (86%), Black 35,228 (6%), Other 41,947 (7%). Hispanic origin 40,586 (7%). 18 and over 425,243 (74%), 62 and over 74,558 (13%). Median age: 34.

boost on gasoline taxes enacted as part of President Clinton's 1993 budget plan. Although Porter had voted against that budget because of its tax increases, he termed the move to repeal the gas tax increase "one of the most mindless things we could possibly do."

Among all House Republicans, Porter had the second-lowest record of support for bills (such as the tax cut package) that stemmed from the "Contract With America," the GOP Conference's 1994 campaign platform. He opposed a sweeping overhaul of federal regulations, in part out of concern for its impact on the environment, and in part because its provisions to reimburse private property owners when their land is subject to wetlands protections had an uncounted price tag.

Porter joined with about 50 other House Republicans in opposing plans to ease federal water regulations and to block the Environmental Protection Agency's power to enforce much major regulation, and he joined with other deficit hawks in opposing a $493 billion expenditure on stealth bombers and funding for a third *Seawolf*-class submarine. He supported an unsuccessful move to hold the Defense Department's spending in fiscal 1997 to the level of the year before.

He was one of just a dozen House Republicans to vote against a proposed constitutional amendment to allow Congress and the states authority to outlaw flag desecration. He also opposed an amendment to limit congressional terms, saying that "it is amazing that anyone would think that simply by changing the document our Founding Fathers left us, all our problems would be solved. Our problems do not lie with a poorly written Constitution." He did, however, support one constitutional change backed by most Republicans — a balanced-budget amendment. Porter also voted for such key GOP legislation during the 104th as overhauls of the welfare system and telecommunications law.

Aside from the Labor-HHS bill, Porter devotes

much of his energies to seeking means via the foreign operations spending bill to punish Turkey for various of its policies he disdains. He attached an amendment at the committee level to the fiscal 1996 bill to prevent Turkey from receiving its full allotment in military loans and economic aid until it ceased blocking humanitarian aid to Armenia. Other amendments, to trim aid to Ankara pending increased political rights for Kurds and resolution of its dispute with Greece over the divided island of Cyprus, were blocked.

Porter sponsored a bill that would have amended the Voting Rights Act to remove a requirement that areas with high numbers of non-English speakers provide ballots in languages other than English. Porter argued that the law "contradicts the value of shared language," and the Judiciary Committee approved the bill in July 1996. But it was never taken up by the House.

At Home: Challenges to Porter from within the right wing of his own party have been his only obstacle to re-election during the 1990s. Richard Rinaolo, a Republican businessman, took on Porter in 1996 for perceived lack of fealty to the Contract With America. But Porter turned him aside with 68 percent of the vote.

In the 1992 and 1994 GOP primaries, Porter's foe was Kathleen M. Sullivan, founder of an organization promoting sexual abstinence among teenagers. Trying to avoid the "single issue" label, Sullivan espoused an agenda of strong conservative positions on economic and social issues. Still, abortion was the defining issue.

Sullivan in 1992 held Porter to 60 percent, his lowest percentage in 10 years. But in the 1994 rematch, Porter climbed up to 66 percent.

The son of a well-known judge in Evanston, Porter returned to the Chicago suburbs after a stint in Washington with the Justice Department in the early 1960s. Porter tried to follow his father into the judiciary in 1970 by running for Cook County Circuit judge. A Republican candidate in the Democratic-dominated county, Porter found his cause was hopeless. But the bid helped boost his credentials within GOP circles. He had no trouble winning a state House seat in 1972 and was re-elected twice.

Meanwhile, Democrat Abner J. Mikva, one of the most liberal House Democrats, had won the old 10th District by scanty margins in 1974 and 1976 and was looking ripe for a challenge. Porter won the 1978 primary over six other Republicans.

Although Porter waged a well-funded campaign, Mikva was not quite ready to be taken: He nudged Porter out by 650 votes. But Mikva was appointed to a federal judgeship a few months later, and Porter won the 1980 special election to fill out his term. Seeking a full term in November 1980, he won by a convincing margin.

When a 1981 redistricting plan placed Porter's Evanston home in the heavily Democratic 9th District, Porter announced that he would move to challenge 10-term GOP Rep. Robert McClory in the new solidly Republican 10th. McClory, then 74, decided to retire, clearing the way for Porter, who defeated an experienced Democratic state legislator and set a pattern of easy November victories.

HOUSE ELECTIONS

1996 General		
John Edward Porter (R)	145,626	(69%)
Philip R. Torf (D)	65,144	(31%)
1996 Primary		
John Edward Porter (R)	33,530	(68%)
Richard Rinaolo (R)	15,563	(32%)
1994 General		
John Edward Porter (R)	114,884	(75%)
Andrew M. Krupp (D)	38,191	(25%)

Previous Winning Percentages: **1992** (65%) **1990** (68%) **1988** (72%) **1986** (75%) **1984** (73%) **1982** (59%) **1980** (61%) **1980**† (54%)

† Special election

CAMPAIGN FINANCE

	Receipts	Receipts from PACs	Expenditures
1996			
Porter (R)	$884,328	$260,801 (29%)	$726,615
Torf (D)	$57,327	$10,800 (19%)	$54,367
1994			
Porter (R)	$654,687	$179,762 (27%)	$538,716
Krupp (D)	$10,308	$2,500 (24%)	$10,214

DISTRICT VOTE FOR PRESIDENT

1996	1992
D 112,105 (50%)	**D** 108,149 (41%)
R 97,434 (43%)	**R** 112,401 (43%)
I 13,418 (6%)	**I** 40,719 (16%)

KEY VOTES

1997	
Ban "partial birth" abortions	Y
1996	
Approve farm bill	Y
Deny public education to illegal immigrants	†
Repeal ban on certain assault-style weapons	N
Increase minimum wage	N
Freeze defense spending	Y
Approve welfare overhaul	Y
1995	
Approve balanced-budget constitutional amendment	Y
Relax Clean Water Act regulations	N
Oppose limits on environmental regulations	Y
Reduce projected Medicare spending	Y
Approve GOP budget with tax and spending cuts	Y

VOTING STUDIES

	Presidential Support		Party Unity		Conservative Coalition	
Year	S	O	S	O	S	O
1996	42	57	79	18	57	41
1995	37	62	81	18	77	22
1994	54	45	71	27	61	39
1993	45	50	71	24	61	36
1992	62	33	73	23	60	31
1991	67	30	69	27	78	22

INTEREST GROUP RATINGS

Year	ADA	AFL-CIO	CCUS	ACU
1996	25	n/a	75	80
1995	25	8	75	48
1994	30	33	83	52
1993	25	0	91	71
1992	30	33	88	74
1991	30	17	80	80

11 Jerry Weller (R)

Of Morris — Elected 1994, 2nd term

Biographical Information

Born: July 7, 1957, Streator, Ill.

Education: U. of Illinois, B.S. 1979; Joliet Junior College, 1977.

Occupation: Congressional aide; state and federal official; hog farmer; sales representative.

Family: Single.

Religion: Christian.

Political Career: Ill. House, 1987-93.

Capitol Office: 130 Cannon Bldg. 20515; 225-3635.

Committees

Ways & Means
Oversight; Social Security

In Washington: By capturing an open Midwestern district that Democrats held for six years, Weller in 1994 earned a ticket back to Washington, where he had served for a time in the 1980s as an aide to Reagan administration Agriculture Secretary John R. Block.

After that executive-branch experience, Weller spent six years in the Illinois House, and when he entered the 104th Congress, he got a seat on the influential (though low-profile) Republican Steering Committee, where members' committee assignments are handed out. He is one of dozens in the Class of 1994 who solidly backed the "Contract With America" and the GOP agenda for overhauling the welfare system, cutting taxes and enacting balanced-budget and term-limits constitutional amendments.

Thanks to his loyalty and political savvy, Weller, after surviving a tough re-election in 1996, won a seat on the prestigious Ways and Means Committee. Also for the 105th, he was elected sophomore class president.

One exception to Weller's steady conservatism in the 104th was his support for increasing the minimum wage. In May 1996, he was one of just 43 Republicans voting to help defeat a GOP leadership-backed amendment to exempt small businesses from a minimum wage increase. Subsequently, he was among the 93 Republicans who supported a 90-cent increase in the wage.

The composition of the 11th District work force helps explain why the minimum wage was a touchy issue for Weller: Nearly one-third of the 11th's workers are blue-collar, a higher proportion than in 16 of Illinois' 20 districts.

Parochial concerns are an important part of Weller's agenda. During the 104th, he bragged about the House approving a measure setting aside 19,000 acres that had been part of the Joliet Arsenal for a tallgrass prairie nature preserve, a veterans cemetery and an industrial park. Weller's predecessor in the 11th, Democrat George E. Sangmeister, had pushed the project for several years. The Chicago Sun-Times faulted Weller for claiming too much credit for getting the legislation enacted.

Noting that other members in the Illinois delegation had grumbled over Weller's "frequent grandstanding," the newspaper added, "The last sentence of [Weller's] two-page release devotes 15 words of credit to Sen. Paul Simon and Sen. Carol Moseley-Braun, who did the heaviest lifting. They overcame big obstacles confronting the bill to transform the arsenal into a nature preserve."

From his seat on the Banking and Financial Services Committee in the 104th, Weller gave voice to concerns in his district about an influx of low-income residents. When the committee in November 1995 considered a bill to overhaul the nation's public housing system, Weller offered an amendment barring Chicago public housing tenants from using federal rent vouchers to move to the southern Cook County suburbs in the 11th.

The amendment provoked lengthy debate, with some Democrats arguing that Weller was motivated by a mindset that "we don't want those people moving into our towns." Weller said the amendment was needed because southern Cook County already had absorbed 70 percent of Chicago housing assistance recipients.

Weller eventually modified his proposal to require that the Housing and Urban Development Department study the concentration of housing assistance recipients in Chicago and Cook County and report to Congress on ways to disperse those tenants. The committee accepted this modification. The legislation died at the end of the 104th Congress, to be revived in the 105th.

Chicago's role as a highway, train and airplane hub gave Weller plenty of issues to follow when he served on the Transportation and Infrastructure Committee in the 104th. In May 1996, he won the Aviation Subcommittee's approval of a proposal to extend for another three years the airlines' exemption from the 1993 4.3-cents-per-gallon increase in the federal fuel tax. Weller also has been a proponent of building a third Chicago-area airport near Kankakee, a city on the southeastern edge of the 11th. Many other politicians

The 11th may be contiguous, but it is not exactly coherent. It reaches from the working-class neighborhoods of far southeast Chicago past suburbs and exurbs to industrial Joliet, then through the farmland and small cities of Will, Kankakee, Grundy and La Salle counties.

With its mix of constituencies, the 11th shapes up as a classic swing district. George Bush carried the district in 1988 with 57 percent; in 1992, the 11th swung to Bill Clinton, even though he won Will, the district's largest county, with just 39 percent. (Ross Perot got 22 percent there.) Clinton won the district again in 1996 with 51 percent.

But Clinton's success did not upend Republican Weller, who has twice lost the portion of Cook County that lies within the 11th but has run stronger in the other four counties.

At the northeast corner of the 11th is a small chunk of Chicago that would have been largely depopulated had Chicago Mayor Richard M. Daley's plan for a third Chicago-area airport gone through. In 1992, he announced plans for an airport in the Lake Calumet area; he said the project would create jobs and clean up the polluted industrial site.

But the thousands of residents who would be displaced — the blue-collar, ethnic community of Hegewisch would have been wiped out — protested; the state legislature, citing cost, blocked the plan; and Daley drew back. The state Department of Transportation subsequently began studying a site in Peotone, in rural Will County, as well as three other sites.

The district also rims the south suburban area of Cook County. There are mainly middle- and working-class communities in Calumet City, Lansing and South Holland, to the east; in the

ILLINOIS 11
South Chicago suburbs and exurbs — Joliet

southern part is comfortable Park Forest. Just south of the Will County line is University Park, a mainly black, middle-class suburb that is the site of Governors State University.

The southern portion of Will County in the 11th has more than a third of the district's population. The loss of much of its industry sent Joliet into a downturn that hit bottom in the early 1980s; it has stabilized now, with regional malls and the Rialto Square performing arts center (an elaborate former movie theater) drawing people to town. There are still a number of factories, including a Caterpillar plant. The Statesville prison north of town is a major employer.

The towns of Mokena and Frankfort are being absorbed into Chicago's south suburbia. Some rural communities to the east, along Interstate 57, are also growing. Farther south, the 11th takes in mainly rural northern Kankakee County, reaching to the edge but not into the city of Kankakee.

To the west, in Grundy County, is Morris, site of a nuclear power plant. Bush won this GOP-leaning county in 1992, but Clinton carried it four years later. Democrats run stronger in La Salle County, which has light industry in La Salle, Ottawa and Streator; Clinton won there handily in 1992 and 1996.

1990 Population: 571,528. White 499,520 (87%), Black 48,897 (9%), Other 23,111 (4%). Hispanic origin 37,049 (6%). 18 and over 417,917 (73%), 62 and over 90,254 (16%). Median age: 33.

have their own idea about where a third airport should go, however, and for now the matter seems becalmed.

Weller has cosponsored legislation to bring sweeping changes to the federal campaign finance system, including a proposal to limit PAC contributions to fundraising within a member's district. Early in the 104th, Weller called campaign finance reform "the big kahuna" in the GOP's effort to change Congress. But after many months of dispute between and among both parties, the drive to alter campaign finance laws faltered in July 1996. The GOP leadership put forth a bill that failed 162-259; many senior members argued that it tampered unnecessarily with a system that works, while many junior members complained that it did not make fundamental change in a system they see as deeply flawed.

During debate on a bill to impose new disclosure requirements on lobbyists, Weller offered an amendment to require lobbyists to list the dates, amounts and recipients of speaking fees paid to journalists. "The public has the right to know who is receiving special interest money whether it is a member of Congress or a member of the media," Weller said, adding that members are prohibited from accepting honoraria. The House rejected the amendment, 193-233.

At Home: Raised on an Illinois farm, Weller studied agriculture at the University of Illinois, and before he graduated he did a stint in the office of Rep. Thomas J. Corcoran, who represented north-central Illinois. During the 1980s he worked at Proctor and Gamble, went to Washington to serve in Block's Agriculture Department and then headed back to Illinois, where he won a state House seat in 1986.

When Democrat Sangmeister decided to retire from the House in 1994, Weller jumped into the race to succeed him. The 11th, which was made decidedly more Republican in the 1990s round of redistricting, included about 30 percent of Weller's legislative district.

Weller's ties to the rural areas of the 11th and his superior fundraising ability enabled him to emerge from a field of six GOP primary candidates to win nomination with 32 percent of the vote. Among those he defeated was Sangmeister's 1992 general-election opponent, Robert T. Herbolsheimer, who ran second with 29 percent. Weller drew support from a range of conservative interests, including the Illinois Farm Bureau, the National Rifle Association and anti-abortion groups.

In the general election, Weller faced Democratic state Rep. Frank Giglio, who himself had emerged from a crowded primary. Theirs was at times a bitter fight. Weller sought to associate Giglio with the then-unpopular Clinton administration and with the Chicago Democratic political machine, which is viewed with suspicion by many voters outside the city.

Giglio accused Weller of not paying his 1994 property taxes, and Weller rebutted with ads dubbing Giglio "40-cent Frank" for frequently using a free tollway pass given to members of a commission that oversees tollway spending. For all the fury, though, the outcome was lopsided, as the Republican tilt of the district and the national GOP surge lifted Weller to a 61 percent victory.

Two years later, what surge there was in the 11th was Democratic; President Clinton carried the district over GOP nominee Bob Dole 51 percent to 38 percent. In House voting, that helped the Democrat, former state Rep. Clem Balanoff.

He was not initially seen as a big threat to Weller; in 1994, Balanoff had lost in the Democratic primary for the 11th. But he turned out to be a dogged campaigner, slamming Weller for supporting Republican measures that he portrayed as harmful to Medicare and other social safety-net programs. Balanoff hardly ever mentioned Weller's name without denouncing Speaker Newt Gingrich in the same breath.

Weller played up his centrist stands, such as support for the minimum wage increase, and he painted Balanoff a "Chicago liberal." Balanoff's base was the small corner of southeast Chicago that is in the district, which ranges west through the city's southern suburbs and into farmland.

Weller dropped nine full points from his tally in 1994, but he still clung to the seat, winning 52 percent to 48 percent.

HOUSE ELECTIONS

1996 General		
Jerry Weller (R)	109,896	(52%)
Clem Balanoff (D)	102,388	(48%)
1994 General		
Gerald C. "Jerry" Weller (R)	97,241	(61%)
Frank Giglio (D)	63,150	(39%)

CAMPAIGN FINANCE

	Receipts	Receipts from PACs	Expend-itures
1996			
Weller (R)	$1,140,081	$439,059 (39%)	$1,116,062
Balanoff (D)	$479,712	$154,328 (32%)	$481,979
1994			
Weller (R)	$885,112	$271,592 (31%)	$877,429
Giglio (D)	$620,793	$205,128 (33%)	$614,142

DISTRICT VOTE FOR PRESIDENT

	1996		1992
D	112,106 (51%)	**D**	108,447 (44%)
R	83,644 (38%)	**R**	90,085 (36%)
I	23,162 (11%)	**I**	50,200 (20%)

KEY VOTES

1997	
Ban "partial-birth" abortions	Y
1996	
Approve farm bill	Y
Deny public education to illegal immigrants	N
Repeal ban on certain assault-style weapons	Y
Increase minimum wage	Y
Freeze defense spending	Y
Approve welfare overhaul	Y
1995	
Approve balanced-budget constitutional amendment	Y
Relax Clean Water Act regulations	Y
Oppose limits on environmental regulations	N
Reduce projected Medicare spending	Y
Approve GOP budget with tax and spending cuts	Y

VOTING STUDIES

	Presidential Support		Party Unity		Conservative Coalition	
Year	**S**	**O**	**S**	**O**	**S**	**O**
1996	41	58	83	16	84	16
1995	17	83	96	4	95	5

INTEREST GROUP RATINGS

Year	ADA	AFL-CIO	CCUS	ACU
1996	5	n/a	87	84
1995	0	17	100	92

12 Jerry F. Costello (D)

Of Belleville — Elected 1988; 5th full term

Biographical Information

Born: Sept. 25, 1949, East St. Louis, Ill.

Education: Belleville Area College, A.A. 1970; Maryville College of the Sacred Heart, B.A. 1972.

Occupation: Law enforcement official.

Family: Wife, Georgia Cockrum; three children.

Religion: Roman Catholic.

Political Career: St. Clair County Board chairman, 1980-88.

Capitol Office: 2454 Rayburn Bldg. 20515; 225-5661.

Committees

Budget

Transportation and Infrastructure
Aviation; Surface Transportation

In Washington: Many members struggle with the debt vs. pork dilemma: A federal debt in the trillions makes voters grouchy, yet they still expect their congressman to bring home goodies from Uncle Sam. The cross-pressure is particularly obvious in Costello's case. Laborers and farmers in his southern Illinois district often scrape to make ends meet, and they are deeply suspicious that their taxes are misspent by Washington bureaucrats. But the 12th District depends heavily on Washington for public works projects and other federal largess to help lift the local economic doldrums.

Costello, with a seat on the Budget Committee, plays the part of fiscal tightwad by touting his support for a balanced-budget constitutional amendment and his votes to eliminate the big-ticket NASA space station. But the real focus of his legislative efforts is the Transportation and Infrastructure Committee, where he toils quietly to secure federal dollars for his district. So far, voters seem to like the juggling act: Costello, nicknamed "Congressman Pork" at home, has easily won re-election.

Costello objected to Republican budget plans during the 104th Congress that would have cut or limited the growth of domestic programs of interest to his core constituents such as Medicare and the Legal Services Corporation. Costello argued that the tax cuts the GOP pursued would hurt lower-income workers. In a rare rhetorical flourish, Costello said, "This [tax cut] bill has been called the 'crown jewel of the Republican Contract With America,' but it appears most of the crown jewels will only go to the rich."

But while he generally echoes the party line in his opposition to key GOP initiatives, Costello is not a certain vote on the party's whip sheets. The 1993 congressional wars over President Clinton's budget were a trial for Costello. The party leadership expected loyalty from Democrats on the Budget Committee. But the initial Clinton plan made Costello squirm: He did not like the proposed Btu tax or inland waterways tax, and he wanted more spending cuts, controls on entitlement spending and a promise that new revenues would go toward deficit reduction. As the House's final vote on the budget approached in August, Costello was said to be wavering. But in the end, he toed the party line, noting that Clinton had dropped the Btu and waterways levies and promised to address entitlements and a deficit-reduction "trust fund."

During the 104th, laboring in the new world of Republican control, Costello found an almost nostalgic worth in the 1993 Clinton budget plan. He thought it had spread the pain of deficit reduction more fairly than the Republican plans, and he went so far as to write an opinion article defending its 4.3 cents per gallon gas tax when the GOP sought to repeal it in 1996. He did support the final versions of Republican legislation to overhaul welfare and telecommunications law.

In criticizing Republican proposals to reduce the deficit without increasing taxes, Costello stressed that deeper spending cuts would choke off some of the federal funds he has worked to bring home. In statements submitted to the Congressional Record — Costello almost never speaks on the House floor — he warned that drastic budget cuts would end research and development of clean coal technologies at Southern Illinois University, kill a rail link between St. Louis' Lambert Airport and St. Clair County (East St. Louis), and force closure of Scott Air Force Base in Belleville and the Chas M. Price Army Support Center in Granite City.

Costello prevailed in the 104th on two votes of direct interest to his district — the only occasions on which he addressed his colleagues from the House floor during the term. California Republican Dana Rohrabacher sought unsuccessfully in 1995 to rescind $4.8 million for a Carterville, Ill., coal gasification research project but was rebuffed, 142-274. Democrat Robert E. Andrews of New Jersey fared even worse on a move to block spending for the military airport program, which is helping underwrite construction of a civilian airport at Scott Air Force Base. During consideration of the

The numbering system is one of the peculiarities of Illinois' House district map for the 1990s. Districts 1 through 13 are all in the Chicago metropolitan area — except the 12th, which is hundreds of miles away in the state's southwest corner.

The 12th also stands out for economic and demographic reasons. This is the most industrial district in southern Illinois, with a belt of factories and refineries on the Mississippi River near St. Louis and a coal-mining region south and east. Blacks (who make up 17 percent of the district's population) are more numerous here than in any other district outside Chicago. The district contains some of the most economically depressed areas in Illinois.

Those factors combine to make this solidly Democratic turf. In 1996, Bill Clinton carried all but one of the nine counties represented in the 12th on his way to a 22-point romp. That same year, Costello won with a career-high 72 percent of the votes.

St. Clair County, with more than two-fifths of the 12th's residents, is its hub. The district's most troubled community, East St. Louis, is here. As late as the 1960s, the city was an industrial center. But the closure of its stockyards set off an economic collapse. In the 1980s, East St. Louis lost a quarter of its population, and now has about 41,000 residents. Most who remain are black and poor; more than half the city's children live below the poverty level.

Belleville, the St. Clair County seat and now its largest city with 43,000 people, is mainly white. It has a mix of poor, working-class and well-off residents, some of whom commute to St. Louis. Nearby is Scott Air Force Base, which is headquarters for the Air Mobility Command and is the district's largest employer.

ILLINOIS 12
Southwest — Carbondale; East St. Louis

To the north, the district takes in the industrial western section of Madison County. Employers include the Laclede Steel plant in Alton and a Shell Oil refinery in Wood River. Alton was the first Illinois city to revive riverboat gambling. Clinton got 57 percent of the votes in the St. Clair County portion of the district and 62 percent in the Madison County part in 1996.

South of St. Clair are Perry and Randolph counties, among Illinois' leading coal producers. Although demand for Illinois coal has remained steady, rapid mechanization during the past decade left thousands of miners looking for work.

Coal also is mined in Jackson County; the county's economy is bolstered by Southern Illinois University in Carbondale, which has 24,000 students and more than 10,000 employees.

At the southern tip of the district is Alexander County and the weary Mississippi River town of Cairo. The scene of racial conflict in the 1960s, the city of about 4,800 residents is something of a microcosm of East St. Louis.

There is farm territory in the western part of the district; wheat is a major crop. This is one area where Democrats' hold is weak. Monroe County was the only county represented in the district that Clinton lost in 1996.

1990 Population: 571,530. White 465,603 (81%), Black 97,185 (17%), Other 8,742 (2%). Hispanic origin 7,527 (1%). 18 and over 421,442 (74%), 62 and over 93,050 (16%). Median age: 32.

fiscal 1996 transportation spending bill, Andrews drew only four other supporters for his amendment.

On social policy issues, Costello reflects his constituency's cultural conservatism. He was one of 10 House members who lobbied to add language expressing tolerance of anti-abortion views to the 1996 Democratic platform. Costello supports gun owners' rights and voted against lifting the ban on homosexuals in the military. A steadfast ally of organized labor, he voted against NAFTA and GATT in the 103rd and for a minimum-wage increase in the 104th.

Costello got a rare moment in the spotlight in 1991. With his son preparing for action near the Kuwait-Iraq border, Costello voted against authorizing the use of military force against Iraq. He was one of only two members with a son or daughter in the Persian Gulf.

At Home: Costello has been mulling a run for Illinois secretary of state in 1998, but his nascent effort may have been stymied by the July 1996 indictment of his lifelong friend Amiel Cueto. Cueto has been charged with trying to block the federal investigation of a convicted racketeer.

The St. Louis Post-Dispatch has reported that sources claim Costello is the "undisclosed business partner, then a public official" who, the grand jury indictment says, provided information to Cueto about the progress of a bill in Congress that would have aided a casino deal in which Cueto was allegedly involved. The "official" also allegedly exerted influence to promote Cueto for the position of St. Clair County state's attorney. Costello denied being Cueto's partner but was named an unindicted co-conspirator in 1997.

The member of a locally prominent political family, Costello was elected chairman of the St. Clair County Commission in 1980. He became well-known in his heavily Democratic region, serving at one point as chairman of the metropolitan St. Louis Council of Governments. His high profile earned him status as heir apparent to Democratic Rep. Melvin Price, an elderly House veteran who did not seek re-election in 1988.

But in the March primary, Madison County Auditor Pete Fields portrayed Costello as an old-style, hardball "boss" in the St. Clair County Democratic machine. A huge financial advantage (and the party structure) helped Costello survive, but with only a 46 percent plurality. That turned out to be an omen for the August 1988 special election forced by Price's death that April.

Costello's GOP foe in the special election was college official Robert H. Gaffner, who had run two futile challenges to Price before a close 1986 contest when Price's health was failing badly. Gaffner copied the line of attack used by Democrat Fields: His ads suggested that voters call Costello and quiz him about his ethics. Costello won with 51.5 percent, shockingly low for the state's most Democratic district outside Chicago. The November election was a replay; Costello got 53 percent.

By 1990, Costello's clouds had lifted. Gaffner tried again, but sank to 34 percent. Costello has won re-election with at least 66 percent of the vote ever since.

HOUSE ELECTIONS

1996 General		
Jerry F. Costello (D)	150,005	(72%)
Shapley R. Hunter (R)	55,690	(27%)
Geoffrey S. Nathan (LIBERT)	3,824	(2%)
1994 General		
Jerry F. Costello (D)	101,391	(66%)
Jan Morris (R)	52,419	(34%)

Previous Winning Percentages: 1992 (71%) **1990** (66%) **1988** (53%) **1988**† (51%)

† *Special election*

CAMPAIGN FINANCE

	Receipts	Receipts from PACs	Expend-itures
1996			
Costello (D)	$574,401	$164,888 (29%)	$506,257
Hunter (R)	$4,809	0	$4,261
1994			
Costello (D)	$677,293	$212,450 (31%)	$499,844
Morris (R)	$44,597	$14 (0%)	$43,779

DISTRICT VOTE FOR PRESIDENT

1996		1992	
D	120,321 (56%)	**D**	132,556 (54%)
R	72,612 (34%)	**R**	69,850 (29%)
I	19,777 (9%)	**I**	42,191 (17%)

KEY VOTES

1997	
Ban "partial-birth" abortions	Y
1996	
Approve farm bill	Y
Deny public education to illegal immigrants	Y
Repeal ban on certain assault-style weapons	Y
Increase minimum wage	Y
Freeze defense spending	Y
Approve welfare overhaul	Y
1995	
Approve balanced-budget constitutional amendment	Y
Relax Clean Water Act regulations	Y
Oppose limits on environmental regulations	Y
Reduce projected Medicare spending	N
Approve GOP budget with tax and spending cuts	N

VOTING STUDIES

	Presidential Support		Party Unity		Conservative Coalition	
Year	S	O	S	O	S	O
1996	66	33	74	25	59	39
1995	60	39	74	23	50	47
1994	73	27	75	23	72	28
1993	71	28	76	24	66	32
1992	32	65	78	18	50	50
1991	34	65	77	22	68	32

INTEREST GROUP RATINGS

Year	ADA	AFL-CIO	CCUS	ACU
1996	70	n/a	25	30
1995	70	83	33	32
1994	50	78	50	38
1993	65	100	9	29
1992	60	83	14	43
1991	55	83	30	15

13 Harris W. Fawell (R)

Of Naperville — Elected 1984, 7th term

Biographical Information

Born: March 25, 1929, West Chicago, Ill.

Education: North Central College, 1947-49; Chicago-Kent College of Law, J.D. 1952.

Occupation: Lawyer.

Family: Wife, Ruth Johnson; three children.

Religion: Methodist.

Political Career: Ill. Senate, 1963-77; candidate for Ill. Supreme Court, 1976.

Capitol Office: 2368 Rayburn Bldg. 20515; 225-3515.

Committees

Education & Workforce
Employer-Employee Relations (chairman); Oversight & Investigations; Workforce Protections (vice)

Science
Energy & Environment

In Washington: Fawell reflects his upscale suburban Chicago constituency when he says he looks at issues "from a businessman's point of view." As chairman of the Employer-Employee Relations Subcommittee of the Education and the Workforce Committee, he champions business interests and is a thorn in the side of organized labor.

During their time in the House majority, conservative Republicans have brought several business-friendly measures to the floor, and Fawell has been on board for every one.

In July 1996 and again in March 1997, he backed a GOP proposal allowing employers to offer workers compensatory time in lieu of overtime pay. Proponents said the bill would help workers balance job and family obligations, but critics said employees might be coerced into accepting comp time when they really wanted overtime pay.

Fawell supported efforts to ease worker safety regulations on small businesses by applying cost-benefit analysis to new regulations issued by the Occupational Safety and Health Administration (OSHA). The idea was roundly booed by pro-labor Democrats such as Major R. Owens of New York, who said it would "put a bounty on the life of every American worker." Fawell said he was taken aback by such "rather extreme statements. . . . What we have here is a group of extremely reasonable suggestions. . . . This should be a sound basis for a bipartisan coming-together."

Once again locking horns with organized labor, Fawell supported legislation allowing non-union companies to set up and control worker-management committees that could "address matters of mutual interest." Labor allies called these committees "sham unions" and warned that they would be captive to employers' interests.

Fawell said the GOP was trying to adapt the National Labor Relations Act of 1935 to modern times. "What we have here, of course, is a fossilized 60-year-old definition of labor organization, colliding head-on with dynamic new concepts of doing business in today's fast evolving, information-centered economy and society."

Fawell introduced legislation in the 104th requiring union officials to obtain annual written consent from members before any portion of their dues could be spent on activities beyond collective bargaining.

Fawell said that he had favored such legislation for years and that it was not being offered in response to the AFL-CIO's $35 million advertising campaign against House Republicans in the 1996 election. Rep. Matthew G. Martinez, D-Calif., countered that corporations routinely spend "uncounted millions of shareholder dollars" to influence the political process. "This is precisely what the AFL-CIO plans to do with its voter education fund," he said, "albeit with a radically different message."

In May 1996, Fawell voted against the initial amendment by Frank Riggs, R-Calif., to increase the minimum wage by 90 cents an hour. Also, he supported a GOP leadership-backed amendment to exempt small businesses from paying the higher minimum. After the Riggs amendment passed and the small-business exemption failed, Fawell voted for the minimum wage increase.

Fawell's contribution to the health care debate came in the form of legislation allowing small businesses to form purchasing cooperatives with other small employers, giving them more leverage with insurance companies when negotiating premiums and benefits. The measure also exempted more insurance plans from state laws that mandate health benefits. The bill was incorporated in the House health insurance overhaul plan that passed in March 1996.

During his years in the minority on the old Education and Labor Committee, Fawell was part of a conservative bloc that consistently voted against labor and some education initiatives that Democrats favored. In 1994, when the committee approved a bill to overhaul the 1970 Occupational Safety and Health Act, Fawell objected, arguing that it would impose unnecessary regulatory burdens on employers, leading to a loss of jobs.

ILLINOIS 13
Southwest Chicago suburbs — Naperville

As a leading critic of wasteful federal spending, Fawell receives little argument from his white-collar suburban constituency. The 13th, which covers southern Du Page County and parts of exurban Cook and Will counties, is a place of wide lawns and spacious houses where business executives live. It is one of the most Republican districts in the country.

George Bush's failure in 1992 to make the most of this advantage contributed to his crushing defeat by Bill Clinton in Illinois. In 1988, Bush took 69 percent of the 13th's vote; in 1992, he slipped all the way to 47 percent. Four years later, Bob Dole did little better, garnering about 50 percent of the district's votes as part of his loss to Clinton in Illinois.

The major demographic changes in late 20th century America have included the emergence of suburban centers as satellite "downtowns" and population explosion in outlying exurbs. The 13th has prime examples of each, in the communities of Oak Brook and Naperville.

Oak Brook, just west of the Cook-Du Page County line, is not especially populous. But its location near the nexus of Interstates 88, 294 and 290 has abetted its development into a leading business center. Its corporate roster includes the headquarters of the McDonald's chain, Ace Hardware Corp., Federal Signal Corp. and the Spiegel mail-order company.

South of Oak Brook along I-88 is a string of suburbs that grew up along the Burlington Northern commuter tracks and long served as the hub of southern Du Page County. (Overall, the county provides about three-fifths of the 13th's population.) With room to spread out, these cities — the largest of which is Downers Grove — gained population; the growth has given Lisle, one of the rare traditional working-class towns in the 13th, a more suburban veneer.

But the spectacular growth has been in Naperville. In 1970, Naperville was a small city amid Du Page and northern Will County farmland; by 1980, it caught up with Downers Grove in population. Then, over the next 10 years, Naperville doubled its population to more than 85,000, making it Illinois' sixth-largest city. It has also become an employment center: Allied Van Lines, Burlington Northern Railroad and Nalco Chemical have headquarters there.

Scientific research is a major source of jobs. Argonne National Laboratory is in southeast Du Page; district residents also work at the Fermi National Accelerator Laboratory, across the line in the 14th District.

Southern Du Page's fast growth has spilled over to the northern Will County city of Bolingbrook. The remainder of the 13th's section of Will County is mainly rural, dotted with towns — Lockport, Romeoville, Plainfield — whose links are mainly with the 11th District city of Joliet.

The 13th also takes in the mainly residential southwest corner of Cook County that includes the fast-growing exurbs of Orland Park and Tinley Park.

1990 Population: 571,531. White 523,801 (92%), Black 18,067 (3%), Other 29,663 (5%). Hispanic origin 16,929 (3%). 18 and over 412,733 (72%), 62 and over 55,223 (10%). Median age: 32.

The bill, which never made it to the House floor, would have required employers with 11 or more employees to establish a committee of workers and managers to review health and safety procedures and recommend improvements. Supporters argued that employment safety rules had to be be strengthened to reduce the high number of work-related accidents.

When the Labor-Management Relations Subcommittee took up a bill in 1994 that aimed to protect workers from technology that could infringe on their rights, Fawell offered an amendment to eliminate an employee's right to sue for compensatory and punitive damages if an employer violated restrictions on electronic monitoring. It was rejected.

Thinking that members should take a dose of the regulatory medicine they give to others, Fawell was an eager sponsor of legislation enacted in the 104th to require Congress to live by the same laws as private industry. The point "of finally applying these laws to members of Congress," Fawell told the Chicago Sun-Times, "was to force them to feel the pain of the impact of the laws they pass."

He was a co-founder of the Porkbusters Coalition, a largely Republican organization that jumps on large spending bills and targets hundreds of projects at a time in an attempt to show that lots of little programs add up to big dollars. He proudly touts the description by Citizens Against Government Waste as having "the best lifetime record of any member of Congress for cutting wasteful spending."

Fawell's close scrutiny of spending does not endear him to members whose favored projects are targeted, but if some regard Fawell as a nitpicker, he seems not to care. Even in the 103rd Congress, when Republicans were in the minority, he scored a budget-cutting hit with the elimination of the agriculture subsidy for honey producers.

In some cases, Fawell is willing to cut projects in his home state. Early in the 103rd, he and the 74 other porkbusters took aim at 747 projects approved by Congress in 1992 worth nearly $2 billion, including $1 million for tree planting in Chicago and a $1.7 million visitor center to be built in Springfield to honor Abraham Lincoln.

But in 1994, Fawell balked when conferees on the energy and water spending bill agreed to cut a $1.1 billion nuclear reactor research project at Argonne National Laboratory in Fawell's district. About 500 scientists at the lab were expected to lose their jobs.

Although Fawell sees eye-to-eye with GOP conservatives on fiscal policy issues, he stakes out a position to the left of his party's majority on a number of other matters. He has supported a five-day waiting period for handgun purchases, voted to ban certain semiautomatic assault-style weapons and opposed an effort in 1996 to repeal that ban. He generally sides with proponents of abortion rights, although he has supported banning a particular abortion technique that opponents call "partial birth" abortion. And he does not favor congressional term limits.

At Home: The political spectrum in the 13th ranges from the moderate to far right within the Republican Party. It is secure ground for Fawell, who since winning a closely contested open-seat primary in 1984 has never seen his election tally drop below 60 percent.

As the campaign treasurer for his longtime friend, veteran Rep. John N. Erlenborn, Fawell was well-positioned in 1984 when Erlenborn announced his retirement after 20 years of service. Fawell picked up most of the incumbent's political network; Erlenborn's chief aide became Fawell's campaign manager.

That help proved invaluable to winning the GOP primary. Fawell, who as a state legislator had promoted measures to aid the disabled, faced two opponents — state Sen. George Ray Hudson and former state Sen. Mark Rhoads — who tried to portray him as a liberal.

With backing from the formal Du Page and Cook County GOP organizations as well as conservative contacts, Hudson seemed at least an even bet to defeat Fawell. But he lost time and momentum after falling off a campaign stage and breaking a leg. Fawell took the nomination with 30 percent of the vote, 7 percentage points ahead of Hudson.

HOUSE ELECTIONS

1996 General		
Harris W. Fawell (R)	141,651	(60%)
Susan W. Hynes (D)	94,693	(40%)
1994 General		
Harris W. Fawell (R)	124,312	(73%)
William A. Riley (D)	45,709	(27%)

Previous Winning Percentages: 1992 (68%) **1990** (66%) **1988** (70%) **1986** (73%) **1984** (67%)

CAMPAIGN FINANCE

	Receipts	Receipts from PACs		Expend-itures
1996				
Fawell (R)	$441,444	$189,353	(43%)	$537,449
Hynes (D)	$147,516	$63,761	(43%)	$130,612
1994				
Fawell (R)	$359,750	$118,627	(33%)	$278,469

DISTRICT VOTE FOR PRESIDENT

1996		1992	
D	104,714 (41%)	**D**	88,324 (32%)
R	126,596 (50%)	**R**	128,627 (47%)
I	21,701 (9%)	**I**	58,125 (21%)

KEY VOTES

1997	
Ban "partial birth" abortions	Y
1996	
Approve farm bill	Y
Deny public education to illegal immigrants	Y
Repeal ban on certain assault-style weapons	N
Increase minimum wage	N
Freeze defense spending	Y
Approve welfare overhaul	Y
1995	
Approve balanced-budget constitutional amendment	Y
Relax Clean Water Act regulations	Y
Oppose limits on environmental regulations	Y
Reduce projected Medicare spending	Y
Approve GOP budget with tax and spending cuts	Y

VOTING STUDIES

	Presidential Support		Party Unity		Conservative Coalition	
Year	S	O	S	O	S	O
1996	43	57	84	14	78	22
1995	29	71	88	11	86	14
1994	51	49	85	15	78	22
1993	43	56	86	14	84	16
1992	70	29	86	13	75	25
1991	75	22	80	16	84	11

INTEREST GROUP RATINGS

Year	ADA	AFL-CIO	CCUS	ACU
1996	10	n/a	100	85
1995	20	0	96	60
1994	25	11	92	81
1993	15	0	82	92
1992	25	17	88	84
1991	15	8	100	84

14 Dennis Hastert (R)

Of Yorkville — Elected 1986, 6th term

Biographical Information
Born: Jan. 2, 1942, Aurora, Ill.
Education: Wheaton College, A.B. 1964; Northern Illinois U., M.A. 1967.
Occupation: Teacher; restaurateur.
Family: Wife, Jean Kahl; two children.
Religion: Protestant.
Political Career: Ill. House, 1981-87.
Capitol Office: 2241 Rayburn Bldg. 20515; 225-2976.

Committees
Commerce
Energy & Power; Health & Environment; Telecommunications, Trade & Consumer Protection
Government Reform & Oversight
National Economic Growth, Natural Resources & Regulatory Affairs; National Security, International Affairs & Criminal Justice (chairman)

Chief Deputy Whip

In Washington: During the eight years he spent in the House Republican minority, there were times when it looked as if Hastert might end up like his mentor, fellow Illinoisan Robert H. Michel, whose skill at the art of legislating lifted him to the post of GOP leader, but who never enjoyed the leverage of being in the majority.

But the Republican sweep of 1994 gave Hastert's legislative life a new lease. With the support of Speaker Newt Gingrich, Hastert, an able and ambitious inside operator, moved into the leadership post of chief deputy whip. In that job, he was swiftly and intimately involved in pushing the "Contract With America" legislative agenda through the House.

He was especially associated with overhauling the "earnings penalty" assessed Social Security recipients between the ages of 65 and 69 who continue to work. He has called this penalty a burden on low- and middle-income seniors who must work to supplement their retirement funds.

In 1996, Hastert saw a partial victory when Congress cleared legislation that would, over seven years, raise the amount seniors may earn without losing any of their benefits from $11,520 to $30,000. Hastert would like to see the limit raised more rapidly.

Health care issues have been a central focus for Hastert ever since he was chosen in 1993 to be the GOP House member on Hillary Rodham Clinton's health care task force. He also was tapped as a negotiator with moderate Democrats crafting a bipartisan alternative to the Clinton health plan. Hastert negotiated with Jim Cooper, D-Tenn., a leading apostate in his party, but the two sides proved too far apart.

Hastert took a dim view of efforts by the congressional Democratic majority to force some sort of health care compromise through the Congress as the 1994 election approached, saying "not too many people [were] going to be fooled."

In the Republican-controlled 104th, Hastert was a key player in legislation to guarantee the "portability" of health insurance coverage. The bill, which Clinton signed in August 1996, allows workers to continue their health-care coverage if they change or lose their jobs.

Conferees spent months negotiating the differences between the House- and Senate-passed versions of the bill, and became stuck, in particular, on a House-passed provision to create something called medical savings accounts (MSAs). House Republicans strongly supported MSAs, which would allow people with high-deductible plans to make tax-deductible contributions into a special account to cover health care costs. Democrats vigorously opposed it. Hastert fought hard to save the provision.

The division was deep, and there was much speculation that conferees would deadlock and the bill would die. But Hastert did not give up.

"There were many times when we would reach an impasse with the House, and [Hastert] just kept quietly convening meetings, having everybody come to the table," said Sen. Nancy Landon Kassebaum, R-Kan., then chairwoman of the Labor and Human Resources Committee. "In a very quiet manner, he kept everything together."

The eventual compromise allowed for the creation of a narrow pilot program that would permit about 750,000 participants to use MSAs. The final deal was negotiated directly between Ways and Means Committee Chairman Bill Archer, Texas Republican, a strong supporter of the plan, and Sen. Edward M. Kennedy, Massachusetts Republican, the measure's toughest foe.

Hastert returned to the health-care debate in the fall of 1996 after the Senate passed the fiscal 1997 spending bill for the Veterans' Affairs Department with three controversial health-related amendments.

The provisions required insurance plans to cover extended stays for mothers and their newborns; provided veterans benefits to children born with spina bifida if either parent had been exposed to the Agent Orange defoliant in Vietnam; and required group health insurance companies to provide the same annual and lifetime limits for mental health coverage as they do

ILLINOIS 14
North Central — Aurora; Elgin; De Kalb

A decade ago, the historically industrial cities of Aurora and Elgin in eastern Kane County were in a prolonged state of Rust Belt decline. However, the cities' location at the edge of metropolitan Chicago, their proximity to such booming satellite cities as Schaumburg and Naperville, and their reasonable land values gave them a new life and boosted their populations during the 1980s.

The growth here and in other Fox River Valley communities reinforced Kane County's dominance in the 14th; it contributes more than half the district's population. The rest of the people are distributed among a section of exurban Du Page County to the east and a mainly rural stretch south and west that includes Kendall, De Kalb, Lee and the northern part of La Salle counties. Exurban and rural Republican tendencies dominate the 14th's politics, offsetting the Democratic habits of some blue-collar whites and minority-group voters. After a tough 1986 contest against a Kane County Democratic official, Hastert has been re-elected to the House seat five times with at least 64 percent.

This GOP lean made the 14th one of George Bush's best Illinois districts in 1992, though he fell well short of his 65 percent showing here in 1988. Bob Dole narrowly won the district in 1996 with 48 percent of the vote, while Ross Perot slid from 22 percent in 1992 to 10 percent.

Aurora, with nearly 100,000 residents, is the district's largest city. It maintains an industrial heritage, with the Caterpillar tractor company and Weyerhauser as major employers. But the growth is in white-collar operations, including Toyota's Midwest headquarters. The city's "Anywhere U.S.A." image led to its being the setting for "Wayne's World," a TV skit and then a pair of movie comedies about two middle-class teenage rock fans.

The economic mix is similar in Elgin, which has about 77,000 residents. Factory workers here still make a variety of products, including Elgin street sweepers. But the largest private employer is First Chicago Corp.'s credit card processing center.

Much of the residential and retail growth has been in new subdivisions on the cities' east sides, leaving aging downtowns behind. Yet urban Kane County has attracted a growing number of Hispanic residents.

Between Elgin and Aurora are St. Charles, Geneva and Batavia, site of the Fermi National Accelerator Laboratory that extends into Du Page County. The 14th's section of Du Page includes West Chicago and part of Bartlett. To the south is lightly populated, conservative-voting Kendall County.

Just west of the Fox River Valley, the 14th leaves the metropolis and enters rural downstate Illinois. The only large break in the farmscape is De Kalb, site of Northern Illinois University (22,500 students). Clinton twice narrowly won De Kalb; in 1996, it was the only county partially or wholly in the 14th that he carried. In Lee County is Dixon, former President Ronald Reagan's boyhood hometown.

1990 Population: 571,530. White 507,488 (89%), Black 23,867 (4%), Other 40,175 (7%). Hispanic origin 56,145 (10%). 18 and over 407,741 (71%), 62 and over 63,855 (11%). Median age: 31.

for physical illnesses, if they had previously covered mental health.

Top Republicans, especially in the House, opposed the provisions, and Hastert and others were dispatched to try to negotiate them out of the bill. But after weeks of closed-door meetings they had no success, and House Republicans gave in. "The Senate was not going to retract on this," said Hastert afterward. "We have to go on now. We have to get out of here."

Hastert has been a career-long advocate of lower taxes and a balanced-budget constitutional amendment. He is an evangelical Christian with conservative views on social-policy questions, and he also is a zealous adherent to the GOP creed that the federal government is prone to overregulate.

Hastert was a logical choice to become chief deputy whip in 1995, not only because he had been one of six GOP deputy whips in the 103rd, but also because he added regional balance to a leadership structure long on Southerners.

In his early years in Washington, Hastert was a protege of Michel's and worked hard to protect his turf for him. He became a key behind-the-scenes operator for the traditional Middle America wing of the House GOP, drawing on skills he had learned in a long apprenticeship in the state legislature (where he was viewed as an ally of moderate GOP Gov. James R. Thompson).

Hastert's daily duties as chief deputy whip involve taking the temperature of his colleagues on legislative proposals coming to the floor. His business is to know which members are persuadable when the leadership needs votes. His ability to push the party line without making colleagues feel they've been arm-twisted has made him one of the more influential House Republicans.

A beefy former wrestling coach who once headed the National Wrestling Congress, Hastert is usually rather reticent in his public persona. But he can get exercised at times, as when he dressed down David A. Kessler, the commissioner of the Food and Drug Administration, in the midst of a hearing on smoking. Hastert called Kessler's refusal to reveal the sources of certain documents damning to the tobacco industry "contempt of Congress" and shouted at him from his seat. Kessler responded: "There are bounds, sir."

Hastert holds a seat on the influential Commerce Committee, and on the Government Reform and Oversight Committee he is chairman of the subcommittee on National Security, International Affairs and Criminal Justice.

At Home: Just as he has worked his way into the GOP leadership circle, Hastert had earlier risen quickly within the Illinois Republican delegation.

That was evident during the redistricting process that preceded the 1992 election: Hastert took the lead in organizing GOP House members behind a plan favoring Republicans that was eventually enacted by a three-judge federal court panel.

The remap left Hastert in 1992 with an exurban-rural district similar to the one that had previously elected him to the House. Hastert has breezed to victory ever since, as he had in two previous re-election campaigns.

Only Hastert's first House general-election contest caused him difficulty. He had already gone a long way in politics without breaking a sweat. Appointed to the Illinois House in 1981 to fill a vacancy, Hastert gained respect for his knowledge of state budget matters. Hastert was selected in 1986 as the 14th District nominee by a Republican convention after GOP Rep. John E. Grotberg was forced to retire because of a terminal illness.

But in the general election, Hastert struggled to maintain the Republican hold on the district. His Democratic foe, Kane County Coroner Mary Lou Kearns, enjoyed some advantages that made the election close.

Whereas Kearns was an official in the district's largest county, Hastert came from the southeast corner of the 14th, away from its population centers. And while Kearns had begun to campaign in summer 1985, Hastert was not nominated until June 1986, leaving him just a little more than four months to summon the normal GOP loyalties.

Hastert was hindered in that effort by the bruised feelings left over from the convention that nominated him. The backers of two other candidates — West Chicago lawyer Tom Johnson and Elgin Mayor Richard Verbic — complained that the convention was stacked in Hastert's favor.

While Hastert struggled to gain his footing, Kearns attacked him for supporting a utility measure in the legislature that she claimed would result in rate increases. But in the final weeks, Hastert's sluggish effort finally came together. He promoted his experience in Springfield, where he was GOP spokesman on the state House Appropriations Committee.

Hastert also went after Kearns, reminding district Republicans that she was a presidential convention delegate in 1984 for Walter F. Mondale. Hastert won with 52 percent. Kearns demurred on a rematch in 1988, and Hastert pinned a little-known Democratic opponent by a nearly 3-1 margin, establishing a solid hold on the seat.

HOUSE ELECTIONS

1996 General		
Dennis Hastert (R)	134,432	(64%)
Doug Mains (D)	74,332	(36%)
1994 General		
Dennis Hastert (R)	110,204	(76%)
Steve Denari (D)	33,891	(24%)

Previous Winning Percentages: **1992** (67%) **1990** (67%) **1988** (74%) **1986** (52%)

CAMPAIGN FINANCE

	Receipts	Receipts from PACs	Expend-itures
1996			
Hastert (R)	$947,512	$555,365 (59%)	$968,055
Mains (D)	$123,760	$2,500 (2%)	$125,997
1994			
Hastert (R)	$689,729	$359,743 (52%)	$696,217
Denari (D)	$56,750	$500 (1%)	$54,330

DISTRICT VOTE FOR PRESIDENT

	1996		1992
D	89,939 (41%)	**D**	83,107 (34%)
R	103,773 (48%)	**R**	105,698 (44%)
I	22,148 (10%)	**I**	52,914 (22%)

KEY VOTES

1997	
Ban "partial birth" abortions	Y
1996	
Approve farm bill	Y
Deny public education to illegal immigrants	Y
Repeal ban on certain assault-style weapons	Y
Increase minimum wage	N
Freeze defense spending	N
Approve welfare overhaul	Y
1995	
Approve balanced-budget constitutional amendment	Y
Relax Clean Water Act regulations	Y
Oppose limits on environmental regulations	N
Reduce projected Medicare spending	Y
Approve GOP budget with tax and spending cuts	Y

VOTING STUDIES

	Presidential Support		Party Unity		Conservative Coalition	
Year	**S**	**O**	**S**	**O**	**S**	**O**
1996	37	62	95	4	98	0
1995	19	80	94	2	94	2
1994	45	50	92	5	94	6
1993	35	64	92	6	93	7
1992	78	19	89	10	88	13
1991	84	14	90	6	95	3

INTEREST GROUP RATINGS

Year	ADA	AFL-CIO	CCUS	ACU
1996	0	n/a	100	100
1995	0	0	100	92
1994	5	0	92	95
1993	5	8	91	100
1992	5	25	75	92
1991	0	8	100	95

15 Thomas W. Ewing (R)

Of Pontiac — Elected 1991; 3rd full term

Biographical Information

Born: Sept. 19, 1935, Atlanta, Ill.

Education: Millikin U., B.S. 1957; John Marshall Law School, J.D. 1968.

Military Service: Army, 1957; Army Reserve, 1957-63.

Occupation: Lawyer.

Family: Wife, Connie Lupo; three children; three stepchildren.

Religion: Methodist.

Political Career: Ill. House, 1975-91, deputy Republican leader.

Capitol Office: 2417 Rayburn Bldg. 20515; 225-2371.

Committees

Agriculture
Department Operations, Nutrition & Foreign Agriculture; Risk Management & Specialty Crops (chairman)

Science
Basic Research; Technology

Transportation & Infrastructure
Aviation; Surface Transportation

In Washington: Four years into his House career, Ewing played an important role in the GOP effort to overhaul federal farm laws, helping to write the bill that brought farm policy more in line with free-market principles. Ewing's seat on the Agriculture Committee is important to his constituents, who grow much of the state's corn and soybeans.

From his position as chairman of the committee's Risk Management and Specialty Crops Subcommittee, Ewing worked to overhaul the current price support programs for peanuts and sugar and then helped to ward off attempts by a coalition of free market conservatives and urban liberals to phase out the programs. Both the peanut and sugar programs prop up prices through a combination of government loans and production limits, which critics claim inflate prices for consumers and businesses that use them in their products.

When the House considered the so-called Freedom to Farm bill in February 1996, both price-support programs were saved by close votes. Ewing led the floor fight to save the sugar program. Opponents of the program introduced an amendment that would have phased out the program over five years, which was a tactical retreat from an earlier version that would have eliminated the program immediately. But Ewing and other sugar defenders said the farm bill already reformed the program, adding that eliminating the price supports entirely would cost jobs and leave the United States dependent on foreign sugar.

"Under our proposal, which preserves the sugar industry of America from unfair competition by subsidized sugar producers around the world, we have freed up production," Ewing told the House. "There are a lot of different prices for sugar around the world. But American sugar is stable in price. The supply is stable." The House voted to preserve the program, 208-217.

Ewing also backs a free market in international trade which he says will benefit American farmers, giving them more places to sell their crops. He introduced legislation in 1996 that would permanently extend most favored nation (MFN) status to 17 nations that currently require annual renewal of MFN. Under MFN status, foreign goods can enter the United States with non-discriminatory tariffs. The 17 nations include former Soviet-bloc republics and China. "The future growth of the American economy depends heavily on increasing exports to eastern Europe and China, and our businesses cannot be crippled by the uncertainty of annual MFN renewal," Ewing said when introducing the bill. "This issue is particularly important to agriculture. With declining budgets and more market-oriented agricultural policies, exports are more important than ever."

When the House in June 1996 held its annual debate over whether to grant MFN to China, Ewing ardently defended the trade status for the Chinese. Opponents argued that Beijing should be denied the trade standing because of its policies on human rights, its threat of military action against Taiwan, and its sale of nuclear weapons components to Pakistan.

But Ewing said that trade with China is extremely important to American farmers. "It is indeed the fastest growing market," he said, adding that, "I firmly believe that when we are involved in China, we can improve conditions in China." The House agreed with him, defeating, 141-286, a resolution that would have ended China's MFN status.

A true believer in regulatory reform, Ewing saw three of his own measures easing certain regulations signed into law during the 104th Congress. One measure would provide judicial review of the 1980 Regulatory Flexibility Act (RFA), which requires federal regulators to conduct an analysis of the impact of any proposed new regulation on small businesses. Ewing said that too often regulators use a loophole in the law that allows them to publish a statement in the Federal Register certifying that their regulation does not affect a significant number of small businesses and therefore allows the agency to avoid

Most counties of downstate Illinois struggled with double-digit unemployment at the height of the recent recession. But two adjacent 15th District counties were islands of economic stability: McLean, which has an unusually thriving business sector, and Champaign, home of the main campus of the University of Illinois.

This relative prosperity, combined with a traditional Republican base in surrounding farm country, makes the 15th a quintessential Midwestern Republican district. Though there are faded industrial areas and liberal academic communities that provide some Democratic votes, they are rarely enough to swing the partisan balance.

However, Clinton won twice in the district with 43 percent in 1992 and 45 percent in 1996. His narrow lead in 1996 was built mainly on his winning margin in Champaign and Vermilion counties. From a Republican standpoint, it was a far cry from 1988, when George Bush garnered 57 percent of the votes and led in 10 of the district's 11 counties.

Bloomington and Normal, in McLean County at the west end of the district, form its largest urban center. The cities have more than 90,000 residents between them. State Farm Insurance, the world's largest auto insurer, has its headquarters in Bloomington; Country Companies, another insurance firm, is based here. Normal has Illinois State University, with 19,300 students; and Diamond-Star Motors, a joint venture of Mitsubishi and Chrysler, builds cars.

The rest of McLean County, as well as De Witt County to the south and Livingston, Ford and Iroquois counties north and east, contain some of the state's most prolific corn and soybean farms. These five counties, which Bob

ILLINOIS 15
East Central — Champaign; Kankakee

Dole carried in 1996, make up the 15th's Republican core.

But a mix of academia, industry and farming makes Champaign County a swing-voting area.

Republican Ewing won the county with 52 percent of the votes in 1996, while Clinton led in the county with 49 percent. The University of Illinois dominates the economic landscape in the twin cities of Champaign and Urbana. Its payroll of 13,000 people supports a student enrollment of slightly more than 36,000. A Kraft food oils plant is the city's largest industrial facility.

Other urban areas of the district are not as economically healthy. Even in Champaign County, Rantoul is coping with the shutdown of Chanute Air Force Base under the 1989 base-closing law.

Vermilion County has been hurt by factory layoffs in Danville and the demise of the tapped-out coal industry nearby. Clinton beat Dole here by more than 3,500 votes.

Kankakee, at the district's northern edge, has been seeking an economic formula since the departure of two large industrial employers in the early 1980s. The city is one-third black, giving it the largest minority population in the 15th.

1990 Population: 571,532. White 512,928 (90%), Black 42,571 (7%), Other 16,033 (3%). Hispanic origin 9,300 (2%). 18 and over 433,424 (76%), 62 and over 87,262 (15%). Median age: 31.

conducting the RFA analyses. A small business owner also was prohibited from asking the courts to review whether the agency had complied with the RFA. Ewing's measure, which was part of a broader bill offering small businesses tax relief, would allow such a court challenge.

"Small businesses in particular felt that the money and time they spent complying with rules and regulations handed down from the federal government were crippling their ability to complete and invest in productive activity," Ewing said.

He also was successful with legislation requiring federal oil spill regulations to differentiate oils made from petroleum from those made from peanuts, olives, corn or other edible bases. The measure ensured that the owners and operators of vessels carrying animal fats and vegetable oils are not required to meet the same environmental regulations as those involving the transportation of petroleum oil.

Ewing said that since edible oils do not pose the same risks to the environment as petroleum oils, they should be treated differently when writing regulations.

The third measure Ewing sponsored that became law in 1996 amended existing labor law to permit 16- and 17-year olds to load paper balers and compactors. This bill allows teenage workers at businesses such as grocery stores to load paper into machines that meet the approval of the American National Standards Institute, a private organization that rates the safety of such equipment. Workers under 18 would still be prohibited from operating or unloading the balers.

The measure revises a Labor Department regulation issued in 1954 that has caused grocery stores to pay large fines, Ewing told the House, just because their teenage employees have tossed empty boxes into paper balers. Even though current machines are much safer than those the regulation was originally written for, the law itself has not been updated, Ewing said. "The Labor Department, in my opinion, has misused their power by fining grocers huge amounts of money for a casual violation, when there is not a real safety concern," he said. "This is an example of what has become a hated symbol of excessive and needless government regulation."

Ewing's pro-business stance tracks with his conservative views on other issues. He opposes abortion and voted to repeal the ban on certain assault weapons. He also votes against labor positions. In May 1996, Ewing opposed raising the minimum wage by 90 cents an hour, but in August, when the wage increase won final passage in the House, he switched and voted "yea." The final version of the wage bill included other provisions sought by Republicans, including $10 billion in business tax cuts over five years, a $5,000 tax credit to offset the cost of adoption and an expansion of Individual Retirement Accounts.

Ewing also supported a GOP effort to allow non-union employees to choose compensatory time off instead of overtime. Union leaders and other critics of the measure said it was a way to cheat workers out of their hard-earned overtime pay, but supporters said it would give workers more flexibility to take time off.

In the 104th Congress, Ewing was the chairman of the Conservative Opportunity Society, a Republican discussion group started by House Speaker Newt Gingrich in the early 1980s.

At Home: Ewing easily won the July 1991 special election to succeed Republican Rep. Edward Madigan, who had become President George Bush's Agriculture Secretary, but there was some question whether he had made the right move. It seemed at the time that he had given up a senior position in the state House (deputy Republican leader) for what might be a short stay in Washington.

Redistricting was around the corner; Illinois was slated to lose two House seats, and a third incumbent would be displaced to make room for a new Hispanic-majority district. Democrats, who controlled the state legislature, conceded that two House Democrats would go, but they also seemed ready to scrap a GOP seat by merging the districts of Ewing and then-GOP leader Robert H. Michel.

But the legislature stalemated over which Democratic incumbents would be hurt by redistricting. A federal court panel took over and enacted a plan drawn up by state GOP officials. Democratic members bore the entire burden of the seat shift; Ewing and Michel were given their own districts in which to run.

Ewing kept most of his GOP base in the new 15th. He lost some rural territory and picked up Democratic Vermilion County, which has a struggling industrial economy. Ewing drew no primary opposition for Madigan's vacated seat, and he had no problem defeating Democratic former state Rep. Gerald Bradley in the July special election. Since then, he has won comfortably, always taking over 55 percent.

HOUSE ELECTIONS

1996 General		
Thomas W. Ewing (R)	121,019	(57%)
Laurel Lunt Prussing (D)	90,065	(43%)
1994 General		
Thomas W. Ewing (R)	108,857	(68%)
Paul Alexander (D)	50,874	(32%)

Previous Winning Percentages: 1992 (59%) **1991**† (66%)

† Special election

CAMPAIGN FINANCE

	Receipts	Receipts from PACs		Expend-itures
1996				
Ewing (R)	$645,573	$344,979	(53%)	$664,934
Prussing (D)	$378,082	$65,209	(17%)	$369,185
1994				
Ewing (R)	$496,254	$219,532	(44%)	$511,926
Alexander (D)	$144,242	$54,138	(38%)	$144,040

DISTRICT VOTE FOR PRESIDENT

1996		1992	
D	100,017 (45%)	**D**	107,962 (43%)
R	98,925 (45%)	**R**	98,372 (39%)
I	19,477 (9%)	**I**	47,259 (19%)

KEY VOTES

1997	
Ban "partial birth" abortions	Y
1996	
Approve farm bill	Y
Deny public education to illegal immigrants	Y
Repeal ban on certain assault-style weapons	Y
Increase minimum wage	N
Freeze defense spending	Y
Approve welfare overhaul	Y
1995	
Approve balanced-budget constitutional amendment	Y
Relax Clean Water Act regulations	Y
Oppose limits on environmental regulations	N
Reduce projected Medicare spending	Y
Approve GOP budget with tax and spending cuts	Y

VOTING STUDIES

	Presidential Support		Party Unity		Conservative Coalition	
Year	**S**	**O**	**S**	**O**	**S**	**O**
1996	34	63	91	6	94	6
1995	17	81	94†	4†	95†	2†
1994	41	54	92	6	94	6
1993	31	69	93	5	89	11
1992	74	25	80	17	71	27
1991	86†	14†	81†	15†	100†	0†

† Not eligible for all recorded votes.

INTEREST GROUP RATINGS

Year	ADA	AFL-CIO	CCUS	ACU
1996	0	n/a	100	100
1995	0	0	96	96
1994	10	0	92	90
1993	5	0	91	100
1992	25	33	88	88
1991	0†	13†	100†	100†

† Not eligible for all recorded votes.

16 Donald Manzullo (R)

Of Egan — Elected 1992, 3rd term

Biographical Information
Born: March 24, 1944, Rockford, Ill.
Education: American U., B.A. 1967; Marquette U., J.D. 1970.
Occupation: Lawyer.
Family: Wife, Freda Tezlik; three children.
Religion: Baptist.
Political Career: Sought Republican nomination for U.S. House, 1990.
Capitol Office: 409 Cannon Bldg. 20515; 225-5676.

Committees
Banking & Financial Services
Domestic & International Monetary Policy
International Relations
Asia & the Pacific; International Economic Policy & Trade
Small Business
Tax, Finance & Exports (chairman)
Joint Economic

In Washington: Manzullo is an enthusiastic supporter of international free trade and a staunch social-issues conservative, a combination that puts him in an interesting position during debates about U.S. policy toward China.

The economy of the 16th District has strengthened in recent years thanks to an expansion of export business, and Manzullo strongly believes that the United States should keep up good commercial relations with China, an important emerging market. But he abhors what he sees as a coercive abortion policy dictated by Chinese rulers bent on controlling the vast nation's population growth.

Manzullo, who sits on the International Relations Committee, has urged a cutoff of U.S. money for the United Nations Population Fund (UNFPA) because, as he said during debate on the fiscal 1996 foreign operations spending measure, "The bill provides $25 million to the UNFPA, but we should not send one penny to an organization that not only condones, but praises China's brutal family planning program."

At the same time, Manzullo argues that expanded trade with China benefits American workers and can lead to advances in human rights in the country. "Change sometimes comes too slowly for Americans, but I am confident that the inevitable triumph of democracy and respect for human rights will happen one day soon in China just as it has in other parts of the world," he once told the House.

Manzullo favors continuing China's most-favored-nation (MFN) trade status, which allows Chinese goods to enter the United States with normal, non-discriminatory tariffs. Opponents of China's MFN status say its government's sins — abuse of human rights, military threats against Taiwan, sales of nuclear weapons components to Pakistan and alleged violations of U.S. trade agreements — should disqualify it from receiving the trade standing.

But Manzullo contends that denying China normal trade relations "jeopardizes the long-term survivability" of high-paying U.S. jobs. "It is expected that China will account for 37 percent of the future growth in United States exports," Manzullo said in June 1996, when the House was considering a resolution to disapprove China's MFN status. "Thus, trade with China is a cornerstone for resolving the most pressing problem in the minds of the forgotten American — stagnant wages and job growth." The House rejected the disapproval resolution, 141-286.

Manzullo's positive outlook on international trade is shaped by the experience of his district, where in the early 1980's, the industrial city of Rockford had a staggering unemployment problem. "Now, thanks to an export-driven recovery over the past decade, Rockford has one of the lowest unemployment rates in the country at 4 percent," he told the House in September 1996. "During my visits to the 16th District, I am constantly amazed at the number of small firms engaged in world trade."

An important Illinois employer, Peoria-based Caterpillar Inc., has special interest in China because of that nation's planned Three Gorges Dam project, which could be the largest earth-moving undertaking in history.

Manzullo is among those in Congress who want the Export-Import Bank to finance loans to China for new sales of heavy equipment for the project. They are concerned that if China does not receive the financing, U.S. companies will miss a golden opportunity for hundreds of millions of dollars in heavy equipment sales to China.

But in May 1996 the Ex-Im Bank decided against issuing letters of interest to China for the project because of environmental and human rights concerns. In his position in the 104th Congress as chairman of the Small Business Subcommittee on Procurement, Exports and Business Opportunities, Manzullo asked the bank to issue the letters of interest. He told the Financial Times that no environmental considerations are required for the letters, and that the bank has "lost sight of its primary mission" — to provide financing for U.S. exporters. Manzullo

ILLINOIS 16
Northwest — Rockford; McHenry

The Yankees and Scandinavian farmers who settled the northern tier of Illinois gave it a lasting Republican tenor. Republicans held the region's House seat throughout the 20th century — until 1990.

After an uncharacteristic fling at Democratic voting in 1990, the 16th returned to its Republican form two years later. GOP challenger Manzullo unseated one-term Democratic Rep. John W. Cox Jr. Both Manzullo and Bob Dole won easily here in 1996, although the congressman had the larger margin.

The rare Republican setbacks in the district in 1990 were in part the results of flawed candidacies. Cox's opponent, John W. Hallock Jr., faced questions about his personal ethics. And then-16th District GOP Rep. Lynn Martin's challenge to Democratic Sen. Paul Simon bombed; she got just 45 percent in her home base.

There is a core Democratic vote in the 16th, much of it centered in industrial Rockford (Winnebago County). But even within Winnebago County (which provides more than 40 percent of the 16th's votes), the Democratic edge is tempered by a Republican suburban and rural vote. And the overall Republican advantage in the 16th is cemented by McHenry County, a GOP bastion in exurban Chicago at the district's eastern end.

Rockford, with nearly 140,000 residents, is Illinois' second-largest city. Democrats rely on the city's blue collar work force. Rockford has about 21,000 black residents, more than three-quarters of the district's black population.

A Chrysler plant and Sundstrand Corp. (a defense contractor based here) are the largest employers of Rockford's residents. Unemployment soared to 20 percent at one point during the early 1980s recession, but the city, with an extensive park system and other municipal amenities, has held on to its population better than some other industrial cities: Rockford had a net loss of fewer than 300 people between 1980 and 1990.

This relative stability pales, though, compared with McHenry County's boom during that period. Located at the northwestern edge of Chicago's exurbia, McHenry increased its population by 24 percent during the 1980s.

This growth brought dramatic change to McHenry's larger towns: McHenry, Crystal Lake, Cary, Algonquin, Woodstock. Motorola Inc. opened in 1994 for a cellular phone assembly plant in Harvard in January 1997 that is expected to employ 6,000 workers. But much of the county remains devoted to the traditional farming pursuits that emboldened the town of Harvard to call itself "the milk capital of the world." McHenry may be one of Illinois' most Republican counties. Dole beat beat Bill Clinton here by 10,000 votes.

The other counties of this Wisconsin-border district are among Illinois' leading dairy producers. Jo Daviess County, in Illinois' northwest corner, leads the state in raising beef cattle. Galena, in rolling hills near the Mississippi River, has a tourist-based economy: It features the home of President Ulysses S. Grant and numerous bed-and-breakfast establishments.

1990 Population: 571,530. White 530,666 (93%), Black 26,845 (5%), Other 14,019 (2%). Hispanic origin 17,567 (3%). 18 and over 415,480 (73%), 62 and over 82,705 (14%). Median age: 33.

chairs the Small Business panel again in the 105th, although it has been renamed the Tax, Finance and Exports Subcommittee.

Manzullo expressed his displeasure with the Export-Import Bank's China decision by offering an amendment to the fiscal 1997 foreign operations spending bill to reduce the agency's budget by $3.1 million. The amendment would have cut the bank's Washington bureaucracy at the same level as cuts in the program account, he told the House. He also was angry that 200 Ex-Im Bank employees received bonuses adding up to nearly $1 million. The bank later admitted that many of the employees were overpaid.

"If Ex-Im declines at this time to support our exporters for the Three Gorges Dam project . . . and if Ex-Im immediately withdraws support for both large and small U.S. exporters for this huge project, then Ex-Im does not need the extra $2 million for outreach activities to small businesses," Manzullo said. "Ex-Im could do more for small businesses by revisiting the Three Gorges Dam decision." But the House rejected his effort to reduce the agency's budget, 176-236.

Though Manzullo shares the Clinton administration's goal of extending America's commercial reach abroad, he typically argues against U.S. military involvement overseas. He voted for a measure in November 1995 that would have prohibited the use of federal funds for the deployment of U.S. troops to Bosnia as part of any peacekeeping operation. Manzullo said that the Bosnians should be arming and defending themselves in the Balkan conflict. "It is unconscionable that President Clinton has refused to lift the Bosnian arms embargo, while making every effort to send 25,000 American troops to protect the very country he has worked to disarm." The House passed the bill, 243-171. But after the warring parties in the conflict signed a U.S.-brokered peace agreement, U.S. troops were sent to Bosnia to help enforce it.

On the domestic front, Manzullo was successful in 1995 in amending the 1990 Clean Air Act to ease a provision aimed at inducing commuters to stop driving to and from work alone. His bill lifted a federal requirement that employers in high pollution zones reduce by 25 percent the number of car trips employees make in commuting to work.

Manzullo's measure leaves it up to the states to decide whether to enforce the mandate, although it stipulates that the emissions reductions that the states agreed to under the act will have to be made up in some other fashion.

On social issues, Manzullo anchors the GOP right. In the 1980s, he picketed clinics in Rockford that performed abortions. He supports the death penalty, favors gunowners' rights, and backed an effort in 1996 to deny public education to the children of illegal immigrants. In 1994, when the House was debating a school aid bill and a dispute arose over whether home-schooling parents should be government-certified, Manzullo said, "The right to choose the form of education for one's children and be free of government interference is at the core of our liberties in this nation." The issue is close to his heart: His wife has taught their three children at home.

At Home: Manzullo first tried for this seat in 1990, losing in the GOP primary to John W. Hallock Jr., a more moderate state legislator. Hallock lost the general election to Democrat John W. Cox Jr. in an upset; the northwestern district had sent a Republican to the House in every election since 1900.

In 1992, it was expected that Republicans would take on Cox behind state Sen. Jack Schaffer, who had party establishment backing and more money than Manzullo. But Manzullo, back for a second try with a corps of volunteers (including conservative Christian activists) and seasoned from his first race, went after Schaffer, accusing him of supporting increased taxes. He also hit Schaffer for supporting a legislative pay raise and accepting contributions from liberal-leaning PACs. Manzullo, who netted 46 percent in the 1990 primary, outran Schaffer in 1992 with 56 percent.

He then had to get by Cox, who had brought a low-key, forthright approach to the job that seemed to have plenty of appeal. Cox at times went against his district's conservative streak — opposing the use of force against Iraq, opposing capital punishment, and supporting abortion rights and the family leave bill that President George Bush vetoed. But Cox embraced a balanced-budget amendment to the Constitution, middle-income tax relief, a modest capital gains tax cut and investment tax credits.

The district, though, reverted to traditional Republican form, electing Manzullo with 56 percent of the vote. He climbed to 71 percent in the big GOP year of 1994, then settled down to a 60 percent victory in 1996 against Democrat Catherine M. Lee, a former Barrington school board president.

HOUSE ELECTIONS

1996 General		
Donald Manzullo (R)	137,523	(60%)
Catherine M. Lee (D)	90,575	(40%)
1994 General		
Donald Manzullo (R)	117,238	(71%)
Pete Sullivan (D)	48,736	(29%)

Previous Winning Percentages: 1992 (56%)

CAMPAIGN FINANCE

	Receipts	Receipts from PACs		Expend-itures
1996				
Manzullo (R)	$782,233	$176,071	(23%)	$786,063
Lee (D)	$357,666	$69,719	(19%)	$391,414
1994				
Manzullo (R)	$584,949	$162,096	(28%)	$579,059
Sullivan (D)	$215,208	$63,007	(29%)	$214,715

DISTRICT VOTE FOR PRESIDENT

1996		1992	
D	99,397 (42%)	**D**	95,102 (37%)
R	111,639 (47%)	**R**	108,949 (42%)
I	24,153 (10%)	**I**	56,169 (22%)

KEY VOTES

1997	
Ban "partial birth" abortions	Y
1996	
Approve farm bill	Y
Deny public education to illegal immigrants	Y
Repeal ban on certain assault-style weapons	Y
Increase minimum wage	N
Freeze defense spending	N
Approve welfare overhaul	Y
1995	
Approve balanced-budget constitutional amendment	Y
Relax Clean Water Act regulations	Y
Oppose limits on environmental regulations	N
Reduce projected Medicare spending	Y
Approve GOP budget with tax and spending cuts	Y

VOTING STUDIES

	Presidential Support		Party Unity		Conservative Coalition	
Year	S	O	S	O	S	O
1996	33	65	92	6	82	18
1995	16	84	95	5	88	12
1994	46	54	94	6	94	6
1993	29	71	95	4	91	9

INTEREST GROUP RATINGS

Year	ADA	AFL-CIO	CCUS	ACU
1996	5	n/a	94	100
1995	0	0	100	100
1994	5	0	92	95
1993	5	0	91	100

17 Lane Evans (D)

Of Rock Island — Elected 1982, 8th term

Biographical Information
Born: Aug. 4, 1951, Rock Island, Ill.
Education: Augustana College (Rock Island, Ill.), B.A. 1974; Georgetown U., J.D. 1978.
Military Service: Marine Corps, 1969-71.
Occupation: Lawyer.
Family: Single.
Religion: Roman Catholic.
Political Career: No previous office.
Capitol Office: 2335 Rayburn Bldg. 20515; 225-5905.

Committees
National Security
Military Procurement; Military Readiness
Veterans' Affairs (ranking)

In Washington: In a Congress controlled by conservatives, Evans is a fairly rare bird: an unabashed pro-labor liberal from a Middle-American district of farms, market towns and small cities.

He sits on two committees with memberships that tilt decidedly to the right — National Security and Veterans' Affairs — yet he is a leading proponent of limiting armaments that he sees as beyond the pale, such as anti-personnel land mines and blinding lasers.

In the 105th Congress, Evans is the ranking Democrat on Veterans' Affairs, where he has fought for increased attention to the medical problems and other needs of soldiers who served in the Vietnam and Persian Gulf wars.

Evans' liberalism has brought him some adverse electoral consequences: In 1996, he heard a GOP challenger denounce his "far-left social agenda and tax-and-spend record," and he won an eighth term with a career-low 52 percent tally.

Evans is the first Vietnam-era veteran to hold the ranking slot on Veterans' Affairs. He was in the Marine Corps during the Vietnam War, and although he was not assigned to Vietnam, he emerged a few years ago as a leading proponent of federal programs benefiting veterans of that conflict. He was the premier House crusader for veterans suffering from diseases linked to Agent Orange, a defoliant used during the Vietnam conflict. His four-year effort paid off with the enactment of legislation on Agent Orange medical compensation in the 102nd Congress.

Evans expanded on that effort in the 104th Congress and won approval of a measure helping certain children of Vietnam veterans who were exposed to Agent Orange; the legislation provides health and vocational benefits to children with the spina bifida birth defect. The provision, included in the fiscal 1997 spending bill funding the Department of Veterans' Affairs (VA), marked the first time that the children of veterans were awarded government benefits.

"I believe that these children are as much veterans of the war as any other person that served or who was wounded during time of war," Evans told the House in September 1996. "Through no choice of their own, they lost their health in service to our country."

A continuing concern of the Veterans' Affairs panel are questions surrounding gulf war syndrome, a mysterious complex of medical problems among Persian Gulf War veterans that is thought to be connected to exposure to Iraqi chemical weapons. Evans has pressed for increased treatment and compensation for veterans with the syndrome, many of whom continue to report symptoms almost six years after the end of the war.

All 700,000 Gulf War veterans are entitled to priority medical care through 1998, and veterans with undiagnosed illnesses also may receive monthly compensation if they can demonstrate that an illness arose within two years of returning from the gulf. But critics of this policy say the two-year window has led the VA to deny compensation to most gulf war veterans.

Evans and Minnesota Democratic Sen. Paul Wellstone have introduced legislation extending the time limit from two years to 10 years, which would make the government responsible for illnesses that develop in veterans through 2001. "It is clear that it may take many years to establish the cause of the mystery illness that is afflicting our vets," Evans said when introducing the bill. "With many vets developing symptoms after the two year period, we have to act now and give them the benefit of the doubt."

Evans made a splash on Veterans' Affairs in December 1992 when he bid for the committee chairmanship, a position held for 12 years by venerable Mississippi Democrat G.V. "Sonny" Montgomery. Evans fell four votes short of taking the chair, and many assumed that his strong showing presaged success against Montgomery in a 1994 rematch. But fate intervened in the form of a House GOP majority, and Evans decided against challenging Montgomery for the ranking spot. Later, Montgomery announced that the 104th Congress would be his last.

Evans' bid for the chairmanship came after

For western Illinois' 17th, the recession of the early 1990s was mild compared with the economic devastation that occurred in the previous decade. Then, the industrial regions centered on the neighboring cities of Rock Island and Moline (at the 17th's western end) and Peoria (across its eastern border in the 18th District) hit the skids.

Layoffs and factory closures in the district's essential industry — farm equipment manufacturing — caused severe hardship. Job-seekers left the area. Although economic stability has slowly and shakily returned, the earlier near-depression conditions had a lasting political impact: The 17th, a former GOP bastion, now leans to the Democrats.

Evans blazed the partisan trail by narrowly capturing this House seat in 1982. He has since won seven re-elections. His most recent re-election bid was the first one that he did not capture at least 55 percent of the votes.

The 17th remains more competitive in major-office contests; for example, Republican Gov. Jim Edgar won every county here with at least 65 percent of the vote. But in 1996, Bill Clinton carried the 17th, finishing first in 11 of the 14 counties that are all or part in the district, beating Bob Dole by 13 percentage points.

Farm machinery is still king in the Quad Cities: Rock Island and Moline in Illinois, Davenport and Bettendorf in Iowa across the Mississippi River. Deere & Co., makers of John Deere tractors, has its headquarters in Moline as well as production and distribution facilities around the region. There is other farm-related industry, including meat packing; the federal arsenal at Rock Island is also a major employer.

ILLINOIS 17
West — Rock Island; Moline

Moline, with about 43,000 residents, is the district's largest city; Rock Island (Evans' base) is next with just over 40,000. Blacks and Hispanics make up more than 10 percent of Rock Island County, the largest minority-group concentration in the district.

Overall, Rock Island County was a boon to Democrats in 1996, giving Clinton 57 percent of its votes and Evans 58 percent.

Galesburg (Knox County) — the hometown of Illinois' late poet laureate, Carl Sandburg — is also broad-shouldered: Its largest employer is a Maytag refrigerator plant. At its southern end, the 17th takes in Quincy (Adams County), a river town that relies on agribusiness for jobs. Some coal is mined in McDonough and Fulton counties at the southeast end of the 17th.

The rest of the district is mainly rich farmland, with corn, hogs and soybeans abundant. Before the rise of Evans and the onset of economic difficulties, the large rural Republican vote usually offset the Democratic urban vote in the 17th.

At the district's north end, Carroll County and the part of Ogle County in the 17th were two of the counties to vote for Dole in 1996. The third, Adams County, is at the far southern end of the district.

1990 Population: 571,530. White 540,954 (95%), Black 18,609 (3%), Other 11,967 (2%). Hispanic origin 17,398 (3%). 18 and over 427,877 (75%), 62 and over 111,381 (19%). Median age: 35.

years of locking horns with the older Montgomery over his handling of issues relating to Vietnam-era veterans. Younger veterans, who believed Montgomery was dragging his feet on compensation for Agent Orange-related diseases, portrayed the chairman, a military officer in World War II and the Korean War, as intent on protecting his generation's programs at the expense of Vietnam veterans. But Montgomery eventually yielded to the demands of the Vietnam vets and allowed Evans' Agent Orange legislation to pass.

Evans also brings his liberal views to the National Security Committee, where he has criticized GOP efforts to allocate more for defense than the Clinton administration requests. He backed an unsuccessful attempt in June 1996 to freeze defense spending at the prior year level.

Evans sponsored a provision to the fiscal 1996 defense bill that would impose a one-year moratorium on U.S. forces' use of anti-personnel land mines. The moratorium, to take effect three years after enactment of the bill, would allow deployment of anti-personnel mines only along international borders or internationally recognized demilitarized zones — and only if the armaments were scattered in areas marked as minefields.

Since 1992, Evans and Vermont Democratic Sen. Patrick J. Leahy have tried to mobilize U.S. government support for an international agreement to ban the use of these small and inexpensive weapons, which annually kill or maim thousands of civilians long after the wars in which they were deployed.

The Pentagon vehemently opposed the provision, and it was dropped by Senate-House conferees. Leahy then inserted the core provision of the land-mine ban into the foreign operations appropriations bill, which was attached to the stopgap spending bill approved by Congress and signed by President Clinton in January 1996.

Evans also joined forces with Leahy and called on the Pentagon to support an international prohibition on waging war with laser weapons that intentionally blind. In an August 1996 letter to Defense Secretary William J. Perry, the two lawmakers said: "We are concerned that the proliferation of such weapons could pose a potent threat to American troops. We dread the day when hundreds of thousands of American servicemen and women return home from combat to face the rest of their lives without eyesight."

Evans opposed almost all of the Republicans' social and economic initiatives in the 104th; voting against an overhaul of the welfare and Medicare systems, a repeal of the assault weapons ban, and efforts to curb government regulations. Evans supports abortion rights and backed the successful Democratic effort to raise the minimum wage.

At Home: Evans' 1982 capture of this traditionally Republican seat was regarded as stunning, but his hard work, engaging manner and constituent service soon ensconced him.

Still, district Republicans try every election to convince voters that Evans is a liberal extremist. So far, he has deflected the charge, but the fire has been withering in the last few years, knocking Evans down to 55 percent in 1994 and 52 percent in 1996.

Evans wins in part because he works tirelessly at home — conducting meetings to study the district's problems, popping up at every county and small-town celebration and making himself available to the local media.

In 1982, Evans emerged from his community legal clinic in Rock Island to make his first run for public office. It was an effort that seemed futile until the March primary that year, when former state Sen. Kenneth G. McMillan, a New Right stalwart, defeated Rep. Tom Railsback, a moderate eight-term Republican.

Railsback's defeat set up a clear ideological choice, one that benefited Evans in the recession year of 1982. Evans, who had worked in the presidential campaign of Massachusetts Sen. Edward M. Kennedy in 1980, urged voters in the economically troubled district to use his candidacy as a way to "send Reagan a message." McMillan defended President Ronald Reagan's economic program, not a winning tack in that year. Evans won with 53 percent of the vote.

The 1984 election brought a rematch. McMillan moderated his rhetoric, trying to appeal to conservative voters in the rural counties of the district and to blue-collar voters in the industrial cities to the north. But Evans improved to 57 percent, carrying nine of the district's 14 counties.

In 1992, Republicans nominated Ken Schloemer, a Moline restaurateur active in Rock Island County civic affairs. Schloemer said Evan's low ratings from some business and farm interest groups, and his advocacy of gay rights in the military, proved he was out of step with the district. Evans took 60 percent.

After an anemic 55 percent showing against an unheralded GOP challenger in 1994, Evans faced an aggressive 1996 foe in Mark Baker, a first-time candidate, but one with broad name recognition in the southern part of the 17th thanks to his work as a newsman on a Quincy TV station. Baker took the usual Republican tack, portraying Evans as a liberal and promising to fight for a balanced budget and lower taxes. Evans retorted that Baker if elected would fall in line with the strongly conservative Republican agenda. He won by 5 points.

HOUSE ELECTIONS

1996 General		
Lane Evans (D)	120,008	(52%)
Mark Baker (R)	109,240	(47%)
1994 General		
Lane Evans (D)	95,312	(55%)
Jim Anderson (R)	79,471	(45%)

Previous Winning Percentages: 1992 (60%) **1990** (67%) **1988** (65%) **1986** (56%) **1984** (57%) **1982** (53%)

CAMPAIGN FINANCE

	Receipts	Receipts from PACs		Expend-itures
1996				
Evans (D)	$632,918	$333,131	(53%)	$629,624
Baker (R)	$508,527	$160,469	(32%)	$506,793
1994				
Evans (D)	$255,019	$146,700	(58%)	$270,939
Anderson (R)	$15,898	$14	(0%)	$15,583

DISTRICT VOTE FOR PRESIDENT

	1996		1992
D	119,907 (51%)	**D**	124,173 (47%)
R	89,452 (38%)	**R**	95,553 (36%)
I	23,176 (10%)	**I**	45,566 (17%)

KEY VOTES

1997	
Ban "partial birth" abortions	N
1996	
Approve farm bill	N
Deny public education to illegal immigrants	N
Repeal ban on certain assault-style weapons	N
Increase minimum wage	Y
Freeze defense spending	Y
Approve welfare overhaul	N
1995	
Approve balanced-budget constitutional amendment	N
Relax Clean Water Act regulations	N
Oppose limits on environmental regulations	Y
Reduce projected Medicare spending	N
Approve GOP budget with tax and spending cuts	N

VOTING STUDIES

	Presidential Support		Party Unity		Conservative Coalition	
Year	S	O	S	O	S	O
1996	75	25	95	5	14	86
1995	85	13	96	3	8	92
1994	77	23	99	1	6	94
1993	69	27	94	3	5	95
1992	11	88	95	5	6	94
1991	15	85	95	4	11	89

INTEREST GROUP RATINGS

Year	ADA	AFL-CIO	CCUS	ACU
1996	95	n/a	19	0
1995	95	100	8	12
1994	100	100	25	0
1993	100	100	0	4
1992	95	100	13	4
1991	100	100	20	5

18 Ray LaHood (R)

Of Peoria — Elected 1994, 2nd term

Biographical Information
Born: Dec. 6, 1945, Peoria, Ill.
Education: Spoon River Community College, 1963-65; Bradley U., B.S. 1971.
Occupation: Congressional aide; teacher; youth bureau director; urban planning commission director.
Family: Wife, Kathleen Dunk; four children.
Religion: Roman Catholic.
Political Career: Ill. House, 1982-83; defeated for re-election to Ill. House, 1982.
Capitol Office: 329 Cannon Bldg. 20515; 225-6201.

Committees
Agriculture
Department Operations, Nutrition & Foreign Agriculture; Forestry, Resource Conservation & Research
Transportation & Infrastructure
Aviation; Surface Transportation
Veterans' Affairs
Benefits

In Washington: In a House Class of 1994 filled with Republicans whose campaigns drew inspiration from Newt Gingrich and the "Contract With America," LaHood is a special case. He is a conservative, to be sure, but no big fan of Speaker Gingrich's style, and sometimes a high-profile critic of the GOP leadership's schemes.

Before his election, LaHood was chief of staff to House Minority Leader Robert H. Michel, who retired in 1994, having steadily lost influence in the GOP Conference to Gingrich, the party's ideological driving force after his 1989 election as minority whip over a candidate Michel backed.

In the initial 73-member GOP class, LaHood is one of just three who did not sign the contract. He voiced concern that its advocacy of tax cuts and defense spending increases would worsen the federal deficit.

In March 1995, LaHood was part of a tiny six-man contingent of Republicans who refused to vote with their leadership on a rescissions package cutting $17 billion from the fiscal 1995 budget. "I didn't vote for the spending cuts because it was going to pay for tax cuts," he said. The rescissions bill passed 227-200.

The next month, LaHood was one of 11 Republicans voting against what party leaders called the "crown jewel" of the contract — a tax relief package worth $189 billion over five years. He cited polls showing that a majority of Americans wanted the money saved from spending cuts to go toward reducing the deficit, not cutting taxes.

Before the vote, LaHood was one of more than 100 Republicans who signed a letter circulated by a fellow GOP freshman, Iowa's Greg Ganske, that called for narrowing the scope of the tax cuts. Ganske wanted to limit eligibility for a $500-per-child tax credit to families earning $95,000 or less a year, rather than giving that credit to families earning up to $200,000, as the contract had promised. By a vote of 246-188, the leadership pushed through the contract tax-cut language.

LaHood carried his objections to the GOP leadership's fiscal policy priorities into the October 1995 debate on the massive budget-reconciliation bill, the centerpiece of the Republican agenda to cut taxes, reduce the size of the federal government and balance the budget. The reconciliation bill passed the House, 227-203, but LaHood was one of just 10 Republicans voting "no."

In 1996, LaHood was an early supporter of efforts to raise the minimum wage, an idea warmly embraced by most Democrats but coolly greeted in the pro-business ranks of the GOP. The Republican leadership pushed an amendment to exempt small businesses from paying the higher minimum, but LaHood was one of just 43 Republicans voting against that proposal.

While such stands separate LaHood from conservative purists in House GOP ranks, he joins with them on many issues. He favored limiting punitive damages in product liability cases, supported overhauling welfare and endorsed efforts to clip the regulatory wings of the Environmental Protection Agency. He opposes abortion, backs a 12-year service-limit for the House and Senate and is a vocal proponent of a balanced-budget constitutional amendment.

In fact, when the House took up the amendment in January 1995, LaHood stood shoulder-to-shoulder with GOP freshmen who wanted it to include a hard-line "tax limitation" provision aimed at making it very tough to raise taxes. That provision was so controversial that GOP leaders decided early on to fall back and push a somewhat weaker version of the amendment, a strategy that angered the freshmen. "They went to their second game plan before they really, you know, went [all] out on their first one," LaHood complained. "We need to let our leadership people know that we were not happy with the way they handled this thing."

LaHood had hoped for a seat on Appropriations, where Michel served for a quarter-century before becoming party leader, but instead he got Agriculture and Transportation. He added Veterans' Affairs in the 105th Congress.

With its modest-sized industrial cities, small towns and farms, the 18th is in some ways a model of middle-class, Middle American conservatism.

In various permutations through a series of redistrictings, this central Illinois district has elected mostly Republican representatives since the Great Depression. Not for nothing did President Richard M. Nixon want to know how his policies would "play in Peoria."

Yet the 18th also has some concerns that make it less than a Republican bastion — including a Peoria-based industrial sector that has lost thousands of jobs in recent years and an economically worried working-class constituency.

Bill Clinton won by pluralities over George Bush in 1992 in Peoria and Tazewell, the 18th's most populous counties; he won four other counties in the Illinois River Valley and even won in the heavily Republican northern part of Sangamon County (Springfield) that is in the 18th. Bush finished first in just six mainly rural counties. In 1994, Republican LaHood carried every county except Putnam, which he lost by nine votes. Clinton carried just five counties, including Peoria, in 1996, and LaHood carried them all. (He won Putman by 71 votes this time.)

The 18th has been a legacy for three congressional generations; LaHood served as chief of staff to his predecessor, former Minority Leader Robert H. Michel, who in turn had taken over the seat from his old boss, Harold Velde.

But if the chain of representation has been stable, the district itself has not. In the 1960s, Peoria (Peoria County) anchored the southern end of the district; in the 1970s, the city was at the district's center. In the 1980s, Peoria was near the northeast corner of a district that ran west to the Mississippi River; in the 1990s, it is in the northwest portion of a mainly north-south district.

ILLINOIS 18
Central — Peoria; part of Springfield

The 18th's economic health is largely dependent on Caterpillar Inc. The manufacturer of earth-moving equipment and other heavy machinery is based in Peoria and employs nearly 18,000 people at its headquarters and plants, the largest of which is in East Peoria (Tazewell County, which also includes the cities of Pekin and Morton).

Caterpillar's slump in the early 1980s contributed to a migration from the region: Peoria, still Illinois' third-largest city with about 113,000 residents, lost about a tenth of its population during the 1980s. The company has rebounded somewhat in recent years, though a labor dispute closed Caterpillar's factories for six months beginning in November 1991 and caused regional hardship.

Democratic leanings in the industrial area usually are negated by the solid GOP rural vote. In the south, the 18th covers much of Sangamon County, including the northern, mainly white-collar portion of Springfield, the state capital.

1990 Population: 571,580. White 535,359 (94%), Black 29,414 (5%), Other 6,807 (1%). Hispanic origin 5,278 (1%). 18 and over 422,030 (74%), 62 and over 96,813 (17%). Median age: 35.

The 18th is home to corn and soybean growers and grain dealers, and Caterpillar Inc., a maker of earth-moving equipment and other heavy machinery, has headquarters in Peoria. LaHood was an early critic of Republican efforts in the 104th to remake federal farm policy along free-market lines. He said the longstanding system of crop subsidies had benefited the American economy and also made the nation self-sufficient in food. "What we don't want to see is American agriculture going overseas so we're dependent on foreign governments and foreign farmers for our agriculture," LaHood said in June 1995. Eventually he voted for the final "Freedom to Farm" bill that cleared Congress in 1996; it made concessions to some commodity interests on subsidies, but gave farmers greater flexibility in deciding what to plant and instituted a system of fixed but declining payments in lieu of subsidies.

LaHood is especially interested in protecting an agriculture research facility in his district, noting that its work helps farmers boost production while possibly reducing reliance on pesticides. "Even if there wasn't an agriculture lab in Peoria, I'd be in support of research," LaHood said.

Local concerns and constituent needs have long been a priority for LaHood, who, as Michel's chief of staff, was based in Peoria. Unlike some in his class who are deeply skeptical of the federal government, LaHood is not bashful about asking for help from Washington: He lobbied for sparing Springfield's Small Business Administration office from closure; he has sought federal loan guarantees for the struggling Toledo, Peoria and Western Railroad, which connects shippers in the 18th to regional carriers; and he has asked that Lake Springfield in his district be included in a federally funded water-treatment program that aims to reduce levels of the pollutant atrazine.

While many of his peers in the Class of 1994 pushed the successful effort in 1995 to ban members from receiving most gifts and meals, LaHood voted for an amendment allowing lawmakers to continue accepting gifts as long as they were disclosed. The amendment was defeated. LaHood said in March 1996 that while touring his district the month before, he frequently found himself having to reject small offerings. "The ordinary citizens, our constituents . . . don't realize that they're not supposed to be giving us different items," he said.

In January 1997, LaHood and Rep. Bob Wise, D-W.Va., introduced legislation to abolish the Electoral College, the institution that officially elects the president and vice president. The legislation would amend the Constitution to allow for those offices to be decided by direct election of the people. "The existence of the college needs to be addressed before we are embroiled in a crisis in which a president is elected without winning the popular vote," LaHood said.

He was one of the organizers behind a weekend retreat for House members and their families to Hershey, Pa., in March 1997. "This is not the solution. It's not a panacea. This is the beginning of people building friendships and building relationships," LaHood said. He and David E. Skaggs, D-Colo., began organizing the retreat in the fall of 1996 after witnessing a particularly heated debate on the floor. "This is an extraordinary opportunity for members of Congress to come together and . . . to start off on the right foot," LaHood said. The weekend drew about 220 members, including both the Democratic and Republican leadership.

At Home: The day after Michel announced his retirement in 1993, LaHood declared his candidacy for the open seat, and from the start he was favored to win. He called himself a conservative on social and fiscal issues, but said he hoped to emulate Michel's willingness to work with Democrats.

LaHood had only two opponents in the primary, and just one, former state Rep. Judy Koehler, represented any threat. Her biggest ammunition was advertising that attacked LaHood for campaigning on taxpayer time. LaHood waited several weeks to respond, telling voters he had taken a leave of absence from Michel's staff to run. With Michel campaigning at his side, LaHood won nomination with 50 percent of the vote.

Democrats nominated lawyer G. Douglas Stephens, who had twice lost to Michel. He agreed with LaHood on many issues. The two differed primarily on the 1994 crime bill, with LaHood contending that it contained too much "pork" in the form of social programs. Stephens tried to paint LaHood as a Washington insider, but LaHood, who was born and educated in the local school district and later worked as a junior high social studies teacher, ran TV ads that showed him walking through a school where he had taught, discussing the importance of teaching values to children. He won with 60 percent of the vote and posted nearly the same tally in winning a second term in 1996.

LaHood worked 12 years for Michel, and before that, in the early 1980s, he was an aide to GOP Rep. Tom Railsback, who represented a neighboring district. In succeeding his boss in the House, LaHood followed in Michel's path: He first won election to Congress in 1956, when his employer, GOP Rep. Harold Velde, retired.

HOUSE ELECTIONS

1996 General		
Ray LaHood (R)	143,110	(59%)
Mike Curran (D)	98,413	(41%)
1994 General		
Ray LaHood (R)	119,838	(60%)
G. Douglas Stephens (D)	78,332	(39%)

CAMPAIGN FINANCE

	Receipts	Receipts from PACs	Expend-itures
1996			
LaHood (R)	$700,220	$299,355 (43%)	$699,963
Curran (D)	$121,816	$87,550 (72%)	$113,363
1994			
LaHood (R)	$743,011	$236,634 (32%)	$697,727
Stephens (D)	$357,711	$141,850 (40%)	$345,701

DISTRICT VOTE FOR PRESIDENT

1996	1992
D 112,588 (44%)	D 116,864 (42%)
R 118,444 (47%)	R 113,656 (41%)
I 20,972 (8%)	I 46,990 (17%)

KEY VOTES

1997	
Ban "partial birth" abortions	Y
1996	
Approve farm bill	Y
Deny public education to illegal immigrants	Y
Repeal ban on certain assault-style weapons	Y
Increase minimum wage	Y
Freeze defense spending	Y
Approve welfare overhaul	Y
1995	
Approve balanced-budget constitutional amendment	Y
Relax Clean Water Act regulations	Y
Oppose limits on environmental regulations	N
Reduce projected Medicare spending	Y
Approve GOP budget with tax and spending cuts	N

VOTING STUDIES

	Presidential Support		Party Unity		Conservative Coalition	
Year	S	O	S	O	S	O
1996	39	61	84	16	76	24
1995	22	77	92	8	94	5

INTEREST GROUP RATINGS

Year	ADA	AFL-CIO	CCUS	ACU
1996	10	n/a	88	80
1995	10	17	88	72

19 Glenn Poshard (D)

Of Carterville — Elected 1988, 5th term

Biographical Information
Born: Oct. 30, 1945, Herald, Ill.
Education: Southern Illinois U., B.S. 1970, M.S. 1974, Ph.D. 1984.
Military Service: Army, 1962-65.
Occupation: Educator.
Family: Wife, Jo Roetzel; two children.
Religion: Baptist.
Political Career: Sought Democratic nomination for Ill. Senate, 1982; Ill. Senate, 1984-89.
Capitol Office: 2334 Rayburn Bldg. 20515; 225-5201.

Committees
Small Business
Government Programs & Oversight (ranking)
Transportation & Infrastructure
Aviation; Water Resources & Environment

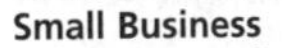

In Washington: Early in his House career, Poshard made a commitment to serve no more than 10 years in the chamber, and after he easily won a fifth term in 1996, Poshard said that was his last House campaign. He did not, however, say he was through with politics altogether, and in March 1997, he launched a bid for governor.

The nature of his opposition was unclear then, and it remained so through the spring, with GOP Gov. Jim Edgar yet to declare whether he would seek re-election in 1998 or run for the Senate seat held by Democrat Carol Moseley-Braun.

Meanwhile, Poshard went about lining up support to take the Democratic nomination — no mean feat for a candidate from outside Cook County (Chicago), which casts the majority of ballots in statewide Democratic primaries. Poshard, in Chicago to kick off his bid, said he would "contend for every inch of every precinct and every ward in this city. I think it is possible for a moderate downstate Democrat to win."

In May, Poshard announced he had endorsements from Democratic Party chairmen in more than three-fourths of Illinois' 102 counties, but missing from the group was the chairman from Cook County, where several potential candidates were waiting to see what Edgar would do.

During his tenure in the House, Poshard never had much trouble winning elections. His likable demeanor and close-to-the-people style impressed working class voters in his politically moderate district.

The factory laborers, miners, and small farmers in the 19th often disagree with the Clinton administration on social and cultural issues, but they cling to a suspicion that on economic matters, the GOP is the rich man's friend.

Poshard's life experiences connect him with these voters. He grew up around coal miners and farmers in rural Southern Illinois, attending a Baptist church that remains a touchstone for his strong religious convictions. He joined the Army at age 17 and served for three years, then enrolled at Southern Illinois University, where he eventually earned a doctorate in education.

After Democrats lost control of the House in 1994, Poshard expressed concern that liberals had come to dominate party dialogue. "I've always believed that the moderate wing of the Democrat Party had a place, that its ideals were more in line with where the average American was."

Poshard opposed the Clinton administration-backed gun control initiatives approved in the Democratic-controlled 103rd Congress, and he said this issue alone was enough to cost Democrats the House in 1994, by discrediting the party in rural districts. In the 104th, when the House GOP majority fulfilled a campaign pledge to try to repeal the ban on certain semiautomatic assault-style weapons, Poshard voted for repeal.

On votes regarding abortion policy, Poshard consistently is among the minority in his party who sides with anti-abortion forces. He voted in the 104th against requiring states to fund Medicaid abortions for poor women, against permitting abortions at overseas military hospitals, and against allowing federal employees' health care plans to cover abortions. He supports banning a particular abortion technique that opponents call "partial-birth" abortion.

In 1990, he cast a lonely vote against the Democratic leadership on the Clean Air Act. Predicting that it would cause coal mine closures and job losses in his district, Poshard was one of just 20 House members to oppose the bill.

But Poshard has warmly embraced his party when it pursues issues he sees as important to ordinary Americans — such as increasing the minimum wage, which he supported in 1996. He also has stood with the Democratic leadership in opposing GOP efforts to allow companies to offer their employees comp time in lieu of overtime pay, an idea opposed by organized labor.

Also, Poshard's views on welfare overhaul ally closely with President Clinton's. Sympathetic to laid-off workers unable to find jobs in his district's troubled industries, Poshard through most of the 104th opposed Republican attempts to

The northern part of the 19th is a familiar landscape of downstate Illinois. At the district's northern edge is its only large city, Decatur, where heavy industry and grain processing plants employ a large blue-collar work force. For miles south, flat land produces corn and soybeans.

The southern part of the district is different. The hilly territory produces coal and timber. Portions of this "border state" area are Appalachian-like. Of the 11 southernmost counties in the 19th, six have poverty rates at or above 20 percent.

This region was settled from the South and has a strong Southern Democratic tradition that tends to predominate in the 19th. Poshard, a native of rural White County, has staked his political success on an agenda that combines a populist economic message with conservative views on social issues.

Poshard defeated fellow Democratic Rep. Terry L. Bruce in a 1992 primary forced by redistricting, then carried every county in the district in that year's general election. He is hugely popular in his base in the southern part of the 19th.

Clinton also carried the 11 southern counties in 1992, and he won 10 of them in 1996 (all except Johnson). Although there is a Republican base in the heavily farmed northern part (which enabled George Bush in 1988 to narrowly carry the areas that now make up the 19th), Clinton ran well there in 1996, winning in Macon, Moultrie, Coles and Shelby counties.

Bob Dole won 10 of the district's 27 counties in 1996, most of them concentrated in the district's midsection. One of these counties, Edwards, was the only county Poshard failed to win.

Four of Illinois' 10 leading coal-producing counties are in the southern part of the 19th. Unemployment is an endemic problem in much of the region. In recent years, mechanization of mining has caused job losses, and passage of the clean air act in 1990 also has cut down on mining of the area's high-sulfur coal.

ILLINOIS 19
Rural — Southern counties; Decatur

At the southern tip of the 19th, Pope County, Illinois' least populous, is almost entirely within the Shawnee National Forest. In nearby Massac and Pulaski counties, river towns near the confluence of the Ohio and Mississippi have seen more prosperous days. Williamson County (Marion), at the district's western edge, benefits from its proximity to Southern Illinois University (in the 12th).

At the top of the district is Decatur (Macon County); with about 85,000 residents, the city is more populous than any of the 19th's other counties. Corn and soybean processors Archer Daniels Midland and A. E. Staley are economic mainstays, although a Caterpillar plant is the city's largest single employer. Industrial downsizing has taken a toll on Decatur. The city usually reinforces the Democratic vote to the south.

In between is mainly farming country, dotted with such small cities as Mattoon and Effingham. Charleston, hometown of GOP Gov. Jim Edgar, is the site of Eastern Illinois University.

1990 Population: 571,530. White 546,051 (96%), Black 22,086 (4%), Other 3,393 (1%). Hispanic origin 2,727 (<1%). 18 and over 429,589 (75%), 62 and over 116,422 (20%). Median age: 36.

impose tough new work requirements on welfare recipients and to set time limits on benefits. In the end, Poshard voted for a compromise welfare bill that Clinton agreed to sign.

Poshard in his first term served on the Education and Labor Committee — a natural given his doctorate and his work in educational administration.

Now he sits on the Transportation and Infrastructure Committee (formerly Public Works), where he argues for infrastructure improvements and other economic development projects in the 19th. Poshard is always looking for ways to help local farmers with water projects and crop diversification to meet new market demands. To boost the 19th's reeling high-sulfur coal industry, he favors federal funding for clean-coal research. He also has worked to make it easier for black lung victims to win disability benefits, and he has defended the Economic Development Administration (EDA) against budget-cutting efforts, saying it provides a "modest helping hand in bringing economic growth to our rural communities."

Through the years, the Public Works Committee was known as a prime spot for pork-barreling, and Poshard is sensitive about being tagged with that label because he feels Congress should exercise fiscal discipline so as not to bequeath future generations a crippling debt. He has voted to kill NASA's multibillion-dollar space station, and has opposed GOP efforts to spend more on defense than Clinton requests.

Although he accepted money from PACs in his first race for the House in 1988, Poshard says he decided to stop after he got into Congress and encountered issues where he wanted to vote differently from the way a PAC donor preferred. Now he supports banning PAC contributions and reducing the limit for individual givers from $1,000 to $500. He also wants to bar members from sending mass-mail newsletters and to cut members' mailing budgets in half, applying all savings to deficit reduction.

At Home: When Democratic Rep. Kenneth J. Gray of the then-22nd District decided not to run in 1988, Poshard was the party's obvious pick. In style and background, there were sharp contrasts between Gray and Poshard. Gray, known for his flashy clothes and boisterous personality, never attended college and had worked as a car dealer and auctioneer. Poshard had embarked on a career in teaching and academic administration after earning his doctorate.

But Poshard comes from working-class roots, and his regular-guy manner was well-received in the district's coal-mining communities and Ohio River towns.

Poshard's first run for office, in 1982, was a primary challenge to a veteran Democratic state senator. Though he fell short, Poshard's ability to address blue-collar concerns impressed fellow Democrats. When the senator died in mid-1984, district party leaders picked Poshard for the vacancy.

Poshard went on to win two state Senate contests on his own. He specialized in education, labor, rural health care and coal-related issues in Springfield. He was named keynote speaker for the 1986 state party convention and chairman of the Senate Labor and Commerce Committee.

When Poshard moved to succeed Gray in 1988, no Democrat stood in his way. His GOP foe, law professor Patrick Kelley, was articulate but little-known outside Carbondale, where he had served two terms on the City Council. Kelley's efforts to frame the election as an ideological contest were easily deflected by Poshard, who does not fit the profile of a liberal. Poshard won with 65 percent.

It appeared in early 1992 that redistricting would halt Poshard's rise. Instead, the ensuing contest raised his reputation as a star campaigner.

With Illinois losing two House seats in 1990 reapportionment, Poshard was thrown into the new 19th District with fellow Democrat Terry L. Bruce. Poshard appeared disadvantaged: Bruce brought more of his former constituents into the district and, as a member of Energy and Commerce, had a stronger fundraising base.

But Poshard was exceedingly strong on his turf and had ties beyond it: His White County boyhood home gave him a beachhead in what had been Bruce's district.

Even more helpful was a campaign theme in tune with the electorate. Anti-insider sentiment in Illinois was high at the time of the March 1992 primary. Though an incumbent himself, Poshard ran as an outsider, declining PAC contributions and tying Bruce to special interests with dealings on Energy and Commerce.

Poshard ran up 90 percent of the vote in the area he had represented, and he even edged Bruce in Bruce's own turf. Only in the northern end of the district, territory new to both, did Poshard run behind. In November, aided by the district's Democratic tilt, Poshard breezed by Republican lawyer Douglas E. Lee.

In the big Republican year of 1994, Poshard won with a comfortable 58 percent, and in his last House campaign in 1996, he took 67 percent.

HOUSE ELECTIONS

1996 General		
Glenn Poshard (D)	158,668	(67%)
Brent Winters (R)	75,751	(32%)
1994 General		
Glenn Poshard (D)	115,045	(58%)
Brent Winters (R)	81,995	(42%)

Previous Winning Percentages: 1992 (69%) **1990** (84%) **1988** (65%)

CAMPAIGN FINANCE

	Receipts	Receipts from PACs	Expend-itures
1996			
Poshard (D)	$263,241	0	$237,030
Winters (R)	$99,643	$4,390 (4%)	$100,055
1994			
Poshard (D)	$166,841	0	$164,541
Winters (R)	$58,816	$2,714 (5%)	$57,702

DISTRICT VOTE FOR PRESIDENT

	1996		1992
D	113,685 (47%)	**D**	131,483 (47%)
R	97,862 (41%)	**R**	95,672 (34%)
I	28,649 (12%)	**I**	50,665 (18%)

KEY VOTES

1997	
Ban "partial birth" abortions	Y
1996	
Approve farm bill	Y
Deny public education to illegal immigrants	Y
Repeal ban on certain assault-style weapons	Y
Increase minimum wage	Y
Freeze defense spending	Y
Approve welfare overhaul	Y
1995	
Approve balanced-budget constitutional amendment	Y
Relax Clean Water Act regulations	Y
Oppose limits on environmental regulations	N
Reduce projected Medicare spending	N
Approve GOP budget with tax and spending cuts	N

VOTING STUDIES

	Presidential Support		Party Unity		Conservative Coalition	
Year	**S**	**O**	**S**	**O**	**S**	**O**
1996	61	39	68	32	63	37
1995	61	39	71	29	56	44
1994	63	37	65	35	69	31
1993	57	43	72	28	61	39
1992	30	70	79	20	48	52
1991	30	70	79	19	57	43

INTEREST GROUP RATINGS

Year	ADA	AFL-CIO	CCUS	ACU
1996	70	n/a	44	45
1995	60	83	54	44
1994	55	56	83	38
1993	60	92	9	38
1992	65	83	25	36
1991	65	75	30	25

20 John M. Shimkus (R)

Of Collinsville — Elected 1996, 1st term

Biographical Information

Born: Feb. 21, 1958, Collinsville, Ill.
Education: U.S. Military Academy, B.S. 1980; Southern Illinois U., 1991-.
Military Service: Army, 1980-86; Army Reserve, 1986-present.
Occupation: Teacher; Army officer; Madison County Treasurer.
Family: Wife, Karen Muth; two children.
Religion: Lutheran.
Political Career: Candidate for Madison County Board, 1988; Collinsville Township Board of Trustees, 1989-97; Madison County treasurer, 1990-97; Republican nominee for U.S. House, 1992.
Capitol Office: 513 Cannon Bldg. 20515; 225-5271.

Committees

Commerce
Energy & Power; Telecommunications, Trade & Consumer Protection

The Path to Washington: A coveted seat on the Commerce Committee was Shimkus' reward for capturing the 20th District seat formerly represented by Democrat Richard J. Durbin, who was elected to the Senate in 1996.

Shimkus took a narrow lead over Democrat Jay C. Hoffman, a state legislator, on election night and held it through the final count, eventually winning by 1,238 votes.

The Commerce Committee, which was Shimkus' first choice, traditionally has been one of the most lucrative panels when it comes to raising campaign funds, and Shimkus — a narrow winner in a district President Clinton carried in 1992 and 1996 — can expect to be a prime target of Democrats in 1998.

Shimkus has seats on two Commerce subcommittees whose work is particularly important to business interests — the Energy and Power subcommittee (which is considering deregulation of the electric utility industry in the 105th) and the Telecommunications, Trade and Consumer Protection subcommittee.

Besides Shimkus, the only other Republican first-termer who got a seat on Commerce was James E. Rogan of California, who also won a close race for an open seat.

Shimkus' drive for Commerce got a boost from Rep. Dennis Hastert, a fellow Illinois Republican who is chief deputy majority whip. A senior member of the Commerce Committee and a member of the Committee on Committees, Hastert pushed for Shimkus, Illinois' lone Republican freshman, to get the coveted appointment.

For Shimkus, who as Madison County treasurer was the only Republican elected countywide (only two Republicans sat in the county legislature elected from districts), being elected to Congress gives him an unaccustomed opportunity to schmooze with his fellow party members.

"Now I have peers of the same political persuasion," he told the Chicago Sun-Times shortly after his election. "I can have a pizza and a beer with them and discuss my job."

Durbin had won the swing district handily since first being elected to Congress in 1982, but when he vacated the 20th to try for the Senate, the seat was up for grabs. Durbin endorsed Hoffman, a state representative, as his successor, and the Republicans favored Shimkus, who had earned a respectable 43 percent against Durbin in 1992.

Hoffman and Shimkus claimed their parties' nominations in March.

More conservative than Durbin, Hoffman emphasized his anti-abortion stance and anti-crime legislation he supported in the Illinois legislature. He had the support of organized labor and tried to link Shimkus to Speaker Newt Gingrich and the conservative House GOP majority.

Shimkus, who also opposes abortion, aimed for the political center. He tried to portray Hoffman as an opponent of tax relief, and campaigned as a pro-business candidate who would fight in Congress to roll back taxes and regulations he said stifle economic growth. Shimkus said he would seek ways to make health care more available for self-employed workers and small-business employees.

As county treasurer, he advocated reducing taxes and balancing the budget through fiscal restraint. He reduced his office staff by one-third and returned pay raises authorized by the county board. He easily won re-election in 1994.

In Washington, he said he would try to consolidate government operations as one way to hold down spending. He would also like to see an income tax cut.

A graduate of West Point who served in Germany before returning to his hometown, Shimkus said one way to fight crime would be to stop drugs from coming into the country. Along those lines, he wants to step up interdiction efforts.

Shimkus serves concurrently in the Army Reserves (where he is a major) and the House.

ILLINOIS 20
West Central — Part of Springfield; Collinsville

The 20th takes in a border-state portion of Illinois; its western edge lies along the Mississippi River, across from Missouri. Its Southern Democratic traditions are maintained by blue-collar voters near the Mississippi, many of the state employees in Springfield and coal industry workers in the southern part of the 20th.

This district is favorable terrain for Democrats, though its prevailing political tone is moderate-to-conservative. Sen. Richard J. Durbin, who represented the 20th from 1983 to 1997, was usually re-elected with comfortable margins, though his races were more competitive after 1992 redistricting. Shimkus' razor-thin victory in 1996 marked a rare occasion that year when a Republican captured an open seat that had been represented by a Democrat. And Bob Dole nearly halved Bill Clinton's winning margin in the 20th from four years earlier though Clinton still carried the district.

The district has a portion of Springfield (the rest is in the 18th District), but otherwise there are no large cities, and there are few minority-group residents.

Population is diffuse in the 20th. The section of Madison County in the district has about 20 percent of the total; the part of Sangamon County (Springfield) in the 20th is close behind. But the remaining residents are spread across 15 counties and parts of two others.

About half of Madison County's residents are in the 20th. Although most of the county's industry is located in the 12th District, the factories provide jobs for many residents in such 20th District communities as Edwardsville, Collinsville and Glen Carbon. Edwardsville is the site of a Southern Illinois University campus (11,000 students).

The southern part of Springfield, the state capital, is the 20th's largest single urban area; about two-thirds of the city's 105,000 residents are in the 20th. Nearly a fifth of these constituents are black, by far the largest minority concentration in the district.

The state government payroll provides economic stability, as do the city's academic institutions, Sangamon State University and Southern Illinois University's medical school. The county also has some industry.

The economy is not nearly as generous in some of the district's less populous areas, which have had bouts of double-digit unemployment in recent years. The jobless rate in sparsely populated Calhoun County, on the Mississippi, is among the highest in Illinois.

Farming is widespread through the district's more rural counties. Adams and Pike counties, in the northwest corner, are major livestock producers. Nearby Scott County, also rural, opted for Dole in 1996, as did Adams. Near the southern end is Illinois' wheat belt.

In Clinton and Washington counties, farms give way to coal mines. A rural Republican vote prevails in Washington. But neighboring Jefferson, a leading coal-producing county, is a Democratic stronghold.

1990 Population: 571,480. White 542,965 (95%), Black 23,928 (4%), Other 4,587 (1%). Hispanic origin 3,749 (1%). 18 and over 424,776 (74%), 62 and over 106,712 (19%). Median age: 35.

HOUSE ELECTIONS

1996 General		
John M. Shimkus (R)	120,926	(50%)
Jay C. Hoffman (D)	119,688	(50%)
1996 Primary		
John M. Shimkus (R)	23,218	(51%)
Carl Oblinger (R)	8,786	(19%)
Bill Owens (R)	6,344	(14%)
Rick Angel (R)	4,436	(10%)
James K. Zerkle (R)	1,180	(3%)
Dave Green (R)	897	(2%)
Patrick Baikauskas (R)	778	(2%)

CAMPAIGN FINANCE

	Receipts	Receipts from PACs		Expend-itures
1996				
Shimkus (R)	$653,501	$225,024	(34%)	$647,796
Hoffman (D)	$815,309	$365,093	(45%)	$812,397

DISTRICT VOTE FOR PRESIDENT

	1996		1992
D	117,896 (48%)	D	130,383 (46%)
R	101,844 (41%)	R	94,532 (34%)
I	26,440 (11%)	I	55,824 (20%)

KEY VOTES

1997
Ban "partial birth" abortions Y

INDIANA

Governor: Frank L. O'Bannon (D)
First elected: 1996
Length of term: 4 years
Term expires: 1/01
Salary: $77,200 — accepts $66,000
Term limit: 2 terms
Phone: (317) 232-4567
Born: Jan. 30, 1930; Louisville, Ky.
Education: Indiana U., B.A. 1952; Indiana U., J.D. 1957
Occupation: Lawyer; publisher.
Family: Wife, Judith Mae Asmus; three children.
Religion: Methodist.
Political Career: Ind. Senate, 1971-88; Ind. lieutenant governor, 1989-97

Lt. Gov.: Joe Kernan (D)
First elected: 1996
Length of term: 4 years
Term expires: 1/01
Salary: $64,000 + $11,600 for serving as head of Senate
Phone: (317) 232-4545

State election official: (317) 232-6531
Democratic headquarters: (317) 231-7100
Republican headquarters: (317) 635-7561

REDISTRICTING

Indiana retained its 10 House seats in reapportionment. The legislature passed the map June 13, 1991; the governor signed it June 14.

STATE LEGISLATURE

General Assembly. First session meets for 90 days between January and April; second session, 30 days between January and March.

Senate: 50 members, 4-year terms
1996 breakdown: 31R, 19D; 36 men, 14 women
Salary: $11,600
Phone: (317) 232-9608

House of Representatives: 100 members, 2-year terms
1996 breakdown: 50R, 50D; 86 men, 14 women
Salary: $11,600
Phone: (317) 232-9400

URBAN STATISTICS

City	Population
Indianapolis	731,327
Mayor Stephen Goldsmith, R	
Fort Wayne	184,221
Mayor Paul Helmke, R	
Evansville	126,000
Mayor Frank F. McDonald II, D	
Gary	116,646
Mayor Scott King, D	
South Bend	105,511
Mayor Joseph Kernan, D	

U.S. CONGRESS

Senate: 0 D, 2 R
House: 4 D, 6 R

TERM LIMITS

For state offices: No

ELECTIONS

1996 Presidential Vote

Bob Dole	47%
Bill Clinton	42%
Ross Perot	11%

1992 Presidential Vote

George Bush	43%
Bill Clinton	37%
Ross Perot	20%

1988 Presidential Vote

George Bush	60%
Michael S. Dukakis	40%

POPULATION

1990 population		5,544,159
1980 population		5,490,224
Percent change		+1%
Rank among states:		14
White		91%
Black		8%
Hispanic		2%
Asian or Pacific islander		1%
Urban		65%
Rural		35%
Born in state		71%
Foreign-born		2%
Under age 18	1,455,964	26%
Ages 18-64	3,391,999	61%
65 and older	696,196	13%
Median age		32.8

MISCELLANEOUS

Capital: Indianapolis
Number of counties: 92
Per capita income: $17,217 (1991)
Rank among states: 32
Total area: 36,185 sq. miles
Rank among states: 38

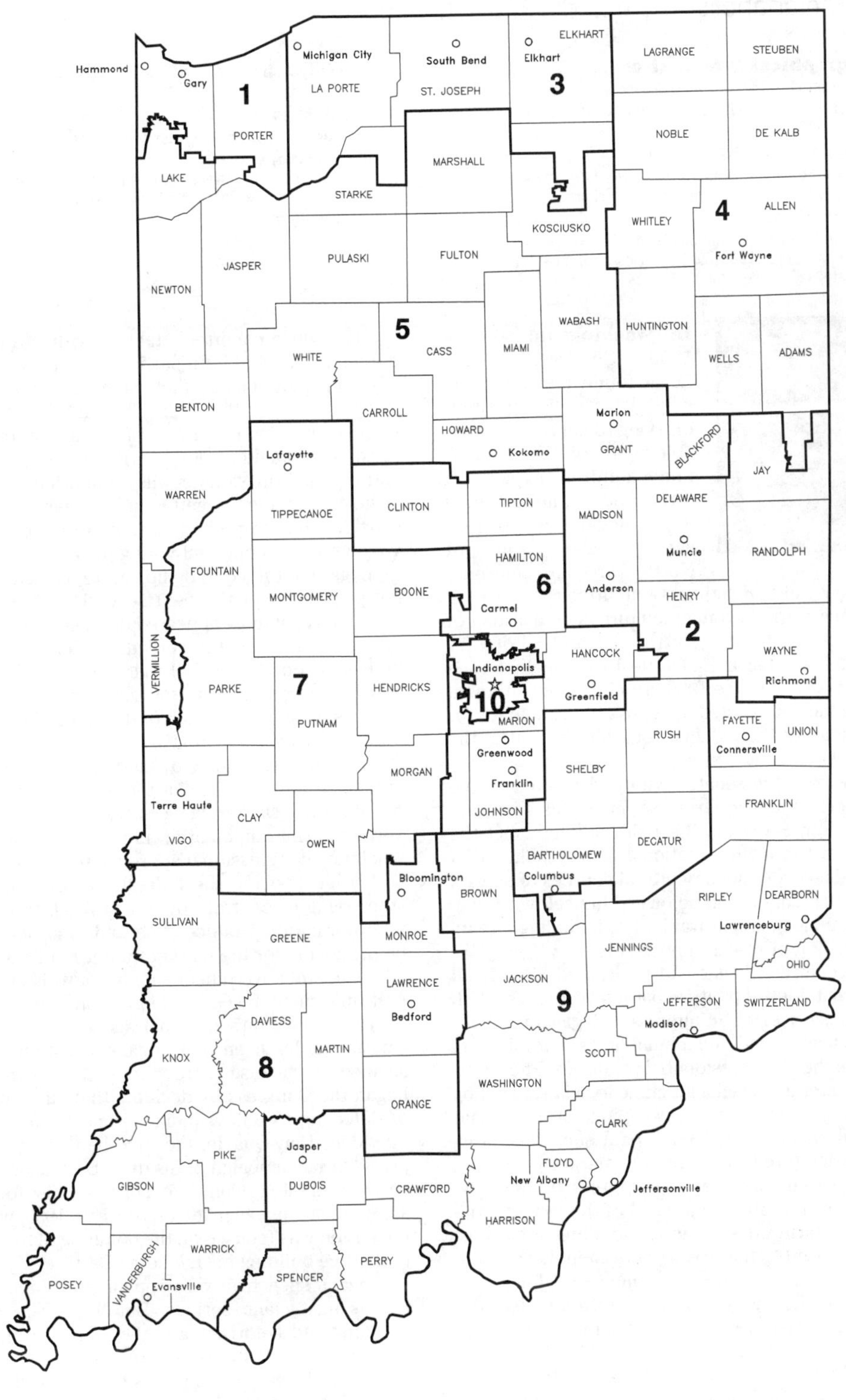
Hammond
Gary
1
PORTER
LAKE
Michigan City
LA PORTE
South Bend
ST. JOSEPH
Elkhart
ELKHART
3
LAGRANGE
STEUBEN
NOBLE
DE KALB
MARSHALL
STARKE
KOSCIUSKO
WHITLEY
4
ALLEN
Fort Wayne
NEWTON
JASPER
PULASKI
FULTON
WABASH
HUNTINGTON
5
WHITE
CASS
MIAMI
WELLS
ADAMS
BENTON
CARROLL
HOWARD
Kokomo
Marion
GRANT
BLACKFORD
JAY
Lafayette
TIPPECANOE
WARREN
CLINTON
TIPTON
MADISON
DELAWARE
Muncie
RANDOLPH
FOUNTAIN
MONTGOMERY
BOONE
HAMILTON
6
Anderson
HENRY
Carmel
2
VERMILLION
PARKE
7
HENDRICKS
Indianapolis
10
MARION
HANCOCK
Greenfield
WAYNE
Richmond
PUTNAM
RUSH
FAYETTE
Connersville
UNION
Greenwood
Franklin
MORGAN
SHELBY
Terre Haute
VIGO
CLAY
OWEN
JOHNSON
FRANKLIN
DECATUR
BARTHOLOMEW
Columbus
Bloomington
BROWN
RIPLEY
DEARBORN
Lawrenceburg
SULLIVAN
GREENE
MONROE
JENNINGS
OHIO
LAWRENCE
Bedford
JACKSON
9
JEFFERSON
SWITZERLAND
Madison
DAVIESS
KNOX
8
MARTIN
SCOTT
WASHINGTON
ORANGE
CLARK
PIKE
Jasper
DUBOIS
FLOYD
New Albany
Jeffersonville
GIBSON
CRAWFORD
HARRISON
WARRICK
PERRY
POSEY
VANDERBURGH
Evansville
SPENCER

Richard G. Lugar (R)

Of Indianapolis — Elected 1976, 4th term

Biographical Information
Born: April 4, 1932, Indianapolis, Ind.
Education: Denison U., B.A. 1954; Oxford U., B.A. 1956, M.A. 1956.
Military Service: Navy, 1957-60.
Occupation: Manufacturing executive; farm manager.
Family: Wife, Charlene Smeltzer; four children.
Religion: Methodist.
Political Career: Indianapolis School Board, 1964-67; mayor of Indianapolis, 1968-75; Republican nominee for U.S. Senate, 1974.

Capitol Office: 306 Hart Bldg. 20510; 224-4814.

Committees
Agriculture, Nutrition & Forestry (chairman)
Foreign Relations
East Asian & Pacific Affairs; European Affairs; Western Hemisphere, Peace Corps, Narcotics and Terrorism
Select Intelligence

In Washington: As the 105th Congress began, Lugar found himself in the painfully familiar position of trying to carve out a suitable niche for his talents. A much-admired expert on foreign policy, he remained in the shadow of the more senior Jesse Helms of North Carolina, chairman of the Foreign Relations Committee.

An expert also on agriculture and chairman of the Agriculture, Nutrition and Forestry Committee, Lugar had little to do in that area after passage of the 1996 farm bill. And, although his name was floated as a possible candidate for secretary of State, Lugar took himself out of the running for that post.

Instead, the senator who had aspired to the presidency a year earlier set his sights comparatively low. He began the 105th talking about the need to formulate a national energy policy that would incorporate agricultural sources of energy, such as ethanol. And he busied himself with relatively minor agricultural issues, including a reauthorization of research programs.

In contrast, Lugar had positioned himself on the front lines of political battles during the 104th Congress, scoring an impressive legislative victory even as he endured a humbling electoral rejection in the GOP presidential primaries. The veteran senator achieved a longtime legislative goal by winning approval of a sweeping farm bill that scaled back decades-old federal subsidies, moving agriculture toward the free market.

The GOP takeover of Congress in 1995 signaled the possible death knell of the Democratic-written farm subsidy and land-idling programs, which dated to the Great Depression. Lugar, himself a corn and soybean farmer who found the government programs too confining, led the charge early in 1995. With provisions of the 1990 farm bill expiring at the end of 1995, Lugar proposed cutting subsidies and export programs by as much as $15 billion over five years, thereby greatly reducing the government's role.

His own committee, stacked with farm program advocates of both parties, responded coolly to the idea. But Lugar's tactical thrust threw farm-state senators on the defensive, and he kept hammering away with various proposals to reduce agriculture spending. Faced with intense partisan and regional divisions on his committee, he nevertheless cobbled together a package that cut subsidies but won committee approval on a 9-8 vote, with one opponent voting present.

Lugar continued to demonstrate his deal-making prowess over the next several months. The farm bill repeatedly appeared doomed, especially after President Clinton vetoed the deficit-cutting budget reconciliation bill that had included key agricultural provisions. But Lugar revitalized the process by adopting much of the House farm bill, known as "Freedom to Farm," and split Senate Democratic resistance by adding conservation and nutrition provisions at the behest of ranking Agriculture Democrat Patrick J. Leahy of Vermont. The combination ultimately won overwhelming congressional approval in March 1996.

"From now on, the federal government will stop trying to control how much food, feed and fiber our nation produces," he said. "Farmers will be producing for the market, rather than restricted by federal government supply controls, for the first time since the Great Depression."

The legislation's eventual success was especially notable, given that Lugar's attention often seemed to be elsewhere during the 104th. He began the Congress by deciding that, after years of deferring to fellow Indianan and former Vice President Dan Quayle, the time had come for a presidential campaign of his own. But Lugar's bid seemed ill-fated from the start — his formal announcement was made on April 19, 1995, when the nation was focused on the bombing of the federal office building in Oklahoma City.

Lugar's speeches were applauded by journalists as meaty and serious. But they were also plodding and colorless, and they failed to ignite the electorate. At times, the candidate seemed to go out of his way to tell voters what they did not want to hear, such as indicating to an unemployed father of five in Maine that there wasn't much the government could do to help parents. After failing to surpass single-digit support in the key early contests, Lugar withdrew in March 1996 and endorsed his fellow senator, Bob Dole of Kansas, the eventual nominee.

The failed campaign was the most recent in a series of political setbacks for Lugar on the national stage. The senator had been had been chafing at his position in the party's leadership queue since George Bush chose Quayle as his running mate in 1988. Lugar himself had been on most people's lists of vice presidential prospects that year, as he had been in 1980.

He had acknowledged White House interest as far back as the early 1970s, when he was mayor of Indianapolis. And while he and Quayle had been friendly, the senior senator had to swallow hard to see his junior colleague promoted over him. That setback came on the heels of another. In 1987, after the Democrats had taken over the Senate and dislodged him as chair of Foreign Relations, Helms asserted his seniority to claim ranking member status on that committee (leaving Lugar the top Republican on Agriculture).

Lugar responded by becoming a cooperative ranking member at Agriculture, at times almost a co-pilot for Democratic Chairman Leahy. He also remained available to President Bush and to the news media on foreign affairs, acting as his party's spokesman on Capitol Hill during the Persian Gulf conflict of 1990-91 and on the foreign policy crises in Yugoslavia and Africa in 1992-93.

And if the intervening years have done little to raise Lugar's popular profile, they continue to burnish his reputation in Washington. He received the Outstanding Legislator award from the American Political Science Association in 1991 and the next year was honored for his contributions to foreign policy by Harvard University's John F. Kennedy School of Government.

Lugar is known as an independent thinker on many issues, a man who has earned bipartisan respect partly by studying at length before taking a position. But he also remains a solid conservative who supported Bush on key votes more often than all but three other Republican senators in 1992. His rating from the liberal Americans for Democratic Action has averaged only 10 over his Senate career. And he had a chance to underscore his anti-abortion position in February 1995 by vociferously opposing a Clinton nominee for surgeon general who had performed abortions.

Yet, he is not adverse to departing from the party line. He is friendly to some forms of environmental legislation and gun control, voting for both the 1993 Brady law, which imposed a waiting period for handgun purchases, and the ban on certain semiautomatic assault-style weapons.

Lugar's environmentalist tendencies are stronger than those of most Senate Republicans, and of many Agriculture Committee members of either party. He worked with Leahy to block changes sought by farm organizations in environmental restrictions in the 1985 farm bill, including the "swampbuster" provisions requiring cutoffs in federal payments to farmers who drain protected wetlands. With Lugar's support, the 1996 farm bill expanded many conservation programs.

Lugar's stand on nutrition issues frustrated some of his more conservative colleagues in the 104th Congress. With some reluctance, he agreed to deep cuts in the food stamp program as part of a sweeping welfare overhaul bill that was ultimately signed by Clinton. But he dug in his heels over the politically sensitive school lunch program, successfully staving off an attempt by House Republicans to turn over partial control of those programs to state officials.

On foreign policy as well, Lugar often charted a centrist course. He has supported foreign aid for the former Soviet Union, and expressed skepticism over revamping America's relationship with the United Nations. Even during the heat of the 1996 presidential race, Lugar backed Clinton's decision to send troops to Bosnia. And in the 105th, Lugar voted for the Chemical Weapons Convention that sought to outlaw the use of chemical weapons. The Senate adopted the measure, 74-26, in April 1997.

Despite his interest in foreign policy, Lugar's main focus in recent years has been on the Agriculture panel. He and Leahy, who swapped positions in 1995, long viewed farm subsidies with distaste. The two lawmakers also shared an interest in slimming down the Agriculture Department bureaucracy. The Bush administration was reluctant to alter policy and fought off efforts to close down some agricultural field offices. But in the 103rd Congress, with the backing of Clinton and Vice President Al Gore, Leahy and Lugar pushed through an overhaul plan that eliminated 7,500 jobs, with more of the cuts taking place at Washington headquarters than at field offices.

Lugar enjoyed national notice (and international importance) during the Gulf crisis of 1990-91 and the rebellion against Ferdinand E. Marcos in the Philippines in 1986. Lugar took the lead among Foreign Relations Republicans on the U.S. response to the August 1990 occupation of Kuwait by forces of Iraqi President Saddam Hussein. After the invasion, Lugar raced out ahead of Bush, whose stated goal was simply to get Iraq to give up Kuwait. "It seems to me important that Saddam Hussein must either leave or be removed," Lugar said.

Lugar also insisted that Congress fulfill what he viewed as its constitutional responsibility to authorize the use of military force. Even before the 101st Congress adjourned in late October, Lugar said, "Congress ought to come back into session to entertain a declaration of war."

Still, Lugar emerged as a Senate point man for Bush's gulf policy. He spoke frequently, in the Senate and to the media, in favor of the January 1991 resolution authorizing military force.

Despite the U.S.-led military rout that liberated Kuwait, Lugar's hopes for Saddam's downfall were not met; instead, the Iraqi strongman used what military might he had left to crush revolts among his nation's Kurdish and Shiite Muslim populations. Lugar nonetheless defended Bush against criticisms that he had stopped short of Saddam's removal and had reacted slowly to the plight of Iraq's minority groups.

Early in 1986, President Ronald Reagan asked Lugar to head a U.S. delegation monitoring the Philippines election between Marcos and challenger Corazon C. Aquino. Lugar concluded that Marcos was stealing the election, and he privately implored Reagan to denounce Marcos. Reagan instead argued there was fraud on both sides. Lugar persisted. Eventually the administration pressured Marcos to quit, in what came to be regarded as one of Reagan's chief foreign policy achievements. But in 1989, Aquino gave Lugar the credit. "Without him," she said, "there would be no Philippine-U.S. relations to speak of by now."

At Home: In 1994, Lugar became the first Indiana senator to be re-elected to a fourth term. A potentially competitive challenge by former Democratic Rep. Jim Jontz fizzled out long before the year's climate assured Lugar a victory.

A tireless campaigner, Jontz hoped to present himself as a middle-class populist and Lugar as an out-of-touch politician who cared more about Peru, the country, than Peru, Ind. But when a follower of political extremist Lyndon H. LaRouche Jr. held Jontz to 54 percent in the Democratic primary, the Democrat's chances of attracting money, staff and party support evaporated.

Lugar relied on his popularity, strong organization and substantial campaign resources to rack up 67 percent of the vote. A statewide poll released after the election showed that more Hoosiers supported a Lugar challenge to Clinton in 1996 than one by Quayle.

Lugar's long record of electoral success is remarkable given his modest gifts as a campaigner. He meets crowds woodenly and his style borders on lecturing. But he has always impressed the Indiana electorate as a man of substance.

Even in 1974, running for the Senate in a Watergate-dominated year with a reputation as "Richard Nixon's favorite mayor," he came within a respectable 75,000 votes against Democrat Birch Bayh. Two years later, against a much weaker Democrat, Sen. Vance Hartke, he won handily. In his 1982 re-election bid, Lugar's personal popularity and massive campaign treasury carried him past his Democratic foe, Rep. Floyd Fithian.

Lugar's record as mayor of Indianapolis still stands as the foundation of his political career. His conservative, efficiency-minded administration won him favorable notices all over Indiana, and he attracted national attention by defeating John V. Lindsay of New York City for vice president of the National League of Cities in 1970.

A Rhodes scholar, Lugar served in the Navy as a briefing officer at the Pentagon before returning home to run the family tool business. He won his first election in 1964, to the Indianapolis School Board. Three years later, he saw an opportunity to take over the mayor's office. The Democrats were divided, and with the help of powerful Marion County GOP Chairman Keith Bulen, he beat incumbent Democrat John Barton.

Lugar's election over Lindsay was national news because he won it in an electorate of big-city mayors, most of them Democrats. He was a spokesman for Nixon administration policies, and the president began to take an interest in him.

He came to regret those ties in 1974, when he was saddled with the Nixon connection. Still, he came close enough to Bayh to become the logical contender in 1976 against Hartke. Hartke had nearly lost six years earlier and was severely damaged by a primary challenger who charged him with foreign junketing and slavish loyalty to the communications industry. Lugar took 59 percent.

SENATE ELECTIONS

1994 General		
Richard G. Lugar (R)	1,039,625	(67%)
Jim Jontz (D)	470,799	(31%)
Barbara Bourland (LIBERT)	17,343	(1%)
Mary Catherine Barton (NA)	15,801	(1%)

Previous Winning Percentages: 1988 (68%) **1982** (54%) **1976** (59%)

KEY VOTES

1997	
Approve balanced-budget constitutional amendment	Y
Approve chemical weapons treaty	Y
1996	
Approve farm bill	Y
Limit punitive damages in product liability cases	Y
Exempt small businesses from higher minimum wage	Y
Approve welfare overhaul	Y
Bar job discrimination based on sexual orientation	N
Override veto of ban on "partial birth" abortions	Y
1995	
Approve GOP budget with tax and spending cuts	Y
Approve constitutional amendment barring flag desecration	Y

CAMPAIGN FINANCE

	Receipts	Receipts from PACs		Expenditures
1994				
Lugar (R)	$3,122,705	$727,662	(23%)	$4,063,703
Jontz (D)	$488,714	$214,424	(44%)	$472,788
Barton (NA)	$8,279	0		$9,926

VOTING STUDIES

	Presidential Support		Party Unity		Conservative Coalition	
Year	S	O	S	O	S	O
1996	31	68	88	10	92	8
1995	26	67	88	7	79	16
1994	45	55	78	22	78	22
1993	34	65	88	12	88	10
1992	87	10	86	12	76	21
1991	93	7	88	11	83	10

INTEREST GROUP RATINGS

Year	ADA	AFL-CIO	CCUS	ACU
1996	5	n/a	85	95
1995	5	0	100	77
1994	10	0	90	76
1993	10	0	100	72
1992	10	17	100	85
1991	10	17	90	76

Daniel R. Coats (R)

Of Fort Wayne — Elected 1990; 1st full term
Appointed to the Senate 1989.

Biographical Information

Born: May 16, 1943, Jackson, Mich.
Education: Wheaton College, B.A. 1965; Indiana U., J.D. 1971.
Military Service: Army Corps of Engineers, 1966-68.
Occupation: Lawyer.
Family: Wife, Marcia Anne Crawford; three children.
Religion: Presbyterian.
Political Career: U.S. House, 1981-88.
Capitol Office: 404 Russell Bldg. 20510; 224-5623.

Committees

Armed Services
Airland Forces (chairman); Personnel; Readiness
Select Intelligence
Labor & Human Resources
Children & Families (chairman); Public Health & Safety

In Washington: Coats has not made clear what profession he will pursue after his congressional career, which he announced in December 1996 would end with the 105th Congress. Had he sought re-election in 1998, he likely would have faced a daunting obstacle in the candidacy of Democratic former Gov. Evan Bayh. But the conservative stalwart will spend his last Congress with active roles in both the social policy and defense arenas as chairman of two important subcommittees.

Coats, a veteran member of the Armed Services Committee, retains for the 105th the chairmanship of the Airland Forces Subcommittee. He also picked up the gavel of the new Children and Families Subcommittee of Labor and Human Resources.

Coats ranks second on the Labor Committee behind James M. Jeffords of Vermont, one of the Senate's more liberal Republicans. When conservatives fretted that Jeffords might prove too moderate a chairman, they turned to Coats to challenge him.

But Coats, after consultation with GOP Senate leaders late in 1996, decided to defer to Jeffords' seniority. Coats also serves on an education task force appointed by Senate Majority Leader Trent Lott.

Coats is best known as a social conservative who seriously examines the implications of his positions, urging other "movement conservatives" to care not only about abortion and school prayer but also about the welfare of children and the poor. During debate about a plan to end the federal welfare entitlement, Coats warned against total faith in the devolution theory regnant in his party, saying, "State officials are fully capable of repeating the same mistakes as federal officials, and state welfare bureaucracies can be just as strong and just as wrong as federal programs."

On education issues, Coats is directly in line with conservative views. He is a forceful and passionate advocate for school choice, arguing that allowing children and parents to choose schools would inject some much-needed competition into stagnant and failing educational systems. An amendment from Coats to repeal the federal Direct Loan Program and require student loan recipients to pay the interest that accrued on their accounts in the first six months after graduation was defeated by the Labor Committee in 1995.

But Coats recognizes that school choice has not engendered consensus support as yet. In February 1997, he noted, "Democrats very effectively spun our proposal into an anti-education initiative. We clearly want to give states more flexibility. But we're not out to demolish the Department of Education anymore."

Coats is not much for compromising his principles in strategic retreat, but unlike some of his younger Senate brethren he is willing to bend and on rare occasion to break ranks with his party; he is not viewed as one-dimensional, even by frequent adversaries. Coats devotes much of his energy to social issues such as abortion. Even on the Armed Services panel — where he has consistently joined the chorus of calling for beefier budgets — Coats made his mark on what was essentially a social matter: gays in the military. He is one of the leading congressional voices in favor of amending the Constitution to allow prayer in public schools.

He coauthored a provision of the 1996 telecommunications law to outlaw obscenity and limit indecency on the Internet — a measure that quickly became First Amendment fodder for the courts. In the 105th, dissatisfied with the broadcast industry's voluntary ratings system, Coats has introduced a bill to require the TV industry to set content-based ratings.

A solid supporter of GOP efforts to cut tax rates, Coats was a leading proponent of the move to grant the president a kind of line-item veto authority. He is a supporter of increased defense spending, noting, "When we're dealing with national security, I'd like to err on the plus side." Coats is far more restrained when it comes to domestic spending. Arguing that funding for programs such as the National Endowments for the Arts and Humanities should be cut in a time of waist-cinching, he said, "We're acting like the entire culture of the United States is going to unravel." Noting the government's dire budgetary straits, he cautioned, "We are fiddling here while Rome burns."

Coats has a stubborn streak, in part exemplified by his self-described "lonely vigil" to grant new power to states to keep out unwanted trash. Coats took up the cause in 1990 and saw a compromise through the Senate, only to watch it dropped in conference with the House on the fiscal 1997 energy and water spending bill.

Coats opposed President Clinton's second nominee for surgeon general, Henry W. Foster Jr., alleging a lack of accuracy as the doctor sought to recall the number of abortions he had performed. "There is a litmus test here, but it is not abortion," Coats said. "The litmus test is truth-telling, and on this point, the president's and Dr. Foster's version of truth differ from day to day."

In endorsing the presidential candidacy of Bob Dole after Indiana's senior senator, Richard G. Lugar, dropped out of the hunt in 1996, Coats warned the party's standard-bearer not to shirk the issues that energize conservatives. Coats has never been one to shrink from them himself. Backing a ban on privately funded abortions in military hospitals overseas, Coats argued in June 1996 that such procedures are subsidized by taxpayers and that "we must not take money from citizens and use it to vandalize their moral values."

When Republicans launched an offensive in 1993 against Clinton's proposal to lift the ban on homosexuals serving in the military, they went looking for someone to take the point. Coats was their volunteer.

According to The Washington Post, the day before the confirmation hearing for Defense Secretary Les Aspin, Republican members of the Armed Services Committee met to discuss their questions. When Strom Thurmond of South Carolina wanted to know who would ask questions on the gay ban, no one spoke up.

"There was kind of a dead silence," Coats told the Post. "Assignments had been handed out, and nobody said anything. I think my exact words were: 'Well, if no one else wants to take it, I'll ask the question.'"

It was a stroke of luck for the GOP. On morning network news shows and elsewhere, Coats expressed forcefully but without strident rhetoric the feelings of many Americans opposed to lifting the ban. Unlike some of his more unyielding Republican colleagues, Coats, though a staunch conservative, brought a record of compromise and thus credibility to the debate.

In 1992, Coats had decided to break ranks with his party and president and become a supporter of a bill mandating that businesses allow their workers unpaid leave for family and medical emergencies. Although he was still concerned about the costs it would impose on businesses, he said he had also felt uncomfortable opposing such a "pro-family" measure. The bill was vetoed by President George Bush in 1992 but signed into law by Clinton early in 1993.

But he was one of only five Republicans to oppose a compromise civil rights bill in 1991 that had Bush's support.

Coats carried the fight against abortion into the health care debate that dominated the second half of the 103rd Congress. When the Labor Committee took up Clinton's health care proposal in June 1994, Coats unsuccessfully offered an amendment that would have ensured that abortion was not part of the basic benefits package except in cases of rape, incest or a threat to the woman's life. The health care overhaul effort failed.

He often finds himself attempting the difficult balancing act of offering economic incentives without spawning government interference. He has called for doubling the personal tax exemption and creating tax credits for low-income families with children younger than 6. He also won adoption of several amendments in 1989 child-care legislation to permit in-home care and to allow requirements that care-providers adhere to certain religious beliefs.

Though it is not unusual for one politician to be carried some distance by the career successes of another, few have come as far this way as has Coats.

Starting as Dan Quayle's aide when Quayle represented northeast Indiana in the House, Coats has moved up behind his boss. When Quayle went to the Senate in 1980, Coats ran for and won his House seat. And after Quayle was elected vice president in 1988, Indiana's retiring GOP Gov. Robert D. Orr appointed Coats to succeed Quayle in the Senate.

At Home: When Orr named Coats to replace Quayle in the Senate a month after the 1988 presidential election, he was formalizing what many Indiana observers had considered a fait accompli. Coats was presumed to be Quayle's choice, just as he had been when Quayle left the House eight years earlier.

As Quayle's district representative from 1978 through 1980, Coats cultivated the role of surrogate congressman. He handled constituents' problems personally, and sometimes stepped in for Quayle to give a "government is too big" speech. When Quayle ran for the Senate in 1980, Coats had a spot on the ballot just below him and shared the highly effective organization both had helped build. Coats actually bested Quayle that November in the 4th.

Democrats in 1990 tried and failed to recruit a front-line Senate candidate such as Rep. Lee H. Hamilton. Instead, they nominated little-known state Rep. Baron P. Hill, a former high school basketball star. Hill gained ground with clever television ads depicting the state as being flooded by Coats' franked mail. He also took a walking tour of the length of the state. Voters warmed to Hill's fiery stump style, which contrasted with Coats' stiff presence in crowds and reliance on television ads and mailings.

In the end, Hill did not have enough money or name recognition to overtake the incumbent. Coats won with 54 percent, although Hill did well enough to merit being mentioned as a possible repeat challenger in 1992.

But Hill decided not to try again. Instead Democrats offered up Indiana Secretary of State Joseph H. Hogsett, a close associate of Gov. Bayh. Hogsett, who had helped run Bayh's gubernatorial campaign, was seen early as a strong threat to Coats. But the threat fizzled as Coats built up a large campaign treasury and a highly organized and effective campaign.

On Election Day, Coats pushed his tally to 57 percent.

When he first ran for the House in 1980, Coats still was a relative newcomer to the district. But he easily surmounted a bitter GOP primary against two candidates with much stronger local roots, winning nomination by carrying every county. In November, Coats smashed Democrat John D. Walda in Walda's second try. Four re-election campaigns produced no surprises.

SENATE ELECTIONS

1992 General		
Daniel R. Coats (R)	1,267,972	(57%)
Joseph H. Hogsett (D)	900,148	(41%)
Steve Dillon (LIBERT)	35,733	(2%)

Previous Winning Percentages: 1990 (54%) **1988*** (62%) **1986*** (70%) **1984*** (61%) **1982*** (64%) **1980*** (61%)

** House elections*

CAMPAIGN FINANCE

	Receipts	Receipts from PACs	Expend-itures
1992			
Coats (R)	$3,642,012	$1,135,005 (31%)	$3,802,077
Hogsett (D)	$1,621,467	$436,042 (27%)	$1,584,173

KEY VOTES

1997	
Approve balanced-budget constitutional amendment	Y
Approve chemical weapons treaty	Y
1996	
Approve farm bill	Y
Limit punitive damages in product liability cases	Y
Exempt small businesses from higher minimum wage	Y
Approve welfare overhaul	Y
Bar job discrimination based on sexual orientation	N
Override veto of ban on "partial birth" abortions	Y
1995	
Approve GOP budget with tax and spending cuts	Y
Approve constitutional amendment barring flag desecration	Y

VOTING STUDIES

	Presidential Support		Party Unity		Conservative Coalition	
Year	S	O	S	O	S	O
1996	29	68	93	4	84	11
1995	23	76	97	2	95	5
1994	42	58	88	11	78	19
1993	29	70	85	12	80	20
1992	75	22	92	8	87	13
1991	85	15	91	9	85	15

INTEREST GROUP RATINGS

Year	ADA	AFL-CIO	CCUS	ACU
1996	10	n/a	100	100
1995	0	0	95	96
1994	5	0	90	92
1993	20	18	100	88
1992	10	33	90	93
1991	5	25	80	100

1 Peter J. Visclosky (D)

Of Merrillville — Elected 1984, 7th term

Biographical Information
Born: Aug. 13, 1949, Gary, Ind.
Education: Indiana U. Northwest, B.S. 1970; U. of Notre Dame, J.D. 1973; Georgetown U., LL.M. 1982.
Occupation: Lawyer.
Family: Separated; two children.
Religion: Roman Catholic.
Political Career: No previous office.
Capitol Office: 2313 Rayburn Bldg. 20515; 225-2461.

Committees
Appropriations
Energy & Water Development; National Security

In Washington: Visclosky has been on the Hill nearly his entire adult life, first as an aide and, since 1985, as a member. Now in his seventh full term, he is not yet 50, and with few political worries at home, he appears to be settling in for the long haul.

At the start of the 105th, Visclosky traded Appropriations subcommittee assignments, moving up to more prestigious panels that oversee spending on defense and on energy and water development. For about two decades, Indiana's interests were well-served on the energy and water panel by Republican John T. Myers; he chaired the subcommittee during the 104th prior to his retirement. Visclosky is now the No. 2 Democrat on the subcommittee, and if his party recaptures a House majority in some not-too-distant future election, he has a good shot at becoming an Appropriations "cardinal."

In the meantime, Visclosky carefully balances competing interests in his constituency. He votes a generally loyal Democratic line, but breaks with his party and his president on some social and fiscal issues. He seeks a middle position between protecting the environment of his lakeshore district and sustaining the viability of the steel industry that dominates its economy. In recent years, he has shown more tightfistedness on certain spending matters, and he is circumspect about the business of bringing home projects to his district. "I'm getting no mileage out of it," he said in 1996. "I don't even talk about it anymore."

Still, part of his work remains seeing that northwestern Indiana gets its share of federal largess. Early in the 104th, Visclosky was singled out for praise by Indiana's senior senator, Republican Richard G. Lugar, when he saved $52 million for a federal courthouse in Hammond from the chopping block when Republicans presented a package of spending cuts in a rescissions bill. Visclosky was one of only six Democrats who voted for the final package, which elicited President Clinton's first-ever veto.

Visclosky voted against many of the signature elements of the GOP's agenda at the start of the party's reign in the majority, including plans to limit congressional terms, block much federal regulatory authority and proffer $189 billion in tax relief. But by the end of the 104th, he had found common ground with Republicans on some social-policy issues. He backed GOP efforts to toughen immigration standards, and he voted to override President Clinton's veto of legislation banning a particular abortion technique that opponents call a "partial birth" abortion (although earlier he had voted against the ban). He opposed the GOP's initial welfare overhaul legislation, but supported the final compromise that Clinton signed over some liberal Democrats' objections.

In March 1997, Visclosky was one of 30 founding members of a group called the New Democratic Coalition, which sought to ply a centrist platform within the party. An aide explained to The White House Bulletin that the group is fiscally conservative, "but they're not as conservative as some of the 'blue dogs' on some of the social issues, such as education, gun control, environmental protection."

Visclosky pays special attention to labor matters; the 1st produces more steel than any other district in the country, but employment in the industry has dropped dramatically in the past 30 years. In 1993, he opposed NAFTA, a reflection of the continuing influence of organized labor in the district and anxiety there about economic decline, job loss and foreign competition. He joined in support of a resolution criticizing Clinton's bailout of the Mexican peso in 1995.

He strongly opposes one of the GOP's showcase initiatives in the field of labor management, a measure that would require that employers grant their employees flexible schedules or compensatory time for extra hours worked. Like many Democrats, Visclosky views this as a move to deny workers lucrative overtime wages.

In 1994, he joined with more than 50 other House members to introduce a "Worker Rights and Labor Standards Trade Act," directing the administration to work through the World Trade Organization to force labor and environmental

INDIANA 1
Northwest — Gary; Hammond

With its large blue-collar work force and 21 percent black population, the 1st is solidly Democratic. Industrial decline and urban decay in Gary and other cities along Lake Michigan cost the 1st nearly 10 percent of its population in the 1980s. Gary itself lost 23 percent, a steeper rate of decline than in any U.S. city during the 1980s. To compensate, 1991 redistricting added a substantial suburban swath in Lake and Porter counties.

Though Porter County, with its pockets of GOP voters, slightly dilutes the 1st's Democratic vote, the district remains firmly Democratic. In 1996's three-way presidential race, Bill Clinton won easily here.

Gary and urban Lake County are Democratic pillars. Minorities have a major impact: Once packed with factory workers of Slavic extraction, Gary is now more than 80 percent black. The Hispanic presence has increased in Hammond and East Chicago.

Gary, named for turn-of-the-century steel baron Elbert H. Gary, has become the heart of U.S. steelmaking. While factories were abandoned in other Rust Belt regions, companies such as USX, Inland Steel and Bethlehem Steel modernized plants here. The 1st produces more steel than any other district in the country.

But the steelmakers' revival came after recessions and the effects of foreign competition had whittled payrolls. And the streamlined, automated factories require fewer workers. Socioeconomic problems are endemic. In 1994, Gary had the fourth-highest homicide rate of cities with populations of more than 100,000.

Hammond, on the Illinois border and the 1st's other urban anchor, has a more varied economy, including a longstanding Lever Bros. bar soap plant. A marina recently was built as part of an economic development effort. An Amoco oil refinery takes up most of the land area in neighboring Whiting.

As the district moves south of the Indiana Toll Road into such communities as Merrillville and Crown Point, the population becomes more white and the employment more white-collar.

Many residents of these suburbs are East European ethnics who have maintained their Democratic loyalties. In recent decades, rivalry between white ethnics and blacks has been a feature of the 1st's Democratic politics. But of late, tension between the two camps has diminished, thanks in part to the governing style of Gary's black former mayor, Thomas V. Barnes.

Porter County's demographics and politics sharply contrast with Lake's. It is racially homogeneous (less than 1 percent black) and growing. Chesterton, Valparaiso and other exurban communities are home to a number of former Lake Countians and to Chicago commuters, who came here seeking cheaper housing.

Although there is a Democratic vote in Portage and Burns Harbor, Porter is friendly to GOP candidates. Bob Dole came within a thousand votes of edging Clinton in the district's portion of Porter County in 1996, though Dole lost in Lake County by more than 2-to-1.

1990 Population: 554,416. White 411,190 (74%), Black 116,863 (21%), Other 26,363 (5%). Hispanic origin 47,320 (9%). 18 and over 400,197 (72%), 62 and over 81,439 (15%). Median age: 33.

reforms in Third World countries. Visclosky called it "immoral for our trading partners to seek competitive advantage by exploiting their workers." Before a WTO meeting in December 1996, Visclosky and 49 of his colleagues sent a letter to Clinton: "We would welcome a clear and unequivocal presidential commitment, along with a public pronouncement that the establishment of a WTO Working Party on worker rights and trade should be included in the new WTO work program."

A "Working Party" may not move mountains, but initiatives of that ilk are Visclosky's stock in trade; he is a low-key, detail-minded legislator, devoted to the notion that politics is about resolving disputes through discussion and compromise.

In 1995, during consideration of a bill to ease federal clean water regulations, Visclosky proposed a bill to create a trust fund for collection of penalties for violations of the act, so the money would remain distinct from the Treasury's general fund. Citing his district's industrial developments as well as its rivers and wetlands, Visclosky stated, "I am keenly aware of the need to balance between protecting the environment and encouraging economic growth." His proposal was shot down, 156-247.

Visclosky waged a persistent fight during the 104th to block aid to enemies of Armenia on the foreign operations spending bill. In committee and on the floor, Visclosky repeatedly attempted to strip funds for Turkey and Azerbaijan. Visclosky, still known by old-timers as "the Slovak kid," highlights his Eastern European heritage for ethnic voters in his district.

Before joining Appropriations, Visclosky looked out for the 1st from the Public Works Committee and the Interior and Insular Affairs Committee. When Public Works wrote a water resources bill in the 99th Congress, Visclosky was able to include about $100 million for flood and erosion control along the district's Lake Michigan shoreline. He also successfully promoted legislation enlarging the Indiana Dunes National Lakeshore, a longtime cause célèbre for Midwest environmentalists and one of the few tourist attractions in northwest Indiana. During the 105th, Visclosky pushed through a provision clarifying that riverboat gambling on Lake Michigan will not be blocked by a 1951 law that prohibits gambling devices on U.S. flagged ships in special maritime and territorial waters.

At Home: After finishing law school in 1973, Visclosky linked his fortunes to Adam Benjamin Jr., then a state senator and rising political star. Visclosky coordinated Benjamin's successful campaign for Congress in 1976 and worked with him in Washington for the next six years.

When Benjamin died in September 1982, Gary's longtime black mayor, Richard G. Hatcher, was the 1st District Democratic chairman, and thus had the legal right to choose the substitute Democratic House nominee. He picked Katie Hall, a black state senator and loyal ally. She won the general election, but when she sought renomination in 1984, Visclosky and white Lake County prosecutor Jack Crawford challenged her.

Everyone knew Hall would face renomination problems. Minorities made up less than one-third of the district's population, and Hall did not build much of a biracial constituency.

But Visclosky initially attracted little attention because Crawford was considered Hall's chief threat: Lake County accounted for 80 percent of the district vote.

In the end, though, Visclosky had greater appeal. To contrast his modestly funded bid with Crawford's high-budget operation, Visclosky put on dozens of "dog and bean" $2 dinners aimed at attracting the young, the elderly and the unemployed. His "Slovak kid" background also helped him, and older voters responded favorably because they remembered his father, John, who had served as Gary's comptroller in the 1950s and as the city's appointed mayor in 1962-63.

An added boost was the endorsement in late 1983 of Pat Benjamin, the congressman's widow, plus support from newspapers in Gary (Hall's home) and Hammond (Crawford's home). Visclosky won over late-deciding white voters whose first priority was defeating Hall. She finished second, Crawford a close third. Visclosky swamped Republican Joseph B. Grenchik, the mayor of Whiting, in November.

In 1986, Hall tried a comeback. She retained her support in the black community, where Visclosky had alienated some voters by failing to close his congressional office on the Martin Luther King Jr. holiday in 1985. But with Hall as his only serious foe in this white-majority district, Visclosky's renomination was all but assured. He won 57 percent to 35 percent. In the 1990 primary, Hall tried again, but slipped to 30 percent.

In the strong GOP year of 1994, Visclosky slipped to 56 percent, but his 1996 tally rebounded to 69 percent.

Visclosky takes care to acknowledge the ethnic diversity of his constituency, faithfully submitting statements to the Congressional Record that commemorate the anniversary of the Armenian genocide and honor black history month.

HOUSE ELECTIONS

1996 General		
Peter J. Visclosky (D)	133,553	(69%)
Michael Edward Petyo (R)	56,418	(29%)
Michael Crass (LIBERT)	3,142	(2%)
1996 Primary		
Peter J. Visclosky (D)	43,140	(84%)
Daniel C. Langmesser (D)	8,216	(16%)
1994 General		
Peter J. Visclosky (D)	68,612	(56%)
John Larson (R)	52,920	(44%)

Previous Winning Percentages: 1992 (69%) **1990** (66%) **1988** (77%) **1986** (73%) **1984** (71%)

CAMPAIGN FINANCE

	Receipts	Receipts from PACs	Expend-itures
1996			
Visclosky (D)	$337,613	$209,590 (62%)	$318,769
Petyo (R)	$48,553	$1,016 (2%)	$47,379
1994			
Visclosky (D)	$299,307	$198,390 (66%)	$290,049
Larson (R)	$172,534	$4,164 (2%)	$172,531

DISTRICT VOTE FOR PRESIDENT

1996		1992	
D	116,355 (58%)	**D**	117,126 (53%)
R	62,595 (31%)	**R**	68,403 (31%)
I	19,532 (10%)	**I**	37,136 (17%)

KEY VOTES

1997	
Ban "partial birth" abortions	Y
1996	
Approve farm bill	Y
Deny public education to illegal immigrants	Y
Repeal ban on certain assault-style weapons	N
Increase minimum wage	Y
Freeze defense spending	N
Approve welfare overhaul	Y
1995	
Approve balanced-budget constitutional amendment	Y
Relax Clean Water Act regulations	N
Oppose limits on environmental regulations	Y
Reduce projected Medicare spending	N
Approve GOP budget with tax and spending cuts	N

VOTING STUDIES

	Presidential Support		Party Unity		Conservative Coalition	
Year	**S**	**O**	**S**	**O**	**S**	**O**
1996	71	24	80	18	41	59
1995	80	19	83	16	48	50
1994	91	9	93	4	36	64
1993	82	17	90	9	45	55
1992	22	78	91	9	38	63
1991	29	71	92	8	32	68

INTEREST GROUP RATINGS

Year	ADA	AFL-CIO	CCUS	ACU
1996	85	n/a	19	15
1995	70	92	25	8
1994	75	78	50	19
1993	75	92	0	17
1992	85	100	50	16
1991	80	92	30	10

2 David M. McIntosh (R)

Of Muncie — Elected 1994, 2nd term

Biographical Information
Born: June 8, 1958, Oakland, Calif.
Education: Yale U., B.A. 1980; U. of Chicago, J.D. 1983.
Occupation: Lawyer; White House aide; national security and public policy analyst.
Family: Wife, Elizabeth Ruth McManis.
Religion: Episcopalian.
Political Career: No previous office.
Capitol Office: 1208 Longworth Bldg. 20515; 225-3021.

Committees
Education & Workforce
Early Childhood, Youth & Families; Postsecondary Education, Training & Life-Long Learning
Government Reform & Oversight
Human Resources; National Economic Growth, Natural Resources & Regulatory Affairs (chairman)
Small Business
Regulatory Reform & Paperwork Reduction

In Washington: The soft-spoken McIntosh seems an unlikely revolutionary, but behind his deadpan demeanor lies a driving resolve to dismantle the federal regulatory structure — a resolve that has made him a powerful and controversial figure during his short time in the House.

McIntosh wields the gavel of a panel with an ungainly name, Government Reform and Oversight's Subcommittee on National Economic Growth, Natural Resources and Regulatory Affairs. During the 104th, McIntosh used his chairmanship to press the case for curbing federal regulations. In the 105th, with the full committee taking the lead in the House's investigation of possible campaign wrongdoing by President Clinton, McIntosh has been an aggressive questioner of Democrats, and he earned national media attention with his probing of a White House database he was certain had been used for political ends.

McIntosh has been among Clinton's most unsparing critics. At a subcommittee hearing in January 1995, he said Clinton was "having a love affair with federal regulation," and he has called administration officials "incompetent."

McIntosh was unsparingly personal in his attacks on President and Hillary Rodham Clinton for their complicity in fundraising tactics he found highly dubious. In March 1997, The Wall Street Journal found that McIntosh also had received contributions shortly after meetings with companies and trade groups. The paper found that almost $200,000 of McIntosh's campaign treasury came from groups or individuals that met with him or subcommittee staff between March 1995 and October 1996.

Although just 36 when elected, McIntosh had one of the longer governmental resumés in the Class of 1994, having worked for Presidents Ronald Reagan and George Bush. In the Bush administration he headed Vice President Dan Quayle's Council on Competitiveness, where he sought to reduce regulation, overhaul the civil justice system and speed up the drug approval process, among other matters.

After Bush left office, McIntosh was a senior fellow at Citizens for a Sound Economy, a free-market advocacy group, and there he helped generate the 1993 grass-roots protest to a proposed energy tax.

McIntosh has been a voice in the chorus of young conservatives pushing the GOP leadership hard on issues from tax cuts to the minimum wage. In 1995 and 1997, he generated letters signed by dozens of GOP members demanding action on tax cuts when it appeared party leaders might be wavering on the issue. McIntosh characterizes tax cuts as "a fundamental Republican principle" and a "solemn pledge."

Complaining in April 1997 of a "sense of malaise" in the House Republican Conference, he argued that "rather than folding, some members ought to exercise leadership, drive a message and fight for a principle. Otherwise, what's the point of being in the majority?" But, in contrast with some of his classmates, he has stayed within GOP ranks when leaders have demanded his vote.

McIntosh was one of the leaders in the 1996 fight against an increase in the minimum wage, offering legislation that would have exempted low-income workers from certain federal payroll taxes so that employers did not bear the burden of a raise. He accepted his loss gracefully, saying, "The conservatives were beaten. That happens."

With conservatives having been beaten up during the 1996 campaign for attempting to slow the growth of Medicare, McIntosh joined in an effort to take Social Security trust funds "off budget," to protect the program under balanced budget plans mandated by constitutional fiat. But the balanced-budget constitutional amendment failed in the Senate in 1997.

During the first 100 days of the 1995 session, McIntosh moved faster than Republican William F. Clinger of Pennsylvania, then the Government Reform and Oversight chairman, to lead GOP efforts to revamp the regulatory process, freeze new rules and slash government paperwork requirements. "The need for a freeze on regula-

McIntosh's successful effort to make the 1994 race a national referendum on Clinton and a Democratic Congress made particular sense in a district with a GOP tradition in presidential elections. Although the 2nd had been represented by a Democrat since 1975, it was one of 51 districts with a Democratic representative that did not vote for Clinton in 1992.

A series of industrial recessions and the financial uncertainties of family farmers had made the district's mainly conservative electorate more receptive to Democrats at other levels. But low voter turnout in usually Democratic Madison and Delaware counties helped McIntosh narrowly carry even those areas of manufacturing-dominated economies.

McIntosh won Madison in 1996 and he improved on his total districtwide. Bob Dole carried the district by a plurality.

Unemployment throughout the 2nd is well below the near-depression levels of the early 1980s, when local auto-related industries laid off thousands. However, the long-term downscaling of the blue-collar work force took its toll: 1990 population in Delaware County (Muncie) was down more than 7 percent from 1980, and Madison County (Anderson) was down nearly that much. Rural areas such as Randolph and Henry counties also saw their economies and populations slip.

In the 1920s, Muncie was the model for "Middletown," a study of small-town American life. Today, with about 71,000 residents, it is the largest city in the 2nd. Muncie's biggest private employer is Borg-Warner Automotive, which makes transmissions. The city's economy also benefits from Ball State University, which has about 19,000 students and employs more than 6,100 people, and from the Ball Corp. The company was founded and has its headquarters in Muncie, although most of its glass canning jars are made elsewhere.

INDIANA 2
East Central — Muncie; Anderson; Columbus

Anderson's economy is heavily reliant on auto components manufacturing; the city is still trying to recover from layoffs and downsizing in that sector during the 1980s. Its largest employers are affiliates of General Motors: The Delco Remy division makes car ignition systems and electrical components; Inland Fisher Guide makes lighting equipment and bumpers. Officials in both Anderson and Muncie want to use their locations on the White River for economic development and recreational purposes.

Although Columbus (Bartholomew County) has a strong industrial base — it is home to the Cummins Engine Co. and Arvin Industries — many of the voters are conservative: Dole took Bartholomew with 52 percent of the vote in 1996 and McIntosh won it with 65 percent. Columbus boasts an array of modern buildings designed by leading architects. Richmond (Wayne County), which Quakers founded in the 19th century, has an opera company.

The land outside the cities is rural and heavily farmed. Soybeans, oats and wheat are major crops in the northern part of the 2nd.

1990 Population: 554,416. White 526,723 (95%), Black 22,887 (4%), Other 4,806 (1%). Hispanic origin 3,322 (1%). 18 and over 416,400 (75%), 62 and over 91,595 (17%). Median age: 34.

tions is beyond debate," he said. When accused of creating problems for the regulatory process, he replied, "I think if we have some gridlock on the regulatory agencies, the American people will stand up and say, 'Yeah! Hallelujah!'"

McIntosh stirred controversy with his proposal, offered with Ernest Istook, R-Okla., that nonprofit recipients of federal grants be barred from federal lobbying. Nonprofit groups argued that McIntosh was trying to stifle debate coming from a sector that tends to favor Democrats. McIntosh and Istook attached their provision to a series of bills during the fiscal 1996 appropriations season, stalling action on whatever underlying bill they touched. With the Senate and Clinton opposed to the move, their proposal eventually died.

Preparatory to a September 1995 hearing on the proposal, McIntosh's staff handed out a news release showing that nonprofit groups belonging to the umbrella advocacy organization Alliance for Justice had received more than $7 million in federal grants. The release was printed on Alliance for Justice letterhead, leaving the impression that the lobbying group had prepared it. McIntosh wrote a letter apologizing to the group, and the ethics committee dismissed two complaints about the incident in March 1996.

McIntosh earned perfect scores during his first term from such groups as the American Conservative Union and the U.S. Chamber of Commerce, while drawing zero ratings from the liberal Americans for Democratic Action and the AFL-CIO.

At Home: McIntosh runs a model constituent service effort, and he was among the quickest in his House class to establish an aggressive media relations effort in his district. Those factors, coupled with a Midas touch as a fundraiser, carried him to re-election in 1996 in a district that had previously gone Democratic. Although transparently ambitious, McIntosh evidently will bypass running for an open Senate seat in 1998.

McIntosh has made many enemies on the left during his career in politics and they all came out in force against him in 1996. But the efforts of labor, environmentalists and gun control and abortion rights activists were not enough to make the candidacy of Democrat Marc Carmichael sing. The former state representative and utility company official fell a million dollars behind McIntosh in the money chase and failed to aggressively court free media opportunities. Carmichael started his campaign way behind and campaigned sluggishly through the summer. McIntosh prevailed with 58 percent of the vote.

McIntosh won election in 1994 by aiming his campaign rhetoric at the man who had put him out of work in 1992: Bill Clinton. In a district where Clinton received only 35 percent of the vote in 1992, McIntosh's opposition to Clinton's policies resonated enough to blunt his opponent's main line of attack, that McIntosh had only recently moved to the district.

Most of McIntosh's ads did not mention his opponent, Indiana Democratic Secretary of State Joseph H. Hogsett, except when the ads "morphed" Hogsett into Clinton. (A candidate roast to benefit the Society for Professional Journalists in Muncie even featured a Clinton impersonator, hired by the McIntosh campaign, who shocked some in the audience with his patter of sexually suggestive lines.)

McIntosh's campaign and the Republican year overcame Hogsett's local roots, formidable fundraising, name identification from a 1992 Senate race and strong campaign skills. McIntosh, remembered by his aunt as the kind of boy who used to sit and read the encyclopedia, had some trouble connecting with local voters. Although polls showed the race close, most of the late deciders went for McIntosh, while Hogsett was hurt by low turnout in Democratic territories such as Madison County (Muncie).

Before reaching the general election, McIntosh had weathered a tough battle for his party's nomination. Local GOP officials initially preferred state Auditor Ann DeVore, who subsequently stunned them by forgetting to file her candidacy papers in the secretary of state's office, located down the hall from her own. McIntosh then faced Bill Frazier, who had four times unsuccessfully challenged retiring Democratic Rep. Philip R. Sharp. Frazier played up his local connections and attacked McIntosh as a carpetbagger. McIntosh called Frazier a perennial loser and highlighted his $450,000 campaign debt to himself. An endorsement by former Gov. Robert D. Orr and targeted mailings helped McIntosh squeeze by with a 473-vote margin.

Growing up in northeastern Indiana, McIntosh was viewed as much older than his years, partly because of his intelligence and partly because he helped care for his three younger siblings after his father's death. Although his mother was a Democratic city judge in Kendallville, McIntosh became attracted to conservative ideas at Yale in the 1970s. At the University of Chicago Law School — where he studied under future Supreme Court Justice Antonin Scalia — McIntosh founded the Federalist Society for Law & Public Policy, a group of conservative lawyers and law students.

HOUSE ELECTIONS

1996 General		
David M. McIntosh (R)	123,113	(58%)
R. Marc "Marc" Carmichael (D)	85,105	(40%)
Paul E. Zimmerman (LIBERT)	4,665	(2%)
1996 Primary		
David M. McIntosh (R)	57,915	(86%)
Daniel A. Holtz (R)	10,727	(27%)
Gregory "Greg" Lunsford (R)	9,418	(14%)
1994 General		
David M. McIntosh (R)	93,592	(54%)
Joseph H. Hogsett (D)	78,241	(46%)

CAMPAIGN FINANCE

	Receipts	Receipts from PACs		Expend-itures
1996				
McIntosh (R)	$1,341,997	$483,576	(36%)	$1,050,616
Carmichael (D)	$210,080	$120,668	(57%)	$182,508
1994				
McIntosh (R)	$1,007,135	$243,945	(24%)	$973,209
Hogsett (D)	$796,169	$302,112	(38%)	$794,684

DISTRICT VOTE FOR PRESIDENT

	1996		1992
D	89,038 (42%)	**D**	81,915 (35%)
R	97,406 (45%)	**R**	101,341 (43%)
I	26,483 (12%)	**I**	50,424 (22%)

KEY VOTES

1997	
Ban "partial birth" abortions	Y
1996	
Approve farm bill	Y
Deny public education to illegal immigrants	Y
Repeal ban on certain assault-style weapons	Y
Increase minimum wage	N
Freeze defense spending	?
Approve welfare overhaul	Y
1995	
Approve balanced-budget constitutional amendment	Y
Relax Clean Water Act regulations	Y
Oppose limits on environmental regulations	N
Reduce projected Medicare spending	Y
Approve GOP budget with tax and spending cuts	Y

VOTING STUDIES

	Presidential Support		Party Unity		Conservative Coalition	
Year	**S**	**O**	**S**	**O**	**S**	**O**
1996	35	63	89	5	88	4
1995	17	80	95	3	95	3

INTEREST GROUP RATINGS

Year	ADA	AFL-CIO	CCUS	ACU
1996	0	n/a	100	100
1995	0	0	100	100

3 Tim Roemer (D)

Of South Bend — Elected 1990, 4th term

Biographical Information

Born: Oct. 30, 1956, South Bend, Ind.

Education: U. of California, San Diego, B.A. 1979; U. of Notre Dame, M.A. 1981, Ph.D. 1985.

Occupation: Congressional aide; adjunct professor.

Family: Wife, Sally Johnston; three children.

Religion: Roman Catholic.

Political Career: No previous office.

Capitol Office: 2348 Rayburn Bldg. 20515; 225-3915.

Committees

Education & Workforce
Early Childhood, Youth & Families; Postsecondary Education, Training & Life-Long Learning

Science
Energy & Environment (ranking)

In Washington: On fiscal and social policy matters, Roemer stands out as one of the more conservative non-Southern House Democrats. He pops up as a player on a range of issues — allocating dollars for space, finding middle ground on the budget, restricting abortion and making the House more "family friendly" — and in his work he draws on his prior experience as a congressional aide and on political lessons learned from his father-in-law, former Democratic Sen. J. Bennett Johnston of Louisiana.

Roemer quickly won prominence as a freshman in the 102nd Congress, when he joined another first-termer, Dick Zimmer, R-N.J., to target NASA's proposed space station, which was coming under criticism for cost overruns, schedule slips and design changes. On two votes in 1992, Roemer and Zimmer made a strong run at killing the orbiting laboratory. That set the stage for a down-to-the-wire battle in 1993, when a Roemer-Zimmer amendment to kill the station failed by a single vote.

That scare prompted a furious, pro-space station lobbying campaign by the Clinton administration, which stressed that it had directed NASA to pursue a simpler, less expensive design for the project, one costing $2.1 billion per year for five years. The full-court press worked: In its next test, the station survived the Roemer-Zimmer killer amendment by 24 votes.

Roemer kept up the pressure. "If it's not killed this year," he said in 1993, "it'll be next year. And if not next year, then the year after."

Roemer has portrayed the station as a pork barrel project drawing funds away from more scientifically worthy NASA undertakings. But Clinton and NASA said the station would advance scientific understanding, facilitate space exploration and promote international cooperation, since the station would be developed with Russia, Canada, Japan and 10 European countries.

When Republicans took control in the 104th, space station supporters wondered if the big new crop of deficit-conscious GOP freshmen would support the big-ticket project. As it turned out, the Republican leadership was foursquare behind it, and attempts to eliminate funding for the station failed 132-287 in 1995 and 127-286 in 1996.

Roemer thought he was getting some compelling new ammunition in 1997, when the Russians, America's principal partners in the station, said they could not meet deadlines for their responsibilities on the project. NASA officials announced in April that startup of construction on the station would be delayed because Russia could not deliver a key component on time.

But when the House considered Roemer's killer amendment in April 1997, it met with a lopsided 112-305 defeat, a margin that seemed to suggest the station's toughest battles were behind it.

During the budget battles of the 104th, Roemer struggled to find middle ground between the Clinton administration and congressional Republicans. Roemer backed a budget proposal fashioned by "blue dog" Democrats; it met the Republican requirement of zeroing out the deficit, but unlike the GOP proposal, it did not provide for tax cuts until the budget was balanced, and it contained more modest reductions in spending growth on entitlement programs such as Medicare and Medicaid.

That plan, though, was greeted coolly by both the White House and congressional Republicans, whose refusal to budge in bargaining eventually led to partial shutdowns of the federal government. But even when agreement seemed unlikely, Roemer searched for compromise.

In the middle of the first, six-day partial shutdown, Roemer was one of 48 Democrats who abandoned the White House position by joining Republicans to pass a bill which temporarily funded the government and also contained a balanced-budget commitment. Clinton had already vetoed a bill that contained such a commitment in addition to a controversial Medicare proposal.

Later, with significant parts of the government again closed, Roemer joined Republican Fred Upton of Michigan to organize a group of House centrists trying to come up with a temporary

INDIANA 3
Northern Tier — South Bend; Elkhart

The 3rd, dominated by industrial cities that line the Indiana Toll Road near the state's northern border, has been something of a barometer of national political trends.

At the onset of the "Reagan Revolution" in 1980, Republicans took this district from the Democrats, as 27-year-old John Hiler ousted House Majority Whip John Brademas. Ten years later, the 3rd offered evidence that the Reagan-Bush era was drawing to a close, as Democrat Roemer ousted Hiler. In 1994, Roemer's moderate ideology helped him survive the GOP tide, although with a less than secure 55 percent of the vote. He edged up to 58 percent in 1996, even as Bob Dole barely carried the district in presidential voting with 46 percent of the votes.

The 3rd long has been politically competitive. Its voters cross the political spectrum, from conservative and Republican Elkhart (Elkhart County) to swing-voting La Porte city and more Democratic South Bend (St. Joseph County) and Michigan City (La Porte County).

La Porte and Michigan City are La Porte County's two urban areas. Michigan City is blue-collar and has most of the county's minorities. Officials in Michigan City have tried to exploit the tourist potential of the city's Lake Michigan location. Much of the development has been in shopping centers and vacation home communities near the Indiana Dunes National Seashore.

To the southeast is the city of La Porte, which also has an industrial base. Employers include a Howmet Corp. plant that makes aerospace castings and a Whirlpool Corp. appliance distribution center.

With just over 105,000 residents, South Bend is the district's population nexus; neighboring Mishawaka adds 42,000 people. Although best-known for the University of Notre Dame, South Bend is also a center for tool-and-die manufacturing and the production of plastics. AM General Division, based in South Bend, makes military vehicles, including the "Humvee" transport. The manufacturing facility is in Mishawaka.

Like many industrial Midwestern locales, St. Joseph County has had its share of shocks. The collapse of the Studebaker Co. in the 1960s was a harbinger of the decline of the U.S. auto industry. The home-grown Bendix Corp. is now part of Allied-Signal Inc., which has headquarters elsewhere.

But the region has shown resilience. While foreign competition has hurt some local manufacturers, St. Joseph County has benefitted from the location in New Carlisle of the super-modern I/N Tek steel plant, a joint venture of Inland Steel Co. and Japan's Nippon Steel Corp.

Elkhart is a center for manufactured housing and recreational vehicle construction, and is known as the band instrument capital. One of the largest in that business is the Selmer Co., which gave Bill Clinton two saxophones just before his 1993 inauguration.

Outside the cities, the landscape shifts to farmland. Elkhart County, with a large Amish population, is the state's largest milk producer.

1990 Population: 554,416. White 502,899 (91%), Black 41,091 (7%), Other 10,426 (2%). Hispanic origin 10,717 (2%). 18 and over 407,768 (74%), 62 and over 86,726 (16%). Median age: 33.

funding measure to reopen the government. The group also tried to work out a balanced budget plan, but the effort collapsed. Although Republicans finally cut a deal with Clinton to reopen the government, it took until May 1997 for the two sides to announce agreement on the outline of a long-term balanced-budget plan.

In budget debates and on other issues, Roemer often rubs elbows with various ideological factions within the House. In March 1997, he decided to form his own group, and he joined with Cal Dooley, D-Calif. and James P. Moran, D-Va.. to unveil the "New Democrat Coalition (NDC)." Claiming 32 charter members in the House, the group promised to respond "to the public's demand for non-bureaucratic but activist government." On the House Democratic ideological spectrum, the NDC falls somewhere between the right-of-center "blue dogs" and the chamber's 100-some reliably liberal members.

The group is a good fit for Roemer, who sees himself as a progressive, but on numerous issues parts company with the Democratic left.

In mid-July 1996 he was one of only 30 Democrats who supported the GOP's third welfare-overhaul proposal. It took another round of Republican compromising with Clinton before the House in late July passed a welfare bill he agreed to sign, and which half the House Democrats (including Roemer) supported.

In the 104th, Roemer became a high-profile proponent of efforts by conservatives to ban a particular abortion technique that opponents call "partial birth" abortion. Congress approved the ban, but Clinton vetoed it.

A father of three youngsters, Roemer also has taken an interest in modifying Congress' sometimes backbreaking schedule to allow members and staff to spend more time with their families. In addition to their ambitious plans for the country, the new House GOP majority in 1995 also came in talking of making the chamber run in a more "family friendly" way. Speaker Newt Gingrich appointed a task force on the issue, chaired by Virginia Republican Frank R. Wolf.

But those intentions immediately fell casualty to the higher priority of plowing through the House GOP's "Contract With America" legislative agenda, a forced march that kept the House in session long hours for weeks on end in the early months of 1995. At one point during the marathon, Roemer complained that "the only time we see our families is when we take a picture of them out of our wallets." He said the House needed to be run more efficiently, with fewer late-night votes. On another occasion Roemer voiced his frustration in verse on the House floor, saying: "Roses are red. Violets are blue. If we're not home by seven, we're in deep stew."

Wrapping up the work of his task force, Wolf issued a grim prognosis, saying, "I personally doubt that a truly family friendly Congress will ever be possible."

At Home: Roemer has won election four times in the politically competitive 3rd, taking as little as 51 percent (in 1990, his first race) and as much as 58 percent, his 1996 tally against Republican state Sen. Joe Zakas.

Roemer's arrival in Washington in 1991 was a homecoming of sorts; he served as an aide to both former Democratic House Majority Whip John Brademas of Indiana and Democratic Sen. Dennis DeConcini of Arizona, and he taught at the American University in Washington.

Shaking off early primary criticism from some fellow Democrats that he was a carpetbagger from the East Coast, Roemer (who was born and raised in Indiana) took aim at GOP Rep. John Hiler, a veteran of several hard-fought re-elections in the 3rd.

As Johnston's son-in-law, Roemer was able to shake the Washington Beltway money tree; he raised more in PAC dollars than Hiler, and ran a sophisticated campaign with help from Johnston's research and media consultants. Roemer raised his name recognition with groups of volunteers called "Roemer's Roamers," who donned T-shirts and performed public services such as picking up trash and playing bingo with the elderly.

Roemer also benefited from the savings and loan scandal. The issue wounded Hiler, who had served on the House committee with responsibility for overseeing the thrift and banking industries.

Effectively steering a middle course during the campaign, Roemer sprinkled a traditional populism with occasional dashes of conservatism. One day he would hold a news conference at a plant rumored to be closing to lambaste the plight of the middle class; the next day he would out-Republican some Republicans by calling for a balanced budget and criticizing President George Bush for reneging on his no-new-taxes pledge. By a two-point margin, Roemer ousted Hiler.

In 1992, Roemer scored a solid re-election victory over Republican Carl H. Baxmeyer, a city planner who in 1987 had waged a strong bid for mayor of South Bend. The Republican wave in 1994 pulled down Roemer's margin but was not enough to place him in serious jeopardy against Warsaw tire salesman Richard Burkett.

HOUSE ELECTIONS

1996 General		
Tim Roemer (D)	114,288	(58%)
Joe Zakas (R)	80,699	(41%)
Bernie Taylor (LIBERT)	2,325	(1%)
1994 General		
Tim Roemer (D)	72,497	(55%)
Richard Burkett (R)	58,878	(45%)

Previous Winning Percentages: 1992 (57%) **1990** (51%)

CAMPAIGN FINANCE

	Receipts	Receipts from PACs		Expend-itures
1996				
Roemer (D)	$468,209	$298,648	(64%)	$525,727
Zakas (R)	$312,146	$35,544	(11%)	$310,084
1994				
Roemer (D)	$400,817	$267,714	(67%)	$350,594
Burkett (R)	$62,585	$14	(0%)	$64,373

DISTRICT VOTE FOR PRESIDENT

1996		1992	
D	86,715 (43%)	**D**	82,483 (38%)
R	91,427 (46%)	**R**	91,708 (43%)
I	20,371 (10%)	**I**	41,358 (19%)

VOTING STUDIES

	Presidential Support		Party Unity		Conservative Coalition	
Year	**S**	**O**	**S**	**O**	**S**	**O**
1996	68	32	64	36	63	37
1995	65	35	64	36	75	24
1994	83	17	85	14	69	31
1993	74	25	81	18	50	50
1992	40	58	70	29	71	29
1991	43	56	75	25	76	24

KEY VOTES

1997	
Ban "partial birth" abortions	Y
1996	
Approve farm bill	Y
Deny public education to illegal immigrants	Y
Repeal ban on certain assault-style weapons	N
Increase minimum wage	Y
Freeze defense spending	Y
Approve welfare overhaul	Y
1995	
Approve balanced-budget constitutional amendment	Y
Relax Clean Water Act regulations	N
Oppose limits on environmental regulations	N
Reduce projected Medicare spending	N
Approve GOP budget with tax and spending cuts	N

INTEREST GROUP RATINGS

Year	ADA	AFL-CIO	CCUS	ACU
1996	60	n/a	56	40
1995	75	75	50	32
1994	65	56	92	14
1993	45	73	55	38
1992	55	58	63	40
1991	50	67	40	30

4 Mark Souder (R)

Of Fort Wayne — Elected 1994, 2nd term

Biographical Information
Born: July 18, 1950, Fort Wayne, Ind.
Education: Indiana U., B.S. 1972; Notre Dame, M.B.A. 1974.
Occupation: Congressional aide; general store owner.
Family: Wife, Diane Zimmer; three children.
Religion: Evangelical.
Political Career: No previous office.
Capitol Office: 418 Cannon Bldg. 20515; 225-4436.

Committees
Education & Workforce
Early Childhood, Youth & Families; Postsecondary Education, Training & Life-Long Learning
Government Reform & Oversight
Human Resources; National Security, International Affairs & Criminal Justice
Small Business
Empowerment (chairman)

In Washington: Souder was vice president of the large and boisterous Republican Class of 1994, and during the 104th Congress he personified the group's often unyielding devotion to conservative principles. Souder's views on a range of issues — cutting taxes, reducing spending, opposing abortion — were so unstinting that they brought him into conflict even with GOP leaders when they decided it was time to compromise to keep the legislative process moving. In 1995, House Majority Leader Dick Armey of Texas joshingly tagged Souder the "designated varmint."

At the start of the 104th, Souder expressed respect, but hardly worship, for Speaker Newt Gingrich, widely hailed within Class of 1994 ranks as the architect of the GOP's electoral success. "He gave us an organizing principle," Souder said in January 1995, "but we are not indebted to Gingrich personally." In October 1995, Souder observed, "Some of the time Gingrich uses us because he really agrees with us. And some of the time he doesn't have a choice." Souder said his conservative classmates wanted "to get something done. We're not just here to blow things up." At the same time, he stressed, "We came here to be different. And we are not going to be housebroken."

After spending time on Capitol Hill, a number of Souder's peers came to accept the legislative maxim that winning half a loaf is better than nothing at all. But the drive to compromise left Souder nonplussed. In April 1996 he observed, "People who like to govern ... actually see it as an accomplishment to strike a deal." Only after the 1996 election reduced the GOP's House majority did Souder begin sounding less hostile to incrementalism.

Souder's skepticism of compromise led him to oppose passage of one of the GOP's top priorities in the 104th, a balanced-budget constitutional amendment. When the House in early 1995 considered a version of the amendment that GOP leaders backed, Souder was one of only two Republicans who voted "no." He was disappointed that the leadership had not insisted on pushing another, more strict version of the amendment—one that would have required a two-thirds supermajority in both chambers for any future tax increase.

"Back home in Indiana, a 60 percent supermajority to pass a tax increase does not seem enough," Souder said on the House floor. "In fact, in Indiana they would like 100 percent of this House to have to approve a tax increase, maybe twice, and maybe if they pass it, even an extra clause for a caning for those who pass the tax increase."

In 1996, Souder stuck with GOP leaders who resisted approving an increase in the minimum wage, even though dozens of Republicans had decided to back the increase. Souder called it a "layoff bill" that would cost low-income workers their jobs. He owns a retail store in his district.

In conjunction with other GOP freshmen in the 104th, Souder and his staff developed a system for poring over spending bills and alerting members to expenditures they deemed wasteful or other provisions they found objectionable. Partly because of "alerts" issued by these fiscal watchdogs, the House in September 1995 rejected the fiscal 1996 spending bill for the Defense Department. Souder and other abortion opponents were angry that bill negotiators had dropped a ban on privately funded abortions in U.S. military hospitals. "We do not want to divide the party," Souder said of the contentious issue of abortion. "But if the leaders don't let us do our thing, we won't let them do their thing."

When a privacy bill came up early in the 104th, Souder successfully offered an amendment to require parental consent before children participated in research surveys. He read into the Congressional Record a questionnaire that one of his children had been handed at school. It included such questions as, "Are you a virgin?" and, "Have you ever had an orgasm?" He complained, "Many things in these surveys imply that it is normal to have as a freshman in high school multiple sexual partners."

Souder's 1994 campaign buttons read "Quayle/Coats/Souder," a reminder of the Republican tradition in the 4th that had been interrupted by Democrat Jill L. Long. Only the third Democrat to represent the district in the last half century, Long had captured the seat in a special House election in 1989.

Long succeeded Daniel R. Coats, an aide to Dan Quayle who moved to his boss' Senate seat when Quayle became vice president in 1989. But Souder was able in 1994 to win back the GOP voters who had defected to Long, largely because of her personal appeal.

Souder solidified his hold on the district in his 1996 re-election bid by gaining 58 percent of the votes. Bob Dole carried the district at the presidential level by 17 percentage points. Still, other moderate Democrats running statewide have found the district receptive at times.

Fort Wayne, which dominates the 10-county 4th, avoided the economic upheaval and population exodus that plagued many large Midwestern cities in the 1980s. The population of Indiana's second-largest city was nearly the same in 1990 as it was a decade earlier, just under 173,000.

The city and its Allen County environs have several large industrial facilities: General Electric has a factory and General Motors builds trucks and buses at a plant just outside town.

But Fort Wayne's economy is buffered from industrial downturns by its large white-collar sector. The city's largest employer is the Lincoln National Life Insurance Co. Much of

INDIANA 4
Northeast — Fort Wayne

the area's manufacturing is technology-oriented: Raytheon (formerly Hughes Electronics), which makes military radios, and ITT Corp.'s aerospace and communications division, producing meteorological instruments, are here.

German-Americans, a rather conservative constituency, remain Allen County's largest ethnic group: Fort Wayne's Germanfest is an annual social highlight.

Fort Wayne's cityscape gives way to some of Indiana's most fertile farms. Allen County leads the state in production of wheat, is No. 2 in oats, and is near the top in soybeans. Lagrange County trails only Elkhart County (in the 3rd) in milk production. Like Elkhart, Lagrange has one of the nation's largest Amish populations. Souder's great-great-grandfather was one of the first Amish settlers in Allen County in 1846.

Small cities dot the 4th's fields. One of them, Huntington, is Quayle's hometown. The town has a walking tour called The Quayle Trail, and in 1993, the Dan Quayle Commemorative Museum opened. Huntington County gave Dole 59 percent in 1996 — even better than four years previous when Quayle had been on the ticket.

1990 Population: 554,416. White 514,933 (93%), Black 30,635 (6%), Other 8,848 (2%). Hispanic origin 8,818 (2%). 18 and over 396,224 (71%), 62 and over 79,975 (14%). Median age: 32.

Souder later got into trouble for making his own implications about sexual practices. In an interview with the Fort Wayne Journal-Gazette, Souder criticized the FBI for its handling of the 1993 siege at the Branch Davidian compound near Waco, Texas. The only law that the FBI clearly established that Davidian leader David Koresh broke, Souder said, is the law against having sex with consenting minors. "Do you send government troops into the large sections of Kentucky and Tennessee and other places where such things occur?" he said.

The remark drew Souder a quick rebuke from Democrat Mike Ward of Kentucky. "I can't decide if I'm more outraged by his thinking that there is such a thing as consensual sex with a minor, or that he says that it goes on commonly in Kentucky," Ward said.

Souder has shown a modicum of interest in foreign affairs, cosponsoring a bill that would withdraw the United States from NAFTA unless certain conditions are met. After a trip to Latin America, he offered an amendment to the fiscal 1997 foreign operations appropriations bill to block aid to Mexico unless it took a number of specific steps to combat illegal drug trafficking. The provision was agreed to by the House but watered down in conference.

At Home: Souder spent most of the decade before his first House election working for Indiana Republican Sen. Daniel R. Coats. With his 1994 defeat of Democratic Rep. Jill L. Long, Souder returned to the GOP a seat once held by Coats and before him by Dan Quayle. Long replaced Coats in the House in 1989 after Coats moved into the Senate seat that Quayle vacated to become vice president.

In winning the 1994 Republican nomination to challenge Long, Souder appealed to various factions in his party and targeted rural areas outside Fort Wayne, the district's population center. Although all the major contenders in the six-candidate primary had strong conservative credentials, Souder's low-key demeanor during the campaign made him appear less hard-line. He was helped by concerns among many Republicans that, as in past years, the GOP nomination would go to a candidate with limited appeal to the electorate in November.

Souder won nomination with 40 percent, but

Long's popularity remained high, and not all Republicans rallied quickly around their candidate. He went on the attack early, starting with summer radio ads that portrayed Long as a Washington insider beholden to special interests. He made every effort to tie her to President Clinton.

Both candidates frequently accused each other of lying. Souder received about 30 bars of soap in the mail after a Long ad said Souder's hands must be dirty from all his mudslinging. Long's toughest ad took Souder to task for having to pay $12,318 in late real estate taxes and penalties on land he partly owned. Souder responded that the bill had been misdirected. In another ad, Souder's mother accused Long of smearing her family.

Because Long was a personally popular Democrat who had won three times in a GOP-dominated district, the race in the 4th was seen as a national bellwether for Republican prospects of taking control of the House. On Election Night, the early returns in the 4th foretold that Democrats nationally would have a long night. Souder eventually won by a decisive 10 points.

During the campaign, Souder emphasized his local roots, partly to offset his years of service with Coats — eight of them in Washington. Souder's great-great-grandfather was one of the first Amish settlers in Allen County, in 1846. The family's original harness shop grew into a series of family businesses, including a log cabin restaurant in which Souder has a financial interest.

Seeking re-election in 1996, Souder won comfortably against Democrat Gerald L. Houseman, a political science professor under whom Souder once studied.

HOUSE ELECTIONS

1996 General		
Mark Souder (R)	121,344	(58%)
Gerald L. Houseman (D)	81,740	(39%)
Ken Bisson (LIBERT)	4,796	(2%)
1996 Primary		
Mark Souder (R)	44,853	(82%)
Phillip D. Marx (R)	10,118	(18%)
1994 General		
Mark Edward Souder (R)	88,584	(55%)
Jill L. Long (D)	71,235	(45%)

CAMPAIGN FINANCE

	Receipts	Receipts from PACs	Expend-itures
1996			
Souder (R)	$434,758	$132,056 (30%)	$438,384
Houseman (D)	$66,860	$21,850 (33%)	$65,093
Bisson (LIBERT)	$5,249	0	$5,067
1994			
Souder (R)	$428,362	$45,209 (11%)	$422,161
Long (D)	$400,346	$283,938 (71%)	$410,299

DISTRICT VOTE FOR PRESIDENT

	1996		1992
D	75,185 (36%)	**D**	69,292 (31%)
R	110,538 (53%)	**R**	102,779 (46%)
I	19,641 (10%)	**I**	49,565 (22%)

KEY VOTES

1997	
Ban "partial birth" abortions	Y
1996	
Approve farm bill	Y
Deny public education to illegal immigrants	Y
Repeal ban on certain assault-style weapons	Y
Increase minimum wage	N
Freeze defense spending	?
Approve welfare overhaul	Y
1995	
Approve balanced-budget constitutional amendment	N
Relax Clean Water Act regulations	Y
Oppose limits on environmental regulations	N
Reduce projected Medicare spending	Y
Approve GOP budget with tax and spending cuts	Y

VOTING STUDIES

	Presidential Support		Party Unity		Conservative Coalition	
Year	**S**	**O**	**S**	**O**	**S**	**O**
1996	35	61	89	8	88	8
1995	20	80	93	6	86	14

INTEREST GROUP RATINGS

Year	ADA	AFL-CIO	CCUS	ACU
1996	10	n/a	75	95
1995	5	8	92	100

5 Steve Buyer (R)

Of Monticello — Elected 1992, 3rd term

Biographical Information

Born: Nov. 26, 1958, Rensselaer, Ind.
Education: The Citadel, B.S. 1980; Valparaiso U., J.D. 1984.
Military Service: Army Reserve, 1980-84; Army, 1984-87; Army Reserve, 1987-present.
Occupation: Lawyer.
Family: Wife, Joni Geyer; two children.
Religion: Methodist.
Political Career: No previous office.
Capitol Office: 326 Cannon Bldg. 20515; 225-5037.

Committees

Judiciary
Crime
National Security
Military Installations and Facilities; Military Personnel (chairman)
Veterans' Affairs
Oversight & Investigations

In Washington: Buyer's status as a veteran of the Persian Gulf War was a political plus as he captured the 5th from Democrats in 1992, and military matters have been a big part of his work in Congress. Now in his third term, Buyer chairs the National Security Subcommittee on Military Personnel, and he serves on the Veterans' Affairs Committee, where he has been active in Congress' study of health problems reported by soldiers who were stationed in the Persian Gulf region.

In the fall of 1996, Buyer got an early start looking into another matter that falls under the purview of the Military Personnel Subcommittee: Floyd D. Spence of South Carolina, the National Security Committee chairman, asked Buyer to help lead the committee's inquiry into allegations that Army drill sergeants at several training bases pressured female recruits for sex. Buyer, along with the two women members of the committee, Florida Republican Tillie Fowler and California Democrat Jane Harman, said they would try to learn why the network of Army policies intended to prevent the harassment of recruits may have broken down and why some of the women were slow to report the incidents.

Buyer, a major in the Army reserves, plainly wanted to make sure the controversy did not give the military a black eye; he praised the Army for "its open, swift and aggressive investigation" of the allegations. Noting that scores of military assignments previously closed to women have been opened in recent years, Buyer said that a congressional review of such changes would be timely. At the same time, he distanced himself from conservatives who said the alleged incidents at training bases demonstrated that expanding the role of women in the military is inherently perilous. "Let's not give any excuses for these thugs to somehow justify their indecent actions," he said.

A big concern for Buyer in the 104th was President Clinton's commitment to deploy U.S. troops in the former Yugoslavia, torn for years by civil war. In October 1995, two days before peace negotiations among the warring Balkan parties were scheduled to begin in Dayton, Ohio, Buyer and Pennsylvania's Paul McHale, a Democrat on National Security, offered a nonbinding House resolution expressing the sense of Congress that negotiators should not assume that U.S. troops would be deployed, and that no deployment should occur unless authorized by Congress. The House approved the resolution, 315-103.

Assistant Secretary of State Richard C. Holbrooke objected to the Buyer-McHale effort, saying, "This kind of resolution is extremely unhelpful. It would weaken the United States; it would weaken the negotiations." Buyer called Holbrooke's comments "gross exaggerations" and said: "If the parties sit down and focus on the real reason they're killing each other and sign a peace agreement, they don't need peacemakers and enforcers."

Once the warring parties crafted a peace agreement in December 1995, Clinton began the deployment of 20,000 U.S. troops to the area. Buyer and Missouri's Ike Skelton, another National Security Democrat, brought another resolution to the floor that supported the troops but disowned the deployment decision and insisted that the United States remain scrupulously neutral among Bosnia's contending parties. The House approved this resolution, 287-141. Buyer backed a second measure that would have denied funds for the Bosnia deployment, but the House rejected that proposal.

Buyer also has used his National Security seat to protect interests at home. In September 1995, his advocacy of building a new fire station at Grissom Air Reserve Base in the 5th drew him into a spat with the ranking Democrat on the Appropriations Committee, David R. Obey of Wisconsin. The argument came as the House debated the fiscal 1996 military construction bill. Obey complained that the bill included 23 projects, amounting to about $150 million, that were not included on the Pentagon's five-year construction schedule. In a letter to House colleagues, Obey singled out the $4.25 million Grissom fire station as a project that was not part of the Pentagon's five-year plan. The 1991 base-closing commission voted to shut down Grissom as an active duty base, leaving the installation to the

INDIANA 5
Northern Rural — Kokomo

The 5th stretches across a mainly rural area that calls itself the "Hoosier Heartland." One would expect such a place to have a Republican tilt, and it does: Bob Dole won the district with 50 percent of the vote in 1996, Bill Clinton took 37 percent, while Ross Perot pulled down 13 percent. Redistricting in 1991 enhanced GOP strength in the 5th, and that helped Buyer narrowly defeat Democratic Rep. Jim Jontz, who had won the district three times.

With economies heavily reliant on auto parts manufacturing, many of the district's small cities have struggled. Like many areas across the Midwest, several 5th District counties declined in population during the 1980s. Industrial Grant County (Marion) lost 8 percent of its population, while Howard County (Kokomo) fell by 7 percent. Warren, a farm county on Indiana's western border, was down by 9 percent.

Kokomo, with about 45,000 people, is the district's largest city. It was long a center for industrial innovation: Kokomo resident Elwood Haynes produced the first successful gasoline-powered car and later invented stainless steel (Haynes International Inc., a producer of metal alloys, is one of Kokomo's major employers). The biggest job-provider in the city is Delco Electronics Corp., known for its automobile sound systems. Much of Kokomo's hopes for economic growth are based on Delco's development of electronic pollution-control systems and safety devices such as air bags. Employment at Chrysler's transmission plant has been steady.

Economic recovery has been difficult in Marion and nearby Gas City. A General Motors auto body stamping plant is the largest employer in Marion. The city is also home to the Ball-Foster Corp., which makes glass containers, and Thomson Consumer Electronics, manufacturer of RCA products.

To the north are a string of smaller working-class cities: Wabash, Peru and Logansport. Their distance from major highways is a hindrance to growth; locals are pushing for a "Hoosier Heartland Highway," which would modernize Routes 24 and 25 that connect these cities with Fort Wayne and Lafayette.

Peru has a colorful past — it was the hometown of songwriter Cole Porter and the base for a children's circus — but it has a tenuous present: Nearby Grissom Air Reserve Base, formerly Grissom Air Force Base, was redesigned and now houses only reserves.

At its northwest corner, the 5th includes small suburbs of central Lake County. In Porter County, only the town of Hebron is in the 5th.

Most of the remaining land in the 5th is farmed. In the district's northeast corner is part of Kosciusko County, which calls itself Indiana's leading agricultural county. This is strong Republican country: Dole beat Clinton here by more than 2-to-1.

To the west, the 5th contains counties that are prolific producers of corn, soybeans and hogs. At its southwest extreme, the 5th's terrain and politics change quickly. Vermillion County, where Indiana's coal-mining territory begins, is heavily Democratic. It was the only county to back Buyer's Democratic challenger in 1996.

1990 Population: 554,415. White 536,008 (97%), Black 11,928 (2%), Other 6,479 (1%). Hispanic origin 7,463 (1%). 18 and over 403,843 (73%), 62 and over 89,590 (16%). Median age: 34.

reserves.

But Buyer said Grissom had been a reserve facility since October 1994, is home to the 434th Air Refueling Wing and also may house helicopters from the Indiana National Guard. The fire station was on the Air Force schedule for construction in 1998, he maintained, and he simply wanted to move up the date by two years.

Obey said the Office of Management and Budget informed him that the project was not on the Pentagon's planning list and that the existing fire station is sufficient at Grissom, where civilian employment has dropped from 3,200 to 700. But moments after the heated discussion ended, the House approved the bill with the fire station funds and sent it to the Senate.

On Veterans' Affairs in the 104th, Buyer was chairman of the Education, Training Employment and Housing Subcommittee, and he became a leading proponent of efforts to direct the Veterans' Affairs Department to ensure comprehensive care for gulf war veterans who might be suffering from "Persian Gulf syndrome," the label given to an array of ailments that many believe stem from exposure to Iraqi chemical weapons. Buyer says he has personal experience with the syndrome: While campaigning for the House in 1992, Buyer suffered from a range of ailments. He told The Dallas Morning News in 1993 that a month after he returned home from the war, he noticed he could not jog short distances "without feeling exhausted." He also had kidney problems, two cases of pneumonia and spent "much of the last month" of the 1992 campaign in bed. He sharply criticized the Pentagon's early response to veterans' complaints of illness, calling a 1995 Pentagon study on the syndrome "a callous attempt by the Pentagon officials to discount the suffering of gulf war veterans and their families."

Buyer's third committee assignment is Judiciary, and there he has lent his voice to GOP assertions that the nation should take a tougher stand against criminals. When the committee in

April 1996 approved a measure that would increase prison sentences by an average of two years for those who commit crimes against children, the elderly or other vulnerable people, Democrats protested that it would interfere with the U.S. Sentencing Commission's ability to set sentencing guidelines. Unmoved, Buyer said Congress should intervene when necessary. He said the commission had rejected directives in the 1994 crime bill to reassess sentences for crimes against the vulnerable. "What we're trying to do is change a trend line here," he said. "There's too much of the coddling and too much 'hug-a-thug' that happens."

At Home: As a captain in the Army Reserves, Buyer was an attorney for troops in the Persian Gulf. Soon after he returned to U.S. soil, he took to the campaign stump against three-term Democratic incumbent Jim Jontz, displaying his combat boots at some stops and scoring Jontz's vote against giving President George Bush authority to commit troops to the gulf.

When the war faded from the news and from the list of viable campaign issues, Buyer did not miss a beat. He seized the theme of "change" that grew out of the House bank and Post Office scandals and successfully painted Jontz as part of a corrupt Washington establishment. Jontz had only four bank overdrafts totaling less than $1,000, not even placing him in the list of the top 200 offenders. Still, Buyer took him to task. Jontz's arguments that he did not try to take advantage of the system — he noted that one overdraft was for a scholarship fund financed by the congressional pay raise he refused — were undermined when a Buyer ad noted that not all of Jontz's pay increase went to the fund, as Jontz's ads had implied.

Some voters also were turned off by Jontz's involvement in environmental issues that primarily affected the Pacific Northwest, not the 5th District. Bill Clinton took a dismal 31 percent in the district's presidential voting, and a strong local showing by independent Ross Perot (23 percent) brought to the polls reform-minded voters who found Buyer's pitch appealing. He took 51 percent in one of the biggest upsets of 1992.

The 5th was traditionally Republican before Jontz's tenure, and it re-elected Buyer easily in 1994 and 1996.

HOUSE ELECTIONS

1996 General		
Steve Buyer (R)	125,191	(65%)
Douglas L. Clark (D)	63,578	(33%)
Tom Lehman (LIBERT)	5,069	(3%)
1994 General		
Steve Buyer (R)	111,031	(70%)
J.D. Beatty (D)	45,224	(28%)
Clayton L. Alfred (I)	3,403	(2%)

Previous Winning Percentages: **1992** (51%)

CAMPAIGN FINANCE

	Receipts	Receipts from PACs	Expend-itures
1996			
Buyer (R)	$369,273	$159,361 (43%)	$227,204
Clark (D)	$15,272	$8,500 (56%)	$6,764
Lehman (LIBERT)	$2,135	0	$2,184
1994			
Buyer (R)	$504,249	$208,512 (41%)	$501,287
Beatty (D)	$178,324	$88,282 (50%)	$181,780

DISTRICT VOTE FOR PRESIDENT

	1996		1992
D	78,270 (37%)	**D**	70,893 (31%)
R	105,906 (50%)	**R**	103,118 (46%)
I	27,470 (13%)	**I**	52,354 (23%)

KEY VOTES

1997	
Ban "partial birth" abortions	Y
1996	
Approve farm bill	Y
Deny public education to illegal immigrants	Y
Repeal ban on certain assault-style weapons	Y
Increase minimum wage	Y
Freeze defense spending	N
Approve welfare overhaul	Y
1995	
Approve balanced-budget constitutional amendment	Y
Relax Clean Water Act regulations	Y
Oppose limits on environmental regulations	N
Reduce projected Medicare spending	Y
Approve GOP budget with tax and spending cuts	Y

VOTING STUDIES

	Presidential Support		Party Unity		Conservative Coalition	
Year	S	O	S	O	S	O
1996	37	63	93	5	98	2
1995	19	80	95	2	100	0
1994	50	50	92	6	94	3
1993	40	59	95	5	98	2

INTEREST GROUP RATINGS

Year	ADA	AFL-CIO	CCUS	ACU
1996	5	n/a	94	95
1995	0	0	100	88
1994	0	11	100	100
1993	0	17	100	100

6 Dan Burton (R)

Of Indianapolis — Elected 1982, 8th term

Biographical Information
Born: June 21, 1938, Indianapolis, Ind.
Education: Indiana U., 1958-59; Cincinnati Bible College, 1959-60.
Military Service: Army, 1956-57; Army Reserve, 1957-62.
Occupation: Real estate and insurance agent.
Family: Wife, Barbara Logan; three children.
Religion: Christian.
Political Career: Ind. House, 1967-69; Ind. Senate, 1969-71; Republican nominee for U.S. House, 1970; sought Republican nomination for U.S. House, 1972; Ind. House, 1977-81; Ind. Senate, 1981-83.
Capitol Office: 2185 Rayburn Bldg. 20515; 225-2276.

Committees
Government Reform & Oversight (chairman)
International Relations
International Operations & Human Rights; Western Hemisphere

In Washington: A tenacious partisan, Burton is the House Republicans' point man in the 1997 investigation of political fundraising that focuses on money brought in by President Clinton's 1996 re-election campaign. The task gives him another crack at exposing misdeeds in a Clinton White House he has already accused of ethics lapses: A highlight of Burton's career in the House minority came when he rose on the House floor in July 1994 to argue that White House Deputy Counsel Vincent W. Foster Jr. was murdered. Of the campaign finance investigation Burton has said, "This thing could end up being much bigger than Watergate."

Burton got the job of running the inquiry by ascending to the chairmanship of the Government Reform and Oversight Committee in the 105th Congress. He had been the third-ranking Republican on the panel in the 104th Congress, when it was chaired by William F. Clinger, R-Pa., who did not seek re-election in 1996. (The committee's No. 2 Republican, Benjamin A. Gilman, chairs the International Relations Committee.)

Despite his pit-bull reputation, Burton in November 1996 promised a fair, objective investigation. "I know some have seen me as an attack dog," he said. "I think they're going to be pleasantly surprised. We're not going to go on any witch hunts. We're going to try to conduct the committee in a bipartisan way. I'm going to try to be a fair as possible."

Nevertheless, as the 105th Congress convened, the Republicans gave Burton exclusive power to issue subpoenas, rejecting a Democratic request that he first secure committee approval, or at least the consent of ranking minority member Henry A. Waxman, D-Calif.

And in April, Burton and the Republicans defeated a Democratic attempt to broaden the scope of the committee's investigation. Although some Repubicans on the panel argued that the probe would eventually widen, whatever Burton himself might prefer, Democrats complained that the committee had been committed to a one-sided inquisition into Clinton's re-election effort that would ignore abuses in congressional campaign financing (not to mention Republican presidential spending).

Burton's attempt to get $3.8 million for this investigation, plus access to a $7.9 million contingency fund, was blocked temporarily in March 1997 when 11 Republicans bucked their party and joined with the Democratic minority to kill the rule bringing the funding resolution to the floor. (The Republican dissenters objected to the overall increased spending for House committees, which was to rise from $156 million to $170 million.)

Burton also ran into some fundraising controversies of his own. A March 1997 story in The Washington Post contained a charge from Mark A. Siegel, a lobbyist for Pakistan and a former Democratic Party official, who accused Burton of threatening to retaliate against him unless he raised money for the chairman's 1996 House race. Siegel later spent about three hours testifying before a grand jury looking into the allegations. "Lies, lies lies," Burton said. "Let them come at me, they won't find anything. They fear Dan Burton because they know Dan Burton will uncover the truth."

That same month, Burton was forced on the defensive after The New York Times reported that he accepted an invitation to play golf with AT&T's chairman at the famed Pebble Beach golf course and accepted a $2,000 contribution from the company's PAC. Burton's committee will award a multibillion dollar federal telecommunications contract currently held by AT&T. "I'm going to tell you, for $2,000, no one is going to buy anyone's vote and certainly not mine," Burton said.

And The Hill newspaper reported in April 1997 that Burton received illegal campaign contributions from Sikh temples and tax-exempt organizations associated with that Asian religion. "Listen real clear," Burton said. "These contributions were in 1992 and 1993. I believe the total was $600, $700 total. It was a mistake. They thought it was intentional, but it was a mistake."

One senior Republican on the committee,

Over the past couple of decades, the farms and undeveloped tracts of Hamilton, Johnson and outer Marion counties have been overtaken by Indianapolis subdivisions. Growth in some areas outside the city's widely looping beltway (Interstate 465) has been explosive. The population of once pastoral Hamilton County has doubled since 1970, and it increased 33 percent in the 1980s, reaching about 110,000 in 1990.

The boom has changed the look but not the politics of the outlying areas that make up the core of the 6th. The wealthy and near-wealthy who have moved here are nearly as conservative as the farmers who live nearby. Republican vote totals are consistently high. Bob Dole won 70 percent of the Hamilton County vote and 60 percent in neighboring Hancock County in 1996. He won the overall district with 63 percent, his best showing in the state. Burton garnered 75 percent, the highest of any House candidate in Indiana that year.

The Democrats in the state House who controlled redistricting in 1991 packed even more Republicans into the 6th than the district contained in the 1980s. Increasingly suburban sections of Morgan and Boone counties, as well as mainly rural Clinton, Tipton, Hancock and a slice of Henry counties, were transferred to the 6th. As a result, the district is not only the most Republican in Indiana but also one of the most GOP-oriented House districts in the nation.

There is almost no minority group constituency: Hamilton's black population in 1990 was less than 1 percent.

The 6th takes in the loyally Republican sections of northern and southern Marion County. The rest of Marion is in the Democratic-held 10th. Leaders in the GOP vote parade are the

INDIANA 6
Central — Suburban Indianapolis

established suburbs of Washington Township and the growth area to the northeast around Geist Reservoir. Castleton and part of the city of Lawrence are also in the district.

The northern sections of Marion County blend with the white-collar suburbs of Hamilton County. Carmel, which is 15 miles from downtown Indianapolis, was a town of about 7,000 people in 1970; now, more than 25,000 live there.

Noblesville and the nearby Morse Reservoir area also have grown significantly. Zionsville, in the southeast corner of Boone County, continues to advertise its quaint appearance even as it is further absorbed into the Indianapolis sphere.

There is suburban wealth in the district's southern reaches, but a number of residents of more modest means also live there. Some working-class Marion County suburbanites work at the Amtrak repair shops in Beech Grove and at Indianapolis International Airport. The 6th also takes in the city of Speedway, host of the Indianapolis 500 auto race.

Johnson County, where population grew by 14 percent in the 1980s, combines suburban sprawl with an industrial presence.

The suburbs have encroached somewhat on Hancock County (Greenfield). However, the northernmost counties, Clinton and Tipton, are still primarily farmland.

1990 Population: 554,416. White 541,811 (98%), Black 5,888 (1%), Other 6,717 (1%). Hispanic origin 4,374 (1%). 18 and over 408,057 (74%), 62 and over 74,996 (14%). Median age: 34.

Christopher Shays of Connecticut, said Burton needed to address the various allegations. "For our investigation to have credibility, people can't question" the chairman's integrity, Shays said. "We have to make sure these issues are resolved. They can't be allowed to continue."

In January 1997, Burton voted against the reprimand and $300,000 penalty the House ethics committee recommended for Speaker Newt Gingrich for violating House rules. In response to all of the Democratic-filed complaints against Gingrich, Burton in December 1995 had introduced a resolution to penalize lawmakers who submit frivolous allegations to the ethics committee. Lawmakers would be subject to a personal fine and would be required to pay legal fees out of their office accounts. "One of the favorite pastimes is to attack Newt to try to discredit him," Burton said. "What I am trying to do is say, 'Enough is enough.'"

Burton also led the unsuccessful fight against a stringent ban on members receiving gifts, meals and lobbyist-financed trips. In November 1995, as the House prepared to vote on gift rules similar to those enacted earlier in the Senate — limiting gifts and meals to $50, with a maximum of $100 from any one source per year, and banning lobbyist-financed trips to golf and tennis outings designed to raise money for charity — he offered a substitute to the proposed restrictions that would have kept the existing gift rules in place and strengthened disclosure requirements. But the House defeated Burton's amendment, 154-276, before adopting an amendment by Gingrich to go further than the Senate, banning all gifts, 422-8. The House adopted the final amended gift ban resolution, 422-6.

Burton spent the first four years of the Clinton administration pillorying the Democratic president with more tenacity than the most partisan of his GOP colleagues. He infuriated Democrats and shocked no small number of Republicans with his July 1994 floor speech questioning presidential counsel Foster's apparent suicide and proposing that Foster was murdered. Burton contended that, regardless of how Foster died, his body had been secretly moved to the spot where U.S. Park Police discovered it.

"Who moved the body?" asked Burton. "We need to find out who moved the body. There was blonde hair, not Mr. Foster's, on his T-shirt and other parts of his garments. Whose hair was it? It was not his. There were carpet and other wool fibers found on the body. Where did they come from?"

In the course of his own investigation, Burton said, he had re-enacted Foster's death in his back yard. "We, at my house, with a homicide detective, tried to re-create a head and fired a .38-inch barrel into that, to see if the sound could be heard from 100 yards away," Burton said.

As chairman of the International Relations Western Hemisphere Subcommittee in the 104th Congress, he co-authored legislation strengthening the U.S. economic embargo of Cuba. The Helms-Burton Act, named for Burton and Senate Foreign Relations Committee Chairman Jesse Helms, R-N.C., allowed U.S. nationals whose properties have been confiscated by Fidel Castro's government to sue foreign companies that knowingly "traffic" in such properties. The bill also barred executives from companies trading in expropriated properties, and their families, from obtaining U.S. visas.

Though the White House initially opposed key aspects of the bill, Clinton's objections melted away in February 1996, after Cuban military planes shot down two civilian aircraft being flown toward the island nation by Cuban-American opponents of Castro, killing four. Clinton signed the bill in March 1996 over the objections of U.S. trading partners.

Burton in March 1996 said sources had told him that the U.S. Air Force had time to intercept the Cuban MiGs after they entered international air space but before they shot down the civilian aircraft.

At Home: Redistricting made the 6th solid Republican terrain in 1982 and helped put Burton in office. After the 1990 census, the district was made even more Republican, further solidifying Burton's hold. He polled three-fourths of the vote in 1996.

Burton, a longtime state legislator, settled an old intraparty score by winning the 1982 GOP primary in the 6th. A decade earlier he had lost to William Hudnut by 81 votes for the House nomination in a nearby district; Hudnut served a term in Congress and later became mayor of Indianapolis. When the 6th was created in 1981, Hudnut hoped to secure the nomination for his GOP ally, state party Chairman Bruce Melchert. Against Melchert, however, Burton won.

Burton and Melchert agreed on most issues, and the competition was mostly amiable. But the Burton-Hudnut feud surfaced at one point, when Burton suggested that the mayor had engineered the last-minute candidacy of political unknown Ricky Bartl to deprive Burton of the first position on the alphabetical ballot.

HOUSE ELECTIONS

1996 General		
Dan Burton (R)	193,193	(75%)
Carrie J. Dillard-Trammell (D)	59,661	(23%)
Fred Peterson (LIBERT)	5,003	(2%)
1994 General		
Dan Burton (R)	136,876	(77%)
Natalie M. Bruner (D)	40,815	(23%)

Previous Winning Percentages: **1992** (72%) **1990** (63%) **1988** (73%) **1986** (68%) **1984** (73%) **1982** (65%)

CAMPAIGN FINANCE

	Receipts	Receipts from PACs	Expend-itures
1996			
Burton (R)	$723,846	$248,337 (34%)	$491,082
Dillard-Trammell (D)	$8,389	$5,000 (60%)	$11,273
1994			
Burton (R)	$560,821	$162,727 (29%)	$455,095

DISTRICT VOTE FOR PRESIDENT

	1996		1992
D	74,997 (28%)	**D**	61,171 (23%)
R	168,010 (63%)	**R**	153,280 (57%)
I	22,398 (8%)	**I**	54,718 (20%)

KEY VOTES

1997	
Ban "partial birth" abortions	Y
1996	
Approve farm bill	Y
Deny public education to illegal immigrants	Y
Repeal ban on certain assault-style weapons	Y
Increase minimum wage	N
Freeze defense spending	N
Approve welfare overhaul	Y
1995	
Approve balanced-budget constitutional amendment	Y
Relax Clean Water Act regulations	Y
Oppose limits on environmental regulations	N
Reduce projected Medicare spending	Y
Approve GOP budget with tax and spending cuts	Y

VOTING STUDIES

	Presidential Support		Party Unity		Conservative Coalition	
Year	S	O	S	O	S	O
1996	35	65	95	4	94	6
1995	17	83	96	2	96	2
1994	28	71	97	1	94	3
1993	25	74	97	2	91	9
1992	75	23	94	4	85	10
1991	75	23	92	6	97	3

INTEREST GROUP RATINGS

Year	ADA	AFL-CIO	CCUS	ACU
1996	10	n/a	94	100
1995	0	0	96	100
1994	0	22	73	100
1993	10	17	91	100
1992	10	25	86	100
1991	5	17	80	100

7 Ed Pease (R)

Of Terre Haute — Elected 1996, 1st term

Biographical Information

Born: May 22, 1951, Vigo County, Ind.

Education: Indiana U., A.B. 1973, J.D. 1977; Indiana State U., 1981-85.

Occupation: College administrator; lawyer.

Family: Single.

Religion: United Methodist.

Political Career: Ind. Senate, 1981-93.

Capitol Office: 226 Cannon Bldg. 20515; 225-5805.

Committees

Judiciary

Courts & Intellectual Property; Immigration & Claims

Transportation & Infrastructure

Aviation; Surface Transportation

The Path to Washington: Affable and soft-spoken, Pease is likely to vote with his conservative brethren on most issues. But he will seek to emulate John T. Myers, his Republican predecessor who retired in 1996, in reaching across the aisle to cut deals with Democrats when necessary to advance his causes.

"I come with strong convictions, but I also come with great respect for people of different convictions," said Pease, who landed a spot on the Transportation and Infrastructure Committee, where deal-making is an art.

One area in which Pease may sometimes break with his GOP peers is education. Although he supports efforts to return more control over education to states and localities, the former Indiana State University administrative vice president would like to see a continued federal role in funding higher education.

Pease, who considers himself a solid conservative, concedes that he breaks with his party's mainstream in his support of increased funding for student loans and grants, as well as environmental safeguards.

Pease supports, in principle, cuts in tax rates, though he did not come out in favor of a specific package. He was more specific about spending cuts, proposing that administrative budgets, except that of the Pentagon, be reduced by 10 percent across the board. He also favored killing the departments of Energy and Commerce.

Social conservatives have an ally in Pease, well-positioned on the Judiciary Committee. He opposes abortion, gun control and affirmative action and supports a constitutional amendment to allow prayer in public schools.

Pease earned a reputation during three terms in the Indiana Senate as a thorough and honest legislator. Lobbyists for both industry and education learned that his vote could not be taken for granted.

His crowning achievements came as chairman of the Judiciary Committee, where he sponsored legislation that allowed more flexibility in sentencing. Pease backed more lenient penalties for juvenile and first-time offenders, arguing that more resources would be available for hardened criminals.

During his House campaign against Democratic state Sen. Bob Hellmann, Pease assured voters in ads that he would not support spending reductions in Social Security, Medicare or veterans' programs.

Pease, who worked hog roasts and chili suppers across the 13-county district in lieu of sharing many stages with Hellmann, complained that he put on 25 pounds during the campaign.

Pease's roots in Vigo County, the most Democratic section of the district, made Hellmann's uphill climb that much steeper.

Pease's biggest electoral challenge came in winning the 15-way GOP primary. The field included several well-known politicians, including John Meyers, a Lafayette lawyer and former GOP district chairman. Concerned that voters might be confused by the candidate's name, retiring Rep. Myers endorsed Pease in the closing weeks. (The incumbent's daughter and son-in-law were already working for Pease.)

Family connections also provided a boost to Pease's fundraising efforts. Pease underwrote most of his primary campaign, with the funds coming from the sale of his Terre Haute house to his second cousin Robert A. Funk, an Oklahoma City businessman. Pease continued to live in the house under a lease.

The Terre Haute Tribune-Star, which revealed the house sale, also reported that Pease received some three dozen contributions totaling more than $10,000 from Oklahoma residents. Pease's house was again in the local press the weekend before the election, when the Lafayette Journal and Courier reported that 10 men were registered to vote at Pease's address.

In keeping with his belief that government programs should be an avenue of last resort, Pease has devoted himself to community service, from lay leadership in his church to the national board of the Boy Scouts.

INDIANA 7

West — Terre Haute; Lafayette

The Wabash River recalls to Hoosier nostalgists the days when western Indiana was settled by newcomers arriving on flatboats and steamers. The 7th, which ranges across this region, has long been identified with Lafayette and Terre Haute, which formed along the river.

However, rapid growth in the suburban counties west of Indianapolis has given the 7th a third population center. Adding to this new suburban clout is the northwest section of Monroe County, which contains expanding communities near Bloomington.

In the Indianapolis orbit is Hendricks County, the largest of the district's suburban counties; its population increased by 18 percent from 1990 to 1996, third-fastest in the state. Growth also is flush to the south in Morgan County and to the north in Boone County, most of which are in the 7th.

Each of these counties is relatively affluent and has a minuscule minority population: just nine blacks were counted among Morgan County's 56,000 residents in 1990. The conservative tone of these counties has strongly reinforced the district's long-held GOP tendencies.

Lafayette and Terre Haute remain the 7th's major urban centers. The tale of these cities is a study in contrasts.

The Lafayette area (Tippecanoe County) has enjoyed economic growth. Some is attributed to Purdue University, which helps attract technology-oriented businesses, in West Lafayette. With nearly 35,000 students, Purdue employs the equivalent of 23,000 full-time workers, the most in the area. Industry also has expanded around Lafayette, including a Subaru-Isuzu plant that employs nearly 3,000 people. Other facilities include an Eli Lilly chemical plant, an Alcoa aluminum plant and a Fairfield plant that makes gear shafts.

While its blue-collar sector provides some Democratic votes, Tippecanoe has held fast to its GOP traditions. But Terre Haute (Vigo County) has a Democratic bent that economic hard times reinforced. Once a hotbed of radicalism — Terre Haute was the hometown of socialist Eugene V. Debs, a five-time presidential candidate — Vigo supported Bill Clinton in 1996 with 47 percent of the vote, the only county lying wholly in the 7th he carried.

Terre Haute (French for "high ground") is coping with long-term industrial decline. At the northern end of Indiana's coal country, the city suffered from the national coal industry's ailments. Today, the largest area employer is Columbia House, the mail-order music distributor. Several factories produce plastics and films; Pfizer has a pharmaceutical plant nearby. Local officials tout the city's colleges: Indiana State University (11,200 students) and the Rose-Hulman Institute.

The rest of the 7th is mainly GOP farmland, dotted with small cities such as Crawfordsville (Montgomery County), which has a large R. R. Donnelley printing plant. Greencastle (Putnam County) contains former Vice President Dan Quayle's alma mater, DePauw University (2,100 students).

1990 Population: 554,416. White 533,827 (96%), Black 10,899 (2%), Other 9,690 (2%). Hispanic origin 4,611 (1%). 18 and over 418,523 (75%), 62 and over 82,291 (15%). Median age: 32.

HOUSE ELECTIONS

1996 General		
Ed Pease (R)	130,010	(62%)
Robert F. Hellmann (D)	72,705	(35%)
Barbara Bourland (LIBERT)	7,125	(3%)
1996 Primary		
Edward A. Pease (R)	22,055	(30%)
John Meyers (R)	12,487	(17%)
Richard "Dick" Thompson (R)	10,792	(15%)
Dan L. Pool (R)	8,157	(11%)
Katherine "Kathy" Willing (R)	6,724	(9%)
Pete Ross (R)	5,020	(7%)
John Lee Smith (R)	3,813	(5%)
Jeffrey "Jeff" Baldwin (R)	2,266	(3%)
Anthony W. "Tony" Duncan (R)	1,014	(1%)

CAMPAIGN FINANCE

	Receipts	Receipts from PACs	Expend-itures
1996			
Pease (R)	$592,680	$193,733 (33%)	$586,488
Hellmann (D)	$340,900	$120,200 (35%)	$340,816

DISTRICT VOTE FOR PRESIDENT

1996		1992	
D	75,428 (35%)	**D**	70,699 (32%)
R	111,832 (52%)	**R**	103,700 (46%)
I	25,844 (12%)	**I**	49,103 (22%)

KEY VOTES

1997

Ban "partial birth" abortions Y

8 John Hostettler (R)

Of Wadesville — Elected 1994, 2nd term

Biographical Information
Born: July 19, 1961, Evansville, Ind.
Education: Rose-Hulman Institute of Technology, B.S.M.E. 1983.
Occupation: Mechanical engineer.
Family: Wife, Elizabeth Ann Hamman; three children.
Religion: General Baptist.
Political Career: No previous office.
Capitol Office: 431 Cannon Bldg. 20515; 225-4636.

Committees
Agriculture
Forestry, Resource Conservation & Research; Livestock, Dairy & Poultry
National Security
Military Installations and Facilities; Military Research & Development

In Washington: Once represented by a moderately liberal Democrat, Indiana's 8th has now twice narrowly elected Republican Hostettler, a pure conservative whose chief prior civic involvement before Congress consisted of work for his church. Even in the strongly conservative GOP Class of 1994, Hostettler's ideological certitude stands out. He has said he draws on his professional experience as a mechanical engineer in his new role as a politician. Engineers, Hostettler explains, believe there is one answer to a problem, and in Congress he tries to find that one correct answer to policy questions.

In the 104th Congress, Hostettler voted with the GOP majority more than 90 percent of the time, and when he split from the party line it was often to take a more conservative stance than his party leaders wanted. In early January 1996, Hostettler was one of 15 Republicans who defied House Speaker Newt Gingrich's directive to vote to reopen the federal government, which had been partially shut down in late 1995 after a breakdown in budget talks between Congress and the White House.

Gingrich canceled appearances at fundraisers for several of the freshmen who went against the leadership on that vote. Hostettler, one of those on the cancellation list, wrote a "Dear Newt" letter telling the Speaker, "I cannot allow my fundraising to be tied in any way to specific votes." Hostettler then invited Majority Leader Dick Armey of Texas to visit his district instead, and Armey accepted. In June 1996, Hostettler was one of only 19 Republicans who voted against the leadership's budget plan for fiscal 1997 and beyond. He and other conservatives complained that the plan forecast a higher deficit in the short term before bringing it into balance in fiscal 2002.

In early 1997, Hostettler was among five GOP lawmakers to vote "present" in the election of Gingrich to be Speaker for the 105th Congress. Some House Republicans were concerned that Gingrich's ethical troubles would diminish his authority. After his vote, Hostettler found he was not wanted at a GOP gala honoring outgoing Republican National Committee Chairman Haley Barbour. Hostettler's office said he decided against attending the gala when organizers told him, "Donors did not want to be seated at a table with any Republicans who had not voted for Newt."

In 1995, Hostettler also voted "no" on two major components of the House GOP's "Contract With America": He opposed a constitutional amendment requiring a balanced budget, saying he did not favor making significant changes to the Constitution and believed the budget could be balanced without it. Also in 1995 (and again in 1997), he opposed a term limits constitutional amendment, preferring that the issue be left to the states.

Prior to Congress, Hostettler's chief experience in the public arena was as a member of the board of deacons at Twelfth Avenue General Baptist Church, where he has taught Bible study and led prayer meetings. His strongly held religious beliefs translate into firmly conservative views on social policy issues such as abortion. Arguing in the 104th against an amendment that would have allowed abortions at overseas military facilities if the government was reimbursed for the cost of the procedure, Hostettler said: "The Supreme Court has told us that we have to allow the killings of preborn children. It has not, however, told us that government has an obligation to provide this service."

He also supported an amendment that would have restricted abortion coverage under taxpayer-subsidized federal employees health care plans. "Unfortunately, ending a pregnancy by an elective abortion may be an option that is available to every woman in this country," Hostettler said. "This fact does not in any way require that the American taxpayer be forced to finance these morally objectionable procedures."

In November 1995, Hostettler successfully amended the spending bill for the District of Columbia to repeal a District ordinance allowing city workers to buy health insurance for their domestic partners. Democrats called the amend-

Heading toward the Ohio River, Indiana leaves the Corn Belt and enters the hilly border South. The political tradition in much of the 8th is of the Southern Democratic variety. Three group traditionally provide much of the 8th's Democratic vote: industrial workers in Evansville and Bloomington; the university communities in those cities; and the miners who work in seven of the district's 12 counties.

In 1992 Democrat Evan Bayh carried every county in the district in his gubernatorial re-election bid. And Bill Clinton won in the district's presidential voting, breaking a dry spell: The 8th had not voted for a Democratic presidential candidate since 1964. Like the rest of the South it went Republican in 1994. Clinton again carried the district in 1996, but only by 2 percentage points.

Evansville, an Ohio River port and the state's third-largest city, is southern Indiana's industrial center. A Bristol-Myers pharmaceutical plant and a Whirlpool refrigerator factory are two of the leading employers; residents also commute east to an Alcoa aluminum plant in Newburgh (Warrick County) and west to a General Electric plastics plant in Mount Vernon (Posey County). Although Evansville has access to Interstate 64, it is the state's only large city without a direct highway link to Indianapolis.

While the city hosts two small colleges, the University of Southern Indiana and the University of Evansville, it is Bloomington — home of Indiana University — that is the district's college town. "IU" has 35,000 students and employs 6,000 people. Although the campus and blue-collar crowds rarely mix — tensions between students and working-class Bloomington youths

INDIANA 8
Southwest — Evansville; Bloomington

were portrayed in the movie "Breaking Away" — they combine politically to give Democrats an edge. A General Electrics refrigerator factory and an Otis Elevator factory are among the city's largest industrial companies.

Past the limestone quarries of Monroe and Lawrence counties is the Naval Surface Warfare Center in Crane (Martin County), one of the district's largest employers, which develops naval systems and produces ammunition. Then come the counties where coal is strip-mined. Increasing mechanization in Indiana coal tonnage came at the expense of jobs. Sullivan County was hit hard, losing 10 percent of its population in the 1980s.

Several of the district's small towns have unique attractions. Vincennes, on the Wabash River, was the site of a key Revolutionary War battle. New Harmony was the scene of 19th-century experiments in communal life led by Father George Rapp and Robert Owen. French Lick, whose ornate but aging hotels denote its past as a resort town, more recently earned fame as the hometown of Larry Bird, who went from basketball stardom at Indiana State University to an all-star career with the Boston Celtics.

1990 Population: 554,416. White 531,232 (96%), Black 17,093 (3%), Other 6,091 (1%). Hispanic origin 3,262 (1%). 18 and over 421,765 (76%), 62 and over 92,412 (17%). Median age: 33.

ment an intrusion by Congress on the city's home rule charter, but Hostettler said the ordinance put traditional families on par with "a person so vaguely defined that it can be a homosexual lover, a same-sex lover, a roommate, a member of one's extended family, a homeless person one invites into their abode to enjoy health benefits and other legal rights by virtue of their so-called partnership with a District of Columbia government employee." The House approved Hostettler's amendment, 249-172.

An early proponent of sweeping welfare reform, Hostettler on the Agriculture Committee urged colleagues to dismantle the federal food stamp program and give states money to deliver food assistance. Although committee members were willing to restrain funding for food stamps, they were not prepared to end federal control over the program. Hostettler said state officials are in a better position than Washington bureaucrats to make program decisions, and he added that it was time to make "tough decisions" to balance the federal budget.

But senior Republicans on the committee, including Chairman Pat Roberts of Kansas, said it would be too risky to turn over the food stamp program to the states at the same time that welfare overhaul would be giving them control of many other social service programs. The committee concurred with him.

Though Hostettler is not very keen on most government spending, he does not object to boosting the nation's defense funding. From his seat on the National Security Committee, he has supported GOP efforts to give more money to the Pentagon than requested by the president. He also voted against a 1996 attempt to freeze defense spending at the prior fiscal year level. The Naval Surface Warfare Center is an important employer in the district.

At Home: Hostettler has had two very close races in the politically competitive 8th. He beat Democratic incumbent Frank McCloskey in 1994 by 4 points and then won even more narrowly in 1996 over a former McCloskey aide, Jonathan Weinzapfel.

Political neophyte Hostettler did not run for the House full time in 1994 until July, when his campaign reported a negative bank balance. He overcame those impediments and several campaign gaffes to accomplish what seemingly stronger Republican candidates had failed to do — defeat McCloskey.

The Democrat was regarded as a good bet to win re-election after Hostettler took 35 percent of the vote to emerge atop a six-person GOP primary field. He owed much of his success to a grassroots organization drawn primarily from area churches. Hostettler was the only one of the GOP hopefuls to be endorsed by Indiana Right to Life.

After the primary, the district's Republican establishment seemed tentative about Hostettler. Some privately said he was too conservative to win the 8th; others were turned off by comments he made during a Kiwanis Club speech that were criticized as anti-Semitic.

Hostettler's inexperience on the campaign trail was plain for all to see. During a meeting with high school students, he appeared to suggest that citizens have the right to the same weapons as the government — including nuclear arms. He later denied he said that, but a teacher nonetheless expressed amazement that Hostettler made the original remarks. Her comment was used in a McCloskey ad that called Hostettler "a risk not worth taking."

Hostettler had to backtrack on comments he made about the minimum wage, saying he would not vote to abolish it and explaining that his original statement reflected only his personal view. (In the House in 1996, he voted against increasing the minimum wage by 90 cents.)

Such difficulties probably would have doomed Hostettler's candidacy in other years. But in 1994, the unpopular Clinton administration was a lead weight dragging down McCloskey. McCloskey tried to focus the campaign on his service to the district, rather than on his votes or ideology. But he barely carried populous Vanderburg County (Evansville), which had boosted him in past close races. Hostettler prevailed overall, 52 percent to 48 percent. The cake at his victory celebration read, "To God Give the Glory."

Hostettler's 1996 race against Weinzapfel had a mainly negative tone. Weinzapfel charged that Hostettler backed GOP plans to "cut" Medicare. Hostettler explained that Republicans want to save Medicare and were merely slowing the rate of projected spending growth on the program.

For his part, Hostettler sought to make an issue of a campaign contribution Weinzapfel received from the Laborers International Union's PAC, which the incumbent alleged was "linked to organized crime."

Weinzapfel also had to do some intraparty fence mending. He angered some Democrats with post-primary criticisms of McCloskey, his former boss. McCloskey had backed Weinzapfel's primary opponent. Hostettler squeaked by to a second term, prevailing by 2 percentage points.

HOUSE ELECTIONS

1996 General		
John Hostettler (R)	109,860	(50%)
Jonathan Weinzapfel (D)	106,201	(48%)
Paul Hager (LIBERT)	3,803	(2%)
1996 Primary		
John Hostettler (R)	38,807	(82%)
Michael Allen McCamish (R)	8,537	(18%)
1994 General		
John Hostettler (R)	93,529	(52%)
Frank McCloskey (D)	84,857	(48%)

CAMPAIGN FINANCE

	Receipts	Receipts from PACs		Expend-itures
1996				
Hostettler (R)	$541,213	$0	(0%)	$528,325
Weinzapfel (D)	$472,265	$184,745	(39%)	$470,027
Hager (LIBERT)	$599	$0		$394
1994				
Hostettler (R)	$318,082	$6,220	(2%)	$309,484
McCloskey (D)	$577,434	$328,843	(57%)	$565,810

DISTRICT VOTE FOR PRESIDENT

1996		1992	
D	99,893 (45%)	**D**	103,697 (43%)
R	96,624 (43%)	**R**	97,070 (40%)
I	23,834 (11%)	**I**	43,181 (18%)

KEY VOTES

1997	
Ban "partial birth" abortions	Y
1996	
Approve farm bill	Y
Deny public education to illegal immigrants	+
Repeal ban on certain assault-style weapons	Y
Increase minimum wage	N
Freeze defense spending	N
Approve welfare overhaul	Y
1995	
Approve balanced-budget constitutional amendment	N
Relax Clean Water Act regulations	Y
Oppose limits on environmental regulations	N
Reduce projected Medicare spending	Y
Approve GOP budget with tax and spending cuts	Y

VOTING STUDIES

	Presidential Support		Party Unity		Conservative Coalition	
Year	**S**	**O**	**S**	**O**	**S**	**O**
1996	38	61	91	5	88	10
1995	21	78	95	3	90	8

INTEREST GROUP RATINGS

Year	ADA	AFL-CIO	CCUS	ACU
1996	20	n/a	88	95
1995	5	8	83	84

9 Lee H. Hamilton (D)

Of Nashville — Elected 1964, 17th term

Biographical Information

Born: April 20, 1931, Daytona Beach, Fla.

Education: DePauw U., B.A. 1952; Goethe U. (Frankfurt, Germany), 1952-53; Indiana U., J.D. 1956.

Occupation: Lawyer.

Family: Wife, Nancy Nelson; three children.

Religion: Methodist.

Political Career: No previous office.

Capitol Office: 2314 Rayburn Bldg. 20515; 225-5315.

Committees

International Relations (ranking)

Joint Economic

In Washington: Hamilton, who is retiring at the end of the 105th Congress, departs as his party's leading voice on foreign affairs, a sometimes lonely advocate in the House for Clinton administration policies abroad. Hamilton came to the Hill with the Great Society Class of 1964, but he appears to shed no tears at the GOP's hunger to dismantle many of that era's social programs; a streak of domestic conservatism that showed itself early in Hamilton's career has come to the fore at its end.

As a House freshman in 1965, Hamilton sent a letter to President Lyndon B. Johnson suggesting that it was "time to pause" in the rush to enact Great Society legislation. After an electoral scare in 1994, when he won a 16th term by just four percentage points, Hamilton posted his highest-ever voting score from the American Conservative Union in 1996, and he joined with Republicans against a majority of Democrats on a number of high-profile votes in the 104th. He supported a move to ease federal clean water regulations, to overhaul federal regulatory procedures in general and to deny education to children of illegal immigrants. He also voted for a ban on a particular abortion technique that opponents call a "partial birth" abortion and joined with the GOP in adding $7 billion to President Clinton's fiscal 1997 defense spending request.

But Hamilton, ranking Democrat on the International Relations Committee, stood firm behind Clinton's policies toward Bosnia. When Senate Majority Leader Bob Dole, R-Kan., spearheaded an effort in the summer of 1995 to lift the arms embargo against Bosnia, Hamilton led the charge against the idea in the House.

Hamilton also appeared on numerous public affairs programs and wrote opinion articles in an effort to sway public opinion — something he criticized Clinton for failing to do. He defended the presidential prerogative to determine the main course of foreign policy, and criticized his colleagues who wanted to circumvent that executive authority.

Once Clinton decided to send troops to Bosnia to maintain a U.S.-brokered peace agreement, Steve Buyer, R-Ind., and Ike Skelton, D-Mo., offered a successful resolution in December 1995 expressing support for the troops but disowning the deployment decision. Hamilton offered a substitute that would have declared support for the troops without slamming Clinton's policy; it failed, 190-237.

"The United States will only be taken seriously in the world if we are seen as reliable," Hamilton said when some Republican members sought to cut off funding for the deployment.

When it was revealed in 1996 that the Clinton administration had given tacit approval to Iranian arms shipments to Bosnia, in violation of the embargo, Hamilton was appointed ranking member of a select subcommittee created to investigate the matter and dismissed the controversy's importance: "Many members knew about the arms shipments at the time and they did not protest."

To Hamilton's many admirers, his caution as a foreign policy-maker is an aid in deterring the nation from rushing into foreign policy mistakes. But over the years he also heard detractors who called his caution indecisiveness.

Revelations that the Reagan administration had secretly sold arms to Iran and diverted the profits to the Nicaraguan contras burst into the news in November 1986. The facts might have emerged sooner if Hamilton, as Intelligence Committee chairman in 1985 and 1986, had not held back from probing early reports of illegal White House activity. Hamilton defended himself by pointing out that administration officials persistently lied about the Iran-contra events.

He did a widely commended job as House chairman of the special committee that investigated the affair. In hindsight, however, some Democrats and outside legal experts criticized Hamilton's support for providing some witnesses with legal immunity for their testimony. They said this undercut efforts to pursue charges against such key operatives as former National Security

INDIANA 9
Southeast Hill Country — New Albany

Much of the 9th has more in common with Kentucky to the south than with the flatlands of Indiana to the north. The district's population centers — New Albany (Floyd County) and Jeffersonville (Clark County) — are just across the Ohio River from Louisville. The inland areas are scenic but remote and dependent on resource industries, such as timber and coal; rural poverty is present in the 9th.

Voting tendencies are those seen in many districts with Southern Democratic roots. Consequently, Hamilton had a close call from the 1994 conservative electorate. After comfortably winning every county in 1992, he lost nine counties and saw his overall total slip to 52 percent.

Hamilton recovered in 1996, and he and Bill Clinton each carried the district. With the seat opening in 1998 with Hamilton's retirement, the Democratic bench in the district appeared deep.

The more Democratic part of the 9th is its hilly southern region. To the north, where the land levels out, patterns are similar to those in the rest of Indiana's farmland.

The towns in Louisville's sphere grew up as shipbuilding centers: The *Robert E. Lee* and other famed riverboats were built in New Albany. Although the largest area employer, a U.S. Census Bureau data preparation center, is white-collar, this remains an industrial region. New Albany's factories include a Pillsbury plant that makes refrigerated dough products. To the east, Clarksville has a Colgate-Palmolive plant topped by a clock 40 feet in diameter that is said to be the second-largest in the world.

Jeffersonville still builds boats, including barges. From 1974 to 1996, it was home to the Hillerich and Bradsby sporting goods factory. Tourist interest in seeing its famous baseball bats led the company to build a new complex back across the river in the original home of the "Louisville Slugger."

Northeast along the Ohio is Madison; its industrial base includes producers of automotive equipment and women's shoes. The local economy is adjusting to the 1995 closure, under the 1989 base-closing law, of the Army's Jefferson Proving Ground, which sprawled across Jefferson and Ripley counties. Upriver is Lawrenceburg (Dearborn County), site of a Joseph E. Seagram whiskey distillery. Although Dearborn's economy has taken some blows — a Schenley distillery closed in 1988 — the county has grown, thanks to its proximity to Cincinnati. Population was up 13 percent in the 1980s.

At the district's extremes are two small industrial cities: In the northeast part of the 9th, Connersville is the site of a Ford auto air conditioning plant and a Frigidaire appliance factory. At the western end of the 9th is Jasper (Dubois County), a city dominated by German-Americans that bills itself as the nation's "wood office furniture capital."

Some coal is mined in Dubois and in Spencer County to the south. In between are forests that attract recreationists to Southern Indiana. But unemployment runs well above the state norm in most of the rural counties.

1990 Population: 554,416. White 541,899 (98%), Black 9,436 (2%), Other 3,081 (1%). Hispanic origin 2,458 (<1%). 18 and over 404,813 (73%), 62 and over 85,684 (15%). Median age: 34.

Council aide Oliver L. North.

In the 103rd, as co-chairman of the Joint Committee on the Organization of Congress, Hamilton helped the committee produce a series of recommendations to revamp the way Congress did business. But their suggestions proved too controversial for most senior Democrats who stood to lose power, and most of the recommendations never even made it to the House floor.

In the Republican-led 104th Congress, many of the reform panel's suggestions were voted on as rule changes the first day the House convened.

Even before his votes for certain GOP-backed measures in the 104th, Hamilton occasionally stepped off his party's line. He was one of only 29 Democrats to vote against a bill requiring unpaid family and medical leave in 1993, and one of 58 Democrats who voted against the rule to bring Clinton's broad anti-crime bill to the floor in 1994.

Still, Hamilton's judicious manner earned him a reputation as one of the wise men of the Democratic Party. In the 1980s he served as chairman of the Intelligence Committee, and as Foreign Relations chairman in the 103rd Hamilton often voiced the House Democratic leadership's positions on foreign policy issues. When the House took up a resolution rebuking the president for allowing U.S. troops to be under U.N. command during the peacekeeping mission in Somalia, Hamilton offered the prevailing amendment that kept the troops there on the White House's timetable.

At Home: Until 1994, Hamilton had easily won re-election for nearly three decades. But the success that Republicans experienced nationwide also spilled into the 9th, contributing to his poorest showing ever.

Despite his personal popularity and his efforts to keep his votes in line with the thinking in his conservative district, Republicans thought they had a chance with state Sen. Jean Leising. But after a late October poll conducted for the Republican National Committee showed Hamilton at 65 percent and Leising at 20 percent, party strategists gave up hope.

As it turned out, their pessimism was uncalled for. The swell of support for Republican candidates that drowned the Democratic House majority nearly pulled Hamilton under, too. He won with just 52 percent of the vote — one of the bigger surprises of the cycle.

Leising was convinced that she could have won if the party had lent her more support, and she tried again in 1996. But Hamilton had his guard up, raising his largest campaign treasury ever, tacking rightward on some issues and not letting any Leising charge go unanswered. He defeated her in the rematch by a more comfortable margin, but still finished well under 60 percent.

The son and brother of ministers, Hamilton has a devotion to work that comes out of his traditional Methodist family. From his days in Evansville High School in 1948, when he helped propel the basketball team to the state finals, to his race for Congress in 1964, he displayed a quiet, consistent determination.

Hamilton practiced law for a while in Chicago, but soon decided to settle in Columbus, Ind. In 1960 he was chairman of the Bartholomew County (Columbus) Citizens for Kennedy. Two years later he managed Birch Bayh's Senate campaign in Columbus.

He was the consensus choice of the local Democratic organization for the 9th District House nomination in 1964 and won the primary with 46 percent of the vote in a field of five candidates. He went on to defeat longtime Republican Rep. Earl Wilson, a crusty fiscal watchdog who had represented the district for almost a quarter of a century.

Hamilton remained in the House even though other political opportunities arose, most notably when Indiana Democrats urged him to challenge junior GOP Sen. Daniel R. Coats in the 1990 special election to fill the remainder of Vice President Dan Quayle's Senate term.

Despite the limits of Hamilton's base in the state's rural southeast, Indiana political observers considered him the party's most promising candidate against Coats. So great was the respect for Hamilton in both the state and national party structures that the nomination was his to refuse.

But refuse it he did.

HOUSE ELECTIONS

1996 General		
Lee H. Hamilton (D)	128,123	(56%)
Jean Leising (R)	96,442	(43%)
Diane Feeney (LIBERT)	2,279	(1%)
1996 Primary		
Lee H. Hamilton (D)	52,737	(86%)
E. Joe Finke (D)	8,415	(14%)
1994 General		
Lee H. Hamilton (D)	91,459	(52%)
Jean Leising (R)	84,315	(48%)

Previous Winning Percentages: **1992** (70%) **1990** (69%) **1988** (71%) **1986** (72%) **1984** (65%) **1982** (67%) **1980** (64%) **1978** (66%) **1976** (100%) **1974** (71%) **1972** (63%) **1970** (63%) **1968** (54%) **1966** (54%) **1964** (54%)

CAMPAIGN FINANCE

	Receipts	Receipts from PACs		Expend-itures
1996				
Hamilton (D)	$985,265	$426,153	(43%)	$967,859
Leising (R)	$450,512	$57,544	(13%)	$451,475
1994				
Hamilton (D)	$527,103	$190,116	(36%)	$578,468
Leising (R)	$242,006	$8,707	(4%)	$241,854

DISTRICT VOTE FOR PRESIDENT

	1996		1992
D	101,434 (44%)	**D**	98,063 (41%)
R	99,915 (44%)	**R**	97,441 (41%)
I	26,154 (11%)	**I**	44,873 (19%)

KEY VOTES

1997	
Ban "partial birth" abortions	Y
1996	
Approve farm bill	Y
Deny public education to illegal immigrants	Y
Repeal ban on certain assault-style weapons	Y
Increase minimum wage	Y
Freeze defense spending	N
Approve welfare overhaul	Y
1995	
Approve balanced-budget constitutional amendment	Y
Relax Clean Water Act regulations	Y
Oppose limits on environmental regulations	Y
Reduce projected Medicare spending	N
Approve GOP budget with tax and spending cuts	N

VOTING STUDIES

	Presidential Support		Party Unity		Conservative Coalition	
Year	**S**	**O**	**S**	**O**	**S**	**O**
1996	63	37	56	44	88	12
1995	69	31	67	33	71	28
1994	82	18	78	22	69	31
1993	85	15	83	17	68	32
1992	33	66	79	20	73	25
1991	43	57	80	20	57	43

INTEREST GROUP RATINGS

Year	ADA	AFL-CIO	CCUS	ACU
1996	45	n/a	56	45
1995	70	75	42	12
1994	60	44	67	38
1993	45	75	36	29
1992	80	75	63	32
1991	65	58	50	15

10 Julia Carson (D)

Of Indianapolis — Elected 1996, 1st term

Biographical Information

Born: July 8, 1938, Louisville, Ky.
Education: Martin U., 1994-95.
Occupation: Clothing store owner; human resource manager; congressional aide.
Family: Divorced; two children.
Religion: Baptist.
Political Career: Ind. House, 1973-77; Ind. Senate, 1977-91; Center Township Trustee, 1991-97.
Capitol Office: 1541 Longworth Bldg. 20515; 225-4011.

Committees

Banking & Financial Services
Housing & Community Opportunity
Veterans' Affairs
Health

The Path to Washington: Carson's rise from poverty to the halls of Congress has been precipitous but not without occasional personal pitfalls. Carson will be a more consistently liberal vote than her predecessor and former boss, Democrat Andrew Jacobs Jr., who retired in 1996.

Jacobs hired Carson away from a secretarial job at the United Auto Workers' Indianapolis local at the start of his Hill career. After working as a caseworker for Jacobs for eight years, Carson launched her own successful political career, first winning election to the Indiana House in 1972. She moved on to the state Senate, where she served on the Finance Committee. She received assignments to the Banking and Financial Services Committee and the Veterans' Affairs Committee for her first term in Congress.

An unreconstructed believer in the power of government to engender good, Carson most recently served as head of the Marion County Center Township Trustee, which administers relief to the poor. Carson campaigned heavily on her achievement in reducing the debt of the trustee's office.

Her GOP opponent, former state Sen. Virginia Blankenbaker, sought to make political hay of the fact that Carson had enjoyed a 63.5 percent increase in salary over the five years she served as trustee. Blankenbaker also noted that Carson's daughter and two grandsons had worked for the agency. And Indiana Legislative Insight, a political newsletter, reported that about two dozen registered voters listed the agency's office as their home address.

Although administrative costs soared under Carson, she was able to trumpet her success in turning around the agency's finances overall. She cut the nearly bankrupt agency's bond debt from $13.66 million when she took office to less than $3 million by 1996. She also cut local taxes and lowered the number of people on relief rolls from 77,000 to fewer than 38,000 in 1995.

She attributed her success in turning the office around to requirements she imposed that put able-bodied recipients to work for vouchers. That policy lent Carson some political cover during the 1996 campaign, when she opposed the federal welfare overhaul law. Carson favors universal access to health care, although she opposes a nationalized delivery system. She also contends that spending money on education is cheaper and more productive than building prisons.

Blankenbaker, who held liberal positions on abortion and capital punishment, sought to portray Carson as too liberal for the district. She ran ads saying that Carson, who is ambivalent about sentencing guidelines, was soft on crime.

Carson's main opponent for the Democratic nomination, former state party Chairwoman Ann DeLaney, also had sought to portray herself as tougher on crime than Carson. But the tactic held less promise for Blankenbaker, whose husband had chaired the city's public safety commission, after an August 1996 incident in Indianapolis, in which several drunken Indianapolis police officers verbally accosted passersby and beat two of them, resulting in indictments and headlines nationwide. These events crippled local GOP candidates. Carson defeated Blankenbaker by 8 percentage points, 53 percent to 45 percent.

Carson was sidelined at the beginning of the 105th Congress because she underwent heart bypass surgery.

Carson, who is the first black to represent Indianapolis in the House, owed her primary victory over DeLaney to her ability to turn out voters in inner-city precincts. Carson has consistently been underrated by pollsters and her opponents, but her organizational skills have left her undefeated politically. Carson worked a variety of jobs as a youngster to help the family make ends meet, including stints as a hairdresser and working on a farm. She eventually landed a job as human resources director at Cummins Electric, using her savings to open a dress shop in Indianapolis that failed and left her saddled with debt. She had her wages garnisheed as a state senator to partially pay off the losses. It was reported in 1990 that she owed $10,000 in property taxes and penalties.

INDIANA 10
Central — Indianapolis

Geographically and figuratively, Indianapolis is at the center of Indiana life. With just over 730,000 residents in 1990, the state capital had more than four times the population of Fort Wayne, Indiana's second-largest city. Indianapolis is the state's banking and commercial hub, and it retains its traditional role as an industrial city.

Under a unitary city-county government instituted in 1970 (it collects all taxes and handles most services except schools and public safety), Indianapolis takes in all of Marion County except for the small cities of Lawrence, Beech Grove, Speedway and Southport. Consolidation brought large blocks of affluent suburbia into the city limits, reinforcing Indianapolis' standing as one of the most conservative large cities in the country. Its largely non-ethnic white population leans Republican. However, the 10th is crafted to take in Indianapolis' most Democratic areas, including many blacks, who comprise 23 percent of the city's population. Bill Clinton's 54 percent tally in 1996 marked his second-best performance in the Hoosier state.

A downtown building boom in the 1980s and a relatively low unemployment rate have made Indianapolis a success story among Midwestern cities. Federal, state and city-county governments employ tens of thousands; the Indiana University-Purdue University campus, Butler University and numerous large health-care complexes are also major employers. Banks, insurance companies and the headquarters for the Eli Lilly pharmaceutical company add to the white-collar base.

Long known for its "500" auto race each Memorial Day weekend, Indianapolis has become a major league sports city and convention site. Construction of the Hoosier Dome, just across the commons from the state Capitol, lured the National Football League Colts from Baltimore in 1984. The Indiana Pacers basketball team plays in nearby Market Square Arena. Indianapolis is also headquarters for the Amateur Athletic Union.

Heavy industry continues to play a role in the city's economy, with blue-collar workers turning out products such as turbine engines and transmissions. GM, Ford and Chrysler all maintain automotive components plants in the city. But Indy's economic picture has not been cloudless. Chrysler and Western Electric closed plants on the east side; the warehousing and light-manufacturing companies that filled the space are less labor-intensive.

In general, the city's economic growth has been in white-collar and service industries that are inaccessible or unappealing to many former industrial workers.

Indianapolis is also bracing for the phase-out of the Army's Fort Benjamin Harrison, scheduled to close by the summer of 1997. The base includes the Defense Finance and Accounting Center. Some of the district's workers commute to the Naval Air Warfare Center in the neighboring 6th.

1990 Population: 554,416. White 380,178 (69%), Black 165,372 (30%), Other 8,866 (2%). Hispanic origin 6,443 (1%). 18 and over 410,605 (74%), 62 and over 77,040 (14%). Median age: 31.

HOUSE ELECTIONS

1996 General		
Julia Carson (D)	85,965	(53%)
Virginia Blankenbaker (R)	72,796	(45%)
Kurt St. Angelo (LIBERT)	3,605	(2%)
1996 Primary		
Julia M. Carson (D)	17,950	(49%)
Ann DeLaney (D)	11,310	(31%)
Jocelyn-Tandy Adande (D)	3,747	(10%)
Mmoja Ajabu (D)	1,492	(4%)
Charles F. Henderson (D)	784	(2%)
Joe L. Turner (D)	611	(2%)
Gale P. Jontz (D)	441	(1%)

CAMPAIGN FINANCE

	Receipts	Receipts from PACs	Expend-itures
1996			
Carson (D)	$575,674	$176,238 (31%)	$572,617
Blankenbaker (R)	$681,946	$197,844 (29%)	$638,275
St. Angelo (LIBERT)	$6,530	0	$6,504

DISTRICT VOTE FOR PRESIDENT

	1996		1992
D	90,139 (54%)	**D**	92,514 (47%)
R	62,469 (37%)	**R**	70,458 (36%)
I	12,587 (8%)	**I**	33,229 (17%)

KEY VOTES

1997

Ban "partial birth" abortions N

IOWA

Governor: Terry E. Branstad (R)
First elected: 1982
Length of term: 4 years
Term expires: 1/99
Salary: $98,200
Term limit: No
Phone: (515) 281-5211
Born: Nov. 17, 1946; Leland, Iowa.
Education: U. of Iowa, B.A. 1969; Drake U., J.D. 1974.
Military Service: Army, 1969-71.
Occupation: Lawyer; farmer.
Family: Wife, Christine Johnson; three children.
Religion: Roman Catholic.
Political Career: Iowa House, 1973-79; lieutenant governor, 1979-83.

Lt. Gov.: Joy Corning (R)
First elected: 1990
Length of term: 4 years
Term expires: 1/99
Salary: $68,740
Phone: (515) 281-3421

State election official: (515) 281-5865
Democratic headquarters: (515) 244-7292
Republican headquarters: (515) 282-8105

REDISTRICTING

Iowa lost one seat in reapportionment, dropping from six districts to five. The legislature passed the map May 11, 1991; the governor signed it May 30.

STATE LEGISLATURE

Bicameral General Assembly. Meets January-May.

Senate: 50 members, 4-year terms
1996 breakdown: 29R, 21D; 39 men, 11 women
Salary: $20,120
Phone: (515) 281-3371

House of Representatives: 100 members, 2-year terms
1996 breakdown: 54R, 46D; 80 men, 20 women
Salary: $20,120
Phone: (515) 281-3221

URBAN STATISTICS

City	Population
Des Moines	193,187
Mayor Arthur Davis, N-P	
Cedar Rapids	108,780
Mayor Lee Clancey, N-P	
Davenport	95,333
Mayor Pat Gibbs, R	
Sioux City	80,505
Mayor Robert Scott, N-P	
Waterloo	66,467
Mayor John Rooff III, R	

U.S. CONGRESS

Senate: 1 D, 1 R
House: 1 D, 4 R

TERM LIMITS

For state offices: No

ELECTIONS

1996 Presidential Vote

Bill Clinton	50%
Bob Dole	40%
Ross Perot	9%

1992 Presidential Vote

Bill Clinton	43%
George Bush	37%
Ross Perot	19%

1988 Presidential Vote

Michael S. Dukakis	55%
George Bush	44%

POPULATION

1990 population		2,776,755
1980 population		2,913,808
Percent change		-5%
Rank among states:		30
White		97%
Black		2%
Hispanic		1%
Asian or Pacific islander		1%
Urban		61%
Rural		39%
Born in state		76%
Foreign-born		2%
Under age 18	718,880	26%
Ages 18-64	1,631,769	59%
65 and older	426,106	15%
Median age		34.0

MISCELLANEOUS

Capital: Des Moines
Number of counties: 99
Per capita income: $17,505 (1991)
Rank among states: 28
Total area: 56,275 sq. miles
Rank among states: 25

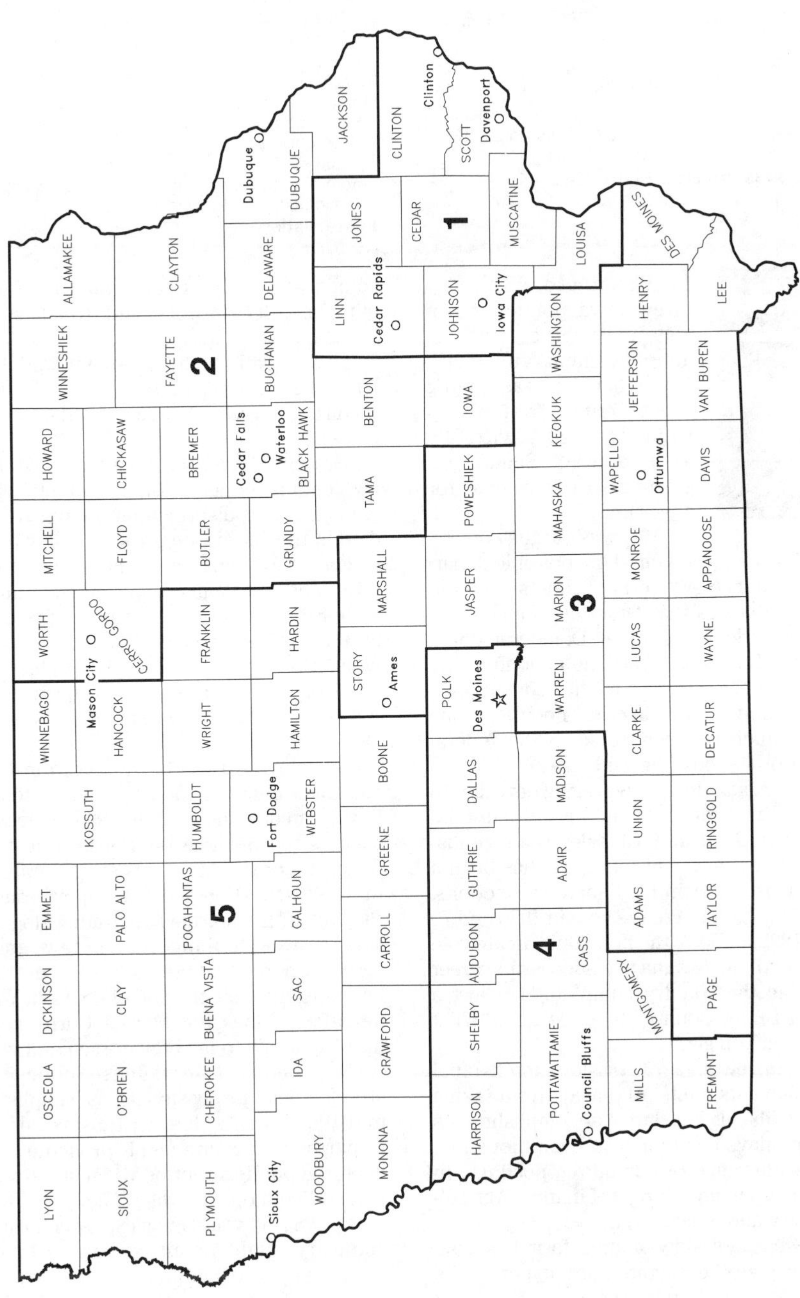
LYON
SIOUX
PLYMOUTH
Sioux City
WOODBURY
MONONA
HARRISON
POTTAWATTAMIE
Council Bluffs
MILLS
FREMONT
OSCEOLA
O'BRIEN
CHEROKEE
IDA
CRAWFORD
SHELBY
MONTGOMERY
PAGE
DICKINSON
CLAY
BUENA VISTA
SAC
CARROLL
AUDUBON
CASS
4
TAYLOR
ADAMS
EMMET
PALO ALTO
POCAHONTAS
5
CALHOUN
GREENE
GUTHRIE
ADAIR
RINGGOLD
UNION
KOSSUTH
HUMBOLDT
Fort Dodge
WEBSTER
BOONE
DALLAS
MADISON
DECATUR
CLARKE
WINNEBAGO
Mason City
HANCOCK
WRIGHT
HAMILTON
STORY
Ames
POLK
Des Moines
WARREN
WAYNE
LUCAS
WORTH
CERRO GORDO
FRANKLIN
HARDIN
MARSHALL
JASPER
MARION
3
APPANOOSE
MONROE
MITCHELL
FLOYD
BUTLER
GRUNDY
TAMA
POWESHIEK
MAHASKA
WAPELLO
Ottumwa
DAVIS
HOWARD
CHICKASAW
BREMER
Cedar Falls
Waterloo
BLACK HAWK
BENTON
IOWA
KEOKUK
JEFFERSON
VAN BUREN
WINNESHIEK
FAYETTE
2
BUCHANAN
LINN
Cedar Rapids
JOHNSON
Iowa City
WASHINGTON
HENRY
LEE
ALLAMAKEE
CLAYTON
DELAWARE
JONES
CEDAR
1
MUSCATINE
LOUISA
DES MOINES
Dubuque
DUBUQUE
JACKSON
CLINTON
Clinton
SCOTT
Davenport

Charles E. Grassley (R)

Of New Hartford — Elected 1980, 3rd term

Biographical Information

Born: Sept. 17, 1933, New Hartford, Iowa.

Education: U. of Northern Iowa, B.A. 1955, M.A. 1956; U. of Iowa, 1957-58.

Occupation: Farmer.

Family: Wife, Barbara Ann Speicher; five children.

Religion: Baptist.

Political Career: Republican nominee for Iowa House, 1956; Iowa House. 1959-75; U.S. House, 1975-81.

Capitol Office: 135 Hart Bldg. 20510; 224-3744.

Committees

Special Aging (chairman)

Agriculture, Nutrition & Forestry
Forestry, Conservation & Rural Revitalization; Production & Price Competitiveness

Budget

Finance
Health Care; International Trade (chairman); Taxation & IRS Oversight

Judiciary
Administrative Oversight & the Courts (chairman); Immigration; Youth Violence

Joint Taxation

In Washington: Grassley threw Iowa politics into a state of suspense with his announcement in early 1997 that he was giving "deep consideration" to bypassing a virtually assured 1998 Senate re-election to run instead for governor.

He was urged on by state GOP leaders, who feared the possible departure of popular Gov. Terry Branstad would increase the chances that Grassley's Senate colleague Tom Harkin or another Democrat could claim the job. But in late April, he announced he would seek re-election, saying his constituents urged him to stay in Washington. "People tell me they need Chuck Grassley to keep the federal government on its toes," he said.

With his longstanding, unwavering devotion to Iowa's agricultural interests and his straight-talking Midwestern demeanor, Grassley is a formidable political presence in his state. He has been a prodigious vote-getter in his Senate re-elections, winning with 66 percent of the vote in 1986 and 70 percent in 1992. Milking the non-sophisticate role for all it's worth, he has made a successful career out of playing the country bumpkin. "I'm just a farmer from Butler County," he once said. "What you see is what you get."

It is not entirely an act. Grassley's intellectual reach does have its limits. And aside from taking on obvious evils, his legislative accomplishments in the Senate have been modest, even though he has had a wide range of committee postings. In the 105th, they include Budget, Finance, Agriculture, Judiciary and Special Aging.

But if Grassley's slow-talking, farm-boy routine reinforces all the Eastern stereotypes of the rural Midwest, the liberals who once dismissed him as a right-wing rube now call him sly like a fox.

Indeed, the independent-minded Grassley has an uncanny knack for honing in on issues that appeal to the average citizen. Grassley first gained attention as the man who ferreted out expensive coffeepots and toilet seat covers bought by the Pentagon.

In the 104th, he hit a nerve in Middle America with his successful pursuit of legislation to require Congress to abide by the same laws it passes.

Grassley had been pushing since 1989 for a law ending congressional exemptions to most labor and anti-discrimination laws. After the bill died in the 103rd Congress, Grassley told his colleagues, "We can't continue to have two sets of laws, one for Pennsylvania Avenue and one for Main Street America." It was the first bill passed by the GOP-controlled 104th Congress. Grassley won an amendment to the Civil Rights Act of 1991 requiring the Senate to abide by the same civil rights and sexual harassment laws as everyone else.

Grassley also has been dogged in his push to cut government spending — and often clever in how he makes his case. In 1996, he tried without success to convince the Senate that the Marine Corps did not need the 12 new generals called for in the fiscal 1997 defense appropriations bill. Playing off the Marines' recruiting slogan that the service was looking for "a few good men," Grassley noted that the ranks of all of the services have shrunk since the end of the Cold War. "Why," he asked, "does the Marine Corps need a few more generals to lead fewer men and women?"

No specialist in defense policy, Grassley struck some professionals as simplistic in the mid-1980s with his criticisms of Defense Department procurement procedures. But he captured public attention when he seized the subject and held on with the tenacity of a bulldog.

In 1984, it was Grassley, as chairman of the Judiciary Subcommittee on Administrative Practices, who publicized the now-infamous $7,600 coffee maker purchased by the Air Force.

In mid-1990, he drew attention with disclosures of further procurement follies: Pentagon purchases of $999 pliers, $1,868 toilet seat covers and a mystifying $343 altar vase. No sweeping congressional investigation followed, but Grassley got his headlines.

In recent years, Grassley's concern with defense fraud has made him a major sponsor of legislation to protect workers who blow the whistle on abuse of tax dollars. After President Ronald Reagan issued a surprise veto, Grassley helped negotiate a compromise that President George Bush signed.

Grassley's first serious legislative attack on defense waste came in the 99th Congress, when he and Arkansas Democrat David Pryor unsuccessfully promoted Pentagon procurement reforms.

But Grassley succeeded in a 1986 attack on dishonest military contractors. He won passage of a bill updating the penalties and enforcement procedures of the federal False Claims Act, a law passed during the Civil War to crack down on suppliers who bilked the Union Army. In 1988, Grassley and Ohio Democrat Howard M. Metzenbaum succeeded in creating a new crime statute to impose tough prison penalties and fines to crack down on fraud in government contracts.

In the 104th Congress, Grassley's position as chairman of Judiciary's Subcommittee on Administrative Oversight and the Courts gave him a new perch from which to take aim at government spending. In January 1996, he raised eyebrows among some members of the bench by sending a detailed questionnaire to about 1,000 circuit and district judges asking for suggestions on where to cut costs.

Grassley remained at the center of the fray over judges in 1997, as conservative groups stepped up efforts to urge the Senate to delay confirming President Clinton's nominees. Majority Leader Trent Lott asked Grassley to serve on a Senate GOP task force to study how to revamp the nominations process. Despite criticism from Democrats, Grassley also remained a strong advocate for cutting judgeships in some judicial circuits with light caseloads. "We may have some circuits that have to have some increases," he said. "But for every judgeship we create, we ought to eliminate one."

Grassley served on another task force looking at ways to streamline the efficiency of the Internal Revenue Service. During the 104th, he sponsored a "taxpayer bill of rights" that was signed into law, giving citizens a variety of new protections against IRS abuses. It allowed taxpayers to sue for as much as $1 million for wrongful collections, an amount 10 times greater than the prior cap on lawsuits.

Parochial concerns always have been a big part of Grassley's focus in the Senate. Pigs and pork often top his agenda. He was commended by the National Pork Producers Council in late 1992 for helping win approval for the sale of pork to the former Soviet Union. He returned to the Agriculture, Nutrition and Forestry Committee in the 104th Congress during the reshuffling following Bob Packwood's resignation. Also, he continues as chairman of the Finance Subcommittee on International Trade, a job that gives him a chance to work to expand overseas markets for Iowa commodities.

During debate in the 104th on overhauling federal farm policy to bring it more into line with free market principles, Grassley sought to ensure that his state's farmers would not be adversely affected. Shortly before voting to pass the GOP-backed "Freedom to Farm" bill in February 1996, he led a group of 14 Republicans who warned that they would oppose any effort to scale back the fixed payments farmers were to receive for seven years in lieu of traditional crop subsidies.

National debates typically take on a local feel with Grassley. As the immigration law overhaul moved through the Judiciary Committee in early 1996, Grassley won a promise from the Immigration and Naturalization Service that it would establish its first office in Iowa to keep up with the state's growing immigrant population. The INS had been handling Iowa cases out of its office in neighboring Nebraska.

Grassley's cost-cutting sniping at the Pentagon sets him apart from the many pro-defense hawks in the GOP, but he usually sides with the party's more conservative element on matters of social policy.

In the 104th, he introduced a bill designed to affirm parents' rights to direct the schooling, discipline, religious instruction and health care of their children; it would allow parents to bring suit against officials whom they believed had unjustly interfered with those responsibilities.

One of the biggest Senate supporters of Bob Dole's presidential bid in 1996, Grassley has been a persistent critic of the Clinton administration, particularly its approach to law enforcement. In November 1995, during hearings on the standoff with the Branch Davidians at their compound near Waco, Texas, he complained of excessive militarization of those agencies. "The swashbucklers were in control," he said of the FBI portion of the operation.

As he took the gavel of the Special Aging Committee in 1997, Grassley pledged to cooperate with the panel's Democrats. He has a long familiarity with issues of concern to senior citizens, having been an original member of the House Select Committee on Aging in the 1970s and also chairman of the Senate Labor Subcommittee on Aging in the mid-1980s.

In his Senate floor votes, Grassley sees eye-to-eye with Harkin less often than most other same-state senators of different parties. In the 104th, the two voted the same way just 37 percent of the time. Only two other Republican-Democrat Senate pairs agreed less often — Minnesota's Rod Grams and Paul Wellstone, and Michigan's Spencer Abraham and Carl Levin.

At Home: Grassley plays to the Iowa audience with understated artistry, blending shrewd political positioning with the homespun simplicity of the farm country he grew up in. This skill enabled him to crush an opponent who appeared to have all the right ingredients for a successful 1992 bid.

In a campaign season dubbed "The Year of the Woman," state Sen. Jean Lloyd-Jones looked strong on paper. Entering the race soon after the confirmation hearings of Supreme Court Justice Clarence Thomas, Lloyd-Jones was one of 10 female Senate nominees to appear on stage at the Democratic National Convention.

But her record in the General Assembly was spotty, and her candidacy never caught hold. For Grassley, it turned out to be one of the easiest Senate races in state history.

Grassley joined the Iowa House in 1959 at age 25, rose to become chairman of its Appropriations Committee and developed a reputation for personal integrity and suspicion of government.

When veteran GOP Rep. H.R. Gross announced his retirement in 1974, Grassley organized the 3rd District's most conservative elements and won the GOP nomination with 42 percent. In November, he eked out 51 percent against an aggressive young Democrat in a Democratic year.

After conservative Republicans helped Roger W. Jepsen to victory over liberal Democratic Sen. Dick Clark in 1978, attention focused on Grassley as a 1980 challenger to Clark's liberal Senate colleague, John C. Culver.

Grassley's announcement of his Senate candidacy mobilized conservatives, who built a strong grass-roots organization across Iowa. Against a well-financed, moderate GOP primary opponent, Grassley won 90 of the state's 99 counties.

Then Grassley ran head-on into Culver, who conducted an insistent and impassioned defense of his liberal Senate voting record and characterized Grassley's legislative record as mediocre. Targeted for defeat by the Moral Majority and the National Conservative Political Action Committee, Culver lashed out at Grassley's New Right supporters, calling them a "poison in the political bloodstream."

But Grassley, an earnest, easygoing farmer, did not fit the part of a fanatic. He disassociated himself from New Right tactics without losing conservative support, and he turned voters' attention to pocketbook issues by charging that Democratic economic policies brought high inflation. Outpolling Ronald Reagan in Iowa, Grassley won 54 percent of the vote.

By 1986, Grassley's crusades against federal waste had built him a constituency that was unaffected by Iowa's massive farm discontent and anti-Reagan feelings. No prominent Democrat wanted to run against him, and the candidate who did, Des Moines lawyer John Roehrick, was never really in the contest.

SENATE ELECTIONS

1992 General		
Charles E. Grassley (R)	899,761	(70%)
Jean Lloyd-Jones (D)	351,561	(27%)
Stuart Zimmerman (NL)	16,403	(1%)

Previous Winning Percentages: 1986 (66%) **1980** (54%) **1978*** (75%) **1976*** (57%) **1974*** (51%)

** House elections*

CAMPAIGN FINANCE

	Receipts	Receipts from PACs	Expend-itures
1992			
Grassley (R)	$2,502,647	$1,002,585 (40%)	$2,322,262
Lloyd-Jones (D)	$415,829	0	$410,894

KEY VOTES

1997	
Approve balanced-budget constitutional amendment	Y
Approve chemical weapons treaty	N
1996	
Approve farm bill	Y
Limit punitive damages in product liability cases	Y
Exempt small businesses from higher minimum wage	Y
Approve welfare overhaul	Y
Bar job discrimination based on sexual orientation	N
Override veto of ban on "partial birth" abortions	Y
1995	
Approve GOP budget with tax and spending cuts	Y
Approve constitutional amendment barring flag desecration	Y

VOTING STUDIES

	Presidential Support		Party Unity		Conservative Coalition	
Year	S	O	S	O	S	O
1996	32	68	92	8	82	18
1995	26	74	92	8	84	16
1994	34	66	87	13	69	31
1993	25	75	90	9	80	20
1992	70	30	81	19	68	32
1991	75	25	83	17	83	18

INTEREST GROUP RATINGS

Year	ADA	AFL-CIO	CCUS	ACU
1996	15	n/a	92	90
1995	5	0	100	91
1994	15	0	90	92
1993	20	0	91	88
1992	30	17	90	74
1991	15	17	60	81

Tom Harkin (D)

Of Cumming — Elected 1984, 3rd term

Biographical Information

Born: Nov. 19, 1939, Cumming, Iowa.
Education: Iowa State U., B.S. 1962; Catholic U., J.D. 1972.
Military Service: Navy, 1962-67; Naval Reserve, 1968-74.
Occupation: Lawyer.
Family: Wife, Ruth Raduenz; two children.
Religion: Roman Catholic.
Political Career: Democratic nominee for U.S. House, 1972; U.S. House, 1975-85; sought Democratic nomination for president, 1992.
Capitol Office: 731 Hart Bldg. 20510; 224-3254.

Committees

Agriculture, Nutrition & Forestry (ranking)
Appropriations
Agriculture, Rural Development & Related Agencies; Defense; Foreign Operations; Labor, Health & Human Services & Education (ranking); VA, HUD & Independent Agencies
Labor & Human Resources
Employment & Training; Public Health & Safety
Small Business

In Washington: The first Democrat in state history to win a third Senate term, Harkin gives Iowans a leading voice on agriculture issues with his ascension to the ranking minority post on the Senate Agriculture, Nutrition and Forestry Committee in the 105th Congress. In addition, he remains as the top Democrat on the Appropriations Subcommittee on Labor, Health and Human Services and Education, where he can not only funnel federal dollars to Iowa but also influence policy on children, health care, disabilities and other issues that have been the focus of his Senate career.

The path to success for Harkin, whose 1992 foray into presidential politics ended soon after his favorite-son victory in the Iowa caucuses, has been one of catering to longtime constituencies such as labor, but not without concessions to prevailing political winds. The Iowa populist campaigned for president as an unapologetic New Deal liberal in late 1991 and early 1992, but he has also been known to temper that liberal image at times.

In the 104th Congress, Harkin and Missouri Republican Christopher S. Bond introduced the first bipartisan welfare legislation, which was modeled after Iowa's successful Family Investment Plan. The plan, which requires recipients to sign an actual contract with the state, has increased the number of welfare recipients landing new jobs and lowered the state's costs. Harkin also voted against same-sex marriages, and he offered his support for a limited capital gains tax cut, traditionally a conservative cause, early in 1995.

But Harkin's most notable departure from the liberal ideology that has marked his tenure has come on the balanced-budget constitutional amendment. He backed the amendment in the 104th and 105th Congresses, saying that if the budget could be balanced, prospects would be brighter for funding government programs that he supports, because fewer dollars would be needed to pay interest on the national debt.

Earlier, Harkin had run hot and cold on the balanced-budget amendment. Skewered by conservative groups for opposing it in his first Senate race against GOP Sen. Roger W. Jepsen in 1984, Harkin voted for the amendment in 1986. But after becoming the first Iowa Democrat to be re-elected to the Senate in 1990, he voted against the amendment in 1994. Facing re-election in 1996, he switched positions again.

Harkin is a close ally of President Clinton's. The president appointed Harkin's wife, Ruth Raduenz, as president and chief executive officer of the Overseas Private Investment Corporation (OPIC). Harkin himself had been quick to endorse Clinton's presidential bid in 1992 after his own fourth-place finish in the New Hampshire primary (and a lack of campaign money) forced him to bow out. Harkin worked hard the rest of the year to win votes for Clinton, especially among his labor union allies.

Harkin's ties to Clinton have made him a passionate defender of the administration in its difficult hours. He backed the nomination of Dr. Henry W. Foster Jr. to be surgeon general, and when Republicans prevented a vote on that nomination in June 1995, Harkin warned of the consequences. "We are going down a very bad road because if we continue this, the worm will turn," he said. "There will be a Democratic Senate and a Republican president, and the shoe will be on the other foot."

Still, Harkin has shown a willingness to part ways with Clinton on several occasions, especially when the president's views contrast with Harkin's populism. He opposed the 1996 reauthorization of the nation's farm programs because he feared poorer farmers might suffer under its system of fixed, declining subsidies; although Clinton, too, had misgivings about that approach, he signed the measure. When Clinton agreed early in 1996 to sign a stopgap spending bill that included cuts in education funding, Harkin called the decision a mistake.

Harkin became a thorn in the administration's side in 1996 when Clinton nominated Alan

Greenspan to serve a second four-year term as chairman of the Federal Reserve Board. Quick Senate confirmation was expected, but Harkin delayed a floor vote for weeks because he wanted to debate the nomination in the context of overall Fed policy. He contended that Greenspan's acceptance of slow growth as the price for low inflation had kept businesses from creating new jobs and increasing workers' incomes. Senate leaders ultimately let Harkin raise questions about that policy to break the logjam on the nomination.

Harkin also has questioned the Clinton administration's foreign policy decisions. He criticized its slow response toward restoring democratic rule to Haiti in the 103rd Congress and said of the 1995 offer of $40 billion in U.S.-backed loan guarantees to Mexico when it faced financial collapse: "We shouldn't go at this like the Lone Ranger. Other countries ought to chip in."

Harkin sees himself as a defender of the interests of the common folk and the disadvantaged against the rich and powerful. When Democrats were in the majority, he used his chairmanships of an Appropriations subcommittee and the Labor and Human Resources Subcommittee on Disability Policy to pursue his causes. But after Republicans took Senate control in 1995, he had to react to their agenda more often than not. Early in the 104th, Harkin and Democrat Joseph I. Lieberman of Connecticut proposed new limitations on the use of the filibuster, an idea they had begun to pursue when in the majority. But Harkin also quickly availed himself of the weapon when Republicans began to push anti-labor proposals.

In one such instance in 1995, Senate Republicans sought to overturn a Clinton directive barring big federal contractors from hiring permanent replacements for strikers. Harkin rallied Democrats to defend the president's directive. Two efforts to end floor debate on the GOP effort failed on party-line votes, and Republicans eventually dropped the "striker replacement" language.

Harkin was a central figure in another labor-related debate as Congress neared adjournment in 1996. He and Democrat Edward M. Kennedy of Massachusetts brought the Senate to a standstill as they fought to remove language from the Federal Aviation Administration reauthorization bill that they said would make it more difficult for employees of Federal Express Corp. to unionize. Harkin and Kennedy ultimately failed in that effort, but their performance as Horatius at the bridge to slow the machine was widely noted.

An advocate for children since the outset of his congressional career, Harkin in the 104th Congress challenged Republican efforts to narrow the federal education role. Resisting cuts in education spending at every opportunity, he succeeded in helping to get $2.7 billion restored in fiscal 1996 for programs such as Head Start, Goals 2000, school-to-work training, dislocated worker training and counseling, and summer youth jobs. In 1996, Harkin helped win the restoration of $2 billion in proposed cuts in education and health care for the fiscal 1997 budget.

Harkin has been a successful activist for increased funding for breast cancer research; two of his sisters died of breast cancer. In the 102nd Congress, he successfully pushed a measure to expand programs under the Individuals with Disabilities Education Act. He also won reauthorization of legislation aimed at protecting the rights of the mentally ill.

Harkin has said that the proudest moment of his years in Congress came in 1990 when President George Bush signed the Americans with Disabilities Act. The law, passed after years of effort and negotiations, extends broad civil rights protections to an estimated 43 million Americans with mental and physical disabilities. During final consideration, Harkin delivered a portion of his floor speech in sign language; it was addressed, he said, to his brother Frank, who is deaf.

Against the backdrop of a long and stressful 1990 re-election contest, Harkin reoriented his issue agenda in the 101st Congress, reflecting the changing focus of Iowa voters. In the mid-1980s, Harkin's extreme views on the importance of helping farmers were a centerpiece of his persona. But as Iowa's farm economy improved, he assumed a higher profile on a number of social policy issues, and he continued as an outspoken liberal voice on foreign policy — always politically correct in dovish Iowa.

Harkin has long been known for his outspokenness on U.S. foreign policy, especially involving Central America and the human rights records of other countries. When the 102nd Congress convened and turned its attention to the Persian Gulf crisis, Harkin led the liberals' charge. In November 1990, Harkin had joined 53 Democratic House members in a lawsuit seeking to prevent Bush from launching a military attack without Congress' approval.

At Home: Harkin's path to re-election in 1996 was similar to the one he traveled in 1990: He faced a well-funded GOP House incumbent. His 1990 foe had been Rep. Tom Tauke, perhaps the strongest candidate Republicans could have nominated that year except for Gov. Terry E. Branstad; in 1996, Rep. Jim Ross Lightfoot heeded the GOP call.

Lightfoot spoiled Harkin's hopes of cruising to re-election against a lesser-known opponent when he filed to run just three weeks before the March 15 deadline. But he did not spoil Harkin's bid for an unprecedented third term.

Tagged as a "liberal" in 60-second radio ads aired by the National Republican Senatorial Committee and accused by Lightfoot's campaign of having an "out-of-touch voting record," Harkin won by his narrowest margin ever. But his ties to Clinton, whose appearance at one

Iowa fundraiser garnered $200,000, helped Harkin outdistance the GOP challenger by 52 percent to 47 percent.

Harkin had been considered highly vulnerable in 1990, but he pulled off a historic win, becoming the first Iowa Democrat ever to be re-elected to the Senate. Harkin took nothing for granted en route to a second term. He opened his re-election battle early in 1989 by announcing his county-by-county campaign chairmen and stockpiled a sizable campaign fund. That did not scare off Rep. Tauke, who also began early, raising money and seeking to build on his bipartisan base in the 2nd District.

Tauke pecked away at Harkin on a variety of issues, accusing him of franking abuses and of voting for excessive spending. But none of the attacks truly took hold, while Harkin stressed his work on legislation to help people with disabilities. The two men also clashed over abortion — Harkin for abortion rights, Tauke opposed — although voters appeared divided on the issue, possibly making it a political wash. In the end Harkin won by a rather comfortable 9 points.

Harkin was no stranger to hard-fought campaigns; his 1984 race against Republican Sen. Roger W. Jepsen was one of that year's heavyweight bouts. Six years earlier, Jepsen had stunned Iowa Democrats by ousting Sen. Dick Clark. There never was much doubt that Jepsen would be vulnerable in 1984, and Harkin, who had proved his campaign skills by securing a Republican House district, was the logical opponent.

Jepsen's problem was that most of the events by which he had distinguished himself in office reflected badly on him. In 1983, for example, he had cited constitutional immunity to escape paying a traffic ticket while driving to work. Conservative organizations flocked to his defense, financing a barrage of TV and radio ads skewering Harkin for opposing a balanced-budget amendment and favoring higher taxes. Harkin came back with charges that Jepsen was freer with tax dollars than any other recent Iowa senator, dubbing him "Red Ink Roger." Though polls showed a tight race, Harkin took 56 percent.

Republicans saw little cause for worry when Harkin first announced for Congress in 1972 against an entrenched GOP incumbent. But they soon found themselves up against one of the more resourceful Democrats in recent Iowa politics.

Harkin projected his concern for agriculture in rural western Iowa and drew publicity with his gimmick of "work days." Republican Rep. William Scherle defeated him, but by the lowest percentage of his House career. Harkin launched his 1974 bid early, built a stronger organization and raised more money. Scherle made more appearances and tried to distance himself from the unpopular Republican administration. But Harkin won narrowly and quickly secured his hold on the seat.

SENATE ELECTIONS

1996 General

Tom Harkin (D)	634,166	(52%)
Jim Ross Lightfoot (R)	571,807	(47%)

Previous Winning Percentages: **1990** (54%) **1984** (56%) **1982*** (59%) **1980*** (60%) **1978*** (59%) **1976*** (65%) **1974*** (51%)

** House elections*

CAMPAIGN FINANCE

	Receipts	Receipts from PACs		Expend-itures
1996				
Harkin (D)	$4,665,182	$1,061,573	(23%)	$5,276,708
Lightfoot (R)	$2,474,871	$553,512	(22%)	$2,439,679

KEY VOTES

1997	
Approve balanced-budget constitutional amendment	Y
Approve chemical weapons treaty	Y
1996	
Approve farm bill	N
Limit punitive damages in product liability cases	N
Exempt small businesses from higher minimum wage	N
Approve welfare overhaul	Y
Bar job discrimination based on sexual orientation	Y
Override veto of ban on "partial birth" abortions	N
1995	
Approve GOP budget with tax and spending cuts	N
Approve constitutional amendment barring flag desecration	N

VOTING STUDIES

	Presidential Support		Party Unity		Conservative Coalition	
Year	S	O	S	O	S	O
1996	85	15	91	9	18	82
1995	90	10	91	9	14	86
1994	90	8	95	3	9	88
1993	92	7	92	6	15	83
1992	18	62	66	3	5	66
1991	19	62	75	3	5	75

INTEREST GROUP RATINGS

Year	ADA	AFL-CIO	CCUS	ACU
1996	80	n/a	38	10
1995	95	92	44	9
1994	100	88	30	0
1993	90	73	27	0
1992	85	91	17	0
1991	100	90	14	0

1 Jim Leach (R)

Of Davenport — Elected 1976, 11th term

Biographical Information

Born: Oct. 15, 1942, Davenport, Iowa.

Education: Princeton U., B.A. 1964; Johns Hopkins U., M.A. 1966; London School of Economics, 1966-68.

Occupation: Propane gas company executive; foreign service officer.

Family: Wife, Elisabeth Ann "Deba" Foxley; two children.

Religion: Episcopalian.

Political Career: Republican nominee for U.S. House, 1974.

Capitol Office: 2186 Rayburn Bldg. 20515; 225-6576.

Committees

Banking & Financial Services (chairman)

International Relations

Asia & the Pacific

In Washington: Having survived his toughest-ever re-election in 1996, Leach is back for a second term as chairman of the House Banking and Financial Services Committee. He hopes to overhaul the nation's banking laws, a goal that eluded him in the 104th Congress. But his first vote of the 105th Congress may make it more difficult for him to achieve that goal.

In January 1997, Leach was one of just nine Republicans who did not vote to re-elect Newt Gingrich as House Speaker. He was the highest-ranking Republican to dissent. Leach voted instead for former House Minority Leader Robert H. Michel, R-Ill. Leach received two votes for Speaker, from Tom Campbell, R-Calif., and Michael P. Forbes, R-N.Y.

Shortly before the vote, Leach issued a statement saying he would not vote for Gingrich, and he called on him to relinquish the Speakership. The House ethics committee was concluding a lengthy investigation of irregularities in Gingrich's political fundraising activities, and by month's end the House would vote to reprimand Gingrich and assess him a $300,000 penalty. "The [Speaker] must be free of any shadow concerning allegiance to the law or to the truth," Leach said. "Accordingly, for the country's sake, I have concluded that the most responsible course of action for the Speaker is to step down and for the members to choose another leader for the House."

Leach, who once quit his job as a junior foreign service officer to protest President Richard M. Nixon's dismissal of Watergate Special Prosecutor Archibald Cox, went on to say: "The charges the ethics committee has brought against the Speaker go to the heart of our constitutional way of life. In America, process is our most important product. Winning does not vindicate taking shortcuts with public ethics, even if it can be suggested that others may have followed similar or less defensible paths."

Leach reached his decision on vacation in a cabin in West Virginia with his family, and he spoke to Gingrich two days before he issued his statement. "I just thought it through and thought it through, and it just seemed to me to be the only appropriate step to take," Leach said later. "What I told the Speaker was that I had written two briefs, one defending a vote for him and one suggesting I couldn't vote for him, and that I felt the second brief, deep down, more compelling."

Though the Republican leadership promised no retaliation, in March 1997 GOP Conference Chairman John A. Boehner, R-Ohio, was given sweeping new authority over overhauling the banking system.

In the 104th, Leach had championed a narrow rewrite of the Depression-era Glass-Steagall Act, which erected walls between banks and other industries. His version would have allowed banks, securities firms and insurance companies to compete in one another's markets.

But he received a ton of brickbats for his efforts. Gingrich instructed him to change the bill to accommodate the insurance agents' lobby. Banks objected to a provision curbing the ability of the Comptroller of the Currency to give banks new powers to sell certain insurance products. The bill nearly came to a vote on the House floor in late 1995, but a revolt by the banking lobby over the insurance provision forced House leaders to shelve the legislation.

The following March, after a Supreme Court decision confirmed the ability of national banks to sell insurance free of interference from the states, banks played hardball in negotiations, and that ultimately yielded a compromise insurance provision pleasing to no one. In addition, the Clinton administration engaged in behind-the-scenes warfare against the bill, which called for shifting some regulatory authority from the Treasury Department to the Federal Reserve Board. The administration also bitterly fought the Comptroller of the Currency provision.

In June 1996, Leach called off a markup of a scaled-back banking bill after a closed-door caucus of committee Republicans asked him to abort the effort amid signals from House Majority Leader Dick Armey, R-Texas, that the measure

IOWA 1
East — Cedar Rapids; Davenport; Iowa City

The 1st is Iowa's most urbanized district, with three of the state's six most populous cities. Cedar Rapids (Linn County) and Davenport (Scott County) grew up around heavy industry, and Iowa City (Johnson County) is home to the University of Iowa.

These urban centers give the 1st a somewhat Democratic tilt. Bill Clinton prevailed by comfortable margins in all three counties in both 1992 and 1996. That helped him win the overall district with 54 percent in 1996. But Leach has kept the 1st in GOP hands by mixing fiscal conservatism with moderate social views. Leach narrowly lost both Johnson and Linn counties in 1996, and won Scott by 14,000 votes.

Cedar Rapids emerged as Iowa's second-largest city in the late 1980s; nearly a third of the district residents live in or near it. Long a center for the grain-processing business, Cedar Rapids has weathered hard economic times of late with help from high technology, such as production of electronic and telecommunications equipment.

Nearly 30 percent of the people in the 1st live in Scott County. Davenport and neighboring Bettendorf, along with the Illinois cities of Rock Island and Moline, make up the Quad Cities. These are old, industrial Mississippi River cities whose economies suffered badly during the 1980s, as did the nearby manufacturing cities of Clinton and Muscatine.

The district was to receive a boost in the spring of 1997 when Canadian-based Ipsco Steel Inc. opened a steel mill in rural Muscatine County. The plant was expected to employ more than 200 people.

Emblematic of the difficulties is a Caterpillar plant outside Davenport that once employed 4,000 people. Briefly abandoned in the 1980s, it has recently found new life, but as a storage warehouse for several local businesses. Davenport and the other river cities are trying to rebound by capitalizing on tourist dollars drawn to riverboat gambling.

Iowa City, the next-largest population center, grew by nearly 18 percent in the 1980s. The city and Johnson County cast just under one-fifth of the district's vote. Once labeled "Berkeley of the Midwest," Johnson County remains a Democratic bastion, although suburban and high-tech influences have moderated its politics. In the past, the 1,800 University of Iowa faculty members were predominantly liberal, while the 27,000-member student body was more conservative. Students' attitudes, particularly on social issues, recently have shifted leftward, and they have become more concerned about whether the economy will afford them gainful employment after graduation.

Export sales by companies such as Stanley Consultants, an engineering consulting firm, and Hon Industries, makers of office furniture, give the 1st's economy an international dimension. But the traditional lifeblood, agriculture, is still important: By one estimate, there are four hogs to every person in the district, and its range of crops includes corn, tomatoes, soybeans and watermelons.

1990 Population: 555,229. White 527,384 (95%), Black 14,624 (3%), Other 13,221 (2%). Hispanic origin 11,102 (2%). 18 and over 413,721 (75%), 62 and over 79,309 (14%). Median age: 32.

probably would not be scheduled for floor consideration. "Unfortunately, while many different approaches to gaining consensus have been suggested, the Treasury Department remains in adamant opposition, and the committee has become entangled in partisan and interest group wrangling," Leach said.

In addition, Banking Committee Democrats complained that they had been shut out of the process under which Leach made multiple revisions to the bill. They were particularly incensed about Leach's efforts to bring the dramatically reshaped Glass-Steagall bill to the floor with barely any consultation with the minority. "There's a lot of resentment towards Jim on both sides of the aisle because of the sentiment that he's left most everybody out of the process," said senior committee Democrat John J. LaFalce of New York.

In the 105th, Leach began backpedaling on some of the contentious issues that doomed his bill in the 104th. An opponent of permitting bank holding companies to engage in non-financial activities, Leach in March 1997 said he would support allowing banking companies and commercial corporations to have limited investments in each other's businesses.

The 104th Congress did enact legislation shoring up the federal fund that insures thrift deposits, but the bill was shaped less by Leach than by senior members of both parties. The effort was attached to the omnibus fiscal 1997 spending bill. Under the new law, the nation's savings and loans will pay into the Savings Association Insurance Fund a one-time assessment, and banks will share responsibility with thrifts for annual interest payments of $780 million on bonds that financed an earlier round of the thrift cleanup. In July 1996, as House Banking marked up the deposit insurance fund bill that eventually was folded into the omnibus spending bill, Leach failed to quash a problematic amendment. Instead, against the chairman's wishes, the panel adopted an amendment by Bill Orton, D-Utah, directing the Federal Reserve to devote $3 billion of its surpluses to help pay off the bonds related to the savings and loan bailout. Orton's amendment could have been ruled out of order as non-germane but Leach didn't do so. However, the amendment was left out of the final bill.

Early in the 104th, Leach chaired a series of hearings into Whitewater, a failed land deal involving the Clintons and the owner of a now defunct Arkansas thrift. It was a payback time for the Republicans, who howled in protest when the Democratic-controlled 103rd Congress gave short shrift to the issue. "Whitewater is about the arrogance of power — conflicts of interest that are self-evidently unseemly," Leach said when his hearings opened in August 1995. "What is remarkable is the hypocrisy of the circumstance. Time after time in the 1980s, politicians posturing in public as defenders of the little guys, found themselves in private advancing the interests of a small number of [thrift] owners who ran their financial institutions . . . like a candy store for insiders."

In the 103rd, Leach was the House GOP's chief Whitewater inquisitor. As the ranking Republican on the Banking Committee, he led the charge for congressional hearings on the matter. In March 1994, Leach took to the House floor for a speech in which he methodically outlined a list of alleged improprieties he discovered in his investigation of Whitewater and related matters. He summed up Whitewater as being "about the arrogance of power — Machiavellian machinations of single-party government."

At Home: Leach was forced on the defensive in 1996 as he tried for an 11th House term, with his Democratic challenger, former state Sen. Bob Rush, charging that the incumbent had become more partisan and less moderate with the GOP takeover. Leach emphasized his centrist stands: he was an early supporter of increasing the minimum wage and opposed repealing the ban on certain semiautomatic assault-style weapons. Getting no help from the top of the GOP ticket — Clinton carried the 1st with a solid 54 percent — Leach held on with 53 percent, his lowest tally since he first won the seat in 1976.

Leach brought a varied background to his first campaign, in 1974, against first-term Democrat Edward Mezvinsky. Leach had studied at Princeton and at the London School of Economics, worked in the Office of Economic Opportunity and in the Foreign Service, was assigned to the Arms Control and Disarmament Agency, then returned to Iowa to run the propane gas manufacturing firm that his family owned.

He held Mezvinsky to 54 percent in 1974, a good showing for a Republican newcomer in a Democratic year. During the next two years, he spoke regularly in the district, held his organization together and built a $200,000 campaign fund.

In 1976 Leach stressed his ties to Robert Ray, Iowa's moderate GOP governor. He described himself as a "Bob Ray Republican" and called Mezvinsky a "Bella Abzug Democrat." Leach won with 52 percent, propelled by a victory in his home base of Scott County (Davenport), which Mezvinsky had taken in 1974.

HOUSE ELECTIONS

1996 General		
Jim Leach (R)	129,242	(53%)
Bob Rush (D)	111,595	(46%)
1994 General		
Jim Leach (R)	110,448	(60%)
Glen Winekauf (D)	69,461	(38%)
Jan J. Zonneveld (I)	2,264	(1%)

Previous Winning Percentages: **1992** (68%) **1990** (100%) **1988** (61%) **1986** (66%) **1984** (67%) **1982** (59%) **1980** (64%) **1978** (64%) **1976** (52%)

CAMPAIGN FINANCE

	Receipts	Receipts from PACs	Expend-itures
1996			
Leach (R)	$371,594	$0 (0%)	$369,864
Rush (D)	$423,567	$128,750 (30%)	$419,647
1994			
Leach (R)	$277,155	$0 (0%)	$268,937
Winekauf (D)	$83,506	$26,500 (32%)	$82,447

DISTRICT VOTE FOR PRESIDENT

1996		1992	
D	135,839 (54%)	**D**	128,655 (46%)
R	92,207 (37%)	**R**	95,660 (35%)
I	19,027 (8%)	**I**	52,983 (19%)

KEY VOTES

1997	
Ban "partial birth" abortions	Y
1996	
Approve farm bill	Y
Deny public education to illegal immigrants	N
Repeal ban on certain assault-style weapons	N
Increase minimum wage	Y
Freeze defense spending	Y
Approve welfare overhaul	Y
1995	
Approve balanced-budget constitutional amendment	Y
Relax Clean Water Act regulations	Y
Oppose limits on environmental regulations	Y
Reduce projected Medicare spending	Y
Approve GOP budget with tax and spending cuts	Y

VOTING STUDIES

	Presidential Support		Party Unity		Conservative Coalition	
Year	S	O	S	O	S	O
1996	58	42	68	31	59	41
1995	40	59	78	21	75	23
1994	63	35	68	31	69	31
1993	55	39	63	28	43	50
1992	52	47	65	33	54	40
1991	59	41	61	35	59	41

INTEREST GROUP RATINGS

Year	ADA	AFL-CIO	CCUS	ACU
1996	40	n/a	69	37
1995	30	8	96	40
1994	40	22	100	33
1993	55	42	82	55
1992	60	33	63	40
1991	60	42	70	35

2 Jim Nussle (R)

Of Manchester — Elected 1990, 4th term

Biographical Information
Born: June 27, 1960, Des Moines, Iowa.
Education: Luther College, B.A. 1983; Drake U., J.D. 1985.
Occupation: Lawyer.
Family: Divorced; two children.
Religion: Lutheran.
Political Career: Delaware County attorney, 1986-90.
Capitol Office: 303 Cannon Bldg. 20515; 225-2911.

Committees
Budget
Ways & Means
Trade

In Washington: As Republicans prepared late in 1994 to take over the House for the first time in 40 years, Nussle was their very public face, a fixture of national media coverage as head of the GOP's transition team. But once the 104th Congress actually got under way, Nussle faded from view, becoming just one of many foot soldiers in the Republican "revolution." He went through divorce proceedings in the 104th, and closed out 1996 with an underwhelming 53 percent re-election tally; in four campaigns, Nussle has yet to top 56 percent of the vote.

An advocate of institutional reform when Republicans were the House minority, Nussle in late 1994 became the point man for incoming Speaker Newt Gingrich's plan to remake the House by instituting numerous changes, including cutting committee staffs and eliminating funding for legislative service organizations. Nussle was even detailed by Gingrich to work with new House Oversight Committee Chairman Bill Thomas, R-Calif., as the panel's jurisdiction and duties were being formulated at the beginning of the 104th — even though Nussle was not a member of the panel.

But as the 105th began, Thomas had joined the inner circle of Gingrich advisers, while Nussle was sufficiently on the outs with Gingrich that he let it be publicly known in the days leading up to the Speakership election that he had not yet decided whether to support the ethically embattled Georgian for another term. Nussle, who served during the 104th as vice chairman of the National Republican Campaign Committee, had been rumored as a contender to be the new chairman of the NRCC, succeeding outgoing Chairman Bill Paxon of New York. But Nussle saw the NRCC job go to Rep. John Linder, Gingrich's neighbor in Georgia.

From his seat on the Ways and Means Committee, Nussle did play a key role on some of the earliest pieces of major legislation pushed by the newly regnant Republicans He served on Gingrich's Welfare Reform Task Force.

When Ways and Means marked up the GOP's first welfare overhaul bill, Nussle mocked an unsuccessful amendment by Barbara B. Kennelly, D-Conn., to require that states, not parents, take responsibility for seeing that children would be cared for when welfare recipients went to work. "Soon we're going to have a Department of Alarm Clocks to wake them up and a Department of Bedtime Stories to tuck them in," he said. "It's not the government's responsibility."

But he supported another Kennelly amendment for personal reasons. When she proposed allowing states to yank driver's licenses or other licenses from parents who fail to pay the child support they owe, Nussle said, "I happen to have a biological father who I never met who did that, and if they still want to enjoy privileges, have a license, that's where we have to start drawing the line." Nussle sometimes engaged in verbal fisticuffs with another panel Democrat, Charles B. Rangel of New York, as Ways and Means considered changes to Medicare as well as welfare.

Nussle led a team of about 30 rural lawmakers who helped win concessions from Gingrich on the doomed Medicare bill that would have allowed rural hospitals a far greater reimbursement per patient treated than the legislation originally allowed.

Nussle also serves on the Budget Committee, and in that role early in 1995 he was called upon by the GOP leadership to help wrangle some wayward members who were anxious over the GOP's massive tax cut plan. About two dozen moderate Republicans, led by Michael N. Castle of Delaware, wanted to delay the tax cuts until there was a guarantee that the government would achieve a balanced budget. Working with Budget Committee Chairman John R. Kasich of Ohio, Nussle helped persuade the moderates to drop their concerns and support stand-alone tax relief.

Nussle received some unfavorable publicity in April 1996 when it was reported that he and Robert S. Walker, R-Pa., "on behalf of the House leadership," sent a memo to committee chairmen requesting that they have their staff gather infor-

IOWA 2
Northeast — Waterloo; Dubuque

The 2nd is dominated by two midsize industrial cities, Waterloo and Dubuque, and a university town, Cedar Falls. But nearly two-thirds of the vote comes from their rural surroundings.

Black Hawk County, with Waterloo and Cedar Falls, is Iowa's fourth-largest metropolitan area and traditionally a strong Democratic base. The county casts more than one-fifth of the 2nd's vote.

Waterloo had the first gasoline-tractor manufacturer, and it now has a large John Deere facility. The city grew up around the farm-implement and meatpacking industries. Hogs are still slaughtered here at the world's largest pork plant. (Neighboring Delaware County is one of the leading hog producing areas in the country.)

Until 1986, the GOP prevailed in House voting in Black Hawk County, despite the industrial and union influences in Waterloo and an academic community at the University of Northern Iowa in Cedar Falls. The majority in Black Hawk seemed politically more akin to those in the surrounding Republican-voting farmlands.

In the mid- to late 1980s, Black Hawk County voters occasionally split their tickets. But in 1988 with Michael S. Dukakis and Dave Nagle and in 1992 with Bill Clinton and Nagle, Democrats easily carried the county. The same was true in 1996 when Clinton won the county, but Republican Nussle did not.

Dubuque is the district's other population center. Together with Dubuque County, the area contributes more than 15 percent of the 2nd's vote. Built on and against the bluffs facing the Mississippi River, Dubuque is Iowa's oldest city. Its economic base shifted from lead mines and lumbering to manufacturing and meatpacking, which suffered in the 1980s. The city is now seeking to lure tourists with a new industry, riverboat gambling. Dubuque also has gotten a lift from people trekking to nearby Dyersville to see the baseball field featured in the movie "Field of Dreams."

Dubuque is predominantly Democratic by registration, but elections reveal the conservative outlook of this ethnic and heavily Catholic city. Clinton won big in Dubuque in 1996, and Nussle fell well short.

Almost 10 percent of the district's vote comes out of Mason City (Cerro Gordo County), on the northwestern edge of the 2nd. The can-do spirit that inspired native son Meredith Willson to compose "The Music Man" helped the city weather the farm crisis; the city has emerged as a health-care hub. Residents here demonstrate their independence at the polls; in 1996 Clinton managed to carry Cerro Gordon County, and Nussle also finished ahead.

While pork, grain and dairy remain integral industries in the 2nd, much of the district is rural, with dairying and a bucolic Northern European flavor. The German-influenced Amana Colonies are in Iowa County and Decorah in Winneshiek County has a fine Norwegian museum.

Overall, Clinton won all but one of the counties in the district (Grundy). Nussle won all but the two most populous — Black Hawk and Dubuque. Despite different party affiliations, both won the district with 53 percent.

1990 Population: 555,494. White 540,713 (97%), Black 9,511 (2%), Other 5,270 (1%). Hispanic origin 3,673 (1%). 18 and over 408,469 (74%), 62 and over 107,097 (19%). Median age: 35.

mation "that expose areas that amplify" their case that President Clinton suffered ethical lapses and that the Democrats operate at the behest of labor unions. A Republican spokesman dismissed the memo as "routine management stuff."

Nussle, who has rarely met a spending bill that he liked, cast one of his rare votes against the GOP leadership in 1996 in support of an amendment that would have frozen defense spending at the previous year's level. He has long been a crusader for deficit reduction, and he and another Midwesterner, Rep. Timothy J. Penny of Minnesota, led a fight in 1993 to offset some spending for aid to victims of flooding in the Midwest. The House leadership blocked Penny and Nussle, whose district was affected by the flooding, from bringing their amendment to the floor but promised to establish a task force to examine ways to fund future disaster relief efforts.

Nussle's efforts to offset flood relief with cuts came back to haunt him in 1994 when his opponent, former Democratic Rep. Dave Nagle, tried to use the issue against him.

Nussle may never again get the attention he received after his Oct. 1, 1991, floor speech in which he decried House leaders' decision not to make public the names of members who had overdrawn accounts at the House bank.

It wasn't what he said that drew attention so much as the fact that he delivered his remarks with a brown paper bag over his head. The moment — captured by C-SPAN and reproduced by the national media — seemed to symbolize the public image problems of the 102nd Congress and Nussle's outspoken reform efforts.

Nussle was chastised by the acting Speaker at the time and criticized by editorial writers at home. But voters did not seem to mind, and, for some, the incident served to break the House into two groups: those members who had overdrafts and those who were damned mad at the first group. Nussle was clearly among the angry ones.

Nussle was also one of the "Gang of Seven" in the 102nd Congress — a group of House Republican first-termers who aggressively agitated for changes in the ways Congress operated.

At Home: When Iowa lost a seat in reapportionment in 1992, Nussle and Democrat Nagle were thrown into battle in the new 2nd, setting the stage for a vicious, expensive campaign — by Iowa standards.

Initially ridiculed for his brown-bag stunt, Nussle continued his reform theme into the campaign, hammering Nagle for four overdrafts at the House bank. He also took a "Lead or Leave" pledge, promising not to run again if the federal deficit was not halved by 1996.

On the issues, the two were polar opposites. And in the end, Nussle's anti-abortion position kept him within a 22-vote margin in heavily Catholic — yet often Democratic — Dubuque County. The remainder of his slim margin came from the more rural counties of the 2nd.

Nussle's 1994 rematch with Nagle was almost as spirited. The outcome, however, wasn't as close. Nussle won with 56 percent.

His victory margin dipped in 1996 against Dubuque County Supervisor Donna L. Smith, an abortion opponent who castigated Nussle for his opposition to an increase in the minimum wage and his association with Gingrich.

Nussle engaged in some fierce campaigning in his first bid for Congress. In 1990, Democrat Eric Tabor charged that Nussle had exaggerated his work experience on his résumé by claiming he had served as a "staff assistant, legal counsel" for Gov. Terry E. Branstad in 1985 and was an "attorney at law" the same year.

In fact, Nussle did not receive his law degree from Drake University until 1985, and he was an unpaid intern in Branstad's office.

But Tabor's campaign blew up in his face just days before the election when it was revealed that an aide had registered his father, mother and sister as Democrats to vote absentee ballots in the district even though they lived in what was then the 4th District.

Tabor moved quickly to staunch the damage by firing the aide. But in the end, voters — by a 1,642-vote margin — chose Nussle.

HOUSE ELECTIONS

1996 General		
Jim Nussle (R)	127,827	(53%)
Donna L. Smith (D)	109,731	(46%)
1994 General		
Jim Nussle (R)	111,076	(56%)
Dave Nagle (D)	86,087	(43%)

Previous Winning Percentages: 1992 (50%) **1990** (50%)

CAMPAIGN FINANCE

	Receipts	Receipts from PACs	Expend-itures
1996			
Nussle (R)	$739,256	$369,190 (50%)	$679,904
Smith (D)	$70,711	$26,125 (37%)	$69,796
1994			
Nussle (R)	$892,653	$367,543 (41%)	$876,142
Nagle (D)	$486,229	$230,172 (47%)	$491,552

DISTRICT VOTE FOR PRESIDENT

1996		1992	
D	129,148 (53%)	**D**	120,228 (44%)
R	91,155 (37%)	**R**	95,005 (35%)
I	21,377 (9%)	**I**	55,279 (20%)

VOTING STUDIES

	Presidential Support		Party Unity		Conservative Coalition	
Year	**S**	**O**	**S**	**O**	**S**	**O**
1996	33	67	96	4	90	10
1995	21	78	95	3	89	5
1994	42	56	93	6	81	19
1993	17	83	89	10	59	41
1992	71	29	89	10	65	35
1991	80	20	85	14	81	19

KEY VOTES

1997	
Ban "partial birth" abortions	Y
1996	
Approve farm bill	Y
Deny public education to illegal immigrants	Y
Repeal ban on certain assault-style weapons	Y
Increase minimum wage	N
Freeze defense spending	Y
Approve welfare overhaul	Y
1995	
Approve balanced-budget constitutional amendment	Y
Relax Clean Water Act regulations	Y
Oppose limits on environmental regulations	N
Reduce projected Medicare spending	Y
Approve GOP budget with tax and spending cuts	Y

INTEREST GROUP RATINGS

Year	ADA	AFL-CIO	CCUS	ACU
1996	5	n/a	94	95
1995	0	0	100	84
1994	25	22	100	70
1993	20	8	91	83
1992	25	25	88	76
1991	20	8	90	85

3 Leonard L. Boswell (D)

Of Davis City — Elected 1996, 1st term

Biographical Information

Born: Jan. 10, 1934, Harrison County, Mo.
Education: Graceland College, B.A. 1969.
Military Service: Army, 1956-76.
Occupation: Farmer.
Family: Wife, Dody; three children.
Religion: Reorganized Church of Jesus Christ of Latter Day Saints.
Political Career: Iowa Senate, 1985-97, president, 1992-97; sought Democratic nomination for U.S. House, 1986; Democratic nominee for lieutenant governor, 1994.
Capitol Office: 1029 Longworth Bldg. 20515; 225-3806.

Committees

Agriculture
Livestock, Dairy & Poultry; Risk Management & Specialty Crops
Transportation & Infrastructure
Aviation; Water Resources & Environment

The Path to Washington: Boswell, who at 63 is the oldest first-term congressman in the 105th, arrives in Congress not only with 12 years of experience in the Iowa Senate — he left as state Senate president — but also with two other lengthy careers under his belt. A working farmer, Boswell is a retired career military man.

Boswell's seasoning probably contributed to his selection as one of three freshmen selected for the Democratic Steering Committee, a leadership arm that plays a key role in determining members' committee assignments.

In addition, Boswell has a seat on the Transportation and Infrastructure Committee. He sought the post in order to play a role on commerce-related issues affecting Iowa, such as the movement of agricultural commodities and other products. Befitting a farm state legislator, Boswell serves on the Agriculture Committee. He is the only Iowa representative on that panel.

Among Boswell's goals is balancing the budget while sparing education, public safety and senior citizens' programs from spending cuts. He stresses his experience in working toward eliminating Iowa's budget deficit while in the state Senate.

Boswell's campaign against Republican Mike Mahaffey, the Poweshiek County attorney and a former state party chairman, was notable for its niceness. Both candidates pledged to avoid negative attacks on each other, and, for the most part, succeeded. The task was made easier by the fact that both men are political centrists.

While the two agreed on many issues, they did have differences — most notably over how to balance the budget. Boswell stressed the need to protect senior citizens' programs, but Mahaffey said it was necessary to look at such programs as Medicare and Social Security to ensure that the entire system does not break down in the future.

Boswell spent much of the campaign criticizing the GOP congressional agenda. He captured the endorsement of the Iowa Farm Bureau, unusual for a Democrat. In the end, Boswell eked out a thin margin of victory over Mahaffey, winning 49 percent to 48 percent. He is the only Democratic representative in the state's five-person House delegation.

The 3rd is a rural, agricultural district that sprawls over Iowa's southern tier from the Mississippi nearly to the Nebraska border, then hooks northward to include suburban areas near Des Moines. Boswell's predecessor, six-term Republican Jim Ross Lightfoot, had been held under 50 percent in 1992 and 60 percent in 1994 but was favored to win re-election in 1996.

But in late February, just weeks before the state's congressional filing deadline, Lightfoot announced that he would challenge Democratic Sen. Tom Harkin, an undertaking that eventually proved unsuccessful. Lightfoot's decision prompted Mahaffey to seek the GOP nomination, and he won the three-person primary.

Two Democrats, state Executive Deputy Attorney General Charlie Krogmeier and Lee County Supervisor Tracy Vance, had already been vying for the right to challenge Lightfoot.

But supporters encouraged Boswell to run. He had gained name recognition through his state Senate service and in two previous attempts at higher office: His 1986 bid for a U.S. House seat fell short in the Democratic primary (which he lost 48 percent to 52 percent), and in 1994 he was the Democratic candidate for lieutenant governor on a ticket that was defeated in a landslide.

Vance subsequently dropped out and backed Boswell, who defeated Krogmeier in the primary by a comfortable margin.

Throughout his campaign, Boswell often flew his own plane to appearances around the vast district. A 20-year Army veteran who rose to the rank of lieutenant colonel, Boswell, served as a pilot in Vietnam and earned two Distinguished Flying Crosses and two Bronze Stars.

After leaving the Army, Boswell returned to Iowa to farm. But community members encouraged him to become active in politics. His first post was on the local elevator board. Supporters then urged him to run for the state Senate, to which he was elected in 1984.

IOWA 3
South Central — Ames; Burlington

Taking in 27 counties, nearly 14,000 square miles and six media markets, the 3rd gives a fair picture of Iowa. Within its borders are relatively well-off urban and suburban areas, depressed rural counties and industrial cities, and scattered towns with high hopes for economic development. Although this area trended Democratic during the 1980s, district voters frequently split their tickets.

The largest city is Ames (Story County), 25 miles north of Des Moines and home to Iowa State University. Coupled with the state Department of Transportation office, the university ensures stability for Ames in hard times.

Story County makes up nearly 15 percent of the 3rd's population and is essentially Democratic. Story voted decisively for Bill Clinton and narrowly for Boswell in 1996.

Roughly one-quarter of the district's residents live in the other four counties near Des Moines, and many of them vote independently.

Some of Iowa's most productive farms are in this area, but the number of Des Moines bedroom communities is growing, and some towns have developed independent economic bases. Newton, in Jasper County, is Maytag Corp.'s headquarters — where F. L. Maytag built the first mechanized washer in 1909. Pella, in Marion County, is home to the windowmaker Pella Corp.

The 3rd's other population concentration is southeast, along the Mississippi River in Des Moines County (Burlington) and Lee County (Fort Madison). They account for 15 percent of the district's residents. These two old manufacturing cities, set in rolling hills and forests, have turned to tourism and riverboat gambling. Clinton and Democratic Sen. Tom Harkin won easily in Des Moines, Lee and Wapello counties in 1996.

The rest of the district's population is spread across Iowa's southern tier, bordering Missouri. Once forest and rough grazing land, much of it was put into production during the 1970s.

Although hard times helped Democratic candidates here in the 1980s, voters moved back toward their traditional Republican roots in 1992. On the western side of the 3rd, several smaller, rural counties — including Page, Taylor, Union, Adams and Ringgold — helped GOP Rep. Jim Ross Lightfoot stave off a tough re-election challenge in 1992 and stuck with him in 1994. Two years later, Democrats Clinton and Boswell won four of those five counties, losing just Taylor. In the 1996 U.S. Senate race, Lightfoot lost his former district to Democratic Sen. Tom Harkin by 52 percent to 46 percent.

Only two southern counties show much potential for growth: Jefferson (Fairfield) and Henry (Mount Pleasant). Maharishi International University, later renamed Maharishi University of Management, which moved to Fairfield in 1974, helped lure several small software companies. Mount Pleasant got a boost when Wal-Mart Stores Inc. opened a regional distribution center there.

1990 Population: 555,299. White 541,358 (97%), Black 5,219 (1%), Other 8,722 (2%). Hispanic origin 4,481 (1%). 18 and over 417,743 (75%), 62 and over 107,335 (19%). Median age: 35.

HOUSE ELECTIONS

1996 General		
Leonard L. Boswell (D)	115,914	(49%)
Mike Mahaffey (R)	111,895	(48%)
Jay B. Marcus (NL)	3,194	(1%)
Edward T. Rusk (WC)	2,534	(1%)
1996 Primary		
Leonard L. Boswell (D)	15,349	(58%)
Charles J. Krogmeier (D)	11,008	(42%)

CAMPAIGN FINANCE

	Receipts	Receipts from PACs	Expend-itures
1996			
Boswell (D)	$650,196	$275,942 (42%)	$634,351
Mahaffey (R)	$444,283	$140,148 (32%)	$439,269
Marcus (NL)	$25,044	0	$24,830

DISTRICT VOTE FOR PRESIDENT

	1996		1992
D	123,246 (50%)	D	120,495 (46%)
R	95,308 (39%)	R	96,515 (37%)
I	21,408 (9%)	I	47,028 (18%)

KEY VOTES

1997

Ban "partial birth" abortions Y

4 Greg Ganske (R)

Of Des Moines — Elected 1994, 2nd term

Biographical Information
Born: March 31, 1949, New Hampton, Iowa.
Education: U. of Iowa, B.A. 1972, M.D. 1976.
Military Service: Army Reserve, 1986-present.
Occupation: Plastic surgeon.
Family: Wife, Corrine Mikkelson; three children.
Religion: Roman Catholic.
Political Career: No previous office.
Capitol Office: 1108 Longworth Bldg. 20515; 225-4426.

Committees
Commerce
Finance & Hazardous Materials; Health & Environment; Oversight & Investigations

In Washington: Before coming to Congress, Ganske made his living in the delicate business of wielding surgical instruments in the operating room. Politics, his new calling, also requires a deft touch from Ganske: He faces pressures to be a loyal soldier in the conservative House GOP majority while representing a traditionally Democratic district where being tagged a "Newt clone" could spell big electoral trouble.

In 1994, Ganske knocked off 36-year Democratic Rep. Neal Smith, who was a member of the "college of cardinals," the powerful group of Appropriations subcommittee chairmen.

On several high-profile issues debated in the 104th Congress, Ganske has stood apart from most of his colleagues in the conservative GOP Class of 1994. He was most visibly a thorn in the paws of Speaker Newt Gingrich and Majority Leader Dick Armey when he joined with Kansas Republican Pat Roberts to oppose the leadership's effort to give a $500-per-child tax credit to families earning up to $200,000 annually. Roberts and Ganske thought that was extravagant, and they fought to limit the credit to families earning up to $95,000. And because of his medical background, Ganske gained attention with his cautious reaction to GOP proposals to restrain the rate of growth in Medicare spending.

Also, Ganske was one of 37 Republicans to vote against a measure increasing defense funding for fiscal 1996, and he was one of 42 Republicans to vote "no" on a bill repealing the ban on certain semiautomatic assault-style weapons. In addition, he bucked the Republican leadership in 1996 by supporting an increase in the minimum wage.

But despite the divergences, Ganske is not to be confused with a liberal. In the main, his views are conservative, particularly on fiscal issues. He voted for most elements of the GOP's "Contract With America," including a balanced-budget constitutional amendment, regulatory relief, an overhaul of the welfare system and a limit on congressional terms.

As part of their effort to balance the budget, the House Republican majority proposed restructuring Medicare and reducing projected spending on the federal insurance program for the elderly by $270 billion over seven years. When the Commerce Committee, on which Ganske sits, began to mark up the Medicare provisions in the fall of 1995, Ganske disclosed that he worried the rate of spending might be restrained too much. Based on his experience treating about 1,000 Medicare beneficiaries, Ganske said he was concerned the reductions would be "bad for the quality of health care."

"If Medicare and Medicaid cuts are too deep, hospitals and doctors will shy away from serving the elderly and the poor or will try to push those costs onto the non-elderly, which could further increase the number of uninsured," he said. "A tourniquet can prevent hemorrhage, but too tightly applied can cause gangrene."

Ganske has also been concerned about potential abuses of Medicare and other patients by health maintenance organizations (HMOs). He pushed a measure in the 104th aimed at preventing HMOs from restricting the medical advice their member doctors can give. Dubbed the Patient Right to Know Act, the bill would outlaw the practice of HMOs barring doctors from informing patients of treatment options not covered by their medical insurance. Although the Commerce Committee approved the bill in July 1996, it went no further. Ganske and Commerce Democratic colleague Edward J. Markey of Massachusetts introduced the bill again in the 105th, and President Clinton said in early 1997 that he would sign the measure if it reached him.

In 1995, when Ganske and Roberts tried to lower the income ceiling for the $500-per-child credit on the GOP tax-cut bill, they got nearly half the Republican Conference to sign a letter to Gingrich asking for an amendment limiting eligibility for the credit to families earning $95,000 or less a year. The $200,000 ceiling drew howls of protest from Democrats, who claimed it was a sign of the GOP being "the party of the rich."

IOWA 4
Southwest — Des Moines; Council Bluffs

Though the 4th sprawls from central Iowa all the way west to the Missouri River, its anchor is Des Moines (Polk County), the region's commercial, financial and governmental center and home to Iowa's influential statewide newspaper, The Des Moines Register.

Nearly 60 percent of the 4th's voters live in Polk County, a dominance that is likely to increase if current population trends continue through the 1990s. Polk grew nearly 8 percent in the 1980s, though the state lost residents.

Des Moines emerged fairly unscathed from the farm and manufacturing recessions that racked Iowa in the 1980s. The relative prosperity helped spawn the phrase "Golden Circle" to describe the towns and suburbs within a 50-mile radius of the city. The web of skywalks in downtown Des Moines, built during a $1 billion development spree during the 1980s, gives it a gleam of success.

Des Moines managed to flourish in part because of its white-collar employment base and its independence from agriculture. It is home to the state government and also is the nation's second-largest insurance center. About 60 insurance companies have headquarters or major offices in the city, led by Principal Financial Group. And Des Moines' role in the state's commerce grew as economies crumbled in the small towns that once offered medical care and other basic services.

Des Moines always has been more like Minneapolis than like Chicago or Milwaukee: It is predominantly white, Protestant and middle-class.

Polk County's Democratic tradition strengthened in recent years. Des Moines' prosperity has created a comfortable middle class that is largely missing disaffected white ethnics and go-go entrepreneurs — two groups that voted Republican in other parts of the country during the 1980s.

Polk has been more reliably Democratic than many parts of the country, supporting Walter F. Mondale, Michael S. Dukakis and Bill Clinton in recent presidential elections. Clinton lost seven of the district's 13 counties in 1996, but overcame that with a nearly 23,000-vote margin in Polk. Ganske won all but two counties — Audubon and Polk, where he neutralized the traditional Democratic turnout and trailed by less than 700 votes.

In past years, Polk's voting pattern and the city's size minimized the influence in the 4th of the western city of Council Bluffs (Pottawattamie County), a GOP stronghold. Built against bluffs, the city was once a bustling crossroads for three westward trails in the early 1800s, and five railroads later met here. Today, many workers cross the Missouri River to work in Omaha in businesses lured by Nebraska's lower tax rates.

The 1980s farm crisis failed to shake the GOP grip on Pottawattamie and the rural counties surrounding it. It voted for Bob Dole in 1996, and was one of the few Iowa counties to give George Bush a solid victory in the 1992.

Farmers in Harrison and Shelby counties have been relatively prosperous, thanks to fertile soil, and Dole carried them, too. To the south and east, land is rough and relatively dry, more suitable for grazing than farming.

1990 Population: 555,276. White 529,118 (95%), Black 15,395 (3%), Other 10,763 (2%). Hispanic origin 8,329 (1%). 18 and over 412,171 (74%), 62 and over 91,013 (16%). Median age: 34.

But the Republican leadership held fast, refusing to allow a vote on Ganske's amendment to lower the income ceiling. And so he ended up as one of just 11 Republicans voting against the rule on the tax cut bill. He also was the only Republican to vote for a Democratic effort to send the bill back to the Ways and Means Committee with directions to change the income level eligibility. When the tax-cut bill came up for passage in the House, though, Ganske swallowed his reservations and supported it.

Although he is generally opposed to abortion, Ganske does support federal family planning programs and has occasionally found himself on the same side as abortion rights supporters. Ganske backed an amendment to the Labor-HHS bill that restored $193.3 million in fiscal 1996 for family planning programs under Title X of the Public Health Service Act. "I will base my vote on this amendment on my view of the best way to decrease the incidence of abortion," Ganske told the House. The amendment was adopted, as Ganske joined 56 other Republicans in voting for it.

Ganske was also one of 49 Republicans who voted to strike a provision in the fiscal 1996 omnibus appropriations bill allowing states to cut off Medicaid funding of abortions in cases of rape or incest. The amendment failed on a 198-222 vote, however.

Although Ganske ran in 1994 as a critic of so-called pork barrel projects, in Congress he has not been averse to seeing Iowa gain a share of federal largess. "I see my primary role as trying to [help] government be more fiscally responsible than it has been in the past," he said. But "it's also part of a congressman's job to represent his district."

Two projects in the 4th ended up on a list of federal programs to be killed when the House in the 104th considered a bill rescinding money from the previous fiscal year. Before the vote, Ganske secured a promise from appropriators that money for one of the projects — a park-and-ride facility to aid mass transit in Des Moines — would be restored. But he was not able to do the same for the other project — a trail center in Council Bluffs — and that earned him a rebuke from the newspaper in Council Bluffs. After the House vote, Ganske helped persuade conferees to restore funding for the trail center as well. Ganske argued that both projects were too far along to be cut.

At Home: Ganske ousted Smith with 53 percent of the vote in 1994 and held off an aggressive Democratic opponent in 1996, winning re-election with 52 percent.

A soft-spoken physician specializing in plastic and reconstructive surgery, Ganske in his 1994 campaign employed all the tools and technology of modern politicking as well as a touch of wit. To underscore his theme that Smith had stayed too long in Congress, Ganske stumped for votes with an antique DeSoto dubbed the Nealmobile. It was a model from 1958, the year the Democratic incumbent first went to Washington.

Smith recognized the seriousness of Ganske's threat to his political career, but at age 74 he was not nimble on the campaign trail. He stressed his seniority and his ability to bring home earmarked projects, but Ganske said those were arguments for kicking him out of office. Ganske argued that for every federal project Smith had brought home, Iowans had paid dearly in the form of higher taxes and a ballooning deficit.

Smith stepped up his campaigning toward the end and went on the attack, attempting to portray Ganske as a wealthy "cosmetic" surgeon trying to buy a seat in Congress. Smith also claimed that Ganske's signature on the Contract With America was a sign that he would help other Republicans in Congress slash Social Security and Medicare to pay for increased defense spending.

Ganske said there was nothing wrong with investing his own money in the campaign, because that enabled him to compete with special-interest PAC money Smith was receiving. In the end, Ganske spent nearly $1.2 million and Smith spent more than $1 million. Ganske also neutralized the wealth issue by noting that Smith had a higher net worth and would earn a hefty congressional pension in retirement. On Election Day, he sent Smith packing by a seven-point margin.

In 1996, Ganske faced a well-known personality in the district, former Des Moines TV weather reporter Connie McBurney. As a Republican freshman in a swing district, Ganske became the target of a hard-hitting campaign by labor unions, which ran television advertisements against him for months. Ganske countered with ads discussing his record in positive terms and alleging that McBurney was being "mysterious" about her positions on issues. McBurney emphasized her outsider status, just as Ganske had in 1994.

Adding to the uncertainty about the outcome was Ganske's temporary absence from the campaign trail in the weeks after Labor Day. He was recuperating from encephalitis and related ailments he contracted while on a medical mission to Peru during the summer congressional recess. Voters did not hold the absence against him, returning him to office by a 5-point margin.

HOUSE ELECTIONS

1996 General		
Greg Ganske (R)	133,419	(52%)
Connie McBurney (D)	119,790	(47%)
1994 General		
Greg Ganske (R)	111,935	(53%)
Neal Smith (D)	98,824	(46%)

CAMPAIGN FINANCE

	Receipts	Receipts from PACs	Expend-itures
1996			
Ganske (R)	$2,337,935	$668,464 (29%)	$2,334,251
McBurney (D)	$878,292	$208,222 (24%)	$853,104
1994			
Ganske (R)	$1,213,634	$156,966 (13%)	$1,195,525
Smith (D)	$565,354	$331,836 (59%)	$1,005,498

DISTRICT VOTE FOR PRESIDENT

1996		1992	
D	127,250 (49%)	**D**	117,863 (43%)
R	107,359 (42%)	**R**	107,745 (39%)
I	20,296 (8%)	**I**	47,835 (18%)

KEY VOTES

1997	
Ban "partial birth" abortions	Y
1996	
Approve farm bill	Y
Deny public education to illegal immigrants	Y
Repeal ban on certain assault-style weapons	N
Increase minimum wage	Y
Freeze defense spending	Y
Approve welfare overhaul	Y
1995	
Approve balanced-budget constitutional amendment	Y
Relax Clean Water Act regulations	Y
Oppose limits on environmental regulations	N
Reduce projected Medicare spending	Y
Approve GOP budget with tax and spending cuts	Y

VOTING STUDIES

	Presidential Support		Party Unity		Conservative Coalition	
Year	**S**	**O**	**S**	**O**	**S**	**O**
1996	42	52	82	15	59	37
1995	24	75	91+	9+	83+	17+

+ Not eligible for all recorded votes.

INTEREST GROUP RATINGS

Year	ADA	AFL-CIO	CCUS	ACU
1996	20	n/a	94	83
1995	10	0	100	72

5 Tom Latham (R)

Of Alexander — Elected 1994, 2nd term

Biographical Information

Born: July 14, 1948, Hampton, Iowa.

Education: Wartburg College, 1967; Iowa State U., 1967-70.

Occupation: Seed company executive; insurance agency marketing representative; insurance agent; bank teller.

Family: Wife, Kathy; three children.

Religion: Lutheran.

Political Career: Franklin County Republican chairman, 1984-91.

Capitol Office: 516 Cannon Bldg. 20515; 225-5476.

Committees

Appropriations
Agriculture, Rural Development, FDA & Related Agencies; Commerce, Justice, State & Judiciary; Legislative

In Washington: When he first ran for the open 5th in 1994, Latham brought in a well-known foe of farm price supports, GOP Rep. Dick Armey of Texas, to campaign for him — an indication that Latham, if elected, would consider supporting fundamental changes in federal farm policy.

Latham won the heavily agricultural northwestern Iowa district with a decisive 61 percent. He was assigned to the Agriculture Committee, giving him a key seat as the new GOP majority undertook to pass a sweeping overhaul of farm programs to bring them more in line with free-market principles. Latham was a strong backer of the "Freedom to Farm" bill, which he said would give farmers greater planting flexibility. The 5th is home to some of the most productive farms in the nation.

"The idea of continuing a convoluted program which restricts options for farmers, which does nothing to change programs that have been in place since the horse-and-buggy days, is simply incomprehensible to me," Latham said during committee debate on the bill, which ultimately was signed into law in the spring of 1996.

With the farm bill in place, Latham was rewarded at the start of the 105th Congress with a seat on the Appropriations Committee, where from his seat on the Agriculture and Rural Development Subcommittee, he can continue to protect and promote the interests of the agriculture-dependent 5th. He also has seats on the Commerce, Justice, State and the Judiciary and the Legislative Branch subcommittees.

Latham said that on Appropriations he would "continue to fight for a balanced budget and the American Dream while ensuring that Iowa taxpayers get a common-sense return on their investment in government."

Latham is likely to use his Appropriations assignment to continue his fight against environmental regulations that he says do economic harm to farmers by improperly designating arable ground as wetlands. He praised provisions in the farm bill that limited the enrollment of agricultural land in the wetlands reserve program.

In early 1995 he had introduced a measure putting a moratorium on new wetlands designations until a farm bill was passed. "Current procedures for the designation of wetlands are extremely flawed," Latham said when introducing the bill. "In too many cases our government overlooks farmer hardships for the sake of pleasing radical environmentalists."

In May 1995, when the House passed a rewrite of the 1972 clean water act, Latham also spoke in favor of provisions relaxing federal wetlands regulations. He and other proponents of deregulation said they simply wished to end protection of areas with marginal ecological benefit.

Latham railed against the existing definitions of wetland areas, saying, "Property owners and the general public no longer know what a wetland is. They expect to see a swamp or marsh or bog, only to be told by regulators that land that is usually dry is a wetland or that a set spot in a field of corn is wetland. This abuse has gone on far too long."

As that rhetoric suggests, Latham takes a staunchly conservative position on most issues. He supported all the major items of the GOP's "Contract With America," favoring a balanced-budget constitutional amendment, overhaul of the welfare system, congressional term limits and tax and spending cuts. He voted against an increase in the minimum wage the first time it came through the House in May 1996, but in August he switched and voted for the final version, which included other provisions sought by Republicans, including $10 billion in business tax cuts over five years, a $5,000 tax credit to offset the cost of adoption and an expansion of Individual Retirement Accounts.

He has told the House that his constituents often stop him and say: "Thank you for trying to at least start some regulatory relief to get the government off our backs. It is bad enough they are deep in our pockets, but please help us get the government off our backs."

Latham likes to recount the story that he and

IOWA 5
Northwest — Sioux City; Fort Dodge

The 5th takes in nearly 18,000 square miles of fertile soil and gently undulating hills. The farms here are some of the nation's most productive, turning out impressive yields of corn, soybeans and hogs.

The bountiful land has allowed the region to remain more like the Iowa of old than any other part of the state. Virtually every town has a working grain elevator, and many adults are involved in the farm-to-market agricultural network. Politically, Iowa's GOP tradition holds sway. The 5th is the only district in which registered Republicans outnumber Democrats; to win statewide, GOP candidates need lopsided margins here.

Yet even here, demographic and political change is evident. The area suffered dramatic population losses during the 1980s as many small-scale farmers sold their land to agribusiness operations. Each of the district's 30 counties lost population, and 18 lost more than 10 percent. In 1996, Bob Dole took 45 percent of the vote, barely beating Bill Clinton.

The smallest population loss was in Woodbury County (Sioux City), which is the district's largest, accounting for about 20 percent of the 5th's population. Once a meatpacking town, Sioux City has evolved into a more service-oriented center for a region that includes part of South Dakota and Nebraska. Some Sioux City businesses have moved across the river to take advantage of more favorable tax laws in South Dakota and Nebraska. But Woodbury County has sprouted numerous bedroom communities to house their employees — who prefer Iowa's schools and government services.

Politically, Sioux City has long leaned Republican. This pattern held during the 1980s, as the shift of voters to the Democrats on economic and peace issues was offset by the declining influence of labor. In 1996, Latham won comfortably in Woodbury County while Clinton edged out Dole.

The district's only other significant population center is Fort Dodge (Webster County). The county is home to less than 10 percent of the 5th's voters — a figure that underscores the region's rural character. An industrial center near large gypsum mines, Fort Dodge emerged as a leader in veterinary pharmaceuticals in the 1980s. The city is in the heart of a region first settled by Irish Catholics. Webster and its heavily Catholic neighbor, Greene County, typically vote Democratic, though Latham carried them both in his re-election bid.

If Iowa has a playground, it is Dickinson County on the Minnesota border. With Spirit Lake and East and West Okoboji lakes, the county attracts tourists, making it the rare Iowa community debating how fast and how much it should grow.

Elsewhere, county fairs are the annual highlight: Clay County's is the nation's second-largest. The September Tulipfest in conservative, Dutch-settled Orange City (Sioux County) is a must-attend event for GOP candidates, and performers attend the annual Donna Reed Festival in her hometown of Denison (Crawford County).

1990 Population: 555,457. White 544,517 (98%), Black 3,341 (1%), Other 7,599 (1%). Hispanic origin 5,062 (1%). 18 and over 405,771 (73%), 62 and over 118,656 (21%). Median age: 36.

his brothers had to spend $12,000 in 1993 to measure dust microns on their small soybean farm outside Alexander, Iowa, in order to comply with the Clean Air Act.

"It was no benefit to the well-being of people or animals or anything," Latham told the Seattle Times in January 1995, speaking of the Clean Air Act provision he said was intended to apply to gigantic grain producers. "It is exactly why any small-business person today is much more concerned about someone from the government walking in and saying they want to help than any competitor down the street."

Latham has also done his share to watch out for Sioux City. He praised the 1995 military construction spending bill for helping fund the resurfacing of the runway used by the 185th Air National Guard; he said the runway was 10 years overdue for reconstruction.

In early 1997, Latham was successful in getting one full-time Immigration and Naturalization Service (INS) officer assigned to Sioux City and the possibility of a second one to be assigned later. He noted that his seat on the Commerce, Justice, State Appropriations Subcommittee helped him secure the INS assignment. The panel has jurisdiction over the INS. "I saw that this was something that many Northwest Iowans felt was needed to address our growing drug and illegal immigration problems," he said.

Latham added that the INS officer assignment augmented an amendment he had successfully attached to a broad immigration bill passed by the House in March 1996. It allowed state and local law enforcement agencies to enter into agreements with the Department of Justice giving them the authority to apprehend illegal aliens.

At Home: Democrats had hopes of capturing the 5th in 1994 when GOP Rep. Fred Grandy left it to run for governor. Before Grandy, a Democrat had held the district, and the party's nominee for the open seat, Sheila McGuire, waged an aggressive campaign that spent more than $700,000. But Latham was a good fit for the district in a strongly Republican year, and he breezed to election.

He touted his agricultural background, his deep roots in the district and his roles as husband and father, and voters felt more comfortable with him than with McGuire. Though she grew up in the district and her family had long operated a local auction company, the unmarried, Harvard-educated Democrat was saddled with an image as a liberal apologist for the unpopular Clinton administration.

Before his contest with McGuire, Latham had capitalized on contacts he had made as Franklin County Republican chairman for seven years to win the Republican nomination over Sioux City state Sen. Brad Banks.

Latham boasted of having held more than 500 meetings with farmers across the district as the co-owner of his family's seed company. He said those discussions, along with his own experience in farming, provided him with the background needed to help represent the district as farm policy was being crafted in Congress.

In the fall campaign, McGuire disputed Latham's claim to be farmer-friendly, portraying him instead as a wealthy businessman who would promote the interests of agribusiness. When Latham brought in Armey to campaign for him, McGuire tried to use the visit to support her claim that her GOP opponent would not look out for Iowa's family farmers.

Latham, who was named a "friend of agriculture" by the Iowa Farm Bureau Federation, cast McGuire as an outsider, citing her research for Harvard as evidence that she was really an East Coast professor who had come back to Iowa only to run for office.

McGuire attempted to use her experience as one of a handful of Iowans on a White House advisory panel on the Clinton health care plan as testimony to her clout and expertise. But when the president's health-reform crusade stirred so much controversy that it fizzled in Congress, her experience on the panel became a factor contributing to her defeat. Latham said that McGuire's work on the plan proved she backed big government and costly bureaucratic programs. He ended up posting a hefty 22-point victory.

He improved on that victory in 1996, winning re-election with almost two-thirds of the vote.

HOUSE ELECTIONS

1996 General		
Tom Latham (R)	147,576	(65%)
MacDonald Smith (D)	75,785	(34%)
1994 General		
Tom Latham (R)	114,796	(61%)
Sheila McGuire (D)	73,627	(39%)

CAMPAIGN FINANCE

	Receipts	Receipts from PACs	Expend-itures
1996			
Latham (R)	$524,817	$299,946 (57%)	$477,173
Smith (D)	$126,651	$56,480 (45%)	$126,516
1994			
Latham (R)	$758,405	$159,887 (21%)	$742,308
McGuire (D)	$730,572	$264,797 (36%)	$719,811

DISTRICT VOTE FOR PRESIDENT

	1996		1992
D	104,775 (44%)	**D**	99,112 (38%)
R	106,615 (45%)	**R**	109,966 (42%)
I	23,051 (10%)	**I**	50,343 (19%)

KEY VOTES

1997	
Ban "partial birth" abortions	Y
1996	
Approve farm bill	Y
Deny public education to illegal immigrants	Y
Repeal ban on certain assault-style weapons	Y
Increase minimum wage	N
Freeze defense spending	Y
Approve welfare overhaul	Y
1995	
Approve balanced-budget constitutional amendment	Y
Relax Clean Water Act regulations	Y
Oppose limits on environmental regulations	N
Reduce projected Medicare spending	Y
Approve GOP budget with tax and spending cuts	Y

VOTING STUDIES

	Presidential Support		Party Unity		Conservative Coalition	
Year	**S**	**O**	**S**	**O**	**S**	**O**
1996	32	67	95	4	94	6
1995	17	80	97	3	93	7

INTEREST GROUP RATINGS

Year	ADA	AFL-CIO	CCUS	ACU
1996	0	n/a	100	95
1995	5	0	96	84

KANSAS

Governor: Bill Graves (R)
First elected: 1994
Length of term: 4 years
Term expires: 1/99
Salary: $76,476
Term limit: 2 terms
Phone: (913) 296-3232
Born: January 9, 1953; Salina, Kan.
Education: Kansas Wesleyan College, B.B.A. 1975; U. of Kansas, attended 1979.
Occupation: Trucking company manager.
Family: Wife, Linda Richey.
Religion: Methodist.
Political Career: Kan. secretary of state, 1987.

Lt. Gov.: Gary Shear (R)
First elected: Appointed 7/96
Length of term: 4 years
Term expires: 1/99
Salary: $21,638
Phone: (913) 296-2213

State election official: (913) 296-4561
Democratic headquarters: (913) 234-0425
Republican headquarters: (913) 234-3416

REDISTRICTING

Kansas lost one seat in reapportionment, dropping from five districts to four. The legislature passed the map May 7, 1992; the governor signed it May 11. Federal court finalized that map with minor changes June 3.

STATE LEGISLATURE

Bicameral Legislature. Meets January-June.

Senate: 40 members, 4-year terms
1996 breakdown: 27R, 13D; 26 men, 14 women
Salary: $65/day salary, $73/day expenses while in session
Phone: (913) 296-7344

House of Representatives: 125 members, 2-year terms
1996 breakdown: 77R, 48D; 90 men, 35 women
Salary: $63/day salary, $73/day expenses while in session
Phone: (913) 296-7633

URBAN STATISTICS

City	Population
Wichita	304,011
Mayor Bob Knight, N-P	
Kansas City	149,800
Mayor Carol Marinovich, N-P	
Topeka	119,883
Mayor Harry "Butch" Felker, N-P	
Overland Park	111,790
Mayor Ed Eilert, R	
Lawrence	65,608
Mayor Bonnie Augustine, N-P	

U.S. CONGRESS

Senate: 0 D, 2 R
House: 0 D, 4 R

TERM LIMITS

For state offices: No

ELECTIONS

1996 Presidential Vote

Bob Dole	54%
Bill Clinton	36%
Ross Perot	9%

1992 Presidential Vote

George Bush	39%
Bill Clinton	34%
Ross Perot	27%

1988 Presidential Vote

George Bush	56%
Michael S. Dukakis	43%

POPULATION

1990 population		2,477,574
1980 population		2,363,679
Percent change		+5%
Rank among states:		32
White		90%
Black		6%
Hispanic		4%
Asian or Pacific islander		1%
Urban		69%
Rural		31%
Born in state		61%
Foreign-born		3%
Under age 18	662,002	27%
Ages 18-64	1,473,001	59%
65 and older	342,571	14%
Median age		32.9

MISCELLANEOUS

Capital: Topeka
Number of counties: 105
Per capita income: $18,511 (1991)
Rank among states: 21
Total area: 82,277 sq. miles
Rank among states: 14

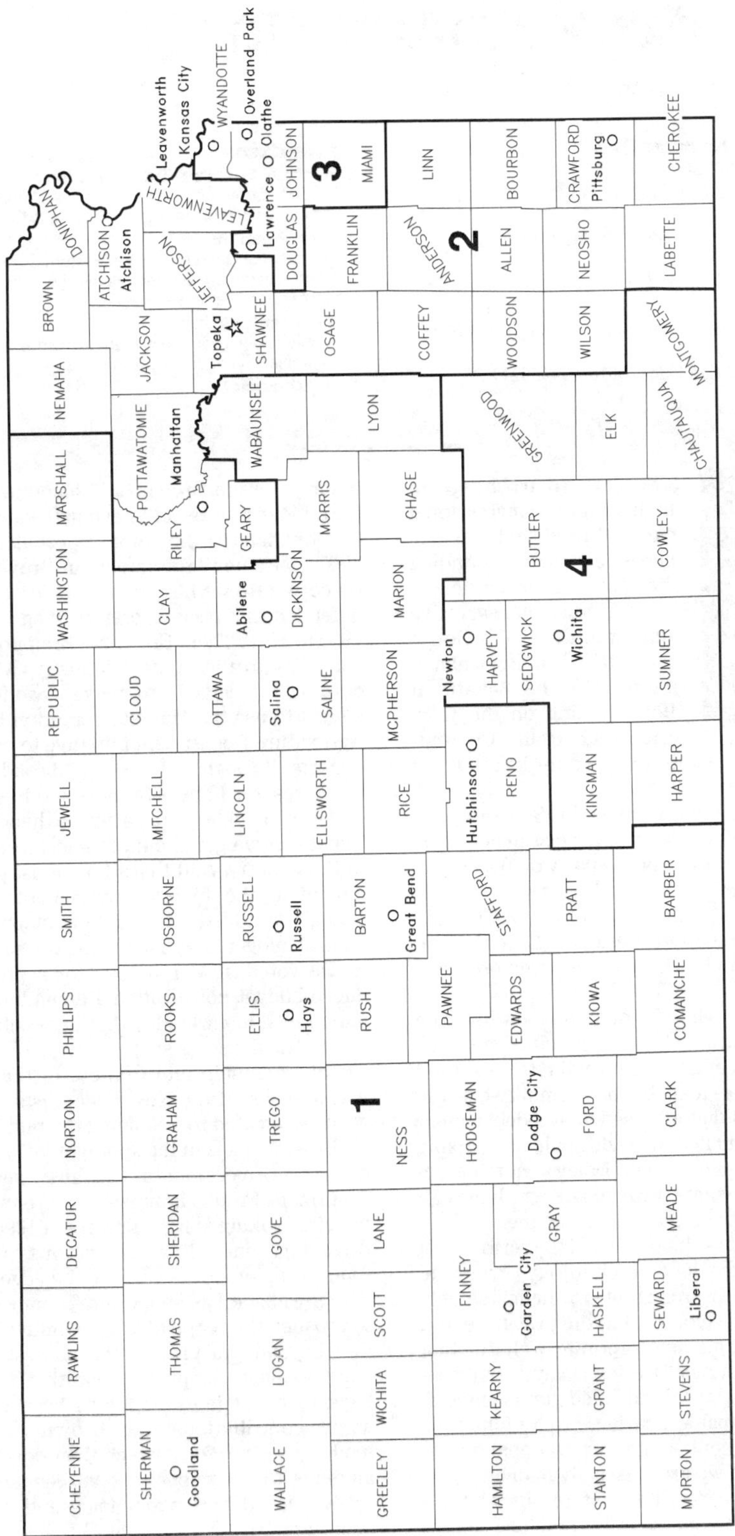
CHEYENNE
RAWLINS
DECATUR
NORTON
PHILLIPS
SMITH
JEWELL
REPUBLIC
WASHINGTON
MARSHALL
NEMAHA
BROWN
DONIPHAN
ATCHISON
Atchison
JEFFERSON
LEAVENWORTH
Leavenworth
Kansas City
WYANDOTTE
Overland Park
Olathe
JOHNSON
Lawrence
DOUGLAS
JACKSON
Topeka
SHAWNEE
POTTAWATOMIE
Manhattan
WABAUNSEE
RILEY
GEARY
CLAY
CLOUD
SHERMAN
Goodland
THOMAS
SHERIDAN
GRAHAM
ROOKS
OSBORNE
MITCHELL
LINCOLN
OTTAWA
Salina
SALINE
Abilene
DICKINSON
MORRIS
LYON
OSAGE
FRANKLIN
MIAMI
3
LINN
ANDERSON
2
COFFEY
BOURBON
ALLEN
WOODSON
CRAWFORD
Pittsburg
NEOSHO
WILSON
CHEROKEE
LABETTE
MONTGOMERY
CHAUTAUQUA
ELK
GREENWOOD
CHASE
MARION
MCPHERSON
Newton
HARVEY
BUTLER
4
SEDGWICK
Wichita
COWLEY
SUMNER
WALLACE
LOGAN
GOVE
TREGO
ELLIS
Hays
RUSSELL
Russell
ELLSWORTH
RICE
Hutchinson
RENO
KINGMAN
HARPER
BARTON
Great Bend
STAFFORD
PRATT
BARBER
GREELEY
WICHITA
SCOTT
LANE
NESS
1
RUSH
PAWNEE
EDWARDS
KIOWA
COMANCHE
HODGEMAN
Dodge City
FORD
CLARK
FINNEY
Garden City
GRAY
MEADE
HAMILTON
KEARNY
GRANT
HASKELL
SEWARD
Liberal
STANTON
STEVENS
MORTON

Sam Brownback (R)

Of Topeka — Elected 1996, 1st term

Biographical Information

Born: Sept. 12, 1956, Garnett, Kan.

Education: Kansas State U., B.S. 1979; U. of Kansas, J.D. 1982.

Occupation: Teacher; lawyer; White House fellow; broadcaster.

Family: Wife, Mary Stouffer; three children.

Religion: Methodist.

Political Career: Kan. secretary of Agriculture, 1986-93; U.S. House, 1995-96.

Capitol Office: 303 Hart Bldg. 20510; 224-6521.

Committees

Commerce, Science & Transportation
Aviation; Communications; Consumer Affairs, Foreign Commerce & Tourism; Manufacturing & Competitiveness

Foreign Relations
International Operations; Near Eastern & South Asian Affairs (chairman); Western Hemisphere, Peace Corps, Narcotics and Terrorism

Governmental Affairs
Oversight of Government Management & the District of Columbia (chairman); Investigations

Joint Economic

The Path to Washington: In his short congressional career, Brownback has displayed a knack for finding the center of the action.

A leading conservative activist in the GOP's House Class of 1994, Brownback jumped to the Senate in 1996, landing on the Governmental Affairs Committee just in time for its high-profile hearings on campaign finance.

Brownback — who assumed his Senate seat in late November 1996, ahead of his classmates — is a staunch conservative, particularly on fiscal matters. He cast the solitary "no" when the Senate Commerce, Science and Transportation Committee voted 19-1 to support President Clinton's nomination of William M. Daley to be Commerce secretary.

Brownback, who favors dismantling the Commerce Department, said Daley had not suggested sufficient cuts. "I believe him to be a good man, an honorable man, but not committed to the specific changes that are needed at a department that has been riddled with difficult and vexing problems," he said. When Daley's nomination came to the full Senate, Brownback and James M. Inhofe, R-Okla., were the lone dissenters.

Brownback has been especially critical of Commerce's Advanced Technology Program, which provides research grants for fledgling technologies under development in the private sector. He sees such grants as "corporate welfare" that the budget cannot bear. During Daley's confirmation hearing, Brownback ridiculed grants made to Fortune 500 companies, saying, "We're funding a program [that benefits large corporations] directly at a time when we are massively in debt."

In attacking corporate welfare, Brownback says, "I'm certainly going to be reaching across the aisle . . . working with whoever, whatever ideology." Indeed, liberal Democrats Edward M. Kennedy and John Kerry of Massachusetts were among a group Brownback joined in 1997 to ask for a bipartisan panel to evaluate such spending.

The Kansas City Star reported in February 1997 that among the targets in Brownback's war on corporate welfare are two federal ventures he defended as Kansas' secretary of agriculture from 1986 to 1993. Then, Brownback supported federal subsidies to the ethanol industry, which distills corn and blends it to make gasohol. He also sought to use the Market Promotion Program, an Agriculture Department initiative to promote U.S. exports through advertising abroad and other measures, for Kansas farmers and businesses.

Brownback says his attitude then was to grab "what can we get ahold of — just like everybody in the country. And that's how most people have looked at the federal government the last 40 years," he added. "I'm looking at balancing the federal budget now. That is the top priority."

He voted in March 1997 for a proposed balanced-budget constitutional amendment, and he announced in early May that he would support a budget deal taking shape between the congressional leadership and Clinton. In the House, he was a leader of the New Federalists, a freshman group dedicated to balancing the budget.

Brownback is in the spotlight in 1997 by virtue of his Governmental Affairs seat. Under Chairman Fred Thompson of Tennessee, the panel is looking at irregularities in 1996 campaign financing, including allegations that some fundraising practices came to the edge of the law.

Brownback has supported Thompson's efforts to broaden the scope of the committee's investigation beyond the presidential contest to include congressional campaigns, but that could come back to haunt him. Questions have been raised about contributions that Brownback's in-laws made to seven PACs, which then donated similar amounts to Brownback's 1996 Senate campaign. Brownback denies wrongdoing and says he has been targeted by Democrats because part of the Governmental Affairs inquiry involves probing the Democratic National Committee's fundraising.

Brownback also sits on the Foreign Relations

Committee. In April 1997, he was one of 26 Republicans voting against ratification of the Chemical Weapons Convention. Also, Brownback is on the Joint Economic Committee.

Brownback holds a gavel on Governmental Affairs, chairing its Subcommittee on Oversight of Government Management and the District of Columbia. Early in 1997, he impressed District supporters by making the city a priority, at least on his subcommittee's hearing schedule.

And Brownback joined Washington Mayor Marion S. Barry Jr. in opposing part of Clinton's initiative to revive the District. The two expressed concern about the structure of an economic development corporation proposed for the city. Brownback called the plan "a Department of Commerce for the District of Columbia." He added: "This isn't a plan for economic revitalization. You're just going to give certain people in groups and areas you favor tax breaks."

When Senate Majority Leader Bob Dole announced in the spring of 1996 that he would resign his Senate seat to run for president, Brownback was quick to act. Already having established an organization for his expected House re-election bid, he instead declared his candidacy to fill the last two years of Dole's term.

But any easy path to the GOP Senate nomination was hampered by a bitter split in the Kansas Republican Party between moderates — such as Gov. Bill Graves — and conservatives. Brownback had gained much of his political support from the conservative wing of the party. While well-known in Washington from his role in the 104th Congress, Brownback was little-known statewide — except to farmers — but reached out aggressively to business and conservative social groups.

Graves named Lt. Gov. Sheila Frahm to fill Dole's seat until a special election. A special primary was set for Aug. 6, the same day as Kansas' regular congressional primaries.

The Brownback-Frahm brawl shaped up as a showdown between the two factions of the state GOP, although the candidates shied away from ideological labels. Frahm called herself a conservative, but she was perceived as having more moderate views on some social issues, such as abortion. Brownback, meanwhile, said he was gaining support from party traditionalists as well as movement conservatives.

August proved fruitful for the state GOP's conservative wing. Not only did Brownback defeat Frahm, but also two conservative House candidates defeated their more moderate primary opponents in competitive open-seat races.

Brownback moved on to his general-election contest with stockbroker Jill Docking. Though a political newcomer, Docking bears a famous name in Kansas politics. Her husband was a lieutenant governor, and his father and grandfather were both governors. Democrats hoped Docking, who espoused a centrist message, would be able to attract moderate Republican voters. But Brownback eventually was able to garner support from prominent moderates such as Graves and Frahm, and he won with 54 percent of the vote.

SENATE ELECTIONS

1996 Special		
Sam Brownback (R)	574,021	(54%)
Jill Docking (D)	461,344	(43%)
Donald R. Klaassen (REF)	29,351	(3%)
1996 Special Primary		
Sam Brownback (R)	187,914	(55%)
Sheila Frahm (R)	142,487	(42%)
Christina Campbell-Cline (R)	12,378	(4%)

Previous Winning Percentages: 1994* (66%)

** House election*

KEY VOTES

1997	
Approve balanced-budget constitutional amendment	Y
Approve chemical weapons treaty	N
House Service:	
1996	
Approve farm bill	Y
Deny public education to illegal immigrants	Y
Increase minimum wage	N
Freeze defense spending	N
Approve welfare overhaul	Y
1995	
Approve balanced-budget constitutional amendment	Y
Relax Clean Water Act regulations	Y
Oppose limits on environmental regulations	N
Reduce projected Medicare spending	Y
Approve GOP budget with tax and spending cuts	Y

CAMPAIGN FINANCE

	Receipts	Receipts from PACs	Expend-itures
1996			
Brownback (R)	$2,269,850	$676,753 (30%)	$2,269,550
Docking (D)	$1,219,383	$278,924 (23%)	$1,199,844
Klaassen (REF)	$28,184	0	$24,183

VOTING STUDIES

	Presidential Support		Party Unity		Conservative Coalition	
Year	**S**	**O**	**S**	**O**	**S**	**O**
House Service:						
1996	30	63	85	7	78	14
1995	22	78	95	4	90	9

INTEREST GROUP RATINGS

Year	**ADA**	**AFL-CIO**	**CCUS**	**ACU**
House Service:				
1996	5	0	93	100
1995	0	8	100	92

Pat Roberts (R)

Of Dodge City — Elected 1996, 1st term

Biographical Information
Born: April 20, 1936, Topeka, Kan.
Education: Kansas State U., B.A. 1958.
Military Service: Marine Corps, 1958-62.
Occupation: Journalist; congressional aide.
Family: Wife, Franki Fann; three children.
Religion: Methodist.
Political Career: U.S. House, 1981-97.
Capitol Office: 302 Hart Bldg. 20510; 224-4774.

Committees
Agriculture, Nutrition & Forestry
Forestry, Conservation & Rural Revitalization; Production & Price Competitiveness
Armed Services
Acquisition & Technology; Airland Forces; Readiness
Select Ethics
Select Intelligence

The Path to Washington: Despite losing clout in the Senate with the departures of veteran Republican deal-makers Bob Dole and Nancy Landon Kassebaum, Kansans can look to Roberts to help fill the void.

Indeed, Roberts is the only member of the state's six-person delegation who started the 105th Congress with more than two years' experience on Capitol Hill.

In 1996, Kansas voters had a chance to remake the state's political landscape. They sent Roberts and his freshman House colleague Sam Brownback into the Senate and elected three new Republicans to the House.

Roberts' election to the Senate caps a 28-year political career. After working as a House aide for 12 years, he served as a representative for 16 — the last two as chairman of the Agriculture Committee. One of the most popular politicians in Kansas, he brings to the Senate a caustic wit, a reliably conservative vote and a fierce dedication to rural causes.

On many social issues, Roberts is likely to weigh in to the right of his predecessor, Kassebaum, who supported abortion rights and some gun control measures.

The major force behind 1996 omnibus farm legislation, Roberts took a seat on the Senate Agriculture Committee, where he can monitor the reforms he helped enact in the 104th.

A former Marine, Roberts also sits on the Intelligence Committee and on the Armed Services Committee, casting a watchful eye on the commitment of U.S. forces around the world.

In late March 1997, Roberts and four other senators made an official trip to North Korea. Amid rumors of widespread famine in the hard-line communist state, Roberts reported that rice and vegetables were available to North Koreans the delegation saw, but "there is no livestock production. There was not a chicken, there was not a pig, there was not a duck, there was not a goose."

A month later, Roberts voted to ratify the Chemical Weapons Convention, saying he was swayed by a Marine general who told him U.S. troops would be better off with the treaty than without.

Roberts' road to the Senate, which at first seemed straight, instead was filled with twists and turns.

When speculation mounted in 1995 that Kassebaum would not seek a fourth term, Roberts — then in his eighth term representing western Kansas' vast, agricultural 1st District — seemed the likely front-runner to replace her.

But on Nov. 13, just a week before Kassebaum's long-anticipated official announcement, Roberts — who for months had been raising money for a potential Senate bid — stunned many observers by pulling his name from consideration. He cited his responsibilities on the Agriculture Committee as a factor that could distract him from the planned campaign.

After two months of frenzied speculation in Kansas political circles about who might emerge as a new front-runner, Roberts reversed course and declared in January 1996 that he would indeed seek Kassebaum's Senate seat. His decision established him again as the leading contender and discouraged other well-known Republicans from challenging him for the GOP nomination.

After easily defeating three little-known opponents in the August GOP primary, Roberts faced Democratic state Treasurer Sally Thompson in the general election. The contest between Roberts and Thompson was overshadowed by the late-starting second Senate race in Kansas — to replace Dole, who had left the Senate in June to focus on his presidential bid.

Thompson tried to convince voters that Roberts had spent too many years in Washington and was out of touch with the concerns of Kansas voters. But voters weren't buying, and Roberts rolled up a big win, taking 62 percent of the vote to Thompson's 34 percent.

Friends view Roberts as pleasantly irascible, although the pressures of his House chairmanship in the 104th seemed to make him more testy, both in Washington and on the campaign trail. He publicly apologized after referring to Thompson during the campaign as a "bitch."

After years in the House minority, Roberts came into his own during the 104th. Known as "The Aggie" by friends and colleagues, he sponsored "Freedom to Farm" legislation, which phased out most New Deal-era crop subsidies, replacing them with a system of fixed, but declining, payments that farmers would receive over seven years, regardless of market prices or their planting decisions. Republicans said the measure would allow farmers to plant for the marketplace, rather than be bound by restrictive government programs, although critics faulted it for eliminating the "safety net" of subsidies to farmers in times of low prices.

Roberts received mixed reviews for his handling of the legislation. Although he eventually produced a product that both met Republican budget-cutting targets and satisfied powerful agricultural organizations — no small feat — he ran into so much opposition that his own committee at one point voted down his proposal.

Later in 1996, however, Roberts mended fences with his own committee, winning bipartisan approval of a major rewrite of pesticide laws. And he won a bruising battle with appropriators by shielding farm programs from cuts in the 1997 agriculture spending bill.

In the House, Roberts sat on the Oversight Committee, which monitored the House's internal operations. He saw one of his longtime complaints about the House resolved in the 104th with the abolition of taxpayer funding for legislative service organizations, which were issue-oriented confederations of like-minded members.

In the Senate, Roberts likewise has an assignment dealing with institutional matters: the Ethics Committee.

Early in the 105th, Roberts called for Congress to wait on campaign finance overhaul until after an investigation into Democratic fundraising practices. "Let's get at the criminal transgressions of existing law first; then we can proceed," he said.

SENATE ELECTIONS

1996 General		
Pat Roberts (R)	652,677	(62%)
Sally Thompson (D)	362,380	(34%)
Mark S. Marney (REF)	24,145	(2%)
Steven Rosile (LIBERT)	13,098	(1%)
1996 Primary		
Pat Roberts (R)	245,411	(78%)
Tom Little (R)	25,052	(8%)
Thomas L. Oyler (R)	23,266	(7%)
Richard L. Cooley (R)	20,060	(6%)

Previous Winning Percentages: 1994* (77%) **1992*** (68%) **1990*** (63%) **1988*** (100%) **1986*** (77%) **1984*** (76%) **1982*** (68%) **1980*** (62%)

* *House elections*

KEY VOTES

1997	
Approve balanced-budget constitutional amendment	Y
Approve chemical weapons treaty	Y
House Service:	
1996	
Approve farm bill	Y
Deny public education to illegal immigrants	Y
Increase minimum wage	Y
Freeze defense spending	N
Approve welfare overhaul	Y
1995	
Approve balanced-budget constitutional amendment	Y
Relax Clean Water Act regulations	Y
Oppose limits on environmental regulations	N
Reduce projected Medicare spending	Y
Approve GOP budget with tax and spending cuts	Y

CAMPAIGN FINANCE

	Receipts	Receipts from PACs	Expend-itures
1996			
Roberts (R)	$2,297,886	$1,216,831 (53%)	$2,305,898
Thompson (D)	$662,523	$203,024 (31%)	$659,066
Marney (REF)	$10,413	0	$10,412

VOTING STUDIES

	Presidential Support		Party Unity		Conservative Coalition	
Year	S	O	S	O	S	O
House Service:						
1996	35	59	90	7	98	0
1995	19	80	94	4	95	1
1994	38	58	93	4	89	3
1993	34	66	91	6	95	5
1992	87	11	93	4	96	4
1991	82	17	90	6	97	3

INTEREST GROUP RATINGS

Year	ADA	AFL-CIO	CCUS	ACU
House Service:				
1996	5	0	94	95
1995	0	0	96	80
1994	0	0	92	100
1993	0	0	100	100
1992	10	17	88	88
1991	5	0	90	83

1 Jerry Moran (R)

Of Hays — Elected 1996, 1st term

Biographical Information
Born: May 29, 1954, Great Bend, Kan.
Education: U. of Kansas, B.S. 1976, J.D. 1981.
Occupation: Lawyer.
Family: Wife, Robba Addison; two children.
Religion: Methodist.
Political Career: Kansas Senate, 1989-97, vice president, 1993-95; majority leader, 1995-97.
Capitol Office: 1217 Longworth Bldg. 20515; 225-2715.

Committees
Agriculture
Forestry, Resource Conservation & Research; General Farm Commodities; Risk Management & Specialty Crops
International Relations
International Economic Policy & Trade
Veterans' Affairs
Health

The Path to Washington: In a year when the world of Kansas politics was turned upside down, Moran's 1996 House campaign was an island of relative tranquility. When eight-term Republican Rep. Pat Roberts decided in January 1996 that he would seek the seat of retiring GOP Sen. Nancy Landon Kassebaum, Moran quickly established himself as the front-runner in the race to succeed Roberts in the House.

Moran, then the state Senate majority leader, said during the campaign that he would provide similar representation to that offered by Roberts, a pragmatic conservative. Like Roberts, he sees himself as able to gain support from both wings of the Kansas Republican Party, which has been sharply split in recent years between moderates and conservatives.

Moran easily overcame two little-known opponents in the GOP primary and moved on to face his Democratic opponent, John Divine, an IBM executive and former mayor of Salina.

With the 1st District's strong Republican base and GOP presidential nominee Bob Dole — whose Russell hometown is in the 1st — topping the ticket, Moran was seen as the likely winner, especially in a year in which Kansas political activists on both sides of the aisle were distracted by two Senate contests and three more competitive House races.

During the campaign, Moran stressed a message of fiscal restraint, limited government and personal responsibility. Divine, meanwhile, said he would help family farmers concerned about domination by large agribusiness corporations.

Roberts repeatedly won election in the 1st with 62 percent of the vote or higher, and Moran kept up the tradition of easy elections, winning with 73 percent of the vote.

In the House, Moran will sit on the Agriculture, International Relations and Veterans' Affairs committees.

Farming is a key concern in the 1st, a vast rural western district, and Roberts chaired the Agriculture Committee in the 104th Congress.

Moran supports the "Freedom to Farm" law, the overhaul of agriculture programs that was enacted during the 104th Congress.

But he says he is concerned that tight budgets could make it hard to get all the funding for farmers promised in that bill. On the Agriculture Committee, he notes, he is well-positioned to deal with unforeseen problems that arise as the new law is carried out.

On International Relations, he hopes to focus on trade issues that affect the district's farms and small manufacturing companies. And on Veterans' Affairs, he plans to stress the importance of VA hospitals, working to ensure that they are adequately funded and that veterans receive proper care.

Another key topic for Moran is likely to be rural health, including how small hospitals are reimbursed by Medicare, the federal health insurance program for the elderly.

A lawyer, Moran defeated an 18-year incumbent to win election to the state Senate in 1988. He was unopposed for a second term in 1992. Moran had started out as a precinct committeeman in 1974 and worked his way through the political ranks in the western part of the state. Moran's state senate service included a stint as chairman of the Judiciary Committee, where his interests included efforts to strengthen Kansas' laws on juvenile crime.

Moran became majority leader in 1995, succeeding Sheila Frahm, who had been elected lieutenant governor the previous year and who in May 1996 was appointed to the U.S. Senate to fill the vacancy created by Dole's resignation.

As a state legislator, Moran says he saw firsthand evidence of the problems caused by federal mandates that were imposed on the states without adequate funding.

He says the unfunded-mandate law enacted during the 104th Congress was a step in the right direction. But he wants Congress to go back and examine all such mandates that are already on the books.

KANSAS 1
Rural West — Salina; Hutchinson; Dodge City

Sprawling across 66 counties and more than two-thirds of Kansas' land area, the "Big First" is larger than a majority of U.S. states (including twenty-three of the twenty-six states east of the Mississippi River). This is wheat-growing and cattle-raising country, dotted with small cities (none with more than 42,500 residents) and otherwise sparsely populated.

While much of the nation was enjoying an economic boom during the 1980s, western Kansas endured a period of "farm crisis" along with the typical vagaries of drought and freeze. These factors, along with continuing farm mechanization and concentration of land ownership, exacerbated population decline: Most counties in the 1st lost people in the 1980s.

But those who want to work in western Kansas can. Unemployment is extraordinarily low: In December 1992, several western counties had jobless rates below 2 percent.

The 1st's voting traditions are heavily Republican. The 1st's GOP proclivities were especially apparent in 1996, with two of its erstwhile congressmen — Robert Dole (1961-1969) and Pat Roberts (1981-1997) — on the ballot for president and senator, respectively. Dole and Moran won majorities in every county.

The two largest population centers are in the 1st's eastern reaches. Salina (Saline County) is a traditional farm-market town, but it has an industrial element. Beech Aircraft has a factory here; food products, car batteries and light bulbs are also produced. Abilene (Dickinson County) is the site of Dwight D. Eisenhower's burial place and his presidential library.

Industry in Hutchinson (Reno County) is largely farm- and food-related. Hutchinson also is the site of the annual Kansas State Fair. The city of McPherson is nearby to the north; Emporia is at the district's eastern edge.

In recent years, the nation's meatpacking industry has dispersed from big-city stockyards to smaller towns closer to the Midwest's cattle ranches. Such southwest Kansas locales as Garden City and Dodge City have benefited from the trend and bucked Kansas' population slump. Finney County (Garden City) had the state's largest population increase (32 percent) during the 1980s, a boost fueled by Mexican and Asian immigrants who came to work in the huge IBP and Monfort beef-processing plants.

An Excel beef plant is the heart of Dodge City's economy. But the town also relies on a tourist trade based on its "Wild West" history. At the district's western edge is a sparsely populated region with some strong GOP allegiances. Dole got 76 percent of the votes in Wallace County, along the Colorado border.

At the district's center is Russell, Dole's hometown. It came as no surprise that Russell County cast the state's highest percentage of the presidential vote for Dole (79 percent). Just west is Ellis County: populated largely by farmers of German and Russian extraction, Ellis developed a Democratic habit that is abetted by the presence of Fort Hays State University. It was the only 1st District county that Bill Clinton carried in 1992, but Dole won it handily.

1990 Population: 619,370. White 583,625 (94%), Black 8,155 (1%), Other 27,590 (4%). Hispanic origin 31,962 (5%). 18 and over 452,729 (73%), 62 and over 124,511 (20%). Median age: 35.

HOUSE ELECTIONS

1996 General		
Jerry Moran (R)	191,899	(73%)
John Divine (D)	63,948	(24%)
Bill Earnest (LIBERT)	5,298	(2%)
1996 Primary		
Jerry Moran (R)	79,119	(76%)
R.W. Yeager (R)	15,376	(15%)
Bert Fisher (R)	9,887	(9%)

CAMPAIGN FINANCE

	Receipts	Receipts from PACs	Expend-itures
1996			
Moran (R)	$510,370	$109,036 (21%)	$430,261
Divine (D)	$84,191	0	$82,631

DISTRICT VOTE FOR PRESIDENT

1996		1992	
D	75,820 (28%)	**D**	81,526 (28%)
R	167,194 (62%)	**R**	123,019 (42%)
I	25,052 (9%)	**I**	85,550 (29%)

KEY VOTES

1997

Ban "partial birth" abortions — Y

2 Jim Ryun (R)

Of Topeka — Elected 1996, 1st term

Biographical Information
Born: April 29, 1947, Wichita, Kan.
Education: U. of Kansas, B.A. 1970.
Occupation: Motivational speaker; author; product consultant; olympic athlete.
Family: Wife, Anne Snider; four children.
Religion: Presbyterian.
Political Career: No previous office.
Capitol Office: 511 Cannon Bldg. 20515; 225-6601.

Committees
Banking & Financial Services
Financial Institutions & Consumer Credit
National Security
Military Personnel; Military Procurement
Small Business
Regulatory Reform & Paperwork Reduction

The Path to Washington: Ryun, a former Olympic runner who once held the world record for the mile, joins a handful of other well-known athletes in Congress. During his 1996 House campaign, he benefited from his high name recognition in Kansas, where his athletic exploits made him a local celebrity.

His arrival in the House resulted from an unusual chain of events. When Senate Majority Leader Bob Dole announced in May 1996 that he would leave the Senate to campaign full time for the presidency, 2nd District freshman Republican Rep. Sam Brownback decided to seek election to the remainder of Dole's unexpired term.

That created an open contest for Brownback's House seat, and Ryun was viewed from the outset as the front-runner. A social and fiscal conservative, Ryun, who had worked as a motivational speaker and been involved in sports camps, gained the backing of the conservative wing of Kansas' divided Republican Party.

But he faced a three-way contest for the nomination, drawing two more-moderate candidates: Douglas S. Wright, a former mayor of Topeka; and Cheryl Brown Henderson, whose family had been involved in the landmark *Brown v. Board of Education* school desegregation case.

With such a late start to the primary campaign, none of the Republican candidates could amass a large campaign treasury. Meanwhile, Democrat John Frieden, a well-funded lawyer who had won a $50 million tax settlement for Kansas military retirees who were being unfairly taxed, faced no primary challenge.

While Ryun highlighted "family values" and economic issues, Wright presented himself as the only candidate in the race with political experience. Henderson made a strong appeal to women voters.

Ryun, who made the U.S. Olympic squad as a high-schooler in 1964 and won the silver medal in the 1,500-meter race at the 1968 Mexico City Games, was aided by the media focus on the 1996 Olympic Games in Atlanta during the weeks leading up to the August primary, which Ryun won with a comfortable 62 percent.

In the general election, Frieden, a moderate-to-conservative Democrat, tried to paint Ryun as too extreme for the district.

In particular, Democrats tried to focus attention on an article Ryun and his wife, Anne, wrote in which they advocated a "courtship" style of dating for young people. They suggested that a boy should seek permission from a girl's father before asking her out and that there should be no dating at all unless the couple's ultimate intention is to marry — rules the Ryuns say they carry out with their own children.

Ryun's campaign, meanwhile, expressed frustration with this focus, contending that while Ryun stands by his writings, his family should be off-limits. Ryun supports a $500-per-child tax credit and calls for cutting the taxes paid by small businesses. His social conservative philosophy includes opposition to abortion and support of school vouchers.

While Frieden had backing from most Democrats and Ryun gained support from conservative Republicans, including conservative Christian and anti-abortion groups, the two fought for the votes of moderate Republicans. Frieden chopped away at much of Ryun's huge early lead in the polls but failed to overtake him; Ryun won with 52 percent of the vote.

Ryun joins several other high-profile former athletes in the House GOP ranks. These include Jim Bunning of Kentucky, a pitcher who was inducted into baseball's Hall of Fame in 1996, and Oklahomans Steve Largent, who starred at wide receiver for the Seattle Seahawks, and J. C. Watts, who quarterbacked the University of Oklahoma Sooners and played professional football.

Ryun will divide his time in the 105th among assignments on the Banking and Financial Services, National Security, and Small Business committees.

Sworn in early to succeed Brownback (who was sworn in early to the Senate), Ryun leapfrogged his classmates in seniority.

KANSAS 2
East — Topeka; Leavenworth; Pittsburg

The 25-county 2nd sweeps from Kansas' eastern corners, touching Nebraska to the north and Oklahoma to the south and making up most of Kansas' border with Missouri in between.

Two-thirds of the residents live in or north of Shawnee County. Topeka (the state capital and the third-biggest city in Kansas, with nearly 120,000 residents), Leavenworth and Manhattan are here. The small city of Pittsburg, with 17,800 residents, is the biggest town in the 2nd's southern reaches. In the 1994 gubernatorial contest, Republican Gov. Bill Graves bested the district's former Democratic Rep. Jim Slattery in all but two counties, a southern one added in redistricting and one in Slattery's old northern base.

In the 1992 presidential race, George Bush barely won the 2nd, and four years later it was the only Kansas district not to give Bob Dole a majority of its votes. (He got 49 percent.) Sam Brownback, who represented this district in the 104th Congress, and Pat Roberts carried every county in the 2nd en route to election to the Senate in 1996, and Ryun lost just three of the district's counties. Republicans run well in the district's more rural northern and south-central regions, while Democrats are strongest in the urbanized north-central area influenced by Topeka and Kansas City, Mo., and in the blue-collar, southeast corner of Kansas.

The 11 northern counties that made up Slattery's longtime base include numerous state employees and a scattering of minority-group concentrations. The coal mines and oil fields of southeastern Kansas long ago drew Southern Democrats and Eastern European immigrants (because of whom this hilly area was nicknamed "the Balkans"). Although these resource industries faded, there is enough remaining manufacturing to sustain a blue-collar Democratic vote.

State government is Topeka's largest employer. Medical centers, including the Menninger Foundation's psychiatric facilities, employ thousands. The economy includes an industrial component. Goodyear Tire and Rubber Co. and the Burlington Northern Santa Fe Railway are leading employers.

To the west is Manhattan with Kansas State University (18,500 students); this agriculture-oriented school gives Riley County a conservative tone that is reinforced by the military community at Fort Riley, which sprawls into Geary County and is home to the Army's 1st Infantry Division.

Geary has a substantial minority population — nearly a quarter is black — and a fair number of Democrats. But the county, like neighboring Riley, votes consistently GOP for higher offices.

At the district's eastern edge is Leavenworth, home to the well-known federal penitentiary and the fort that hosts the Army's Command and General Staff College. Leavenworth County has been drawn into Kansas City, Mo.'s, suburbia; its population grew 17 percent in the 1980s.

To the north and south of Topeka is mainly farmland where soybeans are grown, hogs are raised and mostly Republican votes are cast. Most of the rural counties have suffered the kind of population slump seen in the 1st District.

1990 Population: 619,391. White 558,318 (90%), Black 38,940 (6%), Other 22,133 (4%). Hispanic origin 18,390 (3%). 18 and over 458,157 (74%), 62 and over 104,237 (17%). Median age: 33.

HOUSE ELECTIONS

1996 General		
Jim Ryun (R)	131,592	(52%)
John Frieden (D)	114,644	(45%)
Art Clack (LIBERT)	5,842	(2%)
1996 Primary		
Jim Ryun (R)	48,602	(62%)
Douglas S. Wright (R)	19,410	(25%)
Cheryl Brown Henderson (R)	10,923	(14%)

CAMPAIGN FINANCE

	Receipts	Receipts from PACs	Expend-itures
1996			
Ryun (R)	$415,863	$105,150 (25%)	$415,606
Frieden (D)	$762,090	$181,140 (24%)	$757,637

DISTRICT VOTE FOR PRESIDENT

1996		1992	
D	100,090 (39%)	D	98,527 (36%)
R	125,095 (49%)	R	98,999 (36%)
I	27,751 (11%)	I	75,600 (28%)

KEY VOTES

1997

Ban "partial birth" abortions — Y

3 Vince Snowbarger (R)

Of Olathe — Elected 1996, 1st term

Biographical Information

Born: Sept. 16, 1949, Kankakee, Ill.

Education: Southern Nazarene U., B.A. 1971; U. of Illinois, M.A. 1974; U. of Kansas, J.D. 1977.

Occupation: Lawyer; college instructor.

Family: Wife, Carolyn, two children.

Religion: Nazarene.

Political Career: Kansas House, 1985-97, majority leader, 1993-97.

Capitol Office: 509 Cannon Bldg. 20515; 225-2865.

Committees

Banking & Financial Services
Capital Markets, Securities & Government Sponsored Enterprises

Government Reform & Oversight
Human Resources; National Economic Growth, Natural Resources & Regulatory Affairs

Small Business
Tax & Exports

The Path to Washington: Snowbarger in the 105th Congress is adjusting to life as a freshman after having held one of the top positions in the Kansas legislature: state House majority leader.

To make it to Washington, Snowbarger had to survive not only a fiercely combative primary that reflected the ideological tensions in the Kansas Republican Party, but also a hotly contested general-election campaign.

Republican Jan Meyers hewed to the moderate wing of the party in her six terms of representing the 3rd, which the GOP has held since 1961. Her fiscal conservatism and moderate stances on social issues meshed well with this mostly suburban electorate, and she won each of her elections decisively.

When Meyers decided to retire in 1996, six candidates sought the GOP nomination to succeed her. The two most prominent were Overland Park Mayor Ed Eilert, a moderate backed by Meyers and other leading GOP centrists; and Snowbarger, who drew support from the party's increasingly influential social conservative wing.

Eilert attacked Snowbarger for saying he would vote to repeal the current ban on the manufacture and sale of certain semiautomatic assault-style weapons. Snowbarger argued that the ban is ineffective.

Eilert and Snowbarger traded charges on fiscal policy and other issues, including abortion: Snowbarger is anti-abortion, while Eilert, like Meyers, supports abortion rights. Although he was outspent by almost 3-to-1 by Eilert, Snowbarger had enough grass-roots backing to emerge on top of the pack in the August primary.

Snowbarger squared off in the general with Democrat Judy Hancock, an attorney who had garnered a respectable 43 percent in her 1994 challenge to Meyers.

Hancock also attacked Snowbarger on the gun issue, specifically pointing out his support in the state legislature of a bill that would have allowed people to carry a concealed weapon after obtaining a permit, training and certification. Snowbarger argued that such legislation is "gun control at its finest."

In part because Hancock had no legislative record to attack, Snowbarger tried to make the Democrat's credibility a central issue, especially in the campaign's latter stages. He accused Hancock of having a poor voting record and of overstating her importance in the U.S. trade representative's office during the Carter administration.

Democrats thought Snowbarger's conservatism in this politically moderate district would work to Hancock's advantage. While most Democrats lined up with Hancock and conservative Republicans backed Snowbarger, the two vied for the votes of moderate Republicans.

Snowbarger, though, was able to pick up endorsements from Meyers and other key moderates. In the end, that helped boost Snowbarger to a narrow victory, 50 percent to 45 percent.

Snowbarger hews to the conservative creed that as much power as possible should be devolved from the federal government to the states. His campaign slogan was "Send a leader to Congress," and in seeking the 3rd he stressed his legislative experience, including his dozen years in the state House (the last four of which he spent as majority leader). He touted his work with the business community, citing his efforts to reduce certain business-related taxes. A lawyer, Snowbarger also has a background in areas such as estate planning and landlord-tenant relations.

For his first term in Congress, the Republican leadership gave Snowbarger assignments on three committees: Banking and Financial Services, Government Reform and Oversight, and Small Business, which Meyers chaired in the 104th Congress. Snowbarger, who holds a master's degree in political science in addition to his law degree, said he first ran for office at the suggestion of a student at MidAmerica Nazarene College, where he has taught history, political science and law.

KANSAS 3
Kansas City region — Overland Park; Lawrence

The 3rd, bordering Missouri in eastern Kansas, differs markedly from the state's other districts. Geographically compact, it is almost entirely within the metropolitan sphere of Kansas City, Mo. Its population is mainly in the graceful suburbs of Johnson County, in the grittier urban environs of Kansas City, Kan., and in Lawrence (home to the University of Kansas, which enrolls about 21,000 at its Lawrence campus).

There are sharp contrasts within the 3rd. Non-Hispanic whites make up more than 90 percent of Johnson County's population. But more than a third of the residents in Kansas City (in neighboring Wyandotte County) are black or Hispanic. The 1990 census reported a poverty rate in Johnson County of 3.6 percent; Wyandotte's rate was nearly five times higher.

Johnson County, with more than 350,000 people, dominates the 3rd. It is Republican turf that usually tilts the district to GOP candidates. But Wyandotte County sometimes provides a counterbalance that gives Democrats a chance.

In 1992, Bill Clinton scored a rare Democratic win over George Bush in the 3rd, thanks to Clinton's 55 percent showing in Wyandotte and Bush's mediocre 44 percent plurality in Johnson. In 1996, Clinton amassed 63 percent in Wyandotte (the only Kansas county to give Clinton a majority of its votes), but Dole captured 58 percent in Johnson to attain a majority districtwide. In the House race, Snowbarger's 56 percent in Johnson compensated for his 29 percent showing in Wyandotte.

Johnson has experienced a population boom since the 1960s; from 1990 to 1996, it was Kansas' second-fastest growing county. This rapid growth has turned Overland Park into a satellite city with more than 110,000 residents.

Numerous companies are based in Johnson, which bills itself as "Executive Country." Westwood is home to U.S. Sprint. Residential growth has spread to exurban areas west of Overland Park. Olathe, the county seat, has more than 63,000 residents. Lenexa, a farm town of 2,400 in 1960, is now a city of 34,000.

Bordering to the north is Wyandotte County and Kansas City. Overshadowed by its namesake across the Missouri River, Kansas City, Kan., is an industrial town that has had its share of Rust Belt blues due to factory closures and the long-term decline of urban stockyards. But Kansas City maintains a large industrial base and has attracted some growth in its biotechnology sector. A new federal courthouse here and the transfer of a regional Housing and Urban Development office from Kansas City, Mo., have provided a boost.

To the west, the 3rd takes in Lawrence and most of Douglas County. The county's eastern portions along state Route 10 are becoming increasingly suburban. University-centered Lawrence has some liberal activists, but the outlying farm areas lean Republican.

At the district's southern end is Miami County, which is lightly populated and has a Republican tilt, though that has been tempered by some recent economic troubles.

1990 Population: 619,439. White 540,210 (87%), Black 55,263 (9%), Other 23,966 (4%). Hispanic origin 20,395 (3%). 18 and over 455,833 (74%), 62 and over 77,999 (13%). Median age: 32.

HOUSE ELECTIONS

1996 General		
Vince Snowbarger (R)	139,169	(50%)
Judy Hancock (D)	126,848	(45%)
Randy Gardner (REF)	9,495	(3%)
Charles Clack (LIBERT)	3,752	(1%)
1996 Primary		
Vince Snowbarger (R)	31,341	(44%)
Ed Eilert (R)	28,453	(40%)
Greg J. Schoofs (R)	4,307	(6%)
Anne B. Lyddon (R)	3,378	(5%)
Richard "Rode" Rodewald (R)	2,721	(4%)
Bonnie Rahimian (R)	1,445	(2%)

CAMPAIGN FINANCE

	Receipts	Receipts from PACs	Expend-itures
1996			
Snowbarger (R)	$475,860	$191,881 (40%)	$465,869
Hancock (D)	$839,786	$276,614 (33%)	$840,595

DISTRICT VOTE FOR PRESIDENT

1996		1992	
D	121,172 (42%)	**D**	116,729 (38%)
R	144,916 (50%)	**R**	114,220 (37%)
I	18,173 (6%)	**I**	75,608 (25%)

KEY VOTES

1997

Ban "partial birth" abortions — Y

4 Todd Tiahrt (R)

Of Goddard — Elected 1994, 2nd term

Biographical Information

Born: June 15, 1951, Vermillion, S.D.

Education: Evangel College, B.A. 1975; Southwest Missouri State U., M.B.A. 1989.

Occupation: College instructor; airline company manager.

Family: Wife, Vicki Holland; three children.

Religion: Assembly of God.

Political Career: Republican nominee for Kan. House, 1990; Kan. Senate, 1993-95.

Capitol Office: 428 Cannon Bldg. 20515; 225-6216.

Committees

Appropriations

District of Columbia; Military Construction; Transportation

In Washington: Tiahrt is one of the dozen or so Class of 1994 Republicans who have compiled records of nearly unalloyed conservatism even though they represent politically marginal districts. On more than one occasion in the 104th Congress, he took a stand to the right of House GOP leaders, because he felt they were insufficiently committed to balancing the budget.

He also riled Rules Committee Chairman Gerald B.H. Solomon of New York by insisting on an amendment to the fiscal 1997 Treasury-Postal spending bill that blocked the automatic cost of living adjustment (COLA) that Congress voted itself in 1989. When Tiahrt and other backers of the amendment went before the Rules Committee in July 1996, Solomon was clearly not thrilled with the proposal. He told them what a difficult time he had putting five children through college on a congressional salary. "You have to have a living wage here," Solomon said. "We can't have a Congress just of millionaires."

But the amendment made it to the floor, where it passed overwhelmingly, 352-67.

Despite Tiahrt's independent streak, in the 105th he was awarded a seat on Appropriations. That committee was once the exclusive province of leadership loyalists, but GOP leaders have put some of their politically vulnerable members there, hoping to shore up their re-election prospects. So as Tiahrt exercises his commitment to reduce federal spending, he also may be able to steer some federal dollars to his district.

In October 1995, he touted his success at securing funding on the energy and water spending bill for construction of two flood control levees in his district, saying: "I am an unapologetic advocate for the 4th District of Kansas."

Tiahrt has bucked the GOP leadership on several high-profile votes. He and 11 of his GOP classmates voted "no" in early 1996 when House Speaker Newt Gingrich asked his troops to vote to end a partial government shutdown that had resulted from a breakdown in budget negotiations between Congress and the Clinton White House. Gingrich and many other Republicans worried that the public was blaming the House GOP for the closure, so he sought to end the stalemate.

But Tiahrt and a few others balked. "We've seen no indication on the part of the administration that they're willing to negotiate in good faith," he told the Denver Post in December 1995. "This could be our last, best hope to get a balanced budget. If we don't get it now, it could slip through our fingers. This is what we came here for. . . . It's both a moral and an economic duty."

Tiahrt also jumped ship when it came time in June 1996 to approve the final version of the fiscal 1997 GOP budget agreement. He complained that the agreement allowed the deficit to bump up for two years and contained an additional $4 billion in domestic spending, added at the insistence of the Senate. Tiahrt was among 19 Republicans — 16 of them freshmen — who voted against the plan, which passed only narrowly, 216-211.

And in September 1996, he was among 24 Republicans opposing a $610 billion omnibus spending bill for fiscal 1997. The dissenters complained that the bill was larded with unnecessary spending, but most GOP lawmakers were eager for a deal with President Clinton so they could adjourn Congress and hit the campaign trail.

Tiahrt's main crusade in the 104th, however, was his frustrating battle to close the Department of Energy (DOE), which he said needs to be "privatized, consolidated and eliminated."

At the outset of the 104th, the Republican freshmen embarked on an ambitious project aimed at abolishing several Cabinet departments. Chosen to head a GOP task force that studied ways to dismantle the nation's energy programs, Tiahrt concluded, "It's time to turn the lights out at the Department of Energy." In June 1995, Tiahrt's task force recommended taking away DOE's Cabinet status within six months and abolishing the department in three years.

But the Energy Department counted some powerful defenders among senior Republicans, especially in the Senate, where Budget Chairman Pete V. Domenici of New Mexico gave a cold

KANSAS 4
South central — Wichita

The 4th takes in a 12-county stretch in south-central Kansas. But the district is dominated by Kansas' largest city, Wichita (Sedgwick County). Sedgwick provides more than two-thirds of the district's population; Wichita alone, with more than 300,000 residents, makes up nearly half.

A center for military, commercial and general aviation aircraft production, Wichita has a large number of blue-collar whites with roots in Oklahoma, Texas and elsewhere in the South. Blacks and Hispanics make up about 16 percent of Wichita's population, a modest proportion by big-city standards but huge compared with the rest of the 4th.

The Democratic traditions of the district's Southern whites and the strong partisan affiliation of minority voters have boosted some centrist Democratic candidates for statewide office. But the 4th's overall tone is generally conservative.

Bob Dole easily defeated Bill Clinton here in 1996, carrying all 12 counties partly or wholly within the district. Republican Bill Graves swept the district in his successful 1994 gubernatorial bid. And in his 1994 upset victory over former Democratic Rep. Dan Glickman, Tiahrt carried every county but one. Tiahrt had a more difficult time in 1996. He again won every county but one (Cowley), but kept his seat by only 3 percentage points.

While many industrial cities struggled during the 1980s, Wichita rode the wings of its aviation industry. The decade's big growth in defense spending boosted Boeing's military aircraft lines in Wichita; the national business boom aided Learjet, Cessna and Beech, civilian plane-builders affiliated with larger companies but based in Wichita.

The decline in defense spending is creating local concerns not only about the aviation industry but also the future of McConnell Air Force Base, site of a B-1 bomber fleet. The base employs close to 3,000 active duty members and over 400 civilians. The early 1990s recession and the downward spiral of the nation's passenger airlines already have unsettled aviation's commercial side. Once rock-solid, Boeing cut its Wichita work force by more than 20 percent in 1993.

The city is hardly a one-industry town. The Coleman recreation equipment company and the Pizza Hut restaurant chain are headquartered here, as is Koch Industries, a leader in development of southern Kansas' oil and gas resources. Wichita State University (14,500 students) also is a major employer.

Wichita has developed a growing suburbia. Derby, a few miles south on State Highway 15, has nearly 15,000 residents, almost double its population 20 years ago. There has been some spillover into Butler County (El Dorado).

Much of the rest of the 4th (including rural parts of Sedgwick) is farmland. Sumner County, on the Oklahoma border, is Kansas' leading wheat-growing county. Wheat is also important to Harper and Kingman counties to the west. Cattle graze in sparsely populated Greenwood, Elk and Chautauqua counties to the east.

1990 Population: 619,374. White 549,833 (89%), Black 40,718 (7%), Other 28,823 (5%). Hispanic origin 22,923 (4%). 18 and over 449,241 (73%), 62 and over 99,483 (16%). Median age: 33.

shoulder to shutting down DOE. New Mexico is home to several DOE facilities, including the Los Alamos and Sandia national laboratories.

Undaunted, Tiahrt in the fall of 1995 pounced on Energy Secretary Hazel R. O'Leary when she drew media attention for her high-cost official travels and for paying a private company to monitor coverage of DOE in the media. O'Leary defended her frequent travels overseas, saying they had yielded more than $19 billion in contracts for U.S. businesses. But Tiahrt and more than 70 other Republicans sent Clinton a letter demanding O'Leary's resignation.

Tiahrt's interest in shrinking federal programs does not extend to one project targeted by some other deficit hawks in Congress: NASA's space station. On the Science Committee in the 104th, he opposed efforts to terminate funding for the project. Before coming to Congress, Tiahrt worked in Wichita for Boeing, a space station contractor.

Tiahrt's Appropriations subcommittees include Military Construction and Transportation, and from those venues he can look out for Wichita's military, commercial and general aviation manufacturers. In addition to the military work Boeing does in Wichita, the city also is home to civilian plane builders Learjet, Cessna and Beech. The general aviation sector is rebounding, thanks in large part to a revised aircraft liability law enacted in the 103rd Congress. The Democrat whom Tiahrt ousted from the 4th in 1994, Dan Glickman, was a key shaper of that legislation.

Tiahrt did not mention Glickman when he rose in the 104th to extol the new liability law for helping companies such as Cessna get out from under the burden of lawsuits involving single-engine planes constructed years ago. With litigation costs reduced, Tiahrt said, Cessna could build a new manufacturing plant in Independence, Kansas.

Tiahrt has also endorsed building more B-2 bombers than the 20 planes the Pentagon says are sufficient. The B-2 was one of the projects Tiahrt worked on at Boeing. Despite supporting the high-cost B-2, Tiahrt voted in June 1996 to cap overall defense spending, and he voted to freeze the fiscal 1997 defense budget at the fiscal 1996 level.

At Home: Arguably the biggest surprise winner in the 1994 Republican sweep, Tiahrt ambushed one of Kansas' most successful Democratic vote-getters — nine-term Rep. Glickman — with a campaign that spent modestly and peaked late, not arousing Glickman to worry until it was too late for him to react. Tiahrt also successfully defended the 4th in 1996, winning with 50 percent of the vote despite a determined effort by Democrats to take back the district.

Tiahrt got involved in Republican politics while working as a manager at Boeing. He first took to the campaign trail in 1990, challenging a Democratic state House incumbent. The initial election tally gave Tiahrt a 24-vote lead, but a recount showed him a loser by eight votes. He chaired the 4th District GOP for two years, then in 1992 took on an appointed Democratic state senator. He won that election with 54 percent of the vote.

Tiahrt's entry into the 1994 House race in the 4th did not cause any stir at first. Glickman had survived a close race in 1992 against a Republican who was regarded as more appealing than Tiahrt.

Tiahrt, who was best known in the state Senate for pushing legislation allowing people to carry concealed weapons, won a three-way GOP primary with 54 percent. Glickman's polls throughout the summer showed him leading in the 30-point range, but Tiahrt mobilized a grassroots network that drew heavily from the ranks of the Kansas Republican Coalition for Life, an anti-abortion group affiliated with Phyllis Schlafly's Eagle Forum. Tiahrt kept chipping away at Glickman, linking him to the unpopular Clinton.

With November near, Tiahrt released a poll showing him within 7 percentage points, and a TV debate was hastily arranged for the Sunday before the election. Glickman tried to portray Tiahrt as a product of the radical right, causing Tiahrt to say nine times that Glickman was "practicing the politics of fear and deception." Glickman defended his support for an assault weapons ban and the Brady bill, but those stands alienated some blue-collar voters who had backed him in the past.

In the end, Glickman did relatively well in high-income, traditionally Republican precincts, where some voters did not warm to Tiahrt's close association with conservative religious activists. But Glickman ran only even in the working-class neighborhoods of south Wichita. Tiahrt carried all but one county in the district and prevailed by six points. In celebrating on election night, his supporters sang "What a Mighty God We Serve." Glickman went on to become secretary of Agriculture in the Clinton administration.

In 1996, Tiahrt faced former U.S. Attorney Randy Rathbun, who cast himself as a Democratic moderate. Rathbun gained recognition for handling the Kansas portion of the federal investigation into the 1995 bombing of the Alfred P. Murrah Federal Building in Oklahoma City. In his campaign, Rathbun focused on both crime and education. Tiahrt saw his tally drop to 50 percent, but that was enough to win by 3 percentage points.

HOUSE ELECTIONS

1996 General		
Todd Tiahrt (R)	128,486	(50%)
Randy Rathbun (D)	119,544	(47%)
Seth L. Warren (LIBERT)	8,361	(3%)
1994 General		
Todd Tiahrt (R)	111,653	(53%)
Dan Glickman (D)	99,366	(47%)

CAMPAIGN FINANCE

	Receipts	Receipts from PACs	Expend-itures
1996			
Tiahrt (R)	$921,795	$314,122 (34%)	$903,348
Rathbun (D)	$608,638	$212,341 (35%)	$608,355
1994			
Tiahrt (R)	$203,438	$32,020 (16%)	$199,973
Glickman (D)	$675,993	$298,515 (44%)	$693,534

DISTRICT VOTE FOR PRESIDENT

	1996		1992
D	90,577 (35%)	**D**	93,652 (33%)
R	146,040 (56%)	**R**	113,713 (40%)
I	21,663 (8%)	**I**	75,600 (27%)

KEY VOTES

1997	
Ban "partial birth" abortions	Y
1996	
Approve farm bill	Y
Deny public education to illegal immigrants	Y
Repeal ban on certain assault-style weapons	Y
Increase minimum wage	N
Freeze defense spending	Y
Approve welfare overhaul	Y
1995	
Approve balanced-budget constitutional amendment	Y
Relax Clean Water Act regulations	Y
Oppose limits on environmental regulations	N
Reduce projected Medicare spending	Y
Approve GOP budget with tax and spending cuts	Y

VOTING STUDIES

	Presidential Support		Party Unity		Conservative Coalition	
Year	S	O	S	O	S	O
1996	34	65	92	7	88	12
1995	20	80	97	3	94	5

INTEREST GROUP RATINGS

Year	ADA	AFL-CIO	CCUS	ACU
1996	5	n/a	94	100
1995	0	0	100	100

KENTUCKY

Governor: Paul E. Patton (D)
First elected: 1995
Length of term: 4 years
Term expires: 12/99
Salary: $90,919.44
Term limit: 2 terms
Phone: (502) 564-2611
Born: May 26, 1937; Fallsburg, Ky.
Education: U. of Kentucky, B.S. 1959.
Occupation: Coal company executive.
Family: Wife, Judi; four children.
Religion: Unspecified.
Political Career: Ky. Democratic Party chairman, 1981-83; lieutenant governor, 1991-95.

Lt. Gov.: Stephan L. Henry (D)
First elected: 1995
Length of term: 4 years
Term expires: 12/99
Salary: $69,412
Phone: (502) 564-7562

State election official: (502) 564-7100
Democratic headquarters: (502) 695-4828
Republican headquarters: (502) 875-5130

REDISTRICTING

Kentucky lost one seat in reapportionment, dropping from seven districts to six. The legislature passed the map Dec. 18, 1991; the governor signed it Dec. 20. New map passed by the legislature April 1, 1994, and signed by governor April 13; it became effective after the 1994 general election.

STATE LEGISLATURE

General Assembly. Meets January through mid-April.

Senate: 38 members, 4-year terms
1996 breakdown: 20D, 18R; 36 men, 2 women
Salary: $100/day and $74,80/day expenses
Phone: (502) 564-8100

House of Representatives: 100 members, 2-year terms
1996 breakdown: 64D, 36R; 89 men, 11 women
Salary: $100/day and $74.80/day expenses
Phone: (502) 564-8100

URBAN STATISTICS

City	Population
Louisville	269,063
Mayor Jerry Abramson, D	
Lexington	225,366
Mayor Pam Miller, I	
Owensboro	53,549
Mayor Waymond Morris, N-P	
Covington	43,264
Mayor Denny Bowman, D	
Bowling Green	40,641
Mayor Eldon Renard, N-P	

U.S. CONGRESS

Senate: 1 D, 1 R
House: 1 D, 5 R

TERM LIMITS

For state offices: No

ELECTIONS

1996 Presidential Vote

Bill Clinton	46%
Bob Dole	45%
Ross Perot	9%

1992 Presidential Vote

Bill Clinton	45%
George Bush	41%
Ross Perot	14%

1988 Presidential Vote

George Bush	56%
Michael S. Dukakis	44%

POPULATION

1990 population		3,685,296
1980 population		3,660,777
Percent change		+1%
Rank among states:		23
White		92%
Black		7%
Hispanic		1%
Asian or Pacific islander		<1%
Urban		52%
Rural		48%
Born in state		77%
Foreign-born		1%
Under age 18	954,094	26%
Ages 18-64	2,264,357	61%
65 and older	466,845	13%
Median age		33

MISCELLANEOUS

Capital: Frankfort
Number of counties: 120
Per capita income: $15,539 (1991)
Rank among states: 42
Total area: 40,410 sq. miles
Rank among states: 37

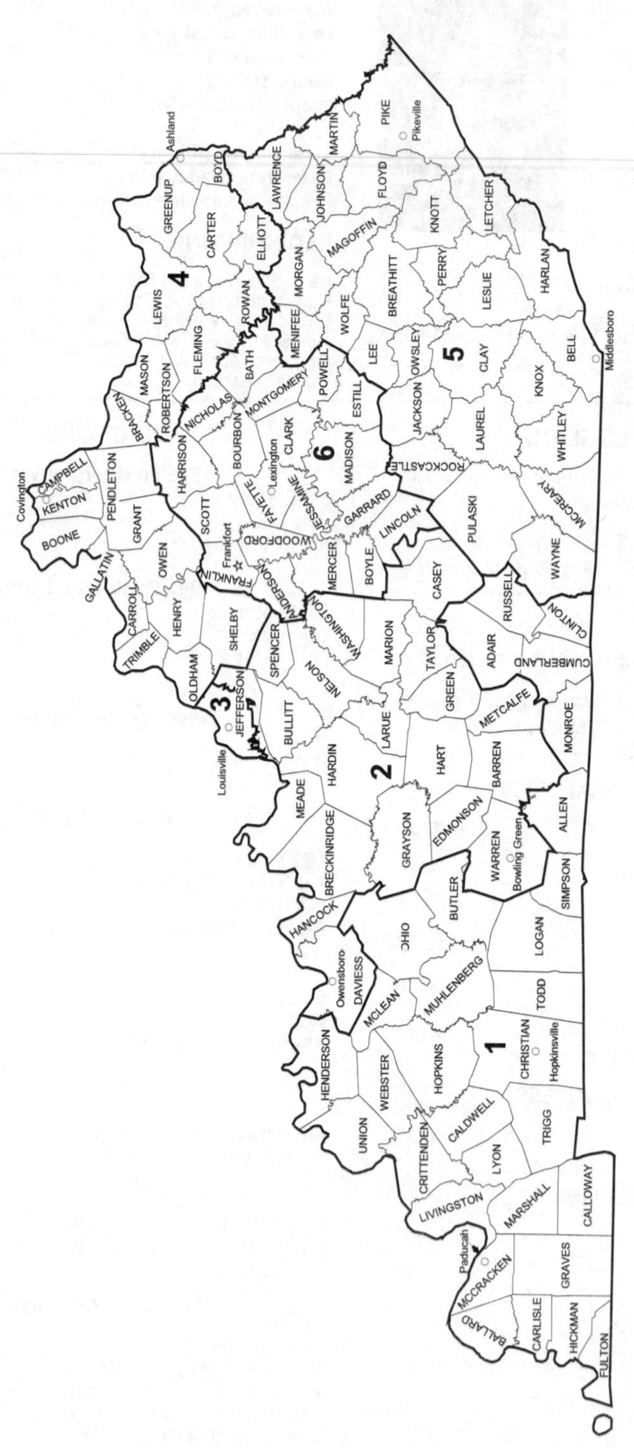
Ashland
Covington
Lexington
Frankfort
Louisville
Owensboro
Bowling Green
Hopkinsville
Paducah
Pikeville
Middlesboro
1
2
3
4
5
6
BOONE
KENTON
CAMPBELL
PENDLETON
GRANT
GALLATIN
OWEN
CARROLL
TRIMBLE
HENRY
OLDHAM
SHELBY
FRANKLIN
SCOTT
HARRISON
BRACKEN
ROBERTSON
MASON
LEWIS
GREENUP
BOYD
CARTER
ELLIOTT
FLEMING
ROWAN
BATH
NICHOLAS
BOURBON
MONTGOMERY
MENIFEE
MORGAN
LAWRENCE
JOHNSON
MARTIN
PIKE
FLOYD
MAGOFFIN
KNOTT
LETCHER
PERRY
BREATHITT
WOLFE
POWELL
CLARK
FAYETTE
WOODFORD
JESSAMINE
ANDERSON
MERCER
BOYLE
GARRARD
MADISON
ESTILL
LEE
OWSLEY
JACKSON
CLAY
LESLIE
HARLAN
BELL
KNOX
LAUREL
WHITLEY
ROCKCASTLE
LINCOLN
PULASKI
MCCREARY
WAYNE
CASEY
RUSSELL
CLINTON
CUMBERLAND
ADAIR
TAYLOR
GREEN
METCALFE
MONROE
MARION
WASHINGTON
NELSON
SPENCER
JEFFERSON
BULLITT
LARUE
HARDIN
HART
BARREN
ALLEN
MEADE
BRECKINRIDGE
GRAYSON
EDMONSON
WARREN
SIMPSON
HANCOCK
OHIO
BUTLER
LOGAN
DAVIESS
MCLEAN
MUHLENBERG
TODD
HENDERSON
WEBSTER
HOPKINS
CHRISTIAN
UNION
CRITTENDEN
CALDWELL
TRIGG
LYON
LIVINGSTON
MARSHALL
CALLOWAY
MCCRACKEN
GRAVES
BALLARD
CARLISLE
HICKMAN
FULTON

Wendell H. Ford (D)

Of Owensboro — Elected 1974, 4th term

Biographical Information

Born: Sept. 8, 1924, Daviess County, Ky.
Education: U. of Kentucky, 1942-43.
Military Service: Army, 1945-46; National Guard, 1949-62.
Occupation: Insurance executive.
Family: Wife, Jean Neel; two children.
Religion: Baptist.
Political Career: Ky. Senate, 1965-67; lieutenant governor, 1967-71; governor, 1971-74.
Capitol Office: 173A Russell Bldg. 20510; 224-4343.

Committees

Commerce, Science & Transportation
Aviation (ranking); Communications; Consumer Affairs, Foreign Commerce & Tourism
Energy & Natural Resources
Energy Research Development Production & Regulation (ranking); Water & Power
Rules & Administration (ranking)
Joint Printing (ranking)

Minority Whip

In Washington: Having already served longer in the Senate than any other Kentuckian — 22 years, six as the No. 2 man in the Democratic leadership— Ford announced in March 1997 that the 105th Congress would be his last. His departure will leave the chamber notably short in the "good old boy" department, depleting the ranks of Southern Democrats whose style combined rustic charm with a courtly manner.

Ford came to Washington in 1975 calling himself "a dumb country boy with dirt between his toes," but he had in fact been in politics for more than a decade and been the state's governor from 1971 through 1974. He would be among the last senators to light up cigarettes in committee hearings and brag about his state as the "the home of good whiskey, fast horses and beautiful women." And he would prove himself among the wiliest practitioners of Senate rules and folkways in his generation.

Ford has needed his political wits about him, as his long career has coincided with a rising tide of Republicanism in his home state. By 1997, he had spent most of his Senate career in the company of a Republican junior senator (Mitch McConnell) and lived to see the state's contingent of Democrats in the House dwindle to one.

For a time in the 1980s, Ford even contemplated giving up the Senate for a return to the governorship. But he decided to stay and pursue a leadership post, finally moving into the job of Majority Whip under Majority Leader George J. Mitchell of Maine in 1991. Ford was seen as something of a conservative counterweight to Mitchell and to Mitchell's successor, Tom Daschle, D-S.D.

A Southern-style Democrat who voted for President George Bush's position 57 percent of the time in his first year as Democratic whip, Ford spoke for the conservative minority within the Democratic conference. But this role as waned in more recent years, as the Senate Democrats have lost a net of nine seats in the South beginning in 1992.

The later Ford has had more than a few partisan moments, as when he became the champion for the "motor voter" bill facilitating registration and for Democratic versions of lobbyist limits and-campaign finance reform. In the 105th Congress, Ford has been especially outspoken in supporting Democratic colleague Mary L. Landrieu's claim to the seat she won in Louisiana in 1996. As the ranking Democrat on the Senate Rules Committee, which he chaired prior to the Republican takeover in 1994, Ford opposed sending Senate investigators to Louisiana to probe charges of vote fraud lodged by Landrieu's Republican opponent, Louis P. "Woody" Jenkins.

When Senate Rules, on a straight party-line vote, launched a full-scale investiation, Ford chided his Republican counterpart, Rules Chairman John W. Warner of Virginia, in highly personal terms while the panel was still in public session. Later, his involvement in the case led to a hallway shouting match with junior committee member Rick Santorum, R-Pa., in full view of tourists.

Such outbursts have not been typical of Ford's career. Although he can be cantankerous, he has been known as an insider and a backroom player, disinclined to public duels. "Why make a speech?" he once said, "when you can sit down with your colleagues and work something out?"

In his accommodating dealmaker mode, Ford had been successful defending Kentucky's traditional interests — especially tobacco. No other issue has required him to negotiate such a fine line between the demands of his party position and those of his state. And with pressure on this industry increasing early in 1997, it seemed fitting that Ford would soon be passing the torch to others.

Even before the successful lawsuit by state attorneys general forced tobacco into bargaining for its future in 1997, Ford had been on the defensive. He had found it necessary in particular to distance himself from the active anti-smoking initiatives of President Clinton. In 1995, for example, Ford split from Clinton as the president declared nicotine an addictive drug and gave the Food and Drug Administration permission to regulate it. The FDA immediately proposed rules to strictly limit teenagers' access to cigarettes and chewing tobacco.

"My farmers lost out to zealots," he declared on the Senate floor after Clinton made the announcement. He called FDA Commissioner David A. Kessler an extremist pulling Clinton to the far left. "Americans are clearly sick and tired of this kind of intrusive over-regulation."

The FDA rules would ban tobacco advertising at sports events, in magazines that reach a significant number of children and teenagers, and within 1,000 feet of schools and playgrounds. The rules would ban tobacco vending machines and free samples.

"No one is against efforts to stop teen smoking," commented Ford, "but turning over the responsibility to the FDA is like asking one of the Hatfields to baby-sit over at the McCoys."

Clinton said he acted to stop the spread of tobacco use among youths because Congress had refused to do so. Within two months, Ford introduced legislation that would prohibit the FDA from regulating tobacco, but would provide some restrictions on advertising and tobacco access. The bill would restrict outdoor ads to 500 feet of schools and playgrounds, and restrict vending machines to supervised locations and free samples to places where youth access is denied.

During the 103rd Congress, Ford opposed Democrat-sponsored, House-passed bills to extend smoking bans to federal buildings and to international flights using U.S. airports. As chairman of the Aviation subcommittee of the Commerce, Science and Transportation panel, Ford was able to keep both measures from reaching the floor.

Ford also got help from GOP Sen. Jesse Helms of North Carolina and other tobacco-state senators to defeat an attack on the federal tobacco price support program during debate on the fiscal 1995 Agriculture appropriations bill. Ford used his status as whip to issue an unsubtle threat to go after one of Brown's parochial interests: "It gets into a position at some point that this amendment passes, the Senate will vote on increased grazing fees," Ford warned. Brown and other Western senators had blocked Clinton administration efforts to raise fees paid by ranchers to graze their livestock on federal lands. Brown's amendment was defeated on a tabling motion.

Ford touts his staunch defense of his rural constituents. As a member of the conference committee which produced the Telecommunications Act of 1996, he helped shaped the compromises that companies provide the same basic telecommunications services to all Americans, regardless of geography or income.

Working with Daschle, Ford also won an amendment to the 1996 farm bill authorizing $300 million over three years for the so-called Fund for Rural America, to help pay for rural development projects such as water and sewage grants.

Ford held sway over the Rules Committee at a time when its focus was changing. From such housekeeping matters as dispensing parking spaces and approving postage stamp disbursements, the panel was moving on to the weightier issues surrounding the Senate's efforts to clean up its image in the wake of the "Keating Five" affair, in which senators were accused of improperly intervening on behalf of an Arizona thrift operator, and allegations of sexual harassment against GOP Sen. Bob Packwood of Oregon.

But as ranking minority member, Ford has had to work harder to gain attention as a government watchdog. Early in the 104th, Ford won voice-vote approval of an amendment that codified an existing rule barring senators and staff members from taking any frequent-flier miles accrued from official travel for their own use. The amendment was to a Republican-led bill to make Congress subject to the same employment laws faced by business.

Ford was a member of a task force during the 104th Congress that designed a compromise gift-ban and lobby registration bill. It is an issue that sets him apart from McConnell, his longtime Kentucky nemesis, who vocally opposes limits on gifts and lobbying.

Ford suffered a stinging loss when he tried to soften the new time limit in the welfare overhaul of 1996. Ford offered an amendment that would have allowed federal welfare funds to be used for non-cash benefits, or vouchers, for families of welfare recipients who exceeded the five-year time limit. Democrats expected enough Republican support to win approval for the proposal, but GOP moderates acknowledged that they were pressed into maintaining the party line. Senators voted to kill the amendment 50-49.

As the 104th Congress got under way, the Supreme Court helped quell a GOP push to repeal one of Ford's pet projects. The high court refused to hear the State of California's case against the "motor voter" law that Ford sponsored and helped push to enactment in the 103rd. It allows people to register to vote when they apply for or renew a driver's license of apply for public assistance. Many Senate Republicans, including McConnell, say the law unfairly imposes requirements on states without providing the funds to pay for them. But as the new motor voters have given no discernable benefit to either party, objections to the law have begun to fade.

Ford, whose grin is often seen through a halo of cigarette smoke, typically pursues his legislative aims through private negotiations in committee, at the conference table or in the cloakroom.

He is a loyal friend of business interests, particularly those important to his state — tobacco, liquor and coal — and the one he knows best, insurance.

Ford owned two Kentucky insurance companies during most of his first decade in the Senate, and recused himself when insurance-related matters came before the Commerce Committee. But he sold his business interests to family members in 1985 and began to work actively in the industry's behalf.

At Home: In announcing his retirement, Ford

said he felt sure he could win a fifth term but did not want to spend the next two years raising the $5 million he estimated he would need. He said he would have to raise $100,000 a week, and "Mrs. Ford won't let me bring anyone home to sleep in our spare bedroom" — a jab at Clinton, who had been criticized for letting big donors use the Lincoln Bedroom at the White House.

Ford has always approached his campaigns with methodical, almost fanatic concentration. Faced with the likelihood of weak opposition in his first Senate re-election (in 1980), Ford still amassed a huge treasury. No serious challenger emerged, but he conducted an exhausting campaign anyway and crushed long-shot Republican Mary Louise Foust.

In 1986, he actually had a reason to be cautious. Two years before, his Democratic colleague, Walter D. Huddleston, had been ousted by McConnell in an upset, and Republicans hoped for a repeat performance. But in the wake of Huddleston's defeat, Ford commissioned a series of polls to test where in the state he might be in danger. He again began raising money early, and by the end of 1985 had more than enough to scare off any top-drawer opposition. He won 74 percent of the vote in 1986.

Armed with an overflowing campaign kitty again in 1992, Ford parried charges by underfunded state Sen. David L. Williams that Ford was a Washington insider whose ascent to the Democratic leadership was accompanied by a leftward veer in his voting record. Outside the rock-ribbed GOP mountain counties, not many voters believed Williams; Ford won without blinking.

While building his insurance business, Ford started in politics as a protégé of Democratic Gov. Bert Combs, for whom he worked as an aide from 1959-63. But that relationship soured. By 1971, after a term in the state Senate and one as lieutenant governor, Ford was ready for the governorship. Combs, however, decided on a comeback.

Their contest for the Democratic nomination was rough. Ford said Combs was the candidate of the "fat cats and the courthouse crowd." Combs said Ford was a "punchless promiser with both hands tied behind him by special interests." Combs had his traditional base in eastern Kentucky, but Ford did better in Louisville and the counties to the west and defeated his old mentor soundly. He had little trouble beating Republican Tom Emberton that fall.

As governor, Ford earned popularity by cutting taxes imposed under his Republican predecessor, Louie B. Nunn. This left him in good stead when he ran for the Senate in 1974 against one-term GOP incumbent Marlow W. Cook. The Ford-Cook race was no more pleasant than the earlier gubernatorial contest. Cook accused Ford of using state contracts as governor to reward his political allies. Ford labeled Cook "marvelous Marlow, the wonderful wobbler." Cook was hurt by his earlier defense of Richard M. Nixon. In a Democratic year, Ford won comfortably.

After deciding not to run for governor in 1983, Ford conducted the race vicariously by helping an ally, Lt. Gov. Martha Layne Collins, win. In 1984, he was notably less successful. He volunteered to chair the state campaign for Democratic presidential nominee Walter F. Mondale, hoping to hold down Reagan's margin and thereby protect uddleston. Mondale lost badly, and Huddleston fell with him.

SENATE ELECTIONS

1992 General

Wendell H. Ford (D)	836,888	(63%)
David L. Williams (R)	476,604	(36%)
James A. Ridenour (LIBERT)	17,366	(1%)

Previous Winning Percentages: **1986** (74%) **1980** (65%) **1974** (54%)

CAMPAIGN FINANCE

	Receipts	Receipts from PACs	Expend-itures
1992			
Ford (D)	$2,317,149	$1,312,902 (57%)	$2,076,069
Williams (R)	$345,291	$19,940 (6%)	$335,304

KEY VOTES

1997

Approve balanced-budget constitutional amendment	N
Approve chemical weapons treaty	Y
1996	
Approve farm bill	Y
Limit punitive damages in product liability cases	N
Exempt small businesses from higher minimum wage	N
Approve welfare overhaul	Y
Bar job discrimination based on sexual orientation	N
Override veto of ban on "partial birth" abortions	Y
1995	
Approve GOP budget with tax and spending cuts	N
Approve constitutional amendment barring flag desecration	Y

VOTING STUDIES

	Presidential Support		Party Unity		Conservative Coalition	
Year	**S**	**O**	**S**	**O**	**S**	**O**
1996	83	17	79	21	74	26
1995	79	21	78	22	82	16
1994	90	8	81	18	59	38
1993	92	8	86	14	80	20
1992	35	65	70	29	82	16
1991	57	43	67	33	95	5

INTEREST GROUP RATINGS

Year	ADA	AFL-CIO	CCUS	ACU
1996	70	n/a	38	40
1995	80	92	47	13
1994	60	75	30	24
1993	60	91	27	24
1992	75	92	10	15
1991	50	75	10	47

Mitch McConnell (R)

Of Louisville — Elected 1984, 3rd term

Biographical Information

Born: Feb. 20, 1942, Sheffield, Ala.
Education: U. of Louisville, B.A. 1964; U. of Kentucky, J.D. 1967.
Occupation: Lawyer.
Family: Wife, Elaine Chao; three children.
Religion: Baptist.
Political Career: Jefferson County judge/executive, 1978-85.
Capitol Office: 361A Russell Bldg. 20510; 224-2541.

Committees

Agriculture, Nutrition & Forestry
Marketing, Inspection & Product Promotion; Research, Nutrition & General Legislation (chairman)
Appropriations
Agriculture, Rural Development & Related Agencies; Commerce, Justice, State & Judiciary; Defense; Energy & Water Development; Foreign Operations (chairman)
Labor & Human Resources
Children & Families; Employment & Training
Rules & Administration
Joint Printing

In Washington: McConnell relishes his role as Darth Vader against efforts aimed at limiting the amount of money that can be spent on congressional campaigns. And no amount of force so far has been capable of defeating him. "This is about the First Amendment to the Constitution," he told a National Press Club audience in March 1997. "Political speech is at the core of the First Amendment."

Simply put, McConnell does not believe that it is constitutional to hold down campaign spending. Most efforts to change the campaign finance system revolve around offering incentives, such as public funds, for candidates who agree to limit the amount of money they spend. McConnell said that voluntary spending limits "are as voluntary as giving your wallet to a robber with a gun to your head," he said.

McConnell has been the Senate's leading opponent of legislation introduced by Sens. John McCain, R-Ariz., and Russell D. Feingold, D-Wis., which would offer incentives to limit spending. In March, he assembled a diverse group of organizations — including the American Civil Liberties Union and the National Rifle Association — to argue against the bill. "There's never been any indication of a public outcry on this issue," McConnell said. "Not a single race has been decided on it."

McConnell has another reason to object to restrictions on fundraising. In the 1998 election cycle, he will chair the National Republican Senatorial Committee.

McConnell's opposition to campaign finance legislation goes back to his first term, when in the 100th Congress he helped beat back a record-setting eight cloture votes on a Democratic bill. In the 101st and 102nd Congresses, McConnell was the Republican floor leader on campaign finance. The bill died in conference in the 101st; President George Bush vetoed a largely similar bill in the 102nd.

McConnell also headed the push to kill the Democrats' effort to change the system in the closing days of the 103rd Congress, blocking a proposal endorsed by President Clinton that again offered public financing as an incentive to hold down spending. In the end, the Republicans successfully filibustered an attempt by the Senate Democratic majority to even go to conference on the legislation. "I make no apologies for killing this turkey of a bill," McConnell said.

McConnell does agree, however, that restrictions on "soft money" — the unregulated sums used for issue-oriented advertisements and party-building activities such as get-out-the-vote drives — might be warranted. Instead of soft money, which can be raised without restrictions, he suggests that Congress drop restrictions on how much financial help political parties can give to their nominees.

As the Senate prepared in March 1997 to launch an investigation of fundraising in the 1996 election cycle, McConnell and Rick Santorum of Pennsylvania, two members of the Rules and Administration Committee, insisted that the GOP-controlled Senate focus solely on the White House and not look at congressional fundraising. With the GOP holding a mere two-seat edge on the Rules Committee, defections by the two Republicans could have killed the measure. Majority Leader Trent Lott initially agreed to McConnell and Santorum's demands, but he changed course after another group of GOP senators insisted that the probe also include Congress.

McConnell's advocacy of the First Amendment goes beyond campaign finance. In December 1995, he voted against a constitutional amendment prohibiting flag burning.

With the Republican takeover of the Senate in 1995, McConnell became chairman of the Appropriations Foreign Operations Subcommittee. In July 1996, he failed to win support for strong sanctions against Myanmar (formerly Burma). The Senate instead voted for milder restrictions in the fiscal 1997 foreign operations spending bill. McConnell initially proposed banning all U.S. investment in Myanmar, which would have forced Unocal Corp., a California-based oil company, to abandon its large stake in a billion-dollar natural gas pipeline under construction in the Andaman Sea off Myanmar. Texaco Inc., also involved in gas exploration in Myanmar, would have had to withdraw as well. With U.S. petroleum interests in Myanmar threatened by McConnell's proposal, and with the Clinton administration firmly opposed to an investment ban, the Senate backed a softer alternative proposed by Maine Republican William S. Cohen, now Defense secretary. The amendment was approved on a voice vote.

McConnell said the administration's stance, along with aggressive lobbying by Unocal, had decided the outcome.

McConnell also sits on the Agriculture, Nutrition and Forestry Committee, where he is chairman of the Research, Nutrition and General Legislation Subcommittee. But his chief interest is tobacco, a key crop in Kentucky. "When it comes to tobacco, I'm prepared to wheel and deal," he said.

As the 105th Congress convened, McConnell gave up the chairmanship of the Senate Ethics Committee. He chaired the panel as it completed its investigation of then-Sen. Bob Packwood, R-Ore. In May 1995, the committee announced that it had found "substantial credible evidence" that Packwood engaged in sexual misconduct at least 18 times with 17 women, that he altered his diaries and that he improperly solicited jobs for his ex-wife in an attempt to reduce his alimony payments. After Packwood declined to call for public hearings, the committee splintered along party lines over whether to hold them. McConnell privately threatened to retaliate by calling for similar public hearings into charges against Democratic senators. Eventually, the dispute spilled onto the Senate floor. "A wedge has been driven through the committee for the first time in this investigation," McConnell said in July.

Amid a growing perception that partisanship would stymie the Ethics Committee and allow Packwood to escape with little more than a reprimand, the committee voted, 3-3, along party lines at the end of July not to hold public hearings. In August, Democrat Barbara Boxer of California moved on the Senate floor for public hearings. The Senate defeated Boxer's motions, 48-52.

The committee, poised to issue a final verdict, then abruptly adjourned its closed-door deliberations a day later. The move was intended to give the staff time to investigate two additional allegations of sexual misconduct, one involving unwanted sexual advances against a 17-year-old minor. Packwood screamed foul. He said his lawyers had been assured that the investigation was complete, the case closed. Then he reversed his position and said he wanted to have public hearings to defend himself. Even some Packwood allies who had earlier supported his move to avoid public hearings felt betrayed.

When the Ethics Committee resumed its deliberations in September, the panel decided to drop its investigation of the two additional charges and voted on the extensive evidence already gathered. The panel unanimously adopted, 6-0, a resolution calling for Packwood's expulsion. The expulsion resolution was the first approved by the committee since 1981, when it voted to expel Harrison A. Williams Jr., D-N.J., who had been convicted in the Abscam scandal. Williams resigned on March 11, 1982, after it became apparent that two-thirds of the Senate would support the resolution.

Before the meeting, Vice Chairman Richard H. Bryan, D-Nev., told McConnell that he planned to introduce a resolution to expel Packwood. McConnell said he would make the motion himself. It was the first time that the committee had discussed punishment, and within half an hour, it became obvious that all the members thought alike on the issue. "The committee has heard enough," McConnell said. "The Senate has heard enough. The public has heard enough."

Packwood, too, finally had enough. The Senate chamber filled up as he prepared to speak. His voice cracking, Packwood tendered his resignation.

At Home: Three things brought McConnell to Congress: bloodhounds, Ronald Reagan and dogged persistence in the face of daunting odds. And three things have kept him there: bloodhounds, infighting between state Democrats and a record of looking out for Kentucky's interests.

He had his easiest race in 1996, defeating former Lt. Gov. Steven L. Beshear, 55 percent to 43 percent, to win a third term in the Democratic state. Beshear, who has also served as state attorney general, tried to paint McConnell as a dangerous ideologue for opposing campaign finance overhaul legislation while supporting much of the conservative Republican congressional agenda. But McConnell fought back, charging that Beshear was beholden to special interests because he had accepted sizable campaign contributions from PACs. McConnell also spent more than $4.5 million, over twice what Beshear spent.

McConnell was the favorite in that race, the opposite of his first try for the Senate in 1984. For much of that year, few people believed McConnell had much chance of defeating two-term Democratic Sen. Walter D. Huddleston. Even some GOP leaders complained that McConnell had a "citified" image that would not play well in most parts of Kentucky; his base was metropolitan Louisville, where he had twice been elected Jefferson County judge, the county's top administrative post.

McConnell's campaign struggled for quite a while; he even lost the endorsement of Marlow Cook, the last Republican to win a Senate election in Kentucky and McConnell's boss when he was a Senate aide in the 1960s. At times, it seemed that McConnell's bid was surviving on little more than his fierce ambition to be a senator, a goal he admitted having harbored for two decades.

Then McConnell hit upon a clever, homey gimmick to get across his claim that Huddleston had limited influence and was often absent from committee meetings. McConnell aired TV ads showing bloodhounds sniffing frantically around Washington in search of the incumbent.

The hound dog gimmick got people talking about a race they had ignored, and many concluded that McConnell had a point — they were not exactly sure what Huddleston had been doing since he went to Congress in 1973. The incumbent, an easygoing mainstream Democrat, had worked behind the scenes on Kentucky issues, such as tobacco and coal, never causing much controversy and never earning much publicity. With President Ronald Reagan crushing Walter F. Mondale by more than 280,000 votes statewide, McConnell had long coattails to latch on to. He won by four-tenths of a percentage point.

In 1990, McConnell was tabbed as one of the most vulnerable Republicans up for re-election. But, unlike his predecessor, McConnell came out early and tough. He brought back the TV bloodhounds, this time to bark up the fact that he had made 99 percent of the votes cast during his first term.

Former Louisville Mayor Harvey I. Sloane emerged from a bloody Democratic primary as one of the best-heeled Senate challengers in the country. But McConnell, a polished debater with a flair for cutting, sometimes snide repartee, kept Sloane on the defensive from the start. Sloane, a non-practicing physician, was also plagued throughout the campaign by revelations that he had prescribed himself sleeping pills during a 20-month period, contrary to accepted medical practice and without renewing his permit for prescribing drugs.

In the final days of the campaign, Sloane appeared to ride the wave of anti-incumbent sentiment to close the gap, but he came up short, losing 48 percent to 52 percent.

A lifelong political overachiever, McConnell was student body president in high school and college and president of the student bar association at law school. After earning his law degree in 1967, he worked for Cook and then served as deputy assistant U.S. attorney general in the Ford administration. In his 1977 campaign for Jefferson County judge, McConnell defeated a Democratic incumbent; four years later, he won re-election by a narrow margin and started laying the groundwork for a statewide campaign.

SENATE ELECTIONS

1996 General		
Mitch McConnell (R)	724,794	(55%)
Steven L. Beshear (D)	560,012	(43%)
1996 Primary		
Mitch McConnell (R)	88,620	(89%)
Tommy Klein (R)	11,410	(11%)

Previous Winning Percentages: 1990 (52%) **1984** (50%)

CAMPAIGN FINANCE

	Receipts	Receipts from PACs	Expend-itures
1996			
McConnell (R)	$3,840,374	$1,293,151 (34%)	$4,669,642
Beshear (D)	$1,879,343	$229,780 (12%)	$2,073,794

KEY VOTES

1997	
Approve balanced-budget constitutional amendment	Y
Approve chemical weapons treaty	Y
1996	
Approve farm bill	Y
Limit punitive damages in product liability cases	Y
Exempt small businesses from higher minimum wage	Y
Approve welfare overhaul	Y
Bar job discrimination based on sexual orientation	N
Override veto of ban on "partial birth" abortions	Y
1995	
Approve GOP budget with tax and spending cuts	Y
Approve constitutional amendment barring flag desecration	N

VOTING STUDIES

	Presidential Support		Party Unity		Conservative Coalition	
Year	S	O	S	O	S	O
1996	39	61	95	5	92	5
1995	24	76	95	5	89	9
1994	35	61	91	8	84	13
1993	28	71	92	6	98	2
1992	77	23	91	8	92	8
1991	93	7	95	5	98	3

INTEREST GROUP RATINGS

Year	ADA	AFL-CIO	CCUS	ACU
1996	10	n/a	85	95
1995	0	0	100	91
1994	5	0	90	92
1993	15	0	100	79
1992	15	18	100	89
1991	0	17	90	90

1 Edward Whitfield (R)

Of Hopkinsville — Elected 1994, 2nd term

Biographical Information

Born: May 25, 1943, Hopkinsville, Ky.
Education: U. of Kentucky, B.S. 1965; Wesley Theological Seminary, 1966; U. of Kentucky, J.D. 1969.
Military Service: Army Reserve, 1967-73.
Occupation: Lawyer; oil distributor; railroad executive.
Family: Wife, Constance B. Harriman; one child.
Religion: Methodist.
Political Career: Ky. House, 1974-75.
Capitol Office: 236 Cannon Bldg. 20515; 225-3115.

Committees

Commerce
Energy & Power; Health & Environment

In Washington: Whitfield generally votes a conservative line, but this former Capitol Hill lobbyist is somewhat less partisan-minded than a number of his peers in the GOP Class of 1994 — in part because the 1st still has many more registered Democratic voters than Republicans.

In the first year of the 104th Congress, Whitfield successfully pushed an amendment on rail workers' severance pay that was a significant victory for the labor movement. Whitfield's amendment was attached to a November 1995 bill killing the Interstate Commerce Commission (ICC), the agency charged with regulating interstate rail traffic, busing and trucking. The measure aimed to ensure that employees of some small and medium-size railroads would receive up to one year of severance pay if they lost their jobs because of a merger or acquisition.

Although Whitfield's worker-severance amendment was fairly narrow in scope — it primarily affected midsize rail lines with revenues between $20 million and $250 million — its approval demonstrated that even in a Republican Congress, railroad labor has clout. Fifty-one Republicans joined a large majority of Democrats in adopting the amendment 241-184.

Later in the 104th, Whitfield voted to increase the minimum wage, another labor priority.

Whitfield did, however, want to exempt small businesses from paying the higher minimum wage, and he supported a measure allowing employers to give workers compensatory time off rather than overtime pay. Critics said that might lead to employees being coerced into accepting comp time when they really wanted overtime pay.

Whitfield came to Congress with a strong grounding in business and railroad issues. He had worked for the ICC in Washington and was a lobbyist for railroad giant CSX Corp. He served as a Democrat in the Kentucky legislature in the mid-1970s, and switched to the GOP just as he launched his 1994 challenge to first-term Democratic Rep. Tom Barlow.

In his first term, Whitfield won a coveted slot on the Commerce Committee. Chairman Thomas J. Bliley Jr. of Virginia was looking to bring friends of the tobacco industry on board, and tobacco is an important crop in the 1st.

When the Clinton administration raised the possibility of the government regulating tobacco like a drug, Whitfield said the move was politically motivated. "I think that [Clinton officials] recognize that he will not be particularly successful in the Southeast and many tobacco-producing areas, and I think they have made a calculated decision to be anti-tobacco nationwide as a way for them to win votes," Whitfield told The Washington Times.

On most floor votes, Whitfield walks closely in step with the GOP's conservative wing. He is a consistent ally of abortion opponents, and he supports constitutional amendments to balance the budget and impose congressional term limits.

He voted in 1996 to repeal the ban on certain semiautomatic assault-style weapons, and he introduced legislation making it easier for guards who work for armored car companies to carry their guns into other states. Under current law, security guards who work for armored car companies must obtain a weapons permit from most states they want to enter. Whitfield's bill would require states to recognize guards' weapons licenses granted in other states and require a criminal background check when an initial license is granted. The bill would eliminate the requirement that renewals be made annually.

Whitfield did take exception when some of the more ardent budget-cutters in his party swung the cost-cutting axe at the Tennessee Valley Authority (TVA), an important entity in Western Kentucky. The 1st is home to a large TVA recreation area and wildlife preserve known as the Land Between the Lakes, which, Whitfield notes, draws two million visitors a year.

He objected when Republicans sought to amend the fiscal 1996 energy and water spending bill to eliminate funds for TVA. Whitfield said TVA was acting on its own to cut costs and deserved to live. "We are trying to redefine the role of govern-

KENTUCKY 1
West — Paducah

Western Kentucky's 1st is the state's version of the Deep South. In the Civil War era, regional sentiment strongly favored the Confederacy — Jefferson Davis was born here in 1808 — and slaves helped cultivate tobacco and cotton crops. Kentucky's eight westernmost counties even plotted to secede and form their own state along with some renegade Tennessee counties.

The Confederate legacy traditionally translated into Democratic votes. But in the 1994 GOP wave that swelled nationwide, the 1st District elected its first Republican representative. By winning then and again in 1996, Whitfield overcame a distinct voter registration deficit: Most counties in Western Kentucky are at least 80 percent Democratic in registration.

The Republican trend had begun to appear in the 1980s when the region drifted toward GOP presidential candidates before opting for Bill Clinton in 1992 and 1996.

Kentucky's redistricting changes, which became law after the 1994 elections, united Adair County in the 1st (a county precinct had been included in the 2nd).

Five television markets reach Western Kentucky, but no city in the 1st has more than 30,000 people. Many of the district's residents are employed in agriculture, from soybeans and tobacco to chicken processing in Mayfield.

Hopkins, Muhlenberg, Ohio and Union counties have a coal-country tradition, but jobs in the mining industry have been waning. In 1980, mining jobs accounted for about a quarter of all jobs in Muhlenberg and Ohio counties, but by 1996 that share had dropped to about 4 percent. Hopkins County has better weathered the post-World War II coal industry decline by evolving into a regional industrial and medical center.

Tourism and recreation also play a role in the regional economy, especially near the Land Between the Lakes Recreation Area. Nearby Murray has become a retirement destination.

The Ohio River port of Paducah (McCracken County) has traditionally been the political and population center of Western Kentucky, but its population has been surpassed by Hopkinsville (Christian County), an agricultural market center dependent on the nearby Fort Campbell military base.

The Atomic Energy Commission plant steered to Paducah by native son Alben W. Barkley — the longtime Democratic senator and then vice president under Harry S Truman — is a major employer, though new uranium-generation technology has cast doubts on its future.

Traditionally, the main source of Republican votes in the 1st comes from the economically disadvantaged mountain counties on the far eastern edge of the district. Bordering Tennessee to the south and the 5th District to the east, counties such as Adair, Clinton, Cumberland, Monroe and Russell have been turning in GOP majorities since the Civil War. Adair County, for example, cast 74 percent of its votes for Whitfield, 68 percent for Sen. Mitch McConnell and 59 percent for Bob Dole in 1996.

1990 Population: 614,226. White 561,481 (91%), Black 47,932 (8%), Other 4,813 (1%). Hispanic origin 4,458 (1%). 18 and over 460,899 (75%), 62 and over 110,855 (18%). Median age: 34.

ment, and we can do that, but we need some time," Whitfield said. "They are reducing the TVA budget this year by 28 percent, but we are not asking many agencies of government to go to zero funding."

In January 1997, Whitfield was not happy when TVA Chairman Craven Crowell unexpectedly announced he favored ending the agency's federal subsidy — which finances TVA's non-power generating functions, such as management of recreation areas — so the agency could concentrate solely on energy production. "We were betrayed," Whitfield said. "We're down there every year fighting for this thing, and he comes around very cavalierly and declares he doesn't want to fool with it anymore."

In the 104th, Whitfield successfully offered two amendments to a bill allowing the sale of a government corporation, the U.S. Enrichment Corp., that markets and produces uranium enrichment services for commercial nuclear power plants in the United States and 11 foreign countries.

One amendment aimed to ensure that pensions of employees at the corporation would not be affected by a sale. Also, the corporation was required to abide by collective bargaining agreements in place on the date of a sale. The other amendment barred the sale of the corporation unless the compensation to the government was deemed "an adequate amount."

In June 1995, Whitfield introduced a bill that he said would equalize incumbents' and challengers' opportunity to raise campaign funds. The measure lowered the amount PACs could contribute per election (either primary or general) from $5,000 to $3,000, and it raised the amount individuals could contribute from $1,000 to $3,000.

At Home: The first Republican ever to represent Western Kentucky's 1st District, Whitfield faced a tough 1996 battle to retain the seat against a strong effort by Democratic lawyer Dennis Null. In spite of Whitfield's votes for some causes espoused by organized labor, unions lumped Whitfield into their effort to oust the House GOP majority, airing a series of television commercials that criticized his support for the GOP's Medicare cost-reduction efforts and unfavorably comparing his and Null's stands on education and pensions.

A Null campaign volunteer came to Whitfield's town meetings dressed in a tuxedo, as if to present the incumbent with an Oscar. The campaign worker carried a sign that read, "Best Supporting Oscar to Ed Whitfield for supporting Newt 91% of the time." But Clinton's victory margin in the 1st was down from his 1992 showing, and in some quarters Null did not profit from his association with the national Democratic Party. Whitfield won a second term with 54 percent of the vote.

Whitfield's challenge to Barlow in 1994 looked like an uphill battle, given that most of the distric's 31 counties are at least 80 percent Democratic in registration. But Barlow became a national GOP target because he had supported the Clinton administration with fair frequency, and because there was a flukish element to his initial House election. In the 1992 Democratic primary, Barlow narrowly prevailed over ethically tainted incumbent Carroll Hubbard Jr., who was caught up in the House bank scandal. The GOP had not anticipated Hubbard's defeat, and Barlow comfortably won his first House term in November.

For much of 1994, though, Whitfield did not look like a hot property. He struggled to win a low-turnout GOP primary against Steve Hamrick, who had lost as the Republican candidate against Barlow in 1992. Whitfield found that his recent conversion to Republicanism did not sit well with some party faithful, nor did the fact that he had recently moved back to Kentucky, after living in Washington and Florida.

But as November approached and national Republican momentum surged, Whitfield quickly closed in on Barlow, overcoming the Democrat's substantial spending advantage. Whitfield dedicated his resources to tying Barlow to the increasingly unpopular Clinton. One Whitfield ad noted that Barlow "votes for Clinton's liberal programs nearly 80 percent of the time." Though his past work identified him with Washington, Whitfield campaigned on "outsider" themes, calling for tighter restrictions on members' free-mailing privileges and demanding that members vote on all prospective pay raises, including cost of living increases. The climate was right for the 1st to shuck its Democratic traditions: Whitfield won with 51 percent of the vote.

HOUSE ELECTIONS

1996 General		
Edward Whitfield (R)	111,473	(54%)
Dennis L. Null (D)	96,684	(46%)
1994 General		
Edward Whitfield (R)	64,849	(51%)
Tom Barlow (D)	62,387	(49%)

CAMPAIGN FINANCE

	Receipts	Receipts from PACs	Expend- itures
1996			
Whitfield (R)	$975,004	$526,844 (54%)	$897,338
Null (D)	$479,545	$177,620 (37%)	$479,210
1994			
Whitfield (R)	$352,431	$53,744 (15%)	$349,472
Barlow (D)	$615,475	$436,407 (71%)	$621,279

DISTRICT VOTE FOR PRESIDENT

1996	1992
D 105,150 (47%)	**D** 116,648 (48%)
R 96,356 (43%)	**R** 96,605 (40%)
I 22,726 (10%)	**I** 30,871 (13%)

KEY VOTES

1997	
Ban "partial birth" abortions	Y
1996	
Approve farm bill	Y
Deny public education to illegal immigrants	Y
Repeal ban on certain assault-style weapons	Y
Increase minimum wage	Y
Freeze defense spending	N
Approve welfare overhaul	Y
1995	
Approve balanced-budget constitutional amendment	Y
Relax Clean Water Act regulations	Y
Oppose limits on environmental regulations	N
Reduce projected Medicare spending	Y
Approve GOP budget with tax and spending cuts	Y

VOTING STUDIES

	Presidential Support		Party Unity		Conservative Coalition	
Year	**S**	**O**	**S**	**O**	**S**	**O**
1996	38	61	88	11	98	2
1995	22	77	90	9	91	6

INTEREST GROUP RATINGS

Year	ADA	AFL-CIO	CCUS	ACU
1996	5	n/a	94	85
1995	10	17	100	92

2 Ron Lewis (R)

Of Elizabethtown — Elected 1994; 2nd full term

Biographical Information

Born: Sept. 14, 1946, Greenup County, Ky.
Education: Morehead State U.; U. of Kentucky, B.A. 1969; Morehead State U., M.A. 1980.
Military Service: Navy, 1972.
Occupation: Bookstore owner; minister; public official.
Family: Wife, Kayi Gambill; two children.
Religion: Baptist.
Political Career: Sought Republican nomination for Ky. House, 1971.

Capitol Office: 223 Cannon Bldg. 20515; 225-3501.

Committees

Agriculture
Forestry, Resource Conservation & Research; Livestock, Dairy & Poultry; Risk Management & Specialty Crops

National Security
Military Personnel; Military Procurement

In Washington: Compared with the man he succeeded in the House, 40-year veteran William H. Natcher, Lewis is likely to have but a fleeting time in Congress. But already he has earned at least a footnote in history, because Lewis' May 1994 special election victory in the historically Democratic 2nd was a harbinger of the Republican successes that six months later would sweep the GOP to its first House majority in four decades.

The typical voter in the 2nd did not have to make a big ideological leap to support Lewis; the culturally conservative views he espouses have always been the norm here. But until 1994, this was dyed-in-the-wool Old South Democratic territory in House voting; Lewis is the first Republican ever to represent this part of Kentucky in the House.

In his maiden speech on the House floor, Lewis acknowledged having big shoes to fill as successor to the late Natcher, who had risen to chairman of the Appropriations Committee. But in case there were any doubts, it soon became clear that Lewis had not come to Washington to be another Natcher. Although he had endorsed a 12-year limit on House service, Lewis drew fire from more ardent term-limits proponents, and he finally settled on a pledge to serve no more than six years.

And while Natcher generally kept himself apart from partisan tussles on the House floor, Lewis is not shy about launching verbal broadsides at the Democrats for "obstructionist" tactics and other misdeeds. In May 1996, Lewis told the House that the minority had "brought false charges against the new Speaker of the House"; had failed to help to reform welfare, and instead "the liberal whiners just wanted to march to the floor and accuse the new Republican freshmen of being extremists and wanting to starve children"; and had failed to save Medicare, instead "the liberal whiners and complainers just stuck their heads in the sand and tried to scare the elderly."

The GOP tapped Lewis to respond to President Clinton's end-of-the-year radio address in December 1995, when the federal government was partially shut down because the White House and the Republican Congress could not agree on a budget. Clinton called on congressional leaders to reopen the government and said he was optimistic that negotiations would soon deliver a balanced-budget agreement. In his response, Lewis urged Clinton to "negotiate in good faith" to end the budget impasse. Working with Congress to develop a balanced-budget plan is "our last, best chance to stop robbing our children," Lewis said.

When the House in October 1995 considered the Republicans' plan to balance the federal budget in seven years, Lewis laid the blame for the nation's debt at the feet of the Democrats, saying that "for 40 years we had a tax-and-spend Congress . . . for 30 years there has been a war on poverty, $5 trillion has been spent. And what have we got? We have more in poverty, we have more welfare, more illegitimacy, lower education, higher crime, more poverty, more drugs."

But Lewis can see good in some federal spending aimed at helping the underprivileged. He opposed a GOP amendment in July 1995 that would have killed all funding for the Appalachian Regional Commission, a Great Society program to build roads and spur economic development in 13 Appalachian states. Telling the House that he grew up in the Appalachians, Lewis said, "I remember the little one-lane roads, the dusty dirt roads, the lack of utilities, the small one-room schools." Because of the commission, he said, there has been "tremendous improvement" in eastern Kentucky and "now there are nice highways, nice schools, utilities reaching into the homes, paved highways." The House rejected the effort to kill the commission, 108-319.

Despite his brief tenure in Congress, Lewis got in ahead of the big GOP Class of 1994, and he is already senior to one-third of his party colleagues on the National Security Committee and to one half on the Agriculture Committee.

From his National Security perch, Lewis is an enthusiastic advocate for the Army Reserves. In April 1996, he marked the Reserves' 88th anniver-

KENTUCKY 2
West central — Owensboro

The wide Democratic registration advantage in the 2nd is misleading. This is a competitive district in state and national elections. The 2nd includes three distinct areas of the state: the outer Bluegrass region in the east, suburban Louisville to the north and the rolling hill country of the Pennyrile in the southwest.

More than two-thirds of the district's voters are registered Democrats. But they have an independent streak and a penchant for backing Republicans for federal office. In 1994, they elected the district's first GOP representative since the Civil War after the death of longtime Rep. William H. Natcher.

That election continued a trend that is evident in good GOP years, in which statewide candidates have a shot at the 2nd's three major population centers: Daviess County (Owensboro), Hardin County (the Fort Knox area) and Warren County (Bowling Green). Republicans have always been able to count on some smaller counties. Casey County backed George Bush in 1992 and Bob Dole 1996. Grayson and Edmonson, centers of Union support during the Civil War, also voted for both Bush and Dole. Dole won the entire district by 8 percentage points in 1996, although Ross Perot took 10 percent of the vote.

Remapping in 1994 had a negligible effect, moving one Adair County precinct from the 2nd to the 1st.

Owensboro, along the Ohio River in the far northwestern edge of the district, is the largest city in the 2nd. Tobacco, oil and coal help make it Western Kentucky's leading trade center.

At the other end of the Green River Parkway lies Bowling Green (Warren County), the district's second-largest city. Metals and machinery are some of Bowling Green's industrial output, but the GM Corvette assembly plant there draws more attention. Western Kentucky University, the largest college in the state west of Louisville, overlooks the city.

Hardin County, home to Fort Knox, is between Owensboro and Louisville. Adjacent to the military reservation is the Treasury Department's Gold Depository, where bars of almost pure gold are locked in a vault behind a door weighing more than 20 tons. Active-duty and retired military help fuel the economies of nearby Radcliff and Elizabethtown.

Closer to Louisville, the 2nd includes some Republican-leaning Jefferson County suburbs and Bullitt County, an extension of Louisville's suburbs. White flight from Louisville fueled a 66 percent population increase in Bullitt in the 1970s, though growth tapered off considerably in the 1980s. The county's sizable blue-collar element frequently bolts the Democratic ticket; Bullitt County went narrowly for Dole in 1996.

Bardstown (Nelson County) claims to be the "The Bourbon Capital of the World." Several distilleries are in the vicinity, including Maker's Mark in Loretto. As if to balance the worldly pleasure that bourbon brings, the names of several area towns connote ethereality, including Holy Cross, Calvary, St. Mary, St. Francis, Saint Catharine and Gethsemane.

1990 Population: 614,833. White 574,373 (93%), Black 33,700 (5%), Other 6,760 (1%). Hispanic origin 5,103 (1%). 18 and over 448,234 (73%), 62 and over 84,999 (14%). Median age: 32.

sary with a tribute on the House floor. His district is home to Fort Knox, and active duty and retired military personnel are an important factor in the local economy. (Lewis himself served in the Navy for a year.)

From his seat on Agriculture, Lewis has been an unflagging supporter of tobacco farmers. He and others from tobacco-growing states reacted angrily in June 1996 to an amendment offered by Illinois Democrat Richard J. Durbin that would have done away with federal crop insurance and extension services for tobacco growers. "We shouldn't single out the farmers who grow tobacco. We shouldn't hurt the many families who are just barely getting by with a few acres of this legal product," Lewis argued. "And we shouldn't pretend that this amendment will stop one person from smoking, because it won't."

Still, Lewis was an early supporter of the Republicans' "Freedom to Farm" bill, which brought federal farm policy more in line with free-market principles. Calling the measure "the most sweeping change in farm policy since the New Deal," Lewis said, "it's good for farmers, it helps us move toward a balanced budget and it doesn't pull the rug out from under the people who feed our nation."

At Home: Lewis has posted three solid election victories in the 2nd, a record Republicans say is proof the GOP has definitively broken this predominantly rural district from its traditional Democratic moorings.

When he ran in the May 1994 special election to fill the vacancy caused by Natcher's death, Lewis, a sometime minister and religious bookstore owner, focused on two issues: his ties to the district and tying his Democratic opponent to the Clinton White House. Against his Democratic opponent, former state Sen. Joseph Prather, Lewis used such messages as "Ron Lewis — he's one of us" and "Kentucky doesn't need another professional politician."

Prather tried to emulate Natcher's no-frills, low-cost campaign efforts. He also expected to benefit from the district's 2-1 Democratic registration edge and its well-established voting habits.

Sensing an opportunity, the national GOP worked closely with Lewis' campaign, pouring about $200,000 into the race in the last few weeks. Prather, who had rejected offers from the national Democratic Party, tried to regroup. He increased his spending dramatically, but it was too late; Lewis won with 55 percent of the vote.

At the time he won the special election, Lewis was already the Republican nominee for the fall. Kentucky Democratic leaders selected David Adkisson, the mayor of Owensboro, as their November nominee.

Learning from the Prather debacle, Adkisson sought help from experienced party leaders and the national party. It was not enough, however. Lewis, benefiting from the voters' attitude of "Let's give the fellow a chance," moved up to 60 percent.

In 1996, former state Senate Majority Leader Joe Wright hoped there was enough residual Democratic sentiment in the 2nd to help him regain it for his party. Wright tried to portray Lewis as doing the bidding of the House Republican leadership. Promising he would be a "common-sense voice" for the district, Wright raised enough money to be competitive.

Tobacco is a big crop in the 2nd, and the Clinton administration's anti-smoking crusade wins Democrats few friends here, but Wright's background helped him deflect voter anger: He is a tobacco farmer and former president of the Burley Tobacco Growers Cooperative Association.

Lewis defended his votes for the GOP agenda, claiming that they were in line with the district's conservatism. He repeated the Republican mantra of 1996, "promises made, promises kept," noting progress toward a balanced budget, enactment of welfare reform and other legislative successes. "What I said I would do is exactly what I've done," he said. In the end, 58 percent of voters endorsed his re-election effort.

HOUSE ELECTIONS

1996 General		
Ron Lewis (R)	125,433	(58%)
Joe Wright (D)	90,483	(42%)
1994 General		
Ron Lewis (R)	90,535	(60%)
David Adkisson (D)	60,867	(40%)
1994 Special		
Ron Lewis (R)	40,126	(55%)
Joseph Prather (D)	32,625	(45%)

CAMPAIGN FINANCE

	Receipts	Receipts from PACs	Expend-itures
1996			
Lewis (R)	$637,567	$214,047 (34%)	$639,397
Wright (D)	$493,964	$61,500 (12%)	$480,101
1994			
Lewis (R)	$384,399	$95,070 (25%)	$393,266
Adkisson (D)	$494,319	$155,550 (31%)	$493,564
1994 Special			
Lewis (R)	$45,719	$1,000 (2%)	$18,546
Prather (D)	$41,125	0	$6,799

DISTRICT VOTE FOR PRESIDENT

	1996		1992
D	95,193 (41%)	D	100,378 (41%)
R	113,373 (49%)	R	109,517 (45%)
I	21,984 (10%)	I	33,987 (14%)

KEY VOTES

1997	
Ban "partial birth" abortions	Y
1996	
Approve farm bill	Y
Deny public education to illegal immigrants	Y
Repeal ban on certain assault-style weapons	Y
Increase minimum wage	N
Freeze defense spending	N
Approve welfare overhaul	Y
1995	
Approve balanced-budget constitutional amendment	Y
Relax Clean Water Act regulations	Y
Oppose limits on environmental regulations	N
Reduce projected Medicare spending	Y
Approve GOP budget with tax and spending cuts	Y

VOTING STUDIES

	Presidential Support		Party Unity		Conservative Coalition	
Year	**S**	**O**	**S**	**O**	**S**	**O**
1996	37	63	95	5	96	4
1995	18	82	98	2	97	2
1994	40†	60†	96†	4†	89†	11†

† Not eligible for all recorded votes.

INTEREST GROUP RATINGS

Year	ADA	AFL-CIO	CCUS	ACU
1996	5	n/a	94	100
1995	0	0	96	96
1994	0†	40†	75	86†
1993	0	0	0	0

† Not eligible for all recorded votes.

3 Anne M. Northup (R)

Of Louisville — Elected 1996, 1st term

Biographical Information
Born: Jan. 22, 1948, Louisville, Ky.
Education: St. Mary's College, B.A. 1970.
Occupation: Teacher.
Family: Husband, Robert Wood Northup; six children.
Religion: Roman Catholic.
Political Career: Ky. House, 1987-96.
Capitol Office: 1004 Longworth Bldg. 20515; 225-5401.

Committees
Appropriations
District of Columbia; Labor, Health & Human Services, Education & Related Agencies; Treasury, Postal Service & General Government

The Path to Washington: Northup managed an upset in a year that generally favored Democrats and in a state that voted to re-elect President Clinton. Northup upended Democratic freshman Rep. Mike Ward, who defied the odds in 1994 by narrowly winning election in a strong Republican year. Northup is the only first-term Republican to win election in a district Bill Clinton carried in 1996 with a majority of the vote, and just one of three GOP members who ousted an incumbent.

As a reward, Northup was given a coveted seat on the Appropriations Committee — a rare assignment for a freshman. From this panel, Northup will be in a good position to lobby for one of her parochial goals: securing federal funding to build a new bridge over the Ohio River, a subject of extensive local debate and planning in Louisville.

Northup says her top priority is to fulfill her pledges to make government smaller, turn control over more programs to the local level and cut taxes. In "everything I do, I'm not going to forget those promises," she says.

Northup says she wants to bring a "family ethic" to Washington's policy debates. The mother of six children — two of whom are adopted — and a state representative for nine years, Northup says Congress often resorts to "number crunching" while failing to understand how spending decisions affect everyday working conditions.

This is one reason Northup says Congress, as part of its effort to implement the welfare reform plan approved in August 1996, needs to spare as much money as possible to assist welfare recipients with young children who want to get jobs.

Northup says she is concerned about the regulatory burden on small businesses in particular, adding that many of the most passionate people she met on the campaign trail were struggling entrepreneurs. Northup plans to work on small-business legislation to provide regulatory relief and reduce the costs of starting a company.

She also supports providing a $500-per-child tax credit and reducing the capital gains tax, a move she says is a necessary incentive for businesses to expand and help create jobs.

In launching her bid against Ward, Northup was not saddled with a problem that plagued the 1994 Republican nominee, Susan B. Stokes, who was defeated by fewer than 500 votes.

An abortion rights supporter, Stokes was hampered by a third-party candidate, Richard Lewis, who ran as the only abortion opponent in the race. Northup opposes abortion and had the backing of some religious conservatives who supported Lewis' 1994 campaign.

An independent poll published in midsummer showed Northup trailing Ward by more than 30 points. But she surpassed Ward in fundraising and began running television ads in late August to boost her name identification.

Northup vociferously attacked Ward as being out of step with the district on a variety of issues. After blasting Ward all year long for opposing Republican legislation to overhaul welfare programs, she claimed that his support for the final version of the legislation, backed by the Clinton White House, was one of the incumbent's many election-year conversions.

She also criticized his opposition to legislation making English the nation's official language. And a third barb accused Ward of being weak on crime for opposing legislation linking prison construction money for states to requirements that prisoners serve virtually all of their sentences. The Northup campaign also tried to tar Ward over his fundraising efforts for his 1994 race against Stokes. Ward fought back, attempting to paint Northup as a potential pawn of House Speaker Newt Gingrich, saying that she would back his plans to reduce the rate of growth for Medicare spending.

But while she takes a conservative view on most issues, Northup has shown an independent streak in the past. Even though tobacco is a key component of Kentucky's economy, Northup led an effort in the state legislature to impose stricter laws against the sale of tobacco to children.

Kentucky's rural and small-town communities have always considered themselves different from Louisville, the state's largest city. In a state where blacks make up just 7 percent of the population, Louisville is 30 percent black. The city also has an exceptionally large Roman Catholic population, a legacy of a massive German immigration in the mid-19th century. And Louisville's Courier-Journal newspaper is a leading liberal voice in a state that generally prefers moderate-to-conservative politicians.

Suspicion of Louisville is usually reflected at the ballot box, when the rest of the state bands together to vote against the Louisville-based candidate. GOP Sen. Mitch McConnell, serving in his third term, has been an exception.

Every first Saturday in May, though, the rest of the state turns to Louisville, to be serenaded with the state's official song, "My Old Kentucky Home," and to witness one of horse-racing's biggest spectacles, the Kentucky Derby.

In a state known for its contentious politics, Louisville is no exception. Court-ordered busing of students in the 1970s inflamed passions throughout Jefferson County, leading to riots and violent demonstrations. And in the 1980s, Louisville became known as "Strike City" for its fractious labor-management relations.

Despite some job losses from industrial decline, labor strength runs deep among the blue-collar, white residents of the South End; it translates into Democratic votes. Blacks who live near downtown in the West End turn in even larger Democratic majorities. Republicans live in the affluent East End by the Ohio River.

Louisville's newer jobs are more service-oriented, with employers such as United Parcel Service, which operates a hub out of Standiford

KENTUCKY 3
Louisville and suburbs

Airport, and Galen (formerly Humana), which runs for-profit hospitals.

In the 1970s, the city of Louisville — with the addition of a few suburbs — held enough population for its own congressional district. But massive white flight to the suburbs has expanded the 3rd District's lines farther into the Jefferson County suburbs. Louisville now accounts for less than half the district vote.

That has meant a shift in the 3rd District balance of power. Before the black Democratic vote became a force in the mid- to late 1960s, Jefferson County was fertile ground for Republicans. And in the 3rd, the pendulum is swinging back in that direction, as the suburbs increasingly flex their muscles.

The 3rd is now more receptive to Republicans, particularly in the higher-income areas (such as the Brownsboro Road-Interchange 71 corridor) outside the city and in areas closer to the Oldham County border. The turf between St. Matthews and Middletown, on the 2nd District border, is Republican, well-educated and affluent. The new suburban majority helped make the 1994 and 1996 congressional elections the closest in more than 20 years. The 3rd was the only district to give Bill Clinton a majority of its votes in 1996 while unseating a Democratic House incumbent.

1990 Population: 613,603. White 494,625 (81%), Black 112,290 (18%), Other 6,688 (1%). Hispanic origin 4,075 (1%). 18 and over 465,371 (76%), 62 and over 103,277 (17%). Median age: 34.

HOUSE ELECTIONS

1996 General

Anne M. Northup (R)	126,625	(50%)
Mike Ward (D)	125,326	(50%)

CAMPAIGN FINANCE

	Receipts	Receipts from PACs	Expend-itures
1996			
Northup (R)	$1,198,759	$282,845 (24%)	$1,181,546
Ward (D)	$886,365	$451,787 (51%)	$880,073

DISTRICT VOTE FOR PRESIDENT

1996		1992	
D	135,312 (53%)	**D**	142,384 (51%)
R	102,525 (40%)	**R**	103,338 (37%)
I	17,267 (7%)	**I**	35,104 (13%)

KEY VOTES

1997

Ban "partial-birth" abortions Y

4 Jim Bunning (R)

Of Southgate — Elected 1986, 6th term

Biographical Information
Born: Oct. 23, 1931, Campbell County, Ky.
Education: Xavier U., B.S. 1953.
Occupation: Investment broker; sports agent; professional baseball player.
Family: Wife, Mary Catherine Theis; nine children.
Religion: Roman Catholic.
Political Career: Fort Thomas City Council, 1977-79; Ky. Senate, 1979-83; Republican nominee for governor, 1983.
Capitol Office: 2437 Rayburn Bldg. 20515; 225-3465.

Committees
Budget
Ways & Means
Social Security (chairman)

In Washington: Bunning, who spent the 104th Congress trying to raise the earnings limit for Social Security recipients, offer an adoption tax credit and wrap up the ethics committee investigation of Speaker Newt Gingrich turns in the 105th toward preparing a 1998 campaign for the Senate. He announced in March 1997 that he would try for the seat being vacated by retiring Democrat Wendell H. Ford.

Bunning was elevated to a Ways and Means subcommittee chairmanship when Republicans took over the House in 1995, but another development in his life — one linked to his career before politics — was really a bigger personal highlight: In August 1996, he became the first member of Congress elected to baseball's Hall of Fame, on the strength of a pitching record that included winning more than 100 games in each major league and pitching a no-hitter in each league, including a perfect game in 1964.

Henry J. Hyde, R-Ill., made the announcement of Bunning's election to the Hall of Fame on the House floor. Hyde told the story of how the Yankees' first base coach, Bob Turley, stole the catcher's signs and let the batters know when Bunning would pitch a fastball. Mickey Mantle came to the plate and Bunning told the coach, "If you whistle, I am going to hit him right in the back with a pitch," Hyde recalled. Turley whistled anyway. "Jim decided to cross everybody up. He threw a slider. It got away from him, and hit Mantle right in the back. The next batter was Yogi Berra. Yogi stepped in, pounded the plate, looked at Jim Bunning and said, 'Hey, Jim, if Turley whistles, I ain't listening.' "

Bunning received a standing ovation when his selection was announced to the House. He acknowledged the applause with emotion. "It's hard to speak after 25 years," he said. "I've been retired from baseball 25 years."

After being elected to the House, Bunning once pitched for the Republicans in the annual congressional baseball game. But his arm was shot, and the Democrats hit his pitches with ease. Finally, Dan Schaefer, R-Colo., replaced him on the mound. "I can tell my grandkids that I once relieved the great Jim Bunning," Schaefer said.

Work on Ways and Means and the House ethics committee kept Bunning hopping in the 104th. Having served his requisite three terms on the ethics committee, he resigned at the start of the 105th Congress — even though the committee was in the final stages of its lengthy investigation into the political fundraising activities of House Speaker Newt Gingrich. Bunning was replaced on the panel by Lamar Smith, R-Texas.

In December 1995, Bunning was the only dissenter on the committee when it proposed a change in House rules that would limit book royalties for members. The House instead voted to bar members from accepting advances for books and to require that book contracts be cleared by the ethics panel. Bunning voted for that weaker rule. "Don't tell the American people that the members of this body cannot be trusted to test their ideas in the marketplace," Bunning said.

As chairman of the Ways and Means Social Security Subcommittee, one of his early tasks was to fulfill a "Contract With America" plank and try to raise the outside earnings limit for Social Security recipients. His bill aimed to increase the annual earnings limit for seniors from $11,280 to $30,000 by 2002.

He also played a leading role in legislation giving middle-income families who adopt a child a $5,000 tax credit. "When it comes to matters involving family, I usually hold fast to the position that government should butt out and mind its own business," Bunning said. "But making adoption simple and more affordable is one instance in which the government can and should step in to make a difference."

Bunning was chief sponsor of a provision outlawing the practice of trying to match a child with adoptive parents of the same race. Lawmakers said the policy could leave children languishing in foster care even though parents of another race were willing to adopt them. Bunning became interested in the issue when two of his daughters

KENTUCKY 4
North and East — Covington; Ashland

Of the state's six congressional districts, the 4th is the least oriented toward Kentucky.

Almost half the district's population is located in the Cincinnati suburbs; Ashland, the 4th's second-largest city, is on the far eastern fringe, near where the Ohio River forms a border with Ohio and West Virginia.

Boone, Campbell (Newport) and Kenton (Covington) counties are associated much more closely with Cincinnati — where much of the area's population commutes to work — than with Lexington or Louisville. The Greater Cincinnati International Airport is actually in Kentucky, a few miles west of Covington.

Newport has battled its reputation as a "sin city" — for its go-go bars and nightclubs, where some of Cincinnati's residents go to blow off steam. Ohioans also escape their state-run liquor stores by buying less expensive alcohol in Covington.

A frequently voiced complaint in Covington is that the state ignores the city because of its close ties to Ohio. But the federal government certainly has not: A regional center of the Internal Revenue Service is the city's largest employer. The peak of tax season adds even more jobs to the district's largest city.

Boone County attracted population spillover from Campbell and Kenton counties in the 1970s and 1980s, growing more than 75 percent over the past two decades.

The politics of these three counties is nominally Democratic but increasingly friendly to Republicans. George Bush won all three easily in 1992, as did Bob Dole in 1996.

For a Democrat to win the 4th, the candidate must remain competitive in these counties and then run up sizable margins in the eight rural-suburban counties closer to Louisville.

Most of these rural counties are Democratic, but suburban Oldham County (at the 4th's western edge, closest to Louisville) is leaning Republican. In the 1970s, Oldham's population swelled by 91 percent, thanks to white-collar out-migration from Louisville and an influx of out-of-state business executives. Population growth tapered off considerably in the 1980s, but Oldham has an unmistakable GOP stamp. Dole carried the county in 1996.

Any Democratic strategy for the 4th also has to factor in the industrial city of Ashland (Boyd County), home to Ashland Oil and AK Steel. Strong unions kept the oil refinery workers and steelworkers of Boyd and neighboring Greenup counties in the Democratic column for decades, but their grip has weakened. Still, Bill Clinton carried Boyd in 1992 and Greenup in both 1992 and 1996.

Before redistricting, these counties clustered by the West Virginia border were part of Eastern Kentucky's heavily Democratic, coal-producing Appalachian district. That voting tradition lives on in sparsely populated and 98 percent Democratic Elliott County. Lewis County marches to its own GOP beat, dating to the time when it was a stop on the Underground Railroad.

The remapping plan passed in 1994 by the Kentucky legislature removed the 4th's portions of Lawrence and Nicholas counties, which the district had shared (respectively) with the 5th and 6th districts.

1990 Population: 614,245. White 597,696 (97%), Black 13,180 (2%), Other 3,369 (1%). Hispanic origin 2,666 (<1%). 18 and over 449,764 (73%), 62 and over 90,033 (15%). Median age: 33.

adopted children and one adopted a black child.

During debate in the Ways and Means Committee, Charles B. Rangel, D-N.Y., a member of the Congressional Black Caucus, led the opposition to the provision.

"Are you telling me that if both Mr. Bunning and I were perfect parents and I was first in line to get a child that happened to be a beautiful, blond-haired, blue-eyed child, I would be able to get the child, and the social service worker could not say that child would be more compatible with Mr. Bunning?" Rangel asked.

Bunning and other proponents said more often the problem is that a parent of one color is eager to adopt a child of another race, and the social worker stands in the way. "That social worker will, because of the color of skin, keep that child in foster care, and that child is at risk in foster care," Bunning said.

To end the controversy, E. Clay Shaw Jr., R-Fla., proposed focusing the bill on the Bunning's biggest concern: discrimination that results in delays in placing children. Ways and Means adopted his amendment by voice vote.

Bunning was chief sponsor of legislation exempting from income taxes the military pay of enlisted personnel serving in Bosnia, Herzegovina, Croatia or Macedonia. "This is not about whether you agree with the policy that put U.S. troops in Bosnia," Bunning said. "The point is they are there and since they are there, we need to do everything in our power to make sure they are treated fairly."

Bunning has been quick to respond to his constituents. As Ways and Means in May 1996 marked up a small-business tax package, later to be combined with legislation raising the minimum wage, Bunning stopped the committee from retroactively closing a loophole that would benefit racehorse owners. Through an error in drafting in a 1990 bill, those owners could write off part of the cost of a horse. Bunning, whose home state is famous for racehorse breeding, argued unsuccessfully that the mistake should not be corrected because owners of other livestock — from cows to llamas to greyhounds — received the write-off. He finally consented to correct the mistake for the future but not retroactively.

Kentucky also is tobacco country, and in July 1995 Bunning responded to the Food and Drug Administration's proposals to regulate tobacco by proposing to eliminate the agency's funding. His amendment to the fiscal 1996 agriculture appropriations bill was rejected by voice vote on the House floor.

Early in the 104th, Bunning's viewpoint was often sought in regard to the baseball strike that snuffed the 1994 World Series and was threatening to cancel the entire 1995 season. While opposed to using the government's emergency powers to enter the dispute, Bunning suggested lifting baseball's exemption from antitrust laws and making it operate more like a normal business. In his earlier career, Bunning helped organize the players' union and negotiated contracts.

At Home: After surviving a redistricting-fueled election scare in 1992, Bunning returned to his winning ways in his next two House races, having no re-election trouble in 1994 or 1996.

The 1992 contest was more challenging. After winning re-election easily in his first three tries, Bunning found himself imperiled by redistricting changes. Sensing an opportunity, Democrats recruited Dr. Floyd G. Poore, a prolific fundraiser coming off a losing 1991 gubernatorial bid.

Given the more than 2-1 Democratic registration edge in the refigured district, Poore was considered a serious threat. But Bunning was able to resurrect enough of the character questions raised during Poore's gubernatorial run to keep the Democrat off balance.

After retiring as an active player in 1971, Bunning tried minor-league managing for a while, then returned to his native Kentucky, where he set up as an investment broker and agent to professional athletes.

He also got involved in civic activities that led him to a seat on the Fort Thomas City Council, where in 1977 he began his rapid political rise. After just two years, Bunning unseated a longtime Democratic state senator. He quickly became the minority leader for the small group of Senate Republicans.

In 1983, Kentucky Republicans, searching for a viable gubernatorial candidate, recruited Bunning. He got a respectable 44 percent. In 1986, after GOP Rep. Gene Snyder announced his retirement in 1986, Republican officials enlisted Bunning. His opponent was Democratic state Rep. Terry Mann, who had lost to Snyder by only 12,000 votes in 1982 and had considerable strength in Bunning's Campbell County political base.

But Bunning built a winning margin in the Cincinnati-area counties of Kenton and Boone and in the populous Louisville suburbs of Jefferson County.

HOUSE ELECTIONS

1996 General		
Jim Bunning (R)	149,135	(68%)
Denny Bowman (D)	68,939	(32%)
1994 General		
Jim Bunning (R)	96,695	(74%)
Sally Harris Skaggs (D)	33,717	(26%)

Previous Winning Percentages: 1992 (62%) **1990** (69%) **1988** (74%) **1986** (55%)

CAMPAIGN FINANCE

	Receipts	Receipts from PACs	Expend-itures
1996			
Bunning (R)	$876,647	$397,458 (45%)	$886,717
Bowman (D)	$55,240	$32,200 (58%)	$55,239
1994			
Bunning (R)	$729,429	$322,437 (44%)	$560,590
Skaggs (D)	$20,142	$5,000 (25%)	$20,141

VOTING STUDIES

	Presidential Support		Party Unity		Conservative Coalition	
Year	**S**	**O**	**S**	**O**	**S**	**O**
1996	33	67	96	4	98	2
1995	19	81	97	2	94	4
1994	31	69	95	4	83	17
1993	26	73	94	4	84	14
1992	77	21	89	6	85	8
1991	76	23	94	4	97	3

KEY VOTES

1997	
Ban "partial birth" abortions	Y
1996	
Approve farm bill	Y
Deny public education to illegal immigrants	Y
Repeal ban on certain assault-style weapons	Y
Increase minimum wage	N
Freeze defense spending	N
Approve welfare overhaul	Y
1995	
Approve balanced-budget constitutional amendment	Y
Relax Clean Water Act regulations	Y
Oppose limits on environmental regulations	N
Reduce projected Medicare spending	Y
Approve GOP budget with tax and spending cuts	Y

INTEREST GROUP RATINGS

Year	ADA	AFL-CIO	CCUS	ACU
1996	5	n/a	81	100
1995	0	0	96	92
1994	5	11	83	95
1993	10	8	91	100
1992	10	27	71	90
1991	10	8	90	100

DISTRICT VOTE FOR PRESIDENT

1996		1992	
D	95,070 (41%)	**D**	92,207 (39%)
R	115,187 (50%)	**R**	105,023 (44%)
I	20,733 (9%)	**I**	39,900 (17%)

5 Harold Rogers (R)

Of Somerset — Elected 1980, 9th term

Biographical Information

Born: Dec. 31, 1937, Barrier, Ky.

Education: Western Kentucky U., 1956-57; U. of Kentucky, B.A. 1962, LL.B. 1964.

Military Service: National Guard, 1956-63.

Occupation: Lawyer.

Family: Widowed; three children.

Religion: Baptist.

Political Career: Pulaski and Rockcastle counties commonwealth attorney, 1969-79; Republican nominee for lieutenant governor, 1979.

Capitol Office: 2468 Rayburn Bldg. 20515; 225-4601.

Committees

Appropriations
Commerce, Justice, State & Judiciary (chairman); Energy & Water Development; Transportation

In Washington: Like several GOP veterans who took Appropriations subcommittee chairs in the 104th Congress, Rogers does not always share the zeal of younger House Republicans for budget slashing. He walks a fine line in moving his subcommittee's bill — which funds the departments of Commerce, Justice and State — trying to hold back on spending while protecting programs he considers important.

Although there was strong support in the GOP Class of 1994 for abolishing the Commerce Department, Rogers disagreed. He did promote spending cuts at Commerce in order to free up money for anti-crime programs at the Justice Department. He stood against conservatives' efforts to kill the Legal Services Corporation, which provides legal aid to the poor, and to eliminate the Economic Development Administration, which provides public works and technical aid grants to state and localities.

Rogers concurs with prevailing conservative sentiment when it comes to U.N. funding. He criticizes many U.N. programs, particularly peacekeeping missions, which he calls "aggressive multilateralism, carried to an extreme. . . ."

Rogers' predominantly rural district is one of the poorest in Kentucky, with many residents struggling to adapt to long-term decline in coal mining and tobacco farming. These economic conditions help explain why Rogers' votes sometimes differ from those cast by GOP colleagues who represent upscale suburban districts.

In May 1996, Rogers was among 93 Republicans supporting a 90-cent increase in the minimum wage, a Democrat-driven proposal the GOP leadership had resisted. (Rogers backed an unsuccessful amendment to exempt small businesses from paying the higher minimum.)

In the 103rd Congress, he split with his party majority to oppose NAFTA and GATT, conveying fears in his constituency that low-wage manufacturing jobs in the 5th might shift abroad with the lifting of international trade barriers.

Rogers got a seat on Appropriations in his second term, and for a decade now, his main work has been on the Commerce, Justice, State Subcommittee, where he became ranking Republican in the 100th Congress and chairman in January 1995.

He took the gavel in difficult times. The GOP had won control of the House on a pledge to cut federal spending and balance the budget, and most Republican freshmen had little patience for party oldtimers who did not embrace revolutionary change. In addition, it was a difficult time for Rogers personally, as his wife, Shirley, was battling cancer. She died in the spring of 1995.

In presenting his panel's fiscal 1996 spending bill to the House, Rogers said proposed increases for federal and state law enforcement made it "the toughest anti-crime appropriations bill this House of Representatives has ever produced," even though the bill overall requested about $4 billion less than President Clinton had wanted.

The measure was also the forum for several policy disputes between Republicans and the White House, including tussles over the fate of programs in the 1994 crime law, the future of the Legal Services Corporation and the scope of U.S. involvement in international peacekeeping.

Because of disputes over policy and funding levels, neither of the Commerce, Justice, State spending bills that Rogers managed in the 104th made it on their own into law. Clinton vetoed the fiscal 1996 bill, and the fiscal 1997 bill was rolled into an omnibus catchall spending bill that cleared just as the session ended.

Rogers and other GOP appropriators sought to use the bill to undo some grant programs created by the 1994 crime law. They wanted to replace a police hiring program with a flexible, anti-crime block grant. "The block grant program allows communities to do what they deem wise," Rogers said, "not what we in Washington deem to be wise for them." But the White House and congressional Democrats strongly resisted block grants.

(Testifying before Rogers' subcommittee in March 1997, Attorney General Janet Reno revealed that she had sought $503 million for

KENTUCKY 5
Southeast — Middlesboro; Pikeville

Appalachian Eastern Kentucky long has been one of the state's most downtrodden areas. Lexington and Louisville are culturally, economically and geographically distant from the 5th District, the state's poorest, sickest and least educated.

With no city that has more than 15,000 residents, the 5th spans 27 counties. The Kentucky legislature in 1994 revised the state's congressional district boundaries; Lawrence, the only county that had previously been split (with the 4th), now is wholly within the 5th. Most of Democratic Eastern Kentucky is within its confines, along with the Republican southeastern region along the Tennessee border.

One tie that binds the district is the staggering poverty that differentiates it from the rest of the state. In 1990, about one in five households lacked a telephone or earned less than $5,000 per year.

The 1970s coal boom brought many former residents from the urban Midwest back to the hills and hollows of Appalachia. But the revival died out as coal production began to shift from the East to the West, where, typically, it is cheaper and easier to mine coal.

The decline of the once mighty coal industry — the state lost 20,000 mining jobs in the 1980s — has brought even harder times to the region's mountain people, who never had it easy to begin with.

Besides the abandoned mines and scarred hillsides, King Coal is leaving behind a legion of crippled miners, whether they suffer from black lung disease or are disabled by some other mine-related injury. Fourteen percent of the people in the district have work-related disabilities that prevent them from working.

The United Mine Workers union (UMW) speaks loudly for these residents and carries a big stick in the coal counties in the eastern half of the district. These counties bordering Virginia and West Virginia traditionally turn in Democratic majorities.

Pitted against the coal counties is a fire wall of mountain counties that have been voting Republican since the 1860s. They used to form the backbone of the old GOP 5th District before it was merged with the Democratic 7th in 1992 redistricting.

Leslie County went for Bob Dole in 1996 as did Clay, Laurel and Pulaski. The Democratic eastern half strongly backed Bill Clinton. In Pike (Pikeville) and Floyd (Prestonsburg) counties — the district's first and third most populous — Clinton won by better than a 2-1 margin.

Bell County (Middlesboro), on the Tennessee border, is one of the few competitive counties. In 1996, voters backed Clinton, although they have also traditionally supported Rogers.

Population in the western section is concentrated in Pulaski (Somerset) and Laurel (London) counties. Like the rest of the west, Somerset — the 5th's second-largest city after Middlesboro — relies heavily on tourism and recreation. Lake Cumberland is nearby, as is the Big South Fork National River and Recreation area.

1990 Population: 614,119. White 606,222 (99%), Black 5,884 (1%), Other 2,013 (<1%). Hispanic origin 1,635 (<1%). 18 and over 441,744 (72%), 62 and over 88,669 (14%). Median age: 32.

block grants in her fiscal 1998 budget submission, but that her request was denied by the Office of Management and Budget before the administration sent the budget to Congress. With a knowing smile, Reno told Rogers she would not be displeased if Republicans put money back into the block grant program. "We'd like very much to work with you," she said.)

Rogers in 1995 joined Commerce Department critics in trying to kill its Advanced Technology Program, which promotes new technologies. But he went to bat for the Economic Development Administration, which was slated for elimination in the fiscal 1996 House budget resolution. Rogers is a staunch defender of the EDA, whose projects and grants have helped communities in his district spur economic development.

The fiscal 1996 House bill included a provision barring funding of U.S. troop participation in U.N. peacekeeping operations commanded by a foreigner unless military advisers inform the president and he informs Congress that such participation is in the country's national security interest. Democrats said the language infringed on the president's ability to conduct foreign policy. Rogers said, "They've got the power to do it, but we've got the power not to pay for it."

Rogers hoped to prevent his subcommittee's fiscal 1997 bill from running aground on policy disputes. He allowed consideration of a Democratic amendment adding $109 million to the $141 million recommended by the subcommittee for the Legal Services Corporation. The House in July 1996 approved the additional funding, 247-179, although Rogers voted against it.

But the measure ran into trouble from an unexpected source. Appropriations Committee Chairman Robert L. Livingston of Louisiana added language requiring Clinton to explain to the Senate any substantial changes to the 1972 Anti-Ballistic Missile Treaty, which the administration was negotiating with several Soviet republics. Livingston said the White House was negotiating secretly, in violation of the Constitution. The provision infuriated Democrats, who said it would undermine negotiations. When Rogers' subcommittee considered the bill, he had the uncomfortable job of asking Livingston to withdraw the missile-treaty language. Later, however, the full Appropriations Commit-tee approved Livingston's amendment.

Tobacco is a subject that can get the easygoing Rogers excited: He is a smoker and views the "right to smoke" as an issue of personal liberty. That is good politics because tobacco-growing still puts a lot of groceries on the table in the 5th. In June 1996 when the House debated an agriculture spending bill, Rogers ardently defended federal support programs for tobacco farmers. Illinois Democrat Richard J. Durbin proposed an amendment to do away with federal crop insurance and extension services for tobacco growers. Rogers said the bill would force small farmers onto welfare rolls and ultimately drive down the price of cigarettes by increasing imports of cheaper, foreign tobacco. "Smoking is not involved here," Rogers said. "What is involved here is singling out, by this sinister amendment, small, poor farmers who . . . have no other way to earn a living for their family." In the end, tobacco supporters barely beat back Durbin's amendment, 210-212.

At Home: Before and after a 1992 battle forced by redistricting, Rogers has usually won reelection handily. In fact, between 1984 and 1992, he never even had a Democratic opponent. But in 1992, redistricting merged Rogers' old rock-ribbed Republican 5th and retiring Democratic Rep. Carl C. Perkins' Democratic 7th.

Rogers started laying groundwork early, amassing a hefty treasury and making contacts in counties new to him as a crowded field of Democratic primary aspirants bickered. By the fall, Rogers' greatest concern was the unpopular Bush-Quayle ticket, which lost the 5th by 6 percentage points. The Democratic nominee, former state Sen. John Doug Hays, was sidetracked in October when it was revealed that his second wife hid a court file on their brief divorce. The file indicated that Hays divorced his first wife in 1991 and remarried three weeks later. Six weeks into that marriage, his second wife filed for divorce. But they reconciled, and she said she hid the file to protect Hays. Rogers carried 16 of the district's 27 counties en route to a 10-point victory.

He won decisively in 1994 and was unopposed in 1996. The week after that election, Rogers was awakened by a smoke alarm in his Somerset, Ky., home; he fled the house barefoot and wearing only a bathrobe. The blaze destroyed the back of the house and many of Rogers' personal effects.

Rogers first made his name locally in the 1960s as a civic activist promoting industrial development in Somerset (Pulaski County). He took over as the commonwealth's attorney in 1969 and continued to play a conspicuous role in politics as the prosecutor for Pulaski and Rockcastle counties. He was unsuccessful as the nominee for lieutenant governor in 1979, but the race helped him build name recognition, which paid off in his House campaign in 1980.

GOP Rep. Tim Lee Carter's retirement touched off a scramble, but Rogers quickly moved to the front of the 11-candidate GOP field. The primary revolved around personalities, geography and political alliances, not issues. Rogers drew barely one-fifth of the vote but carried 11 of the district's 28 counties, most of them around his home base in the center of the old 5th.

HOUSE ELECTIONS

1996 General		
Harold Rogers (R)	117,842	(100%)
1994 General		
Harold Rogers (R)	82,291	(79%)
Walter "Doc" Blevins (D)	21,318	(21%)

Previous Winning Percentages: 1992 (55%) **1990** (100%) **1988** (100%) **1986** (100%) **1984** (76%) **1982** (65%) **1980** (68%)

VOTING STUDIES

	Presidential Support		Party Unity		Conservative Coalition	
Year	**S**	**O**	**S**	**O**	**S**	**O**
1996	39	61	90	9	100	0
1995	23	76	91	4	86	2
1994	47	49	79	19	83	14
1993	47	53	84	14	95	5
1992	67	30	80	19	88	13
1991	70	25	76	21	86	5

CAMPAIGN FINANCE

	Receipts	Receipts from PACs	Expend-itures
1996			
Rogers (R)	$378,785	$200,494 (53%)	$132,717
1994			
Rogers (R)	$618,459	$188,081 (30%)	$348,253
Blevins (D)	$56,113	$31,500 (56%)	$52,377

KEY VOTES

1997	
Ban "partial birth" abortions	Y
1996	
Approve farm bill	Y
Deny public education to illegal immigrants	Y
Repeal ban on certain assault-style weapons	Y
Increase minimum wage	Y
Freeze defense spending	N
Approve welfare overhaul	Y
1995	
Approve balanced-budget constitutional amendment	Y
Relax Clean Water Act regulations	Y
Oppose limits on environmental regulations	N
Reduce projected Medicare spending	Y
Approve GOP budget with tax and spending cuts	Y

DISTRICT VOTE FOR PRESIDENT

1996		1992	
D	95,633 (47%)	**D**	111,887 (48%)
R	87,692 (43%)	**R**	97,432 (42%)
I	18,261 (9%)	**I**	24,344 (10%)

INTEREST GROUP RATINGS

Year	ADA	AFL-CIO	CCUS	ACU
1996	10	n/a	81	95
1995	0	17	92	80
1994	15	56	75	89
1993	20	42	82	83
1992	25	50	88	80
1991	10	25	90	79

6 Scotty Baesler (D)

Of Lexington — Elected 1992, 3rd term

Biographical Information
Born: July 9, 1941, Lexington, Ky.
Education: U. of Kentucky, B.A. 1963, J.D. 1966; George Washington U., M.A. 1996.
Military Service: Army Reserve, 1967-73.
Occupation: Lawyer; farmer.
Family: Wife, Alice Woods; two children.
Religion: Independent Christian.
Political Career: Vice mayor of Lexington, 1974-78; candidate for mayor of Lexington, 1977; Fayette County district judge, 1979-81; mayor of Lexington, 1982-92; sought Democratic nomination for governor, 1991.
Capitol Office: 2463 Rayburn Bldg. 20515; 225-4706.

Committees
Agriculture
Forestry, Resource Conservation & Research; Risk Management & Specialty Crops
Budget

In Washington: Baesler, who hopes to move from the House to the Senate in the 1998 election, goes into his statewide campaign with a voting record that is generally supportive of the policies of the Clinton administration, veering off dramatically only on the subject of tobacco, a mainstay of Kentucky's farm economy. A tobacco grower himself, Baesler has had some harsh words for the administration's crusade against the leaf.

Baesler wrote a letter to Clinton in July 1995 arguing that if the administration moved to regulate tobacco through the Food and Drug Administration (FDA), it could hurt a number of Southern Democrats' re-election bids. "I also feel it will be the straw that breaks the camel's back in terms of driving Southern planters and farmers from the Democratic Party," Baesler wrote.

Interestingly, Clinton carried Kentucky in the 1996 general election, and he even won a plurality of the vote in Baesler's 6th District.

Beyond tobacco, Baesler sees eye-to-eye with Clinton and the majority of House Democrats about two-thirds of the time on House floor votes. He supports abortion-rights advocates on most occasions, although he has voted to ban a particular abortion technique that opponents call "partial birth" abortion.

He has taken the side of labor unions in most of their high-profile disputes with the pro-business House Republican leadership — supporting a minimum wage increase in 1996, and voting against allowing companies to offer their employees comp time in lieu of pay for overtime work. He has supported gun control measures, endorsing a five-day waiting period for handgun purchases and a ban on certain semiautomatic assault-style weapons.

As a freshman in the 103rd Congress, Baesler did make one high-profile break with Clinton on a fiscal-policy vote: In August 1993 he opposed the president's deficit-reducing budget plan, which included tax increases. But not long after that, he got back on the White House's good side by announcing his support for NAFTA. At the start of the 105th, Baesler got a seat on the Budget Committee.

During debate on welfare overhaul in the 104th, Baesler, like most Democrats, was skeptical of GOP proposals. But he came around to compromising a little sooner than most in his party. In mid-July 1996, he was one of only 30 Democrats voting for the Republican welfare proposal on the House floor. Further GOP negotiations with Clinton produced a final compromise bill that the president agreed to sign. It passed the House in late July with 98 Democrats for (including Baesler) and 98 against.

Baesler, though, voted with Democratic liberals in June 1996 to freeze fiscal 1997 defense spending at the prior-year level, and he has been a strong proponent of some programs popular with liberals, such as Clinton's national service program, known as AmeriCorps. Arguing against GOP attempts to kill the program that provides college tuition stipends to students who engage in community service, Baesler called the program "lean and non-bureaucratic" and said it has made a positive difference "for my state of Kentucky and charities all over the country."

Baesler also has defended the Legal Services Corporation (LSC) against conservatives' attacks. The agency provides federal grants to local, nonprofit legal aid organizations. Its critics accuse LSC lawyers of pursuing class-action lawsuits to advance liberal causes instead of helping needy clients with their legal problems. But Baesler said, "Legal Services programs have a proud record of accomplishment in Kentucky and in my district. Central Kentucky Legal Services has been working since 1977 with low-income residents . . . serving an estimated poverty population of 58,000." The LSC has so far survived the efforts of some Republicans to kill it.

When the House was debating the fiscal 1996 energy and water appropriations bill, Baesler came to the defense of the Appalachian Regional Commission (ARC). The agency was created to spur economic development in 13 states in the

The 6th embodies the culture and the economic pursuits that most outsiders associate with the state of Kentucky. This is the heart of the Bluegrass region, which has spawned Kentucky Derby champions and is host to considerable tobacco and liquor interests.

Redistricting, which took effect after 1994, united in the 6th District all of Nicholas County (which had been shared with the 4th).

Lexington, the district's largest city, is known best as the hub of the country's horse-breeding industry. Hundreds of horse farms — ranging in size from just a few acres to more than 6,000 — cover the rich bluegrass pastureland within a 35-mile radius of the city.

Consolidated with Fayette County in 1974, Lexington experienced moderate growth in the 1970s and 1980s, spurred by the arrival of some clean, high-tech industry. By the early 1990s, the growth flattened out, in part because of some job losses associated with IBM's sale of its printer division to Lexmark. But, as the market center of the state's burley tobacco industry and home to the University of Kentucky, the city has been able to avoid an economic free fall.

The areas outside Fayette County experienced more rapid population growth and industrial development in the 1980s and early 1990s. Bourbon distilleries, tobacco and horse farms used to dominate the landscape, but they are being joined by new residential divisions and light industrial sprawl.

In Georgetown (Scott County), a Toyota Camry assembly plant that opened in 1988 has already expanded. Neighboring Woodford County is reaping some of the economic rewards of the plant; it ranks as the state's second-highest in per capita income.

Within commuting distance of Lexington, the

KENTUCKY 6
East central — Lexington; Frankfort

northern portion of Madison County — the district's second-most populous — includes bedroom communities for Lexington workers. Eastern Kentucky University (16,000 students) is in the southern portion of the district in the tobacco market town of Richmond.

The influx of white-collar executives and engineers to Lexington, and the changing landscape in the farming counties to the south and west, have increased GOP competitiveness.

Although residents still favor Democrats when registering to vote, George Bush carried the district in 1992 and Bill Clinton won it in 1996 by just 1 percentage point. Also in 1996, Mitch McConnell won 53 percent in the Senate race and led in 15 of the 19 counties wholly or partly in the 6th. At the congressional level, though, every county but three (Estill, Garrard and Jessamine) opted for Baesler, the former long-time Lexington mayor, in 1996.

Clinton carried Franklin County in 1992 and in 1996 on the strength of state government workers in Frankfort. Chosen as the state capital in a compromise between Lexington and Louisville, this Kentucky River Valley city has always stayed modest-sized.

East of Lexington, Democratic strength is found in the farming counties that remain largely untouched by Lexington sprawl.

1990 Population: 614,270. White 557,435 (91%), Black 49,921 (8%), Other 6,914 (1%). Hispanic origin 4,047 (1%). 18 and over 465,190 (76%), 62 and over 85,226 (14%). Median age: 32.

Appalachian region; some Republicans consider it an unneeded New Deal-era holdover. Baesler, who said his district has eight counties that qualify to receive educational and economic development assistance from the ARC, argued against a GOP amendment to terminate the agency. The amendment was rejected, 108-319.

Baesler also skewered Republicans for the education funding incorporated in the fiscal 1996 spending bill for the Labor, Health and Human Services and Education departments. He said the GOP was proposing to reduce spending on education and training by $36 billion over seven years. "Ask any kid what cuts are. They know cuts hurt. We are being asked to believe that these are the kind of cuts that can heal this nation. I believe these are the kind of cuts that will never heal. They will be with us for generations to come."

These criticisms of the GOP notwithstanding, Baesler reserves a measure of his indignation for Clinton on the subject of tobacco. In the summer of 1995, when Clinton was pondering letting the FDA regulate tobacco products, Baesler introduced a bill that would block FDA regulation and at the same time attempt to curb youth smoking.

Baesler's bill aimed to prohibit the sale of tobacco products to teen smokers in all 50 states and imposed fines for selling tobacco products to minors. "None of us questions the wisdom of preventing children from smoking, but the FDA is absolutely the wrong agency for this task," he said.

When the Clinton administration announced in January 1996 that the Department of Health and Human Services would issue federal regulations prohibiting the sale or distribution of tobacco products to minors, Baesler said he would not oppose them. Under the new regulations, states would have to enforce the new regulations or lose federal grants for substance-abuse prevention.

Baesler, who sits on the Agriculture Committee, also has fought to preserve the federally subsidized crop insurance program for tobacco farmers, which congressional anti-smoking forces and "deficit hawks" want to eliminate.

In February 1996, Baesler voted against the GOP's overhaul of federal agriculture law. The "Freedom to Farm" bill phased out most New Deal-era crop subsidies and brought federal farm policy more in line with free-market principles. It replaced subsidies with a system of fixed, but declining, payments that farmers would receive over seven years regardless of market prices or their planting decisions.

Baesler said that because the bill eliminated price supports for commodities such as wheat and grains, "commodities such as tobacco, peanuts and sugar can expect the same fate after seven years."

When the House considered the fiscal 1997 agriculture spending bill, Baesler reacted angrily to an effort by Illinois Democratic Rep. Richard J. Durbin, a longtime tobacco foe, to do away with federal crop insurance and extension services for tobacco growers.

"We are telling my farmers they cannot have insurance. It has nothing to do with smoking. You are basically telling the farmers in Kentucky and North Carolina, we cannot have the safety net that we need to make sure we do not go broke," Baesler said. "What is the next small farmer we are going to kick in the shins? What is the next small farmer we are going to hurt?"

At Home: In Kentucky, politics vies with basketball as the favorite contact sport, and Baesler has tasted success in both. During the early 1960s, he captained the University of Kentucky basketball team under legendary coach Adolph Rupp.

With Democratic Sen. Wendell Ford retiring in 1998, Baesler hopes to be his party's nominee for the open seat. If he is, he could find himself facing a foe who also has a sports pedigree: GOP Rep. Jim Bunning, a former professional baseball pitcher, is seeking the GOP Senate nomination.

The mayor of Lexington from 1982-92, Baesler tried to make the leap from the Bluegrass region of central Kentucky to the statewide stage in 1991, running for governor. He lost in the primary.

But Baesler immediately regrouped and in 1992 went after the 6th, which was open with GOP Rep. Larry J. Hopkins' retirement. Baesler routed four opponents in the Democratic primary. In November, he took 61 percent of the vote against Republican Charles W. Ellinger, a member of the Urban County Council.

Baesler barely got settled in the House when he announced in April 1994 that he would make a second try in 1995 to become governor of Kentucky. In November 1994, he won the 6th again, taking 59 percent. Then in late December 1994, he pulled the plug on his bid for governor. He said that the intense House schedule planned by the chamber's new GOP majority would keep him too busy in Washington to campaign effectively in Kentucky.

In 1996, Baesler faced a well-funded GOP challenger in state Rep. Ernest Fletcher, a physician and Baptist minister. Baesler won a third term with room to spare, although his 56 percent tally was the lowest of his three House elections.

HOUSE ELECTIONS

1996 General		
Scotty Baesler (D)	125,999	(56%)
Ernest Fletcher (R)	100,231	(44%)
1994 General		
Scotty Baesler (D)	70,085	(59%)
Matthew Eric Wills (R)	49,032	(41%)

Previous Winning Percentages: 1992 (61%)

CAMPAIGN FINANCE

	Receipts	Receipts from PACs		Expenditures
1996				
Baesler (D)	$583,576	$303,750	(52%)	$574,074
Fletcher (R)	$437,953	$46,035	(11%)	$435,065
1994				
Baesler (D)	$203,618	$90,500	(44%)	$223,327
Wills (R)	$23,091	$1,557	(7%)	$23,190

DISTRICT VOTE FOR PRESIDENT

1996		1992	
D	110,256 (46%)	**D**	101,887 (41%)
R	108,150 (45%)	**R**	105,263 (43%)
I	19,425 (8%)	**I**	39,738 (16%)

KEY VOTES

1997	
Ban "partial birth" abortions	Y
1996	
Approve farm bill	N
Deny public education to illegal immigrants	N
Repeal ban on certain assault-style weapons	N
Increase minimum wage	Y
Freeze defense spending	Y
Approve welfare overhaul	Y
1995	
Approve balanced-budget constitutional amendment	Y
Relax Clean Water Act regulations	N
Oppose limits on environmental regulations	N
Reduce projected Medicare spending	N
Approve GOP budget with tax and spending cuts	N

VOTING STUDIES

	Presidential Support		Party Unity		Conservative Coalition	
Year	S	O	S	O	S	O
1996	71	27	68	29	75	24
1995	70	29	58	40	84	14
1994	85	15	82	17	83	17
1993	72	25	84	14	64	34

INTEREST GROUP RATINGS

Year	ADA	AFL-CIO	CCUS	ACU
1996	60	n/a	40	25
1995	65	75	54	28
1994	45	56	92	33
1993	40	75	55	39

LOUISIANA

Governor: Mike Foster (R)
First elected: 1995
Length of term: 4 years
Term expires: 1/00
Salary: $95,000
Term limit: 2 terms
Phone: (504) 342-7015
Born: July 11, 1930; Shreveport, La.
Education: Louisiana State U., B.S. 1951.
Military Service: Air Force, 1952-55.
Occupation: Sugar company executive.
Family: Wife, Alice Cosner; two children, two stepchildren.
Religion: Episcopalian.
Political Career: La. Senate, 1988-96.

Lt. Gov.: Kathleen Babineaux Blanco (D)
First elected: 1995
Length of term: 4 years
Term expires: 1/00
Salary: $85,000
Phone: (504) 342-7009

State election official: (504) 342-4971
Democratic headquarters: (504) 336-4155
Republican headquarters: (504) 383-7234

REDISTRICTING

Louisiana lost one seat in reapportionment, to 7. Legislature passed map May 29, 1992; governor signed June 1. Justice Dept. approved map July 6. Federal court invalidated map used in '92 election Dec. 28, 1993. Governor signed into law April 25, 1994, a new map by Legislature. Federal court invalidated new map July 22, implemented its own map July 25. Supreme Court stayed decision Aug. 11, letting '94 election proceed under Legislature map. The Supreme Court dismissed a challenge to the new map June 29, 1995. Federal court again ruled the state's plan unconstitutional on Jan. 5, 1996, and imposed a new map the same day. The Supreme Court rejected an appeal to overturn the new map June 24, 1996.

STATE LEGISLATURE

Bicameral Legislature. Meets March-June yearly.

Senate: 39 members, 4-year terms
1996 breakdown: 25D, 14R; 37 men, 2 women
Salary: $16,800
Phone: (504) 342-2040

House of Representatives: 105 members, 4-year terms
1996 breakdown: 76D, 28R, 1I; 91 men, 14 women
Salary: $16,800
Phone: (504) 342-7263

URBAN STATISTICS

City	Population
New Orleans	496,938
Mayor Mark Morial, D	
Baton Rouge	219,531
Mayor Tom Edward McHugh, D	
Shreveport	198,525
Mayor Robert Williams, R	
Metairie	149,428
Parish President Michael Yenni, D	
Lafayette	94,440
Mayor Walter Comeaux, D	

U.S. CONGRESS

Senate: 2 D, 0 R
House: 2 D, 5 R

TERM LIMITS

For state offices: Yes
Senate: 3 terms
House: 3 terms

ELECTIONS

1996 Presidential Vote

Bill Clinton	52%
Bob Dole	40%
Ross Perot	7%

1992 Presidential Vote

Bill Clinton	46%
George Bush	41%
Ross Perot	12%

1988 Presidential Vote

George Bush	54%
Michael S. Dukakis	44%

POPULATION

1990 population		4,219,973
1980 population		4,205,900
Percent change		+<1%
Rank among states:		21
White		67%
Black		31%
Hispanic		2%
Asian or Pacific islander		1%
Urban		68%
Rural		32%
Born in state		79%
Foreign-born		2%
Under age 18	1,227,269	29%
Ages 18-64	2,523,713	60%
65 and older	468,991	11%
Median age		31

MISCELLANEOUS

Capital: Baton Rouge
Number of parishes: 64
Per capita income: $15,143 (1991)
Rank among states: 45
Total area: 47,752 sq. miles
Rank among states: 31

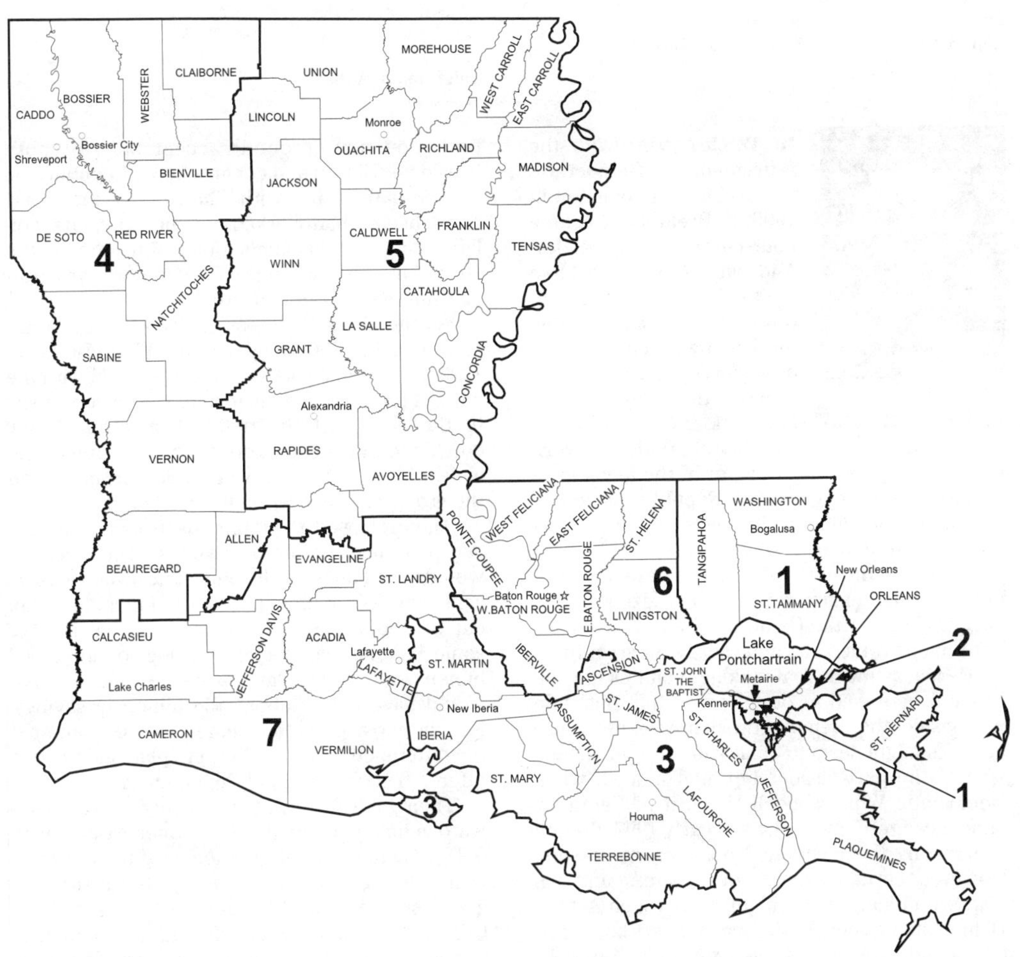
CADDO
BOSSIER
WEBSTER
CLAIBORNE
UNION
MOREHOUSE
WEST CARROLL
EAST CARROLL
LINCOLN
Monroe
OUACHITA
RICHLAND
MADISON
Bossier City
Shreveport
BIENVILLE
JACKSON
FRANKLIN
DE SOTO
RED RIVER
CALDWELL
TENSAS
4
5
WINN
NATCHITOCHES
CATAHOULA
LA SALLE
GRANT
SABINE
CONCORDIA
Alexandria
RAPIDES
VERNON
AVOYELLES
WEST FELICIANA
EAST FELICIANA
ST. HELENA
WASHINGTON
Bogalusa
ALLEN
POINTE COUPEE
TANGIPAHOA
E.BATON ROUGE
EVANGELINE
BEAUREGARD
ST. LANDRY
6
1
New Orleans
Baton Rouge
W.BATON ROUGE
ST.TAMMANY
ORLEANS
LIVINGSTON
CALCASIEU
JEFFERSON DAVIS
ACADIA
Lafayette
IBERVILLE
Lake Pontchartrain
2
ST. MARTIN
ASCENSION
ST. JOHN THE BAPTIST
Metairie
Lake Charles
LAFAYETTE
Kenner
ST. JAMES
New Iberia
ASSUMPTION
ST. CHARLES
ST. BERNARD
CAMERON
7
IBERIA
VERMILION
3
ST. MARY
JEFFERSON
1
3
LAFOURCHE
Houma
PLAQUEMINES
TERREBONNE

John B. Breaux (D)

Of Crowley — Elected 1986, 2nd term

Biographical Information

Born: March 1, 1944, Crowley, La.

Education: U. of Southwestern Louisiana, B.A. 1964; Louisiana State U., J.D. 1967.

Occupation: Lawyer.

Family: Wife, Lois Daigle; four children.

Religion: Roman Catholic.

Political Career: U.S. House, 1972-87.

Capitol Office: 516 Hart Bldg. 20510; 224-4623.

Committees

Special Aging

Commerce, Science & Transportation
Aviation; Communications; Consumer Affairs, Foreign Commerce & Tourism (ranking); Oceans & Fisheries; Surface Transportation & Merchant Marine

Finance
International Trade; Social Security & Family Policy (ranking); Taxation & IRS Oversight

Chief Deputy Whip

In Washington: With the retirement of Democratic Sen. J. Bennett Johnston in 1996, Breaux became Louisiana's senior senator. And with Republican Mike Foster in the governor's office, Breaux also is now the leading voice for Democrats in his state.

With this new status, look for Breaux to do even more of what he has done during a quarter-century in politics — work to move his party to the center of the ideological spectrum and forge ties with Republicans willing to help him advance the interests of constituents and home-state businesses.

Breaux is the sort who cannot get enough of politics, whether fundraising, strategizing or legislating. True to the Cajun tradition, "laissez les bons temps roulez," he makes it seem great fun.

He has as much deal-making talent as anyone in the Senate, and a voting record that puts him just inside the Democratic mainstream. These qualities might seem to qualify him for an elected spot in the party leadership, and indeed, when Democratic Whip Wendell H. Ford of Kentucky announced retirement plans in early 1997, Breaux was among the mentioned possible successors. However, certain aspects of Breaux's and his state's political image might be a tough sell to Democrats nationally: He is a stalwart backer of the oil industry, an unapologetic protégé of controversial former Gov. Edwin W. Edwards and, like Edwards, a roguish charmer, known for once quipping that while his vote could not be bought, "it can be rented."

Although cast into the Senate minority by the 1994 GOP surge, Breaux has a hawk's eyes for legislative opportunity, and that kept him near the center of the action in the 104th Congress. He allied himself with Democratic leaders in seeking changes to the welfare system, Medicaid and the government's job-training programs. But he also joined forces with Rhode Island Republican John H. Chafee during the debate over how to balance the federal budget. Breaux and Chafee tried to find common ground acceptable to both President Clinton and congressional Republicans.

The partnership with Chafee was not a new one. The two had worked together for years, collaborating, for instance, on health care in the 103rd Congress, when the GOP minority frustrated Clinton's overhaul efforts.

As the 104th Congress slogged through difficult budget negotiations with the White House in 1995, Breaux and Chafee grew frustrated with the pace of progress and decided to seek a consensus in the center of the political spectrum. They quickly found six senators from each side of the aisle willing to work toward a compromise, and the group's ranks eventually swelled to 21.

They released their bipartisan balanced-budget plan just before Christmas. The package would have balanced the budget in seven years by achieving $661 billion in savings. It included a tax cut of about $130 billion, Medicare savings of some $154 billion, Medicaid savings of about $62 billion and changes in the welfare system that would have netted about $58 billion in savings. For the most part, the Chafee-Breaux plan split the difference between Clinton's plan and the one offered by congressional Republicans.

Their budget outline also called for a downward adjustment in the Consumer Price Index (CPI), the measure of inflation used to determine cost-of-living adjustments for government programs such as Social Security. A lowering of the CPI would decrease benefits under such programs and increase taxes by slowing the indexing process. The Chafee-Breaux plan would have achieved about $110 billion in savings by lowering the CPI, far more than either the Clinton or GOP plans would have achieved.

Although Clinton and the GOP Congress ultimately failed to work out a long-term budget plan, many of the ideas in the Breaux-Chafee framework continued to surface as the 105th Congress renewed efforts to craft a long-term budget-balancing strategy.

Similarly, Breaux had an impact on the health care debate. The centrist proposal he and Chafee crafted in the 103rd included language that would have prohibited health insurers from refusing coverage or renewal of coverage because of pre-existing medical conditions. Although the broader plan fell by the wayside in the 103rd, the narrow language about pre-existing conditions resurfaced as the foundation of a more modest plan to overhaul the health insurance market. Clinton eventually signed that measure into law.

Because the GOP majority recognizes that Breaux's support can spell the difference between defeat and victory for their proposals, few Democrats can match his ability to get their attention. Early in the 104th, as the Senate neared a vote on a balanced-budget constitutional amendment, Breaux briefly gave GOP leaders a scare when he canceled a news conference at which he was expected to announce he would support the amendment, as he had when the Senate voted on the matter in 1994. Breaux issued a statement saying he was working with fellow undecideds to "address the role of the federal courts in raising taxes and cutting programs under this amendment." Proponents subsequently agreed to include language in the amendment addressing the judicial intervention concern, and Breaux voted for the amendment again in March 1995. (He backed it again in 1997.)

Breaux also helped nudge Republicans toward the center on welfare overhaul in the 104th. Although he worked with Minority Leader Tom Daschle of South Dakota and Maryland Democrat Barbara A. Mikulski to craft the Democratic leadership's alternative welfare plan, Breaux was quick to note the need for compromise with Republicans. "We can't pass a bill without working with them," he said. "They cannot get a bill signed into law without working with us."

Initial efforts to overhaul welfare as part of a broader plan to balance the budget failed in 1995 when Clinton vetoed the GOP-backed bill, but Breaux quickly sought compromise when Republicans offered a new plan in 1996. He and John D. Rockefeller IV, W.Va., voted for the bill on the Senate floor, with the understanding that Democrats would be included in conference discussions, as they were not the first time.

Despite his willingness to work with Republicans, Breaux takes pains not to offend his own party leaders, often negotiating on their behalf — or at least with their blessing. During the health care debate in the 103rd, then-Majority Leader George J. Mitchell of Maine kept in close touch with Breaux, who, along with Chafee, forged the Mainstream Group of Senate moderates. They tried to slow health cost increases through a tax cap limiting businesses' deductions. More than 20 senators embraced the Chafee-Breaux plan, but Mitchell still could not muster the 60 votes needed to stop a filibuster against a health care bill.

Late in 1988, Mitchell picked Breaux for the position that Mitchell himself had parlayed into his leadership victory: chairman of the fundraising Democratic Senatorial Campaign Committee (DSCC). The choice appeared to be an olive branch from Mitchell, who had won the majority leadership over Breaux's home-state colleague, Johnston.

Breaux was ideal for the DSCC job. While Republicans had spoken of using 1990 as a springboard for retaking Senate control in 1992, Democrats actually increased their majority by one seat in 1990, with Breaux raising record sums for his party's candidates.

During the 101st Congress, Breaux was awarded his coveted seat on the Finance Committee, where former Louisiana Democrat Russell B. Long wielded great institutional power as chairman for 14 years. In the 103rd, Breaux was appointed to a spot on the leadership team as chief deputy whip.

Breaux also served a stint as chairman of the Democratic Leadership Conference and, like other moderate-to-conservative Southerners in his party, he very much wants Democrats to have a more centrist image. Considering that, though, Breaux has voted the party line quite often. Notable departures include his stance on issues of gun control and abortion.

Breaux is unabashed about courting business. The quote about his vote being "rented" came in 1981, as he explained that he would support President Ronald Reagan's proposed social spending cuts in return for concessions on natural gas policy and sugar subsidies.

Above all, Breaux is an advocate for Louisiana's interests, especially energy and commercial fishing. In 1990, he helped secure funding to help Louisiana address its coastal erosion problems, a concern not only of environmentalists but also of business. Late in the 101st, during consideration of a deficit-reduction package, Breaux persuaded his Finance colleagues to include a $50 million "wetlands preservation" trust fund, with about $35 million going to Louisiana.

Still, true to his pragmatist style, Breaux is willing to compromise even on some matters that may affect his constituents negatively. In the 104th, Breaux resisted GOP efforts to slash the subsidies for rice, a key farm commodity in Louisiana, as lawmakers debated changes to the nation's farm law. The final bill, though more friendly to rice farmers than at the outset of the debate — thanks to the work of Breaux and other Southerners — left some rice producers skeptical. Still, Breaux voted for the legislation.

And despite a dedication to nuclear power and the petrochemical industry, Breaux also has to balance the safety and environmental concerns of Louisianans. When Environment Committee members offered their first rewrite of the Clean Air Act in April 1989, Breaux was considered a pivotal backer. "Those of us in Louisiana want not only jobs, we want to be able to breathe the air and breathe it safely," he said.

At Home: Breaux learned his trade from one of Louisiana's masters — former Gov. Edwards, who served four terms and was once a member of the House. Breaux was Edwards' junior law partner and served for four years as one of his top congressional aides.

When Edwards first won the governorship in February 1972, he pushed for Breaux to be his successor in the House. With Edwards' organization, Breaux easily paced the field of six Democratic primary candidates, then won the September runoff with 55 percent over TV newscaster Gary Tyler, whom Edwards had defeated to win his first House term seven years earlier.

Breaux does not, however, owe his ascent to the Senate to Edwards' influence. If anything, his one-time mentor made his 1986 bid to replace retiring Democrat Long more difficult. During Edwards' third term, Louisiana's oil industry had foundered, and by the time of the 1986 Senate contest the state's economy was reeling. Many voters were in a mood to blame Democrats. Moreover, Edwards' image had suffered during two trials on corruption charges, even though he was eventually acquitted.

Those circumstances gave the GOP one of its best openings in years. Early in 1986, GOP Rep. W. Henson Moore began airing ads designed to exploit voters' restlessness. Democrats, Moore charged, had squandered the state's resources and prostituted the political system to their own advantage. Republicans, Moore argued, were the party of reform.

If Moore had continued on the same tack, he might have won. But as the all-party September primary approached, he pushed to win more than 50 percent of the vote and avoid a runoff. He shifted his emphasis, beginning a wave of ads and mailings that attacked Breaux directly. "The politician's politician, always putting himself first," one mailer called the Democrat. At the same time, the national GOP mounted a program to purge ineligible voters in black precincts.

None of those tactics sat well with Louisiana's basically Democratic electorate. Moore seemed mean-spirited, especially in contrast with Breaux's Cajun charm. And the "ballot security" program infuriated black voters — a boost for Breaux, since many blacks had considered him too conservative.

The primary was a turning point. Moore came in first, but he did not run as strongly as many had expected. Over the next month, Breaux worked to take the high ground Moore had abandoned, arguing that the state's problems stemmed not from the state government, but from a GOP administration that had followed misguided trade and farm policies. Moore's first allegiance, he charged, was to his party and to President Reagan, not to Louisiana. Breaux won 42 of 64 parishes, taking 53 percent overall.

Six years later, the state GOP was in disarray, coming off a disastrous election year in 1991 that was marked by the defeat of both its endorsed gubernatorial candidate (Rep. Clyde C. Holloway) and the incumbent governor, Democrat-turned-Republican Buddy Roemer, and the embarrassment of having Republican David Duke, a former Ku Klux Klan leader and former Nazi sympathizer, make the gubernatorial runoff against Edwards.

With Breaux's popularity at seemingly unassailable heights, no prominent Republican stepped forward. Breaux won re-election in the five-way primary with 73 percent.

SENATE ELECTIONS

1992 Primary †		
John B. Breaux (D)	616,021	(73%)
Jon Khachaturian (I)	74,785	(9%)
Lyle Stockstill (R)	69,986	(8%)
Nick Joseph Accardo (D)	45,839	(5%)
Fred Clegg Strong (R)	36,406	(4%)

Previous Winning Percentages: 1986 (53%) **1984*** (86%) **1982*** (79%) **1980*** (100%) **1978*** (60%) **1976*** (83%) **1974*** (89%) **1972*** (100%)

** House election*

† In Louisiana the primary is open to candidates of all parties. If a candidate wins 50 percent or more of the vote in the primary, no general election is held. A candidate unopposed in the primary and general election is declared elected and the candidate's name does not appear on the ballot.

CAMPAIGN FINANCE

	Receipts	Receipts from PACs	Expend-itures
1992			
Breaux (D)	$2,449,803	$1,318,635 (54%)	$1,446,199

KEY VOTES

1997	
Approve balanced-budget constitutional amendment	Y
Approve chemical weapons treaty	Y
1996	
Approve farm bill	Y
Limit punitive damages in product liability cases	N
Exempt small businesses from higher minimum wage	N
Approve welfare overhaul	Y
Bar job discrimination based on sexual orientation	Y
Override veto of ban on "partial birth" abortions	Y
1995	
Approve GOP budget with tax and spending cuts	N
Approve constitutional amendment barring flag desecration	Y

VOTING STUDIES

	Presidential Support		Party Unity		Conservative Coalition	
Year	S	O	S	O	S	O
1996	76	22	69	29	82	16
1995	76	23	73	26	93	5
1994	81	15	74	21	78	22
1993	84	13	78	20	80	17
1992	42	58	68	29	76	21
1991	65	33	59	37	83	13

INTEREST GROUP RATINGS

Year	ADA	AFL-CIO	CCUS	ACU
1996	60	n/a	62	20
1995	70	75	56	22
1994	55	63	44	17
1993	40	82	27	24
1992	60	67	10	30
1991	30	67	40	57

Mary L. Landrieu (D)

Of Baton Rouge — Elected 1996, 1st term

Biographical Information

Born: Nov. 23, 1955, Arlington, Va.

Education: Louisiana State U., B.A. 1977.

Occupation: Real estate agent.

Family: Husband, Frank E. Snellings; one child.

Religion: Roman Catholic.

Political Career: La. House, 1980-88; La. treasurer, 1988-96; candidate for governor, 1995.

Capitol Office: 702 Hart Bldg. 20510; 224-5824.

Committees

Agriculture, Nutrition & Forestry
Marketing, Inspection & Product Promotion; Production & Price Competitiveness

Energy & Natural Resources
Energy Research Development Production & Regulation; Forests & Public Land Management; National Parks, Historic Preservation & Recreation

Small Business

The Path to Washington: When Landrieu decided to jump into the Louisiana political gumbo, she already had the benefit of a family name well-known in Pelican State politics. Her father, Moon Landrieu, had been mayor of New Orleans and secretary of Housing and Urban Development in the Carter administration.

It didn't take her long to build a name for herself. She acquired a reputation as a political reformer while serving as a state legislator and later as state treasurer. She comes to the Senate from the "new Democrat" wing of her party, and in her bid for the Senate, she embraced the centrist politics espoused by President Clinton in his two presidential elections.

Given Landrieu's association with reform, it was ironic that her arrival in the Senate was clouded by an investigation into her election. Her Republican opponent in 1996, Louis "Woody" Jenkins, alleged that gambling interests and political associates of New Orleans Mayor Marc Morial had arranged vote buying, multiple voting and other forms of fraud. Although Jenkins said neither Landrieu nor her campaign had been involved in any irregularities, he maintained that tainted votes had enabled her to win.

Jenkins conducted a national campaign of protest, appealing to conservatives for money and attracting attention in conservative media. He called on the Senate to vacate Landrieu's seat and order a new election.

Two attorneys hired by the Senate Rules Committee recommended dismissing most of Jenkins' charges and seeking hard evidence of the others. But the committee, led by Chairman John W. Warner, a Virginia Republican, set aside that recommendation and dispatched a fresh team of investigators to New Orleans in May 1997 to look into the full set of allegations.

The controversy overshadowed several of the critical decisions Landrieu had to make in her early months in the Senate, among them her vote to amend the Constitution to require a balanced federal budget and her vote on a particular abortion method opponents call "partial birth" abortion.

Looking to the longer term, Landrieu had said her top priority in the Senate would be education, including full funding of Head Start, more federal dollars for computers in classrooms and tax credits to help middle-class families pay for college tuition.

On taxes generally, she favors a $10,000-per-year deduction for education expenses and some reduction in capital gains taxes as long it fits within budget constraints.

As a candidate in 1996, Landrieu was a strong supporter of the minimum wage increase enacted that year. But she says she also would like to see better enforcement of laws guaranteeing equal pay for women and increased access to job training programs. Even though more jobs for skilled people have become available in Louisiana, many individuals do not have the skills to fill those jobs, she says.

Landrieu was given a seat on the Energy and Natural Resources Committee, a panel on which her predecessor, J. Bennett Johnston, was once chairman (and retired as the ranking Democrat). Efforts to deregulate utility industries are on that panel's agenda, and Landrieu says she will be protecting Louisiana's interests — which include its large oil and gas industries as well as its energy consumers. Landrieu is also mindful of the support she has received from both industry and environmental groups.

As a member of the Agriculture, Nutrition and Forestry Committee, she plans to promote a research and technology partnership between the private sector and the federal government to help the state's farmers. She was also assigned a seat on the Small Business Committee.

Landrieu's political road to the Senate was not a smooth one. Her bid for governor in 1995 was derailed in the primary by Democratic Rep. Cleo Fields, one of the state's two black members of Congress, who ultimately lost to Republican Mike Foster. Landrieu did not endorse Fields in his runoff against Foster, a decision that would soon return to haunt her.

In her 1996 Senate bid, Landrieu had to battle Democratic Attorney General Richard P. Ieyoub, who quickly wrapped up the support of many of the state's black leaders, including Fields.

Given the oddity of Louisiana's election law, which puts candidates from all parties together on a single primary ballot, Landrieu and Ieyoub appeared for a time to be headed for an all-Democratic runoff. They were running first and second in the summertime polls, with no fewer than six serious Republican candidates dividing the rest of the vote.

In September, however, GOP leaders rallied around Jenkins, enabling him to break out of the pack and consolidate enough of the Republican vote to win a surprising strong plurality in the primary. Landrieu wound up barely eking out a second-place finish over Ieyoub to earn a spot in the runoff with Jenkins.

Landrieu looked becalmed. Ieyoub almost surely would have beaten her in the primary had it not been for news reports that he had used campaign funds for items such as clothing and improvements to his home. Staggering into the runoff with the surging Jenkins, Landrieu suddenly needed to recruit Ieyoub's black supporters. That task was doubly difficult given her strained relations with Fields, who remained an influential leader in the state's black community. After some hesitation, and at the urging of many state and national Democrats, Fields eventually endorsed Landrieu's Senate bid.

Landrieu portrayed herself in her Senate campaign as a fighter for the middle class and working poor. At the same time, she attempted to cast Jenkins as a right-wing extremist. She also was critical of his proposal to abolish the Internal Revenue Service and replace the current tax system with a consumption tax collected by the states. In particular, Landrieu questioned his motives for such a proposal after news reports revealed that the IRS in recent years had placed several liens on his business, Great Oaks Broadcasting, saying he had failed to pay taxes on time.

Jenkins, meanwhile, tried to portray Landrieu as a tax-and-spend liberal. He also criticized her for helping to win parole for a convicted killer. In addition, Jenkins and others, including the retired Roman Catholic archbishop of New Orleans, attacked Landrieu for her support of abortion rights.

Jenkins, who had been a leading opponent of abortion in the state Legislature, said her stand on abortion was out of step with the rest of the state, which has a significant Catholic population and many evangelical Protestants who oppose abortion. Landrieu moderated her stand somewhat by supporting a ban on so-called partial birth abortions.

The candidates met in televised debates that highlighted their many differences. Asked at one point to make one positive statement about his opponent, Jenkins thought a moment and said: "She's nice looking."

Landrieu emerged the winner by 5,788 votes out of 1.7 million cast, the slimmest winning margin ever in a Louisiana Senate race. Jenkins, bidding to be the state's first Republican in the Senate since Reconstruction, refused to concede.

SENATE ELECTIONS

1996 General		
Mary L. Landrieu (D)	852,945	(50%)
Louis "Woody" Jenkins (R)	847,157	(50%)
1996 Primary †		
Louis "Woody" Jenkins (R)	322,244	(27%)
Mary L. Landrieu (D)	264,268	(22%)
Richard P. Ieyoub (D)	250,682	(21%)
David Ernest Duke (R)	141,489	(12%)
Jimmy Hayes (R)	71,699	(6%)
Bill Linder (R)	58,243	(5%)
Chuck McMains (R)	45,164	(4%)
Peggy Wilson (R)	31,877	(3%)
Troyce Guice (D)	15,277	(1%)

† In Louisiana the primary is open to candidates of all parties. If a candidate wins 50 percent or more of the vote in the primary, no general election is held. A candidate unopposed in the primary and general election is declared elected, and the candidate's name does not appear on the ballot.

CAMPAIGN FINANCE

	Receipts	Receipts from PACs	Expend-itures
1996			
Landrieu (D)	$2,899,684	$535,736 (18%)	$2,715,287
Jenkins (R)	$1,969,175	$479,543 (24%)	$1,967,742

KEY VOTES

1997	
Approve balanced-budget constitutional amendment	Y
Approve chemical weapons treaty	Y

1 Robert L. Livingston (R)

Of Metairie — Elected 1977; 10th full term

Biographical Information
Born: April 30, 1943, Colorado Springs, Colo.
Education: Tulane U., B.A. 1967, J.D. 1968.
Military Service: Navy, 1961-63; Naval Reserve, 1963-67.
Occupation: Lawyer.
Family: Wife, Bonnie Robichaux; four children.
Religion: Roman Catholic.
Political Career: Republican nominee for U.S. House, 1976; Republican candidate for governor, 1987.
Capitol Office: 2406 Rayburn Bldg. 20515; 225-3015.

Committees
Appropriations (chairman)

In Washington: Livingston, normally affable but possessed of a hot temper, often dismisses critics' "Chicken Little" complaints that the sky will fall due to Republican spending cuts. But it's at his Appropriations Committee that GOP chickens come home to roost — where members' hard-to-reconcile desires to balance the budget and fund projects back home clash under Livingston's stern gaze. If being in this position has at times stretched Livingston's nerves thin and caused him to make some regrettable remarks, he nevertheless can rightly boast that "What savings there are in the budget came from this committee."

At the start of the 104th Congress, Speaker Newt Gingrich handpicked Livingston for the Appropriations chairmanship over three more senior members. Livingston was one of Gingrich's closest associates in the House, but the Speaker also believed that the Louisianan had been less pickled in the committee's culture of mutual convenience. That meant he might be more likely to play Scrooge instead of Santa when members came calling with funding requests. Even after the panel's senior Republican, Joseph M. McDade of Pennsylvania, was acquitted of ethics charges by a federal jury in 1996 (lifting the cloud that had kept him from the chairmanship), Gingrich refused Livingston's offer to resign. The Speaker still thought Livingston the best man for this uniquely powerful and challenging job.

One reason he thought so was the prospect for a balanced-budget deal with the re-elected President Clinton, a deal that Gingrich knew could unravel in Appropriations unless preserved by a strong chairman loyal to the Speaker. When the deal was struck in May, Livingston was on hand to defend it — despite discretionary spending levels beyond what he would have preferred.

Two years earlier, at the committee's organizational meeting for the 104th Congress, Livingston had displayed his bona fides theatrically by brandishing a series of progressively larger knives that culminated in a machete. His first bill, meant to fund unexpected military maneuvers and natural disasters, ended up slashing $16 billion in recently allocated spending. These so-called rescissions were among the proudest achievements of the new Republican majority.

But the programs Livingston cut so readily were mainly Democratic priorities; the trick became more difficult during the main appropriations season, when he had to carve into programs beloved of Republicans.

Livingston's difficulties in this regard were well illustrated by a supplemental spending bill considered early in 1997. Republicans balked when President Clinton asked for $4 billion to fund military operations, but by the time Appropriations subcommittees had finished their work, they had doubled the package's price tag.

Livingston got into fights early in the 104th with Budget Committee Chairman John R. Kasich, R-Ohio, who stepped into the privileged purview of the appropriators by suggesting not just budget targets but also specific spending cuts. Gingrich brokered a deal between the two with Kasich agreeing to back off but Livingston agreeing to live within the overall budget numbers.

Livingston disagreed strongly with the approach of Agriculture Chairman Pat Roberts, R-Kan., to remaking federal farm policy: weaning farmers from government assistance but only after giving them a boost in funding first. In 1996, Roberts succeeded in passing the "Freedom to Farm" measure. Livingston voted against it, one of only two votes he would cast against high-profile GOP initiatives in the 104th (term limits being the other). Thereafter, in committee, Livingston sought to pare back the first-year payments Roberts had authorized. But with Democrats arguing that this amounted to a broken promise, Livingston restored the funds.

The two chairmen's troubled relationship reached its nadir in July 1995, when Livingston and Roberts' top aide nearly came to blows. Livingston opened a meeting by saying to Roberts: "Some son of a bitch on your staff has been saying bad stuff about my staff in the press, and I'm tired of it." The Roberts aide, objecting to the characterization, confronted Livingston, but the two were separated.

LOUISIANA 1
East — Metairie; part of Florida Parishes

The 1st is conservative territory dominated by the mostly white suburban communities that ring New Orleans. Every proposal considered during the redistricting process of the 1990s spared the 1st from substantial overhaul, including the 1996 court-imposed plan used for that year's elections.

Contributing in part to the district's GOP tendencies is the relative paucity of African-Americans, who make up slightly more than 10 percent of the district's registered voters, the lowest level of any district in a state that is more than 30 percent black.

Jefferson Parish, which is shared with the 2nd and 3rd, anchors the district. The area is made up of affluent New Orleans suburbs such as Metairie, base of the state legislative seat held from 1988 until January 1993 by David Duke, the former Ku Klux Klansman turned GOP conservative who waged high-profile Senate, gubernatorial and presidential campaigns. Nearly half the district resides in Jefferson. The area is packed with white-collar conservatives, many of whom live in the affluent suburbs dotting the southern shore of Lake Pontchartrain (named for Louis XIV's finance minister) and work in New Orleans.

From east Jefferson, the 1st darts across the 23.9-mile Lake Ponchartrain Causeway to take in three of the "Florida Parishes" north of New Orleans: St. Tammany, Washington and Tangipahoa. The eight parishes north of the lake and east of the Mississippi are so named because they were part of Spanish Florida until 1810.

The richest parish in the state, St. Tammany is home to about a quarter of the 1st's registered voters. Once an isolated vacation area for residents escaping the heat and humidity of New Orleans, St. Tammany now is a booming suburban haven, replete with suburbanites who don't mind commuting across the Lake Pontchartrain Causeway to their jobs in New Orleans. St. Tammany's population exploded by more than 70 percent in the 1970s, and its 20 percent growth rate from 1990 to 1995 was the highest in the state. Many of the newcomers are transplants from the East and Midwest who have maintained GOP voting habits.

St. Tammany gave 60 percent of its votes to Bob Dole in 1996, his best performance in the state and one of only two parishes to give him a majority (the other is Jefferson Parish).

To the west of St. Tammany lies Tangipahoa, well-known as a prodigious supplier of strawberries. It is now home to many New Orleans and Baton Rouge commuters, though Tangipahoa farms still produce great amounts of strawberries and bell peppers. The parish economy has diversified and is sustained by Southeastern Louisiana University (14,000 students) and distribution centers for Winn-Dixie and Delchamps supermarkets.

In the district's northeast corner is rural Washington Parish, which bolsters the district's conservative nature and has remained in the 1st since the 1992 redistricting round. Predominantly a farming community that grows watermelons and breeds chickens, Washington Parish bears a striking resemblance to the Mississippi counties it borders.

As of May 19, the Census Bureau had not recalculated population data, racial and ethnic breakdowns and age statistics for districts newly drawn for the 1996 elections.

Livingston's intemperance proved to be a major political handicap on at least one occasion. As Republicans, unable to reach a budget accord with Clinton, voted three days before Christmas 1995 to extend what would prove to be history's longest government shutdown, Livingston thundered on the floor, in his best imitation of Winston Churchill, "We will never, never, never give in. . . . We will stay here until doomsday." He earned roars of approval from his colleagues, but his visage, splashed across the nation's TV screens on many news programs, made him seem the face of Republican intransigence. House Republicans voted to take a Christmas break after all, and the party got the political blame for the partial government shutdown.

Livingston was beside himself with frustration because he had fought so long and hard just to get his bills to the point of being vetoed. His first round of spending measures had routinely been rejected or ignored by the Senate. Some that survived the House-Senate conference were then turned down at the clearing stage by recalcitrant House members. The packages had become magnets for controversy, not only because they upended Democratic spending priorities but because they bore the added weight of policy riders affecting abortion, resource development, and environmental and labor protections.

Although Livingston preferred that his bills stay clean and keep moving through the machinery of approval, he found it necessary to bow to the riders' political force. He was pushed to the limit, however, when one freshman Republican on his committee, Mark W. Neumann of Wisconsin, refused to vote for the defense spending package worked out with the Senate (Neumann thought it spent too much).

Livingston, operating with Gingrich's approval, disciplined Neumann by bumping him from the defense spending subcommittee. But the chairman then found himself bulldogged in Gingrich's office by an angry group of freshmen who were supporting Neumann. While not restored to the subcommittee, Neumann was rewarded for his insubordination with a seat on the Budget Committee. Livingston signed off on the deal, even though it undercut his punishment.

Livingston saved most of his fight, not surprisingly, for Democratic adversaries. He grew weary of Democratic attacks on the legislation he was shepherding; at one markup, sick of the sniping at cuts to programs aiding the less fortunate, he snapped, "We'll play this compassion game all day long, but it won't cut it."

Livingston himself has shown mastery of the traditional ways of Appropriations. Over the years, he has been able to steer more than $1 billion in federal shipbuilding contracts to Avondale Industries, a major employer in his suburban New Orleans district.

And Livingston in 1996 even broke his own edict against policy riders, attaching language to the Commerce-Justice-State spending bill requiring the Clinton administration to explain to Congress its international anti-missile defense negotiations. The possibility of veto did not deter Livingston — "Not when we're talking about the safety and welfare of every man, woman and child" — but he did modify his amendment later, after negotiating with the White House.

At Home: The 1st District did not come close to electing a Republican to the House for a century after Reconstruction, but now that it has one, it seems quite satisfied. Livingston has had no difficulty since winning a 1977 special election.

But Livingston has shown some restlessness in Congress. That in part led to his decision to run for governor in 1987. His visibility among Republicans in the New Orleans area put him in a strong position to finish near the top of a field of five major candidates. But he proved a somewhat plodding candidate; during one TV debate he lost his train of thought and fell silent during a statement on education. He finished third.

A prosperous New Orleans lawyer, former assistant U.S. attorney and veteran party worker, Livingston made his first bid for Congress in 1976, when legendary Democrat F. Edward Hebert retired. Livingston lost narrowly to a labor-backed Democrat, state Rep. Richard A. Tonry.

Livingston did not have to wait long, however, for a second try. Tonry's 1976 primary opponent succeeded in pressing a vote-fraud case against him, and Tonry resigned from the House in May 1977. (He later pleaded guilty to violations of federal campaign finance law and went to prison.)

Ready to run as soon as Tonry resigned, Livingston mounted a well-financed campaign against state Rep. Ron Faucheux, (later the publisher of Campaigns & Elections magazine), who had ousted Tonry in the special Democratic primary. Livingston drew significant blue-collar support as well as backing from more traditional GOP voters in white-collar areas. With organized labor refusing to support Faucheux, Livingston won easily.

He has met no formidable Democratic challenger since, and has been spared harm in Louisiana's redistricting wranglings.

HOUSE ELECTIONS

1996 Primary †		
Robert L. Livingston (R)	unopposed	
1994 Primary †		
Robert L. Livingston (R)	83,928	(81%)
Forest McNeir (D)	12,336	(12%)
Clark Simmons (I)	7,139	(7%)

Previous Winning Percentages: 1992 (73%) **1990** (84%) **1988** (78%) **1986** (100%) **1984** (88%) **1982** (86%) **1980** (88%) **1978** (86%) **1977*** (51%)

** Special election*

† In Louisiana the primary is open to candidates of all parties. If a candidate wins 50 percent or more of the vote in the primary, no general election is held. A candidate unopposed in the primary and general election is declared elected and the candidate's name does not appear on the ballot.

CAMPAIGN FINANCE

	Receipts	Receipts from PACs	Expend-itures
1996			
Livingston (R)	$1,001,655	$642,295 (64%)	$1,042,853
1994			
Livingston (R)	$368,522	$180,544 (49%)	$348,081

DISTRICT VOTE FOR PRESIDENT

1996		1992	
D	103,113 (37%)	**D**	86,886 (31%)
R	152,948 (56%)	**R**	155,422 (56%)
I	17,047 (6%)	**I**	34,494 (13%)

KEY VOTES

1997	
Ban "partial birth" abortions	Y
1996	
Approve farm bill	N
Deny public education to illegal immigrants	Y
Repeal ban on certain assault-style weapons	Y
Increase minimum wage	N
Freeze defense spending	N
Approve welfare overhaul	Y
1995	
Approve balanced-budget constitutional amendment	Y
Relax Clean Water Act regulations	Y
Oppose limits on environmental regulations	N
Reduce projected Medicare spending	Y
Approve GOP budget with tax and spending cuts	Y

VOTING STUDIES

	Presidential Support		Party Unity		Conservative Coalition	
Year	S	O	S	O	S	O
1996	39	61	91	7	98	2
1995	19	80	92	5	98	0
1994	41	54	77	15	83	6
1993	41	59	87	10	95	5
1992	72	11	66	17	73	6
1991	86	14	77	20	100	0

INTEREST GROUP RATINGS

Year	ADA	AFL-CIO	CCUS	ACU
1996	0	n/a	88	95
1995	0	0	96	80
1994	0	25	83	95
1993	0	8	100	96
1992	10	30	83	95
1991	0	8	100	90

2 William J. Jefferson (D)

Of New Orleans — Elected 1990, 4th term

Biographical Information

Born: March 14, 1947, Lake Providence, La.

Education: Southern U. and A&M College, B.A. 1969; Harvard U., J.D. 1972; Georgetown U., LL.M. 1996.

Military Service: Army, 1969-75.

Occupation: Lawyer.

Family: Wife, Andrea Green; five children.

Religion: Baptist.

Political Career: La. Senate, 1980-91; candidate for mayor of New Orleans, 1982, 1986.

Capitol Office: 240 Cannon Bldg. 20515; 225-6636.

Committees

Ways & Means
Social Security; Trade

In Washington: In the 103rd Congress, Jefferson — just in his second term — already had a seat on the Ways and Means Committee and was on a fast track to being a key inside player for Democrats.

But Jefferson reassessed his political future when Republicans seized control of the House in the 1994 election. He lost his place on Ways and Means as Democrats' allotment of committee seats was cut, and he looked into not one but two bids for statewide office — for governor in 1995 and senator in 1996. Ultimately he rejected both, and in 1996 he ran unopposed for a 4th term in the 2nd District. Although his Democrats are still the House minority in the 105th, there was some good news for Jefferson in 1997: He got back onto Ways and Means.

Jefferson first entered the 1995 Louisiana gubernatorial election along with 4th District black Democratic Rep. Cleo Fields and a host of other contenders, all of them white. But just two weeks after the September filing deadline, Jefferson dropped out in favor of Fields for fear of splitting the black primary vote.

"We know for a fact that we don't have a chance if both of us are in the race," Jefferson said at a news conference attended by Fields. Jefferson decided the better route would be to pursue the Senate seat being vacated in 1996 by Democrat J. Bennett Johnston. But in early 1996 Jefferson also backed out of that race.

Upon arriving in Washington in 1991, Jefferson quickly showed his party's leadership that he had skills at shaping legislation behind the scenes, and their desire to diversify the membership of key committees helped him earn a seat on Ways and Means.

After Jefferson was knocked from that perch in 1995, Democratic leaders assigned Jefferson to House Oversight — an insiders' panel that deals with institutional matters — and to the National Security Committee, where he was the only Louisianan and thus had a special responsibility for monitoring the state's defense interests.

In almost every instance, Jefferson has been a steadfast opponent of the Republicans' legislative agenda, voting against their efforts to overhaul the welfare and Medicare systems and to cut taxes and domestic spending. The one exception, however, has been in the area of defense. Jefferson has voted for the GOP-drafted defense bills that have included spending beyond what President Clinton has requested. Jefferson also opposed an effort by House "deficit hawks" to freeze fiscal 1997 defense spending at the prior-year level.

Jefferson has a parochial interest in defense monies; his district is home to Avondale shipyards and Trinity Marine Industries. He was successful with a provision in the fiscal 1996 defense authorization bill that added $600 million to accelerate construction of two military cargo ships originally scheduled for fiscal year 1999, plus $974 million for construction of the first of 12 smaller amphibious landing transports, designated LPDs. Avondale Industries was expected to gain the construction bid for the LPDs. Jefferson said the authorization for accelerated ship construction at Avondale "will have a tremendous impact on the metropolitan New Orleans economy into the next century."

Jefferson is not one of the more vocal members of Congress. He rarely speaks on the House floor, but when he does it is usually to complain about some aspect of the Republicans' agenda. He argued in the 104th that the House majority was cutting child nutrition programs to pay for a tax cut for the wealthy.

"With the near elimination of the school lunch and breakfast programs and the Food Stamp Program, among others," Jefferson told the House, "our colleagues on the other side of the aisle have hit nearly 5 million of America's children, our most previous resource, where it could very well hurt them the most — in their stomachs."

Jefferson belongs to the new generation of

LOUISIANA 2
East — New Orleans

New Orleans' melange of temptations, sensations and attractions gives it a unique mystique in America and lures a steady stream of visitors. But the Crescent City has more on its mind than granting hedonists their fancies.

New Orleans' population declined 11 percent in the 1980s, dropping the city below 500,000 residents for the first time since the early 1940s. In recent years the city has endured budget crunches, rampant crime, teacher strikes, drug problems and racial hostility.

New Orleans' economy is rooted in service industries. A few energy, mining and construction firms have headquarters here, including McDermott International Inc., but retail and hospitality services such as hotels, restaurants and bars employ a majority of the city's workers. The French Quarter is famous for its art galleries and fine dining. Nearby, sports fans descend on the 75,000-seat Louisiana Superdome to root for pro football's Saints and watch other blue-chip sporting events, such as the Sugar Bowl and, periodically, the Super Bowl.

New Orleans is an ethnic potpourri, with blacks, Italians, Irish, Cubans and the largest Honduran population outside Central America. The city also has more than 50,000 college students; schools include the University of New Orleans, Tulane University, Loyola University and Xavier University, the nation's only Catholic college with a predominantly black student population.

The Algiers section, which sits on the west bank of the Mississippi River, is a blend of high- and low-income residents, new condominiums and well-tended historic buildings.

On the east bank, between the Mississippi and Lake Pontchartrain, is a fascinating variety of neighborhoods: comfortable Carrolton, an area of middle-class whites on the city's west side; the wealthy Uptown section, with its professionals and academics; the predominantly black Lower 9th Ward; and fast-growing New Orleans East, reaching into the city's marshland and home to middle-class black and white families.

The district also includes southern parts of Kenner, a growing suburb west of New Orleans that includes the international airport.

Created by court order in 1983, the 2nd was Louisiana's first black-majority House district. Despite its demographics, the 2nd continued to elect white Democrat Lindy (Mrs. Hale) Boggs. But when she decided not to run in 1990, Jefferson became ensconced.

After 1992 redistricting, the 2nd included 85 percent of New Orleans and had a black population of 61 percent. Subsequent remapping plans, including the court-imposed 1996 plan which barely nicked the 2nd but eliminated Louisiana's other majority-black district, preserved the 2nd as a heavily-black district anchored in New Orleans. Just under one-fourth of the district's registered voters reside in Jefferson Parish, which is split with the 1st and 3rd districts.

Republicans have little impact in the 2nd. Registered Democrats outnumber Republicans by nearly 6 to 1. Bill Clinton carried the district in 1996 with 78 percent of the vote, nearly 25 points above his next-best Louisiana district.

As of May 19, the Census Bureau had not recalculated population data, racial and ethnic breakdowns and age statistics for districts newly drawn for the 1996 elections.

black leaders who flow with ease from black communities to halls of power filled with white establishment tradition. A reliable Democratic vote, he was the only member from his state to support Clinton's 1994 crime bill. In the 104th Congress, he supported raising the minimum wage and opposed most of the GOP's efforts to restrict abortion. He has, however, voted with conservatives to ban a particular abortion technique that opponents call "partial birth" abortion. Also, he voted to ban federal recognition of same-gender marriages.

Even on the politically touchy issue of whether employers should have to pay for workers' health care, Jefferson in the 103rd Congress found a way to back the Democratic leadership. During Ways and Means negotiations in the spring of 1994, he won a promise of increased aid for small businesses in return for his support for the so-called employer mandate. His vote helped Ways and Means approve a version of Clinton's health care plan, although the bill later died.

Jefferson now represents Louisiana's only black majority district since a three-judge panel in January 1996 struck down Louisiana's congressional district map. The judges ruled that the Louisiana map — which was drafted with two black-majority districts — was a "racial gerrymander" in violation of the 14th Amendment's equal protection clause. They said race was the main factor used in drawing the black- majority 4th District, which had been represented by Fields. In redrawing all the state's districts, the court made the 4th a white-majority district.

The judges' map was adopted by the state Legislature, and in the 1996 elections Louisiana followed the plan imposed by the judges.

At Home: Jefferson's 1990 election to succeed Democrat Lindy (Mrs. Hale) Boggs was notable on several counts. He became Louisiana's first black congressman since Reconstruction, and his constituency was the last black-majority House district of the 1980s to gain black representation.

In Jefferson, it has a representative whose life has almost literally been a rags-to-riches story. Raised in poverty in rural northeast Louisiana as one of 10 children, he quickly showed brains and ambition.

He was student body president at Southern University in Baton Rouge, winner of a scholarship to Harvard Law School, a law clerk in New Orleans for veteran federal appellate court Judge Alvin Rubin and then a legislative assistant to Sen. Johnston.

In 1979, Jefferson launched his political career by winning a seat in the Louisiana Senate, ousting a white incumbent in a racially mixed New Orleans district that included much of the affluent Uptown area.

When Boggs announced her retirement in 1990, Jefferson was well-positioned to succeed her. With the backing of Mayor Sidney Barthelemy, many of the city's white officials and the Interdenominational Ministerial Alliance (the city's largest organization of black clergy), he ran first in the crowded primary, then beat attorney Marc Morial, the 32-year-old son of the city's first black mayor, Ernest N. "Dutch" Morial, in the bitter November runoff, winning by roughly 5,000 votes.

Morial mocked Jefferson's experience in the Legislature ("We don't want to take Baton Rouge shenanigans to Washington," he said) and hit hard at questions surrounding Jefferson's personal finances.

The two candidates ran virtually neck and neck in the city's black precincts. Jefferson won on the strength of his showing on the largely white, working-class West Bank.

HOUSE ELECTIONS

1996 Primary †		
William J. Jefferson (D	unopposed	
1994 Primary †		
William J. Jefferson (D)	60,906	(75%)
Robert "Bob" Namer (R)	15,113	(19%)
John C. Lawrence (I)	3,036	(4%)
Julius "Uncle Chip" Leahman (D)	2,513	(3%)

Previous Winning Percentages: 1992 (73%) **1990** (53%)

† In Louisiana the primary is open to candidates of all parties. If a candidate wins 50 percent or more of the vote in the primary, no general election is held. A candidate unopposed in the primary and general election is declared elected and the candidate's name does not appear on the ballot.

CAMPAIGN FINANCE

	Receipts	Receipts from PACs	Expend-itures
1996			
Jefferson (D)	$286,711	$168,950 (59%)	$301,082
1994			
Jefferson (D)	$554,568	$311,837 (56%)	$608,567

DISTRICT VOTE FOR PRESIDENT

1996		1992	
D	169,602 (78%)	D	153,342 (69%)
R	40,597 (19%)	R	54,555 (25%)
I	5,405 (3%)	I	13,813 (6%)

KEY VOTES

1997	
Ban "partial birth" abortions	Y
1996	
Approve farm bill	Y
Deny public education to illegal immigrants	N
Repeal ban on certain assault-style weapons	N
Increase minimum wage	Y
Freeze defense spending	N
Approve welfare overhaul	N
1995	
Approve balanced-budget constitutional amendment	N
Relax Clean Water Act regulations	N
Oppose limits on environmental regulations	Y
Reduce projected Medicare spending	N
Approve GOP budget with tax and spending cuts	N

VOTING STUDIES

	Presidential Support		Party Unity		Conservative Coalition	
Year	**S**	**O**	**S**	**O**	**S**	**O**
1996	73	19	85	9	51	43
1995	65	14	73	7	33	50
1994	85	10	86	3	28	67
1993	83	13	91	4	23	73
1992	14	74	81	5	25	65
1991	26	63	82	5	19	68

INTEREST GROUP RATINGS

Year	ADA	AFL-CIO	CCUS	ACU
1996	85	n/a	31	5
1995	70	100	11	9
1994	90	78	33	15
1993	95	92	18	4
1992	85	92	29	0
1991	85	92	20	0

3 W.J. 'Billy' Tauzin (R)

Of Thibodaux — Elected 1980; 9th full term

Biographical Information

Born: June 14, 1943, Chackbay, La.

Education: Nicholls State U., B.A. 1964; Louisiana State U., J.D. 1967.

Occupation: Lawyer.

Family: Wife, Cecile Bergeron; five children.

Religion: Roman Catholic.

Political Career: La. House, 1971-80; candidate for governor, 1987.

Capitol Office: 2183 Rayburn Bldg. 20515; 225-4031.

Committees

Commerce
Finance & Hazardous Materials; Telecommunications, Trade & Consumer Protection (chairman)

Resources
Energy & Mineral Resources; Fisheries Conservation, Wildlife & Oceans

In Washington: As a reward for his August 1995 switch to the Republican Party, Tauzin in the 105th Congress got the chairmanship of the Commerce Subcommittee on Telecommunications, Trade and Consumer Protection, a panel whose work is important to many business interests that are generous givers of campaign contributions.

In his new life as a Republican, Tauzin is a major legislative play-maker, just as he was as a Democrat, on an array of topics. His penchant for Cajun storytelling is paired with a shrewd mind and a knowledge of policy that helps him bargain skillfully on the fiercely competitive Commerce Committee.

After his party switch, Tauzin was eyeing a 1996 Senate bid, for the seat of retiring Democratic Sen. J. Bennett Johnston. But then, the retirement announcement of Texas GOP Rep. Jack Fields made it clear that Tauzin would have a chance to replace Fields in the 105th as a Commerce subcommittee chairman. Tauzin dropped out of the Senate race, saying that Speaker Newt Gingrich and Commerce Chairman Thomas J. Bliley Jr., R-Va., had promised him the telecommunications chairmanship.

But Ohio Republican Michael G. Oxley also wanted that subcommittee chairmanship, and he was next in line behind Fields. In May 1996, Bliley unveiled a Solomonic compromise, splitting the panel's old jurisdiction in two for the 105th. Tauzin gained the telecommunications chairmanship, while Oxley heads a new Finance and Hazardous Materials Subcommittee that oversees the securities market, in addition to such matters as the superfund toxic-waste cleanup.

Tauzin said he planned to hold hearings in the 105th on the technical and legal aspects of cellular phone privacy, the move of TV broadcasters to digital TV transmissions and the new TV content ratings system. Tauzin said he backs the broadcast and cable television industry's voluntary ratings system, although critics have complained that the system is vague and does not provide viewers with sufficient information about the sexual, violence and language content of television programs. Tauzin said the industry's system should be given a chance, and he assailed what he calls the critics' "knee-jerk reaction."

After the November 1994 elections that handed control of the House to the GOP, Tauzin said he would remain a Democrat "for now," declaring that he would stick with his party for at least a year. He didn't even make it to the summer recess. "We have learned over the course of the last year that there is no role for conservatives within the Democratic Party," Tauzin complained at an August 1995 news conference a day after he switched to the GOP. "I decided to go with a party that respects my ideas."

The surest sign that Tauzin was ready to switch came in June 1995, when he and three other Southern House members quit the Democratic Congressional Campaign Committee because they were angry that the campaign group had produced a mailing that lampooned supporters of environmental law rewrites. Tauzin and his colleagues contended that Democratic conservatives suffered persistent snubbing at the hands of the leadership. "They don't understand they have a problem," he said. "I am not helping an organization that eats its own children."

Early in the 104th, Tauzin had helped form a coalition of conservative-to-moderate House Democrats, later known as the "blue dogs," which aimed to take an active role in offering amendments and alternatives on the floor. Tauzin quit the coalition just days before joining the Republican Party.

Tauzin has been a longtime advocate of limiting government in favor of protecting an expansive commitment to private property rights, an issue he also pushes from his seat on the Resources Committee, where he is the No. 2 Republican. He traces his hostility to government bureaucracy to the early 1980s, when economically struggling shrimpers in his district were forced to install expensive devices in their nets to allow endangered sea turtles to escape. Tauzin not only supported every plank of the House

LOUISIANA 3
South Central — Houma; New Iberia

The 3rd begins below Lafayette, in the Cajun heartland of Louisiana, and sweeps east. New Iberia, whose nearby Avery Island produces Tabasco hot sauce, marks a western boundary. The Gulf of Mexico lies to the east and south.

Bayous, grassy marshes and hardwood swamps finger into the gulf for hundreds of miles here, making this a major wetlands area where ecosystems and the economy often intertwine. Alligators, game fish and water birds abound, but so do offshore oil and gas rigs and shrimp boats.

The lushness of the land has belied a Dust Bowl economy during much of the last decade. Exacerbating the problems was Hurricane Andrew, which tore through the district in August 1992 and caused more than $500 million in damage. Everyone feared the worst for sugar cane, the agricultural mainstay here, but farmers rebounded with a record crop.

In the oil and gas industry, no such storybook recovery has been forthcoming. The district, a dominant player in the oil extraction business, has been retrenching ever since Louisiana crude oil prices fell from a 1981 high of $37 a barrel to $10.50 a barrel in 1986. Prices climbed back to about $20 a barrel, but after a modest rally, drilling activity in the 3rd has been sluggish.

Louisiana produces nearly 30 percent of the nation's natural gas, which is abundant in the 3rd. Drilling for gas took up some economic slack here, but lower demand led to a glut and tumbling prices in the early 1990s, and the district economy wobbled again.

Chemical manufacturing has made a big comeback from its 1980s hard times. Many chemical plants operate along the Mississippi River between Baton Rouge and New Orleans. Most of this stretch lies in territory the 3rd picked up in 1992 redistricting (and retained in 1994 and 1996): most of Ascension and all of St. James and St. John the Baptist parishes.

Large black populations in St. James and St. John the Baptist parishes and the presence of labor unions in the chemical plants produce a more liberal tilt here than in the rest of the 3rd. St. James, which is 50 percent black, cast 67 percent of its 1996 presidential votes for Bill Clinton.

The state's easternmost parish, St. Bernard, is a heavily white, working-class area. Republican David Duke, in his unsuccessful 1990 challenge to Democratic Sen. J. Bennett Johnston, amassed 67 percent of St. Bernard's votes, his highest percentage in the state.

Louisiana has had three different congressional district plans in as many election cycles, but the 3rd has escaped major changes. The district remains white-dominated, Catholic, strongly Democratic at the local level and somewhat less so in presidential voting. But in 1996 the 3rd re-elected a Republican congressman (Tauzin, who ran unopposed) and a Democratic president (Clinton, who won the 3rd by 15 percentage points).

As of May 19, the Census Bureau had not recalculated population data, racial and ethnic breakdowns and age statistics for districts newly drawn for the 1996 elections.

GOP's "Contract With America," he also helped draft some of the implementing language on regulatory overhaul and curbs on wetlands provisions that were part of a 1995 rewrite of the clean water law.

Early in the 104th, the House easily passed a private property rights bill to require certain federal agencies to provide financial compensation to landowners for any regulatory action that causes a decrease of at least 20 percent in the fair market value of any portion of their land. Supporters said the legislation was a response to a grassroots movement by landowners who have suffered hardships because government regulators restricted their land use without considering the economic impact. "I believe the fabric of the relationship between those who created this government and this government has been ripped apart for one word more than any other," said Tauzin. "The word is 'arrogance.'"

The House later folded the property rights bill into an omnibus regulatory overhaul bill. Tauzin feared, however, that the Judiciary Committee's version of the contract's regulatory overhaul bill was too broad. He offered an amendment, which passed 301-128, that limited its reach to actions taken under the Endangered Species Act and certain laws pertaining to wetlands and water rights. The regulatory reform measure never made it through the Senate, however.

Stung by a negative public response to their effort to ease certain environmental regulations, Republican leaders pushed hard in 1996 for an overhaul of federal law aimed at protecting the nation's drinking water. Tauzin attributed the deal to election-year pressure to produce. "The Republicans have finally made a decision to deliver on what we can deliver on," he said. He and GOP leaders hoped the bill would help Republicans answer charges on the campaign trail that they oppose environmental protection.

The measure cleared in August 1996 and

included, among other things, a new requirement that community water systems inform the public about the level of contaminants in drinking water.

While Tauzin strongly supports GOP overhauls of the Endangered Species Act and the superfund hazardous waste law, he said in early 1996 that acting on the bills would allow President Clinton and Democratic environmentalists to inflict a rhetorical lashing on the GOP. To defend against such Democratic attacks, Tauzin said GOP leaders should slice off specific aspects of major legislation that are both politically popular and, because of their limited scope, easier to defend on merit. "The only thing that has a chance of surviving is targeted, incremental reform," Tauzin said.

At Home: A poll taken for the Shreveport Times just before his announced party switch indicated that Tauzin would lead the large pack of potential contenders lining up to succeed retiring Sen. Johnston. It also showed him running a couple of points stronger if he campaigned as a Republican. But once the opportunity for the telecommunications chairmanship on Commerce arose, Tauzin decided to stay in the House.

Tauzin first won his House seat in 1980 with the help of an influential ally, Edwin W. Edwards, who was then between terms as governor. Seven years later the two ended up rivals in a hot gubernatorial contest.

Tauzin's decision to run for governor in 1987 came as no surprise; many had expected him to be a strong contender for statewide office someday. But his bid was complicated by Edwards, a colorful figure whose political stock had plummeted as a result of well-publicized indictments (he was eventually acquitted). Both Edwards and Tauzin were popular among southern Louisiana Cajuns and blacks. And while Tauzin was critical of Edwards' candidacy, he also had difficulty distancing himself from his one-time mentor. In the end, there was a surge for Democratic Rep. Buddy Roemer; Tauzin ran fourth.

Most of Tauzin's political efforts have been more successful. His victory in a 1980 special election restored control of the 3rd District to French-speaking, Democratic south Louisiana, after nearly a decade under a Republican from suburban New Orleans, David C. Treen. When Treen vacated the seat after winning the governorship, he tried to pick a successor, James J. Donelon, a Democrat-turned-Republican. Edwards campaigned ardently for Tauzin.

Like Edwards, Tauzin is as comfortable speaking French as English. After practicing law in the bayou towns of Houma and Thibodaux, he won a state legislative seat in 1971. In eight years in the Legislature he emerged as Edwards' protégé, serving as his floor leader in the lower chamber.

Again with Edwards' help, Tauzin finished a strong second in the first round of the special election to fill Treen's House vacancy. Donelon led the four-man field, but not by enough to avoid a runoff. The second round was bitter and expensive. Tauzin won by more than 7,000 votes. GOP leaders did not field a serious candidate after that. And after his switch to the GOP, Democrats were equally reluctant to take him on in 1996. He ran unopposed in the all-party primary.

HOUSE ELECTIONS

1996 Primary †		
W.J. "Billy" Tauzin (R)	unopposed	
unopposed		
1994 Primary †		
W.J. "Billy" Tauzin (D)*	90,536	(76%)
Nick Accardo (I)	28,250	(24%)

Previous Winning Percentages: **1992** (82%) 1 **1990** (88%) **1988** (89%) **1986** (100%) **1984** (100%) **1982** (100%) **1980** (85%) **1980**** ((53%)

**Tauzin was elected as a Democrat from 1980-94.*

*** Special election*

† In Louisiana the primary is open to candidates of all parties. If a candidate wins 50 percent or more of the vote in the primary, no general election is held. A candidate unopposed in the primary and general election is declared elected and the candidate's name does not appear on the ballot.

CAMPAIGN FINANCE

	Receipts	Receipts from PACs	Expend-itures
1996			
Tauzin (R)	$819,148	$557,151 (68%)	$612,332
1994			
Tauzin (D)	$810,673	$514,389 (63%)	$680,211

DISTRICT VOTE FOR PRESIDENT

1996		1992	
D	128,418 (53%)	**D**	115,406 (45%)
R	90,100 (38%)	**R**	105,989 (41%)
I	19,019 (8%)	**I**	36,200 (14%)

KEY VOTES

1997	
Ban "partial birth" abortions	Y
1996	
Approve farm bill	Y
Deny public education to illegal immigrants	Y
Repeal ban on certain assault-style weapons	Y
Increase minimum wage	Y
Freeze defense spending	N
Approve welfare overhaul	Y
1995	
Approve balanced-budget constitutional amendment	Y
Relax Clean Water Act regulations	Y
Oppose limits on environmental regulations	N
Reduce projected Medicare spending	Y
Approve GOP budget with tax and spending cuts	Y

VOTING STUDIES

	Presidential Support		Party Unity		Conservative Coalition	
Year	**S**	**O**	**S**	**O**	**S**	**O**
1996	33	61	82	7	92	2
1995	22	77	95	2	95	2
1994	54	42	50	47	92	8
1993	47	51	48	46	82	11
1992	55	42	55	37	85	10
1991	53	44	50	45	95	5

INTEREST GROUP RATINGS

Year	ADA	AFL-CIO	CCUS	ACU
1996	0	n/a	93	90
1995	5	0	100	83
1994	15	33	100	76
1993	35	42	73	78
1992	40	55	75	71
1991	10	50	80	70

4 Jim McCrery (R)

Of Shreveport — Elected 1988; 4th full term

Biographical Information
Born: Sept. 18, 1949, Shreveport, La.
Education: Louisiana Tech U., B.A. 1971; Louisiana State U., J.D. 1975.
Occupation: Lawyer; congressional aide; government relations executive.
Family: Wife, Johnette Hawkins; two children.
Religion: Methodist.
Political Career: Candidate for Leesville City Council, 1978.
Capitol Office: 2104 Rayburn Bldg. 20515; 225-2777.

Committees
Ways & Means
Health; Human Resources
Joint Economic

In Washington: McCrery turned in a studious and restrained first term on the Ways and Means Committee in the 103rd Congress, but after Republicans gained control of the House in the 104th he became a prominent activist in the committee's social-policy work, in particular challenging some traditional views of the nation's "social safety net" programs, such as Supplemental Security Income (SSI) and welfare.

McCrery's social conservatism riled the more liberal Democrats on Ways and Means, and their sometimes open hostility to his ideas triggered the occasional, unaccustomed flight of partisan rage from the otherwise subdued Southerner.

One notable episode occurred as the House debated the GOP welfare plan in March 1995, when McCrery wondered aloud whether "petulance [is] a proper form of behavior for a member of Congress" after an outburst from Ways and Means' ranking Democrat Sam M. Gibbons, D-Fla. He also once called Democrats "ninnies" and "scaredy cats" during a Ways and Means debate of proposed cuts in Medicare growth. He apologized the next day.

McCrery had little success pushing his ideas about welfare, health and tax policy when Democrats controlled the House, but success came quickly after Republicans gained control of the agenda. His most significant achievement was enactment of a plan to transform the SSI program, which is run by the Social Security Administration. Among other things, the program provides a monthly check to families with disabled children to help them pay medical and other expenses.

The program grew from $1.3 billion for 290,000 beneficiaries in 1989 to an estimated $5 billion for nearly 900,000 beneficiaries in 1995. McCrery set his sights on SSI after educators in his district began complaining that some parents were encouraging their children to misbehave regularly so they could be classified as "disabled" and receive a monthly SSI benefit of more than $400. He drafted a plan to end the cash benefits and replace them with block grants to the states. The final version of his proposal, which was enacted as part of a larger overhaul of the welfare system, will reduce SSI rolls by about 22 percent, according to the Congressional Budget Office.

McCrery, a conferee for Republicans on both their welfare and budget-reconciliation proposals, was a central figure in other GOP fights in the 104th. He was among the most outspoken critics of Democrats' efforts to alter the GOP welfare plan, arguing against vouchers for children whose parents exceed their five-year limit on benefits and against additional benefits for teenagers who have more children after going on welfare. And he was a key advocate of offering "medical savings accounts" to seniors as a way to limit the growth of Medicare.

In his House floor votes during the Bush administration, McCrery almost without exception followed the line laid down by the White House on economic, social policy and foreign policy questions. His one high-profile departure came in October 1990, when he joined with the GOP wing most hostile to tax increases and voted against a budget compromise crafted by the president and House and Senate leaders. The compromise included tax increases.

Although generally loyal to House GOP leaders in the 104th, McCrery at times was a step or two off the leadership line. He openly questioned the size of the tax cuts Republican leaders included in their budget-reconciliation bill, specifically the $500-per-child tax credit. "I'm not convinced that it's desirable to extend this all the way up to $200,000," he said during Ways and Means consideration of the plan in January 1995.

McCrery's hard-line opposition to abortion prompted him to question, and ultimately defeat, a welfare-related proposal once heralded by Ways and Means Chairman Bill Archer, R-Texas. Archer originally proposed giving states an extra 10 percent of their welfare grants for reducing out-of-wedlock births by 2 percent from the previous year, but McCrery said states could qualify for the bonus "simply by performing more abortions." He

LOUISIANA 4
Northwest and west — Shreveport; Bossier City

The 4th has mired Louisiana's redistricting map in a morass of litigation in the 1990s. The version of the 4th used for the 1992 election was a Z-shaped creature that zigzagged through all or part of 28 parishes and five of Louisiana's largest cities, digesting black communities to create the state's second black-majority district.

Although the boundaries were substantially reoriented for the 1994 election, the 4th's black majority was retained and the district still covered a vast distance, sticking to a northwest-to-southeast diagonal from Shreveport to Baton Rouge and resembling, in the words of a state official, "a sash on a beauty queen."

But remapping in 1996 smoothed out the district boundary lines and eliminated the black-majority 4th. Unaccustomed to running in majority-white districts, Democratic Rep. Cleo Fields retired from Congress.

Encompassing northwest and west Louisiana, the current 4th comprises twelve whole parishes and part of another, bordering Arkansas to the north and taking in much of Louisiana's western border with Texas.

Shreveport (Caddo Parish), in the northwest corner of the state, is the third-largest city in Louisiana. About 40 percent of the district's registered voters are from Caddo.

The area economy boomed in the beginning of the 20th century, when oil was discovered near Shreveport. But the city has never fully recovered from the fading of the oil boom. Shreveport's population declined in the 1980s, though its population has inched above 200,000 in the 1990s.

The city's largest employers include General Motors, AT&T, Libbey Glass and Frymaster Corp. The gaming industry — notably Horseshoe, Isle of Capri, and Hannah's casinos — accounts for thousands of jobs in the area.

Shreveport also is home to Centenary College, the oldest chartered institution of higher learning west of the Mississippi. And it is the site of the annual Poulan Weedeater Independence Bowl.

Shreveport has a black population of almost 45 percent, making Caddo a source of Democratic votes. In the 1996 presidential election, Bill Clinton defeated Bob Dole 56 percent to 39 percent in Caddo. But parish voters freely split their tickets, giving Republican McCrery 65 percent of their votes. The general results were similar throughout the district. In fact, of the 30 districts nationally that gave Clinton a majority of their votes while opting for a Republican House member, none of the contested Republicans received a higher percentage than McCrery's 71 percent.

Just across the Red River from Shreveport is Bossier City (population 52,700). The largest single employer for both cities is Barksdale Air Force Base, headquarters for a unit of the Air Combat Command and home to most of the Air Force's fleet of B-52s. Bossier was one of just two parishes in the district that Dole carried.

Fort Polk, the district's other large military installation, is in Vernon parish in the district's southwestern region. Fort Polk employs about 11,000 active-duty and civilian personnel.

Natchitoches, located in its namesake parish in the district's center, is the oldest settlement in the Louisiana Purchase territory.

Claiborne Parish has become a barometer of the overall state's inclinations in presidential campaigns. In the last five presidential elections, the winning candidate's percentages in Claiborne and Louisiana at-large have differed by less than 2 percentage points.

As of May 19, the Census Bureau had not recalculated population data, racial and ethnic breakdowns and age statistics for districts newly drawn for the 1996 elections.

convinced the committee, on a 21-15 party-line vote, to adopt an amendment to require that any increase in abortions be factored into the formula for determining a state's illegitimacy rate.

A stalwart supporter of gunowners' rights, McCrery opposed a five-day waiting-period requirement for handgun purchases and a ban on certain semiautomatic assault-style weapons. He also opposed lifting the ban on homosexuals in the military and voted for legislation that bars federal recognition of same-sex marriages.

McCrery made an unusual splash when he first came to Congress. A 1989 article in the Capitol Hill newspaper Roll Call described McCrery's visit to a topless club in South Carolina, where he wore a dancer's bra on his head. "I'm not going to live like a monk while I'm in Congress," he said.

At Home: Relatively safe in his district since first winning election to the House in a 1988 special election, McCrery, along with some other Republicans in Louisiana's House delegation, toyed with seeking the Senate seat being vacated by retiring Democrat J. Bennett Johnston in 1996.

He ultimately opted out of the race, instead choosing to run in the hospitable confines of the newly drawn 4th District. It is a product of Louisiana's third district map of the 1990s; judges rejected the first two as "racial gerrymanders."

The new lines certainly did not cause McCrery much stress in 1996: He won election to a fifth term outright in the all-party open primary, taking more than 70 percent of the vote.

That was not too far below his high-water mark, 80 percent in 1994.

McCrery's most significant re-election challenge came in 1992, after the initial round of 1990s redistricting matched him against fellow incumbent Jerry Huckaby, an eight-term Democrat.

Although Huckaby chaired the Agriculture Subcommittee on Cotton, Rice and Sugar — commodities of great concern to Louisiana — he had his back to the wall in the new 5th, with its smaller black population and the conservative GOP incumbent from the former 4th District on the ballot.

To win re-election, McCrery had to withstand some unflattering personal publicity: The Advocate, a national gay and lesbian magazine, published an article that said McCrery had had several homosexual affairs. McCrery, recently married, said the story was not true. Voters in the conservative district did not appear to be troubled by the publicity. They gave McCrery a 44 percent to 29 percent lead over Huckaby in the five-candidate, all-party primary.

Huckaby appeared to suffer more lasting damage from his own troubles: He had 88 overdrafts at the House bank; McCrery had none. In the runoff, McCrery breezed past Huckaby, winning with 63 percent of the vote.

McCrery, a former Democrat and once an aide to then-4th District Democratic Rep. Buddy Roemer, was well-positioned to make a bid for the House when Roemer left Congress after his 1987 election as Louisiana governor. McCrery's GOP label, acquired in late 1987 before his House bid began, helped his victory.

McCrery served at one time as assistant city attorney in Shreveport, and more recently had worked in Baton Rouge as a lobbyist for Georgia-Pacific Corp.

He was not well known in the 4th; he stood out in the special election's 10-person primary field largely because he was the only Republican, and he impressed many with his knowledge of legislative issues. And while linking himself to Roemer, he also associated himself with Republican figures, running ads featuring President Ronald Reagan.

McCrery's conservative ties helped him finish atop the large field, sending him into a runoff with Democratic state Sen. Foster L. Campbell Jr. Campbell was a flamboyant, populist-style campaigner whose base was in the 4th's rural northern parishes. But a month before the election, he was seriously injured in a car crash while driving on a closed highway. McCrery won the special election with 51 percent of the vote.

After the special election, McCrery had little time to prepare for November. Fortunately for him, the Democratic effort in the 4th fizzled. Potential challengers stopped in their tracks when Roemer's mother, Adeline, entered the race. She lost badly. And in 1990, McCrery defeated Campbell in a rematch.

HOUSE ELECTIONS

1996 Primary †		
Jim McCrery (R)	94,822	(71%)
Paul M. Chachere (D)	38,015	(29%)
1994 Primary †		
Jim McCrery (R)	106,204	(80%)
Paul Henry Kidd (D)	21,467	(16%)
E. Auston Simmons (I)	5,365	(4%)

Previous Winning Percentages: **1992** (63%) **1990** (55%) **1988** (69%) **1988*** (51%)

** Special election*

† In Louisiana the primary is open to candidates of all parties. If a candidate wins 50 percent or more of the vote in the primary, no general election is held. A candidate unopposed in the primary and general election is declared elected and the candidate's name does not appear on the ballot.

CAMPAIGN FINANCE

	Receipts	Receipts from PACs	Expend-itures
1996			
McCrery (R)	$913,505	$448,425 (49%)	$823,121
1994			
McCrery (R)	$770,648	$335,943 (44%)	$459,098

DISTRICT VOTE FOR PRESIDENT

1996	1992
D 122,776 (52%)	D 150,000 (68%)
R 92,220 (39%)	R 54,230 (25%)
I 17,198 (7%)	I 16,475 (8%)

KEY VOTES

1997	
Ban "partial birth" abortions	Y
1996	
Approve farm bill	Y
Deny public education to illegal immigrants	Y
Repeal ban on certain assault-style weapons	Y
Increase minimum wage	N
Freeze defense spending	N
Approve welfare overhaul	Y
1995	
Approve balanced-budget constitutional amendment	Y
Relax Clean Water Act regulations	Y
Oppose limits on environmental regulations	N
Reduce projected Medicare spending	Y
Approve GOP budget with tax and spending cuts	Y

VOTING STUDIES

	Presidential Support		Party Unity		Conservative Coalition	
Year	**S**	**O**	**S**	**O**	**S**	**O**
1996	35	59	91	6	94	2
1995	18	80	94	3	100	0
1994	53	41	80	13	92	8
1993	44	56	86	12	95	5
1992	77	6	74	6	83	2
1991	84	12	78	15	95	3

INTEREST GROUP RATINGS

Year	ADA	AFL-CIO	CCUS	ACU
1996	0	n/a	100	95
1995	0	0	100	92
1994	5	13	100	90
1993	0	0	100	92
1992	5	10	83	91
1991	0	8	90	85

5 John Cooksey (R)

Of Monroe — Elected 1996, 1st term

Biographical Information

Born: Aug. 20, 1941, Alexandria, La.

Education: Louisiana State U., B.A. 1962, M.D. 1966; U. of Texas, M.B.A. 1994.

Military Service: Air Force, 1967-69; Air Force Reserve, 1969-72.

Occupation: Physician.

Family: Wife, Ann Grabil; three children.

Religion: Methodist.

Political Career: No previous office.

Capitol Office: 317 Cannon Bldg. 20515; 225-8490.

Committees

Agriculture
Forestry, Resource Conservation & Research; General Farm Commodities

Transportation & Infrastructure
Aviation; Public Buildings & Economic Development

Veterans' Affairs
Health

The Path to Washington: Cooksey, the only physician serving his first term in the 105th, spent most of his career as an ophthalmologist and made his first bid for elective office in 1996. Yet, he is no political novice.

Cooksey says he has always been interested in government and has been an active behind-the-scenes player in helping other candidates raise money for their campaigns. Among those he has worked for is fellow Louisiana Republican Rep. Jim McCrery, who won election in the neighboring and newly redrawn 4th District in 1996.

Cooksey also helped lead an effort in the mid-1970s to pass legislation that capped medical malpractice awards in Louisiana at $500,000.

One of his top priorities in Congress will be to try to bring jobs to his largely rural and poor district.

Cooksey says one of the best ways to create a better climate for businesses is to build a four-lane, north-to-south highway in the district. The lack of such a highway is not only a deterrent to bringing new employers to the 5th, he says, but also creates a dangerous situation on the district's two-lane roads, which are heavily traveled by both passenger cars and trucks.

Cooksey will be in a position to lobby for this goal from his seat on the Transportation and Infrastructure Committee. He also was given a spot on the Agriculture Committee. Rice and cotton farming are among the key components of the 5th's agricultural economy. He also proposes providing tax credits to encourage Americans to buy American-made products. He would also like to see domestic free-trade zones, which provide tax breaks to companies that launch manufacturing firms in the zones, expanded to include areas in the 5th District.

In addition, Cooksey proposes giving businesses tax credits for creating vocational and technical programs, particularly for welfare recipients, who he says should be exempted from paying income taxes for a year after getting a job.

Cooksey lines up firmly with conservatives on most issues. He favors a reduction in income, capital gains and estate taxes, elimination of the Education Department, voluntary prayer in public schools, and term limits for members of Congress and federal judges.

He says he also is opposed to abortion but would not back a constitutional amendment banning the procedure. Cooksey says he is concerned about the federal government getting too involved in the issue. "We don't need any more federal bureaucrats," he says.

Cooksey launched his bid for Congress after the state's congressional lines were redrawn in January 1996 by a three-judge federal panel, which ruled that one of Louisiana's congressional districts drawn to favor the election of a minority representative was an unconstitutional racial gerrymander.

The new 5th District includes some of the most conservative areas of the state. But blacks, who generally vote Democratic, make up almost a third of the district's population, and Democrats were counting on the presidential race to draw out more of the black vote.

Cooksey emerged on top of a six-candidate field in the all-party primary but was forced into a runoff with Democratic state Rep. Francis Thompson, who only narrowly got past former Republican Rep. Clyde C. Holloway (1987-93) for second place. Cooksey promoted himself as a "citizen candidate" and attacked Thompson as a career politician. Thompson charged that his opponent was a "rich doctor" who did not understand the district's needs.

"He's sort of a Grey Poupon sort of guy," Thompson charged during the campaign. "I've been in the trenches here for over 30 years."

Cooksey, however, ran a well-organized campaign, distributing thousands of newspapers throughout the district touting his candidacy. He also got assistance from television ads, paid for by the state Republican Party, that attacked Thompson for voting to increase taxes in the state Legislature. Cooksey won with 58 percent of the vote.

LOUISIANA 5
Northeast and central— Monroe; Alexandria.

The 5th, which spans all or part of 20 parishes in northeastern Louisiana, bears little geographic resemblance to its 1994 version, which traversed the entire northern boundary of the state. That district was represented by Republican Jim McCrery, whose Shreveport base was removed from the 5th by remappers in 1996. (McCrery that year ran and won in the northwest-based 4th).

Bill Clinton captured a plurality of votes and won 15 of the 20 parishes in the district in 1996. But the performance of Clinton — governor for 12 years of a state that borders the 5th — belies the district's conservatism. Republicans are on the rise here. Cooksey scored an easy victory, and Bob Dole finished less than 5 percentage points behind Clinton. However, Democrats historically have done well in this rural region when they sweep the sizable black constituency and win the region's numerous white working-class voters.

Monroe (Ouachita Parish), through which Interstate 20 runs, is the district's largest city. Blacks make up almost 56 percent of the city's 54,900 residents. A longtime trading hub of northeast Louisiana, Monroe is an agricultural center that falls squarely between the forest section and the fertile Delta region. The largest employer is Riverwood International, a global paperboard packaging company that employs 1,700 in the Monroe area.

The western part of the district is the hilly timber region where Louisiana's softwood pine is harvested. Union, Lincoln, Caldwell and Jackson parishes are dotted with small lumber and paper mills. Ruston (Lincoln) is home to Grambling State University, one of the nation's prestigious historically black universities.

To the south is Winn Parish, the birthplace of former Gov. and U.S. Sen. Huey P. Long.

In the state's center and the district's southwestern corner lies Rapides Parish, which contains Alexandria, the 5th's second-largest city, with just under 50,000 inhabitants. Alexandria lies on the west bank of the Red River and is nearly equidistant to Shreveport and Baton Rouge. Rapides has shown an affinity for Republican state Rep. Louis "Woody" Jenkins. It was the only parish to support him in all three of his unsuccessful attempts for the U.S. Senate — in 1996 against Democrat Mary L. Landrieu and in 1980 and 1978 as a Democratic challenger to incumbent Democratic Sens. Russell B. Long and J. Bennett Johnston, respectively.

West Carroll, East Carroll and Morehouse parishes, tucked in the state's northeastern corner, are part of Louisiana's Northern Delta region. The alluvial soil and the flat land of the Delta cultivate such row crops as cotton, rice and soybeans. These crops take up nearly 900,000 acres in the eastern reach of the 5th.

Some of the strongest support for former Nazi sympathizer and Republican state Rep. David Duke in his abortive 1991 gubernatorial bid came from the 5th. Of the 11 parishes in which Duke received 55 percent of the vote, nine — including West Carroll, which gave Duke a state high of 69 percent — lie in the 5th.

As of May 19, the Census Bureau had not recalculated population data, racial and ethnic breakdowns and age statistics for districts newly drawn for the 1996 elections.

HOUSE ELECTIONS

1996 General		
John Cooksey (R)	135,990	(58%)
Francis Thompson (D)	97,363	(42%)
1996 Primary †		
John Cooksey (R)	60,853	(34%)
Francis Thompson (D)	50,144	(28%)
Clyde Holloway (R)	48,226	(27%)
Michael Jordan Caire (D)	9,286	(5%)
Ben Marshall (R)	7,106	(4%)
Tim Robinson (R)	5,268	(3%)

† In Louisiana the primary is open to candidates of all parties. If a candidate wins 50 percent or more of the vote in the primary, no general election is held. A candidate unopposed in the primary and general election is declared elected and the candidate's name does not appear on the ballot.

CAMPAIGN FINANCE

	Receipts	Receipts from PACs	Expend-itures
1996			
Cooksey (R)	$898,379	$133,650 (15%)	$898,479
Thompson (D)	$540,761	$79,100 (15%)	$511,183

DISTRICT VOTE FOR PRESIDENT

	1996		1992
D	116,082 (47%)	**D**	95,048 (37%)
R	104,605 (43%)	**R**	127,134 (49%)
I	20,941 (9%)	**I**	36,537 (14%)

KEY VOTES

1997

Ban "partial birth" abortions	Y

6 Richard H. Baker (R)

Of Baton Rouge — Elected 1986, 6th term

Biographical Information
Born: May 22, 1948, New Orleans.
Education: Louisiana State U., B.A. 1971.
Occupation: Real estate broker.
Family: Wife, Kay Carpenter; two children.
Religion: Methodist.
Political Career: La. House, 1972-86.
Capitol Office: 434 Cannon Bldg. 20515; 225-3901.

Committees
Banking & Financial Services
Capital Markets, Securities & Government Sponsored Enterprises (chairman); Housing & Community Opportunity
Transportation & Infrastructure
Surface Transportation; Water Resources & Environment

In Washington: At the start of the 105th Congress, Baker traded in his seat on the Agriculture Committee for one on the Transportation and Infrastructure panel, where he sits on the Surface Transportation and the Water Resources and Environment subcommittees.

Ironically, Baker was threatened with that very switch of assignments in 1995 after bucking the GOP line to oppose the "Freedom to Farm" bill. Republican leaders quashed talk of retribution, so as the Agriculture Committee reshaped federal farm policy to bring it more in line with free-market principles, Baker had a place at the table, looking out for Louisiana's commodity interests. The farm bill passed in 1996.

Now on the Transportation Committee, Baker will be helping write another major reauthorization bill, this one governing the distribution of federal highway and mass transit funds into the next century. Again, Baker can be counted on to lobby for Louisiana's needs and wants.

In September 1995, Baker was one of four Republicans who voted against the Freedom to Farm bill in committee, stalling the legislation. A week later, after a closed-door meeting with committee Republicans, Agriculture Chairman Pat Roberts, a Kansas Republican, said he would adjourn the markup without a consensus and recommend that the Budget Committee and House leadership put the Freedom to Farm proposal into the seven-year budget-reconciliation package anyway.

As Roberts adjourned the markup, Democrats distributed an internal Republican memo. It described a meeting of top GOP strategists at which Speaker Newt Gingrich considered ways to punish the lawmakers for voting against the legislation. Baker would have lost his Agriculture seat and been put on Transportation. But the memo said Gingrich decided against any punishment, observing, "These four guys are not outlaws." Even so, the memo was a big story on Capitol Hill, forcing House Republicans into a damage-control posture. Commenting on the possibility that he would be punished for his vote on the farm bill, Baker said, "I would not have expected our leadership to have responded that way to independent voting necessities."

Indeed, Baker said he would vote against the GOP's budget-reconciliation bill if it included Freedom to Farm, which called for replacing existing crop subsidies with a system of fixed, declining payments to farmers. "I am a likely 'no,' " he said. "I think the consequences of this to my state's economy are very devastating." He was one of 15 lawmakers who signed a letter to Gingrich opposing inclusion of the farm proposal in the budget-reconciliation package. "Transforming current farm programs into strict welfare payments is contrary to the underlying principles of the Republican Conference," the letter said. "Radical farm program reform can be achieved without mailing our farmers 'Freedom to Farm' welfare checks."

As work on the farm bill proceeded, it became more palatable to Baker. He did not desert the party on budget reconciliation in October 1995, and in February 1996 he and his allies successfully fought an amendment that would have phased out government support for the sugar industry, a big player in Louisiana's economy. That amendment failed 208-217, and the next day, Baker voted for the final version of the farm bill.

Baker also sits on the Banking and Financial Services Committee, and after the Republican takeover of the House, he had hoped to become chairman of the Housing and Community Opportunity Subcommittee. In the days surrounding the November 1994 election, he toured a Louisiana housing project and castigated the Department of Housing and Urban Development (HUD). He called the creation of a new Office of AIDS Housing at HUD "unwarranted" and skewered a program to subsidize housing for homeless people with the disease. Soon afterward, Baker referred to HUD as the "worst slum landlord in America" and called for privatizing public housing. However, the Housing Subcommittee chairmanship went to a less-senior Republican, Rick A.

LOUISIANA 6
South Central — Baton Rouge

The 6th has assumed many different forms in Louisiana's three rounds of redistricting since the 1990 census. No Louisiana congressional district except for the 4th has been shaped more dramatically.

The 1992 version of the 6th sprawled across 17 parishes from the Texas border to the state capital, Baton Rouge. The plan in place for the 1994 election reined in some of the 6th's far-flung tentacles, but it still covered all or part of 16 parishes. In its current form, the 6th is more compact, comprising eight full parishes and part of another in lower northeastern Louisiana.

In electoral terms, Baton Rouge is the single biggest influence in the 6th. The city's name is French for "red stick," which purportedly refers to the object that once marked a boundary between two Indian tribes. The entire city of 220,000 is included in the 6th, and East Baton Rouge, the parish that envelops the city, accounts for 60 percent of the district's registered voters. George Bush won the parish in 1992, but Bill Clinton achieved a narrow victory here four years later.

Downtown Baton Rouge, like so many other center cities, has been strapped economically by suburban flight; there has been relatively little major construction here in the past 20 years, and the city's population declined slightly in the 1980s. However, Catfish Town, a city-assisted retail development center that includes newly renovated wharves and warehouses along the Mississippi River, is a site for riverboat gambling. Together with the nearby Naval War Museum, it is attracting tourists.

Baton Rouge remains the center of the South's petrochemical industry. The Exxon Corp. Manufacturing Complex in Baton Rouge has the nation's second-largest chemical manufacturing facility. The petrochemical industry employs more than 14,000 in the area.

Baton Rouge also has a large student population. Louisiana State University enrolls more than 25,000 students, and Southern, the state's largest black university, has a student population of more than 10,000.

One of Baton Rouge's attractions is the 34-story, 450-feet high Capitol building. Former Gov. and U.S. Sen. Huey P. Long, under whose tutelage the building was constructed, was assassinated there in 1935 and is buried in front of the building.

Within its boundaries, the 6th contains a variety of business pursuits linked to the land. Sugar-cane fields dot Point Coupee Parish. Along the Mississippi River border, the 6th picks up much of the timber- and potato-producing parishes of St. Helena and West and East Feliciana.

Some of the most intense support for the 1991 gubernatorial bid of David Duke, the former Ku Klux Klan leader and Nazi sympathizer turned Republican state legislator, came from La Salle and Livingston parishes. Livingston, the district's second most-populous parish, supported Bob Dole in 1996, the only parish in the district to do so. Bill Clinton captured the rest while polling just under 50 percent in the 6th.

As of May 19, the Census Bureau had not recalculated the population data, racial and ethnic breakdowns, and age statistics for districts newly drawn for the 1996 election.

Lazio of New York. Baker wound up chairing the Capital Markets, Securities and Government Sponsored Enterprises Subcommittee.

Baker has sometimes clashed with the chairman of the full Banking Committee, Jim Leach of Iowa. In 1995, for instance, Baker tried to add a provision to Leach's banking overhaul legislation that would allow banks to affiliate with insurance companies. The Baker language would have had the effect of opening the door to a broader rewrite that would offer new powers to a larger array of market players, especially diversified securities firms. He won in committee. But insurance agents, fearing inroads by banks on their business, successfully urged House leaders to strip the Baker language out of their version.

In January 1997, after Leach opposed Gingrich's re-election as Speaker, Baker said he believed that vote would "cause strained relationships between the leadership, the Rules Committee and any product of which Mr. Leach might be the principal advocate."

Though not yet 50 years old, Baker is past the quarter-century mark of involvement in Bayou State politics. By 24, he was already in the state House, where he served for 14 years as a labor-oriented Democrat. But when he switched parties and ran for Congress, Baker began moving to the point on the political spectrum he occupies today — on the right, voting a pro-business line.

Baker's pro-business beliefs led him initially to oppose a minimum wage increase in the 104th Congress. He voted in May 1996 against California GOP Rep. Frank Riggs' amendment to increase the wage by 90 cents an hour, and he also supported a GOP leadership-backed effort to exempt small businesses from paying the higher wage. Riggs' amendment passed, and the small-business exemption failed. In August 1996, when the wage increase won final passage in the House, Baker voted "yea." That final version of the wage bill included other provisions sought by Republicans, including $10 billion in business tax cuts, a $5,000 tax credit to offset the cost of adoption and an expansion of Individual Retirement Accounts.

Baker is a proponent of gunowners' rights, and in recent high-profile floor votes on abortion policy, he has taken the side of abortion foes. He voted in the 104th against requiring states to fund Medicaid abortions for poor women, against permitting abortions at overseas military hospitals, and against allowing federal employees' health care plans to cover abortions. He has supported banning a particular abortion technique that opponents call "partial birth" abortion.

Baker has kept up a political profile beyond his constituency. He chaired George Bush's 1988 and 1992 Louisiana campaigns and led the state's delegation in 1988 at the Republican National Convention in New Orleans. In 1996, he was an early supporter of Texas Sen. Phil Gramm's presidential campaign, but another GOP White House aspirant, commentator Patrick J. Buchanan, won all three delegate slots in Baker's 6th District.

At Home: After Republican Rep. W. Henson Moore announced plans to run for the Senate in 1986, Baker put together an unusual coalition of country-club Republicans and blue-collar Democrats to defeat a better-financed Democratic foe, state Senate President Pro Tempore Thomas Hudson.

It was an odd election. After his years in the state Legislature as a Democrat, Baker switched parties in 1985 at the urging of GOP leaders who saw him as the only candidate who could stop Hudson. Baker had represented a blue-collar Baton Rouge district, while Hudson was from a white-collar constituency.

Baker could not compete with Hudson when it came to endorsements from organized political forces. Only in the rural parishes, where he had Farm Bureau support, did Baker receive help from a significant pressure group.

But Baker had a core of committed GOP volunteers, many of them affluent suburbanites who had backed Moore. Baker also developed an effective appeal to diverse religious groups. He had been a Methodist lay preacher, and he expanded his support among fundamentalists with an endorsement from Baton Rouge-based TV evangelist Jimmy Swaggart, at the time an influential figure. Many Catholics appreciated Baker's opposition to abortion and his support for state aid to parochial schools. In the September open primary, Baker won 51 percent of the vote, avoiding a November runoff.

In 1992, redistricting paired Baker with GOP Rep. Clyde C. Holloway, a conservative who had won three terms in a district that was roughly 85 percent Democratic, but who saw his constituency splintered by the remap. Holloway came in first in the primary, and Baker barely made the runoff, finishing just ahead of Democrat Ned Randolph, the popular conservative mayor of Alexandria, thanks to a strong showing in his home parish, East Baton Rouge, source of the 6th's largest chunk of votes.

In the runoff, Baker carried only two parishes — East Baton Rouge and Livingston — but that was enough to offset his losses across the rest of the 6th.

HOUSE ELECTIONS

1996 Primary †		
Richard H. Baker (R)	117,598	(69%)
Steve Myers (D)	52,092	(31%)
1994 Primary †		
Richard H. Baker (R)	123,953	(81%)
Darryl Paul Ward (D)	24,033	(19%)

Previous Winning Percentages: 1992 (51%) **1990** (100%) **1988** (100%) **1986** (51%)

† In Louisiana the primary is open to candidates of all parties. If a candidate wins 50 percent or more of the vote in the primary, no general election is held. A candidate unopposed in the primary and general election is declared elected and the candidate's name does not appear on the ballot.

CAMPAIGN FINANCE

	Receipts	Receipts from PACs	Expend-itures
1996			
Baker (R)	$568,733	$284,869 (50%)	$554,968
1994			
Baker (R)	$609,698	$244,767 (40%)	$518,945

DISTRICT VOTE FOR PRESIDENT

1996		1992	
D	137,988 (50%)	**D**	92,040 (35%)
R	118,687 (43%)	**R**	135,915 (52%)
I	18,670 (7%)	**I**	35,673 (14%)

KEY VOTES

1997	
Ban "partial birth" abortions	Y
1996	
Approve farm bill	Y
Deny public education to illegal immigrants	Y
Repeal ban on certain assault-style weapons	Y
Increase minimum wage	N
Freeze defense spending	N
Approve welfare overhaul	Y
1995	
Approve balanced-budget constitutional amendment	Y
Relax Clean Water Act regulations	Y
Oppose limits on environmental regulations	N
Reduce projected Medicare spending	Y
Approve GOP budget with tax and spending cuts	Y

VOTING STUDIES

	Presidential Support		Party Unity		Conservative Coalition	
Year	**S**	**O**	**S**	**O**	**S**	**O**
1996	30	59	88	5	100	0
1995	17	79	92	4	94	1
1994	46	51	89	5	92	0
1993	36	62	92	4	93	7
1992	81	9	88	5	94	2
1991	79	14	88	6	92	0

INTEREST GROUP RATINGS

Year	ADA	AFL-CIO	CCUS	ACU
1996	0	n/a	100	95
1995	0	0	96	80
1994	0	13	100	100
1993	0	0	91	100
1992	0	20	86	100
1991	0	8	100	95

7 Chris John (D)

Of Crowley — Elected 1996, 1st term

Biographical Information

Born: Jan. 5, 1960, Crowley, La.

Education: Louisiana State U., B.A. 1982.

Occupation: Transportation business owner.

Family: Wife, Payton Smith.

Religion: Roman Catholic.

Political Career: Crowley City Council, 1984-88; La. House, 1988-96; candidate for lieutenant governor, 1995.

Capitol Office: 1504 Longworth Bldg. 20515; 225-2031.

Committees

Agriculture

Forestry, Resource Conservation & Research; General Farm Commodities

Resources

Energy & Mineral Resources

The Path to Washington: John is the third Crowley politician in recent memory to represent the 7th District. Edwin W. Edwards represented the 7th from 1965 until his election to the governorship in 1972; his successor, John B. Breaux, served until his election to the Senate in 1986.

A conservative Democrat, John came to Washington in 1997 with big plans to reduce government waste and cut the national debt. He acknowledged that his goals might be too far-reaching, but said at the very least he hoped to play the role of a facilitator. "I'm not a press hound, and I don't go looking for quotes. . . . I'm good at negotiating," he said.

John proposed establishing panels charged with pinpointing waste in each government department and cutting program budgets by as much as 10 percent. He also wanted to adopt a page from Louisiana's fiscal procedures by seeing legislation enacted that would require a portion of federal revenues to be dedicated to reducing the national debt.

John has experience in tackling such issues. As an eight-year member of the state House, he served on the Appropriations Committee and Joint Legislative Budget Committee, which oversees all state agency budgets.

To boost economic development, John says he wants to work on ways to bolster trade along the 7th District's inland waterways and ports. He also hopes to increase drilling incentives for offshore oil and gas companies. At the same time, he stresses the importance of making sure that adequate protections for the district's delicate estuaries, fisheries and marshlands are in place. John is well-placed to get involved in energy and environmental issues as a member of the Resources Committee.

John also got a seat on the Agriculture Committee, where he will be looking out for the interest of his district's rice farmers and crawfish industry.

In his House campaign, John promoted his business background and experience in creating jobs as the operator of his family's trucking company.

He received endorsements from two key business groups, the U.S. Chamber of Commerce and the National Federation of Independent Business. He also earned the backing of the man he was seeking to succeed, Democrat-turned-Republican Rep. Jimmy Hayes.

Hayes gave up his seat to run for the Senate post vacated by Democrat J. Bennett Johnston, but Hayes finished fifth in a crowded all-party primary.

With no incumbent running, the 7th drew a crowded field, including John and seven others. As the slate's only legislator, and having run a statewide campaign in 1995 for lieutenant governor (which he lost), John had advantage in name recognition.

The most pointed attacks on John came from one of his Democratic opponents, Tyron Picard, who accused John of mishandling campaign contributions related to his bid for the lieutenant governorship. John denied any wrongdoing and labeled Picard's attack as a desperate move to revive his struggling campaign.

John emerged from the primary in first place but was far short of a majority. John was forced into a runoff with Democratic lawyer Hunter Lundy, whose second-place finish was unsuccessfully challenged by Republican David Thibodaux, who missed a runoff spot by a handful of votes.

Lundy took up where Picard left off, blasting John as a career politician and accusing him of selling his vote in the state legislature. He claimed that John voted against legislation requiring mandatory sentences for people convicted of drunken driving with a child in the car because John had received campaign contributions from alcoholic beverage companies.

John said his votes reflected the views of his district. He also contended that his legislative and business experience provided him better qualifications for the job of congressman than the background of Lundy, a trial lawyer. John won with 53 percent of the vote.

LOUISIANA 7
Southwest — Lake Charles; Lafayette

Literally, the Cajun expression "Lâche pas la patate" means "Don't drop the potato." Figuratively, it comes closer to "Hang in there," and that is what the 7th has been doing with increasing success since the oil bust of the mid-1980s.

The district, which begins in the Cajun core of south-central Louisiana, runs to Texas on the west and borders the Gulf of Mexico on the south. Remapping in 1996 mostly removed territory on or near the Texas border in the northwestern part of the district. Now lying wholly in the 7th is the city of Lafayette; under the 1994 congressional district plan, largely African-American portions of the city had been included in the majority-black 4th district.

Dotted with waterfowl and wildlife refuges, the 7th's gulf edge serves sports and commercial fishermen. Menhaden, which is ground into feed and industrial oil, accounts for a large share of the commercial catch. Back on land, some of the farms north and west of Crowley (Acadia Parish) that grow rice now alternately raise crawfish in fallow rice fields.

Lake Charles (Calcasieu Parish), a refining and chemical-producing hub in the southwest corner of the district, offers a sharp industrial contrast to the 7th's rural areas. A union and Democratic stronghold, the city has seen a rebound in chemical sales abroad. Many refineries have been able to offer hundreds of construction jobs because of environmentally oriented projects undertaken to meet deadlines set in the 1990 Clean Air Act. The chemical manufacturers PPG Industries, Olin Corporation and Condea Vista together employ over 2,700.

The closing of a Boeing repair facility cost Lake Charles 2,000 jobs early in the decade. But Northrop Grumman Corp., which builds JSTARS radar planes, moved in and currently employs 1,500 in the area.

On U.S. Highway 165 in Allen parish lies the small town of Kinder, which houses the Grand Casino Coushatta, a 71,000 square foot facility operated by the Coushatta Indians. Expansion is planned for the facility, Louisiana's largest land-based casino. If they tire of the tables, visitors might head east to sample Cajun fare and the Acadian lifestyle in nearby communities.

In the eastern part of the district is Lafayette, the 7th's largest city with a population of about 100,000. The precipitous drop in oil prices during the early and middle 1980s devastated the Lafayette economy, which has since rebounded and diversified. The two largest private employers in the area are medical facilities, Lafayette General Medical Center and Our Lady of Lourdes Regional Medical Center. Stuller Settings Inc., a jewelry manufacturer in Lafayette, has 1,100 employees.

Lafayette Parish is as close to a political opposite of Lake Charles as this district offers. It was the only parish in the 7th to opt for Bob Dole in 1996. In the House runoff election (which featured two Democrats against one another), Lafayette gave 61 percent to the conservative John.

As of May 19, the Census Bureau had not recalculated population data, racial and ethnic breakdowns and age statistics for districts newly drawn for the 1996 elections.

HOUSE ELECTIONS

1996 General		
Chris John (D)	128,449	(53%)
Hunter Lundy (D)	113,351	(47%)
1996 Primary †		
Chris John (D)	45,404	(26%)
Hunter Lundy (D)	38,605	(22%)
David Thibodaux (R)	38,593	(22%)
Tyron Picard (D)	25,916	(15%)
Jim Slatten (R)	12,467	(7%)
Charlie Buckels (R)	8,302	(5%)
Peter Vidrine (R)	5,071	(3%)
Macklin Schexneider (D)	2,722	(2%)

† In Louisiana the primary is open to candidates of all parties. If a candidate wins 50 percent or more of the vote in the primary, no general election is held. A candidate unopposed in the primary and general election is declared elected and the candidate's name does not appear on the ballot.

CAMPAIGN FINANCE

	Receipts	Receipts from PACs	Expend-itures
1996			
John (D)	$609,190	$121,700 (20%)	$604,865
Lundy (D)	$516,306	$50,800 (10%)	$513,344

DISTRICT VOTE FOR PRESIDENT

	1996		1992
D	147,241 (52%)	D	123,248 (47%)
R	109,404 (38%)	R	100,140 (38%)
I	24,788 (9%)	I	38,285 (15%)

KEY VOTES

1997

Ban "partial birth" abortions	Y

MAINE

Governor: Angus King (I)

First elected: 1994
Length of term: 4 years
Term expires: 1/99
Salary: $70,000 (Actual salary is $65,819.40 after furlough days are taken into account.)
Term limit: 2 consecutive terms
Phone number: (207) 289-3531
Born: March 31, 1944; Alexandria, Va.
Education: Dartmouth College, A.B. 1966; U. of Virginia, J.D. 1969.
Occupation: Energy conservation company owner; television program host; alternative energy company executive; lawyer; congressional aide.
Family: Wife, Mary J. Herman; four children.
Religion: Episcopalian.
Political Career: No previous office.

No Lieutenant Governor

Senate President: Mark W. Lawrence (D)

Salary: $26,215 over 2 years
1st year: $14,962; 2nd year: $11,250
Phone: (207) 287-1500

State election official: (207) 287-4186
Democratic headquarters: (207) 622-6233
Republican headquarters: (207) 622-6247

REDISTRICTING

Maine did not redistrict for the 1990s until after the 1992 election. A new map was issued by state Supreme Judicial Court on June 29, 1993.

STATE LEGISLATURE

Legislature. In even years meets December-June; odd years, January-April.

Senate: 35 members, 2-year terms
1996 breakdown: 19D, 15R,1I; 23 men, 12 women
Salary: $17,475 over 2 years
1st year: $9,975; 2nd year: $7,500
Phone: (207) 289-1500

House of Representatives: 151 members, 2-year terms
1996 breakdown: 81D, 69R, 1I; 117 men, 34 women
Salary: $17,475 over 2 years
1st year: $9,975; 2nd year: $7,500
Phone: (207) 289-1300

URBAN STATISTICS

City	Population
Portland	64,358
Mayor John McDonough, N-P	
Lewiston	39,757
Mayor John Jenkins, D	
Bangor	31,181
Mayor Patricia Blanchette, N-P	
Auburn	24,309
Mayor Lee Young, N-P	

U.S. CONGRESS

Senate: 0 D, 2 R
House: 2 D, 0 R

TERM LIMITS

For state offices: Yes
Senate: 4 Terms
House: 4 Terms

ELECTIONS

1996 Presidential Vote

Bill Clinton	52%
Bob Dole	31%
Ross Perot	14%

1992 Presidential Vote

Bill Clinton	39%
George Bush	30%
Ross Perot	30%

1988 Presidential Vote

George Bush	55%
Michael S. Dukakis	44%

POPULATION

1990 population		1,227,928
1980 population		1,124,660
Percent change		+9%
Rank among states:		38
White		98%
Black		<1%
Hispanic		1%
Asian or Pacific islander		1%
Urban		45%
Rural		55%
Born in state		68%
Foreign-born		3%
Under age 18	309,002	25%
Ages 18-64	755,553	62%
65 and older	163,373	13%
Median age		33.9

MISCELLANEOUS

Capital: Augusta
Number of counties: 16
Per capita income: $17,306 (1991)
Rank among states: 30
Total area: 30,265 sq. miles
Rank among states: 39

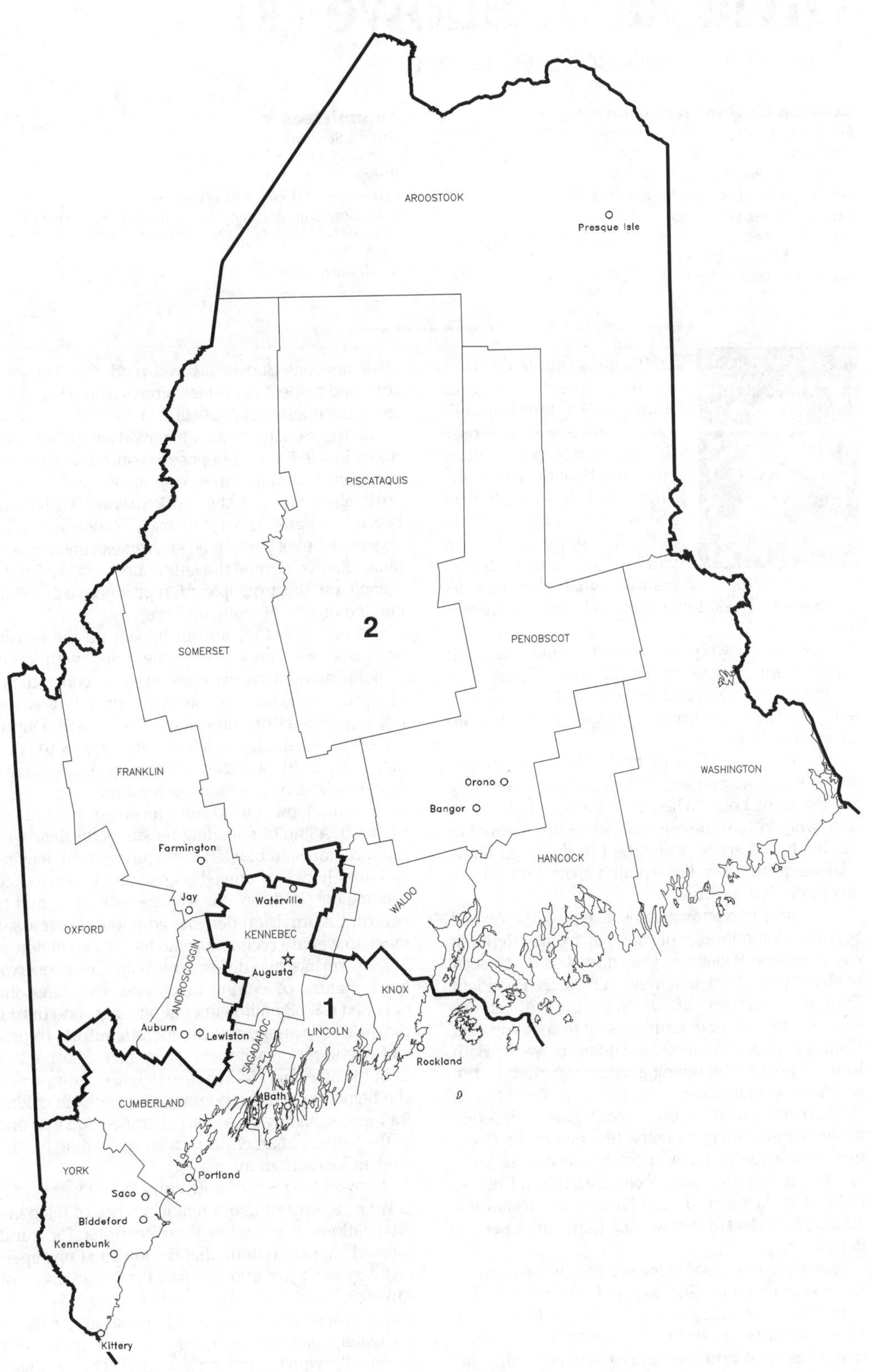
AROOSTOOK
Presque Isle
PISCATAQUIS
2
SOMERSET
PENOBSCOT
WASHINGTON
FRANKLIN
Orono
Bangor
Farmington
HANCOCK
Jay
Waterville
WALDO
OXFORD
KENNEBEC
ANDROSCOGGIN
Augusta
KNOX
1
LINCOLN
Auburn
Lewiston
SAGADAHOC
Rockland
CUMBERLAND
Bath
YORK
Portland
Saco
Biddeford
Kennebunk
Kittery

Olympia J. Snowe (R)

Of Falmouth — Elected 1994, 1st term

Biographical Information

Born: Feb. 21, 1947, Augusta, Maine.

Education: U. of Maine, B.A. 1969.

Occupation: Public official.

Family: Husband, John R. McKernan Jr..

Religion: Greek Orthodox.

Political Career: Maine House, 1973-77; Maine Senate, 1977-79; U.S. House, 1979-95.

Capitol Office: 250 Russell Bldg. 20510; 224-5344.

Committees

Armed Services
Acquisition & Technology; Personnel; Seapower

Budget

Commerce, Science & Transportation
Aviation; Manufacturing & Competitiveness; Oceans & Fisheries (chairman); Surface Transportation & Merchant Marine

Small Business

In Washington: In the 1994 electoral sweep that gave Congress to the Republicans, Snowe was the only GOP moderate newly elected to the Senate. While she finds but a few ideological soul mates among the chamber's Republicans, Snowe works with them to try to restrain what she sees as excesses in legislation advanced by party conservatives.

But Snowe, who fought hard during the 104th Congress for abortion rights and student loans — as well as for the parochial interests of Maine — generally ends up supporting final passage of signature Republican bills.

Snowe served 16 years in the House before her Senate election, and she has close ties to Majority Leader Trent Lott. (When Lott was elected House GOP whip in 1981, he selected her as his deputy.) In the 105th, she serves as counsel to the Republican leadership and is a key conduit from Lott to the moderate GOP faction.

For the 105th Snowe gains a seat on the Armed Services Committee, replacing her former Republican colleague William S. Cohen, who did not seek re-election in 1996 and now serves as President Clinton's secretary of Defense. Snowe can be expected to use her committee seat to try to protect Maine's military interests, including those of Bath Iron Works, a shipbuilding company that is the state's largest employer.

Also in the 105th, Snowe holds a gavel of interest to the Maine fishing industry: She chairs the Commerce, Science and Transportation Subcommittee on Oceans and Fisheries. Along with Susan Collins, Cohen's replacement in the Senate, she forms the nation's first elected two-woman Republican Senate delegation.

Snowe is best known for her unstinting support for abortion rights. She joined Republican Govs. Pete Wilson of California and William F. Weld of Massachusetts in trying to pressure the 1996 Republican platform committee to acknowledge the divergent views party members hold on this issue. (The language Snowe favored read, "We acknowledge and respect the honest convictions that divide us on the question of abortion.")

In the Senate, Snowe's advocacy of abortion rights has led her to oppose a ban on a particular abortion technique that opponents call "partial birth" abortion, and she worked with Washington Democrat Patty Murray to try to block a ban on abortions being performed at overseas military hospitals. Snowe termed the latter ban "another frontal assault on the principle of reproductive freedom and the dignity of women's lives."

Snowe's most significant impact on the legislative process comes when she joins with other Republican moderates to pressure the leadership to compromise its most conservative aims, thus ensuring a GOP majority on critical floor votes. During the 104th, the moderate allies met regularly to coordinate strategy, and they were particularly active during debate on overhauling welfare.

The moderates used their leverage to require a higher baseline of spending by states on their welfare programs, to block conservatives from denying welfare checks to unwed teenage mothers, to add funding for child care for welfare recipients, and to overturn a provision denying additional cash assistance to welfare recipients who have more children.

Snowe has her differences with the conservatives' mantra of cutting taxes and spending. She opposed a $353 million tax cut package, and during the 104th she supported Democratic efforts to protect spending on veterans' programs. She backed Republican efforts to increase defense outlays, and she helped lead her moderate colleagues in calling for more spending on social programs. She was one of the leaders of an effort to restore funding for the student loan program.

Snowe also worked with John D. Rockefeller IV, D-W.Va., to ensure that a major rewrite of telecommunications law included protections for rural folks. "I happen to think that the information superhighway can't just run through the urban areas of America," she said. "The market doesn't work in places where you have a low population density. If companies can't make money in rural areas, they essentially won't serve rural areas." The two succeeded with an amendment to require telecommunications carriers to provide service to rural non-profit health care centers, schools and public libraries.

Snowe also paid close attention to matters of specific concern to Maine. She asked the U.S. trade representative to take steps to make it easier for American potato growers to sell to Canadian processors. And along with the rest of the Maine delegation, she asked the International Trade Commission to investigate potato trade issues in the U.S. and Canada. She also proposed an amendment to limit the number of lobsters that could be landed through dragging with nets — a method banned in Maine.

In the House, Snowe was the longtime co-chairman of the Congressional Caucus for Women's Issues, an advocate for abortion rights and federal research on women's health. Her most publicized stand during the 102nd Congress was an unsuccessful effort to block the closure of Loring Air Force Base, located in Maine's 2nd District. She voiced anti-communist views as a senior member of the House International Relations Committee, and on the Senate Foreign Relations Committee she has sponsored a bill to bar the sharing of sensitive intelligence information. An advocate of U.S. assistance to former Cold War front-line states such as Greece, homeland of her forebears, Snowe is averse to deep cuts in foreign aid. But she has been known for her sallies against what she considers wasteful spending in the foreign policy bureaucracy.

At Home: Snowe's victory marked one of the most notable transitions in the 1994 elections. She won easily to succeed retiring Senate Majority Leader George J. Mitchell, D-Maine, helping and also symbolizing the Republicans' capture of the Senate after eight years of Democratic control.

Snowe's political rise has a storybook quality. She was orphaned at age 9 and raised by an aunt and uncle in blue-collar surroundings. In 1973, her first husband, Maine state Rep. Peter Snowe, was killed in an automobile accident. Snowe was working as a staff aide to Cohen at the time, and she was elected to succeed her late husband in the Legislature. She won election to the state Senate in 1976. Just two years later, Snowe won a close House election to succeed Cohen, who had moved on to the Senate.

In 1990, however, Snowe almost got caught up in a wave of voter dissatisfaction, spurred by a deepening recession that was especially severe in the half of the state Snowe represented. She defeated Democratic state Rep. Patrick K. McGowan by 51 percent to 49 percent after a series of heated exchanges between the two. A 1992 rematch was fought under equally difficult circumstances for Snowe. President George Bush ran third in the state, behind Bill Clinton and Ross Perot. Snowe won with a 49 percent plurality.

Despite her back-to-back House re-election struggles, Snowe was the presumed GOP nominee when Mitchell announced his surprise retirement early in 1994. Having held the House seat in the half of Maine generally considered more Democratic, Snowe was seen as a good bet to pick up the votes she needed in the other half.

Snowe raised more than $2 million, eclipsing Democratic Rep. Thomas H. Andrews' $1.5 million. But that was the least of Andrews' problems. In 1991 he had voted for the base-closing package that shuttered Loring. Snowe never let him forget it, especially because it offered such a handy symbol for his minimalist approach to military outlays in general — a major liability in a state deeply anxious about the future of its defense industry. Snowe prevailed with 60 percent of the vote.

SENATE ELECTIONS

1994 General

Olympia J. Snowe (R)	308,244	(60%)
Thomas H. Andrews (D)	186,042	(36%)
Plato Truman (I)	17,205	(3%)

Previous Winning Percentages: **1992*** (49%) **1990*** (51%) **1988*** (66%) **1986*** (77%) **1984*** (76%) **1982*** (67%) **1980*** (79%) **1978*** (51%)

* *House elections*

CAMPAIGN FINANCE

	Receipts	Receipts from PACs	Expend-itures
1994			
Snowe (R)	$2,309,912	$792,412 (34%)	$2,041,834
Andrews (D)	$1,506,154	$188,347 (13%)	$1,482,060

INTEREST GROUP RATINGS

Year	ADA	AFL-CIO	CCUS	ACU
1996	35	n/a	77	70
1995	40	25	84	39
House Service:				
1994	30	56	0	57
1993	40	42	64	67
1992	50	58	50	60
1991	35	67	40	55

KEY VOTES

1997	
Approve balanced-budget constitutional amendment	Y
Approve chemical weapons treaty	Y
1996	
Approve farm bill	N
Limit punitive damages in product liability cases	Y
Exempt small businesses from higher minimum wage	Y
Approve welfare overhaul	Y
Bar job discrimination based on sexual orientation	Y
Override veto of ban on "partial birth" abortions	N
1995	
Approve GOP budget with tax and spending cuts	Y
Approve constitutional amendment barring flag desecration	Y

VOTING STUDIES

	Presidential Support		Party Unity		Conservative Coalition	
Year	S	O	S	O	S	O
1996	53	47	72	28	79	21
1995	42	58	70	30	61	39
House Service:						
1994	59	40	66	33	75	19
1993	41	59	68	32	66	34
1992	41	59	58	41	69	31
1991	47	47	52	47	89	11

Susan Collins (R)

Of Bangor — Elected 1996, 1st term

Biographical Information
Born: Dec. 7, 1952, Caribou, Maine.
Education: St. Lawrence U., B.A. 1975.
Occupation: Business center director; state deputy treasurer; SBA official; state financial regulation commissioner; congressional aide.
Family: Single.
Religion: Roman Catholic.
Political Career: Republican nominee for governor, 1994.
Capitol Office: 172 Russell Bldg. 20510; 224-2523.

Committees
Special Aging
Governmental Affairs
International Security, Proliferation & Federal Services; Investigations (chairman)
Labor & Human Resources
Children & Families; Public Health & Safety

The Path to Washington: Collins has lived out a dream common among Capitol Hill staffers: She won her old boss's job.

Collins worked a dozen years for GOP Sen. William S. Cohen as an adviser on business issues. After Cohen announced that he would not seek a fourth term in 1996, Collins won the hotly contested race to succeed him, resisting a tide in Maine that carried Democrats to victory in both the state's House districts and in the presidential contest.

Collins' victory made Maine the first state with two female Republican senators. She and colleague Olympia J. Snowe are part of their party's moderate wing, a dwindling but still visible factor in the Senate's legislative work.

Collins holds a seat on the Governmental Affairs Committee, where she chairs the Investigations Subcommittee, and she serves on the Labor and Human Resources Committee and the Special Aging Committee.

Collins, who had never previously held elective office, proved to be a better campaigner in 1996 than she was in 1994, when she lost as the GOP nominee for governor. In that race she finished a poor third, trailing both the Democratic nominee, former Gov. and former U.S. Rep. Joseph E. Brennan, and independent Angus King, who won the race. Many GOP conservatives abandoned Collins in favor of King in that race, turned off by her support for abortion rights and other moderate positions.

The Senate Republican primary in 1996 was an ugly affair, but most of the controversy involved Collins' two opponents, state Sen. W. John Hathaway and wealthy businessman Robert A. G. Monks.

A week before the primary, allegations surfaced that Hathaway had sexually abused his family's adolescent babysitter over an 18-month period in the early 1990s, when the family lived in Alabama. Prosecutors there confirmed that Hathaway had been under investigation; one said he had not been charged out of concern for the child's welfare.

Hathaway accused Monks of planting the story in the media, and he ran TV ads bemoaning Monks' "last-minute character assassination attempt." Monks, who spent $2 million of his own money on the race, denied spreading the story, but acknowledged that he had hired an investigator to look into Hathaway's past.

When the primary ballots were counted, Monks was last with 13 percent, Hathaway second with 31 percent and Collins first with a solid 55 percent.

That sent her into a general-election contest with Brennan, who was back for another try at reviving his political career. This time, though, it was Brennan, not Collins, suffering intraparty troubles.

Some state Democratic leaders had openly urged Brennan not to run for the Senate, questioning his appeal to voters after losses in both the 1990 and 1994 gubernatorial elections. And during the Senate campaign, Sen. Bob Kerrey of Nebraska, chairman of the Democratic Senatorial Campaign Committee (DSCC), knocked Brennan as a lackluster campaigner who had not sharply defined his differences with Collins.

Senate Majority Leader Trent Lott of Mississippi appeared in Maine to tell voters he would work with Collins to ensure a goodly share of federal shipbuilding contracts for Maine, which competes for that business with shipyards in Lott's home state.

The pace of the campaign quickened toward the end, but despite increased activity among unionized workers and senior citizens — two constituencies friendly to Democrats — Brennan polled just 44 percent of the vote, 5 percentage points behind Collins. Two other candidates shared the remaining 7 percent of the vote.

In addition to working for Cohen and on the staff of a Senate subcommittee, Collins spent a year as the New England regional administrator of the Small Business Administration, and she directed the Center for Family Business at Bangor's Husson College. She also worked for Maine Gov. John R. McKernan Jr. in the 1980s as commissioner of the Department of Professional and Financial Regulation.

Like Snowe, Collins supports abortion rights, and she would allow federal funding of the procedure for poor women. She has said she would support banning a particular abortion technique that opponents call "partial birth" abortion, as long as exceptions are made when the life or health of the woman is at risk. However, both of those exceptions were not included in abortion legislation the Senate considered in May 1997. So Collins joined Snowe and two other Republican senators in opposing the legislation, which would permit a "partial birth" abortion to be performed to save the woman's life but not to protect her health. The measure passed, 64-36.

She also opposes capital punishment.

Collins' moderate stance on certain social issues may displease the GOP right, but she stands with gun owners' advocates in supporting repeal of the ban on certain semiautomatic assault-style weapons.

On fiscal policy, too, Collins is in line with party conservatives. She supports a balanced-budget constitutional amendment, and she favors requiring a two-thirds vote of Congress to increase taxes. She also backs a constitutional amendment to limit congressional terms and promises to serve no more than 12 years in the Senate.

She promised if elected to focus on protecting small businesses, saying she would try to reduce estate taxes to make it easier for families to pass on their businesses. She also criticized burdensome regulations and supported putting a seven-year expiration date on new regulations.

SENATE ELECTIONS

1996 General		
Susan Collins (R)	298,422	(49%)
Joseph E. Brennan (D)	266,226	(44%)
John C. Rensenbrink (I)	23,441	(4%)
William P. Clarke (TAX)	18,618	(3%)
1996 Primary		
Susan Collins (R)	53,339	(55%)
W. John Hathaway (R)	29,792	(31%)
Robert A.G. Monks (R)	12,943	(13%)

CAMPAIGN FINANCE

	Receipts	Receipts from PACs		Expend-itures
1996				
Collins (R)	$1,721,825	$598,836	(35%)	$1,621,475
Brennan (D)	$978,848	$321,757	(33%)	$976,805
Rensenbrink (I)	$35,385	0		$33,147
Bost (I)	$9,395	0		$9,857
Clarke (I)	$21,982	0		$20,653

KEY VOTES

1997	
Approve balanced-budget constitutional amendment	Y
Approve chemical weapons treaty	Y

1 Tom Allen (D)

Of Portland — Elected 1996, 1st term

Biographical Information

Born: April 16, 1945, Portland, Maine.

Education: Bowdoin College, B.A. 1967; Oxford U., B.Phil. 1970; Harvard U., J.D. 1974.

Occupation: Policy consultant; lawyer; congressional aide.

Family: Wife, Diana; two children.

Religion: Protestant.

Political Career: Portland City Council, 1989-95; mayor of Portland, 1991-92; sought Democratic nomination for governor, 1994.

Capitol Office: 1630 Longworth Bldg. 20515; 225-6116.

Committees

Government Reform & Oversight
District of Columbia; Human Resources

National Security
Military Procurement; Military Research & Development

The Path to Washington: Allen ran the very model of a Democratic challenge in 1996, mobilizing key elements of his party's base while successfully defining his opponent, freshman GOP Rep. James B. Longley Jr., as ideologically out of step with the district.

As did Longley, Allen will sit on the National Security Committee, where he can keep a lookout for matters of concern to Bath Iron Works, a 1st District shipbuilder that is the state's largest employer.

Allen hopes to make an imprint on campaign finance reform legislation as co-chair (along with Arkansas Republican Asa Hutchinson) of the Bipartisan Campaign Finance Reform Task Force of House Freshmen, which held forums on the issue in the 105th Congress. Allen also is a member of the Government Reform and Oversight Committee, which is investigating campaign fundraising during the 1996 elections.

Allen, a former Portland mayor, was a classmate of President Clinton's at Oxford when both were Rhodes scholars. (During a 1996 campaign appearance in Portland, Clinton said he was "bitter" that Allen's head is still free of gray hairs.) Allen chaired Clinton's Maine campaign in 1992 and was an adviser on agriculture issues during the presidential transition.

Like Clinton, Allen successfully sought the political center during his campaign. The district typically has sent moderate politicians to Congress, and Longley was more of a conservative activist.

With a million-dollar assist from independent expenditure campaigns run by the AFL-CIO, Sierra Club and other groups, Allen portrayed Longley as more representative of the interests of House Speaker Newt Gingrich than of voters in the district.

Longley objected, but his protests proved to be too little, too late. Voters disapproved of Longley's votes in support of GOP efforts to slow the growth of Medicare, Head Start, environmental programs and heating assistance for low-income families. Allen campaigned as the champion of all these causes, while pledging to buck his party if it did not stay on course toward balancing the budget. In the end, he scored a decisive double-digit win over Longley.

Allen worked on Sen. Edmund Muskie's successful 1970 re-election campaign and on his Senate staff before attending Harvard Law School. Like his grandfather and father, Allen served on Portland's City Council. He helped pass the state's first ordinance banning discrimination against gays and lesbians and helped form a downtown corporation that granted low-interest loans to businesses that agreed to locate or expand their operations in the city center.

He hopes to pursue a national child-care initiative to assist working parents. During the 1996 campaign, Allen touted his plan for "Family Learning Accounts," tax-free accounts for college and technical education.

That plan echoed a pledge Allen made during his unsuccessful bid for the Democratic gubernatorial nomination in 1994. He wanted to offer Maine residents who completed two years of community service free tuition at state institutions of higher learning.

The statewide exposure Allen received in that race helped him to overcome state Sen. Dale McCormick in the 1996 Democratic House primary. He and McCormick took similar tacks on most issues and spent more time attacking Longley than attacking one another.

McCormick, who is homosexual, received a great deal of fundraising help from national gay and lesbian organizations, and she was able to outspend Allen appreciably. But despite her aggressive efforts to turn out her supporters, Allen's base in the Portland area propelled him to a narrow primary victory.

Allen supports abortion rights and opposes a ban on a particular abortion technique that opponents call "partial birth" abortion. He wants to strengthen clean air and water laws and supports a national deposit on battery usage, as well as a national bottle recycling bill modeled after a Maine program.

MAINE 1
South — Portland; Augusta

Maine's Democratic core follows Interstate 95 through the heart of the 1st, from industrial Biddeford and Saco in the south through urban Portland and on to blue-collar Waterville in the north.

But the 1st is hardly a sure thing for Democratic candidates. Maine's Yankee Republican heritage still is respected in many suburbs of Portland, inland rural areas and small coastal towns (including Kennebunkport, the vacation hometown of George Bush).

Bush carried the 1st by more than 38,000 votes in 1988. But his fortunes faded here, and he lost to Bill Clinton in 1992 by nearly 30,000 votes. Four years later, Clinton crushed Bob Dole in the 1st by 64,000 votes and 20 percentage points. The 1st's status as a swing district is cemented by a large bloc of independent voters; Ross Perot got 28 percent here in 1992 and again surpassed his national average in 1996.

Powered by the waters of Maine's rivers, industries here have made shoes, textiles, lumber, paper and ships throughout the 20th century.

Portland is Maine's largest city, with about 64,000 people. Working-class communities combine with an environmentalist white-collar vote to provide Democrats with a base that often enables them to carry Cumberland County.

The spread of high-tech industry from Boston brought a modest boom to Portland in the 1980s; high-rise office buildings sprouted, and downtown streets welcomed trendy boutiques and restaurants. But hard times heightened some urban problems.

Impending post-Cold War defense cuts cause concerns in communities that depend on the 1st's military-related employers, such as Brunswick Naval Air Station in Cumberland County and Bath Iron Works, a Navy shipbuilder in Sagadohoc County. The Portsmouth Naval Shipyard often appears targeted for possible closure, and the district was nicked in the 1991 round by the closing of Pease Air Force Base (just across the New Hampshire border) and by cutbacks in the naval shipyard at Kittery.

Kittery is at the tip of York, Maine's southernmost county; Biddeford and Saco, with their large Franco-American populations and Democratic leanings, are in northern York.

In the northern part of the 1st is Augusta, the state capital, which is split rather evenly between white-collar government workers and factory workers. Augusta and the textile city of Waterville usually give Democrats an edge in Kennebec County.

After the 1993 remap, most of Kennebec remained in the 1st, but the county became the only one divided between Maine's two House districts. Three rural communities at the eastern edge of the county and two on its western border were placed in the 2nd District. Waldo County, which had been split between the two districts, was moved wholly into the 2nd. The GOP heartland lies along the northern coast. Lincoln, Knox and Waldo counties consist mainly of coastal towns that help make Maine the No. 1 lobster state.

1990 Population: 613,961. White 604,670 (98%), Black 2,787 (<1%), Other 6,504 (1%). Hispanic origin 3,640 (1%). 18 and over 462,299 (75%), 62 and over 98,007 (16%). Median age: 34.

HOUSE ELECTIONS

1996 General		
Tom Allen (D)	173,745	(55%)
James B. Longley Jr. (R)	140,354	(45%)
1996 Primary		
Tom Allen (D)	26,182	(52%)
Dale McCormick (D)	24,527	(48%)

CAMPAIGN FINANCE

	Receipts	Receipts from PACs		Expend-itures
1996				
Allen (D)	$972,946	$217,560	(22%)	$933,425
Longley (R)	$902,849	$369,155	(41%)	$906,432

DISTRICT VOTE FOR PRESIDENT

1996			1992		
D	165,053	(52%)	D	145,191	(40%)
R	100,851	(32%)	R	115,697	(32%)
I	39,845	(13%)	I	102,828	(28%)

KEY VOTES

1997
Ban "partial birth" abortions — N

2 John Baldacci (D)

Of Bangor — Elected 1994, 2nd term

Biographical Information
Born: Jan. 30, 1955, Bangor, Maine.
Education: U. of Maine, B.A. 1986.
Occupation: Restaurant owner.
Family: Wife, Karen Weston; one child.
Religion: Roman Catholic.
Political Career: Maine Senate, 1982-95; Bangor City Council, 1978-81.
Capitol Office: 1740 Longworth Bldg. 20515; 225-6306.

Committees
Agriculture
Forestry, Resource Conservation & Research; Risk Management & Specialty Crops
Small Business
Tax & Exports (ranking)

In Washington: Before coming to Congress in 1995, Baldacci worked two jobs — as a state senator and as manager of Momma Baldacci's Italian Restaurant — that earned him $12,700 total a year. Given that, he had no qualms in his freshman term about supporting efforts to prevent members from accepting free meals and other gifts.

"Congress is paid a good salary," he said. "There is no need to have somebody else picking up our check when we go out to eat." In 1995, Baldacci was part of a small group of members to sign a pledge not to accept personal favors or gifts from lobbyists. The House overwhelmingly passed a strict gift-ban measure in November 1995.

Baldacci generally has looked favorably on institutional reforms and process-changing proposals emphasized by House Republicans since they took control of Congress in 1995. Speaking of his support for a term-limits amendment, he quipped, "I did enjoy voting for term limits, because I really can't imagine being here for six years at this rate."

But Baldacci often is less happy with other policy preferences of the GOP majority. A member of the small Democratic Class of 1994, he is one of just four freshman Democrats who won districts that were represented in the 103rd by Republicans. Baldacci took over the vast 2nd District, which was left open when Rep. Olympia J. Snowe ran successfully for the Senate.

"We as a national party have taken it for granted that we would remain in control," Baldacci said after the election. "We may not have knocked on enough doors."

In the 104th, Baldacci spoke against GOP plans to reduce taxes for higher-income families, and he criticized the majority's efforts to overhaul the student-aid system. Also, he said it was "irresponsible" for Republicans to eliminate a program that assists low-income individuals with their heating bills. Baldacci supported alternative budget-balancing plans that did not combine deep domestic spending cuts with tax breaks, and in 1996 he voted to freeze defense spending at the previous year's level.

Baldacci spoke against the GOP's plans to overhaul welfare, although he voted for the third version of the bill that was enacted toward the end of the 104th. He voted against a ban on a particular abortion technique that opponents call "partial birth" abortion.

Baldacci expressed regret about the harsh partisan tone of the 104th, saying "I didn't come here to throw bombs at each other. I just think it's unfortunate that we've wasted time in this fashion."

The National Rifle Association has provided financial backing to Baldacci, and in the 104th he did find some common cause with the majority of House Republicans in the area of gunowners' rights. He supported GOP efforts in 1996 to repeal a ban on certain semiautomatic assault-style weapons. He also cast a vote in favor of Georgia Republican Bob Barr's amendment to strip an anti-terrorism law of new police powers, such as allowing authorities to use illegally obtained wiretap evidence in terrorism cases. The NRA worried that the government would abuse such expanded powers, possibly to the detriment of firearms owners.

Baldacci joined with Republicans against a majority of Democrats on another high-profile vote during consideration of the same bill, favoring sharp limitations on the constitutional right to seek federal review of convictions.

Among the solutions he proposes for the 2nd District's unemployment woes are improvements to the local infrastructure, including roads and bridges, which could make it far easier for the district's farmers and fishermen to get their products to market. His seat on the Agriculture Committee provides him some opportunity to assist his farmers. For instance, in 1996, he helped broker a deal that led to the Department of Agriculture agreeing to buy at least eight million pounds of round white potatoes, a common Maine variety, for its nutrition programs.

Baldacci also says he would like to create a

MAINE 2
North — Lewiston; Auburn; Bangor

America's largest congressional district east of the Mississippi, the 2nd accounts for the vast bulk of Maine's territory. Its northern reaches are heavily forested; its people are clustered at the southern end, closer to the state's industrial core.

Heavily dependent on factories, farms and fishing, the 2nd is the less affluent of Maine's House districts.

Pockets of poverty are found in coastal Washington County, which is less accessible to tourists than the seaside regions in the 1st District, and in remote Aroostook County, where economic problems were deepened by the 1991 decision to close Loring Air Force Base. The Air Force base closed before Baldacci took office in 1994. It is now called the Loring Commerce Centre, housing some public and private companies.

Until recently, rural Republican traditions remained sturdy in the 2nd. Then-Rep. Olympia J. Snowe coasted through the 1980s; in 1988, George Bush carried the district by 10 percentage points.

But the recession of the early 1990s soured many voters on Republicans and created opportunities for Democrats and independent candidates. In 1994, Baldacci capitalized on that and took back the seat for the Democrats for the first time in more than two decades. He easily won re-election by 47 percentage points.

In 1996 presidential voting, Bill Clinton won the 2nd with 51 percent; like Baldacci, he led in all 11 counties in the district. Ross Perot captured 16 percent, while Bob Dole improved on the GOP's 1992 showing, but just barely, finishing with about 30 percent.

The 2nd's Democratic base is in Androscoggin County, a part of Maine's industrial belt. The Democratic vote is anchored in blue-collar Lewiston (Maine's second-largest city with nearly 40,000 people). Clinton got 57 percent of the county's vote in 1996 while Baldacci grabbed 73 percent.

The only other city of significant size in the 2nd is Bangor, which has slightly more than 33,000 people. Bangor's heyday as a shipmaking center is over. But its wood-products industry and modest port remain in operation, and its international airport is a refueling station for many transoceanic flights.

Democrats are competitive in local elections, but former GOP Sen. William S. Cohen's hometown is usually more dependable for Republicans seeking higher office. The University of Maine (10,000 students) is nearby in Orono.

The rest of the district is rural, much of it covered with the forests that supply trees to Maine's lumber and paper mills. The district also produces potatoes (mainly in Aroostook County), apples, corn and chickens.

The redistricting plan enacted in 1993 reunited coastal Waldo County in the 2nd; it had been shared with the 1st District in the 1980s. But the 2nd also took in five rural communities in Kennebec County, making it the only county in Maine that is now split between the districts.

1990 Population: 613,967. White 603,690 (98%), Black 2,351 (<1%), Other 7,926 (1%). Hispanic origin 3,189 (1%). 18 and over 456,627 (74%), 62 and over 97,978 (16%). Median age: 34.

free-trade zone around the now-shuttered Loring Air Force Base, which he suggests could serve as an excellent export point for goods bound for the former Soviet Union. Baldacci was given a seat on the Small Business Committee during assignment-shuffling in June 1995.

At Home: Baldacci has earned a reputation at home for being a thoughtful, moderate, cautious legislator. Those same qualities, which are so appealing to Maine voters, may have cost him a ride to the U.S. Senate.

When Republican Sen. William S. Cohen announced his retirement early in 1996, Baldacci appeared well-poised for the position, since neither party had groomed likely successors. But Baldacci, while running a statewide seminar with friends and advisers about whether he should run, twice postponed announcing his decision. His hesitancy drew others into the race, notably Joseph E. Brennan, a former governor and the eventual Democratic nominee. Baldacci chose not to face Brennan, saying he could not run a full-bore race and fulfill his House duties. (Brennan lost the general election to Republican Susan Collins.)

Baldacci easily won a second House term, though, turning aside a challenge from Republican Paul R. Young, a philosophy professor and former state representative. Young had managed Texas Sen. Phil Gramm's abortive GOP presidential bid in the state in 1996 and represented a wing of the party more conservative than the 2nd District electorate. Baldacci ended up beating the underfunded Young by a margin (47 points) that was higher than his total share of the vote had been in 1994.

After Democratic Sen. George J. Mitchell unexpectedly announced his retirement in 1994 and Rep. Olympia J. Snowe declared to succeed him, Baldacci was involved in a seven-person Democratic primary for the open seat. His main competitors were James F. Mitchell, a former state party official and nephew of the senator, and district attorney Janet T. Mills.

Mitchell's familiar name gave him an early edge, but Baldacci worked hard to shore up his Penobscot County (Bangor) base, which he had represented in the state Senate since 1983. Baldacci may also have benefited from the endorsement of author Stephen King, a Bangor resident known more for his horror stories than political stances. Baldacci took 27 percent of the vote to Mitchell's 23 percent.

The four-person Republican primary was won by state Rep. Richard A. Bennett, who had a smooth campaign operation and a solid base in western Maine.

But in the general-election campaign, Bennett, who had represented Oxford in the state legislature since 1990, had trouble expanding his support into populous Bangor, Baldacci's home territory. Two independent candidates siphoned off 14 percent of the vote, and Baldacci prevailed by 5 points over Bennett, winning with a 46 percent plurality.

HOUSE ELECTIONS

1996 General		
John Baldacci (D)	205,439	(72%)
Paul R. Young (R)	70,856	(25%)
Aldric Saucier (I)	9,294	(3%)
1994 General		
John Baldacci (D)	109,615	(46%)
Richard A. Bennett (R)	97,754	(41%)
John M. Michael (I)	21,117	(9%)
Charles FitzGerald (I)	11,353	(5%)

CAMPAIGN FINANCE

	Receipts	Receipts from PACs	Expend-itures
1996			
Baldacci (D)	$594,719	$320,500 (54%)	$581,219
Young (R)	$155,625	$22,581 (15%)	$154,653
Saucier (I)	$3,800	0	$3,565
1994			
Baldacci (D)	$459,016	$152,049 (33%)	$442,226
Bennett (R)	$260,019	$56,647 (22%)	$258,813

DISTRICT VOTE FOR PRESIDENT

1996		1992	
D	147,735 (51%)	**D**	118,229 (38%)
R	85,527 (30%)	**R**	90,807 (29%)
I	46,125 (16%)	**I**	103,992 (33%)

KEY VOTES

1997	
Ban "partial birth" abortions	N
1996	
Approve farm bill	N
Deny public education to illegal immigrants	N
Repeal ban on certain assault-style weapons	Y
Increase minimum wage	Y
Freeze defense spending	Y
Approve welfare overhaul	Y
1995	
Approve balanced-budget constitutional amendment	N
Relax Clean Water Act regulations	N
Oppose limits on environmental regulations	Y
Reduce projected Medicare spending	N
Approve GOP budget with tax and spending cuts	N

VOTING STUDIES

	Presidential Support		Party Unity		Conservative Coalition	
Year	**S**	**O**	**S**	**O**	**S**	**O**
1996	86	14	89	11	47	53
1995	86	14	84	14	44	54

INTEREST GROUP RATINGS

Year	ADA	AFL-CIO	CCUS	ACU
1996	80	n/a	31	10
1995	90	100	33	20

MARYLAND

Governor: Parris N. Glendening (D)
First elected: 1994
Length of term: 4 years
Term expires: 1/99
Salary: $120,000
Term limit: 2 terms
Phone: (410) 974-3901
Born: June 11, 1942; Bronx, N.Y.
Education: Florida State U., B.A. 1964, M.A. 1965, Ph.D. 1967.
Occupation: Professor.
Family: Wife, Frances Anne Hughes; one child.
Religion: Roman Catholic.
Political Career: Hyattsville City Council, 1971-74; Prince George's County Council, 1974-82 (chairman, 1980-81); Prince George's County executive, 1982.

Lt. Gov.: Kathleen Kennedy Townsend (D)
First elected: 1994
Length of term: 4 years
Term expires: 1/99
Salary: $100,000
Phone: (410) 974-2804

State election official: (410) 974-3711
Democratic headquarters: (410) 366-2914
Republican headquarters: (410) 269-0113

REDISTRICTING

Maryland retained its eight House seats in reapportionment. The legislature passed the map Oct. 22, 1991; the governor signed it Oct. 23.

STATE LEGISLATURE

General Assembly. Meets January-April.

Senate: 47 members, 4-year terms
1996 breakdown: 32D, 15R; 40 men, 7 women
Salary: $28,840
Phone: (410) 841-3700

House of Representatives: 141 members, 4-year terms
1996 breakdown: 100D, 41R; 93 men, 48 women;
Salary: $28,840
Phone: (410) 841-3100

URBAN STATISTICS

City	Population
Baltimore	736,014
Mayor Kurt Schmoke, D	
Silver Spring	76,046
County Executive Douglas M. Duncan, D	
Columbia	75,885
County Executive Charles I. Ecker, R	
Dundalk	65,800
County Councilman Donald C. Mason, D	
Bethesda	62,936
County Executive Douglas M. Duncan, D	

U.S. CONGRESS

Senate: 2 D, 0 R
House: 4 D, 4 R

TERM LIMITS

For state offices: No

ELECTIONS

1996 Presidential Vote

Bill Clinton	54%
Bob Dole	38%
Ross Perot	7%

1992 Presidential Vote

Bill Clinton	50%
George Bush	36%
Ross Perot	14%

1988 Presidential Vote

George Bush	51%
Michael S. Dukakis	48%

POPULATION

1990 population		4,781,468
1980 population		4,216,975
Percent change		+13%
Rank among states:		19
White		71%
Black		25%
Hispanic		3%
Asian or Pacific islander		3%
Urban		81%
Rural		19%
Born in state		50%
Foreign-born		7%
Under age 18	1,162,241	24%
Ages 18-64	3,101,745	65%
65 and older	517,482	11%
Median age		33.6

MISCELLANEOUS

Capital: Annapolis
Number of counties: 23
Per capita income: $22,080 (1991)
Rank among states: 5
Total area: 10,460 sq. miles
Rank among states: 42

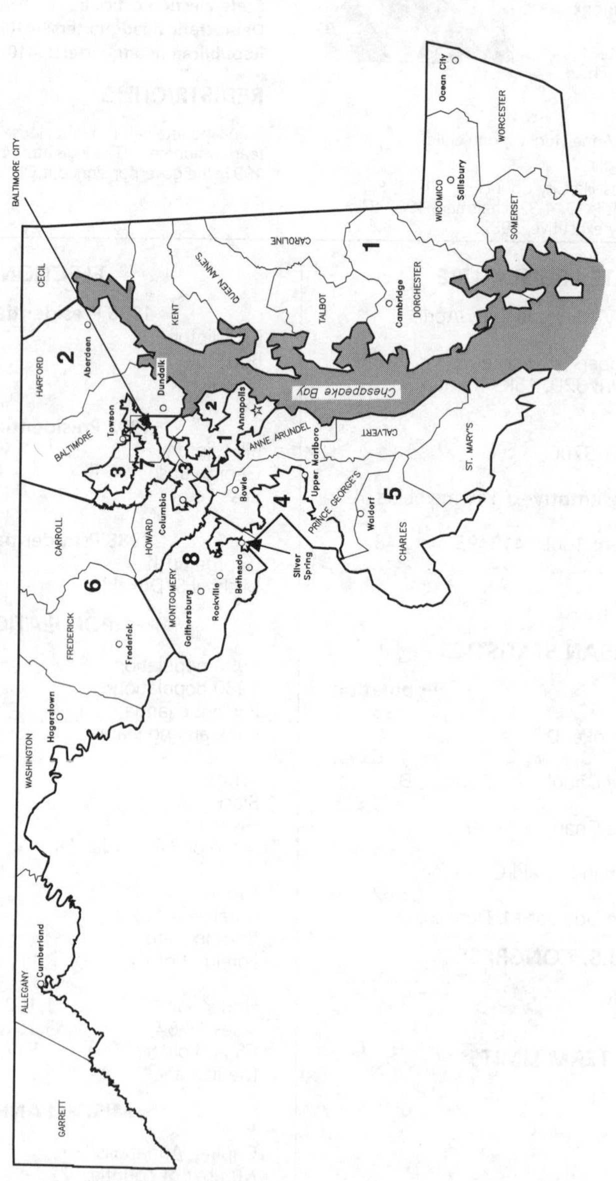
BALTIMORE CITY
CECIL
HARFORD
Aberdeen
2
BALTIMORE
Towson
Dundalk
KENT
QUEEN ANNE'S
CAROLINE
TALBOT
1
Cambridge
DORCHESTER
WICOMICO
Salisbury
SOMERSET
WORCESTER
Ocean City
Chesapeake Bay
Annapolis
ANNE ARUNDEL
CALVERT
ST. MARY'S
5
CHARLES
Waldorf
PRINCE GEORGE'S
Upper Marlboro
4
Bowie
Silver Spring
Bethesda
Rockville
Gaithersburg
MONTGOMERY
8
HOWARD
Columbia
3
CARROLL
6
FREDERICK
Frederick
WASHINGTON
Hagerstown
ALLEGANY
Cumberland
GARRETT

Paul S. Sarbanes (D)

Of Baltimore — Elected 1976, 4th term

Biographical Information

Born: Feb. 3, 1933, Salisbury, Md.
Education: Princeton U., A.B. 1954; Oxford U., B.A. 1957; Harvard U., LL.B. 1960.
Occupation: Lawyer.
Family: Wife, Christine Dunbar; three children.
Religion: Greek Orthodox.
Political Career: Md. House, 1967-71; U.S. House, 1971-77.
Capitol Office: 309 Hart Bldg. 20510; 224-4524.

Committees

Banking, Housing & Urban Affairs (ranking)
Budget
Foreign Relations
African Affairs; European Affairs; International Economic Policy, Export & Trade Promotion (ranking); Near Eastern & South Asian Affairs
Joint Economic

In Washington: When asked a question, Sarbanes is apt to fold his arms, furrow his brow and slip into quiet reflection, sometimes for a very long while. When deliberating thusly, he is rarely deciding where to stand — Sarbanes almost always comes out on the liberal side of debate. Instead, the meditation reflects his methodical and reserved personality.

"It is quite true I don't make decisions off the top of my head," he once explained. "I don't think important decisions ought to be made that way."

Legislatively, Sarbanes' agenda meshes with his style: He concentrates on important, if obscure, details, whether it be the global consequences of Third World debt or the intricacies of deliberations by the Federal Reserve's policy-making committee.

Politically, Democratic leaders turn to Sarbanes when they need a spokesman resistant to partisan fire: In 1987, he was selected for the panel investigating the Iran-contra scandal. In 1995, he was ranking minority member of the Senate Whitewater Committee, where he challenged Republican Sen. Alfonse M. D'Amato of New York at every opportunity. For example, before the White House agreed to turn over notes from a meeting, the Senate had voted along party lines to send the matter to federal court. Sarbanes argued that such a move would be unnecessary.

"They're trying to be forthcoming," he said of the administration. "They're trying to meet the demands of the committee without waiving their attorney-client privilege. We ought not to provoke a constitutional confrontation."

Sarbanes offered a substitute resolution directing the Whitewater Committee to exhaustively explore ways of getting the notes without going to court. It was rejected on a party-line vote. And he argued that the committee hearings into the death of Deputy White House Counsel Vincent W. Foster Jr. and the conduct of the White House staff produced no evidence of wrongdoing.

Sarbanes had hoped to take over the reins of the Banking Committee in the 104th, after the retirement of Donald W. Riegle Jr. of Michigan. But the GOP's takeover of the Senate relegated him to the role of ranking member. In that role, he dissented from Republican-led efforts designed to curb frivolous investor lawsuits. He said the bill went too far.

"Instead of the bill being a stone around the neck of lawyers who fleece investors, it will be a noose around the neck of shareholders with legitimate claims," he said.

On a range of issues, he regularly follows the liberal line against the Republican majority. He voted against the line-item veto, against capping punitive damages in product liability cases, against repealing the national 55 mph speed limit and against overhauling the federal welfare system.

In the past, Sarbanes' painstaking approach and penchant for a narrow legislative focus have frustrated his admirers, who feel he should be more of a leader. One of the Senate's most penetrating intellects, he has the skills to leave opponents sputtering, but he is not a provocateur.

On occasion, Sarbanes does stand in the forefront. In 1991, at the behest of Foreign Relations Committee Chairman Claiborne Pell of Rhode Island, he took the lead on a foreign aid authorization bill and managed to steer a foreign aid conference report through the Senate for the first time since 1985. It was no fault of Sarbanes' that the bill was killed in the House.

Still, Sarbanes often vexes colleagues by targeting minor issues, leading some to conclude that his judgment on the importance of subjects does not always equal his thoroughness in examining them. When he spars at length with witnesses over technicalities, he sometimes seems to miss the big picture by nitpicking minutiae.

For a man who has made politics his life's work, Sarbanes has a curious, if refreshing, distaste for publicity. When he does make headlines, it is generally because he has unearthed a detail offensive to his good-government sensibilities. This was the case in 1989, when Sarbanes held up the consideration of ambassadorial nominees who were major contributors to the GOP. Acknowledging that the practice of rewarding political supporters with ambassadorships has a long bipartisan history, Sarbanes argued that the Bush administration had pursued the practice to excess. (He later would warn President Clinton that his concerns about ambassadorships were bipartisan.)

The nomination of Florida real estate magnate Joseph Zappala to be ambassador to Spain was Sarbanes' test case. "We propose to send as ambassador to Spain [a man] with no particular interest [in] or knowledge of Spain," he said, adding that Mr. Zappala's $145,000 in contributions "appear to be the sole reason" for his selection. While many senators concurred that Zappala's résumé was thin, Foreign Relations narrowly approved his nomination, as did the full Senate.

When Donald P. Gregg was nominated to be ambassador to South Korea, Sarbanes dwelt not on political connections, but on the Iran-contra affair. Sarbanes grilled Gregg, the former national security adviser to Vice President George Bush, about his knowledge of the diversion of funds to the contras. But after a heated debate, the Senate approved his nomination 66-33.

On the select committee investigating the Iran-contra affair in 1987, Sarbanes' performance drew mixed reviews in part because expectations for him were high. His cool, legalistic approach seemed perfect to untangle the complex web of evidence. Many recalled his critical role in the 1974 hearings to impeach President Richard M. Nixon; then a member of the House Judiciary Committee, Sarbanes drafted the most important article of impeachment, charging the president with obstruction of justice.

But what was overlooked about Sarbanes' role in the Watergate hearings was that he had taken center stage for a time precisely because of his cautious nature. The case he built against Nixon was tightly constructed and cogently argued, but he was elected for the job in part because he had avoided the spotlight and withheld an opinion until the committee's work was well under way.

On Foreign Relations and as former chairman of the Banking Subcommittee on International Finance and Monetary Policy, Sarbanes developed a reputation as an expert on the problem of Third World debt and its relationship to U.S. banking and trade. In the 102nd Congress, he managed measures to reauthorize the Export-Import Bank and the Overseas Private Investment Corporation. In the 103rd, he was charged with the relatively thankless task of trying to reshape a 33-year-old law governing the international assistance program.

Also in the 103rd, he joined the Budget Committee and assumed the chairmanship of the Banking Subcommittee on Housing and Urban Affairs, where he could more directly attempt to influence federal spending on urban needs. He and Budget Chairman Jim Sasser of Tennessee were the first to propose an urban aid-fiscal stimulus bill in early 1992, at a time when the economy appeared mired in recession. But their idea for adding $55 billion to the federal deficit found few supporters.

Though he voted in 1993 for Clinton's deficit reduction plan, which included tax increases on the wealthy, he was among the Clinton allies in early 1994 who attempted to quash suggestions that Congress take more action to reduce the deficit. "Sometimes if you take too much medicine too quickly, you don't get better; you get worse," he said.

He tried to steer through housing legislation, with mixed success. He played a key role in passage of a law giving the Department of Housing and Urban Development (HUD) more flexibility to dispose of apartment buildings that had fallen to the government through foreclosures. But a broader bill that would have given HUD and local authorities more say over a range of housing programs died on the Senate floor.

Although Sarbanes may never match Maryland's junior senator, Barbara A. Mikulski, when it comes to bringing home the bacon — she chaired an Appropriations subcommittee when Democrats controlled the Senate — he nonetheless makes an effort to tout his role as leader of the state delegation.

In the 102nd Congress, he won enactment of a bill enlarging the Assateague Island National Seashore. In the 101st, he was the chief Senate sponsor of legislation to clean up the Chesapeake Bay. In 1986, he launched the first filibuster of his career over legislation that would have transferred control over two major Washington, D.C.-area airports from the federal government to a regional authority. Marylanders saw the bill as an economic threat to their state's major airport. Sarbanes talked for five days, with an uncharacteristic enthusiasm that won concessions aimed at providing some protection for Maryland's interests.

At Home: The son of Greek immigrant parents, Sarbanes grew up on Maryland's Eastern Shore, attended Princeton, won a Rhodes scholarship and graduated from Harvard University Law School magna cum laude.

After settling in Baltimore to practice law, Sarbanes entered politics and won a state House seat in 1966. Having developed the quiet, meticulous approach to problem-solving that would mark his Washington career, Sarbanes left the legislature in 1970 to challenge veteran Democratic Rep. George H. Fallon. Running as an anti-war, anti-machine insurgent, Sarbanes defeated the aging chairman of the House Public Works Committee for the Democratic nomination in Baltimore's multiethnic then-4th District. With Democrats enjoying nearly a 4-to-1 registration advantage in the 4th, he had no general-election trouble.

Two years later, redistricting threw him together with another old-time Democrat, Rep. Edward

Garmatz, but Garmatz retired.

By 1976 Sarbanes was ready to move to the Senate, and he did so by unseating one-term Republican J. Glenn Beall Jr. Sarbanes first parried a primary comeback attempt by former Democratic Sen. Joseph D. Tydings, deflecting Tydings' charges that Sarbanes was too liberal.

There were early signs that his 1982 re-election campaign might be more difficult. Emboldened by their 1980 successes, Republicans put Sarbanes on their target list. The National Conservative Political Action Committee (NCPAC) launched a half-million-dollar advertising attack in 1981.

But by early 1982, Sarbanes' opponents had lost their confidence. Many felt the NCPAC campaign had backfired: The Democrat had stepped up his schedule of personal appearances, lashed out at NCPAC as "an alien force" and raised money aggressively.

State GOP leaders failed to enlist a big-name challenger, a problem they would continue to have. That year the nomination went to Prince George's County Executive Lawrence J. Hogan — a former House member who had a chilly relationship with many state GOP activists, stemming from his Watergate-era criticisms of Richard M. Nixon. Hogan carried only three counties.

In 1988, wealthy businessman Thomas L. Blair spent freely and easily won the GOP nomination, only to withdraw in May, citing business obligations. The party conservatives' choice to replace Blair was Alan L. Keyes, a former State Department official who had served as a top assistant to U.N. Representative Jeane J. Kirkpatrick.

Though Keyes had not previously been active in the state party, he drew attention as one of two black Senate contenders in 1988, and he campaigned aggressively. But Keyes also exhibited an independence that alienated some Republicans and never attracted Sarbanes voters.

In 1994, Republicans nominated another Maryland outsider: William Brock, a former Tennessee senator, national GOP chairman and member of the Cabinet under President Ronald Reagan. Brock bumbled questions about when his Maryland residency had begun and never escaped the carpetbagger label. More important, he never gave voters a compelling reason to vote for him.

Brock made the usual "stealth senator" charges about Sarbanes, who tends to keep a low profile in non-election years. But Brock's campaign was equally low-key. Despite heavy personal spending aided by his wealth from the family's candy fortune, Brock managed only 41 percent of the vote.

SENATE ELECTIONS

1994 General		
Paul S. Sarbanes (D)	809,125	(59%)
William Brock (R)	559,908	(41%)
1994 Primary		
Paul S. Sarbanes (D)	382,115	(79%)
John B. Liston (D)	52,031	(11%)
Dennard A. Gayle Sr. (D)	30,665	(6%)
Leonard E. Trout Jr. (D)	19,393	(4%)

Previous Winning Percentages: **1988** (62%) **1982** (64%) **1976** (57%) 1974* (84%) **1972*** (70%) **1970*** (70%)

** House elections*

VOTING STUDIES

	Presidential Support		Party Unity		Conservative Coalition	
Year	S	O	S	O	S	O
1996	90	10	94	6	18	82
1995	90	10	95	4	9	89
1994	95	5	98	2	13	88
1993	96	4	97	2	12	88
1992	27	73	96	4	11	89
1991	30	70	96	4	13	88

KEY VOTES

1997	
Approve balanced-budget constitutional amendment	N
Approve chemical weapons treaty	Y
1996	
Approve farm bill	N
Limit punitive damages in product liability cases	N
Exempt small businesses from higher minimum wage	N
Approve welfare overhaul	N
Bar job discrimination based on sexual orientation	Y
Override veto of ban on "partial birth" abortions	N
1995	
Approve GOP budget with tax and spending cuts	N
Approve constitutional amendment barring flag desecration	N

CAMPAIGN FINANCE

	Receipts	Receipts from PACs	Expend-itures
1994			
Sarbanes (D)	$2,702,116	$932,500 (35%)	$2,698,928
Brock (R)	$3,204,925	$186,718 (6%)	$3,201,650

INTEREST GROUP RATINGS

Year	ADA	AFL-CIO	CCUS	ACU
1996	95	n/a	23	0
1995	100	100	21	0
1994	95	88	20	0
1993	95	91	18	0
1992	100	92	10	0
1991	100	92	10	0

Barbara A. Mikulski (D)

Of Baltimore — Elected 1986, 2nd term

Biographical Information

Born: July 20, 1936, Baltimore, Md.

Education: Mount Saint Agnes College, B.A. 1958; U. of Maryland, M.S.W. 1965.

Occupation: Social worker.

Family: Single.

Religion: Roman Catholic.

Political Career: Baltimore City Council, 1971-77; Democratic nominee for U.S. Senate, 1974; U.S. House, 1977-87.

Capitol Office: 709 Hart Bldg. 20510; 224-4654.

Committees

Appropriations
Commerce, Justice, State & Judiciary; Foreign Operations; Transportation; Treasury & General Government; VA, HUD & Independent Agencies (ranking)

Labor & Human Resources
Aging (ranking); Public Health & Safety

Democratic Conference Secretary

In Washington: Mikulski was the first woman elevated to a leadership post in the Senate, but she decided early in the 105th Congress not to seek to climb another rung on the ladder.

Currently secretary of the Democratic Conference, Mikulski announced in March 1997 that she would not try to succeed Wendell H. Ford of Kentucky (who is retiring in 1998) as minority whip. She said she wanted to concentrate on her 1998 campaign for a third Senate term. Then again, while she will be a strong favorite to win that contest, a bid for whip might have been an uphill fight.

Mikulski entered the leadership ranks after the 1992 elections, when she became assistant floor leader. Top Senate Democrats, sensitive about the lack of diversity in their leadership ranks, turned to Mikulski, the dean of the chamber's five Democratic women. She also got another new responsibility: a seat on the Ethics Committee.

Her assignment was an outgrowth of negative public reaction to the all-male Judiciary Committee's handling of sexual harassment allegations that arose in the process of confirming Clarence Thomas to the Supreme Court in 1991. As the ethics panel began considering the sexual harassment allegations leveled against then-Sen. Bob Packwood of Oregon, Senate leaders made a priority of finding a woman to serve on Ethics.

Mikulski was the first member of the ethics panel to call for public hearings in the Packwood case. "Unless the Senate has public hearings, the public will never believe [that] what we recommend has credibility," she said in March 1995. "The public mood and the whole idea of congressional accountability calls for public hearings."

Other Democrats joined her, and Sen. Barbara Boxer, D-Calif., said in July of that year that she would offer an amendment on the Senate floor calling for public hearings if the Ethics Committee refused to go that route. That led to a threat from Ethics Committee Chairman Mitch McConnell, R-Ky. During one of the panel's closed-door meetings, McConnell told Mikulski to tell Boxer that Republicans would offer companion amendments calling for public hearings into ethics matters involving Senate Minority Leader Tom Daschle, D-S.D., and Edward M. Kennedy, D-Mass.

In September 1995, she joined in the committee's unanimous vote to recommend Packwood's expulsion. "We all had a chance to reflect on this matter and were able to come to a speedy conclusion," she said. The meeting was over so quickly that Mikulski had time the same evening to attend the record-breaking 2,131st consecutive game played by Baltimore Orioles infielder Cal Ripken Jr.

Like most other Democratic women on the Hill, she is a strong supporter of abortion rights. In August 1995, during Senate floor consideration of the fiscal 1996 Treasury-Postal Service spending bill, she fought unsuccessfully against a provision preventing women who are covered under federal health care plans from obtaining abortions through those plans. The House voted to ban abortions except when the life of the woman was threatened. That was too strict a standard for the Senate, which first voted, 52-41, to affirm an Appropriations Committee decision to drop the stricter House-passed language from the bill. Don Nickles, R-Okla., then offered an amendment to ban federal funding of abortions except in cases of rape or incest or to protect the life of the woman. That was adopted 50-44.

After Nickles' amendment was adopted, Mikulski offered an amendment to allow abortions "determined to be medically necessary." Mikulski said this would create a narrow exemption to permit abortions needed to protect a woman's health. Nickles countered that it would permit abortion on demand; the amendment failed, 45-49.

Always pressing for better job opportunities for minorities and women, Mikulski in the 104th criticized the Architect of the Capitol for not doing enough to diversify the large Hill work force under his control. In February 1995, the architect said he would retire rather than seek renomination, a process that would have brought an airing of Mikulski's charges.

In February 1997, she and Sen. Bob Graham, D-Fla., introduced legislation prohibiting health plans from denying coverage and payment for emergency room visits. "Personal health is not something to take chances with," she said. "That's why many people seek emergency assistance when they think something may be seriously wrong with their health. But when the problem turns out to be a non-emergency, the insurance company denies payment. No family should have to second-guess getting the care they need because they are worried about being stuck with an enormous bill."

Mikulski is the ranking minority member of the Aging Subcommittee of the Labor and Human Resources Committee. In May 1996, the panel took up proposed revisions to the Older Americans Act. Republicans said their changes would consolidate food, transportation and employment programs for the elderly by giving states more flexibility in providing services and encouraging competition among groups vying for federal grants in job training and employment services.

Mikulski did not like the way the GOP proposed divvying up the federal funds available under the act. She offered an amendment to retain the existing formula for determining how much money would go to the states. She said a formula change would "cause a serious disruption in services" for those states that would lose funding. But Daniel R. Coats, R-Ind., argued that the new bill updated the formula with new population figures and made payments to the states more equitable for taxpayers. Committee members rejected Mikulski's amendment by a vote of 5-11.

In December 1995, Mikulski helped kill a constitutional amendment prohibiting flag desecration when she decided at the last minute to oppose the measure. The resolution failed by just three votes. She said she did not oppose flag protection but was reluctant to amend the Constitution. "I believe we can and should have a law to end the desecration of our flag," Mikulski said. But amendments to the Constitution should be used "to expand democracy, and not to constrict it," she said.

From her place on the Senate Appropriations Committee — where she is ranking minority member on the VA, HUD and Independent Agencies subcommittee — Mikulski has not been shy about obtaining federal funds for her home state. In July 1995, for example, she successfully proposed an amendment in committee to the fiscal 1996 defense spending bill to continue Baltimore's status as a Navy homeport. It reversed a decision by Navy Secretary John Dalton that effectively eliminated Baltimore's right to compete for short-term Navy repair work. Her measure allowed Baltimore to continue bidding for maintenance contracts.

Mikulski has helped lead the defense of another controversial spending item: NASA's space station. In September 1996, she opposed efforts by Dale Bumpers, D-Ark., who introduced an amendment to the fiscal 1997 VA-HUD spending bill to kill the space station. His amendment was tabled, 60-37. Mikulski argued that medical research with life-saving potential can be performed on the space station.

During a 1993 floor debate on an amendment to kill the space station, Mikulski argued that it had been slimmed down sufficiently by the Clinton administration. "We have cut the cost of the space station without cutting its ability to do significant science," she said. Mikulski's side won the vote 59-40.

With NASA providing thousands of high-paying jobs to Maryland, Mikulski has also been an ardent defender of another "big science" program — the Mission to Planet Earth, a long-term project with a multibillion-dollar price tag that involves using unmanned satellites to collect environmental data about Earth.

She has been one of the Senate's leading advocates of Clinton's AmeriCorps program, trying to fend off Republican attempts to kill it. She voted against the fiscal 1996 VA-HUD appropriations bill in September 1995 because it did not include funding for AmeriCorps. "I believe national service creates an opportunity structure — community service in exchange for a college education," she said. "It fosters the spirit of neighbor helping neighbor that has made our country great."

Mikulski is not above praising Republicans, even though the party's 1995 takeover of the Senate deprived her of the Appropriations subcommittee chairmanship she held in the 103rd Congress. In July 1996, VA-HUD Subcommittee Chairman Christopher S. Bond, R-Mo., proposed a non-controversial spending bill that passed the subcommittee and full committee by voice votes. The measure received lavish praise from Mikulski. "I think you've done a very outstanding job," she told Bond.

She agreed with Republicans who want to streamline the regulatory process at the Food and Drug Administration, speeding up review of new drugs and medical devices. "We have worked to come up with a sensible, moderate plan," Mikulski said in July 1996.

At Home: When she ran to succeed retiring GOP Sen. Charles McC. Mathias Jr. in 1986, many questioned whether the pudgy, 4-foot-11 Mikulski would strike voters as "senatorial." But then-Rep. Mikulski proved her skills, easily outrunning Rep. Michael D. Barnes and outgoing Gov. Harry R. Hughes in the Democratic primary, then drubbing Republican Linda Chavez with 61 percent of the vote.

A self-described "blue-collar senator," Mikulski earned broad popularity with her strong personality and gritty demeanor. In her 1992 reelection campaign, Mikulski took 71 percent of the vote, trouncing Alan L. Keyes, a black conservative activist who had run against Democratic Sen. Paul S. Sarbanes in 1988.

The granddaughter of Polish immigrants, Mikulski first gained a following by discussing the plight of the "forgotten" ethnic residents of America's cities. Mikulski also organized a fight against a highway that would have leveled several Baltimore neighborhoods. She won a City Council seat in 1971 and became prominent in the feminist movement.

In 1974, Mikulski challenged the heavily favored GOP Sen. Mathias and drew 43 percent of the vote. She was well positioned in 1976, when then-Rep. Sarbanes vacated his Baltimore House seat for his first Senate campaign. Mikulski had no trouble winning the Democratic House primary, and she breezed through five general elections.

With Mathias retiring in 1986, Mikulski's vibrant style was a big asset in the Senate primary against two well-known but colorless Democratic rivals. She won by more than 112,000 votes over Barnes; Hughes was a distant third.

Mikulski then had to overcome conservative Chavez, a staff director of the U.S. Commission on Civil Rights under President Ronald Reagan. Though never more than a long shot, Chavez did not go quietly, describing Mikulski as a "San Francisco style" liberal. Mikulski resisted the bait to brawl with an opponent who was no electoral threat and coasted to victory.

Maintaining high approval ratings and compiling a large campaign treasury, Mikulski deterred the most prominent Maryland Republicans in 1992. The GOP nomination went to Keyes, a State Department official during the Reagan presidency who had gained attention for his eloquent opposition to the liberal orthodoxy of most black leaders. When Keyes took 38 percent against Sarbanes, he called it a springboard for a future contest.

But his challenge to Mikulski got off on the wrong foot when it was disclosed that Keyes was paying himself $8,500 a month from his campaign treasury. The practice was legal, but politically dubious in a recession year.

Mikulski played a featured role at the Democratic National Convention, conducting a program featuring female candidates and nominating Tennessee Sen. Al Gore for vice president. Keyes, meanwhile, clashed with the organizers of the Republican National Convention; when they were slow to offer him a speaking slot during TV's prime time, Keyes accused the party of racism. In October, the National Republican Senatorial Committee, citing Keyes' poor showing in opinion polls, cut off funding to his campaign; Keyes declared himself an "independent Republican."

Mikulski ended up carrying all but one of Maryland's counties. Although Maryland was Clinton's best state after Arkansas, Mikulski outran him there by 21 percentage points.

SENATE ELECTIONS

1992 General		
Barbara A. Mikulski (D)	1,307,610	(71%)
Alan L. Keyes (R)	533,688	(29%)
1992 Primary		
Barbara A. Mikulski (D)	376,444	(77%)
Thomas M. Wheatley (D)	31,214	(6%)
Walter Boyd (D)	26,467	(5%)
Don Allensworth (D)	19,731	(4%)
Scott David Britt (D)	13,001	(3%)
James Leonard White (D)	12,470	(3%)
B. Emerson Sweatt (D)	11,150	(2%)

Previous Winning Percentages: 1986 (61%) **1984*** (68%) **1982*** (74%) **1980*** (76%) **1978*** (100%) **1976*** (75%)

** House elections*

KEY VOTES

1997	
Approve balanced-budget constitutional amendment	N
Approve chemical weapons treaty	Y
1996	
Approve farm bill	N
Limit punitive damages in product liability cases	N
Exempt small businesses from higher minimum wage	N
Approve welfare overhaul	Y
Bar job discrimination based on sexual orientation	Y
Override veto of ban on "partial birth" abortions	N
1995	
Approve GOP budget with tax and spending cuts	N
Approve constitutional amendment barring flag desecration	N

CAMPAIGN FINANCE

1992	Receipts	Receipts from PACs		Expend-itures
Mikulski (D)	$2,940,047	$876,062	(30%)	$3,161,104
Keyes (R)	$1,185,385	$31,150	(3%)	$1,175,682

VOTING STUDIES

	Presidential Support		Party Unity		Conservative Coalition	
Year	**S**	**O**	**S**	**O**	**S**	**O**
1996	90	10	92	8	32	68
1995	85	11	82	12	33	56
1994	89	6	89	9	28	69
1993	93	4	92	8	39	61
1992	23	77	87	10	24	74
1991	33	67	91	8	33	65

INTEREST GROUP RATINGS

Year	ADA	AFL-CIO	CCUS	ACU
1996	95	n/a	23	0
1995	90	100	39	4
1994	85	75	33	0
1993	85	100	27	4
1992	100	92	0	0
1991	90	83	20	10

1 Wayne T. Gilchrest (R)

Of Kennedyville — Elected 1990, 4th term

Biographical Information

Born: April 15, 1946, Rahway, N.J.
Education: Wesley College, A.A. 1971; Delaware State U., B.A. 1973; Loyola College (Baltimore, Md.), 1990.
Military Service: Marine Corps, 1964-68.
Occupation: High school teacher.
Family: Wife, Barbara Rawley; three children.
Religion: Methodist.
Political Career: Republican nominee for U.S. House, 1988.
Capitol Office: 332 Cannon Bldg. 20515; 225-5311.

Committees

Resources
Fisheries Conservation, Wildlife & Oceans; National Parks & Public Lands
Transportation & Infrastructure
Coast Guard & Maritime Transportation (chairman); Water Resources & Environment

In Washington: Gilchrest represents a district that wraps around the Chesapeake Bay, and on the Resources Committee he is one of the few Republicans with an avowedly pro-environment bias. This has put him in a delicate but important position.

An itinerant house painter and sometime schoolteacher who capitalized on his "outsider" image to capture the 1st from Democrats in 1990, Gilchrest contends that House Republicans have not built up enough credibility on environmental issues to earn voters' trust in this area. On military and business matters, he says, the GOP has many experts. But, he asks, "Who here has an expertise in the environmental area? The answer is, very few people." Too often, he says, pro-business party colleagues do not study available scientific evidence before proposing major changes in regulations.

After the House passed bills in 1995 that relaxed certain water quality regulations and curtailed the regulatory power of the Environment Protection Agency (EPA), congressional Republicans came under heavy fire from Democrats as "anti-environment," and the label hurt the GOP's standing in public opinion polls. Gilchrest opposed conservatives' efforts to weaken environmental enforcement. This stance is good politics in the 1st; in 1996, Gilchrest won with customary ease.

At the start of the 105th Congress, he became chairman of the Transportation and Infrastructure Committee's Coast Guard and Maritime Transportation subcommittee.

Gilchrest was at the leading edge of the political outsiders who have come to Congress in the 1990s. With an approachable and at times wide-eyed demeanor, he comes across as an idealist, and he has a reputation as a legislator who grapples with issues rather than just voting on them.

After Republicans took control of the House in 1995, conservatives quickly passed a sweeping regulatory reform package that included a measure expanding private property rights at the expense of environmental rules. Gilchrest was one of only eight Republicans opposing it.

And when the majority of Republicans voted for a measure to revise substantially the nation's water pollution laws, Gilchrest was one of 34 Republicans to vote "no." He had been one of three Republicans to oppose reporting the revised clean water act out of the Transportation and Infrastructure Committee in April 1995, arguing that it would gut regulations that provide for clean water. The clean water act overhaul never made it through the Senate.

Gilchrest bucked his party majority in July 1995 on a spending bill that included the budget for the EPA. Republican appropriators had included a provision that would have limited the agency's ability to regulate, among other things, sewer systems, wetlands, water pollution, refineries, and oil and gas manufacturing.

Joining with other moderate Republicans, Gilchrest described these provisions as breaks for polluters. Gilchrest and 50 other Republicans supported an amendment to strike the provision and the resulting 212-206 vote took the GOP leadership by surprise.

On the Resources Committee, Gilchrest fought a proposal by GOP conservatives to overhaul the 1973 Endangered Species Act (ESA). The measure, which the committee approved in October 1995, would have greatly restricted the government's ability to bar development within animal and plant habitats. Proponents, led by California Republican Richard W. Pombo, said federal regulators have used the species act to trample the rights of private property owners under the guise of saving animals and plants from extinction.

Critics of the measure said it would gut the ESA at the behest not of small landowners, but of big corporate interests, including land developers and agribusinesses. Gilchrest offered a substitute amendment, which the committee rejected, that would have maintained strong safeguards against habitat destruction, while encouraging government regulators to reach species protection agreements with private interests.

The 4.3-mile-long Chesapeake Bay Bridge links the mainly rural counties of the Bay's Eastern Shore and the fast-growing suburbia of Anne Arundel County. These regions are different in many ways, but they share a conservative tilt that often benefits Republicans.

George Bush won the 1st easily in 1988 and beat Bill Clinton here by 7 percentage points in 1992. Yet the 1st can be politically competitive, as illustrated by Gilchrest's close 1992 contest against former Democrat Rep. Tom McMillen. Also, Bob Dole beat Clinton in the district by only 4 percentage points in 1996.

Much of the Eastern Shore has a Democratic tradition (albeit of the conservative Southern brand). Annapolis, the state capital, has many government employees. Blacks make up 15 percent of the 1st's population; Annapolis, as well as Salisbury and Cambridge on the Eastern Shore, have large minority communities.

About three-fifths of the district's population is spread across the nine counties of the Eastern Shore. Isolated until the Bay Bridge was completed in the 1950s, most of the region remains rural. The Perdue poultry company has a large work force at its Salisbury headquarters and plants.

But the shore's rustic nature is disrupted on summer weekends when vacationers from the Washington and Baltimore areas head for Ocean City on the Atlantic or villages such as St. Michael's and Crisfield on the bay. The shore's larger communities have some manufacturing. An upswing in cross-bay commuting has boosted the populations of such central areas as Queen Anne's and Talbot counties.

The small town and farm country in the central part of the district is GOP heartland;

MARYLAND 1
Cross Bay — Eastern Shore; Annapolis; Glen Burnie

Gilchrest ran better than 2-to-1 in Talbot and Kent counties in 1996. But he slipped below that in the southernmost part, with its larger working-class and black constituencies. Gilchrest won more narrowly in Cecil County, at the edges of the Baltimore and Philadelphia metropolitan areas in Maryland's northeast corner.

Most of the 1st's other residents are in Anne Arundel County. Annapolis is by far the district's largest urban center. With the capitol, the U.S. Naval Academy, a thriving waterfront area and a stock of well-preserved colonial-era buildings, the city has a large tourist industry.

With a population that is one-third black, Annapolis leans Democratic. But there is a GOP tilt in the affluent suburban areas to the north and west, whose residents commute to Baltimore, Washington and Annapolis. At the county's north end are Glen Burnie and other working-class suburbs that lean Democratic but are rather conservative.

The 1st also covers a small, blue-collar part of Baltimore city that is heavily Democratic but has few voters. In 1996, it was the only part of the district carried by Gilchrest's Democratic challenger.

1990 Population: 597,684. White 498,523 (83%), Black 89,773 (15%), Other 9,388 (2%). Hispanic origin 6,580 (1%). 18 and over 454,906 (76%), 62 and over 91,037 (15%). Median age: 34.

The committee's ESA overhaul bill died, as Speaker Newt Gingrich kept it off the House floor because of concerns that the GOP's profile on environmental issues would hurt party candidates at the polls in November 1996.

In the 105th Congress, critics of the ESA tried a new approach to restrict its reach. Pombo and other California Republicans sought to exempt flood protection projects from the endangered species law. They claimed that because the act requires a cumbersome review of flood-control projects to ensure they do not hurt threatened plants or animals, parties responsible for maintaining levees put off basic maintenance, placing human lives and property at risk.

Gilchrest gave a cool reception to this effort at incremental change, which Resources approved in April 1997 and the House rejected a month later. "I don't believe we should piecemeal the ESA," he said. "This issue can be addressed in broad reform."

Gilchrest has a strong interest in fishing issues. In both the 104th and 105th, he introduced legislation to implement a 1995 international agreement, known as the Declaration of Panama, that would lift the U.S. embargo on Latin American tuna.

Gilchrest says that implementing the international agreement would settle a longstanding dispute between the United States and Mexico, Venezuela and other Latin American nations over access to the $1 billion-a-year U.S. consumer market for canned tuna. It also would clarify the dolphin-safe standard to protect both dolphins and the marine ecosystem as a whole. The Latin American countries have been barred from the U.S. market because they catch tuna with encircling nets, which can also trap dolphins.

"You have these 11 countries who have come together in a global sense and agreed to an environmental solution to an economic problem, and you don't often get that," said Gilchrest.

But opponents, including George Miller of California, the ranking Democrat on Resources, say that Gilchrest's bill would be a step backwards in U.S. efforts to protect dolphins. They say implementing the Panama agreement would set a poor precedent for future trade agreements by compromising domestic environmental laws to satisfy trading partners. The House approved the bill easily in May 1997.

Although Gilchrest at times departs from the GOP script on environmental and gun control votes, his views on fiscal policy are faithfully conservative. He backs a constitutional amendment requiring a balanced budget, and he also favors a constitutional amendment requiring a two-thirds vote in the House and Senate to raise taxes.

Gilchrest in 1996 was not keen on increasing the minimum wage by 90 cents over two years, a proposal pushed by Democrats and backed by some moderate Republicans. He voted for a GOP leadership amendment to exempt small businesses from paying the higher minimum wage, but it failed.

When the minimum wage hike came to the floor on a stand-alone vote in May 1996, Gilchrest was a "no," but then he voted for a measure that increased the wage and also provided that employees need not be paid for the time spent using an employer-owned vehicle to commute. On final passage of the wage increase in August 1996, Gilchrest again was a "yea"; that measure included $10 billion in business tax cuts over five years.

At Home: Gilchrest's easygoing manner may have led the House incumbents he has beaten to underestimate him. Among other occupations, he has labored as a barn builder, forest ranger and chicken slaughterhouse worker. When he first ran for the House in 1988, he was a high school teacher moonlighting as a house painter.

He spent just $300 that year to win the little-sought GOP nomination to oppose Rep. Roy Dyson, a conservative Democrat who looked secure in the 1st. But Dyson's popularity dropped after the suicide of his top House aide and reports of Dyson's ties to contractors involved in a Pentagon procurement scandal. Long-shot Gilchrest got wan support from GOP officials but came within 1,540 votes of winning.

Gilchrest was back for a rematch in 1990, and added to the incumbent's earlier problems, media reports revealed that Dyson, a hawk on military matters, had been a conscientious objector during the Vietnam War. Gilchrest, better-known and better-financed than in 1988, struck voters as an appealing alternative. He won with a solid 57 percent.

In 1992, redistricting carved up Democratic Rep. Tom McMillen's Annapolis-based district and threw him into a cross-bay contest with Gilchrest in the redrawn 1st. Gilchrest again drew on his average-guy appeal. He portrayed McMillen, a former University of Maryland and Washington Bullets basketball star, as a rich Washington insider. With his Eastern Shore advantage offsetting McMillen's western base, Gilchrest won 52 percent. That was his last tough campaign.

HOUSE ELECTIONS

1996 General		
Wayne T. Gilchrest (R)	131,033	(62%)
Steven R. Eastaugh (D)	81,825	(38%)
1996 Primary		
Wayne T. Gilchrest (R)	25,431	(65%)
Thomas E. Anderson (R)	5,739	(15%)
Bradlyn McClanahan (R)	3,224	(8%)
Robert Gawthrop (R)	2,875	(7%)
James M. Plack (R)	1,521	(4%)
James Timothy King (R)	554	(1%)
1994 General		
Wayne T. Gilchrest (R)	120,975	(68%)
Ralph T. Gies (D)	57,712	(32%)

Previous Winning Percentages: 1992 (52%) **1990** (57%)

CAMPAIGN FINANCE

	Receipts	Receipts from PACs		Expend-itures
1996				
Gilchrest (R)	$283,364	$3,356	(1%)	$259,366
Eastaugh (D)	$218,976	$17,500	(8%)	$229,073
1994				
Gilchrest (R)	$157,485	$9,520	(6%)	$153,133
Gies (D)	$31,490	0		$30,612

DISTRICT VOTE FOR PRESIDENT

	1996		1992
D	98,428 (43%)	**D**	93,165 (37%)
R	108,474 (47%)	**R**	109,039 (44%)
I	20,937 (9%)	**I**	47,188 (19%)

KEY VOTES

1997	
Ban "partial birth" abortions	Y
1996	
Approve farm bill	Y
Deny public education to illegal immigrants	Y
Repeal ban on certain assault-style weapons	N
Increase minimum wage	N
Freeze defense spending	Y
Approve welfare overhaul	Y
1995	
Approve balanced-budget constitutional amendment	Y
Relax Clean Water Act regulations	N
Oppose limits on environmental regulations	Y
Reduce projected Medicare spending	Y
Approve GOP budget with tax and spending cuts	Y

VOTING STUDIES

	Presidential Support		Party Unity		Conservative Coalition	
Year	**S**	**O**	**S**	**O**	**S**	**O**
1996	46	54	84	16	76	24
1995	35	65	80	20	81	18
1994	64	36	72	28	78	22
1993	58	41	71	27	61	39
1992	56	42	68	29	71	27
1991	70	30	78	21	86	14

INTEREST GROUP RATINGS

Year	ADA	AFL-CIO	CCUS	ACU
1996	20	n/a	100	80
1995	30	0	83	56
1994	30	22	100	62
1993	30	33	90	63
1992	30	36	75	64
1991	20	17	90	70

2 Robert L. Ehrlich Jr. (R)

Of Lutherville — Elected 1994, 2nd term

Biographical Information
Born: Nov. 25, 1957, Baltimore, Md.
Education: Princeton U., B.A. 1979; Wake Forest U., J.D. 1982.
Occupation: Lawyer; football coach.
Family: Wife, Kendel Sibiski.
Religion: Methodist.
Political Career: Md. House, 1987-95.
Capitol Office: 315 Cannon Bldg. 20515; 225-3061.

Committees
Banking & Financial Services
Financial Institutions & Consumer Credit; Housing & Community Opportunity
Budget

In Washington: Ehrlich's upbringing in a Baltimore row house gives him claim to working-class roots, and on some high-profile issues he stands apart from most of his colleagues in the conservative GOP Class of 1994. He voted against congressional term limits in 1995, for instance, and says he has a "basically pro-choice" stand on abortion.

But on most other issues, Ehrlich is every inch a conservative loyalist. In August 1996, for instance, he was one of only 70 Republicans who voted against increasing the minimum wage, a measure that passed 354-72 with substantial GOP support. He was one of 12 lawmakers who signed a letter announcing support for Newt Gingrich as Speaker in the 105th Congress — an action designed to reassure wavering Republicans. "After reviewing all the available facts," the members wrote, "we agree with [ethics committee Republicans] Porter Goss and Steve Schiff, the two members with the most intimate and detailed knowledge of the situation: We know of no reason why Newt Gingrich would be ineligible to be Speaker."

At the start of the 105th, Ehrlich gained a seat on the Budget Committee, an assignment usually reserved for members on good terms with top party leaders. He pledged that he would work to cut federal spending, noting that he is less eager than some for so-called pork barrel projects. "We don't even think along those lines," he said. "It will never be out of politics, but the more people who come in here with our approach, the less [earmarking] you're going to see." Nevertheless, Ehrlich did join with his fellow Maryland lawmakers in securing a long-sought $3.7 million federal grant for a sewer project in Hanford County.

During his first House term, Ehrlich's interest in barring political advocacy by nonprofit groups brought him into alliance with the Republican right flank. Ehrlich teamed with David M. McIntosh of Indiana, Ernest Istook of Oklahoma and others to propose cutting off federal grants to nonprofit groups that use any portion of their budget — even non-federal funds — to engage in political activities. Ehrlich and his companions argued that liberal advocacy groups indirectly use federal grant money to lobby the government. "Special interests lobby for taxpayers' money and then use that taxpayers' money to create political operations that serve to lobby for even additional money," Ehrlich told the House in 1995. "It is a vicious cycle, it is taxpayer abuse, and it is an outrage." Nonprofit groups said the provision would muzzle their efforts to communicate concerns to government officials and the public.

McIntosh, Istook and Ehrlich tried to attach the grant-cutoff provision to some fiscal 1996 spending bills, including the Treasury-Postal Service funding measure. Speaker Gingrich endorsed their effort, but GOP leaders ultimately decided to take the controversial provision out of the Treasury-Postal bill to speed its passage in the midst of a partial shutdown of the federal government.

A version of the grant-cutoff proposal was also attached to the fiscal 1996 Labor, Health and Human Services spending bill. House Democrats failed to strip it it off on a 187-232 vote, but the matter progressed no further because the Senate never passed a Labor-HHS bill in 1995.

In the 104th, Ehrlich had a seat on the Government Reform and Oversight Committee, and he liked to say, "I was elected to Congress to fight for smaller government, lower taxes and an end to overregulation." On that panel in early 1995 he offered an amendment to freeze federal agencies from implementing regulations proposed since Nov. 20, 1994, until Congress passed all the regulatory changes included in the "Contract With America."

In April 1995, Ehrlich was one of only 11 House Republicans who voted "no" on a rule to bring the GOP's tax cut bill to the floor. He shared the concern of Republican colleagues in the Washington, D.C., area who have a sizable number of federal workers in their districts: They were not happy that the tax bill contained a provision increasing the amount federal employees had to contribute to their pensions. Ehrlich did, however, vote for final passage of the tax bill.

MARYLAND 2
Baltimore and Harford counties

Although Democrats have a big advantage among registered voters in the 2nd, the combination of conservative Democrats and Republican faithful is easily enough to make the district winnable by the GOP.

The 2nd sometimes can be more competitive for Democrats, who have a 2-1 registration advantage, but the district has sufficient Republican territory to provide a base for Ehrlich.

In Baltimore County — home to slightly more than 60 percent of the 2nd's residents — the district takes in middle-class areas of Towson and such upper-income communities as Lutherville, Cockeysville and Hunt Valley, then sweeps north into horse country. The district also includes conservative-minded Harford County, which has experienced a burst of exurban growth.

Bethlehem Steel's complex at Sparrows Point is still Baltimore County's largest employer, but its 6,200 jobs are a fraction of the number employed during steel's heyday. Many of the workers live across the Baltimore Beltway in Dundalk, at the Baltimore city line. Essex and nearby Middle River are largely blue-collar.

To the north, the 2nd moves into more suburban environs, including the county's most affluent communities and its burgeoning employment centers. Diversification has helped keep Baltimore County moving forward even as its heavy-industry sector has declined. The McCormick food company's headquarters are in Hunt Valley; tool manufacturer Black & Decker is based in Towson.

However, several county employers (Lockheed Martin, AAI, Allied-Signal and Westinghouse, for example) rely on defense contracts, a cause for concern in an era of Pentagon cuts. Westinghouse laid off about 4,500 workers earlier this decade. But AAI is trying to diversify and has won a contract to build weather monitoring systems for airports.

Job and other economic concerns dampened the GOP advantage here in 1992. George Bush carried the part of Baltimore County that is in the 2nd by just 44 percent to 38 percent over Bill Clinton. Dole performed slightly better four years later, leading Clinton by 49 percent to 42 percent.

Republican loyalties are stronger to the east in Harford County. Dole beat Clinton by 13 percentage points with Ross Perot pulling down 10 percent of the vote. (Perot won 9 percent in the 2nd, again making it his best district in Maryland.) Harford grew by 25 percent in the 1980s, as commuters poured into subdivisions in such towns as Bel Air and Joppa. Much of Harford's economic base is defense-related: With more than 14,500 employees, the Aberdeen weapons proving ground is by far the region's largest employer.

At its southern end, the 2nd leaps across the Patapsco River into an upscale, strongly Republican corner of Anne Arundel County, including parts of suburban Pasadena and Severna Park.

1990 Population: 597,683. White 547,999 (92%), Black 35,295 (6%), Other 14,389 (2%). Hispanic origin 7,242 (1%). 18 and over 457,201 (76%), 62 and over 88,673 (15%). Median age: 34.

On the issue of abortion, Ehrlich shows a moderate streak. He was one of 44 Republicans voting in September 1995 against an amendment to the defense spending bill to prohibit abortions at U.S. military facilities overseas unless the life of the woman was endangered. Abortion foes hoped to negate an executive order President Clinton issued in 1993 that allowed abortions at overseas facilities if the patients paid for the procedure. The amendment was adopted, however, and Ehrlich voted for final passage of the bill.

In 1996, he voted to allow federal employee health plans to pay for abortions, and to require states to fund Medicaid abortions for poor women in cases of rape and incest. He did, however, vote to ban an abortion technique that opponents call "partial birth" abortion, a measure that passed both houses of Congress but was vetoed by President Clinton. He also voted for legislation banning federal recognition of same-sex marriages.

Ehrlich in the 104th parted ways from most conservatives on the issue of term limits. In 1995 he was one of 40 Republicans opposing a constitutional amendment imposing a 12-year lifetime limit on congressional service in each chamber. But he joined with conservatives in supporting less stringent restrictions on the gifts members could accept. The amendment, which favored full disclosure of the gifts rather than an outright ban, was defeated in 1995.

At Home: Ehrlich won a second term in 1996 after beating back a spirited challenge from Democrat Connie Galiazzo DeJuliis, wife of a local union leader. DeJuliis had strong support from labor unions, which ran advertisements targeting Ehrlich, and she emphasized her support for raising the minimum wage, which Ehrlich opposed. Ehrlich, portraying himself as independent-minded, won easily, despite the Democrats' 2-1 advantage among registered voters in the district.

It was the second time in as many races that Ehrlich had bested the 60 percent mark. The first time came in 1994 after GOP Rep. Helen Delich Bentley left the 2nd to run unsuccessfully for governor.

That race gave voters a choice of candidates with as many similarities as differences. Both Ehrlich and Democratic nominee Gerry L. Brewster attended the same Maryland prep school before graduating from Princeton and earning law degrees. Both represented parts of Baltimore County in the House of Delegates, where they both served on the Judiciary Committee. They were both named "legislators of the year" by the Maryland State Fraternal Order of Police in 1994, the first time the award was shared by two lawmakers. And both claimed cross-party appeal while being viewed as rising stars in their own-parties.

But Ehrlich gained an advantage by stressing the one major thing that was different about the two candidates: where they started out. In his advertising he featured the $13,000 row house where he was raised, and he said he learned life's most important lessons sitting with his family around the dining room table. He portrayed himself as a man from modest circumstances who got some breaks in life — academic and athletic scholarships that helped him attend the expensive private schools.

Brewster's family circumstances were notably more elevated. His father, Democrat Daniel Brewster, served in the House (1959-63) and the Senate (1963-69). In the Democratic primary for the 2nd, Brewster heard the class argument from his main opponent, a state representative from the blue-collar Baltimore area. Brewster narrowly won nomination, while Ehrlich had an easier time getting the GOP nod against two opponents, one of whom was backed by anti-abortion activists. Aided by support from Bentley, Ehrlich defeated his intraparty rivals with 57 percent of the vote.

In the general election campaign, crime and President Clinton joined class as the main points of discussion. Ehrlich said Brewster was not tough enough on criminals, although both men supported the death penalty and tougher sentencing. Brewster also lost support among gun enthusiasts because he had voted in the legislature for a ban on assault-style weapons. Ehrlich opposed the ban.

The race concluded with a barrage of attacks, including charges that Ehrlich had misused election funds, misled people on ethics reports and benefited from illegal fundraising by an indicted state lobbyist. Ehrlich vehemently denied all those accusations, and voters were more in the mood to hear his criticisms of Clinton's tax increases and health care proposal.

HOUSE ELECTIONS

1996 General		
Robert L. Ehrlich Jr. (R)	143,075	(62%)
Connie Galiazzo DeJuliis (D)	88,344	(38%)
1996 Primary		
Robert L. Ehrlich Jr. (R)	29,983	(83%)
Josef Thurston (R)	3,764	(10%)
Walter Boyd (R)	1,570	(4%)
Russell Mirabile (R)	711	(2%)
1994 General		
Robert L. Ehrlich Jr. (R)	125,162	(63%)
Gerry L. Brewster (D)	74,275	(37%)

CAMPAIGN FINANCE

	Receipts	Receipts from PACs		Expend-itures
1996				
Ehrlich (R)	$950,476	$336,310	(35%)	$844,918
DeJuliis (D)	$641,332	$257,361	(40%)	$641,618
1994				
Ehrlich (R)	$568,455	$218,025	(38%)	$562,892
Brewster (D)	$553,908	$108,513	(20%)	$550,471

DISTRICT VOTE FOR PRESIDENT

1996		1992	
D	95,115 (40%)	**D**	98,267 (36%)
R	119,024 (50%)	**R**	121,087 (45%)
I	22,408 (9%)	**I**	52,668 (19%)

KEY VOTES

1997	
Ban "partial-birth" abortions	Y
1996	
Approve farm bill	Y
Deny public education to illegal immigrants	Y
Repeal ban on certain assault-style weapons	Y
Increase minimum wage	N
Freeze defense spending	N
Approve welfare overhaul	Y
1995	
Approve balanced-budget constitutional amendment	Y
Relax Clean Water Act regulations	N
Oppose limits on environmental regulations	Y
Reduce projected Medicare spending	Y
Approve GOP budget with tax and spending cuts	Y

VOTING STUDIES

	Presidential Support		Party Unity		Conservative Coalition	
Year	**S**	**O**	**S**	**O**	**S**	**O**
1996	33	66	92	6	96	4
1995	28	72	89	10	95	5

INTEREST GROUP RATINGS

Year	ADA	AFL-CIO	CCUS	ACU
1996	10	n/a	94	100
1995	20	8	88	64

3 Benjamin L. Cardin (D)

Of Baltimore — Elected 1986, 6th term

Biographical Information
Born: Oct. 5, 1943, Baltimore, Md.
Education: U. of Pittsburgh, B.A. 1964; U. of Maryland, LL.B. 1967.
Occupation: Lawyer.
Family: Wife, Myrna Edelman; two children.
Religion: Jewish.
Political Career: Md. House, 1967-87, speaker, 1979-87.
Capitol Office: 104 Cannon Bldg. 20515; 225-4016.

Committees
Budget
Ways & Means
Health

In Washington: Cardin has been the calm at the center of some storm-tossed congressional moments. He is a liberal through and through, but his unflappable demeanor and ability to work easily with Republicans has earned him a reputation for bipartisanship, despite his key role in one of the most politicized ethics investigations in recent memory.

Cardin was the lead Democrat on a four-member panel that spent the whole of 1996 investigating ethics charges against Speaker Newt Gingrich, centering on accusations that he used tax-exempt foundations to fund a lecture course with partisan underpinnings and purposes. "This was a new way to raise money, a new avenue in which he could promise his contributors a tax exemption to boot," Cardin said.

Cardin had long experience dealing with political combustibles on the ethics committee, having served on task forces that investigated the House bank and Post Office scandals during the 102nd Congress. Democrats respect Cardin's political skills and rewarded the former Maryland House Speaker with a slot on the Ways and Means Committee during the 102nd.

But Cardin's actions in the Gingrich investigation also left him untainted by charges of excessive partisanship that Republicans hurled at some Democrats concerned with the case.

Gingrich admitted to one of the charges and to having lied to the Committee on the Standards of Official Conduct (the ethics committee's formal title). As Gingrich awaited word of his punishment — which proved to be a reprimand and a $300,000 penalty — the ethics committee's ranking Democrat, Jim McDermott of Washington, was forced to recuse himself from the case when accused of leaking a tape recording of a cellular-phone conference call in which Gingrich described his strategy in controlling the story's spin.

Consequently, Cardin became the Democrats' leading public face during the investigation's endgame. He castigated ethics committee Chairwoman Nancy L. Johnson, R-Conn., for having unilaterally cancelled a series of public hearings. But he maintained a good working relationship with Porter J. Goss, the Florida Republican who had chaired the investigative subcommittee.

And Cardin resisted calls from within the Democratic Caucus to hold out for the stiffer penalty of censure, which would have cost Gingrich his Speakership.

Cardin, the only lawyer among the ethics committee Democrats, helped draft the proposals that led to the hiring of a special counsel for the case and the bill of particulars that Gingrich was willing, in effect, to plead to.

Cardin expressed hope that the Gingrich case would reawaken a sense of the need for bipartisanship in Congress, but he was not above making digs at the top House Republican himself. "It will never be put behind him," Cardin said. "It is a part of Mr. Gingrich. He is a reprimanded Speaker, and he needs to deal with it."

After the grueling final weeks of the investigation, Cardin, who had completed his stint on the ethics committee with the January 1997 House vote to reprimand Gingrich, suggested that former members should be allowed to play a formal role in investigations.

Cardin picks up a seat on the Budget Committee for the 105th. In 1995, he helped work with a coalition of conservative Democrats who crafted a package to balance the budget without tax cuts. It was defeated in the House in favor of a Republican bill.

Cardin had helped the Democrats adjust to life in the minority as transition team leader at the start of the 104th. In that role, he denounced the GOP's intention to fire some Hill administrative workers, most of whom had worked for the Democrats, and provide them with no severance or pay for accrued vacation time. The Republicans eventually backtracked and agreed to pay the departing workers for their vacation time.

Although Cardin generally has joined the younger, more liberal members of Ways and

MARYLAND 3
Downtown and ethnic Baltimore; Columbia

The city of Baltimore has long had an ethnically diverse, Democrat-dominated district. Now that district ranges far and wide to take in thousands of city natives who moved to the suburbs.

The 3rd, a reverse-C shape, wends in and out of Baltimore to pick up the Democratic voters who enable Cardin to dominate his House contests. Democratic Sen. Barbara A. Mikulski, a former 3rd District House member, also has run very well here. With its large suburban constituency, the 3rd can be somewhat more competitive in presidential contests. But Bill Clinton easily bested Bob Dole in 1996, with Ross Perot lagging a weak third.

The city still has the largest share (about two-fifths) of the 3rd's residents. At the heart of the district is Baltimore's rejuvenated downtown. Spurred by the success of Harborplace, a retail-and-entertainment complex along the once-forsaken waterfront, Baltimore's downtown has sprouted hotels and office buildings: The USF&G insurance company, NationsBank and Crown Central Petroleum have headquarters here.

Baseball's Orioles play in a stadium just west of downtown. To the south, the 3rd moves through gentrifying Federal Hill, takes in a blue-collar stretch around the harbor leading to Fort McHenry, then hops across the Patapsco River's Middle Branch to mainly black Cherry Hill.

East of downtown is the city's ethnic heartland: Little Italy and Highlandtown (whose Polish and German voters gave Mikulski her political start). There is a working-class accent here: The city is "Bawlamer" and its ball team is the "Eryals." General Motors has a factory in East Baltimore. The 3rd moves north through working-class sections on the city's east edge, then west to pick up some of Baltimore's wealthier communities. The mainly Jewish areas of northwest Baltimore make up Cardin's base.

In its part of Baltimore County (about a third of the total population), the 3rd follows the path of Jewish migration north from wealthy Pikesville to middle-class Reisterstown and west to Randallstown (which has a significant black population). Skimming the city's northern border, the 3rd takes in affluent, less Democratic areas in Ruxton and Towson, growing Perry Hall and modest suburbs such as Parkville.

On the other side of the city, the 3rd includes middle-class suburbs in south Baltimore County and northwest Anne Arundel County near Baltimore-Washington International Airport: Linthicum — site of a Westinghouse facility pinched by defense cuts — and the part of Fort Meade that houses the National Security Agency are here.

The 3rd also includes the eastern portion of Howard County and Columbia, with its planned racial mix and liberal-leaning electorate. The city has become an economic engine in the middle of the Washington-Baltimore metropolitan area. The Rouse development company, which built Columbia and Harborplace, and several high-tech companies are here.

1990 Population: 597,680. White 475,260 (80%), Black 104,380 (17%), Other 18,040 (3%). Hispanic origin 10,264 (2%). 18 and over 459,113 (77%), 62 and over 94,865 (16%). Median age: 34.

Means, he took more of a centrist role when the committee debated health care legislation in the 103rd and 104th congresses. Cardin joined on occasion with Republicans to block or curb some of his Democratic colleagues' more ambitious proposals on private and public health insurance.

He has joined with Health Subcommittee Chairman Bill Thomas, R-Calif., in an attempt to offer more preventive health benefits under Medicare. He also has sought to require health maintenance organizations to offer coverage of "appropriate" emergency room care.

Ways and Means Republicans voted down Cardin's amendments to their welfare overhaul bill to guarantee substance abuse treatment and require states to spend at least as much as they had in fiscal 1994 on Aid to Families With Dependent Children and related programs. Cardin opposed the committee's welfare plan, but voted for a final version that Republicans fashioned to win President Clinton's signature in the summer of 1996.

In the tax-policy arena on Ways and Means, Cardin has supported rolling back Reagan-era tax cuts for the highest income groups, and he has opposed tax cuts (such as the partial exclusion of capital gains income) that would principally benefit the wealthy.

In one instance, Cardin veered from that stance. He joined in early 1993 with Florida Republican E. Clay Shaw Jr. to press for repeal of a tax enacted in 1990 on luxury items, including boats. Though the tax was aimed at the wealthy, it was widely viewed as contributing to a decline in the boat industry, which is critical to Maryland's Chesapeake Bay economy.

But Cardin generally votes a predictably liberal Democratic line in favor of gun control, environmental protections and abortion rights. Cardin got nowhere with an amendment to offer more funding for gang prevention programs in 1995. He sought to pay for them by cutting prison construction grants at the rate of $7.2 million a year but was voted down, 129-295.

And Cardin has not been one to forget the home folk. He opposed a major rewrite of farm law in 1996 because he wanted to see sugar subsidies that hurt a major refinery in his district abolished. In his time on Capitol Hill, he has had a hand in preserving the Coast Guard base at Curtis Bay and restoring Fort McHenry in Baltimore, and he helped secure development assistance for a light rail system in Baltimore and a prototype magnetic levitation train between Baltimore and Washington.

At Home: Like most state legislators, Cardin was perceived as having taken a step up when he moved to Congress from the Maryland House. But Cardin gave up considerable power in doing so. He had served as House Speaker in Annapolis for almost a decade, growing accustomed to calling the legislative shots.

Cardin's legislative talents helped him acquire a leadership role in the Maryland House at an extraordinarily young age. He was 23 when first elected to the legislature, and by age 32 he was chairman of the Ways and Means Committee. Four years later, Cardin became the youngest Speaker in the history of the state House. Cardin was generally popular among his colleagues in Annapolis. Those who viewed him as tough but fair outnumbered critics who complained that he planted pliable allies in chairmanships and rushed favored bills through without debate.

Cardin initially hoped that his strong legislative record would earn him his party's nomination in 1986 to succeed outgoing Democratic Gov. Harry R. Hughes. But William Donald Schaefer, the popular Democratic mayor of Baltimore, also decided to run for governor. Cardin recognized that Schaefer would overshadow him, so he opted to seek the 3rd District seat that Democrat Barbara A. Mikulski was leaving to run for the Senate. (Cardin is still considered a Democratic prospect for the mansion in Annapolis.)

His House elections have been non-events: He drew no significant primary opposition for the open seat in 1986 and has won at least 67 percent in his six general election contests.

Cardin's growing clout in the House and long-standing ties to the state legislature benefited him during the redistricting that preceded the 1992 elections. Although the state map faced major changes to accommodate a second black-majority district, Cardin's interests were protected: He retained a Democratic-leaning district with his base in the heavily Jewish neighborhoods of northwest Baltimore and nearby suburbs.

HOUSE ELECTIONS

1996 General		
Benjamin L. Cardin (D)	130,204	(67%)
Patrick L. McDonough (R)	63,229	(33%)
1996 Primary		
Benjamin L. Cardin (D)	34,496	(90%)
Dan Hiegel (D)	3,720	(10%)
1994 General		
Benjamin L. Cardin (D)	117,269	(71%)
Robert Ryan Tousey (R)	47,966	(29%)

Previous Winning Percentages: **1992** (74%) **1990** (70%) **1988** (73%) **1986** (79%)

CAMPAIGN FINANCE

	Receipts	Receipts from PACs		Expend-itures
1996				
Cardin (D)	$527,180	$305,431	(58%)	$577,270
McDonough (R)	$51,014	$831	(2%)	$49,459
1994				
Cardin (D)	$493,522	$258,658	(52%)	$550,172
Tousey (R)	$13,481	$464	(3%)	$10,439

DISTRICT VOTE FOR PRESIDENT

	1996		1992
D	123,896 (58%)	**D**	136,829 (54%)
R	72,181 (34%)	**R**	82,494 (32%)
I	13,889 (7%)	**I**	34,973 (14%)

KEY VOTES

1997	
Ban "partial-birth" abortions	N
1996	
Approve farm bill	N
Deny public education to illegal immigrants	Y
Repeal ban on certain assault-style weapons	N
Increase minimum wage	Y
Freeze defense spending	?
Approve welfare overhaul	Y
1995	
Approve balanced-budget constitutional amendment	N
Relax Clean Water Act regulations	N
Oppose limits on environmental regulations	Y
Reduce projected Medicare spending	N
Approve GOP budget with tax and spending cuts	N

VOTING STUDIES

	Presidential Support		Party Unity		Conservative Coalition	
Year	**S**	**O**	**S**	**O**	**S**	**O**
1996	80	16	84	13	35	57
1995	87	12	84	14	40	58
1994	74	19	93	4	31	67
1993	83	17	92	5	20	80
1992	17	82	93	5	27	71
1991	32	67	91	8	22	78

INTEREST GROUP RATINGS

Year	ADA	AFL-CIO	CCUS	ACU
1996	75	n/a	25	11
1995	85	100	25	12
1994	75	89	50	10
1993	90	92	18	4
1992	95	83	38	4
1991	75	92	30	0

4 Albert R. Wynn (D)

Of Largo — Elected 1992, 3rd term

Biographical Information
Born: Sept. 10, 1951, Philadelphia, Pa.
Education: U. of Pittsburgh, B.S. 1973; Howard U., 1973-74; Georgetown U., J.D. 1977.
Occupation: Lawyer.
Family: Wife, Jessie Tianaya Jackson; one child.
Religion: Baptist.
Political Career: Md. House, 1983-87; Md. Senate, 1987-93.
Capitol Office: 407 Cannon Bldg. 20515; 225-8699.

Committees
Commerce
Energy & Power; Telecommunications, Trade & Consumer Protection

In Washington: As a liberal-voting member of the Congressional Black Caucus and a believer in a "safety net" for the underprivileged, Wynn not surprisingly was skeptical of GOP efforts in the 104th Congress to overhaul the nation's welfare laws.

When Republicans came forward twice with plans to pass much of the control of the welfare system from the federal government to states, Wynn said the Republican approach "hurts innocent children." He said he favored work requirements for welfare recipients and time limits on benefits — both included in the GOP bills. However, he faulted the measures for lacking common-sense approaches and adequate funding to provide child care and job training to people being moved off the welfare rolls.

Still, Wynn was frustrated with the welfare status quo, like many of the middle-class black suburbanites in his Prince George's County, Md.-based district. A lot of them had left adjacent Washington, D.C., minority neighborhoods plagued by drugs, crime and unemployment.

In the end, Wynn — like President Clinton — decided that reforming welfare, even in a way that catered to GOP priorities, was preferable to the status quo. In July 1996 he voted for the welfare overhaul that cleared Congress and was signed by the president.

Wynn got good news shortly after his 1996 reelection, when he was awarded a seat on the influential Commerce Committee, which has broad legislative responsibilities. The assignment could help Wynn make contacts with businesses that might be interested in locating in the 4th, such as the biotechnology firms that have blossomed in nearby Montgomery County, Md.

Wynn is the first black to represent the Washington suburbs in Congress. His election in 1992 bespoke both the growing clout of black voters in Prince George's and Wynn's skill at appealing across racial lines.

During the 104th, Wynn spent much time serving as a foot soldier in the Democratic campaign to discredit GOP attempts to scale back or eliminate federal government services. Wynn's work in this area is good politics in the 4th, where the GOP's anti-Washington rhetoric rings hollow with the district's many federal employees and government contractors. Wynn rallied against the Republicans' budget proposals, which included plans to reduce the rate of spending growth on Medicare and Medicaid and other programs for the poor.

"They want to eliminate the guarantees that we have for the sick, the elderly, the poor, the blind, and the disabled," Wynn fumed. "They want to take 3.8 million children off the Medicaid rolls and deny them the safety net guarantee that we have now. We have a problem with that. We do not think it is necessary. The reason it is not necessary is because they have hidden in their budget a little poison pill in the form of a $245 billion tax break for the wealthy."

When congressional Republicans failed to reach an agreement with President Clinton over budget priorities, leading to a partial shutdown of the federal government that kept many federal employees home from work, Wynn laid the blame squarely on Republicans.

"My constituents who are federal employees are watching more C-SPAN now than ever," Wynn said on the House floor. "And they are being treated to a sorry spectacle — a bunch of opinionated stuffed shirts sitting around bickering while they are getting paid, while peoples' lives are being disrupted, and while federal employees are losing their paychecks."

In other budget and spending battles of the 104th, Wynn fought to preserve the federal presence in his district. He spoke out against a spending bill that contained cuts in various federal housing programs, calling it a "political meat axe." He opposed a Republican foreign aid bill because it required the president to eliminate one of the government's three foreign policy agencies.

Wynn was particularly critical of a Republican bill that provided a $500-per-child tax credit, pri-

MARYLAND 4
Inner Prince George's County; Silver Spring

The emergence of Prince George's County as one of the nation's few suburban counties with a black majority sparked the creation of the 4th in redistricting for the 1990s. Blacks are about three-fifths of the district's population; most of them live in Prince George's. Taking into account the district's Hispanics, whose numbers have steadily grown in recent years, more than two-thirds of the 4th's residents can be counted as minority group members.

Still, there is a substantial white population, particularly in the southeast section of Montgomery County that contributes more than a quarter of the district's residents. When the first House primary was held in 1992, black Democratic activists worried that a white candidate might maneuver through a large crowd of black contenders. But Wynn used a biracial appeal in both counties to take the nomination.

The Democratic primary is the deciding contest in this district. In the 1992 general election, Wynn got 84 percent of the vote in Prince George's County and 59 percent in Montgomery. In 1996, Wynn secured 90 percent of the vote in Prince George's, and 75 percent in Montgomery. Bill Clinton's showing in the presidential race trailed Wynn only slightly.

Prince George's is in many ways a success story of black upward mobility. For blacks, it is among the nation's leading jurisdictions in business formation, home ownership and education. Many residents work in Washington, D.C., or at a complex in Suitland (which includes the Census Bureau and the National Weather Service) or at Andrews Air Force Base. There are large private employers in Landover, such as the Giant supermarket chain, and in the New Carrollton business center.

The USAir sports arena also is in Landover, home of a pro basketball and hockey franchise until they moved to a new arena in downtown Washington beginning with the 1997-98 season. But the pro football Washington Redskins have relocated from downtown to the new Jack Kent Cooke Stadium near Landover.

For some residents, however, there has been no escaping the drugs and guns that they hoped to leave behind when they moved from the District of Columbia. Drug trafficking and attendant violence plague a number of the 4th's low-income communities, which are mostly inside the Capital Beltway that rings Washington.

The largest concentrations of Hispanics are in working-class and low-income communities in western Prince George's County and in the Silver Spring area of eastern Montgomery County. Takoma Park has a bohemian image: Activists declared it a "nuclear free zone" in the 1980s.

Silver Spring, one of Washington's first suburbs, saw its once-bustling downtown grow seedy as the retail trade moved to regional malls. Developers claimed they would rejuvenate the city with a giant new mall. But local officials pulled the plug on the project when developers failed to attract private investors.

North of Silver Spring, the 4th follows the Route 29 business corridor. The middle- and upper-middle-income communities in this area have a larger white population and are more conservative than the rest of the district.

1990 Population: 597,690. White 200,081 (33%), Black 349,499 (58%), Other 48,110 (8%). Hispanic origin 37,962 (6%). 18 and over 447,123 (75%), 62 and over 54,791 (9%). Median age: 31.

marily because it also contained an increase in the federal employee retirement plan contribution. Wynn tried to put a human face on the often-maligned bureaucrats who staff federal agencies, pointing out that they are "FBI agents, cancer researchers, people that help move our Social Security checks, people who work very hard, who have experienced downsizing . . . ."

In claiming a seat on Commerce, Wynn had to give up seats on the Banking and Financial Services Committee and on the International Relations Committee. On International Relations in the 104th,Wynn fought Republican cuts in foreign policy programs and in the State Department bureaucracy. Like many House Democrats, his foreign policy positions were not always exactly in line with Clinton's. He opposed granting most-favored nation trading status to China, and favored lifting the Bosnian arms embargo to allow the Bosnian Muslims to defend themselves against the Serbs.

At Home: Wynn is an intense, high-energy politician, a style that helped him gain prominence in the state legislature and has carried him to easy House re-election victories.

Wynn's popularity in the 4th drove his 1996 GOP challenger, John B. Kimble, to desperate measures to gain recognition. Kimble offered to pose nude in Playgirl magazine if outspoken New York radio host Howard Stern would help raise $1 million for his campaign. Neither Stern nor Playgirl took him up on the offer, leaving voters to decide the election exclusively on the candidates' political positions. Wynn won with 85 percent.

A loyal Democrat in the state legislature for 10 years, Wynn compiled a record friendly to organized labor and supportive of abortion rights. He developed a close friendship with the man who then represented Prince George's County in Congress, Steny H. Hoyer. (Hoyer still has part of the county in his current 5th District.)

When redistricting for the 1990s created a constituency anchored in Prince George that was designed to elect a black candidate, Wynn moved to take it.

Wynn was not well known in the district's other county, Montgomery, where about one-quarter of the 4th's people live and where there are fewer minority voters. So he plunged into Montgomery with his intensely personal campaign style, hoping that a win there, coupled with sufficient support from his Prince George's base, would be enough to nominate him.

Wynn's principal primary opponent was popular Prince George's State's Attorney Alexander Williams Jr., who had proven his ability to win white votes in past countywide elections but who concentrated his House campaign at home. Williams edged Wynn by a thin 400 votes in Prince George's, and Wynn outpolled Williams in Montgomery by 1,700 votes to take the nomination.

The general election was a foregone conclusion. Republican Michele Dyson, a black business owner from Montgomery County, had the endorsement of the U.S. Chamber of Commerce. But the district's overwhelming Democratic registration and Wynn's name recognition left Dyson in the dust.

He won with 75 percent of the vote and beat her again in 1994 with the same percentage.

HOUSE ELECTIONS

1996 General		
Albert R. Wynn (D)	142,094	(85%)
John B. Kimble (R)	24,700	(15%)
1996 Primary		
Albert R. Wynn (D)	22,270	(85%)
Maria Turner (D)	4,044	(15%)
1994 General		
Albert R. Wynn (D)	93,148	(75%)
Michele Dyson (R)	30,999	(25%)

Previous Winning Percentages: 1992 (75%)

CAMPAIGN FINANCE

	Receipts	Receipts from PACs	Expend-itures
1996			
Wynn (D)	$411,225	$192,635 (47%)	$343,875
1994			
Wynn (D)	$379,024	$226,450 (60%)	$358,607
Dyson (R)	$118,223	$4,014 (3%)	$119,749

DISTRICT VOTE FOR PRESIDENT

1996		1992	
D	151,951 (80%)	**D**	149,262 (74%)
R	30,598 (16%)	**R**	37,716 (19%)
I	5,619 (3%)	**I**	14,160 (7%)

KEY VOTES

1997	
Ban "partial-birth" abortions	N
1996	
Approve farm bill	Y
Deny public education to illegal immigrants	N
Repeal ban on certain assault-style weapons	N
Increase minimum wage	Y
Freeze defense spending	Y
Approve welfare overhaul	Y
1995	
Approve balanced-budget constitutional amendment	N
Relax Clean Water Act regulations	N
Oppose limits on environmental regulations	Y
Reduce projected Medicare spending	N
Approve GOP budget with tax and spending cuts	N

VOTING STUDIES

	Presidential Support		Party Unity		Conservative Coalition	
Year	S	O	S	O	S	O
1996	84	16	90	9	37	63
1995	83	17	92	6	25	73
1994	82	18	95	3	25	72
1993	80	20	97	2	14	86

INTEREST GROUP RATINGS

Year	ADA	AFL-CIO	CCUS	ACU
1996	90	n/a	31	0
1995	95	100	21	12
1994	95	89	42	0
1993	100	100	9	4

5 Steny H. Hoyer (D)

Of Mechanicsville — Elected 1981; 8th full term

Biographical Information

Born: June 14, 1939, New York, N.Y.

Education: U. of Maryland, B.S. 1963; Georgetown U., J.D. 1966.

Occupation: Lawyer.

Family: Widowed; three children.

Religion: Baptist.

Political Career: Md. Senate, 1967-79, president, 1975-79; sought Democratic nomination for lieutenant governor, 1978; Md. Board of Higher Education, 1978-81.

Capitol Office: 1705 Longworth Bldg. 20515; 225-4131.

Committees

Appropriations
Labor, Health & Human Services, Education & Related Agencies; Military Construction; Treasury, Postal Service & General Government (ranking)

House Oversight

Joint Printing

In Washington: In a House where the Republican majority fumes about the excessive size, cost and power of the federal bureaucracy, Hoyer shoulders a heavy burden: speaking well of Uncle Sam's work force.

Because he represents a suburban district just outside of Washington, D.C., Hoyer counts many federal workers among his constituents. He often champions their labors on the Appropriations Committee, where he is ranking member of the Treasury, Postal Service and General Government subcommittee.

Hoyer also has protested GOP efforts to cut back the amount of money Congress spends on itself. In June 1995, the Appropriations Committee approved by voice vote a $1.7 billion legislative branch spending bill. The measure cut $155 million from the comparable fiscal 1995 level of $1.9 billion, primarily through the previously approved reduction of committee staff and by abolishing the Office of Technology Assessment and the Joint Committee on Printing and cutting the General Accounting Office. "This is the beginning of the downsizing of the government," declared Ron Packard, R-Calif., chairman of the Legislative Branch Appropriations Subcommittee. Responded Hoyer: "We ought to stop this self-flagellation. We have a responsibility to be the people's overseers."

Taking on yet another thankless task in the 105th, Hoyer was named the lone Democrat on a task force appointed by the House Oversight Committee to investigate charges of vote fraud in the 1996 election of Democratic Rep. Loretta Sanchez, D-Calif. The election was challenged by the Republican Sanchez defeated, nine-term veteran Robert K. Dornan.

Hoyer suffered a deep personal loss at the outset of the 105th Congress when his wife, Judy, died of cancer in February 1997.

He spoke of his late wife in March 1997 during a debate on legislation to outlaw an abortion procedure that opponents call "partial birth" abortion. "I could not do anything about the cancer that gripped her body, but if I could have done something had she been pregnant with one of our three girls and saved her life, by God, I would have done it," Hoyer said on the House floor. "If the doctor had told me, 'Judy will not be able to have further children if we do not perform an abortion,' I would have said, as much as I love my three daughters, 'Doctor, save Judy's life and our ability to have more children.' "

Before the House passed the bill, Hoyer and James C. Greenwood, R-Pa., offered an amendment allowing any kind of abortion procedure before the fetus reached viability, but banning all post-viability abortions except those needed to save the woman's life or protect her from serious adverse health conditions. The proposal largely mirrored President Clinton's position, which said that any limits on so-called "partial birth" abortions must exempt cases in which a woman's health is at risk. Hoyer offered a motion to send the bill back to committee with instructions to substitute his proposal, but that motion was ruled out of order as non-germane.

In the 104th Congress, Hoyer tried to remove abortion restrictions that were added as riders to various spending bills. He proposed an amendment to the fiscal 1997 Treasury-Postal Service appropriations bill that took out a provision barring women covered by federal employee health plans from obtaining abortions under such plans, except in cases of rape, incest and when the life of the woman was endangered. The amendment failed, 184-238.

Hoyer also used his post on Appropriations to fight Republicans' proposed cuts in spending. In committee, he railed against reductions in education spending in the fiscal 1997 Labor-HHS appropriations bill. In June 1996, Hoyer said the cuts would "undermine our investment in our kids, in our families and our future." Majority Whip Tom DeLay, R-Texas, shot back: "I don't think it's the function of the federal government to educate my kids."

In July 1995, Hoyer tried unsuccessfully to restore $1.1 billion in fiscal 1996 spending to education programs, including money for "Goals 2000" grants, Title I services for educationally disadvantaged children, School-to-Work vocational training and Head Start programs for preschoolers from low-income families. The Appropriations Commit-

MARYLAND 5
Outer Prince George's; Southern Maryland

The 5th has a different makeup from the primarily suburban district that Hoyer represented during his first decade in the House. The creation of the black-majority 4th in 1991 redistricting siphoned off many black Democrats, while pushing Hoyer into less urbanized areas of Prince George's County, southern Anne Arundel County and southern Maryland (Charles, St. Mary's and Calvert counties).

The southern counties have a rural heritage, with tobacco as a major crop. The political tradition is Democratic but conservative, a tendency augmented by an influx of commuters and exurbanites. Winning candidates for major office here usually are conservatives and often are Republicans.

The reshaping of the 5th to include this territory was expected to cause Hoyer trouble, and it did. After years of easy victories, he has failed to crack 60 percent since 1990. In 1996, Hoyer won four of the five counties that, in full or in part, make up the district, losing only Anne Arundel. But only in the 5th's part of Prince George's did Hoyer's margin of victory exceed 5,000 votes or his vote exceed 60 percent.

Prince George's also was the only county in the 5th to back Bill Clinton in 1996. His 61 percent of the vote there enabled him to lead by a 30,500-vote margin in the 5th's portion of the county and to carry the overall district.

P.G. County (as some locals call it) accounts for nearly half the 5th's population. In the northern part of the county, the 5th ducks inside the Capital Beltway to pick up such heavily black communities as Hyattsville. Also in Prince George's County is the University of Maryland's flagship campus at College Park.

The university is among the public employers that boost the district's job base. Up the Interstate 95/Baltimore-Washington Parkway corridor toward Greenbelt and Laurel are NASA's Goddard Space Flight Center and the National Agricultural Research Center. Expansion at the Naval Air Station at Patuxent River is expected to increase employment there to about 32,000 by 1998.

The 5th sweeps east through Bowie, whose location between Washington and Annapolis brought a growth spurt in the 1980s. A new county-owned stadium in Bowie is home to the Baltimore Orioles' Class AA Baysox. The district then sweeps around Andrews Air Force Base into southern Prince George's. The 5th also takes in a portion of southern Anne Arundel County that contributes about 15 percent of the district's residents; upscale communities such as Crofton and Davidsonville are here, but much of the area retains a rural feel.

The southern counties all grew rapidly in the 1980s. Charles County's population grew 39 percent to more than 100,000, as commuters poured into subdivisions along Route 301 and Indian Head Highway. Population in St. Mary's County increased 27 percent. There is much defense-related work in the southern counties. Calvert County's population grew 48 percent, but it is the state's second-least-populous county west of the Chesapeake Bay.

1990 Population: 597,681. White 461,610 (77%), Black 110,953 (19%), Other 25,118 (4%). Hispanic origin 14,520 (2%). 18 and over 450,198 (75%), 62 and over 56,900 (10%). Median age: 31.

tee rejected his amendment, 19-30.

Hoyer tries to make sure Maryland gets its share of federal largess. The fiscal 1996 Treasury-Postal Service appropriations bill earmarked about $5 million for telecommuting projects in his district and state. But Hoyer could not protect nearly $66 million to continue work on a huge Food and Drug Administration building project in the Maryland suburbs. The House approved, 278-146, an amendment to eliminate the money.

Hoyer indirectly was involved in a controversy in July 1995 during a debate on the Treasury-Postal Service bill. David L. Hobson, R-Ohio, offered an amendment to allow the federal government to continue AIDS education programs for federal workers. An opposing pamphlet on the GOP side of the floor misidentified the sponsor, calling on members to defeat the "Hoyer" amendment, because "Hoyer=Sex training for federal workers; Hoyer=condom training; Hoyer=religious indoctrination."

Hoyer got into a fight with Republicans after seeing the handout. "The handout itself was scurrilous, dishonest and clearly contrary to the rules if it had been spoken from the floor."

In response, Speaker Newt Gingrich in September banned anonymous tracts from the House floor, ruling that only members may hand out paper on the floor in an effort to lobby for or against legislation. And the pamphlets, routinely distributed during votes by both Democrats and Republicans to recruit supporters, must bear the name of the member doing the circulating.

"The content of those materials must comport with standards of propriety applicable to words spoken in debate or inserted in the record," the Speaker said. "In order to enhance the quality of debate in the House, the chair would ask members to minimize the use of handouts."

Though generally liberal in his outlook, Hoyer supported the welfare overhaul bill signed by President Clinton in 1996 (after earlier opposing the original Republican version of the legislation). He also has backed a constitutional amendment requiring a balanced budget.

Still, he opposed the House Republican rule, adopted at the start of the 104th Congress, requiring approval of income tax increases by a three-fifths majority. "It's unconstitutional to require by rule a supermajority to pass legislation that is not a constitutional amendment," Hoyer said. "Otherwise, the temporary majority could apply that to any issue. They could require a three-fifths vote, a two-thirds vote, or a three-fourths vote. What if we said to the Republicans, 'You need three-fifths to repeal any funding program'?"

At Home: Hoyer saw much of his black Democratic base in Prince George's County replaced with more conservative voters in redistricting after the 1990 census. In each of the three elections beginning in 1992 he was the target of strong Republican challenges that held him below 60 percent of the vote.

His 1996 challenge came from state Rep. John S. Morgan, who emphasized his support for new prisons and ending parole for violent felons. Hoyer tried to deflect Morgan's characterization of him as a tax-and-spend liberal by emphasizing his support for a balanced budget amendment. Hoyer ended up winning with 57 percent.

In 1994, he faced another aggressive challenger in Donald Devine, former director of the U.S. Office of Personnel Management. Devine ran ads showcasing Hoyer's pronouncement that he is a "tax, tax, spend, spend Democrat." Despite the favorable year for such a tactic, it was still a tough sell in a district that is home to many federal employees whose livelihoods rely on government operations. Hoyer polled 59 percent.

Hoyer was held to a modest victory margin of 9 percentage points in 1992 by a well-known Republican: Lawrence J. Hogan Jr., the son of a former House member and former Prince George's County executive. Hogan's thrust was to hammer at Hoyer's status as a congressional insider. However, Hoyer adroitly pointed out the advantage of his senior status. He took a spot on the Appropriations Military Construction Subcommittee, of benefit to facilities in Southern Maryland.

Hoyer was just out of law school when he was elected to the Maryland Senate in 1966. An ally of Democratic Gov. Marvin Mandel's, Hoyer was chosen Senate president after two terms, becoming the youngest person to take that post.

A 1978 setback briefly slowed Hoyer's rise. After first declaring for governor, he agreed to run for lieutenant governor on a Democratic ticket headed by acting Gov. Blair Lee III. But the ticket was defeated in the primary. Hoyer rebounded by winning a 1981 special House election. The seat had been declared vacant when it became clear that Democratic Rep. Gladys Noon Spellman, who was re-elected in 1980 despite a heart attack that left her in a coma, was unable to serve. Thirty-one candidates, including Spellman's husband, entered the contest to succeed her. But Hoyer was able to call on his past coalition of liberal, labor and black supporters to win the primary. He then defeated Republican Audrey Scott, the mayor of Bowie, with 55 percent and went on to a string of easy general-election wins.

HOUSE ELECTIONS

1996 General		
Steny H. Hoyer (D)	121,288	(57%)
John S. Morgan (R)	91,806	(43%)
1996 Primary		
Steny H. Hoyer (D)	22,598	(84%)
Thomas W. Defibaugh Sr. (D)	4,356	(16%)
1994 General		
Steny H. Hoyer (D)	98,821	(59%)
Donald Devine (R)	69,211	(41%)

Previous Winning Percentages: **1992** (53%) **1990** (81%) **1988** (79%) **1986** (82%) **1984** (72%) **1982** (80%) **1981**† (55%)

† Special election

CAMPAIGN FINANCE

	Receipts	Receipts from PACs		Expend-itures
1996				
Hoyer (D)	$1,239,414	$696,267	(56%)	$1,155,840
Morgan (R)	$238,431	$14,738	(6%)	$236,483
1994				
Hoyer (D)	$1,427,122	$860,152	(60%)	$1,295,542
Devine (R)	$565,371	$59,780	(11%)	$581,198

VOTING STUDIES

	Presidential Support		Party Unity		Conservative Coalition	
Year	**S**	**O**	**S**	**O**	**S**	**O**
1996	86	14	87	13	69	31
1995	78	20	83	14	59	41
1994	86	14	91	5	56	42
1993	93	6	92	7	59	41
1992	27	72	89	8	52	48
1991	33	67	90	7	19	81

DISTRICT VOTE FOR PRESIDENT

1996			1992		
D	117,015	(52%)	**D**	107,618	(45%)
R	94,342	(42%)	**R**	95,356	(40%)
I	14,393	(6%)	**I**	37,441	(16%)

KEY VOTES

1997	
Ban "partial birth" abortions	N
1996	
Approve farm bill	N
Deny public education to illegal immigrants	N
Repeal ban on certain assault-style weapons	N
Increase minimum wage	Y
Freeze defense spending	N
Approve welfare overhaul	Y
1995	
Approve balanced-budget constitutional amendment	Y
Relax Clean Water Act regulations	N
Oppose limits on environmental regulations	Y
Reduce projected Medicare spending	N
Approve GOP budget with tax and spending cuts	N

INTEREST GROUP RATINGS

Year	ADA	AFL-CIO	CCUS	ACU
1996	85	n/a	13	5
1995	80	92	25	8
1994	70	78	42	24
1993	70	92	27	17
1992	90	75	38	17
1991	80	92	30	0

6 Roscoe G. Bartlett (R)

Of Frederick — Elected 1992, 3rd term

Biographical Information

Born: June 3, 1926, Moreland, Ky.

Education: Columbia Union College, B.S. 1947; U. of Maryland, M.S. 1948, Ph.D. 1952.

Occupation: Teacher; engineer; research scientist; small business owner; land developer.

Family: Wife, Ellen Louise Baldwin; 10 children.

Religion: Seventh-Day Adventist.

Political Career: Republican nominee for U.S. House, 1982.

Capitol Office: 322 Cannon Bldg. 20515; 225-2721.

Committees

National Security
Military Personnel; Military Research & Development

Science
Space & Aeronautics; Technology

Small Business
Government Programs & Oversight (chairman)

In Washington: Bartlett marks his 71st birthday during the 105th Congress, but if he is roughly twice as old as many of the conservative young GOP firebrands who have joined the House in the 1990s, he is every bit their equal in ideological fervor.

In the early months of the 104th Congress, Bartlett voted for every item in the "Contract With America" legislative agenda. At the start of the 105th, he was one of 26 Republican holdouts who voted against reprimanding House Speaker Newt Gingrich for ethics violations.

Bartlett's political philosophy is informed by his strongly held religious beliefs and by his Depression-era upbringing, which leads him to extol self-reliance and personal initiative and denounce the intrusiveness of the federal government. During the 104th, when President Clinton said he would veto an early version of the GOP's welfare-overhaul legislation, Bartlett protested. "The welfare state has become a system that encourages family breakdown and government dependence," he told the House. "It fails to hold absentee fathers accountable and traps young people in poverty. When given a chance to change this destructive system, Bill Clinton again proved that he is a say-anything, do-nothing liberal president."

Bartlett opposes abortion; he voted in the 104th against a minimum wage increase; and his hawkishness on eliminating the federal deficit at times exceeds even his own party leadership's. Hoping to keep up pressure for a balanced-budget agreement between Congress and the White House, Bartlett was one of only 45 Republicans voting against a short-term extension of the nation's debt limit.

Although he casts a skeptical eye on government spending, Bartlett, who sits on the National Security Committee, has supported GOP efforts to spend more on defense than Clinton requests. Also a member of the Science Committee, he is a booster of NASA's space station project, which critics say is an overly costly "science pork" endeavor.

Bartlett's support for Second Amendment rights allowing people to keep and bear arms led him to introduce a measure in the 104th stipulating in federal law that Americans have the right to use firearms to defend their families and homes. He told the Baltimore Sun that he fears the rights of gun owners are being destroyed by a flood of local gun-control laws that he says have failed to slow crime. He said his measure was necessary both to overturn oppressive state gun-control laws and to prevent prosecutors from bringing charges against law-abiding citizens who use guns to defend themselves against criminals.

His measure became part of the debate on legislation aimed at repealing the existing ban on certain semiautomatic assault-style weapons. That repeal bill passed the House in March 1996 on a 239-173 vote, but went no further.

From his seat on National Security, Bartlett has latched on to some attention-grabbing issues. He authored a provision in 1996 that he said would end the practice of "Uncle Sam subsidizing smut at defense facilities." The measure, which was enacted into law as part of the fiscal 1997 defense authorization bill, barred the sale of "lascivious" magazines or videotapes on U.S. military bases.

Citing the sale of sexually explicit materials at military post exchanges, Bartlett said, "Most Americans would be shocked to learn that the Defense Department is currently one of the largest purveyors of pornography in the country — at discount prices and without tax."

In early 1997, however, Bartlett's legislation was deemed unconstitutional by U.S. District Judge Shira A. Scheindlin in New York. The ruling came in a suit against the Defense Department by Bob Guccione, the publisher of Penthouse magazine, and others. "In the context of our long and rich First Amendment tradition," the judge wrote, "it becomes clear that sexually explicit material cannot be banned from sale or rental at military exchanges merely because it is offensive."

In the 104th, Bartlett also took up the cause of

MARYLAND 6
Central and West — Frederick; Hagerstown

During the 14 years that Democrat Beverly B. Byron dominated the 6th, local Republicans insisted that it was only her record as one of the most conservative House Democrats that kept the GOP-leaning district from falling into their hands.

The events of 1992 justified their contention. Byron was upset by a more liberal Democrat, Thomas H. Hattery, in the March primary. But in November, the 6th stuck to its conservative form, electing Republican Bartlett by a margin of nearly 20,000 votes. He won again easily in 1994 and in 1996.

The 6th takes in the five westernmost counties along Maryland's northern border — Garrett, Allegany, Washington, Frederick and Carroll — and more than half the population of Howard County. These places include some of the state's most reliably Republican territory. George Bush swept all the counties in 1992; his 48 percent here was by far his best in any state district. Bob Dole was equally successful here in 1996, winning all five counties as well as the district's portion of Howard. Dole's 52 percent in the 6th was also his best showing in the state.

Most of the 6th's people live in the rapidly growing exurban areas of central Maryland. At its southern end, the 6th takes in the recently built subdivisions of western Howard County, then skirts south past the city of Columbia. The growth in the southern part of the 6th drew in a less conservative sort of Democrat who turned against Byron in 1992. But the district's conservative majority, including a number of traditional Democratic voters, rebelled against that result, and the GOP captured the district.

Frederick County's population also blossomed over the past decade. Many residents commute on Interstate 270 to Washington or on Interstate 70 to Baltimore, or to high-tech businesses along those highways. A National Cancer Institute research facility and the Defense Department's Medical Research Center are in the city of Frederick. The Camp David presidential retreat is in Thurmont, in northern Frederick County.

To the east is Carroll County, parts of which have turned into bedroom suburbs of Baltimore. Both Frederick and Carroll counties still have a good deal of farmland and are GOP strongholds.

While development is an issue in central Maryland, slow growth is the problem in the hilly Western Panhandle. The manufacturing sector has diminished. The largest private employer in Hagerstown (Washington County) used to be a Mack Truck factory. Now it is a Citicorp credit card service center, which has taken up some of the employment slack.

In Cumberland (Allegany County), officials are laboring to replace jobs lost in the late 1980s, when Kelly-Springfield (which has headquarters here) closed its tire plant. Hard times give Democrats a chance, but conservatism usually prevails.

With few economic options, Garrett County is trying to make the most of its remote location. Its tourism industry draws visitors to man-made Deep Creek Lake and winter-sport players to its mountain towns.

1990 Population: 597,688. White 560,853 (94%), Black 26,838(4%), Other 9,997 (2%). Hispanic origin 5,495 (1%). 18 and over 447,788 (75%), 62 and over 83,167 (14%). Median age: 34.

Army Specialist Michael New, a medic who was court-martialed in January 1996 for refusing to alter his U.S. Army uniform by wearing a United Nations blue beret and insignia as part of a U.N. peacekeeping mission in Macedonia. "Specialist New took the position that the oath he took when he entered the military was to defend and protect the Constitution of the United States," Bartlett told the House. "He had not taken an oath to defend and protect the charter of the United Nations."

Calling New an American hero, Bartlett and Ohio Democrat James A. Traficant Jr. introduced a non-binding resolution urging Clinton to quash New's conviction. In conservatives' eyes, New's case revealed Clinton's willingness to place U.S. forces under the command of foreign officers, a development they feel may lead to a broader subordination of U.S. interests to the United Nations and other international agencies.

Later, in September 1996, Bartlett successfully sponsored an amendment that would prevent the Pentagon from requiring U.S. troops to wear U.N. uniforms without prior approval by Congress. The House adopted it, 276-130, as part of legislation designed to limit the president's ability to place U.S. troops under U.N. command.

Back in 1994, when Democrats were still the House majority, Bartlett put them on the defensive by bringing attention to a Clinton aide's use of a Marine helicopter to fly to a Maryland golf course, which happened to be in Bartlett's district. Bartlett offered an amendment to the fiscal 1995 executive branch spending bill that would have reduced the White House budget by $13,129.66, the estimated cost of the helicopter outing.

"This is not a partisan amendment," Bartlett asserted, saying he simply wanted the House to go on record that "we believe there should be full disclosure of the use of the presidential helicopters."

The House rejected the amendment.

Democrats pointed out that the aide not only had been fired by the White House but also had agreed to pay for the use of the helicopter.

An engineer and research scientist, Bartlett holds 20 patents for his invention of respiratory support and safety devices used by pilots, astronauts and rescue workers. Although he joins with many of his conservative colleagues in deriding excessive federal spending, he defends government involvement in big-ticket science projects such as the space station and fusion energy research.

During debate in October 1995 on a broad science authorization bill, he argued against cutting the nation's fusion energy research program. "Harnessing fusion power is the most challenging and ambitious scientific endeavor ever undertaken by man," Bartlett told the House. "Not only is fusion one of very few long-term energy options for the future but it is at the cutting edge of scientific research and technology."

Bartlett also has a seat on the Small Business Committee, where in the 105th he is chairman of the Government Programs and Oversight Subcommittee.

At Home: Bartlett's 1992 House campaign unfolded in an unanticipated manner. He narrowly won a quiet, three-way GOP primary and was expecting to face an uphill general-election battle against conservative Democrat Beverly B. Byron, a seven-term incumbent. Bartlett had run against her in 1982 and polled only 26 percent of the vote. But Byron was upset in the primary by challenger Thomas H. Hattery, and in November, Bartlett capitalized on confusion in Democratic ranks to beat Hattery by 8 points.

Bartlett bested Hattery at his own game of negative campaigning. Hattery had sharply criticized Byron's vote for a $35,000 congressional pay raise at a time when the district was suffering high unemployment, and he hit her for extensive overseas travel at taxpayer expense. But Bartlett struck at Hattery for padding his state legislative expense account, and he accused Hattery of failing to buy workers' compensation insurance for the employees at his family-owned printing company. Bartlett essentially set up officeholder Hattery as the nominal incumbent, and with voters in an anti-incumbent mood, that propelled him to a 54 percent victory.

Bartlett made some early stumbles in Congress. In 1993, for instance, while discussing the high percentage of Asian-American scholarship winners in Maryland, he made a reference to Asians not having "normal" American names. Bartlett later contended that his remarks were taken out of context. There was talk he might draw a significant challenge for renomination in 1994, but it came to nothing, and he easily won both the primary and general elections.

In 1996, Bartlett won by 14 points, although Democrat Stephen Crawford, a University of Maryland lecturer, pulled him down to 57 percent.

HOUSE ELECTIONS

1996 General		
Roscoe G. Bartlett (R)	132,853	(57%)
Stephen Crawford (D)	100,910	(43%)
1996 Primary		
Roscoe G. Bartlett (R)	42,704	(85%)
John J. Kubricky (R)	4,183	(8%)
Fredric M. Parker (R)	3,216	(6%)
1994 General		
Roscoe G. Bartlett (R)	122,809	(66%)
Paul Muldowney (D)	63,411	(34%)

Previous Winning Percentages: 1992 (54%)

CAMPAIGN FINANCE

	Receipts	Receipts from PACs		Expend-itures
1996				
Bartlett (R)	$464,344	$123,943	(27%)	$253,966
Crawford (D)	$390,231	$105,700	(27%)	$383,127
1994				
Bartlett (R)	$369,957	$130,871	(35%)	$369,904
Muldowney (D)	$266,365	$49,050	(18%)	$257,690

DISTRICT VOTE FOR PRESIDENT

	1996		1992
D	95,502 (38%)	**D**	88,196 (34%)
R	129,827 (52%)	**R**	125,494 (48%)
I	21,159 (9%)	**I**	46,376 (18%)

KEY VOTES

1997	
Ban "partial birth" abortions	Y
1996	
Approve farm bill	Y
Deny public education to illegal immigrants	Y
Repeal ban on certain assault-style weapons	Y
Increase minimum wage	N
Freeze defense spending	N
Approve welfare overhaul	Y
1995	
Approve balanced-budget constitutional amendment	Y
Relax Clean Water Act regulations	Y
Oppose limits on environmental regulations	N
Reduce projected Medicare spending	Y
Approve GOP budget with tax and spending cuts	Y

VOTING STUDIES

	Presidential Support		Party Unity		Conservative Coalition	
Year	**S**	**O**	**S**	**O**	**S**	**O**
1996	30	70	95	5	96	4
1995	16	83	97	3	99	1
1994	40	60	98	1	100	0
1993	35	65	98	1	95	5

INTEREST GROUP RATINGS

Year	ADA	AFL-CIO	CCUS	ACU
1996	0	n/a	100	100
1995	0	0	100	100
1994	0	0	92	100
1993	5	18	91	100

7 Elijah E. Cummings (D)

Of Baltimore — Elected 1996; 1st full term

Biographical Information

Born: Jan. 18, 1951, Baltimore, Md.

Education: Howard U., B.A. 1973; U. of Maryland, J.D. 1976.

Occupation: Lawyer.

Family: Separated; two children

Religion: Baptist.

Political Career: Md. House, 1983-96, speaker pro tem, 1995-95.

Capitol Office: 1632 Longworth Bldg. 20515; 225-4741.

Committees

Government Reform & Oversight
Civil Service; National Security, International Affairs & Criminal Justice

Transportation & Infrastructure
Aviation; Surface Transportation

In Washington: Cummings entered Congress following a 13-year career in the Maryland House, where he developed a reputation as both a dedicated liberal and a skilled consensus-builder. He rose to the chamber's second-ranking position, Speaker pro tem — the highest state office ever held by a black Maryland lawmaker.

Cummings' opportunity to try for the 7th came because of the surprise departure of Democratic Rep. Kweisi Mfume, who resigned from the House in February 1996 to become president of the NAACP. During nine years representing the heavily black Baltimore district, Mfume became a prominent spokesman for minority interests.

Twenty-seven Democrats and five Republi-cans filed for the March special primary in the 7th. Outpacing his rivals' fundraising, Cummings was able to finance a print and broadcast advertising campaign that helped establish him as the clear front-runner. Also, he collected endorsements from the Sun and the Afro-American newspapers in Baltimore, from the Baltimore Building and Construction Trades Council and its 17 unions, from state House Speaker Casper Taylor and state Senate Majority Leader Clarence Blount, and from a group of political leaders in the Catonsville area of Baltimore County. The county part of the 7th is three-fifths white and more conservative than the rest of the district; it accounts for about one-fifth of the district's population.

Cummings finished comfortably ahead of the Democratic pack, winning nomination with 37 percent of the vote. In an April special election he handily defeated the GOP nominee to earn the right to fill out Mfume's term in the 104th. Cummings also was nominated to seek a full term in November in the overwhelmingly Democratic 7th.

After his special election victory, Cummings said, "I will continue to speak up for those whose voices are rarely, if ever, heard, and stand up for those who cannot stand up for themselves." Once in office, he was assigned to the Transportation and Infrastructure Committee and to the Government Reform and Oversight Committee.

Cummings tried to gain a leadership role at the start of the 105th Congress when he requested the ranking minority seat on the National Economic Growth, Natural Resources and Regulatory Affairs Subcommittee of the Government Reform and Oversight Committee.

Instead, the post went to independent Bernard Sanders of Vermont. In return, Minority Leader Richard A. Gephardt, D-Mo., named Cummings to the Democratic Policy Committee and promised him the next open seat on the panel that makes Democratic committee assignments.

During his first year in the House, Cummings showed every indication that he will be a reliable liberal. He voted against the welfare overhaul bill and against allowing employers to offer their workers compensatory time off in lieu of over-time pay. He voted to kill the space station but favored increasing funding for other science pro-grams by $5.3 billion.

A supporter of abortion rights, he opposed efforts to ban what opponents call a "partial birth" abortion, he favored allowing the federal employee health care plan to pay for abortions, and he backed allowing overseas military hospi-tals to perform abortions. Early in the 105th, he voted in favor of an early release of funds for international family planning, without any abor-tion restrictions.

He is opposed to denying public education to illegal immigrants. And in the 105th, he voted against term limits.

Cummings' first speech on the House floor in April 1996 called for both parties to work togeth-er to solve the nation's problems. "Our world would be a much better world and a much better place if we would only concentrate on the things we have in common instead of concentrating on our differences," he said. "It is easy to find differ-ences, very easy. We need to take more time to find common ground."

Two months later, in June, he criticized Republican plans to roll back the projected growth of Medicare and Medicaid. "The American

MARYLAND 7
Inner-city Baltimore; Western Baltimore County

Downtown Baltimore's resurgence looks like a mirage to residents of the low-income black neighborhoods of West Baltimore and to those living north and east of the city center. The areas' ills — crime, drugs, teen pregnancies, school dropouts, lack of job opportunities — starkly contrast with the vitality of the Inner Harbor.

Baltimore's population reached 939,000 in the 1960s, but the subsequent spread of urban problems sparked an exodus. By 1990, the city's population was 736,000, and an increasing number of middle-class blacks were joining whites in the suburbs.

As a result, the 7th — once wholly within the city — now swings out across western Baltimore County. But by following the black migration west on Liberty Heights Avenue toward Randallstown and down the Baltimore National Pike to Catonsville, the 7th maintains a 71 percent black population.

During his tenure as Baltimore mayor, former Democratic Gov. William Donald Schaefer was berated by black activists for funneling development money into downtown. Since becoming mayor in 1987, Democrat Kurt L. Schmoke has channeled some resources to low-income communities in the flats east of downtown, to row houses along Broadway and to tenements in West Baltimore. But major improvements have been slow.

The picture within the city (which contributes nearly 80 percent of the 7th's population) is not all bleak. Just north of the downtown business district is the gentrified Mount Vernon area, home of the Walters Art Gallery and the Peabody music academy. Farther north are Johns Hopkins University and the Baltimore Museum of Art.

To the west is Druid Hill Park and the Baltimore Zoo. To the east is Waverly and Memorial Stadium, home of the baseball Orioles for 37 years; the team left for a new downtown park in 1992. The National Football League's Baltimore Ravens have been playing there until their downtown facility is completed. To the northeast is Morgan State University.

Though overshadowed by Harborplace, the old retail section west of the downtown hub survives; the Lexington food market and Baltimore Arena are here. There are middle-class black communities along Liberty Heights Road in West Baltimore. The national headquarters of the NAACP is near the city's western border. Over the line in Baltimore County are mainly black suburban settlements in Woodlawn and Lochearn. The Social Security Administration complex and Security Square Mall in Woodlawn are important sources of jobs.

To the south is Catonsville, site of the University of Maryland at Baltimore County. To the north, the 7th reaches to Randallstown, then leaps through a mostly undeveloped area to Reisterstown (both suburbs are shared with the 3rd District). Although black residents have a strong presence in many of the 7th's suburban areas, the Baltimore County portion of the 7th is three-fifths white.

1990 Population: 597,680. White 162,648 (27%), Black 424,132 (71%), Other 10,900 (2%). Hispanic origin 5,268 (1%). 18 and over 448,177 (75%), 62 and over 87,650 (15%). Median age: 32.

people have given us a clear mandate. They have overwhelmingly told us time and time again to protect our neediest citizens, the disabled, the poor, our children and the elderly," Cummings said. "My colleagues on the other side of the aisle have a different vision. Their priorities are jumbled, their budget reflects a flawed economic theory and confusion."

In the state House, Cummings represented a mainly black district in the southern part of West Baltimore, and while he was identified with traditional liberal causes there as well — working for better inner-city health care and education, supporting gun control, and so on — he also worked to get private-sector employers involved in partnerships with government to spur urban economic development and improve city schools. The Sun endorsement noted the role Cummings had played in banning liquor advertisements from inner-city billboards, and it also praised his "skill in developing consensus in a demographically diverse legislature."

Befitting his interests in legal and economic issues, he served as a vice chairman of the Constitutional and Administrative Law and Economic Matters committees in the state House. He touts his legislative efforts to prevent and treat AIDS, foster partnerships between private corporations and elementary schools and create a "boot camp" program to help former prison inmates to find jobs.

On the House floor in February 1997, he talked about the need to connect all schools, especially those in minority communities, to the Internet.

"We must bring the 21st century into every classroom in America," he said. "Technological literacy is essential to succeed in the new economy. We must provide all students access to a computer, good software, and trained teachers. I encourage local businesses, public organizations, educational institutions, parents, teachers, and community members to participate in this effort by volunteering to help link our schools to the information highway, place computer equipment in classrooms, and provide training.

"African-Americans, historically concentrated in agriculture, personal service, and blue-collar occupations, are now disproportionately displaced in the emerging Information Age. There is still very little computer software geared to minorities. There are still relatively few minority firms with a presence on the World Wide Web. Now is the time to commit to helping underserved minority schools. The longer we wait, the wider the gap between these kids and the kids who are technology-fluent expands."

At Home: Born in Baltimore, Cummings was one of seven children of working-class parents who had migrated to the city from a life of farm labor in South Carolina. Growing up in a rental house, he recalls the family scrimping and saving to buy their own home in a city neighborhood that was integrating. They moved there in 1963, when Cummings was 12. "I had never played on grass before," he told a reporter for Baltimore magazine.

Adept early on in the art of politics, Cummings was president of his high school senior class. He graduated Phi Beta Kappa from Howard University and earned a law degree from the University of Maryland in 1976. Six years later, he was elected to the state House. Cummings has two children: a teenage daughter with his wife (from whom he has been separated for years), and a 2-year-old daughter with another woman.

After Mfume announced in December 1995 that he would leave the House to head the NAACP, the Maryland legislature merged the primaries for a special House election in the 7th with the March primaries that had been scheduled to nominate candidates for election to a full term in November.

With a total of 32 candidates campaigning in the special primaries, the weeks leading up to the voting were filled with crowded candidate forums that provided little time for substantive debate. Cummings' most formidable Democratic rival was the Rev. Frank M. Reid III. The pastor of Baltimore's huge Bethel African Methodist Episcopal Church, Reid was a familiar figure to district voters who watched his sermons, televised nationally on Black Entertainment Television. Reid also was supported by his stepbrother, Baltimore Mayor Kurt L. Schmoke.

But on the strength of his array of endorsements, as well as campaign contributions from business and lobbying contacts he made in the legislature, Cummings ran 13 points ahead of Reid, who took 24 percent of the vote. State Sen. Delores G. Kelley, who took 10 percent of the vote, was the only other Democrat in double digits.

The outcome of the April special election was a foregone conclusion in the 7th, which is more than 70 percent black. Cummings won more than 80 percent of the vote against Republican Kenneth Kondner, a white dental technician who had challenged Mfume in the previous three elections. Kondner and Cummings also faced each other in November, and the incumbent won 83 percent of the vote.

HOUSE ELECTIONS

1996 General		
Elijah E. Cummings (D)	115,764	(83%)
Kenneth Kondner (R)	22,929	(17%)
1996 Special		
Elijah E. Cummings (D)	18,870	(81%)
Kenneth Kondner (R)	4,449	(19%)
1996 Special Primary		
Elijah E. Cummings (D)	23,156	(37%)
Frank M. Reid III (D)	14,720	(24%)
Delores G. Kelley (D)	5,918	(10%)
A. Dwight Pettit (D)	4,384	(7%)
Mary W. Conaway (D)	3,003	(5%)
Kenneth Montague (D)	1,899	(3%)
Medgar L. Reid (D)	1,850	(3%)
Clarence Davis (D)	1,171	(2%)
Traci Miller (D)	1,000	(2%)
Salima Siler Marriott (D)	945	(2%)

CAMPAIGN FINANCE

	Receipts	Receipts from PACs	Expend-itures
1996			
Cummings (D)	$741,465	$291,929 (39%)	$691,787

DISTRICT VOTE FOR PRESIDENT

	1996		1992
D	127,850 (81%)	**D**	159,191 (78%)
R	23,757 (15%)	**R**	32,431 (16%)
I	5,207 (3%)	**I**	13,009 (6%)

KEY VOTES

1997	
Ban "partial-birth" abortions	N
1996	
Increase minimum wage	Y
Freeze defense spending	Y
Approve welfare overhaul	N

VOTING STUDIES

	Presidential Support		Party Unity		Conservative Coalition	
Year	**S**	**O**	**S**	**O**	**S**	**O**
1996	76†	24†	94†	6†	18†	82†

† Not eligible for all recorded votes.

INTEREST GROUP RATINGS

Year	ADA	AFL-CIO	CCUS	ACU
1996	92	n/a	22	0

8 Constance A. Morella (R)

Of Bethesda — Elected 1986, 6th term

Biographical Information

Born: Feb. 12, 1931, Somerville, Mass.

Education: Boston U., B.A. 1954; American U., M.A. 1967.

Occupation: Professor.

Family: Husband, Anthony C. Morella; nine children.

Religion: Roman Catholic.

Political Career: Candidate for Md. House, 1974; Md. House, 1979-87; sought Republican nomination for U.S. House, 1980.

Capitol Office: 2228 Rayburn Bldg. 20515; 225-5341.

Committees

Government Reform & Oversight
Civil Service; District of Columbia

Science
Basic Research; Technology (chairman)

In Washington: Although Morella supports President Clinton's policies more often than any other House Republican, and votes along with her party less regularly than anyone else in the GOP Conference, it would be a mistake to think of her as a Democrat in Republican's clothing. She is conservative on fiscal issues and, despite her low "party unity" score, she does vote for the GOP position more often than not.

In a closely divided House, every seat counts in keeping the GOP in control of committees, and Morella's district, due to its party registration and density of federal workers, could easily be in Democratic hands if it weren't for Morella. That helps explain why Republican leaders don't get more worked up about Morella's independent and sometimes liberal voting record, which has earned her five comfortable re-elections.

Sometimes, to be sure, she tests the limits of her party's patience. In January 1997, she was one of nine House Republicans who refused to support Newt Gingrich's bid for re-election as Speaker.

But she voted "present" rather than actively supporting any other candidate, and she did not make a big deal about her decision. This quality of quietness about her moments of reluctance to go along with the party also makes her maverick votes easier to forgive.

Morella does not sit on powerhouse committees where she would come into regular conflict with her party's leaders, and when she does disagree she does not usually raise a public fuss or generally go out of her way to rally support against her party's position.

And if Republicans are unlikely to take Morella into their inner circle, neither do they give her the cold shoulder. She is too personally pleasant to get brusque treatment.

Even as she was voting in 1995 against bills derived from the House GOP's "Contract With America" more often than any other member of the conference, she acknowledged that party leaders were treating her with kid gloves. "I think it has something to do with style," she said. "I don't flaunt it. There are times when I won't speak on an issue because a majority of my colleagues feel the other way."

Morella, who co-chaired the Democrat-dominated House Women's Caucus during the 104th, supports abortion rights (she has opposed GOP attempts to ban a particular abortion technique that opponents call "partial-birth" abortion) and was dismayed when abortion restrictions were attached to a number of spending bills. But her tone was more one of disappointment than anger.

When the House in 1995 took up a controversial spending bill to fund the departments of Labor, Health and Human Services, and Education, Gingrich worked hard to assuage both conservatives and moderates who had reservations about the package. The vote was a nail-biter. Morella voted against the bill — with Barney Frank of Massachusetts yelling encouragement to her from the Democratic side — but not until it was clear that Gingrich had won his majority.

Morella found many other occasions to side with Democrats against her party's signature legislation. She was one of only five Republicans who voted against a welfare bill derived from the "Contract With America," and the only Republican who supported the Democratic alternative. (She did vote for the final, modified welfare overhaul that was enacted in 1996.) She was one of 10 Republicans who voted against the party's massive budget-balancing package in 1995 — even though she had supported the plan's controversial provisions to limit the growth of Medicare spending in a separate stand-alone vote. Morella joined with just seven other Republicans in opposing an omnibus regulatory overhaul bill, and only she and one other Republican opposed a temporary moratorium on new regulations.

Morella, whose district is home to tens of thousands of federal employees, sits on the Government Reform and Oversight Committee, and chairs the Technology Subcommittee of the Science panel. The latter post gives her jurisdiction over several federal agencies in her district,

MARYLAND 8
Montgomery County

A huge federal government presence and a burgeoning private sector spurred a boom in Montgomery County during the 1980s, increasing population by nearly a third to more than 750,000. That put Montgomery ahead of the city of Baltimore as Maryland's largest jurisdiction.

With its steady employment base and large population of educated professionals, Montgomery County is one of the nation's most affluent places. In Potomac, million-dollar homes are interspersed with horse farms. Upscale stores in Chevy Chase and Bethesda anchor a bustling retail trade along Route 355.

Still, the recession of the early 1990s slowed the real estate development and retail sales that keyed Montgomery County's growth. And the county is not entirely dominated by upper-income residents. Most of the county's recent growth has been in middle-income communities in outer suburbs such as Gaithersburg, Germantown and Olney.

Older parts of Rockville, Gaithersburg and the Kensington-Wheaton area have working-class and some low-income areas, home to many of the county's black residents. There are also growing numbers of Hispanic and Asian immigrants.

Public employment underpins Montgomery's economy and sets its political tone. About 60,000 federal employees and 20,000 county workers live in the 8th. Democrats have long dominated local politics here.

Yet Morella has thrived, largely because of her reputation as one of the most liberal House Republicans. And the county is suburban enough to make it a challenge for Democratic presidential candidates. Bill Clinton mastered Montgomery, beating Bob Dole in the 8th by 57 percent to 38 percent (and taking the whole county, some of which is in the 4th District, with 59 percent). But the 1984 and 1988 Democratic tickets won Montgomery narrowly.

Despite Clinton's surge, there are Republicans who view Montgomery County as a potential partisan growth area. They point to the increased importance of such private-sector employers as Marriott International, IBM and Loral Federal Systems, which bought IBM's missile systems operation in Gaithersburg.

Still, many of the county's private employers are research and development companies that rely on federal contracts or assistance. Many of these companies are along the I-270 "technology corridor." Nearby are such federal installations as the National Institutes of Health (Bethesda), the National Institute of Standards and Technology (Gaithersburg) and Department of Energy labs (Germantown). The county is a national center for biotechnology research.

County officials have tried to preserve the remnants of Montgomery's farming heritage in the northern and western areas of the county. Attitudes in these areas are more conservative and Republican voting habits stronger than elsewhere in the county.

1990 Population: 597,682. White 486,990 (81%), Black 49,029 (8%), Other 61,663 (10%). Hispanic origin 37,771 (6%). 18 and over 454,721 (76%), 62 and over 76,602 (13%). Median age: 34.

including the National Institute of Standards and Technology (NIST).

She has found ways to attend to her district's concerns, from trying to boost NIST funding to advocating an end to the government shutdowns that were part of the fallout over budget negotiations during the 105th. Along with Republican Thomas M. Davis III (who represents Washington, D.C., suburbs in Northern Virginia), she opposed a provision of the GOP tax-cut package in 1995 that would have meant a higher pension contribution from federal workers, in effect dooming the bill in the Government Reform Committee and punting it to the Budget Committee. (For the 105th, she serves as Davis' vice chair on the Government Reform Subcommittee on the District of Columbia.)

But Morella explained that her floor vote against the tax package was occasioned by her belief that tax cuts would have contradicted her support for a balanced-budget constitutional amendment. Despite her sometimes liberal leanings, Morella scores high marks from budget watchdog groups such as the Concord Coalition and the National Taxpayers Union.

She opposed GOP attempts to boost defense spending above the level requested by Clinton, and voted against funding the deployment of troops in Bosnia. "Frankly, sending 20,000 of our people to another country where we don't see it's a security risk for us is really perilous," she fretted. Morella would have voted to cut off funding for further production of the B-2 bomber, but missed the vote because she was in China attending a United Nations conference on women.

In addition to expressing the will of her district, as she determines it, on big-picture issues, Morella pushes for smaller items of interest to her suburban constituency. She supported a bipartisan effort to pressure the Federal Communications Commission to require broadcasters to present more educational programming for children, and she pushed for tough child support enforcement provisions in the welfare bill. She also joined with Sens. Barbara A. Mikulski, D-Md., and Kay Bailey Hutchison, R-Texas, in support of a bill to expand use of Individual Retirement Accounts (IRA) to allow families with earnings above $40,000 to enjoy IRA tax benefits.

Morella has never gone out of her way to link up with the national GOP. It was not until 1992, after 30 years as a Republican, that she attended her first national Republican convention. And then she went as a staunch abortion rights supporter opposing a platform plank that described abortion as murder. Morella, who faces some intraparty opposition at home from more conservative Republicans, was nearly denied a 1996 delegate slot by the Maryland GOP convention.

At Home: In 1996, Morella again heard grumblings from conservatives calling her too liberal, and from liberals calling her too conservative. But neither the GOP right nor the Democrats were able to recruit top-tier challengers. Morella won renomination with almost two-thirds of the vote against three other Republicans. In November, Democrat Don Mooers, a former congressional aide and State Department official, held her to her lowest-ever re-election tally: a still very comfortable 61 percent.

Although Democrat Michael D. Barnes held the 8th for four terms prior to his 1986 Senate bid, the district previously had favored such moderate-to-liberal Republicans as Charles McC. Mathias Jr., Gilbert Gude and Newton I. Steers Jr. (Steers had thwarted Morella's first House bid in a 1980 primary.) Morella successfully tied herself to that tradition.

A community college English professor, Morella was involved in environmental and social issues during her eight years in the Maryland House, but the biggest factor in her 1986 House victory was her vivacious personality. She played up her family's immigrant heritage and her working-class upbringing and noted that she and her husband had raised nine children (including her late sister's six).

Her Democratic foe, state Sen. Stewart Bainum, was a millionaire businessman with liberal views. But his wooden campaign style contrasted poorly with Morella's manner. Morella won with 53 percent.

The Montgomery County Democratic Party, which has dominated the affluent but liberal-leaning county for years, worked hard to energize voters in 1992 in behalf of the Clinton-Gore ticket and Democratic Sen. Mikulski's re-election bid. But the party made a tepid effort for Morella's challenger, Edward J. Heffernan, a former House aide making his first try for elective office. Although Clinton and Mikulski easily carried the 8th District, Morella kept the House seat Republican with 73 percent of the vote.

HOUSE ELECTIONS

1996 General		
Constance A. Morella (R)	152,538	(61%)
Don Mooers (D)	96,229	(39%)
1996 Primary		
Constance A. Morella (R)	28,818	(65%)
Barrie S. Ciliberti (R)	11,845	(27%)
John C. Webb Jr. (R)	2,770	(6%)
Luis F. Columba (R)	698	(2%)
1994 General		
Constance A. Morella (R)	143,449	(70%)
Steven Van Grack (D)	60,660	(30%)

Previous Winning Percentages: **1992** (73%) **1990** (74%) **1988** (63%) **1986** (53%)

CAMPAIGN FINANCE

	Receipts	Receipts from PACs	Expend-itures
1996			
Morella (R)	$413,371	$197,549 (48%)	$559,807
Mooers (D)	$201,595	$20,187 (10%)	$196,858
1994			
Morella (R)	$375,061	$186,528 (50%)	$306,968
Van Grack (D)	$15,801	0	$10,802

DISTRICT VOTE FOR PRESIDENT

	1996		1992
D	156,450 (57%)	**D**	156,043 (53%)
R	103,327 (38%)	**R**	103,477 (35%)
I	12,200 (4%)	**I**	35,599 (12%)

KEY VOTES

1997	
Ban "partial birth" abortions	N
1996	
Approve farm bill	Y
Deny public education to illegal immigrants	N
Repeal ban on certain assault-style weapons	N
Increase minimum wage	Y
Freeze defense spending	Y
Approve welfare overhaul	Y
1995	
Approve balanced-budget constitutional amendment	Y
Relax Clean Water Act regulations	N
Oppose limits on environmental regulations	Y
Reduce projected Medicare spending	Y
Approve GOP budget with tax and spending cuts	N

VOTING STUDIES

	Presidential Support		Party Unity		Conservative Coalition	
Year	**S**	**O**	**S**	**O**	**S**	**O**
1996	72	27	55	43	37	61
1995	56	41	63	34	60	34
1994	76	22	45	52	50	47
1993	70	27	47	51	45	52
1992	39	56	46	48	44	44
1991	43	54	39	58	41	57

INTEREST GROUP RATINGS

Year	ADA	AFL-CIO	CCUS	ACU
1996	50	n/a	60	30
1995	45	25	65	25
1994	70	56	83	29
1993	60	67	73	39
1992	70	50	38	35
1991	65	67	60	15

MASSACHUSETTS

Governor: William F. Weld (R)*
First elected: 1990
Length of term: 4 years
Term expires: 1/99
Salary: $90,000 (accepts $75,000)
Term limit: 2 terms
Phone: (617) 727-3600
Born: July 31, 1945; Smithtown, N.Y.
Education: Harvard U., B.A. 1966; Oxford U., 1966-67; Harvard U., J.D. 1970.
Occupation: Lawyer.
Family: Wife, Susan Roosevelt; five children.
Religion: Episcopalian.
Political Career: Republican nominee for Mass. attorney general, 1978; U.S. attorney for Mass., 1981-86; assistant U.S. attorney general, 1986-88.

Lt. Gov.: Argeo Paul Cellucci (R)
First elected: 1990
Length of term: 4 years
Term expires: 1/99
Salary: $75,000
Phone: (617) 727-7200
Born: April 24, 1948; Marlboro, Mass.
Education: Boston College, B.A., 1970, J.D., 1973.
Occupation: Lawyer.
Family: Wife, Janet Garnett; two children.
Religion: Roman Catholic
Political Career: Mass. House, 1977-85; Mass. Senate, 1985-91.

State election official: (617) 727-2830
Democratic headquarters: (617) 426-4760
Republican headquarters: (617) 725-1994.
*Weld was nominated as U.S. envoy to Mexico in May 1997.

STATE LEGISLATURE

General Court. Meeting time varies; usually year-round.

Senate: 40 members, 2-year terms
1996 breakdown: 34D, 6R; 33 men, 7 women
Salary: $46,000
Phone: (617) 722-1455

House of Representatives: 160 members, 2-year terms
1996 breakdown: 134D, 25R, 1I; 122 men, 38 women
Salary: $46,000
Phone: (617) 722-2000

URBAN STATISTICS

City	Population
Boston Mayor Thomas Menino, D	574,283
Worcester Mayor Raymond V. Mariano, D	169,759
Springfield Mayor Michael Albano, N-P	156,983
Lowell Chief Councilman Edward Caulfield, N-P	103,439
New Bedford Mayor Rosemary Tierney, D	99,922

U.S. CONGRESS

Senate: 2 D, 0 R
House: 10 D, 0 R

TERM LIMITS

For state offices: Yes
Senate: 2 Terms
House: 4 Terms

REDISTRICTING

Massachusetts lost one House seat in reapportionment, dropping from 11 districts to 10. The legislature passed the map July 8, 1992; the governor signed it July 9.

ELECTIONS

1996 Presidential Vote

Bill Clinton	61%
Bob Dole	28%
Ross Perot	9%

1992 Presidential Vote

Bill Clinton	48%
George Bush	29%
Ross Perot	23%

1988 Presidential Vote

Michael S. Dukakis	53%
George Bush	45%

POPULATION

1990 population		6,016,425
1980 population		5,737,037
Percent change		+5%
Rank among states:		13
White		90%
Black		5%
Hispanic		5%
Asian or Pacific islander		2%
Urban		84%
Rural		16%
Born in state		69%
Foreign-born		10%
Under age 18	1,353,075	22%
Ages 18-64	3,844,066	64%
65 and older	819,284	14%
Median age		33.6

MISCELLANEOUS

Capital: Boston
Number of counties: 14
Per capita income: $22,897 (1991)
Rank among states: 3
Total area: 8,284 sq. miles
Rank among states: 45

MASSACHUSETTS

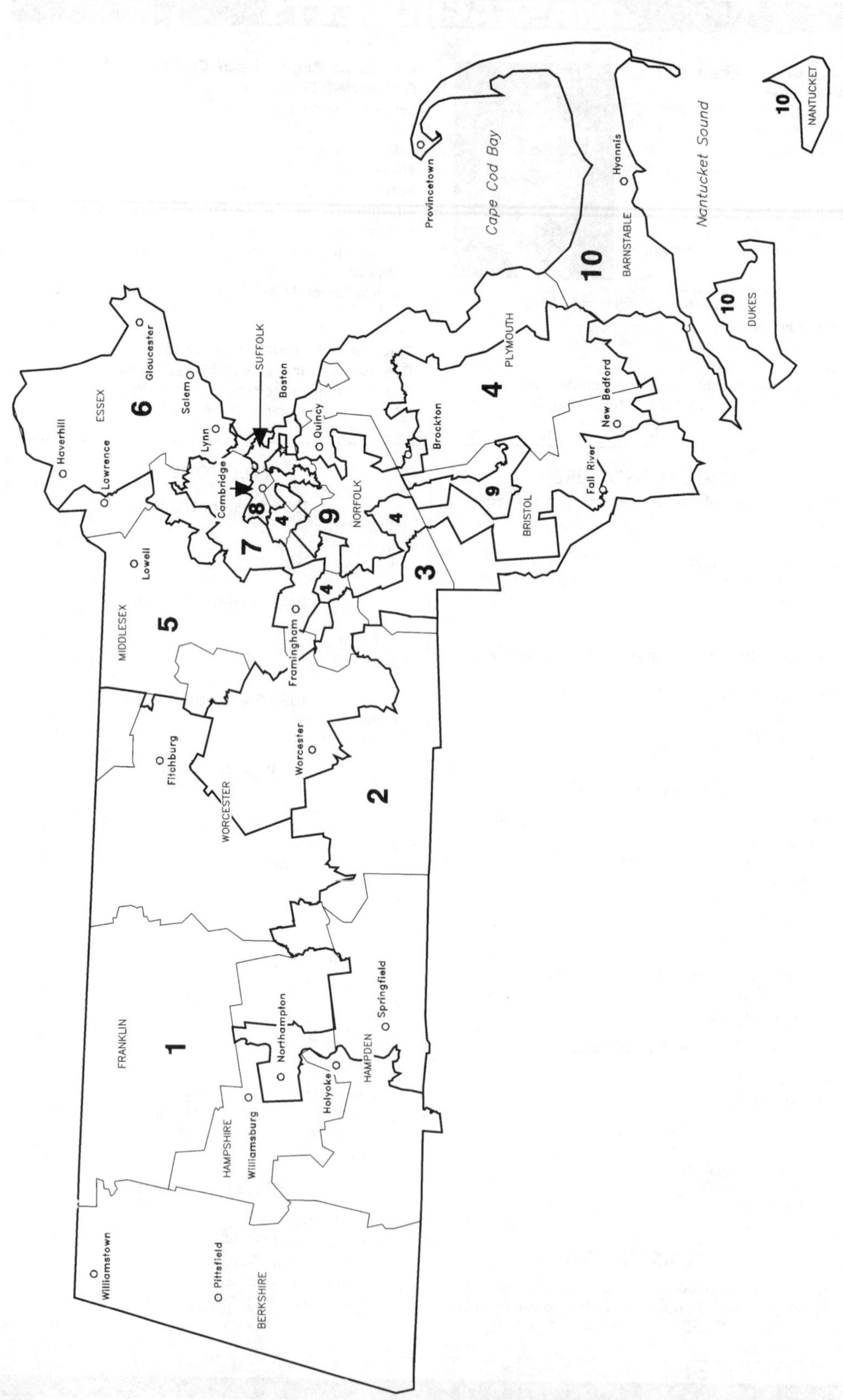

Edward M. Kennedy (D)

Of Boston — Elected 1962; 6th full term

Biographical Information

Born: Feb. 22, 1932, Boston, Mass.

Education: Harvard U., B.A. 1956; International Law School, The Hague (The Netherlands), 1958; U. of Virginia, LL.B. 1959.

Military Service: Army, 1951-53.

Occupation: Lawyer.

Family: Wife, Victoria Reggie; three children, two stepchildren.

Religion: Roman Catholic.

Political Career: Suffolk County assistant district attorney, 1961-62; sought Democratic nomination for president, 1980.

Capitol Office: 315 Russell Bldg. 20510; 224-4543.

Committees

Armed Services
Acquisition & Technology; Personnel; Seapower (ranking)

Judiciary
Constitution, Federalism & Property Rights; Immigration (ranking)

Labor & Human Resources (ranking)
Employment & Training; Public Health & Safety (ranking)

Joint Economic

In Washington: Kennedy's national image is defined by family tragedy, scandals, tabloid headlines and jokes by late-night comedians. But 35 years into his Senate career, Kennedy remains the country's leading liberal, and his perspicacious defense of old Democratic values rallied his party and helped score some big legislative victories during the 104th Congress despite Republican control. The earnestness of his tirades in favor of labor and environmental protections and a social safety net win Kennedy grudging respect even from colleagues who differ with him on the issues.

And, with Democratic leaders drifting rightward in response to the more conservative era on the Hill, Kennedy remains an anchor for his party, helping the minority maintain a focus. "He's as good at what he does as Michael Jordan is at playing basketball," said no less a political observer than President Clinton, in an interview with The New Yorker. "I mean, he can always see the opening. He's got lateral vision, and it's uncanny what he can do."

Kennedy exploited political openings for two major pieces of legislation that were enacted over strong Republican opposition in 1996: an increase in the minimum wage and a bill that mandated health insurance portability, guaranteeing that individuals who lose or leave their jobs can maintain coverage even if they are sick. The two proposals were keynotes of Kennedy's difficult reelection battle in 1994, and he honed his message on the Massachusetts stump. But he was able to shepherd the plans through Congress by dint of procedural knowledge and legerdemain.

The ranking member of the Labor and Human Resources Committee, Kennedy pushed for a minimum wage increase in the 104th even when members of his own party thought it was a lost cause.

Kennedy and other friends of organized labor spent much of the Congress fighting off GOP efforts to scale back worker-safety protections and afford employers the option of giving workers comp time in lieu of overtime pay.

But in March 1996, Kennedy and his allies saw an opening to press the wage increase when Republicans unexpectedly left a parks bill exposed to amendment. Senate Majority Leader Bob Dole, R-Kan., was forced to withdraw the underlying bill, but Kennedy threatened to attach the minimum wage provisions to every bill coming up for a vote. His efforts were heralded in the news media, and the pressure built as dozens of House Republicans broke with their leadership in favor of the politically popular raise. A 90-cent increase, packaged with a $10 billion collection of tax breaks desired by the GOP, was signed by Clinton amid great fanfare in August 1996.

That same month, Clinton also was granted his wish to sign a health insurance bill. The portability law was a much-downsized remnant of Clinton's effort in the 103rd to push a national health care plan, a goal of Kennedy's for decades. Kennedy, in fact, joined with Labor Chairwoman Nancy Landon Kassebaum, R-Kan., in creating a "Teflon coalition" to resist all attempts to expand the bill's scope so much as to doom its chances of passage. (Kennedy introduced for the 105th a comprehensive managed care bill to establish standard regulations for health plans.)

Kassebaum and Kennedy mustered the bill out of committee unanimously, but saw it languish for a year on the Senate calendar. A plug from Clinton in his 1996 State of the Union address helped bring it to the fore; once the bill had its day it passed the Senate, too, unanimously. But the House passed a version containing provisions creating medical savings accounts that Kennedy found unacceptable. He blocked Dole's efforts to convene a conference until he could reach an informal agreement with House Ways and Means Chairman Bill Archer, R-Texas. After Dole's departure from the Senate to concentrate on his presidential bid, Republicans grew hungry for tangible legislative accomplishments to show voters.

Kennedy's coupling with Kassebaum was typical of his methods; although the Reagan-era caricature of Kennedy as a big-government bleeding heart has stuck, he consistently has been able to form alliances with Republican senators. As retired Sen. Alan K. Simpson, R-Wyo., once said, "We don't vote together an awful lot, but we legislate together a lot." When Kennedy broke with his old ally over certain business and family provisions in the 1996 immigration law, he found a new buddy in pro-immigration Republican Spencer Abraham of Michigan, who replaces Simpson as chairman of Judiciary's Immigration panel during the 105th. Kennedy even worked with Lauch Faircloth, R-N.C., one of his most conservative adversaries, on a successful 1996 effort to federalize the crime of church burning. He teamed with Republican Orrin G. Hatch early in the 105th in an unsuccessful effort to provide additional health insurance for uninsured children.

Kennedy saw some big battles go awry during the 104th; he was disappointed that Clinton signed a bill that ended welfare as an entitlement, and his late-session filibuster against a bill that made it harder for Federal Express employees to unionize was broken. Kennedy's charge against a bill blocking recognition of same-gender marriage was lonely and not fruitful. But despite Republican control, the 104th represented for Kennedy a continuation of the upward arc of his late career.

After relinquishing his presidential ambitions some years ago, Kennedy seemed to drop his guard. But public fascination with his personal life did not abate, and his rather libertine ways made Kennedy a near-constant butt of jokes. On Easter Weekend 1991, Kennedy roused his son and nephew out of bed to visit some nightclubs in Palm Beach, Fla. His nephew, William Kennedy Smith, was charged with rape. Although Smith was acquitted, Kennedy appeared a less-than-perfect role model.

For months, Kennedy's public portrait was unflattering: testifying in the rape trial; apologizing for the "faults in the conduct of my personal life"; sitting mutely at the confirmation hearings for Supreme Court Justice Clarence Thomas. Kennedy's near silence was a sharp disappointment to women and others who, in other days, would have counted on him.

But after the rape trial, Kennedy grabbed control of his life in an effort to undo what damage had been done. In July 1992, six months after Smith was acquitted, Kennedy remarried. His new wife is Washington attorney Victoria Reggie, the daughter of old family friends.

In October 1994, Kennedy's name was cleared by the Senate Ethics Committee, which had quietly investigated allegations of harassment and drug use leveled by a former aide in a 1992 book. This vindication anticipated Kennedy's triumph at the polls (when his youngest son, Patrick, also was elected, as a representative from Rhode Island).

Kennedy started his career without any of the leadership pressures that descended on him later. He was 30 years old, his brothers were running the country, and he voted with them while looking out for his state's interests.

In time, he became an innovative and often successful legislator, particularly during the early 1970s, after not only the 1969 Chappaquiddick tragedy but also his most embarrassing Senate defeat, his ouster as majority whip in 1971.

Kennedy had been elected whip in 1969, beating Finance Chairman Russell B. Long, D-La., who had performed erratically in the post. The vote was taken only months after New York Sen. Robert F. Kennedy's assassination, which made the youngest Kennedy the rising star.

But he was bored with the odd parliamentary jobs that make effective leaders. Then that summer, his image was shattered for all time when he drove his car off a bridge at Chappaquiddick and his companion in the car, Mary Jo Kopechne, drowned. When Senate Democrats elected their leaders in 1971, they chose Robert C. Byrd of West Virginia for whip, 31-24.

As he would do more than a decade later upon shelving his national ambitions, Kennedy returned to legislating. As chairman of Labor's Health Subcommittee, he wrote legislation with his House counterpart, Florida Democrat Paul G. Rogers. Together they crafted bills financing research into cancer and heart and lung diseases, family planning and doctor training.

Since 1968, people had looked to Kennedy to run for president. In the fall of 1979, apparently tempted by early polls showing him far ahead of President Jimmy Carter, Kennedy launched his campaign without offering any clear idea of why he wanted to be president. He talked of the need for stronger leadership, but so clumsily as to raise the question of whether he could provide it.

Only in the campaign's second half — by which time Kennedy was essentially beaten — did he present the clear liberal argument he took to the convention. The changes did not bring him any closer to nomination, but they kept him alive as a liberal leader. His stirring Democratic convention speech, with its liberal affirmation that "the work goes on, the cause endures, the hope still lives, and the dream shall never die," helped restore some lost luster.

At Home: Like Chappaquiddick 22 years earlier, the Palm Beach incident renewed doubts about Kennedy's judgment and revived Republican hopes of defeating him at the polls. When a summer 1994 survey showed GOP challenger Mitt Romney within single-digits of the senator, those hopes looked plausible.

Romney, a venture capitalist, tapped personal assets as the basis of his $7.6 million effort. His television spots showed the 62-year-old senator looking tired and haggard, playing up the contrast to the handsome, vigorous challenger. When Romney questioned Kennedy's effectiveness in the Senate, Kennedy toured the state delivering federal checks. He characterized Romney as heartless for putting "profits over people" and questioned his positions in favor of abortion and homosexual rights, given his status in the Mormon Church.

Kennedy punctuated his comeback in two October debates, playing up his experience and making Romney appear unfamiliar with the legislative process. In one of the few bright spots of the season for Democrats, the liberal icon proved his staying power, polling 58 percent.

Kennedy's challenge has been to live up to the standard he set in 1964, when he ran for his first full term less than a year after his brother John's assassination.

Bedridden after an airplane crash, he beat Republican Howard Whitmore Jr. by 74 percent to 25 percent; the victory margin of 1,129,244 votes was the widest in state history.

His 1970 campaign was waged in the shadow of the Chappaquiddick accident the year before. Even some loyally Democratic Bay Staters had doubts, and Kennedy took 62 percent of the vote against Republican Josiah Spaulding.

In 1976, he brushed aside three anti-busing and anti-abortion challengers in the primary, then crushed GOP businessman Michael Robertson by 1 million votes.

In 1982, Kennedy met his first Republican foe able to draw attention on his own. Raymond Shamie, a wealthy inventor, spent more than $1 million in an imaginative campaign in which he offered $10,000 to whoever could "GET TED KENNEDY TO DEBATE RAY SHAMIE." Kennedy accepted Shamie's offer, asking that the reward go to a Catholic school in Hanover. The debate had little impact; Kennedy won 61 percent.

Kennedy burst into politics in 1962 by winning the election to fill the remaining two years of his brother's Senate term. John Kennedy had arranged for family friend Benjamin A. Smith to get the seat when he became president in 1961, and Smith then stepped aside for the younger Kennedy in 1962.

Edward J. McCormack, nephew of House Speaker John W. McCormack, was not as obliging. He derided Kennedy's qualifications, noting his meager experience as an assistant district attorney in Boston and said in a Democratic primary debate: "If your name were Edward Moore [instead of Edward Moore Kennedy], your candidacy would be a joke."

Kennedy easily won the primary. In November, he took 55 percent of the vote against Republican George Cabot Lodge.

SENATE ELECTIONS

1994 General		
Edward M. Kennedy (D)	1,265,997	(58%)
W. Mitt Romney (R)	894,000	(41%)
1994 Primary		
Edward M. Kennedy (D)	391,637	(99%)
Write-ins (D)	4,498	(1%)

Previous Winning Percentages: **1988** (65%) **1982** (61%) **1976** (69%) **1970** (62%) **1964** (74%) **1962†** (55%)

† Special election

CAMPAIGN FINANCE

	Receipts	Receipts from PACs		Expend-itures
1994				
Kennedy (D)	$9,816,808	$7,510	(0%)	$10,540,244
Romney (R)	$7,628,061	$8,500	(0%)	$7,624,491

KEY VOTES

1997	
Approve balanced-budget constitutional amendment	N
Approve chemical weapons treaty	Y
1996	
Approve farm bill	N
Limit punitive damages in product liability cases	N
Exempt small businesses from higher minimum wage	N
Approve welfare overhaul	N
Bar job discrimination based on sexual orientation	Y
Override veto of ban on "partial birth" abortions	N
1995	
Approve GOP budget with tax and spending cuts	N
Approve constitutional amendment barring flag desecration	N

VOTING STUDIES

	Presidential Support		Party Unity		Conservative Coalition	
Year	**S**	**O**	**S**	**O**	**S**	**O**
1996	86	12	93	6	8	92
1995	91	8	93	4	12	84
1994	90	5	92	6	19	78
1993	93	3	95	4	10	90
1992	25	73	95	3	5	92
1991	31	67	92	7	13	88

INTEREST GROUP RATINGS

Year	ADA	AFL-CIO	CCUS	ACU
1996	90	n/a	38	0
1995	100	100	33	4
1994	90	88	20	0
1993	90	82	36	4
1992	100	92	20	0
1991	95	83	20	0

John Kerry (D)

Of Boston — Elected 1984; 3rd term

Biographical Information

Born: Dec. 11, 1943, Denver, Colo.
Education: Yale U., B.A. 1966; Boston College, J.D. 1976.
Military Service: Navy, 1968-69.
Occupation: Lawyer.
Family: Wife, Teresa Heinz; two children, three stepchildren.
Religion: Roman Catholic.
Political Career: Lieutenant governor, 1983-85; Democratic nominee for U.S. House, 1972.
Capitol Office: 421 Russell Bldg. 20510; 224-2742.

Committees

Banking, Housing & Urban Affairs
Financial Services & Technology; Housing Opportunity & Community Development (ranking); Securities
Commerce, Science & Transportation
Communications; Oceans & Fisheries (ranking); Science, Technology & Space
Foreign Relations
East Asian & Pacific Affairs (ranking); International Operations; Western Hemisphere, Peace Corps, Narcotics and Terrorism
Select Intelligence
Small Business

In Washington: Kerry faced the possibility of an abrupt halt to his political career in 1996, when he drew a tough re-election challenger in his state's enormously popular governor, Republican William Weld.

But Kerry prevailed by an impressive 7 percentage points. Battle-hardened from that, his first real electoral test, Kerry now finds his name among those mentioned when speculation arises about potential Democratic aspirants to the White House.

Kerry has played his most notable Senate role in foreign affairs, generally supporting President Clinton and fighting off congressional attempts to weaken the executive's control over foreign policy. And nowhere has Clinton turned to Kerry more than on issues related to Vietnam.

More than 20 years after the last U.S. soldiers pulled out of Vietnam, Kerry finds that the conflict still colors his actions and his life. Kerry teamed up with another decorated Vietnam veteran, Sen. John McCain, R-Ariz., to push for the normalization of relations with Vietnam. Clinton strongly supported the idea, as did a number of U.S. companies eager to tap the Vietnam market.

But without Kerry and McCain's backing, such a measure, pushed by a president dogged by his avoidance of military service, would have had a hard time overcoming strong Republican opposition, which was led by Vietnam veteran Sen. Robert C. Smith of New Hampshire and Majority Leader Bob Dole of Kansas.

Smith and Dole argued that Hanoi had been slow to provide a full accounting for U.S. soldiers still missing in action. Kerry and McCain concluded that Vietnam was being responsive in this regard.

In 1994, Kerry and McCain sponsored an amendment that cleared the way for Clinton to lift the longstanding trade embargo with Vietnam. Yet even as he was helping heal old war wounds, Kerry belied a certain ambivalence. "This is not a reward [for Vietnam]," he said. "It's not a question of taking away leverage, but of giving leverage to us" in pursuing information about American soldiers unaccounted for in Vietnam.

The sense-of-the-Senate amendment came a year after Kerry's Select Committee on POW-MIA Affairs concluded that there was "no compelling evidence" that any American remained alive in captivity in Southeast Asia. But even then, Kerry stated, "This report does not close the issue. It is not meant to."

Clinton normalized relations by executive order in July 1995, but the matter was not put to rest in Congress. The anti-Vietnam sentiment was evident in language that North Carolina Republican Jesse Helms attached to his State Department reorganization bill. A provision in that bill would have restricted the use of funds needed for normalization — a reason Clinton cited for vetoing the measure.

Kerry's views of the Vietnam War inform his foreign policy pronouncements in general, particularly when it comes to sending U.S. troops into battle. In 1991, Kerry voted against the resolution authorizing President George Bush to use force in the Persian Gulf, yet he took pains to note his overall support for confrontation with Iraq.

Kerry went to Vietnam as a Navy officer, protested the war when he returned to the United States and entered politics as an (unsuccessful) anti-war candidate for Congress in 1972. Clinton, whose sidestepping of the draft as a youth diminishes his stature as commander-in-chief, has turned to Kerry for counsel on foreign affairs.

Kerry has come to Clinton's side when Republicans in Congress seem to be trying to limit the executive's control over foreign policy. When senators sparred over the administration's stance toward Haiti, Kerry was among those who warned against handcuffing Clinton. "This is not what the Senate does in relationship with the president, unless it is being asked to play politics," Kerry said.

During the 104th, Clinton depended on Kerry often for legislative support on a number of difficult foreign policy bills, most notably to turn back Helms' bid to reorganize the State Department and close three foreign policy-related agencies.

Kerry argued that the GOP bill would infringe on the president's prerogative to manage the State

Department. In early consideration of the bill, he offered a wide-ranging substitute amendment that would give the president six months from the date of enactment to produce his own consolidation scheme. But Kerry's amendment went too far for the administration, which opposed any consolidation. It was defeated in committee.

Then, with Helms holding up several ambassadorial appointments in an effort to get the administration to negotiate, the Foreign Relations chairman re-offered Kerry's compromise on the floor.

Kerry again pushed the measure. The administration would be able to pry loose its ambassadors at the price of a straight up-or-down Senate vote on a separate measure eliminating a single agency. But the administration dug in its heels over details.

Kerry seemed almost apologetic over the administration's hard-line attitude. "There ought to be an effort to engage in legislative discussions to see whether or not there could be a more bipartisan approach," he told reporters. Eventually, the two sides struck a deal, brokered by Kerry. In return for a vote on his plan, Helms lifted his hold on 15 of Clinton's ambassadorial nominees. The Senate then confirmed all 15 nominees by a single voice vote.

After the bill was passed and cleared for the president, he vetoed it. And the veto was sustained.

Kerry broke with Clinton in 1994 on the use of military force in Bosnia, which the president then opposed. Calling for Clinton to lift the embargo barring Bosnian Muslims from buying Western arms, Kerry admitted that U.S. interests in Bosnia were not as vital as in "other parts of the world where we have chosen to send troops and fight wars."

But he warned against inaction: "The alternative is to do nothing; the alternative is to admit defeat; the alternative is to accept that the United Nations and NATO are impotent in the face of any threat."

Kerry has come to the aid of the Clinton administration on domestic issues as well. During hearings on the Whitewater affair and on White House aide Vincent W. Foster Jr.'s suicide, Kerry sharply questioned witnesses who alleged a cover-up. At the first hearing of the Senate Special Committee on Whitewater, chaired by Sen. Alfonse M. D'Amato, R-N.Y., looking into the Foster suicide, Kerry objected to a demonstration by Sen. Frank H. Murkowski. The Alaska Republican used Foster's briefcase to demonstrate how hard it would have been to misplace the suicide note that administration officials said they did not find for four days.

Kerry countered with his own demonstration of how the torn note might have gone undiscovered, holding the briefcase open to the audience. He complained that Democrats were not told Murkowski would use the briefcase as a prop. He criticized independent counsel Kenneth W. Starr, a Republican heading a separate federal inquiry, for turning the evidence over to the GOP. "It was calculated to attract every camera in this room," Kerry said. "This is an inappropriate way for these hearings to begin."

On domestic policy issues that came up in the 104th, Kerry generally upheld his reputation as a liberal. He cosponsored the Senate Democrats' minimum wage increase in 1996, and, with fellow Massachusetts Democrat Edward M. Kennedy, devised the strategy that ultimately forced reluctant Republicans to allow a vote on the measure.

Kerry antagonized the National Rifle Association by trying to amend anti-terrorism legislation. Arguing that black gunpowder is used in 90 percent of U.S. pipe bombings, Kerry sought to add it to the list of explosives studied by the FBI for the feasibility of adding tracing elements known as taggants. The NRA said black gunpowder was used almost exclusively by antique gun collectors. Kerry's amendment failed.

Kerry was one of only 14 Democrats to vote against a measure intended to prevent states from recognizing same-sex marriages. However, Kerry said his stand was dictated by considerations of constitutionality, not because he favors same-sex unions.

Kerry did part company with fellow liberal Kennedy on welfare overhaul. He voted in August 1996 for the bill that Clinton had announced he would sign into law.

Early in his Senate years, Kerry's reputation suffered somewhat from his apparent preoccupation with image. He got a reputation for caring about how things looked, and when he had corrective jaw surgery it was regarded by some as an effort to improve his appearance.

Kerry also has been seen as overly aware of characteristics he shares with a legendary Massachusetts politician with the same initials. Like John F. Kennedy, Kerry is a product of social privilege (his middle name, Forbes, salutes his mother's blue-blood family). Like Kennedy, Kerry was decorated for his daring as a small-craft commander in the Navy and went quickly into politics in the party of the lower-income classes. But Kerry's career has been more anti-establishment, especially at critical junctures.

At Home: In the grueling Kerry-Weld duel of 1996, each candidate was well-known to voters, yet each labored to distinguish himself from the other. The two shared more similarities than differences. Both were tall, wealthy and patrician. Weld is a descendant of the Cabot family; Kerry is in the Forbes line, and is married to Teresa Heinz, heiress to a ketchup fortune worth at least $600 million (and former wife of the late GOP Sen. John Heinz of Pennsylvania). Both men sport fashionable in-town Boston addresses as well as summer homes. They have similar educational and professional backgrounds. Their wives and children sport similar accomplishments. They even drive the same four-wheel-drive sports utility vehicle.

Kerry emphasized his stands on education, the environment and the minimum wage. He exploited his 20-point lead among women with a press conference attended by all five Democratic women in the Senate. But most of all, Kerry tried to link Weld with House Speaker Newt Gingrich, often noting that Weld was known to refer to him as "Newtie."

Weld relied on his popularity as governor — in his 1994 re-election, he won with 71 percent of the vote. Weld's liberal stands on many issues helped cut into Kerry's base, notably among labor and also in the homosexual community. On the campaign trail, Weld's affable, down-to-earth style contrasted well with Kerry's stiff, aloof persona. And Kerry had to battle allegations of impropriety over the rent-free use of a lobbyist's apartment in Washington.

But Kerry's late spending and solid performance in an extended series of debates bolstered him. He also benefited from the fact that some late-deciding voters who liked both candidates concluded that backing Kerry would keep both men in office.

Kerry first gained attention in 1971, when as a leader of Vietnam Veterans Against the War, he joined with other demonstrators as they threw their medals over the White House fence. Kerry takes pains to explain that he opposed the returning of medals as a tactic and returned none of his own (three Purple Hearts, a Silver Star and a Bronze Star). He threw the medals of a veteran from Worcester, Mass., who could not come to Washington, and also threw several ribbons he had received with his own medals.

He got front-page coverage in 1971 by asking the Senate Foreign Relations Committee, "How do you ask a man to be the last man to die for a mistake?" He tried to exploit the publicity by moving to Lowell and running in the open 5th District in 1972. Kerry won his 10-way primary but lost in the fall to Republican Paul Cronin.

After that defeat, Kerry went to law school and then worked as assistant district attorney in Middlesex County. In 1980, he bowed out of a House campaign in a second suburban district in favor of fellow liberal Barney Frank.

In 1982, he challenged the Democratic establishment by running for lieutenant governor. With help from Ray Flynn, a member of the Boston City Council who later became mayor, he edged out Evelyn Murphy in the primary.

The anti-establishment theme surfaced again in 1984, when he bested Rep. James M. Shannon for the nomination to replace retiring Sen. Paul E. Tsongas.

In the general election, Kerry faced conservative businessman Raymond Shamie, who had won the GOP nomination in a stunning upset over long-time national figure Elliot Richardson. Indications that Shamie had picked up primary votes from working-class Democrats, along with President Ronald Reagan's popularity in lunch-bucket territory, led Kerry to play down foreign policy, talk about economics and mute his anti-war background.

But The Boston Globe ran articles tying Shamie to the ultra-conservative John Birch Society, and Shamie was not helped when some of his supporters questioned Kerry's loyalty as a U.S. citizen. Kerry won with 55 percent.

In 1990, Kerry sought a second term amid a maelstrom of statewide anti-incumbent fervor. However, despite early polls indicating an extremely close race, Kerry took 57 percent of the vote against his GOP challenger, millionaire real estate developer and lawyer Jim Rappaport.

SENATE ELECTIONS

1996 General		
John Kerry (D)	1,334,135	(52%)
William F. Weld (R)	1,143,120	(45%)
Susan C. Gallagher (C)	70,007	(3%)

Previous Winning Percentages: **1990** (57%) **1984** (55%)

CAMPAIGN FINANCE

	Receipts	Receipts from PACs		Expend-itures
1996				
Kerry (D)	$10,342,115	$14,591	(0%)	$10,962,607
Weld (R)	$8,074,417	$800,761	(10%)	$8,002,123
Gallagher (C)	$56,544	$1,700	(3%)	$56,056

INTEREST GROUP RATINGS

Year	ADA	AFL-CIO	CCUS	ACU
1996	95	n/a	31	5
1995	95	100	32	4
1994	95	88	30	0
1993	90	82	45	12
1992	100	83	10	0
1991	95	83	20	5

KEY VOTES

1997	
Approve balanced-budget constitutional amendment	N
Approve chemical weapons treaty	Y
1996	
Approve farm bill	N
Limit punitive damages in product liability cases	N
Exempt small businesses from higher minimum wage	N
Approve welfare overhaul	Y
Bar job discrimination based on sexual orientation	Y
Override veto of ban on "partial-birth" abortions	N
1995	
Approve GOP budget with tax and spending cuts	N
Approve constitutional amendment barring flag desecration	N

VOTING STUDIES

	Presidential Support		Party Unity		Conservative Coalition	
Year	S	O	S	O	S	O
1996	92	8	92	8	18	82
1995	86	13	91	8	12	84
1994	89	10	94	6	16	84
1993	93	7	94	6	24	73
1992	23	77	92	8	8	89
1991	28	72	92	8	10	90

1 John W. Olver (D)

Of Amherst — Elected 1991; 3rd full term

Biographical Information

Born: Sept. 3, 1936, Honesdale, Pa.

Education: Rensselaer Polytechnic Institute, B.S. 1955; Tufts U., M.S. 1956; Massachusetts Institute of Technology, Ph.D. 1961.

Occupation: Professor.

Family: Wife, Rose Richardson; one child.

Religion: Unspecified.

Political Career: Mass. House, 1969-73; Mass. Senate, 1973-91.

Capitol Office: 1027 Longworth Bldg. 20515; 225-5335.

Committees

Appropriations
Military Construction; Transportation

In Washington: Olver has had an uphill struggle trying to garner even a fraction of the power and popularity of his revered predecessor, Republican Silvio O. Conte. In four House elections, Olver has had only one easy ride: The other times he took 50, 52 and 53 percent — the latter of those anemic tallies coming in 1996, when 1st District voters were giving Democrat Bill Clinton a whopping 35-point victory over GOP nominee Bob Dole in the presidential contest.

Returning for the 105th Congress, Olver received a piece of good news: The Democratic leadership put him back on the Appropriations Committee, where Conte served for more than 30 years. Olver had gotten onto Appropriations in the 103rd Congress, but when Republicans won the House majority in 1994, Democrats lost committee slots, and Olver was bumped. During the 104th, Olver served on the Budget and Science committees.

In his redux as the Massachusetts appropriator, Olver serves on the Transportation Subcommittee and the Military Construction Subcommittee. The Transportation assignment may help Olver reap some benefits for his district and state as the 105th works on the massive reauthorization bill funding road, public transit and other transportation projects.

The low-key Olver is a hard worker whose reliance on preparation and mastery of details should serve him well on Appropriations. Unlike the flamboyant Conte, who occasionally donned a pig mask on the House floor to protest pork barrel spending (while effectively funneling millions of federal dollars to his district), Olver tends to work behind the scenes.

At the start of the 104th, however, the GOP's "Contract With America" legislative agenda so offended Olver's liberal sensibilities that he took to the House floor to criticize it every step of the way. He expounded the Democratic dogma, characterizing the Republican budget as extreme, saying it would cut health care, education, job training and environmental programs while increasing spending on defense.

"Republicans say that the war on poverty has been lost, so they are making war on poor children instead," Olver said during one debate.

The normally subdued Olver spoke with unusual passion about his unhappiness with the philosophical direction of the GOP House under the guiding hand of Speaker Newt Gingrich. "We are supposed to be building a better nation, but in the world of Newt Gingrich, we will shamefully throw that responsibility to the states, then cut the dollars that the states need," Olver said on the House floor.

While some Democrats crossed their fingers and endorsed the final package overhauling the welfare system in July 1996, Olver complained about the conservative orthodoxy and opposed GOP proposals from start to finish, saying they would shred the safety net for children. As a proponent of a single-payer health care system, he argued that welfare and health care legislation should be done as a package.

On the health care front during the 104th Congress, Olver endorsed the Kassebaum-Kennedy health insurance "portability" bill "as a small first step."

However, he argued against the Medical Saving Accounts established on a trial basis in the bill, saying that the healthiest individuals would go the MSA route, opting out of the insurance pool and driving up costs for those left. The bill was signed into law by President Clinton; it enables workers to retain health insurance when they change jobs and provides for coverage of individuals with pre-existing medical conditions.

Olver has a strong belief in government's ability to solve society's problems and play a part in economic development. During the 104th, he fought Republican plans to eliminate the Advanced Technology Program, arguing that government should provide seed money to business to promote cutting-edge technology. He also continued his fight to maintain federal aid for home heating fuel for low-income residents, a program important to his rural Northeast district.

MASSACHUSETTS 1
West – Berkshire Hills; Fitchburg; Amherst

The enormous 1st, which is framed by Connecticut on the south, New York on the west and Vermont and New Hampshire on the north, seems more like three districts than one.

Residents of the bucolic Berkshire Hills identify most with New Yorkers; they get their news from Albany and many of their visitors from Manhattan. In the central part of the 1st lies the Connecticut River Valley, a rural region known for its maple syrup and a scenic 63-mile stretch of state Route 2 (the Mohawk Trail), which runs from Greenfield to Williamstown. On the eastern side of the 1st are a handful of medium-sized industrial cities more closely linked to Worcester in the 3rd District.

A theme repeats itself across the district: Major textile industries have died, workers have left, and a handful of educational institutions and small businesses are struggling to revive the region. Shoe factories have closed, and Gardner is no longer a furniture capital. In Pittsfield, General Electric's work force has plummeted from 15,000 in the 1950s. GE's former aerospace plant, now owned by General Dynamics, concentrates on plastics production and employs about 1,000 people. The plastics industry is also lively in Leominster, and paper mills still thrive in the district.

The residents of Western Massachusetts see themselves as a hardy, self-reliant lot. For years this was the only state district sending a Republican to Congress, although ironically, a major contributor to the long tenure of GOP Rep. Silvio O. Conte was his success at producing federal dollars and jobs. After Conte's death, the GOP lost the 1st in a 1991 special election, and it stayed Democratic since.

Olver has held onto the 1st with the help of liberal enclaves such as Amherst, Belchertown, Williamstown and Pelham. Heavily Catholic communities such as Holyoke, Westfield and Pittsfield have many people who like to vote an anti-abortion line, but they will often support Democrats if both parties nominate abortion-rights supporters (as was the case in the 1992 and 1996 House races).

Bill Clinton trailed Olver in most of the district's communities in 1992, but he still carried the 1st. However, in 1996, as Olver struggled to hold onto the 1st, Clinton garnered more than 60 percent of the vote in the district, improving his 1992 showing by 13 percentage points.

The district's schools provide an injection of youth and growth potential to the otherwise aging region. In addition to Williams College, eight of the 30 state college campuses are in the 1st; the largest is the University of Massachusetts at Amherst, with 25,000 students. Its world-class Polymer Research Center has spawned several small businesses.

By the standards of overwhelmingly white Western Massachusetts, a few towns in the 1st have minority populations of some significance. One-third of Holyoke is Hispanic, and there are small black and Asian communities in Fitchburg and Leominster. But the district's predominant non-Yankee groups are Poles, French-Canadians and Italians.

1990 Population: 601,643. White 566,587 (94%), Black 10,183 (2%), Other 24,873 (4%). Hispanic origin 28,927 (5%). 18 and over 457,863 (76%), 62 and over 99,882 (17%). Median age: 33.

In a colorful anecdote on the House floor, Olver expressed what type of government subsidy he opposes. He recounted the story of his father soaking a pack of cigarettes in horse urine to dissuade him from smoking. He then went on to describe the tobacco industry as "the greatest threat to the public health," arguing for the elimination of tobacco crop insurance.

Olver, who as a Massachusetts state legislator was once referred to by a Democratic colleague as a man "who could slap a tax on a galloping horse," in 1994 took the Internal Revenue Service to task for failing to collect billions in taxes owed.

As a member of the Appropriations subcommittee with jurisdiction over the IRS, Olver ordered a General Accounting Office report on IRS enforcement. The report found that in 1992, the agency failed to collect $127 billion from businesses and individuals — nearly 18 percent of what was owed.

In 1996 Olver voted to sustain Clinton's veto of a bill to ban a particular abortion technique that opponents call "partial birth" abortion. He also voted against a bill to ban the federal recognition of same-gender marriages. While Olver's support of abortion rights and gay rights may serve him well in the liberal academic enclaves of his district, it also may cost him votes in the heavily Catholic communities such as Holyoke, Westfield and Pittsfield.

At Home: Barely re-elected in 1996, Olver reminded prognosticators why they should keep an eye on this district, known for its independence. In 1994 Olver was re-elected without primary or general opposition, and people thought he had finally and convincingly established himself in a district whose GOP traditions he had struggled to overcome.

However, going into 1996, Republicans thought Olver was their best chance in Massachusetts to beat a Democratic incumbent, and they came close with Jane Swift, an appealing three-term state senator. Swift, 31, received substantial backing from the Republican National Committee (more than $60,000) while labor interests in the state focused (successfully) on unseating Republican incumbents Peter I. Blute and Peter G. Torkildsen.

Swift cast herself as a moderate Republican and played on the economic anxiety of the district, which has not fully participated in the recovery from the Massachusetts recession. She touted her support for the welfare overhaul and a balanced budget to keep interest rates down. She spent almost $700,000 to Olver's $1 million, and she mustered 47 percent of the vote.

While never a barn-burner in campaigning, Olver, a former chemistry professor, has built a following in the liberal precincts around Amherst, where his activities of handball, cross-country skiing and rock-climbing in a Grateful Dead T-shirt seem fitting. Olver was elected to the state House in 1968. Four years later he bucked the national GOP trend, unseating an incumbent Republican state senator. There he voted for gay rights, for allowing minors access to abortion, for universal health care and for an override of a ballot proposition limiting taxes and spending in Massachusetts state government.

When Conte died, no fewer than 10 Democrats ran to succeed him, including Olver. After winning the 1991 primary with surprising ease, he collected endorsements from his defeated rivals, as well as from labor unions, teachers, environmentalists, women's groups and supporters of abortion rights.

But the Massachusetts GOP was not about to let what was then its only seat in the delegation go without a fight. Its champion was Steven D. Pierce, a former state legislator who had lost the GOP primary for governor to William F. Weld the previous year.

Pierce criticized Olver as an architect of the state's high taxes; Olver fought back by reminding voters that Weld had called Pierce a "right-wing ideologue" during the primary.

Olver benefited from an abortion rights group's campaign against Pierce. The issue may have been pivotal, as Olver won by fewer than 2,000 votes.

His GOP opponent in 1992, former Conte staffer Patrick Larkin, polled 43 percent. Three minor-party candidates split 5 percent. Olver, his campaign hobbled by uncharacteristic misfires, barely recorded a majority.

HOUSE ELECTIONS

1996 General		
John W. Olver (D)	129,232	(53%)
Jane Swift (R)	115,801	(47%)
1994 General		
John W. Olver (D)	150,047	(99%)

Previous Winning Percentages: 1992 (52%) **1991**† (50%)

† Special election

CAMPAIGN FINANCE

	Receipts	Receipts from PACs		Expend-itures
1996				
Olver (D)	$912,454	$315,377	(35%)	$1,005,595
Swift (R)	$695,073	$150,833	(22%)	$693,538
1994				
Olver (D)	$410,961	$241,550	(59%)	$317,317

DISTRICT VOTE FOR PRESIDENT

	1996		1992
D	151,494 (61%)	**D**	130,311 (48%)
R	63,993 (26%)	**R**	72,246 (27%)
I	29,115 (12%)	**I**	68,541 (25%)

KEY VOTES

1997	
Ban "partial birth" abortions	N
1996	
Approve farm bill	N
Deny public education to illegal immigrants	N
Repeal ban on certain assault-style weapons	N
Increase minimum wage	Y
Freeze defense spending	Y
Approve welfare overhaul	N
1995	
Approve balanced-budget constitutional amendment	N
Relax Clean Water Act regulations	N
Oppose limits on environmental regulations	Y
Reduce projected Medicare spending	N
Approve GOP budget with tax and spending cuts	N

VOTING STUDIES

	Presidential Support		Party Unity		Conservative Coalition	
Year	**S**	**O**	**S**	**O**	**S**	**O**
1996	84	15	97	2	6	92
1995	89	11	97	2	8	89
1994	78	22	98	1	3	97
1993	82	17	96	2	14	86
1992	11	87	93	5	10	90
1991	20††	80††	96†	1††	5††	95††

INTEREST GROUP RATINGS

Year	ADA	AFL-CIO	CCUS	ACU
1996	95	n/a	19	0
1995	95	100	17	4
1994	100	89	33	0
1993	95	100	9	9
1992	100	92	25	0
1991	100††	100††	33††	0††

†† Not eligible for all recorded votes.

2 Richard E. Neal (D)

Of Springfield — Elected 1988, 5th term

Biographical Information

Born: Feb. 14, 1949, Worcester, Mass.

Education: American International College, B.A. 1972; U. of Hartford, M.P.A. 1976.

Occupation: Public official; college lecturer.

Family: Wife, Maureen Conway; four children.

Religion: Roman Catholic.

Political Career: Springfield City Council, 1978-84; mayor of Springfield, 1984-89.

Capitol Office: 2236 Rayburn Bldg. 20515; 225-5601.

Committees

Ways & Means
Social Security; Trade

m**In Washington:** After serving on the Banking Committee in his first two terms, Neal in 1993 moved up to Ways and Means. His interest in the details of tax bills and regulation and his preference for working behind the scenes made him a natural for the committee, where the Democratic leadership likes to see detail-minded members not given to grand speechifying. When the Republicans seized control of the House in 1994, placing Democratic committee assignments in jeopardy, Neal had accumulated just enough seniority to remain on Ways and Means.

In the 104th, Neal found himself defending Democratic principles on taxes, Medicare and, most visibly, on welfare. In the early stages of the welfare debate, Neal harshly rebuked Republicans for pushing a welfare proposal that lacked child support enforcement provisions. He voted against the initial Republican bills.

"I have carefully reviewed the Personal Responsibility Act and it includes no child support provisions," Neal, who served as co-chairman of the Democratic welfare task force, said. "Without taking action on child support, we would require young mothers to be responsible while we give fathers a free ride. This is the wrong message to send."

To no avail, he implored President Clinton to extract concessions from the GOP to provide vouchers for individuals forced off the welfare rolls to buy family necessities. And in the end Neal voted for the finished product that Clinton signed.

In the 104th, Neal continued his opposition to a constitutional amendment to require a balanced federal budget, voting against the measure in 1995.

In 1990, Neal had backed a constitutional amendment, but in 1992 he switched at the last minute to oppose the balanced-budget constitutional amendment in the face of the Democratic leadership's stiff lobbying against the measure. That year Neal had even told President George Bush, who telephoned from Air Force One the morning of the vote, that he was planning to vote yes.

During the debate on the Republican plan to cut taxes, Neal argued for the middle ground and a bill that could be "universally supported." He asserted his support of a capital gains tax cut, but he said any package should be targeted to the middle class and geared toward investment. Stressing his experience as a teacher, Neal advocated a bill focused on education with tax deductions for higher education costs and employer-provided education rather than a bill he characterized as benefiting the wealthy and exploding the deficit.

Neal's tenure on the Banking Committee in his first two terms in the House led him to be particularly outraged by GOP plans to offset the tax cuts by allowing the corporations to remove excess funds from overfunded pension plans for any reason. He asserted the approach would put the Pension Benefit Guaranty Corporation at risk and lead to another bailout similar to one created by the savings and loan debacle.

Neal also used his perch on Ways and Means to keep an eye on health care issues. Both the health insurance and medical services industries are major employers in the 2nd, and he consistently opposed GOP plans to reduce the rate of growth in Medicare spending. But he supported a pilot program for tax-free medical savings accounts.

During the 104th, Neal put his effort into a bipartisan plan to re-invigorate personal savings. Along with Republican Senate Finance Chairman William V. Roth Jr. of Delaware, Neal — the House Democratic sponsor — worked to expand Individual Retirement Accounts. The "Super IRA" plan would make all Americans eligible for fully tax-deductible IRAs and create a second option of a non-deductible IRA. The plan would have allowed penalty-free withdrawals for such reasons as education, health care and a first home.

Like many of the Irish Catholics in his constituency, Neal is opposed to abortion in some cases. He has voted against federal funding of abortion except in cases of rape, incest or when the woman's life is in danger and voted to ban a particular abortion technique that opponents call "partial birth" abortion. Neal parts with

The city of Springfield dwarfs all other communities in the 2nd in size, population and economic importance. Located on the banks of the Connecticut River, Springfield was named in 1636 by fur trader William Pynchon after his hometown in England.

Since then, Springfield has laid claim to a string of "firsts," including the first federal armory (approved by Congress in 1794), the first gasoline-powered car, the first Pullman rail car and the first basketball game.

Many of the city's successes of the 1990s are tied to that rich history. Companies such as Spalding Sports Worldwide and Smith & Wesson have kept the economy going as heavy manufacturing has fallen off. And attractions such as the Basketball Hall of Fame and the Springfield Armory National Historic Site have helped lure tourists.

Ultimately, the region's future rests with the insurance and financial services industries. Despite staff reductions in late 1992, Massachusetts Mutual Life Insurance Co. is still one of the district's largest private employers, along with Baystate Health Systems Inc. and Nynex. Some small manufacturers remain, although others are moving to southern locales where the cost of doing business is lower.

Residents in the district also worry about defense spending cutbacks, specifically those affecting United Technologies, the largest private employer in neighboring Connecticut and an important source of jobs for the 2nd as well.

A sizable Hispanic population moved into the 2nd in the 1950s to work in tobacco fields. Although the business has dwindled, West Springfield and Hadley still have laborers picking leaves that form cigar wrappers. The minority population in the 2nd now tops 10 percent.

MASSACHUSETTS 2
West Central – Northampton; Springfield; Sturbridge

Springfield and Chicopee, the second-largest city in the district, together offer a reliable base of votes for any Democratic candidate. Democratic voter registration in the 2nd is four times that of the GOP. Bill Clinton garnered 61 percent districtwide in the 1996 presidential election. Neal, who received 72 percent in the House race, has found a receptive audience to his anti-abortion stance among the large number of Catholic voters in the area.

A drive through the rest of the 2nd is a glimpse of New England at its quaintest. In towns such as Longmeadow, Hadley, Palmer and Ware, village life is still focused on a town green. Two of the "Seven Sisters" schools — Mount Holyoke College and Smith College — add to the traditional New England look. Northampton has a more modern claim to fame: A couple of artists there created an icon of child culture, the Teenage Mutant Ninja Turtles.

Although not as well-known as the nearby Berkshire Hills or Cape Cod along the coast, the 2nd is a popular recreational area. Boating and cross-country skiing are popular, and the brilliant fall foliage always draws a crowd. Virtually every town capitalizes on the scenery with a variety of special events, from Chicopee's World Kielbasa Festival to cider-making at Sturbridge Village.

1990 Population: 601,642. White 539,107 (90%), Black 33,960 (6%), Other 28,575 (5%). Hispanic origin 36,181 (6%). 18 and over 454,404 (76%), 62 and over 101,193 (17%). Median age: 33.

ardent anti-abortion activists, however, on several matters: He voted to allow federal health plans to cover abortions; he voted against legislation to require parental consent for minors who seek abortions; and he voted in the 103rd for "clinic access" legislation aimed at thwarting those who attempt to prevent abortions by employing blockade techniques at clinics.

On Ways and Means, Neal has broadened his range of legislative interests, introducing bills and offering amendments on tax measures, tariff revisions and mutual funds. Like the majority of House Democrats, he bucked President Clinton and voted against NAFTA, which was opposed by labor interests influential in 2nd District Democratic politics.

Neal, a co-chairman of the Ad Hoc Committee for Irish Affairs, also has devoted considerable attention to developments in Northern Ireland, where in 1994 a renunciation of violence by the Irish Republican Army led to dialogue between the IRA's political wing and Great Britain. However, in February 1996 frustration with the pace of progress led the IRA to resume bombing, ending the 18 month cease-fire.

At Home: After elections marked by intraparty squabbling or anti-incumbent sentiment, Neal appears to have a lock on the heavily Democratic 2nd, running unchallenged in the primary and easily dispatching token opposition in the general election for the third election in a row.

Neal began his political career in 1972, as co-chairman of George McGovern's presidential campaign in western Massachusetts. After a five-year stint working as an aide to Springfield Mayor William C. Sullivan, Neal in 1977 was elected to the first of the three terms on the City Council.

In 1983, his preparations to challenge Springfield's Democratic mayor helped persuade the incumbent, Theodore E. Dimauro, to retire. Neal then won the office with a landslide margin that he matched in 1985 and 1987. With about 40 percent of the 2nd District's voters living in Springfield and its suburbs, these electoral successes gave Neal a solid base from which to run for the House. During his tenure as mayor, public criticism of Neal was rare, and usually mild.

Before veteran Rep. Edward P. Boland decided to announce his retirement in 1988, he tipped off Neal to his plans, giving Neal a head start collecting signatures and dollars for his first congressional bid. By the time Boland announced departure plans, Neal had been touring the district's 38 towns and cities for more than a year and had amassed a $200,000 campaign treasury. Neal won the Democratic nomination unopposed and crushed a weak GOP foe, but there was resentment from some politicians and voters who felt Neal inherited the seat rather than earned it.

In 1990, Neal had to deal with political tensions created when Boland all but handed him the seat. Former Mayor Dimauro challenged Neal in the Democratic primary, angrily criticizing Neal's tenure as mayor and battering the freshman as a Washington insider. But any progress Dimauro made evaporated at the end of August when he admitted spreading a rumor about one of the region's largest banks. Dimauro said federal regulators had recommended liquidating the troubled Bank of New England, causing the institution's stock to plunge.

Threatened with lawsuits and criminal prosecution and unable to verify his claim, Dimauro retracted his statement, apologized, and blamed and fired his campaign manager. But his credibility was shot. Neal pulverized Dimauro in the primary, winning all but one community. In January 1991, federal regulators took over the Bank of New England.

Redistricting, anti-incumbent fever and 87 overdrafts at the House bank led to Neal's anemic showing in the 1992 election. Two challengers split the anti-Neal vote in the primary, enabling him to win renomination with a plurality. In November, Neal won 53 percent. His GOP challenger got no help from the top of the ticket, as George Bush took only 29 percent of the presidential vote in the 2nd.

HOUSE ELECTIONS

1996 General		
Richard E. Neal (D)	162,995	(72%)
Mark Steele (R)	49,885	(22%)
Scott Andrichak (I)	9,181	(4%)
Richard Kaynor (NL)	5,124	(2%)
1994 General		
Richard E. Neal (D)	117,178	(59%)
John M. Briare (R)	72,732	(36%)
Kate Ross (NL)	10,167	(5%)

Previous Winning Percentages: **1992** (53%) **1990** (100%) **1988** (80%)

CAMPAIGN FINANCE

	Receipts	Receipts from PACs	Expend-itures
1996			
Neal (D)	$370,806	$259,249 (70%)	$227,105
Steele (R)	$1,383	$16 (1%)	$1,358
1994			
Neal (D)	$501,862	$304,821 (61%)	$318,582
Briare (R)	$60,970	$1,514 (2%)	$60,685

DISTRICT VOTE FOR PRESIDENT

1996	1992
D 147,651 (61%)	**D** 121,750 (46%)
R 66,340 (28%)	**R** 76,244 (29%)
I 25,252 (11%)	**I** 65,924 (25%)

KEY VOTES

1997	
Ban "partial birth" abortions	Y
1996	
Approve farm bill	N
Deny public education to illegal immigrants	N
Repeal ban on certain assault-style weapons	N
Increase minimum wage	Y
Freeze defense spending	Y
Approve welfare overhaul	Y
1995	
Approve balanced-budget constitutional amendment	N
Relax Clean Water Act regulations	N
Oppose limits on environmental regulations	Y
Reduce projected Medicare spending	N
Approve GOP budget with tax and spending cuts	N

VOTING STUDIES

	Presidential Support		Party Unity		Conservative Coalition	
Year	**S**	**O**	**S**	**O**	**S**	**O**
1996	80	19	88	7	18	78
1995	76	24	87	9	28	66
1994	77	21	95	2	25	72
1993	82	16	94	4	16	82
1992	14	85	90	5	15	83
1991	26	71	89	6	19	81

INTEREST GROUP RATINGS

Year	ADA	AFL-CIO	CCUS	ACU
1996	75	n/a	20	11
1995	75	100	25	16
1994	95	89	42	0
1993	95	100	9	9
1992	90	92	13	0
1991	90	100	20	5

3 Jim McGovern (D)

Of Worcester — Elected 1996, 1st term

Biographical Information
Born: Nov. 20, 1959, Worcester, Mass.
Education: American U., B.A. 1981, M.P.A. 1984.
Occupation: Congressional aide.
Family: Wife, Lisa Murray.
Religion: Roman Catholic.
Political Career: Sought Democratic nomination for U.S. House, 1994.
Capitol Office: 512 Cannon Bldg. 20515; 225-6101.

Committees
Transportation & Infrastructure
Surface Transportation; Water Resources & Environment

The Path to Washington: Unlike many new members who have trouble finding their way around the labyrinthine corridors of Capitol Hill, McGovern, a longtime aide to 9th District Democratic Rep. Joe Moakley, is an old hand at both the geography and the substance of the House.

In a 1996 election considered something of an upset, McGovern defeated by a solid margin two-term GOP Rep. Peter I. Blute, one of two Republicans in Massachusetts' 10-member congressional delegation in the 104th Congress.

The 3rd is a serpentine district that takes in the central Massachusetts city of Worcester and then makes its way downward to take in the southeastern fishing community of Fall River. The district's independent nature gave both parties hope for success in the House race.

McGovern hammered away throughout the campaign at Blute's voting record, seeking to link the incumbent to House Speaker Newt Gingrich. Although a relatively moderate Republican, Blute did support most of the Republican leadership's "Contract With America." He was among the Republicans targeted by labor, environmental and other liberal interest groups. In one of the more memorable television moments of the 1996 election cycle, McGovern ran a rhyming advertisement that asked voters the question, "If you wouldn't vote for Newt, why would you ever vote for Blute?"

Although overshadowed by the gargantuan Senate contest between Democratic Sen. John Kerry and Republican Gov. William F. Weld, the McGovern-Blute battle picked up its share of attention: In a year in which President Clinton was expected to do well in Massachusetts, Blute was definitely a top Democratic target.

Blute had garnered 50 percent in knocking off nine-term Democratic Rep. Joseph D. Early in 1992, and he improved to 55 percent two years later. McGovern had unsuccessfully sought the Democratic nomination to face Blute in 1994.

McGovern's interest in politics was sparked as a junior high school student, when Democratic Sen. George McGovern of South Dakota (no relation) ran for president. He found himself having to defend his namesake and got involved in his campaign. Later, as an American University student, he worked for McGovern in his Senate office. George McGovern returned the favor in 1996 by campaigning for Jim McGovern.

In addition, McGovern, a Worcester native, came from a family that followed Democratic politics closely, especially those involving the Kennedys. He remembers his family gathering around to write sympathy cards to Ethel Kennedy in 1968 after her husband, Robert F. Kennedy of New York, was assassinated while seeking the Democratic nomination for president.

McGovern says he has learned a great deal from both Moakley, who also helped out on the campaign trail, and George McGovern. He believes that one of the keys to success on the Hill is building relationships with other members, an area in which he has a head start. Not only has he worked closely with Moakley, but McGovern stresses his experience in working with the Democratic leadership and with members on both sides of the political aisle.

From his seat on the House Transportation and Infrastructure Committee, McGovern aims to increase federal funding for local bridges, roads and sewer systems.

Education is also a paramount issue for McGovern, who hopes to be at the head of any congressional effort to increase education funding. His district includes several leading universities such as Clark and The College of the Holy Cross.

McGovern can also be expected to put a priority on seeking more environmental research and development efforts between the federal government and private industry. He has long supported development of environmental technologies and is looking to secure seed funding in this area for companies in his district. Other topics high on McGovern's agenda are ensuring health care for children and pregnant women, and making pensions portable.

MASSACHUSETTS 3
Central and Southeast — Worcester; coastal towns

Political wags dubbed the snakelike 3rd the "Ivy League" district because it stretches from the town of Princeton in central Massachusetts to Dartmouth on the southeastern coast. (The schools by those names are located in other states.) The nickname is ironic because the 3rd is anchored by two of the state's grittier cities, Fall River and Worcester. Democrats run up large percentages in these two cities, but Republicans can stay competitive in the district by winning in the suburban areas.

Fall River, at the southern end of the 3rd, is a fishing community that often has the highest unemployment of any city in Massachusetts. Split between the 3rd and 4th districts, Fall River long has been a bastion of blue-collar, white ethnic Democrats. Bill Clinton won three-quarters of the vote in Fall River at-large, and McGovern won nearly three-quarters of the votes from the district's share of the city.

To the north of Fall River is Worcester, another working-class city and the population hub of the 3rd, with 170,000 people. It was once a thriving industrial center but did not benefit much from the "Massachusetts Miracle" of the 1980s, which saw a boom in high-technology employment elsewhere in the state. Missing out on the "miracle," however, spared Worcester severe pain when the statewide economy nose-dived in the late 1980s. While other communities were reeling, Worcester plotted for the future.

Building on a foundation of respected hospitals in the region, Worcester is working to expand its role in the medical services field. New laboratories, research institutes and drug-manufacturing plants dot the city; the Biotechnology Research Park is growing. To be completed by decade's end is Medical City, a $200 million downtown project that will include a hospital, a medical office building, offices, restaurants and shops.

In the fall of 1994, Worcester inaugurated its commuter rail station on a line to Boston. By the end of the decade, the city plans to complete renovation on Union Station, which will house the commuter line, Amtrak and retail space. Major additions are under way to the Worcester Centrum, a 15,000-seat arena that draws sporting events and concerts. The expanded 135,000 square-foot facility (called Worcester's Centrum Centre), which will also be used for conventions and meetings, will open in September 1997.

Suburban communities to the north and south of Worcester are likely to have increasing influence on elections in the 3rd. A number of these suburbanites commute to jobs outside the district in Boston or Providence, R.I.

Democratic candidates traditionally have had an overall edge in the areas that make up the 3rd, but "unenrolled" (independent) voters are more numerous than Republicans or Democrats, and a number of them are conservative-leaning. Anti-abortion sentiment is widespread in the 3rd, and the National Rifle Association claims that the largest share of its Massachusetts members live here.

1990 Population: 601,642. White 567,923 (94%), Black 11,024 (2%), Other 22,695 (4%). Hispanic origin 22,454 (4%). 18 and over 458,187 (76%), 62 and over 97,996 (16%). Median age: 34.

HOUSE ELECTIONS

1996 General

Jim McGovern (D)	135,044	(53%)
Peter I. Blute (R)	115,694	(45%)
Dale E. Friedgen (NL)	3,362	(1%)

CAMPAIGN FINANCE

	Receipts	Receipts from PACs	Expend-itures
1996			
McGovern (D)	$812,024	$277,191 (34%)	$806,939
Blute (R)	$1,163,303	$225,700 (19%)	$1,144,540

DISTRICT VOTE FOR PRESIDENT

	1996		1992
D	154,915 (60%)	**D**	122,900 (45%)
R	76,413 (30%)	**R**	84,711 (31%)
I	24,690 (10%)	**I**	63,596 (23%)

KEY VOTES

1997

Ban "partial birth" abortions N

4 Barney Frank (D)

Of Newton — Elected 1980, 9th term

Biographical Information
Born: March 31, 1940, Bayonne, N.J.
Education: Harvard U., B.A. 1962, J.D. 1977.
Occupation: Lawyer.
Family: Lives with Herb Moses.
Religion: Jewish.
Political Career: Mass. House, 1973-81.
Capitol Office: 2210 Rayburn Bldg. 20515; 225-5931.

Committees
Banking & Financial Services
Domestic & International Monetary Policy; Housing & Community Opportunity
Judiciary
Courts & Intellectual Property (ranking)

In Washington: When Frank starts to spray one of his distinctive rapid fire soliloquies around the House chamber, Republicans gnash their teeth, Democrats grin, and staffers watching televised proceedings from their offices all over Capitol Hill reach for their remote controls to turn up the sound. It's showtime, and Frank is more likely than not going to unleash some biting spin about the flaws and inconsistencies he finds in GOP proposals.

Frank was commissioned by the Democratic leadership early in the 104th Congress to monitor the floor and pounce on Republicans with his unique combination of wit and parliamentary acumen. As the term progressed and his committee duties grew heavier (he is a senior member of the Judiciary and the Banking and Financial Services committees), Frank prowled the floor a little less. But he remained a firm partisan, a thorn in the side of Speaker Newt Gingrich particularly, and a stalwart defender of the liberal flame.

But Frank's criticisms are not limited to Republicans alone. After President Clinton signed off on a broad budget pact in May 1997 that would balance the books but cut social programs and offer tax breaks Frank finds regressive, he complained, "We addressed a letter to the Democratic president of the United States and it came back 'addressee unknown.'"

Even though Frank was unhappy with Clinton for having signed the welfare overhaul bill and a measure that blocked federal recognition of same-sex marriages, he worked hard during the 1996 election to keep liberals from sitting out the presidential contest. At the same time, he used his knowledge of parliamentary procedures to force the Republicans to take controversial votes that sometimes split their party.

But for all his smarts and the respect he earns from Republicans as a worthy ideological adversary, the GOP is probably happy to have him as a political foe. Frank was the first member of Congress to announce his homosexuality, and he was reprimanded by the House in 1990 because a household employee he hired was later found to be running a prostitution business out of Frank's Capitol Hill apartment.

In contrast to many bomb throwers, Frank actually manages to get legislation passed. Although most of his recent victories were defensive ones — blocking GOP efforts to raise public housing rents, for instance, and forcing the House to accept Senate repeal of a ban on HIV-positive people in the military — Frank worked amicably with Republicans to enact specific proposals.

In the 104th, Frank served as the ranking member of the Judiciary Subcommittee on the Constitution, where he was a persistent critic of GOP attempts to amend the founding document. (When Republicans split over two competing amendments to protect religious expression in public places such as schools, Frank gleefully noted, "It's a real dilemma for the Republicans. The right hand doesn't know what the far right hand is doing.") But he and Constitution Chairman Charles T. Canady, R-Fla., teamed up on two separate lobby restriction and registration bills, one of which was enacted into law.

Frank, who also worked with Christopher Shays on the lobbying issue, teamed up again with the Connecticut Republican on the issue of defense spending. Their amendment to freeze fiscal 1997 defense spending at the previous year's level (which was $1.9 billion lower), was rejected, 194-219. They also worked on a burden sharing amendment to require European nations to help pay for stationing U.S. forces on their soil.

For Frank, compromise is part of the essence of legislating and he eagerly defends his pragmatic streak against attacks from the ideologically pure on his side. "I think to be unrealistic and unpragmatic is to be disloyal to your ideology," he said. In his 1992 book, "Speaking Frankly," Frank addressed the need for Democrats to reconcile their liberal agenda with mainstream values: "Mainstream liberal Democrats have been intimidated by the left politically to some degree, but morally to an even greater extent."

MASSACHUSETTS 4
Boston suburbs — Newton; New Bedford; part of Fall River

The contorted shape of the 4th is proof positive that the state where the term gerrymander was coined remains true to its tradition of politically motivated mapmaking.

The district begins just over the Boston line in Brookline, juts out west to Sherborn, descends to Fall River and New Bedford on the southern coast and then runs back north to Pembroke. At least there is some political timeliness to the curving lines: They roughly trace the shape of a saxophone, Bill Clinton's instrument of choice.

Clinton won the 4th easily in 1996, as did Frank, partly because many residents are still experiencing hard economic times and they continue to turn to Democrats. Fall River struggles with a declining business base that has resulted in double-digit unemployment. Anderson Little shut down its Fall River clothing plant in 1992; soon thereafter, shoemaker Stride Rite moved out of New Bedford to Louisville, Ky. A local Indian tribe has launched an effort to build a casino.

New Bedford once boasted the largest dollar-volume seafood catch in the nation, thanks to its lucrative scallop industry. But severe restrictions imposed to rebuild a dwindling seafood stock have deepened the region's economic woes. The city lost at least 1,300 jobs in the early 1990s and has had trouble attracting new companies to the area. The early textile mills drew large groups of Portuguese and Cape Verdeans to the coastal communities. Today, Portuguese and Norwegians own most of New Bedford's fleet.

To the northeast, in an area known as the South Shore, cranberry bogs in Carver and Lakeville compete with bogs in Wisconsin. Even some of the wealthiest communities in the 4th suffered tough economic times in the late 1980s and early 1990s, as computer companies such as Wang Laboratories laid off thousands and the credit crunch crippled smaller entrepreneurial firms.

A sign of the times in 1992: lines down the block to get into the food pantry at the Unitarian Church in West Newton. Waiting their turn in this well-to-do suburb were teachers, computer programmers and other professionals trying to feed their families and hang on to their expensive homes. Several years later, the situation was less dramatic but not much improved.

Brookline, another comfortable suburb just over the line from Boston, became famous in 1988 when native Michael S. Dukakis ran for president. As governor, he commuted to work on the trolley line that connects Brookline to downtown. There are now more students and other transient types mixed in with Brookline's homeowners.

Despite the dramatic socioeconomic differences between the district's southern cities and its Boston suburbs, the communities share a loyalty to the Democratic Party. Republicans are numerous only in a handful of upper-crust towns such as Dover, Sherborn and Wellesley.

1990 Population: 601,642. White 562,771 (94%), Black 13,165 (2%), Other 25,706 (4%). Hispanic origin 15,011 (2%). 18 and over 461,073 (77%), 62 and over 97,324 (16%). Median age: 34.

Among the parochial successes Frank enjoyed during the 104th was the creation of a National Whaling Park in New Bedford as part of the 1996 omnibus parks bill, and a bill to allow companies to receive patents for processes of developing substances that are found in nature. Biotechnology is a growing industry in Massachusetts and for that reason Frank in the 105th chose the ranking slot on Judiciary's Courts and Intellectual Property Subcommittee, which deals with patent issues important to biotechnology firms.

Frank opposed the massive rewrite of telecommunications law enacted in 1996, and he particularly took exception with GOP efforts to pass the bill in the dead of night. He led the Democrats' parliamentary attack that forced debate over until the next morning.

Much of his energy was devoted to forcing Republicans to take votes at the committee and floor levels on controversial provisions or ones that revealed their intraparty differences, on issues from abortion and intelligence to term limits. He frequently chides the GOP for legislating federal oversight on some issues, such as prison construction and gambling, in apparent contradiction to their support of states' rights. "We want to make sure that votes are taken on every issue, no matter how controversial they may be," Frank said in January 1995. "We want the Republicans to take responsibility for everything they do."

Frank also prefers that personal matters in his life are in the open, saying simply that he "lives with Herb Moses" and eschewing common euphemisms such as "companion." "I answer every other question I'm asked," he said in disclosing his homosexuality in 1987. "I have nothing to hide, nothing to advertise."

He led the opposition against the same-sex bill, arguing that love between two members of the same sex should be tolerated, if not approved: "If it bothers people, turn your head." Frank even took issues with the bill's official title, the Defense of Marriage Act, saying, "This is not the defense of marriage but the defense of the Republican ticket."

Frank's sexual orientation drew the spotlight early in the 104th when Majority Leader Dick Armey of Texas referred to him as "Barney Fag" during an interview with a group of radio reporters. Armey immediately corrected himself and later apologized for committing a "perceived slur" but he maintained that he had committed no Freudian slip — simply an "unintentional mispronunciation" of Frank's name.

At Home: Massachusetts mapmakers twice have taken aim at Frank's district and two times he has easily survived. His sharp political mind — matched only by his sharp tongue — has made Frank one of the most formidable politicians in the state.

A one-time mayoral aide, Frank relied on political contacts he developed at Boston's City Hall and a large presidential-election turnout in his district to win a ticket to the Statehouse in 1972, where he compiled an unabashedly liberal record in the Legislature.

When Democratic Rep. Robert F. Drinan decided to leave Congress in 1980, bowing to the papal prohibition against priests holding public office, Frank went for the opening. He had to move into the district to run, but his record in the Legislature and high profile in national liberal Democratic circles won him endorsements from Drinan and many liberal organizations.

Frank won the primary by 5 percentage points. But instead of coasting through the general election, he nearly lost under a last-minute flurry of ads by his little-known Republican opponent attacking his liberal stands in the Legislature.

Two years later, Massachusetts had to lose one House seat in redistricting; hostile former colleagues in the Legislature paired him with GOP Rep. Margaret M. Heckler in a district that drew 70 percent of its vote from Heckler's old territory. "If you asked legislators to draw a map in which Barney Frank would never be a congressman again," Frank said, "this would be it."

Heckler's 1981 votes for President Ronald Reagan's economic program gave Frank his issue in the 4th. Hammering at her support for Reagan, appealing to the district's elderly, blue-collar and poor residents, Frank gradually drew former Heckler backers to his side.

Heckler's campaign consisted largely of attacks on Frank's stands in the Legislature in behalf of homosexuals and the creation of an "adult entertainment" zone in Boston. Although Frank's 1980 Republican opponent had used that theme with some success, it made little difference in 1982. He won by nearly 40,000 votes.

After he acknowledged publicly that he is homosexual, Frank prepared for the possibility that his candor about his personal life would generate a political challenge. His GOP opponent, Debra Tucker — a little-known supporter of religious broadcaster Pat Robertson's presidential campaign— tried to make an issue of it, but Frank won in 1988 with 70 percent.

In 1992, redistricting had no real impact on Frank: He has won easily throughout this decade.

HOUSE ELECTIONS

1996 General		
Barney Frank (D)	183,844	(72%)
Jonathan Raymond (R)	72,701	(28%)
1994 General		
Barney Frank (D)	168,942	(99%)

Previous Winning Percentages: 1992 (68%) **1990** (66%) **1988** (70%) **1986** (89%) **1984** (74%) **1982** (60%) **1980** (52%)

CAMPAIGN FINANCE

	Receipts	Receipts from PACs	Expend-itures
1996			
Frank (D)	$373,050	$137,142 (37%)	$334,002
Raymond (R)	$100,746	$7,366 (7%)	$108,348
1994			
Frank (D)	$199,261	$59,850 (30%)	$208,936

DISTRICT VOTE FOR PRESIDENT

1996	1992
D 169,073 (64%)	**D** 144,352 (51%)
R 69,540 (26%)	**R** 75,080 (27%)
I 22,787 (9%)	**I** 63,040 (22%)

KEY VOTES

1997	
Ban "partial birth" abortions	N
1996	
Approve farm bill	N
Deny public education to illegal immigrants	N
Repeal ban on certain assault-style weapons	N
Increase minimum wage	Y
Freeze defense spending	Y
Approve welfare overhaul	N
1995	
Approve balanced-budget constitutional amendment	N
Relax Clean Water Act regulations	Y
Oppose limits on environmental regulations	Y
Reduce projected Medicare spending	N
Approve GOP budget with tax and spending cuts	N

VOTING STUDIES

	Presidential Support		Party Unity		Conservative Coalition	
Year	S	O	S	O	S	O
1996	75	20	92	6	4	96
1995	82	15	89	9	24	75
1994	69	31	94	2	0	97
1993	77	22	96	1	9	91
1992	16	80	93	5	4	96
1991	29	68	90	7	16	84

INTEREST GROUP RATINGS

Year	ADA	AFL-CIO	CCUS	ACU
1996	100	n/a	13	0
1995	100	100	17	4
1994	100	100	25	0
1993	100	100	9	4
1992	100	83	25	0
1991	100	83	20	5

5 Martin T. Meehan (D)

Of Lowell — Elected 1992, 3rd term

Biographical Information
Born: Dec. 30, 1956, Lowell, Mass.
Education: U. of Massachusetts, Lowell, B.A. 1978; Suffolk U., M.A. 1981, J.D. 1983.
Occupation: Lawyer.
Family: Wife, Ellen T. Murphy.
Religion: Roman Catholic.
Political Career: No previous office.
Capitol Office: 2434 Rayburn Bldg. 20515; 225-3411.

Committees
Judiciary
Commercial & Administrative Law; Crime
National Security
Military Readiness; Military Research & Development

In Washington: Meehan has promised to serve only four House terms, and he seems bent on making the most of that time to burnish his image as a reformer, pairing with like-minded Republicans in an effort to overhaul campaign finance laws, restrict lobbying activities and enact congressional term limits. "When members of Congress get here and they have self-imposed limits, they act differently," Meehan said in March 1995. "They're not worried about what kind of chairmanship they're going to get."

Reports in the Massachusetts media often refer to Meehan as the "independent-minded Democrat," and his efforts to promote "reform" causes may help him appeal to non-Democrats if he someday seeks statewide office (as many believe he will).

Meehan keeps his Democratic base happy by voting a liberal line on a range of issues — supporting abortion rights and organized labor and opposing increases in defense spending. In the 104th, he even opposed a widely popular GOP bill banning federal recognition of same-sex marriages, although he missed the actual vote on the bill in July 1996 because he was on his way back to Massachusetts for his own wedding. "I can't imagine that two people could make a commitment to spend the rest of their lives together and never be allowed to have that commitment recognized under the law," Meehan told the House.

But it is on the politically sensitive subject of campaign finance reform that Meehan has been most vocal. In the 104th, he sponsored a measure with Republicans Linda Smith of Washington and Christopher Shays of Connecticut that would outlaw PACs, institute voluntary campaign spending limits and ban so-called soft money (unlimited contributions to political parties). The bill also would have banned fundraising within a 50-mile radius of the Capitol, except for House members from districts near Washington, D.C. Their bill, however, was not to the liking of GOP leaders, and it was never considered by the House.

Ultimately, the Republican majority that had campaigned on cleaning up Congress had no better luck than its Democratic predecessors in changing the campaign finance system. Just before the House in July 1996 rejected a campaign finance overhaul bill proposed by the GOP leadership, Meehan pronounced that the controversial legislation was doomed, and deservedly so. "Since the beginning, the Republican leadership has been wedded to the special-interests corporate contributions that drive their agenda . . . protecting big tobacco, sheltering corporate subsidies, promoting environmental regulation and rolling back environmental laws."

The House rejected the GOP bill, 162-259. It considered a Democratic alternative which, while faring better than the GOP plan, still fell, 177-243,

Early in the 105th, Meehan and Shays were back for another crack at campaign finance overhaul. Their proposal drew bipartisan cosponsorship, but the House GOP leadership again reacted coolly.

Meehan says he was attracted to the issue of campaign finance by former Rep. Mike Synar, a populist Democrat from Oklahoma, who fought for campaign finance reform from his early House days in the mid-1970s until he was defeated in a Democratic primary in 1994. Synar died of cancer in 1996.

Meehan also was a player in a bipartisan bill that aimed to force former congressmen to wait a while longer before lobbying on Capitol Hill. The measure, sponsored by Meehan and New Jersey Republican Dick Zimmer, would have required lawmakers to wait two years, instead of the current one year, before becoming lobbyists. It also would impose a two-year ban on former lawmakers lobbying the executive branch, and a five-year ban on lobbying the committees on which they once served. Ex-lawmakers who become lobbyists also would lose their access to the House and Senate floors, gyms, cloakrooms and dining rooms.

Congress cleared a bill in November 1995 that imposed new reporting requirements on lobbyists, but did not address the issue of lobbying by

MASSACHUSETTS 5
North Central — Lawrence; Lowell

Although located on the northeastern edges of the 5th, the gritty cities of Lawrence and Lowell dominate this otherwise suburban district.

An intense rivalry between the two mill cities dates back to the early 1900s: Lowell, the model "company town," was watched over by paternalistic Yankee Protestants, while immigrant workers in Lawrence labored in unsafe factories and lived in substandard quarters. Ever since, it seems Lawrence has lagged behind the city to the south.

With the help of some federal dollars and arm-twisting in Congress, downtown Lowell was designated a national historic park in 1978. Earning that status was a boost to tourism, and it helped draw business.

But Lowell and its 103,400 people have not been able to escape the 1990s recessionary times. Wang Laboratories, the lifeblood of the city's resurgence that one time employed 10,000, filed for bankruptcy protection and announced massive layoffs in 1992. The company emerged from bankruptcy in 1993 and in 1994 made a lucrative merger with the French firm Groupe Bull. It has since been involved in a series of acquisitions, and now employs about 1,100 in the district.

There are similar troubles elsewhere in the district. Digital Equipment moved a plant from Maynard to New Hampshire, though it remains one of the district's largest employers. The Fort Devens Army Base in Ayer closed in March 1996; the facility now trains Army Reserve and National Guard soldiers.

Lawrence, a city of 70,000, has problems on a scale normally reserved for only the largest of metropolitan areas: arson, drug trafficking, car thefts, teen pregnancy and double-digit unemployment. Police set up barricades in one neighborhood and checked the license of every person entering to try to curtail the drug trade. Minorities make up about 45 percent of the city's population: The largest single group, Hispanics, has begun to flex its political muscle.

Despite the tough times, some of the district's smaller non-traditional businesses are finding profitable niches. Marlborough, on I-495, is home to snack maker Smartfoods and to Stratus Computer.

Businesses in the northern tier of the 5th are competing more successfully with no-sales-tax New Hampshire, thanks to a relaxation of state blue laws that allow merchants within 10 miles of the border to open on Sundays.

Sprinkled through the Merrimack Valley are some of the country's most well-known preparatory schools, including Phillips Academy in Andover and the Groton School and Lawrence Academy, both in Groton. The 5th is also home to Walden Pond in Concord, from where authors Henry David Thoreau and Ralph Waldo Emerson derived inspiration in the 19th century.

Lawrence and Lowell continue to give Democrats a strong anchor in the 5th. In 1996, they were the key to the district's support of Bill Clinton and Meehan, who ran unopposed. But independents, or "unenrolled" voters, outnumber those registered in either major party, which generally makes the district competitive.

1990 Population: 601,643. White 537,800 (89%), Black 13,762 (2%), Other 50,081 (8%). Hispanic origin 49,014 (8%). 18 and over 446,756 (74%), 62 and over 76,460 (13%). Median age: 32.

former members.

Given Meehan's belief that there is too much special interest money fueling Congress, it is no surprise that he has become one of the leading congressional critics of the tobacco industry. When the chief executives of tobacco companies testified in 1994 before a House Commerce subcommittee that nicotine was not addictive, Meehan was so outraged that he asked Attorney General Janet Reno to convene a grand jury to investigate possible perjury charges against the tobacco executives.

In 1995, he and Utah Republican James V. Hansen introduced legislation to gradually remove nicotine from all tobacco products sold in the United States. "Nicotine has been repeatedly and conclusively proven to be a highly addictive drug, and congressional hearings held last year highlighted internal documents from within the tobacco industry which indicated that tobacco companies manipulate nicotine levels in their products," the two members said when introducing the bill. But the measure went nowhere in the 104th.

Meehan told the Boston Globe in September 1995 that his anti-tobacco fervor sprang in part from his father's 25-year smoking habit. He said his father's smoking helped to clog his major heart arteries so drastically that he nearly died before he underwent surgery in 1967.

Meehan, who was 11 at the time, told the newspaper he recalled the day the doctors warned his father to stop smoking immediately if he wished to survive. "What really got me was that he was so addicted that he smoked a cigarette on the way home from being told he was going to die if he didn't stop," Meehan said. His father later did stop smoking.

When the House in June 1996 took up the annual agriculture spending bill, Meehan cosponsored an amendment to do away with federal crop insurance and extension services for tobacco growers. "The tobacco crop insurance subsidies, these are products of a bygone era that have no interest other than the special interest of the big clout that is supporting them," Meehan said. "No longer should the federal government be a willing and knowing partner in the addiction of America's youth. Now is the time to correct a serious disconnect in federal policy." The amendment failed narrowly, 210-212.

After his 1992 election, Meehan stroked Rep. Joe Moakley, dean of the Massachusetts delegation and then-chairman of the Rules Committee, to get good committee slots, and he ended up with a berth on the National Security Committee. He has used his seat to call for increased defense cuts. Meehan voted against the committee's fiscal 1997 defense authorization, which provided $7 billion more than President Clinton had requested for defense. He also supported an unsuccessful effort in June 1996 to freeze fiscal 1997 defense spending at the 1996 level.

In 1994, he offered an amendment to the annual defense authorization bill slicing an additional $200 million from the $2.72 billion approved by the committee for ballistic missile defenses. Meehan opposed continued spending on what he called "exotic missile systems." He said that the country could not "continue spending billions of dollars every year on military programs we don't need without harm to our own economic health." The amendment was rejected, however.

At Home: With three elections under his belt, Meehan has established the 5th as his own — a district that mapmakers had carved up for a Republican. After the state's one-seat loss in reapportionment, GOP Gov. William F. Weld negotiated a 5th District he was counting on to elect Paul W. Cronin in a 1992 matchup with Democratic Rep. Chester G. Atkins. When Meehan trounced Atkins in the September Democratic primary, all bets were off. He branded Atkins an unsavory political insider during the primary campaign, striking a chord with voters when he assailed Atkins for supporting a House pay raise and for having 127 House bank overdrafts.

After he swamped Atkins in the primary, Meehan was favored over GOP businessman and former one-term Rep. Cronin. Meehan, a former prosecutor, portrayed himself as a tough-on-crime Democratic moderate. Cronin argued that as the owner of a fiberglass company he was better suited to represent the business-oriented 5th.

The men lambasted each other's professional qualifications in criticisms often peppered with personal attacks. Cronin accused Meehan of being just a political gopher, paid to hold the coats of the politicians he served. Meehan said Cronin was "a career politician" who had made eight previous runs for office and lost four of them.

Boosted in part by a large turnout in Lowell, Meehan took 52 percent to Cronin's 37 percent, with two independents splitting the rest of the vote. Meehan sailed through 1994 and 1996.

HOUSE ELECTIONS

1996 General		
Martin T. Meehan (D)	183,429	(99%)
1996 Primary		
Martin T. Meehan (D)	23,405	(85%)
Patrick M. Raymond (D)	4,156	(15%)
1994 General		
Martin T. Meehan (D)	140,725	(70%)
David E. Coleman (R)	60,734	(30%)

Previous Winning Percentages: 1992 (52%)

CAMPAIGN FINANCE

	Receipts	Receipts from PACs		Expend-itures
1996				
Meehan (D)	$605,685	$0	(0%)	$308,067
1994				
Meehan (D)	$871,545	$1,400	(0%)	$803,523

DISTRICT VOTE FOR PRESIDENT

	1996		1992
D	143,127 (58%)	**D**	112,959 (42%)
R	76,610 (31%)	**R**	85,260 (32%)
I	24,078 (10%)	**I**	70,391 (26%)

KEY VOTES

1997	
Ban "partial birth" abortions	N
1996	
Approve farm bill	N
Deny public education to illegal immigrants	N
Repeal ban on certain assault-style weapons	N
Increase minimum wage	Y
Freeze defense spending	Y
Approve welfare overhaul	Y
1995	
Approve balanced-budget constitutional amendment	Y
Relax Clean Water Act regulations	N
Oppose limits on environmental regulations	Y
Reduce projected Medicare spending	N
Approve GOP budget with tax and spending cuts	N

VOTING STUDIES

	Presidential Support		Party Unity		Conservative Coalition	
Year	**S**	**O**	**S**	**O**	**S**	**O**
1996	85	13	89	6	8	86
1995	80	18	87	12	26	73
1994	68	29	85	8	11	81
1993	77	22	89	9	16	80

INTEREST GROUP RATINGS

Year	ADA	AFL-CIO	CCUS	ACU
1996	85	n/a	19	0
1995	80	92	38	16
1994	85	67	83	16
1993	90	83	27	17

6 John F. Tierney (D)

Of Salem — Elected 1996, 1st term

Biographical Information

Born: Sept. 18, 1951, Salem, Mass.

Education: Salem State College, B.A. 1973; Suffolk U., J.D. 1976.

Occupation: Lawyer; chamber of commerce official.

Family: Single.

Religion: Unspecified.

Political Career: Democratic nominee for U.S. House, 1994.

Capitol Office: 120 Cannon Bldg. 20515; 225-8020.

Committees

Education & Workforce
Employer-Employee Relations; Postsecondary Education, Training & Life-Long Learning

Government Reform & Oversight
National Economic Growth, Natural Resources & Regulatory Affairs

The Path to Washington: The second time around was the charm for Tierney, as he succeeded in narrowly defeating two-term Republican Rep. Peter G. Torkildsen in 1996, a rematch of their close 1994 battle.

In fact, the 1996 results were even closer than those of two years earlier, when Torkildsen, a moderate Republican, defeated Tierney by 4 percentage points.

In 1996, a good year for Democrats in Massachusetts, Tierney's victory margin was only 360 votes out of more than 265,000 cast.

Education was a paramount issue of Tierney's throughout his campaign, and he was pleased to win a seat on the Education and the Workforce Committee.

He plans to focus on education and job training issues, working with labor, the business community and the educational establishment to match people with appropriate jobs.

Among his other educational focuses is early childhood education, including support for the Head Start program.

Another Tierney interest is the revitalization of downtown areas in cities such as Lynn, the largest community in the district.

The 6th, which includes both factory towns and wealthy suburbs along the North Shore, is a swing district. As evidenced by the close Tierney-Torkildsen races, the district has a substantial bloc of independent voters. ("Unenrolled" or independent voters in Massachusetts are nearly as numerous as registered Democrats and Republicans combined.)

In 1992, Torkildsen, who had served in the state legislature, captured the seat for the Republican Party with 55 percent of the vote. He defeated seven-term Democratic incumbent Nicholas Mavroules, who was tainted by legal problems.

Crime was a central issue in the 1994 Tierney-Torkildsen race. Tierney won endorsements from gun control advocates Jim and Sarah Brady, and accused Torkildsen of waffling on crime. Torkildsen, meanwhile, painted Tierney as too liberal on capital punishment and soft on illegal drugs.

As the 104th Congress began, Torkildsen, along with most other House GOP moderates, supported much of the Republican leadership's "Contract With America." But in his 1996 rematch with Tierney, the incumbent tried to underscore his moderate stances on various issues, including his support for abortion rights. Torkildsen pointed out that in 1995 only four other House Republicans voted against a majority of the GOP more often than he. Torkildsen insisted he was "striking my own chord."

Tierney, who had been gearing up for a November rematch with Torkildsen, had endured a grueling four-candidate Democratic primary in 1994, which he barely won. But this time around, Tierney faced just one primary opponent, little-known lumberyard worker John Gutta, whom he easily dispatched.

Throughout the general-election campaign, Tierney sought to link Torkildsen to House Speaker Newt Gingrich, who was extremely unpopular in Massachusetts. Tierney focused in particular on Republican proposals to restrict funding for Head Start and some other education programs.Working to Tierney's advantage was the involvement of labor unions, which ran television advertisements attacking Torkildsen's record.

Tierney said he has always been interested in politics, in part because of his family. When Tierney was a boy, his uncle served as a ward councilor in the 6th District town of Peabody, and the young Tierney used to help him out by campaigning door-to-door in the community.

Tierney supported what he called a "Contract with the Middle Class, Workers and Small Business People" that included jobs and economic development, improved public schools, universal health care, environmental protection and programs for seniors and children.

He also has an interest in changing the campaign finance system, an area he can explore from his seat on the Government Reform and Oversight Committee.

MASSACHUSETTS 6
North Shore — Lynn; Peabody

The North Shore area is more open to Republican entreaties than most communities in Massachusetts. Republican William F. Weld won the 6th in his 1990 and 1994 campaigns for governor. And in 1992 Republican Peter Torkildsen unseated scandal-plagued Democratic Rep. Nicholas Mavroules and narrowly defeated Tierney two years later before Tierney returned the favor in 1996.

Registered Democrats outnumber Republicans in much of Massachusetts, but the 6th is dominated by independent voters. GOP candidates can succeed by targeting them, holding the votes of wealthy Republican suburbanites who support abortion rights and picking off some conservative Democrats who are angry about high taxes and social programs.

Michael S. Dukakis barely won the 6th in 1988, but Bill Clinton swept the district in 1996 by 28 percentage points, and Tierney nicked Torkildsen in the House race.

The 35 or so cities and towns that constitute the 6th are a melange of scruffy fishing ports, aristocratic suburbs, unspoiled coastland and well-worn factory towns.

Lynn, with 81,000 people, is by far the largest community in the 6th. Lynn's major employer is the General Electric Co., which makes aircraft engines for the F/A-18 Hornet, helicopters and some commercial planes. Employment at the GE plant has dropped from 13,000 workers in 1981 to about 5,100 now. In 1996, Lynn gave Clinton about two-thirds and Democratic Sen. John Kerry 57 percent of its votes. It also gave Tierney a 5,100-vote cushion in the House race.

Although Lynn lies just 10 miles northeast of Boston, the city's officials often feel isolated from the state capital. In 1993 state leaders began debating the prospects of extending a Boston subway line to Lynn.

The coast north of Lynn includes some of the most beautiful landscapes in the state. Each town has its own personality and attitudes. Tourists and fishermen share the coastal communities of Gloucester, Rockport and Marblehead.

Among the three, Gloucester, home to General Mills' Gorton's seafood company and other processing plants, has the largest population and fishing catch, and it gets the most visitors.

Most of the beaches on the North Shore are pristine, protected and open to the public. Manchester-by-the-Sea is something of an exception. A tony town of 5,000 that voted to change its name from just plain Manchester, it discourages outsiders from using its beaches by enforcing a residents-only parking rule. The area has a number of antique shops.

Salem was the site of witch trials in 1692. Bedford, a town of 13,000, was added to the 6th in 1992 redistricting. Located in the southwestern corner of the district, Bedford is home to Hanscom Air Force Base.

The 6th includes most of the territory that made up the original "gerrymandered" district, drawn by the Massachusetts legislature in 1812 and named for then-Governor Elbridge Gerry.

1990 Population: 601,643. White 573,352 (95%), Black 11,405 (2%), Other 16,886 (3%). Hispanic origin 17,373 (3%). 18 and over 480,390 (80%), 62 and over 99,624 (17%). Median age: 35.

HOUSE ELECTIONS

1996 General		
John F. Tierney (D)	133,002	(48%)
Peter G. Torkildsen (R)	132,642	(48%)
Martin J. McNulty (I)	4,195	(2%)
1996 Primary		
John F. Tierney (D)	18,115	(85%)
John Gutta (D)	3,044	(14%)

CAMPAIGN FINANCE

	Receipts	Receipts from PACs		Expend-itures
1996				
Tierney (D)	$779,254	$273,863	(35%)	$776,359
Torkildsen (R)	$1,120,893	0		$1,120,913
Fritz (C)	$10,977	0		$9,304

DISTRICT VOTE FOR PRESIDENT

1996		1992	
D	166,037 (59%)	**D**	134,424 (44%)
R	86,306 (31%)	**R**	96,857 (32%)
I	26,273 (9%)	**I**	75,893 (25%)

KEY VOTES

1997

Ban "partial birth" abortions — N

7 Edward J. Markey (D)

Of Malden — Elected 1976; 11th full term

Biographical Information
Born: July 11, 1946, Malden, Mass.
Education: Boston College, B.A. 1968, J.D. 1972.
Military Service: Army Reserve, 1968-73.
Occupation: Lawyer.
Family: Wife, Susan Blumenthal.
Religion: Roman Catholic.
Political Career: Mass. House, 1973-77.
Capitol Office: 2133 Rayburn Bldg. 20515; 225-2836.

Committees
Commerce
Energy & Power; Finance & Hazardous Materials; Telecommunications, Trade & Consumer Protection (ranking)
Resources
National Parks & Public Lands

In Washington: With his affability, attention to substance and habit of consulting with colleagues, Markey has served as a bridge between Democrats and Republicans on the Commerce Committee.

A senior member of the influential panel, Markey has proved adept at building consensus: In the 104th, he had a hand in shaping broad measures overhauling the telecommunications and securities industries. Markey, the ranking member on the Telecommunications and Finance Subcommittee, worked closely with its chairman, Republican Jack Fields of Texas, to craft a telecommunications bill whose prospects for a time seemed dim until it rebounded and cleared in the 104th. In the 105th, he will work with a new chairman — W.J. "Billy" Tauzin of Louisiana — on the renamed Telecommunications, Trade and Consumer Protection Subcommittee.

Markey displayed his bipartisan stripes early in the 105th, cosponsoring a measure along with Republican Dan Schaefer of Colorado, chairman of the Subcommittee on Energy and Power, that would deregulate the $208 billion electric utility industry. The essential thrust of the bill is to give states more authority to set the terms of electrical service.

A witty sort, Markey is sometimes almost too quick with an apt one-liner or sound bite. But he also is conversant in the mind-numbing details of today's most complex issues. His tendency to actually read about subjects in depth leads him to move methodically. And in the telecommunications field, it has given him a vision of the future of electronic information-sharing that does not hew to the desires or needs of any one industry.

In February 1996, Congress finally approved sweeping telecommunications legislation after years of intense negotiations. The final bill removed the statutory and court-ordered barriers to competition among segments of the industry that were erected over past decades, allowing such multibillion-dollar giants as AT&T and Bell Atlantic to go head-to-head in offering packages of voice, video and data-transferring services. The law also eliminated a provision of the 1984 Cable Act that barred local phone companies from entering the cable TV market in their service area, while easing or eliminating the price controls on cable companies.

"This bill breaks down the last remaining monopolies in the telephone and cable industries and makes possible an information revolution," Markey said upon House approval of the conference agreement.

When the House first considered the bill in August 1995, Markey was successful with two amendments that were also backed by the Clinton administration. The House voted to scale back the bill's proposed deregulation of TV broadcasters and to require TV manufacturers to equip new sets with "v-chips" that could block offensive programs.

As drafted, the bill proposed to remove all the ownership limits on radio stations and ease the limits on TV stations. Companies were to be permitted to own more than one VHF station in a market, TV broadcasters could own the local cable system and local newspapers, and networks could control stations reaching up to half the nation's viewers.

Under these provisions, Markey told his colleagues, it would be legal for a single company in a community "to own the only newspaper, to own the cable system, to own every AM station, to own every FM station, to own the biggest TV station and to own the biggest independent station." He offered an amendment, which the House passed, 228-195, to bar broadcasters from joining forces with the local cable system and to limit network-owned stations' reach to 35 percent of the viewers — up from 25 percent in existing law.

Markey also got the House to back his plan to require v-chip circuitry inside a TV set that could be programmed to block any program that had been labeled electronically as violent, sexually explicit or otherwise unsuitable for children. He gained bipartisan backing for the proposal by teaming up with conservative Indiana Republican Dan Burton.

The four main TV networks hoped to head off the Markey-Burton v-chip amendment by announcing in early August that they had created a $2 million fund to develop blocking technology for parents. The networks also backed an alternative GOP amendment that encouraged the television and video industries to develop blocking technology.

MASSACHUSETTS 7
Northwest suburbs — Woburn; Framingham; Revere

Although the 7th lies outside Boston, the city is the occupational and cultural focal point for most residents of this district. It is a collection of medium-sized cities and towns that almost completely rings Boston, giving the 7th a strong commuter orientation.

The well-educated, liberal-minded suburbanites are reliably Democratic. Bill Clinton ran 37 percentage points ahead of Bob Dole here in 1996. Also, Markey carried the portions of Middlesex and Suffolk counties that make up the 7th by wide margins, winning the district with 70 percent of the vote.

Redistricting in 1992 added Framingham and Natick to the western end of the district, boosting the presence of high technology in the 7th. Route 128, often compared with California's Silicon Valley, has a variety of large and small computer, engineering and telecommunications companies, making Markey's leadership on the issue a natural for the district.

The 7th's largest employer is Lexington-based Raytheon, maker of the Patriot missile system. The company has weathered defense cuts in part by diversifying into commercial products (such as refrigerators, stoves and microwaves) and by delving deeper into the defense sector by attempting to purchase General Motors' Hughes Aircraft Co. division in early 1997.

Waltham, a working-class city once known for its watch factories, has experienced a technological surge in recent years. Smaller new companies — such as Vivo Software Inc, which markets desktop videoconferencing technology — are off Route 128 in Waltham. The Charles River Museum of Industry pays tribute to the city's grand industrial past.

Nearby universities, such as Harvard and the Massachusetts Institute of Technology, have helped fuel the local electronics industry. Graduates of MIT and Harvard founded Wakefield's Boston Technologies in 1986 with just five people. By 1997 the telecommunications company employed nearly 775 workers and was providing voice mail technology to most of Japan's cellular telephone market.

The cities of Medford and Malden are often seen as one metropolitan area, with some shared city services and a rivalry in football. Although many of the residents commute to blue-collar jobs in Boston, the New England processing center for Fleet Bank is a major employer in Malden. Houses in Medford, Malden, Everett and Melrose have been passed on through several generations of Irish and Italian families.

Irish immigrants originally settled in Revere, too, but Southeast Asian immigrants began moving into that coastal city in the 1980s. Revere offers the growing Asian community affordable housing and easy access to jobs in downtown Boston.

Weston, Lincoln and Lexington are the most affluent communities in the 7th, home to professional athletes and media celebrities. Lexington, site of the first Revolutionary War conflict, is popular with out-of-state visitors and Massachusetts students. Re-enactments of the Battle of Lexington are held every April.

1990 Population: 601,642. White 564,252 (94%), Black 13,639 (2%), Other 17,816 (3%). Hispanic origin 17,980 (3%). 18 and over 498,567 (83%), 62 and over 109,360 (18%). Median age: 35.

Supporters of the alternative proposal said it embodied the GOP's principles of parental responsibility and free-market solutions, rather than the bureaucratic approach of the Markey-Burton amendment. But Markey and Burton said only the v-chip would allow parents to block whole categories of programs, eliminating the need to identify individual programs to be blocked from among the thousands carried by broadcasters and cable. The House voted, 222-201, to substitute the GOP proposal for the Markey-Burton amendment.

Minutes later, however, Markey moved to recommit the bill to the Commerce Committee with instructions that it be reported back to the House immediately with the Markey-Burton amendment attached. The motion amounted to an up-or-down vote on the v-chip, something the networks and their allies in the House GOP leadership had hoped to avoid. Such recommittal motions almost never succeed, but this one did, 224-199.

In the 104th, Markey also worked closely with Fields on a bill to modernize regulation of the securities and mutual funds industries; it cleared at the end of the session. The measure streamlined the often overlapping regulation of mutual funds, stock offerings and investment advisers by the states and the Securities and Exchange Commission (SEC).

The bill Fields had first introduced had a much broader scope, but it whipped up great controversy. It would have pre-empted most state securities laws and regulations and allowed stockbrokers to more freely pitch risky investments to institutional clients. Just before a subcommittee markup in March 1996, Fields and Markey met and agreed to scrap the controversial provisions. The new bill then sailed through the House, 407-8, in June 1996.

An impasse between Markey and Texas Republican Sen. Phil Gramm threatened to scuttle the widely backed bill, but both ended up giving ground to reach a deal. Gramm successfully blocked proposed fees on investment advisers and lifted state regulation of larger investment adviser firms.

Markey preserved state regulation of individual adviser representatives and obtained a provision to make it easier for investors to find out if their financial planner has been disciplined by regulators.

Markey's ability to reach across the aisle has allowed him to be a player on major legislation, but he is also not reluctant to play the partisan chip when he disagrees with a measure. One such bill was an attempt to reauthorize the nation's hazardous waste program, known as superfund. The bill went nowhere, partly because Democrats were ready to aim at it as a "bailout bill" for polluters — a charge Republicans refuted. "We really haven't had the commitment required to make it a bipartisan bill," said Markey. "Their intention is to destroy the program and have it out of existence by the year 2000."

Markey also has a forum for his environmental concerns from his seat on the Resources Committee.

Markey's efforts to reveal information about how the U.S. government exposed some Americans to radiation as part of ongoing experiments from the 1940s to the 1970s were rewarded in the 104th when the Energy Department acknowledged that at least 700 Americans were deliberately exposed to radiation in U.S. government tests.

At Home: Markey's only close re-election came in 1984, under unusual circumstances. When Democratic Sen. Paul E. Tsongas quit the Senate that year, Markey was the first Democrat to announce for his seat. His prominence on the nuclear weapons freeze and on nuclear energy issues had earned him a following of anti-nuclear enthusiasts, and they became the core of his campaign.

But Markey's candidacy did not keep several other prominent contenders from entering the Senate contest. In time, it became clear that Markey was at best an even bet against his chief competitors. He decided to drop out of the Senate race and filed again for re-election to his House seat.

Markey had to struggle just to win renomination in his district against former state Sen. Samuel Rotondi, who stayed in the House contest, attacking Markey for indecision. Markey charged that Rotondi had received campaign contributions from executives of utility companies and nuclear industries. Rotondi, he said at a debate, "has so much radioactive money in his Federal Election Commission report it glows in the dark."

Markey won nomination with 54 percent and has not had a primary foe since.

Republicans did not put up any resistance until 1992, when 92 overdrafts at the House bank dented Markey's armor. He still won with 62 percent.

In 1994, Markey's GOP challenger hammered him on the issue of his residence; Markey does not own or rent a home in the 7th, instead using his parents' home in Malden as his residence. He won with his usual ease that year and in 1996.

Before 1984, Markey's only difficult congressional campaign was his first, in 1976. When the critically ill Torbert H. MacDonald announced his retirement that year, virtually every prominent Democrat thought about trying to replace him.

It was clear that a primary with a dozen aspirants would be decided mostly by simple name identification. Markey had received a fair amount of attention for his battles in the legislature with the Democratic leadership, which had once closed his office and banished him to a desk in the hall. Markey took 21 percent of the vote, enough for a comfortable win.

HOUSE ELECTIONS

1996 General		
Edward J. Markey (D)	177,053	(70%)
Patricia Long (R)	76,407	(30%)
1994 General		
Edward J. Markey (D)	146,246	(64%)
Brad Bailey (R)	80,674	(36%)

Previous Winning Percentages: 1992 (62%) **1990** (100%) **1988** (100%) **1986** (100%) **1984** (71%) **1982** (78%) **1980** (100%) **1978** (85%) **1976** (77%)

CAMPAIGN FINANCE

	Receipts	Receipts from PACs		Expend-itures
1996				
Markey (D)	$695,542	$0	(0%)	$351,683
Long (R)	$5,428	$0		$3,033
1994				
Markey (D)	$972,421	$ 0	(0%)	$757,993

DISTRICT VOTE FOR PRESIDENT

1996		1992	
D	171,090 (64%)	**D**	150,102 (50%)
R	72,807 (27%)	**R**	87,432 (29%)
I	19,801 (7%)	**I**	61,965 (21%)

KEY VOTES

1997	
Ban "partial birth" abortions	N
1996	
Approve farm bill	N
Deny public education to illegal immigrants	N
Repeal ban on certain assault-style weapons	N
Increase minimum wage	Y
Freeze defense spending	Y
Approve welfare overhaul	N
1995	
Approve balanced-budget constitutional amendment	N
Relax Clean Water Act regulations	N
Oppose limits on environmental regulations	Y
Reduce projected Medicare spending	N
Approve GOP budget with tax and spending cuts	N

VOTING STUDIES

	Presidential Support		Party Unity		Conservative Coalition	
Year	S	O	S	O	S	O
1996	78	19	95	3	0	98
1995	88	12	96	3	11	89
1994	71	22	95	1	3	97
1993	81	18	96	1	9	89
1992	11	82	91	3	8	88
1991	23	76	94	3	11	89

INTEREST GROUP RATINGS

Year	ADA	AFL-CIO	CCUS	ACU
1996	95	n/a	6	0
1995	80	100	17	8
1994	85	88	33	0
1993	95	92	27	4
1992	100	83	25	0
1991	100	100	20	0

8 Joseph P. Kennedy II (D)

Of Boston — Elected 1986, 6th term

Biographical Information
Born: Sept. 24, 1952, Boston, Mass.
Education: U. of Massachusetts, B.A. 1976.
Occupation: Energy company executive.
Family: Wife, Beth Kelly; two children.
Religion: Roman Catholic.
Political Career: No previous office.
Capitol Office: 2242 Rayburn Bldg. 20515; 225-5111.

Committees
Banking & Financial Services
Domestic & International Monetary Policy; Housing & Community Opportunity (ranking)
Veterans' Affairs
Health

In Washington: After a decade of service on Capitol Hill, Kennedy is looking seriously at a career move many expected he would make some time ago: a bid for the Massachusetts governorship. The chances that Kennedy would seek the statehouse — and that he might win it — improved after Republican Gov. William F. Weld accepted the ambassorship to Mexico.

But coincident with the dispatch of Kennedy's rival was a series of ugly news stories that put a damper on his poll ratings. His first wife blasted Kennedy for having their 12-year marriage, which produced twins, annulled. And his brother Michael became the subject of investigations and screaming headlines after he was implicated for an affair with a family babysitter. Kennedy had profited from his fabled family name, but the ghosts of the family's troubles with women began to haunt him.

The eldest son of the late Sen. Robert F. Kennedy has served on the same committees he joined as a freshman — Banking and Financial Services and Veterans' Affairs. He may not have reached the rank of legislative titan, but Kennedy has been a serious practitioner of the policymaking art, quieting those who once saw him as just a big grin with blue eyes — a dilettante trading on the family name.

Twice now Kennedy has helped protect the top Democrat on the Banking Committee, Texan Henry B. Gonzalez, from challenges to his leadership. The two men share an orientation toward addressing the concerns of minorities and the poor. Gonzalez, however, has an iconoclastic style that does not sit well with some of the other Democrats who are active on the committee. In 1990, when Gonzalez's critics tried to dump him as chairman of the panel (then called Banking, Housing and Urban Affairs), Kennedy drew on his natural political skills to help organize a "war room" operation that lined up key commitments to preserve Gonzalez's job.

When Democrats were organizing for the 105th Congress, Gonzalez faced a challenge to his ranking position on Banking. In the Democratic Caucus, Kennedy said that the committee's Democrats had pulled together to fight GOP initiatives, and he argued that even if Gonzalez had slowed (he is now past 80) , it would be "unconscionable" to dump him. "What are we going to do, take away a ranking membership from a guy who is a folk hero among Democrats?" asked Kennedy. "This guy defines the Democratic Party's values." Gonzalez held on one more time.

With Republicans in the majority, Kennedy spends much of his time trying to thwart or, failing that, at least tone down the GOP's proposals to roll back government regulations and reduce spending for social programs.

When the House in May 1997 passed legislation to overhaul the nation's public housing system, Kennedy offered several losing floor amendments, including a requirement that 75 percent of public housing be reserved for tenants with incomes of less than 30 percent of the area median income. (His proposal reserving 25 percent of units under similar criteria had passed during the 104th.) When Banking marked up its section of the GOP's big budget-reconciliation bill in 1995, Kennedy opposed conservatives' efforts to largely exempt small banks from the Community Reinvestment Act, which encourages banks to lend in the communities where they do business.

To protect cherished social programs from the budget-cutting axe, Kennedy has suggested savings elsewhere in the federal budget. In the fiscal 1997 Interior spending bill, he proposed an amendment to cut $42 million for road construction on federal timber tracts. Kennedy and his allies argued that the road construction program was a subsidy for the nation's timber harvesters and that current road-building practices damaged the environment. His amendment initially succeeded, but it was defeated on a revote.

In the fiscal 1997 VA-HUD spending bill, he tried unsuccessfully to transfer money from NASA's space station project to a variety of programs that help the homeless. He said the amend-

MASSACHUSETTS 8

Parts of Boston and suburbs — Cambridge; Somerville

The 8th, with a population almost 40 percent minority, is an outgrowth of mapmakers' attempt in 1992 to create a district where minorities would have substantial political influence. It links Hispanics in Chelsea, Haitians in Somerville and blacks in the Boston neighborhoods of Dorchester, Roxbury and Mattapan. Blacks are 23 percent of the district's population, Hispanics 11 percent and Asians 6 percent.

The large minority population helps fuel the service economy that dominates the 8th. Many work as custodians, clerical staff, orderlies and cooks at the local hospitals, universities, hotels and government offices. There is a degree of tension in the 8th between these laborers and white-collar professionals who work at the same institutions, but they coexist in reasonable peace partly because of their shared liberalism. The district gave Democrat Bill Clinton his highest percentage vote in the state in 1996.

Two of the world's most renowned universities — Harvard and the Massachusetts Institute of Technology — lie along the banks of the Charles River in Cambridge. Jokingly known as the Kremlin on the Charles, the exceedingly liberal city of 96,000 votes staunchly Democratic.

The two universities employ nearly 19,000 people and educate more than 32,000. Their research activities helped spawn a bevy of highly specialized computer and biotechnology firms in the area.

One of three cities challenging a state ballot initiative approved by voters in 1994 abolishing rent control, Cambridge has grown increasingly crowded. Students and young workers looking for quarters have flocked to nearby Somerville.

Despite the influx of yuppies and a handful of upscale restaurants and boutiques in the 1980s, Somerville remains a working-class, tight-knit community of triple-decker houses, neighborhood pubs and home-style eateries.

More than half the district's residents live in Boston, a city with a metropolitan air but small-town charm, thanks to its many and varied neighborhoods. At least 10 distinct Boston sections are within the 8th. They include: Fenway, home to the Red Sox baseball stadium (Fenway Park) and a large gay population; Mattapan, where black professionals have refurbished single-family homes; Jamaica Plain, a thriving liberal enclave with popular ethnic restaurants and retail shops; Beacon Hill, the historic district of stately brick townhouses behind the Massachusetts Statehouse; and Roxbury, an overwhelmingly poor black neighborhood rife with vacant lots.

The 8th also has Chelsea, a destitute city polluted by toxic waste discharged by oil ships traveling up Chelsea Creek. Things got so dire here in the early 1990s that the city government was put into state receivership and the schools were handed over to Boston University to manage.

Belmont, with its bankers, lawyers and other professionals, is the 8th's only suburban turf. One of the nation's largest concentrations of Armenians lives in neighboring Watertown.

1990 Population: 601,643. White 394,209 (66%), Black 140,276 (23%), Other 67,158 (11%). Hispanic origin 64,055 (11%). 18 and over 505,856 (84%), 62 and over 76,956 (13%). Median age: 30.

ment was critical to "making sure that very poor kids have a roof over their heads." But space station supporters fended him off.

A steadfast pro-labor liberal, Kennedy supported raising the minimum wage by 90 cents an hour and opposed GOP efforts to exempt small businesses from paying the higher wage. He opposed the welfare overhaul bill and voted against legislation barring federal recognition of same-sex marriages. He has opposed banning a particular abortion technique that opponents call "partial birth" abortion. He did end up on the same side as most conservatives on one issue in the 104th when he switched from his previous opposition (in 1990) to support a constitutional amendment banning flag desecration.

In the 103rd Congress, when Democrats held the House majority and Kennedy chaired the Banking Subcommittee on Consumer Credit and Insurance, his most prominent legislative effort was his attempt to end "redlining," the refusal of banks and insurance companies to do business in low-income communities that they deem bad financial risks. He sought to curb a practice sometimes called "reverse redlining" — lenders targeting low-income homeowners, minorities and the elderly for home equity loans on unfair terms that are prone to lead borrowers to default and lose their homes. Provisions to discourage home equity loan abuses eventually made it into law. Kennedy also won passage of language making it easier for consumers to fix errors in their credit reports.

Kennedy has taken a strong interest in the struggle against the British by Catholics living in Protestant Northern Ireland. In a 1988 visit to Northern Ireland, the Irish-Catholic Kennedy traded insults with a British soldier after his car was stopped at gunpoint.

Kennedy has also weighed in on U.S. policy towards Turkey, an outgrowth of the fact that his district includes a sizable population of

Armenian-Americans. During House work on the fiscal 1997 foreign operations appropriations bill, he helped lead efforts to ensure that it contained a provision barring aid to Turkey unless it lifts its blockade of humanitarian aid to Armenia, and another provision capping economic aid to Turkey at $22 million unless the government formally acknowledged that the Armenian population of the Ottoman Empire was subjected to genocide between 1915 and 1923.

At Home: In 1992, 1994 and 1996, Kennedy has polled 83 percent, 100 percent and 84 percent of the vote respectively, in the process spending a total of $3.5 million. His huge campaign budgets — especially the nearly $2 million he spent against nominal opposition in 1996 — has spurred speculation that Kennedy is laying the groundwork for entering the 1998 gubernatorial contest.

This is hardly the first time that "Joe Kennedy" and "governor" have been spoken in the same sentence. From the start of his political career, Kennedy has been a powerhouse at the polls. In early 1989, he rejected a 1990 gubernatorial bid; he also announced that he was separating from his first wife. After Weld's election that year, Democrats again whispered Kennedy's name as a 1994 prospect, but he silenced them in early 1993.

Kennedy was the front-runner in his 1986 House race to replace the retiring incumbent, Speaker Thomas P. O'Neill Jr., but he was not spared a tough campaign. In the Democratic primary, he became the target for a large field of opponents — and some journalists — who questioned his qualifications. Voters were reminded that Kennedy struggled through high school and graduated from college through the aid of correspondence courses. Stories rehashed the 1973 accident that crippled a passenger in the Jeep Kennedy was driving.

Kennedy grew more sure of himself and the issues. He espoused liberal positions on such matters as health care and education but positioned himself as the moderate in a field of liberals. This centrist move provoked a liberal backlash that fueled the campaign of state Sen. George Bachrach, who became Kennedy's closest rival. But Kennedy's moderate posture appealed to blue-collar voters, including many elderly and longtime Kennedy loyalists. Carrying working-class wards by huge margins while running even on Bachrach's home turf of Somerville, Kennedy easily won the 11-candidate primary.

Since then, Kennedy has coasted to re-election every two years. Redistricting gave him the state's first minority-dominated district in 1992, but his relations with the black community are solid, and no serious challenge from that quarter has emerged.

HOUSE ELECTIONS

1996 General		
Joseph P. Kennedy II (D)	147,126	(84%)
R. Philip Hyde (R)	27,303	(16%)
1994 General		
Joseph P. Kennedy II (D)	113,224	(100%)

Previous Winning Percentages: 1992 (83%) **1990** (72%) **1988** (80%) **1986** (72%)

CAMPAIGN FINANCE

	Receipts	Receipts from PACs	Expend-itures
1996			
Kennedy (D)	$2,414,369	$299,854 (12%)	$1,952,906
1994			
Kennedy (D)	$1,396,555	$203,618 (15%)	$839,275

DISTRICT VOTE FOR PRESIDENT

1996	1992
D 141,982 (77%)	**D** 136,582 (68%)
R 31,622 (17%)	**R** 39,284 (20%)
I 8,399 (5%)	**I** 25,503 (13%)

INTEREST GROUP RATINGS

Year	ADA	AFL-CIO	CCUS	ACU
1996	95	n/a	13	0
1995	80	91	17	8
1994	90	75	58	5
1993	95	92	20	4
1992	95	83	25	8
1991	95	100	20	0

KEY VOTES

1997	
Ban "partial birth" abortions	N
1996	
Approve farm bill	N
Deny public education to illegal immigrants	N
Repeal ban on certain assault-style weapons	N
Increase minimum wage	Y
Freeze defense spending	Y
Approve welfare overhaul	N
1995	
Approve balanced-budget constitutional amendment	Y
Relax Clean Water Act regulations	N
Oppose limits on environmental regulations	Y
Reduce projected Medicare spending	N
Approve GOP budget with tax and spending cuts	N

VOTING STUDIES

	Presidential Support		Party Unity		Conservative Coalition	
Year	S	O	S	O	S	O
1996	84	16	93	5	4	92
1995	84	12	91	5	21	77
1994	76	22	94	2	19	78
1993	79	18	93	3	14	86
1992	15	79	85	7	17	81
1991	24	74	94	3	14	86

9 Joe Moakley (D)

Of South Boston — Elected 1972, 13th term

Biographical Information
Born: April 27, 1927, Boston, Mass.
Education: U. of Miami; Suffolk U., J.D. 1956.
Military Service: Navy, 1943-46.
Occupation: Lawyer.
Family: Widowed.
Religion: Roman Catholic.
Political Career: Mass. House, 1953-65; Mass. Senate, 1965-69; sought Democratic nomination for U.S. House, 1970; Boston City Council, 1971-73.

Capitol Office: 235 Cannon Bldg. 20515; 225-8273.

Committees
Rules (ranking)
Legislative & Budget Process

In Washington: For Moakley, the two years of the 104th Congress were perhaps the most painful in his life, both professionally and personally.

Ironically, it may have been the professional setback — the Republican takeover of the House — that ultimately re-energized Moakley, giving him new will to fight.

It all began when the GOP captured the House in the 1994 elections. Until then, Moakley was chairman of the powerful Rules Committee, which decides which bills get to the House floor and how the House will debate each measure.

The GOP takeover essentially made Moakley a spectator on Rules, because the committee traditionally is stacked in favor of the majority, so as to implement its will in scheduling and steering floor action. Rules went from 9-4 Democratic in the 103rd to 9-4 Republican in the 104th.

Along with losing power, Moakley had to endure working longer hours. Republicans undertook one of the most ambitious floor schedules in recent congressional history, and that necessitated numerous late-night Rules meetings to get bills and amendments into the shape Republicans wanted before they took them to the full House.

Moakley began to look ill, and soon he announced that he needed a liver transplant because he had hepatitis B, a disease he believes he contracted while on a fact-finding trip to China in the 1980s. In July 1995, Moakley underwent a 12-hour liver transplant operation.

Around the same time, Moakley's wife, Evelyn Duffy, was battling cancer — a brain tumor that would take her life just a year later. And Moakley had other health difficulties, notably a hip problem that ultimately led him to get a replacement joint in November 1996.

So when reporters gathered for a Moakley news conference in September 1995, most assumed that the well-liked House veteran would be announcing his retirement. Indeed, many of his staff thought the same.

Instead, Moakley declared at the event that he would seek re-election, because, he said, the House needed liberals like him "fighting, kicking and screaming" against the GOP. Moakley said he had planned to announce his retirement, but that Evelyn persuaded him to stay on in office "despite her loneliness and physical condition." She never saw him win his 13th term; her March 1996 death came in their 39th year of marriage.

Moakley himself acknowledged, with his trademark humor, the role the GOP played in his plans. Shortly after the liver surgery, he released a statement which read, "I want to thank the new Republican majority for giving me a fighting spirit to oppose their backward agenda and for giving me the will to live until Willard Scott announces my 100th birthday on the 'Today Show.'"

As chairman of Rules from 1989 through 1994, Moakley carried out the Democratic leadership strategy that antagonized many Republicans — the use of closed rules to limit debate and prevent amendments. Faced with an increasingly confrontational GOP opposition and an increasingly fractured Democratic party, the Democratic leadership relied on restrictive rules to maintain an orderly legislative pace and keep distracting Republican amendments to a minimum.

Although Moakley as chairman executed the will of his party's leaders, he never personally earned a reputation as iron-fisted ruler. Even when Republicans complained about the tyranny of the majority on Rules, they rarely attacked Moakley himself. He is normally an affable fellow, as concerned about people and politics as about the fine print in the bills.

In 1995, with Republicans in charge of the House for the first time in 40 years, Moakley and his Democratic colleagues found they were the aggrieved minority.

Often in his new role as ranking Democrat on Rules, Moakley complained on the House floor about "backhanded" Republican tactics and "gag" rules. When the GOP sent up relatively insignificant bills under open rules, Moakley accused them of disingenuously padding their open-rule count. He even quoted statements that Rules Chairman Gerald B.H. Solomon of New York had

Boston and the 9th will be interesting to watch to assess the Clinton administration's ability to use federal public works dollars to fuel economic revitalization.

Three major projects have been under way in Boston through the 1990s: construction of a third tunnel under Boston Harbor connecting downtown to Logan International Airport; the depression and reconstruction of a north-south highway called the Central Artery; and cleanup of the polluted Boston Harbor. By 1997, cleanup of the Harbor was more than 90 percent complete. The three projects employed 20,000 when they were in full swing.

Basketball's Celtics and hockey's Bruins are already playing in their newly constructed arena, called the Fleet Center.

The projects are especially important to the 9th, where many working-class residents have not had a steady paycheck since the bottom fell out of the commercial real estate market in the late 1980s, halting new construction work. These blue-collar Democrats live primarily in Boston's ethnic neighborhoods.

Italians live in the North End, a compact section near the waterfront where suburbanites trek for some of the region's best food. South Boston, still overwhelmingly white and Irish, was the center of bitter opposition to school busing in the 1970s. Most of the residents of middle-class West Roxbury and Roslindale work downtown at banks, insurance companies, law offices and government agencies.

The 9th takes in nearly all the white sections of Boston. Redistricting in 1992 put most of the city's black, Hispanic and Asian neighborhoods into the 8th to create a minority-influence district.

South of Boston, the 9th includes half the city of Brockton. This former shoe-making capital has struggled since those factories departed in the 1960s. Brockton's population slipped slightly in the 1980s to just under 93,000. Brockton went Republican in the three presidential elections of the 1980s, but Bill Clinton carried it in 1992 and 1996.

MASSACHUSETTS 9

Part of Boston, southern suburbs — Taunton; Braintree; part of Brockton

Despite the presence of Boston, Brockton and (farther south) the city of Taunton, the 9th is evenly divided between urban and suburban communities. Many Boston executives live in and give a conservative flavor to the towns of Milton, Randolph, Medfield and Braintree. These communities (south and west of Boston) are known for their neatly manicured lawns, good schools and predominantly white populations. The state's burgeoning anti-abortion movement is centered in Braintree. Many of the 9th's suburban residents work outside the district, traveling the Route 128 beltway to companies such as Raytheon and Digital Equipment Corp.

In a state where many areas saw significant population decline in the 1980s, Milton held steady and Randolph grew. Adding to Milton's appeal is the nearby Blue Hills Reservation, a 6,500-acre preserve with trails, tennis courts, a golf course and small ski slope. Although Milton is George Bush's birthplace, it went narrowly for Clinton in 1992; Bush won Medfield. Clinton won both in 1996.

1990 Population: 601,643. White 526,931 (88%), Black 40,197 (7%), Other 34,515 (6%). Hispanic origin 27,953 (5%). 18 and over 486,597 (81%), 62 and over 105,018 (17%). Median age: 34.

made when he was in the minority and fighting closed rules.

During a floor fight over a Republican anti-crime proposal carrying the bill number 666, Moakley went to the Bible to find what he considered an apt description for the Republicans. He quoted a passage from the book of Revelations about a "beast rising out of the sea, with 10 horns and seven heads . . . uttering haughty and blasphemous words" that "deceives those who dwell on Earth."

But even when delivering such hyperbole, Moakley rarely lost his sense of humor and perspective. His good nature and political seasoning are useful as he jousts with Solomon, whose short temper is notorious. Moakley allows Solomon's sometimes hard words to slide by, accepting them as just a part of the political process.

Moakley even joked about his own health and political problems. Once while waiting for a Rules meeting to begin, Moakley told his colleagues that his 1996 general-election opponent was a surgeon, Paul Gryska. "I don't know if he wants my job or my business," he said.

In a rare foray into foreign affairs, Moakley took a leading role in responding to atrocities committed by the Salvadoran military in the 1980s, including the slayings of six Jesuit priests. At first, Moakley worked to relax U.S. immigration and deportation policy for Salvadorans. After the murders, Moakley chaired a task force charged with monitoring the government's response. The task force denounced the Salvadoran and military and judicial systems — both of which were heavily subsidized by U.S. aid.

In 1990, the House approved Moakley's call for a cut in military aid to the regime. After a 1993 United Nations' report that mirrored his own, Moakley called for declassifying government records to show how much the Reagan and Bush administrations knew about the case of the murdered priests.

At Home: Moakley is from the same school of party politics as the late Massachusetts Rep. Thomas P. O'Neill Jr., but it took a striking display of independence to elect him to Congress.

He was elected as a state representative by age 25 and knew early on he would like to succeed John W. McCormack in the House. He spent 16 years in the state Legislature and waited for McCormack to retire. But when the Democratic Speaker finally stepped down in 1970, Moakley found himself overmatched in the primary against the more visible Louise Day Hicks, who had nearly been elected mayor of Boston three years earlier on an anti-busing platform. She took the nomination and won in November.

Then things began to turn Moakley's way. Hicks lost her second mayoral try in 1971. The next year the district was substantially rearranged. Moakley, meanwhile, won a seat on Boston's City Council. By 1972, Hicks was highly vulnerable. In the primary, she was held to 37 percent; she won renomination only because five other candidates split the opposition.

Moakley was not one of the primary challengers. In the smartest political gamble of his life, he had decided to run as an independent. Insisting he was a lifelong Democrat, he staked out a position well to Hicks' left. Hicks barely carried the part of Boston remaining in the district, as Moakley cut into the Irish vote and swept the black areas. He won the seat by 5,000 votes.

Since then, only twice has Moakley's re-election tally fallen below 70 percent. In 1982, Republicans drafted state Rep. Deborah R. Cochran, promising to produce her ads. Though she carried several small towns in Bristol and Plymouth counties, Moakley's urban constituents gave him 74 percent of their vote. His 64 percent total was convincing enough to ward off GOP opposition in the next four elections.

Kidney surgery and a looming election made Moakley keenly aware of his mortality in 1992. Electorally, he looked to be endangered by the 90 overdrafts he had written at the House bank. But he quickly confronted the check problem and moved to defuse it: "It seems I should have majored in accounting rather than sheet metal when I was at Southie High," he quipped in April 1992.

Redistricting called for Massachusetts to lose one of its 11 congressional seats. Moakley made it clear he was in no mood for a tough campaign in unfamiliar territory.

As the dean of the delegation and chairman of Rules, Moakley was a valuable asset to Massachusetts officials. And after four decades in politics, he had a long list of allies willing to protect his turf in redistricting. Nicknamed the "clout meister" by one columnist, Moakley ran in a 9th District whose partisan makeup was barely changed by map-carvers. He won with 69 percent, spending more than $1 million along the way.

Since then, he has continued to cruise to victory, winning at or above 70 percent of the vote.

HOUSE ELECTIONS

1996 General		
Joe Moakley (D)	172,009	(72%)
Paul Gryska (R)	66,079	(28%)
1994 General		
Joe Moakley (D)	146,287	(70%)
Michael M. Murphy (R)	63,369	(30%)

Previous Winning Percentages: **1992** (69%) **1990** (70%) **1988** (100%) **1986** (84%) **1984** (100%) **1982** (64%) **1980** (100%) **1978** (92%) **1976** (70%) **1974** (89%) **1972** (43%)

CAMPAIGN FINANCE

	Receipts	Receipts from PACs	Expend-itures
1996			
Moakley (D)	$737,870	$344,471 (47%)	$769,122
Gryska (R)	$257,216	$12,916 (5%)	$232,527
1994			
Moakley (D)	$945,045	$467,267 (49%)	$981,247
Murphy (R)	$178,905	$2,764 (2%)	$178,071

DISTRICT VOTE FOR PRESIDENT

	1996		1992
D	156,335 (62%)	**D**	131,539 (48%)
R	72,614 (29%)	**R**	85,981 (31%)
I	18,714 (8%)	**I**	56,609 (21%)

KEY VOTES

1997	
Ban "partial birth" abortions	Y
1996	
Approve farm bill	N
Deny public education to illegal immigrants	?
Repeal ban on certain assault-style weapons	X
Increase minimum wage	Y
Freeze defense spending	Y
Approve welfare overhaul	N
1995	
Approve balanced-budget constitutional amendment	N
Relax Clean Water Act regulations	N
Oppose limits on environmental regulations	?
Reduce projected Medicare spending	N
Approve GOP budget with tax and spending cuts	N

VOTING STUDIES

	Presidential Support		Party Unity		Conservative Coalition	
Year	**S**	**O**	**S**	**O**	**S**	**O**
1996	68	19	83	6	10	75
1995	44	5	52	2	7	41
1994	78	22	97	0	25	75
1993	74	16	82	2	11	66
1992	15	71	89	2	13	85
1991	32	66	90	7	22	73

INTEREST GROUP RATINGS

Year	ADA	AFL-CIO	CCUS	ACU
1996	65	n/a	25	6
1995	35	100	13	0
1994	95	100	25	0
1993	80	100	9	0
1992	85	92	25	4
1991	90	100	20	5

10 Bill Delahunt (D)

Of Quincy — Elected 1996, 1st term

Biographical Information

Born: July 18, 1941, Quincy, Mass.
Education: Middlebury College, B.A. 1963; Boston College, J.D. 1967.
Military Service: Coast Guard, 1963; Coast Guard reserves, 1963-71.
Occupation: Lawyer.
Family: Divorced; two children.
Religion: Roman Catholic.
Political Career: Quincy City Council, 1971-73; Mass. House, 1973-76; Norfolk Cty district attorney, 1976-97.

Capitol Office: 1517 Longworth Bldg. 20515; 225-3111.

Committees

Judiciary
Commercial & Administrative Law; Courts & Intellectual Property
Resources
National Parks & Public Lands

The Path to Washington: Delahunt can thank the legal system for helping him gain membership in the 105th Congress.

The Democratic front-runner in the battle to succeed retiring 12-term Democratic Rep. Gerry E. Studds, Delahunt was expected to defeat three other contenders in the primary, then move on to face his Republican opponent.

But in a dramatic turn of events, former state Rep. Phil Johnston won what looked like a come-from-behind primary victory. He ran ahead of Delahunt, a longtime Norfolk County district attorney, by fewer than 300 votes.

Johnston's apparent upset of Delahunt set into motion several weeks of confusion in the 10th District. Delahunt called for a recount in parts of the district, prompting Johnston to do the same in other communities.

After more than a week, state election officials upheld Johnston as the winner.

But Delahunt was not ready to call it quits. He took the matter to court, charging that ballots that should have counted for him were mistakenly counted as blank.

A state Superior Court judge concurred, and declared Delahunt the primary winner. Johnston appealed in vain to the state's highest court, which upheld the lower court's ruling.

Among the likely reasons for Delahunt's political near-death experience was negative publicity he suffered during the primary campaign.

In July, a controversy emerged concerning charges to his state campaign fund for restaurant meals and other expenses.

His primary opponents seized upon the issue, but the Delahunt campaign said the expenditures had been found appropriate by the relevant state office.

Awaiting Delahunt after his long-sought primary victory was a general-election showdown with Republican state House Minority Leader Edward Teague, who had easily won his primary and had built a fundraising lead.

Republicans had hopes of winning the 10th, one of Massachusetts' less liberal districts. It seemed possible that Teague would benefit from the turmoil on the Democratic side.

The truncated general-election contest — Delahunt was certified as the winner 28 days before Election Day — was a classic liberal-conservative battle. Delahunt, a longtime public official, focused his campaign on themes such as the economic security of the middle class and support for environmental programs.

Teague highlighted his opposition to tax increases and support for welfare reform and a constitutional balanced-budget amendment. He also took a tough stand on crime.

As it turned out, Delahunt did not suffer much from his protracted fight for nomination. With Massachusetts voting comfortably to re-elect President Clinton, Delahunt won the 10th by 12 percentage points, taking 54 percent of the vote.

Delahunt says he is part of the generation that was inspired to enter politics by another Massachusetts politician, President John F. Kennedy. Delahunt recalls that as a Middlebury College student he was co-chairman of a Vermont students-for-Kennedy group. The other chairman was the late Ronald H. Brown, Clinton's former Commerce Secretary, who was one of Delahunt's fraternity brothers.

Prior to his two decades as Norfolk County district attorney, an elected position, Delahunt served on the Quincy City Council and as a state representative. Delahunt served in the Massachusetts House with three other members of the state's congressional delegation: Democrats John W. Olver, Barney Frank and Edward J. Markey.

Delahunt plans to follow in the footsteps of Studds, a liberal who focused much of his attention on environmental issues important to this coastal district. Delahunt sits on the Resources Committee, where Studds served. In addition, because of his background as a district attorney, Delahunt earned a spot on the Judiciary Committee, where he plans to stay involved with such issues as preventing domestic violence.

MASSACHUSETTS 10
South Shore — Cape Cod; islands

The coastal communities of the 10th have adapted throughout their long history to keep pace with changing economies. The former whaling center converted to textile production after the Civil War, then gave way to fishing and shipbuilding in the 1920s. Today, many of the once bountiful fish stocks that drove the economy are severely depleted, prompting some local innovators to find new ways to survive economically.

A researcher at Woods Hole Oceanographic Institute started his own business to produce a new medicine he developed from squid blood. The Maritime Administration came up with a new idea when it created the nation's first floating classroom by mooring the Southern Cross, a 450-foot ship, at the all-but-abandoned Fore River Shipyard in Quincy.

Since the 10th has never heavily relied on the defense industry and did not partake in the high-tech boom of the 1980s, its economy has stayed more constant than much of the state's. The district lost a small military installation, the South Weymouth Naval Air Station, in the 1995 round of base closures.

The coastal towns, particularly on Cape Cod, rely on tourists to help them survive the long, arduous winters. Though the Cape is referred to as a single locale, it is an eclectic mix, some of them ritzy summer vacation spots, some of them middle-class communities with year-round residents. Provincetown, at the cape's tip, is a liberal, predominantly gay artists' colony. Martha's Vineyard and Nantucket are summer retreats for the rich (and often, famous).

The mainland coastal towns of the 10th are commonly referred to as the South Shore communities. With the exception of a handful of thriving cranberry bogs, most of the South Shore towns consist of bedroom developments for Boston's professionals or Quincy's blue-collar workers. Commuter boats shuttle lawyers and doctors from Hingham and Hull across Boston Harbor to downtown.

Cape Cod, Hingham, Duxbury and Cohasset can offer a trove of votes to the right Republican. GOP Senate candidate Mitt Romney, in an unsuccessful challenge to Democrat Edward M. Kennedy in 1994, took several southern towns, including Duxbury, Chatham, Hingham and Hanover, each of which had gone for Republican George Bush in 1992. Quincy, popularized in the mid-1970s by white Bostonians fleeing the city's forced busing policies, continues its tradition as an ethnic melting pot. Irish and Italian immigrants led the way south; now the Asian-American community is a visible presence in Quincy and has forged a tie with nearby Boston's Chinatown.

The city of Brockton dominates the inland communities of the 10th. Split between the 9th and 10th districts, it has been suffering since the decline of its shoemaking industry in the 1960s.

The 10th overall is one of the Democrats' weaker districts in Massachusetts. But the political milieu in the Northeast was generally opposed to Republicans in 1996. President Clinton won large margins in erstwhile competitive districts like the 10th, where he beat Bob Dole by more than 20 percentage points.

1990 Population: 601,642. White 572,442 (95%), Black 12,519 (2%), Other 16,681 (3%). Hispanic origin 8,601 (1%). 18 and over 480,850 (80%), 62 and over 113,463 (19%). Median age: 36.

HOUSE ELECTIONS

1996 General		
Bill Delahunt (D)	160,745	(54%)
Edward Teague (R)	123,520	(42%)
A. Charles Laws (Green)	10,913	(4%)
1996 Primary		
Bill Delahunt (D)	17,927	(38%)
Phil Johnston (D)	17,808	(38%)
Ian Bowles (D)	10,410	(22%)
Walter S. Murray (D)	1,289	(3%)

CAMPAIGN FINANCE

	Receipts	Receipts from PACs	Expenditures
1996			
Delahunt (D)	$1,081,488	$228,733 (21%)	$1,072,986
Teague (R)	$1,274,616	$162,213 (13%)	$1,391,148

DISTRICT VOTE FOR PRESIDENT

	1996		1992
D	169,805 (56%)	D	133,776 (42%)
R	101,813 (34%)	R	101,936 (32%)
I	28,097 (9%)	I	80,791 (26%)

KEY VOTES

1997	
Ban "partial birth" abortions	N

MICHIGAN

Governor: John Engler (R)
First elected: 1990
Length of term: 4 years
Term expires: 1/99
Salary: $123,800
Term limit: 2 terms
Phone: (517) 373-3400
Born: October 12, 1948; Mt. Pleasant, Mich.
Education: Michigan State U., B.S. 1971; Thomas M. Cooley Law School, J.D. 1981.
Occupation: Lawyer.
Family: Wife, Michelle Dumunbrun; three children.
Religion: Roman Catholic.
Political Career: Mich. House, 1971-79; Mich. Senate, 1979-91, majority leader, 1985-91.

Lt. Gov.: Connie Binsfeld (R)
First elected: 1990
Length of term: 4 years
Term expires: 1/99
Salary: $91,400
Phone: (517) 373-6800

State election official: (517) 373-2540
Democratic headquarters: (517) 371-5410
Republican headquarters: (517) 487-5413

REDISTRICTING

Michigan lost two House seats in reapportionment, dropping from 18 districts to 16. Federal court issued the map March 23, 1992.

STATE LEGISLATURE

Legislature. Meets January-June, September-December.

Senate: 38 members, 4-year terms
1996 breakdown: 22R, 16D; 35 men, 3 women
Salary: $51,895 + $8,925 expenses
Phone: (517) 373-2400

House of Representatives: 110 members, 2-year terms
1996 breakdown: 58D, 52R, 79 men, 31 women
Salary: $51,895 + $8,925 expenses
Phone: (517) 373-0135

URBAN STATISTICS

City	Population
Detroit	1,027,974
Mayor Dennis Archer, D	
Grand Rapids	189,126
Mayor John H. Logie, N-P	
Warren	144,864
Mayor Mark Steenbergh, N-P	
Flint	140,761
Mayor Woodrow Stanley, N-P	
Lansing	127,321
Mayor David Hollister, D	

U.S. CONGRESS

Senate: 1 D, 1 R
House: 10 D, 6 R

TERM LIMITS

For state offices: Yes
Senate: 2 terms
House: 3 terms

ELECTIONS

1996 Presidential Vote

Bill Clinton	52%
Bob Dole	39%
Ross Perot	9%

1992 Presidential Vote

Bill Clinton	44%
George Bush	36%
Ross Perot	19%

1988 Presidential Vote

George Bush	54%
Michael S. Dukakis	46%

POPULATION

1990 population		9,295,297
1980 population		9,262,078
Percent change		+<1%
Rank among states:		8
White		83%
Black		14%
Hispanic		2%
Asian or Pacific islander		1%
Urban		71%
Rural		29%
Born in state		75%
Foreign-born		4%
Under age 18	2,458,765	26%
Ages 18-64	4,675,687	50%
65 and older	1,108,461	12%
Median age		32.6

MISCELLANEOUS

Capital: Lansing
Number of counties: 83
Per capita income: $18,697 (1991)
Rank among states: 20
Total area: 58,527 sq. miles
Rank among states: 23

Isle Royale
KEWEENAW
Lake Superior
KEWEENAW
HOUGHTON
Lake Superior
ONTONAGON
BARAGA
Marquette
GOGEBIC
MARQUETTE
1
ALGER
LUCE
CHIPPEWA
IRON
SCHOOLCRAFT
MACKINAC
DICKINSON
DELTA
MENOMINEE
Lake Huron
EMMET
CHEBOYGAN
1
PRESQUE ISLE
CHARLEVOIX
Lake Michigan
ANTRIM
OTSEGO
MONTMORENCY
ALPENA
LEELANAU
Traverse City
GRAND TRAVERSE
BENZIE
KALKASKA
CRAWFORD
OSCODA
ALCONA
MANISTEE
WEXFORD
MISSAUKEE
ROSCOMMON
OGEMAW
IOSCO
ARENAC
Saginaw Bay
MASON
LAKE
OSCEOLA
CLARE
GLADWIN
HURON
2
4
MIDLAND
BAY
OCEANA
NEWAYGO
MECOSTA
ISABELLA
Midland
Bay City
5
Saginaw
TUSCOLA
SANILAC
MUSKEGON
MONTCALM
GRATIOT
SAGINAW
Muskegon
KENT
GENESEE
OTTAWA
Grand Rapids
IONIA
CLINTON
SHIAWASSEE
Flint
LAPEER
ST. CLAIR
Port Huron
Holland
3
9
10
OAKLAND
Pontiac
MACOMB
Lansing
8
BARRY
EATON
ALLEGAN
LIVINGSTON
11
12
INGHAM
7
WASHTENAW
WAYNE
Kalamazoo
VAN BUREN
Battle Creek
Jackson
13
Benton Harbor
KALAMAZOO
CALHOUN
JACKSON
Ypsilanti
6
Districts 13, 14, 15 and 16 Wayne County, including city of Detroit
St. Joseph
BERRIEN
CASS
ST. JOSEPH
BRANCH
HILLSDALE
LENAWEE
MONROE
16
Ann Arbor

MICHIGAN
DETROIT AREA DISTRICTS

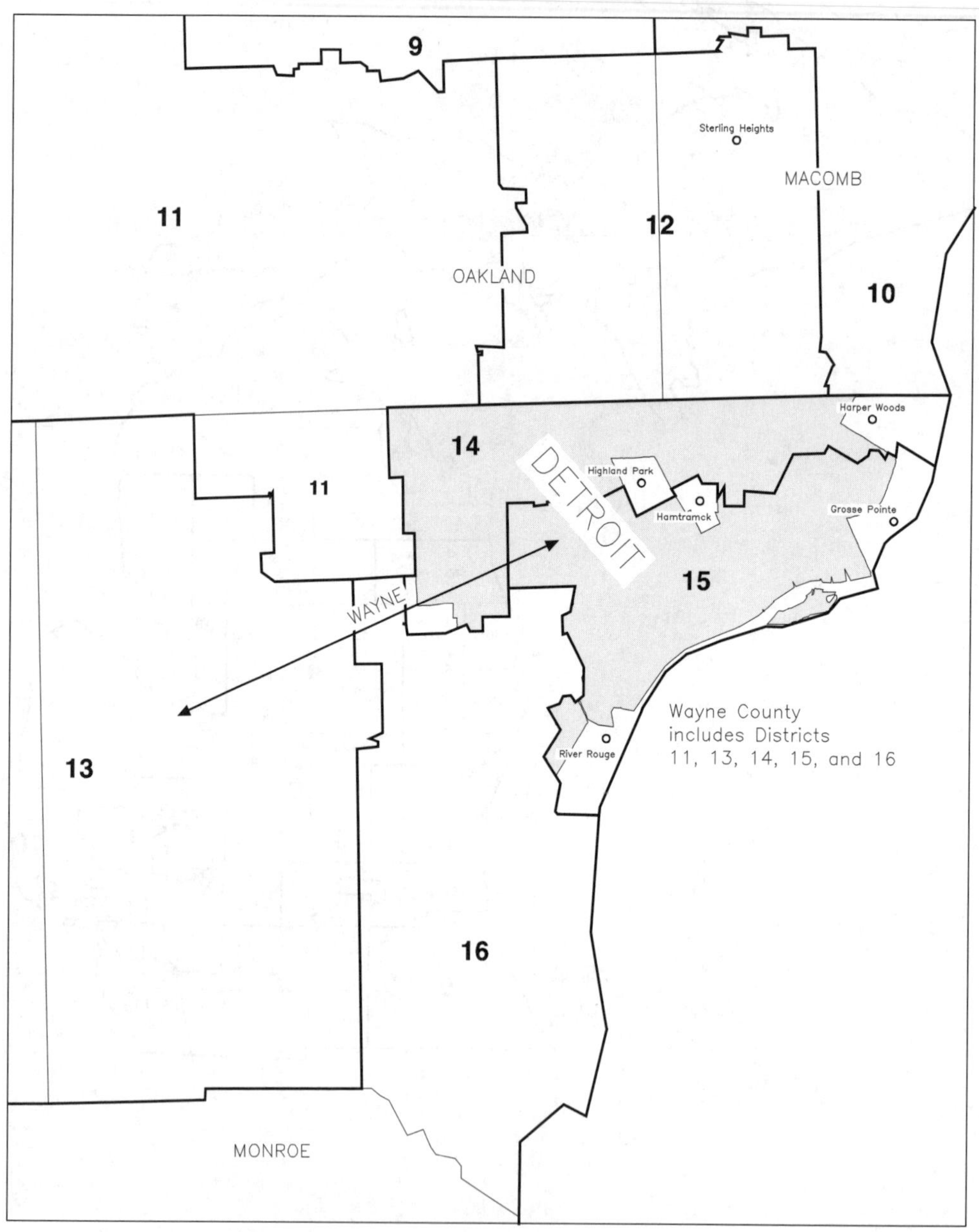

Carl Levin (D)

Of Detroit — Elected 1978, 4th term

Biographical Information
Born: June 28, 1934, Detroit, Mich.
Education: Swarthmore College, B.A. 1956; Harvard U., LL.B. 1959.
Occupation: Lawyer.
Family: Wife, Barbara Halpern; three children.
Religion: Jewish.
Political Career: Detroit City Council, 1970-77, president, 1974-77; Michigan special assistant attorney general; Michigan Civil Rights Commission general counsel.
Capitol Office: 459 Russell Bldg. 20510; 224-6221.

Committees
Armed Services (ranking)
Governmental Affairs
International Security, Proliferation & Federal Services; Investigations
Select Intelligence
Small Business

In Washington: During their years in the Senate, Levin and Maine Republican William S. Cohen often formed a bipartisan team. They alternated as chairman of a subcommittee with jurisdiction over government procurement. They cosponsored the original legislation banning most gifts to lawmakers and imposing new reporting requirements for lobbyists.

In the 105th Congress, Levin and Cohen are linked again. Levin is the new ranking minority member of the Senate Armed Services Committee, Cohen the new secretary of Defense.

The two men have a history of working together on defense issues. In 1996, they jointly declared their strong opposition to additional B-2 fighter planes.

In 1991, after U.S. troops in the war with Iraq had come under missile attack, Republicans stepped up the pressure for a national anti-missile defense. Cohen and Levin helped broker a bipartisan compromise in which Democrats backed deployment of a missile-defense system compatible with the existing treaty on the subject, and Republi-cans shelved, for the time being, their push for space-based anti-missile weapons.

In 1979, Cohen and Levin were part of a bipartisan coalition battled to save the all-volunteer armed forces against an effort to restore the draft. Draft proponents warned that higher pay, more comfortable barracks and other amenities needed to attract recruits would draw money from weapons modernization; too many new recruits were below par in mental aptitude and discipline; and there was no draft to make youth from middle-class and well-to-do families share the burden of national defense. Though Congress restored draft registration, the anti-draft coalition led a successful fight to raise pay and offer new benefits, which helped raise the caliber of recruits.

Levin has been willing to trim the Pentagon's budget. He unsuccessfully tried to cut $48 million for two F-16 fighters from the fiscal 1997 fiscal appropriations bill. The budget requested four of the planes and the Air Force had asked for two more, but the Senate appropriated (and authorized) eight. At the same time, he added a provision requiring a security audit of all U.S. bases and earmarked $14 million for stepped-up protection measures against potential terrorist attacks. He supported efforts in 1996 to cut defense spending by $4 billion and to cut the authorization for a missile defense by $300 million.

And he opposed Republican efforts to pass legislation mandating by 2003 an anti-missile defense system that would protect all 50 states against a relatively small number of attacking missiles and requiring the president to try to negotiate with Russia changes in the 1972 Anti-Ballistic Missile (ABM) Treaty to liberalize some of its restrictions on anti-missile deployments. Levin contended that the bill prematurely would commit the country to an expensive anti-missile deployment.

Despite his liberal bent, Levin's legislative skills earn high marks from more conservative Democrats. "What Carl has in his favor is that he's absolutely honorable, he's very smart, and he's a very effective legislator," said Joseph I. Lieberman of Connecticut. "He has great legislative patience. . . . He'll hang in there."

And Levin's predecessor as ranking Democrat on the Armed Services Committee, Sam Nunn of Georgia, once said Levin's point of view was "pro-defense" but "questioning and probing and skeptical."

Levin has contended that personal relationships often are a larger factor in a member's effectiveness than philosophical positions, especially since many of the ideological lines on defense policy are already blurred. "Personal style is really what's more critical, in the Senate particularly, than where you can label someone on a spectrum," he has said.

Levin and Cohen have worked together on issues other than defense. Since 1979, they swapped the posts of chairman and ranking member of the Senate Governmental Affairs Subcommittee on Government Management, depending on which party controlled the Senate.

They played key roles in crafting legislation intended to make government purchasing agents rely more on competitive bidding and other commercial practices.

The two lawmakers were successful in gaining passage in mid-1994 of legislation to reauthorize the independent counsel law, which expired in December 1992. The law provides for independent prosecutors, operating outside the Justice Department, to investigate alleged wrongdoing by top administration officials.

The law had lapsed after Levin's efforts to pass an extension fell short in the 102nd Congress. He was blocked by Republicans who argued that the Justice Department was capable of investigating executive branch wrongdoing without an independent counsel and who objected that the law was not mandatory for members of Congress. But their main complaint was that Democrats had wielded the law against Republican administrations, pointing to the lengthy, expensive probe by independent counsel Lawrence E. Walsh into the Iran-contra affair.

Levin said that Republicans were "killing the most important single Watergate reform on the books."

And they tasted victory in the 104th Congress when the Senate imposed a new ban on gifts and President Clinton signed a law imposing new reporting requirements for lobbyists. Cohen and Levin's efforts had fallen short in the 103rd Congress, when Senate Republicans filibustered the bill to death. But in the new Congress, Levin and fellow Democrat Paul Wellstone of Minnesota forced Senate Republicans to agree to a vote in July by threatening to attach the bill's provisions to the telecommunications deregulation bill. The Levin-Cohen legislation, which covered both gifts and lobby registration, was split into two bills.

On the lobbying bill, Levin negotiated a compromise with Mitch McConnell of Kentucky, the Republicans' point man on the issue. In the Senate, the bill passed, 98-0.

"Lobbying is part of democratic government, an inherent part of it, a constitutionally protected part of constitutional and democratic government," Levin said. "But the public has a right to know, and the public should know, who is being paid to lobby, how much they are being paid, on what issue."

Levin also helped fashion a compromise on the gift ban, which also passed the Senate unanimously. Since the gift ban was a change in Senate rules, it did not require House approval. The House later enacted its own ban on gifts.

In the 105th Congress, Levin will be one of the five Democrats on a 10-senator task force responsible for recommending changes to the current rules, procedures and practices of the Senate.

Levin is one of six members of Congress who filed suit challenging the constitutionality of the new line-item veto law. The lawmakers contend that the line-item veto is unconstitutional because it gives the "president, acting alone, the authority to 'cancel' and thus repeal provisions of federal law."

"The Constitution does not give the president the power, on his own, to repeal a law," Levin said. "I think it just clearly violates the Constitution."

A federal court judge in April 1997 ruled in favor of the senators, throwing out the line-item veto law. "Under the Constitution, both houses of Congress and the president must be involved in the adoption or repeal of a law," he said after the decision was announced. "The line item veto act allows the president to repeal a law unilaterally. This is not a particularly subtle issue to me; it is black-letter constitutional law."

He fought against GOP efforts to pay the legal fees of former White House Travel Office director Billy Dale. The bill earmarked $500,000 to pay Dale's legal expenses in defending himself against charges that he embezzled $68,000 from the office. Dale was the only employee indicted, but ultimately a jury acquitted him. Levin argued that reimbursing Dale would reverse years of precedent in which Congress had declined to reimburse indicted persons. He said there was nothing improper about Dale's indictment and that the Senate historically had reimbursed only people who had been investigated but not indicted.

On social issues, Levin falls clearly on the left. He voted to confirm Dr. Henry W. Foster Jr. as surgeon general, voted against banning a particular abortion technique that opponents call "partial birth" abortion and opposed a constitutional amendment on flag burning. He opposed efforts to prohibit abortions at overseas medical facilities. He voted to ban job discrimination on the basis of sexual orientation, but did vote to bar federal recognition of same-sex marriages.

Levin's older brother, Sander, is a U.S. representative. They are one of two brother teams serving in the Senate and House. The Hutchinsons of Arkansas, Tim in the Senate and Asa in the House, are the other.

At Home: Every six years Michigan Republicans target Levin, and every six years, their arrows fall far short.

In 1996, Republicans chose Ronna Romney, once married to a son of the late GOP Gov. George W. Romney, over Jim Nicholson, a self-made millionaire who owned and operated a chemical company. At the end of a bitter primary battle, Romney had withstood Nicholson's late television ad assault. Her campaign relied on followers of her radio talk show and organized groups such as the National Rifle Association and Michigan Right to Life. Romney responded with biting television ads of her own that questioned Nicholson's Republican loyalties and conservative credentials.

In the fall, Romney attempted to attack Levin on issues such as his opposition to the balanced-budget amendment to the Constitution. But Levin never lost his lead in the polls or in campaign finance receipts. Running on a ticket headed by Clinton, Levin finally had a campaign in a year favorable to the Democrats. In 1984, Levin had survived a big Reagan presidential victory in Michigan; six years later, Levin won comfortably even as the state's Democratic governor was being ousted from office.

Levin had been anticipating a tough race in 1984 and pumped up his fundraising with dire warnings that the national GOP planned to spend millions of dollars against him. The warnings worked so well that Levin outspent his Republican opponent, former astronaut Jack Lousma, who went heavily into debt in the primary and was strapped for funds in the fall campaign.

But Levin needed more than a monetary advantage as Walter F. Mondale's presidential campaign faded and it became apparent that Ronald Reagan's coattails could cause Levin real problems. He aired a film clip of Lousma warming up a Japanese audience in 1983 by telling them about the Toyota he owned. In Michigan, where Japanese cars meant joblessness for auto workers, Lousma's statement was a major embarrassment. Few were soothed by his plea that the Toyota belonged not to him, but to his son.

The Toyota film clip meshed well with Levin's overall campaign theme; he had billed himself as "A Proven Fighter for Michigan" and stressed his work to limit auto imports, extend unemployment benefits and help relieve the state unemployment compensation debt. Reagan carried Michigan with 59 percent, but Levin held on to win with 52 percent.

In 1990, Levin's political skills were again on view. With national GOP leaders sharpening their knives for him, Levin amassed a daunting campaign treasury and early on aired television ads touting his accomplishments. Only after his opponent, GOP Rep. Bill Schuette, began attacking did Levin fire back, thereby preserving his "nice guy" image. While Democratic Gov. James J. Blanchard lost his bid for a third term, Levin won a decisive 57 percent of the vote.

The big break in Levin's successful 1978 Senate challenge was a major misstep by the GOP incumbent, Robert P. Griffin. Disappointed at losing the contest for Senate Republican leader in 1977, Griffin announced that he would retire the next year and began skipping votes on the floor. He eventually changed his mind about running, but by that time had missed a third of the Senate votes over an entire year. Levin said Griffin was obviously tired of the job, and the voters agreed that the incumbent deserved a rest.

SENATE ELECTIONS

1996 General

Carl Levin (D)	2,195,738	(58%)
Ronna Romney (R)	1,500,106	(40%)

Previous Winning Percentages: 1990 (57%) **1984** (52%) **1978** (52%)

CAMPAIGN FINANCE

	Receipts	Receipts from PACs		Expend-itures
1996				
Levin (D)	$6,021,723	$889,738	(15%)	$5,965,017
Romney (R)	$3,269,294	$227,202	(7%)	$3,287,547

KEY VOTES

1997	
Approve balanced-budget constitutional amendment	N
Approve chemical weapons treaty	Y
1996	
Approve farm bill	N
Limit punitive damages in product liability cases	N
Exempt small businesses from higher minimum wage	N
Approve welfare overhaul	Y
Bar job discrimination based on sexual orientation	Y
Override veto of ban on "partial birth" abortions	N
1995	
Approve GOP budget with tax and spending cuts	N
Approve constitutional amendment barring flag desecration	N

VOTING STUDIES

	Presidential Support		Party Unity		Conservative Coalition	
Year	**S**	**O**	**S**	**O**	**S**	**O**
1996	86	14	94	6	29	71
1995	89	11	96	3	2	96
1994	90	10	92	8	16	84
1993	93	7	97	3	20	80
1992	32	67	91	8	21	76
1991	37	63	90	10	30	70

INTEREST GROUP RATINGS

Year	ADA	AFL-CIO	CCUS	ACU
1996	85	n/a	23	5
1995	100	100	26	0
1994	95	88	20	0
1993	95	91	18	8
1992	100	92	20	0
1991	90	75	0	5

Spencer Abraham (R)

Of Auburn Hills — Elected 1994, 1st term

Biographical Information
Born: June 12, 1952, Lansing, Mich.
Education: Michigan State U., B.A. 1974; Harvard U., J.D. 1979.
Occupation: Lawyer; congressional aide; vice presidential aide.
Family: Wife, Jane; three children.
Religion: Eastern Orthodox Christian.
Political Career: Mich. Republican Party chairman, 1983-90.
Capitol Office: 329 Dirksen Bldg. 20510; 224-4822.

Committees
Budget
Commerce, Science & Transportation
Communications; Consumer Affairs, Foreign Commerce & Tourism; Manufacturing & Competitiveness (chairman); Science, Technology & Space; Surface Transportation & Merchant Marine
Judiciary
Constitution, Federalism & Property Rights; Immigration (chairman)

In Washington: During his first two years in the Senate, Abraham took the Republican line on most major issues, evincing the conservatism for which he was known during his years as a behind-the-scenes strategist in Michigan and Washington.

But Abraham also used his considerable political skills to set himself apart from — and often in front of — his colleagues. He served as one of a handful of advisers to GOP presidential candidate Bob Dole and was credited with persuading him to tout a 15 percent across-the-board tax cut — a proposal that gave Dole's doomed campaign a brief burst of late-summer momentum. On immigration policy, Abraham often disagreed with prevailing party sentiment and established himself as the pre-eminent GOP defender of immigration, successfully disabling more senior members' attempts to stem legal immigration and, for the 105th, taking over as chairman of the Judiciary Subcommittee on Immigration.

At the 1996 Republican National Convention (where he chaired the rules committee), Abraham attributed his high profile to impatience. "I wasn't willing to sit around and wait for seniority to get involved on the front line," he told the Detroit News.

That became evident early in the 104th Congress, when Abraham was chosen to manage Senate floor debate on a key party issue — the balanced-budget constitutional amendment. The measure fell one vote short of passage, but the effort showcased Abraham's ability to gain the favor of Republican leaders. Abraham became a part of the "kitchen cabinet" advising Majority Leader Trent Lott when the 105th Congress began.

The foundation for this relationship and others like it had been established years before, when Abraham served as chief political operative and deputy chief of staff to Vice President Dan Quayle, and when he oversaw the National Republican Congressional Committee (NRCC) during the 1992 election cycle. He also played a pivotal role in the election of his political ally and friend, John Engler, to Michigan's governorship.

During the 104th, Abraham voted with his party more than 90 percent of the time, standing up for efforts to end an arms embargo in Bosnia, cap product liability damages and ban a particular abortion technique that opponents call a "partial birth" abortion. He also was point man for the GOP's unsuccessful plan to dismantle the Commerce Department.

But for all his loyalty to conservative causes, Abraham stood out more for his disagreements. Most prominently, this grandson of Lebanese immigrants tirelessly fought Republicans who wanted to limit legal immigration.

In debate on overhauling immigration policy, Abraham and his allies succeeded in bifurcating the treatment of legal and illegal immigration, thwarting those who wanted to keep them joined in one piece of legislation.

Abraham tangled with Alan K. Simpson of Wyoming, the chairman of the Judiciary Committee's immigration panel in the 104th, in markups on the combined immigration bill. He gathered enough allies to split the bill in two. When the legal immigration bill later came up in subcommittee, Abraham teamed up with liberal Democrat Edward M. Kennedy of Massachusetts to win approval of an amendment that replaced Simpson's cuts in legal immigration with a more limited restructuring of a family reunification system. That bill never made it to the Senate floor.

"We will not allow unhappiness with illegal immigration to cause us to make imprudent changes in legal immigration laws," Abraham said.

Though legal immigration was his passion, Abraham also spoke out on Simpson's measure to stem the number of illegal immigrants coming to the United States. In the Judiciary Committee and on the floor, he offered amendments to rid the bill of a pilot program that would have required employers in some states to verify the immigration status of potential workers by consulting a hotline. Abraham said that likely errors in the identification system would hurt workers, and he called the plan itself a burden on employers. The Judiciary Committee and the Senate did not agree, defeating Abraham's amendment both times it was raised.

Simpson retired at the end of the 104th Congress, and in what The Wall Street Journal called "the biggest policy shift since Madonna became a mother," Abraham took the Immigration Subcommittee reins in 1997. With him wielding the gavel, any new proposals targeting legal immigration will likely get a cool response.

Though immigration has become Abraham's signature issue, he has differed less vocally from the party line on some other matters. He supported efforts to restore some student aid funding and opposed eliminating a program that helps the poor pay heating costs.

He counseled a middle ground on a couple of causes dear to conservatives, suggesting in lieu of a constitutional amendment on term limits that states be allowed to set their own term limits, and proposing that limits on medical malpractice awards not be applied to states that do not want them.

At Home: After a career spent helping Republicans run for office, Abraham won one for himself in 1994. His bid for the Senate was his first outing as a candidate in his own right and the first victory for a Republican Senate candidate in Michigan in 22 years.

Abraham has been a GOP operative since graduating from Michigan State University in 1974. That year he ran the unsuccessful House campaign of Republican Clifford W. Taylor. Two years later, Abraham managed Taylor again and lost again. Both times, the Democratic winner was Bob Carr. It took two decades, but Abraham finally turned the tables by defeating Carr in 1994 to win the Senate seat.

After his first forays into politics, Abraham finished his degree at Harvard Law School and returned to Michigan and his native Lansing. After a short stint as a law professor at the Thomas M. Cooley Law School there, Abraham became chairman of the Michigan state GOP in 1983. His tenure in that job is remembered for two achievements: his careful brokering of the feud between supporters of various candidates in the 1988 presidential cycle (Michigan held a very early straw poll in 1987) and the elevation of Engler to the governorship in 1990.

In that same year, Abraham went to Washington to work for Quayle and then took charge of the NRCC.

Abraham's performance at NRCC and his ties to Quayle were at issue when the party chose a new chairman of the Republican National Committee that winter. Abraham wanted the job as top party operative and spokesman, but he lost to Mississippi's Haley Barbour. Had he gotten the nod, however, Abraham likely would not have been free to run for the Senate when Democratic incumbent Donald W. Riegle Jr. announced that he would retire at the end of the 103rd Congress.

Abraham defeated Ronna Romney in a closely contested GOP primary, then ran his fall campaign against Carr on themes familiar from the many campaigns he had run for others: a forceful attack against liberal Democrats combined with an appeal to traditional family values.

He promoted a plan to "shake up Washington" and joined GOP Senate candidates across the country in a set of pledges, the "Agenda for a Republican Majority," akin to the House GOP's "Contract With America." The pledges included support for tax cuts, welfare reform, tougher anti-crime measures and higher defense spending. One clear difference between Abraham and Carr was on trade, with Carr talking about the need to protect Michigan's autoworkers and Abraham touting free trade. He ran nine percentage points ahead of Carr, taking 52 percent of the vote.

SENATE ELECTIONS

1994 General		
Spencer Abraham (R)	1,578,770	(52%)
Bob Carr (D)	1,300,960	(43%)
Jon Coon (LIBERT)	128,393	(4%)
1994 Primary		
Spencer Abraham (R)	292,399	(52%)
Ronna Romney (R)	270,304	(48%)

CAMPAIGN FINANCE

	Receipts	Receipts from PACs		Expend-itures
1994				
Abraham (R)	$4,477,331	$619,675	(14%)	$4,453,648
Carr (D)	$3,039,175	$831,121	(27%)	$3,040,416
Coon (LIBERT)	$297,526	$216	(0%)	$303,369

INTEREST GROUP RATINGS

Year	ADA	AFL-CIO	CCUS	ACU
1996	15	n/a	92	95
1995	5	0	100	87

KEY VOTES

1997	
Approve balanced-budget constitutional amendment	Y
Approve chemical weapons treaty	Y
1996	
Approve farm bill	Y
Limit punitive damages in product liability cases	Y
Exempt small businesses from higher minimum wage	Y
Approve welfare overhaul	Y
Bar job discrimination based on sexual orientation	N
Override veto of ban on "partial birth" abortions	Y
1995	
Approve GOP budget with tax and spending cuts	Y
Approve constitutional amendment barring flag desecration	Y

VOTING STUDIES

	Presidential Support		Party Unity		Conservative Coalition	
Year	S	O	S	O	S	O
1996	37	63	95	5	95	5
1995	23	77	94	6	89	11

1 Bart Stupak (D)

Of Menominee — Elected 1992, 3rd term

Biographical Information

Born: Feb. 29, 1952, Milwaukee, Wis.

Education: Northwestern Michigan College, A.A. 1972; Saginaw Valley State College, B.S. 1977; Thomas M. Cooley Law School, J.D. 1981.

Occupation: Lawyer; state trooper; patrolman.

Family: Wife, Laurie Ann Olsen; two children.

Religion: Roman Catholic.

Political Career: Mich. House, 1989-91; sought Democratic nomination for Mich. Senate, 1990.

Capitol Office: 1410 Longworth Bldg. 20515; 225-4735.

Committees

Commerce

Finance & Hazardous Materials; Health & Environment; Oversight & Investigations

In Washington: With his stands against abortion and for gunowners' rights, Stupak ranks among the more conservative Democrats in the House. In fact, in states with warmer climes than Michigan, some Democrats of his philosophical ilk have switched to the GOP.

Stupak, though, will have none of that: In 1995, when five House Democrats joined up with the chamber's new GOP majority, Stupak paired with liberal Colorado Democrat Patricia Schroeder to introduce legislation penalizing such fence-jumping. Their measure would have allowed a two-thirds vote of the House to deny party-switchers their seats, and it also required them to return campaign funds provided by their former party.

"I think being a member of a political party is like taking a marriage vow — for better or worse, until death do us part," Stupak wrote in a letter introducing the legislation to his Democratic colleagues.

With assiduous attention to local concerns, Stupak has secured a district that had traditionally voted Republican. The 1st sprawls across both Michigan peninsulas and covers 42 percent of the state's landmass.

Stupak's opposition to abortion reflects the beliefs of most of his fellow Catholics from the Upper Peninsula. He spoke at an anti-abortion rally timed to coincide with the 1996 Democratic National Convention; it was organized by the Christian Coalition and the National Right to Life Committee. A former state trooper, he has been a consistent vote against gun control measures, opposing a five-day waiting period for handgun purchases and a ban on certain semiautomatic assault-style weapons.

Stupak holds a seat on the prized Commerce Committee, where he works well with ranking member and fellow Michigander John D. Dingell, and with panel Republicans.

During debate on the telecommunications bill in the 104th, Stupak pushed an amendment eagerly sought by local governments. It removed a provision from the bill that would have forced cities to charge all telecommunications companies equal fees for the use of public rights-of-way. The amendment was adopted, 338-86. Though Stupak opposed the House-passed version of the telecommunications bill, he voted for the final deal worked out in conference with the Senate.

He also warmed to the Republican-pushed idea of overhauling the welfare system. Like many Democrats, including President Clinton, Stupak opposed the first Republican version of welfare reform, but in the end he embraced the revamped package that Congress passed and Clinton signed into law.

Stupak also cast an early vote for a Republican plan aimed at discouraging illegal immigration by denying a public education to anyone in the United States illegally. That provision was dropped from the final immigration bill.

During the 104th, Stupak's Democratic loyalties were plainest in his votes against many of the signature initiatives unveiled as part of the GOP's "Contract With America," including a $189 billion tax cut package and constitutional amendments to limit congressional terms and require a balanced federal budget. He opposed Republican efforts to add defense dollars to Clinton's budget request, he backed a minimum wage increase and he sided with unions on some other key votes dividing labor and business.

On the environment, a key area of contention between the parties in the 104th, Stupak had a mixed record. He supported the Republican effort to require that cost-benefit analyses be performed before new regulations are imposed. But he voted against GOP legislation to ease clean water regulations and to block the Environmental Protection Agency from enforcing many federal clean air and water laws.

"I'm not necessarily a big fan of the Endangered Species Act," Stupak stated. "But look at all the other environmental attacks that have gone on in this Congress. When you put the whole group together, you have just reversed all the gains in the past 25 years."

In early 1993, Stupak came close to voting

MICHIGAN 1
Upper Peninsula; northern Lower Michigan

Built in 1957, the Mackinac Bridge connects the 1st's two regions — the UP and northern Lower Michigan.

Above the Straits of Mackinac, the UP covers miles of woodland, bordering Wisconsin and Canada. Three of the Great Lakes form its boundaries — Huron to the southeast, Michigan to the south and Superior to the north.

The UP's rugged terrain breeds a special brand of independence, qualities ascribed to the "Yoopers" who live here. They contend with prevailing northwesterly winds that dump several hundred inches of snow every year in the northern reaches of the area. Economic opportunity has been in short supply since the mining industries began to fade at the turn of the century.

The western UP has been hit the hardest. The extraction of copper, iron and timber long supported the area, but mining is almost non-existent and timber jobs have dwindled. Tourism and recreation are the only growth industries.

Known as "Copper Country," these western counties once produced about 90 percent of the copper mined in the United States. But by 1890, most of the purest copper had been mined and prices began to fall.

Calumet, located in the northwestern arm of the UP, was once a booming copper-mining town of 50,000. Now it is a village of 4,000. On Lake Superior, Marquette tells the same story. Some shipping still departs from the city, but many of the ore docks are abandoned. Still, Marquette County is the UP's most populous.

Marquette's economy was hit hard again when K.I. Sawyer Air Force Base showed up on the 1993 base-closure list. The base's payroll for 1,600 military and civilian employees is responsible for about 20 percent of the local economy. It closed in September 1995.

The descendants of the miners, loggers, mill workers and longshoremen retain a union-oriented tradition, thus making the western UP a Democratic stronghold. In each of his races, Stupak has won every county north of the Straits of Mackinac — the dividing line between the UP and Lower Michigan.

The UP's eastern section votes more like the counties south of the bridge. Chippewa and Mackinac counties lean Republican and are more dependent on tourism and farming. The only major city in this area is Sault Ste. Marie (Chippewa), a port city on the Canadian border.

About half the district vote is cast on the Republican turf south of the bridge. The population center of northern Lower Michigan is Traverse City (Grand Traverse County), a GOP stronghold. Tourists and vacationers come for the resorts, golf courses and sandy beaches of Grand Traverse Bay.

Outside the Traverse City area, the communities are conservative, though newly arrived retired autoworkers have boosted the Democratic vote in Cheboygan, Emmet, and Presque Isle counties.

In presidential voting, Bill Clinton won the district in 1992 and 1996, the last time winning all but six of the district's 28 counties.

1990 Population: 580,956. White 558,614 (96%), Black 4,909 (1%), Other 17,433 (3%). Hispanic origin 3,308 (1%). 18 and over 431,643 (74%), 62 and over 108,423 (19%). Median age: 35.

against the budget resolution outlining Clinton's spending and taxing priorities, saying his constituents were not happy with the plan's defense cuts and that they feared a proposed energy tax would raise home heating bills. Adding to local economic anxiety was the fate of the 1st's largest employer, K.I. Sawyer Air Force Base, which was on the 1993 final list of bases recommended for closure. But by August 1993, when Clinton's budget came up for final approval (without the energy tax), Stupak was on board with the administration.

In his first term, Stupak won passage of a measure aimed at stopping the spread of the illegal drug methcathinone, or CAT, which is easy to make. A less potent form of its main ingredient, pure ephedrine, is used in many over-the-counter asthma drugs, making it hard for the Drug Enforcement Administration (DEA) to trace.

The bill required companies manufacturing the pure form of ephedrine to register with the DEA and submit drug sale records. CAT's production arose as a problem in the UP in 1991, when Ann Arbor graduate students shared the "recipe" for making CAT with Marquette-area students.

Stupak joined in 1996 with Republicans in modifying an anti-carcinogen food law once Commerce Committee Chairman Thomas J. Bliley Jr., R-Va., agreed to most of a Clinton administration proposal to ensure that tolerance levels of pesticides protect infants, children, pregnant women and the elderly.

Taking a crack at reform of congressional procedures, Stupak has proposed legislation that would more than double the number of appropriations bills, in order to limit each bill to one government function. As things stand, such disparate programs as housing and the space station are lumped together in the same appropriations measure.

Stupak offered another novel idea when ethics problems threatened to knock House

Speaker Newt Gingrich off his perch at the start of the 105th. Stupak suggested that retired Sen. Bob Dole of Kansas, the GOP nominee for president in 1996, would make a fine compromise choice for Speaker.

That notion drew more jeers than cheers, and Stupak also earned less than rave reviews when a group of congressional and White House staffers were polled for a movie publicity stunt; he was named "Boss from Hell." But he took the news in good stride: "At least we're recognized as one of [Congress'] leaders."

At Home: A lawyer previously in private practice in Menominee, far out on the UP — the Upper Peninsula on the Wisconsin border — Stupak prides himself on his "Yooper" background. (His wife was elevated to the position of Menominee mayor in 1996.) He was a state trooper and served one term in the state House before quitting to run unsuccessfully for the state Senate.

To win election to Congress, Stupak had to survive both a three-way primary and a general-election fight that Republicans worked hard to win.

His November opponent, Philip E. Ruppe, had represented the 1st from 1967 until 1979. In the 1978 race, Ruppe yielded his secure seat to run for the Senate, when it appeared that GOP Sen. Robert P. Griffin would not run again. But Griffin changed his mind, leaving Ruppe with no place to go.

Republican Robert W. Davis inherited the district. He likely would have kept it in 1992, had he not been the third-leading abuser of the House bank (878 overdrafts). He dropped his re-election bid.

Two Republicans and three Democrats (including Stupak) were soon in the race. State and national GOP leaders were concerned that their candidates were not strong enough to hold the seat, so they recruited Ruppe to run again.

Ruppe easily won his primary. Stupak's win was not quite as easy, but he prevailed by carrying the UP, where most Democrats are located.

Stupak then turned his fire on Ruppe, branding him the choice of insiders. With George Bush sinking to 35 percent in the district's presidential voting, Ruppe picked a bad year for a comeback attempt. Stupak won by 10 points.

The GOP in 1994 offered millionaire Gil Ziegler, who attacked Stupak for backing controversial Clinton administration proposals. But Ziegler could not dent Stupak's base in the UP, where he won every county. Stupak improved to 57 percent, with the support of the National Rifle Association and Michigan Right to Life.

In 1996, the GOP failed to recruit several preferred choices to run against Stupak, including the Democrat who had beaten Stupak for the 1990 state Senate nod. (Michigan Republicans, including Gov. John Engler, tried to recruit him for a switch and the House run.) The eventual GOP nominee, Bob Carr, refused PAC money and was unable to trade on the name he shared with a former Democratic House member and the party's 1994 Senate nominee, finishing with just 27 percent.

HOUSE ELECTIONS

1996 General		
Bart Stupak (D)	181,486	(71%)
Bob Carr (R)	69,957	(27%)
Michael C. Oleniczak (LIBERT)	2,830	(1%)
1994 General		
Bart Stupak (D)	121,433	(57%)
Gil Ziegler (R)	89,660	(42%)
Michael McPeak (NL)	2,399	(1%)

Previous Winning Percentages: 1992 (54%)

CAMPAIGN FINANCE

	Receipts	Receipts from PACs	Expend-itures
1996			
Stupak (D)	$497,435	$354,577 (71%)	$458,509
Carr (R)	$5,910	0	$5,834
1994			
Stupak (D)	$681,883	$502,988 (74%)	$678,925
Ziegler (R)	$668,690	$3,829 (1%)	$665,398

DISTRICT VOTE FOR PRESIDENT

	1996		1992
D	125,135 (47%)	**D**	118,879 (42%)
R	107,577 (40%)	**R**	100,997 (35%)
I	31,184 (12%)	**I**	65,339 (23%)

KEY VOTES

1997	
Ban "partial birth" abortions	Y
1996	
Approve farm bill	N
Deny public education to illegal immigrants	Y
Repeal ban on certain assault-style weapons	Y
Increase minimum wage	Y
Freeze defense spending	Y
Approve welfare overhaul	Y
1995	
Approve balanced-budget constitutional amendment	N
Relax Clean Water Act regulations	N
Oppose limits on environmental regulations	Y
Reduce projected Medicare spending	N
Approve GOP budget with tax and spending cuts	N

VOTING STUDIES

	Presidential Support		Party Unity		Conservative Coalition	
Year	**S**	**O**	**S**	**O**	**S**	**O**
1996	73	27	84	16	37	63
1995	71	29	82	16	39	60
1994	72	28	84	15	67	33
1993	72	28	85	13	41	59

INTEREST GROUP RATINGS

Year	ADA	AFL-CIO	CCUS	ACU
1996	75	n/a	25	20
1995	75	92	38	28
1994	70	100	42	24
1993	70	100	9	17

2 Peter Hoekstra (R)

Of Holland — Elected 1992, 3rd term

Biographical Information
Born: Oct. 30, 1953, Groningen, Netherlands.
Education: Hope College, B.A. 1975; U. of Michigan, M.B.A. 1977.
Occupation: Furniture company executive.
Family: Wife, Diane M. Johnson; three children.
Religion: Christian Reformed Church.
Political Career: No previous office.
Capitol Office: 1122 Longworth Bldg. 20515; 225-4401.

Committees
Budget
Education & Workforce
Oversight & Investigations (chairman); Workforce Protections

In Washington: A furniture executive and novice to politics before winning the 2nd in 1992, Hoekstra was a genuine outsider who pretty quickly found himself playing an insider's role in the House's majority party.

Republican leaders liked what they saw of Hoekstra in his freshman term, and after the GOP won control of the House in 1994, he landed a seat on the Budget Committee and the gavel of the Oversight and Investigations Subcommittee on the Economic and Educational Opportunities Committee (now called Education and the Workforce).

Hoekstra helped the leadership out of a pinch in 1995 when he stepped off the Budget Committee to make room for freshman Mark W. Neumann, R-Wis. Neumann's vote against a fiscal 1996 defense spending bill had provoked GOP leaders to remove him from an Appropriations subcommittee position, but they gave him a soft landing onto Budget to tamp down complaints from Neumann's Class of 1994 colleagues that he was being punished for voting his conscience.

By the 105th, Hoekstra was back on Budget (and still a subcommittee chair). In the meantime, the leadership had put him in charge of a task force looking at how to change the way Congress operates.

Hoekstra's first task was to try to develop consensus for legislation strengthening reporting requirements for lobbyists and banning most gifts to lawmakers. Some House Republicans simply wanted to pass the same measures that the Senate did. Others wanted weaker versions. "We're working through that process," Hoekstra said. "The process is not to have one house do all the work and the other house rubber-stamp it because it's easy." In the end, the House passed the Senate version of a lobbying-regulation bill, which President Clinton signed. It approved a more stringent ban on gifts.

Anger over the proposed gift ban disrupted a House Republican Conference in November 1995, with many members objecting to the stringent restrictions. Tensions ran so high that afterward, Hoekstra met with Gerald B.H. Solomon, R-N.Y., chairman of the Rules Committee, to talk about whether to proceed with the scheduled markup of the gift rules proposal the next day. After meeting with Hoekstra, Solomon decided to cancel the Rules markup and use the time to meet with Republicans to discuss how to make the proposed gift restrictions more palatable.

"If we're going to get through this constructively, we've just got to talk to people," Hoekstra said.

Hoekstra supported the House leadership's decision to use an open rule on the lobbying registration bill, even though supporters of the measure said it was a back-door effort to scuttle the legislation. Hoekstra said the open rule on lobbying gave all members a chance to be heard.

The task force then turned its attention to overhauling the campaign finance system. The group rejected efforts championed by fellow Republicans John McCain of Arizona in the Senate and Christopher Shays of Connecticut in the House, which would ban "soft money" and PAC contributions and offer incentives for candidates to limit campaign spending. Instead, the Hoekstra task force proposed: reducing the maximum PAC contribution to candidates from $5,000 per election to between $1,000 and $2,000 per election; doubling the limit on individual contributions from $1,000 to $2,000 per election cycle; and requiring House candidates to raise a majority of their funds from within their district. The 104th Congress did not pass any campaign finance overhaul legislation.

Though Hoekstra's relations with the leadership seem to have been good, at the start of the 105th his vote on re-electing Newt Gingrich as Speaker was in doubt. Shortly before the day of the vote, he joined seven colleagues for dinner. The group talked about how Gingrich's ethics problems were just the latest example of him "doing dumb things" that put the GOP in a bind. They recalled Gingrich's embarrassing $4.5 million book advance, which he later gave up, and

MICHIGAN 2
West — Holland; Muskegon

In terms of GOP hegemony, the 2nd is rivaled only by the 3rd as Michigan's staunchest Republican district. From the fruit and vegetable farmers to the conservative Dutch communities on the 2nd's southern border, Democratic candidates find little sympathy.

The district runs 140 miles along Lake Michigan, from Manistee County south to Allegan County, but the population is concentrated in three counties — Allegan, Muskegon and Ottawa.

The city of Holland, on the border between Allegan and Ottawa counties, is a GOP bastion with a strong Dutch influence. The westernmost point of the "Dutch Triangle" (formed by Holland, Grand Rapids and Kalamazoo), Holland and its environs were settled by immigrants from the Netherlands in the mid-19th century. That heritage is highlighted at an entertainment complex — Dutch Village — where life in the Old Country is replicated, and at the city's two wooden shoe factories. In May, the city hosts a Tulip Festival.

Ottawa County has voted Republican in every presidential election since 1928. In 1988, it voted for George Bush by better than 3 to 1; four years later, it gave Bush 59 percent, 22 points higher than his statewide average. In 1996, even as Democrat Bill Clinton was carrying the state with 52 percent, Ottawa voters were giving 64 percent of their ballots to Republican Bob Dole.

Hoekstra's career as an executive with office furniture maker Herman Miller Inc. was a plus with voters. Three of the nation's four top office furniture makers are based in western Michigan. Two of the companies, Herman Miller and Haworth Inc., have headquarters here. Prince Corp., an automotive parts manufacturer, also is headquartered here and is a large employer.

The 2nd's limited Democratic strength is found north of Ottawa and Allegan counties in and around the industrial city of Muskegon. The city has one of western Michigan's largest, albeit struggling, manufacturing bases.

The black inland precincts and the city's ethnic neighborhoods turn out a strong Democratic vote, though the surrounding suburbs often offset their ballots. Heavily forested Lake and Manistee counties are also sources of Democratic votes, as is the small industrial city of Cadillac (Wexford County).

Tourism, farming and food-processing are the economic mainstays for the rest of the district. Towns along the Lake Michigan shoreline, such as Manistee, are heavily reliant on retirees, Chicago tourists and boaters who sail across the lake into their municipal marinas.

Cherries and asparagus are among the products grown by local farms and processed within the district. Fremont, in Newaygo County, is home to the international headquarters of Gerber baby foods.

1990 Population: 580,956. White 539,604 (93%), Black 25,324 (4%), Other 16,028 (3%). Hispanic origin 17,586 (3%). 18 and over 414,968 (71%), 62 and over 86,799 (15%). Median age: 32.

the two government shutdowns that damaged the House GOP's standing in the 1996 campaign.

Hoekstra recalled for his colleagues that the Speaker seemed to blame his Democratic enemies and errors by his lawyers for the mess.

When Hoekstra returned to his office, he received a phone call from Gingrich, seeking his support. Hoekstra told the Speaker he should apologize to Republicans. On the Speakership vote, though, Hoekstra backed Gingrich.

Hoekstra served notice of his "outsider" status with the first bill he introduced: It would have amended the Constitution to let voters enact legislation themselves. Rules would have been set for placing initiatives on a national ballot. "I'm doing this because I'm frustrated that Congress is not doing some of the stuff that it should be doing," he told the Detroit News.

He also introduced legislation calling for a national referendum on congressional term limits, an idea that was embraced by Ross Perot and his United We Stand America organization.

Hoekstra follows a conservative line on social issues: He is anti-abortion and authored an amendment to the fiscal 1996 omnibus appropriations bill that prevented medical schools from being penalized for refusing to teach abortion procedures to obstetrician/gynecology students.

He voted in the 103rd for a five-day waiting period for handgun purchases, but he opposed a ban on certain semiautomatic assault-style weapons. "Guns are merely an easy target for liberals who need a scapegoat for lax criminal justice standards that they have supported for years," Hoekstra said.

Given his background in furniture, it is no surprise that Hoekstra looks out for business interests. He became a NAFTA supporter after a fact-finding trip to Mexico that he said made him realize Mexico's potential as a market for U.S.-made goods. He said he walked into a plant in Nuevo Laredo and found that all its office furniture was from the company he had worked for in Michigan, Herman Miller Inc. The furniture was made in the United States and exported to Mexico.

Though Hoekstra voted for final passage of

legislation raising the minimum wage in 1996, he opposed the bill when it first came up in the House and supported efforts to exempt small businesses from its provisions.

When what was then known as the House Education and Labor Committee considered legislation in 1994 to revamp the U.S. health care system, Hoekstra tried to protect business. He sponsored amendments to delete a separate health program for seasonal and migrant workers and to strip provisions providing fairly generous benefits to people who retire before age 65 and who earn less than $90,000. Both amendments failed.

Although Hoekstra holds conservative views similar to those of the GOP incumbent he upset in the 1992 primary, Guy Vander Jagt, his personal style is leagues apart. A quiet man who campaigned from his bicycle, Hoekstra brings an almost ascetic approach to his life in Washington. Vander Jagt, in contrast, was a bombastic orator with a reputation for high living; he was featured in a 1990 exposé on ABC of House Ways and Means Committee members cavorting on a Barbados beach with lobbyists.

Hoekstra's strong convictions about balancing the federal budget have been evident in a number of votes. He voted against NASA's space station, against repealing 4.3 cents of the federal gasoline tax and against the omnibus fiscal 1997 appropriations bill. He mounted an unsuccessful effort to strike $240 million in fiscal 1998 funding for the Corporation for Public Broadcasting from the fiscal 1996 Labor-HHS bill. Hoekstra argued that financing for the corporation, one of the few federal programs funded two years in advance, should be considered only after the program was reauthorized. His proposal lost, 136-286.

At Home: The Netherlands-born Hoekstra won his seat by upsetting 26-year veteran Vander Jagt, who was attacked as being too concerned with national party fundraising — he was chairman of the National Republican Congressional Committee — and out of touch with the voters at home.

Lacking name recognition, Hoekstra embarked on a grass-roots campaign. He saved his vacation time to take a county-by-county bicycle tour of the 2nd, which runs 140 miles along Lake Michigan.

Unable to afford TV ads, Hoekstra advertised on radio and campaigned door-to-door. He accepted no PAC funds in the 1992 election cycle.

But Vander Jagt was well-financed and embarked on a last-minute media blitz touting his effectiveness in Washington. The message did not sell, however, and Hoekstra won with 46 percent to Vander Jagt's 40 percent in a three-way race.

It was perhaps to Hoekstra's advantage that the redrawn 2nd included most of one large county and part of a second that were new territory for Vander Jagt. The incumbent carried the district's eight other counties, but these two — Allegan and Ottawa, the district's most populous — chose Hoekstra.

Hoekstra took 63 percent of the vote in the 1992 general election, and he has had no re-election difficulties.

HOUSE ELECTIONS

1996 General		
Peter Hoekstra (R)	165,608	(65%)
Dan Kruszynski (D)	83,603	(33%)
Bruce A. Smith (LIBERT)	3,071	(1%)
1994 General		
Peter Hoekstra (R)	146,164	(75%)
Marcus Pete Hoover (D)	46,097	(24%)

Previous Winning Percentages: 1992 (63%)

CAMPAIGN FINANCE

	Receipts	Receipts from PACs	Expend-itures
1996			
Hoekstra (R)	$218,347	$0 (0%)	$185,831
Kruszynski (D)	$30,395	$8,680 (29%)	$30,962
1994			
Hoekstra (R)	$140,279	$0 (0%)	$134,979
Hoover (D)	$9,794	$7,500 (77%)	$9,792

DISTRICT VOTE FOR PRESIDENT

	1996		1992
D	108,427 (41%)	**D**	95,342 (34%)
R	133,146 (50%)	**R**	127,008 (45%)
I	23,527 (9%)	**I**	58,258 (21%)

KEY VOTES

1997	
Ban "partial birth" abortions	Y
1996	
Approve farm bill	Y
Deny public education to illegal immigrants	Y
Repeal ban on certain assault-style weapons	Y
Increase minimum wage	N
Freeze defense spending	Y
Approve welfare overhaul	Y
1995	
Approve balanced-budget constitutional amendment	Y
Relax Clean Water Act regulations	Y
Oppose limits on environmental regulations	N
Reduce projected Medicare spending	Y
Approve GOP budget with tax and spending cuts	Y

VOTING STUDIES

	Presidential Support		Party Unity		Conservative Coalition	
Year	S	O	S	O	S	O
1996	34	66	91	9	65	33
1995	20	80	91	9	78	22
1994	40	60	94	6	81	19
1993	38	62	86	14	82	18

INTEREST GROUP RATINGS

Year	ADA	AFL-CIO	CCUS	ACU
1996	10	n/a	88	95
1995	5	0	96	84
1994	20	0	100	86
1993	20	8	91	88

3 Vernon J. Ehlers (R)

Of Grand Rapids — Elected 1993; 2nd full term

Biographical Information

Born: Feb. 6, 1934, Pipestone, Minn.

Education: Calvin College, 1952-55; U. of California, Berkeley, A.B. 1956, Ph.D. 1960.

Occupation: Professor; physicist.

Family: Wife, Johanna Meulink; four children.

Religion: Christian Reformed Church.

Political Career: Kent County Commissioner, 1975-83, chairman, 1979-82; Mich. House, 1983-85, assistant Republican floor leader; Mich. Senate, 1985-93, president pro tempore.

Capitol Office: 1717 Longworth Bldg. 20515; 225-3831.

Committees

House Oversight

Science
Energy & Environment; Technology

Transportation & Infrastructure
Aviation; Water Resources & Environment

Joint Library

In Washington: Ehlers has the mien of a quiet scientist — he claimed in his maiden House speech to have been the first physicist ever elected to Congress. Conservative to the core, he has proved increasingly willing to speak his mind in party councils, generally supporting the GOP's stances on social and fiscal issues, but breaking from the Republican herd over the issue of environmental protections.

A loyal ally of Speaker Newt Gingrich, Ehlers brings a scientist's close attention to bear on his congressional tasks. He toes the party line on meat and potatoes Republican fare such as balancing the budget, but leaves the big legislative picture to others. Instead, he delves into such concerns as congressional access to the Internet, the procedures that Americans abroad employ to vote by absentee ballot, and the proper name of a scientific agency. Often called upon by colleagues to lend a scientific perspective to a policy question, Ehlers is occasionally willing to inject personal concerns, such as his severe allergy to animal hair, into House debates.

The son of a minister and a devout Christian himself, Ehlers is the co-author of several books that meld theology and science as guides to managing the environment. They include "Earthkeeping: Christian Stewardship of Natural Resources" and "Earthkeeping in the 90's: Stewardship of Creation." Ehlers supports Republican thought that environmental protections should be tailored to local needs and concerns, but he broke with his colleagues on numerous occasions during the 104th Congress when they set about making regulations, in his opinion, too user-friendly.

"When you have a group of individuals frustrated for 40 years, and they're suddenly given the keys to do it, going overboard is natural," Ehlers commented in 1996. Still, he could not go along with his colleagues' uncorked desire to rewrite regulations, voting against a major overhaul of the clean water act, a move to block the Environmental Protection Agency's ability to enforce key protections, and efforts to reimburse property owners for "takings" when environmental regulations lower the value of their property. All these initiatives passed the House but never became law.

When Republicans realized they had ceded political ground to Democrats on the issue, Gingrich created a task force on the environment composed of both anti-regulatory members and proponents of environmental safeguards. He named Ehlers to the panel from the latter wing.

Ehlers opposed the idea of opening up Alaska's Arctic National Wildlife Refuge to oil drilling, which was contained in the GOP's vetoed fiscal 1996 budget balancing package. He was one of 32 members who wrote a letter to congressional leaders in 1996 to urge cancellation of construction of the Animas-La Plata water project in Colorado, a $475 million system of canals and dams.

He also opposed the big Auburn Dam proposed for Northern California, a potential $949 million expenditure. "The era of the big dam is over," Ehlers declared. "We simply do not have the resources."

Ehlers broke party ranks on a couple of high-profile issues that did not concern the environment during the 104th, supporting an increase in the minimum wage (after initial opposition) and calling for an increase in the student loan program. Ehlers also opposed a constitutional amendment that would have given Congress and the states authority to ban desecration of the flag.

He was the only Republican to vote against a 1995 bill to make it harder for death-row inmates to delay their executions with appeals. That and flag burning aside, Ehlers is generally a reliable vote for the social conservative side on issues including abortion and gunowners' rights. Ehlers was a frequent defender of larger Republican initiatives during the 104th, appearing on the House floor to present the case for the bills to overhaul welfare, Medicaid and Medicare, and the package to balance the budget over seven years. He preached the gospel of giving more power and authority to states, arguing that federal fiat often led to irrational bureaucratic thinking.

MICHIGAN 3
West Central — Grand Rapids

Politically, the Grand Rapids-based 3rd looks a lot like it did when Gerald R. Ford represented the area. The middle-class residents of the city and the farmers and small-town denizens of the surrounding counties make it friendly ground for the GOP.

Kent County is home to more than 85 percent of the district's population. The nearly 190,000 people who live in Grand Rapids make it Michigan's second-largest city. With its diversified economic base, Grand Rapids has weathered recent economic downturns better than most cities its size.

Kent's largest employers count several industries, including auto parts and home products, fabricated metal products, office furniture, avionics systems, automotive stampings and children's apparel. The furniture-making industry is one of Kent County's largest employers. Unlike the furniture industry of North Carolina, western Michigan's furniture makers produce mostly office furniture, much of it the metal variety. Steelcase Inc. employs about 8,400 people in the Grand Rapids area.

Beginning with the 1970s invention of systems furniture, local companies prospered and experienced record growth. That slowed, however, by the early 1990s, as growth in office space stagnated and companies nationwide began to cut their white-collar work forces.

General Motors has a significant presence in Grand Rapids, and another major employer (just east of the city, in Ada) is the Amway Corp., a home- and personal-care products company whose Amway Grand Hotel dominates the city's emerging skyline. The DeVos family, which runs the company, is a leading financial supporter of Republican candidates and causes.

Grand Rapids has a sizable blue-collar work force and, for western Michigan, a high number of black and Hispanic residents, many of whom live in townships north and south of the city. Still, their Democratic votes typically are not enough to offset the GOP wave from the rest of the city and county.

More than one-fifth of the people in the district claim Dutch ancestry, and the strong work ethic and conservative cultural attitudes prevalent among Dutch-Americans are a big factor in commerce and politics.

The local GOP has two wings. The "Dutch Wing" is more conservative, made up of business owners and those affiliated with the several Christian colleges in the 3rd. The "Ford Wing," counting in its number many higher-income executives and younger professionals, holds to a somewhat more moderate brand of Republicanism.

Outside Kent, in Ionia County and part of Barry County, the 3rd is Republican and agriculture-oriented, though not fruit-producing like coastal western Michigan. Ionia County has no town or village with even close to 10,000 residents.

Flat, rural and Republican Barry County is home to Hastings, which boasts the distinction of being listed in a 1993 book as one of America's 100 best small towns.

Bob Dole won the 3rd in 1996 with 53 percent.

1990 Population: 580,956. White 520,262 (90%), Black 43,356 (7%), Other 17,338 (3%). Hispanic origin 16,069 (3%). 18 and over 416,628 (72%), 62 and over 75,777 (13%). Median age: 31.

Ehlers maintains his seats on the Transportation and Infrastructure, Science, and House Oversight committees. On Transportation, he will have a chance to play a hand in the big highway and transit reauthorization bill in the 105th. But most of his time in the 104th was spent on activities without direct political benefit.

Taking note of Ehlers' computer aptitude (he had helped get Michigan's government running on the Internet), Gingrich asked Ehlers to apply his skills to Congress, focusing particularly on making more information about the House available online to the general public. Ehlers offered members training, helped equip their offices with network software and new hardware, and helped offices set up World Wide Web sites to communicate better with constituents.

The goal, he quipped, was to make the system "so simple that an adult can use it."

Ehlers' duties on House Oversight have included serving on task forces looking into electoral disputes surrounding New Hampshire Republican Charles Bass and Democrat Loretta Sanchez of California. He also managed a bill to make it easier for Americans living abroad to vote absentee and to ensure the security of their ballots.

Ehlers offered one amendment to the fiscal 1997 science authorization bill, to block a change in the name of the National Science Foundation to the National Science and Engineering Foundation. Ehlers has a son who is an engineer and expressed respect for the discipline, but contended it would be counterproductive to single out subspecialties and might cause confusion internationally. His arguments prevailed, 339-58.

Ehlers supported a move to amend House administrative procedures that eliminated some anachronistic procedures. "Among the statutes repealed by this bill are the provisions relating to contracting for horses and wagons for the House," Ehlers noted "As someone who is intensely allergic to horses, I am pleased to see that section repealed."

Ehlers' allergies were also brought to bear on a debate about public housing. When Carolyn B. Maloney, D-N.Y., offered an amendment to guarantee elderly public housing dwellers the right to keep pets, Ehlers protested. He said that severe animal hair allergies had led to his being schooled at home until college. Although he said he had never spoken of his "handicap" before, he protested the implications of Maloney's amendment.

"When I first read that pets were being introduced into nursing homes and rest homes, I had an involuntary shudder. I thought if that happens and it appears in all nursing homes and rest homes, I will never be able to go to one," Ehlers worried. But personal appeals from pet-loving members carried the day, and the amendment passed, 375-48.

At Home: In mid-1993, Ehlers was president pro tem of the Michigan Senate and nearing 60; he was looking for a new political challenge and weighing a 1994 campaign for the Senate seat of Democrat Donald W. Riegle Jr. But GOP Rep. Paul B. Henry died of brain cancer on July 31, 1993, and by year's end, Ehlers had won the right to replace Henry in the 3rd.

After receiving his physics doctorate from the University of California at Berkeley at 26, Ehlers stayed in Berkeley as a lecturer and research physicist for six years. In 1966, he traded that liberal atmosphere for the much more conservative, religious-oriented campus of Calvin College in Grand Rapids, Mich., where he had spent three years as an undergraduate.

In Michigan, Ehlers cultivated both his love for science and his interest in politics, devoting more time to the latter pursuit as the years passed. While teaching at Calvin, he took his first steps into public life in 1970 as a member of the West Michigan Environmental Action Council's board of directors. In 1973, he served on the board of the West Michigan Environmental Protection Foundation. In 1974, he was elected to the Kent County Commission, and he was chair of that body from 1979-82.

In 1982, Ehlers won a political job with responsibilities that took him away from Grand Rapids — a state House seat. Over the next dozen years, Ehlers' career in politics shadowed that of Henry's, whom he succeeded in the state House, the state Senate and finally Congress. They became friends at Calvin, where Henry taught political science.

After Henry's death, a large field of Republicans formed to try for the 3rd. Once Ehlers decided against a Senate race and launched a House bid, he moved to the head of the Republican pack. In an eight-way November 1993 primary, Ehlers won the GOP nomination, taking nearly one-third of the vote. The December special election was a waltz in the solidly conservative 3rd, and Ehlers posted landslide wins in his bid for full terms in 1994 and 1996.

HOUSE ELECTIONS

1996 General		
Vernon J. Ehlers (R)	169,466	(69%)
Betsy J. Flory (D)	72,791	(29%)
Erwin J. Haas (LIBERT)	2,994	(1%)
1994 General		
Vernon J. Ehlers (R)	136,711	(74%)
Betsy J. Flory (D)	43,580	(24%)
Barrie Leslie Konicov (LIBERT)	2,960	(2%)

Previous Winning Percentages: **1993†** (67%)

† *Special election*

CAMPAIGN FINANCE

	Receipts	Receipts from PACs		Expend-itures
1996				
Ehlers (R)	$376,952	$101,866	(27%)	$265,960
Flory (D)	$13,043	$6,000	(46%)	$13,042
1994				
Ehlers (R)	$560,624	$154,580	(28%)	$531,562
Flory (D)	$20,402	$8,500	(42%)	$20,402
Konicov (LIBERT)	$29,700	0		$29,699

DISTRICT VOTE FOR PRESIDENT

	1996		1992
D	99,647 (39%)	**D**	94,721 (34%)
R	135,747 (53%)	**R**	128,677 (47%)
I	17,576 (7%)	**I**	52,779 (19%)

KEY VOTES

1997	
Ban "partial birth" abortions	Y
1996	
Approve farm bill	Y
Deny public education to illegal immigrants	Y
Repeal ban on certain assault-style weapons	Y
Increase minimum wage	N
Freeze defense spending	Y
Approve welfare overhaul	Y
1995	
Approve balanced-budget constitutional amendment	Y
Relax Clean Water Act regulations	N
Oppose limits on environmental regulations	Y
Reduce projected Medicare spending	Y
Approve GOP budget with tax and spending cuts	Y

VOTING STUDIES

	Presidential Support		Party Unity		Conservative Coalition	
Year	**S**	**O**	**S**	**O**	**S**	**O**
1996	43	54	79	20	63	37
1995	34	64	80	15	65	32
1994	47	53	76	23	81	19

INTEREST GROUP RATINGS

Year	ADA	AFL-CIO	CCUS	ACU
1996	25	n/a	94	79
1995	20	0	87	68
1994	25	0	100	81
1993	0	0	0	n/a

4 Dave Camp (R)

Of Midland — Elected 1990, 4th term

Biographical Information
Born: July 9, 1953, Midland, Mich.
Education: Albion College, B.A. 1975; U. of California, San Diego, J.D. 1978.
Occupation: Lawyer.
Family: Wife, Nancy Keil; one child.
Religion: Roman Catholic.
Political Career: Mich. House, 1989-91.
Capitol Office: 137 Cannon Bldg. 20515; 225-3561.

Committees
Ways & Means
Human Resources; Trade

In Washington: Camp made a rapid rise to prominence, moving in just six years from serving as a congressional aide to sitting as a junior GOP House member on the influential Ways and Means Committee.

Historically, the parties have put pragmatists and dealmakers on Ways and Means. Before the Republican sweep in 1994, the character of the panel's GOP contingent had begun to change as House Republicans adopted a more confrontational stance toward Democrats. Camp embodies the new-style Ways and Means Republican: His opening bid is almost always firmly conservative.

Overhauling the welfare system was a top priority of the new Republican majority in the 104th, and from his seat on Ways and Means, Camp was a strong critic of the status quo. "Nothing could be crueler or more heartless than the current system," he said. Part of the problem, he believed, was that the current system contained incentives for people to stay on welfare or to engage in inappropriate behaviors. "Federal policy now rewards the formation of never-married families," he said at one committee hearing on welfare. "We intend to reduce the size of the reward."

Camp blamed Democrats for creating a failed system and said the party had "allowed it to fester and cause untold harm to children and families." He expressed skepticism about the Clinton administration's professed commitment to welfare overhaul, suggesting that the president was stalling on the issue.

The first Republican bid to overhaul welfare, put forward in 1995, was tied to a controversial proposal to restrain cost growth in the Medicaid program. Clinton vetoed that bill. By the second session of the 104th, a split had developed within the GOP about whether the two proposals should be linked. Some Republicans argued for continued linkage, figuring that if Clinton maintained his veto stance, the GOP would at least be able to accuse him in the fall campaign with not fulfilling his 1992 pledge to "end welfare as we know it." (GOP presidential nominee Bob Dole was in this camp.)

However, Camp helped circulate a petition urging GOP leaders to move separately on welfare overhaul. That was the course ultimately taken, and after further compromise with the White House, Republicans finally were able to arrive at a plan that Clinton said he would sign. It became law in August 1996.

Even though he favored splitting the welfare and Medicaid issues, Camp defended the GOP's effort to curb Medicare cost growth by about $270 billion over seven years, despite fierce Democratic objections. He said the Republican initiative "officially ends the policy of just raising taxes."

Camp supports a balanced-budget amendment to the Constitution, and he voted for the tax cuts contained in the House GOP's "Contract With America."

Camp carried his fiscal conservatism even further than most in the GOP when he voted against defense spending measures in November 1995 and May 1996, and when he supported a proposal in June 1996 to freeze fiscal 1997 defense spending at the previous year's level. Camp disagreed with GOP leaders' desire to spend more on defense than the Clinton administration had requested.

"In these times of fiscal restraint, I cannot vote for a bill that has $493 million in spending for new B-2 bombers that the Pentagon says it does not need. I also cannot support spending $700 million for another *Seawolf* submarine that is clearly unnecessary."

Camp also has voted to terminate funding for NASA's space station, a multibillion-dollar "big science" project long targeted for criticism by "deficit hawks."

During his freshman term, Camp parted ways with a majority of Republicans in a few high-profile instances. Reflecting economic anxieties in his district, for instance, he voted in 1991 to extend unemployment benefits to the long-term unemployed, a stand that put him at odds with the Bush administration. But in 1993, when Clinton

MICHIGAN 4
North Central-Midland

While the 4th is Michigan's second-largest district in terms of land mass (after the 1st), most of the district's residents live in its southern half. North of Midland, much of the terrain is forested and sparsely populated.

Because there are few cities of size, most of the vote is cast in the small towns and farming communities that traditionally have favored the GOP. But Bill Clinton has done well here. He barely carried the 4th by about 1,200 votes in 1992, then won the district with 47 percent of the vote in 1996 — even though Republican Camp dominated in every county in the House race and got 65 percent.

Midland, site of one of the largest chemical complexes in the United States, is the 4th's population and industrial center. That is where, on 1,900 acres, the Dow Chemical Co. keeps its international headquarters. Dow Corning Corp., another major employer, is the world's largest producer of silicone.

Accordingly, the Dow name is firmly stamped on Midland. Residents can browse at the Grace A. Dow Memorial Library or learn about the man who started it all at the Herbert H. Dow Historical Museum. Their son, Alden, designed many of the city's churches, homes, schools and business complexes. For botanists, there is Dow Gardens.

The company also sets the tone for Midland County's Republican politics. Bob Dole carried Midland in 1996, though he only had a 46 percent plurality. Republican Spencer Abraham easily carried the county in his successful Senate bid in 1994, when GOP Gov. John Engler also won the county by a large margin.

South of Midland, the district is primarily agricultural. The second leading source of votes in the 4th is Saginaw County, although the city of Saginaw belongs to the 5th. The city is heavily Democratic and unionized, but the farmers to the south and west generally favor Republicans. Clinton won here in 1996 with 49 percent.

Clinton County includes a fair number of Lansing commuters, but they, along with farmers and small-town voters, favor Republican candidates.

Owosso (Shiawassee County) and Alma (Gratiot County) are small manufacturing cities. Gratiot tilts Republican, but both produce some Democratic votes. Clinton carried both in 1996.

Tourism and recreation fuel the economy north of these areas. Local residents are more likely to travel farther north toward the Upper Peninsula for vacations, but many autoworkers from Michigan's industrial southeast favor the lakes and woodland of Montcalm and Mecosta counties.

Retirees from the southeastern cities also have made their mark in the far northern portion of the 4th. Counties such as Clare, Gladwin, Ogemaw and Roscommon no longer are routinely Republican. Those four counties went for Democratic Gov. James Blanchard in 1990 and for Clinton in 1992 and 1996. But all four voted for Republican Engler in 1994, and Camp carried them as well.

1990 Population: 580,956. White 564,340 (97%), Black 6,182 (1%), Other 10,434 (2%). Hispanic origin 10,175 (2%). 18 and over 425,655 (73%), 62 and over 87,007 (15%). Median age: 32.

was in the White House and Camp had a solid reelection victory under his belt, he opposed similar unemployment-extension legislation on the grounds that it would put the federal government deeper in the red. "If we are going to help people," urged Camp in opposing the bill, "let us not rob from their children by increasing the budget deficit."

Camp reliably votes a pro-business line. In May 1996, he voted against raising the minimum wage by 90 cents an hour, and he supported a GOP leadership-backed amendment to exempt small businesses from paying the higher wage increase. But in August, when the politically popular increase won final passage in the House, he switched and voted "yea." The final version of the wage bill included business tax breaks and other provisions sought by Republicans.

Camp supports a 12-year limit on congressional terms, but that did not endear him to hardliners in the term limits movement, who pushed to enact a six-year term limit for House members. The organization U.S. Term Limits ran ads in Camp's district attacking his position.

To join Ways and Means at the start of the 103rd Congress, Camp had to give up his seat on the Agriculture Committee, an assignment that reflected the important role that farming plays in his district's economy.

But he maintains an interest in agriculture issues. In 1996, he voted for the GOP-backed "Freedom to Farm" bill that phased out most New Deal-era crop subsidies, replacing them with a system of fixed, but declining, payments that farmers would receive over seven years regardless of market prices or their planting decisions. However, Camp favored successful efforts to revise rather than phase out the sugar and most dairy support programs, which benefit Michigan farmers. He also backed the fiscal 1997 agriculture spending bill, in part because it contained funding for agricultural research programs, which he said are important to maintaining an affordable and plentiful food supply.

Camp takes a dim view of foreign policy initiatives that call for the involvement of U.S. troops abroad. He voted to prohibit funding for the U.S. peacekeeping mission to Bosnia.

At Home: After a two-year stint in Washington as an administrative assistant to his childhood friend, GOP Rep. Bill Schuette, Camp returned to Michigan in 1986 to manage Schuette's re-election campaign and resume his law career.

But in 1988, he decided to run for an open Midland-based state House seat, which he won.

He had barely found his chair in the Legislature when GOP strategists began talking up Schuette to run against Democratic Sen. Carl Levin in 1990; almost in the same breath, they suggested Camp as a replacement for Schuette in the House.

When Schuette announced his campaign for the Senate, he endorsed Camp to succeed him.

But several ambitious Republicans decided to try for the GOP nomination. The result was a heated four-way primary that included Camp, former U.S. Rep. Jim Dunn, and former state Sens. Al Cropsey and Richard J. Allen.

Camp, who ran an unexciting but polished campaign, faced a strong challenge from Cropsey, a hard-line conservative backed by many abortion foes and conservative Christian activists. But like Schuette, Camp enjoyed strong support from GOP establishment figures and from executives at Midland-based Dow Chemical Co. Camp won the nomination on the strength of his Midland base.

The GOP would have been strongly favored in any case, but Camp lucked out when a sparsely attended Democratic primary produced an upset winner, Joan L. Dennison. A dairy farmer who believed the public schools were being run by atheists, Dennison espoused support for some ideas of political extremist Lyndon H. LaRouche Jr. Camp coasted to victory, taking nearly two-thirds of the vote.

Though Michigan lost two House seats in 1990 reapportionment, the redistricting map preserved a district for Camp, and he won his next three general-election victories as handily as his first.

Camp has also seen success on the financial front. In 1995, The Detroit News, in an article drawing on financial disclosure reports by members of the Michigan delegation, reported that Camp, who had owned between $100,000 to $250,000 of stock in Dow Chemical, had increased his financial holdings in the company to between $500,000 and $1 million with his marriage to a Dow lawyer. That put his assets at between $700,000 and $1.73 million, according to the newspaper.

HOUSE ELECTIONS

1996 General		
Dave Camp (R)	159,561	(65%)
Lisa A. Donaldson (D)	79,691	(33%)
1994 General		
Dave Camp (R)	145,176	(73%)
Damion Frasier (D)	50,544	(25%)
Michael Lee (NL)	2,797	(1%)

Previous Winning Percentages: 1992 (63%) **1990** (65%)

CAMPAIGN FINANCE

	Receipts	Receipts from PACs	Expend-itures
1996			
Camp (R)	$595,571	$297,705 (50%)	$555,815
Donaldson (D)	$11,879	$3,500 (29%)	$13,284
1994			
Camp (R)	$584,314	$271,522 (46%)	$444,419
Frasier (D)	$68,976	$11,550 (17%)	$68,801

DISTRICT VOTE FOR PRESIDENT

1996	1992
D 119,427 (47%)	**D** 104,709 (38%)
R 103,912 (41%)	**R** 103,464 (38%)
I 29,938 (12%)	**I** 67,873 (25%)

KEY VOTES

1997	
Ban "partial birth" abortions	Y
1996	
Approve farm bill	Y
Deny public education to illegal immigrants	Y
Repeal ban on certain assault-style weapons	Y
Increase minimum wage	N
Freeze defense spending	Y
Approve welfare overhaul	Y
1995	
Approve balanced-budget constitutional amendment	Y
Relax Clean Water Act regulations	Y
Oppose limits on environmental regulations	N
Reduce projected Medicare spending	Y
Approve GOP budget with tax and spending cuts	Y

VOTING STUDIES

	Presidential Support		Party Unity		Conservative Coalition	
Year	**S**	**O**	**S**	**O**	**S**	**O**
1996	37	63	89	11	71	27
1995	21	76	93	6	83	15
1994	51	49	90	8	86	11
1993	32	68	92	8	84	16
1992	70	30	85	14	73	27
1991	71	29	88	12	95	5

INTEREST GROUP RATINGS

Year	ADA	AFL-CIO	CCUS	ACU
1996	0	n/a	100	95
1995	5	0	100	84
1994	20	11	100	95
1993	5	0	91	92
1992	5	25	75	84
1991	15	8	100	80

5 James A. Barcia (D)

Of Bay City — Elected 1992, 3rd term

Biographical Information
Born: Feb. 25, 1952, Bay City, Mich.
Education: Saginaw Valley State U., B.A. 1974.
Occupation: Congressional aide.
Family: Wife, Vicki Bartlett.
Religion: Roman Catholic.
Political Career: Mich. House, 1977-83, majority whip, 1979-83; Mich. Senate, 1983-93.
Capitol Office: 2419 Rayburn Bldg. 20515; 225-8171.

Committees
Science
Basic Research (ranking); Technology
Transportation & Infrastructure
Surface Transportation; Water Resources & Environment

In Washington: Barcia preaches the virtue of fiscal austerity, and the long-time supporter of such restraining devices as a balanced-budget constitutional amendment and a presidential line-item veto frequently breaks with his party to support conservative measures. But, like a dieter, Barcia sometimes finds the concept of doing without more agreeable than the practice.

Barcia is proud of the federal money he has been able to score for his district. For instance, during consideration of the Safe Drinking Water Act Amendments of 1996, Barcia secured funding for the town of Bad Axe, Mich., to repair its water supply infrastructure.

"These few dollars are the only way for Bad Axe to solve its drinking water crisis," Barcia told his colleagues from the House floor. "If this is pork, pass the platter."

During the 104th, Barcia also succeeded in obtaining federal funds for roads in his district from his perch on the Transportation and Infrastructure Committee. He may do even better during the 105th, as the committee marks up a reauthorization of the major surface transportation law.

In 1995, he saw to it that two Michigan state highways were included among the routes listed in a new National Highway System, and he also won a $3 million study for expansion of a third highway. During consideration of the same bill, Barcia succeeded in changing federal traffic safety compliance standards to allow states to receive federal funding based on their overall safety records. The old standard mandated sobriety checkpoints, which are disallowed by Michigan's constitution.

Barcia also paved the way for yet another Michigan highway to receive federal funding, helping to clear up the area's status of compliance with the Clean Air Act. And he won $1.4 million at the end of the 104th to repair flood damage to federal-aid highways in his district.

Among his non-fiscal priorities is legislation to increase time served by violent criminals. His bill would encourage states to keep prisoners in jail for an average of 85 percent of the length of their sentences. Barcia generally votes with the Republicans on matters pertaining to crime and overhaul of the legal system.

During 16 years in the Michigan Legislature, Barcia was known as a middle-of-the-road Democrat who kept lines open to both unions and management.

In the 104th, Barcia was a reliable vote on labor issues, supporting a boost in the minimum wage and opposing GOP measures letting businesses offer compensatory time in lieu of overtime and making it more difficult for Federal Express employees to unionize.

Keeping up a balancing act between left and right while staying on good terms with the White House is a challenge: Barcia has stood apart from the Clinton administration in a number of high-profile debates — on policies relating to abortion, Bosnia, gun control and the environment. But on Clinton's No. 1 priority — setting new taxing and spending priorities — Barcia has delivered his vote reliably, if not always enthusiastically.

Barcia, who sided with Clinton against the GOP's successful move to add $7 billion to his defense spending request for fiscal 1997, was one of the rare Democrats happy in 1995 when Clinton decided to match the GOP with a balanced-budget plan of his own. Like nearly all Democrats, Barcia was against the GOP's plan to balance the budget, which cut tax rates and reduced the rate of spending growth on Medicare and Medicaid. But he was happy to be able to support a budget that came to balance with a different set of priorities.

"Many of us would be put in a position to support the Republican alternative if the administration didn't come forward with a responsible balanced-budget plan," Barcia said.

Barcia was a reluctant supporter of Clinton's 1993 budget plan, which reduced spending and the deficit and raised taxes. On a key preliminary budget ballot in May 1993, Barcia backed Clinton's plan, but stressed that his vote was a

MICHIGAN 5
East — Saginaw; Bay City

The 5th covers more than 200 miles of Lake Huron shoreline, but population is centered along the Bay City-Saginaw corridor. There, the heavily Democratic vote is usually enough to offset the Republican-voting areas that outline the district.

Saginaw, the largest city in the 5th, has a manufacturing sector that includes a heavy General Motors presence. Accordingly, the United Auto Workers (UAW) union carries a big stick. The city is also home to the Consortium for the International Earth Science Information Network, an environmental data base.

Outside the city, Saginaw County's rich agricultural land produces sugar beets, dry beans, corn and soybeans. The importance of such commodities — along with the auto industry's presence — made NAFTA a touchy subject here. Many sugar beet growers, for example, fear cheap sugar imports from Mexico.

UAW strength and a significant blue-collar base make Saginaw a Democratic stronghold. Democrat Michael S. Dukakis carried Saginaw County by 3,215 votes in the 1988 presidential race. Bill Clinton had a much easier time winning it in 1992 and improved his margin further in 1996, when he led Bob Dole by 16,000 votes.

The second-largest city in the 5th is Bay City (Bay County). Once situated in the midst of a vast pine forest, Bay City was weaned on the lumber industry. Inhabitants used to refer to their home as the "Lumber Capital of the World," and more than 50 mills once operated here.

The city's economy now, like Saginaw's, is more reliant on heavy manufacturing. Bay City's blue-collar workers make boats, auto parts, jet engine components and tubing. The city is also one of the Great Lakes' top-ranked ports in terms of waterborne tonnage.

Bay County voters are even more reliably Democratic than their neighbors in Saginaw County. In the 1992 open-seat House race, Rep. Barcia won 75 percent of the county's vote; in 1996, he upped his total to 81 percent.

Forested Arenac County, north of Bay County, is a popular vacation spot and home to retired autoworkers. Their UAW loyalties are reflected at the ballot box, where Democrats usually prevail.

North of Arenac, Alcona and Iosco counties are preferred weekend destinations for Detroit suburbanites. Military retirees from Wurtsmith Air Force Base help keep Iosco County competitive for the GOP, but in 1992, voters expressed their dissatisfaction over the scheduled shutdown of Wurtsmith by voting for Clinton and Iosco County stayed in the Clinton camp four years later.

The other sizable source of GOP votes in the 5th is in Michigan's Thumb. Once heavily forested, the vast flat reaches of the region produce sugar beets, dry beans, corn, wheat and dairy products; Sanilac and Huron are top dairy counties. Just as Saginaw and Bay City experienced population losses in the 1980s, the counties of the Thumb declined also, though not as dramatically. Along the Lake Huron coastline, small fishing villages and lakeside resorts dot the landscape.

1990 Population: 580,956. White 516,255 (89%), Black 48,758 (8%), Other 15,943 (3%). Hispanic origin 19,611 (3%). 18 and over 418,962 (72%), 62 and over 91,368 (16%). Median age: 33.

"procedural" one to keep the budget moving, "not an endorsement of the details of this package." Approaching the August vote on final passage of the budget, Barcia was a question mark. He ultimately voted "yes" in the 218-216 Clinton victory, but lamented the public's response to the budget debate: Many had griped about cuts in their favorite federal programs yet still complained about being socked with new taxes. "If people want services from their government, then they have to be willing to pay the bills," Barcia said.

Still, on numerous occasions, Barcia has found cause to break with the White House.

He actively sought an override of Clinton's veto of a bill to ban a certain abortion procedure that opponents call a "partial birth" abortion. "As a pro-life advocate I am committed to protecting the rights of unborn children," Barcia said. "My primary concern is that abortion should not be treated like a routine medical procedure." He also broke with the administration over a ban on certain semiautomatic assault-style weapons.

Barcia opposed Clinton's policy in Bosnia every step of the way, voting in favor of lifting an administration-backed arms embargo on the country, a resolution to require prior congressional approval before U.S. troops could be sent there, and a move to cut off funding for the deployment once troops were there.

Barcia also differs with Clinton and most House Democrats over the environment. Although he supports protections for the Great Lakes, Barcia, who once derided the Sierra Club as "anarchists," voted against environmentalists in supporting GOP measures to place a one-year moratorium on new federal regulations, although he later switched his vote; to ease federal clean water regulations; and to compensate private property owners for drops in their land's values when it is classified as protected wetland.

Barcia, who sits on the Science Committee, supports continued funding for NASA's space station project and has made a priority of seeing that the federal government pays the bills for the Consortium for International Earth Science Information Network (CIESIN), a research entity based in Saginaw that works with NASA to make data on environmental science accessible and useful for science, education and policymaking. House Republicans faulted CIESIN in 1993 and hinted that Barcia had sought to protect it by trading Clinton his vote on the budget. That drew a sharp rebuke from Barcia, who said critics of the consortium were ignorant of its accomplishments.

At Home: Elected to the state House at age 24, Barcia served three terms before moving up to the state Senate, where he stayed for a decade. After veteran Democratic Rep. Bob Traxler announced that he would retire in 1992, Barcia launched his House bid.

Barcia made it through a three-way primary with 46 percent of the vote, hearing some criticism that he was a "career politician." The other Democratic hopefuls were to his left, and only after he had the nomination in hand did organized labor get behind him.

Republicans nominated state Rep. Keith Muxlow, a real estate developer and former dairy farmer, but he was an underdog from the start. Unlike Barcia's opponents in the Democratic primary, Muxlow could hardly criticize Barcia for being a career politician. Muxlow had spent 12 years in the state Legislature and was mayor of Brown City for eight years before that.

The local, state and national chambers of commerce endorsed Barcia over Muxlow. Also, Barcia as a state senator had represented a far larger portion of the 5th than Muxlow had as a state representative. Muxlow, outspent 3 to 1, did not have enough money to run TV ads, and he did only a limited amount of radio advertising and direct mail. Barcia took 60 percent of the vote. In 1994 and 1996, he won with ease.

HOUSE ELECTIONS

1996 General		
James A. Barcia (D)	162,675	(70%)
Lawrence H. Sims (R)	65,542	(28%)
Mark Owen (LIBERT)	2,906	(1%)
1994 General		
James A. Barcia (D)	126,456	(65%)
William T. Anderson (R)	61,342	(32%)
Larry L. Fairchild (I)	3,022	(2%)
Susan I. Arnold (NL)	2,323	(1%)

Previous Winning Percentages: 1992 (60%)

CAMPAIGN FINANCE

	Receipts	Receipts from PACs	Expend-itures
1996			
Barcia (D)	$205,435	$132,734 (65%)	$200,556
Sims (R)	$167,729	$3,438 (2%)	$162,739
1994			
Barcia (D)	$267,050	$187,567 (70%)	$205,769
Anderson (R)	$5,862	0	$5,856

DISTRICT VOTE FOR PRESIDENT

1996	1992
D 130,061 (53%)	**D** 118,699 (45%)
R 86,005 (35%)	**R** 84,525 (32%)
I 27,571 (11%)	**I** 60,990 (23%)

KEY VOTES

1997	
Ban "partial birth" abortions	Y
1996	
Approve farm bill	Y
Deny public education to illegal immigrants	N
Repeal ban on certain assault-style weapons	Y
Increase minimum wage	+
Freeze defense spending	Y
Approve welfare overhaul	Y
1995	
Approve balanced-budget constitutional amendment	Y
Relax Clean Water Act regulations	Y
Oppose limits on environmental regulations	N
Reduce projected Medicare spending	N
Approve GOP budget with tax and spending cuts	N

VOTING STUDIES

	Presidential Support		Party Unity		Conservative Coalition	
Year	**S**	**O**	**S**	**O**	**S**	**O**
1996	70	28	68	31	75	25
1995	53	44	71	28	59	40
1994	64	36	68	30	75	25
1993	61	37	74	23	66	34

INTEREST GROUP RATINGS

Year	ADA	AFL-CIO	CCUS	ACU
1996	45	n/a	60	47
1995	70	83	63	52
1994	50	78	67	43
1993	65	100	36	42

6 Fred Upton (R)

Of St. Joseph — Elected 1986, 6th term

Biographical Information
Born: April 23, 1953, St. Joseph, Mich.
Education: U. of Michigan, B.A. 1975.
Occupation: Congressional aide; budget analyst.
Family: Wife, Amey Rulon-Miller; two children.
Religion: Protestant.
Political Career: No previous office.
Capitol Office: 2333 Rayburn Bldg. 20515; 225-3761.

Committees
Commerce
Energy & Power; Health & Environment; Telecommunications, Trade & Consumer Protection
Education & Workforce
Early Childhood, Youth & Families; Postsecondary Education, Training & Life-Long Learning

In Washington: Once a member of the House Republican leadership, Upton now is part of a centrist GOP faction in the chamber that may have a strong say in determining how successful that leadership is.

He is part of the Tuesday Lunch Bunch, a group of Republicans who found themselves marginalized by fervent conservatives when the GOP took control of the House in 1995, but who started reasserting themselves later in the 104th Congress and may hold the balance of power in the 105th because of its smaller Republican majority.

Upton and his allies claimed a measure of credit for the more accommodating atmosphere toward the end of the 104th, as GOP leaders compromised with President Clinton on issues such as the budget, the minimum wage and welfare reform. In 1995 and the early part of the 1996, Lunch Bunch Republicans warned that Democrats were swaying the public to see the GOP as rigidly ideological, bent on rolling back environmental regulations and cutting education programs.

In December 1996, Upton was encouraged by a meeting that a group of GOP pragmatists had with new White House Chief of Staff Erskine Bowles. Upton said the session "sets the stage for real bipartisan cooperation," although he acknowledged that some Republicans still don't like the idea of giving up any ground to Clinton.

"Some members still have a minority mentality, that it is enough just to be against everything," Upton said. "And that does not win."

Earlier, he expressed that philosophy in supporting Clinton's national service program, an idea most Republicans opposed. "We cannot be simple naysayers to proposals and plans simply because a Democrat is in the White House," Upton said.

As the House prepared in 1997 to wrap up the ethics case of Speaker Newt Gingrich, Upton urged Gingrich to move on to the business of legislating. "The Speaker has to redouble his efforts to get this off the front page and to focus on what the country wants us to do here," he said. "The [ethics] issue makes the whole institution look rotten to the core."

Soon after he entered the House in 1987, Upton looked like a man going places in his party. When Gingrich became Republican whip in 1989, he made Upton a deputy whip. In 1990, the young, anti-tax conservatives then gaining strength in House GOP ranks cheered when Upton chided the Bush administration for cutting a budget deal with Democrats that called for higher taxes.

As quickly as he had risen, however, he fell. At the start of the 103rd Congress, Upton resigned his deputy whip post, citing differences with more confrontational conservative GOP leaders such as Gingrich and Dick Armey of Texas.

Those differences surfaced from time to time in the 104th, such as when Upton defied party leaders and backed efforts to lower from $200,000 to $95,000 the income cap for families eligible to receive a $500 per child tax credit

Not that Upton is not a loyal Republican. He supported the planks of the "Contract With America" 91 percent of the time in the 104th. Later in 1995 he toed the party line in supporting the giant budget reconciliation bill, which tried to balance the budget in seven years, partly through reducing the rate of spending growth on Medicaid and Medicare. He backed efforts to overhaul welfare, roll back federal regulations and limit the amount of money consumers can collect when injured by faulty products.

On other social-policy issues, Upton is reliably conservative. He opposed federal recognition of same-sex marriages. He voted to ban a particular abortion technique that opponents call a "partial-birth" abortion, he opposed allowing the federal employee health plan to pay for abortions, and he voted against allowing overseas military hospitals to perform abortions.

But he did support legislation requiring states to pay for abortions for poor women in cases of rape or incest. And he is a vocal advocate of allowing research on fetal tissue, which support-

MICHIGAN 6
Southwest — Kalamazoo; Benton Harbor; St. Joseph

Nestled in the southwestern corner of Michigan, bordered to the west by Lake Michigan and to the south by Indiana, the 6th is prime agricultural and Republican turf.

With 80,000 residents, Kalamazoo is the largest city in the 6th by far. A significant manufacturing sector provides the base for a strong union presence and blue-collar vote. A General Motors body-stamping plant continues to shrink as it prepares to close in 1998.

Other employers make printing and packaging paper, aircraft components, and automotive parts. Large paper manufacturers include James River, Georgia Pacific and Simpson.

The Pharmacia Upjohn, maker of pharmaceuticals, medical equipment and chemicals, has its worldwide headquarters in Portage, just outside the city of Kalamazoo. It employs more than 6,200 people. Three companies, Stryker, Abbot (Ross) Labs and Richard Allen, make medical products.

Education is an economic pillar, led by Western Michigan University, with more than 2,500 students and about 2,900 workers.

The area's Dutch heritage, when combined with corporate managers and the agriculture-oriented townships on the outskirts of Kalamazoo County, helps turn out a moderate-to-conservative vote. Upton easily carried the county in 1992, 1994 and 1996, but Bill Clinton also won here in 1992 and 1996.

The twin cities of Benton Harbor and St. Joseph make Berrien County the second-most populous in the district. The area along the wooded Lake Michigan shoreline, where many affluent Chicagoans maintain second homes and vacation cottages, is known as "Harbor Country."

The cities are more geared toward industry. Separated by the St. Joseph River, more populous Benton Harbor, which is the headquarters of home appliance maker Whirlpool Corp., and St. Joseph eye each other warily. Benton Harbor — once a stop along the Underground Railroad — is more than 90 percent black; St. Joseph is more than 90 percent white. Many of them had moved out of Benton Harbor, formerly a bedroom community for St. Joseph.

Democrats run well in this area, but votes for them usually are negated by the rural voters and retirees of the outlying Republican towns. Berrien County opted for George Bush in 1992 and Bob Dole in 1996.

The flat croplands of Republican Cass and St. Joseph counties form the northeastern edge of the Corn Belt. Dowagiac (Cass) and Three Rivers (St. Joseph) have some industry, but most of the workers are conservative, even those who call themselves Democrats. Cass, which has more hogs than people, backed Clinton over Dole by 46 percent to 41 percent, while St. Joseph residents preferred Dole by 47 percent to 41 percent.

1990 Population: 580,956. White 512,029 (89%), Black 55,474 (8%), Other 13,453 (2%). Hispanic origin 10,506 (3%). 18 and over 426,902 (73%), 62 and over 85,915 (15%). Median age: 33.

ers believe is vital to curing such diseases as Parkinson's, Alzheimer's, diabetes and cancer. Some staunch opponents of abortion argue that allowing fetal-tissue research promotes abortions. When he became president, Clinton repealed the Bush-era administrative ban on fetal tissue research.

Upton voted against the ban on certain semi-automatic assault-style weapons that was enacted in 1994, though he did support the final crime bill that included the ban. He voted to repeal the ban in 1996. He did, however, back the Brady bill's five-day waiting period for handgun purchases.

In 1996, he supported a 90-cent increase in the minimum wage, but only after first voting to exempt small businesses from paying it. And he supported allowing employers to offer their workers compensatory time off rather than overtime pay.

Few pinch pennies as aggressively as Upton. In the 104th he voted to terminate the authorization for the space station and to phase out sugar price supports. He opposed Republican efforts to increase defense spending over Clinton's request. Earlier in his tenure, he voted to kill the superconducting super collider. Upton's commitment to reduce the deficit also put him at odds with GOP advocates of costly weapons systems such as the B-2 bomber and the Strategic Defense Initiative.

When he first came to Congress, Upton drew on his background working for the Office of Management and Budget to carve a niche as a budget-cutter. As a freshman, he joined an effort, led by Republican Tom Tauke of Iowa and Democrat Timothy J. Penny of Minnesota, to shrink the deficit with small cuts in appropriations bills.

Upton is the sponsor of legislation authorizing construction of a temporary nuclear waste depository 100 miles outside Las Vegas at Yucca Mountain in Nevada. The bill has provoked much controversy and fierce opposition from Nevadans in Congress. It did not come up in the House in the 104th Congress, but Upton has said "this bill is coming" in the 105th — even though rumblings in early 1997 indicated that if the measure passes, administration officials will recommend a Clinton veto.

Upton's most-noticed first-term victory

involved blocking an effort to declare a one-time federal holiday on Sept. 17, 1987, honoring the bicentennial of the U.S. Constitution. "We all realize that the Constitution is a working document," Upton said. "If this is true, does it really make sense to celebrate a working document by taking a day off work?"

Upton proudly proclaims that he has not missed a single legislative vote since coming to Congress.

At Home: In 1986, Upton was the only Republican to unseat an incumbent in a primary. But his victory over GOP Rep. Mark D. Siljander was not a total shock.

Much of the local GOP establishment had long disliked Siljander, a Christian conservative activist whose efforts to link religion and politics had often stirred controversy. And Upton was unusually well-positioned to challenge the vulnerable incumbent.

Upton is a member of one of the district's most prominent families — his grandfather was a founder of the Whirlpool appliance company. And although he had never sought office before, Upton had a strong résumé. He spent 10 years as an aide to David A. Stockman during Stockman's tenures as 4th District House member and as President Ronald Reagan's Office of Management and Budget (OMB) director.

Siljander had emerged on the scene in 1981, winning a special election after Stockman's move to OMB. He beat a longtime Stockman ally by mobilizing his fundamentalist backers, and he went on to establish a reputation as a conservative firebrand known to denounce the "perverted" philosophy of "secular humanists." Although his voting record was in line with the majority philosophy of the then-4th, Siljander's style alienated GOP regulars. Upton decided to run when he returned to the district in 1985 after Stockman resigned his OMB post.

Upton generally avoided challenging Siljander's issue positions, instead seeking to convince voters that he was simply a more appealing, less confrontational conservative. He got a break late in the campaign, when Siljander taped an appeal to fundamentalist ministers, implying that the challenge to him was linked to evil forces and calling on voters to "break the back of Satan." The tape helped Upton clinch victory. That November, Upton won with 62 percent of the vote, starting a string of comfortable general-election victories.

Religious activists mounted a 1990 primary challenge to Upton, in the form of conservative state Sen. Ed Fredericks. But Upton won renomination with 63 percent of the vote.

HOUSE ELECTIONS

1996 General		
Fred Upton (R)	146,170	(68%)
Clarence J. Annen (D)	66,243	(31%)
Scott Beavers (LIBERT)	3,370	(2%)
1994 General		
Fred Upton (R)	121,923	(73%)
David Taylor (D)	42,348	(26%)
E.A. Berker (NL)	1,667	(1%)

Previous Winning Percentages: **1992** (62%) **1990** (58%) **1988** (71%) **1986** (62%)

CAMPAIGN FINANCE

	Receipts	Receipts from PACs		Expenditures
1996				
Upton (R)	$625,329	$260,877	(42%)	$399,520
Annen (D)	$12,655	$8,750	(69%)	$12,089
1994				
Upton (R)	$537,130	$228,219	(42%)	$575,406
Taylor (D)	$72,082	$14,325	(20%)	$71,609

DISTRICT VOTE FOR PRESIDENT

1996		1992	
D	103,330 (46%)	D	100,683 (40%)
R	99,884 (44%)	R	97,200 (38%)
I	19,961 (9%)	I	55,667 (22%)

KEY VOTES

1997	
Ban "partial birth" abortions	Y
1996	
Approve farm bill	Y
Deny public education to illegal immigrants	Y
Repeal ban on certain assault-style weapons	Y
Increase minimum wage	Y
Freeze defense spending	Y
Approve welfare overhaul	Y
1995	
Approve balanced-budget constitutional amendment	Y
Relax Clean Water Act regulations	Y
Oppose limits on environmental regulations	Y
Reduce projected Medicare spending	Y
Approve GOP budget with tax and spending cuts	Y

VOTING STUDIES

	Presidential Support		Party Unity		Conservative Coalition	
Year	S	O	S	O	S	O
1996	39	61	82	18	55	45
1995	29	71	85†	15†	76	24
1994	49	51	83	17	64	36
1993	51	49	76	24	66	34
1992	57	43	78	22	73	27
1991	60	40	78	21	86	14

† Not eligible for all recorded votes.

INTEREST GROUP RATINGS

Year	ADA	AFL-CIO	CCUS	ACU
1996	10	n/a	94	85
1995	25	0	100	72
1994	35	33	92	67
1993	35	33	82	67
1992	30	50	88	72
1991	25	25	100	80

7 Nick Smith (R)

Of Addison — Elected 1992, 3rd term

Biographical Information

Born: Nov. 5, 1934, Addison, Mich.

Education: Michigan State U., B.A. 1957; U. of Delaware, M.S. 1959.

Military Service: Air Force, 1959-61.

Occupation: Dairy farmer.

Family: Wife, Bonnalyn Atwood; four children.

Religion: Congregationalist.

Political Career: Somerset Township Board of Trustees, 1962-66; Hillsdale county Board of Supervisors, 1966-68; Mich. House, 1979-83; Mich. Senate, 1983-93.

Capitol Office: 306 Cannon Bldg. 20515; 225-6276.

Committees

Agriculture

Department Operations, Nutrition & Foreign Agriculture; Forestry, Resource Conservation & Research; Livestock, Dairy & Poultry; Risk Management & Specialty Crops

Budget

In Washington: Staunchly conservative on both fiscal and social issues, Smith has won three elections in a district where the plurality of voters have twice supported Bill Clinton for president. Smith's hold on the 7th seems secure enough, although his 1996 re-election tally, 55 percent, was fully 10 points under his 1994 showing.

A member of the Budget Committee, Smith during the 104th Congress played an active role in opposing an increase in the national debt limit. Looking for leverage to force President Clinton to compromise with the GOP on a long-term balanced-budget plan, Smith persuaded 165 of his Republican colleagues to sign a letter in the fall of 1995 warning Clinton that they would not vote to give the federal government more borrowing authority "until legislation is enacted ensuring the government is on a true glide path to a balanced budget by 2002 or sooner."

Without an increase in the debt limit, the administration warned, the government would be at risk of not being able to pay its bills, including interest on Treasury bond obligations, considered among the world's safest investments.

With the debt limit extension caught up in partisan bickering over balancing the budget, the Treasury Department juggled accounts to delay the government's hitting the debt limit ceiling. Smith criticized Treasury Secretary Robert E. Rubin for dipping into civil service retiree trust funds to buy time.

Rubin announced in the fall of 1995 that he would disinvest $61.3 billion in securities from the federal employee thrift plan and the Civil Service Retirement and Disability Fund in order to create room under the $4.9 trillion debt ceiling for issuance of new debt. As chairman of a GOP task force on the debt limit, Smith charged that Rubin violated his legal duties by publicly casting doubt on the country's creditworthiness.

"He intentionally tried to panic U.S. financial markets and recently tried to panic senior citizens with the threat of withholding Social Security and other civil service benefits," Smith said. "His clear message was that unless Republicans give in to White House demands, we could expect bond markets to weaken." Smith called for Rubin's resignation, but Rubin maintained that his actions were legal.

In March 1996, the House approved an increase in the federal debt limit from $4.9 trillion to $5.5 trillion. Smith was one of 30 Republicans voting "no."

As part of the measure raising the debt limit, the House GOP leadership included legislation giving the president line-item veto authority. In voting against raising the debt limit, Smith also voted against the line-item veto. He had expressed reservations about giving the president the power to eliminate selected spending items from appropriations bills. He said the new power would have minimal impact on the deficit and instead would merely transfer power to the president. "I served under three governors while in the state Legislature," said Smith. "Every one of these governors, liberal and conservative, used the leverage of the line-item veto to get the spending they wanted."

Smith has offered a free-enterprise prescription for keeping Social Security solvent. He proposed legislation in July 1996 that would allow workers to invest part of their Social Security payroll tax in a personal retirement savings account that they control, giving people the chance to invest in stocks, which historically have produced a higher rate of return than other investments. "Over time, the assets in workers' accounts will grow very rapidly, producing genuine retirement security," Smith said.

Just as he did during 14 years as a state legislator, Smith persistently advocates tax cuts and government spending restraint. When the House considered the fiscal 1997 spending bill for the legislative branch, Smith joined Indiana Democrat Tim Roemer in offering an amendment, which passed by voice vote, requiring all funds not spent out of House members' office accounts to be used to offset the deficit. Smith habitually returns a chunk of his office allowance unspent.

MICHIGAN 7
South Central — Battle Creek; Jackson

This is a district of conservative small towns and agricultural communities, with a few midsize cities as part of the mix. In 1992's open-seat House race, Democrats did not even bother to offer a candidate. But its politics are changing.

In the House race, Smith's numbers have been steadily dropping. He got 55 percent of the votes in 1996 — his closest call yet and a full 10 percentage points below his 1994 showing. And Bill Clinton has now twice carried this traditionally Republican district in presidential elections. He won the 7th by about 600 votes in 1992, then widened the margin four years later to about 5,700 votes and 2 percentage points. Ross Perot, who garnered 25 percent in 1992, dropped to 11 percent in 1996.

With fewer than 54,000 people, Battle Creek, or "Cereal City," is the largest city in the 7th. It is the home of "Tony the Tiger" of Frosted Flakes fame and breakfast cereal plants employ many of the city's residents. The Kellogg Co., headquartered in Battle Creek, is the top private employer and a prominent force in the city. The federal government also has a heavy local presence; many of the federal employees work at a Veterans Affairs medical center.

Besides the money that Kellogg has poured into civic improvements, the company also has left its imprint on local government. In the early 1980s, Kellogg told Battle Creek in no uncertain terms to merge the city and Battle Creek Township governments. Afraid the company would move its headquarters, the city annexed the township.

With a fair number of blue-collar Democrats, Battle Creek often makes Calhoun County competitive for Democratic candidates. Beyond the city, the vote of corporate executives and outlying small towns tilts Republican. Clinton took 50 percent in Calhoun County in 1996, his best showing in the district, and it was the only county Smith lost.

About an hour's drive east on I-94, the industrial city of Jackson is another source of Democratic votes. Although city of Jackson is smaller in population than Battle Creek, Jackson County is the most populous county wholly within the 7th. Layoffs at the tool-and-die and auto parts shops caused some pain in the city, and Bob Dole barely carried the county by 354 votes in 1996 on the strength of the outlying towns and farming areas. With the auto industry bouncing back, however, the city has experienced some relief.

Dole drew some support from city-based Democrats — a socially conservative lot, with a tendency to pull the lever for the GOP at the presidential level. Unlike Detroit's autoworkers, many of those living here have roots in the surrounding Republican countryside. Dole also carried Eaton County. Small-town conservatives and Republican white-collar executives who work in Lansing (which is in the neighboring 8th District) boosted Dole to 45 percent.

The agricultural counties of Branch, Hillsdale, Jackson and Lenawee had been fertile ground for the GOP. But Dole lost Branch and Lenawee.

1990 Population: 580,957. White 535,970 (92%), Black 32,742 (6%), Other 12,245 (2%). Hispanic origin 14,170 (2%). 18 and over 424,301 (73%), 62 and over 86,007 (15%). Median age: 33.

Smith was less successful in his attempt to cut back government spending by trying to zero-out transportation funds for mass transit programs. When the House took up the fiscal 1996 transportation spending bill, Smith proposed eliminating all $666 million in the bill for those projects, also known as new starts. "By building these projects, we are also committing ourselves to subsidizing these projects in future years, because they cannot operate by themselves," he warned. But House appropriators said that all 30 projects that would share the $666 million were under way. Smith's amendment was defeated, 114-302.

A dairy farmer from a district with a sizable rural constituency, Smith sits on the Agriculture Committee, where in the 104th he weighed into the debate as the GOP sought a sweeping overhaul of federal farm policy. The party's "Freedom to Farm" bill phased out most New Deal-era crop subsidies, replacing them with a system of fixed, but declining, payments that farmers would receive over seven years regardless of market prices or their planting decisions.

To protect dairy farmers in the Midwest, Smith sought to scrap the system of regional fluid milk price supports, known as milk marketing orders, because those orders give greater support to dairy farmers in every other region of the country. He opposed an amendment to the farm bill that aimed to retain price supports and marketing orders for five years.

The final farm bill required the Agriculture Department to consolidate the 33 existing milk marketing orders into 10 to 14 within four years. It also phased out price supports for butter, milk powder and cheese over four years rather than immediately.

Smith is not happy with conservation regulations governing use of the nation's croplands. He backed a November 1995 committee effort reducing the Agriculture Department's role in mandating conservation practices. Smith offered an amendment to change the contentious "swampbuster" program, which penalizes farmers who violate wetlands regulations while receiving government subsidies. His provision, which the committee accepted, would exempt wetlands 1 acre or less in size from swampbuster regulations. Smith said this would ease restrictions on farmers who sometimes must plow around whole fields to avoid damaging small patches of wetland.

But environmentalists strongly criticized the exemption, saying it would impair protection of ducks and other wildlife in the "prairie pothole" regions of the upper Midwest.

Smith has been a critic of "special interest" money in politics since his earliest days in Michigan's Legislature; he refuses PAC contributions and once said, "Lobbyist PAC money too often is nothing short of a bribe." Smith has also pledged not to serve more than six House terms.

At Home: Smith first won the open 7th with 88 percent in 1992 (no Democrat even bothered to file), and he drew a comfortable 65 percent two years later. But in 1996, as Clinton carried the district over GOP nominee Bob Dole 45 percent to 43 percent, Smith received 55 percent, a dozen points better than Democratic challenger Kim H. Tunnicliff, a political science professor at Albion College in south central Calhoun County.

Tunnicliff, elected to the Albion City Council in 1994, portrayed himself as a fiscally conservative and socially moderate centrist sensitive to the needs of the district's agricultural community. But Smith was never threatened.

Smith had a tough fight for the Republican nomination in 1992. His chief adversary in the four-way primary was fellow state Sen. John Schwartz; his name recognition rivaled Smith's, and he raised about twice as much money. The two vied for billing as the most conservative candidate, and Smith nudged ahead on that score when he won the endorsement of Michigan Right to Life (even though Schwartz also opposed abortion).

Smith indirectly benefited from a third candidate's attacks on Schwartz, who was accused in a TV ad of assaulting a veterans hospital security officer with his car after the guard gave him a ticket. Smith went on the offensive against Schwartz over the money issue, using his opposition to PACs to turn Schwartz's bigger campaign treasury into a liability. Smith finished with 43 percent; Schwartz was runner-up with 36 percent.

In the general election, Smith's only obstacle was Libertarian Kenneth L. Proctor.

In 1994, Smith brushed aside a primary challenge from businessman and 7th District GOP Chairman Mark A. Behnke. The November election was suspenseless.

HOUSE ELECTIONS

1996 General		
Nick Smith (R)	120,227	(55%)
Kim H. Tunnicliff (D)	93,725	(43%)
Robert F. Broda Jr. (LIBERT)	3,090	(1%)
1996 Primary		
Nick Smith (R)	40,019	(75%)
Doug Myers (R)	13,595	(25%)
1994 General		
Nick Smith (R)	115,621	(65%)
Kim McCaughtry (D)	57,326	(32%)
Kenneth L. Proctor (LIBERT)	3,311	(2%)

Previous Winning Percentages: 1992 (88%)

CAMPAIGN FINANCE

	Receipts	Receipts from PACs		Expend-itures
1996				
Smith (R)	$265,248	0	(0%)	$263,739
Tunnicliff (D)	$146,323	$40,150	(27%)	$145,511
1994				
Smith (R)	$282,409	0	(0%)	$289,573
McCaughtry (D)	$34,519	$8,000	(23%)	$34,153

DISTRICT VOTE FOR PRESIDENT

1996		1992	
D	104,692 (45%)	**D**	96,940 (38%)
R	99,037 (43%)	**R**	96,336 (38%)
I	24,391 (11%)	**I**	62,673 (25%)

KEY VOTES

1997	
Ban "partial birth" abortions	Y
1996	
Approve farm bill	Y
Deny public education to illegal immigrants	Y
Repeal ban on certain assault-style weapons	Y
Increase minimum wage	N
Freeze defense spending	Y
Approve welfare overhaul	Y
1995	
Approve balanced-budget constitutional amendment	Y
Relax Clean Water Act regulations	Y
Oppose limits on environmental regulations	N
Reduce projected Medicare spending	Y
Approve GOP budget with tax and spending cuts	Y

VOTING STUDIES

	Presidential Support		Party Unity		Conservative Coalition	
Year	**S**	**O**	**S**	**O**	**S**	**O**
1996	34	65	86	11	73	22
1995	18	81	90†	8†	82†	17†
1994	45	51	91	7	89	8
1993	32	62	87	9	84	9

† Not eligible for all recorded votes.

INTEREST GROUP RATINGS

Year	ADA	AFL-CIO	CCUS	ACU
1996	10	n/a	93	95
1995	0	0	96	100
1994	5	13	100	95
1993	10	8	82	88

8 Debbie Stabenow (D)

Of Lansing — Elected 1996, 1st term

Biographical Information
Born: April 29, 1950, Gladwin, Mich.
Education: Michigan State U., B.A. 1972, M.S.W. 1975.
Occupation: Leadership training consultant.
Family: Divorced; two children.
Religion: United Methodist.
Political Career: Ingham County Commissioner, 1975-78, chair, 1977-1978; Mich. House, 1979-91; Mich. Senate, 1991-95; sought Democratic nomination for governor, 1994; Democratic nominee for lieutenant governor, 1994.
Capitol Office: 1516 Longworth Bldg. 20515; 225-4872.

Committees
Agriculture
Forestry, Resource Conservation & Research; General Farm Commodities
Science
Technology

The Path to Washington: A well-known former state legislator and gubernatorial aspirant, Stabenow was the dream nominee in 1996 for Michigan Democrats who were anxious to reclaim the politically marginal 8th District, which had been won in 1994 by Republican Dick Chrysler.

Considered a fiscal conservative, Stabenow began her career in elective politics in 1975 by serving a three-year stint on the Ingham County (Lansing) Commission. In 1978, she was elected to the state House, where she earned a reputation for her work on such issues as domestic violence, child abuse prevention and mental health care.

But it was after Stabenow won a state Senate seat in 1990 that she gained prominence all across Michigan.

In the early 1990s, working in concert with then first-term Republican Gov. John Engler and other members of the state GOP, Stabenow became a vocal and ardent supporter of a measure that drastically reduced property taxes on Michigan residents by ceasing to use that levy as the chief way to finance the state's public school system.

While panned at the time by many Democrats and interest groups, such as the teachers' unions, the move proved popular with voters and catapulted Stabenow to political stardom statewide.

Riding that wave of popularity, Stabenow sought the Democratic gubernatorial nomination to run against Engler in 1994.

But her candidacy stalled in the four-candidate Democratic primary, and Stabenow came in second behind former Rep. Howard Wolpe. Stabenow settled for the nomination for lieutenant governor in what was ultimately a landslide loss.

As a member of Congress, Stabenow said she will back efforts to expand students' access to college and financial aid.

Stabenow is also a strong supporter of Clinton administration proposals to put computers in every classroom in the country.

Stabenow, who said the nation's economic health rides on the country continuing to make technological advances, landed a seat on the Science Committee, where she is likely to push for advanced technology in educational settings.

But in a reflection of how heavily her district still relies on farming, Stabenow also sought and snagged a slot on the Agriculture Committee.

As testament to Stabenow's political stature, Michigan Democratic officials ensured she would have a clean shot at the 8th in 1996 by virtually forbidding any primary opposition.

Stabenow also benefited greatly from more than a year of negative advertising against first-term Republican incumbent Chrysler, who was targeted by independent interest groups, such as the AFL-CIO, upset with his votes to reduce long-term spending on the federal health insurance program for the elderly, to scale back workplace safety laws and to reduce environmental regulations on business.

Democrats had held the 8th District for nearly two decades before Chrysler captured it in 1994, a good year for Republicans, with just 52 percent of the vote.

While organized labor did much of the work of tearing down Chrysler, Stabenow conserved resources and focused her attention on personal appearances and door-to-door contact with voters, particularly those in solidly Republican Livingston County, Chrysler's home turf.

Throughout the campaign, Stabenow tried to tie Chrysler to House Speaker Newt Gingrich, suggesting her opponent did not represent the moderate views of the district.

Chrysler, who touted his work to promote medical savings accounts and make college tuition tax deductible, denounced organized labor's involvement in the campaign and accused the Democratic Party and its allies of trying to "buy the election."

But Chrysler's arguments failed to sway voters, and Stabenow, bolstered by huge margins in Ingham County, won by a convincing 10-point margin.

MICHIGAN 8
Central — Part of Lansing

The 8th reaches from the state capital of Lansing to the outskirts of Flint and Ann Arbor, but the majority of voters live in just two counties, Ingham (Lansing) and Livingston. Between them, they account for nearly 70 percent of the district's population.

Residents of Lansing, the state capital and the district's largest city, live by the area's three Cs: cars, campus and the Capitol. General Motors is the city's largest employer, employing workers who build Pontiacs, Buicks and Oldsmobiles. Ransom Eli Olds founded his Olds Motor Vehicle Co. here in 1897, at first turning out horseless carriages. Districtwide, GM employs more than 16,000 workers.

Other major employers include the state Capitol complex and Michigan State University in East Lansing. The university's 41,500 students are a source of Democratic votes, which, when combined with autoworkers, state employees and the university faculty who live in places such as Okemos Township, tilts Ingham County toward Democrats. Bill Clinton captured 54 percent of the county's votes in 1996, while Stabenow and Democratic Sen. Carl Levin amassed more than 60 percent.

Livingston County retains much of its agricultural character, despite a population influx over the past two decades. Livingston was the state's second-fastest-growing county in the 1970s, and the fastest-growing from 1990 to 1996. Many of these new residents were whites fleeing Detroit, Flint, Lansing and Pontiac.

Much of the vote comes from small towns and farming communities such as Fowlerville and Howell, which celebrates the muskmelon harvest with its annual Melon Festival. The county's traditional conservatism has not been affected by the newcomers. Settled by German Protestant farmers, it was a center of German-American Bund activism in the 1930s. Livingston also is one of the state's most heavily Republican areas: the Democratic candidate has failed to win 40 percent of the vote in Livingston in the last eight presidential elections.

The rest of the district includes parts of Genesee, Oakland, Shiawassee and Washtenaw counties. The Genesee portion takes in the southwestern part of the county, reaching to the Flint city limits. The strongly Democratic heritage of Flint spills over into these areas, and they usually turn out a Democratic vote. Both Clinton and Stabenow carried the Genesee portions of the 8th by double digit margins in 1996.

The northwestern Washtenaw County portion, starting from the edge of Ann Arbor, is mostly small townships and part of the city of Saline. Unlike the Democratic university community in Ann Arbor, these areas generally favor Republicans. Former GOP Rep. Dick Chrysler won the district's portion of Washtenaw in 1994 and 1996, though Clinton narrowly carried it in 1996.

The small segment of Oakland County in the district adds a small number of voters, most of whom lean Republican like the county at-large. But in 1996, Clinton carried the 8th's portion of Oakland (as well as the county at-large).

1990 Population: 580,956. White 525,215 (90%), Black 33,900 (6%), Other 21,841 (4%). Hispanic origin 16,947 (3%). 18 and over 431,535 (74%), 62 and over 64,226 (11%). Median age: 31.

HOUSE ELECTIONS

1996 General

Debbie Stabenow (D)	141,086	(54%)
Dick Chrysler (R)	115,836	(44%)
Doug MacDonald (LIBERT)	3,811	(1%)

CAMPAIGN FINANCE

	Receipts	Receipts from PACs	Expend-itures
1996			
Stabenow (D)	$1,508,161	$382,898 (25%)	$1,497,300
Chrysler (R)	$1,513,297	$478,537 (32%)	$1,515,307

DISTRICT VOTE FOR PRESIDENT

1996		1992	
D	130,353 (49%)	**D**	117,654 (41%)
R	109,277 (41%)	**R**	103,725 (36%)
I	24,447 (9%)	**I**	67,983 (24%)

KEY VOTES

1997

Ban "partial birth" abortions N

9 Dale E. Kildee (D)

Of Flint — Elected 1976, 11th term

Biographical Information
Born: Sept. 16, 1929, Flint, Mich.
Education: Sacred Heart Seminary, B.A. 1952; U. of Detroit, 1954; U. of Peshawar (Pakistan), 1958-59; U. of Michigan, M.A. 1961.
Occupation: Teacher.
Family: Wife, Gayle Heyn; three children.
Religion: Roman Catholic.
Political Career: Mich. House, 1965-75; Mich. Senate, 1975-77.
Capitol Office: 2187 Rayburn Bldg. 20515; 225-3611.

Committees
Education & Workforce
Early Childhood, Youth & Families; Postsecondary Education, Training & Life-Long Learning (ranking)
Resources
Forests & Forest Health; National Parks & Public Lands

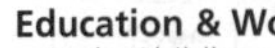

In Washington: Kildee, a staunch liberal, had fundamental disagreements with Republicans in the 104th Congress over their efforts to move many federal education and child welfare programs to the states as block grants. Kildee argues that without federal standards and monitoring, many education and nutrition programs will not serve the groups that most need them. In the House, Kildee has championed social programs to aid the poor, the elderly and the very young. In Michigan, he has filled out tax forms for senior citizens and helped fix their leaky roofs.

But even Kildee, who usually veers to the left on education, welfare and labor votes, made some adaptations to modern times and voted for the final version of a bill overhauling the welfare system, which most liberals opposed. Kildee said he rejected earlier versions because they included provisions he found unacceptable. He contends the measure that President Clinton signed in August 1996 was significantly improved because of pressure applied on the GOP by the White House and congressional Democrats.

In his 1994 election, Kildee saw his vote margin dip to 4 percentage points, causing Republicans to target his district as one they hoped to capture in 1996. But their hopes went unfulfilled as Kildee trounced his 1996 opponent by 20 percentage points.

A senior member of the Education and the Workforce Committee, formerly Economic and Educational Opportunities, Kildee in the 105th Congress assumes the ranking spot on the Postsecondary Education, Training and Life-Long Learning Subcommittee.

A strong proponent of some federal involvement in the nation's schools, Kildee was highly critical of the GOP version of the fiscal 1997 appropriations bill that included funding for the Education Department. He argued that the measure "reduces our commitment to education by an additional $400 million below last year's cut of over $1 billion." He also complained that the measure would eliminate the Goals 2000 program, a federal initiative that Kildee had a hand in passing in the 103rd Congress that aims to help states strengthen education standards. "States are beginning to see some real improvements in their achievement levels under Goals 2000," Kildee told the House. "There is only one reason for eliminating this proposal: political posturing and pressure from certain extreme groups in the outside."

When the Economic and Educational Opportunities Committee in February 1995 considered the first version of a GOP plan to overhaul welfare, Kildee and other panel Democrats tried to change the bill's three proposed block grants that would have given states control over child care, school meals and nutrition for young children and pregnant women. The bill created a school-based Nutrition Block Grant to replace school breakfast and lunch programs and other food programs at schools. The committee defeated, 15-21, an amendment by Kildee to retain current school nutrition programs.

But Republicans insisted that states could more efficiently manage the programs and respond to local needs without federal intervention. When the measure reached the House floor, Kildee asked the Republican sponsors, "Why are we putting this program into a block grant? To save money? To reduce the deficit? No; it appears that the savings will be used to pay for tax cuts for those who are not as needy as our children."

Kildee also wanted to keep a requirement that states continue to use competitive bidding when purchasing infant formula for the Women, Infants and Children (WIC) nutrition program. He said that before Congress enacted the 1989 law requiring states to use competitive bidding, states used a variety of cost containment measures that did not work. "We found that when we required states to use that competitive bidding," Kildee said, "that we saved $1 billion a year . . . that enabled 1-1/2 million more pregnant women and infants to be served each month under the WIC program." The committee rejected Kildee's amendment, though later versions of the welfare bill retained the federal role over WIC.

MICHIGAN 9
East Central — Flint; Pontiac

Conversations about the city of Flint often include mention of the 1989 documentary "Roger and Me." Produced by a local filmmaker, it painted a scathing portrait of General Motors (GM) and the effects of its massive layoffs.

This was the birthplace of GM in 1908, and later, the United Auto Workers (UAW). Thirty years after the first plant opening, the modern labor movement sprouted forth from UAW sit-down strikes that paralyzed two GM factories.

At its employment peak, 80,000 people worked at Flint's GM plants. Today, districtwide, about 62,000 people work in GM facilities. A few years ago abandoned neighborhoods and shuttered businesses reflected the city's population decline and high unemployment.

But the auto industry has begun to bounce back, which has aided Flint's unemployment woes and has boosted auto industry employment districtwide to about 80,000.

Oakland County also has seen a growth of auto-industry related businesses. In addition, Chrysler's move to Auburn Hills further increased the number of autoworkers.

The UAW is still potent, although it suffered in the last few years as members moved in search of jobs. The city continues to be a Democratic bastion, but the outlying Genesee County vote is less partisan.

In 1984, Ronald Reagan won Genesee, but the county has voted for a Democrat for president since then. Clinton captured 61 percent countywide in 1996, and 68 percent of the county's portion in the 9th District. He won the overall district with 52 percent.

Michigan's 1992 remapping radically redrew the district, so that Genesee is divided among the 5th, 8th and 9th districts. Only Flint, Grand Blanc and the southeastern portion of the county remain in the 9th. Flint is still the largest city in the district, but the bulk of the vote now comes from Republican Oakland County.

Pontiac, Oakland's largest city in the 9th, is made up of low-income blacks, Hispanics and socially conservative whites, whose families migrated from the South to work in the auto industry. They lean Democratic but are more independent than their counterparts in Flint.

Outside Pontiac, the townships in the northeastern corner of the county are less developed and more Republican. The GOP vote from areas such as Auburn Hills and Rochester, along with Addison, Orion and Oakland townships, counters the Flint vote and keeps the district competitive for Republicans. In 1992 and 1994, Democratic Kildee faced two of his closest races of his career, in part because his GOP opponents racked up 57 percent and 60 percent, respectively, in Oakland County. But Kildee fared better in 1996, barely winning the county while winning re-election with 59 percent.

Lapeer County, whose southern half is in the district, is also less-than-receptive to Democratic candidates. Eastern Lapeer has a more Democratic cast, a vestige of Flint-UAW spillover, but the county as a whole is more rural than the rest of the district.

1990 Population: 580,956. White 461,400 (79%), Black 103,133 (18%), Other 16,423 (3%). Hispanic origin 16,436 (3%). 18 and over 420,886 (72%), 62 and over 65,534 (11%). Median age: 31.

Kildee also weighed in when the committee debated a bill in May 1996 that would revise funding and disciplinary procedures for the main education program for children with disabilities. Although he ultimately supported it, Kildee said: "We're very nervous about going back to the days when any excuse was taken to exclude special education students from the classroom."

Representing a district that was the birthplace of General Motors, Kildee is strongly pro-labor. He took great exception when Republicans on the Economic and Educational Opportunities Committee in June 1995 ushered a striker replacement bill through the committee. The legislation would have nullified an executive order by Clinton that bars companies with federal contracts of more than $100,000 from permanently replacing striking employees.

Committee Chairman Bill Goodling of Pennsylvania suggested that Clinton's ban would lead to more strikes and more protracted labor disputes, slowing federal contract work. But Democrats argued that the bill would give an unfair advantage to management by giving it the ability to fire striking workers. Kildee said that the striker replacement effort was in keeping with a GOP decision to change the name of the former Education and Labor panel. "You dropped the name of labor from the committee; now you're dumping on labor," he said.

Not surprisingly, Kildee was a proponent of a 90-cent minimum wage increase that the House adopted in August 1996 and opposed a GOP effort to allow companies to offer their employees comp time in lieu of pay for overtime work. Labor unions and thei Democratic allies in Congress argued that the bill might lead to workers being coerced to choose the form of compensation preferred by their employers.

A former divinity student, Kildee has said that his liberal do-gooder outlook on social programs comes from his "deep respect for human life." Although he rarely breaks ranks with his party, his anti-abortion convictions cause him to occasionally vote against Democrats. In 1996, he voted against an amendment allowing abortions at overseas military hospitals and another that would have required states to pay for Medicaid abortions that resulted from rape or incest.

Kildee will also have a place in House history as he currently holds the record for consecutive votes among sitting members, with 5,871 through mid-May 1997. He hasn't missed a vote since Oct. 16, 1985.

At Home: After years of comfortable victories, Kildee has been held below 60 percent in the past three elections, although his 1996 showing was much more solid than his anemic tallies in 1992 and 1994.

His first close call came in 1992, against Megan O'Neill, who had worked in the White House under President George Bush. Kildee had to answer for 100 overdrafts at the House bank, and redistricting dealt him a tough hand: almost half the people in the redrawn 9th were new to him.

O'Neill ran a spirited campaign and gained on Kildee in the final weeks. But even as redrawn, the district retained a Democratic edge (Clinton won it with a plurality in presidential voting), and O'Neill was unable to match Kildee in spending in the home stretch. He won with 54 percent.

Returning in 1994, O'Neill received plenty of help from the national party and again played the outsider theme. She espoused the need for term limits, while criticizing Kildee as a career politician and big-spending Democrat. Kildee had the money to fight back on television and in direct mailings with attacks that said the GOP's "Contract With America," which O'Neill signed, would require slashing entitlements and college loans. O'Neill carried Oakland County with 60 percent of the vote, but Kildee, aided by a strong lead in his home county of Genesee, held on to win with 51 percent.

In 1996, Republicans persuaded former state transportation official Patrick M. Nowak to take on Kildee. Nowak built his campaign around fiscal issues such as balancing the budget, reducing taxes and scaling back the federal government. But Kildee had strong local labor support and favorable Democratic winds at his back. With Clinton carrying a majority of the district's presidential vote, Kildee beat Nowark 59 percent to 39 percent.

As a Democrat from the General Motors town of Flint, Kildee draws his political strength from the labor movement he reliably supports in Washington. The United Auto Workers and the AFL-CIO have deserted him only once, when he first ran for Congress in 1976. Trying to succeed five-term Rep. Donald W. Riegle Jr., who was running for the Senate, Kildee left a state Senate seat he had won only two years before. Labor, which had worked exceptionally hard to help Kildee oust a 26-year state Senate veteran in 1974, felt he should have served out his four-year term. But Kildee insisted on making his move.

Winning was relatively easy, even with division in the ranks of labor. Kildee beat a local union official with 76 percent in the Democratic primary and went on to trounce his general-election opponent. Before 1992, he had never won less than two-thirds of the vote, and often he would take considerably more.

HOUSE ELECTIONS

	Votes	%
1996 General		
Dale E. Kildee (D)	136,856	(59%)
Patrick M. Nowak (R)	89,733	(39%)
Malcolm Johnson (LIBERT)	3,472	(2%)
1994 General		
Dale E. Kildee (D)	97,096	(51%)
Megan O'Neill (R)	89,148	(47%)
Karen Blasdell (NL)	3,240	(2%)

Previous Winning Percentages: **1992** (54%) **1990** (68%) **1988** (76%) **1986** (80%) **1984** (93%) **1982** (75%) **1980** (93%) **1978** (77%) **1976** (70%)

CAMPAIGN FINANCE

	Receipts	Receipts from PACs	Expend-itures
1996			
Kildee (D)	$841,182	$432,909 (51%)	$816,337
Nowak (R)	$444,204	$95,863 (22%)	$443,415
1994			
Kildee (D)	$970,631	$605,558 (62%)	$963,249
O'Neill (R)	$302,758	$50,294 (17%)	$302,174

DISTRICT VOTE FOR PRESIDENT

	1996		1992
D	125,080 (52%)	**D**	117,872 (44%)
R	90,411 (38%)	**R**	92,262 (35%)
I	21,562 (9%)	**I**	55,077 (21%)

KEY VOTES

1997	
Ban "partial birth" abortions	Y
1996	
Approve farm bill	N
Deny public education to illegal immigrants	N
Repeal ban on certain assault-style weapons	N
Increase minimum wage	Y
Freeze defense spending	N
Approve welfare overhaul	Y
1995	
Approve balanced-budget constitutional amendment	N
Relax Clean Water Act regulations	N
Oppose limits on environmental regulations	Y
Reduce projected Medicare spending	N
Approve GOP budget with tax and spending cuts	N

VOTING STUDIES

	Presidential Support		Party Unity		Conservative Coalition	
Year	**S**	**O**	**S**	**O**	**S**	**O**
1996	76	24	85	15	51	49
1995	77	23	91	9	19	81
1994	77	23	93	7	25	75
1993	73	27	92	8	23	77
1992	16	84	96	4	8	92
1991	29	71	95	5	14	86

INTEREST GROUP RATINGS

Year	ADA	AFL-CIO	CCUS	ACU
1996	75	n/a	31	15
1995	75	100	21	24
1994	90	100	42	5
1993	90	100	18	13
1992	90	92	25	4
1991	95	92	10	5

10 David E. Bonior (D)

Of Mount Clemens — Elected 1976, 11th term

Biographical Information
Born: June 6, 1945, Detroit, Mich.
Education: U. of Iowa, B.A. 1967; Chapman College, M.A. 1972.
Military Service: Air Force, 1968-72.
Occupation: Probation officer; adoption caseworker.
Family: Wife, Judy; three children.
Religion: Roman Catholic.
Political Career: Mich. House, 1973-77.
Capitol Office: 2207 Rayburn Bldg. 20515; 225-2106.

Minority Whip

In Washington: Bonior has become Newt Gingrich's Gingrich.

Gingrich, as a Republican backbencher in a Democratic-controlled House, harangued then-Speaker Jim Wright, D-Texas, over alleged ethics violations. Wright eventually resigned.

With Republicans in control of the House in the 104th Congress, Bonior, the minority whip, led the Democratic attacks on the new Speaker. Drawing on bare-knuckled tactics that Gingrich himself employed against Democrats when he was minority whip, Bonior questioned Gingrich's ethical conduct and called for investigations of his past business and professional dealings. One month after the November 1994 election, most Democrats were still nursing their election wounds when Bonior called for an outside investigation into "unanswered questions, ethical allegations and serious conflicts of interest" regarding Gingrich's record.

He questioned the fundraising for a college course Gingrich taught called "Renewing American Civilization." GOPAC, a political group headed by Gingrich, raised money for the course through tax-deductible contributions — something Bonior argued was unjustified because the course was highly political. And since GOPAC's contributors had not been made public, Bonior contended that Gingrich supporters could use the fund to circumvent traditional campaign spending restrictions. Bonior also charged that a House ethics committee investigation into the matter posed a conflict of interest, since Gingrich appointed Republicans to the committee.

Gingrich yielded to some of Bonior's complaints. He arranged to carry over the ethics panel from the 103rd to conduct the investigation, and he agreed to disclose the names of all future — but not past — GOPAC contributors.

Bonior hounded Gingrich when the Speaker announced that he would accept a $4.5 million advance for a book deal about his experiences in Congress. Bonior said the deal was suspicious because Gingrich's publishing company was a corporate holding of publishing magnate Rupert Murdoch, who had interest in legislation before Congress. Gingrich agreed to forgo the advance but not royalties.

Gingrich quickly fired back. "The Democratic leadership is choosing what I think is the most narrow and foolish of partisan tactics," he said in January 1995. "They didn't get any message out of this election."

But Bonior did not let up. In March 1995, he charged Gingrich with improperly using government time and resources to promote his college course and a GOPAC-sponsored conference. Bonior cited five separate occasions, with Gingrich's remarks, later making it into the Congressional Record.

"Newt Gingrich knows full well that you cannot use the Congressional Record to advertise or promote the work of an outside organization," Bonior said. "And the Speaker of the House knows full well that he can't use a 1-800 number on the House floor. I mean, this isn't the Home Shopping Network."

The ethics committee in December 1995 found that Gingrich had violated House rules in touting the college course and the GOPAC conference on the House floor, but took no further action on those charges. At the same time, the panel voted to bring in an outside counsel to investigate charges that Gingrich violated tax laws by raising funds for the college course through tax-exempt foundations.

In February 1996, Bonior filed another complaint, charging the Speaker with commingling "the resources of tax-free foundations, political action committees, his own personal campaign committee and his official resources and staff," and alleging that Gingrich did favors in behalf of donors to GOPAC.

But Bonior received a small taste of his own medicine in March 1996. The conservative Landmark Legal Foundation filed a complaint charging that Bonior violated federal law and House rules by hiring Judy Briggs on March 1, 1991, when the two were engaged to be married,

This is the home of the famed voters of Macomb County. Every four years, national reporters lug their laptops and cameras to the county to get an earful of what working-class America has to say. Political consultants probe their sentiments in focus groups. For presidential candidates, it is a must-stop.

Some of its renown stems from its reputation as an electoral bellwether. In 18 of the past 20 elections for president, governor or U.S. senator, the winner in Macomb has also been the statewide winner. George Bush became one of the exceptions in 1992. But the county reverted to form in 1996, giving Bill Clinton 49 percent of its votes. (He got 48 percent in the portions of Macomb in the 10th District).

Back in 1960, Macomb was solidly Democratic, suburban territory and proved it by delivering an almost 2-1 margin for John F. Kennedy. Voters stayed true to the party through most of the decade, backing Lyndon B. Johnson in 1964 and Hubert H. Humphrey in 1968.

But the late 1960s were a time of political transition for local residents, as they became increasingly disenchanted with the counterculture movement and frightened by the Detroit riots. By 1972, Richard M. Nixon had claimed the county.

As busing and civil rights emerged as prominent local issues, voters associated the national Democratic Party with the policies of the far left. By 1984, Ronald Reagan won by a 2-1 margin.

Strong union loyalties have not been enough to override the social conservatism of the Catholic Italians and Eastern European working-class voters. Democrats are still stigmatized as the party of permissiveness, one that is soft on crime and intent on raising taxes.

MICHIGAN 10
Southeast — Macomb County; Port Huron

Bush won here on those issues in 1988 and in 1992 despite deep discontent among local voters. Japanese trade practices and layoffs weighed heavily on residents' minds. But Clinton managed to wrestle the district back into the Democratic camp in 1996 against Bob Dole.

Bonior, who kept his congressional seat even as voters were choosing Republicans at the top of the ticket, won by 10 percentage points, as Clinton won by eight.

Not all of Macomb County is in the 10th. The district includes the newer subdivisions north of Mount Clemens and Clinton Township, and extends to the grittier neighborhoods, such as East Pointe (formerly called East Detroit), which is shared with the 12th.

The rest of the vote comes from St. Clair County. It leans Republican, though both Clinton and Bonior carried it in 1996. Port Huron, a source of blue-collar voters, is beginning to feel the effects of and commercial spillover from the Detroit metro area. Retailers and developers are moving into the city because it is less developed than areas closer to Detroit and for the potential market of Canadian consumers from nearby Ontario.

1990 Population: 1990 Population: 580,956. White 560,595 (96%), Black 11,755 (2%), Other 8,606 (1%). Hispanic origin 7,430 (1%). 18 and over 434,093 (75%), 62 and over 86,557 (15%). Median age: 33.

and raising her salary by almost $8,000 a month later.

Bonior said that his wife had worked in his office for four years before they were married in May 1991. The ethics committee dismissed the complaint two months later.

In September 1996, after the ethics committee widened its Gingrich probe, Bonior suggested the Georgian should give up his Speakership. "The whole thing is unraveling for the Speaker," Bonior said. "And the Republican Conference should call on the Speaker to step aside."

When the ethics committee recommended reprimanding Gingrich and imposing a $300,000 penalty in January 1997, Bonior did not try to toughen the sanctions. "I have said all along that I will abide by the recommendations of the outside counsel," he said. "If [Gingrich] doesn't step down, we will have to work with him."

In addition to gnawing on Gingrich's ethics, Bonior has attacked the GOP on other fronts. When Republicans in October 1995 voted to roll back projected increases in Medicare spending, Bonior lamented the deed. "With this vote, we turn back 30 years of progress, 30 years of trust and 30 years of hope that our parents and our grandparents will always have the health care they need."

And in May 1996, when Republicans proposed exempting small businesses from paying a new, higher minimum wage, Bonior observed, "Now I can honestly say I have no idea what planet the Republicans are living on."

Bonior continued to dish out the rhetoric early in the 105th Congress. In April 1997, he joined Minority Leader Richard A. Gephardt, D-Mo., and a jar of molasses to complain about the House's slow trickle of action. "It's hard to play ball when the other team doesn't show up," Bonior said. "Democrats are standing up to say, 'Stop the rhetoric and get down to action. If Republicans can't lead, they better get out of the way.'"

In 1996, when House Democrats split 98-98 on

the welfare overhaul plan that President Clinton later signed, Bonior was with the party's steadfast liberals who voted "no." However, he deviates from the liberal orthodoxy of support for abortion rights. Bonior has voted with conservatives to ban the abortion procedure that opponents call "partial birth" abortions. In the 104th Congress, he voted against allowing the federal employee health care plan to pay for abortions, and against requiring states to pay for Medicaid abortions in cases of rape or incest.

A strong supporter of organized labor, Bonior broke with Clinton over NAFTA in the 103rd, leading a vigorous effort to defeat the trade pact in the House. He argued that the treaty would deal a crippling blow to American workers already struggling with a changing global economy, leaving them unable to compete with Mexican workers earning only a fraction of American union labor salaries.

Bonior voted against granting most-favored-nation status to China in June 1996, reviving the pro-labor arguments he used against NAFTA. He charged that China had consistently refused to open its market to U.S. products. "The debate is not about free trade," he said. "It is about fair trade. It is about whether we are going to use the leverage we have as a nation to open up markets in a way that is fair to American workers."

At Home: Bonior's liberal politics have kept him under 60 percent in six of his 10 re-election bids in his blue-collar district. His attacks on Gingrich made him one of the Michigan GOP's top targets in 1996. But after the state party chairwoman, Susy Heintz, failed to attract a high-profile candidate to "bounce Bonior," she resigned her $90,000-a-year position and ran herself.

The state Democratic Party responded by challenging Heintz's ballot petitions, citing irregularities in signature gathering and document handling. The Democrats pushed their challenge all the way to the Michigan Court of Appeals, which eventually ruled that Heintz's petitions were valid.

Heintz said Bonior was too liberal for the district, and she endorsed planks of the House Republicans' "Contract With America," including term limits, state control of welfare and a balanced-budget constitutional amendment.

Bonior fought back with the strong support of organized labor. He argued that Heintz supported proposals that would cut education, worker safety and hazard protections. And he emphasized his constituent service, a hallmark of his tenure in Congress. Bonior was held below 55 percent but won by 10 points, 54 percent to 44 percent.

All of Bonior's re-election campaigns have been supported by organized labor and the Macomb County Democratic organization, but he has not been on the closest of terms with either. In the crowded 1976 contest to find a successor to Democratic Rep. James G. O'Hara, the unions were split and the Macomb Democratic Party favored Bonior's major primary opponent. Bonior narrowly won the primary and general election with an aggressive personal campaign; he went door to door handing out pine tree seedlings.

At the time, Bonior was a two-term state representative, having been elected to the Legislature shortly after completing military duty.

HOUSE ELECTIONS

1996 General		
David E. Bonior (D)	132,829	(54%)
Susy Heintz (R)	106,444	(44%)
Stuart E. Scott (LIBERT)	3,747	(2%)
1994 General		
David E. Bonior (D)	121,876	(62%)
Donald J. Lobsinger (R)	73,862	(38%)

Previous Winning Percentages: **1992** (53%) **1990** (65%) **1988** (54%) **1986** (66%) **1984** (58%) **1982** (66%) **1980** (55%) **1978** (55%) **1976** (52%)

CAMPAIGN FINANCE

	Receipts	Receipts from PACs		Expend-itures
1996				
Bonior (D)	$1,549,061	$862,148	(56%)	$1,513,432
Heintz (R)	$677,206	$122,467	(18%)	$673,996
1994				
Bonior (D)	$1,104,874	$768,648	(70%)	$1,123,472
Lobsinger (R)	$18,884	$14	(0%)	$18,084

DISTRICT VOTE FOR PRESIDENT

1996	1992
D 122,033 (48%)	**D** 100,587 (36%)
R 100,460 (40%)	**R** 115,849 (42%)
I 27,164 (11%)	**I** 60,927 (22%)

KEY VOTES

1997	
Ban "partial birth" abortions	Y
1996	
Approve farm bill	N
Deny public education to illegal immigrants	N
Repeal ban on certain assault-style weapons	N
Increase minimum wage	Y
Freeze defense spending	Y
Approve welfare overhaul	N
1995	
Approve balanced-budget constitutional amendment	N
Relax Clean Water Act regulations	N
Oppose limits on environmental regulations	Y
Reduce projected Medicare spending	N
Approve GOP budget with tax and spending cuts	N

VOTING STUDIES

	Presidential Support		Party Unity		Conservative Coalition	
Year	S	O	S	O	S	O
1996	78	20	95	5	16	84
1995	79	20	95	5	11	87
1994	79	21	97	1	11	86
1993	80	16	93	4	20	77
1992	12	72	79	3	10	71
1991	30	68	94	5	8	89

INTEREST GROUP RATINGS

Year	ADA	AFL-CIO	CCUS	ACU
1996	95	n/a	19	5
1995	95	100	13	12
1994	95	100	25	5
1993	90	100	9	9
1992	80	91	29	0
1991	95	100	20	0

11 Joe Knollenberg (R)

Of Bloomfield Township — Elected 1992, 3rd term

Biographical Information
Born: Nov. 28, 1933, Mattoon, Ill.
Education: Eastern Illinois U., B.S. 1955.
Military Service: Army, 1955-57.
Occupation: Insurance broker.
Family: Wife, Sandie; two children.
Religion: Roman Catholic.
Political Career: Oakland County Republican Party chairman, 1978-86.
Capitol Office: 1511 Longworth Bldg. 20515; 225-5802.

Committees
Appropriations
Energy & Water Development; Foreign Operations, Export Financing & Related Programs; VA, HUD & Independent Agencies
Education & Workforce
Employer-Employee Relations (vice)

In Washington: Knollenberg is one of the most reliable votes for the Republican leadership, supporting the party's fiscal- and social-policy agenda and virtually all the legislation derived from the "Contract With America." His loyalty is such that once when he arrived late to a committee roll call, he declared, "I vote...I vote ...with the majority!"

Knollenberg, who joined the Appropriations Committee when Republicans took over the House in 1995, had his eyes on a powerful subcommittee chairmanship for the 105th: He was in line to chair the Energy and Water Development Subcommittee. But he lost out when Joseph M. McDade of Pennsylvania, the senior GOP appropriator, was cleared of bribery charges in 1996, freeing him to assume a subcommittee chairmanship; McDade chose Energy and Water.

During House consideration of the fiscal 1997 energy and water spending bill, Knollenberg opposed efforts to restore funding for renewable energy research. His argument took an unusual tack: Knollenberg warned that someday there would be a need for renewable energy sources, but he contended that because the need was not immediately pressing, it should be ignored.

"We also know during the next few years, next few decades, that we expect the depletion of our supplies of fossil fuels," Knollenberg said on the House floor. "But that time has not come. And at some point we will have to be prepared for that, but it is not here yet."

The auto industry is a major presence in Knollenberg's district, which is one of the most affluent in the country. Knollenberg succeeded with an insertion in the fiscal 1996 Transportation funding measure that reduced funding by $2 million — money that foes of the corporate average fuel economy (CAFE) standards feared would have gone to help tighten federal mileage standards for vans and light trucks. House Majority Whip Tom DeLay, R-Texas, in a companion move, offered language that flatly bars any further tightening of CAFE requirements for cars or trucks.

"I've always felt very strongly that there was too much zeal about CAFE standards," Knollenberg said. "This was the first opportunity we had to do this."

Knollenberg preaches the virtues of fiscal austerity. "The question is not who is calling for a balanced budget," he declared in 1996. "A balanced budget is about as desirable as world peace. The question is who is willing to make the hard decisions necessary to make a balanced budget a reality."

In addition to his efforts to rein in government spending, Knollenberg still on occasion plays the traditional appropriator's role of picking up goodies for his district. He won funding for a full-time customs agent for the Oakland-Pontiac Airport, and also found $11.6 million for cleanup of the Rouge River. Knollenberg seeks to direct federal gas taxes to roads, a measure that would offer Michigan $200 million more per year.

Also on an appropriations bill, Knollenberg added language barring the department of Housing and Urban Development from interfering with local or state laws declaring English the official language. His effort stemmed from an instance in which HUD considered looking into whether English language policies in Allentown, Pa., amounted to a civil rights violation. (HUD decided not to investigate). "By making it easy for those who come to America, we have ripped the heart out of our national unity. We have shredded our common bond, leaving behind the legacy of our ancestors, new and old, who worked so hard to learn English," Knollenberg said during floor debate on a national English language bill.

He also serves on the Education and the Workforce Committee, and one of his major legislative efforts since the GOP assumed control of the House has been to privatize welfare. When the House took up a major welfare overhaul during the 104th, Knollenberg joined with Arizona Republican Jim Kolbe to offer a substitute package that would have rolled all government programs for the poor — health, food, housing and welfare — into federal block grants, leaving it up

The 11th is the lone Republican stronghold in metropolitan Detroit. Unlike the other suburban districts, which sometimes flirt with local GOP candidates and usually support Republican presidential candidates, the 11th has been reliably Republican — except for 1996, when Bob Dole barely lost the district. A middle- and upper-class district with a 93 percent white population, the 11th covers the southwestern portion of Oakland County (the nation's third wealthiest) and the city of Livonia in Wayne County. Much of the vote is cast in the district's eastern section, where residents tend to be better-educated and more affluent.

More than 70 percent of the district's work force is white collar, more than a third of the people hold college degrees, and the median family income tops $56,000 — the highest of all Michigan districts in each of those categories.

Birmingham and Bloomfield hold the mansions and homes of auto executives and professionals. Birmingham's tony shopping district used to be considered Michigan's version of Rodeo Drive, while Bloomfield Hills was George Romney's hometown in his days as an auto executive (before he was governor and a presidential candidate).

Farmington Hills, Southfield and West Bloomfield are population centers whose recent growth has qualified them for "edge city" status. Located north of 8 Mile Road, Detroit's northern boundary, these municipalities sit in the corridor between Grand River Avenue and the Northwestern Freeway that has served as one of the primary routes for white flight from the city.

MICHIGAN 11
Southeast — Part of Oakland County

While the rest of Oakland County is hostile to Detroit and unreceptive to blacks moving out of the city, Southfield has a relatively large and growing black population. Nearly 30 percent of the city's residents are black; many are middle-class families trying to escape Detroit's high crime rates. As Detroit has declined, businesses have flocked to surrounding suburbs such as Southfield.

Outside of Southfield and nearby Lathrup Village (which is 20 percent black), the rest of the 11th is overwhelmingly white.

The northwestern part of the 11th is covered with lakes and recreation areas. Places such as Novi, South Lyon and Wixom in the southwest have newer subdivisions and are populated with a fair number of socially conservative blue-collar workers.

The Wayne County portion of the 11th consists of Redford Township and part of Livonia. Professionals and middle-level managers give a GOP tilt to Livonia, which is shared with the 13th District.

1990 Population: 580,956. White 540,408 (93%), Black 23,967 (4%), Other 16,581 (3%). Hispanic origin 7,404 (1%). 18 and over 444,245 (76%), 62 and over 89,326 (15%). Median age: 35.

to each state how to allocate the money.

A part of their package lives on, with Knollenberg trying to create a tax credit for donations to human services charities. Taxpayers would be able to designate portions of their federal income tax to a charitable organization engaged in anti-poverty relief. To ensure that the government ultimately saved money, the bill would reduce funding to states by the same amount taxpayers designated to local charities.

"Our welfare delivery system has essentially become a government monopoly," Knollenberg said in 1995. "Our bill revokes the welfare system's monopoly status and replaces it with a public-private partnership."

Knollenberg also has authored a bill that would exempt private-sector volunteers from minimum wage and overtime requirements. "If individuals want to volunteer their time to gain valuable work experience, the federal government should not stop them," he declared.

His opposition to abortion and support for tax cuts, term limits and other signature GOP items have earned him perfect ratings from such groups as the Christian Coalition and the American Conservative Union. But he earns a mark of "zero" from the Human Rights Campaign, an advocacy group for homosexual issues. Knollenberg's son Stephen is gay; he says his son's "sexual orientation is a personal matter" and that he "unequivocally" supports him "with all the love and respect that a family possibly can." (Coincidentally, Kolbe, his partner on welfare legislation, is the only openly gay Republican in Congress.)

Knollenberg sits on the Foreign Operations Appropriations Subcommittee, and in that arena he sides against allowing Pakistan to take control of some U.S. military equipment it has purchased and he voted against funding U.S. troops deployed in Bosnia.

At Home: Knollenberg campaigned in 1992 as an outsider, but he won his seat with an insider's skill, capitalizing on experience gained as Oakland County Republican Party chairman and campaign chairman for Rep. William S. Broomfield. In April 1992, Broomfield announced he would not run for a 19th term.

The 11th is an upscale Republican district in suburban Detroit that abortion rights advocates thought they could win. They persuaded longtime

Oakland County Circuit Judge Alice L. Gilbert to leave the bench to run in the GOP primary. State Sen. Dave Honigman was already in the race, and Gilbert's promoters felt Honigman was taking an ambiguous stand on abortion.

Knollenberg's views on abortion were anything but ambiguous: He opposed abortion in every instance except when continuing a pregnancy would endanger a woman's life.

Millionaires Gilbert and Honigman made extensive use of negative TV ads, chiefly directed at each other. Gilbert attacked her opponent's stance on abortion and faulted Honigman as overly ambitious, while Honigman called her a lazy judge. Knollenberg took some hits on abortion, but escaped much of the name-calling. He could not afford TV ads, but used radio advertising to accuse Gilbert and Honigman of trying to buy the nomination.

The outcome was a big disappointment for abortion rights forces — Gilbert ran third with 27 percent — and a convincing victory for Knollenberg, who took the nomination with 43 percent.

In the general election, Democrat Walter O. Briggs IV made his second run at the seat, hoping that redistricting, which slightly diminished Republican strength in the 11th, would help him improve on his 1990 tally of 34 percent against Broomfield.

Briggs, nephew of respected former Democratic Sen. Philip A. Hart, cast himself as a moderate. He focused on Knollenberg's abortion views and hoped for coattails from a Clinton presidential victory in Michigan. Knollenberg won with a solid 58 percent of the vote, and his re-elections since have come with ease.

HOUSE ELECTIONS

1996 General		
Joe Knollenberg (R)	169,165	(61%)
Morris Frumin (D)	99,303	(36%)
Dick Gach (LIBERT)	5,059	(2%)
Stuart J. Goldberg (NL)	3,047	(1%)
1994 General		
Joe Knollenberg (R)	154,696	(68%)
Mike Breshgold (D)	69,168	(30%)
John R. Hocking (NL)	2,928	(1%)

Previous Winning Percentages: 1992 (58%)

CAMPAIGN FINANCE

	Receipts	Receipts from PACs		Expenditures
1996				
Knollenberg (R)	$636,367	$171,095	(27%)	$608,882
Frumin (D)	$43,590	0		$31,796
1994				
Knollenberg (R)	$621,566	$147,030	(24%)	$507,622
Breshgold (D)	$29,577	$16,854	(57%)	$29,576

DISTRICT VOTE FOR PRESIDENT

	1996		1992
D	134,344 (47%)	**D**	117,274 (37%)
R	131,571 (46%)	**R**	149,109 (47%)
I	19,322 (7%)	**I**	50,675 (16%)

KEY VOTES

1997	
Ban "partial birth" abortions	Y
1996	
Approve farm bill	Y
Deny public education to illegal immigrants	Y
Repeal ban on certain assault-style weapons	Y
Increase minimum wage	N
Freeze defense spending	N
Approve welfare overhaul	Y
1995	
Approve balanced-budget constitutional amendment	Y
Relax Clean Water Act regulations	Y
Oppose limits on environmental regulations	N
Reduce projected Medicare spending	Y
Approve GOP budget with tax and spending cuts	Y

VOTING STUDIES

	Presidential Support		Party Unity		Conservative Coalition	
Year	**S**	**O**	**S**	**O**	**S**	**O**
1996	38	62	93	7	98	2
1995	23	77	95	5	98	2
1994	44	56	95	4	92	6
1993	29	69	94	4	89	11

INTEREST GROUP RATINGS

Year	ADA	AFL-CIO	CCUS	ACU
1996	0	n/a	94	95
1995	0	0	100	88
1994	0	0	92	100
1993	5	0	91	96

12 Sander M. Levin (D)

Of Royal Oak — Elected 1982, 8th term

Biographical Information
Born: Sept. 6, 1931, Detroit, Mich.
Education: U. of Chicago, B.A. 1952; Columbia U., M.A. 1954; Harvard U., LL.B. 1957.
Occupation: Lawyer.
Family: Wife, Victoria Schlafer; four children.
Religion: Jewish.
Political Career: Mich. Senate, 1965-71, minority leader, 1969-70; Democratic nominee for governor, 1970, 1974.
Capitol Office: 2209 Rayburn Bldg. 20515; 225-4961.

Committees
Ways & Means
Human Resources (ranking); Social Security

In Washington: From his perch on the House Ways and Means Committee, Levin in the 104th was part of the Democratic minority that tried to chip away at the GOP majority's grand designs for welfare overhaul — and met with some success in doing so.

The Republicans' initial plans for welfare got a cold reception from Levin and other liberal Democrats, who backed President Clinton's January 1996 veto of an overhaul plan that Republicans had pushed through the House and Senate.

But unlike those who thought the best way to respond to the GOP's welfare effort was to defeat it, Levin tried to reshape it. Like Clinton, Levin quietly accepted the idea of ending the federal guarantee of providing welfare checks to eligible low-income mothers and children. He became an expert on the details of the welfare overhaul and worked with the administration to press Republicans into revising aspects of the bill.

Levin's actions were politically pragmatic. In helping to fashion a welfare bill that he could vote for and that Clinton could sign, Levin recognized the popularity of the issue in Michigan, which had been on the forefront of welfare experiments.

As part of his efforts, Levin sought to rein in what he saw as Republican excesses. Sometimes there were setbacks. In February 1995, the Ways and Means Human Resources Subcommittee rejected, 5-8, a Levin amendment to soften a prohibition on giving cash benefits to a child born out of wedlock to a mother under 18.

But in June 1996, the Ways and Means Committee accepted by voice vote a Levin amendment to guarantee Medicaid coverage for foster children. Levin also won approval of an amendment to keep at 65 the age at which low-income elderly can qualify as "aged" for Supplemental Security Income. The legislation would have increased the qualifying age to 67.

When the conference report on welfare overhaul emerged in August 1996, it included guarantees that Medicaid would remain available for anyone meeting current welfare eligibility requirements. It allowed states to use social services block grant funds to provide non-cash benefits to children whose parents exceeded the five-year time limit on welfare benefits. And it allowed states to provide welfare benefits to unmarried parents under age 18 who followed certain rules.

Those provisions and some other concessions were enough to persuade Clinton to endorse the welfare bill and Levin to vote for it. As evidence of Levin's role, he was one of a handful of lawmakers who attended the Rose Garden ceremony that accompanied the bill signing. "I think we were able to press the Republicans in improving the bill as relates to children," Levin said. "Essentially [Republicans] thought the president would sign anything," Levin said. "They misread him and they misread us."

Levin then worked closely with Republicans to fashion a bill making technical corrections to the welfare overhaul after he became ranking Democrat on the Human Resources Subcommittee in the 105th Congress.

On another issue before Ways and Means, Levin won a small victory in the 104th, then had it snatched away. In May 1996, Levin proposed an amendment to a package of small business tax breaks that allowed an exclusion for employer-paid tuition expenses for graduate as well as undergraduate studies.

The GOP wanted the exclusion to cover only payments for undergraduate work. Shortly after Levin's amendment passed, 18-15, GOP committee aides talked to each Republican who had voted for it. On a revote, the committee killed Levin's amendment, 16-20.

Levin and other Democrats challenged Republican-backed legislation to close a loophole that enabled wealthy individuals to avoid paying taxes by renouncing their citizenship. Democrats charged that the GOP measure, sponsored by Ways and Means Chairman Bill Archer of Texas, would leave some current escape hatches open. Chiding Republicans for being protectors of the wealthy, Levin told them, "I don't understand whose side you're on. These people are just being

MICHIGAN 12
Suburban Detroit — Warren; Sterling Heights

Think of the suburban 12th as a square. The top half contains fast-growing Troy and Sterling Heights. The southwest corner includes some older, racially mixed areas, while the city of Warren anchors the southeastern corner.

The auto industry is the thread that binds the 12th and with the industry comes the United Auto Workers (UAW) as a force. But unlike in the other heavily unionized districts of southeastern Michigan, that does not automatically translate into Democratic votes.

In Troy, a burgeoning high-tech sector revolves around auto industry consulting work that has been farmed out to smaller companies. EDS — one of the largest of these firms — is a major employer; it does computer consulting for General Motors. Another economic presence is Kmart, which keeps its world headquarters in Troy.

On the western side of the district, along what is known as the Golden Corridor, more traditional methods of car-making are evident. From 8 Mile Road — the northern border of Detroit — to Utica in the northern extreme of the 12th, this stretch includes a number of auto plants that make virtually every aspect of the car.

Close by the industrial corridor, in Warren, stands the GM Tech Center, a design and engineering center. Not far from there is a General Dynamics tank assembly plant, where in 1988 Democratic presidential nominee Michael S. Dukakis took his ill-advised tank ride.

With a large number of blue-collar workers, the 12th is fertile ground for Democratic candidates. Bill Clinton took 53 percent of the vote in 1996 and Levin took 57 percent.

Warren, the district's largest city, is a traditional Democratic stronghold, yet socially conservative. Within the city, Republicans have run well in the north, where voters are better off.

A solid Democratic vote is also cast in majority-black Royal Oak Township and in Oak Park, where more than a third of the population is black. A sizable Jewish population in affluent Huntington Woods, Oak Park and Southfield, which is shared with the 11th District, favors Democratic candidates.

Voters in Troy are more likely to be transplants to the area and less likely to be strongly affiliated with a political party than those in the southern half of the 12th. They lean toward the GOP.

Sterling Heights is less transient; a large number of its residents are upwardly mobile, former Warren residents. Republican strength in Troy — supplemented by the white-collar influx — and the swing voters of Sterling Heights allow the GOP to field credible candidates.

Both Clinton and Levin won the portions of the two counties, Macomb and Oakland, that make up the 12th District, running more strongly in the Oakland County portions than in Macomb. In both counties, Clinton polled a majority of the vote in 1996 despite the presence of two major opponents, Bob Dole and Ross Perot.

1990 Population: 580,956. White 541,953 (93%), Black 21,717 (4%), Other 17,286 (3%). Hispanic origin 6,796 (1%). 18 and over 442,863 (76%), 62 and over 89,874 (15%). Median age: 34.

asked to pay [taxes] the same as people who stay in this country."

Levin usually votes a liberal, pro-labor line. He opposes a balanced-budget constitutional amendment and congressional term limits, and he supports gun control and abortion rights, even voting against banning a particular abortion technique that opponents call "partial birth" abortion. He did, however, vote in 1996 for legislation banning federal recognition of same-sex marriages.

Although he identifies with liberals' ideals of greater international cooperation, Levin nonetheless has been confrontational on trade matters when they affect his hard-pressed working-class constituents. In September 1995, he and Rep. Amo Houghton, R-N.Y., introduced legislation renewing the controversial Super 301 section of U.S. trade law, which is a trade weapon the U.S. government uses to force other countries to open their markets to American goods. The law, enacted in 1988, requires the office of the United States Trade Representative to identify countries with barriers to U.S. goods and target them for negotiation and possible retaliation. Some countries, such as Japan, regard Super 301 as protectionist and have complained bitterly about its use.

In the 103rd Congress, Levin joined fellow Michigan Democrat David E. Bonior in a determined effort to defeat NAFTA. On the day of the vote in November 1994, Levin told the House that NAFTA should be renegotiated "to confront economic realities rather than giving a green light to Mexican practices that tilt the playing field against American workers and small businesses." However, he voted for GATT, saying the world trade agreement would open new markets for U.S. goods.

Levin has won considerable respect as a judicious legislator determined to find right answers even if they are not simple answers. This trait was amply demonstrated when Ways and Means in 1994 considered health care reform legislation. Levin knew that the biggest challenge would be paying for health coverage for 35 million uninsured Americans while also reducing the government's overall health care spending. "I'm afraid that the public thinks that everybody will have what they have now and they won't have to pay any new taxes," he said. "Those mathematics don't work out."

Levin's brother, Carl, serves in the Senate. The Levins are one of two brother-brother teams in the 105th Congress. The other team hails from Arkansas, where Tim Hutchinson is a senator and brother Asa serves in the House.

At Home: Levin's 1982 election capped his unexpected return to politics after an eight-year absence from the public eye. He first won office in 1964, taking a state Senate seat in the heavily Jewish Oakland County suburbs north of Detroit. He served as state Democratic Party chairman in the late 1960s and was viewed as one of the party's rising stars in 1970, when he challenged incumbent Republican William G. Milliken for the governorship.

But the low-key, even-tempered manner that had made Levin a successful legislator and party leader was less useful against Milliken. Levin won almost 49 percent of the vote in 1970, but in a second try four years later, he slipped under 47 percent.

After that, Levin's name left the front pages. But when Democratic Rep. William M. Brodhead decided not to run again in 1982, Levin announced for the seat. His well-known name and support from the party establishment helped him overcome five primary opponents.

Levin easily won the old 17th easily through the 1980s, but he has seen more competitive elections in the 1990s, starting with the 1992 race.

In redistricting for the 1990s, a panel of federal judges merged Levin's district with Democratic colleague and friend Dennis M. Hertel's 14th, Hertel decided to retire, but Levin still had some convincing to do. Besides Hertel's constituents, there were voters from other districts added when the map was radically redrawn. Even though Levin spent about $1 million to woo them, he managed only 53 percent against Oakland County commissioner John Pappageorge.

Pappageorge was back in 1994 with the benefits of wider name recognition and a sour political environment for Democrats.

He used the familiar 1994 Republican tactic of trying to tie Levin to an unpopular Clinton, as well as sounding the need for change from the liberal policies of the past. But Levin fought back, accusing Pappageorge of being a right-winger and criticizing his support for the House Republicans' "Contract With America." The victory was Levin's with 52 percent.

In 1996, a more Democratic year, Levin moved up to 57 percent of the vote, his best performance since the 1992 redistricting.

HOUSE ELECTIONS

1996 General		
Sander M. Levin (D)	133,436	(57%)
John Pappageorge (R)	94,235	(41%)
Albert J. Titran (LIBERT)	3,101	(1%)
1994 General		
Sander M. Levin (D)	103,508	(52%)
John Pappageorge (R)	92,762	(47%)

Previous Winning Percentages: 1992 (53%) **1990** (70%) **1988** (70%) **1986** (76%) **1984** (100%) **1982** (67%)

CAMPAIGN FINANCE

	Receipts	Receipts from PACs		Expend-itures
1996				
Levin (D)	$1,329,479	$571,230	(43%)	$1,313,913
Pappageorge (R)	$432,595	$28,915	(7%)	$432,894
1994				
Levin (D)	$1,458,644	$658,315	(45%)	$1,536,445
Pappageorge (R)	$467,227	$74,537	(16%)	$470,616

INTEREST GROUP RATINGS

Year	ADA	AFL-CIO	CCUS	ACU
1996	85	n/a	19	0
1995	90	100	21	8
1994	85	89	50	5
1993	95	100	18	4
1992	95	83	38	4
1991	100	100	30	0

VOTING STUDIES

	Presidential Support		Party Unity		Conservative Coalition	
Year	**S**	**O**	**S**	**O**	**S**	**O**
1996	89	11	93	6	31	69
1995	90	10	92	7	24	75
1994	83	15	95	5	28	72
1993	85	15	96	4	23	77
1992	18	82	96†	4†	30†	70†
1991	28	72	95	5	8	92

† Not eligible for all recorded votes.

DISTRICT VOTE FOR PRESIDENT

1996		1992	
D	127,708 (53%)	**D**	119,055 (42%)
R	91,203 (38%)	**R**	115,065 (41%)
I	20,531 (9%)	**I**	49,519 (18%)

KEY VOTES

1997	
Ban "partial-birth" abortions	N
1996	
Approve farm bill	N
Deny public education to illegal immigrants	N
Repeal ban on certain assault-style weapons	N
Increase minimum wage	Y
Freeze defense spending	Y
Approve welfare overhaul	Y
1995	
Approve balanced-budget constitutional amendment	N
Relax Clean Water Act regulations	N
Oppose limits on environmental regulations	Y
Reduce projected Medicare spending	N
Approve GOP budget with tax and spending cuts	N

13 Lynn Rivers (D)

Of Ann Arbor — Elected 1994, 2nd term

Biographical Information
Born: Dec. 19, 1956, Au Gres, Mich.
Education: U. of Michigan, B.A. 1987; Wayne State U., J.D. 1992.
Occupation: Law clerk.
Family: Husband, Joe Rivers; two children.
Religion: Protestant.
Political Career: Ann Arbor Board of Education, 1985-93, vice president, 1986-87; president 1987-91; Mich. House, 1993-95.
Capitol Office: 1724 Longworth Bldg. 20515; 225-6261.

Committees
Budget
Science
Basic Research; Technology

In Washington: A mother at 18 who worked to help support her family and then earned college and law school degrees in her 30s, Rivers has seen her share of challenges. She likes to tell voters she knows what it's like to have only the skills for a low-wage job, or to be unable to afford health insurance. She entered politics at age 28 as a "mom who got mad at the system," serving first on the Ann Arbor school board and then in the Michigan House.

Her experience as a young mother and her desire to support the Clinton administration caused her in July 1996 to part company with other Democratic liberals — her usual voting companions — and vote for the final version of a bill to overhaul the welfare system. Rivers told The New York Times that she had hoped President Clinton would veto the bill so Democrats in Congress could negotiate for further improvements. "When I saw that that was not going to be the case and that this was probably going to be the last shot we had at welfare reform," she told the newspaper, "I thought it was important that I make it clear that I do support welfare reform, I do support moving people to work, I do support changing the system. I certainly didn't want to be seen as an obstructionist."

Her reluctant support for the welfare bill was emblematic of how dealing with the GOP majority has been a patience-tester for Rivers, because the dominant conservatives do not share her view that the federal government should play an aggressive role in helping people get ahead. Rivers often bluntly expresses her exasperation with the GOP, as in May 1995, when she objected to a proposal to require that federal student loans start accruing interest on the day a student enters school, rather than after graduation.

Citing personal experience, Rivers said, "An education was only available to me because there were student loans, because I could borrow money, because I could get a helping hand. . . . And yet now we see a Republican plan that . . . makes it harder to go to school, that makes it harder to get ahead." She derided Republicans who had benefited from the student loan program, yet were seeking to change it. "What hypocrisy," she said. "I guess it is easy to pull up the ladder of success once you and your children are safely on top."

Rivers similarly denounced a GOP proposal in 1995 to prohibit federal employee health care plans from paying for abortions. "The question here today," she said, "is whether or not we will allow the good burghers who populate Congress to decide the private decisions of American families. . . . They talk about returning to traditional values; well, let's go back to one that is basic to America: 'Mind your own business.' " Rivers has opposed efforts to ban an abortion technique that opponents call "partial birth" abortion.

And Rivers admonished Republicans for their plan to reduce the rate of Medicare spending growth. "Make no mistake, this is not about saving Medicare," she said. "This is about saving the Republicans' political behind. . . . It is only when they have to make good on the promises to the wealthy [to cut taxes] that they have turned to the services to our elderly to get the money. Shame, shame, shame."

Rhetoric like that helps explain why the House Democratic Class of 1994 — a tiny band outnumbered nearly 6-to-1 by Republican freshmen — chose Rivers to serve as class president for 1996. Rivers also was asked to speak at the August 1996 Democratic National Convention during the "families first" segment of the program that preceded first lady Hillary Rodham Clinton's speech. Rivers told the Detroit News that she was probably asked to speak because "part of the theme of the convention is standing up for ordinary people and my life is 100 percent ordinary. I'm married to an autoworker; we had a young marriage, and our kids are ordinary kids." (Rivers' husband, Joe, is a member of the United Auto Workers.)

Rivers does, however, have one thing in common with many of the recently elected Republicans: An interest in institutional reform issues, or what she has called "the deimperialization of Congress." In 1995, she lent her support to

The 13th shares in the Motor City culture. It includes about a half-dozen auto plants scattered across eastern Washtenaw and western Wayne counties. The auto industry is still an important element of the local economy despite the closure in July 1993 of General Motors' Willow Run midsize car division assembly plant. Not surprisingly, Rivers has made labor one of her top priorities in Congress.

Western Wayne County provides more than 60 percent of the district's vote, much of it coming from the cities east of I-275, on the eastern edge of the 13th. Many of these cities, such as Garden City, Inkster, Romulus and Westland, are primarily blue collar, with a heavy dependence on auto industry jobs. These residents turn out a reliably Democratic vote, as do the mostly black voters of Inkster.

Many district residents had been making a habit of crossing over to vote for GOP nominees. But auto industry cutbacks and the recession brought them back to the Democratic fold to vote for Bill Clinton in 1992. He kept their votes again in 1996, topping Bob Dole in the 13th by 23 percentage points, while Rivers beat her Republican opponent by 16 points.

Farther west, closer to Washtenaw County, the townships are less industrialized and more Republican. Canton, Northville and Plymouth generally have higher incomes than their county neighbors who live closer to Detroit; they are receptive to GOP candidates.

Democratic Ann Arbor, the state's seventh-largest city, casts the bulk of Washtenaw County's ballots. Before 1992 redistricting, when the city was part of the old 2nd District,

MICHIGAN 13
Southeast — Ann Arbor; Westland; Ypsilanti

the liberal community of the University of Michigan was a sure-fire source of Democratic votes against then-GOP Rep. Carl D. Pursell. A large number of blacks in Ypsilanti and Ypsilanti Township also boosts local and statewide Democrats.

Traditionally, Washtenaw County as a whole has swung back and forth at the presidential level, as a result of the GOP small towns and farmers who populate the rest of the county. It was the only county in the nation to support both George McGovern in 1972 and Gerald R. Ford in 1976. County voters were not so ambivalent in 1996 when Clinton won the overall county with 59 percent and the district's part of the county with 65 percent.

Many of the Republicans in Washtenaw County now live in the 7th and 8th districts. While the auto industry remains a vital source of jobs, an emerging high-tech corridor has taken shape in the Ann Arbor-Detroit corridor, between I-94 and I-96. Known as "automation alley," this stretch draws on the engineering skills and brainpower of the University of Michigan, and to a lesser extent, Eastern Michigan University in Ypsilanti. Robotics companies have clustered in the area, making factory automation equipment.

1990 Population: 580,956. White 494,938 (85%), Black 64,052 (11%), Other 21,966 (4%). Hispanic origin 10,131 (2%). 18 and over 442,445 (76%), 62 and over 62,132 (11%). Median age: 31.

a Republican initiative barring House members from receiving most gifts from lobbyists. Rivers, who had pledged after her election to accept no gifts, said, "This is not revolutionary, it is not unreasonable, it is not unduly burdensome, it is simply the right thing to do."

Rivers also has suggested that House members save taxpayers' money by footing the bill for their "special order" speeches — orations typically given to a nearly empty House chamber after the day's legislative business ends. She says the speeches cost taxpayers about $7,000 per hour — the price tag for printing them in the Congressional Record and paying overtime to floor staff and Capitol police who must stay on duty whenever members are on the floor. Rivers wants members to pay those costs from their office accounts.

Drawing on her eight years' of service on the Ann Arbor school board, Rivers is an advocate for public schooling and an opponent of conservative education initiatives such as providing parents with vouchers that can be used to pay tuition at private schools. She says that while the federal government must respect local control of schools, Washington should help set standards for education and help localities prepare students to compete in the global marketplace.

As is customary with Michigan Democrats, Rivers places great importance on the concerns of organized labor, especially occupational health and safety issues.

A member of the Budget Committee, Rivers made a passionate speech in late 1996 to her fellow Democrats on why they should elect Louise M. Slaughter of New York as the committee's ranking member. Slaughter had the most seniority for the position, but the Democratic Caucus elected John M. Spratt Jr. of South Carolina over Slaughter, 106-83. Rivers pleaded for Slaughter's election in the name of "diversity." But other Democrats said it was not just a vote on a woman vs. a man, but rather a vote on a moderate vs. a liberal. Rivers also sits on the Science Committee.

At Home: Rivers managed to buck the national Republican trend in 1994, fending off Republican

John A. Schall to keep the 13th in Democratic hands. She replaced veteran Democrat William D. Ford, who retired after 15 terms.

Rivers won a three-way Democratic primary with a solid 56 percent of the vote. Her fall match with the conservative Schall gave voters a clear choice: On abortion, gun control and a range of other issues, the candidates differed sharply.

Schall portrayed Rivers as a tax-and-spend Democrat, calling her "even more liberal than Bill Clinton." He accused her of voting in the state House against a bill to keep guns out of schools and for a measure weakening child pornography laws. Rivers voiced support for tougher crime measures such as requiring criminals to serve their full sentences and increasing the penalties for crimes committed with guns. But she did not back away from her reputation as a liberal, making no apologies for her support of causes such as homosexuals' rights. In the end, she won by 7 percentage points, taking 52 percent of the vote.

Rivers was expected to receive a strong challenge in 1996 from retired GOP businessman Joe Fitzsimmons. The former chairman of an Ann Arbor microfilms firm called UMI, Fitzsimmons ran on a platform of fiscal conservatism. He criticized Rivers as a big spender and faulted her for opposing the balanced-budget constitutional amendment. But Rivers countered that she is a strong advocate of sound fiscal management, and as proof she said she returned nearly $200,000 of her office expense fund by not using franking privileges. She improved on her 1994 showing, taking 57 percent to Fitzsimmons' 41 percent.

Rivers' tenure on the Ann Arbor Board of Education began in 1985, when she was pursuing an undergraduate degree at the University of Michigan. She earned that degree in 1987, then added a law degree from Wayne State University in 1992, the same year she was elected to the state legislature.

HOUSE ELECTIONS

1996 General		
Lynn Rivers (D)	123,133	(57%)
Joe Fitzsimmons (R)	89,907	(41%)
James F. Montgomery (LIBERT)	3,114	(1%)
1994 General		
Lynn Nancy Rivers (D)	89,573	(52%)
John A. Schall (R)	77,908	(45%)
Craig L. Seymour (LIBERT)	3,186	(2%)

CAMPAIGN FINANCE

	Receipts	Receipts from PACs		Expenditures
1996				
Rivers (D)	$1,088,152	$374,199	(34%)	$1,099,549
Fitzsimmons (R)	$1,231,409	$108,282	(9%)	$1,223,433
1994				
Rivers (D)	$640,417	$247,281	(39%)	$610,394
Schall (R)	$354,158	$108,164	(31%)	$348,322

DISTRICT VOTE FOR PRESIDENT

	1996			1992	
D	130,559	(57%)	**D**	125,913	(49%)
R	76,511	(34%)	**R**	86,769	(34%)
I	16,891	(7%)	**I**	42,875	(17%)

KEY VOTES

1997	
Ban "partial birth" abortions	N
1996	
Approve farm bill	N
Deny public education to illegal immigrants	N
Repeal ban on certain assault-style weapons	N
Increase minimum wage	Y
Freeze defense spending	Y
Approve welfare overhaul	Y
1995	
Approve balanced-budget constitutional amendment	N
Relax Clean Water Act regulations	N
Oppose limits on environmental regulations	Y
Reduce projected Medicare spending	N
Approve GOP budget with tax and spending cuts	N

VOTING STUDIES

	Presidential Support		Party Unity		Conservative Coalition	
Year	S	O	S	O	S	O
1996	77	23	91	9	18	82
1995	85	15	94	6	14	85

INTEREST GROUP RATINGS

Year	ADA	AFL-CIO	CCUS	ACU
1996	95	n/a	19	5
1995	95	100	25	16

14 John Conyers Jr. (D)

Of Detroit — Elected 1964, 17th term

Biographical Information
Born: May 16, 1929, Detroit, Mich.
Education: Wayne State U., B.A. 1957, LL.B. 1958.
Military Service: National Guard, 1948-52; Army, 1952-53; Army Reserve, 1953-57.
Occupation: Lawyer.
Family: Wife, Monica Ann Esters; one child.
Religion: Baptist.
Political Career: Candidate for mayor of Detroit, 1989, 1993.
Capitol Office: 2426 Rayburn Bldg. 20515; 225-5126.

Committees
Judiciary (ranking)
Constitution; Courts & Intellectual Property

In Washington: Conyers has taken to his job as ranking Democrat on the Judiciary Committee, even though it means regular defeat. Anchoring the Democratic left in Congress, he met resistance in trying to pull many in his own party that way even when Democrats controlled the House. The role he now plays — cranky idealist fighting the GOP majority to save programs for the poor — seems to suit him.

The soft-spoken Conyers attacks Republicans with politesse, but with relish as well. When Citizen Action, a consumer organization, found that Conyers voted with the policies of Speaker Newt Gingrich less often than any other member of Congress in 1995, Conyers released a statement declaring his delight. "It is easy to vote against him and the special interests he represents," Conyers boasted. "I'm proud to lead the opposition to the Gingrich gang."

Conyers voted "present" rather than accepting the House's 1997 reprimand of Gingrich and the levying of a $300,000 penalty; he felt the punishment for Gingrich's ethics transgressions should have been much more stern. Conyers has referred to Gingrich as the "most unethical Speaker in the nation's history."

In 1996, Conyers complained that "The Republican Party is now completely led by extremists," and he has found very little in the GOP agenda he can support. Conyers opposed the overhaul of welfare, the market-oriented 1996 farm law, a ban on a specific abortion procedure its opponents call "partial-birth" abortion, a major tax cut package, and a proposed constitutional amendment to limit congressional terms.

The focus of Conyers' energy in the 104th was fighting the GOP's anti-crime legislation and other bills that began their legislative journey in the Judiciary Committee. He scored a victory with an amendment to the 1997 version of a balanced-budget amendment that would have kept Social Security surpluses from being counted against the deficit. Conyers' amendment never came to a vote as Chairman Henry J. Hyde, R-Ill., shut down the Judiciary markup rather than risk losing. With the balanced-budget amendment stalled in the House, proponents looked to the Senate for momentum, but the measure died there on a floor vote, killing its prospects for the 105th.

Conyers and Hyde did manage to find common ground on one piece of legislation, which made destruction of religious property a federal crime. The bill they wrote together, which was enacted in 1996, was prompted by a wave of church burnings, mainly hitting African American houses of worship in the South.

Generally, though, Conyers felt that the Republicans were federalizing too many crimes, contradicting their stated philosophy of returning power to the states. He offered numerous amendments, in committee and on the floor, seeking to revise or rewrite GOP crime legislation, but watched most of them sink without a trace.

It was quite a contrast with his experience in the Democratic-controlled 103rd Congress, when Conyers and other black legislators pressed their case with President Clinton as he crafted his 1994 crime bill. He and other members of the Congressional Black Caucus persuaded Crime Subcommittee Chairman Charles E. Schumer, D-N.Y., to amend his bill to provide $2 billion in prevention funds to local governments.

Conyers pressured the Democratic leadership to keep an assault weapons ban in the bill, and he fought to preserve provisions that would allow death penalty defendants to use "racial justice" statistics in their defense. "Without the Congressional Black Caucus signing off on this legislation, it is not going anywhere. Period," boasted Conyers. The Black Caucus got much of what it wanted in the final crime bill, including significant crime prevention funding and the assault weapons ban. But some minority members still were dissatisfied with the final draft, which did not include the racial justice language.

Conyers, who was then chairman of the old Government Operations Committee, had to reconcile his commitment to that provision with his responsibility as a senior Democrat and commit-

MICHIGAN 14
Parts of Detroit; Harper Woods; Highland Park

Henry Ford built his first large factory in Highland Park in 1909, followed by Buick, R. E. Olds and the Fisher brothers. Soon afterward the nascent automobile industry attracted rural Michiganders, residents of Appalachia, Southern blacks and Eastern Europeans, many of whom sought housing in the sea of single- and two-family homes on Detroit's north side.

The industry kept Detroit working and prosperous for much of the century, but over the past few decades, the city has been losing jobs and people rapidly. Many auto industry jobs have moved to Mexico and other non-unionized areas. The residents have moved to the mainly white suburbs that ring the city.

In 1960, the city contained about 1.7 million inhabitants, two-thirds of whom were white. By 1990, the city barely exceeded 1 million residents, three-quarters of whom were black.

But there are signs of economic renewal in the Motor City. Since the federal government designated a large patch of the city as an empowerment zone in 1994, 29 companies have announced plans to spend over $2 billion on business expansion or creation. The largest investor, unsurprisingly, is a car company. Chrysler Corp. announced plans in April 1997 to increase its spending on Jeep Grand Cherokee production in the area by about $1 billion.

Much of the district is centered on the north side of Detroit, taking in Harper Woods, Grosse Pointe Woods and Grosse Pointe Shores on the eastern edge and a handful of precincts from Dearborn Heights (the rest are in the 16th District) on the southwestern fringe. It is generally more residential and better off than the city's other congressional district, the 15th.

Rosedale is home to larger residences that were built for General Motors executives in the 1930s. North of 7 Mile Road, there are racially mixed communities with a relatively high percentage of professionals and white-collar city employees. Toward the west side are some of the city's largest and most politically active black churches.

Politically, this is a Democratic stronghold where Republicans have virtually no presence. In 1994, Conyers' biggest threat was in the primary.

In presidential elections, Democratic nominees regularly rack up the state's highest percentages here and in the 15th District. In statewide politics, Democratic candidates must run up huge margins in Detroit to offset their losses outside of southeastern Michigan. Democratic then-Gov. James J. Blanchard's 1990 upset loss to Republican John Engler was partly attributed to his inability to win big in the Motor City.

The only places where Republicans find quarter are outside the city. The blue-collar and middle-class denizens of Harper Woods lean Republican at the statewide and national levels, but they are swing voters who often split tickets. The doctors, lawyers and auto executives of affluent Grosse Pointe Woods and Grosse Pointe Shores are even more receptive to GOP candidates.

1990 Population: 580,956. White 169,875 (29%), Black 401,444 (69%), Other 9,637 (2%). Hispanic origin 6,127 (1%). 18 and over 408,963 (70%), 62 and over 80,771 (14%). Median age: 31.

tee chairman to help his party and president pass a crime bill. His solution: He voted twice to bring the crime bill to the floor (the first attempt failed) and then opposed the measure on final passage.

In the 104th, Conyers and Schumer attempted to block GOP efforts to abandon the approach of funding specific crime prevention programs and instead provide block grants that states could spend as they saw fit. Republicans scoffed, but their attempt to rewrite the Clinton crime law fell far short of enactment.

Conyers, however, lost an effort to stop the GOP from rejecting a recommendation from the U.S. Sentencing Commission that would have brought the penalty for possessing crack cocaine (used primarily by the poor) more in line with the penalty adherent to powder cocaine (whose users tend to be more upscale). Republicans argued that crack is more addictive and preserved guidelines that allow a drug dealer to sell 100 times more powder than crack before triggering the same mandatory five-year sentence.

Conyers also accused Republicans of overreaching as they crafted an anti-terrorism bill in the wake of the 1995 bombing of an Oklahoma City federal building and other incidents. He spurned the final legislative product, arguing that "What remains is a low-grade crime bill — cats and dogs from the Judiciary Committee . . . that have nothing to do with fighting terrorism."

Conyers also opposed the committee's toughened protections against illegal immigration and a massive overhaul of telecommunications law (Judiciary shared jurisdiction over the latter product with the Commerce Committee). In both cases he thought the bills were drafted to the disadvantage of less wealthy people. He surprised many observers, however, when he voted in a House-Senate conference on the telecommunications bill to accept the Senate's provision banning indecent material from the Internet. (The ban was quickly challenged in the courts.)

Conyers proved his longtime free speech bona fides during consideration of a constitutional amendment enabling Congress and the states to ban desecration of the U.S. flag. "We're going to the heart and soul of the right of the freedom of expression as protected in the Constitution," he warned. "The true test of any nation's commitment to freedom of expression lies in its ability to protect any unpopular expression."

Conyers, a jazz fan, was chairman of the Government Operations Committee (now known as Government Reform and Oversight) for three terms, concluding with the 103rd Congress. For several years he promoted the idea of elevating the Environmental Protection Agency to Cabinet status, but even when Clinton came into office and endorsed the proposal, it did not happen.

One of Conyers' career landmarks came in 1983, when he won creation of a federal holiday to commemorate the Rev. Martin Luther King Jr. He has seen far less success, though, with his plan to authorize a study of the impact of slavery on living African Americans. The study would include recommendations to Congress on possible remedies including reparations.

At Home: The son of an autoworker, Conyers became interested in politics while in law school and worked loyally in the party apparatus. The creation in 1964 of a second black-majority district in Detroit gave him his first opportunity to try for Congress. He ran on a platform of "Equality, Jobs and Peace," pledging to strengthen the United Nations and to exempt low-income families from paying federal income tax.

Among the qualifications Conyers cited for holding office were three years as a district aide to Democratic Rep. John D. Dingell of Michigan and service on a panel of lawyers picked by President John F. Kennedy to look for ways of easing racial tensions in the South. Conyers won the primary by just 108 votes over Richard H. Austin, a Detroit accountant.

For the most part since then, Conyers' House primaries have not been very strenuous. He did not enhance his political reputation, however, with two bids for Detroit mayor. In 1989, Conyers challenged Mayor Coleman A. Young and finished third in the September primary, ceding a runoff berth against Young to accountant Tom Barrow. His second bid, in 1993, also was a flop.

In 1992, Conyers faced re-election after disclosure of his 273 overdrafts at the House bank. And he had to run in a significantly changed district. Though heavily Democratic, much of the territory was new and accustomed to representation from two white Democrats. Blacks retained the balance of power, however, and in a primary against a white state senator, Conyers won easily.

Two Democrats challenged Conyers in the 1994 primary. His closest competitor, Detroit lawyer Melvin "Butch" Hollowell, aggressively promoted himself as a fresh, energetic leader, while blasting Conyers for missing House votes. Conyers ran on his seniority and committee chairmanship and polled 51 percent of the vote, 23 points ahead of Hollowell.

HOUSE ELECTIONS

1996 General		
John Conyers Jr. (D)	157,722	(86%)
William A. Ashe (R)	22,152	(12%)
1994 General		
John Conyers Jr. (D)	128,463	(81%)
Richard Charles Fornier (R)	26,215	(17%)
Richard R. Miller (NL)	2,953	(2%)

Previous Winning Percentages: **1992** (82%) **1990** (89%) **1988** (91%) **1986** (89%) **1984** (89%) **1982** (97%) **1980** (95%) **1978** (93%) **1976** (92%) **1974** (91%) **1972** (88%) **1970** (88%) **1968** (100%) **1966** (84%) **1964** (84%)

CAMPAIGN FINANCE

	Receipts	Receipts from PACs		Expend-itures
1996				
Conyers (D)	$294,627	$162,343	(55%)	$267,039
1994				
Conyers (D)	$577,267	$335,037	(58%)	$575,696

DISTRICT VOTE FOR PRESIDENT

	1996		1992
D	163,629 (86%)	D	180,007 (81%)
R	20,176 (11%)	R	28,937 (13%)
I	4,701 (3%)	I	12,600 (6%)

KEY VOTES

1997	
Ban "partial birth" abortions	N
1996	
Approve farm bill	N
Deny public education to illegal immigrants	N
Repeal ban on certain assault-style weapons	N
Increase minimum wage	Y
Freeze defense spending	?
Approve welfare overhaul	N
1995	
Approve balanced-budget constitutional amendment	N
Relax Clean Water Act regulations	N
Oppose limits on environmental regulations	Y
Reduce projected Medicare spending	N
Approve GOP budget with tax and spending cuts	N

VOTING STUDIES

	Presidential Support		Party Unity		Conservative Coalition	
Year	S	O	S	O	S	O
1996	68	22	91	3	2	88
1995	87	8	94	1	2	97
1994	71	24	92	2	11	75
1993	63	17	70	2	0	57
1992	10	72	69	4	4	79
1991	23	75	91	2	3	89

INTEREST GROUP RATINGS

Year	ADA	AFL-CIO	CCUS	ACU
1996	90	n/a	13	0
1995	90	100	8	8
1994	100	100	25	5
1993	80	100	0	0
1992	90	89	13	0
1991	95	100	20	0

15 Carolyn Cheeks Kilpatrick (D)

Of Detroit — Elected 1996, 1st term

Biographical Information
Born: June 25, 1945, Detroit, Mich.
Education: Ferris State U., A.A. 1965; Western Michigan U., B.S. 1968; U. of Michigan, M.S. 1972.
Occupation: Teacher.
Family: Divorced; two children.
Religion: Baptist.
Political Career: Mich. House, 1979-97; sought Democratic nomination for Mich. Senate, 1994.
Capitol Office: 503 Cannon Bldg. 20515; 225-2261.

Committees
Banking & Financial Services
Financial Institutions & Consumer Credit; General Oversight & Investigations
House Oversight
Joint Library

The Path to Washington: A former schoolteacher and veteran of the state Legislature, Kilpatrick had to take on incumbent Democrat and one-time political ally Barbara-Rose Collins before claiming the 15th, which includes downtown Detroit and some of the city's tonier northeastern suburbs. Kilpatrick is the only first-term House Democrat who unseated an incumbent in a primary election.

Kilpatrick, who served 17 years in the state House before winning her congressional seat, was careful never to criticize Collins directly. Instead she frequently reminded voters of her own legislative experience and commitment to good government, strongly implying that a time for new leadership had arrived.

In Lansing, Kilpatrick had earned a reputation as a careful and thoughtful lawmaker with a knack for working across party lines to get things done.

Allies from her years in the Legislature say she was well-known for her expertise in education, gained during the eight years she taught in Detroit's public school system.

But Kilpatrick also managed to distinguish herself by mastering the nuances of fiscal and appropriations issues. For example, she once led a coalition of Democratic and Republican lawmakers who were seeking to block a proposal from popular Republican Gov. John Engler, who wanted to halt state funding for local transportation programs.

Kilpatrick says she will promote policies designed to support economic development, create new jobs, bolster the wages of working families, and improve the access and affordability of health care, especially for the poor and disadvantaged.

At the urging of Detroit's mayor, Democrat Dennis W. Archer, Kilpatrick is also likely to push for financing for a high-speed rail system and an airport to ease the growing road and air congestion in the city.

Kilpatrick hopes to encourage investment in such projects from her seat on the Banking and Financial Services Committee, where she is expected to be a strong voice for boosting the venture capital available to entrepreneurs and other businesses, particularly in large cities like Detroit.

Kilpatrick also says she is strongly committed to representing the entire district, including upper-class communities such as Grosse Pointe, Hamtramck and Grosse Point Farms.

In recent years, residents of those predominantly white communities have frequently complained that their interests were being ignored in favor of overwhelmingly black Detroit.

Despite her stature in the community and her reputation as an accomplished legislator, Kilpatrick was somewhat reluctant to enter the Democratic primary to run against Collins.

But when Collins became the subject of separate investigations by the House ethics committee and the Justice Department into allegations of ethical and financial misconduct, Kilpatrick felt compelled to step forward.

The road to Washington was not an easy one for Kilpatrick. Five other Democrats filed for a chance at knocking off the incumbent, prompting speculation that such a large field would splinter the vote and give Collins a victory, despite her perceived political weaknesses.

Days before the primary, however, Collins helped to ensure her own defeat when she held a fundraiser at a Detroit strip club that featured male and female exotic dancers.

On primary day, Kilpatrick drew a majority of the vote to trounce Collins, leaving the other candidates in the single digits.

Characteristically, Kilpatrick mended fences with Collins shortly thereafter to promote party unity, then turned her attention to the general election campaign and Republican nominee Stephen Hume.

But in a district where Democrats hold an insurmountable advantage in registered voters, Kilpatrick's November victory over Hume was virtually ensured.

The depopulation of Detroit has been under way for decades, leading the city to be called the Beirut of America, a desolate, burned-out hulk showing few signs of life. By 1992, a local editorial columnist asked, "Has the city of Detroit ceased to exist?"

If it has, a variety of factors contributed over the past four decades. In 1960, Detroit was a metropolis of 1.7 million people. Thirty years later, local officials fretted when a preliminary census count showed fewer than 1 million residents. The final 1990 census numbers confirmed that Detroit had just over 1 million inhabitants.

The domestic automobile industry's woes devastated the economies of southeastern Michigan and Detroit, but some of the population decline can be linked to the 1967 riots, the worst in terms of property damage and deaths this century.

Particularly hard hit was the area that now makes up the 15th. Taking in the older parts of the city, the 15th contains the skeletal remains of an era when Detroit was a manufacturing powerhouse. Even though the 15th contains the city's downtown and waterfront areas, it also houses many downtrodden residents, who live in bombed-out, boarded-up neighborhoods largely clustered south of the Ford Freeway.

The city's downtown and riverfront areas have been the focus of numerous redevelopment projects over the years, aimed at luring residents back. The 73-story Renaissance Center was opened in 1977 to try to revitalize the city's commercial core. Those efforts have met with some success, but the emergence of the outlying suburban cities as commercial centers has made the task even more daunting.

In sharp contrast to the city's mostly poor and working-class blacks are the wealthy white

MICHIGAN 15
Parts of Detroit; Grosse Pointe; Hamtramck; River Rouge

communities of Grosse Pointe Park, Grosse Pointe and Grosse Pointe Farms, nestled in the northeast corner of the district.

Like the rest of the white suburban communities that surround Detroit, residents here are usually hostile toward the city. In 1992, Democratic House primary challenger Tom Barrow appealed to their vote by trying to link then-Rep. Barbara-Rose Collins to former Mayor Coleman A. Young, a tactic that would not have been successful with city-based voters. In this heavily Democratic district, a primary challenge is really the only way to knock off an incumbent in the 15th.

Hamtramck is another white enclave, surrounded on all sides by Detroit. Once home to 50,000 people, many of whom worked at the huge and now-closed Dodge plant at the southern end of town, the city's population has dwindled to fewer than 20,000. Still, a tightknit Polish community exists, leavened by newly arrived Yugoslavs, Albanians and some Middle Eastern immigrants. Other Arab communities of Syrians, Palestinians and Chaldeans exist in southeast Detroit.

River Rouge and Ecorse are grafted on to the 15th's southern extreme; they are populated with autoworkers and steelworkers, many of whom are black.

1990 Population: 580,956. White 153,464 (26%), Black 406,905 (70%), Other 20,587 (4%). Hispanic origin 24,808 (4%). 18 and over 418,224 (72%), 62 and over 97,630 (17%). Median age: 32.

HOUSE ELECTIONS

1996 General		
Carolyn Cheeks Kilpatrick (D)	143,683	(88%)
Stephen Hume (R)	16,009	(10%)
1996 Primary		
Carolyn Cheeks Kilpatrick (D)	27,140	(51%)
Barbara-Rose Collins (D)	16,123	(31%)
Douglass J. Diggs (D)	3,219	(6%)
George Hart (D)	2,440	(5%)
Leon Jenkins (D)	1,454	(3%)
Godfrey Dillard (D)	1,192	(2%)
Henry Edward Stallings II (D)	1,034	(2%)

CAMPAIGN FINANCE

	Receipts	Receipts from PACs	Expend-itures
1996			
Kilpatrick (D)	$180,437	$75,400 (42%)	$174,457

DISTRICT VOTE FOR PRESIDENT

1996	1992
D 142,536 (86%)	D 144,092 (81%)
R 18,003 (11%)	R 26,421 (15%)
I 3,759 (2%)	I 8,278 (5%)

KEY VOTES

1997

Ban "partial birth" abortions	N

16 John D. Dingell (D)

Of Dearborn — Elected 1955; 21st full term

Biographical Information
Born: July 8, 1926, Colorado Springs, Colo.
Education: Georgetown U., B.S. 1949, J.D. 1952.
Military Service: Army, 1944-46.
Occupation: Lawyer.
Family: Wife, Deborah Insley; four children.
Religion: Roman Catholic.
Political Career: Wayne County assistant prosecutor, 1953-55.
Capitol Office: 2328 Rayburn Bldg. 20515; 225-4071.

Committees
Commerce (ranking)

In Washington: Few members lost more power than Dingell when the GOP took over the House in 1995. With a combination of ruthless expansionism and shrewd deal-cutting, Dingell built a remarkable fiefdom out of the Energy and Commerce Committee during his 14 years as chairman. Like Shakespeare's Richard II, Dingell in 1995 was suddenly "eating the bitter bread of banishment"; but unlike many other senior Democrats, Dingell took to his diminished role with élan, working in tandem with Republicans on a wide range of bills, yet standing firm in defense of programs he helped create when they came under attack by conservatives.

"There are other things than being committee chairman that you can do in this place," Dingell commented. "I've learned to live on fairly short rations and do reasonably well. As a result, I have had to learn how to do interesting things like throwing bombs."

Dingell now is the ranking member on the renamed Commerce Committee, where he seems to have a fairly good working relationship with Chairman Thomas J. Bliley Jr., R-Va. The two worked closely during the 104th on telecommunications and insurance legislation, and Dingell has also forged alliances with several other Republicans on matters spanning the legislative globe, including term limits, product liability, waste disposal and electricity deregulation.

But if Dingell has been willing to cut deals, he also holds fast to certain liberal principles, and he has stoutly defended programs such as Medicare. And though Dingell over the years has had run-ins with federal agencies, especially over rules affecting Detroit's auto industry, he believes in activist government and chastises Republicans for attacking government employees as regulatory tyrants. "Washington is not full of crazy, run-amok bureaucrats running around seeking to penalize honest Americans and to create economic hardships," he said in the 104th.

Dingell presided over the House in 1965 when the bill that created the Medicare program was passed, and 30 years later he stood firm in his opposition to GOP attempts to curb its rate of growth. Together with Florida Democrat Sam M. Gibbons, Dingell offered an alternative to the Republican proposal that cut about one-third as much money from projected Medicare spending. It went nowhere, but President Clinton eventually vetoed the GOP plan.

Dingell also objected to a Republican proposal to overhaul Medicaid that included provisions to leave design and enforcement of nursing home standards entirely up to the states. He suggested that, "it could be a short-haired jackass taking care of these people if the state wanted it to."

As much as Dingell objected to the GOP's agenda in the 104th, he was more critical of what he saw as the hasty manner in which Republicans tried to achieve their goals. He was visibly frustrated at his inability to influence the scope and pace of legislative business, even when he supported a Republican bill. For years, Dingell had backed a plan to limit manufacturers' liability for faulty products, but in the 104th he lashed out at GOP leaders for pushing their product-liability measure through without proper deliberation.

Dingell is a regular combatant on the House floor, bringing to bear his command of legislative substance and parliamentary procedure and his long institutional knowledge. He once stated his maxim before the Rules Committee: "If you let me write procedure and I let you write substance, I'll screw you every time."

When Michael G. Oxley, R-Ohio, was working on a plan to overhaul the superfund toxic waste cleanup program, he recognized that winning over Dingell was crucial to garnering sufficient Democratic support for enactment. "We could do it without Dingell, but it would be a lot tougher," Oxley said. Dingell joined with Bliley as a negotiator on the massive telecommunications overhaul of 1996, helping to protect the interests of the regional Baby Bells and succeeding in killing a pet Oxley provision to allow increased foreign ownership of telecommunications outlets.

For the 105th, Dingell has clasped hands with

MICHIGAN 16
Southeast Wayne County; Monroe County

A gray stretch of gritty communities along the Detroit River, the 16th is one of the most industrialized districts in the country.

In a previous incarnation, two rounds of redistricting ago, the Detroit News called it "the most polluted congressional district in the nation." The borders are somewhat different now, but the character is quite similar.

Dearborn, its largest city, is home to the Ford Motor Co. and the factory that was once the largest on Earth. Known simply as "the Rouge," spread over 1,200 acres, its assembly line employed nearly 100,000 workers during its heyday.

The Dearborn Ford facilities now employ about a quarter of that. The tool-and-die shops, foundries, assembly lines and chemical plants of the 16th served as a powerful magnet for U.S. and international job-seekers in the early and mid-20th century. Residents of Appalachia, Germans, Poles, Czechs, Italians, and Southern blacks all migrated here in search of jobs, filling communities such as Melvindale, Wyandotte and Allen Park.

Another wave of migration brought large numbers of Arabs to the Dearborn area. Some Shiite Moslems came during World War I, after Henry Ford opened the massive plant in the southern end of the city. For decades afterwards, Egyptians, Iraqis, Lebanese, Syrians, Palestinians, Jordanians, Saudis and Yemenis would come into the city in spurts.

Today, the Arab business district along Warren Avenue supports the nation's largest Arab-American community.

The migration to the state's ninth largest city has not included blacks. Whites make up 98 percent of Dearborn; relations with majority-black Detroit are strained.

Nearby Dearborn Heights is shared with the Detroit-based 14th District; most of the city is in the 16th. Farther south, just inside the Wayne County limits on the southern edge, is the Flat Rock automotive plant, a joint U.S.-Japanese venture and one of the district's larger employers. The plant also produces Fords and Mazdas.

The Wayne County portion of the district is the most populous. Thoroughly unionized and mostly blue collar, this area regularly turns in Democratic margins. There are some pockets of Republican affluence, mainly in Riverview and Grosse Ile.

Monroe County, south of Wayne, is more politically competitive. Local factories have a union presence, but farther west, the turf is less industrialized and more conservative. Some retirees from the Detroit and Toledo areas have moved to communities on the county's Lake Erie shoreline.

Bill Clinton won Monroe in 1996, but two years before, voters displayed their independence by splitting their tickets and supporting Republican candidates in statewide races while voting to reelect Dingell.

Republican Senate candidate Spencer Abraham carried the county in 1994, as did GOP Gov. John Engler.

1990 Population: 580,956. White 561,164 (97%), Black 8,088 (1%), Other 11,704 (2%). Hispanic origin 14,092 (2%). 18 and over 434,219 (75%), 62 and over 93,030 (16%). Median age: 34.

Republican Sen. Frank H. Murkowski of Alaska in the matter of electricity deregulation, leading a go-slow group that reflects the position of most of the nation's private utilities. Although some Republicans are confident they can have a law in place to create a national utilities market at the turn of the century, Dingell pointedly alludes to efforts to deregulate other industries that took 30 years to complete.

No one understands the slow dance of legislation any better than Dingell, who has the longest continuous service of anyone in the House. Health care has been Dingell's longest crusade; his father, John Dingell Sr., who held the same House seat for 23 years prior to his death, wrote the first national health insurance bill. Dingell has introduced the bill in every Congress since succeeding his father in a 1955 special election.

In the 103rd, buttressed by a Democratic president for whom the issue was central, Dingell spent months trying to forge a compromise health care plan that would satisfy the various Democratic factions on Energy and Commerce. But the task proved too much, even for the man known as one of Congress' savviest arm-twisters. Lacking the votes to move a bill out of his committee, Dingell gave up on trying to find a consensus. Health care legislation reported out of other committees died without a floor vote.

Dingell combined with senior Commerce Democrat Henry A. Waxman to present a united front on a safe drinking water bill during the 104th. Finding themselves stranded together in the minority lifeboat, Dingell would not split from Waxman as he had on environmental issues in the past. They gained increasing leverage as the GOP grew hungry to bulk up its environmental record.

Dingell breaks with most Democrats in his strong support of gun-owners' rights, which led to a rhetorical flare in February 1995 that he came to regret. On the House floor he said that agents of the Bureau of Alcohol, Tobacco and Firearms "are detested, and I have described them properly as jackbooted American fascists." Yet after the April

1995 bombing of a federal building in Oklahoma City, he joined the chorus of Democrats who complained that Republican anti-government rhetoric "provides exactly the kind of stimulus" that leads to violence. "It's coming close to inciting riot."

During his years as chairman, Dingell built a power center that congressional scholars generally regard as one of the more expansive on Capitol Hill in the postwar era. He attracted bright young talent to craft major policy changes in communications, energy, transportation, solid waste disposal and health care. As chairman, Dingell was known for bullying witnesses and badgering members. Having amassed the broadest jurisdiction in the House, Dingell had to spend much of his time defending his committee's turf.

One of his landmark legislative accomplishments came in the 101st Congress with reauthorization of the Clean Air Act. Dingell fought reauthorization through much of the 1980s, championing the interests of the auto industry. In the end, he was credited with holding off action far longer than most lawmakers could have and then driving a decent bargain for automakers.

Much of Dingell's reputation for ruthlessness came from his role as aggressive and merciless investigator in the chair of the Oversight Subcommittee, from which he zealously probed the propriety and performance of federal agencies. On occasion he forced a sluggish federal regulator into action merely by threatening to call him before his subcommittee. And there were also "Dingell-grams," tart rebukes and testy inquiries penned by the chairman and his aggressive staff at a rate of hundreds per year.

At Home: When the elder Dingell died unexpectedly in 1955 while undergoing a routine physical examination, his 29-year-old son stepped in. John Dingell Jr. grew up on Capitol Hill, not in Detroit. It was only when he received his law degree and went to work as an assistant prosecutor that he delved into Detroit politics. But after three years as "my father's ears and eyes," he was ready for the 1955 special election. With backing from organized labor, he trounced a dozen Democratic candidates in the primary and went on to overwhelm his GOP opponent.

Since then, Dingell had to worry about re-election only once, in 1964, when part of his constituency was combined with a larger part of the district held by Democratic Rep. John Lesinski Jr., who had also succeeded his father in the House.

The Dingell-Lesinski primary got national attention because it was thought to be a measure of "white backlash" over recent civil rights legislation. Dingell, whose old district was about one-third black, had voted for the 1964 Civil Rights Act. Lesinski, whose district was nearly all white, was one of four Northern Democrats who had voted against it.

The issue was not brought up in the campaign, but both sides knew it was the main reason Dingell received such strong help from labor, civil rights groups and the state Democratic Party. Dingell won with 55 percent and has had almost no re-election problems since.

HOUSE ELECTIONS

1996 General		
John D. Dingell (D)	136,854	(62%)
James R. DeSana (R)	78,723	(36%)
Bruce W. Cain (LIBERT)	3,155	(1%)
1994 General		
John D. Dingell (D)	105,849	(59%)
Ken Larkin (R)	71,159	(40%)
Noha F. Hamze (NL)	1,968	(1%)

Previous Winning Percentages: **1992** (65%) **1990** (67%) **1988** (97%) **1986** (78%) **1984** (64%) **1982** (74%) **1980** (70%) **1978** (77%) **1976** (76%) **1974** (78%) **1972** (68%) **1970** (79%) **1968** (74%) **1966** (63%) **1964** (73%) **1962** (83%) **1960** (79%) **1958** (79%) **1956** (74%) **1955†** (76%)

† Special election

CAMPAIGN FINANCE

	Receipts	Receipts from PACs		Expend-itures
1996				
Dingell (D)	$1,479,953	$879,060	(59%)	$1,854,280
DeSana (R)	$263,289	$8,977	(3%)	$259,035
1994				
Dingell (D)	$966,924	$752,610	(78%)	$1,075,063
Larkin (R)	$8,644	$14	(0%)	$8,074

DISTRICT VOTE FOR PRESIDENT

1996		1992	
D	122,723 (54%)	**D**	118,079 (44%)
R	78,472 (35%)	**R**	97,968 (36%)
I	24,150 (11%)	**I**	52,963 (20%)

KEY VOTES

1997	
Ban "partial-birth" abortions	Y
1996	
Approve farm bill	Y
Deny public education to illegal immigrants	N
Repeal ban on certain assault-style weapons	Y
Increase minimum wage	Y
Freeze defense spending	Y
Approve welfare overhaul	Y
1995	
Approve balanced-budget constitutional amendment	N
Relax Clean Water Act regulations	N
Oppose limits on environmental regulations	Y
Reduce projected Medicare spending	N
Approve GOP budget with tax and spending cuts	N

VOTING STUDIES

	Presidential Support		Party Unity		Conservative Coalition	
Year	S	O	S	O	S	O
1996	78	22	84	14	51	47
1995	86	11	90	6	17	77
1994	76	17	87	6	36	53
1993	75	17	87	7	39	55
1992	19	74	87	6	31	56
1991	28	67	81	11	51	49

INTEREST GROUP RATINGS

Year	ADA	AFL-CIO	CCUS	ACU
1996	70	n/a	31	25
1995	90	100	17	8
1994	70	75	33	15
1993	70	100	18	10
1992	90	83	25	0
1991	65	92	22	22

MINNESOTA

Governor: Arne Carlson (R)
First elected: 1990
Length of term: 4 years
Term expires: 1/99
Salary: $114,506
Term limit: No
Phone: (612) 296-3391
Born: September 24, 1934; New York, N.Y.
Education: Williams College, B.A. 1957; U. of Minnesota, 1957-58.
Military Service: Army, 1959-60.
Occupation: Computer executive.
Family: Wife, Susan Shepard; three children.
Religion: Protestant.
Political Career: Minneapolis City Council, 1965-67 (majority leader); Minn. House, 1971-79; Minn. auditor, 1979-91.

Lt. Gov.: Joanne Benson (R)
First elected: 1994
Length of term: 4 years
Term expires: 1/99
Salary: $62,980
Phone: (612) 296-3391

State election official: (612) 296-2805
Democratic headquarters: (612) 293-1200
Republican headquarters: (612) 854-1446

REDISTRICTING

A 1993 Supreme Court decision upheld a state-drawn redistricting map and invalidated a plan crafted by the federal courts. The Minnesota delegation was elected under the federal plan in 1992 and used the new state map for the 1994 elections.

STATE LEGISLATURE

Legislature. Meets odd years, January-May; even years, January-March.

Senate: 67 members, 4-year terms
1996 breakdown: 42D, 24R, 1I; 45 men, 22 women
Salary: $29,657.74
Phone: (612) 296-0504

House of Representatives: 134 members, 2-year terms
1996 breakdown: 70D, 64R; 95 men, 39 women
Salary: $29,657.74
Phone: (612) 296-2146

URBAN STATISTICS

City	Population
Minneapolis	368,383
Mayor Sharon Sayles Belton, D	
St. Paul	272,235
Mayor Norm Coleman, D	
Bloomington	86,335
Mayor Coral Houle, N-P	
Duluth	85,493
Mayor Gary Doty, N-P	
Rochester	70,745
Mayor Chuck Canfield, N-P	

U.S. CONGRESS

Senate: 1 D, 1 R
House: 6 D, 2 R

TERM LIMITS

For state offices: No

ELECTIONS

1996 Presidential Vote

Bill Clinton	51%
Bob Dole	35%
Ross Perot	12%

1992 Presidential Vote

Bill Clinton	43%
George Bush	32%
Ross Perot	24%

1988 Presidential Vote

Michael S. Dukakis	53%
George Bush	46%

POPULATION

1990 population		4,375,099
1980 population		4,075,970
Percent change		+7%
Rank among states:		20
White		94%
Black		2%
Hispanic		1%
Asian or Pacific islander		2%
Urban		70%
Rural		30%
Born in state		74%
Foreign-born		3%
Under age 18	1,166,783	27%
Ages 18-64	2,661,382	61%
65 and older	546,934	13%
Median age		32.5

MISCELLANEOUS

Capital: St. Paul
Number of counties: 87
Per capita income: $19,107 (1991)
Rank among states: 17
Total area: 84,402 sq. miles
Rank among states: 12

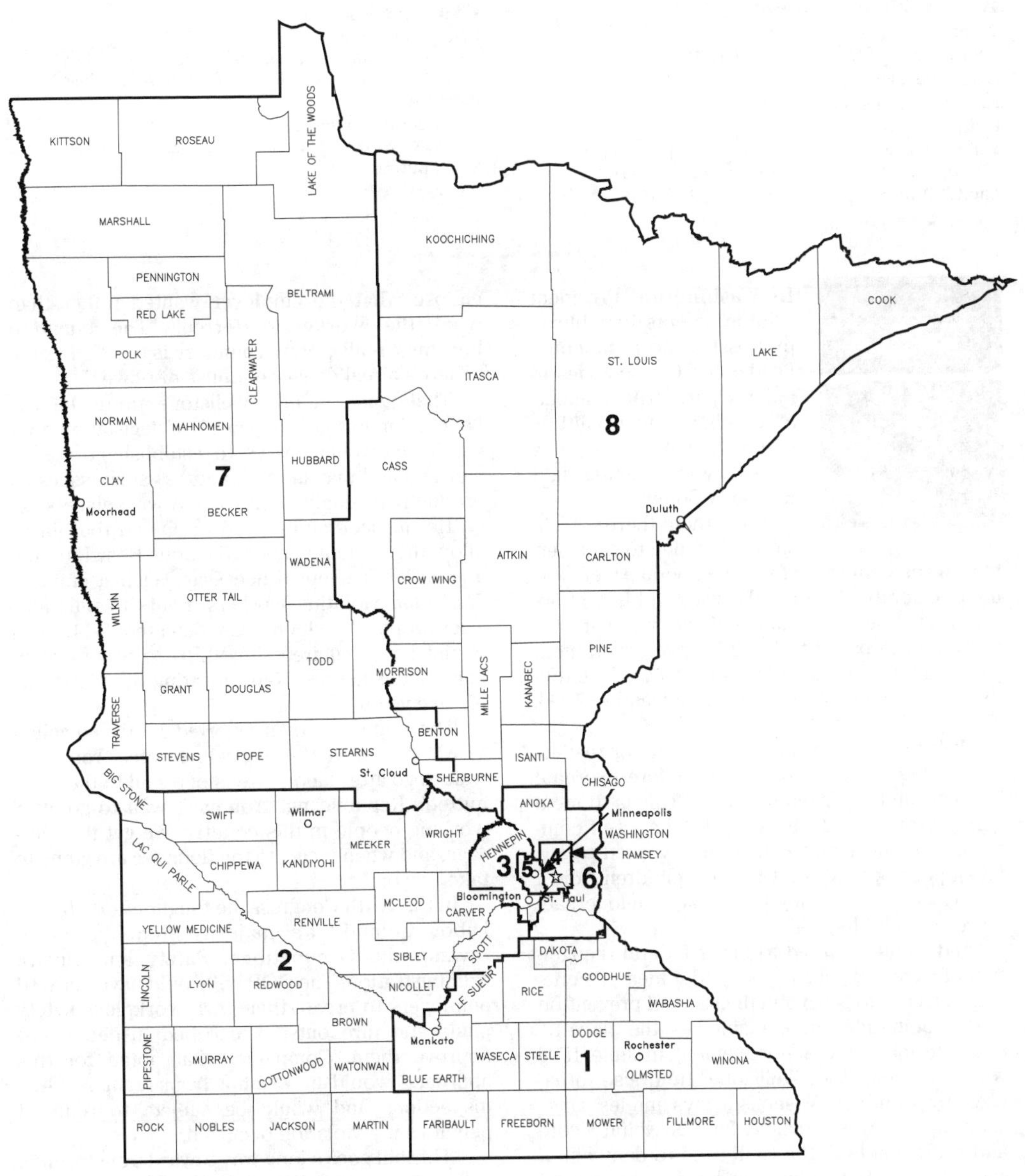
KITTSON
ROSEAU
LAKE OF THE WOODS
MARSHALL
KOOCHICHING
PENNINGTON
RED LAKE
BELTRAMI
COOK
POLK
CLEARWATER
ST. LOUIS
LAKE
ITASCA
NORMAN
MAHNOMEN
8
HUBBARD
CASS
CLAY
7
Moorhead
BECKER
Duluth
AITKIN
CARLTON
WADENA
CROW WING
OTTER TAIL
WILKIN
PINE
TODD
GRANT
DOUGLAS
MORRISON
MILLE LACS
KANABEC
TRAVERSE
BENTON
STEVENS
POPE
STEARNS
ISANTI
St. Cloud
SHERBURNE
CHISAGO
BIG STONE
ANOKA
SWIFT
Wilmar
Minneapolis
WASHINGTON
WRIGHT
MEEKER
HENNEPIN
RAMSEY
LAC QUI PARLE
CHIPPEWA
KANDIYOHI
3
5
4
6
MCLEOD
Bloomington
St. Paul
CARVER
RENVILLE
YELLOW MEDICINE
SCOTT
DAKOTA
SIBLEY
2
GOODHUE
LINCOLN
LYON
REDWOOD
NICOLLET
RICE
LE SUEUR
WABASHA
BROWN
DODGE
Rochester
Mankato
PIPESTONE
MURRAY
COTTONWOOD
WATONWAN
WASECA
STEELE
1
WINONA
OLMSTED
BLUE EARTH
ROCK
NOBLES
JACKSON
MARTIN
FARIBAULT
FREEBORN
MOWER
FILLMORE
HOUSTON

Paul Wellstone (D)

Of St. Paul — Elected 1990, 2nd term

Biographical Information

Born: July 21, 1944, Washington, D.C.

Education: U. of North Carolina, B.A. 1965, Ph.D. 1969.

Occupation: Professor.

Family: Wife, Sheila Ison; three children.

Religion: Jewish.

Political Career: Democratic nominee for Minn. auditor, 1982; Democratic National Committee, 1984-91.

Capitol Office: 136 Hart Bldg. 20510; 224-5641.

Committees

Foreign Relations
European Affairs; International Economic Policy, Export & Trade Promotion; Near Eastern & South Asian Affairs

Indian Affairs

Labor & Human Resources
Children & Families; Employment & Training (ranking)

Small Business

Veterans' Affairs

In Washington: President Clinton co-opts Republican proposals. The Democratic Leadership Council tries to pull the party from its liberal moorings. The Coalition, better known as the "blue dogs," charts a center-right course in Congress.

And then there's Wellstone. He failed to get a perfect 100 percent score from the liberal Americans for Democratic Action only twice in his first six years in the Senate — and in those two years, his score was 95 percent. "I still believe government can be a force for good in people's lives," he told the Star Tribune of Minneapolis in October 1996. "That won't change."

Wellstone was the only senator up for re-election in 1996 who opposed the welfare overhaul bill that Clinton signed into law. "This is to me a very personal point," he said. "I did a lot of community organizing over the years, worked with a lot of poor people, a lot of poor children. And I just can't vote for anything that would create more poor children."

And while he voted to block federal recognition of same-sex marriages — "the idea of same-sex marriage goes beyond the issue of prevention of discrimination," he explained — the place he chose to make the announcement in June 1996 was a "Come Out for Wellstone" fundraiser organized by prominent Wisconsin gays and lesbians.

Wellstone was attacked for his welfare vote and many others as the GOP tried to deny him a second term. But he won re-election by a solid nine-point margin, and as he returned to Washington in 1997, he gave no indication of mellowing with experience.

When the Labor and Human Resources Committee in March 1997 considered legislation to allow businesses to offer workers a choice between overtime pay or compensatory time off for hours worked beyond a traditional 40-hour week, Wellstone, the ranking Democrat on the Employment and Training Subcommittee, worried that companies would coerce employees to choose what the employer wanted rather than what the worker preferred. "The question becomes, really, 'How voluntary is this?'" he said. "There's a real danger of abuse of power."

That same month, Wellstone protested the Labor Committee's approval of legislation that would allow businesses to establish groups of workers and managers to address such issues as productivity, quality control and workplace safety. He unsuccessfully tried to amend the bill to allow the National Labor Relations Board to take any action it deemed necessary against employers found violating workers' rights to unionize. The proposal, which was defeated 7-11, also would have required the NLRB to issue orders barring businesses from repeating the violations for five years.

The committee then reported out the so-called TEAM Act on a 10-8 party-line vote. "You can't wait to go after labor," Wellstone said to the committee's Republicans. "You can't wait to go after working people in this country. We get the message, and when it gets to the floor, we are going to take this on."

In the 104th Congress, he fought efforts by the Labor Committee's majority Republicans to revamp the Occupational Safety and Health Administration. The GOP bill would have allowed employers to create their own workplace safety plans and hire outside, certified inspectors to approve them. Companies that opted for this approach would be exempt from regular OSHA inspections and would be subject to reduced penalties if a violation occurred.

"This bill goes a long way toward transforming OSHA from a regulatory agency into an agency that provides technical assistance," Wellstone complained in March 1996. He said that the bill put too much faith in employers' good will and took too much power away from OSHA.

As the Senate in February 1997 debated a constitutional amendment requiring a balanced federal budget, Wellstone offered an amendment to exempt from balanced-budget calculations federal outlays for programs that provide nutrition, health care and education to children in low-income families. "These vital programs have been neglected," Wellstone said. His amendment was killed, 64-36.

Wellstone is a strong supporter of changing the way congressional campaigns are funded. He has called for public financing of political campaigns and for a national campaign finance awareness day styled after Earth Day. "I hope people in this country turn up the heat," he said. "Because this is the ethical issue of our time. It certainly appears that national political leaders are for sale."

He was one of the first Democrats to call for an independent counsel to investigate White House fundraising practices during Clinton's 1996 re-election campaign. And in March 1997, he was one of only three Democrats to buck his party and vote to kill a resolution stating that only Attorney General Janet Reno has the right to name an independent counsel and urging that if a counsel is named, an inquiry explore fundraising in congressional as well as presidential campaigns.

With Republicans running the Senate in the 104th, Wellstone finally achieved a victory he had been denied when his party held the Senate majority — tightening the rules against senators receiving gifts and meals from lobbyists. "We did something very important," he said after the bill passed in July 1995. "We took a step toward changing the political culture in Washington."

The gift-ban effort had died at the end of the 103rd Congress because of a last-minute Republican filibuster of the conference report. After threatening to attach the gift ban to the telecommunications deregulation bill in the 104th Congress, Wellstone and Carl Levin, D-Mich., won a promise from Senate Majority Leader Bob Dole, R-Kan., to bring up the measure in July 1995.

The Senate passed the ban, 98-0, but not without a floor battle. The resolution originally would have allowed lawmakers to accept meals and gifts worth no more than $20, with a maximum of $50 from any one source. But the Senate approved, 54-46, an amendment by Majority Whip Trent Lott, R-Miss., to raise the individual gift limit to $50 and allow a maximum of $100 in gifts from any one source. The amendment also proposed to exempt gifts under $50 from counting against the $100 limit.

Wellstone then proposed requiring all gifts above $10 to count against the $100 aggregate limit. Supporters told Lott that they would insist on debating the issue and would seek a recorded vote if it was resisted. The threat resonated. Lott accepted Wellstone's modification without floor debate and it passed by voice vote.

His other major success during the 104th Congress came during congressional approval of the fiscal 1997 VA-HUD spending bill. The measure included a provision, co-authored with Pete V. Domenici, R-N.M., requiring group health insurance plans that cover mental illness to set the same annual and lifetime limits on that coverage as they set on physical illness. That mandate, which does not apply to companies with 50 or fewer employees, will be in effect only from Jan. 1, 1998, to Sept. 30, 2001, and will be waived for companies if it causes their premiums to rise 1 percent or more. Both senators had watched close relatives struggle with mental illnesses and had been trying for four years to stop health insurance plans from providing far less coverage for the treatment of mental illnesses than for physical illnesses.

Wellstone can also be a lone wolf. He held up approval of a rescissions bill in July 1995, objecting to spending cuts to the Low Income Home Energy Assistance Program (LIHEAP), education, job training and to a tiny program that offers consumer counseling to senior citizens on medical insurance. "I've been around here for a long time, and I've never dealt with a guy like this," a furious Dole muttered about Wellstone. "Everybody's tired," Wellstone responded. In the end, Wellstone forced the Clinton administration to shift money around to restore $5.5 million for the senior citizens counseling program. He got his floor amendments on LIHEAP and job training programs. Both lost, and the Senate eventually passed the rescissions bill, 90-7.

In July 1996, Wellstone struck again, threatening to block approval of legislation guaranteeing that individuals who lose or leave their jobs could maintain health insurance coverage, even if they are sick. The conference report stalled because of a provision to renew American Home Products' patent of a single drug, Lodine, that otherwise could be sold in less expensive generic form by other manufacturers. Wellstone threatened to hold up the bill unless the drug patent provision was excised. He succeeded in persuading Lott to allow it to be stricken.

In the 105th Congress, Wellstone took a seat on the Foreign Relations Committee, leaving the Energy and Natural Resources Committee, where, as a devout environmentalist, he frequently was at odds with GOP Chairman Frank H. Murkowski of Alaska, and, when the Democrats were in control, J. Bennett Johnston of Louisiana.

Wellstone's style and persistence raised eyebrows in Washington almost from the moment he first arrived at the Capitol in the converted school bus that served as his 1990 campaign symbol. Upon arriving in Washington, Wellstone told reporters that since the age of 19 he had "despised" and "detested" North Carolina Republican Sen. Jesse Helms. In January 1997, Wellstone and Helms once found themselves waiting for the same elevator. Helms made a passing remark about how dramatically radio equipment had changed since his days in the business. "Right?" he asked Wellstone. "He expects me to agree?" Wellstone asked in mock incredulity. "Wrong!" Both men laughed as they entered the elevator together.

At Home: Republican Rudy Boschwitz, the only incumbent senator of either political party to lose a re-election bid in 1990, tried to avenge that loss to Wellstone by waging a comeback in 1996. Supported with a separate advertising campaign financed by the National Republican Senatorial Committee, Boschwitz called Wellstone "ultraliberal" and "embarrassingly liberal," citing his votes on welfare and Clinton's 1993 deficit-reduction package, which raised income taxes on the wealthiest Americans. Boschwitz erected billboards saying, "Old Math: Wellstone = Welfare. New Math: Boschwitz = Workfare."

Wellstone struck back, criticizing Boschwitz for accepting campaign contributions from tobacco interests and for voting against an increase in the minimum wage while backing a pay increase for senators. As the campaign neared the finish line, polls suggested that Boschwitz's cries of "liberal" were falling on deaf ears. Wellstone ended up winning with votes to spare, 50 percent to 41 percent.

That victory was a landslide compared with his initial 1990 win by 2 percentage points over Boschwitz, when Wellstone was boosted by voter disillusionment with Minnesota elected officials, beginning with Republican Sen. Dave Durenberger's hearings before the Senate Ethics Committee and his subsequent denunciation.

Some state legislators also had well-publicized scandals. Questions about GOP Rep. Arlan Stangeland's office phone bill further contributed to Minnesotans' gloom, as did the October surprise of Republican gubernatorial nominee Jon Grunseth, who was edged off the ballot after he was accused of sexual indiscretions.

Touting a fresh, anti-establishment message, Wellstone found himself perfectly positioned to exploit voters' antipathy and topple a senator who as late as mid-October had been considered a safe bet for re-election. It was an upset unrivaled since 1980, when several surprise Republican victories propelled the GOP to a 12-seat pickup and a Senate majority.

A political science professor at Carleton College, Wellstone co-chaired the Rev. Jesse Jackson's 1988 presidential campaign in Minnesota. He had lost his only previous outing as a candidate — a 1982 bid for state auditor.

But his humorous television campaign against Boschwitz caught the imagination of voters. In some of the most original advertisements of the year, Wellstone starred in a Minnesota version of Michael Moore's sardonic documentary "Roger and Me," in which Wellstone, instead of stalking General Motors Corp. Chairman Roger Smith, sought out Boschwitz.

In another ad, Wellstone raced across the state speaking increasingly rapidly, explaining that he had to talk fast because he did not have Boschwitz's $6 million treasury to buy more media time.

On Election Day, Minnesotans revolted against establishment candidates. They threw out 10-year Democratic Gov. Rudy Perpich, voting in maverick Republican Arne Carlson, who had replaced Grunseth as the party's nominee only a week earlier. (Carlson was the winner over Wellstone in the 1982 auditor's race.) Stangeland lost his re-election bid. And Wellstone beat Boschwitz, 50 percent to 48 percent.

SENATE ELECTIONS

1996 General		
Paul Wellstone (D)	1,098,493	(50%)
Rudy Boschwitz (R)	901,282	(41%)
Dean Barkley (REF)	152,333	(7%)
1996 Primary		
Paul Wellstone (D)	194,699	(86%)
Dick Franson (D)	16,465	(7%)
Ed Hansen (D)	9,990	(5%)
Ole Savior (D)	4,180	(2%)

Previous Winning Percentages: 1990 (50%)

KEY VOTES

1997	
Approve balanced-budget constitutional amendment	N
Approve chemical weapons treaty	Y
1996	
Approve farm bill	N
Limit punitive damages in product liability cases	N
Exempt small businesses from higher minimum wage	N
Approve welfare overhaul	N
Bar job discrimination based on sexual orientation	Y
Override veto of ban on "partial birth" abortions	N
1995	
Approve GOP budget with tax and spending cuts	N
Approve constitutional amendment barring flag desecration	N

CAMPAIGN FINANCE

	Receipts	Receipts from PACs		Expend-itures
1996				
Wellstone (D)	$5,991,013	$571,723	(10%)	$5,979,224
Boschwitz (R)	$4,423,974	$1,035,527	(23%)	$4,409,982
Barkley (REF)	$37,725	0		$37,240
Hanson (RES)	$49,489	0		$49,487

VOTING STUDIES

	Presidential Support		Party Unity		Conservative Coalition	
Year	**S**	**O**	**S**	**O**	**S**	**O**
1996	85	15	92	8	11	89
1995	88	12	95	5	7	93
1994	81	18	94	6	3	97
1993	91	8	94	5	5	95
1992	23	75	92	5	8	92
1991	22	75	91	5	8	88

INTEREST GROUP RATINGS

Year	ADA	AFL-CIO	CCUS	ACU
1996	95	n/a	31	5
1995	100	100	32	4
1994	100	100	10	4
1993	100	82	10	4
1992	100	92	10	0
1991	95	83	20	5

Rod Grams (R)

Of Anoka — Elected 1994, 1st term

Biographical Information

Born: Feb. 4, 1948, Princeton, Minn.
Education: Anoka-Ramsey Community College, 1970-72; Carroll College, 1974-75.
Occupation: Contractor; television journalist.
Family: Four children.
Religion: Lutheran.
Political Career: U.S. House, 1993-95.
Capitol Office: 261 Dirksen Bldg. 20510; 224-3244.

Committees

Banking, Housing & Urban Affairs
Financial Institutions & Regulatory Relief; Financial Services & Technology; International Finance (chairman)
Budget
Energy & Natural Resources
Energy Research Development Production & Regulation; National Parks, Historic Preservation & Recreation
Foreign Relations
African Affairs; International Operations (chairman); Near Eastern & South Asian Affairs
Joint Economic

In Washington: Grams' quick rise to the Senate in 1994 after just one term in the House coincided with the zenith of the "Republican revolution."

But Grams, a longtime television newscaster with pronounced conservative views, has asserted himself as more than a foot soldier in the congressional GOP's conservative wing. At times, he has shown more zeal for policies embodied in the House Republicans' "Contract With America" than some of his party leaders.

Grams arrived in the Senate in 1995 just as House Republicans, led by Speaker Newt Gingrich, were rushing a catalog of conservative legislation to passage on the House floor. Grams, who had just spent two years in the House, bridled at the Senate's slower pace.

"When I go home, people ask me how does it feel to be part of the revolution," Grams said. "I tell them I don't know, I'm in the Senate."

In March 1997, though, it was Gingrich who infuriated many conservatives by suggesting that Republicans might consider forgoing tax cuts in order to remove an excuse "liberals" might have used to not support a balanced-budget deal. "Such a retreat would be a horrible mistake," said Grams in a lengthy speech on the Senate floor.

Grams also continues to carry the fight for a cause that was popular in the 104th with House GOP conservatives: closing down some Cabinet departments. His main target has been the Energy Department; he offered legislation to shut it down in the 104th and 105th Congresses.

His targeting of Energy merged with another of his priorities, establishing a temporary repository in Nevada for high-level nuclear waste from power plants in states such as Minnesota that are plagued with storage problems.

In March 1997, Grams was the only senator to vote against Federico F. Peña's confirmation as Energy secretary, a protest against what Grams viewed as foot-dragging on the nuclear waste issue by the Clinton administration.

The conservatives' crusade to close Cabinet departments has not yielded much, nor has Grams' effort on another cause about which he has been quite outspoken: reopening the section of Pennsylvania Avenue in front of the White House to vehicular traffic. The stretch of pavement was blocked off to protect the president against possible terrorism following the April 1995 bombing of a federal building in Oklahoma City.

"We cannot build a protective bubble around the president from which he never emerges," Grams told a Senate Governmental Affairs Committee hearing in June 1996. The Senate approved a non-binding resolution earlier that month calling on the federal government to work with local authorities to develop a plan to reopen the street, but no further action was taken.

As his work on the Pennsylvania Avenue matter shows, Grams has a wide range of interests, and his committee assignments give him latitude to pursue a number of topics.

Appointed to the Budget Committee in March 1996, Grams also is on Banking, Housing and Urban Affairs, chairing its International Finance Subcommittee; Energy and Natural Resources; and Foreign Relations, chairing the International Operations Subcommittee. He also was named in late 1996 as one of two congressional delegates to the United Nations.

Like many of his conservative colleagues, Grams says the United States is justified in withholding some of its scheduled payments to the United Nations to try to force the organization to cut its bureaucracy and costs.

"We have every right to be aggressive in our policies . . . just our size, and if you look at the money we pay. We contribute far more than anybody else," Grams told the Minneapolis/St. Paul Star Tribune during a December 1996 working visit to the United Nations. However, Grams was overheard telling other nations' diplomats that Congress supported a strong United Nations.

Grams got involved during the 104th Congress in a sticky issue much closer to home. He joined with Minnesota Democratic Rep. James L. Oberstar in pushing for legislation allowing increased use of motorized vehicles in the Boundary Waters Canoe Area Wilderness in northern Minnesota, and providing for more local control over the area.

Grams and Oberstar managed in 1996 to get their provision attached to a parks bill that included funding for projects in a number of states and districts. But President Clinton, siding with environmentalists, threatened to veto the parks bill if it included the Boundary Waters language.

The Republican leadership relented, dropping the Boundary Waters provision in September 1996 and leaving Grams fuming about "election year politics." But some Democrats argued it was Grams who was playing politics by pushing the legislation, despite efforts to mediate the issue by Minnesota Democratic Sen. Paul Wellstone, who was up for re-election in 1996.

At Home: Grams' decision to give up broadcasting for politics could not have been better timed. Despite Democratic efforts to cast him as too conservative, Grams benefited from the ethics problems of Democratic Rep. Gerry Sikorski in 1992 to win his one House term, then rode the 1994 Republican tide to his Senate victory.

The aftermath of both these contests underlines Grams' sense of timing. In 1994, William P. "Bill" Luther reclaimed for the Democrats the House seat Grams had vacated to run for the Senate. Just two years after electing Grams to the Senate, Minnesota in 1996 re-elected Wellstone, one of the Senate's most liberal members.

Democrats had scoffed at Grams' House victory as a fluke. Although Sikorski had gotten caught up in the House bank scandal and faced other questions about how he ran his House office, Grams won a four-way race in suburban Minneapolis' 6th District with just 44 percent of the vote to Sikorski's 33 percent.

Grams established a strongly conservative record in the House but never really settled in there. A court-ordered readjustment of the state's districts after the 1992 election made his future look problematic at about the same time veteran moderate Republican Sen. Dave Durenberger was announcing he would retire from the Senate.

Accepting the urgings of national party figures to run statewide, Grams ran a tightly focused Senate campaign, pledging to make government smaller and to crack down on crime. He capitalized on Minnesotans' then-growing disaffection with Clinton.

Grams also gained ground in the campaign's final weeks because of stumbling by Democratic nominee Ann Wynia. A 12-year veteran of the Minnesota House, Wynia was vulnerable to Grams' attacks on her as a career politician. And in a Republican year, Grams' charges that Wynia was too liberal did more damage than the Democrat's effort to portray Grams as too conservative.

Wynia carried the Democratic strongholds of Hennepin (Minneapolis) and Ramsey (St. Paul) counties, but her margins there were thin compared with Wellstone's in 1990. Grams took control in suburban Anoka, Dakota and Washington counties outside the Twin Cities and cruised to victory in the smaller cities and rural venues.

SENATE ELECTIONS

1994 General		
Rod Grams (R)	869,653	(49%)
Ann Wynia (D)	781,860	(44%)
Dean M. Barkley (I)	95,400	(5%)
1994 Primary		
Rod Grams (R)	269,931	(58%)
Joanell M. Dyrstad (R)	163,205	(35%)
Harold Edward Stassen (R)	22,430	(5%)
John J. Zeleniak (R)	8,467	(2%)

Previous Winning Percentages: 1992* (44%)

** House election*

KEY VOTES

1997	
Approve balanced-budget constitutional amendment	Y
Approve chemical weapons treaty	N
1996	
Approve farm bill	Y
Limit punitive damages in product liability cases	Y
Exempt small businesses from higher minimum wage	Y
Approve welfare overhaul	Y
Bar job discrimination based on sexual orientation	N
Override veto of ban on "partial birth" abortions	Y
1995	
Approve GOP budget with tax and spending cuts	Y
Approve constitutional amendment barring flag desecration	Y

CAMPAIGN FINANCE

	Receipts	Receipts from PACs	Expend-itures
1994			
Grams (R)	$2,548,996	$701,180(28%)	$2,439,798
Wynia (D)	$2,688,347	$606,987(23%)	$2,659,423
Barkley (I)	$24,285	0	$24,226

VOTING STUDIES

	Presidential Support		Party Unity		Conservative Coalition	
Year	**S**	**O**	**S**	**O**	**S**	**O**
1996	34	59	97	2	92	8
1995	21	78	98	1	98	2
House Service:						
1994	36	56	88	1	81	3
1993	33	65	95	4	95	5

INTEREST GROUP RATINGS

Year	ADA	AFL-CIO	CCUS	ACU
1996	5	n/a	92	95
1995	0	0	100	96
House Service:				
1994	0	0	91	100
1993	0	0	91	100

1 Gil Gutknecht (R)

Of Rochester — Elected 1994, 2nd term

Biographical Information
Born: March 20, 1951, Cedar Falls, Iowa.
Education: U. of Northern Iowa, B.A. 1973.
Occupation: Real estate broker; school supplies salesman; auctioneer; computer software salesman.
Family: Wife, Mary Catherine Keefe; three children.
Religion: Roman Catholic.
Political Career: Minn. House, 1983-95, floor leader.
Capitol Office: 425 Cannon Bldg. 20515; 225-2472.

Committees
Budget
Science
Basic Research; Technology

In Washington: Gutknecht, who likes to tell voters that his name means "good hired hand" in German, was at times in the 104th Congress a handful for the House GOP leadership. He made a habit of locking arms with other deficit hawks to press for deeper federal spending cuts than even GOP leaders thought advisable.

As the House plowed through its work on fiscal 1997 appropriations bills, Gutknecht persistently — and unsuccessfully — offered amendments calling for across-the-board spending cuts of 1.9 percent. In June 1996, as he sought to trim the cost of the Interior appropriations bill, Gutknecht said, "I do understand that there will be cuts as a result of this 1.9 percent reduction, but if we look down the path, sooner or later we are going to have to pay the price for this. . . . If we cannot make $4.1 billion worth of cuts this year, how are we going to make $47 billion worth of cuts in a couple of years? The answer is we probably are not." The House rejected Gutknecht's amendment, 128-291.

Voters in the 1st are accustomed to having a deficit scold for a congressman. For six terms the district was represented by Democrat Timothy J. Penny, who retired in 1994 after years of trying to goad the House Democratic majority into cutting spending. With Republicans in charge in the 104th, Gutknecht turned in a Penny-like performance aimed at GOP leaders. He was one of only 19 Republicans voting against the party's fiscal 1997 budget plan; he and the other defectors complained that it allowed for a short-term increase in the deficit and included an extra $4 billion for domestic spending — money added at the insistence of moderate GOP senators.

Gutknecht also was in a group of GOP members from rural districts who objected to the Republican leadership's Medicare bill, which aimed to restrain the growth in Medicare spending over seven years. The group held up the bill's passage in October 1995 because of concerns that payment formulas for Medicare providers would discourage physicians from serving rural areas. To satisfy them, the GOP leadership modified the formulas. Gutknecht then backed the bill.

But if Gutknecht gave his party's leaders some headaches, he also established himself as knowledgeable on budget matters — so much so that he earned a seat on the Budget Committee for the 105th Congress.

Gutknecht stands apart from most Republicans by resisting higher Pentagon budgets. In June 1996 he voted for an amendment to freeze fiscal 1997 defense spending at the prior-year level; when it failed, 194-219, he voted against the entire defense spending bill.

Gutknecht says he believes in a strong defense, "but just look at the Defense Department and the amount of waste and duplication and mismanagement that we see." He often mentions his annoyance with the number of Pentagon employees whose work is buying things. Gutknecht once said on the House floor, "I am told according to last count, we had something like 106,000 buyers" at the Pentagon. "We buy about one F-16 fighter aircraft a week. To do that we have 1,646 buyers."

Part of the reason all these buyers are needed, Gutknecht complains, is the regulatory gantlet that complicates federal purchasing. When he sat on the Government Reform and Oversight Committee in the 104th, he supported legislation included in the GOP's "Contract With America" that required agencies to perform detailed cost-benefit analyses before issuing new regulations.

Gutknecht has invested much energy in an effort that is politically appealing even if it annoys some of his colleagues: cutting back on House members' pensions. His idea is to bar members from accruing additional pension benefits after they have served six terms — providing incentive for members to leave after 12 years in office.

Under the current congressional pension system, members who serve 40 years get annual pension payments equal to 80 percent of their top salary over the final five years of their career. At the current rate of pay, that works out to an annual pension of $106,880. Under Gutknecht's plan, the government could not consider any year of

When former Democratic Rep. Timothy J. Penny talked to audiences unfamiliar with the 1st, he described it this way: "It's Redwing Shoes, the Mayo Clinic, Hormel and the valley of the Jolly Green Giant."

The "valley" is still mostly rural, and agriculture — corn, grains, dairy and hog farming — is the major focus. The rolling hills that extend from the Mississippi River to the great bend in the Minnesota River offer farmers some of the state's most productive land.

Except for Rochester and some Mississippi River towns, the population centers in the 1st are devoted to serving the surrounding farms, or in the case of Austin, processing the main local product — hogs.

Austin's economy is fed by the meat-and food-processing plants in the area, and the name Hormel says it all. George A. Hormel founded the company in 1891. At the Mower County Historical Center, visitors can see the original Hormel building, along with steam locomotives and horse-drawn carriages. While there are pockets of Democratic strength (Mower County is the 1st's most consistently Democratic), the district as a whole is Republican with a keen independent streak.

In 1992, the district as it was then configured gave Ross Perot about 27 percent of the vote — more than in any district in Minnesota except the 2nd. In 1988, George Bush won the old 1st with only 51 percent of the vote. With Perot's help, Bill Clinton narrowly carried the district in 1992. Clinton had less trouble winning the district in 1996, beating Bob Dole by 48 percent to 37 percent. Perot received 13 percent of the vote.

The state's redistricting odyssey has not changed the 1st's basic complexion. A 1993 Supreme Court decision upheld a state-drawn redistricting map and invalidated a plan crafted by the federal courts that was used in the 1992 election. However, the new state-drafted districts were in effect for the 1994 congressional election. The 1st changed little, gaining North Mankato. Now all of metropolitan Mankato, the district's second largest city, is in the district.

MINNESOTA 1
Southeast — Rochester; part of Mankato

Redwing Shoes is still a fixture in the 1st. Located in Red Wing, the company employs more than 1,000 people. The district is also known for the world-famous Mayo Clinic, located in Rochester. The 19-story facility is the centerpiece of a booming health-care industry, which employs about 19,000 workers in the Rochester area. And IBM has a Rochester facility that employs about 5,100 people.

Rochester (Olmsted County) has a more white-collar orientation than the rest of the district. Its voters are more reliably Republican than many of the 1st's farmers, who often stray from GOP traditions. Another of the 1st's claims to fame is as the scene of one of the last chapters of Old West history. It was in Northfield (Rice County) that Jesse James and his gang were finally stopped in 1876 when they attempted to rob the Northfield Bank and were ambushed by townfolk. Each Labor Day weekend, thousands attend the "Defeat of Jesse James Days" celebration.

1990 Population: 546,887. White 535,011 (98%), Black 1,758 (<1%), Other 10,118 (2%). Hispanic origin 5,403 (1%). 18 and over 399,240 (73%), 62 and over 90,313 (17%). Median age: 33.

service after 12 years when calculating a member's retirement benefits. The result would be a maximum annual pension payment of $27,254 at current salary levels, Gutknecht has said.

Like many in his party, Gutknecht criticizes Washington for imposing what he sees as unfunded federal mandates on states and localities. In a January 1995 House floor speech, he said that passing legislation to increase the minimum wage would amount to "another unfunded mandate that will kill jobs and hurt productivity." But in May 1996, when a bill increasing the minimum wage by 90 cents reached the House floor, Gutknecht voted for it. (He also supported an unsuccessful GOP effort to exempt small businesses from the minimum wage increase.)

A member of the Science Committee, Gutknecht drew criticism in the medical research community in 1995 when he sent a letter to the National Institutes of Health asking for proof that HIV causes AIDS and that AIDS is contagious. The journal Science subsequently quoted Gutknecht's legislative aide Brian Harte as saying the federal effort to study AIDS based on the HIV-AIDS link "will be seen as the greatest scandal in American history and will make Watergate look like a no-fault divorce." Harte drafted the letter, according to the Minneapolis/St Paul Star Tribune, and Gutknecht signed it.

Gutknecht told the newspaper he was not aiming to try to reduce funding to study AIDS, but he said Congress had not rigorously monitored monies devoted to AIDS research. Gutknecht said he believes there is likely a link between AIDS and HIV. "But it may not be as strong as some people think," he said. "We may be misdiagnosing some other diseases and just calling them AIDS because they happen to be homosexuals or they may happen to have been drug users." Gutknecht later fired Harte for comments he made to the press, the Star Tribune reported.

At Home: Born in Cedar Falls, Iowa, and educated at the University of Northern Iowa in that city, Gutknecht was active in Republican campaigns from an early age. After graduating from college, he became a salesman for a school-supply company, which gave him a chance to hobnob with residents in the small towns of southeast Minnesota.

In 1982, he won election to the Minnesota House, and during a dozen years there he was a loyal team player in the Independent-Republican caucus, attracting attention for his considerable oratorical ability and rising to the post of party floor leader. In the process, he broadened his political horizons: He chaired Jack F. Kemp's 1988 presidential campaign in Minnesota, and in the summer of 1993 he traveled around the state testing the waters for a possible bid for the Senate seat being vacated by Republican Dave Durenberger.

But when Penny announced in August 1993 that he would not seek re-election in the 1st, Gutknecht shifted from an uphill Senate bid to a more winnable campaign for the open House seat.

With his base in the district's leading population center, Rochester, and his ties to the GOP hierarchy, Gutknecht easily won the party's endorsement in the spring district convention and overwhelmed the comeback bid of former GOP Rep. Arlen I. Erdahl (1979-83) in the September primary. In November, he won by 10 points over Democratic state Sen. John C. Hottinger.

Gutknecht's primary campaign against Erdahl had strong generational overtones. The amiable Erdahl, 20 years Gutknecht's senior, was a product of an era when Congress often operated in a collegial and bipartisan manner. He boasted of his ability to work with Democrats in a non-confrontational fashion. But Erdahl was short of money and grass-roots troops. Framing the race as a contest between the past and the future, Gutknecht won nomination with 57 percent.

The general election was closer. As an open Democratic seat in a historically Republican district, the 1st was a top priority for both parties. Gutknecht boasted the virtues of the "Contract With America."

Hottinger pointed to his own 106-point plan to balance the federal budget. And the Democrat had the support of the popular Penny.

But Gutknecht rolled out of Olmsted County (Rochester) with a lead of more than 10,000 votes and padded the margin in Republican counties to the east. Hottinger could not overcome that deficit in the district's scattered Democratic strongholds and in his home base of Mankato. Gutknecht prevailed 55 percent to 45 percent.

In 1996, Gutknecht had to fend off a tough challenge from Winona State University economics professor Mary Rieder. She campaigned as a fiscally conservative Democrat in the Penny mold, but on social issues such as abortion, she ran to the left of Gutknecht, an abortion opponent. Gutknecht raised the specter that Rieder would support higher taxes, and he told voters he had kept his 1994 promise to be a budget-cutter. Rieder made Gutknecht's second race closer than his first, but he won with 53 percent, as the district went Democratic for president by an 11-point margin.

HOUSE ELECTIONS

1996 General		
Gil Gutknecht (R)	137,545	(53%)
Mary Rieder (D)	123,188	(47%)
1994 General		
Gil Gutknecht (R)	117,613	(55%)
John C. Hottinger (D)	95,328	(45%)

CAMPAIGN FINANCE

	Receipts	Receipts from PACs		Expend-itures
1996				
Gutknecht (R)	$954,726	$283,437	(30%)	$927,715
Rieder (D)	$644,547	$236,573	(37%)	$625,244
1994				
Gutknecht (R)	$592,633	$173,550	(29%)	$581,099
Hottinger (D)	$352,406	$149,045	(42%)	$347,084

DISTRICT VOTE FOR PRESIDENT

	1996		1992
D	127,730 (48%)	**D**	110,293 (39%)
R	97,050 (37%)	**R**	97,138 (35%)
I	35,408 (13%)	**I**	75,118 (26%)

KEY VOTES

1997	
Ban "partial birth" abortions	Y
1996	
Approve farm bill	Y
Deny public education to illegal immigrants	Y
Repeal ban on certain assault-style weapons	Y
Increase minimum wage	N
Freeze defense spending	Y
Approve welfare overhaul	Y
1995	
Approve balanced-budget constitutional amendment	Y
Relax Clean Water Act regulations	Y
Oppose limits on environmental regulations	N
Reduce projected Medicare spending	Y
Approve GOP budget with tax and spending cuts	Y

VOTING STUDIES

	Presidential Support		Party Unity		Conservative Coalition	
Year	**S**	**O**	**S**	**O**	**S**	**O**
1996	37	62	88	11	76	18
1995	18	82	95	4	86	14

INTEREST GROUP RATINGS

Year	ADA	AFL-CIO	CCUS	ACU
1996	5	n/a	94	100
1995	0	0	100	96

2 David Minge (D)

Of Montevideo — Elected 1992, 3rd term

Biographical Information
Born: March 19, 1942, Clarkfield, Minn.
Education: St. Olaf College, B.A. 1964; U. of Chicago, J.D. 1967.
Occupation: Lawyer.
Family: Wife, Karen Aaker; two children.
Religion: Lutheran.
Political Career: Montevideo School Board, 1989-92.
Capitol Office: 1415 Longworth Bldg. 20515; 225-2331.

Committees
Agriculture
Forestry, Resource Conservation & Research; General Farm Commodities (ranking)
Budget

In Washington: Representing a politically competitive district, Minge has compiled a voting record with elements that appeal to voters on the right, left and center: He places heavy emphasis on budget-cutting to erase the federal deficit, yet on social-policy issues his views are more in line with Democratic thinking.

In his first bid for the 2nd in 1992, Minge barely won, eking out a 48 percent plurality to capture the district for his party. (GOP Rep. Vin Weber retired.) Since then, his tallies have shown steady improvement — to 52 percent in 1994 and 55 percent in 1996.

Minge has been an active member of the "blue dog" coalition, a group of House Democrats who gained prominence during the 104th for espousing center-right views on the budget, welfare and other issues. The group has tried to steer a path between conservative Republicans, who have made tax-cutting and government downsizing a priority, and the Democratic minority, which seeks to preserve federal services they deem essential.

In the fall of 1995, when congressional Republicans and the Clinton White House were at loggerheads over a multi-year federal budget, the blue dogs produced their own plan for eliminating the deficit. The blue dog budget accepted the GOP notion of containing costs on health care entitlements and welfare, but the blue dogs curbed spending in those areas less aggressively than the GOP, and their plan did not offer a tax cut. The blue dogs' budget prescription never garnered anything close to a majority in the 104th, but their ideas were an important element of continuing budget negotiations in the 105th.

In February 1997, the blue dogs unveiled a five-year budget blueprint similar to their earlier proposal: It called for delaying tax cuts until federal outlays balance with revenues. But the coalition's budget never made it to the House floor, as it was overtaken by the budget agreement reached by the Clinton White House and congressional Republicans in May 1997 that promised a balanced budget by 2002, even with tax cuts. Although Minge voted for the House budget proposal, he was unhappy that the Rules Committee did not allow the centrists to offer an amendment ensuring that deficit projections were on target before tax cuts and spending increases occurred.

In recognition of Minge's involvement and expertise in fiscal policy matters, the Democratic leadership gave him a seat on the Budget Committee in the 105th.

Minge also has set himself up as a "porkbuster," taking aim at appropriations bills with "earmarks" — spending that a lawmaker specifically designates for a particular project, often in his or her district. When the House took up the spending bill for military construction projects in June 1995, Minge and California Republican Ed Royce challenged two of the projects funded by the bill. One, requested by Washington Democrat Norm Dicks, sought $10.4 million for a new physical fitness center at the Bremerton Puget Sound Naval Shipyard, a project the Navy did not request but which Dicks said was part of a five-year service plan.

The second, requested by Pennsylvania Democrat Thomas M. Foglietta, was for $6 million to upgrade the foundry and propeller shop at the Philadelphia Naval Shipyard, a facility that was on the 1991 base closure list. The Navy had not requested the money.

Minge said the Pennsylvania and Washington projects failed basic criteria for funding: that the project be requested by the administration, that it benefit more than one district and that it meet national interests. "The issue is not whether a propeller shop should be maintained or improved. The issue is not whether we should have improved recreation facilities," Minge said. "The issue is whether the funds should be appropriated in the summer of 1995 to do that." But their amendment to cut the funding failed, 158-270.

In another anti-earmark effort, Minge in April 1996 offered a controversial amendment that ran afoul of Transportation and Infrastructure Committee Chairman Bud Shuster's effort to take

MINNESOTA 2
Southwest — Willmar

Much of the landscape of the 2nd District is dotted for mile upon mile with silos and grain elevators, broken up occasionally by small crossroads market centers. The 2nd's largest town, Willmar, has only about 18,000 people.

The 2nd supports a small industrial economy, which includes four 3M facilities — including two in Hutchinson. Turkey growing and processing is big business in Worthington (Nobles County).

But the economy is still driven by farming. Bisected by the broad Minnesota River, the sprawling district, which includes all or part of 27 counties, has some of the best farmland in the state. The well-to-do farmers in the south along the Iowa border enjoy bountiful harvests of corn and soybeans. Moving north along the Minnesota River, dairy farms become more common.

In the spring of 1997, the towns along the Minnesota River suffered from record flooding when a freak April blizzard combined with heavier than average snow melt caused the river to rise out of its banks. The area received federal disaster aid to help residents battle the flooding.

Residents of the 2nd have an independent streak. In 1992, Bill Clinton carried the 2nd with 37 percent of the vote; George Bush took 35 percent and Ross Perot 28 percent. In 1996, Clinton carried the district again with 45 percent, while Bob Dole got 39 percent. Perot garnered only 14 percent in 1996, but it was his highest percentage in the state.

In the prairie counties north of the Minnesota River, the land is sandy and rocky and the politics more unpredictable. Farmers here have to work harder to scratch out a living, and they display a frequent dissatisfaction with any party that is in power.

Many voters in the southern tier of counties are of German ethnic stock. Like those in the adjoining 1st District, they share a strong Republican tradition. At the turn of the century, the Scandinavian settlers here battled constantly with railroads, bankers and grain merchants. Disillusioned by Republicans and Democrats, they were ripe for third-party alternatives.

The economies of some small towns — Morton, Redwood Falls and Granite Falls in the southern part of the district — have benefited from casinos that are owned and operated by the Sioux Indians. The casinos have produced an influx of visitors and jobs; Redwood Falls has built new lodging facilities to accommodate the added traffic.

1990 Population: 546,888. White 538,748 (99%), Black 818 (<1%), Other 7,322 (1%). Hispanic origin 5,222 (1%). 18 and over 390,146 (71%), 62 and over 99,684 (18%). Median age: 34.

transportation trust funds "off budget." Shuster and his allies argued that taking the trust funds off budget would free up money for infrastructure projects that is now hoarded to mask the size of the deficit.

Minge offered an amendment that would have returned the Highway Trust Fund to on-budget status if any of its monies were used for earmarked transportation projects. But Shuster said the amendment was drawn so broadly that Congress would be unable to spend any money on specific highway projects, and the House rejected Minge's proposal, 129-298.

For all his efforts toward deficit reduction, Minge was not bashful about turning to the government when disaster struck at home. The winter of 1996 was particularly harsh for Minnesota and the upper Midwest, capped by an April blizzard, and the spring snowmelt caused rivers to flood their banks on a scale, Minge said, "that has never before occurred in the recorded history of this region of the country."

He told the House that the U.S. Army Corps of Engineers had to help build dikes on streets and highways in an attempt to stave off floodwaters, and President Clinton designated hard-hit areas of Minnesota as disaster areas, qualifying them for aid and assistance from the Federal Emergency Management Agency. "This is not a handout. These are programs that we have established over many decades," Minge said. "I think that we can all be proud as Americans of what this agency is doing and what it is contributing to the well-being of small communities who have been afflicted by these natural disasters."

On behalf of the corn, soybean and dairy farmers in his district, Minge also resisted GOP efforts in the 104th to reduce federal involvement in American agriculture. He sits on the Agriculture Committee and is the ranking member of the General Farm Commodities Subcommittee.

The GOP farm policy overhaul, dubbed the "Freedom to Farm" bill, phased out most New Deal-era crop subsidies and gave farmers greater flexibility in deciding what to plant. In place of the subsidies, the bill provided farmers with fixed, declining payments over seven years, regardless of market prices or their planting decisions.

Many Democrats on the Agriculture Committee said the GOP scheme shredded the economic safety net for farmers, exposing them to financial ruin if commodity prices drop after the seven-year payout ends. "My deepest wish is that we would have a program that we could return to our areas and proudly explain as providing the tools that farmers need to manage their risks," Minge said when the House passed the farm bill in February 1996. He felt "Freedom to Farm" did not do that, and he voted against it.

Minge's stands on social-policy issues mark him as a moderate. He opposed GOP efforts to repeal the ban on certain semiautomatic assault-style weapons, and he has sometimes sided with abortion-rights proponents, voting, for instance, to allow federal employees' health care plans to pay for abortion, and to require states to finance Medicaid abortions for poor women in cases of rape or incest. He has, however, supported a measure to ban a particular abortion technique that opponents call "partial birth" abortion.

Minge voted against the GOP's early efforts to overhaul the welfare system, although when a compromise welfare bill emerged that was acceptable to Clinton, Minge signed on, too. "While not perfect, this bill represents the best opportunity to end the welfare status quo," he told the Minneapolis/St. Paul Star Tribune.

At Home: After GOP Rep. Weber bowed out in 1992, Republicans in the 2nd looked to have a strong prospect to replace him in former state representative Cal R. Ludeman.

Minge, a lawyer and school board member in the town of Montevideo, did not boost his stock much in the Democratic primary, tallying an anemic 53 percent against tepid opposition, even though he carried his party's pre-primary endorsement.

But in the fall campaign, Minge successfully painted his better-known opponent as too radical for the district. "Ludeman has a record of voting based on ideology, not on what is in the best interest of the district," Minge's campaign brochure argued. By a razor-thin 569-vote margin, voters agreed.

Republicans in 1994 nominated the mayor of the town of Redwood Falls, Gary B. Revier. He used national GOP themes to attack Minge, promoting the "Contract With America" while portraying Minge as a liberal pal of the Clinton administration.

But Minge presented himself as a cost-conscious Democrat, and he backed several key tenets of the conservative GOP faith, including congressional term limits, a balanced-budget constitutional amendment and a presidential line-item veto.

Revier took a whistle-stop train trip across the district with GOP Gov. Arne Carlson. Not to be outdone, Minge repeated one of the more successful gimmicks of his 1992 campaign: a cross-district bicycle tour. He ended up beating Revier by seven points, 52 percent to 45 percent.

Revier was back in 1996, this time pushing for cuts in income taxes, inheritance taxes and capital gains taxes. Again he claimed Minge was to the left of the district mainstream. But with two more years of watching Minge operate in Washington, voters liked what they saw even better. Minge moved out to a 14-point victory margin.

HOUSE ELECTIONS

1996 General		
David Minge (D)	144,083	(55%)
Gary B. Revier (R)	107,807	(41%)
Stan Bentz (REF)	10,283	(4%)
1994 General		
David Minge (D)	114,289	(52%)
Gary B. Revier (R)	98,881	(45%)
Stan Bentz (I)	6,535	(3%)

Previous Winning Percentages: 1992 (48%)

CAMPAIGN FINANCE

	Receipts	Receipts from PACs	Expend-itures
1996			
Minge (D)	$633,295	$353,107 (56%)	$616,673
Revier (R)	$285,203	$25,565 (9%)	$284,943
1994			
Minge (D)	$622,552	$361,673 (58%)	$622,920
Revier (R)	$326,991	$52,103 (16%)	$325,853

DISTRICT VOTE FOR PRESIDENT

	1996		1992
D	120,652 (45%)	**D**	102,162 (37%)
R	105,205 (39%)	**R**	97,138 (35%)
I	38,117 (14%)	**I**	78,871 (28%)

KEY VOTES

1997	
Ban "partial birth" abortions	Y
1996	
Approve farm bill	N
Deny public education to illegal immigrants	Y
Repeal ban on certain assault-style weapons	N
Increase minimum wage	Y
Freeze defense spending	Y
Approve welfare overhaul	Y
1995	
Approve balanced-budget constitutional amendment	Y
Relax Clean Water Act regulations	N
Oppose limits on environmental regulations	N
Reduce projected Medicare spending	N
Approve GOP budget with tax and spending cuts	N

VOTING STUDIES

Year	Presidential Support S	Presidential Support O	Party Unity S	Party Unity O	Conservative Coalition S	Conservative Coalition O
1996	73	27	78	21	29	69
1995	74	25	72	27	46	54
1994	68	32	72	28	61	39
1993	66	33	75	21	32	59

INTEREST GROUP RATINGS

Year	ADA	AFL-CIO	CCUS	ACU
1996	70	n/a	38	15
1995	75	75	54	25
1994	60	33	92	14
1993	75	75	55	26

3 Jim Ramstad (R)

Of Minnetonka — Elected 1990, 4th term

Biographical Information
Born: May 6, 1946, Jamestown, N.D.
Education: U. of Minnesota, B.A. 1968; George Washington U., J.D. 1973.
Military Service: Army Reserve, 1968-74.
Occupation: Lawyer; legislative aide.
Family: Single.
Religion: Protestant.
Political Career: Minn. Senate, 1981-91.
Capitol Office: 103 Cannon Bldg. 20515; 225-2871.

Committees
Ways & Means
Oversight; Trade

In Washington: Most of the Republicans who have joined the House in the 1990s are down-the-line conservatives, but Ramstad, a class of 1990 product, is not. On a range of issues — abortion, the environment, defense spending, gun control — he votes a more moderate line than most in his party.

Still, Ramstad consistently hews to the party line in the realm of economic policy, and after Republicans captured control of the House in 1994, he benefited from the conservative party leadership's desire to promote GOP unity by adding more centrist members to key committees. Ramstad won assignment to Ways and Means, where he is shaping Republican tax and trade policies. The step up also kept him in the footsteps of his GOP predecessor in the district, Bill Frenzel, a longtime Ways and Means member.

Keeping loyal to the party leadership's push in the 104th for substantial tax cuts, Ramstad did not join some other GOP moderates in calling for a budget-balancing plan that made fewer spending reductions and deferred tax cuts until the deficit was erased.

As chairman of a Republican task force on legal reform issues, Ramstad helped shape two priorities in the party's "Contract With America," platform: a bill limiting manufacturers' liability for defective products, which President Clinton vetoed; and an overhaul of laws governing investor lawsuits, which was enacted over Clinton's veto.

Despite his support for the GOP economic line, Ramstad showed his moderate stripes on a defense vote early in the 104th. He was one of 24 Republicans supporting a Democratic amendment stipulating that anti-missile defenses for U.S. territory merit a lower priority than maintaining the readiness of U.S. forces and fielding defenses to protect troops in the field. The amendment, adopted 218-212, thwarted a promise Republicans made in their contract to place a high priority on funding for a strategic defense initiative.

Ramstad voted to freeze the fiscal 1997 defense authorization bill at the previous year's spending level, and he opposed GOP efforts to allocate $7 billion more to the Pentagon than the Clinton administration requested. Ramstad also was a vociferous critic of sending U.S. troops to Bosnia, a point of view shared with numerous other Republicans.

Ramstad cited his concern about the federal debt when withholding support for some other items in the contract legislative agenda. He feared the price tag on the Republican plan to accelerate prison construction and found fault with a proposal to compensate property owners when regulations decrease the value of their property, seeing it as a potentially expensive new entitlement program.

Ramstad has consistently opposed funding another big-ticket budget item most Republicans support: NASA's space station.

Ramstad, however, defended spending on some programs GOP conservatives targeted for extinction. He said cutting the Legal Services Corporation was wrong because it would leave the poor without legal representation in civil matters. And the heavy winters in his district were behind his criticism of a proposal to phase out heating aid for low-income families.

Ramstad generally has sided with abortion-rights proponents in House floor votes, although he says he supports "reasonable limits" on access to abortion. He has backed conservatives' efforts to ban a particular abortion technique that opponents call "partial birth" abortion — a procedure he has called "repulsive and extreme."

Ramstad voted in 1996 against repealing the ban on certain semiautomatic assault-style weapons. He had opposed the ban on a stand-alone vote in 1994, but later voted for a broad Clinton-backed anti-crime package that included the ban; he supported the crime package because it included anti-substance abuse programs and legislation he had proposed to crack down on child offenders.

In announcing his support for the assault-weapons ban in 1996, Ramstad said violent crimes traced to military-style assault weapons had been reduced in the year after the ban took effect. The

MINNESOTA 3
Western Twin Cities suburbs — Bloomington; Minnetonka

With its abundance of high-tech industries, white-collar workers, golf courses and middle-class homes, the 3rd is for the most part the very picture of suburban living.

The last round of the state's redistricting pingpong was good news for Ramstad. The 3rd, already a Republican safe haven, became slightly more so when the Supreme Court rejected the federally drawn map that had been used in the 1992 elections. In 1993, the high court ruled that federal courts must stand aside until challenges to redistricting plans run their course in state courts. In 1994 and 1996, candidates ran in districts drawn by the state court in 1992.

In 1992, the district included parts of Dakota, Hennepin, Scott and Washington counties. Under the state plan upheld by the Supreme Court, the 3rd exchanged a piece of Wright County for its share of Washington County, reduced its slice of Dakota County, picked up Republican Plymouth and western Hennepin County communities, and gained the largely Democratic cities of Brooklyn Park and Brooklyn Center.

The 3rd extends beyond the western and southern extremities of the metropolitan area. Suburbanization has touched most of the district except the very farthest reaches, which remain rural.

The district is a popular home for Fortune 500 companies. Several, including Cargill Inc., the world's largest privately owned corporation, are here. Cargill, which is based in Minnetonka and employs about 2,500 people there, is a diversified company that handles everything from wheat and corn processing to financial trading. Other Fortune companies with headquarters in the 3rd include lawn mower manufacturer Toro and grocery chain Super-value. Honeywell has an electronics facility here. And food giant General Mills is headquartered just outside the district lines.

But perhaps most crucial to many local businesses is the fate of the district's largest employer, Northwest Airlines, whose headquarters is just outside the district in Eagan. The 3rd also has another claim to fame — the nation's largest shopping mall. The Mall of America in Bloomington (Hennepin County) measures 4.2 million square feet. Between 30 million and 40 million people visit the mall annually.

A few Democrats can be found in Dakota County, but its comparatively small number of voters will not be enough to loosen the hold the GOP typically has on the 3rd. Ramstad has won the 3rd four times with at least 64 percent of the vote. Republican influence is so strong here that in 1984, home-state Democratic presidential nominee Walter F. Mondale drew less than one-third of the vote in a number of precincts. However, Bill Clinton carried the district, though just barely, in 1992 and won somewhat more comfortably in 1996.

1990 Population: 546,888. White 521,910 (95%), Black 9,751 (2%), Other 15,227 (3%). Hispanic origin 4,945 (1%). 18 and over 401,451 (73%), 62 and over 52,062 (10%). Median age: 32.

majority of Minnesota hunters, he said, do not object to the ban as long as it is not expanded.

In the 103rd, Ramstad was one of 54 Republicans to support a five-day waiting period for handgun purchases.

Ramstad's opposition in the 104th to several GOP initiatives to ease environmental regulations was part of the reason he was one of only 13 Republicans to win the Sierra Club's endorsement for the 1996 election. At the end of the GOP's first year controlling Congress, Ramstad said he disagreed with the direction the House leadership had taken on the environment. He voted against easing federal water pollution control regulations and for maintaining the Environmental Protection Agency's regulatory authority.

Ramstad also worked with a group of moderates to produce a milder rewrite of the Endangered Species Act, and he opposed changing the protected status of the Boundary Waters Canoe Area Wilderness in northern Minnesota.

The minimum wage proved to be a ticklish issue for Ramstad in the 104th. After calling Clinton's proposal to increase the wage a "job killer," Ramstad voted for it. He backed a GOP proposal to exempt small businesses from paying the higher wage, but that failed.

A recovering alcoholic who has devoted much energy to ensure that alcohol and drug education is available to young people, Ramstad speaks often to schools and community groups on the subject. "I really believe that, more than anything else, the chemical abuse problem threatens to undermine the social fiber of our country," he said in 1992.

When Republicans moved in the 104th to stop Social Security payments for recipients disabled by drug or alcohol addictions, Ramstad defended the proposal. Addicts don't need cash, he said, they need treatment. The bill was enacted with restrictions on addicts' benefits..

He had even less success pursuing two other initiatives: a bill creating a two-year commission to review government and private attempts to prevent and treat alcoholism, and including substance abuse treatment in the insurance reform bill passed by the 104th.

At Home: As Frenzel's heir apparent, Ramstad cruised into office in 1990 and has not been threatened at the polls since.

Ramstad painted his 1990 election as a continuation of the Frenzel legacy — a sound move in the affluent suburban Twin Cities district that the moderate Frenzel represented for two decades.

Ramstad's most daunting obstacle in 1990 was the district Independent-Republican convention, where his abortion-rights stance placed him at odds with the anti-abortion delegates who dominate the state's GOP conventions.

But the Republican senator running for re-election that year, abortion foe Rudy Boschwitz, put pragmatism over personal philosophy and wrote convention delegates urging them to unify and support Ramstad. Another anti-abortion Republican, Rep. Vin Weber of the 2nd District, also endorsed Ramstad before the convention.

After seven ballots, Ramstad defeated four other candidates to win the convention endorsement. He easily bested a minor opponent in the primary and then began a push against his Democratic rival, investment executive Lewis DeMars. Ramstad raised a half-million dollars more than DeMars and crushed him 2-1 in the general election.

In 1996, Ramstad was able to return the favor to Boschwitz by endorsing him for the GOP Senate nomination. Ramstad's announcement ended speculation he would try for the job. He had been nudged to make a Senate run in 1994 as well. Instead, Ramstad has chosen to stay with his safe congressional seat where the fundraising potential of his Ways and Means assignment helps ward off challengers.

HOUSE ELECTIONS

1996 General		
Jim Ramstad (R)	205,845	(70%)
Stanley J. Leino (D)	87,359	(30%)
1994 General		
Jim Ramstad (R)	173,223	(73%)
Bob Olson (D)	62,211	(26%)

Previous Winning Percentages: **1992** (64%) **1990** (67%)

CAMPAIGN FINANCE

	Receipts	Receipts from PACs	Expend-itures
1996			
Ramstad (R)	$742,385	$288,567 (39%)	$494,908
Leino (D)	$29,351	$9,000 (31%)	$22,600
1994			
Ramstad (R)	$758,003	$139,231 (18%)	$498,146
Olson (D)	$36,007	$10,500 (29%)	$35,839

DISTRICT VOTE FOR PRESIDENT

1996	1992
D 141,109 (46%)	**D** 122,219 (38%)
R 125,019 (41%)	**R** 120,990 (37%)
I 31,021 (10%)	**I** 80,623 (25%)

KEY VOTES

1997	
Ban "partial birth" abortions	Y
1996	
Approve farm bill	Y
Deny public education to illegal immigrants	Y
Repeal ban on certain assault-style weapons	N
Increase minimum wage	Y
Freeze defense spending	Y
Approve welfare overhaul	Y
1995	
Approve balanced-budget constitutional amendment	Y
Relax Clean Water Act regulations	N
Oppose limits on environmental regulations	Y
Reduce projected Medicare spending	Y
Approve GOP budget with tax and spending cuts	Y

VOTING STUDIES

	Presidential Support		Party Unity		Conservative Coalition	
Year	S	O	S	O	S	O
1996	44	52	74	20	47	51
1995	36	61	81	18	63	31
1994	55	45	82	18	72	28
1993	45	55	82	17	70	30
1992	53	47	78	22	56	44
1991	65	34	81	18	86	14

INTEREST GROUP RATINGS

Year	ADA	AFL-CIO	CCUS	ACU
1996	35	n/a	88	70
1995	30	0	92	64
1994	30	11	100	62
1993	35	33	82	67
1992	30	42	75	68
1991	25	33	80	85

4 Bruce F. Vento (D)

Of St. Paul — Elected 1976, 11th term

Biographical Information

Born: Oct. 7, 1940, St. Paul, Minn.

Education: U. of Minnesota, A.A. 1961; Wisconsin State U., B.S. 1965; U. of Minnesota, 1965-70.

Occupation: Science teacher.

Family: Divorced; three children.

Religion: Roman Catholic.

Political Career: Minn. House, 1971-77.

Capitol Office: 2304 Rayburn Bldg. 20515; 225-6631.

Committees

Banking & Financial Services
Capital Markets, Securities & Government Sponsored Enterprises; Financial Institutions & Consumer Credit (ranking)

Resources
Forests & Forest Health; National Parks & Public Lands

In Washington: A tireless workhorse, Vento has been a stout defender of liberal values from his seats on the Resources and Banking and Financial Services committees. He was behind much of the nation's conservation legislation for two decades and had hoped for greater accomplishment under a Democratic White House. But his hopes were dashed, first by the Clinton administration's deference to Western politicians and then by the Republican takeover of Congress.

Vento estimates that while he chaired the Natural Resources subcommittee overseeing national parks, public lands and forests, he steered into law more than 300 bills protecting the environment.

In addition to his efforts on resources issues, Vento also has been a player on the Banking Committee, raising congressional awareness of issues as diverse as homelessness and the savings and loan crisis. He is ranking Democrat on the Financial Institutions and Consumer Credit Subcommittee.

Vento now is the No. 3 Democrat on the full Banking Committee, and before the start of the 105th Congress, he bid for the ranking Democratic seat held by Henry B. Gonzalez of Texas. John J. LaFalce of New York, the panel's No. 2 Democrat, also ran for the top spot. The effort to topple Gonzalez arose after his absences from committee meetings during the 104th caused even some long-time supporters to seek his ouster. Gonzalez, though, pledged to seek only one final term as top panel Democrat, and he made a stirring speech on his own behalf before the Democratic Caucus.

Buoyed by support from the Congressional Black and Hispanic caucuses, as well as by votes from fellow Texans, Gonzalez won a clear plurality in the three-way race. Gonzalez got 82 votes, LaFalce 62 and Vento 47. Under caucus rules, Vento dropped out and LaFalce and Gonzalez prepared for a runoff. But rather than press his challenge, LaFalce magnanimously withdrew.

From Banking, Vento has weighed in on ways to address the government's management of low-income housing programs. Early in the 105th, the committee approved a sweeping bill to deregulate the public housing industry, mainly by giving the nation's local housing authorities more discretion in areas such as setting rent schedules and tenant eligibility requirements. Supporters of the measure see it as a blueprint for moving people off government dependency. But many panel Democrats argued that the bill would hurt the poor. Vento voted against the bill, even though the committee accepted his amendment to extend the Community Partnerships Against Crime program from one year to five years. The program provides funds to housing authorities to pay for security measures such as fences, security guards and increased police presence.

Vento also tried to increase federal funding to combat homelessness when the House in July 1995 considered the spending bill that funds the Housing and Urban Development Department. Although GOP appropriators agreed to some additional funding for homeless aid, Democratic critics said it was a meager attempt to restore cuts to the housing budget. The House rejected, 160-260, an amendment by Vento to increase homeless assistance by $184 million.

In other banking matters, Vento was part of a bipartisan rump group that helped to refine legislation drafted by Banking Committee Chairman Jim Leach of Iowa to shore up the deposit insurance fund for the thrift industry. The measure was expected to be a compromise that might have restarted the stalled effort to infuse money into the Savings Association Insurance Fund and drive down deposit insurance premiums for thrifts. And although the 104th Congress ultimately passed the legislation, the bill was shaped less by Banking Committee members than by senior members of both parties. The effort was attached to the omnibus fiscal 1997 spending bill.

Early in the 104th, Vento objected to the Banking hearings held to investigate Whitewater, a failed land deal involving the Clintons and the owner of a now-defunct Arkansas thrift. Leach argued that Whitewater was "about the arrogance

MINNESOTA 4
St. Paul and suburbs

The 4th, with its deep roots in the labor movement and its liberal academic communities, is still reliably Democratic, though suburban additions have added a Republican tint.

The economy of the 4th is fueled by the government, education and industry. St. Paul, the capital, is the hub of state government, which employs thousands of unionized workers. The headquarters for the Minnesota Mining and Manufacturing Co., better known as 3M Co., is in a suburb of St. Paul.

The district, which includes Ramsey County and parts of Dakota and Hennepin counties, also has numerous college campuses, including parts of the University of Minnesota.

St. Paul (population 272,000), located in Ramsey County, is a traditionally Democratic city with a large German and Irish-Catholic population. The city developed as a major port and railroading center and still has a strong labor tradition. Many portions of the district are middle- or high-income areas.

St. Paul became more diverse during the 1970s and 1980s, when there was an influx of Hmong refugees from Southeast Asia. In some neighborhoods in mostly northern and eastern sections of the city, some business signs are written in Hmong. The first Hmong elected to public office in the nation was elected to St. Paul's School Board in 1991.

The city's Hispanic population has also increased. On the west side of the city (and in the city of West St. Paul) is a well-organized, solidly Democratic Hispanic community.

The working-class neighborhoods on St. Paul's East Side are drab and solidly Democratic. The precincts here have routinely supported virtually every major statewide Democratic candidate of recent years.

More than 30 years ago, when Eugene J. McCarthy represented St. Paul in the House, nearly 90 percent of the district vote came from the city. But with the growth of the suburbs and a decline in St. Paul's population (from its 1960 peak of 313,000), the city now accounts for just half the district vote.

Most of the suburban vote lies north of the city in Ramsey County. While Vento has no difficulty carrying any section of St. Paul, he sometimes has struggled in several areas in suburban Ramsey. Farther north are the more affluent suburbs of Shoreview, North Oaks and White Bear Lake, which vote Republican more often.

A 1993 Supreme Court decision upheld a state-drawn redistricting map, rejecting a plan crafted by the federal courts and used in the 1992 election. The state plan was used in the 1994 election.

Under the plan approved by the high court, Mendota Heights, which votes Republican, was returned to the 4th. Redistricting also added several other GOP-oriented suburbs in Dakota County, including Sunfish Lake.

1990 Population: 546,887. White 486,882 (89%), Black 23,082 (4%), Other 36,923 (7%). Hispanic origin 15,615 (3%). 18 and over 412,608 (75%), 62 and over 82,652 (15%). Median age: 32.

of power — conflicts of interest that are self-evidently unseemly." But Democrats countered that the hearings amounted to a politically motivated witch hunt. "The timing, the agenda and the witnesses for these hearings have basically dismissed any pretense of objectivity and bipartisan pursuit of the facts," Vento said.

Vento's diligence on legislative matters is well-known in the House. Distracting from his hard work, however, is a trait pointed up by supporters and detractors alike: In making his case, he tends to go on — and on. A former science teacher, Vento can and does explain issues at great length, sometimes testing the patience even of his allies.

Vento spent much energy in the 104th fighting the new GOP landlords of the environment, who tried to rewrite major laws on water quality, hazardous waste and endangered species. Little of the program to ease the burden of environmental regulation was enacted, but it was portrayed in the media as an attempt to roll back important safeguards. Vento claimed that Republicans have "badly overreached" and prompted a backlash. "Environmental issues are not subtle," Vento said. "You talk to a 4-year-old child, they understand water pollution and air pollution."

He objected strongly to a Republican effort on Resources that would have dramatically overhauled the 1973 Endangered Species Act. The measure, which the committee approved in October 1995, would have restricted the government's ability to bar development within animal and plant habitats. Proponents said federal regulators have used the law to trample the rights of private property owners under the guise of saving animals and plants from extinction. But the measure drew opposition from members with environmentalist leanings, who said the committee's bill would gut the act at the behest not of small landowners, but of corporate developers. "This bill is a sell-out to the special interests that make a short term profit and convenience ahead of science, facts, and the preservation of our global life forms," Vento said. The bill never went any further than the committee, however.

Closer to home, Vento fought a proposal by fellow Minnesota Democrat James L. Oberstar, who represents northern Minnesota, and Minnesota Republican Sen. Rod Grams to relax certain restrictions at Minnesota's Voyageurs National Park and the Boundary Waters Canoe Area Wilderness. They wanted more access to the areas for motorboats and all-terrain vehicles.

In response to their measure, Vento proposed his own bill to expand the wilderness areas of the parks and further limit motorized use. A provision of Oberstar's bill was included in omnibus parks legislation in the 104th; but the proposal was dropped when the White House objected.

At Home: The 4th is a strongly Democratic district, and Vento usually wins re-election comfortably, although his recent tallies have fallen below 60 percent.

After running a British-born professor at the University of Minnesota against Vento from 1988 through 1992, Republicans in 1994 and 1996 chose a candidate who reflected the district's sizable blue-collar element, former state Rep. Dennis Newinski.

A longtime union member, Newinski launched his candidacy wearing a hard hat, and he criticized Vento on an array of issues, from his opposition to the use of force in the Persian Gulf to his support for elevator operators in the House office buildings. Newinski lost by 13 points in 1994, but Vento's 55 percent vote share was a career low. In 1996, Vento's margin over Newinski improved to 20 points, as President Clinton carried the 4th over Bob Dole by a 28-point margin.

The son of a Machinists' union official, Vento was a union steward at a plastics plant, then worked in a brewery and on a refrigerator assembly line before becoming a junior high school teacher and state representative.

During his three terms in the Legislature, he echoed the interests of the working-class residents of St. Paul's Phalen Park. A loyal team player, he won the assistant majority leader post under state House Speaker Martin Olav Sabo, now his congressional colleague.

When nine-term U.S. House veteran Joseph E. Karth decided to retire in 1976, he endorsed Vento for his seat; Karth's backing and labor support gave Vento the party endorsement.

Still, Vento faced four foes in the primary. Two were significant: St. Paul attorney John S. Connolly, running as an even more liberal alternative to Vento, and 27-year-old state Auditor Robert W. Mattson, who twice defeated party-endorsed candidates. Vento won a convincing primary victory with 52 percent. The November election was as easy for Vento as it usually had been for Karth.

In 1978, Vento met an aggressive, conservative GOP challenger who held him to 58 percent. But with the same candidate and a much better-financed campaign in 1980, Republicans fared little better, and they did not hold Vento under 60 percent again until 1992.

HOUSE ELECTIONS

1996 General		
Bruce F. Vento (D)	145,831	(57%)
Dennis Newinski (R)	94,110	(37%)
Richard J. Gibbons (REF)	9,323	(4%)
Phil Willkie (GR)	3,615	(1%)
Dan R. Vacek (IG)	2,696	(1%)
1994 General		
Bruce F. Vento (D)	115,638	(55%)
Dennis Newinski (R)	88,344	(42%)
Dan R. Vacek (GR)	6,211	(3%)

Previous Winning Percentages: 1992 (57%) **1990** (65%) **1988** (72%) **1986** (73%) **1984** (74%) **1982** (73%) **1980** (59%) **1978** (58%) **1976** (66%)

CAMPAIGN FINANCE

	Receipts	Receipts from PACs	Expend-itures
1996			
Vento (D)	$570,244	$367,743 (64%)	$559,370
Newinski (IR)	$316,031	$34,815 (11%)	$315,410
1994			
Vento (D)	$329,046	$224,159 (68%)	$339,703
Newinski (R)	$94,343	$2,642 (3%)	$93,457

DISTRICT VOTE FOR PRESIDENT

1996		1992	
D	152,555 (58%)	**D**	148,994 (52%)
R	77,704 (30%)	**R**	79,192 (28%)
I	23,566 (9%)	**I**	58,721 (20%)

KEY VOTES

1997	
Ban "partial birth" abortions	N
1996	
Approve farm bill	N
Deny public education to illegal immigrants	N
Repeal ban on certain assault-style weapons	N
Increase minimum wage	Y
Freeze defense spending	Y
Approve welfare overhaul	Y
1995	
Approve balanced-budget constitutional amendment	N
Relax Clean Water Act regulations	N
Oppose limits on environmental regulations	Y
Reduce projected Medicare spending	N
Approve GOP budget with tax and spending cuts	N

VOTING STUDIES

	Presidential Support		Party Unity		Conservative Coalition	
Year	S	O	S	O	S	O
1996	89	11	96	3	6	92
1995	89	11	96	3	8	90
1994	76	22	95	2	6	94
1993	80	20	95	2	2	95
1992	13	86	95	4	6	92
1991	26	70	94	4	5	86

INTEREST GROUP RATINGS

Year	ADA	AFL-CIO	CCUS	ACU
1996	95	n/a	13	0
1995	95	100	17	4
1994	100	89	27	0
1993	100	100	9	4
1992	100	92	25	0
1991	90	92	10	0

5 Martin Olav Sabo (D)

Of Minneapolis — Elected 1978, 10th term

Biographical Information
Born: Feb. 28, 1938, Crosby, N.D.
Education: Augsburg College, B.A. 1959; U. of Minnesota, 1960.
Occupation: Public official.
Family: Wife, Sylvia Ann Lee; two children.
Religion: Lutheran.
Political Career: Minn. House, 1961-79, minority leader, 1969-73, speaker, 1973-79.
Capitol Office: 2336 Rayburn Bldg. 20515; 225-4755.

Committees
Appropriations
District of Columbia; National Security; Transportation (ranking)

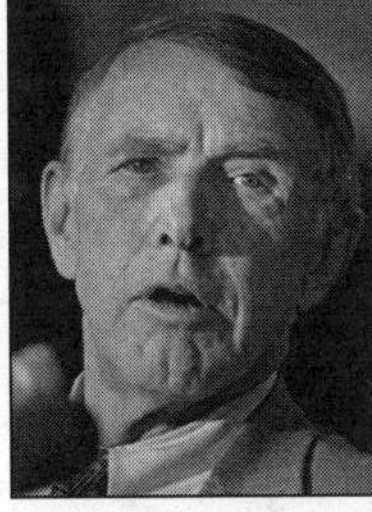

In Washington: After spending the 103rd Congress helping make federal fiscal policy as chairman of the Budget Committee, Sabo was relegated by the Republican-led 104th Congress to a defensive role, fighting budget cutting efforts led by Rep. John R. Kasich, R-Ohio, the new committee chairman.

In the 105th, Sabo steps away from the media swirl and controversy of the Budget Committee, having served there the maximum time permitted under Democratic rules. His new focus is Appropriations' Transportation Subcommittee, where he is ranking Democrat. Upon moving to the post, he said he would strongly support mass transit and alternative means of transportation such as bicycles. He also sits on Appropriations' National Security and District of Columbia subcommittees.

Sabo began the 105th by cosponsoring a bill he had proposed for much of the 1990s, so far to no avail. It would raise the minimum wage to $6.50 an hour by July 1, 2000. Under legislation enacted in 1996, the minimum wage increased from $4.25 to $4.75 an hour in October 1996 and will increase to $5.15 an hour in September 1997. "If we do not follow last year's action . . . the value of the minimum wage, the working wage, will erode," he said. Sabo also reintroduced legislation encouraging companies to limit their executives' compensation to 25 times what the lowest-paid worker earns.

As those two measures attest, Sabo usually toes the liberal line on both fiscal and social issues. He opposed the welfare overhaul bill signed by President Clinton in 1996, he voted against banning federal recognition of same sex marriages and he opposed conservatives' efforts to ban a particular abortion technique called a "partial-birth" abortion.

He is a staunch foe of the balanced-budget amendment. "The Constitution did not create our budget problems, and amending it will not solve them," Sabo has said. "Rather, balancing our budget requires an exercise of political will that is not dependent on the Constitution. The amendment either would be an unenforceable promise that could undermine respect for the Constitution itself, or its enforcement would shift unprecedented budgetary powers away from the people's representatives in Congress to the courts and to the president."

But like many liberals, he has embraced the concept of balancing the budget, albeit not in the ways that Republicans prefer. In the 104th, Sabo joined members of The Coalition, a group of conservative Democrats better known as the "blue dogs," in supporting an alternative to the balanced-budget proposal pushed by the Republicans. Basically, it eschewed the GOP's tax cut plans and thus was able to reduce spending more modestly.

"We can reduce the deficit significantly without resorting to the extreme agenda that the Republican majority tried to enact," he said. "We can balance the budget without abandoning working families, without hurting the most vulnerable Americans and without jeopardizing the country's economic future."

From his perch on the Budget Committee, Sabo was outspoken in his opposition to the GOP plan. "Throughout this budget process, Republicans engaged in a one-sided attack on lower-income Americans," Sabo said. "It's historic but negative."

Early in the process of drafting a fiscal 1996 budget, he tried to eliminate the tax cuts that were a key ingredient of the Republicans' plan. In June 1995, Sabo unsuccessfully tried to instruct House-Senate budget conferees to give up the tax cuts and support smaller reductions in the earned-income tax credit for the working poor. Sabo's motion was defeated, 183-233.

He voted against all the Republican budget proposals and supported the temporary spending bills enacted to end the partial government shutdowns in November 1995 and January 1996. The GOP leadership ultimately yielded ground on the budget to President Clinton and voted to reopen the government. With that episode passed, Sabo

Most residents of the 5th can honestly say they've never left the Democratic fold, no matter how well Republicans have done in national and statewide elections.

Minneapolis residents account for roughly two-thirds of the 5th's voters, and except for those on the southwest side, they predictably choose liberal candidates over conservatives.

The district is home to former Vice President Walter F. Mondale (when he lives in Minnesota) and routinely backs Democratic presidential candidates, even in elections when their nominee is being waxed nationally. When Democrats do well across the country, as Bill Clinton did in 1996, they do even better here; Clinton polled 64 percent of the vote.

Scandinavians remain the most conspicuous ethnic group; it is no coincidence that Sabo includes his middle name, Olav, on all his official papers to eliminate any doubt that he is of Norwegian heritage.

Although many of the flour mills that once lined the Mississippi River at St. Anthony's Falls have moved, the major companies that settled in Minneapolis — Pillsbury and General Mills — have remained and diversified.

They are among the major employers in the Twin Cities, along with the new "brain power" companies that find Minneapolis ideally suited for their needs. Honeywell has its worldwide headquarters here. The white-collar professionals who have been attracted by these "clean" industries help to give the city an image that is reflected in the glistening towers of its downtown area.

Even the presence of Fortune 500 companies could not halt a late 1980s downturn in the regional economy. But it has rebounded since then.

MINNESOTA 5
Minneapolis and suburbs

Minneapolis is not only parks, lakes, glass and chrome. Northwest of the downtown office towers are some poor neighborhoods, home to blacks and some of the city's Chippewa Indian population. East of the Mississippi are older, more traditional blue-collar areas adjoining the main campus of the University of Minnesota.

In 1993, the Supreme Court rejected the federally drawn redistricting map that had been used in the 1992 election. Candidates now run under a state-drawn plan. The recent rounds of redistricting have made the district a bit less Democratic. A number of suburban areas — including Golden Valley and New Hope — were added under the federal plan. The post-1992 state redistricting gave the 5th roughly half of the Republican-oriented suburb of Edina.

Republicans had hoped that these suburbs would mean more GOP votes and a chance to beat Sabo, but that has not happened. Sabo's 64 percent was his best performance since 1990, the election before reapportionment.

While the power of organized labor has waned over the years, it is still a factor in the 5th. So is the district's minority population.

1990 Population: 546,887. White 458,721 (84%), Black 51,602 (9%), Other 36,564 (7%). Hispanic origin 9,654 (2%). 18 and over 435,052 (80%), 62 and over 90,275 (17%) Median age: 33.

had a quieter second year as ranking Democrat on Budget: Republicans in 1996 were willing to compromise with the White House rather than risk election-year voter ire over further government shutdowns.

In contrast to his opposition to the Republicans' budget proposals, Sabo proudly claimed credit for his efforts in pushing through Clinton's 1993 budget plan, which resulted in four years of declining deficits. "Clearly, the 1993 deficit-reduction package has worked," Sabo said in October 1996.

When he took over as Budget chairman in 1993, Sabo was regarded as bright but not as well-versed in the obscure budget procedures as the man he replaced, Democrat Leon E. Panetta. Nevertheless, his patient negotiating and the Democratic majority's desire to stay united behind Clinton gave the president's first budget a successful journey through the House. Democrats voted down every substantive GOP effort to change it.

In late 1993, Sabo continued to play good soldier for the administration on budget matters, helping to defeat a proposal, offered by deficit hawks Kasich and former Democratic Rep. Timothy J. Penny of Minnesota, to cut federal spending by an additional $90 billion over five years. Instead, Sabo helped push through $37 billion in spending cuts, an amount based in large part on a White House plan to cut the federal work force.

In arguing against the Penny-Kasich proposal, Sabo said deeper cuts would harm the Clinton administration's efforts at health care reform. Sabo was a cosponsor of Clinton's health care reform plan and also a single-payer plan introduced in the House.

On Appropriations, Sabo looks out for the major high-technology firms in his district as well as for the University of Minnesota, while advocating development of a federal policy on supercomputers. In April 1996, he sent a letter to the National Science Foundation urging that the National Center for Atmospheric Research (NCAR) in Boulder, Colo., buy an American-made supercomputer rather than a Japanese machine. Supercomputer manufacturer Cray Research is a major employer in Sabo's district.

And the fiscal 1996 transportation appropriations bill included $2 million for an intelligent highway system in Minnesota. During the June 1995 Appropriations Committee markup of the bill, Sabo joined his fellow Democrats in opposing changes in labor law. The top Democrat on the Transportation Appropriations Subcommittee, Ronald D. Coleman, proposed to strike a provision of the bill that would eliminate the labor protections in federal transit law.

The Labor Department now reviews all federal grants to transit agencies to ensure that the money would not be used to the detriment of transit employees. Transit agencies complain that this requirement raises costs and holds up their funding needlessly. Coleman's amendment would have set a 60-day deadline for the department to approve each grant, in keeping with the department's own efforts to streamline and speed its reviews.

His voice wavering with emotion, Sabo said the proposed repeal would exacerbate a national trend toward lower wages for low-skill workers. "This is another fundamental attack on the income of working people of this country." The amendment was defeated, 23-25, with all Democrats and five Republicans voting yes.

Sabo has one semi-official duty in Congress each year, this one in the sports realm: He coaches the Democratic squad in the annual congressional baseball game.

At Home: Sabo has never been a flashy campaigner, but he has been a significant presence in Minnesota politics virtually all his adult life.

When Democrat Donald Fraser left the House for an unsuccessful Senate try in 1978, nearly a dozen candidates began maneuvering to succeed him. But when Sabo announced that he wanted the job, nearly all bowed out of the contest. Those who remained either lost at the endorsing convention or badly trailed his 81 percent primary victory.

Even then, he was already a fixture on the political scene. Elected to the state Legislature at 22, he had served as state House Speaker for six years before trying for Congress. He was seen by most voters as the logical liberal successor to Fraser.

Sabo's first Republican opponent, dentist Mike Till, conducted a much more visible campaign than Republicans usually wage in this heavily Democratic district.

Sabo's winning percentage in 1978 (62 percent) was not quite up to what Fraser had been receiving. But by his second election, Sabo had achieved solid support throughout the area, even in the communities of the district where he was weakest against Till.

Sabo has won handily since then, although his GOP opponent in 1994, Dorothy LeGrand, a black woman who supported abortion rights, held Sabo to 62 percent, his lowest share since he first won the seat in 1978. He polled 64 percent in 1996.

HOUSE ELECTIONS

1996 General		
Martin Olav Sabo (D)	158,275	(64%)
Jack Uldrich (R)	70,115	(28%)
Erika Anderson (GR)	13,102	(5%)
Jennifer Benton (SW)	4,284	(2%)
1994 General		
Martin Olav Sabo (D)	121,515	(62%)
Dorothy LeGrand (R)	73,258	(37%)

Previous Winning Percentages: **1992** (63%) **1990** (73%) **1988** (72%) **1986** (73%) **1984** (70%) **1982** (66%) **1980** (70%) **1978** (62%)

CAMPAIGN FINANCE

	Receipts	Receipts from PACs	Expend-itures
1996			
Sabo (D)	$498,260	$242,438 (49%)	$515,970
Uldrich (R)	$68,843	$4,066 (6%)	$66,821
1994			
Sabo (D)	$460,657	$307,710 (67%)	$333,075
LeGrand (R)	$150,790	$8,992 (6%)	$148,799

VOTING STUDIES

	Presidential Support		Party Unity		Conservative Coalition	
Year	S	O	S	O	S	O
1996	87	13	96	4	18	82
1995	88	11	94†	4†	14†	85†
1994	83	17	97	1	6	94
1993	81	18	96	2	11	84
1992	15	83	96	2	8	92
1991	30	68	91	5	8	89

† Not eligible for all recorded votes.

KEY VOTES

1997	
Ban "partial birth" abortions	N
1996	
Approve farm bill	N
Deny public education to illegal immigrants	N
Repeal ban on certain assault-style weapons	N
Increase minimum wage	Y
Freeze defense spending	Y
Approve welfare overhaul	N
1995	
Approve balanced-budget constitutional amendment	N
Relax Clean Water Act regulations	N
Oppose limits on environmental regulations	Y
Reduce projected Medicare spending	N
Approve GOP budget with tax and spending cuts	N

DISTRICT VOTE FOR PRESIDENT

	1996		1992
D	159,018 (64%)	**D**	168,457 (58%)
R	62,507 (25%)	**R**	70,766 (24%)
I	20,499 (8%)	**I**	52,539 (18%)

INTEREST GROUP RATINGS

Year	ADA	AFL-CIO	CCUS	ACU
1996	90	n/a	13	0
1995	100	100	17	4
1994	95	89	25	10
1993	100	100	9	0
1992	100	92	25	0
1991	90	92	10	0

6 William P. 'Bill' Luther (D)

Of Stillwater — Elected 1994, 2nd term

Biographical Information

Born: June 27, 1945, Fergus Falls, Minn.
Education: U. of Minnesota, B.S. 1967, J.D. 1970.
Occupation: Lawyer.
Family: Wife, Darlene Dunphy; two children.
Religion: Roman Catholic.
Political Career: Minn. House, 1974-76; Minn. Senate, 1976-95, assistant majority leader, 1982-95.
Capitol Office: 117 Cannon Bldg. 20515; 225-2271.

Committees

International Relations
International Economic Policy & Trade
Science
Basic Research; Space & Aeronautics; International Economic Policy & Trade

In Washington: Luther is a career legislator, a throwback to the time when Congress was dominated by Democrats with backgrounds in state and local government. During the 104th Congress, he served as president of the outnumbered Democratic Class of 1994. For the 105th, he has been elected a deputy regional whip.

Quiet and seemingly unassuming, Luther has been able to work with some of the more conservative members of his party on issues such as restraining federal spending and revamping welfare. He is well-connected within the Minneapolis legal establishment and is a prodigious fundraiser; although he favors an overhaul of campaign finance laws, he says he has to work within the existing system.

Luther sides with more liberal members of his party on issues such as abortion, gun control and the environment. He has opposed efforts to ban a particular abortion technique that its opponents call "partial-birth" abortion, and he took exception with a Republican move in 1996 to repeal the ban on certain semiautomatic assault-style weapons. Luther voted against GOP efforts to curtail environmental regulations, including a bill that would have eased many federal water quality protections. He also holds to the view that tax cuts should be put on hold until the federal budget is in balance.

But Luther, who won very narrowly in 1994 and faced a rematch with the same opponent in 1996, compiled a first-term voting record that included support for some of the priorities of the conservative GOP majority. He favored constitutional amendments mandating a balanced budget and congressional term limits, and he endorsed granting the president line-item veto power over spending bills.

Luther, who has heard Republicans attack him as a "tax-and-spend liberal," supported freezing Department of Defense spending at fiscal 1996 levels, and he has risen frequently on the House floor to support amendments cutting funding for a variety of programs, including NASA's space station and the B-2 "stealth" bomber. As it happens, the spending that Luther targets is often for programs dear to GOP conservatives with a strong pro-military or pro-agricultural bent.

Luther cosponsored an amendment in 1995 to ax the Market Promotion Program, which assists U.S. companies in advertising their products overseas.

"Today, after years of overspending, we have no extra money to spend and we must discipline ourselves the way the rest of the world does," Luther said in defending elimination of the promotion program. "We must ask ourselves, not whether there is some value in this program, but rather is it more important to provide this foreign advertisement subsidy or make future investments in our children's education, Head Start, job training and health care for the people of this country?" Luther also thinks that school lunch subsidies and summer jobs programs should be a priority in the budget.

Facing many aggressively conservative House Republicans who wish to reduce the size and scope of the federal government, Luther asks colleagues to end "the partisanship, the bickering" and work toward "bipartisan solutions based on the principles that will help working families."

Luther had the honor in 1996 of authoring an amendment that has become a perennial aspect of congressional housekeeping, blocking an automatic pay increase for members of Congress. He also cosponsored a move, with Minnesota's other member of the Class of 1994, Republican Gil Gutknecht, to cap the number of political appointees in the executive branch at 2,300. The measure was approved by the House but dropped in conference with the Senate.

An influential insider when he was in the Minnesota state Senate, Luther has angled for a more prestigious committee assignment in the House, but with his party in the minority, plum seats are hard to come by. In 1995 he tried without success to get onto the Commerce Committee after one of its Democratic members, W.J. "Billy" Tauzin of Louisiana, switched to the GOP. He was

MINNESOTA 6
Eastern, Southern Twin Cities suburbs

The horseshoe-shaped 6th District wraps around the Twin Cities, taking in surrounding suburbs, plus a bit of farmland farther out. The district includes marginally Democratic areas, some Democratic strongholds and GOP-leaning suburbs. The latest round of redistricting made the area slightly more Democratic.

In the latest round of the state's redistricting pingpong, the Supreme Court in 1993 rejected the federally drawn map that had been used in the 1992 election. The high court ruled that federal courts must stand aside until challenges to redistricting plans run their course in state courts. In 1994 and 1996, candidates ran under a state-drawn plan.

Most of the areas lost by the 6th under the state plan, including the northern and western Hennepin County suburbs, were represented by Republicans in the state Legislature.

The district gained east and central Dakota County and southern Washington County. These areas are developed or emerging suburbs with white-collar voters. However, these voters tend to favor abortion rights and increased funding of education; the Republican Party cannot count on them for reliable support.

The state court also added Farmington, Hastings and Inver Grove Heights, which tend to be more Democratic than their neighbors. (Apple Valley, Eagan and Rosemount in Dakota County were also added for the 1994 elections.)

Anoka County, which casts more than 40 percent of the vote, is the strongest Democratic area in the 6th. It was the cornerstone of former Rep. Gerry Sikorski's congressional victories, and it remained loyal to Walter F. Mondale in 1984 and every Democratic presidential candidate since. But in 1992, the county chose Republican Rod Grams over Sikorski at least in part because of Sikorski's 697 overdrafts at the House bank.

Anoka is a mix of new suburbs, farms and small towns. Lake Wobegon, the mythical town in Garrison Keillor's weekly radio program, "A Prairie Home Companion," is modeled after Keillor's boyhood home in Anoka County.

But the Lake Wobegons of this part of Minnesota are quickly disappearing as the Twin Cities metropolitan area continues to expand farther into the surrounding counties.

The major employer is Northwest Airlines, in Eagan. The airline's headquarters employs about 15,000 people, and its survival is crucial to the economy. Cray Research, which makes supercomputers, and West Publishing Co., the nation's largest publisher of legal books, are also in Eagan.

One of the district's largest employers is United Defense (formerly known as FMC Corp.), a defense contractor in Fridley, a Minneapolis suburb. The Fridley operation is home to the company's Armament Systems Division. The division makes gun and missile launching systems for Navy ships.

Medtronic, which produces heart pacemakers and other medical instruments, employs more than 2,000 workers.

1990 Population: 546,887. White 529,635 (97%), Black 4,732 (1%), Other 12,520 (2%). Hispanic origin 5,928 (1%). 18 and over 377,110 (69%), 62 and over 36,893 (7%). Median age: 30.

also denied a Commerce slot at the start of the 105th; Democratic leaders felt the panel already had sufficient Midwestern representation.

So for his second term, Luther returned to serve on the Science Committee, which is involved in issues of interest to the 6th District's concentration of high-technology and medical-related companies. He also joined the International Relations Committee, giving up a seat on Small Business.

At Home: Luther is linked to the Democrats' historic class of 1974, and not just in his belief in activist government. That was the year when he was first elected to the Minnesota House, a year shy of his 30th birthday.

Over the next two decades, he became a power in the state Legislature, winning election to the state Senate in 1976 and rising to the No. 2 position in the Democratic leadership as assistant majority leader.

Luther has an affable manner on the campaign trail, but in the state Senate he developed a reputation for sharp elbows and aggressive partisanship.

Luther came to Washington with scant experience at being part of a legislative minority. He is used to wielding power, developing what was known in St. Paul as the "Luther machine." One of his protégés became majority leader of the Minnesota House; and Luther's wife, Darlene, was elected state representative in 1992.

Not long after his wife's election, he began laying the groundwork for a run for the suburban Twin Cities House seat that belonged to Democrat Gerry Sikorski before being seized in 1992 by Republican Rod Grams. Luther launched a 1994 campaign for the 6th even before Grams announced in late 1993 that he would run for the Senate rather than seek a second House term.

Well-connected with major Democratic interest groups, Luther raised money quickly. By the end of the 1994 campaign he had spent over $1.1

million, more than any other House candidate in Minnesota, incumbents included.

It was a difficult campaign. Luther lost more than 40 percent of the primary vote to a pair of little-known challengers, one an anti-abortion candidate who also had served in Operation Desert Storm. And in the fall, he weathered a nasty, hard-fought contest with Republican Tad Jude (a former Democrat). In the end, Luther prevailed by a mere 550 votes out of nearly 227,000 ballots cast.

Jude had served as a Democrat for 10 years in the state House, six years in the state Senate and four years as Hennepin County commissioner, switching to the GOP after narrowly losing to Sikorski in the 1992 Democratic House primary.

Neither candidate resided in the district when the campaign began. Luther, who had been living with his family in a working-class suburb northwest of the Twin Cities, established a second residence on the eastern side of the metro area.

Although Jude had the support of the GOP establishment in 1994, he never fully recovered from a divisive primary contest against a pro-abortion rights Republican who attributed Jude's party switch to opportunism. In the general election campaign, Luther emphasized jobs, crime and health care and sought to establish a more moderate image, but even in the strong GOP year of 1994, he fell short.

Luther had an easier go of it in their 1996 rematch, winning comfortably. He raised even more money than he had in 1994, and Jude's campaign was dogged by an ethics case surrounding a misleading TV ad he aired near the close of their first contest. Although the case was eventually dismissed, Jude was distracted throughout the 1996 campaign cycle by an indictment handed down under Minnesota's astringent fair campaign practices law. Luther polled 56 percent of the vote, 12 points ahead of Jude.

HOUSE ELECTIONS

1996 General		
William P. "Bill" Luther (D)	164,921	(56%)
Tad Jude (R)	129,989	(44%)
1994 General		
William P. "Bill" Luther (D)	113,740	(50%)
Tad Jude (R)	113,190	(50%)

CAMPAIGN FINANCE

	Receipts	Receipts from PACs	Expend-itures
1996			
Luther (D)	$1,368,013	$433,010 (32%)	$850,638
Jude (R)	$389,724	$64,590 (17%)	$392,953
1994			
Luther (D)	$1,136,205	$354,445 (31%)	$1,133,977
Jude (R)	$725,340	$156,188 (22%)	$699,413

DISTRICT VOTE FOR PRESIDENT

	1996		1992
D	154,333 (51%)	**D**	125,451 (41%)
R	107,560 (35%)	**R**	96,464 (32%)
I	37,111 (12%)	**I**	81,738 (27%)

KEY VOTES

1997	
Ban "partial birth" abortions	N
1996	
Approve farm bill	N
Deny public education to illegal immigrants	N
Repeal ban on certain assault-style weapons	N
Increase minimum wage	Y
Freeze defense spending	Y
Approve welfare overhaul	Y
1995	
Approve balanced-budget constitutional amendment	Y
Relax Clean Water Act regulations	N
Oppose limits on environmental regulations	Y
Reduce projected Medicare spending	N
Approve GOP budget with tax and spending cuts	N

VOTING STUDIES

	Presidential Support		Party Unity		Conservative Coalition	
Year	**S**	**O**	**S**	**O**	**S**	**O**
1996	81	19	84	16	22	78
1995	74	26	83	17	32	68

INTEREST GROUP RATINGS

Year	ADA	AFL-CIO	CCUS	ACU
1996	80	n/a	19	0
1995	85	92	38	24

7 Collin C. Peterson (D)

Of Detroit Lakes — Elected 1990, 4th term

Biographical Information

Born: June 29, 1944, Fargo, N.D.
Education: Moorhead State U., B.A. 1966.
Military Service: National Guard, 1963-69.
Occupation: Accountant.
Family: Divorced; three children.
Religion: Lutheran.
Political Career: Minn. Senate, 1977-87; sought Democratic nomination for U.S. House, 1982; Democratic nominee for U.S. House, 1984, 1986; sought Democratic nomination for U.S. House, 1988.

Capitol Office: 2159 Rayburn Bldg. 20515; 225-2165.

Committees

Agriculture
Forestry, Resource Conservation & Research; Livestock, Dairy & Poultry (ranking)

Veterans' Affairs
Health

In Washington: With his conservative views on social issues and fiscal matters, Peterson used to look pretty lonely when liberals in his party ran the House. But in the Republican-controlled 104th Congress, he was in the thick of the budget and welfare debates as a leader of the "blue dogs," a group of center-right House Democrats who aimed to find a middle ground between the two parties.

A thorough-going "prairie populist" on farm issues, Peterson also fought in the 104th for revised versions of the sugar and dairy price-support programs and for a farmland conservation program, all of which were included in a broad GOP rewrite of federal agriculture policy. But when the final terms of the farm bill proved unfriendly to Midwest dairy farmers, Peterson voted against it.

It took five campaigns before a persistent Peterson persuaded 7th District voters to send him to Congress, and all of them were waged against GOP incumbent Arlan Stangeland. Peterson's performance in the 104th was evidently a big hit with district voters, because in 1996 they re-elected him with more than two-thirds of the vote, by far the best showing by a 7th District incumbent in the past 20 years.

In explaining his attraction to the blue dogs, Peterson probably summed up many of his constituents' views. "The Republicans generally think that government is bad. And Democrats think that government is good," he told the Minneapolis/St. Paul Star Tribune in May 1995. "The blue dog Democrats think that government a lot of the time is bad, but it can be good."

He also said the coalition was impatient to produce results. "We are the only people willing to work with the Republicans and actually legislate," Peterson said. "The [other] Democrats just trash everything they are trying to do."

This desire for results led the group in the 104th to write its own balanced-budget plans, which traveled a middle road between the two parties. The coalition's budgets did not offer a tax cut like the GOP plan, and they tempered the GOP's spending reductions in health care entitlements and welfare. Although the blue dog budgets did not garner majority support in the House, they were widely credited as serious efforts, and in some respects they helped create momentum for the compromise budget that Clinton and congressional Republicans outlined in May 1997.

Peterson praised President Clinton for signing a measure overhauling the welfare system in August 1996, a move that many liberal Democrats condemned because they feared it would force more children into poverty. Peterson was the only Minnesota Democrat to vote for the House GOP version of the welfare bill approved in July, although he also voted for a Democratic alternative.

The measure, which ended 60 years of federal welfare entitlements for the poor, gives states broad authority over their welfare programs through the creation of a new block grant. Welfare recipients are required to work within two years and are limited to five years of benefits.

"All states and communities are different, and this bill will give them the flexibility to create tailor-made programs that will work for them," Peterson said. "The plan will also give people who are living off of welfare the push they need to break the welfare cycle and take control of their lives and their futures."

On most social issues, however, Peterson is much further to the right than the president. He opposes abortion and supports the rights of gun owners, voting in March 1996 to repeal the ban on certain semiautomatic assault-style weapons. He also backs the Republicans' efforts to protect property owners' rights and to limit federal regulations.

Peterson was an early supporter of a GOP bill to curb unfunded federal mandates, which are requirements that Congress imposes on state and local governments without providing funds to pay for them. He was successful with an amendment during House debate that would require the Congressional Budget Office to estimate the cost

MINNESOTA 7
Northwest — Moorhead; part of St. Cloud

From the prairie wheat fields along the Red River to the hills, forests and lakes in the middle of the state, this vast district is Minnesota's most marginal — economically as well as politically.

While some counties in the 7th, including Kittson, Mahnomen and Beltrami, continue to struggle economically, many of the lake regions are either stable or growing. The area's economy is fueled by farming — dairy, grains and row crops — light manufacturing, tourism and education (the 7th has a number of community colleges). Many farmers struggle to meet high operating costs on land that does not match the quality of the soil farther south. The region's lumber business, once in decline, has revived. And the snowmobile industry has recovered from a spell of dry winters and the 1980s recession.

Politically, the district has been in the marginal category since popular Democrat Bob Bergland left it in 1977 to become Jimmy Carter's secretary of Agriculture. Republican Arlan Stangeland, who represented the 7th from 1977 until 1991, won five of six re-elections with less than 55 percent of the vote. In 1996, Peterson became the first House member to win the district with more than 60 percent of the vote since 1976.

Neither the district's map nor its political landscape changed much under recent redistricting. In 1993, the Supreme Court rejected the federally drawn map that had been used in the 1992 election. The decision upheld a state redistricting plan.

St. Cloud, part of which was placed in the 8th District in the federal plan, is included in the 7th under the state map. The seat of Stearns County, St. Cloud, with 49,000 residents, is the district's largest city and one of the fastest growing in the state. For years, it was a major center for granite quarrying. Today the descendants of the old stonecutters share their ancestors' support of the Democratic Party on economic issues, but they often stray to the GOP when social issues, especially abortion, become paramount.

The state plan also returned a major employer to the 7th: Fingerhut, a mail-order house that sells gadgets and novelty items, is located in St. Cloud. Employing more than 4,000 people, Fingerhut is the district's largest employer.

Apart from St. Cloud and Moorhead, a sister city to Fargo, N.D., there are few population centers. But many of the district's towns are vintage Americana. Sauk Centre — about 40 miles northwest of St. Cloud — was the birthplace of novelist Sinclair Lewis, who used his hometown as the model for his novel "Main Street." Signs along the prime thoroughfare, in fact, call it the "Original Main Street."

The wheat-growing central sections of the district are slightly more populous than the rest and also more Republican. Sugar beets are grown around Moorhead in the Red River Valley, which possesses some of the 7th's most fertile farmland. In the rolling countryside to the east, hunters, fishermen and summer tourists are drawn to hundreds of lakes.

1990 Population: 546,901. White 529,053 (97%), Black 1,198 (<1%), Other 16,650 (3%). Hispanic origin 4,334 (1%). 18 and over 395,127 (72%), 62 and over 96,835 (18%). Median age: 32.

of any legislation that imposed an unfunded mandate of $50 million or more on private business. The measure already included a provision that any legislation that imposed a cost of $50 million or more on a state or local government would be subject to a point of order in either chamber.

"This bill is not perfect but it is a good start," Peterson said. "Personally, I feel it should be tougher and should completely eliminate the practice of unfunded federal mandates. Every dollar spent on a federal mandate is one dollar less in local budgets to fight crime, improve education, or provide public services."

From his Agriculture Committee seat in the 104th, Peterson was heavily involved in the effort to overhaul federal farm policy to bring it more in line with free market principles. Peterson was one of just three Democrats to support the GOP-backed "Freedom to Farm" measure when it was approved in committee in 1996, because he supported the bill's provisions revising (but not eliminating) the sugar and dairy programs. But he voted against the bill when it came back from a House-Senate conference, unhappy that the dairy section of the bill was changed on the House floor to gradually phase out dairy price supports, known as milk marketing orders, rather then ending them immediately. Milk marketing orders are regional price supports that tend to favor Northeastern and Southeastern producers over those in the Upper Midwest.

The final bill required the Agriculture Department to consolidate the 33 orders into 10 to 14 within three years. The bill also phased out price supports for butter, milk powder and cheese over four years rather than immediately. Peterson said the regional price supports hurt Midwest dairy farmers because "they are getting too little money for their milk." He said the inequities in the current program are causing the dairy industry to shift out of the Midwest into places like California. In the 105th Congress, Peterson moved into the ranking minority slot on the Livestock, Dairy and Poultry Subcommittee.

Peterson had also taken the lead in preserving the 36 million acre Conservation Reserve Program, which pays farmers to idle environmentally fragile land. Peterson told the House that many lands in the 7th District fall into this category and, while idle, they provide good habitat for wildlife. A member of the Sportsman's Caucus, Peterson gained the backing of the caucus to keep the program alive.

The 7th is also home to many sugar beet farmers, and Peterson worked to kill an amendment that would have phased out the sugar price-support program, which limits imports to protect U.S. growers.

Peterson also has a seat on the Veterans' Affairs Committee, where he says he will make sure that the the needs of rural veterans' are met.

At Home: Peterson's victory in 1990 owed much to Stangeland's personal baggage. Having been re-elected with more than 55 percent of the vote only once, the Republican had been living on the political edge; in 1990, he went over it.

The end began in January, when The St. Cloud Daily Times reported that Stangeland had used his House credit card to charge several phone calls to or from the phone of a female Virginia lobbyist. A subsequent story revealed that he allowed a lobbyist to use his House parking space. Stangeland denied any wrongdoing, but he was never able to dispel the impression of impropriety.

Peterson might not have run again in 1990 had it not been for Stangeland's problems. After four defeats, his own political image was in disrepair. When Peterson decided to try again in 1990 he was careful to present himself as a "new Collin Peterson," more mellow than in his past campaigns. He ran a virtually error-free campaign and took 54 percent of the vote to oust Stangeland.

Subsequent victories in 1992 and 1994 over a young Republican state legislator, Bernie Omann, were much closer. In 1992, Peterson took just 50 percent as Omann accused him of overusing the congressional franking privilege and of not aiding the state's dairy industry enough.

Two years later, Peterson took the fight to his challenger, cultivating voters in Omann's St. Cloud-area base that he had virtually ignored in 1992. Peterson inched up to 51 percent.

In 1996, Peterson had his first easy campaign. His GOP opponent, Darrell McKigney, who took a leave as legislative director for the "pro-family values" Minnesota Family Council to run against Peterson, had a difficult time finding a salable issue to use against the incumbent. He claimed Peterson is more liberal than he portrays himself, but Peterson's moderate voting record undercut McKigney's argument.

McKigney attacked his opponent for being named the "second biggest spender" in the Minnesota delegation by the National Taxpayers Union. But voters sent Peterson back for another term with a 68 percent tally.

HOUSE ELECTIONS

1996 General		
Collin C. Peterson (D)	170,936	(68%)
Darrell McKigney (R)	80,132	(32%)
1994 General		
Collin C. Peterson (D)	108,023	(51%)
Bernie Omann (R)	102,623	(49%)

Previous Winning Percentages: 1992 (50%) **1990** (54%)

CAMPAIGN FINANCE

	Receipts	Receipts from PACs	Expend-itures
1996			
Peterson (D)	$565,973	$434,063 (77%)	$532,229
McKigney (R)	$182,887	$23,849 (13%)	$181,026
1994			
Peterson (D)	$583,466	$363,530 (62%)	$584,092
Omann (R)	$526,368	$99,571 (19%)	$507,325

DISTRICT VOTE FOR PRESIDENT

1996	1992
D 115,996 (45%)	**D** 103,964 (38%)
R 103,336 (40%)	**R** 103,053 (38%)
I 33,577 (13%)	**I** 63,703 (24%)

INTEREST GROUP RATINGS

Year	ADA	AFL-CIO	CCUS	ACU
1996	55	n/a	63	53
1995	45	75	63	60
1994	45	44	83	52
1993	60	83	27	38
1992	65	75	63	24
1991	65	67	40	15

KEY VOTES

1997	
Ban "partial birth" abortions	Y
1996	
Approve farm bill	N
Deny public education to illegal immigrants	Y
Repeal ban on certain assault-style weapons	Y
Increase minimum wage	Y
Freeze defense spending	Y
Approve welfare overhaul	Y
1995	
Approve balanced-budget constitutional amendment	Y
Relax Clean Water Act regulations	Y
Oppose limits on environmental regulations	N
Reduce projected Medicare spending	N
Approve GOP budget with tax and spending cuts	N

VOTING STUDIES

	Presidential Support		Party Unity		Conservative Coalition	
Year	S	O	S	O	S	O
1996	58	38	60	39	63	37
1995	49	50	49	50	70	29
1994	58	42	58	41	72	25
1993	56	43	67	30	48	52
1992	35	64	82	17	44	54
1991	39	60	76	20	57	43

8 James L. Oberstar (D)

Of Chisholm — Elected 1974, 12th term

Biographical Information
Born: Sept. 10, 1934, Chisholm, Minn.
Education: College of St. Thomas, B.A. 1956; College of Europe (Bruges, Belgium), M.A. 1957.
Occupation: Language teacher; congressional aide.
Family: Wife, Jean Kurth; six children.
Religion: Roman Catholic.
Political Career: Sought Democratic nomination for U.S. Senate, 1984.
Capitol Office: 2366 Rayburn Bldg. 20515; 225-6211.

Committees
Transportation & Infrastructure (ranking)

In Washington: Oberstar remains a consistent supporter of organized labor and differs with the conservative GOP majority on fiscal policy. But as ranking Democrat on the Transportation and Infrastructure Committee, he generally works well with Chairman Bud Shuster, R-Pa.

Oberstar became ranking member of the largest committee in Congress when his classmate, California Democrat Norman Y. Mineta, resigned in October 1995 to work for a defense contractor. He supports the efforts of Shuster to take transportation trust funds "off budget," a move that proponents say would free up money for infrastructure projects that is now hoarded to mask the size of the deficit.

"That means highways. That means improvements. That means benefits to every congressional district in the country," Oberstar says.

With the Transportation Committee in the 105th Congress preparing to allocate an estimated $175 billion in new funding as it rewrites the nation's major surface transportation law, Oberstar joins with Shuster in support of members being able to earmark specific projects for their district. If members left all the funding decisions to state transportation departments, some projects would never get done, Oberstar warns: "You'd be standing out on a highway, hat in hand, for a long time."

Oberstar and Shuster both objected in the 104th when conservatives succeeded in eliminating certain safety laws, including federal speed limits and motorcycle helmet requirements; those changes became law as part of a highway bill. "It is a fact of life — if you drive faster, you kill people," Oberstar argued. On the helmet issue, Oberstar tried to add language denying the use by hospitals of Medicaid funding for patients injured on a motorcycle while not wearing a helmet, but his amendment was ruled non-germane.

Oberstar split from Shuster, however, when he felt the chairman was putting labor protections at risk. The two disagreed about language in the fiscal 1996 transportation spending bill that would have eliminated federal labor protections for mass transit workers. The amendment that killed that language was one of the first significant victories for Democrats during the 104th. (Oberstar strongly supported the Democrats' greatest victory of the Congress, a boost in the minimum wage, as well as every other major position taken on legislation by organized labor.)

The two also clashed when Oberstar raised objections to a shipping deregulation bill after unions worried that it would result in layoffs. Oberstar previously had signed off on the bill and his turnabout on the House floor angered Shuster. "It's a question of welshing on the deal," Shuster complained.

Oberstar chaired the panel's Aviation Subcommittee from 1989 until 1995, when Democrats ruled the House and the committee was known as Public Works and Transportation. During the 104th — when two major air crashes in 1996 focused public attention on airline safety — he joined with subcommittee Chairman John J. "Jimmy" Duncan Jr., R-Tenn., in crafting reauthorizing legislation for the Federal Aviation Administration (FAA). The measure addressed some safety issues, privatized five airports and provided more autonomy for the FAA. But despite rising public concern over the safety of air travel, lawmakers were generally reluctant to add provisions imposing much tighter safety standards, fearing that doing so could lead to severe delays and higher ticket prices.

Oberstar's quest for aviation safety has earned him a reputation as a serious and earnest lawmaker, but that image was questioned by a former Transportation Department inspector general in her 1997 book, "Flying Blind, Flying Safe." Mary Schiavo portrayed Oberstar as interested in safety issues only when cameras were pointed at him and she wrote that hearings he held were empty exercises that yielded no legislation. Oberstar declined comment on the book.

Oberstar has the instincts of a scholar and reformer, but the Transportation and Infrastructure Committee is a place where members

MINNESOTA 8
Northeast — Iron Range; Duluth

If the 8th were somehow dropped onto a map of the East Coast, it would reach from Washington to Connecticut. The district covers about 26,000 square miles and is generally Democratic. The mostly rural area encompasses a vast stretch of land that includes flat farmland, bluffs and lakes. The district's largest city, Duluth (population 85,500), is also the state's fourth largest. From here much of the grain from the Plains states is shipped east.

Singer/songwriter Bob Dylan grew up in Hibbing, which calls itself the "Iron Ore Capital of the World." Hibbing also produced former Boston Celtics great Kevin McHale, who remains a local hero. A local bus line that started in Hibbing in 1914 with one open touring car became the Greyhound Bus Lines. And the nation's only gas station designed by Frank Lloyd Wright is located in Cloquet.

Based in the barren and remote northern reaches of Minnesota, the district has a long Democratic tradition.

Immigrants from Sweden, Finland and Eastern Europe settled here after the turn of the century to work in the iron mines scattered throughout the Mesabi and Vermillion iron ranges. Strongly allied with unions, the workers on the Iron Range today remain unswerving in their allegiance to the Democrats.

The economy is fueled by a variety of industries. Tourism is crucial and the timber industry is also a major employer, both in timber harvesting and in the production of paper and wood products.

In the southern counties farmers grow corn and small grain. Dairy farming slowed in the south during the mid-1980s when many farmers here sold their herds. The federal government paid milk producers to send their herds to slaughter in order to cut milk production and reduce the government's purchases of dairy surpluses.

The economy has taken its knocks. The prolonged slump of the steel industry and the ups and downs of the automobile industry have created job shortages. And domestic steel production has faced intense foreign competition.

But taconite mining has rebounded from a recent slump. It is heavily mechanized and employs fewer people than the old underground mining operations. Yet it was the discovery of new taconite mining technology that helped boost the local economy after the high-quality iron ore mines were largely depleted in the mid-1940s.

Casinos on Indian reservations have been another economic bright spot. The gambling enterprises have brought jobs and spurred sales and construction in many nearby towns. And Northwest Airlines recently opened a maintenance base in Duluth and a ticket reservation center in Chisholm.

The district changed only slightly in the last act of the state's redistricting odyssey. In 1993, the Supreme Court rejected the federally drawn map that had been used in the 1992 election. Under the state-drawn plan in effect in 1994, the 8th gave up a portion of Benton County, traded territory in Sherburne County and gained a portion of Morrison County.

1990 Population: 546,874. White 530,435 (97%), Black 2,003 (<1%), Other 14,436 (3%). Hispanic origin 2,783 (1%). 18 and over 397,582 (73%), 62 and over 101,132 (18%). Median age: 35.

like to dig first and ask questions later; policy analysts take a back seat to pork barrelers. At the same time, Oberstar is only part scholar. The rest of him is Minnesota Iron Range street fighter, a self-described bohunk. He is the son of a miner and a shirt-factory worker, an unrepentant New Deal-style Democrat with deep faith in the job-creating potential of public works and deeper faith yet in his party.

He occasionally beseeches the committee to "rise above" pork barrel thinking and seek innovative ways to address problems. However, he has not been known to turn down a new project for northern Minnesota. He spent years learning how to bring Duluth and the Iron Range a share of the Public Works pie, as an aide and protégé to John A. Blatnik, the Minnesota Democrat who chaired the committee until 1975, when he retired and Oberstar took over his seat.

Although Oberstar consistently opposes the GOP's fiscal-policy prescriptions, he joins conservative Republicans on the issues of abortion and gunowners' rights. Oberstar has proposed a constitutional amendment in the 105th to ban abortions except in cases where the woman's life is endangered. But Oberstar refuses to get cozy with his GOP colleagues, even on this issue. "They call themselves the pro-life party, but that's not true," he said. "They don't support what is needed for the continuum of life — food stamps, the women and infant feeding program — for these same women they purport to care so much about."

And even though Oberstar supported the Republican effort to repeal the ban on certain semiautomatic assault-style weapons, he praised President Clinton for opposing the move. "I respect him for standing up for his principles," Oberstar commented. "It was a good theme for him to strike to show he's a leader."

Oberstar worked with Minnesota Republican Sen. Rod Grams to relax restrictions in two parks in his district to allow wider use. Their legislation put the state's Democratic senator, Paul Wellstone, in an awkward spot as he sought re-election in 1996, because the issue split environmentalists and the generally loyal Democratic voters near the parks who wanted to use their motorized boats. Oberstar objected to a Republican TV ad that flattered him but critiqued Wellstone on the issue. He called the ad "deceitful and divisive" and asked Duluth TV stations not to air it. A provision of Oberstar's bill was included in omnibus parks legislation in the 104th; the proposal was dropped when the White House objected.

At Home: Republicans have not cost Oberstar much sleep since he inherited the 8th in 1974 from Blatnik, his employer and predecessor. But fighting within the Democratic Party has made his life far from tranquil. For years there was a feud between the Blatnik wing of the Democratic Party and the faction headed by the three Perpich brothers, whose leader, Rudy, served as governor of Minnesota.

The battle between the two sides broke into the open in 1974 and flared again in 1980. In 1974, Blatnik tried to anoint Oberstar as his successor, but the result was an acrimonious party-endorsing convention lasting 30 ballots. Eventually Blatnik and Oberstar lost, and the party's endorsement went to state Sen. A. J. "Tony" Perpich. Blatnik then threw all his prestige and power behind Oberstar in the Democratic primary, which Oberstar won.

Six years later, Oberstar faced a second Perpich. This time it was Tony's younger brother, George. When Rudy had been elected lieutenant governor in 1970, George took his seat in the state Senate and carried on the populist Perpich crusade against the mining companies.

At the 1980 nominating convention, George tried to keep the endorsement out of Oberstar's hands, arguing for a neutral party stand. But Oberstar won the endorsement with a fraction more than the 60 percent needed.

Perpich decided not to force a primary, but Duluth City Councilman Thomas E. Dougherty did. Concentrating his campaign in the northern part of the district where unemployment was high, Dougherty picked up votes from Perpich supporters bent on protest. Oberstar was saved by his backing at the southern end of the district, in the Twin Cities media market.

The two faced each other again in 1984 after Oberstar's bid for the Democratic Senate nomination fell short. But the result was not nearly as close. Dougherty, who netted 44 percent of the primary vote in 1980, was beaten by a margin of nearly 2-to-1 in 1984.

Oberstar's Senate candidacy earlier that year had enjoyed support from much of the state's labor movement. But he could not match the strength of his major rival, Secretary of State Joan Growe, the favorite of the liberal activists who dominated the Democratic endorsement process.

Growe got the party endorsement on the 19th ballot at the state convention in June. Oberstar could have continued the fight into a September primary, but he decided instead to run again for his House seat.

HOUSE ELECTIONS

1996 General		
James L. Oberstar (D)	185,333	(67%)
Andy Larson (R)	69,460	(25%)
Stan "The Man" Estes (REF)	16,639	(6%)
Larry Fuhol (LIBERT)	3,688	(1%)
1994 General		
James L. Oberstar (D)	153,161	(66%)
Phil Herwig (R)	79,818	(34%)

Previous Winning Percentages: **1992** (59%) **1990** (73%) **1988** (75%) **1986** (73%) **1984** (67%) **1982** (77%) **1980** (70%) **1978** (87%) **1976** (100%) **1974** (62%)

CAMPAIGN FINANCE

	Receipts	Receipts from PACs	Expend-itures
1996			
Oberstar (D)	$502,907	$370,983 (74%)	$538,159
Larson (R)	$27,150	$1,500 (6%)	$26,951
Fuhol (LIBERT)	$3,155	0	$3,118
1994			
Oberstar (D)	$344,349	$242,900 (71%)	$488,411
Herwig (R)	$31,655	$514 (2%)	$31,673

DISTRICT VOTE FOR PRESIDENT

	1996		1992
D	149,045 (53%)	**D**	138,939 (48%)
R	88,095 (31%)	**R**	81,076 (28%)
I	38,405 (14%)	**I**	70,643 (24%)

KEY VOTES

1997	
Ban "partial birth" abortions	Y
1996	
Approve farm bill	N
Deny public education to illegal immigrants	N
Repeal ban on certain assault-style weapons	Y
Increase minimum wage	Y
Freeze defense spending	Y
Approve welfare overhaul	N
1995	
Approve balanced-budget constitutional amendment	N
Relax Clean Water Act regulations	N
Oppose limits on environmental regulations	Y
Reduce projected Medicare spending	N
Approve GOP budget with tax and spending cuts	N

VOTING STUDIES

	Presidential Support		Party Unity		Conservative Coalition	
Year	**S**	**O**	**S**	**O**	**S**	**O**
1996	75	24	86	11	22	75
1995	77	17	90	7	11	88
1994	72	26	93	4	14	86
1993	72	28	90	9	20	80
1992	17	82	94	5	15	85
1991	30	59	83	8	16	76

INTEREST GROUP RATINGS

Year	ADA	AFL-CIO	CCUS	ACU
1996	80	n/a	20	20
1995	95	100	13	16
1994	80	89	25	15
1993	90	100	18	22
1992	90	92	25	4
1991	85	83	20	11

MISSISSIPPI

Governor: Kirk Fordice (R)
First elected: 1991
Length of term: 4 years
Term expires: 1/2000
Salary: $75,600
Term limit: No
Phone: (601) 359-3150
Born: February 10, 1934; Memphis, Tenn.
Education: Purdue U., B.S. 1956, M.S. 1957.
Military Service: Army, 1957-59; Army Reserve, 1959-77.
Occupation: Construction executive.
Family: Wife, Patricia Owen; four children.
Religion: Methodist.
Political Career: No previous office.

Lt. Gov.: Ronnie Musgrove (D)
First elected: 1995
Length of term: 4 years
Term expires: 1/2000
Salary: $40,800
Phone: (601) 359-3200

State election official: (601) 359-6357
Democratic headquarters: (601) 969-2913
Republican headquarters: (601) 948-5191

REDISTRICTING

Mississippi retained its five House seats in reapportionment. The legislature passed the map Dec. 20, 1991; the governor signed it Dec. 20. Justice Department approved the map Feb. 21, 1992.

STATE LEGISLATURE

Legislature. Meets January-April.

Senate: 52 members, 4-year terms
1996 breakdown: 34D, 18R; 49 men, 3 women
Salary: $10,000
Phone: (601) 359-3202

House of Representatives: 122 members, 4-year terms
1996 breakdown: 86D, 33R, 3 I; 106 men, 16 women
Salary: $10,000
Phone: (601) 359-3360

URBAN STATISTICS

City	Population
Jackson	196,637
Mayor Kane Ditto, D	
Biloxi	46,319
Mayor A.J. Holloway, R	
Greenville	45,226
Mayor Paul Artman, N-P	
Hattiesburg	41,882
Mayor J. Ed Morgan, D	
Meridian	41,036
Mayor John Robert Smith, R	

U.S. CONGRESS

Senate: 0 D, 2 R
House: 2 D, 3 R

TERM LIMITS

For state offices: No

ELECTIONS

1996 Presidential Vote

Bob Dole	49%
Bill Clinton	44%
Ross Perot	6%

1992 Presidential Vote

George Bush	50%
Bill Clinton	41%
Ross Perot	9%

1988 Presidential Vote

George Bush	60%
Michael S. Dukakis	39%

POPULATION

1990 population		2,573,216
1980 population		2,520,638
Percent change		+2%
Rank among states:		31
White		63%
Black		36%
Hispanic		1%
Asian or Pacific islander		1%
Urban		47%
Rural		53%
Born in state		77%
Foreign-born		10%
Under age 18	746,761	29%
Ages 18-64	1,505,181	58%
65 and older	321,284	12%
Median age		31.2

MISCELLANEOUS

Capital: Jackson
Number of counties: 82
Per capita income: $13,343 (1991)
Rank among states: 50
Total area: 47,689 sq. miles
Rank among states: 32

MISSISSIPPI

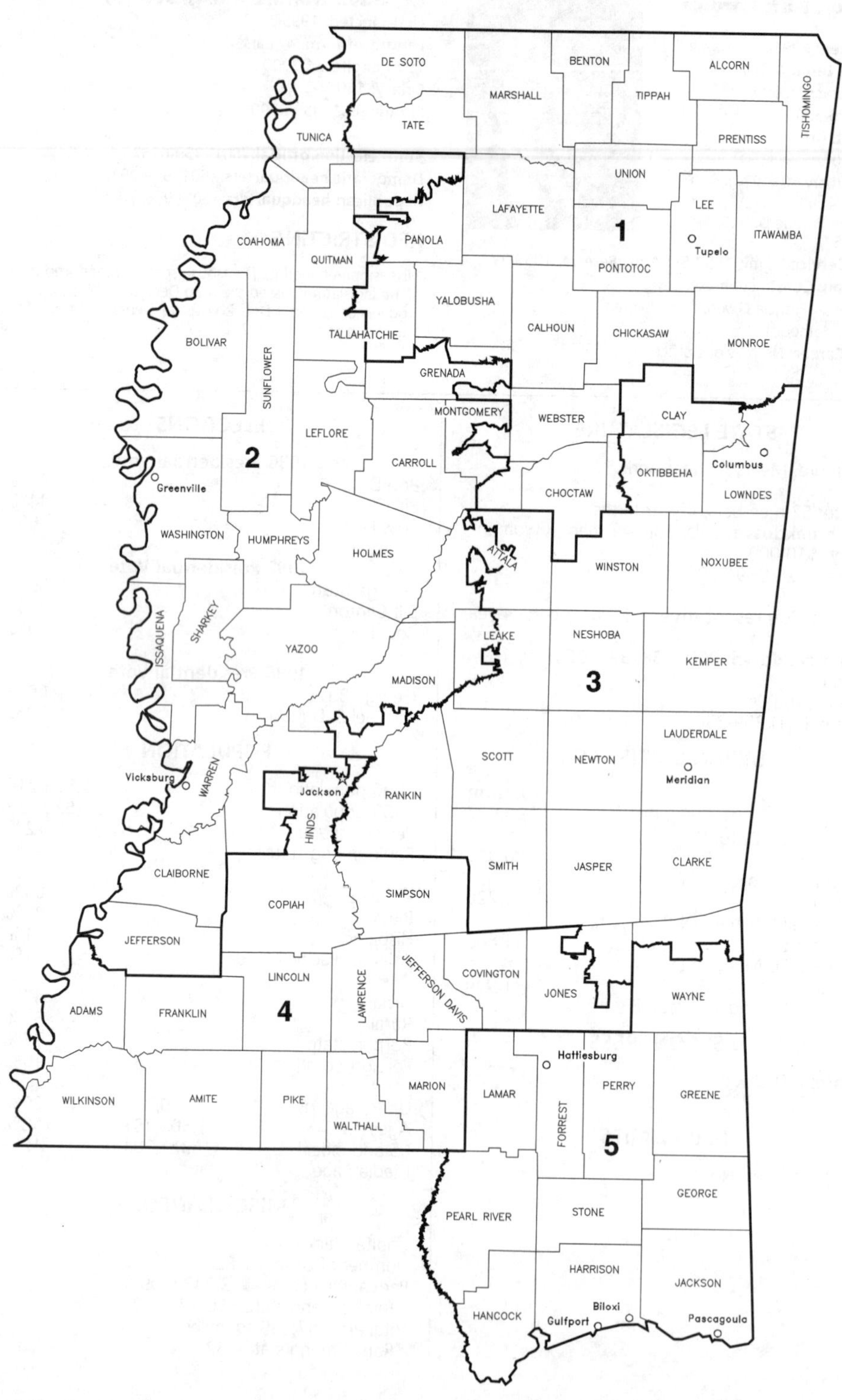

Thad Cochran (R)

Of Jackson — Elected 1978; 3rd term

Biographical Information

Born: Dec. 7, 1937, Pontotoc, Miss.

Education: U. of Mississippi, B.A. 1959; Trinity College (U. of Dublin, Ireland), 1963-64; U. of Mississippi, J.D. 1965.

Military Service: Navy, 1959-61.

Occupation: Lawyer.

Family: Wife, Rose Clayton; two children.

Religion: Baptist.

Political Career: U.S. House, 1973-78.

Capitol Office: 326 Russell Bldg. 20510; 224-5054.

Committees

Agriculture, Nutrition & Forestry
Marketing, Inspection & Product Promotion; Production & Price Competitiveness (chairman)

Appropriations
Agriculture, Rural Development & Related Agencies (chairman); Defense; Energy & Water Development; Interior; Labor, Health & Human Services & Education

Governmental Affairs
International Security, Proliferation & Federal Services (chairman); Investigations

Rules & Administration

Joint Library

Joint Printing

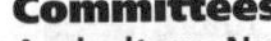

In Washington: Trying to rebound from personal setbacks in the 104th Congress, including losing the Senate majority leader's race to fellow Mississippi Republican Trent Lott, Cochran began the 105th Congress sounding more partisan than usual. When Democrats objected to aspects of a proposed Senate investigation into questionable fundraising tactics by President Clinton's 1996 re-election campaign, Cochran shot back, "I think the Democrats are trying to delay and stonewall this investigation. There is an orchestrated, determined effort under way to drag out this process."

Such rhetoric is not normally heard from the collegial Cochran. In June 1996, when Majority Leader Bob Dole quit the Senate to campaign for president, the race to succeed him went to Lott, partly because Cochran was viewed as operating in the style of the GOP "old bulls" — veteran senators who moved legislation through bipartisanship and comity. Today's more confrontationally conservative Republican senators saw more of what they liked in Lott.

Cochran, while every inch a conservative, typically has preferred to work with Democrats when circumstances dictate and to guard the Senate's more genteel prerogatives against the rough-and-tumble persuasions of the House. The jocular Lott, although just four years younger than Cochran, was an ally of Georgia's Newt Gingrich when both served in the House minority, and that background helps him understand and respond to GOP senators — a number of whom also served in the House — who do not shy away from bare-knuckled partisanship.

Cochran and Lott were longtime rivals in Mississippi politics, dating back to their memberships in rival fraternities at the University of Mississippi. Cochran got to the Senate first, rising to the position of chairman of the Republican Conference — the No. 3 position in leadership. But Lott leapfrogged him in November 1994 by taking on and defeating Alan K. Simpson of Wyoming for the No. 2 position of Republican whip. When Cochran and Lott went head-to-head on June 12, 1996, for the position of majority leader, the verdict was decisive: 44-8 for Lott.

Lott won in part because he was first out of the box; he had made it clear from the beginning of the 104th Congress that he wanted to succeed Dole. By contrast, Cochran waited to announce his candidacy until Dole set his resignation from the Senate. "He probably gave some thought to it, but did not move aggressively to pin down votes," said Richard G. Lugar, R-Ind., a Cochran supporter. In addition to lining up solid support from younger conservatives, Lott reached out adroitly to moderates. After losing, a disappointed Cochran warned his colleagues against becoming overly confrontational. "We will be a stronger party if we appeal to a broad base rather than just a Republican base," he said, because the Democrats' "continued description of our agenda tends to frighten people."

Indeed, through much of the 104th Congress, Cochran used his position as conference chairman to try to moderate the partisan impulses of his colleagues and cushion the sweeping agenda of House Republicans. "We want to work with the House in a cooperative way . . . but we cannot just pick out a day and say we're going to vote on a particular issue," Cochran said early in the 104th. And months later, during the budget showdown with Democrats, he warned that a government shutdown could simply play into Clinton's hands. "What we have to realize . . . is that we cannot produce a budget agreement without the cooperation of the president," he said.

Similarly, during consideration of the 1996 farm bill, Cochran positioned himself as a voice for moderation and stability. As a senior member of the Agriculture, Nutrition and Forestry Committee, he fought successfully to maintain subsidies and price-support programs for Southern crops, including cotton, rice, peanuts and sugar. In this effort, he found himself aligned with Democrats, and often in opposition to House Republicans such as Agriculture Chairman Pat Roberts, R-Kan., who wanted to deregulate farm programs as part of budget-cutting efforts. "The great challenge is to move toward a balanced budget and at the same time preserve those programs that are really important," Cochran said. "Our commodity-support programs work well for America and need to be continued."

It's that sort of attention to parochial interests that has enabled Cochran to come close to defining the modern paradigm of a statewide political success.

Although a relative moderate in a state Republican Party dominated by conservatives, he has established himself or made peace with every important state constituency. Unlike Lott, Cochran has managed to win without alienating the state's sizable black population. In 1988 he decided not to work to defeat then-freshman Democratic Rep. Mike Espy, Mississippi's first black congressman in a century.

In the venerated tradition of Mississippi legislators, Cochran pays close attention to home-state concerns, tending to them by cooperating with Democrats where necessary. In the Democratic-controlled 103rd Congress, he provided the vote needed to end a filibuster on a contentious conference measure to trim the federal work force by providing cash "buyouts" to some workers. The bill contained a provision that would provide $5,000 to as many as 200 Mississippians working on the Advanced Solid Rocket Motor project, a program Congress voted to terminate in 1993.

And in the 104th, Cochran used his position as chairman of the Appropriations agriculture subcommittee to try to steer up to $41 million to cotton farmers who lost crops due to unusually heavy insect damage in 1995. Although that effort failed, he succeeded in earmarking several million dollars for Mississippi agricultural research facilities in appropriations measures.

In the 105th Congress, Cochran occupies a new position — chairman of the Governmental Affairs Subcommittee on International Security, Proliferation, and Federal Services. This newly created subcommittee monitors compliance with the Nuclear Nonproliferation Treaty and oversees international security issues.

Agriculture has always been a major interest of Cochran's. In the past, he has played an important behind-the-scenes role in mediating splits within the Agriculture Committee among various commodity interests. He works well with committee Chairman Lugar. His reasoned, gentlemanly style (he has been called "the Southern Lugar") is well-suited to settling disagreements.

As a junior senator in the early 1980s, Cochran already was writing key farm bills. His influence was significant during work on the 1985 farm bill. Allied with Dole, he worked to develop an overall GOP stance on farm issues out of competing regional interests. At the same time, he hardly overlooked the interests of Mississippi and other Southern farmers, especially those raising cotton or rice. Making full use of their key tactical position, Cochran and a few other Southerners pushed through a radically new and potentially expensive form of price support for growers of the two crops, known as marketing loans. When House Republicans tried to end marketing loans during early consideration of the farm bill in the 104th Congress, Cochran quietly indicated that the Senate wouldn't go along.

Cochran is not immune to the partisan impulse, as shown by his early 1997 flailing at Democrats for their resistance to the fundraising investigation. Another of his harder-edged rhetorical moments came during the Persian Gulf War, a conflict to which many Democrats were reluctant to commit U.S. troops. When U.S.-led military forces drove Iraqi invaders out of Kuwait, Cochran noted that "most of the Democrats in Congress voted to the left of the United Nations — that's something the voters are going to have to consider and will consider."

His conservative inclinations came out clearly on issues before the Judiciary Committee, where he served during his first two years in the Senate. He becomes livid at the mention of language in the Voting Rights Act requiring Southern states to get Justice Department approval before changing their election procedures.

"Local officials have to go to Washington, get on their knees, kiss the ring and tug their forelock to all these third-rate bureaucrats," Cochran once complained. But his effort to make all states comply with the same requirements was rejected by the Senate, 16-74.

Nonetheless, like many of his fellow Republicans on Appropriations, he has avoided strong identification with some elements of the GOP right — "I vote on the social issues because I have to," he once said — and he has been a supporter of funding for food stamps, rural housing and traditionally black colleges. In 1989, he supported continued federal funding for the Martin Luther King Jr. Federal Holiday Commission.

At Home: In each of his first three Senate elections, Cochran made history. In 1978, he became the first Republican to win a Mississippi Senate seat in a century. Six years later, he became the first GOP candidate for any major statewide office to capture a majority of the vote since Reconstruction. In 1990, he became the first statewide Republican to go without Democratic opposition this century.

Seeking a fourth term in 1996, Cochran topped 70 percent of the vote, overwhelming his little-known Democratic opponent, retired farmer James W. "Bootie" Hunt.

The lack of Democratic enthusiasm for challenging Cochran in his last two campaigns can be traced back to his showing in 1984. Facing Democrat William F. Winter, the state's popular governor from 1980 to 1984, Cochran won by a decisive 61 percent to 39 percent.

Cochran has shown a talent for making friends across the political spectrum. Despite his conservative voting record when he served in the House, he drew significant support in most of his House campaigns from blacks, who made up more than 40 percent of his 4th District. After a close first election in 1972, when the presence of a black independent allowed him a narrow victory, he drew more than 70 percent in his 1974 and 1976 campaigns.

His election to the Senate in 1978 was made possible in part by another independent black campaign siphoning off votes from the Democratic nominee, former Columbia Mayor Maurice Dantin. Democrat James O. Eastland retired in 1978 after 36 years in the Senate and endorsed Dantin to succeed him. But a flamboyant campaign by Fayette Mayor Charles Evers, a veteran black activist, drew more attention than Cochran and Dantin combined.

In a state where Democrats must have the black vote, Evers virtually guaranteed GOP success. Drawing 45 percent statewide, Cochran finished nearly 80,000 votes ahead of Dantin.

Many Democrats regarded Cochran's election as a fluke, but he proved his vote-getting ability in 1984 against Winter. Winter's administration was highlighted by passage of a landmark education bill designed to improve the quality of public schools and make Mississippi attractive to new industry.

But Winter dissipated much of the good will when he accepted, then rejected, the University of Mississippi chancellorship in late 1983. By taking more than six weeks after that to decide whether to challenge Cochran, he reinforced an image of indecisiveness. Winter sought to make up ground with an increasingly aggressive campaign. He criticized Cochran as a likable but ineffective "backbencher" whose Senate approach was to "go along to get along."

But with a smooth-running, well-financed campaign operation, Cochran gave Winter few openings. Cochran swept all but a handful of Mississippi's 82 counties, including nearly half of those with majority-black populations.

SENATE ELECTIONS

1996 General		
Thad Cochran (R)	624,154	(71%)
James W. "Bootie" Hunt (D)	240,647	(27%)
Ted C. Weill (I)	13,861	(2%)
1996 Primary		
Thad Cochran (R)	138,813	(95%)
Richard O'Hara (R)	6,762	(5%)

Previous Winning Percentages: **1990** (100%) **1984** (61%) **1978** (45%) **1976*** (76%) **1974*** (70%) **1972*** (48%)

* *House elections*

CAMPAIGN FINANCE

	Receipts	Receipts from PACs	Expend-itures
1996			
Cochran (R)	$787,233	$540,354 (69%)	$828,693

KEY VOTES

1997	
Approve balanced-budget constitutional amendment	Y
Approve chemical weapons treaty	Y
1996	
Approve farm bill	Y
Limit punitive damages in product liability cases	Y
Exempt small businesses from higher minimum wage	?
Approve welfare overhaul	Y
Bar job discrimination based on sexual orientation	N
Override veto of ban on "partial birth" abortions	Y
1995	
Approve GOP budget with tax and spending cuts	Y
Approve constitutional amendment barring flag desecration	Y

VOTING STUDIES

	Presidential Support		Party Unity		Conservative Coalition	
Year	S	O	S	O	S	O
1996	36	54	89	7	87	5
1995	33	66	91	7	96	0
1994	45	55	81	18	91	6
1993	26	74	91	9	98	0
1992	82	15	92	6	89	8
1991	90	9	89	9	95	5

INTEREST GROUP RATINGS

Year	ADA	AFL-CIO	CCUS	ACU
1996	5	n/a	91	94
1995	0	8	95	83
1994	10	13	90	92
1993	0	9	91	84
1992	10	17	100	85
1991	5	25	80	76

Trent Lott (R)

Of Pascagoula — Elected 1988, 2nd term

Biographical Information
Born: Oct. 9, 1941, Grenada County, Miss.
Education: U. of Mississippi, B.P.A. 1963, J.D. 1967.
Occupation: Lawyer.
Family: Wife, Patricia Elizabeth Thompson; two children.
Religion: Baptist.
Political Career: U.S. House, 1973-89.
Capitol Office: 487 Russell Bldg. 20510; 224-6253.

Committees
Commerce, Science & Transportation
Aviation; Communications
Finance
International Trade; Long-Term Growth, Debt & Deficit Reduction; Taxation & IRS Oversight
Rules & Administration

Majority Leader

In Washington: Like Newt Gingrich, with whom he served in the House, Lott can pitch conservative rhetoric with the best of them. But he also is willing to shut up and deal.

Lott's deal-making qualities were evident in the budget agreement congressional leaders and President Clinton announced in May 1997. A letter he wrote to Clinton early in 1997 pleading for cooperation on entitlement changes and other budget sticking points reportedly assuaged the president's fears about whether it was safe to negotiate in good faith with Republicans and helped prompt negotiations. The agreement built on cooperation between the White House and Lott over a chemical weapons treaty and most of Clinton's second-term Cabinet nominations.

Lott, an impeccable dresser who never has a hair out of place, was positioned in 1996 to succeed Bob Dole as majority leader because he had defeated incumbent Whip Alan K. Simpson of Wyoming in 1994. Lott, a decade younger than Simpson and regarded as more conservative and confrontational, had qualities that many junior Republicans thought would be a useful complement to Dole's.

But once he became majority leader, Lott showed a pragmatic streak a mile long. He helped shepherd through legislation overhauling welfare, protecting people from losing health insurance, improving the nation's drinking water systems and raising the minimum wage. "This is the most reform Congress I've ever seen — certainly the most reform-minded Congress in 40 years," Lott said in August 1996.

With Speaker Gingrich weakened by the combination of his ethical problems and a smaller House majority, Lott — who saw his Senate majority increase by two seats — emerged early as the go-to guy in the 105th Congress.

As the Senate convened in January 1997, Lott prevented the body from getting mired in partisan rancor by seating freshman Democrat Mary L. Landrieu of Louisiana and letting the Rules Committee begin an investigation into her disputed 1996 election. He also became the de facto Republican Party leader, with high-profile Haley Barbour stepping down as Republican National Committee chairman. Though reluctant to embrace the title of GOP leader, Lott acknowledged the political reality. "People come here and say, 'You are whether you like it or not,'" he said in March. "I express myself the best I can in public forums, speaking up for the Republican Party. I don't presume to take another role or assume it inappropriately."

Still, he began the 105th with two major defeats. Faced with a Republican rebellion in the ranks, Lott embraced a proposal to widen the scope of the Senate's investigation into campaign fund raising in the 1996 elections. Lott initially planned to push through, over Democratic objections, a resolution giving the Senate Governmental Affairs Committee $4.35 million over nine months to investigate illegal campaign fundraising practices during the 1996 elections.

But at a party luncheon in March shortly before the vote on that plan, at least 10 GOP senators questioned Lott's decision to limit the probe. They complained that it seemed that the Democrats were winning the public relations war, accusing the GOP of covering up their own questionable fundraising habits while digging deeply into the administration's practices. Several Republicans threatened to support a Democratic amendment to include "improper" activities (not just illegal ones) to the committee's investigatory mandate.

So Lott strode out of the luncheon and onto the Senate floor to add his own amendment to review "improper" activities. The final proposal passed, 99-0.

Lott's other major defeat early in the 105th came also in March when the Senate failed, by one vote (66-34), to enact a constitutional amendment requiring a balanced federal budget. Though not mentioning them by name, Lott accused two Democratic freshmen, Tim Johnson of South Dakota and Robert G. Torricelli of New Jersey, of reneging on promises to voters in their 1996 campaigns to support a balanced-budget amendment. Both voted "no."

"This is a question of honesty," Lott said in February, shortly before the vote. "It is a question of truth in government. We wonder why people are cynical, why people wonder about us, why they question us. This is Exhibit A. When you give your word to your constituency in your state during the election campaign . . . and then six months later you say, 'Gee whiz, I have learned something new,' it is hard to take."

Even without the constitutional amendment, Lott went out of his way in early 1997 to indicate a willingness to negotiate a balanced budget with Clinton. Lott's demeanor suggested a determination to avoid repeating the unpleasant experience of the 104th Congress when the House, led by Gingrich, and the Senate, led by Dole, passed their own balanced-budget bill and tried to force Clinton to sign it. When Clinton refused to go along, the resulting stalemate partially shut down the federal government, giving the majority Republicans a public relations headache that lasted into the election season.

The early months of the 105th were marked by a more conscious effort to avoid partisan rancor than was the case in the 104th. Lott has a generally cooperative relationship with Minority Leader Tom Daschle of South Dakota: The two share not only a generational affinity but also a keen understanding of the legislative process based on years as congressional staffers and service in the House before moving up to the Senate.

Despite conservative opposition, Lott in April endorsed a treaty banning production and use of chemical weapons shortly before the Senate ratified it, 74-26.

The next month, the Senate easily endorsed the budget deal, 78-22, after working through more than 50 amendments over a four-day period. Lott had to fight off one amendment that had considerable support: It would have raised the tax on cigarettes by 43 cents a pack and divided the proceeds between deficit reduction and additional health insurance coverage for uninsured children.

Lott called the amendment "clearly a dealbuster," insisting that it would alter the delicate balance between tax cuts and tax increases that budget negotiators had agreed on. If it looked as if the amendment would be adopted, Lott warned, he would pull the budget off the floor. Ultimately Lott's argument prevailed, as the Senate voted 55-45 to table, or kill, the amendment.

In February 1997, Clinton and congressional leaders had met on Capitol Hill and agreed on five priorities for the 105th Congress. The issues included education, juvenile justice, tax cuts, a tax credit for businesses that hire workers from the welfare rolls, and the federal government's responsibility in addressing the financial, educational and public safety woes of the nation's capital. "The atmosphere was the best I've seen it in quite some time," Lott said.

Lott also pledged in the 105th to overhaul the superfund program, which finances the cleanup of toxic waste sites. "Republicans are going to have an environmental agenda," Lott told the U.S. Chamber of Commerce in January, "and I think right at the top of that list is superfund."

He also pushed for legislation allowing businesses to offer workers a choice between overtime pay or time off for hours worked beyond a traditional 40-hour week. The measure also would allow businesses to offer workers "flex-time" schedules. But Lott pulled the bill from the floor in May 1997 after it failed to win the necessary 60 votes to end debate and move to final passage. Democrats and organized labor opposed the measure because they said an unscrupulous employer could use the bill to force employees to take time off rather than money.

Lott's chief of staff, David Hoppe, went to work drafting legislation overhauling the Individuals with Disabilities Education Act, which has had strong bipartisan support in the 21 years since it guaranteed a disabled child's right to a free education and allocated money to help provide it. The law is widely praised for dramatically improving access to education for disabled children. Advocates for the disabled are proud of its record and cautious about making substantive changes to the program. But educators as well as some lawmakers — Republicans in particular — have seized on the need to reauthorize parts of the program as a chance to make sweeping changes. They are particularly interested in giving local school districts more flexibility to reduce costs and to discipline unruly disabled students. Hoppe has drawn praise for his ability to mediate and consider all sides. He has credentials both as a conservative Republican and as the father of a child with Down's syndrome.

And Lott joined Gingrich in telling the National Association of Counties in March that they wanted to turn over more decision-making authority over to the states and counties. "We don't have all the answers in Washington," Lott said. "In fact, we have very few answers here. The best government is the government that is closest to the people. You are where the rubber meets the road."

After the end of the 103rd Congress, Lott had promised Simpson — Dole's choice to remain in the No. 2 slot for the 104th — that he would not run against him for whip, but he changed course and took him on after the 1994 elections made the Republicans the majority party. After defeating Simpson by one vote, 27-26, in November 1994, Lott set his eyes on succeeding Dole as majority leader. Behind the scenes, Lott ran a vigorous campaign for the post for months as Dole launched his presidential run. "[Lott] made it very clear when he was elected whip that he was a candidate for leader," said Robert F. Bennett, R-Utah.

With that, Lott ruffled the feathers of some senators. By moving from Republican Conference secretary to majority whip, Lott jumped over more senior senators, including his rival and fellow Mississippian, Sen. Thad Cochran, who was the Republican Conference chairman. Cochran said that he and Lott met before the election and that he tried to talk Lott out of running for whip. Cochran said he urged Lott to instead support Simpson, a close friend of Cochran's. During that meeting, Cochran said he realized that if Lott ran, his own ambition to be leader someday would be jeopardized.

When Dole left the Senate in June 1996 to concentrate on his presidential campaign, both Lott and Cochran vied to succeed him. Lott cast the race for majority leader as a chance for a more aggressive style of leadership. Cochran presented it as an opportunity for Republican senators to vote against shrill politics and to rebuild public support of Congress. In June, Lott defeated Cochran by a lopsided 44-8 vote, with one abstention.

Although the Republican leadership is dominated by Southerners who share a conservative ideology, Lott also has Judd Gregg of New Hampshire as chief deputy whip and Slade Gorton of Washington as counsel. And after the November 1996 election, he sent a strong signal to Republicans that conservative challenges to centrist GOP chairmen would not be welcomed. Still, he appointed six task forces on education, environment, campaign finance reform, retirement security, health care and the workplace. The heads of the task forces often were more conservative than the committee chairmen who shared jurisdiction.

And along with John Ashcroft of Missouri, Larry E. Craig of Idaho and James M. Jeffords of Vermont, Lott is a member of the Singing Senators quartet, which has serenaded listeners at a variety of party and public functions.

Lott has not been shy about protecting his state's interests. He has threatened to hold up approval of a new surface transportation bill unless the formula governing the distribution of highway aid is changed to give Mississippi a greater share.

During Senate consideration of the fiscal 1995 defense authorization bill, it initially appeared that the Senate would partly reverse one of the Armed Services Committee's most ambitious initiatives — a shift of $601 million that would affect thousands of shipbuilding jobs in Mississippi, Louisiana and California.

At issue was the administration's budget request to spend that amount to buy two "roll on/roll off" cargo ships, large vessels with ramps. The ships would be built in New Orleans and San Diego.

But by a vote of 14-7, the Senate committee had decided to earmark that money instead as a down payment on a $1.4 billion helicopter carrier, designed to haul 2,000 Marines and the helicopters to carry them ashore. This ship would be built by Litton Industries in Mississippi.

The Senate appeared ready to accept an amendment reversing the committee's decision, but Lott and his allies barred final action on the issue, insisting that the Senate first come up with at least partial funding for the helicopter carrier.

In the House from 1973-89, Lott was a key GOP strategist both on the Rules Committee and as minority whip. When he took the No. 2 GOP position in 1981, he was the first Deep South Republican to serve as whip. He was in the vanguard of a younger generation of conservatives, many from Sun Belt states. From 1981 to 1989, Lott was GOP whip under Minority Leader Robert H. Michel of Illinois, and he was tugged between loyalty to Michel, who usually tried to reach accommodation with Democrats on legislation, and kinship with rebellious young conservatives led by Gingrich, with whom Lott had more in common philosophically. Lott typically was loath to cross Michel, a deference to seniority that did not preoccupy Gingrich after he became GOP whip in 1989.

At Home: The 1988 presidential election created a favorable atmosphere for Lott to wage a Senate campaign, and he rose to the occasion. Mississippi, though conservative, was then still traditional Democratic territory that had regularly elected Lott's predecessor, Democratic Sen. John C. Stennis, beginning in 1947. It took a strong campaign for Lott to overcome a skilled opponent, Democratic Rep. Wayne Dowdy, with a solid 54 percent of the vote.

While Dowdy depleted his financial resources to win a tough primary, Lott was free to focus on the fall election. He took the offensive with an early media blitz that Dowdy could not afford to answer for much of the summer. Lott, long identified as a strong supporter of Ronald Reagan's policies, used the airwaves to stress issues that often had been turned against Republicans in the 1980s. To Democrats' dismay, he positioned himself as a champion of Social Security, student loans and public works.

To appeal to rural and blue-collar conservatives often sympathetic to Democrats, Lott stressed his background. Though he had the polished appearance of a blue-suit conservative, Lott reminded voters that his father farmed cotton and drove a school bus. He said Dowdy, whose rumpled appearance and folksy manner belied his family's wealth, was a "millionaire, country-club type."

Dowdy faulted Lott for election-year conversions on issues, and insisted that the Republican was out of step with Mississippi. His late-starting ad campaign included a spot criticizing Lott for having a $50,000 per-year "chauffeur," George Awkward. But Lott blasted the ad, which featured a limousine cruising through the countryside, saying that Awkward was a member of the Capitol security force, funded by a bill Dowdy supported. He added that Awkward showed up for work more often than Dowdy, whose House attendance dropped dramatically during the campaign year.

By summer's end, the sophistication of Lott's effort was apparent, and Democrats were complaining that Dowdy, though a good stump candidate, had an inadequate organization.

But Democrats held out hope that Dowdy's strength might not be apparent until Election Day. Part of that optimism stemmed from his apparent appeal in the black community, which accounts for more than a third of Mississippi's population. While Dowdy was first elected as a champion of the Voting Rights Act, Lott had cast several votes that alienated black leaders, including those against renewal of that act and against the Martin Luther King Jr. holiday.

But Lott came through. In addition to his strong showing among whites, he got a surprising 13 percent of the black vote, according to CBS News-New York Times exit polls.

He was re-elected in 1994 with 69 percent of the vote over an underfunded Democratic challenger, former state Sen. Ken Harper.

Lott suffered a public relations black eye in 1989 when he helped steer the GOP nomination in a Mississippi special House election to a longtime aide rather than to the widow of GOP Rep. Larkin Smith, whose death in a plane crash necessitated the new election. The treatment of Smith's widow was considered by many as brusque and heavy-handed; Republicans lost the House seat Lott had won and held since 1973, and they have failed to regain it.

Lott did not become a Republican until the eve of his first House campaign, in 1972. As Democratic Rep. William M. Colmer's administrative assistant, he had remained a nominal Democrat. But when the venerable Rules chairman — who represented the 5th District — decided to retire in 1972 at age 82, Lott filed in the GOP primary, saying he was "tired of the Muskies and the Kennedys and the Humphreys and the whole lot . . . I will fight against the ever-increasing efforts of the so-called liberals to concentrate more power in the government in Washington."

The wisdom of Lott's switch was soon confirmed. Running that fall against Democrat Ben Stone, chairman of the state Senate Banking Committee, Lott stayed on the offensive by linking Stone with the national Democratic Party. Aided by the Richard M. Nixon landslide and an endorsement from Colmer, Lott carried all but two of the district's 12 counties.

SENATE ELECTIONS

1994 General		
Trent Lott (R)	418,333	(69%)
Ken Harper (D)	189,752	(31%)
1994 Primary		
Trent Lott (R)	72,543	(95%)
Jimmy Ray Bourland (R)	2,023	(3%)
Richard O'Hara (R)	1,453	(2%)

Previous Winning Percentages: **1988** (54%) **1986*** (82%) **1984*** (85%) **1982*** (79%) **1980*** (74%) **1978*** (100%) **1976*** (68%) **1974*** (73%) **1972*** (55%)

** House elections*

KEY VOTES

1997	
Approve balanced-budget constitutional amendment	Y
Approve chemical weapons treaty	Y
1996	
Approve farm bill	Y
Limit punitive damages in product liability cases	Y
Exempt small businesses from higher minimum wage	Y
Approve welfare overhaul	Y
Bar job discrimination based on sexual orientation	N
Override veto of ban on "partial birth" abortions	N
1995	
Approve GOP budget with tax and spending cuts	Y
Approve constitutional amendment barring flag desecration	Y

CAMPAIGN FINANCE

	Receipts	Receipts from PACs	Expend-itures
1994			
Lott (R)	$2,490,825	$1,003,825 (40%)	$2,138,544
Harper (D)	$367,003	$176,399 (48%)	$366,476

VOTING STUDIES

	Presidential Support		Party Unity		Conservative Coalition	
Year	**S**	**O**	**S**	**O**	**S**	**O**
1996	34	66	97	3	97	3
1995	23	77	98	2	100	0
1994	39	58	92	3	97	0
1993	19	79	94	4	98	0
1992	83	17	93	3	97	3
1991	88	10	91	7	93	5

INTEREST GROUP RATINGS

Year	ADA	AFL-CIO	CCUS	ACU
1996	5	n/a	85	100
1995	0	0	100	96
1994	5	0	90	100
1993	5	9	100	92
1992	10	17	90	100
1991	5	27	78	86

1 Roger Wicker (R)

Of Tupelo — Elected 1994, 2nd term

Biographical Information
Born: July 5, 1951, Pontotoc, Miss.
Education: U. of Mississippi, B.S. 1973, J.D. 1975.
Military Service: Air Force, 1976-80; Air Force Reserves, 1980-present.
Occupation: Lawyer; congressional aide.
Family: Wife, Gayle Long; three children.
Religion: Southern Baptist.
Political Career: Miss. Senate, 1987-95.
Capitol Office: 206 Cannon Bldg. 20515; 225-4306.

Committees
Appropriations
Labor, Health & Human Services, Education & Related Agencies; Military Construction; VA, HUD & Independent Agencies

In Washington: Wicker was chosen class president by the freshmen elected in 1994, a group known for its fealty to conservative policies. "We came here on a mission," he said of his class in April 1995. "We've kept our word, we've shifted the direction of debate and we have forever transformed the agenda in this city and for this government."

Yet Wicker, who holds a plum seat on the Appropriations Committee, is not so radical as some of his House peers. A smooth, polished pol, Wicker is happy to pursue change at a pace more incremental than would suit many of his colleagues, and to declare victory at a place short of 100 percent of his original goal.

Wicker does not beat up on President Clinton and decry the way he stopped much of the original GOP agenda through his veto pen. Instead, he celebrates those places where Clinton has had to meet Republicans on terms that would have been unthinkable during the 103rd Congress, as when the president signed the welfare overhaul bill. "Two years ago, there was talk of major government programs like Mrs. Clinton's health care plan," Wicker told constituents in December 1995. "And nobody is talking about that kind of legislation any longer."

In contrast to some other GOP freshmen that winter, Wicker supported Speaker Newt Gingrich's reluctant desire to reopen government services after their partial closure failed to weaken Clinton's resolve in budget negotiations. As the 105th Congress got under way and Gingrich was operating under an ethical cloud, Wicker stood by him and refused to support a reprimand and penalty levied by a vote of the House.

Wicker gave up his class presidency after one year but continued his high-profile cheerleading for the GOP's budget-balancing package and its desire for major cuts in tax rates. Like a number of his classmates, though, Wicker has at times resisted budget-cutting when the target was a program important to his constituents. From his seat on Appropriations, he has evinced the same penchant for pragmatism that was his trademark in the Mississippi state Senate.

"We have dramatically changed the way we do business, but that doesn't mean all federal spending and all programs cease," Wicker said by way of explaining his pursuit of dollars for a flood control project. "If the farmers in Calhoun City are losing land because of flooding and the Corps of Engineers can rectify it, I'm duty-bound to get an appropriation."

In 1995, Wicker joined with other Mississippi Republicans (he once served as staff counsel to Trent Lott, now Senate Majority Leader) in an effort to transfer 1,200 acres of property in his district owned by NASA, plus $10 million in cash, to the state of Mississippi. Wicker and his cohorts maintained that title to the land, which was supposed to have been home to a series of federal projects that were canceled, would appropriately compensate Mississippi for funds presented in anticipation of the failed projects.

When the House considered the fiscal 1996 energy and water development appropriations bill, Wicker opposed a Republican-led effort to kill the Appalachian Regional Commission (ARC). The ARC was created to spur economic development in the 13 states of Appalachia; areas of Wicker's northeastern Mississippi district benefit from the ARC's work. Wicker said his Democratic predecessor, veteran Rep. Jamie L. Whitten, "would be proud of me, and the people who work for economic development in northern Mississippi would be proud of me, too." As a 16-year-old, Wicker had served Whitten as a page.

Wisconsin Republican Scott L. Klug proposed killing all funding for the commission, arguing that it was outdated, but Wicker defended it. "When you start looking at ARC, it's a good product" he said. "It's a little agency with 50 employees. It's a bottom-up approach." Forty Republican freshmen voted against the Klug amendment to kill the agency, which lost 108-319.

Wicker also has supported efforts by appropriators to increase spending on federal highway programs and on airport improvements.

MISSISSIPPI 1
North — Tupelo

Change has slowly crept into this overwhelmingly rural area, awakening the sluggish economy and bringing some jobs and industries that might have been unthinkable to residents 20 years ago.

Once a loyally Democratic district, the area has undergone an economic evolution that has increased Republican white-collar voters. In 1996, Bob Dole carried all but six of the 24 districts that are wholly or partly in the 1st, taking 49 percent of the votes. Wicker solidified his hold on the House seat by getting 68 percent.

In Olive Branch, along the district's northern border with Tennessee, Mazda opened a $20 million parts distribution center in 1996.

Northeastern Mississippi has become a hub for furniture manufacturing, particularly pieces such as recliners. Lee (Tupelo) and Tippah counties rank behind only North Carolina in furniture output. A national furniture market is held twice a year in Tupelo, which is the district's biggest city, with about 34,000 people. Tupelo is still best known as the birthplace of Elvis Presley. The shotgun house where Presley was born is now a tourist attraction.

Another boost to local economic development came with the 1985 opening of the Tennessee-Tombigbee Waterway, a project that longtime Democratic Rep. Jamie L. Whitten and other area legislators strongly advocated. The project has spawned a boom of forestry-related business along the waterway. Small pulp wood and logging companies have sprung up alongside such larger companies as Weyerhaeuser.

The Tenn-Tom cuts through a handful of counties in the northeastern corner of the 1st, connecting the Tennessee and Tombigbee rivers to create an unbroken link to the Gulf of Mexico.

On the western side of the district in Lafayette County is Oxford, site of the University of Mississippi (11,000 students). Popularly known as "Ole Miss," the university is the home of the Center for the Study of Southern Culture. Square Books, on the town square, attracts area literati, including local authors such as Willie Morris and John Grisham. Oxford was the home base for William Faulkner, whose stately home, Rowan Oak, is host to thousands of his admirers each year.

Beyond a handful of built-up areas, the district remains largely rural. It takes in the flat, rich farmland on the edge of the Delta region in northwestern Mississippi and the less fertile plots of the northeastern Hill Country. Although cotton was once the dominant crop in this region, 1st District farmers now also produce soybeans, sweet potatoes, corn, livestock and poultry.

Over the past two decades, the steadiest population growth in the 1st has come in the Memphis, Tenn., suburbs of De Soto County. Population has nearly doubled there since 1970, and De Soto now casts more votes than any other county in the 1st — about 15 percent of the total. White-collar De Soto is unmistakably Republican, having supported GOP presidential candidates since 1976. Dole carried the county with 54 percent of the votes cast in 1996, while Wicker won the county in the House race with 75 percent.

1990 Population: 514,548. White 395,070 (77%), Black 117,126 (23%), Other 2,352 (<1%). Hispanic origin 2,386 (<1%). 18 and over 373,928 (73%), 62 and over 81,130 (16%). Median age: 32.

"Infrastructure spending enables the private sector to create jobs, and that has helped millions of Americans to become taxpayers," Wicker has said. "And it's a heck of a lot better than the government writing someone a check."

Wicker in March 1995 voted against a key plank of the House GOP's "Contract With America," opposing amending the Constitution to limit members' terms in Congress — a stand that separated him from most junior Republicans. A proposal to impose a 12-year service limit in each chamber won a majority in the House, but fell 61 votes short of the two-thirds majority required for passage. But if this was apostasy, Wicker was far from lonely. Three alternative term-limit amendments also considered by the House failed to secure a simple majority. Wicker had the chance to vote against 11 different term limits alternatives in February 1997, and he took advantage of each one.

Wicker, like most members of the Class of 1994, supported a version of the balanced-budget constitutional amendment that would have required a three-fifths majority vote on tax increases. But when that version failed to win approval, Wicker argued that his unhappy classmates should throw their support to a less stringent version. "We just aired our opinions and some people vented their frustrations, but it was important that we did that to see where everybody stood," he said.

Despite some high-profile departures from conservative orthodoxy, Wicker overall is assuredly on the right side of the political spectrum. He helped write Mississippi's strict abortion law and has supported anti-abortion measures at the federal level. Working with Arkansas Republican Jay Dickey, he succeeded in adding a provision to the House's version of the fiscal 1996 spending bill for the Departments of Labor, Education, and Health and Human Services, that prohibited federal funds from being spent on embryo research.

In March 1995, Wicker participated in a Mississippi rally supporting prayer in school, contending that plaintiffs who had filed suit against school prayer "could not have inflicted a deeper wound on the soul of the very core of this community."

As a state senator, Wicker helped push through an education overhaul bill that included a controversial school choice provision, and he actively worked with GOP Gov. Kirk Fordice to pass welfare reform legislation in 1993. But, to the consternation of more ideological conservatives, Wicker supported a 1-cent sales tax increase earmarked for education funding, even to the point of voting with Democrats to override Fordice's veto of the provision.

At Home: Wicker is the first Republican to hold the Mississippi 1st since Reconstruction. For 53 years, the conservative yet historically Democratic district was represented by Whitten, onetime chairman of the Appropriations Committee.

When Whitten retired in 1994, the 1st was ripe for Republican picking. Wicker had to fight his way through a six-person GOP primary and then a runoff against Grant Fox, a former aide to GOP Sen. Thad Cochran. A student body president at the University of Mississippi who went on to become an attorney and state senator, Wicker emphasized his legislative experience and ran a well-financed and tightly organized campaign. He topped the primary field with 27 percent of the vote, then took 53 percent in the runoff against Fox.

In the general election, Wicker faced state Rep. Bill Wheeler, who billed himself as a man of the people, built an energetic grass-roots network and was regarded as having a decent shot at retaining the 1st for Democrats.

But after defeating powerful state House Speaker Tim Ford in a divisive runoff, Wheeler had difficulty reaching out to conservative Democrats. Many of these voters, who usually cast Republican ballots in statewide and national elections, warmed to Wicker's message of reducing the size of government and preserving small-town ideals.

Wicker also benefited from virulent anti-Democratic sentiment and Clinton's low standing in the district. In the end, he won easily, with 63 percent of the vote.

In 1996 he improved to 68 percent over Democrat Henry Boyd Jr.

HOUSE ELECTIONS

1996 General		
Roger Wicker (R)	123,724	(68%)
Henry Boyd Jr. (D)	55,998	(31%)
John A. "Andy" Rouse (LIBERT)	2,281	(1%)
1994 General		
Roger Wicker (R)	80,553	(63%)
Bill Wheeler (D)	47,192	(37%)

CAMPAIGN FINANCE

	Receipts	Receipts from PACs	Expend-itures
1996			
Wicker (R)	$520,547	$273,755 (53%)	$524,101
1994			
Wicker (R)	$745,236	$195,801 (26%)	$729,704
Wheeler (D)	$781,964	$308,496 (39%)	$789,523

DISTRICT VOTE FOR PRESIDENT

	1996		1992
D	78,824 (42%)	D	84,648 (42%)
R	90,596 (49%)	R	101,265 (50%)
I	13,642 (7%)	I	17,979 (9%)

KEY VOTES

1997	
Ban "partial birth" abortions	Y
1996	
Approve farm bill	Y
Deny public education to illegal immigrants	Y
Repeal ban on certain assault-style weapons	Y
Increase minimum wage	N
Freeze defense spending	N
Approve welfare overhaul	Y
1995	
Approve balanced-budget constitutional amendment	Y
Relax Clean Water Act regulations	Y
Oppose limits on environmental regulations	N
Reduce projected Medicare spending	Y
Approve GOP budget with tax and spending cuts	Y

VOTING STUDIES

	Presidential Support		Party Unity		Conservative Coalition	
Year	S	O	S	O	S	O
1996	34	65	96	4	100	0
1995	20	78	96	3	100	0

INTEREST GROUP RATINGS

Year	ADA	AFL-CIO	CCUS	ACU
1996	0	n/a	100	100
1995	0	0	96	80

2 Bennie Thompson (D)

Of Bolton — Elected 1993; 2nd full term

Biographical Information

Born: Jan. 28, 1948, Bolton, Miss.

Education: Tougaloo College, B.A. 1968; Jackson State U., M.S. 1972.

Occupation: Teacher.

Family: Wife, London Johnson; one child.

Religion: Methodist.

Political Career: Hinds County Board of Supervisors, 1980-93; mayor of Bolton, 1973-79; Bolton Board of Aldermen, 1969-73.

Capitol Office: 1408 Longworth Bldg. 20515; 225-5876.

Committees

Agriculture

Department Operations, Nutrition & Foreign Agriculture; General Farm Commodities

Budget

In Washington: Thompson began his political career at age 20, learning the game in a state and local electoral system that was bitterly divided over race.

In the late 1960s, when Thompson began challenging that system, black officeholders were few. Even when a black candidate was elected, white officials sometimes refused to seat the person. "In each instance that I ran for office I had to go to court," Thompson once said.

Since he has been in Congress, Thompson's foremost effort has been to advance and protect minorities. Although not a frequent House orator — he addressed the House only 10 times in the 104th Congress — most of his speeches were directed at issues that had an impact on American minorities. He spoke repeatedly on the benefits of affirmative action, telling the House: "For most of us who are over 45, we never had new textbooks in our community, we never had the opportunity to play in a public playground or swim in a public swimming pool, and so some of us take very seriously the notion of affirmative action because this was the only opportunity that many of us ever received."

And on an even more personal note, he added, "For myself, I wanted to be a lawyer, [but] law school was not an option for me in my state, but nonetheless some other people went. My state went so far as to say we will send you to any school out of state you want to go to as long as you do not want to go to a white school."

Thompson maintains that it was as a result of affirmative action programs and the 1965 Voting Rights Act that he made it to Congress; now he argues for a continuing federal role in seeing that minorities have opportunities to advance.

At the end of the 104th Congress, when Congress cleared an omnibus lands and parks bill, Thompson was able to get funding included for two historically black colleges in Mississippi — his own alma mater, Tougaloo College, and Rust College. The measure included $29 million to rehabilitate and restore historic buildings on the campuses of historically black colleges; Tougaloo received $3 million and Rust $1 million.

Mississippi's 2nd District is one of the poorest in the nation, and Thompson has sought to bring federal money home by helping designate several counties in the Delta area as empowerment zones. He says federal funds have been used to provide job training programs for welfare recipients, to supply capital for small businesses, and to help eliminate drugs from public housing projects.

In a significant and symbolic victory for Southern civil rights activists, Thompson authored two bills in the 103rd Congress that named two Mississippi post offices after leaders in the civil rights movement. The main post office in Jackson is named after the slain civil rights leader, Medgar Evers, and the post office in Ruleville is named after Fannie Lou Hamer. A Mississippi civil rights activist, Hamer was an early mentor to Thompson.

After taking office in 1993, Thompson became a member of the freshman task force on welfare reform, a subject that hits close to home because of his many constituents that live in poverty. Thompson told the House that 40 percent of his constituents receive Aid to Families with Dependent Children [AFDC] and 34 percent receive food stamps.

When Republicans took charge of the House in 1995 and set out their plans for overhauling welfare, Thompson objected every step of the way, complaining that the conservatives' approach would push more children into poverty. He applauded President Clinton's vetoes of two early GOP welfare plans, and was one of his party's unhappy liberals when the president finally agreed to sign a compromise welfare plan Republicans pushed through the House and Senate. Thompson and 97 other Democrats voted "no" on the final welfare bill in July 1996.

Thompson gained a seat on the Budget Committee in the 104th. He arrived on the panel just in time to criticize the GOP's fiscal 1997 budget resolution, which he said included billions in

MISSISSIPPI 2
West central — Mississippi Delta

The 2nd is known both for its rich culture and extreme poverty. The latter has produced an atmosphere that is kinder to Democratic candidates than elsewhere in the state. Bill Clinton took 62 percent here in 1996.

"The Birthplace of the Blues," the Delta was home to many musicians. Muddy Waters was born in Rolling Fork, near Greenville and grew up on a Clarksdale plantation in Coahoma County. Ike Turner and John Lee Hooker are also from Clarksdale, which boasts a blues museum.

Ever since swamp-draining technology and cheap black labor transformed the Delta into an agricultural gold mine in the years after the Civil War, the region has had many more poor rural blacks than affluent white cotton growers.

In the past generation, thousands of Delta blacks, pushed out of work by farm mechanization, moved to Chicago, St. Louis and closer Sun Belt cities such as Little Rock and Memphis.

While a black middle class has always existed in the 2nd, many blacks here live in abject poverty. For years, one of the bleakest pockets was majority-black Tunica County, where half the population lived below the poverty line. This has lessened somewhat with the advent of casino gambling. These days patrons from across the region flock to play in Tunica's casinos, cutting the county's unemployment rate and increasing local government revenues. But some local officials complain that not enough of the gambling money is going back into the county and local citizens have called for increased spending on strapped local schools.

Some residents of the 2nd still make a living off the land. While soybeans has replaced cotton as the largest cash crop, more acreage is devoted to cotton.

More recently, the Delta has become synonymous with "aquaculture" because it produces about 70 percent of the nation's catfish. While the catfish processing industry has provided jobs, many of them are at low wages. Striking workers have gained some concessions from the plant owners. The Catfish Institute, an industry trade group, is based in Belzoni.

The largest city in the 2nd is Greenville, an old riverport and cotton market and the Delta's historical "capital." The city, which has slightly more than 45,000 people and is the seat of Washington County, is one of the few areas of the district that has grown in recent years.

In the southern part of the 2nd, in Warren County, is the city of Vicksburg. It is best known for the Battle of Vicksburg, a 47-day siege in 1863 that resulted in the city's surrender to Union Gen. Ulysses S. Grant. Two regional medical centers are here. And the U.S. Army Corps of Engineers employs about 4,000 people in environmental and water resources projects.

Redistricting for the 1990s added 13 precincts in Jackson, the state capital, to the 2nd. (One more was added just outside the city.) Many of those residents added were poor blacks, leaving more affluent blacks in the more conservative 4th.

1990 Population: 514,845. White 188,309 (37%), Black 324,199 (63%), Other 2,337 (<1%). Hispanic origin 2,731 (1%). 18 and over 345,943 (67%), 62 and over 78,756 (15%). Median age: 29.

spending cuts that would undermine programs providing student loans, job training and other education assistance. "How can individuals break out of poverty through education if they cannot afford to enroll in school or receive job training?" Thompson asked the House.

He also railed against the GOP's plans to reduce the projected growth rate of spending on Medicare, accusing Republicans of cutting costs in that program so as to provide tax breaks. "The Republican plan to cut $270 billion out of Medicare is a cruel and devastating attack on our mothers and grandmothers," Thompson said. "Do you really think that your rich friends need a tax cut this much? I do not think so."

Thompson also has a seat on the Agriculture Committee, where he works to protect his district's interests. Important crops in the 2nd are soybeans and cotton, and much of the nation's catfish are raised here. He voted in 1996 for the Republican-backed "Freedom to Farm" bill, which phased out most New Deal-era crop subsidies, replacing them with a system of fixed, but declining, payments that farmers would receive over seven years regardless of market prices or their planting decisions.

Thompson took to the House floor in 1993 to express his concern over what he saw as attacks on the 1965 Voting Rights Act. The Supreme Court issued a ruling in June 1993 questioning the practice of drawing districts along racial lines in order to elect more minorities. He told the House: "This struggle for redistricting is one where unless we have constitutional guarantees such as the Voting Rights Act, minorities and women and others will not have the protection necessary."

At Home: Thompson was educated in segregated elementary and secondary schools in Mississippi. As a student at Tougaloo College, he met civil rights activist Hamer, who inspired him to pursue a career in politics.

At 20, he ran for alderman in his native Bolton.

He won but was denied a seat by white officials until a court order forced the town to relent. Four years later, he was elected mayor of Bolton, and at 32, he took a seat on the Board of Supervisors for Hinds County, which includes the capital, Jackson.

Thompson has solidified some of the gains made by blacks in their ongoing struggle for power in Mississippi. The House seat he won in a 1993 special election had been held by Mike Espy, who in 1986 became the state's first black in Congress since Reconstruction. Espy resigned in January 1993 to become secretary of Agriculture, a post he held through 1994.

Unlike Espy, Thompson was not seen as a candidate with broad appeal both to blacks and to moderate and conservative whites in the 2nd. His participation in the state's civil rights battles over the past generation made him less attractive to some whites. The 2nd is 63 percent black.

In the 1993 special election, Thompson was thought to have suffered somewhat in the free-for-all Democratic field of contenders in the initial voting in March. Republican Hayes Dent, an adviser to GOP Gov. Kirk Fordice, had finished first in that test with 34 percent. Thompson ran second with 28 percent; in third place, with 20 percent, was Espy's brother, Henry, the mayor of Clarksdale.

With just two weeks to the runoff, campaigning was intense. Unfavorable publicity plagued both candidates. Dent had to answer for a simple-assault conviction from 1983. Stories were revived from the 1980s about whether Thompson's friendship with a state official had helped to prevent an investigation into Thompson's practices as a Hinds County supervisor. But the stories did not prevent Thompson from uniting and galvanizing blacks, who make up 58 percent of the 2nd's voting-age population. Turnout was considered high for a special election (more than 130,000 votes were cast). Thompson won with 55 percent to Dent's 45 percent.

In his 1994 re-election contest, Thompson, who has drawn criticism for his sometimes abrasive style, faced Republican Bill Jordan, a black attorney and ordained minister. Jordan ran a decently funded campaign (spending almost $280,000) and drew support from conservative black voters and whites who reside in agricultural areas such as Washington and Leflore counties. Thompson, spending slightly more than $395,000, ended up winning by 15 points, 54 percent to 39 percent, as a conservative third-party candidate took 7 percent.

In 1996, Republicans tried again with a black nominee: Danny Covington, who was an aide to former 2nd District Rep. Webb Franklin (1983-87), a white Republican. But Covington was swimming against a strong Democratic tide in the district, which gave Clinton 62 percent of its presidential votes. Thompson ran just behind that pace, winning re-election with 60 percent of the vote.

HOUSE ELECTIONS

1996 General		
Bennie Thompson (D)	102,503	(60%)
Danny Covington (R)	65,263	(38%)
William Chipman III (LIBERT)	4,167	(2%)
1994 General		
Bennie Thompson (D)	68,014	(54%)
Bill Jordan (R)	49,270	(39%)
Vince Thornton (MSTAX)	9,408	(7%)

Previous Winning Percentages: 1993† (55%)

† *Special election*

CAMPAIGN FINANCE

	Receipts	Receipts from PACs	Expend-itures
1996			
Thompson (D)	$428,872	$214,075 (50%)	$361,452
Covington (R)	$224,096	$44,066 (20%)	$215,943
1994			
Thompson (D)	$418,006	$220,852 (53%)	$396,502
Jordan (R)	$279,521	$22,897 (8%)	$279,234
Thornton (MSTAX)	$11,761	$350 (3%)	$11,842

DISTRICT VOTE FOR PRESIDENT

1996		1992	
D	104,725 (62%)	**D**	105,052 (58%)
R	58,363 (34%)	**R**	66,350 (37%)
I	5,751 (3%)	**I**	9,805 (5%)

KEY VOTES

1997	
Ban "partial birth" abortions	N
1996	
Approve farm bill	Y
Deny public education to illegal immigrants	N
Repeal ban on certain assault-style weapons	N
Increase minimum wage	Y
Freeze defense spending	N
Approve welfare overhaul	N
1995	
Approve balanced-budget constitutional amendment	N
Relax Clean Water Act regulations	N
Oppose limits on environmental regulations	Y
Reduce projected Medicare spending	N
Approve GOP budget with tax and spending cuts	N

VOTING STUDIES

	Presidential Support		Party Unity		Conservative Coalition	
Year	**S**	**O**	**S**	**O**	**S**	**O**
1996	80	19	88	9	59	33
1995	82	16	94	5	26	74
1994	86	12	88	3	36	61
1993	71†	22†	87†	3†	14†	81†

† *Not eligible for all recorded votes.*

INTEREST GROUP RATINGS

Year	ADA	AFL-CIO	CCUS	ACU
1996	90	n/a	25	5
1995	95	100	8	8
1994	80	88	36	20
1993	94†	100†	20†	6†

† *Not eligible for all recorded votes.*

3 Charles W. 'Chip' Pickering Jr. (R)

Of Laurel — Elected 1996, 1st term

Biographical Information

Born: Aug. 10, 1963, Laurel, Miss.

Education: Mississippi College, 1981-82; U. of Mississippi, B.A. 1986; Baylor U., M.B.A. 1989.

Occupation: Congressional aide; USDA official.

Family: Wife, Leisha Jane Prather; four children.

Religion: Baptist.

Political Career: No previous office.

Capitol Office: 427 Cannon Bldg. 20515; 225-5031.

Committees

Agriculture
Forestry, Resource Conservation & Research; Livestock, Dairy & Poultry

Science
Basic Research; Space & Aeronautics

Transportation & Infrastructure
Aviation; Surface Transportation

The Path to Washington: Pickering arrived in the House with more contacts on Capitol Hill than the typical freshman. He worked for Senate Majority Leader Trent Lott before running for the 3rd District seat in 1996.

Throughout his campaign, Pickering stressed his bonds to the influential Mississippi Republican hierarchy in Washington, including Lott, senior Sen. Thad Cochran and outgoing Republican National Committee Chairman Haley Barbour.

The district, which stretches from the suburbs of the state capital, Jackson, eastward to the Alabama border, had been represented for 15 terms by a conservative Democrat, G.V. "Sonny" Montgomery.

When Montgomery announced his intention to step down, Republicans coveted the seat, hoping that the district's increasingly Republican-leaning voters would be willing to substitute a conservative Republican for a conservative Democrat.

As if to underscore the depth of the Republican Party's strength in the district, nine candidates, including Pickering, plunged into the March Republican primary, while only three Democrats entered their party's race. It was a reversal from earlier decades in the South, when Democratic primaries were the more competitive of the two.

Pickering left his position as an aide to Lott to jump into the race. Although he was only 32 years old, Pickering's extensive ties to powerful figures in Washington and in Mississippi helped him gain a fundraising lead and run early television advertisements.

Pickering's name also resonated in the district and across the state. A generation earlier, his father, Charles Pickering Sr., now a federal judge, had been a key player in the rebirth of the Mississippi Republican Party. Barbour had been executive director when Charles Pickering Sr. chaired the state Republican Party.

The Pickering-Barbour connection resurfaced in 1996: Barbour's nephew, Henry Barbour, served as the younger Pickering's campaign manager.

Though he was the top vote-getter in the primary, Pickering ended up in an April runoff with Bill Crawford, a former state representative. In the runoff, Pickering claimed that he was the truer conservative, and he criticized Crawford for having supported Democrat Ray Mabus in the state's 1987 gubernatorial contest.

Crawford, meanwhile, presented himself as the truer Mississippian and charged that Pickering had raised much of his money from outside the state.

Pickering defeated Crawford and moved on to face Democrat John Arthur Eaves Jr., a lawyer who had also grown up in a political family. His father, John Arthur Eaves Sr., twice ran for governor of Mississippi.

As in the primary, both candidates touted their conservative values, including their support of gunowners' rights and opposition to abortion. Again, Pickering stressed his connections in Washington, and once more he overcame charges that he was an outsider unfamiliar with issues important to Mississippi.

He defeated Eaves convincingly, pulling in 61 percent of the vote.

Pickering had worked on telecommunications issues as an aide to Lott, and he sought a prized seat on the House Commerce Committee.

But instead, he is serving on the Agriculture and Transportation and Infrastructure committees, both of which should be useful assignments for the 3rd District. He also got a seat on the Science Committee.

Pickering was only 3 years old when Montgomery, known as a champion of veterans' issues, was first elected to Congress. Pickering said he hopes to serve with the same dignity and values espoused by his predecessor.

But he stressed different themes, saying that while Montgomery's generation focused on the challenge of fighting the Cold War, he hoped to focus more on issues like telecommunications in order to improve economic development in his district.

MISSISSIPPI 3
East central — Meridian

The 3rd combines east Mississippi Hill Country with suburbs of the city of Jackson in Rankin County. Although former Democratic Rep. G.V. "Sonny" Montgomery (1967-1997) won re-election here with ease, all the building blocks of this district — the rural areas, the small cities and especially the Jackson suburbs — are fertile ground for GOP candidates. In presidential voting, the 3rd is one of the most Republican districts in the country. So Pickering's easy election to the House in 1996 came as no surprise.

Nearly one-fifth of the total district vote is cast in Rankin County, one of the state's fastest-growing areas since 1980. The white-collar professionals here, most of whom have jobs in and around the state capital of Jackson, are among the most faithful Republican voters in the South.

In 1991, Rankin was instrumental in making Kirk Fordice the state's first Republican governor since Reconstruction. Four years later the county gave him a huge margin in his landslide re-election. In the 1996 presidential race, Rankin cast the state's highest percentage for Bob Dole (69 percent).

Due east of Rankin on the Alabama border is Lauderdale County (Meridian), the district's second most populous. During the Civil War, Meridian housed a confederate arsenal and military hospital. General William Tecumseh Sherman and his troops destroyed the city in February 1864, but it quickly rebounded. Today Meridian is an industrial city with Lockheed and General Motors facilities. The Meridian Naval Air Station, 15 miles northeast of the city, trains naval pilots. The station appeared on the Pentagon's 1995 base closing list, but was spared from closure. There are also two Air National Guard facilities in the area. Lauderdale County was just a step behind Rankin in loyalty to Dole, giving him 61 percent of the vote.

In the center of the 3rd is one of Mississippi's most infamous locales: the Neshoba County seat of Philadelphia. Three civil rights workers were murdered near there in 1964. The annual Neshoba County fair is a must stop for any Mississippi politician. In presidential election years, even White House aspirants have been known to include the fair on their itineraries.

In the northeastern corner of the district, Oktibbeha County (Starkville) hosts Mississippi State University and its 13,600 students. Neighboring Lowndes County is the district's third biggest. Columbus, the county seat, is home to the Mississippi University for Women, the nation's first state-supported institution of higher learning for women. Columbus also is the birthplace of playwright Tennessee Williams, and it has more than 100 antebellum homes, some of which are open for viewing each April.

Columbus also has a major Air Force base that provides basic training for prospective pilots, and the military-related population helps boost the GOP in Lowndes County. Dole won 56 percent of the county's presidential vote.

The rest of the district is mostly rural and agricultural. There are a significant number of poultry and poultry-processing businesses, as well as timber companies and oil and gas industries.

1990 Population: 515,314. White 345,115 (67%), Black 161,458 (31%), Other 8,741 (2%). Hispanic origin 2,901 (1%). 18 and over 370,290 (72%), 62 and over 75,457 (15%). Median age: 31.

HOUSE ELECTIONS

1996 General		
Charles W. "Chip" Pickering Jr. (R)	115,443	(61%)
John Arthur Eaves Jr. (D)	68,658	(36%)
Lamen Clemons (I)	2,502	(1%)
1996 Primary Runoff		
Charles W. "Chip" Pickering Jr. (R)	23,939	(56%)
Bill Crawford (R)	18,463	(44%)
1996 Primary		
Charles W. "Chip" Pickering Jr. (R)	15,293	(27%)
Bill Crawford (R)	13,849	(24%)
Mike Gunn (R)	9,958	(18%)
Dutch Dabbs (R)	6,576	(12%)
Dean Kirby (R)	5,077	(9%)
Keith Heard (R)	2,671	(5%)
Jim Yonge (R)	1,546	(3%)
Harold Cross (R)	1,062	(2%)
Michael Lang (R)	690	(1%)

CAMPAIGN FINANCE

	Receipts	Receipts from PACs	Expend-itures
1996			
Pickering (R)	$1,175,126	$430,521 (37%)	$1,167,906
Eaves (D)	$667,780	$16,000 (2%)	$667,567

DISTRICT VOTE FOR PRESIDENT

1996		1992	
D	66,011 (36%)	D	67,552 (34%)
R	107,118 (58%)	R	117,313 (58%)
I	9,786 (5%)	I	16,158 (8%)

KEY VOTES

1997

Ban "partial birth" abortions Y

4 Mike Parker (R)

Of Brookhaven — Elected 1988, 5th term

Biographical Information
Born: Oct. 31, 1949, Laurel, Miss.
Education: William Carey College, B.A. 1970.
Occupation: Funeral director.
Family: Wife, Rosemary Prather; three children.
Religion: Presbyterian.
Political Career: No previous office.
Capitol Office: 2445 Rayburn Bldg. 20515; 225-5865.

Committees
Appropriations
Energy & Water Development; Military Construction
Budget

In Washington: The lead-up to Parker's long-anticipated switch to the Republican Party in November 1995 resembled the dance of the seven veils, as Parker slowly shed every last vestige of his former Democratic clothing.

Parker was rewarded for his move in March 1996 when Republicans created a new slot for him on the Appropriations Committee. Parker is a longtime friend of Budget Committee Chairman John R. Kasich, R-Ohio, and he retains his seat on that panel as a Republican.

As a Democrat on the Budget Committee in 1995, Parker was the only member of his party to support the GOP's budget-balancing blueprint or its implementing legislation. He consulted with Kasich and committee Republicans in their drafting sessions and found himself shut out of closed-door Democratic meetings.

He announced his frustration with the Democratic leadership on the first day of the 104th Congress, when he voted "present" rather than support the bid of Democratic leader Richard A. Gephardt of Missouri for Speaker. Parker said when the Democratic Caucus "wanted the same leadership that got us into this mess, I didn't have a choice." Arms folded tightly in front of him, Parker added, "If you want to go on a boat ride, you don't get the captain of the Titanic to take you out."

Parker's support for the Democratic position on floor votes, which had never been high, plunged dramatically with the GOP takeover of the House. In addition to his votes for the Republican spending and tax cut package, he was one of only four Democrats to support the plan to suppress the growth of Medicare and one of only six Democrats to vote for a preliminary $17 billion package of spending cuts.

The clean water act revisions led to another public rift Parker had with the Democratic leadership. In June 1995, Parker and three other conservative Democrats — W.J. "Billy" Tauzin and Jimmy Hayes of Louisiana and Greg Laughlin of Texas — resigned from the Democratic Congressional Campaign Committee (DCCC) to protest one of its mailings that included a cartoon lampooning GOP-led efforts to rewrite the clean water bill. The cartoon depicted an overweight buffoon representing "pollution lobbies" with his arm around a "good ol' boy" representing Congress. The pair were quaffing a toast under the caption "Let Them Drink Perrier." Parker and his three Democratic colleagues had been involved in helping Republicans draft the clean water legislation. (By the end of 1995, all four had switched to the GOP.) In July, Parker returned more than $16,000 his campaign fund had received from the Democratic National Committee and the DCCC.

Also in July, Parker was a guest on House Speaker Newt Gingrich's National Empowerment Television show, where he said, "I'm a little more conservative than a lot of Republicans." And later that month, Parker resigned from the so-called "blue dog" coalition, a group of nearly two dozen mostly conservative Democrats that formed in early 1995 to pull their party toward the center. Parker said the coalition had been too willing to compromise with liberal Democratic leaders.

When at last he officially joined the Republican Party in November, Parker said, "Although I am not naive enough to believe the Republican Party has all the answers, I do believe it is more in line with the thoughts and beliefs of the people of Mississippi and the people of this country than my former party," Parker said. During his long period of conversion, he said Republicans "paid attention to me, and that is a lot more than I have gotten from the Democrats."

Parker frequently suggested the Democratic leadership had lacked the gumption to discipline him. "I cannot find Democrats who are strong enough or who have the courage of their convictions to kick me out." But it quickly became clear that Parker had been wise to milk his party switching moment for all it was worth — which in his case included a front-page profile in the Washington Post and dogged attention from GOP leaders. Once he made the leap, he seemed to

MISSISSIPPI 4
Southwest — Jackson

The 4th holds a mixture of old Southern charm and New South savvy. Natchez, with a population of just over 19,000, sits on the banks of the Mississippi River in Adams County and embodies the old South. Dripping with Spanish moss, it is home to 500 antebellum mansions ever-popular with tourists.

In the recession of the late 1980s and early 1990s, the southwestern counties of the 4th were hit hard. Although its oil and gas industry suffered, Natchez's economy stayed afloat with other enterprises, with tourism topping the list. The small river city and its antebellum homes attract 150,000 people a year. Other residents find work in the timber industry in such businesses as wood processing and paper production. One such facility in Brookhaven in Lincoln County converts logs into wood chips.

North of Natchez is Jackson, the state capital, in Hinds County. Burned during the Civil War, Jackson has since grown to become the state's largest city, with nearly 200,000 people. Jackson is home to many of the state GOP's financial kingpins. But Bill Clinton carried Hinds County in 1996 with 54 percent of the votes, becoming the first Democratic presidential candidate to win there since 1956.

However, Bob Dole beat Clinton in the 4th District's portion of Hinds, 50 percent to 46 percent. Redistricting for the 1990s had moved less-affluent black sections of Jackson into the 2nd District, leaving the more well-to-do and more conservative black sections of the city in the 4th. Overall, about 56 percent of the city's population is black.

About 40 percent of the 4th District's residents live in Hinds County. Most of the rest hail from rural and small-town areas that have historically been Democratic but are politically and culturally conservative. About 150 miles south of Jackson is the small town of Ovett, where two lesbians brought on the wrath of townspeople when they made plans to start Camp Sister Spirit, a lesbian retreat.

The map for the 1990s gave the 4th most of Republican-leaning Jones County, including the industrial city of Laurel, population 19,000. It has timber-related industry fueled by trees from Mississippi's Piney Woods, and the poultry business is big. Dole got 57 percent of the vote in the district's portion of Jones County in 1996, helping him carry the 4th by 2 percentage points. In the House race, Parker had some fall-out after switching to the GOP, but still won easily with 61 percent.

1990 Population: 513,853. White 301,976 (59%), Black 209,352 (41%), Other 2,225 (<1%). Hispanic origin 2,135 (<1%). 18 and over 367,753 (72%), 62 and over 81,456 (16%). Median age: 32.

fade into the woodwork of the majority.

Parker was active in the 104th in espousing the Parental Rights Act, which he jointly proposed with Oklahoma Republican Steve Largent.

Parker said the legislation was needed because "There is an overzealous bureaucracy that has taken children out of their homes when it shouldn't have happened." The bill, which was a plank in the Christian Coalition's "Contract With the American Family" platform, calls for "clear and convincing evidence" of child abuse before any governmental agency could intervene in a parent-child relationship. Among the parental rights that would be protected under the bill are home education, medical decisions and corporal punishment.

Child advocacy groups are wary of the proposal, fearing it could shield abusive parents. Parker disputes that, and as evidence of his concern for children he cites his personal commitment to helping troubled youths: Testifying before a Judiciary subcommittee in October 1995, Parker said he and his wife have taken in more than a dozen foster children over the past 25 years. But the bill's prospects flagged and eventually expired when anti-abortion groups lined up against it, fearing it would prompt more parents to force their children to have abortions.

Parker has gone to bat against the Department of Energy in behalf of a company in his district, Magnatek, Inc., that employs 1,300 making magnetic ballasts. Parker offered a successful amendment to the fiscal 1996 Interior spending bill to block a rule proposed by DOE that would ban the production and sale of magnetic ballasts, which are used to regulate the amount of electric current flowing into a fluorescent light bulb. According to Parker, the aim of the regulation is to prod manufacturers into producing another kind of ballast — the electronic version — because that technology conserves more energy.

Parker also sought to protect the economy of his district when he joined with other Cotton Belt legislators in writing to Gingrich that the GOP's proposed overhaul of federal agriculture policies would hurt their farmers. The bill was amended in favor of cotton interests and Parker supported the final package.

Parker joined with Sen. Trent Lott, R-Miss., to introduce legislation to require the Army Corps of Engineers to stabilize sections of the Natchez Bluffs overlooking the Mississippi River. The bluffs are made of a fine, powdery soil that virtually liquifies when it becomes wet. Water has apparently infiltrated the special loose soil and caused numerous mudslides.

Parker, who sat on the Transportation and Infrastructure Committee as a Democrat, argued against legislation that dropped federal speed limit and motorcycle helmet requirements. He had cleaned up numerous bodies in his work as a funeral home director and pooh-poohed the arguments that dropping the safety regulations was about freedom. "Everyone likes to talk about freedom," he said. "I found out long ago that the ultimate form of freedom is death."

At Home: Parker's district director commented during the 104th about the difficulty conservative Southern Democrats face in reconciling the desires of their socially conservative "yellow dog" constituents with the aspirations of new black voters. Liberated from that dilemma by his party switch, Parker in 1996 won easily in his first run as a Republican.

Democrats were disappointed that Parker drew no primary opposition, and in November they saw him handily turn aside a black challenger, former Hinds County public works official Kevin Antoine. Antoine cut into the black vote that had fattened Parker's wins as a Democrat, but the newly minted Republican beat him by a 25 point margin.

Parker was a political novice when he began his 1988 campaign for the open 4th — yet he won 55 percent even as George Bush carried the district for president. TV ads early on helped distinguish Parker from more than a dozen contenders, Democrats and Republicans, after Democratic Rep. Wayne Dowdy began a Senate bid. Parker ran second in the primary to Jackson attorney Brad Pigott, who had better party ties. In the runoff, Parker stormed past Pigott with endorsements from the third- and fourth-place primary finishers.

Parker's GOP foe, Thomas Collins, was a POW in Vietnam and was director of the Mississippi Veterans Farm and Home Board. Collins tried to tie Parker to Democratic presidential nominee Michael S. Dukakis, but Parker's ads disassociated him from his party's standard-bearer. That galled some local Democrats, but by stressing the need for "business principles" in Washington, Parker added to his rural base the votes of many business-oriented Republicans in Hinds County.

In the 1994 Democratic primary, Parker drew a challenge from his left by state Treasurer Marshall Bennett. But Parker ran TV ads featuring his mother and a cow, noting his commitment to conservative values. Bennett took 35 percent and a minor candidate 7 percent as Parker won renomination with 58 percent.

HOUSE ELECTIONS

1996 General		
Mike Parker (R)	112,444	(61%)
Kevin Antoine (D)	66,836	(36%)
Kenneth "K.W." Welch (I)	2,262	(1%)
1994 General		
Mike Parker (D)	82,939	(68%)
Mike Wood (R)	38,200	(32%)

Previous Winning Percentages: 1992 (67%) **1990** (81%) **1988** (55%)

VOTING STUDIES

	Presidential Support		Party Unity		Conservative Coalition	
Year	**S**	**O**	**S**	**O**	**S**	**O**
1996	37	62	94	5	98	0
1995†	23	74	94	3	92	5
1994	64	31	59	36	100	0
1993	67	33	59	38	93	5
1992	63	36	62	37	88	13
1991	58	41	50	47	95	3

† Parker switched to the Republican party on Nov. 10, 1995. As a Democrat in 1995 he was eligible for 113 presidential support votes, 566 party unity votes, and 105 conservative coalition votes. As a Republican in 1995 he was eligible for 20 presidential support votes, 69 party unity votes, and six conservative coalition votes. His 1995 scores include votes he cast both as a Democrat and a Republican.

DISTRICT VOTE FOR PRESIDENT

	1996		1992
D	83,425 (46%)	**D**	84,089 (41%)
R	86,880 (48%)	**R**	102,666 (51%)
I	9,611 (5%)	**I**	16,744 (8%)

CAMPAIGN FINANCE

	Receipts	Receipts from PACs	Expend-itures
1996			
Parker (R)	$384,108	$185,638 (48%)	$288,719
Antoine (D)	$44,597	$12,500 (28%)	$44,420
1994			
Parker (D)	$617,819	$284,546 (46%)	$672,593
Wood (R)	$14,022	$264 (2%)	$13,239

KEY VOTES

1997	
Ban "partial birth" abortions	Y
1996	
Approve farm bill	Y
Deny public education to illegal immigrants	Y
Repeal ban on certain assault-style weapons	Y
Increase minimum wage	N
Freeze defense spending	N
Approve welfare overhaul	Y
1995	
Approve balanced-budget constitutional amendment	Y
Relax Clean Water Act regulations	Y
Oppose limits on environmental regulations	N
Reduce projected Medicare spending	Y
Approve GOP budget with tax and spending cuts	Y

INTEREST GROUP RATINGS

Year	ADA	AFL-CIO	CCUS	ACU
1996	0	n/a	100	100
1995	10	0	88	63
1994	20	50	83	67
1993	20	33	73	67
1992	30	25	88	68
1991	20	33	80	75

5 Gene Taylor (D)

Of Bay St. Louis — Elected 1989; 4th full term

Biographical Information

Born: Sept. 17, 1953, New Orleans, La.

Education: Tulane U., B.A. 1976; U. of Southern Mississippi, Gulf Park, 1978-80.

Military Service: Coast Guard Reserve, 1971-84.

Occupation: Sales representative.

Family: Wife, Margaret Gordon; three children.

Religion: Roman Catholic.

Political Career: Bay St. Louis City Council, 1981-83; Miss. Senate, 1983-89; Democratic nominee for U.S. House, 1988.

Capitol Office: 2447 Rayburn Bldg. 20515; 225-5772.

Committees

National Security
Merchant Marine; Military Personnel (ranking); Military Readiness

Transportation & Infrastructure
Surface Transportation; Water Resources & Environment

In Washington: Taylor performs the unusual feat of being a burr under the saddle of both parties' leaders in the House.

A founding member of the "Blue Dog" coalition, a group of Democratic conservatives, Taylor has scored his own party as insufficiently devoted to a balanced budget. When the 104th Congress convened in January 1995, Taylor refused to support the House Democratic leader, Richard A. Gephardt of Missouri, in the election for Speaker. Instead, he voted "present" (as did his Mississippi colleague Mike Parker, who later in the 104th left the Democratic Party and joined the GOP).

In May 1995, Taylor expressed frustration with what he saw as his leadership's failure to present alternatives to the Republican agenda, and he said he might call for new leadership elections if the existing team did not become more proactive. "It's not enough to be against what the other guys are doing," Taylor said.

But there is also no love lost between Taylor and House Speaker Newt Gingrich. When the 105th Congress convened in January 1997, Taylor criticized the resolution reprimanding Gingrich for violating House ethics rules because he felt it should have specified that Gingrich pay the $300,000 penalty levied against him out of personal funds, not campaign coffers or a legal expense fund.

"The Speaker used funds from tax-exempt organizations to promote his political agenda," Taylor told the House. "If a member violates the rules of the House, the member, not their campaign, should be held responsible for whatever fine is levied." Taylor was one of two Democrats voting against the resolution of reprimand.

Taylor's contrariness toward Gephardt early in the 104th fueled speculation that he might join Parker and the other conservative Democrats who switched to the GOP in 1995. By year's end, five Blue Dogs had bolted from the Democratic Party. But as his willingness to criticize Gingrich indicates, Taylor is not a likely GOP convert, despite his conservative views. In fact, his unhappiness with both parties led him once to suggest that he would forsake major-party labels altogether. "I have ruled out a move to the Republican Party," Taylor told the newspaper Roll Call in October 1995. "I have not ruled out a move to a third party."

During the budget battles of 1995, Taylor complained that the Democratic leadership was ignoring party members from fiscally conservative constituencies who put a premium on balancing the budget. "I think our leadership is very busy still trying to end the Vietnam War," Taylor said. "They are stuck in 1975. Someone needs to tell those guys it's 1995."

Taylor also saw red when the Blue Dogs' effort to offer a middle-ground proposal to overhaul the Medicare program was rebuffed by both parties. The coalition's proposal would have squeezed about $170 billion out of projected Medicare costs over seven years — a middle ground between the $270 billion reduction in the Republican bill and the $89 billion trim proposed by Democrats. The Blue Dog plan would have preserved funds the GOP wanted to cut for rural hospitals, but it allowed changes in the Part B fund that covers doctor bills, an idea the Democratic leadership resisted.

Both parties blocked the coalition from offering its alternative when Medicare was considered on the floor in October 1995. The GOP leadership had pushed through a rule for floor debate that barred the coalition's alternative; the Democratic leadership refused to attach the Blue Dog proposal to its motion to recommit the Medicare bill to committee.

"I am furious," said Taylor. "The Republicans came to power promising change, open rules." Then he added: "I've ruled out a move to the Republicans. They are no more fair than the Democrats."

Taylor was also not shy about taking on President Clinton and Gingrich in early 1995 when Clinton initiated a plan to rescue Mexico's failing economy by saying he would offer the country $20 billion in loan guarantees. The Republican leadership backed Clinton's plan, but

MISSISSIPPI 5
Southeast — Gulf Coast; Hattiesburg

At the core of the 5th's economy is defense-related industry, so much so that it would be hard to imagine the district without it.

Some observers estimate that at least half the district's residents have some connection to one of these enterprises. The 5th is home to the state's biggest private employer, Ingalls Shipbuilding, a division of Litton Industries, located in Pascagoula (Jackson County). It employs about 10,000 people.

In 1992, the city of 26,000 saw the opening of Naval Station Pascagoula at Singing River Island. The facility employs about 1,200 military personnel and 160 civilians.

The Gulf Coast counties, with their white sand beaches, resort cities and dockside casino gambling establishments, bear little resemblance to the rest of the state. The Harrison County cities of Gulfport and Biloxi attract thousands of tourists each year. The area is also home to gulf shrimpers and seafood-processing plants. Gulfport is the site of the annual four-day Mississippi Deep Sea Fishing Rodeo held during the week of July 4.

Biloxi is also home of Keesler Air Force Base, the premier training center for the Air Force and one of the four largest bases in the country. Keesler employs about 6,900 military personnel and about 4,000 civilians, and specializes in communications, electronics and medical training. Beauvoir, the last home of Jefferson Davis, the president of the Confederacy, is also in Biloxi.

In neighboring Hancock County is the Stennis Space Center, named for the late Sen. John C. Stennis, who represented the state from 1947 to 1989. The center, a division of NASA, tests rocket engines.

Hattiesburg, the seat of Forrest County, is the sole population center in the northern part of the 5th. The leading employer in the predominantly white-collar town is the University of Southern Mississippi, with 12,000 students.

The tier of counties above the coast — George, Stone, Pearl River, Greene, Perry, Forrest and Lamar — are part of the poorer Piney Woods region, where the economy is driven by the production of wood products, poultry and dairy farming.

In addition, the textile industry has also been a significant employer in rural portions of the district.

Mississippi's long-dormant Republican Party made its initial inroads in the 5th, a solidly conservative region where Democrats are no longer competitive in national elections. Ronald Reagan carried Mississippi in 1980 only because of a 30,000-vote edge in the 5th. Bob Dole easily beat Bill Clinton in the district in 1996, by 56 percent to 35 percent.

Yet while the district has been a GOP beachhead, it is not impregnable. That was made clear by Taylor's special election victory in 1989, his smashing re-election win in 1990 (81 percent of the vote) and his comfortable victories in 1992, 1994 and 1996.

1990 Population: 514,656. White 402,991 (78%), Black 102,922 (20%), Other 8,743 (2%). Hispanic origin 5,778 (1%). 18 and over 368,541 (72%), 62 and over 69,164 (13%). Median age: 31.

many in the rank and file of both parties were against it.

Taylor introduced a resolution in February 1995 calling for an investigation of Clinton's Mexico aid plan. Gingrich issued a parliamentary ruling that blocked the resolution from coming before the House, but Taylor forced a floor vote by appealing the ruling.

Such procedural votes are the cornerstone of the Speaker's power to run the House, and members of the majority party rarely oppose their Speaker's ruling. But some Republicans saw the vote as an opportunity to register opposition to Clinton's Mexico policy. The House upheld Gingrich, 288-143, but 14 Republicans voted against the Speaker. Taylor said he offered the resolution "to demand of the comptroller general the information as to whether or not what President Clinton did last week, when he guaranteed the loan to bail out Wall Street, to bail out the Mexican peso, whether or not that was even legal."

From his seat on the National Security Committee, where he will serve in the 105th as the ranking member on the Military Personnel Subcommittee, Taylor looks after the defense establishment in his Gulf Coast district. The 5th is home to the Naval Station Pascagoula and Ingalls Shipbuilding, the state's largest private employer. Taylor has backed GOP efforts to allocate more money to the Pentagon than Clinton has requested. In 1996, he voted against an effort to freeze defense spending at the prior year level.

Taylor also serves on the committee's Merchant Marine subcommittee, where he looks out for the interests of the shipbuilders, shrimpers and fishermen of his district. Taylor has worked to support the U.S. shipbuilding industry and weaken the influence of foreign shipbuilders. He voted against a measure approved by the House in June 1996 that would implement an international agreement on shipbuilding, even though the House had approved an amendment to extend loan guarantees for U.S. shipbuilders for three years.

Taylor said the original agreement — signed in

1994 by the United States, the European Union, Japan, South Korea, Norway, Sweden and Finland — was bad. He told the House the agreement would not work "because we are counting on about 20 other nations to quit subsidizing their yards unilaterally. It is not going to happen."

In 1996, Taylor also gained a seat on the Transportation and Infrastructure Committee.

At Home: The Democratic Party was cool to Taylor in his first two campaigns for the 5th — in 1988 and in the special election the following year to replace Republican Larkin Smith, who died in an August 1989 plane crash. Taylor drew a respectable 45 percent against Smith in 1988, when both were competing for the seat vacated by Senate aspirant Trent Lott. In the 1989 special election, Taylor amassed 65 percent of the vote in dispatching Lott's longtime Hill aide, Tom Anderson Jr.

A sales representative for a company that manufactured cardboard boxes, Taylor entered politics in 1981 with a bid for the Bay St. Louis City Council. In 1983, he won election to the state Senate. He focused on education issues, such as salary increases and merit pay for teachers.

In 1988, Taylor was considered the strongest candidate in the Democratic field for the open 5th, and he easily defeated Hattiesburg District Attorney Glenn White in a runoff. But he seemed slow to organize for the fall; national party sources concluded that they could better spend their money elsewhere.

Taylor tried to make political capital out of the absence of national Democratic support. He told voters he was being snubbed by party officials for his refusal to moderate his conservative views. But Taylor had trouble raising money and was outspent by Smith by more than 3-to-1.

Taylor was heavily outspent in the 1989 special election as well, but Anderson had an unflattering image as Lott's "anointed" successor. Also, another Democratic candidate, state Attorney General Mike Moore, struck many voters as politically overambitious; he had just been elected attorney general in 1987. Even though Moore was backed by organized labor, Mississippi's main association of educators and Democratic Gov. Ray Mabus, Taylor ran first in the special primary with 42 percent of the vote to Anderson's 37 percent and Moore's 21 percent. The one-on-one runoff matchup with Anderson was a Taylor runaway.

In 1990, Smith won re-election with 81 percent against Smith's widow, Sheila. In 1992, the GOP hoped that Taylor's 1991 vote against authorizing the use of military force in the Persian Gulf would be a political liability in the hawkish 5th. Republicans nominated retired Air Force Gen. Paul Harvey, former commander of Keesler Air Force Base in the district. But Taylor's conservative record continued to hold him in good stead with voters, who re-elected him with 63 percent.

In 1996, Taylor breezed past a primary foe and then faced former state Rep. Dennis Dollar, a one-time Democrat. Dollar argued that as a member of Mississippi's high-profile Republican Party, he would be more effective in Congress than Taylor. Taylor countered that Dollar would be a prisoner of the GOP leadership's agenda. Taylor slipped a bit, to 58 percent, but still defeated Dollar by 18 points.

HOUSE ELECTIONS

1996 General		
Gene Taylor (D)	103,415	(58%)
Dennis Dollar (R)	71,114	(40%)
Le'Roy C. Carney (I)	1,832	(1%)
1996 Primary		
Gene Taylor (D)	14,249	(94%)
Arlon "Blackie" Coate (D)	861	(6%)
1994 General		
Gene Taylor (D)	73,179	(60%)
George Barlos (R)	48,575	(40%)

Previous Winning Percentages: 1992 (63%) **1990** (81%) **1989**† (65%)

† *Special election*

CAMPAIGN FINANCE

	Receipts	Receipts from PACs	Expend-itures
1996			
Taylor (D)	$412,090	$201,264 (49%)	$451,833
Dollar (R)	$466,455	$81,400 (17%)	$462,252
1994			
Taylor (D)	$218,606	$115,720 (53%)	$182,381
Barlos (R)	$73,328	$1,264 (2%)	$71,860

DISTRICT VOTE FOR PRESIDENT

1996		1992	
D	61,035 (35%)	**D**	58,905 (32%)
R	96,880 (56%)	**R**	100,128 (54%)
I	13,431 (8%)	**I**	24,941 (14%)

KEY VOTES

1997	
Ban "partial birth" abortions	Y
1996	
Approve farm bill	N
Deny public education to illegal immigrants	Y
Repeal ban on certain assault-style weapons	Y
Increase minimum wage	Y
Freeze defense spending	N
Approve welfare overhaul	Y
1995	
Approve balanced-budget constitutional amendment	Y
Relax Clean Water Act regulations	N
Oppose limits on environmental regulations	Y
Reduce projected Medicare spending	N
Approve GOP budget with tax and spending cuts	N

VOTING STUDIES

	Presidential Support		Party Unity		Conservative Coalition	
Year	S	O	S	O	S	O
1996	53	47	45	55	86	14
1995	41	59	42	57	88	11
1994	60	40	36	62	97	3
1993	48	52	37	63	91	9
1992	58	42	57	42	83	17
1991	55	42	50	49	86	14

INTEREST GROUP RATINGS

Year	ADA	AFL-CIO	CCUS	ACU
1996	30	n/a	63	80
1995	35	42	63	64
1994	15	56	50	67
1993	25	42	73	79
1992	30	50	50	76
1991	15	33	80	84

MISSOURI

Governor: Mel Carnahan (D)

First elected: 1992
Length of term: 4 years
Term expires: 1/01
Salary: $94,563.60
Term limit: 2 terms
Phone: (573) 751-3222
Born: Feb. 11, 1934; Birch Tree, Mo.
Education: George Washington U., B.A. 1954; U. of Missouri, J.D. 1959.
Military Service: Air Force, 1954-56.
Occupation: Lawyer.
Family: Wife, Jean Carpenter; four children.
Religion: Baptist.
Political Career: Municipal judge, 1961-62; Mo. House, 1963-67; Rolla School Board, 1976-80; Mo. treasurer, 1981-85; lieutenant governor, 1989-93; sought Democratic nomination for Mo. Senate, 1968; sought Democratic nomination for governor, 1984.

Lt. Gov.: Roger Wilson (D)
First elected: 1992
Length of term: 4 years
Term expires: 1/01
Salary: $62,997
Phone: (573) 751-4727

State election official: (573) 751-4875
Democratic headquarters: (573) 636-5241
Republican headquarters: (573) 636-3146

REDISTRICTING

Missouri retained its nine House seats in reapportionment. The legislature passed the map May 16, 1991; the governor signed it July 8.

STATE LEGISLATURE

General Assembly. Meets January-May.

Senate: 34 members, 4-year terms
1996 breakdown: 19D, 15R; 31 men, 3 women
Salary: $24,313.32
Phone: (314) 751-3766

House of Representatives: 163 members, 2-year terms
1996 breakdown: 88D, 75R; 122 men, 41 women
Salary: $26,802.96
Phone: (314) 751-3659

URBAN STATISTICS

City	Population
Kansas City	435,146
Mayor Emanuel Cleaver II, N-P	
St. Louis	396,685
Mayor Clarence Harmon, D	
Springfield	140,494
Mayor Leland Gannaway, N-P	
Independence	112,301
Mayor Ron Stewart, N-P	

U.S. CONGRESS

Senate: 0 D, 2 R
House: 5 D, 4 R

TERM LIMITS

For state offices: Yes
Senate: 4 terms
House: 2 terms

ELECTIONS

1996 Presidential Vote

Bill Clinton	48%
Bob Dole	41%
Ross Perot	10%

1992 Presidential Vote

Bill Clinton	44%
George Bush	34%
Ross Perot	22%

1988 Presidential Vote

George Bush	52%
Michael S. Dukakis	48%

POPULATION

1990 population		5,117,073
1980 population		4,916,686
Percent change		+4.1%
Rank among states:		15
White		88%
Black		11%
Hispanic		1%
Asian or Pacific islander		1%
Urban		69%
Rural		31%
Born in state		70%
Foreign-born		2%
Under age 18	1,314,826	26%
Ages 18-64	3,084,566	60%
65 and older	717,681	14%
Median age		33.5

MISCELLANEOUS

Capital: Jefferson City
Number of counties: 114
Per capita income: $17,842 (1991)
Rank among states: 25
Total area: 69,697 sq. miles
Rank among states: 19

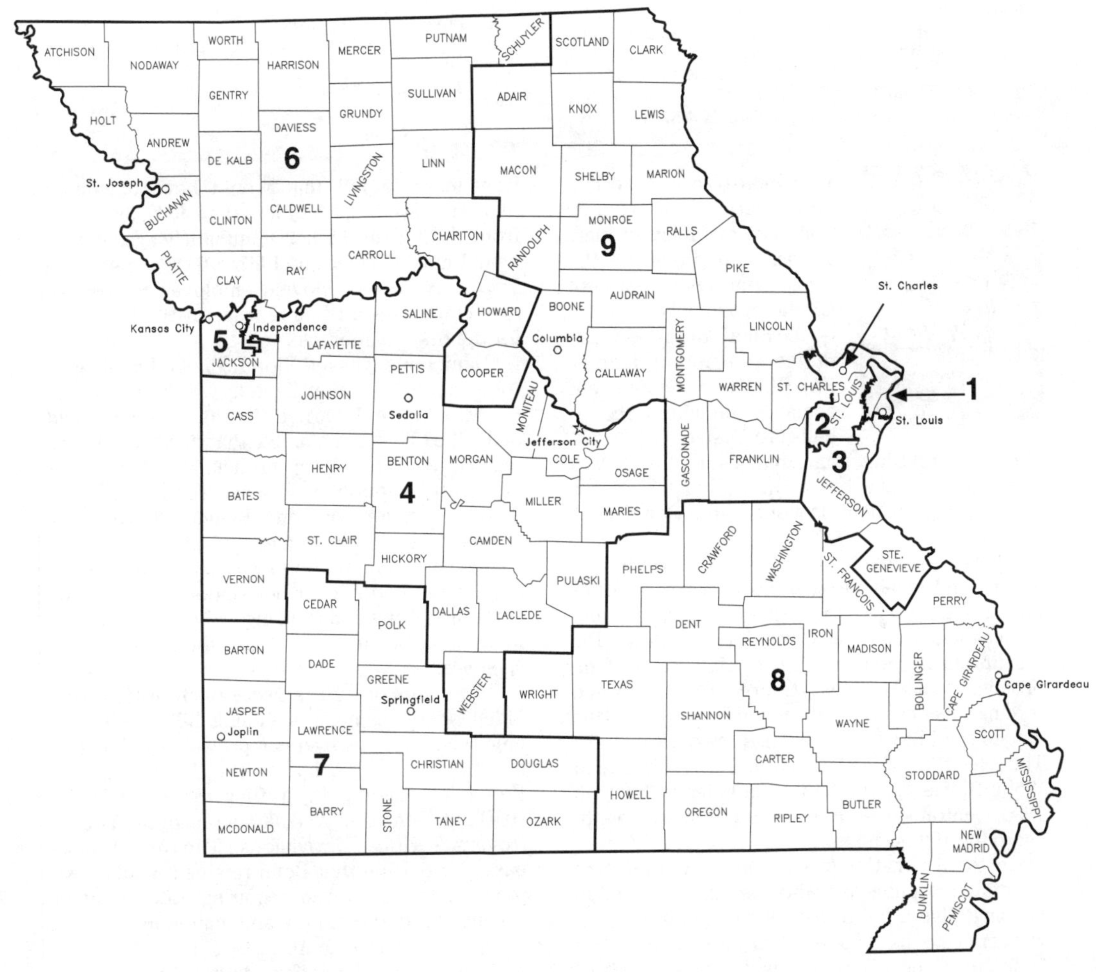
ATCHISON
NODAWAY
WORTH
HARRISON
MERCER
PUTNAM
SCHUYLER
SCOTLAND
CLARK
HOLT
GENTRY
GRUNDY
SULLIVAN
ADAIR
KNOX
LEWIS
ANDREW
DAVIESS
DE KALB
6
LIVINGSTON
LINN
MACON
SHELBY
MARION
St. Joseph
BUCHANAN
CLINTON
CALDWELL
CHARITON
RANDOLPH
MONROE
9
RALLS
PLATTE
CLAY
RAY
CARROLL
PIKE
AUDRAIN
St. Charles
Kansas City
Independence
SALINE
HOWARD
BOONE
LINCOLN
5
JACKSON
LAFAYETTE
Columbia
MONTGOMERY
PETTIS
COOPER
CALLAWAY
WARREN
ST. CHARLES
ST. LOUIS
1
JOHNSON
Sedalia
MONITEAU
2
St. Louis
CASS
Jefferson City
COLE
BENTON
MORGAN
GASCONADE
FRANKLIN
3
HENRY
OSAGE
BATES
4
MILLER
MARIES
JEFFERSON
ST. CLAIR
CAMDEN
PHELPS
CRAWFORD
WASHINGTON
HICKORY
ST. FRANCOIS
STE. GENEVIEVE
VERNON
PULASKI
CEDAR
DALLAS
LACLEDE
PERRY
POLK
DENT
BARTON
IRON
REYNOLDS
MADISON
DADE
GREENE
TEXAS
8
BOLLINGER
CAPE GIRARDEAU
Cape Girardeau
Springfield
WEBSTER
WRIGHT
JASPER
SHANNON
Joplin
LAWRENCE
WAYNE
SCOTT
CARTER
NEWTON
7
CHRISTIAN
DOUGLAS
STODDARD
MISSISSIPPI
HOWELL
BUTLER
BARRY
OREGON
RIPLEY
STONE
TANEY
OZARK
MCDONALD
NEW MADRID
DUNKLIN
PEMISCOT

Christopher S. Bond (R)

Of Mexico — Elected 1986, 2nd term

Biographical Information

Born: March 6, 1939, St. Louis, Mo.

Education: Princeton U., A.B. 1960; U. of Virginia, LL.B. 1963.

Occupation: Lawyer.

Family: Wife, Carolyn Reid; one child.

Religion: Presbyterian.

Political Career: Republican nominee for U.S. House, 1968; Mo. assistant attorney general, 1969-70; Mo. auditor, 1971-73; governor, 1973-77; Republican nominee for governor, 1976; governor, 1981-85.

Capitol Office: 274 Russell Bldg. 20510; 224-5721.

Committees

Appropriations

Agriculture, Rural Development & Related Agencies; Defense; Labor, Health & Human Services & Education; Transportation; VA, HUD & Independent Agencies (chairman)

Budget

Environment & Public Works

Drinking Water, Fisheries & Wildlife; Transportation & Infrastructure

Small Business (chairman)

In Washington: Bond is a conservative who usually does not manifest strongly partisan instincts in the range of issues he pursues. On the two panels he chairs — the Small Business Committee and Appropriations' VA, HUD and independent agencies subcommittee — he is pro-business and pragmatic. In crafting compromises that can win broad support, he has been willing to cross a Republican president or work with a Democratic one.

During the 102nd Congress, Bond worked on legislation to mandate that most businesses offer unpaid family leave to their employees. He and Connecticut Democrat Christopher J. Dodd, the bill's original sponsor, forged a bipartisan compromise. But President George Bush opposed forcing businesses to offer family leave, and he vetoed the bill when it reached his desk in 1992. The election of Bill Clinton, however, ended White House opposition to family leave. Early in 1993, Clinton signed into law a bill nearly identical to the 1992 version.

In the 104th Congress, Bond was one of a handful of Republicans who were instrumental in keeping alive a bill in the Senate to ensure that workers who lose or leave their jobs can maintain health insurance. During consideration in 1996 of the legislation, Bond was one of only five Republicans who joined all of the Senate's Democrats in voting to strip from the bill a controversial provision to allow some individuals to accrue tax-deductible savings accounts dedicated to pay medical expenses. Supporters of the health care legislation, which Congress approved, were concerned that the medical savings accounts provision would kill the bill.

But if Bond was an ally of Democrats in that fight, they saw him as an adversary in another battle in the 104th over raising the minimum wage. Keen on protecting his small-business constituency, Bond offered an amendment to the wage-increase bill that would have exempted businesses with sales of less than $500,000 a year from paying the higher minimum wage. It also would have delayed the bill's effective date until Jan. 1, 1997, and allowed employers to pay all new employees a training wage of $4.25 an hour for the first six months.

Democrats viewed Bond's amendment as a "poison pill," as Labor Secretary Robert B. Reich described it, and warned that its passage would make the bill so unpalatable that they would have to vote against it. With the help of a handful of moderate Republicans, who thought a wage increase was long overdue, Democrats were able to defeat Bond's amendment, 46-52.

Also in the 104th, Bond was deeply involved in a partisan battle over legislation to fund the Veterans Affairs and Housing and Urban Development departments, as well as other independent agencies.

In its version of the fiscal 1996 VA-HUD and independent agencies spending bill, the House approved 17 controversial provisions aimed at limiting the authority of the Environmental Protection Agency. In drafting the Senate's VA-HUD bill, Bond removed all but one of the 17 controversial House provisions. The one House-passed provision that Bond retained would have prevented the EPA from requiring states to adopt a centralized inspection and maintenance program under the Clean Air Act.

However, he also included other language that was more narrowly drawn than the House bill that aimed to constrain the EPA, including a provision to prohibit the agency from vetoing decisions made by the Army Corps of Engineers regarding development permits for wetlands. The Senate bill also made steep reductions in spending for the agency but did not cut as deeply as the House version.

Bond was more in line with House Republicans when it came to funding for the National Service Program, a pet initiative of the Clinton administration. As with the House version, the legislation approved by the Senate Appropriations Committee called for eliminating the program.

Despite this, Bond said he remained open to negotiating the issue with the administration. "When they want to talk about what they are willing to sign, we'll be happy to work with them," Bond said at one point. In the end, the program survived, after Clinton cited the GOP abolition language as one of his reasons for vetoing the spending bill.

In 1996, Bond sought to avoid the partisan battles that had sunk the VA-HUD appropriations bill the year before by crafting legislation that did not include any of the controversial riders and cuts that provoked Democrats and Clinton in 1995.

"We think we have made a good-faith effort to avoid re-opening controversial issues," Bond said during Senate consideration of the bill.

As chairman of the VA-HUD subcommittee, Bond has emerged as one of the Senate's leading authorities on public housing issues.

When some other conservative Republicans in the 104th Congress were pushing to abolish the Department of Housing and Urban Development, Bond led a group of GOP members who instead favored shrinking it and delegating many of its functions to the states. Bond supported a plan to rebuild the department around three major block grants, providing lump sums to the states.

In the Democratic-controlled 103rd Congress, Bond became ranking Republican on the Banking Committee's housing subcommittee. From that position, he worked to achieve bipartisan support for a housing reauthorization bill, though the legislation eventually died on the Senate floor. While he cooperated with HUD Secretary Henry G. Cisneros, Bond urged Cisneros to concentrate on managing HUD's core programs and give local authorities more flexibility rather than developing new federal approaches.

When Republicans took control in the 104th Congress and the Commerce Department was targeted by GOP conservatives for elimination, Bond proposed establishing a new agency that would take over the Commerce Department's duties involving trade issues. Bond indicated in 1995 that he would offer an amendment creating a Cabinet-level international trade agency to legislation eliminating the Commerce Department if it reached the Senate floor, which it did not.

As head of the Small Business Committee, Bond won passage of legislation in the 104th that would have allowed small businesses to take federal agencies to court if they did not comply with a "regulatory flexibility" analysis, which requires agencies to review the impact of new regulations on small businesses under the Regulatory Flexibility Act of 1980.

Bond expressed concern about the House's version of the legislation, which included a controversial provision requiring federal agencies to conduct periodic reviews of rules. The Clinton administration and Senate Democrats said the provision would tie up federal agencies and undermine environmental protection and enforcement of health and safety rules. Bond wanted to avoid loading down the bill with controversial provisions so it could clear the president. "If it's something that will tie the bill up in controversy, maybe we should put it off to a later date," he said.

The legislation was approved by Congress after it was included in a bill lifting the federal statutory debt limit.

Bond, who sits on the Environment and Public Works Committee, got involved in the panel's 1997 work reauthorizing the nation's surface transportation programs. Early in the 105th Congress, Bond helped committee Chairman John H. Chafee, R-R.I., craft a highway reauthorization proposal aimed at ensuring more highway spending.

Early in the 105th, Bond weighed in on the public debate over cloning. The issue gained interest with news in February 1997 that scientists in Scotland had successfully cloned an adult sheep. Bond sponsored a bill permanently banning federal funding for research on human cloning. "I believe there are some areas of science that ought to be off limits," Bond said.

As a former governor, Bond often lobbies for Washington to defer to the wishes of state governments. He joined Democrat John D. Rockefeller IV, a former governor of West Virginia, to advocate giving states a set amount of money to help keep families together and prevent children from needing foster care. The idea, part of an urban aid tax bill that Bush vetoed in 1992, was backed by Clinton and included in the budget reconciliation bill of 1993 that became law.

Bond sponsored legislation in 1996 aimed at aiding GOP Gov. Tommy G. Thompson of Wisconsin in his high-profile effort to overhaul his state's welfare programs. The legislation would have allowed Wisconsin to put into place its welfare reform proposal by granting the state waivers from many federal laws and regulations.

While Bond's influence over issues has grown, he has not managed to move up the leadership ladder of his party. Before the 102nd Congress opened in 1991, he lost 26-17 to Bob Kasten of Wisconsin in a bid for Republican Conference secretary. After Kasten's 1992 re-election defeat reopened the job, Bond tried again, but lost to Mississippi Republican Trent Lott, 20-14.

At Home: In his six statewide races, Bond has never been an overwhelming favorite of Missouri voters. He has won by more than 10 percentage points only once — his first contest, the 1970 state auditor race. In five subsequent statewide runs, he has reached 55 percent only once (his 1972 election as governor), and he lost one race (his 1976 gubernatorial re-election bid).

Still, in 1992, Missouri Democrats did not field a prominent candidate to oppose him. The winner of the 14-candidate Democratic primary was St. Louis County Council member Geri Rothman-Serot, the ex-wife of former Democratic Lt. Gov. Kenneth J. Rothman.

Rothman-Serot sought to capitalize on the "Year of the Woman" sensation that had charged the campaigns of other women trying for the Senate in 1992. But Bond had prepared well. His campaign treasury was four times larger than Rothman-Serot's. His approval ratings remained healthy; his image as a pragmatic conservative did not engender strong partisan antipathy among Democrats. Rothman-Serot's liberal stands and her reluctance to court rural conservatives reminded some Democrats of Bond's 1986 challenger, then-Lt. Gov. Harriett Woods.

On Election Day, Bond was the GOP's only victorious statewide candidate. He took 52 percent of the vote, 7 percentage points ahead of Rothman-Serot.

(Travails in Bond's personal finances were not disclosed until after the campaign. In the spring of 1993, Bond sued his investment adviser, whom he accused of squandering his $1.3 million blind trust. He was forced to sell his million-dollar home in Washington.)

Bond broke into politics in 1968, seeking a seat in the U.S. House from northeastern Missouri. Although he lost, it was the year the modern GOP in Missouri was born. Richard M. Nixon carried the state, and John C. Danforth was elected attorney general. Bond took a job with Danforth, later his Senate colleague, and in 1970 won the office of state auditor. Two years later, he was elected the state's first GOP governor since World War II.

He had a troubled first term. Democrats in the legislature found him aloof; Republicans chafed at his efforts to abolish patronage jobs. In 1976, he lost to Democrat Joseph P. Teasdale, but he avenged this loss in 1980. In his second term, Bond warmed up to the legislature and generally won points for being more accessible.

In 1986, Bond battled Woods in a bitter contest for the Senate seat vacated by retiring Democrat Thomas F. Eagleton. Bond offered himself as a budget-conscious conservative and painted Woods as a liberal with values out of sync with most Missourians. She called Bond a passive governor, an aloof aristocrat and a likely rubber stamp for President Ronald Reagan.

Woods' campaign foundered when she ran a TV ad depicting a weeping farmer describing how he was foreclosed by a company on whose board Bond served. The ad provoked a backlash, damaging Woods' attempts to win conservative rural Democrats.

Bond, too, had past problems with members of his party. Many conservatives remembered his support for Gerald R. Ford over Reagan at the 1976 national GOP convention and never really considered him one of their own. But any doubts they might have had about Bond were drowned out by their antipathy toward Woods; Bond won with 53 percent. He was the only Republican in the country to capture an open Democratic seat in 1986.

SENATE ELECTIONS

1992 General		
Christopher S. Bond (R)	1,221,901	(52%)
Geri Rothman-Serot (D)	1,057,967	(45%)
Jeanne F. Bojarski (LIBERT)	75,048	(3%)
1992 Primary		
Christopher S. Bond (R)	337,795	(83%)
Wes Hummel (R)	70,626	(17%)

Previous Winning Percentages: 1986 (53%)

CAMPAIGN FINANCE

	Receipts	Receipts from PACs	Expend-itures
1992			
Bond (R)	$4,069,717	$1,420,459 (35%)	$4,577,895
Rothman-Serot (D)	$1,113,647	$306,860 (28%)	$1,112,187

KEY VOTES

1997	
Approve balanced-budget constitutional amendment	Y
Approve chemical weapons treaty	N
1996	
Approve farm bill	Y
Limit punitive damages in product liability cases	Y
Exempt small businesses from higher minimum wage	Y
Approve welfare overhaul	Y
Bar job discrimination based on sexual orientation	N
Override veto of ban on "partial birth" abortions	Y
1995	
Approve GOP budget with tax and spending cuts	Y
Approve constitutional amendment barring flag desecration	Y

VOTING STUDIES

	Presidential Support		Party Unity		Conservative Coalition	
Year	**S**	**O**	**S**	**O**	**S**	**O**
1996	37	63	95	5	100	0
1995	35†	63†	89†	7†	91†	5†
1994	47	48	75	21	88	9
1993	31	65	83	14	83	15
1992	70	23	76	14	66	24
1991	85	11	86	12	85	15

† Not eligible for all recorded votes.

INTEREST GROUP RATINGS

Year	ADA	AFL-CIO	CCUS	ACU
1996	10	n/a	100	90
1995	5	8	100	70
1994	20	13	100	83
1993	25	10	100	80
1992	25	33	100	76
1991	20	27	70	81

John Ashcroft (R)

Of Springfield — Elected 1994, 1st term

Biographical Information

Born: May 9, 1942, Chicago, Ill.

Education: Yale U., A.B. 1964; U. Chicago, J.D. 1967.

Occupation: Lawyer.

Family: Wife, Janet Elise Roede; three children.

Religion: Assembly of God.

Political Career: Republican nominee for U.S. House, 1972; Mo. auditor, 1973-75; Mo. assistant attorney general, 1975-76; Mo. attorney general, 1976-85; Mo. governor, 1985-93.

Capitol Office: 316 Hart Bldg. 20510; 224-6154.

Committees

Commerce, Science & Transportation
Aviation; Communications; Consumer Affairs, Foreign Commerce & Tourism (chairman); Manufacturing & Competitiveness; Surface Transportation & Merchant Marine

Foreign Relations
African Affairs (chairman); European Affairs; Near Eastern & South Asian Affairs

Judiciary
Constitution, Federalism & Property Rights (chairman); Youth Violence

In Washington: Ashcroft is a straight-laced conservative with a strong moral bent. He honed his political instincts during a long career in Missouri state government, including two terms as governor, and in the Senate he quickly became a leading advocate of congressional term limits, school discipline and relying on religious organizations to solve welfare-related problems. His legislative proposals in these areas have met with mixed success — at times his ideas are too much even for some conservative colleagues in the chamber — but with his generally quiet demeanor, Ashcroft does not seem an extremist.

In fact, his highest visibility on the national media stage has come for singing in a barbershop quartet with three other Republican senators — James M. Jeffords of Vermont, Majority Leader Trent Lott of Mississippi and Larry E. Craig of Idaho. To that group, dubbed "The Singing Senators," Ashcroft brings his background as a former touring gospel singer. The group's material is a medley of patriotic and gospel tunes, mixed with a little country.

During the 104th Congress' welfare debate , Ashcroft was among a group of conservatives who pushed to include tougher measures to reduce out-of-wedlock births, give states control over more programs, cut aid to non-citizens and tighten work requirements on welfare recipients. Although conservatives did not get everything they wanted, they saw much of their agenda included in the welfare legislation that President Clinton signed in August 1996. Ashcroft would have liked to have taken it further. He tried to cut welfare benefits by 20 percent for parents who did not have their children fully immunized. Another of his amendments, resisted by some even in his own party, would have given states complete control of the food stamps program.

However, he succeeded in amending the bill to allow state governments to use federal funds to contract with religious organizations to deliver services to the needy.

Ashcroft's get-tough approach came though when Congress sought in 1996 to revise the Individuals with Disabilities Education Act (IDEA), the nation's main special education program. Ashcroft said disabled students did not need special protections under the law that made it more difficult to discipline them than other students. While disabled students are entitled to an education, Ashcroft said, they should not "use a law designed to shield them as a weapon of aggression to attack the educational protection of the rest of the students." He pledged to amend the bill more to his liking on the Senate floor. When Senate leaders showed little interest in a protracted floor fight, the bill died for the 104th, though a revised version passed in the 105th.

Ashcroft has been a leader in the Republican effort to allow businesses to offer employees compensatory time off in lieu of overtime pay. Organized labor opposes the idea, warning that employees might be coerced into choosing whatever the employer prefers. Ashcroft's interest persisted into the 105th Congress, even after he had left the Labor and Human Resources Committee.

Term limits are a top priority for Ashcroft. "Term limits would end congressional stagnation and careerism and bring a healthy infusion of new ideas and new people," he has said. Ashcroft called himself one of the few senators "who have been term-limited," noting that certain elected state officials in Missouri are allowed only two terms. He joined with another GOP first-termer, Fred Thompson of Tennessee, in introducing a bill to impose limits of two six-year terms in the Senate and six two-year terms in the House. But he has failed in his efforts to bring term limits to a vote in the Senate.

Ashcroft's conservatism led him to try to require that all applicants to federally funded job training programs submit to mandatory random drug tests. He explained that the nation could not afford to train candidates who were habitual drug users. However, the initiative failed when the job training bill died at the end of 1996.

He tried to reduce funding to the National Endowments for the Arts and Humanities by 50 percent over five years. But the attempt, offered with Judd Gregg, R-N.H., was rejected by the Labor and Human Resources Committee.

Concerned about efforts in Oregon to legalize assisted suicide, Ashcroft has proposed banning federal dollars from being used to help commit a suicide. Such a restriction was necessary "to preserve the integrity of our federal programs serving the elderly and seriously ill," Ashcroft said in introducing the bill with Byron L. Dorgan, D-N.D. The legislation did not pass in the 104th, but there was renewed discussion of it in 1997.

At Home: When Republican John C. Danforth of Missouri decided not to seek re-election to a fourth term in the Senate, state party elders did not have to look very far to find a replacement with statewide appeal. Ashcroft, riding the popularity built during his two terms as governor, breezed to victory in the GOP primary and handily defeated Democratic Rep. Alan Wheat in the general election.

Although born in Chicago, Ashcroft was raised in Springfield, Mo., and still lives in nearby Ballwin. Springfield is the world headquarters of the Assembly of God church, a leading force on the fundamentalist side of contemporary American Protestantism. Ashcroft is a member of the Assembly of God and made much of his early reputation in the area as a touring gospel singer. After an unsuccessful run for the U.S. House in 1972, Ashcroft served in a series of state government jobs until 1976, when he was elected state attorney general (replacing Danforth, who had just been elected to the Senate). After a second term as attorney general, Ashcroft was elected governor in 1984, succeeding Republican Christopher S. Bond (now Missouri's senior senator). Ashcroft won a second term in 1988 and was barred from seeking a third by state law.

With Danforth and Bond, Ashcroft is credited with guiding the Missouri GOP into an era of unprecedented prominence in a state where Democrats had long dominated. Ashcroft, however, has been steadfastly more conservative than the other two, especially on social issues.

Outside Missouri, the best-known event of Ashcroft's governorship was a lawsuit brought by his attorney general, *Webster v. Reproductive Health Services*, that asserted a state's right to limit access to abortion. The case went to the Supreme Court and occasioned an important redefinition of individual rights to abortion and governmental restrictions on those rights.

Wheat, a six-term House member, prevailed in the August primary to become the first black statewide candidate in Missouri's history. But Jackson County Executive Marsha Murphy did far better than initially expected and nearly took the nomination away. Wheat's effort in the primary depleted his finances, and he showed little strength among the rural whites critical to the party's statewide majorities.

Ashcroft, meanwhile, put his campaign on autopilot (he received more than 83 percent of the GOP primary vote) and guarded his resources while coasting to victory. Wheat carried the Democratic cities of St. Louis and Kansas City in November, but lost every county in the state.

SENATE ELECTIONS

1994 General		
John Ashcroft (R)	1,060,149	(60%)
Alan Wheat (D)	633,697	(36%)
Bill Johnson (LIBERT)	81,264	(5%)
1994 Primary		
John Ashcroft (R)	260,065	(83%)
Joyce Lea (R)	15,228	(5%)
Joseph A. Schwan (R)	14,713	(5%)
Ronald G. Halstead (R)	11,339	(4%)
Doug Jones (R)	11,303	(4%)

KEY VOTES

1997	
Approve balanced-budget constitutional amendment	Y
Approve chemical weapons treaty	N
1996	
Approve farm bill	Y
Limit punitive damages in product liability cases	Y
Exempt small businesses from higher minimum wage	Y
Approve welfare overhaul	Y
Bar job discrimination based on sexual orientation	N
Override veto of ban on "partial birth" abortions	Y
1995	
Approve GOP budget with tax and spending cuts	Y
Approve constitutional amendment barring flag desecration	Y

CAMPAIGN FINANCE

	Receipts	Receipts from PACs	Expenditures
1994			
Ashcroft (R)	$4,182,215	$1,079,496 (26%)	$4,063,927
Wheat (D)	$3,461,649	$950,944 (27%)	$3,505,701
Johnson (LIBERT)	$19,230	$200 (1%)	$18,956

VOTING STUDIES

	Presidential Support		Party Unity		Conservative Coalition	
Year	**S**	**O**	**S**	**O**	**S**	**O**
1996	29	69	97	2	89	11
1995	24	76	97	2	96	2

INTEREST GROUP RATINGS

Year	ADA	AFL-CIO	CCUS	ACU
1996	5	n/a	100	100
1995	0	0	100	91

1 William L. Clay (D)

Of St. Louis — Elected 1968, 15th term

Biographical Information
Born: April 30, 1931, St. Louis, Mo.
Education: St. Louis U., B.S. 1953.
Military Service: Army, 1953-55.
Occupation: Real estate and insurance broker.
Family: Wife, Carol Ann Johnson; three children.
Religion: Roman Catholic.
Political Career: St. Louis Board of Aldermen, 1959-64; St. Louis Democratic Committee, 1964-67.
Capitol Office: 2306 Rayburn Bldg. 20515; 225-2406.

Committees
Education & Workforce (ranking)

In Washington: When he came to Congress more than a quarter-century ago, Clay was labeled a black militant. Over the years, he has gradually adjusted his political focus and rhetoric to match his slightly less black and more conservative district, but he remains a strident liberal on the issues he cares deeply about — especially civil rights and labor. These days, Clay finds himself mainly on the losing side of those issues, trying time and time again to halt the march of the House Republican majority.

The situation is especially difficult for Clay because he would have assumed the chairmanship of the Education and Labor Committee had the Democrats kept their majority in the 104th Congress. Instead, he became ranking minority member of the committee, whose name the GOP has shifted twice, always conspicuously omitting "labor" — the Economic and Educational Opportunities Committee in the 104th, and now in the 105th the Education and the Workforce Committee.

There was no surprise in Clay's support of the AFL-CIO's plan to spend $35 million in the 1996 campaigns targeting House Republicans. "The $35 million is a drop in the bucket. Big labor's money is insignificant when compared" with fundraising by Republicans, Clay said. "Why would the American workers not spend money to get them out of office?"

One of the few things that gave Clay cause for a smile in the last two years came in November 1996 when conservative Rep. Gary A. Franks of Connecticut, one of only two black House Republicans, lost his re-election bid. In the 103rd Congress, Clay reprimanded Franks for a voting record he called "inimical to the permanent interests of black folk."

"It would probably be better for all concerned," wrote Clay in a seven-page open letter to Franks, "if you did resign [from the Black Caucus] forthwith, admitting that you never should have joined the ranks of black legislators who fight to protect the rights of black people."

Clay's voting record remains that of a traditional liberal. He voted in the 104th against banning a particular abortion technique that opponents call a "partial-birth" abortion, against overhauling the welfare system and against exempting small businesses from paying a higher minimum wage. He also opposed the health care overhaul bill, which included medical savings accounts, and voted against the anti-terrorism bill. He voted against term limits, the Republican tax cut plan, and the GOP's plan to balance the federal budget by 2002 in part by reducing the rate of growth in spending on Medicare and Medicaid.

A rare legislative victory for Clay in the 104th came when lawmakers voted to raise the minimum wage over the objections of top GOP lawmakers. "The Republican leadership fought this effort," Clay said. "They would not allow a hearing, tried to gut the legislation, then postponed its effective date by one month in 1996. . . . At every turn Republicans have felt compelled to nickel-and-dime low-wage workers and their families."

For the most part, however, Clay was relegated to using his ranking position to rail against Republican proposals.

He opposed a GOP plan to allow employers to offer their workers compensatory time off rather than overtime pay. He said a choice between compensatory time and overtime could never be truly voluntary. Employers could make a compensatory time preference an unwritten condition of employment, he said, or they could simply channel extra work only to those workers willing to accept compensatory time. "This bill places the rights of businesses above the rights of workers," he said.

In February 1995, he complained about the Republican proposal to combine nutrition and child care programs into three huge new block grants. Merging the Special Supplemental Nutrition Program for Women, Infants and Children (WIC) into such a block grant would "potentially starve hundreds of thousands of children and imperil the health of their mothers," Clay said.

He took exception to a health care bill sponsored by Harris W. Fawell, R-Ill., to allow small

MISSOURI 1
North St. Louis; Northeast St. Louis County

Almost everything that outsiders identify with the city of St. Louis is in the 1st. The Gateway Arch, Laclede's Landing, Busch Stadium and Forest Park all lie north of the line that divides the two city-dominated districts.

The other, equally familiar St. Louis is also here: the crime-ridden streets, the rundown neighborhoods, the closed factories and businesses. Parts of the downtown area have declined so far that they shock even visitors accustomed to inner-city blight.

Blacks and whites have fled the city. The well-off have gone to distant suburbia and the less affluent to neighborhoods just outside the city limits. Blacks have also begun to move to the predominantly white neighborhoods of south St. Louis, and, as a consequence, many south St. Louis whites have headed for the suburbs. Once the nation's third-largest city, St. Louis has seen its population shrink to less than half its 1950 total. It fell by 12 percent during the 1980s; with about 400,000 residents in the 1990 census, it has fallen behind Kansas City as Missouri's most-populous city. Politically, the 1st is Missouri's most reliably Democratic district.

The St. Louis area has been rocked in recent years by plant closings and layoffs. Chrysler closed one of its two St. Louis County assembly plants. McDonnell Douglas Corp. has cut thousands of workers and is slated to be merged into the Boeing Corp. Trans World Airlines, whose domestic hub is at St. Louis' Lambert International Airport, has emerged from bankruptcy but still is in severe financial straits. General Dynamics Corp. moved its corporate headquarters to Northern Virginia in 1992.

One positive note for downtown came in mid-1994, when TWA moved its corporate headquarters there and transferred its reservations office and customer relations department to another downtown building.

North St. Louis is not uniformly dilapidated. There remain pockets of stable, older residential areas, such as the Central West End and adjacent neighborhoods north and east of Forest Park, as well as the Mark Twain and Walnut Park neighborhoods near the northern city limits. But most of north St. Louis is in decay. Some of the worst areas lie just north and west of downtown. Much of the central city has become plagued by shootings and drug deals.

The city has waged an ambitious program to renovate its historic buildings. Monumental Union Station, for example, has been rehabilitated into an upscale marketplace with shops, restaurants, nightclubs and a hotel.

The 1st also takes in many of the blacks who have left the city for nearby St. Louis County suburbs. Affluent black professionals live in University City, Clayton and Florissant. Clayton was once the prototypical prosperous suburb, but its profile has been changing of late, as tony shops relocate west to more-affluent locales.

The rest of the 1st is composed largely of white working-class conservatives who work in the auto assembly and aerospace manufacturing facilities ringing the city.

1990 Population: 568,285. White 262,955 (46%), Black 297,331 (52%), Other 7,999 (1%). Hispanic origin 5,090 (<1%). 18 and over 418,731 (74%), 62 and over 94,234 (17%). Median age: 32.

businesses to form purchasing cooperatives with other small employers, giving them more leverage with insurance companies when negotiating premiums and benefits. It also would have exempted more insurance plans from state laws that mandate health benefits. Fawell said his proposal would "make insurance affordable and accessible to millions of Americans who are without coverage today." But Clay, in March 1996, argued that the bill would "leave many individuals now protected by stricter state insurance rules and aggressive state regulators much worse off."

At an Economic and Educational Opportunities Committee meeting in June 1995, Clay criticized legislation that would amend U.S. labor law to make clear that businesses can establish voluntary workplace "teams." He contended that the measure would erode workers' job security and was really aimed at undermining organized labor.

Through his many years in the House, Clay has had a number of confrontations with the House ethics committee. The most contentious was in 1992, when the panel found that he had overdrawn his account at the House bank 328 times. Clay blasted the committee for the way it handled the issues; he was furious over what he saw as the panel's piecemeal release of the names of the overdraft offenders.

In the 104th Congress, Clay voted for a less stringent alternative to a proposed ban on most gifts and meals to lawmakers. The proposal, which was defeated, would have allowed House members to continue receiving the gifts, meals and trips, as long as they were disclosed.

At Home: Clay's career has thrived on confrontation. His own campaign literature once noted that he had been "arrested, convicted of contempt of court [and] served 110 days in jail" for demonstrating at a St. Louis bank.

That incident took place years before his election to the House in 1968. But it was one of a string of such confrontations that gave him a reputation as a civil rights activist. In 1954, while going through military training at Fort McClellan in Alabama, Clay found the post swimming pool and barber shop closed to blacks, and the non-commissioned officers' club off-limits when there were white women present. He led blacks to swim en masse in the pool, boycott haircuts and picket the club.

After returning to St. Louis, Clay became active in the NAACP and CORE, the Congress on Racial Equality. He was elected to the city's Board of Aldermen in 1959 and became an official in the politically active Pipefitters Union in 1966. While keeping his identification as a civil rights militant, he moved closer over the years to the patronage politics of the local Democratic Party.

Redistricting by the Missouri legislature in 1967 placed most of St. Louis' 257,000 blacks in the 1st District, ending years of fragmentation of the black vote. Democrat Frank M. Karsten, the 1st District representative for 22 years, decided to retire rather than seek re-election in 1968.

With the backing of most local black leaders, Clay emerged from a racially divided four-way primary with a 48 percent plurality. In the general election, he ran on a platform geared to the district's 55 percent black majority. He called for more federal money for jobs, housing, health and education, and for changes in police agencies and the court system to eliminate bias against blacks. Clay won 64 percent against black Republican Curtis C. Crawford to become Missouri's first black congressman.

As Clay extended his tenure in the House, the population in his district dwindled steadily. The 1st lost one-quarter of its people during the 1970s, and redistricting in 1981 gave Clay nearly 200,000 new constituents, many of them blue-collar workers in largely white sections of St. Louis County. In Clay's old district, two-thirds of the population was black; in the redrawn 1st, blacks barely formed a majority, and more whites than blacks were registered to vote.

A sizable number of Clay's new constituents fiercely objected to his support for abortion and for busing of students to integrate schools. In 1982, anti-Clay Democrats coalesced behind a white primary challenger, state Sen. Al Mueller, an opponent of abortion and busing.

Mueller carried the St. Louis County portion of the 1st, but Clay, strongly backed by organized labor, crushed him in the city en route to a 61 percent victory districtwide.

For someone who has spent nearly 30 years in Washington, Clay remains unusually active in local politics. He clashed repeatedly with St. Louis' former mayor, Vincent C. Schoemehl Jr. In 1992, Clay worked energetically for Schoemehl's opponent in the Democratic gubernatorial primary, then-Lt. Gov. (and now-Gov.) Mel Carnahan.

That kind of high profile has at times put some stress on Clay's political organization (many call it Clay's "machine"). In 1994, he drew three credible if little-known primary challengers, and although his nearest foe captured only 20 percent of the vote, Clay was renominated with just 53 percent of the vote. In 1996, Clay crushed his solo primary opponent, and, as always, won the general election with ease.

HOUSE ELECTIONS

1996 General		
William L. Clay (D)	131,659	(70%)
Daniel F. O'Sullivan Jr. (R)	51,857	(28%)
Tamara Millay (LIBERT)	4,137	(2%)
1996 Primary		
William L. Clay (D)	44,971	(78%)
Patrick J. Cacchione (D)	12,537	(22%)
1994 General		
William L. Clay (D)	97,061	(63%)
Donald R. Counts (R)	50,303	(33%)
Craig W. Williamson (LIBERT)	5,654	(4%)

Previous Winning Percentages: **1992** (68%) **1990** (61%) **1988** (72%) **1986** (66%) **1984** (68%) **1982** (66%) **1980** (70%) **1978** (67%) **1976** (66%) **1974** (68%) **1972** (64%) **1970** (91%) **1968** (64%)

CAMPAIGN FINANCE

	Receipts	Receipts from PACs	Expend-itures
1996			
Clay (D)	$301,267	$212,315 (70%)	$366,550
O'Sullivan (R)	$78,374	$14,416 (18%)	$77,978
1994			
Clay (D)	$438,179	$284,300 (65%)	$349,528
Counts (R)	$9,461	$14 (0%)	$7,408

DISTRICT VOTE FOR PRESIDENT

	1996		1992
D	144,349 (74%)	**D**	161,794 (69%)
R	38,561 (20%)	**R**	44,980 (19%)
I	9,738 (5%)	**I**	29,586 (13%)

KEY VOTES

1997	
Ban "partial birth" abortions	N
1996	
Approve farm bill	N
Deny public education to illegal immigrants	N
Repeal ban on certain assault-style weapons	?
Increase minimum wage	Y
Freeze defense spending	Y
Approve welfare overhaul	N
1995	
Approve balanced-budget constitutional amendment	N
Relax Clean Water Act regulations	N
Oppose limits on environmental regulations	Y
Reduce projected Medicare spending	N
Approve GOP budget with tax and spending cuts	N

VOTING STUDIES

	Presidential Support		Party Unity		Conservative Coalition	
Year	**S**	**O**	**S**	**O**	**S**	**O**
1996	66	20	84	4	12	84
1995	85	8	91	2	6	92
1994	60	24	74	12	8	83
1993	78	19	83	10	16	84
1992	9	86	80	9	10	77
1991	24	69	80	10	3	86

INTEREST GROUP RATINGS

Year	ADA	AFL-CIO	CCUS	ACU
1996	80	n/a	19	6
1995	100	100	13	4
1994	85	100	18	14
1993	100	100	0	0
1992	95	91	13	0
1991	90	100	20	0

2 James M. Talent (R)

Of Chesterfield — Elected 1992, 3rd term

Biographical Information
Born: Oct. 18, 1956, St. Louis, Mo.
Education: Washington U., B.A. 1978; U. of Chicago, J.D. 1981.
Occupation: Lawyer.
Family: Wife, Brenda Lyons; three children.
Religion: Presbyterian.
Political Career: Mo. House, 1985-93, minority leader, 1989-93.
Capitol Office: 1022 Longworth Bldg. 20515; 225-2561.

Committees
Education & Workforce
Employer-Employee Relations
National Security
Military Personnel; Military Procurement
Small Business (chairman)

In Washington: Fresh off his 1996 re-election to a third term, Talent began the 105th Congress as chairman of the House Small Business Committee and immediately pledged to cut taxes for small businesses and to reduce regulations that he sees as bureaucratic "red tape."

"Time and time again, I hear disturbing stories of the burden of outrageous regulations — regulations that offer no tangible benefit to the general public and yet continue to plague small business owners," Talent said. He also has pledged to use his chairmanship to work on revitalizing low-income communities. He endorsed enterprise zones, with cuts in capital gains taxes and government regulations, to spur economic development. In the 104th Congress, he joined GOP Rep. J.C. Watts of Oklahoma in introducing legislation creating 100 "renewal communities" that would be exempted from certain business regulations and capital gains taxes in order to encourage economic growth. State and local sales taxes also would be eliminated in these areas.

Talent arrived in Washington with substantial legislative experience, having served eight years in the Missouri House, half of that time as minority leader.

Drawing on that background, he moved quickly in Congress to make a contribution to the conservative GOP view on welfare reform. In the 104th, he advocated a tougher welfare overhaul bill than the one that eventually made it through Congress and onto President Clinton's desk.

In 1994, he sponsored legislation to cut off federal assistance for unmarried mothers younger than 21 and eventually under age 25. Talent's legislation was even more stringent than the welfare reform proposal in the House GOP's "Contract With America."

"I'm concerned that the contract bill may not go far enough in changing the incentives in the existing welfare system," Talent said in December 1994. "I'm going to work to make sure we do not shift the focus off of illegitimacy."

In the House Economic and Educational Opportunities Committee (now the Education and the Workforce Committee), he joined Rep. Tim Hutchinson, R-Ark., in the 104th to reduce from 12 weeks to four the amount of time welfare recipients could apply job searches to their work requirements — except in areas where unemployment exceeds the national average. He and Hutchinson also pushed through an amendment that would require able-bodied welfare recipients to work an average of 25 hours a week in fiscal 1999, increasing to 35 hours by fiscal 2002.

Talent criticized elements in the National Governors' Association's welfare overhaul proposal as too lenient. He said the NGA proposal would not do enough to reduce out-of-wedlock births or require states to move a significant amount of their caseload into jobs. "I've said over and over again for two years that real welfare reform means doing something about the problem of illegitimacy," he said.

He also objected to the NGA's proposals to make it easier for states to meet requirements that they move a certain percentage of welfare recipients into the workplace and to let states decide whether to use federal money to provide welfare checks for children born to welfare recipients. This latter point, known as the family cap, was an emotional issue throughout the welfare debate.

Talent also sits on the National Security Committee, a choice slot from which to monitor the interests of McDonnell Douglas Corp. The company has been headquartered in the 2nd and provides thousands of paychecks, but is planning to merge with Seattle-based Boeing Co. Talent has been a vocal critic of the Clinton administration's defense budgets.

Complaining that "systematic underfunding of the troops" is resulting in the "hollowing of the force," Talent said the "little things" in the armed forces, such as training and equipment, are disappearing. "Pretty soon you find that they cannot do what they were supposed to do, or they cannot do it as well. Or what is even more crucial, they cannot do it with the minimum loss of life."

MISSOURI 2
Western St. Louis County; Eastern St. Charles County

The suburban 2nd has some of Missouri's most affluent suburbs and some of the fastest-growing communities in the country. Republicans clearly dominate, but enough independent voters and blue-collar households remain to give Democratic candidates some audience.

Separate from the city of St. Louis since 1876, St. Louis County, the most populous jurisdiction in Missouri, makes up about 80 percent of the 2nd's population. The county has steadily filled with St. Louisans fleeing the urban center.

The heaviest concentration of Republicans is along the U.S. 40 corridor, across the heart of the 2nd. Communities such as Ladue and Frontenac have some of the area's wealthiest residents; the GOP vote is unshakable.

The affluent suburban vote has been spreading as the St. Louis suburbs have expanded west and northwest. Municipalities such as Chesterfield, Town and Country, and Ballwin are attracting the suburbanites who used to settle in Webster Groves, Kirkwood and other suburbs closer to the city. In the western part of the county, where subdivisions give way to unincorporated areas and farmland, affluent new arrivals mix with longtime residents of less lofty incomes and less predictable voting habits.

The southwestern part of the 2nd is home to the ghost town of Times Beach, site of one of the worst U.S. environmental disasters. Residents were threatened by health problems associated with dioxin-tainted soil.

The auto industry is a major employer in the district. At the southeastern corner, the district takes in the Chrysler assembly plant at Fenton. Two plants operated at the Fenton site until mid-1991, when Chrysler closed one, laying off about 4,000 workers. The second plant continues to make minivans. Ford's Hazelwood plant is here. General Motors' Wentzville facility, in the 9th District, employs many residents of the 2nd.

The 2nd has been the headquarters of the McDonnell Douglas Corp., but the aerospace giant plans to merge with the Boeing Co. McDonnell Douglas also has a plant adjacent to St. Louis' Lambert International Airport and is one of the largest employers here. These workers lend a blue-collar tinge to the "North County." Traditional working-class communities such as St. Ann, Overland, Bridgeton and Olivette are Democratic strongholds. The 2nd also takes in two-thirds of reliably Democratic Florissant.

About 20 percent of the district lies over the Missouri River in St. Charles County, which in each of the past two decades has grown about 50 percent.

The city of St. Charles served as Missouri's first capital from 1821 to 1826. The historic buildings on South Main Street have been restored, including the original Capitol. McDonnell Douglas manufactures the Harpoon missile at its St. Charles plant.

The rest of the 2nd in St. Charles County is rural. Soybeans and corn grow in the rich soil of the northern flood plain. In the summer of 1993, however, the floods that ravaged the Midwest devastated this area, which lies between the Missouri and Mississippi rivers.

1990 Population: 568,306. White 535,626 (94%), Black 21,149 (4%), Other 11,531 (2%). Hispanic origin 5,803 (1%). 18 and over 420,651 (74%), 62 and over 72,790 (13%). Median age: 34.

He joined with House Minority Leader Richard A. Gephardt, D-Mo., in seeking a review of the Pentagon's 1996 decision to choose Lockheed Martin Corp. and Boeing to build the demonstration aircraft for the Joint Strike Fighter program. The decision froze McDonnell Douglas out.

During 1994 House consideration of the annual defense authorization bill, Talent argued for an amendment to fund six C-17 cargo jets, built by McDonnell Douglas. The House Armed Services Committee had proposed buying only four. Talent said the C-17, which had struggled with performance and budget problems, "is at the crux of our plans for the American military over the next few years."

Across the waterfront of social-policy issues, Talent hews to a conservative line. He opposes abortion except in cases of rape, incest or threat to a woman's life. He voted against a bill that makes it a federal offense to use physical force or threats to prevent women from entering abortion clinics. Talent said the bill should not have singled out abortion protesters, but should have included violent acts on all types of picket lines. He would like to eliminate affirmative action in favor of initiatives to create economic opportunity for the disadvantaged. He voted against the family and medical leave bill.

Talent backs term limits and balanced-budget constitutional amendments, and he voted against banning certain semiautomatic assault-style weapons and against a five-day waiting period for handgun purchases. He supported GOP efforts to roll back federal environmental regulations. His rating from the AFL-CIO is typically at or near zero, while the U.S. Chamber of Commerce rates his voting record at or near perfect.

At Home: After breezing to re-election in 1994 against a weak Democratic challenger, Talent in 1996 faced a rematch with former Rep. Joan Kelly Horn, the Democrat he had ousted in 1992. Just as

Talent tried to portray Horn as too liberal for the district in his initial race, Horn in the rematch told voters that Talent was too conservative.

Horn also charged that Talent's support of efforts to locate a nuclear waste dump at Yucca Mountain in Nevada meant that the materials would be transported through the district along Interstate 70 or the Union Pacific railroad tracks. While that issue got the attention of a few voters (the district includes Times Beach, the town razed during the 1980s because of dioxin contamination). But over his four years in the 2nd, Talent had built up a bulwark of conservative support that Horn found unassailable. He won with a decisive 61 percent tally.

Republicans initially targeted Horn in 1992 because she had won the 2nd in 1990 by only 54 votes. Horn was further weakened by redistricting before the 1992 election; it removed several Democratic neighborhoods from a district that already had a record of voting for Republican presidential and statewide candidates.

But Talent still did not have an easy path to his initial victory. In the GOP primary, he faced Bert Walker or, more precisely, George Herbert Walker III — a cousin of then-President George Bush. Walker deployed two Cabinet members and roughly $600,000 in his campaign for the nomination, but Talent, with far less money and far more grass-roots support, beat him soundly.

The primary drained Talent's campaign treasury. Horn, a former political consultant, was a relatively strong candidate despite the redrawn 2nd's GOP slant. She had money to use against Talent and had tended to district concerns during her term.

But Talent allied himself with the popular yen for change, backing term limits and claiming that Horn flip-flopped to vote against a balanced-budget constitutional amendment she had helped sponsor. Talent eked out a 2 percentage point win, then rolled up two-thirds of the vote in the big GOP year of 1994 before facing Horn the second time in 1996.

Talent entered politics in 1984. After finishing law school and clerking for a Chicago judge, he returned to the St. Louis area and ran for the Missouri House, capturing a vacant seat in safe Republican territory. In 1988, he was elected minority floor leader. In the legislature, he was known as a strong fiscal and social conservative — even bucking GOP Gov. John Ashcroft on proposed education reforms that included a tax increase.

HOUSE ELECTIONS

1996 General		
James M. Talent (R)	165,999	(61%)
Joan Kelly Horn (D)	100,372	(37%)
Anton Charles Stever (LIBERT)	2,737	(1%)
1994 General		
James M. Talent (R)	154,882	(67%)
Pat Kelly (D)	70,480	(31%)
Jim Higgins (LIBERT)	4,925	(2%)

Previous Winning Percentages: 1992 (50%)

CAMPAIGN FINANCE

	Receipts	Receipts from PACs	Expend-itures
1996			
Talent (R)	$1,168,958	$277,433 (24%)	$1,165,81
Horn (D)	$385,763	$144,336 (37%)	$381,873
1994			
Talent (R)	$957,340	$250,249 (26%)	$773,953
Kelly (D)	$144,981	$15,700 (11%)	$135,867

DISTRICT VOTE FOR PRESIDENT

1996		1992	
D	115,386 (41%)	**D**	114,792 (36%)
R	138,136 (49%)	**R**	126,788 (40%)
I	22,756 (8%)	**I**	73,048 (23%)

KEY VOTES

1997	
Ban "partial birth" abortions	Y
1996	
Approve farm bill	Y
Deny public education to illegal immigrants	Y
Repeal ban on certain assault-style weapons	Y
Increase minimum wage	N
Freeze defense spending	N
Approve welfare overhaul	Y
1995	
Approve balanced-budget constitutional amendment	Y
Relax Clean Water Act regulations	Y
Oppose limits on environmental regulations	N
Reduce projected Medicare spending	Y
Approve GOP budget with tax and spending cuts	Y

VOTING STUDIES

	Presidential Support		Party Unity		Conservative Coalition	
Year	S	O	S	O	S	O
1996	30	66	90	6	86	10
1995	15	85	97	2	97	3
1994	50	49	94	5	97	3
1993	33	65	91	7	86	9

INTEREST GROUP RATINGS

Year	ADA	AFL-CIO	CCUS	ACU
1996	10	n/a	100	100
1995	0	0	100	96
1994	5	0	100	95
1993	10	8	82	96

3 Richard A. Gephardt (D)

Of St. Louis — Elected 1976, 11th term

Biographical Information

Born: Jan. 31, 1941, St. Louis, Mo.

Education: Northwestern U., B.S. 1962; U. of Michigan, J.D. 1965.

Military Service: Air National Guard, 1965-71.

Occupation: Lawyer.

Family: Wife, Jane Ann Byrnes; three children.

Religion: Baptist.

Political Career: St. Louis Board of Aldermen, 1971-76; sought Democratic nomination for president, 1988.

Capitol Office: 1226 Longworth Bldg. 20515; 225-2671.

Minority Leader

In Washington: Gephardt has his eye on two elections: 1998, when the Democrats will try to reclaim the House majority; and 2000, when the Democrats will choose a nominee to succeed Bill Clinton in the White House.

In late 1996 and during the early months of the 105th Congress, Gephardt aggressively marketed the Democratic Party — and by extension, himself — as both progressive and reasonable.

In November 1996, after being re-elected as minority leader, Gephardt reiterated his support for the Democrats' "Families First" agenda, including a "sensibly" balanced budget, environment and education programs, and revised pension laws. And in January 1997, Gephardt stressed that he would not support a budget agreement that appeared to benefit wealthy Americans at the expense of children, the elderly and middle-class families.

True to that warning, when the House in May 1997 considered a budget plan that had been worked out between President Clinton and congressional Republicans, Gephardt voted "no." He said the plan cut spending to subsidize tax cuts for well-off Americans. "This budget isn't fair," Gephardt told the House. "At a time when we are asking average, hard-working Americans to tighten their belts, we shouldn't be telling the wealthiest Americans that not only don't they have to participate, they'll actually get a huge tax cut." He was the only member of the top House Democratic leadership to vote against the budget outline, which passed 333-99.

Earlier in 1997, Gephardt had hinted his crankiness about some aspects of the White House and Republican effort to reach a budget agreement, particularly in the matter of adjusting the Consumer Price Index (CPI). Some economists argue that the CPI overstates actual inflation, and adjusting it downward would make it easier to balance the budget by reducing automatic cost-of-living increases in entitlement programs. Gephardt, however, came out against the idea in February 1997, writing in a letter to Clinton: "Because of the singularly important place that Social Security holds in the lives of retired Americans...I will oppose any effort to place this [CPI] decision into a politically brokered budget agreement." A slight adjustment of the CPI was assumed in the budget deal.

In his floor speech opposing the budget, Gephardt maintained that the agreement would lead to the deficit ballooning after 2002 because of the impact of the plan's tax cuts. He said the plan was "a budget of many deficits — a deficit of principle, a deficit of fairness, a deficit of tax justice, and, worst of all, a deficit of dollars."

As the budget discord showed, relations between Gephardt and the Clinton-Gore administration are not always the best. On several issues — protecting entitlements, trade privileges for China, abortion policy — Gephardt has his own views, and in some cases they highlight distinctions between himself and Vice President Al Gore, the likely front-runner for the 2000 Democratic presidential nomination.

Gephardt has voted to ban a particular abortion technique that its opponents call "partial birth" abortion; Clinton vetoed the ban.

And Gephardt has come out against renewing most favored nation trade status for China, which the Clinton administration supported. Gephardt is a longtime advocate of "fair trade" (as opposed to the "free trade" bent of Clinton and congressional Republicans). In 1993, Gephardt was an opponent of NAFTA, for which Clinton and Gore lobbied aggressively.

It was Gephardt who, on Jan. 4, 1995, the opening day of the 104th Congress, executed the official transfer from Democratic to Republican rule in the House. "With resignation but with resolve, I hereby end 40 years of Democratic rule of this House," he said when passing the gavel to Gingrich. "You are now my Speaker. Let the great debate begin."

Gephardt spent the 104th trying to mold the Democrats into a cohesive, unified minority and trying to occupy the political middle ground. The party used some of the same guerrilla-type tactics

For years, south St. Louis has been a collection of white working-class neighborhoods that reflect the European heritage of their residents. While the city's high-crime and low-income areas are primarily associated with north St. Louis (in the 1st District), the south has not been immune. Crime has risen in south St. Louis and spilled over the city limits into St. Louis County.

With its declining population, the city now accounts for less than a third of the vote in the 3rd. Much of that vestige still has a heavily ethnic European cast. Italians are clustered in The Hill, where family-owned businesses have survived for generations. Bevo Mill and Carondelet are old-line German communities. Mounting threats of crime have energized powerful neighborhood associations to arrest the decline of housing values in south St. Louis. In some neighborhoods, these groups rival the Democratic ward machines for power and organization.

McDonnell Douglas Corp., Anheuser-Busch, Monsanto, Barnes Hospital and the area automobile assembly plants have been major employers of the 3rd's blue-collar workers. But McDonnell Douglas plans to merge with Boeing, the nation's other major aircraft manufacturer.

The wards along the Mississippi, near the Anheuser-Busch brewery, are home to the poorest whites. Affluent whites live in the St. Louis Hills neighborhood, in the southwest part of the city. It is the city's only Republican area. For the most part, south St. Louis is residential and middle class. Monsanto and Mallinckrodt chemical facilities and barge operations along the Mississippi are important to the 3rd's economy. But the most prominent enterprise in this part of the city is Anheuser-Busch, one of the city's biggest employers.

MISSOURI 3
South St. Louis; southeast St. Louis County; Jefferson and Ste. Genevieve counties

Looking to escape from typical urban ills in many north St. Louis neighborhoods, blacks have been moving into the south wards. Whites, in turn, have sought the St. Louis County suburbs, in communities such as Lemay, Afton and Concord.

Some kept on going until they reached Jefferson County, where the population ballooned from about 146,000 to more than 171,000 during the 1980s. The southern part of Jefferson remains predominantly rural. Farmers in the Hillsboro area regularly truck their produce to markets in downtown St. Louis. Jefferson backed George Bush in 1988, but Bill Clinton won in both 1992 and 1996. Gephardt's 15,000-vote margin in the county trailed only his 23,000-vote margin in the portion of the city of St. Louis in the 3rd.

Ste. Genevieve County has escaped the rapid residential expansion of its neighbors. Founded by French lead miners in the 1720s, the city of Ste. Genevieve was the first permanent settlement in Missouri. Its roots are evident in restored French homes downtown. The Mississippi Lime Co. tops the list of city employers, but much of the county's land is devoted to corn, soybeans and hogs.

1990 Population: 568,326. White 547,496 (96%), Black 13,342 (2%), Other 7,488 (1%). Hispanic origin 6,513 (1%). 18 and over 428,779 (75%), 62 and over 100,122 (18%). Median age: 34.

Gingrich specialized in when Republicans were in the minority. A case in point came in June 1995, when Democrats brought the House to a crawl, demanding repeated roll call votes and forcing the chamber into its first all-night session of the year after Republicans added party-switcher Greg Laughlin of Texas to the powerful Ways and Means Committee but did not add another Democrat. "It's a shameless attempt to stack the deck on House committees," Gephardt said.

The first months of the 104th were tough for Gephardt and House Democrats, as the GOP pushed through its "Contract With America" agenda. But as the Congress wore on, Democrats got the better of the GOP on some issues, including protecting the environment and most especially increasing the minimum wage. The Democrats forced an unwilling GOP leadership to deal with that issue by relentlessly pressing their message and coordinating with well-funded outside groups, mostly organized labor. With the help of some GOP moderates, the wage increase passed.

And time and time again, Gephardt returned to his basic theme that Republicans were cutting vital federal programs to provide tax cuts for the wealthy. "Republicans always revert to form; they always want to help people at the top," Gephardt said. "They believe wealth trickles down."

While Gingrich was plagued throughout his first term as Speaker by ethical questions, Gephardt also came under some scrutiny. Jennifer Dunn, R-Wash., asked the ethics committee in February 1996 to check whether Gephardt had filed contradictory information about his acquisition of a vacation home in North Carolina. In 1991, Gephardt traded property in Duck, N.C., for beachfront property in nearby Corolla, thus taking advantage of a capital gains tax exemption permitted for investment properties. But Dunn noted that Gephardt listed the Duck property on his congressional financial disclosure forms as a "vacation home" and reported no rental income.

In September 1996, Democrats offered a resolution requiring the ethics committee to release special counsel James M. Cole's report on Gingrich. It was tabled, 225-179. John Linder, R-Ga., then offered a resolution calling on a special counsel to look into the charges against Gephardt. Linder's resolution was tabled, 395-9.

At month's end, Gephardt filed an amended disclosure form listing rental income of $25,000 to $50,000 on the property for 1992. A day later, the ethics committee dismissed the complaint against him, although it upbraided him for failing to properly disclose income from a vacation property.

At Home: For the third time in four elections, Gephardt in 1996 finished below 60 percent in 1996. But he still had a comfortable advantage over Republican Deborah Lynn Wheelehan, an office manager. He outraised her by better than 52 to 1 and beat her 59 percent to 39 percent.

In 1994, first-time candidate Gary Gill depicted Gephardt as the embodiment of Congress' ills, beholden to the special interest groups that helped fill his campaign treasury. Gephardt retaliated with negative TV and radio ads which said that by signing the GOP's contract, Gill showed he wanted to cut Social Security benefits. Vastly outspent, Gill lost, 58 percent to 40 percent.

Gephardt polled 57 percent in 1990 but might really have had to sweat if state and national Republicans had been able to run their preferred candidate, St. Louis County Election Board member Stephen Doss. Instead, a number of St. Louis County Republicans lined up behind former Webster Groves City Council member Malcolm L. "Mack" Holekamp. Both filed for the GOP primary and, after several weeks of finger-pointing, Doss quit the race. At that point, the national GOP lost interest in the contest, and Holekamp, though a feisty challenger, had trouble raising money.

Gephardt first was elected to Congress in 1976 on the strength of his reputation as a young activist on the machine-dominated St. Louis Board of Aldermen. While on the board, he had sponsored zoning laws to preserve ethnic neighborhoods, building a constituency among German-American working-class communities on the city's South Side. He also supported a constitutional amendment to restrict abortions, a position that he abandoned later in his career.

In the 1976 Democratic primary, Gephardt defeated state Sen. Donald J. Gralike, head of an electrical workers local. Gephardt's November opponent was Republican Joseph L. Badaracco, who had served eight years as a St. Louis alderman, six of those as board president. Badaracco stressed his reputation for honesty in city politics and portrayed Gephardt as a rich downtown lawyer groomed for Congress by the pin-striped establishment. Gephardt promised to emulate the moderate approach of Democratic Rep. Leonor K. Sullivan, who was retiring. He won with ease.

HOUSE ELECTIONS

1996 General		
Richard A. Gephardt (D)	137,300	(59%)
Deborah Lynn "Debbie" Wheelehan (R)	90,202	(39%)
Michael H. Crist (LIBERT)	3,966	(2%)
1996 Primary		
Richard A. Gephardt (D)	45,619	(75%)
Joseph C. Keller (D)	12,390	(20%)
Leif O. Johnson (D)	2,690	(4%)
1994 General		
Richard A. Gephardt (D)	117,601	(58%)
Gary Gill (R)	80,977	(40%)
Bradley Ems (LIBERT)	5,362	(3%)

Previous Winning Percentages: **1992** (64%) **1990** (57%) **1988** (63%) **1986** (69%) **1984** (100%) **1982** (78%) **1980** (78%) **1978** (82%) **1976** (64%)

CAMPAIGN FINANCE

	Receipts	Receipts from PACs	Expend-itures
1996			
Gephardt (D)	$3,309,642	$1,169,422 (35%)	$3,110,509
Wheelehan (R)	$62,960	$4,325 (7%)	$62,504
1994			
Gephardt (D)	$2,509,186	$1,010,316 (40%)	$2,621,479
Gill (R)	$198,235	$14,619 (7%)	$196,461

DISTRICT VOTE FOR PRESIDENT

1996		1992	
D	116,377 (49%)	**D**	120,866 (44%)
R	93,134 (39%)	**R**	87,406 (32%)
I	25,626 (11%)	**I**	64,511 (24%)

KEY VOTES

1997	
Ban "partial-birth" abortions	Y
1996	
Approve farm bill	N
Deny public education to illegal immigrants	N
Repeal ban on certain assault-style weapons	N
Increase minimum wage	Y
Freeze defense spending	Y
Approve welfare overhaul	N
1995	
Approve balanced-budget constitutional amendment	N
Relax Clean Water Act regulations	?
Oppose limits on environmental regulations	Y
Reduce projected Medicare spending	N
Approve GOP budget with tax and spending cuts	N

VOTING STUDIES

	Presidential Support		Party Unity		Conservative Coalition	
Year	S	O	S	O	S	O
1996	73	16	81	6	33	63
1995	79	14	88	5	22	70
1994	86	9	93	0	17	64
1993	86	9	91	4	30	68
1992	16	76	88	4	33	58
1991	30	68	90	5	22	70

INTEREST GROUP RATINGS

Year	ADA	AFL-CIO	CCUS	ACU
1996	85	n/a	27	6
1995	85	100	30	12
1994	80	89	33	5
1993	90	100	9	8
1992	85	78	25	0
1991	75	92	30	0

4 Ike Skelton (D)

Of Lexington — Elected 1976, 11th term

Biographical Information

Born: Dec. 20, 1931, Lexington, Mo.

Education: Wentworth Military Academy, A.A. 1951; U. of Edinburgh (Scotland), 1953; U. of Missouri, A.B. 1953, LL.B. 1956.

Occupation: Lawyer.

Family: Wife, Susan Anding; three children.

Religion: Christian Church.

Political Career: Lafayette County prosecuting attorney, 1957-60; Mo. special assistant attorney general, 1961-63; Mo. Senate, 1971-77.

Capitol Office: 2227 Rayburn Bldg. 20515; 225-2876.

Committees

Select Intelligence
Technical & Tactical Intelligence

National Security
Military Personnel; Military Procurement (ranking)

In Washington: When Democrats controlled the House, Skelton was a key member of the centrist Democratic coalition on the Armed Services Committee that acted as a counterweight to the panel's liberal chairman, Ronald V. Dellums of California. Under Republican rule, Skelton finds he has much in common with the GOP leadership on his committee (now called National Security), who share his support for higher defense budgets and continued production of the B-2 "stealth" bomber, and who echoed his concerns about sending U.S. troops to Bosnia as peacekeepers.

An avid student of military history, Skelton is unabashedly pro-defense, but he also is not reluctant to challenge Pentagon civilians and the military brass. And he is favorably disposed toward some causes that some hawkish conservatives have been slow to embrace. For instance, he supported an active U.S. role in helping former Soviet states dismantle their nuclear, chemical and biological weapons arsenals. And he expressed strong concern about reports of sexual harassment of women at Army training bases, including Fort Leonard Wood, located in Skelton's district.

Now the ranking member of the Military Procurement Subcommittee, Skelton had been chairman of the Military Forces and Personnel Subcommittee before Republicans took over the House in 1995. In that position, he urged caution in reducing the nation's post-Cold War defense commitment, and he criticized some of President Clinton's plans to cut military spending.

Skelton's desire to protect military spending was on display in February 1995, when the House considered an "enhanced rescissions" bill that would have allowed the president to kill or reduce any dollar item in a spending bill, Skelton offered an amendment to exempt from recission any defense program costing $50 million or more. Skelton said he aimed to protect national defense from any president who might cut defense spending too much. But opponents argued that all discretionary spending ought to be vulnerable to the bill's provisions, and his amendment was overwhelmingly rejected, 52-362.

Also in 1995, Skelton was a key member of a group that persuaded the House to fund production of additional B-2 bombers. His district includes Whiteman Air Force Base, home of the B-2 fleet. Skelton waged a successful effort in the 1980s to convince the Air Force to station the bomber at Whiteman.

Proponents of the radar-evading plane managed to add increased funds for B-2 procurement as part of the fiscal 1996 Pentagon funding request, even though defense officials maintained that the 20 planes previously funded were enough. Opponents of the added funds included many deficit-minded Republicans, such as Budget Committee Chairman John R. Kasich of Ohio, a longtime B-2 critic. But Skelton and his allies prevailed, defeating the amendment to kill the funding on a 203-219 vote.

Opposed to sending U.S. troops to Bosnia, Skelton predicted that future historians would look back on the operation as the "American folly of 1995." But he shied away from cutting off funds for the troop deployment. In December 1995 he sponsored a resolution with Indiana Republican Steve Buyer that expressed support for the troops, but disowned President Clinton's deployment decision and insisted that the United States remain scrupulously neutral among Bosnia's contending parties. The House approved their resolution, 287-141.

Skelton told the House he was worried that the Clinton administration had formally agreed to coordinate the arming and the training of the Moslem forces. "This policy defies common sense, because it will cause U.S. troops to be viewed as favoring one side over the other," he said. "It will destroy our impartiality and puts our troops in danger."

Skelton is not unwilling to challenge the defense establishment if serious shortcomings appear, as seemed to be the case in the fall of 1996 when published reports alleged that Army drill instructors at several training bases had pressured female recruits for sex. Some conservatives suggested that the training incidents highlighted the peril of laws and Pentagon policies broadening the role of women in

MISSOURI 4
West Central — Kansas City suburbs; Jefferson City

The 4th is splayed two-thirds of the way across the state, stretching south and east from suburban bedroom communities in Jackson County (Kansas City) to encompass rural farmland, resort areas and small cities — including the state capital of Jefferson City. The easternmost point of the 4th in Osage County is just 75 miles from St. Louis.

Voters in the 4th are conservative, and the GOP presidential nominee usually fares well. Bob Dole carried the district in 1996, leading in 14 of its 23 counties, though he beat Bill Clinton only by 5 percentage points. Ross Perot racked up 12 percent.

But the district is more conservative Democratic than rock-ribbed Republican, and the right kind of Democrat can do quite well, as Skelton's comfortable re-elections demonstrate. For Democrats perceived as liberal, the 4th can be forbidding. Rep. Alan Wheat lost every county in the district in his failed 1994 Senate bid.

Moderate Democrats running for statewide office can find support in the western portion of the 4th. Toward the east, however, voter tendencies take a Republican turn. Democrats in competitive contests rarely top one-third of the vote in Cole, Miller and Osage counties.

Much of the 4th is devoted to small farming. While the farm economy has brightened considerably since the mid-1980s, it remains unsettled. Here, as elsewhere in the state, young people are leaving the farms to find steadier employment.

Corn, wheat and soybeans are grown in the rich soil along the Missouri River, on the 4th's northern frontier, as well as in the west. Livestock and dairy production dominate the southern part of the district, where the terrain turns hilly and rocky. The floods ravaging the Midwest in the summer of 1993 put much of northern Missouri under water.

The greatest growth in the 1980s within the 4th was registered in the Lake of the Ozarks resort area and in the suburbs outside Kansas City (especially the growing Cass County suburbs to the south). Retirees have been drawn to the Lake of the Ozarks area, in the center of the district.

State government has been a fairly reliable source of jobs in Cole County, just slightly less populous than Cass. Jefferson City also has some light industry. Chesebrough Ponds makes Q-Tips at its Jefferson City plant.

Military installations have been a major factor in the economy. Whiteman Air Force Base in Johnson County houses the first wing of B-2 stealth bombers, and the Army's Fort Leonard Wood is in Pulaski County. The Pentagon's 1991 base-closing plan prompted the 1994 closure of Richards-Gebaur Air Force Base in Cass County.

Sedalia (Pettis County) once was a railhead of the Missouri Pacific Railroad and an entertainment mecca for rail workers. Ragtime composer Scott Joplin got his start in a Sedalia club. Every June, Sedalia holds the Scott Joplin Ragtime Festival, attracting artists from across the country.

1990 Population: 569,146. White 542,723 (95%), Black 18,271 (3%), Other 6,214 (1%). Hispanic origin 8,152 (1%). 18 and over 420,347 (74%), 62 and over 98,757 (17%). Median age: 34.

the military.

But Skelton focused on the alleged transgressions of the drill instructors, noting the tremendous power that they wield over recruits under their command, who typically are in their late teens. "No one is more powerful in America than a drill sergeant — their word is law," Skelton fumed. "The few drill sergeants who break that trust do irreparable harm, not just to their service, and not just to their victims, but to the respect that Americans have for people in uniform."

Skelton also split with some House conservatives in his support of the Nunn-Lugar program, aimed at helping former Soviet states dispose of their nuclear arsenal. He opposed an amendment to the fiscal 1997 defense bill that would have barred assistance to Russia and Belarus unless the president certified to Congress that those countries were abstaining from several military and diplomatic activities, including modernizing their nuclear forces, conducting offensive military operations in Chechnya or providing intelligence information to Cuba.

Skelton was among those arguing that the Nunn-Lugar program held out promise of eliminating potential military threats to the United States and should not be linked to Russian behavior in other areas of policy. The House rejected the amendment, 202-220.

When he chaired the Armed Services subcommittee dealing with personnel issues, Skelton was in the middle of the fierce 1993 debate on homosexuals in the military. Clinton set off a firestorm in January 1993 by proposing to revoke the military's "gay ban." Skelton, who said he had qualms about lifting the ban, ended up supporting a compromise that Clinton worked out with military officials and key congressional Democrats. Clinton settled for a modest revision of the policy under which homosexual conduct in the military still would be prohibited, but military recruits no longer would be asked if they were homosexual.

Skelton disagreed with the liberal majority of House Democrats on many social issues. He opposes abortion in most cases and voted in the 104th to repeal the ban on certain semiautomatic assault-style weapons.

Skelton also was one of only 29 Democrats in the 103rd Congress to vote against the family and medical leave act. But he did agree with most Democrats in the 104th that the minimum wage should be raised.

At Home: In 11 general elections, Skelton has never won less than 55 percent in his conservative-leaning district. His toughest race occurred in 1982, when redistricting threw him together with freshman Republican Rep. Wendell Bailey.

Mapmakers gave Skelton a head start in the 1982 race. When Bailey's old 8th District was dismembered, the largest single block of his constituents was added to Skelton's 4th. So Bailey decided that was the place to seek a second term. But for every one of his old constituents in the new district, there were nearly two of Skelton's.

The Skelton-Bailey match was billed as a referendum on Reaganomics in the rural heartland. The candidates responded appropriately: Skelton called Bailey a "rubber stamp" because he supported nearly all of Reagan's budget and tax proposals, and Bailey countered that Skelton's mixed record of support for Reaganomics showed him to be a liberal who occasionally waffled to appease conservatives.

Bailey was relying on the gregarious, hard-charging style he developed as a car salesman to help him pull Democrats away from the less dynamic Skelton. But Skelton, a small-town lawyer with a sincere, low-key style, benefited from greater familiarity with the new district's voters. Of the seven counties that had been part of Bailey's old 8th District, Bailey carried six. But Skelton had represented 13 counties and managed to carry 12 of them. That brought him victory with 55 percent.

Skelton's only other tough House election was his first, in 1976, when he won the seat of retiring Democratic Rep. William Randall. As a rural state legislator with a narrow political base, Skelton did not look particularly well-positioned when the campaign began. Only two counties in his state Senate district were within the borders of the 4th District as it was then drawn. His major rivals for the Democratic nomination were state senators from the Kansas City suburbs, which cast about 40 percent of the district vote.

Skelton emphasized his rural roots and campaigned successfully for farm and small-town support. He ran third in the suburbs, but with the rural vote he won nomination with 40 percent.

Independence Mayor Richard A. King was the GOP nominee. A protégé to then-Gov. (and now Sen.) Christopher S. Bond, King tied his campaign to the GOP ticket of Bond and Senate candidate John C. Danforth. Skelton cited his farm background and fiscal conservatism. And the top of the GOP ticket did not give King much coattail pull. Danforth carried the 4th, but Bond lost it. Skelton won with 56 percent.

In 1996, Skelton won 64 percent against former Missouri Lt. Gov. Bill Phelps, who had worked as a life insurance executive in Houston after losing the 1980 GOP gubernatorial primary. Phelps returned to his native state in 1996 and won the GOP House primary in the 4th. But Skelton referred to Phelps as "Pecos Bill" and said he had abandoned Missourians.

HOUSE ELECTIONS

1996 General		
Ike Skelton (D)	153,566	(64%)
Bill Phelps (R)	81,650	(34%)
Edwin "Ed" Hoag (LIBERT)	5,573	(2%)
1994 General		
Ike Skelton (D)	137,876	(68%)
James A. Noland Jr. (R)	65,616	(32%)

Previous Winning Percentages: 1992 (70%) **1990** (62%) **1988** (72%) **1986** (100%) **1984** (67%) **1982** (55%) **1980** (68%) **1978** (73%) **1976** (56%)

CAMPAIGN FINANCE

	Receipts	Receipts from PACs	Expend-itures
1996			
Skelton (D)	$680,816	$369,147 (54%)	$770,607
Phelps (R)	$326,078	$60,500 (19%)	$316,989
Hoag (LIBERT)	$161	0	$0
1994			
Skelton (D)	$415,058	$218,500 (53%)	$427,184
Noland (R)	$16,666	$264 (2%)	$15,666

DISTRICT VOTE FOR PRESIDENT

1996		1992	
D	100,159 (41%)	**D**	94,951 (37%)
R	111,158 (46%)	**R**	96,752 (38%)
I	29,038 (12%)	**I**	65,231 (25%)

KEY VOTES

1997	
Ban "partial birth" abortions	Y
1996	
Approve farm bill	Y
Deny public education to illegal immigrants	N
Repeal ban on certain assault-style weapons	Y
Increase minimum wage	Y
Freeze defense spending	N
Approve welfare overhaul	Y
1995	
Approve balanced-budget constitutional amendment	Y
Relax Clean Water Act regulations	Y
Oppose limits on environmental regulations	X
Reduce projected Medicare spending	N
Approve GOP budget with tax and spending cuts	N

VOTING STUDIES

	Presidential Support		Party Unity		Conservative Coalition	
Year	S	O	S	O	S	O
1996	66	34	57	42	100	0
1995	53	45	49	50	88	10
1994	78	22	67	29	97	0
1993	73	25	70	27	86	14
1992	57	38	66	31	83	15
1991	52	47	65	32	92	5

INTEREST GROUP RATINGS

Year	ADA	AFL-CIO	CCUS	ACU
1996	40	n/a	60	50
1995	40	75	61	42
1994	35	56	67	62
1993	35	80	45	43
1992	45	67	86	65
1991	30	67	60	47

5 Karen McCarthy (D)

Of Kansas City — Elected 1994, 2nd term

Biographical Information
Born: March 18, 1947, Haverhill, Mass.
Education: U. of Kansas, B.S. 1969, M.B.A. 1986; U. of Birmingham, England, 1974; U. of Missouri, Kansas City, M.A. 1976.
Occupation: Teacher.
Family: Divorced.
Religion: Roman Catholic.
Political Career: Mo. State House, 1977-95.
Capitol Office: 1232 Longworth Bldg. 20515; 225-4535.

Committees
Commerce
Energy & Power; Telecommunications, Trade & Consumer Protection

In Washington: McCarthy is a former president of the National Conference of State Legislatures and a 12-year chairman of the Missouri House Ways and Means Committee, and after one term watching her operate in the House, Democratic leaders evidently liked what they saw: She won promotion in the 105th to the influential Commerce Committee. Her seat on its Energy and Power Subcommittee gives her a say in Congress' consideration of high-stakes legislation to deregulate the electric utility industry.

McCarthy's philosophy blends a generous portion of mainstream Democratic liberalism with a dash of sympathy for conservatives' thinking on certain topics, such as the GOP creed that state and local governments should have more authority.

In the 104th, she was an early supporter of Republican efforts to prevent Washington from putting mandates on state and local governments without providing funds to meet those mandates. The effort to bar "unfunded mandates" drew criticism from some liberal Democrats, who accused conservatives of seeking to undermine or eliminate federal environmental, labor and public-health laws.

But McCarthy told the House in 1995 that as "a former state legislative leader, I am very sensitive to the potential financial and administrative burdens that federal unfunded mandates place on state governments."

Early in the 104th Congress, McCarthy was one of 72 Democrats voting in favor of amending the Constitution to require a balanced budget. She backed a version of the measure that would have required a balanced budget by 2002, or two years after ratification, whichever was later.

"I was elected to end the practice of irresponsible federal deficit spending," she said. "I believe the adoption of a balanced-budget amendment to the Constitution is the first step in the process toward greater fiscal responsibility."

McCarthy had considerable background in one of the big issues tackled by the 104th: welfare reform. In the Missouri legislature, she successfully sponsored legislation that provided job training programs and day-care services to women on welfare as part of an effort to move them into the work force.

She took a dim view of the Republican approach to overhauling welfare, saying, among other things, that it would make "punitive reductions in food stamp benefits." She supported a Democratic alternative that she said "ensures that families working their way out of poverty will be able to put food on the table."

However, when compromise welfare legislation emerged from a House-Senate conference in July 1996, McCarthy voted for it, even though many liberal Democrats insisted that the measure would add more than 1 million children to the poverty ranks.

President Clinton signed the welfare bill, which ended the 61-year-old federal guarantee to provide welfare checks to all eligible low-income mothers and children. Instead, states will receive predetermined lump-sum federal payments known as block grants, and they will have broad authority to determine eligibility and benefits.

McCarthy's liberal colors are most plain in her reaction to GOP spending priorities and proposals for tax cuts. As a member of the Science Committee in the 104th, she criticized the Republicans for funding NASA's space station while cutting back on child nutrition programs.

"The Republicans claim they received a clear electoral message [in 1994] that the nation was ready for change. Well, we have begun to see what their definition of change means," she said. "If you are a poor, hungry child in America, then you have to wait in line behind the space station and tax breaks for the wealthy before you can receive a nutritious meal." She complained that the GOP majority wanted "to cut child nutrition programs, loans for college students and programs for the elderly, as well as increase taxes on federal employees, to pay for tax cuts that mainly accrue to the top wage earners in this country."

She consistently votes against increases in the

MISSOURI 5
Kansas City and eastern suburbs; Independence

From its fountains and skyscrapers to its barbecue joints and sports complex, one-time cow town Kansas City is now a modern, frontline U.S. city. It passed St. Louis as Missouri's most populous city in the 1990 census — because it has lost population more slowly.

While Kansas City remains a nationally prominent market for feeder cattle and hard winter wheat, the city's economy is far more diverse than its longtime image implies. The stockyards' heyday ended decades ago. Diversity enabled Kansas City to weather economic doldrums better than many urban areas.

The district is solidly Democratic: Bill Clinton carried the 5th by wide margins in both 1992 and 1996. That helped Democrat Alan Wheat, who is black and had always attracted biracial support, maintain a steady hold on the white-majority district for six terms, and made McCarthy the heavy favorite once she won the primary in 1994.

Long a center for automobile production, metropolitan Kansas City is one of the nation's largest auto producers. Ford has an expanding plant north of the city in Claycomo (in the 6th District); General Motors' Fairfax assembly plant is just across the Missouri River in Kansas. Many autoworkers live in blue-collar neighborhoods in Kansas City and in nearby Independence.

Other blue-collar workers who live in the district work at Kansas City International Airport, north of the city. Trans World Airlines has a large base there, where it overhauls its aircraft.

With many regional offices in the city and across the Kansas border, the federal government is one of the area's largest employers. The steel, transportation and communications industries are significant as well. Hallmark Cards is a hometown corporation and has spent millions on commercial redevelopment within the city. It built Crown Center, which includes an array of restaurants, shops, pricey apartments and a luxury hotel. Hallmark and other major corporations received some unflattering attention in 1991 with their "screening committee" to dub an acceptable mayoral candidate. Ultimately, City Council member Emanuel Cleaver, who had been snubbed by the corporate elite, won the election, becoming Kansas City's first black mayor.

Though Kansas City has not suffered the flight of people and businesses that has drained St. Louis, its population has declined to about 435,000 — fewer people than were living in the city 30 years ago. For a generation there has been steady out-migration to Jackson County suburbs and into Johnson County, Kan.

But Kansas City has not capitulated. Yuppies have been lured back to the central city by projects such as the restoration of the Quality Hill section, one of Kansas City's oldest areas, and of City Market, an outdoor market in use since the 1800s. And the city boasts an outstanding housing stock around the University of Missouri-Kansas City.

To the east, the 5th includes Independence (population 112,300), the fourth most populous city in Missouri and hometown of Harry S Truman.

1990 Population: 569,130. White 416,843 (73%), Black 134,608 (24%), Other 17,679 (3%). Hispanic origin 18,032 (3%). 18 and over 428,226 (75%), 62 and over 93,429 (16%). Median age: 33.

defense budget, and in June 1996 she supported a bipartisan effort to freeze the fiscal 1997 defense budget at the prior year level.

On most social-policy issues, McCarthy votes with the liberal side of her party, supporting a woman's right to abortion and opposing efforts to repeal the ban on certain semiautomatic assault-style weapons. She did, however, vote for a measure barring federal recognition of same-sex marriages.

She also votes for labor causes, reflecting the views of Kansas City's sizable blue-collar workforce. McCarthy supported the successful Democratic effort to raise the minimum wage in 1996, and she has opposed a GOP effort to allow companies to offer employees compensatory time off in lieu of overtime pay. Proponents say the plan would give workers more flexibility to take time off, but organized labor and most congressional Democrats worry that employees might be coerced into accepting time off when they really want overtime pay.

McCarthy joined the Transportation and Infrastructure Committee in June 1995, and she backed a proposal by Chairman Bud Shuster, a Pennsylvania Republican, to place the transportation trust funds "off-budget." Shuster and other proponents of this move say it is dishonest for Congress to allow money to build up in the trust funds (which are financed by taxes on gasoline, airplane tickets and cargo) and then count those monies as part of the annual budget in order to mask the size of the federal deficit. They argue that the trust funds were meant to be spent on infrastructure needs, not hoarded.

"In my state of Missouri, we have more than $1.7 billion in unmet highway needs, including 261 lane miles of 4-lane highway needs, and 136 bridges in need of major repair or replacement," McCarthy told the House. This measure "will remove the transportation trust funds from the artificial constraints that prevent needed money from being released." The House passed the bill, 284-143, in April 1996, but it did not make it into law in the 104th Congress.

At Home: A former English teacher, economic analyst for an investment banking firm and 18-year veteran of the Missouri House, McCarthy was regarded as a favorite to win the 5th when black Democratic Rep. Alan Wheat left it for an unsuccessful 1994 Senate campaign.

Her status as front-runner, however, did not discourage competition. Ten others ran in the Democratic primary, and there were some fireworks. Jackie McGee, a black candidate and one of McCarthy's colleagues in the state legislature, blasted a local black political organization for backing McCarthy. McGee reportedly described the organization, Freedom Inc., as "a bunch of Uncle Toms who are only concerned about how much money they can get for an election." Another candidate, Edward "Gomer" Moody, seemed to be fanning anti-Semitism when he made an issue out of the fact that another candidate had changed his name from Myron Silverstein to Myron Sildon.

McCarthy's well-financed and well-organized campaign stayed above the fray, and she rolled to nomination with 41 percent of the vote.

In the general election, McCarthy faced an appealing political outsider, conservative black Republican Ron Freeman. A former professional football player who worked for seven years as an urban youth coordinator for the Fellowship of Christian Athletes, Freeman was a forceful speaker and an energetic campaigner. He had fundraising support from Jack F. Kemp. Freeman's positions — for welfare reform, school vouchers, term limits and a balanced-budget amendment, against abortion, universal health care and gay-rights legislation — were backed by a compelling personal story of early poverty overcome through determination, hard work and faith.

While the population of the 5th is 73 percent white, the district showed its willingness to vote across racial lines during Wheat's 12-year tenure.

But for all of Freeman's personal appeal, his message was simply too conservative for the district, which is dominated by the urban Democrats of Kansas City. Aided by her contacts in the Kansas City business community and support from national women's and labor groups, McCarthy enjoyed a $350,000 financial advantage. She ended up winning by a comfortable margin, 57 percent to 43 percent.

In 1996, she rolled up two-thirds of the vote to win a second term.

HOUSE ELECTIONS

1996 General		
Karen McCarthy (D)	144,223	(67%)
Penny Bennett (R)	61,803	(29%)
Kevin Hertel (LIBERT)	4,110	(2%)
Tom Danaher (NL)	3,835	(2%)
1994 General		
Karen McCarthy (D)	100,391	(57%)
Ron Freeman (R)	77,120	(43%)

CAMPAIGN FINANCE

	Receipts	Receipts from PACs	Expend-itures
1996			
McCarthy (D)	$488,706	$280,050 (57%)	$220,339
1994			
McCarthy (D)	$885,192	$328,571 (37%)	$866,808
Freeman (R)	$488,579	$74,810 (15%)	$458,373

DISTRICT VOTE FOR PRESIDENT

1996	1992
D 127,432 (58%)	D 134,932 (52%)
R 71,231 (33%)	R 67,503 (26%)
I 17,446 (8%)	I 55,763 (22%)

KEY VOTES

1997	
Ban "partial birth" abortions	N
1996	
Approve farm bill	N
Deny public education to illegal immigrants	N
Repeal ban on certain assault-style weapons	N
Increase minimum wage	Y
Freeze defense spending	Y
Approve welfare overhaul	Y
1995	
Approve balanced-budget constitutional amendment	Y
Relax Clean Water Act regulations	N
Oppose limits on environmental regulations	Y
Reduce projected Medicare spending	N
Approve GOP budget with tax and spending cuts	N

VOTING STUDIES

	Presidential Support		Party Unity		Conservative Coalition	
Year	S	O	S	O	S	O
1996	82	15	86	13	22	75
1995	83	17	84	13	34	64

INTEREST GROUP RATINGS

Year	ADA	AFL-CIO	CCUS	ACU
1996	80	n/a	25	5
1995	80	92	38	24

6 Pat Danner (D)

Of Kansas City — Elected 1992, 3rd term

Biographical Information
Born: Jan. 13, 1934, Louisville, Ky.
Education: Northeast Missouri State U., B.A. 1972.
Occupation: Congressional aide; federal official.
Family: Husband, Markt Meyer; four children.
Religion: Roman Catholic.
Political Career: Sought Democratic nomination for U.S. House, 1976; Mo. Senate, 1983-93.
Capitol Office: 1207 Longworth Bldg. 20515; 225-7041.

Committees
International Relations
International Economic Policy & Trade
Transportation & Infrastructure
Aviation; Surface Transportation

In Washington: An opponent of abortion and a supporter of gunowners' rights, Danner is perhaps the most conservative woman in the Democratic Caucus. She is a member of The Coalition, the group of center-right Democrats better known as the "blue dogs" who have exerted a rightward pull on their party in debates on a range of issues, including fiscal policy and welfare overhaul. Danner captured the 6th from a Republican in 1992, and she is ever-mindful that many of her northern Missouri constituents — even those calling themselves Democrats — have a conservative mindset.

She attracted attention halfway through her freshman term by dropping out of the Congressional Caucus for Women's Issues. There was speculation that she withdrew to avoid being associated with the caucus' advocacy of abortion rights, but Danner said she simply was not getting good value for the $1,800 membership fee.

On 104th Congress floor votes involving abortion policy, Danner consistently sided with abortion opponents. She voted against requiring states to fund Medicaid abortions for poor women, against permitting abortions at overseas military hospitals, and against allowing federal employees' health care plans to cover abortions. She supports banning a particular abortion technique that opponents call "partial birth" abortion.

In February 1997, Danner did vote to approve President Clinton's request for an earlier-than-scheduled release of funds for international family planning and population control programs. Many abortion foes opposed Clinton's request, arguing that the money would help organizations that perform or promote abortion abroad. But some Republicans and the large majority of Democrats — including some in the party who, like Danner, oppose abortion — were satisfied that existing U.S. laws would prevent the family planning funds from being used for abortions.

Efforts to limit gunowners' rights draw an automatic "no" from Danner. As a freshman she opposed a five-day waiting period for handgun purchases, she opposed a ban on certain semiautomatic assault-style weapons and she voted against the Clinton-backed crime bill that included that ban. In 1996, she supported repeal of the assault-weapons ban.

Early in the 103rd Congress, when both Danner and Clinton were new to Washington, she stood with the administration on its first two key economic votes, one setting out Clinton's budget blueprint and another proposing a $16 billion economic stimulus package. But Democratic leaders soon learned they would have a difficult time keeping Danner in line. She turned against Clinton's budget on a key vote in May 1993 and voted against the final version in August. Standing apart from the Clinton administration's efforts to lower trade barriers, she raised concerns about loss of U.S. sovereignty in opposing NAFTA and GATT in the 103rd.

Since Republicans took control of Congress in 1995, Danner has concurred with a number of elements in their legislative agenda, including constitutional amendments mandating a balanced federal budget and imposing congressional term limits. In November 1995, Danner was one of 28 Democrats voting for a Republican-backed measure that sought to block Clinton from deploying U.S. forces to Bosnia unless Congress approved funds for the operation.

Danner co-authored the first measure handled through the "Corrections Day" procedure, which the new GOP majority introduced in 1995 to spotlight regulations deemed unreasonable by conservatives and expedite elimination of them. Danner's legislation required federal agencies, when issuing regulations, to make a distinction between petroleum and edible vegetable oils. Both kinds of oils had been subject to the same regulations.

But in one area of policy — labor-management issues — Danner's Democratic stripes are

The 6th encompasses prosperous suburbs east and north of Kansas City and struggling farms along the Iowa border. The economic disparities are mirrored in its political diversity: It is the state's most marginal district.

George Bush carried what was then the 6th in 1988, but just barely. In 1992, Democrat Bill Clinton carried all but two of the 28 counties wholly or partly within the 6th. That year, Democratic gubernatorial nominee Mel Carnahan carried all but four counties, while GOP Sen. Christopher S. Bond won all but three district counties. However, Republican John Ashcroft carried every county in his 1994 Senate race. Clinton carried the district again in 1996, polling 46 percent. He carried 19 of the 27 counties this time around.

The substantial population losses in the 1980s in the district's northern tier reflect the devastation of the farm economy. Northwestern Missouri still is recovering from the mid-1980s farm crisis. Erosion, drought and flooding have taken their toll. Some soybean and corn farmers and their families wound up on welfare. In towns such as Princeton (Mercer County), businesses that sold farm equipment are boarding up. Being far from the state's four-lane highways perpetuates the sense of isolation. The floods that ravaged the Midwest in the summer of 1993 put much of northern Missouri under water, damaging homes, businesses and farmland.

Farther west, farming is becoming more of a part-time occupation, as many farmers take second jobs. Small to medium-size companies dot the region. Agricultural research critical to the local economy is conducted at Northwest Missouri State University in Maryville (Nodaway County).

MISSOURI 6
Northwest — St. Joseph

The river city of St. Joseph (Buchanan County) gained a place in history as the eastern end of the Pony Express. A booming supply depot for gold prospectors heading to California in the 1800s, St. Joseph had more than 100,000 people in 1900. But the city shrank steadily as the stockyards declined, and people looked to jobs and metropolitan life in Kansas City, 35 miles south. Things seemed to hit bottom in the 1960s with the exodus of meatpacking companies, and St. Joseph's 1990 population (about 71,900) was its lowest in 100 years.

Attempting to right itself, the city's business sector has diversified. Recent location decisions by new and existing businesses have offered some hope of improvement. But it suffered a blow in 1993 when ConAgra closed its Monfort pork plant, which employed 1,050.

Times have not been as hard in the southwestern part of the 6th, where Kansas City area workers opting for a more bucolic exurb moved into surrounding counties. Platte and Clay counties registered double-digit percentage gains in population in the 1980s.

Kansas City International Airport is another vital employer. An export facility at the airport, which is considered a focus of agricultural exports, ships cattle by air to the Far East.

1990 Population: 569,131. White 549,059 (96%), Black 11,997 (2%), Other 8,075 (1%). Hispanic origin 8,478 (2%). 18 and over 421,046 (74%), 62 and over 96,559 (17%). Median age: 34.

fairly pronounced. She voted in 1993 in favor of legislation requiring employers to provide unpaid family and medical leave, and she has consistently taken the side of organized labor in its high-profile disputes with the pro-business Republican leadership — on raising the minimum wage and exempting small businesses from paying the higher minimum, on allowing companies to offer comp time in lieu of overtime pay, and on letting non-union companies set up and control labor-management teams.

She opposed the GOP's initial welfare-overhaul legislation, but voted in July 1996 for the compromise plan that Clinton signed into law.

Also, Danner's zeal for deficit reduction outstrips that of many Republicans, as evinced by her votes to kill NASA's space station and the superconducting super collider (projects that many conservatives backed), and her vote in 1996 to freeze spending on defense.

Danner serves on the Transportation and Infrastructure Committee, and on its Surface Transportation Subcommittee, giving her a ringside seat as the 105th Congress tackles reauthorization of the nation's highway and mass-transit programs. She supports the proposal — by committee Chairman Bud Shuster, a Pennsylvania Republican, to take the transportation trust funds off-budget, a move proponents say will end the practice of hoarding trust fund monies to mask the size of the deficit, thus freeing up funds for public works projects.

Following the widespread Midwest flooding of 1993, Danner joined with a bipartisan group of Missouri and Illinois members in pressing for funds to help individuals repair damaged levees that were not built by the federal government and thus were ineligible for repair by the Corps of Engineers.

In the 104th, Danner sponsored a bill with fellow Missourian Bill Emerson to protect donors and distributors of food for the needy from legal liability for mishaps or illnesses resulting from the donations. The measure requires states to adopt laws to protect those who donate food in good faith (while not providing protection in cases of gross negligence or intentional harm). After Emerson died in 1996, the legislation was renamed the Bill Emerson Good Samaritan Food Donation Act. It cleared both houses of Congress and was signed into law by Clinton.

Danner also sits on the International Relations Committee. Of Lebanese descent, Danner in 1996 joined other Lebanese-American legislators in urging Clinton administration officials to seek aid for Lebanon, which was in need of food, water, medicine and housing.

At Home: Danner's strategy for winning the 6th in 1992 was to hammer the GOP incumbent while cloaking herself in the image of a beloved local political figure.

A state senator since 1983, she frequently invoked the memory of former Democratic Rep. Jerry Litton, for whom she had been chief district aide. Litton, who represented the district from 1973 to 1976, died in a plane crash after winning the 1976 Democratic Senate nomination.

The first sign of trouble for GOP incumbent Tom Coleman came in 1990, when a little-known Democratic challenger held him to 52 percent. That prompted eight Democrats to file for the 6th in 1992, with Danner and state Rep. Sandra Reeves leading the field. Reeves, who favored abortion rights, accused Danner of misleading voters by suggesting that Danner, too, supported abortion rights. The charge, however, did not damage Danner; she won the nomination by more than 25 percentage points.

In November, Danner benefited from the public's perception of Coleman as being aloof and inaccessible. The ranking Republican on the Agriculture Committee, he was hobbled by discontent among farmers over a lingering slump in the agricultural economy.

Playing on anti-Congress sentiment, Danner attacked Coleman for his vote for a congressional pay raise and his use of franked mailings. Coleman waged a heavy TV ad campaign assailing Danner's voting record in the legislature and questioning her ethics. But unlike Coleman's 1990 opponent, Danner was amply funded and well-known. Between Danner and her son, then-state Sen. Steve Danner, 20 of the 26 counties wholly within the 6th were represented by a Danner in the state Senate. Danner outran Coleman by 10 percentage points, and she has won re-election easily since then.

HOUSE ELECTIONS

1996 General		
Pat Danner (D)	169,006	(69%)
Jeff Bailey (R)	72,064	(29%)
Karl H. Wetzel (LIBERT)	5,212	(2%)
1996 Primary		
Pat Danner (D)	42,450	(77%)
Larry E. Kinnamon Jr. (D)	12,782	(23%)
1994 General		
Pat Danner (D)	140,108	(66%)
Tina Tucker (R)	71,709	(34%)

Previous Winning Percentages: 1992 (55%)

CAMPAIGN FINANCE

	Receipts	Receipts from PACs	Expend-itures
1996			
Danner (D)	$437,415	$323,727 (74%)	$112,970
1994			
Danner (D)	$510,082	$354,836 (70%)	$474,038
Tucker (R)	$42,425	$12,514 (29%)	$42,378

DISTRICT VOTE FOR PRESIDENT

1996	1992
D 115,417 (46%)	**D** 110,064 (40%)
R 105,320 (42%)	**R** 89,005 (32%)
I 29,287 (12%)	**I** 75,185 (27%)

KEY VOTES

1997	
Ban "partial birth" abortions	Y
1996	
Approve farm bill	Y
Deny public education to illegal immigrants	Y
Repeal ban on certain assault-style weapons	Y
Increase minimum wage	Y
Freeze defense spending	Y
Approve welfare overhaul	Y
1995	
Approve balanced-budget constitutional amendment	Y
Relax Clean Water Act regulations	Y
Oppose limits on environmental regulations	N
Reduce projected Medicare spending	N
Approve GOP budget with tax and spending cuts	N

VOTING STUDIES

	Presidential Support		Party Unity		Conservative Coalition	
Year	S	O	S	O	S	O
1996	63	37	67	33	63	37
1995	56	44	64	36	68	32
1994	69	29	80	19	75	22
1993	72	28	87	13	52	48

INTEREST GROUP RATINGS

Year	ADA	AFL-CIO	CCUS	ACU
1996	55	n/a	56	45
1995	70	75	67	48
1994	70	78	58	29
1993	60	92	27	25

7 Roy Blunt (R)

Of Bolivar — Elected 1996, 1st term

Biographical Information

Born: Jan. 10, 1950, Niangua, Mo.

Education: Southwest Baptist U., B.S. 1970; Southwest Missouri State U., M.A. 1972.

Occupation: University president; teacher.

Family: Wife, Elizbeth Roseann; three children.

Religion: Baptist.

Political Career: Greene County clerk, 1972-84; Republican nominee for lieutenant governor, 1980; Mo. secretary of state, 1985-93; sought Republican nomination for governor, 1992.

Capitol Office: 508 Cannon Bldg. 20515; 225-6536.

Committees

Agriculture
Livestock, Dairy & Poultry

International Relations
International Economic Policy & Trade; Western Hemisphere

Transportation & Infrastructure
Aviation

The Path to Washington: Blunt's 1996 election to the House revived a political career that had seemed over in 1992. After two terms as Missouri's secretary of state, he ran for the Republican nomination for governor in 1992 and lost to William L. Webster, who in turn was defeated by Democrat Mel Carnahan.

A former high school government and history teacher, Blunt entered politics in 1973 when GOP Gov. (now Sen.) Christopher S. Bond appointed him Greene County clerk. In 1980, Blunt won the Republican primary for lieutenant governor, but he lost in the general election. He was elected secretary of state in 1984 and held that post for eight years, serving under GOP Gov. (now Sen.) John Ashcroft.

After losing the Republican gubernatorial primary in 1992, Blunt disavowed talk of challenging Carnahan in 1996 and instead settled into a post as president of Southwest Baptist University in Bolivar, where he had received his bachelor's degree two decades earlier at the age of 20.

But when four-term GOP Rep. Mel Hancock announced his retirement, Blunt re-entered the public arena, announcing his candidacy for the open congressional seat. His opponent in the primary — the pivotal contest in this strongly Republican district — was Gary Nodler, a former aide to Hancock's predecessor, GOP Rep. Gene Taylor (1973-1989). Nodler narrowly lost the 1988 Republican primary to Hancock in the race to succeed Taylor.

Blunt touted his experience in running a state agency and private university. Nodler cited his background as a congressional aide and his experience in private business.

With superior name recognition and a bigger bank account, Blunt captured the nomination with 56 percent of the vote. Both Nodler and Taylor quickly announced support for Blunt at a news conference outside the Gene Taylor Library in Sarcoxie.

Blunt's easy (65 percent) victory over Democratic nominee Ruth Bamberger, a professor of political science at Drury College in Springfield, came as no surprise.

In the 105th Congress, Blunt will have a chance to get involved in a panoply of issues from his committee posts on Agriculture, Transportation and Infrastructure, and International Relations.

As befits the nature of the district, Blunt is a consistent supporter of conservative policies. He supports a balanced-budget constitutional amendment, favors passing legislation requiring a three-fifths majority of both houses of Congress to raise taxes, overhauling welfare, instituting medical savings accounts and lowering taxes on capital gains.

He also opposes the family leave law, a higher minimum wage, abortion and a five-day waiting period for handgun purchases. He wants to eliminate the federal government's Goals 2000 program for education.

Blunt supports a constitutional amendment to limit senators to two six-year terms and House members to either three or four two-year terms.

He is willing to look at Medicare and other "sacred cows" in the federal budget in order to eliminate the deficit. He supports efforts to flatten the tax code, eliminating many deductions and brackets, but backs a tax break for individuals who buy their own health insurance.

Blunt is a critic of government regulations he sees as burdensome, and he wants to require that rules be enacted only after businesses and state or local governments prove incapable of solving the problems on their own.

He supports GOP-led efforts to shrink the federal government and shift programs such as welfare and Medicaid to the states and localities. He characterizes many environmental regulations on business as excessive and believes the federal government should compensate land-owners for the loss of the use of their land.

Blunt is no supporter of changing the way congressional campaigns are financed. He opposes public financing and new limits on contributions.

MISSOURI 7
Southwest — Springfield; Joplin

Two decades of rapid growth have helped lift southwestern Missouri from poor hillbilly hideaway to burgeoning resort region with a growing industrial base. Since the 1970s, this part of Missouri has outpaced the rest of the state in population growth.

The 7th boomed during the 1980s as a stream of retirees and other newcomers settled in the resort area around Table Rock Lake. Branson (Taney County) has become a magnet for country music fans, attracting 4 million visitors a year to its many theaters and studios.

The recreational trade nourishes local services and industries. Bass Pro Shops, which manufactures and sells fishing boats and other sporting goods, is based in Springfield (Greene County), the district's industrial and commercial center. Nationwide customers of Bass Pro's mail-order catalog are lured to the Springfield store much as devotees of L.L. Bean descend on its site in Maine.

Springfield's major employers include Aarons Automotive Products, Hudson Foods, MCI, Kraft Foods and Southwest Missouri State University, which enrolls over 16,000 students. More than 40 percent of the 7th's residents live in Greene and neighboring Christian County; the latter experienced a 38 percent population increase from 1990 to 1996, highest in the state.

Joplin is the district's other population center. An old lead and zinc mining town, Joplin is now a manufacturing and trucking center. Nearby Carthage, the Jasper County seat, competes for attention with its larger neighbor. Leggett & Platt, which makes box springs and other bedding and furniture components, has its headquarters and three manufacturing plants in Carthage.

Wheat, soybeans and corn are grown in the 7th's western counties. The more hilly Ozark counties raise beef and dairy cattle. Poultry farming and production also contribute to the economy.

The rural and agricultural character of the Ozarks has not entirely yielded to development and modernization. Many small, isolated communities are legacies of the region's settlers — Scots-Irish mountaineers from eastern Tennessee, western Virginia and Kentucky. Many of these rural counties struggle economically.

Southwestern Missouri is a breeding ground for statewide GOP politicians. The last Republican governor, secretary of state, attorney general and state treasurer all had roots in the southwest. George Bush in 1992 and Bob Dole in 1996 carried every county in the 7th, and it was the only Missouri district to give Dole a majority of its votes. Favorite son John Ashcroft, a former governor, swept every county in his landslide 1994 Senate bid.

The area's Republican lineage dates from the Civil War. Though there was some slave trading on Springfield's town square, most Ozark settlers had no use for slavery on their small, hilly farms; pro-Union sentiment was strong. The GOP preference in the Joplin area was cemented when President Woodrow Wilson lowered tariffs on lead and zinc and crippled the mining industry.

The 7th's conservatism also is reflected in its politically active religious organizations. The national headquarters of the Assemblies of God, the nation's largest Pentecostal church, is in Springfield, and the Pentecostal Church of God's international headquarters is in Joplin. Southwest Baptist University in Bolivar (Polk County) has about 3,200 students.

1990 Population: 568,017. White 552,934 (97%). Black 5,295 (1%), Other 9,788 (2%). Hispanic origin 4,443 (1%). 18 and over 428,827 (75%), 62 and over 105,271 (19%). Median age: 35.

HOUSE ELECTIONS

1996 General		
Roy Blunt (R)	162,558	(65%)
Ruth Bamberger (D)	79,306	(32%)
Mike Harman (LIBERT)	6,543	(3%)
1996 Primary		
Roy Blunt (R)	42,401	(56%)
Gary Nodler (R)	33,426	(44%)

CAMPAIGN FINANCE

	Receipts	Receipts from PACs	Expend-itures
1996			
Blunt (R)	$995,345	$202,072 (20%)	$985,764
Bamberger (D)	$105,364	$18,700 (18%)	$103,747

DISTRICT VOTE FOR PRESIDENT

	1996		1992
D	93,537 (37%)	**D**	96,621 (37%)
R	129,249 (51%)	**R**	118,817 (45%)
I	27,580 (11%)	**I**	48,824 (19%)

KEY VOTES

1997

Ban "partial birth" abortions Y

8 Jo Ann Emerson (R)

Of Cape Girardeau — Elected 1996, 1st term

Biographical Information
Born: Sept. 16, 1950, Washington, D.C.
Education: Ohio Wesleyan U., B.A. 1972.
Occupation: Public affairs executive; lobbyist.
Family: Widowed; four children.
Religion: Presbyterian.
Political Career: No previous office.
Capitol Office: 132 Cannon Bldg. 20515; 225-4404.

Committees
Agriculture
Forestry, Resource Conservation & Research; General Farm Commodities
Small Business
Regulatory Reform & Paperwork Reduction
Transportation & Infrastructure
Surface Transportation; Water Resources & Environment

The Path to Washington: Voters in southeastern Missouri's 8th District continue to be represented by an Emerson, but not the one who occupied the seat for 16 years.

Rep. Bill Emerson, whose election in 1980 ended 50 years of Democratic hegemony over the conservative-leaning district that still sends Democrats to local office, died of lung cancer in 1996. His widow, Jo Ann, picked up his banner and carried it into the fall election.

Emerson is no stranger to politics. She served as senior vice president of public affairs for the American Insurance Association, director of state relations for the National Restaurant Association, and deputy director of communications for the National Republican Congressional Committee (NRCC).

Actually, she won twice in November, prevailing in a special election as a Republican to fill out her husband's unexpired term, and winning a full term in the 105th Congress as an independent.

She had to run as an independent because the filing deadline for the primary had closed before her husband died, and Missouri Secretary of State Bekki Cook said state law prohibited her from reopening nominations.

Republican Party officials mulled a lawsuit, but instead began encouraging Emerson's widow to circulate petitions and file to run in the general election as an independent, since that deadline had not closed. She garnered the endorsements of the House Republican leadership, the NRCC and the Missouri Republican Party.

While Emerson had the support of the Republican establishment, the GOP primary became a contest between two little-known Republicans, who initially had filed to challenge the incumbent congressman. The winner was Coast Guard veteran Richard A. Kline, who was given little chance to win the election.

The Democrats, on the other hand, put up an attractive nominee, timber company owner Emily Firebaugh, and hoped to bring the district's voters back to their Democratic roots.

Firebaugh emphasized her long ties to the district and contrasted them with Emerson, who lived and worked in Washington.

Firebaugh received a boost from President Clinton, who made Cape Girardeau in the 8th District his first stop on his post-convention bus trip. She also hoped that many Democrats who for years had crossed party lines to vote for Emerson would return home.

But Emerson wrapped herself in her husband's mantle — the campaign was called "Team Emerson" — and pledged to continue his legacy.

She pledged in her campaign literature, for example, to "continue her late husband's winning fight to secure funding to improve highways . . . and the Cape Girardeau Mississippi River Bridge."

The GOP leadership assigned Emerson to the two panels on which her husband served: Transportation and Infrastructure, and Agriculture. Her husband had been in line to chair the Agriculture Committee. She also has a seat on the Small Business Committee.

Emerson said she wants to expand markets for crops grown in the district, including soybeans, rice, and cotton. She supports NAFTA and wants to go after other barriers to farm exports.

She opposes abortion and is a staunch defender of gunowners' rights and private property rights. She backs a balanced-budget constitutional amendment and the congressional Republicans' effort to balance the federal budget by 2002, in part by cutting the growth in Medicare and Medicaid spending.

On health care, she wants to allow small businesses and the self-employed to deduct the entire cost of health insurance, and she supports efforts to allow people to buy insurance even if they had a serious illness.

During the campaign, she pledged to back constitutional amendments to outlaw flag burning, outlaw abortion, allow voluntary prayer in public schools, impose term limits on lawmakers, and require a two-thirds majority of both houses of Congress to raise taxes.

MISSOURI 8
Southeast — Cape Girardeau

Within the borders of the 8th is some of the state's most bountiful farmland, and the district's agricultural diversity is matched by its political breadth. The 8th spans the spectrum from solidly Republican counties in the west and northeast along the Mississippi River to "yellow dog" Democratic territory in the southeastern Bootheel.

The 8th's growth during the 1980s came primarily in its northernmost counties, not far from metropolitan St. Louis. Washington and St. Francois counties both had double-digit growth as commuters settled into bedroom communities. Both counties solidly backed Bill Clinton in 1992 and 1996, and narrowly supported Jo Ann Emerson's Democratic opponent.

In the southeastern corner is the Bootheel, a cluster of counties that look and vote like the Old South. Predominantly a wheat-growing region until the mid-1920s, the Bootheel was transformed when cotton growers and black sharecroppers from Mississippi, Alabama and Tennessee, driven north by the boll weevil, discovered the area's rich delta land and settled. The seven counties in the southeastern corner — Mississippi, New Madrid, Pemiscot, Dunklin, Butler, Stoddard and Scott — grow 35 percent of the state's cash crops. In 1996, Clinton won five of the seven, losing only Butler and Stoddard.

The Bootheel is the northernmost area in the country where cotton and rice grow. The port at New Madrid has Missouri's only rice mill; it opened in 1988. Dunklin is the nation's No. 3 watermelon-harvesting county and is in the top 50 for peach production.

Soybeans and corn have supplanted cotton as the Bootheel's leading crops, but the Southern Democratic habits forged during cotton's heyday have persisted. A search of the Bootheel counties' courthouses would reveal only the occasional Republican. But in statewide contests, these Democratic strongholds are largely offset by Republican votes from Cape Girardeau and Perry counties. Cape Girardeau (its namesake city is Rush Limbaugh's hometown) was Bob Dole's best Missouri county in 1996; he received more than 56 percent of the vote there.

Above the Bootheel, along the Mississippi River, dairy production and beef cattle fuel the economy. Livestock, timber and fruit production flourish in other parts of the 8th. Wright is Missouri's foremost dairy county. Oregon County breeds feeder pigs for Iowa slaughterhouses. Apples are grown in the Mark Twain National Forest.

Even the ground beneath the 8th yields riches. The vast majority of the nation's lead — and most of the world's — is mined in southeast Missouri. The discovery of a "New Lead Belt" called the Viburnum Trend during the late 1950s revitalized an industry that dates back to the early 1700s, when French explorers mined in Mine La Motte (Madison County). Most of today's lead mining is centered in the New Lead Belt of western Iron County and Reynolds County.

The Ozark forests once provided the timber that built St. Louis. Small lumber mills in the area still produce pallets and other wood products. The Ozarks also attract recreation-seekers who fish and canoe in the Eleven Point and Current rivers and in the Ozark National Scenic Riverways.

1990 Population: 568,385. White 538,611 (95%), Black 25,155 (4%), Other 4,619 (1%). Hispanic origin 2,907 (1%). 18 and over 418,339 (74%), 62 and over 109,113 (19%). Median age: 35.

HOUSE ELECTIONS

1996 General		
Jo Ann Emerson (I)	112,472	(50%)
Emily Firebaugh (D)	83,084	(37%)
Richard A. Kline (R)	23,477	(11%)
Greg Tlapek (LIBERT)	2,503	(1%)
1996 Special†		
Jo Ann Emerson (R)	132,804	(63%)
Emily Firebaugh (D)	71,625	(34%)
Greg Tlapek (LIBERT)	5,326	(3%)

† On Election Day, Emerson was elected to a full term and to fill out the remainder of the term of Bill Emerson, R, who died June 22, 1996.

CAMPAIGN FINANCE

	Receipts	Receipts from PACs	Expend-itures
1996			
Emerson (I)	$833,907	$402,294 (48%)	$806,205
Firebaugh (D)	$834,518	$258,221 (31%)	$831,533

DISTRICT VOTE FOR PRESIDENT

1996		1992	
D	101,339 (45%)	**D**	109,858 (46%)
R	96,457 (43%)	**R**	89,238 (37%)
I	25,089 (11%)	**I**	41,558 (17%)

KEY VOTES

1997

Ban "partial birth" abortions Y

9 Kenny Hulshof (R)

Of Columbia — Elected 1996, 1st term

Biographical Information

Born: May 22, 1958, Sikeston, Mo.

Education: U. of Missouri, B.S. 1980; U. of Mississippi, J.D. 1983.

Occupation: Public defender; prosecutor; assistant attorney general.

Family: Wife, Renee Lynn Howell.

Religion: Roman Catholic.

Political Career: Sought Republican nomination for Boone county prosecutor, 1992; Republican nominee for U.S. House, 1994.

Capitol Office: 1728 Longworth Bldg. 20515; 225-2956.

Committees

Ways & Means
Oversight; Social Security

The Path to Washington: As befits someone who defeated a cantankerous critic of the House Republican majority, Hulshof was feted when the GOP organized for the 105th Congress. He landed a seat on the Ways and Means Committee, a rare appointment for a first-termer, and was elected president of the freshman class.

Those honors were a thank-you from Republicans for ousting 10-term Democratic Rep. Harold L. Volkmer, who flourished during the 104th Congress as an outspoken opponent of the newly ascendant GOP.

Having come within 11,000 votes of defeating Volkmer in 1994, Hulshof spent the next two years preparing for a rematch. He almost did not get it.

Harry Eggleston, a wealthy ophthalmologist, reached into his own pocket for more than $300,000 and challenged Hulshof for the GOP nomination in 1996.

Hulshof pointed to his strong showing in 1994 as proof he could cut into Volkmer's base because he lived one of the district's Democratic areas, Boone County, which includes Columbia. Eggleston countered that he could improve GOP turnout because he lived in the more Republican part of the district, the St. Louis suburbs.

On primary day, Hulshof edged Eggleston by fewer than 200 votes and went on to his rematch with Volkmer.

Two years earlier, Hulshof had held Volkmer to 50 percent of the vote. His performance was especially remarkable because Hulshof did not enter the race until the original nominee, Rick Hardy, withdrew in June, citing depression. (Hardy had held Volkmer to a career-low 48 percent in 1992.)

In the fall campaign, Hulshof touted his crime-fighting prowess as a former assistant district attorney, noting that he helped send seven convicted killers to death row. He called for new limits on death row appeals and for amending the 1994 crime bill to provide for block grants that would give states more control over spending, as proposed unsuccessfully by House Republicans in the 104th Congress.

In a district with a large rural population, Hulshof emphasized his growing up on a farm, his activity in Future Farmers of America and earning a degree in agricultural economics from the University of Missouri. He supports compensating farmers and other landowners if their property values are reduced by federal regulations.

Hulshof emphasized his opposition to abortion and his support of gunowners' rights, and accused Volkmer of casting the deciding vote for President Clinton's controversial 1993 deficit reduction package, which passed the House by a 218-216 margin.

Hulshof has called for applying cost-benefit analyses to new federal regulations, adopting a balanced-budget amendment to the Constitution, and imposing term limits on members of Congress.

In the closing weeks of the campaign, Hulshof seized on a radio comment in which Volkmer said residents were not overtaxed. Hulshof contrasted that with his own call for a tax credit for families with children, a tax credit for taxpayers who cared for elderly parents or grandparents at home, a cut in estate taxes, and a repeal of the 1993 tax increase on the Social Security benefits of higher-income senior citizens. He also hit Volkmer for his votes to raise lawmakers' pay.

Volkmer, who bows to no one in his support of gun owners' rights and his opposition to abortion, touted his own conservative credentials while attempting to push Hulshof to the far right.

He reminded voters that Hulshof signed the House GOP's "Contract With America" in 1994 and criticized what he said were Republican efforts to cut Medicare, Medicaid and education funding, and roll back environmental protections.

As in 1994, the final outcome was close. But this time, Hulshof finished on top with a 49 percent plurality, two points ahead of Volkmer.

MISSOURI 9
Northeast — Columbia

Stark contrasts of prosperity and penury define the 9th. Population in the southeastern part of the district skyrocketed in the 1980s and 1990s as the St. Louis suburbs expanded into adjacent counties. St. Charles County grew by 77 percent from 1980 to 1996. And the populations of Lincoln and Warren counties increased by more than 50 percent.

Many of the new arrivals commute to St. Louis; others work at the General Motors assembly plant in Wentzville or at McDonnell Douglas Corp. in St. Charles and St. Louis counties. Local concerns revolve around bridges and roads to support the population crunch.

But the blossoming at this end of the district is countered by bleak conditions in the northern counties, where farm families find it increasingly hard to survive. The agricultural depression of the 1980s has abated elsewhere but lingers in many parts of the 9th. Young people, leaving their hometowns for more reliable employment, often cross the border to work in Iowa or Illinois.

Agriculture remains the mainstay of the 9th's economy. Winter wheat, corn and soybeans are grown throughout the district. St. Charles County still has some wheat and corn fields. Cattle and hogs are raised across the district. Vineyards in Gasconade and Warren counties grow grapes for area wineries that date back more than 150 years. Among Missouri's first settlers were Virginians and Kentuckians who found the rich soil to their liking. Those settlers had pro-Southern sympathies during the Civil War, but they could not pull Missouri into the Confederacy; their descendants still vote Democratic.

Their support for the national party faded in the early 1980s. Of the core Little Dixie counties in the 9th — Ralls, Pike, Monroe, Audrain, Callaway, Randolph and Boone — Ronald Reagan won four in 1980 and all seven in 1984. But the farm crisis brought them back to the Democrats. Michael S. Dukakis won six of the counties in 1988 and Bill Clinton won all seven in 1992 and 1996.

The economy in Boone County is steadied by the University of Missouri in Columbia (22,000 students), the oldest state university west of the Mississippi River, and by the Ellis Fischel State Cancer Center in Columbia.

Boone voters have a penchant for splitting their tickets. In 1988, Boone voted Democratic for president and Republican for governor. Four years later, the county voted Democratic for president and governor but Republican for Senate. And in 1996, Boone again opted for Clinton, but it favored Hulshof by 55 percent to 38 percent over 20-year Democratic incumbent Harold L. Volkmer.

East of Boone is Callaway County, whose residents declared it a kingdom unto itself in defiance of the Union during the Civil War. Many state government employees who work in Jefferson City live here. On the banks of the Mississippi lies Hannibal, where a cement industry provided jobs for Italians, Hungarians, Czechs and other European immigrants in the 19th century. Hannibal is best known as the birthplace of Mark Twain (Samuel Clemens) and attracts more than 250,000 visitors a year to view his boyhood home and "Tom Sawyer's fence."

The district was hard hit by the floods that ravaged the Midwest in 1993. Much of northern Missouri was under water, as homes, businesses and farmland were damaged.

1990 Population: 568,347. White 539,981 (95%), Black 21,060 (4%), Other 7,306 (1%). Hispanic origin 4,222 (1%). 18 and over 417,301 (73%), 62 and over 85,744 (15%). Median age: 32.

HOUSE ELECTIONS

1996 General		
Kenny Hulshof (R)	123,580	(49%)
Harold L. Volkmer (D)	117,685	(47%)
Mitchell J. Moore (LIBERT)	7,140	(3%)
1996 Primary		
Kenny Hulshof (R)	19,259	(50%)
Harry Eggleston (R)	19,091	(50%)

CAMPAIGN FINANCE

	Receipts	Receipts from PACs	Expend-itures
1996			
Hulshof (R)	$680,860	$117,425 (17%)	$686,450
Volkmer (D)	$536,780	$332,544 (62%)	$542,368

DISTRICT VOTE FOR PRESIDENT

	1996		1992
D	111,939 (44%)	**D**	109,995 (41%)
R	106,770 (42%)	**R**	90,669 (34%)
I	30,628 (12%)	**I**	65,032 (25%)

KEY VOTES

1997

Ban "partial-birth" abortions Y

MONTANA

Governor: Marc Racicot (R)
First elected: 1992
Length of term: 4 years
Term expires: 1/01
Salary: $55,288
Term limit: 8 years in a 16-year period
Phone: (406) 444-3111
Born: July 24, 1948; Thompson Falls, Mont.
Education: Carroll College, B.A. 1970; U. of Montana, J.D. 1973.
Military Service: Army, 1973-76.
Occupation: Lawyer.
Family: Wife, Theresa Barber; five children.
Religion: Roman Catholic.
Political Career: Candidate for Mont. Supreme Court, 1980; candidate for Mont. District Court, 1982, 1984; Mont. attorney general, 1989-93.

Lt. Gov.: Judy Martz (R)
First elected: 1996
Length of term: 4 years
Term expires: 1/01
Salary: $40,310
Phone: (406) 444-5551

State election official: (406) 444-4732
Democratic headquarters: (406) 442-9520
Republican headquarters: (406) 442-6469

STATE LEGISLATURE

Legislature. Meets January-April.

Senate: 50 members, 4-year terms
1996 breakdown: 34R, 16D; 41 men, 9 women
Salary: $57 per day in session
Phone: (406) 444-4880

House of Representatives: 100 members, 2-year terms
1996 breakdown: 65R, 35D; 74 men, 26 women
Salary: $57 per day in session
Phone: (406) 444-4819

URBAN STATISTICS

City	Population
Billings	81,151
Mayor Charles Tooley, N-P	
Great Falls	55,097
Mayor Bob Deming, N-P	
Missoula	42,918
Mayor Mike Kadas	
Butte/Silver Bow	33,336
Mayor Jack Lynch, D	
Helena	24,569
Mayor Colleen McCarthy, N-P	

U.S. CONGRESS

Senate: 1 D, 1 R
House: 0 D, 1 R

TERM LIMITS

For state offices: Yes
Senate: 8 years in a 16-year period
House: 8 years in a 16-year period

ELECTIONS

1996 Presidential Vote

Bob Dole	44%
Bill Clinton	41%
Ross Perot	14%

1992 Presidential Vote

Bill Clinton	38%
George Bush	35%
Ross Perot	26%

1988 Presidential Vote

George Bush	52%
Michael S. Dukakis	46%

POPULATION

1990 population		799,065
1980 population		786,690
Percent change		+2%
Rank among states:		44
White		93%
Black		<1%
Hispanic		2%
Asian or Pacific islander		1%
Urban		53%
Rural		47%
Born in state		59%
Foreign-born		2%
Under age 18	222,104	28%
Ages 18-64	470,464	59%
65 and older	106,497	13%
Median age		33.1

MISCELLANEOUS

Capital: Helena
Number of counties: 56
Per capita income: $16,043 (1991)
Rank among states: 39
Total area: 147,046 sq. miles
Rank among states: 4

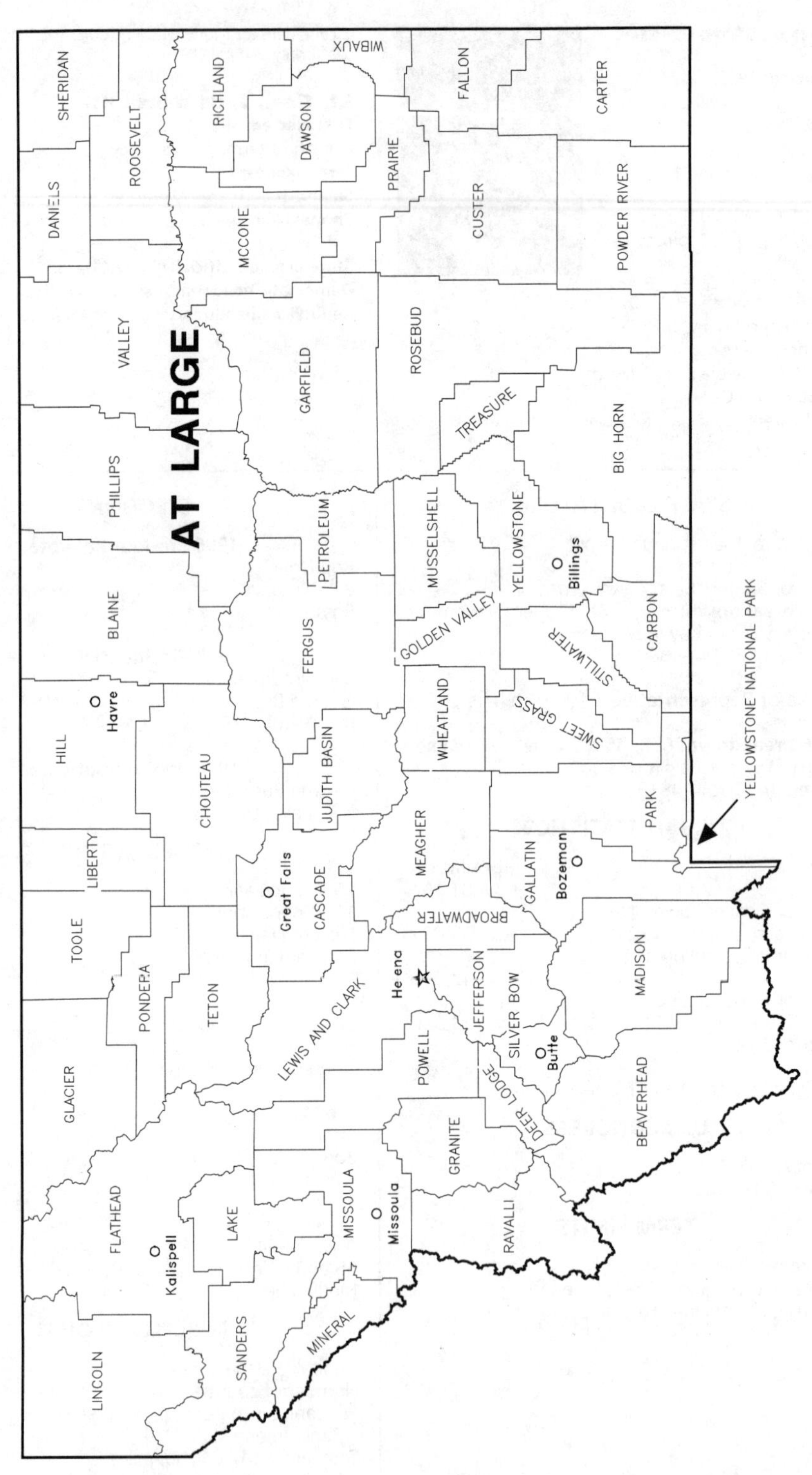
AT LARGE
SHERIDAN
DANIELS
ROOSEVELT
RICHLAND
DAWSON
WIBAUX
FALLON
CARTER
PRAIRIE
MCCONE
CUSTER
POWDER RIVER
VALLEY
GARFIELD
ROSEBUD
TREASURE
BIG HORN
PHILLIPS
PETROLEUM
MUSSELSHELL
YELLOWSTONE
Billings
BLAINE
FERGUS
GOLDEN VALLEY
STILLWATER
CARBON
YELLOWSTONE NATIONAL PARK
HILL
Havre
CHOUTEAU
JUDITH BASIN
WHEATLAND
SWEET GRASS
PARK
LIBERTY
CASCADE
Great Falls
MEAGHER
GALLATIN
Bozeman
TOOLE
PONDERA
TETON
BROADWATER
Helena
LEWIS AND CLARK
JEFFERSON
MADISON
SILVER BOW
Butte
GLACIER
POWELL
DEER LODGE
BEAVERHEAD
GRANITE
FLATHEAD
Kalispell
LAKE
MISSOULA
Missoula
RAVALLI
LINCOLN
SANDERS
MINERAL

Max Baucus (D)

Of Helena — Elected 1978; 4th term

Biographical Information
Born: Dec. 11, 1941, Helena, Mont.
Education: Stanford U., A.B. 1964, LL.B. 1967.
Occupation: Lawyer.
Family: Wife, Wanda Minge; one child.
Religion: United Church of Christ.
Political Career: Mont. House, 1973-75; U.S. House, 1975-78.
Capitol Office: 511 Hart Bldg. 20510; 224-2651.

Committees
Agriculture, Nutrition & Forestry
Forestry, Conservation & Rural Revitalization; Marketing, Inspection & Product Promotion (ranking)
Environment & Public Works (ranking)
Transportation & Infrastructure (ranking)
Finance
Health Care; International Trade; Taxation & IRS Oversight (ranking)
Select Intelligence
Joint Taxation

In Washington: Now in his fourth Senate term, Baucus has spent his career trying to balance competing interests and loyalties. He is the top Democrat on the Environment and Public works Committee, but he diverges from the White House to protect home-state ranchers and miners. He also has been a crucial swing vote for the GOP on such hot-button issues as welfare reform and the balanced-budget constitutional amendment.

But through it all, Baucus has remained fiercely committed to one guiding principle above party loyalty or ideological purity, a motto that graces his Senate office desk, "Montana Comes First." It is that credo that likely enabled him to endure one of the toughest re-election races he has faced.

In fact, it was an environmental bill, the Safe Drinking Water Act Amendments of 1996, that was Baucus' most significant accomplishment of the 104th Congress. True to form, Baucus strongly advocated incorporating provisions into the law to reduce paperwork burdens and regulatory mandates on small, rural drinking water systems.

But Baucus, who chaired the Environment panel in the 103rd, comes from a state deeply divided on many environmental and natural resource issues. And particularly on land-use issues, Baucus has ended up opposite environmentalists and the Clinton administration, most notably in recent years on the effort to overhaul grazing fees. During his stint as Environment chairman, the panel made headway on several key initiatives, including the Safe Drinking Water Act, the clean water act and legislation to overhaul the superfund law governing cleanup of the nation's hazardous waste sites. But none of the bills became law. The 103rd Congress, led on both sides of the Capitol by Democrats and working with a new Democratic president, failed to enact much significant environmental legislation.

Baucus generally has agreed with the administration's approach to revamping traditional pollution control laws such as the drinking water, clean water and superfund laws. And he supported Clinton's moves to block the 104th Congress from enacting property rights legislation and opening the Arctic National Wildlife Refuge to oil drilling. Baucus' tendency to put his rural constituents first has drawn the ire of environmentalists, who charge that Baucus is more interested in getting re-elected than in protecting the environment. A Montana environmentalist and frequent Baucus critic told the Great Falls Tribune he thinks it is "more important" to Baucus "to be a U.S. senator than to do the right thing." Another criticized him in the Billings Gazette as "the leading opponent of 1872 Mining Law reform among Senate Democrats," referring to the 19th century law to encourage frontier mining that environmentalists criticize as a virtual giveaway of precious resources on federal land.

In 1993, Baucus opposed the Clinton administration's plan to raise grazing fees and impose tough environmental standards on ranchers who graze their cattle on federal land. He joined a group of Democratic and Republican Western senators in a filibuster against the 1994 Interior appropriations bill to protest grazing fee language in the legislation. The group was successful in forcing the administration to remove the offending language from the bill. This eventually led to a White House announcement in late 1994 that it was dropping its plan to raise grazing fees and deferring to Congress on the issue.

The issue was resurrected but not resolved in the 104th Congress in response to the Interior Department's August 1995 adoption of tougher grazing regulations. In March 1996, the Senate passed a pro-ranching industry grazing reform bill, which Baucus supported, that drew a veto threat from the Clinton administration. Although the House approved similar legislation, it also drew fire from the White House; when House Republicans' attempts to draft a compromise failed to attract administration support, grazing reform died for the 104th.

Baucus has spent much of his time in the Senate working on a Montana wilderness bill. In the 103rd Congress, he supported a plan that he had developed in the 102nd with his Montana colleague, GOP Sen. Conrad Burns, which would have designated 1.2 million acres as wilderness and released 4 million acres for multiple-use activities. But Burns took a harder line in the 103rd, deciding against setting aside so much land as wilderness, and the two never reached agreement on a plan to put forth in the Senate.

Baucus also emerged as a key player during negotiations on the budget-reconciliation bill of 1993. It was his opposition to a provision that he believed would unfairly affect his constituents in Montana that brought him the most attention.

The second-ranking Democrat on the Finance Committee, Baucus forced the panel's other Democrats to hold a proposed increase in the transportation fuels tax to below 5 cents per gallon. He opposed a bigger increase because he said it would impose an unfair burden on larger states, where residents and businesspeople must drive long distances. The committee approved a 4.3-cents-per-gallon increase, which was eventually included in the final bill.

As the ranking Democrat on the Transportation and Infrastructure Subcommittee of Senate Environment, Baucus played a leading role in the 104th on another transportation issue as cosponsor of the National Highway Designation Act of 1995. In addition to the measure's road-building provisions, Baucus made sure it eliminated the national speed limit and allowed states to set their own limits; as a result, Montana dropped its daytime speed limit altogether.

Baucus' subcommittee also is taking the lead on one of the biggest bills slated to move in the 105th Congress, reauthorization of the Intermodal Surface Transportation Efficiency Act of 1991. Baucus told the Lewiston, Mont., Gazette in September 1996 that he will "fight like a bearcat, a wolverine" against proposals to change the law's formula for allocating federal highway dollars that would hurt Montana and other large, thinly populated states.

Despite his previous efforts to appease his constituents, Baucus faced much grief for reversing his career-long opposition to gun control by voting in the 103rd for the Brady bill, which imposed a waiting period and background check for the purchase of a handgun, and the 1994 crime bill, which included a ban on certain semiautomatic assault-style weapons.

In March 1995, he also reversed his position on a balanced-budget constitutional amendment. Baucus was one of only three Democrats who switched from their previous opposition to such an amendment to support for it. The amendment fell just short of the two-thirds majority required for passage. Baucus in 1997 again joined just a handful of Democrats in voting for the amendment, which again failed by a close margin.

Baucus was the only Democrat on the Senate Finance Committee in the 104th to vote for the controversial welfare reform package, which Clinton later signed. Baucus also was the only Democrat on the Agriculture Committee to support legislation later incorporated into the welfare overhaul to cut food stamp spending and impose work requirements on food stamp recipients.

In the 101st Congress, the Clean Air Act gave Baucus his first major chance to redress the assessment of him as a senator whose interests seldom strayed beyond his state's borders. As the new chairman of the Environmental Protection Subcommittee, he had a choice position at an opportune time. With the guidance of then-Senate Majority Leader George J. Mitchell of Maine, Baucus steered the clean air bill through committee, managed it on the floor and chaired the House-Senate conference. The conference negotiations took three months, but the agreement produced the first clean air rewrite in 13 years.

An issue that came in over Baucus' transom in the 102nd Congress that he has since pursued was trade with China. With an eye firmly on his state's wheat exports, Baucus supported President George Bush and opposed efforts to rescind China's most-favored-nation trade status as a way of expressing U.S. displeasure with the human rights situation in that country. Baucus continued through the 104th Congress to be one of Senate's staunchest supporters of MFN status for China, even proposing that China be granted permanent MFN status.

At Home: Considered by many pundits to be the most vulnerable Senate Democrat up for reelection in 1996, Baucus spent more than $3.7 million to eke out the narrowest victory of his political career against Lt. Gov. Dennis Rehberg, winning a nasty campaign with 50 percent of the vote.

The Helena Independent Record called the race "one of the nastiest in at least modern Montana history" and reported that GOP Gov. Marc Racicot "scolded both major Senate candidates for their negative campaigns." The low point of the heated campaign, according to the Billings Gazette, came five days before the election, when in a nationally televised debate Rehberg accused Baucus — falsely — of being "Montana's most famous deadbeat dad." In fact, Baucus had disputed the amount of child support he owed his ex-wife in 1993, but he continued to make the payments. The day after the debate, the Gazette reported, Rehberg supporter Racicot "chewed out" Rehberg's campaign manager for the tone the race had taken.

Combined with earlier aggressive attack ads aimed at Baucus by the National Republican Senatorial Committee, the strategy backfired and it was Rehberg's negative ratings, not Baucus', that increased over the course of the campaign.

In addition to effectively counterattacking Rehberg, Baucus also dusted off a winning strategy from the past, reprising the districtwide walk he took in his successful first bid for Congress. Baucus this time traversed the entire state to underscore his commitment to protecting Montanans' interests in Washington.

The son of a wealthy Helena ranching family, Baucus rose rapidly in Montana politics. After working in Washington as a lawyer for the Securities and Exchange Commission, he returned home to serve as coordinator of the state constitutional convention in 1972. The same year, he won his state legislative seat.

In 1974, Baucus moved up to the U.S. House, dislodging Republican Richard G. Shoup, who was trying for a third term. To gain publicity for the race, Baucus walked 631 miles across his congressional district. He managed to impress the labor-oriented Democrats who dominate the party in western Montana, and he did little to antagonize Republicans. He was a comfortable winner over Shoup in 1974 and an easy winner in 1976.

Meanwhile, he was focusing on the Senate. His hopes were temporarily frustrated in early 1978 by Democratic Gov. Thomas L. Judge, a political rival. After the death of veteran Democrat Lee Metcalf, the governor bypassed Baucus and appointed Paul Hatfield, chief justice of the Montana Supreme Court, to succeed Metcalf.

But Baucus already had begun his 1978 Senate campaign, and he did not step aside for Hatfield. The newly appointed senator could not match Baucus' head start in organizing. Baucus easily won the primary. That fall, he had a hard-nosed Republican competitor in financier Larry Williams, who castigated him as too liberal. But just as Williams seemed on the verge of overtaking him, Baucus' Democratic allies released their "bombshell" — a picture of the "conservative" Williams in shaggy hair and love beads, taken before he moved from California to Montana. Baucus kept his distance from the issue, but the AFL-CIO made sure the picture was all over Montana in the weeks before the election. Baucus won comfortably.

Heading into 1984, Baucus organized and raised money at a feverish pace. His preparations daunted Republican recruiting efforts: No well-known GOP figure stepped forward to take on the incumbent. Former state Rep. Chuck Cozzens won the GOP primary.

Cozzens had trouble attracting the attention he needed to be viewed as a credible challenger to Baucus. He tried to solve that problem by airing a series of radio advertisements calling Baucus a "wimp" who "talks out of both sides of his mouth." But the "wimp" portrayal backfired; many editorial writers and even some Republicans criticized Cozzens for running a mudslinging campaign. In spite of President Ronald Reagan's 60 percent showing in Montana, Baucus took 57 percent of the vote.

In 1990, national Republicans, fresh from their 1988 upset in Montana of Democratic Sen. John Melcher, hungrily eyed Baucus' slot. But things went right for Baucus from the start.

Lt. Gov. Allen C. Kolstad, the putative GOP front-runner, was held under 44 percent in the June primary, while Baucus breezed to renomination. In the general election, Baucus' polished, energetic campaign style complemented his superior campaign operation. In contrast, Kolstad's effort was lackluster and ineffective. Baucus won 68 percent, the best showing of any Montana Senate candidate since Mike Mansfield won a second term in 1958.

SENATE ELECTIONS

1996 General

Max Baucus (D)	201,935	(50%)
Dennis Rehberg (R)	182,111	(45%)
Becky Shaw (REF)	19,276	(5%)
Stephen Heaton (NL)	4,168	(1%)

Previous Winning Percentages: **1990** (68%) **1984** (57%) **1978** (56%) **1976*** (66%) **1974*** (55%)

** House elections*

CAMPAIGN FINANCE

	Receipts	Receipts from PACs	Expend-itures
1996			
Baucus (D)	$3,449,478	$1,352,466 (39%)	$3,748,502
Rehberg (R)	$1,369,530	$333,744 (24%)	$1,358,165
Rankin (I)	$11,263	0	$10,717

KEY VOTES

1997	
Approve balanced-budget constitutional amendment	Y
Approve chemical weapons treaty	Y
1996	
Approve farm bill	Y
Limit punitive damages in product liability cases	N
Exempt small businesses from higher minimum wage	N
Approve welfare overhaul	Y
Bar job discrimination based on sexual orientation	Y
Override veto of ban on "partial birth" abortions	N
1995	
Approve GOP budget with tax and spending cuts	N
Approve constitutional amendment barring flag desecration	Y

VOTING STUDIES

	Presidential Support		Party Unity		Conservative Coalition	
Year	**S**	**O**	**S**	**O**	**S**	**O**
1996	90	10	73	27	45	55
1995	79	21	68	32	51	49
1994	89	11	86	14	50	50
1993	89	10	80	15	54	39
1992	35	65	83	17	45	55
1991	40	58	83	17	45	55

INTEREST GROUP RATINGS

Year	ADA	AFL-CIO	CCUS	ACU
1996	85	n/a	46	20
1995	75	83	47	13
1994	85	100	20	0
1993	85	73	20	16
1992	95	75	20	4
1991	70	58	20	24

Conrad Burns (R)

Of Billings — Elected 1988, 2nd term

Biographical Information

Born: Jan. 25, 1935, Gallatin, Mo.
Education: U. of Missouri, 1952-54.
Military Service: Marine Corps, 1955-57.
Occupation: Radio and television broadcaster.
Family: Wife, Phyllis Kuhlmann; two children.
Religion: Lutheran.
Political Career: Yellowstone County Commission, 1987-89.
Capitol Office: 187 Dirksen Bldg. 20510; 224-2644.

Committees

Special Aging

Appropriations
Agriculture, Rural Development & Related Agencies; Energy & Water Development; Interior; Military Construction (chairman); VA, HUD & Independent Agencies

Commerce, Science & Transportation
Aviation; Communications (chairman); Consumer Affairs, Foreign Commerce & Tourism; Science, Technology & Space; Surface Transportation & Merchant Marine

Energy & Natural Resources
Forests & Public Land Management (vice-chairman); National Parks, Historic Preservation & Recreation

Small Business

In Washington: Burns tossed in his hat for the only contested GOP Senate leadership slot heading into the 105th Congress, taking on Georgian Paul Coverdell for the opening to be Republican Conference secretary. Burns is best known as a battler against the Clinton administration in what he would term "the War on the West," and he sought to play up his regional appeal, arguing that he could help diversify the Senate's nearly all-Southern GOP leadership team. But he found that most of his colleagues are more interested in waging a war on taxes than a war for the West, and Burns, who has not always been completely zealous on that front, lost to Coverdell, 41-14.

And so Burns returns to his knitting on his myriad subcommittees, where his interests run from bison through latrines to computers. The former Marine retains the chairmanship of the Military Construction Subcommittee on the Appropriations Committee and for the 105th gains the gavel of the Commerce, Science and Transportation Subcommittee on Communications.

Like a number of his colleagues who have sizable rural constituencies, Burns hopes that the burgeoning telecommunications industry can help isolated communities compete economically with more urban areas. His championing of the computer network infrastructure has made him an unlikely hero of the so-called digerati; although his office still has to issue denials to media outlets stating that Burns, a former tobacco chewer, does not use the spittoons on the Senate floor, he has been highlighted in the hip computer magazine Wired.

His main push in the electronic arena for the 105th would change administration policy on exporting encrypted software. The Clinton administration has resisted allowing commercial export of technology that makes electronic communication more secure. Burns maintains this puts U.S. companies at a disadvantage in the global market. "I believe we're on the verge of exporting entire industries overseas," he warned in April 1997.

Burns lent an air of social-issue concern to the debate over telecommunications policy during the 104th. Although most interest in this area was expended over a provision of the revised law that sought to ban obscenity from the Internet, Burns was concerned about the requirement that nonprofit organizations such as hospitals and migrant health centers be granted lower rates. He said this could also apply to clinics operated by Planned Parenthood that perform abortions. His contention that the group was too controversial to be included in the massive legislation seemed to fall on deaf ears, though.

With momentum building to revise the estate tax code, Burns states firmly his belief that "the estate tax's roots go back to socialism. It goes to expropriation of people's property." But he voted in May 1995 against a move to endorse $312 billion in House-passed tax cuts, and a month later he was one of a dozen Senate Republicans who sent an appeal to Budget Committee Chairman Pete V. Domenici, R-N.M., urging him to resist tax-cut fervor in negotiating the budget resolution with the House.

Burns, who served during the 104th as chairman of the Commerce Subcommittee on Science, Technology and Space, defended funding of NASA's space station, saying it represented "one-seventh of 1 percent of the federal budget" and comparing the decision to fund it with Thomas Jefferson's decision to finance the Lewis and Clark expedition.

Burns served for three years in the Marine Corps in Okinawa, Japan and Korea; sleeping in hot Quonset huts left a lasting impression. Burns says he worries that an all-volunteer force competing with private industry has to upgrade family housing, especially given the increase in married personnel since his days as an $82 a month corporal. One priority for Burns in the fiscal 1996 military construction spending bill was an $8.5 million earmark for new latrines and a training support facility for the Army National Guard at Fort Harrison, Mont.

Among other home-state concerns Burns attended to were a $20 million increase in payments to barley growers he sought during consideration of the fiscal 1997 agriculture spending bill and a decrease in funding for the program to reintroduce Canadian wolves to Yellowstone National Park, across the state border in Wyoming. Burns also proposed a measure to require the federal government to test Yellowstone bison for brucellosis, a disease which he feared was spreading to cattle owned by ranchers in his state.

Burns criticized the administration's timber policy and cosponsored a bill that would have turned over all 270 million acres of public land administered by the Bureau of Land Management to the states. He also offered a bill to cut total federal land management costs by 30 percent, entailing the sales of some BLM land. But Burns said he would not pursue such large-scale plans during the 105th. He said he'd been advised by Montana GOP Gov. Marc Racicot that "the state just does not have the capacity to assume management of Bureau of Land Management lands at this time."

Burns tried the patience of Judiciary Committee Chairman Orrin G. Hatch, R-Utah, by stalling the confirmation of two appointees to the 9th Circuit Court of Appeals. Burns and Washington Republican Slade Gorton joined in an effort to split the 9th Circuit into two, removing several northwestern states from the San Francisco-based court. California Democrat Dianne Feinstein succeeded in substituting a plan to study such a split that passed the Senate.

Gorton and Burns, who both sit on the Energy and Natural Resources Committee, have made clear their opposition to sales of their region's federal power operations, including the Bonneville Power Administration.

Burns sponsored the "Rodeo Freedom Act of 1995," which would have prevented the Food and Drug Administration from regulating advertising at or sponsorship of rodeo events. Although the bill did not mention tobacco companies, they were the apparent beneficiary of the legislation. "This is not a product issue," Burns explained. "It is an issue of personal freedom, and the right of Westerners to enjoy their recreational pursuits."

Such a stance is in keeping with Burns' backroads image. He came to office with an appealing and folksy style, and tried in his first four years to achieve results by bridging differences. He was rewarded in the 103rd Congress with a seat on the Appropriations Committee.

However, Burns made it clear during the 103rd that he would not give in to the Clinton administration or liberal colleagues on the Hill on one of the most contentious and longest-running issues in the state: wilderness preservation. He threatened to filibuster the 1994 Interior appropriations bill "until there is no more blood left," adding, with characteristic cowboy flair, that a proposed grazing fee increase "turns the management of our nation's rangeland over to a bunch of inside-the-Beltway bureaucrats who don't know a good stand of grass from a manicured lawn."

A former rancher and farm broadcaster with little political experience, Burns sought credibility as a legislator while maintaining the crowd-pleasing image that helped him overcome Democratic Sen. John "Doc" Melcher in the biggest Senate upset of 1988. He has made no effort to dispel the countrified persona he projected at a freshman orientation session — to which he wore aged cowboy boots and a leather belt with a "C" on the buckle. After a tree-planting ceremony near the Lincoln Memorial, Burns walked over to a police horse and examined its mouth to see how old the animal was; a syndicated story on the incident was carried by Burns' hometown newspaper, The Billings Gazette.

"Thanks, Conrad, thanks for telling the world what hicks we are," the Gazette has written. The harshest criticism came over Burns' glib remark that "there are awful good folks" in Montana, including some who "can read and write."

At Home: Burns began the 1994 election cycle high on the Democrats' target list. Critics said he had accomplished little in the Senate since his 1988 ouster of Melcher, a weak two-term incumbent. Besides, Montana had not returned a Republican incumbent to the Senate in this century.

But Burns would break that record, and do it easily. He spent most of the year stockpiling money (he wound up raising more than $3 million), while Democrats scrapped for the nomination against him. Melcher was back in hopes of a rematch, but he was unable to shed his baggage or live down the fact that he had remained in Washington as a lobbyist after losing in 1988.

The Democratic nomination went to Jack Mudd, former dean of the law school at the University of Montana, who was making his first bid for public office. Mudd had to contend with a late primary entry by Becky Shaw, who contested his claim to the votes of abortion rights supporters and received 21 percent in the June primary.

Burns took the unusual step of buying air time late in the primary to denigrate Mudd and highlight Shaw's position on abortion in what appeared to be a bid to help anti-abortion Melcher split the field and win the nomination. Burns denied any intent to influence the Democratic outcome.

In the fall, Burns embarrassed himself by telling a newspaper editorial board a story about a farmer who used a racial epithet when referring to African-Americans. Burns also reported his own complaints about living in Washington, a city with a large black-majority population.

But none of this seemed to faze his supporters. Mudd, meanwhile, was unable to break out of the corporate lawyer frame fashioned for him by Melcher in the primary. Outspent 3-to-1, he never reached a competitive level of name recognition. Burns wound up winning with 62 percent of the vote.

When he entered the 1988 Senate contest, Burns had served less than two years in his only elective office, Yellowstone County (Billings) commissioner. He had no broad expertise on national or international issues. And he seemed to be a fallback candidate, recruited by the National Republican Senatorial Committee (NRSC) for a state party that had failed to find a well-known elected official to challenge Melcher.

But Burns actually had a much stronger political base than most observers recognized, including Melcher. His broadcasts on the Northern Agricultural Network, which he cofounded, had given him a statewide following and high name recognition.

Melcher, for his part, was a veterinarian widely known as "Doc" who had built his popularity with his own folksy charm. But he was a stumbling campaigner, and his Senate voting record, which often earned him 100 percent ratings from the Americans for Democratic Action, left him vulnerable to charges that he was to the left of the state mainstream.

The NRSC spotted this vulnerability early on and promoted Burns, to a disbelieving political and media establishment, as their "upset special." The campaign committee poured in enough to buy plenty of TV ad time in a state where air time is inexpensive.

Burns benefited from an article in the Great Falls Tribune detailing Melcher's interest in Philippine issues; Burns had labored to draw attention to the fact that the incumbent had visited the Philippines three times in five years. Burns also gained from the publicity attending a Billings campaign visit by Republican presidential nominee George Bush in late October.

But the event that may have clinched the win for Burns was President Ronald Reagan's veto of a wilderness bill, written by Melcher, just days before the election. The bill, which had long been stalled in Congress, had been an albatross for Melcher, endearing him neither to development interests, which opposed wilderness legislation in general, nor environmentalists, who wanted more land protected than the bill provided. Then, when Reagan vetoed the bill, it appeared to reinforce Burns' claim that Melcher lacked the clout to get his proposals enacted. Burns won with 52 percent of the vote.

SENATE ELECTIONS

1994 General		
Conrad Burns (R)	218,542	(62%)
Jack Mudd (D)	131,845	(38%)

Previous Winning Percentages: 1988 (52%)

CAMPAIGN FINANCE

1994	Receipts	Receipts from PACs	Expend-itures
Burns (R)	$3,065,090	$1,316,194 (43%)	$3,157,084
Mudd (D)	$1,120,638	$320,782 (29%)	$1,107,591

KEY VOTES

1997	
Approve balanced-budget constitutional amendment	Y
Approve chemical weapons treaty	N
1996	
Approve farm bill	Y
Limit punitive damages in product liability cases	Y
Exempt small businesses from higher minimum wage	Y
Approve welfare overhaul	Y
Bar job discrimination based on sexual orientation	N
Override veto of ban on "partial birth" abortions	Y
1995	
Approve GOP budget with tax and spending cuts	Y
Approve constitutional amendment barring flag desecration	Y

VOTING STUDIES

	Presidential Support		Party Unity		Conservative Coalition	
Year	S	O	S	O	S	O
1996	29	71	97	3	95	5
1995	26	74	95	5	96	4
1994	42	55	82	15	91	6
1993	24	75	92	8	85	15
1992	85	15	94	6	95	5
1991	89	11	93	7	95	5

INTEREST GROUP RATINGS

Year	ADA	AFL-CIO	CCUS	ACU
1996	5	n/a	85	100
1995	0	0	100	83
1994	0	13	70	92
1993	20	18	91	96
1992	5	25	100	89
1991	5	17	90	86

AL Rick Hill (R)

Of Helena — Elected 1996, 1st term

Biographical Information
Born: Dec. 30, 1946, Grand Rapids, Mich.
Education: St. Cloud State U., B.A. 1968.
Occupation: Surety bonding and insurance company owner.
Family: Wife, Betti Christie; three children.
Religion: Assembly of God.
Political Career: Mont. Republican Party chairman, 1991-92.
Capitol Office: 1037 Longworth Bldg. 20515; 225-3211.

Committees
Banking & Financial Services
Capital Markets, Securities & Government Sponsored Enterprises; Housing & Community Opportunity
Resources
Forests & Forest Health; National Parks & Public Lands
Small Business
Government Programs & Oversight

The Path to Washington: Hill brings to Congress a decidedly more conservative viewpoint than the man he succeeds in the House, liberal Democrat Pat Williams (who retired in 1996).

But Hill will likely find himself occupied with some of the same issues that Williams worked on in Congress, even if their approach to those matters differs greatly.

Hill says that with nearly one-third of Montana's land owned by the federal government, his primary focus in Congress will be to improve the management of those lands, repair deteriorating parks, and protect the state's oil, gas and coal resources.

He also wants to work on resolving decades-old conflicts over wilderness lands. He says the federal government has held up numerous cases involving wilderness lands while failing to manage the land properly. Hill supports the idea of earmarking park fees to support infrastructure improvements, particularly at Yellowstone National Park, instead of spending the money on operations.

Hill says he supports timber harvesting as a land management tool and favors allowing exploratory drilling for oil and gas along the Rocky Mountain Front without opening the area to wholesale development.

Hill will be in position to work on these issues as a member of the Resources Committee. A former owner of a surety bond firm and an insurance company, Hill sits on the Banking and Small Business committees.

Hill, who served as state Republican Party chairman and head of the state worker's compensation fund, generally follows a conservative line.

He opposes abortion, except to save the life of the woman, and favors banning a particular abortion technique opponents call "partial birth" abortion. A term-limits advocate, Hill promises to serve only three terms in the House.

He also supports a balanced-budget constitutional amendment. Hill was the only Republican freshman to vote in May 1997 against the fiscal 1998 budget resolution that aims to balance the budget by 2002. The measure passed 333-99.

To help curb federal spending, Hill says Japan and Germany should contribute more of the cost of maintaining U.S. troops in their countries. He also supports the abolition of federal highway demonstration projects and a phaseout of farm subsidies.

Hill began the race for Congress long before Williams announced that he would retire after 18 years. He faced two opponents in the primary, one of whom, Dwight MacKay, was backed by GOP Sen. Conrad Burns. After polls showed him trailing his primary opponents, Hill managed to pull ahead in the final days by pouring $100,000 of his own money into television ads.

Hill emerged on top again in the general election after a hard-fought battle with Democrat Bill Yellowtail, a former state senator and former regional director for the Environmental Protection Agency.

Montana has been a competitive arena for both parties in congressional elections, and the race remained close through much of the fall, only turning Hill's way toward the end.

Throughout the campaign, skeletons came tumbling out of both candidates' closets. Weeks before the primary, Yellowtail revealed that 20 years earlier he had slapped the woman who was his wife at the time. He also had his state Senate wages garnished for failing to pay child support and had burglarized a camera store as a student at Dartmouth College.

Despite his promise not to use Yellowtail's past as an issue in the general-election campaign, Hill did say that a candidate's handling of his family responsibilities reflected on his integrity, and the Republican touted his own efforts in raising his sons after his divorce. But about a month before the election, Hill's campaign was rocked by local news reports that revealed he had an affair while still married to his first wife, which she said led to the couple's divorce in 1980.

Hill also was attacked in a TV ad campaign by

Only the invisible hand of the U.S. census would have dared join the rugged west of Montana's old 1st District and the eastern plains of the 2nd. Because the state's population grew little during the 1980s (up 2 percent, to 799,065), reapportionment cost Montana a House seat, bringing western labor Democrats and eastern Republican ranchers into an at-large constituency. A match made in heaven this is not. (However, if current population trends hold — Montana's population grew more than 10 percent from 1990 to 1996 — it could regain the second House seat after the 2000 Census.)

In economic and political terms, eastern and western Montana seem more like separate states than two halves of the same. The west is mountains, mines, lumber mills and tourism; the east is flat country, largely given over to wheat and cattle. Throughout the 1980s, the west was represented in the House by Democrat Pat Williams, a labor liberal. The east elected Republican Ron Marlenee, a crusty conservative. When Williams and Marlenee faced off in 1992, Williams won by less than 4 percentage points.

But the politics of Montana — where there is now no daytime speed limit on interstate highways — have been difficult to pigeonhole ever since this state elected the first woman, Jeanette Rankin, to Congress in 1916. Bill Clinton edged George Bush in Montana in 1992, becoming the first Democratic presidential candidate since 1964 to carry the state. Montana was among Ross Perot's best states in 1992 and 1996. And in 1996 the state soundly elected Republican Hill to the House and overwhelmingly re-elected GOP Gov. Marc Racicot while re-electing Democratic Sen. Max Baucus.

The current political behavior of eastern and western Montana is rooted in their historic economic underpinnings.

The mountains of western Montana begat lumber mills and mines early in this century. While the prodigious lodes of copper, zinc and lead in Butte's "richest hill on Earth" produced some of the nation's wealthiest mine owners, they also spawned strong unions to represent the miners.

Though forestry and mining have not always provided a steady living, union-inspired Democratic voting habits have been quite regular in most western counties. Nowhere is this clearer than in heavily unionized Silver Bow County (Butte) and its neighbor Deer Lodge County (Anaconda). In 1996, Clinton won 63 percent in Silver Bow and 66 percent in Deer Lodge; Perot nearly defeated Bob Dole in the latter county.

Clinton in 1992 carried the two western counties with sizable urban centers — Missoula County (Missoula) and Lewis and Clark County (Helena). He narrowly lost the latter in 1996.

Missoula, lying at the hub of several agricultural valleys, is a lumber-processing center and home to the University of Montana. Helena, the capital, got its start when gold was discovered in Last Chance Gulch during the Civil War.

MONTANA
At large

There are pockets of GOP strength in the west, most notably Flathead County in the north (where visitors to Glacier National Park help sustain Kalispell and Whitefish). Dole defeated Clinton by nearly 20 percentage points in Flathead in 1996.

While population grew a bit in western Montana during the 1980s, ranching and wheat-growing counties in the east suffered a net loss. Most of these counties usually turn in healthy GOP margins, but their vote tallies are small. In 1996, Dole won 75 percent of the mere 746 votes cast in Garfield County.

Farther east are Montana's two largest cities, Billings (Yellowstone County) and Great Falls (Cascade County). Billings has generally been the more dependable of the two for Republicans — both Dole and Hill comfortably carried the territory in 1996. Cascade voters went Democratic for president and Republican for Congress.

From its start as a market center for sugar beets and other farm products, Billings grew in the 1970s to become headquarters for many energy ventures. Also fueling economic growth in urban areas such as Billings and Great Falls are regional health care centers that have opened in the past several years, attracting patients from neighboring states. In Great Falls, cheap hydroelectric power drawn from nearby falls on the Missouri River spurred industrial development early in the century, as well as a surviving tradition of union activism.

About 140 miles northeast of Billings is the small town of Jordan (Garfield County), near the site of an 81-day standoff in 1996 between federal authorities and an anti-tax group called The Freemen.

The GOP also is strong in Gallatin County in the south (site of Bozeman and Montana State University).

A new phenomenon drawing attention to Montana — and giving a boost to Democrats — is the state's status as a getaway for the rich and famous. And an increasing number of professionals are relocating to Montana, where they use new technology to telecommute.

A new kind of economic pressure is gripping the state, however, as corporations snap up and subdivide property along streams and rivers known for their trout fishing and natural beauty. The battle over whether to impose tougher restrictions on development, which many Montanans complain has driven up property taxes in the state, has ignited a fierce debate.

1990 Population: 799,065. White 741,111 (93%), Black 2,381 (<1%), Other 55,573 (7%). Hispanic origin 12,174 (2%). 18 and over 576,961 (72%), 62 and over 126,919 (16%). Median age: 34.

the AFL-CIO, which claimed he supported cuts in student loans.

But Hill managed to overcome the negative publicity by amassing a larger campaign treasury than Yellowtail. He had more money to spend on television ads and claimed that Yellowtail was "a dangerous liberal." Hill won by the comfortable margin of 52 percent to 43 percent.

HOUSE ELECTIONS

1996 General		
Rick Hill (R)	211,975	(52%)
Bill Yellowtail (D)	174,516	(43%)
Jim Brooks (NL)	17,935	(4%)
1996 Primary		
Rick Hill (R)	48,560	(44%)
Dwight MacKay (R)	39,651	(36%)
Alan Mikkelsen (R)	22,736	(20%)

CAMPAIGN FINANCE

	Receipts	Receipts from PACs		Expend-itures
1996				
Hill (R)	$977,435	$236,511	(24%)	$943,062
Yellowtail (D)	$648,399	$181,217	(28%)	$635,282

DISTRICT VOTE FOR PRESIDENT

	1996		1992
D	167,922 (41%)	**D**	154,507 (38%)
R	179,652 (44%)	**R**	144,207 (36%)
I	55,229 (14%)	**I**	107,225 (26%)

KEY VOTES

1997

Ban "partial birth" abortions Y

NEBRASKA

Governor: Ben Nelson (D)
First elected: 1990
Length of term: 4 years
Term expires: 1/99
Salary: $65,000
Term limit: 2 consecutive terms
Phone: (402) 471-2244
Born: May 17, 1941; McCook, Neb.
Education: U. of Nebraska, B.A. 1963, M.A. 1965, J.D. 1970.
Occupation: Lawyer.
Family: Wife, Diane Lyle; four children.
Religion: Methodist.
Political Career: Neb. director of insurance, 1975-76; Democratic nominee for U.S. Senate, 1996.

Lt. Gov.: Kim Robak (D)
First elected: 1994
Length of term: 4 years
Term expires: 1/99
Salary: $47,000
Phone: (402) 471-2256

State election official: (402) 471-2554
Democratic headquarters: (402) 475-4584
Republican headquarters: (402) 475-2122

REDISTRICTING

Nebraska retained its three House seats in reapportionment. The legislature passed the map June 5, 1991; the governor signed it June 10.

STATE LEGISLATURE

Unicameral Legislature. Meets January-May in odd years, January-April in even years.

Legislature: 49 nonpartisan members, 4-year terms
1996 breakdown: 36 men, 13 women
Salary: $12,000
Phone: (402) 471-2271

URBAN STATISTICS

City	Population
Omaha	335,795
Mayor Hal Daub, R	
Lincoln	191,972
Mayor Mike Johanns, R	
Grand Island	39,457
Mayor Ken Gnadt, R	
Bellevue	30,982
Mayor Inez Boyd, I	
Kearney	24,396
Mayor Peter G. Kotsiopulos, I	

U.S. CONGRESS

Senate: 1 D, 1 R
House: 0 D, 3 R

TERM LIMITS

For state offices: Yes
Unicameral legislature: 2 terms

ELECTIONS

1996 Presidential Vote

Bob Dole	54%
Bill Clinton	35%
Ross Perot	11%

1992 Presidential Vote

George Bush	47%
Bill Clinton	29%
Ross Perot	24%

1988 Presidential Vote

George Bush	60%
Michael S. Dukakis	39%

POPULATION

1990 population		1,578,385
1980 population		1,569,825
Percent change		+<1%
Rank among states:		36
White		94%
Black		4%
Hispanic		2%
Asian or Pacific islander		1%
Urban		66%
Rural		34%
Born in state		70%
Foreign-born		2%
Under age 18	429,012	27%
Ages 18-64	926,305	59%
65 and older	223,068	14%
Median age		33

MISCELLANEOUS

Capital: Lincoln
Number of counties: 93
Per capita income: $17,852 (1991)
Rank among states: 24
Total area: 77,355 sq. miles
Rank among states: 15

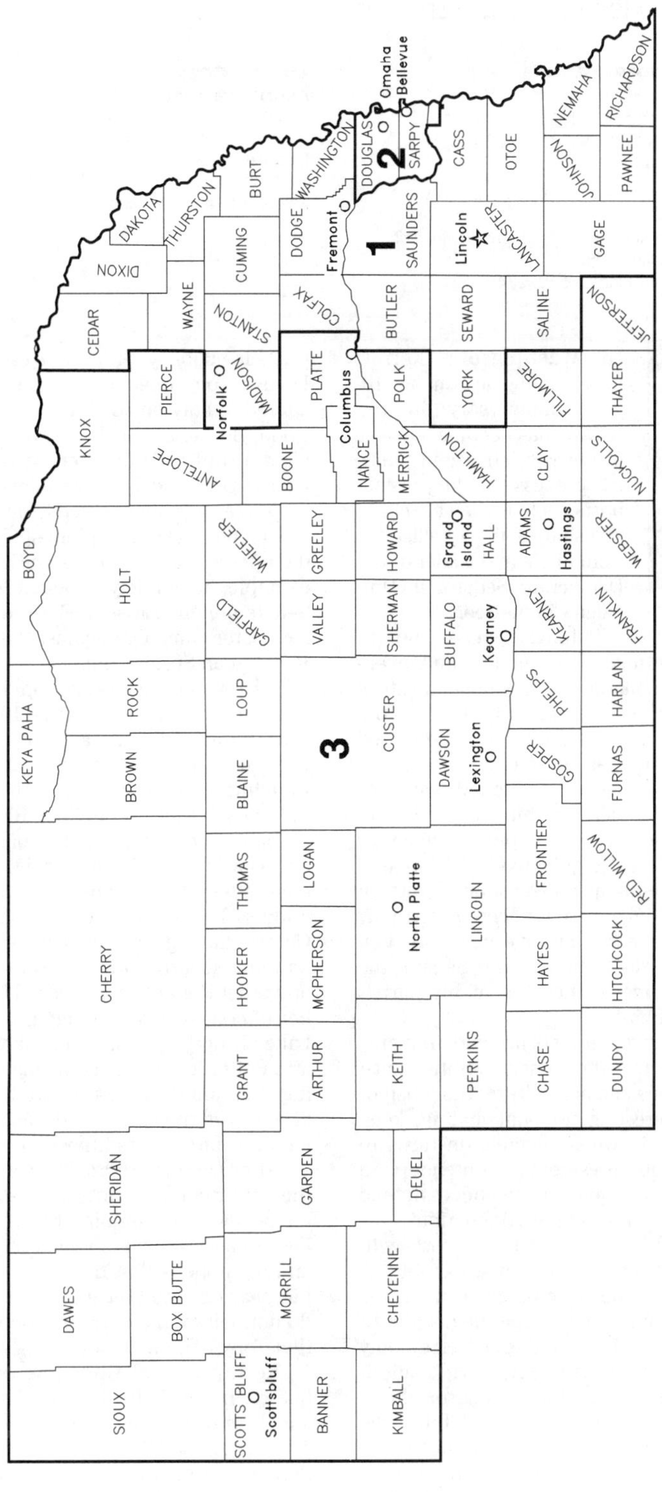
1
2
3
Omaha
Bellevue
Fremont
Lincoln
Norfolk
Columbus
Grand Island
Hastings
Kearney
Lexington
North Platte
Scottsbluff
RICHARDSON
NEMAHA
PAWNEE
JOHNSON
OTOE
CASS
SARPY
DOUGLAS
WASHINGTON
BURT
THURSTON
DAKOTA
DIXON
CEDAR
WAYNE
CUMING
DODGE
SAUNDERS
LANCASTER
GAGE
JEFFERSON
SALINE
SEWARD
BUTLER
COLFAX
STANTON
MADISON
PIERCE
KNOX
ANTELOPE
PLATTE
BOONE
NANCE
MERRICK
POLK
YORK
FILLMORE
THAYER
NUCKOLLS
CLAY
HAMILTON
HALL
ADAMS
WEBSTER
FRANKLIN
KEARNEY
BUFFALO
HOWARD
GREELEY
WHEELER
GARFIELD
VALLEY
SHERMAN
CUSTER
PHELPS
HARLAN
GOSPER
FURNAS
DAWSON
BOYD
HOLT
KEYA PAHA
ROCK
BROWN
LOUP
BLAINE
THOMAS
LOGAN
LINCOLN
FRONTIER
RED WILLOW
HITCHCOCK
HAYES
CHERRY
HOOKER
MCPHERSON
GRANT
ARTHUR
KEITH
PERKINS
CHASE
DUNDY
SHERIDAN
GARDEN
DEUEL
DAWES
BOX BUTTE
MORRILL
CHEYENNE
SIOUX
SCOTTS BLUFF
BANNER
KIMBALL

Bob Kerrey (D)

Of Lincoln — Elected 1988, 2nd term

Biographical Information
Born: Aug. 27, 1943, Lincoln, Neb.
Education: U. of Nebraska, B.S. 1966.
Military Service: Navy, 1966-69.
Occupation: Restaurateur.
Family: Divorced; two children.
Religion: Congregationalist.
Political Career: Governor, 1983-87; sought Democratic nomination for president, 1992.
Capitol Office: 141 Hart Bldg. 20510; 224-6551.

Committees
Agriculture, Nutrition & Forestry
Marketing, Inspection & Product Promotion; Production & Price Competitiveness (ranking)
Finance
Health Care; International Trade; Taxation & IRS Oversight
Select Intelligence (ranking)

In Washington: Kerrey, now coming up on his 10-year anniversary in the Senate, has become a player in the legislative and political process, holding visible posts such as the vice chairmanship of the Intelligence Committee and leader of the Democratic Senatorial Campaign Committee.

But the world of Washington seems not to have changed him much. He remains unconventional, at times enigmatic, a man whose life story and "star quality" set him apart even in the Senate, which has more than its share of outsized personalities. Kerrey has mesmerized Nebraska voters for years: a telegenic wounded war hero who returned from Vietnam, built a successful business career and became a popular vote-getter in a Republican state. He defeated a GOP incumbent for the governorship, had a romance with an actress (Debra Winger), renounced a virtually guaranteed second term as governor, and then won election and re-election to the Senate, the latter victory coming in the face of his party's national 1994 drubbing.

Kerrey's legislative interests are wide-ranging, including intelligence, the budget, entitlements, telecommunications and agriculture. His grasp of issues and his interesting personal qualities keep his name in the mix when speculation turns to potential Democratic presidential contenders, in 2000 or beyond. Kerrey made an unsuccessful bid for his party's 1992 presidential nomination.

Starting in 1995, Kerrey got to network with donors across the country as chairman of the Democratic Senatorial Campaign Committee (DSCC). These contacts may help if he decides to wage another White House bid, but Kerrey only reluctantly agreed to run the DSCC. He made it plain he did not relish the fundraising or cheerleading aspects of the post. "When I think the Democratic Party is wrong, I'll continue to say so," he said after being named DSCC chairman.

The Democrats' Senate showing in 1996 was not stellar: Republicans added a net of two seats to their majority. Still, after cajoling by Minority Leader Tom Daschle of South Dakota, Kerrey agreed to stay on as DSCC chairman for another cycle. But he is aided by a vice chairman known as a prolific fundraiser, freshman Democrat Robert G. Torricelli of New Jersey.

Kerrey has never shied from playing "skunk at the picnic," and his plain-spokenness certainly did not disappear with his DSCC role. In 1996, for example, he publicly knocked Maine Democratic Senate nominee Joseph E. Brennan for running a lackluster campaign against the eventual winner, Republican Susan Collins.

Kerrey has been the top Democrat on the Intelligence Committee since 1995. The panel has a tradition of bipartisanship, and Kerrey had a good working relationship with the committee's Republican chairman in the 104th, Arlen Specter of Pennsylvania. Republican Richard C. Shelby of Alabama is chairman in the 105th Congress.

In early 1997, Kerrey struggled to maintain the committee's bipartisan tradition during consideration of President Clinton's nominee to head the Central Intelligence Agency, former White House national security adviser Anthony Lake. Shelby and other Republicans pressed Lake about a number of controversial foreign policy decisions, and Lake abruptly withdrew his name from consideration after a week of confirmation hearings, saying Republicans had politicized the process. Shelby said the committee was making legitimate inquiries into Lake's fitness to run the CIA.

After Lake's withdrawal, Kerrey also criticized the confirmation process. "I believe this committee needs to remain bipartisan," Kerrey said. ". . . I've got a great deal of respect for Senator Shelby, and my hope is that the next nominee will get a fair hearing. And I have to, very respectfully, say I do not believe the current process — the process that Tony Lake went through — was fair."

Kerrey and Shelby have worked together before. In the 104th Congress, Shelby was chair and Kerrey ranking member of Appropriations' Treasury, Postal Service and General Government Subcommittee; there were some tense moments on that panel, too. During consideration of the fiscal 1996 treasury-postal spending bill, they found themselves competing over who could cut more from construction projects after Kerrey offered an amendment that some Republicans said targeted GOP-favored projects too heavily. Kerrey left the Appropriations Committee and joined the Finance Committee for the 105th Congress.

In the fiscal policy arena, Kerrey has a conservative streak. He was one of only three Democrats to vote for the GOP budget resolution when it first passed the Senate in 1995. But after the GOP plan emerged from conference with the House, he and the two other Democratic backers, Charles S. Robb of Virginia and Sam Nunn of Georgia, dropped their support for the proposal because Senate Republicans agreed to a much bigger package of tax cuts.

Kerrey later signed on to an unsuccessful effort by a group of moderate Republicans and Democrats to develop a bipartisan plan to balance the budget by 2002. The group proposed a much smaller tax cut package than the one GOP leaders backed, as well as deeper cuts in the growth of entitlement programs than those advocated by Clinton and congressional Democrats.

In 1993, Kerrey became the critical vote to approve the Clinton administration-backed budget-reconciliation conference report, a plan that raised taxes and reduced the deficit. In exchange for Kerrey's vote, Clinton agreed to set up a commission to recommend how to limit entitlement spending.

While the commission's efforts ultimately came to little, Kerrey has remained a strong advocate of focusing attention on reining in entitlement spending. He introduced a series of bills in the 104th Congress with former Sen. Alan K. Simpson, R-Wyo., to increase the retirement age to 70, reduce the cost of living allowance for Social Security recipients and encourage workers to place into personal savings plans some payroll taxes that would otherwise go to Social Security. The aim of the legislation was to save the Social Security system from insolvency when the baby boom generation starts to retire. "Now is the time, not later. Mathematics are not on our side. Demographics are not on our side," Kerrey said.

Kerrey, who lost part of his right leg in Vietnam and was awarded the Medal of Honor, has been a vocal supporter of Clinton's push to restore full diplomatic relations with Vietnam. After Clinton announced in July 1995 that he was normalizing relations with Vietnam, Kerrey chastised conservatives who opposed this move and threatened to withhold funds for a U.S. embassy in Hanoi. "Leave us alone, for God's sake," an emotional Kerrey said after a White House ceremony announcing the decision. "Let us go forward with the pride [with which] we fought this war. We fought it for freedom, and now we're going to try to extend freedom back there. Leave this one alone. Go on to something else."

Even for a man known to speak his mind, Kerrey raised some eyebrows in 1997 when he criticized a drive led by a former Senate colleague and fellow disabled war veteran, Kansas Republican Bob Dole, to build a World War II memorial on the National Mall. Kerrey said he did not think anything should be built on the proposed spot.

Kerrey has been careful to tend to parochial interests. From his seat on the Agriculture Committee, he reacted coolly in the 104th to GOP-backed legislation overhauling federal farm programs to bring them more in line with a free market. Kerrey was among a group of Midwestern Democrats who sought to maintain a safety net for farmers when prices fell. He ultimately voted against the "Freedom to Farm" bill, which phased out most New Deal-era crop subsidies and replaced them with fixed declining payments.

And as the 104th Congress rewrote telecommunications law, Kerrey was concerned that rural people not get left behind on the information superhighway. In late 1995, Kerrey and Sen. Byron L. Dorgan, D-N.D., threatened to filibuster the conference report, which was still being negotiated, unless it included Senate language giving the Federal Communications Commission broad authority to compel companies to serve remote areas. Kerrey also emerged as the consumer groups' point man on telecommunications. During debate, he echoed administration concerns about provisions lifting price controls on cable, easing ownership restrictions on broadcasters and limiting the Justice Department's influence over the Baby Bells' expansion.

Kerrey's popularity in Nebraska was little affected by the failure of his brief bid for the Democratic presidential nomination in 1992. During that campaign, he delivered one of the most damning lines about Clinton's draft record, warning that in the fall under a GOP onslaught, Clinton was "going to be opened up like a soft peanut." After dropping out of the race, Kerrey dismissed his prior remarks as "political hyperbole" and pledged to campaign hard for Clinton if he emerged as the nominee.

At Home: An unconventional style and disregard for the accepted rules of political behavior vaulted Kerrey into the governorship in 1982 and sent him to the Senate six years later.

Although Kerrey was known locally as a war hero and a successful restaurateur, he was a political novice when he ran against Republican Gov. Charles Thone in 1982. However, Thone had a reputation for being bland and indecisive. Employing an aggressive campaign style and a wry, self-deprecating sense of humor, Kerrey attracted publicity and scored a narrow upset.

Kerrey soon showed he was unafraid to buck political trends: He became a critic of President Ronald Reagan, who in 1984 would carry 71 percent of the Nebraska vote. Kerrey attacked Reagan's economic and farm policies and accused the president of taking an approach to foreign affairs that "drapes euphemism and simplistic slogans over the realities of war."

But it was Kerrey's relationship with Winger,

not his political agenda, that left the most enduring impression from his gubernatorial tenure. Kerrey, who was divorced, met Winger in 1983 while she was making a movie in Lincoln.

While Kerrey's public romance made him something of a dashing figure, it also led to criticisms that he was long on style and short on substance. Although he cut an activist image early in his term, pushing deficit reduction and banking-law reform, his relationship with the unicameral Legislature soured somewhat.

Still, Kerrey was heavily favored to win a second term; his job approval rating hung at about 70 percent. He thus sealed his reputation for unpredictability when he announced he would not run for re-election in 1986. Although some observers tied the decision to distress over his breakup with Winger, Kerrey cited business obligations and a desire to spend more time with his two children.

With both Senate seats held by Democrats, it appeared that Kerrey might have plenty of quality time before seeking higher office. However, Democratic Sen. Edward Zorinsky died in March 1987; Republican Gov. Kay A. Orr picked an obscure businessman, David K. Karnes, as a replacement. Knowing his political base was much stronger than Karnes', Kerrey entered the 1988 contest for a full Senate term.

As it turned out, Kerrey got unexpected help from a would-be Republican rival. Four-term 2nd District GOP Rep. Hal Daub, angered that Orr had passed him over in favor of Karnes, entered the GOP Senate primary. Bolstered by his brief incumbency and the support of the state party, Karnes held on to win with 55 percent. But he was bloodied and entered the fall campaign against Kerrey as a distinct underdog.

Kerrey, who had token opposition for the Democratic nomination, had already filled the airwaves with image-building biographical ads. He stuck to his own script for the general election, touting his support for catastrophic health insurance, parental leave legislation and an overhaul of the welfare system. He called for a mix of spending cuts and tax increases to reduce the deficit.

Karnes, meanwhile, had spent much of his money on the primary and was $200,000 in debt by the end of June. He also made a disastrous gaffe: In discussing improved agricultural technology, Karnes said, "We need fewer farmers at this point in time," a remark that provoked jeers from a state-fair audience. Karnes immediately retreated, saying he had misspoken, but the damage was done. Kerry won by 15 percentage points.

In 1994, Republicans nominated business executive Jan Stoney, and she received strong backing from the national party and prominent conservative figures such as actor Charlton Heston. But her efforts to tie Kerrey to Clinton were hard to sell considering the incumbent's reputation for independent thinking. Kerrey took 55 percent, 10 percentage points ahead of Stoney.

SENATE ELECTIONS

1994 General		
Bob Kerrey (D)	317,297	(55%)
Jan Stoney (R)	260,668	(45%)

Previous Winning Percentages: 1988 (57%)

CAMPAIGN FINANCE

	Receipts	Receipts from PACs		Expend-itures
1994				
Kerrey (D)	$4,400,801	$1,275,087	(29%)	$4,471,081
Stoney (R)	$1,896,787	$168,250	(9%)	$1,871,778

KEY VOTES

1997	
Approve balanced-budget constitutional amendment	N
Approve chemical weapons treaty	Y
1996	
Approve farm bill	N
Limit punitive damages in product liability cases	?
Exempt small businesses from higher minimum wage	N
Approve welfare overhaul	N
Bar job discrimination based on sexual orientation	Y
Override veto of ban on "partial birth" abortions	N
1995	
Approve GOP budget with tax and spending cuts	N
Approve constitutional amendment barring flag desecration	N

VOTING STUDIES

	Presidential Support		Party Unity		Conservative Coalition	
Year	**S**	**O**	**S**	**O**	**S**	**O**
1996	81	14	85	12	32	68
1995	81	17	78	20	37	60
1994	89	10	83	17	47	53
1993	80	19	77	21	59	39
1992	25	58	74	9	18	58
1991	32	52	70	13	45	35

INTEREST GROUP RATINGS

Year	ADA	AFL-CIO	CCUS	ACU
1996	85	n/a	23	5
1995	80	75	39	0
1994	80	88	40	24
1993	75	64	45	8
1992	90	91	25	0
1991	75	78	29	5

Chuck Hagel (R)

Of Omaha — Elected 1996, 1st term

Biographical Information
Born: Oct. 4, 1946, North Platte, Neb.
Education: U. of Nebraska, Omaha, B.A. 1971.
Military Service: Army, 1967-68.
Occupation: Investment bank executive; international business consultant.
Family: Wife, Lilibet Ziller; two children.
Religion: Episcopalian.
Political Career: No previous office.
Capitol Office: 346 Russell Bldg. 20510; 224-4224.

Committees
Special Aging
Banking, Housing & Urban Affairs
Financial Services & Technology; International Finance; Housing Opportunity & Community Development
Foreign Relations
East Asian & Pacific Affairs; European Affairs; International Economic Policy, Export & Trade Promotion (chairman)

The Path to Washington: Hagel came from behind twice in his 1996 campaign for the Senate, first to upset Nebraska Attorney General Don Stenberg in the Republican primary, and then in November to thump Democratic Gov. Ben Nelson, who from the outset had been seen as the favorite to hold the state's open Senate seat for his party.

Nelson was thought to be one of the top recruiting successes of fellow Nebraskan Bob Kerrey, chairman of the Democratic Senatorial Campaign Committee. The popular governor — re-elected with 74 percent of the vote in 1994 despite the national Republican trend — agreed to run for the seat being vacated by retiring Democratic Sen. Jim Exon.

The GOP primary campaign began with Stenberg enjoying far greater statewide name recognition than Hagel. But by spending lavishly from his personal resources, wealthy businessman Hagel spread his name and message through television advertising. "I produce opportunities," Hagel said of his business experience. "I build jobs." He swept to nomination with more than 60 percent of the vote.

In the fall campaign, Hagel again invested aggressively in himself. With a fervor worthy of Jack F. Kemp, the 1996 GOP vice presidential nominee, Hagel made the centerpiece of his bid the argument that federal tax cuts would stimulate economic growth. And this growth, he contended, would do more to address problems in society than any government program could.

Besides endorsing Republican presidential nominee Bob Dole's proposed 15 percent tax cut, Hagel proposed a package of additional cuts including a phase-out of the capital gains tax, a $500-per-child tax credit and the elimination of estate and gift taxes.

To offset revenue losses, Hagel called for eliminating the departments of Energy, Education, Commerce, and Housing and Urban Development. He also called for a 25 percent cut in the budget of every regulatory agency.

Hagel endorsed a constitutional amendment requiring a balanced budget and one requiring a two-thirds majority in both chambers of Congress to raise taxes. He supported efforts to send welfare and Medicaid to the states.

On crime, he ticked off the litany of conservative solutions: the death penalty, the end of parole for violent criminals and mandatory life in prison for anyone convicted of a third violent felony.

In the general-election campaign, Nelson echoed arguments against Hagel that had first been laid out by Stenberg. He said Hagel had left the state and became a Washington insider, even toying with the idea of running for public office in his adopted state of Virginia, only to return to Nebraska to run for the Senate. Nelson referred to himself as a lifelong Nebraskan.

Nelson also challenged Hagel's tax-cutting proposals, arguing that they would increase the federal deficit. Nelson pointed to his own record of proposing six balanced state budgets in a row. He also defended the Education Department against Hagel's plan to eliminate it.

And in answer to Republican criticisms that he was breaking his pledge to serve out his four-year term as governor, Nelson said the voters could decide whether to hold him to that pledge or let him serve them in the Senate.

On Election Day, the voters' verdict was decisively clear. Hagel won by an impressive 14-point margin, taking 56 percent of the vote to Nelson's 42 percent.

Though new to the Senate, Hagel is an old hand in the ways of Washington; he spent nearly two decades in the nation's capital as a Republican political operative and a highly successful entrepreneur.

As a young man, Hagel spent a year as an infantryman in Vietnam, where he was seriously wounded twice. He returned to Nebraska with two Purple Hearts, worked as a bartender and radio newscaster, and finished college.

His Washington years began in 1971, when he started a six-year stint on the staff of Rep. John Y. McCollister, R-Neb. (1971-77), followed by four years as a corporate lobbyist, the last year of which he spent working on Ronald Reagan's 1980 presidential campaign.

Hagel became deputy administrator of the Veterans' Administration — the highest-ranking Reagan administration job to go to a Vietnam vet. He was a leading backer of the then-controversial Vietnam Memorial in Washington. In 1982, he resigned from the post because of disagreements with VA Administrator Robert P. Nimmo, a friend of Reagan's who was intent on cutting programs and who complained that veterans groups were greedy.

Within months, Hagel entered the nascent cellular telephone business, and by early 1987, his work in that field had made him wealthy.

He spent two years at the helm of the United Service Organizations, a nonprofit organization providing assistance to military personnel, then ran a consortium of companies set up to apply business methods to government problems. In 1990, he was chief operating officer of the Economic Summit of Industrialized Nations.

After the summit, Hagel became president and chief executive officer of the Private Sector Council, a Washington group involved in bringing business methods to government work. He left the council and returned to Nebraska in 1992 to become president of an investment banking firm.

In the Senate, Hagel applies his knowledge of business and finance to his work on the Banking, Housing and Urban Affairs Committee. On the Foreign Relations Committee, he is chairman of the Subcommittee on International Economic Policy, Export and Trade Promotion. He is also a deputy whip, one of three from the GOP Class of 1996.

SENATE ELECTIONS

1996 General		
Chuck Hagel (R)	379,933	(56%)
Ben Nelson (D)	281,904	(42%)
John W. DeCamp (LIBERT)	9,483	(1%)
1996 Primary		
Chuck Hagel (R)	108,612	(62%)
Don Stenberg (R)	65,813	(38%)

CAMPAIGN FINANCE

	Receipts	Receipts from PACs	Expend-itures
1996			
Hagel (R)	$3,612,338	$486,034 (13%)	$3,564,316
Nelson (D)	$2,179,131	$909,486 (42%)	$2,159,653
Dunn (NL)	$5,330	0	$6,599

KEY VOTES

1997	
Approve balanced-budget constitutional amendment	Y
Approve chemical weapons treaty	Y

1 Doug Bereuter (R)

Of Lincoln — Elected 1978, 10th term

Biographical Information

Born: Oct. 6, 1939, York, Neb.

Education: U. of Nebraska, B.A. 1961; Harvard U., M.C.P. 1966, M.P.A. 1973.

Military Service: Army, 1963-65.

Occupation: Urban planner; professor; state official.

Family: Wife, Louise Anna Meyer; two children.

Religion: Lutheran.

Political Career: Neb. Legislature, 1975-79.

Capitol Office: 2184 Rayburn Bldg. 20515; 225-4806.

Committees

Banking & Financial Services
Financial Institutions & Consumer Credit; Housing & Community Opportunity

International Relations
Asia & the Pacific (chairman); International Economic Policy & Trade

In Washington: Coming from an agricultural state, Bereuter has long understood that export opportunities are integral to the economic success of American farmers. He brings an internationalist outlook to his work on the Banking and Financial Services Committee and on the International Relations Committee, where he serves as chairman of the Asia and the Pacific Subcommittee.

Bereuter said he chose the Asia and Pacific chair because of the importance of the Pacific Rim to Nebraska. "Asian and Pacific nations comprise Nebraska's No. 1 market for exports," he told the Lincoln Star soon after he took over the committee at the start of the 104th Congress.

Bereuter is in general agreement with the Clinton administration on the importance of lowering trade barriers and keeping China as a trading partner, but he also has had sharp disagreements with the White House on some other foreign policy matters.

A hard-working, deliberate and pragmatic member, Bereuter takes a more moderate stance than many in his party on certain social and labor issues. He voted in the 104th against a GOP measure repealing a ban on certain semiautomatic assault-style weapons and in the 105th for a Democratic effort to release international family planning funds early. He was an early GOP supporter of increasing the minimum wage (although he did vote to exempt small businesses from paying the higher wage). And in July 1995 he joined with 51 other Republican moderates to oppose conservatives' efforts to bar the Environmental Protection Agency from enforcing certain environmental laws.

Bereuter's consensus-building inclinations were most evident during the House's July 1995 debate over whether to agree with President Clinton's intention to grant most-favored nation trading status to China. With some conservatives pushing again for revocation of MFN — an effort that fails annually — Bereuter worked with congressional critics of China and drafted a measure calling on Clinton to urge China to improve its human rights and trade practices and to curtail its military buildup and export of arms. But it stopped short of requiring trade sanctions. The House passed the measure overwhelmingly, 416-10.

The House then tabled, or killed, 321-107, a resolution that would have halted MFN status for China. Under MFN, Chinese goods are permitted to enter the United States at low, non-discriminatory tariff rates. Bereuter, who supports granting MFN to China, felt that an outright vote against MFN could be dangerous for Chinese-American relations. Bereuter said he drafted the alternative bill to give lawmakers something to vote for and to vent their displeasure at the Chinese on human rights and other issues, without toppling MFN.

Early in 1997, Bereuter also focused on China's pending reabsorption of Hong Kong; the tiny British colony was to go back under Chinese rule in July 1997. Bereuter introduced legislation to make the changes necessary in various U.S. laws to reflect the changeover from British rule to Chinese sovereignty called for under a 1984 Sino-British accord.

But the first section of his bill also spelled out U.S. concerns about the transition, in language intended to send a stiff warning to China about human rights and other controversies. Under the 1984 accord, the people of Hong Kong are to retain their "current lifestyle and legal, social, and economic systems" for the next 50 years. But in early 1997, China signaled that protest rallies would not be allowed in Hong Kong without prior police approval, and the Chinese indicated to journalists that criticism of the government or advocacy for Taiwan or Tibet would not be protected speech.

Bereuter said that concerns over Hong Kong will complicate the already troubled annual debate over China's trade status with the United States. "It will make it understandably more difficult to pass MFN," he said.

Another sore spot in U.S.-Chinese relations has been Beijing's belligerence toward Taiwan. In

NEBRASKA 1
East — Lincoln; Norfolk

Not long ago, Lincoln was a sleepy town that came to life only during the Legislature's sessions and on autumn Saturdays when the University of Nebraska played football. Back then, Cornhusker crowds nearly matched the city's population. Today, however, Lincoln is thriving: Its population has nearly doubled over the past 40 years to 192,000. A diversified employment base makes Lincoln (Lancaster County) a picture of economic health.

The city's boom has been led by the expanding state and city governments and by the university, which has 24,000 students. Lincoln has three major hospital complexes, and the white-collar base features banks and insurance companies. In addition, Lincoln (like Omaha) is fast becoming a telecommunications hub. Gallup Organization Inc., the polling company, is in Lincoln. Lincoln does have industrial employers, including a Goodyear factory that makes rubber belts and hoses. There are also a number of food-processing companies.

The 1st has pockets of population growth elsewhere. Norfolk (Madison County) is known for pursuing industry; beef products, electronic components and steel products are made here. The district includes Omaha exurbs to the north (Washington County) and south (most of Cass County), as well as Dakota County suburbs of Sioux City, Iowa (where IBP, the nation's largest beef processor, has headquarters), and Dodge County.

The more sparsely populated rural sections of the 1st contain some of the nation's most productive farmland. Counties in the northern part of the 1st are among Nebraska's leaders in hog and milk production; York County, to the west, is a leading corn producer. Farming in the rural parts of Lancaster County outside Lincoln makes the county the biggest sorghum producer.

The rural Republican vote gives the GOP an advantage in the 1st. In 1992, Madison County gave 57 percent to George Bush, and in 1996, the county gave 63 percent of its vote to Bob Dole.

But Lancaster, which casts more than 40 percent of the district's total vote, tends to be a swing county. The county went for Dole in 1996, though Bill Clinton was close behind, losing by less than 1,500 votes out of more than 97,000 cast. In 1992, George Bush won Lancaster over Clinton by just 193 votes, out of more than 104,000 cast.

Bereuter took Lancaster easily in the House race, winning with 65 percent of the votes in 1996.

The strongest Democratic counties are at opposite corners of the district. In the northeast are Dakota County, with a large blue-collar contingent and some Hispanic and Asian residents, and Thurston County, made up almost entirely of Winnebago and Omaha Indian reservations. In the southwest is rural Saline County, dominated by people of Czech heritage with a longstanding Democratic tradition.

1990 Population: 526,297. White 507,343 (96%), Black 5,544 (1%), Other 13,410 (3%). Hispanic origin 7,106 (1%). 18 and over 389,852 (74%), 62 and over 91,091 (17%). Median age: 33.

March 1996, the Chinese tested missiles near Taiwan, an action interpreted as intending to frighten the island nation before its presidential election. Although the Clinton administration deployed a pair of aircraft carrier battle groups to the seas near Taiwan, many conservative lawmakers said that was not enough. Bereuter backed a House resolution committing the United States to defend Taiwan if it is attacked.

Bereuter said the administration sent confusing signals during the first phase of the Taiwan crisis. "In part, the resolution springs from the fact that the administration's early statements on the crisis were vague and ambiguous," he said. "If it weren't for that, the deployment of the carriers might not have been necessary."

Bereuter also joined with his GOP colleagues on International Relations to condemn the Clinton administration's tacit acceptance of Iran's arming of the Bosnian Muslims during the civil war in the former Yugoslavia, in defiance of an international arms embargo. The House passed a resolution in May 1996 launching a formal probe of the administration's secret policy; it created an eight-member International Relations select subcommittee, of which Bereuter was a member, to investigate the affair. Republicans charged that the administration had misled Congress, broke faith with U.S. allies in Europe and allowed Iran to gain a foothold in Europe. Rejecting assertions by Democrats that information on Iran's shipments to Bosnia was widely available, Bereuter said no one in Congress was informed that the White House was "dumb enough" to permit the Iranian role.

Bereuter also brings his diligence to the Banking and Financial Services Committee, where he sponsored a bill in the 104th to scale back bank regulations and consumer protection laws. Bereuter and other proponents said the measure would curb rules and paperwork that impose costly regulatory burdens on banks —

costs he says that are passed on to consumers. "This is relief which will benefit consumers through new, better and less expensive products and [benefit] financial institutions with less paperwork, less red tape and less needed bureaucracy," Bereuter said.

Included in the omnibus fiscal 1997 appropriations bill, the banking measure contained an overhaul of the law governing credit reporting, simplified disclosure requirements under the Truth in Lending Act and streamlined application processes for automated teller machines. The measure was much less than the banking industry had originally hoped for, but objections by the White House caused the bill to be steadily diluted. The administration had voiced particular opposition to provisions that would have weakened community reinvestment and consumer laws.

A city planner by profession, Bereuter also has been active on the Banking Committee on housing and development issues. He praised a measure passed by the House in May 1997 that aimed to overhaul the nation's public housing system by giving local housing authorities more power and requiring residents to take more responsibility for pursuing goals such as finding a job or getting an education.

Democrats complained that some of the measure's provisions were too prescriptive, and they took particular exception to provisions that would require public housing residents to perform eight hours of community service a month. But Republicans said the bill would usher in a new era of improved public housing by granting more authority to local agencies.

"Rather than centralizing decision-making in Washington, the bill provides greater flexibility for local elected officials to work with public housing agencies to determine the housing needs of the community and decide the best way to meet these needs," Bereuter told the House.

At Home: Bereuter's background is unusual for a Nebraska politician. He held the state's top city planning post under moderate GOP Gov. Norbert Tiemann from 1969 to 1971. Then he served one four-year term in the Legislature, winning a reputation as one of the more liberal members by sponsoring a land-use planning bill. Farming and ranching interests regarded the bill as an intrusion into private-property decisions.

Bereuter used conservative rhetoric during his 1978 House campaign, but he was still seen as a moderate in Lincoln. His big margin in Lancaster County (Lincoln) pushed him past a conservative state senator in the GOP primary.

In November he drew united Republican support and a large independent vote to collect 58 percent against Hess Dyas, a former state Democratic Party chairman.

Thereafter he won every two years with 64 percent or better, until 1992, when redistricting added some of the Omaha metropolitan area to his Lincoln-based district.

He slipped to 60 percent that year, but has improved steadily since then and won with 70 percent in 1996.

HOUSE ELECTIONS

1996 General		
Doug Bereuter (R)	157,108	(70%)
Patrick J. Combs (D)	67,152	(30%)
1994 General		
Doug Bereuter (R)	117,967	(63%)
Patrick Combs (D)	70,369	(37%)

Previous Winning Percentages: 1992 (60%) **1990** (65%) **1988** (67%) **1986** (64%) **1984** (74%) **1982** (75%) **1980** (79%) **1978** (58%)

CAMPAIGN FINANCE

	Receipts	Receipts from PACs	Expend-itures
1996			
Bereuter (R)	$405,151	$271,889 (67%)	$394,292
Combs (D)	$59,119	$35,550 (60%)	$59,666
1994			
Bereuter (R)	$348,290	$200,907 (58%)	$334,598
Combs (D)	$178,985	$86,500 (48%)	$178,046

DISTRICT VOTE FOR PRESIDENT

1996		1992	
D	87,713 (38%)	**D**	80,700 (33%)
R	114,560 (50%)	**R**	107,092 (43%)
I	25,973 (11%)	**I**	59,979 (24%)

KEY VOTES

1997	
Ban "partial birth" abortions	Y
1996	
Approve farm bill	Y
Deny public education to illegal immigrants	Y
Repeal ban on certain assault-style weapons	N
Increase minimum wage	Y
Freeze defense spending	N
Approve welfare overhaul	Y
1995	
Approve balanced-budget constitutional amendment	Y
Relax Clean Water Act regulations	Y
Oppose limits on environmental regulations	Y
Reduce projected Medicare spending	Y
Approve GOP budget with tax and spending cuts	Y

VOTING STUDIES

	Presidential Support		Party Unity		Conservative Coalition	
Year	**S**	**O**	**S**	**O**	**S**	**O**
1996	51	49	82	18	82	18
1995	32	68	86	14	83	17
1994	55	45	77	22	81	17
1993	53	47	80	19	84	16
1992	68	30	77	21	73	25
1991	79	21	77	22	78	22

INTEREST GROUP RATINGS

Year	ADA	AFL-CIO	CCUS	ACU
1996	20	n/a	81	60
1995	20	8	92	58
1994	15	11	100	71
1993	10	8	91	88
1992	20	33	88	79
1991	10	17	100	85

2 Jon Christensen (R)

Of Omaha — Elected 1994, 2nd term

Biographical Information

Born: Feb. 20, 1963, St. Paul, Neb.

Education: Midland Lutheran College, B.A. 1985; South Texas College, J.D. 1989.

Occupation: Insurance agent; insurance marketing director; farm products company executive.

Family: Divorced.

Religion: Christian Missionary Alliance.

Political Career: No previous office.

Capitol Office: 413 Cannon Bldg. 20515; 225-4155.

Committees

Ways & Means
Health; Social Security

In Washington: A winner in 1994 by just 1,766 votes, Christensen expected a tough 1996 re-election campaign, and he moved quickly to find a role in the 104th Congress that would boost his stature and enhance his fundraising.

Between his election in November and Congress' convening in January, Christensen raised $80,000 and donated it to the National Republican Congressional Committee, according to the Omaha World Herald. When GOP elders handed out committee assignments, Christensen got a plum: a seat on Ways and Means, whose work on tax and health policy is keenly watched by insurer Mutual of Omaha and the city's other major businesses.

"When you've got 73 freshmen you're competing with for one [committee] seat, and you want to be that one person, you've got to do everything to stand out, to be a leader," Christensen told the Omaha paper in February 1995. "Everything I did was part of that plan." (In the end, two other freshmen made it with Christensen onto Ways and Means.)

As it turned out, Christensen's Democratic challenger in 1996, high-profile Omaha lawyer James Martin Davis, raised more than $416,000. But that was less than one-fourth the staggering sum of nearly $1.8 million that Christensen raised for his campaign. He easily won a second term, despite being targeted by organized labor and environmentalists as too conservative for the 2nd.

Across a range of economic and social issues, Christensen's House voting record shows consistent loyalty to the GOP leadership. He was sharply critical of President Clinton in late 1995 for vetoing the GOP's plan to balance the budget, calling the veto "politics and rhetoric."

Where he parts ways with the leadership, it typically has been in defiance of their pleas for pragmatism. His commitment to reining in federal spending led to a protracted refusal to support raising the ceiling on the national debt. He was unmoved by warnings that failure to raise the debt limit would force the government into default, halting Social Security checks and throwing the financial markets into turmoil. "I will not vote for a bill that raises the ceiling," Christensen said. "We'd better find some alternative way to reduce outlays."

In November 1995 he was one of only seven Republicans voting "no" on a bill to increase the debt limit temporarily. In an early March vote, he was one of 45 GOP "nays." He finally yielded in late March, joining an overwhelming majority in supporting a long-term debt-limit extender. That bill included sweeteners aimed at attracting conservatives' support, including an increase in the Social Security earning limit and a measure giving small businesses more latitude to wage court challenges to federal regulations.

In June 1996, Christensen bucked the GOP leadership again, throwing in with 18 other Republicans — most of them freshmen — to vote against the fiscal 1997 budget resolution. The defectors complained that the measure forecast a temporary spike in the deficit in 1997 and 1998 before forcing it down to zero in 2002. Many also were unhappy that Senate Republicans had added more spending for domestic programs in the budget, and that the House GOP leadership went along. Despite the defections, the resolution passed, 216-211.

Christensen's crusade for fiscal austerity was on display in June 1995 when he tried to persuade the House to eliminate funding for the staffers who oversee operation of the automatic elevators in House office buildings. Christensen said his amendment would save taxpayers $263,000 per year in salaries and benefits, and he told his colleagues, "The time has come for members of Congress to start pushing their own buttons. Yes, that grievous, arduous task of pushing your own elevator button." But the House rejected his effort, 177-246.

On a bigger-ticket item, Christensen voted in 1996 and 1997 to terminate funding for NASA's space station. Both times, the station survived with ease.

He found merit, however, in the work of the

NEBRASKA 2
East — Omaha; Sarpy County suburbs

Omaha grew up as a blue-collar city: a railroad center, a Missouri River port and a place where cattle became steaks. To outsiders, this broad-shouldered, gritty image remains. But Omaha (Douglas County) has become mainly a place of white-collar jobs and new downtown office buildings. The county is also reliably Republican, voting for the GOP White House candidate every time but once in the post-Roosevelt era. In 1996, Bob Dole won the county with 51 percent of the vote. In 1994, the 2nd tossed out its Democratic incumbent in favor of the conservative Christensen.

Omaha's economic health is reflected in its continued growth: Its 1990 population topped 335,000, up by 7 percent since 1980. Once rural Sarpy County, which borders Douglas County to the south, continued to blossom: Now with more than 102,000 people, it is the state's third most populous.

As its core has filled with people through the years, the Omaha-based 2nd has become more compact. It now covers just Douglas and Sarpy counties and a tiny slice of Cass County, including the city of Plattsmouth.

Metropolitan Omaha's economy is a mix of new and old. One of the largest employers is the Strategic Air Command at Offutt Air Force Base in Sarpy County, another GOP stronghold. A large telemarketing and credit-processing industry has been established in Omaha. Telecommunications is also a burgeoning industry. Yet the Mutual of Omaha insurance company, long a community pillar, remains its largest private employer. Downtown includes the corporate headquarters for ConAgra — the agricultural products giant that is among the top Fortune 500 companies — and the Union Pacific Railroad. While most of Omaha's stockyards are now obsolete, more than 20 food processing companies are here.

Blue-collar jobs historically drew an ethnic population — including large numbers of Irish, Italians, Germans and Eastern Europeans — to Omaha's south side. Mainly Roman Catholics, they set the 2nd's political tone. It has a Democratic tradition, and victory here is essential for Democrats to win statewide. While narrowly losing to Christensen, former Democratic Rep. Peter Hoagland managed to carry Douglas County in 1994.

However, the longtime partisan leanings are tempered by a strong conservative streak, especially on social issues. Many working-class residents vote with more affluent residents, which has enabled recent GOP presidential candidates to carry the 2nd. George Bush won the county by 13 percentage points over Bill Clinton in 1992. In 1996, Dole carried the overall district, beating Bill Clinton by 15 percentage points.The city is 13 percent black, a large proportion by Nebraska standards; more than three-fourths of the state's entire black population lives in Omaha.

Long known mainly for the Boys Town orphanage, western Omaha is now heavily residential, with some new, affluent subdivisions. Nearby, onetime crossroads communities are now burgeoning cities. Bellevue, with nearly 31,000 people, is Nebraska's fourth-largest city.

The area benefits from Omaha's status as Nebraska's cultural and sports capital. The area still hosts the World Series of college baseball each spring. But Ak-Sar-Ben (Nebraska spelled backward) is being converted to a business center after years as a race track.

1990 Population: 526,567. White 460,519 (87%), Black 50,907 (10%), Other 15,141 (3%). Hispanic origin 14,865 (3%). 18 and over 379,331 (72%), 62 and over 64,581 (12%). Median age: 31.

Overseas Private Investment Corporation (OPIC), and opposed a GOP effort in June 1995 to do away with it. OPIC is a small agency that provides loans and political risk insurance to American companies doing business abroad. Christensen noted that OPIC takes in more money than it spends, showing a net income of $167 million in 1994.

"In my opinion, OPIC is an example of how a federal agency should be run," he said. "Its elimination would hurt U.S. interests and result in higher deficits."

Christensen also wants the government to continue its commitment to the impact aid program, which provides payments in lieu of taxes to local jurisdictions that educate children of military personnel, among others. The program is important in Christensen's district because one of its largest employers is the Pentagon's Strategic Air Command. A Christensen campaign ad claimed that he cared so much about impact aid that he "went against his own party to fight for it." In the final days of the 104th, lawmakers agreed to increase spending for virtually every federal education program, including impact aid.

Christensen's social policy stands mirror the views of the Christian conservative activists who have been a crucial bloc of support for him and many other GOP House candidates in recent elections. He opposes abortion except to save the life of the woman and once told an anti-abortion rally that a vote for President Clinton "is a vote for abortion."

He voted in March 1996 to repeal the ban on certain semiautomatic assault-style weapons. He has introduced a bill, dubbed the Hard Times for Gun Crimes Act, which embodies his belief that firearms are not a problem in our society, but rather the criminals who use them. The bill would dramatically increase the penalties for possessing, brandishing or discharging a firearm during the commission of a felony. "We should work now, today, to stop coddling criminals and start crushing them," Christensen said.

At Home: When he ran for the 2nd in 1994, Christensen was 31 and just five years out of South Texas College's law school, with experience in the insurance and fertilizer businesses but a novice at politics.

Applying his sales and marketing skills to a new field of endeavor, he campaigned tirelessly, knocking on thousands of doors across the district and hounding Democratic incumbent Peter Hoagland. Once he showed up at a Hoagland district meeting before the incumbent, and greeted people as they entered the room. He also trekked to Washington, sat in the front row of spectators at Ways and Means, and stared at Hoagland.

Hoagland had won narrowly in 1992, and Christensen was among three contenders for the Republican nomination in 1994. The others — state Sen. Brad Ashford and Ron Staskiewicz, the GOP nominee in 1992 — got about one-fourth of the primary vote, and Christensen roared to the front with a 53 percent tally.

The general-election campaign was one of the nastiest in the country. Hoagland accused Christensen in a TV ad of having told a couple during door-to-door campaigning that Omaha public school textbooks taught immoral values. Christensen denied that the incident took place, took a lie detector test and passed it. Hoagland said he hadn't concocted the story and also passed a lie detector test, but he pulled the TV ad after the couple featured in it reported receiving anonymous telephone death threats. Hoagland labeled Christensen a right-wing religious extremist; Christensen attacked Hoagland as a Clinton clone.

With Hoagland spending more than $1.1 million and Christensen more than $950,000, the two slugged it out to a near-standoff. But the national Republican tide lifted Christensen to a narrow victory.

In 1996, Democrats thought they had a good shot with Davis, a Vietnam veteran, former Secret Service agent and ex-federal prosecutor. He campaigned as a moderate-to-conservative Democrat, arguing that Christensen was slavishly following the House Republican leadership rather than representing his constituents' views.

But Christensen said he had stayed in close touch by returning to the district every weekend, and he used his immense campaign treasury to make a case over the airwaves that he had voted in line with Nebraskans' wishes to get the country on firm fiscal footing.

His support among "cultural conservatives" was evidently not affected by the very public breakup in late 1995 of his marriage, which included an admission by his wife that she had committed adultery. Christensen beat Davis by 17 points, taking 57 percent of the vote.

HOUSE ELECTIONS

1996 General		
Jon Christensen (R)	125,201	(57%)
James Martin Davis (D)	88,447	(40%)
Patricia A. Dunn (NL)	4,369	(2%)
1996 Primary		
Jon Christensen (R)	40,830	(97%)
1994 General		
Jon Christensen (R)	92,516	(50%)
Peter Hoagland (D)	90,750	(49%)

CAMPAIGN FINANCE

	Receipts	Receipts from PACs	Expend- itures
1996			
Christensen (R)	$1,771,220	$627,125 (35%)	$1,722,490
Davis (D)	$416,128	$179,937 (43%)	$384,582
1994			
Christensen (R)	$966,568	$163,406 (17%)	$953,163
Hoagland (D)	$1,195,716	$778,250 (65%)	$1,105,892

DISTRICT VOTE FOR PRESIDENT

1996	1992
D 84,666 (38%)	D 78,697 (32%)
R 116,892 (53%)	R 115,244 (48%)
I 18,935 (9%)	I 48,652 (20%)

KEY VOTES

1997	
Ban "partial birth" abortions	Y
1996	
Approve farm bill	Y
Deny public education to illegal immigrants	Y
Repeal ban on certain assault-style weapons	Y
Increase minimum wage	N
Freeze defense spending	N
Approve welfare overhaul	Y
1995	
Approve balanced-budget constitutional amendment	Y
Relax Clean Water Act regulations	Y
Oppose limits on environmental regulations	N
Reduce projected Medicare spending	Y
Approve GOP budget with tax and spending cuts	Y

VOTING STUDIES

	Presidential Support		Party Unity		Conservative Coalition	
Year	S	O	S	O	S	O
1996	33	62	92	5	86	10
1995	17	83	97	3	92	8

INTEREST GROUP RATINGS

Year	ADA	AFL-CIO	CCUS	ACU
1996	5	n/a	88	100
1995	0	0	96	92

3 Bill Barrett (R)

Of Lexington — Elected 1990, 4th term

Biographical Information
Born: Feb. 9, 1929, Lexington, Neb.
Education: Hastings College, B.A. 1951.
Military Service: Navy, 1951-52.
Occupation: Real estate and insurance broker.
Family: Wife, Elsie Carlson; four children.
Religion: Presbyterian.
Political Career: Neb. Legislature, 1979-91, speaker, 1987-91.
Capitol Office: 2458 Rayburn Bldg. 20515; 225-6435.

Committees
Agriculture
Forestry, Resource Conservation & Research; General Farm Commodities (chairman)
Education & Workforce
Postsecondary Education, Training & Life-Long Learning; Workforce Protections

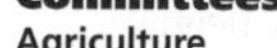

In Washington: After serving just two terms in the House, Barrett took the gavel of the Agriculture Committee's General Farm Commodities Subcommittee in the GOP-controlled 104th Congress, and from there he helped push through the biggest changes in the nation's farm programs since the New Deal.

When Barrett and Agriculture Committee Chairman Pat Roberts of Kansas presented the draft of the Republican plan to overhaul federal agriculture policy, Barrett summed it up thusly: "It would make farmers plant for the marketplace instead of the government."

Despite his junior status in the House, such a leadership role is nothing new for Barrett, who before coming to Washington had a 12-year career in Nebraska's unicameral Legislature, rising to become Speaker of the body. Serving on the Agriculture Committee in the House is a natural fit for Barrett, whose 3rd District is one of the largest and most rural constituencies in the country, encompassing 66 counties.

In the fall of 1995, when the committee first took up the measure overhauling farm programs, Barrett and Roberts ran into criticism not only from committee Democrats but also from some in the GOP. The sweeping measure, known as "Freedom to Farm," aimed to phase out the New Deal-era crop subsidy system that required farmers to plant certain commodities and compensated them if market prices on those crops dropped. Instead, farmers who signed contracts with the government would receive fixed, but declining, payments every year for seven years, regardless of market prices or their planting decisions.

The bill was backed by many rural lawmakers such as Barrett, who said its package of $43.2 billion over seven years was the best deal farmers could expect from a Congress bent on budget-cutting. Farmers would benefit, Barrett said, by being freed from many planting restrictions and by receiving guaranteed payments for seven years, even if market conditions were favorable.

"We're in a different world now," said Barrett. "The day may be coming when we don't have a farm program, certainly as we have it today."

But panel Democrats assailed the plan for potentially shredding the economic safety net protecting farmers in times of low prices. They said farmers might be left with no government program at all after seven years. Republican members with cotton growers in their districts were especially unhappy with "Freedom to Farm," which sought to eliminate the lucrative cotton marketing loan program. Four Republicans on Agriculture and all the committee's Democrats voted against Roberts' bill, bringing it down to defeat. Roberts never brought the bill back up in committee, instead rolling it into the GOP's broad seven-year budget-balancing reconciliation measure Congress passed in late 1995.

But President Clinton vetoed the reconciliation measure in December 1995. So in February 1996, the farm legislation came to the House floor as a stand-alone bill. It included concessions to growers of certain crops, including one of particular concern to Barrett: sugar.

Barrett, who told the House he has 550 sugar beet farmers in his district, fought to preserve price supports and import restrictions on sugar, arguing that elimination of the subsidy would put sugar growers at risk of being driven out of business by a flood of less-expensive sugar imported from overseas.

Critics said the price supports inflate domestic sugar prices, and they pushed an amendment to phase out the sugar program over five years.

Objecting to this amendment, Barrett said, "If the program is repealed, U.S. producers would be exposed to a highly subsidized world sugar market, costing the United States in the end. Our sugar program allows U.S. producers to compete against unfair trade practices and subsidies from other countries." Barrett and other sugar allies beat back the amendment, 208-217.

Barrett cosponsored another amendment, offered by moderate Republican Sherwood Boehlert of New York, that provided a seven-year reauthorization of the Conservation Reserve

As ever, agriculture is king in the 3rd. To the east are the state's most productive corn-growing regions and several leading hog-raising counties; the west has the biggest wheat farms. Western Nebraska is also a national leader in production of sugar beets and dry beans.

On the plains in the northern and central parts of the 3rd, the old saw that there are more cows than people is a gross understatement. Vast Cherry County, with fewer than 7,000 people, has tens of thousands more cattle than people.

In this part of Nebraska, one can drive for hours along straight, flat roads without passing any community larger than a village. Between 1980 and 1990, 63 of the 66 counties in the 3rd lost population.

The 3rd is traditionally the most Republican district in the state. In 1992, Bush carried the district with 50 percent, down from 67 percent four years earlier. Bush's decline was no help to Bill Clinton, who finished third in the district with 24 percent, behind Ross Perot's 27 percent. Republican nominee Bob Dole actually improved upon Bush's score in 1996. Dole garnered 59 percent, Clinton took 29 percent and Perot dropped to 12 percent.

The only city in the 3rd with more than 30,000 people is Grand Island (Hall County), a retail center for the surrounding farmlands. Grand Island's major industries are farm implements and meatpacking.

North of Grand Island are the only counties in the district where Democrats have had a significant advantage among registered voters (Sherman, Greeley and Howard counties). Another, Nance, has a slimmer Democratic edge. But Dole and Barrett won all the counties in the district in 1996.

NEBRASKA 3
Rural West — Grand Island; North Platte

The smaller population centers of Kearney, North Platte and Scottsbluff are strung along the Platte River west of Grand Island. Much of Kearney's growth has come from its campus of the University of Nebraska.

West of Kearney along the Platte is Lexington, a town of 6,600. It struggled in the mid-1980s farm crisis but was revitalized in 1990 with the opening of an IBP meat-packing plant.

North Platte, located in the valley where the North and South Platte rivers meet, was the home of William F. "Buffalo Bill" Cody. It tries to coax Omaha-to-Denver travelers into staying awhile by putting on Buffalo Bill shows and rodeos. The Union Pacific runs through North Platte and is its biggest employer. Corn and livestock are raised in the valley, with wheat fields to the west and huge cattle ranches to the north.

The Oregon and Mormon trails run through Scottsbluff, which has the only sizable Hispanic population in western Nebraska, a legacy of the migrant labor used over a period of several decades to harvest sugar beets. Great northern beans are a major crop in the farm areas surrounding Scottsbluff. The major employers are the Regional West Medical Center, a health management organization, and Lockwood Corp., a farm equipment manufacturer.

1990 Population: 525,521. White 512,696 (98%), Black 953 (<1%), Other 11,872 (2%). Hispanic origin 14,998 (3%). 18 and over 380,190 (72%), 62 and over 108,148 (21%). Median age: 35.

Program, which pays farmers to idle environmentally sensitive land. "The Conservation Reserve Program, which was established in 1985, helps to protect our soil and water. It is an extremely important matter that we continue the program," Barrett said. "It has a wide spectrum of interests, and farmers and environmentalists and sportsmen and the public sector, frankly, get large benefits from the program, and the House should not dismiss our responsibility to reauthorize the program." The House passed the amendment, 372-37.

The vote on final passage of "Freedom to Farm" was 270-155, with Barrett among the majority of Republicans in support.

Barrett takes an internationalist stance on free trade and foreign aid, seeing them as important vehicles to promote export sales of Nebraska corn and wheat. He has agreed, therefore, with the Clinton administration's free-trade advocacy. Barrett supported the president's push for NAFTA in 1993, saying he was reassured by Mexico's promise not to dump sugar products in the U.S. market. He also backed GATT in 1994.

When the House considered the fiscal 1996 agriculture spending bill, he opposed an effort led by "deficit hawks" in his own party to undermine the Market Promotion Program (MPP), which assists companies in promoting their products overseas. The House rejected an amendment to eliminate $110 million for the program, which critics call "corporate welfare" because it channels money to major agribusiness concerns and trade associations to help them pay for overseas television and print advertising campaigns.

Urging a "no" vote on the amendment, Barrett said, "The MPP is just one of the few tools that we have that has been instrumental in assisting the United States in increasing and enhancing agricultural exports."

Again citing the agricultural trade advantages, Barrett backed the Clinton administration's decision to provide most-favored-nation (MFN) trading status for China. Under MFN, granted to all but a handful of countries, Chinese goods enter the United States with non-discriminatory status. Barrett told the House that as "agricultural subsidies decline, we must allow and encourage expansion of markets for U.S. agricultural commodities. MFN to China leaves important trade avenues open, benefiting family farms, ranches and businesses." And he noted that "currently, China is the largest importer of American wheat."

Barrett also sits on the Education and the Workforce Committee (called Economic and Educational Opportunities in the 104th), where he was critical of Clinton's executive order banning the use of permanent replacement workers by companies with federal contracts of $100,000 or more. Barrett called the executive order "unconstitutional," adding that it is "a direct challenge to the prerogatives of the Congress to set labor law."

Barrett praised a provision in the fiscal 1996 Labor-HHS spending bill that prohibited funds in the bill from being used to implement the executive order. "The president's order — in the opinion of many — is nothing but a backroom deal to coddle favor with labor unions, and is a direct challenge to decades of well-established labor law which permits the use of permanent replacement workers," Barrett said.

At Home: Barrett won only narrowly in 1990 when the 3rd was open, but he has topped 70 percent in each of his three re-elections.

When GOP Rep. Virginia Smith retired in 1990, Barrett struggled to hold the traditionally Republican 3rd. His 51 percent tally over Democratic state Sen. Sandra K. Scofield was unexpectedly anemic in a district where two-thirds of the 1988 presidential vote went to George Bush.

A small-town real estate and insurance executive, Barrett was a member of the state Republican Committee for eight years and served as state GOP chairman from 1973 to 1975. He had represented his south-central Nebraska legislative district since 1979.

But Barrett had trouble in the Republican primary, winning nomination with barely 30 percent against two competitors. And in the general election, Barrett was hampered by weak mates on the GOP ticket. Embattled Republican Gov. Kay A. Orr posted a mediocre re-election performance in western Nebraska, sealing her defeat at the hands of Democrat Ben Nelson. And Democratic Sen. Jim Exon rolled up a big win over his Republican challenger, former 2nd District Rep. Hal Daub.

Barrett also found that his greatest strength, his position as Speaker of Nebraska's Legislature, was also something of a liability in a year when many voters were in an anti-incumbent mood. While Barrett's position gave him a boost in stature over unicameral colleague Scofield, it also let Scofield link him to some of the more unpopular Orr policies.

Still, Barrett carried 41 of the district's 62 counties, generally dominating the eastern two-thirds of the 3rd. That enabled him to overcome Scofield's strength in her western Nebraska base.

HOUSE ELECTIONS

1996 General		
Bill Barrett (R)	167,758	(77%)
John Webster (D)	48,833	(23%)
1994 General		
Bill Barrett (R)	154,919	(79%)
Gil Chapin (D)	41,943	(21%)

Previous Winning Percentages: 1992 (72%) **1990** (51%)

CAMPAIGN FINANCE

	Receipts	Receipts from PACs	Expend-itures
1996			
Barrett (R)	$263,068	$147,466 (56%)	$203,582
Webster (D)	$15,508	0	$15,190
1994			
Barrett (R)	$280,264	$131,051 (47%)	$232,013
Chapin (D)	$40,085	$22,100 (55%)	$54,519

DISTRICT VOTE FOR PRESIDENT

	1996		1992
D	64,382 (29%)	**D**	57,467 (24%)
R	132,015 (59%)	**R**	121,342 (50%)
I	26,370 (12%)	**I**	65,473 (27%)

KEY VOTES

1997	
Ban "partial birth" abortions	Y
1996	
Approve farm bill	Y
Deny public education to illegal immigrants	Y
Repeal ban on certain assault-style weapons	Y
Increase minimum wage	N
Freeze defense spending	N
Approve welfare overhaul	Y
1995	
Approve balanced-budget constitutional amendment	Y
Relax Clean Water Act regulations	Y
Oppose limits on environmental regulations	N
Reduce projected Medicare spending	Y
Approve GOP budget with tax and spending cuts	Y

VOTING STUDIES

	Presidential Support		Party Unity		Conservative Coalition	
Year	**S**	**O**	**S**	**O**	**S**	**O**
1996	41	59	92	8	96	4
1995	20	80	95	4	94	4
1994	46	51	94	5	97	3
1993	40	60	91	9	91	9
1992	85	15	91	8	85	13
1991	84	14	92	6	97	0

INTEREST GROUP RATINGS

Year	ADA	AFL-CIO	CCUS	ACU
1996	0	n/a	94	95
1995	0	0	100	84
1994	5	11	92	95
1993	5	0	91	92
1992	10	25	88	84
1991	0	8	90	89

NEVADA

Governor: Bob Miller (D)

First elected: 1990 (Assumed office 1988)
Length of term: 4 years
Term expires: 1/99
Salary: $90,000
Term limit: 2 terms
Phone: (702) 687-5670
Born: March 30, 1945; Chicago, Ill.
Education: U. of Santa Clara, B.A. 1967; Loyola U. (Los Angeles, Calif.), J.D. 1971.
Military Service: Air Force Reserve, 1967-73.
Occupation: Lawyer.
Family: Wife, Sandy Searles; three children.
Religion: Roman Catholic.
Political Career: Clark County deputy district attorney, 1971-73; Las Vegas Township justice of the peace, 1975-78 (appointed 1975-76); Clark County district attorney, 1979-86; lieutenant governor, 1987-89.

Lt. Gov.: Lonnie Hammargren (R)
First elected: 1994
Length of term: 4 years
Term expires: 1/99
Salary: $20,000
Phone: (702) 687-3037

State election official: (702) 687-3176
Democratic Party Chairman: (702) 323-8683
Republican headquarters: (702) 258-9182

REDISTRICTING

Nevada retained its two House seats in reapportionment. Legislature passed the map June 11, 1991; governor signed it June 20.

STATE LEGISLATURE

Legislature. Meets January-June.

Senate: 21 members, 4-year terms
1996 breakdown: 12R, 9D; 16 men, 5 women
Salary: $130 per day for 60 days plus salary for official meetings during interim
Phone: (702) 687-5742

Assembly: 42 members, 2-year terms
1996 breakdown: 25D, 17R; 27 men, 15 women
Salary: $130 per day for 60 days plus salary for official meetings during interim
Phone: (702) 687-5739

URBAN STATISTICS

City	Population
Las Vegas	258,204
Mayor Jan Laverty Jones, N-P	
Reno	133,850
Mayor Jeff Griffin, N-P	
Paradise	124,682
County Commissioner Yvonne Atkinson Gates, D	
Sunrise Manor	95,362
County Commissioner Yvonne Atkinson Gates, D	
Henderson	64,942
Mayor Robert Groesbeck, N-P	

U.S. CONGRESS

Senate: 2 D, 0 R
House: 0 D, 2 R

TERM LIMITS

\For state offices: Yes
Senate: 3 terms
Assembly: 6 terms

ELECTIONS

1996 Presidential Vote

Bill Clinton	44%
Bob Dole	43%
Ross Perot	9%

1992 Presidential Vote

Bill Clinton	37%
George Bush	35%
Ross Perot	26%

1988 Presidential Vote

George Bush	59%
Michael S. Dukakis	38%

POPULATION

1990 population		1,201,833
1980 population		800,493
Percent change		+50%
Rank among states:		39
White		84%
Black		7%
Hispanic		10%
Asian or Pacific islander		3%
Urban		88%
Rural		12%
Born in state		22%
Foreign-born		9%
Under age 18	296,948	25%
Ages 18-64	777,254	65%
65 and older	127,631	11%
Median age		33.3

MISCELLANEOUS

Capital: Carson City
Number of counties: 16
Per capita income: $19,175 (1991)
Rank among states: 15
Total area: 110,561 sq. miles
Rank among states: 7

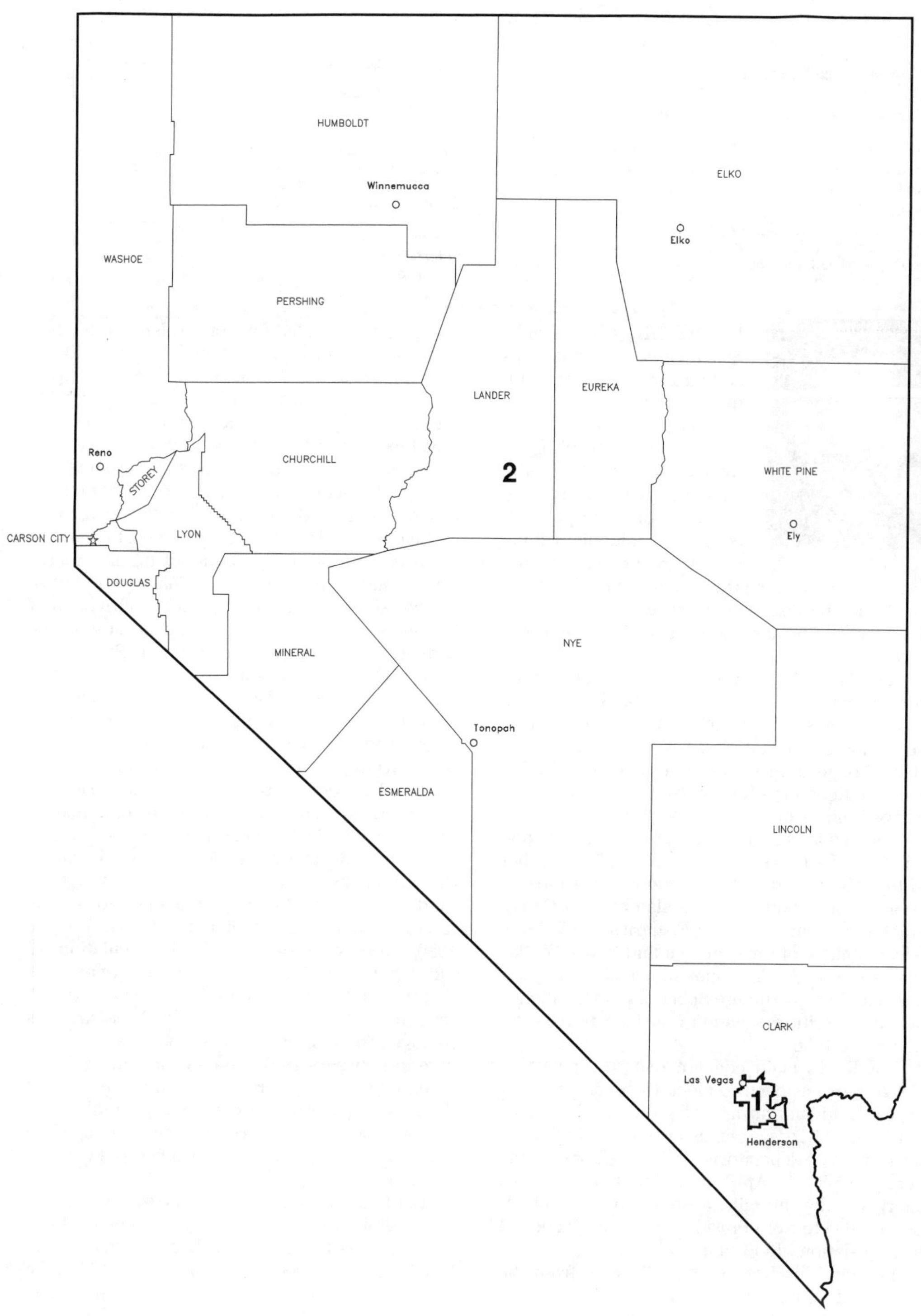
HUMBOLDT
Winnemucca
ELKO
Elko
WASHOE
PERSHING
LANDER
EUREKA
Reno
CHURCHILL
STOREY
2
WHITE PINE
Ely
CARSON CITY
LYON
DOUGLAS
NYE
MINERAL
Tonopah
ESMERALDA
LINCOLN
CLARK
Las Vegas
1
Henderson

NEVADA

Harry Reid (D)

Of Searchlight — Elected 1986, 2nd term

Biographical Information

Born: Dec. 2, 1939, Searchlight, Nev.

Education: Southern Utah State College, A.S. 1959; Utah State U., B.A. 1961; George Washington U., J.D. 1964; U. of Nevada, Las Vegas, 1969-70.

Occupation: Lawyer.

Family: Wife, Landra Gould; five children.

Religion: Mormon.

Political Career: Nev. Assembly, 1969-71; lieutenant governor, 1971-75; Democratic nominee for U.S. Senate, 1974; candidate for mayor of Las Vegas, 1975; U.S. House, 1983-87; Henderson City attorney.

Capitol Office: 528 Hart Bldg. 20510; 224-3542.

Committees

Special Aging

Appropriations
Energy & Water Development (ranking); Interior; Labor, Health & Human Services & Education; Military Construction; Transportation

Environment & Public Works
Drinking Water, Fisheries & Wildlife (ranking); Transportation & Infrastructure

Select Ethics

Indian Affairs

In Washington: Reid's recent career demonstrates certain institutional imperatives of the Senate. His staunch resistance to a nuclear waste depository in Nevada shows how the chamber gives voice to the concerns of underpopulated states, while his willingness to work with Republicans on particular issues is an example of the need for bipartisan compromise in an era when majority rule means accruing 60 filibuster-proof votes.

Reid is up for re-election in 1998. Should he survive (he had $1 million in the bank at the end of 1996), he is a likely candidate for the position of Democratic whip, which will be open in the 106th Congress after the retirement of Wendell Ford of Kentucky. Reid currently co-chairs the party's Policy Committee in the Senate.

His regular committee assignments are a good mix for a Western senator. He is ranking member of the Energy and Water Development Appropriations Subcommittee, and is also the top Democrat on the Drinking Water, Fisheries and Wildlife Subcommittee of Environment and Public Works. Reid sits on the Environment panel's Transportation and Infrastructure Subcommittee, which is helping rewrite the nation's surface transportation in the 105th.

But Reid's main concern over the past two Congresses has been to block the designation of Yucca Mountain, an arid ridge about 100 miles northwest of Las Vegas, as an interim high-level nuclear waste depository. A Yucca bill passed the Senate, 65-34, in April 1997, but that total fell short of the margin needed to override a promised veto from President Clinton. "We killed bad legislation," Reid said.

Reid and his Democratic colleague from the Silver State, Richard H. Bryan, launched a three-month filibuster against similar legislation in the spring and summer of 1996. The vote in the 104th also fell short of a veto-proof two-thirds majority, and the House never took up the Yucca bill.

In July 1996, a federal court ruled that the federal government is obliged under a 1982 law to take possession of the nuclear waste piling up in storage pools at the nation's nuclear power facilities. In January 1997, 46 states and 33 electric utilities filed suit to force the Energy Department to begin taking control of their waste; they sought to suspend $3 billion in payments to a federal fund designed to remedy the nuclear waste program.

Senate GOP leaders made passage of the Yucca bill a top priority early in the 105th, and Senate Energy and Natural Resources Chairman Frank H. Murkowski, R-Alaska, delayed the confirmation of Energy Secretary Federico F. Peña because of the administration's opposition to Yucca. But despite the mounted forces seeking to create a site at Yucca, Clinton and the Nevadans believe that the environmental hazards of shipping and storage are too great. They also contend that the temporary storage bill is written in such a way that will stick Nevada with the hazardous waste on a permanent basis.

Reid also has been a longstanding opponent of a balanced-budget amendment to the Constitution. In both 1995 and 1997, he offered language that would have excluded Social Security trust funds from deficit-ending considerations. The trust funds have been declared "off budget" since 1990, but they are still included in calculations of the deficit, masking its true size. Reid contends that the funds will amount to nothing more than a "roomful of IOUs" unless Social Security is removed from deficit calculations. In a party-line vote in February 1997, Republicans killed Reid's amendment, 55-44. But the threat to Social Security lent cover to Democrats who killed the constitutional amendment by a single vote, while attracting early attack ads against Reid in his home state.

But Reid's intransigence is narrow; on a broad range of issues, he has been willing to shake hands across the aisle with Republicans to help legislation keep moving. During the 104th, he signed onto a safe drinking water bill sponsored by Republican Dirk Kempthorne of Idaho that passed the Senate unanimously. He also worked with Don Nickles, R-Okla., on legislation to limit manufacturer liability for defective products and to overhaul the federal regulatory structure. Reid saw the Senate kill an amendment he offered with Arizona Republican Jon Kyl that would have extended the president's authority to order some underground nuclear weapons tests until a test-ban treaty then under negotiation went into effect.

Reid supported a budget-balancing plan worked out by a bipartisan group of senators, led by John H. Chafee, R-R.I., and John B. Breaux, D-La., but the bill failed. Reid opposed the GOP's 1996 farm legislation, but supported Republican efforts to overhaul welfare, ban a particular abortion procedure its opponents call "partial birth" abortion, and allow Congress and the states the power to ban desecration of the U.S. flag.

He voted against the GOP's doomed effort in 1995 to balance the federal budget with an omnibus change in entitlements and tax rates. Going down to defeat with the bill was a provision sponsored by Reid to prohibit states from collecting income tax on the retirement income of people who move out of state. The amendment would have been a boon especially for people who move from high income tax states — California, for example — to states without an income tax such as Nevada.

Reid served as ranking Democrat on the Military Construction Appropriations Subcommittee during the 104th (Nevada Republican Barbara F. Vucanovich chaired the counterpart House panel). Nevada benefited with $16 million in the fiscal 1996 bill, including $9 million for a reserve center in Las Vegas the administration did not request.

For several years, the House and Senate have battled each other over whether to increase the fees that ranchers pay to graze their animals on federal land. In the past, Western senators have rallied enough votes to block an increase, and Reid has been a staunch defender of the ranchers' interests.

The landscape appeared to change with Clinton's appointment of Bruce Babbitt as secretary of the Interior. Babbitt made grazing reform one of his top priorities and eventually released a plan to boost fees and impose tougher environmental standards by executive order. In 1993, Reid helped round up votes for a successful effort led by Sen. Pete V. Domenici, R-N.M., to bar the administration from spending money to implement the plan for a year.

But Reid was then asked to broker a compromise. He wrote legislation that would have nearly doubled grazing fees and overhauled land management policies by abolishing rancher-dominated grazing advisory boards, ending the practice of giving ranchers ownership of stock ponds they dig on federal land and other water facilities, and tying the length of ranchers' leases to their environmental stewardship. But after three failed attempts to cut off a Domenici-led filibuster on the Interior spending bill, Reid dropped the compromise.

Reid also reached an impasse over longstanding efforts to rewrite the 1872 Mining Law. Reid, whose state includes some of the nation's largest gold mines, was among those balking at the draft proposal. He offered an alternative that would have required companies to pay fair market value for mining rights on federal land but would not have imposed royalties.

Fearing that no compromise would be reached, the House inserted a one-year moratorium on issuing new mining patents into the fiscal 1995 Interior Appropriations bill. "We are not going to work out anything this year," Reid said after reluctantly agreeing to the moratorium, which has been extended each year since, so as not to hold up the spending bill.

Reid has taken on a range of issues in the "human needs" category — help for battered women; a children's bill of rights to aid prosecution of sexual abuse; and limiting the use of certain chemicals used on test animals to measure toxicity. Reid began pushing for additional funds to research women's diseases when three women who suffered from interstitial cystitis showed up at his office asking for help.

At the start of the 105th, Reid added another title to his portfolio: vice chairman of the Select Ethics Committee.

During two terms in the House before he moved into the Senate, Reid staked out a conservative position on a few highly publicized issues, then voted with the majority of Democrats much of the rest of the time. Reflecting the cultural values of his state and his own Mormonism, he shared Ronald Reagan's opposition to the Equal Rights Amendment and legalized abortion. He also supported the MX missile program.

At Home: Although Reid has fashioned a long career in Nevada politics, he is hardly a premier vote-getter. His early fundraising success scared off big-name challengers in 1992, yet he still struggled to win both the primary and the general election with bare majorities.

Charles Woods, a wealthy, eccentric broadcast executive, fared unexpectedly well in the primary. An Alabama native, Woods had run early in the year in the Democratic presidential primaries, then shifted to the Senate.

Reid largely ignored Woods' candidacy, allowing the challenger to saturate the airwaves with advertising that stressed the need to elect a businessman like himself to the Senate. Woods appeared in his own ads, making no effort to hide the vivid scars from a World War II plane crash that disfigured his face and hands.

Although Reid prevailed by 14 percentage points, he was held to 53 percent, as Woods swept most of Nevada's rural "cow counties." Reid rolled up his winning margin in the state's major population centers, Clark (Las Vegas) and Washoe (Reno) counties.

A similar voting pattern recurred in the general election. Reid, who had saved his money for the fall campaign, outspent rancher Demar Dahl, the

GOP nominee, by a margin of more than 5-to-1. But Reid won the race with an unspectacular 51 percent, to Dahl's 40 percent.

Reid's self-made career has been part skyrocket and part slow, hard climb. He was born into modest circumstances in remote Searchlight. He worked his way through school, including a stint as a policeman in the U.S. Capitol while attending law school in Washington. Within five years he was a successful lawyer in booming Las Vegas, well on his way toward becoming a millionaire and a freshly elected member of the state Legislature — all before he was 30.

In 1970, he ran successfully for lieutenant governor on a ticket with his former high school boxing coach, Mike O'Callaghan, who was elected governor. After one term in the No. 2 job, at age 34, Reid came within 625 votes of election to the U.S. Senate. It was 1974, and the Watergate scandal almost lifted Reid past the state's Republican former governor, Paul Laxalt.

A year later, Reid lost a bid to be mayor of Las Vegas. Then, in 1977, O'Callaghan appointed him chairman of the Nevada Gaming Commission. While Reid held that job, the FBI uncovered evidence of organized-crime influence in the Nevada gaming industry, and one reputed mobster accused Reid of being on the take.

Reid was cleared of charges that he intervened in behalf of organized-crime figures before the Gaming Commission. When he left the commission in 1981, Reid was praised for helping to eliminate criminal elements from the gaming industry. Politically, he was alive again.

In the 1982 House race, Reid faced an articulate Republican, former state Rep. Peggy Cavnar. But she had embarrassed the Las Vegas GOP establishment by defeating its hand-picked candidate in the primary. Reid's superior financial resources and organization resulted in a 58 percent win. Reid again beat Cavnar convincingly in a 1984 rematch.

In 1986, Reid squared off against former Democratic Rep. Jim Santini in one of the year's most closely watched Senate races. Retiring Sen. Laxalt had helped woo Santini to the GOP in 1985 and helped clear the way for him to have the GOP nomination. President Reagan helped raise money for Santini, and Laxalt campaigned extensively for him. But Reid minimized their impact by tapping the state's distrust of Washington with an "us vs. them" campaign. Reid carried only two of the state's 16 counties. But one of them was Clark, his political base and home to a majority of Nevada voters.

SENATE ELECTIONS

1992 General		
Harry Reid (D)	253,150	(51%)
Demar Dahl (R)	199,413	(40%)
Joe S. Garcia Jr. (IA)	11,240	(2%)
Lois Avery (NL)	7,279	(1%)
H. Kent Cromwell (LIBERT)	7,222	(1%)
1992 Primary		
Harry Reid (D)	64,828	(53%)
Charles Woods (D)	48,364	(39%)
"None of these candidates"	4,429	(4%)
Norman Hollingsworth (D)	3,253	(3%)
God Almighty (D)	1,869	(2%)

Previous Winning Percentages: 1986 (50%) **1984*** (56%) **1982*** (58%)

** House elections*

CAMPAIGN FINANCE

	Receipts	Receipts from PACs	Expend-itures
1992			
Reid (D)	$2,142,152	$871,102 (41%)	$2,725,713
Dahl (R)	$481,653	0	$471,371

KEY VOTES

1997	
Approve balanced-budget constitutional amendment	N
Approve chemical weapons treaty	Y
1996	
Approve farm bill	N
Limit punitive damages in product liability cases	N
Exempt small businesses from higher minimum wage	N
Approve welfare overhaul	Y
Bar job discrimination based on sexual orientation	Y
Override veto of ban on "partial birth" abortions	Y
1995	
Approve GOP budget with tax and spending cuts	N
Approve constitutional amendment barring flag desecration	Y

VOTING STUDIES

	Presidential Support		Party Unity		Conservative Coalition	
Year	**S**	**O**	**S**	**O**	**S**	**O**
1996	78	22	79	21	53	47
1995	75	25	74	25	49	51
1994	90	10	85	12	41	59
1993	88	12	86	14	49	49
1992	37	62	75	22	45	55
1991	51	49	75	25	60	38

INTEREST GROUP RATINGS

Year	ADA	AFL-CIO	CCUS	ACU
1996	85	n/a	31	15
1995	80	100	37	9
1994	85	100	20	4
1993	60	82	18	24
1992	80	73	10	23
1991	65	92	10	33

Richard H. Bryan (D)

Of Las Vegas — Elected 1988, 2nd term

Biographical Information

Born: July 16, 1937, Washington, D.C.

Education: U. of Nevada, B.A. 1959; U. of California, Hastings Law School, LL.B. 1963.

Military Service: Army, 1959-60.

Occupation: Lawyer.

Family: Wife, Bonnie Fairchild; three children.

Religion: Episcopalian.

Political Career: Nev. Assembly, 1968-72; Nev. Senate, 1972-78; Democratic nominee for Nev. attorney general, 1974; Nev. attorney general, 1978-82; governor, 1982-88.

Capitol Office: 269 Russell Bldg. 20510; 224-6244.

Committees

Banking, Housing and Urban Affairs
Financial Institutions & Regulatory Relief (ranking); Housing Opportunity & Community Development; Securities

Commerce, Science and Transportation
Aviation; Consumer Affairs, Foreign Commerce & Tourism; Manufacturing & Competitiveness (ranking); Science, Technology & Space; Surface Transportation & Merchant Marine

Finance
Health Care; Long-Term Growth, Debt & Deficit Reduction; Taxation & IRS Oversight

Select Intelligence

In Washington: Both Bryan and his senior Senate colleague, Harry Reid, run a bit against type. Although Nevada's politics have a strong conservative flavor that favors Republicans, both senators are middle-of-the road Democrats.

And while Nevada is best known for the neon glitz of its entertainment capitals, Las Vegas and Reno, it sends two low-key, businesslike men to the Senate.

Bryan is no wallflower, though, when it comes to defending home-state interests; he has been a vociferous critic of the proposal to build a repository for high-level nuclear waste at remote Yucca Mountain in the western Nevada desert.

In 1987, Congress cleared legislation designating Yucca Mountain as the only potential site for the nuclear waste dump. Bryan was then Nevada's governor, and his vocal opposition to the move helped him unseat one-term Republican Sen. Chic Hecht in 1988. And at the rate the issue is proceeding in Congress, Bryan may still be fighting the fight when his Senate seat next comes up for election in 2000.

Bryan has not been able to forestall the federal government from proceeding with a test tunnel for a permanent repository — an Energy Department study on the project's viability is expected by 2000.

But through early 1997, he and Reid had fought to a draw associated efforts to construct an interim waste dump near Yucca Mountain to house spent fuel rods that are piling up in temporary storage facilities at the nation's commercial nuclear power plants.

The issue reached full boil in 1996. Senate Energy and Natural Resources Committee Chairman Frank H. Murkowski, R-Alaska, was determined to push through a bill mandating the temporary waste site in Nevada. But the Nevadans stood firm, bolstered by a veto threat from President Clinton, who said the temporary site would undermine the studies on a long-term repository. The Senate ultimately skirted delaying tactics by Bryan and Reid in July 1996 and passed the bill, 63-37. But that was four votes shy of a veto-proof majority, and the House declined to take up the bill. The Senate in April 1997 passed a similar bill, 65-34, again short of what was needed to assure a veto override.

The debates enabled Bryan to unleash fiery rhetoric that is atypical for him. He frequently referred to Yucca Mountain measures as "screw Nevada" bills. "What [proponents] want more than anything else, what they would sacrifice their first- and second-born for, is to get nuclear waste stored in Nevada," he said in May 1996.

Most of the time, Bryan is better known for an image of composure and probity, which he projected as the top Democrat on the Senate Ethics Committee during the deliberations on sexual harassment charges against Oregon Republican Sen. Bob Packwood in the 104th Congress. Despite the potentially explosive nature of the investigation, Bryan played down partisanship for the most part.

When the Ethics Committee announced in May 1995 that it had found credible evidence of misconduct by Packwood, Bryan said, "We have not made a conclusion about guilt or innocence. We have reached a milepost on the road. That is all we have done."

Bryan did have one open rift with Ethics Committee Chairman Mitch McConnell of Kentucky that July, after the Democrat called for public hearings on the Packwood charges. But that September, they joined in the committee's decision to call for Packwood's expulsion from the Senate, which spurred him to resign.

Bryan also served during the 104th Congress on the so-called Whitewater committee that probed the Clintons' business dealings during Bill Clinton's tenure as governor of Arkansas.

Little else in Bryan's Senate career has approached that sort of drama. His manner befits his sober-sided committee assignments.

Bryan's willingness to take on thankless duties for the Democratic leadership, such as ethics, has had some benefits for him. At the start of the 105th Congress, he obtained a coveted seat on the Finance Committee, giving up a place on Armed Services that he had held briefly. He also moved off the Ethics Committee.

Meanwhile, he maintained his position on the committees on Banking, Housing and Urban Affairs, Commerce, Science and Transportation, and Select Intelligence. He is ranking Democrat on the Banking Subcommittee on Financial Institutions and Regulatory Relief and a newly created Commerce Subcommittee on Manufacturing and Competitiveness.

In his first Senate term, Bryan established himself as a serious legislator through his work on energy issues, particularly his quest to raise federal standards for automobile fuel efficiency.

Heavy lobbying by the auto industry and the administration of President George Bush stalled Bryan's attempt at the end of the 101st Congress. The Senate fell three votes short of the 60 needed to limit debate on a bill that would have required automakers to increase 1988 Corporate Average Fuel Economy (CAFE) levels by 20 percent by 1995 and by 40 percent by 2001. The existing standard is 27.5 miles per gallon.

The legislation got a boost after the August 1990 Iraqi invasion of Kuwait set off renewed debate about U.S. energy policy. Bryan said his bill would save 2.8 million barrels of oil per day and lead automakers to produce fleets with an average rating of 40 mpg.

Bryan redoubled his efforts at the start of the 102nd Congress, when prospects for moving new CAFE legislation improved amid efforts by Congress and the White House to come up with a new national energy policy. But despite several months of maneuvering, including threats of filibusters and Senate floor amendments, the fuel efficiency mandates were left out of the energy bill that finally cleared Congress. As part of a deal worked out by Energy and Natural Resources Chairman J. Bennett Johnston of Louisiana, Bryan agreed to drop his proposal, noting the financial problems the auto industry was then suffering. "Pretty clearly the economic climate makes for some additional obstacles," he said.

The compromise on the energy bill afforded Bryan and five other like-minded senators a victory on another issue — keeping Alaska's Arctic National Wildlife Refuge closed to oil and gas drilling. The Bush administration had argued vigorously for opening up the refuge, but Bryan countered that this option was "fatally flawed."

"It is worshiping at the shrine of production," Bryan said. "We cannot drill our way out of our dependence on oil."

Bryan's support of CAFE standards helped sway him to oppose GATT in the lame-duck session of the 104th Congress. The European Union claims that the CAFE standards are discriminatory because they use fleetwide averaging, thus helping manufacturers such as the American Big Three that produce a whole range of cars, some below the standards and some above. The Europeans primarily produce low-mileage, expensive vehicles.

"There is a legitimate issue here," Bryan said. "If, indeed, this allows a back-door assault on our legitimate environmental laws, then we have given away too much."

Bryan retains a seat on the Commerce subcommittee that handles consumer issues, a panel he chaired prior to the Republican takeover of the Senate in 1995. In the 101st Congress, he oversaw the reauthorization of the Consumer Product Safety Commission, the first stand-alone reauthorization of the watchdog agency since 1981.

The bill, a long-sought victory for consumer activists, was aimed at jump-starting the commission, which for a decade had seen its budget and staff cut and its role as a consumer watchdog diminished by Reagan administration appointees. After some effort, Bryan succeeded in keeping the reauthorization measure free of product-specific provisions that had stopped earlier bills.

Bryan also has pushed for legislation to combat fraud committed in connection with telephone sales.

Bryan's overall voting record is well inside the Democratic mainstream. In 1996, he joined with a majority of Senate Democrats against a majority of Republicans on 82 percent of party-line votes. He backed Clinton on 78 percent of the votes on which the president took a position.

However, Bryan's conservative posture on some high-profile issues separates him from liberal Senate Democrats. He has been a consistent supporter of a constitutional amendment to require a balanced budget, and he has also backed a cut in the capital gains tax. He has opposed banning certain semiautomatic assault-style weapons and imposing a five-day waiting period for handgun purchases. He has supported a constitutional amendment to ban flag desecration. He was also one of the 10 Democratic senators to support the January 1991 resolution authorizing the president to use force in the Persian Gulf.

At Home: Bryan first ran for the Senate in the middle of his second term as governor. He had first been elected governor in 1982, and in 1986 he was re-elected with 72 percent of the vote. As he rode to that easy win, it was widely assumed that he would run in 1988 against Hecht, who had been a surprise winner in 1982.

Bryan began his political career as a public defender and prosecutor in Clark County (Las Vegas). He also had served a decade in the state Assembly and Senate before winning his first statewide office, attorney general, in 1978. In his first term as governor, he built his reputation as a fiscal conservative when he cut hundreds of state government jobs in a budget-balancing drive.

By the time Bryan sought the Senate, Hecht offered an irresistible target. Elected with 50 percent against scandal-tainted Democratic incumbent Howard W. Cannon, Hecht had been battered by the nuclear waste controversy. When Hecht finally turned against putting the dump in Nevada, the momentum in Congress for choosing the state was unstoppable. For years before, Hecht had viewed the dump as a patriotic duty and as a potential source of federal money and jobs.

Hecht also had to compensate for an unimposing personal presence and a tendency to utter malapropisms. (He once said the state should not become "a nuclear suppository.")

Bryan emphasized those perceptions of Hecht in the 1988 campaign. At one point he referred to the state's senior senator as being "unable to find the men's room." But Hecht's campaign team used some of its $2 million treasury for a TV blitz that portrayed a humble, hard-working Hecht, devoted to helping the little guy, making Bryan come off as harsh and a touch arrogant.

Bryan righted his campaign by summer, moving belatedly to counter Hecht's efforts on the airwaves and shifting his aim to issues. He kept up the heat on the nuclear waste dump.

Hecht had to deal with a state GOP rife with internal disputes involving new leaders associated with the party's rising religious-conservative wing. Hecht was distracted when the Clark County GOP chairman impugned Bryan's marital fidelity on a radio program. But Hecht pressed his case, raking Bryan for trying to leave the governorship in midterm and for being too close to the power elements of the national Democratic Party.

Bryan never managed to knock Hecht flat. The race was close to the end. At one point on election night, at least one TV network projected Hecht the winner. But Bryan ended up nearly 43,000 votes ahead of his party's presidential ticket and won by 4 percentage points, 50 percent to 46 percent.

Early in the 1994 election cycle, national Republicans regarded Bryan as a vulnerable incumbent, citing polls indicating that voters might be receptive to another candidate. But they failed to recruit a top-drawer challenger, and Bryan was not seriously threatened in his bid for a second term, despite an acutely anti-Clinton climate across the state. Bryan had distanced himself from Clinton by his high-profile defiance of White House pressure to back the 1993 deficit-reduction bill that raised taxes.

He ran up a huge fundraising advantage over the GOP nominee, first-time candidate Hal Furman — a consultant, lobbyist and former Interior Department deputy assistant secretary — who was hamstrung by an expensive September primary against a quixotic millionaire. Bryan won a second term by 11 percentage points.

SENATE ELECTIONS

1994 General		
Richard H. Bryan (D)	193,804	(53%)
Hal Furman (R)	156,020	(42%)
Anna Nevenich (I)	6,666	(2%)
Bob Days (LIBERT)	5,964	(2%)
Neal A. Grasteit (IA)	5,450	(1%)

Previous Winning Percentages: 1988 (50%)

CAMPAIGN FINANCE

	Receipts	Receipts from PACs	Expend-itures
1994			
Bryan (D)	$3,029,661	$1,250,009 (41%)	$3,021,834
Furman (R)	$885,824	$80,492 (9%)	$885,430

KEY VOTES

1997	
Approve balanced-budget constitutional amendment	Y
Approve chemical weapons treaty	Y
1996	
Approve farm bill	N
Limit punitive damages in product liability cases	N
Exempt small businesses from higher minimum wage	N
Approve welfare overhaul	Y
Bar job discrimination based on sexual orientation	Y
Override veto of ban on "partial birth" abortions	N
1995	
Approve GOP budget with tax and spending cuts	N
Approve constitutional amendment barring flag desecration	Y

VOTING STUDIES

	Presidential Support		Party Unity		Conservative Coalition	
Year	**S**	**O**	**S**	**O**	**S**	**O**
1996	78	22	82	18	50	50
1995	78	21	80	19	44	56
1994	82	15	83	14	44	47
1993	81	19	83	17	61	39
1992	32	68	78	22	47	50
1991	47	53	78	22	73	28

INTEREST GROUP RATINGS

Year	ADA	AFL-CIO	CCUS	ACU
1996	85	n/a	38	10
1995	100	92	42	9
1994	75	88	30	12
1993	60	73	36	29
1992	80	67	10	19
1991	70	83	20	38

1 John Ensign (R)

Of Las Vegas — Elected 1994, 2nd term

Biographical Information

Born: March 25, 1958, Roseville, Calif.
Education: U. of Nevada, Las Vegas, 1976-79; Oregon State U., B.S. 1981; Colorado State U., D.V.M. 1985.
Occupation: Veterinarian; casino manager.
Family: Wife, Darlene Sciaretta; two children.
Religion: Christian.
Political Career: No previous office.
Capitol Office: 414 Cannon Bldg. 20515; 225-5965.

Committees

Resources
National Parks & Public Lands; Water & Power
Ways & Means
Health; Human Resources

In Washington: Fewer than 1,500 votes separated Ensign and the Democratic incumbent he ousted in 1994, and during the 104th Congress the conservative Republican had two top priorities: Amass a huge campaign treasury to finance what was sure to be a tough 1996 re-election campaign and show Nevada voters he was lobbying hard to try to keep Congress from putting a nuclear waste repository in their state.

House GOP leaders boosted Ensign's fundraising prospects by giving him a seat on the Ways and Means Committee, whose work is vital to the business community. In 1996, Ensign spent $1.9 million on his campaign, nearly $700,000 of it from PACs. That was triple the amount spent by his Democratic challenger, and it helped Ensign to a six-point re-election victory.

In seeking campaign cash, Ensign also benefits from his ties to the gambling industry: His stepfather is chief operating officer of Circus Circus, a casino chain in Las Vegas, and Ensign was a general manager of hotel and casino properties before opening a veterinary hospital.

Throughout the 104th, Ensign warily eyed the progress of a proposal to build an interim storage site for nuclear waste at Nevada's Yucca Mountain. He called the waste-site matter "the most important political issue in my state," and he warned the GOP leadership that if it became law, "it could potentially cost two Republican House seats" — his and Nevada's 2nd District, which was open in 1996.

The Yucca bill would allow as much as 60,000 metric tons of nuclear waste to be brought to a temporary dump 100 miles outside Las Vegas; the waste would come from the 34 states where commercial nuclear waste now is stored temporarily.

Ensign has urged consideration of two other nuclear waste storage sites — Savannah River, S.C., and Hanford, Wash. On the Resources Committee, he has argued that those sites are built, have a work force trained to handle harmful radioactive waste and have benefited from the use of commercial nuclear power. "Nevada has never had the benefit of this [nuclear power]," Ensign said, "and therefore, it should not be dumped on a small state just because that small state only has two representatives in the House."

Despite strong objections from Nevada's two senators, the Senate passed the Yucca proposal in July 1996. But the matter then stalled, partly because political considerations came more into play as the fall election approached.

The Yucca bill passed the Senate in April 1997, but the margin was two votes short of the 67 needed to override a promised veto by President Clinton.

The gambling industry is Nevada's largest employer, and Ensign has sought to protect it from critics who say gambling in various forms is becoming too prevalent in America. When GOP Rep. Frank R. Wolf of Virginia and others pushed in the 104th to create a national commission to study the gambling industry and its social and economic impact, Ensign objected. "I see no reason why the federal government should be involved in a study of a legal, state-regulated industry," he said in July 1996.

The proposal put GOP congressional leaders in a tight spot, because some in the party consider gambling undesirable, even immoral, while others such as Ensign think the gambling industry is a perfectly appropriate free-enterprise endeavor. A bill creating a nine-member National Gambling Impact and Policy Commission cleared Congress in 1996 only after Republicans settled a dispute about the commission's subpoena power; they limited such power to documents.

In Ways and Means, Ensign helped stop efforts to add a tax on gambling to legislation making technical corrections to a bill raising the minimum wage.

In the social- and fiscal-policy arenas, Ensign usually stands with his party's conservative majority. But he has deviated when parochial interests were compelling. In May 1996, he was one of 93 Republicans supporting a Democratic-backed effort to raise the minimum wage. The work force in the 1st has many minimum wage casino employees. Ensign supported a GOP lead-

For the second time this century, Las Vegas is undergoing a transformation. Once a dusty railroad stop on the Union Pacific Line, the town evolved after World War II into Sin City, a garish neon pleasure haven where gambling flourished and visiting businessmen could hop a private plane to a rural bordello.

The gaming industry is still king — it is the building block of the local economy — but glitzy hotels boasting albino tigers, flaming manmade volcanoes and entertainer Wayne Newton no longer monopolize local business headlines.

Economic diversification is the city's new buzzword, and it is coming none too soon. Some of the older casinos, such as the Dunes, have gone under. Meanwhile, high-tech companies have joined such well-known gambling establishments as Bally's, Caesar's Palace, the Golden Nugget and the Mirage on the local business roster.

Attracted by low taxes and a pro-business environment, nearly 100 companies relocated to the Las Vegas area in the 1980s. The jobs they offered were a magnet for newcomers: 275,000 people moved to the Las Vegas Valley in that time. Several thousand people a month have moved to Nevada in the 1990s. The business district continues to boom, and large technology companies have opened satellite offices in the area.

While Chamber of Commerce officials drool, many longtime residents are clamoring for a development slowdown. The valley is experiencing air quality problems, traffic congestion, crowded schools and strained water resources.

Mormon conservatism flavors Clark County politics, but within the city limits of Las Vegas, Democrats have the edge. The 1st encompasses the downtown areas and the city of Henderson, to the southeast, which despite recent development maintains its blue-collar image. In 1994,

NEVADA 1
South — Las Vegas

Ensign had to overcome a huge Democratic voter registration advantage to defeat incumbent Democratic Rep. James P. Bilbray by fewer than 1,500 votes. Ensign's winning margin widened in 1996 to more than 11,000 votes, even as Bill Clinton won with 51 percent in the presidential race.

Unionized service workers, many of whom work in the glittery resort hotels along "The Strip" just south of Las Vegas, include a number of blacks who live on the city's west side. Democrats also can tap the city of North Las Vegas (which is 37 percent black) for votes. Under the 1980s map, North Las Vegas was divided between the 1st and 2nd districts. Now, virtually all of it is in the 1st.

Henderson supports itself with chemical manufacturing. Green Valley, home to professionals, young families and California transplants, is a GOP oasis. Workers at Nellis Air Force Base, northeast of Las Vegas, and at the Energy Department's Nevada Test Site also tend to favor GOP candidates.

Rural portions of Clark County were pared from the 1st in 1991 redistricting, creating a constituency that is almost exclusively urban.

Overall, Clark County casts more than half the vote in Nevada, so winning there has become crucial to statewide victory. Clinton carried only two of the state's 17 counties in 1992 and 1996, but won statewide both times.

1990 Population: 600,957. White 477,946 (80%), Black 62,809 (10%), Other 60,202 (10%). Hispanic origin 73,184 (12%). 18 and over 456,137 (76%), 62 and over 82,602 (14%). Median age: 34.

ership-backed amendment to exempt small businesses from the wage increase, but it failed.

The 1st also is home to many retirees and veterans, and in November 1995 Ensign joined 25 other Republicans in rejecting a bill funding the Department of Veterans Affairs because they felt it did not include enough for veterans' medical care. The House returned the measure to a conference committee instructing it to increase funding for veterans' medical care by $213 million.

Also on Ways and Means, Ensign has tried to change the Medicaid funding formula to help areas with fast-growing populations, such as Las Vegas. And he amended the GOP's health insurance portability bill to include tax deductions for long-term care expenses. His amendment would make those expenses, other than insurance premiums, deductible after they exceeded 7.5 percent of a taxpayer's adjusted gross income.

Ensign also strongly backed overhauling the welfare system. Speaking on the subject, Ensign often referred to his mother, praising her determination and self-sufficiency. "My mom, when my parents were divorced when I was about 3 years of age, would have made more money going on welfare because she had no child support," Ensign once told the House. "She had three kids to raise. But I saw my mom each and every single day get up and go to work, and that taught me a work ethic that we are robbing from welfare families today."

Ensign says his biological father (whose name he does not use or mention) abandoned him, his siblings and mother. His mother made change in a Reno casino for $12 a day. The family shared a house with another fatherless family and never went on welfare. "You just didn't do it. You did whatever it took as a family to work together to get through it." (His mother later remarried.)

At Home: Ensign had never sought political office before his 1994 House bid. But his business background — as a hotel/casino manager and owner of an animal hospital — gave him some community standing, and after state GOP leaders encouraged him to take on four-term Democratic Rep. James P. Bilbray, Ensign assembled an impressive organization of volunteers and embarked on an energetic precinct-walking effort.

Ensign's message was similar to that of many GOP challengers in 1994. He signed the Republican "Contract With America" and promoted a "tough on crime" platform emphasizing "truth in sentencing," advocating stiff and fixed sentences as a deterrent to violent crime.

Ensign easily won the September GOP primary. In the general election, he could not keep pace with Bilbray's fundraising — the incumbent spent more than $900,000 — but Ensign did get help from gambling industry sources and ultimately spent $687,000.

Although redistricting for the 1990s gave the 1st more registered Democrats, a number of them are conservative, including working-class union members and culturally traditional voters affiliated with Las Vegas' many churches. Ensign got backing from gun owners upset with Bilbray's vote for the 1994 crime bill, which banned certain types of semiautomatic assault-style weapons. ("Nevadans like their guns," Ensign noted.)

After the primary, Ensign began airing TV ads tweaking Bilbray for upgrading to first class on official flights home from Washington. But it was a series of front-page stories in late September in the Las Vegas Review-Journal that ruined Bilbray. The newspaper reported that a longtime Bilbray confidant and political adviser, Don Williams, stood to realize a $7 million return on a land investment if a bill sponsored by Bilbray to expand the boundaries of the Red Rock Canyon National Conservation Area was enacted.

Bilbray denied that he knew of Williams' land holdings when he drew up the bill, which had widespread support in the Las Vegas area, or of Williams' proposal to the Bureau of Land Management that he swap his land for property in southwest Las Vegas. An Ensign TV ad chastised Bilbray for not disclosing his friend's holdings. In the end, Ensign squeezed past Bilbray by just a fraction.

That narrow defeat prompted Democrats to make Ensign a top target in 1996. His challenger was state Sen. Bob Coffin, who emphasized his conservatism and independence even as he courted traditional Democratic constituencies in the labor and black communities.

Trying to capitalize on the fact that Ensign backed the House's "Contract With America" legislative agenda 100 percent of the time, the Democratic Congressional Campaign Committee marked the two-year anniversary of the contract's debut by offering satellite footage of Ensign signing the document. Coffin said, "John Ensign found himself bound to the Contract With America, which cut education, Medicare and Medicaid for a majority of the constituents and cut taxes for people with great wealth. . . . The only contract I'm going to sign is with the state of Nevada and the voters of the 1st Congressional District."

But if district voters were angry at the GOP, they took it out on the party's presidential nominee Bob Dole. He lost the 1st by 14 points to Clinton, as Ensign won 50 percent to 44 percent.

HOUSE ELECTIONS

1996 General		
John Ensign (R)	86,472	(50%)
Bob Coffin (D)	75,081	(44%)
Ted Gunderson (IA)	4,572	(3%)
James Dan (LIBERT)	3,341	(2%)
Richard Eidson (NL)	3,127	(2%)
1994 General		
John Ensign (R)	73,769	(48%)
James P. Bilbray (D)	72,333	(48%)
Gary Wood (LIBERT)	6,065	(4%)

CAMPAIGN FINANCE

	Receipts	Receipts from PACs	Expend- itures
1996			
Ensign (R)	$1,989,386	$698,949 (35%)	$1,904,413
Coffin (D)	$601,069	$263,831 (44%)	$592,726
1994			
Ensign (R)	$735,800	$138,144 (19%)	$687,194
Bilbray (D)	$894,220	$306,960 (34%)	$913,708

DISTRICT VOTE FOR PRESIDENT

1996		1992	
D	91,265 (51%)	D	98,801 (44%)
R	65,984 (37%)	R	70,586 (31%)
I	15,937 (9%)	I	56,058 (25%)

KEY VOTES

1997	
Ban "partial birth" abortions	Y
1996	
Approve farm bill	Y
Deny public education to illegal immigrants	Y
Repeal ban on certain assault-style weapons	Y
Increase minimum wage	Y
Freeze defense spending	Y
Approve welfare overhaul	Y
1995	
Approve balanced-budget constitutional amendment	Y
Relax Clean Water Act regulations	Y
Oppose limits on environmental regulations	N
Reduce projected Medicare spending	Y
Approve GOP budget with tax and spending cuts	Y

VOTING STUDIES

	Presidential Support		Party Unity		Conservative Coalition	
Year	S	O	S	O	S	O
1996	39	59	79	20	67	31
1995	18	81	88	11	83	16

INTEREST GROUP RATINGS

Year	ADA	AFL-CIO	CCUS	ACU
1996	5	n/a	88	85
1995	0	0	100	96

2 Jim Gibbons (R)

Of Reno — Elected 1996, 1st term

Biographical Information

Born: Dec. 16, 1944, Sparks, Nev.

Education: U. of Nevada, Reno, B.S. 1967, M.S. 1973; Southwestern U., J.D. 1979.

Military Service: Air Force, 1967-71; Nev. Air National Guard, 1975-95.

Occupation: Airline pilot; lawyer; geologist.

Family: Wife, Dawn Snelling; three children.

Religion: Protestant.

Political Career: Nev. Assembly, 1989-93, minority whip, 1993; Republican nominee for governor, 1994.

Capitol Office: 1116 Longworth Bldg. 20515; 225-6155.

Committees

National Security
Military Readiness; Military Research & Development

Resources
Energy & Mineral Resources; National Parks & Public Lands

Select Intelligence
Technical & Tactical Intelligence

The Path to Washington: It did Gibbons no harm that he shared the November 1996 ballot with his own amendment to the state constitution requiring a two-thirds vote of the legislature for any tax increase. In tax-sensitive Nevada, both the amendment and its author won handily.

Gibbons, who had drafted the measure in 1993 while still a state assemblyman, promised to take his brand of fiscal restraint to Washington, bolstering the ranks of Republican budget-cutters.

But Gibbons also drew some sharp distinctions with House GOP leaders. For one thing, he supports abortion rights. In February 1997, Gibbons was the only freshman Republican and one of just 44 GOP members to join a majority of Democrats in passing a bill authorizing the early release of $385 million for international family planning programs. But Gibbons joined the majority of Republicans in passing a subsequent bill to deny funds to overseas organizations that use private money to perform or promote abortions.

And in the closing weeks of his campaign, mindful of the retirees from California flooding into his state, Gibbons said he did not support a Republican plan to limit the growth of the Medicare program.

From his seat on the Resources Committee, Gibbons will join Nevada's other representative, Republican John Ensign, in opposing efforts to set up a temporary repository for nuclear waste at Yucca Mountain in the state. The measure passed the Senate in the 104th Congress but did not come up for a vote in the House, another bill passed the Senate in April 1997, but the margin was two votes short of the 67 needed to override a promised veto by President Clinton.

A former Air Force combat pilot — he won a Distinguished Flying Cross in Vietnam and served in the Persian Gulf War with the Nevada Air National Guard — Gibbons also won assignments on the National Security and Select Intelligence committees.

Thanks to a race for governor in 1994, which he lost to incumbent Democratic Gov. Bob Miller, Gibbons was the best known of the Republican candidates who jumped into the House race when veteran Republican Rep. Barbara F. Vucanovich in 1996 announced her retirement after seven terms.

He also had the broadest résumé. Educated as a geologist, then as a lawyer, Gibbons spent four years in the Air Force at the height of the Vietnam War, 20 in the Air National Guard and the past decade as a Delta Air Lines pilot. He was in the state Assembly for four years.

In the primary, Gibbons faced former House Counsel Cheryl A. Lau and former Lander County District Attorney Patty Cafferata, Vucanovich's daughter-in-law.

Gibbons had defeated Lau in 1994 to win the Republican gubernatorial nomination. Lau came to Washington in 1995 to work for the new House Republican majority, but left a year later to return to her native state and run for Vucanovich's seat. Cafferata ran for governor in 1986, losing to Democrat Richard H. Bryan, now Nevada's senior U.S. senator. Adding to the twists and turns was the fact that, unlike Gibbons, the two women, Lau and Cafferata, opposed abortion rights.

In a race decided mainly on the tax issue, Gibbons won and became the favorite in the Republican-leaning district that takes in the entire state except for the city of Las Vegas and some of its suburbs. But the Democrats put up a fight with former state Sen. Thomas "Spike" Wilson, chairman of Nevada's ethics commission.

Gibbons campaigned on a host of conservative issues, calling for lower taxes, a balanced budget, term limits and fewer federal regulations. Gibbons backed Republican presidential nominee Bob Dole's proposed 15 percent income tax cut, and most of the GOP's budget plan.

He also emphasized crime issues, calling for a reserve police officers training corps, like the ROTC for the military, in which students would receive college scholarships if they agree to serve in law enforcement after graduation.

In the end, Gibbons won going away, running up 59 percent of the vote to Wilson's 35 percent.

Campaigning in the 2nd is an awesome undertaking. It contains 99.8 percent of the land area (nearly 110,000 square miles) of the nation's seventh-largest state.

While redistricting enlarged the 2nd so it now encompasses all but Las Vegas and its immediate environs, the district's population nexus is in the north, in the Reno (Washoe County) area. Reno is older, more conservative and less reliant on the gambling industry than Las Vegas. Proximity to California and the Pacific Northwest make warehousing an important part of the local economy.

Formerly a GOP stronghold, Reno has seen its politics moderated by an influx of environmentally conscious newcomers. (Its population grew 33 percent in the 1980s.) Catholics make up a significant portion of the electorate, but they tend not to be as politically active as their Mormon brethren in Clark County. Two statewide Democrats — Sen. Richard H. Bryan and Gov. Bob Miller — carried Washoe in their respective 1994 re-election bids.

The state capital, Carson City, is in the 2nd, as is Lake Tahoe, a year-round resort area astride the California-Nevada line that attracts visitors to its golf courses, casinos and chalets. The rural Cow Counties cover most of the state but hold few of its residents: Several of these enormous counties are home to fewer than 10,000 people. Agriculture and ranching are the main pursuits, and huge expanses of uninhabited mountain and desert land are used as military test ranges.

Yucca Mountain looms ominously over Nye County — the state's fastest growing in population from 1990 to 1995 — as the site Congress has proposed for a federal nuclear waste dump. Nevadans share a bipartisan resentment of what they call the "Screw Nevada" dump bill, which Congress passed in 1987.

Resentment of the federal government — which owns nearly 90 percent of the district's land — is most adamant in the conservative-voting

NEVADA 2
Reno, the 'Cow Counties' and part of Clark County

"Cows." Federal water and grazing regulations generate animosity, as do airspace restrictions that local pilots face near the bombing ranges.

Retired military personnel are numerous in Hawthorne (Mineral County), site of the Hawthorne Army Ammunition Plant. State politicians rarely miss the small town's annual armed forces parade. A modern-day mining boom has spurred growth in a number of rural communities to the north, particularly in Elko (Elko County), Lovelock (Pershing County) and Battle Mountain (Lander County).

The location of Ely (White Pine County) on U.S. 50 makes it a regional center for commerce and business. The highway, snaking across central Nevada past Carson City, became known as "the loneliest road in America" after a Life magazine article claimed travelers needed survival skills to cross this stretch of empty and desolate desert.

In 1996, Bob Dole carried every county lying wholly in the 2nd except Mineral — as well as the district's portion of Clark County — to carry it by 7 percentage points. Storey County, which includes the famous 19th century mining center of Virginia City, backed Ross Perot in 1992. White Pine County, where a unionized work force once mined copper and other minerals from huge pits, voted for Bill Clinton in 1992 but gave Dole a two-vote margin in 1996.

1990 Population: 600,876. White 534,749 (89%), Black 15,962 (3%), Other 50,165 (8%). Hispanic origin 51,235 (9%). 18 and over 448,748 (75%), 62 and over 76,899 (13%). Median age: 33.

HOUSE ELECTIONS

1996 General		
Jim Gibbons (R)	162,310	(59%)
Thomas "Spike" Wilson (D)	97,742	(35%)
Dan Hansen (IA)	8,780	(3%)
Lois Avery (NL)	4,628	(2%)
Louis R. Tomburello (LIBERT)	3,732	(1%)
1996 Primary		
Jim Gibbons (R)	33,332	(42%)
Cheryl A. Lau (R)	19,243	(24%)
Patty Cafferata (R)	19,192	(24%)
Bob Seale (R)	3,129	(4%)
Pat McMillan (R)	1,465	(2%)
Mike Schaefer (R)	1,188	(2%)

CAMPAIGN FINANCE

	Receipts	Receipts from PACs		Expend-itures
1996				
Gibbons (R)	$754,380	$192,815	(26%)	$724,036
Wilson (D)	$608,762	$143,550	(24%)	$606,227
Hansen (IA)	$28,259	0		$28,258

DISTRICT VOTE FOR PRESIDENT

1996		1992	
D	112,709 (40%)	**D**	90,347 (33%)
R	133,260 (47%)	**R**	105,242 (39%)
I	28,049 (10%)	**I**	76,522 (28%)

KEY VOTES

1997

Ban "partial birth" abortions — Y

NEW HAMPSHIRE

Governor: Jeanne Shaheen (D)
First elected: 1996
Length of term: 2 years
Term expires: 1/99
Salary: $86,235
Term limit: No
Phone: (603) 271-2121
Born: January 28, 1947; St, Charles, Mo.
Education: Shippensburg U., B.A. 1969; U. of Mississippi, M.S.S. 1973.
Occupation: Campaign manager; teacher.
Family: Husband, William H. Shaheen; three children.
Religion: Protestant
Political Career: Democratic Nominee for N.H. Senate, 1978; N.H. Senate, 1991-97.

No lieutenant governor

Senate President: Joseph Delahunty (R)
Phone: (603) 271-2111
Salary: $125

State election official: (603) 271-3242
Democratic headquarters: (603) 225-6899
Republican headquarters: (603) 225-9341

REDISTRICTING

New Hampshire retained its two House seats in reapportionment. The legislature passed the map March 24, 1992; the governor signed it March 27. Justice Department approved the map June 12.

STATE LEGISLATURE

General Court. Meets January-July.

Senate: 24 members, 2-year terms.
1996 breakdown: 15R, 9D; 16 men, 8 women
Salary: $100/year + mileage
Phone: (603) 271-2111

House of Representatives: 400 members, 2-year terms
1996 breakdown: 255R, 143D, 2I; 277 men, 123 women
Salary: $100/year + mileage
Phone: (603) 271-3661

URBAN STATISTICS

City	Population
Manchester	98,332
Mayor Raymond J. Wieczorek, R	
Nashua	79,662
Mayor Donald Davidson, N-P	
Concord	36,006
Mayor William Veroneau, N-P	
Derry	29,603
Council Chairman Gordon Graham, N-P	
Rochester	26,630
Mayor Harvey Bernier, I	

U.S. CONGRESS

Senate: 0 D, 2 R
House: 0 D, 2 R

TERM LIMITS

For state offices: No

ELECTIONS

1996 Presidential Vote

Bill Clinton	49%
Bob Dole	39%
Ross Perot	10%

1992 Presidential Vote

Bill Clinton	39%
George Bush	38%
Ross Perot	23%

1988 Presidential Vote

George Bush	62%
Michael S. Dukakis	36%

POPULATION

1990 population		1,109,252
1980 population		920,610
Percent change		+20%
Rank among states:		40
White		98%
Black		1%
Hispanic		1%
Asian or Pacific islander		1%
Urban		51%
Rural		49%
Born in state		44%
Foreign-born		4%
Under age 18	278,755	25%
Ages 18-64	705,468	64%
65 and older	125,029	11%
Median age		32.8

MISCELLANEOUS

Capital: Concord
Number of counties: 10
Per capita income: $20,951 (1991)
Rank among states: 9
Total area: 9,279 sq. miles
Rank among states: 44

NEW HAMPSHIRE

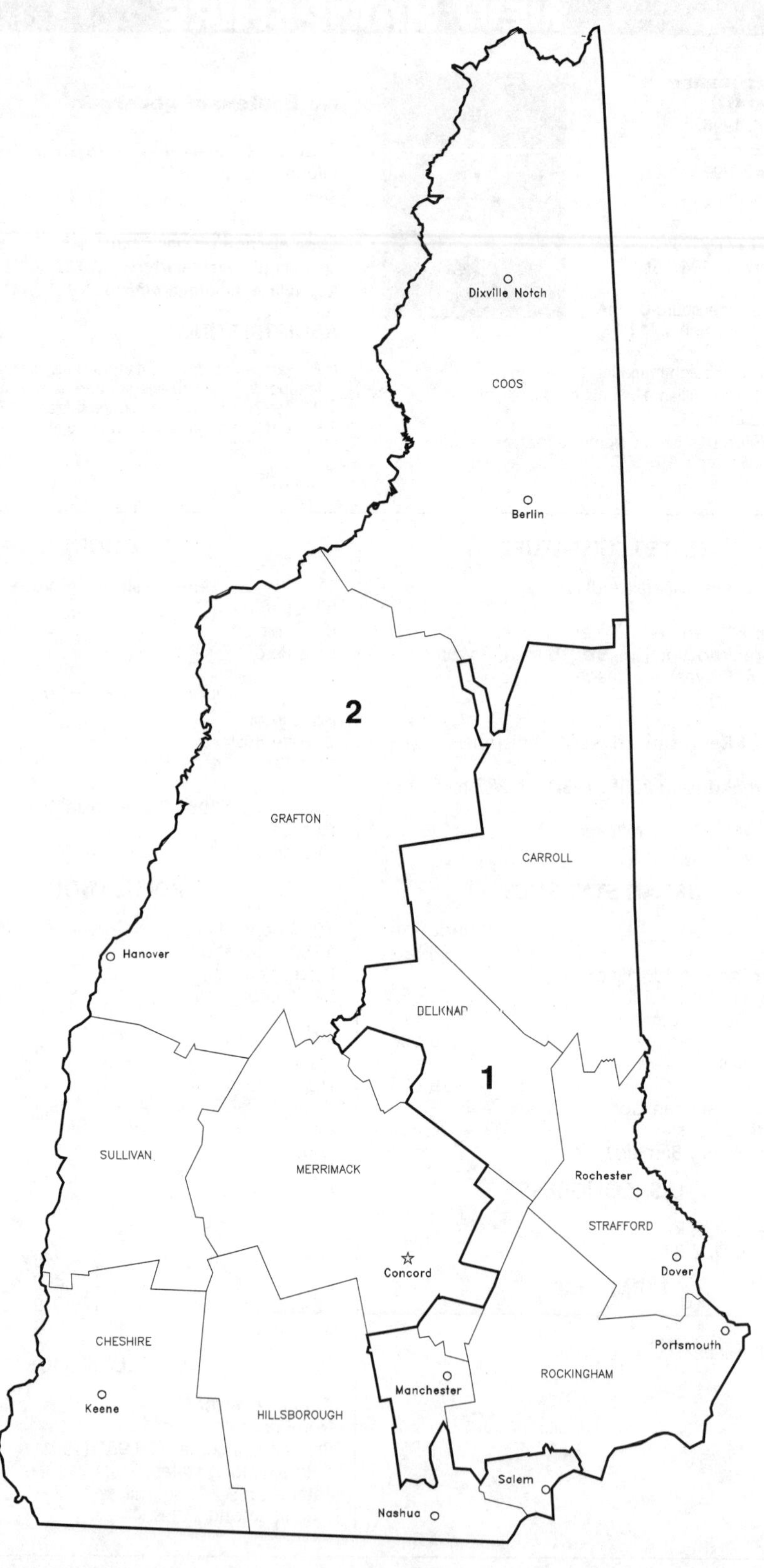
Dixville Notch
COOS
Berlin
2
GRAFTON
CARROLL
Hanover
BELKNAP
1
SULLIVAN
MERRIMACK
Rochester
STRAFFORD
Dover
Concord
CHESHIRE
Portsmouth
Manchester
ROCKINGHAM
Keene
HILLSBOROUGH
Salem
Nashua

Robert C. Smith (R)

Of Tuftonboro — Elected 1990; 2nd term

Biographical Information

Born: March 30, 1941, Trenton, N.J.

Education: Trenton Junior College, A.A. 1963; Lafayette College, B.A. 1965; California State U., Long Beach, 1968-69.

Military Service: Navy, 1965-67.

Occupation: Real estate broker; high school teacher.

Family: Wife, Mary Jo Hutchinson; three children.

Religion: Roman Catholic.

Political Career: Gov. Wentworth Regional School Board (Wolfeboro, N.H.), 1978-84; sought Republican nomination for U.S. House, 1980; Republican nominee for U.S. House, 1982; U.S. House, 1985-90.

Capitol Office: 307 Dirksen Bldg. 20510; 224-2841.

Committees

Armed Services
Acquisition & Technology; Seapower; Strategic Forces (chairman)

Environment & Public Works
Superfund, Waste Control & Risk Assessment (chairman); Transportation & Infrastructure

Governmental Affairs
Investigations; International Security, Proliferation & Federal Services

Select Ethics (chairman)

In Washington: Smith, a bedrock conservative, has seen his influence ebb and flow in recent years with the shifting ideological tides of the country and Congress.

The burly former high school teacher with the sharp tongue and aggressive political style has never quite made it into the Senate's clubby inner circle. In 1993, the combination of a new Democratic president and a Democratic Congress confined Smith to the political margin. But the Republican sweep of 1994 brought the mainstream closer to Smith's views.

The 1996 elections resulted in a more conservative Senate under the leadership of Mississippian Trent Lott. It remains to be seen whether Smith can turn his strong beliefs into effective legislative action. To date, his trademark has been passionate advocacy on a few heartfelt causes.

In the 104th Congress, Smith sponsored legislation to outlaw a certain late-term abortion procedure that opponents call "partial-birth" abortion. In a floor speech, Smith described in detail the particulars of the method, calling it "grisly" and "disgusting." Smith has called abortion "one of the great issues of the day, much as slavery was 100 years ago."

In foreign affairs, too, Smith has exhibited an unyielding style. When Republican Sen. John McCain of Arizona, a former prisoner of war in Vietnam, helped lead the Senate to vote in favor of normalizing diplomatic relations with Vietnam, Smith vehemently resisted.

He said no improvement should be contemplated until Vietnam came forward with more information about Americans missing or dead from the seven-year war. Smith, also a Vietnam veteran, gained national attention for his work seeking information about prisoners of war and those listed as missing in action.

Although he signed on to a 1993 report that found "no compelling evidence" of POWs still alive in captivity, Smith gained the support of some family and veterans' groups by arguing that the possibility must be thoroughly investigated. In January 1994, when the Senate supported President Clinton on lifting the economic embargo against Vietnam, Smith said the move was "equivalent to getting down on your knees and hoping and praying that the Vietnamese will give us all this information."

Smith also railed against Clinton's policy on Bosnia. In 1994, he voted for lifting the arms embargo to help supply Bosnia's Muslims in their civil war against the Bosnian Serbs. But when Clinton brokered a fragile peace in the region in late 1995, Smith passionately argued against sending U.S. troops to enforce the agreement:

"American soldiers, air crews, Marines and sailors will now be placed in harm's way because this administration failed to do what so many of us urged — permit the legal government of Bosnia, permit the people of Bosnia to defend their country, and their lives."

As a member of the Armed Services Committee, Smith supported higher levels of defense spending, while seeking to freeze or cut the federal budget in virtually every other area. In December 1994, when Clinton proposed adding $25 billion to his defense spending plan over six years, Smith scoffed.

"The president sees the political handwriting on the wall with the Republican control of Congress," Smith said. "He knows we are going to seize this issue of inadequate defense spending and give him no mercy, and he is trying to counter it. But it is not enough. It is a Band-Aid where you need a tourniquet."

Smith's unswerving advocacy of increased defense spending is one instance where he abandons strict fiscal conservatism. Another is on protecting businesses from costs associated with the superfund hazardous waste law.

Smith used his chairmanship of the Environment and Public Works Subcommittee on Superfund, Waste Control and Risk Assessment to advance the view that businesses should not be held to "retroactive liability" for causing pollution. In the 104th, he sponsored legislation to strike the part of the superfund law that holds polluters liable for dumping hazardous wastes before the law took effect in 1980.

Smith said the revisions could increase the government's share of the cost of the program from $1.5 billion to as much as $2.2 billion. He conceded that finding that much funding would be difficult, but argued that it was unfair to make businesses liable for waste disposed of legally before superfund was enacted.

On some occasions, Smith's down-the-line conservatism gives way to regional priorities. For example, while classic conservative support for free trade dictated a yes vote on NAFTA, Smith opposed it, out of a desire to protect local industries whose jobs might be threatened by competition south of the border.

And while generally pro-business when it comes to curbing environmental regulation, Smith joined with environmentalists on acid rain. In New Hampshire, where lakes and streams show signs of damage from the pollution problem, the issue cuts across party and ideological lines.

Notwithstanding his opposition to NAFTA, Smith has received consistently low grades from organized labor for his voting patterns. In May 1995, Smith sponsored an amendment to a routine highway bill that would have exempted highway projects from the provisions of the Davis-Bacon Act, a favorite target of Smith's that is considered sacrosanct by organized labor.

The law requires the government to pay the "prevailing wage" on contracts in whatever region of the country it is doing business. Smith argued that repeal of the Davis-Bacon Act would save taxpayers up to 15 percent on federal highway projects. In 1994 Smith opposed including Davis-Bacon Act wage thresholds in a defense procurement reform bill. Two months earlier, a Senate panel rejected a Smith amendment that would have repealed the Davis-Bacon Act as it applied to sewage treatment plant construction.

Smith came to the Senate in 1990, filling the seat of Republican Gordon J. Humphrey, who retired. In succeeding Humphrey, he brought his obstreperous brand of conservatism — which often caused him trouble in the House — to a chamber more accustomed to individualism and to accommodating members with iconoclastic views.

In the Senate, Smith was able to get a seat on the Armed Services Committee, where he could team up with other conservative ideologues on defense and foreign policy issues. Smith was one of only four senators — all Republicans — who voted against the 1991 treaty signed by President George Bush that reduced conventional forces and called for the destruction of weapons by the United States and the Soviet Union. He was one of three Republican senators who criticized the 1992 defense authorization bill as cutting too much of the funding for the Strategic Defense Initiative.

In the House, Smith was a vocal opponent of congressional pay raises. When the House voted in February 1989 to block a proposed 51 percent salary increase for members of Congress, Smith was both a big winner and a big loser.

He was a winner because he helped lead the fight against a procedure that would have allowed the raise to be enacted without a House vote.

"Would I like to have a $45,000 raise? You're damned right I would," Smith said. "But that's not the way to get it. If we can't convince the American people we should have a raise, then we shouldn't have it."

While such statements did not always make Smith the most popular representative in the cloakroom, they have served him very well in fiscally conservative New Hampshire, a state that has a 98 percent white population, that has neither an income nor sales tax, and that prides itself on its bare-bones state and local governments.

At Home: But the same pay raise issue that helped Smith elevate his political profile enough to win the Senate seat in 1990 gave his 1996 opponent, former Democratic Rep. Dick Swett, an opening that almost made Smith a one-term senator.

Swett hammered Smith for hypocrisy in voting for a Senate pay raise in 1991 after saying he would not. He accused Smith of voting to cut funding for environmental protection and claimed that Smith's views on issues such as abortion are too far to the right even in New Hampshire, a traditional Republican stronghold. Swett said his "centrist positions" were more in line with those of state voters.

Smith's campaign relied on a formidable fundraising base and a consistent message to counter Swett's charges. He revisited the gun control issue that helped Republican Charles Bass defeat Swett in the 1994 House race: Swett's vote in 1994 for a ban on certain assault weapons, which he cast despite a promise to oppose the legislation.

Smith also cast his opponent as a liberal. One of Smith's early television ads claimed that the Clinton administration's health care overhaul plan, which Swett cosponsored during the 103rd Congress, would have allowed "the federal government to take over health care" and "could have prohibited you from choosing your own doctor" — claims long denied by supporters of the failed legislation.

In the end, the vote was close enough that several TV networks declared Swett the winner on Election Night. Later returns reversed the fortunes, and Smith returned to serve a second Senate term.

A small-town real estate agent and one-time teacher, New Hampshire's senior senator has cultivated the image of a real-life "Mr. Smith Goes to Washington." But he also exhibited a good bit of political savvy in 1990 in navigating his crossing from one side of Capitol Hill to the other.

In three terms of representing New Hampshire's 1st District, Smith had forged a reputation as an ardent Congress-basher and hard-right conservative immersed in few issues other than accounting for Vietnam MIAs.

But when Humphrey announced in early 1989 that he would not seek re-election, Smith moved quickly to assume the mantle. He announced his candidacy, wrapped up the support of key Republican leaders and began to project a more moderate position on several key issues.

In the Republican primary, Smith's well-heeled campaign rolled up nearly two-thirds of the vote against Tom Christo, a wealthy lawyer specializing in computer law who was backed by the National Abortion and Reproductive Rights Action League. Smith ran just as well in the general election, crushing the comeback bid of former Democratic Sen. John A. Durkin (1975-80).

Durkin tried hard, mocking Smith as "Bumbling Bob" and the "abominable no-man" and portraying him as a simplistic ideologue who would be intellectually over his head in the Senate. But Smith was able to give as good as he got, accusing Durkin of being a tax-and-spend liberal who supported the federal bailout of New York City but opposed the Kemp-Roth tax cut.

Heavily outspent, Durkin was in no position to compete effectively in the final days of the campaign. In Republican New Hampshire, the result was a rout, as Smith took nearly two-thirds of the vote.

Smith's early campaigns were far more modest: short on money, long on Rotary Club luncheons. But they gave him a chance to demonstrate his persistence. On his first House try, in 1980, Smith lost in the Republican primary. On his second try, in 1982, he won the primary but lost the general election to Democratic Rep. Norman E. D'Amours (1975-85). On his third try, in 1984, when D'Amours ran for the Senate, Smith finally won the seat.

In beating the highest-ranking Democrat in state government, Executive Councilor Dudley Dudley, he returned the eastern New Hampshire House seat to the GOP for the first time in a decade.

Unlike D'Amours, whose roots were in ethnic Manchester, Smith reflected small-town Yankee New Hampshire. It was there that he wrote his brief political resume as a member and chairman of the Wolfeboro School Board. In private life, he was a civics and gym teacher at the local junior high school.

Rather than embellish his modest credentials when he ran for the House, Smith presented himself as a citizen-politician who understood New Hampshire's common-sense values. Each campaign played up the down-home manner of the big, burly baseball coach and emphasized his fervent conservatism.

It is a combination that has played well for Smith with the voters. Dismissing Dudley in 1984 as "Dudley Dudley, Liberal Liberal," Smith was elected to the House by a margin of nearly 3-to-2. A pair of comfortable re-election victories followed before Smith mounted his successful Senate campaign in 1990.

SENATE ELECTIONS

1996 General

Robert C. Smith (R)	242,257	(49%)
Dick Swett (D)	227,355	(46%)
Ken Blevens (LIBERT)	22,261	(5%)

Previous Winning Percentages: 1990 (65%) **1988*** (60%) **1986*** (56%) **1984*** (59%)

** House elections*

CAMPAIGN FINANCE

	Receipts	Receipts from PACs	Expend-itures
1996			
Smith (R)	$1,708,376	$875,951 (51%)	$1,718,413
Swett (D)	$1,759,089	$348,388 (20%)	$1,558,563

KEY VOTES

1997	
Approve balanced-budget constitutional amendment	Y
Approve chemical weapons treaty	N
1996	
Approve farm bill	Y
Limit punitive damages in product liability cases	Y
Exempt small businesses from higher minimum wage	Y
Approve welfare overhaul	Y
Bar job discrimination based on sexual orientation	N
Override veto of ban on "partial birth" abortions	Y
1995	
Approve GOP budget with tax and spending cuts	Y
Approve constitutional amendment barring flag desecration	Y

VOTING STUDIES

	Presidential Support		Party Unity		Conservative Coalition	
Year	**S**	**O**	**S**	**O**	**S**	**O**
1996	29	71	94	4	92	8
1995	18	82	97	3	91	7
1994	19	79	95	4	88	13
1993	11	87	94	4	90	10
1992	73	27	92	8	89	11
1991	85	14	93	6	85	15

INTEREST GROUP RATINGS

Year	ADA	AFL-CIO	CCUS	ACU
1996	5	n/a	92	100
1995	0	0	100	100
1994	5	14	80	100
1993	15	9	91	100
1992	5	25	90	96
1991	10	17	70	90

NEW HAMPSHIRE

Judd Gregg (R)

Of Rye — Elected 1992, 1st term

Biographical Information

Born: Feb. 14, 1947, Nashua, N.H.

Education: Columbia U., A.B. 1969; Boston U., J.D. 1972, LL.M. 1975.

Occupation: Lawyer.

Family: Wife, Kathleen MacLellan; three children.

Religion: Congregationalist.

Political Career: N.H. Governor's Executive Council, 1979-81; U.S. House, 1981-89; governor, 1989-93.

Capitol Office: 393 Russell Bldg. 20510; 224-3324.

Committees

Appropriations
Commerce, Justice, State & Judiciary (chairman); Defense; Foreign Operations; Interior; Labor, Health & Human Services & Education

Budget

Labor & Human Resources
Aging (chairman); Children & Families

Chief Deputy Whip

In Washington: There are many GOP senators as conservative as Gregg, but not so many with his extensive background in politics: He is the only Republican senator to have served in the House and as a governor.

Gregg's particular blend of ideological commitment and government experience makes him a useful ally to the Senate GOP leadership.

Gregg enjoys a close relationship with Majority Leader Trent Lott of Mississippi. They served together in the House through 1988, when Gregg ran for governor and Lott for the Senate. During his House tenure, Gregg was an early participant in the Conservative Opportunity Society, a group founded by Rep. Newt Gingrich with the aim of toppling the House Democratic majority.

At the start of the 104th Congress, when Lott was Senate majority whip, he named Gregg to be chief deputy whip, and Gregg assumed a seat on the Appropriations Committee. After Majority Leader Bob Dole left the Senate to run for president in June 1996, Lott assumed the top Senate post. In a mid-Congress shuffle of committee assignments, Gregg ended up chairman of an Appropriations subcommittee.

While on most issues Gregg sees eye-to-eye with his party's conservative firebrands, he is more prone than some of them to regard legislating as a give-and-take process that involves accommodating competing interests.

In April 1997, Gregg concurred with Lott in voting to ratify a treaty that aimed to prevent the use of chemical weapons worldwide. Many on the GOP right, including some in the party's Senate leadership, said the treaty would compromise U.S. sovereignty as well as military and trade secrets. But President Clinton argued that unless the United States ratified the treaty it would be unable to participate in its enforcement. To win over skeptics, he offered assurances that the United States could pull out of the treaty if the national interest was threatened. In the end, 29 of 55 GOP senators voted for the treaty.

When Dole was majority leader, he named Gregg to head a commission studying the future of entitlement programs such as Medicare and Medicaid. The commission issued a plan that called for reducing projected spending on Medicare by up to $120 billion, on Medicaid by $115 billion and on welfare by $89 billion. The group also proposed financial incentives to encourage seniors to choose less expensive health care coverage.

The commission's proposed Medicare savings distinguished it from a budget plan passed by House Republicans in 1995, which called for about $270 billion in Medicare savings and also proposed about $245 billion in tax cuts.

Gregg favored more modest Medicare savings and a smaller tax cut. "In the Senate I think we'll go to $63 billion in tax cuts, which is what the president wants," Gregg predicted on a television news program in February 1995. "I don't think we should go over what he asked for."

Gregg moved through his subcommittee another proposal Clinton supported: doubling (to $300 million) the money spent to combat terrorism, an idea that grew out of the 1995 bombing of a federal office building in Oklahoma City. But many GOP conservatives balked at giving law enforcement expanded powers contained in the measure. The anti-terrorism package enacted in the 104th was a scaled-back version.

Texas Republican Phil Gramm's move to the Finance Committee during the 104th gave Gregg an opening to chair Appropriations' Commerce, Justice, State and Judiciary Subcommittee. Gregg said he agreed philosophically with the staunchly conservative Gramm, but said he "may not be as aggressive in some accounts," which was taken as a signal that he would not swing such a big budget-cutting ax at programs such as legal services for the poor.

Nevertheless, the spending bill that came out of Gregg's subcommittee in 1996 became embroiled in controversy, in part because it cut funding for U.S. dues to the United Nations and for the Commerce Department's Advanced Technology Program. Though normally willing to consider compromise, Gregg dug in his heels in this instance. Under pressure to make a deal with the White House on an omnibus spending bill in 1996, the GOP leadership "unceremoniously removed" Gregg from negotiations, as Gregg put it. "I was too disruptive to the process, because I kept saying we should be concerned about our tax dollars," Gregg said. "The American taxpayers were being fleeced."

Although there is a strong strain of libertarianism in his state's GOP's heritage, Gregg also carries his conservatism into the social-issue arena: As governor, he vetoed bills liberalizing abortion rights provisions of state law. In the Senate, he is an ally of anti-abortion forces and has voted to ban a particular abortion technique opponents call "partial birth" abortion.

At Home: Gregg's ascent in New Hampshire politics has proceeded like clockwork, although his timing was nearly thrown off in 1992 when he ran into stiff opposition in his effort to return to Washington after a four-year hiatus as governor.

A tenacious campaigner and scion of a family famous in New Hampshire politics, Gregg had won convincingly in four House races and two gubernatorial contests since the fall of 1980.

But in 1992, New Hampshire's economic woes fired up an angry electorate, helping Bill Clinton carry the state for president and putting pro-business Democrat John Rauh in a position to give Gregg his toughest electoral fight ever in his bid to replace retiring GOP Sen. Warren B. Rudman.

As governor and as a Senate candidate, Gregg took the heat for the state's economic troubles. In the Republican primary, wealthy developer Harold Eckman pounded away at Gregg with a lavishly financed media campaign that held Gregg to a bare majority of the vote.

Rauh, a millionaire businessman who moved to Sunapee, N.H., from Ohio in 1986, continued the attack in the fall. He repeatedly reminded voters that Gregg had presided over some of the worst fiscal times in New Hampshire's history.

While acknowledging the state's economic hardships, Gregg frequently noted that he had kept a tight lid on spending and remained staunchly opposed to state income and sales taxes. The race went down to the wire. Gregg lost most of the counties in his old congressional district on the rural western side of New Hampshire. But he won the populous southeast corner of the state and the Republican "North Country" by enough votes to take the Senate seat.

Gregg has devoted almost his entire adult life to public service. He practiced law only a short time before launching his political career in 1978 by unseating a GOP incumbent for a seat on the five-member state Executive Council. Two years later, Gregg won the House seat of retiring GOP Rep. James C. Cleveland.

With a strong base in the populous Nashua area and the quiet support of his father (former Gov. Hugh Gregg), he won the nine-way GOP primary with 34 percent of the vote. From then until 1992, Gregg coasted at the polls, winning every primary and general election with at least 60 percent of the vote.

SENATE ELECTIONS

1992 General		
Judd Gregg (R)	249,591	(48%)
John Rauh (D)	234,982	(45%)
Katherine M. Alexander (LIBERT)	18,214	(4%)
Larry Brady (I)	9,340	(2%)
1992 Primary		
Judd Gregg (R)	57,141	(50%)
Harold Eckman (R)	43,264	(38%)
Jean T. White (R)	10,642	(9%)
Mark W. Farnham (R)	2,295	(2%)

Previous Winning Percentages: **1986*** (74%) **1984*** (76%) **1982*** (71%) **1980*** (64%)

* *House elections*

KEY VOTES

1997	
Approve balanced-budget constitutional amendment	Y
Approve chemical weapons treaty	Y
1996	
Approve farm bill	N
Limit punitive damages in product liability cases	Y
Exempt small businesses from higher minimum wage	Y
Approve welfare overhaul	Y
Bar job discrimination based on sexual orientation	N
Override veto of ban on "partial birth" abortions	Y
1995	
Approve GOP budget with tax and spending cuts	Y
Approve constitutional amendment barring flag desecration	Y

CAMPAIGN FINANCE

	Receipts	Receipts from PACs		Expend-itures
1992				
Gregg (R)	$990,836	$367,605	(37%)	$875,675
Rauh (D)	$834,000	0		$833,967
Blevens (I)	$0	0		$484

VOTING STUDIES

	Presidential Support		Party Unity		Conservative Coalition	
Year	**S**	**O**	**S**	**O**	**S**	**O**
1996	34	64	90	8	89	11
1995	22	76	93	5	88	5
1994	40	56	83	16	78	22
1993	22	72	87	10	71	27

INTEREST GROUP RATINGS

Year	ADA	AFL-CIO	CCUS	ACU
1996	5	n/a	92	75
1995	0	0	95	87
1994	15	0	90	79
1993	10	0	91	92

1 John E. Sununu (R)

Of Bedford — Elected 1996, 1st term

Biographical Information

Born: Sept. 10, 1964, Boston, Mass.

Education: Massachusetts Institute of Technology, B.S. 1986, M.S. 1987; Harvard U., M.B.A. 1991.

Occupation: Small business owner; corporate financial officer; management consultant; design engineer.

Family: Wife, Catherine Halloran; two children.

Religion: Roman Catholic.

Political Career: No previous office.

Capitol Office: 1229 Longworth Bldg. 20515; 225-5456.

Committees

Budget

Government Reform & Oversight
Government Management, Information & Technology; National Economic Growth, Natural Resources & Regulatory Affairs

Small Business
Government Programs & Oversight

The Path to Washington: Sununu is the son of one of New Hampshire's most famous politicians. His father, John H. Sununu, served as governor from 1983 to 1989 and went on to become White House chief of staff to President George Bush.

The family name undoubtedly was an asset for the younger Sununu in his 1996 campaign for the open 1st, particularly in the hard-fought Republican primary. But making his first bid for elective office, he tried to emphasize his background in business and mechanical engineering rather than his political connections.

Sununu says he understands the importance of small businesses and their contributions to job creation. He points to his experience helping manage a manufacturing firm.

He plans to focus his efforts in Congress on finding ways to help small businesses and working families. This includes a pledge to oppose any increase in individual or business tax rates.

He also backs reductions in capital gains and inheritance taxes and a $500-per-child tax credit.

Among other proposals to cut spending and help balance the federal budget, Sununu advocates eliminating a handful of Cabinet departments, including Energy, Commerce, Education, and Housing and Urban Development. He also says agriculture, sugar and marketing subsidies to large corporations should end.

Education was a topic of much debate during Sununu's campaign. While he calls for abolishing the Education Department and sending money directly to states and communities in the form of block grants, Sununu does not favor any reductions in education funding.

Sununu will pursue his agenda on three committees: Budget, Government Reform and Oversight, and Small Business.

Like most of the Republicans elected in recent years, he backs term limits for members of Congress. He also says members should reform the congressional pension and mail systems.

Given his name identification and political connections, Sununu walked into the contest for the 1st with an instant edge. But his task proved much more difficult than expected.

When three-term GOP Rep. Bill Zeliff left the district to run for governor (he lost in the primary), seven other Republicans joined Sununu in seeking the party nod. Democratic lawyer Joseph F. Keefe was unopposed for his party's nomination. Sununu's main competition for the Republican nomination was Manchester Mayor Raymond J. Wieczorek and Jack Heath, who had resigned as news director for WMUR-TV, New Hampshire's only statewide television station.

With no major policy differences between the candidates, Sununu's challenge was to stay above the fray as Heath and Wieczorek questioned his commitment to cutting taxes and balancing the budget. The sheer number of Republicans in the race, however, elevated the importance of name identification.

That helped Sununu squeak by Wieczorek to clinch the GOP nod.

Even though the Republican Party has long dominated politics in New Hampshire, Sununu had to contend with a remarkably strong Democratic year in 1996 in the Granite State. President Clinton won a comfortable victory over Republican presidential candidate Bob Dole, and Democrat Jeanne Shaheen easily won the contest to succeed retiring two-term GOP Gov. Stephen Merrill. And two Republican incumbents, Sen. Robert C. Smith and Rep. Charles Bass, beat back strong challenges from Democrats.

Both Sununu and Keefe courted moderate voters while claiming the other represented the extreme end of his party. Keefe tried in vain to link Sununu to House Speaker Newt Gingrich. He also claimed that at age 32, Sununu lacked the experience to serve in Congress.

Sununu shot back that his business experience was better tailored to the needs of district residents than the liberal Keefe's background as a lawyer.

Sununu won a bare majority, with Keefe close behind at 47 percent and Libertarian Gary A. Flanders getting 3 percent.

NEW HAMPSHIRE 1
East — Manchester

The 1st qualifies as New Hampshire's urban district. It covers barely one-quarter of the state's land area yet contains seven of the 11 largest communities in New Hampshire, including the largest, Manchester, which has about 100,000 residents.

As in the neighboring 2nd, most of the district's population lives in the southern tier within 30 miles of the Massachusetts border, with the largest concentration of voters in the "Golden Triangle." It is an area extending roughly from Nashua and Salem on the south to Manchester on the north that straddles the line between the two most populous counties in the state, Hillsborough and Rockingham.

Within the Triangle are many of the high-tech companies and bedroom communities (all within easy commuting range of Boston) that have helped New Hampshire nearly double its population since 1960.

The southern half of the Triangle along the Massachusetts line is in the 2nd District. But the 1st includes many of the faster-growing towns that stretch to the north along Interstate 93 and Route 3. During the 1980s, Derry grew by 57 percent, Londonderry by 45 percent, Merrimack by 44 percent. Each town currently boasts a population in excess of 19,000.

The 1st is gradually recovering from the economic slump that gripped New Hampshire in the early 1990s. The district's biggest hit occurred along the Atlantic seacoast with the 1991 closure of Pease Air Force Base in Newington. Commuter airlines use the facility, but that has not offset the loss of thousands of jobs. The region avoided another blow when the government decided in 1993 to keep open the Portsmouth Naval Shipyard in nearby Kittery, Maine.

The economic uncertainties helped Democrats in 1992 and 1996 carry more than their usual beachheads in Durham (Strafford County), the home of the University of New Hampshire, and the gentrified seaport of Portsmouth (Rockingham County). Bill Clinton in 1992 and 1996 not only swept old mill towns such as Rochester and Somersworth but also carried the historic Yankee town of Exeter, site of the Phillips Exeter Academy. And he carried Manchester, where the huge Franco-American vote is nominally Democratic but subject to blandishments from the city's conservative newspaper, the Manchester Union Leader.

Bush's vote percentage in the 1st from 1988 to 1992 dropped more than 25 percentage points, one of his most precipitous drops in a congressional district nationwide. In 1996, Clinton carried the district by 9 percentage points.

Carroll County, which anchors the northern end of the district, has voted for a Democratic presidential candidate in only one election this century — in 1912, when it opted for Woodrow Wilson. Despite Democratic gains throughout the state in 1996, Carroll again favored a Republican for president, albeit by a Lilliputian margin.

In 1992 redistricting, the 1st shed a half-dozen towns on its western fringe.

1990 Population: 554,360. White 543,105 (98%), Black 4,052 (1%), Other 7,203 (1%). Hispanic origin

HOUSE ELECTIONS

1996 General		
John E. Sununu (R)	123,939	(50%)
Joseph F. Keefe (D)	115,462	(47%)
Gary A. Flanders (LIBERT)	8,176	(3%)
1996 Primary		
John E. Sununu (R)	14,797	(28%)
Raymond J. Wieczorek (R)	14,319	(27%)
Jack Heath (R)	13,814	(26%)
Tom Colantuono (R)	5,070	(9%)
Vivian Clark (R)	2,195	(4%)
Toni Pappas (R)	2,096	(4%)
George A. Lovejoy (R)	853	(2%)

CAMPAIGN FINANCE

	Receipts	Receipts from PACs	Expend-itures
1996			
Sununu (R)	$609,524	$146,864 (24%)	$545,865
Keefe (D)	$586,642	$203,715 (35%)	$580,749

DISTRICT VOTE FOR PRESIDENT

	1996		1992
D	121,602 (49%)	D	101,415 (38%)
R	101,295 (40%)	R	104,653 (39%)
I	23,898 (10%)	I	61,571 (23%)

KEY VOTES

1997

Ban "partial birth" abortions Y

2 Charles Bass (R)

Of Peterborough — Elected 1994, 2nd term

Biographical Information
Born: Jan. 8, 1952, Boston, Mass.
Education: Dartmouth College, A.B. 1974.
Occupation: Congressional aide; architectural products executive.
Family: Wife, Lisa Levesque; two children.
Religion: Episcopalian.
Political Career: Sought Republican nomination for U.S. House, 1980; N.H. House, 1983-89; N.H. Senate, 1989-93.
Capitol Office: 218 Cannon Bldg. 20515; 225-5206.

Committees
Budget
Select Intelligence
Human Intelligence, Analysis & Counterintelligence
Transportation & Infrastructure
Aviation; Surface Transportation

In Washington: Bass' qualified support of abortion rights sets him apart from the majority of Republicans in Congress, and it was partly the reason he drew opposition from the GOP right when he sought renomination to a second term in 1996. Bass quashed that primary challenge and also narrowly won in the general election by stressing his work to downsize the federal government, promote business interests and stand up for gunowners' rights.

Devoted to the low-tax credo of the New Hampshire Republican Party, Bass got a seat on the Budget Committee in the 104th, and quickly sought to impose that doctrine at the federal level by supporting a version of a balanced-budget constitutional amendment that would have required a three-fifths vote in both the House and Senate to approve any tax increase. He said the three-fifths limitation "not only ensures a balanced budget, but helps ensure that it is done through a shrinking of government and not a growth in taxes."

At the start of the 105th Congress, Bass received two other plum committee assignments: a seat on the Intelligence Committee and one on the Transportation and Infrastructure Committee, which is considering a major reauthorization of federal highway and mass transit programs.

Throughout the 104th, Bass usually was a loyal vote for the GOP leadership in its tussles with the Clinton administration over federal spending. In June 1996, though, he did break ranks, joining 59 other Republicans supporting an effort to freeze fiscal 1997 defense spending at the prior-year level. He also voted against a National Security Committee proposal for more B-2 bombers. "We are standing here on the threshold of authorizing an additional $553 million to pay for a bomber program that has not been in the existing budget," Bass warned the House. "This budget-busting program has the potential to add over $30 billion to the defense budget."

One of Bass' budget-cutting moves earned him some criticism at home: He voted against restoring funding to the Low Income Home Energy Assistance Program, which helps low-income families pay heating and cooling bills and weatherize their homes.

Bass typically has sided with business in its legislative disputes with organized labor. He twice has voted for a GOP proposal to allow businesses to offer workers compensatory time off instead of pay for overtime work. In May 1996, he opposed increasing the minimum wage by 90 cents an hour, and prior to that vote, he backed a GOP leadership effort to exempt small businesses from paying the higher minimum wage. In August 1996, though, when the wage increase won final passage, Bass voted "yea." The final version of the wage bill included other provisions sought by Republicans, including $10 billion in business tax cuts over five years, a $5,000 tax credit to offset the cost of adoption and an expansion of Individual Retirement Accounts.

Like a number of his peers in the Class of 1994, Bass called for abolishing the departments of Energy and Commerce. "I truly doubt most people can pinpoint exactly what the Commerce Department really does," he once said, and he called the Energy Department "low on efficiency, high on mismanagement, and lacking in mission."

The issue of gun owners' rights played a big part in Bass' 1994 victory over Democratic Rep. Dick Swett, who voted in May 1994 to ban certain semiautomatic, assault-style weapons. Gunowners rallied to Bass, and in the 104th he voted to repeal the assault weapons ban, saying he did not believe it addressed the problem of crime.

While Bass generally shares the view of GOP conservatives that the federal government discourages economic development by saddling business with too many regulations, his record in the environmental area is mixed. Early in the 104th he joined the GOP effort to relax many of the regulations under the clean water act, but in July 1995 he was one of 51 Republicans supporting a Democratic effort to strike legislative language limiting the regulatory authority of the Environmental Protection Agency (EPA). He also sided with environmentalists on a June 1996 vote

NEW HAMPSHIRE 2
West — Concord; Nashua

Through most of the century, the 2nd has been regarded as one of the most rock-ribbed Republican districts in the country. Only once before 1990 did the district elect a Democrat to Congress — that was in 1912 during the GOP-Bull Moose bloodletting and it only lasted for two years.

But in recent years, the 2nd has been quite politically competitive. In 1990, western New Hampshire voters elected Democrat Dick Swett to the House. Two years later they not only re-elected him overwhelmingly but also gave Bill Clinton a 10,000-vote plurality. That helped Clinton become the first Democratic presidential candidate since Lyndon B. Johnson in 1964 to carry the Granite State.

In 1994, the 2nd returned to its historic congressional roots, ousting Swett in favor of Republican Bass. In 1996, Bass and Clinton both won the district, each taking about 50 percent of the vote. Clinton won all eight counties represented in the district while Bass carried all but Cheshire County. Votes for independent presidential candidate Ross Perot dropped from 23 percent in 1992 to 10 percent in 1996.

New Hampshire's sharp economic downturn in the early 1990s affected normal voting patterns — shaking loose a number of Republican-oriented rural voters while bringing back to the Democratic fold blue-collar voters in old mill towns such as Berlin (Coos County) and Claremont (Sullivan County).

In 1994, Swett carried many of the small cities across the 2nd but lost rural portions of the district to Bass. The most reliable source of Democratic votes in the 2nd has been the liberal college town of Hanover (Grafton County), home of Dartmouth College. It is arguably the only recession-proof community in the district.

The economy of the heavily forested "North Country" is closely tied to paper manufacturing and wood products. The populous southern tier along the Massachusetts border has experienced ups and downs with high-tech industries deeply involved in computers and defense electronics. In between, many of western New Hampshire's picturesque small towns depend on tourist dollars — from summer vacationers at the myriad lakes to wintertime skiers in the White Mountains.

Loaded with well-educated, upwardly mobile refugees from "Taxachusetts," many of the towns along the southern tier remained reliably Republican during the recession. The largest city in the 2nd, Nashua (with almost 80,000 residents) in Hillsborough County voted for Clinton in 1994 and 1996.

Newcomers in the northern part of the district, including the state capital of Concord (Merrimack County) and the college town of Keene (Cheshire County), are as likely to be attuned to environmental concerns as they are to taxes.

Yet it is hard to see the 2nd becoming a nest of Yankee bolshevism. Three of the four counties that conservative commentator Patrick J. Buchanan carried in the 1996 New Hampshire presidential primary were wholly or predominately within the 2nd, including his top two counties percentage-wise, Coos (41 percent of the vote) and Hillsborough (30 percent).

1990 Population: 554,892. White 544,328 (98%), Black 3,146 (<1%), Other 7,418 (1%). Hispanic origin 5,562 (1%). 18 and over 414,613 (75%), 62 and over 77,176 (14%). Median age: 33.

involving protection of a threatened seabird species, the marbled murrelet.

Early in the 105th, Bass introduced a measure aimed at protecting a huge swath of forest land in northern New England and New York. The bill would authorize the states to manage the largely privately held forest that runs from the Canadian border to the Catskills. He also re-introduced a measure that President Clinton vetoed in the 104th Congress that would prevent the government from taking land for the Silvio O. Conte Fish and Wildlife Refuge from unwilling property owners. He said the bill would address landowners' fears that the Fish and Wildlife Service will abuse its power of eminent domain.

It is Bass' periodic votes with abortion-rights advocates that most clearly distinguish him from the bulk of Republicans in Congress. In March 1996, he was one of 49 Republicans voting to allow states to use Medicaid funds to finance abortions for pregnancies resulting from rape or incest. In July 1996 he backed a Democratic amendment allowing abortions at overseas military hospitals, if the woman paid for the procedure. He has, however, voted to outlaw a particular abortion technique that opponents call "partial birth" abortion.

At Home: Bass' 1994 victory over Swett returned western New Hampshire's House seat not only to Republican hands but also to the Bass family. His father, Perkins Bass, represented the same district from 1955 to 1963. Bass comes from a line of New Hampshire political notables — his father's father, Robert P. Bass, was governor from 1911 to 1913 — but in spite of that, it took Charles two tries to win a seat in Congress.

His first attempt came in 1980, when the seat came open with the retirement of GOP Rep. James C. Cleveland (1963-81). Bass had served several years as chief of staff to Republican Rep.

David F. Emery of Maine, but he was outmaneuvered by another New Hampshire "blue blood," Judd Gregg. Representing the populous Nashua area on the Executive Council, Gregg had a larger base of support than his GOP primary rivals. And quietly aided by his prominent father, former Gov. Hugh Gregg (1953-55), he boasted better political contacts. Gregg won the primary with one-third of the vote, while Bass finished third.

For the next dozen years, Bass helped run a small manufacturing business in the southwest corner of the state while fashioning a political career in the New Hampshire Legislature. But he irked many Republicans after the 1990 election by bolting from GOP ranks in the state Senate and voting with Democrats in an unsuccessful effort to elect a leader. In 1992 he was beaten for renomination in the Republican primary by a conservative challenger.

When he decided to go for Swett's seat in 1994, Bass benefited from a split on the GOP right between two candidates who almost evenly divided nearly half the primary vote. Bass easily outpolled a lesser-known rival for moderate Republican votes to win nomination with 29 percent.

Meanwhile, Swett — a surprise 1990 winner in the historically Republican district — was clearly vulnerable because of his controversial vote for the assault weapons ban. And Bass did his best to tie Swett in voters' minds to the then-unpopular Clinton, running advertising that showed the two embracing. Bass was sometimes joined on the campaign trail by his father, who helped him amplify his campaign slogan: "From New Hampshire ... for New Hampshire." The slogan was a not-so-subtle slap at Swett, who was raised in New Hampshire but lived in California for many years and is the son-in-law of Democratic Rep. Tom Lantos of California.

Swett fought back gamely, charging that Bass was trying to inherit a seat he did not earn. But the Democrat was swimming against a strong 1994 GOP tide, and Bass won by 5 percentage points.

In 1996, Bass drew four Republican primary opponents, the most aggressive of them the man who ran second to him in the 1994 primary, Mike Hammond, a former congressional aide and state co-chairman for Patrick J. Buchanan's 1996 presidential campaign. But Hammond's effort to tear down Bass on the abortion issue had limited appeal; the incumbent got 66 percent to Hammond's 26 percent, then headed into a general-election contest against former state Rep. Deborah "Arnie" Arnesen, the 1992 Democratic nominee for governor.

Arnesen said Bass had shifted too far to the right since being elected to Congress and no longer represented the views of the district. Bass portrayed Arnesen as big-government liberal and liked to remind voters that when she ran for governor, she proposed instituting an income tax, a plan she said she offered in order to help reduce property taxes. Bass won a second term, taking 50 percent to Arnesen's 43 percent.

HOUSE ELECTIONS

1996 General		
Charles Bass (R)	122,957	(50%)
Deborah "Arnie" Arnesen (D)	105,824	(43%)
Carole Lamirande (I)	10,753	(4%)
Roy Kendel (IA)	3,726	(2%)
1996 Primary		
Charles Bass (R)	30,525	(66%)
Mike Hammond (R)	12,138	(26%)
Dana Albert (R)	1,539	(3%)
Robert J. Kulak (R)	985	(2%)
Tom Alciere (R)	546	(1%)
1994 General		
Charles Bass (R)	83,121	(51%)
Dick Swett (D)	74,243	(46%)
John Lewicke (LIBERT)	2,986	(2%)

CAMPAIGN FINANCE

	Receipts	Receipts from PACs	Expend-itures
1996			
Bass (R)	$691,374	$260,627 (38%)	$625,147
Arnesen (D)	$719,967	$208,757 (29%)	$706,623
Lamirande (I)	$6,932	0	$7,091
1994			
Bass (R)	$450,208	$78,131 (17%)	$448,431
Swett (D)	$956,780	$357,002 (37%)	$1,029,471

DISTRICT VOTE FOR PRESIDENT

	1996		1992
D	124,564 (50%)	**D**	107,625 (41%)
R	95,191 (38%)	**R**	97,831 (37%)
I	24,490 (10%)	**I**	59,766 (23%)

VOTING STUDIES

	Presidential Support		Party Unity		Conservative Coalition	
Year	**S**	**O**	**S**	**O**	**S**	**O**
1996	34	66	91	9	78	20
1995	25	75	90	9	90	9

INTEREST GROUP RATINGS

Year	ADA	AFL-CIO	CCUS	ACU
1996	0	n/a	100	100
1995	15	0	96	72

KEY VOTES

1997	
Ban "partial birth" abortions	Y
1996	
Approve farm bill	Y
Deny public education to illegal immigrants	Y
Repeal ban on certain assault-style weapons	Y
Increase minimum wage	N
Freeze defense spending	Y
Approve welfare overhaul	Y
1995	
Approve balanced-budget constitutional amendment	Y
Relax Clean Water Act regulations	Y
Oppose limits on environmental regulations	Y
Reduce projected Medicare spending	Y
Approve GOP budget with tax and spending cuts	Y

NEW JERSEY

Governor: Christine Todd Whitman (R)
First elected: 1993
Length of term: 4 years
Term expires: 1/98
Salary: $130,000 (By law, governor's salary is $130,000; Whitman accepts $85,000.)
Term limit: 2 consecutive terms
Phone: (609) 292-6000
Born: September 26, 1946; New York, N.Y.
Education: Wheaton College, B.A. 1968.
Occupation: Newspaper columnist; radio talk show host; teacher.
Family: Husband, John Whitman; two children.
Religion: Unspecified.
Political Career: Somerset County Board of Chosen Freeholders, 1982-88 (director; deputy director); New Jersey Board of Public Utilities president, 1988-90; Republican nominee for U.S. Senate, 1990.

No lieutenant governor

Senate President: Donald T. DiFrancesco (R)
Salary: $46,666
Phone: (609) 292-5199

State election official: (609) 292-3760
Democratic headquarters: (609) 392-3367
Republican headquarters: (609) 989-7300

REDISTRICTING

New Jersey lost one House seat in reapportionment, dropping from 14 districts to 13. Legislature established bipartisan commission Jan. 13, 1992; commission issued map March 20.

STATE LEGISLATURE

Legislature. Meets year-round.

Senate: 40 members, 4-year terms
1996 breakdown: 24R, 16D; 39 men, 1 woman
Salary: $35,000
Phone: (609) 292-5199

General Assembly: 80 members, 2-year terms
1996 breakdown: 50R, 30D; 63 men, 17 women
Salary: $35,000
Phone: (609) 292-5339

URBAN STATISTICS

City	Population
Newark	275,221
Mayor Sharpe James, D	
Jersey City	228,537
Mayor Bret Schundler, R	
Paterson	140,891
Mayor Martin G. Barnes, R	
Elizabeth	110,002
Mayor J. Christian Bollwage, D	
Woodbridge	93,086
Mayor James McGreevey, D	

U.S. CONGRESS

Senate: 2 D, 0 R
House: 6 D, 7 R

TERM LIMITS

For state offices: No

ELECTIONS

1996 Presidential Vote

Bill Clinton	54%
Bob Dole	36%
Ross Perot	9%

1992 Presidential Vote

Bill Clinton	43%
George Bush	41%
Ross Perot	16%

1988 Presidential Vote

George Bush	56%
Michael S. Dukakis	43%

POPULATION

1990 population		7,730,188
1980 population		7,364,823
Percent change		+5%
Rank among states:		9
White		79%
Black		13%
Hispanic		10%
Asian or Pacific islander		4%
Urban		89%
Rural		11%
Born in state		87%
Foreign-born		13%
Under age 18	1,799,462	23%
Ages 18-64	4,898,701	63%
65 and older	1,032,025	13%
Median age		34.5

MISCELLANEOUS

Capital: Trenton
Number of counties: 21
Per capita income: $25,372 (1991)
Rank among states: 2
Total area: 7,787 sq. miles
Rank among states: 46

NEW JERSEY

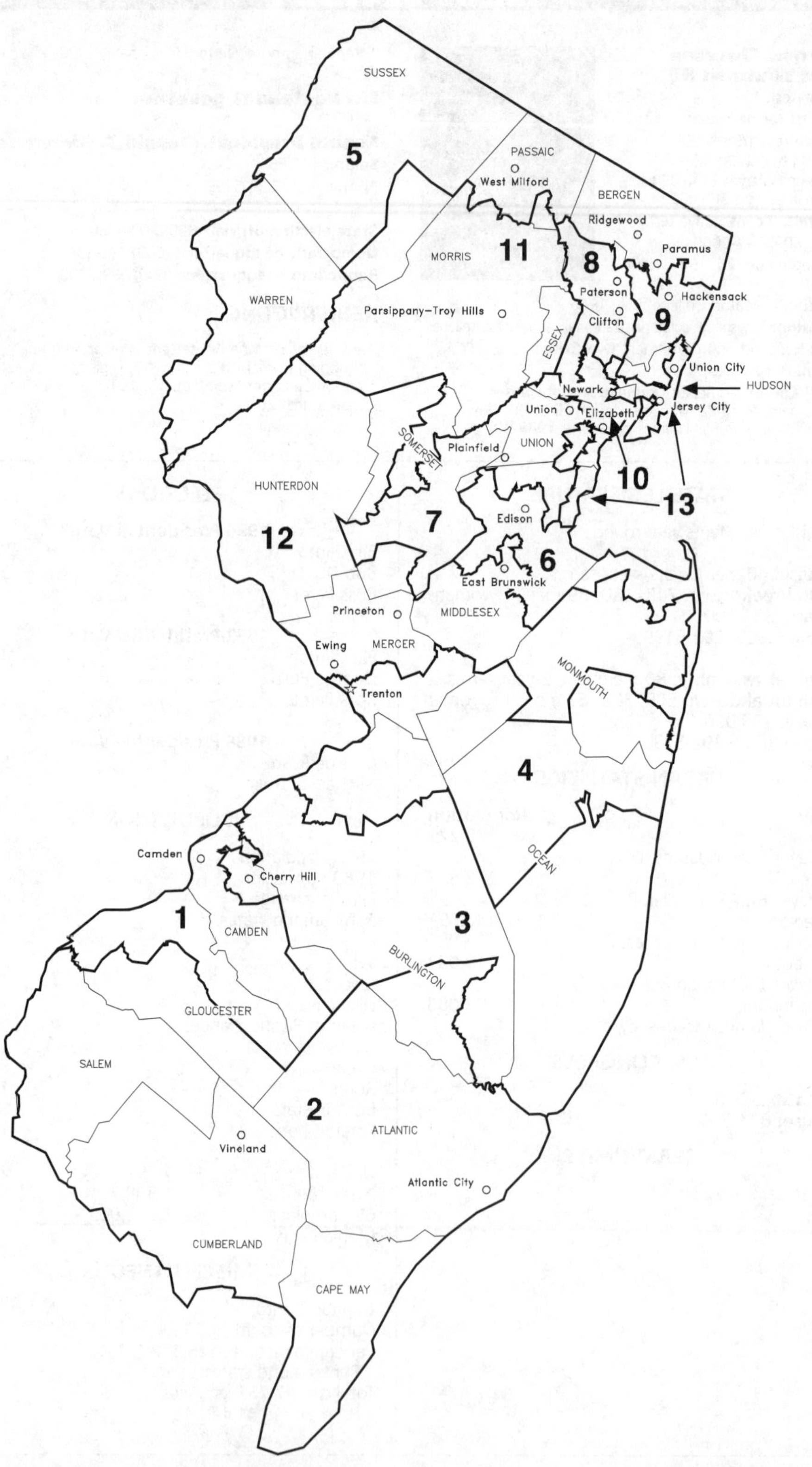
SUSSEX
5
PASSAIC
West Milford
BERGEN
Ridgewood
Paramus
11
MORRIS
8
Paterson
Hackensack
WARREN
Parsippany–Troy Hills
Clifton
9
ESSEX
Union City
HUDSON
Newark
Union
Elizabeth
Jersey City
SOMERSET
Plainfield
UNION
10
HUNTERDON
13
7
Edison
12
6
East Brunswick
Princeton
MIDDLESEX
Ewing
MERCER
MONMOUTH
Trenton
4
OCEAN
Camden
Cherry Hill
1
CAMDEN
3
BURLINGTON
GLOUCESTER
SALEM
2
ATLANTIC
Vineland
Atlantic City
CUMBERLAND
CAPE MAY

Frank R. Lautenberg (D)

Of Cliffside Park — Elected 1982; 3rd term

Biographical Information
Born: Jan. 23, 1924, Paterson, N.J.
Education: Columbia U., B.S. 1949.
Military Service: Army, 1942-46.
Occupation: Computer firm executive.
Family: Separated; four children.
Religion: Jewish.
Political Career: No previous office.
Capitol Office: 506 Hart Bldg. 20510; 224-4744.

Committees
Appropriations
Commerce, Justice, State & Judiciary; Defense; Foreign Operations; Transportation (ranking); VA, HUD & Independent Agencies
Budget (ranking)
Environment & Public Works
Drinking Water, Fisheries & Wildlife; Superfund, Waste Control & Risk Assessment (ranking)
Select Intelligence

In Washington: Lautenberg moved into a new role in the 105th Congress, taking over as ranking Democrat on the Senate Budget Committee, working under Republican Chairman Pete V. Domenici of New Mexico.

In May 1997, when the White House and congressional Republican leaders came to terms on a plan designed to balance the federal budget by 2002, Lautenberg endorsed the agreement, albeit without evincing great enthusiasm. Nonetheless, because Lautenberg is generally seen as a fiscal-policy liberal, his willingness to stand with Domenici as the plan was announced was taken as a sign that the agreement probably would be broadly acceptable among Senate Democrats. Indeed, the budget resolution passed, 78-22, in late May. It gave the GOP tax and spending cuts and gave President Clinton more money for certain domestic priorities, including funds to provide health insurance for uninsured children and to restore certain federal benefits denied legal immigrants under the 1996 welfare overhaul bill.

During the 104th, Lautenberg was often sharply critical of Republican budget practices. He voted in 1995 against the GOP's budget-reconciliation bill, which tried to balance the federal budget by 2002 in part by reducing the rate of spending growth on Medicare and Medicaid, and he has opposed the balanced-budget constitutional amendment. He also voted against the welfare overhaul legislation.

Lautenberg has resisted major funding reductions in the area of environmental protection. He has been a strong advocate for financing cleanup. For the fiscal 1996 VA-HUD appropriations bill, for example, he unsuccessfully tried to add $432 million to the nearly $1 billion for the superfund hazardous waste cleanup fund; $328 million to the $2.3 billion to help local communities build sewage treatment plants; and another $1 million to the $1 million for the Council on Environmental Quality, which provides environmental advice to the White House and federal agencies. Lautenberg proposed to offset these costs by limiting any proposed tax cuts to families earning more than $150,000 per year.

"If forced to choose between a tax break for the rich and strengthening environmental protections," Lautenberg said, "I'm convinced most Americans would strongly support the environment."

On another issue, he pushed through an amendment to the Omnibus Fiscal 1997 Appropriations bill (including Treasury-Postal Service-General Government) that bars anyone convicted of domestic violence — including spouse or child abuse — from possessing a firearm. The legislation survived a spirited resistance on the floor backed by the National Rifle Association.

"I believe that this legislation will save the lives of many battered wives and abused children," Lautenberg said. "We had to overcome intense opposition from one of the most powerful special interests in American politics."

And Lautenberg won approval of an amendment to the fiscal 1997 transportation appropriations bill that fully funded the administration's request for $188.5 million for airport security. Lautenberg was a member of the President's Commission on Aviation Security, formed after the bombing of Pan Am Flight 103.

Lautenberg was a member of the bipartisan Senate task force empaneled to work out new gift and lobby regulations during the 104th Congress. The legislation had been killed by a Republican-led filibuster at the end of the 103rd Congress. The Senate voted to ban most gifts from lobbyists. It also passed legislation toughening lobbying regulation requirements; an identical bill passed the House and was signed into law by President Clinton.

"When lobbyists take a senator to dinner, they are not just buying a meal for a nice person," Lautenberg said during debate on the bill. "The meal involves time, and time means access. Ordinary citizens do not have that access."

Lautenberg was a major mover of the fiscal 1994 highway bill from his post as chairman of the Transportation Subcommittee on Senate Appropriations. Along with Rep. Bob Carr, D-Mich., his House Appropriations counterpart in the 103rd, Lautenberg waged a battle to streamline the way in which dollars were divvied up in the $13.9 billion spending bill. To the consternation of some members on both sides of the aisle, both Carr and Lautenberg sought to take some of the politics out of the legislation. Lautenberg, in particular, argued that unauthorized projects should not receive funding. The final bill lowered the amount of money directed to members' pet transportation projects and did not provide for any new highway or bridge projects that were not authorized.

Lautenberg's attention to the state has been his hallmark — he was first elected in 1982 by pledging to put "New Jersey first." And he has tried to fulfill this pledge by concentrating on the responsibilities he has assumed in transportation and pollution policy.

But learning to make the system work should not be confused with liking it. Lautenberg came to politics from a business career, and, like many self-made men, he has trouble dealing with the slow grind of legislation. The tough, hard-driving entrepreneur has elbowed his way into issues where his presence was not always welcome. While he generally has done so without alienating colleagues, there have been exceptions.

As Republican Christine Todd Whitman in 1993 pilloried Democratic Gov. James J. Florio for tax increases he imposed, Lautenberg very publicly opposed Clinton's 1993 budget-reconciliation bill, saying the measure did not contain enough spending cuts.

In 1989, Lautenberg showed he had learned to play hardball when he steered a smoking ban on domestic airline flights through the Senate. A former two-pack-a-day smoker himself, he counseled tobacco farmers to "grow soybeans or something." This brought down the wrath of Republican Jesse Helms of North Carolina and other tobacco state senators, who howled that Lautenberg had bypassed their committees by attaching the ban to an appropriations bill. Lautenberg snapped: "The committee system is safe. The flying public is not."

Further engendering the ire of the tobacco state contingent, he shepherded an amendment through the Senate in 1993 to ban smoking in most federal buildings.

New Jersey has long resented the arrival of New York City's sludge on its shores, and Lautenberg has helped enact legislation to prevent recurrences. He has also pressed for laws against ocean dumping of plastics that do not degrade like organic materials. Allied with environmentalists, he was deeply involved in the 1994 effort to reauthorize the superfund program. Lautenberg worked behind the scenes with the Clinton administration to craft a fragile overhaul bill aimed at hastening the pace of cleanup at some of the nation's worst superfund sites. But the clock ran out on the compromise measure, and the bill died with the end of the 103rd Congress.

Like most in the New Jersey delegation, Lautenberg has been heavily involved in efforts to protect New Jersey's ability to export garbage to landfills in other states.

In the 102nd Congress, Lautenberg pushed a bill through the Senate to expand the EPA's authority to monitor and help improve indoor air quality, but the House did not act on it. He also steered passage of a bill to reauthorize programs aimed at reducing levels of radon, a colorless, odorless gas that can cause lung damage, but the House failed to act on this as well.

In the 103rd, Lautenberg's other subcommittee chairmanship, the Transportation Subcommittee on Appropriations, allowed him to push for more transportation funds for densely populated East Coast states, especially New Jersey, and to fight attempts to eliminate federal funding for Amtrak.

At Home: Lautenberg survived the 1994 GOP sweep that engulfed many of his Democratic colleagues. This was no small feat, particularly in light of the statewide gains that New Jersey Republicans have made in recent years.

State Assembly Speaker Garabed "Chuck" Haytaian, a conservative who took few cues from moderate GOP Gov. Whitman, struggled to formulate a campaign message beyond the general notion of lower taxes. Though he drew little visible support from Whitman, Haytaian did his best to tar Lautenberg as a free-spending liberal. Lautenberg touted transportation projects that he brought back to the state and emphasized his status as an independent Democrat unafraid to cross the president.

By the campaign's final months, Haytaian's chief obstacle appeared to be his lack of familiarity to New Jersey voters. Still, Haytaian benefited from a national mood receptive to Republicans. The contest tightened down the stretch, and in the end, Lautenberg managed to win re-election with 50 percent of the vote, to 47 percent for Haytaian.

Lautenberg's races have always been close. In 1988, he beat back an aggressive challenge from Republican Pete Dawkins, who was the national GOP's premier "résumé candidate" for the Senate. Dawkins' life had been an unbroken string of accomplishments — winner of the Heisman Trophy (while playing for the Army in 1958), a Rhodes scholar, the Army's youngest brigadier general, a high-ranking Pentagon official, a Wall Street financial executive. He tried to mold his golden image to political advantage, describing himself as a potential national leader. He denigrated Lautenberg as "the junior senator."

But Dawkins soon found his superstar image challenged. An article in a Manhattan business magazine described him as a failure in a variety of military and business positions, who still was promoted because of the public relations value of his all-America image. It was said that he had shopped for a state in which to seek public office and settled on New Jersey, moving in just before announcing his Senate candidacy.

Dawkins spent $1 million-plus in the spring to get his name in front of voters, but he entered the fall trailing Lautenberg in the polls. At that point, Lautenberg went on the attack, beginning with an unusual ad showing Dawkins himself making a flowery statement about the glories of New Jersey. "Be Real, Pete" was superimposed on the film clip, conveying Lautenberg's theme that Dawkins was a carpetbagger and a phony.

The two then got into a tit-for-tat war of negativism that sank to its lowest when Dawkins charged multimillionaire Lautenberg with using his Senate seat for personal profit. Lautenberg's lead weathered the fierce exchanges, and in spite of George Bush's solid victory in New Jersey, Lautenberg won with 54 percent of the vote.

While Lautenberg had been involved for years as a Democratic activist and fundraiser — his $90,000 contribution to George McGovern's campaign in 1972 earned him a place on President Richard M. Nixon's "enemies list" — he had never sought office before his 1982 bid for the seat vacated by appointed Republican Sen. Nicholas F. Brady.

After winning with a plurality in a Democratic primary, he came from behind to defeat Republican Rep. Millicent Fenwick.

Both candidates were wealthy. But while Fenwick inherited her fortune, Lautenberg, the son of an immigrant silk mill worker, was a self-made man. The Democrat spent about $4 million of his own money to drive home that contrast. At one campaign stop, he pointed to the gap between his front teeth and said, "If my parents had money I wouldn't have this. I keep it as a badge of my roots."

Irreverent, witty and eccentric, Fenwick was frequently profiled and quoted in the national media and was a heroine to numerous good-government causes. She started out with a sizable lead over Lautenberg.

But Lautenberg overcame Fenwick's reformist credentials and personal popularity by painting her and the GOP as insensitive to working-class people. He touted himself as an expert on creating jobs, talking about how he had turned his company, Automatic Data Processing, from a three-man business into one of the world leaders in computer services.

To erase organized labor's doubts about him, Lautenberg advocated a minimum tax on corporations and elimination of the third year of President Ronald Reagan's tax cut for those earning more than $40,000 per year. Labor finally went along with him against Fenwick, overlooking the absence of unions at his company. Lautenberg said no one had tried to organize the firm.

With the endorsements of several major newspapers, the unions and such liberal forces as the National Organization for Women, Lautenberg showed that Fenwick's lead was soft. He hammered on her votes for the 1981 Reagan economic package. She could not equal his media effort, as she would not dip as heavily into her wealth and refused donations from political action committees. Lautenberg rejected her request that each side limit spending to $1.6 million. He won with 51 percent of the vote.

SENATE ELECTIONS

1994 General		
Frank R. Lautenberg (D)	1,033,487	(50%)
Garabed "Chuck" Haytaian (R)	966,244	(47%)
1994 Primary		
Frank R. Lautenberg (D)	151,416	(81%)
Bill Campbell (D)	26,066	(14%)
Lynne A. Speed (D)	9,563	(5%)

Previous Winning Percentages: 1988 (54%) **1982** (51%)

KEY VOTES

1997	
Approve balanced-budget constitutional amendment	N
Approve chemical weapons treaty	Y
1996	
Approve farm bill	N
Limit punitive damages in product liability cases	N
Exempt small businesses from higher minimum wage	N
Approve welfare overhaul	N
Bar job discrimination based on sexual orientation	Y
Override veto of ban on "partial birth" abortions	N
1995	
Approve GOP budget with tax and spending cuts	N
Approve constitutional amendment barring flag desecration	N

VOTING STUDIES

	Presidential Support		Party Unity		Conservative Coalition	
Year	**S**	**O**	**S**	**O**	**S**	**O**
1996	90	10	91	7	11	87
1995	87	13	94	6	7	93
1994	81	18	84	16	19	78
1993	85	15	86	14	20	80
1992	22	78	92	8	5	95
1991	31	69	89	11	10	90

INTEREST GROUP RATINGS

Year	ADA	AFL-CIO	CCUS	ACU
1996	95	n/a	15	0
1995	100	100	16	0
1994	95	88	30	4
1993	95	82	45	24
1992	100	92	30	4
1991	95	67	10	5

CAMPAIGN FINANCE

	Receipts	Receipts from PACs		Expend-itures
1994				
Lautenberg (D)	$6,443,199	$1,248,189	(19%)	$7,278,332
Haytaian (R)	$5,110,518	$450,300	(9%)	$5,110,378

Robert G. Torricelli (D)

Of Englewood — Elected 1996, 1st term

Biographical Information

Born: Aug. 26, 1951, Paterson, N.J.
Education: Rutgers U., A.B. 1974, J.D. 1977; Harvard U., M.P.A. 1980.
Occupation: Lawyer.
Family: Divorced.
Religion: Methodist.
Political Career: U.S. House, 1983-97.
Capitol Office: 113 Dirksen Bldg. 20510; 224-3224.

Committees

Governmental Affairs
International Security, Proliferation & Federal Services; Investigations
Judiciary
Antitrust, Business Rights & Competition; Constitution, Federalism & Property Rights; Youth Violence
Rules & Administration

The Path to Washington: The man they call "The Torch" didn't take long to light up the Senate.

In March 1997, only three months into his Senate career, he cast the deciding vote against a proposal to amend the Constitution to require a balanced federal budget.

It was no surprise that the sure-footed and media-savvy Torricelli — the last of four undecided Democratic freshmen who had campaigned in favor of the measure or voted for it in the House — ended up in the limelight. Previously, Torricelli's congressional reputation had been shaped as much by his forceful fundraising style and celebrity romance with Bianca Jagger as by his accomplishments on the House International Relations Committee.

"My impression was Torricelli was clearly very cagey and enjoyed every minute of it," said amendment supporter John B. Breaux, D La.

Torricelli finally announced his decision to oppose the constitutional amendment after losing, 34-66, in an attempt to amend the measure to permit deficits for a "capital budget" dedicated to infrastructure projects and to make it easier to waive balanced-budget requirements in times of recession or a national security emergency.

"At the end of the day ... I was chosen to serve in the United States Senate to exercise my best judgment," Torricelli said. "The balanced-budget amendment has good aspects, but it is simply not good enough in dealing with fundamental constitutional change for our country."

Torricelli remains in the spotlight as a member of the Governmental Affairs Committee, which, under Chairman Fred Thompson, R-Tenn., is looking at irregularities in 1996 campaign financing, including allegations that some fundraising practices came up to the edge of the law.

Like his fellow Democrats, Torricelli hoped to expand the focus of the inquiry beyond the White House and Democratic National Committee. When allegations surfaced in May 1997 that Haley Barbour, while chairman of the Republican National Committee, used a tax-exempt foundation to funnel $2.2 million from a Hong Kong businessman into GOP campaigns, Torricelli called it "a real test for Chairman Thompson and for the fundamental integrity of the committee's investigation."

But Torricelli has been known to spark controversy himself. Exuding intelligence and a brash self-assurance, he muscled his way into several major policy debates during seven terms in the House. Along the way he attracted allies — mainly Democrats who admired his intensity and partisan zeal — and detractors, including Republicans nettled by his rhetoric and some "good government" types who saw his aggressive fundraising as emblematic of the system he is probing as part of Thompson's committee.

Torricelli also has made news with his focus on Latin America. During the 1980s, he opposed American assistance to anti-communists in Nicaragua and El Salvador, and in March 1995, he disclosed that a Guatemalan colonel who had been on the CIA payroll was responsible for the murder of an American innkeeper in Guatemala.

After the latter incident, House Republicans charged that Torricelli had violated the House secrecy oath imposed at the start of the 104th Congress. Torricelli said he had not gotten the information from anyone connected with the Intelligence Committee, but through other sources. The House ethics committee in July 1995 said Torricelli should not be punished because the oath was vague.

Torricelli has continued to look south in the Senate. He was one of five dissenters in March 1997 when the chamber significantly weakened a House-passed resolution threatening Mexico's status as a drug-war ally. Torricelli charged that any step short of decertification would permit the United States and Mexico to continue the "silent conspiracy" in which both nations falsely claim that progress is being achieved in the drug war. "Mexico pretends to be interdicting narcotics," Torricelli said. "We pretend to believe them.

"It is argued that to decertify Mexico would offend Mexican sensibilities," Torricelli added. But he said that was less important than affirming the "unmistakable truth that Mexico is not an ally in the drug war."

Torricelli, though, sided with the Clinton administration on another key foreign policy issue in early 1997, voting in April to ratify the Chemical Weapons Convention.

Torricelli is a staunch supporter of Israel and a strong critic of Fidel Castro, a reflection of two powerful voting blocs in New Jersey: Jews and Cuban-Americans.

In addition to Governmental Affairs, Torricelli sits on the Judiciary and Rules committees. If his House tenure is a guide, he is likely to compile a liberal voting record on social issues, tempered with bouts of fiscal conservatism.

Torricelli's environmental record, which includes opposing the dumping of waste off the New Jersey coast and supporting efforts to preserve a forest along the New York-New Jersey border, has won him favor with the Sierra Club.

He is a supporter of gun control, including a five-day waiting period for handgun purchases, and the ban on certain semiautomatic assault-style weapons. He also supported efforts to ban anyone convicted of domestic violence from buying a handgun. And he backed the 1994 crime bill, which authorized $30.2 billion over six years; mainly to hire more police officers, build prisons and help communities prevent crime. He also favors the death penalty.

Torricelli is a strong ally of organized labor. He opposed NAFTA and three times between 1989 and 1994 got a perfect score from the AFL-CIO.

In moving up to the Senate, Torricelli won — some would say survived — one of the nastiest campaigns in New Jersey history.

When Democratic Sen. Bill Bradley announced his retirement, Torricelli — who had long been known to harbor aspirations for higher office and whose desire for a change seemed to intensify when the 1994 election relegated Democrats to the House minority — jumped into the race. His November foe was GOP Rep. Dick Zimmer. The race was one of the most expensive in the nation.

Though both candidates were relatively moderate, Zimmer insisted that Torricelli was "liberal and not worth it," while Torricelli called Zimmer "a mouthpiece for [Speaker] Newt Gingrich's extreme right" because the Republican had voted for the House GOP's "Contract With America" 94 percent of the time.

The rhetorical barbs obscured the fact that on certain social issues, at least, the two men were not very far apart. Both, for instance, supported a woman's right to choose abortion.

Zimmer was endorsed by New Jersey's GOP Gov. Christine Todd Whitman, but Torricelli began his Senate quest with a $1 million campaign treasury and a base in Bergen County, where Republicans traditionally fare well. Polls taken after Bradley's announcement showed that while Torricelli was not well-known statewide, he was not linked in the public's mind to former Gov. James Florio, a Democrat who raised taxes and lost a 1993 re-election bid.

In the end, Torricelli was helped by Clinton's strong showing in the state and won with 53 percent of the vote.

SENATE ELECTIONS

1996 General		
Robert G. Torricelli (D)	1,519,154	(53%)
Dick Zimmer (R)	1,227,351	(43%)
Richard J. Pezzullo (NJC)	50,971	(2%)

Previous Winning Percentages: **1994*** (63%) **1992*** (58%) **1990*** (57%) **1988*** (67%) **1986*** (69%) **1984*** (63%) **1982*** (53%)

** House elections*

KEY VOTES

1997	
Approve balanced-budget constitutional amendment	N
Approve chemical weapons treaty	Y
House Service:	
1996	
Approve farm bill	Y
Deny public education to illegal immigrants	Y
Increase minimum wage	Y
Freeze defense spending	Y
Approve welfare overhaul	Y
1995	
Approve balanced-budget constitutional amendment	Y
Relax Clean Water Act regulations	N
Oppose limits on environmental regulations	Y
Reduce projected Medicare spending	N
Approve GOP budget with tax and spending cuts	N

CAMPAIGN FINANCE

	Receipts	Receipts from PACs	Expend-itures
1996			
Torricelli (D)	$9,211,508	$952,153 (10%)	$9,134,854
Zimmer (R)	$8,212,612	$1,197,917 (15%)	$8,238,181

VOTING STUDIES

	Presidential Support		Party Unity		Conservative Coalition	
Year	**S**	**O**	**S**	**O**	**S**	**O**
House Service:						
1996	67	18	62	19	51	35
1995	75	17	78	14	38	56
1994	72	21	83	9	42	42
1993	91	6	83	9	43	55
1992	25	66	82	10	48	40
1991	33	60	81	10	38	54

INTEREST GROUP RATINGS

Year	ADA	AFL-CIO	CCUS	ACU
House Service:				
1996	70	0	31	21
1995	80	83	25	13
1994	65	78	58	6
1993	85	100	20	9
1992	85	83	33	16
1991	60	92	30	20

1 Robert E. Andrews (D)

Of Bellmawr — Elected 1990; 4th term

Biographical Information

Born: Aug. 4, 1957, Camden, N.J.

Education: Bucknell U., B.A. 1979; Cornell U., J.D. 1982.

Occupation: Professor.

Family: Wife, Camille Spinella; two children.

Religion: Episcopalian.

Political Career: Camden County Board of Chosen Freeholders, 1987-90, director, 1988-90; sought Democratic gubernatorial nomination, 1997.

Capitol Office: 2439 Rayburn Bldg. 20515; 225-6501.

Committees

Education & Workforce
Postsecondary Education, Training & Life-Long Learning; Workforce Protections

International Relations
Asia & the Pacific; Western Hemisphere

In Washington: After working to mend fences with members of his own party who had spurned him for his conservative leanings, Andrews spent the early part of 1997 campaigning for the Democratic nomination to take on New Jersey's GOP Gov. Christine Todd Whitman.

Heading into the June 3 primary, Andrews was regarded as the favorite against Woodbridge Mayor and state Sen. Jim McGreevey and a third Democrat, ex-Morris County Prosecutor Michael Murphy. But with a strong showing in northern Jersey, McGreevey scored an upset victory.

The Andrews for Governor Committee had formed in November 1996, but the campaign did not really pick up steam until three months later, when former Democratic Gov. James J. Florio (1989-93) said he would not try for a comeback and endorsed Andrews.

Although Whitman looked to be a formidable candidate for re-election, Andrews thought he could make a case to voters that their property taxes had risen as a direct result of the income-tax cuts Whitman instituted. Also, he hoped to capitalize on unhappiness with Whitman's effort to cap what upscale school districts spend so as to minimize costs borne by the state to bring poorer school districts up to the spending levels of affluent ones. In the primary, however, Andrews did not generate as much support as he expected in his south Jersey base, and he lost to McGreevey by 2 percentage points.

Andrews, who took the 1st after Florio left it for the governorship, has been influenced by the voter anger over taxes that rained down on Florio after he pushed through a big tax increase early in his tenure as governor. The tax hike was instrumental in Florio's defeat at Whitman's hands.

Andrews promised in his 1990 House campaign to oppose all tax increases during his first term. In 1993, he voted against President Clinton's five-year deficit-reduction plan, which included tax increases.

Andrews spent much of 1994 pushing a spending-cut proposal that came to be known as the "A-to-Z" plan, after its sponsors, Andrews and New Hampshire Republican Bill Zeliff. The plan would have set aside 56 hours of debate time on the House floor to spending-cut amendments. Zeliff and Andrews said their proposal was intended to combat the frustration felt by House members, who usually were blocked from offering spending-cut amendments by restrictive floor debate rules or committee processes.

But the Democratic leadership said the plan would force members to cast hasty votes on ill-conceived proposals that had not been examined in committee. In the end, Andrews and Zeliff failed to get their proposal out of committee.

Andrews' high profile on the A-to-Z plan did not sit well with some other Jersey Democrats. In a 1994 Philadelphia Inquirer article, Rep. Robert Menendez called Andrews a "grandstander." In the same article, Rep. Donald M. Payne said Andrews was a "political opportunist" with no future in the House Democratic leadership.

Andrews re-introduced his A-to-Z plan in the 104th Congress. But what had seemed like an extreme spending cut measure when the House was under Democratic rule was suddenly mild compared with proposals of some GOP members, who were advocating cutting entire departments.

Yet by taking the lead as a Democrat committed to taxing less and spending less, Andrews helped prod his party toward the center — a position that Clinton himself hustled to occupy in preparation for his 1996 re-election campaign.

Andrews supported Clinton's fiscal year 1997 budget, and generally he was more in sync with his House Democratic colleagues in the 104th and 105th than he had been earlier, voting with the party majority to uphold abortion rights, oppose repeal of the ban on certain semiautomatic assault-style weapons and increase the minimum wage. He opposed a GOP-backed effort to allow companies to offer their employees comp time in lieu of overtime pay, he voted with most Democrats to freeze defense spending at the fiscal 1996 level, and he joined a majority of Democrats in opposing a GOP effort to deny pub-

NEW JERSEY 1
Southwest — Camden

More than two-thirds of the 1st District hails from Camden County, an amalgam of older suburbs, developing countryside and the city of Camden.

Once a major industrial center and Delaware River port, Camden now is one of the nation's most distressed cities. More than 70 percent of its children live below the poverty line. Businesses and middle-class residents have fled in droves to the suburbs, decimating the tax base.

City officials are counting on the redeveloped Camden waterfront, featuring an aquarium and the 25,000-seat Sony-Blockbuster amphitheater, to lure tourists from the suburbs and neighboring Philadelphia. The new Delaware River Port Authority headquarters building opened in 1996, and plans call for building a restaurant and nightclub along the water.

Camden once was the hub of Camden County's powerful Democratic machine. Democratic Gov. James J. Florio, who was defeated in 1993 by Republican Christine Todd Whitman, was a product of its farm system. But as population has decreased precipitously over the past three decades, suburban GOP strength has made the county more competitive.

The city now holds less than 20 percent of county residents. Most of the county is in the 1st, with the exception of Cherry Hill and several smaller municipalities that are in the 3rd District.

Along the Delaware River, the cities are gritty and industry-oriented. The factories and oil storage yards of mostly working-class and poor Pennsauken, on the northern tip of the 1st, give it a Democratic character. Democrats also can find refuge in the older blue-collar towns farther south along the Black Horse Pike. East of Camden, the district becomes more suburban and Republican.

Republicans have experienced gains in the growing southern portion of Camden County and in suburban Gloucester County, which is shared with the 2nd. Roughly a quarter of the district's population hails from Gloucester County.

Commercial growth in and around Cherry Hill has spurred runaway population growth in Camden County locales such as Washington, middle-class Gloucester and white-collar Voorhees townships, though the growth is beginning to stabilize. Many residents moved to escape the older suburbs closer to Camden, but others sought the relatively easy access to Center City Philadelphia or Cherry Hill.

Not so long ago, Voorhees was a farming hamlet. But the population has skyrocketed over the past two decades. R.F. Power Products Inc., a computer company that had considered moving to Silicon Valley, opted instead to stay in Voorhees and move into a new manufacturing facility there in 1996.

Winslow Township and Berlin Township have also experienced some residential growth recently.

1990 Population: 594,630. White 465,929 (78%), Black 94,014 (16%), Other 34,687 (6%). Hispanic origin 37,350 (6%). 18 and over 435,857 (73%), 62 and over 84,651 (14%). Median age: 32.

lic education to illegal immigrants.

In March 1995, Andrews did cause liberals to bristle when he was one of nine House Democrats to support the GOP welfare bill — an amended version of the "Contract With America" proposal to cut benefits to legal immigrants and give states authority over a wide range of social services, from welfare to school lunches. But Andrews voted in mid-July 1996 against a later GOP version of welfare overhaul. Later that month, he voted for the final welfare bill, which Clinton had agreed to sign.

That Democrats were viewing Andrews more favorably was evident by early 1997. According to a Philadelphia Inquirer article about Andrews' gubernatorial run, Menendez was "instrumental" in helping Andrews "make inroads" in North Jersey. The article also said Andrews and Democrat Robert G. Torricelli had "buried the hatchet" during Torricelli's successful 1996 Senate race.

When asked about his apparently improved relations with previous critics, Andrews told the Inquirer: "I've always fought for the values Democrats care about. . . . Once people got to know my record and me, they saw I share the same values with everyone in our party."

Andrews cosponsored a bill in 1997 to eliminate the Overseas Private Investment Corp., an organization that gives federally subsidized loans and insurance to U.S. companies to spur foreign investment. Andrews labeled the operation "corporate welfare."

Andrews also has led a drive to get the equal rights amendment ratified. Andrews believes when the amendment passed in 1972 there should have been no time-limit on states for ratification. He has introduced a resolution that would require Congress to verify the constitutional amendment if it is approved by three more states, and has targeted Virginia, Illinois and Florida as potential supporters of the amendment.

Andrews played an important role in the move toward direct student loans. In 1993 he pushed through a plan to have the federal government provide direct loans to college students, a shift from the established practice of having the government guarantee loans that students obtain from private banks.

At Home: In 1990, anger toward Florio among those he used to represent in Congress gave a scare to Andrews, his heir apparent.

Florio, who left the 1st in January 1990 to become governor, ignited a statewide voter revolt when he raised taxes shortly after taking that office. Running to keep the vacant 1st in Democratic hands in November, Andrews had to sweat out a victory in a contest that originally figured to be a cakewalk for him.

Also that November, Andrews won the special election to fill Florio's vacant seat for the balance of the 101st Congress.

After Florio moved to Trenton, Andrews, director of the Camden County Board of Chosen Freeholders, looked like a good bet to succeed him in the 1st. A political ally of the governor's, Andrews was known as a young reformer in the Florio mold. He lined up the backing of the Camden County Democratic Party organization and brushed off faint primary opposition.

His GOP opponent, businessman Daniel J. Mangini, backed into the nomination after a better-known candidate could not be found. While Mangini, a Gloucester County freeholder, directed his understaffed, underfunded effort from the back of an appliance store, Andrews was headquartered in the spacious end unit of a Somerdale shopping center. Andrews outraised Mangini by more than 6-to-1.

But the $2.8 billion increase in sales and income taxes that Florio pushed through the Legislature in June leveled the playing field. Democrats at every level, alarmed at bumper stickers and signs across the state with exhortations such as "Flush Florio," attempted to distance themselves from the governor.

Mangini repeatedly referred to Andrews as "Florio's handpicked protege," but Andrews held steady and refrained from directly repudiating the governor, though he did take a "no new taxes" pledge for his first term.

The "Florio factor" did not prove powerful enough to offset Andrews' money and organization. The Democrat carried all three counties in the 1st, winning with 54 percent.

Andrews' first foray into electoral politics came in 1986, after he had practiced law at several area firms and taught law at Rutgers University. He was elected to the Camden County Board and two years later was chosen freeholder director by the board.

Andrews won at least two-thirds of the vote in his three House re-elections.

HOUSE ELECTIONS

1996 General		
Robert E. Andrews (D)	160,413	(76%)
Mel Suplee (R)	44,287	(21%)
Michael Edmondson (LIBERT)	2,668	(1%)
1994 General		
Robert E. Andrews (D)	108,155	(72%)
James N. Hogan (R)	41,505	(28%)

Previous Winning Percentages: 1992 (67%) **1990** (54%) **1990†** (55%)

† Special election

DISTRICT VOTE FOR PRESIDENT

1996	1992
D 132,808 (59%)	**D** 118,060 (48%)
R 61,379 (27%)	**R** 78,095 (32%)
I 25,098 (11%)	**I** 48,157 (20%)

VOTING STUDIES

	Presidential Support		Party Unity		Conservative Coalition	
Year	**S**	**O**	**S**	**O**	**S**	**O**
1996	76	23	82	17	43	57
1995	62	27	63	27	48	39
1994	68	28	64	29	72	28
1993	74	25	81	14	50	50
1992	38	58	78	18	50	48
1991	35	64	78	18	41	59

KEY VOTES

1997	
Ban "partial birth" abortions	N
1996	
Approve farm bill	N
Deny public education to illegal immigrants	N
Repeal ban on certain assault-style weapons	N
Increase minimum wage	Y
Freeze defense spending	Y
Approve welfare overhaul	Y
1995	
Approve balanced-budget constitutional amendment	Y
Relax Clean Water Act regulations	N
Oppose limits on environmental regulations	Y
Reduce projected Medicare spending	N
Approve GOP budget with tax and spending cuts	N

INTEREST GROUP RATINGS

Year	ADA	AFL-CIO	CCUS	ACU
1996	65	n/a	31	25
1995	60	73	48	36
1994	45	67	83	26
1993	60	83	27	25
1992	70	83	38	32
1991	70	92	10	15

CAMPAIGN FINANCE

	Receipts	Receipts from PACs	Expend-itures
1996			
Andrews (D)	$629,607	$303,127 (48%)	$414,266
Suplee (R)	$9,011	$16 (0%)	$9,010
1994			
Andrews (D)	$706,980	$336,368 (48%)	$674,366
Hogan (R)	$81,020	$514 (1%)	$78,028

2 Frank A. LoBiondo (R)

Of Vineland — Elected 1994, 2nd term

Biographical Information
Born: May 12, 1946, Bridgeton, N.J.
Education: St. Joseph's U., B.S. 1968.
Occupation: Trucking company operations manager.
Family: Wife, Jan Dwyer; two children.
Religion: Roman Catholic.
Political Career: Cumberland County Board of Freeholders, 1985-88; N.J. House, 1988-94; Republican nominee for U.S. House, 1992.
Capitol Office: 222 Cannon Bldg. 20515; 225-6572.

Committees
Small Business
Empowerment; Tax & Exports
Transportation & Infrastructure
Coast Guard & Maritime Transportation ; Water Resources & Environment

In Washington: LoBiondo rallied his district's most fervent conservatives to reach the House, upsetting state Sen. William L. Gormley, the party establishment's more moderate choice for the open 2nd, in the 1994 GOP primary.

While LoBiondo votes a generally conservative line in the House, on several high-profile controversies he has stepped off the line laid down by party leaders to side with more moderate House Republicans.

In October 1995, for instance, he was one of only six Republicans — four of them from New Jersey — voting against the GOP leadership's plan to restructure the Medicare program and reduce its projected cost growth by $270 billion over seven years. The New Jersey members felt the bill would harm their state's hospitals, which have a sizable caseload of Medicare patients. Later that month, LoBiondo was one of 10 Republicans who refused to back the GOP's huge budget-balancing reconciliation bill, which included the Medicare overhaul. In January 1996, he joined 26 other Republicans in opposing final passage of the $265 billion defense authorization bill for fiscal 1996. He joined 24 other Republicans in voting to send the fiscal 1996 VA-HUD appropriations bill back to conference with instructions to add funding for VA medical care. And in May 1996 he was one of 43 Republicans voting to defeat a GOP leadership-backed amendment to exempt small businesses from a minimum wage increase.

Because of the 2nd's considerable ocean frontage and wetlands areas, environmental matters are a concern to many voters, and in this issue realm, too, LoBiondo has more moderate inclinations than many of his GOP colleagues from the South and West. In May 1995, he and 33 other Republicans voted "no" on a party-backed bill rewriting the clean water act; among its aims was relaxing regulations governing the discharge of wastes and storm water into waterways. Then, in July 1995, he and 50 other Republicans helped pass a Democratic-sponsored amendment to strike language limiting the regulatory authority of the Environmental Protection Agency (EPA). Conservatives sought the limits on grounds that the EPA had been overzealously enforcing regulations and discouraging business development.

In February 1996, LoBiondo was among 19 Republicans opposing the GOP's sweeping revision of federal farm policy, which phased out most New Deal-era crop subsidies and gave farmers greater flexibility in deciding what to plant. He opposed the measure because it continued government subsidies for certain crops — peanuts, sugar and tobacco — and provided funding for the Market Promotion Program, which LoBiondo called a form of "corporate welfare." The program provides subsidies to commodity producers and food processors, many of which are large corporations, to help them advertise their products overseas.

LoBiondo is in step with his party's majority on most other issues, including the balanced-budget constitutional amendment, gunowners' rights, welfare overhaul and congressional term limits. In March 1996 he voted to repeal the ban on certain semiautomatic assault-style weapons, a priority of the National Rifle Association, which backed LoBiondo's initial bid for Congress in 1994.

On term limits, LoBiondo and eight other House members told the Clerk of the House to remove their names from the House roll if they stay longer than promised. "Term limits is about changing Congress — it is about changing the status quo," LoBiondo said on the House floor in March 1995. "It will create elections for open seats. It will ensure that we have new members of Congress, who come here with different backgrounds, different experiences, and fresh ideas. The concept of our democracy is that real people — average citizens — make the decisions that will affect us as a nation. Term limits will ensure that more members of the House and the Senate have that real world experience."

Flag desecration infuriates him, as he once told the House: "Our flag is more than just a piece

NEW JERSEY 2
South — Atlantic City; Vineland

The Mason-Dixon Line does not cross the Delaware River, but if it did, the 2nd would fit right in with the South. Like the rest of South Jersey (Burlington and all counties south of it), the 2nd is generally less affluent than the northern half of the state, median home values are lower and the area is less densely populated.

Though New Jersey is known better as an urban and suburban state, agriculture is a leading industry in the 2nd. The district is also known for its dislike of gun control measures.

Taking in all of Atlantic, Cape May, Cumberland and Salem counties — along with part of Gloucester County and one township from Burlington — the 2nd covers the bottom portion of New Jersey.

The towns along the Delaware River are more industrialized, and many residents work in the chemical plants across the river from Wilmington and in refineries on the Jersey side, just south of Philadelphia.

Farther inland, in Salem and Cumberland counties, there are pockets of rural poverty in an agricultural area that was once one of the nation's leading egg producers. Produce and small manufacturing are now large parts of the local economy. There is glass-making in Vineland and Millville.

The 2nd's best-known city is Atlantic City (Atlantic County). Once known as "Sodom by the Sea" for its seedy nightlife, this resort town fell on hard times before gambling was legalized in the mid-1970s.

But while glitzy casinos and hotels have sprouted up on the Boardwalk and property values have soared, the prosperity has been slow to trickle down to the mainly black and poor residents of the city. The city is awaiting the completion of a convention center that is aimed at luring business travelers to Atlantic City.

The shore communities south of Atlantic City, in Cape May County, have fared much better. From north to south, the county takes in family-oriented Ocean City, wealthy Avalon and Stone Harbor, then rowdier Wildwood.

On the southern tip, the city of Cape May has prospered as GOP-voting retirees have flocked to this old seaside resort of Victorian homes and small cottages.

The coastal character — and vast pinelands west of the shoreline — places environmental issues at the forefront of political discourse. In Cape May County, wetlands preservation is a volatile issue. Federal flood insurance and ocean dumping are also weighty concerns to residents of the hurricane-sensitive shore communities.

Politically, the 2nd has a Republican tilt. Ronald Reagan and George Bush easily carried it in 1984 and 1988, but in statewide elections, Democrats have fared well. Sen. Bill Bradley won every county in the district in his tight 1990 victory.

The district's split nature was evident in 1996. Democrat Bill Clinton won in the 2nd by 14 percentage points, faring especially well in Atlantic and Cumberland counties, even as LoBiondo swept to victory.

In the more industrial towns such as Bridgeton, Millville and Vineland — which has a significant number of Hispanic and black voters — and in Atlantic City, Democrats have an advantage.

1990 Population: 594,630. White 480,000 (81%), Black 83,902 (14%), Other 30,728 (5%). Hispanic origin 39,494 (7%). 18 and over 450,384 (76%), 62 and over 105,491 (18%). Median age: 34.

of cloth. It embodies us as a nation — our values and our beliefs. That is why we cannot tolerate any deliberate desecration of the American flag."

LoBiondo supports banning a particular abortion technique that opponents call "partial birth" abortion. However, in March 1996 he and 48 other Republicans backed a Democratic-led effort to retain a requirement that states fund Medicaid abortions in cases of rape and incest and to protect the life of the woman. Abortion foes wanted to give states new authority to set their own abortion funding policies on rape and incest.

LoBiondo's district includes the gambling haven of Atlantic City, and soon after arriving in the House he signaled his intent to protect the pillar of the resort's economy, founding the Congressional Gaming Caucus with Nevada Republican Reps. John Ensign and Barbara F. Vucanovich.

At the start of the 105th Congress, LoBiondo moved from the Banking Committee to the Transportation and Infrastructure Committee, where he can watch out for New Jersey interests as the panel reauthorizes the nation's surface transportation law.

At Home: Everyone knew Republicans had a good chance of winning the 2nd when veteran Democratic Rep. William J. Hughes decided not to seek re-election in 1994. For 10 terms, Hughes' moderate image and personal popularity had offset his district's Republican voter-registration advantage; LoBiondo managed just 41 percent against him as the GOP nominee in 1992.

But the expected Republican beneficiary of Hughes' exit was state Sen. Gormley, the longtime boss of the Atlantic County GOP and chairman of the Senate Judiciary Committee. Favored by the state's old-line GOP establishment, Gormley's primary bid was better-funded than LoBiondo's comeback attempt.

But LoBiondo, a state assemblyman, adroitly used Gormley's long public record against him, tagging him a "closet Democrat" because of his past work with Democrats such as Gov. James J. Florio. He hammered Gormley for being the only Republican in the state Legislature who supported Florio's 1990 ban on assault weapons, and the NRA financed a radio ad campaign against Gormley. In the end, LoBiondo won nomination going away, taking 55 percent of the vote to Gormley's 35 percent; 10 percent went to a candidate running on an anti-abortion theme.

With Hughes' departure, there was confusion in Democratic ranks. John Mruz, a longtime aide to Hughes, was first to join the race. But he pulled out when Ruth Katz, a former member of President Clinton's transition team, came home to the district after 14 years in Washington and declared herself ready to spend up to $1 million to win the seat. Amid rumblings that Katz was a carpetbagger, attorney Louis N. Magazzu decided to run and quickly picked up support from county organizations. Katz dropped out a short time later.

Magazzu jokingly referred to himself as "Lou Who?" early in the campaign, and he suffered throughout from a lack of name recognition and a treasury vastly smaller than LoBiondo's. Magazzu campaigned on a moderate platform stressing crime control, welfare overhaul, spending reduction and congressional reform, but he never found an issue that would galvanize opposition to LoBiondo. Meanwhile, LoBiondo dismissed his opponent as a tax-and-spend Democrat, and benefiting from the national GOP tide, he won election with nearly two-thirds of the vote.

Katz came back in 1996 and had a clear passage to the Democratic nomination. Fueling her campaign with more than a quarter-million dollars in personal money, she tried to paint LoBiondo as a loyal follower of Speaker Newt Gingrich and therefore too extreme for New Jersey.

"The one constant in Frank LoBiondo's voting record is his unwavering support for the interests of Newt Gingrich," she said. "And those interests have come at the expense of the people of South Jersey."

LoBiondo argued that he voted the way the district wanted him to. "I'm pleased that much of what we talked about in South Jersey has been successful in Washington," he said. "We got welfare reform, congressional reform, and we're balancing the budget. We brought common sense, real world South Jersey values to Washington, D.C. That's the record I'm running on."

Katz made it competitive financially but not electorally; LoBiondo won handily, polling 60 percent of the vote.

HOUSE ELECTIONS

1996 General		
Frank A. LoBiondo (R)	133,131	(60%)
Ruth Katz (D)	83,890	(38%)
1994 General		
Frank A. LoBiondo (R)	102,566	(65%)
Louis N. Magazzu (D)	56,151	(35%)
1994 Primary		
Frank A. LoBiondo (R)	23,152	(55%)
William L Gormley (R)	14,989	(35%)
Robert D. Green (R)	4,364	(10%)

CAMPAIGN FINANCE

	Receipts	Receipts from PACs		Expend-itures
1996				
LoBiondo (R)	$935,426	$235,811	(25%)	$890,526
Katz (D)	$831,006	$48,857	(6%)	$806,232
Headrick (TLL)	$3,417	0		$3,417
1994				
LoBiondo (R)	$912,195	$151,575	(17%)	$757,681
Magazzu (D)	$169,283	$30,001	(18%)	$168,428

DISTRICT VOTE FOR PRESIDENT

1996		1992	
D	117,605 (50%)	D	101,718 (41%)
R	84,100 (36%)	R	97,696 (39%)
I	27,616 (12%)	I	50,870 (20%)

KEY VOTES

1997	
Ban "partial birth" abortions	Y
1996	
Approve farm bill	N
Deny public education to illegal immigrants	Y
Repeal ban on certain assault-style weapons	Y
Increase minimum wage	Y
Freeze defense spending	Y
Approve welfare overhaul	Y
1995	
Approve balanced-budget constitutional amendment	Y
Relax Clean Water Act regulations	N
Oppose limits on environmental regulations	Y
Reduce projected Medicare spending	N
Approve GOP budget with tax and spending cuts	N

VOTING STUDIES

	Presidential Support		Party Unity		Conservative Coalition	
Year	**S**	**O**	**S**	**O**	**S**	**O**
1996	44	56	76	24	53	47
1995	31	69	83	16	72	28

INTEREST GROUP RATINGS

Year	ADA	AFL-CIO	CCUS	ACU
1996	25	n/a	81	70
1995	25	42	79	80

3 H. James Saxton (R)

Of Mount Holly — Elected 1984; 7th full term

Biographical Information
Born: Jan. 22, 1943, Nicholson, Pa.
Education: East Stroudsburg State College, B.A. 1965; Temple U., 1967-68.
Occupation: Real estate broker; elementary school teacher.
Family: Divorced; two children.
Religion: Methodist.
Political Career: N.J. Assembly, 1976-82; N.J. Senate, 1982-84.
Capitol Office: 339 Cannon Bldg. 20515; 225-4765.

Committees
National Security
Military Installations and Facilities; Military Procurement
Resources
Fisheries Conservation, Wildlife & Oceans (chairman)
Joint Economic (chairman)

In Washington: Saxton stands with GOP fiscal conservatives who support a balanced-budget constitutional amendment and with his party's pro-defense stalwarts who back higher budgets for the Pentagon.

He embraces, though, another cause that is less popular on the Republican right but is important to many residents of the coastal 3rd District: environmental protection.

Saxton is chairman of the Resources Committee's Fisheries Conservation, Wildlife and Oceans Subcommittee. The full committee is headed by Republican Don Young of Alaska, and in the 104th, it was an ideological battleground, populated by Western conservatives eager to reverse what they saw as years of bias against development under Democratic-controlled Congresses. The fight played out in debates on a series of land and water issues, including efforts to rewrite the endangered species law, overhaul mining regulations, address the health of the nation's forests and protect the nation's drinking water.

Compounding divisiveness on the committee was the widely held perception that Young was using his prerogatives as chairman to route environmental reform bills around Saxton's subcommittee, lest Saxton try to put a more environment-friendly stamp on conservatives' proposals. Young basically circumvented the subcommittee when he created a special task force, headed by second-term conservative California Republican Richard W. Pombo, to rewrite the Endangered Species Act. Saxton had cosponsored a reauthorization of the law in 1995 that fell short of conservatives' calls for dramatic change. Saxton acknowledges the constraints his subcommittee faces, but still he says he has a "good working relationship with Young."

Early in the 104th, a Republican-led effort that included a coalition of private property rights activists laid out a case for changing the endangered species law. Proponents of change came armed with anecdotes which they said showed that species such as the fairy shrimp and the kangaroo rat were being protected at great expense to individual landowners and to the economy as a whole.

But supporters of the act — including environmental organizations and many Democrats — cited the bill as evidence of their claim that the congressional Republican majority was anti-environment. A number of GOP moderates warned that this notion might take hold in the electorate and cause problems for Republican candidates in 1996.

Pombo wanted to rewrite the act to include language that a property owner could compel compensation from the federal government if an action under the act resulted in a 50 percent decrease in the value of his land. Government critics — particularly in the West and the South — contend that federal regulators often trample on Fifth Amendment protections against government confiscation of property without just compensation. Saxton opposed the property rights language, calling it an anti-environment budget-buster. "There is deep disagreement on the issue between Richard Pombo and me," he said. "It seems to me that some of the Westerners are locked into an unforgiving position."

Also, Saxton in 1995 fought his party's broad rewrite of clean water regulations. Water quality is a sensitive issue in New Jersey. In the late 1980s, some state beaches were plagued by overflows of municipal sewage and medical waste. "Our environment was perceived to have gone south, and the economy went south as well," Saxton said.

Saxton persuaded every member of the state's delegation except one — Republican Bob Franks — to oppose the GOP water bill on final passage. Saxton offered an amendment that would have stripped the bill of some provisions that environmentalists most strongly opposed, but it was rejected, 184-242.

Saxton did get a provision included in a measure aimed at protecting tap water that became law in August 1996. He and California Democrat Henry A. Waxman added language requiring com-

NEW JERSEY 3
South central — Cherry Hill

On the surface, the Camden and Burlington County suburbs would seem to have little in common with the shore communities of Ocean County. But both share an affinity for Republicans and concerns about the spiraling growth that is affecting their quality of life.

Only four Camden County municipalities are included in the 3rd, but they include Cherry Hill, which has grown over the past three decades as a result of out-migration from Philadelphia and Camden.

The new housing developments, office parks and shopping malls have changed the complexion of this once rural hamlet. But there has been a price: traffic congestion.

The young, mostly white suburbanites who live here lean Republican, but they are an independent lot. In 1996, voters split their tickets for Bill Clinton and Republican Saxton, as they did throughout the district. Overall, Clinton got 50 percent in the 3rd, while Saxton got 64 percent.

A much larger share of the 3rd District vote is cast in the suburbs of Burlington County. Democrats run well in the industrial towns along the Delaware River, and in Willingboro, a Levittown-style community that is more than 50 percent black.

The communities of Cinnaminson and Delran are more affluent, though not as upscale as Moorestown. High-tech and defense contractors are leading employers in the area, as is McGuire Air Force Base.

West of these towns, suburban sprawl takes over. Population has exploded in places such as Mount Laurel and Evesham, which are near highways used by white-collar employees commuting to Trenton, Philadelphia and corporations in north Jersey.

Away from the riverfront, the vote is more Republican. Although Clinton carried the portions of Burlington County in the district with 51 percent and 17,000-vote margin in 1996, Saxton won by a margin of better than 2-to-1.

After Burlington County, the second-largest population cluster is in rapidly growing Ocean County (which is split between the 3rd and 4th districts). Many live in the Toms River area, and the rest are scattered in smaller, seaside communities. Retirees are an important constituency; there are age-restricted housing developments in Berkeley Township.

Retirees have not been the only ones moving to GOP-inclined Ocean County. The 1950s extension of the Garden State Parkway to the shore area made the area attractive for commuters and spawned Parkway bedroom communities. Closer to the fragile Atlantic coastline, barrier beach development has pitted builders against environmentalists.

1990 Population: 594,630. White 528,533 (89%), Black 47,565 (8%), Other 18,532 (3%). Hispanic origin 15,477 (3%). 18 and over 451,821 (76%), 62 and over 108,169 (18%). Median age: 36.

munity water systems to inform the public about the level of contaminants in drinking water and the health effects of contaminants that exceed Environmental Protection Agency (EPA) standards.

The "right to know" language was a priority for environmentalists, including pro-environment Republicans. It remained in the final version of the bill, prompting Saxton to comment, "We have proven on numerous occasions that when [GOP moderates] push for something, we could get it done."

In addition to his sympathy for environmental causes, Saxton shows a moderate streak on some other issues. In March 1996, he was one of 42 Republicans to vote against repealing a ban on certain assault-style weapons. He also backed a Democratic effort to raise the minimum wage by 90 cents over two years, after initially opposing it.

His record on abortion is mixed. He opposes allowing the federal employees' health plan to cover abortions, and he objects to abortions at overseas military hospitals. But he was one of only 49 Republicans voting in 1996 to require states to fund Medicaid abortions for poor women who are victims of rape or incest.

On a key litmus test on fiscal policy for conservatives, Saxton supported the House GOP's "Contract With America" initiative to cut taxes by $189 billion over five years, including a $500-per-child tax credit for families earning as much as $200,000 a year and a reduction in the capital gains tax.

Some of these tax breaks were included in the broad budget-reconciliation bill, which the House passed in October 1995. Saxton, however, was one of 10 Republicans voting against that bill, because he believed its provisions restructuring Medicare would harm New Jersey's Medicare-dependent hospitals.

Saxton serves in the 105th as chairman of the Joint Economic Committee, which gives him a platform to continue to push for legislation prohibiting federal agencies from assisting or encouraging pension fund managers to make economically targeted investments (ETIs). These are investments selected not only for their profit potential but also for their larger benefits to the overall economy.

Saxton argues that some ETIs in social policy areas, such as public housing projects, do not yield as great a return as other investments.

Therefore, he says, such ETIs violate sections of the 1974 Employee Retirement Income Security Act, which requires fund managers to give "undivided loyalty" to pension beneficiaries. The House approved his bill, 239-179, in September 1995.

Saxton also has a seat on the National Security Committee, where his profile has always been rather low and his interests mainly parochial; he was occupied in the early 1990s with trying to protect military bases in his district from closure.

He supports GOP leaders on the committee who push for more defense spending than the Clinton administration requests. And he backed a bill, passed by the House in September 1996, aimed at limiting the president's ability to place U.S. troops under U.N. command. The measure would deny funding for U.S. participation in any U.N. military operation, unless Congress authorized such a mission or the president declared in advance that it was in the national security interest. "When U.S. lives are at stake, the American public expects and demands that Americans are at the helm," Saxton said.

At Home: Saxton struggled to win the nomination for the seat left open by the 1984 death of GOP Rep. Edwin B. Forsythe. But after surviving a tough primary, he has had little trouble in this heavily Republican district.

A state legislator for eight years, Saxton came into his first House race with the backing of the strong GOP organization in Burlington County, the most populous in the district. But the district also includes Camden and Ocean counties, and each supplied a candidate.

M. Dean Haines and his Ocean County organization gave Saxton his stiffest challenge. Assemblyman John A. Rocco of Camden County also ran, but his differences with his county GOP organization resulted in it endorsing Saxton. The lesser known Haines concentrated his efforts on Ocean County, where turnout was traditionally high. Saxton, with his large state Senate constituency, ran ads on Philadelphia TV stations to reach voters in Camden and Burlington counties.

The strategy paid off. With Saxton and Haines winning on their home turf, the contest was decided in Camden County. Saxton's second-place showing behind Rocco there allowed him to win the primary by about 1,400 votes.

In 1990, Saxton faced aggressive young Democrat John H. Adler, a former Cherry Hill City Council member. With many voters furious over former Democratic Gov. James J. Florio's $2.8 billion tax package and looking for victims at the polls, the House race attracted a decade-high turnout. Although the state climate was hostile toward Democrats, Adler managed to hold Saxton under 60 percent for the first time.

Saxton won with 59 percent in 1992 and since then has stayed well above the 60 percent mark.

HOUSE ELECTIONS

1996 General		
H. James Saxton (R)	157,503	(64%)
John Leonardi (D)	81,590	(33%)
Janice Presser (LIBERT)	3,037	(1%)
1994 General		
H. James Saxton (R)	115,750	(66%)
James Smith (D)	54,441	(31%)
D. James Hill (UWS)	3,015	(2%)

Previous Winning Percentages: 1992 (59%) **1990** (58%) **1988** (69%) **1986** (65%) **1984** (61%)

CAMPAIGN FINANCE

	Receipts	Receipts from PACs	Expend-itures
1996			
Saxton (R)	$676,788	$305,958 (45%)	$533,850
Leonardi (D)	$23,154	$3,750 (16%)	$21,957
1994			
Saxton (R)	$611,801	$237,114 (39%)	$356,108
Hill (UWS)	$793	0	$2,143

DISTRICT VOTE FOR PRESIDENT

1996	1992
D 133,773 (50%)	**D** 114,503 (40%)
R 100,849 (38%)	**R** 113,583 (40%)
I 28,143 (11%)	**I** 54,989 (19%)

KEY VOTES

1997	
Ban "partial birth" abortions	Y
1996	
Approve farm bill	N
Deny public education to illegal immigrants	Y
Repeal ban on certain assault-style weapons	N
Increase minimum wage	N
Freeze defense spending	?
Approve welfare overhaul	Y
1995	
Approve balanced-budget constitutional amendment	Y
Relax Clean Water Act regulations	N
Oppose limits on environmental regulations	Y
Reduce projected Medicare spending	N
Approve GOP budget with tax and spending cuts	N

VOTING STUDIES

	Presidential Support		Party Unity		Conservative Coalition	
Year	S	O	S	O	S	O
1996	39	58	84	14	76	16
1995	26	73	90	9	89	10
1994	63	37	81	17	89	11
1993	50	50	82	16	91	9
1992	73	25	79	18	88	10
1991	69	29	76	19	86	11

INTEREST GROUP RATINGS

Year	ADA	AFL-CIO	CCUS	ACU
1996	15	n/a	94	84
1995	15	17	79	84
1994	15	22	100	67
1993	20	42	82	79
1992	15	50	75	80
1991	10	27	67	74

4 Christopher H. Smith (R)

Of Robbinsville — Elected 1980, 9th term

Biographical Information
Born: March 4, 1953, Rahway, N.J.
Education: Trenton State College, B.A. 1975.
Occupation: Sporting goods executive.
Family: Wife, Marie Hahn; four children.
Religion: Roman Catholic.
Political Career: Republican nominee for U.S. House, 1978.
Capitol Office: 2370 Rayburn Bldg. 20515; 225-3765.

Committees
International Relations
International Operations & Human Rights (chairman); Western Hemisphere
Veterans' Affairs
Health

In Washington: On a range of issues — labor-management matters, the environment, gun control, and fiscal policy — Smith in the 104th Congress set himself apart from GOP conservatives. This has been Smith's custom during his career in the House, which helps explain why he has such a firm grip on his politically competitive district.

But if he appeals to moderate and independent voters in the 4th with his support for a minimum wage increase and his opposition to repealing the ban on certain semiautomatic assault-style weapons, Smith is mostly known in Washington as a vehement, high-profile opponent of abortion. In fact, Smith often has given House GOP leaders heartburn by refusing to brook compromise on abortion policy, even when disputes are holding up bills that the leadership wants to move through the pipeline.

Smith sees his work against abortion and his interests in international affairs as springing from the same concern for human rights. He has a platform from which to be heard on international human rights issues as chairman of the International Operations and Human Rights Subcommittee on the International Relations Committee. He also sits on the Veterans' Affairs Committee, where he is the No. 2 Republican.

Smith's fight against abortion has long been at the top of his legislative agenda, and his arguments typically cut to the quick. When the House debated an amendment to lift the ban on military personnel obtaining privately funded abortions at overseas military facilities, Smith argued against it. He said the amendment "would facilitate the killing of children by dismemberment and chemical poisoning."

Smith also has been a vocal advocate of a GOP measure banning a particular abortion technique that opponents call "partial birth" abortion. The bill would make it a federal crime for a doctor to perform the abortion unless it was deemed necessary to save the woman's life. The bill defined the procedure as an abortion in which the doctor "partially vaginally delivers a living fetus before killing the fetus and completing the delivery."

When the House cleared the measure in March 1996, Smith said that if President Clinton vetoed the bill "then he alone will have empowered abortionists to kill babies in this way." Clinton vetoed the measure in April 1996, and the Senate failed to override. The House passed an identical measure in March 1997, but despite several new faces and vote switches, the Senate in May still came up just short of the two-thirds majority needed for a veto override.

Smith's main quest to restrict abortions overseas has come on the foreign operations spending bill, which includes funding for international family planning activities. Smith managed to delay the measure in both 1995 and 1996, as he placed abortion-related restrictions on family planning aid. That battle centers on efforts by abortion opponents to reinstate the policy of the Reagan and Bush administrations, which denied funds to groups that refused to promise they would not perform or promote abortions abroad, even with their own money. Clinton reversed that so-called Mexico City policy — unveiled at a 1984 population conference in the Mexican capital — with an executive order on his second day in office.

In 1995, the first year Republicans had control over foreign aid spending, Smith added a provision that would have banned funding for any organization providing abortions overseas, and for the U.N. Population Fund unless it withdrew from China, which has been criticized for using coercive family planning techniques.

Smith said his amendment was intended to erect "a wall of separation" between abortion and family planning. The measure remained stalled for months, as both the Senate and the White House objected to Smith's provision. An agreement was finally brokered in January 1996 providing that funds for family planning programs would be reduced by 35 percent from the fiscal 1995 level of $548 million unless a separate bill authorizing those programs became law by July 1. No authorization bill was enacted, however.

The next year, Smith tried again. During House consideration of the foreign operations bill in

NEW JERSEY 4
Central — Trenton

Stretching from Trenton to the Atlantic Ocean, the 4th covers the state's midsection, an area where the Garden State begins to make the transition from South Jersey to North Jersey.

The motto of the state capital — and the district's largest city — is "Trenton Makes, the World Takes." That catchy phrase refers to the city's industrial heritage, but nowadays, the city makes less and takes a lot more federal aid.

Minorities make up more than half the city's population, though there are a few remaining white ethnic enclaves such as the Italian section of Chambersburg.

Hispanics and blacks, when combined with the contingent of state employees, help Trenton turn out a fairly sizable Democratic vote. It is usually enough to put Mercer County into the Democratic column in statewide elections. Mercer backed Bill Clinton in 1992, though he lost the district. But in 1996, Clinton won both Mercer and the district, beating Bob Dole by 14 percentage points districtwide.

Countering Trenton is a burgeoning suburban voice, made up mostly of Trenton expatriates. These white suburbanites are more independent voters who, at the federal level, tend to prefer GOP candidates.

Many blue-collar Irish and Italians settled in Hamilton Township after leaving Trenton. Its population has boomed as Trenton's declined; now it is only slightly smaller.

Ocean County is the site of the largest concentration of voters in the district. If a Democratic candidate comes out ahead in Mercer, that lead is likely to be blunted by the Republican advantage in Ocean County.

Retirement communities have sprouted up in Lakewood, and in Brick and Manchester townships, sparking creation of new service industries geared to the elderly. Ocean County — which the 4th shares with the 3rd District — houses one of the heaviest concentrations of retirees in the Northeast. These retirees also come out in droves on Election Day. The largest employer in the area is Lakehurst Naval Air Warfare Center, which employs 3,000 military and civilian personnel. It was targeted for closure in 1995, but local protests helped save it..

Parts of Monmouth and Burlington counties round out the district. The Monmouth County portion includes some fast-growing inland communities such as Howell, where white-collar employees commute to Trenton or New York City. In 1996, Dole outdistanced Clinton by more than 2,000 ballots in Monmouth County.

The Burlington County portion is slightly smaller than Monmouth's but more Democratic. The industrial areas closer to the Delaware River favor Democrats, but farther east, Republicans fare better because of places such as Mansfield, a community where posh housing developments are growing in number, facilitated by access to Princeton, Philadelphia and Trenton.

1990 Population: 594,630. White 497,624 (84%), Black 74,309 (12%), Other 22,697 (4%). Hispanic origin 31,141 (5%). 18 and over 451,927 (76%), 62 and over 115,364 (19%). Median age: 35.

June 1996, he was successful with an amendment cutting aid to overseas groups that spend their own money on abortions. Although conferees ultimately abandoned Smith's language, Republicans succeeded in imposing tight funding limits on family planning programs. The final version provided $385 million for family planning activities, but none of the money could be spent until July 1, 1997, unless both chambers voted to release the aid by Feb. 28, 1997. In one of the key early votes of the 105th, the House and Senate did just that, handing the Clinton administration a victory.

Abortion-rights backers prompted the vote saying that the agreement on the 1996 foreign operations bill provided for a vote on whether to release the money on March 1, 1997. House Republican leaders also agreed to permit a second vote on a Smith bill linking early disbursement of the family planning money to the reinstatement of the policy of barring international family planning groups from using their own funds to perform abortion. "Make no mistake about it, the consequence of approving Mr. Clinton's resolution is a fat payday for abortion providers," Smith said.

Ultimately, a narrow majority of lawmakers adopted the position that the resolution had more to do with family planning than abortion. The measure to release the funds early carried on a 220-209 vote. The House then approved Smith's legislation on a 231-194 vote. The Senate, which in February 1997 agreed to release the funds, did not take up Smith's measure.

Smith's human rights politics include supporting additional funding for international child health care. When his International Relations subcommittee in April 1997 approved a two-year bill authorizing the programs of the State Department and related agencies, Smith added $20 million for a program to combat child labor abroad.

Smith's visibility on abortion and international relations issues sometimes masks his broad disagreements with other GOP positions. Smith was the only Republican in November 1995 to vote against the conference report on the GOP's deficit-reducing budget-reconciliation bill. And he was one of 10 Republicans, four of whom were from New Jersey, to vote against it when it first passed the House in late October. The reconciliation bill included provisions aimed at reducing the growth in Medicare spending, and restructuring the Medicare program. Smith, and other members of the New Jersey delegation, wanted more protection for Medicare-dependent hospitals.

Smith has also opposed GOP efforts to change labor laws, voting against a measure that would allow companies to offer employees comp time in lieu of pay for overtime work. He was an early supporter of a minimum wage increase in 1996, and he opposed a GOP effort to exempt small businesses from paying the higher wage.

At Home: Smith became ensconced in the 4th with surprising ease, demolishing Democratic hopes of recapturing a district that was long theirs. Smith's diligent constituent work and well-run campaigns were important, but the secret of his success is his moderate voting record. Though steadfast in the anti-abortion activism that drew him into politics, his attention to the interests of blue-collar workers and organized labor has given Smith considerable crossover appeal.

Even redistricting, which gave him a constituency about one-third new in 1992, failed to faze Smith. Democrat Brian M. Hughes, son of former Democratic Gov. Richard J. Hughes, tried to convince voters in the reconfigured 4th that Smith's high-profile House opposition to abortion came at the expense of local interests.

But that is a charge Democrats throw at Smith every two years, so far to no avail. Without a fresh issue to keep voters' attention, Hughes struggled to stay in the public eye. When local media finally got interested in the contest, it was mostly to detail charges of resume padding that were leveled against Hughes. Smith breezed through with 62 percent.

In 1980, Smith ousted 13-term Democratic Rep. Frank Thompson Jr. solely because of Thompson's involvement in Abscam. In 1978, as a political novice running almost exclusively on his contacts in the anti-abortion movement, Smith had failed to draw even 40 percent against Thompson. On the second try, after Thompson's bribery indictment, Smith won with 57 percent.

Despite that solid showing, Smith was viewed as nearly certain to fall in 1982 to Democrat Joseph P. Merlino, the former president of the New Jersey Senate. As it turned out, Merlino came across in areas outside Trenton as a gruff, horse-trading pol. After one debate, when Smith approached him to exchange pleasantries, Merlino growled, "Beat it, kid." Smith won with 53 percent.

In 1984, Democrats tried again with a protege of Merlino, former Mercer County Freeholder James C. Hedden. Hedden took Smith seriously, accusing his opponent of being obsessed with abortion. But Smith soared to 61 percent and has not won less than that since.

HOUSE ELECTIONS

1996 General		
Christopher H. Smith (R)	146,404	(64%)
Kevin John Meara (D)	77,565	(34%)
Robert Figueroa (LIBERT)	3,000	(1%)
1994 General		
Christopher H. Smith (R)	109,818	(68%)
Ralph Walsh (D)	49,537	(31%)

Previous Winning Percentages: 1992 (62%) **1990** (63%) **1988** (66%) **1986** (61%) **1984** (61%) **1982** (53%) **1980** (57%)

CAMPAIGN FINANCE

	Receipts	Receipts from PACs	Expend-itures
1996			
Smith (R)	$328,861	$101,127 (31%)	$284,776
1994			
Smith (R)	$309,663	$93,431 (30%)	$271,108
Walsh (D)	$22,418	$7,500 (33%)	$16,217

DISTRICT VOTE FOR PRESIDENT

	1996		1992
D	127,043 (51%)	D	105,335 (40%)
R	92,445 (37%)	R	109,907 (41%)
I	26,840 (11%)	I	50,768 (19%)

VOTING STUDIES

	Presidential Support		Party Unity		Conservative Coalition	
Year	S	O	S	O	S	O
1996	44	52	79	18	69	22
1995	31	68	83	14	86	14
1994	53	45	64	34	72	25
1993	52	46	69	28	89	11
1992	61	38	61	37	83	17
1991	62	37	58	40	73	24

KEY VOTES

1997	
Ban "partial birth" abortions	Y
1996	
Approve farm bill	Y
Deny public education to illegal immigrants	Y
Repeal ban on certain assault-style weapons	N
Increase minimum wage	Y
Freeze defense spending	N
Approve welfare overhaul	Y
1995	
Approve balanced-budget constitutional amendment	Y
Relax Clean Water Act regulations	N
Oppose limits on environmental regulations	Y
Reduce projected Medicare spending	N
Approve GOP budget with tax and spending cuts	N

INTEREST GROUP RATINGS

Year	ADA	AFL-CIO	CCUS	ACU
1996	30	n/a	75	80
1995	20	50	63	64
1994	30	56	83	70
1993	30	67	64	71
1992	40	67	75	68
1991	45	75	40	60

5 Marge Roukema (R)

Of Ridgewood — Elected 1980, 9th term

Biographical Information
Born: Sept. 19, 1929, West Orange, N.J.
Education: Montclair State College, B.A. 1951.
Occupation: High school government and history teacher.
Family: Husband, Richard Roukema; two children.
Religion: Protestant.
Political Career: Ridgewood Board of Education, 1970-73; Republican nominee for U.S. House, 1978.
Capitol Office: 2469 Rayburn Bldg. 20515; 225-4465.

Committees
Banking & Financial Services
Financial Institutions & Consumer Credit (chairwoman); Housing & Community Opportunity
Education & Workforce
Employer-Employee Relations; Postsecondary Education, Training & Life-Long Learning

In Washington: Roukema is now the longest-serving woman in the House, and since 1995 she has chaired the Banking Committee's Financial Institutions and Consumer Credit Subcommittee.

But Roukema remains best-known as a frank voice of moderation within the Republican Party, one of a relatively small number of GOP lawmakers who concur with liberals on abortion rights and other social policy causes, while strongly supporting fiscal conservatism. This stance sets her apart from the majority of House Republicans, who hew to the right on social as well as fiscal matters.

Roukema's beliefs reflect the affluent New Jersey district she represents, and the GOP leadership rarely tries to press her into line. They learned long ago that she's not likely to change her mind.

She does, however, frequently speak it. In early 1997, Roukema called on her party to appoint an interim Speaker until the ethics committee had completed its work and made its recommendations on the ethical situation of the incumbent Speaker, Newt Gingrich.

Ignoring that call, Gingrich stood for re-election before the ethics committee report was released. Roukema voted for him, but later, after voting for the ethics committee's recommendation to reprimand Gingrich and assess him a $300,000 penalty, she said he should pay the sum with personal funds instead of from campaign coffers, a course of action most Democrats favored but one that Gingrich took only after considerable reflection. Gingrich got a personal loan from former Senate Majority Leader Bob Dole. For part of the penalty; he was to pay the rest with personal funds.

Another example of Roukema's cage-rattling came in early 1996, as President Clinton and congressional Republicans battled over the budget, prolonging a partial government shutdown. Roukema and 15 other Republicans sent a letter to their party leaders that was, according to a report in the Los Angeles Times, one of the final catalysts in persuading the GOP leadership to compromise with Clinton on the budget.

The Roukema letter contained an implicit warning that the GOP could lose control of the House floor if she and other moderates began supporting Democrats in their efforts to force the government to reopen.

If Roukema had had her way in 1989, Gingrich would not have won the race for minority whip, which put him on track to become Speaker. In that 1989 contest, Roukema's choice for GOP whip was Edward Madigan of Illinois, a low-key, pragmatic conservative from the GOP's "Old Bull" wing, which winced at Gingrich's confrontational brand of conservatism. Madigan lost by two votes.

Fittingly perhaps, Roukema's biggest legislative achievement to date carried the signature of a Democratic president. Roukema would have received more notice for the Family and Medical Leave Act had it been signed when first passed, when George Bush held the presidency.

But Roukema's efforts over eight years on what she called "a bedrock family issue" met with stiff resistance from conservatives in Congress. Bush vetoed the measure twice, and solid GOP voting in Congress sustained both vetoes. Passed again in 1993, the bill became the first legislative trophy of Bill Clinton's presidency.

Roukema was the lead Republican sponsor of the bill, which requires large and medium-sized businesses to provide unpaid leave to new parents, disabled workers and those caring for a seriously ill family member. Her work led to moderating revisions that allowed the bill to win passage for the first time in 1990, only to be vetoed by Bush, as it was again in 1992.

After years of fighting for the family leave legislation, Roukema in mid-1990 revealed a personal facet to her commitment. In 1976, when she was a graduate student, she had dropped out of her academic program to care for her 17-year-old son Todd, who was dying of leukemia. "What would I have done if not only did I have the tragedy and trauma of caring for my child," she asks, "but also had to worry about losing a job

NEW JERSEY 5
North and West — Ridgewood

The 5th has little in common with the stereotype of New Jersey as the "Turnpike State." In fact, the New Jersey Turnpike actually stops short of entering the district in Bergen County.

This is one of the state's least densely populated districts, stretching from Warren County north to the New York border, then all the way across the northern tier to the Hudson River. No municipality has more than 30,000 residents. It includes some of the state's most scenic, most wealthy and most Republican areas.

But in presidential elections, at least, GOP support has been slipping. George Bush racked up 66 percent of the district's vote in 1988, then slid to 50 percent four years later. In 1996, Bob Dole carried the 5th with 47 percent.

Northern Bergen County provides the bulk of the vote. These affluent voters are so heavily Republican that Democrats often have a hard time finding candidates to run in legislative races.

Property values and income levels are among the highest in the state. Alpine is home to sports stars and celebrities. Less famous denizens include the corporate executives and white-collar New York commuters who live in places such as Ridgewood and Oradell. It is only fitting that the company that makes the car of choice for many upscale buyers — BMW — keeps its U.S. headquarters in Woodcliff Lake. Park Ridge also serves as a corporate headquarters site for Sony in the United States.

The district also includes Warren County and parts of Passaic and Sussex counties.

The mountains of Warren and affluent Sussex counties are dotted with sparsely populated small towns. Phillipsburg, situated across the Delaware River from Easton, Pa., has some industry and is Warren County's only town with as many as 15,000 residents.

The scenic back country of western Sussex attracts some tourists, especially around the Delaware Water Gap region. Much of the county remains rural, despite a 13 percent jump in population in the 1980s as affluent young professionals stretched the New York metropolitan orbit even farther west.

The small towns and boroughs of Sussex are much like those in Warren, but even more Republican. Sussex and Warren were two of the five New Jersey counties Dole carried in 1996.

The less-populous portion of upper Passaic County contributes four municipalities to the 5th. It is more Republican and less industrialized than its southern section, which is mostly in the 8th District. It includes West Milford Township, which, at about 25,000 in population, barely beats out suburban Paramus (Bergen County) as the 5th's most populous.

1990 Population: 594,630. White 556,154 (94%), Black 7,906 (1%), Other 30,570 (5%). Hispanic origin 16,567 (3%). 18 and over 452,587 (76%), 62 and over 91,998 (15%). Median age: 36.

and the roof over my head?"

In the 104th Congress, Roukema was sponsor of the House version of the Kassebaum-Kennedy health insurance "portability" bill, which made it easier for people to keep continuous health care coverage when moving from job to job, and made it very difficult for insurance companies to refuse coverage for "pre-existing" health conditions.

Conservative Republicans included a variety of provisions of their own liking to the health care legislation, including a highly controversial plan to allow people to establish medical savings accounts to pay health care costs independent of insurance coverage.

The House defeated Roukema's measure, which was offered as a substitute amendment to the leadership-backed proposal. But after much struggling between congressional Republicans and the Clinton White House, Roukema could take satisfaction in the fact that the health insurance bill as enacted was closer to what she had proposed than to the House Republican measure.

In the Democratic-controlled 103rd Congress, Roukema had offered her own health care overhaul legislation when the Education and Labor Committee's Labor-Management Relations Subcommittee took up a bill closely resembling Clinton's proposed health care overhaul.

Her substitute measure called for incremental changes, not the more ambitious reform contemplated by the administration. It would have required employers to offer — but not pay for — health insurance for their workers. It would have allowed businesses with fewer than 50 employees to band together to voluntarily increase their bargaining power with insurance companies for better policies and prices.

It also would have held down what insurance companies could charge for their policies. And, under most circumstances, it would have prevented insurers from excluding people with pre-existing conditions from purchasing a policy.

Roukema, who was the subcommittee's ranking Republican, said her bill would "address the most glaring faults of our system," without tearing apart what is good about health care in the United States. Her plan was rejected, however, on a party-line vote.

Roukema also has been one of the most tenacious supporters of helping parents collect child support payments they are owed. Provisions giving states more power to track down and collect from non-paying parents were included in the welfare overhaul bill that became law in 1996.

In her votes on spending taxpayer's money, Roukema exceeds the conservatism of many in the GOP who disdain her moderation on social-policy issues. The Concord Coalition, a group advocating fiscal discipline to eliminate the deficit, has named her one of the top 10 most "deficit-conscious" members of the House.

She voted for measures to restrain or freeze defense spending, opposing GOP-led efforts to give the Pentagon more money than requested by the Clinton administration. She has opposed two big-ticket projects favored by many in her party, the superconducting super collider (which was killed) and NASA's space station (which survives).

Roukema has long been a leader of House Republican women who support abortion rights. In the 104th, she voted to maintain a requirement that states fund Medicaid abortions for poor women in cases of rape, incest and to protect the life of the woman; she voted to permit abortions at overseas military hospitals; and she voted to allow federal employees' health care plans to cover abortions. She has, however, sided with efforts to ban a particular abortion technique that opponents call "partial birth" abortion.

Roukema voted for two gun control measures passed in the 103rd Congress that were strongly backed by the Clinton administration. Before her vote on banning 19 types of semiautomatic assault-style weapons, Roukema said, "We do not pretend that an assault weapon ban will end all crime, or even all gun violence. But taken in step with a strong crime bill, this can start to end the national epidemic of violence." In 1996, she was one of just 42 House Republicans to vote against repealing the assault-weapons ban.

At Home: It took Roukema two tries to topple a Democratic incumbent. But after her narrow victory in 1980, redistricting gave her a constituency that is very happy with her brand of moderate GOP representation.

The Democratic Legislature's 1981 remap paired her with fellow Republican Jim Courter in a GOP-friendly 5th District. Courter decided to run in the 12th, giving Roukema a clear shot. She won in 1982 with 65 percent and has not drawn less than 71 percent in any election since then.

Elections were much more difficult for Roukema in her original district. The old 7th was less Republican, and she had to run twice there to unseat liberal Democratic Rep. Andrew Maguire. In her first challenge, in 1978, she was a former teacher returning to politics five years after leaving the Ridgewood Board of Education. She attacked Maguire for being "anti-defense" and lost by 8,815 votes.

In 1980, she focused on complaints that Maguire, a critic of big oil companies during the 1979 gasoline shortage, was anti-business. With a

HOUSE ELECTIONS

1996 General		
Marge Roukema (R)	181,323	(71%)
Bill Auer (D)	62,956	(25%)
Lorraine L. La Neve (NJC)	4,093	(2%)
1996 Primary		
Marge Roukema (R)	20,682	(75%)
George Matreyek (R)	5,076	(18%)
Roger Bacon (R)	1,820	(7%)
1994 General		
Marge Roukema (R)	139,964	(74%)
Bill Auer (D)	41,275	(22%)
William J. Leonard (I)	3,746	(2%)
Roger Bacon (LIBERT)	2,882	(2%)

Previous Winning Percentages: 1992 (72%) **1990** (76%) **1988** (76%) **1986** (75%) **1984** (71%) **1982** (65%) **1980** (51%)

CAMPAIGN FINANCE

	Receipts	Receipts from PACs	Expend-itures
1996			
Roukema (R)	$515,185	$302,940 (59%)	$496,610
Auer (D)	$31,440	$4,700 (15%)	$28,002
Childers (ROP)	$671	0	$549
1994			
Roukema (R)	$494,801	$235,286 (48%)	$497,345
Auer (D)	$6,634	$5,500 (83%)	$160

DISTRICT VOTE FOR PRESIDENT

1996		1992	
D	115,346 (43%)	**D**	99,733 (34%)
R	127,415 (47%)	**R**	146,004 (50%)
I	23,659 (9%)	**I**	48,666 (17%)

KEY VOTES

1997	
Ban "partial birth" abortions	Y
1996	
Approve farm bill	Y
Deny public education to illegal immigrants	Y
Repeal ban on certain assault-style weapons	N
Increase minimum wage	Y
Freeze defense spending	Y
Approve welfare overhaul	Y
1995	
Approve balanced-budget constitutional amendment	Y
Relax Clean Water Act regulations	N
Oppose limits on environmental regulations	Y
Reduce projected Medicare spending	Y
Approve GOP budget with tax and spending cuts	Y

VOTING STUDIES

	Presidential Support		Party Unity		Conservative Coalition	
Year	**S**	**O**	**S**	**O**	**S**	**O**
1996	51	46	64	31	43	55
1995	44	51	69	27	61	33
1994	62	31	64	29	61	31
1993	45	49	67	29	59	39
1992	48	45	66	30	56	35
1991	54	41	56	37	62	35

INTEREST GROUP RATINGS

Year	ADA	AFL-CIO	CCUS	ACU
1996	50	n/a	56	53
1995	35	8	65	36
1994	35	17	100	50
1993	35	33	70	54
1992	50	42	71	68
1991	35	55	67	50

6 Frank Pallone Jr. (D)

Of Long Branch — Elected 1988; 5th full term

Biographical Information

Born: Oct. 30, 1951, Long Branch, N.J.

Education: Middlebury College, B.A. 1973; Tufts U., M.A. 1974; Rutgers U., J.D. 1978.

Occupation: Lawyer.

Family: Wife, Sarah Hospodor; two children.

Religion: Roman Catholic.

Political Career: Long Branch City Council, 1982-88; N.J. Senate, 1984-88.

Capitol Office: 420 Cannon Bldg. 20515; 225-4671.

Committees

Commerce
Energy & Power; Finance & Hazardous Materials; Health & Environment

Resources
Fisheries Conservation, Wildlife & Oceans

In Washington: At the outset of the 105th Congress, Pallone left the influential Commerce Committee to accommodate House Democratic leaders, who had six prospects in mind for the panel but only five seats vacant. Pallone gave up Commerce with assurances that he would get back on as soon as another seat came open, and that opening came very quickly — when New Mexico Democrat Bill Richardson left the House in February 1997 to become U.S. representative to the United Nations.

Pallone also keeps his seat on the Resources Committee, which he gained in June 1995.

Commerce and Resources both give Pallone a chance to pursue his interest in environmental matters. The 6th District includes a part of the Jersey shore, and many residents vividly recall New Jersey's late-1980s problems with municipal sewage overflowing onto beaches and forcing their closure.

When the House in May 1995 debated a GOP measure relaxing clean water act regulations dealing with the discharge of wastes and storm water into waterways, Pallone offered a number of amendments aimed at preserving current water pollution restrictions. All his proposals were rejected. One Pallone amendment would have removed from the bill a provision waiving secondary treatment requirements for certain water treatment plants that discharge into deep ocean waters; a second established uniform national standards for beach water quality.

Pallone has been among the Democrats most assertive in portraying the GOP as anti-environment — a line of attack that did some damage in the 1996 elections. As Pallone sees it, Republicans aim "to gut successful environmental laws" such as the clean water act, the Clean Air Act, the superfund hazardous waste law, and the Safe Drinking Water Act. The GOP, he said in 1996, "voted against adequate funding for our nation's toxic waste cleanup programs. They voted to stop the EPA from protecting Americans from exposure to arsenic, dioxin, lead and other cancer-causing pollutants and to allow corporate polluters to dump as many as 70,000 chemicals into our nation's rivers, lakes and streams and, finally, to allow industry to pollute our drinking water."

Pallone also fumed about a GOP effort to include a provision in the final version of the fiscal 1996 spending bill for the Department of Commerce that he said would undermine the federal ban against dumping trash and sludge at sea.

Pallone said the conference report contained language directing the National Oceanographic and Atmospheric Administration to spend money to evaluate and begin a demonstration project on the "deep ocean isolation of wastes." He told the House that the federal Ocean Dumping Ban Act of 1988 makes it illegal to dispose of waste at sea. "This is the second attack on ocean protection we've seen by this Congress," Pallone said. "Earlier this year, the House passed a so-called Clean Water Act reauthorization that allowed sewage to be dumped into the ocean. Now we have a conference report that spends taxpayer money to authorize the use of the ocean floor as a landfill. Frankly, I've had it. I'm sick and tired of Republican efforts to gut our environmental laws in order to benefit special interests."

Pallone told the Newark Star-Ledger that he considers "ocean-related issues" the No. 1 concern in his district. "I think a lot of times people feel like pollution is being dumped on them," he said in October 1996.

From his Commerce seat, Pallone also fought a GOP effort to wipe out a recent expansion in federal pipeline safety regulations. The committee in May 1995 approved a bill that would apply the new Republican-drafted "risk assessment" rule — requiring that the cost of regulations be no greater than the probable reduction in risk — to operators of natural gas and hazardous liquid pipelines. The pipeline safety programs are funded by fees on pipeline operators.

Pallone said the consequences of pipeline accidents are too great to risk the changes required under the bill. An apartment complex in

NEW JERSEY 6
Central — Part of Edison; New Brunswick; Long Branch

From industrial Middlesex County to the shore communities of Monmouth County, the 6th has been one of the more competitive districts in New Jersey, although recent trends have favored Democrats.

This mostly middle-class and independent-voting slice of New Jersey is a crucial component of any successful statewide effort.

The 1992 presidential campaign emphasized the district's competitive nature. Both Bill Clinton and George Bush made concerted efforts here, but in the Monmouth County portion, neither could gain a decisive advantage: Bush won by about 1,100 votes. Four years later, Clinton had widened the margin to more than 16,000 votes and nearly doubled that in the Middlesex County portion.

Jobs and the economy are pressing issues in Middlesex County, where almost 60 percent of the district population comes from 13 towns. Democrats traditionally run well in the county, though residents have been known to split their tickets.

Edison — a part of which is in the 7th District — is the largest city in the district, and home to some manufacturing concerns and corporate headquarters. Some of Edison's white-collar employees live nearby in Metuchen.

Black voters and the Rutgers University community boost Democrats in New Brunswick. Across the Raritan River, Republicans are competitive in more affluent Piscataway and Highland Park. Suburban ticket-splitting and independent voting is more prevalent in populous Old Bridge and Sayreville.

The inland portion of Monmouth County is suburban, and less affluent and Republican than the rest of the county, which is divided into the 4th, 6th and 12th districts. In the 4th and 12th parts, Republicans carried the House and presidential races relatively easily in 1992. But in the 6th's, Bush barely squeaked by, while Pallone won by more than 7,000 votes.

Most of the suburban, Republican turf of Middletown — the largest town in Monmouth County — is in the 6th, but a part of it is in the 12th District. The more working-class Red Bank is fertile ground for Democrats.

In coastal Monmouth County, the environment weighs heavily in political debates. Ocean dumping, beach erosion and hurricane protection are matters of import to locals. The coastal region begins with the Sandy Hook part of the Gateway National Recreation Area, which extends like a thin finger from the top of Monmouth County.

Democrats also tend to find votes in the working-class Bayshore area, made up of small fishing towns to the west of Sandy Hook, although voters here are also prone to split their tickets.

Farther south, the shore communities used to attract the 19th century elite. President James A. Garfield was brought to his summer cottage in Long Branch in 1881 after he was shot; he died there a few weeks later. The aging seaside resort of Asbury Park — glorified by singer and local hero Bruce Springsteen — has faded in prominence. The black community in Asbury Park helps keep it in the Democratic column. Deal is a wealthier, residential community.

1990 Population: 594,630. White 486,512 (82%), Black 66,850 (11%), Other 41,268 (7%). Hispanic origin 36,492 (6%). 18 and over 465,699 (78%), 62 and over 88,181 (15%). Median age: 33.

his district was destroyed in March 1994 by a gas explosion. The committee did include a provision he sponsored that would establish civil and criminal penalties for dumping solid waste within a petroleum or natural gas pipeline right-of-way. Dumping in the vicinity of a pipeline was suspected of having caused the Edison, N.J., explosion.

In the 104th Congress, Pallone was the ranking Democrat on Commerce's Energy and Power Subcommittee, where he weighed in early on the looming issue of electric utility deregulation, a big agenda item in the 105th.

He introduced a bill late in the 104th that would predicate any legislation on utility restructuring on changing the Clean Air Act to bring old coal-fired plants under tighter federal air quality standards. Pallone is worried that in a deregulated utilities marketplace, emissions from coal-fired power plants in the Midwest would increase, polluting the air in the Northeast. Others argue that reopening the Clean Air Act while members are trying to enact sweeping energy legislation would make the task that much more daunting.

Pallone generally votes a loyal Democratic line, with some high-profile exceptions. In 1993, he deserted Clinton in two key battles: on passage of the budget and NAFTA. Citing environmental and labor concerns, Pallone also opposed GATT.

In the 104th, he broke from many in the liberal wing of his party and voted for a balanced-budget constitutional amendment and for overhauling the welfare system.

Like most Democrats, though, he opposed repealing the ban on certain semiautomatic assault-style weapons, and he supported a freeze on defense spending. He shifted from his longtime anti-abortion stance in the 101st Congress and now generally sides with abortion-rights advocates. After the Supreme Court's *Webster* decision giving states more authority to regulate abortion, Pallone said, "I have come to the conclusion that it is inappropriate for me to impose my religious beliefs on those who do not share those beliefs or whose circumstances demand that other choices be available."

At Home: While 1992 redistricting may have set Pallone in unfamiliar territory, he has gained a solid hold on the 6th, winning a fifth term in 1996 with more than 60 percent of the vote.

When some members of New Jersey's House delegation got together to draw up their version of the new congressional map for the 1990s, Pallone was conspicuously absent. So, too, was Pallone's district when a final plan was handed down in March 1992.

It was partly a reflection of Pallone's lone wolf status, earned when he angered Democrats by criticizing the congressional pay raise of 1989. It was also rooted in the political reality of reapportionment. (New Jersey lost one seat.)

Pallone's 3rd District was merged with Democratic Rep. Bernard J. Dwyer's 6th. Instead of his old Monmouth County-based "shore" district, Pallone had to run in 1992 in a district rooted in unfamiliar Middlesex County. He dodged a bullet when Dwyer retired, but state Rep. Bob Smith took Dwyer's place in the primary.

Endorsed by Dwyer, Smith ran a high-spending, hard-hitting campaign, portraying Pallone as ineffective. But Pallone artfully positioned himself as an outsider; his campaign slogan was "Our best hope — their worst nightmare." He painted Smith, a former county party chairman in Middlesex County, as an insider. Pallone won the primary by 18 points.

In the general election, both Pallone and the Republican nominee, state Sen. Joseph M. Kyrillos, wooed the district's mostly moderate, independent, middle-of-the-road voters. Kyrillos distanced himself from the national party line on social issues such as abortion, while Pallone stressed his outsider credentials.

But as George Bush's prospects faded, so did Kyrillos'. With a 2-1 fundraising advantage, Pallone won by 52 percent to 45 percent. He improved to 60 percent in 1994 and hit 61 percent in 1996 against GOP state Rep. Steve Corodemus.

Pallone was a protégé of veteran Democratic Rep. James J. Howard, who was chairman of the Public Works Committee until he died in 1988, leaving the 3rd open. For the special election, many Democratic insiders, including Howard's widow, lined up behind Pallone, who had won reelection to the state Senate in 1987 with 60 percent of the vote. He won the Democratic House nomination without a contest and faced Republican Joseph Azzolina, a former state legislator, in the general election.

Though both candidates had name-recognition problems outside their home areas, Pallone enjoyed an advantage because of his work on environmental issues in the pollution-conscious 3rd. Pallone won with 52 percent of the vote.

In 1990, Democrats across New Jersey hunkered down, fearing the wrath of voters angry about Democratic Gov. James J. Florio's $2.8 billion tax increase. Pallone's little-known Republican challenger, lawyer Paul A. Kapalko, milked anti-tax fury for all it was worth and Pallone survived by only 4,258 votes.

HOUSE ELECTIONS

1996 General		
Frank Pallone Jr. (D)	124,635	(61%)
Steven J. Corodemus (R)	73,402	(36%)
Keith Quarles (LIBERT)	2,044	(1%)
1994 General		
Frank Pallone Jr. (D)	88,922	(60%)
Mike Herson (R)	55,287	(38%)
Charles H. Dickson (CAP)	1,774	(1%)

Previous Winning Percentages: 1992 (52%) **1990** (49%) **1988** (52%) **1988†** (52%)

† Special election

CAMPAIGN FINANCE

	Receipts	Receipts from PACs	Expend-itures
1996			
Pallone (D)	$735,687	$485,351 (66%)	$658,367
Corodemus (R)	$320,856	$16,066 (5%)	$319,354
Quarles (LIBERT)	$7,528	0	$7,527
1994			
Pallone (D)	$672,935	$471,210 (70%)	$672,626
Herson (R)	$256,328	$7,099 (3%)	$252,307

DISTRICT VOTE FOR PRESIDENT

1996		1992	
D	122,759 (55%)	**D**	110,821 (44%)
R	74,600 (33%)	**R**	98,397 (39%)
I	22,167 (10%)	**I**	41,646 (17%)

KEY VOTES

1997	
Ban "partial-birth" abortions	N
1996	
Approve farm bill	N
Deny public education to illegal immigrants	N
Repeal ban on certain assault-style weapons	N
Increase minimum wage	Y
Freeze defense spending	Y
Approve welfare overhaul	Y
1995	
Approve balanced-budget constitutional amendment	Y
Relax Clean Water Act regulations	N
Oppose limits on environmental regulations	Y
Reduce projected Medicare spending	N
Approve GOP budget with tax and spending cuts	N

VOTING STUDIES

	Presidential Support		Party Unity		Conservative Coalition	
Year	S	O	S	O	S	O
1996	81	19	91	9	25	75
1995	77	23	89	11	37	63
1994	71	29	89	11	39	61
1993	74	26	90	10	32	68
1992	29	71	82	18	33	67
1991	33	66	75	24	54	46

INTEREST GROUP RATINGS

Year	ADA	AFL-CIO	CCUS	ACU
1996	90	n/a	25	10
1995	85	83	33	24
1994	70	78	67	14
1993	90	92	36	13
1992	90	83	38	28
1991	60	92	10	30

7 Bob Franks (R)

Of New Providence — Elected 1992, 3rd term

Biographical Information
Born: Sept. 21, 1951, Hackensack, N.J.
Education: DePauw U., B.A. 1973; Southern Methodist U., J.D. 1976.
Occupation: Newspaper owner.
Family: Single.
Religion: Methodist.
Political Career: N.J. Assembly, 1980-92; N.J. Republican Party chairman, 1988-92.
Capitol Office: 225 Cannon Bldg. 20515; 225-5361.

Committees
Budget
Transportation & Infrastructure
Railroads; Surface Transportation; Water Resources & Environment

In Washington: Franks is another one of the socially moderate, fiscally conservative Republicans not uncommon in the party's northeastern ranks. But on occasion he has tacked further to the right than most of his regional colleagues.

In 1995, for instance, he was the only Garden State Republican who supported an overhaul of the clean water act, defying the efforts of fellow New Jersey GOP Rep. H. James Saxton to rally the state's Republican delegation against the bill. The measure was particularly controversial in New Jersey, which in the late 1980s saw some of its beaches fouled by municipal sewage overflows.

In the opening months of the 104th Congress, Franks voted for "Contract With America" legislation 95 percent of the time, and in October 1995 he supported the GOP's budget-reconciliation bill, which provided for a balanced budget by 2002 in part by making controversial reductions in the rate of spending growth on Medicare and Medicaid.

As a freshman in the 103rd Congress, Franks got a seat on the Budget Committee, and he used it to contend that President Clinton's economic policies were "Florio II". Democrats in Washington, he said, were pursuing the same kind of high-tax, big-government course that made James J. Florio a one-term governor in New Jersey. Franks argued that the federal budget needed a dose of the fiscal medicine being administered by Republican Christine Todd Whitman, who ousted Florio in November 1993: cutting taxes and rigorously prioritizing programs.

Franks' line of thinking was widely fashionable after Republicans captured Congress in 1994; Gov. Whitman was chosen to deliver the GOP response to Clinton's January 1995 State of the Union address. Earlier, Franks had been named by Speaker-to-be Newt Gingrich to a 10-member GOP team overseeing the transition from Democratic to Republican rule in the House. Franks had particular responsibility for reallocating Hill office space, and in that capacity he got involved in GOP efforts to sell one of the House office buildings as a symbol of congressional staff downsizing. But for various logistical reasons, none of the bigger office buildings proved a good candidate to put up for sale, and the best the Republicans could do was offer up a small building that was partly occupied by the House day care center.

"Better government at less cost" was Franks' mantra, and he faulted regulations and mandates imposed from Washington "with no consideration of their impact on jobs." In 1995, he and Paul E. Gillmor, R-Ohio, proposed a constitutional amendment barring unfunded mandates.

Franks' zeal for conservative fiscal policies has endeared him to GOP leaders. In 1996, he and Jennifer Dunn of Washington represented rank-and-file House Republicans at weekly strategy meetings that Senate Majority Leader Trent Lott, Gingrich and Republican National Committee Chairman Haley Barbour designed to coordinate Republican House and Senate campaigns with the presidential campaign of GOP nominee Bob Dole.

At the same time, however, Franks takes care not to stray too far to the right for his politically competitive district, which Clinton carried over Dole by 51 percent to 40 percent in 1996. In the 103rd Congress, he voted to require employers to provide unpaid family and medical leave, and he was one of just seven in his freshman GOP class who voted for a five-day waiting period for handgun purchases and for a ban on certain semiautomatic assault-style weapons. In the 104th, he voted against repealing the assault weapons ban, he backed efforts to increase the minimum wage and he opposed exempting small businesses from paying the higher wage. Franks generally sides with abortion-rights proponents, although he has supported banning a particular abortion technique that opponents call "partial birth" abortion.

Franks also tends to the home front through his work on the Transportation and Infrastructure Committee, where he tries to make sure New Jersey gets its share of federal transportation funds. The 105th Congress will be apportioning billions in this area as it crafts a new surface

Before GOP Rep. Matthew J. Rinaldo unexpectedly announced his post-primary retirement in 1992, it was assumed that he easily would win re-election to the 7th. Redistricting had removed urban, industrial and Democratic Elizabeth, though it hardly had been a problem for Rinaldo in the past since the Republican suburbs usually drowned out Elizabeth's vote.

After Rinaldo dropped out, Democrats had hopes they might capture the 7th in an open race. But Republican Franks held the seat for his party with 53 percent, carrying the four counties that make up the 7th — Essex, Middlesex, Somerset and Union (a part of each is in the district).

Democratic fortunes in the 7th have steadily improved in presidential contests. In 1988, George Bush won 60 percent of the vote in the areas that make up the district; four years later, he dropped to 45 percent, but that beat Bill Clinton's 41 percent. In 1996 Clinton carried the 7th with 51 percent and led in the parts of all four counties in the district, even as Franks won re-election.

Roughly half the vote is cast in Union County. Predominantly black and Democratic Plainfield is the most populous place in the county's portion of the 7th, followed closely by Union Township (a small part of the township is in the 10th).

North of Plainfield, the towns are mostly suburban, white and Republican. Summit, Westfield and Cranford are bedroom communities for New York City and Newark. Local officials in the greater Plainfield area have been engaged in a two-decade effort to lobby the federal government for flood control measures to protect the heavily populated Green Brook basin at the foot of the Watchung Mountains. In 1973, a torrential rainstorm sent water pouring down the steep mountain ridges into the flatlands below. Green Brook and other normally placid streams swelled up, killing six people and causing more than $30 million in property damage.

NEW JERSEY 7
North and Central — Parts of Woodbridge and Union

About a quarter of the district's population comes from each of Middlesex and Somerset counties. Middlesex contributes only two whole municipalities and parts of two others, but these areas constitute a significant voting bloc. Included are one of New Jersey's largest suburbs, middle-class Woodbridge, and part of Edison. (Most of Edison is in the neighboring 6th District.)

Farther west, in southern Somerset County, corporate and industrial growth along Interstate 287 and U.S. 22 has led to population increases in Bridgewater and Hillsborough. Somerset generally backs Republican candidates. But Democratic votes can be found in the industrial boroughs, such as Manville and Bound Brook, to the south.

The Johns Manville plant that gave Manville its name attracted large numbers of Poles and other Slavic immigrants in the 1930s and '40s. By 1982, though, the company was forced to file for bankruptcy after being slapped with tens of thousands of asbestos-related lawsuits. In 1985, the factory shut down.

A small portion of western Essex County is in the 7th's northern tip. It includes parts of two towns, Maplewood and affluent Millburn. Pharmaceutical companies and high-tech ventures are among area employers.

1990 Population: 594,629. White 497,273 (84%), Black 60,532 (10%), Other 36,824 (6%). Hispanic origin 29,712 (5%). 18 and over 467,393 (79%), 62 and over 101,000 (17%). Median age: 36.

transportation authorization bill.

Franks pursues constituent concerns such as airport noise, flood control, and highway and commuter rail improvements. He helped obtain $500,000 in the fiscal 1997 transportation appropriations bill to restore the defunct West Trenton Railroad Line from Somerset County to Mercer County.

He introduced a bill relocating the Federal Aviation Administration to New Jersey so it could experience airport noise up close and in person. The FAA in 1987 rerouted air traffic along the East Coast, increasing the noise over New Jersey.

"After a few months of being in one of the most noise-impacted counties in the nation, perhaps the FAA will become more amenable to finally solving New Jersey's aircraft noise problem," Franks said.

Members from New York, where the FAA now is located, vowed to fight the bill. "Should Congressman Franks succeed in his relocation efforts, the state of New York could lose approximately 600 jobs," said Rep. Susan Molinari of neighboring Staten Island. "I fail to see how reopening the debate over the relocation of the eastern regional FAA offices effectively addresses the very real air noise concerns."

But Franks and Molinari later joined forces and appeared together at Newark Airport to announce legislation they said would force the FAA to reduce aircraft noise in both Staten Island and New Jersey. The lawmakers said the FAA had been misleading them, saying the other side wanted to shift the noise across the Hudson River.

"Instead of being pitted against each other, New York and New Jersey are working together to solve what the FAA seems to be unable to," Molinari said.

Franks also won approval of an amendment to legislation removing the FAA from the Transportation Department, exempting it from federal procurement and personnel regulations, and taking the aviation trust funds off budget. Franks' amendment created an FAA ombudsman on airplane noise.

After the crash of two New Jersey Transit commuter trains that killed three people, Franks joined labor union officials at Newark's Penn Station and announced he would introduce legislation banning overnight split shifts for train crews. Investigators for the National Transportation Safety Board said their preliminary review showed that operator fatigue might have contributed to the crash.

At Home: Franks first gained widespread public notice in 1991 by spearheading the Republicans' anti-tax, anti-Florio campaign that resulted in the GOP capturing both chambers of New Jersey's Legislature.

He had not anticipated that 1992 would find him a candidate for the House; many believed he was preparing to run for governor in 1993. But the GOP nomination for the 7th virtually fell into his lap when veteran Rep. Matthew J. Rinaldo unexpectedly announced his retirement after the primary.

A state assemblyman for 13 years and a former GOP state chairman, Franks was well-positioned to succeed Rinaldo. The Democratic nominee, real estate developer Leonard R. Sendelsky, lacked Franks' name recognition, but he was one of the state's top Democratic fundraisers. And having held no previous political office, he could claim the popular "outsider" label. But Franks had gained sufficient anti-status-quo credentials with his efforts to roll back Florio's much loathed $2.8 billion 1990 tax increase. He won 53 percent to Sendelsky's 43 percent, and in 1994 posted an even more comfortable margin of victory.

Franks had strong opposition in 1996 in the form of lawyer Larry Lerner, who spent about $500,000 of his own money on the race. The AFL-CIO targeted Franks, and Lerner, like many Democratic challengers, attempted to link him to Gingrich and the conservative Republican revolution that had fallen into disfavor with moderate voters. But some transportation unions contributed to Franks even as the national labor federation was running advertisements criticizing his voting record. Franks ran five points behind his 1994 tally, but still won comfortably, 55 percent to 42 percent.

Franks' involvement in the GOP dates to his junior high school days in Chicago, when he volunteered on Charles H. Percy's unsuccessful 1964 bid for governor of Illinois. His introduction to New Jersey politics came in 1967 when he worked on Thomas H. Kean's campaign for the Legislature. Later he played a leading role in Kean's successful 1981 gubernatorial bid, and in 1987, Kean named Franks state GOP chairman.

HOUSE ELECTIONS

1996 General		
Bob Franks (R)	128,821	(55%)
Larry Lerner (D)	97,285	(42%)
Dorothy De Laura (NJC)	4,076	(2%)
1994 General		
Bob Franks (R)	98,814	(60%)
Karen Carroll (D)	64,231	(39%)
James J. Cleary (LAWR)	2,331	(1%)

Previous Winning Percentages: 1992 (53%)

CAMPAIGN FINANCE

	Receipts	Receipts from PACs		Expend-itures
1996				
Franks (R)	$1,196,918	$278,004	(23%)	$1,305,753
Lerner (D)	$808,625	$73,752	(9%)	$801,815
1994				
Franks (R)	$709,685	$148,101	(21%)	$542,564
Carroll (D)	$15,949	$2,500	(16%)	$15,667

DISTRICT VOTE FOR PRESIDENT

1996		1992	
D	130,313 (51%)	**D**	115,846 (41%)
R	101,647 (40%)	**R**	125,592 (45%)
I	19,793 (8%)	**I**	40,708 (14%)

KEY VOTES

1997	
Ban "partial birth" abortions	Y
1996	
Approve farm bill	N
Deny public education to illegal immigrants	Y
Repeal ban on certain assault-style weapons	N
Increase minimum wage	Y
Freeze defense spending	Y
Approve welfare overhaul	Y
1995	
Approve balanced-budget constitutional amendment	Y
Relax Clean Water Act regulations	Y
Oppose limits on environmental regulations	Y
Reduce projected Medicare spending	Y
Approve GOP budget with tax and spending cuts	Y

VOTING STUDIES

	Presidential Support		Party Unity		Conservative Coalition	
Year	**S**	**O**	**S**	**O**	**S**	**O**
1996	52	48	71	28	39	59
1995	39	60	80	19	70	30
1994	54	45	76	23	67	31
1993	56	44	77	22	64	36

INTEREST GROUP RATINGS

Year	ADA	AFL-CIO	CCUS	ACU
1996	35	n/a	81	63
1995	25	17	92	52
1994	25	0	91	62
1993	35	50	82	67

8 Bill Pascrell Jr. (D)

Of Paterson — Elected 1996, 1st term

Biographical Information

Born: Jan. 27, 1937, Paterson, N.J.

Education: Fordham U., B.A. 1959, M.A. 1961.

Military Service: Army, 1961; Army Reserves, 1962-67.

Occupation: City official; teacher.

Family: Wife, Elsie Marie Botto; three children.

Religion: Roman Catholic.

Political Career: N.J. House, 1988-97; mayor of Paterson, 1990-97.

Capitol Office: 1722 Longworth Bldg. 20515; 225-5751.

Committees

Small Business
Empowerment

Transportation & Infrastructure
Surface Transportation; Water Resources & Environment

The Path to Washington: A veteran state legislator and local official, Pascrell was his party's first choice to take on Rep. Bill Martini in 1996, two years after the freshman Republican's narrow victory ended 34 years of Democratic hegemony in the 8th District. The 1996 race was another close one: Pascrell toppled Martini with 51 percent of the vote.

With his son, William J. Pascrell III, running the campaign, Pascrell campaigned around the district trying to link Martini to House Speaker Newt Gingrich and the conservative House Republican majority.

Since upsetting freshman Democrat Herb Klein by just 1,800 votes in 1994, Martini had tried to steer a moderate path, bucking his party to support an increase in the minimum wage and opposing efforts to repeal the ban on certain semiautomatic assault-style weapons. He had the backing of the Sierra Club.

But he voted for provisions in the House Republicans' "Contract With America" 91 percent of the time and supported the Republicans' balanced-budget plan, which made cuts in the projected growth of Medicaid and Medicare.

Though Martini had the support of some local labor unions, most notably those representing transportation workers, he was one of the targets of the AFL-CIO's $35 million advertising campaign during the fall.

Pascrell had the backing of the New Jersey labor federation, and state union leaders eagerly embraced him. He called for programs to retrain workers, saying that concern about jobs was the number one issue on voters' minds in the district, which is a melange of suburbs and blue-collar towns. The district has suffered in recent years from the same sort of industrial decline that has afflicted numerous Northeastern cities.

During the campaign, Pascrell talked about being the grandson of Italian immigrants and a U.S. Army veteran. As is permitted by New Jersey law, he simultaneously served as mayor of Paterson, the city where he grew up, and as a state representative.

In 1996, his mayoral colleagues elected him "mayor of the year," a bipartisan honor that he touted as proof of his record in helping Paterson rebound from an exodus of manufacturing jobs

He also said his colleagues' support was evidence of his desire to go beyond party politics and work with lawmakers on both sides of the aisle to solve problems.

As a state lawmaker, he supported the still-unpopular tax increase advanced by Democratic Gov. James J. Florio in 1990. But as a congressional candidate, he boasted of his effort to eliminate a $1 million deficit in the Paterson city budget, and of how he reduced his own salary by $3,000 and did not take a pay raise.

He has called for middle-class tax cuts and a reduction in the capital gains tax if there is a way to ensure that some of the proceeds are used to promote economic growth. He also supports a balanced-budget constitutional amendment.

To pay for these tax breaks and to balance the budget, Pascrell said Congress should scale back the tax breaks and other benefits that go to corporations — so-called corporate welfare.

He supports family leave and the five-day waiting period requirement to purchase handguns, opposes the welfare overhaul enacted in the 104th, and supports additional defense cuts.

A former teacher and president of the Paterson Board of Education, Pascrell used his state legislative position to bring back extra state aid to Paterson. He developed drug education programs, authored state legislation to put first-time drug offenders in boot camps, and tried to curb the proliferation of pay phones in an attempt to hinder drug dealing in his city.

The 8th District had been represented for more than two decades by Democrat Robert A. Roe, who chaired the House Public Works and Transportation Committee. Martini had a seat on the renamed Transportation and Infrastructure Committee, and Pascrell landed a position there as well. He also got a seat on the Small Business Committee.

NEW JERSEY 8
North — Paterson

After surveying the Great Falls of the Passaic River in the late 18th century, Treasury Secretary Alexander Hamilton figured it would be an ideal place to develop some home-grown industry, independent of England. So he created the Society for Establishing Useful Manufactures to build facilities to harness the water power in Paterson, now the third-largest city in New Jersey.

The industrial complex was slow to develop, but by the mid-19th century, Paterson had attracted a wave of English, Irish and Dutch immigrants to staff its silk mills. A second wave would bring Italians, Poles and Slavs to work the looms.

Hamilton's vision thrived, and "Silk City" (as Paterson became known) developed into one of the world's leading textile producers. The city's mills also produced the first Colt revolvers, and by the late 19th century, Paterson was a leading producer of locomotives. The engine used in "The Spirit of St. Louis," the plane Charles Lindbergh piloted on his transatlantic voyage, was manufactured in Paterson.

But the introduction of rayon and other 20th century synthetic fabrics triggered an economic free fall from which the city has never fully recovered. Today, Paterson suffers from chronic unemployment, poverty and the side effects of industrial decline. The 1989 movie "Lean on Me" focused on the city's troubled Eastside High School and and principal Joe Clark's efforts to reverse its decline. At the behest of local officials, Congress in 1996 designated Great Falls as a historic district.

The city's large minority population — three-fourths of the residents are black or Hispanic — coupled with its deep-seated labor tradition, make Paterson (Passaic county) a reliable source of Democratic votes.

The white ethnics who left this area moved to Passaic County suburbs such as Wayne and Clifton, one of New Jersey's largest and oldest suburban communities.

Along with suburban Essex County voters, these independent-minded suburbanites increasingly allow GOP candidates to remain competitive in the 8th, despite Democrats' substantial registration advantage here. The Essex County portion of the district — about a third of the 8th's population — is mainly suburban turf, from the more affluent areas such as Montclair and South Orange to the blue-collar and middle-class towns of Nutley and Belleville. Italian Catholics make up a notable segment; there are also pockets of Jewish voters. Pascrell lost Essex County by 3,300 votes but won Passaic County by 9,600 votes.

Bloomfield, Essex County's largest city in the 8th, even played a role in the 1988 presidential election. It was at a local flag factory that Bush met with makers of Old Glory in order to publicize a controversy surrounding Democratic nominee Michael S. Dukakis and the Pledge of Allegiance.

Democrats run strongest in local and state political contests. At the presidential level, the GOP is more competitive. George Bush won this district by 9 percentage points in 1988, but prospects for Republican presidential candidates have dimmed since then. Bill Clinton edged Bush in the 8th in 1992, then overwhelmed Bob Dole four years later with 58 percent of the vote.

1990 Population: 594,629. White 444,372 (75%), Black 77,145 (13%), Other 73,112 (12%). Hispanic origin 105,764 (18%). 18 and over 461,457 (78%), 62 and over 104,868 (18%). Median age: 35.

HOUSE ELECTIONS

1996 General		
Bill J. Pascrell Jr. (D)	98,861	(51%)
Bill Martini (R)	92,609	(48%)

CAMPAIGN FINANCE

1996	Receipts	Receipts from PACs		Expend-itures
Pascrell (D)	$970,189	$221,876	(23%)	$952,722
Martini (R)	$1,422,638	$497,459	(35%)	$1,393,134

DISTRICT VOTE FOR PRESIDENT

	1996		1992
D	125,017 (58%)	D	107,304 (46%)
R	73,994 (34%)	R	99,974 (43%)
I	12,929 (6%)	I	27,797 (12%)

KEY VOTES

1997

Ban "partial birth" abortions	Y

9 Steven R. Rothman (D)

Of Fairlawn — Elected 1996, 1st term

Biographical Information

Born: Oct. 14, 1952, Englewood, N.J.

Education: Syracuse U., B.A. 1974; Washington U., J.D. 1977.

Occupation: Lawyer.

Family: Divorced; two children.

Religion: Jewish.

Political Career: Mayor of Englewood, 1983-89; Democratic nominee for Bergen County Freeholder, 1989; Bergen County surrogate court judge, 1993-96.

Capitol Office: 1607 Longworth Bldg. 20515; 225-5061.

Committees

International Relations
International Economic Policy & Trade

Judiciary
Crime

The Path to Washington: Though he faced determined opposition in the primary and general elections, Rothman won both handily to take the House seat that Democratic Rep. Robert G. Torricelli gave up in 1996 for a successful Senate bid.

After Torricelli announced he would seek the Senate seat being vacated by retiring Democrat Bill Bradley, Rothman quickly jumped into the race for the 9th and won the party endorsement.

But former Fair Lawn Mayor Robert Gordon challenged Rothman in the primary, calling him a tool of the party bosses. Gordon also outspent Rothman better than 2 to 1, putting in more than $350,000 out of his own pocket. Despite the monetary disadvantage, Rothman won nomination with 79 percent of the vote.

In the general election, Rothman faced Bergen County Clerk Kathleen A. Donovan, the kind of socially moderate, fiscally conservative Republican who, like Gov. Christine Todd Whitman and 5th District Rep. Marge Roukema, usually runs well in New Jersey.

Donovan also had been chairwoman of the Port Authority of New York and New Jersey, a bistate authority that runs the region's airports and many of its bridges and tunnels.

Rothman again won with room to spare, this time taking 56 percent of the vote, 14 points ahead of Donovan. In a district where the cost of television advertising is prohibitive, Rothman went door-to-door, talking up his record as mayor of Engle-wood and as judge of the Bergen County Surrogate Court.

On many issues, Rothman is a classic Democrat, supporting abortion rights, gun control and Pentagon spending cuts. He opposes term limits and the welfare overhaul bill signed into law by President Clinton during the 104th Congress.

Rothman, however, campaigned as a fiscal conservative, highlighting his efforts as mayor of Englewood to reduce the city's tax rate, while attacking Donovan for her use of the Port Authority helicopter and limousine.

He also tried to link Donovan to House Speaker Newt Gingrich, whom polls showed was very unpopular in New Jersey. Rothman repeatedly reminded audiences that Donovan's first vote as a congresswoman would likely be to reelect Gingrich as Speaker.

Although the district, with its affluent New York City suburbs in Bergen and Hudson counties, has shown some willingness to support Republicans, it routinely had given Torricelli more than 55 percent of the vote.

Donovan countered Rothman's attacks with her record of moderation, and endorsements from such groups as the Sierra Club and New Jersey Education Association. She stressed her opposition to the House Republicans' balanced-budget plan, which relied on cuts in the projected growth of Medicaid and Medicare.

Once elected, Rothman spent his first few days in Washington lobbying his Democratic colleagues before they filled the vacancies on House committees. He landed a seat on International Relations, where Torricelli played a major role in foreign affairs. He also serves on the Judiciary Committee.

He found an apartment in Washington; he will continue to live in Fair Lawn, N.J., where he has joint custody of his two children, and commute to the Capitol. In fact, in the midst of the Democratic organizational meetings, he flew back to New Jersey to attend a parent-teacher conference.

Rothman said he would try in Congress to create special education accounts, in which the interest on money deposited would be tax-free if the proceeds were used to help pay a child's college costs.

Like Torricelli, he is expected to be a vote for gun control. He backs the ban on certain semiautomatic assault-style weapons and the five-day waiting period for handgun purchases. He also supports the death penalty and opposes parole for violent criminals. During the campaign, he touted his record in reducing crime in Englewood.

NEW JERSEY 9
North — Fort Lee; Hackensack

Sports fans and concertgoers are familiar with the Meadowlands stadium complex in East Rutherford, but otherwise, there is little to distinguish the 9th from other suburban New Jersey districts.

By one measure — money — the 9th stands out. With more than half the population of Bergen County, one of the country's wealthiest counties, the district is more affluent than its suburban and urbanized north Jersey counterparts. It covers southeastern Bergen County and part of Hudson County, with prestigious Bergen addresses clustered in Englewood and the northern reaches of the 9th. The blue-collar areas are in the south.

The George Washington Bridge, connecting Manhattan's 181st Street and the New Jersey Palisades, is a fitting symbol for the 9th. Opened in 1931, the span spurred the growth of Bergen County.

South of posh Englewood, Fort Lee is home to affluent Asian-Americans, including a thriving Japanese community. Farther west from the Hudson River, the Jewish voters of Teaneck and Fair Lawn — part of which is in the 5th District — help turn out a Democratic vote, despite the towns' relative affluence. Hackensack has some affluent sections, but is more blue-collar, with a large black population.

Beginning south of the city of Hackensack, the Hackensack Meadowlands area is a 30-mile commercial and residential engine, experiencing increasing development amid the swamps of the region.

The southern reaches of the 9th contain working-class towns with large numbers of white ethnics, in places such as North Arlington, Lyndhurst and Kearny (Hudson County). Most of Kearny is in the 9th, with the exception of about 300 residents who live in the 13th.

Hudson County contributes less than a fifth of district voters and contains a mix of Hispanics and white ethnics, drawn from parts of Jersey City, Kearny, North Bergen and all of Secaucus.

The Jersey City segment is carved from the northern part of the city; it includes many Hispanics. The 9th is one of three districts that splice into Jersey City, the other two being the majority-minority 10th and 13th districts.

The 9th has no single dominant industry. Englewood houses some corporate headquarters; Secaucus has attracted new restaurants, offices, hotels and shopping outlets. It is also a warehousing and distribution center.

The politics of the 9th are firmly Democratic. Bergen, as a whole, has backed Republicans, namely George Bush in 1992 and Gov. Christine Todd Whitman in 1993, but Republican strength is derived from the county's northern tier, which lies in the 5th district. Bill Clinton won 48 percent in the 9th's portion of Bergen in 1992, and four years tallied 60 percent there. Rothman carried Bergen by about 18,700 votes against a highly touted Republican challenger.

1990 Population: 594,630. White 497,644 (84%), Black 38,517 (6%), Other 58,469 (10%). Hispanic origin 67,913 (11%). 18 and over 480,677 (81%), 62 and over 115,521 (19%). Median age: 37.

HOUSE ELECTIONS

1996 General		
Steven R. Rothman (D)	117,646	(56%)
Kathleen A. Donovan (R)	89,005	(42%)
Arthur B. Rosen (NJI)	2,730	(1%)
1996 Primary		
Steven R. Rothman (D)	17,016	(79%)
Robert Gordon (D)	3,715	(17%)
Lynne Athay Dow (D)	680	(3%)

CAMPAIGN FINANCE

	Receipts	Receipts from PACs	Expend-itures
1996			
Rothman (D)	$809,178	$252,600 (31%)	$797,632
Donovan (R)	$827,043	$193,324 (23%)	$789,894

DISTRICT VOTE FOR PRESIDENT

1996		1992	
D	138,109 (60%)	**D**	122,676 (48%)
R	71,678 (31%)	**R**	102,578 (40%)
I	17,007 (7%)	**I**	31,527 (12%)

KEY VOTES

1997

Ban "partial birth" abortions N

10 Donald M. Payne (D)

Of Newark — Elected 1988, 5th term

Biographical Information

Born: July 16, 1934, Newark, N.J.
Education: Seton Hall U., B.A. 1957.
Occupation: Community development executive.
Family: Widowed; three children.
Religion: Baptist.
Political Career: Essex County Board of Chosen Freeholders, 1972-78; sought Democratic nomination for Essex County executive, 1978; sought Democratic nomination for U.S. House, 1980; Newark Municipal Council, 1982-88; sought Democratic nomination for U.S. House, 1986.
Capitol Office: 2244 Rayburn Bldg. 20515; 225-3436.

Committees

Education & Workforce
Early Childhood, Youth & Families; Employer-Employee Relations (ranking)
International Relations
Africa; International Operations & Human Rights

In Washington: As chairman of the Congressional Black Caucus in the 104th Congress, Payne — previously known as a low-key, behind-the-scenes lawmaker — emerged as a vocal critic of the new Republican majority across a wide spectrum of issues, including affirmative action and welfare overhaul.

Payne's first challenge upon taking charge of the Black Caucus was dealing with its abolition as an official creature of Congress. One of the House's legislative support organizations (LSOs), it lost its taxpayer funding as House Republicans, intent on cutting congressional staff and expenses, eliminated all LSOs. House members in the Black Caucus kept the group going by contributing staff and resources, but for the first time in its 25-year history, the caucus had to battle being a minority within the House minority. "The struggle continues, which is the bad news; the good news is that we feel up to it," Payne said.

Although the CBC might not be in a position to push legislation through the House, Payne said, it would try to block enactment of bills it saw as harmful to blacks. One of the caucus' defensive successes came on affirmative action.

Early in the 104th, the caucus formed a task force to examine GOP affirmative action plans. "I am outraged by the efforts of the Republican majority to try to repeal affirmative action programs and attempt to turn the clock back on progress that had been made throughout the years," Payne said in a House floor speech.

In June 1995, CBC officials went to the White House to discuss the issue. "We wanted to communicate . . . in the strongest possible terms that there can be no abandonment of affirmative action," Payne told the Washington Times. The caucus got a measure of credit for President Clinton's subsequent announcement that he would seek to "mend, not end" affirmative action.

However, Payne's opposition to the 104th Congress' effort to, in Clinton's words, "end welfare as we know it," proved less successful. He argued passionately that unless Congress was willing to spend money to create new jobs, the GOP's welfare plan would have disastrous results.

"Without . . . opportunity for employment, opportunity for day care, opportunity for an adequate salary . . . taking this punitive approach to drop people from the welfare rolls will certainly do more harm," Payne said in July 1996.

Despite the Black Caucus' opposition, Congress passed and Clinton signed a welfare overhaul that ended the federal guarantee of assistance to low-income mothers and children. The law sets work requirements for welfare recipients and limits them to five years of benefits.

On the minimum wage, however, Payne backed a winner. With assistance from moderate Republicans, Democrats pressured the House GOP leadership to bring a wage-increase bill to the floor, where it passed. Payne said that raising the wage from $4.25 to $5.15 was a "small effort to help hard-working Americans struggle to keep themselves and their families out of poverty."

In May 1996, Payne faulted the Judiciary Committee for taking too long to schedule hearings after a string of 25 arsons at predominantly black churches in the first half of the year. Payne accused the committee of foot-dragging, noting that several weeks of hearings had been held to look into law officers' actions at the Branch Davidian compound near Waco, Texas, and at Ruby Ridge, Idaho. "We should have the same effort put into church burnings," Payne told The Boston Globe. "There is a disparity in the way justice is being dispensed in this country."

Payne cosponsored the "Church Arson Prevention Act," which made it clear that federal officials can investigate church burnings, and removed a bar on federal intervention in cases with less than $10,000 damage. Clinton signed the bill six days after it passed the House in June.

Payne also criticized Supreme Court rulings striking down what it saw as "racially gerrymandered" House districts in Texas and North Carolina. "The court ignored our nation's long, anguished history of racial discrimination," he said, noting a "dangerous parallel between the

NEW JERSEY 10
Parts of Newark and Jersey City

At midcentury, Newark was a city of nearly a half-million people. Nine percent of the state's population lived here; it was a commercial center that held about 15 percent of all jobs in New Jersey.

As the century winds down, Newark tells a different story. Population has declined to about 275,000. The city is still the most populous in the state — and the largest employment center — but its share of New Jersey's jobs is only about 4 percent.

The decade after the riots of the late 1960s saw a steep decline in the number of jobs and an increase in the number of whites moving out of the city. As the Irish and Italians who used to vie for political power fled to the suburbs, blacks became a majority and, accordingly, grabbed the reins of power at City Hall; an African-American has held the mayoralty since 1970. Districtwide, blacks make up about 60 percent of the population.

Blacks and whites have lived an uneasy coexistence in Newark, but both communities are as one in their inurement to the political intrigue and ethical improprieties of local politics.

In political circles, Essex County Democrats have been stabbing each other in the back since the late 1970s, when the county switched to a county executive form of government, thus diminishing the influence of local party bosses.

Redistricting split the city between the 10th and 13th districts, but more than half the residents of Newark live in the 10th. The 10th District portion is made up of the primarily black central, south and west wards and the racially mixed north section of the city. The central ward was decimated in the riots of 1967 and has never fully recovered. There have been efforts to revitalize the area, but the desperate living conditions and deep poverty continue.

From Newark, the district extends into the Essex County suburbs that combine with the city to make up nearly 60 percent of the district's voters.

Outside the city are some racially mixed, working-class suburbs such as Irvington and Montclair (which is shared with the 8th District).

Orange and populous East Orange are majority-black. More affluent are South and liberal West Orange, although most of both places are in the 8th.

Union County adds about 30 percent of the vote. Democratic and blue-collar Elizabeth makes up one-third of this portion, even though it is divided between the 13th and the 10th. Republicans can find votes in Rahway and Roselle.

Parts of two Democratic Hudson County municipalities — Jersey City and Bayonne — round out the 10th. This section of Jersey City includes about one-fourth of New Jersey's second-largest city; the Bayonne segment consists of about 5,000 residents. Like virtually everywhere else in the district, which is far and away the most Democratic in the state, they churn out healthy Democratic margins.

1990 Population: 594,630. White 194,097 (33%), Black 357,671 (60%), Other 42,862 (7%). Hispanic origin 72,877 (12%). 18 and over 444,087 (75%), 62 and over 83,709 (14%). Median age: 32.

redistricting decisions of 1996, which threaten to disenfranchise African-Americans," and the court''s 1896 ruling in *Plessy v. Ferguson*, approving the segregation of blacks under the "separate but equal" doctrine.

From his seat on the International Relations Committee, Payne continues to speak out on foreign affairs issues of concern to many blacks, most notably regarding Haiti and Africa.

In the 103rd Congress, Payne was one of the Black Caucus' point men on Haiti, pressing the Clinton administration to restore Jean-Bertrand Aristide — ousted in a 1991 military coup — as the nation's president. Payne joined five other members of Congress in April 1994 in front of the White House to protest the administration's Haiti policy. They were arrested for civil disobedience.

After Clinton sent U.S. troops to the island in September 1994 and restored Aristide to power, Payne became a booster of the administration's policy. He visited the island in April as peacekeeping duties were turned over to the United Nations, and later acted as an international observer overseeing the Haitian elections.

Although Payne opposed authorizing the use of force against Iraq in 1991, he has been more positive about U.S. military involvement in some other places, as the Haiti episode showed. Payne in late 1992 supported President George Bush's decision to send U.S. troops as part of a U.N. peacekeeping mission to Somalia.

"I think the question today is whether the United States of America is going to be a participant in the new international order, the new world order, where the United Nations will be the police people of the world," Payne told the House.

He criticized as "disgraceful" the Clinton administration's response to the civil war in Rwanda, and he has faulted what he sees as Clinton's failure to develop a coherent foreign policy toward Africa. In 1994, when the administration hastily planned a White House conference on

Africa, Black Caucus members boycotted the event, complaining that the guests were only invited a few days before it was held.

"During the Cold War, the United States stayed engaged in Africa to fight off the threat of communism," Payne said. "Now we have a chance to help Africa eradicate the problems of health care, eradicate illiteracy, eradicate AIDS, fight disease and continue to move to democratization."

Payne also serves on the Education and the Workforce Committee, where he is ranking Democrat on the Employer-Employee Relations Subcommittee. Payne's district is centered on Newark, which, like many cities, is struggling with high rates of poverty and unemployment.

Concern about a dearth of job opportunities helped persuade Payne to vote against NAFTA in 1993. He said more than 50 industries in New Jersey were identified as being at risk under NAFTA, potentially affecting more than 250,000 workers. "Considering the bleak condition of our urban economy, the prospect of losing a single American job is unacceptable," Payne said.

At Home: Perseverance enabled Payne to pull himself up from poverty and become a successful businessman and community and political leader in his hometown of Newark. It took the same kind of perseverance – three campaigns — to win election in the black-majority 10th: His path was blocked by the legendary Democratic Rep. Peter W. Rodino Jr., who held the seat for 40 years. Rodino, chairman of the Judiciary Committee, achieved national fame during the 1974 Watergate hearings, but it was Rodino's steadfast advocacy of civil rights legislation that earned him the loyalty — and votes — of many black residents in the 10th.

Insisting that the time had come for Newark-area blacks to be represented by one of their own, Payne challenged Rodino in the 1980 Democratic primary and again in the 1986 primary. However, black good will toward Rodino, combined with his base in Newark's mainly Italian North Ward, enabled the incumbent to win easily. Payne got 23 percent of the vote in 1980 and 36 percent in 1986.

But when Rodino said the 1986 contest would be his last, local Democrats got behind Payne, a longtime party insider who had served on the Essex County Board and was in his second term on the Newark Municipal Council. Payne's only opposition came in the Democratic primary from City Council colleague Ralph T. Grant Jr. But Payne's advantages — party support, a sizable campaign treasury and recognition earned in his earlier campaigns — easily brought him the nomination. Payne's November victory was a formality in the overwhelmingly Democratic district.

A high school history teacher and football coach after college, Payne moved into business in 1963 as community affairs director for the Newark-based Prudential Insurance Co. Later, he was vice president of a computer forms company founded by his brother.

The head of a "storefront YMCA" in inner-city Newark in the late 1950s, Payne became the first black president of the National Council of YMCAs in 1970 and later served two four-year terms as chairman of the YMCA's International Committee on refugees. While participating in all these activities, the widowed Payne was raising two children and building his political career.

HOUSE ELECTIONS

1996 General		
Donald M. Payne (D)	127,126	(84%)
Vanessa Williams (R)	22,086	(15%)
1996 Primary		
Donald M. Payne (D)	35,002	(82%)
Brian Connors (D)	4,421	(10%)
Cecil J. Banks (D)	3,062	(7%)
1994 General		
Donald M. Payne (D)	74,622	(76%)
Jim Ford (R)	21,524	(22%)
Rose Monyek (IFH)	1,598	(2%)

Previous Winning Percentages: 1992 (78%) **1990** (81%) **1988** (77%)

CAMPAIGN FINANCE

	Receipts	Receipts from PACs	Expend-itures
1996			
Payne (D)	$388,323	$224,567 (58%)	$404,017
Williams (R)	$20,933	$100 (0%)	$20,902
1994			
Payne (D)	$269,445	$139,739 (52%)	$309,623
Ford (R)	$21,545	$14 (0%)	$18,180

DISTRICT VOTE FOR PRESIDENT

	1996		1992
D	135,825 (82%)	**D**	125,922 (71%)
R	21,649 (13%)	**R**	35,930 (20%)
I	5,704 (3%)	**I**	14,854 (8%)

KEY VOTES

1997	
Ban "partial birth" abortions	N
1996	
Approve farm bill	N
Deny public education to illegal immigrants	N
Repeal ban on certain assault-style weapons	N
Increase minimum wage	Y
Freeze defense spending	Y
Approve welfare overhaul	N
1995	
Approve balanced-budget constitutional amendment	N
Relax Clean Water Act regulations	N
Oppose limits on environmental regulations	Y
Reduce projected Medicare spending	N
Approve GOP budget with tax and spending cuts	N

VOTING STUDIES

	Presidential Support		Party Unity		Conservative Coalition	
Year	**S**	**O**	**S**	**O**	**S**	**O**
1996	78	22	96	2	6	94
1995	88	9	96	1	4	95
1994	73	26	94	2	3	94
1993	78	19	95	1	5	89
1992	10	85	92	3	4	92
1991	24	72	95	2	0	97

INTEREST GROUP RATINGS

Year	ADA	AFL-CIO	CCUS	ACU
1996	95	n/a	19	0
1995	100	100	8	4
1994	95	100	18	5
1993	100	100	10	0
1992	95	91	13	0
1991	95	100	20	0

11 Rodney Frelinghuysen (R)

Of Morristown — Elected 1994, 2nd term

Biographical Information

Born: April 29, 1946, New York City, N.Y.
Education: Hobart College, B.A. 1969; Trinity College (Hartford, Conn.), 1971.
Military Service: Army, 1969-71.
Occupation: Public official.
Family: Wife, Virginia T. Robinson; two children.
Religion: Episcopalian.
Political Career: Morris County freeholder, 1974-83, director, 1980; N.J. Assembly, 1983-95.
Capitol Office: 228 Cannon Bldg. 20515; 225-5034.

Committees

Appropriations
Energy & Water Development; Foreign Operations, Export Financing & Related Programs; VA, HUD & Independent Agencies

In Washington: Frelinghuysen typically takes a more moderate stance on environmental and social policy issues than many of his colleagues in the GOP Class of 1994, reflecting the views of the upscale suburbanites who dominate the 11th. Theirs is a more genteel brand of Republicanism than that of the House's harder-edged conservative revolutionaries from Southern and Western districts.

In April 1996, Frelinghuysen was one of only 18 Republicans voting against a bill that facilitated opening preserves in the National Wildlife Refuge System to hunting and fishing. Conservative advocates of the measure said it would "give back the refuge system to the people," while opponents said it would upset the balance between recreation and the protection of wildlife.

In May 1995, Frelinghuysen sided with most of the New Jersey House delegation — and against 195 of 229 House Republicans — in voting against a bill aimed at relaxing clean water act regulations dealing with the discharge of wastes and storm water into waterways. Frelinghuysen's vote was influenced by New Jersey's late-1980s problems with municipal sewage overflowing onto beaches and forcing their closure; he was serving in the state Assembly at the time.

Asking House colleagues not to relax federal water quality standards, Frelinghuysen said, "We don't want to go down that road, potentially undoing what we've worked so hard to achieve."

He first tried to amend the bill to enable states, such as New Jersey, that have created their own wetlands programs to keep them in force without having to resubmit them for review under the bill's new requirements. But the House rejected this idea, 181-243.

Frelinghuysen nonetheless has had harsh words for the Environmental Protection Agency's management of the superfund hazardous waste cleanup program. Since the program began in 1980, he said, only 75 sites out of about 1,300 had been removed from the national cleanup list, largely because of costly and protracted litigation over who is liable for sites' cleanup costs. "Superfund has been a major, vulgar, super waste of taxpayer dollars," he said.

He introduced a bill in December 1995 mandating that all superfund site cleanups be managed by the Army Corps of Engineers, which he said has the experience to handle large construction projects. Under Frelinghuysen's bill, the EPA would still be involved in the scientific analysis of the sites, but would no longer handle the cleanup itself.

In July 1995, Frelinghuysen was the only member of the New Jersey House delegation who supported conservatives' efforts to cut the EPA's funding by 32 percent and limit the agency's authority to enforce a range of environmental laws.

Frelinghuysen's support of abortion rights is in step with the views of New Jersey's top Republican, Gov. Christine Todd Whitman, but not with the majority of House Republicans. One of six GOP first-termers who won a prized seat on Appropriations in the 104th, Frelinghuysen is the sole abortion rights supporter in that group.

He voted in the 104th to maintain a requirement that states fund Medicaid abortions for poor women in cases of rape, incest or danger to the life of the woman; he voted to permit privately financed abortions at overseas military hospitals; and he voted to allow federal employees' health care plans to cover abortions.

He also voted to restore funding for federal family planning programs, which fall under Title X of the Public Health Service Act. Although no Title X funds can be used for abortions, conservative Republicans argued that some clinics that provide federally funded family planning services also perform abortions, creating the potential for federal monies to indirectly finance abortion.

"This debate is about whether or not we believe it is a national priority to provide low-income women with family planning information, education and services," Frelinghuysen said. "I respectfully submit that it is a national priority."

Similarly, Frelinghuysen in February 1997 voted to approve a Clinton administration request for the

NEW JERSEY 11
North — Morris County

The 11th covers all of Morris County and parts of four other counties, but the district best can be described by one word: Republican.

Frelinghuysen first swept the largely white-collar district with more than 70 percent of the vote in 1994, then was re-elected with 66 percent in 1996. And in 1993, Morris County gave more than 60 percent of its vote to GOP gubernatorial candidate Christine Todd Whitman, who defeated Democratic incumbent James J. Florio.

The district's Republican stance has a long history: Dean A. Gallo, Frelinghuysen's late predecessor, easily won five terms here. Both Ronald Reagan and George Bush won more than two-thirds of the vote here in 1984 and 1988, respectively. In 1996, the 11th gave Bob Dole his best showing in the state — 49 percent of the district vote.

More than two-thirds of the district vote comes from Morris County. The middle-class Parsippany-Troy Hills community is the largest in the district; it is occasionally receptive to Democratic candidates.

Central and northern Morris County are mostly white and affluent, populated by well-educated white-collar professionals, bankers, lawyers and stockbrokers who live in upscale places such as Chatham, Kinnelon and Mendham. Harding is especially well-off, even by Morris County standards.

Minorities make up a tiny portion of the 11th's population. Morristown has a relatively large black community; Hispanics live in blue-collar Dover and Victory Gardens.

Toward the west, the county has lost some of its pastoral landscape to newer tract developments, which are rapidly altering the area's character.

Eastern Morris is home to a number of Fortune 500 companies that keep headquarters in local corporate office complexes.

During the 1980s, a number of corporate complexes sprouted up across the county, but the recession and white-collar downsizing have left the area with a glut of vacant office space. Large companies such as Novell and AT&T have begun to move facilities into the area, however, easing the pain somewhat.

After Morris County, Essex County is the most-populous portion with about 66,000 residents. This handful of western municipalities is wealthier than the county as a whole. Livingston, hometown of former GOP Gov. Thomas H. Kean, is Republican but contains a large Jewish community that leans Democratic.

A grab bag of towns from Somerset and Sussex counties also are grafted onto the 11th, along with Bloomingdale, the lone town from Passaic County. Somerset adds Bernards township, Raritan borough, Somerville and Bridgewater — which is shared with the 7th District. Hopatcong and Sparta are the largest towns from Sussex County.

1990 Population: 594,630. White 548,691 (92%), Black 15,995 (3%), Other 29,944 (5%). Hispanic origin 24,567 (4%). 18 and over 458,657 (77%), 62 and over 79,766 (13%). Median age: 35.

early release of $385 million for international family planning programs — a move supporters said would keep open dozens of family planning clinics in poor countries around the world.

Frelinghuysen has shifted his position on whether to ban an abortion technique that opponents call "partial birth" abortion. He voted against the ban in March and September 1996, but voted for the ban in March 1997.

Frelinghuysen went against most in his party when he voted in March 1996 against repealing the ban on certain semiautomatic assault-style weapons; he was one of 42 GOP "no" votes.

Although Frelinghuysen is on the GOP left on social issues, in the opening months of the 104th he voted for all the major tenets of the "Contract With America," including measures backing constitutional amendments for a balanced budget and term limits, overhauling the federal welfare program, scaling back the federal regulatory process and providing a $189 billion tax cut over five years. Frelinghuysen also favored a constitutional amendment to ban flag desecration. "Burning our flag is simply wrong, and should be outlawed," he said.

He sometimes has clashed with organized labor. In July 1995, he supported a failed effort to eliminate federal labor protections for mass-transit workers. The protections require the Labor Department to approve how federal grants are used, which effectively requires transit agencies to negotiate with their unions before making any major changes that affect employees.

Frelinghuysen and his allies argued that the labor protections are costly, outdated and allow unions to take transit grants hostage until transit agencies make wage concessions, raising the cost of operations. Their opponents said eliminating the protections would cause thousands of blue-collar transit workers to lose their right to collective bargaining.

Frelinghuysen in 1996 initially opposed but subsequently backed one cause dear to organized labor: raising the minimum wage. He endorses another idea that unions fight: allowing companies to offer their employees comp time in lieu of overtime pay.

In the 105th Congress, Frelinghuysen switched one of his Appropriations subcommittee assignments, leaving the District of Columbia panel for Foreign Operations. Frelinghuysen said he sought to move to the panel that provides foreign assistance funds because of the importance of export financing programs to many New Jersey companies with international business interests. He also sits on subcommittees with more direct parochial ties: Energy and Water Development and Veterans Affairs, Housing and Urban Development.

Frelinghuysen is not bashful about using his Appropriations seat to bring federal money to New Jersey. According to statements from his office, the fiscal 1997 bounty included $57 million allocated for fusion energy research at the Princeton Plasma Physics Laboratory and $30 million in military base projects contained in the House version of the military construction bill.

At Home: The Frelinghuysen family has a record of public service stretching back to the Revolutionary War era. Four Frelinghuysens have served in the Senate, one as secretary of State. A Frelinghuysen founded what is now Rutgers University, and Rodney Frelinghuysen's father, Peter, served in the House for 22 years, until 1975.

Following college and a stint in the Army during the Vietnam War, Rodney Frelinghuysen went to work for Dean Gallo, then a Morris County freeholder and later a member of the House. Frelinghuysen became a freeholder himself in 1974. In 1982 he lost a GOP primary for the 12th District House seat to Jim Courter, then in 1983 he won a state Assembly seat. In 1990 he tried again for the 12th, running third in a GOP primary won by Dick Zimmer. When Republicans won control of the New Jersey legislature in 1991, Frelinghuysen became chairman of the Appropriations Committee.

When he finally won election to the House in 1994, victory had a bittersweet taste, because it came following the death of his friend and political mentor Gallo. Ill health forced Gallo to abandon his campaign for a sixth term in August 1994. Gallo anointed Frelinghuysen, who had been managing the re-election bid, as his successor.

After New Jersey GOP insiders overwhelmingly ratified Gallo's choice at a special nominating convention, Frelinghuysen enjoyed a fairly smooth ride to victory in the Republican-dominated 11th. Gallo died two days before the November election, which Frelinghuysen won with 71 percent over Democrat Frank Herbert, a former state senator. In 1996, Frelinghuysen took 66 percent against Democrat Chris Evangel, a municipal bond analyst.

HOUSE ELECTIONS

1996 General		
Rodney Frelinghuysen (R)	169,091	(66%)
Chris Evangel (D)	78,742	(31%)
Ed De Mott (NJC)	2,870	(1%)
Austin S. Lett (LIBERT)	2,618	(1%)
1994 General		
Rodney Frelinghuysen (R)	127,868	(71%)
Frank Herbert (D)	50,211	(28%)

CAMPAIGN FINANCE

	Receipts	Receipts from PACs	Expend-itures
1996			
Frelinghuysen (R)	$603,258	$194,069 (32%)	$581,895
Evangel (D)	$167,930	$2,500 (1%)	$181,050
1994			
Frelinghuysen (R)	$414,455	$81,620 (20%)	$243,923
Herbert (D)	$50,074	$12,250 (24%)	$43,614

DISTRICT VOTE FOR PRESIDENT

	1996		1992
D	116,466 (42%)	D	97,697 (33%)
R	136,025 (49%)	R	153,731 (52%)
I	21,382 (8%)	I	46,418 (16%)

KEY VOTES

1997	
Ban "partial birth" abortions	Y
1996	
Approve farm bill	N
Deny public education to illegal immigrants	Y
Repeal ban on certain assault-style weapons	N
Increase minimum wage	N
Freeze defense spending	N
Approve welfare overhaul	Y
1995	
Approve balanced-budget constitutional amendment	Y
Relax clean water act regulations	N
Oppose limits on environmental regulations	N
Reduce projected Medicare spending	Y
Approve GOP budget with tax and spending cuts	Y

VOTING STUDIES

	Presidential Support		Party Unity		Conservative Coalition	
Year	S	O	S	O	S	O
1996	53	46	79	20	76	18
1995	34	66	87	13	88	12

INTEREST GROUP RATINGS

Year	ADA	AFL-CIO	CCUS	ACU
1996	30	n/a	87	75
1995	15	0	88	60

12 Michael Pappas (R)

Of Rocky Hill — Elected 1996, 1st term

Biographical Information
Born: Dec. 29, 1960, New Brunswick, N.J.
Education: Seton Hall U., attended 1979.
Occupation: Insurance agent.
Family: Divorced; one child.
Religion: Christian.
Political Career: Franklin Township Council, 1982-87; mayor of Franklin Township, 1983-84; Somerset County freeholder, 1984-97.
Capitol Office: 1710 Longworth Bldg. 20515; 225-5801.

Committees
Government Reform & Oversight
Civil Service; Human Resources
National Security
Military Procurement; Military Research & Development
Small Business
Government Programs & Oversight

The Path to Washington: Voters in the 12th have usually been represented in the House by moderate Republicans, such as the previous occupant of this seat, Dick Zimmer. But Pappas is a staunchly conservative Republican — an ardent foe of abortion and a strong supporter of gun-owners' rights.

A member of the Somerset County government, he was the only abortion opponent in a four-way 1996 primary for the GOP nomination to succeed Zimmer, who lost in New Jersey's open-seat Senate race to Democratic Rep. Robert G. Torricelli.

The two leading contenders in the Republican primary, state Sen. John Bennett and state Rep. Leonard Lance, were moderate supporters of abortion rights, in the mold of Zimmer and Gov. Christine Todd Whitman. Indeed, a majority of the Republican primary voters appeared to show moderate stripes. Bennett and Lance combined polled 60 percent of the vote. But Pappas, with 38 percent, finished first. Bennett took 34 percent to finish second.

Pappas' conservatism gave Democrats an opening in the traditionally Republican district, and they attempted to drive through it with Lambertville Mayor David N. Del Vecchio. Emphasizing his support for abortion rights, and his fiscally conservative record, Del Vecchio attempted to add moderate Republicans and independents to his Democratic base.

During the campaign, it was Del Vecchio, not Pappas, who sent out a release trumpeting the National Rifle Association's characterization of the Republican nominee as "a true believer."

For his part, Pappas tried to push Del Vecchio to the left, insisting that he was a tax-and-spend liberal, and trying to link him to former Democratic Gov. James J. Florio, whose 1990 tax increase still riles many New Jersey voters.

As a sign of how seriously both major parties were taking the election, both Bill Clinton and Bob Dole visited the district.

In the end, though, the district's Republican heritage was too much for Del Vecchio. However, he did manage to hold Pappas well below the 65 percent support that Zimmer averaged during his three congressional races. Pappas edged Del Vecchio by 50 percent to 47 percent.

Pappas' political career began at age 19 when he joined the Franklin Township Planning Board. He was elected to the town council two years later and became a member of the Somerset County Board of Chosen Freeholders two years after that.

During the campaign, Pappas eagerly embraced Dole's proposal to reduce the federal income tax by 15 percent across the board, and he can be expected to support tax-cutting efforts in the 105th Congress.

Pappas also is expected to vote more in line with the conservatives who dominate the House Republican conference than with his New Jersey GOP colleagues, who largely tend to occupy slots in the party's moderate wing.

For example, four New Jersey lawmakers were among only 10 Republican House members who voted in 1995 against their party's reconciliation bill, which was designed to reach a balanced budget by 2002. Pappas said he would have supported the measure.

He backs constitutional amendments requiring a balanced budget and requiring a two-thirds majority of both houses of Congress to raise taxes. GOP presidential candidate Malcolm S. "Steve" Forbes Jr. campaigned for him.

Pappas' election to Congress was welcomed by fellow New Jersey Rep. Christopher H. Smith, one of the House's leading opponents of abortion.

Just as he succeeded Zimmer in the House, Pappas lobbied to succeed him on the House Ways and Means Committee. Zimmer was the only New Jersey Republican on the powerful panel.

Instead, Pappas was named to the Government Reform and Oversight, National Security and Small Business committees.

NEW JERSEY 12
North and central — Flemington; Princeton

Reaching from the Delaware River, on its western border, almost to the Atlantic Ocean, the 12th meanders across New Jersey's midsection.

The district, which comprises all of Hunterdon County and parts of four other counties, generally prefers Republican candidates. More than a third of the population lives in Republican-leaning Monmouth County. Mostly middle-class or affluent, this portion includes rapidly growing towns such as Manalaplan and Marlboro. Voters favor Republican candidates down to the local level, particularly so in wealthy Rumson and Shrewsbury. The district border stops just short of the fragile strip of Atlantic coastline, which belongs to the neighboring 6th District.

Hunterdon, Mercer and Middlesex counties each contribute about one-fifth of the district's population. The Mercer portion includes the affluent, white-collar Trenton suburbs and middle-class, blue-collar Ewing. Colonial Princeton — home to the Ivy League institution of the same name and its 6,400 students — is a source of Democratic votes cast by the liberal academic community. In the 1996 elections, Clinton and Pappas' Democratic opponent posted double-digit margins in the district's portion of Mercer.

Commercial and residential spillover from the Princeton and Route 1 corridor has brought new growth in southern Middlesex County, especially in Plainsboro and South Brunswick. The 12th's border in Middlesex stretches as far north as upscale East Brunswick, the district's largest city.

Hunterdon is the lone county wholly contained in the 12th. Here the green pastureland and riverside hamlets breed a brand of Republicanism that permeates every level of governance. Pappas carried Hunterdon by 12,700 votes and 61 percent; he won the entire district by just 10,200 votes. In 1996, Bob Dole and unsuccessful U.S. Senate candidate Dick Zimmer scored higher percentages in Hunterdon than in any other Garden State county.

The river towns, such as Frenchtown and Lambertville, are filled with quaint antique shops and bed-and-breakfasts. Flemington, the county seat, is a shopping outlet center. The 1980s rousted this sleepy county to the reality of soaring land values and development as it became a popular East Coast weekend getaway destination and second-home community.

Northern Somerset County adds some lightly populated, wealthy communities, including Far Hills and Peapack, from the hunt country.

The old-money towns and affluent suburbs of the 12th give Republicans an advantage; George Bush won here with 61 percent in 1988. But Bill Clinton only narrowly lost the district in 1992 and then won it by 18,000 votes in 1996, even as Pappas kept the House seat in GOP hands.

1990 Population: 594,630. White 532,833 (90%), Black 31,114 (5%), Other 30,683 (5%). Hispanic origin 15,792 (3%). 18 and over 455,824 (77%), 62 and over 83,469 (14%). Median age: 35.

HOUSE ELECTIONS

1996 General		
Michael Pappas (R)	135,811	(50%)
David N. Del Vecchio (D)	125,594	(47%)
Virginia A. Flynn (LIBERT)	3,955	(1%)
1996 Primary		
Michael Pappas (R)	11,069	(38%)
John Bennett (R)	9,894	(34%)
Leonard Lance (R)	7,630	(26%)
Luis de Agustin (R)	481	(2%)

CAMPAIGN FINANCE

	Receipts	Receipts from PACs	Expend-itures
1996			
Pappas (R)	$615,549	$153,115 (25%)	$591,536
Del Vecchio (D)	$477,433	$150,138 (31%)	$475,370

DISTRICT VOTE FOR PRESIDENT

1996		1992	
D	140,033 (48%)	**D**	121,447 (40%)
R	121,837 (42%)	**R**	130,651 (43%)
I	23,315 (8%)	**I**	50,477 (17%)

KEY VOTES

1997

Ban "partial birth" abortions Y

13 Robert Menendez (D)

Of Union City — Elected 1992, 3rd term

Biographical Information
Born: Jan. 1, 1954, New York, N.Y.
Education: St. Peter's College, B.A. 1976; Rutgers U., J.D. 1979.
Occupation: Lawyer.
Family: Wife, Jane Jacobsen; two children.
Religion: Roman Catholic.
Political Career: Union City Board of Education, 1974-78; mayor of Union City, 1986-92; N.J. Assembly, 1987-91; N.J. Senate, 1991-92.
Capitol Office: 405 Cannon Bldg. 20515; 225-7919.

Committees
International Relations
Africa (ranking); Western Hemisphere
Transportation & Infrastructure
Surface Transportation; Water Resources & Environment
Chief Deputy Whip

In Washington: Menendez, the son of Cuban immigrants, takes pride in being the first Hispanic to represent New Jersey in the House, but in Congress he tries to be a voice for all the constituents in the ethnically diverse, heavily urbanized 13th. (Union City is the most densely populated municipality in the nation's most densely populated state.) In the 105th Congress, Menendez has a chance to use that voice on a wider playing field in his new role as one of four chief deputy whips for House Democrats. The leadership picked him to replace Bill Richardson of New Mexico, who resigned from the House in 1997 to become ambassador to the United Nations.

Menendez has been a steady supporter of the Clinton administration. As a freshman in the 103rd Congress, he called the president's five-year deficit-reduction plan "fair to everyone," and he supported Clinton's effort to overhaul the nation's health care system, noting that 25 percent of his district's residents did not have health insurance.

With Republicans running the show in the 104th Congress, Menendez voted a staunchly liberal line, siding with abortion rights advocates, organized labor and gun control proponents against the House's conservative majority.

Having voted in the 103rd for a five-day waiting period for handgun purchases and a ban on semiautomatic assault-style weapons, he opposed a GOP-backed initiative in 1996 to repeal the assault-weapons ban. "Street thugs are not my idea of a well-regulated militia," he once said.

One of his rare breaks with the White House came on the issue of welfare overhaul. He was one of only two New Jersey House members who voted in 1996 against the final welfare bill eventually signed into law by Clinton. "I didn't run for Congress to vote to increase poverty and suffering, and it's a sad day when members of Congress happily and without shame would do so," Menendez said.

Previously, Menendez had turned away from Clinton on NAFTA, arguing that lower Mexican tariffs would lead U.S. companies to invest less in creating jobs domestically.

Jobs were also on Menendez's mind when he spoke out against the Pentagon's proposal to close a post in Bayonne as part of the final round of base closings. He said the Army's study of the facility's economic impact and the military value was "replete with faulty analysis."

On the International Relations Committee, Menendez is active on issues important to his Cuban-American constituents. He spoke out against an amendment on a bill to reauthorize the State Department that would have promoted international cultural contacts with Cuba. Menendez charged that such exchanges would provide Fidel Castro's regime with desperately needed hard currency.

He also has proposed legislation to provide U.S. financial aid to Cuba in the event Castro is no longer in power and there is a transitional government committed to democracy. He said his program of financial, educational and humanitarian assistance would send a signal of U.S. "solidarity" with Cuba's "enslaved" people.

In the 104th, Menendez opposed efforts to eliminate $11 million in the fiscal 1997 Commerce, Justice, State appropriations bill for TV Marti, the station that beams U.S. programs to Cuba. "I am shocked that this cut could survive the Republican-led Appropriations Committee and the Republican-led House," he said.

He backed the Helms-Burton bill designed to punish foreign companies that invest in Cuba. He helped broker a deal with Clinton to sign a modified version of the legislation, completing negotiations with the White House shortly after Cuban military planes shot down two civilian aircraft being flown toward the island nation by Cuban-American opponents of Castro, killing four. Menendez said the deal sent a "very strong bipartisan message that we will not allow our citizens to be gunned down in cold blood."

He also responded to the shooting by calling on Clinton to revoke the visas of Cuban officials working in the Cuban Interest sections in Washington and New York, and for the United Nations to impose economic sanctions.

Not far from the place that welcomed the tired, the poor and the huddled masses yearning to be free rests Jersey City, a modern-day melting pot. Ellis Island, the one-time processing point for countless numbers of immigrants, and the Statue of Liberty are appropriately situated a short ferry ride from the city's Liberty State Park. Although the subject is of some dispute, city boosters say the statue is within city limits.

Legendary political boss Frank "I Am the Law" Hague's machine controlled Hudson County politics from 1917 to the late 1940s, oiled by the votes of those white, working-class European immigrants. But now more than half the votes in Jersey City come from minorities, many of whom came in a second wave of immigration, primarily from Spanish-speaking countries.

About half of Jersey City — the state's second-largest city — is in the 13th, with the rest shared between the 9th and 10th districts. This portion consists mainly of the city's eastern parts, including the downtown area, which has experienced some gentrification as young professionals have moved across the Hudson River.

There are Russian immigrants living downtown and scattered pockets of Indian, Korean and Filipino immigrants, but blacks and Hispanics together make up more than half the city's population.

The local Hispanic community is far from monolithic; it consists of immigrants from more than 20 countries. The 13th as a whole has a Hispanic population of 41 percent, though Hispanics constitute a much smaller percentage of registered voters. Yet Democrat Robert Menendez won the 13th seat in 1992 to become New Jersey's first Hispanic House member.

NEW JERSEY 13
Parts of Jersey City and Newark

The Hispanic communities are scattered across the district, as far south as Elizabeth (Union County) and Perth Amboy (Middlesex County). Union City, North Bergen, Guttenberg and especially West New York have politically active Cuban communities that tend to vote Republican at the presidential level and Democratic in local elections.

Outside those Republican votes, the GOP presence is muted. The various Hispanic communities and large numbers of blue-collar whites favor Democrats. Bill Clinton outpolled Bob Dole by a ratio of more than 3-to-1 in the district in 1996 while Menendez did better than that.

Another Hudson County locale that has been gentrified is Hoboken, where young professionals have taken over the city's eastern section. The city may be better known, though, as Frank Sinatra's birthplace and the setting for the 1954 film "On the Waterfront."

From Hudson County, the 13th extends to Newark (Essex County) to siphon Puerto Rican and Italian voters from the city's north and east wards.

Middlesex and Union counties also contribute voters, but on a smaller scale. All of Perth Amboy and Carteret along with a small portion of suburban Woodbridge make up about 10 percent of the district. Parts of Elizabeth and Linden round out the Union County contingent.

1990 Population: 594,630. White 400,803 (67%), Black 81,305 (14%), Other 112,522 (19%). Hispanic origin 246,715 (41%). 18 and over 454,356 (76%), 62 and over 87,646 (15%). Median age: 32.

"A country that cannot observe international law is not a country that should be receiving aid from the United Nations, which promotes international law," he said.

In the fiscal 1996 foreign operations appropriations bill, he sponsored an amendment to reduce aid to Moscow by the amount it spends to help complete a nuclear plant in Cuba. Several lawmakers said the plant had safety problems that could ultimately pose a risk to the southeastern United States.

And, in an unusual move, Clinton selected Menendez to present an anti-Cuba resolution to the U.N. Human Rights Commission in Geneva. Usually, diplomats are chosen for the task. The resolution, which criticized Cuba for jailing and harassing dissident groups and for not cooperating with a U.N. investigator assigned to document human rights abuses, was approved by a wide margin. "The resolution outlines the concerns of the United States and other countries that are with us in regard to the human rights questions in Cuba," Menendez told the Star-Ledger of Newark.

He also is interested in Northern Ireland. Early in 1994, he urged the Clinton administration to grant an entry visa to Gerry Adams, president of Sinn Fein, the Irish Republican Army's political arm. He said the visa issue is "symbolic of our commitment to an honest and fair resolution of the Northern Ireland question."

While serving on International Relations gives Menendez a role in world affairs, he tends to matters close to home from his seat on the Transportation and Infrastructure Committee.

He has worked to obtain federal funds to dredge the Port of New York and New Jersey, saying that the port would lose business and jobs to Canada if it was not dredged.

He crossed swords with Transportation Chairman Bud Shuster after the Pennsylvania Republican overcame organized labor's opposition and pushed through an ocean shipping bill in 1996.

The bill, which would partially deregulate the shipping industry, was backed by many large carriers and shippers who want more leeway in setting their rates. But many port authorities and labor leaders opposed it, fearing that it could cost jobs and lead to a consolidation of the shipping industry.

Menendez said lawmakers and lobbyists who opposed the legislation were threatened with reprisals. He first made the assertion on the House floor during the May debate on the bill.

The message from Shuster's committee, Menendez said, was: "If you continue to mount opposition to this bill, there will be consequences to it." He said the committee leadership threatened to use its power over such issues as the dredging of ports to force opponents to knuckle under. "The breadth and scope and intensity with which it was done, I think, was unusual," said Menendez, who voted against the bill.

At Home: As chairman of the state Assembly's taxation subcommittee in 1990, Menendez carried then-Gov. James J. Florio's $2.8 billion income tax bill, despite the risk of political consequences. He argued that the measure benefited his Hudson County constituency by easing a disproportionate property tax burden, boosting aid for municipalities, especially for schools, and stabilizing the tax base.

For his troubles, Menendez suffered no electoral consequences. He was appointed to fill a state Senate vacancy in early 1991 and the following November was elected to that seat.

Menendez is a lifelong Democrat, unusual for a Cuban-American politician, and an affiliation that he says reflects his belief in an activist government. He won his first election to the School Board in 1974 while still in college. He became mayor of Union City in May 1986 and simultaneously served in the Legislature beginning in January 1987.

Redistricting for the 1990s nearly doubled the 13th's Hispanic population, but that may not have been the most important factor in Democratic Rep. Frank J. Guarini's decision to retire after 14 years in the House. It did provide Menendez with a strong incentive to consider the race. And once Guarini decided to step down, Menendez found himself with a virtually clear field for the primary and general election.

He faced Jersey City lawyer Robert P. Haney Jr. in the Democratic primary and a host of candidates in the general election, including Republican Fred J. Theemling Jr., who had lost twice to Guarini. Menendez won the primary with 68 percent of the vote and the general with 64 percent. In both cases, turnout was light, which could be attributable to typically low voter participation among Hispanics.

Running for re-election in 1996, he easily dispatched a primary challenge from an anti-abortion Democrat and polled more than three-fourths of the vote against Republican nominee Carlos E. Munoz.

HOUSE ELECTIONS

1996 General		
Robert Menendez (D)	115,459	(79%)
Carlos E. Munoz (R)	25,427	(17%)
Herbert H. Shaw (PAC)	2,136	(1%)
Mike Buoncristiano (LIBERT)	2,094	(1%)
1996 Primary		
Robert Menendez (D)	34,685	(93%)
Christopher Curioli (D)	2,685	(7%)
1994 General		
Robert Menendez (D)	67,688	(71%)
Fernando A. Alonso (R)	24,071	(25%)
Frank J. Rubino Jr. (WTP)	1,494	(2%)
Herbert H. Shaw (PAC)	1,319	(1%)

Previous Winning Percentages: 1992 (64%)

CAMPAIGN FINANCE

	Receipts	Receipts from PACs	Expend-itures
1996			
Menendez (D)	$908,485	$247,050 (27%)	$379,469
Buoncristiano (LIBERT)	$18,769	0	$18,449
1994			
Menendez (D)	$626,358	$213,700 (34%)	$488,448
Alonso (R)	$6,160	$14 (0%)	$6,159

DISTRICT VOTE FOR PRESIDENT

	1996		1992
D	117,241 (72%)	**D**	95,144 (54%)
R	35,482 (22%)	**R**	64,727 (37%)
I	8,509 (5%)	**I**	14,911 (9%)

KEY VOTES

1997	
Ban "partial birth" abortions	N
1996	
Approve farm bill	Y
Deny public education to illegal immigrants	N
Repeal ban on certain assault-style weapons	N
Increase minimum wage	Y
Freeze defense spending	Y
Approve welfare overhaul	N
1995	
Approve balanced-budget constitutional amendment	N
Relax Clean Water Act regulations	N
Oppose limits on environmental regulations	Y
Reduce projected Medicare spending	N
Approve GOP budget with tax and spending cuts	N

VOTING STUDIES

	Presidential Support		Party Unity		Conservative Coalition	
Year	**S**	**O**	**S**	**O**	**S**	**O**
1996	77	19	91	5	25	71
1995	83	15	87	11	28	72
1994	79	21	95	4	31	69
1993	81	17	90	8	41	59

INTEREST GROUP RATINGS

Year	ADA	AFL-CIO	CCUS	ACU
1996	85	n/a	19	5
1995	90	100	21	17
1994	90	89	50	5
1993	90	100	18	9

NEW MEXICO

Governor: Gary E. Johnson (R)
First elected: 1994
Length of term: 4 years
Term expires: 1/99
Salary: $90,000
Term limit: 2 consecutive terms
Phone: (505) 827-3000
Born: January 1, 1953; Minot, N.D.
Education: U. of New Mexico, B.S. 1975.
Occupation: Construction company owner.
Family: Wife, Dee Simms; two children.
Religion: Lutheran.
Political Career: No previous office.

Lt. Gov.: Walter Bradley (R)
First elected: 1994
Length of term: 4 years
Term expires: 1/99
Salary: $65,500
Phone: (505) 827-3050

State election official: (505) 827-3621
Democratic headquarters: (505) 842-8208
Republican headquarters: (505) 298-3662

REDISTRICTING

New Mexico retained its three House seats in reapportionment. Legislature passed the map Sept. 18, 1991; governor signed it Oct. 4.

STATE LEGISLATURE

Legislature. Meets January-March in odd years; January-February in even years.

Senate: 42 members, 4-year terms
1996 breakdown: 25D, 17R; 32 men, 10 women
Salary: $124/day
Phone: (505) 986-4714

House of Representatives: 70 members, 2-year terms
1996 breakdown: 42D, 28R; 50 men, 20 women
Salary: $124/day
Phone: (505) 247-4321

URBAN STATISTICS

City	Population
Albuquerque	384,736
Mayor Martin Chavez, D	
Las Cruces	62,126
Mayor Ruben Smith, N-P	
Santa Fe	56,551
Mayor Debbie Jaramillo, D	
Roswell	44,654
Mayor Thomas E. Jennings, N-P	
Farmington	33,997
Mayor Thomas C. Taylor, R	

U.S. CONGRESS

Senate: 1 D, 1 R
House: 0 D, 3 R

TERM LIMITS

For state offices: No

ELECTIONS

1996 Presidential Vote

Bill Clinton	49%
Bob Dole	42%
Ross Perot	6%

1992 Presidential Vote

Bill Clinton	46%
George Bush	37%
Ross Perot	16%

1988 Presidential Vote

George Bush	52%
Michael S. Dukakis	47%

POPULATION

1990 population		1,515,069
1980 population		1,302,894
Percent change		+16%
Rank among states:		37
White		76%
Black		2%
Hispanic		38%
Asian or Pacific islander		1%
Urban		73%
Rural		27%
Born in state		52%
Foreign-born		5%
Under age 18	446,741	29%
Ages 18-64	905,266	60%
65 and older	163,062	11%
Median age		31.3

MISCELLANEOUS

Capital: Santa Fe
Number of counties: 33
Per capita income: $14,844 (1991)
Rank among states: 46
Total area: 121,593 sq. miles
Rank among states: 5

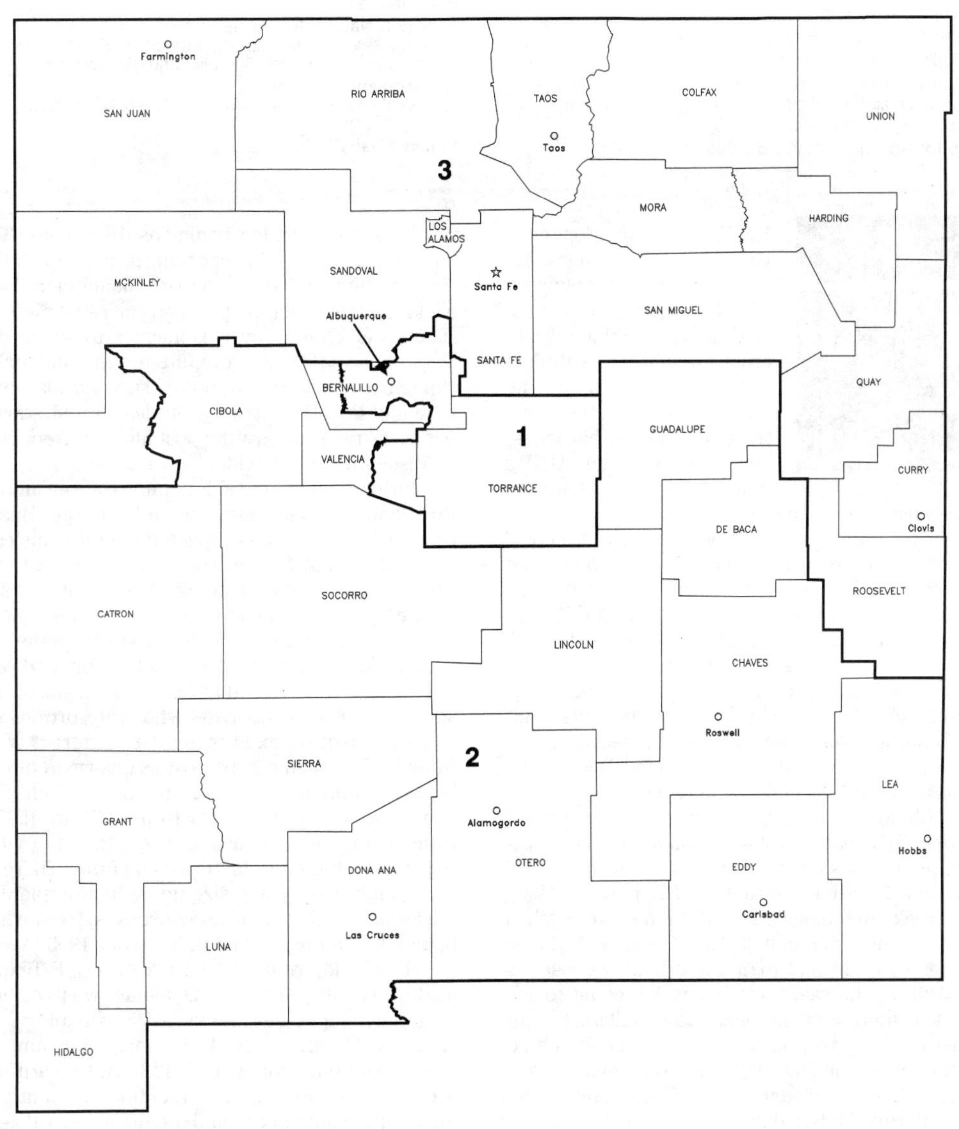
Farmington
SAN JUAN
RIO ARRIBA
TAOS
Taos
COLFAX
UNION
3
MORA
HARDING
LOS ALAMOS
MCKINLEY
SANDOVAL
Santa Fe
SAN MIGUEL
Albuquerque
SANTA FE
QUAY
BERNALILLO
CIBOLA
1
GUADALUPE
VALENCIA
CURRY
TORRANCE
Clovis
DE BACA
ROOSEVELT
CATRON
SOCORRO
LINCOLN
CHAVES
Roswell
2
SIERRA
LEA
Alamogordo
GRANT
Hobbs
OTERO
DONA ANA
EDDY
Carlsbad
Las Cruces
LUNA
HIDALGO

Pete V. Domenici (R)

Of Albuquerque — Elected 1972, 5th term

Biographical Information

Born: May 7, 1932, Albuquerque, N.M.

Education: U. of Albuquerque, 1950-52; U. of New Mexico, B.S. 1954; U. of Denver, LL.B. 1958.

Occupation: Lawyer.

Family: Wife, Nancy Burke; eight children.

Religion: Roman Catholic.

Political Career: Albuquerque City Commission, 1966-70, chairman and ex-officio mayor, 1967-70; Republican nominee for governor, 1970.

Capitol Office: 328 Hart Bldg. 20510; 224-6621.

Committees

Appropriations
Commerce, Justice, State & Judiciary; Defense; Energy & Water Development (chairman); Interior; Transportation

Budget (chairman)

Energy & Natural Resources
Energy Research Development Production & Regulation (vice-chairman); Forests & Public Land Management

Governmental Affairs
International Security, Proliferation & Federal Services; Investigations

Indian Affairs

In Washington: For many years, Domenici has pursued the political holy grail of a balanced federal budget, laboring diligently to erase the deficit. As Budget Committee chairman, he has been on hand for a protracted series of battles — some within the GOP's inner ranks — over how to make his vision a reality.

In May 1997, it was Domenici who received much of the credit from other Republicans when he and a team of GOP negotiators ended more than a month of closed-door talks with the Clinton administration by announcing an agreement to balance the budget by 2002. The sprawling pact bore Domenici's stamp of pragmatism by containing something for both sides — tax cuts that Republicans sought for more than a decade, along with limited new money for selected Democratic priorities such as children's health care.

Although Domenici had been an architect of earlier GOP balanced-budget plans, he took special pride in his latest achievement. He compared his previous efforts to those of Sisyphus, the king in Greek mythology forever doomed to push a heavy stone uphill only to have it roll back down. "I feel it's more real than any others because it's bipartisan," he said. "You know it's going to get implemented; we're not going to be talking to ourselves, talking another language." Domenici's hard work paid off in late May when the Senate easily passed the budget agreement, 78-22. The House had approved it two days earlier, 333-99.

Domenici has dedicated much of his career to tracking the federal budget; he knows more about it and has more staff devoted to it than just about anyone else in Congress. Yet he often has remained at odds with his party's leadership in seeking to restrain spending for its own sake, rather than to free up money to pay for tax cuts that other, more conservative Republicans desire.

Domenici is conservative, but not nearly enough so to suit some of his colleagues. As a result, he has been left behind as the Senate GOP has moved rightward in choosing its leaders. At the start of the 102nd Congress, Oklahoman Don Nickles, a product of the Reagan revolution of 1980, was chosen over Domenici to chair the Republican Policy Committee. In mid-1996, Domenici considered trying to succeed his long-time ally Bob Dole as majority leader, but stayed out of the race and saw the post filled by Trent Lott of Mississippi, a more ideological figure.

During 12 years of GOP administrations under Presidents Ronald Reagan and George Bush, Domenici at times was expected to muffle his call to cut the budget. After the 1992 election of Bill Clinton, he was free to attack a Democratic White House for inadequate efforts to shrink the deficit.

At the start of the 104th Congress, Domenici was advising Republicans to settle for a "down payment" on a balanced budget as he squared off against House Republicans who were promising an assortment of tax cuts in their "Contract With America." Reclaiming his post as chairman of the Budget Committee (which he held when the Senate was in GOP hands from 1981 to 1987), Domenici made it clear that — contract notwithstanding — deficit reduction came first. "There is no commitment to any size tax-reduction plan in the Senate, and there is no consensus, from what I can tell," Domenici said in February 1995.

House Majority Leader Dick Armey, R-Texas, made it equally clear that Domenici was not driving the budget bus, however. In an interview after the November 1994 election, for example, Armey said that Domenici "will have to learn" to accept the conservative contention that cutting the capital gains tax would augment federal revenues and not add to the deficit.

The budget that Domenici's committee produced in May 1995 did include tax cuts, but at $170 billion they were less than half the size of the House's $353 billion. At his insistence, the budget also made the cuts conditional on passage of a deficit-reducing budget-reconciliation bill and required the Congressional Budget Office (CBO) to confirm that the bill was big enough to balance the budget by 2002 before Congress could approve the tax cuts. As a sign of the respect accorded Domenici on fiscal matters, the plan that passed the Senate was virtually unchanged from the version he had drawn up.

"We are bent today and tomorrow on what kind of legacy we are going to leave our children," Domenici said. "Will it be a legacy of debt, of a diminished standard of living, a legacy which says, 'You will have to work 30 percent to 40 percent of your working lives to pay our bills?' "

But Domenici subsequently assumed a role he would occupy at times during the 104th Congress: that of the good soldier who accommodated the wishes of others. The House-Senate conference on the budget agreement became a war of wills within the GOP, with Domenici and Dole facing Armey and other Republican revolutionaries who wanted hefty tax cuts. When the deal was done, the old guard ceded to the new guard, giving House Republicans enough in tax cuts to meet many of the promises they had made.

Throughout the process, Domenici fended off criticism from Democrats who questioned whether he had abandoned his reputation as a seeker of bipartisan compromise. He also worked to build an alliance with Ohio Republican John R. Kasich, his younger, brasher counterpart chairing the House Budget Committee. The two got off to a shaky start but eventually became comrades in arms. At the announcement of the May 1997 budget deal, a grateful Kasich said Domenici "has helped me grow up and become wiser in my job."

Until that deal was struck, Domenici's biggest frustrations on the budget had come from the White House. He had been adamant that the administration use CBO's economic assumptions rather than the more optimistic projections of its own Office of Management and Budget. That led to bitter clashes in late 1995 and early 1996 with White House Chief of Staff Leon E. Panetta, and Domenici became disgusted with what he saw as Democratic demagoguery. His desire to remain at the bargaining table could not avert a government shutdown when the negotiations stalled.

Having failed to win the budget battle, Domenici emerged in 1996 determined to help Dole defeat Clinton in the presidential election. He implored Republican colleagues to remain loyal when Dole trailed in the polls in July and later defended Dole's uncharacteristic support of a 15 percent tax cut.

Even as he has sought to reduce federal spending, Domenici has doggedly sought money for New Mexico, something that has helped him become far and away his state's dominant political figure.

He has been such an ardent protector of the Department of Energy that some agency employees affectionately refer to him as "St. Pete." As chairman of the Senate Appropriations Committee's Energy and Water panel, he was instrumental in securing a $375 million increase for the department in fiscal 1997, including a boost in funding for nuclear weapons research at DOE's Sandia and Los Alamos national laboratories in New Mexico. He also has brought home funds for DOE's Waste Isolation Pilot Plant nuclear waste repository, for Albuquerque's Petroglyph National Monument and for rural water and sewer systems.

Domenici also has taken up the cause of ranchers who graze livestock on public lands, an emotional issue in the rural West. In the 104th, he countered a series of stringent regulations put forth by Interior Secretary Bruce Babbitt with legislation backed by the ranching industry. That measure drew heavy criticism from environmentalists as well as Domenici's Democratic colleague Jeff Bingaman; it cleared the Senate but failed to come to a vote in the House.

Domenici took on an array of other challenges. He teamed with liberal Minnesota Democrat Paul Wellstone to attach a provision to the fiscal 1997 VA-HUD spending bill requiring group health insurance plans that cover mental illness to set the same limits on that coverage as they set on physical illness. Both senators had watched close relatives struggle with mental illness.

Earlier, he offered a successful amendment to the GOP's welfare legislation striking a proposal to deny federal funding for cash benefits for children born to welfare recipients. The debate over the so-called "family cap" pitted Domenici against Texas Sen. Phil Gramm, who also tangled with Domenici on other issues. Gramm led the early conservative criticism of the 1997 budget deal.

Over Gramm's objections, Domenici won approval for an amendment to the fiscal 1996 Commerce, Justice, State appropriations bill that scrapped replacing the Legal Services Corporation with a block grant program and restored $340 million in funding for the agency.

Domenici also has been aggressive in promoting a character education program taught in New Mexico schools called "Character Counts" and touting a variety of good-government proposals, such as moving to a two-year budget cycle. He worked with Democrats in 1995 to pass, and override a presidential veto of, a bill seeking to curb class-action lawsuits in behalf of shareholders whose stocks perform below expectations.

In his first six years as Budget chairman during the 1980s, Domenici worked to build unity on his committee, heeding colleagues' wishes on everything from meeting times to spending priorities. But Domenici's earnest temperament sometimes produced irritated outbursts that worked against his consensus-building efforts. He is an intense presence, a sensitive man who appears genuinely distressed when a colleague is angry at him. He does not suffer criticism lightly, and can bristle at reporters and others who question his actions.

Domenici's record as chairman loomed over his bid to become majority leader at the start of the 99th Congress. His fellow Republicans saw him as hard-working and intelligent, but without the flair for firm direction that an eventual majority saw in Dole.

In 1981, Domenici led the Budget Committee

balancing the budget than in providing the fiscal stimulus sought by "supply side" conservatives (Reagan budget director David A. Stockman called him "a Hooverite"). He feared the full Reagan tax-cut program would deepen the deficit, and later, when the red ink began to mount, he worked with Finance Chairman Dole and Majority Leader Howard H. Baker Jr. to pass the $98 billion tax-increase bill of 1982.

Before the Republican takeover of the Senate in 1981 thrust the Budget chair on Domenici, he had been a legislative dabbler, stubborn and intense about promoting a variety of issues but not widely identified with any. Much of his hardest work was oriented to New Mexico.

At Home: Seeking a first term in 1972, Domenici had the advantage of speaking Spanish in a state that was 37 percent Hispanic. He also had a Hispanic-sounding surname, even though he was born Pietro Vichi Domenici, the son of an immigrant Italian grocer. He drew more votes in Hispanic northern New Mexico than Republicans normally do.

Domenici's background was in municipal government. After law school, he had made his first political foray by winning a seat on the Albuquerque City Commission, and later became chairman, the equivalent of mayor. As a city official, he prided himself on neighborhood meetings he held to hear residents' complaints.

Counting on his Bernalillo County (Albuquerque) base, which cast a third of the vote in the state, Domenici ran for governor in 1970. Although he dominated a six-way primary in which he was seen as a moderate, Domenici did not get the boost he needed from Bernalillo County in the fall. He carried it by only 8,909 votes, not enough for him to win statewide against Democrat Bruce King, the state House Speaker. King had the party registration advantage and was better known statewide.

Undeterred, Domenici came back in 1972, this time running for the Senate seat being vacated by Democrat Clinton P. Anderson. His Democratic opponent was former state Rep. Jack Daniels, who had also run for governor in 1970 but lost to King in the Democratic primary.

Daniels, a wealthy banker, differed little from Domenici on the issues. But Domenici pointed out that Daniels had stood on the same platform as Sen. George McGovern that year and pledged to back him as the Democratic presidential nominee. While Daniels had repudiated McGovern's call for reduced defense spending, the association hurt him. Domenici won with 54 percent.

Domenici's percentage dropped slightly in 1978. The Democratic candidate, state Attorney General (and later one-term governor) Toney Anaya, was Hispanic. Domenici had taken most of the heavily Hispanic counties in 1972, but six years later he lost most of them. In addition, his 1972 plurality of 31,240 votes in Bernalillo shrank to 6,766 in 1978.

Domenici's next two elections reaffirmed his popularity with voters. In 1984 and 1990 he tallied more than 70 percent. In 1996, as Clinton carried New Mexico, Domenici polled 65 percent against former Santa Fe Mayor Art Trujillo.

SENATE ELECTIONS

1996 General		
Pete V. Domenici (R)	357,171	(65%)
Art Trujillo (D)	164,356	(30%)
Abraham J. Gutmann (GREEN)	24,230	(4%)
Bruce M. Bush (LIBERT)	6,064	(1%)

Previous Winning Percentages: 1990 (73%) **1984** (72%) **1978** (53%) **1972** (54%)

CAMPAIGN FINANCE

	Receipts	Receipts from PACs	Expend-itures
1996			
Domenici (R)	$3,264,601	$1,154,329 (35%)	$3,110,548
Trujillo (D)	$163,728	$12,800 (8%)	$163,613
Gutmann (GREEN)	$12,062	0	$12,025
Bush (LIBERT)	$5,655	0	$5,655

KEY VOTES

1997	
Approve balanced-budget constitutional amendment	Y
Approve chemical weapons treaty	Y
1996	
Approve farm bill	?
Limit punitive damages in product liability cases	Y
Exempt small businesses from higher minimum wage	Y
Approve welfare overhaul	Y
Bar job discrimination based on sexual orientation	N
Override veto of ban on "partial birth" abortions	Y
1995	
Approve GOP budget with tax and spending cuts	Y
Approve constitutional amendment barring flag desecration	Y

VOTING STUDIES

	Presidential Support		Party Unity		Conservative Coalition	
Year	S	O	S	O	S	O
1996	41	56	86	9	89	5
1995	25	72	93	7	91	7
1994	53	47	78	22	94	6
1993	34	66	83	14	85	12
1992	82	18	88	11	89	11
1991	93	6	88	11	88	10

INTEREST GROUP RATINGS

Year	ADA	AFL-CIO	CCUS	ACU
1996	20	n/a	83	85
1995	5	8	100	78
1994	25	13	90	84
1993	20	9	100	80
1992	15	17	78	78
1991	10	17	90	76

Jeff Bingaman (D)

Of Santa Fe — Elected 1982, 3rd term

Biographical Information
Born: Oct. 3, 1943, El Paso, Texas.
Education: Harvard U., A.B. 1965; Stanford U., J.D. 1968.
Military Service: Army Reserve, 1968-74.
Occupation: Lawyer.
Family: Wife, Anne Kovacovich; one child.
Religion: Methodist.
Political Career: N.M. attorney general, 1979-83.
Capitol Office: 703 Hart Bldg. 20510; 224-5521.

Committees
Armed Services
Acquisition & Technology; Airland Forces; Strategic Forces (ranking)
Energy & Natural Resources
Energy Research Development Production & Regulation; National Parks, Historic Preservation & Recreation (ranking)
Labor & Human Resources
Children & Families; Public Health & Safety
Joint Economic

In Washington: For some time, Bingaman has been seen as having the potential to become "the next Sam Nunn" on the Senate Armed Services Committee, and now that the Georgia Democrat has retired, Bingaman's chance has arrived. The two have much in common: Each is a serious, studious lawmaker well-versed on issues and well-regarded by colleagues on both sides of the aisle.

But as Bingaman has shown with increasing regularity, he can display a strong partisan streak. He made an unprecedented, for him, number of journeys into the rhetorical ring during the 104th Congress, assailing Republican plans for Medicaid, education and taxes before and during the 1995-1996 budget impasse.

After the Senate Finance Committee passed a plan in October 1995 to realign the earned-income tax credit, Bingaman criticized the move. Citing a U.S. Treasury analysis, he argued that the result would raise taxes on thousands of New Mexico workers earning less than $28,500 a year.

His comments on the subject — and on a variety of subsequent economic initiatives affecting low-income residents — were strikingly at odds with those voiced by his much higher-profile home-state colleague, Republican Pete V. Domenici.

In March 1995, Bingaman was one of six Democrats who switched from supporting a balanced-budget constitutional amendment to opposing it. He said the proposal would have placed the burden of balancing the budget on working families — an opinion he continued to sound as the Republican budget-balancing bill moved through Congress that year.

Bingaman has attributed his growing tendency toward outspokenness to his unhappiness with the GOP agenda. "I feel much better [speaking out] than just getting along and going along and saying, 'Whatever you guys want to pass, I'm happy to agree to it,' " he explained in an interview.

Unlike some Democrats, however, Bingaman has carefully picked his spots to gripe. In December 1995, he surprised the Senate by holding up consideration of one of the GOP's legislative priorities, a constitutional amendment to ban destruction of the U.S. flag.

His stated objections stemmed not from the amendment itself — which he opposes — but from having the Senate take up the matter while delaying the START II arms-reduction deal and the appointments of ambassadors to 18 countries. When Majority Leader Bob Dole sought to quell his objections by assuring him that supporters were "one phone call away" from a solution, Bingaman politely but firmly responded, "I do believe it's important to make that one additional phone call."

With his return in the 105th Congress to the Labor and Human Resources Committee — he stepped off the panel in the 104th — Bingaman is expected to become a player on education and pocketbook issues for working families.

With Democrat Edward M. Kennedy of Massachusetts, Bingaman has been a leading proponent of pension reform. In the 104th, he sponsored legislation to set up a clearinghouse that would manage portable pension accounts for the employees of private companies.

He also has been involved in the Democratic effort to create more high-wage jobs. Bingaman led a task force on the subject that came out with its report just as the issue was heating up on the Republican presidential campaign trail in early 1996. The task force called for changing the tax system in favor of businesses that contribute designated amounts to employee pension, health care and profit-sharing plans and set aside 2 percent of their payroll for worker training and education. The Clinton administration paid scant attention, but Bingaman remains committed to the idea.

Bingaman's interest in economic issues extends to competitiveness with Pacific Rim nations. He is expected to use his position as ranking Democrat on the Joint Economic Committee as a way to focus more public attention on strengthening trade ties with Asia.

As a longtime member of Armed Services, Bingaman has been a proponent of the need to convert and reinvest defense resources toward creating private sector jobs. His state is home to two of the

Energy Department's national laboratories, Sandia and Los Alamos, that have sought new missions with the end of the Cold War.

Bingaman argues that defense research has an important effect on the civilian economy, particularly the computer, semiconductor and aviation industries. He is a leader in the push toward dual-use technologies — those that have commercial and defense use.

In the 104th, he became increasingly exasperated with GOP criticism of technology-transfer initiatives enabling businesses to take advantage of the labs' expertise; Republicans said there was little evidence the programs are working. "When you see Congress making a U-turn and trying to pretend these problems will be resolved without our assistance, you do get frustrated," he said at one point.

But Bingaman does not automatically support defense research. During the 101st and 102nd Congresses, he argued that the Strategic Defense Initiative (SDI), the space-based shield to protect against a missile attack, was not feasible under current technology and violated the 1972 Anti-Ballistic Missile Treaty with the Soviet Union. In August 1990, Bingaman joined Democratic Sen. Richard C. Shelby of Alabama on an amendment to the fiscal 1991 defense authorization bill diverting money from Brilliant Pebbles, a system of small interceptor missiles that was the current favorite of those advocating rapid deployment of a space-based SDI.

Bingaman has become known for his efforts to make the Pentagon more efficient. He sponsored an amendment in 1995 to cap the Pentagon's renovation cost at $1.1 billion, or $100 million below the current ceiling. He also has tried to speed up the rate at which Defense Department pays its bills.

During debate on the fiscal 1996 military construction appropriations bill, Bingaman denounced the "pork-laden" measure as "a mockery of all the protestations about deficit reduction coming from Congress." But his efforts to cut the bill by $300 million were rebuffed.

That matter notwithstanding, Bingaman's colleagues usually pay attention to what he has to say. "When Jeff gets into an issue, he knows it," observed Michigan's Carl Levin, Armed Services' ranking Democrat.

Bingaman has worked assiduously on defense matters close to home. He banded together with the rest of New Mexico's congressional delegation on a successful 1995 effort to persuade the Defense Base Closure and Realignment Commission not to gut Albuquerque's Kirtland Air Force Base by transferring 6,850 jobs. Bingaman and others argued that closing the base would only shift costs rather than save money.

On another issue important to New Mexico, livestock grazing on federal lands, Bingaman emerged as a key figure during the 104th. As a member of the Energy and Natural Resources Committee, he introduced a measure calling for a higher grazing fee increase and more restrictions on the use of rangelands than a competing bill sponsored by Domenici and backed by the ranching industry. Although the committee rejected Bingaman's proposal, Domenici reworked his legislation to address Bingaman's concerns.

Bingaman's break with Domenici on the grazing issue — he had previously resisted efforts to raise fees — marked a departure from his tendency to adapt his liberal leanings to the conservative tilt of the Westerners he represents. On gun control, he supported a five-day waiting period for the purchase of a handgun, but he opposed a ban on certain semiautomatic assault-style weapons.

At Home: When he launched his 1982 Senate campaign, Bingaman was in his third year as New Mexico's attorney general, little-known outside the legal and political communities but politically unscarred. Whether by luck or shrewdness, he remained relatively fresh through the primary (against former Democratic Gov. Jerry Apodaca) and then against GOP Sen. Harrison Schmitt.

In the primary, the ex-governor was hamstrung by reports that he had ties to underworld figures. Bingaman did not directly mention Apodaca's problems, but he gave voters a not-so-subtle reminder with his slogan, "a senator we can proudly call our own."

Bingaman was endorsed by the state AFL-CIO, then narrowly won the support of the party convention. In the primary, he swept to nomination by a margin of nearly 3-to-2.

Incumbent Schmitt, a former Apollo astronaut, lacked Apodaca's political baggage. But he appeared more interested in pet subjects such as 21st century technology than in the state's struggling economy. Bingaman lambasted Schmitt for supporting supply-side economics, sharp increases in defense spending and cuts in Social Security payments. With statewide unemployment at 10 percent, Schmitt's ties to President Ronald Reagan were a campaign liability.

Long before 1988, national GOP operatives were portraying Bingaman as one of their top targets. His low-profile manner had left him with a fairly fuzzy image after one term in the Senate, and the GOP wanted to define it, claiming that Bingaman lacked stature and had achieved little in Congress.

But the GOP line lost credibility when the party chose a nominee with his own stature problems who was no more compelling on the stump than Bingaman. GOP state Sen. Bill Valentine managed less than 40 percent of the vote.

In 1994, Republicans thought they might have a sleeper on their hands with Colin R. McMillan, a former George Bush appointee to the Pentagon. Using much of his own money, McMillan pulled down Bingaman's numbers with ads attacking his stance on grazing fees and his support for President Clinton's 1993 budget.

But New Mexico's Democratic tendencies helped save Bingaman from the "war on the West" arguments that critically wounded other Western Democrats. McMillan could not make sufficient inroads in Democratic counties, and Bingaman won with 54 percent of the vote.

McMillan's aggressive, high-spending campaign against Bingaman marked a departure from the way New Mexico campaigns traditionally have been conducted, something that distressed Bingaman. One McMillan television spot displayed Bingaman's disembodied head popping out of the Capitol dome and bouncing away. That portrayal and others like it led the senator to introduce a bill in 1996 requiring political candidates to appear personally in ads attacking their opponents as well as giving the targets of those ads free air time to respond.

Bingaman grew up in the isolated New Mexico mining town of Silver City, the son of a professor and nephew of John Bingaman, a confidant of Democratic Sen. Clinton Anderson. At Stanford Law School, Bingaman worked for Robert F. Kennedy's 1968 presidential campaign. Returning to New Mexico, he served as counsel to the 1969 state constitutional convention, joined a politically connected law firm and ran successfully for attorney general in 1978.

SENATE ELECTIONS

1994 General

Jeff Bingaman (D)	249,989	(54%)
Colin R. McMillan (R)	213,025	(46%)

Previous Winning Percentages: **1988** (63%) **1982** (54%)

CAMPAIGN FINANCE

	Receipts	Receipts from PACs	Expend-itures
1994			
Bingaman (D)	$2,855,038	$1,030,243 (36%)	$3,227,352
McMillan (R)	$1,549,197	$151,612 (10%)	$1,537,563

KEY VOTES

1997	
Approve balanced-budget constitutional amendment	N
Approve chemical weapons treaty	Y
1996	
Approve farm bill	N
Limit punitive damages in product liability cases	N
Exempt small businesses from higher minimum wage	N
Approve welfare overhaul	N
Bar job discrimination based on sexual orientation	Y
Override veto of ban on "partial birth" abortions	N
1995	
Approve GOP budget with tax and spending cuts	N
Approve constitutional amendment barring flag desecration	N

VOTING STUDIES

	Presidential Support		Party Unity		Conservative Coalition	
Year	S	O	S	O	S	O
1996	83	15	87	12	37	63
1995	91	9	83	16	32	65
1994	89	11	84	16	53	47
1993	85	13	79	20	49	49
1992	40	50	70	23	39	55
1991	51	48	78	20	65	35

INTEREST GROUP RATINGS

Year	ADA	AFL-CIO	CCUS	ACU
1996	95	n/a	15	0
1995	90	100	42	0
1994	60	75	50	16
1993	70	73	36	20
1992	75	92	20	4
1991	65	67	20	19

1 Steven H. Schiff (R)

Of Albuquerque — Elected 1988, 5th term

Biographical Information

Born: March 18, 1947, Chicago, Ill.

Education: U. of Illinois, Chicago Circle, B.A. 1968; U. of New Mexico, J.D. 1972.

Military Service: Air National Guard, 1969-91; Air Force Reserves, 1991-present.

Occupation: Lawyer.

Family: Wife, Marcia Lewis; two children.

Religion: Jewish.

Political Career: Candidate for district judge, 1978; Bernalillo County district attorney, 1981-89.

Capitol Office: 2404 Rayburn Bldg. 20515; 225-6316.

Committees

Government Reform & Oversight
Human Resources; National Security, International Affairs & Criminal Justice

Judiciary
Commercial & Administrative Law; Crime

Science
Basic Research (chairman); Energy & Environment

In Washington: Despite having worked studiously on crime and science matters since he joined the House in 1989, Schiff has been more in the public eye lately for his efforts in a couple of matters he would just as soon not have seen arise.

One of those issues was the furor concerning House Speaker Newt Gingrich's use of charitable donations to pay for college courses that served as Republican recruiting tools. Schiff, a former district attorney in Albuquerque, was a member of a four-person subcommittee of the House ethics committee that investigated the allegations filed against Gingrich.

In December 1996, the panel voted unanimously to formally charge the Speaker with House rules violations, touching off a flurry of negotiations between Gingrich's lawyers and special counsel James M. Cole.

With these discussions bumping up against the scheduled start of the 105th Congress, members were put in the difficult position of deciding whether to re-elect Gingrich as Speaker without knowing the precise nature of the sanction he would draw from the ethics committee.

Into this void stepped Schiff and fellow subcommittee Republican Porter J. Goss of Florida, who took the unusual step of sending a letter to House Republicans stating that they knew of no reason why Gingrich should not continue as Speaker.

Angry Democrats accused Goss and Schiff of violating House rules that bar ethics committee members from talking publicly about a pending case. Schiff responded that the letter helped stave off a politically motivated postponement of a vote on the penalty while keeping the House focused on its business.

In the end, Gingrich publicly admitted that he had broken House rules, and the House voted to reprimand him and require him to pay $300,000. Schiff said the sizable assessment was his idea, meant to communicate that Gingrich should be held to a higher standard than other politicians. "He holds a unique position," Schiff told the Baltimore Sun. "He's simply not just a member of the House."

It was surprising to see Schiff's late jump into the public fray about Gingrich. Methodical and analytical, he had kept his own counsel during most of the investigation, and on other ethics committee matters. He is known for going by the book; one of his aides said he regularly drives 1 mph below the speed limit even on the most barren stretches of New Mexico's highways.

Another matter that has shoved Schiff reluctantly into the spotlight has been his effort to push the Pentagon for information about the so-called Roswell Incident, the 1947 crash of a mysterious object on a remote ranch in what is now Schiff's district. The crash made headlines after the public information officer for the Roswell Army Air Base issued a press release saying that the wreckage of a flying saucer had been recovered. That version of events was quickly retracted, with officials saying that what had crashed was simply a weather balloon. But the incident has long been a favorite of UFO believers and has even spawned the establishment of a UFO museum in Roswell.

Pressure from Schiff prompted the Air Force to revisit the incident and issue a report in September 1994 that concluded the object was probably a top-secret Army Air Force balloon designed to monitor Soviet nuclear testing. However, in July 1995, Schiff released a General Accounting Office report that said numerous key documents relating to the crash were missing.

Schiff, who says he is a skeptic when it comes to UFOs, said he risked ridicule in pressing for the new investigation because citizens have a right to the information. "I don't think it matters whether the subject of their inquiry is extraterrestrial creatures or radiation experiments or any other subject. The people are entitled to know what their government did."

In May 1997, Schiff again drew unsolicited attention when he underwent the second of two surgeries for skin cancer. His medical problem kept him away from Washington in the early

NEW MEXICO 1
Central —Albuquerque

Albuquerque's postwar emergence as New Mexico's commercial hub and a GOP stronghold was fueled by the development of a prosperous military-aerospace industry. Despite a Democratic edge in registration, the GOP has maintained its hold on the House seat by offering fiscally conservative, defense-oriented moderate candidates.

However, the existence of a large state and local government work force and a big minority population gives Democrats a foothold in Bernalillo County, alongside Republican-voting white-collar professionals employed in the area's defense and aerospace industries. About 38 percent of the 1st District's population is Hispanic. The city and the county together cast about one-third of the state vote.

Before World War II, Albuquerque was a lightly populated regional trade center, better known as a health resort where tubercular patients could alleviate their suffering by taking advantage of the dry climate.

Since the A-bomb was developed in 1945 (less than 100 miles north at Los Alamos), Albuquerque has seen its population multiply from 35,000 people in 1940 to about 385,000 today. The district has a high concentration of scientists and engineers. A large employer is Sandia National Laboratories, which specializes in nuclear and solar research and testing. Also in the 1st is Kirtland Air Force Base, which survived a proposed Pentagon downsizing attempt in 1995. Defense and aviation technology companies such as Honeywell and General Electric are here as are scores of newer electronics, computer and communications companies.

Teachers also form an important bloc; the University of New Mexico and Albuquerque public school system account for 23,000 jobs.

Much of the GOP vote is cast in the city's heavily white, upper-middle-class Northeast Heights section. The Hispanic-majority South Valley, on the south and west sides of the Rio Grande, boosts Democratic totals.

Until 1992, Bernalillo County had supported the GOP presidential nominee in all but one election since 1952. Then Bill Clinton took 46 percent of the county's vote, making him the first Democrat to win here since Lyndon B. Johnson in 1964. And Clinton carried the county again in 1996, winning Bernalillo and the 1st District with 48 percent. His showing demonstrates that despite the county's GOP tendencies, strong Democratic candidates can win here. In 1994, Bernalillo's support helped propel Democratic Sen. Jeff Bingaman to a second term.

Bernalillo serves as the population center of the district, but rural Torrance County, with 3,300 square miles, has most of the land area. Torrance accounts for only about 2 percent of the district vote.

Portions of three other counties make up the balance of the 1st. About 13,000 voters — mainly professionals — live in Albuquerque bedroom communities in eastern Valencia County, and about 11,000 voters hail from a primarily rural section of Sandoval County.

1990 Population: 505,491. White 392,124 (78%), Black 13,434 (3%), Other 99,933 (20%). Hispanic origin 192,384 (38%). 18 and over 371,875 (74%), 62 and over 64,551 (13%). Median age: 32.

months of the 105th as he underwent follow-up treatments in Albuquerque.

Schiff has moderate tendencies on some issues. He voted in 1996 and 1997 against a GOP-backed proposal to allow employers to offer their workers compensatory time in lieu of overtime pay. He voted against denying public education to illegal immigrants, and he supported an increase in the minimum wage (though he also sought to exempt small businesses from paying the higher minimum).

But Schiff casts his share of votes with the right wing of his party. Despite his support of limited abortion rights, he voted with anti-abortion forces on several occasions during the 104th Congress. And Schiff has been uniformly conservative on crime. A proponent of tough anti-crime measures and critic of gun control, he voted in 1996 to repeal the ban on certain semiautomatic assault-style weapons, and in 1993 he opposed passage of the five-day waiting period for purchase of a handgun. He prefers tougher penalties for crimes committed with a gun. In the 104th Congress, Schiff also pushed into law a measure making health-care fraud punishable by a fine or imprisonment.

As chairman of the Science Committee's Basic Research Subcommittee, Schiff is in a position to influence federal spending priorities in an area of considerable interest to his scientifically inclined district. The 1st is home to Sandia National Laboratories, a nuclear and solar research and testing center, and other high-tech concerns.

Schiff has in the past been a supporter of "big science," voting consistently in favor of continued funding for NASA's space station and the now-defunct superconducting super collider project. He has expressed concerns about efforts by GOP conservatives to shut down the Department of Energy and has argued that the government must clearly define the post-Cold War missions of Sandia and DOE's other national labs.

An Air Force Reserves colonel, Schiff spent several days in the Bosnia theater in February 1996 as a judge advocate general involved with international legal matters. In 1991 he was called for active service during the Persian Gulf crisis; he did not go overseas but volunteered to serve three days drafting wills and performing other legal aid for reservists.

Like others in New Mexico's congressional delegation, Schiff has been protective of the state's federally driven economy. In 1995, he joined the other members in a successful effort to save Albuquerque's Kirtland Air Force Base, one of the hubs of the city's economy. The Pentagon had targeted Kirtland for a substantial reduction in jobs.

In April 1997, Schiff joined fellow Republicans Sen. Pete V. Domenici and Rep. Joe Skeen to introduce legislation adjusting the boundaries of Albuquerque's Petroglyph National Monument to allow for an extension of a road improving access to and from the city's booming West Side. The legislation prompted objections from some local activists despite the lawmakers' contention that the measure would not harm the monument's prehistoric and historic rock drawings.

At Home: Schiff won his 1988 House election on a pledge to deliver constituent service, a rather modest agenda for a Republican who toppled two family dynasties to win in a politically competitive district. But constituent service had been the hallmark of his GOP predecessor, Manuel Lujan Jr.

When Lujan announced his plans to leave the House after 20 years (he later served as George Bush's Interior secretary), a dozen candidates jockeyed to succeed him, including his brother, former state GOP Chairman Edward Lujan, and Democrat Tom Udall, the son of former Interior Secretary Stewart Udall and nephew of former Arizona Rep. Morris K. Udall.

Schiff had been contemplating a Senate bid but quickly shifted to the open House seat. In eight years as a popular district attorney in Bernalillo County, Schiff had become a familiar face in the media; he directed the prosecution of numerous high-profile criminal cases. Outspent in the House primary by nearly 2-to-1, Schiff came under fire for his willingness to plea-bargain. But the charge did not stick because Schiff's image as a law-and-order figure was well-known to voters.

Schiff defeated Lujan in the primary by four percentage points, and he posted the same victory margin again in November over Udall.

In 1990, the Democratic nominee, Secretary of State Rebecca Vigil-Giron, was sent reeling by revelations that she had exaggerated her academic record, defaulted on a student loan and watched her roommate forge a signature on her 1986 ballot petition. Schiff took 70 percent and also won with ease in 1992 and 1994.

Democrats initially hoped Schiff might be vulnerable in 1996. His Democratic opponent was John Wertheim, a youthful and energetic campaigner who had been active in state political circles. Wertheim sought to highlight his similarities with President Clinton while making an issue of Schiff's involvement in the Gingrich case.

Although Clinton visited the district three times and carried it by 5 percentage points over Bob Dole, Schiff took 57 percent of the vote, finishing 20 points ahead of Wertheim.

HOUSE ELECTIONS

1996 General		
Steven H. Schiff (R)	109,290	(57%)
John Wertheim (D)	71,635	(37%)
John A. "Jack" Uhrich (GREEN)	7,694	(4%)
Betty Turrietta-Koury (I)	4,459	(2%)
1994 General		
Steven H. Schiff (R)	119,996	(74%)
Peter L. Zollinger (D)	42,316	(26%)

Previous Winning Percentages: 1992 (63%) **1990** (70%) **1988** (51%)

CAMPAIGN FINANCE

	Receipts	Receipts from PACs	Expend-itures
1996			
Schiff (R)	$599,401	$148,723 (25%)	$603,316
Wertheim (D)	$286,974	$68,168 (24%)	$285,999
Uhrich (GREEN)	$12,517	0	$12,120
Turrietta-Koury (I)	$12,376	0	$12,374
1994			
Schiff (R)	$461,451	$146,843 (32%)	$458,653
Zollinger (D)	$6,069	0	$5,944

VOTING STUDIES

	Presidential Support		Party Unity		Conservative Coalition	
Year	S	O	S	O	S	O
1996	51	41	71	22	78	12
1995	30	70	85	13	91	8
1994	53	47	79	19	89	11
1993	51	47	81	17	82	14
1992	67	31	72	26	85	15
1991	67	33	64	33	86	14

DISTRICT VOTE FOR PRESIDENT

	1996		1992
D	94,334 (48%)	**D**	95,677 (46%)
R	84,044 (43%)	**R**	81,046 (39%)
I	9,625 (5%)	**I**	33,032 (16%)

KEY VOTES

1997	
Ban "partial birth" abortions	Y
1996	
Approve farm bill	Y
Deny public education to illegal immigrants	N
Repeal ban on certain assault-style weapons	Y
Increase minimum wage	Y
Freeze defense spending	N
Approve welfare overhaul	Y
1995	
Approve balanced-budget constitutional amendment	Y
Relax Clean Water Act regulations	Y
Oppose limits on environmental regulations	Y
Reduce projected Medicare spending	Y
Approve GOP budget with tax and spending cuts	Y

INTEREST GROUP RATINGS

Year	ADA	AFL-CIO	CCUS	ACU
1996	25	n/a	80	63
1995	15	25	92	64
1994	15	44	83	80
1993	5	8	91	88
1992	25	58	88	72
1991	20	33	80	65

2 Joe Skeen (R)

Of Picacho — Elected 1980, 9th term

Biographical Information

Born: June 30, 1927, Roswell, N.M.

Education: Texas A&M U., B.S. 1950.

Military Service: Navy, 1945-46; Air Force Reserve, 1949-52.

Occupation: Sheep rancher; soil and water engineer; flying service operator.

Family: Wife, Mary Jones; two children.

Religion: Roman Catholic.

Political Career: N.M. Senate, 1961-71, minority leader, 1965-71; N.M. Republican Party chairman, 1962-65; Republican nominee for lieutenant governor, 1970; Republican nominee for governor, 1974, 1978.

Capitol Office: 2302 Rayburn Bldg. 20515; 225-2365.

Committees

Appropriations

Agriculture, Rural Development, FDA & Related Agencies (chairman); Interior; National Security

In Washington: Skeen laid to rest years of rumors about his health in March 1997 when he revealed he had Parkinson's disease, the same degenerative nerve disorder afflicting Attorney General Janet Reno. But he vowed to press on with unfinished legislative business and not let the illness prevent him from seeking a 10th House term in 1998.

Skeen has plenty of business on his hands. With the Republican takeover of the House in 1994, he entered the exclusive "college of cardinals," the 13 subcommittee chairmen of the House Appropriations Committee. Holding the gavel of the Appropriations panel on agriculture and rural development, he faces the challenge of reconciling his desire to fund farm programs with his new responsibility as chairman to be a leader in his party's efforts to cut federal expenditures and bring the budget to balance.

The first spending bill Skeen oversaw — the fiscal 1996 agriculture appropriations bill — provided $3.2 billion less in budget authority than President Clinton had requested and $5.8 billion less than what had been appropriated in fiscal 1995. Part of the decrease was due to favorable marketplace conditions, which had temporarily reduced the annual demand for crop subsidies, but part also reflected the determination of Skeen and other Republicans to make spending cuts across the board.

For Skeen, however, the belt-tightening was often painful. A longtime sheep rancher, he made little secret of his preference to restore subsidies to wool and mohair producers instead of taking an ax to programs that were popular among his rural constituents.

"The good news is that I'm chairman of the Agriculture Subcommittee," he said in May 1995. "And the bad news is that I'm chairman of the Agriculture Subcommittee."

In addition to making cuts, Skeen found himself caught in a conflict over the bill with agriculture authorizers. In October 1995, then-House Agriculture Chairman Pat Roberts, R-Kan., accused Skeen's panel of tampering with spending levels for mandatory programs under the jurisdiction of Roberts' committee.

A letter signed by Roberts and 32 other House Republicans to their colleagues assailed the appropriations bill for "budget gimmickry." That prompted Skeen to fire off a letter of his own accusing Roberts of spreading "misinformation" and defending his subcommittee's spending measure as "a good bill and one you can defend back home."

Skeen likes to stress his support for politically sensitive nutritional programs, such as food stamps and school lunches. And his rhetoric separates him from many younger Republicans who crusade to prune down government. "You just can't keep chopping, chopping, chopping," he said in May 1996.

Skeen began his House career on the Agriculture Committee, where he earned a reputation as a battler in behalf of cattle, sheep and peanut growers in his state. He moved to Appropriations in the 99th Congress, taking seats on the Agriculture and Interior subcommittees.

He has continued to fight the rangeland's wars, especially in resisting the perennial effort to raise the grazing fees charged ranchers on lands run by the Bureau of Land Management (BLM). Advocates of higher fees say the current below-market charges amount to a government giveaway that contributes to the deficit. Skeen has argued that the fees are actually too high — given the amount of work ranchers must do to keep up federal rangelands as part of their grazing permit.

In the 104th Congress, Skeen supported legislation to turn over control of the BLM's lands to states. He also introduced a measure that would give local irrigation districts jurisdiction over federally controlled irrigation facilities and land. The legislation was intended to benefit about two dozen districts in the West, including three in southern New Mexico.

Despite his belief that the federal government can be insensitive to rural Westerners' special perspective on land-management issues and

NEW MEXICO 2
South — Little Texas; Las Cruces; Roswell

Southern New Mexico was once firmly Democratic, but traditional party ties have eroded here. During the 1970s, the area developed a strong habit of voting Republican in statewide contests, as ranchers and other Southern-style Democrats came to resent their party's national program.

In 1991, redistricting wrought more changes. To try to make the district more competitive for Democrats, the state's Democratic Legislature drew district lines to include more liberal voters. The population of Hispanics jumped from 34 percent to 42 percent.

In addition, the 2nd District lost Curry, Quay and Roosevelt counties, all Democratic but conservative. The district picked up De Baca and Guadalupe, where ranching is the mainstay.

In what was once resolutely GOP country, Bill Clinton beat George Bush in the district by 1 percentage point in 1992, then repeated the feat against Bob Dole four years later.

Other Democratic strongholds are in the Mexican Highlands, along the Arizona border, where copper and lead mines have attracted union labor. But they have provided less than 10 percent of the vote.

"Little Texas," the southeastern corner of New Mexico, accounts for about 50 percent of the 2nd. This region, settled by Texans early in the 20th century, is more culturally and economically attuned to conservative, Baptist West Texas than to the more liberal capital city of Santa Fe. Most of the land is devoted to grazing cattle or sheep. But oil and military projects have reshaped voting habits in a GOP direction. The oil- and gas-producing centers of Chaves and Lea counties are conservative bastions.

Near Carlsbad in Eddy County are the nation's most productive salt mines. Democratic miners occasionally influence county elections. The subterranean salt beds will be the site of the nation's first nuclear waste dump, the controversial Waste Isolation Pilot Plant. Many in the Carlsbad area support the project, expected to inject millions of dollars into the stagnant local economy. However, delays already have pushed its opening back 10 years — its operations are now scheduled to begin by 1998. Meanwhile, the safety of the Carlsbad nuclear repository has ignited a firestorm of criticism statewide.

To the west are Otero and Dona Ana counties, which account for more than one-third of the 2nd's population. Otero County favors the GOP. Dona Ana, which includes Las Cruces, has a Hispanic majority, giving the Democrats a substantial base. Clinton won Dona Ana handily in 1992 and 1996, and Republican Skeen narrowly lost there in 1996. Parts of Dona Ana, Otero and Sierra counties hold the sprawling White Sands Missile Range.

Holloman Air Force Base in Otero County also provides GOP strength. Just north of Otero, in the southeastern corner of Socorro County, the world's first atomic bomb was exploded in 1945.

Billy the Kid stood trial in the tiny village of Mesilla, in Las Cruces, but escaped. The village also served briefly as the Confederate capital of the Arizona Territory.

1990 Population: 504,659. White 423,661 (84%), Black 10,662 (2%), Other 70,336 (14%). Hispanic origin 212,355 (42%). 18 and over 350,557 (69%), 62 and over 72,656 (14%). Median age: 31.

other concerns, he also has looked to Uncle Sam for help for troubled mining industries in his home state. And on the Appropriations Committee, he works to bring home New Mexico's share of federal dollars.

As part of the fiscal 1996 agriculture appropriations bill, he was able to secure $500,000 for rangeland research in southern New Mexico. The bill also contained money for research into eradicating the broom snakeweed and locoweed, a menace in New Mexico and the Southwest.

Skeen is one of the few House members willing to entertain the idea of locating a nuclear waste site in his district. The Waste Isolation Pilot Plant, to be located in underground salt caverns near the 2nd District city of Carlsbad, would make the site the first permanent facility to store defense-generated waste. It is designed to store plutonium-tainted waste from nuclear weapons production factories in Colorado, Idaho and other states.

After years of deadlock, the House in 1992 voted to begin limited trial storage at the facility. The legislation, which would transfer the repository to the Energy Department and set certain conditions — including Environmental Protection Agency oversight — before site testing could begin, became law at the end of the 102nd Congress. Plans call for the plant to receive its first waste in late 1997 or early 1998, but lawsuits could delay the opening.

At Home: Skeen hasn't had too much trouble holding his largely rural district, even though Democratic strength in the 2nd has grown in recent years. One reason is that many of the nominally Democratic older residents in the southeast oil-patch corner of the state known as "Little Texas" remain conservative and disposed to back Republicans such as Skeen.

Skeen's long run in politics began in the New Mexico Senate, where he served from 1961 to 1971 and for six years was minority leader. He failed in a 1970 bid for lieutenant governor and then narrowly lost carefully planned campaigns for governor in 1974 and 1978. His luck turned in the "Sagebrush Rebellion" year of 1980, when he won election to the House without even being on the ballot. He is one of the few write-in candidates ever elected to Congress.

Skeen's unusual victory came after Democratic Rep. Harold E. Runnels, who was unopposed for re-election, died on Aug. 5, 1980. Runnels' death set off three months of complex maneuvering, with Skeen and Runnels' widow, Dorothy, mounting unsuccessful court challenges to win a spot on the ballot against the substitute Democratic nominee, David King.

Skeen and Mrs. Runnels pursued separate write-in campaigns, aided by negative publicity that hit King. A former state finance commissioner, King moved to the district only after Harold Runnels' death, and there were complaints that his choice was arranged by his uncle, Democratic Gov. Bruce King.

Skeen based his campaign on the contention that no one should be appointed to Congress. His write-ins totaled 38 percent of the vote, enough to win the three-way contest.

Skeen then went on a streak of comfortable re-elections. But in 1992, he got a serious opponent with officeholding credentials and name recognition: Dan Sosa Jr. Sosa had served 17 years on the state's Supreme Court, including five as chief justice, before retiring in 1991. And Sosa, a Hispanic, hoped to benefit from the fact that 1992 redistricting added more than 65,000 Hispanics to the 2nd, making its population 42 percent Hispanic.

Sosa ran a campaign against the status quo and longtime incumbency. He also faulted Skeen for his opposition to family and medical leave legislation and for voting no on civil rights and extended unemployment compensation legislation.

But Skeen was able to draw on a deep reservoir of support that he had built with years of steady attention to constituents. He won with 56 percent of the vote, running 16 points ahead of George Bush in the district.

Skeen received the same percentage of the vote in 1996 against Democratic state Rep. Shirley Baca of Las Cruces, despite the fact that President Clinton narrowly carried the district. In the GOP primary, Skeen had handily defeated Las Cruces businessman and political newcomer Gregory Sowards.

HOUSE ELECTIONS

1996 General		
Joe Skeen (R)	95,091	(56%)
E. Shirley Baca (D)	74,915	(44%)
1996 Primary		
Joe Skeen (R)	17,520	(70%)
Gregory E. Sowards (R)	7,450	(30%)
1994 General		
Joe Skeen (R)	89,966	(63%)
Benjamin Anthony Chavez (D)	45,316	(32%)
Rex Johnson (GREEN)	6,898	(5%)

Previous Winning Percentages: 1992 (56%) **1990** (100%) **1988** (100%) **1986** (63%) **1984** (74%) **1982** (58%) **1980** (38%)

CAMPAIGN FINANCE

	Receipts	Receipts from PACs	Expend-itures
1996			
Skeen (R)	$505,836	$255,366 (50%)	$539,969
Baca (D)	$192,413	$45,446 (24%)	$191,794
1994			
Skeen (R)	$336,005	$155,370 (46%)	$384,687
Chavez (D)	$216,563	$16,500 (8%)	$221,676

VOTING STUDIES

	Presidential Support		Party Unity		Conservative Coalition	
Year	S	O	S	O	S	O
1996	42	58	89	11	98	2
1995	20	80	95+	4+	100+	0+
1994	53	47	82	17	100	0
1993	45	51	78	11	80	5
1992	76	24	67	32	92	8
1991	75	25	69	30	89	11

+ Not eligible for all recorded votes.

DISTRICT VOTE FOR PRESIDENT

	1996		1992
D	80,307 (46%)	**D**	70,646 (41%)
R	77,369 (45%)	**R**	68,754 (40%)
I	12,104 (7%)	**I**	31,782 (19%)

KEY VOTES

1997	
Ban "partial birth" abortions	Y
1996	
Approve farm bill	Y
Deny public education to illegal immigrants	Y
Repeal ban on certain assault-style weapons	Y
Increase minimum wage	N
Freeze defense spending	N
Approve welfare overhaul	Y
1995	
Approve balanced-budget constitutional amendment	Y
Relax Clean Water Act regulations	Y
Oppose limits on environmental regulations	N
Reduce projected Medicare spending	Y
Approve GOP budget with tax and spending cuts	Y

INTEREST GROUP RATINGS

Year	ADA	AFL-CIO	CCUS	ACU
1996	5	n/a	100	90
1995	0	0	96	76
1994	0	11	75	95
1993	5	17	91	87
1992	20	42	88	76
1991	0	17	90	85

3 Bill Redmond (R)

Of Los Alamos — Elected 1997, 1st term

Biographical Information

Born: Jan. 28, 1954, Chicago, Ill.

Education: Murray State U., 1973-75; Lincoln Christian College, B.A. 1979; Lincoln Christian Seminary, M.Div. 1988.

Military Service: Army, 1984-92.

Occupation: Minister; teacher; roller rink manager.

Family: Wife, Shirley Raye; two children.

Religion: Christian.

Political Career: N.M. Republican Central Committee; Republican nominee for U.S. House, 1996.

Capitol Office: 2268 Rayburn Bldg.; 225-6190.

The Path to Washington: A conservative Republican in a district that has long been a Democratic stronghold, Redmond won his seat in the face of formidable odds by running what amounted to a 30-month campaign.

He began laying the groundwork in December 1994, shortly after Democrat Bill Richardson was elected to a seventh term. He took a leave of absence from his job as minister at a Santa Fe church to stump at candidate forums and on radio shows across the ethnically diverse and expansive district. In the November 1996 election, Richardson overwhelmingly won an eighth term. Redmond's 56,580 votes were the most for a Republican nominee in the 3rd in a dozen years, but they still amounted to only a 31 percent share of the total vote.

Redmond, however, got a second chance. As post-election speculation mounted that Richardson might receive a Cabinet-level position in a second Clinton administration, Redmond lined up commitments from GOP officials with an eye toward a special election. He kept "Redmond for Congress" as the message on his telephone answering machine.

Richardson eventually was named U.S. Representative to the United Nations, partly in recognition of the fact that while serving in the House, he had scored negotiating successes on a string of politically sensitive diplomatic missions. When the special election was called, the parties nominated candidates without a primary, Redmond came to the March 1997 meeting of 3rd District party leaders as one of seven contenders. Others had longer political résumés, but Redmond came away with the backing of 70 of the 132 Republican representatives present.

In the May special election, Redmond's Democratic opponent was Eric P. Serna, a member of the state Corporation Commission who had long hoped to move into Richardson's seat. But even members of Serna's own party questioned his electability, pointing to ethics allegations that Serna tried to dismiss as insignificant. Redmond ran radio and television advertisements questioning his opponent's integrity while campaigning on his support of the House Republican agenda, including school vouchers and elimination of the capital gains tax and estate tax. Serna tried paint Redmond as "a radical right-wing preacher who wants to impose his extreme values and social agenda on all of us." But Serna was hurt by the emergence of the Green Party, a rising force in state politics.

Its nominee for the 3rd, Carol Miller, drew 17 percent of the vote, siphoning support from Serna in strongly Democratic areas, including Santa Fe, the district's largest city. Serna finished with 40 percent, trailing Redmond's 43 percent.

Redmond wants to continue Richardson's tradition of holding town meetings in the district, although he said he will approach the sessions differently. "Bill Richardson played Santa Claus instead of allowing people to see legislation and make comments on legislation," he said.

Redmond's views on the environment, a topic of considerable interest in his district, also stand in sharp contrast to those of Richardson. Redmond wants the Endangered Species Act to be "more respectful of private property rights," and he also supports legislation to compensate landowners whose property values are reduced because of a federal regulatory action. Like many rural legislators, he favors repealing the ban on certain semiautomatic assault-style weapons.

Redmond hopes to improve access to education and health care for Indians. He also plans to work to adjust the boundaries of Petroglyph National Monument to extend an east-west roadway. Residents of the city's rapidly growing west side say the move will improve access and clear up traffic congestion, but some local activists protest it will harm the monument's prehistoric rock drawings.

Redmond faces an uphill fight in holding on to his seat in 1998. Democrats have vowed to field a candidate who can win Green support. Given Democrats' 2-to-1 voter registration advantage over Republicans in the district, Redmond would appear to have a tough time winning re-election if his opposition is not split.

NEW MEXICO 3
North and East Central — Farmington; Santa Fe

With more than half its voters either Hispanic or Indian, the 3rd is more liberal and more Democratic than either of the state's other districts. It contains eight of the 10 New Mexico counties that Michael S. Dukakis carried in 1988. In 1992, Bill Clinton took 51 percent of the 3rd's vote, and 53 percent in 1996.

However, 1991 redistricting made the district a bit less Democratic, trading a chunk of Hispanic territory for a piece of conservative GOP turf. Richardson now represents a constituency that is about 35 percent Hispanic, down from 39 percent in the 1980s. Anglos make up about 40 percent; the remainder is American Indian. The population is divided between the Hispanic counties of northern New Mexico and some energy-rich Indian lands along the Arizona border.

Areas of the 3rd, particularly Cibola, McKinley and Mora counties, are plagued with high unemployment and poverty. In most of the counties that ring the Santa Fe-Taos area, between one-third and one-half of the residents, many of whom are unskilled minorities, live in poverty. Unemployment levels here routinely run about 10 percent for most of these counties; the Mora County jobless rate hovered above 30 percent for much of the 1980s. And although programs have targeted alcoholism, it remains a problem in poorer pockets of the 3rd.

The scenery in parts of the 3rd is breathtaking, making it a trendy tourist spot. Taos, home of Taos Ski Valley and many art galleries and specialty shops, attracts thousands of tourists.

The 3rd gained some conservative farming and ranching territory when it picked up Curry, Quay and Roosevelt counties in 1991 redistricting. Curry is home to Cannon Air Force Base and a considerable number of military retirees who make this area a conservative bastion.

The centerpiece of the region is Santa Fe, the third-largest city in the state. The city has evolved into a regional arts center, supporting more than 150 art galleries and hundreds of shops that peddle distinctive Southwestern and Indian art styles. Artists, state employees, Hispanics, Indians and Anglo liberals combine to make the city a Democratic stronghold; Democrats outnumber Republicans here by about 3-to-1.

The rest of the Hispanic north is primarily mountainous, semi-arid grazing land that supports some subsistence farming.

An economic oasis is the Anglo community of Los Alamos, where the atomic bomb was developed during World War II. One of the most prosperous counties in the country, it has well-educated and largely Republican voters.

In Indian country, voters turn out in small numbers and divide more closely at the polls. However, American Indians, most of them Navajo, usually vote Democratic.

The largest county in the region is San Juan, where a conservative Anglo population settled around Farmington (population 34,000) to tap the vast supply of oil, gas and coal in the Four Corners area. San Juan went solidly for George Bush in 1988 and 1992.

1990 Population: 504,919. White 330,243 (65%), Black 6,114 (1%), Other 168,562 (33%). Hispanic origin 174,485 (35%). 18 and over 345,896 (69%), 62 and over 61,140 (12%). Median age: 31.

HOUSE ELECTIONS

1997 Special *		
Bill Redmond (R)	43,472	(43%)
Eric P. Serna (D)	40,424	(40%)
Carol A. Miller (GREEN)	17,079	(17%)

** Nearly complete, unofficial returns.*

DISTRICT VOTE FOR PRESIDENT

	1996		1992
D	98,854 (53%)	D	95,294 (51%)
R	71,338 (38%)	R	63,024 (34%)
I	10,528 (6%)	I	27,081 (15%)

NEW YORK

Governor: George E. Pataki (R)
First elected: 1994
Length of term: 4 years
Term expires: 1/99
Salary: $130,000
Term limit: No
Phone: (518) 474-8390
Born: June 24, 1945; Peekskill, N.Y.
Education: Yale U., B.A. 1967; Columbia U., J.D. 1970.
Occupation: Lawyer; farm owner.
Family: Wife, Elizabeth Rowland; four children.
Religion: Unspecified.
Political Career: Mayor of Peekskill, 1982-84; N.Y. Assembly, 1985-92; N.Y. Senate, 1993-95.

Lt. Gov.: Betsy McCaughey (R)
First elected: 1994
Length of term: 4 years
Term expires: 1/99
Salary: $110,000
Phone: (518) 474-4623

State election official: (518) 474-6220
Democratic headquarters: (518) 462-7407
Republican headquarters: (518) 462-2601

REDISTRICTING

New York lost three House seats in reapportionment, dropping from 34 districts to 31. Legislature passed map June 9, 1992; governor signed June 11. Justice Department approved July 2.

STATE LEGISLATURE

Legislature. Officially meets year-round; usually meets January-June.

Senate: 61 members, 2-year terms
1996 breakdown: 35R, 26D; 53 men, 8 women
Salary: $57,500
Phone: (518) 455-3216

Assembly: 150 members, 2-year terms
1996 breakdown: 96D, 52R, 2 vacancies; 117 men, 31 women
Salary: $57,500
Phone: (518) 455-4218

URBAN STATISTICS

City	Population
New York City	7,322,564
Mayor Rudolph Giuliani, R	
Buffalo	328,175
Mayor Anthony Masiello, D	
Rochester	231,636
Mayor Bill Johnson, D	
Yonkers	188,082
Mayor John Spencer, R	
Syracuse	163,860
Mayor Roy Bernardi, R	

U.S. CONGRESS

Senate: 1 D, 1 R
House: 18 D, 13 R

TERM LIMITS

For state offices: No

ELECTIONS

1996 Presidential Vote

Bill Clinton	60%
Bob Dole	31%
Ross Perot	8%

1992 Presidential Vote

Bill Clinton	50%
George Bush	34%
Ross Perot	16%

1988 Presidential Vote

Michael S. Dukakis	52%
George Bush	48%

POPULATION

1990 population		17,990,455
1980 population		17,558,072
Percent change		+2%
Rank among states:		2
White		74%
Black		16%
Hispanic		12%
Asian or Pacific islander		4%
Urban		84%
Rural		16%
Born in state		68%
Foreign-born		16%
Under age 18	4,259,549	24%
Ages 18-64	11,367,184	63%
65 and older	2,363,722	13%
Median age		33.9

MISCELLANEOUS

Capital: Albany
Number of counties: 62
Per capita income: $22,456 (1991)
Rank among states: 4
Total area: 49,108 sq. miles
Rank among states: 30

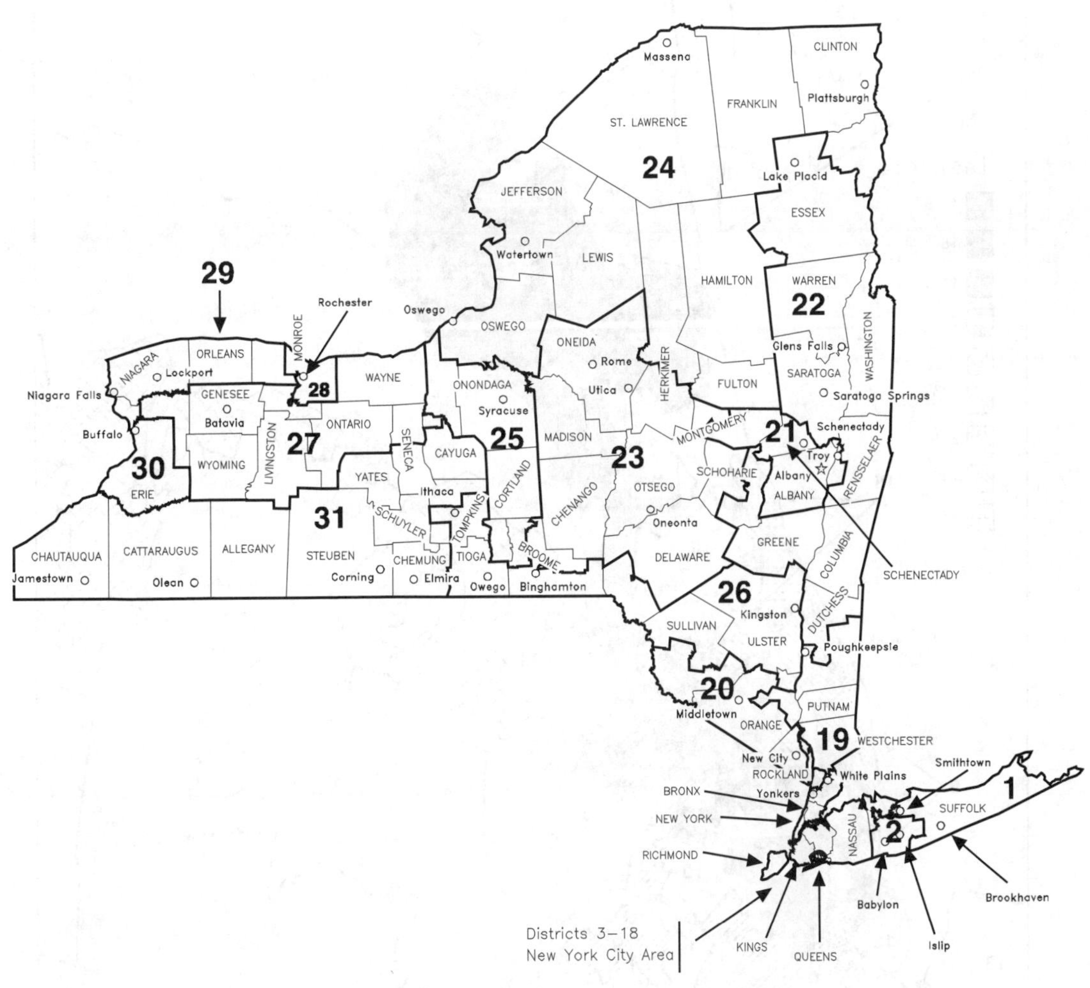
CLINTON
Massena
Plattsburgh
FRANKLIN
ST. LAWRENCE
24
Lake Placid
JEFFERSON
ESSEX
Watertown
LEWIS
HAMILTON
WARREN
29
22
Rochester
Oswego
OSWEGO
ONEIDA
Glens Falls
ORLEANS
MONROE
NIAGARA
Lockport
WAYNE
Rome
HERKIMER
SARATOGA
WASHINGTON
Niagara Falls
GENESEE
28
ONONDAGA
Utica
FULTON
Saratoga Springs
Batavia
Syracuse
ONTARIO
Buffalo
27
LIVINGSTON
SENECA
25
MADISON
MONTGOMERY
21
Schenectady
30
WYOMING
CAYUGA
23
SCHOHARIE
Troy
RENSSELAER
YATES
CORTLAND
OTSEGO
Albany
ERIE
Ithaca
ALBANY
31
SCHUYLER
CHENANGO
Oneonta
TOMPKINS
GREENE
CHAUTAUQUA
CATTARAUGUS
ALLEGANY
STEUBEN
TIOGA
BROOME
DELAWARE
COLUMBIA
SCHENECTADY
CHEMUNG
Jamestown
Olean
Corning
Elmira
Owego
Binghamton
26
Kingston
DUTCHESS
SULLIVAN
ULSTER
Poughkeepsie
20
PUTNAM
Middletown
ORANGE
19
WESTCHESTER
New City
Smithtown
ROCKLAND
White Plains
1
BRONX
Yonkers
SUFFOLK
NEW YORK
2
NASSAU
RICHMOND
Brookhaven
Babylon
Districts 3–18
New York City Area
KINGS
QUEENS
Islip

NEW YORK
NEW YORK CITY AREA DISTRICTS

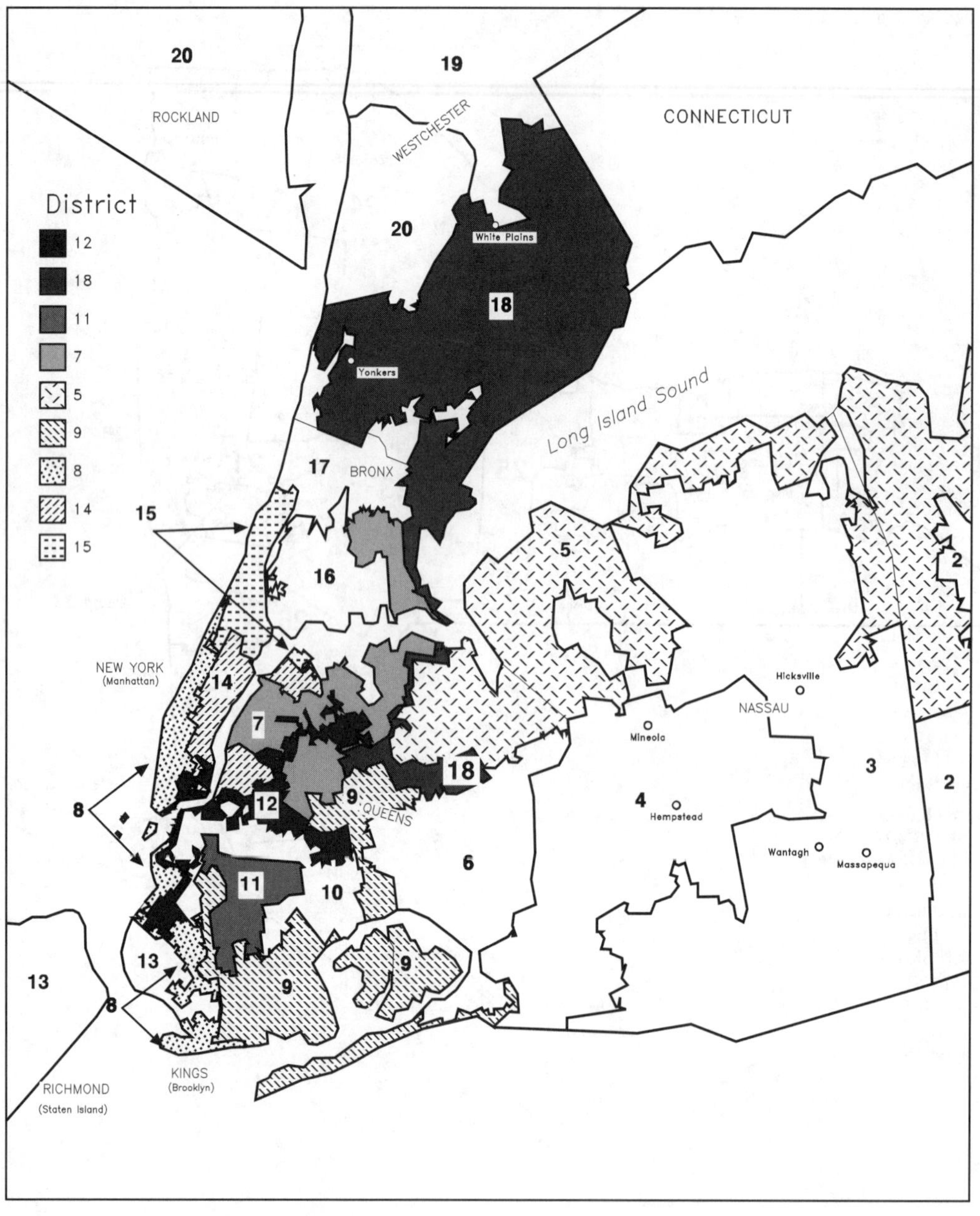

Daniel Patrick Moynihan (D)

Of Pindars Corners — Elected 1976, 4th term

Biographical Information

Born: March 16, 1927, Tulsa, Okla.

Education: City U. of New York, City College, 1943; Tufts U., B.N.S. 1946, B.A. 1948; Fletcher School of Law and Diplomacy, M.A. 1949, Ph.D. 1961.

Military Service: Navy, 1944-47; Naval Reserve, 1947-66.

Occupation: Professor; writer.

Family: Wife, Elizabeth Brennan; three children.

Religion: Roman Catholic.

Political Career: Sought Democratic nomination for N.Y. City Council president, 1965.

Capitol Office: 464 Russell Bldg. 20510; 224-4451.

Committees

Environment & Public Works
Superfund, Waste Control & Risk Assessment; Transportation & Infrastructure

Finance (ranking)
International Trade (ranking); Social Security & Family Policy; Taxation & IRS Oversight

Rules & Administration

Joint Library

Joint Taxation

In Washington: Two framed magazine covers hang on the wall of Moynihan's Russell Building office. One is a 1979 issue of The Nation, titled "Moynihan: The conscience of a neoconservative." The other is a 1981 issue of The New Republic. Its headline: "Pat Moynihan, neo-liberal."

Moynihan, easily one of the sharpest intellects in the Senate, always has been a puzzle.

A seer on welfare — which many years ago led to his being branded a racist — he was a lonely voice in opposition while President Clinton and the Republicans who control Congress enacted massive welfare overhaul legislation in the 104th Congress.

"I fear we may be now commencing the end of the Social Security system. The one thing not wrong with welfare was the commitment of the federal government to help with the provision of aid to dependent children," Moynihan said during the debate on the welfare bill. "We are abandoning that commitment today."

Only 21 senators voted against the final version of the welfare bill, and Moynihan was one of them. He bristled at Clinton's decision to sign the measure, having urged the president to veto any bill that eliminated a poor family's entitlement to cash assistance.

"If this administration wishes to go down in history as one that abandoned, eagerly abandoned, the national commitment to dependent children, so be it," Moynihan said. "I would not want to be associated with such an enterprise."

It was ironic that Moynihan was among the dissenters when Congress and the president enacted the historic 1996 welfare legislation. Moynihan, after all, had been the chief architect of the last major welfare overhaul, in 1988. And he had been the intellectual father of President Richard M. Nixon's unsuccessful 1969 plan for overhauling the system.

The 1969 proposal would have replaced Aid to Families with Dependent Children, the main federal welfare program, with the Family Assistance program, which would have provided the unemployed with $1,600 a year for a family of four, plus food stamps valued at $800. The working poor would have qualified for benefits, too. The unemployed would have been required to take job training or lose their portion of the benefit. The proposal passed the House but died in the Senate.

And it was Moynihan who foresaw the growth in single-parent families in inner cities. Writing in his 1965 report, "The Negro Family," he argued that this trend would deepen poverty and intensify anti-social behavior and that it would be preferable for the government to practice "benign neglect" than pursue destructive welfare programs. At the time, Moynihan was vilified as a racist and his social views created a gulf between him and some minority-group leaders.

In the end, Moynihan was sadly vindicated. "To be as candid as can be," he told the Syracuse Herald American shortly before being renominated for the Senate in 1994, "I wish it had turned out I was wrong. We have such awful problems about all kinds of families."

On other issues as well, Moynihan continues to go his own way. He was the only Democrat to oppose holding public hearings on the sexual misconduct charges against then-Sen. Bob Packwood, R-Ore. The Senate voted narrowly against the hearings in August 1995, but Packwood resigned the following month.

He was one of six members of Congress to go to court to challenge the legality of the line-item veto law, which permits presidents to strike specific expenditures, entitlements and narrowly focused tax breaks while otherwise signing a measure into law. A federal judge in April 1997 ruled the veto unconstitutional.

Though usually a supporter of abortion rights, he voted to ban a particular abortion technique that opponents call "partial birth" abortion, legislation vetoed by Clinton.

And he is a strong advocate of adjusting the Consumer Price Index, which he says overstates inflation. "If we fail to make this correction, it will cost the Treasury a trillion dollars in the next 12 years," Moynihan said. "If we do it, we can move out of this protracted fiscal crisis that is so draining on the country."

No surprise, then, that his brief tenure as chairman of the Finance Committee during the 103rd Congress was noteworthy as much for the fits it gave the new Clinton administration as for its legislative achievements — enactment of a $500 billion deficit-reduction bill and two massive trade measures: NAFTA (which Moynihan opposed) and GATT.

Moynihan had big shoes to fill in following Lloyd Bentsen of Texas, who gave up the chairmanship of Finance to serve as Treasury secretary for Clinton. And it was more than just the stylistic change from "board chairman" Bentsen in his custom-tailored suits to perennially rumpled Harvard professor Moynihan. Where Bentsen was cool and detached, Moynihan could be pedantic and quirky. While Bentsen resisted quixotic crusades, Moynihan has seemed to revel in them during his long career in government and academia. And while Bentsen focused on economic growth issues such as trade and taxes, Moynihan made his mark overhauling social programs such as welfare and Social Security.

Still, at least for Clinton, Finance was where the action was. With its narrow 11-9 party split and jurisdiction over trade, taxes, health and welfare programs, it would in large part determine the outcome of the president's agenda.

Strange, then, that at times Clinton seemed to ignore Moynihan. The senator had made it clear to New Yorkers that his top priority in any health care bill was to change the federal reimbursement formula for Medicaid, which paid half of New York's costs but paid a higher percentage of the costs incurred by many other states. Clinton's proposed health care bill did not change the formula. Moreover, it contained another provision that, in seeking to increase the supply of general practitioners in comparison to specialists, would have hurt New York's many teaching hospitals. Moynihan, who despite his scholarly manner can be rhetorically zealous, characterized the proposal's effect on those hospitals as "a sin against the Holy Ghost."

Moynihan struck back. During a discussion of health reform, he proclaimed, "We don't have a health care crisis. We DO have a welfare crisis." Still, Moynihan came through for the president on the budget bill — no easy task, since it involved holding together all 11 of the committee's often fractious Democrats. And while Clinton later told a group of Texas supporters that he raised taxes too much in the bill, Moynihan was unrepentant.

"The president may in retrospect think that he made a mistake," Moynihan said. "I think we did the right thing."

Moynihan's success in shepherding through the budget bill should not have been that much of a surprise. While he is best known and much appreciated for his high oratory, he has demonstrated considerable ability to turn bills into law. On the 1991 Intermodal Surface Transportation Efficiency Act, he cut deals over the state allocation of highway money with a facility that belied his reputation as a deep thinker who was not practical enough to be a legislative heavyweight.

Not that the deep thinker reputation is undeserved. At certain moments, listening to him is both an education and a treat, as when he interrupts routine debate with a personal discourse on the impossibility of free trade with a country like Mexico that lacks an independent judiciary, or discusses an algebraic formula for determining national income and explains in comprehensible terms how it works.

Impressed colleagues do not always appreciate his manner, though; his digressions can cross the border to pomposity and appear as self-aggrandizement wrapped in disheveled, professorial tweed.

And Moynihan still can demonstrate a tin ear for what is politically achievable. In 1990 and 1991, he proposed to cut Social Security taxes to stop the building of surpluses that were masking the true size of the federal deficit. The Senate voted it down both times.

Then, during the health debate in 1994, he proposed a tax on firearm ammunition as a potential financing mechanism, complete with the catchy line, "Guns don't kill people. Bullets do." Cooler heads were required to convince him the last thing that the health care measure needed was opposition from the National Rifle Association.

At Home: It is said that a New Yorker sees Sen. Alfonse M. D'Amato for a passport and Moynihan for a history of immigration. Moynihan may not have the populist appeal of his earthier colleague, but his unique style and avoidance of scandal has protected him from the sort of electoral scrape that D'Amato barely survived in 1992.

It also enabled him to withstand the powerful GOP swell in 1994 that ousted Democratic Gov. Mario M. Cuomo. As Republicans concentrated their efforts on defeating the three-term governor, they largely ignored Moynihan. His opponent, first-time candidate Bernadette Castro, a former sofa-bed company executive and now state parks commissioner, was outspent by more than 3-to-1. Moynihan did feel the tug of the year's big GOP vote: His 55 percent tally was his lowest-ever re-election score. Still, he beat Castro by 13 percentage points.

He had drawn a more-noticed, but even less successful, primary challenger: black activist and 1992 Senate candidate Al Sharpton. Beyond New York City, Sharpton went nowhere, losing 3-1 statewide.

Moynihan's election results powerfully attest to his political popularity. After unseating Republican Sen. James L. Buckley in 1976, Moynihan found the Republicans unable to attract any first-tier candidates in 1982. He won 65 percent of the vote against little-known state Rep. Florence Sullivan. In 1988, he defeated

Republican lawyer Robert R. McMillan with 67 percent — breaking his own state record for Senate vote percentage.

Moynihan has risen from Manhattan's ethnic, blue-collar precincts to the heights of academia and government. His father, a hard-drinking journalist, walked out on the family when the senator was 6; his mother ran a saloon near Times Square. Moynihan walked into the entrance exam for City College with a longshoreman's loading hook in his back pocket.

After establishing himself as an academic — he taught his personal combination of economics, sociology and urban studies at Harvard and at the Joint Center for Urban Studies — Moynihan turned to government service in the 1960s and became one of the few officials to serve at the Cabinet or sub-Cabinet level in four successive presidential administrations.He worked in the Labor Department for Presidents John F. Kennedy and Lyndon B. Johnson, and as an urban affairs expert for Nixon. In the latter role, Moynihan was the architect of the ill-fated Nixon "family assistance" welfare proposal, whose history he detailed in a book. He also caused himself great trouble when he counseled "benign neglect" toward minorities.

He fared far better as ambassador to India and to the United Nations under Nixon and President Gerald R. Ford. Moynihan's service at the United Nations clearly helped his political prospects in New York, although he denied any connection. His staunch defense of Israel earned him support among New York's sizable Jewish constituency, and his televised militancy at the United Nations in 1975 allowed him to begin the 1976 campaign as a celebrity, rather than just an articulate Harvard professor. "He spoke up for America," one campaign advertisement said. "He'd speak up for New York."

Three well-known figures of the Democratic left split the primary vote: Rep. Bella Abzug, former U.S. Attorney General Ramsey Clark and New York City Council President Paul O'Dwyer. Clark and O'Dwyer took a combined 19 percent, enough to sink Abzug, who finished 10,000 votes behind Moynihan.

Moynihan started with a strong lead over Buckley in the polls, and he neither said nor did anything in the fall to fracture his tenuous party harmony. He spent much of his time in Massachusetts, teaching at Harvard to protect his tenure. When he did speak out, he called Buckley a right-wing extremist out of step with the state's politics — citing Buckley's initial opposition in 1975 to federal loan guarantees for New York City. He sailed to victory over Buckley by a half-million votes, polling 54 percent.

SENATE ELECTIONS

1994 General		
Daniel Patrick Moynihan (D,L)	2,646,541	(55%)
Bernadette Castro (R,C,TCN)	1,988,308	(42%)
Henry F. Hewes (RTL)	95,954	(2%)
1994 Primary		
Daniel Patrick Moynihan (D)	526,766	(75%)
Al Sharpton (D)	178,231	(25%)

Previous Winning Percentages: 1988 (67%) **1982** (65%) **1976** (54%)

CAMPAIGN FINANCE

	Receipts	Receipts from PACs	Expend-itures
1994			
Moynihan (D)	$5,245,823	$1,260,776 (24%)	$5,784,736
Castro (R)	$1,582,667	$25,923 (2%)	$1,581,901

KEY VOTES

1997	
Approve balanced-budget constitutional amendment	N
Approve chemical weapons treaty	Y
1996	
Approve farm bill	Y
Limit punitive damages in product liability cases	N
Exempt small businesses from higher minimum wage	N
Approve welfare overhaul	N
Bar job discrimination based on sexual orientation	Y
Override veto of ban on "partial birth" abortions	Y
1995	
Approve GOP budget with tax and spending cuts	N
Approve constitutional amendment barring flag desecration	N

VOTING STUDIES

	Presidential Support		Party Unity		Conservative Coalition	
Year	S	O	S	O	S	O
1996	78	19	87	10	18	79
1995	75	16	84	12	19	79
1994	84	16	92	8	16	84
1993	93	7	95	5	15	85
1992	35	65	90	10	34	66
1991	35	65	92	7	25	75

INTEREST GROUP RATINGS

Year	ADA	AFL-CIO	CCUS	ACU
1996	90	n/a	31	10
1995	90	100	22	0
1994	100	88	20	0
1993	90	91	27	4
1992	100	83	10	0
1991	95	92	10	0

Alfonse M. D'Amato (R)

Of Island Park — Elected 1980, 3rd term

Biographical Information

Born: Aug. 1, 1937, Brooklyn, N.Y.

Education: Syracuse U., B.S. 1959, J.D. 1961.

Occupation: Lawyer.

Family: Divorced; four children.

Religion: Roman Catholic.

Political Career: Nassau County public administrator, 1965-68; Town of Hempstead tax receiver, 1969-71; Hempstead town supervisor, 1971-77; Nassau County Board of Supervisors, 1971-81, presiding supervisor, 1977-81.

Capitol Office: 520 Hart Bldg. 20510; 224-6542.

Committees

Banking, Housing & Urban Affairs (chairman)

Finance

Health Care; International Trade; Taxation & IRS Oversight

In Washington: After more than a year playing bulldog inquisitor from the chairmanship of the Senate committee investigating Whitewater, a kinder, gentler D'Amato emerged as he prepared to run for re-election in 1998.

First, D'Amato weighed in on the side of Republican moderates who said House Speaker Newt Gingrich and his conservative allies went too far during their first year in the House majority. "Newt Gingrich is very smart, very capable, but I think he misread the '94 election results," D'Amato said in the summer of 1996. "They voted for evolution, not revolution. I think the House Republican agenda as put forth in the last session was one that sent the wrong message."

Then, he announced that he would not try to resume Whitewater hearings in the 105th Congress, saying that special prosecutor Kenneth W. Starr should be free to work undisturbed. "It seems to me we've done our job," he told The New York Times right after the November 1996 elections. "Now it's time for us to let the special prosecutor do his. In my opinion, we should let the special prosecutor do his work and don't second-guess him."

On the home front, D'Amato raised millions of dollars and appeared in television commercials touting a statewide environmental bond issue, and he engineered an agreement with state legislative leaders in Albany to give longer hospital stays to women who have mastectomies. He also pushed for legislation to prevent banks from charging automatic teller fees for customers from other banks.

He took the lead in pressing Swiss banks to acknowledge their role in helping finance Nazi Germany and to make financial amends to Holocaust victims. "There are two heroes in Washington on this whole question — President Clinton and Sen. D'Amato," said Elan Steinberg, executive director of the World Jewish Congress.

He shepherded through the nomination of Andrew M. Cuomo as secretary of Housing and Urban Development. "I commend my fellow New Yorker for his record of public service," D'Amato said. The younger Cuomo had been mentioned as a potential Democratic challenger to D'Amato in 1998, and his father, former New York Gov. Mario M. Cuomo, lost in 1994 to D'Amato's handpicked GOP gubernatorial candidate, George E. Pataki.

And D'Amato finished 1996 with almost $7 million in his campaign bank account, more than the combined total of the other four leading fundraisers in the Senate who face election in 1998.

D'Amato began the 104th Congress as chairman of the Senate Banking Committee and the special panel looking at Whitewater. He chaired the National Republican Senatorial Committee (NRSC), which had a hand in the GOP's pickup of two Senate seats in the November 1996 election. He also moved to the Finance Committee, giving up his beloved seat on Appropriations, as part of an effort to prevent Texan Phil Gramm, who was challenging Bob Dole for president, from claiming a post on the tax panel.

D'Amato drew brickbats for running the Senate investigation of President and Hillary Rodham Clinton's Whitewater dealings even as he championed Dole's presidential campaign. Senate Republicans, in their report released in June 1996, portrayed Mrs. Clinton as the chief culprit in White House attempts to impede investigations. D'Amato stopped short of accusing her of criminal wrongdoing, leaving the issue to Starr. The scathing GOP report raised the question of whether only an exculpable rendering from Starr could remove the cloud of suspicion from Mrs. Clinton. The White House said the answer lay with the public's final verdict on the Senate investigation, an inquiry they derided as a "kangaroo court."

D'Amato's support of Dole even led to dissension in his own party. D'Amato used New York's arcane election law to try to keep all the other Republican challengers off the presidential primary ballot. Supporters of publisher Malcolm S. "Steve" Forbes Jr. campaigned against D'Amato as much as Dole.

The senator also ran into another spate of ethical problems. In September 1996, the Senate Ethics Committee cleared him of wrongdoing for any special treatment he may have received from a New York brokerage firm that earned him a lucrative, one-day stock profit. The Congressional Accountability Project, a group affiliated with consumer advocate Ralph Nader, had asked the committee to look into D'Amato's stock dealings with Stratton Oakmont, a firm based in Lake Success, N.Y. A Securities and Exchange Commission (SEC) report prepared by an independent consultant found that Stratton Oakmont in a 1993 transaction gave D'Amato "atypical" treatment that resulted in the senator making a one-day profit of $37,125. At the time, the brokerage firm was under investigation by the SEC and D'Amato was ranking Republican on the Senate Banking Committee, which has jurisdiction over the SEC.

That was the second ethics complaint D'Amato had faced. In 1991, the Ethics Committee rebuked him for operating his office in an "improper and inappropriate manner."

More unwelcome scrutiny hit D'Amato in early 1997 when Federal Election Commission records revealed that he diverted $1.9 million in NRSC funds to Pataki's re-election campaign. The maneuver prompted some donors to demand refunds.

In April 1995, D'Amato drew a wave of unflattering publicity for ridiculing the Japanese-American judge in the O.J. Simpson murder trial. In a conversation with New York radio talk show host Don Imus, D'Amato criticized Judge Lance Ito for his handling of the Simpson trial and used an exaggerated Japanese accent to imitate the judge. Complaining to Imus that the trial was going to run forever, D'Amato, in his rendition of a Japanese accent, said: "Judge Ito loves the limelight. He is making a disgrace of the judicial system. Little Judge Ito. . . . "

The remarks drew numerous complaints from anti-discrimination organizations and from New York Japanese-Americans. It was noted that Ito, a third-generation Japanese-American, has no foreign accent. D'Amato ultimately apologized. "If I offended anyone, I'm sorry," he said in a statement. "I was making fun of the pomposity of the judge and the manner in which he's dragging the trial out."

As befits a representative from New York, which has a large Jewish population, D'Amato is a staunch supporter of Israel and a fierce opponent of Arab countries that would destroy the Jewish state. He was the chief Senate sponsor of legislation signed by Clinton in August 1996 that penalizes foreign companies assisting the oil industries of Iran or Libya. The law required the president to impose two of six possible sanctions on foreign companies that invest at least $40 million in the oil industries of Iran or Libya. Also, foreign companies that sell petroleum-related goods and technology to Libya would face the same penalties.

During his years on the Appropriations Committee, D'Amato pursued federal aid in a brazen and persistent manner that earned him the nickname "Senator Pothole." In a state that has sent to the Senate such national figures as Robert F. Kennedy, Robert F. Wagner, Jacob K. Javits and Daniel Patrick Moynihan, D'Amato always has been concerned with the provincial.

And as a legislator, D'Amato is known for his grandstanding style. In 1992 and earlier in 1986 (both election years), D'Amato used filibusters to little effect, other than the generating of huge amounts of publicity. In 1992, the issue was an urban aid tax bill. D'Amato blocked a final vote on the bill for 15 hours and 15 minutes, the sixth-longest live filibuster in Senate history, because the bill did not include a provision intended to prevent the loss of 850 jobs at a Smith-Corona typewriter plant in upstate New York. The House adjourned while D'Amato droned on, and the bill died. In 1986, D'Amato held up consideration of a must-pass omnibus appropriations bill in an attempt to block an amendment to halt production of the T-46 trainer airplane built by the Fairchild Republic Co. on Long Island. The filibuster forced a partial federal shutdown, and D'Amato won a temporary reprieve for the T-46, but in the end the program was canceled.

In the 103rd, D'Amato got considerable media attention — not all of it favorable — for singing a version of "Old McDonald's Farm" on the Senate floor during consideration of the crime bill. "With a pork, pork here and a pork, pork there . . ." sang D'Amato, leading Newsweek to observe, "and on his farm he had an ass, E-I-E-I-O."

At Home: D'Amato's many critics may never stop declaiming his ethical standards or his parochial agenda. But after his come-from-behind victory in 1992, no one can doubt D'Amato's survival skills. With the 1994 election of his protégé Pataki as governor, D'Amato's standing in New York GOP politics has never been more exalted.

The 1992 campaign was just another loop in D'Amato's roller-coaster career. A local official little known outside his Nassau County base when he entered the 1980 Senate race, D'Amato upset four-term GOP Sen. Javits in the primary and then won by a narrow plurality over Democratic Rep. Elizabeth Holtzman. But D'Amato's home-state orientation and his straight talk — delivered with his distinctive "Long Island" accent — quickly made him a popular figure; in 1986, he swept up 57 percent against consumer activist Mark Green.

D'Amato then appeared to fall fast; his low approval ratings early in 1992 marked him as the most vulnerable GOP incumbent that year. Arcane New York election laws barred a prospective GOP primary challenger with a venerable family name in state and national politics, Laurence Rockefeller, from the September primary ballot.

But the eventual Democratic nominee, state Attorney General Robert Abrams, was stuck in a primary brawl with 1984 vice presidential nominee Geraldine A. Ferraro, black activist Al Sharpton and New York City Comptroller

Holtzman, seeking a rematch with D'Amato. Abrams won by 1 point and entered the six-week general-election campaign bruised and broke.

D'Amato had used the primary respite to remind voters of his legislative efforts in behalf of New York interests. Though behind in the polls after the Democratic primary, he had a bulging campaign treasury that he quickly put to use.

Seeking to bolster his Republican base, D'Amato ran a barrage of TV ads branding Abrams as "hopelessly liberal." Abrams returned fire, hanging the scandal cloud over D'Amato. But Abrams also made a major gaffe. At a rally, he responded to heckling by D'Amato supporters by calling the senator a "fascist." D'Amato, near tears, demanded an apology, called the epithet an ethnic slur and ran ads with images of Benito Mussolini to underline the point.

Although New York's presidential vote went heavily to Clinton, D'Amato held on, winning by just under 81,000 votes. D'Amato's narrow win recalled his first Senate bid in 1980. His decision to run that year was a surprise. Then a township presiding supervisor and product of the Nassau County Republican machine, D'Amato gambled that the conservative wave spurred by Ronald Reagan's presidential campaign would enable him to unseat Javits, one of the Senate's most liberal Republicans. D'Amato also made an issue of Javits' age (76) and infirmity (he suffered from a progressive motor neuron disease). D'Amato won with votes to spare.

Javits' insistence on a last hurrah may have ensured D'Amato's election. Running as the nominee of New York's Liberal Party, Javits pulled off more than 10 percent of the vote. Although Holtzman tried to link D'Amato to alleged corruption in the Nassau GOP, he won by 45 percent to 44 percent.

While Pataki's election sealed D'Amato's preeminent role in the state GOP, he had earlier stumbled in his efforts to assume a power-broker role in New York Republican politics. In 1988, he gave his presidential endorsement to Senate colleague Bob Dole of Kansas, who was swamped by George Bush in the New York primary. A political feud with former federal prosecutor Rudolph W. Giuliani led D'Amato to endorse another candidate for New York mayor in 1989. But Giuliani won the primary in a landslide (he lost narrowly in the general election). D'Amato scored an intraparty victory in early 1991 when his longtime aide William Powers was elected chairman of the state GOP.

During the 1992 campaign, he mended fences with Giuliani. But the truce with Giuliani was short-lived: Giuliani was elected mayor in 1993, and one year later he endorsed Democrat Cuomo for re-election, arguing that Pataki would be little more than a D'Amato clone. "He would establish a government of D'Amato, for D'Amato and by D'Amato," said Giuliani on CNN. Giuliani was the only prominent Republican officeholder in the state who refused to climb aboard D'Amato's Dole bandwagon before the 1996 New York primary. But with Giuliani facing re-election in 1997 and D'Amato doing likewise in 1998, the two again have appeared of late to be patching up their differences.

SENATE ELECTIONS

1992 General

Alfonse M. D'Amato (R, C, RTL)	3,166,994	(49%)
Robert Abrams (D, L)	3,086,200	(48%)
Norma Segal (LIBERT)	108,530	(2%)

Previous Winning Percentages: 1986 (57%) **1980** (45%)

CAMPAIGN FINANCE

	Receipts	Receipts from PACs	Expend-itures
1992			
D'Amato (R)	$6,533,230	$922,922 (14%)	$9,175,533
Abrams (D)	$6,764,365	$590,769 (9%)	$6,408,981

KEY VOTES

1997

Approve balanced-budget constitutional amendment	Y
Approve chemical weapons treaty	Y
1996	
Approve farm bill	Y
Limit punitive damages in product liability cases	N
Exempt small businesses from higher minimum wage	N
Approve welfare overhaul	Y
Bar job discrimination based on sexual orientation	Y
Override veto of ban on "partial birth" abortions	Y
1995	
Approve GOP budget with tax and spending cuts	Y
Approve constitutional amendment barring flag desecration	Y

VOTING STUDIES

	Presidential Support		Party Unity		Conservative Coalition	
Year	S	O	S	O	S	O
1996	46	49	85	13	84	11
1995	29	70	90	10	88	11
1994	34	65	79	18	81	16
1993	28	69	82	15	78	20
1992	58	38	59	36	42	45
1991	79	21	75	25	80	20

INTEREST GROUP RATINGS

Year	ADA	AFL-CIO	CCUS	ACU
1996	25	n/a	69	75
1995	15	0	89	78
1994	20	38	80	92
1993	35	50	91	80
1992	30	70	60	52
1991	15	67	50	86

1 Michael P. Forbes (R)

Of Quogue — Elected 1994, 2nd term

Biographical Information
Born: July 16, 1952, Riverhead, N.Y.
Education: State U. of New York at Albany, B.A. 1983.
Occupation: Chamber of commerce manager.
Family: Wife, Barbara Ann Blackburn; two children.
Religion: Roman Catholic.
Political Career: No previous office.
Capitol Office: 416 Cannon Bldg. 20515; 225-3826.

Committees
Appropriations
Commerce, Justice, State & Judiciary; Foreign Operations, Export Financing & Related Programs; Treasury, Postal Service & General Government

In Washington: Forbes began the 104th Congress with a seat on the House Appropriations Committee, a reward for defeating a four-term Democratic incumbent. In the early months of 1995, he voted for every plank in the House GOP's "Contract With America" platform. But by the start of his second term, Forbes was risking pariah status among his GOP colleagues by announcing he would oppose Newt Gingrich's re-election as Speaker. He was the first Republican publicly to break ranks.

Forbes made his announcement after coming off a tough re-election campaign in which he had to defend himself against charges that he was a Gingrich clone — a detriment in New York.

After reading the documents from the House ethics committee, which investigated the funding of some of Gingrich's political activities, Forbes said in December 1996 that Gingrich should not seek re-election as Speaker. "I'm physically sick over it, and I'm sick he's making us do this, but he'll be a Speaker who's weighed down," Forbes told The New York Times. "We need leadership that will not be cowering, contrite or hiding from the media so we can aggressively pursue a balanced budget and tax reform."

Forbes also made his case at a closed-door House Republican conference in January, where he was surrounded by empty seats. Praising the Speaker for being the architect of the Republican revolution, Forbes urged Gingrich to step down, arguing that he could not carry forward the GOP agenda as a result of the swirling ethics controversy. Forbes said that Gingrich already had made his place in history and that it was time for a new leader to step in who could drive the Republican agenda. Utter silence followed his statement, as compared to the applause that met with others' equally emphatic defenses of Gingrich. "I'm one you don't put the applause meter up on," Forbes said later.

He eventually voted for Iowa Republican Jim Leach for Speaker. Asked if he expected to be punished for that vote, Forbes said, "If this becomes a place where there is retribution for an act of principle, the place won't work. There are people not happy with the way this played out, but the leadership knows this was an act of conscience. It also has work to do. It does not have time to spend sharpening knives."

Nevertheless, Forbes quickly was disinvited from a gala honoring outgoing Republican National Committee (RNC) Chairman Haley Barbour and Co-Chairman Evelyn McPhail after some longtime donors said they did not want to sit with lawmakers who voted against the Speaker.

Forbes' vote on the speakership was not his first defection from the GOP line. After the contract phase early in the 104th, when House Republicans voted nearly in lock step, Forbes parted from the Republican majority on several sensitive issues.

He voted in 1996 for a 90-cent increase in the minimum wage, and he also sided with labor unions in opposing legislation allowing employers to offer compensatory time off to workers in lieu of overtime.

Later in 1995 and beyond, Forbes had some differences with his party leadership in the area of environmental policy. He was one of just 34 Republicans voting against a bill rewriting the clean water act. He said the measure went "too far," lifting strict regulations on pollutants discharged from sewage treatment and industrial plants into rivers, streams, bays and oceans. Although he said the 1972 law could use some reform, Forbes added, "It does not mean Congress has a license to gut a law that has done so much good and is working to safeguard our environment."

In July 1995 he was one of 51 Republicans voting to strike language that would have limited the regulatory authority of the Environmental Protection Agency. In April 1996, he was one of 18 Republicans opposed to a bill that facilitated opening preserves in the National Wildlife Refuge System to hunting and fishing. And in June 1996, he took the environmentalists' side on a vote

NEW YORK 1
Eastern Suffolk County — Brookhaven; Smithtown

Located more than 100 miles from downtown Manhattan, Long Island's lightly populated East End presents a tableau of the Suffolk County of 40 years ago. Farms, fishing villages and the vacation homes of the wealthy (in such enclaves as the Hamptons and Shelter Island) remain this region's most prominent features.

Nonetheless, suburban sprawl has thoroughly overtaken the closer-in areas on the western side of the 1st. Brookhaven Town, the 1st's core jurisdiction, increased in population more than ninefold between 1950 and 1990, from 44,500 to 408,000.

Suburbanization has not greatly changed the Republican tilt that dates to the 1st District's rural days. Yet two Democrats — Otis G. Pike and George J. Hochbrueckner — represented the area for 26 of the 34 years between 1961 and 1995, and Bill Clinton carried the district in 1996. There is a small minority population on which to build a Democratic base, and the district has large numbers of Irish- and Italian-Americans, many with blue-collar, urban roots. The 1st has some industrial employment, including a defense-production base that has become tenuous in the post-Cold War era. A reliance on seasonal employment in many of the 1st's exurban and rural areas provides modest incomes for many district residents.

Constituents' environmental concerns can also aid Democratic candidates. In recent years, local residents fought alongside Hochbrueckner to decommission a nuclear power plant in Shoreham and pushed to clean up the ocean waters that are vital to the 1st's fishing and tourism industries.

The bulk of the 1st's residents live in a part of Smithtown, at the district's western end, and in Brookhaven, which covers a large swath spanning the width of Suffolk County. The North Shore area along Long Island Sound has several well-off subdivisions, but most of the 1st's suburbs are middle class. Coram, with just over 30,000 residents, is the largest of Brookhaven's many sizable suburban communities. The mainly residential area includes the State University at Stony Brook (11,000 students), a center for scientific research and home of a major teaching hospital. In the exurbs to the east is Brookhaven National Laboratory. The economy suffered a blow when Northrop Grumman pulled out of Calverton, near Riverhead. Local officials are hoping to redevelop some of the property; most of the rest will be turned into a nature preserve named for Pike.

Five less-populous towns — Riverhead, East Hampton, Shelter Island, Southampton and Southold — make up the East End. There are still many potato and duck farms here; small vineyards also have been established on Long Island's North Fork, which has a climate and soil similar to the Burgundy region of France.

The beaches along the 1st's southern edge are summer playgrounds; parts of Fire Island are long-established retreats for New York's gay community. But these coastal areas are vulnerable to damage by storms, such as the fierce nor'easters that hit during the winter of 1992-93.

1990 Population: 580,338. White 539,824 (93%), Black 23,691 (4%), Other 16,823 (3%). Hispanic origin 27,210 (5%). 18 and over 433,173 (75%), 62 and over 81,669 (14%). Median age: 33.

involving protection of a threatened sea bird species, the marbled murrelet.

On social issues, though, Forbes generally sticks with his party's staunch conservatives. In January 1997 he declared his solidarity with the anti-abortion demonstrators marching on the Capitol and the Supreme Court on the 24th anniversary of the *Roe v. Wade* decision legalizing abortion. Forbes and at least seven other lawmakers said they were marching to show their support for legislation that would ban a particular abortion technique that opponents call a "partial birth" abortion.

And in March 1996, he voted to repeal the ban on certain semiautomatic assault-style weapons. That issue was especially controversial on Long Island, where in December 1993 a gunman wielding such a weapon killed six and injured 19 others on a Long Island Rail Road commuter train.

Forbes risked the ire of colleagues from New York when in November 1995 he opposed their efforts to secure federal funds for rebuilding Pennsylvania Station, the main train depot for thousands of Long Island Rail Road commuters. "We do not need this kind of pork," Forbes said. "I have to tell you that it is a new time, it is a new place. We are supposed to be ferreting out this kind of excessive spending."

But Forbes does not have a blanket policy against seeking federal funding for parochial needs: On Appropriations he has sought additional monies for the government to research the "red tide," a marine phenomenon of concern to Long Island beach communities.

Also, he obtained $500,000 — money transferred from another project — to buy vans to transport senior citizens and the mentally retarded in his district, and he lined up $502,000 in federal grants to help local volunteer firefighters who battled a major 1995 fire.

In July 1996, the explosion of TWA Flight 800 focused attention on Forbes' eastern Long Island district. The area around the town of East Moriches was a staging ground for media and emergency personnel after the disaster, and Forbes was among the politicians who received publicity for their comments on the search-and-recovery efforts.

At Home: Forbes knew Capitol Hill well before 1st District voters sent him there in 1994. He had served as chief of staff to two Republican members: Rep. (now Sen.) Connie Mack of Florida and Sen. Alfonse M. D'Amato of New York. He also served in New York as regional administrator for the Small Business Administration during the Bush administration, and as regional manager for the U.S. Chamber of Commerce.

A Suffolk County native who got involved in local political affairs in his teenage years, Forbes was tapped by county GOP officials to run in the 1st after several better-known political figures turned down a chance to take on Democratic Rep. George J. Hochbrueckner, who had scratched out four wins in the Republican-leaning district.

Before facing Hochbrueckner, Forbes had to win Republican and Conservative party primaries, which he did comfortably, taking 56 percent against two GOP foes and 74 percent against another Conservative.

For much of the fall race, Hochbrueckner did not appear to face any greater danger than he had in previous years when Republicans fell short of ousting him. Fund raising was plainly a mismatch: The incumbent took in more than $740,000, swamping Forbes' receipts of $270,000. But from the time of his first election in 1986, Hochbrueckner had never faced voters in a year when national and state winds were blowing so foul for his Democratic Party. Forbes campaigned aggressively, focusing his attack on Hochbrueckner's vote for President Clinton's tax-raising deficit-reduction bill, contending that the 1st is one of the most highly taxed parts of the country. The challenger also stressed that he knew Capitol Hill and could hit the ground running. Meanwhile, Democratic Gov. Mario M. Cuomo was going down to defeat at the hands of GOP nominee George E. Pataki. It was too much for Hochbrueckner to overcome; Forbes won with 53 percent of the vote.

Democrats had high hopes of defeating Forbes in 1996 as the GOP tide ebbed. But Hochbrueckner declined a rematch, and the Democrats scrambled to find someone else. They finally came up with a viable challenger in Suffolk County Legislator Nora Bredes, who helped lead the successful fight against the Shoreham nuclear power plant. But Forbes raised plenty of money early, and Bredes' feisty and aggressive campaign could not overcome her late start, though she did have help from actors Alec Baldwin and Kim Basinger, who hosted a fundraiser at their East End home. Forbes improved his winning tally slightly from his first race, taking 55 percent.

HOUSE ELECTIONS

1996 General		
Michael P. Forbes (R,C,INDC,RTL)	116,620	(55%)
Nora Bredes (D,SM)	96,496	(45%)
1994 General		
Michael P. Forbes (R,C,RTL,WTP)	90,491	(53%)
George J. Hochbrueckner (D,LIF)	80,146	(47%)

CAMPAIGN FINANCE

	Receipts	Receipts from PACs	Expend-itures
1996			
Forbes (R)	$1,040,813	$321,938 (31%)	$918,162
Bredes (D)	$425,479	$147,954 (35%)	$394,083
1994			
Forbes (R)	$270,215	$62,608 (23%)	$265,930
Hochbrueckner (D)	$741,038	$373,022 (50%)	$719,102

DISTRICT VOTE FOR PRESIDENT

	1996		1992
D	118,187 (51%)	**D**	96,890 (38%)
R	83,956 (36%)	**R**	101,160 (40%)
I	25,850 (11%)	**I**	54,128 (21%)

KEY VOTES

1997	
Ban "partial birth" abortions	Y
1996	
Approve farm bill	Y
Deny public education to illegal immigrants	Y
Repeal ban on certain assault-style weapons	Y
Increase minimum wage	Y
Freeze defense spending	N
Approve welfare overhaul	Y
1995	
Approve balanced-budget constitutional amendment	Y
Relax Clean Water Act regulations	N
Oppose limits on environmental regulations	Y
Reduce projected Medicare spending	Y
Approve GOP budget with tax and spending cuts	Y

VOTING STUDIES

	Presidential Support		Party Unity		Conservative Coalition	
Year	**S**	**O**	**S**	**O**	**S**	**O**
1996	41	54	72	22	84	8
1995	30	68	83	14	87	12

INTEREST GROUP RATINGS

Year	ADA	AFL-CIO	CCUS	ACU
1996	15	n/a	73	84
1995	15	18	79	80

2 Rick A. Lazio (R)

Of Brightwaters — Elected 1992, 3rd term

Biographical Information

Born: March 13, 1958, West Islip, N.Y.
Education: Vassar College, B.A. 1980; American U., J.D. 1983.
Occupation: Lawyer.
Family: Wife, Patricia; two children.
Religion: Roman Catholic.
Political Career: Suffolk County Legislature, 1990-93.
Capitol Office: 2444 Rayburn Bldg. 20515; 225-3335.

Committees

Banking & Financial Services
Capital Markets, Securities & Government Sponsored Enterprises; Housing & Community Opportunity (chairman)
Commerce
Finance & Hazardous Materials; Health & Environment

In Washington: The 105th Congress convened with Lazio as a new member of the Commerce Committee, but some unfinished business from the 104th occupied much of his attention early in 1997.

While obtaining the coveted Commerce seat, Lazio received a waiver at the request of Speaker Newt Gingrich, R-Ga., that allowed him to also keep his seat on the Banking and Financial Services Committee — and to continue chairing its Housing and Community Opportunity Subcommittee.

The chairmanship led Lazio to become the prime sponsor of legislation to overhaul the nation's public housing system and the Department of Housing and Urban Development. Though similar bills passed both chambers during the 104th, negotiators could not craft a compromise, and the housing overhaul measure died. Lazio introduced similar legislation in 1997.

The housing overhaul measure consolidated many existing housing programs into two block grants to be distributed to public housing authorities; the aim was to save money while giving local authorities more control of their programs. The measure also requires residents to take more responsibility for pursuing goals such as finding a job or getting an education and, in some cases, to perform eight hours of community service a month to keep their public housing.

The House bill also repealed both the U.S. Housing Act of 1937 — the foundation of public housing programs — and the so-called Brooke Amendment of 1968, which generally requires that public housing tenants pay no more than 30 percent of their incomes in rent. Lazio's bill would give tenants the option of paying 30 percent of their income in rent or a flat monthly fee that they could negotiate with their housing authority.

"For the sake of decent standards of housing for the poor, more local discretion is needed," Lazio told the House. "Single dimension, lowest income housing simply has not worked."

Democrats took particular exception to the provision that would require all unemployed, able-bodied, adult public housing residents who are not covered by a state's welfare law to perform community service. Democrats said it discriminates against the poor by mandating that public housing residents work without pay; they called it the equivalent to involuntary servitude. But Lazio and Banking Committee Chairman Jim Leach, R-Iowa, said the community service requirement was aimed at encouraging greater community involvement and that housing was part of the compensation. Democrats unsuccessful tried to remove or alter the community service requirement.

The housing overhaul proposal generated spirited debate on the House floor in May 1997, but in the end, it passed easily 293-132, with 71 Democrats voting for it.

Even though no housing overhaul bill cleared in the 104th Congress, Lazio and his fellow Republicans were successful in changing HUD. The agency's fiscal 1997 budget request called for merging more than 20 programs into three, the first phase of a plan to consolidate more than 60 programs, phase out 29 inactive programs and shut down 37 others. That would reduce HUD employment from the current 11,600 employees to 10,447, en route to a planned 7,500 by 2001. "The cultural changes are amazing," Lazio said. "We're talking about things that we never dared to talk about before."

Still, Lazio supports a federal involvement in housing. He opposed plans by a House Appropriations subcommittee to slash funding in the fiscal 1996 spending bill for HUD. The measure also provided funding for NASA. "Is it appropriate to spend billions on the space station if it means we're failing to deliver on our responsibilities to help those who can't be part of the marketplace?" asked Lazio, who voted to kill the space station in the 104th Congress.

He is not shy about trying to obtain federal funds for his district, helping to secure money for the Central Islip courthouse and the Dowling College National Aviation and Transportation Center, and for protecting Long Island's South

NEW YORK 2
Western Suffolk County; Islip; Babylon

Western Suffolk County's well-established, middle-class suburbs have a pronounced GOP tilt. But district voters are not fervently partisan Republicans. Democratic Rep. Thomas J. Downey managed to keep the 2nd's partisan tendencies in check for 18 years before Lazio defeated him in 1992.

Voters in this affluent suburban district tend to favor Lazio's moderate brand of Republicanism, but Democratic candidates do have a base here that is sizable by suburban Long Island standards.

While the district's mainly white-collar work force includes many who commute to New York City, there is a blue-collar constituency, including a number of workers dependent on Long Island's defense-related industries that have been hit hard by funding cutbacks. Non-Hispanic whites account for about 80 percent of the district, a considerably smaller share than in the adjacent 1st and 3rd districts.

The district's demographic composition makes the 2nd politically competitive. George Bush carried the 2nd in 1988 and 1992 (by just 1,332 votes in his re-election bid), while Democratic Sen. Daniel Patrick Moynihan as well as then-Gov. Mario M. Cuomo won districtwide in the 1980s and early '90s. Bill Clinton polled 54 percent of the vote here in 1996 even as Lazio won by a nearly 2-to-1 margin.

The 2nd has more than 56,000 Hispanics — the largest Hispanic population among the Long Island districts — and as many blacks. More than a third of the 45,000 residents of Brentwood (the largest community in Islip town) are Hispanics; blacks make up three-quarters of the nearly 14,000 residents of North Amityville in Babylon town.

Islip and Babylon — the two townships that make up the southwest corner of Suffolk County — took full part in the post-World War II suburban boom, but they hit a plateau in the 1970s. Islip, where population jumped from about 71,500 in 1950 to 279,000 in 1970, gained a net of just 20,000 people over the next 20 years. Babylon, which had 45,000 residents in 1950, topped 200,000 in 1970 but stuck there.

Islip town — which takes in such communities as Brentwood, West Islip, Central Islip and Bay Shore — contains much of the district's employment base. Hauppauge, the seat of Suffolk County's government, is shared with the 1st District; the 2nd has the county office complex and much of the community's commercial real estate.

While Babylon town is made up mainly of residential communities — the largest of which, with just over 42,000 residents, is West Babylon — there is some industry: AIL Systems makes defense electronics in Deer Park. But defense industry employment has been faltering since a Fairchild Republic Aircraft plant in Farmingdale closed in the late 1980s.

The northern part of the 2nd also takes in parts of Huntington town and Smithtown. These areas have large Jewish populations and Democratic leanings.

1990 Population: 580,337. White 496,052 (85%), Black 56,722 (10%), Other 27,563 (5%). Hispanic origin 56,302 (10%). 18 and over 437,435 (75%), 62 and over 70,884 (12%). Median age: 33.

Shore coastline. He obtained money for the National Cancer Institute to conduct a five-year study of Long Island's high breast cancer rates. He introduced legislation in the 105th to reimburse Suffolk County the more than $5 million it spent for costs associated with the crash of TWA Flight 800 in July 1996. "The president has made a commitment that the county would not be left holding the proverbial bag on this," he said.

Though he has a reputation for being a moderate — he voted with a majority of his party against a majority of Democrats just 75 percent of the time in 1996 — Lazio stood with the GOP on many high-profile issues. He voted for term limits, to overhaul the welfare system, to ban a particular abortion technique that opponents call a "partial birth" abortion and to allow employers to offer their workers compensatory time off rather than overtime pay.

At the same time, he voted to allow the federal employee health care plan to pay for abortions and to require states to pay for abortions in cases of rape or incest; he supported President Clinton's AmeriCorps program; and he voted against repealing the ban on certain semiautomatic assault-style weapons. He supported raising the minimum wage, but also voted to exempt small businesses from paying the higher salaries. The Sierra Club and League of Conservation Voters endorsed him.

Lazio showed his independent streak soon after joining the House. At a Budget markup in March 1993, he was the only committee Republican to vote against a GOP alternative budget prepared by John R. Kasich of Ohio, then the ranking Republican (and now Budget chairman). Then in September 1993, Lazio was one of only 24 Republicans to vote for the final installment of money for the savings and loan bailout, which the House narrowly passed, 214-208. "It's a politically difficult vote," Lazio said when the $18.3 billion infusion for the Resolution Trust Corporation was dodging bullets in the Banking Committee that April.

In 1994, Lazio came under intense pressure to stick with his party and reject the rule allowing consideration of Clinton's big crime bill. But the bill contained a Lazio-backed ban on assault weapons; the year before, a gunman wielding a semiautomatic weapon killed six and injured 19 others on a Long Island Rail Road train. In a telephone call, Clinton urged a "yes" vote. But Lazio voted no, and the bill stalled. The White House later scaled down the bill somewhat, and Lazio got another telephone plea, this time from Attorney General Janet Reno.

Ultimately he supported the revised bill, which passed. In the 103rd, Lazio voted for the Brady bill, which imposes a waiting period for handgun purchases, and for bills mandating family leave and safeguarding access to abortion clinics.

In joining the Commerce Committee, Lazio gave up his position on the Budget Committee. On Commerce, he succeeds fellow Long Island Republican Daniel Frisa, who landed the high-profile post as a freshman but lost his re-election bid in 1996. Commerce and Banking, Lazio's two committees, are two of the top panels for attracting campaign contributions.

At Home: In 1992, 18-year Democratic incumbent Thomas Downey was well-known in Washington for his attention to national issues such as welfare reform, unemployment and arms control. But Lazio turned Downey's high profile against him.

Lazio, who had served three years in the Suffolk County Legislature (representing Downey's old district), did not draw an opponent in the 1992 GOP primary, so he was free to concentrate his much smaller campaign treasury on Downey, who had 151 overdrafts at the House bank. Lazio zeroed in on that, and also reminded voters that Downey took a junket to Barbados in 1990 that received negative national publicity.

Downey counterattacked, pointing to Lazio's support of a plan to borrow money to cover a county revenue shortfall, and saying Lazio's refusal to support a sales tax increase to raise the money was just a political move for the campaign. But Downey's maneuvers and superior funding did not prove enough; Lazio prevailed with 53 percent of the vote. He has not been seriously challenged since.

HOUSE ELECTIONS

1996 General		
Rick A. Lazio (R,C)	112,135	(64%)
Kenneth J. Herman (D,INDC)	57,953	(33%)
Alice Cort Ross (RTL)	4,506	(3%)
1994 General		
Rick A. Lazio (R,C,WTP)	100,107	(68%)
James Manfre (D,LIF)	41,102	(28%)
Alice Cort Ross (RTL)	5,567	(4%)

Previous Winning Percentages: 1992 (53%)

CAMPAIGN FINANCE

	Receipts	Receipts from PACs	Expend-itures
1996			
Lazio (R)	$1,318,712	$475,694 (36%)	$696,180
Herman (D)	$19,989	0	$14,487
1994			
Lazio (R)	$613,563	$223,185 (36%)	$484,133
Manfre (D)	$96,381	$17,000 (18%)	$87,156

DISTRICT VOTE FOR PRESIDENT

1996		1992	
D	108,598 (54%)	**D**	91,430 (40%)
R	68,710 (34%)	**R**	92,762 (40%)
I	20,419 (10%)	**I**	44,603 (19%)

KEY VOTES

1997	
Ban "partial birth" abortions	Y
1996	
Approve farm bill	Y
Deny public education to illegal immigrants	Y
Repeal ban on certain assault-style weapons	N
Increase minimum wage	Y
Freeze defense spending	N
Approve welfare overhaul	Y
1995	
Approve balanced-budget constitutional amendment	Y
Relax Clean Water Act regulations	N
Oppose limits on environmental regulations	Y
Reduce projected Medicare spending	Y
Approve GOP budget with tax and spending cuts	Y

VOTING STUDIES

	Presidential Support		Party Unity		Conservative Coalition	
Year	**S**	**O**	**S**	**O**	**S**	**O**
1996	46	53	75	23	76	24
1995	34	66	82	17	77	23
1994	72	28	77	23	83	17
1993	59	41	74	26	82	18

INTEREST GROUP RATINGS

Year	ADA	AFL-CIO	CCUS	ACU
1996	15	n/a	87	75
1995	25	25	83	68
1994	20	33	100	57
1993	40	58	73	71

3 Peter T. King (R)

Of Seaford — Elected 1992, 3rd term

Biographical Information

Born: April 5, 1944, Manhattan, N.Y.

Education: St. Francis College, B.A. 1965; U. of Notre Dame, J.D. 1968.

Military Service: National Guard, 1968-73.

Occupation: Lawyer.

Family: Wife, Rosemary; two children.

Religion: Roman Catholic.

Political Career: Hempstead Town Council, 1978-81; Nassau County comptroller, 1981-93.

Capitol Office: 403 Cannon Bldg. 20515; 225-7896.

Committees

Banking & Financial Services
Capital Markets, Securities & Government Sponsored Enterprises; Financial Institutions & Consumer Credit; General Oversight & Investigations

International Relations
Asia & the Pacific; International Operations & Human Rights

In Washington: It is no surprise that King's favorite movie is "High Noon." A two-decade veteran of the rough-and-tumble local politics in Nassau County, Long Island, he relishes political showdowns. He believes confrontation and partisanship are natural elements of the legislative and political business. He describes politics as a contact sport, "somewhere between roller derby and a 25-round fight."

King takes on all comers, both within and without the Republican Party. He announced in November 1996 that he would oppose Newt Gingrich's re-election as Speaker in the Republican Conference and claimed that a majority of House Republicans wanted Gingrich to step aside. "We have got to get our best team on the field right away and move as quickly as we can," King said. "As long as we have Newt on the field, we will have Newt's problems holding us back. A lot of the charges against him are unfair. But life is unfair. Newt is a big boy. He knows that after a while, appearances become reality."

King said 15 to 20 colleagues quietly encouraged him to lead the anti-Gingrich charge. "They said they agree with me in calling on Newt to step aside, but that does not mean they are going to stand with me," King said. "It could go from a very little support to a lot very quickly. I figured if somebody got out front, it would embolden others to do the same." On that count, King figured wrong: Gingrich won overwhelming support in the party conference.

After that, King fell in line behind the Speaker. In fact, as Gingrich's ethical problems led other Republicans to reconsider their support for him, King was contemptuous toward them. "I don't have too much patience for Republicans who are anguishing right now," he said. "My question is, 'Where were you when we were voting on him as our nominee?' "

Not only did King vote to re-elect Gingrich, but also he later voted against the ethics committee's recommended reprimand and $300,000 penalty against the Speaker for his ethical transgressions.

But later, in March 1997, King went after Gingrich in an article he wrote for the conservative magazine, The Weekly Standard. "As roadkill on the highway of American politics, Newt Gingrich cannot sell the Republican agenda," King wrote. "So instead of replacing Newt, the Republican leadership has replaced the agenda." King told Newsday that he wrote the article to stop Gingrich's drift to the political center.

These were not King's first public tiffs with the House Republican leadership. In the spring of 1996, he was part of the band of Republicans, mostly from the Northeast, who were pushing for a House floor vote on raising the minimum wage. GOP leaders, opposed to the increase, portrayed it as a Democratic payoff to labor unions, provoking a harsh rebuke from King. "Instead of going for solid working people, people who work hard, are patriotic and put their kids through school, the people who would be role models for Republican campaign commercials, we're driving them away," King complained. "We're driving them toward Clinton. We're going to turn ourselves into a party of barefoot hillbillies who go to revival meetings."

King voted in May 1996 for California Republican Rep. Frank Riggs' initial amendment to raise the minimum wage, and he opposed GOP leaders' efforts to exempt small businesses from its provisions. He also sided with labor in opposing legislation that would allow employers to offer comp time rather than overtime pay to their workers.

Still, King can be a fierce GOP partisan, tormenting House Democrats. In July 1996, he filed an ethics complaint against Jim McDermott of Washington, then the ranking Democrat on the House ethics committee. King said McDermott should recuse himself from considering complaints against Gingrich because Steven J. Jost, a fundraiser McDermott once employed, was involved in filing ethics complaints against the Speaker. King also said McDermott had violated House rules by making public statements about the ethics process.

NEW YORK 3
Eastern Nassau County — Oyster Bay

During 22 years (1971-93) of representing much of eastern Nassau County, Republican Rep. Norman F. Lent faced few serious election challenges. The elements of this successful GOP track record in the 3rd — made up mainly of Lent's former turf — remain firmly in place. The 3rd's suburban population is more than 90 percent non-Hispanic white; it has more pockets of affluence than of poverty.

In addition, a Republican machine has controlled Nassau County politics for decades. Its most prominent alumnus, third-term GOP Sen. Alfonse M. D'Amato, hails from Island Park in the southwest part of the 3rd.

Yet the economic problems of the early 1990s hit home in the 3rd and loosened the GOP grip in 1992. The impact of the national recession on the 3rd's mainly white-collar work force was amplified by the district's dependence on a declining defense industrial base. Consider the Grumman Corp., a contractor that built the F-14 fighter planes made famous by the movie "Top Gun" and constructed the lunar module that landed the astronauts on the moon. Acres of small single-family homes were built near its sprawling Bethpage facility to house the engineers who came to work for the defense giant. Grumman since has been bought by the Northrop Co., becoming Northrop Grumman, and sharply scaled back its local presence.

Pockets of Democratic support in the communities of Plainview, Old Bethpage and Syosset make the district appear more friendly to the party than it really is. Even as voter anger over a declining economy, burdensome property taxes and high electric utility rates sparked a mini-revolt and enabled Bill Clinton to carry the district in 1992, Nassau County Comptroller Peter T. King still polled 50 percent of the vote and kept the congressional seat in GOP hands. Clinton won again in 1996 with 53 percent of the vote but King polled 55 percent.

The 3rd reaches a finger into northwest Nassau County, taking in such well-off communities as Plandome Manor, Manhasset and North Hills. The district then broadens to cover much of eastern Nassau County.

The Long Island Expressway (LIE) roughly bisects this area. To the north is estate country in such communities as Brookville and Old Westbury. The Sagamore Hill estate of President Theodore Roosevelt is near Long Island Sound. The State University College at Old Westbury, C. W. Post College and the New York Institute of Technology are in the north part of the 3rd.

The bulk of the 3rd's people are in the portions of Hempstead Town and Oyster Bay south of the LIE. This is mainly white-collar suburbia, with many commuters to the financial and corporate offices of Manhattan.

The 3rd has just over half the residents of Levittown, the development that sparked Long Island's suburban boom in the 1940s and '50s. The district has a large number of Italian-American and Jewish residents: Massapequa, in the southeast corner, was once nicknamed "Matzo-Pizza" for its ethnic mix, though it is now mainly Italian.

1990 Population: 580,337. White 547,567 (94%), Black 11,702 (2%), Other 21,068 (4%). Hispanic origin 25,545 (4%). 18 and over 455,840 (79%), 62 and over 99,657 (17%). Median age: 37.

The ethics panel said King had not sufficiently substantiated his conflict-of-interest allegation. The panel also admonished all its members for public statements "concerning the work of the ethics committee that could be viewed as inconsistent with the letter or spirit of our very restrictive rules."

From his seat on the Banking Committee during hearings on Whitewater in the 103rd Congress, King swapped barbs with California Democrat Maxine Waters. She told him to shut up after he questioned the credibility of Hillary Rodham Clinton's chief of staff, Margaret Williams. The next day, King took to the House floor: "She's not going to tell me to shut up," he said. Responded Waters: "The day is over when men can intimidate and badger women."

During the 1993 debate on NAFTA, which King supported, he caused a stir by saying that President Clinton had promised to oppose any Democratic efforts to criticize the congressman's support of the trade pact.

On most issues (including abortion, which he stoutly opposes), King votes a conservative line. On the International Relations Committee, he takes a page from the playbook of a fellow product of the Nassau County Republican organization, U.S. Sen. Alfonse M. D'Amato, expressing strong support for Israel and Jewish causes. That helps him win support from liberal Jewish voters in the 3rd who otherwise would be likely to vote Democratic.

For example, King led the fight to overturn millions of dollars in contracts awarded by the U.S. Department of Housing and Urban Development (HUD) to the Rev. Louis Farrakhan's Nation of Islam for security services in public housing. HUD wound up canceling some contracts and deciding not to renew others.

He went after the Nation of Islam again in October 1995, asking for a federal investigation of whether the group violated regulations barring the solicitation of funds at public gatherings on the Mall in Washington, D.C.. He said the Nation of Islam passed around large cardboard boxes seeking contributions during its Million Man March event. "Political correctness reared its ugly head," King wrote Interior Secretary Bruce Babbitt (whose agency oversees the Mall). "Once again, Louis Farrakhan and the Nation of Islam have received special treatment from the federal government."

King opposes term limits, and in November 1995 he was one of only six lawmakers to vote against a proposed House rule banning members and staff from accepting gifts, meals and trips except for those from family members and friends.

As befits his Irish background, King also has been an avid and outspoken supporter of the Irish Republican Army (IRA) and its efforts to oust the British from Northern Ireland. In March 1996, he praised Clinton's decision to grant a visa to Gerry Adams, the leader of Sinn Fein, the political wing of the IRA, to attend St. Patrick's Day celebrations in the United States. King, a personal friend of Adams', said through a spokesman that Clinton "recognizes the value of keeping Sinn Fein in the peace process."

At Home: When 22-year GOP Rep. Norman F. Lent announced in June 1992 that he was not seeking re-election, King, the Nassau County comptroller and an unsuccessful candidate for New York attorney general six years earlier, moved with characteristic dispatch to establish himself as his successor. Defying the "outsider" pitch in vogue with so many candidates in the 1990s, King said that with his government experience he could get things done in Washington.

He coasted through the primary. The general election proved more difficult, as King drew a strong and well-financed opponent in Democrat Steve A. Orlins, a senior consultant to American Express. Although the district usually is Republican turf, Orlins held a potent trump card: a huge campaign treasury, four times as big as King's, including $775,000 from his own resources. This allowed Orlins to bombard the district with mass mailings and radio ads.

True to form, however, King came out firing. He accused Orlins of being "a carpetbagging millionaire" who was "trying to buy the election." Orlins, who grew up on Long Island, had lived in Manhattan until he rented a house in the district in July. He countered that as part of the long-dominant Nassau Republican machine, King had to take his share of responsibility for the county's $130 million deficit and high tax rates.

King's history of local involvement helped him hold the district's GOP votes. Although he fell short of a majority, he turned back Orlins' challenge by 4 percentage points.

In 1994, King's Democratic opponent was Glen Head lawyer Norma Grill. She spent $415,000 — more than half of it her own — but got only 40 percent of the vote. In 1996, Democrats offered Dal LaMagna, a wealthy businessman who owned a beauty products company and handed out tweezers imprinted with the slogan, "Vote for Tweezerman." King won, 55 percent to 42 percent.

HOUSE ELECTIONS

1996 General		
Peter T. King (R,C,FDM)	127,972	(55%)
Dal LaMagna (D,INDC)	97,518	(42%)
John O'Shea (RTL)	4,129	(2%)
1996 Primary		
Peter T. King (R,C,FDM)	7,593	(88%)
Robert Previdi (R)	1,014	(12%)
1994 General		
Peter T. King (R,C)	115,236	(59%)
Norma Grill (D)	77,774	(40%)

Previous Winning Percentages: 1992 (50%)

CAMPAIGN FINANCE

	Receipts	Receipts from PACs	Expend-itures
1996			
King (R)	$660,058	$360,568 (55%)	$645,951
LaMagna (D)	$1,083,554	$7,136 (1%)	$1,083,576
1994			
King (R)	$536,956	$206,018 (38%)	$516,548
Grill (D)	$433,656	$55,593 (13%)	$415,561

DISTRICT VOTE FOR PRESIDENT

1996	1992
D 136,326 (53%)	**D** 126,112 (44%)
R 96,255 (38%)	**R** 121,176 (42%)
I 18,975 (7%)	**I** 40,450 (14%)

KEY VOTES

1997	
Ban "partial birth" abortions	Y
1996	
Approve farm bill	Y
Deny public education to illegal immigrants	Y
Repeal ban on certain assault-style weapons	N
Increase minimum wage	Y
Freeze defense spending	?
Approve welfare overhaul	Y
1995	
Approve balanced-budget constitutional amendment	Y
Relax Clean Water Act regulations	Y
Oppose limits on environmental regulations	N
Reduce projected Medicare spending	Y
Approve GOP budget with tax and spending cuts	Y

VOTING STUDIES

	Presidential Support		Party Unity		Conservative Coalition	
Year	**S**	**O**	**S**	**O**	**S**	**O**
1996	49	51	82	16	80	14
1995	25	74	91	8	95	5
1994	45	54	91	8	83	17
1993	47	53	92	8	93	7

INTEREST GROUP RATINGS

Year	ADA	AFL-CIO	CCUS	ACU
1996	20	n/a	69	79
1995	5	25	79	64
1994	5	22	83	81
1993	15	42	82	92

4 Carolyn McCarthy (D)

Of Mineola — Elected 1996, 1st term

Biographical Information
Born: Jan. 5, 1944, Brooklyn, N.Y.
Education: Glen Cove Nursing School, L.P.N. 1964.
Occupation: Nurse..
Family: Widowed; one child.
Religion: Roman Catholic.
Political Career: No previous office.
Capitol Office: 1725 Longworth Bldg. 20515; 225-5516.

Committees
Education & Workforce
Employer-Employee Relations; Postsecondary Education, Training & Life-Long Learning
Small Business
Government Programs & Oversight; Tax & Exports

The Path to Washington: A personal tragedy pushed McCarthy into politics, and her compelling story made her one of the media's most sought-after freshmen in the early days of the 105th Congress.

A nurse and mother living in Nassau County, Long Island, her life was shattered when a crazed gunman opened fire on a Long Island Rail Road commuter train in 1993. Among the victims were her husband, who was killed, and her adult son, who was seriously injured and remains partially disabled.

McCarthy became an advocate for stricter gun control laws, and during the 104th Congress asked her representative, freshman Republican Daniel Frisa, to oppose GOP-led efforts to repeal the ban on certain semiautomatic assault-style weapons enacted as part of the 1994 crime bill.

Frisa rebuffed her pleas and supported the repeal, which passed the House but never came up for a vote in the Senate. Frisa explained his vote on the assault weapons ban by saying the original bill was flawed.

Following that rebuff, McCarthy decided to challenge Frisa. A lifelong Republican, McCarthy tried to mount a primary challenge, but Nassau Republican officials discouraged her. Nassau Democrats then eagerly offered her their ballot line, which she accepted. Although the district was drawn to favor Republicans, it does have some elements that make it winnable for Democrats, including a significant minority community and a number of working-class residents.

McCarthy also received support from the national Democratic Party. She landed a coveted prime time speaking role at the party's national convention in Chicago.

"This journey will make a difference when our neighborhoods pull together, when government listens to us again, when all of us, Democrats and Republicans, come together to solve our problems," McCarthy said in her convention address.

Her challenge attracted national attention and enough money to wage a strong campaign against the well-financed Frisa.

Frisa had scored an upset primary victory two years earlier, defeating freshman Republican Rep. David A. Levy in what was an embarrassment for the Nassau County Republican Organization, one of the last of the dominant party organizations. Levy was the only House Republican incumbent defeated for re-election in 1994.

Like many Democrats, McCarthy attempted to tie Frisa to Speaker Newt Gingrich and the House Republicans' efforts to scale back the projected spending increases in Medicaid and Medicare in order to balance the federal budget.

Gingrich was so unpopular on Long Island that two other Nassau County Republicans, Sen. Alfonse M. D'Amato and Rep. Peter T. King, went public with their criticism of the Speaker.

Like many Republicans, Frisa, who backed the House Republicans' "Contract With America" 98 percent of the time, began backing away from the party line as Election Day drew near. For example, he supported raising the minimum wage over objections of the GOP leadership.

Despite the Republican tint of the district, McCarthy won by a stunning 16-point margin, taking 57 percent of the vote. Frisa helped her by virtually disappearing in the final days of the campaign, shunning appearances and interviews.

McCarthy had hoped for a major committee assignment in Washington, setting her sights on Commerce or Judiciary, where she could continue her crusade for gun control. She also would have liked to serve on Ways and Means or Appropriations.

But with Democrats still in the House minority, those seats were hard to come by. Most of them went to more senior Democrats who had been bumped off prestigious committees when Republicans won control of the House in 1994. McCarthy instead got seats on the Education and the Workforce Committee and the Small Business Committee.

After McCarthy won, she said she visited her husband's grave at the cemetery and exclaimed: "Hey Den! My God, Dennis. Look at me now. Who would've ever thought?"

NEW YORK 4

Southwest Nassau County — Hempstead; Mineola

The 4th shares many Republican traits with the neighboring 3rd District. The 4th has some of New York City's longest established suburbs. Its middle- to upper-income residents head to work on the Long Island Rail Road and such congested routes as the Southern State Parkway and Long Island Expressway. The district, which includes the Nassau County seat of Mineola, is a stronghold for the county's GOP organization.

Yet the 4th does have some elements that can make the district winnable for a Democrat. Nearly a quarter of the district's residents are black or Hispanic, the largest minority group constituency of any Long Island House district.

There are a number of working-class residents who work at John F. Kennedy International Airport (across the district line in Queens), the Belmont Park horse track in Floral Park, and such large shopping centers as Roosevelt Field and Green Acres. Some of the district's wealthiest communities, in its southwestern corner, are mainly Jewish and lean Democratic.

These constituencies provide Democrats with a foothold in the 4th. This base — combined with the national recession, cutbacks in the region's defense and banking industries and fiscal problems in the Republican-controlled county government — enabled Bill Clinton to carry the district in 1992 and 1996, the latter by a margin of 20 percentage points.

More than 80 percent of the 4th District's population is in the sprawling township of Hempstead; the remainder is in North Hempstead. The foundation of Republican success is the nearly all white, middle- and upper-middle-income suburbs, such as Valley Stream, New Hyde Park, Garden City and Franklin Square.

The ethnic mix of the district includes many Italian- and Irish-Americans. Rockville Centre is the seat of suburban Long Island's Roman Catholic diocese.

The district's black population, and much of its Democratic vote, is mainly in such east side communities as Roosevelt, Uniondale, Hempstead and New Cassel. While these are largely middle-class areas, their poverty rates are well above the district's average.

The other Democratic bloc is at the other end of the district and income scale, in the largely Jewish "Five Towns" of Inwood, Lawrence, Cedarhurst, Woodmere and Hewlett. Nearby Atlantic Beach makes up the 4th's coastline, the shortest of any suburban Long Island district.

At the district's eastern end is about half the historic suburban development of Levittown. The largest employment hub is between Garden City and Uniondale. It includes the Roosevelt Field shopping complex and the former site of the Mitchell Field airport, which now supports the Nassau County Veterans' Memorial Coliseum and the campuses of Hofstra University and Nassau Community College. Adelphi University is also in the district.

1990 Population: 580,338. White 454,297 (78%), Black 94,141 (16%), Other 31,900 (5%). Hispanic origin 43,751 (8%). 18 and over 450,745 (78%), 62 and over 104,547 (18%). Median age: 36.

HOUSE ELECTIONS

1996 General

Carolyn McCarthy (D,INDC)	127,060	(57%)
Daniel Frisa (R,C,FDM)	89,542	(41%)
Vincent P. Garbitelli (RTL)	3,252	(1%)

CAMPAIGN FINANCE

	Receipts	Receipts from PACs	Expenditures
1996			
McCarthy (D)	$1,087,082	$262,855 (24%)	$967,221
Frisa (R)	$1,025,927	$538,600 (52%)	$893,147

DISTRICT VOTE FOR PRESIDENT

1996		1992	
D	132,140 (56%)	**D**	119,947 (47%)
R	84,065 (36%)	**R**	106,016 (41%)
I	14,493 (6%)	**I**	30,476 (12%)

KEY VOTES

1997

Ban "partial birth" abortions N

5 Gary L. Ackerman (D)

Of Queens — Elected 1983; 7th full term

Biographical Information
Born: Nov. 19, 1942, Brooklyn, N.Y.
Education: Queens College, B.A. 1965.
Occupation: Teacher; publisher and editor; advertising executive.
Family: Wife, Rita Gail Tewel; three children.
Religion: Jewish.
Political Career: Sought Democratic nomination for N.Y. City Council at large, 1977; N.Y. Senate, 1979-83.
Capitol Office: 2243 Rayburn Bldg. 20515; 225-2601.

Committees
Banking & Financial Services
Capital Markets, Securities & Government Sponsored Enterprises; Financial Institutions & Consumer Credit
International Relations
International Operations & Human Rights; Western Hemisphere (ranking)

In Washington: Although he knows he faces certain defeat in the conservative-dominated House, the affable and liberal Ackerman has taken on the task of fighting efforts to pass a constitutional amendment to ban desecration of the U.S. flag. Some members consider it politically risky to oppose the flag amendment, but Ackerman's poll performance has improved through the 1990s, from 52 percent in 1992 to 55 percent in 1994 to 64 percent in his 1996 race.

Ackerman, dean of the Long Island delegation in the House, also boosted his stature in the 5th by working well with Long Island Republicans on matters of parochial concern.

Ackerman's sense of irony and renowned wit were on full display when the House considered the flag desecration amendment in June 1995. During the debate, supporters argued that a constitutional amendment was needed to protect the flag, as a national symbol, from physical mistreatment. But Ackerman and other opponents countered that the amendment would undermine the freedom of expression guaranteed under the Bill of Rights. He argued the measure would lead to excessive litigation because states could come up with different definitions of "desecration" and "flag."

To make this point, Ackerman came to the House floor with boxer shorts, pantihose, napkins, hats and ties, all decorated with the familiar red, white and blue and the stars and stripes of the flag. As he held up each item, Ackerman asked his colleagues whether they thought it was a flag and whether it was an act of desecration to use it. "How about American flag napkins?" he inquired. "If you blow your nose in one, have you broken the law? Violating the Constitution is nothing to sneeze at. And how about American flag plates? If you put your spaghetti in it, do you go to the can?" Ackerman asked.

"Desecraters cannot destroy the flag," Ackerman told the House. "You cannot destroy a symbol unless you destroy what it represents." The House, however, easily approved the proposed constitutional amendment, 312-120. In the Senate, though, the amendment fell short of the two-thirds majority necessary for approval. Proponents promised another try in the 105th.

He has said leading opposition to the amendment is a dirty job that someone has to do. "It's a very tough side of the issue to be on, especially if you consider yourself a patriotic person, which I am," Ackerman told Newsday in May 1997.

From his seat on the International Relations Committee, where he is ranking member of the Western Hemisphere Subcommittee, Ackerman challenged GOP efforts in the 104th to limit foreign aid spending and reorganize and reduce the federal government's foreign-affairs work force.

After stern objections from Ackerman and many other Democrats, the House in June 1995 passed a GOP-backed foreign aid funding and State Department reorganization measure. It called for consolidating three separate foreign affairs agencies within the State Department.

Ackerman and his allies said the measure unwisely slashed funding for overseas programs and downsized the foreign policy bureaucracy. "Now a wave of neo-isolationism has taken over and this Congress is preparing to walk away from our responsibilities as a world leader," Ackerman told the House.

Ackerman offered an amendment to prevent the agencies' consolidation from going forward until the Congressional Budget Office and Office of Management and Budget made studies of the costs and benefits of the proposal. But Republicans said the amendment would gut their reorganization plan, and it was defeated, 177-233.

The foreign aid and State Department bill was ultimately vetoed by President Clinton in April 1996, and the House failed to override.

One of Ackerman's priorities in the 104th was winning reinstatement of a federally funded program to test newborns for HIV, which can cause AIDS, and to tell mothers the results. Ackerman introduced the measure along with conservative Oklahoma Republican Tom Coburn, a doctor. The Centers for Disease Control had conducted a

One of the noted wits in the House, Democrat Ackerman used humor to express his displeasure with the 1992 redistricting plan that created the elongated, politically competitive 5th.

Congressional districts are supposed to be compact and contiguous. When state legislators showed the proposed remap to Ackerman, he asked how the shore-hugging district — which is connected in three places only by the waters of Long Island Sound — could be contiguous. By that reasoning, Ackerman said, Maine, New Jersey and Florida, connected only by the Atlantic Ocean, are contiguous.

But the 5th remained as drawn, one of several irregularly shaped districts on the new New York map. And its difficult navigability turned out to be just one of Ackerman's problems in 1992. Almost exactly half the district's population lives in suburban Long Island; even the portion of the New York City borough of Queens (Ackerman's base) that is in the 5th is more suburban than urban. As a result, Democrats do not have a lock on the district.

The 1992 election results indicated that the 5th had the potential to be a political swing district. Ackerman edged a local Republican official by just 7 percentage points; Bill Clinton's majority win here was strong by suburban Long Island standards but weak compared with other New York City-based districts. But by 1996, Ackerman appeared to have made the district his own, winning easily with 64 percent of the vote. And Clinton also improved, taking 60 percent.

The portion of Queens that makes up the western end of the 5th is the Democratic base: Ackerman won 61 percent here in 1992, 63 percent in 1994, and 72 percent in 1996. It has many Jewish residents and a large number of Asians (including a Chinese-American constituency centered on the community of Flushing). Flushing, one of Queens' "downtown" centers, is the most urbanized area of the district and has some low-income population.

NEW YORK 5
Northeast Queens; northern Nassau and Suffolk counties

Among the major employers in the Queens part of the 5th are Queens College of the City University of New York in South Flushing and the Long Island Jewish Medical Center in New Hyde Park.

Just across the Nassau County border are two peninsulas that contain some of the nation's wealthiest communities, including Sands Point, Kings Point and Great Neck. Despite its affluence, this area, which has a large Jewish population, is usually strong for Democrats. The U.S. Merchant Marine Academy is in Kings Point. Unisys, a maker of high-tech defense systems, is in Great Neck; Canon USA is based in Lake Success.

The exurban part of the district on Suffolk County's North Shore provides a sharp political contrast. Taking in most of the town of Huntington before terminating in the western part of Smithtown, the Suffolk County portion of the 5th votes steadily Republican. Melville, at Suffolk's western border, is a commercial center. The newspaper Newsday and the Long Island offices of Chase Manhattan and Chemical Bank are there.

1990 Population: 580,337. White 487,569 (84%), Black 20,140 (3%), Other 72,628 (13%). Hispanic origin 42,440 (7%). 18 and over 462,505 (80%), 62 and over 109,899 (19%). Median age: 38.

study that involved testing infants for HIV, but the CDC tested infants anonymously. As a result, Ackerman said, some babies with the virus went without treatment.

The "Baby AIDS" measure was attached to the Ryan White Act, which provides federal grants to cities and states to treat and support AIDS patients. "For years, our country has been testing newborn infants anonymously to determine whether or not they have their mother's antibodies for HIV and then allowing those infants and mothers to go home from the hospital, never being told that the child tested positive, never allowing . . . that newborn infant to access the medical system so that his or her young life might be made a little bit more comfortable," Ackerman said when the House passed the Ryan White Act in September 1995.

But Senate conferees opposed the mandatory testing language and instead pushed for encouraging voluntary HIV testing of pregnant women. They said newborns are less likely to be infected if the mother's health status is known before child birth, because women can be treated to reduce transmission risk. Conferees finally agreed that states would share $10 million to promote voluntary counseling, testing and treatment for pregnant women. The agreement would trigger mandatory testing of newborns unless progress is made in preventing transmission to them. Clinton signed the Ryan White measure in May 1996.

During his early years in the House, Ackerman was known mainly for his idiosyncrasies: his glib wit, considerable girth, goatee, boutonniere and unusual residence (a houseboat docked in a Potomac River marina).

Now, though, as chairman of the Long Island Caucus, Ackerman is just as much known in the House and at home for leading the charge on a number of endeavors important his region, including: obtaining a hefty grant from the National Cancer Institute for Long Island breast cancer research; combating an effort by the Office of Management and Budget to decrease federal aid by lumping Nassau and Suffolk counties under the same metropolitan statistical status as New York City; dealing with a railroad strike on Long Island in 1994; and gaining $250,000 in the fiscal 1997 energy and water spending bill for a coastal erosion study on Long Island's north shore.

Ackerman also has a seat on the Banking and Financial Services Committee, where he sits on subcommittees dealing with capital markets, securities, consumer credit and other issues important to New York's financial sector.

At Home: After winning a 1983 special election, Ackerman cruised through four re-elections in the then-7th District. His mainly urban constituency included many loyally Democratic Jewish and Hispanic voters. But in 1992, redistricting removed much of his base in the New York City borough of Queens and gave him more conservative voters in suburban Long Island.

Ackerman opted to run in the mainly suburban 5th. He avoided a showdown with Democratic Rep. James H. Scheuer, who had many constituents in the new district. He decided to retire.

But Ackerman suffered a double blow from the House bank investigation. He had 111 overdrafts, and some members with more overdrafts accused him of taking advantage of his seat on the ethics committee to leak a preliminary list of the worst bank offenders. Ackerman unequivocally denied leaking the list, but he quit the ethics committee anyway, declaring it a "thankless task."

A Democratic primary revealed that Ackerman had some weaknesses. He won nomination with 62 percent, but opponent Rita Morris, a grandmotherly college librarian who had never run for office, carried the Suffolk County part of the 5th.

Suffolk was the base of Ackerman's GOP foe, County Legislator Allan E. Binder. Binder ran on a theme of congressional reform and pounded Ackerman on ethics issues. However, the much better-financed Ackerman prevailed by 7 percentage points, his big margin in Queens offsetting Binder's advantage in Suffolk. Binder tried again in 1994, but he was upset in both the Republican and Conservative primaries by first-time candidate Grant M. Lally, a young lawyer from Nassau County. Lally spent more than $300,000 of his own money on the race, and while Ackerman against lost Suffolk, he crushed Lally in Nassau and Queens and won by 12 percentage points.

Lally was back for a rematch in 1996, but he fell well short of his previous mark, as Ackerman took 64 percent.

Ackerman came to the House to succeed Democratic Rep. Benjamin S. Rosenthal, who died in early 1983. A former social studies teacher, Ackerman had run-ins with the Queens Democratic machine as a publisher of a weekly newspaper, and he had lost as an independent in a 1977 challenge to a City Council incumbent. But he won a state Senate seat in 1978 and convinced Democratic leaders in 1983 that he was the party's best hope in a House race against a wealthy independent, pollster Douglas Schoen, and a less competitive GOP candidate. Ackerman won the special election with 50 percent of the vote.

HOUSE ELECTIONS

1996 General		
Gary L. Ackerman (D,L,INDC)	125,918	(64%)
Grant M. Lally (R,C,FDM)	69,244	(35%)
Andrew J. Duff (RTL)	2,623	(1%)
1994 General		
Gary Ackerman (D,L)	93,896	(55%)
Grant M. Lally (R,C)	73,884	(43%)
Edward Elkowitz (RTL)	2,862	(2%)

Previous Winning Percentages: 1992 (52%) **1990** (100%) **1988** (100%) **1986** (77%) **1984** (69%) **1983**† (50%)

† Special election

CAMPAIGN FINANCE

	Receipts	Receipts from PACs	Expend-itures
1996			
Ackerman (D)	$1,175,151	$358,500 (31%)	$1,123,926
Lally (R)	$172,597	$3,466 (2%)	$170,326
1994			
Ackerman (D)	$1,358,352	$426,907 (31%)	$1,376,467
Lally (R)	$446,197	$18,301 (4%)	$442,726

DISTRICT VOTE FOR PRESIDENT

	1996		1992
D	132,454 (60%)	**D**	131,095 (52%)
R	71,659 (32%)	**R**	88,586 (35%)
I	13,354 (6%)	**I**	30,475 (12%)

KEY VOTES

1997	
Ban "partial birth" abortions	N
1996	
Approve farm bill	N
Deny public education to illegal immigrants	N
Repeal ban on certain assault-style weapons	N
Increase minimum wage	Y
Freeze defense spending	?
Approve welfare overhaul	Y
1995	
Approve balanced-budget constitutional amendment	N
Relax Clean Water Act regulations	N
Oppose limits on environmental regulations	Y
Reduce projected Medicare spending	N
Approve GOP budget with tax and spending cuts	N

VOTING STUDIES

	Presidential Support		Party Unity		Conservative Coalition	
Year	S	O	S	O	S	O
1996	86	10	90	4	31	63
1995	80	17	87	6	23	76
1994	74	18	90	4	25	64
1993	83	10	90	3	30	66
1992	13	57	76	1	6	52
1991	25	64	86	3	8	78

INTEREST GROUP RATINGS

Year	ADA	AFL-CIO	CCUS	ACU
1996	85	n/a	31	0
1995	90	100	25	13
1994	90	71	50	0
1993	80	100	20	13
1992	70	91	33	0
1991	85	100	20	10

6 Floyd H. Flake (D)

Of Queens — Elected 1986, 6th term

Biographical Information

Born: Jan. 30, 1945, Los Angeles, Calif.

Education: Wilberforce U., B.A. 1967; Payne Theological Seminary, 1968-70; Northeastern U., 1974-75; St. John's U., 1982-85; United Theological Seminary, D.M. 1995.

Occupation: Minister.

Family: Wife, M. Elaine McCollins; four children.

Religion: African Methodist Episcopal.

Political Career: No previous office.

Capitol Office: 1035 Longworth Bldg. 20515; 225-3461.

Committees

Banking & Financial Services
Capital Markets, Securities & Government Sponsored Enterprises; Domestic & International Monetary Policy (ranking)

Small Business
Empowerment

In Washington: A handsome and elegantly dressed minister who speaks in the captivating cadences of the black church, Flake's major contribution to the legislative process is his frequent oratory on the House floor, preaching that old-time liberal Democratic religion.

"I find it the height of hypocrisy," Flake thundered to his colleagues during an April 1996 debate on raising the minimum wage 90 cents, "when members of this body stand before the United States of America and proclaim that persons who are making $4.25 an hour, if we move it beyond $5, that will cause inflation in America. Let me tell my colleagues what causes inflation in America. The hundreds of people who are CEOs of major corporations collecting millions of dollars, getting their golden parachutes and moving out to their various places, moving jobs outside this country so that they can benefit by low wages from persons who are not Americans and yet shipping back to America the products they produce and selling them at the highest possible price."

Flake sometimes refers to his own experiences as he defends federal programs against proposed Republican budget cuts. As the GOP sought in the 104th to cut back on the student loan program and eliminate the Department of Education, Flake said such reductions could have prevented him from going to college.

"I am one of 13 children born to parents of fifth and sixth grade educations," Flake said in May 1995. "Without the National Defense Student Loan Program, I would not have even had the opportunity to go to college in the first place. It was a loan. I paid it back. Others will do the same thing if given the opportunity."

And in April 1996, as he again urged Congress to raise the minimum wage, he argued that students, too, needed the higher pay. "I stand here as a product of the family of 13 children, parents who could not afford to send me to college, and the only way I could get through was to work," Flake said. "I do not see anything wrong with trying to provide a wage that allows a student to be able to work their way through school. . . . Pay them a good enough salary so that . . . if we reduce the scholarships, they will know they can work their way through."

Flake is a senior member of the Banking and Financial Services Committee and ranking Democrat on the Domestic and International Monetary Policy Subcommittee. He also sits on the Small Business Committee.

On Banking, Flake tried to soften efforts by House Republicans in the 104th Congress to overhaul the nation's housing programs. In November 1995, the Banking panel gave voice-vote approval to an amendment he sponsored with Joseph P. Kennedy II, D-Mass., to retain a Housing and Urban Development program giving local authorities funds to demolish, replace or restore uninhabitable public housing projects.

When Republicans held the White House, Flake was critical of administration efforts to bail out the failed savings and loan industry, portraying the rescue operation as a handout to wealthy financial interests. But just as he became chairman of the General Oversight Subcommittee in the 103rd Congress, Democrats moved into the White House, and Flake became responsible for helping advance President Clinton's effort to finish the cleanup.

A vocal advocate for minorities and the poor, Flake at the same time works to promote the interests of New York's big banking and financial interests, which provide jobs in his district. He teamed with then-ranking Republican Rep. Jim Leach of Iowa to persuade the Banking Committee to modify a Clinton program designed to encourage lending in distressed communities. Flake and Leach shifted one-third of the funds from community development banks to mainstream lending institutions.

In September 1996, he introduced legislation with Bob Franks, R-N.J., to mint a coin commemorating the 50th anniversary of Jackie Robinson becoming the first black to play major league baseball. "He was the first of many Negro League stars to play in the big leagues, and he suffered

The southeast portion of Queens has sent an African-American to the House only since 1986; up until then, the white-run Democratic machine had dominated Queens politics. But a challenge to black representation here appears unlikely. Redistricting for the 1990s boosted the black population from 50 percent to 56 percent. Hispanics (about 17 percent) contribute to the minority-group voting bloc.

The 6th provides a dependable partisan base for Flake and other Democrats. In 1996, Bill Clinton dominated the 6th, winning 85 percent of the votes. Any political action here is going to be in the Democratic primaries.

With an eastern border that follows the line between the New York City borough of Queens and suburban Nassau County, the 6th is one of the most economically sound minority-majority districts. Its poverty rate is less than the rate for New York state as a whole; the poverty rates for blacks and Hispanics are about half the figures for those groups statewide.

More than a generation ago, such communities as Springfield Gardens and St. Albans were settled by a burgeoning Roman Catholic middle class. Today, the economic profile of these areas is not much different: Its brick homes house many civil servants, teachers and small-business owners. But the demographics are completely different. Instead of Irish- and Italian-Americans, most of the residents now are blacks.

John F. Kennedy International Airport, by far the district's largest employer, provides a steady job base. It is also the district's most prominent geographical feature: Originally named Idlewild for the marshlands on which it was built, Kennedy Airport occupies a huge swath of the 6th along the north shore of Jamaica Bay.

NEW YORK 6
Southeast Queens — Jamaica; St. Albans

Despite its overall middle-class veneer, the 6th does have some areas that are much less well off. South Jamaica, where such urban problems as low high school graduation rates, welfare dependency, crime and drugs are rife, is the focus of efforts by economic development advocates (including Flake). The 6th's portion of the Rockaway peninsula — across Jamaica Bay from the airport with no direct land link to the rest of the district — has several public housing projects.

Much of the district's mainly middle-class white population is in its northeast end, in such communities as Bellerose and Queens Village, and near its western border, in Ozone Park. These areas are mainly Irish and Italian, with a scattering of Jewish residents. They lean Democratic, though the Republican vote is heavier than in the rest of the 6th. The Aqueduct horse track is in South Ozone Park.

1990 Population: 580,337. White 170,071 (29%), Black 326,335 (56%), Other 83,931 (14%). Hispanic origin 98,209 (17%). 18 and over 432,187 (74%), 62 and over 79,944 (14%). Median age: 32.

the strains of racism throughout major league ballparks," Flake said. "By successfully bearing this burden, he in fact became a symbol of victory for African Americans, and he carried the torch of equality that lit the flame of equality in America."

Flake has inspired comparisons to another black clergyman elected to Congress from New York — the late Rep. Adam Clayton Powell Jr. For a time, the parallel with Powell, who faced legal and ethical problems during much of his early House career, seemed to be getting uncomfortably close.

In April 1991, the government's case against Flake — which consisted of charges that he embezzled funds from a housing project run by his church and evaded taxes — was dismissed after a federal judge barred prosecutors from presenting what one called "the heart" of the case to the jury.

Despite that victory, the entire episode made Flake "damaged goods" in the eyes of many Democrats, hurting his prospects for advancement in Washington. When two New York Democrats left the Appropriations Committee prior to the 103rd Congress, Flake made a bid for the panel. Instead, two more junior New Yorkers — Nita M. Lowey and Jose E. Serrano — were tapped for the vacancies.

At Home: Flake has a diverse background in corporate marketing and in education. He was an administrator at Lincoln University and Boston College. But it was his long tenure as pastor of the Allen African Methodist Episcopal Church — and the economic and social programs that he sponsored in that role — that gave Flake a base for a political career.

Black leaders had targeted the 6th after 1982 redistricting gave it a black majority. But the opportunity to cash in on that demographic edge did not occur until 1986, after the death of white Democratic Rep. Joseph P. Addabbo.

The special election that June occurred at a time of chaos within the white-run Queens Democratic machine, brought on by a corruption scandal and the suicide of county Democratic leader Donald M. Manes. Black state Assemblyman Alton R. Waldon Jr. had support from surviving fragments of the Democratic organization enabling him to edge out Flake, who was making his political debut.

But Waldon was aided by a filing technicality that prevented Flake from appearing on absentee ballots. Flake's followers, angered by the absentee ballot flap, believed the election was stolen by a corrupt Queens machine.

That sentiment gave Flake momentum going into the September primary to choose a nominee for a full term in the 100th Congress. Fusing his support in the black church with elements of black organized labor, Flake defeated Waldon and went on to an easy general election win.

In 1988, Flake drew no significant opposition. His only difficulty was of a personal nature. In May, a woman who had worked for Flake at his Queens church accused Flake of harassing her to quit after she broke off a sexual affair with him. Flake denied the accusations.

In 1990, Flake carried his tax-evasion indictment into the campaign, but it proved no hindrance, as he won re-election with 73 percent of the vote.

Even after surviving his legal battles, Flake had other problems in 1992. First, he continued a feud with the Queens Democrats by organizing a slate of primary candidates to challenge party regulars for elective and party positions, after they endorsed his opponent in the Democratic primary. The party organization retaliated by challenging the ballot status of Flake and the slated challengers. An out-of-court compromise was reached under which most of the challengers withdrew and Flake stayed on the ballot.

His primary challenger, black businessman Simeon Golar, campaigned vigorously, but managed only 25 percent of the vote. Flake won big in November and has not been pressed since.

HOUSE ELECTIONS

1996 General		
Floyd H. Flake (D)	102,799	(85%)
Jorawar Misir (R,C,INDC,FDM)	18,348	(15%)
1994 General		
Floyd H. Flake (D)	68,596	(80%)
Denny D. Bhagwandin (R,C)	16,675	(20%)

Previous Winning Percentages: 1992 (81%) **1990** (73%) **1988** (86%) **1986** (68%)

CAMPAIGN FINANCE

	Receipts	Receipts from PACs	Expend-itures
1996			
Flake (D)	$160,853	$107,658 (67%)	$165,311
Misir (R)	$12,043	0	$7,689
1994			
Flake (D)	$279,248	$167,240 (60%)	$227,256

DISTRICT VOTE FOR PRESIDENT

1996		1992	
D	128,071 (85%)	**D**	115,253 (75%)
R	15,946 (11%)	**R**	27,855 (18%)
I	4,380 (3%)	**I**	9,335 (6%)

KEY VOTES

1997	
Ban "partial birth" abortions	Y
1996	
Approve farm bill	N
Deny public education to illegal immigrants	N
Repeal ban on certain assault-style weapons	N
Increase minimum wage	Y
Freeze defense spending	Y
Approve welfare overhaul	?
1995	
Approve balanced-budget constitutional amendment	N
Relax Clean Water Act regulations	N
Oppose limits on environmental regulations	Y
Reduce projected Medicare spending	N
Approve GOP budget with tax and spending cuts	N

VOTING STUDIES

	Presidential Support		Party Unity		Conservative Coalition	
Year	S	O	S	O	S	O
1996	70	11	80	5	22	61
1995	80	12	85	5	18	77
1994	74	14	86	1	14	72
1993	72	21	91	3	11	77
1992	10	76	87	3	10	83
1991	23	65	87	4	0	95

INTEREST GROUP RATINGS

Year	ADA	AFL-CIO	CCUS	ACU
1996	80	n/a	8	6
1995	85	100	21	4
1994	95	78	45	0
1993	90	92	22	5
1992	90	92	13	0
1991	100	100	20	0

7 Thomas J. Manton (D)

Of Queens — Elected 1984, 7th term

Biographical Information

Born: Nov. 3, 1932, New York, N.Y.

Education: St. John's U., B.B.A. 1958, LL.B. 1962.

Military Service: Marine Corps, 1951-53.

Occupation: Lawyer.

Family: Wife, Diane Mason Schley; four children.

Religion: Roman Catholic.

Political Career: N.Y. City Council, 1970-84; sought Democratic nomination for U.S. House, 1972, 1978.

Capitol Office: 2235 Rayburn Bldg. 20515; 225-3965.

Committees

Commerce

Finance & Hazardous Materials (ranking); Telecommunications, Trade & Consumer Protection

In Washington: Behind-the-scenes politics is Manton's natural orientation; as chairman of the Democratic organization in Queens, he is deeply involved in parochial politics. Despite his political punch at home, he has never gained much broader notice, either as a power broker in New York State politics or as a mover and shaker in Washington.

Instead, Manton does his job with little fanfare, attracting even less attention these days because Republican takeover of the House cost him two subcommittee chairmanships. One area in which he excels is fundraising; he finished the 1996 campaign with more than half a million dollars in the bank. Manton has good access to political contributors owing to his seat on the Commerce Committee, which has wide-ranging legislative responsibilities.

When the new Republican majority reorganized House committees for the 104th, it axed the Merchant Marine panel, where Manton had chaired the Fisheries Subcommittee. Also, Manton was bumped off the House Administration Committee, which the GOP shrank and renamed House Oversight; Manton had chaired the Personnel and Police Subcommittee there. He lost another "insider" outpost when the Democratic Steering and Policy Committee was reformulated by new Minority Leader Richard A. Gephardt.

While most New York City Democrats vote a reliably liberal line, Manton is a bit more conservative — his party unity scores usually are in the 80 percent range — reflecting the traditional cultural values of white working-class ethnics in his district. Many of his departures from the party line come on abortion-related issues. In the 104th, he voted to ban a particular abortion technique that opponents call a "partial-birth" abortion, to prevent federal employee health care plans from paying for abortions, to bar abortions at overseas military hospitals, and to allow states not to fund Medicaid abortions for poor women in cases of rape or incest. In the 103rd, he voted to require parental notification of minors' abortions and against legislation safeguarding access to clinics where abortions are performed.

Like many other urban liberals, Manton took a dim view in the 104th of conservatives' early proposals for overhauling the welfare system, finding them too stringent. But in the end, when compromises produced a bill that President Clinton said he found acceptable, Manton voted for it.

On most other issues, Manton's views have mirrored those of Democrats to his left. In the 103rd, he backed Clinton's budget bill, the family and medical leave act and the "motor voter" bill to expand voter registration. In the 104th, he supported a minimum wage increase, voted against repealing the ban on certain semiautomatic assault-style weapons and opposed limits on awards to consumers injured by faulty products. In 1997 he voted against a term limits constitutional amendment.

In March 1995, Manton unsuccessfully tried to amend legislation making it harder for dissatisfied investors to sue companies. The measure would require the loser to pay the winner's attorneys' fees if the court found that the litigant had pursued a meritless case and that the payment of legal costs would be just. Manton's amendment would have required the loser to pay the winner's attorneys fees only if his arguments were frivolous. Manton's amendment was rejected 167-254.

Bringing a slice of his district's life to the House floor, Manton on several occasions has delivered orations meant to appeal to the Greek-Americans who have moved to Astoria, a community in northwest Queens near the Triboro Bridge.

For example, in March 1996, he rose on the House floor to celebrate Greek Independence Day. "We as Americans, as well as each of the new and older democracies of the world, owe much to the country of Greece because of their important role in fostering the freedom and democracy we know today," he said. "The relationship between Greece and the United States is one based on mutual respect and admiration. The democratic principles used by our Founding Fathers to frame

Democrats have a strong registration advantage in the 7th, a multiethnic, mainly middle-class, urban district that connects northern Queens with the southern Bronx. There is a substantial minority presence: More than a fifth of the residents are Hispanic, with blacks and Asians (including a Chinese-American concentration in Flushing) each making up about a tenth of the population.

Yet the Democratic vote here is somewhat less dependable than in most of New York City. Non-Hispanic whites make up just under 60 percent of the 7th's population but vote in greater numbers than its minority-group residents. Many of these whites are of working-class backgrounds and of ethnic groups that have conservative tendencies on social issues.

This district was the setting for the 1970s TV show "All in the Family" and Archie Bunker, its conservative, blue-collar protagonist.

The 7th supported Ronald Reagan in the 1980s, even in 1984 when Geraldine A. Ferraro — who then represented much of the 7th District in the House — was the Democratic vice presidential nominee. The 7th only narrowly returned to the Democratic side in the 1988 presidential contest, but Bill Clinton won it by wide margins in both 1992 and 1996.

Manton had little trouble winning in 1996 either, polling 71 percent of the vote. He received 72 percent in Queens, where he is county Democratic chairman, and 69 percent in The Bronx.

The 7th owes its irregular shape in Queens (which has about three-quarters of the district's population) to the Hispanic-majority 12th District, which winds around northern Queens to pick up pockets of Hispanic residents.

At the 7th's western end is Long Island City,

NEW YORK 7
Parts of Queens and the Bronx — Long Island City

which faces Manhattan across the East River. This longtime industrial center still has blue-collar employers, including the Swingline stapler company, but has lost many of its factories in recent years.

A Citicorp skyscraper, the tallest building in Queens, is in Long Island City. The Astoria Film Center, a studio used since the silent-movie days, is nearby, as is much of Astoria's Greek community. Sunnyside has Amtrak and Long Island Rail Road yards.

The 7th picks up a largely Irish section in Jackson Heights, then wraps around the 12th to take in much of its own Hispanic population in such areas as East Elmhurst and Corona. Bordering Flushing Bay are LaGuardia Airport and Flushing Meadow Park, site of Shea Stadium (home of the New York Mets), the National Tennis Center (home of the U.S. Open), and the 1939 and 1964-65 world's fairs.

To the east, the district covers residential College Point and Whitestone, then moves across the Bronx-Whitestone Bridge. The 7th's portion of the Bronx is shaped roughly like the numeral "7." Italian-Americans are the predominant ethnic group. The Bronx section has a large hospital complex that includes Yeshiva University's Albert Einstein College of Medicine.

1990 Population: 580,337. White 406,394 (70%), Black 58,788 (10%), Other 115,155 (20%). Hispanic origin 123,495 (21%). 18 and over 472,528 (81%), 62 and over 116,640 (20%). Median age: 37.

our Constitution were born in ancient Greece. In turn, our Founding Fathers and the American Revolution served as ideals for the Greek people when they began their modern fight for independence in the 1820's. The Greeks translated the United States Declaration of Independence into their own language so they, too, could share the same freedoms of the United States."

In July 1995 he spoke during a House special order marking the 21st anniversary of the partitioning of Cyprus between Greek and Turkish Cypriots, an event that Greeks continue to denounce. "The division of Cyprus has the distinction of being one of the most intractable in the world today," he said. "Since Turkey first invaded Cyprus in 1974, 1,619 people including eight Americans last seen alive in the occupied areas of Cyprus have never been accounted for. We must not let the passage of years weaken our resolve to pressure the Turkish government to provide answers to the families of the missing. We cannot forget their suffering continues."

Manton represents one of the nation's top garbage-producing areas — a fact that put him in the forefront of the early 1990s debate on whether to allow states to restrict the import of out-of-state garbage. When the Energy and Commerce Committee took up a measure to that effect, Manton worked to weaken it by grandfathering increased numbers of existing intra-state garbage contracts. "The legislation has the potential to impose untold economic harm on communities that export some . . . municipal solid waste and on other communities that import waste as a means of economic development," Manton said.

A former policeman, Manton touts his sponsorship of federal disability pay to law enforcement officials injured in the line of duty, which was passed as part of omnibus anti-crime legislation in 1990. He also has supported levying the federal death penalty against those who commit gun murders, and he favors imposing mandatory prison sentences for many crimes.

At Home: Although Manton served for 14 years on the New York City Council, he had some initial trouble gaining political stature. He twice lost House nomination races during the 1970s. During his first successful House campaign, in 1984, Manton was overshadowed by his predecessor, Democrat Geraldine A. Ferraro, who was then Walter F. Mondale's vice presidential running mate.

Soon thereafter, Manton obtained prominence in his own right, taking over as Queens Democratic chairman and stabilizing a party organization that had been wracked by scandal. Manton's party position provided him with a ready-made organization for a series of easy re-elections to the House.

However, with voter skepticism about politicians on the rise in 1992, Manton's image as a political insider provided fodder for his Republican opponent, aggressive first-time candidate Dennis C. Shea, a 31-year-old lawyer who once served as legal counsel to Republican Sen. Bob Dole of Kansas. Shea portrayed Manton as a local party boss who busied himself in Congress taking overseas junkets, enjoying perks and voting for House pay raises. He also played up Manton's 17 overdrafts at the House bank.

Manton's precinct organization in the Queens part of the redrawn 7th District delivered for him; he took 59 percent of the vote there. But in the part of the Bronx added to Manton's base in redistricting, he edged Shea with just 52 percent. Overall, Manton's 57 percent tally was his lowest election tally since his 1984 race.

Republicans did not follow up in 1994, however, failing to nominate anyone against Manton. He crushed a Conservative Party candidate and in 1996 dispatched his GOP challenger with 71 percent.

The 1984 contest marked a turnaround for Manton. In 1972, as a junior member of the New York City Council, Manton unsuccessfully challenged longtime Democratic Rep. James J. Delaney in the House primary. He tried again for the seat when Delaney retired in 1978; Ferraro defeated him decisively.

But when Mondale tapped Ferraro in 1984, Manton, by then a veteran councilman, became a front-runner to replace her. He eked out a narrow primary win and then defeated conservative Republican Serphin R. Maltese, whose vigorous campaign held the heavily favored Manton to 53 percent. By 1986, Manton had a firm grip on his district (then numbered the 9th).

Manton won the Queens Democratic post in October 1986. He succeeded an interim replacement to Donald Manes, the Queens borough president and longtime party chairman who committed suicide earlier that year following his implication in a city corruption scandal.

HOUSE ELECTIONS

1996 General		
Thomas J. Manton (D)	78,848	(71%)
Rose Birtley (R,C,INDC)	32,092	(29%)
1994 General		
Thomas J. Manton (D)	58,935	(87%)
Robert E. Hurley (C)	8,698	(13%)

Previous Winning Percentages: 1992 (57%) **1990** (64%) **1988** (100%) **1986** (69%) **1984** (53%)

CAMPAIGN FINANCE

	Receipts	Receipts from PACs	Expend-itures
1996			
Manton (D)	$531,149	$293,323 (55%)	$374,982
Birtley (R)	$62,190	$4,236 (7%)	$62,209
1994			
Manton (D)	$614,706	$409,848 (67%)	$360,940

DISTRICT VOTE FOR PRESIDENT

	1996		1992
D	99,813 (68%)	**D**	91,803 (56%)
R	37,230 (25%)	**R**	57,783 (35%)
I	7,437 (5%)	**I**	15,118 (9%)

KEY VOTES

1997	
Ban "partial birth" abortions	Y
1996	
Approve farm bill	N
Deny public education to illegal immigrants	N
Repeal ban on certain assault-style weapons	N
Increase minimum wage	Y
Freeze defense spending	Y
Approve welfare overhaul	Y
1995	
Approve balanced-budget constitutional amendment	N
Relax Clean Water Act regulations	N
Oppose limits on environmental regulations	Y
Reduce projected Medicare spending	N
Approve GOP budget with tax and spending cuts	N

VOTING STUDIES

	Presidential Support		Party Unity		Conservative Coalition	
Year	**S**	**O**	**S**	**O**	**S**	**O**
1996	73	24	77	19	65	33
1995	68	32	82	15	47	50
1994	83	14	86	6	47	50
1993	84	11	82	10	50	45
1992	30	63	84	9	40	52
1991	35	58	86	6	22	76

INTEREST GROUP RATINGS

Year	ADA	AFL-CIO	CCUS	ACU
1996	65	n/a	33	26
1995	65	92	38	29
1994	70	75	45	15
1993	70	100	9	17
1992	85	83	29	8
1991	80	92	20	10

8 Jerrold Nadler (D)

Of Manhattan — Elected 1992; 3rd full term

Biographical Information
Born: June 13, 1947, Brooklyn, N.Y.
Education: Columbia U., A.B. 1969; Fordham U., J.D. 1978.
Occupation: State official; lawyer.
Family: Wife, Joyce L. Miller; one child.
Religion: Jewish.
Political Career: N.Y. Assembly, 1977-92; candidate for Manhattan Borough President, 1985; candidate for New York City Comptroller, 1989.
Capitol Office: 2448 Rayburn Bldg. 20515; 225-5635.

Committees
Judiciary
Commercial & Administrative Law (ranking); Constitution
Transportation & Infrastructure
Railroads; Surface Transportation

In Washington: Nadler's left-of-center views are shared by most of his politically active constituents in the 8th, a West Side Manhattan district with many liberal Jewish voters and a sizable group of politically active gays and lesbians.

Nadler gained the seat after Democratic Rep. Ted Weiss died of heart failure the day before the 1992 primary. By dint of his adiposity and his strong advocacy of liberal causes, Nadler made an immediate impression on Capitol Hill. He has continued Weiss' tradition of supporting gay and women's rights, and of favoring less spending on defense and more on the poor.

A Judiciary Committee member, Nadler began the 105th Congress as ranking Democrat on the Commercial and Administrative Law Subcommittee. The panel has jurisdiction over bankruptcy law, administrative law, laws governing federal contracting and the Legal Services Corporation (LSC), which provides legal counsel to the poor.

"I look forward to working with my colleagues on both sides of the aisle to ensure the fair and efficient administration of justice, the protection of consumers, sensible and effective safeguards for the environment and public health, and the right to competent legal representation for the rights of all Americans," Nadler said in January 1997 as he assumed his ranking position.

He defends the LSC against critics who feel that the agency litigates not just in behalf of needy citizens but as an advocate of liberal social causes. While some conservatives want to abolish the LSC, Nadler would like to repeal some of the existing restrictions on the types of cases Legal Services lawyers can handle.

In the 104th Congress, he was the co-author of an unsuccessful Democratic alternative to the GOP-backed counterterrorism bill. The Democrats acted after Rep. Bob Barr, R-Ga., successfully stripped several key provisions from the bill, including ones to allow the administration to designate certain groups as terrorist, deny them entry visas and bar them from fundraising in the United States; to expedite deportation of aliens suspected of terrorism; to make it easier to use illegally obtained wiretap evidence in terrorism cases; and to make it easier to prosecute those who provide guns later used in a violent crime.

The Democratic substitute amended rather than deleted these provisions. And it dropped the Republican bill's restrictions on federal appeals by death row inmates and other prisoners. The amendment failed, receiving just 129 votes.

Nadler is an opponent of the death penalty, and he tried unsuccessfully to replace the federal death penalty provisions in the 1994 crime bill with a requirement for life imprisonment without parole. He was able to insert a modification to the "three strikes and you're out" provision in the crime bill to allow inmates older than 70 who had served 30 years to be released if they posed no threat to society. Prison officials and other critics of the "three strikes" provision, which mandates life imprisonment for three-time felons, had warned that federal prisons might become high-cost geriatric wards.

He has been particularly sensitive to the concerns of the gay community, a priority that also is good politics for him. In the 1994 Democratic primary, Nadler turned back a challenge from an openly gay, openly HIV-positive New York City councilman, Thomas K. Duane.

Nadler condemned the Clinton administration's failure to lift the ban on homosexuals in the military, saying, "The new 'don't ask, don't tell, don't get caught' policy represents a reaffirmation of the policy of official bigotry by the United States, with changes only in the methods by which that bigotry will be enforced."

And on a 1994 education bill, Nadler lambasted the authors of an amendment that would have mandated a cutoff of federal funds to any school district that used instructional materials depicting homosexuals. "Do we not believe in local control of education?" he asked. "Or are we in favor of local control only when local school officials agree with us and with our prejudices?"

Later in 1994, Nadler introduced a bill to earmark $1.8 billion to find a cure for AIDS. He said he

NEW YORK 8
West Side Manhattan; parts of southwest Brooklyn

A strong strain of liberalism prevails on the West Side of Manhattan. Containing nearly three-fifths of the 8th's population, this area gives Democrats a lock on the district. This part of the island is Nadler's base, as it was the base for his predecessor, the late Ted Weiss. The West Side has many liberal-voting Jewish residents and one of the nation's largest concentrations of gays and lesbians. The portion of Brooklyn that has the remainder of the 8th's population does not look very different. Like the Manhattan side, this is a thoroughly urban area of apartment dwellers; Jews are a large constituency.

But while most of Manhattan's Jewish residents lead mainly secular lifestyles, the Brooklyn part of the 8th has large communities of Hasidic Jews, whose religion-centered lives and orthodox reading of the Old Testament set a more conservative political tone. Though Democrats have a huge registration advantage, these communities are not averse to supporting socially conservative Republicans who meet a major condition: strong support for Israel. One such figure, Sen. Alfonse M. D'Amato, was backed by key Hasidic leaders during his 1992 campaign against a liberal Jewish Democrat.

Although Democrats still typically dominate the Brooklyn part, their numbers are slightly lower than in Manhattan. Nadler won 84 percent of the vote in the Manhattan part of the 8th and 78 percent in Brooklyn in 1996.

The district's liberal leaning belies its status as a world center of finance and commerce. The Wall Street financial district is at the southern tip of Manhattan in the 8th, as are the twin towers of the World Trade Center, the site of a terrorist bomb attack in February 1993. The Empire State Building, in midtown, long reigned as the world's tallest skyscraper.

The 8th also is a world-famous cultural center. Here are Lincoln Center, the Broadway theater district and Madison Square Garden, home of the New York Knicks and Rangers. Greenwich Village, a longtime magnet for artists, is home to New York University; the gay community, once a strong force in the Village, has moved to Chelsea.

Much of the 8th's low-income population, including a number of blacks and Hispanics, lives in its far northern part, near Columbia University (in the 15th District). In midtown near the river is a working-class area, initially populated by Irish-Americans, that was long known as one of the city's roughest areas.

After crossing the Brooklyn-Battery Tunnel and skimming along the Brooklyn waterfront, the 8th takes in mainly residential areas, including the orthodox Jewish center of Borough Park and part of ethnically mixed, racially tense Bensonhurst. At its southern end, the district meets the Atlantic Ocean at Brighton Beach, the setting for some of Neil Simon's autobiographical plays and home to a large number of Russian immigrants. Coney Island, whose century-old amusement park is a place of faded glory, has a population mix of minorities and Jews, many of them elderly.

1990 Population: 580,337. White 466,355 (80%), Black 49,725 (9%), Other 64,257 (11%). Hispanic origin 73,580 (13%). 18 and over 486,296 (84%), 62 and over 103,793 (18%). Median age: 37.

wanted the same type of concentrated government effort in finding an AIDS cure as was directed to the invention of the nuclear bomb.

Thinking again of his constituents, he introduced a bill that would index federal tax brackets to reflect regional differences in the cost of living. He said the cost of living in New York City is more than 2 1/2 times as great as in some other areas of the country. "So pretending that a New York City family earning $50,000 per year is high-income is a joke — a bad joke, if you happen to be a New Yorker," he said.

He opposed legislation that would prohibit states from taxing the retirement income of former residents. He argued that the measure was unfair to the states where the retirees worked, because the workers benefited from government services during their careers while their pension funds were shielded from taxation. Many New York City retirees move to Florida, which has no income tax.

On another local issue, Nadler managed to amend the fiscal 1996 transportation appropriations bill to prohibit the use of federal funds to relocate the West Side Highway. The proposed relocation of that road project would have allowed an unobstructed view of the Hudson River for residents of a new luxury housing development promoted by Donald Trump. Nadler is a member of the Transportation and Infrastructure Committee.

When the House passed legislation in 1995 designed to wean Amtrak from dependence on federal subsidies, Nadler weighed in with an amendment to force Amtrak to open up its Northeast corridor tracks to more freight trains. Under a contract between Conrail and Amtrak, Conrail has the exclusive rights for freight business on those tracks — an arrangement Nadler called an unfair "giveaway to big business."

But Rep. Bud Shuster, R-Pa., chairman of the House Transportation and Infrastructure Committee, responded that doing so would increase freight traffic in the busiest rail corridor in the country. And, he said, Congress has no business abrogating a contract between two corporate entities. The House defeated the amendment.

Nadler also unsuccessfully argued against a Transportation Committee decision to sell Governors Island in New York Harbor. The island was sold by the Manhatas Indians in 1637 for a reported price of two ax heads, some nails and other small objects. It is best known as the site of international summit meetings during the 1980s and 1990s. It has been home to a Coast Guard facility since 1966. The Coast Guard has indicated it is preparing to shut down the facility.

Nadler argued that the ramifications of the sale had not been thoroughly explored. "I don't necessarily object to selling Governors Island," he said. "I object to the haste with which it's being undertaken."

He has used his position on the Transportation Committee to seek improvements to the Port of New York and New Jersey. He supports expanding Brooklyn's port and building a rail freight tunnel. In 1996, he successfully proposed an amendment to the water resources development act that instructed the Army Corps of Engineers to look at the New York side of the harbor as it studies the need to deepen port channels.

His impact, however, was most keenly felt within his own party caucus. The "Nadler rule" prohibits ranking Democrats of full committees from also heading subcommittees.

At Home: Brooklyn-born, Nadler spent his early years on a New Jersey poultry farm. His family moved back to New York City after the farm failed.

His early political ventures found him organizing anti-war students to campaign for Eugene J. McCarthy in the 1968 New Hampshire presidential primary, warning tenants about lead paint and campaigning for Weiss in an early unsuccessful bid for Congress. In 1976, Nadler narrowly won an open seat in the state Legislature and served for 16 years. In Albany, he authored several laws concerning domestic violence and child support.

When Weiss died on the eve of the September 1992 Democratic primary, voters renominated him nonetheless, giving party officials the right to pick a successor. That set off a scramble among the district's ample cadre of Democratic activists, with six candidates jumping into the frenetic nine-day race for the nomination.

Nadler quickly became the presumptive leader. While other potential nominees such as former Rep. Bella S. Abzug were better-known to the public, Nadler had longstanding ties to the insiders who would cast the votes. Once gaining the party nomination, he then easily won the general election.

In the 1994 primary, Duane faulted the party gathering that awarded Nadler the nomination in 1992. He attempted to run to Nadler's left while trying to attract gay voters. Against Nadler, the quintessential organizational politician, he did not even come close. Nadler won the primary by a 2-1 ratio.

Nadler had another primary challenge in 1996, but won easily and coasted to another term in November.

HOUSE ELECTIONS

1996 General		
Jerrold Nadler (D,L)	131,943	(82%)
Michael Benjamin (R,FDM)	26,028	(16%)
George A. Galip Jr. (C)	2,381	(1%)
1996 Primary		
Jerrold Nadler (D,L)	28,466	(84%)
Brian W. Steel (D)	3,903	(12%)
Matthew W. Sperling (D)	1,668	(5%)
1994 General		
Jerrold Nadler (D,L)	109,946	(82%)
David L. Askren (R)	21,132	(16%)
Margaret V. Byrnes (C)	3,008	(2%)

Previous Winning Percentages: 1992 (81%) **1992†** (100%)

† Special election

CAMPAIGN FINANCE

	Receipts	Receipts from PACs	Expend-itures
1996			
Nadler (D)	$798,015	$248,837 (31%)	$780,423
Benjamin (R)	$134,322	$1,166 (1%)	$121,422
1994			
Nadler (D)	$797,183	$295,672 (37%)	$791,767
Askren (R)	$16,009	$14 (0%)	$16,172

DISTRICT VOTE FOR PRESIDENT

1996		1992	
D	147,864 (78%)	**D**	169,005 (77%)
R	30,141 (16%)	**R**	37,614 (17%)
I	5,142 (3%)	**I**	12,216 (6%)

KEY VOTES

1997	
Ban "partial birth" abortions	N
1996	
Approve farm bill	N
Deny public education to illegal immigrants	-
Repeal ban on certain assault-style weapons	N
Increase minimum wage	Y
Freeze defense spending	Y
Approve welfare overhaul	N
1995	
Approve balanced-budget constitutional amendment	N
Relax Clean Water Act regulations	N
Oppose limits on environmental regulations	Y
Reduce projected Medicare spending	N
Approve GOP budget with tax and spending cuts	N

VOTING STUDIES

	Presidential Support		Party Unity		Conservative Coalition	
Year	S	O	S	O	S	O
1996	72	22	93	4	4	92
1995	86	12	96	2	4	96
1994	72	26	88	4	6	83
1993	75	24	92	3	7	86

INTEREST GROUP RATINGS

Year	ADA	AFL-CIO	CCUS	ACU
1996	100	n/a	7	0
1995	100	100	8	0
1994	100	100	17	5
1993	95	100	9	8

9 Charles E. Schumer (D)

Of Brooklyn — Elected 1980, 9th term

Biographical Information
Born: Nov. 23, 1950, Brooklyn, N.Y.
Education: Harvard U., B.A. 1971, J.D. 1974.
Occupation: Lawyer.
Family: Wife, Iris Weinshall; two children.
Religion: Jewish.
Political Career: N.Y. Assembly, 1975-81.
Capitol Office: 2211 Rayburn Bldg. 20515; 225-6616.

Committees
Banking & Financial Services
Capital Markets, Securities & Government Sponsored Enterprises; Financial Institutions & Consumer Credit
Judiciary
Crime (ranking); Immigration & Claims

In Washington: Schumer finished his 1996 campaign with a balance of $5 million — more than any other House candidate — and said in April 1997 that he would challenge Republican Sen. Alfonse M. D'Amato in 1998. Schumer's spring announcement ended months of speculation that he would run statewide, either against D'Amato or Republican Gov. George E. Pataki. Schumer said the Senate race was "the right fit."

During the first two years Bill Clinton occupied the White House, Schumer was at the center of congressional anti-crime efforts. The Democratic-controlled 103rd Congress imposed a five-day waiting period for handgun purchases, banned certain semiautomatic assault-style weapons and cleared a massive anti-crime bill that included federal grants for municipalities to hire up to 100,000 new police officers.

But with the Republican takeover of Congress in 1994, Schumer spent the last two years of Clinton's first term trying to prevent the GOP from undoing everything he had accomplished earlier. As ranking Democrat on House Judiciary's Crime Subcommittee, he fought GOP efforts to repeal the assault-weapons ban and undo the 1994 crime bill. Schumer, third-ranking Democrat on the full Judiciary Committee, retained his ranking spot on the Crime Subcommittee in the 105th Congress; he was the only Democrat on the committee who chose not to shift to a new ranking subcommittee seat.

In March 1996, the House voted, 239-173, to repeal the assault-weapons ban passed in the 103rd, even though proponents of repeal knew they did not have much chance in the Senate, which never took up the measure. Schumer charged that the House vote was a political payoff to the National Rifle Association, whose support for GOP candidates in 1994 played a part in the party winning a House majority. "[Speaker] Newt Gingrich bent his knee and is kissing the ring of the NRA," Schumer said.

A year earlier, Schumer had fought GOP efforts to rewrite other parts of the 1994 crime bill. He said Republicans simply were trying to erase a political success for Clinton and his party. "It's a political one-upsmanship game," he said.

The Republicans proposed combining funds authorized for hiring new police officers and for a number of other crime prevention programs into a $10 billion block grant program. The GOP goal was to give local governments more flexibility in deciding how to spend the money.

In February 1995, Schumer offered an amendment on the House floor to keep $7.5 billion for the "cops on the streets" program, leaving $2.5 billion for the GOP's proposed block grants. Schumer and other Democrats pointed out that many communities already were hiring new police officers under the program. But some Republicans cited communities that could not afford to pay the 25 percent matching requirement for the street-cops grants, or that needed money for other crime-fighting purposes. After considerable debate, lawmakers rejected the Schumer proposal, 196-235.

Schumer played a seminal role in crafting the $30.2 billion anti-crime measure that cleared Congress in August 1994 after a tortured journey through the House and Senate. He used his chairmanship of Judiciary's Crime Subcommittee to craft a bill that included extensive crime-prevention funding favored by liberals and strict punitive measures favored by conservatives. But a division of the NRA, angered by the bill's assault-weapons ban, ran a full-page ad in USA Today calling Schumer "the criminal's best friend."

Schumer was unfazed, saying, "I wear this like a badge of honor."

After a coalition of Republicans and members of the Congressional Black Caucus united to vote down the rule needed to bring the crime bill to the floor, Schumer accused Republicans of trying to kill the bill for political gain. "It's clear what the Republican leadership wants," he said. "No bill at any cost."

But after the Clinton administration and Democratic leaders agreed to shrink the bill's price tag, enough Republicans reversed their

NEW YORK 9
Parts of Brooklyn and Queens — Sheepshead Bay; Forest Hills

Contiguity, a supposed criterion for congressional districts, may be in the eye of the beholder. But it would be hard to find a more geographically disparate district anywhere than the 9th, which takes in widely separated parts of Brooklyn and Queens.

One of the most interesting of the many abstract designs on the current map, the 9th reaches a point in the Park Slope section of central Brooklyn, then follows a narrow corridor south before broadening out along that borough's waterfront. It jumps across an inlet to the Rockaways, running the length of the narrow peninsula that forms the southern part of Queens. It also heads back across Jamaica Bay (touching several islands that make up a wildlife refuge) to the mainland and follows another narrow band north, before broadening out across a swath of west-central Queens.

The only connections between the three regions are the two auto causeways to and from the Rockaways and the broad waters of Jamaica Bay. At the south side of the mainland, the district's pieces are separated by about a mile across the 10th District. But at the northern extremes, the Queens and Brooklyn branches of the 9th are more than four miles apart, with parts of the 10th, 11th and 12th districts in between.

It is only when the demographics of the 9th are considered that its design begins to make sense. Under the mandates of the Voting Rights Act, remappers drew the 9th around the minority-group concentrations in the intervening districts, two of which are majority black, the other majority Hispanic. As a result, the population is about 82 percent non-Hispanic white.

The lack of a large minority base does not keep the 9th from being a regularly Democratic district that is tailor-made for Schumer. Like the all-Brooklyn district Schumer represented during the 1980s, the mostly middle-class and residential 9th has large Jewish and ethnic populations (mainly Italian- and Irish-Americans) that give it a strong Democratic flavor. Schumer polled 75 percent of the vote in 1996 while Bill Clinton garnered 66 percent in the presidential race.

There are pockets of social conservatism, however, and racial tension is not unknown. The Howard Beach community in Queens is still living down a 1986 incident in which a gang of whites chased a black man onto a highway, where he was struck by a car and killed.

From its Brooklyn tip in Park Slope, an upscale community hard by sprawling Prospect Park, the 9th takes in the Brooklyn College campus and such middle-class areas as Sheepshead Bay and Canarsie. It then crosses the Marine Parkway Bridge to Queens, running the length of the peninsula from Breezy Point to Far Rockaway.

Cross Bay Boulevard carries the district back to the mainland at Howard Beach, then north to Woodhaven. At the northeast corner of the 9th are two of its wealthiest communities, Forest Hills and Kew Gardens.

1990 Population: 580,338. White 508,396 (88%), Black 19,156 (3%), Other 52,786 (9%). Hispanic origin 49,220 (8%). 18 and over 469,579 (81%), 62 and over 134,443 (23%). Median age: 39.

votes to move the bill to the floor and pass it.

Even though the Republican majority made it a tough task, Schumer in the 104th backed the Clinton administration's attempt to pass strong anti-terrorism legislation in the wake of the April 1995 bombing of a federal office building in Oklahoma City. Schumer was enraged after the House passed an amendment by Bob Barr, R-Ga., to eliminate language banning terrorist organizations from raising money in the United States, making it harder for the federal government to keep people linked to terrorist organizations out of the country, and making it easier to convict people who sold or traded a gun to someone who used it to commit a felony or terrorist act. Observed Schumer: "Hamas [the militant Islamic group] has found a new best friend in America: the National Rifle Association."

Schumer went after the NRA again in July 1995, as he objected to House hearings into the 1993 Bureau of Alcohol, Tobacco and Firearms (ATF) raid of the Branch Davidian compound in Waco, Texas. The hearings were being conducted by the Judiciary Crime Subcommittee and the Government Reform and Oversight Subcommittee on National Security.

"From the beginning, these hearings have had the odor of bias hanging over them," Schumer said. "And over the last week, we've discovered where that smell is coming from — the National Rifle Association."

Florida Republican Bill McCollum, the Crime Subcommittee chairman, hit back hard at Schumer for suggesting that the hearings were being orchestrated by the NRA as part of its long-running feud with the ATF. "The Clinton administration, Schumer and perhaps others run the risk of fanning the flames of conspiracy theories," McCollum said.

Although the Crime Subcommittee is where Schumer has concentrated much energy of late, he also is active on the Banking Committee, where he is the fourth-ranking Democrat. In July 1996, he joined with Financial Institutions

Subcommittee Chairwoman Marge Roukema, R-N.J., in sponsoring legislation to strengthen and write into law current regulations that require automatic teller machine (ATM) operators to display, at the point of transaction, fees that are imposed upon a consumer who is not a customer of the bank owning the machine. The bill would beef up current disclosure requirements to require ATM owners to display the new surcharges both with a sign and on the electronic screen of the machine, and it would require that a consumer be allowed to cancel the transaction.

He has other interests as well. During the February 1996 debate on reauthorizing farm programs, Schumer sponsored an amendment to eliminate price supports for sugar. He and Dan Miller, R-Fla., proposed phasing out the program over five years, a tactical retreat from an earlier version that would have eliminated the program immediately. The amendment barely failed, 208-217. Schumer later voted against the final version of the farm bill.

As a member of the majority, Schumer thrived not only in the public eye, but also in the back rooms that are the incubators of legislative accomplishment. He is shrewd and tough, sees the big picture but attends to detail, and can make necessary compromises. A keen mind and an abundance of energy have enabled him over the years to put his imprint on housing, trade, immigration, crime, farm and banking policy.

At Home: Schumer began his political career as a state Assembly aide to Brooklyn Democrat Stephen J. Solarz, who moved to the House in 1974. After winning three Assembly terms on his own, Schumer won a House seat in 1980, succeeding Elizabeth Holtzman, and renewed his alliance with Solarz.

However, by the end of the 1980s, Schumer and Solarz were rivals for local and national political stature. Their relationship was further undercut by speculation that the two might be thrown together in redistricting. Untested at the polls over the decade in their heavily Democratic districts, both Schumer and Solarz piled up more than $2 million in campaign funds in case they were matched up in 1992.

But the face-off never happened. The redistricting plan dismembered Solarz's former 13th District, and part of his constituency was placed in the new 9th, where Schumer planned to run. But Schumer had a substantial territorial advantage there — the district maintained his largely Jewish turf in southeast Brooklyn — and Solarz opted instead for a major gamble: He ran in the newly created Hispanic-majority 12th and lost a six-way primary to Puerto Rican activist Nydia M. Velázquez. Schumer made out much better. He faced no major-party challenger in either the primary or general elections, winning a seventh term with nearly 90 percent over a Conservative Party candidate. He has continued to pile up big re-election scores through the decade.

HOUSE ELECTIONS

1996 General		
Charles E. Schumer (D,L)	107,107	(75%)
Robert J. Verga (R,INDC,FDM)	30,488	(21%)
Michael Mossa (C)	5,618	(4%)
1994 General		
Charles E. Schumer (D,L)	95,139	(73%)
James McCall (R,C)	35,880	(27%)

Previous Winning Percentages: **1992** (89%) **1990** (80%) **1988** (78%) **1986** (93%) **1984** (72%) **1982** (79%) **1980** (77%)

CAMPAIGN FINANCE

	Receipts	Receipts from PACs		Expend-itures
1996				
Schumer (D)	$3,318,153	$307,502	(9%)	$487,841
Verga (R)	$37,325	$16	(0%)	$36,351
1994				
Schumer (D)	$274,394	$97,900	(36%)	$157,108
McCall (R)	$8,435	$5,714	(68%)	$13,831

DISTRICT VOTE FOR PRESIDENT

	1996		1992
D	113,939 (66%)	**D**	121,110 (59%)
R	47,498 (28%)	**R**	66,917 (33%)
I	8,248 (5%)	**I**	17,574 (9%)

KEY VOTES

1997	
Ban "partial birth" abortions	N
1996	
Approve farm bill	N
Deny public education to illegal immigrants	N
Repeal ban on certain assault-style weapons	N
Increase minimum wage	Y
Freeze defense spending	Y
Approve welfare overhaul	N
1995	
Approve balanced-budget constitutional amendment	N
Relax Clean Water Act regulations	N
Oppose limits on environmental regulations	Y
Reduce projected Medicare spending	N
Approve GOP budget with tax and spending cuts	N

VOTING STUDIES

	Presidential Support		Party Unity		Conservative Coalition	
Year	S	O	S	O	S	O
1996	80	16	86	9	22	69
1995	81	12	83	10	26	67
1994	79	17	86	5	31	69
1993	81	17	93	3	16	84
1992	18	76	90	5	13	81
1991	28	70	89	6	19	78

INTEREST GROUP RATINGS

Year	ADA	AFL-CIO	CCUS	ACU
1996	90	n/a	31	5
1995	80	100	32	4
1994	90	75	58	5
1993	95	100	9	9
1992	95	82	25	0
1991	85	92	20	0

10 Edolphus Towns (D)

Of Brooklyn — Elected 1982, 8th term

Biographical Information
Born: July 21, 1934, Chadbourn, N.C.
Education: North Carolina A&T State U., B.S. 1956; Adelphi U., M.S.W. 1973.
Military Service: Army, 1956-58.
Occupation: Professor; hospital administrator.
Family: Wife, Gwendolyn Forbes; two children.
Religion: Independent Baptist.
Political Career: Brooklyn Borough deputy president, 1976-82.

Capitol Office: 2232 Rayburn Bldg. 20515; 225-5936.

Committees
Commerce
Energy & Power; Finance & Hazardous Materials; Health & Environment
Government Reform & Oversight
Human Resources (ranking)

In Washington: Now in his eighth term, Towns has reached the upper tier of seniority among Democrats on the Commerce Committee, a panel with wide-ranging legislative interests and only two other black members. While he has gone to bat for pharmaceutical companies, the tobacco industry, alarm-service providers and other business interests, Towns also pleads for attention to economically disadvantaged people who cannot find affordable health care. This is a tough sell at a time when many legislators are focused instead on trying to restrain the cost of government-financed health care,

Towns champions what he calls "progressive science" — which emphasizes preventive medicine — and a sampling of bills he has introduced highlight his priorities in this regard.

He has proposed improving health care in medically disadvantaged communities by developing comprehensive managed care programs. He has proposed trying to reduce infant mortality by improving health care services provided to pregnant women under Medicaid. He introduced the Medicaid Women's Basic Health Coverage Act of 1997, which would pay for mammography and pap smears, which are used to detect cancer.

In February 1996, Towns took the National Cancer Institute to task for withdrawing its previous recommendation that women under 50 get annual mammograms — a procedure that diagnoses breast cancer. "Both early detection and screening in younger women can be beneficial in combating this disease," Towns said. "If you can recommend an appropriate daily allowance for vegetables in the American diet, you should be able to recommend lifesaving screenings for American women." In February 1997, he introduced a resolution seeking accurate guidelines for breast cancer screenings.

During the 103rd Congress' debate on health care reform, many liberals like Towns gave President Clinton credit for putting the issue at center stage, even though they favored setting up a more sweeping "single payer" system instead of Clinton's "managed competition" concept. But Towns was such an insistent critic of Clinton's proposal that at times his views sounded indistinguishable from those of conservatives committed to killing the administration's reform efforts.

Towns also expressed concern that changes in the nation's health care delivery system might impede pharmaceutical manufacturers' ability to develop new drugs. Preserving the profitability of that industry is of great importance to Towns, since the Pfizer pharmaceutical company is located in his district. Drug companies, along with tobacco companies, are among Towns' biggest campaign contributors.

The son of a North Carolina sharecropper, Towns has been a reliable vote for tobacco interests, opposing a public smoking ban in the 103rd Congress and opposing a June 1996 effort aimed at killing federally subsidized crop insurance for tobacco farmers.

On another front, Towns successfully amended the telecommunications deregulation bill that passed in the 104th to require the Bell operating companies to wait six years, not five, before providing alarm-monitoring services. The amendment was sought by the alarm services industry.

And in 1996, he intervened with the Federal Communications Commission to prevent the giant cable television company Tele-Communications Inc. from moving into the direct broadcast service market. TCI needed an extension in order to build a DBS system, but the commission voted against it, marking the first time such a request was rejected. Wrote Towns before the vote: "It is my understanding the FCC is considering transferring, for a nominal fee, the license . . . to a cable consortium headed by John Malone at TCI. The public will be harmed by the elimination of competitive alternatives."

When Democrats last controlled the House, Towns was chairman of a subcommittee on the Government Operations Committee. That panel was reconstituted by the new GOP majority in 1995 as the Government Reform and Oversight Committee, and there in the 104th Towns fought a

NEW YORK 10
Parts of Brooklyn —Bedford-Stuyvesant; Brooklyn Heights

During the 1980s, Towns represented a Brooklyn district in which blacks made up just a plurality of the population; a large Hispanic constituency comprised a competing power bloc. But in the 1992 redistricting, many of these constituents were drawn off into the new Hispanic-majority 12th District, which forms the western and northern borders of the 10th. However, the 10th could be affected by a February 1997 federal court ruling declaring the 12th an unconstitutional racial gerrymander.

Blacks make up more than three-fifths of the 10th's population; non-Hispanic whites and Hispanics are roughly one-fifth each. This breakdown appears enough to ensure the election of a black representative. In 1992, Towns faced a primary challenge from Susan Alter, a white city councilwoman with a largely black constituency. Towns won with 62 percent of the vote.

If there is political action here, it is almost certain to be in the Democratic primary. More than 80 percent of the 10th's registered voters are Democrats. Towns polled 91 percent of the vote in 1996; Bill Clinton received 90 percent.

The district is roughly the shape of an upside-down U. It runs from just inside Brooklyn's industrial waterfront along New York Bay to the Queens border and the shores of Jamaica Bay. Connecting the east and west parts of the district is Atlantic Avenue, one of Brooklyn's main east-west thoroughfares and commercial corridors.

In the central part of the district is Bedford-Stuyvesant, a mainly low-income black area. Though troubles abound, the community has been a target for economic revival efforts since the 1960s, when Sen. Robert F. Kennedy promoted an urban industrial park regarded as a forerunner of the "enterprise zone" concept.

To the east is the even more devastated East New York, which has one of New York City's highest murder rates. The 10th then follows Pennsylvania Avenue south to the Belt Parkway and Jamaica Bay. Nearby is Starrett City, a high-rise apartment complex that is racially integrated. But there are parts of working-class Canarsie, which has a large Italian-American population, where blacks are known to be unwelcome. The 10th also has an appendage that reaches into mostly black East Flatbush.

The predominantly white and affluent parts of the 10th are on its west side. This section includes the landmarked brownstones of Brooklyn Heights, Boerum Hill and part of Park Slope, and middle-class, Italian-American Carroll Gardens. Much of Brooklyn's civic life — including Borough Hall, its court houses, St. Francis College and the Brooklyn campus of Long Island University — is here.

The biggest problem here is the district's aging infrastructure. One of the oldest areas of the city, its water and sewer lines are prone to collapse. Heavy truck traffic is eroding the Brooklyn-Queens Expressway and residential streets leading up to the Brooklyn and Manhattan bridges (located in the 12th District, which hugs the waterfront).

1990 Population: 580,335. White 155,496 (27%), Black 352,521 (61%), Other 72,318 (12%). Hispanic origin 114,153 (20%). 18 and over 414,607 (71%), 62 and over 69,073 (12%). Median age: 30.

losing battle against Republican efforts to streamline federal grant regulations.

When the committee in April 1996 approved legislation to permit local governments to consolidate disparate federal grants into more flexible spending plans, Towns said he feared the waiver provisions would allow local agencies to subvert labor, environmental and safety laws under the pretext of increased efficiency. Under the bill, recipients could seek waivers of regulations and laws that would inhibit the implementation of their plans.

"This bill guts crucial federal laws that create standards of protection for every American, and that's wrong," he said. Towns proposed an amendment prohibiting the waiver of any federal law, although waivers of regulations would still be allowed. Republican Constance A. Morella of Maryland, however, amended the Towns proposal to allow statutory waivers that deal with procedural or administrative changes. Towns' proposal, with the underlying Morella amendment, was adopted in committee, 25-17.

Highlighting his concern about "environmental racism" — including the siting of potentially health-threatening facilities in minority communities — Towns introduced legislation in 1993 to ban the construction of new waste incinerators.

Another interest for Towns has been college athletics and the rights of student athletes. In the early 1990s he pushed and ultimately won passage of the Student Athlete Right to Know Act. Towns worked with two former professional basketball players, then-Rep. Tom McMillen, D-Md., and then-Sen. Bill Bradley, D-N.J., in helping to enact the law requiring colleges to disclose the graduation rates of their scholarship athletes.

Towns endured a spate of negative publicity as the House bank controversy unfolded in the 102nd Congress. He had 408 overdrafts at the bank, and the House ethics committee cited him as having abused banking privileges. Towns explained that a receptionist in his office had embezzled $28,000 from his account to support a drug habit and hid his accounts. "I was the victim," he said.

In 1993, Towns received a letter from federal authorities informing him that the investigation into his accounts had been closed. But publicity from the incident, combined with 1991 news reports that the Congressional Black Caucus (which Towns chaired from 1991-93) had used funds from the office account of a retiring member to pay delinquent taxes, contributed to a perception that Towns and the caucus should have been paying closer attention to their financial affairs. When Republicans took control of the House in 1995, they abolished funding for legislative support organizations such as the Black Caucus, partly on the grounds that their finances had been managed sloppily.

When the House in 1995 approved stringent new rules banning most gifts from lobbyists, Towns was one of only six lawmakers to oppose the resolution.

At Home: After winning a 1982 primary in a newly drawn, majority-minority district (then the 11th), Towns settled in for a decade of political quiet. Towns' calm was disrupted in 1992, when Democratic City Council member Susan D. Alter staged a primary challenge in the redrawn and renumbered 10th District.

A 12-year City Council member, Alter — who in 1980 lost a primary for an open House seat — touted her record on community-level issues. She argued that Towns was too busy cultivating special interest contacts and assailed Towns for being high on the House bank overdraft list.

Redistricting had boosted the district's black population share to 61 percent. Alter, a white candidate, dealt with the demographics by emphasizing that she represented a black-majority council district. But most of the 10th's black leaders stuck with Towns; some challenged Alter's decision to run in a district drawn to preserve black representation. Towns won with 62 percent of the vote, more than doubling Alter's total.

If the remap of 1992 caused him some discomfort, Towns had the remap of 1982 to thank for paving his way into the House. New York's Legislature wanted to make the 11th a largely Hispanic district, but black Democrats in Brooklyn objected to the plan and the Justice Department ultimately threw it out. The final version, creating a constituency almost evenly split between blacks and Hispanics, was much more congenial to Towns.

The new district included some Brooklyn territory that had been represented by white Democratic Rep. Frederick W. Richmond. But Richmond, who had been indicted (and later was convicted) of income-tax evasion and marijuana possession, resigned from the House in 1982.

A social worker who served as deputy Brooklyn borough president, Towns bid for the open 11th and drew support from both party regulars and a rival faction calling for reform. Towns fended off two Hispanic primary contenders to win nomination with 50 percent. He easily won in November, setting a pattern of general election landslides in the Democratic stronghold.

HOUSE ELECTIONS

1996 General		
Edolphus Towns (D,L)	99,889	(91%)
Amelia Smith Parker (R,C,FDM)	8,660	(8%)
1994 General		
Edolphus Towns (D,L)	77,026	(89%)
Amelia Smith Parker (R)	7,995	(9%)
Mildred K. Mahoney (C)	1,489	(2%)

Previous Winning Percentages: **1992** (96%) **1990** (93%) **1988** (89%) **1986** (89%) **1984** (85%) **1982** (84%)

CAMPAIGN FINANCE

	Receipts	Receipts from PACs	Expend-itures
1996			
Towns (D)	$569,271	$265,583 (47%)	$533,824
1994			
Towns (D)	$469,185	$244,777 (52%)	$453,427

VOTING STUDIES

	Presidential Support		Party Unity		Conservative Coalition	
Year	**S**	**O**	**S**	**O**	**S**	**O**
1996	76	20	88	3	8	84
1995	74	17	86	5	17	70
1994	67	15	79	2	11	58
1993	74	20	86	2	5	86
1992	11	64	70	4	10	60
1991	21	69	83	3	3	86

KEY VOTES

1997	
Ban "partial birth" abortions	N
1996	
Approve farm bill	N
Deny public education to illegal immigrants	N
Repeal ban on certain assault-style weapons	N
Increase minimum wage	Y
Freeze defense spending	Y
Approve welfare overhaul	N
1995	
Approve balanced-budget constitutional amendment	N
Relax Clean Water Act regulations	N
Oppose limits on environmental regulations	Y
Reduce projected Medicare spending	N
Approve GOP budget with tax and spending cuts	N

INTEREST GROUP RATINGS

Year	ADA	AFL-CIO	CCUS	ACU
1996	85	n/a	20	0
1995	85	92	14	14
1994	85	100	25	0
1993	95	100	10	5
1992	80	82	14	0
1991	90	100	13	0

DISTRICT VOTE FOR PRESIDENT

	1996		1992
D	134,057 (90%)	**D**	125,206 (83%)
R	9,059 (6%)	**R**	19,177 (13%)
I	2,511 (2%)	**I**	5,711 (4%)

11 Major R. Owens (D)

Of Brooklyn — Elected 1982, 8th term

Biographical Information
Born: June 28, 1936, Memphis, Tenn.
Education: Morehouse College, B.A. 1956; Atlanta U., M.L.S. 1957.
Occupation: Librarian.
Family: Wife, Maria Cuprill; five children.
Religion: Baptist.
Political Career: N.Y. Senate, 1975-83.
Capitol Office: 2305 Rayburn Bldg. 20515; 225-6231.

Committees
Education & Workforce
Early Childhood, Youth & Families; Workforce Protections (ranking)
Government Reform & Oversight
Government Management, Information & Technology; Postal Service

In Washington: "I am one of those who is not ashamed to be called a liberal," Owens said on the House floor in March 1997. "In fact, I am proud of it. I am a liberal, I am progressive, all of those kinds of things that people seem to shrink away from. Our group has not disappeared. We really represent the majority of Americans."

It's hard to verify that claim, but it is worth noting that, despite Republican majorities in both the House and Senate, liberals such as Owens did not see the 104th Congress enact legislation allowing employers to offer their workers compensatory time off rather than overtime pay, and the left was able to celebrate passage into law of a 90-cent increase in the minimum wage.

Those issues were of particular concern to Owens, who is ranking member of the Workforce Protections Subcommittee of the House Education and the Workforce Committee (formerly Economic and Educational Opportunities). On that panel, one of the most ardent backers of labor — Owens — leads the Democratic defense against one of business' strongest supporters — subcommittee Chairman Cass Ballenger, R-N.C.

A member of the House Progressive Caucus, the most left-leaning of the congressional policy groups, Owens is diligent, passionate — and sometimes even belligerent — about issues affecting people he believes are oppressed or discriminated against. "We have a situation in America where we cannot take care of, or we refuse to take care of, a large part of the population of our children," Owens said in March 1997. "We have already dropped any discussion of a universal health plan. Beyond the children, there are 40 million Americans who are not covered, and that number is increasing all the time. We are not even discussing it. This is an era where those who have the most are in charge. In the last election, unfortunately, large numbers of people did not bother to come out and exercise their democratic right and vote, so there is a great deal of contempt for people out there who have needs and did not bother to go vote to protect their rights or their needs."

He has been a strong supporter of federal aid for the disabled. In January 1995, he unsuccessfully tried to add to the Republicans' unfunded mandates bill an exemption for laws that protect the health of disabled people. The House rejected the amendment, 149-275.

And he had problems in May 1996 with a Republican plan to revise funding and disciplinary procedures for the Individuals with Disabilities Education Act, which provides state grants to help ensure access to public education for children with disabilities. The Economic and Educational Opportunities Committee passed the bill, 32-5. "The current law did not need to be overhauled," Owens complained during the markup. "This bill is an attack to establish a beachhead" for Republicans to "attempt a total annihilation of federal support for special education." Interrupted Randy "Duke" Cunningham, R-Calif.: "Do we have to sit here and listen to this demagoguery?"

Owens was most active in supporting organized labor in its fight against several GOP-sponsored bills. In June 1996, for example, Owens criticized the Economic and Educational Opportunities Committee's 20-16 approval of comp time legislation. Owens declared he would tell his constituents: "The Republicans are coming for your overtime pay."

The issue was re-fought in March 1997, after the Republicans gave the bill the number HR 1, denoting its high priority.

"HR 1 is called, rightly by the Democrats, the Paycheck Reduction Act, or some of us call it the Employer Cash Enhancement Act," Owens said. "It deals with changing the Fair Labor Standards Act, which has existed since Franklin Roosevelt and the New Deal. The act did not fall from heaven. It was the result of exploitation of workers by employers in large numbers, exploitation in terms of low payment of wages in general and working workers around the clock, late hours each day, weekends, Sundays, Saturdays."

The House passed the bill, 222-210, but not

NEW YORK 11
Central Brooklyn — Flatbush; Crown Heights; Brownsville

The concentration of black residents in the central core of Brooklyn allowed House mapmakers to construct the 11th as a rather compact district; its minority majority is one of the largest of any of the House districts. Seventy-four percent of the 11th's residents are African-American. People of Hispanic origin top 10 percent of the population. Non-Hispanic whites make up 19 percent.

The 11th follows the overwhelmingly Democratic pattern of minority-dominated districts nationwide. More than 80 percent of the registered voters are Democrats. In 1990 and 1992, Owens ran without Republican opposition; in 1996, he received 92 percent of the vote. Bill Clinton did almost as well; he won 91 percent.

The heart of the 11th is Flatbush. Through the years immediately after World War II, this was a mainly white, working-class area whose residents identified with such early TV characters as the Kramdens, of "The Honeymooners" fame.

Today, Flatbush has a sizable black plurality and a number of Hispanics; much of the white population (about a third of Flatbush's total) is elderly. Though there is some poverty, this remains a working-class area, as does much of adjacent, predominantly black East Flatbush. A large medical complex that includes Kings County Hospital, Kingsbrook Jewish Medical Center and the State University of New York Health Sciences Center is in Flatbush.

To the north, across Eastern Parkway, is Crown Heights, where a black majority and a Hasidic Jewish community have a tense relationship. When the car of an assistant to an orthodox rabbi struck and killed a black child in 1991, rioting broke out, and a Jewish theological student was killed.

Ebbets Field, the home of baseball's Brooklyn Dodgers, was in Flatbush. The team's departure for Los Angeles after the 1957 season deprived the borough of much of its national identity. The stadium site is now a housing project.

At the eastern extreme of the 11th is Brownsville, its most economically troubled community. Many of its residents are on some kind of government income support, especially public assistance.

However, the rapid depopulation that occurred during the 1970s was reversed in the last decade, in part because of an influx of immigrants from the Caribbean, including many Jamaicans, Haitians and Guyanans. (West Indians have also located in many other black communities in the 11th.)

Much of the district's white population lives on its west side, in heavily Jewish, middle-class Kensington and Midwood and in well-to-do Park Slope.

Such attractions as the Brooklyn Museum, Botanical Garden and Academy of Music are in this west section, which rims sprawling Prospect Park (mostly in the 9th District).

1990 Population: 580,337. White 108,289 (19%), Black 429,728 (74%), Other 42,320 (7%). Hispanic origin 67,014 (12%). 18 and over 414,564 (71%), 62 and over 60,151 (10%). Median age: 31.

before Owens tried to exempt workers paid less than $10 an hour. His amendment failed, 182-237.

In April 1996, he was on the short side of a party-line 7-5 vote as the Workforce Protections Subcommittee approved legislation designed to ease Occupational Safety and Health Administration regulations on small businesses. Observed Owens: "Take a minute to meditate on the workers who will die and the mothers and fathers who will suffer if this legislation is enacted."

And when the Economic and Educational Opportunities Committee in March 1996 approved by voice vote legislation that would not require employees to pay commuting time to workers who use company cars to travel to and from work, Owens argued that the measure would allow employers to require workers to work for free. "At a time when corporations are making historic profits, while working families are seeing their wages decline, the Republicans are seeking to enact legislation that literally steals both time and money from workers," Owens said.

He has even brought the rhythm of the streets to Congress, expressing his frustration through rap music. During the 1990 budget-summit talks between the White House and congressional leaders, the Congressional Record reported his lyrics: "At the big white D.C. mansion/There's a meeting of the mob/And the question on the table/Is which beggars will they rob."

Owens said he liked rap for the same reasons it has mass appeal. "Rap is a way that angry young men are getting things off their chest," he said. "So it seemed a good way to get some things off my chest."

For years, he expressed frustration about the nation's policy toward Haiti. First he blasted President George Bush's policy of repatriating Haitian boat people intercepted at sea, calling it a "David Duke immigration policy." As head of the Congressional Black Caucus' Haiti Task Force, Owens emerged as a vocal critic of President Clinton, who continued Bush's policy. In 1994,

Owens was arrested in front of the White House along with five other members who were protesting the repatriation policy.

The only trained librarian in Congress, Owens has emphasized the importance of libraries. He has drawn on his library background for non book issues. During one committee session, he suggested that a variation of the Dewey Decimal System be used on child-welfare program information.

At Home: Owens cofounded the black "reform" faction of the Brooklyn Democratic Party, and his 1982 primary victory over an organization stalwart testified to the movement's progress.

A community organizer in Brooklyn's economically depressed Brownsville section in the mid-1960s, Owens was tapped by Mayor John V. Lindsay to head New York City's Community Development Agency.

In 1974, Owens made his first bid for elective office. Leading a slate of candidates opposing incumbents backed by the Brooklyn Democratic machine, he won a state Senate seat that he would hold for eight years.

When Owens set his sights on the House in 1982, he faced a tough opponent, state Sen. Vander Beatty, who as deputy Democratic leader in the state Senate had built a patronage empire in the Brooklyn black community. But Owens capitalized on Beatty's unsavory connections: A longtime Beatty ally, former City Councilman Samuel Wright, was convicted of extortion and conspiracy in 1978. Owens emphasized his own reputation for honesty and his scandal-free tenure as community development chief. He won by a narrow margin.

Beatty challenged the result, accusing Owens' forces of forging signatures on voter registration cards. Although an acting state Supreme Court judge in Brooklyn ordered a second vote, Owens ultimately triumphed in the New York Court of Appeals, which canceled the rerun and cleared his path to Congress.

Since then, Owens has faced only one foe of note. In the 1986 primary, he met Congress of Racial Equality Chairman Roy Innis, who had drawn attention with his brashly conservative stands against crime. Owens romped to victory.

In 1994, however, Owens found himself the target of a younger generation of insurgent black Democrats. Eric Adams, a transit officer and leader of the city's black police officers association, filed to run. Adams was endorsed by the Nation of Islam. But he was removed from the ballot after the state elections board upheld a challenge to his qualifying petitions.

Republicans have never posed a threat to Owens, whose solidly Democratic district has more African-Americans than any other in New York. In 1996, for example, Owens polled 92 percent of the vote against GOP nominee Claudette Hayle.

Owens' actor son Geoffrey is also in the public eye. He had a recurring role on TV's long-running "The Cosby Show."

HOUSE ELECTIONS

1996 General		
Major R. Owens (D,L)	89,905	(92%)
Claudette Hayle (R,C,INDC,FDM)	7,866	(8%)
1994 General		
Major R. Owens (D,L)	61,945	(89%)
Gary S. Popkin (R,LIBERT)	6,605	(9%)
Michael Gaffney (C)	1,150	(2%)

Previous Winning Percentages: **1992** (94%) **1990** (95%) **1988** (93%) **1986** (91%) **1984** (91%) **1982** (91%)

CAMPAIGN FINANCE

	Receipts	Receipts from PACs	Expend-itures
1996			
Owens (D)	$157,145	$132,550 (84%)	$129,983
1994			
Owens (D)	$285,303	$136,754 (48%)	$295,986

DISTRICT VOTE FOR PRESIDENT

1996		1992	
D	116,390 (91%)	**D**	104,678 (87%)
R	7,832 (6%)	**R**	11,709 (10%)
I	1,719 (1%)	**I**	3,916 (3%)

KEY VOTES

1997	
Ban "partial birth" abortions	N
1996	
Approve farm bill	N
Deny public education to illegal immigrants	N
Repeal ban on certain assault-style weapons	N
Increase minimum wage	Y
Freeze defense spending	Y
Approve welfare overhaul	N
1995	
Approve balanced-budget constitutional amendment	N
Relax Clean Water Act regulations	N
Oppose limits on environmental regulations	Y
Reduce projected Medicare spending	N
Approve GOP budget with tax and spending cuts	N

VOTING STUDIES

	Presidential Support		Party Unity		Conservative Coalition	
Year	S	O	S	O	S	O
1996	77	19	95	2	2	94
1995	82	13	93	2	3	93
1994	63	23	79	2	3	72
1993	73	25	92	2	2	93
1992	11	85	89	4	6	92
1991	21	77	87	3	0	97

INTEREST GROUP RATINGS

Year	ADA	AFL-CIO	CCUS	ACU
1996	95	n/a	19	0
1995	100	100	9	8
1994	90	100	18	0
1993	95	100	0	0
1992	85	92	13	0
1991	100	100	11	0

12 Nydia M. Velázquez (D)

Of Brooklyn — Elected 1992, 3rd term

Biographical Information

Born: March 22, 1953, Yabucoa, P.R.

Education: U. of Puerto Rico, B.A. 1974; New York U., M.A. 1976.

Occupation: Professor.

Family: Divorced.

Religion: Roman Catholic.

Political Career: N.Y. City Council, 1984-85; defeated for re-election to N.Y. City Council, 1984.

Capitol Office: 1221 Longworth Bldg. 20515; 225-2361.

Committees

Banking & Financial Services
Domestic & International Monetary Policy; Housing & Community Opportunity

Small Business
Empowerment (ranking)

In Washington: Velázquez is the first Puerto Rican woman elected to Congress, the beneficiary of a district designed to expand Hispanic representation in Congress. Born in the sugar cane region of Puerto Rico, she was also the first Hispanic woman to serve on the New York City Council.

Velázquez began the 105th Congress with a new assignment — ranking Democrat on the Empowerment Subcommittee of the Small Business Committee — to complement her continued service on the Banking and Financial Services Committee. She also serves amid uncertainty: A federal court in February 1997 said her district, which reaches across three boroughs to take in a Hispanic majority, was an unconstitutional racial gerrymander. "I'm very disappointed," said Velázquez, who planned to appeal. "It's a sad day for communities of color."

Velázquez worked as a liaison between the Puerto Rican government and Latino communities in the United States from 1986 until her first House election in 1992. In Congress, she has been a vocal advocate for the concerns of immigrants at a time of growing public anger not only about illegal immigration, but also about the cost of providing services to people who come to this country legally.

In the 104th Congress, she voted against a Republican-sponsored measure to allow states to deny public education to illegal aliens. When the House considered overhauling the nation's immigration laws, she challenged a provision forbidding illegal aliens from collecting certain benefits on behalf of their U.S.-born children. Velázquez questioned how these children would obtain their lawful benefits, but her amendment to delete the provision was defeated, 151-269, in March 1996. That same month, she voted against a measure requiring employees to verify that their workers were in the country legally.

Also in March 1996, she blasted legislation that would make English the official language of the U.S. government and require the government to conduct all official business in English. "It fuels the fire of anti-immigrant hatred, encouraging racism and discrimination," she said.

Like most other New York City Democrats, Velázquez compiles a liberal voting record. During her first four years in office, the liberal Americans for Democratic Action gave her favorable ratings of 95, 100, 100, and 100. She voted in the 104th against overhauling welfare, against repealing the ban on certain semiautomatic assault-style weapons, against limiting punitive damages in product liability cases, against banning a particular abortion technique that opponents call "partial-birth" abortion, against limiting congressional terms, against banning the federal recognition of same-sex marriages, and against balancing the budget largely through restraining the rate of growth in spending on Medicaid and Medicare.

"Many seniors will have to make hard choices between food on their table or the medical attention that they desperately need to survive," she said in June 1995. "Republicans argue that these cuts are necessary to save the system. However, the very same Republican budget that cuts Medicare contains a $288 billion tax giveaway for the most affluent Americans. Senior citizens have worked hard and contributed all their lives to this country. They deserve affordable health care. Let us end these shameless cuts and consider real health care reform."

Like her fellow New York lawmaker, Jose E. Serrano, who also is of Puerto Rican ancestry, Velázquez voted against tightening the U.S. economic embargo of Cuba.

As befits her liberal leanings, she was a strong supporter of raising the minimum wage. "The latest polls show that 85 percent of Americans are in favor of raising the minimum wage," she said in April 1996 as the House GOP leadership continued to resist efforts by Democrats and some moderate Republicans to allow a minimum wage bill to reach the floor. "I will say to my Republican colleagues, they have lost the battle in the court

NEW YORK 12

Lower East Side of Manhattan; parts of Brooklyn and Queens

The 12th district, drawn to create a second Hispanic majority district, likely will look different before the 1998 elections. A federal court in February 1997 ruled that the district was an unconstitutional racial gerrymander.

The district was born as a result of an ongoing influx that began just after World War II. Hispanic population had grown by 1990 to nearly a quarter of the city's total. Yet only the South Bronx House district had sent a Hispanic to Congress.

Drawing a new Hispanic-majority district, however, was no easy matter. Unlike blacks, who often live in geographic concentrations, Hispanic immigrants settled in disparate low- and middle-income communities scattered across the city's five boroughs. Mapmakers had to go block-by-block to build a district that could reasonably assure a Hispanic's election. The result was the 12th, one of the most unusually shaped House districts in the nation's history. It follows a wildly meandering path through parts of three New York City boroughs: Queens, Brooklyn and Manhattan.

Along with its geographic sampling, the 12th also has an ethnic variety that the generic term Hispanic — which applies to nearly three-fifths of the district's residents — fails to capture. Puerto Ricans, by far the largest single group, make up nearly half the Hispanic population. The other groups came from Mexico, the Caribbean, and Central and South America.

The district's design had its desired effect in 1992: Velázquez, a Puerto Rican activist, won out over a crowded Democratic primary field that included non-Hispanic Democratic Rep. Stephen J. Solarz, whose district was eliminated under reapportionment. She then easily won the general election in this overwhelmingly Democratic district.

But voter participation in the 12th is greatly dampened by such factors as residents' recent immigration status and poverty. In 1996, Velázquez received fewer votes than any other winning congressional candidate in the state, even though she polled 85 percent.

The district's northeastern terminus is well into Queens (the borough has slightly more than a quarter of the 12th's population). The district's parts of Jackson Heights, Corona and Elmhurst are largely Hispanic.

The district then moves southwest through Woodside and Maspeth and into Brooklyn, which has just over half the 12th's population. Hispanics share this section with blacks in East New York and Bushwick and with Hasidic Jews in Williamsburg; Sunset Park, at the southern end, is racially and ethnically mixed.

From there, the 12th crosses the East River — on the Brooklyn and Manhattan bridges and the Brooklyn-Battery Tunnel — to Manhattan's Lower East Side.

The Manhattan portion (about a fifth of the district) is the only one where Hispanics are in the minority. Here Asians are the largest racial group; the district takes in most of Chinatown. There are also remnants of the Lower East Side's once abundant Jewish population.

1990 Population: 580,340. White 196,368 (34%), Black 79,265 (14%), Other 304,707 (53%). Hispanic origin 335,817 (58%). 18 and over 417,933 (72%), 62 and over 60,819 (10%). Median age: 30.

of public opinion. . . . Instead of following the will of the American people, they are following the will of corporate America and the fat cats who have funded their campaigns. That is immoral."

An opponent of NAFTA, she also sided with organized labor in March 1997 when she voted against legislation allowing companies to offer their employees compensatory time off in lieu of overtime pay.

She has taken to the House floor on a number of other occasions to criticize Republican budget proposals. In March 1995, she accused the GOP of voting to cut the school lunch program. "With a five-year, $5 billion program cut, the GOP will raise the nutritional deficit of thousands of school age kids," she said. "Republicans need to understand that in their callous and inhuman proposal, they will be hurting the most vulnerable of Americans — our nation's children."

And in September 1995, she strongly backed the Legal Services Corporation, calling Republican efforts to eliminate it "one of the most shameful attacks on the working poor that I have ever witnessed." She continued: "The Constitution says we are all entitled to equal protection under the law, but in today's society some of us seem to be more equal than others. You see, in this country if you have the money to hire a good lawyer, you can make your way through our legal system. If you are poor, new to this country, or don't understand the legal system, however, you will lose regardless of whether you are right or wrong. That's why the efforts of the Legal Services Corporation are so important. They are in over 900 communities, working to make sure that those who need help have a fighting chance."

In June 1996, she introduced legislation that she said would put an end to "cruel policies" of health maintenance organizations. "Across this country, Americans are joining managed care plans in order to cut costs," she said. "However, while ultra-wealthy HMOs are making multibillion-dollar profits, working-class families are paying for these profits with their health and, in some cases, their lives. Health care companies should make people healthier, not sicker, yet HMO patients are routinely denied access to specialists and refused compensation for emergency room visits."

Velázquez was part of a group of 20 Latino women that met with Hillary Rodham Clinton in April 1993 to discuss health care reform. "I want Hillary to get the real picture when it comes to Latinas and health care," Velázquez said before the meeting.

Since the Clintons were looking to fully computerizing medical records as a way of cutting health costs, Velázquez stressed the importance of privacy. "People may fear seeking professional help if they feel their records could be leaked," Velázquez said.

During her first House campaign, an anonymous source faxed to the New York Post hospital records showing that she had attempted suicide in 1991. The records also revealed that she had been battling depression with alcohol and pills.

"It was a sad and painful experience for me — and one I thought was now in the past," she said at a news conference in Brooklyn at the time. Friends said her depression stemmed from being torn between duty to her ailing parents in Puerto Rico and her work with the New York Hispanic community. She said counseling had helped her overcome her depression.

At Home: In 1992, Velázquez secured election in the newly drawn Hispanic-majority 12th by winning a hard-fought Democratic primary over five contenders, including nine-term Rep. Stephen J. Solarz.

Velázquez's local name recognition had increased dramatically shortly before her 1992 race, when she ran a Hispanic voter registration effort financed by the Puerto Rican government. She said the effort registered 200,000 voters nationwide, but critics contended that she targeted the Brooklyn sections that later became part of her congressional district.

Her biggest obstacle in the 1992 primary was Solarz, whose district had been dismantled in redistricting. Solarz targeted his ads to the Hispanic media, hired Hispanic advisers and learned a few Spanish phrases. But as an unknown to many of his would-be constituents, he was branded a carpetbagger and wealthy outsider.

Velázquez, if the local favorite, was not the only Latino candidate. With four other Hispanics in the primary, many predicted that Solarz would benefit from a split vote among Hispanics. But Velázquez got 33 percent to Solarz's 28 percent. General elections are an afterthought in the heavily Democratic district.

HOUSE ELECTIONS

1996 General		
Nydia M. Velazquez (D,L)	61,913	(85%)
Miguel I. Prado (R,C,RTL)	9,978	(14%)
Eleanor Garcia (SW)	1,283	(2%)
1994 General		
Nydia M. Velazquez (D,L)	39,929	(92%)
Genevieve R. Brennan (C)	2,747	(6%)
Eric Ruano-Melendez (PHA)	589	(1%)

Previous Winning Percentages: 1992 (77%)

CAMPAIGN FINANCE

	Receipts	Receipts from PACs	Expend-itures
1996			
Velazquez (D)	$294,751	$104,402 (35%)	$236,564
Prado (R)	$32,869	$600 (2%)	$23,991
1994			
Velazquez (D)	$624,095	$189,989 (30%)	$605,787

DISTRICT VOTE FOR PRESIDENT

	1996		1992
D	80,852 (84%)	**D**	67,114 (68%)
R	10,249 (11%)	**R**	25,622 (26%)
I	2,296 (2%)	**I**	5,121 (5%)

KEY VOTES

1997	
Ban "partial birth" abortions	N
1996	
Approve farm bill	N
Deny public education to illegal immigrants	N
Repeal ban on certain assault-style weapons	N
Increase minimum wage	Y
Freeze defense spending	Y
Approve welfare overhaul	N
1995	
Approve balanced-budget constitutional amendment	N
Relax Clean Water Act regulations	N
Oppose limits on environmental regulations	Y
Reduce projected Medicare spending	N
Approve GOP budget with tax and spending cuts	N

VOTING STUDIES

	Presidential Support		Party Unity		Conservative Coalition	
Year	S	O	S	O	S	O
1996	78	20	94	4	2	94
1995	83	11	93	2	3	94
1994	71	28	94	2	6	92
1993	68	27	95	2	7	93

INTEREST GROUP RATINGS

Year	ADA	AFL-CIO	CCUS	ACU
1996	100	n/a	6	0
1995	100	100	8	13
1994	100	100	17	0
1993	95	100	0	0

13 Susan Molinari (R)

Of Staten Island — Elected 1990; 4th full term

Biographical Information

Born: March 27, 1958, Staten Island, N.Y.

Education: State U. of New York, Albany, B.A. 1980, M.A. 1982.

Occupation: Political aide.

Family: Husband, Bill Paxon; one child.

Religion: Roman Catholic.

Political Career: N.Y. City Council, 1985-90.

Capitol Office: 2411 Rayburn Bldg. 20515; 225-3371.

Committees

Budget

Transportation & Infrastructure
Aviation; Railroads (chairman); Water Resources & Environment

Conference Vice Chairman

In Washington: After enjoying a highly successful 104th Congress, Molinari announced in May 1997 that she would leave the House by August to become co-anchor of a new CBS Saturday morning news program. Molinari said the "opportunity with CBS News is one I became more and more intrigued with, and, ultimately, decided I couldn't pass up."

The announcement came on the heels of a congressional session in which Molinari was in the spotlight more than ever before. In 1995, her party assumed control of the House, and she joined the ranks of the leadership, winning election as vice chair of the Republican Conference. She also got a subcommittee gavel, heading a panel on the Transportation and Infrastructure Committee. In May 1996, she and her husband, New York Rep. Bill Paxon, had a baby girl, Susan Ruby Paxon; Molinari was just the third member of Congress ever to give birth. And in August, Susan Ruby was on display as her mother delivered the keynote address at the Republican National Convention in San Diego.

Molinari started the 105th Congress as conference vice chairwoman, and both she and Paxon are members of the GOP leadership group that meets regularly to map strategy.

Molinari's views on abortion and gun control are well to the left of those of most congressional Republicans, so her prominence in the party is often cited as evidence that the GOP is a "big tent" with room for people of divergent views. In other policy arenas, though, Molinari is for the most part a loyal conservative.

As the House Republican leadership scrambled before the 105th to ensure Rep. Newt Gingrich's re-election as Speaker despite his ethical troubles, Molinari and Conference Secretary Jennifer Dunn of Washington kept tabs on wavering voters. She rushed to Gingrich's defense after the House ethics committee counsel, James M. Cole, issued his report. She called Gingrich's transgression an innocent mistake that anyone could have made, given the "arcane tax law."

She has promoted Republican efforts to allow companies to give their employees compensatory time off in lieu of overtime pay, a bill that is strongly opposed by labor unions. The measure would "make men's and women's lives a little easier as they tend to their families and keep things going," Molinari said in January 1997. The comp-time bill passed the House for a second time in 1997, but it faced a presidential veto threat.

Molinari voted in the 104th to overhaul welfare, backed a constitutional amendment requiring a balanced budget and endorsed the Republicans' budget-reconciliation plan to eliminate the federal deficit by the year 2002 in part by restraining the rate of spending growth on Medicare and Medicaid.

She supported the GOP leadership against an effort by Democrats and some moderate Republicans to strip from the fiscal 1996 VA-HUD appropriations bill 17 riders curtailing the authority of the Environmental Protection Agency. The amendment initially passed but was defeated on a revote. In the end, most of the riders were missing from the final spending bill that cleared Congress but was vetoed by President Clinton.

As chairman of the Railroads Subcommittee, Molinari again was on the opposite side of some of her moderate GOP colleagues as the Transportation and Infrastructure Committee marked up legislation in June 1995 to streamline Amtrak. The bill was designed to give Amtrak more autonomy to change its operations by contracting out services, and making deep cuts in the railroad's federal subsidies.

But the legislation ran into trouble when fellow New Yorker Jack Quinn, a Buffalo Republican, pushed through an amendment that would protect existing labor contracts, requiring Amtrak to negotiate new job agreements before contracting out work. Molinari contended that the amendment would destroy Amtrak's ability to survive, by not granting it the freedom it needs to restructure its operations. Eventually, both sides agreed to leave Amtrak's current labor contracts in place while new agreements were sought on

NEW YORK 13
Staten Island; part of southwest Brooklyn

With Staten Island — the most suburban of the five boroughs — making up nearly two-thirds of its population, the 13th stands out among New York City's House districts. It is the only Republican district in the otherwise Democratic-dominated city. Bob Dole got 40 percent of the district's vote in 1996, 10 points better than anywhere else in the city, though Bill Clinton still won with 51 percent.

The 13th, with a working population of mainly middle- to upper-middle-class commuters, has the lowest poverty rate of any district wholly in New York City. Italian-Americans, many of them social conservatives, make up the largest ethnic group in the 13th (which also includes part of Brooklyn across the New York Bay Narrows); Irish-Americans are also a large constituency. The non-Hispanic white population is more than 85 percent; there are few minority voters to provide a Democratic base.

Although there are some Democratic pockets in the more working-class ethnic parts of Brooklyn, the district seems tailor-made for Republican Molinari. It also has been hospitable to the family. Guy Molinari served in the House from 1981 until he was elected Staten Island borough president in 1989; he was succeeded by his daughter, Susan.

If some community activists have their way, the 13th will no longer be the most Republican district in New York City — because Staten Island would no longer be part of New York City. Staten Island voters approved a secession referendum in 1993, but that is just the first step in a tortuous path toward breaking away.

Staten Island has always been distant, both physically and psychologically, from the rest of the city. It is the least populous of the boroughs, with about 380,000 residents, and the most remote (its only land link to the city is the Verrazano-Narrows Bridge, opened in 1964, which connects it with Brooklyn; the Staten Island Ferry is still the only direct route to Manhattan).

Residents have become increasingly angry over the use of Staten Island as a literal dumping ground: Its Fresh Kills landfill, one of the world's largest facilities, receives much of the city's garbage. Secession opponents say Staten Island, which has few major employers, lacks the tax base to go it alone.

But supporters argue otherwise, citing such recent business locations as the headquarters of Teleport Communications Group, which provides telecommunications services for large corporations and came here in 1994.

Staten Island's Navy homeport was shut down, having been placed on the 1993 base-closing list. Although Molinari fought to preserve funding for the project, a result of the Reagan-era plan to greatly expand the U.S. naval force, Staten Island lost out to Norfolk, Va.

The Brooklyn portion of the 13th includes Bay Ridge — setting for the 1977 disco movie "Saturday Night Fever" — and part of Bensonhurst, a mainly Italian community and the site of unrest after the murder of a black youth in 1989.

1990 Population: 580,337. White 502,925 (87%), Black 32,474 (6%), Other 44,938 (8%). Hispanic origin 43,336 (7%). 18 and over 449,571 (77%), 62 and over 97,316 (17%). Median age: 35.

severance pay and subcontracting.

Because of Molinari's support of abortion rights, there were some anguished cries from conservative religious activists when GOP presidential nominee-apparent Bob Dole announced she would give the 1996 convention keynote address. Molinari in the 104th voted to require states to fund Medicaid abortions for poor women and to allow federal employees' health care plans to cover abortions.

She joined with House Democrats in blocking a move to end funding of the federal government's main family planning programs during consideration of the fiscal 1996 spending bill covering the Department of Health and Human Services. "Where are these women now going to go?" Molinari wondered. "Family planning works to save lives. . . . We must give poor women a place to go." About a fifth of the House Republicans voted with the Democrats in preserving the programs.

And in June 1995, Molinari opposed an effort to stop medical personnel at overseas military installations from performing abortions. The fiscal 1996 defense authorization bill renewed the ban on abortions at overseas bases. The debate, Molinari said, "is about equal protection under the law for women who serve our country."

However, Molinari sides with abortion foes in support of banning a particular abortion technique that opponents call "partial birth" abortion.

On gun control, Molinari has supported a five-day waiting period for handgun purchases and a ban on certain semiautomatic assault-style weapons. In August 1994, she joined a group of centrist Republicans who negotiated with the White House to make changes in the the Clinton-backed crime bill. She was one of 42 Republicans who voted to bring the modified bill to the floor, and she voted for its final passage. In 1996, she opposed a Republican-backed proposal to repeal the assault weapons ban.

The 13th District is made up largely of middle-

and upper-middle-class "ethnics," some of whom have family ties to the war-torn region of the former Yugoslavia. Molinari has traveled to Croatia to get a personal impression of the tensions and strife in the Balkans. She led a 15-member delegation to Bosnia in December 1995 and opposed Clinton's decision to send troops there. "I still do not agree with the policy of sending 20,000 American troops precisely because of what I heard from the political leaders" in Bosnia, she said.

Molinari's grandfather was a fixture in Staten Island politics, and she occupies the House seat that her father, Guy V. Molinari, held from 1981 until 1990, when he resigned to become Staten Island borough president. Many sons have succeeded their fathers in the House, but Molinari is one of few daughters to do so. Illinois Republican Winnifred Mason Huck was elected in 1922 to replace her father, William Mason, who died in midterm, but she served only that partial term. In 1992, Democrat Lucille Roybal-Allard of California joined the list; she succeeded longtime Rep. Edward R. Roybal.

At Home: Guy Molinari's victory for Staten Island borough president forced a 1990 special election in a House district where Democrats once were competitive. But there was little doubt that the major effect of the transition in the then-14th District would be a change in the House nameplates to read "Ms. Molinari" rather than "Mr. Molinari."

Susan Molinari entered the House contest with huge advantages over any potential Democratic candidate. Her father blazed a path for her, winning strongly both in his Staten Island base and in the Brooklyn part of the district. In winning two terms on the New York City Council, Molinari had established herself as a popular officeholder.

After stints with the Republican Governors' Association and the Republican National Committee, Molinari ran for the council in 1985 and won. Her status on the council was singular: She was the only Republican in the city's legislative body. "I was the only Republican among 34 Democrats, which made me minority leader," she joked in 1995. Several well-known Democrats expressed interest in the March 1990 House special election, but Democratic leaders put their muscle behind lawyer and party insider Robert Gigante. From the outset, he trailed far behind Molinari in name identification, and he lacked the financial resources to build recognition.

Hoping to make up the difference with a splash in the media, Gigante wound up splattering himself. In an early campaign forum, Gigante described himself as more typical of the district voter by noting that he and his wife had four children while Molinari, who recently had married her first husband, had none. A reporter for the Staten Island Advance then criticized the Democrat for trying to make family size a qualification for office. Molinari won easily, taking 58 percent to Gigante's 34 percent. She has won easily ever since.

HOUSE ELECTIONS

1996 General		
Susan Molinari (R,C,FDM)	94,660	(62%)
Tyrone G. Butler (D,L)	53,376	(35%)
Kathleen Marciano (RTL)	3,396	(2%)
Anita Lerman (INDC)	2,337	(2%)
1994 General		
Susan Molinari (R,C)	96,491	(71%)
Tyrone G. Butler (D,L)	33,937	(25%)
Elisa Disimone (RTL)	4,655	(3%)

Previous Winning Percentages: 1992 (56%) **1990** (60%) **1990+** (58%)

+ *Special election*

CAMPAIGN FINANCE

	Receipts	Receipts from PACs	Expend-itures
1996			
Molinari (R)	$936,459	$497,462 (53%)	$557,586
Butler (D)	$54,499	$14,750 (27%)	$53,459
1994			
Molinari (R)	$453,426	$217,713 (48%)	$481,588
Butler (D)	$22,147	$500 (2%)	$21,618

DISTRICT VOTE FOR PRESIDENT

1996		1992	
D	92,619 (51%)	**D**	82,796 (39%)
R	72,233 (40%)	**R**	100,761 (48%)
I	12,095 (7%)	**I**	26,317 (13%)

KEY VOTES

1997	
Ban "partial birth" abortions	Y
1996	
Approve farm bill	Y
Deny public education to illegal immigrants	N
Repeal ban on certain assault-style weapons	N
Increase minimum wage	?
Freeze defense spending	N
Approve welfare overhaul	Y
1995	
Approve balanced-budget constitutional amendment	Y
Relax Clean Water Act regulations	Y
Oppose limits on environmental regulations	N
Reduce projected Medicare spending	Y
Approve GOP budget with tax and spending cuts	Y

VOTING STUDIES

	Presidential Support		Party Unity		Conservative Coalition	
Year	S	O	S	O	S	O
1996	33	47	69	13	67	16
1995	27	73	91	9	92	8
1994	60	40	83	16	83	17
1993	52	47	80	20	84	16
1992	65	33	77	21	81	19
1991	62	33	72	26	76	24

INTEREST GROUP RATINGS

Year	ADA	AFL-CIO	CCUS	ACU
1996	20	n/a	92	88
1995	10	0	96	68
1994	20	44	92	71
1993	25	42	100	71
1992	35	58	88	64
1991	30	58	70	70

14 Carolyn B. Maloney (D)

Of Manhattan — Elected 1992, 3rd term

Biographical Information

Born: Feb. 19, 1948, Greensboro, N.C.
Education: Greensboro College, A.B. 1968.
Occupation: Legislative aide; teacher.
Family: Husband, Clifton H.W. Maloney; two children.
Religion: Presbyterian.
Political Career: N.Y. City Council, 1982-93.
Capitol Office: 1330 Longworth Bldg. 20515; 225-7944.

Committees

Banking & Financial Services
Domestic & International Monetary Policy; Financial Institutions & Consumer Credit

Government Reform & Oversight
Government Management, Information & Technology (ranking); National Security, International Affairs & Criminal Justice

Joint Economic

In Washington: As the House prepared to investigate campaign finance abuses in the 1996 elections, Maloney found herself in the middle of the debate as a member of the Government Reform and Oversight Committee, which is conducting the probe.

In March 1997, when the House debated whether to fund the investigation into Democratic fundraising practices, Maloney suggested that a $7.9 million reserve fund being proposed instead be transferred to the Federal Election Commission, which has asked for additional funding to handle an ever-increasing caseload. "Instead of using this as a slush fund, we should use it for the FEC," Maloney said.

Also in March, she and and three Republican lawmakers announced that they had formed a coalition to rally support for an independent commission to recommend changes to campaign financing regulations. Maloney said the coalition's proposed approach was comparable to the independent base closing commission that was formed by Congress in 1988 to tackle the politically sensitive task of identifying military facilities that could be closed to save money.

In the 104th Congress, Maloney showed her partisan side on more than one occasion. In July 1996, she objected to the Government Reform and Oversight Committee's approval of legislation establishing an Office of the Inspector General in the White House. Maloney called the measure "bureaucratic and costly, unconstitutional, and a clear attempt to embarrass the president."

And in February 1995, she fought legislation prohibiting the executive branch from implementing most regulations that had been issued since the previous fall. She joined other Democrats on the Government Reform and Oversight Committee in protesting the possible health and safety consequences of such a moratorium. She proposed legislation exempting drinking water standards from the moratorium, but the committee rejected her motion, 15-26.

From her perch as ranking minority member of the Government Management, Information and Technology Subcommittee, Maloney was involved in broadening the federal Freedom of Information Act (FOIA).

She sponsored legislation to require federal agencies to release information on Nazi war criminals who are on a special "watch" list and are banned from entering the United States. The measure would prohibit the government from denying FOIA requests on alleged Nazi war criminals on the grounds of national security. The bill would require the government to release information on such war criminals unless doing so could reveal the identity of an intelligence agent requiring protection or place at risk a person who gave confidential information. Maloney argued that former U.N. Secretary General Kurt Waldheim never would have risen to that post if the public had access to then-secret U.S. government files on his World War II activities. The bill passed the House in September 1996.

In July, as the Government Reform and Oversight Committee passed legislation making computerized records subject to FOIA, Maloney successfully proposed an amendment requiring agencies to report annually the number of pending requests and how long it would take to meet them.

Maloney also sits on the Banking and Financial Services Committee, where, in May 1996, she successfully amended legislation overhauling federal housing programs. Her amendment gave senior citizens in public housing the right to own household pets. The original bill let housing authorities set guidelines — including prohibition — for pet ownership.

Current law allows pets only in developments designated as senior housing. Maloney's amendment allowed housing authorities to set rules regarding pets, but would preclude them from prohibiting the elderly — regardless of whether they live in senior housing — from owning pets.

Vernon J. Ehlers, R-Mich., objected to Maloney's amendment. He said that he had to be home-schooled until college because of severe

A bastion of urban liberalism, the House district centered on Manhattan's East Side presented a paradox during the 1980s. Voters strongly supported all Democratic presidential candidates, including landslide losers such as Walter F. Mondale in 1984. Yet during this same period, the district sent a liberal Republican, Bill Green, to the House.

But Green, who had won eight House contests, could not buck the Democratic surge in 1992. The 14th District, which backed Bill Clinton by a wide margin, also chose Democrat Maloney over Green for the House seat.

Green, in fact, was able to narrowly carry his Manhattan base (shared with then-City Council member Maloney). But he was undone by a redistricting plan that added two working-class areas, in Queens and Brooklyn, where voters had more regularly Democratic habits in House contests. Maloney's wide margins in these areas carried her to victory.

In 1996, the district went overwhelmingly for Clinton (70 percent) and Maloney (72 percent).

The East Side of Manhattan has a Republican heritage. Known as the "Silk Stocking" district, its avenues were once lined with the mansions of Republican industrialists. (Most have long since been replaced by apartment buildings; others, such as the Frick mansion owned by a steel magnate, have been preserved as museums.)

But by the 1960s, young urban liberals, Jewish voters and other Democratic support groups had gained dominance. The social and cultural liberalism of even some wealthy residents gave rise to the term "limousine liberal." Today, the only Republicans who have a shot in the 14th are liberals like Green. Democrats have a 3-1 voter registration advantage here.

NEW YORK 14
East Side Manhattan; Parts of Queens and Brooklyn

The East Side district has many of the office towers that make up the skyline, including the Citicorp and AT&T buildings. The U.N. building, the Chrysler Building, Grand Central Station and the main New York Public Library touch on 42nd Street. Such landmarks as Rockefeller Center and the Metropolitan Museum of Art are in the 14th, as is all of Central Park (which the 14th crosses to take in a small piece of the West Side).

The district's population is 80 percent non-Hispanic white. The largest minority-group concentrations are at the north end, near Harlem, and south in the Lower East Side, which has a large Hispanic population. The 14th also takes in part of Chinatown, as well as the East Village, a nexus for artists and counterculturalists.

The rest of the 14th is one of those marvels of New York redistricting. It crosses the East River to parts of Astoria in Queens and Greenpoint in Brooklyn, which are three miles apart on either side of the 7th District.

Despite being more conservative than the Manhattan side, these parts were decisive in a Democrat winning the 1992 House race. The mainly ethnic residents (Greeks and Italians in Astoria, Poles and Italians in Greenpoint) generally stick with their Democratic traditions, but there is a strain of social conservatism.

1990 Population: 580,337. White 498,371 (86%), Black 26,844 (5%), Other 55,122 (9%). Hispanic origin 63,398 (11%). 18 and over 515,981 (89%), 62 and over 107,359 (18%). Median age: 39.

animal hair allergies. "When I first read that pets were being introduced into nursing homes and rest homes, I had an involuntary shudder," he said. "I thought if that happens, and it appears in all nursing homes and rest homes, I will never be able to go to one."

Maloney's amendment passed, 375-48, and the overall legislation passed, 315-107.

She is a strong supporter of abortion rights. In August 1995, she backed efforts to include a provision in the fiscal 1996 Labor-Health and Human Services spending bill requiring states to provide federally funded abortions for poor women in cases of rape or incest. The legislation would have given states the option to decide whether to pay for abortions, but Jim Kolbe, R-Ariz., sought to make it mandatory. Supporters of the Kolbe amendment tried to convince their colleagues that voting it down would punish women victimized by violence. If a poor woman was denied access to an abortion, Maloney said, "she will be forced to spend nine months reliving the crime." But the amendment was defeated, 206-215.

Maloney and other members of the Congressional Women's Caucus met with several high-ranking Army officials in November 1996 in response to complaints about sexual harassment at military bases. "I truly believe that this is the most serious peacetime scandal in the military," Maloney said.

In March 1997, she introduced legislation to set up a commission to investigate the military justice system, including procedures concerning reports of sexual misconduct, harassment and discrimination.

Maloney has introduced a new Equal Rights Amendment to the Constitution, and she wants to expand the family leave law and provide for Medicare-funded mammographies for women age 65 or older.

As a freshman, Maloney opposed President

Clinton's deficit-reduction bill in May 1993, a move that raised eyebrows because she had campaigned on a platform of reduced government spending. After being personally lobbied by Clinton, she voted for final passage three months later. She also gained notice for trying, albeit unsuccessfully, to eliminate a $2.5 million rifle marksmanship program.

Maloney ruffled feathers on both sides of the aisle with her Northern Rockies Ecosystem Protection Act, which sought to classify 16 million acres in five states as wilderness. Western representatives, in retaliation, offered mock legislation to designate Manhattan, which Maloney represents, as a natural wilderness.

She was named to the Joint Economic Committee for the 105th Congress.

At Home: Maloney's victory over seven-term incumbent Republican Bill Green contained many of the elements that energized voters in 1992: a female Democrat who upset a powerful, entrenched incumbent, thanks in large part to a newly drawn congressional district. Her resounding re-election wins in 1994 and 1996 demonstrated her firm hold on the affluent and heavily Democratic district.

Green, an affable, liberal Republican with a liberal-leaning constituency, had defeated in the past such visible names as former Rep. Bella S. Abzug and then-Manhattan Borough President Andrew Stein. Running in the so-called Silk Stocking district, long dominated by landed Republican gentry, Green is heir to a family supermarket fortune.

Maloney herself is no pauper, though she was vastly outspent by Green. A former teacher, Maloney early in the campaign used the slogan "there are too many millionaires and not enough women" in the House of Representatives, referring to Green and her primary challenger, real estate tycoon Abraham J. Hirschfeld. But she and her husband, a successful businessman, also are worth $3 million to $5 million, with most assets in real estate holdings, according to her financial disclosure form.

Maloney also profited from a high level of name recognition as a 10-year veteran of the City Council.

In 1994, City Councilman Charles Millard, a moderate Republican, sought to reclaim the district for the GOP. First elected to the council in 1991, he had distinguished himself as a staunch advocate of homosexual rights and as something of a character: He was known for giving council speeches in verse. He also had the Liberal Party line, which had gone to Maloney in 1992.

The result was not close. Running on a ticket with Democratic Gov. Mario M. Cuomo, who won New York City comfortably, Maloney prevailed by nearly 2-1. In 1996, Maloney breezed to re-election with 72 percent against a weak GOP opponent.

HOUSE ELECTIONS

1996 General		
Carolyn B. Maloney (D,L)	130,175	(72%)
Jeffrey E. Livingston (R)	42,641	(24%)
Thomas K. Leighton (INDC,GREEN)	3,512	(2%)
Joseph A. Lavezzo (C)	2,188	(1%)
1994 General		
Carolyn B. Maloney (D,IN)	98,479	(64%)
Charles Millard (R,L)	54,277	(35%)

Previous Winning Percentages: 1992 (50%)

CAMPAIGN FINANCE

	Receipts	Receipts from PACs	Expend-itures
1996			
Maloney (D)	$705,991	$266,942 (38%)	$599,406
Livingston (R)	$154,621	$5,641 (4%)	$152,503
1994			
Maloney (D)	$1,040,044	$461,393 (44%)	$1,032,181
Millard (R)	$999,298	$1,829 (0%)	$988,112

DISTRICT VOTE FOR PRESIDENT

	1996		1992
D	144,885 (70%)	**D**	159,750 (69%)
R	46,970 (23%)	**R**	53,675 (23%)
I	6,623 (3%)	**I**	16,419 (7%)

KEY VOTES

1997	
Ban "partial birth" abortions	N
1996	
Approve farm bill	N
Deny public education to illegal immigrants	N
Repeal ban on certain assault-style weapons	N
Increase minimum wage	Y
Freeze defense spending	Y
Approve welfare overhaul	N
1995	
Approve balanced-budget constitutional amendment	N
Relax Clean Water Act regulations	N
Oppose limits on environmental regulations	Y
Reduce projected Medicare spending	N
Approve GOP budget with tax and spending cuts	N

VOTING STUDIES

	Presidential Support		Party Unity		Conservative Coalition	
Year	**S**	**O**	**S**	**O**	**S**	**O**
1996	84	14	93	4	12	82
1995	84	12	92	4	14	78
1994	74	23	91	6	22	78
1993	79	21	91	4	16	84

INTEREST GROUP RATINGS

Year	ADA	AFL-CIO	CCUS	ACU
1996	85	n/a	20	5
1995	80	100	21	0
1994	100	78	58	0
1993	95	100	27	4

15 Charles B. Rangel (D)

Of Manhattan — Elected 1970, 14th term

Biographical Information
Born: June 11, 1930, New York, N.Y.
Education: New York U., B.S. 1957; St. John's U., LL.B. 1960.
Military Service: Army, 1948-52.
Occupation: Lawyer.
Family: Wife, Alma Carter; two children.
Religion: Roman Catholic.
Political Career: N.Y. Assembly, 1967-71; sought Democratic nomination for N.Y. City Council president, 1969.

Capitol Office: 2354 Rayburn Bldg. 20515; 225-4365.

Committees
Ways & Means (ranking)
Trade
Joint Taxation

In Washington: At the start of the 105th Congress, Rangel finally got something he had wanted for a long time: the top Democratic seat on the House Ways and Means Committee. He had, however, hoped for more — that as the panel's No. 1 Democrat, he would be chairman, not just the ranking minority member.

It was not for lack of Rangel's trying that Democrats failed to win back control of the House in the 1996 election.

He identified 30 House districts with a black population of at least 20 percent and offered to help Democratic candidates campaign in black communities and conduct get-out-the-vote campaigns. He was on the road for much of the fall, visiting candidates whose districts fit the profile and others who requested his help.

With the 1996 retirement of Florida's Sam M. Gibbons (ranking Democrat on Ways and Means in the 104th), Rangel knew that he was next in line for the Ways and Means gavel if his party could topple the GOP majority. As he stumped in districts around the country, "I was campaigning to be chairman of the Ways and Means Committee," Rangel said. "I don't know how well I would have done if I was campaigning to become the ranking member." He raised more than $1.35 million, much of it from the same PACs that gave to the National Republican Congressional Committee (NRCC). "I would call right behind them and say, 'I see you donated to the NRCC. I know in the interests of good government, you would like to donate to the DCCC [Democratic Congressional Campaign Committee], too.' "

With his raspy voice and partisan bite, Rangel made a memorable impression in his numerous media appearances, and Republicans sought to cast him as a sort of menacing poster boy in arguing for continued GOP control of the House. Speaker Newt Gingrich, addressing the American International Automobile Dealers Association in May 1996, cited the contrast between Rangel and Ways and Means Committee Chairman Bill Archer, R-Texas. "The difference in those two people — the difference in philosophy, difference in tax level, difference in attitude towards job creation, difference in attitude towards small business — is literally as wide as you can get in Washington, D.C.," Gingrich said.

And in September 1996, Majority Whip Tom DeLay, R-Texas, warned that if Democrats again took control of the chamber, "they will reverse the great progress we have made over the last two years." Singling out Rangel and John D. Dingell, D-Mich., the ranking Democrat of the Commerce Committee, DeLay said, "If Democrats regain control of the Congress, you can forget about tax relief for working families."

Despite Rangel's campaign efforts and President Clinton's re-election victory, the Democrats remained in the minority and Rangel had to settle for the ranking member slot. He also is the top Democrat on the Joint Committee on Taxation and a member of the Democratic Steering Committee.

The outcome of the 1996 election was just the latest in a string of disappointments for Rangel. In 1987, he was defeated in his bid for the majority whip's job. Then he was subjected to one of the longer investigations of the House bank scandal. At the start of the 103rd, he was denied the committee platform from which he had battled vigorously against illegal drugs — the chairmanship of the Select Committee on Narcotics — when the House voted against reauthorizing the non-legislative committee. And in 1995, when the GOP took control of the House, Rangel lost his chairmanship of a Ways and Means subcommittee.

Still, Rangel looked forward with relish to his work in the 105th. "This is going to be exciting as hell for me," he said after the 1996 election.

At times in the 104th, Rangel's relationship with Archer was less than positive. They engaged in a testy exchange in February 1995, when the House passed legislation allowing self-employed Americans to deduct 25 percent of the cost of health care premiums. The benefit was funded by eliminating a tax break for companies that sell

NEW YORK 15
Northern Manhattan — Harlem; Washington Heights

One of the original seats of black political power, the Upper Manhattan area centered on Harlem has been transformed in recent decades: There has been a major influx of Hispanics, mainly from Puerto Rico and the Dominican Republic, with a large sampling of other Latin American ethnicities.

Hispanics make up a large plurality (46 percent) of the population in the 15th, which blankets Upper Manhattan from 96th Street to its northern tip. But in part because of low Hispanic voter participation rates, the non-Hispanic blacks who make up about 37 percent of the population continue to have the political upper hand.

Since first sending an African-American to Congress, the Harlem-based district has had just two House members, both Democrats: the flamboyant Adam Clayton Powell Jr., who won a landmark election in 1944, and the low-key Rangel, who unseated the ailing and scandal-plagued Powell in 1970. Rangel has held the seat since.

Democrats have a lock on the constituency covered by the 15th. Throughout his career, Rangel has often received the endorsement not only of the local Democrats, but of the minuscule Republican organization as well.

At the turn of the 20th century, Harlem, about 10 miles north of New York City's original hub, was an upscale suburb with a nearly all-white population. But in 1904, blacks — steered by a black real estate agent named Philip A. Payton Jr. — began to move in. By the 1920s, the height of its cultural "renaissance," Harlem was mainly black and upscale. By the 1940s, the trickle of low-income blacks arriving there became a flood, turning much of Harlem into the economically troubled area it remains.

The largest concentration of blacks in the 15th is in west-central Harlem. Puerto Ricans dominate in East Harlem; West Harlem and Washington Heights farther north have large Dominican communities. Most of the 15th's non-Hispanic whites live in three areas: its south end in the Upper East and West sides; the Inwood section at the north end; and a longtime Italian-American community in East Harlem.

Large parts of the 15th have the array of social problems plaguing low-income minority communities. More than a third of its residents live in poverty. Harlem has some relatively affluent areas, such as Strivers' Row and Lenox Terrace. There has been some reversal of the outflow of upwardly mobile blacks in such areas as Mount Morris Park, where once-grand brownstones are being restored.

On the west side of the 15th are the campuses of Columbia University and the City College of New York. The district contains such historic sites as the massive Cathedral of St. John the Divine and the tomb of Ulysses S. Grant. The George Washington Bridge connects Upper Manhattan with New Jersey.

An incongruous appendage to the 15th is Rikers Island, located off Manhattan in the East River. A New York City prison complex occupies the island.

1990 Population: 580,337. White 160,127 (28%), Black 272,063 (47%), Other 148,147 (26%). Hispanic origin 269,051 (46%). 18 and over 437,484 (75%), 62 and over 81,239 (14%). Median age: 32.

broadcast stations to minorities.

"How dare anyone say it is a good idea to tie up this bill with this vicious act," Rangel said. He told Archer there were hundreds of corporate tax preferences that could have been terminated instead. An angry Ways and Means session led to a sharply worded written exchange. Rangel charged that "a wave of scapegoating is sweeping the country. . . . Just like under Hitler, people say they don't mean to blame any particular individuals or groups . . . but in the U.S., those groups always turned out to be minorities and immigrants."

Archer replied with a letter, saying he was "appalled" by Rangel's accusation and adding that "invoking the name of Hitler injects an utterly invalid and totally uncalled-for extremism into a legitimate congressional debate."

In October 1995, Rangel criticized proposed cuts in the projected growth of Medicare by saying, "What the Republicans are saying is that if you are sick, if you are poor or if you are old, you are not entitled to anything."

He said he will work on compromises with Republicans, but only if congressional Democrats are allowed a hand in writing the legislation. "What is there for me to say if the Republicans say, 'We've worked it out with the president'?" Rangel said. "That's not bipartisanship, that's being a potted plant."

Rangel, who supported Iowa Sen. Tom Harkin for president in 1992, has had his differences with Clinton. He made it very clear early in the 105th Congress that he would not support efforts to sharply reduce the projected growth of Medicare. "$100 billion in cuts and no blood on the floor? How do you do it?" he asked Secretary of Health and Human Services Donna E. Shalala in February 1997.

And Rangel, who in the 104th tried repeatedly without success to amend the welfare overhaul bill as it moved through the House, criticized Clinton's decision in July 1996 to sign the final version. "The truth is, the Republicans would throw 2 million people into poverty and my president would only throw 1 million people into poverty," he said.

And while he fights for traditional Democratic constituencies such as the poor, cities and organized labor, Rangel also is sensitive to the needs of business, especially New York City's financial community. With an eye on the large number of Puerto Ricans who live in New York, Rangel in May 1996 unsuccessfully opposed legislation that paid for a package of tax breaks by curbing the tax credit for U.S. manufacturing firms that do business in Puerto Rico or other U.S. territories. "We pay for this bill by going to the poorest people with the weakest political posture," Rangel said.

At Home: Rangel's 1970 primary victory over flamboyant Democratic Rep. Adam Clayton Powell was big news. It was not until 1994 that Rangel had another race of note: the Democratic primary challenge by Powell's son, City Council member Adam Clayton Powell IV.

In name and appearance, Powell reminded many voters of his late father. Rangel took the challenge seriously, aggressively rebutting Powell's claims that he was out of touch with the district. Rangel retorted that the only things Powell had in common with his father were his name and his poor attendance record, citing criticism of Powell's City Council service. Rangel ended up winning renomination by 28 percentage points.

A high school dropout, Rangel joined the Army and fought in the Korean War. He then returned to Manhattan and entered college in his mid-20s. He got his law degree in 1960 and the next year was appointed assistant U.S. attorney for the Southern District of New York.

In 1966 Rangel won a seat in the New York Assembly. Three years later, he made a quixotic bid for citywide office by running for City Council president in the Democratic primary on a ticket headed by U.S. Rep. James H. Scheuer. Rangel ran last in a field of six but received publicity in black areas as the only citywide black candidate.

Rangel bounced back the next year, applying the coup de grâce to Powell's fading political career. The veteran Democrat had been "excluded" from the 90th Congress on charges that he had misused committee funds for parties and travel to the Caribbean. The Supreme Court ruled the exclusion unconstitutional, and Powell was seen as a martyr by constituents. But when he took a seat in the 91st Congress and then spent most of the following year out of the country, that view changed.

Rangel had the backing of a coalition of younger black politicians who were tired of Powell's behavior and wanted someone who would work harder for blacks and for New York: He portrayed Powell as an absentee representative and promised to work full time for his constituents. Although the anti-Powell vote was split four ways, Rangel's coalition of younger blacks and liberal whites prevailed.

HOUSE ELECTIONS

1996 General		
Charles B. Rangel (D,L)	113,898	(91%)
Edward R. Adams (R)	5,951	(5%)
Ruben Dario Vargas (C,INDC)	3,896	(3%)
1994 General		
Charles B. Rangel (D,L)	77,830	(97%)
Jose Suero (RTL,IF)	2,812	(3%)

Previous Winning Percentages: **1992** (95%) **1990** (97%) **1988** (97%) **1986** (96%) **1984** (97%) **1982** (97%) **1980** (96%) **1978** (96%) **1976** (97%) **1974** (97%) **1972** (96%) **1970** (87%)

CAMPAIGN FINANCE

	Receipts	Receipts from PACs	Expenditures
1996			
Rangel (D)	$1,285,828	$711,089 (55%)	$1,086,065
1994			
Rangel (D)	$1,350,357	$763,025 (57%)	$1,437,297
Suero (R)	$2,860	0	$2,782

DISTRICT VOTE FOR PRESIDENT

	1996			1992	
D	135,845	(89%)	**D**	124,594	(86%)
R	7,658	(5%)	**R**	15,589	(11%)
I	2,377	(2%)	**I**	4,726	(3%)

KEY VOTES

1997	
Ban "partial birth" abortions	N
1996	
Approve farm bill	N
Deny public education to illegal immigrants	N
Repeal ban on certain assault-style weapons	N
Increase minimum wage	Y
Freeze defense spending	Y
Approve welfare overhaul	N
1995	
Approve balanced-budget constitutional amendment	N
Relax Clean Water Act regulations	N
Oppose limits on environmental regulations	Y
Reduce projected Medicare spending	N
Approve GOP budget with tax and spending cuts	N

VOTING STUDIES

	Presidential Support		Party Unity		Conservative Coalition	
Year	**S**	**O**	**S**	**O**	**S**	**O**
1996	77	16	92	3	8	90
1995	83	9	89	2	5	80
1994	72	18	82	2	8	64
1993	76	22	90	3	5	91
1992	12	84	90	4	15	81
1991	25	71	92	2	0	97

INTEREST GROUP RATINGS

Year	ADA	AFL-CIO	CCUS	ACU
1996	95	n/a	13	0
1995	85	100	14	8
1994	95	100	18	5
1993	95	100	0	0
1992	95	92	25	0
1991	95	100	20	0

16 Jose E. Serrano (D)

Of the Bronx — Elected 1990; 4th full term

Biographical Information
Born: Oct. 24, 1943, Mayaguez, P.R.
Education: Dodge Vocational H.S., 1961.
Military Service: Army Medical Corps, 1964-66.
Occupation: Public official.
Family: Wife, Mary Staucet; five children.
Religion: Roman Catholic.
Political Career: N.Y. Assembly, 1975-90; sought Democratic nomination for Bronx borough president, 1985.

Capitol Office: 2342 Rayburn Bldg. 20515; 225-4361.

Committees
Appropriations
Agriculture, Rural Development, FDA & Related Agencies; Legislative Branch (ranking)

In Washington: When the House Democratic leadership set about making key committees "look more like America" in 1993, the Puerto Rico-born Serrano received a seat on the Appropriations Committee. When America voted in 1994 to put Republicans in charge of the House, Serrano got bumped off Appropriations as his party's allotment of seats on the panel was cut.

But in an odd twist of circumstance, more good news for the GOP put Serrano back on Appropriations midway through the 104th Congress: After Mississippi Democratic Rep. Mike Parker switched parties, the GOP leadership added two seats to Appropriations — one for their new convert Parker, and one for the Democrats to fill. Serrano reclaimed his place.

Serrano was a 15-year veteran of the New York Assembly before coming to Washington, and he looks for ways to play the role of legislative insider. In the 105th Congress, though, he failed in his quest to be selected one of his party's four chief deputy whips. The whip post came open after Bill Richardson, D-N.M., left the House to become ambassador to the United Nations. Democratic leaders chose Robert Menendez of New Jersey over Serrano to succeed Richardson.

Serrano remains a vice chairman of the Democratic Steering Committee, the leadership panel that makes committee assignments. And in the 105th, he became ranking member on Appropriations' Legislative Branch Subcommittee, which handles funding for Congress' own operations.

On that subcommittee in the 104th, Serrano successfully fought efforts by Republicans to require the Architect of the Capitol to study the feasibility of placing a "debt clock" on the grounds of the U.S. Capitol to continuously flash the accumulated national debt. The provision was added by the subcommittee over Democratic objections in June 1996. But as the full committee considered the bill later that month, subcommittee chairman Ron Packard, R-Calif., moved to strip the provision from the bill. Packard's motion was adopted by voice vote.

Packard was eyeing the fact that Serrano had come to the full committee armed with 10 amendments that he planned to offer if Republicans persisted in pushing the debt clock. Serrano's amendments proposed studying the feasibility of placing an array of "clocks" on the Capitol grounds that would flash figures on a variety of statistics, including the number of reported cases of child abuse, of homeless families and of children lost to drugs. These subjects are "just as important as finding out how much we owe," Serrano explained.

In returning to Appropriations, Serrano resigned his seat on the Judiciary Committee. Shortly after moving to Judiciary, he ridiculed efforts by the Republican majority to limit congressional terms. "This has to be one of the silliest issues to come before this country in a long, long time," he said in February 1995. "I think instead of dealing with poverty in America, we're dealing with a parking spot."

During his 15 months on Judiciary, Serrano was a leading voice against Republican efforts to restrict immigration. In September 1995, he challenged legislation aimed at significantly limiting legal immigration and cracking down on those who enter or stay in the country unlawfully. "Shame on us," said Serrano, charging his colleagues with using immigrants as scapegoats. "It is easier to beat up on a dishwasher than it is to beat up on the Pentagon."

In October 1995, he fought efforts to make English the official language of the United States and to ban federally sponsored bilingual education programs. Serrano argued that the drive to succeed economically provides ample incentive for learning English. "When Hispanics sit around the dinner table, we don't plot how to make Spanish the official language," he said.

He splits from most Hispanics in Congress (including Menendez) on the issue of relations with Cuba. While Cuban-American critics of Fidel Castro's regime support tougher economic sanctions against Cuba, Serrano in the 105th Congress

One of the most economically devastated areas in the United States, the mostly Hispanic South Bronx had by the 1970s become a metaphor for the nation's urban ills. Its stretches of refuse-strewn lots and burned-out buildings provided backdrops for visiting politicians of both parties, who prescribed varying solutions to revive the inner cities. Residents have complained bitterly that these photo sessions have resulted in no improvements for the low-income communities of the South Bronx.

But the fragile seedlings of an economic turnaround have begun to take root in parts of the area that forms the 16th. Like frontier settlements, several developments of single-family homes and low-rise apartments have been built on vacated lots by subsidized economic development organizations and occupied by working-class, minority families. These areas, together with more settled, middle-class Hispanic communities in the eastern part of the 16th, provide hope for improvement.

The South Bronx, overtaken by the post-World War II influx of Hispanics to New York City, has since 1970 elected Democrats of Puerto Rican origin to the House. That year, Herman Badillo became the first Puerto Rican to serve in Congress. In 1979, he was succeeded by Robert Garcia, who resigned after being convicted in the Wedtech scandal. His conviction later was overturned on appeal. In 1990, Serrano stepped in and has easily held the seat since.

Once largely the province of working-class white ethnics, Jews and blacks, the 16th's territory is now 60 percent Hispanic. About a third of the residents are non-Hispanic blacks; fewer than 5 percent are non-Hispanic whites, one of the lowest proportions in any district.

NEW YORK 16
South Bronx

Overwhelming Democratic strength here is consistent with other mainly minority districts. Another consistent pattern is low voter turnout, a result of such factors as recent immigration status, political alienation and poverty.

A range of inner-city problems affects the residents of the 16th. It has the lowest median family income of the 435 House districts. More than 40 percent of all residents (and nearly half the Hispanic residents) live in poverty. Less than half of the people 25 or older have high school diplomas.

The hardest-pressed communities, such as Mott Haven, Melrose, Morrisania and East Tremont, are in the south and central parts of the district. Some of the new developments are scattered here among the ruins of urban decay. Across the Bronx River, in Soundview and Clason Point, are communities of middle-class Hispanic homeowners.

Once a major factory area, the South Bronx still has a handful of industrial employers, as well as two large wholesale food centers, the Hunts Point and the Bronx terminal markets; Yankee Stadium is near the latter, though owner George Steinbrenner has threatened to take the team out of the borough. The 16th comes to a northern point in Bronx Park, site of the Bronx Zoo and the New York Botanical Garden.

1990 Population: 580,338. White 116,116 (20%), Black 244,636 (42%), Other 219,586 (38%). Hispanic origin 349,190 (60%). 18 and over 385,188 (66%), 62 and over 51,111 (9%). Median age: 27.

reintroduced legislation to repeal two measures, including the Helms-Burton Act just enacted in 1996, that tightened the U.S. embargo against Cuba.

"It is inhumane to starve the Cuban people, punishing them with a trade embargo designed to bend their government to our political will," Serrano said.

He also introduced legislation removing restrictions on American citizens traveling to Cuba, and he backed allowing the United States and Cuba to open news bureaus in each other's countries. Cable News Network already has received permission from the Cuban government for a bureau in Havana. Serrano said that increased exchanges of information between Cubans and Americans will spur a peaceful democratic transition in Cuba.

In the 105th Congress, Serrano also introduced a constitutional amendment to repeal the 22nd Amendment, which limits the president to two four-year terms, and a measure, sponsored by Republican Alfonse M. D'Amato of New York in the Senate, to award a congressional gold medal to Frank Sinatra for his contributions to humanitarian causes and the entertainment industry.

In the 103rd, Serrano served as chairman of the Congressional Hispanic Caucus. In that role, he frequently rose to object to numerous amendments aimed at curtailing benefits for illegal and, in some cases, legal immigrants. His defense of the nation's immigrants grows out of strong personal experience. His colleagues still remember a moving speech Serrano delivered on the House floor shortly after he was sworn in. In the speech he recalled how his parents, now deceased, immigrated to the United States from Puerto Rico when he was 7.

During Serrano's term as caucus chairman, he often found himself on the House floor trying to deflect members' anger about immigrants. Some lawmakers, particularly from border states, argued that providing benefits to illegal immigrants was bankrupting state and federal coffers.

One of the first vehicles for this debate was President Clinton's National Service bill. In July 1993, the House rejected an amendment by California Republican Bill Baker to require charities and other National Service participants to have a written policy of providing no services to illegal aliens and to report illegals to the Immigration and Naturalization Service. "This doesn't strengthen the country," Serrano responded. "It just makes us look like really bad people."

At Home: Although Serrano's state Assembly career had made him a fixture in New York Hispanic politics, his avenues for advancement had looked narrow before 1989. Democratic Rep. Robert Garcia, first elected in 1978, was still in his 50s and seemed unlikely to leave his House seat soon.

But Garcia's career was shattered by his October 1989 conviction on charges of extortion. The case involved Wedtech Corp., a Bronx defense contractor that had aggressively pursued business under minority set-aside programs in the 1980s. Wedtech's lobbying techniques included bribes to several politicians.

Garcia resigned his seat in what was then the 18th District in January 1990, and a March election was set to fill his unexpired term. Serrano moved quickly to stake his claim.

Serrano breezed to the Democratic House nomination despite some dissent from African-American activists incensed at references to the 18th, then nearly half black, as a "Puerto Rican" seat. Bronx Republican officials, who seldom contest Democratic dominance in the South Bronx, probed that rift by running black businessman Simeon Golar. But Serrano ran away with 92 percent of the vote in the special election. He won a full term with 93 percent that November.

As a politician in a place plagued by unemployment and crime, Serrano has touted his own up-from-poverty story. An immigrant who was raised in a housing project, Serrano graduated from a vocational high school and served in the Army. Thereafter, he worked for a New York City bank and took a position on a community school board in the Bronx that helped him develop a core group of political allies.

In 1974, those contacts helped him win a state Assembly seat. By 1983, he was chairman of the Assembly Education Committee, a post from which he could look out for schools in New York City in general and for his minority constituents in particular.

Serrano twice sought the office of Bronx borough president. In 1985, he nearly upset incumbent Democrat Stanley Simon in a primary. Two years later, Serrano failed to become the party's appointed interim replacement for Simon, who also had been convicted in the Wedtech case and forced from office.

In 1992, the already well-entrenched Serrano gained insurance from a House redistricting plan that made his district more Hispanic.

HOUSE ELECTIONS

1996 General		
Jose E. Serrano (D,L)	95,568	(96%)
Rodney Torres (R)	2,878	(3%)
1994 General		
Jose E. Serrano (D,L)	58,572	(96%)
Michael Walters (C)	2,257	(4%)

Previous Winning Percentages: 1992 (91%) **1990** (93%) **1990**† (92%)

† Special election

CAMPAIGN FINANCE

	Receipts	Receipts from PACs	Expend-itures
1996			
Serrano (D)	$75,611	$58,352 (77%)	$149,752
1994			
Serrano (D)	$172,030	$91,563 (53%)	$125,441

DISTRICT VOTE FOR PRESIDENT

	1996		1992
D	117,624 (94%)	**D**	100,602 (81%)
R	4,825 (4%)	**R**	18,834 (15%)
I	1,862 (2%)	**I**	4,042 (3%)

KEY VOTES

1997	
Ban "partial birth" abortions	N
1996	
Approve farm bill	N
Deny public education to illegal immigrants	N
Repeal ban on certain assault-style weapons	N
Increase minimum wage	Y
Freeze defense spending	Y
Approve welfare overhaul	N
1995	
Approve balanced-budget constitutional amendment	N
Relax Clean Water Act regulations	N
Oppose limits on environmental regulations	Y
Reduce projected Medicare spending	N
Approve GOP budget with tax and spending cuts	N

VOTING STUDIES

	Presidential Support		Party Unity		Conservative Coalition	
Year	**S**	**O**	**S**	**O**	**S**	**O**
1996	78	18	95	4	12	86
1995	84	12	93	3	8	90
1994	71	26	94	2	8	89
1993	74	23	94	1	9	89
1992	9	89	90	3	4	92
1991	19	71	86	3	5	89

INTEREST GROUP RATINGS

Year	ADA	AFL-CIO	CCUS	ACU
1996	95	n/a	19	0
1995	100	100	13	4
1994	95	78	42	0
1993	100	100	0	4
1992	95	91	13	0
1991	100	100	10	0

17 Eliot L. Engel (D)

Of the Bronx — Elected 1988, 5th term

Biographical Information
Born: Feb. 18, 1947, Bronx, N.Y.
Education: Hunter-Lehman College, B.A. 1969; Lehman College, M.A. 1973; New York Law School, J.D. 1987.
Occupation: Teacher; guidance counselor.
Family: Wife, Patricia Ennis; three children.
Religion: Jewish.
Political Career: Bronx Democratic district leader, 1974-77; N.Y. Assembly, 1977-88.
Capitol Office: 2303 Rayburn Bldg. 20515; 225-2464.

Committees
Commerce
Finance & Hazardous Materials; Oversight & Investigations; Telecommunications, Trade & Consumer Protection

In Washington: During his first six years in the House, Engel voted a reliably liberal line and established a name for himself as a foreign-policy activist.

Then, in the middle of the 104th Congress, the Democratic leadership rewarded Engel for his loyalty and labors by giving him a seat on the influential Commerce Committee, affording him an opportunity to pursue a range of domestic-policy concerns.

His Commerce subcommittee assignments are Telecommunications, Trade and Consumer Protection; and Finance and Hazardous Materials. His interests include providing adequate radio bands to accommodate police and fire departments; securing funds for hospitals that serve many Medicaid patients; and ensuring that the transfer of refuse across state lines is uninhibited (a vital matter for garbage-exporting New York).

To join Commerce, Engel had to give up his seat on the International Relations Committee, but he retains his longstanding interest in global affairs, a matter that is akin to constituent service for Engel, as he represents one of the most ethnically and racially diverse districts in the nation.

The 17th, based in the borough of the Bronx, is divided about evenly among whites, blacks and Hispanics. It includes dozens of ethnic groups, including Irish, Italians and East Europeans. Like Engel, many of the district's residents are Jewish.

Engel is a liberal interventionist — he believes the United States should weigh in when it can put a stop to humanitarian tragedies. He was an early advocate of U.S. intervention in the civil war in the former Yugoslavia. In February 1993, he joined a bipartisan group of lawmakers who urged the Clinton administration to take sides in Bosnia against the Serbs, who were being accused of perpetrating widespread atrocities in the name of "ethnic cleansing" — the forced removal of Muslims from their communities.

Engel called on the administration to drop its opposition to lifting the United Nations arms embargo against Bosnia, and he supported limited airstrikes on Serbian positions.

Engel told the House in May 1994 that by standing aside in the Bosnian war, the United States and Europe were showing the Serbs that aggression, brutality and genocide paid. "Here it is 50 years after the Nazi era, and we are seeing the same kinds of atrocities committed on civilian populations, and the world wrings its hands. Nobody can agree and so nobody does anything."

(Later, in the 104th Congress, it was revealed that the Clinton administration knew and tacitly approved of arms transfers from Iran to the Bosnian Muslims.)

When the House in November 1995 passed a GOP-backed measure seeking to block Clinton from deploying U.S. peacekeeping troops to Bosnia unless Congress agreed to fund the mission, Engel opposed the restriction.

Soon afterward, talks in Dayton, Ohio, between the warring parties in the former Yugoslavia produced a laboriously negotiated peace accord. Engel subsequently kept up the pressure on the Serbs, arguing against lifting international sanctions on Serbia until the human rights situation there improved.

In early 1994, Engel urged more U.S. involvement in Haiti, saying the "despotic" government of Lt. Gen. Raoul Cedras had been free "to commit one atrocity after another." In October 1994, he supported Clinton's decision to threaten military force to chase Cedras out of Haiti, and the subsequent deployment of U.S. troops to keep the peace until Haitians restored democratic rule.

During a lengthy House debate over whether Clinton should have sought congressional approval before sending troops to Haiti, Engel said that since the troops were there already and had encountered little difficulty, they should complete their mission.

Engel is a strong supporter of Israel, whose well-being is a big concern of Jewish residents in the 17th, many of whom live in a massive high-rise complex known as Co-Op City.

In the spring of 1997, Engel called on Clinton to suspend non-humanitarian aid to the Palestin-

NEW YORK 17
North Bronx; parts of southern Westchester

Reflective of the demographic changes the borough of the Bronx has undergone in recent years, the 17th is one of the most ethnically and racially diverse congressional districts. Blacks, with a more than two-fifths plurality, make up the largest racial group in the 17th (which takes in nearly all of the northern part of the Bronx as well as urbanized parts of Yonkers, Mount Vernon and New Rochelle in Westchester County). But Hispanics and non-Hispanic whites are just behind, almost tied with about a third of the population each.

The non-Hispanic white constituency subdivides among dozens of ethnic groups, with long-standing communities of Italian- and Irish-Americans, Eastern Europeans and Jews.

Many white ethnics are traditionally Democratic but hold conservative views on social issues. They provided the political base for such figures as former Rep. Mario Biaggi, who held the North Bronx district for nearly two decades before running afoul of the law in 1988.

But the 17th, as reconfigured in 1992, is a majority-minority district where the liberal views of Engel may be more welcome. Like Biaggi, Engel supports the various foreign policy causes of his district's European ethnics. But he must maintain a liberal voting record and build multiracial coalitions to overcome primary challenges by minority-group candidates.

Any serious House contest in the 17th will almost have to be in the primary. Nearly three-quarters of the registered voters are Democrats. Bill Clinton won with 85 percent of the vote here in 1996.

There are some low-income pockets in the 17th, including some housing projects located in an odd arm that follows the Major Deegan Expressway into an area of the South Bronx adjacent to (but not including) Yankee Stadium. The poverty rate for Hispanic residents in the 17th, about 30 percent, is on par with New York state's rate.

But by and large, this is a middle- to working-class district where the city meets the suburbs. The poverty rate for blacks in the 17th is well below that for the state. A composite of the district can be found in middle-income Co-Op City, a massive complex of high-rise apartments in the eastern part of the 17th. It has a large Jewish population that is Engel's political base, but also many black and Hispanic residents.

At the western border of the Bronx is its most affluent and suburban community, heavily Jewish Riverdale. Just to the north, though, is much of the western part of the city of Yonkers, which is two-thirds minority and mainly low-income. The concentration of minorities in this section has led to a drawn-out federal court battle over housing discrimination in Yonkers.

On its east side, the 17th takes in a part of Mount Vernon that is three-quarters black, a small and racially mixed part of Pelham, and a part of New Rochelle (including its downtown) that is two-thirds black.

1990 Population: 580,337. White 233,703 (40%), Black 243,182 (42%), Other 103,452 (18%). Hispanic origin 168,791 (29%). 18 and over 438,290 (76%), 62 and over 97,471 (17%). Median age: 33.

ian Authority until it complied with its "solemn commitment to halt violence and terrorism." Also, Engel believes Jerusalem should serve as the undivided capital of Israel. In 1995, he supported moving the U.S. embassy from Tel Aviv to Jerusalem.

Always on guard against anti-Semitism or insensitivity to Jewish concerns, Engel condemned a proposed shopping mall on the site of the Auschwitz death camp in Poland. His office received anti-Semitic calls and faxes after he spoke in the House against a proposal to deny raises to federal agents involved in the sieges at Waco, Texas, and Ruby Ridge, Idaho.

Engel's involvement in the problems of Northern Ireland also has a constituent link: His district's many Irish-Americans include a number of activists who favor expanded rights for the Catholic minority and an eventual end to British rule of Northern Ireland.

Although his district is predominantly middle-class, it does have some pockets of low-income residents. Engel felt these communities were especially threatened by the GOP's budget-cutting plans in the 104th. He steadfastly opposed Republican attempts to overhaul welfare, including the compromise bill that Clinton signed.

After the 1994 election, Engel had predicted that Clinton would try to enhance his popularity by making some moves to the center, as he did on welfare. "I frankly think in the White House they're looking at what's good for Clinton," he said. "I don't think they're necessarily looking at what's good for the party."

Engel has been a strong defender of the Corporation for Public Broadcasting — a favorite budget-cutting target of conservatives. "If we cut the legs out from under public television," he said in the 104th, "we will not be hurting the imaginary liberal elite. We will be hurting children and families who often rely on public broadcasting for their source on news and education."

He also found frequent occasion in the 104th to stick up for organized labor in battles with the business-minded GOP majority. When Republicans tried to repeal the 1931 Davis-Bacon Act, which requires the government to pay prevailing wages (usually union-scale) on construction contracts, he called the effort "shameful union-bashing." He opposed a GOP bill to allow establishment of employer-employee teams to negotiate labor issues in non-union shops, faulted another Republican proposal to allow employers to permanently replace striking workers, and voted to increase the minimum wage. Many of those issues went through the Economic and Educational Opportunities Committee, where Engel served until moving to Commerce.

At Home: Engel won election to the House in 1988 by defeating former 10-term Democrat Mario Biaggi, who had been convicted earlier that year on federal charges of bribery and extortion. Engel had a relatively routine re-election in 1990, then stifled Biaggi's unlikely last hurrah in 1992.

Redistricting in 1992 made the 17th a majority-minority district. In 1994, Engel was tested by Willie Colon, an international salsa star who was backed by some prominent black leaders. Colon sought to ride an ad hoc black-Hispanic coalition against Engel, who is white. But Engel maintained support from many area Hispanic elected officials and refused to cede the Hispanic or black vote. He ended up winning the primary with 61 percent.

A low-key figure during more than a decade in the New York Assembly, Engel held positions that served him well in his initial House race. He had chaired a committee on drug and alcohol abuse and a subcommittee that handled moderate-income housing issues. Nevertheless, it was the gamble of his career when Engel mounted a primary challenge to Biaggi. Biaggi was about to be tried in a federal case involving alleged bribes by Wedtech Corp. (a defunct Bronx defense contractor), and he had been convicted of accepting illegal gratuities in a separate 1987 case. But he remained highly popular in the 19th, where he was known as a decorated former police officer and neighborhood hero. So most Democrats stood aside when he defiantly announced he would seek re-election in 1988.

In August, Biaggi was convicted and resigned his seat. His name remained on the ballot, however, for both the primary and the general election (the latter because he regularly received the endorsement of district Republicans). Engel won both contests, taking 50 percent of the primary vote and then winning the general election with 56 percent to Biaggi's 27 percent.

In 1991, Biaggi was given early release from his jail sentence because of heart and neurological problems. But a year later, he pronounced himself hale and determined to reclaim his seat.

Biaggi retained a loyal core of supporters, but his comeback try, likely doomed in any election year, was especially ill-timed in 1992, when the House bank scandal had voters stirred up about corruption in Congress. Engel touted his record of delivering for the district and said Biaggi had "weaseled his way out of prison" with health complaints. Engel won the primary by nearly 3-1.

HOUSE ELECTIONS

1996 General		
Eliot L. Engel (D,L)	101,287	(85%)
Denis McCarthy (R,C,RTL)	15,892	(13%)
Dennis Coleman (INDC)	2,008	(2%)
1996 Primary		
Eliot L. Engel (D,L)	14,366	(77%)
Herbert Moreira Brown (D)	4,314	(23%)
1994 General		
Eliot L. Engel (D,L)	73,321	(78%)
Edward T. Marshall (R)	16,896	(18%)
Kevin Brawley (C)	2,187	(2%)
Ann M. Noonan (RTL)	2,075	(2%)

Previous Winning Percentages: 1992 (80%) **1990** (61%) **1988** (56%)

CAMPAIGN FINANCE

	Receipts	Receipts from PACs	Expend-itures
1996			
Engel (D)	$411,814	$206,493 (50%)	$374,074
1994			
Engel (D)	$462,713	$279,150 (60%)	$464,001
Marshall (R)	$211,374	$514 (0%)	$211,374

DISTRICT VOTE FOR PRESIDENT

1996		1992	
D	126,832 (85%)	**D**	120,286 (76%)
R	16,117 (11%)	**R**	30,133 (19%)
I	3,841 (3%)	**I**	7,945 (5%)

KEY VOTES

1997	
Ban "partial birth" abortions	N
1996	
Approve farm bill	N
Deny public education to illegal immigrants	N
Repeal ban on certain assault-style weapons	N
Increase minimum wage	Y
Freeze defense spending	Y
Approve welfare overhaul	N
1995	
Approve balanced-budget constitutional amendment	N
Relax Clean Water Act regulations	N
Oppose limits on environmental regulations	Y
Reduce projected Medicare spending	N
Approve GOP budget with tax and spending cuts	N

VOTING STUDIES

	Presidential Support		Party Unity		Conservative Coalition	
Year	S	O	S	O	S	O
1996	80	15	91	4	22	75
1995	86	13	96	3	10	89
1994	78	19	89	3	11	86
1993	77	15	86	2	11	77
1992	16	75	85	5	25	73
1991	27	71	93	4	14	86

INTEREST GROUP RATINGS

Year	ADA	AFL-CIO	CCUS	ACU
1996	95	n/a	25	0
1995	100	100	8	8
1994	100	100	18	0
1993	90	100	0	5
1992	95	91	25	4
1991	90	100	30	15

18 Nita M. Lowey (D)

Of Harrison — Elected 1988, 5th term

Biographical Information

Born: July 5, 1937, Bronx, N.Y.
Education: Mount Holyoke College, B.A. 1959.
Occupation: Public official.
Family: Husband, Stephen Lowey; three children.
Religion: Jewish.
Political Career: N.Y. assistant secretary of state, 1985-87.
Capitol Office: 2421 Rayburn Bldg. 20515; 225-6506.

Committees

Appropriations
Foreign Operations, Export Financing & Related Programs; Labor, Health & Human Services, Education & Related Agencies

In Washington: Lowey is a high-profile defender of abortion rights and other liberal causes, and her position on the Appropriations Committee puts her in the thick of the battle as conservative Republicans try to cut off funding for federal programs and policies they dislike. Her visibility, along with her prowess at fund-raising and vote-winning, have earned her mention as a possible Senate candidate. In May 1997, Lowey, however, took herself out of the running in 1998, when GOP Sen. Alfonse M. D'Amato is up for re-election.

Lowey fought and lost one intraparty battle as Democrats were organizing for the 105th Congress. She pushed for the election of fellow New York Democrat Louise M. Slaughter as ranking minority member of the House Budget Committee. Slaughter's boosters noted that no other committee had a woman in the ranking slot. But Slaughter lost to Rep. John M. Spratt Jr. of South Carolina, 106-83. "Women clearly don't have a proportionate share of power in the House," Lowey said. "They are sorely under-represented. We have to work to ensure that women are better represented."

From her seat on Appropriations, Lowey has been an aggressive critic of efforts by anti-abortion Republicans to incorporate language reflecting their views into appropriations bills.

Lowey initially won a victory during the markup of the fiscal 1997 Labor-HHS spending bill when Appropriations' Labor-HHS-Education Subcommittee approved her amendment to allow federal researchers to use human embryos in medical studies. It also would have upheld a ban on creating embryos specifically for research purposes. But the full Appropriations Committee stripped out the amendment and the House voted, 167-256, against Lowey's attempt to resurrect her proposal.

She strenuously objects to banning a particular abortion technique that opponents call "partial-birth" abortion. Lowey has said the technique is used in extreme circumstances — when the woman's life is in danger or when the fetus has abnormalities that likely would kill it soon after birth. "This procedure is not about choice, it's about necessity," she said. "This legislation will criminalize abortion, harass doctors and prevent women from getting the medical care they need."

She waved the abortion-rights banner again during debate on the fiscal 1997 appropriations bill for the Treasury Department and related agencies. The House rejected, 184-238, an amendment by Steny H. Hoyer, D-Md., to allow health plans offered to federal employees to include abortion coverage. Current law prohibits such coverage, and the bill continued that ban through fiscal 1997.

"American women shouldn't have their constitutional rights taken away simply because they work for the government," Lowey said.

Supporters of the ban countered that because federal funds are used to pay part of health care premiums for federal workers, the plans should not offer abortion as a service. It is important "that taxpayers are not forced to subsidize the killing of baby boys and girls by abortion," argued Christopher H. Smith, R-N.J.

In the fiscal 1996 Labor-HHS appropriations bill, she strongly supported an amendment by Jim Kolbe, R-Ariz., to maintain provisions in existing law that required states to provide Medicaid funding for the abortions of low-income women in instances of rape, incest or danger to the life of the woman. Under the bill, states no longer were required to provide funding in instances of rape and incest.

"Rape is horrible," said Henry J. Hyde, R-Ill. speaking in favor of the tighter restrictions. "The only thing worse than rape is abortion. That's killing."

Proponents of Kolbe's amendment said the restrictions in the bill heaped further abuse on women who already had been victimized by rape. Said Lowey: "It's draconian; it's extreme; it's cruel, and it's unfair."

Beyond the abortion policy arena, Lowey promotes efforts to combat sexual harassment and physical abuse of women. She tried twice (unsuc-

NEW YORK 18
Parts of Westchester, Bronx and Queens counties

The 18th is one of many jigsaw-puzzle pieces in New York's district map. It stretches from the southern part of Westchester County (which has two-thirds of the district's population), down a ribbon of the East Bronx bordering Long Island Sound, across the mouth of the East River and down a narrow corridor into central Queens.

Before 1992 redistricting, Democrat Lowey's constituency was wholly within Westchester. The remap removed mainly black, Democratic-voting communities on the urban southern edge of Westchester. But it replaced them with heavily Jewish parts of Queens, where Lowey took 71 percent of the vote in 1992, cinching her victory over the Republican she unseated four years earlier, former Rep. Joseph J. DioGuardi. She did even better in 1996, polling 75 percent of the Queens vote.

The Westchester portion of the district is more competitive: Lowey won 53 percent there in 1992 but she improved to 61 percent in 1996. This section has some of the most affluent communities in New York state. Most — including such places as Bronxville and Harrison — lean Republican, though Scarsdale, with its large Jewish population, often goes Democratic. The 18th's coastal location along the Long Island Sound also breeds an environmental consciousness that has benefited Lowey.

The most Democratic sections are in the low- to middle-income areas of the large cities, including parts of New Rochelle and White Plains, the county's seat and commercial center. The 18th has the largest portion of Yonkers, Westchester's most populous city (which is split among three districts).

While Yonkers provides some Democratic votes from its ethnic white, working-class population, it is not a liberal place; it was involved in a lengthy federal court battle over whether there was intentional housing discrimination. The part of the city in the 18th (mainly on the east side) is nearly 90 percent non-Hispanic white, while the southwest part in the 17th District is two-thirds minority.

While there is much commuting to New York City, the portion of Westchester in the 18th has several large employers, including the headquarters of Texaco (White Plains) and Pepsico (Purchase). There is a significant retail trade, much of it in White Plains. Educational institutions include Iona College in New Rochelle and exclusive Sarah Lawrence College in Yonkers.

On its east side, the district takes in an edge of the Bronx, including Pelham Bay Park and City Island. This area's small population, mainly working-class Italian-Americans, leans Republican. Lowey took in 53 percent in 1996 and Bob Dole, who polled just 35 percent in the 18th District, received 42 percent here.

The 18th then enters Queens via the Throgs Neck Bridge and follows a winding path through urban Flushing, which gives it much of its Asian population. After enveloping the southern part of Flushing Meadow Park, the district spreads west to take in the community of Rego Park and east to Utopia, site of St. John's University.

1990 Population: 580,337. White 470,717 (81%), Black 43,506 (7%), Other 66,114 (11%). Hispanic origin 60,202 (10%). 18 and over 467,381 (81%), 62 and over 117,660 (20%). Median age: 38.

cessfully) to get money for programs addressing violence against women into the fiscal 1996 spending bill for the departments of Commerce, Justice and State and the federal judiciary.

With claims of sexual harassment in the Army garnering attention in the media, Lowey — who co-chairs the Congressional Caucus for Women's Issues — met with her colleagues in that group and Army officials to suggest that the military set up a system outside the regular chain of command for soldiers to report allegations of sexual harassment. She said the group also had talked to the other military services to discuss the problem. "It is hard to believe that this activity . . . has not occurred in the other branches as well," she said.

She was outspoken about reports that women employees at Mitsubishi Motor Manufacturing of America had endured sexual harassment and discrimination. "Quite frankly, Mitsubishi has a public relations disaster on its hands," Lowey said.

Aiming to trump conservatives who profess a desire to cut federal spending, Lowey came forward during debate on the fiscal 1996 agriculture appropriations bill with a proposal to block farm subsidies from going to people with more than $100,000 in off-farm income. "At a time of tight budgets . . . it doesn't make sense to me to have millionaires collecting farm subsidies," she said.

But rural members — even some staunchly conservative "deficit hawks" in the GOP — argued that payments to farmers are intended to stabilize the agricultural economy and should go to all growers regardless of their wealth. "It has nothing to do with a farmer's income," said Jack Kingston, R-Ga. The House rejected Lowey's amendment, 158-249.

She also joined with Christopher Shays, R-Conn., in an unsuccessful attempt to eliminate peanut programs.

Lowey has had better luck playing the inside game. At the start of the 102nd Congress, she wanted a seat on the Appropriations Committee, which she got by aggressively lobbying the Democratic leadership. When the GOP took over after the 1994 elections and vowed to trim committee rosters, Lowey's seat looked to be at risk. But rather than trust her own leaders to negotiate on her behalf, Lowey went directly to the decision-makers, pleading her case to incoming House Speaker Newt Gingrich and Appropriations Chairman Robert L. Livingston of Louisiana. She argued that by sparing only a few more Democratic committee seats, the incoming regime could maintain important diversity on Appropriations. Her seat was saved, along with that of California Hispanic Esteban E. Torres.

While waging her issue crusades and pursuing institutional politics, Lowey has been careful not to neglect her district, which, since 1992 redistricting, includes not only much of upscale Westchester County but also some blue-collar neighborhoods in Queens and the Bronx. From her perch at Appropriations she helped city residents by winning an increase in funding to renovate Grant's Tomb and by preserving funding for renovation of Penn Station. For Westchester, she and Democratic Sen. Daniel Patrick Moynihan managed to obtain more than $4 million for development of downtown Yonkers.

At Home: Lowey made a stunning political debut in 1988 when she unseated two-term GOP Rep. Joseph J. DioGuardi in the then-20th District. Her outgoing personality and district-oriented legislative efforts enabled her to settle in quickly, and her fundraising skills have made her tough to beat ever since. She defeated a poorly funded Republican candidate in 1990, brushed aside a comeback attempt by DioGuardi in 1992, faced down a challenge by wealthy lawyer Andrew C. Hartzell Jr. in 1994, and had no problems defeating lawyer Kerry J. Katsorhis in 1996.

By the time she entered the political arena, Lowey had spent years as a Democratic activist. In 1974, Lowey, then a homemaker in Queens, worked in the lieutenant governor's campaign of a neighbor, Mario M. Cuomo. Cuomo lost the primary but later was appointed by then-Democratic Gov. Hugh L. Carey as New York secretary of state and hired Lowey to work in his department's anti-poverty division.

By the mid-1980s, Cuomo was governor; Lowey was the top aide to Secretary of State Gail Schaffer and a resident of the Westchester suburb of Harrison. Meanwhile, DioGuardi in 1984 had captured a swing Westchester House district that long had been held by Democrats.

In 1988, Lowey aimed for DioGuardi. She survived a primary against Hamilton Fish III, publisher of The Nation magazine and son of a House member, and businessman Dennis Mehiel.

Lowey raised $1.3 million, a huge treasury for a challenger. DioGuardi outspent her, but his fundraising also turned into his downfall. A newspaper reported in October that a New Rochelle auto dealer had funneled $57,000 in corporate contributions to DioGuardi's campaign through his employees. DioGuardi denied knowledge of the pass-through scheme, but the revelations damaged him. Despite DioGuardi's effort to brand her as an extreme liberal, Lowey won narrowly.

HOUSE ELECTIONS

1996 General		
Nita M. Lowey (D)	118,194	(64%)
Kerry J. Katsorhis (R,C)	59,487	(32%)
Concetta M. Ferrara (INDC)	4,283	(2%)
Florence T. O'Grady (RTL)	3,758	(2%)
1994 General		
Nita M. Lowey (D)	91,663	(57%)
Andrew C. Hartzell Jr. (R,C)	65,517	(41%)
Florence T. O'Grady (RTL)	2,873	(2%)

Previous Winning Percentages: **1992** (56%) **1990** (63%) **1988** (50%)

CAMPAIGN FINANCE

	Receipts	Receipts from PACs	Expend-itures
1996			
Lowey (D)	$1,390,131	$229,227 (16%)	$1,138,456
Katsorhis (R)	$253,498	$1,216 (0%)	$238,826
1994			
Lowey (D)	$1,314,605	$251,171 (19%)	$1,343,347
Hartzell (R)	$429,716	$7,464 (2%)	$427,491

INTEREST GROUP RATINGS

Year	ADA	AFL-CIO	CCUS	ACU
1996	90	n/a	31	0
1995	90	100	25	4
1994	85	89	42	10
1993	90	92	18	4
1992	100	92	25	0
1991	100	100	20	0

KEY VOTES

1997	
Ban "partial birth" abortions	N
1996	
Approve farm bill	N
Deny public education to illegal immigrants	N
Repeal ban on certain assault-style weapons	N
Increase minimum wage	Y
Freeze defense spending	Y
Approve welfare overhaul	Y
1995	
Approve balanced-budget constitutional amendment	N
Relax Clean Water Act regulations	N
Oppose limits on environmental regulations	Y
Reduce projected Medicare spending	N
Approve GOP budget with tax and spending cuts	N

VOTING STUDIES

	Presidential Support		Party Unity		Conservative Coalition	
Year	S	O	S	O	S	O
1996	86	14	93	5	10	90
1995	86†	13†	96†	4†	13†	87†
1994	82	18	97	2	11	89
1993	84	16	95	3	18	82
1992	13	87	96	3	15	85
1991	24	74	95	3	8	92

† Not eligible for all recorded votes.

DISTRICT VOTE FOR PRESIDENT

1996		1992	
D	121,676 (58%)	**D**	117,937 (50%)
R	73,335 (35%)	**R**	94,754 (40%)
I	10,244 (5%)	**I**	22,019 (9%)

19 Sue W. Kelly (R)

Of Katonah — Elected 1994, 2nd term

Biographical Information

Born: Sept. 26, 1936, Lima, Ohio.

Education: Denison U., B.A. 1958; Sarah Lawrence College, M.A. 1985.

Occupation: Professor; teacher; hospital administrative aide; medical researcher; retailer.

Family: Husband, Edward W. Kelly; four children.

Religion: Presbyterian.

Political Career: No previous office.

Capitol Office: 1222 Longworth Bldg. 20515; 225-5441.

Committees

Banking & Financial Services
Financial Institutions & Consumer Credit; Housing & Community Opportunity

Small Business
Regulatory Reform & Paperwork Reduction (chairman)

Transportation & Infrastructure
Surface Transportation; Water Resources & Environment

In Washington: Kelly is essentially a moderate Republican in the mold of her predecessor, GOP Rep. Hamilton Fish Jr. But Kelly, who runs as both an environmentalist and an abortion-rights supporter, must remain alert to political pressure from the right. Her efforts to strike a balance between conservatism and moderation in Congress have spawned some controversy at home.

The 19th District had a history of centrist Republican representation under Fish, but his retirement in 1994 opened the door to stiff competition between moderate and conservative elements in the local GOP. To win the open seat, Kelly had to get past six conservative men in the Republican primary, including former Rep. Joseph J. DioGuardi. In 1996, she again faced DioGuardi in the GOP primary.

In the first months of the 104th Congress, Kelly ran in harness with the GOP leadership on the "Contract With America" agenda; her votes included support for a broad bill making it more difficult for federal agencies to issue health, safety and environmental regulations. In May 1995, she supported a conservative-backed bill revising the 1972 clean water act, even though many environmentalists portrayed the measure as a "a polluter's bill of rights." Defending her stand, Kelly said "There are certain laws that become sacred cows, and it's very important that we sometimes address sacred cows."

That kind of talk warmed conservatives' hearts, but it disappointed moderates, who felt she had sold out to the GOP right. Her Mount Kisco district office was picketed by environmental activists, and there were critical editorials in some local newspapers.

In July 1995, Kelly's record took on a greener tinge as she was one of 51 Republicans supporting an effort to strike legislative language limiting the regulatory authority of the Environmental Protection Agency. "We must not jeopardize the flow of federal funds for important environmental programs that control combined sewer overflows, protect important wetlands or clean our drinking water," she said.

In early 1996, Kelly voted for two environmentally minded amendments to the omnibus farm bill. One included funding for a conservation reserve program, which pays farmers to idle ecologically sensitive land, and the other provided $210 million to buy land and provide for environmental protections in the Florida Everglades. Also in 1996, Kelly was assigned to the 13-member steering committee of a GOP environmental task force set up by Speaker Newt Gingrich and co-chaired by fellow upstate New York Republican Sherwood Boehlert. The group was established at a time when opinion polls were indicating that the public viewed the GOP as too cozy with corporate and industrial interests, to the detriment of the environment.

She helped push through legislation protecting Sterling Forest, a vast undeveloped parcel of land along the New York-New Jersey border, and a measure authorizing $11 million to restore and preserve wildlife habitats along the Hudson River.

For the most part, Kelly has been a consistent supporter of abortion rights. She and 48 other Republicans backed a Democratic-led effort in March 1996 to retain a requirement that states fund Medicaid abortions in cases of rape and incest and to protect the life of the woman. Abortion foes wanted to give states new authority to set their own abortion funding policies on rape and incest.

Also in March 1996, she was one of only 15 House Republicans voting against a GOP initiative to ban a procedure that opponents call "partial birth" abortion. But she switched sides in March 1997 and voted with the Republican majority for a ban.

Kelly also was the only one of the seven Class of 1994 GOP women to join the Congressional Women's Caucus, which in past yeats helped draft the Family and Medical Leave Act, the Violence Against Women Act and bills authorizing federal funding of abortions for poor women.

On fiscal policy, Kelly has few disagreements

NEW YORK 19
Hudson Valley — Poughkeepsie

From its southern edge in Westchester County, the 19th links the densely packed New York City constituencies to the spacious districts of upstate New York. Though it takes in part of White Plains and Poughkeepsie, the 19th is largely exurban and even partially rural.

For 26 years, the 19th provided a comfortable base for GOP Rep. Hamilton Fish Jr., though it is not the state's most Republican district. The New York City-oriented Westchester part of the 19th, which provides just under half the population, can be competitive. In 1994, Republican Kelly defeated retiring Rep. Fish's Democratic son and namesake, 48 percent to 41 percent, in Westchester. In 1996, Kelly lost the Westchester portion of the district to Democratic challenger Richard S. Klein by just under 2,000 votes.

Much of the 19th's Democratic vote comes from White Plains and working-class communities along the Hudson River. A General Motors plant closed in September 1996 under a corporate restructuring plan. The town that housed the plant, North Tarrytown, changed its name to Sleepy Hollow, after the Washington Irving story about Ichabod Crane and the Headless Horseman, in the hope of attracting tourists. Ossining is the site of the Sing Sing correctional facility; its location on the Hudson gave rise to the warning about being "sent up the river." In Buchanan, near Peekskill, is the Indian Point nuclear power plant. Minority groups make up a higher proportion of the population in these areas than in the rest of the Westchester part of the 19th.

That portion is otherwise made up mainly of white-collar and middle- to upper middle-class homeowners. During its boom years, International Business Machines — which has its corporate headquarters in Armonk and an international marketing office in White Plains — spurred rapid residential growth in exurban northern Westchester. IBM's layoffs earlier in 1988-91 hurt the region economically.

Among other employers based here is the Reader's Digest Co. in Pleasantville. The Rockefeller family estate, much of it now a state park, is in Pocantico Hills.

Putnam County has experienced some exurban growth, but much of it remains relatively rural. The same can be said about eastern Dutchess County, estate country that has a number of horse farms. Across the Hudson, the 19th takes in a piece of Orange County that includes the U.S. Military Academy at West Point.

The population in the Dutchess County portion is concentrated near its western border with the Hudson. IBM's fallout also has shaken this area. Vassar and Marist colleges are in Poughkeepsie.

The Dutchess County town of Hyde Park is just north of the 19th, but it remains a historic touchstone for the Fish political dynasty. The late Rep. Hamilton Fish Sr. was one of the most fervent opponents of the New Deal policies of President Franklin D. Roosevelt, whose Hyde Park estate was in Fish's House district.

1990 Population: 580,337. White 516,568 (89%), Black 42,260 (7%), Other 21,509 (4%). Hispanic origin 30,293 (5%). 18 and over 444,315 (77%), 62 and over 78,595 (14%). Median age: 34.

with her more conservative party brethren. She is in a position to demonstrate her support of the Republican mantra of less taxes and regulations as the new chairwoman of the Small Business Subcommittee on Regulatory Reform and Paperwork Reduction, which oversees the IRS, OSHA and Small Business Administration.

She supports a balanced budget constitutional amendment, the presidential line-item veto and elimination of the capital gains tax. She began the 105th Congress by introducing legislation exempting homeowners from capital gains taxes when they sell their principal residence.

Kelly got attention at home for working to preserve federal "impact aid" for a school district in the 19th. Impact aid goes to local school systems that are affected by the presence of federally owned property, which cannot be taxed. Kelly said that 93 percent of the lands within the Highland Falls-Fort Montgomery School District, which is adjacent to the United States Military Academy at West Point, are non-taxable, making it difficult for the school system to raise revenue.

Kelly also lobbied hard for a measure to restore local control over the disposal of municipal solid waste. The bill came in response to a 1994 Supreme Court decision that prevented local governments from directing waste to specific incinerators, landfills or dumps. Kelly was concerned about the financial troubles of a resource recovery agency in her district. It was built with the belief that a steady stream of waste would be available to it to meet its financial obligations. She told the House in January 1996 that because of the Supreme Court decision, the facility had a $3 million shortfall in 1995 and expected more of the same "unless corrective action is taken." The House, however, went against her wishes on the issue by a 150-271 vote.

At Home: Although Kelly's 1994 campaign for Congress was her first bid for elective office, she had toiled for more than three decades to elect GOP candidates to local, state and national office. As a candidate she could draw on a variety of life experiences, including raising four children, volunteering as a rape crisis counselor and patient advocate at St. Luke's Hospital in New York City, teaching junior high science and math and running a florist business.

In the seven-way GOP primary, Kelly topped her all-male cast of competitors with 23 percent of the vote. DioGuardi, who served in the House from 1985-89, was second with 20 percent. He pressed on to November as the nominee of the Conservative and Right to Life parties, calling himself "the true conservative Republican in this race" and deriding Kelly as "a Democrat in disguise."

In addition to her problems with the right, Kelly also saw retiring incumbent Fish abandon party loyalty and endorse the Democratic nominee, his son, Hamilton Fish III. Kelly and the elder Fish had not been on good terms; he complained that she had worked for his 1992 Democratic challenger and even picketed his local congressional office.

According to the Poughkeepsie Journal, in October 1992, Fish's campaign manager told a newspaper editorial board that Fish would oppose abortions "for some lady who doesn't want to get fat." Angry at the implication that women seek abortions for cosmetic reasons, the newspaper said Kelly gave the names of pro-abortion-rights Republicans to Fish's Democratic opponent, Neil McCarthy. In addition, Kelly, dressed in a black cloak resembling an Iranian chador, demonstrated outside Fish's office holding a sign that read: "Fish = Women in the Dark Ages," according to The Reporter Dispatch of White Plains, Westchester County.

Kelly got the backing of the national GOP: New York Rep. Bill Paxon, chairman of the National Republican Congressional Committee, affirmed the committee's support for her as the party's nominee. And she benefited from the surging GOP gubernatorial campaign of George E. Pataki, whose state Senate district was in the 19th. With Hudson Valley Republicans streaming to the polls to elect Pataki over Democratic Gov. Mario M. Cuomo, Kelly won with 52 percent of the vote. Fish took 37 percent and DioGuardi 10 percent.

Returning to challenge Kelly in the 1996 GOP primary, DioGuardi again called himself the true conservative in the race, and he ignored a request from Speaker Newt Gingrich that he not run. DioGuardi gained the support of anti-abortion Republican Reps. Christopher H. Smith of New Jersey and Robert K. Dornan of California for his campaign. The House GOP leadership, which backed Kelly, came down on both Smith and Dornan for supporting DioGuardi; Dornan, for example, initially was kept off the conference committee of the defense authorization bill.

DioGuardi topped 40 percent in the primary and again continued his campaign into the general election as the nominee of the Conservative and Right to Life parties. Kelly also faced a well-financed Democratic challenger, physician Richard S. Klein, who spent more than $250,000 of his own money on the race. DioGuardi took 12 percent and Klein 39 percent, and that pulled Kelly down below her 1994 showing, as she won a second term with a 46 percent tally.

HOUSE ELECTIONS

1996 General		
Sue W. Kelly (R,FDM)	102,142	(46%)
Richard S. Klein (D,L)	86,926	(39%)
Joseph J. DioGuardi (C,RTL)	27,424	(12%)
William F. Haase (INDC)	4,104	(2%)
1996 Primary		
Sue W. Kelly (R,C,FDM)	11,693	(53%)
Joseph J. DioGuardi (R,C,RTL)	9,245	(42%)
Jim Russell (R)	1,198	(5%)
1994 General		
Sue W. Kelly (R)	100,173	(52%)
Hamilton Fish Jr. (D)	70,696	(37%)
Joseph J. DioGuardi (C,RTL)	19,761	(10%)

CAMPAIGN FINANCE

	Receipts	Receipts from PACs	Expend-itures
1996			
Kelly (R)	$976,613	$406,647 (42%)	$906,904
Klein (D)	$631,973	$97,100 (15%)	$630,471
DioGuardi (C,RTL)	$494,448	$30,685 (6%)	$496,133
1994			
Kelly (R)	$570,938	$99,770 (17%)	$570,821
Fish (D)	$591,003	$80,536 (14%)	$566,601

DISTRICT VOTE FOR PRESIDENT

	1996		1992
D	116,560 (48%)	D	104,950 (40%)
R	98,502 (41%)	R	109,965 (42%)
I	20,782 (9%)	I	45,088 (17%)

KEY VOTES

1997	
Ban "partial birth" abortions	Y
1996	
Approve farm bill	Y
Deny public education to illegal immigrants	Y
Repeal ban on certain assault-style weapons	Y
Increase minimum wage	Y
Freeze defense spending	Y
Approve welfare overhaul	Y
1995	
Approve balanced-budget constitutional amendment	Y
Relax Clean Water Act regulations	Y
Oppose limits on environmental regulations	Y
Reduce projected Medicare spending	Y
Approve GOP budget with tax and spending cuts	Y

VOTING STUDIES

	Presidential Support		Party Unity		Conservative Coalition	
Year	S	O	S	O	S	O
1996	47	53	83	17	84	16
1995	37	62	84	15	89	10

INTEREST GROUP RATINGS

Year	ADA	AFL-CIO	CCUS	ACU
1996	10	n/a	88	70
1995	30	33	92	64

20 Benjamin A. Gilman (R)

Of Middletown — Elected 1972, 13th term

Biographical Information

Born: Dec. 6, 1922, Poughkeepsie, N.Y.

Education: U. of Pennsylvania, B.S. 1946; New York Law School, LL.B. 1950.

Military Service: Army, 1943-45; National Guard, 1981-present.

Occupation: Lawyer.

Family: Wife, Georgia Nickles Tingus; three children; two stepchildren.

Religion: Jewish.

Political Career: N.Y. Assembly, 1967-73; assistant N.Y. attorney general, 1953-55.

Capitol Office: 2449 Rayburn Bldg. 20515; 225-3776.

Committees

Government Reform & Oversight
Human Resources; Postal Service

International Relations (chairman)

In Washington: Gilman takes a moderate stance on many domestic policy issues. So after Republicans won control of the House in 1994, there was speculation that party conservatives might want one of their faithful in the chair at International Relations, instead of Gilman. But Gilman's 20-plus years of House seniority counted for something, and GOP leaders were confident enough that Gilman would be loyal. He ascended to the chair.

Gilman has a more internationalist perspective than many on the Republican right, and as chairman he has tried to maintain that line while not alienating party conservatives. When drafting his first foreign aid reauthorization bill, Gilman faced pressure from the GOP leadership to reduce foreign aid spending and downsize the foreign affairs bureaucracy. Swallowing the cuts was tough for Gilman. "I have been a staunch supporter of the programs we are authorizing [in the foreign aid bill]," Gilman said. "Continuing to provide humanitarian and development assistance is in our national interest."

Democratic control of the White House makes Gilman's job that much harder. The executive branch does, after all, play the lead role in foreign affairs, and not since the Truman administration has a congressional Republican majority dealt with a Democratic president in the foreign policy arena. Adding to Gilman's discomfort is the fact that his counterpart in the Senate is Foreign Relations Chairman Jesse Helms, R-N.C., a staunch conservative who is often deeply at odds with the Clinton administration.

As chairman, one of Gilman's main duties is to get the House to accept a foreign aid reauthorization. This is a daunting task: such a bill has not cleared Congress since 1985. A foreign aid bill failed to make it into law in the 104th, as Clinton vetoed it as part of legislation reauthorizing the State Department. As passed by the House, the foreign aid and State Department bill eliminated three foreign affairs agencies and cut foreign aid. Although the measure eventually was modified to require elimination of just one of the three agencies, Clinton complained that it infringed on the president's foreign policy prerogatives.

The measure had prompted intense partisan disputes. When the House failed in April 1996 to get the two-thirds vote needed for the override, Gilman said the veto made a mockery of the administration's claim that it is reinventing government, because Clinton objected to the elimination of one agency. "The only thing this administration has reinvented are new excuses to maintain the status quo," he said.

But early in the 105th, Gilman seemed intent on having less rancor. When his committee began marking up the foreign aid and State Department measure in May 1997, comity abounded. Gilman won praise from Indiana Democrat Lee H. Hamilton, the committee's ranking member, for his willingness to accommodate the administration and committee Democrats.

Despite his recent conciliatory ways, Gilman has had his share of disagreements with the Democrats and Clinton. In fact, his attacks on Clinton's policies in Haiti and Bosnia have earned him points with GOP conservatives.

Late in the 104th, Gilman and his committee subpoenaed 51 documents from the White House related to Haiti, but Clinton refused to hand over 47 of them, invoking executive privilege. Committee Republicans demanded the documents as part of a yearlong probe into political violence in Haiti. Gilman complained that the White House had made "extraordinary use" of executive privilege in withholding the documents. The White House told Gilman the papers "implicate [the president's] ability to conduct the nation's foreign affairs."

Gilman fired back, accusing the president of a "blatant abuse of power to cover up a massive foreign policy failure in Haiti." In 1994, Clinton had ordered U.S. troops into Haiti to restore President Jean-Bertrand Aristide to power. Since then, some Republicans have repeatedly charged that the administration has turned a blind eye to violence by Haiti's U.S.-trained security forces

NEW YORK 20
Rockland and parts of Westchester, Orange and Sullivan counties

The 20th, near the outer edge of New York City's sphere, has a Republican lean but not a full tilt. Its Rockland and Orange county subdivisions have been populated since World War II largely by relocated New York City residents, many of them Irish- and Italian-Americans and Jews. Many brought Democratic voting traditions that were tempered by their new exurban lifestyles. A moderate, such as Gilman, can draw out a solid GOP vote. But in races featuring more conservative GOP candidates, the 20th is somewhat more competitive.

Gilman took 57 percent of the vote in 1996, a 10 percentage point drop from his 1994 total. But the district went overwhelmingly Democratic in the presidential election, enabling Bill Clinton to defeat Bob Dole here by 17 percentage points, 54 percent to 37 percent. In Rockland County — which has just less than half the district's population — Clinton's winning margin was just slightly higher.

The 20th actually starts fairly close in to New York City, in the Westchester County suburbs. It takes in the northeast corner of Yonkers (including its affluent Beech Hill section), Greenburgh (a mainly middle-class town that includes part of the Central Avenue retail corridor) and such mainly comfortable riverside communities as Hastings-on-Hudson, Dobbs Ferry and Tarrytown. A 17 percent combined black and Hispanic population contributes to making this the most Democratic part of the 20th. Gilman lost Westchester County in 1996.

But Gilman usually dominates in his home base of Rockland County. Though Rockland does not have a single urban center — its population is spread among such communities as Spring Valley, Pearl River, Nyack, Congers, New City and Suffern — it is rather thoroughly developed: More than 90 percent of the population is classified by the Census Bureau as urban.

Rockland has a number of employers, the largest of which is a facility of the Lederle Laboratories pharmaceutical company in Pearl River. But many residents drive across the Tappan Zee Bridge to offices in Westchester or make the long commute into New York City.

The county has a large Jewish population that includes several long-established Hasidic communities. The district's parts of Orange and Sullivan counties, which take in some of the Catskill Mountains' "borscht belt" resorts, have unusually large Jewish populations for less urbanized areas.

Orange County contributes about a third of the 20th's population; its largest towns are Warwick and Middletown. On the county's north side is Stewart Airport, a former Air Force base that is now a major cargo terminal. Much of the county is rural, with dairy, stud horse and onion farms.

Sullivan County has less than 5 percent of the 20th's population but has its most famous latter-day cultural site. The Woodstock music festival was held in a farm field near the town of Bethel in 1969. The 25th anniversary concert, Woodstock '94, was held 45 miles northwest in Saugerties (in the 26th District).

1990 Population: 580,338. White 502,759 (87%), Black 47,504 (8%), Other 30,075 (5%). Hispanic origin 35,263 (6%). 18 and over 429,329 (74%), 62 and over 79,090 (14%). Median age: 34.

toward Aristide's political opponents.

Earlier in 1996, Gilman had blocked $5 million in funding for the U.S.-backed police force in Haiti. Gilman said he opposed releasing the money until several conditions were met, including a commitment by Aristide's government to bar human rights violators from joining the new police force and a pledge to cooperate with an FBI investigation of political murders. Eventually Gilman agreed to release half of the $5 million on the "expectation" that human rights violators and others with criminal backgrounds would be barred from participating in the police training program.

Gilman also went head-to-head with the administration over its tacit acceptance of Iran arming the Bosnian Muslims during the civil war in the former Yugoslavia, even as the administration was arguing publicly for continuation of an arms embargo in the region. Gilman charged that the administration allowed Iran to "establish a substantial beachhead in the Balkans," underscoring his point by displaying a large photo of an Iranian Cultural Center now open in the Bosnian capital of Sarajevo. The House voted in May 1996 to launch a formal probe, by an eight-member select International Relations subcommittee, of the administration's actions in the Iran-Bosnia affair.

A notable success for Gilman in the 104th was winning enactment — over the objections of U.S. allies and trading partners — of legislation to penalize foreign companies that aid the oil industries of Iran or Libya. Although administration officials had expressed concern over the measure, Clinton signed the bill in August 1996.

Sponsored by Gilman, the legislation was intended to punish Iran and Libya for their sponsorship of global terrorism and for their efforts to acquire weapons of mass destruction. It was championed by the American Israel Public Affairs Committee and other groups that regard Iran as the main threat to Middle East stability. Gilman has been a longtime supporter of Israel. Any opposition to the bill vanished in the aftermath of the July 1996 explosion of TWA Flight 800, which killed all aboard. In the immediate aftermath of the crash, terrorism was strongly suspected, although federal officials have struggled to identify the cause.

One of the few remaining "Rockefeller Republicans" in the New York House delegation, Gilman holds liberal views on most social issues. In the 104th, he consistently took the abortion rights side against conservatives trying to restrict access to abortion. In the 105th, he was one of only eight Republicans to oppose a measure banning a particular abortion technique that opponents call "partial birth" abortion. He also is sympathetic to organized labor, and has opposed a GOP bill that would allow companies to offer their employees comp time in lieu of pay for overtime work. In 1996, Gilman was an early supporter of increasing the minimum wage, and he was one of just 43 Republicans voting against a GOP leadership-backed amendment to exempt small businesses from the wage increase.

Gilman also sits on the Government Reform and Oversight Committee, where he is the No. 2 Republican.

At Home: Although many House incumbents from New York saw their districts drastically reshaped in redistricting that preceded the 1992 elections, Gilman got off lightly. Retaining his political base in exurban Rockland and Orange counties, Gilman won with his customary ease in 1992 and 1994, and although he dipped to 57 percent in 1996, that was still almost 20 points ahead of his Democratic challenger.

Gilman earned his initial House nomination after quietly working his way through the ranks of appointive and elective office. A former New York state assistant attorney general, Gilman in 1966 won an Assembly seat from Orange County. After three terms in the Assembly, Gilman challenged Democratic Rep. John G. Dow for the House. Viewed as a moderate, Gilman defeated conservative builder Yale Rapkin for the GOP nod. Gilman won with a comfortable plurality, even though Rapkin siphoned off 13 percent as the Conservative Party candidate.

After deflecting a 1974 comeback attempt by Dow, Gilman's re-elections went smoothly until his district was combined with that of Democratic Rep. Peter A. Peyser's in 1982 redistricting. It was an angrier campaign than Gilman had been used to. Peyser criticized him for opposing a nuclear-weapons freeze and for backing military aid to El Salvador. The usually soft-spoken Gilman fired back, calling Peyser — who had been a GOP House colleague of Gilman's before switching parties — an "ultra-liberal."

Gilman's close ties to his geographically dominant Rockland-Orange base paid off: He carried those two counties solidly. Gilman was almost able to carry a usually Democratic, heavily Jewish portion of Sullivan County that had been placed in the district for the first time. Peyser took the Westchester County portion, his home base, but it was not enough.

HOUSE ELECTIONS

1996 General		
Benjamin A. Gilman (R)	122,479	(57%)
Yash P. Aggarwal (D,L)	80,761	(38%)
Robert F. Garrison (RTL)	6,356	(3%)
Ira W. Goodman (INDC)	5,016	(2%)
1994 General		
Benjamin A. Gilman (R)	120,334	(67%)
Gregory B. Julian (D)	52,345	(29%)
Lois M. Colandrea (RTL)	5,612	(3%)

Previous Winning Percentages: **1992** (66%) **1990** (69%) **1988** (71%) **1986** (69%) **1984** (69%) **1982** (53%) **1980** (74%) **1978** (62%) **1976** (65%) **1974** (54%) **1972** (48%)

CAMPAIGN FINANCE

	Receipts	Receipts from PACs		Expend-itures
1996				
Gilman (R)	$778,749	$230,805	(30%)	$682,959
Aggarwal (D)	$211,968	$2,500	(1%)	$210,670
1994				
Gilman (R)	$525,650	$212,370	(40%)	$547,731
Julian (D)	$35,048	$1,307	(4%)	$35,766

DISTRICT VOTE FOR PRESIDENT

	1996		1992
D	130,458 (54%)	D	116,294 (45%)
R	89,378 (37%)	R	107,107 (41%)
I	18,211 (8%)	I	37,011 (14%)

KEY VOTES

1997	
Ban "partial birth" abortions	N
1996	
Approve farm bill	Y
Deny public education to illegal immigrants	N
Repeal ban on certain assault-style weapons	Y
Increase minimum wage	Y
Freeze defense spending	N
Approve welfare overhaul	Y
1995	
Approve balanced-budget constitutional amendment	Y
Relax Clean Water Act regulations	N
Oppose limits on environmental regulations	Y
Reduce projected Medicare spending	Y
Approve GOP budget with tax and spending cuts	Y

VOTING STUDIES

	Presidential Support		Party Unity		Conservative Coalition	
Year	S	O	S	O	S	O
1996	59	38	63	36	78	22
1995	38	62	78	21	80	17
1994	71	28	45	54	69	31
1993	69	31	52	47	68	32
1992	41	58	42	57	56	44
1991	50	50	39	61	57	43

INTEREST GROUP RATINGS

Year	ADA	AFL-CIO	CCUS	ACU
1996	35	n/a	63	45
1995	30	25	79	60
1994	35	89	67	52
1993	55	83	45	46
1992	75	92	50	32
1991	60	92	20	30

21 Michael R. McNulty (D)

Of Green Island — Elected 1988, 5th term

Biographical Information
Born: Sept. 16, 1947, Troy, N.Y.
Education: College of the Holy Cross, A.B. 1969.
Occupation: Public official.
Family: Wife, Nancy Ann Lazzaro; four children.
Religion: Roman Catholic.
Political Career: Green Island supervisor, 1970-77; Democratic nominee for N.Y. Assembly, 1976; mayor of Green Island, 1977-83; N.Y. Assembly, 1983-89.
Capitol Office: 2161 Rayburn Bldg. 20515; 225-5076.

Committees
Ways & Means
Oversight; Trade

In Washington: In his early House years, McNulty toiled quietly as a vote-counter in the Democratic whip structure, and at the start of his third term in 1993, he was rewarded with a prized seat on the Ways and Means Committee. The new Republican majority snatched the prize away in 1995; the GOP cut the number of Democratic seats on Ways and Means, and McNulty was bumped.

But one year into the 104th Congress, McNulty returned to Ways and Means, thanks to a chain of events set off by Jimmy Hayes, a Louisiana Democrat who in December 1995 jumped to the Republican Party.

To reward Hayes, the GOP leadership wanted to add a seat to the Republican side on Ways and Means and give it to him. But earlier in the year, when another Democrat, Texas Rep. Greg Laughlin, had switched to the GOP and was awarded a place on Ways and Means, Democrats howled that it was unfair for the GOP to give itself an additional seat on the panel without increasing the minority's contingent by one as well. After Hayes' switch, the Republican Conference appointed him to Ways and Means and also gave Democrats a new seat, making the panel's partisan ratio 23-16. The Democrat benefiting from all this was McNulty, who got the new Democratic slot.

Though McNulty has his share of differences with party doctrine, on issues important to organized labor his Democratic stripes are quite bright. Three times in his House career he has received a 100 percent score in the AFL-CIO's rating of members' floor votes. In the 104th Congress, for instance, he voted to raise the minimum wage and against allowing employers to offer their workers compensatory time off instead of overtime pay. In the 103rd Congress, he opposed NAFTA.

McNulty also lines up from time to time with his party's most liberal elements. He voted in the 104th against the final welfare overhaul bill, against efforts to allow states to deny public education to illegal aliens and against repealing the ban on certain semiautomatic assault-style weapons. He supported President Clinton's cherished AmeriCorps program, and he was on board for most of Clinton's early legislative endeavors, backing his budget, tax and economic stimulus bills in 1993 and voting for the family and medical leave and "motor voter" bills.

Nonetheless, McNulty's party unity vote scores in the 104th were not exactly astronomical. He voted with a majority of Democrats against Republicans 65 percent of the time in 1995 and 78 percent of the time in 1996. Those were his lowest party unity scores since coming to Washington in 1989.

Those scores can be attributed in part to the GOP majority's attempts to enact anti-abortion legislation and McNulty's support of those efforts. In the 104th, for example, he voted for banning a particular abortion technique that opponents call a "partial birth" abortion, against allowing the federal employees' health plan to pay for abortions, and against allowing overseas military hospitals to perform abortions.

McNulty says he does not support an outright ban on abortion, but he opposes public funding of the procedure except in cases of rape or incest or danger to a woman's life. (In the 104th, he voted to require states to fund Medicaid abortions for poor women in those limited instances.)

He wants to require parental notification when minors seek abortions at federally funded clinics, and he voted in the 103rd against a measure designed to promote safe access to clinics where abortions are performed. He did, however, support lifting the ban on abortion counseling in federally funded clinics.

McNulty has backed the conservative Republican view on several other contentious issues. He voted in 1996 to ban federal recognition of same-sex marriages. He supports a constitutional amendment requiring a balanced budget. In February 1997, he also sided with the Republicans in voting to limit congressional terms.

NEW YORK 21
Capital District — Albany; Schenectady; Troy

With government employment and manufacturing as its economic mainstays, New York's Capital District has long provided Democrats — including McNulty and his predecessor, the late Samuel S. Stratton — with a solid political base.

Yet the 21st is no liberal stronghold. Its minority population is not large, and its major ethnic groups are Irish- and Italian-Americans, many of whom are conservative on social issues. McNulty is one of the few New York Democrats who seeks and receives the endorsement of the state's Conservative Party.

The 21st covers most of the Albany-Schenectady-Troy metropolitan area. Albany, the capital, is the district's largest city with more than 100,000 residents. It has the 21st's largest minority concentration; more than half the district's blacks live there. It also is home to one of the last, great big-city political machines. The Democratic organization has lost a bit of its clout since the heyday of Dan O'Connell and Mayor Erastus Corning II, but still gets the vote out and usually elects its candidates.

Thanks to its political organization, Albany provides the foundations for Democratic wins in the 21st; despite pockets of Republican votes in the suburbs (the largest of which is adjacent Colonie), Albany County usually goes Democratic. It was the only upstate county to favor Democratic Gov. Mario M. Cuomo over Republican George E. Pataki in 1994. The county gave Bill Clinton 61 percent of the vote in 1996, compared with the 53 percent he received elsewhere in the district. The state bureaucracy and regional federal offices in Albany provide economic stability (even though fiscal problems have forced some public agencies to trim their payrolls). Nearly half of all employment in Albany is in the public sector.

Albany County, on the west bank of the Hudson River, has a longstanding industrial sector that includes the arsenal in Watervliet. But its private-sector growth has been in such fields as health care and insurance. The state university campus in Albany (14,400 students) is the largest higher educational institution in the 21st; others include Rensselaer Polytechnic Institute (6,400 students) in Troy and Union College (2,300 students) in Schenectady.

Industrial employment remains more integral in Troy, across the Hudson in Rensselaer County, and west along the Mohawk River in Schenectady and Amsterdam (Montgomery County). General Electric makes power-generating equipment and has its research and development center in Schenectady but has cut its work force deeply over the past decade. Overall industrial employment in Schenectady County declined by more than a third during the 1980s. The blow was cushioned by an aggressive economic development effort that attracted smaller manufacturers and service providers.

But Montgomery County has been struggling since its major employer, a Mohawk Carpet plant, moved south in the 1960s. It has the lowest median household income among the district's counties.

1990 Population: 580,337. White 529,568 (91%), Black 36,352 (6%), Other 14,417 (2%). Hispanic origin 11,963 (2%). 18 and over 451,775 (78%), 62 and over 106,092 (18%). Median age: 34.

McNulty was one of only two Democrats on the Ways and Means Committee who voted in May 1996 to suspend 4.3 cents of the federal gasoline tax for seven months. The issue became a mainstay of Republican presidential nominee Bob Dole's campaign after gas prices shot up.

In June 1996, McNulty again showed his independence on the committee. He was one of only two Ways and Means members to oppose legislation aimed at punishing foreign firms that aid the oil industries of Iran and Libya. Ways and Means had scrapped several key provisions from a sanctions bill initially passed by the House International Relations Committee, and McNulty said he favored that panel's stronger legislation. As passed by Ways and Means, the legislation required the president to impose two of six possible sanctions on foreign companies that make an investment of at least $40 million in a single year in Iran's energy sector. Foreign entities that sell Libya petroleum-related goods or technology would face the same six possible penalties, including a ban on trade with the United States and the denial of U.S. government procurement contracts. The president would have the option of waiving the restrictions in the national interest. But Ways and Means scrapped a provision requiring that the sanctions also be imposed on foreign entities that sell petroleum-related equipment to Tehran. The committee also dropped the bill's mandatory sanctions on foreign companies that invest in Libya's oil sector. And it exempted existing contracts from possible sanctions.

McNulty is not one of the House's more high-profile members. In the 104th Congress, he spoke on the House floor only four times. In the 103rd Congress, he spoke on the floor only 12 times.

At Home: Running in a district dominated by Albany, a Democratic stronghold, McNulty has won five times with more than 60 percent of the vote.

But his conservatism attracted a 1996 primary

challenge from Lee H. Wasserman, an environmental activist. Wasserman argued that McNulty did not represent the Democratic Party, citing his 63 percent support score for the House Republicans' "Contract With America." That was the highest score among New York Democrats. Wasserman drew the support of the Sierra Club, the League of Conservation Voters and the National Abortion and Reproductive Rights Action League.

McNulty countered with the support of the House Democratic leadership and the still-potent Albany County Democratic organization. And he argued that he stood against Speaker Newt Gingrich when the Republicans tried to cut federal spending for social programs. For example, McNulty voted against the GOP's budget-reconciliation bill that tried to balance the budget by the year 2002 in part by reducing projected growth in spending on Medicare and Medicaid.

Wasserman also ran in the fall as the nominee of the state's Liberal Party, but McNulty had little trouble defeating him and GOP nominee Nancy Norman, who was back for a rematch of their 1992 race.

McNulty's initial contest with Norman in 1992 was most notable for the paradox of his getting the Conservative Party endorsement while Norman, an abortion rights supporter, was backed by the Liberal Party. McNulty also had the Conservative line in 1990, 1994 and 1996.

McNulty said in 1988 that serving in Congress had been a lifelong goal. But he did not expect to have the chance that year, because longtime Democratic Rep. Samuel S. Stratton had filed for re-election in what was then the 23rd District.

When New York's candidate filing deadline passed, McNulty had already re-upped to run for a fourth term in the state Assembly. But Stratton, a 30-year House member who was in ill health, suddenly announced his retirement. The 23rd's Democratic leaders met within hours of the announcement and chose McNulty to replace him on the ballot.

While taking typically Democratic positions on most domestic issues, McNulty said he had no major differences on defense policy with the hawkish Stratton, a defense specialist and high-ranking member of the Armed Services Committee. With endorsements from Stratton and environmentalist groups, McNulty defeated local Republican official Peter Bakal with 62 percent. Two years later, he won the Conservative Party endorsement and topped GOP public relations consultant Margaret Buhrmaster with 64 percent.

Deeply rooted in Albany County politics, McNulty's family is virtually dynastic in its home base of Green Island. His grandfather was elected town tax collector in 1914 and went on to serve as town supervisor, county board chairman and county sheriff. McNulty's father was supervisor for eight years, mayor for 16 years and county sheriff for six.

McNulty joined his elders in 1969, winning a seat on the town board at age 22. While in this post, he waged his only unsuccessful campaign, a 1976 challenge to a Republican assemblyman. He recouped the next year by winning a contest for Green Island mayor, then won the first of three state Assembly terms in 1982.

HOUSE ELECTIONS

1996 General		
Michael R. McNulty (D,C,INDC)	158,491	(66%)
Nancy Norman (R,FDM)	64,471	(27%)
Lee H. Wasserman (L)	16,794	(7%)
1996 Primary		
Michael R. McNulty (D,C,INDC)	23,842	(57%)
Lee H. Wasserman (D,L)	17,957	(43%)
1994 General		
Michael R. McNulty (D,C)	147,804	(67%)
Joseph A. Gomez (R)	68,745	(31%)
Timothy J. Wood (RTL)	4,125	(2%)

Previous Winning Percentages: 1992 (63%) **1990** (64%) **1988** (62%)

CAMPAIGN FINANCE

	Receipts	Receipts from PACs	Expend-itures
1996			
McNulty (D)	$536,133	$241,474 (45%)	$628,000
Norman (R)	$6,514	$750 (12%)	$6,953
Wasserman (L)	$393,762	$23,435 (6%)	$392,588
1994			
McNulty (D)	$285,700	$182,218 (64%)	$217,642
Gomez (R)	$29,261	$1,664 (6%)	$25,773

DISTRICT VOTE FOR PRESIDENT

1996		1992	
D	151,714 (58%)	**D**	140,251 (48%)
R	79,804 (30%)	**R**	99,094 (34%)
I	26,840 (10%)	**I**	51,086 (18%)

KEY VOTES

1997	
Ban "partial birth" abortions	Y
1996	
Approve farm bill	N
Deny public education to illegal immigrants	N
Repeal ban on certain assault-style weapons	N
Increase minimum wage	Y
Freeze defense spending	Y
Approve welfare overhaul	N
1995	
Approve balanced-budget constitutional amendment	Y
Relax Clean Water Act regulations	N
Oppose limits on environmental regulations	Y
Reduce projected Medicare spending	N
Approve GOP budget with tax and spending cuts	N

VOTING STUDIES

	Presidential Support		Party Unity		Conservative Coalition	
Year	S	O	S	O	S	O
1996	67	27	78	16	37	59
1995	53	41	65	31	65	32
1994	69	23	78	15	58	39
1993	79	21	84	15	75	25
1992	27	72	87	10	54	46
1991	31	68	93	6	35	65

INTEREST GROUP RATINGS

Year	ADA	AFL-CIO	CCUS	ACU
1996	60	n/a	33	22
1995	60	83	52	44
1994	55	63	60	42
1993	60	100	18	21
1992	90	91	38	13
1991	80	100	10	10

22 Gerald B.H. Solomon (R)

Of Glens Falls — Elected 1978, 10th term

Biographical Information

Born: Aug. 14, 1930, Okeechobee, Fla.

Education: Siena College, 1949-50; St. Lawrence U., 1952-53.

Military Service: Marine Corps, 1951-52.

Occupation: Insurance executive.

Family: Wife, Freda Parker; five children.

Religion: Presbyterian.

Political Career: Queensbury town supervisor, 1968-72; Warren County Legislature, 1968-72; N.Y. Assembly, 1973-79.

Capitol Office: 2206 Rayburn Bldg. 20515; 225-5614.

Committees

Rules (chairman)
Legislative & Budget Process; Rules & Organization of the House

In Washington: To help execute their legislative battle plan in the 104th Congress, the new GOP leaders of the House needed a loyal lieutenant willing to usher the conservative agenda through the Rules Committee. The man for the job was Solomon, a partisan and combative ex-Marine who as Rules chairman has been a good soldier for the "Republican revolution." Only in a couple of areas near and dear to his constituency — dairy and labor matters — has Solomon stepped away from his party's line.

In January 1997, when Speaker Newt Gingrich was reprimanded by the House for ethics transgressions and assessed a $300,000 penalty, Solomon was one of 26 Republicans who voted against the sanctions. And in April 1997, Solomon drew applause at a closed-door Republican caucus when he yelled from the back of the room that Gingrich should not pay the fine with personal funds.

That same month on the House floor, Solomon demanded that the words of Georgia Democratic Rep. John Lewis be stricken from the official record when Lewis referred to Gingrich as having been fined for "lying to Congress."

And in December 1995 Solomon thwarted the House ethics committee's proposal to restrict earnings that members can receive from books they publish. In response to its investigation of Gingrich, who had received a $4.5 million advance for two books, the ethics panel proposed placing advances and royalties under the same limits as all outside earned income: 15 percent of a member's salary.

But Solomon won approval of a rule that allowed him first to offer an amendment to the ethics committee proposal. Solomon's amendment required all members' book contracts to be approved by the ethics committee and banned advances, but it permitted unlimited royalties.

"Is there a problem or conflict involved with members' receiving income from books that are purchased by persons the author does not even know?" Solomon asked. "Does earning royalty income detract from the time a member can devote to his official duties? The answer . . . is no." Solomon's amendment passed, and the Solomon-amended rule was adopted, 259-128.

Solomon also was in the center of efforts to derail other proposed changes in the way Congress operates. After the Senate enacted rules banning lobbyist-financed trips and limiting gifts and meals from lobbyists to $50, some House members sought similar restrictions. But the rule as devised by Solomon first required a vote on keeping the existing gift limit of $250. If that substitute failed, lawmakers then would vote on a total ban on gifts, meals and trips, before allowing the Senate's $50 limit to come to the floor. Since it would be politically impossible for legislators to oppose a total ban, the only way to avoid having to cast that vote would be to support the $250 limit. However, lawmakers rejected the substitute and voted for the total gift ban.

In addition, after the Senate passed legislation imposing new reporting requirements for lobbyists, House supporters wanted to enact the identical bill, thus clearing it for the president rather than sending a separate version to a conference committee. But Solomon reported out an open rule, thus inviting amendments.

Solomon said the amendments were not meant to kill the legislation. "I have an obligation to try to bring reconciliation to the issue," he said. Solomon voted for all four amendments offered to the lobby bill, but all lost and the House cleared the bill for President Clinton.

When Solomon's committee tackled campaign finance in July 1996, the panel proposed "without recommendation" a rule governing debate of a bill to raise contribution limits. Such an action had not happened since before World War II, if at all. The Rules Committee resolution usually recommends that the House pass a measure. "The members of the committee reflect the exact feeling of the Republican Conference, which is totally divided," Solomon said. "Usually if they vote against a Gerald Solomon rule, they will catch hell. This way they won't catch hell."

Solomon's combativeness occasionally gets him

NEW YORK 22
Rural East — Glens Falls; Saratoga Springs

The 22nd runs nearly 200 miles south to north, from the Dutchess County estate country at the edge of the New York City metropolis, around Albany and on to the Adirondack mountain region not far from Canada. It takes in most of New York's eastern border with the New England states.

This largely rural and conservative district has held more strongly to its Yankee Republican voting traditions than its New England neighbors. The 22nd is carried overwhelmingly by Solomon, one of the most outspoken conservative in the House.

In 1994, Solomon carried all of the four full and five partial counties in the 22nd with between 71 percent and 76 percent of the vote. In 1996, Solomon still carried all nine counties represented in the 22nd even as Bill Clinton managed to win the district over Bob Dole by 45 percent to 40 percent.

The 22nd is 97 percent non-Hispanic white; it has the smallest minority population among New York districts. The district's population hub is in its center, in the Albany-Schenectady-Troy metropolitan area. This district has none of those cities, but much of their GOP suburbia. Many unionized state workers live in those suburbs, accounting for Solomon's moderation on labor issues.

Saratoga County, just north of Albany at the confluence of the Hudson and Mohawk rivers, has by far the district's largest population share (with about 30 percent of the district's residents). The ongoing suburbanization of the southern part of the county, in such communities as Halfmoon and Clifton Park, was reflected in Saratoga County's 18 percent population increase during the 1980s. Across the Hudson, the 22nd takes in much of Rensselaer County. But its largest bloc of Democratic votes, in industrial Troy, is snatched away by the 21st District, leaving the 22nd with its suburbs and dairy lands.

In northern Saratoga County is the resort town of Saratoga Springs. Nearby is a Revolutionary War battlefield, one of many 18th century historical sites in the district. The Saratoga Race Track opens for a well-attended limited run every summer.

The district follows Interstate 87 (the Adirondack Northway) into mountainous, scenic Adirondack Park and the resort areas of Lake George and Lake Champlain. In Essex County at the northwest corner of the district is Lake Placid, site of the 1932 and 1980 Winter Olympics. Though tourism is heavy, this area — dependent on seasonal employment and on factory jobs in the Warren County city of Glens Falls — has its share of economic problems.

The southern end of the 22nd is made up of mainly rural territory in Schoharie, Greene, Columbia and northern Dutchess County. Near the south edge of the district is Hyde Park and the estate of President Franklin D. Roosevelt, the patrician Democrat who in his time was regarded by much of the area's landed gentry as a "traitor to his class."

1990 Population: 580,337. White 560,652 (97%), Black 12,548 (2%), Other 7,137 (1%). Hispanic origin 8,807 (2%). 18 and over 434,538 (75%), 62 and over 89,550 (15%). Median age: 34.

into trouble. In February 1996, a New York state representative, Richard Brodsky, chairman of the Assembly Environmental Conservation Committee, was disturbed that the state Department of Environmental Conservation proposed settling a major environmental violation by General Electric, a key employer in Solomon's district, by asking the company to spend $200,000 to erect a boat launch.

Solomon took exception to Brodsky's queries. "New York state has had enough of media-hungry liberals looking for political gain at the expense of business and jobs for New Yorkers," Solomon wrote to Brodsky. "As chairman of the Rules Committee, I could easily retaliate by involving myself in the activities in your Assembly district."

Brodsky was far from cowed. He filed a complaint with the House ethics committee. While the ethics panel in May said that it believed Solomon's statement that he did not intend to retaliate, the panel warned the lawmaker in a letter that "a reader of your letter to Mr. Brodsky could form the impression that you did intend to retaliate against him."

Solomon and another Democrat, Rep. Patrick J. Kennedy of Rhode Island, got into a heated exchange on the House floor during March 1996 debate on repealing the ban on certain semiautomatic assault-style weapons. "You'll never know what it's like, because you didn't have someone in your family killed," said an emotional Kennedy, whose uncles were assassinated in the 1960s. Solomon angrily retorted, "My wife lives alone five days a week in a rural area in upstate New York. She has a right to defend herself when I'm not there, son. And don't you ever forget it." Away from the floor microphone, he continued, "Let's just step outside." The House voted to repeal the assault weapons ban, but the Senate did not act.

Solomon sometimes acts impetuously. Shortly after taking over the Rules Committee in January 1995, he replaced a portrait of former Chairman Claude Pepper, D-Fla., with one of former Chairman Howard W. Smith, D-Va., on the committee room walls. Pepper was a champion of liberal causes; Smith used his chairmanship to block civil rights legislation. Solomon removed Smith's portrait after complaints from the Congressional Black Caucus. "They informed me that the portrait was an offensive symbol of a painful past for African-Americans," Solomon said. "I would never never knowingly display any symbol offensive to them in any way." In January 1997, Solomon returned Pepper to the wall.

A former insurance executive, Solomon remains a strong supporter of the industry. In July 1996, he attempted to amend the fiscal 1997 appropriations bill for the Treasury Department and related agencies by barring the Comptroller of the Currency from issuing regulations allowing banks further rights to enter the insurance business. If the comptroller issued any such regulations, the amendment would have cut off funding for the comptroller's office. The House defeated the amendment, 107-312.

He is the House champion of a constitutional amendment to outlaw flag desecration. In February 1997, he announced plans to resurrect the amendment, which was defeated in 1995.

Solomon did not respond warmly to one major GOP initiative in the 104th: an overhaul of federal farm policies to bring them more in line with free market principles. He ultimately voted for the "Freedom to Farm" bill, but only after winning approval for an amendment to protect New York dairy farmers. Solomon's amendment, which passed 258-164 in February 1996, phased out the federally set price for milk over five years. But his amendment retained regional price supports for milk and continued the practice of government purchases of cheese to keep dairy prices high.

And Solomon's conservatism sometimes lapses on issues of concern to labor, perhaps a concession to the thousands of unionized New York state employees who live in his district. In the 104th, he was an early supporter of efforts (driven by Democrats and moderate Republicans) to increase the minimum wage.

At Home: In Solomon's mainly rural eastern New York district, Yankee Republican traditions have proved sturdier than in the neighboring New England states. He never has been seriously threatened since his easy win to unseat Democratic Rep. Ned Pattison in 1978.

Pattison had been one of the upset Democratic winners in the Watergate year of 1974, becoming the first Democrat to represent the then-29th District in the 20th century. He held the seat in 1976, when a Republican and a Conservative Party candidate split the vote against him. But in Solomon, Pattison faced a popular state legislator who had GOP and Conservative support. Solomon's Assembly constituency lay entirely within the 29th, so he had a solid base.

Pattison hurt himself with an interview in Playboy magazine, in which he admitted that he had smoked marijuana: Conservatives referred to him as "Pot-tison." Solomon went on to win with 54 percent and has tallied much larger margins in his nine reelection campaigns.

A co-founder of an insurance and investment firm, Solomon started in politics in 1968, winning election as Queensbury town supervisor. He held that post and served simultaneously in the Warren County Legislature. In 1972, he won the Assembly seat that he held until his election to the House.

HOUSE ELECTIONS

1996 General		
Gerald B.H. Solomon (R,C,RTL,FDM)	144,125	(60%)
Steve James (D)	94,192	(40%)
1994 General		
Gerald B.H. Solomon (R,C,RTL)	157,717	(73%)
L. Robert Lawrence (D)	57,064	(27%)

Previous Winning Percentages: 1992 (65%) **1990** (68%) **1988** (72%) **1986** (70%) **1984** (73%) **1982** (74%) **1980** (67%) **1978** (54%)

CAMPAIGN FINANCE

	Receipts	Receipts from PACs	Expenditures
1996			
Solomon (R)	$569,959	$510,450 (90%)	$640,080
James (D)	$277,400	$17,750 (6%)	$273,887
1994			
Solomon (R)	$347,744	$254,632 (73%)	$444,067
Lawrence (D)	$17,453	0	$17,363

DISTRICT VOTE FOR PRESIDENT

	1996		1992
D	117,779 (45%)	**D**	99,988 (36%)
R	105,244 (40%)	**R**	116,238 (42%)
I	34,415 (13%)	**I**	62,533 (22%)

KEY VOTES

1997	
Ban "partial birth" abortions	Y
1996	
Approve farm bill	Y
Deny public education to illegal immigrants	Y
Repeal ban on certain assault-style weapons	Y
Increase minimum wage	Y
Freeze defense spending	N
Approve welfare overhaul	Y
1995	
Approve balanced-budget constitutional amendment	Y
Relax Clean Water Act regulations	Y
Oppose limits on environmental regulations	N
Reduce projected Medicare spending	Y
Approve GOP budget with tax and spending cuts	Y

VOTING STUDIES

	Presidential Support		Party Unity		Conservative Coalition	
Year	**S**	**O**	**S**	**O**	**S**	**O**
1996	37	63	92	4	98	2
1995	17	78	95	3	95	4
1994	32	60	91	3	83	11
1993	28	68	93	4	93	7
1992	70	26	88	9	83	13
1991	71	25	89	8	95	3

INTEREST GROUP RATINGS

Year	ADA	AFL-CIO	CCUS	ACU
1996	5	n/a	81	95
1995	0	18	96	96
1994	0	38	67	95
1993	15	40	80	96
1992	15	58	63	96
1991	15	45	56	90

23 Sherwood Boehlert (R)

Of New Hartford — Elected 1982, 8th term

Biographical Information

Born: Sept. 28, 1936, Utica, N.Y.
Education: Utica College, A.B. 1961.
Military Service: Army, 1956-58.
Occupation: Congressional aide; public relations executive.
Family: Wife, Marianne Willey; four children.
Religion: Roman Catholic.
Political Career: Sought Republican nomination for U.S. House, 1972; Oneida County executive, 1979-82.
Capitol Office: 2246 Rayburn Bldg. 20515; 225-3665.

Committees

Select Intelligence
Technical & Tactical Intelligence
Science
Basic Research
Transportation & Infrastructure
Railroads; Water Resources & Environment (chairman)

In Washington: When the 104th Congress began, Boehlert, like others in the small band of moderate-to-liberal House Republicans, found himself in the minority of the majority. Most of the moderates went along with the bulk of the conservative GOP agenda; Boehlert, for instance, voted with a majority of his party against a majority of the Democrats 75 percent of the time in 1995, his highest party unity score since arriving in the House in 1983.

But on environmental issues at least, Boehlert in the 104th tried to hold ground against party colleagues — many from the South and West — who were eager to roll back environmental protections they saw as onerous to business. He assembled enough Republicans to block some of the conservatives' ambitions to weaken the Environmental Protection Agency (EPA), and he was a key player in the closing days of the 104th as Congress enacted new environmental laws on pesticide regulation, safe drinking water and fisheries management.

With Republican takeover of the House in 1995, Boehlert became chairman of the Transportation and Infrastructure Committee's Water Resources and Environment Subcommittee. In 1996, when Speaker Newt Gingrich of Georgia sensed that Democrats were scoring political points by portraying the GOP as anti-environment, he named Boehlert and Richard W. Pombo, R-Calif., as co-chairs of an environmental task force.

As the 105th Congress convened, Boehlert said, "Moderates came into their own in 1996. In 1997, moderates will make the difference."

The hardy band of Republican environmentalists first made their presence felt in the spring of 1995. GOP leaders, as part of their drive to scale back government regulation, had approved the attachment of 17 legislative riders to the VA-HUD appropriations bill, all of them designed to bar or restrict various regulatory activities by the EPA. Led by Boehlert, 51 Republicans joined the Democratic minority and struck the riders from the bill. The Republican leadership brought the bill back later and, in a re-vote, killed the amendment to strip the riders on a 210-210 tie. Later, though, the riders were dropped from the final spending bill.

Boehlert also played a major role in killing a $949 million dam near Auburn, Calif., calling it an environmentally destructive boondoggle. Rep. John T. Doolittle, R-Calif., in whose district the dam would have been built, contended that it was vital to residents of the Sacramento Valley. At the start of the 105th, Doolittle proposed a change in House GOP rules making subcommittee chairmanships subject to the approval of the entire Republican Conference. The measure was seen as a way of gaining leverage over moderate subcommittee chairmen like Boehlert. But the proposal was defeated by a 2-1 margin.

Boehlert scored another success for environmentalists in the 105th, when he successfully amended a measure that would have waived provisions of the Endangered Species Act for flood control projects. Sponsors of the measure, California Republicans Pombo and Wally Herger, said the species law had contributed to flooding in their districts because it inhibits routine maintenance of levees. The law requires a review of flood projects aimed at ensuring that they do not hurt threatened plants or animals. They argued the review is so cumbersome that it delays basic levee maintenance, placing human lives and property at risk, but opponents claimed it was meant to curtail the species act.

When the bill reached the floor in May 1997, the House approved, 227-196, an amendment by Boehlert that all but gutted the bill, prompting Pombo to pull it from the floor. Boehlert said the vote demonstrated the resiliency of an environmentally sensitive coalition in the House.

Environmental protection is a longstanding interest of Boehlert's. He was a leader in the 1980s fight against acid rain, reflecting not only his parochial concern for the acidic Adirondack lakes, but also his general worry about his party's image. "A lot of people have the traditional belief

NEW YORK 23
Central — Utica; Rome

The 23rd, which takes in four full counties and parts of five others in central New York, is a demographic sampler. It has a few cities, including Utica and Rome in Oneida County, many more small towns and rural stretches that make up most of this large district's land area.

A Republican heritage in this upstate region allows most GOP candidates to carry the 23rd, though in 1996 Bob Dole managed to lose every one of the nine counties that make up the district. Boehlert's record as a moderate has appealed to the mix of farm, Main Street and urban voters; he never has been seriously challenged.

Oneida County, Boehlert's home base, has more than 40 percent of the district's population. The biggest concentration is in the short stretch of the Mohawk River Valley that connects Utica and Rome.

Blue-collar jobs continue to be important in these aging industrial cities: The largest private-sector employer is the Oneida silverware company. But the manufacturing sector has declined over the years. Utica's poverty rate is above 20 percent. Local officials look to service industry jobs and such high-tech fields as fiber optics and photonics for growth.

Much of the high-tech work is done at the Air Force's Rome Laboratory, which was removed from the 1995 base closing list after a massive lobbying campaign. In 1993, however, the base closing commission voted to shut Griffiss Air Force Base, costing the region about 4,500 jobs. Since then, a local redevelopment corporation has signed 24 leases with area companies for space at the base, and the Defense Finance Accounting Service located a 400-person facility there. The region also has gotten a boost from New York state's only casino, run by the Oneida Nation; it employs more than 2,300.

The remainder of Oneida County is mainly rural. Although there is some Democratic vote in the cities, the county usually sets a Republican tone for the district. Boehlert took 64 percent of the vote here in 1996. Other areas of the 23rd have concerns about the post-Cold War defense budget. A Simmonds plant in Chenango County makes military jet engines. The area of Broome County in the southern end of the 23rd is affected by cutbacks in nearby Binghamton's defense-related industries.

There are other industrial facilities, including Remington Arms and Chicago Pneumatic Tool plants in Herkimer County. The district's educational institutions include Colgate University in Hamilton (Madison County; 2,900 students), Hartwick College in Oneonta (Otsego County; 1,500 students) and the state university in Oneonta (5,600 students). Oneonta hosts the National Soccer Hall of Fame; Canestota in Madison County is home to the International Boxing Hall of Fame.

But the best known of the halls of fame, baseball, is located in Cooperstown at the south end of Otsego Lake (the source of the Susquehanna River). It was here that James Fenimore Cooper wrote the stories of frontier days that gave central New York its nickname — the "Leatherstocking Region."

1990 Population: 580,337. White 556,069 (96%), Black 16,565 (3%), Other 7,703 (1%). Hispanic origin 8,922 (2%). 18 and over 436,162 (75%), 62 and over 103,010 (18%). Median age: 34.

that Republicans don't give a damn about the environment," he said in 1989. "Well, a lot of people are wrong."

When Democrats controlled the House, Boehlert often sided with them rather than his fellow Republicans. In the 103rd Congress, he was one of 38 Republicans to support the ban on certain semiautomatic assault-style weapons, and in the 104th he opposed conservatives' efforts to repeal the ban. He consistently sides with abortion-rights proponents, even voting in the 104th against a ban on a particular abortion technique that opponents call a "partial birth" abortion. Generally a pro-labor vote in 1996, he supported an increase in the minimum wage.

Boehlert clashed with a neighboring Republican, Rep. John M. McHugh, over the 1993 round of base closings. The Air Force proposed scaling back operations at Griffiss Air Force Base, in Boehlert's district, and expanding Plattsburgh, in McHugh's. Boehlert called for closing Plattsburgh and instead expanding Griffiss, launching a series of attacks on the other New York base, to the dismay of New York state officials eager to present a united front. In the end, the base closing commission voted to expand McGuire Air Force Base in New Jersey and scale back Griffiss and close Plattsburgh, costing upstate New York more than 7,000 jobs.

In 1995, however, Boehlert was more successful, helping to stave off an effort by the Air Force to shut down Rome Laboratory.

Boehlert's willingness to stray from the more conservative GOP script is no surprise considering his background. He was weaned on politics when New York Gov. Nelson A. Rockefeller, a liberal Republican, was at his apogee.

In the House, Boehlert's challenges to party orthodoxy have hindered his efforts to land a position on either the Ways and Means or the Appropriations committees. In 1993, he was passed over for a seat on Appropriations in favor of his neighbor, Republican James T. Walsh of the Syracuse area. In 1995, when a second New York Republican seat opened on Appropriations, it went to freshman Michael P. Forbes.

Still, he joined his fellow Republicans on the Capitol steps in the fall of 1994 to affix his name to the "Contract With America." Boehlert said at the time that he was not wedded to passing all the items in the contract, but he agreed that the issues should come to the House floor and be voted on.

Boehlert also sits on the Science and Select Intelligence committees.

A part owner of the Utica Blue Sox of the Class A New York-Pennsylvania League, Boehlert has created the Congressional Minor League Caucus, which has lobbied in favor of major league baseball's antitrust exemption.

At Home: Boehlert has proven the appeal of his left-of-center Republican philosophy by winning re-election handily over the years. In 1996, he easily disposed of two primary challengers who objected to his support of abortion rights, then cruised to an eighth term in November.

Boehlert's last serious electoral test came in 1992, when he faced a surfeit of challengers but still won with 64 percent, a solid showing in a poor Republican year. One of his opponents was quite well known: Randall Terry, leader of the controversial anti-abortion group Operation Rescue, who ran as the Right to Life Party candidate. But Terry was distracted by his organization's national efforts — he was arrested during the summer for violating court orders restricting his protest activities at the Democratic and Republican national conventions — and did not actively campaign against Boehlert.

This present electoral security was hard-won for Boehlert, a longtime congressional aide whose House ambitions were deferred for a decade after an initial defeat in 1972. That year, Boehlert had hoped to succeed his boss, retiring GOP Rep. Alexander Pirnie, but he lost to Donald J. Mitchell in a Republican primary.

Boehlert swallowed his disappointment and went to work for Mitchell. In 1977, he left Washington to run Mitchell's Utica office; then in 1979 he restarted his own political career by winning the Oneida County executive post.

By 1982, Mitchell was ready to retire. Boehlert was driving along an interstate highway in Oneida County when he heard the news. He pulled into a rest stop, called a radio station and announced his candidacy.

As county executive he had earned high marks from labor unions, and he was one of only two New York state Republicans to get the state AFL-CIO's endorsement in the 1982 elections. After winning the Republican primary comfortably, Boehlert capitalized on a huge organizational and financial advantage over Democrat Anita Maxwell, a dairy farmer who had lost badly to Mitchell in 1976. He won with 56 percent.

HOUSE ELECTIONS

1996 General		
Sherwood Boehlert (R,FDM)	124,626	(64%)
Bruce W. Hapanowicz (D)	50,436	(26%)
Thomas E. Loughlin Jr. (INDC)	10,835	(6%)
William Tapley (RTL)	7,790	(4%)
1996 Primary		
Sherwood Boehlert (R,FDM)	15,115	(65%)
Francis A. Giroux (R)	5,824	(25%)
William Tapley (R,RTL)	2,206	(10%)
1994 General		
Sherwood Boehlert (R)	124,486	(71%)
Charles W. Skeele Jr. (D)	40,786	(23%)
Donald J. Thomas (RTL)	11,216	(6%)

Previous Winning Percentages: **1992** (64%) **1990** (84%) **1988** (100%) **1986** (69%) **1984** (73%) **1982** (56%)

CAMPAIGN FINANCE

	Receipts	Receipts from PACs	Expend-itures
1996			
Boehlert (R)	$678,597	$317,654 (47%)	$610,166
1994			
Boehlert (R)	$334,884	$183,487 (55%)	$336,183
Skeele (D)	$10,670	0	$12,774

DISTRICT VOTE FOR PRESIDENT

1996		1992	
D	102,487 (46%)	**D**	92,549 (37%)
R	87,809 (40%)	**R**	99,497 (40%)
I	29,094 (13%)	**I**	55,902 (23%)

KEY VOTES

1997	
Ban "partial birth" abortions	N
1996	
Approve farm bill	Y
Deny public education to illegal immigrants	N
Repeal ban on certain assault-style weapons	N
Increase minimum wage	Y
Freeze defense spending	N
Approve welfare overhaul	Y
1995	
Approve balanced-budget constitutional amendment	Y
Relax Clean Water Act regulations	N
Oppose limits on environmental regulations	Y
Reduce projected Medicare spending	Y
Approve GOP budget with tax and spending cuts	N

VOTING STUDIES

	Presidential Support		Party Unity		Conservative Coalition	
Year	**S**	**O**	**S**	**O**	**S**	**O**
1996	56	43	68	32	76	22
1995	47	53	75	25	79	21
1994	71	28	57	41	61	36
1993	74	26	59	40	70	30
1992	42	58	50	49	58	40
1991	58	41	46	54	62	38

INTEREST GROUP RATINGS

Year	ADA	AFL-CIO	CCUS	ACU
1996	50	n/a	69	50
1995	40	33	63	40
1994	50	67	75	38
1993	60	83	55	38
1992	75	75	50	40
1991	45	75	40	40

24 John M. McHugh (R)

Of Pierrepont Manor — Elected 1992, 3rd term

Biographical Information
Born: Sept. 29, 1948, Watertown, N.Y.
Education: Utica College of Syracuse U., B.A. 1970; State U. of New York, Albany, M.P.A. 1977.
Occupation: City official; legislative aide; insurance broker.
Family: Separated.
Religion: Roman Catholic.
Political Career: N.Y. Senate, 1985-93.
Capitol Office: 2441 Rayburn Bldg. 20515; 225-4611.

Committees
Government Reform & Oversight
National Security, International Affairs & Criminal Justice; Postal Service (chairman)
International Relations
Africa; Asia & the Pacific
National Security
Military Installations and Facilities; Military Research & Development

In Washington: McHugh is responsible for overseeing something that virtually every American has an opinion on — mail service. As chairman of the Postal Service Subcommittee on the Government Reform and Oversight Committee, McHugh has taken an active role in assessing all manner of matters related to the nation's mail.

From his subcommittee perch, he has proposed legislation that would lend legitimacy to the popular billpayer's refrain "the check's in the mail." His measure would make it a federal law that bills are considered paid on the day they are postmarked, thus shielding consumers from any late fees accrued after they have mailed a bill payment. The measure, McHugh said, is about "protecting innocent citizens who submit their payments in a timely manner, but who through no fault of their own may be assessed late fees and interest charges because those payments are received or processed late."

Bankers, retailers and mortgage holders called the measure a regulatory nightmare that would force them to revert to manually entering billing information, costing them millions of dollars in lost interest payments and straining relations between creditors and consumers. The measure did not make much headway in the 104th.

McHugh was more successful advancing legislation to create an independent Office of Inspector General for the Postal Service. He said it was a problem that the Postal Service's postal inspector general was not organizationally separate from the service's other law enforcement operations. Because the Postal Service inspector general and the chief postal inspector were one and the same, McHugh told the House, the postal service inspector general could not impartially investigate and audit the Postal Inspection Service.

"As a $60 billion federal agency with nearly 870,000 employees, the Postal Service must be overseen by a strong watchdog," McHugh said. "The creation of an independent Office of Inspector General will help our nation's Postal Service operate in an effective and efficient manner." The provision was included in the omnibus fiscal 1997 spending bill approved at the end of the 104th Congress.

In the 104th, McHugh also held a series of hearings on legislation to overhaul the Postal Service by streamlining its bureaucracy and creating a new framework for establishing postal rates. Postmaster General Marvin T. Runyon said such an overhaul is necessary so that the Postal Service can compete with private delivery companies such as Federal Express and electronic transmission mechanisms such as the World Wide Web. McHugh agreed, saying that unless changes are made, "the Postal Service could find itself a communications company bound by outdated legislative constrictions and simply unable to compete."

McHugh is continuing to pursue the overhaul legislation in the 105th.

McHugh's overall voting record is moderately conservative. His sympathies for some concerns of organized labor were evident in his 1996 vote to increase the minimum wage, and in his opposition to a plan to allow employers to offer employees compensatory time off instead of overtime pay. Labor groups felt that businesses would exploit that option to avoid paying overtime. Also, McHugh was one of only 40 Republicans to vote in 1993 for the family and medical leave bill.

McHugh's district, which borders Canada in extreme northern New York, is the state's largest — larger than nine states — and one of its poorest, with an unemployment rate above the national average. Labor unions are influential in some of the industrialized areas of the district.

McHugh also breaks with many GOP conservatives in his opposition to a term-limits constitutional amendment.

But on most other subjects, McHugh fits in comfortably with his party's conservative philosophy. In the 104th, he sided with abortion opponents on a number of key votes, and he supports the rights of gun owners. He backed a GOP-led effort to repeal the 1994 ban on certain semiauto-

NEW YORK 24
North Country — Plattsburgh; Watertown; Oswego

The 24th, which forms the northern border of New York state, is one of the East's most sprawling congressional districts. It covers all of eight counties and parts of two others. Beginning in the east along Lake Champlain, the 24th tracks north to the Canadian border, west along the St. Lawrence River, then south along Lake Ontario as far as Oswego. Its southern edge reaches east to the outskirts of metropolitan Albany. The Adirondack Mountains make up much of the district's middle.

Although there is blue-collar industry along its waterways, the 24th is a mainly rural district that holds strongly to a Yankee Republican tradition. The importance of defense-related facilities — including the Army's Fort Drum — and the lack of a significant minority population reinforce GOP strength.

Republican McHugh easily won the open House seat in 1992 and has held on to it since. GOP Sen. Alfonse M. D'Amato swept the 24th's counties, winning most with 60 percent or more in 1992. Republican George E. Pataki was equally dominant in the 24th in his successful 1994 gubernatorial bid.

Despite the district's GOP tendencies, Republican presidential candidates have not fared well recently because of its rather stagnant economy, a result of its reliance on heavy industry and its remote location. Economic concerns took a toll on George Bush in 1992, who carried the district by the barest of margins. Bob Dole fared even worse in 1996, winning only the two smallest counties in the 24th. Bill Clinton carried the district by 14 percentage points, while independent Ross Perot took 15 percent.

The counties that form the 24th's western border, Oswego, Jefferson and St. Lawrence, are its most populous. Oswego has a number of industrial employers, including an electricity-generating plant and a paper mill, and there is a State University of New York campus within the city limits. In 1995, the Miller Brewing Co. closed a plant it has operated in the Oswego County town of Fulton.

Industry in Jefferson County is centered in Watertown, the 24th's largest city. But Fort Drum, home of the Army's 10th Mountain Division, is the driving economic force.

Massena, in St. Lawrence County, depends on the factories of the Aluminum Company of America (ALCOA), Reynolds Metals and General Motors. An organized labor presence makes St. Lawrence and Franklin counties the most Democratic areas in the 24th. Clinton won both easily in 1996.

Fort Drum, which received a heavy investment in new facilities during the 1980s, looks secure despite the recent squeeze on government defense dollars.

The interior of the 24th includes some of New York's leading dairy farming areas (including parts of Jefferson and St. Lawrence counties) and the mountain-and-lake country of the Adirondacks, where much of the economy is recreation — and tourist-oriented.

1990 Population: 580,338. White 553,432 (95%), Black 15,043 (3%), Other 11,863 (2%). Hispanic origin 9,424 (2%). 18 and over 426,525 (73%), 62 and over 82,732 (14%). Median age: 31.

matic assault-style weapons, and he also favors a balanced-budget constitutional amendment and increases in the defense budget.

McHugh has a seat on the National Security Committee, where he serves as chairman of a working group on morale, welfare and recreation — one of several panels that operate under the regular subcommittee structure. McHugh's district is home to the Army's Fort Drum; another large military facility in the area, Plattsburgh Air Force Base, was slated for shutdown by the 1993 base closure commission.

McHugh praised provisions in the fiscal 1996 defense authorization measure aimed at improving the quality of life of military personnel, saying that these programs, such as family support, child care, commissaries, gymnasiums and other recreational facilities "are a direct investment in readiness because they aid in retaining quality people in our Armed Forces."

As a complement to his National Security responsibilities, McHugh joined the International Relations Committee at the start of the 105th.

A major parochial concern of McHugh's is the health of the dairy farming operations that are an important part of the economy in the 24th. He was one of 10 Republicans to vote against his party's massive deficit-reducing, budget-reconciliation bill in October 1995 because he was upset with the way its agricultural provisions changed the federal dairy program. "It is clearly an attempt to . . . shift dairy production from the Northeast to other regions of the country with no benefit to the federal Treasury," McHugh said.

The reconciliation bill included provisions ending milk marketing orders, which are regional price supports. Established decades ago to stimulate milk production outside the upper Midwest, the federal orders set minimum prices for processors to pay farmers for milk. Critics say the orders are outdated, since rapid refrigerated transportation now enables milk to travel long distances. But the orders are strongly supported by dairy producers in the East.

The dairy provisions were revisited when an omnibus farm bill went to the House floor in February 1996, and there they were changed more to McHugh's liking. He backed an amendment by fellow upstate New York Republican Gerald B. H. Solomon that would end butter, cheese and powdered milk price supports after a five-year phase-down. It also consolidated the 33 milk marketing orders into no more than 10 to 14 by the end of 2000 and guaranteed that California continue to set its own standards for pricing and milk solids. McHugh ended up voting for both the House and final version of the broad farm bill.

At Home: McHugh is a career politician who got his start as an assistant to the city manager of his hometown of Watertown, the largest city in the 24th. From there he moved to the staff of state Sen. H. Douglas Barclay, where his duties included acting as a liaison to local governments in the district — a job that helped McHugh prepare for a successful run for the state Senate when Barclay retired.

In Albany, McHugh worked in the GOP-majority Senate to pass legislation to help farmers, and he pushed to form a compact of Northeastern states that would have let dairy farmers charge higher milk prices. When Martin decided to retire from the House, McHugh jumped into the race.

He beat his more conservative, anti-abortion primary opponent, local business owner and Hamilton town Supervisor Morrison J. Hosley Jr., with 70 percent of the vote. In the general election, the two strongest candidates he faced were Hosley, who ran on the Conservative and Right to Life tickets, and Democrat Margaret M. Ravenscroft, a retired math teacher. Even against their combined strength, McHugh won with 61 percent of the vote. Since then, his re-elections have been walkaways.

HOUSE ELECTIONS

1996 General		
John M. McHugh (R,C)	124,240	(71%)
Donald Ravenscroft (D)	43,692	(25%)
William H. Beaumont (INDC)	6,750	(4%)
1994 General		
John M. McHugh (R,C)	124,645	(79%)
Danny M. Francis (D)	34,032	(21%)

Previous Winning Percentages: 1992 (61%)

CAMPAIGN FINANCE

	Receipts	Receipts from PACs	Expend-itures
1996			
McHugh (R)	$350,165	$181,253 (52%)	$172,883
1994			
McHugh (R)	$116,998	$84,420 (72%)	$53,187

DISTRICT VOTE FOR PRESIDENT

	1996		1992
D	102,009 (49%)	**D**	85,078 (38%)
R	72,305 (35%)	**R**	86,357 (38%)
I	30,047 (15%)	**I**	54,537 (24%)

KEY VOTES

1997	
Ban "partial birth" abortions	Y
1996	
Approve farm bill	Y
Deny public education to illegal immigrants	Y
Repeal ban on certain assault-style weapons	Y
Increase minimum wage	Y
Freeze defense spending	?
Approve welfare overhaul	Y
1995	
Approve balanced-budget constitutional amendment	Y
Relax Clean Water Act regulations	Y
Oppose limits on environmental regulations	N
Reduce projected Medicare spending	Y
Approve GOP budget with tax and spending cuts	N

VOTING STUDIES

	Presidential Support		Party Unity		Conservative Coalition	
Year	S	O	S	O	S	O
1996	42	57	82	15	82	12
1995	25	71	90	7	94	4
1994	51	49	94	6	89	11
1993	38	58	87	10	84	14

INTEREST GROUP RATINGS

Year	ADA	AFL-CIO	CCUS	ACU
1996	10	n/a	81	79
1995	15	33	83	75
1994	10	33	92	90
1993	20	58	73	83

25 James T. Walsh (R)

Of Syracuse — Elected 1988, 5th term

Biographical Information
Born: June 19, 1947, Syracuse, N.Y.
Education: St. Bonaventure U., B.A. 1970.
Occupation: Marketing executive; social worker.
Family: Wife, DeDe Ryan; three children.
Religion: Roman Catholic.
Political Career: Syracuse Common Council, 1978-88, president, 1986-88; sought nomination for Onondaga County executive, 1987.
Capitol Office: 2351 Rayburn Bldg. 20515; 225-3701.

Committees
Appropriations
Agriculture, Rural Development, FDA & Related Agencies; Legislative Branch (chairman); VA, HUD & Independent Agencies

In Washington: Walsh has a new legislative assignment in the 105th Congress, but his focus remains where it was in the 104th — inside the Beltway.

After two years as chairman of Appropriations' District of Columbia Subcommittee, Walsh shed no tears about moving on from overseeing the crisis-riddled municipal affairs of the nation's capital. His new chair on Appropriations is at the Legislative Branch Subcommittee, which has jurisdiction over the budget of Congress itself.

As chairman of the D.C. subcommittee, Walsh helped create a financial control board to oversee the District's finances. He also pressed the District to cut spending, imposing a cap on the size of the local government's deficit. The Walsh-led GOP majority also broadened the congressional ban on the District using federal funds to pay for abortions for poor women, so that there is now a ban on using locally generated tax dollars to fund abortions, except in cases of rape or incest or when the woman's life is threatened.

But Walsh also found himself in the position of having to beat back an attempt by fervent budget-cutters in the GOP to reduce the District's federal allocation, which is essentially a payment in lieu of taxes. "The Constitution placed responsibility for the District under the Congress," he said. "We should not shirk our responsibilities to our nation's capital."

During Walsh's first year as subcommittee chairman, Congress failed to pass a spending bill for the District, instead folding its allocation into a catch-all appropriations bill. Walsh and his fellow House Republicans insisted on including a provision to provide public tax dollars for District residents attending private schools. Senate Republicans refused to go along with the voucher program.

Walsh had prepared for his role as the District's leading critic during the 103rd, when he was ranking minority member of the subcommittee. His skepticism of the D.C. government's handling of financial affairs rose out of his experience on the Syracuse Common Council, where the longtime mayor, Lee Alexander, pleaded guilty and was sentenced to 10 years in federal prison for extorting more than $1 million from consultants he awarded no-bid contracts.

At his first Appropriations subcommittee hearing in 1993, Walsh heard from then-Mayor Sharon Pratt Kelly and then-Council President John A. Wilson Jr., a week before Wilson's suicide. What piqued Walsh's interest was Wilson's complaint that the council did not get to approve no-bid consultant contracts because the mayor broke them up into several pieces, all below the threshold that would trigger review. Kelly said she was following the law.

"The law has been challenged in court and the court has consistently upheld the executive branch's prerogative with respect to that," Kelly said.

Wilson cut in. "I don't care what anybody says, when you give somebody $700 million to spend anyway they want to spend it, with no review by anybody, somebody is going to get into trouble," he said.

Answered Walsh: "I understand the difficulties of it. But we experienced a problem in Syracuse . . . . There is no doubt that the council's review does slow the process down. But it is supposed to."

Though Walsh usually sides with his Republican colleagues on key issues, his support cannot be taken for granted. In the 104th, he was one of the House Republicans who successfully pressured the party leadership for a vote on raising the minimum wage. A former Peace Corps volunteer, he opposed efforts to eliminate AmeriCorps, President Clinton's national service program. Representing an area with a high infant mortality rate, Walsh supports federal funding for the Women, Infants and Children (WIC) program, food stamps and other nutrition programs. He opposed efforts to eliminate the Emergency Food Assistance Program.

During the fight on the 1994 crime bill, he backed a provision allowing the use of racial statistics in capital cases, thus allowing prisoners to

NEW YORK 25
Central — Syracuse

Syracuse, the dominant city in the 25th, is in the center of Onondaga County. Onondaga has more than 80 percent of the district's population, and the traditional Republican advantage there gives GOP candidates a jump on carrying the district.

The economic evolution of Syracuse was similar to that of many Northern industrial towns, but its politics were all upstate New York. While the ethnic populations of other blue-collar cities were drafted into Democratic machines, it was a Republican organization that for years held the loyalties of the various Syracuse constituencies, including large Irish, Italian, Polish and Jewish populations. The electorate's GOP leanings were reinforced by the typical upstate antipathy toward Democratic New York City.

The Republican machine has faded and the decline of the city's once-thriving industrial sector has helped the Democratic Party gain ground. Aided by minority-group residents who make up more than a quarter of the city's population, Democrats dominated the mayor's office until 1993.

The sizable Republican base that remains in the city is coupled with a strong GOP lean in suburban and outlying areas, and that tips the partisan balance in Onondaga County. County voters gave large pluralities to Republican Sen. Alfonse M. D'Amato in 1992 and GOP Gov. George E. Pataki in 1994, but supported Bill Clinton in both 1992 and 1996. Clinton polled 51 percent in Onondaga County in 1996, compared to the 47 percent he received elsewhere in the district. Walsh won re-election with 55 percent.

Once the nation's leading producer of salt, Syracuse grew into a thriving but grimy center for such industries as glass, steel and chemicals. But the manufacturing sector faded, with service industries picking up some slack.

The city's clearer skies make Syracuse somewhat more livable, though it is harder for some blue-collar workers to make a living. Today, Syracuse University competes with Lockheed Martin to be the area's top employer and has surpassed the Carrier Corp. (a division of United Technologies), which helped finance the university's domed stadium.

The largest of Syracuse's suburbs is middle-class Clay; smaller, more affluent towns include Manlius and Pompey.

To the west, the 25th skims the north edge of the Finger Lakes to take in part of Cayuga County. This is a mainly rural Republican area, though there are some working-class Democratic votes in Auburn, which produces auto components, climate-control equipment and recycled steel. Clinton carried Cayuga County in 1996.

South of Syracuse, the district follows I-81 into Cortland County, a hilly dairy farming area that has some industry.

At the southern end of the 25th are a chunk of Broome County northwest of Binghamton and a lightly populated piece of Tioga County. That part of Tioga was the only county represented in the district that Bob Dole won in 1996.

1990 Population: 580,337. White 528,110 (91%), Black 38,527 (7%), Other 13,700 (2%). Hispanic origin 7,950 (1%). 18 and over 435,923 (75%), 62 and over 90,166 (16%). Median age: 33.

challenge the death penalty as discriminatory. Most Republicans opposed the provision. He also was part of the moderate Republican group that supported the final crime bill after President Clinton cut some of the crime-prevention programs; the group's backing was crucial to the measure's passage. A hunter and a gun owner, Walsh is a member of the Congressional Sportsmen's Caucus and voted against a ban on certain semiautomatic assault-style weapons. But he backed a five-day waiting period on handgun purchases.

In 1993, he was one of only three Republicans to back Clinton's economic stimulus package, and he backed two other measures primarily pushed by Democrats — the family and medical leave bill and the "motor voter" bill, which was designed to increase voter registration.

"My responsibility is to my district," Walsh told the Syracuse Herald American shortly before announcing his 1994 re-election campaign. "I tend to be pragmatic when it comes to issues that affect my home community. I run with the Republican designation, and I think I'm as good a Republican as anybody down here. But I'm not afraid to be independent."

Along those lines, while supporting Republican efforts to cut federal spending, Walsh has used his seat on Appropriations to obtain funding for local projects. From Appropriations' Agriculture Subcommittee, for example, he has kept federal research funds flowing to Cornell University. He has also secured funding for cleanup of Onondaga Lake and for watershed protection programs in the Finger Lakes.

Walsh sides with his party's conservative majority in opposing abortion, and he supports a balanced-budget constitutional amendment. In 1995 he backed the GOP's budget reconciliation bill, which projected a balanced budget by 2002, partly through reductions in the rate of spending growth on Medicare and Medicaid. He also voted to overhaul the welfare system.

During his first campaign for the House in 1988, Walsh promised to seek a seat on the Agriculture

Committee. Capitalizing on contacts with senior Republicans who had served with his father (GOP Rep. William F. Walsh, 1973-79), Walsh became the only Republican freshman to win assignment to Agriculture in 1989 and brought the concerns of Northeastern dairy farmers to the discussions on the 1990 farm bill.

In 1996, when the farm bill was reauthorized, he joined an effort led by Rules Committee Chairman Gerald B.H. Solomon, R-N.Y., that beat back the attempt of Midwestern legislators to eliminate a system of regional price supports, known as milk marketing orders. The final bill required the Agriculture Department to consolidate the 33 orders into 10 to 14 within three years. The bill also phased out price supports for butter, milk powder and cheese over four years rather than immediately, as other Republicans originally wanted.

Walsh is chairman of the Friends of Ireland and chaired a congressional delegation that visited Northern Ireland with Clinton in 1995.

At Home: Though Walsh's overall voting record has clear moderate tinges, his 98 percent support of the "Contract With America" in 1995 and his 25 percent favorable rating from the AFL-CIO earned him the enmity of organized labor and a spot on the unions' hit list for the 1996 election. The AFL-CIO ran television and radio advertisements in the 25th criticizing Walsh's record. He was also one of the lawmakers hit with the unions' video voter guide.

But Democratic challenger Marty Mack, former mayor of Cortland, never got himself into a position to take advantage of Walsh's perceived weakness. Mack had trouble raising enough money for a big-time campaign, and his political base of Cortland was outside Walsh's home base of Onondaga County, where most of the district's voters live. Despite the union campaign, Walsh wound up winning by than 10 percentage points.

Indeed, Walsh has never been seriously threatened at the polls, reaching or topping 55 percent in all five of his House campaigns.

Walsh first campaigned for the House in 1988 after four-term Republican Rep. George C. Wortley — with a nudge from GOP officials — decided to retire. Although the then-27th District had a Republican lean, its tone was centrist: Staunch conservative Wortley had barely survived a 1986 challenge by Democrat Rosemary S. Pooler.

Pooler, set for a rematch with Wortley, instead faced the stronger and more moderate Walsh. A consumer advocate and former state public service commissioner, Pooler blamed the GOP presidential administration for the loss of local blue-collar jobs. But Walsh portrayed Pooler as an extreme liberal and turned an expected close race into a runaway.

HOUSE ELECTIONS

1996 General		
James T. Walsh (R,C,INDC,FDM)	126,691	(55%)
Marty Mack (D)	103,199	(45%)
1994 General		
James T. Walsh (R,C)	113,949	(58%)
Rhea Jezer (D,CHGC)	83,853	(42%)

Previous Winning Percentages: 1992 (56%) **1990** (63%) **1988** (57%)

CAMPAIGN FINANCE

	Receipts	Receipts from PACs	Expend-itures
1996			
Walsh (R)	$744,775	$268,052 (36%)	$698,021
Mack (D)	$345,678	$165,444 (48%)	$326,595
1994			
Walsh (R)	$427,838	$134,545 (31%)	$415,314
Jezer (D)	$206,423	$44,850 (22%)	$205,818

DISTRICT VOTE FOR PRESIDENT

	1996		1992
D	121,304 (51%)	**D**	108,334 (41%)
R	90,753 (38%)	**R**	95,476 (36%)
I	23,516 (10%)	**I**	58,239 (22%)

KEY VOTES

1997	
Ban "partial birth" abortions	Y
1996	
Approve farm bill	Y
Deny public education to illegal immigrants	Y
Repeal ban on certain assault-style weapons	Y
Increase minimum wage	Y
Freeze defense spending	N
Approve welfare overhaul	Y
1995	
Approve balanced-budget constitutional amendment	Y
Relax Clean Water Act regulations	Y
Oppose limits on environmental regulations	N
Reduce projected Medicare spending	Y
Approve GOP budget with tax and spending cuts	Y

VOTING STUDIES

	Presidential Support		Party Unity		Conservative Coalition	
Year	S	O	S	O	S	O
1996	47	52	79	21	94	4
1995	25	74	89	10	94	5
1994	69	29	73	26	86	14
1993	49	51	78	20	89	11
1992	64	35	65	33	83	13
1991	70	28	67	32	76	22

INTEREST GROUP RATINGS

Year	ADA	AFL-CIO	CCUS	ACU
1996	20	n/a	81	68
1995	10	25	96	76
1994	20	44	91	67
1993	35	67	64	67
1992	25	75	75	72
1991	25	50	70	63

26 Maurice D. Hinchey (D)

Of Saugerties — Elected 1992, 3rd term

Biographical Information

Born: Oct. 27, 1938, New York, N.Y.

Education: State U. of New York, New Paltz, B.S. 1968, M.A. 1970.

Military Service: Navy, 1956-59.

Occupation: State employee.

Family: Wife, Ilene Marder; three children.

Religion: Roman Catholic.

Political Career: Democratic nominee for N.Y. Assembly, 1972; N.Y. Assembly, 1975-93.

Capitol Office: 2431 Rayburn Bldg. 20515; 225-6335.

Committees

Banking & Financial Services
Domestic & International Monetary Policy; Housing & Community Opportunity

Resources
Forests & Forest Health (ranking); National Parks & Public Lands

Joint Economic

In Washington: Hinchey is a member of the Progressive Caucus — perhaps the furthest left of all the Hill's policy caucuses — and his voting record reads as the diary of a faithful Democrat and reliable supporter of the Clinton administration on nearly every issue.

He voted with a majority of Democrats against a majority of Republicans 93 percent of the time in 1996, the third-highest party unity score in the New York delegation, and the highest of any upstate Democrat; only two New York City liberals outdid him.

In addition to backing President Clinton in his fiscal-policy wars with the GOP majority in Congress, Hinchey invariably has taken the side of labor unions in their high-profile disputes with the pro-business Republican leadership — on raising the minimum wage, on allowing companies to offer comp time in lieu of overtime pay, and on changing the National Labor Relations Act to let non-union companies set up and control labor-management teams. He received a 100 percent favorable rating from the AFL-CIO for each of his first three years in office.

Hinchey is in the corner of abortion-rights activists, even in their difficult battle to prevent imposition of a ban on a particular abortion technique that opponents call "partial birth" abortion. He opposes amending the Constitution to mandate congressional term limits or a balanced federal budget. One of his few breaks with Clinton came on the welfare overhaul issue. Hinchey was one of 98 Democrats who would not support the final compromise welfare bill, even after the president said he would sign it. Also, as befits a strong supporter of labor, he broke with the Clinton administration when it pushed NAFTA through Congress.

Hinchey's seat on the Resources Committee is his platform for espousing strong support for environmental protections. He tried in the 104th Congress to designate as wilderness 5.7 million acres of federal land in Utah, but the committee designated 1.8 million acres as wilderness and released for potential development 1.4 million acres. Hinchey also wanted to allow federal officials to continue barring development on additional lands considered but rejected for formal wilderness designation. In the 103rd Congress, he voted against efforts to open parts of the California desert to certain recreational activities.

Also in the 103rd, Hinchey echoed Clinton's hopes to overhaul the nation's health care system. "We need to have the courage and foresight that our predecessors in the House had when they passed Social Security, when they passed the G.I. bill and when they passed Medicare," he said in a speech on the House floor.

As a member of the Banking Committee, Hinchey chides Republicans and moneyed interests in general for protecting the wealthy and overlooking the needs of average working people. "The disparity in income between those at the top and those at the bottom of the ladder is a cancer that will ultimately sap the vitality of our economic system, exacerbating the social problems that are already plaguing our society," he said in November 1993.

At a 1996 hearing of the Banking Subcommittee on Domestic and International Monetary Policy, Hinchey heard Federal Reserve Board Chairman Alan Greenspan call for public and private leaders to increase on-the-job training and continuing education to narrow the gap between rich and poor and stabilize jobs. "It's technology that is creating this dispersal of incomes," Greenspan said. "The best and most effective way to address it is to bring up the skills of our population."

Responded Hinchey: "I closed my eyes for a moment . . . and thought I heard the voice of Robert Reich." Greenspan replied that he and the Labor secretary were surprised to find they agreed on many training issues.

Only on gunowners' rights does Hinchey deviate from the traditional liberal line. He was the only New York Democrat voting in 1996 to repeal the ban on certain semiautomatic assault-style weapons, and the only New York Democrat to

NEW YORK 26
South — Kingston; Binghamton; Ithaca

The elongated 26th reaches from high above Cayuga Lake's waters to the banks of the Hudson River. Most of the population is found in pockets at the district's extremes: the Ithaca and Binghamton areas to the west, and the Hudson Valley region — which includes the cities of Kingston, Newburgh and Beacon — on the eastern edge.

Although the 26th, like most upstate districts, has a Republican heritage, its demographics have made it a political swing district. A Democratic hold on the region's House seat was established by longtime Rep. Matthew F. McHugh in 1974 and continued by Hinchey, but the 26th can still go Republican in contests for major office.

With Cornell University (18,900 students) and Ithaca College (5,700 students) fostering a liberal academic community, Tompkins County is one of the Democrats' strongholds in New York. Hinchey received 66 percent of the vote in the part of the county in the 26th. The part of Broome County in the 26th takes in the "Triple Cities" of Binghamton, Johnson City and Endicott; its mix of high-tech employees and a traditional blue-collar constituency make Broome politically competitive. Hinchey polled 56 percent of the vote here.

Ulster County (Kingston) has industry, but much rural territory. Both Hinchey and his 1996 GOP opponent, Sue Wittig, live in Ulster; Hinchey won the home-county showdown by a 55-42 percent margin. Overall, Hinchey won six of the eight counties that makeup the 26th District, losing just two small rural counties.

One thing that binds this diverse district is its reliance on a major employer: International Business Machines (IBM), which was founded in Endicott. IBM's pre-eminence in mainframe computer technology made it a corporate giant; it also led the transition of Broome County's traditional smokestack economy to a high-tech base. But IBM's failure to keep up with rapid changes in the industry caused huge financial losses and unprecedented job cutbacks. And the Binghamton area, whose defense contractors produce such products as aircraft components and flight simulators, has been further battered by post-Cold War budget cuts.

But economic development officials base hopes for future high-tech growth on the region's skilled work force and the presence of such academic institutions as Cornell, home of a supercomputing center, and the state university campus in Binghamton (11,900 students).

The economy in less-populous areas relies largely on farming (Ulster County's crops include apples and wine grapes) and recreation. The portion of Sullivan County in the district includes much of the Catskill Mountain resort area, a longtime magnet for middle-class Jews and Italians from the New York City area. Gambling proponents have been rebuffed in their efforts to put casinos here.

Although the original Woodstock music festival in 1969 was held 45 miles to the southeast, Saugerties, in Ulster County, hosted Woodstock '94, the 25th anniversary event, in August 1994.

1990 Population: 580,338. White 525,498 (91%), Black 33,076 (6%), Other 21,764 (4%). Hispanic origin 24,829 (4%). 18 and over 446,405 (77%), 62 and over 91,776 (16%). Median age: 33.

vote against the ban in the first place in the 103rd Congress. He did break with most gun-rights proponents to support the Brady bill's five-day waiting period for handgun purchases. A member of the Congressional Sportsmen's Caucus, Hinchey received some unwelcome attention during his first House term when he was charged with carrying a loaded handgun in his baggage at Washington National Airport. He eventually pleaded no contest and was given a suspended sentence.

At Home: After winning two extremely close races against Republican Bob Moppert in 1992 and 1994, Hinchey faced a new opponent in 1996 and won with votes to spare.

In 1992, as Clinton was carrying the 26th by 10 percentage points, Hinchey edged Moppert by 8,819 votes. Two years later, with Republican gubernatorial nominee George E. Pataki sweeping the counties in the district against Gov. Mario M. Cuomo, Hinchey survived once more, winning by slightly more than 1,200 votes.

An 18-year state assemblyman, Hinchey ran in 1992 to succeed retiring nine-term Democratic Rep. Matthew F. McHugh. Hinchey won by emphasizing his reputation as a legislative activist and calling for efforts to reinvigorate the flagging local economy.

He started as the underdog in the Democratic primary, facing Binghamton Mayor Juanita M. Crabb, a well-known politician who once had been talked about as a potential running mate for Cuomo. But Hinchey prevailed by pushing a New Deal-like plan to revitalize the economy of the recession-hit region — and by holding on to his Ulster County base.

The general election matched Hinchey against Moppert, a conservative six-year Broome County legislator and owner of a Binghamton moving company.

Moppert attacked Hinchey as a "professional politician," but Hinchey's nine terms in the state

Legislature had made him enormously popular in his heavily Republican Assembly district, where he won re-election by strong margins.

The close race and competitive nature of the district made Hinchey a top GOP target for 1994. But despite a more conducive environment for the GOP, Moppert's effort failed to ignite. His fundraising was not nearly as robust as it was in 1992; he needed a late $60,000 contribution from the national GOP to fuel his campaign.

Hinchey attacked Moppert for signing the House GOP's "Contract With America"; Moppert went to Washington and presented one of the contract's 10 legislative proposals. Moppert, in turn, did his best to tie Hinchey not only to Clinton but also to Cuomo, who would go down to defeat in his quest for a fourth term. In Moppert's ads, he criticized Hinchey for backing Clinton's budget-reconciliation bill as well as for casting 54 votes in the Assembly for Cuomo-backed tax increases.

In 1996, Hinchey faced businesswoman Sue Wittig. Her candidacy got an early boost when radio station owner and farmer Bud Walker pulled out in advance of the GOP primary, avoiding a potentially bloody intraparty fight. But Hinchey got a break early on as well when Ulster County District Attorney E. Michael Kavanagh, who would have been potentially his strongest GOP opponent, decided to sit out the race.

Like Moppert, Wittig tried to tie Hinchey to both Clinton and Cuomo. She also embraced Republican presidential nominee Bob Dole's proposed 15 percent tax cut and the Republican Congress' commitment to balance the budget by 2002. Unlike Moppert, Wittig also had the nomination of the state's anti-abortion Right to Life Party.

But Hinchey argued that Wittig was too conservative in a state like New York, where even the Republican Gov. Pataki supports abortion rights. And he trumpeted his ability to bring home federal grants for his district. Boosted by a strong Clinton showing in New York, Hinchey beat Wittig by 13 points, winning a third term with 55 percent of the vote.

HOUSE ELECTIONS

1996 General		
Maurice D. Hinchey (D,L)	122,850	(55%)
Sue Wittig (R,C,RTL,FDM)	94,125	(42%)
Douglas Walter Drazen (INDC)	5,531	(2%)
1994 General		
Maurice D. Hinchey (D,L)	95,492	(49%)
Bob Moppert (R,C)	94,244	(48%)
Thomas F. Kovach (RTL)	4,772	(2%)

Previous Winning Percentages: 1992 (50%)

CAMPAIGN FINANCE

	Receipts	Receipts from PACs	Expend-itures
1996			
Hinchey (D)	$979,210	$426,648 (44%)	$994,042
Wittig (R)	$586,837	$191,659 (33%)	$586,078
Drazen (INDC)	$13,417	0	$13,419
1994			
Hinchey (D)	$750,508	$336,516 (45%)	$738,098
Moppert (R)	$275,465	$73,884 (27%)	$278,962

DISTRICT VOTE FOR PRESIDENT

	1996		1992
D	121,168 (51%)	**D**	116,525 (45%)
R	82,419 (35%)	**R**	91,625 (35%)
I	25,316 (11%)	**I**	52,886 (20%)

KEY VOTES

1997	
Ban "partial birth" abortions	N
1996	
Approve farm bill	N
Deny public education to illegal immigrants	N
Repeal ban on certain assault-style weapons	Y
Increase minimum wage	Y
Freeze defense spending	Y
Approve welfare overhaul	N
1995	
Approve balanced-budget constitutional amendment	N
Relax Clean Water Act regulations	N
Oppose limits on environmental regulations	Y
Reduce projected Medicare spending	N
Approve GOP budget with tax and spending cuts	N

VOTING STUDIES

	Presidential Support		Party Unity		Conservative Coalition	
Year	**S**	**O**	**S**	**O**	**S**	**O**
1996	77	22	93	7	20	78
1995	88	11	96	2	5	93
1994	78	21	97	1	14	86
1993	81	16	92	3	14	80

INTEREST GROUP RATINGS

Year	ADA	AFL-CIO	CCUS	ACU
1996	95	n/a	19	5
1995	95	100	13	8
1994	95	100	33	5
1993	95	100	18	4

27 Bill Paxon (R)

Of Amherst — Elected 1988, 5th term

Biographical Information

Born: April 29, 1954, Buffalo, N.Y.

Education: Canisius College, B.A. 1977.

Occupation: Public official.

Family: Wife, Susan Molinari; one child.

Religion: Roman Catholic.

Political Career: Erie County Legislature, 1978-82; N.Y. Assembly, 1983-89.

Capitol Office: 2412 Rayburn Bldg. 20515; 225-5265.

Committees

Commerce

Energy & Power; Finance & Hazardous Materials

In Washington: Nearing the end of his first decade in the House, Paxon is identified with no major piece of legislation, even though he serves on the influential Commerce Committee, which is active on a range of issues. Yet Paxon's impact on Capitol Hill has been just as great as if he had been deeply involved in the intricacies of lawwriting.

For if Newt Gingrich was the general of the Republican revolution, Paxon was its quartermaster. As chairman of the National Republican Congressional Committee (NRCC) from 1993 through 1996, Paxon recruited and helped finance many of the candidates who propelled the GOP to its first House majority since he was born in 1954, and then returned a GOP majority to the chamber for the first time since 1928.

Paxon's political acumen has earned him a place in the top counsels of the House Republican leadership. And when those leaders gather to map out strategy, Paxon is the only legislator likely to find his wife in the room with him; he is married to Rep. Susan Molinari of the Staten Island-based 13th District, vice chairman of the House Republican Conference and the keynote speaker at the 1996 Republican National Convention. The two had a daughter on May 10, 1996, Susan Ruby Paxon, who was prominently displayed during Molinari's convention speech.

Paxon's foes regard his focus on matters electoral with a mixture of fascination and horror. Democratic Rep. Louise M. Slaughter, who represents an adjoining upstate New York district, once described Paxon this way: "Legislation does not interest him. His interest is just to rid the world of Democrats. He puts politics above policy. I've always seen him as someone whose only goal was to raise money and beat Democrats. He's extraordinarily good at those things."

Still, any assessment of his record as NRCC chairman must note his tendency toward hyperbolic wishful thinking, as when he insisted before the 1996 elections that Republicans would pick up 30 seats in the House. They lost nine.

A close ally of Gingrich, Paxon was part of the inner circle that helped direct the campaign to reelect him as Speaker in 1997 in the face of his ethics problems. In December 1996, he was among the GOP lawmakers who strategized with Gingrich on a cellular phone conference that was taped by a Florida couple and leaked to The New York Times. Gingrich critics cited the tape as evidence that the Speaker had reneged on a promise to the House ethics committee that he would not try to influence the resolution of the investigation into his political fundraising.

Once the tape became public, Gingrich partisans howled that it was recorded illegally, and Paxon led the attack against ethics committee vice chairman Jim McDermott, D-Wash., widely rumored to have leaked the tape to the Times. Paxon said McDermott had "likely committed a felony" in dealing with an intercepted cellular telephone conversation, and he charged that a group of Democrats — not just McDermott alone — were involved in circulating the tapes. Paxon said it was no coincidence that Democrats began complaining about the schedule for release of the final report on ethics charges against Gingrich at the same time the tape was leaked. "The Democrats are guilty of orchestrating events," Paxon said of the leaked tape. He specifically singled out Minority Whip David E. Bonior, D-Mich., Gingrich's chief accuser before the ethics panel. "Did Bonior know about this?" Paxon asked. "It's important for him to come out of hiding."

During the 104th Congress, each Democratic defection to the GOP side and every Democratic retirement gave Paxon occasion to gloat happily to the media. But he suffered a spate of bad publicity in July 1995 with a campaign flyer that attacked 28 House Democrats. Twenty-two of the members pictured on a "wanted" poster were either black, Hispanic, Jewish or female. Democratic Congressional Campaign Committee Chairman Martin Frost of Texas called the poster "race baiting pure and simple."

The poster said the 28 were "wanted" for not supporting the House GOP's "Contract With

NEW YORK 27
Suburban Buffalo and rural west — Amherst

During 1992 redistricting, Paxon lobbied former colleagues in the state Legislature to save his congressional seat rather than merge his district with another incumbent's. Not only was Paxon's district not eliminated, he wound up in the suburban-and-rural 27th, which is as solidly a Republican district as he could have designed himself.

Still, there are some pockets of Democratic strength here. Despite the presence of Jack F. Kemp — who used to represent this area — on the national Republican ticket, Bill Clinton won the district by 344 votes in 1996. Clinton won Kemp's former home county of Erie by 15 votes.

The 27th takes in the northeastern suburbs of Buffalo, some suburbia to the south and west of Rochester and a largely farming region stretching 100 miles across northwestern New York.

Amherst, a Buffalo suburb at the western end of the 27th, is the district's anchor; with more than 111,000 residents, it has nearly a fifth of the residents of the 27th. The main campus of the State University of New York at Buffalo (24,500 students) is here. Greater Buffalo International Airport, just across the Buffalo city line (in the 30th District), is another jobs producer.

Unlike Buffalo, the Erie County suburbs in the 27th have little blue-collar industry and a small minority population. Republicans usually run well in Amherst (Paxon's hometown) and even better in the towns east and south, where the landscape quickly shifts from suburban to exurban to rural.

The New York Thruway links Erie County to the Rochester suburbs of Monroe County. The largest of these communities in the 27th is Chili, with about 25,000 residents. Republicans usually carry these mainly middle-class suburbs.

Between and to the east are the dairy, vegetable and grain farms of rural western New York. Wyoming County is heavily agricultural, but it has a facility that is distinctly unbucolic: the state penitentiary at Attica, the site in 1971 of one of the worst prison riots in U.S. history.

In Ontario and Seneca counties, the 27th moves into the part of the Finger Lakes region, including some of its vineyards and the cities of Geneva and Seneca Falls (site of a convention in 1848 that is regarded as the origin of the women's rights movement and now is home to a national historic site and a women's hall of fame).

The western end of Wayne County (which borders Lake Ontario) is within Rochester's sphere; in its southern reaches are several towns that grew up along the Erie Canal. Palmyra is where Joseph Smith received his vision and began what became the Mormon Church.

The easternmost part of the district extends into Cayuga County and the city of Auburn, which is divided among three Republicans: Paxon, Amo Houghton and James T. Walsh. There is a major correctional facility there as well.

1990 Population: 580,337. White 554,426 (96%), Black 14,748 (3%), Other 11,163 (2%). Hispanic origin 7,391 (1%). 18 and over 433,948 (75%), 62 and over 90,096 (16%). Median age: 34.

America," but by the Republicans' own count, more than 170 Democrats "failed the Contract With America test." Paxon said the mailing was "about ideology and voting records. Any insinuation that it is anything other than that is outrageous."

After the 1994 election, Paxon made it plain that Republicans expected the business community to show its gratitude for the GOP majority pursuing a business-friendly agenda. "Our members have felt they were carrying the legislative water for many of these groups who then gave their money to the other side," Paxon said. "It's very difficult for me to argue that people should open their arms to those who are embracing their opponents. I certainly am not going to embrace someone who's constantly stabbing me in the back. We're making sure that the members know who's wielding the knife."

Despite his emphasis on bringing the GOP success at the ballot box, Paxon has had some time for legislative work. In the 104th, he supported efforts in the farm bill rewrite to preserve the milk marketing orders that favored New York dairy farmers. He fought efforts to severely restrict the ability of New York to send its trash to other states for disposal.

On the telecommunications deregulation bill, he backed efforts to make it easier for the Bell operating companies to enter the long distance market, saying that the market would create competition for local phone service. "We're looking at a lot of these issues through old glasses, and the prescription has changed," Paxon said. "The world's moving much faster than we could ever try to figure out."

Paxon later criticized telecommunications companies for continuing to give campaign money to Democrats. "Their Washington operatives have not gotten the message," he said. "They are still trying to keep those organizations from contributing in a way that's beneficial to their members."

As befits a member of the Republican leadership, Paxon is a reliable vote for his party on the House floor. His party unity score has never been below 89 percent.

At Home: Just as Paxon's NRCC set its sights on the House Democratic leadership in 1994, Paxon found himself facing a well-financed, energetic Democratic challenger in 1996: United Auto Workers regional director Thomas M. Fricano.

Hammering at the Contract With America and buoyed by the strong support of organized labor, Fricano remained on the attack throughout the campaign, accusing Paxon of ignoring the residents of the district in order to follow Speaker Gingrich.

In response, Paxon basically ignored Fricano, airing commercials touting his record in office and meeting in private with groups of constituents. He spent more than $1.5 million on his re-election and won with 60 percent of the vote — down 15 points from his 1994 tally, but a comfortable win nonetheless.

Paxon's fundraising helped spare him a political scare following the 1990 census, when the New York Legislature began redrawing congressional districts. The state was losing three seats, and one of those was earmarked for Western New York. The most junior member in the region, Paxon was the most likely to be sacrificed. But he contributed or raised more than $40,000 in campaign funds to help New York Republicans defend their majority in the state Senate and promised to raise even more money in the future.

The Senate Republicans dug in and insisted that Paxon's district be saved. In the end, Paxon kept his seat, and the dean of the New York congressional delegation, Frank Horton, found himself sharing a district with Democrat Slaughter. Horton decided to retire.

When GOP Rep. Jack F. Kemp left the House to run for president in 1988, Paxon was touted as his heir apparent in the then-31st District. Though only 34 years old, he was already a political veteran. The son of an Erie County family court judge, Paxon was elected at age 23 as the youngest-ever member of the Erie County Legislature. Twice re-elected to county office by huge margins, he then easily won an open Assembly seat in 1982.

Paxon established his conservative credentials in Albany, promoting efforts to cut state welfare costs and often opposing efforts to expand state regulation. He also gained the ranking position on the Assembly corrections committee. Like Gingrich in the U.S. House, Paxon in the Assembly was part of a group of conservative GOP lawmakers who challenged not only the Democratic majority but their own moderate GOP leaders.

His move to the House in 1988 did not go as smoothly as expected. He weathered a vigorous challenge from Democratic Erie County Clerk David Swarts, who denounced Paxon as an ideologue with a reflexive opposition to business regulation. The well-known Democrat's aggressive effort made the contest close in Erie County. But Paxon had breathing room in the district's more rural precincts, and he won 53 percent overall.

HOUSE ELECTIONS

1996 General		
Bill Paxon (R,C,RTL,FDM)	142,568	(60%)
Thomas M. Fricano (D,SM)	95,503	(40%)
1994 General		
Bill Paxon (R,C,RTL)	152,610	(75%)
William A. Long Jr. (D)	52,160	(25%)

Previous Winning Percentages: 1992 (64%) **1990** (57%) **1988** (53%)

CAMPAIGN FINANCE

	Receipts	Receipts from PACs	Expend-itures
1996			
Paxon (R)	$1,443,755	$668,971 (46%)	$1,553,754
Fricano (D)	$659,984	$208,843 (32%)	$656,490
1994			
Paxon (R)	$768,628	$374,410 (49%)	$642,531
Long (D)	$62,797	$26,600 (42%)	$62,746

DISTRICT VOTE FOR PRESIDENT

	1996		1992
D	112,453 (44%)	**D**	90,194 (33%)
R	112,109 (44%)	**R**	115,432 (42%)
I	29,135 (11%)	**I**	67,721 (25%)

KEY VOTES

1997	
Ban "partial birth" abortions	Y
1996	
Approve farm bill	Y
Deny public education to illegal immigrants	Y
Repeal ban on certain assault-style weapons	Y
Increase minimum wage	N
Freeze defense spending	N
Approve welfare overhaul	Y
1995	
Approve balanced-budget constitutional amendment	Y
Relax Clean Water Act regulations	Y
Oppose limits on environmental regulations	N
Reduce projected Medicare spending	Y
Approve GOP budget with tax and spending cuts	Y

VOTING STUDIES

	Presidential Support		Party Unity		Conservative Coalition	
Year	**S**	**O**	**S**	**O**	**S**	**O**
1996	30	57	90	2	88	0
1995	18	82	98	1	96	3
1994	35	65	98	2	92	8
1993	29	70	96	3	95	5
1992	80	20	94	5	96	4
1991	75	23	90	7	97	3

INTEREST GROUP RATINGS

Year	ADA	AFL-CIO	CCUS	ACU
1996	0	n/a	100	100
1995	0	0	100	88
1994	0	0	92	100
1993	5	0	100	100
1992	10	33	75	92
1991	10	17	80	85

28 Louise M. Slaughter (D)

Of Fairport — Elected 1986, 6th term

Biographical Information

Born: Aug. 14, 1929, Harlan County, Ky.
Education: U. of Kentucky, B.S. 1951, M.P.H. 1953.
Occupation: Market researcher; legislative aide.
Family: Husband, Robert Slaughter; three children.
Religion: Episcopalian.
Political Career: Monroe County Legislature, 1975-79; N.Y. Assembly, 1983-87.
Capitol Office: 2347 Rayburn Bldg. 20515; 225-3615.

Committees

Rules
Rules & Organization of the House

In Washington: Slaughter, who lost her coveted position on the House Rules Committee when the GOP took control of the House in 1995, regained that post in the 105th Congress when one of the Democratic seats — the minority party has only four — came open with the retirement of California's Anthony C. Beilenson. But that news only partly salved Slaughter's hurt at losing for the second time in a bid for a more prominent position in the Democratic hierarchy, as she was beaten by South Carolina's John M. Spratt Jr. in their late 1996 contest for the ranking seat on the Budget Committee.

On the Rules Committee, Slaughter will renew her rivalry with fellow New Yorker Gerald B.H. Solomon, who now chairs the panel. In 1992, she engaged in a well-publicized spat with Solomon after asking on the House floor that the Family Planning Amendments Act be brought up. When Solomon, then in the GOP minority, began to complain about the Democrats' rules, Slaughter called for regular order, which would have ended the Republican's soliloquy.

"What did you say?" Solomon queried angrily. "You had better not do that, ma'am. You will regret that as long as you live. Who do you think you are?" The remarks later were revised and never appeared in the Congressional Record.

In her attempt to become the top Democrat on the Budget Committee for the 105th, Slaughter thought she might benefit from the fact that no other House committee has a woman in the ranking seat. But the race between her and Spratt turned less on gender than on ideology. He won, 106-83, with a coalition of centrist and conservative Democrats against her liberals. Two years earlier, Slaughter narrowly lost a race for vice chairman of the Democratic caucus to Barbara B. Kennelly of Connecticut, 93-90. In that matchup between two northerners, Slaughter's Kentucky roots helped win her some Southern Democratic votes. But Kennelly, who had more seniority and had served as a deputy whip, had a slightly stronger claim that it was her turn to move up.

Spratt's victory over Slaughter rankled some House Democratic women, who questioned how a party that owed so much of its 1996 election success to female voters could not have a female ranking member on any House committee. "Half of our governing body of the United States doesn't have representation," Slaughter said.

Slaughter had reached her three-term limit on the Budget Committee but could run for the ranking slot because the Democratic leadership appointed her to another term on the panel. However, after losing to Spratt, she left Budget altogether.

In the 104th Congress, Slaughter served on the Government Reform and Oversight Committee, where she clashed with Rep. David M. McIntosh, R-Ind., a freshman who had landed the chairmanship of the panel's National Economic Growth, Natural Resources and Regulatory Affairs Subcommittee. McIntosh was a cosponsor of legislation banning nonprofit groups that receive federal funds from lobbying the federal government. Before a public hearing, he handed out a news release printed on what appeared to be Alliance for Justice stationery, identifying the advocacy group's members and the amount of federal funds they received. Slaughter cried "forgery" and unsuccessfully offered a resolution on the floor asking the Speaker to investigate McIntosh's conduct. The resolution was tabled. McIntosh later wrote a letter of apology to the organization.

Slaughter also filed two complaints on behalf of the Alliance for Justice against McIntosh with the ethics committee, which dismissed the allegations but admonished McIntosh privately and warned him against doing it again.

Slaughter has been active on issues that she sees as of specific concern to women, always showing her liberal colors. She was one of seven House women who marched on the Senate in October 1991 to urge a delay in the vote on the nomination of Clarence Thomas to the Supreme Court. A bacteriologist with a master's degree in public health, she has scored some successes on

NEW YORK 28
Rochester and most of suburban Monroe County

Rochester's location on Lake Ontario and the Erie Canal made it an industrial center by the early 19th century. Yet unlike many Northern cities with blue-collar bases, Rochester long held to a Republican tradition typical of upstate New York. Only in recent years has the city — which dominates the 28th — began leaning toward some Democrats. Bill Clinton's winning margin of nearly 20 percentage points in the district in 1996 was unusually large.

Known early on as the "Flour City" (for its grain mills) and then the "Flower City" (for its commercial nurseries), Rochester grew to be New York's third-largest city with a push from a pair of giant corporations: Eastman Kodak (founded in the 1880s) and the Xerox Corp. (which began producing copying machines in the 1940s).

These companies spawned a large white-collar managerial class that leaned Republican. They also pursued a rather paternalistic management style that rubbed off on Rochester's civic life. The Republicans who long dominated Rochester politics were generally moderates: Barber B. Conable Jr., who served a Rochester-based district from 1965 to 1985, and Frank Horton, who served in a nearby district from 1963 to 1993, were typical.

Fred J. Eckert, Conable's staunchly conservative GOP successor, lasted but one term before his 1986 loss to Slaughter.

Still, to carry the 28th, Democrats must do well within the city (which has about two-fifths of the 28th's population). More than half the registered voters in the city are Democrats, but Republicans hold a wide plurality among registrants in suburban Monroe County. While the city has a large blue-collar population, the suburbs are mainly white-collar. Rochester's population is nearly one-third black and nearly a tenth Hispanic, but less than 5 percent of the suburban population is black or Hispanic.

Kodak remains the district's largest employer, but it has undergone downsizing in recent years. In addition to Xerox, other big employers include the Bausch and Lomb optical company. Among the region's smaller companies are high-tech startups that benefit from their proximity to the major corporations and the area's major academic institutions, Rochester Institute of Technology (13,000 students) and the University of Rochester (8,000 students).

While the jobless rate has remained relatively moderate in recent years, much of the job slack has been picked up by service industries, which generally provide lower salaries than the manufacturing sector. This transition has exacerbated the problems of Rochester's low-income residents: The city's poverty rate tops 20 percent.

The recent recession took an unusually hard toll on white-collar workers, but the Monroe County suburbs in the 28th are relatively affluent compared with the city. The most populous suburbs, Greece and Irondequoit, are north of the city; Pittsford, the wealthiest suburb, is southeast.

1990 Population: 580,337. White 472,733 (81%), Black 81,107 (14%), Other 26,497 (5%). Hispanic origin 24,703 (4%). 18 and over 439,156 (76%), 62 and over 90,688 (16%). Median age: 33.

health matters. Her bill to increase education about the health risks of exposure to the anti-miscarriage drug DES, which caused cancer and abnormalities in the offspring of some women who took the drug, was enacted in 1992. She also attached an amendment to a 1990 homeless-aid bill to provide incentive grants for states to help ensure that homeless children could attend school. The 1994 crime bill had a Slaughter-sponsored provision requiring that sex offenders released from prison let law enforcement authorities know their new addresses.

In the 104th Congress, she pushed through an amendment to a House crime bill that made rape or serious sexual assault a federal crime if the accused rapist had ever been convicted of rape before, and had crossed state lines before or after committing the crime. Any rapist then convicted in federal court would get life in prison without parole. The provision passed the House, 411-4, but the bill died in the Senate. It was reintroduced as a free-standing bill in the 105th Congress.

Other bills she introduced in the 104th included measures to provide protection from sexual predators; to authorize money to buy four properties to add to the Women's Rights National Historical Park in Seneca Falls, N.Y.; to authorize a review of federal programs that study environmental health risks to women; to express Congress' disapproval of the trafficking of Burmese women and children into Thailand for the purpose of prostitution; and to promote equity in women's health care services through expanded extend research for several diseases, standards for more female scientists at federal agencies and departments, and preventive medical programs for women.

She has been active on trade issues as well, going to bat in behalf of Eastman Kodak, Xerox, Bausch and Lomb, and other companies in her district that are trying to expand into overseas markets. She voted for GATT but answered the call of her close allies in organized labor to oppose NAFTA.

And she has not been shy about trying to bring home federal funds, including $6 million for a high-technology incubator facility, which will help embryonic companies with office space, support services and technical assistance; and $4 million for a wave surge barrier in Rochester Harbor to enable a multimillion-dollar waterfront development project to get underway.

When President Clinton unveiled his proposed health care overhaul, Slaughter challenged elements that she said would jeopardize Rochester's successful managed-competition plan.

A gun control proponent, Slaughter also has introduced legislation that would require anyone buying explosives to first receive a federal permit, and would put purchasers of explosives through the same computerized background check established under the law that mandates a five-day waiting period for handgun purchases.

At Home: Given the demographics of her district, Slaughter is not going to win by decisive margins, but she regularly winds up with a comfortable edge on Election Day.

In 1996, she faced investment banker Geoffrey Rosenberger, who spent lavishly from his own pocket, embraced the conservative Republican agenda and tried to paint Slaughter as an old-fashioned liberal. In 1994, she faced Monroe County (Rochester) legislator Renee Forgensi Davison. In both cases, Slaughter was targeted by her neighbor, Republican Rep. Bill Paxon, chairman of the National Republican Congressional Committee. And in both elections, she walked away with 57 percent of the vote.

Slaughter's charm, grass-roots organization and fundraising skill weighed heavily in her narrow 1986 upset of conservative GOP Rep. Fred J. Eckert. Although Eckert had won the seat in 1984, he was far more conservative than his predecessor, veteran GOP Rep. Barber B. Conable Jr. Democratic PACs that had targeted Eckert for defeat helped Slaughter raise nearly $600,000. Depicting Eckert as a right-wing obstructionist and parrying Eckert's efforts to portray her as an ultraliberal, Slaughter won with 51 percent.

The same advantages, plus her rapid rise to a prestigious committee position, enabled Slaughter to breeze past her next two Republican opponents.

Redistricting before the 1992 election appeared to further solidify her position. The newly drawn 28th District took in all of Rochester, is contained wholly within Monroe County and showed a Democratic tilt.

Yet Slaughter saw her 1992 vote drop a bit, to 55 percent. Her problem was a locally well-known Republican opponent, Monroe County Legislator William P. Polito, who worked to take advantage of an anti-Congress mood.

Slaughter moved to Rochester from her native Kentucky in the 1950s, when her husband went to work as an executive with a local corporation. She entered public life as a Monroe County legislator and as an assistant to Mario M. Cuomo, then New York's secretary of state. In 1982, she ousted a GOP incumbent to move to the state Assembly, and she served there two terms before going to Congress.

HOUSE ELECTIONS

1996 General		
Louise M. Slaughter (D)	133,084	(57%)
Geoffrey Rosenberger (R,C,FDM)	99,366	(43%)
1994 General		
Louise M. Slaughter (D)	110,987	(57%)
Renee Forgensi Davison (R,C)	78,516	(40%)
John A. Clendenin (IF)	6,464	(3%)

Previous Winning Percentages: 1992 (55%) **1990** (59%) **1988** (57%) **1986** (51%)

CAMPAIGN FINANCE

	Receipts	Receipts from PACs	Expend-itures
1996			
Slaughter (D)	$827,367	$375,416 (45%)	$868,969
Rosenberger (R)	$673,669	$33,082 (5%)	$663,441
1994			
Slaughter (D)	$806,231	$425,505 (53%)	$790,778
Davison (R)	$169,819	$21,046 (12%)	$165,922

DISTRICT VOTE FOR PRESIDENT

	1996		1992
D	136,427 (55%)	**D**	119,055 (44%)
R	88,279 (36%)	**R**	103,544 (38%)
I	17,841 (7%)	**I**	48,467 (18%)

KEY VOTES

1997	
Ban "partial birth" abortions	N
1996	
Approve farm bill	N
Deny public education to illegal immigrants	N
Repeal ban on certain assault-style weapons	N
Increase minimum wage	Y
Freeze defense spending	Y
Approve welfare overhaul	N
1995	
Approve balanced-budget constitutional amendment	N
Relax Clean Water Act regulations	N
Oppose limits on environmental regulations	Y
Reduce projected Medicare spending	N
Approve GOP budget with tax and spending cuts	N

VOTING STUDIES

	Presidential Support		Party Unity		Conservative Coalition	
Year	**S**	**O**	**S**	**O**	**S**	**O**
1996	82	15	91	6	18	78
1995	86	13	95	3	11	89
1994	82	18	97	1	14	86
1993	74	25	95	4	20	80
1992	16	84	96	3	17	83
1991	25	73	93	3	24	73

INTEREST GROUP RATINGS

Year	ADA	AFL-CIO	CCUS	ACU
1996	90	n/a	25	5
1995	90	100	17	4
1994	95	75	50	0
1993	100	100	27	4
1992	95	92	25	4
1991	95	100	20	5

29 John J. LaFalce (D)

Of Tonawanda — Elected 1974, 12th term

Biographical Information
Born: Oct. 6, 1939, Buffalo, N.Y.
Education: Canisius College, B.S. 1961; Villanova U., J.D. 1964.
Military Service: Army, 1965-67.
Occupation: Lawyer.
Family: Wife, Patricia Fisher; one child.
Religion: Roman Catholic.
Political Career: N.Y. Senate, 1971-73; N.Y. Assembly, 1973-75.

Capitol Office: 2310 Rayburn Bldg. 20515; 225-3231.

Committees
Banking & Financial Services
Financial Institutions & Consumer Credit; Housing & Community Opportunity
Small Business (ranking)

In Washington: LaFalce has a reputation as one of the smarter members of the House — and for not being shy about letting people know it. He took that trait, and his characteristic intensity, into a November 1996 effort to wrest the top Democratic seat on the Banking and Financial Services Committee from the incumbent, Henry B. Gonzalez of Texas.

LaFalce failed to win the ranking spot, but the remarkably graceful manner in which he conceded to Gonzalez probably sets him up as the front-runner for the job in the 106th Congress. Gonzalez already has pledged that this Congress will be his last atop the Democratic side of the committee, which also oversees housing and urban affairs issues.

The No. 2 Democrat on Banking, LaFalce challenged Gonzalez when the Democratic Caucus gathered to set assignments for the 105th Congress. The committee's third-ranking Democrat, Bruce F. Vento of Minnesota, also entered the race.

LaFalce complained that Gonzalez missed too many important meetings of the committee in the 104th and was uninterested in leading the Democratic charge into battles with the Republican majority. He said Gonzalez had not been a factor in committee business since losing the gavel, and his frequent absences forced LaFalce and Vento to take up the slack.

Even when Democrats controlled the House and Gonzalez chaired the committee, LaFalce and Vento said, the panel's successes came in spite of his sometimes erratic style, which included missing leadership meetings and not responding to leadership messages.

"For far too long, I believe the Banking Committee has failed to fulfill its promise," LaFalce wrote in a campaign letter to fellow Democrats. "Few Banking Committee products get to the House floor; many fail when they get there or receive such tepid support they have no momentum; few go on to become law."

LaFalce gained the support of the House Democratic Steering Committee, which voted 29-12 to make Gonzalez the committee's ranking member emeritus and voted 22-19 to recommend LaFalce for the top Democratic seat over Vento. But after an emotional plea to the full party caucus, Gonzalez emerged with 82 votes. LaFalce got 62 and Vento received 47. Under caucus rules, Vento dropped out and LaFalce and Gonzalez prepared for a runoff. But rather than press his challenge, LaFalce magnanimously withdrew, a move that colleagues greeted with a roar of cheers and applause. "I think I would have had a good shot at getting most of Vento's votes, but that's not the way to do things," LaFalce said after the caucus meeting. "I think everybody was tremendously relieved. I feel very good about what's transpired."

Observed one of LaFalce's supporters on the panel, fellow New Yorker Charles E. Schumer: "You couldn't end up with a better ending. To continue the fight would not be good for the committee. It was a real class act."

During the 104th Congress, LaFalce eagerly tangled with the new Banking chairman, Jim Leach of Iowa. In May 1996, when Leach tried to push banking overhaul legislation to the House floor, panel Democrats said no. They complained that they had been shut out of the process as the measure went through multiple redraftings. "How can we help him bring anything to the floor when we don't know what it is and we've had no input?" LaFalce asked.

LaFalce, who chaired the Small Business Committee when Democrats controlled the House, moved over to become the panel's ranking member in the 104th, with Kansas Republican Jan Meyers wielding the gavel. He remains in that post for the 105th, now paired with a new chairman, James M. Talent of Missouri, who is a harder-edged conservative than was Meyers.

There were some rough spots, but Meyers and LaFalce usually managed to cooperate on legislative business. In July 1996, the committee, by voice vote, reauthorized a number of Small Business Administration programs through fiscal

The many industrial workers in the Buffalo-Niagara Falls region provide a political base for LaFalce and other Democratic candidates in the 29th. However, the district also has a piece of GOP-leaning Buffalo suburbia and Rochester suburbs at its eastern extreme; in between is some solidly Republican rural turf. Many traditional Democratic voters in the Buffalo area are socially conservative white "ethnics" with roots in Italy, Eastern Europe and Ireland.

These factors make the 29th potentially competitive. LaFalce (a leading Democratic opponent of abortion) has maintained his party's grasp on the seat. He polled 62 percent in 1996 against a weak opponent, reversing a trend that saw him win his first seven re-election campaigns with an average of 77 percent, and his next three campaigns with a 55 percent average. In the presidential race, Bill Clinton beat Bob Dole, 51 percent to 35 percent.

Four years earlier, working-class unhappiness with the two major parties led to an exceptional turnout for Ross Perot in Niagara County; Clinton won 37 percent, compared with 32 percent for Bush and 31 percent for Perot. In 1996, Perot took just 14 percent in the county, while Clinton bested Dole, 49 percent to 35 percent.

Most of the district's residents live in northwest Erie County and all of Niagara County (each of these jurisdictions provides about 40 percent of the 29th's population).

The 29th takes in the northwest corner of the city of Buffalo. Though it has a small part of downtown and the Peace Bridge that connects the city with Fort Erie, Ontario, this is a mainly residential area, where Italian-Americans make up the predominant constituent group.

To the north are such mixed blue- and white-collar suburbs as Tonawanda and Grand Island.

NEW YORK 29
Northwest — Part of Buffalo; Niagara Falls

Like the rest of Buffalo, the area is adjusting from being dependent on heavy industry to one based on service and light manufacturers.

The natural grandeur of Niagara Falls makes its namesake city one of the world's leading tourist stops. But the Niagara River also made the region a major industrial center. Its chemical industry provides thousands of jobs but has given the area a bad ecological reputation. A community had to be abandoned in 1978 because of toxic dumping in the city's Love Canal; part of the area has been cleaned up and reoccupied.

Though there has been some retrenchment, blue-collar industry is still central: Occidental Chemical, du Pont and Carborundum factories are in Niagara Falls, as is a Nabisco Shredded Wheat factory. General Motors sold its Lockport facility. Its new owner, Delphi Harrison Thermal Systems, makes air conditioning systems, radiators and other automobile components for GM and other manufacturers.

The remainder of Niagara and Orleans County to the east are largely rural, with many dairy and produce farms. Orleans is by far the most Republican part of the district, and was the only county in the 29th whose voters preferred Dole over Clinton in 1996.

1990 Population: 580,337. White 537,547 (93%), Black 26,118 (5%), Other 16,672 (3%). Hispanic origin 16,241 (3%). 18 and over 441,716 (76%), 62 and over 102,578 (18%). Median age: 34.

1998. The package included several amendments negotiated by LaFalce and Meyers aimed at watering down provisions intended to privatize some of SBA's loan collection and liquidation functions. Earlier, though, LaFalce's initial opposition to the package compelled Meyers to suspend markup of it. LaFalce decried the lack of a previous hearing on the bills. He called the pending business "voluminous and complex legislation that is little understood" by the committee members.

As Small Business chairman from 1987 to 1995, LaFalce labored to change the panel's image as a backwater and give it a role in setting tax and regulatory policy. He expanded the reach of the panel, and he found ways to improve the availability of capital and credit to small businesses. He once conceded that "99 out of 100" issues in which he got Small Business involved were outside the committee's jurisdiction, adding, "I can either say we'll tend to our knitting or we can become the aggressive ombudsman of the small-business community."

LaFalce is among the band of House Democrats opposed to abortion, and he has warned that the party's advocacy of abortion rights could create a lasting rift with ethnic and working-class voters. In recent high-profile floor votes on abortion policy, LaFalce consistently has taken the side of abortion opponents. He voted in the 104th against requiring states to fund Medicaid abortions for poor women, against permitting abortions at overseas military hospitals, and against allowing federal employees' health care plans to cover abortions. He supports banning a particular abortion technique that opponents call "partial-birth" abortion.

On most other issues, though, LaFalce is a reliable liberal. He voted against the welfare overhaul bill signed into law by President Clinton in 1996 and against repealing the ban on certain semiautomatic assault-style weapons. He was an early supporter of increasing the minimum wage — and an opponent of GOP efforts to exempt small businesses from paying the higher wage.

At Home: LaFalce was expecting to face a strong challenge in 1996 from Erie County Comptroller Nancy Naples, whose support of abortion rights could have drained off Democrats and independents upset by LaFalce's anti-abortion stance. But Naples withdrew from the race shortly after she entered, citing her mother's health as a concern. Instead, the Republicans wound up with Orleans County Legislator David B. Callard, who represents one of the least populous areas of the district. LaFalce won easily, 62 percent to 38 percent.

His strong performance in 1996 contrasted markedly with his previous three contests, in which he tallied no more than 55 percent of the vote.

LaFalce was never really at risk in 1990 — he beat his GOP opponent by 24 points — but his 55 percent showing was a big drop from his 73 percent romp in 1988. LaFalce blamed his slippage on complacency and his absence from the district during the 101st Congress' long session.

However, there also was evidence of dissatisfaction in LaFalce's blue-collar base. In 1992, Republicans recruited a higher-profile candidate to challenge LaFalce in the redrawn 29th District. Lawyer William E. Miller was young and aggressive and had a well-known name: His late father, a longtime House member from the area, was the vice presidential candidate on the 1964 GOP ticket with Barry Goldwater.

Miller ran hard on an anti-incumbent theme. He tried to tar LaFalce, as a senior Banking Committee member, with some responsibility for the savings and loan scandal. He also contrasted his support for abortion rights with LaFalce's anti-abortion position.

LaFalce fought back vigorously. He said he was an early advocate of banking law reform and blamed the thrift crisis on regulatory failures by Republican administrations. The final outcome was a 54 percent to 42 percent LaFalce win.

Miller tried again in 1994, but despite the year's favorable GOP climate, the outcome was little different: LaFalce won 55 percent to 43 percent.

LaFalce, a lawyer in his hometown of Buffalo, burst into politics in 1970 with an upset victory for the state Senate. When a redistricting plan gave him an impossible district to run in two years later, he moved down to the state Assembly, where he served one term.

In 1974, when GOP Rep. Henry P. Smith retired, LaFalce campaigned in a semi-suburban district that had not been won by a Democrat in 62 years. He carried 60 percent of the vote, then proceeded to win with even greater margins through the 1980s.

HOUSE ELECTIONS

1996 General		
John J. LaFalce (D,L)	132,317	(62%)
David B. Callard (R,C,RTL,FDM)	81,135	(38%)
1994 General		
John J. LaFalce (D,L)	103,053	(55%)
William E. Miller (R,C)	80,355	(43%)
Patrick Murty (RTL)	3,296	(2%)

Previous Winning Percentages: **1992** (54%) **1990** (55%) **1988** (73%) **1986** (91%) **1984** (69%) **1982** (91%) **1980** (72%) **1978** (74%) **1976** (67%) **1974** (60%)

CAMPAIGN FINANCE

	Receipts	Receipts from PACs	Expend-itures
1996			
LaFalce (D)	$571,924	$287,074 (50%)	$443,052
Callard (R)	$123,957	$500 (0%)	$123,958
1994			
LaFalce (D)	$471,041	$252,505 (54%)	$825,314
Miller (R)	$221,128	$1,264 (1%)	$219,273

DISTRICT VOTE FOR PRESIDENT

1996	1992
D 120,808 (51%)	**D** 103,528 (40%)
R 82,823 (35%)	**R** 86,732 (33%)
I 28,004 (12%)	**I** 70,231 (27%)

KEY VOTES

1997	
Ban "partial birth" abortions	Y
1996	
Approve farm bill	N
Deny public education to illegal immigrants	N
Repeal ban on certain assault-style weapons	N
Increase minimum wage	Y
Freeze defense spending	Y
Approve welfare overhaul	N
1995	
Approve balanced-budget constitutional amendment	N
Relax Clean Water Act regulations	N
Oppose limits on environmental regulations	Y
Reduce projected Medicare spending	N
Approve GOP budget with tax and spending cuts	N

VOTING STUDIES

	Presidential Support		Party Unity		Conservative Coalition	
Year	**S**	**O**	**S**	**O**	**S**	**O**
1996	82	16	88	9	24	75
1995	80	16	84	11	23	74
1994	82	12	86	10	47	42
1993	72	25	84	10	39	61
1992	27	70	86	9	29	65
1991	32	67	89	8	22	78

INTEREST GROUP RATINGS

Year	ADA	AFL-CIO	CCUS	ACU
1996	80	n/a	25	5
1995	75	100	25	16
1994	80	78	58	15
1993	75	100	9	17
1992	85	100	25	12
1991	90	83	30	10

30 Jack Quinn (R)

Of Hamburg — Elected 1992, 3rd term

Biographical Information

Born: April 13, 1951, Buffalo, N.Y.

Education: Siena College, B.A. 1973; State U. of New York, Buffalo, M.A. 1983.

Occupation: Teacher.

Family: Wife, Mary Beth McAndrews; two children.

Religion: Roman Catholic.

Political Career: Town of Hamburg Council, 1982-84; Hamburg town supervisor, 1985-93.

Capitol Office: 331 Cannon Bldg. 20515; 225-3306.

Committees

Transportation & Infrastructure
Railroads; Surface Transportation; Water Resources & Environment

Veterans' Affairs
Benefits (chairman)

In Washington: The first Republican in decades to represent downtown Buffalo, Quinn, like many House GOP moderates, responded to his party leaders' pleas for unity in the first part of the 104th Congress. He voted for "Contract With America" legislation 92 percent of the time in early 1995. He supported the GOP's plan to balance the budget, with its controversial reductions in the rate of spending growth on Medicare and Medicaid.

Then came 1996, and, also like many moderates, Quinn began moving back toward the middle. His party unity score dipped from 84 percent in 1995 to 68 percent in 1996. He led the eventually successful effort within the House Republican Conference to bring to the floor legislation raising the minimum wage. And in the fall election campaign, he emphasized his independence rather than his fealty to House Speaker Newt Gingrich and the GOP.

"The voters in Buffalo understood, and have ample opportunity to know, I vote independently," Quinn said. "The cookie-cutter Quinn-is-Gingrich — they've got the wrong guy. We have a pretty independent record, and we reminded the voters of that."

After the election, Quinn said he hoped Republicans would see that their legislative and political success was the result of moving toward the middle and passing measures raising the minimum wage, making health insurance "portable," and the like. He also expressed hope that GOP leaders, with a smaller majority in the 105th, would pay greater heed to party moderates. "Our votes are more important now than ever to get anything done," Quinn said.

In the 105th, Quinn chairs the Veterans' Affairs Subcommittee on Benefits, which was created by combining two benefits-related panels — the Education, Training, Employment and Housing Subcommittee and the Compensation, Pension, Insurance and Memorial Affairs Subcommittee.

In the 104th, Quinn's most strident declaration of independence came during the second session, when he led a group of two dozen House Republicans demanding that their leadership allow a vote on legislation raising the minimum wage. "We believe people who work a 40-hour week ought to earn a wage they can live on," Quinn said in April 1996.

House Republican leaders eventually caved in to the insurgents' demands. But they punished Quinn and gave another endangered incumbent, Frank Riggs of California, the chance to propose the minimum wage amendment.

Quinn's independence was on display in other votes as well. He opposed efforts to allow states to deny public education to illegal aliens. A supporter of both the Brady bill's five-day waiting period for handgun purchases and the ban on certain semiautomatic assault-style weapons, he voted against a Republican-backed effort to repeal the ban in 1996. "We can't talk about getting tough on crime without banning assault weapons that have no use other than to kill a lot of people in a hurry," Quinn said in voting for the original assault weapons ban.

He strongly backed labor in the summer of 1995 as the House Transportation and Infrastructure Committee worked on legislation reauthorizing Amtrak. Quinn won approval of two amendments designed to protect employees during the railway's transformation into a private company. The first amendment would require Amtrak to seek approval from its unions for any change in severance benefits. The second one would preserve existing Amtrak labor contracts, requiring the railway to negotiate new contracts before contracting out work. Opponents argued that the amendment would destroy Amtrak's ability to survive by denying it the freedom to restructure its operations and subcontract some of its services. Committee chairman Bud Shuster, R-Pa., abruptly ended a markup session once Quinn's second proposal passed.

The two sides eventually worked out a compromise that would maintain current labor con-

NEW YORK 30
West — Buffalo

The 30th, dominated by its part of Buffalo, provided a paradoxical result in the 1992 election. The district, with its large, economically worried working-class population, went to Bill Clinton by a wide margin; George Bush finished behind independent candidate Ross Perot.

Yet even as the district was resoundingly rejecting Bush, it elected Republican Quinn to the House. His win was a major upset: Over the previous 18 years, the territory covered by much of the 30th had elected Democrat Henry J. Nowak without a serious GOP challenge.

Quinn's moderation has helped him get re-elected in 1994 and 1996. The latter victory, 55 percent to 45 percent, was particularly impressive in that it came against a strong Democratic nominee, state Rep. Francis Pordum. And it came when Clinton carried the district with 57 percent of the vote to just 29 percent for Bob Dole.

Political alienation is one lingering effect of the decline of the region's traditional heavy industry base. Decades of Rust Belt decline corroded Buffalo's morale and national image. Though still one of the nation's 50 largest cities with just over 328,000 people, Buffalo lost 29 percent of its population in the 1970s and 9 percent in the 1980s.

The city is slowly resurrecting its economic prospects. The U.S.-Canada free-trade agreement enacted in 1989 is paying business dividends for Buffalo; there was a major upswing in its financial industry. The unemployment rate, as high as 15 percent in the early 1980s, dipped to nearly 6 percent at the end of 1992; it was 9 percent in early 1997. Buffalo attracts record-breaking crowds to AAA-level minor league games at its downtown stadium, North AmeriCare Park. A new hockey facility, Marine Midland Arena, opened in 1996 for the Buffalo Sabres.

Still, the city's transition has hardly been painless for blue-collar whites or the large low-to middle-income black constituency. The manufacturing jobs in the Buffalo area declined by 45,000 between 1980 and 1991. The once-dominant steel industry is now a fragment: Much of the steel-making center in Lackawanna is a wasteland. Though service industry jobs grew by even more than manufacturing jobs fell, many of them provide a fraction of the wages to which unionized factory workers were accustomed.

About two-thirds of the city of Buffalo, including most of its downtown, is in the 30th. Black residents make up about 43 percent of the Buffalo section. Polish-Americans are the largest ethnic group in both Buffalo and Cheektowaga. South Buffalo has a large Irish population.

South of the city along Lake Erie are the industrial parts of Lackawanna and Hamburg, which provide a usually dependable Democratic vote.

But the southern and eastern reaches of the 30th are suburban and exurban areas, some of which provide a Republican counterweight. Orchard Park is the site of Rich Stadium, home of football's Buffalo Bills.

1990 Population: 580,337. White 472,761 (81%), Black 97,103 (17%), Other 10,473 (2%). Hispanic origin 8,922 (2%). 18 and over 441,308 (76%), 62 and over 104,483 (18%). Median age: 34.

tracts while setting in motion procedures to negotiate new agreements. Under the new process, management and labor would have 254 days to reach an agreement, and if they could not agree by the end of that period, the existing contracts would be voided, and unions could strike.

But in other cases, Quinn toed the GOP line. He voted to ban a particular abortion technique that opponents call a "partial-birth" abortion, to limit punitive damages in product liability cases, and to overhaul welfare, and in favor of a constitutional amendment to limit congressional terms.

While in the minority in the 103rd Congress, Quinn was one of only 11 Republicans to support the Clinton administration on a vote to bring the crime bill to the House floor for consideration in August 1994. Many Republicans complained that the bill spent too much money on prevention programs, and after the vote, even Quinn concurred. "This bill is porked up," he said. After $3 billion was cut from the package, Quinn was one of 46 House Republicans to vote in favor of final passage.

He also cut against the grain of his party in voting against NAFTA and GATT, despite the fact that the economy of his border district improved after enactment of a U.S.-Canada free trade agreement in 1989.

Quinn was part of a bipartisan group of representatives that worked on a line-item veto bill in 1994; their legislation formed the basis for a bill that passed the House early in the 104th Congress.

At Home: Quinn says he became a Republican almost by chance — his uncle, a local GOP elections official, happened to be the one who sent him his voter registration papers. But a Republican he is, and the combination of his support for the Contract With America and the district's Democratic demographics made him vulnerable at the polls in 1996.

Democrats were able to recruit a first-tier candidate in state Rep. Francis Pordum, whose moderate-to-conservative record in the state Legislature had strong appeal in the district. Pordum attempted to link Quinn with Speaker Gingrich, even going so far as to have a campaign aide in a Gingrich mask stand outside a school where the two candidates were debating.

"Do you want to have a Congress led by Newt Gingrich and his policies?" Pordum asked during the campaign. "Jack Quinn's first vote if he's re-elected will be for Newt Gingrich."

But Quinn emphasized his overall moderate record and his long record of constituent service. He served as principal for a day of a local elementary school. He picked up strong support from transportation unions, even as the state AFL-CIO was backing Pordum. He pointed to his leadership in pushing the minimum wage bill.

In the end, despite President Clinton's strong showing in the state, Quinn won re-election by 10 percentage points.

Quinn was chief executive (supervisor) of the Democratic suburb of Hamburg when, in 1992, he took on Erie County Executive Dennis Gorski for the House seat being vacated by retiring Democratic Rep. Henry J. Nowak. The main pitch of Quinn's campaign was an 11-point reform platform, calling for limits on franked mailings, members' travel, Congress' budget, closed debating rules and PAC contributions. After securing the GOP nomination with little fuss, Quinn quickly went on the attack, telling voters that Gorski was a typical politician who represented "more of the same."

Quinn battered Gorski for not releasing the 1993 county budget before the election, implying that Gorski was hiding bad fiscal news. Quinn also made the most of reports that much of Gorski's campaign fund came from contributions from county employees. Quinn ended up taking 52 percent of the vote.

Erie County Democratic officials pleaded unsuccessfully with their prospective 1994 candidates to pledge that they would not seek a primary if they lost the party's endorsement. As a result, Buffalo Common Council member David A. Franczyk emerged from the three-way September primary with a near-empty campaign treasury to face Quinn, who had no primary opposition. Quinn rolled to an easy November victory.

HOUSE ELECTIONS

1996 General		
Jack Quinn (R,C,INDC,FDM)	121,369	(55%)
Francis Pordum (D,PS)	100,040	(45%)
1994 General		
Jack Quinn (R,C)	124,738	(67%)
David A. Franczyk (D,L)	61,392	(33%)

Previous Winning Percentages: 1992 (52%)

CAMPAIGN FINANCE

	Receipts	Receipts from PACs	Expend-itures
1996			
Quinn (R)	$697,457	$296,289 (42%)	$752,713
Pordum (D)	$524,610	$179,772 (34%)	$520,826
1994			
Quinn (R)	$541,545	$201,439 (37%)	$488,083
Franczyk (D)	$194,153	$23,575 (12%)	$193,717

DISTRICT VOTE FOR PRESIDENT

	1996		1992
D	137,095 (57%)	**D**	119,115 (46%)
R	69,388 (29%)	**R**	68,172 (26%)
I	28,123 (12%)	**I**	73,333 (28%)

KEY VOTES

1997	
Ban "partial birth" abortions	Y
1996	
Approve farm bill	Y
Deny public education to illegal immigrants	N
Repeal ban on certain assault-style weapons	N
Increase minimum wage	Y
Freeze defense spending	?
Approve welfare overhaul	Y
1995	
Approve balanced-budget constitutional amendment	Y
Relax Clean Water Act regulations	Y
Oppose limits on environmental regulations	Y
Reduce projected Medicare spending	Y
Approve GOP budget with tax and spending cuts	Y

VOTING STUDIES

	Presidential Support		Party Unity		Conservative Coalition	
Year	S	O	S	O	S	O
1996	57	42	68	29	73	18
1995	30	65	84	11	90	7
1994	60	35	78	17	83	17
1993	47	53	84	15	91	9

INTEREST GROUP RATINGS

Year	ADA	AFL-CIO	CCUS	ACU
1996	35	n/a	81	58
1995	20	33	92	72
1994	30	56	91	76
1993	30	67	64	83

31 Amo Houghton (R)

Of Corning — Elected 1986, 6th term

Biographical Information
Born: Aug. 7, 1926, Corning, N.Y.
Education: Harvard U., A.B. 1950, M.B.A. 1952.
Military Service: Marine Corps, 1945-46.
Occupation: Glassworks company executive.
Family: Wife, Priscilla Dewey; four children, three stepchildren.
Religion: Episcopalian.
Political Career: No previous office.
Capitol Office: 1110 Longworth Bldg. 20515; 225-3161.

Committees
International Relations
Africa
Ways & Means
Health; Trade

In Washington: Not many corporate chief executive officers cap their careers by joining the House, relegating themselves to a process in which 435 people have an equal vote in deciding what happens. But Houghton, former CEO for Corning Glass Works and scion of one of the nation's wealthiest families, has done just that.

At age 60, Houghton abandoned plans to work as a missionary in Africa and headed to Capitol Hill instead. Now in his sixth term, he eschews the partisan sniping so often heard in congressional debate these days; indeed, he was one of the organizers of the bipartisan civility retreat in Hershey, Pa., early in the 105th Congress. Occupying a seat on the Ways and Means Committee, he specializes in a few areas (often involving business concerns) and votes a moderate line on issues such as abortion and federal support for the arts. Houghton's authority in Congress never will match the sway he enjoyed at Corning, but the Republican takeover of the House at least promoted him to service in the majority.

Despite his business background, Houghton often deviates from the conservative GOP script. His party unity score on floor votes has topped 70 percent only once in his career: that was his 80 percent score in 1995, the first year of the new GOP majority and its "Contract With America" agenda, when the typical Republican had a party unity score in the 90s.

In 1994, Houghton had supported President Clinton's position on floor votes 68 percent of the time, and his GOP party unity score was only 57 percent.

In the 104th, Houghton was a member of the group of moderate Republicans that successfully pressured the House Republican leadership to bring to the floor a bill increasing the minimum wage; it was enacted. Houghton also opposed efforts to exempt small businesses from paying the higher wage. "The center of the Republican Party is back," Houghton said after the vote.

Even so, Houghton lined up behind some of his party's top priorities early in the 105th Congress. He reversed his position and voted in favor of legislation allowing employers to offer their employees compensatory time off in lieu of overtime pay. He voted to ban a particular abortion technique that opponents call "partial birth" abortion. He backed a constitutional amendment limiting congressional terms.

Houghton's vote on the partial-birth abortion issue is a rare departure from his pro-abortion rights stance. In the 104th Congress, he voted to allow federal employee health plans to pay for abortions, to require states to pay for Medicaid abortions in cases of rape or incest, and to allow overseas military hospitals to perform abortions.

He voted for the GOP plan to reduce projected spending growth on Medicare and for his party's budget-reconciliation package in October 1995. But before supporting the Medicare package, he sought unsuccessfully to ensure protection for Medicare-dependent hospitals in New York. And he quietly expressed concerns that Republicans would look like protectors of the rich if they insisted on a $500-per-child tax credit for families earning up to $200,000 a year, which was a key contract provision. But Ways and Means Chairman Bill Archer, R-Texas, persuaded Houghton not to bring up the issue in committee.

Houghton voted against the initial GOP tax cut package in April 1995, one of only 11 Republicans to do so. And he opposed efforts to repeal 4.3 cents of the federal gasoline tax. In January 1996, he was part of a group of Republican moderates proposing a plan to balance the budget in six years but without a tax cut.

A member of the Ways and Means Trade Subcommittee, Houghton has endorsed giving Clinton fast-track authority to expand NAFTA to Chile. "If we don't pass 'fast track' with Chile and get past this partisanship, we'll be blocked out of Latin America," he said. And in September 1995, he cosponsored an amendment to renew the controversial Super 301 section of U.S. trade law, a trade weapon used by the United States to pressure countries to open their markets to American

NEW YORK 31
Southern Tier — Jamestown; Corning; Elmira

The 31st stretches across the bottom of New York state — the Southern Tier — for more than 100 miles, from Lake Erie on the west to Elmira in the east. This hilly, mainly rural country strongly favors Republicans.

Although the landscape is dotted with small industrial cities, Democrats rarely make inroads here, and those who do tend to be conservative. Republican Houghton's 72 percent in 1996 was typical of his strong showings since winning an open seat in 1986. His predecessor, Democrat Stan Lundine, held the Southern Tier's House seat for a decade, but he was an exception. Lundine gave up the seat to run for lieutenant governor on Gov. Mario M. Cuomo's ticket.

Voters here did support Bill Clinton in the 1996 presidential election, giving him 44 percent of the vote to Bob Dole's 41 percent. But Clinton did not achieve a majority in any of the eight counties (of 10 in the district) that he carried.

The nation's economic problems have been felt in parts of the 31st, with most counties in the district having small net population losses during the 1980s. Officials hope that completion of the Southern Tier Expressway (Route 17) will spur economic development.

Chautauqua County, at the district's western end, is the 31st's most populous; it has about a quarter of the district's residents. Jamestown, the 31st's largest city, with a population of nearly 35,000, is a furniture-making center. The county gave Clinton 48 percent of the vote in 1996.

Republicans often dominate in the counties to the east, including Cattaraugus; its big town is industrial Olean, also home to St. Bonaventure University (2,800 students). Agribusiness plays an important role in neighboring Allegany County. Welch's, a grape-growing cooperative best known for its juice products, is based in Wellsville. Clinton carried Cattaraugus by less than 100 votes in 1996; Dole triumphed by 1,500 votes in Allegany.

Steuben County contains Corning, one of America's better-known company towns. Houghton's family long has controlled Corning Inc., which produces utilitarian dishes, cookware and medical glass products; its Steuben Glass Works makes more costly decorative crystal pieces. Houghton was chief executive officer of Corning before he ran for the House.

The Corning Glass Center, a major tourist attraction, began a $50 million facelift in 1996.

Hornell is where workers build and refurbish New York City subway cars. The Elmira area (Chemung County) also is industrial. Its largest employers are Hardinge Brothers, which makes precision machines, and a Toshiba Display Devices facility.

To the north, the 31st moves into the vineyards and vacation lands of the Finger Lakes region. The large Taylor and Great Western wineries are here, along with numerous small family-run operations. The district also takes in part of Auburn, the commercial center of Cayuga County.

1990 Population: 580,337. White 556,495 (96%), Black 13,485 (2%), Other 10,357 (2%). Hispanic origin 8,614 (1%). 18 and over 428,519 (74%), 62 and over 100,899 (17%). Median age: 34.

goods. The law, which was enacted in 1988, requires the office of the United States Trade Representative to identify countries with barriers to U.S. goods and target them for negotiation and possible retaliation. Ways and Means approved the amendment by voice vote.

Houghton was a leading supporter of the Office of Technology Assessment, the congressional advisory agency eliminated in the fiscal 1996 Legislative Branch Appropriations bill. In June 1996, as the House considered amendments to the spending bill, Vic Fazio, D-Calif., proposed earmarking $18.6 million for the technology office, which the bill proposed to eliminate. Houghton instead proposed transferring the office to the Congressional Research Service. Houghton's substitute passed, setting up a final vote on the revised Fazio amendment.

Republicans lobbied against the amendment and, with the tally showing a 213-214 defeat, presiding officer John Linder, R-Ga., gaveled the vote to a close before two Democratic supporters of the amendment cast their votes. In the ensuing uproar, Republicans quickly adjourned the House.

Still, a perception of unfairness set in. At a National Republican Congressional Committee fundraiser that evening, Houghton said, Gingrich talked to him and sent him a note. "He said, "This thing got out of control. I'm sorry about it,'" according to Houghton. The next morning, the GOP leadership huddled and decided to hold a revote. This time the House voted 220-204 to salvage the OTA. But the Senate version of the bill eliminated the technology office, and, eventually, so did the conference report.

Houghton also has tried to defend the National Endowment for the Arts (NEA) against Republican efforts to kill the agency. As the House in March 1995 took up a spending rescissions bill, Houghton opposed efforts to cut an additional $10 million from the NEA over the $5 million in reductions already included in the legislation. Houghton described arts programs as "quintessential to the community in which you live." The amendment to cut $10 million from the NEA was rejected, 168-260. The rescissions bill then passed by a vote of 227-200.

In 1994, Houghton provided a crucial vote to tip the balance in favor of a ban on certain semi-automatic assault-style weapons that was sought by the Clinton administration and strongly opposed by the National Rifle Association. "I am a member of the NRA," he said, "but I think it's the right thing to do."

Later, Houghton was one of only 11 Republicans to join Democratic leaders in an ill-fated attempt to bring to the House floor a crime bill that included the assault weapons ban. After the White House agreed to cost-cutting alterations in the bill, Houghton was one of 46 Republicans voting for final passage. (The assault weapons ban stayed in the legislation.)

In the 104th, Houghton picked up a seat on the International Relations Committee, where he sits on the Africa Subcommittee. During a May 1995 meeting of the committee, Houghton successfully offered an amendment to the foreign affairs agencies consolidation bill to transfer $57 million in aid authorized for Russia and the former Soviet republics to hard-hit African assistance programs.

At Home: Houghton's easy manner and non-ideological approach seem to suit his constituents in upstate New York's Southern Tier. Since taking 60 percent of the vote in 1986 to win an open House seat previously held by a Democrat, Houghton has dominated. He is carrying on the traditions of a patrician family that for years has run Steuben County's Corning Inc. Houghton served 19 years as chief executive officer of Corning Glass. Then, at age 60, he entered the public sector, as had his father and grandfather.

Houghton's political opportunity appeared suddenly in 1986, when Democratic incumbent Stan Lundine of the Southern Tier's then-34th District was tapped by then-New York Gov. Mario M. Cuomo to run for lieutenant governor.

Before Lundine's departure, Houghton had been spending much of his time on efforts to provide economic relief for Zimbabwe. When the congressional vacancy appeared, he switched his sights closer to home.

Houghton was popular in his hometown of Corning, where Corning Glass is the major employer. The company is involved in an array of local civic endeavors, and it helped finance restoration of the city after a devastating flood in 1972. While he had never been particularly active in local Republican affairs, he had little trouble securing the GOP nomination.

Seeking across-the-board appeal, Houghton pointed to his experience at creating jobs. The Democratic nominee, Cattaraugus County District Attorney Larry Himelein, portrayed Houghton as an elitist and hoped for support from voters who considered the Republican too much of a Brahmin. But Houghton ably deflected criticism. A 3-1 margin in his Steuben County base propelled him to the first in a long string of easy

HOUSE ELECTIONS

1996 General		
Amo Houghton (R,C,FDM)	139,734	(72%)
Bruce D. MacBain (D)	49,502	(25%)
LeRoy Stewart Wilson (RTL)	6,031	(3%)
1994 General		
Amo Houghton (R,C)	121,178	(85%)
Gretchen S. McManus (RTL)	21,747	(15%)

Previous Winning Percentages: 1992 (71%) **1990** (70%) **1988** (96%) **1986** (60%)

CAMPAIGN FINANCE

	Receipts	Receipts from PACs	Expend-itures
1996			
Houghton (R)	$546,570	$322,377 (59%)	$699,270
MacBain (D)	$3,674	$1,000 (27%)	$1,849
1994			
Houghton (R)	$440,674	$233,125 (53%)	$356,525

DISTRICT VOTE FOR PRESIDENT

	1996		1992
D	98,264 (44%)	**D**	82,959 (34%)
R	91,208 (41%)	**R**	97,447 (40%)
I	30,268 (14%)	**I**	62,325 (26%)

KEY VOTES

1997	
Ban "partial birth" abortions	Y
1996	
Approve farm bill	Y
Deny public education to illegal immigrants	N
Repeal ban on certain assault-style weapons	N
Increase minimum wage	Y
Freeze defense spending	N
Approve welfare overhaul	Y
1995	
Approve balanced-budget constitutional amendment	Y
Relax Clean Water Act regulations	Y
Oppose limits on environmental regulations	Y
Reduce projected Medicare spending	Y
Approve GOP budget with tax and spending cuts	Y

VOTING STUDIES

	Presidential Support		Party Unity		Conservative Coalition	
Year	**S**	**O**	**S**	**O**	**S**	**O**
1996	58	38	70	21	75	16
1995	37	59	80	15	88	9
1994	68	27	57	36	75	17
1993	56	41	65	31	86	11
1992	66	32	64	33	79	19
1991	71	27	58	37	65	30

INTEREST GROUP RATINGS

Year	ADA	AFL-CIO	CCUS	ACU
1996	20	n/a	63	60
1995	30	33	91	52
1994	20	11	100	68
1993	20	33	100	79
1992	30	50	88	68
1991	20	50	70	70

NORTH CAROLINA

Governor: James B. Hunt Jr. (D)
Elected: 1992*
Length of term: 4 years
Term expires: 1/01
Salary: $103,012
Term limit: 2 consecutive terms
Phone: (919) 733-4240
Born: May 16, 1937; Greensboro, N.C.
Education: North Carolina State U., B.S. 1959, M.S. 1962; U. of North Carolina, J.D. 1964.
Occupation: Lawyer; cattle rancher.
Family: Wife, Carolyn Leonard; four children.
Religion: Presbyterian.
Political Career: Lieutenant governor, 1973-77; governor, 1977-85*; Democratic nominee for U.S. Senate, 1984.

Lt. Gov.: Dennis Wicker (D)
First elected: 1992
Length of term: 4 years
Term expires: 1/01
Salary: $87,000
Phone: **(919) 733-7350**

State election official: (919) 733-7173
Democratic headquarters: (919) 821-2777
Republican headquarters: (919) 828-6423

REDISTRICTING

North Carolina gained one House seat in reapportionment, increasing to 12. Legislature passed map Jan. 24, 1992; Justice Dept. approved it Feb. 6. In 1993, Supreme Court ruled a lawsuit contesting the map's constitutionality could be heard, remanding it to federal court. Federal court on Aug. 1, 1994, ruled the map was not unconstitutional. However, Supreme Court on June 13, 1996, ruled that it was unconstitutional. The legislature approved a new map in March 1997; federal approval was pending.

STATE LEGISLATURE

Bicameral General Assembly. Meets January-July.

Senate: 50 members, 2-year terms
1996 breakdown: 30D, 20R; 44 men, 6 women
Salary: $13,951
Phone: (919) 733-7350

House of Representatives: 120 members, 2-year terms
1996 breakdown: 61R, 59D; 97 men, 23 women
Salary: $13,951
Phone: (919) 733-3451

URBAN STATISTICS

City	Population
Charlotte	395,934
Mayor Pat McCroy, R	
Raleigh	207,951
Mayor Tom Fetzer, N-P	
Greensboro	183,894
Mayor Carolyn Allen, N-P	
Winston-Salem	143,485
Mayor Martha S. Wood, N-P	
Durham	136,611
Mayor Sylvia S. Kerckhoff, N-P	

U.S. CONGRESS

Senate: 0 D, 2 R
House: 6 D, 6 R

TERM LIMITS

For state offices: No

ELECTIONS

1996 Presidential Vote

Bob Dole	49%
Bill Clinton	44%
Ross Perot	7%

1992 Presidential Vote

George Bush	43%
Bill Clinton	43%
Ross Perot	14%

1988 Presidential Vote

George Bush	58%
Michael S. Dukakis	42%

POPULATION

1990 population		6,628,637
1980 population		5,881,766
Percent change		+13%
Rank among states:		10
White		76%
Black		22%
Hispanic		1%
Asian or Pacific islander		1%
Urban		50%
Rural		50%
Born in state		70%
Foreign-born		2%
Under age 18	1,606,149	24%
Ages 18-64	4,218,147	64%
65 and older	804,341	12%
Median age		33.1

MISCELLANEOUS

Capital: Raleigh
Number of counties: 100
Per capita income: $16,642 (1991)
Rank among states: 34
Total area: 52,669 sq. miles
Rank among states: 28

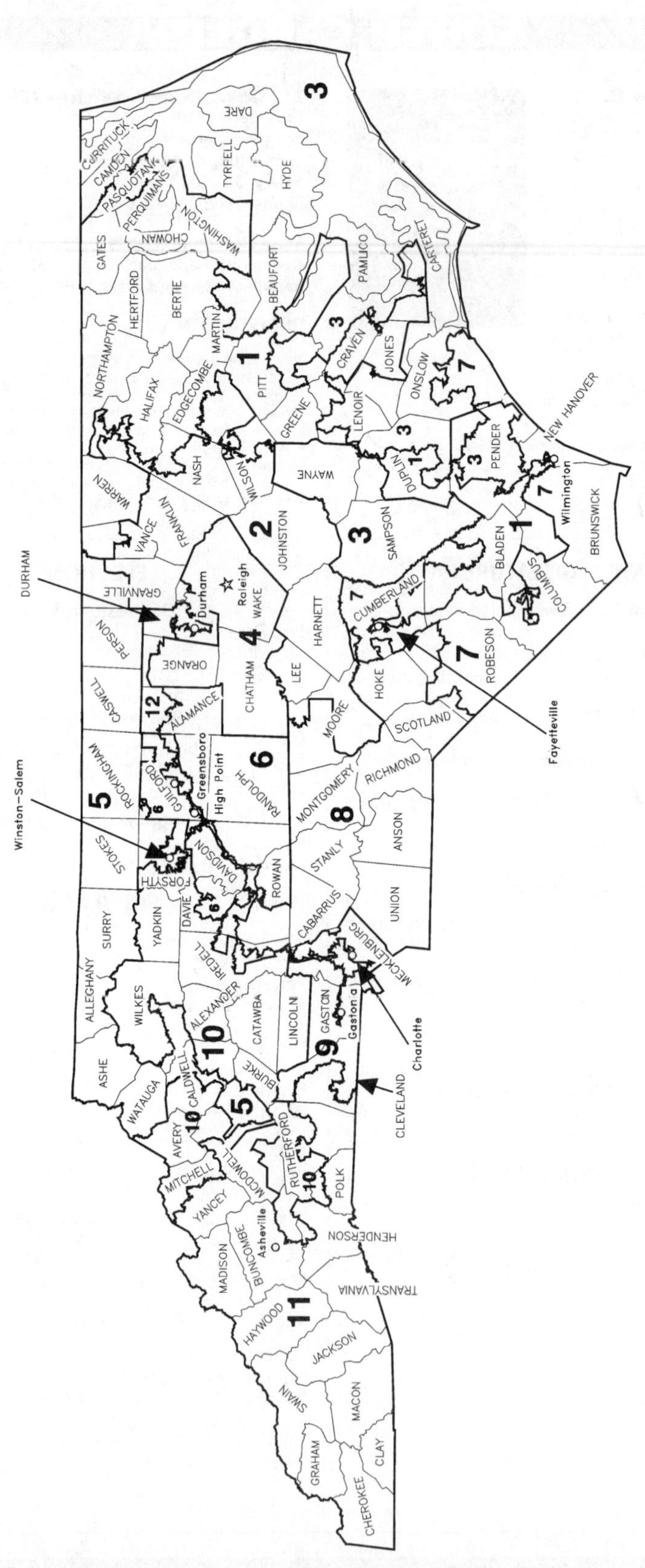

Jesse Helms (R)

Of Raleigh — Elected 1972, 5th term

Biographical Information

Born: Oct. 18, 1921, Monroe, N.C.

Education: Wingate College, 1938-39; Wake Forest U., 1939-40.

Military Service: Navy, 1942-45.

Occupation: Journalist; broadcasting executive; banking executive; congressional aide.

Family: Wife, Dorothy Jane Coble; three children.

Religion: Baptist.

Political Career: Raleigh City Council, 1957-61.

Capitol Office: 403 Dirksen Bldg. 20510; 224-6342.

Committees

Agriculture, Nutrition & Forestry
Marketing, Inspection & Product Promotion; Production & Price Competitiveness

Foreign Relations (chairman)
International Operations; Near Eastern & South Asian Affairs; Western Hemisphere, Peace Corps, Narcotics and Terrorism

Rules & Administration

In Washington: Long known as the Senate's icon of conservatism, Helms displayed two faces in the 104th Congress — legislative roadblock, and later, conciliatory negotiator. Though the 1994 elections brought Helms considerably more power, installing him as chairman of the Senate Foreign Relations Committee, he endured both successes and failures in the 104th, often locking horns with the Clinton administration. Early in the 105th Congress, Helms flexed his legislative muscle and won key concessions from the White House during consideration of the Chemical Weapons Convention.

Helms ardently opposed the pact, an international treaty to ban chemical and biological weapons that was supported by a number of GOP heavy-hitters, including George Bush, Colin Powell and Bob Dole. Helms said the treaty would do nothing to reduce the dangers of chemical weapons and often noted that "rogue nations" such as Iraq, Syria, Libya and North Korea were not signatories to the treaty. Helms utilized the power of his chairmanship not only to obstruct action for months, but also to extract concessions from the president after allowing the chemical weapons pact to leave his committee.

In the end, Helms won support from the administration for legislation that would reduce the number of foreign policy agencies, long one of Helms' top priorities, but opposed by Clinton. In the 104th, Clinton vetoed a hard-fought Helms measure that would have moved the functions of one of three agencies — the Agency for International Development, the Arms Control and Disarmament Agency or the United States Information Agency — into the State Department. The plan reflected Helms' desire for a streamlined foreign policy structure in the absence of a Soviet threat. Helms delayed consideration of numerous foreign service nominees while Senate Democrats filibustered the reorganization measure.

The administration's reorganization proposal was made public the same day Helms agreed to allow a Senate vote on the chemical weapons pact, which Helms and the White House insist was merely coincidental. The proposal also will give Helms a strong voice in deciding whether the United States will pay its U.N. debt, another Helms priority. Clinton's move was widely seen as an effort to help bridge his differences with Helms.

Helms, often branded by his critics as "Senator No," signaled that the weapons pact would not receive a Senate vote unless the administration made certain modifications, many of which were criticized by Foreign Relations Ranking Democrat Joseph R. Biden Jr. of Delaware, as "treaty killers." Similar warning shots had been fired previously toward Clinton. Two years before, just before becoming committee chairman, Helms made national news with a suggestion that Clinton would not be safe if he visited North Carolina. Helms opined in November 1994 that Clinton was not up to the job of commander-in-chief, and he said people in the armed services shared his view.

In stark contrast to his sharp criticisms of Clinton, Helms has been outright friendly to Madeleine K. Albright, secretary of State for the president's second term. Albright won Helms' admiration in 1996 when she accused Cuba of "cowardice" after Cuban military planes shot down two civilian aircraft being flown toward the island nation by Cuban-American opponents of Castro.

Since her unanimous confirmation by the Senate as the highest female officeholder in U.S. history, Albright has enjoyed a cordial relationship with Helms, making numerous public appearances with him. At one event in North Carolina, Albright gave Helms a T-shirt that declared "Someone at the State Department loves me" and told the audience they were "developing a pretty good friendship."

For decades, communists around the world have had few foes as implacable as Helms. And one of Helms' priorities as Foreign Relations chairman was a Cuba sanctions package he sponsored with Rep. Dan Burton, R-Ind. The legislation invoked economic sanctions aimed at punishing foreign businesses that invest in Cuba. Initially, the bill found strong opposition from the Clinton administration, whose international allies complained about the harsh sanctions.

But on Feb. 24, 1996, the bill received a tremendous boost from an unlikely source — Castro's own military. That day, Cuban fighters shot down a pair of civilian aircraft, killing four Americans from an anti-Castro group. Anger at Castro was running so high that Clinton had little choice but to go along with the conference report. Although U.S. allies that trade with Cuba continued to issue strong objections to the bill, there remained a bipartisan desire to punish Castro. The conference report passed the Senate overwhelmingly, 74-22, on March 5.

Helms has effectively used the bully pulpit of his chairmanship to influence the debate on other foreign policy issues. He blasted Colombia's drug trafficking problems and built an ultimately successful campaign to decertify the country as a drug-fighting ally in 1996. Helms has also decried human rights abuses in China, calling for revocation of most-favored-nation status for the communist country, an annual debate in Congress. He also has threatened, and introduced legislation, to withhold payment of U.S. debts to the United Nations until its bureaucracy is reorganized and wasteful spending is eliminated. Without reforms, Helms believes, the United Nations poses a risk to U.S. sovereignty.

Helms' critics portray him as an extremist, but time and again he has proved that he knows the issues that energize the Middle American, overwhelmingly white constituency that has carried him through many campaigns. He opposes abortion and affirmative action and has been unwavering in his support for school-sponsored prayer.

During the 1995 welfare overhaul debate, Helms sought to require all able-bodied, nonelderly food stamp recipients to work 40 hours per week to earn their benefits. After it failed decisively, he offered a scaled-down version in 1996 calling for a 20-hour per week commitment. That lost, too, though the final version signed into law included a similar work requirement.

One of the centerpieces of Helms' lengthy social-issue agenda may be his crusade against homosexuality. During the Ryan White AIDS program reauthorization in 1995, Helms unsuccessfully sought to prohibit any funds from being used to promote homosexuality. Helms later fought vigorously against legislation that would ban most discrimination against homosexuals in the workplace. The bill would compel people who believe homosexuality is immoral to suppress their feelings under threat from the government, he said. "At the heart of this debate is the moral and spiritual survival of this nation," he warned the Senate before lawmakers defeated the measure 49-50.

Paired with Helms' ardent opposition to homosexuality is his distaste for the National Endowment for the Arts (NEA). Helms has repeatedly tied Congress in knots over his amendments to kill the NEA or at least ban funding for sexually explicit projects. During consideration of the fiscal 1996 Interior appropriations bill, the Senate approved a pair of provisions proposed by Helms to bar federal spending for arts projects that "denigrate the objects or beliefs of the adherents of a particular religion" or "depict or describe, in a patently offensive way, sexual or excretory activities or organs."

Helms' conservatism does not necessarily preclude support for key programs that benefit North Carolina. Helms, a former chairman of the Agriculture Committee, was instrumental in protecting peanut price supports as the Senate's top negotiator during consideration of the farm bill in 1996. Helms helped craft a compromise that would bar peanut producers from getting loans for a year rather than having producers' loan rates cut, saving a major program for North Carolina peanut farmers under a bill that overhauled agriculture subsidies.

At a time when many politicians shy from close relationships with tobacco companies, Helms has steadfastly protected his state, the country's top tobacco producer. He has been especially critical of the Food and Drug Administration's plans to regulate access to cigarettes and restrict tobacco advertising. Helms has pledged to propose legislation to block FDA action if a lawsuit filed by tobacco producers against the proposed regulations is rejected by the courts.

Helms turns 77 in the 105th Congress, and he seems undiminished in his battles despite his past health problems. In 1991, he was diagnosed with a rare bone disease, and he revealed that he was in treatment for prostate cancer. In June 1992, he underwent quadruple-bypass heart surgery.

At Home: During his quarter-century as one of the Senate's most fiery conservatives, Helms has drawn national attention in each of his election campaigns. As he went for a fifth term and faced a rematch of his bitter and racially charged 1990 campaign with Harvey B. Gantt, a black former mayor of Charlotte, 1996 was no exception.

But the election turned out to be dull in comparison to the 1990 contest, which is remembered mostly for Helms' television ads that charged racial quotas cost white jobs. The controversial ad featured a pair of white hands crumpling a rejection notice. Gantt recalls the contest as being "scurrilous and racist" and insists that he's a wiser and more experienced candidate as a result.

Helms never gave Gantt the opportunity to gain any momentum in 1996. He carefully kept his distance from the media, refused to appear at any public events with Gantt and would not participate in any debates (his policy since since 1984). In fact, despite running against each other in two elections, Helms and Gantt have never personally met or even shaken hands. Helms kept a low profile throughout the contest and did minimal campaigning, but raised a huge sum of money — over $7.8 million. Overall, the candidates spent about

$16 million. The bulk of Helms' war chest paid for television spots, on which his campaign relied heavily to communicate with North Carolina voters.

Helms mainly took the high road in 1996. He used television to mute his image as a conservative activist and build his image as a senior statesman and powerful chairman of the Foreign Relations Committee. His commercials included testimonials from his grandchildren, painting Helms as the quintessential Southern gentleman, a sensitive and caring family man. He occasionally appeared with foreign dignitaries, touting his influence in boosting the North Carolina economy by increasing state exports, including tobacco.

However, Helms did launch an airwaves attack on Gantt both early and late. In the primary, Helms attacked both Gantt and his chief opponent, wealthy pharmaceuticals executive Charlie Sanders, for favoring racial preferences in hiring, opposing voluntary prayer in public schools and supporting the extension of health insurance to homosexual partners. But the next week Helms pulled the ad and fired his media consultant.

Helms again attacked Gantt via TV, labeling him "liberal" and trying to tie Gantt to Clinton's unpopularity, and especially administration efforts to regulate tobacco, a sensitive issue in some parts of North Carolina. Helms also went after Gantt on gay rights and the death penalty. But these ads, and ultimately the entire campaign, did not get as hot as those of 1990, though the result was essentially the same — Helms winning with 53 percent.

Observers have differing opinions about the changing demographics of North Carolina. It is indisputable that the state has grown immensely, adding 700,000 new residents since 1990. A question remains, however, whether the new voters have significantly changed the political landscape. In 1994, the state appeared to have grown markedly more conservative, evidenced by the 1994 Republican capture of four House seats previously held by Democrats (which was partially reversed in 1996, when Democrats took back two of those seats). But Gantt's election hopes hung on the new voters and whether or not they would reject Helms' brand of conservatism. Even a slight change in the landscape could spell trouble for Helms, whose winning percentage has never been more than 55 percent in his five campaigns.

Helms' closest call came in 1984, a monumental campaign that had found him at his weakest and his challenger, Gov. James B. Hunt Jr., in a strong position to win. Helms' political organization, the National Congressional Club, suffered severe setbacks in 1982, losing every one of five congressional contests it targeted in the state. Further, Helms was plagued by negative publicity over his 1982 vote for raising the cigarette tax and unsuccessful efforts to block creation of a federal holiday for the Rev. Dr. Martin Luther King Jr.

Helms drew support from conservatives nationwide to invest $16.5 million into the race, establishing a new record at that time for the most money spent by a Senate candidate. Helms sought to link Hunt to Democratic presidential candidate Walter F. Mondale and his national party. Aided by President Reagan's coattails, Helms won another term and the North Carolina GOP captured the governorship and three new House seats.

Ironically, for much of his adult life, Helms was a Democrat, even while he delivered conservative editorials for 12 years on WRAL-TV in Raleigh. He left the Democratic Party in 1970 and won his Senate seat as a Republican just two years later.

SENATE ELECTIONS

1996 General		
Jesse Helms (R)	1,345,833	(53%)
Harvey B. Gantt (D)	1,173,875	(46%)

Previous Winning Percentages: 1990 (53%) **1984** (52%) **1978** (55%) **1972** (54%)

CAMPAIGN FINANCE

1996	Receipts	Receipts from PACs	Expend-itures
Helms (R)	$7,808,820	$1,021,560 (13%)	$7,798,520
Gantt (D)	$8,128,548	$406,338 (5%)	$8,012,980

KEY VOTES

1997	
Approve balanced-budget constitutional amendment	Y
Approve chemical weapons treaty	N
1996	
Approve farm bill	Y
Limit punitive damages in product liability cases	Y
Exempt small businesses from higher minimum wage	Y
Approve welfare overhaul	Y
Bar job discrimination based on sexual orientation	N
Override veto of ban on "partial birth" abortions	Y
1995	
Approve GOP budget with tax and spending cuts	Y
Approve constitutional amendment barring flag desecration	Y

VOTING STUDIES

	Presidential Support		Party Unity		Conservative Coalition	
Year	S	O	S	O	S	O
1996	25	75	96	3	95	3
1995	20	76	91	3	86	7
1994	18	76	91	5	81	13
1993	11	84	89	3	83	5
1992	62	15	71	3	71	3
1991	84	11	78	5	90	5

INTEREST GROUP RATINGS

Year	ADA	AFL-CIO	CCUS	ACU
1996	5	n/a	85	100
1995	0	0	100	100
1994	0	14	80	100
1993	10	18	80	100
1992	5	13	100	100
1991	5	20	88	100

Lauch Faircloth (R)

Of Clinton — Elected 1992, 1st term

Biographical Information
Born: Jan. 14, 1928, Clinton, N.C.
Education: Roseboro H.S., graduated 1945.
Military Service: Army, 1954-55.
Occupation: Farm owner; land developer.
Family: Divorced; one child.
Religion: Presbyterian.
Political Career: N.C. Highway Commission, 1961-73, chairman, 1969-73; N.C. secretary of commerce, 1977-83; sought Democratic nomination for governor, 1984.
Capitol Office: 317 Hart Bldg. 20510; 224-3154.

Committees
Appropriations
District of Columbia (chairman); Labor, Health & Human Services & Education; Military Construction; Transportation; Treasury & General Government
Banking, Housing & Urban Affairs
Financial Institutions & Regulatory Relief (chairman); Housing Opportunity & Community Development; Securities
Small Business

In Washington: Whether acting as a fierce Republican attack dog on Whitewater or taking a hard line stance as the senator who controls the purse strings of the financially troubled District of Columbia, Faircloth has made his name as an unrelenting critic of the Clinton administration and one of the Senate's most conservative — and outspoken — members.

As the chairman of the Senate Appropriations subcommittee in charge of the District's budget, Faircloth opened the 105th by firmly rejecting the $3.9 billion Clinton plan for the District as a taxpayer bailout for the mismanaged federal city.

Signaling the new tack he intended to take on District affairs, Faircloth also raised eyebrows by advocating that Congress replace the current self-rule government with a city manager appointed by a permanent financial control board.

Faircloth told The Washington Post in March 1997, "It's time to cut out the euphemisms. It's time to stop worrying about stepping on toes. There are many privileges of living in the capital of the U.S. Voting for mayor simply won't be one of them. If that bothers you, then you need to move."

Faircloth first presented his partisan credentials in the second session of the 103rd Congress as he aggressively attacked President Clinton's role in Whitewater, the land investment that the Clintons were involved in when they were in Arkansas.

During Senate Banking, Housing and Urban Affairs Committee hearings held on the matter in the summer of 1994, Faircloth was among the most openly partisan of the GOP inquisitors. And he was the only member to aggressively probe into unanswered questions surrounding the July 1993 suicide of White House deputy counsel Vincent W. Foster Jr. — questions that were too unseemly or uncomfortable for others to ask.

Faircloth attracted a lot of publicity related to the Whitewater controversy that summer after he reportedly met with Judge David B. Sentelle of the U.S. Court of Appeals for the District of Columbia, who had long political ties to Faircloth and senior North Carolina Sen. Jesse Helms. The meeting, which Helms also attended, took place just as Sentelle and a federal panel he led were deciding whether to replace Whitewater special prosecutor Robert B. Fiske Jr., with Kenneth W. Starr, a move the panel made in August 1994. Faircloth had been critical of Fiske. Early in 1995, Starr reopened the probe into the Foster suicide.

Hearings resumed in July 1995 under the auspices of the Senate Special Committee on Whitewater, which was charged with pursuing a narrow inquiry into White House behavior after Foster's death. Faircloth continued to hammer away at the administration — and particularly at first lady Hillary Rodham Clinton — over the course of the 14-month probe.

Faircloth gained visibility early in his term by teaming with Helms to oppose the nomination of Roberta Achtenberg, a lesbian nominated as an assistant secretary of Housing and Urban Development. He was one of four Banking Committee members to vote against her. But her confirmation was affirmed by the full Senate.

As chairman in the 104th Congress of the Senate Banking subcommittee responsible for overseeing HUD, Faircloth took aim both at the department and at Housing Secretary Henry Cisneros. He introduced legislation to eliminate HUD outright, calling the department "a monster that refuses to die," and advocated abolishing public housing in favor of issuing tenants rent vouchers. Faircloth also pressed for hearings on whether Cisneros concealed information from the FBI in his background check for the post.

Faircloth continued the attack in the 105th Congress, telling Secretary-designate Andrew Cuomo at his January 1997 Senate confirmation hearing that "HUD has failed."

Faircloth does have at least one friend in the administration, however, White House Chief of Staff Erskine Bowles, a North Carolina businessman.

Faircloth also made his mark in the welfare reform debate. In the 103rd Congress, he introduced legislation to deny public or subsidized housing and all benefits under the Aid to Families With Dependent Children and food stamps programs to unwed mothers under age 21, raising the limit to under age 25 in 1998. He continued to push conservative initiatives as debate continued in the next Congress, and joined other conservatives in threatening to filibuster the welfare bill in the summer of 1995 unless it contained provisions to deny welfare checks to unwed teenage mothers and for children born to mothers already on welfare. When some of the language added to the bill to quell the conservative uprising was stripped from the version adopted by the Senate in September 1995, Faircloth was the lone GOP senator to oppose it. Faircloth eventually voted for the landmark welfare bill enacted the following year, though he had initially opposed it as well because he said it was not tough enough.

At Home: Faircloth campaigned in 1992 using themes and strategies honed by Helms' former campaign organization, the National Congressional Club (now called the National Conservative Club), whose operatives helped run Faircloth's race. His campaign against Democratic Sen. Terry Sanford was billed from the beginning as a grudge match.

A multimillionaire farmer and business owner without a college degree, Faircloth was a lifelong Democrat who had enjoyed a symbiotic political alliance with Sanford, which began in the 1950s. Faircloth backed Sanford's successful bid for governor in 1960 and was named to the highway commission. In 1984, after serving as state commerce secretary under Democratic Gov. James B. Hunt Jr., Faircloth ran for governor — with the help of Sanford. Faircloth placed third in the Democratic primary.

The political bedfellows parted ways in 1986. Both were eyeing the Senate seat open after the death of Republican John P. East, and they apparently gave each other mixed signals about their plans.

Sanford's decision to enter the race stunned Faircloth. The two hardly spoke to each other again. After supporting Helms' 1990 re-election bid, Faircloth switched parties on Valentine's Day 1991, saying he was too conservative to remain a Democrat.

He immediately began plotting for a race against Sanford. In the primary, Faircloth outspent his three opponents and had support from allies of then-Gov. James G. Martin, a moderate Republican. For the general election, Faircloth personally kept a low profile, barring reporters from many of his events and prompting critics to dub him the "stealth candidate." His campaign was based on hard-hitting TV ads against Sanford, financed in part by $752,000 in loans from his own pocket. He wound up spending nearly $3 million, about $500,000 more than Sanford. Faircloth lambasted Sanford as too liberal for North Carolina, highlighting his votes against the Persian Gulf War and for federal spending.

On most big issues, Faircloth aligned himself with the conservative wing of the national GOP, supporting school choice, a capital gains tax cut, a "flexible freeze" on spending, a line-item veto and tougher criminal penalties. He opposed gun control, the family leave bill, new environmental protection laws and abortion in all cases except rape, incest and to save the woman's life.

Faircloth ran nearly 104,000 votes ahead of Sanford, posting a 4 percentage point victory.

SENATE ELECTIONS

1992 General		
Lauch Faircloth (R)	1,297,892	(50%)
Terry Sanford (D)	1,194,015	(46%)
Bobby Yates Emory (LIBERT)	85,948	(3%)
1992 Primary		
Lauch Faircloth (R)	129,159	(48%)
Sue Myrick (R)	81,801	(30%)
Eugene Johnston (R)	46,112	(17%)
Larry E. Harrington (R)	13,496	(5%)

CAMPAIGN FINANCE

	Receipts	Receipts from PACs	Expend-itures
1992			
Faircloth (R)	$2,961,865	$365,783 (12%)	$2,952,102
Sanford (D)	$2,410,525	$838,515 (35%)	$2,486,380

KEY VOTES

1997	
Approve balanced-budget constitutional amendment	Y
Approve chemical weapons treaty	N
1996	
Approve farm bill	Y
Limit punitive damages in product liability cases	Y
Exempt small businesses from higher minimum wage	Y
Approve welfare overhaul	Y
Bar job discrimination based on sexual orientation	N
Override veto of ban on "partial birth" abortions	Y
1995	
Approve GOP budget with tax and spending cuts	Y
Approve constitutional amendment barring flag desecration	Y

VOTING STUDIES

	Presidential Support		Party Unity		Conservative Coalition	
Year	S	O	S	O	S	O
1996	20	76	94	4	87	11
1995	21	77	94	3	88	7
1994	23	73	96	2	100	0
1993	12	87	96	3	93	7

INTEREST GROUP RATINGS

Year	ADA	AFL-CIO	CCUS	ACU
1996	5	n/a	92	95
1995	0	0	95	100
1994	5	0	90	100
1993	15	9	67	100

1 Eva Clayton (D)

Of Littleton — Elected 1992; 3rd full term

Biographical Information

Born: Sept. 16, 1934, Savannah, Ga.

Education: Johnson C. Smith U., B.S. 1955; North Carolina Central U., M.S. 1962; U. of North Carolina, 1967.

Occupation: Consulting firm owner; non-profit executive; state official; university official.

Family: Husband, Theaoseus Clayton; four children.

Religion: Presbyterian.

Political Career: Sought Democratic nomination for U.S. House, 1968; N.C. assistant secretary of natural resources, 1977-81; Warren County Commission, 1982-92, chairman 1982-90.

Capitol Office: 2440 Rayburn Bldg. 20515; 225-3101.

Committees

Agriculture

Department Operations, Nutrition & Foreign Agriculture (ranking); Forestry, Resource Conservation & Research

Budget

In Washington: Clayton made history in her 1992 House election and quickly moved into the role of a leader within her class and party. She was the first black woman elected to the House from North Carolina and one of the first two blacks (along with Melvin Watt) to be elected to Congress from the state since 1901.

With support from newly elected Democratic women as well as the Congressional Black Caucus, Clayton won election as president of her freshman class for 1993. After Democrats lost control of the House in 1994, Clayton was asked to join Minority Leader Richard A. Gephardt's new Democratic Policy Committee, a vehicle for mobilizing Democrats to counter the new Republican majority. At the start of the 105th Congress, the Democratic leadership tapped Clayton for another strategic assignment, assigning her to the Budget Committee.

The district Clayton represents is largely rural, with a black-majority population; many of its residents are struggling economically. Not surprisingly, she has stood firmly against efforts by the GOP majority to reduce the cost of federal social programs targeted at the poor.

From start to finish in the 104th, Clayton opposed Republicans' efforts to overhaul the welfare system by requiring all able-bodied adult welfare recipients to work, setting maximum lifetime limits on benefits, and converting some federal programs into block grants to be sent to the states.

She was particularly antagonistic toward GOP attempts to find substantial cost savings in the food stamp program, and to deny food stamp benefits to certain able-bodied adults who could not find work.

Clayton was among those liberals who looked on with disappointment when President Clinton, after vetoing two earlier GOP welfare proposals, finally agreed in August 1996 to sign a third version that Republicans had revised to mollify some White House complaints.

She was, however, pleased with a victory for liberals on another front in the 104th — passage in 1996 of a bill to increase the minimum wage. Clayton joined party leaders in the winter of 1995 to propose the wage increase, accurately predicting that the issue could be useful for Democrats.

"This is the right issue for us," she said. "This is the issue Democrats should go down fighting for." Republican leaders opposed a wage hike, but its political appeal was so strong that many in their own ranks came out in favor of the Democratic-driven proposal. The final version of the wage bill included some sweeteners for the GOP, including $10 billion in business tax cuts over five years, a $5,000 tax credit to offset the cost of adoption and an expansion of Individual Retirement Accounts.

Clayton also objected to another of the GOP's major legislative endeavors in the 104th, overhauling federal farm policy. The Republicans' "Freedom to Farm" bill phased out most New Deal-era crop subsidies, replacing them with a system of fixed, but declining, payments that farmers would receive over seven years regardless of market prices or their planting decisions.

Clayton opposed the measure, believing that the existing regime of crop subsidies provided a safety net especially important to the poor, small-scale farmers in her district. When the farm bill was debated on the House floor, she found that crop subsidies helpful to her district were facing fire not only from free-market GOP conservatives but also from some urban liberals in her own party.

In one debate, Clayton lectured Democratic Rep. Nita M. Lowey of New York, who had criticized the peanut program. "You may not know who those farmers are, but I do know, and many of them are minority farms, many of them are low-income farms, because you can have a small lot of land and still farm." Clayton explained that peanuts crops are popular with many poor and minority farmers because they don't require much land and are relatively inexpensive to maintain.

In its final form, the farm bill scaled back the peanut program, but did not eliminate it altogether. Still, Clayton opposed the bill on final passage.

She takes exception with the majority in her party who criticize tobacco subsidies. In 1996, she joined members from other tobacco states to help

NORTH CAROLINA 1
East — Parts of Rocky Mount, Fayetteville and Greenville

When the Justice Department finally approved the radical redrawing of North Carolina's congressional districts in 1992, black voting power was concentrated in two districts, one rural and one urban.

The 1st is primarily rural and agricultural, stretching from the Virginia border almost to South Carolina, winding through 28 counties to patch together the black communities of northeastern North Carolina down to Wilmington and Fayetteville.

The state's map had to be redrawn after the Supreme Court declared the 12th District an unconstitutional gerrymander in June 1996. The plan passed by the state legislature in March 1997 was still subject to judicial approval. If approved, the 1st District's black population would slip from 57 percent to 50 percent.

Covering 2,039 miles around its perimeter, the 1st takes in nine whole counties and parts of 19 more. The main body is located on the Virginia border; from there, it snakes south in widely varying directions.

The northern part includes the mostly poor blacks of Bertie, Hertford and Northampton counties. Roanoke Rapids (Halifax County), a textile and wood products center, and populous Rocky Mount (Nash County) are shared with the 2nd District.

Pitt County (Greenville), which is divided between the 1st and the 3rd, has some pharmaceutical and paper products manufacturing, but its main employer is government.

On the western edge of Lenoir County, the district narrows into a thin corridor along the Lenoir and Wayne County borders. From there, it expands into Duplin County, skirting Sampson County without crossing in, and breaks north through Bladen County into Cumberland County.

Once in Cumberland — which is also parceled into the 7th and 8th districts — the 1st District takes in some of Fayetteville, which is dominated by Fort Bragg and Pope Air Force Base. The Cumberland County segment is the second-biggest population source. Black neighborhoods from Wilmington (New Hanover County) are also a source of votes in the southern extremity.

The 1st is staunchly Democratic; nearly 90 percent of the district's voters are registered Democrats. Blacks make up 57 percent of the district's population, but that figure is somewhat deceiving. When it comes to voter registration numbers — a better voting pattern indicator — whites make up about half of the electorate.

The white voters of the 1st claim the Democratic roots of their forefathers but often support GOP candidates at the state and national levels. A fair number are "Jessecrats," conservative Democratic supporters of GOP Sen. Jesse Helms. Republicans can also find quarter in some of the increasingly affluent coastal turf of Beaufort and Craven counties. In 1996, Bob Dole led in Greene and the portions of Beaufort County in the district.

1990 Population: 552,394. White 229,853 (42%), Black 316,273 (57%), Other 6,268 (1%). Hispanic origin 4,101 (1%). 18 and over 399,878 (72%), 62 and over 92,837 (17%). Median age: 33.

fend off an amendment to an agriculture spending bill that would have denied federal crop insurance and other government services to tobacco growers.

Penalizing growers, Clayton said, was unfair, since they have a fraction of the wealth of the tobacco companies. "This is not about smoking. This is about discriminating against the poorest of the poor of that industry. Our colleagues are not attacking the big boy. They really are attacking the small farmer."

Going against the Clinton administration, Clayton opposed NAFTA in the 103rd Congress, saying the trade pact would hurt the ability of small farmers in her district to remain competitive and would lead to the loss of low-wage jobs. She told the House that only 58 percent of the people age 25 or older in her district had earned high school diplomas.

Although many members from rural districts are proponents of gunowners' rights, Clayton voted in the 103rd for two gun-control measures backed by Clinton: requiring a five-day waiting period for handgun purchases, and banning certain semiautomatic assault-style weapons. In 1996, she voted against a GOP-led effort to repeal the assault-weapons ban.

At Home: Since winning the 1st District in 1992, Clayton has scored two easy re-elections, but throughout her tenure in the House she has had to contend with legal wranglings over the shape of the 1st, which was drawn with a 57 percent black-majority population.

Even before the 1992 election, the district became the target of a lawsuit when five white plaintiffs from Durham argued that the obvious race-conscious cartography of the state's map violated their constitutional right to equal protection.

The case eventually made it all the way to the Supreme Court in *Shaw v. Reno*. The high court, however, did not resolve the dispute with its 1993 decision. Instead it indicated that districts drawn exclusively to aggregate black voters might go too far. The case went back to a federal court in North Carolina, which upheld the district's lines in August 1994, saying even though it had been racially gerrymandered, it was still constitutional. The case once again was appealed to the Supreme Court, which in

1996 threw out North Carolina's congressional map. That left state legislators with the task of constructing a new map.

In March 1997, the legislature approved a new map recasting the 1st, dropping its black population to 50 percent, and also altering the boundaries of the 12th District (held by Watt), reducing its black population from 57 percent to 46 percent. That map was under judicial review through the spring.

Clayton first got to Congress with the help of organized labor, women's groups, ministers and minority activists across her rural, 28-county district.

When five black candidates and two whites entered the 1992 Democratic primary in the 1st, it was far from clear who would come out on top.

Clayton, a Warren County commissioner during the 1980s, was less well-known in the regional news media than were several of the other candidates, but wooing the media never became a priority. Instead, she looked to grass-roots supporters who were familiar with her work in the community as far back as 1968, when she first ran for Congress.

Contacts from her community experiences coupled with financial backing from national women's organizations helped Clayton make the Democratic runoff against state Rep. Walter B. Jones Jr., whose father had held the 1st until his death in September 1992.

Clayton won the runoff by 10 points over Jones. (Jones later switched to the GOP and in 1994 he was elected to represent the 3rd District.) Clayton's runoff victory paved the way to four wins over Republican Ted Tyler. She beat him twice in 1992— in a special election to fill out the remainder of the unexpired term and then in the general election for a full term — and again in 1994 and 1996. Clayton won each of the three races with more than 55 percent of the vote.

HOUSE ELECTIONS

1996 General		
Eva Clayton (D)	108,759	(66%)
Ted Tyler (R)	54,666	(33%)
1994 General		
Eva Clayton (D)	66,827	(61%)
Ted Tyler (R)	42,602	(39%)

Previous Winning Percentages: 1992 (67%) **1992†** (57%)

† Special election

CAMPAIGN FINANCE

	Receipts	Receipts from PACs	Expend-itures
1996			
Clayton (D)	$287,161	$120,844 (42%)	$300,049
Tyler (R)	$24,918	$750 (3%)	$26,248
1994			
Clayton (D)	$440,813	$213,570 (48%)	$417,700
Tyler (R)	$20,346	$14 (0%)	$16,572

DISTRICT VOTE FOR PRESIDENT

	1996		1992
D	105,487 (64%)	**D**	111,398 (61%)
R	51,766 (31%)	**R**	53,026 (29%)
I	8,259 (5%)	**I**	18,040 (10%)

KEY VOTES

1997	
Ban "partial birth" abortions	N
1996	
Approve farm bill	N
Deny public education to illegal immigrants	N
Repeal ban on certain assault-style weapons	N
Increase minimum wage	Y
Freeze defense spending	Y
Approve welfare overhaul	N
1995	
Approve balanced-budget constitutional amendment	N
Relax Clean Water Act regulations	N
Oppose limits on environmental regulations	Y
Reduce projected Medicare spending	N
Approve GOP budget with tax and spending cuts	N

VOTING STUDIES

	Presidential Support		Party Unity		Conservative Coalition	
Year	**S**	**O**	**S**	**O**	**S**	**O**
1996	84	14	92	6	37	61
1995	88	11	93	4	20	80
1994	81	18	93	2	22	78
1993	76	23	93	2	14	86

INTEREST GROUP RATINGS

Year	ADA	AFL-CIO	CCUS	ACU
1996	100	n/a	13	5
1995	100	100	13	8
1994	100	89	42	0
1993	100	100	9	0

2 Bob Etheridge (D)

Of Lillington — Elected 1996, 1st term

Biographical Information

Born: Aug. 7, 1941, Sampson County, N.C.

Education: Campbell U., B.S. 1965; North Carolina State U., attended 1967.

Military Service: U.S. Army, 1965-67.

Occupation: Hardware store owner; tobacco farmer.

Family: Wife, Faye Cameron; three children.

Religion: Presbyterian.

Political Career: Harnett County commissioner, 1973-77; N.C. House, 1979-87; superintendent of public instruction, 1988-96.

Capitol Office: 1641 Longworth Bldg. 20515; 225-4531.

Committees

Agriculture
General Farm Commodities; Risk Management & Specialty Crops

Science
Basic Research

The Path to Washington: Like many of his fellow Democrats in the Class of 1996, Etheridge brings significant political experience to Washington, having served in both local and state government since entering politics more than two decades ago.

Most recently, Etheridge was North Carolina's superintendent of public instruction, a position he occupied for two four-year terms.

During his tenure as the state's top educator, Etheridge championed the needs of educationally disadvantaged students and worked to strengthen curricula in the state's school system.

Before that, Etheridge served eight years in the North Carolina General Assembly, where he chaired the House Appropriations Committee.

A hardware store owner and part-time tobacco farmer, Etheridge first entered politics in 1972, winning election to the Harnett County Board of Commissioners, where he served for four years, the last two as chairman.

In Congress, Etheridge says he will continue to be a voice for programs aimed at assisting poor and otherwise disadvantaged children.

He has also pledged to pursue policies to expand students' access to higher education.

Reflecting the importance of farming to his district, however, Etheridge sought and received a seat on the Agriculture Committee, where the interests of tobacco farmers will be among his concerns.

Etheridge also serves on the Science Committee.

While in tune with the Clinton administration on most educational and social policies, Etheridge adamantly opposed to White House proposals to regulate tobacco as a drug and may find himself frequently at odds with the executive branch on this issue.

When state and national Democrats in 1996 went looking for a well-known, seasoned candidate to take on freshman Republican Rep. David Funderburk, they did not have to look far to find Etheridge, who was limited to two terms as the state school chief.

Funderburk, formerly an ambassador to Romania during the Reagan administration, was viewed as vulnerable by Democrats. The incumbent was a zealous supporter of the conservative agenda promulgated by House Republicans in the 104th Congress.

Borrowing a page from the 1996 Democratic script, Etheridge said that if Funderburk received a second term, he would undermine entitlement programs such as Social Security, Medicare and Medicaid.

Etheridge also benefited from the fact that Funderburk was one of more than 60 lawmakers whom the AFL-CIO set out to defeat. As a result, Funderburk faced an unremitting storm of negative television commercials attacking him for supporting House Republican proposals that purportedly would weaken the nation's environmental regulations, reduce funding for worker safety initiatives and decrease spending on education programs such as Head Start, Safe and Drug-Free Schools, and Title I for the educationally disadvantaged.

In the campaign's closing weeks, Etheridge produced a television commercial reviving a year-old story about Funderburk that had seriously undermined his credibility.

The ad stemmed from a 1995 auto accident in North Carolina in which Funderburk initially claimed his wife was driving, then later accepted legal responsibility by pleading no contest to a charge of driving left-of-center.

Witnesses to the accident said they saw Funderburk driving the vehicle. Funderburk and his wife, however, continued to insist that she was driving.

Having given Funderburk two years to show his stuff in Congress, voters in the 2nd decided they had seen enough, and Etheridge won with a comfortable 53 percent tally, even as Republican presidential candidate Bob Dole was soundly winning the 2nd.

NORTH CAROLINA 2
North Central — Parts of Durham and Rocky Mount

The half-moon shaped 2nd is home to features of North Carolina's past, present and future economies. The crescent's northern edge holds the high-tech industry of Research Triangle Park; the southern edge contains resorts and retirement communities. They are connected by a rich tobacco-producing region.

In the 1950s, an unusual coalition of academic, political and business leaders decided that North Carolina needed to diversify its economic base beyond the traditional furniture, tobacco and textile industries. They developed the idea of Research Triangle Park, a new industrial area where emerging high-tech industries could tap the brainpower of nearby Duke University (Durham), the University of North Carolina (Chapel Hill) and North Carolina State University (Raleigh).

Today, in the 2nd District's portion of southern Durham County, that vision is the source of thousands of jobs in biotechnology, supercomputers, microelectronics and pharmaceuticals.

Outside the Research Triangle, tobacco, the state's traditional cash crop, is a crucial component of the local economy. The tobacco fields of Nash, Edgecombe, Harnett and Wilson counties make it the district's chief agricultural commodity. The golfing resorts of Pinehurst and Southern Pines (Moore County) attract vacationers and affluent retirees to the Sandhills area of the district's southwestern fringe.

Unlike the white-collar executives and engineers attracted to Durham County — many of whom hew to Durham's progressive political traditions — the newcomers to Moore County are more reliably Republican. Bob Dole carried Moore in 1996 with 56 percent. Moore also went decisively for GOP Sen. Jesse Helms in 1996.

With only four counties wholly contained in the 2nd, along with parts of nine others, the district includes parts of a number of smaller cities.

Rocky Mount, shared with the 1st, is a food processing and textile center. Also shared with the 1st is tobacco-oriented Wilson and a sliver of Halifax County reaching into Roanoke Rapids.

The politics of the 2nd are as varied as its economic interests. Party registration figures give Democrats a big advantage on paper, but many of those small-town voters are Democrats in name only. The district voted for Helms in 1990 and 1996. The 2nd, which until 1994 had not elected a Republican congressman since the beginning of the century, was the nation's only district in 1996 to unseat a Republican incumbent (David Funderburk) while giving Dole a majority in the presidential race.

Blacks constitute about 22 percent of the 2nd's population, boosting Democratic fortunes. More than a third of Franklin and Granville county residents are black. Bill Clinton and Etheridge easily carried both areas in 1996.

North Carolina's new redistricting plan — which passed the state legislature in March 1997 and was pending judicial approval — would likely provide a boost for Etheridge. It would increase the 2nd District's black population to 27 percent.

1990 Population: 552,378. White 421,058 (76%), Black 121,229 (22%), Other 10,091 (2%). Hispanic origin 6,478 (1%). 18 and over 420,128 (76%), 62 and over 87,205 (16%). Median age: 34.

HOUSE ELECTIONS

1996 General

Bob Etheridge (D)	113,820	(53%)
David Funderburk (R)	98,951	(46%)
Mark D. Jackson (LIBERT)	2,892	(1%)

CAMPAIGN FINANCE

	Receipts	Receipts from PACs	Expend-itures
1996			
Etheridge (D)	$732,100	$234,785 (32%)	$730,969
Funderburk (R)	$1,029,627	$364,077 (35%)	$1,037,080

DISTRICT VOTE FOR PRESIDENT

1996		1992	
D	90,701 (42%)	**D**	85,542 (40%)
R	111,502 (52%)	**R**	98,516 (46%)
I	12,496 (6%)	**I**	30,643 (14%)

KEY VOTES

1997

Ban "partial birth" abortions Y

3 Walter B. Jones Jr. (R)

Of Farmville — Elected 1994, 2nd term

Biographical Information
Born: Feb. 10, 1943, Farmville, N.C.
Education: North Carolina State U., 1962-65; Atlantic Christian College, A.B. 1967.
Military Service: N.C. National Guard, 1967-71.
Occupation: Lighting company executive; insurance benefits company executive.
Family: Wife, Joe Anne Whitehurst; one child.
Religion: Roman Catholic.
Political Career: N.C. House, 1983-93; sought Democratic nomination for U.S. House, 1992.
Capitol Office: 422 Cannon Bldg. 20515; 225-3415.

Committees
Banking & Finance Services
Capital Markets, Securities & Government Sponsored Enterprises; Housing & Community Opportunity
National Security
Military Readiness; Military Research & Development
Resources
Fisheries Conservation, Wildlife & Oceans; National Parks & Public Lands
Small Business
Empowerment; Tax & Exports

In Washington: Jones likes to tell the story that when he told his father about his support for term limits, his father said, "Son, I didn't do a very good job of raising you." Jones' father, Walter B. Jones Sr., served in Congress for 26 years, representing many areas that are now in his son's district.

Jones also carries a different party label than his father, who was a lifelong Democrat. The younger Jones served in the state House as a Democrat for 10 years, but after losing a 1992 bid for the Democratic nomination in the 1st District, he switched to run for the 3rd as a Republican in 1994.

Jones seems quite at home in the conservative ranks of his adopted party. He supported all the major items of the "Contract With America," and in the 104th Congress he went to the House floor 132 times to promote a range of party efforts — to overhaul welfare, cut taxes, balance the budget and strengthen national defense. He supported a balanced-budget constitutional amendment that included a provision requiring a three-fifths vote by Congress to approve any tax increase — a stricter version of the amendment than the one the House approved in 1995.

In 1996, Jones was among the GOP freshmen who objected to their party's fiscal 1997 budget resolution, which envisioned the deficit increasing in the short term before heading toward zero by 2002. Class members were unhappy that the Senate had insisted on adding more spending for domestic programs into the budget. "There's a concern that we always have to be the ones to give in," Jones said. "We're tired of that." But when the budget plan came up for a final approval, Jones stuck with the GOP leadership and voted for it.

One area of federal spending that Jones has not been reluctant to support is defense. A member of the National Security Committee, he has backed the committee's advocacy of higher defense budgets. Expressing his support for the fiscal 1997 defense bill, Jones noted that it provided troops with a 3 percent pay raise, an increased housing allowance and $900 million more than President Clinton requested for military construction. Jones said improving the quality of life for U.S. servicemen is "extremely" important to him because his district includes the Marine Corps Air Station Cherry Point, Camp Lejeune Marine Corps training base and Seymour Johnson Air Force Base.

Indeed, Jones has not been reticent about speaking up for federal programs that are important to his district. During Congress' February 1996 debate on rewriting farm law, he spoke against an amendment that would have phased out the federal price support program for peanut growers by 2002. The program boosts peanut prices through a combination of government loans and production limits.

Hoping to protect peanut growers in the 3rd, Jones urged defeat of the amendment. "Further reductions to the price-support level or elimination of the program altogether will cause the economic ruin of America's 15,000 peanut farm families and the thousands of rural communities they support," he told the House. The House rejected the amendment, 209-212.

Jones has been vocal about protecting another important crop in his district — tobacco. President Clinton in the summer of 1995 declared teenage cigarette addiction a "national epidemic" and authorized the first federal crackdown on the sale and promotion of tobacco products to minors. The president also suggested that the Food and Drug Administration (FDA) regulate cigarettes and smokeless tobacco as drugs because of nicotine's potential to be addictive. Jones fumed that Clinton and the FDA were conducting a "witch hunt" against the tobacco farmer. "This is big brother at its worst. What next, prohibition of alcohol, caffeine, chocolate?" he railed on the House floor. "The government has no business in those decisions and the FDA and commissioner have no authority to classify nicotine as a drug."

Jones joined other farm-state lawmakers in pushing to create a new migrant worker program permitting the admission of up to 250,000 foreigners per year to harvest U.S. crops. Supporters of the amendment, which was offered to a broad

NORTH CAROLINA 3
East — Goldsboro; part of Greenville; Outer Banks

In a state full of disfigured congressional districts, the 3rd ranks as one of the most tortuously drawn. It includes the Tidewater region as far south as Onslow County then juts west before sweeping into the tobacco-producing areas of the Coastal Plain.

The fragile barrier islands of the Outer Banks bring tourism dollars into the 3rd, particularly during the summer. Development is a serious concern of the year-round residents of the northern islands, around Nags Head, but it is a less vexing issue farther south where the islands are less accessible and much of the land is designated as a protected seashore.

On the mainland, tourism is also a prominent economic feature of Albemarle and Pamlico sounds, as is fishing and the seafood canning industry.

Onslow County (Jacksonville), the southern edge of the 3rd's coastline, is economically dependent on the Camp Lejeune Marine Corps training base. The 1991 deployment of troops to the Persian Gulf War so drained Onslow's economic lifeblood that then-Gov. James G. Martin, a Republican, declared the county an "economic emergency area."

Farther inland, the business of the 3rd is agriculture. A finger reaches into Pitt County (Greenville), home to a growing industrial base. Turkey-producing Duplin County is the gateway to the tobacco country of Sampson and Wayne counties. All of rural and agricultural Sampson is included in the 3rd, along with most of Wayne County, where the landscape is dominated by huge tobacco warehouses and fields.

Goldsboro, the Wayne County seat, was another economic emergency area after the pilots of Seymour Johnson Air Force Base left for the Persian Gulf. Almost one-fifth of the district's residents live in Wayne County, making it the most populous jurisdiction in the 3rd.

Eastern North Carolina has long been a Democratic stronghold, but in recent years dissatisfaction with state and national Democratic candidates has translated into Republican gains.

The district signaled an allegiance to the GOP by ousting Democratic Rep. H. Martin Lancaster in 1994 and replacing him with Republican Jones. Terry Sanford won every county east of Raleigh in his 1986 Senate race, but in his 1992 re-election effort, his only strength in the east came in the heavily black northeastern counties of the 1st District. In the 3rd, blacks make up slightly more than 20 percent of the population.

GOP Senate candidate Lauch Faircloth carried many of the state's southeastern counties in his successful 1992 bid against Sanford, including Onslow and Wayne counties, where voters remembered Sanford's vote against authorizing force in the Persian Gulf. Bob Dole did well here in 1996, carrying all but three counties in the 3rd and beating Bill Clinton by 14 percentage points. Many white Democrats abandoned their party at the congressional level in 1994 and 1996 in favor of Jones, a conservative former Democrat.

1990 Population: 552,387. White 423,398 (77%), Black 118,640 (21%), Other 10,349 (2%). Hispanic origin 8,659 (2%). 18 and over 413,263 (75%), 62 and over 79,197 (14%). Median age: 32.

immigration bill, said it was needed so growers would have the necessary labor at harvest time. Although existing law allows farmers to petition for migrant workers, supporters of the guest worker plan said the current program is too cumbersome for growers.

Jones told the House that "if it was not for the migrant workers, our farmers would not be able to harvest their crops." But opponents of the provision said it would boost rather than deter illegal immigration; they accused agriculture businesses of trying to ensure a supply of cheap, pliant labor. The House in March 1996 defeated the measure, 180-242.

Jones is a member of the Resources Committee, and in one showing of bipartisanship, he joined in an effort with other House members who represent coastal districts to block a proposal to lift the ban on offshore oil and gas drilling. Jones, whose district includes the tourist-rich barrier islands of the Outer Banks, and the other lawmakers also endorsed a permanent ban on all offshore drilling in environmentally sensitive coastal areas.

In the 104th, Jones successfully pushed a measure allowing U.S. prosecution of war crimes involving an American national or member of the U.S. armed forces, whether as victim or perpetrator. Under the bill, the United States could impose fines and imprisonment on perpetrators, and the death penalty if the victim died. Congress cleared the measure in August 1996.

The legislation brought the United States into compliance with the Geneva Conventions of 1949, which were initially submitted to Congress in the 1950s. At that time, the executive branch and Congress concluded that existing federal and state criminal laws were sufficient, and that implementing legislation was not necessary. "In the absence of a military commission or an international criminal tribunal, the United States currently has no means by which we can try and prosecute perpetrators of war crimes in our courts," Jones said. "A modern-day Adolf Hitler could move to the United

States without worry."

At Home: Jones' first try for Congress came in 1992, the year his father died after more than a quarter-century in the House. That campaign was in the 1st District, which was fashioned in redistricting as one of two new black-majority districts in North Carolina. Jones finished first with 38 percent in a seven-way Democratic primary, sending him into a runoff with the top vote-getter among the primary's black candidates, Eva Clayton. Jones lost the runoff by 10 points, and Clayton went on to win the 1st that November.

In his 1994 campaign, Jones, a newly minted Republican, got the GOP nomination in the 3rd without a fight. He still found it useful to trade on the name his father had built up. Billboards throughout the district displayed Jones' name with the "Jr." in tiny letters at the bottom, or not at all.

Jones' target, four-term Democratic Rep. H. Martin Lancaster, countered by touting an endorsement he received from the elder Jones' longtime administrative assistant, Floyd J. Lupton, even featuring him in TV ads.

Jones focused his efforts on portraying Lancaster as a faithful supporter of the unpopular Clinton administration. One of his most effective and highly publicized tools was a TV advertisement that featured a shot of Lancaster and Clinton jogging together.

Lancaster tried to make hay by publicizing a picture from 1991 that showed Jones at a fund-raiser with presidential candidate Bill Clinton. Democrats also called attention to Federal Election Commission records showing that Jones gave $250 to Clinton's campaign committee. Jones shrugged off the revelations, saying he was a Democrat at the time and only interested in hearing about his party's potential nominee. He added that he ended up supporting George Bush.

Lancaster was grappling with the problem that many district voters were unhappy with Clinton for suggesting that health care reform be financed in part from a cigarette tax increase and for his support of lifting the ban on homosexuals in the military. Redistricting had also weakened Lancaster. Although he won in his redrawn district in 1992, the 3rd had lost black voters to the two new black-majority districts, and their absence was keenly felt in 1994, when many conservative but traditionally Democratic voters swung to the GOP. Compared with Lancaster's disadvantages, issues such as Jones' party switch and his not living in the district were relatively minor. Jones prevailed with 53 percent of the vote.

In 1996, Jones improved to 63 percent of the vote against Democrat George Parrott, a small businessman who had served six years as a special assistant in the North Carolina secretary of State's office. Parrott was a friend of Jones' at one time and had supported the incumbent's 1994 campaign. But disagreements between the two prompted Parrott to launch his ill-fated challenge.

HOUSE ELECTIONS

1996 General		
Walter B. Jones Jr. (R)	118,159	(63%)
George Parrott (D)	68,887	(37%)
1994 General		
Walter B. Jones Jr. (R)	72,464	(53%)
H. Martin Lancaster (D)	65,013	(47%)

CAMPAIGN FINANCE

	Receipts	Receipts from PACs	Expend-itures
1996			
Jones (R)	$640,522	$240,751 (38%)	$593,793
Parrott (D)	$41,550	$7,600 (18%)	$37,255
1994			
Jones (R)	$485,823	$68,067 (14%)	$477,463
Lancaster (D)	$887,963	$427,479 (48%)	$941,904

DISTRICT VOTE FOR PRESIDENT

	1996		1992
D	74,760 (40%)	**D**	74,639 (39%)
R	100,862 (54%)	**R**	89,038 (46%)
I	12,321 (7%)	**I**	28,223 (15%)

KEY VOTES

1997	
Ban "partial birth" abortions	Y
1996	
Approve farm bill	Y
Deny public education to illegal immigrants	Y
Repeal ban on certain assault-style weapons	Y
Increase minimum wage	N
Freeze defense spending	N
Approve welfare overhaul	Y
1995	
Approve balanced-budget constitutional amendment	Y
Relax Clean Water Act regulations	Y
Oppose limits on environmental regulations	N
Reduce projected Medicare spending	Y
Approve GOP budget with tax and spending cuts	Y

VOTING STUDIES

	Presidential Support		Party Unity		Conservative Coalition	
Year	S	O	S	O	S	O
1996	30	70	92	7	94	6
1995	18	82	95	4	95	5

INTEREST GROUP RATINGS

Year	ADA	AFL-CIO	CCUS	ACU
1996	5	n/a	94	100
1995	0	0	96	96

4 David E. Price (D)

Of Chapel Hill — Elected 1986, 5th term

Did not serve 1995-97.

Biographical Information

Born: Aug. 17, 1940, Erwin, Tenn.

Education: Mars Hill College, 1957-59; U. of North Carolina, B.A. 1961; Yale U., B.D. 1964, Ph.D. 1969.

Occupation: Professor.

Family: Wife, Lisa Kanwit; two children.

Religion: Baptist.

Political Career: N.C. Democratic Party chairman, 1983-84; U.S. House, 1987-95; Democratic nominee for U.S. House, 1994.

Capitol Office: 2162 Rayburn Bldg. 20515; 225-1784.

Committees

Appropriations

Treasury, Postal Service & General Government; VA, HUD & Independent Agencies

The Path to Washington: Price, a former four-term House member who was swept out of office in the Republican wave of 1994, avenged that loss in 1996 to end his involuntary exile from Congress.

A political scientist who went to divinity school and holds a Ph.D. from Yale, Price earned his old job back by ousting Republican Fred Heineman, the sometimes controversial freshman who blindsided Price by 1,215 votes in 1994. The 4th was one of the bellwethers of the Democrats' efforts to reverse their 1994 electoral debacle, particularly in the South.

Price returns to a House much different from the one he left. For instance, Price is serving as a member of the minority party. Democrats were the majority party for 40 years before 1994.

Price again sits on the Appropriations Committee, where he served before his 1994 defeat. From that post, Price may have a chance to influence spending that could have an impact on the Research Triangle, the concentration of universities, research facilities and high-technology firms in the Raleigh-Durham-Chapel Hill area.

Sizing up his expectations early in the 105th, Price, a self-described moderate, said the political atmosphere has seldom been better for centrist lawmakers of both parties to reach across the aisle to get things done.

In addition to his calls for bipartisanship, however, Price says he now has a better understanding of how Washington looks to his constituents.

After Price's loss to Heineman in 1994, many Democrats quietly said the former Duke professor had become aloof and too removed from the realities people face. In hindsight, Price agrees and says he has been chastened by the experience and will focus more attention on solving people's everyday problems.

Price says his priorities will be pushing for tax credits for college tuition, saving Medicare from insolvency and revamping the health care insurance system with incremental changes instead of a dramatic overhaul as proposed by President Clinton in 1993. Price also is firmly committed to balancing the budget and remains a solid supporter of the death penalty.

If voters in the 4th District were trying to send Price a wake-up call in 1994, then it appeared he took their message to heart in 1996. In his comeback, Price waged an aggressive grass-roots campaign, emphasizing door-to-door canvassing and plenty of personal contact with voters.

While he spent a significant amount of time in the community, Price pulled his punches somewhat until fairly late in the election season because Heineman was ill for several weeks and unable to campaign. But when Heineman, a former Raleigh police chief, recovered sufficiently to return to the campaign trail, Price unloaded on him. For example, Price ran a television commercial suggesting Heineman was out of touch with reality because the Republican said in 1995 that families earning between $300,000 and $750,000 a year qualified as middle class. "Earth to Fred," the advertisement's announcer said.

Heineman also faced attacks from the AFL-CIO, which weighed in with advertisements accusing the incumbent of voting to cut student loans, and the League of Conservation Voters, which accused him of voting to weaken environmental regulations.

Heineman aired television ads that reminded voters that Price voted in 1989 to increase salaries of all House members from $89,500 to $120,000 over two years.

But voters in the Democratic-leaning district, unimpressed with Heineman's record in his freshman term, reversed their 1994 judgment and sent Price back to Congress by a solid 10-point margin.

Price served as the state Democratic Party chairman in 1983 and 1984. The contacts he established in that post proved invaluable in his congressional bid in 1986, when he fended off three Democratic primary opponents and squared off with freshman Republican Bill Cobey, who had eked out a victory two years earlier. Price smashed the incumbent by 12 points, the largest margin of victory achieved by a House challenger that year.

NORTH CAROLINA 4
Central — Raleigh; Chapel Hill

The 4th has been described as the most progressive of the state's 10 majority-white congressional districts. Located on the eastern edge of the Piedmont plateau, it voted for black Democratic Senate nominee Harvey B. Gantt in his 1990 and 1996 challenges to GOP Sen. Jesse Helms; Democrats make up about two-thirds of all the voters here. But the 4th's propensity for Democrats is not uniform — the district elected a Republican House member in 1994 and had the state's closest presidential race in 1996.

The Democratic base draws deeply from the Research Triangle area, two corners of which are in the 4th. The University of North Carolina (24,400 students) is in Chapel Hill (Orange County); Raleigh (Wake County) has North Carolina State University (27,500 students).

The large numbers of white-collar and professional jobs in the region make it one of the state's most affluent districts.

Orange County (most of which lies in the 4th) has a more liberal bent than the rest of the district, due primarily to the university community of Chapel Hill. Bill Clinton won 61 percent of Orange's vote in 1996, while Gantt and Democratic Gov. James Hunt got more than two-thirds of the vote.

Wake County, the state's second-fastest growing from 1990 to 1996, accounts for about three-fourths of the district's vote. Many of those ballots are cast by people with jobs in or around the state government complex in Raleigh, the state capital. State employees give the county a Democratic tilt, but high-growth suburbs outside Raleigh gradually are redefining local politics. In 1994, GOP Rep. Fred Heineman's 11,000-vote margin in Wake overcame Price's lead in Orange and Chatham. But Price captured Wake by nearly 10,000 votes in their 1996 rematch, sealing his victory.

One suburban town, Cary, grew so fast in the 1980s that it surpassed Chapel Hill in population. Before the opening of Research Triangle Park in the early 1960s, Cary was a sleepy hamlet, surrounded by undeveloped fields and farmland. But its proximity to the Triangle and its location along the Interstate 40 corridor spurred a population boom from 7,600 people to 43,900 between 1970 and 1990. Many of Cary's residents are white-collar executives who work at the biotechnology, pharmaceutical, supercomputer and electronics industries of Research Triangle Park (outside the 4th in southern Durham County) or in Wake County's office parks.

On the western edge of the 4th, largely rural Chatham County is the least populous county in the district, but is reliably Democratic. Its agrarian landscape includes some textile industry, along with Chapel Hill spillover growth along its northern border with Orange County.

The 4th's racial composition and Democratic tilt would remain intact under the redistricting plan passed by state legislature in March 1997, which was still subject to judicial approval. The plan would remove territory in western Chatham and eastern Wake from the 4th and add the rest of Orange County, some of Person County on the Virginia border, and all of heavily Democratic Durham County. The new district would include just 65 percent of the residents now in the 4th.

1990 Population: 552,387. White 426,361 (77%), Black 111,162 (20%), Other 14,864 (3%). Hispanic origin 7,217 (1%). 18 and over 428,984 (78%), 62 and over 57,298 (10%). Median age: 31.

HOUSE ELECTIONS

1996 General		
David E. Price (D)	157,194	(54%)
Fred Heineman (R)	126,466	(44%)
David Allen Walker (LIBERT)	4,132	(1%)

Previous Winning Percentages: **1992** (65%) **1990** (58%) **1988** (58%) **1986** (56%)

CAMPAIGN FINANCE

	Receipts	Receipts from PACs	Expend-itures
1996			
Price (D)	$1,153,067	$299,986 (26%)	$1,168,542
Heineman (R)	$994,967	$338,752 (34%)	$980,249

DISTRICT VOTE FOR PRESIDENT

	1996			1992	
D	141,076	(49%)	**D**	126,616	(47%)
R	130,659	(45%)	**R**	105,555	(39%)
I	14,403	(5%)	**I**	38,854	(14%)

KEY VOTES

1997

Ban "partial birth" abortions N

5 Richard M. Burr (R)

Of Winston-Salem — Elected 1994, 2nd term

Biographical Information
Born: Nov. 30, 1955, Charlottesville, Va.
Education: Wake Forest U., B.A. 1978.
Occupation: Marketing manager.
Family: Wife, Brooke Fauth; two children.
Religion: Methodist.
Political Career: Republican nominee for U.S. House, 1992.
Capitol Office: 1513 Longworth Bldg. 20515; 225-2071.

Committees
Commerce
Energy & Power; Health & Environment; Oversight & Investigations

In Washington: Burr is a staunch conservative and a loyal supporter of the House GOP leadership, and from his seat on the Commerce Committee he makes a particular effort to protect and promote the tobacco industry, traditionally a power in the 5th's largest city, Winston-Salem, and in North Carolina generally.

He is a down-the-line vote for the GOP agenda and business interests. He was a steadfast opponent of raising the minimum wage, even voting against the final version of the bill in August 1996, when passage was assured and a number of other Republicans switched to support it. He favors allowing employers to offer their workers compensatory time off rather than overtime pay, an idea opposed by organized labor. He voted in 1996 to repeal the ban on certain semiautomatic assault-style weapons; he opposes abortion; he supports higher funding for the Pentagon than the Clinton administration has requested, and he backs a balanced-budget constitutional amendment.

He did, however, have kind words in the 104th for one federal expenditure. When President Clinton signed the National Highway System legislation in November 1995, Burr pointed out how the bill helps pave the way for two new North Carolina interstates, I-73 and I-74.

On Commerce, Burr takes every chance to defend tobacco interests, which he says were the target of an "all-out assault" during the Democratic-controlled 103rd Congress. In those days, liberals used the old Energy and Commerce Committee as a forum to pillory tobacco companies for alleged transgressions, including adjusting the level of nicotine in cigarettes to make them addictive. But all that changed in the GOP-controlled 104th; House Speaker Newt Gingrich gave the Commerce Committee chair to Thomas J. Bliley Jr. of Virginia, a longtime friend of the tobacco industry who, like Burr, represents a city (Richmond) where cigarette manufacturing is a big business.

Burr says that many in his district want to continue raising tobacco because the local soil is not conducive to other agriculture, and because most tobacco farms are too small to grow land-intensive crops such as grains. He is resolutely opposed to increased cigarette taxes. In June 1996, Burr and other tobacco allies barely fended off an effort on the House floor to bar funding for tobacco crop insurance and to prevent any money in the annual agriculture appropriations bill from going to pay employees of the federal tobacco extension service program, which advises farmers on the best way to grow their crop. Pro-tobacco forces, which prevailed 212-210, said the language would bankrupt small tobacco farmers because tobacco companies would turn to cheaper foreign tobacco to make their products.

In the summer of 1995, Burr and other tobacco-state lawmakers reacted angrily to a proposal by the federal Food and Drug Administration (FDA) to regulate nicotine as a drug. Some lawmakers called for the resignation of FDA Commissioner David A. Kessler. Burr said, "Kessler and the FDA are out of control."

Burr also is down on the FDA because he says the agency inhibits the development of new drugs and medical devices. In early 1996, he introduced a bill that would allow drug companies to send doctors copies of certain studies on the benefits of using FDA-approved drugs in unapproved ways. Doctors can already prescribe drugs for uses not described on the FDA-approved label, but pharmaceutical companies are barred from promoting these off-label uses. Burr's bill would allow the pharmaceutical companies to distribute studies on these other uses.

"We should allow doctors to have as much information as humanly possible," Burr told the Winston-Salem Journal. "You might use the word promotion; I would use the word education."

Burr and James C. Greenwood, R-Pa., introduced legislation to speed FDA's approval process for legal drugs, biotechnology products and medical devices. In July 1996, the two lawmakers announced they would modify their bills in order to quell opposition, but critics of the

NORTH CAROLINA 5
Northwest — Winston-Salem

Beginning in the 1970s, voters in the 5th started a march toward the Republican side, creating a quadrennial panic among local Democratic officeholders, who feared being dragged down by their party's national ticket. A recession-induced interruption in 1992 marked the first time Democrats saw a break in that procession, but a Republican takeover of the 5th in 1994 reignited that march. In 1996, not only did Burr win re-election with 62 percent of the vote, but Bob Dole polled 51 percent.

The last Republican to hold this seat, Rep. Wilmer D. Mizell, was defeated in 1974 by Democratic Rep. Stephen L. Neal, who did not seek re-election in 1994.

The heart of the district is Winston-Salem, an old-time tobacco town dominated by the leaf since Richard Joshua Reynolds built his first plug chewing tobacco factory in the 1870s. The city remains a tobacco-producing center, where the R. J. Reynolds conglomerate still keeps its tobacco and Planters LifeSavers headquarters, but it has strayed from its industrial origins.

In the 1980s, downsizing in the tobacco industry and the gradual erosion of the manufacturing base translated into slower growth for Winston-Salem than in North Carolina's other major cities. The city of Winston-Salem is about 40 percent black, but most of the black neighborhoods were excised from the 5th during 1992 redistricting and added to the majority-minority 12th District.

Textiles are also an important component of the local economy, but nowadays, tobacco and textiles take a back seat to service industries, now the largest employment sector. Health care is a major industry in Forsyth County.

Forsyth County cast 30 percent of the district's vote in the 1996 presidential election, and most of those tallies went to the Republican side. Dole defeated Bill Clinton by almost 8,000 votes in the county, while Burr defeated Democratic challenger Neil Grist Cashion Jr. by 21,835 votes, a better than 2-1 margin.

Republicans have traditionally run well in the GOP hill country in the western reaches of the 5th, between the Blue Ridge and Appalachian mountains. Early settlers of the area set up small farms with dairy cows, poultry, apple trees and tobacco, and developed a strong antagonism toward the flatland tobacco planters who were wealthier, politically powerful and Democratic.

From mountainous Watauga County, the 5th shoots east and south to take in parts of Republican Wilkes County, and parts of furniture- and textile-producing Burke and Caldwell counties.

The mostly rural counties of the northern tier, along the Virginia border, are typified by small textile towns such as Mount Airy. The fictional town of Mayberry, the setting for the long-running "Andy Griffith Show," loosely was based on Griffith's memories of growing up in this Surry County town. Surry and neighboring Stokes County backed George Bush in 1992. Both counties gave more than half their votes to Dole in 1996.

One exception to the Republican trend is rural Caswell County, a Democratic area in the eastern reaches of the 5th, where blacks make up about 40 percent of the electorate. Clinton carried the county in 1996, and Burr won by just 306 votes. Democrats also do well in the portion of Granville in the 5th; that was the only county where Cashion beat Burr.

1990 Population: 552,386. White 463,183 (84%), Black 83,824 (15%), Other 5,379 (1%). Hispanic origin 4,259 (1%). 18 and over 428,782 (78%), 62 and over 91,914 (17%). Median age: 35.

Republican effort were unmollified.

He faulted Democrats for criticizing GOP efforts to overhaul the welfare system, saying on the House floor that "they are afraid to admit the Great Society failed." By opposing the GOP scheme of converting welfare into block grants for the states, "my Democrat colleagues and the Clinton administration are trying to convince the American people that Big Brother government knows what's better for a community than the people who live there," Burr said. "They call this proposal mean-spirited and callous. In reality, the only mean spirited thing in this whole debate is the current state of our welfare system."

Burr did stray from the party line in a November 1995 vote to send the bill funding the Veterans Affairs and the Housing and Urban Development Departments back to conference with instructions to add funding for veterans medical care. Burr was one of just 25 Republicans who joined with nearly every Democrat in rejecting the conference report.

He weighed in on the side of lawmakers who lamented a decline in civility in the House, joining a group of representatives in January 1996 in promising to stop the name-calling and to start treating each other with respect. "This is legislating by the Golden Rule," Burr said. "Members should treat others on the House floor with the same level of respect and consideration for which we regard the office. To do anything less degrades the entire institution of Congress."

In November 1995, he supported efforts by some conservative Republicans to weaken a proposed ban on most gifts to lawmakers. The amendment by Dan Burton, R-Ind., would have enabled House members to continue to accept lobbyist-paid gifts, trips and meals, but would have strengthened disclosure requirements. The amendment was defeated and the House went on to ban most gifts and meals.

At Home: Burr took 46 percent of the vote against durable Democratic Rep. Stephen L. Neal in 1992, and Neal's retirement in 1994 finally cleared the way for Republicans to win a seat the party had been trying hard to regain since Neal upset GOP Rep. Wilmer D. Mizell, a former major league baseball pitcher, in the Watergate election of 1974.

Burr was unopposed for the GOP nomination in 1994, and in November he won election with 57 percent of the vote. But the fall contest was harder-fought than the final margin indicated, as the Democratic nominee, state Sen. A. P. "Sandy" Sands, waged an aggressive, well-funded campaign unmarred by major gaffes.

Businessman Burr, a graduate of Winston-Salem's Wake Forest University who served as co-chair of North Carolina Taxpayers United, ran against Washington, President Clinton and career politicians — a platform used successfully by Republicans in race after race in 1994. He stressed issues in the House GOP's "Contract With America," including support for a balanced-budget constitutional amendment, congressional term limits, welfare overhaul and institutional reform of Congress.

Sands attacked the contract as "pie-in-the-sky promises" that would bring on huge cuts in veterans benefits and in entitlement programs such as Social Security. In signing the contract, he said, Burr was pledging to the GOP leadership that he would obey the party line over the interests of the district.

In response, Burr sent out more than 60,000 pieces of mail to senior citizens in the 5th, signed by his parents, senior citizens themselves. Burr also had plenty of criticism for Sands, faulting his vote in the state Senate for a 3-cent tobacco-tax increase. To capitalize on anti-Washington sentiment, he said Sands if elected would become "an extension" of problems caused by Clinton and the House Democratic majority. In the end, Sands' effort was no match for anti-administration sentiment in the 5th, which was fueled by the White House's proposal to increase the cigarette tax 75 cents per pack to help finance Clinton's health care proposal.

In 1996, the Democrats did not wage a strong effort to recapture the 5th, and Burr won with 62 percent.

HOUSE ELECTIONS

1996 General		
Richard M. Burr (R)	130,177	(62%)
Neil Grist Cashion Jr. (D)	74,320	(35%)
Barbara J. Howe (LIBERT)	4,193	(2%)
1994 General		
Richard Burr (R)	84,741	(57%)
A.P. "Sandy" Sands (D)	63,194	(43%)

CAMPAIGN FINANCE

	Receipts	Receipts from PACs	Expenditures
1996			
Burr (R)	$855,362	$247,589 (29%)	$697,067
Cashion (D)	$186,806	$17,765 (10%)	$185,998
1994			
Burr (R)	$753,525	$189,490 (25%)	$741,986
Sands (D)	$767,956	$300,940 (39%)	$759,742

DISTRICT VOTE FOR PRESIDENT

1996		1992	
D	86,896 (41%)	**D**	97,821 (43%)
R	106,865 (51%)	**R**	99,087 (44%)
I	15,332 (7%)	**I**	30,560 (13%)

KEY VOTES

1997	
Ban "partial birth" abortions	Y
1996	
Approve farm bill	Y
Deny public education to illegal immigrants	Y
Repeal ban on certain assault-style weapons	Y
Increase minimum wage	N
Freeze defense spending	N
Approve welfare overhaul	Y
1995	
Approve balanced-budget constitutional amendment	Y
Relax Clean Water Act regulations	Y
Oppose limits on environmental regulations	N
Reduce projected Medicare spending	Y
Approve GOP budget with tax and spending cuts	Y

VOTING STUDIES

	Presidential Support		Party Unity		Conservative Coalition	
Year	**S**	**O**	**S**	**O**	**S**	**O**
1996	32	68	96	4	96	4
1995	20	78	95	4	95	5

INTEREST GROUP RATINGS

Year	ADA	AFL-CIO	CCUS	ACU
1996	5	n/a	88	100
1995	0	8	96	88

6 Howard Coble (R)

Of Greensboro — Elected 1984, 7th term

Biographical Information

Born: March 18, 1931, Greensboro, N.C.

Education: Appalachian State U., 1949-50; Guilford College, A.B. 1958; U. of North Carolina, J.D. 1962.

Military Service: Coast Guard, 1952-56; Coast Guard Reserve, 1960-81.

Occupation: Lawyer; insurance claims supervisor.

Family: Single.

Religion: Presbyterian.

Political Career: N.C. House, 1969; secretary, N.C. Department of Revenue, 1973-77; Republican nominee for N.C. treasurer, 1976; N.C. House, 1979-83.

Capitol Office: 2239 Rayburn Bldg. 20515; 225-3065.

Committees

Judiciary
Courts & Intellectual Property (chairman); Crime

Transportation & Infrastructure
Coast Guard & Maritime Transportation; Surface Transportation

In Washington: In the 105th Congress, Coble is the chairman of Judiciary's Courts and Intellectual Property Subcommittee, which has such issues as "cyber copyrights," computer data encoding and patent law under its bailiwick.

Although these may sound like rather dry and technical topics, much is at stake in some of the matters over which Coble's panel presides. He said he had already heard himself described as a "puppet of the Japanese industrial complex," when the House in April 1997 considered a measure he sponsored to overhaul U.S. patent law.

Coble shares many of the conservative views of the new generation of Southern Republicans, but it is more than his years that set him apart from the aggressive younger members. A back-slapping, amiable man with a penchant for cigars and a tough game of tennis, Coble usually has skirted partisan confrontation.

Such confrontation, however, may be tougher for Coble to avoid in the 105th. The ranking member on his Judiciary subcommittee is liberal Massachusetts Democrat Barney Frank, one of the more quick-witted and partisan members of the House.

Coble's first taste of legislative skirmishing came during debate on the patent bill, which the House passed in April 1997. Coble said the measure would bring the U.S. patent system in line with that of other countries and increase the competitiveness of American companies. As introduced, the bill would amend current law to convert the federal government's Patent and Trademark Office into a wholly owned government corporation; it would also provide for the publication of patents 18 months after they are filed. Under existing law, patent applications are not released to the public until after the patent is issued.

California Republican Dana Rohrabacher took particular exception to the 18-month publication date for patents, arguing unsuccessfully that the bill would allow individuals and foreign businesses to have too easy access to the ideas of American inventors. Rohrabacher termed the measure the "Steal American Technology Act" and implied that Japanese companies support the bill so they can get easier access to American ideas.

But Coble argued that the bill provided a more level playing field for American inventors. "Foreign companies are . . . able to study our latest technological developments abroad, but are not required to reveal their work to our inventors on these same terms here," he said. "Eighteen-month publication therefore levels the international playing field."

But opponents also argued that the bill's supporters are changing a system that already works, in order to please big corporations at the expense of the little guy. Although Coble was able to fend off a substitute amendment by Rohrabacher that would have killed the 18-month publication release provision, he could not stop an amendment offered by Democrat Marcy Kaptur of Ohio. The House approved her language barring in most cases publication of patent applications of small businesses, independent inventors and universities until their patents are granted. This is the victory of the "little guy over the big guy," Rohrabacher said after Kaptur's amendment passed.

Coble blamed the bill's opponents for misrepresenting the content of the bill and confusing and misleading other members, "who do not and should not be expected to understand all of the intricacies of a complex and arcane topic such as patent law." Then he added, "If we wait much longer, I anticipate that our detractors will attempt to convince the American public that I, as a lifetime member of the VFW, am conspiring with the other Bolsheviks down at the VFW Hall in Greensboro, N.C., to destroy the United States and subvert her national economy."

Coble's main quest during his seven terms in the House has been to call for an end to congressional and executive branch pensions. His objections to the pension program date to his first

Many of North Carolina's districts are cartographically imaginative, but the 6th is exceptional. It is split in half by a thin reed that is the 12th District; the two halves of the 6th District connect at only a single point.

Almost 40 percent of the district's population lives in middle-class Guilford County (Greensboro), home to two corners of the Piedmont Triad. Greensboro is the third-largest city in North Carolina; its economy is a blend of manufacturing and service industries.

Textile giants such as Burlington Industries and Cone Mills employ thousands, as does AT&T Technologies. It is home to an American Express regional credit card service center, tobacco processing, insurance services and six colleges and universities.

Furniture-making High Point is in the southwestern part of Guilford County. The third corner of the Triad, Winston-Salem, is outside 6th District confines, in the neighboring 5th District.

Guilford County's relatively large managerial class produces a Republican vote, though it is far from monolithic. Bill Clinton carried the county in 1992, but Bob Dole won it in 1996. Dole, in fact, carried every county in the 6th, racking up 59 percent of the vote. Coble also won easily with 73 percent.

Before the 1992 redistricting, all of Greensboro and surrounding Guilford County was included in the 6th. Now the 6th excludes the city's black neighborhoods, which were added to the majority-minority 12th District. The 12th divides the 6th along the I-85 population corridor.

NORTH CAROLINA 6
Central — Part of Greensboro

Textile-oriented Alamance County produces hosiery, upholstery and drapery fabrics, textured yarn and other finished fabrics.

North of the interstate, the Alamance turf belongs to the 12th. Some of the factory-outlet town of Burlington is in the 6th, but most of its black residents are in the 12th. Less-developed southern Alamance is in the 6th.

With a union-resistant textile industry, Alamance usually stays in the Republican fold, despite a Democratic registration edge. Ronald Reagan won with comfortable margins in 1980 and 1984, and George Bush carried the county in 1992. Dole also won it handily in 1996.

Randolph County (Asheboro) and Davidson County produce furniture, textiles and Republican votes.

Bush scored more than 50 percent in each county in 1992; Dole won each by more than 2-to-1 in 1996.

Parts of Davie and Rowan counties — mostly those parts outside the population centers — are also included in the 6th. Both backed Dole by more than 60 percent in 1996.

1990 Population: 552,385. White 504,464 (91%), Black 41,329 (7%), Other 6,592 (1%). Hispanic origin 3,784 (1%). 18 and over 428,096 (77%), 62 and over 84,176 (15%). Median age: 35.

term. In 1985, he introduced legislation to reduce retirement pay for House members, a move that some colleagues regarded as demagoguery. In a February 1993 letter to then-White House budget director Leon E. Panetta, he suggested eliminating the federal contribution to the congressional pension plan as a further spending cut for the Clinton economic team to consider. He is one of the few members of Congress who does not participate in the pension program, calling it "a taxpayer ripoff."

Early in the 105th, he again introduced legislation to end pensions for most members of Congress. In 1993, he had introduced a "triple play for taxpayers' relief." One bill of the triple play would eliminate the pension for congressmen who were not yet vested. Another bill would have required former presidents to waive the right to other pensions in order to receive presidential pensions. A third would have denied pensions to former presidents until they reached the prevailing retirement age under Social Security rules.

Coble said, "The vast majority of Americans struggle to make ends meet and often are unable to save for their own retirement. [Yet] they are forced to contribute to the retirement packages of former presidents . . . Speakers and members of Congress."

Before he took the Intellectual Property chair, Coble in the 104th Congress chaired the Transportation and Infrastructure Committee's Coast Guard and Maritime Transportation Subcommittee, where he managed a bill reauthorizing the Coast Guard. The measure, which passed the House in May 1995, allowed the Coast Guard to close nearly two dozen of its small-boat rescue stations. The Coast Guard had been trying for several years to cut costs by consolidating its smaller rescue stations, but Congress resisted.

Some opponents tried to prevent the rescue stations from closing, saying it would result in loss of life from small-boat accidents. But Coble said he was confident that the closures would not compromise safety. In an era of downsizing, no one knows better than the Coast Guard which stations can be closed, he added.

Although Coble is a faithful backer of his party's positions, he took exception to the leadership's handling of a vote to investigate President Clinton's commitment of $20 billion to help bail out the Mexican economy. The vote came in February 1995 when Mississippi Democrat Gene Taylor introduced a resolution calling on the U.S. comptroller general to investigate Clinton's commitment of the money. Taylor asserted that his was a privileged resolution because Clinton's unilateral action abrogated the authority of Congress. But Speaker Newt Gingrich ruled against him, and when Taylor appealed the ruling of the chair, the House upheld Gingrich, 288-143. Fourteen Republicans sided with Taylor, including Coble.

Gingrich later read the riot act to the 14 dissenters for voting against the leadership, "We were taken to the woodshed," Coble said afterwards.

Coble also pays attention to parochial interests, particularly textiles and tobacco. More than 30,000 of his constituents work in the textile industry, and he has consistently demanded protectionist relief for the industry. "The only place free trade exists is in an economics textbook," he has said.

He was unhappy in the summer of 1995 when the Food and Drug Administration suggested that nicotine is a drug that should be regulated. Coble responded angrily to the FDA's suggestions. "I think tobacco has become the convenient whipping boy on Capitol Hill," he told the New York Times in July 1995. "It is lawfully grown, lawfully packaged and lawfully marketed, and I am getting annoyed by these efforts to make it seem like there is something illegal about tobacco."

At Home: Coble started 1984 thinking about a run for governor. He had gained some notice among Republicans statewide, not only while in the state legislature but also as an assistant U.S. attorney and as secretary of the Department of Revenue under GOP Gov. James E. Holshouser Jr. in the mid-1970s. But he bypassed a statewide bid to challenge freshman Democrat Robin Britt in the 6th.

Despite his reputation, it took all of Coble's efforts just to make himself the GOP nominee. Former state Sen. Walter C. Cockerham, a millionaire construction company owner, had been stumping in the district and courting Republican votes for several months before Coble entered the race. But armed with the support of most local GOP leaders, Coble pulled through the primary by a scant 164 votes.

He then stressed his fiscal conservatism against Britt, whom he sought to paint as an extravagant liberal. Coble criticized Britt for having gone against President Ronald Reagan on two of every three votes cast in 1983. Tapping into the flow of conservative Democrats who crossed party lines for Reagan, Coble won by 2,662 votes.

Britt immediately plotted a comeback. The 1986 results were even closer than those of 1984; only 79 votes separated the winner and the loser on Election Day. Britt appealed the election results, but his challenge proved unsuccessful. Coble has had little to worry about since.

HOUSE ELECTIONS

1996 General		
Howard Coble (R)	167,828	(73%)
Mark Costley (D)	58,022	(25%)
Gary Goodson (LIBERT)	2,693	(1%)
1994 General		
Howard Coble (R)	98,355	(100%)

Previous Winning Percentages: **1992** (71%) **1990** (67%) **1988** (62%) **1986** (50%) **1984** (51%)

CAMPAIGN FINANCE

	Receipts	Receipts from PACs	Expend-itures
1996			
Coble (R)	$592,230	$226,109 (38%)	$498,224
Costley (D)	$43,957	$2,000 (5%)	$32,829
1994			
Coble (R)	$343,124	$130,705 (38%)	$350,981

DISTRICT VOTE FOR PRESIDENT

	1996		1992
D	75,053 (33%)	**D**	75,652 (32%)
R	134,393 (59%)	**R**	120,684 (51%)
I	18,413 (8%)	**I**	38,448 (16%)

KEY VOTES

1997	
Ban "partial birth" abortions	Y
1996	
Approve farm bill	Y
Deny public education to illegal immigrants	Y
Repeal ban on certain assault-style weapons	Y
Increase minimum wage	N
Freeze defense spending	N
Approve welfare overhaul	Y
1995	
Approve balanced-budget constitutional amendment	Y
Relax Clean Water Act regulations	Y
Oppose limits on environmental regulations	N
Reduce projected Medicare spending	Y
Approve GOP budget with tax and spending cuts	Y

VOTING STUDIES

	Presidential Support		Party Unity		Conservative Coalition	
Year	S	O	S	O	S	O
1996	30	70	95	5	88	12
1995	20	80	93	7	86	14
1994	28	72	97	3	83	17
1993	25	75	95	5	73	27
1992	75	25	92	8	75	25
1991	70	30	89	8	86	11

INTEREST GROUP RATINGS

Year	ADA	AFL-CIO	CCUS	ACU
1996	15	n/a	88	90
1995	0	0	92	88
1994	5	22	83	95
1993	5	0	91	96
1992	10	25	75	92
1991	15	25	80	90

7 Mike McIntyre (D)

Of Lumberton — Elected 1996, 1st term

Biographical Information
Born: Aug. 6, 1956, Lumberton, N.C.
Education: U. of North Carolina, B.A. 1978, J.D. 1981.
Occupation: Lawyer.
Family: Wife, Dee Strickland; two children.
Religion: Presbyterian.
Political Career: No previous office.
Capitol Office: 1605 Longworth Bldg. 20515; 225-2731.

Committees
Agriculture
General Farm Commodities; Risk Management & Specialty Crops
National Security
Military Procurement

The Path to Washington: After a November 1972 Fayetteville victory party for newly elected Democratic Rep. Charlie Rose, high school student McIntyre told his father that he wanted to be the next congressman from the 7th District. Twenty-four years later, McIntyre fulfilled his ambition, succeeding Rose, who retired after 12 terms.

A lawyer who had never held elective office, McIntyre won election to Congress in 1996 after many years of community activism and behind-the-scenes involvement in local politics.

In 1987, for example, McIntyre was appointed to a statewide commission on children and youth that submitted recommendations to the state legislature. In 1989, he was appointed to another two-year stint on a similar panel, this one devoted to studying family issues.

McIntyre, a self-described moderate, also chaired the Lumberton Area Chamber of Commerce's legislative committee and served on the chamber's board of directors and its executive committee. Also active in North Carolina's legal community, McIntyre served in various leadership positions with the state bar association, primarily working on youth and education issues.

The road to Congress was not an easy one for McIntyre, who finished a strong enough second in a crowded Democratic primary to force a runoff with the top vote-getter, Rose Marie Lowry-Townsend, a well-known American Indian and teachers' union president who was expected to walk away with the nomination.

With less than a month to campaign for the runoff election, McIntyre criss-crossed the district, stressing his years of community activism in an effort to convince the local party faithful that he would be the Democrats' best choice to defend the seat.

In the days just before the runoff, McIntyre was able to win the backing of several influential leaders in the district's black community, whose support was enough to tip the race in his favor. McIntyre won the nomination with 52 percent.

In the general election, McIntyre faced Republican Bill Caster, a New Hanover County (Wilmington) commissioner and retired Coast Guard officer, who also had scored a primary upset by knocking off Robert C. Anderson, a three-time GOP nominee who had held Rose to a career-low 52 percent in 1994.

Caster, who was promised a subcommittee chairmanship by House Speaker Newt Gingrich if he picked up the seat for Republicans, made drug enforcement and interdiction one of his major campaign themes.

Caster attempted to label McIntyre a stereotypical tax-and-spend Democrat.

But McIntyre's message of protecting education, balancing the budget and creating jobs had broader appeal with voters. Moreover, McIntyre's conservative stance on other issues such as abortion, gunowners' rights and military spending resonated with many voters of this largely conservative district and inoculated him from Caster's attacks. McIntyre, who is a member of the center-right Democratic coalition known as the "blue dogs," beat Caster comfortably, 53 percent to 46 percent, even as Republican presidential candidate Bob Dole was carrying the district.

For successfully defending the 7th, the Democratic leadership awarded McIntyre seats on the Agriculture and National Security committees.

From his position on Agriculture, McIntyre looks out for his district's tobacco farmers, many of whom feel threatened by suggestions that nicotine should be regulated as a drug. While he supported proposals to crack down on underage smoking, McIntyre contended that the district's heavy reliance on agriculture, especially tobacco, would force him to strenuously oppose any proposals aimed at regulating it.

With a large military presence in the 7th District, including Fort Bragg and a significant population of retired military personnel, McIntyre will find the National Security assignment helpful in tending to defense and veterans' issues that concern his constituents.

NORTH CAROLINA 7
Southeast — Part of Fayetteville

Former Democratic Rep. Charlie Rose took a risk in 1991 by voting against authorizing the use of military force in the Persian Gulf. It was an extremely controversial stand in North Carolina's military-dependent southeastern region.

Cumberland County is the 7th's most-populous county, and it has a heavy military cast. It is home to more than 50,000 troops stationed at Fort Bragg and Pope Air Force Base and to thousands of military retirees.

When 75 percent of the troops stationed here were deployed in the gulf war, the county took the equivalent of an economic Scud missile. Local business suffered: Unemployment claims and food stamp applications soared, sales tax revenues plummeted and mobile home sales were cut in half. Then-GOP Gov. James G. Martin declared Cumberland and three other counties economic emergency areas.

One of the other economic emergency areas was coastal Onslow County (Jacksonville), the site of Camp Lejeune Marine Corps training base. Like Cumberland, the Onslow economy depends heavily on the troops who spend their paychecks on the local service industries. McIntyre's Republican opponent easily carried the 7th's share of Onslow in 1996, as did Bob Dole in the presidential election.

As a whole, the district has a Democratic tilt — Democrats make up 70 percent of registered voters — that is usually reflected at the local and statewide levels. But in recent years, the vote has drifted toward the GOP at the national level. Clinton edged George Bush by 500 votes here in the 1992 presidential race. But Dole won the 7th by 8,000 votes four years later, even as McIntyre held the House seat for Democrats.

New Hanover County, in the Cape Fear region, is the district's second most-populous. Population is centered in Wilmington, a 250-year-old port city nestled between the Cape Fear River and the Atlantic Ocean. The restoration of its waterfront area has brought tourism and some white-collar prosperity into this old fishing center. And the newly completed I-40, which connects Wilmington to the Raleigh-Durham area, is expected to further boost the economy in years to come.

GOP strength is more pronounced in New Hanover County than in the rest of the 7th. Dole carried the 7th's portion of the county with 56 percent. McIntyre lost the county in the House race by 22 percentage points and 10,000 votes, garnering only 38 percent of the votes there.

Blacks make up a sizable chunk of the region's population, but most are taken in by the fingers of the primarily minority 1st District, which reaches in all directions through the 7th. The 7th's other significant minority are American Indians, who represent 7 percent of the district's residents. About half of North Carolina's 80,000 American Indians live in Robeson County, which is shared with the 8th. The Lumbee Indians, named for the river which flows through the county, are especially numerous here and tend to vote Democratic. Robeson was crucial to McIntyre's victory; it gave him 81 percent and a nearly 15,000-vote margin.

1990 Population: 552,386. White 394,855 (71%), Black 103,428 (19%), Other 54,103 (10%). Hispanic origin 16,241 (3%). 18 and over 414,413 (75%), 62 and over 60,924 (11%). Median age: 29.

HOUSE ELECTIONS

1996 General		
Mike McIntyre (D)	87,487	(53%)
Bill Caster (R)	75,811	(46%)
1996 Primary Runoff		
Mike McIntyre (D)	16,285	(52%)
Rose Marie Lowry-Townsend (D)	14,868	(48%)
1996 Primary		
Rose Marie Lowry-Townsend (D)	15,925	(30%)
Mike McIntyre (D)	12,327	(23%)
Glenn Jernigan (D)	9,920	(19%)
George W. Breece (D)	5,688	(11%)
Timothy M. "Tim" Dunn (D)	4,868	(9%)
Marcus W. Williams (D)	3,162	(6%)
Howard M. Greenebaum (D)	794	(2%)

CAMPAIGN FINANCE

	Receipts	Receipts from PACs	Expend-itures
1996			
McIntyre (D)	$491,852	$126,421 (26%)	$490,063
Caster (R)	$333,767	$ 96,088 (29%)	$332,746

DISTRICT VOTE FOR PRESIDENT

	1996		1992
D	71,849 (44%)	D	70,664 (43%)
R	79,843 (49%)	R	70,136 (43%)
I	11,961 (7%)	I	22,216 (14%)

KEY VOTES

1997	
Ban "partial birth" abortions	Y

8 W.G. 'Bill' Hefner (D)

Of Concord — Elected 1974, 12th term

Biographical Information
Born: April 11, 1930, Elora, Tenn.
Education: Sardis H.S., graduated 1948.
Occupation: Broadcasting executive.
Family: Wife, Nancy Hill; two children.
Religion: Baptist.
Political Career: No previous office.
Capitol Office: 2470 Rayburn Bldg. 20515; 225-3715.

Committees
Appropriations
Military Construction (ranking); National Security

In Washington: Like the poet Juvenal's black swan, Hefner is an increasingly rare specimen — a loyally Democratic white from a politically competitive Southern House district. In his opposition to the GOP's legislative agenda and his work as the top Democrat on an Appropriations subcommittee, Hefner expresses an abiding concern for the "little guy," and that emphasis has carried him successfully through 12 House elections.

Like other Democrats new to life in the minority, Hefner was not afraid during the 104th Congress to let fly with some rhetorical barbs, although his manner was congenial and his barbs were softened by a cover of folksiness. Here, for instance, is Hefner on the $189 billion GOP tax cut plan in 1995: "This package is like the lady that had the ugly baby that was so ugly, she had to tie a pork chop around its neck to get the dog to play with it. That it how bad this bill is."

Although Hefner was an active presence on the floor during the 104th, most of his energies were devoted to his work as ranking member of Appropriations' Military Construction Subcommittee. Hefner, who chaired the panel for the dozen years leading up to the Republican takeover, got along well with the panel's new GOP leaders in the 104th. The subcommittee's chairman for the 105th is Republican Ron Packard of California, who is also an agreeable sort.

The subcommittee's spending bill is usually the least controversial in the House, although certain funding projects drew wary glances from deficit hawks during the 104th. The panel oversees locally popular military facilities projects such as housing, hospitals and road improvements. Hefner has used his senior position to press for a better quality of life for soldiers. (He also serves on Appropriations' National Security Subcommittee.)

Hefner went along with GOP efforts to boost military construction spending above the level requested by the Pentagon — although he opposed such moves on the larger general defense spending package. But he sometimes criticized GOP priorities in an era of diminished funds. About a missile defense system, Hefner said, "If you buy something like Star Wars, it is going to come from someplace, and it is going to come from the unsexy sector, like barracks . . . if you talk about Star Wars and B-1s and B-2s . . . they are sexy items, but they do not get the job done."

Even in complaint, Hefner remained genial and was often humorous. At an Appropriations meeting, Hefner complained, "Mr. Chairman, the committee is not in order. We're having trouble sleeping over here." And, like many members, Hefner had complaints about the alternatively hectic and erratic floor schedule during the 104th. Hefner joshed the presiding member in March 1995, "Just in the spirit of being family-friendly, I was just curious to know what time we might be able to go home and watch the Andy Griffith reruns, if it would be possible."

But Hefner is not a rickety Old South solon of the Hollywood stereotype; he defends many tenets of the national Democratic faith and even speaks up for President Clinton, never wildly popular in the 8th. He supported several of the GOP's major policy offerings, including tougher restrictions on illegal immigrants, easing of federal regulations and a balanced-budget constitutional amendment. But he was strictly opposed to other signature GOP elements, including a term-limits amendment, the tax-cut plan and the unsuccessful Medicare overhaul.

During floor debate over the Republican plan to revamp welfare in March 1995, Hefner railed against it. And when another version was considered in July 1996, Hefner had no kinder words to say, taking particular exception to an amendment by Bob Ney, R-Ohio, that would have limited adults to three months' receipt of food stamps until they reached age 50, unless they worked at least half the time. Hefner called it "the most mean-spirited amendment that I have ever seen on any bill. If this is what you have to do to get re-elected to this Congress, I do not want to be a part of this body any longer." The stricture was softened in the final package, which Hefner found

NORTH CAROLINA 8
South Central — Kannapolis, part of Fayetteville

Geography and jobs determine politics in the 8th. Along the I-77 and I-85 corridors, the textile-producing counties are wealthier and vote Republican. The poorer, rural counties that make up the district's eastern portion are Democratic.

The Republican voters of the 8th can be divided into two groups. The textile workers of Rowan and Cabarrus counties are centered in the towns of Concord, Kannapolis and Salisbury. They make textiles and textile machinery, and there is some tobacco processing.

Only part of Salisbury (Rowan County) is in the 8th, but all of Kannapolis is included. All of Cabarrus County (Concord), on the southern border of Rowan, is within 8th District confines.

Farther south, the Republican vote is of a suburban variety, in the Charlotte orbit (Mecklenburg County). Only a tiny part of Mecklenburg itself is in the 8th; the real lode of GOP votes is found in the bedroom communities of Union County, which is the district's second most populous county after Cabarrus.

The vote here has become increasingly Republican over the past two decades. Many of these voters live in Charlotte satellites such as Indian Trail, Stallings, and Monroe, the Union County seat. Concord has also seen some spillover from Charlotte. Democrat Hefner got only 42 percent in Union County in 1996, losing the county by a nearly 5,000-vote margin.

Hefner won re-election to the House seat with 55 percent of the votes, even as Bob Dole carried the district's western section by a wide enough margin to carry the overall district with 49 percent.

Anson County and the counties east of the Pee Dee River are more rural and agriculture-oriented; they also have a higher percentage of black voters than the rest of the 8th. Under a new map approved in 1997 by the North Carolina General Assembly, which was still pending judicial approval, the total black population of the district would grow to 28 percent.

Blacks and American Indians currently make up a majority in the Democratic stronghold of Hoke County.

A small portion of Robeson County — home to a significant number of Lumbee Indians — is grafted onto the district's far southeastern fringe. Most of the county's Democratic-voting Indians are in the 7th District.

In 1996, Bill Clinton and Hefner carried Anson, Hoke, Richmond and Robeson handily. Neighboring Cumberland County is home to Fort Bragg and a chunk of black voters. The county was parceled among the 1st, 7th and 8th districts, all of which delve into the city of Fayetteville. (The 1st would lose its share of Cumberland under the proposed new map.)

Moore County, in the Sandhills region, was once Democratic, but it is now an anomaly in the Democratic east. A steady stream of retirees to resorts and golfing communities has made it a Republican bastion. The county would move into the 6th District under the proposed new map.

1990 Population: 552,387. White 402,406 (73%), Black 128,417 (23%), Other 21,564 (4%). Hispanic origin 7,771 (1%). 18 and over 403,678 (73%), 62 and over 79,038 (14%). Median age: 33.

sufficiently satisfying to support. It's been two decades since Hefner cleared 60 percent at the polls, and he stated a clear-eyed concern that a vote against the welfare bill could be used politically against him.

Hefner voted along with most Democrats when there was a chance to express concern for organized labor's side of things, for instance on the bill to increase the minimum wage. He opposed a GOP initiative to allow employers to offer workers compensatory time off in lieu of overtime pay for extra hours worked; Hefner feared this could be used to coerce employees to take the time when they really wanted the money. Although GOP members tried to assure him that workers could seek redress from the Labor Department, headed during the first Clinton administration by Robert B. Reich, Hefner said, "I have an idea that 90 percent of the people in North Carolina do not have any idea who Mr. Reich is. I just think this is not a very good deal for the average working folks in the country."

Although military concerns absorb most of Hefner's energies, he does press for one pet issue: a return to public prayer. He has introduced legislation that would amend the Constitution to allow sanctioned prayer in schools and other public institutions. Hefner, a former gospel singer, has been known to sing renditions of his favorite hymns during political rallies.

After Missouri Republican Bill Emerson died in June 1996, Hefner paid tribute to him on the House floor with the words of Missouri gospel songwriter Albert B. Bromley: "I'll meet you in the morning with a how do you do, and we'll sit down by the river and with rapture our acquaintance renew, and you're going to know me in the morning by the smile that I wear, when I meet you in the morning in the city that is built four square."

First elected in 1974 on a promise to restore "Christian morality" to government, Hefner opposes abortion except in cases of rape, incest or when a woman's life is in danger, and he has backed conservatives' efforts to ban a particular abortion technique that opponents call "partial birth" abortion. In the 103rd, he supported a five-day waiting period requirement before the purchase of a handgun, but he joined 76 other Democrats in voting against a bill to ban certain semiautomatic assault-style weapons, and he backed a GOP move to repeal the ban in March 1996. (Hefner did vote in August 1994 for a broad anti-crime initiative pushed by the Clinton administration that included the assault weapons ban.)

An uncharacteristic explosion of temper in August 1992 left no doubt about Hefner's party loyalties. Flamboyant GOP Rep. Robert K. Dornan of California denounced Democratic presidential candidate Bill Clinton on the House floor as a "womanizer/adulterer" and a "draft dodger." After his speech, Hefner, who had undergone heart bypass surgery only two months earlier, confronted and almost came to blows with Dornan.

At Home: After almost being dragged under by GOP presidential victories in 1984 and 1988, Hefner survived the conservative surge that brought Republicans control of Congress in 1994. His staunchly conservative GOP opponent, businessman Sherrill Morgan, spent about $190,000 of his own money on his effort. A good portion of this was aimed at TV ads that accused Hefner of successfully pushing for federal funding to develop recreation areas and land acquisition in a national forest in order to boost the value of property he owned near it. Hefner denied the allegation, noting that the value of the property did not increase. Hefner, who scraped by with 51 percent in 1984 and 1988, took 52 percent against Morgan.

In 1984, Hefner's GOP opponent was Harris D. Blake, a hardware store owner and former member of the Moore County Board of Education who had challenged him two years earlier. Hefner eked out a victory over Blake by clinging to his base among the traditionally Democratic counties at the district's southern end.

Two years later, Hefner climbed up to 58 percent, but 1988 brought more trouble. Lawyer Ted Blanton put himself in a position to ride a wave of GOP presidential votes, and it carried him to 49 percent overall; Hefner again survived because of his strong base in the Democratic counties in the district's southern end.

In 1996, Hefner took advantage of an improved performance by Clinton and other top-of-the-ticket Democrats in the 8th to post an 11-point victory over former educator and rental housing owner Curtis Blackwood. Blackwood had bumped off Morgan in a GOP runoff, but his underfunded fall campaign never found its legs.

Hefner's hymn-singing and his pledges in 1974 to revive Christian morality might have been seen as an incautious church-state mixture in some places, but not in the Bible Belt 8th. As a promoter and singer of gospel music in the Carolinas and Virginia, Hefner had made many local and statewide TV appearances. With his excellent name recognition, he gradually won back thousands of conservative Democrats who had drifted toward GOP Rep. Earl B. Ruth. Hefner's blend of inspiration, entertainment and politicking helped him soundly defeat Ruth.

HOUSE ELECTIONS

1996 General		
W.G. "Bill" Hefner (D)	103,129	(55%)
Curtis Blackwood (R)	81,676	(44%)
Thomas W. Carlisle (NL)	2,103	(1%)
1994 General		
W.G. "Bill" Hefner (D)	62,845	(52%)
Sherrill Morgan (R)	57,140	(48%)

Previous Winning Percentages: **1992** (58%) **1990** (55%) **1988** (51%) **1986** (58%) **1984** (51%) **1982** (57%) **1980** (59%) **1978** (59%) **1976** (66%) **1974** (57%)

CAMPAIGN FINANCE

	Receipts	Receipts from PACs	Expend-itures
1996			
Hefner (D)	$636,583	$378,503 (59%)	$555,614
Blackwood (R)	$154,066	$5,116 (3%)	$151,081
1994			
Hefner (D)	$642,894	$378,444 (59%)	$669,622
Morgan (R)	$321,395	$1,014 (0%)	$320,520

DISTRICT VOTE FOR PRESIDENT

1996		1992	
D	80,557 (43%)	D	81,697 (42%)
R	91,316 (49%)	R	85,758 (44%)
I	14,603 (8%)	I	27,019 (14%)

KEY VOTES

1997	
Ban "partial-birth" abortions	Y
1996	
Approve farm bill	Y
Deny public education to illegal immigrants	Y
Repeal ban on certain assault-style weapons	Y
Increase minimum wage	Y
Freeze defense spending	N
Approve welfare overhaul	Y
1995	
Approve balanced-budget constitutional amendment	Y
Relax Clean Water Act regulations	Y
Oppose limits on environmental regulations	Y
Reduce projected Medicare spending	N
Approve GOP budget with tax and spending cuts	N

VOTING STUDIES

	Presidential Support		Party Unity		Conservative Coalition	
Year	S	O	S	O	S	O
1996	71	29	75	24	94	6
1995	74	25	75	16	67	24
1994	79	21	90	7	67	28
1993	79	19	88	8	64	32
1992	13	53	61	8	38	21
1991	34	59	79	16	78	19

INTEREST GROUP RATINGS

Year	ADA	AFL-CIO	CCUS	ACU
1996	55	n/a	38	30
1995	75	83	42	9
1994	65	89	45	19
1993	65	92	27	13
1992	40	88	17	6
1991	55	91	40	10

9 Sue Myrick (R)

Of Charlotte — Elected 1994, 2nd term

Biographical Information

Born: Aug. 1, 1941, Tiffin, Ohio.

Education: Heidelberg College, 1959-60.

Occupation: Advertising executive.

Family: Husband, Ed Myrick; two children, three stepchildren.

Religion: Evangelical Methodist.

Political Career: Candidate for Charlotte City Council, 1981; Charlotte City Council, 1983-85; sought Republican nomination for mayor of Charlotte, 1984; mayor of Charlotte, 1987-91; sought Republican nomination for U.S. Senate, 1992.

Capitol Office: 230 Cannon Bldg. 20515; 225-1976.

Committees

Rules

Rules & Organization of the House

In Washington: Upscale Sun Belt conservatives are an increasingly influential voting bloc in the national Republican Party, and Myrick, a former mayor of Charlotte, embodies that constituency. Her status as the only woman from a Southern district in the GOP House Class of 1994 helped attract the attention of her classmates and the Republican leadership, and she has served as a liaison between those two camps.

At times that has been a challenging role for Myrick, who is staunchly conservative but also understands that loyalty to party leaders sometimes demands compromise. Myrick has struck the balance well enough that at the start of the 105th Congress, she was rewarded with a seat on the Rules Committee.

One clash of principle and pragmatism confronted Myrick in early 1996, when the collapse of budget talks between the White House and Congress had resulted in a partial shutdown of the federal government. Republican leaders, seeing that their party was being blamed for the shutdown, urged compromise, but some GOP freshmen were loath to come to terms with President Clinton. Myrick, then a member of the Budget Committee, decided to back the leadership's decision to deal with Clinton on the budget and get the government open again.

In June 1996, though, Myrick was one of 19 Republicans — 16 of them freshmen — who voted against their party leadership on the fiscal 1997 budget resolution. The defectors complained that the measure forecast a temporary spike in the deficit in 1997 and 1998 before forcing it down to zero in 2002. Many also were unhappy that Senate Republicans had added more spending for domestic programs in the budget, and that the House GOP leadership went along. Despite the defections, the resolution passed, 216-211.

Myrick's rhetoric often does not seem to leave much room for pragmatism. In 1995, she told the Washington Times, "I ran on a campaign of, 'If you want pork, don't send me,' because I am not going to bring home the bacon. I'm there to make the decisions that need to be made. I'm going to take a lot of heat, but we've got to do it. . . . We'll make the cuts necessary. It is a fact that government is not there to take care of all of us."

From her seat on the Budget Committee, Myrick had a role in framing the House GOP's demands going into the 1995 budget debate, and she particularly pressed the freshmen's view that any agreement should erase the deficit within seven years. Portraying her aversion to federal red ink as a "pro-family" stand, Myrick urged members in 1995 ". . . to vote for a balanced budget . . . on behalf of our children and our children's children."

Myrick's emphasis on "traditional values" led her to join the Congressional Family Caucus, founded in 1995 by Oklahoma Republican Tom Coburn, whose legislative priorities include restoring voluntary school prayer, reaffirming parental rights, establishing abstinence-based sex education, enacting tougher laws against obscenity and child pornography and eliminating the federal financing of abortion. "The Family Caucus will do its part to help restore the moral foundation on which this great nation was built . . . a foundation that strengthens family ties and encourages traditional values, personal responsibility and the rule of law," Myrick said.

Myrick employs a "pro-family" argument in promoting a GOP initiative to allow companies to offer employees compensatory time off in lieu of overtime pay, a measure the House passed in both 1996 and 1997.

Citing the desire of many working parents for schedule flexibility, Myrick said, "Comp time is pro-family, pro-worker, and when we really think about it, a pro-child approach to provide relief to the hard-working men and women across our nation who struggle daily to support their families." Many labor unions and their congressional Democratic supporters fear that companies would coerce employees into taking time off, even if a worker really wanted overtime pay.

Late in the 104th Congress, Myrick expressed support for a constitutional amendment that

NORTH CAROLINA 9
West Central — Part of Charlotte

The boom times of the 1970s and 1980s transformed Charlotte into the economic colossus of North Carolina and a rival to Atlanta in regional economic clout.

With a highly diversified economy, Charlotte serves as a supply, service and distribution center for the Piedmont regions of North and South Carolina. The city's big banking concerns have expanded their influence beyond the Southeast, becoming prominent players in financial affairs all along the Eastern seaboard. Adding to its emerging stature as a nationally prominent city is the recent arrival of the Charlotte Hornets professional basketball team and Carolina Panthers professional football team.

The Uptown central business district has the headquarters of the Duke Power Co., NationsBank and First Union Bank as well as numerous other banking and insurance operations. Many of the white-collar executives who work in the downtown office towers commute from the affluent southeastern part of the city, the base of the old-line GOP establishment.

The city's Republican leanings are leavened by working-class Democratic allegiances and a black community that accounts for one-third of the population. The city weathered racial tensions over busing in the early 1970s, and in 1983 Charlotte elected its first black mayor, Harvey B. Gantt. He won virtually all the black vote and also drew significant white support.

Attending Charlotte's economic prosperity has been rampant growth in the city and surrounding Mecklenburg County, leading to problems with traffic congestion and scraps between established neighborhoods and developers. The county once had substantial rural areas, particularly in the north, but the pastoral lands are giving way to suburban sprawl.

Politically, Mecklenburg is a mixed bag. Blacks and working-class whites keep the county competitive for Democrats at the state and local levels. In 1990, Gantt, the Democratic nominee against GOP Sen. Jesse Helms, carried 58 percent of the county's vote. Mecklenberg was the only county in the district that Gantt won in 1996. Former Democratic Gov. James B. Hunt Jr. won Mecklenburg with 53 percent in his successful 1992 bid to recapture the office, and won the county with ease again in 1996.

Presidential elections are a different story. The county has gone Republican in the past five White House contests. Overall, Bob Dole easily carried the district in 1996 with 56 percent.

The 9th used to contain the county in its entirety, but 1992 redistricting divided it between the 9th and 12th districts (with a small part in the 8th). Most of the county's blacks, who live north and west of the central city, are included in the black-majority 12th.

Mecklenburg County has roughly two-thirds of the 9th's population, and, without Charlotte's black votes, the district is a GOP stronghold.

The 12th cuts a thin line west through the 9th, into Gastonia (Gaston County) to siphon out more black votes. Most of the Republican, textile-oriented county is in the 9th, though, accounting for about one-quarter of the district's voters.

1990 Population: 552,387. White 492,424 (89%), Black 49,308 (9%), Other 10,655 (2%). Hispanic origin 5,820 (1%). 18 and over 421,616 (76%), 62 and over 69,897 (13%). Median age: 33.

would narrow the scope of the "speech and debate" clause of Article I. That clause exempts lawmakers from prosecution or legal claim for "any Speech or Debate in either House" — language that courts have interpreted broadly as allowing congressmen to say what they please in the line of duty. Myrick's proposal would allow members of Congress to be held liable for false statements or false communications they make. As punishment for violators, Myrick proposed fines of up to $10,000.

Early in the 105th, though, Myrick voted "no" when the House reprimanded Speaker Newt Gingrich and assessed him a $300,000 penalty for providing "inaccurate, incomplete and unreliable statements" to the House ethics committee regarding his political fundraising activities.

During her first year in Washington, Myrick, along with Kansas Rep. Sam Brownback, headed a task force of freshman Republicans that scrutinized the Department of Housing and Urban Development (HUD) and recommended terminating the agency in five years. The task force proposed creating an agency to oversee the dismantling of HUD and replacing public housing programs with a voucher system.

In another effort at fiscal austerity, Myrick opposed a plan to move a statue of three women suffragists to the Capitol Rotunda. The Italian marble statue — a triple bust of Lucretia Mott, Susan B. Anthony and Elizabeth Cady Stanton that commemorates their role in getting women the vote in 1920 — was residing on a lower floor in the Capitol. In July 1995, the Senate passed a resolution to authorize moving the statue up into the Rotunda, which is home to the busts of famous American men. But when House GOP leaders tried to pass the resolution by unanimous consent, Myrick objected. The resolution authorized using funds from the office of the Architect of the Capitol to move the statue, but Myrick said that was not a "judicious" use of taxpayer money.

She said she supported moving the statue, but wanted private-sector money to cover the relocation expenses.

Congress again approved the relocation of the statute in the fall of 1996, but only if the move was paid for with private funds. It also specified that the relocation would be good for only a year, after which a bipartisan commission would select the statue's permanent home. But a new wrinkle developed in the spring of 1997 when a black women's group argued that any monument commemorating the women's suffrage movement should include Sojourner Truth, a 19th century black abolitionist and feminist. Despite their concerns, the statue was moved in May 1997 after $75,000 in private funds were raised.

While some fiscally conservative GOP women in Congress are moderates on social issues, Myrick sticks to the right down the line. She opposes abortion, voted to repeal the ban on certain semiautomatic assault-style weapons and favors the death penalty.

At Home: After five-term GOP Rep. Alex McMillan announced his retirement from the 9th in 1994, Myrick's background as a Charlotte City Council member, two-term mayor and 1992 candidate for the GOP Senate nomination gave her wide name recognition going into a five-way House primary.

But she struggled in the first-round voting, finishing first with a 34 percent tally. Before the runoff, though, news broke that her opponent, state House Minority Leader David Balmer, had included falsehoods in his résumé. Myrick rolled to nomination with 68 percent of the vote. In November, she met only modest resistance from the Democratic nominee, retired pharmacist and businessman Rory Blake, and won election with 65 percent. In 1996, she won a second term with 63 percent against the spirited but long-shot challenge of Democrat Michael C. "Mike" Daisley, a Charlotte lawyer.

Myrick seems secure in the 9th, but before she won election to the House, her political career had ups and downs. She lost her first campaign for City Council in 1981, then won that office in 1983. In 1985 she lost a mayoral bid, but in 1987 she won the office, ousting Harvey B. Gantt. She won re-election in 1989, but feuded with conservative religious activists. When she sought the Republican Senate nomination in 1992, she failed to carry Charlotte and took 30 percent statewide, running 18 points behind nominee and eventual winner Lauch Faircloth.

Like two other North Carolinians in Congress – Sen. Faircloth and Democratic Rep. W.G. "Bill" Hefner – Myrick does not have a college degree. She is a mother of two, stepmother of three and ran a company doing advertising, marketing and public relations.

HOUSE ELECTIONS

1996 General		
Sue Myrick (R)	147,755	(63%)
Michel C. "Mike" Daisley (D)	83,078	(35%)
1994 General		
Sue Myrick (R)	82,374	(65%)
Rory Blake (D)	44,379	(35%)

CAMPAIGN FINANCE

	Receipts	Receipts from PACs	Expend-itures
1996			
Myrick (R)	$544,223	$233,202 (43%)	$547,194
Daisley (D)	$64,614	$6,050 (9%)	$63,598
Knight (LIBERT)	$4,720	0	$4,720
1994			
Myrick (R)	$669,525	$169,148 (25%)	$663,405
Blake (D)	$88,351	$35,550 (40%)	$85,458

DISTRICT VOTE FOR PRESIDENT

	1996		1992
D	88,996 (38%)	**D**	80,953 (33%)
R	130,152 (56%)	**R**	131,335 (53%)
I	13,892 (6%)	**I**	36,706 (15%)

KEY VOTES

1997	
Ban "partial birth" abortions	Y
1996	
Approve farm bill	Y
Deny public education to illegal immigrants	Y
Repeal ban on certain assault-style weapons	Y
Increase minimum wage	N
Freeze defense spending	N
Approve welfare overhaul	Y
1995	
Approve balanced-budget constitutional amendment	Y
Relax Clean Water Act regulations	Y
Oppose limits on environmental regulations	N
Reduce projected Medicare spending	Y
Approve GOP budget with tax and spending cuts	Y

VOTING STUDIES

	Presidential Support		Party Unity		Conservative Coalition	
Year	**S**	**O**	**S**	**O**	**S**	**O**
1996	33	66	95	4	92	8
1995	17	82	97	2	95	4

INTEREST GROUP RATINGS

Year	ADA	AFL-CIO	CCUS	ACU
1996	10	n/a	88	100
1995	0	0	100	96

10 Cass Ballenger (R)

Of Hickory — Elected 1986; 6th full term

Biographical Information
Born: Dec. 6, 1926, Hickory, N.C.
Education: U. of North Carolina, 1944-45; Amherst College, B.A. 1948.
Military Service: Navy Air Corps, 1944-45.
Occupation: Plastics company executive.
Family: Wife, Donna Davis; three children.
Religion: Episcopalian.
Political Career: Catawba County Board of Commissioners, 1966-74, chairman, 1970-74; N.C. House, 1975-77; N.C. Senate, 1977-86.

Capitol Office: 2182 Rayburn Bldg. 20515; 225 2576.

Committees
Education & Workforce
Employer-Employee Relations; Workforce Protections (chairman)
International Relations
International Operations & Human Rights; Western Hemisphere

In Washington: Ballenger brings the perspective of a conservative businessman to Congress, and he has a chance to push his philosophy into policy as chairman of the Workforce Protections Subcommittee on the Education and the Workforce Committee.

When Democrats controlled Congress, Ballenger frequently was at odds with the proposals advanced by the pro-labor liberals running what was then called the Education and Labor Committee. Now those liberals gnash their teeth at many of the pro-business measures advanced by Ballenger.

Chief among his concerns is an effort aimed at curtailing the regulatory powers of the Labor Department's Occupational Safety and Health Administration (OSHA). Created by Congress in 1970 to help ensure the safety and health of U.S. workers, OSHA has become the target of virulent criticism by many in the business community, who contend the agency is often punitive in its actions and damaging to businesses.

Early in the 104th, Ballenger introduced a bill with sweeping OSHA revisions that would have required the agency to work with businesses mostly as a safety consultant rather than as an enforcer. The measure would have required workers to report hazardous conditions to their employers before contacting OSHA, and much of the agency's budget would have been shifted from enforcement to educational programs. Labor activists picketed and demonstrated at Ballenger's district offices, contending the bill would lead to unhealthy and unsafe workplaces.

Yet Ballenger, who has long had a reputation as being a foe of the safety agency, found himself under pressure from the members of the GOP Class of 1994, who were even more zealous about reining in OSHA. "I keep telling those wild freshmen of mine that we haven't accomplished anything if we don't get the president to sign it," Ballenger said.

But House leaders decided not to give the sweeping OSHA bill top priority, and Ballenger concluded that it would never be enacted. So in 1996, he put forth a measure seeking more limited changes to the workplace safety agency. This bill would apply cost-benefit analysis to new regulations issued by OSHA.

It would also give the secretary of Labor the right to waive any fines against businesses of 250 or fewer employees if a minor safety violation is corrected quickly, or if the money for the fine is used to fix the problem. Also, OSHA inspectors could issue no citations for paperwork violations unless an employer "has willfully or repeatedly violated" a regulation or if the violation had exposed a worker to a safety hazard.

"It doesn't help workers when OSHA spends its time and a company's time and money issuing penalties for insignificant problems, instead of preventing truly serious hazards," Ballenger said. His subcommittee approved the measure in April 1996.

Ballenger also is in charge of pushing the GOP's so-called "comp time" legislation, a high priority for the party. It would allow companies to offer their employees compensatory time off instead of pay for overtime work. The measure made it through the House in the 104th but went no further. To underscore its importance, the Republican leadership gave Ballenger the honor of introducing it as the first bill in the 105th. It passed the House on a 222-210 vote in March 1997, but met stiff resistance from Senate Democrats later in the spring, and faced a presidential veto threat.

Labor unions and their Democratic supporters oppose the measure on the grounds that it gives too much power to the employer, but Ballenger says the measure makes clear that it is the worker, not the employer, who decides whether to take overtime pay or comp time.

The crux of the dispute is whether the bill would allow employers to coerce workers into accepting compensatory time instead of the time-and-a-half pay for work beyond 40 hours a week that existing law requires for most workers. Ballenger and other supporters said the measure would simply give employees something that

NORTH CAROLINA 10
West — Hickory; Lincolnton

Splashed across the western Piedmont Plateau and the Appalachian and Blue Ridge mountains is North Carolina's most rock-ribbed Republican district: the 10th.

In 1990, GOP Sen. Jesse Helms posted his best showing in any district in what was the 10th before redistricting in 1992, capturing 66 percent of the vote. Helms also did well here six years later in his rematch against Democrat Harvey B. Gantt. He won Catawba County, the largest county wholly contained in the 10th, with 62 percent, 9 points above his statewide average. In presidential voting, Bob Dole won the 10th with 60 percent of the vote, one of his better showings nationally. Dole easily won every county or portion of a county that makes up the 10th.

Ballenger also carried every county in the House race, most of them by more than 2-to-1. He coasted to a 6th term, winning 70 percent of the votes.

The 10th is composed of six whole counties and parts of 11 more. It is small-town North Carolina: No city has more than 30,000 residents. Textiles, furniture and agriculture form the backbone of the economy.

From the main body of the district, three heads sprout forth: one in the north, one reaching northwest to the Tennessee border and one stretching west toward Asheville, but stopping short.

Catawba County is in the main cluster of counties. The furniture-making industry — particularly upholstered furniture — employs a large segment of the work force in Hickory (the largest city entirely in the 10th). There also is production of cotton and synthetic yarns.

Neighboring Iredell County — split among the 8th, 10th and 12th districts — is mostly rural and agricultural, with some manufacturing. It is the second most populous jurisdiction in the 10th.

Northeast of Catawba County, the district takes in parts of Davie and Forsyth counties and all of Yadkin County. The Forsyth portion is west of Winston-Salem.

Textile- and furniture-oriented Davie and textile- and tobacco-producing Yadkin are diehard Republican bastions. Yadkin was one of just 13 North Carolina counties to back Barry Goldwater in 1964. Both counties went for Dole by better than 2-to-1 in 1996.

West of Yadkin County, the district line makes a loop through Republican Wilkes County. A section of the 5th District slices down into the 10th; beyond it are more Republican votes in mountainous Avery and Mitchell counties, on the Tennessee border.

A segment of the 10th reaches into the woodlands of Western North Carolina, taking in parts of Buncombe, Henderson, McDowell, Polk and Rutherford counties. Forestry, tourism and recreation are staples of the local economies here. Buncombe is competitive for both parties, although Dole still carried it with 54 percent. The other counties lean Republican.

1990 Population: 552,386. White 517,542 (94%), Black 30,155 (5%), Other 4,689 (1%). Hispanic origin 3,991 (1%). 18 and over 421,456 (76%), 62 and over 83,185 (15%). Median age: 35.

polls suggest 75 percent of them want: a choice between money and time off.

"This really is motherhood and apple pie," Ballenger said. "They just haven't recognized it yet."

Ballenger was also an opponent in the 104th of raising the minimum wage, arguing that it would hurt small businesses by increasing labor costs and ultimately costing jobs. Congressional Democrats began to agitate in early 1996 for a wage increase of 90 cents over two years. Ballenger's response was to join with Arkansas Republican Tim Hutchinson and offer a proposal to leave the minimum wage at $4.25 but revamp the earned-income tax credit to raise hourly wages to $7 for families with one child and $8 for families with two or more children.

The proposal, however, highlighted divisions in GOP ranks. In proposing the alternative, Republicans were essentially conceding that working people need help, if not through a higher minimum wage then through another mechanism. The minimum wage increase eventually cleared the House in August 1996, after it was combined with other provisions sought by Republicans, including $10 billion in business tax cuts over five years, a $5,000 tax credit to offset the cost of adoption and an expansion of Individual Retirement Accounts.

Acknowledging a deep interest in foreign policy, especially in Central America, Ballenger is also a member of the International Relations Committee.

In the years when Congress hotly debated U.S. support for the Nicaraguan contras, Ballenger took a personal interest in the region; he and his wife had performed volunteer work in Guatemala in the 1970s. In October 1987, they went to Nicaragua to help restart Radio Catolica, the voice of the Catholic Church. Shortly after Radio Catolica resumed broadcasting, the Sandinista government renewed its censorship of the station. Incensed, Ballenger took to the House floor to denounce the government and called those sympathetic to it "witless peaceniks."

In the 104th Congress, he was asked to join an

eight-member International Relations select subcommittee to investigate the Clinton administration's tacit acceptance of letting Iran arm the Bosnian Muslims, in defiance of an international arms embargo on warring parties in the former Yugoslavia. Republicans charged that by not revealing what it knew about the Iranian arms transfer, the administration misled Congress, broke faith with U.S. allies in Europe and allowed Iran to gain a foothold in Europe. Democrats countered that Republicans were conducting a political witch-hunt on behalf of the GOP presidential nominee Bob Dole.

The health of the nation's textile industry is a special concern to Ballenger. His district leads the nation in textile workers, and helping the industry was one reason Ballenger gave his support to NAFTA in the 103rd Congress.

He told the House that his plastics company was a supplier to the textile industry for 40 years and that when his company lost customers, "they did not go to Mexico, they went to the Far East." Ballenger said that since 1987, reduced trade barriers with Mexico had increased demand for North Carolina-made goods and services and that dropping all trade barriers would clearly increase state exports.

At Home: The 10th District was open in 1986 because its veteran incumbent, Republican James T. Broyhill, had been appointed to the Senate. Both Ballenger and his chief GOP rival, George S. Robinson, promised to emulate Broyhill.

Ballenger was a state senator who had founded a plastics company and built it into a 250-employee business. He reminded audiences that he had been on the state advisory budget commission under two GOP governors and had once served on a White House panel on economic affairs. Robinson, a pro-business state representative from Broyhill's hometown of Lenoir, was president of a lumber company.

Robinson's backers pointed out that their candidate, who at age 40 was roughly 20 years younger than Ballenger, would be able to build seniority the way Broyhill had. But Ballenger enhanced his link with Broyhill by endorsing him in his Senate primary fight, then chastising Robinson for not doing the same. (Robinson subsequently did.)

Ballenger also accused Robinson of having ties to the National Congressional Club, GOP Sen. Jesse Helms' political organization, which was backing Broyhill's primary foe. The claim irked some Robinson supporters all the way through November. Robinson had no official links to the club and did have ties to Broyhill: He started his political career as Broyhill's campaign driver.

Ballenger, a former Catawba County commissioner, had a strong base in what was then the district's second-largest county, and he ran harder than Robinson in the populous city of Gastonia. In November, Ballenger won a comfortable 57 percent against Democrat Lester D. Roark, a former mayor of Shelby.

In subsequent elections, Ballenger has won easily, never falling below 61 percent.

HOUSE ELECTIONS

1996 General		
Cass Ballenger (R)	158,585	(70%)
Ben Neill (D)	65,103	(29%)
Richard Kahn (NL)	2,909	(1%)
1994 General		
Cass Ballenger (R)	107,829	(72%)
Robert Wayne Avery (D)	42,939	(28%)

Previous Winning Percentages: **1992** (63%) **1990** (62%) **1988** (61%) **1986*** (57%)

** Elected to a full term and to fill a vacancy at the same time.*

CAMPAIGN FINANCE

	Receipts	Receipts from PACs	Expend-itures
1996			
Ballenger (R)	$257,800	$157,718 (61%)	$244,447
Neill (D)	$17,995	$2,500 (14%)	$17,993
1994			
Ballenger (R)	$259,352	$124,998 (48%)	$221,536

DISTRICT VOTE FOR PRESIDENT

1996		1992	
D	71,027 (31%)	**D**	76,021 (32%)
R	136,759 (60%)	**R**	127,067 (53%)
I	17,926 (8%)	**I**	35,546 (15%)

KEY VOTES

1997	
Ban "partial birth" abortions	Y
1996	
Approve farm bill	Y
Deny public education to illegal immigrants	Y
Repeal ban on certain assault-style weapons	Y
Increase minimum wage	N
Freeze defense spending	N
Approve welfare overhaul	Y
1995	
Approve balanced-budget constitutional amendment	Y
Relax Clean Water Act regulations	Y
Oppose limits on environmental regulations	N
Reduce projected Medicare spending	Y
Approve GOP budget with tax and spending cuts	Y

VOTING STUDIES

	Presidential Support		Party Unity		Conservative Coalition	
Year	S	O	S	O	S	O
1996	33	67	95	5	98	0
1995	17	82	95	3	95	3
1994	35	62	95	2	86	8
1993	29	71	93†	6†	86	14
1992	69	27	90	6	83	10
1991	79	17	93	3	100	0

INTEREST GROUP RATINGS

Year	ADA	AFL-CIO	CCUS	ACU
1996	0	n/a	100	100
1995	0	0	96	88
1994	5	0	92	90
1993	11†	0	100	87†
1992	10	27	75	92
1991	10	17	90	95

† Not eligible for all recorded votes.

11 Charles H. Taylor (R)

Of Brevard — Elected 1990, 4th term

Biographical Information

Born: Jan. 23, 1941, Brevard, N.C.

Education: Wake Forest U., B.A. 1963, J.D. 1966.

Occupation: Tree farmer.

Family: Wife, Elizabeth Owen; three children.

Religion: Baptist.

Political Career: N.C. House, 1967-73, minority leader, 1969-71; N.C. Senate, 1973-75, minority leader, 1973-75; Republican nominee for U.S. House, 1988.

Capitol Office: 231 Cannon Bldg. 20515; 225-6401.

Committees

Appropriations

Commerce, Justice, State & Judiciary; District of Columbia (chairman); Interior

In Washington: Taking the gavel in the 105th Congress at the Appropriations' Subcommittee on the District of Columbia, Taylor enters the "college of cardinals" — the 13 Appropriations subcommittee chairmen who hold considerable sway on spending bills.

With fellow North Carolinian Lauch Faircloth chairing the D.C. subcommittee of the Senate Appropriations Committees, the two panels that handle finances for the nation's capital are in Southern hands for the first time since two Democrats, Sen. Lawton Chiles of Florida and Rep. William H. Natcher of Kentucky, ruled the roost during the 94th Congress, 1975-76.

But Faircloth and Taylor are a lot more conservative than Chiles and Natcher were. "The District's ox is in a ditch and we've got to get it out," Taylor told The Washington Post early in his tenure as subcommittee chairman.

When President Clinton in January 1997 proposed his own plan to restructure the District of Columbia's finances, Taylor said he would consider the idea but summarized it as "throwing money at difficult problems."

Taylor landed a coveted seat on Appropriations in the 103rd Congress, becoming the first North Carolina lawmaker to sit on that panel in more than four decades.

A wealthy tree farmer, Taylor has his differences with those who would rather preserve trees than harvest them. It was Taylor who in March 1995 added a provision to a rescissions bill that would have required the sale of more than 6 billion board feet of lumber from dead or diseased trees over two years from lands managed by the Forest Service and the Bureau of Land Management. He said it would create thousands of jobs for workers displaced by restrictions on tree cutting and described it as emergency legislation aimed at clearing poor-quality timber that could spread disease and fuel wildfires. "It is an opportunity for us to provide forest health," Taylor said.

Opponents noted that the bill also allowed cutting live, healthy trees as part of a salvage operation. "The Taylor amendment is a timber lobbyist's dream," said Appropriations' Interior Subcommittee ranking Democrat Sidney R. Yates of Illinois. A Yates amendment to strip the salvage timber language from the bill was defeated on a 150-275 vote.

In May 1995, Taylor took to the House floor to defend the timber salvage measure. "Our forests are deteriorating in health because we are not managing them along the lines of our best scientific knowledge in forests," he said. "We have a well-funded special interest of environmental groups in Washington that take in over $600 million, and they take in that money by scaring people into thinking the last tree is going to be cut tomorrow or some other fantasy in order to bring those hundreds of millions of dollars in to themselves."

Clinton vetoed the initial rescissions bill in June. Following negotiations with the White House, Congress cleared a second version of the bill in July, which Clinton signed. The latter legislation also contained a timber salvage provision.

Nevertheless, responding to the objections of environmentalists in the Pacific Northwest who contended that timber companies were overcutting healthy trees, Elizabeth Furse, D-Ore., tried to eliminate the program in June 1996. Taylor argued that it was a necessary step to protect the health of the nation's timber and preventing forest fires. Furse's amendment to the fiscal 1997 interior appropriations bill failed, 209-211.

Earlier that month, Yates tried to amend the bill in subcommittee to cut $14 million from the timber management budget. "This is a $14 million gift to the timber industry in the form of new subsidies," Yates said. Countered Taylor: "Mr. Yates would like us to have no harvesting in the forest industry. The levels we have now will barely allow us to continue harvesting." Yates' amendment failed on a voice vote.

Taylor is a reliable conservative vote on most issues. "We know that the government will mess up a one-car funeral," he said in March 1996 as he

NORTH CAROLINA 11
West — Asheville

In the 1980s, the mountains of Western North Carolina were the stage for arguably the most competitive congressional district in the nation. In 1980, 1982, 1984, 1986 and 1990, voters tossed out their incumbent. Every contest between 1982 and 1990 was decided by fewer than 5,000 votes.

The 11th District is slightly more Democratic than it was in the 1980s, but as voters proved in the 1992 House race, party affiliation counts for little. Taylor has managed to hold the district for four terms, winning it with 60 percent in 1994 — the first time in two decades that a candidate has received a percentage that high. He polled 58 percent in 1996.

Most of the mountainous district is covered by the Cherokee, Nantahala and Pisgah national forests or the Great Smoky Mountains National Park. Accordingly, the local political and economic agenda often revolves around development and natural resource issues. Tourism and recreation revenues also have a disproportionate impact on local economies, especially in the poorer, far western tip of the state.

The heart of Western North Carolina is Asheville (Buncombe County). Known as "The Land of the Sky" for its location high in the Blue Ridge Mountains, the city is the biggest in the 11th.

An expanding health care industry and some light manufacturing anchor Asheville's economy, and the city is also a hub for the southern Appalachian and Cherokee arts and crafts produced in the region.

Asheville and surrounding communities have found recent years especially prosperous, due to a wave of newcomers who have discovered the region's low property taxes and temperate climate. Retirees and business executives seeking a second home have fueled a building boom in towns such as Flat Rock and Hendersonville in Henderson County, and in Tryon (Polk County), where upscale condominiums are popping up on mountainsides and in the piney woods. The University of North Carolina-Asheville has responded to the influx by setting up the North Carolina Center for Creative Retirement.

The combination of retirees and traditional mountain Republicans keeps the 11th competitive, despite a wide Democratic registration advantage. Two traditional sources of Democratic support — labor unions and black voters — are mostly absent from Asheville, but populous Buncombe County still tends to support Democrats for local and statewide office, though Taylor managed to carry it in both 1994 and 1996. Buncombe usually leans Republican in presidential elections, although it did back Bill Clinton in his two presidential races. About 30 percent of the 11th District's residents live here.

The second-most populous county in the 11th is Henderson. Retirees have helped move Henderson and Polk into the GOP column; both counties supported George Bush in 1988 and 1992 and Bob Dole in 1996. Outside Buncombe County, there is some labor strength in the paper and pulp mill towns.

1990 Population: 552,387. White 502,058 (91%), Black 39,767 (7%), Other 10,562 (2%). Hispanic origin 3,633 (1%). 18 and over 430,457 (78%), 62 and over 116,213 (21%). Median age: 38.

voted for an amendment by Bob Barr, R-Ga., that weakened legislation designed to give the government a stronger hand in fighting terrorism.

Early in the 105th Congress, Taylor opposed reinstating the tax on airline tickets. He voted against reprimanding Speaker Newt Gingrich for ethics violations. He opposed all efforts to raise the minimum wage, even voting against the final version, whose approval was a fait accompli.

A consistent opponent of abortion, he voted to outlaw a particular technique that opponents call a "partial-birth" abortion, opposed efforts to allow overseas military hospitals to perform abortions, and voted against enabling the federal employee health care plan to pay for abortions. He also voted against recognizing same-sex marriages.

Having opposed the five-day waiting period for handgun purchases in 1993 and the ban on certain semiautomatic assault-style weapons in 1994, he voted to repeal the assault weapons ban in 1996.

Taylor also has tried to protect the rights of property owners. In the 103rd Congress, he emerged at the forefront of a burgeoning property-rights movement in Congress when he won passage of an amendment that he offered with Rep. W.J. "Billy" Tauzin, D-La., to legislation authorizing the National Biological Survey, an inventory of plant and animal species in the United States. The amendment required the government to obtain written permission from a landowner before entering private property.

In his freshman term, he was a member of the "Gang of Seven," Republicans from the class of 1990 who confronted Democrats and tweaked protocol with full-disclosure demands during the House bank overdraft scandal that first arose in September 1991 and steamed well into 1992. The leadership eventually closed the bank, and full disclosure of overdrafters came despite an ethics committee recommendation to the contrary.

Though he was the lowest-profile member of the gang, Taylor was involved enough to get political mileage out of the perk-bashing effort in his 1992 re-election campaign.

Yet while urging Congress to tighten its belt and bashing congressional perks, Taylor has managed to curry favor with his constituents by bringing home federal largess. In the 104th, he secured $5 million for a new Blue Ridge Parkway headquarters and $1.8 million for a Forest Service Cradle of Forestry Interpretive Center. Taylor said the projects would help spur tourism and jobs in the mountains of Western North Carolina.

At Home: This seat changed between Democratic and Republican hands five times in the six elections from 1980 through 1992, with Democratic Rep. James McClure Clarke and GOP Rep. Bill Hendon each getting knocked out on two separate occasions (Clarke in 1984 and 1990, Hendon in 1982 and 1986). Each of those races was decided by fewer than 5,000 votes.

But Taylor polled 55 percent of the vote in 1992, his first re-election try, and has won by solid margins since. In 1996, he received 58 percent against James Mark Ferguson, a farmer. That was just slightly less than the 60 percent he got against Democrat Maggie Palmer Lauterer in 1994.

A former television reporter who had wide name recognition walking into the race, Lauterer was backed by several national organizations, including EMILY's List. But Taylor had the help of a strong mountain- and small-town base, and his percentage in 1994 was the largest garnered in the 11th in two decades.

Taylor first showed his formidable re-election skills in 1992. Redistricting before the election made the district tougher for him by excising a chunk of Republican voters, but he assiduously courted the residents of the small cities and mountain hamlets that dot Western North Carolina; by Taylor's count he held more than 70 town meetings in his first term.

He touted his role as a freshman renegade in the Gang of Seven. He also cultivated a folksy image, contrasting himself to his patrician Democratic challenger, Asheville lawyer and former state Rep. John S. Stevens. Taylor ended up winning 13 of the district's 16 counties en route to a 10-point victory.

When Taylor ousted Democrat Clarke in 1990, he won by only 2,673 votes, taking 51 percent. Taylor's victory was notable in that it came in a non-presidential year. His best opportunity to get to Congress had appeared to be in 1988, as George Bush polled 59 percent in the 11th (as then configured); despite the coattails, Taylor fell 1,500 votes short in that first try against Clarke. Running as a challenger who was pegged as pro-development, Taylor took issue with Clarke's bill designating 90 percent of the Great Smoky Mountains National Park a wilderness area.

But Taylor softened some of his rough edges for the rematch, toning down his attacks on the low-key and grandfatherly Clarke and presenting himself as a folksy family man in shirt sleeves.

Taylor won his first elective office— a state House seat — in 1966, right after taking a law degree at Wake Forest University. He served six years in the House and later in the state Senate, becoming minority leader in both chambers.

HOUSE ELECTIONS

1996 General		
Charles H. Taylor (R)	132,860	(58%)
James Mark Ferguson (D)	91,257	(40%)
Phil McCanless (LIBERT)	2,307	(1%)
1994 General		
Charles H. Taylor (R)	115,826	(60%)
Maggie Palmer Lauterer (D)	76,862	(40%)

Previous Winning Percentages: 1992 (55%) **1990** (51%)

CAMPAIGN FINANCE

	Receipts	Receipts from PACs	Expend-itures
1996			
Taylor (R)	$759,160	$166,434 (22%)	$481,658
Ferguson (D)	$46,919	$250 (1%)	$46,884
1994			
Taylor (R)	$1,006,234	$234,431 (23%)	$999,467
Lauterer (D)	$607,669	$158,064 (26%)	$607,128

VOTING STUDIES

	Presidential Support		Party Unity		Conservative Coalition	
Year	S	O	S	O	S	O
1996	30	62	90	4	100	0
1995	16	81	96	3	97	1
1994	36	63	92	6	92	6
1993	27	71	93	5	86	14
1992	76	19	89	8	88	10
1991	84	16	91	7	95	5

DISTRICT VOTE FOR PRESIDENT

1996		1992	
D	96,926 (43%)	**D**	105,064 (43%)
R	106,511 (47%)	**R**	104,383 (43%)
I	20,658 (9%)	**I**	34,646 (14%)

KEY VOTES

1997	
Ban "partial-birth" abortions	Y
1996	
Approve farm bill	Y
Deny public education to illegal immigrants	Y
Repeal ban on certain assault-style weapons	Y
Increase minimum wage	N
Freeze defense spending	N
Approve welfare overhaul	Y
1995	
Approve balanced-budget constitutional amendment	Y
Relax Clean Water Act regulations	Y
Oppose limits on environmental regulations	N
Reduce projected Medicare spending	Y
Approve GOP budget with tax and spending cuts	Y

INTEREST GROUP RATINGS

Year	ADA	AFL-CIO	CCUS	ACU
1996	5	n/a	87	100
1995	0	8	96	88
1994	5	33	75	100
1993	5	8	82	100
1992	15	25	86	87
1991	10	17	90	90

12 Melvin Watt (D)

Of Charlotte — Elected 1992, 3rd term

Biographical Information

Born: Aug. 26, 1945, Steele Creek, N.C.
Education: U. of North Carolina, B.S. 1967; Yale U., J.D. 1970.
Occupation: Lawyer.
Family: Wife, Eulada Paysour; two children.
Religion: Presbyterian.
Political Career: N.C. Senate, 1985-87.
Capitol Office: 1230 Longworth Bldg. 20515; 225-1510.

Committees

Banking & Financial Services
Capital Markets, Securities & Government Sponsored Enterprises; Financial Institutions & Consumer Credit
Judiciary
Constitution; Immigration & Claims (ranking)

In Washington: Adjusting to life in the House minority was tough for many Democrats, but Watt seemed energized by the Republican takeover: In debate on the House floor, his is one of the most frequently and passionately heard Democratic voices in defense of civil liberties. Despite his traditionally liberal voting record on many issues, though, Watt cultivates an image as someone who works well with his district's business community and votes an often tight-fisted fiscal line.

Watt serves on the Banking and Financial Services Committee, where he has an interest not only in banking issues, but also in the housing and urban affairs matters under the committee's jurisdiction. He also sits on Judiciary, where he is ranking member of the Immigration and Claims Subcommittee.

A civil rights lawyer for 22 years before winning election to Congress, Watt is the product of a fatherless household and was brought up in rural Mecklenburg County in a tin-roofed shack without running water or electricity. He attended a segregated high school and then moved on to the University of North Carolina at Chapel Hill, where he graduated Phi Beta Kappa, and then to Yale University, where he received a law degree and a coveted spot on the Yale Law Review.

During the 104th Congress, Watt voted against such Republican priorities as the balanced-budget constitutional amendment, the GOP-engineered welfare overhaul legislation that President Clinton signed and the proposed ban on an abortion procedure that its opponents call "partial birth" abortion. But Watt won praise from the Concord Coalition, a balanced-budget advocacy organization, for his 1996 voting record; the group rated Watt the most fiscally prudent member of the North Carolina delegation, noting his opposition to taking transportation trust funds off-budget, his opposition to repealing a portion of the gasoline tax, and his support for a budget blueprint mapped by a conservative Democrats known as "blue dogs" that would have brought the budget into balance without cutting tax rates.

Watt expended a good deal of energy during the 104th railing against GOP crime initiatives. His most notable effort was an attempt during March 1996 consideration of an anti-terrorism bill to retain habeas corpus appeals by state inmates to federal courts. He joined in a strange-bedfellows coalition with staunchly conservative Republican Helen Chenoweth of Idaho, who shared his concern about civil liberties.

Watt argued that the bill's provisions placing restrictions on death row appeals were a betrayal of the Founding Fathers' commitment to individual rights. "We can't sacrifice our constitutional principles because we're angry at people for bombing," Watt said. But this argument did not sway many members and the Watt-Chenoweth amendment was defeated, 135-283.

That vote actually represented a diminution of support from an earlier Watt attempt on different crime legislation to allow defendants federal review if they could produce "clear and convincing" new evidence of innocence. That amendment was beaten, 151-280.

Watt's concern for the point of view of the Founding Fathers was evident in his attempt to attach the Fourth Amendment to a bill allowing officers to obtain evidence through illegal search and seizures, so long as they had been operating in good faith. The Fourth Amendment protects Americans from "unreasonable search and seizures." But bill sponsor Bill McCollum of Florida successfully pleaded, "Don't wipe out the bill by voting for the Constitution," and Watt's move to get Congress to endorse the Fourth Amendment was turned aside, 121-303.

Watt also launched lonely crusades against a federal version of Megan's Law, which requires state and local law enforcement agencies to disclose information about sex offenders upon their release from prison. "An individual, having paid their debt to society by serving time and having complied with their sentence, ought to be able...to get on with their lives," Watt said. But the bill was enacted over that objection.

NORTH CAROLINA 12
The I-85 Corridor – Parts of Charlotte, Greensboro and Durham

The 12th is best described as the mother of all gerrymanders, a congressional district so notorious in its design that it sparked an editorial in The Wall Street Journal and drew criticism from 1992 GOP presidential candidate Patrick J. Buchanan during a campaign stop in North Carolina.

The Supreme Court twice jumped into the fray, declaring the district an unconstitutional gerrymander in June 1996. The district was redrawn by the North Carolina General Assembly in March 1997. If approved in federal court, the new district would slip from 57 percent black to 46 percent black. Under the new boundaries, the 12th would still include Charlotte, Greensboro and Winston-Salem.

The scandal was in the shape. Known as the "I-85 District," the serpentine 12th winds across the Piedmont Plateau mostly along the Interstate 85 corridor, linking small parts of 10 counties and including all of none.

The district was the Democratic-controlled legislature's response to the 1992 Justice Department mandate that North Carolina have two majority-minority districts. In an effort to avoid significantly weakening white Democratic incumbents, the 12th was stretched to extremes.

The predominantly black neighborhoods in Durham, Greensboro, Winston-Salem, Charlotte and Gastonia provide much of the vote.

Durham is the 12th's eastern frontier. Tobacco processing was once the big game in town here, but nowadays, Duke University is Durham County's largest single employer. Besides Duke, the district takes in several of the state's historically black colleges and universities.

Durham has long been home to a black political and economic elite, whose rise was nurtured by an organization that used to be known as the Durham Committee for Negro Affairs. Now referred to simply as the Durham Committee, the group has been a locus of power in black politics since pre-World War II days.

More than half the district's residents live in either Guilford or Mecklenburg (Charlotte) counties. The 12th only covers part of Charlotte, but it is the population anchor of the district; it contains more black voters than any city in the 12th.

Any candidate for the 12th must be careful, though, not to couch his message in Charlotte-oriented terms, for voters in other cities along I-85 have expressed concern about a Charlotte-dominated district that would be less attuned to their local interests.

Throughout its existence, the 12th has routinely given Watt and Bill Clinton two-thirds of the votes cast.

Economically, the 12th is widely diverse. Since it courses through six of the state's 10 largest cities, it relies on the fortunes of the state's traditional industries — tobacco, textiles and furniture. In Charlotte, banking and financial concerns dominate the local economy.

1990 Population: 552,387. White 230,889 (42%), Black 312,791 (57%), Other 8,707 (2%). Hispanic origin 4,772 (1%). 18 and over 411,687 (75%), 62 and over 77,540 (14%). Median age: 32.

He also complained about a bill that would have increased prison sentences an average of two years for those who commit crimes against children or the elderly, saying it would interfere with the U.S. Sentencing Commission's ability to set guidelines. The commission was created, Watt contended, to force Congress to "resist temptations to beat ourselves on the chest and proclaim as politicians how tough we are on crime." The Judiciary Committee rejected his attempt to limit the bill to requiring the commission to review its guidelines. He also failed with an effort to reduce penalties for crack cocaine and methamphetamine to make them equivalent to the penalties that apply to powder cocaine. "Crack cocaine happens to be used by poor people, mostly black people, because it's cheap," Watt said. "Powder cocaine happens to be used by wealthy white people."

Watt's sense of fairness was also upset by the GOP's bill to toughen immigration enforcement, enacted at session's end in 1996. He tried to eliminate a program that allotted 10,000 visa slots for immigrants who have at least $1 million and pledge to create at least 10 jobs in the U.S. "We are allowing rich people to buy their way into our country," Watt complained. He also argued against mandating a 14-mile triple fence in California along part of the Mexican border, saying it could endanger Border Patrol officers trapped and attacked between the layers. Both those efforts, along with an amendment to strengthen the ability to sue for discrimination under an ultimately unsuccessful affirmative action overhaul, were defeated.

Though Watt usually is in league with his party's liberals, he does show an independent streak from time to time. During debate in the 103rd on a bill that would provide stiffer penalties for so-called "hate crimes," he took a position that was contrary to that of most Democrats on Judiciary. Watt argued that the criminal justice system is not equipped to determine a defendant's state of mind.

And when freshmen Democrats met in March 1993 to finalize a proposal on campaign finance law that targeted PACs, Watt stood up and said he could not support a plan that would have hurt his 1992 campaign and that of many other black candidates. Taking PAC money, he said, is a necessity for minority members, who often represent poor districts that are not fertile ground for fundraising. Less than half of his campaign funds had come from PACs to that time; nearly three-quarters of the money he has raised for subsequent bids has come from PACs.

At Home: Watt's political career has been cast in the shadow of criticism of his district, perhaps the most maligned configuration newly drawn for the 1990s. The 12th snakes across the center of North Carolina along Interstates 85 and 77 to pull together a black-majority constituency. Almost from the day it was drawn, the district was a subject of litigation, and in June 1996 it was deemed an unconstitutional gerrymander by the Supreme Court. Given that decision's late date, the existing lines were used again in November 1996 voting, when Watt easily won a third term. He may have a tougher time in the future, because as redrawn in March 1997 by the North Carolina legislature, the 12th's percentage of black residents drops from 57 to 46.

Watt was dubbed "the most effective freshman legislator" during his only other stint in elective office, a 1985-87 term in the North Carolina Senate. He was appointed to that job by local Democrats after their candidate died at the end of the campaign.

HOUSE ELECTIONS

1996 General		
Melvin Watt (D)	124,675	(71%)
Joseph A. "Joe" Martino Jr. (R)	46,581	(27%)
Roger L. Kohn (LIBERT)	1,874	(1%)
1994 General		
Melvin Watt (D)	57,655	(66%)
Joseph A. "Joe" Martino (R)	29,933	(34%)

Previous Winning Percentages: 1992 (70%)

CAMPAIGN FINANCE

	Receipts	Receipts from PACs	Expend-itures
1996			
Watt (D)	$133,797	$94,150 (70%)	$148,001
Martino (R)	$7,206	$16 (0%)	$6,902
1994			
Watt (D)	$273,380	$199,008 (73%)	$253,715
Martino (R)	$15,529	$514 (3%)	$14,700

DISTRICT VOTE FOR PRESIDENT

1996		1992	
D	124,533 (70%)	**D**	127,941 (66%)
R	45,348 (25%)	**R**	49,105 (25%)
I	7,803 (4%)	**I**	16,936 (9%)

KEY VOTES

1997	
Ban "partial birth" abortions	N
1996	
Approve farm bill	N
Deny public education to illegal immigrants	N
Repeal ban on certain assault-style weapons	N
Increase minimum wage	Y
Freeze defense spending	Y
Approve welfare overhaul	N
1995	
Approve balanced-budget constitutional amendment	N
Relax Clean Water Act regulations	N
Oppose limits on environmental regulations	Y
Reduce projected Medicare spending	N
Approve GOP budget with tax and spending cuts	N

VOTING STUDIES

	Presidential Support		Party Unity		Conservative Coalition	
Year	S	O	S	O	S	O
1996	84	16	95	2	16	82
1995	87	11	94	4	9	90
1994	73	27	95	2	3	94
1993	79	21	97	2	7	93

INTEREST GROUP RATINGS

Year	ADA	AFL-CIO	CCUS	ACU
1996	90	n/a	19	0
1995	100	100	4	4
1994	100	100	17	10
1993	100	100	9	0

NORTH DAKOTA

Governor: Edward T. Schafer (R)
First elected: 1992
Length of term: 4 years
Term expires: 12/2000
Salary: $71,040
Term limit: No
Phone: (701) 328-2200
Born: Aug. 8, 1946; Bismarck, N.D.
Education: U. of North Dakota, B.S., B.A. 1969; U. of Denver, M.B.A. 1970.
Occupation: Distributing company owner; real estate developer.
Family: Wife, Nancy Jones; two children; two stepchildren.
Religion: Episcopalian
Political Career: Republican nominee for U.S. House, 1990.

Lt. Gov.: Rosemarie Myrdal (R)
First elected: 1992
Length of term: 4 years
Term expires: 12/2000
Salary: $58,380
Phone: (701) 328-2916

State election official: (701) 328-2905
Democratic headquarters: (701) 255-0460
Republican headquarters: (701) 255-0030

STATE LEGISLATURE

Legislative Assembly meets January-April in odd-numbered years.

Senate: 49 members, 4-year terms
1996 breakdown: 30R, 19D; 43 men, 6 women
Salary: $90/day in session + $180/month year-round; $62.50/day not in session
Phone: (701) 328-2916

House of Representatives: 98 members, 2-year terms
1996 breakdown: 72R, 26D; 79 men, 19 women
Salary: $90/day in session + $180/month year-round; $62.50/day not in session
Phone: (701) 328-2916

URBAN STATISTICS

City	Population
Fargo	74,084
Mayor Bruce Furness, N-P	
Grand Forks	49,425
Mayor Patricia Owens, N-P	
Bismarck	49,256
Mayor Bill Sorensen, N-P	
Minot	34,544
Mayor Orlin W. Backes, N-P	

U.S. CONGRESS

Senate: 2 D, 0 R
House: 1 D, 0 R

TERM LIMITS

For state offices: No

ELECTIONS

1996 Presidential Vote

Bob Dole	47%
Bill Clinton	40%
Ross Perot	12%

1992 Presidential Vote

George Bush	44%
Bill Clinton	32%
Ross Perot	23%

1988 Presidential Vote

George Bush	56%
Michael S. Dukakis	43%

POPULATION

1990 population		638,800
1980 population		652,717
Percent change		-2%
Rank among states:		47
White		95%
Black		1%
Hispanic		1%
Asian or Pacific islander		1%
Urban		53%
Rural		47%
Born in state		73%
Foreign-born		1%
Under age 18	175,385	27%
Ages 18-64	372,360	58%
65 and older	91,055	14%
Median age		32.4

MISCELLANEOUS

Capital: Bismarck
Number of counties: 53
Per capita income: $16,088 (1991)
Rank among states: 38
Total area: 70,702 sq. miles
Rank among states: 17

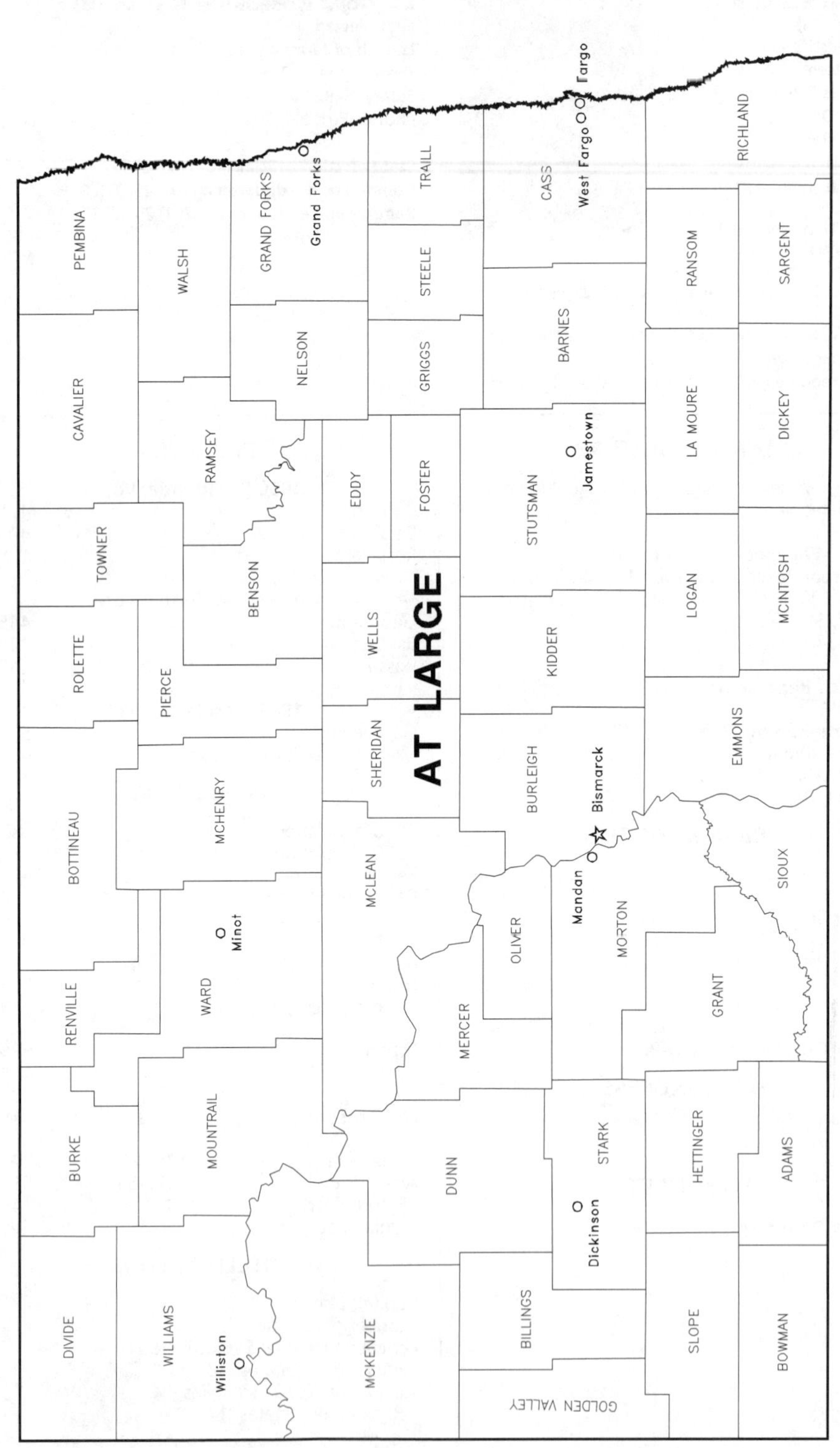

AT LARGE
PEMBINA
WALSH
GRAND FORKS
Grand Forks
TRAILL
CASS
West Fargo
Fargo
RICHLAND
CAVALIER
RAMSEY
NELSON
STEELE
GRIGGS
BARNES
RANSOM
SARGENT
TOWNER
BENSON
EDDY
FOSTER
STUTSMAN
Jamestown
LA MOURE
DICKEY
ROLETTE
PIERCE
WELLS
KIDDER
LOGAN
MCINTOSH
BOTTINEAU
MCHENRY
SHERIDAN
BURLEIGH
Bismarck
EMMONS
Mandan
SIOUX
RENVILLE
WARD
Minot
MCLEAN
OLIVER
MORTON
GRANT
MERCER
BURKE
MOUNTRAIL
DUNN
STARK
Dickinson
HETTINGER
ADAMS
DIVIDE
WILLIAMS
Williston
MCKENZIE
BILLINGS
GOLDEN VALLEY
SLOPE
BOWMAN

Kent Conrad (D)

Of Bismarck — Elected 1986; 2nd full term

Biographical Information

Born: March 12, 1948, Bismarck, N.D.

Education: U. of Missouri, 1967; Stanford U., A.B. 1971; George Washington U., M.B.A. 1975.

Occupation: Management and personnel director.

Family: Wife, Lucy Calautti; one child.

Religion: Unitarian.

Political Career: Candidate for N.D. auditor, 1976; N.D. tax commissioner, 1981-87.

Capitol Office: 530 Hart Bldg. 20510; 224-2043

Committees

Agriculture, Nutrition & Forestry
Forestry, Conservation & Rural Revitalization (ranking); Research, Nutrition & General Legislation

Budget

Select Ethics

Finance
Health Care; International Trade; Taxation & IRS Oversight

Indian Affairs

In Washington: North Dakota has long been fertile soil for populist politicians, and Conrad showed again in the 104th Congress that he is an energetic tiller, as he fumed about the GOP push to overhaul federal farm policy. Conservative Republicans said they were aiming to bring Uncle Sam's agriculture programs in line with free-market principles and give farmers greater flexibility in deciding what to plant. Conrad saw things differently. He denounced Republican plans to phase out New Deal-era crop subsidies as "radical proposals that will devastate America's farm families and damage the nation's successful food policy." The subsidies, of course, had been a fixture of farm life in North Dakota for decades.

The central idea of the GOP's "Freedom to Farm" proposal was to replace crop subsidies with a schedule of fixed payments that would decline over seven years, giving farmers a sort of "soft landing" into an agricultural open market. But Conrad likened the proposal to a welfare plan, one that would give farmers too much during times of high commodity prices and too little when prices dropped. "The freedom to farm proposal will take hundreds of thousands of farmers over the cliff," he said.

Conrad and his Democratic allies from the prairie states were not able to halt the march of "Freedom to Farm," which, after modifications to mollify some commodities groups, passed the Senate in February 1996 and became law. Conrad could at least claim a measure of success in the Republican agreement to leave the old "permanent law" governing agriculture on the books — which means that traditional subsidies could eventually be revived.

Conrad first found himself in the spotlight in the 104th during the early 1995 consideration of the balanced-budget constitutional amendment. His vote was much wooed by both sides. Conrad, who had placed the issue of the deficit at the center of his political mission during his first Senate campaign in 1986, prolonged the suspense until the very end. "This to me is the most important vote I may ever cast in the United States Senate, and I want it to be a vote that can stand the test of time," he said.

Ultimately, he voted no. Both Conrad and fellow North Dakota Democrat Byron L. Dorgan had insisted on language within the amendment to protect Social Security. They objected to including the surplus in Social Security trust funds in the calculations of deficit reduction, saying that lawmakers someday might feel compelled to reduce Social Security benefits to meet a constitutional mandate to balance the budget. The GOP leadership offered to pass a separate bill that would have gradually removed the Social Security funds from the deficit calculations, but that did not satisfy the two North Dakotans. Again in 1996 and 1997 when the balanced-budget amendment came to the Senate floor, Conrad and Dorgan voted no.

Conrad's opposition to the amendment recalled the pledge he made when he was first elected to the Senate. He promised to serve only one term if the deficit was not reduced by 80 percent. Though the deficit was never cut by anything close to that much, he managed both to live up to his pledge and still return to the Senate.

Although polls indicated in 1992 that he could have broken his campaign pledge and sought reelection, he did not do so. Instead, he technically kept his vow by standing for election to the seat that became vacant with the death in September 1992 of North Dakota's senior senator, Quentin N. Burdick. Conrad won, and his Washington career remained on track.

During the Congress vs. Clinton budget wars that partially shut down the federal government in late 1995 and early 1996, Conrad tried to play a mediating role. He allied with a bloc of moderate Republicans and Democrats pushing alternative deficit-reduction plans with smaller spending cuts and a smaller tax cut package than advocated by conservative Republicans. The moderates' efforts never bore fruit, and while the warring parties were able to get the government running again, the job of settling on a long-term budget-balancing plan was left to the 105th Congress.

Over the years, Conrad has offered a variety of ideas for reducing the deficit. In 1991, he proposed freezing most domestic spending, while protecting agriculture, education, health care and veterans' programs. That plan was narrowly defeated in the Budget Committee, as was a 1992 Conrad offering that incorporated a spending freeze, restraints on entitlements and a tax increase for millionaires.

Sometimes he finds politically popular ways to save taxpayer money. He introduced a successful amendment to a 1994 defense procurement bill that barred contractors from being reimbursed for their entertainment expenses. At other times his deficit-reduction efforts are more symbolic: Conrad voted against President George Bush's nominee for Treasury secretary, Nicholas F. Brady, after Brady expressed the belief that the nation's economy could grow out of the deficit.

In the social-policy realm, Conrad had success in the 104th Congress pushing a plan to enable parents to install an electronic device, known as a "v-chip," to keep violent or offensive programs off their televisions. "Parents are increasingly unhappy that they have limited ability to control what their children watch on television," he said. Congress ultimately adopted v-chip provisions as part of a broad telecommunications bill.

Conrad also lobbied vigorously, and with some success, to moderate GOP proposals to overhaul welfare. He especially opposed efforts to turn food stamps into a block grant program that would be run by the states, hailing the food stamp program as "the most important part of our arsenal to fight the battle against poverty in America." Facing opposition from other rural lawmakers of both parties, GOP leaders agreed to keep food stamps a federal program.

Conrad has cast himself as a farm-belt populist throughout his political career. Before his first run for the Senate, he served as North Dakota's tax commissioner, a post from which he took on big business.

In his first Senate term, Conrad quickly found the power centers for protecting North Dakota interests, making his way to the Agriculture and Budget committees. Conrad was elected the year after the 1985 farm bill was passed, and farm programs were clearly viewed as under siege.

Conrad's other committee assignment in his first term was Energy, which he gave up in the 103rd Congress in favor of Finance. There he seeks to advance rural health, protect the farm belt's tax interests and battle the deficit.

He has been willing to take on his own party's bigwigs to advance home state interests. In 1993, for example, President Clinton proposed a tax based on the heat content, or British thermal units (Btu), of most forms of energy, in his first major deficit-reduction effort. The measure had significant implications in North Dakota, and Conrad fought to exempt farm production, which would have been hit hard. The Btu tax ultimately died.

Also, Conrad has joined with other Western senators — many of them Republicans and some Democratic — in resisting Clinton administration efforts to raise grazing fees on federal lands. In September 1996, he was one of nine Democrats voting with 41 Republicans to table a proposal to increase some fees for grazing on federal land. Conrad also voted against NAFTA.

Frequently and with persistence, Conrad has attempted to attach aid for North Dakota farmers to other bills. In 1990, he offered an amendment to an aid bill for Panama and Nicaragua that would have allowed farmers in drought-stricken areas to avoid repaying certain crop subsidies. Senators voted 52-43 to kill the amendment, but Conrad persisted. As the Senate prepared to clear the bill late in the evening, he offered his amendment again. Colleagues persuaded him to withdraw it.

Conrad also has an abiding interest in shifting money to domestic programs from overseas and has argued that American allies should bear a bigger share of their defense burden. During consideration of the 1989 defense appropriations bill, he offered an amendment to return 30,000 troops stationed in Europe and transfer to education programs the $1 billion he said would be saved. "We are paying for their defense umbrella even though we have to borrow money from them to do it," he said. His amendment was rejected 23-76.

In 1990, the Senate accepted Conrad's amendment to cut by 10,000 the number of U.S. military personnel stationed in Japan.

Some of Conrad's votes on abortion reflect the culturally conservative side of the populist tradition. In September 1996, he was one of only 12 Democrats voting to override Clinton's veto of a ban on a particular abortion technique opponents call "partial birth" abortion. He also opposed allowing federal employees' health care plans to cover abortion. But he split with abortion foes in February 1997 to endorse early release of funds for international family-planning programs.

Conrad's most ambitious foray into the health care arena came in the 103rd Congress, when he was a central figure in the failed effort to overhaul the nation's medical-care delivery system. He opposed the so-called employer mandate feature of Clinton's bill, which would have required employers to help pay for their employee's health benefits. "I come from a state with many small businesses that do not supply health insurance," he said in April 1994. "This has to be structured in a way that won't put people out of business."

Conrad participated in the bipartisan group of centrist senators that attempted to resuscitate the initiative late in the 103rd, a group that included Sens. John B. Breaux, D-La., and John H. Chafee, R-R.I. Their measure relied on marketplace competition and changes in insurance practices rather than government mandates to boost coverage. This modest approach also failed.

At Home: Conrad spent 1992 pioneering a way for members who have taken the term limit pledge to stay in Congress even after their time's up: Just switch seats.

During his 1986 race against GOP Sen. Mark Andrews, Conrad promised not to seek re-election unless the trade and budget deficits were dramatically reduced during his term in office. By early 1992, Conrad appeared to be backing off that pledge, joking that he had written it under the influence of a 104-degree fever. But Conrad ended up keeping his word, announcing his retirement in April 1992. While his decision met with approval in North Dakota, political cynics suggested that he simply may have been biding his time until another office came open. Sidelined, Conrad endorsed Dorgan for his seat.

But on Sept. 8, 1992, Burdick died, leaving two years in his Senate term and an election in December. Democrats urged Conrad to run, and he was unchallenged for the party's nomination.

His Republican opponent was state Rep. Jack Dalrymple, who tried to haunt Conrad with his 1986 promise and accused him of reneging on a pledge to return campaign contributions he had collected before deciding to run for Burdick's seat. Voters were unmoved: Conrad won with 63 percent of the vote.

That showing left Republicans pessimistic about their chances of upsetting Conrad in 1994. Nevertheless, as a buffer against Clinton's high unpopularity in North Dakota, Conrad aired a TV ad in which he said, "A majority of the time, I vote with the Republican leader, Bob Dole." Conrad took 58 percent against Ben Clayburgh, a 70-year-old orthopedic surgeon and former Republican National Committee member.

The troubles besetting North Dakota's farms and small towns gave Conrad an opening against Andrews in 1986. On Election Day, Conrad carried only one of the state's four major population centers; his victory was built in the countryside.

Conrad's chief Senate campaign issue was the Reagan administration's farm policy, which was wildly unpopular in a state where farms and small-town banks were failing left and right.

Though Andrews had largely opposed Reagan agricultural policies, he had voted for the 1985 farm bill, which many farmers believed hurt them. Storming around the state with then-Rep. Dorgan, Conrad relentlessly pressed the point, bringing up Andrews' vote whenever the opportunity arose.

In addition to the farm situation, there was a growing perception that Andrews had lost touch with his base. Part of the way into the campaign, Andrews was stung by news stories revealing that a close friend of his had hired private detectives to investigate first Dorgan and then Conrad. Andrews denied any involvement, but the publicity hurt him all the same. Possibly as troubling to voters was a multimillion-dollar lawsuit that Andrews and his wife, Mary, had pursued against family physicians after Mary Andrews was crippled by meningitis.

Andrews was further hurt by the delay in ending Congress' 1986 session. By the time Andrews did return home, Conrad had taken a slight lead in the polls, and Andrews had to try to make up lost ground. He could not, and Conrad won with 50 percent of the vote.

SENATE ELECTIONS

1994 General		
Kent Conrad (D)	137,157	(58%)
Ben Clayburgh (R)	99,390	(42%)

Previous Winning Percentages: 1992† (63%) **1986** (50%)

† Conrad retired after serving one term in the Senate. He was re-elected in a special election to fill the remainder of the term of Quentin N. Burdick, D, who died Sept. 8, 1992.

CAMPAIGN FINANCE

	Receipts	Receipts from PACs		Expend-itures
1994				
Conrad (D)	$1,837,573	$1,429,114	(78%)	$1,927,866
Clayburgh (R)	$990,519	$54,607	(6%)	$961,192

KEY VOTES

1997	
Approve balanced-budget constitutional amendment	N
Approve chemical weapons treaty	Y
1996	
Approve farm bill	N
Limit punitive damages in product liability cases	N
Exempt small businesses from higher minimum wage	N
Approve welfare overhaul	Y
Bar job discrimination based on sexual orientation	Y
Override veto of ban on "partial birth" abortions	Y
1995	
Approve GOP budget with tax and spending cuts	N
Approve constitutional amendment barring flag desecration	N

VOTING STUDIES

	Presidential Support		Party Unity		Conservative Coalition	
Year	S	O	S	O	S	O
1996	83	17	87	13	39	61
1995	81	16	85	13	32	67
1994	89	11	84	15	53	47
1993	80	18	81	18	51	49
1992	32	67	69	29	61	37
1991	36	63	72	26	43	58

INTEREST GROUP RATINGS

Year	ADA	AFL-CIO	CCUS	ACU
1996	85	n/a	23	15
1995	90	100	42	9
1994	85	75	40	12
1993	80	82	9	24
1992	90	75	20	12
1991	75	75	20	43

Byron L. Dorgan (D)

Of Bismarck — Elected 1992, 1st term

Biographical Information
Born: May 14, 1942, Regent, N.D.
Education: U. of North Dakota, B.S. 1965; U. of Denver, M.B.A. 1966.
Occupation: Public official.
Family: Wife, Kimberly Olson; three children.
Religion: Lutheran.
Political Career: N.D. tax commissioner, 1969-80; Democratic nominee for U.S. House, 1974; U.S. House, 1981-93.
Capitol Office: 713 Hart Bldg. 20510; 224-2551.

Committees
Appropriations
Defense; Energy & Water Development; Interior; Legislative Branch (ranking)
Commerce, Science & Transportation
Aviation; Communications; Manufacturing & Competitiveness; Science, Technology & Space; Surface Transportation & Merchant Marine
Energy & Natural Resources
Forests & Public Land Management (ranking); Water & Power
Indian Affairs
Assistant Floor Leader

In Washington: As North Dakota tax commissioner in the 1970s, then in the House for a dozen years and now from the bully pulpit of the Senate, Dorgan has been a contemporary echo of the prairie populism that swept his state in the early 1900s. "People feel powerless," Dorgan once said, "and they feel powerless because they're preyed upon by bigger interests."

With its tolerance for lengthy orations, the Senate gives Dorgan ample opportunity to rail at the large and distant forces — corporations, foreign governments, international financial institutions — that, he says, care not a whit for the common folk.

Dorgan expressed interest in taking his populist outlook into a Senate leadership post in early 1997, after Minority Whip Wendell H. Ford of Kentucky said he would retire at the end of the 105th Congress. But with Tom Daschle of neighboring South Dakota serving as minority leader, regional pressures could work against him.

Dorgan has been one of the Senate's most outspoken critics of the Federal Reserve Board, which he believes does not put enough emphasis on achieving economic growth, and instead is preoccupied with keeping a lid on inflation. The Fed does that by raising interest rates, a policy that Dorgan complains makes credit more expensive for farmers, other businessmen and consumers who borrow money.

After President Clinton reappointed Alan Greenspan to a third term as Fed chairman in 1996, Dorgan was one of seven senators to vote against his confirmation. Greenspan and his colleagues on the Fed, said Dorgan, "view themselves as a set of human brake pads whose mission is to slow down the economy."

In late 1994, Dorgan joined a demonstration protesting an interest rate increase by the Fed. He said that "behind a locked door," the Fed had made a decision whose cost to the public was "20 times the size of tax increases contemplated by Congress" in the past decade.

Dorgan is a strong defender of his region's agricultural interests. He says he understands the need for foreign markets for his state's vast production of wheat, but he fiercely protects farm interests against international competition. In 1994, he agreed not to block Senate confirmation of several Clinton appointees for trade positions only after the administration made a deal with Canada limiting that country's wheat exports. American wheat farmers had complained that the Canadian government was unfairly subsidizing and pricing its wheat exports.

In the 104th Congress, Dorgan opposed the GOP's "Freedom to Farm" bill that phased out most New Deal-era crop subsidies, replacing them with a system of fixed, but declining, payments that farmers would receive over seven years regardless of market prices or their planting decisions. He proposed his own farm bill, which contained smaller payments, but retained subsidies for farmers when crop prices fell.

Dorgan tries to be a scourge of big corporations and a defender of the disenfranchised. When the Senate considered legislation to overhaul product liability law in the 104th, Dorgan offered an amendment to remove a cap on punitive damage awards in lawsuits; he said the cap protected manufacturers at the expense of consumers harmed by defective products. In 1996, he voted to raise the minimum wage.

In the 103rd, Dorgan took exception with the Clinton administration's free-trade initiatives, NAFTA and GATT, which were strongly backed by most corporate interests. Dorgan said passage of GATT would result in job losses for Americans by encouraging companies to move overseas for cheap labor. It is not fair, he said, to make American workers "compete against a 12-year-old working 12 hours a day for 12 cents an hour."

He is also no fan of most Republican tax and budget proposals, including a balanced-budget amendment to the Constitution, which he has opposed since the GOP took control of Congress. In March 1995, Dorgan and his North Dakota colleague Kent Conrad became national news celebrities in the lead-up to the Senate vote on the amendment. Dorgan had voted for the amendment in 1994, but in 1995, he and Conrad said they would support it only if it included language to protect Social Security. Republicans would not agree to that, and both North Dakotans voted "no" as the amendment fell barely short of the two-thirds majority required for passage. Both also opposed the amendment in 1996 and 1997.

In some instances, Dorgan has voted for GOP-backed proposals. He voted for legislation to ban an abortion technique that opponents call "partial birth" abortion. After Clinton vetoed the ban in 1996, Dorgan backed an unsuccessful override effort. He joined Republicans in supporting welfare overhaul legislation that Clinton signed, and he voted for a Republican bill to crack down on illegal immigration.

At the beginning of the 105th, Dorgan won a seat on the Appropriations Committee, where he can look out for North Dakota's needs. The state had a lot of needs after severe spring 1997 flooding inundated Grand Forks and other areas along the path of the Red River.

At Home: For most of the 1980s, Dorgan was regarded as a senator-in-waiting — waiting for the retirement of North Dakota's very senior Democratic senator, Quentin N. Burdick. But when Dorgan did finally move up, it was to replace junior Democratic Sen. Kent Conrad. Conrad announced in April 1992 that he was retiring to fulfill an earlier pledge that he would not seek re-election unless the federal deficit was reduced. (In the end, though, Conrad stayed in the Senate: after Burdick died in September 1992, he won a special election to replace him.)

After Conrad's unexpected spring 1992 declaration, Dorgan jumped into the race and went on to win with ease over the Republican, Fargo City Commissioner Steve Sydness. Sydness tried to make an issue of Dorgan's 98 overdrafts at the House bank, but that did not seriously hurt Dorgan.

Dorgan had been pushed to run for the Senate before but had declined. Heading into the 1986 election, some polls suggested he could defeat GOP Sen. Mark Andrews. When Dorgan demurred, Conrad, his one-time protege and successor as state tax commissioner, ran and won. Heading into 1988, Dorgan backers hoped to pressure Burdick into retiring, but he wouldn't budge.

Dorgan's stands are rooted partly in the populism of the state's old Non-Partisan League and partly in the small-town values of his upbringing. His father was active in the Democratic-leaning Farmers' Union in Regent, N.D., where Dorgan grew up and where, he likes to say, he graduated in the top five in his high school class — of nine.

Dorgan was working in the state tax department in 1969 when he caught the eye of Democratic Gov. William Guy; when the incumbent tax commissioner died in 1969, Dorgan, then 27, got the post. As tax commissioner, Dorgan spoke out on local issues such as property tax revision and on global ones such as military spending. He sued out-of-state corporations to force them to pay taxes. The voters loved it.

Dorgan made it clear he had higher political ambitions by taking on then-Rep. Andrews in 1974. Dorgan held Andrews to 56 percent.

In 1980, GOP Sen. Milton R. Young retired, and Andrews was nominated to succeed him. Dorgan ran for Andrews' House seat. Although favored from the start, Dorgan sought to temper his liberal reputation by supporting an anti-abortion constitutional amendment and decrying government waste. That was astute; the state went easily for Ronald Reagan, but Dorgan took 57 percent and went on to a string of easy House re-elections.

SENATE ELECTIONS

1992 General		
Byron L. Dorgan (D)	179,347	(59%)
Steve Sydness (R)	118,162	(39%)
Tom Asbridge (I)	6,448	(2%)

Previous Winning Percentages: 1990* (65%) **1988*** (71%) **1986*** (76%) **1984*** (79%) **1982*** (72%) **1980*** (57%)

* *House elections*

CAMPAIGN FINANCE

	Receipts	Receipts from PACs	Expend-itures
1992			
Dorgan (D)	$1,054,618	$785,943 (75%)	$1,124,512
Sydness (R)	$507,163	$154,553 (30%)	$498,107

KEY VOTES

1997	
Approve balanced-budget constitutional amendment	N
Approve chemical weapons treaty	Y
1996	
Approve farm bill	N
Limit punitive damages in product liability cases	Y
Exempt small businesses from higher minimum wage	N
Approve welfare overhaul	Y
Bar job discrimination based on sexual orientation	Y
Override veto of ban on "partial birth" abortions	Y
1995	
Approve GOP budget with tax and spending cuts	N
Approve constitutional amendment barring flag desecration	N

VOTING STUDIES

	Presidential Support		Party Unity		Conservative Coalition	
Year	S	O	S	O	S	O
1996	80	20	84	16	37	63
1995	85	14	87	11	32	68
1994	81	19	86	14	44	56
1993	72	17	76	16	32	56
House Service:						
1992	25	75	78	20	44	56
1991	30	69	75	23	51	49

INTEREST GROUP RATINGS

Year	ADA	AFL-CIO	CCUS	ACU
1996	85	n/a	38	20
1995	90	100	47	13
1994	85	75	20	8
1993	65	78	10	23
House Service:				
1992	70	83	38	28
1991	75	75	40	25

AL Earl Pomeroy (D)

Of Valley City — Elected 1992, 3rd term

Biographical Information
Born: Sept. 2, 1952, Valley City, N.D.
Education: U. of North Dakota, B.A. 1974; U. of Durham (England), 1975; U. of North Dakota, J.D. 1979.
Occupation: Lawyer.
Family: Wife, Laurie Kirby; one child.
Religion: Presbyterian.
Political Career: N.D. House, 1981-85; N.D. insurance commissioner, 1985-93.
Capitol Office: 1533 Longworth Bldg. 20515; 225-2611.

Committees
Agriculture
Forestry, Resource Conservation & Research; Risk Management & Specialty Crops
Budget

In Washington: As is their custom, North Dakotans again voted Republican for president in 1996, but at the same time, Democrat Pomeroy gained a third House term without showing any reluctance to criticize the GOP's fiscal and farm policies.

When House Republicans released their first budget plan in May 1995, Pomeroy, a member of the Budget Committee, called it "abhorrent," describing it to the Baltimore Sun as "apocalypse now." Pomeroy had equally harsh words for the Republicans' 1996 overhaul of federal agriculture policy, seeing it as a "stepping-stone to utter elimination of farm programs" with great potential to harm farmers.

Early in the 104th Congress, the Agriculture Committee, where Pomeroy also sits, approved a measure to pare back the nation's food stamp program. The measure would have allowed states to manage the program, setting a single set of eligibility and work requirements. Proponents of the change argued it was time to make "tough decisions" to balance the budget. Pomeroy shot back: "When you cut food stamps, it doesn't sound like a tough decision. It sounds like a stupid decision."

Pomeroy came to Capitol Hill with experience in the state legislature and in agriculture and insurance, including an eight-year stint as North Dakota's insurance commissioner.

The son of a Valley City farm retailer who sold feed, seed and fertilizer, Pomeroy is a lawyer and a former grain-bin builder. Agriculture, particularly growing of wheat for durum (used in pasta), accounts for about half of North Dakota's economy.

From his seat on Agriculture in the 104th, Pomeroy gave a cold eye to the GOP's plan to phase out New Deal-era crop subsidies and give farmers greater flexibility in deciding what to plant. The sweeping measure, dubbed "Freedom to Farm," largely did away with the decades-old system of farmers planting specific crops and being paid subsidies when market prices for their commodities dropped below set levels. Under the new plan, farmers who sign seven-year contracts with the government receive fixed, but declining, payments every year, regardless of market prices or their planting decisions.

Many Democrats on the Agriculture Committee said the GOP plan could shred the economic safety net for farmers, leaving them financially ruined when prices drop. "I think Freedom to Farm is essentially a bait-and-switch proposition," said Pomeroy. "By the year 2003, you've got nothing — no check, no protection against price collapse."

When the House passed the measure in February 1996, Pomeroy voted no. "Even the most efficient farmers have no control over falling market prices," he said. "Leaving no protection for farmers when prices hit the floor will, over time, push family farmers out of business."

Before the farm bill passed, Pomeroy and others successfully fended off an effort to phase out the sugar support program over five years. North Dakota's eastern region grows sugar beets, and farmers feared that without Washington-imposed price supports and import restrictions, they would be driven out of business by a flood of less-expensive sugar imported from overseas.

Critics of the sugar support program said that it drives up the cost of sugar, but their amendment to phase out the program fell short, 208-217.

Pomeroy also fought an effort by some GOP Agriculture members to create a new guest worker program, making it easier for agricultural companies to bring in temporary foreign workers to harvest the nation's crops.

The committee voted in March 1996 to attach the guest worker program to a larger immigration bill moving through the House. Richard W. Pombo, R-Calif., offered the amendment creating the guest worker program, arguing that farmers cannot find enough domestic workers to harvest crops. Pomeroy sharply disagreed. "It's about allowing some large farm operators access to the cheapest employees they can possibly find," he said. He blasted lawmakers who decry illegal immigration but support a large guest worker program, saying, "You can't have it both ways." The program was killed when the immigration bill reached the House floor.

Although Pomeroy concurs with making a prior-

NORTH DAKOTA
At large

The prevailing wisdom that North Dakotans are divided equally among Republican, Democrat and Independent no longer seems to be true. In recent years, the state has been swinging to the Republicans. A popular Republican governor, first elected in 1992, won re-election overwhelmingly in 1996. The state House now strongly favors Republicans, and the GOP also controls the state Senate.

Although Republicans dominate at the local level, voters send Democrats to Washington. Many struggling farmers may now view the state Democratic Party as the modern vehicle for an old force in North Dakota politics, the agrarian populist movement. The original organized expression of that populism was the Non-partisan League, which early in this century spoke for the "little man" and his suspicions of concentrated business interests — railroads, banks and grain companies.

The state's two Democratic senators, Kent Conrad and Byron L. Dorgan, drew national attention leading up to the March 1995 vote on the balanced-budget constitutional amendment. Both senators voted against the amendment — dooming it — when Republicans declined their appeal to include language protecting Social Security.

But the two senators and North Dakota's lone member of the House, Democrat Pomeroy, who has also voted against the balanced-budget amendment, are not out of step with their state. North Dakota has never been a place where people complain about government spending. Many residents rely on Social Security and many others live on farms, which have depended on federal aid.

Yet when it comes to presidential politics, the state opts for the GOP. The last Democrat to carry North Dakota was Lyndon B. Johnson. Republicans have consistently exceeded their national average here since then, though they failed to win a majority in 1992 and 1996. Bob Dole won the state in 1996 with 47 percent. Ross Perot fell to 12 percent after tapping the state's independent streak with 23 percent in 1992.

The state had faced hard times in the 1980s as a weakness in the agricultural economy and a drop in farmland values causing many small farms to disappear from the map. North Dakota has the unwelcome distinction of being the only state with fewer residents than there were in 1930.

There had been signs that North Dakota agriculture was getting back on an even keel in the 1990s, albeit with large-scale, highly mechanized operations playing a more dominant role. But the state endured rough weather in the winter of 1996-97, when massive snowstorms buried homes up to their rooftops. With the spring thaw, the Red River rose high up out of its banks, flooding Fargo and Grand Forks and all the small towns in between — forcing 100,000 people to flee their homes. Grand Forks was evacuated and fires erupted even while water was flowing down the city streets. Congress struggled to respond to the spring devastation with federal disaster aid.

Much of North Dakota's population exodus has occurred in the western portion of the state. Too dry for a good wheat crop, the arid buttes and rolling grasslands attracted cattle ranches. There also is some energy development, although the area oil industry was hit hard by the slide in oil prices during the 1980s.

The coal industry in the southwestern part of the state also has been through rough times, although it got a boost from the Great Plains coal gasification plant in Beulah (Mercer County). The plant did not fulfill grand expectations of transforming huge amounts of coal to natural gas. But private interests bought it from the federal government in 1988 and turned a profit one year later.

Still, within the state, population migration in recent years has been from west to east. The population centers are both on the Red River, which defines North Dakota's eastern border with Minnesota. Fargo (Cass County) grew 21 percent in the 1980s to a population of 74,000.

To the north are the 49,000 residents of Grand Forks (Grand Forks County). With major medical facilities and the two major state universities (the University of North Dakota in Grand Forks and North Dakota State University in Fargo), eastern North Dakota offers most of the state's available white-collar jobs.

The east is also the state's most prosperous agricultural area; the moisture in the soil allowed the region to endure even the great dust storms of the 1930s. The Red River flows through a region that produces wheat, sugar beets and potatoes.

The two other population centers are in the central part of the state: Bismarck (Burleigh County) and Minot (Ward County). Bismarck is the state capital. Also, representatives of the United Tribes (from all over the Americas) gather here for the International Powwow in the fall.

One of North Dakota's two major Air Force bases, Grand Forks, was on the Defense secretary's May 1993 list of military facilities recommended for closure, but the base-closing commission declined to close it. In 1995, the Pentagon recommended cutting about 1,700 jobs at the base.

1990 Population: 638,800. White 604,142 (95%), Black 3,524 (1%), Other 31,134 (5%). Hispanic origin 4,665 (1%). 18 and over 463,415 (73%), 62 and over 107,200 (17%). Median age: 32.

ity of balancing the budget, he voted in 1995 against a GOP-backed balanced-budget constitutional amendment, expressing concern that money reserved for future Social Security payouts might have to be diverted to balance the budget.

This is essentially the same position North Dakota's two Democratic senators have taken in explaining their opposition to the balanced-budget amendment. Kent Conrad and Byron L. Dorgan have sought to include language in the amendment to protect Social Security, a concession the GOP would not make.

In 1995, Pomeroy slammed the House-passed GOP budget-reconciliation bill, which aimed to balance the budget in seven years and offered a $245 billion tax cut. "The effects of this $245 billion tax cut are enormous," Pomeroy said. "The rich get a windfall, and we sacrifice health programs for seniors, nutrition programs for kids, the safety net for family farmers, and even pension security for millions of Americans." President Clinton vetoed the measure in December.

One of Pomeroy's main concerns at the start of 1997 was getting federal disaster aid for his state, which was hit with such severe flooding in April that Grand Forks had to be evacuated. Fargo was also under water. Congress moved to put together a supplemental spending bill that included billions of dollars to help flood victims affected by the swollen Red River.

At Home: Pomeroy's move to the House came as a surprise. In 1992, with his second term as state insurance commissioner ending, Pomeroy decided to leave politics and announced that he and his wife were joining the Peace Corps, with a likely billet to Russia. But on the day of the state Democratic convention, the couple set aside dreams of cultural exploration abroad.

Two days earlier a political scramble had been touched off when Democratic Sen. Conrad announced that he was retiring rather than renege on a 1986 campaign promise not to seek re-election unless the deficit was reduced. Democratic Rep. Dorgan jumped into the race to succeed him, leaving his House seat open. Hours before the nominations were to begin, Pomeroy, a well-known 12-year veteran officeholder, accepted party entreaties to run for Dorgan's seat.

Pomeroy had four successful elections under his belt as well as a couple of years' experience in Washington as the national spokesman for insurance regulators. At age 28, he bucked the 1980 Reagan landslide and won election to North Dakota's state House. After two terms, he moved on to the insurance commissioner's post in 1984.

Unopposed in the primary and a solid November favorite, Pomeroy took 57 percent against GOP businessman John T. Korsmo.

In 1994, Pomeroy faced GOP state Rep. Gary Porter, who waged an aggressive campaign, painting Pomeroy as a loyal supporter of Clinton and the Democratic congressional leadership and criticizing his vote for a broad anti-crime crime bill because it banned certain types of semiautomatic assault-style weapons. The nationwide GOP tide was a cause for worry for Pomeroy, but he ran seven points ahead of Porter, tallying 52 percent.

Pomeroy's 1996 Republican challenger, state tourism director Kevin Cramer, argued that North Dakota was being shortchanged in Congress because its members are in the Democratic minority. Pomeroy contrasted his record to what he called the GOP's radical agenda. This time the spread was 12 percentage points, with Pomeroy taking 55 percent of the vote.

HOUSE ELECTIONS

1996 General		
Earl Pomeroy (D)	144,833	(55%)
Kevin Cramer (R)	113,684	(43%)
Kenneth R. Loughead (I)	4,493	(2%)
1994 General		
Earl Pomeroy (D)	123,134	(52%)
Gary Porter (R)	105,988	(45%)
James Germalic (I)	6,267	(3%)

Previous Winning Percentages: 1992 (57%)

CAMPAIGN FINANCE

	Receipts	Receipts from PACs	Expend-itures
1996			
Pomeroy (D)	$983,193	$604,261 (61%)	$971,332
Cramer (R)	$434,866	$61,999 (14%)	$434,082
1994			
Pomeroy (D)	$810,801	$521,965 (64%)	$813,900
Porter (R)	$821,095	$26,964 (3%)	$818,392

DISTRICT VOTE FOR PRESIDENT

1996		1992	
D	106,905 (40%)	D	99,168 (32%)
R	125,050 (47%)	R	136,244 (45%)
I	32,515 (12%)	I	71,084 (23%)

KEY VOTES

1997	
Ban "partial birth" abortions	Y
1996	
Approve farm bill	N
Deny public education to illegal immigrants	N
Repeal ban on certain assault-style weapons	N
Increase minimum wage	Y
Freeze defense spending	Y
Approve welfare overhaul	Y
1995	
Approve balanced-budget constitutional amendment	N
Relax Clean Water Act regulations	N
Oppose limits on environmental regulations	Y
Reduce projected Medicare spending	N
Approve GOP budget with tax and spending cuts	N

VOTING STUDIES

	Presidential Support		Party Unity		Conservative Coalition	
Year	S	O	S	O	S	O
1996	78	19	78	20	65	31
1995	79	20	80	18	57	42
1994	76	21	84	14	72	28
1993	76	24	86	13	50	45

INTEREST GROUP RATINGS

Year	ADA	AFL-CIO	CCUS	ACU
1996	80	n/a	31	11
1995	80	92	39	23
1994	65	38	75	14
1993	65	92	20	21

OHIO

Governor: George V. Voinovich (R)
First elected: 1990
Length of term: 4 years
Term expires: 1/99
Salary: $115,762.50
Term limit: 2 terms
Phone: (614) 644-0813
Born: July 15, 1936; Collinwood, Ohio.
Education: Ohio U., B.A., 1958; Ohio State U., J.D., 1961.
Occupation: Lawyer.
Family: Wife, Janet Allan; three children.
Religion: Roman Catholic.
Political Career: Ohio assistant attorney general, 1963-64; Ohio House, 1967-71; Cuyahoga County auditor, 1971-76; Cuyahoga County Commission, 1977-78; lieutenant governor, 1979; mayor of Cleveland, 1979-90; Republican nominee for U.S. Senate, 1988.

Lt. Gov.: Nancy Hollister (R)
First elected: 1994
Length of term: 4 years
Term expires: 1/99
Salary: $59,842
Phone: (614) 466-3396

State election official: (614) 466-2585
Democratic headquarters: (614) 221-6563
Republican headquarters: (614) 228-2481

REDISTRICTING

Ohio lost two House seats in reapportionment, dropping from 21 districts to 19. The legislature passed the map March 26, 1992; the governor signed it March 27.

STATE LEGISLATURE

General Assembly. Meets January-July in odd years, January-June in even years.

Senate: 33 members, 4-year terms.
1996 breakdown: 21R, 12D; 25 men, 8 women
Salary: $42,427
Phone: (614) 466-4900

House of Representatives: 99 members, 2-year terms
1996 breakdown: 60R, 39D; 78 men, 21 women
Salary: $42,427
Phone: (614) 466-3357

URBAN STATISTICS

City	Population
Columbus	632,910
Mayor Gregory S. Lashutka, R	
Cleveland	505,616
Mayor Michael R. White, D	
Cincinnati	364,114
Mayor Roxanne Qualls, D	
Toledo	332,943
Mayor Carty Finkbeiner, N-P	

U.S. CONGRESS

Senate: 1 D, 1 R
House: 8 D, 11 R

TERM LIMITS

For state offices: Yes
Senate: 2 terms
House: 4 terms

ELECTIONS

1996 Presidential Vote

Bill Clinton	47%
Bob Dole	41%
Ross Perot	11%

1992 Presidential Vote

Bill Clinton	40%
George Bush	38%
Ross Perot	21%

1988 Presidential Vote

George Bush	55%
Michael S. Dukakis	44%

POPULATION

1990 population		10,847,115
1980 population		10,797,630
Percent change		+<1%
Rank among states:		7
White		88%
Black		11%
Hispanic		1%
Asian or Pacific islander		1%
Urban		74%
Rural		26%
Born in state		74%
Foreign-born		2%
Under age 18	2,799,744	26%
Ages 18-64	6,640,410	61%
65 and older	1,406,961	13%
Median age		33.3

MISCELLANEOUS

Capital: Columbus
Number of counties: 88
Per capita income: $17,916 (1991)
Rank among states: 23
Total area: 41,330 sq. miles
Rank among states: 35

OHIO

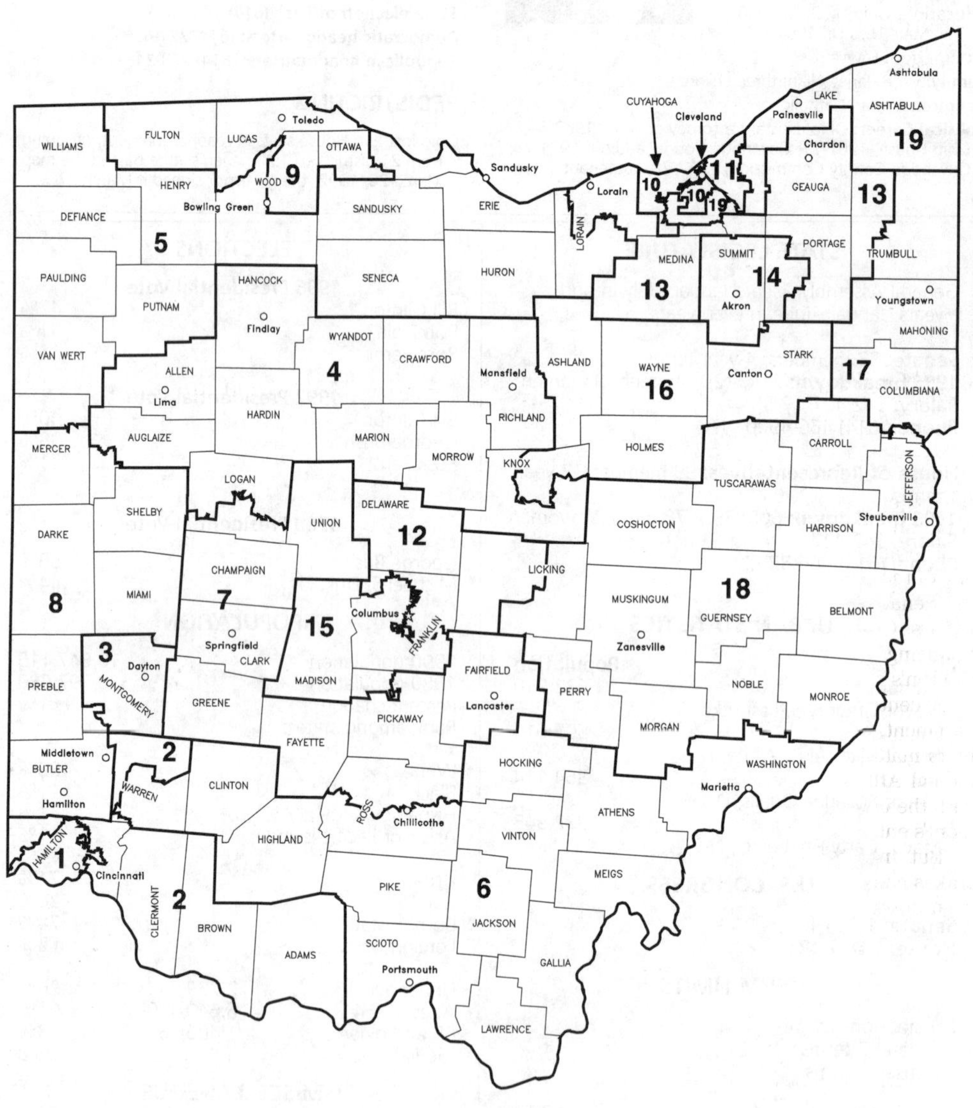

WILLIAMS
FULTON
LUCAS
Toledo
OTTAWA
9
WOOD
Sandusky
HENRY
Bowling Green
DEFIANCE
5
SANDUSKY
ERIE
PAULDING
PUTNAM
HANCOCK
SENECA
HURON
Findlay
VAN WERT
ALLEN
Lima
WYANDOT
4
CRAWFORD
Mansfield
ASHLAND
HARDIN
RICHLAND
AUGLAIZE
MARION
MERCER
MORROW
KNOX
LOGAN
SHELBY
UNION
DELAWARE
12
DARKE
CHAMPAIGN
LICKING
MIAMI
7
8
Columbus
15
FRANKLIN
3
Springfield
Dayton
CLARK
PREBLE
MONTGOMERY
MADISON
FAIRFIELD
GREENE
PICKAWAY
Lancaster
PERRY
FAYETTE
Middletown
BUTLER
2
HOCKING
CLINTON
WARREN
Hamilton
ROSS
Chillicothe
HAMILTON
1
HIGHLAND
VINTON
Cincinnati
2
CLERMONT
BROWN
PIKE
6
ADAMS
SCIOTO
JACKSON
Portsmouth
GALLIA
LAWRENCE
CUYAHOGA
Cleveland
10
Lorain
11
10
19
LORAIN
MEDINA
SUMMIT
13
14
Akron
Ashtabula
LAKE
Painesville
ASHTABULA
19
Chardon
GEAUGA
13
PORTAGE
TRUMBULL
Youngstown
MAHONING
STARK
Canton
17
COLUMBIANA
WAYNE
16
HOLMES
CARROLL
TUSCARAWAS
JEFFERSON
Steubenville
COSHOCTON
HARRISON
18
MUSKINGUM
GUERNSEY
BELMONT
Zanesville
NOBLE
MONROE
MORGAN
WASHINGTON
Marietta
ATHENS
MEIGS

John Glenn (D)

Of Columbus — Elected 1974; 4th term

Biographical Information
Born: July 18, 1921, Cambridge, Ohio.
Education: Muskingum College, B.S. 1962.
Military Service: Marine Corps, 1942-65.
Occupation: Astronaut; soft drink company executive.
Family: Wife, Anna Margaret Castor; two children.
Religion: Presbyterian.
Political Career: Sought Democratic nomination for U.S. Senate, 1970; sought Democratic nomination for president, 1984.

Capitol Office: 503 Hart Bldg. 20510; 224-3353.

Committees
Special Aging
Armed Services
Airland Forces (ranking); Readiness; Strategic Forces
Governmental Affairs (ranking)
Investigations (ranking)
Select Intelligence

In Washington: On Feb. 20, 1997 — the 35th anniversary of his historic orbit around the planet — Glenn announced that he would not run for re-election to the Senate in 1998.

Glenn said his decision was based not on politics or the atmosphere in Congress but on the fact that he would be 83 if he served out another full term. Despite all the technological advances since he became the first American to orbit the Earth in 1962, Glenn quipped, "there is still no cure for the common birthday."

The announcement came as Glenn confronts one of the most challenging roles he has played in the Senate: top Democrat on the Governmental Affairs Committee, which is investigating the financing of 1996 campaigns, including President Clinton's re-election bid.

A centrist Democrat with a technocrat's temperament, Glenn is well suited to the nuts-and-bolts matters normally on the docket at Governmental Affairs. His passion for detail mixes well with the committee's mission to study the government's entrails.

But in the committee's high-visibility, high-stakes campaign finance inquiry, it remains to be seen how the typically non-confrontational, nonpartisan Glenn will work with committee Chairman Fred Thompson, R-Tenn., whose handling of the committee could have bearing on his prospects to contend for the Republican presidential nomination in 2000.

Glenn has spent most of his career focusing on a handful of issues. Indeed, colleagues who admire his character and dedication wonder if he might have accomplished more had he not always been so narrowly focused. But Glenn is simply not the sort to roam the legislative landscape.

Respected as an American icon throughout his prominent public life, Glenn has tried to live by the words he issued even after his dismal 1984 bid for the presidency: "You keep climbing." But Glenn's entanglement in the Keating Five scandal made his climb a steeper one. The Senate Ethics Committee's investigation into his dealings with savings and loan operator Charles H. Keating Jr. concluded that Glenn had not done anything improper or illegal, but the episode took some luster off Glenn's public image.

Glenn was caught up early in the investigation of five lawmakers suspected of doing favors for a wealthy campaign contributor. Of the five senators (the others were Democrats Alan Cranston of California, Donald W. Riegle Jr. of Michigan and Dennis DeConcini of Arizona, and Republican John McCain of Arizona), Glenn may have been Keating's oldest friend in the Senate. They had both personal and political connections. The two met in 1970, when Glenn first ran for the Senate.

Glenn emphasized that he ended virtually all contacts with Keating after federal regulators informed senators that criminal charges might be filed in the case. His only action after that was to set up a lunch meeting in January 1988 between Keating and then-House Speaker Jim Wright of Texas.

The Ethics Committee concluded that Glenn "exercised poor judgment" in arranging the luncheon, but that his actions "did not reach the level requiring institutional action against him."

In the 103rd Congress, Glenn played a pivotal role in helping the Clinton administration pass several measures key to its "reinventing government" initiative. As chairman of Governmental Affairs, he oversaw the portions of the bill dealing with financial and personnel management.

Glenn won Senate passage of two of the plan's main provisions, one to streamline federal purchasing procedures, the other to trim the federal work force by about 250,000 employees, partially through worker buyouts. Under Glenn's tutelage, the panel also approved a measure to revise the Paperwork Reduction Act, a bill aimed at reducing the government's volume of paper.

In the 103rd, Glenn also was responsible for moving a measure through the committee to revamp the Hatch Act. The bill, a version of which was later approved by the Senate and the House, gave federal employees greater latitude to participate in political activities during non-work hours, while tightening on-the-job restrictions.

When the 104th Congress convened, Glenn was no doubt pleased to see some of his longtime favorites on the GOP's legislative agenda: the Paperwork Reduction Act, the "unfunded mandates" measure and congressional compliance with workplace laws.

In the 103rd, Glenn, along with Idaho Republican Dirk Kempthorne, sponsored a measure that would make it harder for Congress to impose mandates on state and local governments without providing funding to carry out the edicts.

The legislation required any congressional committee reporting an authorization bill mandating a federal program to ask the Congressional Budget Office to estimate its cost. The CBO was required to provide a detailed report on any legislation that would impose net costs on local governments of more than $50 million. While the bill never made it into law in the 103rd, similar legislation moved quickly into law in the 104th.

Congress enacted another item early in the 104th that Glenn had advocated: a measure to force Congress to comply with federal labor and worker safety laws other employers must obey.

Despite his successes, the 103rd was not all roses for Glenn. He failed in his efforts, in spite of the president's support, to elevate the Environmental Protection Agency to a Cabinet-level position. The Senate approved the bill in May 1993, but the House, caught up in a dispute over risk assessment, failed to take action.

Glenn's mastery of detail has been useful in the legislative arena, but that and other of his personal traits made him a flop on the presidential campaign trail. Advertised as the main competitor to Walter F. Mondale for the 1984 Democratic nomination, Glenn proved poor at public speaking, made weak showings in a succession of primaries and caucuses, and dropped out of the race.

Just when Glenn seemed resigned to finishing out his political career in the Senate, Massachusetts Democratic Gov. Michael S. Dukakis began to hint strongly in 1988 that he might make Glenn his running mate. Instead, Dukakis chose Texas Sen. Lloyd Bentsen, who he hoped could put the state in the Democratic column for president. Ever the good sport, Glenn introduced Bentsen at the convention in what, ironically, was perhaps his best-ever national speech — one that generated more audience response than Bentsen's.

On Governmental Affairs, Glenn was an active chairman. He played a key role in the passage of legislation to create the Cabinet-level Department of Veterans Affairs. But he unsuccessfully advocated new agencies — created from components of the Commerce Department and the Office of the U.S. Trade Representative — to enhance U.S. competitiveness in trade and industrial policy.

Since the start of the 99th Congress, Glenn has served on the Armed Services Committee. Through most of his career, he has tilted to the hawkish side on national security matters. But his overall record is that of a centrist who, despite his background as a test pilot, has not hesitated to oppose weapons systems if he deems them too expensive.

Glenn has generally enjoyed good working relations with Republicans on the committee. During the 102nd Congress, when many in Congress were calling for a repeal of military policies that excluded women pilots from combat, Glenn and McCain led the majority of the committee's members in opposing an immediate repeal. They preferred to wait for the outcome of additional studies before a decision was made. No repeal was enacted in the 102nd, but Clinton overturned the exclusion rule himself early in 1993.

As U.S. troops began to fight in the Persian Gulf in January 1991, Senate Majority Leader George J. Mitchell appointed Glenn chairman of a Democratic task force to review legislative proposals for aiding military families. Congress subsequently cleared a package of new benefits — including a broad range of tax, health, pay and other benefits for returning troops — for veterans and military personnel.

Glenn also promoted legislation in the 102nd and 103rd to repeal the honoraria ban on federal employees, which prohibits them from accepting writing or speaking fees. In February 1995, the Supreme Court ruled that the honoraria ban does not apply to rank-and-file federal employees who work in the executive branch.

Aiming to close the gap between federal and private-sector salaries, Glenn sponsored an overhaul of the federal pay system in 1990. The new plan gives federal workers raises equal to average annual salary increases in the private sector.

Glenn is the acknowledged expert in Congress on the nuclear proliferation issue, urging foreign nations not to use materials or technology to build nuclear weapons. Glenn's anti-proliferation efforts brought him into frequent conflict with the Reagan administration. Throughout the 1980s, Glenn fought President Ronald Reagan over efforts to send military aid to India and Pakistan, to sell nuclear-power materials to China and to offer nuclear fuel to the Japanese. He continued that stance under President George Bush.

At Home: Glenn drew no punishment in the Keating Five investigation, but the whiff of scandal weakened his popularity in Ohio and gave Lt. Gov. Mike DeWine a fighting chance against him in 1992. (DeWine joined Glenn in the Senate in 1994, when he beat Democrat Joel Hyatt to succeed Democratic Sen. Howard M. Metzenbaum, who retired.)

Against Glenn in 1992, DeWine sounded the most common candidate klaxon, running as the candidate of "change." His strategy from the start was to focus attention on what he considered Glenn's twin albatrosses: the Keating affair and the seemingly irreducible $3 million debt remaining from his 1984 presidential bid. Glenn, seeking his fourth six-year term at age 71, appeared vulnerable.

But DeWine, who had served four terms in the

House and spent most of his adult life in politics, had some trouble coming across as a political outsider. And although he held statewide office, DeWine was not well-known to most Ohioans.

As DeWine sought to tar Glenn with the Keating and debt questions, he also questioned the incumbent's accomplishments during his tenure. "After 18 years in the Senate, what on Earth has John Glenn done?" DeWine inquired, implying that Glenn's terrestrial achievements did not measure up to his pioneering in space.

Glenn decided to engage DeWine early, criticizing him for his opposition to abortion rights and his overdrafts at the House bank and accusing him of having an undistinguished congressional record. On Election Day, Glenn won nearly every county in a swath across industrial northern and eastern Ohio, and he did well in rural, usually Republican southern Ohio as well. He won by 51 percent to 42 percent.

That was Glenn's first brush with electoral difficulty since his earliest days in politics. His career in Congress was delayed for a decade, first by an injury and then by an unexpected defeat.

In 1962, still basking in the glow of his space exploits, Glenn decided to challenge 74-year-old Sen. Stephen M. Young in the 1964 Democratic primary. But he did not get very far: A bathroom fall injured his inner ear, and he had to drop out of the primary.

Glenn's political ambitions then temporarily subsided. He plunged into business, serving on the boards of Royal Crown Cola and the Questor Corp., overseeing four Holiday Inn franchises he partly owned, lecturing and filming television documentaries.

In 1970, with Young retiring, Glenn decided to run for the seat, competing for the Democratic nomination against Metzenbaum, then a millionaire businessman and labor lawyer. Initially a strong favorite, Glenn found that his frequent absences from Ohio over the preceding six years had hurt him with state Democrats. Glenn, whose celebrity status was bringing out large crowds, was overconfident. Meanwhile, Metzenbaum erased his relative anonymity through saturation television advertising. On primary day, Glenn lost the nomination by 13,442 votes.

Metzenbaum was beaten in the general election by Republican Robert A. Taft Jr. Three years later, however, he made it to the Senate as an appointee, chosen by Democratic Gov. John J. Gilligan to fill a vacancy. Metzenbaum immediately began campaigning for a full term in his own right, and Glenn — who made up for his previous mistake by becoming a regular on the political circuit — challenged him for the nomination.

The underdog Glenn of 1974 proved to be much tougher than the favored Glenn of 1970. Glenn was able to even the score with Metzenbaum, winning the primary by 91,000 votes. In the fall, Glenn crushed a weak Republican foe, Cleveland Mayor Ralph J. Perk.

Six years later, Glenn had only nominal opposition for a second term. His win, with 69 percent of the vote, marked him as a 1984 presidential contender. His bid for the Democratic nomination fell flat, though, despite his image as a hero and as a moderate alternative to Mondale. Refocusing on Ohio two years later, Glenn easily won a third Senate term over GOP Rep. Thomas N. Kindness.

SENATE ELECTIONS

1992 General

John Glenn (D)	2,444,419	(51%)
Mike DeWine (R)	2,028,300	(42%)
Martha Kathryn Grevatt (I)	321,234	(7%)

Previous Winning Percentages: 1986 (62%) **1980** (69%) **1974** (65%)

CAMPAIGN FINANCE

	Receipts	Receipts from PACs		Expend-itures
1992				
Glenn (D)	$3,946,713	$1,190,451	(30%)	$3,999,271
DeWine (R)	$3,048,971	$588,975	(19%)	$3,053,156

KEY VOTES

1997	
Approve balanced-budget constitutional amendment	N
Approve chemical weapons treaty	Y
1996	
Approve farm bill	N
Limit punitive damages in product liability cases	Y
Exempt small businesses from higher minimum wage	N
Approve welfare overhaul	N
Bar job discrimination based on sexual orientation	Y
Override veto of ban on "partial birth" abortions	N
1995	
Approve GOP budget with tax and spending cuts	N
Approve constitutional amendment barring flag desecration	N

VOTING STUDIES

	Presidential Support		Party Unity		Conservative Coalition	
Year	S	O	S	O	S	O
1996	88	12	90	10	18	82
1995	89	8	86	12	33	63
1994	92	5	89	9	22	75
1993	97	3	90	9	37	59
1992	30	68	83	17	37	58
1991	41	56	83	14	38	63

INTEREST GROUP RATINGS

Year	ADA	AFL-CIO	CCUS	ACU
1996	95	n/a	23	10
1995	80	100	37	5
1994	80	75	33	4
1993	85	73	27	13
1992	80	75	10	11
1991	90	75	0	10

Mike DeWine (R)

Of Cedarville — Elected 1994, 1st term

Biographical Information

Born: Jan. 5, 1947, Springfield, Ohio.
Education: Miami U. (Ohio), B.S. 1969; Ohio Northern U., J.D. 1972.
Occupation: Lawyer.
Family: Wife, Frances Struewing; eight children.
Religion: Roman Catholic.
Political Career: Greene County prosecuting attorney, 1977-81; Ohio Senate, 1981-83; U.S. House, 1983-91; lieutenant governor, 1991-95; Republican nominee for U.S. Senate, 1992.

Capitol Office: 140 Russell Bldg. 20510; 224-2315.

Committees

Select Intelligence
Judiciary
Antitrust, Business Rights & Competition (chairman); Youth Violence
Labor & Human Resources
Employment & Training (chairman); Public Health & Safety

In Washington: DeWine is a conservative on most fiscal and social issues, and in the 105th Congress, business interests wished him all the best in his efforts to pass legislation allowing companies to offer employees comp time in lieu of pay for overtime work. DeWine shepherded that measure in his role as chairman of Labor and Human Resources' Employment and Training Subcommittee.

But if first-termer DeWine fits in comfortably with the Senate's conservative Republican majority, there is a streak of moderation in his record that sets him a bit apart from the chamber's other recent arrivals who have taken up residence on the GOP's right flank.

For instance, on the Judiciary Committee in the 104th, DeWine took a more moderate stance on immigration matters than some in his party, opposing efforts to limit legal immigration. Immigration Subcommittee Chairman Alan K. Simpson, R-Wyo., proposed cutting the overall number of family reunification visas, and he sought to eliminate provisions in existing law that put a priority on reuniting families by giving immigration preference to adult children of legal immigrants. Critics portrayed this plan as inconsistent with promoting "family values," observed DeWine, "I think this constriction takes a very pessimistic view of this country."

On another matter, when the Labor Committee in February 1996 considered a Republican measure to constrain the Occupational Safety and Health Administration (OSHA), DeWine offered an amendment striking a portion of the bill that would have limited OSHA's inspection practices. The bill aimed to bar OSHA from inspecting a workplace unless an employee had filed a complaint. Existing law permits OSHA to inspect a workplace whether or not a complaint has been filed, and DeWine's amendment sought to retain that authority for OSHA.

In early 1997, DeWine also backed legislation to reauthorize the National Endowment for the Arts and the National Endowment for Humanities, saying he believes they play an important role in early childhood education. Many conservatives want to abolish the agencies.

A family tragedy spurred DeWine's interest in highway safety and organ donation. In 1993, when he was campaigning for the Senate, DeWine's 22-year-old daughter Becky was killed when her car collided with a pickup truck on a rain-slick highway near the DeWines' home. The incident prompted DeWine to speak strongly against efforts in the 104th to repeal national interstate highway speed limits. He urged senators to resist the politically popular course of backing repeal. "The old adage had it right. Speed does in fact kill. Everyone in this chamber knows that," he said.

DeWine joined Sen. Byron L. Dorgan, D-N.D., who also lost a daughter, to establish the congressional organ donation caucus, which publicizes donor programs. Becky DeWine's eyes were donated after her death.

It was a more conventional issue for a conservative, the "comp time" bill, that put DeWine in the spotlight early in the 105th. The bill permitted private-sector employers to give workers the option of being compensated with pay or time off when they work more than 40 hours in a week. The measure also allowed businesses to offer "flex-time" schedules. DeWine said the measure would give workers more control over their work schedules.

But organized labor and its Democratic allies in Congress strenuously opposed the bill, arguing that it could lead to unscrupulous businesses coercing workers to take whatever form of compensation the company preferred.

DeWine responded, "It's voluntary. The employee doesn't have to enter this." But he showed a willingness to compromise. In May 1997 he said he would support certain changes to the bill, such as clarifying that it would not interfere with arrangements worked out by labor unions and employers under collective bargaining agreements. But Democratic resistance to the bill was still so stubborn that GOP leaders were having trouble even getting the Senate to end debate on the matter so a vote could be set.

DeWine, who has eight children, also focuses much legislative attention on children's issues. He won approval in the 104th for an additional $50 million for pediatric research in the National Institutes of Health budget. And he fought to rewrite a federal law that requires agencies to make "reasonable efforts" to keep children in their own homes before resorting to foster-care placement. Although some in his party were pushing "parental rights" initiatives to restrict social workers from investigating allegations of child abuse, DeWine charged children were too often forced to "live with parents who are parents in name only. We send them back to homes that are homes in name only — to people who inflict pain, suffering, torture and abuse."

At Home: DeWine's 1994 election to the Senate was a testament to the slow-but-steady approach to success in Ohio politics.

The race was DeWine's third run for statewide office in five years and capped a political career that began shortly after his graduation from law school. His years of preparation for office have included stints as a county prosecutor, a state senator, a House member and lieutenant governor.

Nonetheless, in a race against Democratic Sen. John Glenn in 1992, DeWine tried to run as an outsider. He lost. Back for a second Senate bid in 1994 matchup, DeWine faced political novice Joel Hyatt, a legal entrepreneur and son-in-law of retiring Democratic Sen. Howard M. Metzenbaum. In that race, DeWine stressed his experience. All his years of service, DeWine said, added up to a proven record, while with Hyatt, "all you have is his word on it" — a sly rephrasing of the familiar line from Hyatt Legal Services' long-running commercial. He won 53 percent to 39 percent.

DeWine has never lacked drive or ambition. After law school, he spent three years as an assistant county prosecutor before running against his boss and beating him in 1976. In 1980, he won a seat in the Ohio Senate. Two years later he began his congressional career, winning the west central 7th District with 56 percent despite a statewide Democratic trend. After three easy re-elections, he considered a bid for governor before settling for the No. 2 job behind GOP Gov. George V. Voinovich.

Two years later, DeWine challenged Glenn and held him to 51 percent (DeWine took 42 percent, and an independent 7 percent). With his victory in 1994, DeWine seemed to verify an axiom of Ohio politics: You have to lose a statewide race before you can win one (it has been four decades since a candidate won the governorship or a Senate seat without first running statewide and losing).

For a time, however, it was far from certain that 1994 would be DeWine's year for running and winning. Many Republicans found him too conservative or too uninspiring. But when DeWine's campaign got under way, it was apparent he had learned from his years in the trenches. His ads played up his down-home origins, showing him wearing flannel shirts and a crooked grin. But behind that persona was a organized and efficient campaign that ran smoothly through a long primary and general-election haul.

SENATE ELECTIONS

1994 General		
Mike DeWine (R)	1,836,556	(53%)
Joel Hyatt (D)	1,348,213	(39%)
Joseph J. Slovenec (I)	252,031	(7%)
1994 Primary		
Mike DeWine (R)	422,366	(52%)
Bernadine Healy (R)	263,559	(32%)
Gene J. Watts (R)	83,103	(10%)
George H. Rhodes (R)	42,633	(5%)

Previous Winning Percentages: **1988*** (74%) **1986*** (100%) **1984*** (77%) **1982*** (56%)

* House elections

CAMPAIGN FINANCE

	Receipts	Receipts from PACs	Expend-itures
1994			
DeWine (R)	$6,344,528	$1,423,379(22%)	$6,274,663
Hyatt (D)	$4,274,071	$597,505 (14%)	$4,773,905
Slovenec (I)	$192,888	0 (0%)	$192,867

KEY VOTES

1997	
Approve balanced-budget constitutional amendment	Y
Approve chemical weapons treaty	Y
1996	
Approve farm bill	Y
Limit punitive damages in product liability cases	Y
Exempt small businesses from higher minimum wage	Y
Approve welfare overhaul	Y
Bar job discrimination based on sexual orientation	N
Override veto of ban on "partial birth" abortions	Y
1995	
Approve GOP budget with tax and spending cuts	Y
Approve constitutional amendment barring flag desecration	Y

VOTING STUDIES

	Presidential Support		Party Unity		Conservative Coalition	
Year	**S**	**O**	**S**	**O**	**S**	**O**
1996	41	59	88	12	92	8
1995	30	70	87	13	82	18

INTEREST GROUP RATINGS

Year	ADA	AFL-CIO	CCUS	ACU
1996	15	n/a	85	85
1995	0	8	89	70

1 Steve Chabot (R)

Of Cincinnati — Elected 1994, 2nd term

Biographical Information

Born: Jan. 22, 1953, Cincinnati, Ohio.
Education: College of William and Mary, B.A. 1975; Northern Kentucky U., J.D. 1978.
Occupation: Lawyer.
Family: Wife, Donna Daly; two children.
Religion: Roman Catholic.
Political Career: Independent candidate for Cincinnati city council, 1979; Republican candidate for Cincinnati city council, 1983; Republican nominee for U.S. House, 1988; Cincinnati city council member, 1985-90; Hamilton county commissioner, 1990-95.
Capitol Office: 129 Cannon Bldg. 20515; 225-2216.

Committees

International Relations
Africa; International Economic Policy & Trade
Judiciary
Commercial & Administrative Law; Crime
Small Business
Empowerment

In Washington: The 1st is supposed to be the more Democratic of Cincinnati's two districts, but Chabot captured it with a solid 56 percent in 1994 and held it for the GOP in 1996. In Congress, he votes a consistently conservative line, at times showing more zeal than House GOP leaders for cutting federal spending.

Chabot even stuck to his campaign pledge to restrain federal spending in one instance when his own constituency stood to benefit from Washington largess: During House consideration of a transportation spending bill in July 1995, he advocated deleting $666 million for mass transit grants, even though $2 million of the money would have gone to study a possible light rail system for Cincinnati.

Local civic leaders, including the mayor, grumbled about Chabot's effort to kill the grants, but Chabot felt many of the projects in the bill were a waste of money. "It might actually just be cheaper if we just bought people cars," he said. The effort to spike the money lost on a 114-302 vote.

"There is still too much pork in Congress, but we're heading in the right direction," Chabot told the Christian Science Monitor in October 1995. "Our goal is to convince fellow members that this should be the new standard by which we judge ourselves, not just voting for the parochial interests of our districts." In the long run, he said, Cincinnati will benefit more from prosperity spawned by a balanced budget than from continued federal handouts.

Chabot's fiscal austerity has led him to buck the GOP leadership's wishes on several high-profile votes. In early January 1996 he was one of 15 Republicans defying House Speaker Newt Gingrich's directive to vote to end a partial closure of the federal government that had stemmed from an impasse in budget talks between Congress and the White House. In June 1996, Chabot and 18 other Republicans voted "no" on the final version of the fiscal 1997 GOP budget agreement, complaining that it showed a short-term increase in the deficit and included $4 billion in extra domestic spending.

In September 1996, he was among 24 Republicans opposing a $610 billion omnibus spending bill for fiscal 1997. Deficit hawks complained that the bill was larded with unnecessary spending, but most GOP lawmakers were eager to get a deal with President Clinton so they could adjourn Congress and hit the campaign trail.

Chabot swung his budget-cutting ax at the National Endowment for the Humanities, offering an amendment in July 1995 to cut the agency's entire $99.5 million budget. "These types of programs, if they are going to be funded, should be funded privately through philanthropy, not federal tax dollars," Chabot said. The House rejected his amendment, voting instead to phase out the agency over two years.

Unlike some GOP conservatives, Chabot carries his skepticism about federal spending into Congress' deliberations on the Pentagon budget. In June 1996, he was one of 60 Republicans to support a proposal to freeze the fiscal 1997 defense budget at prior-year levels. He has also voted to kill funding for NASA's space station.

The debate in the 104th about overhauling immigration law prompted Chabot, a member of the Judiciary Committee, to raise concerns about concentrating power in the hands of the central government. He took particular exception to a proposal that employers be required to call the federal government to verify that prospective employees are legally eligible to work.

Chabot called the proposal "1-800-BIG BROTHER" and tried to strip it from the immigration bill. California Republican Elton Gallegly, who proposed the worker verification system, said it was needed to stop illegal aliens from unlawfully gaining jobs. Under the proposal, employers would call a toll-free government line to verify the name and Social Security number of a new employee. The Judiciary Committee did not endorse a verification system, but it approved pilot programs in five states to test the idea.

Even a pilot program made Chabot unhappy. "I don't like the concept that a business owner

Nestled snugly in the southwestern corner of the state, the 1st reaches out to take in almost every Democrat in the Cincinnati area, leaving the surrounding 2nd District solidly Republican. But the increasing muscle of suburban conservatives in the 1st has offset, somewhat, the district's Democratic inclination.

Cincinnati's black population helped former Democratic Rep. Thomas A. Luken build a majority here in the 1980s, and 1992's round of redistricting gave the 1st a 30 percent black population, compared with 16 percent in the previous decade.

The 1st includes about 85 percent of Cincinnati's 364,000 residents. In order to win, Democrats must receive heavy support from the city's black community — blacks make up 44 percent of this part of Cincinnati and only 14 percent of the rest of the district.

Bill Clinton carried the district twice — by a scant 155 votes in 1992, and by more than 14,000 votes four years later. But Clinton's re-election did not impede Republican Chabot from winning his own second term in 1996 with 54 percent of the vote.

Forming another dominant political bloc are the German Catholics who have defined the city's cautious, conservative personality for more than 100 years. Once clustered in the West Side section of the city known as "Over-the-Rhine," the German-Americans gradually moved out to suburbs such as Cheviot and Green Township. These voters have moved steadily toward the GOP in recent years.

At the bottom of Walnut Hill, in the flat Ohio River basin, is downtown Cincinnati, with the

OHIO 1
Hamilton County — Western Cincinnati and suburbs

Taft Museum and wharves for old stern-wheelers such as the Delta Queen. Construction of Riverfront Stadium and Coliseum (home of baseball's Reds and football's Bengals) in the early 1970s symbolized a downtown renewal project designed to lure suburban dollars back to the city.

A major Ohio River port and a regional center of commerce, the city is headquarters for the giant Procter & Gamble Co.; Milacron, a world leader in the production of machine tools; and Federated Department Stores Inc., which owns Macy's.

Cincinnati's diverse economy prevented it from suffering the degree of hardship that hit other industrial cities in the state in the early 1980s recession, although the region has not been immune from the string of defense cutbacks. The 1980s buildup boosted the revenues of numerous area defense contractors, the largest being General Electric Co., which provides jobs for blue-collar workers in the western section of the city. Renamed GE Aircraft Engines, the company has laid off numerous workers in recent years as it tries to move toward commercial work.

1990 Population: 570,900. White 391,483 (69%), Black 171,871 (30%), Other 7,546 (1%). Hispanic origin 3,421 (1%). 18 and over 420,468 (74%), 62 and over 91,686 (16%). Median age: 32.

would have to get the federal government's OK before they hire someone," he said. When the immigration bill reached the House floor in March 1996, Chabot paired with liberal John Conyers Jr. of Michigan, Judiciary's ranking Democrat, in an effort to strike the pilot programs. Their amendment failed, 159-260, and the final immigration bill cleared by the 104th included the pilot programs.

In the same vein, Chabot was one of four Republicans on Judiciary to vote in June 1995 against an anti-terrorism bill. He opposed provisions that would have broadened federal jurisdiction over violent crimes and expanded the FBI's ability to tap the phones of suspected terrorists.

Chabot called the bill an "overreaction" to the April 1995 bombing of a federal building in Oklahoma City. "I'm concerned there's the possibility there are groups outside of what I would consider terrorists that fall under the purview of this bill," Chabot said. "There are some pro-life groups who some in this administration might consider their tactics terrorist."

Chabot, a death penalty proponent, once said it is not widely perceived as a crime deterrent "because of the length of time that people remain on death row at taxpayer expense. The people in this country are sick and tired of paying for cable TV and . . . for food and lawyers for those who have killed innocent people."

In 1995 he supported a measure aimed at curbing death row appeals. The bill limited the opportunities for death row prisoners to challenge their state convictions in federal court through so-called habeas corpus petitions. Chabot said existing rules allow prisoners to "play games with our legal system from their prison cells for year after year after year."

During Judiciary debate on GOP anti-crime legislation, Chabot sought to ban weightlifting equipment and strength training in federal prisons. He said it was foolish to let prisoners get stronger when they might turn that strength against new victims after their release from jail.

Chabot also serves on the Small Business Committee and on the International Relations Committee, where he has been highly critical of the Clinton administration's support for international family planning organizations.

A vocal opponent of abortion, Chabot supported an amendment to the fiscal 1996 foreign aid spending bill reinstating the so-called Mexico City policy, which prohibits funding for organizations that perform abortions in foreign countries. Clinton had signed an executive order scrapping the Mexico City policy and other abortion-related federal policies soon after taking office.

At Home: Chabot began his political career on the Cincinnati City Council, the launching pad for several of his predecessors in the 1st, including the Democrat he defeated in 1994 and the one to whom he lost in 1988.

Chabot's first House bid was an energetic door-to-door campaign against Democrat Thomas A. Luken in 1988, in which he polled 44 percent of the vote. After five years on the council, Chabot in 1990 moved to the Hamilton County Board of Commissioners, where he was serving when he ran for the House again in 1994.

To this second congressional bid he brought more campaign experience and vastly greater resources. This time, he parlayed voter anger at all things Washington into a solid majority.

In 1990, the 1st passed from Thomas Luken, who retired, to his son, Charles Luken, and in subsequent redistricting, the district was drawn with the younger Luken in mind. The 1st contains almost all of Cincinnati's black residents, who make up 30 percent of the district's population. But when Luken unexpectedly announced after the 1992 primary that he was quitting Congress after just one term, a divisive Democratic special primary pitted a black state senator against David Mann, a wealthy local businessman.

Mann won the primary and then took the seat with a skimpy 51 percent in November. In Congress, his votes for NAFTA and against some of Clinton's fiscal policy proposals angered organized labor and other Democratic groups. In 1994, he barely survived another tough primary and entered the general election weakened.

Mann aggressively sought to distance himself from Clinton, running one ad boasting that he had opposed "Clinton's government takeover of health care." Chabot responded with an ad showing Mann's face transforming into Clinton's while a voiceover proclaimed: "A vote for this Mann is another vote for this man." Chabot painted Mann as an opportunist who blew with the political winds, and he stressed the message of lower taxes, less government and change in Washington.

Chabot emphasized his blue-collar beginnings and Catholic roots, reaching out to the mostly white voters of Cincinnati's working-class neighborhoods and western suburbs. He appealed to independent voters with his calls for congressional reform. With national trends strongly favoring the GOP, Chabot won by 12 percentage points.

In 1996, Chabot faced Democrat Mark Longabaugh, a former aide to House Democratic leader Richard A. Gephardt, and 1992 director of the Clinton-Gore campaign in Ohio; he had also run unsuccessfully for the Cincinnati City Council in 1995. Organized labor lent its voice to the effort to topple Chabot (who had opposed a minimum wage increase in 1996). But with Republicans portraying Longabaugh as an itinerant operative lacking Chabot's local roots, Chabot won by 11 points. Clinton carried the 1st in presidential voting.

HOUSE ELECTIONS

1996 General		
Steve Chabot (R)	118,324	(54%)
Mark P. Longabaugh (D)	94,719	(43%)
John G. Halley (NL)	5,381	(2%)
1994 General		
Steve Chabot (R)	92,997	(56%)
David Mann (D)	72,822	(44%)

CAMPAIGN FINANCE

	Receipts	Receipts from PACs	Expend-itures
1996			
Chabot (R)	$1,068,043	$366,866 (34%)	$983,163
Longabaugh (D)	$551,612	$201,338 (36%)	$544,875
1994			
Chabot (R)	$555,743	$71,576 (13%)	$542,829
Mann (D)	$1,012,740	$368,363 (36%)	$1,001,393

DISTRICT VOTE FOR PRESIDENT

	1996		1992
D	110,666 (50%)	**D**	104,494 (43%)
R	96,352 (43%)	**R**	104,339 (43%)
I	12,863 (6%)	**I**	34,531 (14%)

KEY VOTES

1997	
Ban "partial birth" abortions	Y
1996	
Approve farm bill	Y
Deny public education to illegal immigrants	Y
Repeal ban on certain assault-style weapons	Y
Increase minimum wage	N
Freeze defense spending	Y
Approve welfare overhaul	Y
1995	
Approve balanced-budget constitutional amendment	Y
Relax Clean Water Act regulations	Y
Oppose limits on environmental regulations	N
Reduce projected Medicare spending	Y
Approve GOP budget with tax and spending cuts	Y

VOTING STUDIES

	Presidential Support		Party Unity		Conservative Coalition	
Year	**S**	**O**	**S**	**O**	**S**	**O**
1996	34	63	84	13	65	31
1995	20	80	94	6	86	14

INTEREST GROUP RATINGS

Year	ADA	AFL-CIO	CCUS	ACU
1996	15	n/a	88	100
1995	0	0	96	100

2 Rob Portman (R)

Of Cincinnati — Elected 1993; 2nd full term

Biographical Information

Born: Dec. 19, 1955, Cincinnati, Ohio.

Education: Dartmouth College, B.A. 1979; U. of Michigan, J.D. 1984.

Occupation: Lawyer; White House aide.

Family: Wife, Jane Dudley; three children.

Religion: Methodist.

Political Career: Presidential associate counsel/White House Legis. Affairs director, 1989-91.

Capitol Office: 238 Cannon Bldg. 20515; 225-3164.

Committees

Government Reform & Oversight
Government Management, Information & Technology

Ways & Means
Oversight; Social Security

In Washington: A serious, detail-oriented lawmaker, Portman gained attention in the 104th Congress by successfully pressing unfunded mandates legislation, a high Republican priority and one of the few items in the House GOP's "Contract With America" to be signed into law.

And as the 105th got under way, Portman — who sits on the powerful House Ways and Means Committee — was delving into another topic of great interest within his party: scrutinizing the operations of the Internal Revenue Service.

Almost as soon as he won a 1993 special election to succeed Republican Rep. Bill Gradison, who resigned from Congress for an executive post in the insurance industry, Portman began an assault on unfunded mandates — federal requirements that states take certain actions without financial assistance from Washington.

Portman, who had learned his way around Congress by serving as director of legislative affairs when George Bush was president, argued that the proliferation of such mandates were tying the hands of state officials and draining their resources. "It's really a reasonable concept to a lot of people to think that Congress should have to make its decisions on an informed basis and then provide funding," he said in December 1994. "I see it as good government — honest, good accountability."

In the 104th, Portman was tapped by the newly empowered House GOP leaders to take the lead on unfunded mandates legislation. Working with Sen. Dirk Kempthorne, R-Idaho, and others, he moderated the original Contract With America language, which would have barred virtually all unfunded federal mandates.

Instead, the House and Senate bills sought to discourage the passage of such mandates in Congress by requiring that lawmakers take an additional vote when passing any bill that would impose unfunded costs of $50 million or more on state and local governments. The bill would not affect anti-discrimination laws that contained unfunded mandates.

Thanks to such moderating language, Republicans were able to win overwhelming support for the measure in both chambers, and President Clinton signed it into law. It was a rare legislative success in 1995 for House Republicans, who saw numerous elements of their conservative agenda stall after passing in the House.

During the congressional debate on the unfunded mandates bill, some states-rights advocates worried that it would do little to stop Congress from continuing to impose expensive mandates. But in the months after the measure became law, there was feedback from state officials expressing satisfaction that Washington had become more attuned to the problem of mandates.

Portman, who immersed himself in the details of the legislative language while the bill was being considered, conceded that the law would not put an absolute end to mandates. "There still is a tendency to expand the federal role," he said. "But the important thing is that people are considering the impact on state and local governments."

Portman feels strongly enough about respecting state prerogatives that he has been willing to buck the GOP leadership on some big issues. In 1995, he voted against Republican-sponsored provisions of the revamped crime bill, arguing that the federal government was putting undue pressure on states to stiffen criminal penalties. And he emerged as a strong, and often successful, advocate for increased state flexibility during debate over sweeping welfare legislation.

But on most social and fiscal issues, Portman remains firmly in the GOP camp. He opposes abortion, supported repealing a ban on certain semiautomatic assault-style weapons and voted to deny public education to illegal immigrants.

He also takes a conservative stance on most business-labor issues. He opposed an increase in the minimum wage when the House first passed the bill in May 1996, and he supported a measure to exempt small businesses from paying the higher wage. But when the wage bill returned to the House in August, he voted for it. The final version

OHIO 2
Southwest and Eastern Cincinnati and suburbs

Redistricting in 1992 turned the formerly politically mixed 2nd into a Republican bastion. The map shifted most of the Democratic eastern part of Cincinnati out of the 2nd; in exchange, the 2nd added rural western Hamilton County, a reliably Republican area. The 2nd also picked up all of Adams County and the northern and western parts of Warren County, two mostly rural counties, from the old 6th District.

The net effect of these changes has been the creation of a district that is one of the most solidly Republican in the state, and one with a distinct split between its suburban and rural elements.

About 53,000 of the 364,000 residents in the city of Cincinnati remain in the 2nd. About 5 percent of those city residents who are in the district are black; overall, the city is 38 percent black. Not quite 60 percent of the district's vote is cast in the Hamilton County area.

Cincinnati's wealthy Republican establishment — including the Taft family — has exercised a great deal of political influence over the years. But that influence is now concentrated more in the suburbs than in the city.

The Cincinnati area has less heavy industry than the urban centers of northeastern Ohio. But manufacturing plants dot the Mill Creek Valley, which links downtown with northern suburbs and extends into the district.

More than 150,000 of the 2nd's residents and 23 percent of its voters are in fast-growing Clermont County just east of Hamilton County. It grew 34 percent in the 1970s and 9 percent in the 1980s. Clermont has become more Republican as it has moved closer to Cincinnati's metropolitan orbit.

The outlying counties of the 2nd — Brown, Adams and Warren — have considerably less political pull than Hamilton and Clermont, casting about one-fifth of the district vote. The suburbanization of Clermont County is moving it more into sync with Hamilton, dropping further the influence of rural counties.

Almost 60 percent of Warren County's residents are in the 2nd, living along the county's western and northern sides. Northern Warren is in Dayton's media market, making it the only portion of the district to be outside Cincinnati's gravitational pull.

Bob Dole easily won the 2nd with 58 percent of the vote in 1996, his best showing in the state. He narrowly carried Adams and Brown counties but won handily elsewhere.

1990 Population: 570,902. White 551,917 (97%), Black 12,889 (2%), Other 6,096 (1%). Hispanic origin 2,931 (1%). 18 and over 417,784 (73%), 62 and over 79,924 (14%). Median age: 33.

included other provisions sought by Republicans, including $10 billion in business tax cuts over five years, a $5,000 tax credit to offset the cost of adoption and an expansion of Individual Retirement Accounts.

Portman also backs a GOP effort to allow companies to offer their employees comp time in lieu of pay for overtime work.

The issue of mandates helped Portman define himself as a pragmatic conservative -- a lawmaker willing to reach across the aisle without sacrificing his own beliefs. That approach may serve him well in the 105th as he works with members of both parties in his role as co-chairman of The National Commission on Restructuring the Internal Revenue Service, a 17-member commission of presidential and administration appointees.

He expressed hope in early 1997 that Congress could put aside partisan differences and emphasize tax fairness issues. "It's an opportunity that only comes around maybe once in a generation," he said.

Portman said he thinks the commission has several advantages over earlier groups, including its bicameral and bipartisan makeup. And he said he planned to try to build a cooperative relationship with the agency by visiting IRS service centers and talking with employees.

Another issue important to Portman is open government. As soon as he arrived in Congress in May 1993, he threw his support behind a GOP effort to make members' signatures public on petitions to force floor votes. Under a House precedent, the signatures were kept secret until a majority (218) had signed them. Portman said: "It amazes me that at a time when the American people are demanding more openness in government, there exists a secret process that allows some members of the House to have unfair control over whether or not a bill will be considered by Congress."

Looking out for his district during consideration of the fiscal 1994 energy and water spending bill, Portman decried cuts to a program providing for environmental restoration of Defense Department nuclear waste sites. The Fernald nuclear plant is located in the 2nd. He said his constituents must live with the "nightmare of nuclear byproducts" created by the careless disposal of nuclear waste that can contaminate ground water.

At Home: Portman seems assured of longevity in the House — the 2nd is Ohio's most

Republican district. He won it with 70 percent of the vote in a 1993 special election after Gradison resigned to become president of the Health Insurance Association of America.

Portman's biggest challenge in getting to Congress was the March 1993 special primary election. He faced a former Republican representative, Bob McEwen, and a wealthy home builder, Jay Buchert. Portman won the nomination with 35 percent of the vote to McEwen's 29 percent and Buchert's 25 percent.

In the May special general election. Portman overwhelmed Democrat Lee Hornberger, a lawyer from Cincinnati. Portman won by 40 percentage points.

Just 18 hours after polls closed at 7:30 p.m. on May 4, he was sworn into the House, and two hours later, he cast his first vote, opposing the proposed rule for floor debate on the "motor voter" bill. His staff denied he bought airline tickets for Washington before the polls closed, but a campaign spokesman conceded: "I knew what the flight schedule was."

In his re-elections since then, Portman has topped 70 percent of the vote.

Fresh from law school in 1984, Portman arrived in Washington to practice international trade law for Patton, Boggs & Blow, a prominent and politically well-connected firm. He stayed just two years, but the stint was long enough for Portman to catch flak for it when he ran for Congress. In the GOP primary, he was criticized over some of the firm's clients, who have included Haiti's autocratic Duvalier family.

In 1987, Portman went home to Cincinnati to practice law, returning to Washington two years later to work in the Bush White House, first as an associate counsel and later as a deputy assistant to the president and director of the White House's Office of Legislative Affairs. After leaving the White House, he returned to the Cincinnati law firm.

HOUSE ELECTIONS

1996 General		
Rob Portman (R)	186,853	(72%)
Thomas R. Chandler (D)	58,715	(23%)
Kathleen M. McKnight (NL)	13,905	(5%)
1994 General		
Rob Portman (R)	150,128	(77%)
Les Mann (D)	43,730	(23%)

Previous Winning Percentages: 1993† (70%)

† Special election

CAMPAIGN FINANCE

	Receipts	Receipts from PACs	Expend-itures
1996			
Portman (R)	$432,052	$4,950 (1%)	$256,544
1994			
Portman (R)	$409,772	$520 (0%)	$250,860
Mann (D)	$6,545	$6,000 (92%)	$2,503

DISTRICT VOTE FOR PRESIDENT

	1996	1992
D	91,432 (34%)	78,957 (28%)
R	155,859 (58%)	146,098 (53%)
I	20,146 (8%)	52,006 (19%)

KEY VOTES

1997	
Ban "partial birth" abortions	Y
1996	
Approve farm bill	Y
Deny public education to illegal immigrants	Y
Repeal ban on certain assault-style weapons	Y
Increase minimum wage	N
Freeze defense spending	Y
Approve welfare overhaul	Y
1995	
Approve balanced-budget constitutional amendment	Y
Relax Clean Water Act regulations	Y
Oppose limits on environmental regulations	N
Reduce projected Medicare spending	Y
Approve GOP budget with tax and spending cuts	Y

VOTING STUDIES

	Presidential Support		Party Unity		Conservative Coalition	
Year	**S**	**O**	**S**	**O**	**S**	**O**
1996	35	61	89	8	90	10
1995	24	76	91	8	88	9
1994	44	54	90	6	81	11
1993	35†	65†	89†	10†	86†	14†

INTEREST GROUP RATINGS

Year	ADA	AFL-CIO	CCUS	ACU
1996	10	n/a	94	100
1995	0	0	100	80
1994	10	0	100	86
1993	6†	0†	89†	94††

† Not eligible for all recorded votes.

3 Tony P. Hall (D)

Of Dayton — Elected 1978, 10th term

Biographical Information

Born: Jan. 16, 1942, Dayton, Ohio.
Education: Denison U., A.B. 1964.
Occupation: Real estate broker.
Family: Wife, Janet Dick; one child.
Religion: Presbyterian.
Political Career: Ohio House, 1969-73; Ohio Senate, 1973-79; Democratic nominee for Ohio secretary of state, 1974.
Capitol Office: 1436 Longworth Bldg. 20515; 225-6465.

Committee

Rules
Rules & Organization of the House (ranking)

In Washington: A former Peace Corps volunteer in Thailand, Hall is Congress' leading activist on the issue of hunger. Insisting that everyone on the planet has a "right to food," Hall asks the United States to act assertively to feed the hungry and comfort the afflicted in places such as Ethiopia, Somalia and Rwanda.

Hall, who went on a three-week hunger strike in 1993 to protest the elimination of the Select Committee on Hunger he chaired, is a born-again Christian whose deeply held religious beliefs inform both his concern for the poor and his opposition to abortion and the death penalty.

"There are over 2,500 verses in the Scriptures that deal with the hungry, the sick, the elderly, the orphans, the widows, the old," Hall said before traveling to visit Rwandan refugees in 1996. "God's very clear to us. We're to be involved with the poor. We're to help them. This is not maybe."

Hall's humanitarian agenda has seen setbacks in recent years as GOP majorities moved to curtail spending; he fumed at the Republicans' 1995 welfare bill, saying "this proposal makes absolutely no sense." But even in the minority, he can sometimes win battles on the floor by appealing to members' consciences.

When House Republicans in June 1995 pushed an appropriations bill that cut foreign aid spending, Hall got the House to pass an amendment adding $109 million to a new account dedicated to child survival and disease prevention in Africa and Central America. Many in Congress "simply don't understand what foreign aid does," Hall said. "It saves lives, and it provides markets." The following month, Hall again took the floor as the House considered the agriculture spending bill, which contained a provision capping the number of participants in the government's nutrition program for women, infants and children (WIC). Hall's amendment, which eliminated the cap and allowed all eligible recipients to use the program, passed with votes from 81 Republicans.

Hall's influence was also felt on the floor in February 1997, when he defied expectations and helped pass an international family planning bill that contained no restrictions on abortion. In one of the first high-profile votes of the 105th Congress, Hall — saying he was convinced that the bill's funds would not promote abortion — helped deliver the votes of a group of anti-abortion Democrats. They provided the margin of victory as the bill narrowly passed, 220-209.

Hall's leadership of the anti-abortion wing of his party was solidified in the summer of 1996, when Democrats were preparing the platform for their national convention. A group led by Hall asked for — and won — a key abortion clause that said, "we respect the individual conscience of each American on this difficult issue."

His party was thus able to avoid the kind of messy dispute Republicans endured in drafting platform language on abortion. The Democrats even allowed Hall to speak at the convention; he talked about "the needs of the vulnerable in our nation — the poor and the sick, the elderly, the children and the unborn."

Hall also showed his cultural conservatism in 1993, when he opposed lifting the ban on homosexuals in the military — a vote Hall said he "agonized" over. "I detest the hate and the meanness" often directed at gays and lesbians, Hall said, but "I cannot support their lifestyle and their agenda."

His greatest visibility came at the start of the 103rd Congress in 1993, when he lost the platform he had used to call attention to famine in the world. The Select Committee on Hunger, which Hall had chaired since 1989, was one of four select panels Democrats abolished as part of an effort to trim the House's operating expenses.

Hall pleaded with the Democratic leadership for a floor vote on the panel's fate, but was turned down. After the committee died, Hall embarked on a 22-day, water-only fast — during which he lost 23 pounds but gained intense media attention. He ended his protest after the Agriculture Department and the World Bank announced they would call conferences on the issue of hunger.

Hall also won approval from the House Administration Committee (now called House

OHIO 3
Southwest — Dayton

With a large blue-collar work force and a population that is 40 percent black, Dayton is a Democratic island in a sea of rural western Ohio Republicanism. Most of Dayton's suburbs yield GOP majorities, but the urban vote has kept the 3rd Democratic in most elections. About a third of the district is in Dayton.

The Dayton area, lifelong home of the Wright brothers, claims to be the birthplace of aviation, the refrigerator, the cash register and the electrical automobile starter. Much of the high-skill industry in the region is a legacy of these local inventions. General Motors is the biggest private employer, with nearly a dozen factories — two of which weathered a 17-day strike in 1996. The city is the headquarters of AT&T Global Information Solutions, formerly the NCR Corp. Dayton is also home to the Mead Corp. paper empire and the Lexis-Nexis data base service that Mead launched, but later sold.

In the early 1970s, the Dayton area was one of the most affluent manufacturing centers of Ohio outside the Cleveland suburbs. But there have been severe economic problems since then. GM's large Frigidaire division, Firestone Tire and Rubber, and McCall Publishing Co. have all left. The service and high-tech industries have displaced manufacturing as major employers.

The city boasts a large, thriving military industry, increasingly rare in this era of base closings. Wright-Patterson Air Force Base, most of which is in the 7th's Greene County, is one of the nation's largest military installations. In 1995, the "Dayton accord," which led to a cessation of hostilities in the former Yugoslavia, was negotiated at the base. The aerospace research at Wright-Patterson has been a magnet for private-sector firms. The number of aerospace and advanced technology companies in the 3rd exploded from fewer than 100 in 1982 to more than 800 in 1993. These companies now employ about 25,000 people.

But the other job losses have forced many people out of the area. Dayton's population declined 16 percent in the 1970s and 6 percent more in the 1980s, to 182,000, its lowest level in more than 60 years.

The 3rd encompasses all of Montgomery County except for a chip off the southwest corner ceded to the 8th District. Surrounding the city are much-better-off suburbs. Dayton's per capita income is only 60 percent of the rest of the district's; 34 percent of its family households are headed by women, compared with 13 percent in the rest of the district.

South of Dayton are such GOP-inclined white-collar suburbs as Kettering, which is about one-third of Dayton's size with 61,000 residents. Its residents are as white as their collars; 97 percent are white non-Hispanics and less than 1 percent are black. Less than 3 percent of its families live in poverty. The fast-growing townships north of Dayton, a scattering of cities with 10,000 to 14,000 residents, are largely blue-collar suburban. This is a swing-voting area.

The 3rd voted Republican in the 1988 presidential election, but Bill Clinton gained a narrow 41 percent plurality in 1992. Four years later he carried the district more convincingly, beating Bob Dole 50 percent to 41 percent.

1990 Population: 570,901. White 460,661 (81%), Black 101,809 (18%), Other 8,431 (1%). Hispanic origin 4,533 (1%). 18 and over 429,073 (75%), 62 and over 87,630 (15%). Median age: 33.

Oversight) to establish the Congressional Hunger Caucus, a legislative support organization (LSO). But after Republicans won the House in 1994, budget-conscious conservatives moved to abolish all LSOs. Hall had another outlet, though: His fast had also led to the creation of the Congressional Hunger Center — a nonpartisan clearinghouse that helps direct aid and develop policy.

Hall has long shown a knack for drawing attention to hunger issues. He and other House members once organized a media-savvy gourmet luncheon serving only food culled from Capitol Hill trash cans. Consistent with this effort is Hall's promotion of "gleaning" programs, which gather food that otherwise might be wasted by restaurants, grocers, commercial harvests or events such as the 1996 Olympic Games in Atlanta. Hall also introduced in 1995 a toll-free nationwide hotline that links callers to nearby food banks. In Dayton, he helped prod the local Democratic Party into opening its doors to homeless families unable to get beds at the shelter across the street.

Hall's only committee assignment is Rules, but he has never been inclined toward the stratagems and back-room maneuvering that characterize most of the committee's work. However, when Democrats were the House majority, he handled his share of the committee's floor responsibilities, serving occasionally as the party spokesman when the House considered rules governing debate on a bill. When the party's allotment of seats on Rules dropped from nine to four in 1995, Minority Whip David E. Bonior of Michigan, stepped aside to allow Hall to stay on the panel.

While cruising his cable TV channels in 1994 at a New York City apartment he had rented, Hall was stunned when he stumbled across a sexually explicit program. With parents in mind, the following year he introduced a bill that would require cable companies to offer a basic package that did not include "indecent" material.

One of Hall's concerns is the vast Wright-

Patterson Air Force Base, partly in the 3rd. He helped secure $7.4 million in the fiscal 1997 defense authorization bill to build an engineering lab at the base. Also, Hall helped bring a 600-job postal service center to Dayton, and worked to safeguard a planned aviation national park devoted to the city's Wright Brothers.

In July 1995, months before the Bosnian peace accords were negotiated at Wright-Patterson, Hall spent five days meeting with relief workers in Bosnia. Upon his return, Hall called for a cease-fire in the war so children could be immunized against six diseases. After negotiators in Dayton endorsed the idea, President Clinton — with Hall alongside — announced that the United States would help launch a UNICEF effort to immunize children and repair schools in the region.

Hall also has moved to get the federal government involved in helping convert the Energy Department's Mound Plant in Miamisburg, Ohio, to private use. In January 1996, he got the House to agree to a defense bill amendment that accelerated the pace of cleanups at facilities like the Mound Plant, which formerly produced triggers for nuclear weapons.

Hall rode an emotional roller-coaster during the four years his son, Matthew, battled leukemia; at one point in 1995, the Hall family tried faith healing at a Pentecostal church in Toronto. Matthew died in July 1996, six months after doctors had given him two weeks to live. He was 15.

At Home: Hall was the clear choice of organized labor and the Montgomery County Democratic Party when liberal GOP Rep. Charles W. Whalen decided to retire in 1978. Once a small-college football all-star at Denison University — he played tailback in a single-wing offense — Hall had represented Dayton in the Ohio legislature for nearly a decade, and his father, a Republican, had served as Dayton's mayor for five years.

Hall had gained some statewide recognition during a 1974 campaign for Ohio secretary of state, narrowly losing to Ted W. Brown. To reach Washington, Hall had to defeat Republican Dudley P. Kircher, a former Chamber of Commerce official who was considerably more conservative than Whalen. Hall emphasized his legislative experience and called Kircher the "voice of big business." Strong support from labor helped Hall offset Kircher's $130,000 spending edge. The Democrat took 70 percent of the vote in Dayton, allowing him to win narrowly districtwide.

Redistricting gave Hall a safer seat in 1982. Republicans did not field a candidate that year or in 1984. In the two ensuing elections, he faced Ron Crutcher, a black Republican who got some national media attention, but was trounced.

In 1992, Republicans recruited Persian Gulf War veteran Peter Davis, hoping to capitalize on Hall's 1991 opposition to using force against Iraq. Davis ran TV ads saying Hall was more interested in fighting famine than in tending the district's needs. Davis was better funded than Hall's past opponents, and he held the incumbent to his lowest tally since 1980 — but that was still a very comfortable 60 percent.

Physician David A. Westbrock was Hall's opponent in 1994, and after Dayton Mayor Mike Turner decided not to enter the GOP fray in 1996, Westbrock again was the nominee. But Hall scored easy victories in both elections.

HOUSE ELECTIONS

1996 General		
Tony P. Hall (D)	144,583	(64%)
David A. Westbrock (R)	75,732	(33%)
Dorothy H. Mackey (NL)	5,088	(2%)
1994 General		
Tony P. Hall (D)	105,342	(59%)
David A. Westbrock (R)	72,314	(41%)

Previous Winning Percentages: 1992 (60%) **1990** (100%) **1988** (77%) **1986** (74%) **1984** (100%) **1982** (88%) **1980** (57%) **1978** (54%)

CAMPAIGN FINANCE

	Receipts	Receipts from PACs		Expend-itures
1996				
Hall (D)	$311,302	$225,900	(73%)	$247,426
Westbrock (R)	$405,056	$35,736	(9%)	$403,972
1994				
Hall (D)	$253,112	$183,605	(73%)	$292,838
Westbrock (R)	$220,230	$8,354	(4%)	$218,384

DISTRICT VOTE FOR PRESIDENT

1996		1992	
D	115,165 (50%)	**D**	107,798 (41%)
R	94,999 (41%)	**R**	104,414 (40%)
I	18,193 (8%)	**I**	47,612 (18%)

KEY VOTES

1997	
Ban "partial birth" abortions	Y
1996	
Approve farm bill	N
Deny public education to illegal immigrants	Y
Repeal ban on certain assault-style weapons	N
Increase minimum wage	Y
Freeze defense spending	N
Approve welfare overhaul	N
1995	
Approve balanced-budget constitutional amendment	N
Relax Clean Water Act regulations	N
Oppose limits on environmental regulations	?
Reduce projected Medicare spending	N
Approve GOP budget with tax and spending cuts	N

VOTING STUDIES

	Presidential Support		Party Unity		Conservative Coalition	
Year	S	O	S	O	S	O
1996	67	28	70	18	47	43
1995	67	26	75	16	39	50
1994	77	18	85	9	44	53
1993	61	24	79	11	43	50
1992	28	69	80	11	40	56
1991	35	61	86	11	38	62

INTEREST GROUP RATINGS

Year	ADA	AFL-CIO	CCUS	ACU
1996	65	n/a	33	15
1995	75	100	29	22
1994	85	78	33	19
1993	70	100	11	19
1992	60	67	25	25
1991	75	75	30	10

4 Michael G. Oxley (R)

Of Findlay — Elected 1981; 8th full term

Biographical Information
Born: Feb. 11, 1944, Findlay, Ohio.
Education: Miami U. (Oxford, Ohio), B.A. 1966; Ohio State U., J.D. 1969.
Occupation: FBI agent; lawyer.
Family: Wife, Patricia Pluguez; one child.
Religion: Lutheran.
Political Career: Ohio House, 1973-81.
Capitol Office: 2233 Rayburn Bldg. 20515; 225-2676.

Committees
Commerce
Finance & Hazardous Materials (chairman); Telecommunications, Trade & Consumer Protection

In Washington: Oxley is one of those Republican members who, after years of laboring in the minority to influence the course of legislation, finally got a chance to run the show in the 104th. While he demonstrated he had the skills for the job, he encountered his share of frustrations. And his ultimate reward for steering a Commerce subcommittee through difficult shoals was less than he had cause to hope.

Oxley served during the 104th as chairman of the Commerce, Trade and Hazardous Materials Subcommittee. In the 105th, he hoped to move up to head the more prestigious Telecommunications and Finance Subcommittee; he was next in line behind that panel's retiring chairman. But Oxley's ambition was thwarted after W.J. "Billy" Tauzin of Louisiana, an active Commerce Committee Democrat, switched parties. As a reward for joining the GOP, Tauzin received a promise from Speaker Newt Gingrich and Commerce Committee Chairman Thomas J. Bliley Jr., R-Va., that he could chair the telecommunications panel, a powerful magnet for campaign contributions.

Refusing to give in, Oxley gave tens of thousands of dollars in campaign funds to junior members of the committee as part of his active effort to derail the deal with Tauzin. In May 1996, Bliley unveiled a Solomonic compromise, splitting the panel's old jurisdiction in two for the 105th. Tauzin now reigns over telecommunications issues, but Oxley's new Finance and Hazardous Materials Subcommittee oversees the securities market, in addition to retaining control over such matters as superfund toxic-waste cleanup that kept Oxley busy in between rounds of palace intrigue during the 104th.

Cleanup of toxic sites has been slowed by a tangle of litigation over superfund, and authorization for the program ended in 1994. A superfund bill in 1994, when Democrats controlled the House, enjoyed bipartisan support, but died anyway. In 1995, Chairman Oxley found that he faced stubborn resistance to his overhaul plan not only from the Democratic minority but also from members of his own party's leadership as well as key business interests.

"Any member of Congress who has the status quo in one hand and our bill in the other is going to go with our bill," Oxley claimed. He sought to weaken a provision of the old law that required companies to pay for cleaning up waste they dumped even before such dumpings became illegal. All the top GOP leaders wanted this "retroactive liability" eliminated, but Oxley could not find the funds to make up for an estimated $1.3 billion in lost annual revenue, and he offered instead a rebate provision that sought to split the difference between responsible companies, their insurance companies and the funding needs of the program.

Oxley's bill drew criticism from environmentalists and the Clinton administration, who felt it went too far in streamlining the program, giving too much authority over it to the states, and relaxing cleanup standards. The measure never even made it onto the House floor.

Oxley also played an important role in shaping the massive telecommunications law overhaul during the 104th. (He will serve as Tauzin's vice chairman for the 105th.) A free trader, Oxley hoped to allow unlimited foreign ownership of U.S. telecommunications companies. His provision, adopted by the Telecommunications Subcommittee, was struck from the final bill. A later attempt to revive it never made it past the subcommittee.

Oxley, a longtime ally of the Bell operating companies, argued against Democratic fears of media concentration. The maximum audience reach of any given broadcast owner was allowed to increase under the telecommunications bill, but not as much as Oxley wanted. "They're very fearful of bigness," he complained. "'Bigness is bad' — I think every Democrat was born with that on their forehead."

He won out in the struggle to lift cable television price controls, though. Arguing against a bipartisan amendment to maintain some measure of regulation over cable costs, Oxley said, "We

OHIO 4
West Central — Mansfield; Lima; Findlay

The 4th is a solid block of Ohio Corn Belt counties dominated by farms and small towns. The land supports corn, soybeans, livestock — and Republicans. Not one of the 11 counties in the 4th has supported a Democratic presidential candidate since 1964. Two of the three largest — Allen and Hancock — have backed the GOP national ticket since the Roosevelt-Landon contest of 1936.

Democrats have oases of support in the 4th, but they are few and far between. They can normally count on votes in Richland County, especially in Mansfield, the district's largest city. And Lima (population 46,000) sometimes votes Democratic. But the rest of the county's solidly Republican outlying areas overwhelm Lima's sentiments.

Auglaize County in the 4th's southwestern corner is Democratic in the west and Republican in the east. The west is populated by descendants of Germans who settled in the 19th century; they never caught the conservatism that swept through much of the rest of the area.

Economically, corn and soybeans are king in this district, which sprawls across two of Ohio's area codes. The bulk of this district's industry is in its past.

Marion (population 34,000) — named after Revolutionary War Gen. Francis Marion, the "Swamp Fox" — used to make steam shovels and steam rollers, but now instead grows popping corn. Lima and Findlay both emerged as small manufacturing centers at the end of the 19th century when oil and gas were found nearby.

Lima was one of the original refinery centers for John D. Rockefeller's Standard Oil. Although the petroleum boom passed long ago, Findlay (population 36,000), as headquarters of Marathon Oil, is still the 4th's most prosperous part — and the most Republican part of this Republican district.

Close ties to the automobile industry caused economic hardships in Mansfield and Lima during the 1982 recession. They made a partial recovery in the latter 1980s and were not set back much by the 1990s recession, though the Mansfield auto plant's employment slipped. Smaller auto-related companies have taken up some of the slack.

One of the brighter spots in the district's industrial base is its General Dynamics plant, which opened in Lima in 1982 and became its second-largest employer behind a Ford plant. The General Dynamics facility, which has laid off several hundred employees as the Pentagon has downsized, builds the Army's M-1 Abrams tank. British Petroleum still operates an oil refinery here that it opened in the 1920s. Many of Logan County's jobs depend on a new Honda plant in East Liberty and another in Marysville, within the neighboring 7th District.

Knox County in the 4th's southeast corner is within Columbus' range, making Knox less culturally isolated than many of its neighbors.

Bob Dole did well across the district in 1996, although Bill Clinton came fairly close in several counties.

1990 Population: 570,901. White 539,111 (94%), Black 26,333 (5%), Other 5,457 (1%). Hispanic origin 5,262 (1%). 18 and over 417,141 (73%), 62 and over 91,326 (16%). Median age: 34.

don't need more bureaucrats telling the American public what they cannot pay for MTV and other entertainment services." That sentiment prevailed on the House floor and the amendment died, 148-275.

A promise to limit the liability of manufacturers who make faulty products was part of the House GOP's "Contract With America," and a bill to do so was introduced early in the 104th Congress in the Judiciary Committee. But Oxley introduced his own bill and teamed up with Bliley to try to grab back jurisdiction.

Oxley often wins perfect ratings for his voting record from the U.S. Chamber of Commerce and his rating from the AFL-CIO rarely rises into the double digits. Now and then, though, Oxley will cast a vote with Democrats. He supported the 1990 budget agreement that raised taxes, for instance, and he opposes term limits. A former FBI agent, he sometimes has responded to calls for gun control. In the 103rd Congress, for example, he voted for a five-day waiting period for handgun purchases. And he opposed an ultimately successful amendment to a 1996 anti-terrorism bill that stripped the measure of several new law enforcement powers.

At Home: Oxley traces his conservative roots to his Midwestern upbringing. Born in rural Findlay, Ohio, he sported a flat-top haircut in high school and thrived in athletics. As a college student at Miami University in Ohio in the mid-1960s, he recalls jousting with liberal professors. Barry Goldwater's "The Conscience of a Conservative" and free-market economist Milton Friedman were important influences. "In college," Oxley said in a 1995 interview, "I became the class conservative."

While many of his generation were protesting the Vietnam War or participating in the social revolution, Oxley, the son of a county prosecutor, took a more traditional path. After graduating from law school in 1969, he signed on as an agent for the FBI, later receiving a commendation for his role in a tense, high-profile arrest of two suspected bank robbers who were members of the

Black Panthers. The pair were hiding from the law at a womens' college dormitory in Amherst, Mass.

After serving since 1973 in the Ohio General Assembly, Oxley got an opening to run for Congress in April 1981, when GOP Rep. Tennyson Guyer died. Oxley was an early favorite in the special election to succeed him, but he faced stiff primary competition. Running in the early days of Ronald Reagan's presidency, the Republican candidates tried to out-Reagan one another. Robert J. Huffman, a Reagan backer in the 1976 presidential race, branded Oxley a late-comer because he had supported George Bush for president in 1980. Oxley won narrowly.

Winning the Republican nomination had traditionally been tantamount to election in this Republican Corn Belt district. But in state Rep. Dale Locker, the Democrats fielded their best possible candidate. Locker was a farmer and chairman of the state House Agriculture and Natural Resources Committee, ideal credentials for the 4th District.

Oxley outgunned Locker financially, spending $275,000 and flooding the media with advertisements in the closing days of the campaign. But his efforts nearly failed because he was unable to develop the personal rapport with voters that had made the 4th District safe for Guyer. Carrying only six of the district's 12 counties, Oxley struggled to a 341-vote victory. A recount delayed his swearing-in for nearly a month.

Locker weighed a rematch in 1982 but backed off when the state legislature fashioned new district boundaries to Oxley's advantage. Oxley won a full term with 65 percent and has not been pressed since.

HOUSE ELECTIONS

1996 General		
Michael G. Oxley (R)	147,608	(65%)
Paul McClain (D)	69,096	(30%)
Michael McCaffery (NL)	11,057	(5%)
1994 General		
Michael G. Oxley (R)	139,841	(100%)

Previous Winning Percentages: **1992** (61%) **1990** (62%) **1988** (100%) **1986** (75%) **1984** (78%) **1982** (65%) **1981†** (50%)

† Special election

CAMPAIGN FINANCE

	Receipts	Receipts from PACs	Expend-itures
1996			
Oxley (R)	$640,721	$433,734 (68%)	$639,496
McClain (D)	$27,494	$10,950 (40%)	$27,230
1994			
Oxley (R)	$467,781	$300,240 (64%)	$279,829

DISTRICT VOTE FOR PRESIDENT

1996		1992	
D	88,089 (37%)	**D**	77,918 (31%)
R	117,491 (50%)	**R**	118,088 (46%)
I	28,051 (12%)	**I**	58,957 (23%)

KEY VOTES

1997	
Ban "partial birth" abortions	†
1996	
Approve farm bill	Y
Deny public education to illegal immigrants	Y
Repeal ban on certain assault-style weapons	Y
Increase minimum wage	N
Freeze defense spending	N
Approve welfare overhaul	Y
1995	
Approve balanced-budget constitutional amendment	Y
Relax Clean Water Act regulations	Y
Oppose limits on environmental regulations	N
Reduce projected Medicare spending	Y
Approve GOP budget with tax and spending cuts	Y

VOTING STUDIES

	Presidential Support		Party Unity		Conservative Coalition	
Year	S	O	S	O	S	O
1996	37	63	88	6	96	2
1995	17	81	93	4	96	1
1994	47	51	88	8	86	8
1993	43	52	87	11	93	5
1992	86	11	86	10	96	2
1991	79	20	83	16	95	5

INTEREST GROUP RATINGS

Year	ADA	AFL-CIO	CCUS	ACU
1996	5	n/a	100	100
1995	0	0	96	76
1994	0	0	92	95
1993	5	8	100	88
1992	5	17	86	96
1991	5	8	100	80

5 Paul E. Gillmor (R)

Of Old Fort — Elected 1988, 5th term

Biographical Information

Born: Feb. 1, 1939, Tiffin, Ohio.
Education: Ohio Wesleyan U., B.A. 1961; U. of Michigan, J.D. 1964.
Military Service: Air Force, 1965-66.
Occupation: Lawyer.
Family: Wife, Karen Lako; five children.
Religion: Methodist.
Political Career: Ohio Senate, 1967-89, minority leader, 1978-80, 1983-84, president, 1981-82, 1985-88; sought Republican nomination for governor, 1986.

Capitol Office: 1203 Longworth Bldg. 20515; 225-6405.

Committees

Commerce
Finance & Hazardous Materials; Telecommunications, Trade & Consumer Protection

In Washington: Gillmor came to Capitol Hill in 1989 with abundant experience as an inside legislative operator — 22 years in the Ohio Senate, including six as the chamber's president. After two terms in Congress, he landed a seat in 1993 on the influential Energy and Commerce Committee, renamed simply the Commerce Committee by Republicans when they took control of the House in 1995.

Though Commerce attracts a good share of attention with its work, Gillmor generally does not, preferring to function behind the scenes.

On occasion he makes his views well known. When the telecommunications deregulation bill was introduced in May 1995, Gillmor touted it on the House floor. "If this legislation is enacted, the law will begin to foster economic and technological development, instead of hamper it," he said. "The bill will provide consumers and businesses new communications services, an increase in choices in the marketplace, more competition and better prices." He introduced a separate measure allowing public utilities to offer telecommunications services such as telephone and cable television.

When Gillmor does surface, it is usually as an ally of the House GOP leadership. For example, during the intraparty debate over whether Republicans should re-elect Newt Gingrich as Speaker for the 105th Congress despite his ethical problems, Gillmor signed a letter with 11 other lawmakers endorsing Gingrich.

Gillmor was most visible during the 104th Congress on the subject of unfunded mandates. And he wanted to go further than the Republican Congress did; instead of a law curtailing the mandates, he advocated a constitutional amendment. "There is legislation pending to curtail unfunded mandates by statute," he said in January 1995. "I support that. I cosponsored it last year, and I am cosponsoring it again this year. But the weakness of a statute is that it can be changed by a simple majority vote. And the only real long-term protection is by a constitutional amendment."

During the 103rd, when Democrats were in the majority, Gillmor strenuously argued his view that liberals in Congress were imposing mandates on the states without providing funds to fulfill them. "The federal government has long had its foot on the necks of the states and its hands rummaging through their wallets," he said. He hauled out a prop he called a "Mandate-O-Meter" to illustrate "how onerous a piece of legislation would be to state and local governments."

For example, Gillmor said in 1993, implementing the "motor voter" legislation to expand voter registration would cost Ohio $20 million a year — money that could have paid for more teachers, scholarships, state troopers or any number of causes he deemed more worthy than "some new mandated government forms and an expanded role for the omnipresent federal bureaucracy."

In February 1995, he spoke on the House floor in favor of legislation requiring federal agencies to use cost-benefit analysis before imposing new regulations. "This legislation very simply puts common sense into the way the government regulates," he said. "All of us have heard the horror stories from businesses and municipalities about the federal regulations and the way that they have strangled their budgets only to have minuscule benefits result."

Other than his early support in the 104th for legislation raising the minimum wage, he has been a reliable conservative vote. He favors a term-limits constitutional amendment and opposes abortion. He supports a balanced-budget constitutional amendment (although he also defended two targets of budget-cutters — NASA's space station and price supports for sugar). He voted to overhaul welfare and to allow employers to offer compensatory time off instead of overtime pay. He backed efforts to repeal the ban on assault weapons. He supported an amendment to a proposed change in House rules that would allow lawmakers to continue receiving lobbyist-paid gifts, meals and gifts that are fully disclosed.

Gillmor's Ohio experience with internal legislative affairs and his willingness to engage in con-

OHIO 5
Northwest — Bowling Green; Sandusky

This Republican district is a mixture of fertile, flat farmland and small towns. It spread its wings a bit in redistricting for the 1990s, tacking a county and a half onto its eastern and western ends, though it shed a bit of land up north.

Added to the 5th were Van Wert County and half of Mercer County — agricultural areas that run along the western border with Indiana — and, to the east, the rest of Huron County and part of Lorain County (near Cleveland). The district lost its section of Fulton County and part of Wood and Ottawa counties (near Toledo) to the 9th District.

The district's Republican nature has been slipping in recent presidential elections. Bob Dole won here in 1996, albeit just 44 percent to 42 percent over Bill Clinton as Ross Perot took 13 percent of the vote. Dole won eight of the district's 14 counties while Gillmor swept them all.

The nature of the 5th's population concentrations changed slightly in remapping. The Lake Erie port of Sandusky (population 30,000) is still the district's largest community. But Tiffin, a city of 19,000 in Seneca County, now is the district's second most-populous city.

An additional 95,000 people live in seven other cities throughout the district, with populations ranging from 11,000 to 18,000. The other residents of the 5th live in smaller towns and rural areas.

The district's western counties are almost exclusively devoted to agriculture. Packing plants operated by Heinz and Campbell attest to the quality of the region's tomatoes. The district's population is 96 percent white, but the Mexican-American farmworkers who live in migrant camps during harvest season have added an ethnic element to this otherwise homogeneous region. The 5th is 3 percent Hispanic compared to the statewide Hispanic population of about 1 percent.

Erie County, midway between Cleveland and Toledo on Lake Erie, long has been a major recreation area. Sandusky, the county seat, is a fishing market and coal port. In the surrounding countryside, fruit orchards and vineyards abound. German immigrants established wineries in Sandusky a century ago, and they remain a key feature of the local economy.

The sizable blue-collar element occasionally pushes Erie County into the Democratic column. Clinton carried the county by 4,500 votes in 1996. But even though the county's residents cast a larger share of the votes than any other county's, it is only 12 percent of the total. Erie is but a Democratic ripple in the large Republican pond. Clinton's edge in Erie was all but canceled out by Dole's 4,300-vote margin in Putnam, which overall accounted for just 4 percent of the total vote in the district.

Wood County, which sprawls from the outskirts of Toledo deep into the Ohio Corn Belt, accounts for a tenth of the district's voters. The county is consistently Republican; Dole bested Clinton by 1,100 votes in 1996.

1990 Population: 570,901. White 547,282 (96%), Black 11,957 (2%), Other 11,662 (2%). Hispanic origin 17,643 (3%). 18 and over 411,006 (72%), 62 and over 88,928 (16%). Median age: 33.

servative saber rattling played a part in his being advanced for a committee leadership position when Republicans were organizing for the 103rd. In December 1992, forces allied with Gingrich pushed Gillmor as a candidate to replace Bill Thomas of California as the ranking Republican on the House Administration Committee. Thomas was viewed as too conciliatory with Democrats, and Gingrich and his allies saw Gillmor as a potentially appealing candidate — conservative but not too hard-line, and hailing from a northern industrial state, rather than the Sun Belt base of the Gingrich wing.

Gillmor, though, was less than thrilled about being caught up in an intraparty power struggle for the dubious honor of leading the GOP side on a committee that dealt chiefly with the internal business of the House. "It's not a plum, it's something you do for the good of the institution and the caucus," he said at the time. "I don't look at it as a committee where you make a lot of friends."

Despite his lack of interest, Gillmor posted a strong showing in the race for the job. Thomas kept his ranking seat by a vote of 87-72. Then Gillmor got the slot on Energy and Commerce, an exclusive committee assignment. That meant he had to quit House Administration altogether, and also give up his seat on Banking. In the 104th, Gingrich reformulated House Administration, renaming it House Oversight, and he allowed Thomas to chair the panel.

Gillmor is the House sponsor of legislation establishing a coin to commemorate Thomas Alva Edison on the 150th anniversary of his birth, 1997. Under the bill, 350,000 silver one-dollar coins and 350,000 silver half-dollar coins would be minted. A surcharge would be placed on all coin sales and go to seven organizations to help maintain or expand exhibits about Edison, including the Edison Birthplace Association in Milan, Ohio.

He also has introduced legislation creating education savings accounts, modeled after Individual Retirement Accounts. The bill would create a tax break for contributions to an education savings account. The tax deduction would be limited to $1,500 per account for children under age 19. Funds used for purposes other than those permitted by the legislation would be subject to a 10 percent surtax. Funds could be transferred to the savings account from an IRA and could be transferred back to the IRA without penalty.

During the three-way presidential contest in 1992, Gillmor filed legislation that would have prevented the House from choosing a president in the event no candidate received a majority of electoral votes, as provided for in the 12th Amendment to the Constitution. He supported establishing a two-way presidential runoff to take place three weeks after the general election.

At Home: A state legislator who comes to Congress is uniformly regarded as having received a promotion. Gillmor, however, had to sacrifice a good bit of power when he left Columbus for Washington. As president of the Ohio Senate for six of his last eight years there, Gillmor was the highest-ranking Republican in state government.

When he decided to seek the House seat of retiring GOP Rep. Delbert L. Latta in 1988, Gillmor knew well that his biggest challenge would be in the primary: As Senate president in the early 1980s, Gillmor had a say over the redistricting plan that made the 5th a GOP stronghold.

The GOP primary was indeed a bruising one. The 30-year incumbent wanted to hand the seat to his son, 32-year-old lawyer Robert E. Latta. The resulting face-off turned bitter and personal; Gillmor won narrowly.

During Gillmor's years in the state Senate, he represented more than two-thirds of Latta's House territory, and the two men competed for dominance of the local political scene. When Gillmor announced he would run for the House, Rep. Latta briefly threatened to drop his retirement plans and seek re-election.

The younger Latta campaigned aggressively, aided by his father's ready-made organization. However, Gillmor towered over the newcomer in personal recognition. Gillmor not only had his own solid political base in most of the 5th, but also was known throughout the district from his 1986 bid for the GOP gubernatorial nomination. (Although he lost statewide, he carried the 5th in that primary.)

Gillmor ran a media-oriented campaign, highlighting his legislative experience. He stressed his fiscal conservatism and cited his successes as the Senate Republican leader. He was known as an accessible, consensus-oriented leader able to move legislation despite the GOP's narrow Senate majority.

Those credentials boosted Gillmor to victory, but just barely. He won the primary by 27 votes — the smallest margin in any 1988 House contest.

In the general election, though, the district's Republican tendencies kicked in for Gillmor. His foe was wealthy Democratic attorney Thomas Murray, who had gotten just 35 percent against Del Latta in 1986. Although Murray spent $850,000, mainly on TV ads, Gillmor topped 60 percent. By 1990, Gillmor was solidly established in the 5th.

HOUSE ELECTIONS

1996 General		
Paul E. Gillmor (R)	145,692	(61%)
Annie Saunders (D)	81,170	(34%)
David J. Schaffer (NL)	11,461	(5%)
1994 General		
Paul E. Gillmor (R)	135,879	(73%)
Jarrod Tudor (D)	49,335	(27%)

Previous Winning Percentages: 1992 (100%) **1990** (68%) **1988** (61%)

CAMPAIGN FINANCE

	Receipts	Receipts from PACs	Expend-itures
1996			
Gillmor (R)	$341,773	$260,194 (76%)	$327,472
Saunders (D)	$24,475	$11,600 (47%)	$23,710
Schaffer (NL)	$954	$2,000	$6,170
1994			
Gillmor (R)	$335,506	$248,885 (74%)	$210,789

DISTRICT VOTE FOR PRESIDENT

1996		1992	
D	102,296 (42%)	**D**	87,883 (33%)
R	107,909 (44%)	**R**	109,020 (41%)
I	32,152 (13%)	**I**	66,648 (25%)

INTEREST GROUP RATINGS

Year	ADA	AFL-CIO	CCUS	ACU
1996	15	n/a	73	84
1995	5	8	100	80
1994	15	33	100	86
1993	15	30	100	82
1992	20	50	75	80
1991	10	25	70	65

VOTING STUDIES

	Presidential Support		Party Unity		Conservative Coalition	
Year	S	O	S	O	S	O
1996	39	58	88	8	75	6
1995	21	77	92	7	94	1
1994	63	36	67	32	86	11
1993	47	47	72	26	93	5
1992	73	26	75	21	90	6
1991	73†	26†	67†	30†	95	5

† Not eligible for all recorded votes.

KEY VOTES

1997	
Ban "partial birth" abortions	Y
1996	
Approve farm bill	Y
Deny public education to illegal immigrants	Y
Repeal ban on certain assault-style weapons	Y
Increase minimum wage	Y
Freeze defense spending	?
Approve welfare overhaul	Y
1995	
Approve balanced-budget constitutional amendment	Y
Relax Clean Water Act regulations	Y
Oppose limits on environmental regulations	Y
Reduce projected Medicare spending	Y
Approve GOP budget with tax and spending cuts	Y

6 Ted Strickland (D)

Of Lucasville — Elected 1992, 2nd term
Did not serve 1995-97.

Biographical Information

Born: Aug. 4, 1941, Lucasville, Ohio.
Education: Asbury College, B.A. 1963; U. of Kentucky, M.A. 1966; Asbury Theological Seminary, M.A. 1967; U. of Kentucky, Ph.D. 1980.
Occupation: Professor; psychologist.
Family: Wife, Frances Smith.
Religion: Methodist.
Political Career: Democratic nominee for U.S. House, 1976, 1978, 1980; U.S. House, 1993-95.
Capitol Office: 336 Cannon Bldg. 20515; 225-5705.

Committees

Commerce
Finance & Hazardous Materials; Health & Environment

The Path to Washington: For the past several years, Strickland, who in 1997 returned to the House as a freshman for the second time, has been on a political seesaw.

In 1992, he scored a nearly 2 percentage point victory to win the 6th District House seat. In 1994, he lost re-election by less than 2 percentage points to Republican businessman Frank A. Cremeans.

In 1996, the balance tipped in Strickland's favor. In a nationally watched rematch viewed as something of a referendum on the 104th Congress, he defeated Cremeans — again by 2 percentage points.

In his first term, Strickland sat on the Education and Labor and Small Business committees. But for the 105th Congress, the Democratic leadership gave him a seat on the influential Commerce Committee, from which he hopes to protect government business for a uranium enrichment plant operated by Lockheed Martin in his poor, largely Appalachian district.

In addition, representing a district where many families scrape by without health insurance, Strickland hopes to be involved in health care legislation — a longtime interest of his.

A psychologist and college professor who once worked with inmates at Ohio prisons, Strickland also has a deep interest in education issues.

He ran for Congress three previous times before hitting the jackpot in 1992. His first victory resulted in part from post-census redistricting that put two veteran GOP incumbents — Reps. Bob McEwen and Clarence E. Miller — in the same district. Strickland narrowly defeated the eventual GOP nominee, McEwen (who beat Strickland in 1980), who had gone through a tough primary and had sustained political damage from having 166 overdrafts at the House bank.

Strickland followed a moderately liberal line during his first term. He supported abortion rights and publicly backed the Clinton administration's "don't ask, don't tell" policy on homosexuals in the military.

The district's well-organized religious community turned enthusiastically to Cremeans, a conservative, during the 1994 campaign. But the issue of taxes may have been Strickland's final undoing that year.

At a candidates' debate just days before the 1994 election, Strickland was asked a question about how to pay for universal health care, an idea he supported. In the course of his response, Strickland said that some taxes might have to be raised.

The Cremeans campaign seized on the comment and used it successfully in last-minute television ads to which Strickland had no time to respond.

In their heated and acrimonious 1996 rematch, taxes were again a key theme. Cremeans once again ran footage of Strickland's tax-raising comment. But this time, Strickland shot back with charges that Cremeans had raised taxes on the working poor by supporting a cut in the earned-income tax credit.

While many Republican candidates tried, as the 1996 elections neared, to distance themselves from the "Contract With America" of two years earlier, Cremeans continued to embrace the document's promises and to stick up for the priorities of the Republican-controlled House.

Cremeans was perhaps best-known during his House tenure for his outspoken support of Republican presidential candidate Malcolm S. "Steve" Forbes Jr.

Strickland, who trailed Cremeans in campaign spending, benefited from an expensive ad campaign by labor unions targeting Cremeans on the issue of containing cost growth in the Medicare program.

While Cremeans criticized the ads as inappropriate, Strickland maintained that the union campaign was part of a history of interest-group involvement in congressional races — including, he said, the effort by conservative Christian groups in behalf of Cremeans in 1994.

OHIO 6
South — Portsmouth; Chillicothe; Athens

The 6th is the state's largest district, taking in all of Ohio's southeast corner and reaching across to fast-growing Warren County in Ohio's southwest. What suburbs it had near Dayton and Cincinnati were stripped away in the 1992 redistricting, leaving behind a collection of some of Ohio's poorest rural areas.

Scioto County is the 6th's most populous, with 80,000 residents and 14 percent of the total. It contains Portsmouth, the district's largest city (population 23,000). While steel and bricks have been staples of Portsmouth's economy throughout the century, the district's economic linchpin is the nearby uranium-enrichment facility (in Pike County), which processes uranium for use as reactor fuel.

In Chillicothe (20,000 of whose 22,000 residents are in the 6th), 44 miles due north of Portsmouth in Ross County, nearby forests support a large paper plant.

Athens County has a number of government employers, including Ohio University, with about 19,100 students, that cushions it somewhat from adverse economic conditions. It is also heavily Democratic. Athens was one of just two Ohio counties in 1972 to vote for Democratic presidential candidate George McGovern, and it has given majorities to the Democratic presidential candidate in the last three elections. Athens County was integral to Strickland's successful 1996 comeback. He carried Athens with 65 percent and by 7,122 votes; he lost the rest of the district by 1,026 votes.

Many of the poorer voters in other counties along the Ohio River still call themselves Democrats — a remnant of Civil War days when Confederate sympathies were strong in this area — but nowadays their conservative outlook leads them toward Republicans.

The counties immediately east of the Cincinnati area are rural Republican country. Clinton and Highland counties lie on the outer fringe of the Corn Belt. Wilmington, the Clinton County seat, houses a major hub operation of the Seattle-based delivery service Airborne Express. Despite the name affinity, Clinton County is heavily Republican; it gave a solid majority to Bob Dole in 1996.

Farther east the land is poorer, the Appalachian Mountains rise and GOP strength begins to ebb. Seven of the eight poorest counties in the state (in terms of proportion of families in poverty) are in the 6th: Pike, Scioto, Jackson, Meigs, Lawrence, Vinton and Gallia. Of those seven, Bill Clinton carried all but Jackson and Gallia in 1992, then made a clean sweep of them in 1996.

One-fifth of the 6th's land area is contained within the three regions of the Wayne National Forest in the district's eastern Appalachian section, including almost all of Lawrence County on Ohio's southern edge.

The 6th is a battleground region in congressional contests — the winner in the last three House elections has taken 51 percent of the vote — as well as in presidential races. George Bush edged Clinton here in 1992 by less than 1 percentage point; then Clinton beat Dole by just 3 percentage points in 1996.

1990 Population: 570,901. White 554,194 (97%), Black 12,086 (2%), Other 4,621(1%). Hispanic origin 2,180 (<1%). 18 and over 421,059 (74%), 62 and over 90,625 (16%). Median age: 33.

HOUSE ELECTIONS

1996 General

Ted Strickland (D)	118,003	(51%)
Frank A. Cremeans (R)	111,907	(49%)

Previous Winning Percentage: 1992 (51%)

CAMPAIGN FINANCE

	Receipts	Receipts from PACs	Expend-itures
1996			
Strickland (D)	$680,167	$315,418 (46%)	$714,172
Cremeans (R)	$1,788,241	$585,756 (33%)	$1,786,582

DISTRICT VOTE FOR PRESIDENT

1996		1992	
D	105,482 (45%)	**D**	98,768 (40%)
R	99,309 (42%)	**R**	100,162 (40%)
I	28,650 (12%)	**I**	49,796 (20%)

KEY VOTES

1997

Ban "partial birth" abortions Y

7 David L. Hobson (R)

Of Springfield — Elected 1990, 4th term

Biographical Information
Born: Oct. 17, 1936, Cincinnati, Ohio.
Education: Ohio Wesleyan U., B.A. 1958 Ohio State U., J.D. 1963.
Military Service: Ohio Air National Guard, 1958-63.
Occupation: Financial executive.
Family: Wife, Carolyn Alexander; three children.
Religion: Methodist.
Political Career: Candidate for Ohio House, 1982; Ohio Senate, 1982-91, majority whip, 1986-88, president pro tempore, 1988-90.

Capitol Office: 1514 Longworth Bldg. 20515; 225-4324.

Committees
Appropriations
Military Construction; National Security; VA, HUD & Independent Agencies
Budget

In Washington: Though just in his fourth House term, Hobson is in his early 60s — older than most Republicans who have come to the House in recent years. He arrived in Washington with years of experience in politics and finance, and, drawing on that background, he brings to the legislative process the instincts of a deal-maker.

That streak of pragmatism distinguishes Hobson from the younger generation of more ideologically pugnacious Republicans who helped sweep the GOP to a House majority in the 1994 election. From his seat on the Budget Committee, Hobson has stayed in step with the times by faithfully supporting the efforts of GOP conservatives who seek dramatic and specific cuts in federal spending. But if Hobson's stance on budget matters is fairly hard line, he has been willing to negotiate with Democrats on some other issues, and even to support President Clinton on key votes from time to time.

Hobson's blend of attributes looked good enough to the GOP leadership that he was named the Speaker's designee on the Budget Committee in the 104th, advancing him to the No. 2 spot on the panel and giving him a seat at the table in leadership deliberations. Hobson, who supported Texas Republican Tom DeLay's successful race for majority whip, also was named an assistant whip.

At the start of the 105th, Hobson got excused from one onerous chore he had taken on for the leadership: sitting on the House ethics committee. In January 1997, shortly before the panel was to vote on whether to sanction Speaker Newt Gingrich for violating House rules, the committee's top Democrat, Jim McDermott of Washington, got embroiled in a controversy over the leaking to The New York Times of a tape of an intercepted cellular phone conservation between Gingrich and some of his top House lieutenants. McDermott recused himself from the committee's deliberations on the Gingrich case, and Hobson followed suit to keep the panel's ratio at four Republicans and four Democrats; membership on the ethics committee is traditionally balanced evenly between the two parties.

Hobson's six-year service on the committee was to have ended with the 104th Congress, but he had agreed to stay on until the Gingrich case was concluded.

In his role as the Speaker's designee on the Budget Committee, Hobson, who also sits on the Appropriations Committee, serves as a liaison between the two panels. During the winter of 1995-96, he was in the thick of the budget imbroglio between the Clinton White House and the GOP Congress. A firm believer in a balanced budget, Hobson helped to write the GOP's seven-year balanced-budget plan, which included a controversial proposal to reduce the projected rate of spending growth on Medicare and Medicaid.

When it became clear in early 1996 that Clinton and the GOP leadership could not agree to a balanced-budget plan, Hobson was more willing than many junior Republicans to back away from the tactic of trying to pressure Clinton into a deal by shutting down the government or threatening to put the federal Treasury into default. Hobson said that seeking a partial agreement with the White House was "the quickest way to get some things done" before the November elections. "The feeling is half a loaf is better than fighting the rest of the year over a non-loaf," Hobson said.

Although he is a balanced-budget disciple who argues for spending restraint, Hobson uses his Appropriations Committee seat to direct some federal money home. He often catalogs in news-releases the funds he has secured for the 7th District. A particular priority for Hobson is Wright-Patterson Air Force Base, which lies partially in the 7th and is a major district employer. He sits on Appropriations' National Security subcommittee, and in the fiscal 1997 defense spending bill he said he was able to obtain $7 million for the Aeronautical Systems Center's Simulation and Analysis Facility, a project that should help Wright-Patterson be chosen as the program office

OHIO 7
West central — Springfield; Lancaster

This district resembles a gaping mouth that is set to swallow Columbus whole. Its nine counties surround Columbus' district (the 15th) on three sides.

The 7th is bisected by U.S. Route 40. The northern section contains a third of the district's land but casts only 15 percent of its vote. Champaign, Logan and Union to the north are rural counties that combine agriculture and small industry and have been GOP strongholds for generations. They backed Republican Alfred M. Landon for president in his 1936 landslide loss to Franklin D. Roosevelt.

South of Route 40, the people are concentrated in Democrat-tilted Clark County (Springfield) and in Greene County, which extends into Dayton's eastern suburbs.

Springfield's site along Route 40 (the old National Road) enabled it to develop into the area's leading population center, with 74,000 residents. The city's economy suffered substantially in the early 1980s but got a boost in 1983 when International Harvester (now Navistar) consolidated its truckmaking operations here.

Greene County has a working-class mix of blacks and Southern whites. Wright-Patterson Air Force Base, in the county's far southwest corner, is responsible for a substantial amount of military-related employment. The base employs more people than any other military installation in the nation — about 23,000 military and civilian jobs are connected to the base.

The Air Force continues to bolster Wright-Patterson by consolidating several "commands" into a new one based here: the Air Force Materiel Command, which controls one-fifth of the Air Force's budget. The base is the largest single-site employer in the state.

Up north, the economic picture is rosier in Union County than in many of Ohio's other rural areas. Lying just northwest of Columbus, this is an attractive site for industries seeking open land, low taxes and — despite the county's name — no history of unions.

Much of the area's economic stimulus has come from an unusual source: Japan. Honda opened a motorcycle plant in Marysville in the western part of Union County in 1979, and three years later the company opened its first American auto plant there. Honda employs more than 6,500 people between the two facilities, making it the largest private employer in the region. (Other Honda plants in adjoining districts employ about 5,900 more people.) The Marysville auto plant is the only builder of Accord coupes, sedans and station wagons, and Honda exports tens of thousands of the cars, many of them to the Japanese market.

Fairfield County, in the 7th's far southeast corner, has grown in recent years, as bedroom communities blossomed along Route 33, a four-lane highway connecting Lancaster with the thriving city of Columbus, 30 miles northwest.

Bob Dole won the 7th in 1996, taking 48 percent of the vote to Bill Clinton's 41 percent. Dole was especially strong in Union County, beating Clinton by almost 2-to-1.

1990 Population: 570,902. White 534,087 (94%), Black 30,347 (5%), Other 11,089 (2%). Hispanic origin 3,745 (1%). 18 and over 421,456 (74%), 62 and over 82,366 (14%). Median age: 34.

site for the Joint Strike Fighter, the next generation of fighter aircraft to be used by the Air Force, Navy and Marines.

"Other Wright-Patt funds in the bill include $1.25 million to complete design work for a new building at the U.S. Air Force Museum, $20 million for the Joint Logistics Systems Center and $27.5 million for a computer system that tracks Air Force maintenance information," Hobson wrote.

In the 105th Congress, he will serve as vice chairman of Appropriations' Military Construction Subcommittee, while continuing to serve on the National Security Subcommittee and the VA, HUD and Independent Agencies Subcommittee.

Hobson also knows his way around the subject of health care, having specialized in that area when he was the No. 2 leader of the GOP majority in the Ohio Senate. He was successful in the 104th with legislation he had proposed for three years that would make it possible for medical providers to submit patient bills to insurance companies electronically. That method of transmission, Hobson said, would move transactions more quickly and securely and with less opportunity for fraud. The measure was included in a broader bill guaranteeing the "portability" of health insurance — allowing workers to maintain their insurance coverage if they lose or leave their jobs.

On abortion-related issues in the 104th Congress, Hobson typically sided with opponents of abortion — voting against allowing abortions at overseas military hospitals, against allowing federal employees' health plans to cover abortions, and against an effort to require states to fund Medicaid abortions for poor women in cases of rape or incest.

But Hobson supports certain family planning programs. He spoke against an amendment to the fiscal 1997 Labor-HHS spending bill that would have required parents to give written permission before their children could receive federally funded family planning services. Hobson said the amendment would limit access to family planning services and was a health care issue, not an abortion issue. "I believe limited access to these services will lead to more abortions," Hobson said. "Through family planning services, unintended pregnancies have been reduced."

Also, in February 1997 Hobson was one of 44 Republicans to back legislation allowing the Clinton administration to begin spending $385 million in international family planning funds that had already been appropriated. Opponents argued that voting for the measure showed support for promoting abortion abroad, but those in favor of releasing the funds argued that it was simply a vote for family planning programs. The latter view prevailed as the House approved the resolution, 220-209.

At Home: When former GOP Rep. Mike DeWine (now a U.S. senator) embarked on what would be a successful 1990 bid for lieutenant governor, Hobson ran for the House and upheld his reputation as DeWine's heir apparent.

Hobson's election marked the second time he had followed in DeWine's footsteps. He was appointed in December 1982 to the state Senate seat DeWine gave up to run for the House. Elected in 1984, Hobson was chosen by his GOP colleagues as Senate majority whip two years later. In November 1988, the same month he won re-election, Hobson moved up to president pro tem, the Senate's second-ranking position.

Hobson was a business success before entering politics; he served as chairman of financial corporations and on the boards of a bank, an oil company and a restaurant company. In the legislature he compiled a lengthy list of successes and earned widespread praise in the state and district media.

Appointed early in his career to the Senate Health Committee, Hobson led an investigation into the scandal-plagued state Department of Mental Retardation that brought the ouster of the agency's director. He also drew up a measure to provide respite care for sufferers of Alzheimer's disease and wrote a comprehensive bill for the detection and treatment of AIDS.

Hobson's record on health issues and his sizable voter base — he already represented more than half of the 7th District in the state Senate – made him the strong favorite in the 1990 House contest.

The Democratic nominee was Jack Schira, a retired Air Force colonel who took 26 percent in a 1988 challenge to DeWine. Schira was a determined but poorly funded candidate who borrowed against his home and credit cards to finance his campaign. Hobson carried all of the district's counties, winning with 62 percent of the vote. His 1992, 1994 and 1996 re-elections were uneventful.

HOUSE ELECTIONS

1996 General		
David L. Hobson (R)	158,087	(68%)
Richard K. Blain (D)	61,419	(26%)
Dawn Marie Johnson (NL)	13,478	(6%)
1996 Primary		
David L. Hobson (R)	61,210	(86%)
Richard A. Herron (R)	10,239	(14%)
1994 General		
David L. Hobson (R)	140,124	(100%)

Previous Winning Percentages: 1992 (71%) **1990** (62%)

CAMPAIGN FINANCE

	Receipts	Receipts from PACs	Expend-itures
1996			
Hobson (R)	$670,446	$306,083 (46%)	$620,093
Blain (D)	$9,950	$4,900 (49%)	$9,824
1994			
Hobson (R)	$286,524	$154,457 (54%)	$191,660

INTEREST GROUP RATINGS

Year	ADA	AFL-CIO	CCUS	ACU
1996	0	n/a	88	90
1995	10	0	96	68
1994	20	22	83	67
1993	15	17	91	79
1992	15	33	88	80
1991	10	25	80	80

VOTING STUDIES

	Presidential Support		Party Unity		Conservative Coalition	
Year	S	O	S	O	S	O
1996	38	62	89	9	94	6
1995	23	77	91	9	95	5
1994	58	42	82	18	83	17
1993	49	51	83	17	82	18
1992	67	33	85	15	88	13
1991	77	23	85	15	95	5

DISTRICT VOTE FOR PRESIDENT

1996	1992
D 100,475 (41%)	**D** 84,111 (34%)
R 115,697 (48%)	**R** 112,517 (45%)
I 25,440 (10%)	**I** 54,050 (22%)

KEY VOTES

1997	
Ban "partial birth" abortions	Y
1996	
Approve farm bill	Y
Deny public education to illegal immigrants	Y
Repeal ban on certain assault-style weapons	Y
Increase minimum wage	Y
Freeze defense spending	N
Approve welfare overhaul	Y
1995	
Approve balanced-budget constitutional amendment	Y
Relax Clean Water Act regulations	Y
Oppose limits on environmental regulations	N
Reduce projected Medicare spending	Y
Approve GOP budget with tax and spending cuts	Y

8 John A. Boehner (R)

Of West Chester — Elected 1990, 4th term

Biographical Information
Born: Nov. 17, 1949, Cincinnati, Ohio.
Education: Xavier U., B.S. 1977.
Military Service: Navy, 1969.
Occupation: Plastics and packaging executive.
Family: Wife, Debbie Gunlack; two children.
Religion: Roman Catholic.
Political Career: Ohio House, 1985-91.
Capitol Office: 1011 Longworth Bldg. 20515; 225-6205.

Committees
Agriculture
General Farm Commodities; Livestock, Dairy & Poultry
House Oversight
Republican Conference Chairman

In Washington: First elected in 1990, Boehner quickly established himself as both a belligerent critic of congressional perks and as an ardent follower of conservative GOP leader Newt Gingrich. Smart moves both: After Republicans won the House majority in 1994, Boehner became a key lieutenant to the House Speaker, and Boehner's colleagues elected him chairman of the Republican Conference.

Boehner facilitated Gingrich's moves early in the 104th Congress to centralize power over the GOP's message and strategy in the Speaker's office. As conference chairman he devoted himself to helping keep the party's troops marching toward fulfillment of the "Contract With America" in early 1995.

And, along with the rest of the House GOP leadership, Boehner drew criticism when the public began to sour on some elements of the Republican "revolution." The success of President Clinton's "three E's" campaign mantra of 1996 — promising to protect the environment, education and the elderly — was rooted in the public's anxiety about policies pushed by House conservatives such as Boehner.

As conference chairman, Boehner is in charge of getting information to GOP members. The conference writes and distributes "floor preps," which spell out the provisions of legislation on the House floor that day and any amendments expected.

Part of Boehner's job also is to help GOP members explain to their constituents what is happening in Washington. This is the area where Boehner encountered the most trouble in the 104th.

He is easily the most-quoted member of the House GOP leadership, in part because he is the most accessible to reporters. When the House is voting, he can usually be found just outside the chamber, grabbing a quick smoke and chatting with journalists. But while he is comfortable with the press, he is usually very controlled in what he says, sticking to the party line on most issues.

As the 104th unfolded and polls showed the public responding negatively to some of the House GOP's actions, Boehner, as lead party messenger, met with increasing criticism from colleagues who believed that if they could just "get the message out" voters would be sunnier about the GOP agenda.

Boehner also drew negative publicity — and motivated proponents of campaign finance law overhaul — after he distributed campaign-contribution checks from tobacco concerns to members on the House floor. House Republicans passed a rule in the 105th Congress that bans anyone from distributing campaign checks in and around the House chamber.

In late 1995 and early 1996, when deadlocked budget negotiations between Clinton and Congress resulted in partial government shutdowns, the court of public opinion mostly blamed Republicans. Unable to counter Democratic attacks that the GOP wanted to slash Medicare spending, Boehner found that his position in the leadership was weakened.

There was even talk that Boehner might face a challenge in the leadership elections for the 105th. But by the time that voting came around in late 1996, the party was focused on a bigger matter: whether Gingrich's ethics problems would sidetrack his Speakership; Boehner was re-elected conference chair.

Boehner, like others in the leadership, was drawn into the Gingrich ethics drama. It was Boehner's cellular phone, which he used while vacationing in Florida, that enabled a couple of Democratic activists to eavesdrop on a conference call among top House Republicans discussing how Gingrich's agreement with the ethics committee prohibited him from orchestrating a counterattack to charges.

John and Alice Martin taped the conversation and brought it to Washington, where they say they gave it to Jim McDermott, D-Wash., then the ranking Democrat on the ethics committee. That tape made its way to national news outlets. Boehner immediately called on Attorney General Janet Reno to investigate the matter, and in late April 1997, the Martins pleaded guilty to illegally intercepting a cellular telephone call.

Boehner also told a Fox news program that if, as widely suspected, McDermott leaked the tape to the media, "he should resign the Congress immediately. This is ridiculous."

OHIO 8
Southwest —Hamilton; Middletown

Butler County is the anchor of this southwestern Ohio district, which has changed shape several times in recent redistrictings but always remained solidly Republican.

Butler contains more than half the district's population and two medium-sized manufacturing centers along the Great Miami River — Hamilton (population 61,000) and Middletown (population 46,000). Steel, paper, automobile bodies, machine tools and a variety of other metal products are made in the two cities.

Most of what few minorities there are in this district live in the two cities; Hamilton is 7 percent black and Middletown is 11 percent black. The rest of the district is about 1 percent black. All other minorities make up about 1 percent of the district. But both Hamilton and Middletown have lost population in recent years. Most of Butler County's 291,000 residents live not in the two cities but in suburban communities and small towns such as Oxford, the home of Miami University. Union Township, also in Butler County, is one of the state's fastest-growing suburbs. Many residents here commute to Cincinnati or Dayton.

The expansion in Butler County's suburban territory has escalated a rightward trend in the local Republican Party.

Ronald Reagan carried Butler in 1980 with 62 percent of the vote, and increased that to 73 percent in 1984. In 1988, George Bush carried Butler with 69 percent of the vote, well above his statewide average of 55 percent. He beat Bill Clinton here by 19 percentage points in 1992, winning 49 percent of the vote. While Bob Dole lost Ohio in 1996, he won the 8th District with 52 percent. In recent years the county has elected some of the state's most conservative Republican legislators.

The other half of the 8th's residents live outside Butler County in a string of fertile Corn Belt counties running north along the Indiana border and east toward Springfield. The land is flat and the roads are straight. Once leaving the Miami Valley in northern Butler, a motorist can drive north through the 8th along Route 127 without more than an occasional slight turn of the steering wheel.

Corn and soybeans are major cash crops in the rural counties. Poultry and livestock also are money-makers. In recent years, Darke and Mercer counties have been the leading Ohio counties in farm income.

Mercer, the southern half of which remains in the 8th, was settled by German Catholics and is the only county in the district with much of a Democratic heritage; Democrats also have a chance in Darke County. But Mercer likes its Democrats conservative. It has not backed the party's presidential candidate since 1968.

Shelby County and a bit of southwestern Auglaize County were added to the 8th in the last redistricting. Shelby voted heavily for Bush and Ross Perot in 1992, giving them 44 percent and 29 percent of the vote, respectively, to Clinton's 26 percent. Dole won the county with only 48 percent four years later.

1990 Population: 570,901. White 549,313 (96%), Black 15,892 (3%), Other 5,696 (1%). Hispanic origin 2,763 (<1%). 18 and over 415,676 (73%), 62 and over 80,274 (14%). Median age: 32.

During the days leading up to Gingrich's re-election as Speaker in January 1997, Boehner and others in the leadership hit the television talk-show circuit, making the case for him to continue in office.

But reporters began examining who might take over if Gingrich should fall. Several reports noted the tension between Boehner and Majority Whip Tom DeLay of Texas, both of whom see themselves as the true representative of the conservatives in the GOP conference. While the jostling for position calmed after Gingrich's re-election, the Boehner-DeLay relationship bears watching.

As a freshman in the 102nd Congress, Boehner received national media attention for his reformist efforts, most notably as a member of the GOP's Gang of Seven (which castigated the Democratic leadership over the House bank scandal) and as an advocate of a constitutional amendment prohibiting a congressional pay raise from taking effect without an intervening election.

Boehner's interest in such institutional matters helped earn him a spot on the House Administration Committee. Republicans renamed the panel House Oversight for the 104th, and Boehner remains there.

In winning the conference chair in late 1994, Boehner defeated Duncan Hunter of California. Although the two are close in age, Hunter has served in the House since 1981, and the outcome was seen as a victory for younger-generation Republicans, many of whom won election in the 1990s by exploiting anti-Congress sentiment that Boehner helped spawn with the House bank crusade. The fact that Hunter had run up 399 overdrafts at the House bank also probably diminished his appeal to newer House members. Boehner got 122 votes to Hunter's 102.

Boehner votes a conservative line, supporting tax cuts and regulatory relief and siding with opponents of abortion and proponents of gunowners' rights. He voted in 1996 against a minimum wage increase, and in the debate on a balanced-budget constitutional amendment, he preferred the most hard-nosed option, one that would have required a three-fifths vote by both chambers to raise taxes.

"We should balance the budget by downsizing government and not by raising taxes," Boehner said.

But unlike some deficit-conscious Republicans, Boehner supported two big-ticket science projects targeted by budget-cutters: the superconducting super collider (which was killed) and the space station (which survives). And while some GOP "deficit hawks" believe the Pentagon must share in the belt-tightening being asked of domestic programs, Boehner has supported GOP leaders' efforts to spend more on defense than the Clinton administration requests.

Occupied mostly with institutional and political affairs, Boehner so far has not made a name as a legislative draftsman. He has a seat on the Agriculture Committee, and although sympathetic to sugar price supports and some other subsidy programs, he voted in the 104th for the GOP rewrite of farm laws, the "Freedom to Farm" bill. It phased out most New Deal-era crop subsidies (although scaled-back sugar supports survived), bringing federal farm policy more in line with free-market principles and giving farmers greater flexibility in deciding what to plant.

At Home: In the reliably Republican 8th, the GOP primary surprise in 1990 was not that embattled Rep. Donald E. "Buz" Lukens was ousted but that Boehner emerged victorious. A state representative and local businessman, Boehner was barely a blip on the radar screen at the beginning of the campaign.

Lukens was doomed after his May 1989 conviction on a misdemeanor charge stemming from a sexual liaison with a 16-year-old girl. He finally resigned the seat after a second allegation of sexual misconduct that October.

Former six-term GOP Rep. Thomas N. Kindness started out as the heavy primary favorite, but Boehner made up for his lack of name recognition by running a smart and aggressive primary campaign.

While Kindness focused his sights on the wounded incumbent, Boehner ignored Lukens and chipped away at Kindness, framing him as a shady lobbyist who abandoned the district after losing a 1986 challenge to Democratic Sen. John Glenn. Boehner used his financial resources to outspend Kindness by more than 5-to-1.

Kindness responded to the barrage of negative ads by describing Boehner as "an immature yuppie." But Boehner stuck to his theme and suggested that Kindness might have conflicts of interest on issues involving his former clients. Boehner won with 49 percent; Kindness trailed with 32 percent.

The general election was not as close or nasty, with Boehner sweeping every county against the Democratic nominee, former Hamilton Mayor Gregory V. Jolivette.

Though Lukens had ceased to be an issue, he threw a monkey wrench into the race late in the fall campaign. His resignation triggered a series of cumbersome electoral problems, forcing the governor to rescind his order for a special election. The seat remained vacant for the remainder of the 101st Congress.

In 1992, Boehner easily dispatched Fred Sennet, a college instructor from Fairfield. He ran unopposed in 1994 and won 70 percent in 1996.

HOUSE ELECTIONS

1996 General		
John A. Boehner (R)	165,815	(70%)
Jeffrey D. Kitchen (D)	61,515	(26%)
William Baker (NL)	8,613	(4%)
1994 General		
John A. Boehner (R)	148,338	(100%)

Previous Winning Percentages: 1992 (74%) **1990** (61%)

CAMPAIGN FINANCE

	Receipts	Receipts from PACs	Expend-itures
1996			
Boehner (R)	$1,322,349	$561,646 (42%)	$1,312,440
Kitchen (D)	$20,855	$9,000 (43%)	$20,853
1994			
Boehner (R)	$709,466	$216,076 (30%)	$713,223

DISTRICT VOTE FOR PRESIDENT

1996		1992	
D	88,930 (37%)	D	75,189 (29%)
R	125,201 (52%)	R	120,847 (47%)
I	25,999 (11%)	I	59,937 (23%)

KEY VOTES

1997	
Ban "partial birth" abortions	Y
1996	
Approve farm bill	Y
Deny public education to illegal immigrants	Y
Repeal ban on certain assault-style weapons	Y
Increase minimum wage	N
Freeze defense spending	N
Approve welfare overhaul	Y
1995	
Approve balanced-budget constitutional amendment	Y
Relax Clean Water Act regulations	Y
Oppose limits on environmental regulations	N
Reduce projected Medicare spending	Y
Approve GOP budget with tax and spending cuts	Y

VOTING STUDIES

	Presidential Support		Party Unity		Conservative Coalition	
Year	S	O	S	O	S	O
1996	34	66	96	3	98	2
1995	19	81	97	1	96	0
1994	37	60	95	2	92	3
1993	34	66	96	2	95	2
1992	87	11	94	3	94	6
1991	84	14	96	4	97	0

INTEREST GROUP RATINGS

Year	ADA	AFL-CIO	CCUS	ACU
1996	0	n/a	94	100
1995	0	0	100	88
1994	5	0	83	100
1993	0	0	91	100
1992	5	17	88	96
1991	0	0	100	95

9 Marcy Kaptur (D)

Of Toledo — Elected 1982, 8th term

Biographical Information
Born: June 17, 1946, Toledo, Ohio.
Education: U. of Wisconsin, B.A. 1968; U. of Michigan, M.U.P. 1974; Massachusetts Institute of Technology, 1981.
Occupation: Urban planner; White House aide.
Family: Single.
Religion: Roman Catholic.
Political Career: No previous office.
Capitol Office: 2311 Rayburn Bldg. 20515; 225-4146.

Committees
Appropriations
Agriculture, Rural Development, FDA & Related Agencies (ranking); Legislative; VA, HUD & Independent Agencies

In Washington: Kaptur has waged a steady, determined and largely unsuccessful effort to halt the Clinton administration's push for lowering trade barriers. She took a leading role in the 103rd Congress in opposing NAFTA and GATT. After both trade agreements were implemented, she introduced legislation in the 104th requiring U.S. withdrawal from NAFTA unless the trade pact met specific standards on job growth, public health and the trade deficit.

Her profile on trade issues was high enough that independent presidential candidate Ross Perot asked her to be his running mate in the 1996 election. Perot shares Kaptur's disdain for NAFTA. Kaptur declined his offer, saying that although she and Perot had been allies on a number of issues, "it is my hope to continue serving our northwest Ohio community and our state as long as the voters give me the honor."

In the 105th, Kaptur serves as ranking Democrat on the Appropriations Agriculture Subcommittee, where she can look after the wheat, corn and soybean farmers in her district. Kaptur won a coveted slot on the Appropriations Committee late in the 101st Congress, after several years of striving for it.

But what Kaptur relishes most is her role as a defender of U.S. manufacturing jobs — jobs that were certain to disappear under NAFTA, she said, as companies moved to Mexico in search of cheap labor. In her own hometown of Toledo, an auto parts plant shut down and some personnel and equipment were sent to Matamoros, Mexico. Ohio has lost more than 100,000 jobs to Mexico, she said.

By the time the vote on NAFTA was taken in November 1993, those opposed to it knew that the Clinton administration's lobbying on behalf of the pact had paid off. Kaptur wiped away tears as she listened to Michigan Democrat David E. Bonior give one of the closing speeches. Bonior, the majority whip, had led the anti-NAFTA forces in the House.

Although she failed to stop the trade deal, Kaptur continued to remind the House of its consequences. In a 1994 floor speech on the "Post-NAFTA Era," Kaptur listed the names of U.S. companies that had moved south since the agreement was approved.

In early 1995, Kaptur and Oregon Democrat Peter A. DeFazio called for the United States to withdraw from NAFTA. Their appeal came on the heels of an unanticipated 35 percent drop in the value of the Mexican peso and a proposal by the Clinton administration to implement a $20 billion bailout plan for the country, $9 billion of which would come from the U.S. Treasury.

"There is a new kind for foreign aid afoot in our land. It is called NAFTA," Kaptur told the House. "Because of the instability in Mexico, our taxpayers, with no vote occurring here in the Congress of the United States, our taxpayers are being asked to foot a multibillion-dollar bailout of the Mexican peso."

She was so critical of Clinton's decision to shore up the Mexican economy that she introduced a resolution in March 1995 calling on the president to make available to Congress within 14 days documents relating to the bailout. The House overwhelmingly approved the resolution, 407-21.

Although the resolution had little impact, it was clearly intended to send a signal to the president about the the bailout's unpopularity. "Today's vote should signal a political change to those powerful special interests that have for too long written the rules of banking and trade, who have given away our jobs, and then had to call on our U.S. Treasury to bail out their mistakes," Kaptur said. "The American people have a right to know how their money is being risked and spent."

She also worked hard in November 1994 to prevent House approval of GATT. She and others who were opposed to the world trade agreement based much of their criticism on the powers that would be vested with a new World Trade Organization that would monitor trade activity and resolve disputes. Kaptur is a strong supporter of labor unions, which put up a solid front

OHIO 9
Northwest — Toledo

Toledo's fortunes have tended to rise and fall with the health of the automobile industry. But by the beginning of the 1990s, it was Wall Street, not Detroit, that had undermined Toledo's economy.

The city had climbed back from the depths of the early 1980s recession by mid-decade, and there was some cause for optimism. A Jeep plant, with over 4,800 employees, and a General Motors transmission factory with its 4,800 employees were operating at full capacity. In 1986, unemployment in Toledo slipped below 10 percent.

Undergirding Toledo's economy are the several crude oil and gas pipelines that terminate there and the refineries they feed.

In recent years, the city has experienced an increase in manufacturing job growth. Millions have been spent to improve the city's Toledo Express Airport. The Burlington Air Express delivery company opened a $50 million terminal and sorting center there in 1991, creating more than 800 jobs.

Almost three-fifths — about 333,000 — of the district's residents live in Toledo, an important port city that sits at the mouth of the largest river that flows into the Great Lakes, the Maumee. Even so, about 50 percent of the district's land mass is agricultural. Wheat, soybeans and corn are among the crops grown.

The city, built on the site of a remote 18th century fort, is now a lonely Democratic outpost in rural, Republican northwestern Ohio. Democrats outnumber Republicans in surrounding Lucas County (which holds an additional 129,000 residents) by more than 2-to-1.

A smaller black population keeps Democratic majorities in Toledo lower than those in Dayton or Cleveland. Jimmy Carter carried the city in 1980, but with only 49 percent of the vote. Democrats Walter F. Mondale and Michael S. Dukakis carried on the tradition in 1984 and 1988. And Bill Clinton won it handily in 1992 and 1996.

Toledo is an ethnic city. There are major concentrations of Germans, Irish, Poles and Hungarians. While traditionally Democratic, most blue-collar ethnics there vote Republican at least occasionally.

To the east of the city are blue-collar, traditionally Democratic suburbs. Republicans are concentrated in the more affluent suburbs on Toledo's west side, where Ottawa Hills has one of the highest per capita incomes of any community in Ohio.

All of Fulton County was included in the 9th in 1992 redistricting. Fulton is one of the most Republican counties in Ohio, but part of it is in Toledo's orbit and contains some solid Democratic precincts. Bob Dole won the county by 2,000 votes in 1996, the only part of the district that he carried.

The 9th now includes about a third of Wood County's land mass and about half of its people. The part of Wood County in the district includes 15,000 of Bowling Green's 28,000 residents, along with Bowling Green State University and its 17,500 students.

1990 Population: 570,901. White 484,770 (85%), Black 69,444 (12%), Other 16,687 (3%). Hispanic origin 19,347 (3%). 18 and over 421,341 (74%), 62 and over 86,721 (15%). Median age: 32.

against GATT. But many lawmakers who typically side with labor, including some who voted against NAFTA, accepted the Clinton administration's promises of booming U.S. export and job growth resulting from the new GATT pact. The House passed it, 288-146.

Kaptur's preoccupation with the two international trade pacts reflects her concern for her district. Toledo's economic health long has been dependent on the auto industry and labor remains a strong influence in the city.

She also has been a consistent critic of the Clinton administration's decision to continue most-favored-nation (MFN) trade status for China. Under MFN, Chinese goods are permitted to enter the United States at the low, non-discriminatory tariff rates available to most nations. Those who oppose giving China the trade status say the country has little regard for human rights, exports goods made from prison and child labor and engages in unfair trading practices. But their efforts to place even certain conditions on China's MFN designation have been largely unsuccessful. "A vote not to disapprove will signify a triumph of commercialism over balanced foreign policy and a triumph of fascism over liberty," Kaptur told the House during the June 1996 China MFN debate.

But many lawmakers worried that cutting off MFN would only serve to antagonize China and deny U.S. businesses a chance to compete in the world's hottest export market. The House rejected, 141-286, a resolution that would have withdrawn China's MFN status.

From her Appropriations seat, Kaptur successfully added a provision to the fiscal 1997 agriculture spending bill that required farmers in good weather to either plant a crop or undertake certain conservation measures in order to receive government subsidies. "This amendment basically says to receive a federal payment you must work for it," Kaptur said. "If we expect welfare recipients to work for federal payments, why shouldn't farm payments go only to those who work."

Kaptur's most notable divergence from the majority of the Democratic Caucus — and from most Democratic women in the House, where she is now the second most senior woman — is on certain abortion-related questions.

Kaptur opposes the use of federal funds for abortions. In 1996, she voted against an amendment that would have allowed privately financed abortions at overseas military hospitals. She supports banning a particular abortion technique that opponents call "partial birth" abortion. But in 1996, she supported maintaining a requirement that states fund Medicaid abortions for poor women in cases of rape, incest or a threat to the life of the woman.

In making her successful bid for the Appropriations Committee in 1990, Kaptur played her gender and geography cards. She noted that the committee had just one Democratic woman, Lindy (Mrs. Hale) Boggs of Louisiana, who was retiring at the end of the 101st Congress; she also stirred other Rust Belt members to quash a move by Californians for a sixth Appropriations seat.

At Home: Kaptur's victory over GOP Rep. Ed Weber was one of the Democrats' surprise 1982 successes. Although a poised and aggressive candidate, she had to overcome a late start and a poorly financed, underorganized campaign with little help from the national party.

Kaptur took the Democratic nomination essentially by default in February 1982 when the local party gave up on trying to find a proven vote-getter to challenge the popular Republican incumbent. At that point in the election year, national GOP strategists were pointing to Weber as a symbol of the way their first-term House members were entrenching in Democratic territory.

But Kaptur began hammering away at Weber's voting record, using his support for President Ronald Reagan's economic policies during a recession as evidence of insensitivity to Toledo's economic plight. Weber never shifted in his public backing for Reagan's program; that was his undoing in a region with double-digit unemployment.

Overconfident, he failed to exploit one vulnerability in Kaptur's record. Although she was a Toledo native, Kaptur had spent many years away, most recently as the assistant director of urban affairs for President Jimmy Carter. But with Weber ignoring the issue, neither Kaptur's absence nor her Carter connection proved to be any problem.

In 1984, Republicans nominated Frank Venner, a longtime TV newscaster. Although he had no previous political experience, Venner was a familiar figure to a generation of Toledo voters. But he had trouble translating his avuncular, non-ideological TV image into a partisan campaign. He had plenty of campaign money, but neither a strong organization nor a potent local issue to use against Kaptur. Fortified by support from labor and the district's large ethnic population, Kaptur won 55 percent. That was her last close race.

HOUSE ELECTIONS

1996 General		
Marcy Kaptur (D)	170,617	(77%)
Randy Whitman (R)	46,040	(21%)
Elizabeth A. Slotnick (NL)	4,677	(2%)
1994 General		
Marcy Kaptur (D)	118,120	(75%)
R. Randy Whitman (R)	38,665	(25%)

Previous Winning Percentages: 1992 (74%) **1990** (78%) **1988** (81%) **1986** (78%) **1984** (55%) **1982** (58%)

CAMPAIGN FINANCE

	Receipts	Receipts from PACs	Expend-itures
1996			
Kaptur (D)	$401,736	$222,534 (55%)	$253,432
Whitman (R)	$45,363	$516 (1%)	$44,641
1994			
Kaptur (D)	$499,886	$243,769 (49%)	$309,247
Whitman (R)	$9,864	$14 (0%)	$9,500

DISTRICT VOTE FOR PRESIDENT

1996		1992	
D	125,976 (55%)	**D**	118,818 (47%)
R	76,532 (34%)	**R**	81,881 (33%)
I	22,951 (10%)	**I**	50,155 (20%)

KEY VOTES

1997	
Ban "partial birth" abortions	?
1996	
Approve farm bill	Y
Deny public education to illegal immigrants	Y
Repeal ban on certain assault-style weapons	N
Increase minimum wage	Y
Freeze defense spending	Y
Approve welfare overhaul	Y
1995	
Approve balanced-budget constitutional amendment	Y
Relax Clean Water Act regulations	N
Oppose limits on environmental regulations	Y
Reduce projected Medicare spending	N
Approve GOP budget with tax and spending cuts	N

VOTING STUDIES

	Presidential Support		Party Unity		Conservative Coalition	
Year	S	O	S	O	S	O
1996	71	24	80	15	31	69
1995	71	25	83	13	35	60
1994	76	19	83	10	58	42
1993	69	27	83	13	66	32
1992	23	75	86	10	50	48
1991	29	67	85	8	41	54

INTEREST GROUP RATINGS

Year	ADA	AFL-CIO	CCUS	ACU
1996	75	n/a	33	15
1995	75	92	29	16
1994	60	100	40	20
1993	70	92	18	26
1992	75	100	14	8
1991	85	82	30	5

10 Dennis J. Kucinich (D)

Of Cleveland — Elected 1996, 1st term

Biographical Information
Born: Oct. 8, 1946, Cleveland, Ohio.
Education: Case Western Reserve U., B.A., M.A..
Occupation: Video producer; public power consultant.
Family: Single; one child.
Religion: Roman Catholic.
Political Career: Cleveland City Council, 1969-71; mayor of Cleveland, 1977-79; Cleveland City Council, 1983; Democratic nominee for U.S. House, 1972; independent candidate for U.S. House, 1974; sought Democratic nomination for U.S. House, 1988, 1992; Ohio Senate, 1995-97.
Capitol Office: 1730 Longworth Bldg. 20515; 225-5871
.

Committees
Education & Workforce
Early Childhood, Youth & Families
Government Reform & Oversight
Human Resources; National Economic Growth, Natural Resources & Regulatory Affairs

The Path to Washington: Kucinich arrives in Congress best known for his tenure two decades ago as the "boy mayor" of Cleveland.

During his brief, stormy service as mayor (1977-1979), the city fell into financial default.

Kucinich lost his 1979 re-election bid to George V. Voinovich, who is now governor of Ohio. But in the intervening years, both Cleveland and Kucinich have rebounded. The man who wore a bulletproof vest to throw out the first pitch of the Indians' 1978 baseball season seized a state Senate seat from a Republican incumbent in 1994, capping his political comeback in 1996 by ousting two-term Republican Rep. Martin R. Hoke in the Cleveland-based 10th District.

It was the persistent Kucinich's first congressional election success after four previous House races since 1972.

Perseverance is one of Kucinich's most enduring personality traits. At freshman class orientation in November 1996, he handed out cards depicting himself as a 4-foot 9-inch, 97-pound third-string quarterback in a 1960 school photo.

The race between Hoke and Kucinich drew national attention, as Democrats sought to recapture a seat they had lost in 1992. The 10th, an urban and suburban district that includes many voters of Eastern European descent, leans Democratic.

In 1992, Hoke defeated Democratic incumbent Mary Rose Oakar, who had been damaged by ethics troubles. Democrats took aim at Hoke in 1994, but missed their chance to defeat him when their candidate was also dogged by ethics questions.

In 1996, the equation was different. In his television advertisements, Hoke tried to paint negative images of Kucinich's tenure as mayor. But Kucinich, who sought to link Hoke with House Speaker Newt Gingrich, drew on strong grass-roots support from many district residents.

Kucinich also benefited from an expensive barrage of labor union-funded ads attacking Hoke, particularly on the issue of GOP efforts to reduce the spending growth of Medicare.

On the road to his acrimonious showdown with Hoke, Kucinich trounced three primary opponents in the state's March primary, winning more than three-quarters of the vote.

In the fall campaign, Kucinich benefited from a perception that even Republicans saw Hoke as imperiled.

In September 1996, The Associated Press reported that Rep. Bill Paxon of New York, chairman of the National Republican Congressional Committee (NRCC), said Hoke was one of six Republican House members likely to lose if the election was held then. The NRCC subsequently denied that Paxon had made the remark.

But in early October, Hoke took another hit from a surprising source: Fellow Ohio Republican Rep. Steven C. LaTourette, a freshman from the neighboring 19th District, was quoted in the Cleveland Plain Dealer as saying Hoke would lose his race.

Hoke ran well ahead of Republican presidential candidate Bob Dole and spent almost $1.5 million, more than twice as much as Kucinich, but the Democratic challenger upended him, 49 percent to 46 percent.

Kucinich made a splash in January 1997 by entertaining a congressional dinner audience with a mocking imitation of Newt Gingrich's college course on renewing American civilization.

In the 105th Congress, Kucinich will sit on the House Government Reform and Oversight and Education and the Workforce committees.

Kucinich, a close ally of labor unions, is a strong critic of international trade pacts such as NAFTA and GATT. He maintains that they have undermined domestic jobs and has said he will push legislation to reform or repeal the agreements.

Unions in Cleveland have been hurt by the loss of manufacturing jobs, and Kucinich has expressed an interest in being involved in the effort to expand job training programs for skilled workers.

OHIO 10
Cleveland — West Side and suburbs

The 1996 election of Kucinich put the 10th back where it was designed to be: in Democratic hands. The district was drawn for the 1990s with the safety of Democratic Rep. Mary Rose Oakar in mind, but she was upset in 1992 by Republican Martin Hoke. He won again in 1994, but could not hold on in 1996, as the 10th went Democratic in presidential voting by a 15-point margin.

The line between the 10th and 11th districts generally divides Cleveland's white and black populations. The 10th is the white district, containing the state's largest concentration of ethnic voters. Poles, Czechs, Italians, Irish and Germans are the largest groups.

The city's steel industry fueled the ethnic influx around the turn of the century, with immigrants settling near the West Side mills. Steel manufacturing, automobile and aluminum plants combine with smaller businesses to make up the employment base today.

But many of the younger people who work there bought homes in the suburbs. In 1980, Cleveland was still Ohio's most populous city, but by decade's end its population had declined by 12 percent. This population loss, combined with the addition of more western Cleveland suburbs in redistricting, means more than half the electorate now lies outside the city limits.

The downtown area was gerrymandered in order to divvy up sources of campaign contributions, not votes. Its businesses are split between the 10th and 11th districts. The city's economic problems of the 1970s, notably its near bankruptcy under then-Mayor Kucinich, made it a national symbol of urban decay. But Cleveland today is stronger than many industrial cities of the Frost Belt, mainly because of its transition to a service economy. The city also boasts of having the nation's fourth-largest concentration of Fortune 500 company headquarters.

To offset auto and steel slumps, a consortium of the city's largest companies mapped out a long-term, diversified plan for growth — and a number of small, high-tech companies already have been attracted. Condominiums are being built near the BP America headquarters, and old dry-goods warehouses are being converted to homes — the first downtown housing to go up in a generation. Several art deco theaters have been restored, and Cleveland's Lake Erie waterfront is receiving a face-lift. Even the Cuyahoga River — which was once so polluted that it caught fire — has been revived. Baseball's Indians and basketball's Cavaliers play at new facilities (Jacobs Field and Gund Arena, respectively).

Still, children and grandchildren of European immigrants have moved out of Cleveland to inner suburbs such as Parma, due south of the city. In recent years they have moved again. Parma's population declined in the 1970s and '80s, as residents left their ranch homes of the 1950s for the open spaces of outer suburbs such as Strongsville.

But even with the population loss, Parma (population 88,000) still is the eighth-largest city in Ohio. Nearby steel mills and automobile plants give it a strong union presence.

1990 Population: 570,903. White 537,301 (94%), Black 11,982 (2%), Other 21,620 (4%), Hispanic origin 22,966 (4%). 18 and over 435,467 (76%), 62 and over 104,152 (18%). Median age: 35.

HOUSE ELECTIONS

1996 General		
Dennis J. Kucinich (D)	110,723	(49%)
Martin R. Hoke (R)	104,546	(46%)
Robert B. Iverson (NL)	10,415	(5%)
1996 Primary		
Dennis J. Kucinich (D)	37,895	(77%)
Ed Boyle (D)	9,221	(19%)
Donald B. Slusher Jr. (D)	1,253	(3%)
C. River Smith (D)	703	(1%)

CAMPAIGN FINANCE

	Receipts	Receipts from PACs	Expend-itures
1996			
Kucinich (D)	$754,928	$285,108 (38%)	$692,867
Hoke (R)	$1,427,123	$39,465 (3%)	$1,480,181

DISTRICT VOTE FOR PRESIDENT

	1996		1992
D	118,165 (51%)	**D**	107,460 (42%)
R	82,815 (36%)	**R**	92,849 (36%)
I	26,883 (12%)	**I**	58,095 (22%)

KEY VOTES

1997	
Ban "partial birth" abortions	Y

11 Louis Stokes (D)

Of Shaker Heights — Elected 1968, 15th term

Biographical Information
Born: Feb. 23, 1925, Cleveland, Ohio.
Education: Case Western Reserve U., 1946-48; Cleveland-Marshall College of Law, J.D. 1953.
Military Service: Army, 1943-46.
Occupation: Lawyer.
Family: Wife, Jeannette Francis; four children.
Religion: African Methodist Episcopal Zion.
Political Career: No previous office.
Capitol Office: 2365 Rayburn Bldg. 20515; 225-7032.

Committees
Appropriations
Labor, Health & Human Services, Education & Related Agencies; VA, HUD & Independent Agencies (ranking)

In Washington: For Stokes, like many senior Democrats, the 104th Congress was a period of adjustment. A courtly fellow, Stokes had grown quite used to life in the majority, having Republicans address him respectfully as he chaired several different panels. But suddenly he was on the outs, and as ranking minority member of the VA-HUD Appropriations Subcommittee he watched the GOP majority tear into the budgets of housing programs he had helped create.

During the 103rd Congress, Stokes chaired the subcommittee, which doles out funds for a grab-bag of agencies including the Veterans Administration, the Department of Housing and Urban Development, NASA and the Environmental Protection Agency. He enjoyed good relations with Jerry Lewis of California, the panel's senior Republican. But when Lewis assumed the gavel, he was operating under a mandate to slash spending, which piqued Stokes and soured their relations, at least temporarily.

A typical frustrating moment for Stokes came in 1995, as he was defending public housing, which was subject to deep cuts under the GOP's spending bill. Stokes noted that he and his brother Carl, a former Cleveland mayor and then ambassador to Seychelles before his death in 1996, had grown up in public housing. Were it not for such assistance, Stokes said, he and his brother "would be either in jail or dead, we'd be some kind of statistic." To which Appropriations Committee Chairman Robert L. Livingston replied, "We can play this compassion game all day but it won't cut it."

The VA-HUD bill is one of the two largest pots of domestic discretionary spending, and it carried more than its fair share of weight as GOP budget-cutters sought savings. The cuts began early in the 104th with a package of rescissions in spending programs approved when Democrats controlled Congress. The suddenly outgunned Democrats could do little but complain. Stokes called the cuts "unconscionable," "reprehensible," "appalling," and a "prescription for disaster." But all six amendments he offered at the committee level were turned back on party-line votes. "You have to try," Stokes reasoned.

As the fiscal 1996 spending season began, Stokes led the way in trying to restore funding for programs covered by the VA-HUD bill and he also offered several amendments to the Labor-HHS-Education spending package (he also sits on Appropriations' Labor-HHS Subcommittee). He sought several times to change the GOP legislation to restore funding for housing and social services and overturn limits but, predictably, these efforts bore no fruit.

Stokes' new role led to friction with Lewis, who had genially referred to Stokes as "my chairman" during the 103rd and grew disappointed with Stokes' attacks on his legislation. Stokes felt he had been shut out and voted against Lewis' position on almost every floor amendment considered to the fiscal 1996 VA-HUD bill.

But Stokes got his revenge. He joined with New York Republican Sherwood Boehlert to offer an amendment to strike 17 policy riders on the bill that would have blocked the EPA from enforcing major portions of such laws as the Clean Air and clean water acts. Boehlert was one of 51 Republicans to vote to strip the riders, enough to provide Stokes and the Democrats with a heartening 212-206 victory.

That victory proved short-lived, though, as the following week Lewis called the amendment up for a revote. Several Democratic supporters missed the vote and the Stokes amendment died on a tie, 210-210 vote. Stokes warned members: "This vote will never go away. This vote will stay with all of us for a very long time."

His words proved prophetic; his move succeeded on a third vote (a motion to instruct House members to strip it during conference with the Senate), but the bill and its riders died anyway under a presidential veto, and the affected programs had to be funded under an omnibus spending bill. But perhaps more importantly, the EPA riders proved to be a public relations flop, and the

OHIO 11
Cleveland — East Side and suburbs

One of the axioms of Ohio politics is that to win statewide, a Democratic candidate must build a 100,000-vote edge in Cuyahoga County. Most of that lead has to be built in the 11th, which is anchored in Cleveland's heavily black East Side. Bill Clinton amassed a 125,500-vote margin over Bob Dole here in 1996, helping him walk away with Ohio's 21 electoral votes.

This compact district — one of the smallest in the state — includes poor inner-city areas as well as upper middle-class territory farther from the downtown area. Nineteen percent of the 11th's families — and almost a third of those in its section of Cleveland — live below the poverty line. Conditions improve out toward the city's eastern suburbs, where blue- and white-collar occupations are more common in the diverse black population.

Devastated by the riots of the 1960s, inner-city neighborhoods of Hough and Glenville can claim some new residential and commercial development, but they still bear the scars of poverty.

Out toward the lake, this area includes the middle-class, white ethnic neighborhoods of Collinwood and St. Clare, inhabited by Italians, and Poles, Yugoslavs and other Eastern Europeans.

Overall, the 11th is 59 percent black and heavily Democratic. During the past decade, it has been one of the most Democratic districts in the state.

Any hopes that Stokes would be made vulnerable when his district was extended east to take in some white working-class areas — his old 21st District was 62 percent black — were dashed in 1992 when he pulled down 69 percent of the vote in a field of four, compared with 80 percent against a single opponent in 1990.

New to Stokes' territory is Euclid, a white, ethnic, working-class city of 55,000 east of Cleveland. Euclid was described by a local observer as "Democratic, but hardly comfortable with the black part of this district." A Democrat from Euclid running against Stokes as an independent in 1992 hoped — in vain — to capitalize on this sentiment.

Some of the 11th's other major suburbs are Cleveland Heights, Shaker Heights and University Heights (populations, 54,000, 31,000 and 15,000, respectively).

With a large proportion of Jews and young professionals, these are among Ohio's most liberal communities. North of Shaker Heights is Cleveland Heights, many of whose integrated neighborhoods are a short walk from University Circle, home of Case Western Reserve University and Cleveland's cultural hub.

From the circle area, commuters drive along historic Euclid Avenue to their jobs downtown. While the avenue now bears the marks of poverty, it was known as "Millionaires' Row" at the turn of the century. Few of the old mansions remain. The one belonging to John D. Rockefeller, founder of Standard Oil, was razed after his death in 1937.

1990 Population: 570,901. White 226,986 (40%), Black 334,348 (59%), Other 9,567 (2%). Hispanic origin 6,402 (1%). 18 and over 424,718 (74%), 62 and over 102,401 (18%). Median age: 34.

GOP retreated from its efforts to radically overhaul environmental enforcement laws.

In 1996, Lewis bent over backwards to placate Stokes, spending hours in meetings with him in search of mutually acceptable legislation. Stokes termed it "a 360-degree difference" from the previous year. Such moves led to enmity among Republicans who thought Lewis had grown too accommodating toward the Democrats.

Like some other veteran appropriators, Stokes opposed the initiative that granted the president a version of line-item veto authority. He refused to applaud as Clinton praised the idea in an address to Congress and he found the statutory approach to such a major shift in power depressing.

Stokes also joined with Martin R. Hoke, a Republican from Cleveland, in seeking legislative avenues of redress as the town's professional football team made plans to move to Baltimore. The Browns moved anyway; Cleveland hopes to secure a new franchise for the city.

For the 105th, Stokes was appointed to a task force empowered to look into revising the methods by which the House polices ethics infringements among its members; the impetus for establishing the task force was the politicized investigation of Speaker Newt Gingrich.

It is a familiar role for Stokes, a former ethics committee chairman. In 1989, Stokes was picked by the Democratic leadership to a similar task force reviewing ethics — a panel established in the wake of the House investigation of Speaker Jim Wright of Texas. Stokes had first established an image as a troubleshooter as chairman in 1977 of the committee investigating the assassinations of John F. Kennedy and Martin Luther King Jr.

In 1981, with the case of the last figure in the Abscam bribery scandal, valued leadership lieutenant John P. Murtha, D-Pa., pending before the ethics committee, Speaker Thomas P. O'Neill Jr. of Massachusetts replaced Chairman Charles E. Bennett of Florida with Stokes, a committee member who had often expressed concern for the accused in House ethics cases. The committee ultimately recommended no action against Murtha, provoking its counsel to resign. Stokes continued as ethics chairman until 1985.

In 1991, with Congress searching to define its ethical standards in the wake of several financial and personal scandals, Stokes was asked again to chair the ethics committee. But as the House bank scandal unfolded that fall, Stokes recused himself. In a letter to Speaker Thomas S. Foley of Washington, Stokes wrote, "I have admitted that on occasions . . . my account was overdrawn." Not until the panel released its report in April 1992 was it known that Stokes had 551 overdrafts.

Stokes served on the Intelligence Committee between 1983 and 1989, rising to the chairmanship during the 100th Congress. He was a strong critic of the Reagan administration's actions in the Iran-contra affair.

At Home: While the House bank uproar swirled about his colleagues in 1992, Stokes had remained mum about his overdrafts. By the time the ethics committee report revealed that he had 551, the Ohio filing deadline for candidates had passed, leaving him unopposed in the primary in his heavily Democratic district.

Stokes faced three foes that November, including Republican Beryl E. Rothschild, the mayor of University Heights, and Edmund Gudenas, a Euclid City Council member. They combined to hold Stokes to a career-low 69 percent in his redrawn district. In 1994, he rebounded to 77 percent, and he topped 80 percent in 1996.

Stokes is feeling some pressure from a new generation of black leaders emerging in Cleveland, symbolized by the 1989 election of Michael White as mayor. But the Stokes family name still carries great weight in city politics, thanks to the long record of civic involvement by Stokes and his younger brother Carl. Carl grabbed the spotlight in the mid-1960s when he first ran for mayor of Cleveland. He served two terms as mayor (1967-71), later was elected to the Cleveland Municipal Court and went on to ambassadorial work before his death in 1996.

Louis Stokes' first victory was won as much in court as on Cleveland's East Side. Representing a black Republican, he charged in a 1967 suit that the Ohio legislature had gerrymandered the state's congressional districts, dividing the minority vote and preventing the election of a black candidate. Stokes won an appeal before the U.S. Supreme Court, forcing the lines to be redrawn.

Stokes had plenty of company in the 1968 contest for the open 21st: 13 other candidates filed to run in the Democratic primary. The outcome was little in doubt, though. Aided by his brother in City Hall and by his reputation as a civil rights lawyer, Stokes won with 41 percent of the primary vote. That November, he became the first black congressman from Ohio by defeating Charles P. Lucas — the Republican he had represented in court the previous year.

Stokes is now past 70, and he gave serious thought to retiring in the 104th Congress. But he announced he would "stay and fight" the GOP majority and easily won a 15th term in 1996.

HOUSE ELECTIONS

1996 General		
Louis Stokes (D)	153,546	(81%)
James J. Sykora (R)	28,821	(15%)
Sonja Glavina (NL)	6,665	(4%)
1994 General		
Louis Stokes (D)	114,220	(77%)
James J. Sykora (R)	33,705	(23%)

Previous Winning Percentages: **1992** (69%) **1990** (80%) **1988** (86%) **1986** (82%) **1984** (82%) **1982** (86%) **1980** (88%) **1978** (86%) **1976** (84%) **1974** (82%) **1972** (81%) **1970** (78%) **1968** (75%)

CAMPAIGN FINANCE

	Receipts	Receipts from PACs	Expend-itures
1996			
Stokes (D)	$318,954	$115,186 (36%)	$361,175
1994			
Stokes (D)	$437,673	$165,800 (38%)	$382,332

VOTING STUDIES

	Presidential Support		Party Unity		Conservative Coalition	
Year	**S**	**O**	**S**	**O**	**S**	**O**
1996	65	16	75	4	12	71
1995	86	6	91	1	3	93
1994	71	27	91	2	8	89
1993	82	12	91	3	14	73
1992	10	87	92	2	6	92
1991	24	74	90	4	0	100

KEY VOTES

1997	
Ban "partial birth" abortions	N
1996	
Approve farm bill	X
Deny public education to illegal immigrants	?
Repeal ban on certain assault-style weapons	?
Increase minimum wage	Y
Freeze defense spending	Y
Approve welfare overhaul	N
1995	
Approve balanced-budget constitutional amendment	N
Relax Clean Water Act regulations	N
Oppose limits on environmental regulations	Y
Reduce projected Medicare spending	N
Approve GOP budget with tax and spending cuts	N

DISTRICT VOTE FOR PRESIDENT

1996		1992	
D	154,612 (79%)	**D**	169,877 (73%)
R	29,060 (15%)	**R**	37,880 (16%)
I	9,536 (5%)	**I**	23,423 (10%)

INTEREST GROUP RATINGS

Year	ADA	AFL-CIO	CCUS	ACU
1996	65	n/a	17	0
1995	90	100	17	9
1994	100	100	18	10
1993	90	100	0	4
1992	95	92	14	0
1991	100	100	22	0

12 John R. Kasich (R)

Of Westerville — Elected 1982, 8th term

Biographical Information
Born: May 13, 1952, McKees Rocks, Pa.
Education: Ohio State U., B.S. 1974.
Occupation: Legislative aide.
Family: Wife, Karen Waldbillig.
Religion: Christian.
Political Career: Ohio Senate, 1979-83.
Capitol Office: 1111 Longworth Bldg. 20515; 225-5355.

Committees
Budget (chairman)
National Security
Military Readiness; Military Research & Development

In Washington: When the Republican-led Congress and President Clinton agreed in May 1997 to a long-term plan to balance the budget, Kasich was one of its main architects, and when the House that same month overwhelmingly passed the plan, he was given much of the credit.

Kasich has been trying to "get to zero" for the whole of his career, offering up detailed alternative packages years before assuming the mantle of Budget Committee chairman.

But if Kasich has zeal and vision, he also has a tendency to run late, thrash his arms, talk in sports metaphors, and sometimes anger and perplex important colleagues. Just in his mid-40s, Kasich is generally the youngest person in the room when high-level decisions are being made, and he is still remembered around Washington for trying to bully his way onstage at a 1991 Grateful Dead concert. At the same time, he has embraced his Christian faith with a renewed ardor since his parents were killed by a drunk driver in 1987. The many facets of Kasich's personality confound his senior colleagues, and anyone else who might expect a Budget chairman to be a more conventional, green-eyeshade type.

"People who want to separate themselves from the world are just weird," Kasich said in a 1997 New Yorker profile. "I like baseball, I swear a lot, I like Pearl Jam — and I have a personal relationship with God. But I think He likes Pearl Jam, too. ... I'm not sure gravitas is what all these Washington fuddy-duddy stiffs think it is."

Kasich's energy and commitment to the central Republican ideal of eliminating deficit spending have made him a hero to younger members; he was elected the only honorary member of the Class of 1994. Indeed, some see him as a potential Speaker or national or statewide candidate; others in the party hope his overheated personality will cool with the passage of time.

Ironically, Kasich was the most hesitant among House GOP leaders to embrace the notion in 1995 of creating a budget that would reach balance in seven years; he feared that a seven-year budget would be seen as more gimmicky than the traditional five-year model. At a meeting of the top leadership in February 1995, Kasich asked where it was "engraved in stone" that the budget had to be balanced in seven years. Speaker Newt Gingrich asked for a show of hands in favor of carving it in stone, the stone-carvers won, and Kasich had his marching orders.

Kasich happily found that once the seven-year die was cast, it lent new purpose to the budget debate. "We have a crusade attitude," he said. Kasich had been presenting his own, detailed budget plans to Congress since joining the Budget Committee in 1989, steadily building support from an initial, 30-393, drubbing.

The experience of jawboning colleagues into publicly backing spending cuts they desperately hoped to avoid proved invaluable once he became House Budget chairman. He had learned that most Republicans, like Democrats, have wish lists for government spending.

Shortly after the 1994 election that gave the GOP control of the House, Kasich declared that, "The most important thing will be the vote on that balanced-budget amendment. Once that's done, guys can't say 'Why are we doing this? What's the reason here?'" Yet the defeat of the amendment in 1995 gave new impetus to Kasich's efforts. (The House adopted it, but the Senate killed it by a single vote.) Democrats had taunted the GOP that they didn't present the specifics to back up such a constitutional mandate. With the amendment history for the 104th, Kasich accepted the dare to show that balance could be achieved.

"In seven years we will, in fact, balance this budget and save this country and save the next generation," Kasich announced. He views the budget wars more as a fight about moving control of programs out of Washington than over simply reducing the deficit. Kasich complained that the Clinton "administration simply does not trust the American people. They simply do not have confidence that people across this country, in the towns and villages, cities, of our great country,

OHIO 12
Central — Eastern Columbus and suburbs

Columbus has not suffered from the kind of economic collapse that has afflicted most of Ohio's industrial cities in recent years. It is primarily a white-collar town, one whose diverse industrial base is bolstered by the state government complex, a major banking center and numerous scientific research companies.

No longer is Columbus recognized only as the home of the Ohio State University football team; an economic renaissance in the early 1990s led some national publications to list the city as one of the most progressive and prosperous.

According to marketers, Columbus is a mirror for the nation, so average that it serves as a favored test bed for all sorts of fast-food menu items and other consumer products.

More than three-quarters of the 12th District's residents live in Columbus and its Franklin County suburbs. Democrats must do very well in the city to have a chance districtwide. Bill Clinton barely won the district in 1996, even as Kasich handily won re-election.

Forty-five percent of Columbus is in the 12th; the rest is to the west in the 15th District. The 12th's section of Columbus is more heavily black, poorer and less well-educated than the other. About 43 percent of the 12th's 284,000 Columbus residents are black, compared with just 6 percent in the 15th's western half of the city. Nearly 18 percent of its families live below the poverty level, compared with 8 percent of the 15th's section.

As one moves east from the state Capitol building along Broad Street, the black Democratic vote goes down and the Republican vote goes up. Only 4 percent of the 12th's Franklin County suburbs of Columbus are black.

About three miles east of the Capitol is affluent Bexley, an independent community of 13,000 surrounded by the city.

While usually Republican, Bexley has a large Jewish population and sometimes votes for Democratic candidates. Two miles farther east is Whitehall, another independent town, with 21,500 largely blue-collar residents who frequently split their tickets.

Whitehall is the site of the Defense Logistic Agency's Defense Construction Supply Center, which has about 5,000 employees. The Columbus Defense Distribution Depot and the Defense Construction Supply Center are expected to lose about 700 jobs by 2001.

Farther out from Whitehall are newer suburbs. Some of these, such as Reynoldsburg and Gahanna, are predominantly blue collar. Major employers include Lucent Corporation, a telecommunications equipment manufacturer, Nationwide Insurance and The Limited, a retail clothing chain. There have been some setbacks: Nearly 2,000 employees lost their jobs when a McDonnell Douglas plant closed in 1994.

Boasting more than 80 million square feet of warehouse space and proximity to several national arteries, the Columbus area has become one of Ohio's most active trucking and distribution points. The rest of the 12th is rural and Republican, with some light industry.

1990 Population: 570,902. White 427,286 (75%), Black 132,718 (23%), Other 10,898 (2%). Hispanic origin 4,834 (1%). 18 and over 416,053 (73%), 62 and over 66,229 (12%). Median age: 31.

are capable of running their own lives."

His plan offered much larger tax cuts than the counterpart Senate package, it "flat-lined" defense spending, it privatized or eliminated many agencies, and it significantly stunted the growth of Medicare. Kasich fought a losing rhetorical war over the use of the word "cut" to describe the drop in Medicare's projected spending. "We're sick and tired of having a 5 percent increase described as a cut," he complained. But as if to illustrate the difficulty, he instituted an office policy fining anyone on his staff who said "cuts," only to find himself the first to feed the kitty.

Kasich continued his long quest, in alliance with top National Security Committee Democrat Ronald V. Dellums of California, to block further production of the B-2 "stealth" bomber. The two joined forces on an amendment to delete $493 billion for the plane from the fiscal 1996 defense bill. "I don't think facts had anything to do with the outcome," Kasich groused. "We could have announced that the B-2 couldn't fly . . . and it wouldn't have made a difference." The amendment was grounded, 210-213.

Kasich continually ran into roadblocks put up by members protecting industries germane to their districts' economies. "Agriculture is a mess," Kasich declared in exasperation. "I got the reconciliation blues, mama." He locked horns with Ways and Means Committee Chairman Bill Archer, R-Texas, over the issue of deleting "corporate welfare" breaks. "I am sick and tired of hearing you use that phrase," Archer said. "OK," Kasich said. "How about 'inappropriate corporate subsidies?'"

The Budget Committee had traditionally just sketched out the big picture, leaving details to the other money panels. But, despite his antics, credibility was hugely important to Kasich. He didn't want anyone questioning the validity of his numbers, and so he set out $100 billion in specific discretionary spending cuts as a model.

"Kasich was determined to turn his Budget

Committee into an all-powerful policy directorate for the rest of the House committees," according to "Mirage," a 1997 book about the budget process. Appropriations Chairman Robert L. Livingston, R-La., took umbrage at Kasich's "recommendations," and the two got into shouting matches in policy meetings. Eventually, Kasich was reined in and moped to his Budget colleagues. But they recognized he had won a tremendous victory, getting appropriators to agree to his broad numbers if not his specific cuts.

In the end, Kasich's defeat lay not at the feet of turf battles with his GOP colleagues, but upon Clinton's veto pen. After protracted partial government shutdowns from late 1995 into 1996, Kasich and the GOP were blamed for not coming to terms with Clinton on a long-term budget plan. Although discretionary spending was cut by Livingston and the Senate in the absence of an overarching budget plan, some of that gain was lost just before the 1996 elections, when Republicans gave Clinton more of the billions he desired for his priority programs.

As the 105th Congress got under way, some budget players were optimistic the GOP and Clinton could bridge the gap that had separated them. In the early months of 1997, progress was glacial. But by the end of April, things began to look up as Republicans and the White House both agreed to compromise.

The balanced-budget deal, which was negotiated behind closed doors, gave Republicans tax cuts and spending cuts, but much smaller ones then they had initially demanded. And it gave Clinton limited money for selected priorities, including an additional $16 billion over five years to provide health insurance for up to five million uninsured children and an additional $9.7 billion to restore certain federal benefits for about two-thirds of the legal immigrants scheduled to lose them under the 1996 welfare system overhaul. Kasich was all smiles when the House overwhelmingly passed the agreement May 21 by a 333-99 vote.

At Home: After narrowly winning the 12th in 1982, Kasich has restored the Republican tradition of the district. It had been interrupted by the 1980 win of Democrat Bob Shamansky, who caught GOP Rep. Samuel Devine napping.

Before the 1982 election, a redistricting plan, passed by the legislature in which Kasich served, added a rural, predominantly Republican area to the 12th while removing some heavily black wards on the east side of Columbus. Although Shamansky carried Franklin County (Columbus), his margin there could not overcome Kasich's lead in the rural counties. He won with 51 percent.

After his 1974 graduation from Ohio State, Kasich moved quickly into politics, working as an aide to a staunchly conservative GOP state senator. At age 26 in 1978 he made his debut as a candidate, upsetting a veteran Democratic state senator with an energetic grass-roots campaign. In 1980, he chaired the Ohio presidential campaign of Rep. Phillip M. Crane, R-Ill., who offered himself (unsuccessfully) as an equally conservative but younger alternative to Ronald Reagan. In 1982, President Reagan bore no grudge, campaigning for Kasich against Shamansky.

HOUSE ELECTIONS

1996 General		
John R. Kasich (R)	151,667	(64%)
Cynthia L. Ruccia (D)	78,762	(33%)
Barbara Ann Edelman (NL)	7,005	(3%)
1996 Primary		
John R. Kasich (R)	47,585	(88%)
Ramona Whisler (R)	6,517	(12%)
1994 General		
John R. Kasich (R)	114,608	(66%)
Cynthia L. Ruccia (D)	57,294	(33%)

Previous Winning Percentages: **1992** (71%) **1990** (72%) **1988** (79%) **1986** (73%) **1984** (70%) **1982** (51%)

CAMPAIGN FINANCE

	Receipts	Receipts from PACs	Expend-itures
1996			
Kasich (R)	$1,882,613	$487,413 (26%)	$1,578,812
Ruccia (D)	$269,751	$145,518 (54%)	$273,184
1994			
Kasich (R)	$529,788	$198,490 (37%)	$560,117
Ruccia (D)	$261,834	$179,350 (68%)	$258,299

DISTRICT VOTE FOR PRESIDENT

1996	1992
D 118,352 (47%)	**D** 104,187 (40%)
R 113,804 (45%)	**R** 108,618 (42%)
I 16,290 (7%)	**I** 46,943 (18%)

KEY VOTES

1997	
Ban "partial birth" abortions	Y
1996	
Approve farm bill	Y
Deny public education to illegal immigrants	Y
Repeal ban on certain assault-style weapons	N
Increase minimum wage	N
Freeze defense spending	N
Approve welfare overhaul	Y
1995	
Approve balanced-budget constitutional amendment	Y
Relax Clean Water Act regulations	Y
Oppose limits on environmental regulations	N
Reduce projected Medicare spending	Y
Approve GOP budget with tax and spending cuts	Y

VOTING STUDIES

	Presidential Support		Party Unity		Conservative Coalition	
Year	S	O	S	O	S	O
1996	41	59	88	9	82	14
1995	20	79	94	5	91	8
1994	46	53	81	19	86	14
1993	32	65	80	17	86	14
1992	71	26	71	25	79	19
1991	77	23	81	17	97	3

INTEREST GROUP RATINGS

Year	ADA	AFL-CIO	CCUS	ACU
1996	15	n/a	94	95
1995	0	0	96	92
1994	10	11	92	76
1993	0	8	100	92
1992	15	42	86	84
1991	15	8	100	85

13 Sherrod Brown (D)

Of Lorain — Elected 1992, 3rd term

Biographical Information
Born: Nov. 9, 1952, Mansfield, Ohio.
Education: Yale U., B.A. 1974; Ohio State U., M.A. 1979, M.A. 1981.
Occupation: Teacher.
Family: Divorced; two children.
Religion: Lutheran.
Political Career: Ohio House, 1975-83; Ohio secretary of state, 1983-91; defeated for re-election as Ohio secretary of state, 1990.
Capitol Office: 328 Cannon Bldg. 20515; 225-3401.

Committees
Commerce
Energy & Power; Health & Environment (ranking)
International Relations
Asia & the Pacific

In Washington: Brown was educated at Yale and holds two graduate degrees, but few can match his populist fervor when he thinks jobs are at risk in his labor-dominated, industrial district.

During his time in Congress, Brown often has seized on trade issues, arguing that free-trade agreements prevent the United States from responding to unfair or immoral trade practices by rivals — and thus end up costing America jobs. In the 103rd Congress, Brown vigorously opposed NAFTA and GATT. Then in the 104th, he became a standard-bearer for those in the House who insist China is not entitled to normal trade privileges because of its human rights record — a faction that includes Minority Leader Richard A. Gephardt.

In a letter to members as the House debated denying most-favored-nation (MFN) trade status to China in June 1996, Brown wrote, "MFN is a referendum on China's policies — unfair trade, nuclear proliferation, occupation of Tibet, intimidation of Taiwan, suppression of religion, forced abortion, slave labor, and now, smuggling assault weapons into California." Brown took to the floor of the House and held up toys he said were made by Tibetan children in a Chinese sweatshop. The MFN opponents ultimately failed.

Brown was also quick to criticize the World Trade Organization (WTO), created by the GATT treaty he had bitterly fought in 1994. When the WTO ruled in favor of Venezuela and Brazil, which had contended that U.S. clean air rules for gasoline violated international law, Brown pounced. "Our environment wasn't the only loser in the WTO," he said in April 1996. "Workers in America's refineries lost, too . . . because they will have to compete with dirty gas imports. It was our first loss, but it will not be our last. "

That environment/trade issue was a natural for Brown, who is now the ranking Democrat on the Commerce Committee's Health and Environment Subcommittee and sits on International Relations' Asia and the Pacific Subcommittee. The latter has been his chief forum for hammering China.

Brown won the coveted Commerce seat in his first term, when the panel was called Energy and Commerce, after campaigning hard for the assignment. He even parted with a favored baseball card — that of 1950s Boston Red Sox outfielder Jimmy Piersall, who suffered from a mental illness. Brown gave the card to influential California Democrat Vic Fazio, with the note: "Don't be crazy. Vote for Sherrod Brown for Energy and Commerce."

When the Republicans swept to congressional majorities in the 1994 election, they claimed 13 seats in Ohio's House delegation. Brown survived, but won by just a narrow plurality. While many Democrats struggled to adapt to being out of power, Brown quickly became a feisty member of the minority.

In early 1995, he showed his independence from the standard Democratic line by supporting politically popular constitutional amendments to balance the budget and limit congressional terms.

Nor was he hesitant to confront his party's own leader. As President Clinton appealed for Democrats to support a rescue plan for Mexico's failing economy in January 1995, Brown derided the plan for using "$40 billion of taxpayer money." He also voted later to override Clinton's veto of a bill that placed curbs on "frivolous" lawsuits by a company's shareholders.

But his headiest moment may have come in June 1995, when Clinton abruptly shifted gears and offered a new, 10-year balanced budget. Its proposed spending restraints on entitlement programs stunned and infuriated many Democrats. "Maybe we should reopen Pennsylvania Avenue," Brown said at a Democratic Caucus meeting, a remark reprinted in newspapers the next day. (The street in front of the White House had earlier been closed to traffic after a rifle-wielding man fired at the president's residence.) Brown later issued a statement saying his remark was "inappropriate."

On the Commerce Committee, Brown has staked out a few environmental issues. He spon-

OHIO 13
Northeast — Suburbs of Cleveland, Akron and Youngstown

Lying squarely in the midst of industrial northern Ohio, the 13th has all the problems of a declining Frost Belt economy. Heavily dependent on the automobile and steel industries, populous Lorain County approached Depression-era conditions in the early 1980s.

The district centers on two distinct communities: Lorain-Elyria and a band of suburbs in northern Summit and southern Cuyahoga counties, which revolve around Cleveland but are beginning to look south to Akron as well. The Ohio Turnpike is all that connects the two; they are completely separate communities.

The 13th also includes sparsely populated land off to the east in Portage, Geauga and Trumbull counties. To the southwest is Medina County. The geography makes it tough for a House challenger to build name recognition.

Economically, the most serious trouble spot in the district is the once-booming port city of Lorain. But while the local economy there has been battered — Lorain's Ford plant will stop making Thunderbirds and Mercury Cougars in 1997 — the old New Deal political coalition is alive and well. Blue-collar ethnics, blacks and Hispanics in Lorain combine with those in nearby Elyria and academics in the college town of Oberlin, about 10 miles south, to produce Democratic majorities. Districtwide, Bill Clinton won the 13th in 1996 with 46 percent of the vote.

As one of the traditional immigration centers on the Great Lakes, the city of Lorain has an ethnic diversity that matches Cleveland's West Side. Fifty-six different ethnic groups have been counted within its borders. Today, Hispanics make up 17 percent of Lorain's population, a far higher share than any other city in Ohio.

Oberlin roughly divides the district's urban, Catholic Democrats in the north and its rural, Protestant Republicans in the south. Founded in 1833, Oberlin College was the first coeducational institution of higher learning in the country and among the first to admit black students. The Yankees who founded Oberlin and other towns in this part of Ohio took strong anti-slavery stands in the 19th century. Their descendants continue to crusade for social reforms.

The Summit County area south of Cleveland is a checkerboard of industrial and residential suburbs upon which much of the city's industry has scattered. Twinsburg is home to the Revco drug chain, one of the 13th's biggest employers.

Evidence of the Cleveland area's recovering economy can be seen in its increasing growth toward surrounding counties. On the northern edge of Medina County, Brunswick has new suburban development. To the east, Cleveland's growth has seeped into the northern part of Portage County — Streetsboro has seen a surge of development in recent years — but the rest of Portage remains quite rural. Trumbull County, farther east, orients itself south toward the 17th District cities of Youngstown and Warren.

1990 Population: 570,894. White 534,340 (94%), Black 25,954 (5%), Other 10,600 (2%). Hispanic origin 16,567 (3%). 18 and over 413,086 (72%), 62 and over 76,067 (13%). Median age: 33.

sored a bill to encourage the cleanup of "brownfields" — abandoned industrial sites that may be chemically tainted — by offering grants and loans to potential purchasers and freeing them of some liability risks. Brown also offered the measure as an amendment to the superfund waste cleanup overhaul when the Commerce, Trade and Hazardous Materials Subcommittee marked up that bill late in 1995. But it was voted down, and the superfund bill itself was not taken up by the full committee.

When Commerce in 1996 debated a far-reaching bill that would have ended federal Medicaid guarantees, Brown tried to amend it to require states to follow existing federal guidelines for breast cancer treatment. (Brown started a breast cancer task force in the 13th District, which has a high incidence of the illness.) That attempt failed, but he did get a provision inserted into the Safe Drinking Water Act, a $7.6 billion rewrite the president signed in 1996. Brown's language, written with Bart Stupak, D-Mich., allows the Environmental Protection Agency to test certain drinking-water chemicals that mimic estrogen and may cause cancer.

Like many other Democrats, Brown has positioned himself as a defender of Medicare. He praised a group of angry senior citizens who disrupted the Commerce Committee's markup of a Medicare overhaul in October 1995, saying "they were arrested because they wanted to speak their minds." Brown also offered a bill that would provide protections for Medicare beneficiaries who enroll in managed-care health plans. That bill went nowhere, but he signed on to a similar measure offered in the 105th Congress by Rep. Tom Coburn, R-Okla.

Brown stepped in when Revco Inc., a pharmaceutical company based in the 13th, was targeted for a takeover by Rite Aid Corp. in 1996. His letter to the Federal Trade Commission said the merger would cost jobs and raise drug prices in northeast Ohio; Brown cheered later that year when the FTC voted to block the merger in federal court. But Revco has proved a popular target, and Brown found himself penning a similar letter to the FTC in February 1997 when the CVS drugstore chain made a bid to acquire the company.

As a freshman in the 103rd Congress, Brown probably worked harder than anyone else in the class of 1992 to defeat NAFTA — lobbying fellow freshmen, taking the House floor time and again to detail the pact's flaws and publishing a newsletter that kept track of anti-NAFTA activities.

In one typical NAFTA speech in 1993, Brown — himself an Ivy Leaguer — denounced "the trendy Harvard economists and UCLA economists and The New York Times editorial board and the Chicago Tribune and the Cleveland Plain Dealer and all these large papers. . . . They all say people like us who oppose NAFTA simply do not understand economics. [But] we understand what ordinary people are faced with if this passes. . . . It is those people that lose their jobs, not the economists in Georgetown."

House approval of NAFTA in November 1993 left Brown sour: "Nothing has changed here in the last eight months," he groused after the vote. "This big freshman class apparently did not make much difference."

At Home: Brown's first House victory in 1992 marked a successful return for the one-time "boy wonder" of Ohio politics. In 1974, just before his 22nd birthday, Brown was elected to the state House, where he served four terms. In 1982, he was elected secretary of state, a post to which he was re-elected in 1986 and from which he was expected to vault to higher office.

But Brown lost re-election in 1990 to Republican Robert A. Taft II, the latest in a long line of politically successful Ohio Tafts. Brown had proposed a two-month, unpaid leave of absence from his job to take an educational trip to Japan, and Taft hammered him with ads that proclaimed "Sayonara, Sherrod."

Brown's House win in 1992 came at the expense of Republican Margaret R. Mueller, a millionaire social worker who had lost three times to Democratic Rep. Dennis E. Eckart. To reach the general election, Brown had survived an eight-way Democratic primary for the open seat, created as mapmakers eliminated two Ohio districts. Brown was his party's clear front-runner, although he had moved into the 13th to run.

Although 1994 was an especially bad year for the Ohio Democratic Party, Brown won a second term by holding off Republican Gregory A. White, the Lorain County prosecutor. White hammered Brown for his early support of a single-payer health care reform plan, but Brown poured endless hours of personal politicking into the race, as well as nearly $1 million — much of it from PACs. That was enough to bring victory, albeit with just a plurality of the vote.

Observers were expecting an equally tense rematch in 1996, but White dropped out of the race in January and the GOP diverted few resources to the race afterward. Kenneth C. Blair Jr., a trucking company executive and school board member, won a four-way GOP primary in March. Blair tried to paint Brown as too liberal for the 13th, but Brown echoed Clinton's mantra of protecting "Medicare, Medicaid, education and the environment," frequently pointing to the cleanup of Lake Erie as an example of a federal program that worked. Brown won with 60 percent.

HOUSE ELECTIONS

1996 General		
Sherrod Brown (D)	146,690	(60%)
Kenneth C. Blair Jr. (R)	87,108	(36%)
David Kluter (NL)	8,707	(4%)
1994 General		
Sherrod Brown (D)	93,147	(49%)
Gregory A. White (R)	86,422	(46%)
Howard Mason (I)	7,777	(4%)
John Michael Ryan (I)	2,430	(1%)

Previous Winning Percentages: 1992 (53%)

CAMPAIGN FINANCE

	Receipts	Receipts from PACs	Expend-itures
1996			
Brown (D)	$975,675	$510,561 (52%)	$607,543
Blair (R)	$56,923	$3,253 (6%)	$54,064
1994			
Brown (D)	$966,836	$619,932 (64%)	$974,225
White (R)	$574,910	$59,504 (10%)	$570,331
Mason (I)	$11,954	0	$11,593

DISTRICT VOTE FOR PRESIDENT

	1996		1992
D	116,305 (46%)	**D**	101,104 (38%)
R	98,272 (39%)	**R**	94,651 (36%)
I	35,414 (14%)	**I**	70,624 (27%)

KEY VOTES

1997	
Ban "partial birth" abortions	N
1996	
Approve farm bill	N
Deny public education to illegal immigrants	N
Repeal ban on certain assault-style weapons	N
Increase minimum wage	Y
Freeze defense spending	Y
Approve welfare overhaul	N
1995	
Approve balanced-budget constitutional amendment	Y
Relax Clean Water Act regulations	N
Oppose limits on environmental regulations	Y
Reduce projected Medicare spending	N
Approve GOP budget with tax and spending cuts	N

VOTING STUDIES

	Presidential Support		Party Unity		Conservative Coalition	
Year	**S**	**O**	**S**	**O**	**S**	**O**
1996	81	15	94	4	6	92
1995	83	15	91	7	23	73
1994	64	36	91	8	36	64
1993	72	26	91	5	23	77

INTEREST GROUP RATINGS

Year	ADA	AFL-CIO	CCUS	ACU
1996	95	n/a	13	0
1995	85	92	38	32
1994	75	78	67	14
1993	95	100	18	9

14 Tom Sawyer (D)

Of Akron — Elected 1986, 6th term

Biographical Information
Born: Aug. 15, 1945, Akron, Ohio.
Education: U. of Akron, B.A. 1968, M.A. 1970.
Occupation: Teacher.
Family: Wife, Joyce Handler; one child.
Religion: Presbyterian.
Political Career: Ohio House, 1977-83; mayor of Akron, 1984-86.
Capitol Office: 1414 Longworth Bldg. 20515; 225-5231.

Committees
Commerce
Finance & Hazardous Materials; Oversight & Investigations; Telecommunications, Trade & Consumer Protection

In Washington: Sawyer's move onto the Commerce Committee at the start of the 105th Congress finally gives this diligent and detail-minded Democrat a place on a plum committee, something he had sought for a number of years.

The committee's broad legislative reach affords Sawyer the chance to weigh in on an array of issues and will broaden his campaign fundraising contacts, an important consideration for the six-term veteran, as the 1996 election marked his second straight sub-55 percent tally.

One of the foremost issues on Commerce's radar screen in the 105th — an overhaul of the nation's laws that regulate electric utilities — is of particular interest to Sawyer. Any change in those laws could have a lasting impact on the coal-burning utilities in his home state.

And in another area where Commerce legislates — health care policy — Sawyer has been active. He and fellow Ohioan David L. Hobson, a Republican, persuaded the House to add a paperwork-related provision to a broader health insurance measure in the 104th Congress. Their language seeks to speed the transmission of insurance data to doctors and hospitals by electronic means, thus eliminating paperwork and reducing opportunities for fraud.

When Democrats ran the House, Sawyer was a subcommittee chairman on the Post Office and Civil Service Committee. But in the 104th, the new GOP majority abolished that panel, and Sawyer occupied himself on two other committees: Economic and Educational Opportunities, and Transportation and Infrastructure. (In 1997 he relinquished those slots to move to Commerce, an "exclusive" committee under House Democratic rules). Also in the 104th, he was tapped to head a Democratic task force on retirement that issued a report late in 1996 on steps that should be taken to protect Americans' retirement security.

For the most part, though, Sawyer maintained a low profile during his first term in the minority. Even in his role as a member of the House ethics committee — whose leaders, Republican Nancy L. Johnson of Connecticut and Democrat Jim McDermott of Washington, and other members battled openly about the investigation of Speaker Newt Gingrich — Sawyer served quietly and stayed above the fray. It was Sawyer's thoughtful demeanor, combined with the respect he enjoys from members from both parties, that made him a logical choice in 1993 to fill a Democratic vacancy on the politically sensitive committee.

A former teacher who once chaired the Education Committee in the Ohio House, Sawyer in his freshman House term got a seat on the Education and Labor Committee, the scene of many partisan battles. Sawyer distinguished himself as a serious-minded debater not given to polarizing rhetoric. "You've got to be patient," Sawyer once said with reference to his committee work. "You get into a position where you're trusted by sufficient numbers of others in those areas where you hope to make a difference."

In 1995, Republicans renamed the committee Economic and Educational Opportunities, and it was there that Sawyer got engaged in one of the few issues that thrust him into the center of the action in the 104th. The panel moved a bill, known as the TEAM Act, that would have allowed employee-management teams in nonunion workplaces to discuss wage and employment issues. Both in committee and on the House floor, Sawyer offered an amendment that instead would have updated the nation's labor laws to specify how employers could participate in employee teams without making them forums for negotiations on wages and working conditions.

Both the committee and the House defeated Sawyer's amendment — the House vote was 221-204 — but President Clinton vetoed the legislation in 1996.

On the postal committee in the 102nd and 103rd Congresses, Sawyer carved a policy niche for himself as overseer of the decennial census, devoting his energies to issues great and small that revolved around the counting of U.S. citizens.

The 14th is in a part of Ohio that was built on rubber — tires in particular. At one time, nearly 90 percent of America's tires were manufactured here.

Within the district's confines in Akron — once referred to as the "premier factory town in America" — are the corporate headquarters of the Goodyear and Goodrich tire companies. Bridgestone-Firestone, which once loomed as a symbol of rubber's economic dominance in the 14th, moved its corporate headquarters to Nashville in 1992.

The 14th became one of the most Democratic districts in the state on the strength of votes from the blue-collar workers who kept the rubber factories humming.

But the district's economy is changing. While the major rubber companies are still important employers, the jobs with a future are largely white-collar. The last quarter-century has seen a steady transfer of manufacturing from the old, high-wage factories in Akron to new plants in lower-wage areas of the Sun Belt. Many Akron residents have left: The city's 1990 population of 223,000 was less than it was more than a half-century ago.

But city leaders are hopeful about revitalization efforts. Akron's AA minor-league baseball team, the Akron Aeros, opened its first season in a new downtown stadium in 1997, and the city is renovating recreational areas along the Ohio & Erie Canal.

Sawyer and other Akron leaders have fought to forge a high-tech future for the city, and they have had enough success that Akron's unemployment rate in recent years has been lower than that of some other industrial centers in northern Ohio.

What has kept the city alive through these

OHIO 14
Northeast – Akron

tough years is this: While the tire companies have quit manufacturing here, their headquarters and labs have remained, employing engineers, scientists and executives who work more with polymers these days than with rubber.

Population flight out of Akron has meant that the city is now smaller than its britches. It is an area with public facilities and a housing stock built to handle far more people than live here. The city is doing better than others in the area.

In the boom years of the rubber industry before World War II, Akron was a mecca for job-seeking Appalachians. The annual West Virginia Day was one of the city's most popular events, and it was said that more West Virginians lived in Akron than in Charleston.

These days, the Appalachian descendants combine with blacks, ethnics and the academic community at the University of Akron to keep the city reliably Democratic. North of Akron, suburbs and farmland in northern Summit County provide Republican votes.

Usually, they are too few to overcome the Democratic advantage in Akron and swing the 14th to the GOP. Both Jimmy Carter in 1980 and Michael S. Dukakis in 1988 won Akron by a wide enough margin to carry Summit County narrowly. Bill Clinton won the county's vote by comfortable margins in both 1992 and 1996.

1990 Population: 570,900. White 500,576 (88%), Black 62,400 (11%), Other 7,924 (1%). Hispanic origin 3,419 (1%). 18 and over 433,423 (76%), 62 and over 93,084 (16%). Median age: 34.

But with the Republican takeover of the House, Sawyer lost both the clout and even the committee assignment needed to continue in that role. The GOP decision to reorganize the House, shrinking the number of committees and subcommittees, caused a cascade of displaced Democrats, and Sawyer was a casualty. When the music stopped and the Post Office and Civil Service panel was merged into a new Government Reform and Oversight Committee, he lost his seat altogether.

Before 1995, Sawyer worked hard at policing the accuracy of the 1990 census and the calculations that followed, a task that fell to him as chairman of the panel's Subcommittee on Census and Population. When evidence pointed to an undercount with a bias against minorities, Sawyer pressed for an adjustment of the head count, but he was rebuffed by the Bush administration and in the courts.

Before yielding his gavel in the GOP takeover, Sawyer was directing his subcommittee toward the task of overseeing the Census Bureau's efforts to produce a more sophisticated and accurate census in 2000.

At Home: Sawyer has not lost an election in a political career than spans more than two decades and includes stints as mayor of Akron and as a state legislator in addition to his 10 years in the House, but his hold on the 14th District has been tested in his past two bids for re-election. He received 52 percent of the vote in 1994 and 54 percent in 1996.

In 1996, Sawyer's GOP challenger was former U.S. attorney Joyce George, an abortion rights supporter who was heavily courted for the campaign by prominent Republicans, including Speaker Gingrich. But after winning by just a four-point margin in 1994, Sawyer moved out to a 12-point victory over George, who finished with 42 percent; a Natural Law Party candidate got four percent. Sawyer had the advantage of sharing the

Democratic ballot with Clinton, who beat GOP nominee Bob Dole by 20 points in the district's presidential voting.

Previously, Sawyer's two closest calls at the polls came against the same Republican: former Summit County prosecutor Lynn Slaby, who held Sawyer to 52 percent in 1994 and 54 percent in 1986.

In his 1994 rematch with Sawyer, Slaby did his best to link Sawyer to Clinton, whose popularity was then at a low point. Slaby's attempts to appeal to labor won him the endorsement of a local union or two, but Sawyer held on despite the heavy GOP tide and his 1993 vote for NAFTA — a move that angered labor and earned him a nominal primary challenge.

Two decisive, late-campaign moves helped him prevail. The first was a bold ad he put on the air in the campaign's final days, essentially labeling Slaby a liar for an assertion he made that Sawyer wished to slash Social Security. The second was a well-honed eleventh-hour effort to appeal to the district's black voters: Hours before the polls opened, Sawyer had Martin Luther King III trolling the district in an effort to inspire black voters to come to the polls.

Sawyer first won the district in 1986 after surviving a primary battle between the new Akron and the old Akron. On one side was Sawyer, the city's young mayor and an apostle of high technology. From a white-collar background, he was the son of a prominent Akron businessman. On the other side was Democratic state Sen. Oliver Ocasek — a 60-year-old, Humphrey-style, pro-labor war horse.

When Sawyer announced his House bid, some Akron residents were upset. His election to the mayoralty in 1983 ended nearly 20 years of GOP rule, and he had promised to serve at least one full four-year term as mayor. But he was running for higher office after only three years. Sawyer, though, received a key boost when retiring Democratic Rep. John F. Seiberling endorsed his candidacy.

Sawyer proved to be the consummate media-age politician. While Ocasek was garrulous and emotional and boasted ties to old-time labor leaders, Sawyer was reserved, methodical and adept at the task of nuts-and-bolts organization. He emerged from the primary with a comfortable 49 percent to 39 percent victory.

Sawyer then had to get past Slaby, the Republicans' most prominent local officeholder. Although Slaby ran a well-funded campaign in which he emphasized his blue-collar roots, he could not get an angle on Sawyer. When Slaby called his foe a tax-and-spend liberal, Sawyer noted that Akron had not raised taxes during his mayoralty. Sawyer took the open seat with 54 percent and won re-election comfortably until 1994.

HOUSE ELECTIONS

1996 General		
Tom Sawyer (D)	124,136	(54%)
Joyce George (R)	95,307	(42%)
Terry E. Wilkinson (NL)	8,976	(4%)
1996 Primary		
Tom Sawyer (D)	32,297	(80%)
Ken Mack (D)	4,382	(11%)
John B. Nicholas (D)	3,866	(10%)
1994 General		
Tom Sawyer (D)	96,274	(52%)
Lynn Slaby (R)	89,106	(48%)

Previous Winning Percentages: 1992 (68%) **1990** (60%) **1988** (75%) **1986** (54%)

CAMPAIGN FINANCE

	Receipts	Receipts from PACs	Expend-itures
1996			
Sawyer (D)	$522,163	$316,725 (61%)	$523,412
George (R)	$291,433	$23,339 (8%)	$279,210
1994			
Sawyer (D)	$563,931	$291,149 (52%)	$595,448
Slaby (R)	$282,424	$30,196 (11%)	$256,758

DISTRICT VOTE FOR PRESIDENT

1996		1992	
D	121,987 (53%)	**D**	119,144 (46%)
R	76,354 (33%)	**R**	81,603 (31%)
I	30,442 (13%)	**I**	60,338 (23%)

KEY VOTES

1997	
Ban "partial birth" abortions	N
1996	
Approve farm bill	N
Deny public education to illegal immigrants	N
Repeal ban on certain assault-style weapons	N
Increase minimum wage	Y
Freeze defense spending	N
Approve welfare overhaul	Y
1995	
Approve balanced-budget constitutional amendment	N
Relax Clean Water Act regulations	N
Oppose limits on environmental regulations	Y
Reduce projected Medicare spending	N
Approve GOP budget with tax and spending cuts	N

VOTING STUDIES

	Presidential Support		Party Unity		Conservative Coalition	
Year	**S**	**O**	**S**	**O**	**S**	**O**
1996	85	11	91	7	37	63
1995	90	10	91	9	37	63
1994	90	8	97	2	28	64
1993	87	12	96	3	30	66
1992	17	83	95	3	15	85
1991	31	69	91	6	14	86

INTEREST GROUP RATINGS

Year	ADA	AFL-CIO	CCUS	ACU
1996	90	n/a	25	0
1995	90	100	29	0
1994	90	78	50	5
1993	85	92	30	9
1992	95	83	38	4
1991	90	92	30	0

15 Deborah Pryce (R)

Of Dublin — Elected 1992, 3rd term

Biographical Information

Born: July 29, 1951, Warren, Ohio.
Education: Ohio State U., B.A. 1973; Capital U., J.D. 1976.
Occupation: Judge; lawyer.
Family: Husband, Randy Walker; one child, one stepchild.
Religion: Presbyterian.
Political Career: Franklin County Municipal Court judge, 1985-92.
Capitol Office: 221 Cannon Bldg. 20515; 225-2015.

Committees

Rules
Legislative & Budget Process

In Washington: Pryce has made waves in Congress from the start. She had automatic visibility as one of just three women in the GOP Class of 1992, and her first-term colleagues named her their "interim leader" for the early weeks of the 103rd Congress. As Republicans moved into the House majority in 1995, Pryce got a sweet spot: a seat on the powerful Rules Committee.

The GOP leadership made a special point of giving Pryce a high profile during the 104th Congress' debate on welfare overhaul. Her job was to counter Democratic portrayals of the GOP as hard-hearted toward poor people on welfare, particularly women. Pryce, along with Republicans Enid Greene of Utah and Nancy L. Johnson of Connecticut successfully offered an amendment to the GOP welfare bill that increased federal money for child care programs by $160 million a year over five years.

But Pryce's most prominent effort in the 104th came in another area: She authored the most controversial section of a GOP bill aimed at promoting adoption. Pryce did not get her way: The adoption measure that became law did not include a section sponsored by Pryce that rewrote the 1978 Indian Child Welfare Act.

Pryce got into the issue because of a wrenching adoption situation in her district. Jim and Colette Roast, who had adopted twin girls, were faced with losing them because the girls were part Indian. The Pomo tribe had learned of the girls' heritage after the adoption was completed; it filed suit to revoke the adoption and give custody of the girls to the tribe.

The Indian Child Welfare Act had been enacted to help tribes stem the flow of Indian children who were then being adopted by non-Indians. The tribes said the exodus threatened their cultural integrity. In the case of the Roasts, the Pomo tribe asserted interest in the twins because a relative of the girls' biological father was a Pomo Indian.

Pryce pushed for a dramatic overhaul of the law. She wanted to bar a tribe from getting involved in an adoption process unless one of the child's biological parents had a significant relationship with the tribe — ancestry alone would not be enough for the tribe to claim rights to a child.

She faced a formidable foe: Resources Committee Chairman Don Young, R-Alaska, opposed the changes Pryce sought, and his committee voted to strip the bill of the Indian adoption section.

But Pryce used her power as a member of the Rules Committee to get the most favorable possible ground rules for debating the bill on the House floor. Despite the fact that Resources had killed the Indian section of the adoption legislation, Pryce persuaded GOP leaders to include the Indian provisions in the bill they put onto the House floor for consideration in May 1996.

Young was given a chance to strip the provisions out of the measure. After an emotional debate, his amendment failed 195-212, and Pryce's provisions were part of the bill sent to the Senate.

But in that chamber, Pryce ran into vehement opposition from Sen. John McCain, R-Ariz., then chairman of the Indian Affairs Committee. His committee deleted her Indian adoption section from the bill, and the rest of the measure went on to become law.

Pryce began the 105th promising to continue her fight on the issue.

On fiscal policy and regulatory matters, Pryce covers all the conservative bases: She supports a balanced-budget constitutional amendment and a presidential line-item veto, and she complains of onerous federal mandates. She parted ways with most of her female House colleagues on the 1993 vote to require businesses to provide family and medical leave. Pryce said, "As we try to work our way out of this recession . . . now is not the time to shove restrictive federal mandates down the throats of American businesses."

She is unabashedly partisan in money debates. As President Clinton's first budget came up for a final House vote in August 1993, Pryce crisply said: "For the Democrats, it is the American people who have too much money. For us

OHIO 15
Central — Western Columbus and suburbs

Columbus is no tourist attraction. Swarms of visitors descend on the city only at Ohio State Fair time in August and on the half-dozen Saturdays in the fall when the Ohio State Buckeyes are playing football at home.

But the area has gained a reputation as a good place to raise a family. During the 1970s, it was the only major urban center in Ohio to gain population. It now boasts 633,000 residents overall, with about 348,000 of them in the 15th.

In the 1980s recession years, the service-industry-oriented economy of Columbus stumbled, but its suffering paled in comparison to that of many other Ohio cities.

In redistricting for the 1990s, the 15th picked up what parts of Madison County it did not already have and also gained the northwestern corner from Pickaway County. While Madison compares with Franklin in size, it is far less densely populated. Madison County has only about 80 residents for each of its 465 square miles; Franklin County has about 1,780 people for each of its 540 square miles.

Consequently, Franklin County holds 92 percent of the district's residents and Madison County contains only 6 percent. The other 2 percent are in Pickaway County to the south.

Of the two districts that divide Ohio's capital, Columbus, the 15th — on Columbus' western side — traditionally has been the more Republican.

Although the district includes most of the academic community at Ohio State University, the Democratic vote there is offset by the solid Republican areas in northern Columbus and the rock-ribbed Republican suburbs west of the Olentangy and Scioto rivers. In Upper Arlington and similar affluent suburbs, it is not unusual for Republican presidential candidates to draw more than two-thirds of the vote.

Apart from the large university vote — Ohio State has about 55,000 students — the major pocket of Democratic strength in the district is on the near West Side of Columbus. Sandwiched between the Scioto River and the Central Ohio Psychiatric Hospital are neighborhoods of lower-income whites of Appalachian heritage.

The 15th includes far less of the heavily black East Side of Columbus than it did in the 1980s. Only 6 percent of the 15th's portion of Columbus is black, compared with 43 percent of the 12th District's section.

The 15th includes the blue-collar communities in the southeast portion of Franklin County, which enhance the Democratic vote, but just slightly.

The 15th does not include the heart of downtown Columbus, with the state Capitol and the offices of Ohio's major banking and commercial institutions. But with nearly two-thirds of Franklin County's land area, the district contains most of the region's expanding service base, which includes several large high-technology research centers.

1990 Population: 570,902. White 527,361 (92%), Black 27,884 (5%), Other 15,657 (3%). Hispanic origin 5,459 (1%). 18 and over 443,164 (78%), 62 and over 70,267 (12%). Median age: 31.

Republicans, it is the government that has too much." She showed similar pith on Clinton's health care plan, saying in early 1994: "It's like a bungee cord with a lot of frayed rope. It may work, but why take the chance?"

Pryce again flung partisan barbs in March 1994, as she endorsed an effort by Oklahoma Republican Ernest Istook to get the ethics committee to investigate the House Post Office. Democrats said a probe might compromise prosecutors' efforts, but Pryce accused the majority of "allowing our wounds to fester in the minds of the public to the point that this body begins to decay."

In 1994, Pryce, a former judge, gained national publicity with her proposal to prohibit federal prison inmates from training on free weights or studying martial arts. "Taxpayer dollars," she said, "are being used to build bigger and better thugs."

Pryce has parted company with the GOP majority on the issue of banning certain semiautomatic assault-style weapons. She supported the ban in the 103rd and opposed efforts to repeal it in the 104th. She did, however, side with conservatives in opposing a five-day waiting period for handgun purchases.

Abortion was a hot topic in Pryce's 1992 campaign, and in the House Pryce has struggled to find a middle ground. Early in the 103rd she sided with abortion rights forces on a vote to lift the "gag rule" barring staff at federally funded family planning clinics from discussing abortion. But later she voted to continue the so-called Hyde amendment ban on federally funded abortions, after working to get rape and incest exceptions into the restriction.

Since then, Pryce has sided with abortion-rights supporters on several occasions: She voted to maintain a requirement that states fund certain Medicaid abortions for poor women; she voted to allow federal employees' health care plans to cover abortions; and she voted in 1997 for an early release of funds for international family planning programs, a Clinton administration request that was opposed by anti-abortion forces.

But Pryce has consistently supported banning a particular abortion technique that opponents call "partial birth" abortion, and she voted against allowing women in federal prisons to obtain abortions unless their life is threatened by the pregnancy.

At Home: The 15th came open in 1992 when veteran GOP Rep. Chalmers P. Wylie decided to retire. Pryce jumped into the race along with more than a half-dozen other Republicans. Her troubles began when she sought her party's nomination at the Franklin County GOP Convention, where she allowed several anti-abortion members of the central committee to believe she had joined their camp. (Her main adversaries for the party endorsement supported abortion rights in at least a limited form.)

With help from the anti-abortion faction, Pryce eked out the endorsement — and ran unopposed in the GOP primary. But soon after the central committee gave her its blessing, Pryce clarified her views. Pryce said she supported abortion rights generally but opposed abortion personally and favored letting states impose "reasonable restrictions" on the availability of abortions.

Anti-abortion activists howled that they had been deceived, and they were without a candidate: The Democratic nominee, state Rep. Richard Cordray, was in the abortion rights camp. The result was the entry of Linda S. Reidelbach, a GOP political novice and abortion opponent who ran as an independent.

Pryce campaigned on a combined theme of reform and deep spending cuts to reduce the deficit. She won the endorsement of the Columbus Dispatch, chiefly on the expectation that she would work to reduce government's overall presence. Cordray hoped Pryce and Reidelbach would split the conservative vote, but he managed only 38 percent and Reidelbach, 18 percent. Pryce's 44 percent was enough to win.

Pryce's winning tally soared to 71 percent in 1994 and stayed there in 1996.

HOUSE ELECTIONS

1996 General		
Deborah Pryce (R)	156,776	(71%)
Cliff Arnebeck (D)	64,665	(29%)
1996 Primary		
Deborah Pryce (R)	35,034	(86%)
Craig Z. Lortz (R)	5,920	(14%)
1994 General		
Deborah Pryce (R)	112,912	(71%)
Bill Buckel (D)	46,480	(29%)

Previous Winning Percentages: 1992 (44%)

CAMPAIGN FINANCE

	Receipts	Receipts from PACs	Expend-itures
1996			
Pryce (R)	$522,293	$226,093 (43%)	$384,780
Arnebeck (D)	$9,700	$3,300 (34%)	$9,629
1994			
Pryce (R)	$603,820	$248,280 (41%)	$443,007

VOTING STUDIES

	Presidential Support		Party Unity		Conservative Coalition	
Year	S	O	S	O	S	O
1996	39	58	87	11	84	12
1995	25	71	87	9	92	6
1994	55	45	85	9	83	11
1993	46	54	86	13	93	7

KEY VOTES

1997	
Ban "partial birth" abortions	Y
1996	
Approve farm bill	Y
Deny public education to illegal immigrants	Y
Repeal ban on certain assault-style weapons	N
Increase minimum wage	N
Freeze defense spending	N
Approve welfare overhaul	Y
1995	
Approve balanced-budget constitutional amendment	Y
Relax Clean Water Act regulations	Y
Oppose limits on environmental regulations	N
Reduce projected Medicare spending	Y
Approve GOP budget with tax and spending cuts	Y

DISTRICT VOTE FOR PRESIDENT

	1996		1992
D	105,796 (44%)	**D**	95,627 (36%)
R	114,367 (48%)	**R**	119,355 (45%)
I	17,415 (7%)	**I**	52,413 (20%)

INTEREST GROUP RATINGS

Year	ADA	AFL-CIO	CCUS	ACU
1996	5	n/a	94	85
1995	10	0	100	72
1994	15	11	100	67
1993	10	8	82	88

16 Ralph Regula (R)

Of Navarre — Elected 1972, 13th term

Biographical Information
Born: Dec. 3, 1924, Beach City, Ohio.
Education: Mount Union College, B.A. 1948; William McKinley School of Law, LL.B. 1952.
Military Service: Navy, 1944-46.
Occupation: Lawyer; businessman.
Family: Wife, Mary Rogusky; three children.
Religion: Episcopalian.
Political Career: Ohio Board of Education, 1960-64; Ohio House, 1965-67; Ohio Senate, 1967-73.
Capitol Office: 2309 Rayburn Bldg. 20515; 225-3876.

Committees
Appropriations
Commerce, Justice, State & Judiciary; Interior (chairman); Transportation

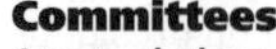

In Washington: Regula served as ranking Republican on the Interior Appropriations Subcommittee for a decade, and his dreams of attaining its chairmanship were fulfilled in the 104th Congress by the Republican takeover of Capitol Hill. But as with most answered prayers, there was some price to pay for Regula, as he found himself buffeted by attacks from the left and right on environmental and arts issues.

The bulk of Regula's spending bill goes to funding the Interior Department, but he also oversees the budget of the National Endowments for the Arts and Humanities. His subcommittee's first bill, for fiscal 1996, died a thousand deaths, being twice sent back to conference by the House, vetoed by President Clinton, and finally supplanted by an omnibus spending package. Regula's legislation, it seemed, had something to offend everyone.

"Every group in the House has a veto," Regula complained. "The combination of the environmentalists, fiscal conservatives and Democrats will stop it."

Many Republicans expressed concern that Regula might distinguish himself as chairman mainly by accommodating the Democrats too much. When Democrats ruled the House, Regula worked well with top Interior Appropriations Democrat Sidney R. Yates of Illinois, and the Ohioan struck a far more conciliatory posture toward liberals than did conservative firebrands in the GOP Conference.

Regula swiftly sought to quiet such fears, declaring just before the start of the 104th Congress that "my environmental record is not all that great" and seeking out policy advice from such conservative public policy groups as the Heritage Foundation.

Regula had long voted a conservative line on federal taxation and spending issues, and he established his ideological bona fides as chairman early during consideration of a spending rescissions package. He offered up for budget cuts programs under his dominion such as the NEA and NEH, endangered species protection and home weatherization assistance.

Regula helped broker a deal on the NEA, an agency that draws particular animosity from many conservatives. He approved slashing the agency's funding but saved it from abolition by helping to midwife a compromise by which it would be zeroed out after two years. With that deadline approaching in the 105th, Regula hopes he can keep his word. "It's an easy one to point to and say this is not a legitimate role of government," he said. But he acknowledges that the NEA has many powerful allies and that the Senate never signed on to the plan to kill it by fiscal 1998.

Regula often complained that a Clinton administration hungry for more dollars for the programs he oversees was unyielding. But Clinton's objections to the fiscal 1996 bill stemmed more from policy riders than dollar amounts. Clinton disdained one proposal to turn over management of the Mojave National Preserve to a more user-friendly land shepherd than the National Park Service, and another to increase timber harvesting in Alaska's Tongass National Forest. The president also insisted on the continuation of the annual mining patents freeze first authored by Regula but attacked by many pro-mining Western conservatives.

But before the bill could reach its date with Clinton's veto pen, it had to clear Congress, and the House twice rejected the deal worked out by Regula in conference with the Senate. A coalition of deficit hawks on the Republican side and environmentalists among the Democrats deemed the measure unworthy because it did not contain the freeze on mining patents, which the coalition regarded as a giveaway of public land.

Regula is a longtime critic of the patenting system under the 1872 Mining Law that allows miners to purchase federal land for as little as $2.50 an acre. He was the author of a provision of the fiscal 1995 interior spending bill that placed a one-year freeze on such claims. He voted in September 1995 along with 90 other Republicans to send the bill back to conference to renew that

OHIO 16
Northeast — Canton

Although it has undergone a variety of changes over the years, the 16th is still centered on Stark County and the city of Canton. That is just as it was when William McKinley represented it more than a century ago, before he became governor of Ohio and then president.

While it is a working-class city like nearby Akron and Youngstown and often votes Democratic in local elections, Canton does not share in the solidly Democratic tradition of the rest of northeastern Ohio. That is partly a result of the conservative mentality brought to the community by the family-run Timken Co. — a large steel and roller-bearing company.

With sizable black and ethnic populations, Canton proper (population 84,000) goes Democratic on occasion. But the suburbs in surrounding Stark County are more receptive to Republicans. Since 1920, only four Democratic presidential candidates have carried the county — which accounts for nearly two-thirds of the district's population: Franklin D. Roosevelt, Lyndon B. Johnson and Bill Clinton (twice). In 1996, Clinton took 46 percent in Stark County to Bob Dole's 38 percent. That helped him barely carry the district even as Regula easily won re-election.

Besides Timken, Canton is the national headquarters of the Hoover Co., the vacuum cleaner manufacturer, and Diebold Inc., a producer of bank safes and commercial security equipment. But it is more famous as the home of the Professional Football Hall of Fame and for the front porch from which McKinley ran his 1896 presidential campaign. McKinley, who was assassinated in 1901, is buried in a park on the west end of Canton in a large memorial that roughly resembles the Taj Mahal. The Hall of Fame is at the other end of the park.

The portion of the 16th outside Stark County tends to be rural and Republican. Wooster (population 22,000), the Wayne County seat, is the site of Rubbermaid's corporate headquarters. Nearby Orrville (population 8,000) is the home of the Smucker family, which markets jams and peanut butter.

The 16th was extended south in 1982 by redistricting to annex Holmes County, and west in 1992 to pick up Ashland County and part of Knox County.

Many of Holmes' 33,000 residents are Amish, and motorists driving through the county have to be careful not to plow into the back of a horse-drawn buggy. Houses without electricity are common in the county, and the income level is less than 70 percent of the state's average — just $9,191 per capita. Although tourism and leather and noodle factories have brought new employment to the agricultural area, much business is still conducted in small Amish family-owned shops that sell buggies and other necessities.

Ashland County is a very rural, very Republican area that usually rewards statewide GOP candidates with 60 percent or more of the vote. But Dole got only 53 percent.

1990 Population: 570,902. White 538,938 (94%), Black 27,419 (5%), Other 4,545 (1%). Hispanic origin 3,612 (1%). 18 and over 419,742 (74%), 62 and over 94,741 (17%). Median age: 34.

freeze, even though he was managing the bill on the floor. Two months later, the House rejected a conditional freeze worked out in conference with the Senate; this time, Regula voted in favor of his own bill but saw it rejected anyway.

Regula was an opponent of a moratorium on offshore oil drilling annually contained in his bill, calling the environmental concerns a "red herring." "The Lord spills more through seepage," Regula contended, but he saw the moratorium extended through the efforts of members of his own party from the coasts.

Regula stepped more lightly in the fiscal 1997 spending bill, and if his second product still was not to Yates' liking, it had a much less bumpy road. Many Republicans felt their party had been burned by Democrats and the media because of environmental votes they took in 1995, so they slowed their attack in 1996.

Regula votes with his party most of the time and supported GOP signature initiatives to overhaul welfare, balance the budget, and make the telecommunications and agriculture industries more respondent to their respective marketplaces. He did break from the GOP on a few key votes, though.

Democrats won a rare victory early in the 104th on an amendment to reorder the priorities of the GOP's defense bill, putting troop readiness and resupply ahead of development of a national missile system. Regula and four Republican committee chairmen supported the move, helping to put it over the top, but the underlying bill was never taken up by the Senate.

Regula supported the 90-cent increase in the minimum wage, which Democrats hail as one of their salient victories of the 104th, and he also joined with about 50 Republicans in helping to kill some environmental riders on the fiscal 1996 VA-HUD spending bill. The 17 riders, which would have blocked enforcement of major sections of such laws as the Clean Air and clean water acts, were put to three votes in the House before finally being put to rest.

With Speaker Newt Gingrich taking a particular interest in the fate of the District of Columbia, suggesting that Washington be made part of Maryland for voting purposes, Regula revived an old idea from his service earlier in the decade on the D.C. Appropriations Subcommittee. Although in 1990 Maryland Democratic Gov. William Donald Schaefer backed Regula's proposal to annex the District back into Maryland, in 1996 the state's new governor, Democrat Parris N. Glendening, suggested that Congress could give the city to Gingrich's district in Georgia.

One of Regula's minor but persistent crusades is for federal recognition of President William McKinley, his hometown's most famous native. A graduate of the McKinley School of Law, Regula observes McKinley's January birthday by giving red carnations to his colleagues. He is always on the watch to block efforts by Alaska GOP Sen. Ted Stevens to rename Mount McKinley in Alaska Mount Denali.

At Home: Regula has been a political force in northeast Ohio since winning a House seat in 1972. Between 1978 and 1988 — a period of great economic difficulty for the industrial areas of his district — Regula never dropped below 66 percent of the vote at election time.

But in 1990, Regula could not avoid a general anti-incumbent mood that affected most House incumbents in Ohio; nor could he totally escape voter wrath over his vote for a congressional pay raise. Running against Democrat Warner D. Mendenhall, an underfinanced college professor, Regula won with 59 percent, his lowest-ever reelection tally.

In 1992, with anti-incumbent sentiment still prevalent, Mendenhall returned, raising nearly half his money from PACs. But Regula, who does not accept PAC contributions, worked hard to avoid an upset. He skipped the Republican National Convention to campaign, and spent a career-high $209,000. His efforts paid off, as his tally rose to 64 percent.

Regula came to the House after eight years in the state legislature, where he specialized in writing conservation bills. His state Senate constituency included a large part of Stark County, the heart of the 16th, and when GOP Rep. Frank T. Bow retired in 1972 after 22 years in Congress, Regula won Bow's endorsement.

Redistricting that year removed part of Democratic Mahoning County from the 16th, making it more Republican. Regula defeated Democrat Virgil Musser with 57 percent of the vote.

HOUSE ELECTIONS

1996 General		
Ralph Regula (R)	159,314	(69%)
Thomas E. Burkhart (D)	64,902	(28%)
Brad Graef (NL)	7,611	(3%)
1996 Primary		
Ralph Regula (R)	55,380	(84%)
Vince Yambrovich (R)	10,404	(16%)
1994 General		
Ralph Regula (R)	137,322	(75%)
J. Michael Finn (D)	45,781	(25%)

Previous Winning Percentages: 1992 (64%) **1990** (59%) **1988** (79%) **1986** (76%) **1984** (72%) **1982** (66%) **1980** (79%) **1978** (78%) **1976** (67%) **1974** (66%) **1972** (57%)

CAMPAIGN FINANCE

	Receipts	Receipts from PACs		Expend-itures
1996				
Regula (R)	$181,992	$0	(0%)	$154,379
Burkhart (D)	$4,409	$3,050	(69%)	$3,552
1994				
Regula (R)	$168,218	$1,520	(1%)	$120,279

DISTRICT VOTE FOR PRESIDENT

	1996		1992
D	100,880 (43%)	**D**	95,193 (37%)
R	99,395 (42%)	**R**	98,953 (39%)
I	33,382 (14%)	**I**	60,824 (24%)

KEY VOTES

1997	
Ban "partial birth" abortions	Y
1996	
Approve farm bill	Y
Deny public education to illegal immigrants	Y
Repeal ban on certain assault-style weapons	Y
Increase minimum wage	Y
Freeze defense spending	N
Approve welfare overhaul	Y
1995	
Approve balanced-budget constitutional amendment	Y
Relax Clean Water Act regulations	Y
Oppose limits on environmental regulations	Y
Reduce projected Medicare spending	Y
Approve GOP budget with tax and spending cuts	Y

VOTING STUDIES

	Presidential Support		Party Unity		Conservative Coalition	
Year	S	O	S	O	S	O
1996	48	52	86	14	94	6
1995	24	76	90	10	91	8
1994	59	41	76	24	89	11
1993	58	42	79	21	91	9
1992	55	44	73	27	81	19
1991	69	30	70	29	86	14

INTEREST GROUP RATINGS

Year	ADA	AFL-CIO	CCUS	ACU
1996	15	n/a	81	75
1995	10	8	100	71
1994	15	11	92	86
1993	30	50	73	71
1992	35	67	100	72
1991	20	58	60	55

17 James A. Traficant Jr. (D)

Of Poland — Elected 1984, 7th term

Biographical Information

Born: May 8, 1941, Youngstown, Ohio.
Education: U. of Pittsburgh, B.S. 1963; Youngstown State U., M.S. 1973, M.S. 1976.
Occupation: County drug program director; sheriff.
Family: Wife, Patricia Choppa; two children.
Religion: Roman Catholic.
Political Career: Mahoning County sheriff, 1981-85.
Capitol Office: 2446 Rayburn Bldg. 20515; 225-5261.

Committees

Science
Space & Aeronautics
Transportation & Infrastructure
Aviation; Public Buildings & Economic Development (ranking)

In Washington: Traficant makes quite a spectacle on the House floor as, with fist pounding and hair askew, he pours out a message that is equal parts working-class anxiety and disbelieving pique. The switch of party control in the House has not changed the pitch of his preachings — he was angry in the majority, and he remains so in the minority. After President Clinton's 1996 State of the Union address, Traficant said, "I think the nation needs a strong, viable third party alternative, because I really don't see that much difference between the two parties,"

Traficant sees eye-to-eye with most Democrats on labor initiatives such as increasing the minimum wage. And he continues his attacks on corporate "fat cats." But he has found a fair number of policy proposals on the agenda of the Republican majority that he can embrace. Traficant's support of positions taken by Clinton and his party were among the lowest registered by a Democrat in the 104th Congress.

One of only nine House Democrats to vote for the GOP's first welfare overhaul package, derived from the House GOP's "Contract With America," Traficant announced that the prevailing welfare system had "destroyed our country. . . . Anybody who supports the status quo is anti-family, anti-kids and, damn it, anti-American."

He joined with Republicans on such central legislation as the plan to cut taxes by a total of $189 billion, to boost defense spending, to repeal a portion of the gasoline tax and to ban a particular abortion procedure its opponents call "partial birth" abortion. During debate over a constitutional amendment to allow laws banning flag desecration, Traficant argued: "This isn't about the flag debate. Today it's about pride, it's about respect, it's about values. Burn your bra, burn your pantihose, burn your BVDs . . . but let the flag alone."

Traficant supported Republican attempts to ease environmental regulations, saying the 1995 bill to revise federal clean water standards would "restore common sense" in deciding which lands require federal protection. He maintained, "This nation has gotten so environmentally overzealous that if a dog accidentally passes water on a parking lot, some government agent might deem it to be a wetland."

Traficant is a committed disbeliever in the notion of foreign aid. He is the House's most impassioned defender of American-made goods and during the 104th he moved to attach "buy American" language to bills covering, for example, Amtrak, agriculture payments and intelligence gathering. The House passed, 367-9, his bill calling on the Commerce Department to establish a toll-free hotline so consumers could call to determine if a product was made in the United States, but the Senate never took it up.

Traficant is convinced that his working-class constituents — many of whom had high-paying factory jobs that are gone for good — are being ripped off by the global economy. After AT&T announced a layoff of 40,000 workers, Traficant noted, "Uncle Sam keeps saying, 'Do not worry, because NAFTA and GATT are going to replace those jobs with high-technology jobs.' Right. The only high technology job I see is that new Slurpee machine at 7-Eleven."

In addition to his scorn for trade agreements, Traficant disdained U.S. efforts to prop up the Mexican peso. (He blasted congressional leaders for supporting Clinton's Mexico aid package, wondering, "Who the hell are they to say, 'Go ahead, Mr. President?'") Traficant supported the GOP's efforts to toughen immigration enforcement and deny public education to illegal aliens. Griping that illegal immigrants receive social services, he announced, "It is time to put American military troops on our border. . . . We have got millions of illegal immigrants, many of them running over our borders with backpacks full of cocaine and heroin. Beam me up. Whoever created this immigration policy is in fact smoking dope."

In his House speeches, Traficant regularly accuses his adversaries of "smoking dope." Also, he frequently claims that Congress and other vil-

Once called America's "Little Ruhr," after Germany's Ruhr Valley, in recognition of its industrial productivity, the Youngstown-Warren area now is a symbol of industrial decline. Many of the giant steel furnaces that once lighted the eastern Ohio sky are dark. Most of the workers who have not retired or left the area are looking for other jobs.

Located on the state's eastern border with Pennsylvania, the region was long a steel center serving Cleveland and Pittsburgh. Only a decade or so ago the steel plants in the Mahoning River Valley employed more than 50,000 workers. Now the work force is a fraction of that.

The 17th has begun to diversify its economy, but many of the gains made in the late 1980s have been lost. Youngstown (population 96,000) lost 17 percent of its population in the 1980s, and for those who stayed, an unemployment rate approaching 20 percent has not been uncommon. In the 1980s, the city was one of only five in the nation to drop from the ranks of those with 100,000 or more people.

Troubles have plagued one of Youngstown's few corporate bright spots. Phar-Mor, a national chain of discount drug stores with headquarters in Youngstown, declared bankruptcy in 1992. Plans to merge with Shopko Stores Inc. were scrapped in April 1997.

With its remaining blue-collar base, the 17th is one of Ohio's solidly Democratic areas in most elections. Bill Clinton's 58 percent showing in 1996 was his second highest in the state, trailing only the Cleveland-based 11th District.

Mahoning and Trumbull were among the 10 Ohio counties that voted for Jimmy Carter in 1980, and both have been in the Democratic column since.

OHIO 17
Northeast — Youngstown, Warren

Most Democratic candidates build comfortable majorities in the string of declining ethnic communities along the Mahoning River. Italians dominate in Niles and Lowellville. Eastern Europeans and Greeks are the most important groups in Campbell. In the two largest cities — Youngstown and Warren — blacks are part of the demographic mixture, making up 38 and 21 percent of those cities, respectively.

The GOP vote increases as one moves south beyond the industrial Mahoning Valley, though the numbers are too small to make much of a difference districtwide. Rural Columbiana County is a swing region, influenced by Pennsylvania and West Virginia. But it is enough smaller than Mahoning and Trumbull counties that it lacks much political pull in the 17th.

For years there has been local and even some national publicity about a hazardous-waste incinerator in East Liverpool, along the West Virginia border. Construction of the incinerator was completed in 1992, but commercial operation of the facility was complicated by legal actions initiated by environmental groups and others concerned that emissions from waste burning pose a safety threat. The controversy has diminished somewhat since then.

1990 Population: 570,900. White 509,008 (89%), Black 55,796 (10%), Other 6,096 (1%). Hispanic origin 7,693 (1%). 18 and over 428,405 (75%), 62 and over 110,092 (19%). Median age: 36.

lains are "so damn dumb they could throw themselves on the ground and miss." But of all his rhetorical formulations, none recurs so often as "beam me up," his pet term for indignation and befuddlement. Traficant said "beam me up" more than 95 times in floor speeches during the 104th.

Traficant complained that some hospitals engaged in cost cutting were also "building luxury suites for the fats cats," providing "gourmet food" for "VIPs" while patients are "line-itemed for toilet paper and aspirin. Beam me up. Mr. Speaker, the truth is the CEOs of these HMOs keep lining their pockets with cash. I say they should be handcuffed to a chain link fence and flogged. Then sent to jail. Think about it. I yield back the balance of those line-itemed toilet paper bills."

Traficant is often profane. Proclaiming his opposition to Clinton's budget proposal in May 1993, Traficant said, "I am not for this damn plan. And I say, as a Democrat, shove this big tax increase up your compromise." After one 1993 Traficant tirade on trade that included two "hells" and one "damn," the member presiding over the House said, "The chair would admonish the gentleman from Ohio not to use profane language in his speeches" — an admonition Traficant religiously ignores.

His colorful speeches are frequently clipped onto network news programs, bringing him attention disproportionate to his influence in the House. But Traficant's efforts to secure a seat on a powerful committee were greeted with bemusement by Democratic insiders. He has, though, risen to the senior ranks of the Science Committee and the Transportation and Infrastructure Committee; he is ranking member of Transportation's Public Buildings and Economic Development Subcommittee. He has secured more than $100 million in recent years for the Mahoning Valley in the shape of grants or loans for law enforcement, small businesses, an airport and an art museum.

One of Traficant's early legislative successes came in 1987, when he won approval of a $30 million program to provide counseling for people faced with mortgage foreclosure because of circumstances beyond their control, such as job layoffs. The measure harked back to the incident that first made him a local legend: In 1982, during his tenure as Mahoning County (Youngstown) sheriff, Traficant went to jail for three days rather than serve several laid-off factory workers with foreclosure orders.

That act helped give Traficant such a loyal following that he has weathered legal problems that might have sunk other politicians. In 1987, a federal tax court ruled that Traficant took $108,000 in bribes from organized-crime figures while serving as sheriff, and it held him liable for back taxes, interest and civil penalties. But Traficant — who was acquitted in 1983 on federal criminal charges involving the same allegations — brushed off questions of corruption and portrayed himself as a victim of the Internal Revenue Service (IRS).

Even allowing for his mercurial nature and his flair for the dramatic, Traficant startled colleagues by announcing plans to run in the 1988 Democratic presidential primaries (while seeking House re-election) to promote the Rust Belt's interests. Traficant made the ballot only in a handful of House districts in Ohio and Pennsylvania. Still, he topped 30,000 votes in the Ohio primary (just over 2 percent of the total) and earned a delegate to the Democratic National Convention.

At Home: Traficant's style is great theater, and, judging from his re-election margins, smart politics. No Republican opposed him in 1996, and his raw vote total was the highest of any House candidate in the country. A former football star at the University of Pittsburgh, he ran an anti-drug program in Mahoning County before being elected sheriff in 1980. He became a hero to the district's hard-hit factory workers, but he quickly alienated virtually every government official in the area by claiming that most were controlled by organized crime.

Those allegations took on an ironic cast when Traficant himself was indicted for bribery. A conviction seemed certain: The FBI had tape recordings of him accepting $163,000 from underworld figures. Traficant, despite a lack of legal training, defended himself in court, putting on a tour de force against federal prosecutors. He said he took the money only to get evidence against the mobsters, and the jury believed him. After a seven-week trial, he was acquitted, touching off a celebration by his fans in Youngstown and generating national media attention.

In 1984, Traficant's popularity spurred him to challenge GOP Rep. Lyle Williams, a genial ex-barber with a knack for reaching the working-class majority. Although Traficant was underfinanced and had to overcome the hostility of Democratic leaders — one nemesis sought to get him committed to a mental institution — Traficant drew large crowds with his attacks on banks, big business and the IRS. Williams warned that Traficant would embarrass the district. But the 17th's continuing high unemployment was a lead weight on the Republican, and Traficant won with 53 percent.

HOUSE ELECTIONS

1996 General		
James A. Traficant Jr. (D)	218,283	(91%)
James M. Cahaney (NL)	21,685	(9%)
1994 General		
James A. Traficant Jr. (D)	149,004	(77%)
Mike G. Meister (R)	43,490	(23%)

Previous Winning Percentages: 1992 (84%) **1990** (78%) **1988** (77%) **1986** (72%) **1984** (53%)

CAMPAIGN FINANCE

	Receipts	Receipts from PACs	Expend-itures
1996			
Traficant (D)	$187,053	$116,385 (62%)	$156,597
1994			
Traficant (D)	$144,972	$73,750 (51%)	$145,793
Meister (R)	$8,287	$14 (0%)	$8,522

DISTRICT VOTE FOR PRESIDENT

1996	1992
D 142,949 (58%)	**D** 133,213 (50%)
R 67,977 (28%)	**R** 68,417 (26%)
I 31,765 (13%)	**I** 64,936 (24%)

VOTING STUDIES

	Presidential Support		Party Unity		Conservative Coalition	
Year	S	O	S	O	S	O
1996	57	43	50	49	92	8
1995	41	59	52	48	77	23
1994	68	32	80	20	67	33
1993	66	33	85	15	64	36
1992	21	78	89	9	42	58
1991	26	74	82	17	46	54

KEY VOTES

1997	
Ban "partial birth" abortions	Y
1996	
Approve farm bill	N
Deny public education to illegal immigrants	Y
Repeal ban on certain assault-style weapons	N
Increase minimum wage	Y
Freeze defense spending	N
Approve welfare overhaul	Y
1995	
Approve balanced-budget constitutional amendment	N
Relax Clean Water Act regulations	Y
Oppose limits on environmental regulations	N
Reduce projected Medicare spending	N
Approve GOP budget with tax and spending cuts	N

INTEREST GROUP RATINGS

Year	ADA	AFL-CIO	CCUS	ACU
1996	55	n/a	44	50
1995	55	75	63	48
1994	65	100	42	33
1993	75	92	45	21
1992	85	90	50	8
1991	85	100	20	15

18 Bob Ney (R)

Of St. Clairsville — Elected 1994, 2nd term

Biographical Information

Born: July 5, 1954, Wheeling, W.Va.

Education: U. of Ohio, 1972-74; Ohio State U., B.S. 1976.

Occupation: State health and education program manager; local safety director; educator.

Family: Two children.

Religion: Roman Catholic.

Political Career: Ohio House, 1981-83; defeated for re-election to Ohio House, 1982; Ohio Senate, 1985-95.

Capitol Office: 1024 Longworth Bldg. 20515; 225-6265.

Committees

Banking & Financial Services
Domestic & International Monetary Policy; General Oversight & Investigations; Housing & Community Opportunity

House Oversight

Transportation & Infrastructure
Surface Transportation; Water Resources & Environment

Joint Library

Joint Printing

In Washington: Organized labor finds few friends in the GOP Class of 1994, but some of the first-term Republicans occasionally take the union side in legislative debate, and Ney falls in that category. He comes from working-class origins — his father was a camera operator for a TV station, and his mother worked in a liquor store. Also, Ney is responding to the political realities of his eastern Ohio district, which has much of what remains of Ohio's coal and steel industries and includes a sizable Democratic vote. The 18th is an ethnic melting pot, with a large Catholic population, including descendants of Eastern European and Greek immigrants.

In July 1995, Ney helped organized labor score its first major victory in the Republican-controlled House; he joined Texas Democrat Ronald D. Coleman to thwart an effort to eliminate federal labor protection for mass transit workers. Conservative House appropriators had included language to scuttle the protection as they were working on the fiscal 1996 transportation spending bill. Ney and Coleman warned that passage of the language would cause thousands of transit workers to lose their right to collective bargaining. Proponents of the measure portrayed existing labor protection as outdated and costly. Disputing that claim, Ney said, "There are 100 reasons why transit costs can go up. . . . I do not think we need to lay that blame upon the worker."

At issue was section 13(c) of the Federal Transit Act, which requires the Labor Department to approve how federal grants are used. The roots of 13(c) go back to 1964, when Congress first offered local governments money to take over financially beleaguered private bus and rail lines. Because many states barred public employees from joining unions or bargaining collectively, Congress enacted 13(c) to ensure that unionized transit workers did not lose their bargaining rights when they moved to the public sector.

In an outcome that surprised the GOP leadership, Ney and Coleman won, 233-186, when they offered an amendment to block conservatives from eliminating 13(c) protection.

Ney also was an early Republican proponent of increasing the minimum wage, a politically popular proposal that the Democratic minority pushed onto the legislative agenda in 1996, to the dismay of the House GOP leadership. Ney was one of just 43 Republicans who opposed an effort by GOP leaders to exempt small businesses from paying the higher minimum wage.

In September 1995, Ney was the only Republican in the Ohio House delegation — and one of just 22 in the whole House GOP — to oppose a conservative-backed bill aimed at fostering employer-employee teams to address health and safety concerns and other employment issues. Ney and other foes of the bill said it really aimed to undermine organized labor. Supporters said more workplace cooperation is needed for U.S. companies to compete in the international marketplace. The House narrowly adopted the controversial measure, 221-202.

In another nod to labor, Ney spoke in June 1995 against a provision in the fiscal 1996 budget resolution that sought to save about $4.4 billion over seven years by assuming that the 1934 Davis-Bacon Act would be repealed. The Davis-Bacon Act requires construction firms that work for the government to pay the prevailing local wage, which is often set by union contracts.

"Some have called the Act a special interest 'dole-out' that is earmarked specifically for organized labor," Ney said, "But this is an unfair assessment. If there is any clear evidence with respect to the Davis-Bacon Act, it is that the act has effectively taken the wages of working men and women out of the federal construction bidding process."

But if Ney has differences with GOP conservatives on some labor-related issues, he joins arms with those in his party who criticize what they see as excessive regulating by the Environmental Protection Agency (EPA). Overregulation of the coal industry, Ney says, has "taken food off of the

OHIO 18
East — Steubenville; Zanesville

In 1994 voters here opted to send a Republican House member to Washington for the first time in 48 years. Two years later, Ney retained the seat, winning by 4 percentage points.

Redistricting in 1992 added more farmers and a more GOP-inclined population to the 18th. Even so, Democrats still have strong presence here — legacies of the coal and steel that left the region's air and waters polluted. Cramped along the steep banks of the Ohio River, Steubenville (population 22,000) long had some of the nation's foulest air pollution. But jobs in the smoke-belching plants along a 50-mile stretch of the Ohio River take priority over clean air, a fact that successful politicians quickly learn.

Locals boast that there was not an air pollution alert in Steubenville in the 1980s. But the clearing skies are a gloomy sign for the local economy. For years the unemployment rate in Steubenville and surrounding Jefferson County has been in or near double digits, a situation expected to get worse later this decade as new Clean Air Act regulations make the high-sulfur coal that the area mines less desirable.

West of Jefferson is economically depressed Harrison County. The closing in 1985 of a pottery plant that employed about 1,000 people pushed up the already high unemployment rate.

In Jefferson, Belmont and Monroe counties, the steelworking and coal-mining Democrats of the district generally show strong party allegiance, though they tend to shy away from supporting liberals. This part of Ohio resembles West Virginia and eastern Kentucky. Some cattle are raised, but the hilly terrain makes farming generally unprofitable. Under the hills, however, there are extensive coal deposits.

As one moves west, the district becomes less Democratic, and the tractors of Republican farmers replace the giant shovels of Democratic coal miners.

A sweep of counties added to the 18th's southwest end in the 1992 redistricting — Muskingum, Perry, Morgan and about half of Licking — are similar to the nearby farming counties that were already part of the district.

Licking County is a pocket of prosperity. The areas around Newark are a growing center for manufacturing and research, with Owens-Corning and Diebold as major employers. Dow Chemical also has a large research facility here. The city is scrambling to come up with a conversion plan for Newark Air Force Base, whose shutdown was announced in March 1993, though it was not immediately closed.

The addition of Muskingum County has added the city of Zanesville to the 18th. With 27,000 residents, Zanesville is now the largest city completely in the district. It was the state capital in the early 1800s and was once the country's pottery capital. Zanesville benefitted economically from the construction in 1996 of a state prison in Noble County and the expansion of a national auto parts store.

Bill Clinton lost all of the 18th's southwest counties in 1992, except for Perry. He won elsewhere in the district, finishing with 43 percent. Clinton carried the district in 1996 by 12 percentage points, barely losing three of its 14 counties.

1990 Population: 570,900. White 554,522 (97%), Black 13,483 (2%), Other 2,895 (1%). Hispanic origin 1,937 (<1%). 18 and over 421,743 (74%), 62 and over 104,287 (18%). Median age: 35.

tables of people in southern Ohio." And he believes that Ohioans and other Midwesterners have "suffered tremendously" under the Clean Air Act, specifically its provisions targeting acid rain. "The Clean Air Act was a liberal, overzealous, too-far-reaching measure," he said.

Ney strongly supported the GOP's regulatory overhaul initiative (outlined in the "Contract With America") that sought to restrain federal agencies' regulatory powers. He said the measure would "correct the faults that have occurred because of an overstretched bureaucratic arm" and prevent "unelected bureaucrats" from running the government "lock, stock and barrel."

Ney also shares the conservative social views of the GOP majority. He opposes abortion, favors repealing the ban on certain semiautomatic assault-style weapons and voted for welfare overhaul.

Despite his periodic straying from the party line on labor matters, Ney has solid enough conservative credentials that the House leadership made him the only Class of 1994 member on the House Oversight Committee, which handles the chamber's internal affairs. In the 105th Congress, he is vice chairman of the committee. Also for the 105th, Ney got a seat on the Transportation and Infrastructure Committee, giving him input as the panel works on the massive surface transportation reauthorization bill. He is one of five deputy whips in his class, and he also serves on the Banking and Financial Services Committee.

At Home: Raised in a middle-class family, Ney worked his way through Ohio State University and then taught English in Iran before the fall of the shah. (He still can speak Farsi.)

He worked in municipal government, then in 1980 got his start in elective politics at age 26 by toppling a Democrat who was well-known in Washington, albeit with a tarnished reputation — former Rep. Wayne L. Hays. The chairman of the House Administration Committee, Hays resigned from Congress in 1976 after news broke that he had kept a secretary on the House payroll who served primarily as his mistress. Hays re-entered politics in 1978, winning a seat in the Ohio House, but in 1980, a big Republican year, he was sent into retirement by Ney. In 1982, a good year for Democrats, Ney lost his state House seat, but in 1984, he won election to the state Senate.

As chairman of the Senate's Finance Committee, Ney earned a reputation as a bipartisan player. In 1992, he was a leading supporter of a health care reform bill that was initially sponsored by a state House Democrat. The measure, designed to make it easier for workers to get insurance even if they switched jobs, became law.

After nine-term Democratic Rep. Douglas Applegate's retirement opened the 18th District in 1994, Ney had an advantage in the six-person GOP primary: He was well-known to many in the district, having represented 50 percent of it at one time or another during his state legislative career. Armed with more money and higher name identification than his rivals, Ney walked away with the Republican nomination and was crowned the general-election front-runner against Democratic state Rep. Greg L. DiDonato.

DiDonato, like Ney, campaigned as an abortion foe and strongly opposed any efforts to regulate firearms. A main difference between the two men was in style, with Ney projecting a smooth, polished manner and DiDonato exhibiting a more "regular-Joe" persona.

Although the United Mine Workers (UMW) backed DiDonato, Ney could make a pitch for working-class votes by citing his efforts in the state legislature to mitigate the effects of the federal clean air act on Ohio's steel and coal industries. Ney had pushed legislators to provide state funds to help companies comply with required reductions in sulfur emissions. The UMW had supported Ney in his state Senate campaigns, and Ney's House bid was endorsed by the National Education Association.

Ney called for a balanced-budget amendment and term limits for members. He signed the "Contract With America," but did not make it a centerpiece of his campaign. DiDonato and Ney traded ugly insults over the airwaves; ultimately DiDonato suffered more political fallout from the skirmishes. Ney sought to move to higher ground, challenging DiDonato to sign a "clean campaign" pledge. DiDonato turned him down, but Ney pulled his negative television ads anyway. He won with 54 percent.

In 1996, Ney saw his victory margin drop in the face of a stiff Democratic challenge from state Sen. Robert L. Burch. He argued that Ney had abandoned his roots as a moderate by supporting the agenda of much more conservative Republicans in Congress. Ney said he had continued to work in a bipartisan manner. Burch was boosted by a 12-point Bill Clinton win in the 18th's presidential voting, but Ney eked out 50 percent, 4 points ahead of Burch.

HOUSE ELECTIONS

1996 General		
Bob Ney (R)	117,365	(50%)
Robert L. Burch (D)	108,332	(46%)
Margaret Chitti (NL)	8,146	(3%)
1994 General		
Bob Ney (R)	103,115	(54%)
Greg L. DiDonato (D)	87,926	(46%)

CAMPAIGN FINANCE

	Receipts	Receipts from PACs	Expend-itures
1996			
Ney (R)	$887,317	$504,846 (57%)	$879,110
Burch (D)	$283,013	$173,902 (61%)	$263,417
1994			
Ney (R)	$603,937	$245,500 (41%)	$600,426
DiDonato (D)	$438,354	$159,099 (36%)	$434,905

DISTRICT VOTE FOR PRESIDENT

	1996		1992
D	112,757 (48%)	**D**	110,494 (43%)
R	86,254 (36%)	**R**	87,429 (34%)
I	36,095 (15%)	**I**	58,578 (23%)

KEY VOTES

1997	
Ban "partial birth" abortions	Y
1996	
Approve farm bill	Y
Deny public education to illegal immigrants	Y
Repeal ban on certain assault-style weapons	Y
Increase minimum wage	Y
Freeze defense spending	Y
Approve welfare overhaul	Y
1995	
Approve balanced-budget constitutional amendment	Y
Relax Clean Water Act regulations	Y
Oppose limits on environmental regulations	N
Reduce projected Medicare spending	Y
Approve GOP budget with tax and spending cuts	Y

VOTING STUDIES

	Presidential Support		Party Unity		Conservative Coalition	
Year	S	O	S	O	S	O
1996	39	61	89	9	88	12
1995	22	78	90	9	89	10

INTEREST GROUP RATINGS

Year	ADA	AFL-CIO	CCUS	ACU
1996	10	n/a	88	85
1995	10	33	88	84

19 Steven C. LaTourette (R)

Of Madison — Elected 1994, 2nd term

Biographical Information

Born: July 22, 1954, Cleveland, Ohio.

Education: U. of Michigan, B.A. 1976; Cleveland State U., J.D. 1979.

Occupation: Lawyer.

Family: Wife, Susan Koprowski; four children.

Religion: Methodist.

Political Career: Candidate for Lake County prosecutor, 1984; Lake County prosecutor, 1989-94.

Capitol Office: 1239 Longworth Bldg. 20515; 225-5731.

Committees

Banking & Financial Services
Domestic & International Monetary Policy; General Oversight & Investigations

Government Reform & Oversight
National Economic Growth, Natural Resources & Regulatory Affairs; National Security, International Affairs & Criminal Justice; Postal Service

Transportation & Infrastructure
Public Buildings & Economic Development; Surface Transportation; Water Resources & Environment

In Washington: When it comes to opposing abortion and supporting gunowners' rights, LaTourette is every bit as conservative as the majority of his colleagues in the GOP Class of 1994. But on some other issues, he has voted a more moderate line, reflecting the politically competitive nature of his suburban Cleveland constituency.

LaTourette's approach won positive reviews from the electorate when he sought a second term in 1996: He won by a 14 point margin over his Democratic challenger. Two years before, LaTourette captured the 19th with just 48 percent of the vote, five points better than Democratic Rep. Eric D. Fingerhut.

The son of a certified public accountant, LaTourette had a middle-class upbringing. After law school he worked as a public defender, a job that he says taught him what it was like to have "nobody like you." As a county prosecutor he gained notice for prosecuting a cult-related, mass murder case.

Given this background, LaTourette seems an unlikely conduit for irreverent humor, but that's what he became for a brief time early in his freshman House term, when he allowed humor columnist Dave Barry to do a volunteer stint as a press assistant in his office. Barry's influence was noticeable in a March 1995 floor speech LaTourette gave on tort reform. "As a lawyer, I am the last person to suggest that everybody in my profession is a money-grubbing, scum-sucking toad. The actual figure is only about 73 percent," LaTourette told the House. "I am of course just pulling the Speaker's honorable leg. The vast majority of lawyers are responsible professionals, as well as, in many ways, human beings."

On a more serious note, shortly after his 1994 election, LaTourette told the Cleveland Plain Dealer he was looking forward to working with President Clinton, adding that he had a "bit of anxiety" that GOP leaders might "give in to the temptation for revenge."

LaTourette broke with his party's leadership in October 1995 when he was one of just 10 Republicans to vote against the House version of the GOP's seven-year balanced budget plan. He said he agreed with balancing the budget but "could not in good conscience support that version of the budget because it contained numerous favors to special interests." He did, however, vote for the final version of the budget after changes by a House-Senate conference addressed a number of his concerns, including Medicaid funding formulas, protections for pension funds and quality standards for nursing homes.

LaTourette also split from the GOP majority in June 1996 to oppose an increase in the defense budget. He and 59 other Republicans supported an amendment to freeze fiscal 1997 defense spending at fiscal 1996 levels. They argued that exempting the Pentagon from the budget squeeze affecting other agencies would undermine Congress' ability to deal with the deficit. With the help of hawkish Democrats, the GOP leadership defeated the freeze amendment, 219-194.

LaTourette was one of the 24 Republicans who launched a drive to get their party's leadership to schedule a vote on increasing the minimum wage. Pro-business conservatives resisted at first, but in May 1996, the House voted 281-144 to increase the minimum wage by 90 cents over two years. He also opposed a GOP effort that would have exempted small businesses from paying the higher wage. That measure was defeated, 196-229.

Early in 1995, LaTourette voted with his party's majority for a measure aimed at easing many federal water pollution control regulations. Later, though, he was one of 51 Republicans who voted to block conservatives from restricting the Environmental Protection Agency's ability to carry out certain regulations. LaTourette has spoken often about the importance of environmental research, particularly on the Great Lakes. The northern border of the 19th is Lake Erie. He praised House appropriators in July 1995 for saving the funding of the Great Lakes Environmental Research Laboratory, which LaTourette said helps the government meet its scientific and management responsibilities under the Great Lakes

OHIO 19
Cleveland suburbs — Ashtabula and Lake counties

The 19th is one of the most politically competitive districts in the Cleveland area, and one of the most strangely shaped in Ohio. Its western fingers reach around and up into Cleveland's western suburbs, squeeze east and then north to Lake County along Lake Erie's shore. The district ends up in Ashtabula County in Ohio's far northeastern corner.

The combination of the competition and geography makes the 19th difficult to campaign in: It is full of Republicans and Democrats, autoworkers and farmers. The district's 1992 presidential vote was indicative of its diversity. Bill Clinton beat George Bush by three percentage points, 40 percent to 37 percent, while Ross Perot received 23 percent. Clinton won more decisively in 1996, while Republican LaTourette won re-election by a comfortable margin.

Brook Park, the 19th's westernmost city, is an autoworkers' community just west of Parma. The city is blue-collar, usually Democratic, overwhelmingly white and very sensitive to the ups and downs of the automobile industry. Many of its 23,000 residents settled here to work at the city's large Ford plant. Starting with Brook Park, the 19th forms a small bowl around three sides (west, south and east) of Parma.

Heading east, a ribbon of the tiny village of Oakwood connects to the band of Republican eastern Cleveland suburbs that head straight north into Lake County. These suburbs are substantially better off economically than those on the western side. Median household income in such areas as Pepper Pike and Gates Mills hovers around $100,000, compared with $37,000 in Brook Park and $18,000 in Cleveland proper.

The far northeastern communities of the 19th, reliant on the steel, chemical and automobile industries for jobs, are among the most depressed parts of the state. But there is growth: As migration from Cleveland moved eastward between 1950 and 1970, the population of Lake County more than doubled. The rapid growth has slowed, but the suburbs continue to grow farther east, obliterating the truck gardens and vineyards along Lake Erie.

Mentor (population 47,000), one of the area's fastest growing cities, traditionally has been an industrial Democratic area, but its growth is coming from Republicans moving in. The county's Republican farmers and suburbanites are no longer canceled out politically by ethnic Democrats in the western part of the county. LaTourette's re-election in 1996 was based largely on his getting 63 percent in Lake County.

Lake County casts about 36 percent of the 19th's ballots; Cuyahoga County casts just under half. The remaining votes are in Ashtabula County, where agriculture is king. Employment here has recovered only modestly since the early 1980s, when the jobless rate hit 20 percent.

The steel and chemical plants along Lake Erie have been severely hurt by foreign competition, and it is hard to find signs of revival. Ashtabula has been reliably Democratic in past elections, but a strong GOP county organization has kept the party's candidates close.

1990 Population: 570,901. White 552,620 (97%), Black 10,214 (2%), Other 8,067 (1%). Hispanic origin 4,982 (1%). 18 and over 436,566 (76%), 62 and over 106,606 (19%). Median age: 36.

Water Quality Agreement with Canada.

He also has been a booster of funding for the Great Lakes Fishery Commission, which he credits with helping the Great Lakes' $4 billion fishing industry. He told the House the commission is helping eradicate the sea lamprey, a "slimy eel-like thing" that can destroy 10 to 40 pounds of fish during its parasitic period. Before the commission's founding, the sea lamprey had "virtually destroyed the entire region's prosperous recreational and commercial fisheries," he said.

A member of the Transportation and Infrastructure Committee, LaTourette backed a move in 1996 by committee Chairman Bud Shuster, R-Pa., to place transportation trust funds "off budget." Funds collected through an 18.4-cent tax on gasoline and a 10-percent tax on airline tickets go into four trust funds and are supposed to be spent on infrastructure repairs. But calculations of the federal balance sheet take the trust funds into consideration, thus reducing the apparent size of the deficit. Taking the trust funds "off-budget," proponents say, will free up for infrastructure projects money that now is hoarded.

LaTourette said that by not spending all the money on transportation projects in the states, the "federal government is essentially stealing from Americans each time they travel." He said the Ohio Department of Transportation estimates that Ohio sends about $1 billion in federal gas taxes to Washington annually, but gets back only about $600 million. "Of the remaining millions, $345 million is used to hide the size of the deficit," LaTourette said, "while the rest of the money disappears into . . . a bureaucratic black hole inside the Beltway," he complained.

During consideration of the 1995 transportation spending bill, LaTourette sought to shift $6 million from the secretary of Transportation's office to the Coast Guard in order to keep open 23 small-boat rescue stations. He said the proposed consolidation of stations would cost lives, but opponents said the Coast Guard should not have to maintain facilities it said it did not need. The House rejected LaTourette's amendment, 183-234.

For the 105th, LaTourette added a seat on the Banking and Financial Services Committee to his portfolio. He also serves on the Government Reform and Oversight Committee.

LaTourette typically concurs with GOP conservatives on social-policy issues. He consistently votes with anti-abortion forces, supported repeal of the ban on certain semiautomatic assault-style weapons and backed welfare overhaul.

At Home: In 1994, LaTourette unseated Fingerhut by yanking the rug out from under the issue Fingerhut yearned to call his own — congressional reform — and by capitalizing on his own credentials as a popular Lake County prosecutor. LaTourette billed himself as a law-and-order Republican concerned with such projects as a local domestic-violence task force. He also played up his image as a family man who had weathered the painful divorce of his parents and who agonized about running for Congress. One of the main drawbacks of the campaign, he was quoted as saying, was that it was preventing him from attending his son's soccer games.

LaTourette made his first try for county prosecutor in 1984, and after losing came back four years later for a second try. He succeeded, booting out a 12-year incumbent who was criticized for his poor conviction rate.

Not long after, LaTourette won the convictions of several people in a highly publicized cult-related mass murder trial. The name recognition he built during six years as prosecutor — particularly in predominantly Democratic Lake County — was a big boost when he decided to run against Fingerhut for the House in 1994.

In the 19th, which stretches from suburban Cleveland to the Pennsylvania border, Democrats outnumber Republicans by about 2-to-1. But Fingerhut, who had won the open seat in 1992 on a pledge to work for congressional reform, had a hard time running for re-election on that platform. LaTourette called him a hypocrite for his extensive use of the congressional frank to send taxpayer-financed mailings.

Dubbing Fingerhut an out-of-touch liberal, LaTourette hammered him for supporting Clinton's 1993 budget, which reduced the deficit but also raised taxes. Fingerhut countered by criticizing LaTourette's opposition to gun control and by accusing him of accepting too many plea bargains as prosecutor. Local newspapers chided both candidates for the negative campaign, exemplified by one Fingerhut TV ad that flashed a mug of LaTourette with the word "LIE" splayed across it. LaTourette won a 48 percent plurality, as two independents siphoned off 9 percent of the vote.

In 1996, LaTourette's Democratic challenger was Tom Coyne Jr., longtime mayor of Brook Park, the district's westernmost city. He tried to make a negative of the stands that LaTourette had taken in agreement with Speaker Newt Gingrich and the GOP leadership. But even as Clinton won the 19th by 9 percentage points over Republican Bob Dole in presidential voting, LaTourette posted a 55 percent to 41 percent victory.

HOUSE ELECTIONS

1996 General		
Steven C. LaTourette (R)	135,012	(55%)
Tom Coyne Jr. (D)	101,152	(41%)
Thomas A. Martin (NL)	10,655	(4%)
1994 General		
Steven C. LaTourette (R)	99,997	(48%)
Eric D. Fingerhut (D)	89,701	(43%)
Ronald E. Young (I)	11,364	(6%)
Jerome A. Brentar (I)	5,180	(3%)

CAMPAIGN FINANCE

	Receipts	Receipts from PACs	Expend-itures
1996			
LaTourette (R)	$1,018,974	$348,867 (34%)	$1,025,247
Coyne (D)	$568,709	$187,552 (33%)	$568,352
1994			
LaTourette (R)	$723,906	$137,763 (19%)	$712,925
Fingerhut (D)	$991,241	$412,262 (42%)	$981,882
Young (I)	$41,640	$29 (0%)	$42,785

DISTRICT VOTE FOR PRESIDENT

	1996		1992
D	127,913 (48%)	**D**	114,357 (40%)
R	102,239 (39%)	**R**	106,950 (37%)
I	31,542 (12%)	**I**	66,429 (23%)

KEY VOTES

1997	
Ban "partial birth" abortions	Y
1996	
Approve farm bill	Y
Deny public education to illegal immigrants	Y
Repeal ban on certain assault-style weapons	Y
Increase minimum wage	Y
Freeze defense spending	Y
Approve welfare overhaul	Y
1995	
Approve balanced-budget constitutional amendment	Y
Relax Clean Water Act regulations	Y
Oppose limits on environmental regulations	Y
Reduce projected Medicare spending	Y
Approve GOP budget with tax and spending cuts	N

VOTING STUDIES

	Presidential Support		Party Unity		Conservative Coalition	
Year	**S**	**O**	**S**	**O**	**S**	**O**
1996	44	53	84	15	90	10
1995	28	71	90	9	93	7

INTEREST GROUP RATINGS

Year	ADA	AFL-CIO	CCUS	ACU
1996	15	n/a	88	80
1995	15	25	96	80

OKLAHOMA

Governor: Frank Keating (R)
First elected: 1994
Length of term: 4 years
Term expires: 1/99
Salary: $70,000
Term limit: 2 terms
Phone: (405) 521-2342
Born: February 10, 1944; St. Louis.
Education: Georgetown U., A.B. 1966; U. of Oklahoma, J.D. 1969.
Occupation: Lawyer.
Family: Wife, Cathy; three children.
Religion: Roman Catholic.
Political Career: Okla. House, 1972-74; Okla. Senate, 1974-81; U.S. attorney for Northern District of Oklahoma, 1981-85; assistant secretary of the Treasury, 1985-88; associate attorney general, 1988-89; acting deputy secretary of the Department of Housing and Urban Development, 1989-93.

Lt. Gov.: Mary Fallin (R)
First elected: 1994
Length of term: 4 years
Term expires: 1/99
Salary: $62,500
Phone: (405) 521-2161

State election official: (405) 521-2391
Democratic headquarters: (405) 239-2700
Republican headquarters: (405) 528-3501

REDISTRICTING

Oklahoma retained its six House seats in reapportionment. The legislature passed the map May 24, 1991; the governor signed it May 27.

STATE LEGISLATURE

Legislature. Meets February-May yearly.

Senate: 48 members, 4-year terms
1996 breakdown: 33D, 15R; 42 men, 6 women
Salary: $32,000
Phone: (405) 524-0126

House of Representatives: 101 members, 2-year terms
1996 breakdown: 65D, 36R; 92 men, 9 women
Salary: $32,000
Phone: (405) 521-2711

URBAN STATISTICS

City	Population
Oklahoma City	444,719
Mayor Ronald J. Norick, N-P	
Tulsa	367,302
Mayor M. Susan Savage, D	
Lawton	80,561
Mayor John T. Marley, N-P	
Norman	80,071
Mayor William Nations, N-P	

U.S. CONGRESS

Senate: 0 D, 2 R
House: 0 D, 6 R

TERM LIMITS

For state offices: Yes
No more than 12 years combined (Senate and/or House) service

ELECTIONS

1996 Presidential Vote

Bob Dole	48%
Bill Clinton	40%
Ross Perot	11%

1992 Presidential Vote

George Bush	43%
Bill Clinton	34%
Ross Perot	23%

1988 Presidential Vote

George Bush	58%
Michael S. Dukakis	41%

POPULATION

1990 population		3,145,585
1980 population		3,025,290
Percent change		+4%
Rank among states:		28
White		82%
Black		7%
Hispanic		3%
Asian or Pacific islander		1%
Urban		68%
Rural		32%
Born in state		63%
Foreign-born		2%
Under age 18	837,007	27%
Ages 18-64	1,884,365	60%
65 and older	424,213	13%
Median age		33.2

MISCELLANEOUS

Capital: Oklahoma City
Number of counties: 77
Per capita income: $15,827 (1991)
Rank among states: 40
Total area: 69,919 sq. miles
Rank among states: 18

OKLAHOMA

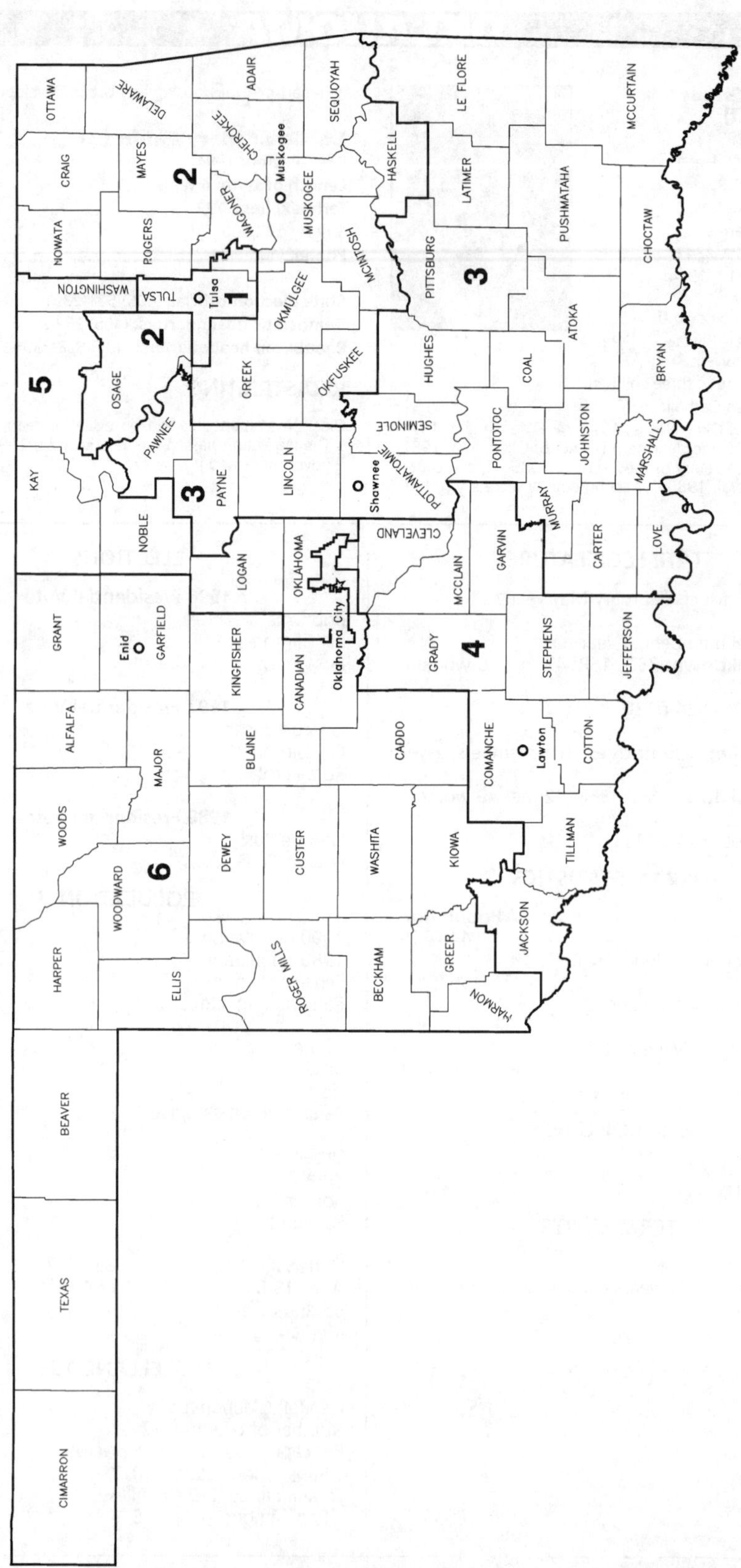
OTTAWA
DELAWARE
ADAIR
SEQUOYAH
LE FLORE
MCCURTAIN
CRAIG
MAYES
CHEROKEE
Muskogee
MUSKOGEE
HASKELL
LATIMER
PUSHMATAHA
NOWATA
ROGERS
WAGONER
MCINTOSH
PITTSBURG
CHOCTAW
WASHINGTON
TULSA
Tulsa
OKMULGEE
ATOKA
OSAGE
CREEK
OKFUSKEE
HUGHES
COAL
BRYAN
PAWNEE
SEMINOLE
PONTOTOC
JOHNSTON
MARSHALL
KAY
PAYNE
LINCOLN
Shawnee
POTTAWATOMIE
MURRAY
NOBLE
LOGAN
OKLAHOMA
CLEVELAND
MCCLAIN
GARVIN
CARTER
LOVE
GRANT
Enid
GARFIELD
KINGFISHER
CANADIAN
Oklahoma City
GRADY
STEPHENS
JEFFERSON
ALFALFA
MAJOR
BLAINE
CADDO
COMANCHE
Lawton
COTTON
WOODS
DEWEY
CUSTER
WASHITA
KIOWA
TILLMAN
WOODWARD
HARPER
ELLIS
ROGER MILLS
BECKHAM
GREER
JACKSON
HARMON
BEAVER
TEXAS
CIMARRON
1
2
2
3
3
4
5
6

Don Nickles (R)

Of Punca City — Elected 1980, 3rd term

Biographical Information
Born: Dec. 6, 1948, Ponca City, Okla.
Education: Oklahoma State U., B.B.A. 1971.
Military Service: National Guard, 1970-76.
Occupation: Machine company executive.
Family: Wife, Linda Morrison; four children.
Religion: Christian.
Political Career: Okla. Senate, 1979-81.
Capitol Office: 133 Hart Bldg. 20510; 224-5754.

Committees
Budget
Energy & Natural Resources
Energy Research, Development, Production & Regulation (chairman); National Parks, Historic Preservation & Recreation
Finance
Health Care; Social Security & Family Policy; Taxation & IRS Oversight (chairman)
Governmental Affairs
International Security, Proliferation & Federal Services; Investigations
Rules & Administration
Assistant Majority Leader

In Washington: Nickles, with his youthful vigor and staunchly conservative opinions, entered the Senate in 1981 as a rising star of the Republican right. And rise he did, chairing the party's senatorial campaign committee for the 1990 elections, winning the job of Policy Committee chairman in fall 1990 and stepping into the party's No. 2 job of majority whip in 1996.

Although not viewed as one of the Senate's master legislators, Nickles has won the trust and good will of many Republicans, which helps explain his steady progress on the leadership ladder.

But no portrait of Nickles can be complete without considering the career of an even stronger Republican comer — Mississippi Sen. Trent Lott. The two conservatives have similar views and their ascendancy has paralleled the rise of a young generation of conservative activists. But along the way, Lott shouldered past Nickles, becoming majority whip in December 1994 and then taking the leader's job after Bob Dole left the Senate in June 1996 to campaign for president. Nickles wanted to run for majority leader, but sizing up his prospects against Lott, he decided to try for the whip slot instead.

"It was possible to win the leader's job," he said. "It was more probable to win at whip." He took that post with no opposition.

With Lott and Nickles in the No. 1 and No. 2 positions, conservatives in the 105th Congress enjoy a forceful lock on the Senate GOP hierarchy.

As the only member of the Republican leadership on the Governmental Affairs Committee, Nickles was drawn into a key role in the committee's investigation of campaign fundraising that was sure to preoccupy the 105th Congress.

Though committee Chairman Fred Thompson of Tennessee was willing to conduct broad hearings into congressional as well as presidential fundraising, Nickles was intent on keeping the probe focused on the White House and the Democratic National Committee. He strongly opposed Democratic subpoenas aimed at such groups as the Christian Coalition and the National Right to Life Committee.

"We need to find out who is breaking the law in the last election cycle. There's allegations of very serious improprieties by the administration, by the Democratic National Committee," he told a television interviewer in March. "I don't think we should be on, you know, a witch hunt, trying to dig up something."

Nevertheless, Nickles is aware that on some issues, political realities can dictate a course of compromise. The GOP's image took a beating in the budget wars of the 104th Congress, as the conservatives' strategy of trying to bully Clinton into an agreement on their terms yielded a partial government shutdown that the public blamed on Republican intransigence. With Clinton back for a second term in 1997, Nickles joined other Republicans who gritted their teeth in anticipation of giving some ground on the budget. "We don't have any choice but to work with" Clinton, said Nickles, using the exact same words as fellow conservative Sen. Phil Gramm, R-Texas, during a hearing on the budget early in the 105th.

Nickles is an approachable figure who combines boyish looks with a friendly and even-tempered disposition. But his easygoing manner belies a fierce conservatism on many issues. He is an advocate of cutting the federal budget and barring tax increases while maintaining substantial funding for the military. He has been at the forefront of efforts in the Senate to block government funding for abortions, and he favors a constitutional amendment outlawing abortion. He played a pivotal role in the 104th in the debate over funding abortions for federal workers under federal health care plans. Nickles supported House-passed language that would have banned federal funding of abortions except when the life of the woman was at stake. After objections from other Republicans, he won an amendment that added funding in cases of rape or incest. He successfully fought off an amendment allowing abortions "determined to be medically necessary," arguing that it would permit abortions on demand.

In early 1995, Nickles called on the White House to withdraw the nomination of Dr. Henry W. Foster Jr., Clinton's choice to replace Dr. Joycelyn Elders as surgeon general, in the wake of disclosures that Foster had performed abortions when he was a practicing obstetrician and gynecologist and did research on drugs that induce abortions. Nickles also accused Foster of trying to mislead Congress about his record by saying he had performed fewer abortions than records showed. Douglas Johnson, legislative director of the National Right to Life Committee, said Nickles was able to tap the resources of the Policy Committee to help collect and disseminate information about Foster's record that was used in the successful floor fight against the nomination.

He had led the charge in 1993 against the confirmation of Elders. Many conservatives were troubled by Elders' outspoken views on sex education and birth control, and when they organized a campaign against her, Nickles was ready to lead the Senate blocking maneuvers. He used procedural tactics to delay Elders' confirmation hearing, and later a Senate floor vote. Although Elders eventually won confirmation, she remained controversial and was eventually forced out of the position in late 1994.

Nickles serves on the Finance Committee, and his conservatism extends to fiscal issues as well. He supports budget cuts, a balanced-budget constitutional amendment and a presidential line-item veto, and he generally opposes tax increases. He is one of the most vocal critics of the earned-income tax credit (EITC) and worked during the 104th Congress to cut it back. "The credit is growing like Topsy," said Nickles of the EITC, designed as an incentive to get low-income workers to stay on the job and off welfare. "The EITC is not a tax cut. It is the federal government's fastest growing and most fraud-prone welfare program."

A former business executive, Nickles stands out as a supporter of business interests. He was a determined opponent of increasing the minimum wage, one of the Democrats' top legislative priorities of 1996. Shortly after his election to the whip's post, Nickles made it clear that he and fellow conservatives were more than willing to sacrifice the small-business tax cuts that accompanied the wage increase bill passed by the House. When the wage bill finally passed the Senate, Nickles infuriated Democrats by threatening to block appointment of senators to a House-Senate conference until Democrats stopped blocking a conference on a Republican health care bill. The threat also bothered some Republicans, who thought the party had caught enough rhetorical flak over its reluctance to raise the wage.

Nickles was coordinator of the Senate GOP's regulatory overhaul efforts in the 104th. He originally backed a temporary moratorium on all new federal regulations. But Democrats threatened a filibuster, and Nickles looked instead for a substitute that could gain bipartisan support. He settled on a 45-day congressional review of new regulations, reviving the concept of the legislative veto. The bill passed on a 100-0 vote.

His ability to compromise is evident as Nickles joined Lott and several Finance Committee Democrats on a bill that would reduce the federal estate tax. Lott and many other conservatives would like to eliminate the tax altogether, but they concede that that goal is unrealistic.

"It's one of the most unfair, one of the most punitive taxes we have on the code today," Nickles said at a news conference when the bill was introduced. "It makes it very, very difficult, if you want to build a business or pass on a farm or a ranch to second and third generations."

As whip, Nickles has continued a practice that Lott favored during his time in the post: Twelve deputy whips are responsible for using printed cards to keep tabs on how five or six Republicans will vote on close issues.

On one major issue early in the 105th Congress, however, even his whip organization sharply divided — ratification of a treaty banning chemical weapons. Nickles and five of his deputies voted against the treaty; seven others, including chief deputy whip Judd Gregg of New Hampshire, voted for it. The issue similarly split the party's elected leadership — only Lott voted for the treaty.

Like most members from the "energy belt," Nickles backs most priorities of the oil, gas and nuclear power industries. As chairman of the Energy Research, Development, Production and Regulation Subcommittee of the Energy and Natural Resources Committee, he will be involved in the debate on electric power deregulation, a major issue facing the 105th Congress.

He is a fighter for home state oil and gas interests. In 1992, he successfully battled a proposal to make oil refiners supply a certain percentage of so-called alternative fuels, such as ethanol and methanol. The following year, combining his instincts on energy and taxes, he was a leading opponent of the 4.3-cents-per-gallon increase in the gasoline tax. That increase is once again a topic of debate, with members of both parties calling for an election-year repeal.

Nickles' election to the GOP leadership in the 102nd had been part of a move by younger Senate conservatives to increase their role in setting the party's legislative agenda: He defeated the more senior, and on some issues more moderate, Sen. Pete V. Domenici of New Mexico by a 23-20 vote in the Republican Conference.

Previously, Nickles had served as chairman of the National Republican Senatorial Committee during the 1990 election cycle. Although the GOP suffered a net loss of one seat in that cycle, his election to leadership indicated that Nickles was not held personally responsible, at least not by his fellow conservatives.

At Home: Nickles began his 1992 re-election campaign as a strong favorite, and he retained that status throughout, eventually winning by 21 percentage points over former state House Speaker Steve Lewis.

Lewis was a credible opponent. He had won statewide notice for steering through the Legislature a landmark education and tax reform bill. In 1990, he had run a close third in the Democratic gubernatorial primary. But Nickles raised more than twice as much money as Lewis, and the challenger was never able to dent the incumbent's popularity. Nickles became the only Republican in Oklahoma history ever elected to a third Senate term. And his 59 percent tally had been topped by a Republican Senate candidate only once before, in 1924, by William B. Pine.

Nickles had shown similar strength in winning his second term in 1986. When that campaign began, Nickles was regarded as one of the most vulnerable Republicans facing re-election. He had been aided in 1980 by Ronald Reagan's coattails. And unlike his first contest, in which he defeated former Oklahoma City District Attorney Andy Coats, this one presented him with a formidable Democratic opponent: 1st District Rep. James R. Jones.

Some of Nickles' media efforts were aimed at reinforcing his conservative, clean-cut image, but the core of his campaign was a series of ads portraying Jones as a liberal and accusing him of persistently voting for congressional pay raises. Jones did not respond immediately to Nickles.

But with polls indicating that the liberal label was sticking, Jones attempted to refute Nickles' claims. He cited House vote studies that placed him as a Democratic moderate and quoted Washington sources who said Nickles was distorting Jones' record.

But Jones' delayed reaction to Nickles' attacks placed him on the defensive during the crucial late weeks of the campaign. Nickles won with a solid 55 percent of the vote.

After a brief stint in the state Legislature, Nickles in 1980 became the youngest member of the Senate. He had been active in Republican politics for several years, but not until 1978 did he run for public office, winning a seat in the state Senate. Just two years later, he entered the 1980 Republican primary to replace retiring GOP Sen. Henry Bellmon.

Nickles' calls for a return to traditional family values drew a favorable response from Oklahoma's large evangelical community. Boosted by organizational support from conservative Christian groups, Nickles startled political observers by topping a five-man field in the GOP primary and then winning the runoff in a walk.

The general election pitted Nickles against Coats, whose role in the prosecution of a famous Oklahoma City murder case made his name a household word in central Oklahoma. But Coats was on the defensive much of the time, seeking to convince voters that he was not a closet liberal, as Nickles alleged.

Nickles' organization mounted successful voter registration drives to shore up Republican strength and helped spread his conservative themes to sympathetic Democrats. Aided by Reagan's strong showing in the state, Nickles won with 54 percent of the vote.

SENATE ELECTIONS

1992 General

Don Nickles (R)	757,876	(59%)
Steve Lewis (D)	494,350	(38%)
Roy V. Edwards (I)	21,225	(2%)
Thomas D. Ledgerwood II (I)	20,972	(2%)

Previous Winning Percentages: 1986 (55%) **1980** (54%)

CAMPAIGN FINANCE

	Receipts	Receipts from PACs	Expend-itures
1992			
Nickles (R)	$3,235,075	$1,148,233 (35%)	$3,316,336
Lewis (D)	$1,456,533	$274,668 (19%)	$1,455,848

KEY VOTES

1997	
Approve balanced-budget constitutional amendment	Y
Approve chemical weapons treaty	N
1996	
Approve farm bill	Y
Limit punitive damages in product liability cases	Y
Exempt small businesses from higher minimum wage	Y
Approve welfare overhaul	Y
Bar job discrimination based on sexual orientation	N
Override veto of ban on "partial birth" abortions	Y
1995	
Approve GOP budget with tax and spending cuts	Y
Approve constitutional amendment barring flag desecration	Y

VOTING STUDIES

	Presidential Support		Party Unity		Conservative Coalition	
Year	**S**	**O**	**S**	**O**	**S**	**O**
1996	34	66	99	1	97	3
1995	22	78	97	2	93	7
1994	24	73	92	6	88	13
1993	18	81	94	5	85	12
1992	77	20	90	5	87	11
1991	89	9	88	9	93	8

INTEREST GROUP RATINGS

Year	ADA	AFL-CIO	CCUS	ACU
1996	0	n/a	100	100
1995	0	0	100	100
1994	5	0	90	100
1993	5	0	91	96
1992	0	8	89	96
1991	0	25	100	95

James M. Inhofe (R)

Of Tulsa — Elected 1994; 1st full term

Appointed to the Senate 1994.

Biographical Information

Born: Nov. 17, 1934, Des Moines, Iowa.
Education: U. of Tulsa, B.A. 1973.
Military Service: Army, 1954-56.
Occupation: Real estate developer; insurance executive.
Family: Wife, Kay Kirkpatrick; four children.
Religion: Presbyterian.
Political Career: Okla. House, 1967-69; Okla. Senate, 1969-77; Republican nominee for governor, 1974; Republican nominee for U.S. House, 1976; mayor of Tulsa, 1978-84; defeated for re-election as mayor of Tulsa, 1984; U.S. House, 1987-94.
Capitol Office: 453 Russell Bldg. 20510; 224-4721.

Committees

Armed Services
Airland Forces; Readiness (chairman); Strategic Forces
Environment & Public Works
Clean Air, Wetlands, Private Property & Nuclear Safety (chairman); Superfund, Waste Control & Risk Assessment; Transportation & Infrastructure
Indian Affairs
Select Intelligence

In Washington: As a newly minted senator accustomed to the partisan trench warfare he waged for nine years in the House, conservative activist Inhofe at first chafed at the Senate's more deliberate pace. He soon learned that it can be ground to a standstill by a determined minority.

Frustrated over the power of the Democratic minority to derail the "Contract With America" legislation sent over from the hard-charging new GOP majority in the House, Inhofe complained in 1995 that despite Republicans' commitment to "a revolution in this country, in the Senate you can't do it with just a majority; it takes 60 votes."

But no one could accuse Inhofe of not doing his part: In the 104th Congress, he voted the party line on major initiatives 100 percent of the time, on issues such as the balanced-budget constitutional amendment, term limits, banning so-called partial birth abortions and the assault weapons ban.

In some cases, Inhofe joined forces with like-minded colleagues to offer conservative alternatives to legislation under consideration. He supported the tougher welfare overhaul proposal that would have denied benefits to unwed teenage mothers offered by Phil Gramm, R-Texas, and Lauch Faircloth, R-N.C., as an alternative to Senate Finance Committee bill in May 1995.

In what the Oklahoma City Sunday Oklahoman called "perhaps his finest hour," Inhofe led a splinter group of Republicans who broke with then-Majority Leader Bob Dole, R-Kan., and opposed President Clinton's plan to send 20,000 American ground troops to Bosnia in December 1995 to enforce a Balkan peace pact.

But the effort failed as the Senate voted 47-52 against the resolution Inhofe and Kay Bailey Hutchison, R-Texas, offered opposing Clinton's decision to dispatch the troops, and rejected, 22-77, Inhofe's effort to bar funds for the mission.

A staunchly pro-defense lawmaker whose state has several military installations, Inhofe is a vigorous proponent of creating a national missile defense system. From his seat in the 104th Congress on the Armed Services Committee he urged the Pentagon to move ahead with building a regional missile defense system. In the 105th Congress, he was named chairman of the panel's readiness subcommittee, where he oversees issues affecting Oklahoma's military bases.

A former businessman who worked in aviation, real estate and insurance, Inhofe gets the opportunity in the 105th Congress to frame the highly charged debate over stricter new air quality standards proposed in November 1996 by the Environmental Protection Agency. He is chairman of the Clean Air, Wetlands, Private Property and Nuclear Safety Subcommittee of the Environment and Public Works Committee.

Inhofe's subcommittee opened the 105th delving into what he and other critics have characterized as the faulty science behind the proposed standards and the burdens they could impose on state and local governments.

At Home: Inhofe's fiery conservatism has made him a hero to Tulsa's hard-core conservatives, including important energy interests and religious fundamentalists. That loyalty was enough to help him through a controversial mayoral career and four close House elections, but it did not look sufficient to sustain a statewide campaign — until 1994.

That was when Republicans enjoyed perhaps their best year ever in the Sooner State, electing a governor and a 5-1 majority in the House. The crowning glory was Inhofe's 15 percentage point rout of Democratic Rep. Dave McCurdy to succeed retiring Democratic Sen. David L. Boren.

A licensed commercial pilot, Inhofe has experienced turbulence in his political and professional life. He was a veteran of the Oklahoma Legislature but lost a 1974 campaign for governor (won by Boren) and a 1976 campaign for Congress before being elected mayor of Tulsa in 1978. He served three two-year terms as mayor before losing a re-election bid in an upset in 1984, then bounced back just two years later to win election to the House district dominated by Tulsa.

In 1988, his campaign for re-election was complicated when he sued his brother over a stock sale involving the family insurance business. In 1992 there was more litigation and a court-ordered payment to the Federal Deposit Insurance Corporation of $588,238. In four House campaigns in the state's most Republican district, Inhofe never got more than 56 percent of the vote.

Inhofe made perhaps the biggest splash of his career in 1993 by leading the effort to loosen rules governing the discharge of bills from committee. Previously, members who signed a discharge petition were not publicly identified until a House majority had signed. Inhofe argued that this arrangement made it easier for the Democratic leadership to pressure members not to sign petitions. When the rules were changed, independent presidential aspirant Ross Perot appeared at a news conference praising Inhofe and being photographed with him. Not many weeks later, Inhofe launched his first statewide race in 20 years.

McCurdy had been the favorite since Boren announced he would leave in midterm to become president of the University of Oklahoma. McCurdy fit the general mold of conservative Democratic politics, equal parts populist and business-friendly, and his bid discouraged virtually all would-be rivals in the Democratic Party.

But in all his years of positioning, McCurdy had made one error that turned out to be fatal. He became associated with Bill Clinton, largely because both were leaders in the centrist Democratic Leadership Council (DLC). And McCurdy supported Clinton's presidential campaign and some of his White House initiatives.

That facilitated the Republican strategy, which was to run the 1994 Senate race as a referendum on Clinton. No matter what McCurdy said about having differences with the president, Inhofe could top it. Inhofe had opposed virtually every move Clinton had made and could recite the list.

McCurdy tried to chip away at Inhofe's integrity by making an issue of a fine that Inhofe had paid on a 1986 election law violation. Inhofe also had to overcome disclosures that he graduated from college 14 years later than he had claimed. But nothing seemed to matter except the big Republican tide and the TV ads that showed McCurdy's face changing into Clinton's.

Inhofe continued to benefit from the crushing defeat he delivered to McCurdy when he ran for re-election to a full six-year term in 1996; strong Democratic opposition did not emerge.

Inhofe was further helped by the national Democratic Party's early decision to back James Sears Bryant, a wealthy sports attorney and former state representative. But Bryant ran into controversy when a radio station reported that his law firm owed $210,000 in unpaid taxes, and he dropped out of the Democratic primary race.

That cleared the way for Jim Boren, a political scientist, humorist and cousin of the former senator, to claim the Democratic nomination. He did not go quietly, but he went nonetheless, losing by 17 percentage points.

SENATE ELECTIONS

1996 General		
James M. Inhofe (R)	670,610	(57%)
Jim Boren (D)	474,162	(40%)
Bill Maguire (I)	15,092	(1%)
Agnes Marie Regier (LIBERT)	14,595	(1%)
1996 Primary		
James M. Inhofe (R)	116,241	(75%)
Dan Lowe (R)	38,044	(25%)

Previous Winning Percentages: 1994† (55%) **1992*** (53%) **1990*** (56%) **1988*** (53%) **1986*** (55%)

† *Special election*
* *House elections*

KEY VOTES

1997	
Approve balanced-budget constitutional amendment	Y
Approve chemical weapons treaty	N
1996	
Approve farm bill	Y
Limit punitive damages in product liability cases	Y
Exempt small businesses from higher minimum wage	Y
Approve welfare overhaul	Y
Bar job discrimination based on sexual orientation	N
Override veto of ban on "partial birth" abortions	Y
1995	
Approve GOP budget with tax and spending cuts	Y
Approve constitutional amendment barring flag desecration	Y

CAMPAIGN FINANCE

	Receipts	Receipts from PACs	Expend-itures
1996			
Inhofe (R)	$2,706,849	$1,117,944 (41%)	$2,510,946
Boren (D)	$312,183	0	$311,171

VOTING STUDIES

Year	Presidential Support S	Presidential Support O	Party Unity S	Party Unity O	Conservative Coalition S	Conservative Coalition O
1996	27	71	99	0	95	3
1995	24	75	96	2	91	9
1994	0†	100†	0†	0†	0†	0†
House Service:						
1994	40†	49†	88†	1†	89	3
1993	30	68	94	3	93	7
1992	81	17	92	4	92	4
1991	68	27	90	6	97	3

† *Not eligible for all recorded votes.*

INTEREST GROUP RATINGS

Year	ADA	AFL-CIO	CCUS	ACU
1996	0	n/a	100	100
1995	0	0	100	100
1994	0	0	0	0
House Service:				
1994	0	0	0	100
1993	10	8	91	100
1992	10	36	75	96
1991	5	9	90	100

1 Steve Largent (R)

Of Tulsa — Elected 1994; 2nd full term

Biographical Information

Born: Sept. 28, 1955, Tulsa, Okla.
Education: U. of Tulsa, B.S. 1976.
Occupation: Marketing consultant; professional football player.
Family: Wife, Terry; four children.
Religion: Protestant.
Political Career: No previous office.
Capitol Office: 426 Cannon Bldg. 20515; 225-2211.

Committees

Commerce
Energy & Power; Finance & Hazardous Materials; Telecommunications, Trade & Consumer Protection

In Washington: With a background in professional football and a keen interest in fiscal policy, Largent calls to mind another Republican who graduated from the gridiron to politics, serving first in Congress, then the Cabinet and in 1996 receiving his party's vice presidential nomination. Indeed, before Jack F. Kemp got the nod to run on the GOP ticket with Bob Dole, some of Largent's House freshman colleagues were talking up the telegenic young Oklahoman for the No. 2 spot.

One difference between Largent and Kemp is Largent's close identification with conservative Christian activists in the GOP. A Bible Belt product, Largent capitalized on his fame as a wide receiver for the Seattle Seahawks to promote the "family values" he holds. In Congress, Largent pursues both economic and social policy interests, rising one day to call for reforms in the budget process and the next to denounce same-sex marriages, proclaiming that "No culture that has embraced homosexuality has ever survived."

Largent has snagged some prize committee assignments — a seat on the Budget Committee in his first term and on Commerce in his second. He serves on Commerce's Energy and Power Subcommittee, which in the 105th is wrestling with the issue of deregulating the electric utility industry.

The Commerce plum came Largent's way even though he has had some differences with GOP elders. Approaching the January 1997 vote on re-electing Newt Gingrich, R-Ga., as House Speaker, Largent was among several Republicans who expressed reservations about supporting Gingrich until ethics charges against him were settled. In late 1996 on the Fox television network, Largent responded to a question about the possibility of Illinois Republican Henry J. Hyde being elected Speaker by saying that such a scenario would allow House Republicans "to work more constructively."

Gingrich called Largent to have a few words, and Largent subsequently said he was caught off-guard by the interviewer's question and did not mean to imply he would not support Gingrich for Speaker. Largent did vote for Gingrich, but didn't seem very happy about it. He told the Tulsa World: "It's a lose-lose situation, no matter what you do." Gingrich was later reprimanded by the House and assessed a $300,000 penalty for violating ethics rules. Largent backed the reprimand.

Gingrich's ethical troubles seemed to distract GOP leaders early in the 105th, prompting Largent to complain that the House lacked a clear legislative agenda. "The last two years they beat us to death. This year they are boring us to death," Largent told The Atlanta Journal and Constitution in February 1997. "We don't have a bold game plan.... You just get this creeping feeling that either people were not very serious about the 'Contract With America' and the 1994 election or we're somehow sliding back to where we came in."

In the 104th Congress, when Largent was on the Budget Committee, he often did not concur with his party's leadership on key budget votes. In early January 1996 he was one of 15 Republicans who defied Gingrich's directive to vote to end a partial closure of the federal government. The shutdown stemmed from the late 1995 impasse in budget talks between Congress and the White House. GOP leaders came to worry that the public was blaming Republicans for the standoff, but Largent and his allies wanted to hold out longer, hoping to force President Clinton to agree to a balanced budget on GOP terms.

An exasperated Gingrich then canceled appearances at fundraisers for several of the freshmen who had voted against him, and a public spat ensued. Some of the freshmen whom Gingrich stiffed asked Largent to be their stand-in guest, and thanks in part to his "star quality" from sports — he is in the professional football Hall of Fame — Largent proved to be a good draw.

In June 1996, Largent voted "no" on the final version of the fiscal 1997 GOP budget agreement, complaining that it showed a short-term increase in the deficit and included $4 billion in extra domestic spending. Largent was among 19

OKLAHOMA 1
Tulsa; part of Wagoner County

The precipitous fall of oil prices from the early to mid-1980s had a resounding impact on the city that not long ago was calling itself "The Oil Capital of the World." But by diversifying its economy, Tulsa has rebounded, propelled by its thriving aerospace and aviation industries.

American Airlines is the city's largest employer, providing about 10,000 jobs. American's national headquarters for flight reservations is in Tulsa, and the company's maintenance depot is at Tulsa International Airport. Tulsa also is a deepwater port accessible to the Gulf of Mexico, a status it gained in 1971 with the opening of the Arkansas River Navigation System.

McDonnell Douglas Corp. and Boeing North American (formerly Rockwell International) are leading companies in Tulsa, although the receding defense budget has curtailed their expansion. Together, they employ about 2,000.

Tulsa has become a manufacturing hub of flight simulators for military and civilian use. With several technical schools and aviation academies, it also has developed a worldwide reputation as an aviation training center.

Once a post office on the Pony Express trail, Tulsa was transformed by the discovery of oil nearby in 1901 and 1905. Oil drove Tulsa's economic development until the last decade. The repercussions of the 1980s price drop can be seen in the grand estates in southeast Tulsa, whose values plummeted with the oil fortunes that built them.

But with the local economy on the mend, real estate prices are beginning to rise. Young professionals are moving into some of the older, established neighborhoods in the central section of the city and are renovating single-family homes.

Tulsa was a forerunner in the trend of Sun Belt cities evolving into Republican-voting bastions. Tulsa County has gone Republican in all but two presidential elections since 1920. North Tulsa's predominantly black neighborhoods provide Democrats with their best turf.

But Tulsa's conservatism differs from Oklahoma City's more viscerally anti-government brand. Tulsa, for example, strongly backed a landmark 1990 education and tax reform law. That year, Democratic gubernatorial nominee David Walters crushed his conservative GOP opponent, who sought the law's repeal. In 1991, a ballot measure to repeal the law lost in Tulsa County by more than 2-to-1.

Tulsa's fundamentalist community is in the east, anchored by Oral Roberts University (3,600 students), a tourist attraction. Its 200-foot glass and steel prayer tower and 60-foot bronze "Praying Hands" sculpture are big draws.

Southeast of Tulsa, the 1st takes in the city of Broken Arrow, home to many Tulsa workers who commute via the Broken Arrow Expressway. Broken Arrow also has a sizable fundamentalist community. In 1970, Broken Arrow had fewer than 12,000 people; its population now tops 58,000.

1990 Population: 524,264. White 436,341 (83%), Black 50,149 (10%), Other 37,774 (7%). Hispanic origin 12,288 (2%). 18 and over 386,158 (74%), 62 and over 72,438 (14%). Median age: 33.

Republicans who voted against the plan, which passed only narrowly, 216-211.

And in September 1996, he was among 24 Republicans voting against a $610 billion omnibus spending bill that funded nine Cabinet departments and numerous agencies for fiscal 1997. Deficit hawks said the huge bill was larded with unnecessary spending, but most GOP lawmakers wanted a deal with Clinton so they could adjourn Congress and hit the campaign trail.

Although Largent backed most efforts to cut federal spending, he opposed one cut that hit close to home. He voted against an amendment to the fiscal 1997 interior spending bill that would have cut more than $130 million in federal funding for fossil energy research. Oklahoma is home to numerous oil and natural gas producers, and Largent rejected the argument that fossil energy research is a form of "corporate welfare." He told the House that the people that benefit from such research and development are "the marginal well, the stripper well, the producer, the mom-and-pop operation, the rancher, the farmer." The House agreed, rejecting the amendment, 196-224.

Largent's biggest splash in the social policy realm came in 1996, when Congress enacted legislation he supported that barred federal recognition of same-sex marriages. The impetus for the measure was a court case in Hawaii involving three homosexual couples suing for the right to marry, citing a sexual discrimination clause in the state's constitution. The bill also shielded states from having to recognize same-sex marriages sanctioned by any other state. Arguing that marriage should be the "exclusive territory" of monogamous heterosexual couples, Largent said that homosexuals' efforts to marry "may eventually be the final blow to the American family."

Earlier in the 104th, Largent teamed with Mississippi Republican Mike Parker to propose a "parental rights" bill designed to give parents more control — and the government less — over major decisions in their children's lives. Among the parental rights protected under the bill were home education, medical decisions and corporal punishment. The measure, however, drew fire from all sides. Child advocacy groups worried that it would make it more difficult to intervene in cases of suspected child abuse, and opponents of abortion feared the measure would allow parents to compel their daughters to have abortions.

An unwavering supporter of the "Contract With America," Largent voted for regulatory reform, an overhaul of the welfare system, tax cuts, constitutional amendments on term limits and a balanced budget. He also opposed a minimum wage increase. Like many of his 1994 classmates, Largent believes he must change the government before it changes him. He once said he would like his political epitaph to read: "Brilliant but Brief."

At Home: Though Largent's 1994 House campaign was his first bid for public office, he started building relationships with conservative political and business leaders even before his 1989 retirement from professional football.

Largent got to know Jack Kemp through Kemp's son Jeff, who was once the Seattle Seahawks' quarterback. Largent held fundraisers for state politicians in his native Tulsa, where he played college football in the mid-1970s. And when 1st District GOP Rep. James M. Inhofe decided to run for the Senate in 1994, GOP Sen. Don Nickles urged Largent to go for the 1st.

Other Republican hopefuls sniped at Largent's money-raising techniques, which included a pair of fundraisers in Seattle. Tulsa County Clerk Joan King Hastings, one of five others in the GOP primary, suggested that Largent run for Congress in Washington State. But none of this had an appreciable impact on Largent. While his ties to conservative Christian groups drew notice, all the candidates took socially conservative stands. Largent won nomination with 51 percent of the vote.

In the general election, Largent faced a well-financed and well-organized Democrat, Tulsa oilman Stuart Price. He attempted to overcome Largent's lead in name recognition through early and extensive television advertising. Liberal-minded women's groups and public-education advocates sided with Price, repulsed by Largent's anti-abortion position, his opposition to a Tulsa school bond issue and his support for tuition vouchers. Price tried to cast a negative light on Largent's religious beliefs, noting that Largent had referred to opponents of conservative religious activism as "the enemy" during a prayer breakfast.

But Price was dragged down by virulent anti-Clinton sentiment among voters. Price had served as state finance chairman for Clinton's 1992 presidential campaign. The Largent campaign hit Price for his support of abortion rights, and a Largent campaign official told reporters at one event that Price "supports homosexual rights." In the end it was a runaway, with Largent rolling up 63 percent. He improved on that in his 1996 re-election.

Largent was sworn into the House on Nov. 29, 1994, filling the seat Inhofe left early to join the Senate, where Democrat David L. Boren had resigned Nov. 15. Largent actually cast a vote in the 103rd Congress — opposing GATT — and his first floor speech came with outgoing Democratic Speaker Thomas S. Foley in the chair.

HOUSE ELECTIONS

1996 General		
Steve Largent (R)	143,415	(68%)
Randolph John Amen (D)	57,996	(28%)
Karla Condray (I)	8,996	(4%)
1994 General		
Steve Largent (R)	107,085	(63%)
Stuart Price (D)	63,753	(37%)

CAMPAIGN FINANCE

	Receipts	Receipts from PACs	Expend-itures
1996			
Largent (R)	$423,759	$157,547 (37%)	$345,612
Amen (D)	$8,785	0	$9,377
1994			
Largent (R)	$661,081	$153,476 (23%)	$610,211
Price (D)	$547,239	$53,550 (10%)	$546,570

VOTING STUDIES

	Presidential Support		Party Unity		Conservative Coalition	
Year	S	O	S	O	S	O
1996	29	68	92	4	88	8
1995	15	83	92	3	87	10
1994†	0	100	-	-	-	-

† Largent was sworn in Nov. 29, 1994. He was eligible for one presidential support vote, no party unity votes and no conservative coalition votes in 1994.

DISTRICT VOTE FOR PRESIDENT

1996		1992	
D	79,518 (37%)	**D**	73,495 (30%)
R	115,997 (54%)	**R**	122,189 (49%)
I	19,087 (9%)	**I**	52,088 (21%)

KEY VOTES

1997	
Ban "partial birth" abortions	Y
1996	
Approve farm bill	Y
Deny public education to illegal immigrants	Y
Repeal ban on certain assault-style weapons	Y
Increase minimum wage	N
Freeze defense spending	N
Approve welfare overhaul	Y
1995	
Approve balanced-budget constitutional amendment	Y
Relax Clean Water Act regulations	Y
Oppose limits on environmental regulations	X
Reduce projected Medicare spending	Y
Approve GOP budget with tax and spending cuts	Y

INTEREST GROUP RATINGS

Year	ADA	AFL-CIO	CCUS	ACU
1996	10	n/a	86	100
1995	0	0	100	100

2 Tom Coburn (R)

Of Muskogee — Elected 1994, 2nd term

Biographical Information
Born: March 14, 1948, Casper, Wyo.
Education: Oklahoma State U., B.S. 1970; Oklahoma U., M.D. 1983.
Occupation: Physician; optical firm manager.
Family: Wife, Carolyn Denton; three children.
Religion: Baptist.
Political Career: No previous office.
Capitol Office: 429 Cannon Bldg. 20515; 225-2701.

Committees
Commerce
Energy & Power; Health & Environment; Oversight & Investigations
Science
Energy & Environment

In Washington: Coburn, who has pledged to serve no more than three terms, appeals to 2nd District voters as a "citizen legislator." Almost without exception, Coburn has emphasized in floor speeches that he lends to policy debates perspective as a physician, and he frequently laments that Washington is a little short on "good old Oklahoma English." Even in the Class of 1994, widely noted for its ideological purity, Coburn has stood out as a vehement defender of fiscal restraint and social conservatism.

Coburn, who sits on the Commerce Committee, knows with assurance the stars that guide his course — but his unyielding stance on issues ranging from AIDS and abortion to broadcast content and drinking water standards have sometimes stirred controversy.

Coburn often fashions himself rhetorically as an emissary from the "real world" that lies beyond the Beltway. During debate on a bill to allow states to reject same-gender marriages, Coburn essayed his district's feelings on the matter, reporting that his constituents believe "homosexuality is immoral, that it is based on perversion, that it is based on lust. . . . It is discrimination towards the act, not towards the individual."

He got himself into some hot water with remarks about the February 1997 broadcast of a widely acclaimed dramatic film about the Holocaust, "Schindler's List," on NBC. Coburn maintained that the broadcast took network television "to an all-time low with full frontal nudity, violence and profanity being shown in our homes." His comments earned the ire even of prominent Republicans, who castigated him for failing to recognize the historical accuracy of the film. Coburn took to the House floor and said, "I feel terrible that my criticism of NBC . . . has been misinterpreted as a criticism of 'Schindler's List' or the millions of Jews who died senselessly during the Holocaust."

The Academy Award-winning film was the first broadcast presentation to receive a TV-M rating — unsuitable for viewers under age 17 — under the broadcast industry's new voluntary ratings system. Finding that system wholly inadequate, Coburn has introduced legislation to impose a content-based ratings system. He opposed a provision in the 1996 telecommunications law to require a "v-chip" in television sets, designed to allow parents to block objectionable programming.

Coburn sponsored an alternative to the v-chip that would have encouraged, but not required, the television and video industries to develop blocking technology, in effect leaving the problems in the hands of the free market. The House accepted his substitute, 222-201, but later voted to require v-chips anyway.

Coburn's opposition to government regulation and intrusion was illustrated most clearly during consideration of an anti-terrorism bill in 1996. Coburn backed a successful amendment offered by Bob Barr, R-Ga., to strip the bill of new law enforcement powers that many members feared would impinge on individual liberty.

"Terrorism in this country obviously poses a serious threat to us as a free society," Coburn acknowledged. "But there is a far greater fear that is present in this country, and that is fear of our own government. . . . We should not do anything to promote further lack of confidence in our own government."

Coburn has devoted much of his energy to social issues, but he has been a persistent deficit hawk as well. He scored political points at home by returning his salary during the partial government shutdowns of 1995 and 1996; but when House GOP leaders came up with a plan to reopen the government, Coburn was one of 15 Republicans to vote against it. House Speaker Newt Gingrich, R-Ga., told the Republican Conference that he needed to give a little in negotiations with President Clinton over a balanced-budget plan, likening the move to using sugar and a stick in training a dog. "Well, this dog's got distemper!" Coburn barked. He was also one of 19 House Republicans to vote against the fiscal 1997 budget resolution.

OKLAHOMA 2
Northeast — Muskogee

The 2nd is Oklahoma's most imaginatively shaped district. It starts in the "Green Country" of northeast Oklahoma, but after curling underneath Tulsa County, it squirms between the 1st and 3rd districts to collect much of rural, Democratic Osage County.

Democrats traditionally have done well here, but in 1994, the GOP tide rolled across the 2nd, and voters elected their first Republican representative since 1920. In 1996, Clinton scored his second consecutive win here, though Democrats failed to dislodge Coburn.

In recent years, tourism and recreation have joined the traditional engines of the 2nd's economy, agriculture and energy. The 2nd has part of the state's largest lake (Eufaula) and takes in several others, including Grand Lake O' the Cherokees, Fort Gibson, Tenkiller and Keystone. Accompanying the growth in the tourism industry has been a wave of retirees moving to the resort areas, where real estate prices are low. The population of Delaware County, which contains most of Grand Lake, grew by 17 percent during the 1980s.

But recreation has not supplanted the more time-honored enterprises. Soybeans, wheat and beef cattle are the district's main agricultural products. Many farmers raise both crops and livestock, helping them weather fluctuations in the farm economy. Eastern counties such as Adair, Delaware and Ottawa feature poultry production; several poultry and meat companies are close by, just over the Arkansas border.

The farm crisis of the 1980s did not spare rural areas in the 2nd. Small towns such as Stigler (Haskell County) suffered the same fate as many other farm state communities, with farm-implement dealers and other agriculture-related businesses struggling and sometimes failing.

Muskogee — with 37,700 people, the 2nd's largest city — dredges silica sand from the Arkansas River beds for use in its glass industry. The Department of Veterans Affairs serves several states from Muskogee.

Two of the 2nd's fastest-growing counties during the 1980s were Wagoner (15 percent) and Rogers (19 percent), which border Tulsa County and are absorbing Tulsa's exurbanization. They are GOP strongholds. Along the 2nd's southern tier, voters resemble their "Little Dixie" neighbors, lending Democrats generous margins.

For many American Indians, northeast Oklahoma was the end of the Trail of Tears — the U.S. Army's forced march in 1838 of Cherokees away from their homes in the Southeast. The largest Indian population in Oklahoma is concentrated within the 2nd's boundaries; the Cherokee Nation has its headquarters in Tahlequah (Cherokee County), and members of other tribes are scattered through surrounding counties.

Humorist Will Rogers, who was part Cherokee, was born near Claremore (Rogers County). His life and works are commemorated at the Will Rogers Memorial and celebrated each November during Will Rogers Days.

1990 Population: 524,264. White 404,216 (77%), Black 26,568 (5%), Other 93,480 (18%). Hispanic origin 5,946 (1%). 18 and over 382,426 (73%), 62 and over 94,676 (18%). Median age: 35.

As the 104th Congress wore on, Coburn acknowledged that in some areas the political winds had shifted against the GOP. During consideration of a safe drinking water bill in 1996, he said, "The political dynamic is, get environmental bills passed so you don't get beat up at home." Coburn, who had supported 1995 efforts to limit the Environmental Protection Agency's (EPA) enforcement powers and to ease federal clean water regulations, offered an amendment to the drinking water bill that would have made it more difficult for the EPA to regulate carcinogenic byproducts of chlorine and other chemicals used to disinfect tap water. Commerce Committee Chairman Thomas J. Bliley Jr., R-Va., feared that Coburn's amendment would unravel a deal carefully worked out with the Senate and helped to kill it in subcommittee.

Coburn was quoted by the Newark Star-Ledger as saying that cryptosporidium, a drinking water pathogen, might be useful in identifying people with compromised immune systems.

In debate on the fiscal 1996 spending bill for the departments of Labor, Health and Human Services and Education, Coburn favored a change in policy to allow federal grants to go to medical schools that have been denied accreditation because they do not provide abortion training. The stricture, Coburn complained, "isn't accreditation for quality medical care. This is social and political engineering. . . . They're trying to provide more abortionists." Coburn argued that abortion training requirements are redundant, since obstetricians and gynecologists are trained to evacuate a womb in case of emergency. On a 235-189 vote, his viewpoint prevailed. Coburn was a founder of the Congressional Family Caucus and is frequently on the floor arguing for passage of a ban on a particular abortion technique that opponents call a "partial-birth" abortion.

On Commerce, Coburn voiced concerns about reauthorizing funding for the federal government's AIDS program. He felt program funds should not go to states without requirements for HIV testing of newborns, or to states that bar insurance companies from not covering AIDS victims. During the conference with the Senate, he helped work out a plan to require mandatory HIV testing if measures included in the Senate version proved ineffective in reducing the incidence of AIDS.

At Home: The 2nd was considered a solidly Democratic seat going into 1994, but Coburn narrowly defeated Virgil R. Cooper, a 71-year-old retired middle school principal who had snitched the Democratic nomination from incumbent Mike Synar in a September runoff.

Media-shy, Cooper spent less than $20,000 in the primary, using no television advertising and no paid staff and campaigning in large part by placing business cards under the wiper blades of parked cars. Cooper's toppling of Synar was a big break for Coburn, a well-funded, well-known family doctor and Sunday school teacher. Though no Republican had represented the district since 1922, GOP recruiters saw Coburn as a dream candidate.

Coburn had never before sought public office, his only previous elected posts being the presidency of both his Oklahoma State University senior class and his University of Oklahoma medical school class. Before becoming a doctor, he ran a small business manufacturing optical supplies. In contrast to the bachelor Synar, Coburn could point to a wife of 25 years and three children. And after setting up his medical practice in Muskogee in 1986, he had made a favorable impression on many locals by delivering more than 3,000 babies. He continues to deliver children during weekend visits to the district.

Coburn got a relatively late start in the race for the Republican nomination — he entered the contest in mid-June — but he managed to raise $85,000 in only five weeks. In the August primary, he handily defeated Jerry Hill, the party's 1992 nominee, and one other candidate. In November, Coburn had to tread lightly around Cooper's folk-hero appeal, but the Democrat was reluctant to appear in head-to-head debate, and Coburn won 52 percent of the voters with a pitch that he would be more adept at articulating the district's views in Washington.

A week before the 1996 primary, Cooper endorsed Coburn for re-election — one of several blows dealt to Democratic challenger Glen D. Johnson, the Speaker of the Oklahoma House. Johnson was highly touted by national Democrats as one of their top recruits, but he failed to catch fire as a candidate outside his state House district.

Johnson tried to portray Coburn as too close to Gingrich and out of step with the district on issues such as Medicare funding. But Coburn had demonstrated his independence with certain votes and was able to cast Johnson as a career politician. Ads run against Coburn by organized labor appeared to backfire and lend credence to his charge that Johnson was a "tax and spend" Democrat of the kind the district had rejected in ousting Synar. Coburn outspent Johnson and every other House candidate in the state on his way to a 10-point margin of victory.

HOUSE ELECTIONS

1996 General		
Tom Coburn (R)	112,273	(55%)
Glen D. Johnson (D)	90,120	(45%)
1994 General		
Tom Coburn (R)	82,479	(52%)
Virgil R. Cooper (D)	75,943	(48%)

CAMPAIGN FINANCE

	Receipts	Receipts from PACs	Expend-itures
1996			
Coburn (R)	$1,452,829	$622,794 (43%)	$1,354,299
Johnson (D)	$1,055,755	$219,945 (21%)	$1,053,616
1994			
Coburn (R)	$608,233	$163,301 (27%)	$604,924
Cooper (D)	$75,200	$18,950 (25%)	$75,202

DISTRICT VOTE FOR PRESIDENT

	1996		1992
D	97,343 (47%)	**D**	96,510 (43%)
R	81,604 (40%)	**R**	81,375 (36%)
I	25,892 (13%)	**I**	49,107 (22%)

KEY VOTES

1997	
Ban "partial birth" abortions	Y
1996	
Approve farm bill	Y
Deny public education to illegal immigrants	Y
Repeal ban on certain assault-style weapons	Y
Increase minimum wage	N
Freeze defense spending	N
Approve welfare overhaul	Y
1995	
Approve balanced-budget constitutional amendment	Y
Relax Clean Water Act regulations	Y
Oppose limits on environmental regulations	N
Reduce projected Medicare spending	Y
Approve GOP budget with tax and spending cuts	Y

VOTING STUDIES

	Presidential Support		Party Unity		Conservative Coalition	
Year	**S**	**O**	**S**	**O**	**S**	**O**
1996	29	71	90	9	82	14
1995	18	80	91	6	86	11

INTEREST GROUP RATINGS

Year	ADA	AFL-CIO	CCUS	ACU
1996	10	n/a	80	89
1995	0	0	96	100

3 Wes Watkins (R)

Of Stillwater — Elected 1996, 9th term

Also served 1977-1990 as a Democrat.

Biographical Information

Born: Dec. 15, 1938, DeQueen, Ark.

Education: Oklahoma State U., B.S. 1960, M.S. 1961.

Military Service: Okla. National Guard, 1971-67..

Occupation: Communications executive; homebuilding contractor; economic developer.

Family: Wife, Lou Rogers; three children.

Religion: Presbyterian.

Political Career: Okla. Senate, 1975-77; U.S. House, 1977-90; candidate for governor, 1990.

Capitol Office: 2312 Rayburn Bldg. 20515; 225-4565.

Committees

Ways & Means
Human Resources; Oversight

The Path to Washington: A longtime Democrat, then an independent and now a Republican, Watkins in 1996 persuaded Oklahomans to give him a second chance in the House seat he held for 13 years. Watkins had served in Congress as a Democrat from 1977 until 1990, succeeding House Speaker Carl Albert when he retired after 30 years in Congress.

When Watkins' former House seat came open in 1996, he switched to the GOP and won it. A grateful House Republican leadership gave Watkins a place on the Ways and Means Committee for the 105th Congress.

Watkins had left Congress to run for governor in 1990, narrowly failing to capture the Democratic nomination. The experience, in which he did not receive the help he counted on from people who owed him political favors, left him embittered about the party.

He supported independent Ross Perot's presidential bid for a brief time in 1992, then made a repeat run for governor as an independent in 1994, again unsuccessfully. He finished with 24 percent, well behind Republican Frank Keating and Democrat Jack Mildren, but he carried his old district and did well enough statewide for some Democrats to blame him for their candidate's defeat.

When Democrat Rep. Bill Brewster, who had succeeded Watkins in the House, announced at the end of 1995 that he would not seek re-election, Watkins appeared to take less time deciding whether to run than in deciding which party he would run with.

Watkins chose the GOP, saying that the national party's positions in favor of gunowners' rights and a balanced-budget amendment to the Constitution suited him best.

"If I were a political opportunist, I would be running as a Democrat," Watkins stated in June 1996. "But the national Democratic Party is controlled by extreme liberals and does not represent Oklahoma's traditional and conservative moral values."

His wife Lou, who represented Oklahoma on the Democratic National Committee for four years, has followed Watkins in his party peregrinations.

During his previous House tenure, Watkins was always more concerned with the needs of his district than with questions of party loyalty. Although he held a position in the House Democratic leadership as an assistant party whip and a member of the Steering and Policy Committee, Watkins' interest in national issues was secondary to his strong devotion to directing federal resources to his district.

Watkins is the product of a classic "Okie" Depression childhood; his family traveled west three times from neighboring Arkansas to California before he was 10 years old.

During a decade on the House Appropriations Committee, Watkins inserted uncounted earmarks into spending bills to benefit his hard-scrabble district. Two of his pet projects were fingered by the Reagan administration in a 1988 list of "pork" cited as evidence of the need for a presidential line-item veto.

Among his many projects were advanced technology and international trade centers at Oklahoma State University, his alma mater and former employer. His ties to Payne County (Stillwater), home of the university, helped him carry the district in 1996. Although his Democratic opponent, state Sen. Darryl Roberts, carried the majority of the district's counties, Watkins won big where it counted, in the more populous counties in the north end of the district.

The district's core, "Little Dixie," was thought to be an unshakable bastion of Democratic support. Roberts, a former prosecutor and Vietnam veteran, centered his campaign on party loyalty, contending that voters confused by Watkins' party affiliations could not count on him to maintain consistent positions. But Watkins held insurmountable advantages in fundraising and name recognition, and he polled 51 percent to return to office and guarantee the Oklahoma GOP its first ever all-Republican congressional delegation.

OKLAHOMA 3
Southeast — "Little Dixie"

The only district in the state that lacks a major urban area, the 3rd sprawls across southeastern Oklahoma, with a three-county appendage on its northern end. The largest city in the 3rd, Stillwater (Payne County) has 36,700 people. Only two other cities in the district, Shawnee (Pottawatomie) and Ardmore (Carter), have more than 20,000 people.

Oklahoma's southeastern district historically has been its most reliably Democratic. Since Oklahoma became a state in 1907, the "Little Dixie" region had not elected a Republican to the House until 1996, when it elected Watkins, who formerly represented the district as a Democrat.

The area was settled largely by migrants from Texas and Arkansas, and its voters are conservative "yellow dog" Democrats. The 3rd was one of two Oklahoma districts Bill Clinton won in 1992 and 1996. But Republican Sen. James M. Inhofe scored a narrow victory here in his successful 1996 bid for a full term.

In elections for offices below the presidency, most voters in the 3rd harbor little sympathy for the GOP. The most reliable territory for a Republican is along the district's northern corridor, which has more in common with more Republican northern Oklahoma than with Little Dixie. Bob Dole in 1996 won just three of the district's 21 counties (including Payne and Pottawatomie, the district's most populous), all in the northern corridor.

Although the 3rd has a significant energy industry, with several counties producing oil and natural gas, Little Dixie largely missed out on the oil discoveries that brought wealth — and Republicanism — to central and western Oklahoma.

Wracked by rural depression in the 1920s and again in the 1980s, this region is the least prosperous area of Oklahoma today. Primarily rural, the 3rd relies on farming and livestock to fuel its economy. Beef cattle, chickens and hogs are raised throughout the 3rd. Tyson Foods, with headquarters in nearby Springdale, Ark., has a $50 million hog-breeding complex in Holdenville (Hughes County). Bryan, Hughes and Love are among the nation's leading peanut-growing counties.

Timber is harvested in the Ouachita National Forest, in the southeastern part of the 3rd. In the south, truck farmers send their produce to the Campbell Soup factory just over the border in Paris, Texas. Ardmore has a large, modern BF Goodrich factory that produces Michelin tires. Many district residents who live on the outskirts of Oklahoma City work at Tinker Air Force Base (in the 4th District).

Oklahoma's maximum-security prison is in McAlester (Pittsburg County). The inmates' two-day rodeo in late summer has become a popular attraction. Lake Texoma in the southwest is a summer vacation destination.

The names of Coal and Pittsburg counties are reminders that coal once was mined in abundance in eastern Oklahoma; Latimer and Le Flore counties also have significant coal reserves. Coal mining now accounts for a fraction of its previous share of the area's economy, but some high-sulfur bituminous coal is still mined in those counties.

1990 Population: 524,264. White 437,177 (83%), Black 21,186 (4%), Other 65,901 (13%). Hispanic origin 7,291 (1%). 18 and over 388,310 (74%), 62 and over 99,042 (19%). Median age: 34.

HOUSE ELECTIONS

1996 General		
Wes Watkins (R)	98,526	(51%)
Darryl Roberts (D)	86,647	(45%)
Scott Demaree (I)	6,335	(3%)
1996 Primary		
Wes Watkins (R)	12,740	(79%)
Evelyn L. Rogers (R)	1,262	(8%)
Ken B. Privett (R)	1,045	(6%)
Bill E. Henley (R)	584	(4%)
Darrel D. Tallant (R)	467	(3%)

Previous Winning Percentages*: **1990** (100%) **1988** (100%) **1986** (78%) **1984** (78%) **1982** (82%) **1980** (100%) **1978** (100%) **1976** (82%)

**Elected as a Democrat from 1976-1990.*

CAMPAIGN FINANCE

	Receipts	Receipts from PACs	Expend-itures
1996			
Watkins (R)	$1,133,772	$322,257 (28%)	$1,106,300
Roberts (D)	$619,508	$135,900 (22%)	$542,286

DISTRICT VOTE FOR PRESIDENT

1996		1992	
D	92,007 (47%)	**D**	94,763 (42%)
R	77,287 (40%)	**R**	77,054 (34%)
I	24,580 (13%)	**I**	55,974 (24%)

KEY VOTES

1997

Ban "partial birth" abortions Y

4 J.C. Watts Jr. (R)

Of Norman — Elected 1994, 2nd term

Biographical Information

Born: Nov. 18, 1957, Eufaula, Okla.
Education: U. of Oklahoma, B.S. 1981.
Occupation: Property management company owner; professional football player; youth minister.
Family: Wife, Frankie Jones; five children.
Religion: Southern Baptist.
Political Career: Okla. corporation commissioner, 1991-95.
Capitol Office: 1210 Longworth Bldg. 20515; 225-6165.

Committees

National Security
Military Personnel; Military Procurement
Transportation & Infrastructure
Aviation; Surface Transportation

In Washington: No end of attention has been showered on the celebrated — and pilloried — GOP Class of 1994, and in that class, no individual has drawn more of the spotlight than Watts. Minister Watts is a gifted and sometimes moving orator, and he became a leading national spokesman for Republican programs and policy during his first House term. An undeniable part of his appeal to party leaders is the fact that he is black — now, with the 1996 defeat of Connecticut Rep. Gary A. Franks, the only black Republican in Congress.

Asked by an audience member of a CBS news program in May 1995 how Republicans were going to address minority issues, House Speaker Newt Gingrich replied, "Part of it is bringing in members like J.C. Watts from Oklahoma."

Gingrich and other GOP leaders have found several occasions in which to prominently showcase Watts, most notably in February 1997, when he was tapped to offer the official Republican response to President Clinton's State of the Union address. Watts highlighted GOP support for "family values" and a balanced-budget constitutional amendment and emphasized the party's credo of returning power to citizens and local governments. "The strength of America is not in Washington; the strength of America is at home in lives well-lived in the land of faith and family," Watts said.

His nationally televised speech brought him a new level of exposure, and with that a new degree of scrutiny — some of it unflattering. In an interview with The Washington Post, he complained about "race-hustling poverty pimps" — African-American leaders who, Watts said, have a vested interest in keeping blacks dependent on the government. "What scares them the most is that black people might break out of that racial group thing and start thinking for themselves," he said.

Watts' comments angered black leaders, particularly Rep. Jesse L. Jackson Jr., D-Ill. He also earned poor notices in the press for sending a letter touting his speech, inviting donors to applaud him by returning a pre-printed card that read, "J.C., what a great speech! Here's some help to rebuild your campaign fund."

Such missteps in the spotlight added to fears among some GOP leaders that Watts was not completely ready for prime time; party leaders helped to squash talk that Watts might take over the GOP chairmanship in 1997, working from the recent Democratic model of having an elected official act as national spokesman. Still, Watts was prominently featured as a speaker at rallies for the 1996 presidential candidacy of Bob Dole, and he served as a co-chairman of that year's national platform committee.

Watts' speech to the GOP convention in 1996 may have been the best-received of the entire confab. In it, he urged blacks and other minorities to place their hope in Dole. "Compassion can't be measured in dollars and cents," he said. "It does come with a price tag, but that price tag isn't the amount of money spent. The price tag is love — being able to see people as they can be and not as they are."

In the 104th, Gingrich asked Watts to co-chair a task force on minority issues, and his work there led to legislation that he is cosponsoring in the 105th with Small Business Committee Chairman James M. Talent, R-Mo., aimed at improving inner-city life. Their package calls for "community renewal" through school vouchers, tax cuts and reduced government regulations and has an undetermined price tag. It is a program that largely emphasizes charity and private contributions over federal involvement and is an attempt by the GOP to offer an upbeat "empowerment" alternative before a promised assault on federal affirmative action programs.

Watts, who sits on the National Security Committee, joins the Transportation and Infrastructure Committee in the 105th, in time to help rewrite the main federal surface transportation law. He is taking a leave during the 105th from the Banking and Financial Services Committee.

Watts is a reliable Republican vote on fiscal as well as social issues and supported the signature

The 4th District made history in 1994 by electing Watts, making him the first black Republican elected to Congress from a Southern state since Reconstruction.

Watts described the district in his nationally televised response to President Clinton's 1997 State of the Union address: "We raise cattle back home, we grow some cotton and wheat, peanuts, and we drill for oil."

He represents a district in which the military is a ubiquitous force and which is home to Altus Air Force Base, in Jackson County, one of the Air Force's principal pilot training bases. The Army's Fort Sill is on the northwest side of Lawton (Comanche County). The district stretches north and east into Oklahoma County (Oklahoma City) to snare within its confines Tinker Air Force Base. With a combined civilian and military staff of almost 27,000, Tinker is the largest single-site employer in the state.

Agriculture and energy are the other dominant industries. Tillman and Jackson counties are among the nation's leaders in cotton harvesting. Jackson, Comanche, Stephens and Grady counties also grow wheat.

Despite price fluctuations, the energy industry has become important to the 4th's economy over the past 20 years. The gas- and oil-producing Anadarko Basin extends down from the 6th District into Comanche and Stephens counties. Halliburton employs about 3,000 people in Duncan (Stephens County) for oil-drilling research, development and manufacturing for its worldwide drilling enterprise.

With a population of about 81,000, Lawton is the third-largest city in Oklahoma (although it trails No. 2 Tulsa by more than 280,000).

OKLAHOMA 4
Southwest; part of Oklahoma City

Connected by an interstate turnpike to Oklahoma City and to Wichita Falls, Texas, Lawton is the commercial center of southwest Oklahoma. Goodyear's tire and rubber plant, one of the largest factories in the state, employs more than 1,800.

The city of Norman has slightly more than 80,000 people and is home to the University of Oklahoma (20,000 students). The university's new energy center conducts research into oil-drilling techniques and alternative fuels. The university and such government-sponsored research programs as the National Severe Storm Laboratory are attracting high-tech industries.

On the southern border, the Red River, which marks the frontier between Texas and Oklahoma, has spawned considerable aggravation and acrimony over the years because of its capricious disregard for the states' boundaries. The river changes course whenever it floods, which results in hundreds of acres of farmers' land ending up in the other state. Some disputes have led to gunfire.

Bedroom communities have sprouted along I-44 from Chickasha into Oklahoma County. Suburban Moore, outside the Oklahoma City limits in Cleveland County, grew by 15 percent in the 1980s; it is strongly Republican.

1990 Population: 524,265. White 441,223 (84%), Black 37,708 (7%), Other 45,334 (9%). Hispanic origin 21,023 (4%). 18 and over 381,702 (73%), 62 and over 68,635 (13%). Median age: 31.

elements of the House GOP's "Contract With America," including a tax-cut package, a welfare overhaul plan and term limits. He proudly notes his relations with conservative Christian groups.

But Watts is willing to question the party line on occasion. He was one of 25 Republicans who voted to send the fiscal 1996 spending bill for the Veterans Administration back to conference with a demand for more health care spending for veterans. And Watts has counseled a "go slow" approach to revamping affirmative action programs. He acknowledges that many Republicans want to end affirmative action "cold turkey," but thinks such an approach unwise.

Watts has made it clear that he is chary of the "certain connotation" that comes from being a black Republican. "They can't say that J.C. Watts has danced to anybody's music except his own," he once remarked. Watts is the first African-American member not to join the Congressional Black Caucus since its inception.

Watts has played an active part in trying to recruit blacks to the GOP, particularly as candidates. "I am willing to help in that arena if and when and however I can." But he added that he brings more to the table than merely being black. Watts insisted in 1995 that if the GOP governs according to its principles, there would be more blacks in Congress who are Republicans than Democrats by the year 2000.

His district is home to Tinker Air Force Base, which survived the 1995 round of base closings. The base is the largest single-site employer in the state. Calling on the president to accept the base closure commission's final list, Watts said on the House floor that its work "was fair to every individual in the country. Some win, some lose." In February 1995, Watts and three other members of the Oklahoma delegation announced that Tinker had won Defense Department approval to maintain the nation's B-2 bomber fleet, and Watts opposed an attempt to cut off funding for further production of the plane in 1995.

As a teenager, Watts fathered a daughter out of

wedlock. He offered The Washington Monthly testimony that this proved his political consistency, since the child had not been aborted and "she never received one dime of government assistance" because she was raised by his family (she was adopted shortly after birth by his uncle).

At Home: Julius Caesar Watts first won fame as a star quarterback for the University of Oklahoma in 1979 and 1980. He was named most valuable player in the Orange Bowl two years in a row.

After six years in the Canadian Football League, Watts and his family settled in Norman, where he worked in real estate and petroleum marketing. A Democrat most of his life, Watts became a Republican in 1989, then won election in 1990 to the state's Corporation Commission, which regulates the energy industry. That made him the first black elected to statewide office in Oklahoma history.

Watts entered the 1994 House race to succeed Democrat Dave McCurdy (who ran for the Senate) with high name recognition and good access to campaign funds. He already had a track record of doing well with voters in the 4th, garnering 56 percent of the district's vote in his 1990 race for the Corporation Commission.

As predicted, Watts was the leading vote-getter in August's five-candidate GOP primary, but his 49 percent forced him into a September runoff with state Rep. Ed Apple. With both business and military experience (the 4th has several major military installations, including Tinker), Apple made the runoff closer than many expected. Watts won by four percentage points.

In November, Watts faced David Perryman, a Chickasha lawyer and former Grady County Democratic chairman. Perryman finished second in the Democratic primary, but mustered a strong grass-roots effort and bested Cleveland County District Attorney Tully McCoy in the runoff.

If Perryman was somewhat more liberal than the November electorate, Watts was more conservative. His platform included opposition to all abortions except to save the life of the woman, and Watts told The New York Times that abortion is "a scriptural issue, not a political issue." The force of the national Republican sweep was felt fully in Oklahoma, where GOP candidates won the Senate and gubernatorial races and five of six House races. Watts took 52 percent of the vote to 43 percent for Perryman.

Democrats hoped in vain they could recover the district in 1996, with state Rep. Ed Crocker running an aggressive, negative campaign. Watts' illegitimate daughter became an issue, as were some tax debts and apparent sweetheart deals rung up by the incumbent. But Crocker carried baggage of his own because of his questionable draft status during the Vietnam War and was comparatively underfunded. Watts was sufficiently confident that he spent a great deal of the fall campaign season stumping for other candidates around the country; he won with 58 percent.

HOUSE ELECTIONS

1996 General		
J.C. Watts (R)	106,923	(58%)
Ed Crocker (D)	73,950	(40%)
Robert T. Murphy (LIBERT)	4,500	(2%)
1994 General		
J.C. Watts (R)	80,251	(52%)
David Perryman (D)	67,237	(43%)
Bill Tiffee (I)	7,913	(5%)

CAMPAIGN FINANCE

	Receipts	Receipts from PACs	Expend-itures
1996			
Watts (R)	$1,374,562	$442,872 (32%)	$1,363,291
Crocker (D)	$350,765	$140,896 (40%)	$350,073
Murphy (LIBERT)	$5,655	0	$5,591
1994			
Watts (R)	$579,371	$156,949 (27%)	$568,942
Perryman (D)	$226,178	$72,129 (32%)	$222,946

DISTRICT VOTE FOR PRESIDENT

	1996		1992
D	75,291 (40%)	**D**	72,613 (33%)
R	92,011 (49%)	**R**	90,467 (41%)
I	20,376 (11%)	**I**	53,921 (25%)

KEY VOTES

1997	
Ban "partial birth" abortions	Y
1996	
Approve farm bill	Y
Deny public education to illegal immigrants	Y
Repeal ban on certain assault-style weapons	Y
Increase minimum wage	N
Freeze defense spending	N
Approve welfare overhaul	Y
1995	
Approve balanced-budget constitutional amendment	Y
Relax Clean Water Act regulations	Y
Oppose limits on environmental regulations	N
Reduce projected Medicare spending	Y
Approve GOP budget with tax and spending cuts	Y

VOTING STUDIES

	Presidential Support		Party Unity		Conservative Coalition	
Year	S	O	S	O	S	O
1996	32	67	91	7	92	2
1995	15	80	90†	4†	86	5

† Not eligible for all recorded votes.

INTEREST GROUP RATINGS

Year	ADA	AFL-CIO	CCUS	ACU
1996	0	n/a	100	100
1995	0	0	100	96

5 Ernest Istook (R)

Of Oklahoma City — Elected 1992, 3rd term

Biographical Information
Born: Feb. 11, 1950, Ft. Worth, Texas.
Education: Baylor U., B.A. 1971; Oklahoma City U., J.D. 1977.
Occupation: Lawyer.
Family: Wife, Judy Bills; five children.
Religion: Mormon.
Political Career: Warr Acres City Council, 1983-87; Okla. House, 1987-93.
Capitol Office: 119 Cannon Bldg. 20515; 225-2132.

Committees
Appropriations
Labor, Health & Human Services, Education & Related Agencies; National Security; Treasury, Postal Service & General Government

In Washington: When the GOP took over Congress in 1995, sophomore Istook was well-positioned to lead on a number of issues important to the most conservative wing of the Republican Party. Arriving in 1993 to a Washington run by Democrats in the Capitol and the White House, Istook endured frustrations that sharpened his edge for second-term attacks on federal spending and unyielding attempts to legislate on moral issues such as abortion and school prayer.

Istook was named to the Appropriations Committee as a freshman and he has brought a contemporary conservative attitude to that post. Instead of taking the traditional tack of using the seat to secure funds for his district and his state, he has concentrated most of his efforts on either blocking spending he views as unnecessary or trying to attach policy changes to fast-moving spending bills.

Istook's desires to curb lobbying by groups whose politics he does not favor, to ban federal funding of almost all abortions, and to allow prayer in public schools, sometimes have trouble winning broad acceptance even within the conservative GOP Conference. To help build support for his proposals, during the 104th Congress he helped found and direct the Conservative Action Team, a caucus devoted to reining in government regulation and expenses and pursuing legislation promoting a conservative ideal of family and social life. Istook was a rare Republican who bucked his party's leaders and voted against the GOP budget resolution and omnibus spending plan in fiscal 1997 out of anger that they cost too much money.

His highest-profile effort during the 104th was an attempt to find a legislative home for his language that would ban groups from receiving federal grants if they devote more than 5 percent of their budgets to lobbying and other "political advocacy" efforts. He contends that these groups in effect use federal money to plump for their agenda — spending federal dollars in pursuit of more federal dollars.

Istook had the backing of House GOP leaders on the issue, and he succeeded in adding this provision to the fiscal 1996 spending bill covering the departments of Labor, Health and Human Services, and Education. An attempt to remove the language on the floor failed, 187-232, but the stricture was unacceptable to key senators on the relevant subcommittee.

So Istook tried again on the bill that funded the Treasury Department and the Postal Service. The Senate version contained a narrower provision about lobbying by larger nonprofit groups, but the bill got tied up for weeks until House conservatives recognized it was too weak a vehicle to carry the Istook language. President Clinton and other Democrats viewed the effort as an attempt to gag groups aligned with their agenda. Once the Istook provision was dropped, the Treasury-Postal bill was cleared quickly.

But Istook and his main allies, freshman Republicans David M. McIntosh of Indiana and Robert L. Ehrlich Jr. of Maryland, refused to say die. They added versions of the language to two different continuing resolutions and a more general lobbying bill. They had their moments — a 211-209 House vote in March 1996 to add a softened reporting requirement, for instance — but they could never make it over the hump into law.

Such persistence paid off for Istook, though, in restricting federal funding of abortions. Istook sought to block Medicaid payments for abortions performed in cases of rape or incest, restoring a ban that Congress had lifted in the wake of Clinton's election. GOP leaders removed his language from a rescissions bill early in the 104th, for fear of offending a small but important block of Republican abortion rights supporters. But they promised Istook he could revisit the issue, which he did on the fiscal 1996 Labor-HHS bill.

Istook argued that it was a states' rights issue, because 36 states had laws on their books that conflicted with the existing Medicaid language. An amendment offered by Jim Kolbe, R-Ariz., to retain the prevalent funding requirement that states pay for abortions for victims of rape or

OKLAHOMA 5
North Central — Part of Oklahoma City

As it sweeps from Oklahoma City north to the Kansas border, the 5th collects Republican-minded voters all along the way. Democrats may still have a registration edge in the 5th, but this is unmistakably GOP terrain. It was Bob Dole's best Oklahoma district in 1996, and four years earlier it had been the state's best performer for George Bush. Only the small portion of Osage County in the district can be described as Democratic territory — and even that went for Dole and Istook in 1996.

Oklahoma City enjoyed modest population growth of about 10 percent in the 1980s; much of this increase came in the city's more affluent northwest section, which is in the 5th. The district takes in such well-to-do suburbs as Nichols Hills, as well as medium-income suburbs such as Bethany. Remappers shifted the poorer black neighborhoods that had been in the 5th over to the 6th District. Dole carried the Oklahoma City portion of the 5th by a ratio of more than 2-to-1 over Bill Clinton in 1996.

Oklahoma City's growth did not stop at the city limits. It spread north to Edmond and west — along the Northwest Expressway — into Canadian County. Edmond's population expanded by more than 50 percent in the 1980s; with just over 52,000 people, it is now the sixth-largest city in Oklahoma. Canadian County experienced similarly rapid growth. Its population rose by 32 percent in the 1980s, faster than any other county in the state.

Since the discovery of a large oil pool underneath Oklahoma City in the 1930s, much of the city's economy has revolved around the oil industry. But the sharp drop in oil prices from the early to mid-1980s forced "O.K. City" (as locals call it) to diversify. The aviation industry is a significant area employer, with the Federal Aviation Administration's training facility at the city's airport (in the 6th). The military has a prominent presence, with Tinker Air Force Base on the city's outskirts (in the 4th). Others work in state government, health care, trucking and meatpacking.

The 5th's northeastern anchor is Bartles-ville (Washington County), the home of Phillips Petroleum. Oil has been of paramount importance to the local economy since 1897. Now, Bartlesville is a genteel community of 34,000, boasting modern architecture — including an office and apartment building designed by Frank Lloyd Wright — a symphony orchestra, ballet and an annual Mozart festival.

Energy and agriculture are key components of the 5th's economy. Farmers grow wheat and soybeans and raise beef cattle. Phillips and Conoco have refineries in the district.

Guthrie (Logan County) was Oklahoma's first capital. The town, which is renovating its Victorian-era buildings, has been restored to resemble the early 20th century. To the north in Noble County, Perry's annual Cherokee Strip Celebration commemorates the 1893 land run that led to its founding. The Cherokee Strip is a 12,000-square-mile area that makes up much of what is now north-central Oklahoma.

1990 Population: 524,264. White 453,965 (87%), Black 29,186 (6%), Other 41,113 (8%). Hispanic origin 16,718 (3%). 18 and over 388,030 (74%), 62 and over 80,604 (15%). Median age: 33.

incest was turned back by the House, 206-215.

Istook suffered a setback on the same bill when the House blocked his effort to gut federal family planning. For fiscal 1997, he tried again with a provision that would have required parental consent for minors to receive family planning services. "The federal government is inviting them [teenagers] to go against the moral guidance of their parents on the most intimate and personal of issues," Istook complained. Most Democrats and many moderate Republicans joined ranks to defeat his proposal.

The Labor-HHS bill was not the only forum for fights over abortion, though. Istook, who gained a seat on Appropriations' National Security Subcommittee in 1995, joined the battle on that panel's bill for fiscal 1996 over whether to allow abortions to be performed at military hospitals overseas. The Senate proposed allowing abortions to save the life of the woman or cases of rape or incest, to which Istook replied that exceptions should be allowed only if "it's truly a case of rape or incest, and not a spurious claim by a woman intent on getting an abortion," which he would test by requiring that such incidents be reported to military authorities. Democratic Sen. Daniel K. Inouye of Hawaii called that proviso "an insult to women" and the conference report was cleared without it.

Istook also spent a good deal of his time at loggerheads over a religious liberty amendment with Judiciary Committee Chairman Henry J. Hyde, R-Ill., the original sponsor of the ban on Medicaid funding of most abortions. Hyde offered a constitutional amendment that would have prevented discrimination against religious expression; it aimed to overturn restrictions on such expressions in public settings like football games and government offices, as well as schools. Istook wanted to specify that the Constitution does not prevent prayer in public schools, but religious conservatives split over which was the best approach, helping to doom the possibility that a measure would be voted on.

Istook failed on some more homey attempts to attend to the interests of his district. He wanted to block a requirement that contractors repairing the damage from the April 1995 Oklahoma City federal building bombing had to pay "prevailing," or union, wages, and he wanted to make it easier for states to collect sales taxes from tribal businesses. He said Oklahoma was losing out on $13 million in fuel taxes from its 18 tribal-owned gas stations.

In line with his efforts to balance the federal budget, Istook for the most part has refrained from earmarking funds for Oklahoma. Apparently, local officials and constituent groups such as the chamber of commerce were slower to change their mindset because Istook remarked in August 1996 that "You still have folks back home whose expectations reflect the old way of doing business." On a 251-160 vote, the House stripped $5 million for an oil research project in his district that he had included in the fiscal 1996 Interior spending bill.

During the 1993 appropriations process, Istook did find something for the home folks. When the Transportation Appropriations Subcommittee was earmarking funds for bus facilities, Istook got in line. He said at the time that he would prefer a standardized formula for awarding the money, but if earmarks were in, Oklahoma should get its share. He secured $1 million for his district.

At Home: Campaigning on an anti-pork platform, Istook won the 5th in 1992 after denying renomination to eight-term GOP Rep. Mickey Edwards, who was damaged by 386 House bank overdrafts. Istook said he did not intend "to be a pork barreler. Things for Oklahoma will be things that are deserved for Oklahoma."

Istook was neither the best-known nor the best-financed of the three leading candidates in the 1992 GOP primary for the 5th. Edwards had represented the Oklahoma City-based district since 1977. And former U.S. Attorney Bill Price had been the GOP's 1990 nominee for governor.

The primary was billed as a match between two heavyweights, Edwards and Price. Both spent lavishly on TV ads. Meanwhile, Istook ran a ground-level campaign that relied less on media ads and more on targeting likely GOP voters through direct mail and phone banks. He also refrained from personally attacking Edwards. Price's ads assailed the incumbent for his lengthy tenure as well as his problems with the bank. Price ran first in the primary, but it was Istook who made the runoff, not Edwards (he ran third with 26 percent). In the runoff, Istook carried all seven counties wholly or partly contained in the 5th, defeating Price by 12 percentage points.

The Democratic nominee was Laurie Williams, an oil and gas lawyer from Oklahoma City making her first bid for political office. She labeled Istook an "extremist," taking issue in particular with his anti-abortion position. But the Republican tilt of the 5th was enough for Istook to win with 53 percent. Re-election has come easily since then.

HOUSE ELECTIONS

1996 General		
Ernest Istook (R)	148,362	(70%)
James L. Forsythe (D)	57,594	(27%)
Ava Kennedy (I)	6,835	(3%)
1994 General		
Ernest Istook (R)	136,877	(78%)
Tom Keith (I)	38,270	(22%)

Previous Winning Percentages: 1992 (53%)

CAMPAIGN FINANCE

	Receipts	Receipts from PACs	Expend-itures
1996			
Istook (R)	$308,059	$129,057 (42%)	$306,411
Forsythe (D)	$35,469	$2,500 (7%)	$40,483
1994			
Istook (R)	$345,117	$119,142 (35%)	$274,179

DISTRICT VOTE FOR PRESIDENT

1996		1992	
D	68,163 (31%)	**D**	61,842 (25%)
R	128,746 (59%)	**R**	129,465 (51%)
I	20,704 (10%)	**I**	59,681 (24%)

KEY VOTES

1997	
Ban "partial-birth" abortions	Y
1996	
Approve farm bill	Y
Deny public education to illegal immigrants	Y
Repeal ban on certain assault-style weapons	Y
Increase minimum wage	N
Freeze defense spending	N
Approve welfare overhaul	Y
1995	
Approve balanced-budget constitutional amendment	Y
Relax Clean Water Act regulations	Y
Oppose limits on environmental regulations	X
Reduce projected Medicare spending	Y
Approve GOP budget with tax and spending cuts	Y

VOTING STUDIES

	Presidential Support		Party Unity		Conservative Coalition	
Year	**S**	**O**	**S**	**O**	**S**	**O**
1996	32	67	95	4	98	2
1995	16	82	92	3	91	4
1994	36	59	92	4	81	8
1993	30	69	90	6	75	18

INTEREST GROUP RATINGS

Year	ADA	AFL-CIO	CCUS	ACU
1996	10	n/a	94	100
1995	0	0	96	96
1994	5	11	83	95
1993	10	0	100	100

6 Frank D. Lucas (R)

Of Cheyenne — Elected 1994; 2nd full term

Biographical Information

Born: Jan. 6, 1960, Cheyenne, Okla.
Education: Oklahoma State U., B.S. 1982.
Occupation: Farmer; rancher.
Family: Wife, Lynda Bradshaw; three children.
Religion: Baptist.
Political Career: Republican nominee for Okla. House, 1984, 1986; Okla. House, 1989-94.
Capitol Office: 107 Cannon Bldg. 20515; 225-5565.

Committees

Agriculture
Forestry, Resource Conservation & Research; General Farm Commodities; Livestock, Dairy & Poultry
Banking & Financial Services
Capital Markets, Securities & Government Sponsored Enterprises; Domestic & International Monetary Policy

In Washington: The world's attention was riveted on Lucas' district when a bomb destroyed the Alfred P. Murrah Federal Building in downtown Oklahoma City. The blast killed 168 people, including a number of children in the building's day care center.

The bombing on the morning of April 19, 1995, was doubly shocking because it occurred in a small Midwestern city, the sort of place most regard as safe from terrorist violence. As Lucas told the House: "At two minutes after nine o'clock, America's heartland lost its innocence."

Much of Lucas' legislative agenda in the 104th Congress was driven by the event. Thirteen days after the bombing, the House passed a resolution offered by Lucas that condemned the bombing and offered condolences to the victims' families. "I, like you and the nation as a whole, will never forget the scene or the devastation — the death, the suffering — and most of all, the innocent children," Lucas said.

After two suspects were indicted for the bombing, the judge in the case moved the trial to Denver, ruling that the two could not get a fair trial in Oklahoma. Lucas then added a provision to an anti-terrorism bill moving through the House to provide closed-circuit television access to any trial that has been moved more than 350 miles from where the original trial would have taken place. He said it was a burden to the survivors and victims' families in Oklahoma City to have to travel so far to see the accused stand trial. Existing law prohibited the use of cameras in federal courtrooms.

The provision was included in the final version of the first anti-terrorism bill that passed the House in April 1996. "I believe all Americans who must endure such a tragedy, like the people of Oklahoma, deserve the opportunity to view the trial in their state," Lucas told the House. Although the judge at first said he would not allow any cameras in the courtroom, he later relented and allowed a closed-circuit site to be set up in Oklahoma City only for survivors and victims' family members.

Lucas also backed the anti-terrorism measure because it limited the rights of death-row inmates to make lengthy challenges to their convictions in federal court, known as habeas corpus appeals. Lucas told the House that he is now a champion of habeas corpus reform. "This is not because I have had a change of heart, but because of the heartbreak of the people of my state," he said. "An important part of the healing process for the survivors will be to see that those who committed this heinous crime are punished."

From his seat on the Agriculture Committee, Lucas in the 104th kept close tabs on the progress of the GOP leadership's proposal to overhaul federal farm policy. The party's "Freedom to Farm" bill phased out most New Deal-era crop subsidies, replacing them with a system of fixed but declining payments that farmers would receive over seven years regardless of market prices or their planting decisions.

Lucas backed the final version of the farm bill, saying, "Agriculture is truly at a crossroads. It is time we break the bonds of the old and ring in a market-oriented program that will guide us into the next century."

When the committee first debated the bill, Democratic critics said that paying farmers even when market conditions were good would spur taxpayer protests about undeserving farmers getting government handouts. But Lucas and other supporters said farmers who collect subsidies in good years could use that money to invest for leaner times. "My gosh, what's wrong with giving a farmer a chance to prosper once in a while?" asked Lucas. "For every one of those exceptional years, there will be a number that are not exceptional." The provision remained in the bill.

The farm bill revised but did not eliminate price support programs for two crops important in Lucas' district — cotton and peanuts. Lucas opposed a proposal to eliminate marketing loans for cotton producers after 1998. "This amendment to rip the heart out of the current cotton program represents probably the greatest step backwards

In terms of economy, occupation, personality and politics, the 6th spans a wider range than any other Oklahoma district. From inner-city black neighborhoods and booming suburbs in and around Oklahoma City to the wild frontier of the Panhandle, the 6th encompasses all aspects of Oklahoma. It is massive: Covering more than 25,000 square miles, the 6th District is larger than 10 states.

The 6th also includes the portion of Oklahoma City (Oklahoma County) where the Alfred P. Murrah Federal Building once stood. In an event that horrified the nation, the building was destroyed in April 1995 by a truck bomb. It killed 168 people, including a number of children in the building's day care center. The city plans to turn the site into a park with a memorial to the victims. Two years after the blast, the area remained fenced off, and the fence had become a memorial of its own as people left tributes on it to those who perished. The Journal Record Building across the street was also damaged; the city considered turning it into a museum commemorating those who died.

Oklahoma City is split among three districts. The 6th's portion includes the most famous symbols of the state's oil wealth: working wells on the grounds of the state Capitol. Also included in the 6th are most of the city's 71,000 blacks. State government offices and the Federal Aviation Administration's Aeronautical Center at Will Rogers World Airport are major employers, but many residents also work at Tinker Air Force Base and General Motors (both in the 4th District) and AT&T (5th District).

Western Oklahoma traditionally is the state's most conservative region. Residents share an aversion to most government activity other than

OKLAHOMA 6
West and Panhandle; part of Oklahoma City

military expenditures and agricultural subsidies. Part of the Dust Bowl, western Oklahoma was devastated in the 1930s and 1940s. It made great strides in the two subsequent decades, becoming a region of huge wheat farms and cattle ranches. But the double shock in the 1980s of falling energy prices and the farm credit crisis dealt the district another economic setback. Most counties in the 6th lost population then, many by more than 10 percent.

The historical origins of Oklahoma's settlers indicate the state's voting patterns. Northern Oklahoma's settlers came from Kansas and Nebraska, importing their Republican voting habits. The northern tier of the 6th is the most solid GOP territory in the state. Many of these counties went for Bob Dole in 1996.

Texans settled the southwestern part of Oklahoma. Like the area they left, the southern part of the district is dominated by conservative, "yellow dog" Democrats. Bill Clinton carried the four southernmost counties in 1996.

Agriculture and energy are mainstays. Hard red winter wheat is grown across the district, especially in the north and northwest. Beef cattle also are raised in the 6th. In the south, cotton and peanuts are key commodities. Much of the energy production in the district is in the Panhandle, where there are huge gas fields.

1990 Population: 524,264. White 410,590 (78%), Black 69,004 (13%), Other 44,670 (9%). Hispanic origin 22,894 (4%). 18 and over 381,952 (73%), 62 and over 91,759 (18%). Median age: 34.

in American [agricultural] policy that any member of Congress has proposed in many years," Lucas told the House.

He also argued against an attempt to phase out the peanut price support program, which boosts peanut prices through a combination of government loans and production limits. Lucas said the amendment should be titled, "The 'How many rural economies can we wreck?' amendment of 1996." Telling the House the peanut program had been reformed under the farm bill, Lucas said eliminating the program "will cause the economic ruin of thousands of farm families, rural banking systems, and the country towns they support."

Like many conservative Republicans, Lucas feels that private property owners' rights are often disregarded in the pursuit of enforcing environmental regulations. He backed a GOP effort in early 1995 to extend a moratorium until Dec. 31, 1996, for new animal and plant listings under the Endangered Species Act (ESA). Lucas worried that the Fish and Wildlife Service would put the Arkansas River shiner on the endangered list.

He said this little bait fish "might have the power to stop those in the agriculture industry from irrigating their land or protecting their crops." He said the ESA "is flawed because of its lack of human compassion. Economic impact and private property rights must be taken into account in future draftings of the act."

Lucas, who also sits on the Banking and Financial Services Committee, supports a balanced-budget constitutional amendment, and in 1996 he opposed increasing the minimum wage. He voted to repeal the ban on certain semiautomatic assault-style weapons.

At Home: Lucas' interest in politics extends to his days at Oklahoma State University, when he was president of the local chapter of College Republicans while working on a degree in agriculture economics. After graduating, he returned to Cheyenne and soon entered politics. He ran unsuccessfully for the state House in 1984 and 1986, losing in a district where Democrats made up 92 percent of the registered voters.

In 1988, Lucas' luck turned: He won a state House district that covered an area stretching from the Panhandle to the outskirts of Oklahoma County. In the Legislature, he served on committees that dealt with taxes, agriculture, energy, small business and government reform. He also was chairman of the state House Republican Caucus.

When 10-term Democratic Rep. Glenn English resigned the 6th in early 1994 to head a rural electric lobbying association in Washington, Lucas had to fight through a special primary and runoff to secure the GOP nomination. Among five Republicans in the primary, Lucas ran second, trailing state Sen. Brooks Douglass. But in the runoff he surged past Douglass, taking 56 percent of the vote.

That left Lucas battle-hardened for his special-election contest with conservative Democrat Dan Webber Jr., a former aide to Oklahoma Democratic Sen. David L. Boren, who supported Webber's bid.

Lucas campaigned on the theme that he was "from western Oklahoma and for western Oklahoma." He stressed his work in agriculture and contrasted his lifelong residence in the 6th with the background of Webber, who grew up in Oklahoma but had spent years in Washington as a congressional aide. Lucas ran TV ads showing Webber's home in Washington and District of Columbia license plates.

Webber tried to counter Lucas' portrayal of him as a Washingtonian by stressing that he held conservative values and issue positions. But his efforts to win more local support were to no avail. Four days before the May election, local members of Ross Perot's United We Stand America announced that 86 percent of them preferred Lucas.

Despite Boren's efforts on Webber's behalf, Lucas won 54 percent. When Lucas sought election to his first full term in November 1994, Democrats did not put up much of a fight. Their nominee, black minister Jeffrey S. Tollett, was soundly defeated.

In 1996, Lucas faced Democrat Paul M. Barby, the son of a prominent ranching family and a member of the Board of Regents for Oklahoma Colleges, who had helped lead a successful fight against a ballot initiative to cut property taxes. Barby campaigned on education, energy and farming issues, but what attracted attention to his bid beyond the Oklahoma Panhandle was that he is an acknowledged homosexual.

Barby said he decided to run in part to protest "the three Gs" slogan that conservative Republican James M. Inhofe employed in his successful 1994 Senate bid — "God, gays and guns." Although Lucas said that Barby's personal wealth could make him a serious contender, Lucas won 64 percent to 36 percent.

HOUSE ELECTIONS

1996 General		
Frank D. Lucas (R)	113,499	(64%)
Paul M. Barby (D)	64,173	(36%)
1994 General		
Frank D. Lucas (R)	106,961	(70%)
Jeffrey S. Tollett (D)	45,399	(30%)
1994 Special		
Frank D. Lucas (R)	71,354	(54%)
Dan Webber Jr. (D)	60,411	(46%)

CAMPAIGN FINANCE

	Receipts	Receipts from PACs		Expend-itures
1996				
Lucas (R)	$423,038	$212,837	(50%)	$439,969
Barby (D)	$482,394	$20,000	(4%)	$476,471
1994				
Lucas (R)	$188,985	$88,115	(47%)	$146,806
Tollett (D)	$22,796	$1,250	(5%)	$22,760
1994 Special				
Lucas (R)	$359,153	$50,965	(14%)	$306,888
Webber (D)	$333,611	$68,840	(21%)	$254,105

DISTRICT VOTE FOR PRESIDENT

	1996		1992
D	75,783 (41%)	**D**	73,843 (34%)
R	86,670 (47%)	**R**	92,379 (43%)
I	20,149 (11%)	**I**	49,106 (23%)

KEY VOTES

1997	
Ban "partial birth" abortions	Y
1996	
Approve farm bill	Y
Deny public education to illegal immigrants	Y
Repeal ban on certain assault-style weapons	Y
Increase minimum wage	N
Freeze defense spending	N
Approve welfare overhaul	Y
1995	
Approve balanced-budget constitutional amendment	Y
Relax Clean Water Act regulations	Y
Oppose limits on environmental regulations	N
Reduce projected Medicare spending	Y
Approve GOP budget with tax and spending cuts	Y

VOTING STUDIES

	Presidential Support		Party Unity		Conservative Coalition	
Year	**S**	**O**	**S**	**O**	**S**	**O**
1996	34	66	95	4	98	0
1995	17	83	97	2	98	1
1994	49†	51†	93†	7†	100†	0†

† Not eligible for all recorded votes.

INTEREST GROUP RATINGS

Year	ADA	AFL-CIO	CCUS	ACU
1996	0	n/a	100	100
1995	0	0	100	88
1994	0†	17†	89	100†

† Not eligible for all recorded votes.

OREGON

Governor: John Kitzhaber (D)
First elected: 1994
Length of term: 4 years
Term expires: 1/99
Salary: $80,000.04
Term limit: 2 terms
Phone: (503) 378-3111
Born: March 5, 1947; Colfax, Wash.
Education: Dartmouth College, B.A. 1969; U. of Oregon, M.D. 1973.
Occupation: Physician.
Family: Wife, Sharon LaCroix.
Religion: Unspecified.
Political Career: Ore. Senate,1981-95, president, 1985-93; Ore. House, 1979-81.

No lieutenant governor

Secretary of State: Phil Keisling (D)
First elected: 1992 (appointed 1/91)
Length of Term: 4 years
Term expires: 1/01
Salary: $61,500
Phone: (503) 378-4139

State election official: (503) 378-4144
Democratic headquarters: (503) 224-8200
Republican headquarters: (503) 620-4330

REDISTRICTING

Oregon retained its five House seats in reapportionment. Federal court approved the map Dec. 2, 1991; that map became law Dec. 16, after the legislature failed to act.

STATE LEGISLATURE

Legislative Assembly. Meets January-June or January-July.

Senate: 30 members, 4-year terms
1996 breakdown: 20R, 10D; 21 men, 9 women
Salary: $998/month + $75/day (7 days a week) in session; $400-$550/month in expenses not in session
Phone: (503) 378-8168

House of Representatives: 60 members, 2-year terms
1996 breakdown: 31R, 29D; 46 men, 14 women
Salary: same as Senate
Phone: (503) 378-8551

URBAN STATISTICS

City	Population
Portland	437,319
Mayor Vera Katz, D	
Eugene	112,669
Mayor Ruth Bascom, D	
Salem	107,786
Mayor Mike Swaim, N-P	
Gresham	68,235
Mayor Gussie McRobert, N-P	
Beaverton	53,310
Mayor Rob Drake, N-P	

U.S. CONGRESS

Senate: 1 D, 1 R
House: 4 D, 1 R

TERM LIMITS

For state offices: Yes
Senate: 2 terms
House: 3 terms
No more than 12 years combined

ELECTIONS

1996 Presidential Vote

Bill Clinton	47%
Bob Dole	39%
Ross Perot	9%

1992 Presidential Vote

Bill Clinton	42%
George Bush	33%
Ross Perot	24%

1988 Presidential Vote

Michael S. Dukakis	51%
George Bush	47%

POPULATION

1990 population		2,842,321
1980 population		2,633,105
Percent change		+8%
Rank among states:		29
White		93%
Black		2%
Hispanic		4%
Asian or Pacific islander		2%
Urban		70%
Rural		30%
Born in state		47%
Foreign-born		5%
Under age 18	724,130	25%
Ages 18-64	1,726,867	61%
65 and older	391,324	14%
Median age		34.5

MISCELLANEOUS

Capital: Salem
Number of counties: 36
Per capita income: $17,592 (1991)
Rank among states: 27
Total area: 97,073 sq. miles
Rank among states: 10

OREGON

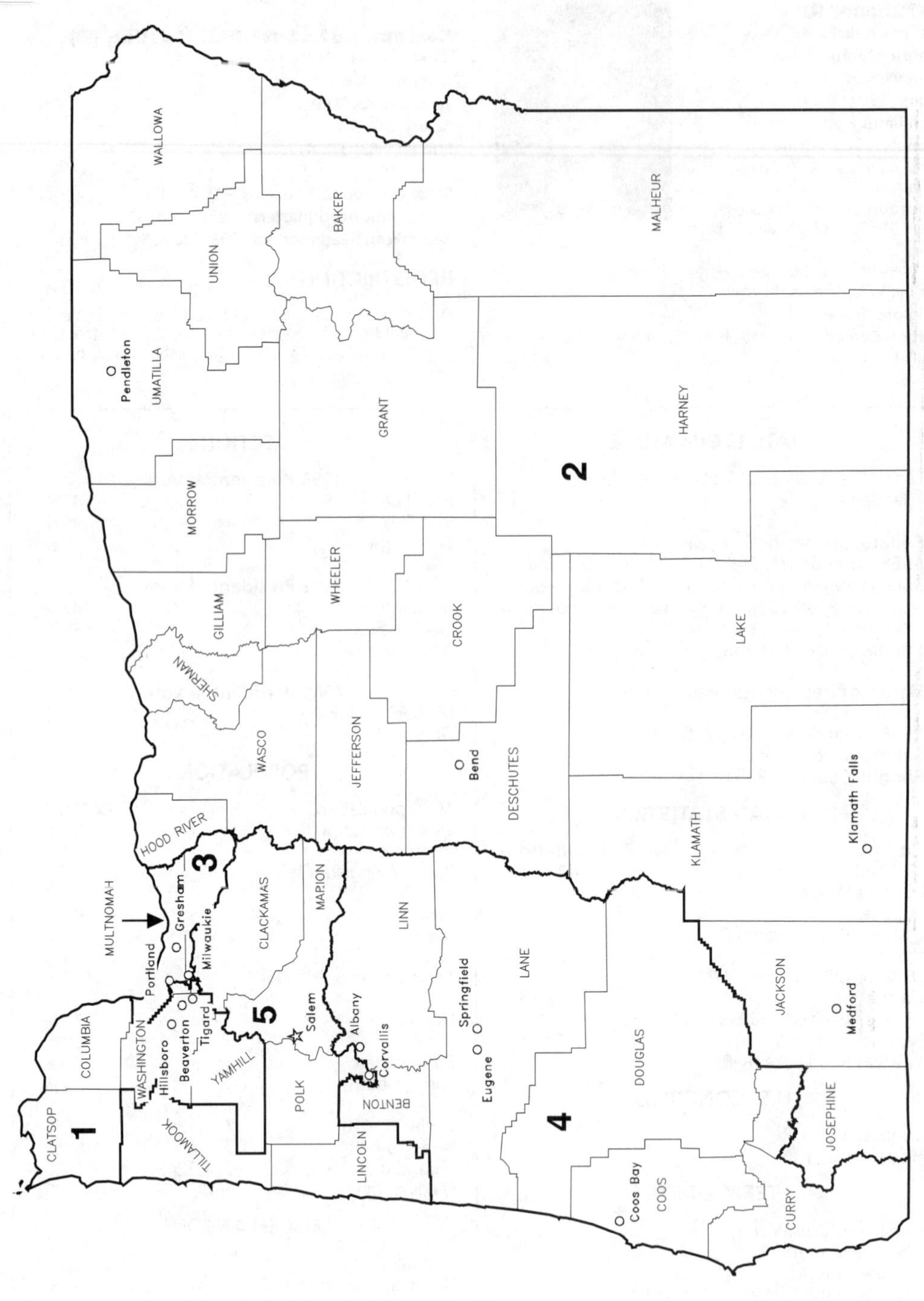

WALLOWA
BAKER
MALHEUR
UNION
UMATILLA
Pendleton
GRANT
HARNEY
2
MORROW
WHEELER
GILLIAM
CROOK
LAKE
SHERMAN
WASCO
JEFFERSON
Bend
DESCHUTES
Klamath Falls
HOOD RIVER
KLAMATH
3
MULTNOMAH
Gresham
Portland
Milwaukie
CLACKAMAS
MARION
LINN
LANE
Springfield
JACKSON
Medford
COLUMBIA
WASHINGTON
Hillsboro
Beaverton
Tigard
5
Salem
Albany
Corvallis
Eugene
DOUGLAS
YAMHILL
POLK
BENTON
CLATSOP
1
TILLAMOOK
LINCOLN
4
JOSEPHINE
Coos Bay
COOS
CURRY

Ron Wyden (D)

Of Portland — Elected 1996, 1st term

Biographical Information
Born: May 3, 1949, Wichita, Kan.
Education: Stanford U., A.B. 1971; U. of Oregon, J.D. 1974.
Occupation: Lawyer; professor.
Family: Wife, Laurie Oseran; two children.
Religion: Jewish.
Political Career: U.S. House, 1981-96.
Capitol Office: 717 Hart Bldg. 20510; 224-5244.

Committees
Special Aging
Budget
Commerce, Science & Transportation
Aviation; Communications; Surface Transportation & Merchant Marine
Energy & Natural Resources
Energy Research Development Production & Regulation; Forests & Public Land Management; Water & Power
Environment & Public Works
Drinking Water, Fisheries & Wildlife

In Washington: Wyden's January 1996 victory in Oregon's vote-by-mail special Senate election was a big psychological boost to the Democratic Party. After losing control of Congress in 1994 and enduring GOP conservatives' efforts to dictate policy in 1995, Democrats cited Wyden's success as proof that voters were coming to regard the Republican agenda as too extreme.

The GOP put on a brave face about the loss, noting that Oregon had been trending Democratic anyway. But the Oregon loss, coming shortly after the GOP was blamed for resisting a budget compromise with President Clinton, played a part in leading congressional Republicans to cooperate more with Democrats to produce tangible legislative results, such as the welfare overhaul bill. That image makeover helped boost GOP congressional candidates in November 1996 — enough so that the party added to its Senate majority and voters in Oregon filled their open Senate seat with the Republican Wyden had defeated in January, Gordon H. Smith.

Wyden was elected to fill the unexpired term, ending in January 1999, of veteran GOP Sen. Bob Packwood, who resigned in 1995 in the face of certain expulsion on charges of sexual harassment and other personal misconduct. Wyden prevailed by 48 to 46 percent over Smith, the state Senate president. Smith got his chance for a comeback when Oregon's senior senator, Mark O. Hatfield, announced his retirement.

It didn't take Wyden long to make an impact on the Senate. Heading into 1996, Majority Leader Bob Dole was struggling to line up the votes to pass a balanced-budget constitutional amendment, which had failed by a single vote in 1995. The switch from Packwood, who had supported the amendment, to Wyden, who opposed it, spelled doom for Dole's dream.

In the Senate, Wyden is building on the reputation he established during 15 years in the House as a liberal populist whose legislative efforts focus on health, consumer and environmental protection issues. He has a knack for finding the spotlight and using it to draw attention to abuses and wrongs done to his constituents.

For instance, Wyden has criticized managed care providers that place so-called gag rules on doctors to restrict them from discussing with their patients certain treatment options that might fall outside the scope of their health plan. As the 104th Congress was winding down, Wyden tried to prohibit the practice by offering an amendment to an appropriations bill, and the amendment nearly passed. A frustrated Majority Leader Trent Lott was forced to pull the bill from the floor, prompting Wyden briefly to threaten to offer his amendment to every measure that came to the floor.

The crash of a ValuJet passenger airplane in Florida, followed by the midair explosion of TWA Flight 800 in New York, prompted some sharp talk from Wyden about airline safety. He called for the Federal Aviation Administration (FAA) to disclose the safety records of individual air carriers so consumers could weigh that information in making air travel plans. He questioned the FAA's ability to fulfill its dual role of investigating crashes and promoting the airline industry. He also called for better organization of government and private safety efforts. "Who's in charge here?" he asked after the TWA crash. "My sense is there's no clear line of responsibility."

Wyden won election to the Senate by portraying himself as a reasonable-thinking alternative to the conservative Smith on such issues as education, the environment, revamping Medicare and balancing the budget. He also had the good fortune of running during a low point in the popularity of the GOP agenda — just after Republicans had been tarred by the contentious budget battles and partial federal government shutdown.

While serving in the House, Wyden compiled an unabashedly liberal record, voting for gun control and abortion rights and against most elements of the GOP "Contract With America." In 1995, Wyden voted against Republican plans to reduce projected Medicare spending by $270 billion over seven years. He opposed legislation that would have limited the Environmental Protection Agency's regulatory authority and voted against a proposal that would have eased federal water pollution control standards.

The GOP takeover of the House deprived Wyden of the vehicle he had used to generate attention for sometimes obscure crusades: the chair of the Small Business Subcommittee on Regulation, Business Opportunities and Technology. Republicans killed the panel after they won the House majority.

When he chaired that subcommittee, Wyden made a habit of holding high-profile hearings to investigate alleged wrongdoing — in the cosmetics industry and by plastic surgeons and diet companies, for instance.

At Home: A former high school basketball star, the gangly Wyden is soft-spoken but extremely competitive. He entered politics as a citizen activist: He was Oregon executive director for the Gray Panthers, an organization promoting senior citizens' interests, when he first was elected to the House in 1980.

After that victory, Wyden enjoyed easy re-elections in his Portland-based 3rd District, and by the mid-1980s he was being discussed as a possibility for statewide office. He got his chance after Packwood announced his retirement in 1995, leading to the first national vote-by-mail election.

Wyden initially drew two opponents in the Democratic primary: his party colleagues in the Oregon House delegation, five-term Rep. Peter A. DeFazio and second-term Rep. Elizabeth Furse.

One potential hurdle for Wyden was his support for passage of NAFTA (both DeFazio and Furse opposed it). That stand angered many in Oregon's influential organized labor movement. Wyden stumbled, most notably on a televised quiz that drew much attention: He could not quote the price of a loaf of bread or a gallon of milk in Portland, and he could not name the Canadian prime minister or find Bosnia on a map. But Wyden was better funded and better known than his primary opponents. Furse dropped out of the race, and Wyden won with 50 percent, six points ahead of DeFazio.

A Mormon from Pendleton in rural northeastern Oregon, Smith made a fortune in business as a grower and packer of peas and other vegetables. He spent heavily on the Senate race — about $4 million overall, including an estimated $2 million out of his own pocket.

Just after the primary, Smith pounced with TV ads depicting Wyden as an out-of-touch liberal. Wyden responded with ads flailing Smith for pollution and unsafe conditions at his plants and for expensive tastes (including an antique set of four golf clubs that cost him $1.25 million). The war of negatives escalated and included an ad sponsored by the Teamsters Union that held Smith responsible for the death of an employee's child (killed in a fall at the plant). Smith responded with a testimonial from the child's family.

Smith carried three-fourths of the state's 36 counties, but his percentages were disappointing in the populous Portland suburbs and exurbs, where many independents and Republicans had preferred the moderate conservatism of Packwood and Hatfield. But while Wyden carried only nine counties, they included the four most-populous, led by Multnomah (Portland), where he crushed Smith by 2-to-1.

SENATE ELECTIONS

1996 Special		
Ron Wyden (D)	571,739	(48%)
Gordon H. Smith (R)	553,519	(46%)
Karen E. Shilling (AM)	25,597	(2%)
Gene Nanni (LIBERT)	15,698	(1%)
1996 Special Primary		
Ron Wyden (D)	212,532	(50%)
Peter A. DeFazio (D)	187,411	(44%)
Anna Nevenich (D)	11,201	(3%)
Michael Donnelly (D)	8,340	(2%)

Previous Winning Percentages: 1994* (73%) **1992*** (77%) **1990*** (81%) **1988*** (99%) **1986*** (86%) **1984*** (72%) **1982*** (78%) **1980*** (72%)

** House elections*

KEY VOTES

1997	
Approve balanced-budget constitutional amendment	N
Approve chemical weapons treaty	Y
1996	
Approve farm bill	Y
Limit punitive damages in product liability cases	N
Exempt small businesses from higher minimum wage	N
Approve welfare overhaul	Y
Bar job discrimination based on sexual orientation	Y
Override veto of ban on "partial birth" abortions	N
House Service:	
1995	
Approve balanced-budget constitutional amendment	N
Relax Clean Water Act regulations	N
Oppose limits on environmental regulations	Y
Reduce projected Medicare spending	N
Approve GOP budget with tax and spending cuts	N

CAMPAIGN FINANCE

	Receipts	Receipts from PACs	Expend- itures
1996 Special			
Wyden (D)	$2,786,218	$471,710 (17%)	$2,752,879
Smith (R)	$3,748,118	$438,754 (12%)	$3,732,250

VOTING STUDIES

	Presidential Support		Party Unity		Conservative Coalition	
Year	**S**	**O**	**S**	**O**	**S**	**O**
1996*	95	5	92	8	24	76
House Service:						
1995	83	17	89	10	28	72
1994	79	19	94	4	33	67
1993	77	22	95	4	11	89
1992	17	81	90	8	19	79
1991	31	68	94	5	24	73

** Wyden was sworn in on Feb. 6, 1996, replacing Bob Packwood, R, who resigned. In 1996, he was eligible for 56 presidential support votes, 186 party unity votes, and 37 conservative coalition votes.*

INTEREST GROUP RATINGS

Year	ADA	AFL-CIO	CCUS	ACU
1996	95	n/a	38	15
House Service:				
1996	0	0	0	0
1995	90	100	29	12
1994	80	78	58	0
1993	95	92	18	4
1992	95	73	25	0
1991	85	83	30	5

Gordon H. Smith (R)

Of Pendleton — Elected 1996, 1st term

Biographical Information
Born: May 25, 1952, Pendleton, Ore.
Education: Brigham Young U., B.A. 1976; Southwestern U., J.D. 1979.
Occupation: Frozen food company executive; lawyer.
Family: Wife, Sharon; three children.
Religion: Mormon.
Political Career: Ore. Senate, 1993-97, president, 1995-97; Republican nominee for U.S. Senate, 1996 special election.
Capitol Office: 359 Dirksen Bldg. 20510; 224-3753.

Committees
Budget
Energy & Natural Resources
Energy Research Development Production & Regulation; Forests & Public Land Management; Water & Power
Foreign Relations
European Affairs (chairman); International Operations; Near Eastern & South Asian Affairs

The Path to Washington: A millionaire businessman from northeastern Oregon, Smith had an arduous climb to Congress, running two separate Senate campaigns in 1996.

He started the year by narrowly losing to Democratic Rep. Ron Wyden in a special election to fill the seat left vacant by Republican Bob Packwood, who resigned from the Senate in September 1995 after allegations of ethical and sexual misconduct.

But Smith got a second chance when Oregon's other veteran Republican senator, Mark O. Hatfield, announced he would retire at the end of the 104th Congress. Since Smith had just made himself known to voters statewide, most Republicans saw him as a logical choice to defend the seat for the party.

Owner of a frozen foods packaging company in Pendleton, Smith first entered politics in 1992, winning a seat in the state Senate. When Republicans won control of the chamber in 1994, he was elected Senate president.

In that post he showed a penchant for conciliation and deal-making. He was instrumental, for instance, in crafting a compromise in 1995 that provided state money for expansion of Portland's light-rail commuter system. Smith also was a key Republican player in the establishment of Oregon's state health care plan for low-income residents, an initiative that included funding for abortion services — even though Smith opposes the procedure except in cases of rape, incest or danger to the life of the woman.

But Smith is a staunch conservative on fiscal issues, and some of his votes in the state Senate gave Democrats an opening to portray him as too extreme. For instance, he was one of only a handful of lawmakers to vote against a measure aimed at toughening sanctions against employers who violate minimum wage laws.

Using ammunition such as that, Democrats in both Senate campaigns portrayed Smith as outside Oregon's mainstream. Wyden repeatedly attacked Smith during the special election for receiving support from the Oregon Citizens Alliance (OCA), which has waged high-profile battles against abortion and homosexuals' rights.

Smith also came under heavy criticism for environmental violations at his food plant, and for his personal spending — including such things as a million-dollar collection of antique Scottish golf clubs.

After putting out an estimated $2 million of his own money trading negative television commercials with Wyden, Smith narrowly lost.

When Hatfield announced his retirement, Smith initially said he would not run again in 1996. But national Republicans, anxious to prevent Democrats from picking up a second seat previously held by the GOP, assured Smith he would not have to invest more of his personal fortune in another attempt.

Smith returned to the campaign trail, redoubling his efforts to portray himself as a reasonable centrist. Despite his opposition to abortion in most instances, he said he would not pursue a constitutional amendment banning abortion if elected to the Senate. And he pledged not to allow his views on abortion or other contentious issues to prevent him from seeking the "greater good."

Such rhetoric sparked a challenge to Smith in the Republican primary from Lon Mabon, chairman of the conservative Oregon Citizens Alliance. Mabon said he was taking on Smith to make sure conservatives had a voice in the election.

But Mabon's message failed to attract even 10 percent of the primary vote, as Smith breezed to nomination against Mabon and three others with a 78 percent tally.

That set the stage for a fall campaign pitting Smith against Democrat Tom Bruggere, himself a millionaire and successful businessman.

Although Bruggere, a founder and former chief executive officer of the Portland-area high-tech firm Mentor Graphics, was making his first bid for elected office, he came highly touted by state and national Democrats as a fresh face with deep pockets.

Bruggere cruised through the primary season to

grab the Democratic nomination and then took aim at Smith by recycling charges first used by Wyden that the Republican was too far right on issues such as the environment and abortion rights.

But with the experience of the previous campaign under his belt, Smith deftly blunted most of Bruggere's criticisms, promising to work for a balance between economic development, job creation and environmental protection.

When Bruggere charged that Smith was a "chronic corporate polluter" in eastern Oregon, Smith responded with charges that his opponent was digging for damaging information about Smith's wife and her relatives for use in the campaign.

In the closing days of the race, Smith reached out to moderate voters in the highly populous Portland metropolitan area by vowing to support federal funding for abortions for low-income women in cases of rape or incest or when necessary to save the woman's life. He won with 50 percent, 4 percentage points ahead of Bruggere.

In his second month in the Senate, Smith voted for the early release of $385 million for international family planning programs — a move supporters said would keep open dozens of family planning clinics in poor countries around the world.

The 53-46 vote to release the funds March 1 — four months earlier than scheduled under legislation passed in the 104th — was a victory for abortion-rights advocates, but most supporters framed the issue in terms of family planning rather than abortion. That argument, advanced by Republican abortion-rights supporter Olympia J. Snowe of Maine, convinced at least one Republican abortion opponent, Smith, to vote for the early release of the money.

He said he believed that in four months' time, family planning services would prevent enough unwanted pregnancies to prevent 1.6 million abortions from being performed. "Like Mr. Hatfield I am pro-life," Smith said. "I will vote yes" to the release.

Smith sits on the Foreign Relation Committee and serves as chairman of the Subcommittee on European Affairs. He also has seats on the Budget Committee and on Energy and Natural Resources.

SENATE ELECTIONS

1996 General		
Gordon H. Smith (R)	677,336	(50%)
Tom Bruggere (D)	624,370	(46%)
Brent Thompson (REF)	20,381	(1%)
Gary Kutcher (PACIFIC)	14,193	(1%)
1996 Primary		
Gordon Smith (R)	224,428	(78%)
Lon Mabon (R)	23,479	(8%)
Kirby Brumfield (R)	15,744	(5%)
Jeff Lewis (R)	13,359	(5%)
Robert J. Fenton (R)	8,958	(3%))

CAMPAIGN FINANCE

	Receipts	Receipts from PACs	Expend-itures
1996			
Smith (R)	$3,840,273	$757,905 (20%)	$3,764,272
Bruggere (D)	$3,318,883	$406,731 (12%)	$3,301,736

KEY VOTES

1997	
Approve balanced-budget constitutional amendment	Y
Approve chemical weapons treaty	Y

1 Elizabeth Furse (D)

Of Hillsboro — Elected 1992, 3rd term

Biographical Information
Born: Oct. 13, 1936, Nairobi, Kenya.
Education: Evergreen State College, B.A. 1974.
Occupation: Community activist.
Family: Husband, John C. Platt; two children.
Religion: Protestant.
Political Career: No previous office.
Capitol Office: 316 Cannon Bldg. 20515; 225-0855.

Committees
Commerce
Energy & Power; Finance & Hazardous Materials; Health & Environment

In Washington: Furse came to Congress in 1993 as a community activist and political neophyte, but she has honed her legislative skills quickly. She now can claim solid credentials as a budget-cutter, environmentalist and liberal champion on social issues.

Furse's voting record, a fusion of progressive politics and fiscal discipline, is partly a response to her tenuous political position: She has never won more than 52 percent of the vote. Furse belongs to a recent vintage of deficit-conscious Democrats who work to safeguard certain social priorities while acknowledging that the GOP has shifted the terms of the budget debate.

The child of British parents, Furse grew up in South Africa, where her mother was a founder of the Black Sash, a women's anti-apartheid group. Furse became a U.S. citizen in 1972, working as a community organizer in the Watts neighborhood of Los Angeles and on behalf of Northwestern Indian tribes. In 1985 she founded the Oregon Peace Institute, which tries to resolve conflict through non-violence.

As a freshman in 1993, Furse won three committee assignments — Banking, Finance and Urban Affairs; Merchant Marine and Fisheries; and Armed Services — but in the 104th Congress she dropped them all for a chance to serve exclusively on the Commerce Committee. In 1997, Furse shifted to Commerce's Energy and Power Subcommittee because that panel will be a major player in the proposed deregulation of electric utilities. She also moved to the Health and Environment Subcommittee to better protect the Oregon Health Plan, which she believes could suffer under GOP funding formulas for Medicaid.

Though Furse no longer serves on Armed Services (now called National Security), she maintains an interest in the defense budget. She has annually cosponsored a "burden-sharing" amendment to the defense authorization bill that requires European nations to help pay the cost of stationing U.S. troops on their soil. The House passed the provision in both 1995 and 1996 (though the Senate agreed to it in 1996 only).

The House also passed a Furse amendment to the 1995 defense spending bill that cut $22 million from Air Force procurement for the C-17 transport plane — a project Furse has targeted relentlessly, arguing that cheaper aircraft could be modified to serve as cargo planes. When the same appropriations bill returned to the floor in 1996, Furse successfully offered an amendment that cut $35 million by streamlining the Pentagon's Transportation Command. In 1994, Furse also got the House to agree to cut $150 million from the ballistic missile defense program.

Those cost-cutting efforts — along with her votes for welfare overhaul and for the austere alternative budgets offered by conservative Democrats — have made her a darling among balanced-budget boosters such as the Concord Coalition, the National Taxpayers Union and Citizens Against Government Waste, which appointed her to its advisory board.

Still, Furse's ranking among the House's most budget-conscious Democrats has not deterred her from securing money for home-state programs, such as a light-rail project in Portland and salmon recovery efforts that bolster the Northwest's fishing industry.

An ardent supporter of abortion rights, Furse chose Jan. 22, 1997 — the 24th anniversary of the *Roe v. Wade* ruling — to publish a column in the Washington Times describing a decision she faced in 1961, when she was 25. Furse was told she could undergo a hysterectomy rather than give birth to a child that her doctor said would probably be blind, deaf and brain-damaged. "What a terrible set of choices: I could risk a back-alley abortion, carry a severely damaged fetus to term or lose my fertility forever," Furse wrote.

"I chose the final option. . . . I returned home to my two children knowing that my family would never become any larger." Furse said she broke her long silence on the episode because "there is a new generation of women who must hear the tragic stories of what life for women was like before *Roe v. Wade*."

Furse has spoken on other women's concerns

The Portland-based 1st starts on the western bank of the Willamette River, which splits Oregon's largest city. The district's urban component is downtown Portland (Multnomah County) and nearby neighborhoods that tend to be liberal and affluent; to the west are fast-growing Republican suburbs.

Metropolitan Portland has drawn California exiles and other out-of-staters searching for "livability" — less congestion, a moderate cost of living, a big city that still has a sense of community. Portlanders flock downtown to Saturday Market beneath the Burnside Bridge and attend events in Pioneer Courthouse Square and Waterfront Park. Each June the "City of Roses" hosts its popular Rose Festival.

In the past two decades, businesses and people have streamed into the suburbs west of Portland. The 1st is dominated by suburban Washington County; with 312,000 people, it is the state's second-most-populous county. Washington was the state's fastest-growing county in the 1980s; its population increased almost 27 percent. During remapping, Republicans lobbied hard to include in the 1st the GOP-heavy Clackamas County city of Lake Oswego.

The high-tech businesses that sprouted along U.S. 26 in Washington County during the 1980s suffered a decline, leaving empty office space, but the high-tech industry now appears to be on the rebound. Bedroom communities of Portland such as Beaverton, Tigard and Hillsboro have become satellite cities with their own economies. Electronics and computer companies such as Intel, Fujitsu and Sumitomo provide thousands of jobs and continue to expand. Nike, the sports-shoe manufacturer, has its futuristic headquarters in Beaverton. Portland's light-rail line is slated to connect the downtown with Hillsboro, 18 miles to the west, by the late 1990s.

OREGON 1
Western Portland and suburbs

Republicans outnumber Democrats in suburban Washington County. But the Republicans here are some of the most liberal in the country, and they are more than willing to cast split ballots.

Outside the Portland metropolitan area, the 1st becomes rural and more Democratic. The fishing and logging counties of Columbia and Clatsop are the strongest Democratic areas of the 1st outside Portland, although many of those Democrats are more conservative than Portland's affluent liberals. Columbia County has voted for every Democratic presidential nominee since 1932; Clatsop County went for Adlai E. Stevenson in 1956 and has remained in the Democratic column for president.

Both the district's logging and salmon industries are threatened as the local economy has moved from industries that rely on brawn to those that favor brains. The last of the big canneries closed in Astoria in the mid-1980s. Tourism buoys the local economy of some coastal communities, such as Seaside and Cannon Beach. Oregon's modest wine industry is centered in the Tualatin and northern Willamette valleys of Yamhill County, which tends to vote Republican.

Bill Clinton won 50 percent of the district's presidential vote in 1996. In the House race, Furse's winning margin was based largely on her 68 percent showing in Multnomah County.

1990 Population: 568,461. White 529,999 (93%), Black 4,498 (1%), Other 33,964 (6%). Hispanic origin 22,569 (4%). 18 and over 425,695 (75%), 62 and over 78,899 (14%). Median age: 34.

with similar intensity. Several women came forward in 1995 with allegations of sexual harassment by a fellow Oregonian, GOP Sen. Bob Packwood. When the Senate appeared unlikely to air their complaints in a public hearing, Furse repeatedly called for Packwood to agree to the hearings or resign. Facing wilting pressure, Packwood resigned in September 1995.

Furse also offered a bill directing the National Institutes of Health to study the effects that environmental factors have on women's health; the measure was enacted as part of the fiscal 1997 Labor-Health and Human Services spending bill. And to address what she saw as pension inequities facing women, Furse proposed legislation that would change pension law to protect women in divorce proceedings and simplify spousal consent rules for survivor annuities. No action was taken on the bill, but she plans to keep pushing it.

Furse votes a strong environmentalist line and has been an outspoken defender of the Endangered Species Act, so she was probably not surprised when the League of Private Property Voters ranked her among the 12 members of Congress "most threatening" to property rights. But she may be recognized most for leading the drive to overturn a controversial provision, tacked on to an unrelated rescissions bill in 1994, that allowed the harvest of downed and diseased timber on federal land.

Opponents of that "timber salvage rider" said loggers were abusing the law to overcut healthy trees. When the Interior spending bill came to the floor in June 1996, Furse offered an amendment to repeal the rider. Her amendment was defeated by a tiny margin, 209-211, but it had the support of 50 Republicans, and it served notice that the tide had turned: Later in the year, Congress did not renew the salvage waiver.

Furse, whose daughter has diabetes, points out that the illness accounts for 27 percent of the Medicare budget. She co-founded the Congressional Diabetes Caucus and assembled more than 250 cosponsors for two bills; they would expand Medicare coverage to include self-training for diabetics and blood testing strips. The bills were abruptly dropped from consideration on the House floor a half-hour before the 104th Congress adjourned in September 1996, but she has reintroduced them.

In the 103rd Congress, Furse supported the White House on all key budget votes and on gun control, abortion rights and gays in the military. Her only break with President Clinton came over NAFTA, which she voted against, saying it would "ride roughshod over our environmental laws."

At Home: Furse probably will never be able to relax in her politically marginal, largely suburban district. She won the seat in 1992 with 52 percent, then barely held on to it two years later, surviving a recount to post a narrow 301-vote victory. Not surprisingly, in 1996, a year after Furse briefly ran for the Senate, Republicans targeted her seat. In a rematch with her 1994 opponent, Furse survived, but once again with only 52 percent.

After Democrat Les AuCoin left the House in 1992 to run for the Senate, Furse — who had never served in government — provided a contrast to 1st District GOP nominee Tony Meeker, the Oregon state treasurer. Meeker, long an opponent of abortion, never sought to obscure his lengthy government experience. But Furse was well-funded, campaigned on her support for abortion rights and benefited from the year's Democratic surge in the Northwest. She was helped by an 18,000-vote edge in the Multnomah County portion of the 1st.

Abortion was once again the focus of Furse's difficult 1994 campaign against conservative GOP businessman Bill Witt, another staunch abortion foe. But Furse was happy to stress social issues, including her opposition to a controversial anti-gay rights initiative on the Oregon ballot. Witt criticized Furse's efforts to cut defense spending, and the strong Republican tide that year nearly swept him into office: Furse looked solid on Election Day, but a large proportion of the nearly 63,000 absentee ballots cast in the race vaulted Witt within a hairsbreadth of victory.

When Packwood resigned from the Senate in September 1995, Furse jumped into the race to serve out his term, as did Democratic Reps. Peter A. DeFazio and Ron Wyden. Furse said a woman in Packwood's seat "sounds like justice," and the women's fundraising group EMILY's List backed her.

But Gov. John Kitzhaber declared that the Dec. 5 primary would be conducted entirely with mail-in ballots — an unprecedented step that meant candidates had to raise money quickly to get advertising on the air before the ballots were sent out in mid-November. Three weeks after getting into the race, Furse dropped out, saying she would be unable to raise her target of $750,000 in time. Wyden, who had a strong fundraising advantage, won the primary and then the general election in January 1996.

Encouraged by Furse's tiny margin of victory in 1994, a crowd of Republicans lined up for the chance to deny her a third term. Witt, who had earlier dropped out of the race for the seat of retiring GOP Sen. Mark O. Hatfield, once again won the House primary, this time with a 32 percent plurality. Oregon Republicans made Witt the leader of their party's delegation to the Republican National Convention that summer. Furse's rematch with Witt was somewhat less centered on abortion than their 1994 contest; on the stump, Witt focused more on his flat-tax proposal. But Furse received a ringing endorsement from the Portland Oregonian and won in November with 52 percent of the vote.

HOUSE ELECTIONS

1996 General		
Elizabeth Furse (D)	144,588	(52%)
Bill Witt (R)	126,146	(45%)
Richard Johnson (LIBERT)	6,310	(2%)
1994 General		
Elizabeth Furse (D)	121,147	(48%)
Bill Witt (R)	120,846	(48%)
Brewster Gillett (AM)	6,695	(3%)
Daniel E. Wilson (LIBERT)	5,161	(2%)

Previous Winning Percentages: 1992 (52%)

CAMPAIGN FINANCE

	Receipts	Receipts from PACs	Expend-itures
1996			
Furse (D)	$1,356,538	$442,412 (33%)	$1,370,710
Witt (R)	$885,307	$210,349 (24%)	$880,871
1994			
Furse (D)	$1,145,731	$431,158 (38%)	$1,132,394
Witt (R)	$542,368	$84,181 (16%)	$541,456
Gillett (AM)	$2,985	0	$2,779

DISTRICT VOTE FOR PRESIDENT

	1996		1992
D	145,540 (50%)	**D**	136,630 (44%)
R	112,152 (38%)	**R**	99,304 (32%)
I	21,304 (7%)	**I**	73,134 (24%)

KEY VOTES

1997	
Ban "partial birth" abortions	N
1996	
Approve farm bill	#
Deny public education to illegal immigrants	N
Repeal ban on certain assault-style weapons	N
Increase minimum wage	Y
Freeze defense spending	Y
Approve welfare overhaul	Y
1995	
Approve balanced-budget constitutional amendment	N
Relax Clean Water Act regulations	N
Oppose limits on environmental regulations	Y
Reduce projected Medicare spending	N
Approve GOP budget with tax and spending cuts	N

VOTING STUDIES

	Presidential Support		Party Unity		Conservative Coalition	
Year	**S**	**O**	**S**	**O**	**S**	**O**
1996	78	19	88	6	12	86
1995	82	14	93	5	14	82
1994	79	19	94	4	22	78
1993	80	19	98	1	2	95

INTEREST GROUP RATINGS

Year	ADA	AFL-CIO	CCUS	ACU
1996	80	n/a	33	5
1995	90	100	33	20
1994	95	78	67	5
1993	95	100	10	4

2 Bob Smith (R)

Of Burns — Elected 1982, 7th term
Did not serve 1995-1997.

Biographical Information
Born: June 16, 1931, Portland, Ore.
Education: Willamette U., B.A. 1953.
Occupation: Public relations firm owner; cattle rancher; businessman.
Family: Wife, Kaye Tomlinson; three children.
Religion: Presbyterian.
Political Career: Ore. House, 1961-73, speaker, 1969-73; Ore. Senate, 1973-83, minority leader, 1977-83; U.S. House, 1983-95.
Capitol Office: 1126 Longworth Bldg. 20515; 225-6730.

Committees
Agriculture (chairman)
Resources
National Parks & Public Lands; Water & Power

The Path to Washington: Smith, who represented Oregon's 2nd District for 12 years before voluntarily stepping down in 1994, was lured out of retirement in 1996 only after receiving a personal guarantee from House Speaker Newt Gingrich that he would be rewarded with the Agriculture Committee chairmanship in the 105th Congress, provided he won and Republicans retained control of the House.

He won and they won and Smith holds the gavel at Agriculture, where he was a senior member before leaving Congress.

Smith brings a steady hand and historical perspective to the committee, which has seen the departure of some key senior Republicans including former chairman Pat Roberts of Kansas, who ran successfully for the Senate; Missouri Rep. Bill Emerson, who died of lung cancer in 1996; and Wisconsin Rep. Steve Gunderson, who retired.

Smith says the Agriculture Committee's highest priority in the 105th is reducing trade barriers to U.S. agricultural products.

"American farmers and ranchers, the most productive in the world, can prosper only where there is free and fair world trade," Smith said in March 1997. He added that U.S. agricultural exports totaled $60 billion in 1996 and do much to ameliorate the U.S. trade deficit. To underscore the need for open agricultural markets, Smith in the 105th led trade missions to Mexico and Chile.

Smith had some disagreements with the Clinton administration in the 105th over the Conservation Reserve Program (CRP), a program established in the 1985 farm bill and reauthorized in the 1996 farm bill. Under the CRP, landowners enter into contracts with the Department of Agriculture to place highly erodible cropland in long-term conservation practices. The landowners receive annual rental payments for doing this.

In 1997, Smith criticized the Agriculture Department for waiting too long to tell farmers if their enrolled acreage — much of which was due to expire later in the year — would be enrolled in the CRP for the coming year. He sought a one-year "technical correction" that purported to give farmers time to prepare the ground to plant fall crops if the Agriculture Department eventually rejected the acreage for enrollment in CRP.

Another of the committee's focuses is forestry, a particularly salient issue for Smith, whose district contains ten national forests. Smith is especially concerned about the role and effectiveness of management in forest protection; in January 1997 he held a forest management hearing in his district to underscore this.

Overall, however, the committee is likely to assume a lower profile in the next two years, particularly because Congress finished work in 1996 on two major pieces of agriculture legislation: an omnibus farm measure dubbed the "Freedom to Farm" bill and a rewrite of a pesticides law.

Although Smith now finds himself leading one of Capitol Hill's most influential committees, his return to politics was unplanned.

Smith's name first surfaced in connection with a possible return to Congress in the spring of 1996 when he tried to persuade freshman Republican Rep. Wes Cooley — who had succeeded Smith — to step aside in favor of another GOP candidate.

Cooley, a rancher and former state legislator, had come under scrutiny earlier that year for a series of allegations, including charges that he and his wife, Rosemary, had concealed their wedding date so she could continue receiving nearly $900 a month in veterans' benefits after the 1965 death of her first husband, a Marine captain who was killed in a plane crash.

Playing the role of respected party elder, Smith quietly worked behind the scenes for weeks to try to ease Cooley out of the picture while simultaneously looking for other GOP candidates who could receive the support of the district's diverse Republican majority.

Although several potential Republican candidates emerged, Cooley refused to step aside.

Finally, Gingrich and other national GOP leaders, nervous about the possibility of losing a seat that had elected just two Democrats since 1933, turned to Smith and persuaded him to come out

OREGON 2
East and Southwest — Medford; Bend

The 2nd is enormous, covering more than two-thirds of Oregon and bordering Washington, Idaho, Nevada and California. It is the state's most reliably Republican district, and the only one the Republican presidential candidate won in 1992 and 1996.

For the most part, people in the 2nd work the land, whether that means timber, livestock, crops or fruit. In a district where the federal government owns three-quarters of the acreage, loggers' jobs ride on court action restricting timber harvesting in national forests. Fishermen who make their living catching salmon on the Columbia River have also been snagged by endangered-species action.

Given the sprawling nature of the 2nd, any House candidate has to focus on a few widely scattered population centers. Although the district's two most-populous counties, Jackson and Deschutes, both registered double-digit growth in the 1980s, most of the counties in the 2nd lost population during the last decade. But from 1990 to 1996, only one Oregon county (Sherman, in the district's northern area) lost population.

With about 47,000 people, Medford (Jackson County) is the largest city in the 2nd. Medford is surrounded by pear, cherry and apple orchards of the fruit-growing Rogue River Valley. Less than 20 miles southeast of Medford is Ashland, which has hosted the Oregon Shakespeare Festival since 1935.

Population in Deschutes County has soared since 1970, as nearby skiing areas lured people to build summer homes and vacation condominiums. In 1986, Democratic gubernatorial candidate Neil Goldschmidt referred to Bend, the county's population center, as "the middle of nowhere." Deschutes has grown faster than any other county in the state since then.

Bend has attracted high-tech and light industry, emblematic of central Oregon's effort to diversify its economy and reduce its dependence on timber. Deschutes County also grows potatoes, mint and hay.

Although Bush lost Jackson and Deschutes counties in 1992, GOP Sen. Gordon H. Smith easily carried them in his narrow loss in the special January 1996 Senate election and in his razor-thin victory in November. Bob Dole also carried Jackson and Deschutes in 1996.

Beef cattle graze on public land throughout eastern Oregon. Alfalfa and hay grow on the dry, thinly settled plateau. In the north, most people live along or near the irrigated Columbia River Valley, where wheat ripens on steep golden hillsides. Umatilla is one of the leading wheat-harvesting counties in the nation. Pears, cherries and apples grow near the Hood River, a popular wind-surfing destination. Potatoes are grown and processed for export around Hermiston. Near Hermiston is the Umatilla Army Depot, where the Army stores nerve and mustard gas weapons that are destined for incineration.

1990 Population: 568,464. White 532,857 (94%), Black 1,658 (<1%), Other 33,949 (6%). Hispanic origin 30,470 (5%). 18 and over 418,063 (74%), 62 and over 106,398 (19%). Median age: 36.

of retirement by offering him chairmanship of the Agriculture panel. In short order, Cooley agreed to step aside, clearing the way for Smith's return. (In March 1997, Cooley was found guilty of lying about his military record in official voters' pamphlets. He was sentenced to two years' probation and ordered to pay fines and perform community service.)

But the Democrats were not going to concede with seat to Smith without a fight. They had an attractive candidate of their own — Mike Dugan, a district attorney from central Deschutes County who cast a moderate image. Dugan urged voters to reject Smith and the Republican Party for their willingness to engage in blatant "political backroom dealmaking."

But such arguments seemed to have little effect, and Smith, with wide name recognition and popularity and an ideology palatable to district residents, scored an overwhelming victory over Dugan and a minor-party candidate in November.

Smith, like some other prominent Oregon politicians, attended Willamette University in Salem, the state capital. In the early 1950s, Smith and former Oregon Sen. Bob Packwood were students, and former Oregon Sen. Mark O. Hatfield was a political science professor at Willamette.

Except for the two-year lacuna in his House service, Smith has served continuously in legislative office since 1961, the year he entered the Oregon House of Representatives. In 1969 he became Speaker, a position he held until entering the state Senate in 1973. Smith became minority leader of that legislative body in 1977, holding the post until his election to Congress.

Smith's congressional entrance in 1983 was in part due to good fortune. Due to above-average population growth in the 1970s, Oregon earned an additional congressional seat in the post-Census reapportionment.

Freshman Republican Denny Smith — who is no relation to Bob Smith — had represented the vast, eastern 2nd the previous two years, instead chose to run in the new 5th District, which comprised territory in the Willamette Valley.

That left the solidly Republican 2nd without an incumbent in 1982, and Smith entered the race to represent that district. After easily winning the GOP primary, he faced Democrat rancher Larryann Willis in the general. In a bad year for congressional Republicans nationwide, Smith comfortably defeated Willis with 56 percent of the vote.

Smith again easily turned back a 1984 challenge from Willis, and his subsequent elections were without suspense. He topped two-thirds of the vote in 1990 and 1992.

HOUSE ELECTIONS

1996 General

Bob Smith (R)	164,062	(62%)
Mike Dugan (D)	97,195	(37%)
Frank Wise (LIBERT)	4,581	(2%)

Previous Winning Percentages: **1992** (67%) **1990** (68%) **1988** (63%) **1986** (60%) **1984** (57%) **1982** (56%)

CAMPAIGN FINANCE

	Receipts	Receipts from PACs	Expend-itures
1996			
Smith (R)	$438,403	$265,963 (61%)	$412,394
Dugan (D)	$266,177	$110,500 (42%)	$264,902

DISTRICT VOTE FOR PRESIDENT

1996		1992	
D	103,116 (38%)	**D**	97,672 (35%)
R	130,406 (48%)	**R**	106,839 (38%)
I	30,093 (11%)	**I**	74,539 (27%)

KEY VOTES

1997

Ban "partial birth" abortions Y

3 Earl Blumenauer (D)

Of Portland — Elected 1996; 1st full term

Biographical Information

Born: Aug. 16, 1948, Portland, Ore.
Education: Lewis and Clark College, B.A. 1970, J.D. 1976.
Occupation: Lawyer; public official.
Family: Wife, Janice Babcock; two children.
Religion: Unspecified.
Political Career: Ore. House, 1973-77; candidate for Portland City Council, 1980; Multnomah County Commission, 1978-86; candidate for mayor of Portland, 1992; Portland City Council, 1986-96.
Capitol Office: 1113 Longworth Bldg. 20515; 225-4811.

Committees

Transportation & Infrastructure
Railroads; Water Resources & Environment

In Washington: Blumenauer won the Portland-based 3rd District in a May 1996 special election and it took him a little over nine months to land a committee assignment — on the Transportation and Infrastructure panel — that dovetails with his major area of expertise before coming to Congress. During eight years on the Multnomah County (Portland) Board of Commissioners, Blumenauer concentrated on transportation and land use issues, and during 10 years on the Portland City Council, he was an advocate of improving urban planning and was active in establishing Portland's commuter light rail system.

After entering the House, Blumenauer got a seat on the Economic and Educational Opportunities Committee; he left that panel (now called Education and The Workforce) in March 1997 to move to Transportation and Infrastructure, where he is the No. 2 Democrat on the Railroads Subcommittee and also serves on the Water Resources and Environment Subcommittee.

In Congress, one of Blumenauer's first House floor speeches highlighted an annual conference, Rail Volution, that took place in Washington in September 1996.

"We are talking about light rail, intercity rail, managing the auto and transportation infrastructure, mixed use development," Blumenauer said. "At a time when we are concerned about making our communities livable while dealing with the deficit, the Rail Volution message was a breath of fresh air: spending wiser, not raising taxes, making change, solving problems rather than creating them, and viewing citizen input as a valuable tool, not citizens as an enemy. This is an important message for us in Congress to hear and to act upon."

On the Transportation Committee, Blumenauer will have a ringside seat as the 105th Congress works on the five-year bill reauthorizing the nation's transportation programs. The legislation is a follow-on to the last major reauthorization, which was called the Intermodal Surface Transportation and Efficiency Act, better known by its acronym, ISTEA.

"We need ISTEA and the money that it brings," Blumenauer said in a 1996 floor speech. "But more important, to deal with the problems of our increasingly mobile populations, is the flexibility that that legislation entails. More important than money is the local planning framework that is involved. And most important of all is the public involvement that is entailed. Our citizens, our constituents, know what they need. If we engage them in the process of planning for our future, they will respond with innovation and nontraditional solutions. We in Congress talk a lot about empowerment and doing more with less. ISTEA is a chance to deliver on that promise."

In keeping with that theme, Blumenauer said he wanted to create the Livability Caucus, which would focus on issues such as providing transportation options that allow individuals to choose the most cost-effective way of traveling, using renewable energy, looking for less expensive and more environmentally friendly solutions to alleviating congestion than simply building new roads or widening existing ones, and promoting non-polluting modes of travel. He called for federal programs to put mass transit on equal footing with solutions that involve car commuting.

He also planned to organize a Bike Caucus, to call attention to that mode of transportation. Blumenauer does not have a car in Washington and often bicycles to work.

He introduced legislation in both the 104th and 105th Congress to encourage states to adopt laws to seize the cars of repeat drunk drivers. The measure was based on a law he championed on the Portland City Council.

Blumenauer's predecessor in the 3rd was Democrat Ron Wyden, who left the House after winning a special Senate election. Shortly after arriving in Washington, Blumenauer followed Wyden in another respect: He won the annual House Gym basketball free-throw tournament, hitting 78 percent of his shots. The previous year, Wyden had won the contest, shooting 94 percent.

Blumenauer votes a steadily liberal, pro-labor

OREGON 3
East and North Portland and eastern suburbs

Socially and politically, Portland is two cities. The 3rd District portion east of the Willamette River is a working-class town. Blue-collar neighborhoods abut middle-class suburbs. The section west of the river is generally more affluent and elegant.

In an area with little cultural diversity — the Portland metropolitan area is more than 90 percent white — northeast and southeast Portland are veritable melting pots. The Albina section is home to many of Portland's blacks; it is the poorest area in the city. There are also Asian and Hispanic communities east of the river. Some young white professionals live in the Irvington, Alameda and Laurelhurst sections of East Portland.

Democratic candidates take comfortable margins in the 3rd, thanks to blacks in the Albina section, blue-collar whites in North Portland and the many elderly residents of the east side.

But many voters in the 3rd are conservative, white, working-class "Reagan Democrats," particularly in such areas as the St. Johns section of North Portland, East County, the Clackamas County suburb of Milwaukie, and the cities of Gresham and Troutdale east of Portland.

New to the 3rd for the 1990s is a section west of the Willamette River in southwest Portland that includes the large homes and winding streets of Dunthorpe, one of Portland's most expensive neighborhoods. Democrats are few and far between here, but the small number of Republican voters in this area does not alter the 3rd's overall Democratic cast.

While Portland's commercial center remains west of the Willamette, the city has been investing of late in some east side projects. The Lloyd Center, one of the country's oldest urban malls, has had significant renovation. The Oregon Museum of Science and Industry has moved from southwest Portland to a new, larger east side home under the Marquam Bridge. Pro basketball's Portland Trail Blazers moved into a larger east side arena at the new Oregon Convention Center.

Over the last decade there was growth in the east side suburbs of Multnomah County, a few of which are as sumptuous as the in-town residential areas west of the Willamette. Gresham, the eastern terminus of Portland's light-rail line, is the largest of the 3rd's suburban cities.

Gresham tripled in size during the 1970s and grew in the 1980s to a population of 68,200; it is now Oregon's fourth-largest city. Gresham's annual Mount Hood Festival of Jazz draws national and international artists each August.

Once outside the suburbs, Multnomah and Clackamas counties quickly turn rural. There are a few farms along the Columbia River, the 3rd's northern boundary. Visitors to the underwater viewing room at the Bonneville Lock and Dam can observe migrating fish ascending a fish ladder.

Mount Hood National Forest occupies most of the district's eastern part.

1990 Population: 568,465. White 496,062 (87%), Black 33,709 (6%), Other 38,694 (7%). Hispanic origin 17,946 (3%). 18 and over 428,542 (75%), 62 and over 90,244 (16%). Median age: 34.

line, siding with a majority of Democrats against Republicans 91 percent of the time in 1996 floor votes. One of those votes was in support of an effort by Reps. Christopher Shays, R-Conn., and Barney Frank, D-Mass., to freeze defense spending for fiscal 1997. The measure failed, 194-219. Blumenauer backed President Clinton 82 percent of the time in 1996, but he was one of 98 Republicans who refused to go along with the compromise welfare overhaul bill, which Clinton signed into law after vetoing two earlier Republican-backed proposals.

In keeping with his populist spirit, Blumenauer in March 1997 introduced legislation giving a communitiy the option of making an offer to buy its professional sports team if the owner wants to move it out of town. "I believe that any community which owns its team will create for itself traditions of the sort which seldom, if ever, flow from the suites of owners who care more about profit margins than about their communities," Blumenauer said.

At Home: Long considered a rising star in Oregon politics, Blumenauer was all but assured of victory in the 3rd after Wyden left it after his election to the Senate in January 1996.

In a three-way, vote-by-mail Democratic special primary April 2. Blumenauer far outdistanced state Sen. Shirley Gold and registered nurse Anna Nevenich. On May 21, Blumenauer sailed past Republican nominee Mark Brunelle, winning the right to serve through the end of the 104th Congress. Blumenauer, who reminded his supporters to "vote Earl, vote often," also prevailed in the same-day regular primary.

A liberal activist in politics since his teenage years in the late 1960s, Blumenauer was just one year out of college in 1971 when he testified before a congressional subcommittee in support of a constitutional amendment to lower the voting age to 18. The next year, at age 24, he was elected to the Oregon House, He quickly rose to prominence, becoming chairman of the Revenue Committee and helping to shape legislation on issues such as collective bargaining, campaign reform, transportation, taxation and the environment.

Blumenauer was elected to the Multnomah County (Portland) Board of Commissioners in 1978 and he served in that post for eight years. In 1986, he was elected to the Portland City Council.

His political climb has not been without some stumbles. He failed in a 1980 City Council bid, and in 1992 he ran unsuccessfully for mayor of Portland. But once on the council, he routinely racked up huge re-election margins, and in the fall of 1995, when Wyden announced for the Senate seat being vacated by disgraced Republican Bob Packwood, Oregon Democratic officials did not have to look far for a House candidate with high name recognition and broad appeal.

A Portland native and lifelong resident of the 3rd District, Blumenauer won virtually unanimous endorsement from organizations and officials prominent in Oregon Democratic politics, including many who had supported Wyden through his eight House terms. Perhaps most notable among Blumenauer's credits was the cross-party endorsement he received from retiring five-term Republican Sen. Mark O. Hatfield.

In November 1996, Blumenauer had no trouble winning a full term, taking 67 percent of the vote against Republican Scott Bruun.

HOUSE ELECTIONS

1996 General		
Earl Blumenauer (D)	165,922	(67%)
Scott Bruun (R)	65,259	(26%)
Joe Keating (PACIFIC)	9,274	(4%)
Bruce Alexander Knight (LIBERT)	4,474	(2%)
1996 Primary		
Earl Blumenauer (D)	50,747	(78%)
Shirley Gold (D)	13,812	(21%)
1996 Special		
Earl Blumenauer (D)	50,125	(70%)
Mark Brunelle (R)	17,085	(24%)
Joe Keating (PACIFIC)	2,916	(4%)
Victoria P. Guillebeau (S)	1,604	(2%)
1996 Special Primary		
Earl Blumenauer (D)	53,275	(72%)
Shirley Gold (D)	17,674	(24%)
Anna Nevenich (D)	2,433	(3%)

CAMPAIGN FINANCE

	Receipts	Receipts from PACs	Expend-itures
1996			
Blumenauer (D)	$539,320	$157,707 (29%)	$507,414
Bruun (R)	$11,438	0	$11,823

DISTRICT VOTE FOR PRESIDENT

	1996		1992
D	147,066 (57%)	**D**	146,835 (53%)
R	72,121 (28%)	**R**	72,338 (26%)
I	18,556 (7%)	**I**	58,900 (21%)

KEY VOTES

1997	
Ban "partial birth" abortions	N
1996	
Freeze defense spending	Y
Approve welfare overhaul	N

VOTING STUDIES

	Presidential Support		Party Unity		Conservative Coalition	
Year	**S**	**O**	**S**	**O**	**S**	**O**
1996†	82	13	91	6	9	91

INTEREST GROUP RATINGS

Year	ADA	AFL-CIO	CCUS	ACU
1996†	78	n/a	20	0

† Not eligible for all recorded votes.

4 Peter A. DeFazio (D)

Of Springfield — Elected 1986, 6th term

Biographical Information

Born: May 27, 1947, Needham, Mass.
Education: Tufts U., B.A. 1969; U. of Oregon, 1969-71, M.S. 1977.
Military Service: Air Force, 1967-71.
Occupation: Congressional aide.
Family: Wife, Myrnie L. Daut.
Religion: Roman Catholic.
Political Career: Lane County Commission, 1982-86; sought Democratic nomination for U.S. Senate, 1996 special.
Capitol Office: 2134 Rayburn Bldg. 20515; 225-6416.

Committees

Resources
Water & Power (ranking)
Transportation & Infrastructure
Aviation; Surface Transportation

In Washington: DeFazio has made it his business vigorously to confront the House's conservative Republican majority, accusing the GOP, among other things, of promoting corporate welfare and spending excessively on the military.

He sought during the 104th to move to a bigger stage, running for the Senate after incumbent Republican Bob Packwood resigned rather than face certain expulsion on charges of sexual harassment and other personal misconduct.

But in a December 1995 special primary, DeFazio lost the Democratic nomination to eight-term Democratic Rep. Ron Wyden (who went on to win the seat).

In 1996, DeFazio gave thought to seeking Oregon's other Senate seat, after incumbent Republican Mark O. Hatfield announced his retirement. But DeFazio declared in February 1996 that he would instead run for re-election to the House. He said he did not want to repeat 1995's fundraising efforts.

DeFazio has kept busy in the House jabbing at Republican policies as a vocal member of the Progressive Caucus, a group of the chamber's most liberal Democrats. The group in October 1995 took exception to GOP plans to balance the budget, portraying them as "grossly promoting greed over the well being of middle and low-income Americans."

DeFazio has devoted special attention to the Pentagon, where he believes many taxpayer dollars could be saved. He has been especially critical of the military's Operational Support Aircraft (OSA) account for executive travel. He and Republican "deficit hawk" Mark W. Neumann of Wisconsin were successful with an amendment to the fiscal 1996 defense appropriations bill that reduced funds for the account by $50 million. The amendment was prompted by reports that an Air Force general used support aircraft to fly to the United States from Italy with his cat. "It's time to subject the generals and admirals to the same kind of critical review we've given to welfare queens and deadbeat dads," DeFazio said.

He has also focused on potential budget savings at the Selective Service System, arguing that the agency is an outmoded vestige of the Cold War. DeFazio offered an amendment to the fiscal 1996 appropriations bill for the Veterans Administration to cut funding for the agency and to end the registration of young men for a potential military draft. Arguing that selective service is unnecessary in light of the breakup of the Soviet Union, DeFazio said: "The fiscal-conservative, government-efficiency types have been overwhelmed by the right-wing Cold War ideologues." But the House rejected his amendment, 175-242, in July 1995.

DeFazio holds a seat on the Resources Committee, where he is ranking Democrat on the Water and Power Subcommittee. He also has been active through the years on what is now the Transportation and Infrastructure Committee (formerly called Public Works and Transportation).

DeFazio, like many of his Democratic colleagues, rebel at Republican efforts to overhaul key environmental laws. When the House in May 1995 passed a measure substantially revising the nation's key water pollution law, DeFazio was aghast. The measure would have eased many anti-pollution requirements of existing law, which critics argued were unnecessarily costly. DeFazio was among the Democrats charging that the bill would give polluters free rein. "A vote for this bill is a vote to turn back the country to the days when our rivers were more like open sewers and industrial cesspools than they were precious resources," said DeFazio. The measure passed the House, but it went no further.

But DeFazio must manage more of a juggling act when it comes to forest and resource management questions. His district and state include strongly conflicting interests on those issues — the loggers who oppose restrictions on cutting and the environmentalists who want restrictions; the shippers who profit from timber exports and the mill workers who want to keep the logs for their saws. DeFazio opposed a GOP-backed tim-

Loggers, fishermen and environmentalists combine to give the 4th a potentially combustible political mix.

Many of the district's communities have been dependent on the wood products industry; others have made their livings in salmon fishing. But roughly half the district vote is cast in Lane County (Eugene), home to the University of Oregon and a sizable environmentalist faction.

A politician running districtwide has the precarious task of balancing the economic needs of loggers and fishermen against others' concerns for protection of the environment.

Most of the ancient, old-growth forest that is the habitat of the threatened northern spotted owl is in the Cascade Range in the eastern part of the 4th. Congress in 1995 allowed the sale of salvage timber (dead or diseased trees) for two years, requiring federal agencies to sell billions of board feet in large tracts of federal forest. The measure exempted the timber sales from the requirements of certain environmental and land management laws and specified that the sales may not be halted by the courts. Logging on federal lands has long been subject to numerous legal challenges by environmentalists.

Roseburg (Douglas County), which calls itself the Timber Capital of the Nation, is perhaps the district's most timber-dependent community. Mill closures and other timber-related cutbacks boosted its unemployment rate. An influx of newcomers, many of them retirees from California, has helped keep the population in the Roseburg area from dropping precipitously.

Along the Pacific Coast, Coos County (Coos Bay) has also seen once-thriving timber mills close. And fishermen in coastal towns such as

OREGON 4
Southwest — Eugene

Charleston, Bandon and Port Orford have seen declining salmon runs.

With a university and some light industry, Eugene has weathered the timber decline better through economic diversity. But a large segment of Eugene's economy is still linked to timber processing.

For the workers and their families whose lives are tethered to the lumber industry, jobs and growth are more important than environmental preservation. Industrial employment has been unsteady in Eugene and its timber-dominated neighbor, Springfield.

Eugene in the 1960s and 1970s was a mecca for the back-to-nature counterculture. Many students stayed after graduation. As they moved into workaday society, they learned how to influence local politics; they usually elect liberal Democrats.

But the electoral history of Lane County is mixed. Lane went Democratic in the 1976 presidential election and Republican in 1968, 1972 and 1980, though it has been in the Democratic column in every presidential race since 1984.

Agriculture also contributes to the 4th's economy. There are some dairy farms on the south coast (Bandon prides itself on its cheddar cheese and cranberries). In the north, ryegrass is grown in the fertile Willamette Valley.

1990 Population: 568,465. White 545,768 (96%), Black 2,659 (<1%), Other 20,038 (4%). Hispanic origin 13,409 (2%). 18 and over 424,702 (75%), 62 and over 98,733 (17%). Median age: 35.

ber salvage provision that was added to a fiscal 1995 rescissions bill; it required the sale of more than 6 billion board feet of lumber from dead or diseased trees over two years from federal lands. Supporters of the provision said it would create thousands of jobs for workers displaced by restrictions on tree cutting. But opponents, like DeFazio, noted that the provision also allowed cutting live, healthy trees as part of salvaging. An amendment to strip the salvage timber language from the bill was defeated on a 150-275 vote.

A new area of concern for the West is a push by some in Congress to deregulate the electric utility industry. The Pacific Northwest has long enjoyed relatively cheap electricity because of its abundant hydroelectric power, and members from states in the region worry that deregulation could raise electric rates. DeFazio advocates a go-slow approach on the issue by Congress, preferring that states take the lead. In a February 1997 letter to colleagues, DeFazio implored, "Maybe we ought to let the states continue to experiment, so we'll have a better idea about the risks, the costs and the potential benefits of deregulation."

DeFazio shares with many of his constituents a skepticism about international entanglements, particularly in the trade arena. In the 103rd Congress, he was the only Oregonian in the House to vote against both NAFTA and GATT.

At Home: Initially, DeFazio, Wyden, and 1st District Democratic Rep. Elizabeth D. Furse all expressed interest in Packwood's seat. Once Packwood resigned, Democratic Gov. John Kitzhaber announced an election schedule: He set a primary for Dec. 5 and a general election for Jan. 30, 1996, with both to be entirely vote-by-mail events — a first in congressional elections.

In the early jostling, DeFazio sought to portray Wyden's appeal as limited to his Portland base, offering himself as the kind of Democrat who could appeal to small-town and rural voters. In the contest for support from organized labor,

DeFazio's 1994 opposition to NAFTA gave him an edge over Wyden, who supported passage.

Furse soon dropped her Senate bid, citing difficulty raising money, and DeFazio asserted that her absence from the contest would help him gain labors' solid backing. But Furse's departure from the race improved Wyden's chances of getting a hefty vote from the metropolitan Portland area, where he and Furse were both expected to draw their strongest support. Wyden's fundraising prowess and name recognition helped him win the primary; he took 50 percent of the vote, six points ahead of DeFazio.

When DeFazio first won election to Congress in 1986, his strength and his weakness as a candidate were the same: He was identified with Jim Weaver, his predecessor in the 4th. In the end, the Weaver connection was more help than hindrance. DeFazio portrayed himself as heir to Weaver's populist appeal, but kept apart from Weaver's personal quarrels and financial entanglements. DeFazio first went to work for Weaver in 1977, fresh from a graduate program in gerontology at the University of Oregon. He handled senior citizens' issues in Weaver's Eugene office, spent two years in Washington as his legislative aide, then returned to Eugene as Weaver's constituent services director. After that, DeFazio won election to the Lane County (Eugene) Commission in 1982.

As an elected official, DeFazio proved to be less abrasive than Weaver but equally aggressive. He sued to nullify contracts between Oregon utilities and the Washington Public Power Supply System, whose failed nuclear projects had resulted in utility rate increases. He also led the fight against a 1983 proposal for a Eugene city income tax.

When Weaver announced he would not seek re-election in 1986, DeFazio stepped in. He had ties to environmentalists and liberals in Eugene's university community, a residence in the timber-oriented suburb of Springfield, and name familiarity throughout Lane County. DeFazio had primary opposition from state Sen. Bill Bradbury, popular in the coastal areas, and state Sen. Margie Hendriksen, who had labor and feminist support. But DeFazio edged Bradbury by just under 1,000 votes with Hendriksen a close third.

Republicans nominated Bruce Long, who had taken 42 percent against Weaver in 1984. Long sought to cultivate the many voters Weaver had alienated over the years; time and again, he described DeFazio as "Jim Weaver Jr." Allegations that Weaver had used campaign funds to play the commodities market made DeFazio's ties to the incumbent seem all the more undesirable.

But DeFazio had no connection with Weaver's financial troubles, and he deflected the "clone" critique by insisting that he was an independent thinker who had picked up experience in Weaver's office. DeFazio called Long a dogmatic conservative lacking sympathy for district voters.

Long was better financed than in 1984, but his media efforts could not overshadow DeFazio's Lane County base and strong organization. DeFazio took 54 percent and since then he has won re-election with ease.

HOUSE ELECTIONS

1996 General		
Peter A. DeFazio (D)	177,270	(66%)
John D. Newkirk (R)	76,649	(28%)
Tonie Nathan (LIBERT)	4,919	(2%)
William "Bill" Bonville (REF)	3,960	(1%)
1994 General		
Peter A. DeFazio (D)	158,981	(67%)
John D. Newkirk (R)	78,947	(33%)

Previous Winning Percentages: 1992 (71%) **1990** (86%) **1988** (72%) **1986** (54%)

CAMPAIGN FINANCE

	Receipts	Receipts from PACs	Expend-itures
1996			
DeFazio (D)	$253,164	$178,212 (70%)	$301,211
Newkirk (R)	$10,613	$516 (5%)	$10,609
1994			
DeFazio (D)	$290,182	$164,559 (57%)	$221,718
Newkirk (R)	$10,673	$214 (2%)	$10,767

DISTRICT VOTE FOR PRESIDENT

1996	1992
D 122,392 (45%)	**D** 123,387 (42%)
R 108,782 (40%)	**R** 93,889 (32%)
I 26,826 (10%)	**I** 74,447 (26%)

KEY VOTES

1997	
Ban "partial birth" abortions	N
1996	
Approve farm bill	N
Deny public education to illegal immigrants	N
Repeal ban on certain assault-style weapons	N
Increase minimum wage	Y
Freeze defense spending	Y
Approve welfare overhaul	Y
1995	
Approve balanced-budget constitutional amendment	Y
Relax Clean Water Act regulations	N
Oppose limits on environmental regulations	Y
Reduce projected Medicare spending	N
Approve GOP budget with tax and spending cuts	N

VOTING STUDIES

	Presidential Support		Party Unity		Conservative Coalition	
Year	S	O	S	O	S	O
1996	67	28	87	11	18	80
1995	74	22	87	9	19	77
1994	56	35	83	9	31	58
1993	66	32	84	10	25	75
1992	12	84	85	7	21	75
1991	26	70	88	8	27	68

INTEREST GROUP RATINGS

Year	ADA	AFL-CIO	CCUS	ACU
1996	95	n/a	19	5
1995	90	92	25	16
1994	70	75	75	29
1993	100	100	9	13
1992	90	82	25	9
1991	80	100	20	11

5 Darlene Hooley (D)

Of West Linn — Elected 1996, 1st term

Biographical Information
Born: April 4, 1939, Williston, N.D.
Education: Pasadena Nazarene College, 1957-59; Oregon State U., B.S. 1961.
Occupation: Teacher.
Family: Husband, John Hooley; two children.
Religion: Lutheran.
Political Career: West Linn City Council, 1977-81; Ore. House, 1981-87; Clackamas County Commission, 1987-97.
Capitol Office: 1419 Longworth Bldg. 20515; 225-5711.

Committees
Banking & Financial Services
General Oversight & Investigations; Housing & Community Opportunity
Science
Energy & Environment

The Path to Washington: Hooley in 1996 became the third person and the second Democrat in six years elected to represent this quintessential swing district that stretches to the south and west of Portland.

But supporters contend that Hooley's strong diplomatic skills and a non-confrontational leadership style may be just the right fit for the politically marginal area.

A former schoolteacher, Hooley entered politics in 1977 as a member of the West Linn City Council.

Four years later, she was elected to the Oregon House of Representatives and served in that chamber for six years. There she earned a reputation for being a serious and conciliatory lawmaker more interested in formulating policy than engaging in partisan and ideological confrontations.

Hooley was instrumental in establishing Oregon's recycling laws and played a key role in reforming the state's welfare system.

In 1987, Hooley was appointed to the Clackamas County Commission, a position to which she was re-elected twice. Hooley held the rotating chairmanship of the three-member commission in 1990, 1993 and 1996. She oversaw the establishment of a pilot project that sought to counsel welfare recipients and reduce the number of people on public assistance.

As a member of Congress, Hooley has pledged to work to protect funding for early childhood education programs, such as Head Start, while also promoting policies to increase access to college.

Hooley has said she will work to preserve Social Security and Medicare for senior citizens, and protect abortion rights for women.

Hooley supports balancing the budget, but says she would oppose efforts to cut taxes before doing so.

She has, however, indicated that she would be in favor of tax policies aimed at economic development and creating new jobs.

On environmental issues, Hooley says she will adamantly oppose any efforts to weaken clean air and clean water regulation. But cognizant of the district's heavy reliance on timber, agriculture and fishing, Hooley contends that the federal government should set standards but not dictate to local governments and industry how to meet such standards.

Hooley was assigned to the Banking and Financial Services Committee and the Science Committee.

In the primary campaign, Hooley easily outpaced two lesser-known Democrats to claim the party's nomination and the right to take on conservative Republican freshman Rep. Jim Bunn.

Hooley quickly won the aid of national Democrats who targeted Bunn as vulnerable because of his modest winning percentage in 1994 and his strong support of much of the conservative House agenda.

Bunn also became one of the more than 60 lawmakers who drew the wrath of the AFL-CIO for his votes to reduce funding for worker safety programs and the National Labor Relations Board.

Hooley displayed a knack for attracting attention and raising money. For example, she received early backing from EMILY's List, an influential political group of pro-abortion rights Democratic women, among other groups.

With her campaign well-tuned and well-financed, Hooley used her time and money to promote proposals such as tuition deductions for college students and their families and improved vocational programs for those needing professional retraining.

Another proposal that Hooley discussed was investing more money in programs aimed at preventing juvenile crime and rehabilitating minors already in the judicial system.

Meanwhile, Bunn found himself flooded by a barrage of negative ads that portrayed him as too conservative for the district and frequently sought to tie him to House Speaker Newt Gingrich. Hooley won with 51 percent of the vote.

OREGON 5
Willamette Valley, Pacific Coast — Salem; Corvallis

Oregon's four major industries — timber, agriculture, fishing and tourism — are all represented in the 5th, whose shape bears a passing resemblance to that of the state fish, the chinook salmon.

Politically, the district is marginal. It combines traditional Democrats in coastal Tillamook and Lincoln counties with Republicans in Marion County and large numbers of independent voters in some of Clackamas County's Portland suburbs.

Some old-growth forests are in Mount Hood National Forest in the eastern part of the district. Logging families and owners of small, family-run mills in places such as Mill City, Detroit and Molalla have no use for the environmental protections aimed at preserving the northern spotted owl — or for politicians sympathetic to the owl.

Forty percent of the 5th's population is in Marion County (Salem), usually a dependable Republican base. But Bill Clinton in 1996 edged Bob Dole by a 45 percent to 43 percent margin, becoming the first Democratic presidential candidate since 1964 to win Marion. Democrat Hooley also won Marion in 1996, but Republican Gordon H. Smith romped to 55 percent in his successful bid for the U.S. Senate.

Clackamas, Marion and Polk counties are at the heart of the Willamette Valley, Oregon's most productive agricultural area. It is the center of Oregon's greenhouse and nursery crop industry, the state's second-largest agricultural commodity group. Trees and shrubs are grown, primarily for export.

The area is renowned for its fruits and berries, as well as its grass seeds. Willamette hops from Marion and Clackamas go into some of the country's finest beers. Polk County grows cherries and wine grapes; wineries dot Polk and Marion counties. Marion is among the nation's top counties for snap beans.

Along the coast, tourism and fishing fuel the economy. The resort town of Newport (Lincoln County) is also a vibrant fishing community known for its Dungeness crabs. Sport fishing is popular in such coastal towns as Lincoln City, Waldport and Yachats. To the north in Tillamook County, timber and dairy interests predominate. The Tillamook County Creamery Association produces a famous cheddar cheese.

The district reaches into Portland's Clackamas County suburbs; West Linn is one of Oregon's wealthiest communities. Along the Clackamas River is Oregon City, the western terminus of the Oregon Trail, 2,000 miles from Independence, Mo. Incorporated in 1844, Oregon City is the oldest city west of the Rockies.

The 5th contains only a corner of Benton County, but that includes the city of Corvallis, the district's only major city outside of Salem. It is the home of Oregon State University and numerous political activists who make Corvallis the most liberal area in the 5th. Clinton and Hooley carried this area handily in 1996.

1990 Population: 568,466. White 532,101 (94%), Black 3,654 (1%), Other 32,711 (6%). Hispanic origin 28,313 (5%). 18 and over 421,189 (74%), 62 and over 90,921 (16%). Median age: 34.

HOUSE ELECTIONS

1996 General		
Darlene Hooley (D)	139,521	(51%)
Jim Bunn (R)	125,409	(46%)
Lawrence Knight Duquesne (LIBERT)	5,191	(2%)
1996 Primary		
Darlene Hooley (D)	27,930	(51%)
Loren W. Collins (D)	14,899	(27%)
Sharon Scott (D)	11,461	(21%)

CAMPAIGN FINANCE

	Receipts	Receipts from PACs	Expend-itures
1996			
Hooley (D)	$1,021,007	$267,892 (26%)	$1,019,312
Bunn (R)	$573,710	$267,625 (47%)	$553,726

DISTRICT VOTE FOR PRESIDENT

	1996		1992
D	131,527 (47%)	D	116,790 (40%)
R	114,691 (41%)	R	103,387 (35%)
I	24,442 (9%)	I	73,071 (25%)

KEY VOTES

1997

Ban "partial birth" abortions N

PENNSYLVANIA

Governor: Tom Ridge (R)
First elected: 1994
Length of term: 4 years
Term expires: 1/99
Salary: $105,000
Term limit: 2 terms
Phone: (717) 787-2500
Born: August 26, 1945; Munhall, Pa.
Education: Harvard U., B.A. 1967; Dickinson School of Law, J.D. 1972.
Military Service: Army, 1968-70.
Occupation: Lawyer.
Family: Wife, Michele Moore; two children.
Religion: Roman Catholic.
Political Career: Erie assistant district attorney, 1979-82; U.S. House, 1983-95.

Lt. Gov.: Mark Schweiker (R)
First elected: 1994
Length of term: 4 years
Term expires: 1/99
Salary: $83,000
Phone: (717) 787-3300

State election official: (717) 787-5280
Democratic headquarters: (717) 238-9381
Republican headquarters: (717) 234-4901

REDISTRICTING

Pennsylvania lost two House seats in reapportionment, dropping from 23 districts to 21. Commonwealth court judge issued map Feb. 24, 1992; state Supreme court approved March 10.

STATE LEGISLATURE

General Assembly. Biennial session; meets year-round.

Senate: 50 members, 4-year terms
1996 breakdown: 30R, 20D; 44 men, 6 women
Salary: $57,367 + expenses
Phone: (717) 787-5920

House of Representatives: 203 members, 2-year terms
1996 breakdown: 104R, 99D; 178 men, 25 women
Salary: $57,367 + expenses
Phone: (717) 787-2372

URBAN STATISTICS

City	Population
Philadelphia	1,585,577
Mayor Edward Rendell, D	
Pittsburgh	369,879
Mayor Tom Murphy, D	
Erie	108,718
Mayor Joyce Savocchio, D	
Allentown	105,301
Mayor William Heydt, R	
Scranton	81,805
Mayor James P. Connors, R	

U.S. CONGRESS

Senate: 0 D, 2 R
House: 11 D, 10 R

TERM LIMITS

For state offices: No

ELECTIONS

1996 Presidential Vote

Bill Clinton	49%
Bob Dole	40%
Ross Perot	10%

1992 Presidential Vote

Bill Clinton	45%
George Bush	36%
Ross Perot	18%

1988 Presidential Vote

George Bush	51%
Michael S. Dukakis	48%

POPULATION

1990 population		11,881,643
1980 population		11,863,895
Percent change		+<1%
Rank among states:		5
White		89%
Black		9%
Hispanic		2%
Asian or Pacific islander		1%
Urban		69%
Rural		31%
Born in state		80%
Foreign-born		3%
Under age 18	2,794,810	24%
Ages 18-64	7,257,727	61%
65 and older	1,829,106	15%
Median age		35

MISCELLANEOUS

Capital: Harrisburg
Number of counties: 67
Per capita income: $19,128 (1991)
Rank among states: 16
Total area: 45,308 sq. miles
Rank among states: 33

PENNSYLVANIA

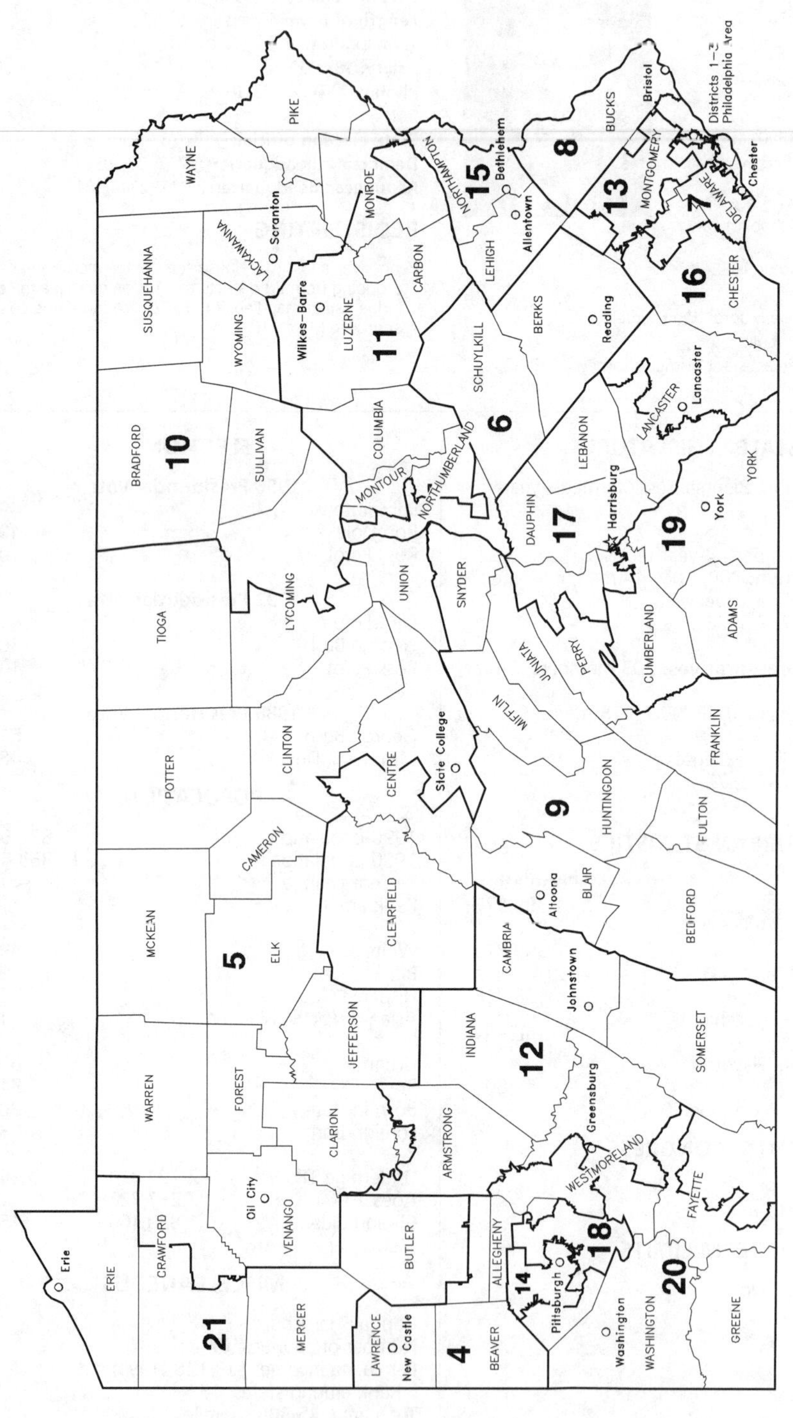

PHILADELPHIA AREA DISTRICTS

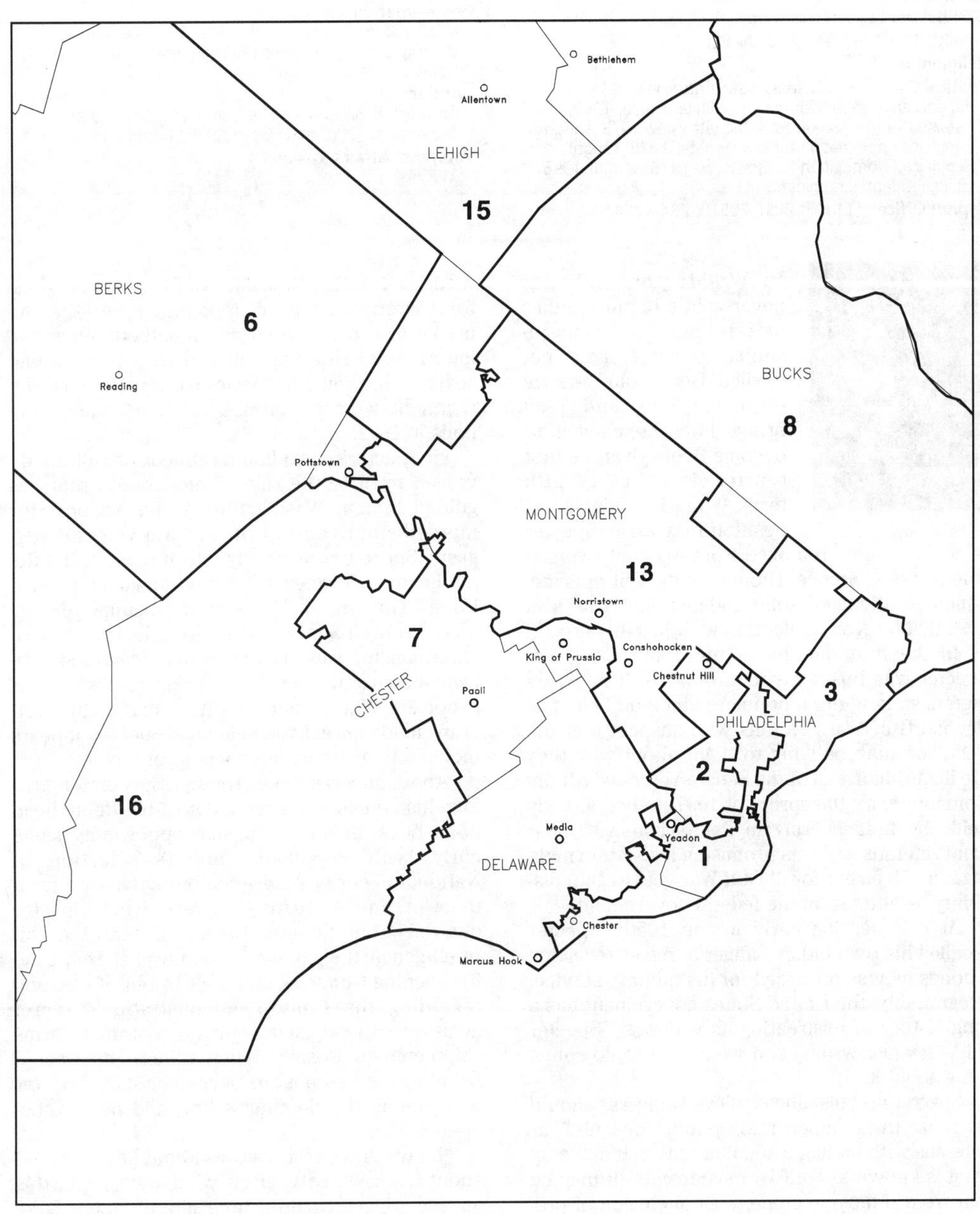

Arlen Specter (R)

Of Philadelphia — Elected 1980, 3rd term

Biographical Information

Born: Feb. 12, 1930, Wichita, Kan.

Education: U. of Pennsylvania, B.A. 1951; Yale U., LL.B. 1956.

Military Service: Air Force, 1951-53.

Occupation: Lawyer; professor.

Family: Wife, Joan Levy; two children.

Religion: Jewish.

Political Career: Philadelphia district attorney, 1966-74; Republican nominee for mayor of Philadelphia, 1967; defeated for re-election as district attorney, 1973; sought Republican nomination for U.S. Senate, 1976; sought Republican nomination for governor, 1978; sought 1996 GOP presidential nomination.

Capitol Office: 711 Hart Bldg. 20510; 224-4254.

Committees

Appropriations
Agriculture, Rural Development & Related Agencies; Defense; Foreign Operations; Labor, Health & Human Services & Education (chairman); Transportation

Governmental Affairs
International Security, Proliferation & Federal Services; Oversight of Government Management & the District of Columbia; Investigations

Judiciary
Antitrust, Business Rights & Competition; Immigration; Technology, Terrorism & Government Information

Veterans' Affairs (chairman)

In Washington: Although never wildly popular either in Washington or Pennsylvania, Specter has bedeviled Democrats' efforts to defeat him, and 1998 brings him the chance to become Pennsylvania's first senator elected to a fourth term. While formidable opposition may arise, Specter is now six years removed from his controversial role in the Clarence Thomas-Anita Hill episode, which so alienated some independent voters in 1992 that he won re-election with just 49 percent.

In the first months of the 105th Congress, Specter was busily laying groundwork in Washington, staking out a popular stance on behalf of Persian Gulf War veterans who suspect that the Pentagon may be lying to them about why they are ill. As chairman of the Senate Veterans' Affairs Committee, by the spring of 1997 he had already held one field hearing in Pennsylvania to hear from veterans and was promising legislation making it much easier for ill Gulf War vets to gain disability benefits from the federal government.

At one hearing early in the 105th, Specter recalled his own father's anger at never receiving a bonus he was promised for his military service. "Regrettably, the United States government has a long history of mistreating its veterans," Specter said. "It's just wrong, and we intend to do something about it."

Specter and his allies believe Congress should liberalize the compensation policy for Gulf War veterans with undiagnosed illnesses that make up what is known as Gulf War syndrome. "It may be that we will have to come to a conclusion of presumptive disability as we did with Agent Orange in the Vietnam War," Specter said.

This was comfortable territory for the ex-prosecutor, who likes to display his cross-examination skills in hearings. And it was surely a less polarizing display of those skills than the one the nation witnessed during the 1991 confirmation hearings for Clarence Thomas' appointment to the Supreme Court. Specter's unsympathetic questioning of Anita Hill, who alleged that Thomas had sexually harassed her years earlier, incurred the wrath of women's groups and hurt him at the polls in 1992.

In Specter's hard-line treatment of Hill, he diverged from to the rule of moderation that has guided him in Washington. As his support for more liberal treatment of Gulf War veterans suggests, Specter is markedly left of most of his Republican colleagues on many social and fiscal issues. On Veterans' Affairs, for example, he replaces retired Sen. Alan Simpson, R-Wyo., whose chairmanship was marked by a noticeable skepticism aimed at the very veterans programs Specter espouses. Where Simpson often charged that veterans made unrealistic demands, Specter appears inclined to give them the benefit of the doubt.

About once a session, though, Specter tends to give his colleagues a reminder of his Republican bona fides. In the 105th, that opportunity came early, with President Clinton's selection of National Security Adviser Anthony Lake to head the CIA. In the 104th Congress, when Specter chaired the Senate Select Committee on Intelligence, the panel had sharply criticized Lake for keeping Congress and the CIA out of the loop regarding the Clinton administration's secret decision to lend tacit approval to Iranian arms shipments to Bosnia. When Clinton nominated Lake for the CIA post in December 1996, Specter was among the nominee's first and most vehement critics.

"I have grave reservations about Mr. Lake and about his sensitivity, given what went on in this matter," Specter said. Three months later, Lake withdrew his name from consideration as it became increasingly clear the skepticism about his fitness for the job was spreading from Republicans to Democrats.

While Specter's role as former Intelligence Committee chairman boosted his prominence in the Lake nomination fight, Specter appeared to derive little benefit from the post when he actually held it. Indeed, his marquee bid to reform the intelligence community flopped at the end of 1996 when Congress passed a watered-down version of the House and Senate reform bills. Specter and his House counterpart, Larry Combest, R-Texas, had sought to broaden the powers of the director of Central Intelligence. Under the existing system, they argued, the director had responsibility for the vast U.S. intelligence community but little power to control major elements of it. Most of the community comes under Pentagon control, including the Defense Intelligence Agency and the spy satellite agencies.

The overhaul effort, however, drew fierce resistance not only from the Pentagon but also from the House and Senate defense committees, which saw the proposal as a turf-grab. The friction spilled over into other areas, as when Specter sought unsuccessfully to haul then-Defense Secretary William J. Perry before his committee to explain why the military failed to respond to intelligence warnings that preceded the terrorist bombing of a U.S. military barracks in Dhahran, Saudi Arabia in June 1996. Perry refused to appear, saying he reported to the Armed Services Committee, and that panel backed him up.

Perhaps because of those frustrations, Specter appears ready to call the Pentagon to account in a number of areas. When the Air Force said none of its officers were culpable for failings prior to the Saudi bombing, Specter responded tartly, "The Department of Defense has become an excuse factory, as opposed to standing up and being accountable and responsible."

From his Veterans' Affairs perch, Specter has ordered an investigation of the Pentagon's handling of the Gulf War illness issue, headed by Philadelphia attorney Michael J. Rotko. At a February 1997 hearing, Specter said he was dissatisfied, for example, with a report that failed to identify any clear explanation for the disappearance of military logs intended to track chemical weapons incidents during the 1991 Gulf conflict.

"The Department of Defense is entitled to the benefit of the doubt for a reasonable number of coincidences, but they've passed their quota," Specter said.

But criticizing and investigating government missteps, such as the Pentagon's losing its military logs, is much easier than passing legislation to prevent them. In March 1997, the Senate overwhelmingly rejected a Specter measure that would have amended the Constitution to allow Congress and the states to limit spending on political campaigns. The resolution, backed by Specter and Sen. Ernest F. Hollings, D-S.C., effectively would have overturned the 1976 Supreme Court ruling in *Buckley v. Valeo* that said restrictions on campaign spending infringe on the First Amendment right of free speech.

In March 1997, Specter was a key figure in the deliberations on a Senate Governmental Affairs Committee probe into campaign finance irregularities in the 1996 campaign. Where some Republicans wanted to focus on the White House, Specter became a catalyst for a leadership shift in favor of a bipartisan probe. Specter announced that he would vote against a draft GOP resolution that, in effect, limited the inquiry to Clinton. "The public is going to respond badly" if there were a limited inquiry, Specter said. "Appearances always count."

Specter's bipartisanship on campaign financing recalls how he angered some colleagues by opposing conservative jurist Robert H. Bork's nomination to the Supreme Court in the 1980s.

Medical issues have become a priority for Specter, not only as chairman of the Senate Appropriations Subcommittee on Labor, Health and Human Services and Education but also as the survivor in June 1993 of a frightening operation to remove a tumor from his brain. The problem was not diagnosed until a procedure known as magnetic resonance imaging was used — prompting Specter to become an outspoken proponent of health tests no matter what the expense.

In March 1997, Specter pressed Health and Human Services Secretary Donna E. Shalala to issue new guidelines advising that women in their 40s get mammography screening to detect breast cancer. "What I'm looking for is a prompt ruling that mammograms are warranted," Specter said.

Like most Republicans, Specter supports a balanced-budget amendment to the Constitution and a presidential line-item veto. But he remains one of the Senate's more liberal Republicans, particularly on social issues. A proponent of abortion rights, Specter switched his vote to support a ban on a particular abortion technique that opponents call "partial birth" abortion. Calling it one of the most difficult votes he had cast in the Senate, Specter said: "The line of the law is drawn, in my legal judgment, when the child is partially out of the womb of the mother. It is no longer abortion; it is infanticide."

Specter has used his seat on Appropriations' Foreign Operations Subcommittee as a platform for his ardent support for Israel.

Specter offered himself as a candidate for the 1996 GOP presidential nomination, but found few takers. Arguing for a more inclusive party, he took to the road late in 1994, campaigning as a fiscal conservative and social libertarian. Specter formally declared in March 1995, saying "Neither this nation or this party can afford a Republican candidate so captive to the demands of the intolerant right that we end up re-electing a president of the incompetent left." But by November 1995, low on funds and barely visible in opinion polls, he announced he was putting his campaign on ice.

At Home: Specter's political career has had more ups and downs than that of the average politician. He lost races for four separate offices between his election as Philadelphia district attorney in 1965 and his election to the Senate in 1980.

But since then, he has weathered every challenge that Democrats and conservative Republicans could throw at him.

Specter's roots in Philadelphia politics reach to the early 1960s, when he was an assistant district attorney and a hard-working young reformer. Then, he was the bright young star of Pennsylvania GOP politics, but he lost his momentum in defeats for mayor of Philadelphia in 1967 and for re-election as the city's district attorney in 1973. When Specter lost two statewide primaries, in 1976 and 1978, it appeared that his triumphs were behind him.

But he decided to make one more try when Republican Richard S. Schweiker announced he would retire in 1980. This time, Specter had the good fortune of running against a Democrat, former Pittsburgh Mayor Pete Flaherty, who was also a two-time statewide loser. Specter narrowly carried Philadelphia and won by immense margins in its suburbs, enough to offset Flaherty's showing in the west.

Specter swept to re-election in 1986 with money, high name recognition and a moderate Republican image. With a weak campaign by his Democratic rival, Rep. Bob Edgar, Specter won by more than 450,000 votes.

Democrats, though, viewed him as beatable in 1992. Even before he was criticized for grilling Hill, he was mocked in the major motion picture "JFK" as the chief author of the "single-bullet theory" in the Warren Commission report on President John F. Kennedy's assassination. Making matters worse was a brewing primary challenge from the right.

Specter and the state's right wing have never had an easy co-existence. His vote against confirming Bork prompted some to tag him "Benedict Arlen." But conservatives never jelled behind the primary challenge of state Rep. Stephen F. Freind, author of the state's restrictive abortion law, whom many considered a single-issue candidate.

Democrats nominated Lynn Yeakel, president of a Philadelphia-based women's fundraising organization. Weak in early polls, Yeakel rocketed from nowhere to the top of the five-candidate field in the final month of the primary. Polls taken soon after the primary showed her within striking distance of Specter.

But Yeakel squandered her momentum over the summer. Her campaign was beset with internal problems. And she committed several gaffes such as botching the name of one central Pennsylvania county when she visited.

Specter, meanwhile, stressed his longtime image as a social-issues moderate and attempted to explain his role in the Thomas confirmation hearings. And as always, he campaigned extensively; his office noted that since his election in 1980, he had made over 1,600 trips home.

Yeakel closed ground in the fall, working to dispel the notion that she was a single-issue candidate. But by then, Specter's campaign was in high gear, and he won by 3 percentage points.

SENATE ELECTIONS

1992 General		
Arlen Specter (R)	2,358,125	(49%)
Lynn Yeakel (D)	2,224,966	(46%)
John F. Perry III (LIBERT)	219,319	(5%)
1992 Primary		
Arlen Specter (R)	683,118	(65%)
Stephen F. Freind (R)	366,608	(35%)

Previous Winning Percentages: 1986 (56%) **1980** (51%)

CAMPAIGN FINANCE

	Receipts	Receipts from PACs		Expend-itures
1992				
Specter (R)	$6,869,894	$1,409,209	(21%)	$8,854,815
Yeakel (D)	$5,021,067	$371,721	(7%)	$5,028,669

KEY VOTES

1997	
Approve balanced-budget constitutional amendment	Y
Approve chemical weapons treaty	Y
1996	
Approve farm bill	Y
Limit punitive damages in product liability cases	N
Exempt small businesses from higher minimum wage	N
Approve welfare overhaul	Y
Bar job discrimination based on sexual orientation	Y
Override veto of ban on "partial birth" abortions	Y
1995	
Approve GOP budget with tax and spending cuts	Y
Approve constitutional amendment barring flag desecration	Y

VOTING STUDIES

	Presidential Support		Party Unity		Conservative Coalition	
Year	**S**	**O**	**S**	**O**	**S**	**O**
1996	59	41	63	36	66	34
1995	49	51	65	34	67	30
1994	55	44	55	43	59	38
1993	42	47	54	31	61	27
1992	45	55	41	57	37	58
1991	68	32	67	33	75	25

INTEREST GROUP RATINGS

Year	ADA	AFL-CIO	CCUS	ACU
1996	50	n/a	77	50
1995	55	33	79	36
1994	55	38	60	46
1993	45	45	100	57
1992	65	83	60	30
1991	40	58	50	71

Rick Santorum (R)

Of Pittsburgh — Elected 1994, 1st term

Biographical Information

Born: May 10, 1958, Winchester, Va.

Education: Pennsylvania State U., B.A. 1980; U. of Pittsburgh, M.B.A. 1981; Dickinson School of Law, J.D. 1986.

Occupation: Lawyer; legislative aide.

Family: Wife, Karen Garver; three children.

Religion: Roman Catholic.

Political Career: U.S. House, 1991-95.

Capitol Office: 120 Russell Bldg. 20510; 224-6324.

Committees

Special Aging

Agriculture, Nutrition & Forestry
Forestry, Conservation & Rural Revitalization (chairman); Research, Nutrition & General Legislation

Armed Services
Acquisition & Technology (chairman); Airland Forces; Seapower

Rules & Administration

In Washington: In just two years in the Senate, Santorum has emerged as one of the august body's most bare-knuckled lawmakers. Young, brash and conservative, he is known for pushing relentlessly for such Republican causes as paring back welfare benefits and passing a balanced-budget constitutional amendment, while discomforting colleagues with a no-holds-barred approach to getting his way.

The freshman's quick initiation as a Senate insider came when he pitched in as floor manager of a sweeping welfare overhaul bill in 1995. Santorum, who had focused on welfare issues during his four years in the House, was tapped by GOP leaders to fill in for embattled Finance Committee Chairman Bob Packwood, R-Ore.

Despite his youth and relative inexperience, he went toe-to-toe with veteran Democrats, tossing off detailed explanations of welfare's woes and working with GOP moderates to ensure passage. Elated by an overwhelming Senate vote in September 1995, he said: "I do not think anyone, in as short a time as two years ago, would have expected us to pass a bill as dramatic, progressive and as focused . . . to try to help people out of poverty." The welfare legislation was vetoed twice by President Clinton, but a somewhat scaled-back version was finally enacted in 1996.

To conservatives, this former House member and Newt Gingrich ally was a breath of fresh air, bringing hard-nosed tactics and a sense of urgency to the genteel, discursive Senate. But to many Senate veterans, Santorum simply seemed a boor. When he accused Clinton of telling "bald-faced untruths" to the American public, veteran Sen. Robert C. Byrd, D-W.Va., mourned that such talk would lead the Senate to be seen as "just a miserable lot of bickering juveniles."

But by far the biggest controversy to embroil Santorum erupted when he took on a senior member of his own party: Appropriations Chairman Mark O. Hatfield of Oregon. After Hatfield voted in 1995 against the balanced-budget amendment, Santorum joined Connie Mack, R-Fla., in calling for the 28-year veteran to be stripped of his chairmanship.

In the staid Senate, revenge is rarely sought so openly, and even many conservative senators saw Santorum's gambit as a dangerous precedent. The incident reinforced Santorum's reputation for confronting, not conciliating, even within his own party. Hatfield kept his chair, but Santorum got some results. To appease restless freshmen after the Hatfield episode, Republicans adopted several rule changes intended to make chairmen more beholden to the party. Hatfield retired voluntarily after the 104th Congress.

Santorum was in the spotlight again in May 1997 with his unyielding push of a measure to ban a particular abortion technique that opponents call "partial birth" abortion. Santorum outlined the procedure in graphic detail, illustrating his remarks with pictures of the process. He said the procedure involves "killing a little baby that hasn't hurt anyone, that just wants a chance." The Senate passed the bill, 64-36, short of the 67-vote majority needed to override a promised veto.

Santorum deserves his reputation as a staunch conservative, but he can break from his party line. In the House, for example, he joined pro-labor Democrats in voting against NAFTA, which was highly unpopular in the Rust Belt Pittsburgh-area district Santorum then represented. During the Senate welfare debate in the 104th, Santorum worked with California Democrat Barbara Boxer, one of the Senate's most liberal members, to fashion two child welfare amendments. And despite his budget-cutting desires, he also worked to restore funding in fiscal 1996 for the Low Income Home Energy Assistance Program, which is popular among Northeastern voters.

Santorum, a member of the Agriculture Committee, also kept his constituents in mind when he took on sugar and peanut price-support programs in the farm bill. He contended that they interfered with the marketplace, echoing criticisms of food manufacturers such as Pennsylvania-based Hershey Foods Corp. The senator briefly blocked committee approval of the farm bill, but ultimately settled for a compromise that would pare back the supports somewhat instead of ending them altogether. "You got to get what you can get," Santorum said later.

During his two House terms, Santorum generally followed the path defined by Gingrich, then GOP whip. He opposed Clinton budget proposals that included new taxes, and backed Republican deficit-cutting packages that focused on spending reductions. He opposed abortion, the Family and Medical Leave Act of 1993 and the crime bill of 1994, and he also fought congressional perks.

He made a name for himself in the 103rd Congress by helping organize the "Gang of Seven" — GOP freshmen who pressed for full disclosure of overdrafts at the House bank. The resulting scandal fed the national anti-incumbent mood, which by 1994 was aimed at Democrats and helped oust them from control of Congress.

At Home: Santorum's 1994 victory over short-term Democratic Sen. Harris Wofford made the Republican, then 36, the youngest member of the Senate and a symbol of the electorate's rapidly changing mood. Legendary for his hard-charging political style, Santorum ran a fiery campaign that fed on widespread voter discontent with Washington — as Wofford's own campaign had done three years earlier.

Wofford's use of the health care issue in his 1991 special election victory had inspired much of Clinton's emphasis on it in 1992. But when no health care legislation came close to being enacted in the 103rd, both Wofford and Clinton saw their stock tumble. And Wofford, who had played far less of a role in the policy debate than some had expected, was unluckily on the ballot in 1994 (seeking a full term in his own right after finishing that of the late GOP Sen. John Heinz).

Santorum had first gained notice by ousting 14-year veteran Democratic Rep. Doug Walgren in 1990 with a door-to-door campaign in a firmly Democratic district. He raised only about $250,000 for the race, but estimated that he had knocked on 25,000 doors. In 1992, Santorum was among the top targets of national Democrats. A dozen lined up for the Democratic primary, but the nomination went to a controversial party-switcher who fell below 40 percent in November.

In the 1994 Senate campaign, Santorum's only rival in the primary was an underfinanced black minister from Philadelphia. Santorum was able to husband his resources for the fall, eventually raising more than $6.5 million to supplement his usual high-energy, ground-level campaigning.

By contrast, the academic and patrician Wofford, a former president of Bryn Mawr College, seemed lackluster. He spent much of the campaign warning that Santorum was a far-right-wing ideologue. But he seemed uncomfortable with the hardball tactics.

Santorum worked hard to paint his opponent as an out-of-date liberal. He also capitalized on voter anger in rural western and central Pennsylvania over Wofford's support for gun control measures such as the 1993 law mandating a five-day waiting period to purchase a handgun and the 1994 crime bill, which included a ban on certain semiautomatic assault-style weapons. Santorum won with 49 percent to Wofford's 47 percent.

SENATE ELECTIONS

1994 General		
Rick Santorum (R)	1,735,691	(49%)
Harris Wofford (D)	1,648,481	(47%)
Diane Blough (PAT)	69,825	(2%)
Donald C. Ernsberger (LIBERT)	59,115	(2%)
1994 Primary		
Rick Santorum (R)	667,115	(82%)
Joe Watkins (R)	150,969	(18%)

Previous Winning Percentages: 1992* (61%) **1990*** (51%)

* *House elections*

KEY VOTES

1997	
Approve balanced-budget constitutional amendment	Y
Approve chemical weapons treaty	Y
1996	
Approve farm bill	N
Limit punitive damages in product liability cases	Y
Exempt small businesses from higher minimum wage	Y
Approve welfare overhaul	Y
Bar job discrimination based on sexual orientation	N
Override veto of ban on "partial birth" abortions	Y
1995	
Approve GOP budget with tax and spending cuts	Y
Approve constitutional amendment barring flag desecration	Y

CAMPAIGN FINANCE

	Receipts	Receipts from PACs		Expend-itures
1994				
Santorum (R)	$6,850,767	$1,237,564	(18%)	$6,732,849
Wofford (D)	$5,918,433	$1,023,544	(17%)	$6,300,560
Blough (PAT)	$7,366	0		$6,632

VOTING STUDIES

	Presidential Support		Party Unity		Conservative Coalition	
Year	**S**	**O**	**S**	**O**	**S**	**O**
1996	39	59	91	7	89	8
1995	24	75	95	4	89	9
House Service:						
1994	51	41	76	16	81	6
1993	45	54	77	16	77	23
1992	70	28	80	16	79	21
1991	72	28	88	12	97	3

INTEREST GROUP RATINGS

Year	ADA	AFL-CIO	CCUS	ACU
1996	15	n/a	77	95
1995	5	8	100	83
House Service:				
1994	15	22	100	81
1993	20	50	73	70
1992	20	58	88	83
1991	15	42	80	80

1 Thomas M. Foglietta (D)

Of Philadelphia — Elected 1980, 9th term

Biographical Information
Born: Dec. 3, 1928, Philadelphia, Pa.
Education: St. Joseph's College, B.A. 1949; Temple U., J.D. 1952.
Occupation: Lawyer.
Family: Single.
Religion: Roman Catholic.
Political Career: Philadelphia City Council, 1955-75; Republican nominee for mayor of Philadelphia, 1975.
Capitol Office: 242 Cannon Bldg. 20515; 225-4731.

Committees
Appropriations
Foreign Operations, Export Financing & Related Programs; Transportation

In Washington: Foglietta's political career, now into its fifth decade, has taken several interesting twists and turns. Once a Republican city council member who fought Philadelphia's powerful Democratic machine, Foglietta was elected to the House as an independent in 1980 and soon after became a Democrat.

During his first decade in Congress, his constituency was predominantly white ethnic, with a minority component of blacks and Hispanics. But with redistricting and re-election in 1992, Foglietta became the only white to represent a black-majority House district; blacks make up 52 percent of the people in the 1st. In the 1994 and 1996 Democratic primaries, Foglietta drew black challengers, but the veteran incumbent won overwhelmingly, stressing his efforts to preserve jobs in Philadelphia and the value of his seat on the Appropriations Committee, an assignment he gained in the 103rd Congress.

In the early months of 1997, there was speculation that Foglietta's career might take yet another turn — this time in an overseas direction. Foglietta was mentioned in media reports as a possible Clinton choice to be the U.S. ambassador to Italy.

Foglietta has long shown an interest in international relations. In the early 1990s he was out front in arguing for American involvement in restoring a democratically elected government in Haiti. He joined a congressional delegation investigating human rights abuses there, and he said the United States had "reached the ultimate last resort" when U.S. peacekeepers aboard the USS Harlan County were turned away from Haiti. After President Clinton in September 1994 reached an accommodation with Haiti's military leaders in which they agreed to step down, Foglietta praised Clinton for his efforts.

In the 1980s, Foglietta was a vigorous supporter of elements in South Korea that were pushing the country's rulers to restore full democratic procedures. He and several other Americans attracted international publicity in 1985 when they were roughed up by government police at the Seoul airport while accompanying exiled opposition leader Kim Dae Jung on his re-entry into South Korea.

At the start of the 105th Congress, Foglietta took a seat on Appropriations' Foreign Operations Subcommittee. He also serves on Appropriations' Transportation Subcommittee, where the work has obvious importance to commuter and commercial traffic in the Philadelphia area.

Foglietta's highest-profile pursuit in recent years has been his vigorous work in behalf of the Philadelphia Naval Shipyard, an aged facility that once hummed with work maintaining battleships and aircraft carriers. As far back as the 100th Congress, Foglietta was lobbying to keep the shipyard off the list of bases recommended for closure by an independent commission that Congress set up to review the Pentagon's facilities needs. When the commission in 1991 recommended closing the shipyard, the facility's advocates pursued a legal challenge, saying the Navy suppressed information that supported keeping the shipyard open. Republican Sen. Arlen Specter of Pennsylvania argued the shipyard's case before the U.S. Supreme Court in 1994, but the court unanimously rejected his complaint and allowed the closure to proceed.

Learning to make the best of a bad situation, Foglietta has funneled tens of millions of federal dollars the shipyard's way since it was slated for closure. Foglietta secured a $50 million loan for defense conversion in the fiscal 1993 defense spending bill.

In a more austere climate under Republican control, Foglietta nevertheless won another earmark for the facility in the fiscal 1996 military construction bill. (Foglietta sat on the Appropriations Military Construction Subcommittee during the 104th.) Self-described "porkbusters" Ed Royce, R-Calif., and David Minge, D-Minn., targeted the $6 million appropriation to upgrade the Philadelphia shipyard's foundry and propeller shop, along with a Washington state earmark, but their amendment to kill the projects

PENNSYLVANIA 1
South and central Philadelphia; part of Chester

Many of the personalities and places commonly associated with Philadelphia can be traced to the 1st District. Broad Street courses the 1st, beginning at the Montgomery County border. It cuts through the Oak Lane and Olney sections and the Democratic-voting poor and working-class black neighborhoods of North Philly. Temple University is situated by Cecil B. Moore Avenue.

Broad Street also marks the Center City border with the 2nd District. Center City, west of Broad Street — including City Hall — is in the 2nd. The 1st District portion of Center City is east of City Hall, in the 5th Ward. However, the waterfront area of the 5th Ward belongs to the 3rd District.

Besides the historical presence of the Liberty Bell and Independence Hall, the 1st boasts the pop cultural landmarks of South Philly. At 9th and Passyunk Avenues, tourists, locals and political candidates find it difficult to pass up a cheesesteak at Pat's or across the street at Geno's. Right down the street is the famous Italian Market where vendors hawk fresh vegetables, meats, cheeses and fish.

Italian culture permeates much of South Philly. There are Catholic churches that still say Mass in Italian; bocce courts can be found at Marconi Plaza park.

These are the neighborhoods of Hollywood's "Rocky Balboa" and of the late Mayor Frank Rizzo, where Rizzo's tough law-and-order stance had great appeal. When Irish-Americans controlled the Democratic Party decades ago, Italian-Americans mostly sided with the GOP. Now they mostly vote Democratic.

Veterans Stadium and the CoreStates Arena, homes to the city's professional sports teams, are at Broad and Pattison. Past the stadiums, the row houses end and the Philadelphia Naval Shipyard begins. All the shipyard's functions but the foundry and prop shop are now closed, and local officials are scrambling to find a job-providing function for the rest. Oil refineries line the Schuylkill River just before it empties into the Delaware River.

The one 1st District ward west of the Schuylkill is in southwest Philadelphia. In the late 19th century, the large factories located here attracted Irish, Italian and black immigrants. But as the General Electric, Fels Naptha and American Tobacco Co. factories shut down, the adjoining areas such as Elmwood and Kingsessing went into decline. The bleak economic landscape for those who did not move away manifested itself in racial turmoil. Today, the whites, blacks, and the recently arrived Vietnamese and Cambodians eye each other with suspicion.

Outside the city limits, south of the Philadelphia International Airport, the 1st takes in bits of Delaware County along Interstate 95. Working-class whites in Glenolden and Tinicum retain the GOP loyalties taught to them by the Republican county machine.

Black voters in the blighted city of Chester, almost all of which is in the district, boost the district's minority population to just over half.

1990 Population: 565,842. White 213,114 (38%), Black 296,314 (52%), Other 56,414 (10%). Hispanic origin 55,891 (10%). 18 and over 412,588 (73%), 62 and over 86,364 (15%). Median age: 31.

failed, 158-270.

"I think we have a responsibility to provide transportation to people, safe transportation and not be totally overcome with saving money," Foglietta declared at the start of the 104th. True to his word, he tried unsuccessfully to add $135 million for transit operating subsidies to the fiscal 1996 transportation spending bill. Working in tandem with Pennsylvania Republican Jon D. Fox, Foglietta sought money to offset the desired transit expenditures with cuts in Federal Aviation Administration accounts, but their move was rebuffed, 122-295.

Even before the 1st became majority-black, Foglietta aggressively courted support from minority voters, who were a sizable component of the Democratic electorate in the old 1st. In the 102nd Congress, he formed the Congressional Urban Caucus, which has lobbied for more money for jobs programs and against funding for NASA's space station.

Foglietta, who opposed the GOP plan to overhaul welfare, decried Republican efforts to wield the budget axe in places that have a direct impact on his inner-city constituents, such as children's nutrition and summer jobs programs. "From every sign that we can see, this Congress has declared war on America's cities," said Foglietta "It's aimed at the class of people who live in the cities."

At Home: Foglietta shed his lifelong GOP label and fought his way through a complicated political situation to secure his first term in Congress in 1980. Running as an independent usually guarantees failure. But the circumstances of that autumn were far from usual. Democratic incumbent Michael "Ozzie" Myers, indicted in the Abscam bribery scandal, had been renominated nonetheless. Anti-Myers Democrats were looking for a candidate, and Foglietta was available. When Myers was convicted on bribery charges and expelled from the House a month before the election, Foglietta was positioned to win. Once elected, he acknowledged his political debt by voting with Democrats to organize the 97th Congress.

To gain a second term in 1982 as a Democrat, Foglietta survived a tough primary that pitted him against not only U.S. Rep. Joseph F. Smith but also against the organization of former Mayor Frank Rizzo, still a powerful figure in the 1st. As a Republican, Foglietta had unsuccessfully challenged Rizzo for mayor in 1975.

Redistricting paired Foglietta and Smith. Rizzo's support helped make Smith competitive in South Philadelphia, but it also brought out a large vote for Foglietta from blacks and from Center City liberals antagonistic toward Rizzo.

Foglietta was challenged in the 1984 and 1986 primaries by Jimmy Tayoun, who, in the state House and then the Philadelphia City Council, became famous for tending to the personal needs of his constituents. One Tayoun campaign leaflet noted that he "keeps faith with the Bill Barrett tradition of personal evening service." Barrett, who represented the 1st for 29 years following World War II, was a bit player in Washington but was very popular in Philadelphia because he returned there every night to hold evening office hours.

Foglietta prevailed on the backing of black voters and young, liberal Center City professionals. Tayoun's most faithful backers were old-line, working-class whites, including many Irish and Polish voters in the "river wards" along the Delaware River.

The crucial votes were in the Italian community of South Philadelphia. Tayoun voiced more conservative views on social issues, but Foglietta's roots in the Italian community are deep. His father was a Republican city councilman, and Foglietta followed in those footsteps, serving on the City Council for two decades. Against Tayoun, he won renomination in the 1984 primary with 52 percent.

Two years later, Tayoun sought to make his primary rematch with the incumbent at least partly a referendum on Philadelphia's controversial Mayor W. Wilson Goode. But his effort to link the two politicians failed. Foglietta raised his vote share to 60 percent and expanded his base from liberals, blacks and Italians to include some non-Italian ethnics as well.

The demographic changes that 1992 redistricting wrought on the 1st so far have posed no problem for Foglietta. He has not been seriously threatened at the polls, although the majority-black composition of the district has encouraged repeated primary challenges. In 1994 he defeated a black former TV reporter for the Democratic nomination by a margin of more than 2-1.

HOUSE ELECTIONS

1996 General		
Thomas M. Foglietta (D)	145,210	(88%)
James D. Cella (R)	20,734	(12%)
1996 Primary		
Thomas M. Foglietta (D)	36,426	(73%)
John L. Braxton (D)	13,237	(27%)
1994 General		
Thomas M. Foglietta (D)	99,669	(82%)
Roger F. Gordon (R)	22,595	(18%)

Previous Winning Percentages: 1992 (81%) **1990** (79%) **1988** (76%) **1986** (75%) **1984** (75%) **1982** (72%) **1980** (38%)

CAMPAIGN FINANCE

	Receipts	Receipts from PACs	Expend-itures
1996			
Foglietta (D)	$378,598	$225,724 (60%)	$485,748
Cella (R)	$6,285	$16 (0%)	$4,603
1994			
Foglietta (D)	$474,985	$239,470 (50%)	$486,812

DISTRICT VOTE FOR PRESIDENT

	1996		1992
D	148,833 (83%)	**D**	149,699 (73%)
R	21,828 (12%)	**R**	39,042 (19%)
I	7,517 (4%)	**I**	17,021 (8%)

KEY VOTES

1997	
Ban "partial birth" abortions	Y
1996	
Approve farm bill	N
Deny public education to illegal immigrants	N
Repeal ban on certain assault-style weapons	N
Increase minimum wage	Y
Freeze defense spending	Y
Approve welfare overhaul	N
1995	
Approve balanced-budget constitutional amendment	N
Relax Clean Water Act regulations	N
Oppose limits on environmental regulations	Y
Reduce projected Medicare spending	N
Approve GOP budget with tax and spending cuts	N

INTEREST GROUP RATINGS

Year	ADA	AFL-CIO	CCUS	ACU
1996	85	n/a	20	5
1995	100	100	17	4
1994	95	89	25	0
1993	95	92	0	0
1992	80	91	33	0
1991	95	100	11	0

VOTING STUDIES

	Presidential Support		Party Unity		Conservative Coalition	
Year	S	O	S	O	S	O
1996	81	13	90	4	8	84
1995	89	7	94	2	7	91
1994	78	18	92	1	8	86
1993	78	18	92	3	7	89
1992	16	76	83	3	13	77
1991	23	72	92	3	5	89

2 Chaka Fattah (D)

Of Philadelphia — Elected 1994, 2nd term

Biographical Information

Born: Nov. 21, 1956, Philadelphia, Pa.

Education: Community College of Philadelphia, A.A. 1976; U. of Pennsylvania, M.A. 1986.

Occupation: Public official.

Family: Wife, Patricia Renfroe; three children.

Religion: Baptist.

Political Career: Democratic candidate for Philadelphia City commissioner, 1978; Pa. House, 1983-89; Pa. Senate, 1989-95.

Capitol Office: 1205 Longworth Bldg. 20515; 225-4001.

Committees

Education & Workforce
Employer-Employee Relations; Postsecondary Education, Training & Life-Long Learning

Government Reform & Oversight
National Economic Growth, Natural Resources & Regulatory Affairs; Postal Service (ranking)

In Washington: Before winning election to the House in 1994, Fattah served 12 years in the Pennsylvania legislature, part of that time in a state Senate where Republicans were a majority. Fattah was known for working hard to overcome the disadvantage of being a minority-party lawmaker; he mobilized his colleagues in the black caucus to employ attention-getting rhetoric and delaying tactics to influence the legislative agenda.

As it turned out, that experience was good preparation for Fattah's life in Washington, where he again is serving in the minority. A frequent and blunt critic of the House GOP majority, he routinely pillories conservatives for abandoning the poor, the young and the elderly to cater to the wishes of the wealthy. His political smarts were recognized early on: In December 1994, Fattah was elected whip of the Congressional Black Caucus.

During debate in early 1995 on a GOP proposal to overhaul the welfare system, Fattah said: "We have some tough cowboys here on the floor of the House. This is a new interesting kind of wagon train in which the cowboys have decided to throw the women and infants and the children and the senior citizens out of the wagon train so they can get where they are going faster. It is cruel."

And when the House considered a fiscal 1995 rescissions bill that included cuts to the prenatal care program for poor women called Healthy Start, Fattah lambasted the GOP's spending priorities. "It is interesting that we could not find any dollars from the military to cut even though we spend more than the rest of the world combined on our Armed Forces," he said. "We could not find in any of the billions in corporate welfare any room to cut, but somehow we have zeroed in on children, we have zeroed in on Healthy Start, on college scholarships, on summer job programs."

Fattah regards himself as upholding a tradition in American government of "careful, deliberative change," and so he resists what he sees as overzealous Republican efforts to drastically shrink the role of the federal government. "At its core, the Republican political philosophy is a repudiation of government," he told The St. Petersburg Times in February 1995. "This is the gang that wants to change things overnight; they call themselves revolutionaries. We want to guard against radical changes in policy that could have a disastrous effect on the country . . . and would be difficult to undo."

Upon arriving in Washington, Fattah was assigned to the Government Reform and Oversight Committee and the Small Business panel. He had hoped for a seat on Economic and Educational Opportunities so he could pursue his interest in education issues affecting minorities. Before long, though, he got that wish: After Rep. Mel Reynolds, D-Ill., resigned from the House in October 1995 following his conviction on sexual misconduct charges, Fattah got his seat on the Opportunities Committee (which was renamed Education and the Workforce in the 105th Congress.)

Fattah takes issue with Republicans who oppose federal affirmative action programs, once calling them the "David Duke faction" in the House. He opposed a GOP effort in early 1995 to finance a health insurance tax break for the self-employed by eliminating a tax deferral currently given to those who sell to minority-owned businesses, particularly in the radio, TV and cable markets. Fattah noted that of the 18,655 broadcast licenses issued by the FCC, 322 are owned by minorities — a sixfold increase since the tax-deferral incentive was put in place. "Tonight, under the guise of helping the self-employed," Fattah told the House, "some want to snatch the rug out from under a program that has been very meaningful for the tens of millions of African-Americans and Hispanic-Americans throughout this country."

On floor votes, Fattah is a consistent liberal, and he commended President Clinton for standing up to the GOP during the 1995-96 budget wars. Fattah admonished Republicans for inflexibility

PENNSYLVANIA 2
West Philadelphia; Chestnut Hill; Yeadon

William Penn's statue atop City Hall stands like a sentinel over Philadelphia. From his vantage point, he views a variety of neighborhoods across the 2nd, all with one thing in common: an affinity for Democrats. Bill Clinton won the 2nd with 86 percent in 1996; his highest tally in any Pennsylvania district.

Republicans need not apply in the 2nd; Democrats enjoy an overwhelming districtwide edge in voter registration. Here, the Democratic primary is the only forum for political redress.

Stretching west from City Hall, the 2nd begins under the skyscrapers of Center City's 8th Ward. Many of the white-collar professionals who labor here by day live outside the district, but some prefer to live nearby in ritzy Rittenhouse Square. The whites of this area are not a large part of the district vote, but their wealth allows them to weigh in disproportionately in any political campaign.

From there, the 2nd crosses the Schuylkill River and immediately encounters two massive edifices, the U.S. Postal Service building and the 30th Street train station. Traveling westbound on Walnut Street, past the campuses of Drexel University and the University of Pennsylvania, a sea of row houses seems to continue indefinitely. These are the neighborhoods of West Philly.

Two generations ago, Irish, Greeks and Jews lived under de facto ethnic segregation in these areas. Today, West Philly is nearly all black. Some of these working-class and lower middle-class neighborhoods are gripped by urban blight; others are well-maintained.

It was the western edge of West Philadelphia that drew notoriety in May 1985, when an ill-conceived police battle against the cult group MOVE led to a fire that burned down two square blocks of row houses.

Farther north, City Line Avenue forms a border with Montgomery County. The middle-class and affluent sections of Overbrook are on the city side, while the posh Main Line begins across the street.

Cutting a wide swath through the northern part of the 2nd is vast and verdant Fairmount Park, which flanks the Schuylkill River and contains the city's art museum, zoo and "Boathouse Row."

Adjoining the park to the northwest is Germantown. Once home to Philadelphia's upper crust, it and nearby Mount Airy now are racially diverse and mostly middle-class. The park runs as far north as the Montgomery County border, where it ends in affluent Chestnut Hill.

Farther north along the Schuylkill River, Roxborough and Manayunk are older neighborhoods experiencing a wave of gentrification. Although longtime residents complain about the upscale restaurants and shops that now occupy Manayunk's Main Street, the businesses have revitalized what was a dying area.

The 2nd abruptly halts at the city's Montgomery County border, but it reaches a finger into Darby, Lansdowne and Yeadon, which are black, Democratic sections of Delaware County.

1990 Population: 565,650. White 196,070 (35%), Black 352,111 (62%), Other 17,469 (3%). Hispanic origin 8,872 (2%). 18 and over 439,005 (78%), 62 and over 99,760 (18%). Median age: 33.

in the budget talks, saying they "lack the maturity to be productive participants in shaping the course of public policy in our land."

But he did disagree with Clinton on giving the president line-item veto authority, questioning the assertion that it would help restrain federal spending. A line-item veto has been in place in Pennsylvania since 1982, Fattah said, and during that time the state's total debt has tripled. He cited a finding by the Congressional Budget Office that line-item vetoes in states have not primarily been used to hold down state spending or deficits but rather to advance the spending priorities of the governors wielding the veto authority. "While the president may know the most efficient way to run the executive branch, he does not know the most efficient way to run the Congress," Fattah said. "Indeed, a future president may want to make Congress less effective in its oversight of the executive branch."

Fattah also opposed Clinton's decision to sign the final version of the welfare overhaul bill that ended the 60-year-old federal guarantee of aid to the poor. "I strongly disagree with [Clinton] on this," Fattah said in early August 1996, though he tempered his criticism with a suggestion that the president was politically boxed in on the issue. "Some people might picket him in Chicago [at the Democratic national convention] next week," Fattah told the Associated Press, "but they should have been protesting Congress for the last two years because that is where this bill came from."

Fattah was one of six House members — three Republicans and three Democrats — voting in late 1995 against a measure banning House members and staff from accepting all gifts, meals and trips except for gifts from personal friends and family and campaign contributions. Fattah did vote for a proposal that would have kept the existing gift rules in place but strengthened disclosure requirements. He was also one of 48

Democrats to vote in July 1996 against an amendment denying lawmakers their annual cost of living adjustment, which would have been about $3,000 in fiscal 1997. Supporters of the pay freeze said members should not get a pay increase until the federal budget is balanced. The House adopted it, 352-67.

With an eye on increasing members' efficiency early in their first terms, Fattah introduced a bill in June 1996 to require outgoing members to vacate their offices a month before their terms expire, so incoming freshmen could have their office and staff in place by the time they are sworn in. His measure would cut off funding for outgoing members on Dec. 1 and begin funding for the new members at the same time.

Under existing House rules, departing members can remain in their offices until mid-December, and they retain their office allowances through Dec. 31. Members-elect are given temporary desks and phone lines, often in an out-of-the way basement. Fattah said it is the outgoing members who should be forced to work in those basement offices. "In the 104th Congress, we got to hire our staffs on Jan. 2, and went to work on Jan. 3," Fattah said. "We will see a lot of freshmen in the next couple terms. This [bill] behooves the institution. It is not self-serving."

At Home: The outcome of the May 1994 Democratic primary in the 2nd District signaled a generational shift in Philadelphia's black political community, as Fattah, then 37, toppled incumbent Democrat Lucien E. Blackwell, a longtime labor leader and veteran party war horse.

Fattah had demonstrated the limits of his obedience to Democratic Party bosses in 1991, when he temporarily quit the party and opposed city councilman Blackwell in the special election to replace Rev. William H. Gray III, who left the 2nd in 1991 to become president of the United Negro College Fund. Running on the Consumer Party ballot line, Fattah polled 28 percent, but Blackwell won election with 39 percent.

Redistricting before the 1992 election reduced the 2nd's black population from 80 percent of the total to 62 percent. That put Blackwell at risk, because his appeal was strongest among West Philly's poor and working-class blacks. The redrawn 2nd was more receptive to the smoother, college-educated Fattah, a modern-style media-savvy politician who tried to reach across racial lines. By contrast, Blackwell, nicknamed "Lucien the Solution," for his focus on delivering favors and protecting local interests, seemed parochial and outdated.

Still, there were those who called Fattah foolhardy and arrogant when he announced his intention to challenge Blackwell's renomination in 1994. The incumbent had the backing of Philadelphia Mayor Ed Rendell and City Council President John Street. But Fattah mounted an impressive campaign, using political polls, heavy radio advertising and a strong grass-roots operation built on a solid base of support in his state Senate district. He won the primary with 58 percent of the vote. That November, Fattah crushed the GOP nominee. In 1996, he faced no primary challenge and breezed through the general election.

HOUSE ELECTIONS

1996 General		
Chaka Fattah (D)	168,887	(88%)
Larry G. Murphy (R)	23,047	(12%)
1994 General		
Chaka Fattah (D)	120,553	(86%)
Lawrence R. Watson (R)	19,824	(14%)

CAMPAIGN FINANCE

	Receipts	Receipts from PACs	Expend-itures
1996			
Fattah (D)	$400,417	$149,700 (37%)	$412,478
1994			
Fattah (D)	$514,789	$154,951 (30%)	$492,348
Watson (R)	$2,840	$14 (0%)	$2,828

DISTRICT VOTE FOR PRESIDENT

	1996		1992
D	173,709 (86%)	D	184,284 (80%)
R	20,659 (10%)	R	31,836 (14%)
I	5,979 (3%)	I	14,510 (6%)

VOTING STUDIES

	Presidential Support		Party Unity		Conservative Coalition	
Year	**S**	**O**	**S**	**O**	**S**	**O**
1996	81	16	95	2	6	88
1995	82	11	91	1	5	89

KEY VOTES

1997	
Ban "partial-birth" abortions	N
1996	
Approve farm bill	N
Deny public education to illegal immigrants	N
Repeal ban on certain assault-style weapons	N
Increase minimum wage	Y
Freeze defense spending	Y
Approve welfare overhaul	N
1995	
Approve balanced-budget constitutional amendment	N
Relax Clean Water Act regulations	N
Oppose limits on environmental regulations	Y
Reduce projected Medicare spending	N
Approve GOP budget with tax and spending cuts	N

INTEREST GROUP RATINGS

Year	ADA	AFL-CIO	CCUS	ACU
1996	95	n/a	25	0
1995	95	100	13	4

3 Robert A. Borski (D)

Of Philadelphia — Elected 1982, 8th term

Biographical Information
Born: Oct. 20, 1948, Philadelphia, Pa.
Education: U. of Baltimore, B.A. 1972.
Occupation: Stockbroker.
Family: Wife, Karen Lloyd; five children.
Religion: Roman Catholic.
Political Career: Pa. House, 1977-83.
Capitol Office: 2267 Rayburn Bldg. 20515; 225-8251.

Committees
Transportation & Infrastructure
Coast Guard & Maritime Transportation; Railroads; Water Resources & Environment (ranking)

In Washington: Following more than a dozen years in Washington, Borski is ensconced as a parochial politician focused on the concerns of his Northeast Philadelphia constituents. When it comes to matters of moving people and goods, from port dredging to inland waterways, Borski has worked closely with another Pennsylvanian, Bud Shuster, the Republican chairman of the Transportation and Infrastructure Committee. With the nation's main transportation law up for reauthorization during the 105th, Borski is well-positioned as the large panel's third-ranking Democrat to enter the fray over funding priorities.

Despite his good relations with Shuster, Borski's posture toward him is not always go-along-to-get-along. He opposed Shuster's effort during the 104th Congress to make environmental protections under the clean water act less stringent. And Borski has reliably sided with his party over the GOP on most key issues. He supported the 1996 increase in the minimum wage, opposed Republican attempts to balance the budget partially at the expense of Medicare's growth, and voted to uphold many of President Clinton's more prominent vetoes of GOP priorities, such as increased defense spending, during the 104th.

His willingness to be of service to his party is exemplified by his accepting a thankless slot on the ethics committee; there, he took part in the tumultuous investigation of Speaker Newt Gingrich, R-Ga., that spilled over into the 105th.

During the 103rd Congress, Borski even joined with other party members in voting against requiring federally funded clinics to notify the parents of minors seeking abortions, a rare departure from a voting record on abortion that has generally been in step with the culturally conservative ethnic Catholics who make up most of his district. During the 104th, Borski supported an ultimately unsuccessful attempt to ban a particular abortion technique that opponents call a "partial birth" abortion.

Borski opposed the balanced-budget constitutional amendment approved by the House in 1995, saying that he would only support a capital budget that allowed deficit spending for long-term investments. He also opposed a move during the 104th to amend the Constitution to ban flag burning. Although virulently opposed to the gesture, he said, "The issue of free speech inherent in the flag-burning argument is far too important to be politicized or trivialized through name-calling and scare tactics."

Borski has tried to push the Transportation and Infrastructure Committee to move beyond its traditional focus on roads and bridges, and to pay more attention to the transportation needs of urban areas, particularly mass transit. Borski opposed the fiscal 1996 transportation spending bill, calling it "backward-looking" because it raised highway spending while cutting funds for airport improvements and mass transit programs.

Borski has also concentrated on safety issues. Shuster succeeded in lifting the federal speed limit during the 104th, but Borski objected in the strongest terms. "If we decide to eliminate the speed limit laws, we will be choosing death for thousands of our citizens every year," Borski warned fellow members from the well of the House in September 1995.

On a parochial level, Borski during the 104th secured more than $62 million in funds for dredging, environmental infrastructure construction, wetlands restoration and other environmental and transportation spending for his home region.

During the 102nd, he wrote language in the highway bill to bar the use of triple trailers on state highways that do not already allow them. In the 103rd, Borski and the Oversight Subcommittee he chaired prodded the Federal Aviation Administration to force foreign airlines operating in this country to come closer to compliance with U.S. safety standards.

Borski is now the ranking member of the Transportation Subcommittee on Water Resources and Environment — a term that Borski

PENNSYLVANIA 3
Northeast Philadelphia

In a Democratic and racially diverse city, the 3rd stands alone in its racial homogeneity and its status as the only Philadelphia district where Republicans often fare well.

The body of the 3rd is known as the Great Northeast, named for its geographic expanse. This part of Philadelphia borders suburban Montgomery and Bucks counties, and many of its communities have taken on suburban traits of their own. Yet this is the only congressional district wholly contained within Philadelphia.

The mostly white residents who migrated to Northeast neighborhoods established themselves in the past two generations as the black population grew in other parts of the city. And as many residents began to equate the national Democratic Party with policies that provide preferential treatment for minorities, Republican voter registration swelled.

Democrats outnumber Republicans in the 3rd, but in the 1980s, the Republican presidential ticket carried Northeast three times. Bill Clinton broke the losing streak in 1992, carrying the district easily over George Bush. He expanded on his victory margin in 1996.

Philadelphia's handful of Republican state legislators and GOP City Council members used to hail from this area. Now area voters usually elect Democrats there, too.

Conservative social attitudes and concern about crime inspire loyalty to tough law-and-order candidates — such as former Mayor Frank Rizzo. Also welcome is the presence of city police officers and firefighters, many of whom live in the Northeast. Holmesburg Prison is here, as is the Philadelphia Police Academy.

With scores of hospitals, the Northeast Philadelphia Airport and three bridges that connect to New Jersey, infrastructure issues are also of particular concern to 3rd District residents.

Besides large numbers of Catholics, the Great Northeast boasts a large Jewish population, many of whom live west of Roosevelt Boulevard in Bustleton and Somerton.

South of Cottman Avenue, the district begins to lose its suburban feel. The Irish and Polish residents of the Democratic wards by the Delaware River are crowded in row houses under Interstate 95. Union ties bind voters here to the Democratic Party, but they often part company on social issues.

Huge losses of industrial jobs in Kensington, Bridesburg and Port Richmond have affected these white ethnic communities. In such lower-income neighborhoods as Kensington, economic uncertainty translated into racial tensions among whites, blacks and Hispanics, although neighborhood-based human relations groups have been exercising a positive influence.

The southern border of the 3rd reaches as far south as Christian Street in South Philadelphia. It snakes close to the river while taking in Penn's Landing, Philadelphia's revitalized waterfront area. Some of the boutiques, shops and restaurants of funky South Street are also in the 3rd District confines.

1990 Population: 565,866. White 505,152 (89%), Black 27,493 (5%), Other 33,221 (6%). Hispanic origin 26,543 (5%). 18 and over 437,241 (77%), 62 and over 118,551 (21%). Median age: 35.

defines in the broadest sense. He supported legislation in 1996 that would have directed the Federal Emergency Management Agency (FEMA) to develop a national snow removal policy. "I will be working with FEMA to make sure the snow removal policy meets the needs of the entire nation," Borski said. "The problems faced by Philadelphia and other Northeastern cities must be addressed in a fair and consistent manner." Although passed by the House at the end of the 104th, the measure was never taken up by the Senate.

At Home: Borski may not cut a high profile in Washington, but his concentration on local issues and his assiduous courtship of constituents so far has given him a firm grip on a once-Republican seat, winning in 1996 with 69 percent of the vote

Redistricting and a challenge from an old nemesis gave a scare to Borski in 1992, but in the end he was re-elected with 59 percent of the vote.

His 1992 opponent, former GOP Rep. Charles F. Dougherty, was the man Borski beat for the seat 10 years earlier. It was Dougherty's second attempt to win back the seat. After Borski won re-election easily in 1984, Dougherty tried a comeback in 1986, only to lose the GOP primary.

In 1992, Dougherty returned to run in a district made slightly less Democratic by redistricting. He criticized Borski for his 33 overdrafts at the House Bank and mocked the incumbent's low-key demeanor and party fealty. Even The Philadelphia Inquirer piled on, when, in an endorsement of Dougherty, the paper said the challenger "simply has more backbone than most of the munchkins on Capitol Hill — and that includes Borski."

Dougherty kept the pressure on to the end, but Borski showed an unexpected strength in winning by 20 percentage points.

Borski launched himself toward Congress by managing another congressional candidate's campaign — the unsuccessful 1981 special-election effort of Philadelphia Democratic Party Chairman David Glancey in the old 3rd District. Borski emerged from the effort with greater visibility and a determination to run for Congress himself. In 1982, when redistricting grafted his state legislative base in the blue-collar "river ward" of Bridesburg onto Dougherty's territory in Philadelphia's semi-suburban Northeast, Borski made his move.

More experienced Democrats stayed out, convinced that Dougherty was too strong. But with economic discontent strong in blue-collar Philadelphia, the clean-cut Borski seemed a good vehicle for protesting hard times. He won by 2,664 votes.

HOUSE ELECTIONS

1996 General		
Robert A. Borski (D)	121,120	(69%)
Joseph M. McColgan (R)	54,681	(31%)
1996 Primary		
Robert A. Borski (D)	26,211	(91%)
John R. Kates (D)	2,687	(9%)
1994 General		
Robert A. Borski (D)	92,702	(63%)
James C. Hasher (R)	55,209	(37%)

Previous Winning Percentages: 1992 (59%) **1990** (60%) **1988** (63%) **1986** (62%) **1984** (64%) **1982** (50%)

CAMPAIGN FINANCE

	Receipts	Receipts from PACs	Expend-itures
1996			
Borski (D)	$403,329	$225,913 (56%)	$317,799
McColgan (R)	$96,530	$5,850 (6%)	$95,008
1994			
Borski (D)	$443,530	$254,476 (57%)	$323,957
Hasher (R)	$125,360	$9,464 (8%)	$120,616

DISTRICT VOTE FOR PRESIDENT

1996	1992
D 114,664 (61%)	**D** 124,944 (52%)
R 51,763 (28%)	**R** 75,474 (31%)
I 18,876 (10%)	**I** 39,617 (17%)

KEY VOTES

1997	
Ban "partial birth" abortions	Y
1996	
Approve farm bill	N
Deny public education to illegal immigrants	N
Repeal ban on certain assault-style weapons	N
Increase minimum wage	Y
Freeze defense spending	Y
Approve welfare overhaul	Y
1995	
Approve balanced-budget constitutional amendment	N
Relax Clean Water Act regulations	N
Oppose limits on environmental regulations	Y
Reduce projected Medicare spending	N
Approve GOP budget with tax and spending cuts	N

VOTING STUDIES

	Presidential Support		Party Unity		Conservative Coalition	
Year	S	O	S	O	S	O
1996	81	18	82	14	37	63
1995	80	17	88	10	31	68
1994	86	14	93	5	44	53
1993	85	11	89	8	48	50
1992	28	70	91	8	40	60
1991	36	59	89	9	38	54

INTEREST GROUP RATINGS

Year	ADA	AFL-CIO	CCUS	ACU
1996	80	n/a	20	10
1995	80	100	22	16
1994	65	89	33	29
1993	70	100	20	13
1992	80	83	29	16
1991	60	91	10	30

4 Ron Klink (D)

Of Murrysville — Elected 1992, 3rd term

Biographical Information
Born: Sept. 23, 1951, Canton, Ohio.
Education: Meyersdale H.S., graduated 1969.
Occupation: Television journalist.
Family: Wife, Linda Hogan; two children.
Religion: United Church of Christ.
Political Career: No previous office.
Capitol Office: 125 Cannon Bldg. 20515; 225-2565.

Committees
Commerce
Oversight & Investigations (ranking); Telecommunications, Trade & Consumer Protection

In Washington: Representing a district whose economy is still struggling to rebound from the decline of its industrial base, Klink combines the strong pro-labor views of an earlier generation of Democratic politicians with the kind of aggressive and media-savvy style that you would expect from someone who entered elective office after a career in television news.

At the start of his second House term, Klink got a seat on the influential Commerce Committee. Although he had to endure the frustration of seeing the panel's agenda driven by its new Republican leadership, he did what he could to focus attention on the need for jobs in his district.

When Commerce began a major overhaul of the nation's telecommunications laws in the 104th, Klink was a skeptic: He opposed the bill in committee and when it came to the House floor for a vote. But in the end, he supported the final bill, which was a product of negotiations between the House, the Senate and the White House, because he said it would create 140,000 jobs in Pennsylvania over ten years.

In 1996, Klink became the ranking Democrat on Commerce's Oversight and Investigations Subcommittee. The panel has broad oversight authority over a swath of federal agencies, including the Environmental Protection Agency (EPA). In 1995, when GOP conservatives pushed for hearings to examine the impact of the Clean Air Act, Klink did not share their degree of antipathy toward the legislation, but he did say that the hearings were useful in informing the EPA of the impact of job losses in Pennsylvania and the importance of "common sense" environmental regulations.

As a freshman in the Democratic-controlled 103rd, Klink served on the Education and Labor Committee, a seat he gave up to move to Commerce in the 104th. But labor's concerns are never far from his mind.

The 4th District, which at one time was known for its steel-producing capacity and strong union influence, was disproportionately affected by the crumbling of heavy industry in the early 1980s. But the blue-collar presence here remains strong, and organized labor is still a political force.

"I have been a union negotiator," Klink once said. "I have sat across the table from negotiators — hired guns, we called them — who would come in from out of town. They would sit there and they would stare you in the eye and say, 'Unless you accept these concessions, we will hire replacement workers. You will all be on the street.' "

Klink opposed NAFTA in the 103rd Congress, saying the trade pact would lead to hundreds of thousands of U.S. job losses and massive environmental degradation, and would contribute to political and financial abuses in Mexico. He also voted against GATT.

Early in the 104th, when Mexico's currency collapsed and President Clinton proposed a U.S.-backed bailout, it was hard for Klink and other NAFTA opponents not to gloat. "We do not want to say we told you so. We would prefer to be here taking up another issue, enjoying the prosperity. . . . But instead what has happened is all of those people who rushed down to Mexico to make investments are now asking the people who live in our districts to bail out the peso." Proponents of the rescue plan, though, were ultimately able to point out that Mexico paid off the loans arranged by the Clinton administration.

Democrats such as Klink who are closely attuned to organized labor's concerns were often at odds with the GOP majority in the 104th. But with the 1996 elections approaching and Republicans in Congress worried about their anemic standing in public opinion polls, even many conservatives had a difficult time opposing a Democratic-driven proposal to increase the minimum wage — contributing to one of the biggest Democratic victories in the 104th. To help make the case for the minimum wage increase, Klink referred to his region's traumatic industrial past.

"I come from an area in southwestern Pennsylvania where we have coal fields and steel mills. And when we did not have workers' protection, when we did not have minimum wage, we saw people working for next to nothing. We saw them going

PENNSYLVANIA 4
West — Beaver County; part of Westmoreland County

The mostly abandoned steel mills that line the Beaver and Ohio rivers in western Pennsylvania haunt the 4th District towns that once lived and breathed by them.

In Aliquippa, a seven-mile-long steelworks employed 15,000 at its peak. Today, it is a shadow of that. So, too, is the town, which has about one-third of the population it did in the 1950s. Across the river in Ambridge, there is a similar story of economic struggle.

The hard-luck Beaver Valley and the district's largest city, New Castle (Lawrence County), also have experienced the decline of heavy manufacturing in the past generation. Union strength remains unbroken, though, making the district solidly Democratic.

Bill Clinton handily won both Beaver and Lawrence counties in 1992, helping him to win the district by 17 percentage points. Four years later, Clinton's lead had narrowed to 5 percentage points in the district. Republican Bob Dole had cut into Clinton's margin in both counties. Dole seemed to take advantage of Ross Perot's slide in popularity from 21 percent of the district's vote in 1992 to less than half that four years later.

Beaver County, dotted by boroughs and townships with evocative (if not imaginative) names such as Big Beaver, Little Beaver, Beaver Falls, South Beaver and Raccoon, is the district's most populous county.

In 4th District congressional politics, Beaver and Lawrence counties are suspicious of candidates who do not hail from the region. Observers say that voters here would be more inclined to support a candidate from over the border in Youngstown, Ohio, than a candidate from rival Westmoreland County, which is miles to the east, on the other side of Pittsburgh. Westmoreland is connected to the rest of the 4th by only a thin corridor of land in northern Allegheny County.

Traditionally, the representative of the 4th has hailed from the district's western region. Beaver County has been accustomed to throwing around its weight in elections ever since the late 19th century, when local product Matthew Quay was a U.S. senator and head of a powerful local political machine. But in the 1992 House contest, voters in the western region set aside their geographic bias and supported Klink, who is from Westmoreland County.

The Allegheny River divides Westmoreland County from Allegheny County. On the Allegheny County side are Natrona Heights and Tarentum; on the eastern side of the river in Westmoreland are Lower Burrell and Arnold. Farther south, the 4th takes in Jeannette, but the district stops short of one of southwestern Pennsylvania's population centers, the city of Greensburg. Roughly one-fourth of the district's registered Democrats hail from Westmoreland.

A thorough search will turn up some Republicans, located mostly in farming communities or in Butler County, whose southern tier is in the 4th. (The rest of Butler is in the 21st.) Butler County last voted Democratic for president in 1964.

1990 Population: 565,792. White 544,659 (96%), Black 17,973 (3%), Other 3,160 (1%). Hispanic origin 2,633 (<1%). 18 and over 431,903 (76%), 62 and over 112,761 (20%). Median age: 37.

into the coal mines. Children were forced to work. They would go in before the sun came up each morning, go into the mines, and come out at night when the sun was down, never seeing daylight."

Klink generally supports his party on economic issues. He used strong words to help oppose the GOP's "Contract With America" tax cuts. "This is not about a Republican tax break," he said. "This is about a Republican rape of the poor and the middle class in order to reward the wealthy." He also fought some of the GOP's budget-cutting proposals, such as the elimination of federal nursing home standards.

But on social issues, he takes a more conservative line. Unlike most of his Democratic colleagues, Klink is a strong opponent of abortion. Klink has urged his party to moderate the pro-abortion rights plank in its national platform order to accommodate social conservatives.

Klink twice opposed Republican attempts to reform the welfare system with work requirements and time-limited benefits. But like many social conservatives in the party, he joined President Clinton in supporting the final welfare reform program that was enacted.

At Home: Klink's general-election victory was all but assured in April 1992, when he won a four-way primary battle that resulted in the ouster of the little-regarded Joe Kolter, an old-fashioned labor Democrat who had spent a career in politics.

Kolter's reputation had been marred by two widely read, unflattering profiles. One, a 1990 story in The Wall Street Journal, painted Kolter as an incumbent preoccupied with re-election whose primary legislative interest was securing money for local highway and airport construction projects. The other article, in the Pittsburgh Press, printed transcripts from portions of a leaked audiotape in which Kolter planned to manipulate the electorate — at one point on the tape he called himself "a political whore."

Klink's chances got even better when organized labor withdrew its support for Kolter after the congressman missed a key vote on extending unemployment benefits. In the summer of 1993, it also came to light that Kolter was one of two congressmen implicated by court documents in a scheme of skimming cash from the House Post Office. Kolter already had lost his seat to Klink by then.

Klink came in for a good share of criticism from his primary opponents. Although he had covered the region for 14 years as a reporter for Pittsburgh's KDKA-TV, a network affiliate, he had never held elective office. His lack of political experience generated some unfavorable comment that he was just a "talking head" with little substantive policy knowledge.

But Klink published a booklet outlining his ideas for turning the district's economy around, and he stressed his opposition to abortion. He won the Democratic nomination with 45 percent of the vote; his closest rival took 22 percent, and Kolter ran third with 19 percent.

In the general election, Klink rolled to victory over his Republican opponent with 78 percent of the vote. His two re-elections have each come with 64 percent of the vote.

HOUSE ELECTIONS

1996 General		
Ron Klink (D)	142,621	(64%)
Paul T. Adametz (R)	79,448	(36%)
1994 General		
Ron Klink (D)	119,115	(64%)
Ed Peglow (R)	66,509	(36%)

Previous Winning Percentages: 1992 (78%)

CAMPAIGN FINANCE

	Receipts	Receipts from PACs	Expend-itures
1996			
Klink (D)	$518,531	$318,825 (61%)	$506,560
Adametz (R)	$17,255	$1,000 (6%)	$17,028
1994			
Klink (D)	$482,569	$322,807 (67%)	$467,285
Peglow (R)	$88,939	$53 (0%)	$88,576

DISTRICT VOTE FOR PRESIDENT

	1996		1992
D	107,000 (47%)	**D**	118,701 (48%)
R	96,495 (42%)	**R**	76,193 (31%)
I	23,373 (10%)	**I**	50,647 (21%)

VOTING STUDIES

	Presidential Support		Party Unity		Conservative Coalition	
Year	S	O	S	O	S	O
1996	62	37	73	25	61	37
1995	73	26	77	22	58	42
1994	72	28	81	17	53	47
1993	65	33	83	16	52	48

KEY VOTES

1997	
Ban "partial-birth" abortions	Y
1996	
Approve farm bill	N
Deny public education to illegal immigrants	Y
Repeal ban on certain assault-style weapons	Y
Increase minimum wage	Y
Freeze defense spending	N
Approve welfare overhaul	Y
1995	
Approve balanced-budget constitutional amendment	N
Relax Clean Water Act regulations	Y
Oppose limits on environmental regulations	Y
Reduce projected Medicare spending	N
Approve GOP budget with tax and spending cuts	N

INTEREST GROUP RATINGS

Year	ADA	AFL-CIO	CCUS	ACU
1996	65	n/a	20	30
1995	75	100	29	16
1994	50	100	33	43
1993	65	92	30	25

5 John E. Peterson (R)

Of Pleasantville — Elected 1996, 1st term

Biographical Information
Born: Dec. 25, 1938, Titusville, Pa.
Education: Titusville High School, graduated 1956.
Military Service: Army Reserves, 1958-64.
Occupation: Supermarket owner.
Family: Wife, Saundra; one child.
Religion: Methodist.
Political Career: Pleasantville Borough Council, 1969-77; Pa. House, 1977-85; Pa. Senate, 1985-97.
Capitol Office: 1020 Longworth Bldg. 20515; 225-5121.

Committees
Education & Workforce
Early Childhood, Youth & Families; Postsecondary Education, Training & Life-Long Learning
Resources
Fisheries Conservation, Wildlife & Oceans; Forests & Forest Health

The Path to Washington: Unlike many of the new breed of Republican House members, Peterson comes to Capitol Hill with a wealth of legislative experience. Before winning the seat vacated by retiring Republican Rep. William F. Clinger in 1996, he served for nearly two decades in the Pennsylvania legislature.

In Harrisburg, Peterson showed himself to be a team player who could scale the political ladder. In his final years in the state Senate, Peterson chaired the Public Health and Welfare Committee as well as the Republican Policy Committee. For the 105th Congress, Peterson drew seats on the Resources Committee and the Education and the Workforce Committee.

Peterson's winning tally in November 1996 was a solid 60 percent. But his victory did not come without difficulty. In the spring, he had to survive a crowded primary field that included Bob Shuster, the son of GOP Rep. Bud Shuster, the powerful chairman of the House Transportation and Infrastructure Committee who represents a neighboring Pennsylvania district. In the fall, Peterson had to weather charges of sexual harassment that emerged less than a month before the election.

In each case, Peterson showed a willingness to play political hardball. He fired an early shot across young Shuster's bow in the primary, challenging the validity of some of the names on his nominating petitions (albeit unsuccessfully).

And in mid-October, when the Harrisburg Patriot News ran a story reporting complaints by several women of unwelcome sexual advances by Peterson, he responded on several fronts. He denied the allegations, attributing them to negative campaigning by his Democratic opponent, state Rep. Ruth C. Rudy. Meanwhile, Peterson's wife wrote an open letter to district voters hailing her husband as "the most honest, decent and caring person I have ever known."

The counterattack proved effective. On the way to his comfortable victory, Peterson ran virtually even with Rudy in her populous home base of Centre County (State College), in the southeast corner of the district. Peterson lost just one other county in his landslide victory.

Rudy came to the race politically well-connected: She was a member of the Democratic National Committee for 16 years and a past president of the National Federation of Democratic Women. She represented a state House district heavily Republican in registration. In the race with Peterson, she introduced herself to voters in outlying counties through "work days."

But in both the primary and general election, Peterson enjoyed a major asset: geography. His state Senate district covered roughly the western half of the sprawling congressional district, which itself is one of the largest east of the Mississippi. And over the years, Peterson had cultivated his legislative constituency.

For more than a quarter-century, he ran a grocery store in his hometown of Pleasantville and in the meantime got extensively involved in local politics. He served as a district assistant to former GOP Rep. Albert Johnson (1963-1977) before launching his own political career, which has included six years as head of the Pleasantville Borough Council, nearly eight years in the Pennsylvania House and a dozen years in the state Senate.

Peterson should find himself in the mainstream of Republicans on Capitol Hill. He opposes abortion except in cases of rape, incest or when the life of the woman is in danger. A supporter of gunowners' rights, Peterson advocates repeal of both the Brady law mandating a five-day waiting period for handgun purchases and the ban on certain semiautomatic assault-style weapons. He favors a "flatter tax" on incomes, a balanced-budget amendment and 12-year federal term limits.

With his background as a grocer, Peterson has claimed a personal understanding of the concerns of small-business owners, particularly in dealing with government paperwork. He has described himself as "a good bureaucracy fighter. I don't get angry," he has said, "but I'm persistent."

PENNSYLVANIA 5
Northwest, Central — State College

The 5th is Pennsylvania's largest congressional district in land area, including all or part of 17 counties.

To get a rough idea of the size of the 5th, take a ride on meandering Route 6, which runs along the northern tier of the district. It is a faster ride on I-80, which nearly bifurcates Pennsylvania, but the old road affords more time to notice the scores of hamlets that dot the rural landscape.

The road also cuts through the heartland of the Allegheny National Forest Region, an area covering about a half-million acres of woodland. It runs by Pine Creek Gorge in Tioga County — the attraction known as "Pennsylvania's Grand Canyon" — and continues all the way past Warren, on the western outskirts of the district.

With hundreds of thousands of acres of state game land, hunting and fishing are sacred pursuits for many people here. In some areas, schools close for the first day of hunting season.

Tourism and recreation are the district's economic mainstays, but beyond those industries, there is not much else.

Population is sprinkled fairly lightly through the rural counties. The only sizable concentration of people is in Centre County, where the borough of State College is home to Pennsylvania State University.

A sleepy college town three decades ago, State College has grown to form the nucleus of an emerging metropolitan area. The university has spawned a small high-tech industrial complex outside town that adds to the area's white-collar base.

Centre County as a whole tends to vote Republican, but the university community keeps it competitive for Democrats. In 1992, Bill Clinton and Democratic Senate nominee Lynn Yeakel both carried Centre County, and Clinton again won the county in 1996. But Republican Reps. Tom Ridge and Rick Santorum both won Centre in 1994 in their successful bids for governor and senator, respectively.

Neighboring Clinton County is nominally Democratic; in 1996, it supported Clinton by a comfortable margin. West of Clinton County, paper mill workers help give Elk County a Democratic lean.

The counties of the northern tier, on the New York border, are less receptive to Democrats. They form the top segment of the GOP voting bloc known as the Republican "T." The "T" is rooted in the strongly Republican counties that begin on the Maryland border and rise north, before fanning out east and west on the northern tier. McKean, Potter, Tioga and Cameron counties opted for Bob Dole in 1996.

Jefferson is also solid Republican territory. But the county's politics take a back seat to its most famous resident, Punxsutawney Phil, the groundhog who becomes a national media star every Feb. 2; Phil was featured in the 1993 movie "Groundhog Day."

Another 5th District icon is Edwin Drake, the 19th century Jed Clampett who drilled America's first crude oil well near Titusville (Venango County), about fifteen miles north of Oil City.

1990 Population: 565,813. White 553,157 (98%), Black 5,600 (1%), Other 7,056 (1%). Hispanic origin 3,456 (1%). 18 and over 431,688 (76%), 62 and over 95,173 (17%). Median age: 33.

HOUSE ELECTIONS

1996 General		
John E. Peterson (R)	116,303	(60%)
Ruth C. Rudy (D)	76,627	(40%)
1996 Primary		
John E. Peterson (R)	22,000	(38%)
Daniel S. Gordeux (R)	16,230	(28%)
Bob Shuster (R)	10,734	(18%)
Patrick Conway (R)	9,334	(16%)

CAMPAIGN FINANCE

	Receipts	Receipts from PACs	Expend-itures
1996			
Peterson (R)	$865,989	$228,650 (26%)	$858,637
Rudy (D)	$451,052	$97,821 (22%)	$446,613

DISTRICT VOTE FOR PRESIDENT

	1996		1992
D	79,986 (40%)	D	78,049 (36%)
R	91,602 (46%)	R	89,373 (42%)
I	25,685 (13%)	I	48,093 (22%)

KEY VOTES

1997

Ban "partial birth" abortions — Y

6 Tim Holden (D)

Of St. Clair — Elected 1992, 3rd term

Biographical Information
Born: March 5, 1957, St. Clair, Pa.
Education: Bloomsburg U., B.A. 1980.
Occupation: Sheriff.
Family: Wife, Gwen Kieres.
Religion: Roman Catholic.
Political Career: Schuylkill County sheriff, 1985-93.
Capitol Office: 1421 Longworth Bldg. 20515; 225-5546.

Committees
Agriculture
Forestry, Resource Conservation & Research; Livestock, Dairy & Poultry
Transportation and Infrastructure
Public Buildings & Economic Development

In Washington: Holden hails from a tradition of working-class Democrats who worry about holding on to their jobs and their guns and about how much Uncle Sam takes out of their wallets.

One of the more conservative northern Democrats, Holden disagrees with many in his party on social issues. In House floor votes he reliably casts his lot with abortion opponents, and he also is a steadfast supporter of gunowners' rights. In the 103rd Congress he voted against a five-day waiting period for handgun purchases, and he opposed a ban on certain semiautomatic assault-style weapons (although he voted for a broad anticrime bill that included the ban). In 1996, he supported a Republican initiative to repeal the assault-weapons ban.

During the 104th Congress' debate on welfare overhaul, Holden had reservations about what the GOP majority wanted to see welfare become, but in mid-July 1996, he was one of only 30 Democrats to back the Republican welfare proposal. The GOP further modified its plan until President Clinton agreed to sign it. That compromise bill was approved by the House in late July 1996, with Holden one of the 98 Democrats voting for it.

Holden is a member of the "Blue Dog" coalition, a group of center-right House Democrats who mostly represent Southern districts. On welfare, the budget and other issues, they have sought a middle course: to the right of the Democratic Party's liberals, but more centrist than the conservative GOP majority.

Yet Holden is certainly not beyond the Clinton administration's reach on budget issues. In August 1993, he switched to vote for Clinton's budget, which had been revised to include a gasoline tax rather than a broad-based Btu energy tax. He had initially voted "no" on Clinton's deficit reduction plan because, he said, the Btu energy tax would have hurt his rural district.

Holden's Democratic stripes are clearest on issues important to organized labor. He has consistently taken the side of labor unions in their high-profile disputes with the pro-business Republican leadership — on raising the minimum wage, on allowing companies to offer comp time in lieu of overtime pay, and on changing the National Labor Relations Act to let non-union companies set up and control labor-management teams.

In the 103rd Congress, he opposed NAFTA, believing it would lead to U.S. jobs being exported to Mexico, where labor is cheaper. He also opposed GATT.

A former sheriff, Holden likes Clinton's community policing program that was included in the 1994 crime bill with a goal of putting 100,000 more police officers on the street over six years. House Republicans in early 1995 sought to replace the community policing program with a block grant program so local officials could spend federal dollars as they saw fit to reduce crime. Holden objected. "I have spent 14 years in law enforcement, seven as a county sheriff. And I believe in my heart that if we are going to win the war against crime, to make a significant contribution to reducing crime, we need more police officers on the street."

Holden also took a swipe at what he saw as Republican parliamentary high-handednesss when the House in August 1995 was to consider a broad bill overhauling the telecommunications industry. GOP leaders sent the bill to the floor under a rule that allowed only eight amendments. They also planned to conduct the entire debate late at night. The scheduling caused opponents of the bill, like Holden, to cry foul.

"This bill will impact the life of every American — whether they talk on the telephone, listen to the radio, watch television or send a fax," said Holden. "So how does the House of Representatives deal with this bill? By debating it into the dark of night under a rule which allows for almost no amendments. This process is seriously flawed."

Although not a particularly verbose member — Holden went to the floor only 17 times in the 104th Congress — he will speak out when he feels

PENNSYLVANIA 6
Southeast — Reading

The story of the 6th is a tale of two counties, both hit hard by deindustrialization. Berks County, the more populous of the two, learned to diversify its economy. Schuylkill County, the poorer cousin to the north, never truly weaned itself from King Coal.

Reading, the largest city in Berks and the district, is no longer recognized as a major railroad or manufacturing center. It remains more industrialized than most of the state but now features a large and diverse economic base where no single employer dominates the work force. Where there once were steel and textile mills, now there are factory outlet stores. Bargain hunters often board buses to make the pilgrimage to the city that bills itself as "the outlet capital of the world."

The city has seen an influx of Hispanics looking for work, which in turn sparked a migration of whites to the surrounding suburbs. Because of this migration, the outlying areas — once mainly agricultural and always supportive of Republicans — now turn in even bigger numbers for GOP candidates. In 1996, Berks County opted for Bob Dole. That helped him win the overall district by 3 percentage points even as Democrat Holden gathered his highest percentage ever, 59 percent.

In southern Berks, residential developments have sprouted because the completion of Route 422 made it feasible to commute to jobs in the Philadelphia area.

Schuylkill County is divided by the physical presence of Broad Mountain. To locals, "north of the mountain" means the coal belt that begins north of Pottsville, or what remains of it.

The domes of Eastern Orthodox churches built by the Eastern European miners in the late 19th century still dominate the roof lines of small, church-filled towns such as St. Clair. The "Molly McGuires," a secret organization that battled mine companies and their agents to provide better working and living conditions in the coal fields, were drawn from the ranks of Irish and Welsh immigrant miners.

Today, the county's coal tradition is a vein for tourism. Visitors can take a ride in an open mine car deep into Mahanoy Mountain or visit the Museum of Anthracite Mining in Ashland.

The decline of the coal industry has tracked the decline of traditional Republican strength in Schuylkill. Once a GOP stronghold, Schuylkill has become more receptive to Democrats in recent years.

Pottsville, the largest city in the county, is where the county's remaining coal operations do business. It is home to the family-owned Yuengling brewery, America's oldest. Schuylkill County residents refer to it as "Vitamin Y."

Along the Susquehanna River, the 6th also takes in a strip of Northumberland County that includes Sunbury, another former manufacturing and railroad city that has fallen on hard times. The southeastern tip of the district dips into Montgomery County, to take in part of Pottstown.

1990 Population: 565,760. White 538,487 (95%), Black 13,870 (2%), Other 13,403 (2%). Hispanic origin 18,862 (3%). 18 and over 435,116 (77%), 62 and over 114,327 (20%). Median age: 36.

Pennsylvania's interests are threatened. He said the Republicans' intention to make Medicaid a block grant program for the states would cause Pennsylvania to lose $9 billion over seven years in the Medicaid program. "Pennsylvania has the second highest senior citizen population in the country, next to Florida," Holden told the House. "Forty-five percent of all Medicaid expenditures in the Commonwealth of Pennsylvania are for the senior citizens and nursing homes."

He was equally disturbed by the GOP plan to cut projected Medicare spending by $270 billion over seven years, saying that would have "a devastating effect" on health care for citizens in Pennsylvania. "The American people also know that the Republican plan only puts in $90 billion to make [Medicare] solvent to 2006, and the rest of the money is being used for a tax break and to balance the budget on the backs of senior citizens. That is wrong," Holden said.

Holden sits on the Agriculture Committee, and in the 104th he voted in February 1996 against passage of the GOP's "Freedom to Farm" bill that phased out most New Deal-era crop subsidies, replacing them with a system of fixed, but declining, payments that farmers would receive over seven years regardless of market prices or their planting decisions.

In the 105th Holden shifted off the Government Reform and Oversight Committee to take a seat on Transportation and Infrastructure. That affords him input in Congress' work on a massive reauthorization bill funding highway, public transit and other transportation projects.

At Home: Holden's Pennsylvania roots run deep. He was born in the 6th District town of St. Clair, went to school about an hour north of his hometown and came back to be sheriff.

When Holden shows up at a fire hall barbecue or a high school football game, he moves with the easy affability of someone who has spent most of his life at such events.

His family has a tradition of public service: His father, Joseph "Socks" Holden, served as a Schuylkill County commissioner for almost two decades beginning in 1959. And his great-grandfather, John Siney, founded the Miner's Benevolent Association, the forerunner of the United Mine Workers union.

Although redistricting for the 1990s made the 6th more competitive for the GOP, Holden held it for the Democrats in the open-seat race of 1992, and he has posted comfortable re-election tallies of 57 and 59 percent.

In the 1992 Democratic primary to succeed retiring Democratic Rep. Gus Yatron, Holden benefited from the fact that two candidates from the more-populous eastern half of the 6th split the vote in that area, allowing him to win nomination with a plurality of 39 percent. He hails from the less populated Schuylkill County portion of the district.

Then during the 1992 general election, Holden emphasized his "man of the people" roots, contrasting himself with his GOP opponent, John E. Jones, a lawyer and judge from Schuylkill County.

"I'm not an elitist. I'm not personally wealthy, and I don't just come around when I'm running for office," Holden said.

Jones had a big financial advantage over Holden, outspending him by more than $150,000. He tried to paint Holden as a lightweight liberal who would bring little in intellect or leadership to the job of U.S. representative. But Holden appealed to voters with his deep local roots, and by presenting himself as a "conservative Democrat" who would work to keep high-paying jobs in the district. He won with 52 percent of the vote.

Even though 1994 was a big year for the GOP nationally, the Republican challenge to Holden was not strong, and he moved up to 57 percent.

In 1996, though, he drew an aggressive challenge from Republican Christian Y. Leinbach, a former Berks County (Reading) GOP chairman and member of Republican Sen. Rick Santorum's staff. Leinbach's campaign spent about $420,000, and GOP presidential nominee Bob Dole carried the 6th by three points over Clinton.

But Holden's voting record gave Leinbach few openings to exploit, and he saw Holden roll to victory by a convincing 18-point margin.

HOUSE ELECTIONS

1996 General		
Tim Holden (D)	115,193	(59%)
Christian Y. Leinbach (R)	80,061	(41%)
1994 General		
Tim Holden (D)	90,023	(57%)
Fred Levering (R)	68,610	(43%)

Previous Winning Percentages: 1992 (52%)

CAMPAIGN FINANCE

	Receipts	Receipts from PACs	Expend-itures
1996			
Holden (D)	$692,499	$366,763 (53%)	$609,346
Leinbach (R)	$420,627	$53,867 (13%)	$419,013
1994			
Holden (D)	$678,727	$361,586 (53%)	$675,274
Levering (R)	$133,127	$5,464 (4%)	$132,889

DISTRICT VOTE FOR PRESIDENT

	1996		1992
D	83,762 (42%)	**D**	78,326 (36%)
R	89,679 (45%)	**R**	89,791 (41%)
I	25,137 (13%)	**I**	50,207 (23%)

KEY VOTES

1997	
Ban "partial birth" abortions	Y
1996	
Approve farm bill	N
Deny public education to illegal immigrants	Y
Repeal ban on certain assault-style weapons	Y
Increase minimum wage	Y
Freeze defense spending	Y
Approve welfare overhaul	Y
1995	
Approve balanced-budget constitutional amendment	N
Relax Clean Water Act regulations	Y
Oppose limits on environmental regulations	Y
Reduce projected Medicare spending	N
Approve GOP budget with tax and spending cuts	N

VOTING STUDIES

	Presidential Support		Party Unity		Conservative Coalition	
Year	S	O	S	O	S	O
1996	57	37	59	36	76	22
1995	59	41	71	29	73	27
1994	68	32	75	25	72	28
1993	65	35	80	19	57	43

INTEREST GROUP RATINGS

Year	ADA	AFL-CIO	CCUS	ACU
1996	45	n/a	63	47
1995	60	92	46	46
1994	45	100	58	43
1993	60	92	27	38

7 Curt Weldon (R)

Of Aston — Elected 1986, 6th term

Biographical Information

Born: July 22, 1947, Marcus Hook, Pa.
Education: West Chester State College, B.A. 1969.
Occupation: Teacher; consultant.
Family: Wife, Mary Gallagher; five children.
Religion: Protestant.
Political Career: Mayor of Marcus Hook, 1977-82; Delaware County Council, 1981-86; Republican nominee for U.S. House, 1984.
Capitol Office: 2452 Rayburn Bldg. 20515; 225-2011.

Committees

National Security
Military Readiness; Military Research & Development (chairman)
Science
Energy & Environment; Technology

In Washington: Weldon pushed hard in the 104th Congress to build congressional and grass-roots support for an anti-ballistic missile defense system. As chairman of the National Security Committee's Military Research and Development Subcommittee, he warns that the Clinton administration underestimates the threat the United States faces from ballistic missiles — armed with nuclear, chemical or biological warheads — in the hands of nations that are hostile to U.S. interests. It is unwise, Weldon and his allies argue, to assume that such rogue regimes will be dissuaded from attacking the United States by threat of massive American retaliation. Better, he says, to develop a U.S. defensive capacity.

Diligent, persistent and politically smart, Weldon has been successful in the past in getting things he wants. For several years, he worked to preserve the V-22 Osprey tilt-rotor aircraft program, a job-provider at the big Boeing plant in Weldon's district. Osprey prototypes crashed in 1991 and 1992, raising the possibility that the plane would be judged expendable. Weldon lobbied extensively for continuation of the Osprey program. He got good news in 1994 when a Pentagon review board recommended limited production of the aircraft.

Liberal Democrats have criticized the concept of an anti-missile system as a swipe at Moscow that may goad Russia into halting the destruction of nuclear-armed missiles pursuant to earlier arms reduction agreements. But Weldon, who is proficient in Russian, maintains that his tough line on anti-missile defense meshes with his efforts to forge a partnership with Russia. He has labored to foster a working relationship between Congress and the Duma, Russia's legislature.

When the GOP-led National Security Committee marked up its first defense bill for fiscal 1996, members added a provision requiring deployment of a nationwide anti-ballistic missile system by 2003 and added $763 million to President Clinton's fiscal 1996 missile defense request. Clinton vetoed the bill in December 1995, citing specifically his objections to the provision mandating the defense shield by 2003.

Republicans failed to override the veto, and eventually they removed the objectionable provision in order to get the bill signed into law. But Weldon would not cry uncle. "This is not the end of the fight, this is the beginning of what promises to be a war," he vowed.

Weldon and fellow National Security Republican Duncan Hunter of California formed a caucus of 70 lawmakers examining missile defense. Arguing that the status quo of no missile defense "is unacceptable," Weldon said, "It is our job in government to protect our citizens."

Weldon and Hunter hope to generate grass-roots pressure in favor of missile defense to prod wavering members. As proof of the lengths Weldon will go to convince members of the importance of the defense shield, he enlisted the aid of rock guitarist Jeff "Skunk" Baxter in his anti-missile campaign. The bearded, pony-tailed Baxter is a founding member of the group Steely Dan and also played with the Doobie Brothers. He is an avid student of high technology who, Weldon said, advises the Energy Department's Lawrence Livermore Laboratory on lasers. Baxter agreed to join Weldon to highlight some of the technology breakthroughs that U.S. anti-missile defenses could exploit and to chair a new Civilian Advisory Board on Ballistic Missile Defense.

Certain that Clinton would veto the fiscal 1997 defense bill if it contained the national missile defense system language, Weldon and other proponents decided to move the language as a separate bill. Called the "Defend America Act," it was slated for House action in May 1996. But the GOP leadership quickly pulled the bill from the floor when faced with united opposition from Democrats and some wavering Republicans. Skeptics noted that the Congressional Budget Office estimated the cost of the missile defense system to be $10 billion over five years, whereas supporters had said it could be built for $5 billion.

Weldon also took the unusual step in July 1996 of seeking a court order to force Clinton and then-

Delaware County, the anchor of the 7th District, provides a textbook example of a suburban Republican machine. There are more than a few working-class towns in the district, but in elections from the township level to the presidency, most voters pull the GOP lever.

From the 1920s to the mid-1970s, local politics were ruled by the "war board," a secretive group officially called the Delaware County Republican Board of Supervisors. The current GOP organization is a looser confederation, but party discipline and patronage still keep most of the 7th's voters in line.

That is what made George Bush's countywide defeat in 1992 so hard for local GOP officials to swallow. Bush visited Delaware County several times; its national prominence as a middle-class bastion makes it a must-stop for GOP statewide or presidential candidates. But Bill Clinton won the county again in 1996, and this time led in the entire district, even as Weldon easily won re-election.

Normally, one of the few places in Delaware county where Democrats find sanctuary is Swarthmore, where Swarthmore College is located. The academic community at the prestigious Quaker-founded institution provides a liberal island in a sea of Republicanism.

Closer to Philadelphia, older suburbs such as Norwood, Ridley Park and Upper Darby are mostly white and working class. Marcus Hook, an old oil refinery town along the Delaware River, also fits that description. The only concentrations of blacks in the county — in Yeadon, Darby and the city of Chester — are sliced out of the 7th and pieced onto Philadelphia-based congressional districts.

Surrounding these areas, farther out on

PENNSYLVANIA 7
Suburban Philadelphia — Part of Delaware County

West Chester Pike, are more comfortably middle-class places such as Springfield and Newtown Square. In the district's southwest corner, Birmingham and Thornbury townships are less developed. The white-collar professionals in wealthy Radnor Township and on Philadelphia's affluent Main Line are less attuned to the GOP organization but remain staunchly Republican. (Most of the Main Line is in the neighboring 13th, in Montgomery County.)

Upper Merion Township stands out as the lone portion of Montgomery County attached to the district; it features King of Prussia, a fast-growing Philadelphia exurb. Spurring economic and residential development in the King of Prussia corridor is the "Blue Route," a highway connecting I-95 in southern Delaware County with the Schuylkill Expressway near King of Prussia.

The 7th also contains a portion of Chester County. Tredyffrin Township holds the majority of its population and includes the old-money mansions in Paoli and the newer residential developments of Chesterbrook. Farther west are less populous but emerging exurban townships such as East Whiteland, West Pikeland and West Vincent.

1990 Population: 565,746. White 530,827 (94%), Black 21,685 (4%), Other 13,234 (2%). Hispanic origin 5,305 (1%). 18 and over 440,851(78%), 62 and over 104,385 (18%). Median age: 36.

Defense Secretary William J. Perry to accelerate the development of two anti-missile defense systems to meet deadlines set by the GOP Congress. The fiscal 1996 defense act required that a prototype of the Army's Theater High-Altitude Air Defense (THAAD) system be ready for an emergency by 1998 and that the system be up and running by 2000. A prototype of the Navy's comparable "Upper Tier" system must be ready by 1999, with the system deployed by 2001.

Less than a week after the bill became law, however, the Pentagon announced that it did not intend to meet the deadlines and, in fact, was slowing down the pace of the Army and Navy programs to accelerate development of other anti-missile projects. Weldon denounced the administration's action as "a blatant effort to ignore the requirements of the . . . bill."

Weldon pursued Russian Studies in college and has led various bipartisan delegations to Russia. He has proposed setting up an Internet "hotline" over which members of the two national legislatures could communicate with simultaneous translation. He also wants to organize joint committees of members from Congress and the Russian Duma to discuss issues of mutual interest, including energy, budget and finance, environment, and defense and foreign policy. "The idea is to build relationships [working on important but not necessarily contentious issues] so that, when we get to the more difficult issues, we will . . . have built up some trust and understanding," Weldon explains.

Weldon takes exception with many GOP conservatives who regard environmental regulations as burdensome to business. In 1995 he voted against a majority of his party in opposing a controversial rewrite of the clean water act, and he supported a move to block limitations on the Environmental Protection Agency's ability to enforce environmental laws.

Simply by showing up for the October 1995 vote on budget reconciliation, Weldon achieved something that was hard to come by in the 104th: bipartisan applause. At the end of a contentious debate about spending priorities, Robert S.

Walker, R-Pa., announced that Weldon was present for "this historic vote," just one week after undergoing heart bypass surgery. A standing ovation ensued. Weldon, who cast his vote for the GOP budget, said it was "too important for the future or our children and grandchildren to miss."

Weldon voted with a majority of House Democrats against passage of NAFTA. The son of a factory worker, he has tried through the years to stay on decent terms with thc labor interests in his district. He backed the Democratic-led effort to raise the minimum wage in 1996 and was one of just 43 Republicans who opposed a GOP leadership's attempt to exempt small businesses from paying the higher wage.

While plenty of members aim to set the world on fire when they come to Congress, Weldon spends considerable time promoting fire prevention. He founded the Fire Services Caucus, the largest caucus in Congress. Weldon had to endure some political heat, however, when he used campaign funds to buy his own vintage fire truck.

At Home: Weldon's first victory in the Republican 7th ended 12 years of Democratic control. The man frustrating the GOP had been Bob Edgar, who left the 7th open in 1986 to wage a Senate bid that ended in defeat. Weldon was the unanimous choice of local Republicans to bid for the House seat vacated by Edgar. The youngest of nine children, Weldon is a former volunteer fireman, teacher and mayor of his hometown, Marcus Hook , making him a good fit for the 7th's conservative mix of blue-and white-collar workers.

Weldon rose to prominence as the architect of Marcus Hook's revival. A small working-class city at the 7th's southern end, it was gripped by economic decline and gang warfare when Weldon became GOP mayor in 1977. Ordering a series of tough police raids, he broke up the Pagan motorcycle gang and ended its illicit drug trafficking.

Weldon's accomplishments caught the eye of the powerful Delaware County GOP, and in 1981, with machine backing, Weldon won a County Council seat. He was elected chairman by popular ballot in early 1984.

In 1984, Weldon ran against Edgar, taking on a task that had undone five Republicans before him. Weldon lost by only 412 votes, and his near-miss made him the favorite when Edgar's departure for a Senate race opened up the 7th in 1986. Weldon took the seat with 61 percent of the vote that year and has won re-election easily since then.

In 1990, Democrats hoped to sidetrack Weldon by calling attention to his role in a Delaware County economic development agency he founded and chaired. According to a June 1989 audit by the Department of Housing and Urban Development, the agency misspent at least $1.6 million in federal funds. Weldon said he had a largely absentee role in the agency's management and that a disgruntled former agency employee was trying to make him appear guilty of a cover-up. Voters seemed to accept Weldon's explanation; he won by a ratio of nearly 2-to-1.

HOUSE ELECTIONS

1996 General		
Curt Weldon (R)	165,087	(67%)
John Innelli (D)	79,875	(32%)
1996 Primary		
Curt Weldon (R)	49,999	(83%)
Rob McHonagle (R)	9,882	(17%)
1994 General		
Curt Weldon (R)	137,480	(70%)
Sara Nichols (D)	59,845	(30%)

Previous Winning Percentages: **1992** (66%) **1990** (65%) **1988** (68%) **1986** (61%)

CAMPAIGN FINANCE

	Receipts	Receipts from PACs	Expend-itures
1996			
Weldon (R)	$567,696	$235,266 (41%)	$362,252
Innelli (D)	$51,492	$7,250 (14%)	$50,562
1994			
Weldon (R)	$397,378	$164,820 (41%)	$349,639
Nichols (D)	$140,542	$750 (1%)	$149,028

DISTRICT VOTE FOR PRESIDENT

1996		1992	
D	116,638 (45%)	**D**	111,518 (39%)
R	112,412 (44%)	**R**	123,954 (44%)
I	23,645 (9%)	**I**	49,802 (18%)

KEY VOTES

1997	
Ban "partial birth" abortions	Y
1996	
Approve farm bill	Y
Deny public education to illegal immigrants	Y
Repeal ban on certain assault-style weapons	Y
Increase minimum wage	Y
Freeze defense spending	N
Approve welfare overhaul	Y
1995	
Approve balanced-budget constitutional amendment	Y
Relax Clean Water Act regulations	N
Oppose limits on environmental regulations	Y
Reduce projected Medicare spending	Y
Approve GOP budget with tax and spending cuts	Y

VOTING STUDIES

	Presidential Support		Party Unity		Conservative Coalition	
Year	**S**	**O**	**S**	**O**	**S**	**O**
1996	39	48	74	13	82	12
1995	21	71	79	12	79	13
1994	63	33	77	19	81	19
1993	47	51	86	13	95	2
1992	68	31	82	16	83	17
1991	54	41	71	24	76	22

INTEREST GROUP RATINGS

Year	ADA	AFL-CIO	CCUS	ACU
1996	15	n/a	85	84
1995	15	18	83	78
1994	10	33	92	74
1993	25	55	55	73
1992	25	83	88	80
1991	30	55	60	65

8 James C. Greenwood (R)

Of Erwinna — Elected 1992, 3rd term

Biographical Information
Born: May 4, 1951, Philadelphia, Pa.
Education: Dickinson College, B.A. 1973.
Occupation: State official.
Family: Wife, Christina Paugh; four children.
Religion: Presbyterian.
Political Career: Pa. House, 1981-87; Pa. Senate, 1987-93.
Capitol Office: 2436 Rayburn Bldg. 20515; 225-4276.

Committees
Commerce
Finance & Hazardous Materials; Health & Environment; Oversight & Investigations
Education & Workforce
Early Childhood, Youth & Families; Postsecondary Education, Training & Life-Long Learning

In Washington: In the GOP conference, Greenwood has emerged as a centrist, favoring gun control, abortion rights, family planning programs and an increase in the minimum wage. An emissary to leadership meetings, Greenwood represents a group of GOP moderates known as the "Tuesday Lunch Bunch."

Although he is a moderate on social issues, he takes a harder line on economic policy, supporting a balanced-budget constitutional amendment and a line-item veto. He also worked hard in the 104th on the GOP's plan to reduce projected spending on Medicare and backed the proposed medical savings accounts as a way to cut health care costs for seniors. Greenwood has also taken the lead on other medical issues important to his party, such as restructuring the Food and Drug Administration.

Greenwood was on the House task force that drafted the changes to Medicare to reduce its spending by $270 billion over seven years. The savings were to be obtained by reducing payments to providers, encouraging seniors to switch to managed care and requiring well-to-do beneficiaries to pay more for part of their coverage.

A key component of the GOP Medicare plan were medical savings accounts (MSA), a sort of individual retirement account that individuals could establish for health care. Under the proposal that Greenwood helped to draft, Medicare would contribute a certain amount of money toward a beneficiary's purchase of high-deductible catastrophic health insurance. Leftover money would be placed in beneficiaries' medical savings accounts, from which they could pay the deductibles for their catastrophic coverage or other health care costs.

Greenwood and other proponents of the accounts said they would drive down medical costs by giving account holders a financial incentive to get the most for their health care dollars. Critics contended that the accounts would attract only the healthiest and wealthiest Medicare beneficiaries, leaving sicker, frailer elderly people in what could become a financially strapped fee-for-service program.

The medical savings accounts gave added fuel to the Democrats to object to the GOP's entire Medicare proposal. "If no matter what we do, we can't keep the MSAs in reconciliation, we still have a bill that saves Medicare and reduces the deficit," Greenwood said, defending the plan. "We could revisit MSAs. The leadership position is that we have to save it and it's a critical issue, but everything doesn't blow up without it."

President Clinton ended up vetoing the GOP's deficit-reducing reconciliation bill in December 1995, in part because he thought the reductions in Medicare spending were too high.

The next year, Greenwood was asked by Commerce Committee Chairman Thomas J. Bliley Jr. to take the lead on a measure to overhaul the way the Food and Drug Administration (FDA) does business. A senior member of Commerce, Greenwood also has a seat on its Health and Environment Subcommittee.

Greenwood and other members of the committee drafted three measures streamlining the FDA — one dealing with pharmaceuticals, one with medical devices and one with food products. Greenwood approached the bills in a bipartisan fashion and said his goal was "to get a bill on the president's desk that he will sign." But in May 1996 he was taken to task by FDA Director David A. Kessler who said the three bills, which also aimed to expedite the agency's drug and medical devices approval process, would put public health at risk. Greenwood said that two-thirds of the drugs the agency had approved over the past few years had been available overseas years earlier. "Americans are dying of red tape," he told Kessler. None of the three bills were marked up in the 104th, however.

Greenwood was more successful with a measure to identify methods to prevent head trauma and to minimize the dysfunction that can result from such an injury. His measure authorized $24 million to conduct brain injury research and to increase access to care for victims of such injuries. "The tragedy of traumatic brain injury can be a living hell for victims and their families," Greenwood

PENNSYLVANIA 8
Northern Philadelphia suburbs — Bucks County

Population growth and development have changed some of the character of the 8th. Once a GOP stronghold, Bucks County has become more competitive. Although it continues to vote locally for Republicans, the 8th backed Bill Clinton in both 1992 and 1996.

Former Democratic Rep. Peter H. Kostmayer had held the seat for all but two years from 1977 until January 1993, thanks to tenacious constituent service and the votes of independents and Democrats from lower Bucks County. His environmentalist credentials also had some appeal among moderate Republicans. But voters threw out Kostmayer in 1992, even as Bill Clinton narrowly won the district with 40 percent. Greenwood has been re-elected handily since then, while Clinton improved his showing to 45 percent in 1996.

Part of the reason for Kostmayer's upset was the selection of Greenwood, whose moderate brand of Republicanism had countywide appeal from the landed gentry and farmers of Upper Bucks to the newly arrived independent voters. These newcomers, who include business executives from New Jersey and Manhattan, have fueled a two-decade population boom that has altered some of the area's rural charm.

Places such as Newtown Township experienced exponential growth in the 1980s; New Hope, a quaint artists' colony along the Delaware River, has turned into a tourist mecca.

The lure was Bucks County's rich history and rolling countryside. Established in 1682 as one of Pennsylvania's three original counties, Bucks contains mansions such as Pennsbury Manor, the Georgian-style mansion and plantation William Penn built for himself and his second wife. Washington Crossing was the site from which, on Christmas Day 1776, George Washington crossed the Delaware River to attack Hessian mercenaries in Trenton.

In the early 20th century, New York intellectuals and prominent writers such as Dorothy Parker and Pearl S. Buck found refuge in Bucks County.

Much of the countryside in upper Bucks remains largely undeveloped and heavily Republican. Democrats can stay competitive in the county's midsection in communities such as Warminster and Doylestown. Lower Bucks is more fertile ground for Democrats, with its grittier ambiance and closer association with Philadelphia. Levittown's tightly spaced homes, built after World War II, attracted thousands of ethnic Democrats moving from the big city.

Democratic strength surged in the 1980s as lower Bucks struggled with industrial problems typified by the massive layoffs in the remaining work force at the USX (formerly U.S. Steel) Fairless Works.

As a whole, the 8th contains all of Bucks County and about 25,000 residents in Montgomery County. One of five districts that take in some slice of Montgomery, the 8th has a portion of the county that includes Horsham and part of Lower Moreland Township.

1990 Population: 565,787. White 537,517 (95%), Black 15,995 (3%), Other 11,679 (2%). Hispanic origin 9,162 (2%). 18 and over 421,078 (74%), 62 and over 76,344 (13%). Median age: 34.

said. The Senate cleared the bill in July 1996.

Although he has been given some high profile health care assignments by his party leadership, Greenwood often differs with a majority of his party on certain social issues. In explaining his opposition to congressional restrictions on abortion, Greenwood has said his philosophy is that "the federal government should be involved in fewer things rather than more." Yet Greenwood, reflecting his suburban constituency, wants government to play an active role in areas such as promoting child immunization and toxic waste cleanup, ensuring access to family planning services and regulating firearms. He opposed the March 1996 effort by the GOP House to repeal the ban on certain assault weapons.

Not only does he vote to preserve family planning and abortion services, he often takes the lead on fending off his party's efforts to cut them.

When the House in February 1997 debated a resolution releasing money for international family planning aid, Greenwood led a small band of Republicans in favor of the effort to allow the Clinton administration to release the funds. The resolution would make $385 million in already appropriated family planning aid available on March 1 without any abortion restrictions. A narrow majority of lawmakers adopted the position, strongly endorsed by the Clinton administration, that the resolution had more to do with family planning than abortion.

"They [the opponents] had a nonstop mantra that this was about abortion," said Greenwood. "We had a nonstop mantra that it was not an abortion vote." The measure carried on a 220-209 vote, marking a rare defeat in the House for abortion opponents, who had mounted an intensive campaign to kill the measure because it included no abortion restrictions.

Greenwood was also successful in restoring funds for domestic family planning programs when the House took up the annual spending bill for the Health and Human Services Department in August 1995. After contentious negotiations between GOP moderates and conservatives, Greenwood was permitted to offer an amendment aimed at restoring $193.3 million in fiscal 1996 for family planning under Title X of the Public Health Service Act.

Under existing law, no Title X funds can be used to fund abortion services. However, conservatives have argued that some clinics provide family planning services and perform abortions, creating a circumstance whereby federal money could indirectly be used for that purpose. Family planning proponents argued that the program helps prevent unwanted pregnancies and, therefore, abortions. Greenwood said the debate "was about the right of women, poor women in this country to plan their families." The House agreed, adopting his amendment, 224-204.

Members on the Commerce Committee normally have an easy time raising PAC money from the many interests with a stake in committee business, but early in his first term, negative publicity persuaded Greenwood to swear off PAC money.

In his 1992 challenge to Democratic Rep. Peter H. Kostmayer, Greenwood had tacked play money to a large U.S. map to show how far the incumbent had traveled to collect PAC funds. Greenwood asked Kostmayer to join him in refusing PAC contributions, but when Kostmayer declined, Greenwood said he had to keep the PAC door open, too. But after media reports in February 1993 disclosed that Greenwood attended a retreat for House GOP members financed by lobbyists (some of whom were at the conference) howls of protest from his district prompted Greenwood to say he would pay for the trip personally and quit taking PAC contributions.

At Home: In 1992, Greenwood ran successfully on a platform of change against a 14-year incumbent, despite his own 12-year political career. Kostmayer tried to tag Greenwood as "just another politician," but Greenwood responded that he had been "fired in the oven of the political process, but I haven't shattered." He lumped Kostmayer with a Congress whose "me first" attitude was symbolized by "bounced checks, international junkets [and] deluxe perks." Kostmayer had 50 overdrafts at the House bank. Greenwood also was helped by an upsurge in local GOP voter registration. He won with 52 percent. Kostmayer pondered a rematch but declined. Greenwood easily won re-election.

In 1996, he had a primary challenge and then faced his 1994 opponent, teacher John P. Murray, again. He won by 24 percentage points.

During six years in the state House and six in the state Senate, Greenwood was active on a variety of issues. He helped pass a collective bargaining law that addressed a state problem with teacher strikes, played a large role in passing a solid waste act that mandated recycling and set up a state superfund for environmental compensation, and worked on housing and children's legislation.

It was romance that got Greenwood into politics: His girlfriend's father was a state legislator, and Greenwood worked for him as a legislative assistant and campaign manager. He won his state House seat in 1980 and moved to the Senate in 1986.

HOUSE ELECTIONS

1996 General		
James C. Greenwood (R)	133,749	(59%)
John P. Murray (D)	79,856	(35%)
Richard J. Piotrowski (LIBERT)	6,991	(3%)
David A. Booth (CONSTL)	5,714	(3%)
1996 Primary		
Jim Greenwood (R)	18,376	(60%)
Tom Lingenfelter (R)	12,088	(40%)
1994 General		
James C. Greenwood (R)	110,499	(66%)
John P. Murray (D)	44,559	(27%)
Jay Russell (LIBERT)	7,925	(5%)
Robert J. Cash (I)	4,191	(3%)

Previous Winning Percentages: 1992 (52%)

CAMPAIGN FINANCE

	Receipts	Receipts from PACs	Expend-itures
1996			
Greenwood (R)	$564,303	0	$614,221
Murray (D)	$69,410	$31,450 (45%)	$67,321
Piotrowski (LIBERT)	$5,665	0	$5,675
1994			
Greenwood (R)	$432,390	$9,950 (2%)	$360,600
Murray (D)	$30,950	$13,200 (43%)	$29,945

DISTRICT VOTE FOR PRESIDENT

	1996		1992
D	107,483 (45%)	**D**	101,630 (40%)
R	99,442 (42%)	**R**	99,269 (39%)
I	25,568 (11%)	**I**	56,261 (22%)

KEY VOTES

1997	
Ban "partial birth" abortions	N
1996	
Approve farm bill	Y
Deny public education to illegal immigrants	Y
Repeal ban on certain assault-style weapons	N
Increase minimum wage	Y
Freeze defense spending	Y
Approve welfare overhaul	Y
1995	
Approve balanced-budget constitutional amendment	Y
Relax Clean Water Act regulations	N
Oppose limits on environmental regulations	Y
Reduce projected Medicare spending	Y
Approve GOP budget with tax and spending cuts	Y

VOTING STUDIES

	Presidential Support		Party Unity		Conservative Coalition	
Year	**S**	**O**	**S**	**O**	**S**	**O**
1996	49	51	76	21	78	20
1995	37	62	82	15	82	15
1994	65	29	69	28	78	22
1993	43	56	79	20	80	20

INTEREST GROUP RATINGS

Year	ADA	AFL-CIO	CCUS	ACU
1996	25	n/a	88	60
1995	20	0	88	60
1994	20	11	100	70
1993	20	8	82	83

9 Bud Shuster (R)

Of Everett — Elected 1972, 13th term

Biographical Information
Born: Jan. 23, 1932, Glassport, Pa.
Education: U. of Pittsburgh, B.S. 1954; Duquesne U., M.B.A. 1960; American U., Ph.D. 1967.
Military Service: Army, 1954-56.
Occupation: Computer industry executive.
Family: Wife, Patricia Rommel; five children.
Religion: United Church of Christ.
Political Career: No previous office.
Capitol Office: 2188 Rayburn Bldg. 20515; 225-2431.

Committees
Select Intelligence
Human Intelligence, Analysis & Counterintelligence
Transportation & Infrastructure (chairman)

In Washington: Back for a second crack at running the show in the 105th Congress, Republicans are devoting their attention to passing workable legislation, and few in their ranks are better-equipped to play the old-fashioned legislative game than Shuster, czar of the Transportation and Infrastructure Committee.

Shuster has prepared his expansive fiefdom to run smoothly as it rewrites the nation's main highway and mass transit law, which will authorize as much as $180 billion in new spending. One potential distraction, however, does loom over Shuster, in the form of ethics questions.

In an era of budget belt-tightening, Shuster unapologetically seeks to fill his committee's plate to heaping. He threw himself in front of the fiscal 1998 budget deal negotiated in May 1997 between President Clinton and GOP leaders, upset that it did not include more highway funding. On the House floor, Shuster offered an amendment to the budget pact boosting transportation spending by $12 billion over the next five years. Opponents held their breath as votes were tallied on Shuster's amendment; in the end, it barely lost, 214-216.

"I hope they put on my tombstone, 40 years from now: 'He helped build America,'" Shuster once said. The most famous monument to the chairman's soft spot for asphalt, the Bud Shuster Highway that runs for a brief stretch beside the Pennsylvania Turnpike through his home town, was upgraded in 1996 to interstate status, making it eligible for more federal dollars.

That change came as part of legislation creating a new National Highway System that Shuster shepherded to passage in the 104th. Another of his accomplishments was a law abolishing the Interstate Commerce Commission, the nation's oldest regulatory agency. Shuster's fights against labor protections for railway workers, his criticisms of environmental and other federal regulatory mandates, and his solidly conservative voting record lend him cover as he sometimes bucks the GOP leadership with moves meant to ensure that the tap of federal transportation dollars never runs dry. "There's no such thing as a Republican or a Democratic bridge," said Shuster in early 1993, "or a Republican or a Democratic airport."

Preparatory to rewriting the surface transportation law in the 105th, Shuster expanded the ranks of his committee to 73 members — up from 64 during the 104th — making it the largest congressional committee ever assembled. That helps explain why Shuster came so close to passing his May 1997 budget amendment, despite the leadership's opposition: If Shuster can keep his committee in line, he is a third of the way to a majority on the House floor even before he approaches anyone "outside the family."

Shuster, a tenacious campaigner for his projects, saw a decade's worth of work yield a House floor victory in the 104th, as members voted 284-143 to take the nation's transportation trust funds "off budget." The four trust funds — covering programs for highways and mass transit, aviation, harbors and inland waterways — are financed by user fees. Shuster contends that taking the trust fund money off budget would make it more likely to be spent for its intended purpose, rather than hoarded to mask the size of the deficit. "Deficit hawks" such as Budget Committee Chairman John R. Kasich, R-Ohio, opposed Shuster's proposal, but the Pennsylvanian took a dim view of negotiating with his ilk. "You don't persuade Kasich," Shuster said. "You beat Kasich."

For Shuster, the trust fund issue is another bargaining chip in his single-minded efforts to secure more funds for pavement projects. When he took over the Transportation Committee in 1995, Shuster drafted a daily plan for the coming twelve months and managed for the most part to stick to it. This disciplined approach owes something to Shuster's three years as an infantry lieutenant in peacetime Army service in the mid-1950s, and he also notes that when he worked as a computer executive, he learned to think of time in terms of "microseconds and nanoseconds."

Shuster is masterful at moving bills through his committee and the House floor, but he has

PENNSYLVANIA 9
South Central — Altoona

This south-central Pennsylvania region long has been a passageway from the East to Pittsburgh and beyond. Transportation has historically been its primary focus, in particular the railroad industry.

The district's largest city, Altoona (Blair County), once prospered as a rail center despite its relatively inaccessible location in the Allegheny Mountains. Johnstown is only 40 miles to the west, but between the cities loomed the Alleghenies.

Crossing the southern Alleghenies was difficult in the mid-19th century. But the old Pennsylvania Railroad overcame the harsh landscape by devising engineering marvels such as Horseshoe Curve, just west of Altoona.

The Pennsylvania Railroad also nurtured the city of Altoona, but as the rail industry declined, population withered. When the railroad workers left, they took their Democratic loyalties with them. In 1996, Bob Dole carried Blair County with 53 percent of the votes.

Today, the remnants of the railroad industry serve as a tourism draw. Besides Horseshoe Curve, railroad buffs can visit the Railroaders Memorial Museum in Altoona or the Allegheny Portage Railroad National Historic Site. The Allegheny Portage was part of an early attempt to link Philadelphia with Pittsburgh and the West.

The Pennsylvania Turnpike, the nation's first superhighway, crosses the southern section of the 9th District's tortured topography. Its epitome is Breezewood, known as the "Town of Motels." Though Bedford County features 14 historic covered bridges, travelers recognize it better for the garish display of neon signs adorning the hotels and fast-food restaurants of the turnpike's Interchange 12, at Breezewood.

Before the turnpike's opening in 1940, Bedford County was a destination point, rather than a stopover. The pure and soothing waters of Bedford Springs attracted not only the afflicted, but the elite. President James Buchanan made the resort his summer White House.

The 9th consists mostly of small villages scattered among the mountains. It has little industry; its farmers raise cattle for beef and milk. The isolation and agricultural character of the region breeds a strong sense of conservatism. The 11 counties contained wholly or in part in the district all backed Dole in 1996. Snyder County, the 9th's easternmost, on the Susquehanna River, voted for him by a ratio of nearly 2-to-1.

Much of Franklin County lies in a broad valley dotted with prosperous farms and well-tended towns such as Mercersburg, Buchanan's boyhood home. Dole got 57 percent there.

Clearfield County's industrial tradition sometimes gives Democrats an edge, but its voting habits are as anomalous to the district as its location in the extreme northwest. The district includes all of Clearfield, save for one township that is in the 5th.

The 5th and the 9th districts also share Centre County, home to the Pennsylvania State University in State College. Although State College is not in the 9th, outlying towns such as Port Matilda and Philipsburg are included.

1990 Population: 565,803. White 556,077 (98%), Black 6,654 (1%), Other 3,072 (1%). Hispanic origin 2,470 (<1%). 18 and over 425,600 (75%), 62 and over 104,203 (18%). Median age: 35.

gotten hung up at times in dealings with the Senate and the Clinton administration. Clinton signed the $6.5 billion National Highway System bill with reluctance because of its provisions to lift the federal speed limit and motorcycle helmet requirements. Both chambers had favored lifting the speed and helmet mandates, and that view prevailed in conference despite Shuster's objections. "I opposed it but got rolled," he complained.

Some of Shuster's handicraft never made it to the Senate floor, much less to conference, including the trust fund maneuver. His initiatives to deregulate ocean shipping and ease federal clean water regulations were never even taken up by a Senate committee. Shuster refused to iron out controversies by compromising with opponents, and he saw his water bill derided as a "polluter's bill of rights" and "the Dirty Water Act."

Shuster worked with House Appropriations Transportation Subcommittee Chairman Frank R. Wolf, R-Va., to include language on the fiscal 1996 spending bill to block Amtrak funding unless a stalled Shuster plan to revamp the railroad was enacted. That plan, too, passed the House but was later blocked. Shuster says he wants to save Amtrak but opposes Clinton administration plans to include it in the massive surface transportation bill, where it would fight for the same pot of money as highways and mass transit systems.

In addition to the Shuster Highway, he has pushed projects including a $90 million upgrade for Route 220 from Altoona to Tyrone; a Franklin County exit off Interstate 81; a $5.5 million Route 36 bypass around the town of Loysburg; and $3.2 million for a bus-testing facility in Altoona. Sometimes his projects have generated flak. A column by humorist Dave Barry in early 1992 lampooned an automated pedestrian sidewalk that Shuster sought for Altoona.

That May, the Altoona Mirror ran a story intimating that Shuster inserted money in the 1991 transportation bill for an experimental monorail project that was likely to be developed by a company employing Shuster's daughter and a former aide. Shuster denied any ethics wrongdoing.

But Shuster's ethical woes multiplied after he assumed the chairmanship. Publicity surrounding a Justice Department review of potential illegal gratuities Shuster received from Ann Eppard, a transportation lobbyist and his former chief aide, earned him poor press during the 1996 Pennsylvania primary season, and that did not help his son Bob Shuster's bid for the 5th District GOP nod. Shuster's re-election campaign paid Eppard $3,000 a month in consulting fees while raising tens of thousands of dollars from officials from Eppard clients; complainants contended those clients received favorable treatment from the Transportation Committee.

And as the 105th got under way, Shuster found himself under investigation by a federal grand jury for allegedly using his position to help two Boston businessmen whose properties were threatened by a federally funded highway project in that city. The two had contributed thousands to Shuster's congressional campaign committee.

Shuster's interests are not confined to public works. Indeed, during the 102nd Congress he had something of a profile in the media as the ranking -Republican on the Intelligence Committee. Shuster's consecutive three-term tenure on Intelligence ended with the 102nd, but he again secured a seat on the panel in the 104th.

Shuster's one big thrust at a top leadership position, minority whip, was thwarted by Trent Lott of Mississippi in 1981. Starting as a distinct underdog, Shuster campaigned with his typical intensity and closed the gap. But Lott held on to win by a 96-90 vote of the House GOP Conference.

At Home: Although Shuster has some detractors in local political circles, even in the GOP organization of the 9th's most populous county, Blair (Altoona), he remains untouchable at the polls. In 1996, he won overwhelmingly against Democratic journalist Monte Kemmler, his first opponent since 1984.

In 1984, Shuster drew an interesting Democratic challenger in 62-year-old Nancy Kulp, who played Miss Jane Hathaway on "The Beverly Hillbillies" television comedy in the 1960s. Retired from show business and living on a Pennsylvania farm, Kulp accused Shuster of voting down the line with Reagan and ignoring the needs of farmers, veterans and elderly constituents.

Shuster counterattacked vigorously. Among his salvos was a radio commercial featuring the leading actor from the series, Buddy Ebsen. In the ad Ebsen said he had "dropped her a note to say, 'Hey, Nancy, I love you dearly, but you're too liberal for me — I've got to go with Bud Shuster.'" Voters agreed; Shuster won re-election with two-thirds of the vote.

Before entering politics, Shuster had a successful business career with the Radio Corporation of America and as an independent electronics entrepreneur. When GOP Rep. J. Irving Whalley announced his retirement in 1972, Shuster embarked on a self-generated campaign and won the Republican primary over a state senator with significant party backing. He took 62 percent in November, the first of many easy wins.

HOUSE ELECTIONS

1996 General		
Bud Shuster (R)	142,105	(74%)
Monte Kemmler (D)	50,650	(26%)
1994 General		
Bud Shuster (R)	146,688	(100%)

Previous Winning Percentages: **1992** (100%) **1990** (100%) **1988** (100%) **1986** (100%) **1984** (67%) **1982** (65%) **1980** (100%) **1978** (75%) **1976** (100%) **1974** (57%) **1972** (62%)

CAMPAIGN FINANCE

	Receipts	Receipts from PACs	Expend-itures
1996			
Shuster (R)	$1,219,644	$537,067 (44%)	$1,213,304
Kemmler (D)	$112,925	$9,850 (9%)	$113,294
1994			
Shuster (R)	$674,610	$334,485 (50%)	$776,175

DISTRICT VOTE FOR PRESIDENT

1996		1992	
D	70,189 (36%)	**D**	66,929 (33%)
R	102,831 (53%)	**R**	97,772 (48%)
I	21,237 (11%)	**I**	40,204 (20%)

KEY VOTES

1997	
Ban "partial birth" abortions	Y
1996	
Approve farm bill	Y
Deny public education to illegal immigrants	Y
Repeal ban on certain assault-style weapons	Y
Increase minimum wage	N
Freeze defense spending	N
Approve welfare overhaul	Y
1995	
Approve balanced-budget constitutional amendment	Y
Relax Clean Water Act regulations	Y
Oppose limits on environmental regulations	N
Reduce projected Medicare spending	Y
Approve GOP budget with tax and spending cuts	Y

VOTING STUDIES

	Presidential Support		Party Unity		Conservative Coalition	
Year	S	O	S	O	S	O
1996	34	63	92	7	92	8
1995	14	83	93	4	90	7
1994	45	54	92	7	92	6
1993	22	75	90	6	82	11
1992	74	26	86	10	92	8
1991	68	28	75	20	92	3

INTEREST GROUP RATINGS

Year	ADA	AFL-CIO	CCUS	ACU
1996	0	n/a	100	100
1995	0	0	96	87
1994	0	0	92	100
1993	10	8	70	96
1992	5	17	88	100
1991	15	42	90	95

10 Joseph M. McDade (R)

Of Scranton — Elected 1962, 18th term

Biographical Information
Born: Sept. 29, 1931, Scranton, Pa.
Education: U. of Notre Dame, B.A. 1953; U. of Pennsylvania, LL.B. 1956.
Occupation: Lawyer.
Family: Wife, Sarah Scripture; five children.
Religion: Roman Catholic.
Political Career: No previous office.
Capitol Office: 2107 Rayburn Bldg. 20515; 225-3731.

Committees
Appropriations
Energy & Water Development (chairman); Interior; National Security

In Washington: McDade, acquitted of the charges that cost him the Appropriations Committee chairmanship in the 104th Congress, did not get his wish to take over the chair for the 105th. Instead, the GOP leadership gave him the consolation prize of chairing the Energy and Water Development Subcommittee, and a couple of honorific titles — vice chairman of the full Appropriations Committee, and vice chairman of its National Security Subcommittee.

In addition to coming to terms with the fact that the Appropriations chair will likely never be his, McDade is also coping with Parkinson's disease, a progressive nerve disorder. Diagnosed with the malady early in 1996, he was hospitalized twice during his seven-week trial.

As the House GOP was preparing to organize for the 105th, McDade, the longest-serving Republican in the chamber, was planning to challenge Robert L. Livingston, R-La., who was Appropriations chairman in the 104th. But many younger Republicans did not see McDade as the kind of member who should be given a plum role. McDade was unknown to most of the Class of 1994 (he showed up for only 51 percent of floor votes in 1996), whereas they had gotten used to dealing with Livingston. Also, McDade was viewed as one of the veteran "old bulls" of the committee system, whom the newcomers viewed as more resistant to change than younger chairmen like Livingston. Republican Conference Chairman John A. Boehner of Ohio noted that Livingston "would have a significant amount of support" in his bid to stay on as chairman.

When it became apparent that his efforts would fail, McDade dropped his challenge and instead accepted the vice chairmanship. McDade said he wanted to chair the National Security Subcommittee, but Livingston did not want to bump C.W. Bill Young of Florida. Instead, McDade was told he could take any of three vacant subcommittee chairmanships. He picked Energy and Water Development, which was led in the 104th by John T. Myers of Indiana, who retired. McDade also got the vice chair title on the National Security Subcommittee.

In the 104th, Livingston had promised to give up the Appropriations chairmanship if McDade was acquitted of the bribery and racketeering charges against him. After the verdict came down in McDade's favor, Livingston submitted a letter of resignation to Speaker Newt Gingrich, R-Ga., in August 1996. But Gingrich, while praising McDade, announced that "on the recommendation of Joe McDade, I have rejected the resignation and asked Bob to remain as chairman through the remainder of the 104th Congress."

After an eight-year legal battle, McDade had been acquitted Aug. 1, 1996, of charges that he accepted gifts from defense contractors in return for helping them get federal contracts. A jury found that McDade, when he was ranking Republican on the House Defense Appropriations Subcommittee, was not guilty of peddling influence in exchange for $100,000 in illegal gifts, favors and bribes. In the trial, federal prosecutors in Philadelphia attempted to prove that McDade extorted those items from five defense firms and a lobbyist seeking government contracts between 1983 and 1988. In return, they charged, McDade helped the businesses get $68 million in federal contracts.

The case turned on the relationship between McDade and United Chem-Con Corp., which moved to a town in his district with an 85 percent unemployment rate. The electronics company opened a metal manufacturing company in the 10th just as the Navy was preparing to award a contract to build 40-foot steel cargo containers. The now-defunct firm won that contract. Prosecutors alleged that McDade accepted gifts and money in exchange for helping companies like United Chem-Con get fat government contracts. Prosecutors claimed that McDade was given free trips to places like Montego Bay, Jamaica, and Seattle for an NCAA Final Four basketball game; a series of free airplane rides from United Chem-Con and other companies currying favor for contracts; and $10,250 in "sham contri-

PENNSYLVANIA 10
Northeast — Scranton

The city of Scranton dominated the politics of northeastern Pennsylvania in the early part of this century. But as the coal-and-railroad town declined in population, the political influence of Scranton and Lackawanna County has slipped.

The rest of the region no longer takes its cue from Scranton, the most populous city in the 10th. While Lackawanna retains its traditional Democratic loyalties, Republicans have solidified their position in the outlying counties. Lackawanna was the lone county in the 10th to support Bill Clinton for president in 1992 and 1996. In the latter race, Clinton emerged from Lackawanna with a 19,447-vote plurality, enough to enable him to capture the 10th even though he lost the other eight counties that make up the district.

The county's Democratic majority casts its vote in Scranton and in some of the outlying blue-collar towns such as Moosic, home of a Class AAA minor league baseball team. Republicans can be found in more affluent suburbs such as Clarks Summit and Dalton.

At one time, Scranton was known as the "Anthracite Capital of the World." The city entered the Industrial Age by manufacturing iron. From an outpost of 650 people in 1840, Scranton grew to 260,000 in 1950. But the coal industry was already beginning to peter out in the 1940s, and the city's fortunes have declined through most of the postwar era.

Scranton has attempted to diversify its economic base, but the turnaround has been slow. There are some signs of improvement, though: The city has begun to appear on some lists of the "most livable places," thanks mostly to its affordable housing and relatively low crime rate. Business publications tout the city as a good place to relocate or start a new business.

Local civic boosters say the city's economic vitality has been restored by the Steamtown National Historic Site, a railroad park and retail complex. The controversial historic site and its adjacent $100 million mall have been pilloried as an example of federal pork barrel politics run amok. But what outsiders see as pork looks like a potential godsend to Scrantonians.

The population growth that the 10th saw during the 1980s came to the east of Lackawanna County. There, on the New Jersey border, Pike County has experienced spectacular growth as business executives who commute to New York have moved to the area. Pike's population boomed by 55 percent in the 1970s and 53 percent in the 1980s. Pocono Mountain resorts and ski areas boost Monroe County's economy. Only part of Monroe County is in the 10th, but it is an especially scenic portion that includes the Delaware Water Gap National Recreation Area.

North and west of Scranton are reliably Republican and agricultural Bradford and Susquehanna counties. Democrats can be found on the far western edge of the district in Williamsport, the 10th's second-largest city and home to the annual Little League World Series.

1990 Population: 565,681. White 554,920 (98%), Black 6,215 (1%), Other 4,546 (1%). Hispanic origin 4,337 (1%). 18 and over 428,771 (76%), 62 and over 113,630 (20%). Median age: 36.

butions" from United Chem-Con employees who were then illegally reimbursed for the donations. The prosecution called his intent criminal, charging him with violating the 1970 Racketeer Influenced and Corrupt Organizations (RICO) act — a law originally aimed at drug kingpins and members of the Mafia.

The defense argued that McDade was not doing anything different from anyone else on the Hill. "The government wants us to believe that when you become a congressman, you become a monk," said Sal Cognetti Jr., the Scranton lawyer who headed McDade's defense. "He was on trial for being a congressman."

McDade acknowledged that he should have reimbursed companies for the free airplane rides he was given, but he said it was an honest mistake. Gifts such as a green golf jacket should have been reported, but he said his office didn't realize the jacket was priced in excess of $100, the legal reporting limit. And the so-called sham contributions were donations at a fundraiser, he said.

Some House Republicans said McDade was the victim of overzealous Justice Department prosecutors. Jerry Lewis, R-Calif., chairman of the Veteran Affairs, Housing and Urban Development Appropriations Subcommittee, said, "Joe McDade is a national asset who has almost been destroyed by this process."

But after the trial, McDade raised eyebrows during the August Republican National Convention when defense contractors, including Tenneco and General Dynamics, and other businesses threw a party for him.

Before the 104th, McDade served for 10 years as ranking Republican on the Defense Subcommittee, where he was instrumental in channeling the immense sums within that jurisdiction. He enjoyed special inside leverage thanks to his friendly pairing with that subcommittee's Democratic chairman, fellow Pennsylvanian John P. Murtha.

They worked together to bring Pennsylvania a

$963 million modernization contract for an aircraft carrier in 1990. The fiscal 1992 defense bill included $60 million for 80 armored ammunition carriers built in York, as well as a provision continuing the longstanding congressional campaign to ensure the purchase of U.S.-mined coal to heat U.S. bases in Europe. McDade points to his ability to secure appropriations for the Tobyhanna Army Depot, the largest employer in the region.

His most visible — and controversial — achievement in recent years has been the securing of more than $80 million over the years for the Steamtown National Historic Site, a 40-acre park and steam railroad museum in the 10th. The project has been derided as a prime example of pork-barrel spending and criticized for its high cost and dubious historical value.

In the 103rd, members began to show their irritation with the project. The House passed a bill to authorize the Steamtown site — a typically necessary step never taken in this case. But in so doing the bill would have imposed strict limits on the use of money appropriated for it. The Senate never acted on it.

At Home: With the indictment still hanging over him in early 1996, McDade faced his first GOP primary challenger since 1982, a self-described "country lawyer" with the attention-grabbing name of Errol Flynn. On paper, Flynn's candidacy did not look formidable. He was a little-known, first-time candidate with a skimpy campaign fund. Flynn reported raising barely $30,000 before the primary. But he campaigned energetically, particularly in the more rural areas of the district outside McDade's base of Lackawanna County (Scranton).

The challenger basically argued that he was all that McDade was not. Flynn touted his experience as a small-town community activist and a small-business man. "It's time for us to join the Republican Revolution of 1994 and fight for a leaner, more efficient government," Flynn argued. "The era of pork-barrel spending has ended."

Many district Republicans seemed to agree, but not enough to dislodge McDade. The incumbent swept Lackawanna County by a ratio of more than 2-to-1, and that compensated for the fact that he was outpolled in much of the rest of the district, which encompasses all or portions of nine counties. McDade won renomination for an 18th term with 53 percent of the vote.

In the fall, after being acquitted, McDade faced environmental lawyer Joe Cullen. The Democrat was buoyed by McDade's anemic primary showing, and, like Flynn, he harped on the incumbent's long tenure and his reputation as a pork-barrel politician. McDade registered his poorest November showing in 30 years, but he still polled 60 percent of the vote.

A lawyer and former municipal solicitor in his home city, McDade first came to the House in 1963, succeeding Republican William W. Scranton, after whose ancestors the city of Scranton is named. Handpicked by Scranton for the 1962 House nomination, McDade won an unspectacular election victory, and he narrowly held on in the big Democratic year of 1964. By 1966, however, he had enlisted the support of organized labor and started a long skein of easy victories.

HOUSE ELECTIONS

1996 General		
Joseph M. McDade (R)	124,670	(60%)
Joe Cullen (D)	75,536	(36%)
Thomas J. McLaughlin (REF)	8,311	(4%)
1996 Primary		
Joseph M. McDade (R)	17,155	(53%)
Errol Flynn (R)	15,043	(47%)
1994 General		
Joseph M. McDade (R)	106,992	(66%)
Daniel J. Schreffler (D)	50,635	(31%)
Albert A. Smith (LIBERT)	5,196	(3%)

Previous Winning Percentages: **1992** (90%) **1990** (100%) **1988** (73%) **1986** (75%) **1984** (77%) **1982** (68%) **1980** (77%) **1978** (77%) **1976** (63%) **1974** (65%) **1972** (74%) **1970** (65%) **1968** (67%) **1966** (67%) **1964** (51%) **1962** (52%)

CAMPAIGN FINANCE

	Receipts	Receipts from PACs	Expend-itures
1996			
McDade (R)	$564,409	$273,015 (48%)	$724,776
Cullen (D)	$206,370	$37,000 (18%)	$204,185
McLaughlin (REF)	$6,628	0	$6,315
1994			
McDade (R)	$311,731	$223,113 (72%)	$415,387
Schreffler (D)	$16,145	0	$12,395

DISTRICT VOTE FOR PRESIDENT

	1996		1992
D	95,696 (45%)	**D**	88,150 (38%)
R	91,613 (43%)	**R**	95,820 (42%)
I	24,300 (11%)	**I**	46,878 (20%)

KEY VOTES

1997	
Ban "partial birth" abortions	Y
1996	
Approve farm bill	Y
Deny public education to illegal immigrants	Y
Repeal ban on certain assault-style weapons	N
Increase minimum wage	Y
Freeze defense spending	?
Approve welfare overhaul	?
1995	
Approve balanced-budget constitutional amendment	Y
Relax Clean Water Act regulations	Y
Oppose limits on environmental regulations	N
Reduce projected Medicare spending	Y
Approve GOP budget with tax and spending cuts	Y

VOTING STUDIES

	Presidential Support		Party Unity		Conservative Coalition	
Year	S	O	S	O	S	O
1996	24	33	45	7	41	2
1995	21	72	83	8	90	2
1994	62	28	61	23	86	6
1993	46	28	59	18	68	11
1992	57	22	51	27	65	13
1991	68	25	56	36	70	19

INTEREST GROUP RATINGS

Year	ADA	AFL-CIO	CCUS	ACU
1996	5	n/a	67	75
1995	5	25	91	65
1994	20	38	89	83
1993	20	56	82	74
1992	15	75	86	76
1991	30	56	44	65

11 Paul E. Kanjorski (D)

Of Nanticoke — Elected 1984, 7th term

Biographical Information
Born: April 2, 1937, Nanticoke, Pa.
Education: Temple U., 1957-62; Dickinson School of Law, 1962-65.
Military Service: Army, 1960-61.
Occupation: Lawyer.
Family: Wife, Nancy Hickerson; one child.
Religion: Roman Catholic.
Political Career: Sought Democratic nomination for U.S. House special election, 1980; sought Democratic nomination for U.S. House, 1980.

Capitol Office: 2353 Rayburn Bldg. 20515; 225-6511.

Committees
Banking & Financial Services
Capital Markets, Securities & Government Sponsored Enterprises (ranking); Domestic & International Monetary Policy
Government Reform & Oversight
Government Management, Information & Technology; National Economic Growth, Natural Resources & Regulatory Affairs

In Washington: A generation ago, the Democratic Party in Pennsylvania was dominated by the sort of people Kanjorski represents — white, ethnic, working-class, culturally conservative people, many of them Catholics. But as blue-collar employment waned and minorities and activist liberals became more influential, old-style Democrats such as Kanjorski often found themselves at odds with national party doctrine.

Then came the 1994 election, bringing to power ideologically conservative Republicans who wanted to eliminate entire government departments, roll back federal regulations and trim social programs. Living under Republican rule helped remind many conservative Democrats why they were Democrats in the first place. Some of them felt more comfortable in the 104th defending their party on the House floor and fighting GOP proposals they said went too far.

Kanjorski made a particular point of defending President Clinton against a series of ethics charges. The Banking and Government Reform and Oversight committees, where Kanjorski sits, both became the battlegrounds over Whitewater and other scandals involving the White House. Kanjorski called the prolonged investigations into the Whitewater real estate deal a circus, and borrowed from Winston Churchill to say, "Never before in the history of our nation has so much been spent by so many to produce so little."

Government Reform grew increasingly partisan during its investigation into the president's financial dealings, the White House travel office firings and the White House's gathering of FBI files on top Republicans. When Chairman William F. Clinger took to the House floor to discuss the FBI files case and accused the White House Counsel of lying about Hillary Rodham Clinton's role, Kanjorski defended the first lady and blasted fellow Pennsylvanian Clinger.

"You didn't have the nerve to go up in the press gallery and make those charges because you would be subject to lawsuit," he charged. (After some of his comments were stricken from the official record, Kanjorski apologized for contributing to a breakdown in the House's comity.)

Kanjorski, though, was no automatic apologist for the administration. When a White House aide testifying in the travel office case invoked a right to ask that cameras be barred from the hearing, Kanjorski called the decision "the dumbest thing I have heard in a long time.... You have created an aura now that there's something here that should be looked into."

Kanjorski was a foot soldier in the Democratic effort to block enactment of the GOP's "Contract With America" platform, or, failing that, at least to portray the Republican agenda in an unfavorable light. He won approval in committee of an amendment to exempt Social Security from the GOP's legislation to bar "unfunded mandates" imposed on the states. Later, he tried unsuccessfully to win exemption for federal mandates that established data bases to track sex offenders.

Kanjorski tried to amend the GOP version of a line-item veto proposal to allow the president to eliminate "corporate welfare" tax breaks as well as spending items. He also had a role in taking on Speaker Newt Gingrich; his proposal to ban members' acceptance of book royalties was a swipe at Gingrich, who got embroiled in a controversy regarding royalties for a book he wrote.

Kanjorski often takes his voting cues from a powerful political patron, fellow Pennsylvanian and Appropriations power-broker John P. Murtha. In August 1994, when the Clinton administration was scrambling to line up votes to pass a rule allowing consideration of its huge crime bill package, the Pennsylvania troika of Murtha, Kanjorski and Democratic Rep. Austin J. Murphy, all backed the president — even though all three opposed the crime bill. At one point in the 104th when Democrats were worried that the 1996 election would further erode their strength in the House, Murtha organized a seminar for at-risk Democrats and brought in Kanjorski as a guest lecturer because his winning percentages often approached 70 percent.

Kanjorski has differences with Democratic

PENNSYLVANIA 11
Northeast — Wilkes-Barre

Voters in the 11th know how to pick a winner when it comes to presidential politics. "Reagan Democrats" here helped send Ronald Reagan to the White House in 1980 and 1984, and opted for George Bush in 1988. The district gave Bill Clinton a 42 percent plurality in 1992 (in line with his national percentage), and gave him 48 percent in 1996 (slightly below his 49 percent national percentage).

In the House race, Kanjorski has repeatedly won re-election with at least two-thirds of the votes cast.

This region long had been Democratic territory, primarily because of Luzerne County's Democratic influence. In the 11th's largest city, Wilkes-Barre, and in other Wyoming Valley towns, the Democratic tradition dates back to the days when the anthracite coal mining industry dominated the local economy.

But as the costs of mining anthracite coal rose and the use of oil and natural gas for heating homes increased, the local industry began a steep decline. So did the region's population, and along with it, Democratic hegemony.

Luzerne County, with its rich ethnic stew of East Europeans, Italians, Irish and Welsh, still casts more than half the district's vote. Much of the county vote comes from Wilkes-Barre's outlying towns such as Pittston and Kingston, but Hazleton, in southern Luzerne County, also is of some size.

Politics takes a back seat to football in neighboring Columbia County. Berwick is a hard-core gridiron town, where residents shoehorn into Crispin Field to forget about the demise of the coal industry and to watch the Berwick Bulldogs, annually one of the nation's finest high school teams.

Another vestige of the coal industry in Columbia County is the decades-old mine fire that still burns beneath the borough of Centralia. The threat of cave-ins and explosions scared most residents away over the years, and the rest were bought out by the federal government.

Jim Thorpe, a Carbon County coal region town on the eastern side of the 11th, has fared much better. Once a haven for the wealthy — locals boast that 13 of America's 70 millionaires lived here in the late 19th century — this picturesque Lehigh River town fell on hard times when the demand for anthracite coal waned in the 1930s and 1940s. In hopes of reviving the town, officials in 1954 changed the town's name from Mauch Chunk to that of the famed Olympic athlete Jim Thorpe, who died in 1953 and is buried here. Today, tourism is thriving since the town became a demonstration preservation project for the Interior Department.

Elsewhere in the county, in Panther Valley coal towns such as Lansford and Nesquehoning, the economic outlook is not as promising.

Northeast of Carbon County, the Monroe County portion of the district includes some of the southern Pocono Mountain resort areas.

1990 Population: 565,913. White 556,762 (98%), Black 5,283 (1%), Other 3,868 (1%). Hispanic origin 4,119 (1%). 18 and over 441,306 (78%), 62 and over 126,417 (22%). Median age: 37.

leadership, especially on social policy issues such as abortion. In the 104th, he voted to ban an abortion technique that its opponents call "partial birth" abortion, and he voted not to allow federal employee health plans to cover abortion. In the 103rd, he voted to ban federal funding for abortion in most circumstances and to require parental notification of minors' abortions. Kanjorski has voted against lifting the ban on homosexuals in the military and against federal recognition of same-gender marriages. Like most centrist Democrats, Kanjorski voted for the welfare reform bill that Clinton signed in 1996.

Kanjorski is an unstinting supporter of organized labor. In the 104th, he voted to raise the minimum wage, and in the 103rd, he opposed passage of NAFTA, casting doubt on the administration view that the impact of domestic job losses could be offset with worker retraining. "The question is, where are the jobs we are going to retrain these people for? It is fun to retrain people, but to retrain them and not have a job for them is not a very successful thing for the government to do."

In the 103rd, when Democrats ran the House, Kanjorski's seniority on the Banking Committee earned him the chair of its Subcommittee on Economic Growth. He proposed legislation, which did not get very far, to encourage banks to lend money to small businesses by making it easier for the banks to sell those loans at a profit to Wall Street firms or to a new quasi-government entity.

Kanjorski also sought to help small banks by working to roll back rules intended to prevent banks from "redlining" poor and minority neighborhoods where they do not want to lend. In 1991 he worked to curtail the scope of the 1977 Community Reinvestment Act, but the law's supporters succeeded in blocking any changes.

The savings and loan bailout also drew Kanjorski's attention. He complained that taxpayers throughout the country, including those in Pennsylvania, had to pay to bail out reckless lenders from the Sun Belt. "My taxpayers are not happy," he once said, "that well into the next century they will be paying for fraud, abuse, excessive powers and improper regulation by thrifts and their state regulators in California and Texas. . . . We paid once when California and Texas S&Ls paid high rates to siphon-off investment capital away from our region. . . . While our infrastructure deteriorated, theirs was improved with federallv insured deposits."

In the 104th, Kanjorski became ranking Democrat on the Capital Markets, Securities and Government Sponsored Enterprises Subcommittee of the renamed Banking and Financial Services Committee.

At the start of the 102nd, Kanjorski sought a higher-profile platform for espousing his ideas — a seat on the Budget Committee. But he fell short by one vote. His appearance on an ABC-TV news show in 1990, where he was quoted as a congressional scold of junketing Ways and Means Committee members, came only a few months before the Budget Committee selections.

At Home: Kanjorski owed his first House victory to an intestinal parasite and a sunny beach. Those are peculiar agents of change, but politics in the 11th can be peculiar. In one five-year span (1980-85), five different people represented it.

The outcome of Kanjorski's 1984 primary challenge to incumbent Democrat Frank Harrison might have been different if not for the discovery that water supplies in parts of the 11th were contaminated with the giardiasis parasite. As people boiled their water to make it drinkable, Harrison flew off on congressional excursion to Central America.

Kanjorski pounced on Harrison with a largely self-financed blitz of clever ads portraying him as an aloof globe-trotter. One ad showed a picture of a sunny Costa Rican beach and noted Harrison's visit there, then switched to a shot of a teakettle on a stove and concluded, "It's enough to make you boil." Harrison tried to ignore Kanjorski and stressed his experience in Washington, but Kanjorski leaped from long shot to victor.

In November, Kanjorski was rated the favorite over Republican Robert P. Hudock. But Hudock enlivened things by accusing Kanjorski of charging excessive fees for his private legal work in behalf of local communities seeking federal grants. Hudock also accused Kanjorski of taking payment from citizens and businesses seeking relief money from Washington after Hurricane Agnes hit the area in 1972.

Kanjorski responded that his firm charged competitive fees, and he said he had helped bring more than $50 million in federal aid to the 11th. He noted that he had often provided free legal services, including working without pay as Nanticoke's assistant city solicitor for 14 years.

An opponent of abortion and gun control and an advocate of prayer in schools, Kanjorski was viewed by most voters as sharing their values, not those of the national Democratic Party. So even though Ronald Reagan carried the district for president, Kanjorski won with 59 percent.

In 1986, Kanjorski was not as much the focus as was his GOP challenger, Marc L. Holtzman. In a district that is aging, heavily Catholic and struggling economically, Holtzman was 26 years old, Jewish and wealthy. He stressed that his contacts with conservative leaders would allow him to recruit industry into the district. In the end, Holtzman spent more than $1.3 million, but he drew only 29 percent of the vote. Kanjorski has not been seriously challenged since then.

HOUSE ELECTIONS

1996 General		
Paul E. Kanjorski (D)	128,258	(68%)
Stephen A. Urban (R)	60,339	(32%)
1994 General		
Paul E. Kanjorski (D)	101,966	(67%)
J. Andrew Podolak (R)	51,295	(33%)

Previous Winning Percentages: 1992 (67%) **1990** (100%) **1988** (100%) **1986** (71%) **1984** (59%)

KEY VOTES

1997	
Ban "partial birth" abortions	Y
1996	
Approve farm bill	N
Deny public education to illegal immigrants	Y
Repeal ban on certain assault-style weapons	Y
Increase minimum wage	Y
Freeze defense spending	Y
Approve welfare overhaul	Y
1995	
Approve balanced-budget constitutional amendment	N
Relax Clean Water Act regulations	N
Oppose limits on environmental regulations	Y
Reduce projected Medicare spending	N
Approve GOP budget with tax and spending cuts	N

DISTRICT VOTE FOR PRESIDENT

	1996		1992
D	97,377 (48%)	**D**	91,671 (42%)
R	76,952 (38%)	**R**	84,203 (39%)
I	25,595 (13%)	**I**	42,960 (20%)

CAMPAIGN FINANCE

	Receipts	Receipts from PACs	Expend-itures
1996			
Kanjorski (D)	$351,236	$199,985 (57%)	$342,141
Urban (R)	$45,261	0	$43,761
1994			
Kanjorski (D)	$322,370	$218,945 (68%)	$304,520
Podolak (R)	$55,721	$765 (1%)	$57,006

VOTING STUDIES

	Presidential Support		Party Unity		Conservative Coalition	
Year	**S**	**O**	**S**	**O**	**S**	**O**
1996	68	32	78	22	55	45
1995	76	24	83	16	37	61
1994	82	18	87	12	47	53
1993	73	27	89	11	48	52
1992	31	69	85	15	46	54
1991	37	63	85	14	59	41

INTEREST GROUP RATINGS

Year	ADA	AFL-CIO	CCUS	ACU
1996	65	n/a	25	30
1995	80	100	29	16
1994	55	89	42	29
1993	70	100	18	21
1992	80	83	25	16
1991	50	92	10	25

12 John P. Murtha (D)

Of Johnstown — Elected 1974; 12th full term

Biographical Information

Born: June 17, 1932, New Martinsville, W.Va.
Education: U. of Pittsburgh, B.A. 1962.
Military Service: Marine Corps, 1952-55, 1966-67; Marine Corps Reserve, 1967-90.
Occupation: Car wash owner and operator.
Family: Wife, Joyce Bell; three children.
Religion: Roman Catholic.
Political Career: Democratic nominee for U.S. House, 1968; Pa. House, 1969-74.
Capitol Office: 2423 Rayburn Bldg. 20515; 225-2065.

Committees

Appropriations
Interior; National Security (ranking)

In Washington: As the ranking Democrat on Appropriations' National Security Subcommittee, Murtha straddles a line. A pro-defense hawk, he finds a lot to like in the GOP's drive to boost the Pentagon's budget above what the Clinton administration feels is necessary. But as a partisan Democrat, Murtha also feels some pull to defend the White House against Republican attack.

Since Republicans took control of Congress, where Murtha has often ended up is trying to broker agreement between President Clinton and Congress. Such was the case when House and Senate negotiators were wrapping up work on the fiscal 1996 defense spending bill, which spent $7 billion more than Clinton had wanted. "We're driven by the guys who want more money for defense," Murtha said. "We're trying to get it down to where [the president] might sign it."

The measure included several provisions that the president opposed, including $493 million to continue production of the B-2 "stealth" bomber beyond the 20 planes the Pentagon says are sufficient; and $700 million on top of Clinton's $3 billion request to develop and purchase anti-missile defenses.

The next year, the House passed a defense bill that added $11 billion to Clinton's funding request, but pressures grew to reduce the price tag to make room for more money in bills funding domestic programs. Republican appropriators said they were willing to shift about $1 billion from defense to domestic programs. Murtha said his bottom line was a shift of $2 billion. In the end, the defense bill added $9.7 billion to Clinton's request. It became the vehicle in late September 1996 for a catchall appropriations bill that included five other spending bills.

Murtha also threw his weight behind a Clinton defense priority known as the Nunn-Lugar program (after former Democratic Sen. Sam Nunn of Georgia and Republican Sen. Richard G. Lugar of Indiana), which is intended to help former Soviet states dismantle their nuclear, chemical and biological weapons. When the House in May 1996 considered the defense authorization bill, Republicans offered an amendment that would effectively have barred assistance to Russia and Belarus under the Nunn-Lugar program.

Murtha spoke up for Nunn-Lugar, insisting that it eliminates potential military threats to the United States and should not be held hostage to Russian behavior in other areas of policy. "The program has been successful," Murtha declared. "They are demilitarizing nuclear weapons." The GOP amendment was rejected, 202-220.

Also in the 104th, Murtha led opposition in the House to a measure that would have repudiated the Clinton administration's support of a U.N. mandated arms embargo on the former Yugoslav republics. Critics of the embargo wanted to let the Bosnian Muslim government obtain arms to offset the country's well-armed ethnic Serbs. The House overwhelmingly passed the measure, 298-128, in early August 1995, and Clinton vetoed it. "Congress is going in the opposite direction from the president of the United States," Murtha lamented.

But with characteristic bluntness, Murtha also rapped the administration for failing to consult with Congress on foreign affairs. He said that if the White House had met with key members weeks before the House took up the embargo issue — rather than just hours before — the vote might have gone differently. "They should have immediately started working with members on their plan a long time ago," Murtha said. "We should have regular meetings, at least once every six months." (Later, it emerged that the Clinton administration had long known and acquiesced to the fact that the Bosnian Muslims were being supplied arms in defiance of the embargo — but never shared this information with Congress.)

In November 1995, when representatives of the warring Yugoslav parties were meeting in Dayton, Ohio, to craft a peace agreement, Murtha spoke strongly against a GOP-led effort to bar the use of funds for a U.S. troop deployment to Bosnia without prior congressional approval.

PENNSYLVANIA 12
Southwest —Johnstown

Pennsylvania's Laurel Highlands are the setting for the 12th, a region once noted for its coal, iron and steel industries but nowadays better known for its chronic hard luck.

Johnstown, the biggest city in the 12th, is famous for the floods that have devastated the town three times in a century. The Great Flood of 1889 was the worst, when an earthen dam outside town collapsed, sending 20 million tons of water surging through the Conemaugh Valley. The town was virtually destroyed and 2,200 people were killed. In 1936, another flood struck, killing 25. The most recent flood, in 1977, took the lives of 85 residents.

The early 1980s recession took a similarly heavy toll on Johnstown's economy, flattening what remained of the city's coal and steel industries and sending unemployment rates over 27 percent, the nation's highest at the time.

Johnstown has attempted to bounce back, partly by capitalizing on its flood history. In 1989, the city stressed the centennial anniversary of the Great Flood; tourists can visit the Johnstown Flood Museum.

Besides the hard times, another constant has been the Democratic tradition of Johnstown and Cambria County. There were defections to Ronald Reagan in 1980, but four years later voters registered their unhappiness with Reagan's unwillingness to impose mandatory steel quotas by backing Walter F. Mondale.

In 1992 and 1996, Bill Clinton won comfortably in Cambria as did Murtha. So did the Democrats' unsuccessful 1994 Senate and gubernatorial candidates.

The eastern portions of Westmoreland and Fayette counties in the 12th are also fonts of Democratic votes. Fayette is a rural, Democratic stronghold where unions are king and Republicans need not apply. Westmoreland is less reliably Democratic. For beer connoisseurs, most notable in the Westmoreland County part of the 12th is Latrobe, home to the Rolling Rock brewery.

In politically competitive Armstrong County, Democrats run best in Kittanning, a commercial center along the Allegheny River.

Rural Somerset is the only county entirely within the 12th where Republicans have an edge. Bob Dole won the county in 1996 by more than 2,000 votes, although county residents also backed Murtha by a ratio of almost 2-to-1.

Clarion County, at the northern extreme of the 12th, votes Republican, but virtually all of the county (except New Bethlehem) belongs to the 5th District.

Indiana County is a mixture of farms and mines, which bills itself as the "Christmas tree capital of the world" for its abundance of blue spruces, and Scotch, Norway and white pines. But St. Nick is not the real hero; it is the hometown boy whose statue stands in front of the county courthouse — actor Jimmy Stewart.

1990 Population: 565,794. White 556,028 (98%), Black 7,302 (1%), Other 2,464 (<1%). Hispanic origin 2,175 (<1%). 18 and over 431,900 (76%), 62 and over 115,464 (20%). Median age: 36.

Clinton previously had pledged to help police a peace agreement with 20,000 U.S. ground troops as part of a NATO force.

Murtha said he believed the president should wait for congressional authorization before sending the troops, but then he added that with peace negotiations going on it was "a delicate time" for the House to vote against deployment, which potentially could disrupt the peace process.

Telling House colleagues about his visits to the war-torn country, former Marine Murtha praised Clinton for getting the parties to negotiate. "The point is they would not have stopped fighting and killing, and, if my colleagues stood there and looked at the blood on the ground, they would have understood how serious it was," he said. "They would not have stopped if it had not been for the intervention of the president of the United States." Still, the House voted 243-171 to bar any deployment prior to congressional approval. The Senate, however, rejected the measure.

Early in the 104th Congress, when Republican appropriators drafted a measure to rescind money from the previous fiscal year (when the Democrats were in charge), Murtha challenged the Republicans to direct the savings from spending cuts toward deficit reduction. He offered an amendment during committee action that called for applying all money saved by cutting spending to deficit reduction, blocking the use of savings to pay for a tax cut. The amendment was rejected, 23-32.

Appropriations Committee Chairman Robert L. Livingston of Louisiana insisted the GOP had no plan to cut discretionary spending in fiscal 1995 to pay for any tax cut. Countered Murtha: "I know what you've been saying all day. I just hope we can put it in writing."

In addition to his belief in the need for a robust defense budget, Murtha also sides with a majority of Republicans on a number of social issues. In the 104th, he cast votes against abortion and for a repeal of the ban on certain types of semiautomatic assault-style weapons.

But when it comes to labor issues, Murtha sticks with his Democratic roots. In the 104th, he backed a successful effort to raise the minimum wage by 90 cents, and he has opposed a GOP proposal that would allow employers to offer comp time in lieu of overtime. Labor unions warn that the measure could lead workers to be coerced into taking time off when they really want money.

At Home: When longtime GOP Rep. John P. Saylor died in 1973, the Cambria County (Johnstown) Democratic organization seized its chance to recapture a nominally Democratic district. They found an attractive candidate in Murtha, a personable state legislator who had won a Bronze Star and two Purple Hearts as a Marine in Vietnam.

Murtha won narrowly over Harry M. Fox, a former Saylor aide, in a 1974 special election that focused on the Republicans' Watergate problems. He handily dispatched Fox the following November and won easily for nearly a decade.

In 1982, Pennsylvania's Republican-controlled legislature combined Murtha's district with that of fellow Democrat Don Bailey. The primary paired two excellent campaigners and close friends with similar pro-labor views.

The merged district contained about the same number of former constituents of each candidate, making it a battle between two organizations. Murtha's proved superior. In addition, he convinced voters that he could better help the economically depressed district through his greater seniority and influence with the House leadership. He won renomination with 52 percent, to Bailey's 38 percent.

Murtha was not seriously challenged again until 1990, when he was almost blindsided. His Democratic primary foe, lawyer Kenneth B. Burkley, made the contest a referendum on Murtha's use of congressional power. Murtha, Burkley argued, might be an influential member of Congress, but he was using his clout to secure his own financial well-being rather than to help his economically struggling constituency.

Burkley's campaign was both feisty and irreverent. He mocked the value of Murtha's incumbency by appearing at abandoned factories and vacant storefronts in the 12th with a cardboard likeness of the incumbent. He offered a $1,000 reward to anyone who could get Murtha to debate him. And Burkley capped his low-budget campaign with a mailing titled "John P. Murtha's Wheel of Fortune." A takeoff on the TV game show, the mailing portrayed Murtha as a junketeer and congressional pay-raiser.

Tapping defense contractors and lobbyists, heavy industry and unions, Murtha financed a massive blitz that accused Burkley of lies and distortion, while pointing to a variety of economic development projects within the district that Murtha had helped make possible. "Experience ... Makes It Happen," read the Murtha billboards. Burkley ended up carrying his home base, populous Westmoreland County on the outskirts of Pittsburgh, but Murtha won elsewhere to score a 51 percent to 43 percent primary victory.

HOUSE ELECTIONS

1996 General		
John P. Murtha (D)	136,815	(70%)
Bill Choby (R)	58,643	(30%)
1994 General		
John P. Murtha (D)	117,825	(69%)
Bill Choby (R)	53,147	(31%)

Previous Winning Percentages: 1992 (100%) **1990** (62%) **1988** (100%) **1986** (67%) **1984** (69%) **1982** (61%) **1980** (59%) **1978** (69%) **1976** (68%) **1974** (58%) **1974†** (50%)

† Special election

CAMPAIGN FINANCE

	Receipts	Receipts from PACs	Expend-itures
1996			
Murtha (D)	$681,976	$417,563 (61%)	$785,486
Choby (R)	$22,798	$16 (0%)	$22,867
1994			
Murtha (D)	$907,875	$511,779 (56%)	$913,004
Choby (R)	$35,846	$14 (0%)	$35,782

DISTRICT VOTE FOR PRESIDENT

	1996		1992
D	93,515 (46%)	**D**	102,777 (47%)
R	81,106 (40%)	**R**	72,671 (33%)
I	25,753 (13%)	**I**	44,852 (20%)

KEY VOTES

1997	
Ban "partial birth" abortions	Y
1996	
Approve farm bill	Y
Deny public education to illegal immigrants	Y
Repeal ban on certain assault-style weapons	Y
Increase minimum wage	Y
Freeze defense spending	N
Approve welfare overhaul	Y
1995	
Approve balanced-budget constitutional amendment	N
Relax Clean Water Act regulations	N
Oppose limits on environmental regulations	Y
Reduce projected Medicare spending	N
Approve GOP budget with tax and spending cuts	N

VOTING STUDIES

	Presidential Support		Party Unity		Conservative Coalition	
Year	**S**	**O**	**S**	**O**	**S**	**O**
1996	76	23	63	34	86	10
1995	68	29	63	34	72	23
1994	81	14	83	11	69	19
1993	85	9	83	13	77	20
1992	39	54	81	13	67	27
1991	44	52	82	15	62	35

INTEREST GROUP RATINGS

Year	ADA	AFL-CIO	CCUS	ACU
1996	55	n/a	25	25
1995	65	100	33	24
1994	50	78	55	38
1993	50	100	27	22
1992	65	92	63	28
1991	40	92	30	26

13 Jon D. Fox (R)

Of Abington — Elected 1994, 2nd term

Biographical Information

Born: April 22, 1947, Abington, Pa.

Education: Pennsylvania State U., B.A. 1969; Widener U., J.D. 1975.

Military Service: Air Force Reserve, 1969-75.

Occupation: Lawyer.

Family: Wife, Judithanne Wilbert.

Religion: Jewish.

Political Career: Montgomery County assistant district attorney, 1976-80; Abington Township Board of Commissioners, 1980-84; Pa. House, 1985-91; Montgomery County Board of Commissioners, 1991-95; Republican nominee for U.S. House, 1992.

Capitol Office: 435 Cannon Bldg. 20515; 225-6111.

Committees

Banking & Financial Services
Domestic & International Monetary Policy; Housing & Community Opportunity

International Relations
Asia & the Pacific

Transportation & Infrastructure
Aviation; Railroads

In Washington: No one would confuse Fox for a liberal, but there are aspects of his voting record that set him noticeably apart from the more ideologically fervent GOP conservatives who first entered the House with him in 1994. Fox nearly always lines up with GOP conservatives on budget and tax issues. During his freshman term, he took the House floor 230 times to talk up Republican efforts to balance the budget, restrain Medicare spending, overhaul the welfare system and provide a middle-class tax cut.

But on numerous other matters — the environment, gun control and abortion, for instance — Fox reflects the centrist impulses of his upscale suburban constituency. Just one example from 1996: He was an early supporter of Democratic-driven legislation to increase the minimum wage, a politically popular measure the GOP leadership reluctantly brought up for a floor vote in May 1996. Republican leaders tried to mitigate the impact of the increase by exempting small businesses from paying it, but Fox was one of just 43 Republicans throwing cold water on that idea, helping kill it.

At the polls, Fox needs every inch of the center ground he can take. The Democrats came at him hard in 1996, and he won a second term by only 84 votes. Fox knew a thing or two about surviving close elections, because he had won narrowly in 1994 against a Democratic incumbent, Marjorie Margolies-Mezvinsky. Two years earlier, she had barely beaten Fox on a promise not to raise taxes (and in winning had become the first in her party to take the 13th since World War I).

But in August 1993, House Democratic leaders, facing defeat on a crucial vote, pressed her to support the conference report on Clinton's budget-balancing plan, which included a tax increase. She'd said earlier she would vote "no" but at the last minute switched and cast the vote that passed the measure. Her vote figured prominently in her 1994 defeat in a rematch with Fox.

Not surprisingly, Fox talks about tax-cutting in many of his floor speeches. He told Republicans in November 1995 that their motto "should be this: 'There is no such thing as government money, only taxpayers' money.' The burden of proof is on those who would increase taxes."

Unlike many conservative Republicans, though, Fox has a generally positive attitude toward government expenditures for mass transit. Many white-collar professionals in the 13th take commuter trains into Philadelphia on the Pennsylvania Railroad's Main Line. In July 1995, Fox and Philadelphia Democrat Thomas M. Foglietta tried to increase funding for mass transit when the House considered a transportation spending bill. They wanted to add $135 million to the operating subsidies for mass transit by rescinding $135 million that had been appropriated for facilities and equipment at the Federal Aviation Administration. They said the bill cut too much for mass transit operating assistance, nearly a 40 percent reduction. But the House rejected the Fox-Foglietta plan, 122-295.

In 1997, Fox got a new committee seat, on Transportation and Infrastructure, that gives him input in setting funding priorities for the nation's highway and mass transit programs, which are to be reauthorized in the 105th Congress.

Again unlike the majority of House Republicans, Fox voted against two efforts in 1995 to reduce federal regulatory involvement in environmental protection. In May 1995, he was one of just 34 Republicans opposing a measure that revised the 1972 Clean Water Act to ease numerous federal water pollution regulations. In July 1995, he was one of 51 Republicans who supported an amendment that lifted provisions prohibiting the Environmental Protection Agency from enforcing key environmental laws.

Fox was one of 60 in his House class to get contributions from the National Rifle Association in 1995, but in March 1996 he was the only one of that group who opposed repealing the ban on certain semiautomatic assault-style weapons. Just 42 Republicans voted against repealing the law.

Neither staunch abortion foes nor proponents of abortion rights are fully satisfied with Fox's

PENNSYLVANIA 13
Northwest Philadelphia suburbs — the Main Line

Anchored solely in Montgomery County, the 13th includes Lower Merion Township, home to Philadelphia's aristocracy. The area is known as the Main Line, for the Pennsylvania Railroad's Main Line of Public Works, along which doctors, lawyers and old-money families built their posh estates. The white-collar professionals of Bryn Mawr, Narberth and Ardmore still ride into the city on the commuter trains that run along this line. A smaller portion of the Main Line is contained in the 7th District.

Though some Democratic-voting blacks have moved out of Philadelphia into areas such as Abington and Cheltenham, the county is overwhelmingly white and Republican. In 1992, the county experienced a bout of ballot topsy-turvy as it deserted George Bush, backed GOP Sen. Arlen Specter and elected Democrat Marjorie Margolies-Mezvinsky to Congress. In 1994, it returned to form, voting Republican for governor, senator and House. But district voters remain fickle. In 1996, they voted for Bill Clinton, giving him 50 percent to Bob Dole's 41 percent. Of the five Pennsylvania districts that opted both for Clinton and a Republican representative, the 13th gave Clinton his highest winning percentage. Fox, meanwhile, won his second term by only 84 votes.

As a wealthy, suburban county that borders a troubled big city, Montgomery follows developments in Philadelphia with interest and concern. When redistricting plans surfaced in the state legislature that would have grafted part of the county into a city-based district, county legislators fought hard to kill the proposals.

Norristown, the county seat, has the largest concentration of minorities in the county. At the end of each workday when the white-collar legal community departs, Norristown reverts to a small borough with some big-city problems. Hatfield and Lansdale are other population centers.

The western portion of the county, especially along the Route 422 corridor, is coming to grips with problems associated with rapid growth. New residential developments are sprouting to house employees of the pharmaceutical companies that have relocated to Upper Providence Township.

Local infrastructure improvements have made the surrounding region accessible and attractive to commuters and businesses. Even in the former farmland communities of Lower Salford, Worcester and Franconia, the loosely organized lobby of Pennsylvania Dutch farmers, jokingly referred to as the "Mennonite-Industrial Complex," is seeing its influence diminish.

Central Montgomery County already experienced that growth, particularly around Fort Washington. There the Northeast extension of the Pennsylvania Turnpike toll road begins its way to Allentown, Wilkes-Barre and Scranton.

1990 Population: 565,793. White 514,755 (91%), Black 34,507 (6%), Other 16,531 (3%). Hispanic origin 6,825 (1%). 18 and over 439,132 (78%), 62 and over 104,795 (19%). Median age: 36.

voting record on abortion and family-planning issues. In May 1996 he voted to ban abortions at overseas military hospitals; in July 1996 he voted against allowing federal employees' health plans to pay for abortions. He also would ban a particular abortion technique opponents call "partial birth" abortion.

Fox did, however, vote to restore Title X federal funding for family planning, and in March 1996 he opposed an effort to allow states to deny Medicaid funds to pay for abortions for poor women in cases of rape or incest. "I support a woman's right to choose. I support family planning," Fox told the Philadelphia Daily News in August 1995. "But I don't believe the government should pay for abortions except through Medicaid in cases of rape, incest or when the mother's life is in danger." In early 1997, he rejected abortion foes' pleas to block early release of federal funds for international population-control programs.

Fox, a former assistant district attorney in Montgomery County, cultivates a tough-on-crime image. In May 1996, the House approved a bill he sponsored that increased sentences for those convicted of tampering with or harassing juries and witnesses. Fox told colleagues that as the federal penalties for serious crimes have increased, the penalties for tampering with a witness or jury have not kept pace. Under his bill, those convicted of jury tampering could receive either a 10-year prison sentence or the maximum penalty that the defendant in the case would have faced. It would not apply to death penalty cases.

Again staking out a moderate position, Fox opposed efforts by GOP conservatives to cut back the budget of the Legal Services Corporation (LSC), which funds legal aid clinics serving the poor. When the House in July 1996 considered the spending bill for the Justice Department, Fox and West Virginia Democrat Allan B. Mollohan were successful with an amendment helpful to the LSC. Some on the GOP right argue that LSC lawyers spend more time filing class action suits and defending the likes of drug dealers and murderers than they do representing the civil litigation needs of the poor. But cutting Legal Services would leave the poor without meaningful access to the courts, Fox said. A contingent of 56 Republicans defied the position of the GOP leadership and voted for the amendment, which passed, 247-179.

Fox, who also gained a seat on the International Relations Committee in 1997, ventured into foreign policymaking in the 104th when he joined the effort to have the U.S. embassy in Israel moved from Tel Aviv to Jerusalem. Fox, the only member of his House class who is Jewish, noted in October 1995, "In every other country across the world, the United States has its embassy in the capital of the country; not so, of course, in Israel" — because Palestinians dispute Israel's claim to the city. Fox praised Israel as "the only democracy in the Middle East, a country that has been America's best friend."

He also sits on the Banking Committee.

At Home: Fox's interest in politics extends back to his days in student government at Penn State University. After law school and a stint as assistant district attorney in Montgomery County, he served four years as a township commissioner, six years as a state representative and four years as a county commissioner before winning a seat in Congress on his second try, in 1994. Through the years he built up a support network within the powerful Montgomery County GOP organization; he also heard criticism from opponents that he always seemed to be angling for a higher office.

Fox's first House bid came in 1992, when longtime GOP Rep. Lawrence Coughlin retired from the 13th. In this district and nationally, it turned out to be a good year for female Democratic candidates; Margolies-Mezvinsky won by 1,373 votes.

In 1994, Fox first had to make it through a five-way GOP primary. His principal opposition came from state Rep. Ellen Hartley, who said she could better compete with the incumbent for the support of women voters. Fox was nominated with 37 percent of the vote, to Hartley's 25 percent.

Campaigning for re-election, Margolies-Mezvinsky sought to depict her high-profile vote for Clinton's budget as a trade: She cast the crucial vote, and Clinton held a presidential seminar on deficit reduction in her district in the fall of 1995. But Fox hit "The Vote" time and again, arguing that it would increase taxes within the 13th by $1.5 billion over five years and chiding the incumbent for breaking trust with the district's voters.

Margolies-Mezvinsky responded by citing a list of tax increases that Fox had backed throughout his political career. But in the end, Margolies-Mezvinsky could not escape the stigma of "The Vote." Fox was elected with a 49 percent plurality, four percentage points ahead of the incumbent.

In 1996, the Democrats turned to Montgomery County Commissioner Joseph M. Hoeffel, who had been the Democratic challenger to Coughlin in 1984 and 1986. Hoeffel's tactic was to link Fox to House Speaker Newt Gingrich, not a popular figure among the district's moderate and independent voters. Fox protested that he was "the most independent of the 73 freshman Republicans, representing Montgomery County, not the Beltway leadership." Hoeffel's strategy, aided by a nine-percentage-point Clinton win in the district, almost worked. Fox held on, just barely.

HOUSE ELECTIONS

1996 General		
Jon D. Fox (R)	120,304	(49%)
Joseph M. Hoeffel (D)	120,220	(49%)
Thomas Patrick Burke (LIBERT)	4,930	(2%)
1994 General		
Jon D. Fox (R)	96,254	(49%)
Marjorie Margolies-Mezvinsky (D)	88,073	(45%)
Lee D. Hustead (LIBERT)	7,183	(4%)
Frank W. Szabo (I)	3,278	(2%)

CAMPAIGN FINANCE

	Receipts	Receipts from PACs		Expend-itures
1996				
Fox (R)	$1,663,100	$483,301	(29%)	$1,659,723
Hoeffel (D)	$704,328	$182,001	(26%)	$697,490
1994				
Fox (R)	$1,023,009	$165,749	(16%)	$1,015,330
Margolies-Mezvinsky (D)	$1,609,938	$656,716	(41%)	$1,620,110

DISTRICT VOTE FOR PRESIDENT

1996		1992	
D	125,348 (50%)	**D**	119,042 (44%)
R	103,445 (41%)	**R**	107,811 (40%)
I	19,920 (8%)	**I**	44,280 (16%)

KEY VOTES

1997	
Ban "partial birth" abortions	Y
1996	
Approve farm bill	Y
Deny public education to illegal immigrants	Y
Repeal ban on certain assault-style weapons	N
Increase minimum wage	Y
Freeze defense spending	Y
Approve welfare overhaul	Y
1995	
Approve balanced-budget constitutional amendment	Y
Relax Clean Water Act regulations	N
Oppose limits on environmental regulations	Y
Reduce projected Medicare spending	Y
Approve GOP budget with tax and spending cuts	Y

VOTING STUDIES

	Presidential Support		Party Unity		Conservative Coalition	
Year	**S**	**O**	**S**	**O**	**S**	**O**
1996	44	56	76	23	65	33
1995	25	74	84	15	84	14

INTEREST GROUP RATINGS

Year	ADA	AFL-CIO	CCUS	ACU
1996	35	n/a	81	65
1995	20	17	83	80

14 William J. Coyne (D)

Of Pittsburgh — Elected 1980, 9th term

Biographical Information

Born: Aug. 24, 1936, Pittsburgh, Pa.

Education: Robert Morris College, B.S. 1965.

Military Service: Army, 1955-57.

Occupation: Accountant.

Family: Single.

Religion: Roman Catholic.

Political Career: Pa. House, 1971-73; sought Democratic nomination for Pa. Senate, 1972; Pittsburgh City Council, 1974-81.

Capitol Office: 2455 Rayburn Bldg. 20515; 225-2301.

Committees

Ways & Means
Human Resources; Oversight (ranking)

In Washington: Many Democrats with records as liberal as Coyne's have made it their business since 1995 to confront aggressively the conservative House Republican majority, taking the floor to denounce GOP policies as unwise and heartless.

Coyne, however, has maintained his reputation as one of the House's quieter members. To be sure, he nearly always votes against Republican proposals, and sometimes he even makes his disapproval known in a short speech on the House floor.

But rhetorical fisticuffs are typically not the specialty of this low-key and unobtrusive Democratic loyalist. On the Ways and Means Committee, where he was given a seat in 1985, the spotlight seldom finds him. A corporate accountant before he entered politics, Coyne is not the center-stage type. He lobbies for the city of Pittsburgh and leaves grand strategizing to the party leadership.

At the start of the 103rd Congress, Coyne won another reward for loyal service, as he was picked to fill one of the Budget Committee seats reserved for Ways and Means members. He served two terms there, looking out for Pittsburgh's business and financial interests, lining up more money for a transportation project linking the city to its airport and securing funding for a Software Engineering Institute and for a pediatric clinic research center. (He left Budget in the 105th.)

The Republicans' drive for a fundamental reordering of federal budget priorities has moved even the normally undemonstrative Coyne to some occasional strong words. He described the proposed balanced-budget constitutional amendment as a "fiscal placebo instead of an honest and realistic plan for reducing the federal deficit."

In another rare floor speech, he said that GOP budget proposals in the 104th cut into Medicare, environmental programs, and community development programs important to Pittsburgh in order to support unwise tax cuts. "This tax giveaway to the wealthiest individuals in the U.S. is made possible only by taking a meat axe to programs serving children, seniors and the poor."

Coyne said he supported an alternative budget fashioned by the House Progressive Caucus and the Congressional Black Caucus, although he also commended separate budgets proposed by President Clinton and by a group of conservative Democrats.

Coyne also took a dim view of Republican efforts to overhaul the welfare system with new work requirements for recipients and maximum lifetime limits on benefits. Echoing the liberal Democratic line, Coyne said the GOP welfare plan was "tough on children and weak on work. This plan will punish children who happen to be born into poverty. At the same time, this plan cuts child care funding and other programs that are essential if an adult on welfare is to get a job and leave the welfare rolls."

Even after Republicans revised their welfare bill to the point that President Clinton said he would sign it, Coyne voted "no" on final passage, ending up on the losing end of a 328-101 tally.

On that occasion and many others in the 104th, Coyne sided with the House's most forthright liberals. He was one of only 67 members (including only one Republican) to oppose a bill to bar federal recognition of same-sex marriages, and to allow states to refuse to recognize such marriages even if they were sanctioned by other states.

He also has opposed a constitutional amendment banning desecration of the U.S. flag.

Democratic control of the White House has brought progress on some proposals Coyne has made to change the tax code to benefit cities. For several years Coyne advocated extending tax breaks for small-issue industrial development bonds (IDBs) in order to permit state and local governments to offer low-cost financing to small manufacturers. Routine renewal of the IDB exemption was snuffed out when President George Bush vetoed two tax bills in the 102nd Congress, and the exemption expired in 1992. But the permanent exemption was enacted after Clinton included it in his 1993 budget.

PENNSYLVANIA 14
Pittsburgh and suburbs

Once referred to as "hell with the lid off," Pittsburgh has undergone an economic transformation that has produced many new white-collar and service-oriented jobs. But the decline of manufacturing means the city has far fewer high-wage, working-class jobs than existed in days past.

No one calls Pittsburgh "the smoky city" anymore. Gone are the pollution and grime created by the steel mills and heavy industry that hugged the Allegheny, Monongahela and Ohio rivers. In their places are medical centers and universities, parks and skyscrapers. Pittsburgh often ranks high on media lists of "most livable places."

The "Golden Triangle" area, where the Allegheny and Monongahela meet to form the Ohio River, is a thriving downtown with a large corporate community. Companies such as USX, Aluminum Company of America, Westinghouse and H.J. Heinz have headquarters in the city where such industrial giants as Andrew Carnegie, Andrew Mellon and H.J. Heinz made their fortunes. The USX Tower, a 64-story edifice, is one of the largest buildings between New York and Chicago.

The Fort Duquesne Bridge, one of hundreds of bridges and tunnels that connect the city's valleys and ridges, is a gateway to Three Rivers Stadium and Pittsburgh's North Side.

The economic and cultural renaissance of recent years has made for a more sophisticated city, but Pittsburgh retains its traditional ethnic character. About 80 distinct neighborhoods dot the city, including the Oakland academic-medical complex — the site of Carnegie-Mellon University, the University of Pittsburgh and Children's Hospital — and the East European, working-class enclaves on the South Side. Italians live in Bloomfield; Poles and Germans, in Lawrenceville; and Jews, in Squirrel Hill. There are black neighborhoods in Homewood and East Liberty.

Pittsburgh's Democratic tradition is another constant. In statewide elections, lopsided Democratic margins provided by Pittsburgh and Philadelphia can offset the GOP advantage elsewhere in Pennsylvania.

Unions remain a force, contributing to Pittsburgh's huge Democratic majority. Within the city — all of which is in the 14th — Democrats outnumber Republicans by more than 6-to-1.

Republicans have a better time in the northern and western suburbs that make up about one-third of the 14th's population. There, the Democratic voter registration advantage is much less decisive. The suburbanites are generally younger, more affluent and less bound by traditional party loyalties than city residents.

In many of these areas, Republicans control local offices. The fast-growing North Hills area, partly in the 14th, is filled with executives from Pittsburgh's burgeoning high-tech industry.

1990 Population: 565,787. White 455,246 (80%), Black 100,771 (18%), Other 9,770 (2%). Hispanic origin 4,385 (1%). 18 and over 449,638 (79%), 62 and over 117,747 (21%). Median age: 36.

And with the Clinton administration's desire to promote high-speed rail construction, Coyne's proposal to make state and local financing for these projects tax-exempt was enacted as part of the president's 1993 budget. Pittsburgh is the world headquarters for MagLev Inc., a company developing a high-speed rail prototype system.

In the 104th Congress, Coyne voted to take transportation trust funds "off-budget," a move proponents say will free up money for infrastructure projects that is now hoarded to mask the size of the deficit. A big booster of this idea is a Pennsylvania colleague of Coyne's, Republican Bud Shuster, chairman of the Transportation and Infrastructure Committee. Shuster is mostly a highways man, while Coyne would like to see more generous spending on mass transit.

Coyne is also a strong supporter of organized labor, and has sided with unions in high-profile disputes with the pro-business Republican majority — support a higher minimum wage, opposing allowing companies to offer comp time in lieu of overtime pay, and opposing a GOP proposal to let non-union companies set up and control labor-management teams.

Earlier, Coyne voted against NAFTA and supported legislation requiring employers to provide unpaid family and medical leave.

He also dabbles in health issues. After the Pittsburgh Post-Gazette cataloged hospital and pharmacists' errors in dispensing medication, Coyne proposed legislation to create a national network to track deaths caused by medication.

Powerful Pennsylvania Democrat John P. Murtha is chiefly responsible for Coyne's having a place on Ways and Means. Coyne did little campaigning on his own, but Murtha made it clear that Coyne was his choice to give the Pennsylvania steel industry some representation on the influential tax-writing panel.

Coyne had four competitors for one remaining seat, including Michael A. Andrews, a Texan favored by then-Majority Leader Jim Wright. But after some complicated horse-trading that produced an alliance between Murtha and former Ways and Means Chairman Dan Rostenkowski of Illinois, Coyne won by one vote.

At Home: Coyne's political career never has

forced him to stray very far from his inner-city Pittsburgh roots. He still lives in the house where he was born. Before coming to Congress, he was active in Pittsburgh politics for a decade, working loyally with the city Democratic organization.

Elected to the state House in 1970, Coyne lost a state Senate bid in 1972. In 1973, he was elected to the City Council, and while on the council he also served as city chairman of the Pittsburgh Democratic Party.

When the 14th opened up in 1980 with the retirement of longtime Democratic Rep. William S. Moorhead, Coyne had the connections to claim it. The city Democratic organization helped him easily defeat Moorhead's son in the primary. He cruised past the GOP nominee that fall.

Coyne has gotten very good at winning elections, typically pulling in more than 70 percent of the vote. But his re-election campaigns in recent years have grown a bid more arduous. Redistricting for the 1990s slightly reduced the Democratic advantage in the 14th, and Coyne drew a primary challenger in 1992 who demanded that the district elect someone to Congress who would "do something." Coyne flattened him with 76 percent of the vote, but two years later saw his November vote share fall to 64 percent, noticeably below his usual 70-percent-plus tallies.

Coyne's 1996 primary opponent, City Councilman Dan Cohen, tried a similar tactic. Cohen was considered a serious challenger, in no small part because he had raised about $250,000 in campaign money by the end of 1995. Coyne responded with a slogan: "Results. Not Talk." It proved to be effective; he won the primary with two-thirds of the vote. In November, Coyne's re-election tally was 61 percent — still very comfortable but a career low.

HOUSE ELECTIONS

1996 General		
William J. Coyne (D)	122,922	(61%)
Bill Ravotti (R)	78,921	(39%)
1996 Primary		
William J. Coyne (D)	47,334	(66%)
Dan Cohen (D)	24,364	(34%)
1994 General		
William J. Coyne (D)	105,310	(64%)
John Robert Clark (R)	53,221	(32%)
Edward L. Stewart (PAT)	3,826	(2%)
Paul Scherrer (WL)	1,819	(1%)

Previous Winning Percentages: 1992 (72%) **1990** (72%) **1988** (79%) **1986** (90%) **1984** (77%) **1982** (75%) **1980** (69%)

CAMPAIGN FINANCE

	Receipts	Receipts from PACs	Expend-itures
1996			
Coyne (D)	$727,359	$369,382 (51%)	$1,027,674
Ravotti (R)	$213,933	$20,116 (9%)	$212,284
1994			
Coyne (D)	$329,481	$207,813 (63%)	$185,539
Clark (R)	$9,904	$14 (0%)	$9,747

DISTRICT VOTE FOR PRESIDENT

	1996		1992
D	126,687 (59%)	**D**	145,419 (58%)
R	70,450 (33%)	**R**	66,016 (26%)
I	15,415 (7%)	**I**	38,460 (15%)

KEY VOTES

1997	
Ban "partial birth" abortions	N
1996	
Approve farm bill	N
Deny public education to illegal immigrants	N
Repeal ban on certain assault-style weapons	N
Increase minimum wage	Y
Freeze defense spending	Y
Approve welfare overhaul	N
1995	
Approve balanced-budget constitutional amendment	N
Relax Clean Water Act regulations	N
Oppose limits on environmental regulations	Y
Reduce projected Medicare spending	N
Approve GOP budget with tax and spending cuts	N

VOTING STUDIES

	Presidential Support		Party Unity		Conservative Coalition	
Year	**S**	**O**	**S**	**O**	**S**	**O**
1996	81	19	93	5	10	90
1995	91	8	95	4	9	90
1994	74	24	98	1	3	92
1993	83	17	98	1	7	93
1992	19	81	96	3	19	81
1991	28	70	93	4	16	81

INTEREST GROUP RATINGS

Year	ADA	AFL-CIO	CCUS	ACU
1996	100	n/a	19	0
1995	100	100	13	4
1994	100	89	25	0
1993	95	100	0	4
1992	95	92	50	4
1991	80	83	20	0

15 Paul McHale (D)

Of Bethlehem — Elected 1992, 3rd term

Biographical Information

Born: July 26, 1950, Bethlehem, Pa.

Education: Lehigh U., B.A. 1972; Georgetown U., J.D. 1977.

Military Service: Marine Corps, 1972-74; Marine Corps Reserve, 1974-present.

Occupation: Lawyer; adjunct professor.

Family: Wife, Katherine Pecka; three children.

Religion: Roman Catholic.

Political Career: Sought Democratic nomination for U.S. House, 1980; Pa. House, 1983-91; sought Democratic nomination for Pa. Commonwealth Court, 1989.

Capitol Office: 217 Cannon Bldg. 20515; 225-6411.

Committees

National Security
Military Readiness; Military Research & Development

Science
Energy & Environment; Technology

In Washington: After defeating a Republican incumbent in 1992, McHale barely won a second term in 1994, and during the 104th Congress he expended a great deal of energy on congressional reform issues, working with like-minded members in the GOP majority on matters such as fuller disclosure of lobbying practices and curbs on members' spending on official mailings.

These efforts by McHale, along with his endorsement of welfare reform and his support for traditional Democratic positions — abortion rights, gun control and a minimum wage increase — yielded electoral success in 1996, as McHale defeated his GOP challenger by 14 points.

McHale gained considerable notice in the 104th for taking the lead, along with Connecticut Republican Christopher Shays, on a bill designed to close loopholes in the existing 1946 lobbying law that had enabled many congressional lobbyists to avoid registration. Under the McHale-Shays measure, which the House cleared in November 1995, any lobbyist receiving at least $5,000 in a six-month period from a single client must register with the clerk of the House and the secretary of the Senate. Lobbyists also must list the congressional chambers and federal agencies they contact, the issues they lobby on, and how much money they spend. "Lobbying is a constitutionally protected activity, but one best exercised with maximum public exposure," McHale told the House. "In politics, as elsewhere, sunshine is the best disinfectant."

McHale also joined up with two other Republicans — Michael N. Castle of Delaware and Linda Smith of Washington — in sponsoring an amendment to the fiscal 1996 legislative branch spending bill that would have frozen members' office expenses and franked mail accounts at the prior year level, reducing the amount by $4.6 million. McHale said that in 1994, members sent out over six times more mail than they received. "Two hundred sixty-seven million pieces of mail were sent out by Congress during that period," he told the House in June 1995, adding, "We are making tough choices in balancing the budget. We have a moral and political responsibility to share in carrying that burden." The amendment was narrowly rejected, 213-215.

McHale had another idea on how to reduce congressional spending: eliminate 140 House seats by 2002. In July 1995, he introduced legislation to reduce the House from 435 to 295 members, saying it is just too big. "With such large numbers, some House members barely recognize each other," McHale said. "Members have little effect on each other's opinions. They have come to depend too heavily on party identity when dealing with one another." But in a statement explaining the proposal, McHale acknowledged that his colleagues were not likely to embrace the plan, considering their "general desire to remain in office."

McHale's extensive military record — he has served a quarter-century in the U.S. Marine Corps and Marine Reserves, and did two tours of duty in the Persian Gulf — helped earn him a seat on the National Security Committee, where he has been an unflinching booster of his service branch. When the House considered the fiscal 1997 defense authorization bill, McHale complained that it included a provision killing the design of a plane wanted by the Marine Corps.

The defense bill approved the funding of the so-called Joint Strike Fighter program, an effort to develop an airplane, to be built in three versions, as a replacement late in the next decade for 1970s-vintage jets currently used by the Air Force, Navy and Marine Corps. The committee version of the bill would have killed a planned variant of the plane, one that could take off and land vertically — something the Marines want to replace their aging Harrier jets. McHale said the provision would "deliver a crippling blow to the future of Marine Corps aviation" and complained that "this attack upon Marine Corps aviation came completely without warning, without member involvement and without service consultation."

Also from his National Security seat, McHale argued against committing U.S. troops to the con-

PENNSYLVANIA 15
East — Allentown; Bethlehem

In 1992, residents of the Lehigh Valley shucked the Republican congressman who had represented them since 1978 and voted for a Democratic presidential nominee for the first time since 1976. They have stayed in the Democratic column in the presidential and congressional races since then.

The Valley previously had strayed to the GOP despite having all the makings of a Democratic stronghold. In the 1980s, the area's heavy industrial tradition, strong unions and sizable ethnic population could not overcome disaffection with the liberal image of the national Democratic Party.

The Republican trend was partly because the district's largest city, Allentown (Lehigh County), had fared better than most of Pennsylvania's other older, industrial cities. Although singer Billy Joel chose Allentown in 1982 to represent the plight of the newly unemployed, the recession did not hit the city quite as hard as some other places because of its diversified economy. Even after Mack Trucks moved one of its main plants to South Carolina in 1987 — in search of lower, non-union wages — the city's then-thriving small companies helped brace the economy.

Two hundred and fifty years ago, Germans settled this region, and their work ethic carries down to the present. Many of the newer businesses depend on the high-quality craftsmanship of the Pennsylvania Dutch, who are conservative and union-resistant. But the German influence has been diluted in recent years by a steady, westward migration from New Jersey and New York into the region.

On the New Jersey border, industrial Northampton County eagerly returned to its Democratic roots in 1992 and has generally stayed there since.

Northampton boasts a slightly stronger industrial heritage, mainly in Bethlehem and Easton. Bethlehem Steel's smokestacks dominate the Bethlehem city landscape. Though employment at the steel mills is a fraction of what it was in World War II, the company is still a pillar of the local economy. Easton produces chemicals and paper products.

At Christmastime, Bethlehem sheds its gritty, steel town veneer and transforms into a shining city of glittering trees and candlelit windows. The scene is completed with a Star of Bethlehem that sparkles from atop South Mountain. The Christmas spirit dates back to the mid-1700s, when Moravian Protestants first established a communal church-village. Moravian College, one of the oldest in America, traces its roots to the 18th century.

Lehigh and Northampton counties provide the bulk of the district vote, but a small nub of northwestern Montgomery County is grafted onto the southern portion of the district. This Republican section backed Bob Dole in the 1996 presidential race.

1990 Population: 565,810. White 531,721 (94%), Black 12,175 (2%), Other 21,914 (4%). Hispanic origin 26,766 (5%). 18 and over 434,888 (77%), 62 and over 102,494 (18%). Median age: 35.

flict in the former Yugoslavia — a position opposed by the White House, which emphasized that peace negotiations among the governments of Bosnia, Serbia and Croatia would not produce results without the assurance that U.S. troops would participate.

He and Indiana Republican Steve Buyer introduced a resolution expressing the sense of Congress that peace negotiators should not assume that U.S. troops would be deployed and that no deployment should occur unless approved by Congress. The House approved it, 315-103, on Oct. 30, 1995, two days before the peace negotiations were to begin.

But after the successful outcome of the peace negotiations, McHale voted against a measure in December 1995 that would have prohibited the use of federal funds for the deployment of U.S. ground troops in Bosnia as part of a peacekeeping operation. Instead, he backed a resolution that disowned the deployment, which was already under way, but expressed support for the troops. McHale said that even if members opposed the deployment, they still needed to provide the resources necessary to accomplish the mission, urging the House to give "strong support for our soldiers." That measure passed, 287-141.

As evidenced by that episode and by some of his other votes — his backing of a balanced-budget constitutional amendment, for instance — McHale clearly is not unwilling to go against the White House. But when his party really needs his vote, McHale often antes up. He pleased the White House in August 1993 by abandoning his earlier opposition to President Clinton's budget plan and voting with the razor-thin majority that gave it final approval in the House.

McHale had voted against Clinton's deficit reduction package in May 1993 because, he said, the proposed "Btu tax" on the energy content of fuels would devastate the manufacturing base in his district, home to Bethlehem Steel, Mack Trucks and five of the nation's remaining cement manufacturers. But once the Btu tax was dropped, McHale agreed to support Clinton's budget.

McHale has also been a Clinton ally on some controversial social policy issues. In the 103rd, he voted for two gun control measures pushed by the administration, and he voted against a Republican effort in the 104th to repeal one of the laws, a ban on certain semiautomatic assault-style weapons.

On the divisive issue of abortion, he keeps to the middle. In the 104th, he voted for a measure banning a particular abortion technique that opponents call a "partial-birth" abortion, and he voted against allowing federal employee health care plans to cover abortion. But he voted in favor of allowing women at overseas military facilities to have abortions if they paid for the procedure themselves, and he also supported a requirement that states pay for abortions for poor women in cases of rape or incest.

A member of the Science Committee, McHale voted in the 104th for continued funding of the space station project and for an unsuccessful Democratic proposal to increase spending on scientific research by more than $5 billion.

At Home: McHale barely made it back to Congress in 1994, winning re-election by a mere 471 votes. His campaign drew criticism for passivity, especially on the fundraising front. He was slow to raise money, and by Election Day had been outspent by Republican businessman Jim Yeager by roughly $100,000. But McHale took dramatic steps to distance himself from the Clinton administration. He appeared before a model of the Liberty Bell to declare that he could not be bought, bullied or bribed by the president, party leaders or special interests.

In 1992, McHale had won by a 5-point margin over seven-term GOP Rep. Don Ritter. McHale called Ritter ineffective, saying the district needed "someone who is a leader in Congress, not someone on the sidelines." McHale benefited from a sizable anti-status quo vote in the 15th that also showed up in Ross Perot's 22 percent tally in the district's presidential voting.

McHale campaigned and did more vigorous fundraising in 1996. His GOP opponent, real estate agent Bob Kilbanks, mounted a low-budget, door-to-door effort, drawing his strongest support from a cadre of abortion opponents and gunowners' rights advocates.

Also on the district's ballot was Nicholas R. Sabatine, the candidate of Perot's Reform Party. Sabatine, the national chairman of the Patriot Party (a Reform Party ally), supported for term limits and some other conservative themes. Sabatine received 3 percent of the vote, Kilbanks 41 percent, and McHale took a third term with 55 percent.

HOUSE ELECTIONS

1996 General		
Paul McHale (D)	109,812	(55%)
Bob Kilbanks (R)	82,803	(41%)
Nicholas R. Sabatine (REF)	6,931	(3%)
1994 General		
Paul McHale (D)	72,073	(48%)
Jim Yeager (R)	71,602	(47%)
Victor Mazziotti (PAT)	7,227	(5%)

Previous Winning Percentages: 1992 (52%)

CAMPAIGN FINANCE

	Receipts	Receipts from PACs	Expend-itures
1996			
McHale (D)	$374,776	$221,725 (59%)	$366,847
Kilbanks (R)	$264,657	$55,787 (21%)	$263,747
Sabatine (REF)	$23,686	0	$22,041
1994			
McHale (D)	$285,097	$174,874 (61%)	$284,930
Yeager (R)	$330,081	$48,370 (15%)	$325,713
Mazziotti (PAT)	$25,081	0	$25,080

DISTRICT VOTE FOR PRESIDENT

	1996		1992
D	96,364 (47%)	**D**	92,363 (42%)
R	85,719 (41%)	**R**	81,349 (37%)
I	22,123 (11%)	**I**	47,740 (22%)

KEY VOTES

1997	
Ban "partial birth" abortions	Y
1996	
Approve farm bill	N
Deny public education to illegal immigrants	Y
Repeal ban on certain assault-style weapons	N
Increase minimum wage	Y
Freeze defense spending	Y
Approve welfare overhaul	Y
1995	
Approve balanced-budget constitutional amendment	Y
Relax Clean Water Act regulations	N
Oppose limits on environmental regulations	Y
Reduce projected Medicare spending	N
Approve GOP budget with tax and spending cuts	N

VOTING STUDIES

	Presidential Support		Party Unity		Conservative Coalition	
Year	**S**	**O**	**S**	**O**	**S**	**O**
1996	72	28	77	23	53	47
1995	73	27	78	22	55	45
1994	78	22	84	16	69	31
1993	86	14	88	11	55	45

INTEREST GROUP RATINGS

Year	ADA	AFL-CIO	CCUS	ACU
1996	70	n/a	38	20
1995	75	92	38	12
1994	45	67	83	24
1993	65	92	36	25

16 Joseph R. Pitts (R)

Of Kennett Square — Elected 1996, 1st term

Biographical Information
Born: Oct. 10, 1939, Lexington, Ky.
Education: Asbury College, A.B. 1961; West Chester U., M.Ed. 1972.
Military Service: Air Force, 1963-69.
Occupation: Nursery owner; teacher.
Family: Wife, Virginia M. Pratt; three children.
Religion: Protestant.
Political Career: Pa. House, 1972-96.
Capitol Office: 504 Cannon Bldg. 20515; 225-2411.

Committees
Budget
Transportation & Infrastructure
Aviation; Railroads; Surface Transportation

The Path to Washington: Pitts should fit nicely into the conservative mold of the man he succeeded, veteran Republican Robert S. Walker, who retired in 1996. An Air Force combat pilot during the Vietnam War, Pitts hews to the right on fiscal policy as well as social issues.

He arrived on Capitol Hill after nearly a quarter-century in the Pennsylvania House, where in his final years he chaired the Appropriations Committee. That high-profile position gave him a forum to promote his pro-business, smaller government philosophy, which included calls for privatization of parts of state government, such as Pennsylvania's liquor control system.

Tax reform has also been a major concern for Pitts. In 1992, he proposed a state constitutional amendment that he called "The Taxpayer's Bill of Rights," which would have set limits on state and local jurisdictions' ability to increase their taxes or spending. In 1997, Pitts called for a cut in the capital gains tax and repeal of the estate tax.

Over the years, Pitts has been equally outspoken on social issues. He has been a staunch foe of abortion and wrote Pennsylvania's law allowing families to educate their children at home. His congressional campaign literature in 1996 described him as "a champion, some say 'the' champion, of traditional values in Harrisburg."

Pitts has a quiet, unassuming temperament, but his views have made him a lightning rod for controversy even among Republican constituents. When he was running for renomination to an 11th term in the state House in 1992, he lost more than 40 percent of the GOP primary vote to a challenger who was pro-abortion rights, and his 1994 primary was even closer.

But Pitts' outspokenness has also created a base of support, which he tapped to win the crowded GOP congressional primary in April 1996 with a plurality of the vote.

His toughest opposition in the primary came from Chester County Commissioner Karen Martynick, a vociferous supporter of abortion rights. The only woman and abortion rights supporter in the five-candidate field, Martynick drew the backing of several women's and environmental groups.

Martynick tried to depict Pitts as a pampered political insider. But he was able to claim that he was more than a career politician by pointing to the 116 combat missions he flew during the Vietnam War, his years as a high school basketball coach as well as a teacher of math and science, his ownership of a small landscape nursery, and his experience in legislative budget-writing.

The race was expected to have strong geographical overtones. The 16th District is split almost evenly between Pitts' home base of Chester County, which includes portions of suburban Philadelphia, and Lancaster County to the west. But both Pitts and Martynick ran more visible campaigns than the pair of candidates from Lancaster County. And on primary day, Pitts swept both counties and finished with 45 percent; Martynick was a distant second with 26 percent.

Pitts' primary victory proved tantamount to election in the heavily Republican district — the "Pennsylvania Dutch" seat has not elected a Democrat since the Civil War — although his Democratic opponent, weekly newspaper publisher James G. Blaine, mounted a spirited campaign.

The Democrat boasted a historical name. He was a descendant of James G. Blaine, the 19th century House Speaker and GOP presidential nominee in 1884. And the modern-day Blaine reached deep into his pockets to finance his campaign. He depicted himself as a non-politician and ran a series of ads attempting to establish himself as a moderate alternative to Pitts.

But that argument had limited appeal. While Blaine drew a higher share of the vote than any Democrat has in the district in more than a quarter-century, he still lost to Pitts by 22 points, 37 percent to 59 percent.

Republican House leaders gave Pitts a couple of plum committee assignments: Budget and Transportation and Infrastructure, which is chaired by fellow Pennsylvanian Bud Shuster.

PENNSYLVANIA 16
Southeast — Lancaster

Rapid growth and development are redefining the character of the two formerly rural counties that make up the 16th. But development has not altered the historical partisan preference of either Chester or Lancaster counties.

In these two counties — especially Chester — over the past two decades, rural Republicanism has been superseded by a new brand: suburban Republicanism. In Chester County, the state's sixth-fastest growing in population from 1990 to 1996, the mushroom farmers of Kennett Square cast their GOP ballots along with the managers, scientists and executives who moved to such places as Birmingham Township in the 1980s. West Goshen Township, by West Chester University, also has experienced recent growth.

Scenic farm country and a favorable business climate made Lancaster County one of the state's fastest-growing areas in the 1980s. The strong work ethic of the local labor force makes the county a preferred location for companies looking to start new plants in proximity to the East Coast's major markets.

This is the heart of Pennsylvania Dutch Country, which was etched into popular consciousness by the 1985 movie "Witness." The Amish "plain people" featured in the movie still farm the area, though increasing property values and suburban encroachment have driven many away. Some sects cling closer to the old ways than others. They range from the Old Order Amish, who in effect live in the mid-19th century, to the "black bumper Mennonites," who use electricity and drive cars but paint chrome bumpers black.

Besides setting the county's conservative political tone, they affect the county's economy, for tourists flock to Dutch Country to gawk at the horse-and-buggies, eat at the family-style restaurants and browse at the quilt shops.

Slightly more than half the district's residents live in Lancaster County. Not all of the county is in the 16th — the northwestern part is in the 17th — but the city of Lancaster and affluent suburbs such as Manheim Township and Warwick Township are in the 16th.

The Amish and Mennonites are joined in their support of Republican candidates by the affluent communities outside the city of Lancaster. Household incomes for the business executives of Manheim and Warwick townships far outpace those in the rest of the county.

Bob Dole carried Lancaster County in 1996 with 60 percent, 7 percentage points higher than his overall district average. Democratic strength in the district is limited to municipalities such as Coatesville and Phoenixville in Chester County. There are also pockets of Democratic support in the city of Lancaster.

But this is solidly Republican turf: Dole's robust 53 percent in the district marked his second-best showing in Pennsylvania. Only in the adjacent 17th District did he do better.

1990 Population: 565,835. White 517,422 (91%), Black 29,578 (5%), Other 18,835 (3%). Hispanic origin 21,706 (4%). 18 and over 416,976 (74%), 62 and over 81,737 (14%). Median age: 33.

HOUSE ELECTIONS

1996 General		
Joseph R. Pitts (R)	124,511	(59%)
James G. Blaine (D)	78,598	(37%)
Robert S. Yorczyk (REF)	6,485	(3%)
1996 Primary		
Joseph R. Pitts (R)	26,515	(45%)
Karen Martynick (R)	15,314	(26%)
Stephen R. Gibble (R)	11,777	(20%)
Pat Sellers (R)	2,696	(5%)
Brad S. Fischer (R)	2,386	(4%)

CAMPAIGN FINANCE

	Receipts	Receipts from PACs	Expend-itures
1996			
Pitts (R)	$632,652	$180,568 (29%)	$616,874
Blaine (D)	$467,975	$12,000 (3%)	$405,264
Yorczyk (REF)	$3,947	0	$3,947

DISTRICT VOTE FOR PRESIDENT

1996		1992	
D	80,459 (37%)	D	72,719 (32%)
R	114,148 (53%)	R	109,037 (49%)
I	18,008 (8%)	I	43,279 (19%)

KEY VOTES

1997

Ban "partial birth" abortions Y

17 George W. Gekas (R)

Of Harrisburg — Elected 1982, 8th term

Biographical Information

Born: April 14, 1930, Harrisburg, Pa.

Education: Dickinson College, B.A. 1952; Dickinson School of Law, LL.B. 1958, J.D. 1958.

Military Service: Army, 1953-55.

Occupation: Lawyer.

Family: Wife, Evangeline Charas.

Religion: Greek Orthodox.

Political Career: Pa. House, 1967-75; Republican nominee for Pa. House, 1974; Pa. Senate, 1977-83; assistant district attorney.

Capitol Office: 2410 Rayburn Bldg. 20515; 225-4315.

Committees

Judiciary
Commercial & Administrative Law (chairman); Crime

In Washington: Name the issue, and when the roll is called, Gekas almost certainly can be found voting on the conservative side. Indeed, he remains best known in the House for his career-long crusade for the death penalty.

But in today's Republican-majority House, the fact that Gekas has had a long career in politics sets him a bit apart from the many recently arrived conservative Republican revolutionaries. Gekas holds a chairmanship now — on Judiciary's Commercial and Administrative Law Subcommittee — and more than once in the 104th Congress, he found himself working to tone down proposals emanating from zealous colleagues in the ranks of the GOP right.

Going back a number of years, Gekas and other conservatives on Judiciary had been complaining that the Legal Services Corporation was not a legal aid organization for the poor, but a tool of the left that spent taxpayers' money on class-action lawsuits and other efforts to advance a leftist agenda. LSC foes, though, made little headway under Democratic rule.

At last in the majority in 1995, Gekas sought to abolish the LSC in four years and convert its funding into a block grant for the states during that period. But in the changed context of the 104th, that position was regarded as too gradualist by a sizable corps of conservative members, who called for outright elimination of the organization. After one meeting with a group of fervent LSC critics, Gekas lamented, "I failed to get through to them."

And when the Judiciary Committee marked up immigration legislation, Gekas sought to add some softening touches. He said the bill could penalize immigrants seeking to reunite with their families living legally in the United States. He offered an amendment to restore visas for single adult children of citizens and permanent residents. Although that particular amendment was not adopted, the committee did alter the bill to address his concerns. Similarly, the committee accommodated Gekas' concerns about provisions in the bill that increased the amount of training and experience that people need to qualify for skilled worker immigrant visas.

Also, Gekas showed some sensitivity to his opponents' concerns about procedure when the House was considering a bill to provide for a cost-benefit analysis of new regulations. Some Republicans wanted to include separate legislation providing for the review and possible termination of existing federal regulations. Gekas, though, asked that they withdraw their amendment so hearings could be held on the new provisions.

When the Judiciary Committee took up term limits in 1995, Gekas offered an amendment that would have applied a 12-year limit only to consecutive terms served (as opposed to a 12-year lifetime limit favored by sponsor Rep. Bill McCollum of Florida). With the support of Democrats, Gekas' proposal was adopted. But when Democrats began saying they would offer a similar amendment on the House floor, Gekas backed away from supporting his own proposal.

But if 14 years in the House (and 14 before that in the Pennsylvania legislature) and the responsibilities of a chairmanship make Gekas a bit more accommodating of others' views, he is, as ever, a reliable party man on fiscal and social-policy issues, reflecting the ingrained conservatism of his central Pennsylvania district.

His fiscal conservatism was on display in May 1997 when the House took up a fiscal 1997 supplemental spending bill to provide aid to the flood-ravaged Midwest. Gekas offered an amendment to the emergency spending bill that would guarantee that government agencies would keep operating even if all 13 annual appropriations bills were not finished by the start of the fiscal year in October. Republicans want the provision in order to avoid any potential repeat of the politically disastrous 1995 government shutdown. But President Clinton vowed to veto the measure if the Gekas language remained, fearing an erosion of his leverage in the appropriations process. Even so, the House passed the amendment, 227-197.

PENNSYLVANIA 17
South Central — Harrisburg

One of the few places where Democrats can be found in the 17th is in Harrisburg, or more precisely, on the 65-acre state Capitol complex in Harrisburg. For outside the legislative chambers and the state government buildings, Democrats are few and far between. Harrisburg, the district's largest city, with just over 52,000 people, is about 100 miles west of Philadelphia and 150 miles east of Pittsburgh in Republican-minded central Pennsylvania.

Its modest skyline is dominated by a magnificent Capitol building topped with a dome inspired by the design of St. Peter's Basilica in Rome. Inside, ornate tiles and murals decorate the corridors and chambers. A grand stairway of Italian marble — modeled after the Opera House of Paris — is the centerpiece of the Rotunda.

Operating within these walls are many Democratic-voting state government workers and legislative staffers. The city's large black community — which accounts for more than half of Harrisburg's population — enhances the Democratic tilt.

As a whole, though, Dauphin County turns in Republican margins. The Harrisburg suburbs and outlying conservative small towns provide about 80 percent of the county vote. They helped George Bush carry Dauphin in 1988 and 1992, and Bob Dole carry it in 1996.

To get the real flavor of Dauphin County, most visitors skip Harrisburg and go to Hershey, otherwise known as "Chocolatetown, U.S.A." The massive chocolate factory stands at the center of town, emanating the most pleasing of industrial odors. The neat and well-tended company town even has street lights shaped like the bite-size Hershey's Kisses.

Another well-known site in Dauphin County is Three Mile Island, site of a 1979 nuclear accident that had a profound impact on many Americans' attitudes toward nuclear energy.

Besides Dauphin, the only other county wholly within the 17th is Lebanon County, in Pennsylvania Dutch Country. The bologna-making techniques of the Germans who first settled the area are still in evidence in the handful of bologna factories that operate here. True bologna connoisseurs know not to miss the annual Bologna Fest in August.

Like the rest of Dutch Country, Lebanon County evinces a strong strain of conservatism. With a 2-to-1 GOP voter registration advantage, the county gave Bill Clinton a mere 29 percent of the vote in 1992, and only 35 percent in 1996.

Across the scenic and shallow Susquehanna River on the western side of the 17th, the district takes in parts of Republican Perry and Cumberland counties. At its southeastern extreme, the district includes part of Republican Lancaster County, which has some of the suburbs of the city of Lancaster.

The district's Republican nature has benefitted Gekas, who has received at least 70 percent of the votes in all of his re-election bids.

1990 Population: 565,742. White 516,393 (91%), Black 37,793 (7%), Other 11,556 (2%). Hispanic origin 10,619 (2%). 18 and over 427,245 (76%), 62 and over 92,724 (16%). Median age: 34.

The man who once vowed to use "every parliamentary maneuver known to mankind" to ensure enactment of a death penalty bill has made capital punishment a personal crusade. At every twist and turn of the legislative process — particularly when he was in the minority — Gekas was there with a fistful of amendments, seeking to add the death penalty as punishment for an array of crimes.

During debate in the spring of 1994 on a broad anti-crime bill, Gekas was able to get an amendment approved that, among other things, eliminated a requirement that juries be told they are never required to impose the death penalty. Gekas argued that the bill's proposed legal procedures, such as requiring consideration of both aggravating and mitigating factors, would make it too hard to impose capital punishment.

Gekas introduced a measure in 1993 that would make the killing of foreign tourists a federal crime punishable by death. There had been a rash of slayings of foreign tourists visiting the United States, and Gekas said such killings could affect U.S. trade and diplomatic relations abroad.

He was an early advocate of expanding the list of capital crimes to include such actions as terrorist murders committed in the United States or against U.S. citizens abroad.

His first death penalty victory came in 1988 when heightened concern about illegal drug trafficking persuaded 299 House members to support capital punishment for drug-related murders.

Gekas does not believe that stronger gun controls will solve the problem of violent crime. In the 103rd Congress, he opposed a five-day waiting period requirement for the purchase of a handgun. Also, he opposed a measure banning 19 types of semiautomatic assault-style weapons, saying that only a fraction of crimes are committed with the firearms targeted under the bill. "Criminals today are laughing at what we're doing here," Gekas said. In 1996, he supported an unsuccessful effort to repeal the assault weapons ban.

Gekas sees tougher penalties as having a deterrent effect on crime, and he has carried that belief into his efforts to impose tougher penalties on "animal rights terrorists" — protesters who destroy animal research facilities. When the House took up a bill that would make it a federal crime to obstruct the entrance to an abortion clinic, he was angry that he was not allowed to offer an amendment extending the bill "to nuclear facility demonstrators, to animal rights demonstrators, to tree lumberjack demonstrators, to other kinds of facilities which also are recipients of the indignation of the public."

In the 104th Congress, Gekas was a dependable conservative vote on a host of issues before Judiciary — voting to repeal federal bilingual ballots requirements, requiring criminals to pay restitution to their victims, overhauling the welfare system, opposing abortion and the like.

His conservative credentials on fiscal policy also are firm. Gekas praised the House Republicans' "Contract With America" tax cut legislation as "truly a middle-class tax cut." He consistently sides with business in its legislative disputes with organized labor. In May 1996, he voted against raising the minimum wage by 90 cents an hour, although in August, when the wage increase won final passage in the House, he switched and voted "yea." The final version of the wage bill included other provisions sought by Republicans, including $10 billion in business tax cuts over five years, a $5,000 tax credit to offset the cost of adoption and an expansion of Individual Retirement Accounts.

At Home: A member of Harrisburg's small but influential Greek community, Gekas took the traditional path to political success in central Pennsylvania. He went to a local college and law school, became an assistant district attorney, then moved on to the state Capitol.

Gekas fashioned his state legislative career around a hard-line stand against crime. He managed capital punishment legislation, chaired the state Senate Judiciary Committee and wrote a tough mandatory sentencing bill.

Gekas encountered remarkably few obstacles on his path to Congress in 1982. He launched his campaign after Democratic Rep. Allen Ertel announced for governor and after the GOP-controlled General Assembly approved new district lines favoring the election of a Republican.

In the primary, Gekas was endorsed by the GOP in Dauphin County (Harrisburg) and won nomination handily over a candidate backed by the Lycoming County GOP. Gekas rolled over his November opponent, Dauphin County Commissioner Larry J. Hochendoner, who had lost to Gekas in a 1976 state Senate contest. With a 3-1 spending advantage, Gekas ran media ads almost daily showing him at an eatery waiting on tables and serving pizza.

Since his 1982 victory, Gekas has always racked up more than 70 percent of the vote in his re-elections, often running unopposed.

HOUSE ELECTIONS

1996 General		
George W. Gekas (R)	150,678	(72%)
Paul Kettl (D)	57,911	(28%)
1994 General		
George W. Gekas (R)	133,788	(100%)

Previous Winning Percentages: 1992 (70%) **1990** (100%) **1988** (100%) **1986** (74%) **1984** (73%) **1982** (58%)

CAMPAIGN FINANCE

	Receipts	Receipts from PACs	Expend-itures
1996			
Gekas (R)	$97,429	$78,266 (80%)	$110,578
Kettl (D)	$1,827	$500 (27%)	$1,476
1994			
Gekas (R)	$90,126	$64,645 (72%)	$86,839

DISTRICT VOTE FOR PRESIDENT

1996		1992	
D	81,189 (37%)	**D**	73,654 (32%)
R	116,456 (54%)	**R**	115,598 (50%)
I	17,995 (8%)	**I**	41,103 (18%)

KEY VOTES

1997	
Ban "partial birth" abortions	Y
1996	
Approve farm bill	Y
Deny public education to illegal immigrants	Y
Repeal ban on certain assault-style weapons	Y
Increase minimum wage	N
Freeze defense spending	N
Approve welfare overhaul	Y
1995	
Approve balanced-budget constitutional amendment	Y
Relax Clean Water Act regulations	Y
Oppose limits on environmental regulations	N
Reduce projected Medicare spending	Y
Approve GOP budget with tax and spending cuts	Y

VOTING STUDIES

	Presidential Support		Party Unity		Conservative Coalition	
Year	S	O	S	O	S	O
1996	35	65	95	4	98	2
1995	19	78	93	4	94	3
1994	41	59	93	7	94	3
1993	31	68	90	8	86	14
1992	74	20	90	6	83	13
1991	74	25	84	14	97	3

INTEREST GROUP RATINGS

Year	ADA	AFL-CIO	CCUS	ACU
1996	0	n/a	100	100
1995	5	0	100	76
1994	10	11	92	95
1993	5	0	91	92
1992	15	18	88	88
1991	5	25	100	90

18 Mike Doyle (D)

Of Pittsburgh — Elected 1994, 2nd term

Biographical Information
Born: Aug. 5, 1953, Pittsburgh, Pa.
Education: Penn State U., B.S. 1975.
Occupation: Insurance company executive; state legislative aide.
Family: Wife, Susan Erlandson; four children.
Religion: Roman Catholic.
Political Career: Swissvale Borough Council, 1977-81.
Capitol Office: 133 Cannon Bldg. 20515; 225-2135.

Committees
Science
Energy & Environment; Technology
Veterans' Affairs
Health

In Washington: Doyle is one of just four Democrats who swam against the national GOP tide in 1994 to capture a House seat that had been in Republican hands. Although his victory was a bright spot for Democrats on an otherwise gray election day, Doyle won by using some of the "time for a change" rhetoric popularized by GOP conservatives. The voters who elected him, Doyle said, were sending "a clear message: They wanted government waste and inefficiency eliminated; they wanted the pork-barrel, spendthrift ways of the past to change; they wanted our deficit brought down."

Doyle's voting record during his first term was consistent with his pledge to be a different kind of Democratic drummer. On House floor votes, he sided with his party and President Clinton just about two-thirds of the time, and he supported roughly half the bills derived from the House GOP's "Contract With America." Doyle's opposition to abortion is in keeping with the desires of his district, as is his support for organized labor.

Still, his instincts are sufficiently in line with the prevailing wisdom on the Democratic side of the aisle that he was named a sophomore class whip at the start of the 105th Congress. In his second term, he continues his service on the Science and Veterans' Affairs committees. Those assignments are relevant to a district that includes advanced medical research companies and world-renowned hospitals as well as numerous veterans in "The Deer Hunter" country of the Monongahela Valley.

In the electoral climate of 1994, there were only 13 Democrats hardy enough to win first House terms. Doyle had this advice for Clinton and House Democratic leaders in 1995: "We as a party need to define ourselves. If we oppose the Republican welfare plan, it better be with a Democratic welfare reform plan. I didn't come down here to point fingers and vote against guys with Rs after their names," Doyle told the Minneapolis Star Tribune.

Early in the 104th Congress, Doyle supported a welfare overhaul plan offered by Nathan Deal of Georgia, who at that point had not yet left the Democratic Party to become a Republican. Doyle also supported the Republican welfare bill that was enacted toward the end of the 104th.

In January 1995, Doyle actively promoted a proposed balanced-budget constitutional amendment offered by Charles W. Stenholm, D-Texas, and Dan Schaefer, R-Colo. Doyle was one of 66 Democrats to sign a letter to House Speaker Newt Gingrich offering support for the Stenholm-Schaefer plan, which won House approval.

But Doyle has challenged the GOP on its spending priorities, arguing that the wrong programs are being protected in a time of fiscal austerity. For example, he questioned the wisdom of increasing spending on certain missile defenses at the same time the House was voting to kill a program to assist the poor in paying their heating bills. He also thought that revenue shortfalls might better be made up by raising mining royalties on federal land than by cutting energy research programs.

From his seat on the Science Committee, Doyle resists calls from conservatives to eliminate the Energy Department. The committee voted in 1995 to preserve the agency, but to streamline its functions.

Doyle unsuccessfully offered an amendment before Science's Energy and Environment Subcommittee in June 1995 to restore $800 million in spending cuts to energy research and development programs. He argued that the proposed cuts of $1.4 billion would "virtually destroy" government research on fossil fuels, energy conservation and renewable energy sources such as wind power.

He continued fighting for fossil energy on the House floor, offering an amendment to the fiscal 1997 science authorization bill that would have restored $122 million in energy research and development funding. It was defeated, 173-245.

Doyle carefully kept his energy spending desires within budgetary frameworks that would not raise the deficit. He was relentless in finding

PENNSYLVANIA 18
Pittsburgh suburbs; Clairton; McKeesport

The story of the Mon Valley is surely one of America's grandest boom-and-bust tales. The denizens of the Monongahela Valley were at the forefront of establishing America as the world's industrial giant in the years leading up to and through World War II. But in the post-industrial decades since, this once-proud region has withered.

It all began in 1851, when the first steel mill opened. Production expanded so rapidly that the local labor pool was quickly exhausted, forcing U.S. Steel to place advertisements in European newspapers seeking workers.

Thousands of Hungarians, Irish, Italians, Poles, Russians, Serbs and Ukrainians were among those who heeded the call; by the late 1940s, U.S. Steel employed 80,000 here.

The company controlled all facets of life. Transportation systems were designed to move workers efficiently at shift changes. Local government and politics were dictated by U.S. Steel policies, particularly before the United Steelworkers union came into existence in 1942.

But after World War II expansion, the steel industry began its downward spiral. And as the steel works began closing, the towns that lived and breathed with the industry drew their last gasps.

By the mid-1980s, declining population and loss of industry slashed the tax bases of such Allegheny County towns as Homestead, Duquesne and McKeesport. Clairton — the setting for the movie "The Deer Hunter" — had to furlough its entire police force and turn off the street lights. Just as telling was the closing of the McKeesport McDonald's restaurant.

These desperate conditions were reflected in the Valley's voting patterns. Angry and unemployed workers voted for Democrat Walter F. Mondale in 1984; one local steelworkers official said, "In this area, if Ronald Reagan bought a cemetery, people would quit dying." In 1988, Michael S. Dukakis posted even bigger victory margins in areas that now make up the 18th.

Today, despite the massive job losses, the steelworkers union, building trades council and the United Mine Workers still hold sway; Democrats make up more than two-thirds of the 18th's registration.

The steelworkers who were able to find new employment — mostly in lower-paying service jobs — proved steadfast in their support of Democratic candidates in 1991, when Harris Wofford won 57 percent here in the special Senate election against Allegheny County native Dick Thornburgh, the former governor and U.S. attorney general. Bill Clinton easily beat George Bush here in 1992 and Bob Dole in 1996, though Dole narrowed the margin.

Outside the Mon Valley, the 18th contains northern, eastern and southern Pittsburgh suburbs.

Located entirely within the bounds of Allegheny County, the 18th also includes the middle-class areas of Penn Hills, Shaler and Monroeville, along with the old-money GOP communities of Fox Chapel and Mount Lebanon.

1990 Population: 565,781. White 516,212 (91%), Black 43,969 (8%), Other 5,600 (1%). Hispanic origin 3,299 (1%). 18 and over 447,927 (79%), 62 and over 126,757 (22%). Median age: 38.

ways to argue around opponents to his priorities.

Faced with a letter from an interest group noting the high levels of pollution resulting from coal and oil use, Doyle posited, "I could not state a better argument for fossil energy R&D than this. This [opposition] statement makes it sound as if fossil research was trying to find more ways to make it harmful to use these fuels when that is the very purpose of these programs, to find more efficient ways and cleaner ways to burn fossil fuel."

Doyle opposed the tax cuts sought by Republicans as part of their budget-balancing plan, noting that deficit spending had soared after major tax cuts were enacted in the early 1980s.

At Home: Doyle won a battle of former legislative aides in 1994 to return to Democratic hands the suburban Pittsburgh 18th, which was held for two terms by Republican Rick Santorum before he moved up to the Senate.

A longtime chief of staff to state Sen. Frank A. Pecora, Doyle capitalized on the district's Democratic nature to defeat Republican John McCarty, a former aide to the late Sen. John Heinz who tried to cast the contest as a referendum on their respective patrons.

Before Congress, Doyle had a long record of involvement in suburban Pittsburgh politics. After taking a degree in community development from Penn State, he returned to his hometown of Swissvale (just east of Pittsburgh) in the mid-1970s. He entered the insurance business, became involved in community affairs as executive director of the Turtle Creek Valley Citizens Union and was elected to the Swissvale Borough Council, where he served as finance and recreation chairman.

In 1979, he became chief of staff to Pecora, who like Doyle was a recent convert to the Democratic Party. In 1992, Pecora fought through a crowded Democratic primary to win the right to challenge Santorum, only to lose decisively in November.

With Santorum running statewide in 1994, Doyle tried his hand at the open 18th, and he survived a seven-person primary, winning the Democratic nomination with 20 percent of the vote. Doyle stressed that unlike some of the other Democratic contenders, he was not a lawyer. "Sending another lawyer to Washington is like trying to put out a fire with gasoline" he said in one campaign ad.

In the general election, Doyle was not well-known across the district, but neither was GOP nominee McCarty. And while the candidates had some issue differences, neither campaigned as strongly ideological. "There's not a whole lot of areas where we don't agree," McCarty said, "so it comes down to background."

The race never emerged from the shadow of Pennsylvania's high-profile Senate and gubernatorial contests, and that led to a re-emergence of the district's Democratic leanings, which Santorum had twice countered with high-energy, aggressively conservative House campaigns. Doyle beat McCarty by 10 percentage points.

In 1996, the Pittsburgh Post-Gazette thought Republican lawyer David B. Fawcett held greater potential than Doyle and his "solid but uninspired leadership." Although the paper endorsed Fawcett, it was embarrassed when he doctored one of its photographs to depict Doyle with money bags in his hands. Neither this tactic nor the endorsement helped Fawcett much and Doyle won re-election by a 16-point margin, taking 56 percent of the ballots cast.

HOUSE ELECTIONS

1996 General		
Mike Doyle (D)	120,410	(56%)
David B. Fawcett (R)	86,829	(40%)
Richard Edward Caligiuri (I)	6,859	(3%)
1996 Primary		
Mike Doyle (D)	45,967	(74%)
Joseph Rudolph (D)	15,822	(26%)
1994 General		
Mike Doyle (D)	101,784	(55%)
John McCarty (R)	83,881	(45%)

CAMPAIGN FINANCE

	Receipts	Receipts from PACs	Expend-itures
1996			
Doyle (D)	$532,747	$284,127 (53%)	$528,291
Fawcett (R)	$346,020	$27,950 (8%)	$343,898
1994			
Doyle (D)	$385,317	$173,082 (45%)	$381,733
McCarty (R)	$362,833	$79,436 (22%)	$362,091

DISTRICT VOTE FOR PRESIDENT

1996		1992	
D	119,926 (52%)	**D**	137,507 (52%)
R	89,563 (39%)	**R**	80,795 (31%)
I	19,687 (9%)	**I**	46,754 (18%)

KEY VOTES

1997	
Ban "partial birth" abortions	Y
1996	
Approve farm bill	N
Deny public education to illegal immigrants	Y
Repeal ban on certain assault-style weapons	N
Increase minimum wage	Y
Freeze defense spending	Y
Approve welfare overhaul	Y
1995	
Approve balanced-budget constitutional amendment	Y
Relax Clean Water Act regulations	Y
Oppose limits on environmental regulations	Y
Reduce projected Medicare spending	N
Approve GOP budget with tax and spending cuts	N

VOTING STUDIES

	Presidential Support		Party Unity		Conservative Coalition	
Year	**S**	**O**	**S**	**O**	**S**	**O**
1996	66	34	66	34	63	37
1995	66	34	74	26	66	34

INTEREST GROUP RATINGS

Year	ADA	AFL-CIO	CCUS	ACU
1996	55	n/a	44	32
1995	75	83	50	36

19 Bill Goodling (R)

Of Jacobus — Elected 1974, 12th term

Biographical Information
Born: Dec. 5, 1927, Loganville, Pa.
Education: U. of Maryland, B.S. 1953; Western Maryland College, M.Ed. 1956; Pennsylvania State U., 1960-62.
Military Service: Army, 1946-48.
Occupation: Public school superintendent.
Family: Wife, Hilda Wright; two children.
Religion: Methodist.
Political Career: Dallastown School Board president, 1964-67.

Capitol Office: 2263 Rayburn Bldg. 20515; 225-5836.

Committees
Education & Workforce (chairman)
Early Childhood, Youth & Families; Employer-Employee Relations; Postsecondary Education, Training & Life-Long Learning
International Relations
International Operations & Human Rights

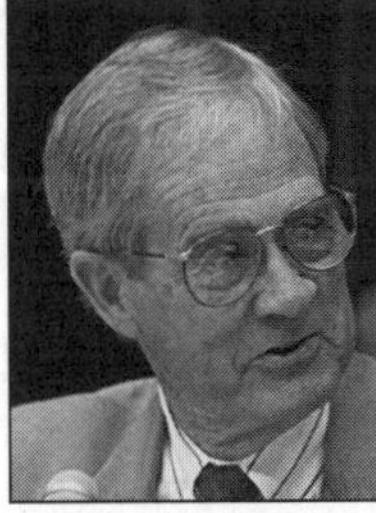

In Washington: When Democrats controlled the House, Goodling was ranking Republican on the Education and Labor Committee. After the GOP won the House majority in 1994, Goodling became chairman of the Economic and Educational Opportunities Committee for the 104th Congress. Now in the 105th, Goodling chairs the Education and the Workforce Committee. It is the same committee in all three instances; the name-changing reflects the GOP's effort to underscore that it wants Congress to look at both schools and jobs with employers' needs in mind, rejecting the traditional Democratic orientation toward teachers and big labor unions.

Whatever the committee's name, Goodling has been his party's standard-bearer on a host of issues that pit conservatives against organized labor and other liberal elements in the Democratic Party. For example, after the GOP leadership in May 1996 reluctantly consented to floor consideration of a higher minimum wage, Goodling tried unsuccessfully to amend the bill to exempt small businesses' (those with annual sales of $500,000 or less) new hires. That proposal was labeled a "poison pill" by President Clinton, who threatened to veto any legislation containing it. The House rejected the Goodling amendment, 196-229.

Goodling and House Republican leaders maintained that the proposal would merely reinstate a provision enacted by a Democratic Congress in 1989 but nullified by subsequent administrative interpretations. But Secretary of Labor Robert B. Reich branded the proposal "a dramatic leap backward from current law — effectively exempting virtually all new employees of two-thirds of all firms."

The uproar over the amendment — dubbed "the Goodling surprise" by Charles E. Schumer, D-N.Y. — was due in part to its sudden appearance late in the legislative process. Republicans had not had much time to research the proposal, and that compromised their ability to defend it against Democratic attack. Goodling maintained that the intentions and effect of his amendment were being badly distorted. Just before his amendment went down to defeat, he complained: "If we tell the Big Lie enough times, we will believe it ourselves. If we tell it more, we will have others believe it."

Goodling's committee approved legislation in June 1995 to nullify an executive order by Clinton barring companies with federal contracts of more than $100,000 from permanently replacing striking employees. The 22-16 party-line vote came after nearly two hours of partisan debate. Clinton had issued the executive order in March 1995 after the 103rd Congress failed to pass legislation barring private firms from permanently hiring replacements for strikers. Goodling said Clinton's action "sidestepped" the legislative process and ran counter to the legislative intent expressed by Congress. He also suggested that Clinton's ban would lead to more strikes and more protracted labor disputes, slowing federal contract work.

In the 104th and again in the 105th, Goodling helped lead the fight for legislation allowing private employers to offer their employees a choice between compensatory time off and overtime pay. The House passed the measure, 222-210, in March 1997. A similar bill had passed the House in the 104th as a top priority of the chamber's new majority, but it moved no further.

Opponents argued that workers could be coerced into accepting one form of compensation rather than the other and they could be subject to discrimination or harassment for not heeding the company's wishes. Clinton threatened to veto the bill.

To counterattacks from organized labor, Goodling proposed an amendment on the House floor to exempt employees who worked less than 1,000 hours for a single employer and to reduce, from 240 hours to 160, the compensatory time a company could allow an employee to "bank" in a year. The amendment passed, 408-19. The House also approved, 390-36, an amendment by Allen Boyd, D-Fla., to "sunset" the legislation five years after it becomes law.

PENNSYLVANIA 19
South Central — York

Republicans running statewide in Pennsylvania are boosted by electoral dominance in a T-shaped part of the state that begins on the Maryland border and rises north, where it fans out along the New York border. The 19th is at the base of the "T."

This placid farm country rests on the western fringe of Pennsylvania Dutch Country, taking in all of sparsely populated Adams and populous York counties, and most of Cumberland County to the north. The Susquehanna River forms the eastern border with the 16th and 17th districts.

Democrats are limited to what passes for urbanized areas in the reliably Republican 19th. More than half the population lives in suburbs, small towns or rural areas.

With its solidly Republican character, about the only skirmishing that occurs here is when hundreds of Civil War enthusiasts stage reenactments at Gettysburg National Military Park, site of one of the war's bloodiest battles.

The counties of the 19th stayed true to their Republican roots even as Bill Clinton captured the Keystone State in the last two presidential elections. GOP nominee Bob Dole captured 52 percent of the vote in the district in 1996.

In Adams County, the heavy Republican vote is leavened somewhat by Gettysburg College. With 7,000 residents, Gettysburg is the largest town in Adams County. The others are rural farming villages. Still, Dole polled 52 percent in the county, his districtwide percentage.

Democrats are mostly concentrated in York, the district's largest city and the nation's capital for a brief period in 1777-78 when the British occupied Philadelphia. Then, nearby forges turned out munitions for patriot troops. More recently, local industries have been making barbells and assembling Harley-Davidson motorcycles. Clinton polled 39 percent in York County, slightly higher than his overall 38 percent in the district.

A relatively short ride from Baltimore along Interstate 83, York — and its suburbs such as Springettsbury Township — experienced moderate growth in the 1980s as newcomers in search of lower taxes and affordable real estate moved in. One sure sign of York's status in the Baltimore orbit is an Orioles baseball store.

Another source of Democratic votes in York County is the pretzel and potato chip makers of Hanover. Outside these areas, however, the conservative Pennsylvania Dutch ethic dominates the rural countryside.

Among Cumberland County's population centers is Carlisle, a supply center for expeditions against the French during the French and Indian War, and later an active station along the Underground Railroad.

The West Shore suburbs — across the Susquehanna from Harrisburg — are home to state employees and blue-collar workers who live in Lemoyne and New Cumberland. The 17th District creeps across the river to grab East Pennsboro Township, Mechanicsburg and Shiremanstown, but affluent Camp Hill, home to the Book of the Month Club, is in the 19th.

1990 Population: 565,831. White 542,646 (96%), Black 14,769 (3%), Other 8,416 (1%). Hispanic origin 7,489 (1%). 18 and over 432,100 (76%), 62 and over 91,193 (16%). Median age: 34.

A former teacher, principal and school board president, Goodling through his years in the House minority supported an array of federal education programs, including the school lunch program, Head Start and Even Start. But as chairman, he has hewn to the conservative line on the educational front as well.

Goodling objected to the Clinton administration's education-loan program that bypassed banks to lend money directly to students. He said the Education Department had little or no experience at collecting money. "All they do is hand out the money," he said in November 1995. "Getting it back is a lot harder."

In February 1995, Goodling and his fellow Republicans came under fire for proposing to replace school breakfast and lunch programs with block grants to the states. Clinton said it would be a "terrible mistake," and House Minority Leader Richard A. Gephardt called it "mean-spirited."

Goodling countered the criticism: "The federal government simply cannot dictate every detail for every state and every local community and expect that the money is going to be spent in the best and most effective way possible."

Still, Goodling can point to some accomplishments in his time with the gavel. Congress in May 1996 cleared legislation making it easier for schools to show that they have met new federal nutritional guidelines for their lunch and breakfast programs. The bill eased Agriculture Department regulations designed to implement a 2-year-old congressional mandate to make school meals more nutritious and to lower their salt and fat content. Schools could use "any reasonable approach" to comply.

"As long as schools are serving healthy, nutritious meals, it shouldn't matter how individual schools meet the dietary guidelines," said Goodling, who sponsored the bill. "The bottom line is that schools know best what children will eat."

He agreed to try to work with Clinton on education issues in the 105th Congress after meeting with the president at the White House in February 1997.

Goodling said he indicated to Clinton that he agreed with two and one-half of the president's three goals for education. "I agree every 8-year-old must be able to read; I agree every 12-year-old must be able to log on to the Internet; and I agree with one-half of his goal concerning the lifetime learning of all Americans," Goodling said. "However, I believe it is demeaning to the 75 percent of Americans who do not receive a college degree to say that all 18-year-olds must go to college."

At a hearing with Education Secretary Richard W. Riley in March 1997, Goodling said, "Before we can consider major new initiatives to expand the federal role in education, I think we first need to take a step back and ask, 'What is working and what isn't in the programs we have now?'" Goodling said the committee ought to continue its study of all the 760 federal education programs before weighing Clinton's initiatives.

Meanwhile, he is working to try to reauthorize and revise the Individuals with Disabilities Education Act (IDEA), introducing legislation virtually identical to a measure that died in the Senate in 1996. The education legislation has had strong bipartisan support in the 21 years since it guaranteed a disabled child's right to a free education and allocated money to help provide it. Goodling has tried to rewrite the federal funding formula and to give schools more leeway to discipline unruly students who are disabled.

In November 1995, after House approval of a rule banning most gifts to members, Goodling issued a news release praising the new regulations. "I absolutely support a strict gift ban prohibiting the acceptance of any gift, regardless of value," he declared. "This reform should help restore the public's faith in Congress."

His news release said he backed the resolution. But the official Congressional Record did not concur: It listed Goodling as one of six members who voted against the resolution, which passed with 422 votes. "He's dead certain he voted for it," said a Goodling spokesman. "We're at a loss to explain what happened."

At Home: Goodling had a surprisingly difficult primary in 1996, polling only 55 percent against Charles Gerow, the state chairman of Citizens Against Government Waste. Gerow argued that it was time for a change, and rekindled the ethics allegations that had hurt Goodling in 1992 (when he had to defend his 430 overdrafts at the House bank). Once he won the 1996 primary, however, Goodling had little trouble in the overwhelmingly Republican district, receiving 63 percent of the vote against policy analyst Scott L. Chronister.

Until his first run for Congress in 1974, Goodling had held just one elective office — on the Dallastown School Board. But he had a locally famous name. He was bidding to succeed his father, George A. Goodling, who had held the seat for six terms in the 1960s and '70s.

The younger Goodling emerged as the winner in a seven-way primary in 1974, outdistancing the favored John W. Eden, who once had challenged Goodling's father. In November, he won with 51 percent and did not have another tough election until 1992, when against two opponents he prevailed with a 45 percent plurality.

HOUSE ELECTIONS

1996 General		
Bill Goodling (R)	130,716	(63%)
Scott L. Chronister (D)	74,944	(36%)
Francis Worley (FWC)	3,194	(2%)
1996 Primary		
Bill Goodling (R)	24,014	(55%)
Charles Gerow (R)	19,700	(45%)
1994 General		
Bill Goodling (R)	124,496	(100%)

Previous Winning Percentages: **1992** (45%) **1990** (100%) **1988** (77%) **1986** (73%) **1984** (76%) **1982** (71%) **1980** (76%) **1978** (79%) **1976** (71%) **1974** (51%)

CAMPAIGN FINANCE

	Receipts	Receipts from PACs		Expend-itures
1996				
Goodling (R)	$298,134	$3,016	(1%)	$305,541
Chronister (D)	$65,794	$31,999	(49%)	$63,803
1994				
Goodling (R)	$56,406	$5,920	(10%)	$50,718

DISTRICT VOTE FOR PRESIDENT

1996		1992	
D	81,301 (38%)	**D**	74,445 (34%)
R	112,205 (52%)	**R**	104,258 (47%)
I	18,970 (9%)	**I**	43,759 (20%)

KEY VOTES

1997	
Ban "partial birth" abortions	Y
1996	
Approve farm bill	Y
Deny public education to illegal immigrants	Y
Repeal ban on certain assault-style weapons	Y
Increase minimum wage	N
Freeze defense spending	N
Approve welfare overhaul	Y
1995	
Approve balanced-budget constitutional amendment	Y
Relax Clean Water Act regulations	†
Oppose limits on environmental regulations	N
Reduce projected Medicare spending	Y
Approve GOP budget with tax and spending cuts	Y

VOTING STUDIES

	Presidential Support		Party Unity		Conservative Coalition	
Year	**S**	**O**	**S**	**O**	**S**	**O**
1996	37	63	86	11	86	12
1995	17	79	89	8	86	9
1994	46	54	89	9	81	14
1993	41	57	85	13	86	11
1992	72	28	83	14	81	19
1991	68	23	70	20	78	8

INTEREST GROUP RATINGS

Year	ADA	AFL-CIO	CCUS	ACU
1996	10	n/a	94	95
1995	5	0	96	84
1994	10	33	92	90
1993	10	17	90	87
1992	10	33	75	83
1991	20	25	70	73

20 Frank R. Mascara (D)

Of Charleroi — Elected 1994, 2nd term

Biographical Information

Born: Jan. 19, 1930, Belle Vernon, Pa.
Education: California University of Pennsylvania, B.S. 1972.
Military Service: Army, 1946-47.
Occupation: Accountant; educator.
Family: Wife, Delores; four children.
Religion: Roman Catholic.
Political Career: Washington County Controller, 1974-79; Washington County Commission chairman, 1980-95; sought Democratic nomination for U.S. House, 1992.
Capitol Office: 314 Cannon Bldg. 20515; 225-4665.

Committees

Transportation & Infrastructure
Surface Transportation; Water Resources & Environment
Veterans' Affairs
Benefits

In Washington: However much Bill Clinton talks about forging a modern-style, baby-boomer "New Democrat" image for his party, Mascara serves to remind that the House Democratic Caucus still includes a contingent of older-fashioned, pro-labor, pro-public works, ethnic New Deal Democrats from districts that are struggling to adapt to new economic realities. Mascara's blue-collar constituents, hurt by declining employment in the steel and coal industries, are hard-pressed to find a role in the global marketplace.

In his floor speeches, Mascara often refers to his district's economic woes. Once, when rising to support an increase in the minimum wage, he said, "As my colleagues know, I represent southwestern Pennsylvania, an area of the country that lost 200,000 jobs in the 1980s when the winds of change blew through the steel mills and the coal mines. Many of my constituents are now left to subsist on $4.25 per hour, or $8,840 per year, hardly a living wage and nowhere near enough to raise a family."

Mascara first won his House seat at an age when most people are planning their retirement; he is a generation older than most of the members first elected with him in 1994, and the limited-government, less-regulation philosophy espoused by many younger members is a world apart from Mascara's beliefs, which are shaped by his working-class roots. Mascara's father died as a result of a steel mill accident, and his grandfather died in a mining accident; Mascara paid for the headstone on his grandfather's grave in Belle Vernon, Pa., which carries the epitaph "Coal Miner."

Early in the 104th Congress, Mascara objected to a GOP measure to impose a temporary moratorium on the implementation of federal regulations. With Democrat Bob Wise of West Virginia, he offered an amendment to the measure and told the House that passing it was a matter of "life and death."

Their amendment would have exempted aircraft, mine and nuclear safety regulations from the moratorium. "We know firsthand about one of the world's most dangerous occupations, working in the mines," Mascara told the House. "While in good times our communities have benefited economically from the mining industry, they have also experienced the tragedy of mining accidents and poor health that can result from years of breathing coal dust." The amendment was rejected, 194-228.

Mascara also voted against a provision of the GOP's "Contract With America" that required federal agencies to perform a battery of analyses, tests and cost comparisons to justify any new federal regulation. And although he voted for a contract item making it more difficult for Congress to impose new regulations without providing funds for state and local governments to comply, he tried to amend the "unfunded mandates" bill to exempt child support enforcement laws.

"I am sure my colleagues on both sides of the aisle would agree that our job is to insure that state and local governments collect every dollar possible from deadbeat dads, or any parent who has shirked their responsibilities and left their family to live off of welfare," Mascara told the House. But his amendment was rejected, 158-259.

Although Mascara finds little to like in the GOP's fiscal-policy agenda, he is one of the more conservative voices in his party on social issues, often siding with culturally conservative Republicans. He opposes abortion, he voted to repeal the ban on certain semiautomatic assault-style weapons and he favors a constitutional amendment to prohibit flag desecration.

Unlike most of the liberal Democrats in the House, Mascara was keen on overhauling the welfare system. In mid-July 1996, he was one of just 30 Democrats voting on the House floor for a Republican welfare plan; later in the month, the GOP made enough concessions in that plan to secure a pledge from Clinton that he would sign it. Also, during the debate on overhauling immigration law, Mascara voted for a GOP measure denying public education to illegal immigrants.

Mascara initially was assigned to the Govern-

PENNSYLVANIA 20
Southwest — The Mon Valley; Washington

With West Virginia on its southern and western borders, the 20th is Pennsylvania's own version of Appalachia. Much of the district is rural, poor and, like its neighbor, traditionally Democratic.

Politics in the 20th is not for the weak of heart. From the industrial areas along the Monongahela River to the coal fields of Fayette and Greene counties, hardball politics is the rule. Then-United Mine Workers President W. A. "Tony" Boyle was convicted here in the 1969 murder of union rival Joseph A. "Jock" Yablonski.

Part of the reason is the sense of economic desperation that often grips the region. Coal mining has always been subject to boom-and-bust cycles, and with mining's increasing mechanization and the shift of production from Eastern mines to those out West, unemployment is high in Fayette and Greene coal country. The UMW's clout has diminished, but the union remains an important political force.

Along the Monongahela, the slow demise of the steel industry has led to massive job losses from Donora to Brownsville, the borough that marks the unofficial end to the industrialized Mon Valley.

But Washington County has witnessed recent economic development with the construction near Canonsburg of a 600-acre technological park called Southpointe. Outside of Pittsburgh and Philadelphia, this is the most reliably Democratic region in the state.

In 1992, Washington, Fayette and Greene counties voted for Bill Clinton by ratios of more than 2-to-1. He fell short of that mark four years later in all but Fayette, though he easily won all three counties. Mascara won in Fayette and Greene counties by a nearly 2-to-1 ratio in 1996.

The population centers of the 20th are the city of Washington (Washington County) and Greensburg (Westmoreland County). The city of Washington is home to the county's old factory-owning families and occasionally supports Republicans. Peters Township, a white-collar bedroom community for Pittsburgh commuters on the Allegheny County line, also is receptive to GOP candidates.

Greensburg, Westmoreland's county seat, has no major military installation, but it was perhaps the U.S. town most tragically touched by the Persian Gulf War. Eleven reservists of the 14th Quartermaster Detachment, based in Greensburg, were killed by an Iraqi Scud missile attack one week after arriving in Saudi Arabia.

The 20th is one of three House districts that take in a part of Westmoreland. Allegheny County is shared by four districts. The only counties wholly contained in the 20th are Washington, where more than one-third of the people in the 20th live, and Greene. The Allegheny portion of the district, where Mascara got 41 percent of the vote in 1996, was the only county he did not carry.

1990 Population: 565,815. White 544,113 (96%), Black 17,889 (3%), Other 3,813 (1%). Hispanic origin 2,877 (1%). 18 and over 436,822 (77%), 62 and over 114,810 (20%). Median age: 37.

ment Reform and Veterans' Affairs committees, then in the summer of 1995, when Texan Greg Laughlin switched to become a Republican, he got Laughlin's seat on the Transportation and Infrastructure Committee.

There one of his causes is pushing for completion of a local highway project, the Mon-Fayette Expressway. Mascara said he and his constituents believe that once the highway is built, "like the playing field in the movie 'Field of Dreams' . . . businesses and jobs will follow."

In 1996, Mascara strongly supported Transportation Committee Chairman Bud Shuster, a Pennsylvania Republican, in his effort to move four transportation trust funds "off budget." Mascara concurred with Shuster's assertion that the funds should be spent on highways and other infrastructure projects, not hoarded to reduce the size of the federal deficit.

"Americans pay 18.4 cents federal tax on every gallon of gas they purchase and a 10-percent excise tax on all airline tickets," Mascara said. "Last year alone, these taxes added up to nearly $30 billion. I find it simply inexcusable that the government refuses to release these funds at a time when our nation's infrastructure is crumbling."

The 1995 base closure and realignment list contained some good news for Mascara and the 20th, sparing two local military bases — the 911th Air Reserve Station at Pittsburgh International Airport and the Charles E. Kelley Support Facility in Oakdale, Pa.

At Home: Mascara's home turf is Washington County, which has more than one-third of the people in the 20th District. An Army veteran and accountant, he served as Washington County Controller from 1974-79 and was chairman of the county Board of Commissioners from 1980 until he took his House seat in 1995.

Mascara first tried for the House in 1992, waging a Democratic primary challenge to veteran incumbent Austin J. Murphy. Murphy's stock started dropping when he was reprimanded by the House in 1987 for ethical lapses ranging from allowing another member to vote for him on the

House floor to keeping a "ghost employee" on his payroll.

By early 1992 there were rumors Murphy might retire, and Mascara and three other Democrats got busy running to succeed him. But Murphy did not step down, and even though it was revealed that he had written overdrafts at the House bank, he won renomination with 36 percent of the vote; Mascara finished second with 34 percent. A few days after the primary, news broke that Murphy was being investigated in connection with misdeeds at the House Post Office, and he squeaked to re-election in November with a 51 percent tally.

When Murphy decided not to seek a 10th term in 1994, Mascara was ready to run again. He stressed his experience as a mediator between management and labor, claiming credit for helping resolve labor disputes at a local hospital and a steel mill. He took 54 percent against two opponents in the Democratic primary and, given the Democratic traditions of the district, was rated a favorite over GOP nominee Mike McCormick, an investment adviser and political newcomer.

Their contest, however, was more competitive than expected, as McCormick tapped what benefited Republican candidates nationally: voter anger with the political status quo in Washington. Mascara's margin of victory was 6 percentage points, a showing that McCormick felt warranted his making another try for the House. But in the 1996 rematch, Mascara widened his advantage slightly, taking 54 percent of the vote, 8 percentage points ahead of McCormick.

HOUSE ELECTIONS

1996 General		
Frank R. Mascara (D)	113,394	(54%)
Mike McCormick (R)	97,004	(46%)
1994 General		
Frank R. Mascara (D)	95,251	(53%)
Mike McCormick (R)	84,156	(47%)

CAMPAIGN FINANCE

	Receipts	Receipts from PACs	Expend-itures
1996			
Mascara (D)	$573,937	$343,408 (60%)	$577,217
McCormick (R)	$383,715	$28,650 (7%)	$381,404
1994			
Mascara (D)	$497,196	$175,550 (35%)	$489,508
McCormick (R)	$363,327	$20,893 (6%)	$363,080

DISTRICT VOTE FOR PRESIDENT

	1996		1992
D	109,281 (50%)	**D**	121,815 (51%)
R	85,022 (39%)	**R**	69,802 (29%)
I	23,649 (11%)	**I**	48,249 (20%)

KEY VOTES

1997	
Ban "partial birth" abortions	Y
1996	
Approve farm bill	N
Deny public education to illegal immigrants	Y
Repeal ban on certain assault-style weapons	Y
Increase minimum wage	Y
Freeze defense spending	Y
Approve welfare overhaul	Y
1995	
Approve balanced-budget constitutional amendment	N
Relax Clean Water Act regulations	Y
Oppose limits on environmental regulations	Y
Reduce projected Medicare spending	N
Approve GOP budget with tax and spending cuts	N

VOTING STUDIES

	Presidential Support		Party Unity		Conservative Coalition	
Year	S	O	S	O	S	O
1996	70	30	70	29	75	24
1995	71	29	80	20	57	43

INTEREST GROUP RATINGS

Year	ADA	AFL-CIO	CCUS	ACU
1996	60	n/a	38	35
1995	80	100	42	40

21 Phil English (R)

Of Erie — Elected 1994, 2nd term

Biographical Information
Born: June 20, 1956, Erie, Pa.
Education: U. of Pennsylvania, B.A. 1979.
Occupation: State legislative aide.
Family: Wife, Christiane Weschler.
Religion: Roman Catholic.
Political Career: Erie County Controller, 1986-89; Republican nominee for Pa. treasurer, 1988.
Capitol Office: 1721 Longworth Bldg. 20515; 225-5406.

Committees
Science
Energy & Environment
Small Business
Empowerment
Ways & Means
Human Resources; Oversight

In Washington: When the House in May 1996 passed a 90-cent increase in the minimum wage, 93 Republicans voted for it. But four months earlier, when President Clinton in his State of the Union speech called on Congress to lift the wage floor, only one Republican stood and applauded: English.

The political composition of the 21st helps explain English's early support for raising the minimum wage. Organized labor has substantial electoral clout in the district, and in his two winning House elections, English hasn't had many votes to spare: He took 49 percent in 1994, and in 1996 won with 51 percent. English has quite a ways to go to match the popularity that his GOP predecessor in the 21st enjoyed with blue-collar voters: Tom Ridge won 65 percent or better in his five House re-elections, before moving up to Pennsylvania's governorship in 1994.

In addition to supporting a higher minimum wage, English also has taken labor's side on some other issues: He was one of only 44 Republicans to support a labor effort in July 1995 to protect the collective bargaining rights of mass transit workers, and in November 1995 he voted to ensure that employees of some small and medium-size railroads would receive severance pay if they lost their jobs because of a merger or acquisition. In September 1995, English was one of 22 Republicans opposed to a conservative-led effort to modify the 1935 National Labor Relations Act to enable non-union companies to establish worker-management groups to discuss business matters. The bill, known as the Teamwork for Employees and Management Act, was opposed by organized labor, which argued that the groups would become "company unions" captive to employers' demands.

In July 1996, English voted for a GOP-backed bill to allow businesses to offer their employees comp time in lieu of overtime pay. But when Republicans brought a slightly modified version of the bill to the floor in March 1997, English opposed it. Organized labor expressed fears that employees might be coerced into taking comp time when they really wanted overtime pay.

English in the 104th broke with most of his GOP colleagues to support the federal government's low-income energy assistance program, which helps poor families pay their heating bills. The program has long been a target of conservative budget-cutters, who see it as a relic from the energy crisis of the 1970s. English disagreed, telling the House that the program brings "life-saving heat" to nearly 6 million poor families. "To put it quite simply, this program insures many families in my district that they do not have to choose between eating or heating," he said.

To be sure, there is plenty in English's voting record for a partisan Democrat to dislike. He supported all the major items of the GOP's "Contract With America," and from his seat on the high-profile Ways and Means Committee, English has been a steadfast advocate of conservatives' efforts to overhaul welfare and restrain Medicare spending.

The Medicare debate caused some fireworks in English's district. He supported the GOP plan to cut $270 billion from projected Medicare spending growth over seven years. Democrats said this would drastically hurt Medicare beneficiaries, and English became a target of Project '95, a coalition of labor and consumer groups opposed to the GOP's Medicare plan. During Congress' October 1995 Columbus Day recess (just before Ways and Means was to vote on the Medicare proposal), Project '95 drove a steamroller down an Erie street with a poster-sized picture of English stuck to its side. The steamroller mowed down six gray-wigged mannequins.

That same month, English criticized Democrats for claiming that the Republicans were cutting the federal health insurance program to pay for tax cuts. "You have heard and will continue to hear that Republicans are cutting Medicare to pay for tax cuts," English told the House. "Members of this body who oppose saving Medicare have fabricated the Medicare-tax-cut connection because it is useful politically."

At town meetings and other gatherings in his

The state's third-largest after Philadelphia and Pittsburgh, Erie is Pennsylvania's forgotten big city. Even among Great Lakes neighbors Cleveland and Buffalo, Erie is a lesser light. But it is the population center of the 21st.

Local politics are Democratic, with two ethnic groups — Italians and Poles — vying for power. Actually, the first considerable immigration to the city was that of the Pennsylvania Dutch, followed by Italians, Poles and Russians. Italians settled on the West Side and Poles on the East Side. Together, the blue-collar communities worked on East Side assembly-line jobs at General Electric and other heavy industries.

More recently, though, younger Italians have begun a move out of the 6th Ward, toward such suburbs as Summit and Millcreek townships, where their traditional Democratic loyalties have weakened.

That mobility has largely been absent in the Polish community. The Polish East Side is now larger than the city's Italian community, and more Democratic. Organized labor is a force.

Local politics sometimes reflects the divisions between the two communities. In 1982, when a Pole defeated an Italian for the Democratic House nomination, many disappointed Italians supported Republican Tom Ridge in November, helping him win. His cordial relations with labor enabled him to stay in Congress until he won the governorship in 1994.

The independent and GOP voters outside the city make Erie County politically competitive. Ronald Reagan carried it in 1980 and 1984, but Democratic presidential candidates have carried it since then. With Ridge leading the GOP ticket, Erie County voted Republican for governor, senator and House in 1994.

Outside Erie County, where Democrats have

PENNSYLVANIA 21
Northwest — Erie

a healthy voter registration advantage, Republicans fare better. South of Erie, Crawford County toes the Republican line. The dairy farmers and retirees in the Conneaut Lake area backed Bob Dole in 1996. The county is divided between the 21st and 5th districts, but the 21st District portion includes what passes for the county's largest city, Meadville.

Butler County, another favorable area for Republicans, also backed Dole. The small city of Butler has a Democratic tradition, but the outlying areas are Republican. Most of the county is in the 21st, with the exception of some southern boroughs and townships that belong to the 4th.

The tone is more Democratic in industrial Mercer County. Shenango Valley steel towns such as Farrell, Hermitage, Sharon, Sharpsville and Wheatland vote Democratic like much of the rest of western Pennsylvania, and have been equally hard-hit by steel industry decline. The less-populous and industrial eastern section of the county is Republican.

Mercer and Erie counties both went heavily for Bill Clinton in 1996, allowing him to win the district by 9 percentage points. Both counties opted for the Democrat in the House race, too. But Republican English kept his losses to a minimum there and led by a big enough margin in Butler and Crawford counties to win re-election by less than 3,000 votes.

1990 Population: 565,802. White 538,923 (95%), Black 21,849 (4%), Other 5,030 (1%). Hispanic origin 4,471 (1%). 18 and over 425,058 (75%), 62 and over 100,741 (18%). Median age: 34.

district, English aggressively made the case that Republicans were not undermining Medicare, but working to "preserve and protect" it.

He sponsored a "lockbox" amendment to the Medicare bill that provided for placing all Medicare Part B cost-savings in a trust fund that would not be tapped until 2003. Ways and Means Democrats dismissed the scheme as an accounting gimmick aimed at drawing attention away from their accusation that Medicare savings would in fact help finance tax cuts. English also introduced a bill to create an independent commission to plot a strategy for Medicare.

Early in the 104th, English was critical of Democrats' notions for changing welfare, saying the Democratic plan "has cash flow problems. . . . [U]nder it, cash flows to minors, cash flows to aliens, cash flows to welfare families who have additional kids, and states are even required to pay cash to some who are not working."

By the spring of 1996, he was sounding a bit more conciliatory toward Clinton and congressional Democrats, saying "I'm not willing to let the perfect be the enemy of substantial reform. I would rather be able to say that I got something done. I might lose this election. I would like to be part of reforming the welfare system." In July 1996, Congress finally approved a welfare plan Clinton had agreed to sign; English voted for it.

After his narrow re-election in 1996, English said that he and most other members of the GOP class of 1994 had come to realize that "the public wanted us to slow our pace and be less partisan."

English was one of a handful in his class who expressed qualms about supporting Newt Gingrich for a second term as Speaker in early 1997, when the House ethics committee was wrapping up a probe that led to Gingrich being reprimanded for violating House ethics rules. English, though, ended up backing Gingrich.

At Home: The son of a patrician family, English has been a political animal since his youth. By his early 20s, he was a member of the GOP state committee. By age 30, he had held several jobs as a legislative aide in Harrisburg, including work for the Transportation and Labor and Industry committees of the Pennsylvania Senate.

English returned to Erie and won the office of city controller on a pledge to be a watchdog over the Democrat-dominated city government. In 1988, at the midpoint of his four-year term in that job, he sought the office of state treasurer. He ran an attention-getting campaign with a lighter side: Accusing his Democratic opponent of ducking debates with him, English showed up at one news event with a Peking duck. But while English impressed GOP officials with his knowledge of state fiscal issues, he lost by nearly 500,000 votes.

Thereafter, he switched roles, moving from candidate to strategist. He did not seek re-election as Erie city controller, traveling instead to the Pittsburgh suburbs to help a little-known underdog, Rick Santorum, organize his 1990 upset of Democratic Rep. Doug Walgren. Santorum returned the favor in 1994 during his successful Senate bid, stumping with English in the 21st.

For most of the early 1990s, English was back in Harrisburg, serving as chief of staff for Republican state Sen. Melissa Hart and honing his expertise on tax and social welfare issues.

When Ridge left the 21st to run for governor in 1994, English took up the candidate's mantle again. He encountered little trouble winning his party's nomination, while Democrats had a crowded, hotly competitive primary. Their eventual nominee, with 23 percent of the vote, was Bill Leavens, executive director of the Shenango Valley Chamber of Commerce. A business-oriented moderate, he said he had been approached by some GOP activists to run for Ridge's seat because they assumed he was a Republican.

Leavens tried to energize district Democrats by framing his contest against English in terms of class differences. He boasted of being the son of a Polish-American millworker and said English had never held a private sector job.

English responded with calls for a middle-class tax cut and his 18-point "Invest in Pennsylvania" plan for spurring business and industrial development. And he criticized Leavens as a "Clinton clone." In the end, the one-two punch of the national Republican tide and Ridge's successful gubernatorial campaign helped English prevail by a two-point margin.

In 1996, English faced lawyer Ronald A. DiNicola, who has a background similar to Ridge. Like Ridge, DiNicola has working-class roots, served in the military and earned a degree at Harvard University before becoming a lawyer. DiNicola, though, went on to practice law in California. He maintained a practice on the West Coast, even after moving back to Erie.

English intimated that his opponent was a carpetbagger, and he was able to mitigate the impact of negative advertising sponsored by the AFL-CIO by calling attention to his stands on issues such as the minimum wage increase. Even though Clinton won the 21st by 9 percentage points in presidential voting, English squeaked by again by 2 percentage points.

HOUSE ELECTIONS

1996 General		
Phil English (R)	106,875	(51%)
Ronald A. DiNicola (D)	104,004	(49%)
1994 General		
Phil English (R)	89,439	(49%)
Bill Leavens (D)	84,796	(47%)
Arthur E. Drew (I)	6,588	(4%)

CAMPAIGN FINANCE

	Receipts	Receipts from PACs	Expend-itures
1996			
English (R)	$1,256,083	$672,296 (54%)	$1,262,645
DiNicola (D)	$494,528	$184,373 (37%)	$478,871
1994			
English (R)	$464,166	$143,115 (31%)	$450,795
Leavens (D)	$471,524	$134,550 (29%)	$465,191

DISTRICT VOTE FOR PRESIDENT

1996		1992	
D	106,063 (49%)	**D**	105,538 (45%)
R	87,431 (40%)	**R**	81,003 (35%)
I	22,508 (10%)	**I**	47,923 (20%)

KEY VOTES

1997	
Ban "partial birth" abortions	Y
1996	
Approve farm bill	Y
Deny public education to illegal immigrants	Y
Repeal ban on certain assault-style weapons	Y
Increase minimum wage	Y
Freeze defense spending	?
Approve welfare overhaul	Y
1995	
Approve balanced-budget constitutional amendment	Y
Relax Clean Water Act regulations	Y
Oppose limits on environmental regulations	Y
Reduce projected Medicare spending	Y
Approve GOP budget with tax and spending cuts	Y

VOTING STUDIES

	Presidential Support		Party Unity		Conservative Coalition	
Year	**S**	**O**	**S**	**O**	**S**	**O**
1996	46	53	79	18	76	16
1995	26	72	89	9	89	8

INTEREST GROUP RATINGS

Year	ADA	AFL-CIO	CCUS	ACU
1996	10	n/a	88	74
1995	15	25	92	84

RHODE ISLAND

Governor: Lincoln C. Almond (R)
First elected: 1994
Length of term: 4 years
Term expires: 1/99
Salary: $69,900
Term limit: 2 terms
Phone: (401) 277-2080
Born: June 16, 1936; Pawtucket, R.I.
Education: U. of Rhode Island, B.S. 1958; Boston U., J.D. 1961.
Military Service: Navy Submarine Service Reserve.
Occupation: Lawyer.
Family: Wife, Marilyn A. Johnson; two children.
Religion: Episcopalian.
Political Career: Republican candidate for U.S. House, 1968; U.S. attorney; Republican nominee for governor, 1978.

Lt. Gov.: Bernard A. Jackvony (R)
First elected: Appointed 1/97
Length of term: 4 years
Term expires: 1/99
Salary: $52,000
Phone: (401) 277-2371

State election official: (401) 277-2345
Democratic headquarters: (401) 736-7200
Republican headquarters: (401) 453-4100

REDISTRICTING

Rhode Island retained its two House seats in reapportionment. The legislature passed the map May 14, 1992. The governor took no action on it, and the map became law May 22.

STATE LEGISLATURE

Legislature. Meets January-May.

Senate: 50 members, 2-year terms
1996 breakdown: 41D, 9R; 39 men, 11 women
Salary: $5/day
Phone: (401) 277-6655

House of Representatives: 100 members, 2-year terms
1996 breakdown: 84D, 16R; 72 men, 28 women
Salary: $5/day
Phone: (401) 277-2466

URBAN STATISTICS

City	Population
Providence	160,728
Mayor Vincent A. Cianci Jr., I	
Warwick	85,427
Mayor Lincoln Chafee, R	
Cranston	76,060
Mayor Michael A. Traficante, R	
Pawtucket	72,644
Mayor Robert Metivier, D	
East Providence	50,380
Mayor "city manager" Paul Lemont, D	

U.S. CONGRESS

Senate: 1 D, 1 R
House: 2 D, 0 R

TERM LIMITS

For state offices: No

ELECTIONS

1996 Presidential Vote

Bill Clinton	60%
Bob Dole	27%
Ross Perot	11%

1992 Presidential Vote

Bill Clinton	47%
George Bush	29%
Ross Perot	23%

1988 Presidential Vote

Michael S. Dukakis	56%
George Bush	44%

POPULATION

1990 population		1,003,464
1980 population		947,154
Percent change		+6%
Rank among states:		43
White		91%
Black		4%
Hispanic		5%
Asian or Pacific islander		2%
Urban		86%
Rural		14%
Born in state		91%
Foreign-born		9%
Under age 18	225,690	22%
Ages 18-64	627,227	63%
65 and older	150,547	15%
Median age		34.0

MISCELLANEOUS

Capital: Providence
Number of counties: 5
Per capita income: $18,840 (1991)
Rank among states: 19
Total area: 1,212 sq. miles
Rank among states: 50

Woonsocket
1
PROVIDENCE
North Providence
Pawtucket
Providence
Cranston
BRISTOL
Warwick
Bristol
2
KENT
NEWPORT (PT)
NEWPORT (PART)
NEWPORT (PT)
NEWPORT (PART)
Newport
WASHINGTON
Kingston
Westerly

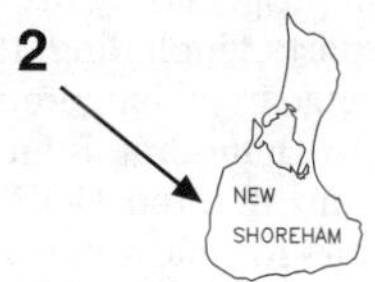

John H. Chafee (R)

Of Warwick — Elected 1976; 4th term

Biographical Information

Born: Oct. 22, 1922, Providence, R.I.
Education: Yale U., B.A. 1947; Harvard U., LL.B. 1950.
Military Service: Marine Corps, 1942-45, 1951-52.
Occupation: Lawyer.
Family: Wife, Virginia Coates; five children.
Religion: Episcopalian.
Political Career: R.I. House, 1957-63, minority leader, 1959-63; governor, 1963-69; defeated for re-election as governor, 1968; secretary of the Navy, 1969-72; Republican nominee for U.S. Senate, 1972.
Capitol Office: 505 Dirksen Bldg. 20510; 224-2921.

Committees

Environment & Public Works (chairman)
Finance
Health Care; International Trade; Social Security & Family Policy (chairman)
Select Intelligence
Joint Taxation

In Washington: Chafee, a former Navy secretary and Marine, has to navigate difficult waters with the Senate under Republican control. Long a maverick vote within the GOP Conference, he managed during the 104th Congress to remain a player on budget, health and environmental issues despite working in a chamber dominated by colleagues who don't agree with him on very much.

"Moderate doesn't mean you're wishy-washy on the issues," Chafee states. "It means you're more thoughtful." As the Senate has grown more conservative with each election cycle, Chafee simply continues his "you can't win them all" approach more carefully, looking for opportunities to join with Democrats to alter Republican legislation he finds too harsh.

Chafee ranks second among Republicans on the Finance Committee, and in the 105th he retains the chairmanship of the Environment and Public Works Committee despite sometimes open grousing from conservatives. (Senate Majority Leader Trent Lott of Mississippi, has appointed an environmental task force for the 105th chaired by private property rights advocate Republican Larry E. Craig of Idaho.) Chafee has pressed his swing vote on Finance to maximum advantage, and has artfully placated conservative opposition to his policy positions on Environment, in part by delegating lots of authority to more aggressively anti-regulatory subcommittee chairmen.

Chafee had Robert C. Smith, R-N.H., take the lead during the 104th on the effort to revamp the troubled superfund hazardous waste program. Chafee wanted legislation to repair a program plagued by inefficiency and delay, describing superfund as "a caricature of a federal program." But the bill died without Senate action, despite attempts by leaders in both chambers to forge a bipartisan consensus.

Environment and Public Works has major jurisdiction during the 105th over reauthorizing the nation's surface transportation law. But if the 104th is any indication, Chafee is likely to let John W. Warner, R-Va., chairman of the Transportation and Infrastructure Subcommittee, take the lead in the Senate. During the 104th, Chafee let Warner manage all through conference a bill designating routes in a new National Highway System.

Chafee, whose state receives $2.34 for every dollar it puts into transportation trust funds, is reluctant to tinker with the current funding formula. (Chafee moved to make a Rhode Island rail project eligible for federal funds during consideration of the 104th's highway bill, and he opposes changes to the airline tax that might hurt flyers in his state.) Chafee blocked a House-passed initiative in 1995 that would have taken transportation funds "off budget" because of his concern that the resultant increase in highway spending would exacerbate the deficit, which is Chafee's primary concern. For the 105th Chafee unveiled a plan that would spend all new revenue that comes into the Highway Trust Fund but not its previously accrued balance.

Chafee also blocked a bill passed by the House that would have rewritten federal clean water law. "The so-called clean water bill that they sent over went way beyond what was acceptable to me and way beyond what was acceptable in the Senate as a whole," Chafee said.

When he thinks regulations become too burdensome, Chafee expresses concern that "paralysis by analysis" takes the place of sensible environmental protection. And early in the 105th, Chafee warmed the hearts of conservatives by announcing his uneasiness about new clean air regulations under consideration by the Environmental Protection Agency. But Chafee opposed many sweeping changes to environmental regulation proposed by his colleagues and House counterparts, including the clean water bill and a change in endangered species law. He joined with Ohio Democrat John Glenn to offer a substitute for an ill-fated GOP bill to require risk assessments for many new regulations (their alternative failed narrowly, 48-52). And he called a bill to provide new rights to private property owners "a loser." He worried aloud that Republicans had misplayed their hand on the environment and handed the Democrats an issue "on a silver platter."

Chafee complained at times that he was under fire from all sides — from conservatives on his committee and his environmental allies as well. On the broader range of issues, Chafee did what he could to tinker with bills he found objectionable but generally supported GOP priority legislation on final passage. (He did oppose a ban on a particular abortion procedure its opponents call "partial birth" abortion, and he was the Republican senator most likely to vote in favor of President Clinton's priorities in 1996.)

Some centrist Republicans in the House openly hoped that the Senate would moderate legislation passed more quickly by their chamber, but Chafee resisted the role of backstop, choosing to pick his shots carefully. "I don't want to sign on to say that every fight the moderates lost in the House, count on me to take it up in the Senate," he said.

At the same time, Chafee was willing to vote in favor of the GOP's massive budget-balancing package in 1995 with the full confidence that Clinton would veto it and the provisions he disdained might be revisited. "We know this isn't the last station," Chafee commented.

Chafee did join in 1996 with Louisiana Democrat John B. Breaux, with whom he had fashioned a health care alternative during the 103rd, to create an alternative to that year's GOP budget resolution. Their proposal roughly split the difference between the White House and the vetoed 1995 budget bill on tax cuts and reductions in projected entitlement spending. Their group had the blessing of the White House and top GOP senators, and the package drew bipartisan support, but it failed, 46-53.

Chafee leveraged his position as one of the only Republican moderates left on the Finance Committee to tweak as best he could welfare, Medicaid and Medicare overhaul bills. "The conservatives push, too, so there's nothing wrong with us making a push," Chafee said of the dwindling band of Senate GOP moderates who represented swing votes under narrow majority rule. In some cases, he worried, "what they're doing is not only bad policy, it's bad politics for the Republican Party."

During opening remarks when the Finance Committee took up a plan to overhaul Medicaid, Chafee declared, "I'm for flexibility, but if providing flexibility means no longer protecting the most vulnerable, I don't think we're headed in the right direction." Chafee joined with Finance Democrats to create numerous 10-10 tie votes in favor of losing amendments to require states to maintain the program as an entitlement and address nursing home standards, low-income mothers, children, infant mortality rates and the uninsured. The underlying bill died.

Chafee was not willing to provide his tie-making vote to impede GOP bills from reaching the floor. On the budget-balancing package, Chafee said, "We felt that this was just an incredible historic moment to achieve a balanced budget," acknowledging that "to succeed you've got to give some." He did manage to strike from the budget package on the floor a prohibition against states spending federal funds for abortions except in cases of rape, incest or danger to a woman's life.

He was willing at times to trade his support to gain assurance that some changes he wanted would be made. He thus won approval during consideration of the welfare bill of requirements that states provide benefits for poor pregnant women, children under age 12 and the disabled, and that federal funds be used to cover pre-pregnancy family planning. Moderate Republicans joined with Democrats on the floor to strike language that would have allowed states control over the food stamp program by receiving money in a block grant.

Because of his frequent departures from the party line, Chafee at the end of 1990 was ousted from his post as chairman of the Senate Republican Conference, the No. 3 position in the GOP leadership.

At Home: Chafee's affability and moderate record have carried him through 40 years of politics in Rhode Island, enabling him to win most of the time and to recover from occasional defeat. Some thought he would be vulnerable in 1994 because he was insufficiently conservative for many Republicans and too Republican for a strongly Democratic state. But instead he grew stronger politically throughout the year and wound up with 65 percent of the vote — easily his best showing ever.

The Democratic challenger, state legislator Linda J. Kushner, committed $400,000 of her own funds but was still outspent by more than 2 to 1. Yet her real problem lay in lacking a rationale for ousting the incumbent in a year when Republicans were pushing the limits of party success nearly everywhere — including New England.

Chafee had faced a far tougher challenge in 1988, when he dispatched a telegenic and talented campaigner, Lt. Gov. Richard A. Licht. The 40-year-old nephew of the man who had ousted Chafee from the governorship in 1968, Licht got an early start organizing and fundraising; he had raised more than Chafee by the start of 1988. Before winning statewide, Licht had built a solid record as a legislator on issues of wide voter appeal, such as child care and protection of open spaces.

But Chafee turned some of Licht's assets against him. He seized on Licht's campaign treasury to portray himself as the fiscal underdog in the race. Democrat Michael S. Dukakis easily carried Rhode Island for president that year, but Chafee was re-elected with a comfortable 55 percent.

Chafee's survival was a closer question in 1982, when Democratic former state Attorney General

Julius C. Michaelson came within 8,200 votes of victory simply by emphasizing that Chafee belonged to the party of Ronald Reagan and that Reagan was no friend of Rhode Island.

Chafee fought off Michaelson by reasserting his value to Rhode Island. He boasted of his role in negotiations that persuaded General Dynamics' Electric Boat division to keep its large shipyard in the state.

Chafee's position on the Finance Committee and his efforts to ease the burden on American businesses abroad helped him build a campaign treasury twice the size of Michaelson's. The challenger, general counsel to the state AFL-CIO, depended heavily on union support.

The close result was not unusual for Chafee. When he ran for governor in 1962, after serving as state House minority leader, he won by 398 votes over Democratic incumbent John A. Notte Jr.,who had damaged himself by advocating a state income tax. That issue was to cause Chafee trouble six years later.

As a three-term governor in the 1960s, Chafee pushed for an increase in Rhode Island's social and welfare spending, calling it "a state version of the Great Society." He won re-election easily in 1964 and in 1966.

In 1968, however, running against Democrat Frank Licht, he got caught on the wrong side of a dispute over state taxes. Chafee insisted an income tax was necessary to prevent a boost in the sales tax. Licht disagreed, and he upset Chafee by 7,808 votes.

After his defeat, Chafee was appointed Navy secretary in the Nixon administration. That seemed likely to help the 1972 Senate campaign he was planning against Democratic Sen. Claiborne Pell. When he left the Pentagon to begin the campaign, he looked strong.

But it did not turn out that way. Though Pell has always been accused of aloofness, he knew what to do that year, running superb TV advertising and speaking a collection of European languages to voters in the ethnic neighborhoods of Providence and the mill towns. And the old tax issue was still a partial liability for Chafee. Even the rare Republican presidential victory in the state that fall did not help him. Pell won 54 percent of the vote.

That might have been the end of Chafee's political career, had Democrats not done everything but throw the state's other Senate seat at him in 1976 by fighting with each other all year.

Gov. Philip W. Noel was the front-runner for the 1976 Democratic Senate nomination, but he crippled himself by making comments in a wire service interview that sounded like racial slurs. He had to resign as the party's national platform chairman, and he went on to lose the Senate primary by 100 votes to Cadillac dealer Richard P. Lorber, who spent lavishly of his own money and accused Noel not only of racial insensitivity but of bossism.

Noel then refused to back Lorber in the general election, allowing Chafee to resurrect his old coalition of the early early 1960s — Republicans, independents and dissident Democrats. He won every town in the state except one.

SENATE ELECTIONS

1994 General		
John H. Chafee (R)	222,856	(65%)
Linda J. Kushner (D)	122,532	(35%)
1994 Primary		
John H. Chafee (R)	27,906	(69%)
Thomas R. Post Jr. (R)	12,517	(31%)

Previous Winning Percentages: 1988 (55%) **1982** (51%) **1976** (58%)

CAMPAIGN FINANCE

	Receipts	Receipts from PACs	Expend-itures
1994			
Chafee (R)	$2,146,027	$996,926 (46%)	$1,896,589
Kushner (D)	$822,799	$124,300 (15%)	$805,867

KEY VOTES

1997	
Approve balanced-budget constitutional amendment	Y
Approve chemical weapons treaty	Y
1996	
Approve farm bill	N
Limit punitive damages in product liability cases	Y
Exempt small businesses from higher minimum wage	Y
Approve welfare overhaul	Y
Bar job discrimination based on sexual orientation	Y
Override veto of ban on "partial birth" abortions	N
1995	
Approve GOP budget with tax and spending cuts	Y
Approve constitutional amendment barring flag desecration	N

VOTING STUDIES

	Presidential Support		Party Unity		Conservative Coalition	
Year	**S**	**O**	**S**	**O**	**S**	**O**
1996	59	39	64	36	68	32
1995	50	50	75	24	74	26
1994	76	19	44	51	41	56
1993	57	43	56	41	46	54
1992	62	38	59	40	55	45
1991	62	35	52	45	45	52

INTEREST GROUP RATINGS

Year	ADA	AFL-CIO	CCUS	ACU
1996	40	n/a	92	60
1995	30	8	89	35
1994	65	25	67	30
1993	55	27	82	52
1992	40	17	80	44
1991	60	45	40	24

Jack Reed (D)

Of Cranston — Elected 1996, 1st term

Biographical Information
Born: Nov. 12, 1949, Providence, R.I.
Education: U.S. Military Academy, B.S. 1971; Harvard U., M.P.P. 1973, J.D. 1982.
Military Service: Army, 1967-79; Army Reserves, 1979-91.
Occupation: Lawyer.
Family: Single.
Religion: Roman Catholic.
Political Career: R.I. Senate, 1985-91; U.S. House, 1991-97.
Capitol Office: 320 Hart Bldg. 20510; 224-4642.

Committees
Special Aging
Banking, Housing & Urban Affairs
Financial Institutions & Regulatory Relief; International Finance; Housing Opportunity & Community Development
Labor & Human Resources
Children & Families; Public Health & Safety

The Path to Washington: The son of working-class parents, Reed stands in stark contrast to the man he succeeded in the Senate, wealthy patrician Claiborne Pell. But while their backgrounds are dramatically different, both are classic liberals. Reed will vote much as Pell did.

Reed's father was a custodian, his mother a factory worker in South Providence. At his Catholic prep school, he was an overachieving, 124-pound defensive back who won admission to West Point in 1967. He later commanded a company of the Army's 82nd Airborne Division.

At 29, Reed left the Army for Harvard Law School. He took a job at Rhode Island's biggest corporate law firm and a year later, in 1984, was elected to the state Senate.

In 1990, he ran for the House, emerging from a pack of Democratic hopefuls and then in November defeating Republican Gertrude M. "Trudy" Coxe, a well-known environmentalist. He took the 2nd District seat that GOP Rep. Claudine Schneider (1981-91) had given up to wage an unsuccessful challenge to Pell.

Reed easily won two House re-elections, building up a reputation as a nice guy who delivered crackerjack constituent service. Before long he was widely regarded as heir-apparent to Pell, whose health was failing.

In the 104th Congress, Reed did battle with the GOP majority on some high-profile issues. During work on a welfare overhaul bill, he tried but failed to ensure that welfare block grants to the states would grow automatically when the national unemployment rate rose above 6 percent. He opposed the GOP on welfare until late July 1996, when Republicans made enough adjustments in their legislation to elicit a promise from President Clinton that he would sign it.

On immigration law overhaul, Reed voted against a Republican proposal to deny public education to illegal immigrants, a provision that passed the House but then died. Reed succeeded in amending the immigration bill to include a provision that bars people who renounce their U.S. citizenship from avoiding taxes when re-entering the country.

When Pell announced in September 1995 his plans to retire, Reed was well-prepared to expand his campaign operation into the state's other district, where, because of Rhode Island's small size, his name recognition already was high.

He avoided a potentially contentious primary when Joseph Paolino Jr., a former Providence mayor and former U.S. ambassador to Malta, passed up the race, running instead for Reed's open House seat. Reed wound up with only token opposition in the Senate primary.

In the fall campaign, Reed's opponent was state Treasurer Nancy J. Mayer, a socially moderate, fiscally conservative Republican in the mold of the state's GOP senior senator, John H. Chafee.

Mayer said she would bring the fiscal acumen she had demonstrated at the state level to Washington and put it to work trying to eliminate the federal deficit.

However, her campaign had problems from the beginning. She managed to get the official party endorsement by only one vote over conservative businessman Thomas R. Post Jr., who had unsuccessfully challenged Chafee two years earlier. The deciding vote was cast by the state party chairman, John A. Holmes Jr.

Although Mayer was an easy winner in the primary over Post and another even more conservative candidate, she entered the general-election campaign a decided underdog, with Reed enjoying a comfortable lead in public opinion polls.

Reed stayed well ahead despite negative advertising paid for by the National Republican Senatorial Committee, which sought to convince voters that Reed was a tax-and-spend liberal. The ads did not have the desired impact, in part because Reed had always worn his party label proudly in his previous campaigns, to no ill effect at the polls.

In fact, Reed turned the GOP ads to his advantage during a debate with Mayer. When she pledged to back an overhaul of the campaign finance system, including banning "soft money," the unregulated contributions that both political parties used to run attack ads in the fall campaign. Reed countered that Mayer should have stopped the NRSC's ad campaign against him if she believed soft money was wrong. "You could have taken a stand," he told her. "You could have stood up and said, 'This is wrong.'"

The final outcome was a rout for Reed, as he took 63 percent of the vote.

During his first week in the Senate, Reed left Washington to tour Bosnia and neighboring regions involved in the conflict there. He told The Providence Journal-Bulletin that he was looking at how soon the United States realistically could plan to bring home its peacekeeping troops.

Reed's committee assignments primarily will involve him in domestic policy concerns: He serves on Banking, Housing and Urban Affairs; Labor and Human Resources; and Special Aging.

Reed opposes "means testing" for Medicare and favors the creation of a commission to determine what should be done to stabilize the system when Baby Boomers start to become eligible. "One of the strengths of the system is that it doesn't depend on the income of people or their illness" he said. "Everyone is covered." Otherwise, he told The Journal-Bulletin, "we'll get to the point increasingly where the affluent will sense that they're putting a lot of money [and] if you're poor you get it and if you're rich you don't get much."

Reed also opposes Republican-backed legislation that would allow companies to offer their employees comp time in lieu of overtime pay, saying it "undermines longstanding wage protections." Organized labor, a major force in Rhode Island politics, opposes the idea.

Reed's early moves in the Senate were consistent with his past loyalty to the liberal Democratic line. In March 1997 he voted against a balanced-budget constitutional amendment, and he joined a coalition of Democratic senators and citizen-activist groups in calling for public financing of congressional elections.

SENATE ELECTIONS

1996 General		
Jack Reed (D)	230,676	(63%)
Nancy J. Mayer (R)	127,368	(35%)
Donald W. Lovejoy (I)	5,327	(1%)
1996 Primary		
Jack Reed (D)	59,336	(86%)
Don Gil (D)	9,554	(14%)

Previous Winning Percentages: 1994* (68%) **1992*** (71%) **1990*** (59%)

* *House elections*

KEY VOTES

1997	
Approve balanced-budget constitutional amendment	N
Approve chemical weapons treaty	Y
House Service:	
1996	
Approve farm bill	N
Deny public education to illegal immigrants	N
Increase minimum wage	Y
Freeze defense spending	N
Approve welfare overhaul	Y
1995	
Approve balanced-budget constitutional amendment	N
Relax Clean Water Act regulations	N
Oppose limits on environmental regulations	Y
Reduce projected Medicare spending	N
Approve GOP budget with tax and spending cuts	N

CAMPAIGN FINANCE

	Receipts	Receipts from PACs	Expend-itures
1996			
Reed (D)	$2,688,136	$1,031,702 (38%)	$2,732,011
Mayer (R)	$787,231	$132,368 (17%)	$773,789

VOTING STUDIES

	Presidential Support		Party Unity		Conservative Coalition	
Year	**S**	**O**	**S**	**O**	**S**	**O**
House Service:						
1996	80	19	88	12	27	71
1995	82	18	91	8	26	74
1994	90	9	96	3	28	72
1993	82	17	96	4	23	75
1992	14	86	94	5	17	83
1991	29	71	92	7	27	70

INTEREST GROUP RATINGS

Year	ADA	AFL-CIO	CCUS	ACU
House Service:				
1996	80	0	31	5
1995	90	100	25	12
1994	85	78	50	5
1993	90	100	18	9
1992	90	92	13	4
1991	95	92	20	0

1 Patrick J. Kennedy (D)

Of Providence — Elected 1994, 2nd term

Biographical Information
Born: July 14, 1967, Brighton, Mass.
Education: Providence College, B.A. 1991.
Occupation: Public official.
Family: Single.
Religion: Roman Catholic.
Political Career: R.I. House, 1989-95.
Capitol Office: 312 Cannon Bldg. 20515; 225-4911.

Committees
National Security
Military Personnel; Military Research & Development
Resources
Fisheries Conservation, Wildlife & Oceans; National Parks & Public Lands

In Washington: In keeping with his family's ideological lineage, Kennedy usually votes a liberal line in the House. His most-visible moment in the 104th Congress came during a floor debate on repealing the assault weapons ban, when he passionately lectured gun-rights advocates that they had no understanding of gun violence "because you didn't have someone in your family killed."

But there are instances when Kennedy chooses a path different from that of his older kin in Congress — his father, Massachusetts Democratic Sen. Edward M. Kennedy, and his cousin, Massachusetts Democratic Rep. Joseph P. Kennedy II. Unlike them, this younger Kennedy has some problems with the prevailing desire among Democrats to cut defense spending to make more room in the budget for domestic programs.

Kennedy has a seat on the National Security Committee, and he had tough words for Cuban leader Fidel Castro in February 1996, when two civilian planes piloted by anti-Castro Cuban-Americans were shot down off the coast of Cuba. Kennedy said the United States should not rule out "the use of military force in responding to this act of wanton aggression." In the 104th, Kennedy supported legislation pushed by Indiana Republican Dan Burton to tighten the economic blockade of Cuba. The measure allowed Cuban-American claimants to sue foreign firms that purchased or leased factories, farms and other assets that were seized when Castro took power.

During debate on the bill, Burton read a statement from Patrick Kennedy stating, "We will not back away from being partners in our common fight for freedom begun by my uncle, President [John F.] Kennedy." It was during Kennedy's administration, in 1961, that Cuban exiles trained by the CIA launched an ill-fated invasion of the island nation.

Defense dollars help fuel the economy of Kennedy's district, which is home to naval facilities in and around Newport that employ about 10,000 people. In the 104th he voted for higher defense budgets sought by Republicans, and in June 1996 he opposed an effort to freeze defense spending for fiscal 1997 at the prior-year level. Although 60 Republicans bucked their party line to support the freeze, the GOP leadership gained the backing of Kennedy and 57 other Democrats to defeat it, 194-219.

When National Security took up the fiscal 1996 defense authorization bill, Kennedy joined Connecticut Democrat Rosa DeLauro in trying to push through an amendment favorable to General Dynamics' Electric Boat Division, the Connecticut shipyard that employs workers in his district. Eventually, the amendment was dropped. "We didn't have the votes," Kennedy said.

Kennedy allied with a majority of Republicans on a contentious social-policy issue, voting to outlaw a particular abortion technique that opponents call a "partial birth" abortion. His father and cousin both opposed the ban, which cleared Congress but was vetoed by President Clinton.

However, on other matters relating to abortion policy, Kennedy consistently sides with those who believe a woman has a right to terminate her pregnancy. He voted in July 1996 to allow federal employee health plans to cover the cost of abortion. He voted in May 1996 to repeal the law that bars overseas military hospitals from performing abortions for U.S. servicewomen. And in March 1996, he voted to require states to pay for Medicaid abortions in cases of rape or incest.

Kennedy also sided with the liberal wing of his party on a number of other issues. He voted against the welfare overhaul bill, against a term limits constitutional amendment, against efforts to roll back federal regulations, and against a balanced budget constitutional amendment. He scored a perfect 100 percent from the AFL-CIO in his first year in office and raised more money from union PACs than anyone else in the Class of 1994.

Kennedy, who at age 27 was the youngest person elected to the 104th Congress, voices the concerns of his generation about the affordability of higher education. He lambasted Republicans in the

RHODE ISLAND 1
East — Part of Providence; Pawtucket; Newport

The 1st binds the genteel Newport communities in southern Rhode Island with ethnic Providence neighborhoods and the blue-collar industrial towns of the Blackstone Valley in the north.

The Rhode Island portion of the Blackstone Valley, a highly industrialized, 15-mile region, is anchored on the south by Pawtucket and on the north by Woonsocket, a heavily French-Canadian wool- and textile-manufacturing city along the Massachusetts border. Pawtucket was the site of the first factory in America and is now home to about 250 manufacturing plants. The valley's economy includes metalworking and jewelry companies among much light manufacturing.

Moving south, the 1st takes in part of Providence, along with its smaller suburbs. Within the capital city, the 1st includes all of the heavily Italian Fourth Ward and most of the Italian Fifth Ward; both generally vote Democratic. On the more affluent East Side of Providence, the votes of upper-income conservatives are partially offset by liberals around Brown University; this section also has communities of immigrants from Portugal and the Cape Verde Islands.

Providence dominates the district, casting 70 percent of the vote. And Bill Clinton dominated Providence, winning with 64 percent. That was higher than the 55 percent he captured elsewhere in the 1st District. Kennedy, who was re-elected with 69 percent of the vote, took 71 percent in Providence.

South of Providence, the pristine coastal preserves along the scenic Narragansett Bay and Atlantic Ocean dominate.

Fishing, shipping and naval operations are vital to the coastal economy. In Portsmouth, defense contractor Raytheon has become an important employer with its work in sonar technology for Navy submarines. The company gained notice in 1991 because its Patriot missiles, which were made at other New England facilities, were used in the Persian Gulf War. But because of defense cuts, Raytheon has eliminated more than 1,100 jobs in Rhode Island since 1989.

Some of the smaller seacoast villages around the bay are wealthy residential areas that tend to favor the GOP, but the neighboring larger towns, such as Newport and Tiverton, vote Democratic.

Newport, renowned for the ostentatious wealth of its 19th century social elite, lures tourists with its restored palatial mansions. It is home to the Newport Navy Base, which maintains and houses several ships and contains the Naval Education and Training Center and the Naval Undersea Warfare Center, a large research and development complex. The naval operations employ about 10,000 civilian and military employees. The center has been designated as one of four "superlab" sites nationwide.

Clinton captured 53 percent of Newport's vote in 1996, while Kennedy received 65 percent.

1990 Population: 501,677. White 465,599 (93%), Black 16,361 (3%), Other 19,717 (4%). Hispanic origin 18,967 (4%). 18 and over 392,873 (78%), 62 and over 92,969 (19%). Median age: 34.

104th for supporting lower taxes while at the same time proposing cutbacks in student loans. "Eighty-nine percent of the American people oppose cuts to student financial aid programs. They want their children to pursue higher education and achieve their dreams," Kennedy said. "The Republicans offer a tax cut to the rich and then try to pay for it on the backs of students."

Senior citizens are another focus for Kennedy. Demographically speaking, his district is one of the oldest in the country, with 19 percent of the people age 62 or over. He was highly critical of the GOP effort to restrain the growth in spending on Medicare, accusing the GOP of supporting $270 billion in Medicare savings over seven years in order to pay for a $245 billion tax cut. "Better than 52 percent of that tax cut is going to go to individuals and families earning $100,000 or more," Kennedy told the House. "Republicans should be ashamed of themselves."

Kennedy also had harsh words for the GOP when the House in August 1996 passed a bill declaring English the official language of the federal government. He accused bill sponsors of "immigrant bashing" in an election year. "This bill is playing directly to the politics of fear and prejudice that this Congress is so well known for," he said.

He issued a similar verdict on a GOP bill to ban federal recognition of same-sex marriages and allow states to do the same. "This is not about defending marriage. It is about finding an enemy. It is not about marital union. It is about disunion, about dividing one group of Americans against another," Kennedy told the House. ". . . the spirit behind this bill further fans the flames of prejudice and bigotry that this 104th Congress has done a pretty good job at fanning thus far."

But he was most fervent during the March 1996 debate on repealing the assault-weapons ban, which passed the House. Fuming on the floor at proponents of repeal, a choked-up Kennedy, who had two uncles killed by assassins, said, "Families like mine know all too well what the damage of weapons can do. All I have to say to you is, you play with the devil, you die with the devil. You will never know what it's like because you don't have someone in your family killed. It's not the person who's killed. It's the whole family that's affected."

His speech provoked an equally heated response from New York Republican Gerald B.H. Solomon. "My wife lives alone five days a week in a rural area of upstate New York," Solomon shouted. "She has a right to defend herself when I'm not there, son. And don't you ever forget it." Away from the floor microphone, Solomon continued, "Let's just step outside."

At Home: Although Democrats are dominant in the 1st, moderate Republican Ronald K. Machtley won it three times. When he announced plans to run for governor in 1994 and Kennedy made known his plans to try for the House, Democratic insiders anointed him the front-runner, confident that the Kennedy name would ensure victory.

But those same insiders began to worry when the Republican nominee, Kevin Vigilante, started to gain momentum. A physician with a record of volunteer service that included work at a clinic for indigent women, Vigilante stressed his middle-class roots and the fact that he worked his way through college and medical school. He noted that Kennedy had never held a job outside of his part-time position as a state legislator. Kennedy had won election to the state House of Representatives in 1988, while still an undergraduate at Providence College. In September, Vigilante pulled to within 10 points of Kennedy in local polls and was getting support from the national Republican Party, which saw great symbolic value in the defeat of a Kennedy.

But with a $1 million campaign treasury and a forthright defense of his family name, Kennedy prevented Vigilante from closing the gap. Kennedy told voters that his family connections would be useful in bringing federal funds into the 1st, and Clinton visited the district in October to campaign for Kennedy, helping to validate his claims of clout. He won with 54 percent of the vote, to 46 percent for Vigilante. Their race later was chronicled by Boston filmmaker Joshua Seftel in a PBS documentary titled "Taking on the Kennedys."

Despite the competitive 1994 race and the district's past willingness to elect Republicans, state Republican officials had a hard time coming up with a candidate in 1996. Kennedy raised more than $1 million and won more than two-thirds of the vote.

HOUSE ELECTIONS

1996 General		
Patrick J. Kennedy (D)	121,781	(69%)
Giovanni D. Cicione (R)	49,199	(28%)
1994 General		
Patrick J. Kennedy (D)	89,832	(54%)
Kevin Vigilante (R)	76,069	(46%)

CAMPAIGN FINANCE

	Receipts	Receipts from PACs	Expend-itures
1996			
Kennedy (D)	$1,170,107	$316,590 (27%)	$1,051,719
Cicione (R)	$23,238	$600 (3%)	$23,237
1994			
Kennedy (D)	$1,065,747	$290,933 (27%)	$1,065,597
Vigilante (R)	$784,333	$144,838 (18%)	$803,371

DISTRICT VOTE FOR PRESIDENT

	1996		1992
D	115,039 (61%)	**D**	107,702 (50%)
R	49,031 (26%)	**R**	61,011 (28%)
I	20,359 (11%)	**I**	47,733 (22%)

KEY VOTES

1997	
Ban "partial birth" abortions	Y
1996	
Approve farm bill	N
Deny public education to illegal immigrants	N
Repeal ban on certain assault-style weapons	N
Increase minimum wage	Y
Freeze defense spending	N
Approve welfare overhaul	N
1995	
Approve balanced-budget constitutional amendment	N
Relax Clean Water Act regulations	N
Oppose limits on environmental regulations	Y
Reduce projected Medicare spending	N
Approve GOP budget with tax and spending cuts	N

VOTING STUDIES

	Presidential Support		Party Unity		Conservative Coalition	
Year	**S**	**O**	**S**	**O**	**S**	**O**
1996	73	24	85	14	35	65
1995	76	22	86	10	34	64

INTEREST GROUP RATINGS

Year	ADA	AFL-CIO	CCUS	ACU
1996	85	n/a	13	10
1995	90	100	25	16

2 Bob Weygand (D)

Of North Kingstown — Elected 1996, 1st term

Biographical Information

Born: May 10, 1948, Attleboro, Mass.
Education: U. of Rhode Island, B.F.A. 1971, B.S. 1976.
Occupation: Landscape architect; architectural firm executive.
Family: Wife, Frances; three children.
Religion: Roman Catholic.
Political Career: R.I. House, 1985-93; lieutenant governor, 1993-97.
Capitol Office: 507 Cannon Bldg. 20515; 225-2735.

Committees

Budget

Small Business
Government Programs & Oversight; Tax & Exports

The Path to Washington: Weygand, having made a mark in state-level politics in Rhode Island, got an opening to come to Washington in 1996 when Democratic Rep. Jack Reed announced he would run for the seat being vacated by retiring Sen. Claiborne Pell. Weygand, the state's lieutenant governor, lined up support from Rhode Island's powerful labor unions and quickly jumped into the race.

He was the best-financed of the candidates and the favorite to win the primary. But shortly before the filing deadline, a formidable new Democratic candidate entered: Joseph A. Paolino Jr., a former Providence mayor and former U.S. ambassador to Malta. Like Weygand, Paolino had run statewide; he lost the 1990 Democratic gubernatorial primary.

Paolino's entry drove several other candidates from the Democratic field. He won the endorsement of the state Democratic convention and went on to spend more than $250,000 of his own money on the primary, in which he contrasted his support for abortion rights with Weygand's anti-abortion stance.

Still, Weygand won the primary by a solid margin, and in this heavily Democratic district had little trouble dispatching Republican physician Rick Wild in November. Wild, an anti-abortion conservative, had defeated a more moderate candidate, state Sen. Robin Porter, in the GOP primary. While Rhode Islanders have elected middle-of-the-road Republicans such as Sen. John H. Chafee to office, Wild was no Chafee-style Republican. Weygand rolled to a 2-1 victory.

Weygand's initial fame in politics came in June 1991, when he played a key role in a successful FBI investigation of Brian J. Sarault, then the mayor of Pawtucket. Sarault offered a bribe to Weygand, who agreed to cooperate with federal authorities and be fitted with a hidden microphone. Wearing the listening equipment, Weygand met with Sarault in the mayor's office. Minutes after Weygand left the room with the incriminating tape, FBI officials burst into the office and arrested Sarault, who was convicted and sent to prison.

"He's created a political career out of his situation with Sarault," state House Majority Leader George Caruolo, a fellow Democrat, told the Providence Journal-Bulletin.

Weygand got his start in politics as a member of the East Providence Planning Board before winning a seat in the state House in 1984. After eight years of service (the last six as chairman of the House Corporations Committee), Weygand was elected lieutenant governor in 1992 and re-elected in 1994 easily, even as Republican Lincoln C. Almond captured the governorship.

Weygand hoped for a seat on the House Commerce Committee, while acknowledging that the chance was slim of landing the coveted position as a freshman. Instead, he got places on the Budget Committee and the Small Business Committee.

Except for his opposition to abortion, Weygand fits right in with the liberal majority in the House Democratic caucus. He opposes the death penalty, congressional term limits, and a constitutional amendment requiring a balanced budget. He opposed President Clinton's decision to sign the 1996 welfare overhaul bill.

A strong supporter of organized labor, which reciprocated the favor in his congressional campaign, Weygand said he supports legislation prohibiting companies from hiring permanent replacements for strikers, and he opposes GOP-sponsored legislation that would make it easier to create employee-management teams. He opposes repeal of the Davis-Bacon Act, which requires federal contractors to pay a locale's prevailing wage, usually the union wage. Weygand said he would have voted against NAFTA, which organized labor opposed.

RHODE ISLAND 2
West — Western Providence; Warwick

Stretching from the rolling hillsides of upstate Rhode Island through the Providence metropolitan area and on to quiet fishing villages in the south, the 2nd is reliably Democratic. In the past six presidential elections, the district has gone Republican only once, in 1984 for Ronald Reagan.

The largest concentration of voters in the 2nd is in Providence, the state capital and a Democratic stronghold. The city's population slid from 268,000 in 1925 to about 161,000 in 1990. As working-class white ethnics departed, the minority population increased; blacks and Hispanics made up one-third of the city's population in 1990.

The 2nd takes in about two-thirds of Providence, including the business district, where pedestrian shopping areas have had some success at reviving downtown. Also included is South Providence, once a mixed Irish and Jewish middle-class neighborhood that is increasingly black and Hispanic; Federal Hill and Silver Lake, where Italian-Americans predominate; and Elmhurst, a middle-class, ethnic community near Providence College.

Outside Providence, there are small GOP pockets. Scituate to the east and East Greenwich to the south were the only communities in the state to favor George Bush in 1992.

Just south of Providence along Interstates 95 and 295 are the district's next two largest cities, Warwick and Cranston. With significant white-collar populations, especially in Warwick, both cities are swing areas on the few occasions statewide races are closely contested.

Nearby Quonset Point, in the town of North Kingstown, is home to one of the district's largest private employers, General Dynamics' Electric Boat Division (930 employees). Workers here assemble the hulls for nuclear submarines that are to be completed in Electric Boat's Groton, Conn., facility. Many residents in the southwestern Rhode Island town of Westerly commute to Groton to work on the submarines. Defense cuts have hurt the facility, which used to employ 5,000. But in 1996 Congress agreed that Electric Boat would help build a new class of attack submarines along with Newport News Shipbuilding and Dry Dock Co.

Westerly, an old shipping center that now blends light manufacturing with its fishing trade, is somewhat more Democratic than most of the other towns on Rhode Island's western border; many of them are old Yankee enclaves that vote Republican. Westerly, which is home to a large Italian-American population, gave Clinton comfortable wins in 1992 and 1996.

A 40-minute drive from Providence, Westerly is located in Washington County, the state's fastest-growing county. Washington County, with coastal cities and maritime commerce as well as the inland marshes known as the "Great Swamp," grew 18 percent during the 1980s. Much of the growth stems from residential development along the shoreline.

In the town of Kingston is the University of Rhode Island, the state's largest (13,700 students) and one of the district's top employers.

1990 Population: 501,787. White 451,776 (90%), Black 22,500 (4%), Other 27,511 (5%). Hispanic origin 26,785 (5%). 18 and over 384,901 (77%), 62 and over 86,417 (17%). Median age: 34.

HOUSE ELECTIONS

1996 General		
Bob Weygand (D)	118,827	(64%)
Rick Wild (R)	58,458	(32%)
Thomas J. Ricci (I)	3,139	(2%)
Gail Alison Casman (I)	2,199	(1%)
1996 Primary		
Bob Weygand (D)	19,898	(48%)
Joseph R. Paolino (D)	15,689	(38%)
Kathryn O'Hare (D)	4,876	(12%)
Joseph J. McGair (D)	904	(2%)

CAMPAIGN FINANCE

	Receipts	Receipts from PACs	Expend-itures
1996			
Weygand (D)	$818,915	$348,925 (43%)	$785,547
Wild (R)	$421,820	$20,448 (5%)	$416,771

DISTRICT VOTE FOR PRESIDENT

	1996		1992
D	118,012 (59%)	D	105,597 (45%)
R	55,652 (28%)	R	70,590 (30%)
I	23,364 (12%)	I	57,312 (25%)

KEY VOTES

1997

Ban "partial birth" abortions Y

SOUTH CAROLINA

Governor: David Beasley (R)
First elected: 1994
Length of term: 4 years
Term expires: 1/99
Salary: $101,959
Term limit: 2 consecutive terms
Phone: (803) 734-9818
Born: February 26, 1957; Florence, S.C.
Education: U. of South Carolina, B.A. 1979, J.D. 1983.
Occupation: Lawyer; banker; farmer.
Family: Wife, Mary Wood Payne; three children.
Religion: Southern Baptist.
Political Career: S.C. House, 1978-92.

Lt. Gov.: Bob Peeler (R)
First elected: 1994
Length of term: 4 years
Term expires: 1/99
Salary: $44,737
Phone: (803) 734-2080

State election official: (803) 734-9060
Democratic headquarters: (803) 799-7798
Republican headquarters: (803) 798-8999

REDISTRICTING

South Carolina retained its six House seats in reapportionment. Federal court issued a map May 1, 1992. Federal court on July 13, 1993, invalidated map used in 1992. On March 30, 1994, a new map with minor changes became law without governor's signature. Justice Department approved the map April 28, 1994.

STATE LEGISLATURE

General Assembly. Meets January-June.

Senate: 46 members, 4-year terms
1996 breakdown: 26D, 20R; 43 men, 3 women
Salary: $10,400
Phone: (803) 734-2806

House of Representatives: 124 members, 2-year terms
1996 breakdown: 70R, 53D, 1I; 96 men, 28 women
Salary: $10,400
Phone: (803) 734-2010

URBAN STATISTICS

City	Population
Columbia	98,052
Mayor Robert D. Coble, D	
Charleston	80,414
Mayor Joseph P. Riley Jr., D	
North Charleston	70,218
Mayor R. Keith Summey, N-P	
Greenville	58,282
Mayor Knox White, R	
Spartanburg	43,467
Mayor James E. Talley, N-P	

U.S. CONGRESS

Senate: 1 D, 1 R
House: 2 D, 4 R

TERM LIMITS

For state offices: No

ELECTIONS

1996 Presidential Vote

Bob Dole	50%
Bill Clinton	44%
Ross Perot	6%

1992 Presidential Vote

George Bush	48%
Bill Clinton	40%
Ross Perot	12%

1988 Presidential Vote

George Bush	62%
Michael S. Dukakis	38%

POPULATION

1990 population		3,486,703
1980 population		3,120,820
Percent change		+12%
Rank among states:		25
White		69%
Black		30%
Hispanic		1%
Asian or Pacific islander		1%
Urban		55%
Rural		45%
Born in state		68%
Foreign-born		1%
Under age 18	920,207	26%
Ages 18-64	2,169,561	62%
65 and older	396,935	11%
Median age		32

MISCELLANEOUS

Capital: Columbia
Number of counties: 46
Per capita income: $15,420 (1991)
Rank among states: 43
Total area: 31,113 sq. miles
Rank among states: 40

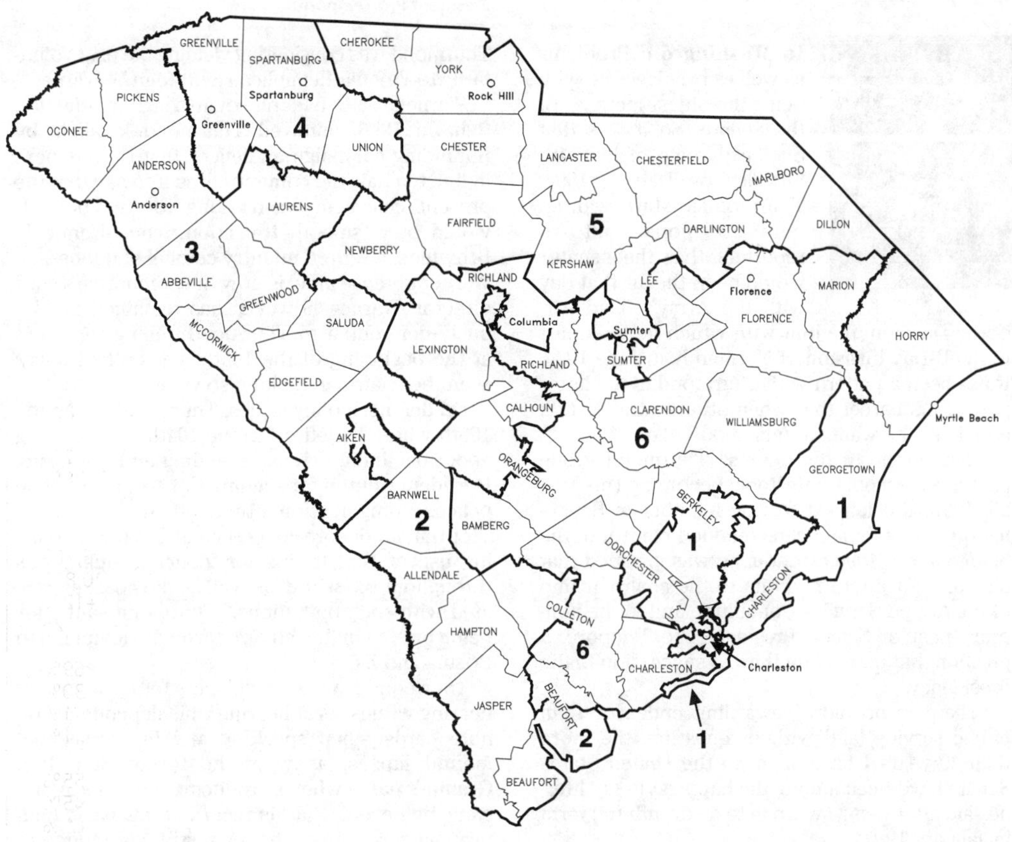
GREENVILLE
CHEROKEE
SPARTANBURG
YORK
Spartanburg
Rock Hill
PICKENS
OCONEE
Greenville
4
UNION
CHESTER
ANDERSON
LANCASTER
CHESTERFIELD
MARLBORO
Anderson
LAURENS
FAIRFIELD
5
DARLINGTON
DILLON
3
NEWBERRY
KERSHAW
ABBEVILLE
RICHLAND
LEE
Florence
MARION
GREENWOOD
SALUDA
Columbia
FLORENCE
MCCORMICK
LEXINGTON
Sumter
HORRY
RICHLAND
SUMTER
EDGEFIELD
CALHOUN
CLARENDON
WILLIAMSBURG
Myrtle Beach
AIKEN
6
ORANGEBURG
GEORGETOWN
BARNWELL
BERKELEY
1
2
BAMBERG
1
DORCHESTER
ALLENDALE
CHARLESTON
COLLETON
HAMPTON
6
Charleston
CHARLESTON
JASPER
BEAUFORT
1
2
BEAUFORT

Strom Thurmond (R)

Of Aiken — Elected 1954; 7th full term

Appointed to the Senate 1956; Did not serve April-Nov. 1956.

Biographical Information

Born: Dec. 5, 1902, Edgefield, S.C.

Education: Clemson U., B.S. 1923.

Military Service: Army Reserve, 1924-41; Army, 1942-46; Army Reserve, 1947-60.

Occupation: Lawyer; teacher; coach; education administrator.

Family: Separated; three children.

Religion: Baptist.

Political Career: Edgefield superintendent of education, 1929-33; S.C. Senate, 1933-38; S.C. Circuit Court of Appeals, 1938-46; governor, 1947-51; States' Rights nominee for president, 1948; sought Democratic nomination for U.S. Senate, 1950.

Capitol Office: 217 Russell Bldg. 20510; 224-5972.

Committees

Armed Services (chairman)

Judiciary

Administrative Oversight & the Courts; Antitrust, Business Rights & Competition; Constitution, Federalism & Property Rights

Veterans' Affairs

President Pro Tempore

In Washington: Problems as well as privileges go with being the oldest member of the Senate. So it was that on the passing of his 94th birthday on Dec. 5, 1996, Thurmond's staff wanted only to point out to reporters that the senator would be in the air that day with the Army's 82nd Airborne Division, the unit with which he took part in the D-Day invasion of Normandy in June 1944. It has been a pattern with Thurmond in the latter part of his career that when others want to talk about age, he wants to talk about vigor.

Early in the 105th Congress, Thurmond strode past a remarkable milestone: becoming (on May 25, 1997) the longest-serving member in Senate history. After Republicans retained control of the Senate in the 1996 election, he was gratified that his colleagues returned him to the chairmanship of the Armed Services Committee and to the honorary post of Senate President Pro Tempore, a position that places him third in succession to the presidency.

"There is no more rewarding endeavor than public service, and without question, the more than 40 years I have spent in the United States Senate have been among the happiest in my life," he said after being sworn in to a seventh full term in January 1997.

Many find it hard to comprehend that Thurmond is still an active player nearly 70 years after his career in public office first began, and nearly half a century after he waged a third-party candidacy for president, against Harry S Truman.

Speculation has it that Thurmond will end his record-breaking run voluntarily in this term. That notion was in the air even as South Carolina voters re-elected him in 1996, giving him a 53 percent share of the vote that was well below his poll performance in previous years. At the end of January, he was hospitalized for 11 days with the flu. And two years after he beat back an attempt by GOP colleagues to ease him out of the Armed Services chairmanship, rumors were circulating that Thurmond was considering yielding the post voluntarily to Virginia Republican Sen. John W Warner.

Warner, who had his own tough re-election fight in 1996, annoyed Thurmond loyalists by reminding campaign audiences that he was next in line to chair the committee, as if to say that the present chairman wasn't long for the post. It would be a smooth transition, since Romie L. Brownlee, a retired infantry colonel and longtime Warner defense aide, is now the committee's staff director. Warner, however, has remained assiduously deferential to Thurmond, telling reporters at the beginning of the 105th that he had never seen the chairman looking so vigorous.

On defense policy issues, Thurmond began the 105th where he left off in the 104th: complaining about declining defense spending and criticizing President Clinton for sending U.S. troops into one peacekeeping mission after another.

"I remain deeply concerned about the increasing use of U.S. troops for 'policing' operations throughout the world, as well as the costs associated with such operations," Thurmond said after being briefed in the fall of 1996 on deployments to Bosnia and Zaire.

Thurmond may draw whispers for his difficulty hearing witnesses at hearings, his dependence on note cards when speaking and his occasional mental lapses, as when he forgot Sen. Phil Gramm's name when introducing the senator at a campaign event. But his record on his basic military agenda shows he can still get concrete results. His stance on Clinton's defense budgets during 1995 and 1996, when he first held the chairmanship, was that spending was too low. The Republican-controlled Congress responded by adding $18 billion to Clinton's defense budgets during those years. Much of that additional money went for weapons purchases, an area that Thurmond says has been given short shrift at the expense of foreign adventures.

"The administration keeps promising that procurement funding will increase, but it never does," Thurmond said.

Early in 1997, Thurmond warmly endorsed former Republican Sen. William S. Cohen for secretary of Defense, but not without getting in a plug for the GOP agenda on military matters. Thurmond said he hoped Cohen would "lead the Clinton administration to provide more adequately for the security of the nation and those who serve in our military forces."

When a rival committee sought to elbow in on Armed Services Committee territory in the 104th, Thurmond vigorously protected his turf. The fight revolved around efforts by the House and Senate Intelligence committees to expand the power of the CIA director at the expense of the secretary of Defense. Such a move would inevitably have increased the power of the intelligence panels over matters now handled by the House and Senate defense committees. Thurmond and Sen. Sam Nunn of Georgia, now retired but then the committee's ranking Democrat, successfully blocked the overhaul legislation.

"In my view, this is an unnecessary expansion of bureaucracy at a time when virtually every other area of the government is shrinking," Thurmond said. The reorganization bill that passed was a shadow of its former self, lacking the additional positions and powers for the CIA that it originally contained.

And when Pennsylvania Republican Sen. Arlen Specter, chairman of the Senate Intelligence Committee, called Defense Secretary William Perry before his panel to answer questions on the July 1996 terrorist bombing of a U.S. barracks in Saudi Arabia, Thurmond again stepped in, backing up Perry's insistence on reporting to the Armed Services Committee.

Thurmond's tenure as chairman has not been without its setbacks. A presidential veto, and a partisan battle about national missile defense policy, kept Thurmond's first defense authorization bill in limbo well beyond the beginning of the fiscal year in October 1995. With a defense appropriations measure already in place, the delay left some to wonder whether there was a need for an authorization bill at all.

The inability of the Republicans, and Thurmond, to establish a firm policy to build a system that could protect the United States from limited long-range missile attack has been a persistent failure. The problem has been twofold: a general public suspicion — bolstered by Congressional Budget Office estimates — that the missile shield would be hugely expensive; and a lack of any intense public fear that rogue states such as North Korea or Libya would ever launch such an attack.

Thurmond's age may have indirectly contributed to the delays in passage of the bill. One concession he made in hanging on to his chairmanship in the 104th was agreeing to give wider leeway to his subcommittee chairmen, some of whom were much more strident on defense policy issues such as the missile defense measure. Another factor may have been staff inexperience. Not only were the Republicans generally running things in the Senate for the first time in eight years, but Thurmond's committee staff in 1995 was known for fairly frequent turnover, due in part to the senator's regimented management style, and for a lack of intellectual weight in the top-ranking positions.

Also under Thurmond's management, the Armed Services Committee early in 1996 found itself under attack from many senior officers concerning its handling of the case of Navy Cmdr. Robert Stumpf. A Navy aviator decorated in the Persian Gulf War and a former leader of the elite "Blue Angels" flying team, Stumpf had been confirmed by the Senate for promotion to captain. Belatedly, the Navy admitted it had neglected to tell lawmakers about Stumpf's attendance at the notorious 1991 Tailhook convention, where Navy aviators engaged in drunken and lewd behavior.

When Thurmond and Nunn wrote Navy Secretary John Dalton that the committee would not have confirmed Stumpf had it known, Dalton pulled Stumpf's promotion. That brought the committee criticism for excessive political correctness and ignoring a man's stellar career because of one blemish. Panel members delivered lengthy floor statements defending their action.

Through it all Thurmond continues to enjoy the perks — and suffer the indignities — of age. As president pro tempore, Thurmond got a seat at the head table when House and Senate leaders lunched with Clinton after the president's second inaugural. South Carolina GOP Gov. David Beasley signed a bill to clear the way for a Strom Thurmond statue on the state Capitol grounds.

On the other hand, there is the seemingly endless stream of age-related jokes. Jay Leno cracked that under one GOP fundraising plan, $45,000 was good for breakfast with Bob Dole; $30,000 got a donor lunch with House Speaker Newt Gingrich "and for the people who weren't very wealthy, for 10 bucks you could down a glass of Metamucil with Strom Thurmond."

Even with his lower re-election percentage in 1996, Thurmond still finished 9 points ahead of his Democratic challenger, and his campaign-year efforts showed that he still has a finger on the South Carolina pulse. Representing a relatively low-income state, Thurmond decided to vote for the minimum wage increase in July 1996, one of seven Republicans up for re-election to do so. He also criticized a Department of Energy nuclear waste plan that he said threatened to turn the state's Savannah River nuclear weapons facility "into some sort of nuclear junkyard."

At Home: Thurmond has punctuated his long political career with turns and reversals, but he has always seemed to carry his constituents with him.

They supported him in 1948 when, as governor, he bolted the Democratic Party to run as the States' Rights candidate for president. As a senator in 1964 he announced that he was joining the GOP because the Democrats were "leading the evolution of our nation to a socialistic dictatorship." And despite the state's historical partisan leanings, he easily won re-election two years later.

Since the mid-1960s, black voting strength has grown in South Carolina, and Thurmond has adjusted again. It must be said, however, that his efforts to help black communities have never brought him much of the black vote; his long record of opposing civil rights bills is not that easily forgotten.

But for two decades now, Thurmond has been regarded as a medical political marvel. As a 75-year-old in 1978 being challenged for re-election by a man barely half his age, Thurmond traveled the state with his wife and four young children in a camper called "Strom Trek," handing out family recipes, riding parade elephants and sliding down firehouse poles. (Thurmond and his wife separated in 1991.)

Thurmond learned politics from one of his father's friends, Democratic Sen. Benjamin "Pitchfork Ben" Tillman. Early in his career he was a populist, representing poor white farmers from the upcountry against the Tidewater establishment. After starting out in 1929 as superintendent of education in the town of Edgefield, he moved up to the state Senate during the Depression years. In 1946, after returning from World War II, he was elected governor. He was in his second year in office when the Democratic National Convention decided to adopt a strong civil rights plank, and Thurmond offered himself as a regional candidate for president on the States' Rights Democratic ticket. He carried South Carolina, Alabama, Mississippi and Louisiana.

Thurmond made a first try for the Senate in 1950, but lost the Democratic primary to incumbent Olin D. Johnston. Four years later, however, he won — the first and so far the only senator to be elected as a write-in candidate. Sen. Burnet R. Maybank had died and the 31-member State Democratic Committee froze Thurmond out by choosing state Sen. Edgar A. Brown. Thurmond focused his campaign on whether "31 men" or the voters should make the decision. His write-in campaign defeated Brown by nearly 60,000 votes.

True to a 1954 promise, Thurmond resigned in 1956 and ran for re-election without benefit of incumbency. No one filed against him — a circumstance that repeated itself in 1960, when it was time to run for a full six-year term. After Thurmond's party switch, the Democratic nominees in 1966 and 1972 could not hold him under 60 percent.

In 1978 Thurmond finally met a stiff re-election challenge from Charles "Pug" Ravenel, who had won the Democratic primary for governor four years before but been ruled ineligible for failure to meet residency requirements. A media-oriented "New South" politician, Ravenel tried to remind blacks of the senator's segregationist past. But Ravenel suffered from a carpetbagger's image. He had left the state to be an investment banker in New York, returning shortly before his 1974 gubernatorial bid. Thurmond won 56 percent.

The 1984 and 1990 campaigns were no problem for Thurmond, with the hapless Democratic nominees losing by 30-plus points. In 1996, Thurmond faced a well-financed Democratic foe in Elliott Close, a real estate developer and textile heir. Spending lavishly from his own pocket, Close called himself a "new conservative" for the next century, and in one of his TV ads, the message on Thurmond was "It's about time for him to come home." He faulted Thurmond for refusing to debate, but Thurmond said he didn't want to give his challenger any free publicity, leaving surrogates to dismiss Close as "a nice fellow who inherited some money." Close finished with 44 percent.

SENATE ELECTIONS

1996 General		
Strom Thurmond (R)	619,739	(53%)
Elliott Close (D)	510,810	(44%)
Richard T. Quillian (LIBERT)	12,988	(1%)
1996 Primary		
Strom Thurmond (R)	132,157	(60%)
Harold Worley (R)	65,670	(30%)
Charles E. Thompson (R)	20,188	(10%)

Previous Winning Percentages: 1990 (64%) **1984** (67%) **1978** (56%) **1972** (63%) **1966** (62%) **1960†** (100%) **1956†*** (100%) **1954†** (63%)

** Thurmond was elected as a write-in candidate in 1954. He resigned April 4, 1956, and was elected to fill the vacancy caused by his own resignation in a 1956 special election.*

† Thurmond was elected as a Democrat in 1954-60.

CAMPAIGN FINANCE

	Receipts	Receipts from PACs		Expend-itures
1996				
Thurmond (R)	$2,335,746	$782,308	(33%)	$2,385,185
Close (D)	$1,919,735	0		$1,913,574

KEY VOTES

1997	
Approve balanced-budget constitutional amendment	Y
Approve chemical weapons treaty	N
1996	
Approve farm bill	Y
Limit punitive damages in product liability cases	Y
Exempt small businesses from higher minimum wage	Y
Approve welfare overhaul	Y
Bar job discrimination based on sexual orientation	N
Override veto of ban on "partial birth" abortions	Y
1995	
Approve GOP budget with tax and spending cuts	Y
Approve constitutional amendment barring flag desecration	Y

VOTING STUDIES

	Presidential Support		Party Unity		Conservative Coalition	
Year	S	O	S	O	S	O
1996	39	61	97	3	95	5
1995	26	74	97	3	96	4
1994	39	60	93	6	97	3
1993	27	71	91	6	98	2
1992	78	22	94	6	95	5
1991	88	10	92	7	98	3

INTEREST GROUP RATINGS

Year	ADA	AFL-CIO	CCUS	ACU
1996	5	n/a	92	95
1995	0	0	100	96
1994	5	13	80	96
1993	10	10	82	83
1992	10	25	100	89
1991	10	25	70	90

Ernest F. Hollings (D)

Of Charleston — Elected 1966; 5th full term

Biographical Information

Born: Jan. 1, 1922, Charleston, S.C.

Education: The Citadel, B.A. 1942; U. of South Carolina, LL.B. 1947.

Military Service: Army, 1942-45.

Occupation: Lawyer.

Family: Wife, Rita "Peatsy" Liddy; four children.

Religion: Lutheran.

Political Career: S.C. House, 1949-55; lieutenant governor, 1955-59; governor, 1959-63; sought Democratic nomination for U.S. Senate, 1962; sought Democratic nomination for president, 1984.

Capitol Office: 125 Russell Bldg. 20510; 224-6121.

Committees

Appropriations
Commerce, Justice, State & Judiciary (ranking); Defense; Energy & Water Development; Interior; Labor, Health & Human Services & Education

Budget

Commerce, Science & Transportation (ranking)
Aviation; Communications (ranking); Manufacturing & Competitiveness

In Washington: If Hollings runs for re-election in 1998 — and signs in early 1997 suggested he would — he will be 76 years old seeking his sixth full Senate term. Although he has lost a good deal of clout now that Republicans control Congress, Hollings remains a force to be reckoned with, particularly in the areas of trade and telecommunications.

Hollings chaired the Commerce, Science and Transportation Committee from 1987 until 1995, when the GOP regained the majority in the Senate. He now serves as the committee's ranking Democrat, the same post he holds on the Commerce-Justice-State Appropriations Subcommittee. So Hollings is usually still in the room when those panels make major decisions, allowing him to bring his considerable legislative skill to bear.

Hollings has been a prominent, if unpredictable, player in many of the important policy debates of his era: poverty, civil rights, the budget deficit, arms control, the defense buildup in the 1980s, the defense retrenchment and telecommunications. But, though his mind may be nimble, his acerbic tongue usually leaves the deeper impression. Rarely does a year or two pass without Hollings making headlines by offending someone or other with an off-the-cuff remark.

Hollings angered Budget Committee Chairman Pete V. Domenici, R-N.M., by calling him "son" at a May 1995 markup. (Domenici is 65.) Hollings apologized early in 1994 for widely reported comments disparaging African "potentates" who travel to Geneva for trade talks. "Rather than eating each other, they'd just come up and get a good square meal," he was quoted as saying. He dismissed the incident as a joke.

It was this image of Hollings as impolitic, even mean-spirited, that often isolated him from his colleagues and diverted attention from his long record of legislative triumph. As Hollings began to adjust anew to life in the minority party, he quickly got a taste of what it's like to be cut out of the legislative process. Within weeks of taking Hollings' gavel as chairman of the Commerce panel, Larry Pressler, R-S.D., held a Republicans-only hearing on yet another attempt by the committee to rewrite the nation's communications laws. The Republicans then withdrew for several weeks to write their own version of the bill before bringing Hollings and other Democrats into the process.

Although he was insulted about not being consulted initially, Hollings had the last laugh. In negotiations with Pressler, particularly when the bill went to conference with the House, Hollings often snookered the outmatched Pressler, striking numerous provisions that he or the White House objected to. The final product bore a greater resemblance to the bill Hollings sponsored during the 103rd than to Pressler's Republicans-only first draft.

No less a Republican insider than Dennis Hastert of Illinois, the House chief deputy whip, complained, "A lot of people felt Pressler really didn't match Hollings step for step and that Hollings drove the negotiations on that side." Pressler ended up losing his 1996 re-election bid, and the new Commerce chairman with whom Hollings is working is John McCain of Arizona.

Hollings has been associated with some major legislative endeavors aimed at balancing the budget, chief among them the 1985 Gramm-Rudman-Hollings law (usually labeled just Gramm-Rudman), which set up a mechanism for automatic spending cuts if deficit targets were not met. He has run hot and cold on adding a balanced-budget amendment to the Constitution, turning colder under GOP Senate control. He voted for the amendment in 1994 but switched to oppose it in March 1995. By the 1997 vote, Hollings had sufficiently turned against the idea that when proponent Orrin G. Hatch, R-Utah, displayed a stack of 28 unbalanced presidential budgets, Hollings derisively referred to the prop as the "Reagan-Bush memorial deficit pile." His grand scheme for getting the country's fiscal house in order is to replace income taxes with a nationwide value-added tax on consumer goods.

Hollings, a former trial lawyer, is a key point man aiding efforts by the Trial Lawyers Association of America to keep legislation from passing that would impose federal limits on a manufacturer's responsibility for harm caused by faulty products. The Senate lacked the votes to close debate on product liability legislation in 1994. During the 104th, Hollings turned Republican federalist rhetoric against the idea, complaining that the GOP was seeking to enshrine a federal standard in an area that has always been reserved for the states. "It goes against the grain of everything before this Congress," Hollings stated. President Clinton vetoed the product liability bill in 1996.

Hollings, who has been unembarrassed over the years about sending appropriations home to South Carolina, proved at the end of the 104th that he is happy to pull legislative strings for a friend. Hollings attached a provision to an otherwise non-controversial reauthorization of the Federal Aviation Administration to make it harder for Federal Express employees to unionize. Hollings explained that he was grateful for the company's airlift of hay to drought-stricken South Carolina farmers a decade earlier. As he was watching the hay being unloaded, the senator remembered thinking, "If I can ever do [them] a favor, return it, I'll be glad to do it." Although prolabor Democrats cried foul, the plan was enacted.

Hollings sometimes leads a parade of one, as when he delayed a waiver early in the 105th allowing confirmation of Clinton's trade representative, Charlene Barshefsky, by trying to enlarge Congress' role in trade negotiations. Hollings displayed his bill-stalling abilities in September 1994 when he forced the Senate to postpone consideration of the bill to implement GATT until after the elections. Hollings had long criticized U.S. free-trade policies as contributing to a decline in the nation's industrial base. His hope in putting the bill off was to give opposition a chance to ripen, even though the delay harmed Clinton's already shaky political standing shortly before the fall elections. The bill ultimately was passed and signed by Clinton in early December.

Hollings has not worried much about displaying distance from Clinton. In the 103rd, he was one of six Democrats to cross party lines and help to kill legislation to ban employers from replacing striking workers. He and three other Democrats also broke ranks with the party by voting against Clinton's National Service program. But Hollings fought hard during the 104th to restore funding for Clinton's "cops on the beat" program and sponsored provisions, with New Hampshire Republican Judd Gregg, to create new law enforcement powers to combat terrorism (provisions supported by Clinton but killed by the House).

Hollings supports overhauling campaign finance law — a front-burner issue in the 105th. Hollings has long pushed a constitutional amendment to give Congress and the states the power to limit spending on political campaigns. In March 1997, the Senate rejected the proposal, 38-61, giving it even less support than in previous Congresses.

Hollings also supported the Republican-backed constitutional amendment to make possible the banning of flag desecration. But he showed a liberal streak at times during the 104th, voting for a ban on job discrimination based on sexual orientation and opposing a ban on a particular abortion procedure that its opponents call "partial birth" abortion. However, early in the 105th, Hollings changed his mind and voted to outlaw the controversial method in an April vote.

At Home: Those positions may cause Hollings some grief as he seeks re-election in an increasingly Republican state. Hollings had a scare in 1992, and among the challengers already lined up for 1998 is conservative GOP Rep. Bob Inglis.

Hollings started building his political career in South Carolina at a time of emotional argument about racial issues. He succeeded in combining old-time rhetoric with a tangible record of moderation. Modern times have brought new issues to the fore, but Hollings has kept up a balancing act, appealing to traditionally Democratic-voting rural and small-town whites, as well as rural and urban blacks, while clinging to enough of the business- and defense-minded GOP vote to survive in a state that has evolved into one of the national Republican Party's premier bastions.

As a candidate in the late 1950s, Hollings firmly espoused states' rights and condemned school integration. In his inaugural speech as governor in 1959, Hollings criticized President Dwight D. Eisenhower for commanding a "marching army, this time not against Berlin, but against Little Rock." But as chief executive of the state, he quietly integrated the public schools.

In fact, despite grumblings about his rhetoric, blacks provided Hollings' margin of victory in 1966, when he won his Senate seat against a more conservative GOP opponent. Since then, he never has faced a credible candidate to his left, and blacks have generally supported him.

Hollings twice won unanimous election to the state House speakership and in 1954 moved up to lieutenant governor. In 1958, Democratic Gov. George B. Timmerman was ineligible to succeed himself. Hollings won a heated three-way race for the nomination, defeating Donald S. Russell, former University of South Carolina president and a protege of ex-Gov. James F. Byrnes.

As governor, Hollings worked hard to strengthen his state's educational system, establishing a commission on higher education. Barred from seeking a second gubernatorial term in 1962, he challenged Democratic Sen. Olin D. Johnston but failed to draw much more than one-third of the vote.

The senator died in 1965, however, and Donald Russell — by then governor — had himself appointed to the seat. That provided the issue for Hollings' comeback in 1966. He ousted Russell in the special primary to finish Johnston's term.

He won a full term two years later.

Hollings rolled over weak opponents in 1974 and 1980. For 1986, Republicans tried to stir up talk that Hollings was bored with the Senate and dispirited by the failure of his 1984 bid for the Democratic presidential nomination. But Hollings discredited the rumor early on by stumping all over the state and raising a hefty campaign treasury. Well-known Republicans ducked, leaving the nomination to a little-known former U.S. attorney. He was crushed in the race.

Support from black voters proved vital for Hollings when he sought a fifth full term in 1992. It was a roller-coaster of an election cycle for Hollings, in which he first looked vulnerable, then secure, then vulnerable again. In the heady days after the 1991 Persian Gulf War, Republicans thought that Hollings' vote against the use of force would seriously undermine his prospects for re-election in strongly pro-defense South Carolina. But voters' focus seemed to drift from the war in early 1992, and the campaign of the presumed GOP nominee, former Rep. Thomas F. Hartnett, did not draw rave reviews for its vigor and fundraising.

Over time, though, Hartnett's portrayal of Hollings as an arrogant, entrenched incumbent began to resonate with voters. And ironically, Hartnett benefited from the travails of his party's presidential ticket, because it needed to shore up its Southern base. President George Bush, who could take South Carolina for granted in 1988, paid attention to the state in 1992, helping mobilize the GOP faithful.

Hartnett prevailed in two-thirds of the state's 15 most populous counties. Hollings' pro-business image and his efforts to boost military spending in the state helped him hold down his losses in white-collar, retirement and military-dependent areas, but it was strong support from traditionally Democratic rural and small-town South Carolina that re-elected him. In the end, Hollings won with 50 percent, three percentage points ahead of Hartnett.

SENATE ELECTIONS

1992 General

Ernest F. Hollings (D)	591,030	(50%)
Thomas F. Hartnett (R)	554,175	(47%)
Mark Johnson (LIBERT)	22,962	(2%)

Previous Winning Percentages: **1986** (63%) **1980** (70%) **1974** (70%) **1968** (62%) **1966†** (51%)

† Special election

CAMPAIGN FINANCE

	Receipts	Receipts from PACs	Expend-itures
1992			
Hollings (D)	$2,736,893	$1,052,164 (38%)	$3,642,045
Hartnett (R)	$907,376	$153,311 (17%)	$886,816

KEY VOTES

1997	
Approve balanced-budget constitutional amendment	N
Approve chemical weapons treaty	Y
1996	
Approve farm bill	N
Limit punitive damages in product liability cases	N
Exempt small businesses from higher minimum wage	N
Approve welfare overhaul	Y
Bar job discrimination based on sexual orientation	Y
Override veto of ban on "partial birth" abortions	N
1995	
Approve GOP budget with tax and spending cuts	N
Approve constitutional amendment barring flag desecration	Y

VOTING STUDIES

	Presidential Support		Party Unity		Conservative Coalition	
Year	**S**	**O**	**S**	**O**	**S**	**O**
1996	80	17	80	18	58	39
1995	75	24	75	24	68	28
1994	81	13	78	19	69	28
1993	73	27	76	20	59	41
1992	38	62	58	42	55	45
1991	56	44	63	37	65	35

INTEREST GROUP RATINGS

Year	ADA	AFL-CIO	CCUS	ACU
1996	70	n/a	46	20
1995	75	75	37	35
1994	50	71	40	22
1993	55	91	27	42
1992	35	50	60	63
1991	55	75	40	62

1 Mark Sanford (R)

Of Charleston — Elected 1994, 2nd term

Biographical Information

Born: May 28, 1960, Fort Lauderdale, Fla.
Education: Furman U., B.A. 1983; U. of Virginia, M.B.A. 1988.
Occupation: Real estate investor; investment banker.
Family: Wife, Jennifer Sullivan; three children.
Religion: Episcopalian.
Political Career: No previous office.
Capitol Office: 1223 Longworth Bldg. 20515; 225-3176.

Committees

Government Reform & Oversight
Government Management, Information & Technology; Postal Service
International Relations
Africa; Western Hemisphere
Joint Economic

In Washington: At times, businessman Sanford has held the conservative line as tightly as anyone in the House GOP. For instance, when many Republicans dropped their earlier reservations and voted in August 1996 for a politically popular bill increasing the minimum wage, Sanford said "no."

But Sanford stands apart from many Southern Republicans because of his generally positive attitude toward environmental regulation and his support for freezing spending on defense. Considering the special nature of the Southern district he represents, however, those positions make political sense.

The 1st includes much of South Carolina's Atlantic Ocean coast, taking in resorts such as Isle of Palms and Myrtle Beach. Beaches and waterways help the 1st draw tourists and retirees, so even as pressure grows to build and develop, there is an awareness that protecting environmental quality is good for business.

Sanford was one of only 34 Republicans voting in 1995 against a conservative-led effort to rewrite the clean water act; critics of the law wanted to relax regulations dealing with the discharge of wastes and storm water into waterways. He also supported a Democratic effort to strike language limiting the regulatory authority of the Environmental Protection Agency (EPA). The language, which conservatives sought to include in the 1995 bill funding the EPA, would have restricted the agency's ability to regulate emissions from industrial facilities, raw sewage overflows and arsenic and radon in drinking water.

Sanford's opposition to increased defense spending is reflective of changing attitudes in his district, which was long enamored of the military. The 1st includes part of Charleston, historically a center of U.S. naval operations, including the huge Charleston Naval Station and Naval Shipyard. But the military presence in Charleston is declining dramatically as part of the Pentagon's 1990s base-closing campaign. Sanford can safely vote to restrain defense spending because so much less of it now comes his district's way.

He voted against the final fiscal 1996 defense spending bill, and was one of 60 Republicans voting to freeze the fiscal 1997 defense budget at the previous year's level. After that freeze amendment failed, Sanford was the only South Carolina House member to vote against the entire defense spending bill — even though the National Security Committee, which drafted the bill, is chaired by Republican Floyd D. Spence, dean of the state's House delegation.

Restraining defense spending is a component of Sanford's overall zeal for balancing the budget, He was one of 15 GOP members — 12 of them freshmen — who bucked the GOP leadership in early 1996 and voted against reopening the federal government, which had partially closed when budget negotiations between the White House and Congress broke down.

Also, he was one of 19 Republicans who opposed the fiscal 1997 budget resolution because it forecast a short-term increase in the deficit and called for an additional $4 billion for domestic programs. The Senate pushed for the extra spending, angering conservatives in the House.

Early in the 104th Congress, Sanford supported the toughest version of a balanced-budget constitutional amendment — one that would have required a three-fifths majority vote in both the House and Senate to increase taxes, engage in deficit spending or raise the public debt limit.

Explaining his stand, Sanford — who often peppers his floor speeches with historical allusions — said, "Rome collapsed in 476 A.D. The Byzantine Empire collapsed in 1453. The Italian Renaissance came to an end in 1550. The Dutch Empire ended in 1759. . . . What you would find is that in every instance, civilizations reached a crossroads in which they had to decide, do we go back to what made us competitive and a world power in the first place, or do we stay on this happy but ultimately unsustainable cycle of upward government spending and upward gov-

SOUTH CAROLINA 1
East — Part of Charleston; Myrtle Beach

The 1st encompasses two of South Carolina's growth hot spots: Charleston and its suburbs, which were part of the district in the 1980s, and, up the Atlantic Coast, newly added Myrtle Beach (Horry County). Remapping in 1992 shifted the 1st north and east to make way for the black-majority 6th.

A 1980s boom in tourism and federal spending at Charleston's many military installations and industries produced a vibrant economy and fueled population growth of more than 40 percent in some parts of the 1st.

In 1992, the military directly or indirectly supplied one-third of the payroll and one-fourth of the jobs in the southern counties of Berkeley, Charleston and Dorchester. But military downsizing hit Charleston with a vengeance in 1993. Two major military installations — the Charleston Naval Station and the Charleston Naval Shipyard — were closed. The city plans to have the abandoned bases converted into private houses in an attempt to build tourism.

To counter dismal projections of military and civilian job losses, city leaders were able to save some smaller facilities, such as a Navy hospital and a parts supply center. And in 1995 the Pentagon recommended steering some new personnel to Charleston as part of the realignment of other bases, although that did not immediately happen.

The Charleston area is now faced with having to convert its economy. Charleston created the Charleston Regional Development Alliance to garner new businesses for the area. It quickly attracted more than 40 new companies, including Nucor Steel, Mikasa and National Car Rental.

So far, at both ends of the district, layoffs have been absorbed by growth in the non-military sector. Charleston's historic district and nearby beaches are a cash cow; 5 million tourists visit the area annually, leaving an estimated $850 million a year behind. A growing health care industry, anchored by the Medical University of South Carolina, employs about 23,000.

Myrtle Beach thrives on tourism as well, drawing visitors to its surf, myriad golf courses and honky-tonk amusements. Beaches of the "Grand Strand" — 60 miles of shoreline from the North Carolina border down into Georgetown County — feature waters warmed by the Gulf Stream, just a few miles offshore.

In redistricting, the 1st saw much of its black population, both rural and urban, go into the 6th District. That left the 1st with demographics most GOP candidates can only dream about. Support for Republicans is high among the white, affluent suburbanites around Charleston as well as among the district's conservative-minded military personnel and many retirees. Sanford won his first House term with 66 percent, then was re-elected in 1996 without Democratic opposition.

Despite the district's overall right-of-center tilt, there is a moderate shading on some issues. Widespread support for protecting the area's waterways, marshes, beaches and wildlife has spawned a strong environmental movement.

1990 Population: 581,133. White 453,332 (78%), Black 116,817 (20%), Other 10,984 (2%). Hispanic origin 8,032 (1%). 18 and over 427,354 (74%), 62 and over 67,599 (12%). Median age: 31.

ernment consumption?"

Another way to curtail government spending, Sanford believes, is to limit members' tenure in Congress. He calls himself a "citizen legislator" and says he will serve six years in the House, no more. Enacting a three-term limit would "most directly [affect] this culture of spending that we have in Washington," he has said.

Dismissing the argument that term limits would rob Congress of valuable experience built up over the years by veteran members, Sanford told the Minneapolis/St. Paul Star Tribune in March 1995, "It's not like we're dealing with brain surgery. Probably there's a six-month learning curve, and even after a year you don't have it down pat. But over time, you begin to erode your sense of the outside world."

When House Republicans scheduled a floor vote in March 1995 on a term limits constitutional amendment, it fell short of the two-thirds majority required for adoption. The issue came back to the floor in early February 1997, and again proponents were disappointed.

Sanford would like to allow states to decide individually on term limits. But the Supreme Court ruled in May 1995 that the only legal way to set term limits is through a constitutional amendment, not through state-by-state initiatives.

Sanford's personal commitment to limiting his time in Washington is dramatized by his choice of living quarters: his office in the Longworth Building. Sanford sleeps on a futon in the office and his family still lives in Charleston.

And he called attention to his disdain for congressional perks by crusading with other GOP first-termers to eliminate the traditional delivery of ice to each congressional office. Sanford said that halting the ice flow would "save the taxpayers $500,000 per year and is just another step in making Congress more like a citizen legislature." The ice deliveries were stopped in April 1995.

Sanford holds seats on the International

Relations Committee, the Government Reform and Oversight Committee, and the Joint Economic Committee.

At Home: During the 1994 campaign, Sanford and his supporters donned hunting camouflage, declaring "open season" on career politicians who masquerade as citizen legislators. That pitch helped Sanford muscle past six other Republican hopefuls for the open 1st, including the presumed front-runner, former state GOP Chairman Van Hipp. Sanford ran second to Hipp in the primary and then beat him 52 percent to 48 percent in a runoff. In November, Sanford coasted to election. Seeking a second term in 1996, he drew no Democratic opponent.

Sanford's 1994 House bid was his first try for public office; a young businessman, he was part owner of two real estate businesses and helped manage his family's farm. The 1st was open because four-term GOP Rep. Arthur Ravenel Jr. decided to run for governor. Hipp's past party activism earned him billing as the favorite; the only question was which of the other six candidates might force a runoff.

While others focused attention on undermining Hipp, Sanford spent his time blasting Congress, investing some of the $150,000 he gave his own campaign to air commercials criticizing the institution. He plastered the district with billboards promising he would serve no more than six years. In the primary, Sanford tallied 19 percent of the vote, well behind Hipp's 31 percent, but enough to earn second place and make the runoff.

In the second-round voting, Sanford found the party apparatus and local conservative Christian activists arrayed against him. But he got the endorsements of all but one of the Republican candidates who were eliminated in the primary.

Continuing his call for citizen legislators, he emphasized that as a businessman he knew how to meet a payroll and stick to a budget. And when Hipp started attacking him, Sanford urged him to "take the McDonald's pledge and give the voters a break today by stopping the name-calling." Republican voters gave him a 4-point victory.

Democrats nominated an appealing candidate in state Rep. Robert Barber, a moderate legislator whose popular restaurant in Charleston boosted his name recognition. He criticized Sanford for signing the House GOP's "Contract With America" and backing a flat tax proposal.

But voters in the increasingly Republican 1st were in no mood in 1994 to listen to any Democrat, even a moderate one. Pledging to cut spending on welfare, crop subsidies, Amtrak and congressional staff, and to hold entitlement spending growth to 2 percent annually, Sanford rolled to an impressive 66 percent victory.

HOUSE ELECTIONS

1996 General		
Mark Sanford (R)	138,467	(96%)
Joseph F. Innella (NL)	5,105	(4%)
1994 General		
Mark Sanford (R)	97,803	(66%)
Robert Barber (D)	47,769	(32%)
Robert Paine (LIBERT)	1,836	(1%)

CAMPAIGN FINANCE

	Receipts	Receipts from PACs	Expend-itures
1996			
Sanford (R)	$308,006	$0 (0%)	$97,231
1994			
Sanford (R)	$552,761	$1,071 (0%)	$544,574
Barber (D)	$439,036	$87,450 (20%)	$437,530

DISTRICT VOTE FOR PRESIDENT

	1996		1992
D	71,958 (37%)	**D**	62,513 (33%)
R	107,330 (56%)	**R**	102,194 (53%)
I	11,456 (6%)	**I**	26,711 (14%)

KEY VOTES

1997	
Ban "partial-birth" abortions	Y
1996	
Approve farm bill	Y
Deny public education to illegal immigrants	N
Repeal ban on certain assault-style weapons	Y
Increase minimum wage	N
Freeze defense spending	Y
Approve welfare overhaul	Y
1995	
Approve balanced-budget constitutional amendment	Y
Relax Clean Water Act regulations	N
Oppose limits on environmental regulations	Y
Reduce projected Medicare spending	Y
Approve GOP budget with tax and spending cuts	Y

VOTING STUDIES

	Presidential Support		Party Unity		Conservative Coalition	
Year	**S**	**O**	**S**	**O**	**S**	**O**
1996	43	54	84	16	61	35
1995	24	76	89	11	77	23

INTEREST GROUP RATINGS

Year	ADA	AFL-CIO	CCUS	ACU
1996	10	n/a	81	95
1995	15	0	92	88

2 Floyd D. Spence (R)

Of Lexington — Elected 1970, 14th term

Biographical Information
Born: April 9, 1928, Columbia, S.C.
Education: U. of South Carolina, A.B. 1952, L.L.B. 1956.
Military Service: Naval Reserve, 1947-88; Navy, 1952-54.
Occupation: Lawyer.
Family: Wife, Deborah Williams; four children.
Religion: Lutheran.
Political Career: S.C. House, 1957-63; Republican nominee for U.S. House, 1962; S.C. Senate, 1967-71, minority leader, 1967-71.
Capitol Office: 2405 Rayburn Bldg. 20515; 225-2452.

Committees
National Security (chairman)
Military Procurement
Veterans' Affairs
Oversight & Investigations

In Washington: With a ferocity that belies his genial demeanor, Spence, as chairman of the National Security Committee, regularly attacks President Clinton's defense program for underfunding the U.S. military while over-extending it on humanitarian missions overseas. But increasingly, Spence's critiques have had an undertone of frustrated resignation, because GOP defense hawks are not finding it easy to arouse public support for substantially higher defense budgets. Even in his own party's House ranks, Spence encounters many "deficit hawks" — members so preoccupied with eliminating federal red ink that they cast a hostile eye on costly weapons systems.

Spence brags that in his time as chairman, National Security has made a "historic" break from the pattern of declining defense budgets that had prevailed since the mid-1980s. "Even the additional funds . . . will not solve all that is wrong with the Clinton defense plan," Spence declared in the 104th Congress. "But it will allow us to slow the hemorrhaging by applying resources against many of the most pressing readiness, modernization and quality-of-life problems."

In his quest to allocate more money to the Pentagon than the Clinton administration requests, Spence meets resistance from many Democrats and some Republicans who balk at increasing any kind of government spending when there is much emphasis on getting the deficit to zero by the early 21st century.

The most visible example of internal GOP dissent on defense spending is the sustained effort by Budget Committee Chairman John R. Kasich — who is also the No. 4 Republican on National Security — to eliminate funding for building more B-2 "stealth" bombers beyond the 20 planes that the administration says are sufficient.

Kasich and the ranking Democrat on National Security, liberal Californian Ronald V. Dellums, sought to amend the fiscal 1996 defense authorization bill to strike an extra $553 million that the committee had added to build future B-2s. Their amendment was rejected, 203-219.

In addition to such intracommittee quarrels over extra dollars for defense, there were also rumblings in the 104th that some younger Republicans on National Security felt Spence did not have a firm enough hand on the committee's tiller. In late 1995, Spence dismissed speculation in the media that his chairmanship was at risk. "I think I would know. I have support from everybody. I think it's ridiculous," he said. Later House Speaker Newt Gingrich sent Spence a note saying he was "outraged" and "appalled" that there was some doubt about Spence's leadership, adding "you have my full confidence and support."

When he took the National Security gavel in 1995, Spence did not have a reputation as a master strategist on defense policy. When Democrats controlled the House, Spence had ascended the GOP seniority ladder on the old Armed Service Committee without developing a prominent profile. Serious health problems distracted him in the 1980s. In his college days Spence was an athlete, but in later years he developed an obstructive lung disease that left him so breathless he could barely speak; he required a wheelchair and portable oxygen supply. In May 1988, doctors in Jackson, Miss., replaced Spence's damaged lungs with those of a man who had been killed in a traffic accident. His health has seemed steady ever since; Spence turns 70 in the 105th Congress.

In his first year as chairman, Spence and committee Republicans ran into some heavy seas after approving a change in the pension calculation for retiring military personnel. The impetus for the recalculation was to save money; the committee was trying to meet Budget Committee targets for the GOP's deficit-reducing budget-reconciliation bill. On a party-line vote in August 1995, National Security voted to change the system for figuring pensions for retiring personnel who entered service before Sept, 8, 1980. Under the plan, pensions would have been based on an average of pay in the last 12 months of service, not on pay in the last month, which is typically higher.

The committee plan provoked protest from Defense Secretary William J. Perry, the Joint

SOUTH CAROLINA 2
Central and South — Columbia suburbs; Hilton Head

Winding downward from the state capital, Columbia, to the Atlantic Ocean, the 2nd illustrates the contrasts that growth has brought to South Carolina. Anchored at either end by the first- and third-richest counties in the state — Lexington and Beaufort, respectively — the 2nd also contains the poorest county, Allendale, in its midsection. The population of Atlantic Coast towns skyrocketed during the 1980s, while inland counties such as Hampton and Allendale struggled to retain population.

More than three-fourths of the votes cast in the 2nd come from the thriving ends of the district. To the north, Columbia (Richland County) and its bedroom communities in nearby Lexington County flourished during the 1980s, as service businesses and midsize companies that produce everything from software to nuclear casings kept the area's economy vibrant. However, the main sources of jobs here continue to be state, federal and local government agencies, as well as the University of South Carolina (25,500 students); together these employ nearly 60,000 people and provide a fairly stable base of white-collar jobs.

At the southern end of the 2nd, Beaufort County is another bastion of affluence. The swank resorts of Hilton Head Island abound with retirees and vacationers sweating in the sun; only five miles away, recruits sweat at the Parris Island Marine Corps camp. The enormous popularity of Hilton Head caused its population to boom by 111 percent during the 1980s.

Growth and wealth at both ends of the 2nd — as well as a 1992 redistricting map that shifted the district's percentage of black residents down to 25 percent — have put it firmly in the GOP column. Lexington County, with its mix of white-collar professionals and blue-collar social conservatives, gave Bob Dole 63 percent of its votes in 1996. Beaufort County, which a generation ago was rural and Democratic, is now reliably Republican as well, giving Dole 51 percent.

Between the poles of the 2nd, however, lie some of the poorest areas of South Carolina, places that were passed over by the boom of the 1980s and remain mired in rural poverty. In Allendale County, one in three people lives below the poverty line; in Hampton and Jasper counties, one in four falls below the line. Tenant farming and sharecropping are long-lived traditions in these black-majority, thinly settled counties.

Although South Carolina's GOP has made considerable progress in recent years luring white voters who once called themselves Democrats, there are still a number of die-hard white Democrats in the middle part of the 2nd. Their votes, in combination with the district's 25 percent black population, enabled Bill Clinton to carry Jasper, Hampton, Allendale and Calhoun counties in 1996. However, those Democrats' voices were drowned out by Republicans to their north and south.

1990 Population: 581,099. White 425,249 (73%), Black 145,761 (25%), Other 10,089 (2%). Hispanic origin 8,323 (1%). 18 and over 431,261 (74%), 62 and over 72,336 (12%). Median age: 31.

Chiefs of Staff and rank-and-file military who stood to lose some money in retirement. Several Republicans also opposed the idea, including Senate Majority Leader Bob Dole, who called it a "breach of faith" with military personnel.

Spence abandoned the pension-recalculation plan and proposed to satisfy Budget Committee targets by selling materials in the National Defense Stockpile. In announcing this alternative, however, Spence created more trouble for himself. Committee Democrats were offended by a statement in Spence's news release congratulating Republicans for coming up with the alternative plan and an accompanying letter to Defense Secretary Perry chastising the administration for its criticism and reticence to help the GOP.

"The press release claims that the Committee Republicans persevered and ultimately succeeded' in changing this initiative," said Dellums. "Let the record show that if that is the case, they have persevered and ultimately succeeded in undoing their own work." Spence then apologized to committee Democrats, explaining that his criticism of the administration was not aimed at them.

In December 1995, Clinton vetoed the fiscal 1996 defense spending bill, in part because it spent more than he desired, but also because he opposed a provision that would have mandated deployment of a nationwide anti-missile defense system by 2003. The missile defense language was ultimately dropped as conferees crafted a second spending bill Clinton signed in early 1996.

Spence and fellow missile defense proponents believe support for such a system would be overwhelming if public attention could be focused on the fact that the United States cannot fend off an incoming ballistic missile warhead. Spence recalls a focus group organized in Columbia, S.C., by GOP pollster Frank Luntz's firm in which 16 people expressed astonishment that the United States could not block a missile aimed at its territory. "They were incredulous," Spence said. "They were angry and wanted to know who was responsible for us being left naked."

But given the problems that missile defense language caused in reaching agreement on the fiscal 1996 defense spending bill, Spence omitted the language when he drafted the fiscal 1997 defense bill. The GOP leadership moved the missile-defense language as a free-standing bill, but the "Defend America Act" was pulled from consideration when high cost estimates from the Congressional Budget Office alarmed some deficit-conscious conservatives.

Spence was able to secure money to develop a system to protect U.S. territory from a limited number of attacking missiles and for systems to protect U.S. and allied forces in the field.

Whatever his difficulties, Spence could claim success in the 104th in his overarching goal to increase defense spending, as both the fiscal 1996 and 1997 bills included more than Clinton sought.

The GOP quest for a more robust defense budget is opposed by ranking Democrat Dellums, who chaired the committee in the 103rd Congress. Spence and Dellums come from opposite coasts and opposite ends of the ideological spectrum.

Despite their differences, the two men have worked together. They joined forces in July 1996 to scale back legislation proposed by the Intelligence Committee that would have expanded the power of the director of Central Intelligence at the expense of the secretary of Defense. Spence and Dellums and the committee came down squarely on the Pentagon's side in the long-running turf war over reorganizing intelligence agencies.

Spence's only other committee assignment is also military-related: Veterans' Affairs.

At Home: It is usually to a challenger's advantage to campaign against an incumbent of infirm health. But in 1988, Democrats never could get a handle on the health issue against Spence, even though his illness, transplant surgery and recovery limited his campaigning.

In the fall, Democratic challenger Jim Leventis had to campaign in the context of flattering media attention of the recovering Spence as a medical marvel who had won a reprieve from death.

Leventis was a strong, well-financed contender. A 50-year-old attorney and banker, he boasted personal or professional contacts with many in the business and political elite of Columbia, the 2nd's largest city. In crucial Lexington County, suburban home of Columbia's professional class, Spence amassed 68 percent of the vote, overcoming Leventis' modest margins in Richland County (Columbia) and majority-black Orangeburg County. Overall, Spence took 53 percent. That was his last competitive election.

After his days as a star athlete at the University of South Carolina and then practice as a lawyer, Spence won a state House seat as a Democrat. But he quit the party in 1962, complaining it was too liberal, and ran for Congress as a Republican. Spence was a consensus choice for the 1962 GOP nomination in the open 2nd. But he narrowly lost to a conservative Democrat, state Sen. Albert W. Watson. Watson himself switched parties in 1965 and in 1970 ran for governor as a Republican. Spence tried again for Congress, stressing his opposition to the busing decisions of the U.S. Supreme Court. He took 53 percent against Democrat Heyward McDonald, and his re-election tally did not dip that low again until the 1988 contest.

HOUSE ELECTIONS

1996 General		
Floyd D. Spence (R)	158,229	(90%)
Maurice T. Raiford (NL)	17,713	(10%)
1994 General		
Floyd D. Spence (R)	133,307	(100%)

Previous Winning Percentages: **1992** (88%) **1990** (89%) **1988** (53%) **1986** (54%) **1984** (62%) **1982** (59%) **1980** (56%) **1978** (57%) **1976** (58%) **1974** (56%) **1972** (100%) **1970** (53%)

CAMPAIGN FINANCE

	Receipts	Receipts from PACs	Expend-itures
1996			
Spence (R)	$340,486	$259,650 (76%)	$303,421
1994			
Spence (R)	$179,401	$145,670 (81%)	$149,321

DISTRICT VOTE FOR PRESIDENT

1996		1992	
D	89,629 (41%)	**D**	82,964 (36%)
R	117,914 (54%)	**R**	119,122 (52%)
I	10,856 (5%)	**I**	25,592 (11%)

KEY VOTES

1997	
Ban "partial birth" abortions	Y
1996	
Approve farm bill	Y
Deny public education to illegal immigrants	Y
Repeal ban on certain assault-style weapons	Y
Increase minimum wage	N
Freeze defense spending	N
Approve welfare overhaul	Y
1995	
Approve balanced-budget constitutional amendment	Y
Relax Clean Water Act regulations	Y
Oppose limits on environmental regulations	N
Reduce projected Medicare spending	Y
Approve GOP budget with tax and spending cuts	Y

VOTING STUDIES

	Presidential Support		Party Unity		Conservative Coalition	
Year	S	O	S	O	S	O
1996	35	65	95	4	100	0
1995	18	81	95	3	97	1
1994	53	46	87	11	92	8
1993	41	59	89	10	95	5
1992	76	24	82	17	98	2
1991	74	19	75	18	86	8

INTEREST GROUP RATINGS

Year	ADA	AFL-CIO	CCUS	ACU
1996	5	n/a	88	100
1995	0	0	96	92
1994	5	33	82	95
1993	5	17	82	96
1992	15	42	75	92
1991	10	25	80	95

3 Lindsey Graham (R)

Of Seneca — Elected 1994, 2nd term

Biographical Information
Born: July 9, 1955, Seneca, S.C.
Education: U. of South Carolina, B.A. 1977, M.P.A. 1978, J.D. 1981.
Military Service: Air Force, 1982-88, 1990; Air National Guard, 1989-present.
Occupation: Lawyer.
Family: Single.
Religion: Southern Baptist.
Political Career: S.C. assistant attorney, 1988-92; S.C. House, 1992-95.

Capitol Office: 1429 Longworth Bldg. 20515; 225-5301.

Committees
Education & Workforce
Postsecondary Education, Training & Life-Long Learning (vice); Workforce Protections
International Relations
International Economic Policy & Trade; International Operations & Human Rights
National Security
Military Personnel; Military Procurement

In Washington: Graham is the first Republican to represent South Carolina's 3rd District since 1877, and his 1994 victory was part of a regionwide conservative surge that gave the GOP its first majority of the South's House seats since Reconstruction. He fits comfortably on the Republican right, espousing conservative views on social issues, pledging to spend taxpayers' dollars sparingly and supporting political reforms such as congressional term limits.

Graham, who says he will not serve more than 12 years in the House, believes that limiting terms would "change the motivation" of people in Congress. "They will be less interested in trying to find a pork-barrel project to [help them] get . . . reelected, and more interested in trying to make the world better where [they] are going to go back to, and that is home," he once told the House. (Asked to justify his support of South Carolina GOP Sen. Strom Thurmond's bid for a seventh full term in 1996, Graham said, "I am looking at institutional changes. There is no use picking on one person.")

Early in the 105th Congress, when the House considered 11 versions of a term limits amendment to the Constitution, Graham voted for every one, including a proposal offered by Republican Bill McCollum of Florida to limit House and Senate members to 12 years in office, not counting time already served. The tally on that plan was 217-211 — 69 votes short of the two-thirds majority needed for passage. Graham had introduced his own term limits proposal, one establishing three four-year terms for the House and limiting senators to two six-year terms. The House did not consider his plan, however.

Graham also strongly supported a measure approved in 1995 that prohibited House members and their staff from accepting gifts, meals and trips, except for those from family members and friends. "It's not about whether you can be bought," Graham said of the gift-ban measure. "It's about adopting the values the people want. In South Carolina you cannot take anything of value from a registered lobbyist, and the government still works," he told The Washington Times. Lawmakers' ethics are a sensitive issue in South Carolina, which a few years back saw its state legislature rocked by a bribery-for-votes scandal.

In the fiscal-policy arena, Graham at times has taken an even harder line than the GOP leadership on restraining federal spending. In early 1996, when the Republican Congress was grappling with the Clinton administration over the terms of a budget plan, Graham was one of 12 members of the Class of 1994 to disobey House Speaker Newt Gingrich and vote against reopening the federal government.

Early in the 104th, Graham supported passage of a balanced-budget constitutional amendment that allowed for tax increases only with the concurrence of a three-fifths majority in each chamber. The GOP leadership felt the restrictive tax provision would cost the amendment support, but Graham warned that Congress needed to act decisively to restrain the impulse of Washington to tax and spend. Otherwise, he told the House, "everybody in the country begins to look to the federal government to solve every problem they have" and "over time you ruin the character of your people." Ultimately, GOP leaders allowed a vote on the version of the balanced-budget amendment Graham backed, and it failed to garner the two-thirds majority needed for passage.

Although Graham typically seeks to limit the scope of the federal government, in one area he is a notable opponent of cutbacks. During June 1995 debate on a defense authorization bill, Graham objected to cutting $50 million in funding for the production of tritium — a radioactive form of hydrogen gas that is a critical element of nuclear warheads. The gas must be replenished because it decays. The 3rd District is home to the Savannah River Nuclear Complex, a longtime tritium producer.

In the 105th, Graham gained appointment to the National Security Committee, where he sits on the Military Procurement Subcommittee, which authorizes most of Savannah River's annual budget. Early in 1997, he spoke against

SOUTH CAROLINA 3
West — Anderson; Aiken

As South Carolina has grown in recent years, it has grown steadily more Republican. That trend is clear in the 3rd, a one-time "yellow dog" Democratic district where GOP candidates now typically win up-ballot contests. Graham is the first Republican to hold the seat since Reconstruction.

Nearly half the district vote is cast in three counties — Anderson, Pickens and Oconee — that are part of South Carolina's "upcountry" and have a diverse economic base. The biggest, Anderson, benefits from its proximity to the Greenville-Spartanburg area, just a few miles up Interstate 85 in the 4th District.

Northern and foreign industries find wages, taxes and living costs in the upcountry hospitable. The plants and businesses have brought in an increasingly skilled and white-collar work force.

Now, towns once dependent upon cotton mills churn out a variety of products, including tires, auto parts and refrigerators. At the same time, many textile mills have converted to high-tech fiber manufacturers; in the city of Anderson, Clarks Schwabel makes the skin for stealth fighters.

Clemson University and its 17,000 students provide economic insurance for Pickens County, and a conservative pull comes from its agriculture- and engineering-oriented faculty. Bob Dole won the county by more than 2-to-1 in 1996, as did Graham.

Growth, prosperity and a large business community in the northern part of the 3rd have boosted GOP fortunes, though Democrats still dominate local political offices.

Dole won all but two counties — sparsely populated Abbeville and McCormick — in the 3rd, winning the district with 54 percent of the vote. Graham also carried all but those two counties in 1996, winning with 60 percent, the same percentage with which he won in 1994.

Traditional Democratic voting habits still hold sway in the rural midsection of the district, where a sizable black population and less prosperity have kept the GOP from building momentum. Abbeville, McCormick and Edgefield were the only counties not to support George Bush in 1992. McCormick even refused to back GOP Sen. Strom Thurmond when he easily won re-election in 1990, perhaps to spite state officials for changing the name of their local lake — Clark's Hill — to Thurmond Lake. McCormick did opt for Thurmond in 1996.

At its southern end, the 3rd includes most of the people in Aiken County, although 1992 redistricting put the eastern half of the county in the 2nd. Known as the polo center of the South — matches are every Sunday at Whitney Field — the town of Aiken is a picture of gentility preserved, with more than 70 historic homes and gardens, six golf courses and three racetracks.

Aiken is Thurmond's home base, and the white-collar commuters to Augusta, Ga., and Ph.D.s working at the Savannah River Nuclear Complex make it solidly Republican. Dole won by nearly 2-to-1 here, while Graham did better than that.

1990 Population: 581,116. White 454,983 (78%), Black 122,444 (21%), Other 3,689 (1%). Hispanic origin 3,071 (1%). 18 and over 435,177 (75%), 62 and over 91,186 (16%). Median age: 34.

President Clinton's proposed fiscal 1998 budget, complaining that it would cut funding for Savannah River by $128 million. "If the numbers are left unchanged, the site would be forced to lay off up to 2,000 employees and suffer serious deficiencies in existing cleanup missions vital to the nation," Graham said. He also took a seat on the International Relations Committee in the 105th.

In his first term, Graham was an early and vocal critic of increasing the minimum wage. At a hearing of the Economic and Educational Opportunities Committee in January 1995, he told Labor Secretary Robert B. Reich that "I didn't promise to raise the minimum wage, and I was elected overwhelmingly," The Washington Times reported. In May 1996, Graham voted against raising the minimum wage by 90 cents an hour, but in August, when the wage increase won final passage in the House, he voted "yea." The final version of the wage bill included other provisions sought by Republicans, including $10 billion in business tax cuts over five years, a $5,000 tax credit to offset the cost of adoption and an expansion of Individual Retirement Accounts.

Graham also supported a measure to allow non-union companies to set up and control worker-management committees that could "address matters of mutual interest." Labor groups opposed the bill, arguing that it would erode workers' job security and was really aimed at undermining organized labor. But supporters said that more employer-employee cooperation is needed for companies to remain competitive in the international marketplace. The House passed the bill, 221-202, in September 1995.

On social policy issues, Graham hews to the right. He opposes abortion, he voted to repeal the ban on certain semiautomatic assault-style weapons and he favors amending the Constitution to outlaw flag desecration. "If you feel the need to burn something," he once said, "burn your congressman in effigy, burn me, do not burn the flag."

At Home: Graham captured a traditionally Democratic district when it was open in 1994 and easily defended it for the GOP in 1996.

He is one of the few in the House Class of 1994 with military experience, though his work in uniform was primarily as a lawyer. He graduated from the University of South Carolina in 1981 (having earned degrees in psychology and law), worked for two years in the legal office of Shaw Air Force Base in Sumter, S.C., and then was chief prosecutor for the Air Force in Europe from 1984 to 1988. Returning to South Carolina, he was assistant county attorney in Oconee County and city attorney for Central, S.C. As a member of the Air National Guard, he was called to active duty during Desert Shield and Desert Storm; posted in South Carolina, his responsibilities included processing wills.

In 1992 he won a seat in the state House, and there he successfully pushed legislation barring homosexuals from the state's National Guard.

Graham saw an opportunity for political advancement early in 1994, when 10-term Democratic Rep. Butler Derrick decided to retire. Derrick had once predicted that his district would go Republican when he left, and he turned out to be correct. In the GOP primary, Graham proved an able organizer and fundraiser, and he won 52 percent of the vote against a lawyer and a county council member. The primary turnout hinted at the difficulty Democrats would face in holding the district in November: The Republican contest drew over 6,000 more voters than a hotly competitive Democratic primary. State Sen. James Bryan secured the Democratic nomination in a runoff.

In the fall campaign, Bryan highlighted his humble origins, which included putting himself through college and law school, partly by working as a guard at a maximum security prison. But Graham was not without an interesting life story. At age 20, he had become the legal guardian of his teenage sister after his parents died.

Bryan thought he had an opening when Graham enthusiastically supported the GOP's "Contract With America." Bryan attacked the contract's credibility and charged that Graham was allowing himself to be a tool of his national party. But in a district where even Derrick had posted some lukewarm re-election tallies in his later campaigns, the voters' mood in 1994 was decidedly favorable for Republican Graham. Bryan refused to rule out voting for legislation that would restrict firearms, and the National Rifle Association mailed a letter in Graham's behalf to its members in the district. Although Bryan won his home county of Laurens and carried traditionally Democratic Abbeville and McCormick, Graham ran up huge margins in Oconee, Pickens and Aiken counties, and he won overall with a decisive 60 percent tally.

He earned the same vote share in 1996, running against Democratic lawyer Debbie Dorn, the daughter of former Democratic Rep. William Jennings Bryan Dorn, who held the 3rd from 1947 to 1949 and from 1951 to 1975.

HOUSE ELECTIONS

1996 General		
Lindsey Graham (R)	114,273	(60%)
Debbie Dorn (D)	73,417	(39%)
1994 General		
Lindsey Graham (R)	90,123	(60%)
James Bryan (D)	59,932	(40%)

CAMPAIGN FINANCE

	Receipts	Receipts from PACs	Expend-itures
1996			
Graham (R)	$683,213	$226,297 (33%)	$644,451
Dorn (D)	$132,561	$24,850 (19%)	$128,230
1994			
Graham (R)	$573,225	$116,287 (20%)	$551,212
Bryan (D)	$444,083	$76,250 (17%)	$443,965

DISTRICT VOTE FOR PRESIDENT

	1996		1992
D	71,855 (39%)	D	69,365 (35%)
R	99,859 (54%)	R	102,458 (52%)
I	13,176 (7%)	I	26,609 (13%)

KEY VOTES

1997	
Ban "partial birth" abortions	Y
1996	
Approve farm bill	Y
Deny public education to illegal immigrants	Y
Repeal ban on certain assault-style weapons	Y
Increase minimum wage	N
Freeze defense spending	N
Approve welfare overhaul	Y
1995	
Approve balanced-budget constitutional amendment	Y
Relax Clean Water Act regulations	Y
Oppose limits on environmental regulations	N
Reduce projected Medicare spending	Y
Approve GOP budget with tax and spending cuts	Y

VOTING STUDIES

	Presidential Support		Party Unity		Conservative Coalition	
Year	S	O	S	O	S	O
1996	34	65	96	4	98	2
1995	20	80	93	5	95	5

INTEREST GROUP RATINGS

Year	ADA	AFL-CIO	CCUS	ACU
1996	0	n/a	100	100
1995	5	0	96	96

4 Bob Inglis (R)

Of Greenville — Elected 1992, 3rd term

Biographical Information
Born: Oct. 11, 1959, Savannah, Ga.
Education: Duke U., A.B. 1981; U. of Virginia, J.D. 1984.
Occupation: Lawyer.
Family: Wife, Mary Anne Williams; five children.
Religion: Presbyterian.
Political Career: No previous office.
Capitol Office: 320 Cannon Bldg. 20515; 225-6030.

Committees
Budget
Judiciary
Commercial & Administrative Law; Constitution

In Washington: A true political outsider whose first-ever campaign ambushed a popular Democratic incumbent, Inglis has sought as ardently as any other Republican "revolutionary" to alter legislative life in the nation's capital.

Inglis would like to ban PACs and end members' free mailing privileges, but what he feels most strongly about is limiting congressional terms. Inglis says that members who are truly reform-minded must be willing to stand up for term limits, even though it may not be in their own self-interest. (He once quipped that asking Congress to vote for term limits was a little like asking the chicken to vote for Colonel Sanders.) Inglis in the 104th and 105th congresses saw efforts to pass a term-limits constitutional amendment fall short, but he is sticking by his promise to serve no more than three terms in the House, so he will leave the chamber at the end of the 105th.

He does not, however, want to leave politics. His exit from the House coincides with a South Carolina Senate race, open on the Republican side, that Inglis announced in January 1997 he would enter. Inglis laid the philosophical groundwork for such a move during one of his many floor speeches on the subject of term limits.

Rebutting the argument that term limits would drain the talent pool in the House, Inglis contended, "We are not going to lose the talent; we are going to redirect it. All the folks we are hearing about we are going to lose, they might be the president of the United States if we forced them out of here, or might be a great senator, or maybe a governor."

Inglis often argues by homey example, and he reasons that since the average American changes jobs every six years, members of Congress should stick to the same standard. He contends that a high turnover rate will not only lead to a Congress that is more in tune with its constituents but one that is more efficient as well, as new members come in with proposals they know they'll have to hurry to enact.

Even the Supreme Court's May 1995 decision to nullify term limits that had been approved through state ballot initiatives could not dent Inglis' optimism.

"One of the ways you increase the passion for an issue is to have an adverse decision like this," Inglis said of the Supreme Court's judgment.

Should South Carolina voters choose to send Inglis to the Senate, they will be electing an ardent and occasionally graphic opponent of abortion, and someone who overall is one of the most unblinking adherents of the contemporary conservative agenda.

Inglis serves on the Budget and Judiciary committees, where he has often tangled with Democrats. He is a reliable vote for his party's leaders, though he has candidly expressed unease on occasions when party loyalty butts up against his principles. He admitted that his support of South Carolina Republican Sen. Strom Thurmond's run in 1996 for a seventh full term was "an obvious inconsistency" with his drum beating for term limits. More significantly, he wavered about supporting Newt Gingrich for Speaker in the 105th Congress.

"The more troubling question is how the Speaker came to mislead the [ethics] committee about these allegations" of campaign finance irregularities, Inglis said. "It's a troubling matter." In the end, Inglis voted for Gingrich to serve as Speaker.

Typically, though, Inglis can be heard railing against any kind of "business as usual" attitude in the legislative process. He would have colleagues weigh every federal spending proposal against the advice a constituent once offered: "Run the Congress as though you are bankrupt."

In 1996, Inglis likened highway demonstration projects to "holy water" sprinkled by members wastefully within their districts. Inglis argued that in highway systems as in many other areas he believed states could determine their own needs better than federal legislators. He earlier had voted to kill the superconducting super collider and NASA's space station, even though suppliers for both projects were in his district. "Pork is

SOUTH CAROLINA 4
Northwest — Greenville; Spartanburg

The nucleus of the 4th is Greenville County, the most populous county in the state and a showpiece of New South industrialism.

The city of Greenville developed as a textile center after the Civil War. Although employment in the mills and clothing manufacturers declined as that industry moved farther south, the city has not suffered the same depressing fate as other textile-dependent areas. Instead, civic leaders lured Frost Belt and overseas investment to the area, ensuring a robust economy and driving the steady population growth of Greenville and Spartanburg counties.

They call the stretch of interstate between those two cities "the autobahn" because of the foreign-owned industries along it. This is where BMW chose to build its first U.S. plant, near Michelin, Hoechst Celanese, Hitachi, General Electric and other multinational corporations.

Greenville County has a history of conservatism dating to its Tory leanings during the American Revolution. It was one of the first areas in the state to embrace Republicanism after World War II.

Growth in such white-collar occupations as engineering and management have made the area increasingly affluent, and that has intensified its GOP leanings. Bob Dole won the 4th with 56 percent in 1996, while Inglis cruised to a third term with 71 percent.

Beneath an apparently unified conservative voting population, however, there are two distinct camps in the local GOP: mainstream, business-oriented conservatives and intensely conservative Christian fundamentalists focused around Greenville-based Bob Jones University. Former Democratic Rep. Liz J. Patterson held the 4th for six years by appealing to the business crowd. But in 1992, Inglis united the GOP and ousted her.

Democrats in Greenville County tend to be conservative and often vote for GOP candidates. A small band of liberal Democrats in the city of Greenville does not offer much of a launching pad for left-leaning candidates.

Spartanburg County scored a coup with the 1992 announcement that BMW would build its U.S. assembly line here; it employs about 2,000 people. Textile work is still big, with Milliken and Co. the leader in that industry. Agriculture also plays a role; Spartanburg's sprawling orchards hold bragging rights to the second biggest peach crop in the South.

Rank-and-file textile workers and farm laborers give Spartanburg firmer Democratic loyalties than Greenville has. Patterson carried the county in 1992. But in statewide and national races, voters here typically opt for the GOP, if not by the margins that Greenville provides. In 1996, Dole got 54 percent in Spartanburg and 59 percent in Greenville; Inglis won both easily.

Rural Union County usually delivers its votes to Democrats, though it too went for Inglis in 1996.

1990 Population: 581,113. White 460,805 (79%), Black 114,332 (20%), Other 5,976 (1%). Hispanic origin 4,655 (1%). 18 and over 437,837 (75%), 62 and over 86,874 (15%). Median age: 34.

pork," he said.

Inglis sees the social-policy agenda of the Clinton administration as a political call to arms for conservatives: "Right now there is a cultural war in this country to determine whose set of values rule," he said in 1993. "Unfortunately, we have a number of people at the White House that believe that the basic unit of society is not the family, it is the social worker and his or her client."

Inglis is closely allied with social conservatives; when the Federal Election Commission filed a 1996 lawsuit against the Christian Coalition for allegedly violating election laws by trying to elect Republicans, Inglis' 1992 race was singled out as an example of the group illegally acting "in coordination, cooperation and/or consultation" with a candidate's campaign.

Inglis strongly backed a 1996 law that defined marriage as the union of a man and a woman, worrying that if the government recognized same-gender marriages it would have to recognize polygamy as well.

He refers to abortion as "the critical moral question of our day" and describes women who have had abortion as victims, frequently expressing "compassion for the victims of abortion that are walking around today." Inglis supports a parental notification requirement for minors' abortions and opposes federal funding of abortions for low-income women. He wishes to ban a particular abortion technique that opponents call "partial-birth" abortion, referring to doctors who perform it as "hired assassins." When the Judiciary Committee considered a ban in 1995, Inglis challenged a medical doctor who was testifying to explain the difference between the procedure and an infant having its head chopped off.

Inglis' views of foreign affairs are shaped by a skeptical attitude about the ability to impose peace and humanitarian principles on other nations. Referring to atrocities in Bosnia, Inglis stated that "This is the normal inhumanity of man against man, normal hatred." He also expressed outright opposition to a U.S. role in the former Yugoslavia, circulating a letter among members in

1995 seeking to block President Clinton from sending troops there.

"I think if you are going to wage peace, you do not send in the U.S. Army. The U.S. Army goes into places to crush, kill and destroy," Inglis said. "If there is a peace, there is no need for peacekeepers. They have peace."

Completing a record of near-total opposition to Clinton's major objectives, Inglis also voted against NAFTA in 1993 and GATT in 1994. He said NAFTA would "create a positive investment climate in Mexico while ours is becoming more and more negative" because of federal taxes and regulations borne by U.S. businesses.

Inglis did, however, share a stage with Clinton when the president came to Greeleyville in 1996 to decry a series of church burnings. Inglis believed that such an issue should not be politicized.

At Home: A summa cum laude graduate of Duke University with a law degree from the University of Virginia, Inglis at 31 became the youngest partner in one of Greenville's most prestigious law firms. He generated substantial income for the firm with his successful practice in commercial law.

Inglis began plotting his quest for Congress after 1990, betting that voters' anti-incumbent sentiment would continue to build. He waged an intensive door-to-door effort that countered the strong ties Democratic Rep. Liz J. Patterson had established in the district. Through force of personality and a moderate voting record, she had neutralized the solid GOP tilt of the 4th.

Inglis accepted no PAC money, while nearly three-fifths of Patterson's contributions came from PACs. He advertised himself as "un-bought and not for sale," a "citizen statesman, not a professional politician." Throughout the campaign, Inglis was seen as a long shot, but Clinton was intensely unpopular in the 4th, and that created a climate that Patterson's personal appeal could not overcome. George Bush carried the 4th with 55 percent, and Inglis won with 50 percent.

After the election, Patterson blamed her stunning loss on negative campaigning by Inglis and the Christian Coalition, which distributed thousands of leaflets opposing her. Inglis, brushing aside that charge, said he had campaigned not so much against Patterson as against Congress itself.

In both his re-election campaigns, Inglis topped 70 percent of the vote.

HOUSE ELECTIONS

1996 General		
Bob Inglis (R)	138,165	(71%)
Darrell E. Curry (D)	54,126	(28%)
C. Faye Walters (NL)	2,501	(1%)
1994 General		
Bob Inglis (R)	109,626	(73%)
Jerry Fowler (D)	39,396	(26%)

Previous Winning Percentages: 1992 (50%)

CAMPAIGN FINANCE

	Receipts	Receipts from PACs	Expend-itures
1996			
Inglis (R)	$300,543	$0 (0%)	$143,966
Curry (D)	$16,153	$6,000 (37%)	$15,643
1994			
Inglis (R)	$406,691	$0 (0%)	$184,079
Fowler (D)	$15,598	$500 (3%)	$6,311

DISTRICT VOTE FOR PRESIDENT

1996		1992	
D	74,174 (37%)	**D**	65,092 (33%)
R	111,706 (56%)	**R**	107,983 (55%)
I	11,496 (6%)	**I**	24,136 (12%)

KEY VOTES

1997	
Ban "partial birth" abortions	Y
1996	
Approve farm bill	Y
Deny public education to illegal immigrants	Y
Repeal ban on certain assault-style weapons	Y
Increase minimum wage	N
Freeze defense spending	N
Approve welfare overhaul	Y
1995	
Approve balanced-budget constitutional amendment	Y
Relax Clean Water Act regulations	Y
Oppose limits on environmental regulations	N
Reduce projected Medicare spending	Y
Approve GOP budget with tax and spending cuts	Y

VOTING STUDIES

	Presidential Support		Party Unity		Conservative Coalition	
Year	S	O	S	O	S	O
1996	33	65	94	5	90	6
1995	17	83	96	4	92	8
1994	38	62	85	14	92	8
1993	25	75	84	14	89	11

INTEREST GROUP RATINGS

Year	ADA	AFL-CIO	CCUS	ACU
1996	10	n/a	87	100
1995	0	0	96	92
1994	5	22	67	100
1993	10	8	82	100

5 John M. Spratt Jr. (D)

Of York — Elected 1982, 8th term

Biographical Information
Born: Nov. 1, 1942, Charlotte, N.C.
Education: Davidson College, A.B. 1964; Oxford U., M.A. 1966; Yale U., LL.B. 1969.
Military Service: Army, 1969-71.
Occupation: Lawyer.
Family: Wife, Jane Stacy; three children.
Religion: Presbyterian.
Political Career: No previous office.
Capitol Office: 1536 Longworth Bldg. 20515; 225-5501.

Committees
Budget (ranking)
National Security
Military Procurement

In Washington: For years an influential centrist on matters military, Spratt is well accustomed to being perched between members to his left and to his right on the National Security Committee. In the 105th, he carries his political and legislative smarts into a new arena, serving as top Democrat on the Budget Committee.

Four years after losing out in a bid to become Budget chairman, Spratt defeated, 106-83, the more liberal Louise M. Slaughter of New York to take the panel's ranking spot in 1997. Some liberal members called it unjust that women would not serve as ranking member of any congressional committees for the 105th. Spratt said he was "sympathetic" to that plea, calling the diversity argument "powerful"; but he added, "You don't have to defer to that principle in every case."

In his new role, Spratt complained early in the 105th about Republican reluctance to put up an alternative to President Clinton's fiscal 1998 budget. But Spratt then played a leading role in negotiating the massive 1997 budget compromise. It gave Republicans tax cuts and spending cuts (although much smaller ones then they had initially demanded), and it gave Clinton limited money for selected priorities, including an additional $16 billion over five years to provide health insurance for up to five million uninsured children and an additional $9.7 billion to restore certain federal benefits for legal immigrants scheduled to lose them under the 1996 welfare overhaul.

Spratt pushed the House to accept the agreement, but acknowledged, "We have...a choice between gridlock and compromise, and what we have before us is just that — it is compromise. It is not a perfect solution." The House passed it in May 1997 by a 333-99 vote.

On National Security, he has often taken issue with GOP spending priorities, while maintaining his rhetorical zeal for a strong defense.

He handed the GOP its first setback as the majority party in February 1995. When a Republican defense bill came to the floor, Spratt offered an amendment stipulating that anti-missile defenses for U.S. territory merit lower priority than maintaining the readiness of U.S. forces and fielding defenses to protect troops in the field. The amendment was adopted 218-212, with 24 Republicans voting with the Democrats.

For nearly a decade, Spratt had been the kingpin among centrist House Democrats on the missile defense issue. Introduced to it by a staff member, Spratt nourished his curiosity through a network of contacts in the defense scientific community, managing the anti-missile issue while higher-ranking panel Democrats wrestled with the broader issues of fashioning a defense program that would unite Democrats. Spratt favors both theater defenses and preservation of the Anti-Ballistic Missile (ABM) Treaty, but he opposes space-based weapons.

That history lent him credibility as he upended the GOP bill's emphasis on strategic defenses. Spratt's amendment continued the Democratic ploy of hammering at the potential budgetary impact of a nationwide anti-missile defense. Still, Speaker Newt Gingrich was nonchalant about the defeat: "After something like 145 votes, we finally lost one. We think that's pretty remarkable."

During the 104th, Spratt's efforts to cajole his Democratic colleagues into supporting defense programs they had traditionally opposed generally met with more success than his efforts to sway Republicans to take the edge off of their proposals.

During consideration of the fiscal 1996 defense authorization bill, Spratt offered an amendment to stipulate that nothing in the package was intended to violate the 1972 ABM Treaty. Although senior Republicans vehemently insisted that the bill did not mandate abrogation of the treaty, Spratt contended that some provisions telegraphed an intention to scrap it. He preferred to negotiate treaty amendments with Russia, arguing that it would be cheaper to persuade Russia to scrap parts of its nuclear arsenal than to build defenses against those missiles. Republicans countered that the country needed to be protected against attack by other nations and defeated Spratt's amendment, 185-242.

SOUTH CAROLINA 5
North Central — Rock Hill

Touching on four distinct regions of South Carolina, the 5th extends from the hills of Cherokee County south to the low country around Sumter. To command a districtwide media presence, a candidate has to buy time in four cities outside the district: Greenville, Columbia, Florence and Charlotte, N.C.

This geographic diversity makes it difficult to pigeonhole the district's personality. In the west, rural counties such as Newberry, Chester, Lancaster and Kershaw produce cotton for the textile mills that historically have dominated this region's economy.

The small but growing cities of Rock Hill and Sumter add urbane, progressive immigrants from the North to the population mix. In the east, residents of Chesterfield, Dillon and Marlboro counties depend heavily on tobacco farming.

Linking the two rural parts of the district is their common struggle with declining economies. About 20 percent of the tobacco-producing counties live in poverty, and modernization has stripped many mills in the west of their plentiful, low-skill jobs.

To the north, the city of Rock Hill provides population and suburban affluence to the district. Once heavily textile-dependent, county residents now gravitate north toward white-collar jobs in Charlotte. In fact, the area's biggest challenge may be to avoid surrendering its identity to Charlotte's yuppies, who traverse I-77 searching for bedroom communities.

Native industry here still includes textile mills; many have converted from weaving cotton to producing high-tech fibers for industrial uses.

Rock Hill grew modestly during the 1980s but is experiencing faster growth in the 1990s. The settlement in the Catawba Indians' claim to 144,000 acres in two counties — which stymied investment as buyers worried about a proposed lawsuit against 62,000 individual landowners — has helped to unleash a pent-up drive for development.

In national elections, increasing affluence has persuaded some areas to abandon their Democratic heritage.

Bob Dole reaped 52 percent of the 1996 vote in York County while barely beating Bill Clinton districtwide. And Spratt has had an increasingly difficult time holding on to the "yellow dog" Democrats, mostly mill and agricultural workers who inherited ideological proclivities from their parents and grandparents. In 1996, Spratt recovered from his career-low showing two years earlier but still lost three of the district's 13 counties

York County's days as a hotbed of religious conservatism have been fading, however, since television evangelist Jim Bakker's downfall and incarceration forced him to abandon his PTL headquarters in Fort Mill; some of Bakker's supporters since have moved elsewhere.

Other conservative votes in the district come from the counties of Sumter (home of Shaw Air Force Base) and Kershaw.

1990 Population: 581,131. White 396,287 (68%), Black 179,155 (31%), Other 5,689 (1%). Hispanic origin 3,233 (1%). 18 and over 422,575 (73%), 62 and over 83,253 (14%). Median age: 32.

Outside the defense arena, Spratt showed a conservative side with his opposition to a particular abortion technique that opponents call a "partial birth" abortion and his efforts to shield children from "violence and vulgarity" on television. He joined with James P. Moran, D-Va., in sponsoring legislation that would have yanked licenses from TV stations that aired violent programs during hours when many children were watching. Although that provision went nowhere, Spratt was a cosponsor of the 1996 telecommunications law's requirement that most new TV sets come with a "v-chip" to allow parents to block out objectionable programming.

Spratt supported a constitutional amendment to balance the federal budget in both 1994 and 1995 and got behind GOP efforts to give the president a form of line-item veto power. He pushed Republicans to speed up the process of enacting the latter bill and also sought, unsuccessfully, to extend that veto to tax incentives.

He supported GOP attempts to ease federal regulations, but grew cautious when it appeared that Republican efforts might endanger the cleanup of hazardous waste. In January 1995, some 1,800 containers of hazardous waste awaiting incineration in his district caught fire and virtually melted the metal building that housed them. Much of the waste handled at that incinerator came from out of state, and Spratt worried about South Carolina's ability to regulate that waste without federal help.

Spratt has been a leading advocate for the textile industry that helps fuel the 5th's economy. He was persuaded to vote for NAFTA in 1993 when the Clinton administration gained an agreement from the Philippines and some other developing countries to accept a phaseout of existing U.S. textile import quotas over 15 years, rather than 10 years. Spratt opposes China's most-favored-nation trading status in part because of its textile policies.

As the 103rd Congress began, Spratt unsuccessfully sought the Budget Committee chairmanship, running as a moderate against liberal Rep. Martin Olav Sabo of Minnesota. Within the liberal-tilted Democratic Caucus, Sabo had a clear edge; he defeated Spratt by a vote of 149-112.

At Home: With his lofty academic credentials (Davidson, Oxford, Yale) and background in law and banking, Spratt is not the obvious choice for a district where many of the Democratic voters come from poor textile towns and dusty farms.

Spratt did not have a close race until 1994. Republican Larry L. Bigham, a Rock Hill restaurant owner whose only political experience was service on a local school board and an unsuccessful state Senate bid, distributed bumper stickers reading, "Stop the Clinton-Spratt agenda."

When Bigham and the electoral climate looked increasingly dangerous for Spratt, he guaranteed a $200,000 loan to his campaign. The money helped Spratt continue his attacks on the House GOP's "Contract With America," which Bigham signed, and to stress his own conservative views and service to the district. Spratt sent a targeted mailing to senior citizens, telling them that the contract threatened Medicare and Social Security. He squeezed by with 52 percent.

Spratt improved on that total in a 1996 rematch with Bigham. He continued the argument that Republicans like Bigham would harm Medicare, while Bigham charged that Spratt voted with liberals in Washington. Spratt touted his efforts at keeping Shaw Air Force Base off the closure list and, with Clinton running stronger in the district and more blacks turning out than had been the case in 1994, Spratt won by an 11-point margin.

In 1982, when Democratic Rep. Ken Holland announced his retirement just before the filing deadline, Spratt jumped for the Democratic nomination, as did former Holland aide John Winburn and state Rep. Ernie Nunnery.

Winburn had Holland's contacts and Nunnery had a base in Chester County, but Spratt's banking interests and his law practice gave him strong connections in political and business circles. Many Democratic leaders quietly backed him. And when Winburn called Spratt "a millionaire banker, lawyer and hobby farmer" who could not relate to ordinary people, Spratt persuasively argued that his work with small-town clients and depositors had given him an understanding of their circumstances. Spratt finished first in the primary with 38 percent of the vote, then took 55 percent in a runoff against Winburn.

In November, Republican John Wilkerson, a longtime friend and legal client of Spratt's, accused the Democrat of being too liberal for the district. But Spratt appealed to the district's prevailing partisan loyalties and had a clear organizational edge. When he visited county courthouses, rural areas and factories, he often had a locally popular political figure close at hand. One source described Wilkerson's core supporters as "the country club boys — the fellows who put ice in their whiskey." Spratt won two-thirds of the vote.

HOUSE ELECTIONS

1996 General		
John M. Spratt Jr. (D)	97,174	(54%)
Larry L. Bigham (R)	81,360	(45%)
1994 General		
John M. Spratt Jr. (D)	77,311	(52%)
Larry L. Bigham (R)	70,967	(48%)

Previous Winning Percentages: 1992 (61%) **1990** (100%) **1988** (70%) **1986** (100%) **1984** (92%) **1982** (68%)

CAMPAIGN FINANCE

	Receipts	Receipts from PACs	Expend-itures
1996			
Spratt (D)	$792,499	$427,113 (54%)	$855,622
Bigham (R)	$380,404	$2,235 (1%)	$373,117
1994			
Spratt (D)	$674,280	$256,050 (38%)	$643,947
Bigham (R)	$215,265	$14 (0%)	$213,775

VOTING STUDIES

	Presidential Support		Party Unity		Conservative Coalition	
Year	S	O	S	O	S	O
1996	72	27	79	20	75	25
1995	68	31	76	22	73	25
1994	81	18	89	9	78	22
1993	82	16	85†	13†	82	18
1992	34	66	83	15	79	21
1991	40	59	82	15	73	27

† Not eligible for all recorded votes.

KEY VOTES

1997	
Ban "partial birth" abortions	Y
1996	
Approve farm bill	Y
Deny public education to illegal immigrants	Y
Repeal ban on certain assault-style weapons	N
Increase minimum wage	Y
Freeze defense spending	Y
Approve welfare overhaul	Y
1995	
Approve balanced-budget constitutional amendment	Y
Relax Clean Water Act regulations	N
Oppose limits on environmental regulations	Y
Reduce projected Medicare spending	N
Approve GOP budget with tax and spending cuts	N

DISTRICT VOTE FOR PRESIDENT

	1996		1992
D	82,386 (46%)	**D**	81,197 (43%)
R	83,243 (47%)	**R**	85,971 (45%)
I	11,824 (7%)	**I**	23,437 (12%)

INTEREST GROUP RATINGS

Year	ADA	AFL-CIO	CCUS	ACU
1996	60	n/a	31	25
1995	65	83	46	16
1994	65	88	50	24
1993	55	83	45	25
1992	75	67	50	28
1991	50	83	30	21

6 James E. Clyburn (D)

Of Charleston — Elected 1992, 3rd term

Biographical Information
Born: July 21, 1940, Sumter, S.C.
Education: South Carolina State College, B.S. 1962.
Occupation: State official.
Family: Wife, Emily England; three children.
Religion: African Methodist Episcopal.
Political Career: S.C. Human Affairs commissioner, 1974-92; sought Democratic nomination for S.C. secretary of state, 1978, 1986.
Capitol Office: 319 Cannon Bldg. 20515; 225-3315.

Committees
Transportation & Infrastructure
Aviation; Surface Transportation
Veterans' Affairs
Oversight & Investigations

In Washington: Clyburn, the first black to represent South Carolina in Congress in nearly a century, enjoyed only one term — the 103rd Congress — in the House majority. Now he is a minority in a minority, faithfully standing up for workplace protections and social spending, using his voice and his vote in often-uphill struggles to protect old liberal priorities from the designs of the GOP.

Clyburn has a pragmatic streak, though, and he finds areas of agreement with the Republican leadership of the Transportation and Infrastructure Committee, a panel that works in a more bipartisan fashion than most others on the Hill. Clyburn joins with Transportation Chairman Bud Shuster, R-Pa., in calling for removing highway trust funds from the general budget. Taking the trust funds "off-budget," proponents say, will free up money for infrastructure projects that is now hoarded to mask the size of the deficit. Clyburn also supports establishment of a capital budget to allow deficit spending for long-term projects.

In the 105th, Clyburn is in a good position to address his concerns about improving rural roads, a subject of interest in the non-urban parts of his district: He is a senior Democrat on the Surface Transportation Subcommittee, which gets first crack at a major rewrite of highway and mass transit law during the 105th.

Clyburn also serves on the Veterans' Affairs Committee, and he objected to GOP plans in the fiscal 1996 budget to reduce spending for veterans' health programs. The controversial bill, which ended up being vetoed, was rejected by the House in November 1995 and sent back to conference with instructions to increase funding for veterans' medical care by $213 million.

The vote was a disappointment to Republican leaders but a victory for Clyburn, a persistent critic of GOP priorities in the budget and on other issues. Clyburn opposed Republican efforts to cut taxes, ease federal regulations and lift a ban on certain semiautomatic assault-style weapons. He consistently sided in the 104th with abortion-rights proponents in their battles with abortion foes, and he opposes banning a particular abortion technique that opponents call "partial-birth" abortion.

Clyburn has accused Republicans of trying to roll back workplace protections, and he typically concurs with the views of organized labor. He opposes a GOP initiative that would allow businesses to offer employees comp time in lieu of overtime pay and he voted against a measure that made it harder for Federal Express truck drivers to unionize.

Clyburn reserved some of his strongest criticism for Republican policies on affirmative action and welfare. He opposed each version of the GOP's welfare overhaul bill, including the final plan that earned the support of Clinton and half the House Democrats.

"Welfare reform should not mean help denied," Clyburn told his House colleagues in a floor speech. He contended that Republicans had forgotten the parable about teaching a man to fish, and argued that enforcement of child support payments needed to be toughened. "I think we can all agree that the welfare system is in need of reform. But the Republicans' idea of welfare reform is to callously toss welfare recipients off the government rolls without much thought to getting or keeping them on payrolls."

Clyburn served as co-chairman of a Congressional Black Caucus task force that was created to block Republican efforts to overhaul affirmative action policies.

Clyburn accepted the Supreme Court's June 1995 decision that federal affirmative action programs must meet strict standards, which the Justice Department interpreted as meaning programs must respond to specific discrimination rather than to general racism. "We have a court decision," Clyburn said, "and that ought to guide us." But he was vocal in support of affirmative action, taking to the floor for "special orders" to defend it with his caucus colleagues. (Clyburn's orations on the floor are infrequent, typically

SOUTH CAROLINA 6

Central and South — Florence; parts of Columbia and Charleston

After drawing a 6th District with more nooks and crannies than an English muffin, mapmakers saw it perform as expected in 1992, electing South Carolina's first black representative since George Washington Murray left office in 1897. To make the 6th a majority-minority seat, the line-drawers sheared off white and increasingly Republican Horry County from the old 6th and shifted the district south and inland to increase its black population.

The redrawn district, under legal challenge as a "racial gerrymander," sprawls over all or part of 16 counties in the eastern half of South Carolina. It starts near the North Carolina border and runs southward well below Charleston.

Along the way, district lines capture urban black precincts in Columbia and Charleston, and they take in predominantly rural counties that either have a sizable black minority or are black-majority. Overall, the district's black population exceeds 60 percent, although blacks make up 58 percent of registered voters.

South Carolina's first black-majority district is also its most poverty-ridden. Of the six poorest counties in the state, five are within Clyburn's jurisdiction. Twenty-three percent of the district's families live in poverty, more than double the poverty rate in most of the state's other districts. The district's median family income is less than $23,000; in every other South Carolina district, that figure is at least $29,000. The counties of Lee, Bamberg, Marion and Williamsburg lost population in the 1980s as residents left farms or as textile jobs disappeared. For those who stay in these rural areas, agriculture remains an important part of life.

Many residents of the 6th work outside the district. Richland County residents commute to Columbia for jobs in state government. Many in the 6th have collected paychecks from neighboring military installations, including Charleston Naval Base in the 1st, Shaw Air Force Base in the 5th and Fort Jackson in the 2nd. Shaw and Fort Jackson seem safe from military downsizing, but the Charleston naval facility has closed.

The most populous jurisdiction wholly within the 6th is Florence County, with 114,000 residents. A railhead since the Civil War, Florence has drawn new plants and industries in recent years, and the city has become an important regional medical center. Hoffman-LaRoche, a major pharmaceutical company, relocated its research and development facility here. Metalworking and the manufacture of plastics, paperboard and textiles also sustain Florence's economy.

Not surprising given its demographics, the majority of voters in the 6th support Democratic candidates on every level. Republican strength in the 6th lies in suburban areas surrounding the cities of Columbia and Charleston, as well as in Florence, the one county Clyburn failed to carry in his first race. Florence is also the only county he failed to carry in 1996.

1990 Population: 581,111. White 216,318 (37%), Black 361,375 (62%), Other 3,418 (<1%). Hispanic origin 3,237 (1%). 18 and over 412,292 (71%), 62 and over 82,904 (14%). Median age: 31.

coming in after-hours special-order speeches commemorating veterans and civil rights heroes.)

During his political career in South Carolina, Clyburn saw "the system" become more open to blacks, an evolution confirmed when 1992 redistricting created the majority-black 6th District. Covering all or part of 16 counties, it is a blend of urban and rural turf, like several other new majority-minority seats first drawn in 1992.

After the Supreme Court in 1993 first raised questions about whether oddly shaped majority-minority districts were "racial gerrymanders," Clyburn said it was vital to correct past political discrimination against blacks. "We should not be so distressed about the geometric correctness or abstract artistic value of a congressional district, but instead glory in our ability to fashion peaceful and tolerable remedies to one of our longstanding social ills."

A number of these districts have since been declared unconstitutional gerrymanders by the courts, and Clyburn's own district remains under dispute.

Members from these racially mixed districts, Clyburn once said, "have a different style of politics" from members whose constituents are strictly inner-city. "We are a little more prone to seek consensus."

Clyburn did vote in the 104th for two constitutional amendments widely backed by conservatives, one to mandate a balanced budget and another imposing congressional term limits. And although he did not like all its provisions, he voted in 1996 for the GOP-backed "Freedom to Farm" bill, which brought federal farm policy more in line with free-market principles.

At Home: When Democratic Gov. John West named Clyburn as a special assistant for human resources in 1971, Clyburn was the first black to serve as a gubernatorial appointee in more than 70 years. Three years later, he became the state's Human Affairs commissioner, a position he held until running for the House in 1992.

Clyburn, the son of a minister, always had his eye on moving up. In 1978 and 1986, he unsuccessfully sought the Democratic nomination for secretary of state. Running for Congress was a lifelong dream. "If conditions were different, I would have done it at 32," he once said, "rather than 52," a reference to the hard realities of race in South Carolina in the early 1970s.

In the human affairs office, Clyburn brought conflicting parties together to deal with such problems as racial tension and sexual harassment. He earned a reputation as an able conciliator and established close ties with those in the political power structure.

After 1992 redistricting made the 6th majority-black, white Democratic incumbent Robin Tallon said he would seek re-election. But he backed out, saying he did not want to provoke a racially divisive campaign. Clyburn and four other black Democrats ran in the primary. While all had some political experience, none could match Clyburn's name recognition in the black community or his high-level contacts in the white Democratic Party establishment.

Taking 56 percent of the vote, Clyburn won the nomination without a runoff. In November, he rolled up 65 percent. His 1994 and 1996 re-election bids were similarly smooth.

HOUSE ELECTIONS

1996 General		
James E. Clyburn (D)	120,132	(69%)
Gary McLeod (R)	51,974	(30%)
1996 Primary		
James E. Clyburn (D)	48,807	(88%)
Ben Frasier Jr. (D)	6,950	(12%)
1994 General		
James E. Clyburn (D)	88,635	(64%)
Gary McLeod (R)	50,259	(36%)

Previous Winning Percentages: 1992 (65%)

CAMPAIGN FINANCE

	Receipts	Receipts from PACs	Expend-itures
1996			
Clyburn (D)	$251,145	$176,400 (70%)	$196,440
McLeod (R)	$41,099	$250 (1%)	$39,395
1994			
Clyburn (D)	$444,335	$197,075 (44%)	$445,461
McLeod (R)	$13,290	$14 (0%)	$13,047

DISTRICT VOTE FOR PRESIDENT

	1996		1992
D	116,283 (66%)	**D**	118,394 (62%)
R	53,411 (30%)	**R**	59,799 (31%)
I	5,578 (3%)	**I**	12,322 (7%)

KEY VOTES

1997	
Ban "partial birth" abortions	N
1996	
Approve farm bill	Y
Deny public education to illegal immigrants	N
Repeal ban on certain assault-style weapons	N
Increase minimum wage	Y
Freeze defense spending	N
Approve welfare overhaul	N
1995	
Approve balanced-budget constitutional amendment	Y
Relax Clean Water Act regulations	N
Oppose limits on environmental regulations	Y
Reduce projected Medicare spending	N
Approve GOP budget with tax and spending cuts	N

VOTING STUDIES

	Presidential Support		Party Unity		Conservative Coalition	
Year	**S**	**O**	**S**	**O**	**S**	**O**
1996	82	15	90	9	63	33
1995	84	15	92	7	37	62
1994	85	10	93	4	36	61
1993	82	18	90	5	45	55

INTEREST GROUP RATINGS

Year	ADA	AFL-CIO	CCUS	ACU
1996	95	n/a	25	5
1995	90	92	29	16
1994	75	88	45	15
1993	90	100	27	13

SOUTH DAKOTA

Governor: William J. Janklow (R)
Elected: 1994*
Length of term: 4 years
Term expires: 1/99
Salary: $82,271
Term limit: 2 consecutive terms
Phone: (605) 773-3212
Born: September 13, 1939; Chicago, Ill.
Education: U. of South Dakota, B.A. 1964, J.D. 1966.
Military Service: Marine Corps, 1956-59.
Occupation: Lawyer.
Family: Wife, Mary Dean; three children.
Religion: Lutheran.
Political Career: S.D. attorney general, 1975-79; governor, 1979-87*; sought Republican nomination for U.S. Senate, 1986.

Lt. Gov: Carole Hillard (R)
Length of term: 4 years
Term expires: 1/99
Salary: $59,740
Phone: (605) 773-3212

State election official: (605) 773-3537
Democratic headquarters: (605) 335-7337
Republican headquarters: (605) 224-7347

STATE LEGISLATURE

Legislature. Meets January-February in even years, January-March in odd years.

Senate: 35 members, 2-year terms
1996 breakdown: 22R, 13D; 30 men, 5 women
Salary: $4,267 for first session; $3,733 for second.
Phone: (605) 773-3251

House of Representatives: 70 members, 2-year terms
1996 breakdown: 47R, 23D; 56 men, 14 women
Salary: Same as upper chamber
Phone: (605) 773-3251

URBAN STATISTICS

City	Population
Sioux Falls	100,836
Mayor Gary Hansen, R	
Rapid City	54,523
Mayor Edward McLaughlin, R	
Aberdeen	24,927
Mayor Timothy G. Rich, N-P	

U.S. CONGRESS

Senate: 2 D, 0 R
House: 0 D, 1 R

TERM LIMITS

For state offices: Yes
Senate: 2 four-year terms
House: 4 two-year terms

ELECTIONS

1996 Presidential Vote

Bob Dole	47%
Bill Clinton	43%
Ross Perot	10%

1992 Presidential Vote

George Bush	41%
Bill Clinton	37%
Ross Perot	22%

1988 Presidential Vote

George Bush	53%
Michael S. Dukakis	47%

POPULATION

1990 population		696,004
1980 population		690,768
Percent change		+1%
Rank among states:		45
White		92%
Black		<1%
Hispanic		1%
Asian or Pacific islander		<1%
Urban		50%
Rural		50%
Born in state		70%
Foreign-born		1%
Under age 18	198,462	29%
Ages 18-64	395,211	57%
65 and older	102,331	15%
Median age		32.5

MISCELLANEOUS

Capital: Pierre
Number of counties: 67
Per capita income: $16,392 (1991)
Rank among states: 36
Total area: 77,116 sq. miles
Rank among states: 16

SOUTH DAKOTA

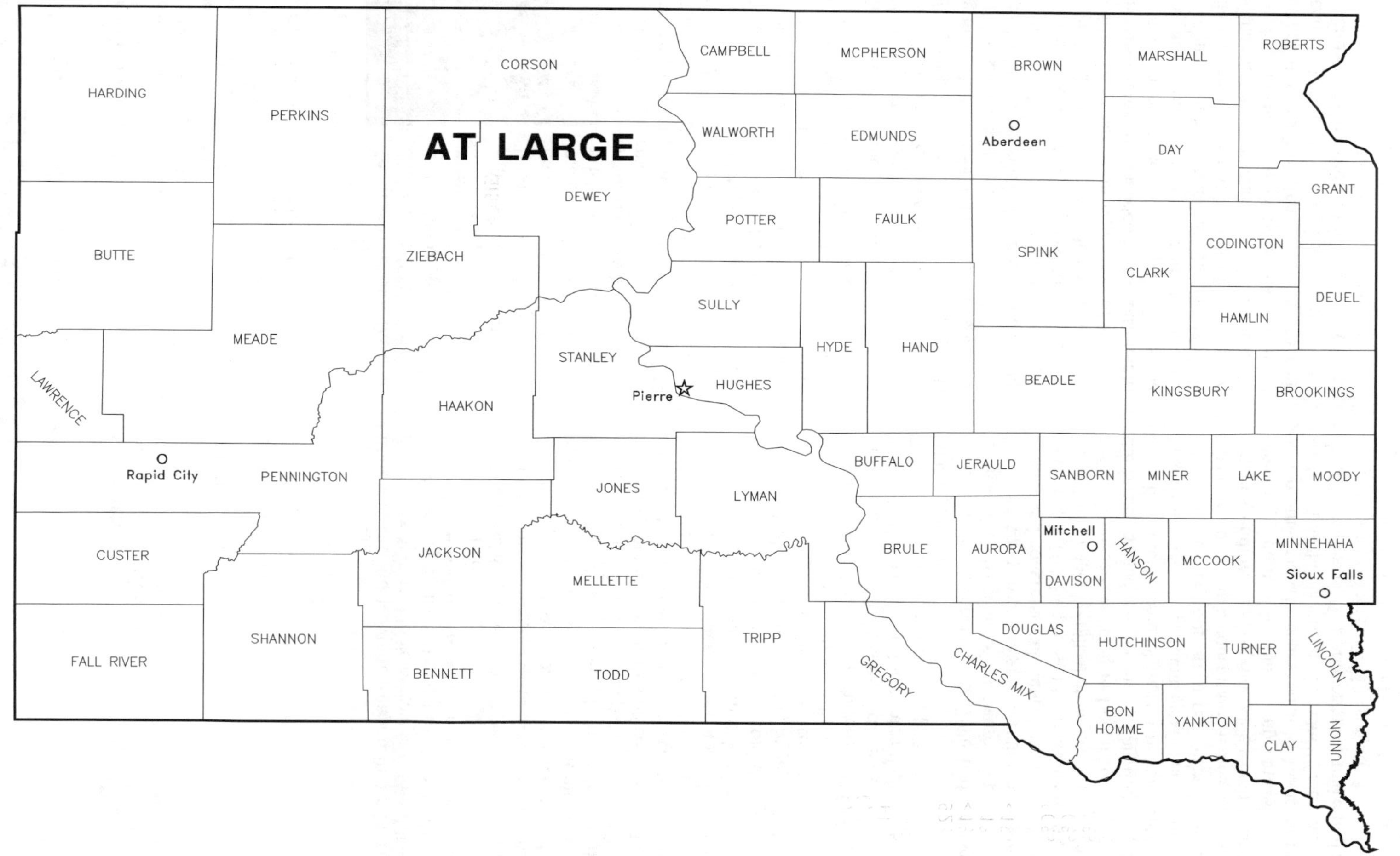

Tom Daschle (D)

Of Aberdeen — Elected 1986, 2nd term

Biographical Information
Born: Dec. 9, 1947, Aberdeen, S.D.
Education: South Dakota State U., B.A. 1969.
Military Service: Air Force, 1969-72.
Occupation: Congressional aide.
Family: Wife, Linda Hall; three children.
Religion: Roman Catholic.
Political Career: U.S. House, 1979-87.
Capitol Office: 509 Hart Bldg. 20510; 224-2321.

Committees
Agriculture, Nutrition & Forestry
Forestry, Conservation & Rural Revitalization; Production & Price Competitiveness

Minority Leader

Conference Chairman

In Washington: Daschle entered the 104th Congress in a tenuous position, the unproven leader of a newly disenfranchised minority. But he surprised skeptics by skillfully uniting his caucus not only to thwart many GOP initiatives but to push several Democratic priorities into law.

Daschle's performance in the December 1994 minority leader's race was underwhelming: He sweated out a 24-23 victory over Connecticut's Christopher J. Dodd, a late entrant into the race. But by the end of the 104th, Daschle was a unanimous choice to continue as leader. Making his victory even sweeter was the fact that West Virginia's Robert C. Byrd — a former Democratic leader himself and a Daschle critic early in the 104th — nominated him for the post. "I did not support Tom Daschle in 1994, in the main, because I did not think he was tough enough to deal with the likes of Bob Dole," Byrd told colleagues. "I am here today to tell you that I was totally wrong about this young man. He has steel in his spine, despite his reasonable and modest demeanor."

Daschle has won such plaudits by balancing his affable, low-key personality with a determined partisan streak and a willingness to stand and fight. In April 1997, he upbraided Senate Rules Committee Chairman John W. Warner of Virginia when he called for an expanded investigation into charges of voter fraud in the 1996 Louisiana Senate race (won by Democrat Mary L. Landrieu over conservative Republican Louis "Woody" Jenkins). Daschle accused Warner of pushing the Louisiana matter to romance the GOP right wing, whose relationship with Warner has been so chilly that it might threaten his efforts to gain influence in the Senate. "I think everyone in this town knows what's going on," Daschle told reporters. "John Warner wants to be the next chairman of the Armed Services Committee. . . . I think the Republicans are trying to steal this election."

Daschle also has not hesitated to employ the filibuster, the most potent weapon in a minority party's arsenal, to block or reshape Republican initiatives. He at times refused to allow GOP legislation to proceed unless Democrats were guaranteed a vote on their priorities.

The most prominent payoff from that strategy came in the spring of 1996, when Democrats forced and won a vote on increasing the minimum wage. Its passage followed warnings from Daschle that if the GOP would not agree to the Democrats' demand to bring up the wage bill, "We are simply going to shut this place down." Then-Majority Leader Dole tried on three consecutive days to cut off debate, but failed to muster the required 60 votes. When Dole complained about the tactics, according to former Wyoming GOP Sen. Alan K. Simpson, Daschle told the majority leader, "'Welcome to the Senate, Senator Dole.'"

In early 1997 Daschle was preoccupied with trying to broaden the scope of the Senate Governmental Affairs Committee's investigation into campaign fundraising practices. Daschle pressed the GOP to look at allegations of Republican and Democratic improprieties in the 1996 campaign.

Like many lawmakers, Daschle had received money raised by some of the figures implicated in the controversy over foreign contributions to presidential and congressional campaigns; he ended up returning $5,000. He pressed for consideration of a campaign spending bill that many Republicans actively opposed, warning in December 1996 that the Senate would not accomplish anything significant "if we don't effectively deal with our campaign finance laws today. . . . Campaign finance reform is first and foremost our strongest desire." He has advocated enacting a constitutional amendment to rein in spending, a remedy not widely embraced by other supporters of retooling campaign laws.

On other volatile issues, such as Medicare and welfare, Daschle has offered moderate alternatives to GOP proposals. He also worked to find a middle ground between abortion-rights supporters and proponents of a ban on a particular abortion technique opponents call "partial birth" abortion. Daschle would ban abortions of any viable fetus except when the pregnancy would threaten a woman's life or risk "grievous injury to her personal health." The Senate rejected his proposal in May 1997.

Daschle has preached inclusiveness in shaping his party's goals and plotting strategy. That style has led him to reach out to House Democrats, particularly Minority Leader Richard A. Gephardt of Missouri, a friend of Daschle's. The two helped oversee the development of a modest Democratic agenda called "Families First." Aimed at middle-class working families, it would protect pensions and provide targeted tax breaks for education. One challenge Daschle faces in the 105th is navigating the political jockeying between Gephardt and Vice President Al Gore over their party's presidential nomination in 2000.

Shortly after becoming Democratic leader, Daschle sought to establish his credentials as an independent leader by putting some distance between Senate Democrats and the White House. "My first responsibility is to my caucus," he said. "I believe that it's important for us to create our own identity. . . . We will not be led by the [Clinton administration]; we will not view ourselves as an extension of them. But I think to the degree we can, we certainly have every interest in working closely with them."

As budget talks between Republicans and the White House began in the spring of 1997, Daschle joined Gephardt in urging that not too many concessions be made on Medicare and tax cuts. They also prodded the administration to demand that Republicans offer a balanced-budget plan. When the talks produced a deal in May, Daschle initially denounced the closed-door negotiating process as "atrocious" and suggested he might oppose the agreement. But after meeting with his Senate troops and learning that most supported it, Daschle softened his rhetoric, and ultimately he voted for the budget when it passed the Senate, 78-22, on May 23.

For all of his public criticism of Republicans, Daschle has developed a comfortable working relationship with Dole's successor as majority leader, Trent Lott of Mississippi. On legislative days, the two leaders have met often, sometimes hourly, to resolve sticking points. Daschle has praised Lott's willingness to roll up his sleeves and search for common ground, but has said the two "mix it up both privately and publicly."

At the start of the 104th, with Republicans setting the Senate agenda, Daschle was in the tough spot of needing to establish his authority as Democratic leader, but finding that the most important measure up for debate — a balanced-budget constitutional amendment — was a proposal he had supported in the past. The amendment was most decidedly not backed by Byrd, and he led the Democratic charge against it, upstaging Daschle. After Daschle failed to win passage of a measure designed to prevent Social Security funds from being raided to balance the budget, he voted in March 1995 against the constitutional amendment, which fell just short of the two-thirds majority required for passage. The amendment again narrowly failed two years later.

Daschle's early efforts to solidify his position as leader were complicated by reports in the media questioning whether he had intervened with federal officials to stop them from grounding unsafe airplanes. Daschle issued a report in February 1995 that said his action in behalf of B&L Aviation of Rapid City, S.D., was simply a case of a conscientious senator responding to a constituent concern. Nine months later, the Senate Ethics Committee dismissed allegations that he had done anything improper.

Daschle has gone the extra mile to cultivate close relations with reporters, holding news conferences in his office almost every weekday. He outlines the Senate schedule, fields questions and includes a few plugs for the Democratic agenda. Such sessions have been the province of the majority leader, but Dole avoided them outright and Lott has held them less frequently than Daschle.

Daschle's legislative specialties have hewed closely to home state interests and political needs: agriculture, which is a requirement, not an elective, for farm state lawmakers; veterans issues, a cause that tends to transcend ideology; Indian affairs, important in South Dakota because of its Native American population; and health care, particularly the special concerns of rural regions. In the 103rd Congress, he was a strong supporter of Clinton's health care reform effort and a key player in trying to sell the reform measure to his Senate colleagues.

A member of the Agriculture Committees in both the House (where he served four terms) and now in the Senate, Daschle is a "prairie populist" who aggressively defends the interests of his state's farmers in debates on crop subsidies and other federal support. During consideration of the GOP's so-called "Freedom to Farm" bill in early 1996, he appeared to lose an opportunity to keep the system of crop subsidy payments to farmers intact when he and other Democrats hesitated on accepting a compromise offer from Dole.

The offer would have kept the payments at a reduced level while preserving permanent farm law and steered money into nutrition, rural development and conservation programs, all top Democratic priorities. For Republicans, the deal would have represented a wholesale retreat from their original goal of phasing out subsidies over seven years. But after receiving the offer, Daschle said some details remained murky, and said he wanted to see the proposal in writing. Republicans ultimately withdrew the offer; Daschle blamed the breakdown on the GOP. The version of "Freedom to Farm" that ultimately passed did phase out most New Deal-era crop subsidies over seven years, during which time farmers would receive fixed but declining payments regardless of their planting decisions.

After barely winning his House seat in 1978, Daschle immediately began building a political base inside Congress. One of the first people he sought out was then-Rep. Morris K. Udall, D-Ariz., who encouraged him to seek election as his region's representative to the Democratic whip organization. In 1983, Daschle won a seat on the Democratic leadership's Steering and Policy Committee and became a protege of Maine Democratic Sen. George Mitchell. When then-Majority Leader Mitchell announced his retirement in 1994, Daschle immediately began seeking to succeed him.

At Home: When Daschle began planning his 1986 Senate campaign, he was considered one of the Democrats' surest bets. The farm economy was on the ropes, and GOP Sen. James Abdnor had a reputation as bumbling and ineffective.

But Abdnor's consultants moved aggressively to inoculate the senator against charges of ineffectiveness, starting an extensive TV ad campaign in late 1985. Abdnor, whose amiable and low-key nature had endeared him to voters for nearly three decades, scored a strong primary victory.

Daschle then faced the challenge of framing the general election as a referendum on Abdnor's politics, not his personality. Abdnor handed him an issue shortly after the primary, when he stumbled at a forum by suggesting that farmers might have to "sell below cost" to compete. But the race tightened considerably in the fall, with two visits by President Ronald Reagan and a bevy of personal attacks on Daschle. In his ads, Abdnor linked Daschle with actress and former anti-war activist Jane Fonda, who had been pictured with Daschle at a fundraiser. Abdnor also hoped to tie Daschle to Fonda's efforts, in her health books, to discourage the consumption of red meat. Promoting vegetarianism in meat-producing South Dakota is a political felony.

Daschle's massive effort to turn out the farm vote, along with his late October charge that Abdnor had voted to cut Social Security, gave him a narrow victory.

His re-election in 1992 was much easier. He beat teacher Charlene Haar by 2-to-1. Although he is a favorite to win again in 1998, Daschle likely will hear GOP catcalls that his national stature has led him to lose touch with constituents' concerns. Daschle also will have to juggle the demands of being minority leader with the task of campaigning in a distant, vast and increasingly Republican state.

Daschle won his House seat originally on sheer energy. In a year, he and his first wife rang more than 40,000 doorbells as they campaigned to win the 1978 Democratic primary over former Rep. Frank Denholm and then defeat Republican nominee Leo Thorsness by just 139 votes.

Daschle had become familiar with politics and legislation while working for Sen. James Abourezk as a legislative assistant. He moved back to South Dakota in late 1976 to become field director for Abourezk and to prepare his 1978 House campaign.

In 1982, reapportionment forced a merger of South Dakota's two districts, and he met the state's other House incumbent, Republican Clint Roberts. The contest matched the state's two parties and its two regions. Daschle represented the Corn Belt territory of eastern South Dakota; Roberts spoke for the western ranching counties. Roberts tried to pin the Eastern label on Daschle, noting that while he had been running a ranch, Daschle had been on a government payroll. But Daschle told voters that what the state needed in Congress was not a farmer, but someone who knew how to write farm bills. Roberts took virtually every county in his old district, but Daschle got 59 percent in his eastern territory, for 52 percent overall.

SENATE ELECTIONS

1992 General		
Tom Daschle (D)	217,095	(65%)
Charlene Haar (R)	108,733	(33%)
Gus Hercules (LIBERT)	4,353	(1%)
Kent Hyde (I)	4,314	(1%)

Previous Winning Percentages: 1986 (52%) **1984*** (57%) **1982*** (52%) **1980*** (66%) **1978*** (50%)

* House elections

CAMPAIGN FINANCE

1996	Receipts	Receipts from PACs	Expend-itures
Daschle (D)	$2,838,866	$1,350,572 (48%)	$2,878,375
Haar (R)	$479,045	$71,491 (15%)	$478,421
Hercules (LIBERT)	$8,840	$0	$8,839

KEY VOTES

1997	
Approve balanced-budget constitutional amendment	N
Approve chemical weapons treaty	Y
1996	
Approve farm bill	N
Limit punitive damages in product liability cases	N
Exempt small businesses from higher minimum wage	N
Approve welfare overhaul	N
Bar job discrimination based on sexual orientation	Y
Override veto of ban on "partial birth" abortions	N
1995	
Approve GOP budget with tax and spending cuts	N
Approve constitutional amendment barring flag desecration	N

VOTING STUDIES

	Presidential Support		Party Unity		Conservative Coalition	
Year	**S**	**O**	**S**	**O**	**S**	**O**
1996	93	7	94	6	24	76
1995	92	8	92	7	35	63
1994	94	6	91	9	38	63
1993	92	7	89	9	51	44
1992	25	75	82	18	37	63
1991	27	73	90	9	38	63

INTEREST GROUP RATINGS

Year	ADA	AFL-CIO	CCUS	ACU
1996	90	n/a	38	0
1995	95	100	37	4
1994	80	63	40	4
1993	75	91	20	12
1992	95	75	20	22
1991	85	83	10	24

Tim Johnson (D)

Of Vermillion — Elected 1996, 1st term

Biographical Information

Born: Dec. 28, 1946, Canton, S.D.

Education: U. of South Dakota, B.A. 1969, M.A. 1970; Michigan State U., 1970-71; U. of South Dakota, J.D. 1975.

Military Service: Army, 1969.

Occupation: Lawyer.

Family: Wife, Barbara Brooks; three children.

Religion: Lutheran.

Political Career: S.D. House, 1979-83; S.D. Senate, 1983-87; Clay County deputy state's attorney, 1985; U.S. House, 1987-97.

Capitol Office: 502 Hart Bldg. 20510; 224-5842.

Committees

Agriculture, Nutrition & Forestry
Production & Price Competitiveness; Research, Nutrition & General Legislation

Banking, Housing & Urban Affairs
Financial Institutions & Regulatory Relief; Financial Services & Technology; Securities

Budget

Energy & Natural Resources
Energy Research Development Production & Regulation; Forests & Public Land Management

The Path to Washington: Johnson holds a unique position in the Senate relative to other freshmen who have come over from the House: He already is familiar with his entire state's needs, having served a decade as South Dakota's at-large House member. And he has an influential ally in Tom Daschle, South Dakota's other senator and the chamber's top Democrat.

This close relationship paid off for Democrats early in the 105th Congress, when Republicans again attempted to pass a balanced-budget constitutional amendment. Johnson was one of four freshman Senate Democrats — along with Robert G. Torricelli of New Jersey, Mary L. Landrieu of Louisiana and Max Cleland of Georgia — who had supported the idea in their 1996 campaigns and initially signaled to Daschle that they were not inclined to change their positions.

But Daschle, aided by President Clinton, Treasury Secretary Robert E. Rubin and senior Senate Democrats, patiently led Johnson and Torricelli into the opposition camp. Their votes ensured defeat of the amendment.

In a February 1997 announcement, Johnson cited the issue of "protecting" Social Security as his reason for opposing the version of the balanced-budget amendment before the Senate. The measure had been massaged by Republicans and a handful of Democrats to allay such fears, but many Democrats and a few conservative House Republicans criticized it for not excluding Social Security's trust funds from balanced-budget calculations — in effect, enshrining the current practice of using surplus Social Security revenues to offset the budget deficit.

"In the past I have supported a version similar to this amendment," Johnson said in a statement, "but I cannot [support this version] knowing that it will jeopardize Social Security, as well as the ability of the government to set aside funds for disasters, recessions or other crises."

Proponents of the amendment were stung by Johnson's decision to oppose it.

"This is a question of honesty," Majority Leader Trent Lott said on the Senate floor. "It is a question of truth in government. We wonder why people are cynical, why people wonder about us, why they question us. This is exhibit A. When you give your word . . . during the election campaign . . . and then six months later you say, 'Gee whiz, I have learned something new,' it is hard to take."

Johnson dismissed Lott's criticisms, saying he had cast a vote of conscience and didn't need a Mississippian lecturing him about how to represent South Dakotans.

In the November 1996 election, Johnson was the only challenger to beat a sitting senator. He was rewarded for his victory over three-term Republican Larry Pressler with seats on the Agriculture, Nutrition and Forestry; Banking, Housing and Urban Affairs; Budget; and Energy and Natural Resources committees.

Johnson endured a hard-fought, closely contested battle against Pressler in which he was the target of relentless televised attacks branding him a liberal. Johnson responded by characterizing Pressler as out of touch and captive to special interests. As an example, he seized upon news accounts disclosing that Pressler spent hundreds of thousands of dollars on travel, meals and lodging without fully accounting for their connection to his campaign, saying it was "a long way from Humboldt to Hong Kong," referring to the Republican's South Dakota hometown.

The race broke all spending records in the sparsely populated state, with television ads first appearing well over a year before Election Day.

Pressler's own polls showed that his attempts to cast Johnson as too liberal for the generally Republican state were not hitting home, perhaps because they already knew Johnson from his House tenure and had never thought of him as a left-winger.

Capitalizing on his role as Senate Commerce Committee chairman, Pressler raised a good-sized chunk of his campaign treasury from telecommunications interests grateful for his role in enacting a law deregulating the industry. He touted the bill as a job creator in his early campaign advertising. But Johnson scored points by noting that after passage of the telecommunications bill, there was a rash of sales of South Dakota TV stations, and telephone and cable rates in the state had risen.

The two also took different tacks on the GOP's "Freedom to Farm" bill that passed in the 104th. It phased out most New Deal-era crop subsidies, replacing them with a system of fixed, but declining, payments that farmers would receive over seven years regardless of market prices or their planting decisions.

Pressler backed the legislation, but Johnson said its market-oriented approach might prove too generous to farmers in good times and too parsimonious when crops or prices are poor.

In the end, Johnson prevailed narrowly, winning 51 percent to 49 percent.

During his years in the House, Johnson exhibited a cerebral, low-key manner. He usually sided with his party's majority, but compiled a more moderate record than Daschle. He was a tenacious advocate for his state's farmers, and aggressively sought federal funds for local water projects, bridges and roads.

In the 103rd Congress, Johnson chaired the House Agriculture Environment, Credit and Rural Development Subcommittee, where much of his work centered on overhauling the federally backed crop insurance program.

In the Senate, Johnson joins Daschle in a variety of agriculture-related causes that are important to farm-state senators of both parties, such as protection of the ethanol industry. He sits on two Agriculture subcommittees: Production and Price Competitiveness, and Research, Nutrition and General Legislation.

Johnson also is likely to be active on matters involving senior citizens, an important constituency in South Dakota. He sponsored legislation in the House that would have penalized companies found to charge excessive prices for prescription drugs and has vowed to continue working on the issue.

During the 1996 campaign, Johnson touted his efforts to protect Social Security and his support of proposals to reduce or eliminate the tax burden on senior citizens who work during their retirement years.

Johnson has opposed federal funding of abortion, and he has a mixed record on gun control issues. In the House, he supported a five-day waiting period requirement for handgun purchases, saying the wait created "only negligible inconvenience to law-abiding handgun owners." On a bill banning 19 types of semiautomatic assault-style weapons, Johnson voted "no," although in August 1994 he supported the Clinton-backed crime bill, which included an assault weapons ban. However, he voted in 1996 to repeal the ban.

Johnson voted for the compromise welfare overhaul bill that was enacted in the 104th Congress, after opposing two previous Republican-backed versions that Clinton vetoed.

SENATE ELECTIONS

1996 General		
Tim Johnson (D)	166,533	(51%)
Larry Pressler (R)	157,954	(49%)

Previous Winning Percentages: 1994* (60%) **1992*** (69%) **1990*** (68%) **1988*** (72%) **1986*** (59%)

* House elections

KEY VOTES

1997	
Approve balanced-budget constitutional amendment	N
Approve chemical weapons treaty	Y
House Service:	
1996	
Approve farm bill	N
Deny public education to illegal immigrants	Y
Repeal ban on certain assault-style weapons	Y
Increase minimum wage	Y
Freeze defense spending	Y
Approve welfare overhaul	Y
1995	
Approve balanced-budget constitutional amendment	Y
Relax Clean Water Act regulations	Y
Oppose limits on environmental regulations	Y
Reduce projected Medicare spending	N
Approve GOP budget with tax and spending cuts	N

CAMPAIGN FINANCE

	Receipts	Receipts from PACs	Expend-itures
***1996**			
Johnson (D)	$2,866,518	$847,621 (30%)	$2,990,554
Pressler (R)	$4,091,490	$1,513,835 (37%)	$4,468,434

VOTING STUDIES

	Presidential Support		Party Unity		Conservative Coalition	
Year	S	O	S	O	S	O
House Service:						
1996	65	29	76	20	51	49
1995	76	23	81	18	46	53
1994	81	18	89	10	58	36
1993	73	26	85	13	50	45
1992	29	71	81	17	40	60
1991	34	66	80	19	54	46

INTEREST GROUP RATINGS

Year	ADA	AFL-CIO	CCUS	ACU
House Service:				
1996	55	0	33	37
1995	85	75	50	28
1994	55	67	75	24
1993	65	92	36	21
1992	70	67	50	32
1991	65	83	40	20

AL John Thune (R)

Of Pierre — Elected 1996, 1st term

Biographical Information
Born: Jan. 7, 1961, Pierre, S.D.
Education: Biola U., B.S. 1983; U. of South Dakota, M.B.A. 1984.
Occupation: Municipal league executive; congressional aide.
Family: Wife, Kimberley; two children.
Religion: Protestant.
Political Career: No previous office.
Capitol Office: 506 Cannon Bldg. 20515; 225-2801.

Committees
Agriculture
Department Operations, Nutrition & Foreign Agriculture; General Farm Commodities
Transportation & Infrastructure
Surface Transportation; Water Resources & Environment

The Path to Washington: Thune fits the general profile of candidates that South Dakotans have chosen to send to Washington in recent years — young and ambitious, yet experienced in government.

Thune doesn't plan to climb too far up the House seniority ladder, though. A supporter of term limits, he has pledged to serve no more than three terms.

One of only two members of the GOP Class of 1996 who captured previously Democratic House seats outside the South, Thune was rewarded prior to the start of the 105th Congress by his classmates, who selected him to serve as their liaison to the House GOP leadership.

South Dakota's at-large House seat, which Democrat Tim Johnson left to run successfully for the Senate, had been held by Democrats since the state went down to a sole congressional district in 1982. Thune picked up committee assignments allowing him to look out for the state's concerns: slots on the Transportation and Infrastructure and Agriculture committees.

Thune took an independent tack from Republican orthodoxy on tax cuts. Thune said that he could not support Republican presidential candidate Bob Dole's 15 percent tax cut plan until the federal budget was in balance. Thune did, however, sign a pledge not to increase income taxes. He supports a constitutional amendment to require a balanced federal budget.

During a summer debate with Democratic nominee Rick Weiland, Thune refused to state whether he would vote to return Newt Gingrich as Speaker. Distancing himself from party leaders helped Thune establish centrist credentials at home. (When the 105th convened, Thune did back Gingrich for Speaker.)

Weiland, a longtime aide to South Dakota Democratic Sen. Tom Daschle, tried to appeal to traditional Democratic constituencies as a supporter of unions and rural development. But he was unable to seize the political center in a state in which Republicans hold a comfortable edge in voter registration. Weiland angered many even within his own party with an advertisement accusing his primary opponent of being disloyal for having made financial contributions to Republican candidates in the past. In the end, Thune showed impressive crossover appeal. Though Dole won the state by just three points and Johnson unseated three-term GOP Sen. Larry Pressler, Thune rolled to a 21-point victory, winning 60 of 66 counties.

Thune ran in the GOP primary as a supporter of many of the tenets of the Republicans' "Contract With America."

He defeated by a wide margin Lt. Gov. Carole Hilliard, who had big leads in early polls and who ran more as a media candidate than the hard-stumping Thune. But Hilliard lacked the funds to parlay her advantage in name recognition into a winning candidacy, and her efforts were greatly hindered by the refusal of her boss, Republican Gov. William J. Janklow, to endorse her.

By contrast, Thune was able to tout the unqualified support of his own old boss and political mentor, former Sen. James Abdnor (1981-87).

Thune served as a legislative assistant to Abdnor during the 99th Congress, specializing in tax and small-business issues. He continued to work for Abdnor (who lost to Daschle in 1986) after President Ronald Reagan appointed him head of the Small Business Administration. Thune later held an appointment as deputy staff director of the Senate Small Business Committee.

In 1989, Thune returned to South Dakota, where he served as executive director of the state GOP and later as state railroad director under the late GOP Gov. George Mickelson. In 1993, Thune was appointed executive director of the South Dakota Municipal League, an association of local governments. He left his position to mount his House bid. During the primary, Thune made an ethical misstep by failing to file a personal financial disclosure form, which he dismissed as an "oversight." Thune has pledged not to accept a pay raise or participate in the congressional pension system. He also says he will forgo publicly funded overseas trips.

The contrasts of beauty and poverty in South Dakota are striking. Its varied and breathtaking landscape, with stark mountains, desert canyons, and sweeping farmland and grassland, has helped make tourism the second-largest industry.

But the violent battles that raged a century ago between white settlers and American Indians left a terrible legacy. Unemployment and poverty are rife on South Dakota's numerous Indian reservations. More than half the people live below the poverty level; nearly one-quarter of the work force is jobless.

Wounded Knee is located in Shannon County. More than 200 Sioux were massacred there in one day in 1890 after their chief, Sitting Bull, had been killed. Shannon County is by many measures one of the nation's most impoverished counties; more than 50 percent of the county's residents live below the poverty level, higher than any other county nationwide.

State lawmakers declared 1990 a Year of Reconciliation, and then-Gov. George Mickelson invited tribal representatives to sit cross-legged in the Capitol rotunda and smoke the peace pipe. The state has renamed Columbus Day, calling it Native American Day, and state officials drafted an elementary and high school curriculum to include Indian studies. South Dakota ranks 45th in terms of population among the 50 states, but it has the fourth-highest percentage of Indians in its population.

The Missouri River, running north to south through the center of South Dakota, divides not only the geography and economy of the state, but also its political predilections.

The flat, rich farmland east of the river holds two-thirds of the state's population and nourishes an agricultural economy based on corn and soybeans. Voters in the east tend to support Democrats. "West River" is rolling, arid grassland suited for grazing and ranching. Mining, including gold mining, is also a feature of the western mountains. Most western voters are Republicans.

While Ronald Reagan carried South Dakota for president with more than 60 percent of the vote in 1980 and 1984, disenchantment with GOP farm policy began to set in mid-decade, whittling down George Bush's South Dakota margin in 1988. Ross Perot's 22 percent showing in 1992 cut into both major-party nominees: Bush won the state with just 41 percent, the lowest percentage received by a Republican presidential candidate here since 1932. Then, in 1996, Bob Dole carried the state by just 4 percentage points. It was the closest a GOP presidential candidate has come to losing South Dakota since Gerald Ford won the state by fewer than 2 percentage points in 1976.

SOUTH DAKOTA
At large

Corn's primacy in South Dakota's economy is symbolized by the Corn Palace in Mitchell, an auditorium whose exterior is festooned with mosaics made from colored cobs.

Not far from Mitchell is the focal point of eastern South Dakota and the state's largest metropolis, Sioux Falls (Minnehaha County). The city grew 24 percent in the 1980s — while the rest of the state was losing population — to about 101,000, as it transformed from meatpacking town to regional commerce hub. Though meatpacker John Morrell & Co. is still a major employer, the city has become a service center whose banks, insurance companies, medical facilities and retailers are affected by the health of the agricultural economy, if not entirely dependent on it. Clinton won Minnehaha County in 1996 with 48 percent.

On the western side of the Missouri, the towns are fewer, and there is still something of the old Wild West feel. Much of the majestic, high plains scenery in the 1990 Academy Award-winning film "Dances With Wolves" was shot here.

Near the western border of the state is South Dakota's second-largest city, Rapid City (Pennington County), with a population of more than 54,000. Originally a market for surrounding ranchers and farmers, it has prospered in recent years partly thanks to tourism: The Badlands, the Black Hills and Mount Rushmore are nearby.

In neighboring Lawrence County, legalized gambling has helped rejuvenate the town of Deadwood, once a gold-mining boom town. Calamity Jane and Wild Bill Hickok are buried at Mount Moriah Cemetery in Deadwood. Video lottery gambling has skyrocketed in the state in recent years, bringing with it much controversy. Mindful of the revenue it generates for the cash-strapped state, voters in 1994 — by a 51 percent to 49 percent margin — approved a ballot initiative backing continuation of the lottery. "Wolves" star Kevin Costner, who is a partial owner of a Deadwood casino, is building a gambling resort on the city's outskirts, in the Black Hills.

Dole won Pennington County with 54 percent of the vote, and he carried every other county west of the Missouri River except five — all of them dominated by votes from Indian reservations.

1990 Population: 696,004. White 637,515 (92%), Black 3,258 (<1%), Other 55,231 (8%). Hispanic origin 5,252 (1%). 18 and over 497,542 (71%), 62 and over 120,737 (17%). Median age: 33.

HOUSE ELECTIONS

1996 General		
John Thune (R)	186,393	(58%)
Rick Weiland (D)	119,547	(37%)
Stacey Nelson (REF)	10,397	(3%)
Kurt Evans (I)	6,866	(2%)
1996 Primary		
John Thune (R)	41,322	(59%)
Carole Hillard (R)	28,139	(41%)

CAMPAIGN FINANCE

	Receipts	Receipts from PACs	Expend-itures
1996			
Thune (R)	$786,915	$175,509 (22%)	$773,125
Weiland (D)	$894,720	$346,270 (39%)	$890,708

DISTRICT VOTE FOR PRESIDENT

1996		1992	
D	139,333 (43%)	**D**	124,888 (37%)
R	150,543 (46%)	**R**	136,718 (41%)
I	31,250 (10%)	**I**	73,295 (22%)

KEY VOTES

1997

Ban "partial birth" abortions	Y

TENNESSEE

Governor: Don Sundquist (R)
First elected: 1994
Length of term: 4 years
Term expires: 1/99
Salary: $85,000
Term limit: 2 consecutive terms
Phone: (615) 741-2001
Born: March 15, 1936; Moline, Ill.
Education: Augustana College (Rock Island, Ill.), B.A 1957.
Military Service: Navy, 1957-59.
Occupation: Printing, advertising and marketing executive.
Family: Wife, Martha Swanson; three children.
Religion: Lutheran.
Political Career: U.S. House, 1983-95.

Lt. Gov.: John S. Wilder (D)
First elected: 1971
Length of term: 2 years (elected by the state Senate)
Term expires: 1/99
Salary: $49,500
Phone: (615) 741-2368

State election official: (615) 741-7956
Democratic headquarters: (615) 327-9779
Republican headquarters: (615) 292-9497

REDISTRICTING

Tennessee retained its nine House seats in reapportionment. The legislature passed the map May 6, 1992; the governor signed it May 7.

STATE LEGISLATURE

General Assembly. Meets for 90 days over 2 years, beginning in January.

Senate: 33 members, 4-year terms
1996 breakdown: 18D, 15R; 30 men, 3 women
Salary: $16,500
Phone: (615) 741-2730

House of Representatives: 99 members, 2-year terms
1996 breakdown: 61D, 38R; 84 men, 15 women
Salary: $16,500
Phone: (615) 741-2901

URBAN STATISTICS

City	Population
Memphis	610,337
Mayor W. W. Herenton, D	
Nashville-Davidson	488,374
Mayor Philip N. Bredesen, D	
Knoxville	165,121
Mayor Victor Ashe, R	
Chattanooga	152,466
Mayor Gene Roberts, R	
Clarksville	75,494
Mayor Donald W. Trotter, N-P	

U.S. CONGRESS

Senate: 0 D, 2 R
House: 4 D, 5 R

TERM LIMITS

For state offices: No

ELECTIONS

1996 Presidential Vote

Bill Clinton	48%
Bob Dole	46%
Ross Perot	6%

1992 Presidential Vote

Bill Clinton	47%
George Bush	42%
Ross Perot	10%

1988 Presidential Vote

George Bush	58%
Michael S. Dukakis	42%

POPULATION

1990 population		4,877,185
1980 population		4,591,120
Percent change		+6%
Rank among states:		17
White		83%
Black		16%
Hispanic		1%
Asian or Pacific islander		1%
Urban		61%
Rural		39%
Born in state		69%
Foreign-born		1%
Under age 18	1,216,604	25%
Ages 18-64	3,041,763	62%
65 and older	618,818	13%
Median age		34

MISCELLANEOUS

Capital: Nashville
Number of counties: 95
Per capita income: $16,325 (1991)
Rank among states: 37
Total area: 42,144 sq. miles
Rank among states: 34

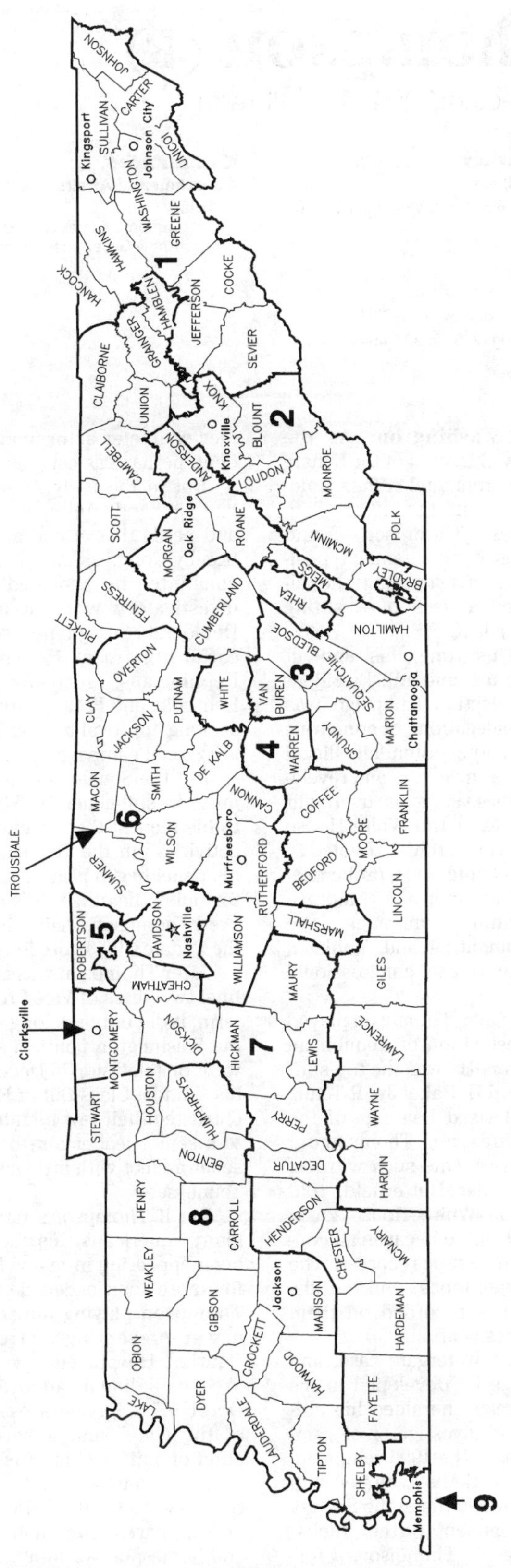
JOHNSON
CARTER
SULLIVAN
Kingsport
Johnson City
UNICOI
WASHINGTON
GREENE
HAWKINS
HANCOCK
1
COCKE
HAMBLEN
JEFFERSON
GRAINGER
CLAIBORNE
SEVIER
UNION
KNOX
Knoxville
BLOUNT
2
CAMPBELL
ANDERSON
Oak Ridge
LOUDON
MONROE
SCOTT
MORGAN
ROANE
POLK
McMINN
MEIGS
BRADLEY
FENTRESS
CUMBERLAND
RHEA
PICKETT
HAMILTON
BLEDSOE
Chattanooga
OVERTON
SEQUATCHIE
3
CLAY
PUTNAM
WHITE
VAN BUREN
MARION
JACKSON
GRUNDY
WARREN
4
DE KALB
SMITH
MACON
CANNON
COFFEE
FRANKLIN
TROUSDALE
6
WILSON
Murfreesboro
RUTHERFORD
MOORE
BEDFORD
SUMNER
LINCOLN
ROBERTSON
5
DAVIDSON
Nashville
WILLIAMSON
MARSHALL
CHEATHAM
MAURY
GILES
Clarksville
MONTGOMERY
DICKSON
HICKMAN
7
LEWIS
LAWRENCE
STEWART
HOUSTON
HUMPHREYS
PERRY
WAYNE
BENTON
DECATUR
HARDIN
HENRY
CARROLL
8
HENDERSON
McNAIRY
CHESTER
WEAKLEY
GIBSON
Jackson
MADISON
HARDEMAN
OBION
CROCKETT
HAYWOOD
LAKE
DYER
FAYETTE
LAUDERDALE
TIPTON
SHELBY
Memphis
9

Fred Thompson (R)

Of Nashville — Elected 1994; 1st full term

Biographical Information
Born: Aug. 19, 1942, Sheffield, Ala.
Education: Memphis State U., B.S. 1964; Vanderbilt U., J.D. 1967.
Occupation: Lawyer; actor.
Family: Divorced; three children.
Religion: Protestant.
Political Career: Assistant U.S. attorney, 1969-72.
Capitol Office: 523 Dirksen Bldg. 20510; 224-4944.

Committees
Governmental Affairs (chairman)
Judiciary
Constitution, Federalism & Property Rights; Technology, Terrorism & Government Information; Youth Violence

In Washington: As the new chairman of the Senate Governmental Affairs Committee in the 105th Congress, Thompson found himself in a familiar position: investigating the alleged abuses of a sitting president.

This time, his subject was a Democrat, President Clinton, whose 1996 re-election campaign was buffeted in early 1997 by allegations of numerous infractions, including accepting potentially illegal contributions from overseas investors and revelations of other irregularities, such as overnight stays and exclusive coffees at the White House for big donors. The Senate in March 1997 voted to give Thompson's panel $4.3 million to probe allegations of both "illegal" and "improper" fundraising activities of Clinton's campaign, the Democratic National Committee and, unlike a related investigation in the House, congressional campaigns.

More than two decades ago, Thompson played a central role in the investigation of Republican President Richard M. Nixon. He was the top staff lawyer to then-Sen. Howard H. Baker Jr., R-Tenn., during the sometimes-televised hearings of the Senate Watergate Committee, and Thompson at times interrogated witnesses. One such witness, White House aide Alexander Butterfield, told Thompson that the Nixon White House knew what was said in the Oval Office because all conversations there were secretly tape recorded. The revelation of the "Watergate tapes" and the discussions of illegal activities recorded on them ultimately led to Nixon's resignation.

Thompson's role in the Watergate case, and the clean but tough image he developed in his first two years in the Senate, heralded his ultimate selection as the head investigator of campaign fundraising practices in the 1996 campaign. Majority Leader Trent Lott, R-Miss., tapped him for the job despite his junior status in the Senate, and the high-profile assignment further fueled speculation that the telegenic Thompson, a former character actor, may one day run for president, perhaps as early as 2000.

But in the early months of 1997, Thompson had his hands full coping with the controversies and perils that attend any high-stakes investigation by Congress. At the outset, he asked that his committee be allocated $6.5 million to do its investigatory work, a much larger sum than Democrats thought necessary, and so he heard an earful from them. He also angered conservative Republicans, such as Mitch McConnell of Kentucky and Rick Santorum of Pennsylvania, by seeking approval to peer into fundraising by congressional campaigns.

But the Senate vote to give Thompson's committee a still-generous $4.3 million and to assent to his request that its inquiry include "improper" activities put the Tennessean on solid footing as his panel began issuing subpoenas and preparing for public hearings. "It's a stamp of approval for Fred Thompson," said Thad Cochran, R-Miss., of the Senate's 99-0 vote in early March.

After Thompson was elected in 1994 to fill the final two years of Vice President Al Gore's Senate term, it did not take long for him to get a place in the Washington political spotlight. When Clinton went on television in December 1994 to announce his "Middle Class Bill of Rights," the Republicans entrusted their few minutes of response time not to a senior leader but to Thompson, a freshman senator-elect with little name recognition outside Tennessee.

But if Thompson's name was not familiar to many Americans, his face surely was. He had been appearing in major Hollywood productions for more than a decade. Moviegoers first saw Thompson playing himself, an underdog attorney representing actress Sissy Spacek in "Marie." He played a variety of authority figures, including an admiral in "The Hunt for Red October," a business executive in "Barbarians at the Gate" and a hard-nosed White House chief of staff in Clint Eastwood's "In the Line of Fire." Thompson got rave reviews for his response to Clinton's tax speech, delivering his brief remarks with such a blend of seriousness and homespun warmth that some commentators immediately began predicting a major national role for the 52-year-old lawyer-actor and first-term senator from Nashville.

During his first two years in Congress, Thompson focused on many of the institutional issues he regarded as symbolic of congressional arrogance and remoteness. He sponsored a term-limits measure that fell two votes short of the 60 needed to halt debate on the Senate floor; he wrote language that denied lawmakers automatic cost-of-living adjustments in their pay; and he joined forces with John McCain, R-Ariz., and Russell D. Feingold, D-Wis., in their quest for changes to campaign finance laws.

The Senate fell six votes short of the 60 needed to close debate on that campaign finance measure, known as the McCain-Feingold bill, in June 1996. Clinton has advocated that measure as the best chance for compromise on campaign finance in the 105th Congress, and Thompson also has embraced the legislation again.

At Home: In Hollywood, Thompson learned how to get into character; on the campaign trail, he used the same technique. This time his role was that of the outsider, and it helped him score easy victories over former Rep. Jim Cooper in his first race and win re-election to his first full term over a lesser-known candidate in 1996.

During his first campaign, Thompson moved around Tennessee in a pickup truck, usually dressed in a flannel shirt or other casual clothes. In one late September appearance, for instance, he attended a tobacco rally in New Tazewell, where he chomped on a wad of chewing tobacco and had a cigar protruding from his shirt pocket.

He contrasted his background — a one-time night worker in a bicycle factory and son of a used-car salesman — with that of the 40-year-old Cooper, the son of a former governor, a prep-school graduate who became a Rhodes scholar at Oxford University and obtained a law degree from Harvard and who was elected two years after graduating to the first of six House terms.

Thompson did have a fair claim to insider status himself, a fact Cooper tried to exploit. Apart from his time as a staff member for Baker, Thompson had worked for years as a Washington lobbyist with some high-profile clients, including the Teamsters Union pension fund.

Cooper, however, was never able to pin the insider tag on Thompson, who also benefited from extremely effective advertising that for the most part was devoid of the negative tones of many of the season's campaigns. And Cooper, who had built a reputation in the House as a pragmatic centrist Democrat, had trouble energizing the more liberal core constituencies of his party, including black voters and organized labor.

He began as the clear favorite to succeed appointed Democratic Sen. Harlan Mathews in the seat vacated by Gore. But he saw his initial advantage in fundraising (he had nearly $4 million) all but erased by a late influx of dollars for Thompson. Cooper changed campaign and media advisers late in the season and, at the end, appeared to be in free fall. Thompson wound up winning 60 percent of the vote.

In 1996, Thompson used his formidable campaign treasury to run feel-good TV ads and tallied 61 percent, this time defeating Democratic lawyer J. Houston Gordon. Thompson was so confident that he took time off campaigning to help GOP presidential nominee Bob Dole prepare for the October presidential debates.

SENATE ELECTIONS

1996 General		
Fred Thompson (R)	1,091,554	(61%)
J. Houston Gordon (D)	654,937	(37%)
1996 Primary		
Fred Thompson (R)	266,549	(94%)
Jim Counts (R)	16,715	(6%)

Previous Winning Percentages: 1994† (60%)

† Special election

KEY VOTES

1997	
Approve balanced-budget constitutional amendment	Y
Approve chemical weapons treaty	N
1996	
Approve farm bill	Y
Limit punitive damages in product liability cases	Y
Exempt small businesses from higher minimum wage	Y
Approve welfare overhaul	Y
Bar job discrimination based on sexual orientation	N
Override veto of ban on "partial birth" abortions	Y
1995	
Approve GOP budget with tax and spending cuts	Y
Approve constitutional amendment barring flag desecration	Y

CAMPAIGN FINANCE

	Receipts	Receipts from PACs	Expend-itures
1996			
Thompson (R)	$4,232,418	$1,080,345 (26%)	$3,469,369
Gordon (D)	$800,607	$88,600 (11%)	$795,969

VOTING STUDIES

	Presidential Support		Party Unity		Conservative Coalition	
Year	S	O	S	O	S	O
1996	36	64	95	4	89	8
1995	31	69	92	8	88	12

INTEREST GROUP RATINGS

Year	ADA	AFL-CIO	CCUS	ACU
1996	0	n/a	100	85
1995	5	8	89	83

Bill Frist (R)

Of Nashville — Elected 1994, 1st term

Biographical Information
Born: Feb. 22, 1952, Nashville, Tenn.
Education: Princeton U., B.A. 1974; Harvard U., M.D. 1978.
Occupation: Surgeon.
Family: Wife, Karyn McLaughlin; three children.
Religion: Presbyterian.
Political Career: No previous office.
Capitol Office: 565 Dirksen Bldg. 20510; 224-3344.

Committees
Budget
Commerce, Science & Transportation
Aviation; Communications; Manufacturing & Competitiveness; Science, Technology & Space (chairman); Surface Transportation & Merchant Marine
Foreign Relations
African Affairs; East Asian & Pacific Affairs; International Economic Policy, Export & Trade Promotion
Labor & Human Resources
Children & Families; Public Health & Safety (chairman)
Small Business

In Washington: Frist gave constituent service a new meaning in September 1995, when he administered cardio-pulmonary resuscitation to a heart attack victim from Tennessee who had collapsed on his way to meet the senator at his Dirksen Building office.

That dramatic incident was just one of the times that Frist's background as a heart and lung transplant surgeon gave him a special role in his first two years in elective office. During the 104th Congress, he had a hand in a variety of health-related issues and played a prominent role in several of them.

When a conference on reauthorizing the Ryan White CARE Act, the government's key AIDS program, stalled in the spring of 1996, then-Senate Labor and Human Resources Chairwoman Nancy Landon Kassebaum, R-Kan., turned to Frist. He helped work out a deal with Rep. Tom Coburn, R-Okla., a fellow physician.

And when Republicans first met with political trouble in the fall of 1995 over what Democrats portrayed as a GOP attempt to cut Medicare, Frist was enlisted to star in his party's televised counterattack. In one ad, he appeared inside a hospital and assured viewers that the Democrats' criticism "sounds scary, but it's simply not true."

Such an assignment plays to Frist's strengths: Like Majority Leader Trent Lott of Mississippi, he is a telegenic, affable politician who can articulate conservative views without sounding bellicose.

Unlike Lott, though, Frist has shown no interest in becoming a creature of Washington. He has joined fellow Tennessee Republican Fred Thompson in backing term limits, contending they would bring a more diverse and talented membership to Congress. He also has sponsored legislation to end the tradition of free airport parking and other legislative perks for senators.

Frist has compiled a solidly conservative voting record, and has made clear his disdain for increased spending on non-defense programs as well as his strong opposition to abortion.

On some other health matters, though, his posture is more moderate. With Democrat Bill Bradley of New Jersey, Frist championed a provision in the fiscal 1997 VA-HUD appropriations bill that requires health insurance plans with maternity coverage to cover at least 48 hours of hospitalization for mothers and newborns after conventional deliveries and 96 hours after Caesarean deliveries.

Frist will delve further into the debate over health in the 105th as chairman of Labor's subcommittee on Public Health and Safety. During the 104th, he chaired the subcommittee on disability policy, a role that found him struggling to reach a compromise with the House in the session's final days on the Individuals With Disabilities Education Act. Frist had hailed the Senate version of the bill as a carefully crafted compromise among diverse interests that preserved the civil rights of disabled students. The measure died in the 104th but will be considered again in the 105th.

On Medicare, Frist was appointed chairman of a Republican working group during the 104th and repeatedly expressed alarm about the impending bankruptcy of the program's trust fund. "We must not fall back on the traditional approach of raising payroll taxes and ratcheting down provider fees," he said in February 1996. "We must reintroduce private sector principles into this public program."

At the start of the 105th, Frist joined with GOP moderates in cosponsoring a measure that would provide greater portability for Medicare beneficiaries who buy Medicare supplemental insurance or private Medigap policies.

Frist found himself in a tough spot in the spring of 1995 as the Labor Committee considered President Clinton's nomination of Dr. Henry W. Foster Jr. to be surgeon general. Frist had been a professional colleague of Foster's in Nashville, but Frist knew that supporting Foster's nomination would anger abortion opponents, many of whom had supported him in his 1994 campaign. Foster acknowledged performing abortions in his 35-year career as an obstetrician/gynecologist.

But Frist's personal ties to Foster won out over political calculations. In late May, Republican James M. Jeffords of Vermont joined Frist and the panel's Democrats to send the nomination to the floor on a 9-7 vote. In June, Frist voted with all the Senate's Democrats and 10 other Republicans to shut off a threatened filibuster of Foster's nomination. But efforts to cut off debate failed, derailing Foster's nomination.

At Home: In the end it was not Frist's wealth that enabled him to defeat three-term Democratic Sen. Jim Sasser in 1994. Nor was it Frist's fame as a heart surgeon, although he did include a picture of himself holding a human heart in his campaign literature, and he assembled former patients to endorse him at his first news conference.

Frist won because he was unmistakably the outsider and because Sasser could not stop looking like the sort of Democratic career politician who drew many voters' wrath in 1994. But even in that year's wave of Republican triumph, Frist's achievement stood out. He took down the state's senior senator, denying Sasser not only his fourth term but also his opportunity to be the Democratic leader in the Senate (a job he was expected to win in party caucus after the election). And he won by 14 percentage points.

An earnest political outsider, Frist was an ideal messenger for an electorate angry at Washington. He had never sought office before and had shown little interest in politics, going much of his adult life without even voting.

Frist sometimes revealed too much of himself. In his autobiography, he owned up to a youthful obsession with science that drove him to adopt cats from animal shelters so he could perform medical experiments on them. But on balance, his lack of political polish seemed to work to his benefit. As a famous doctor with ample personal resources, he could plausibly deny interest in politics as a career.

And, as he himself would ask his audiences on the stump, "Who better than a heart surgeon to take out that bleeding-heart liberal Jim Sasser?"

Frist's father had founded the giant health care conglomerate Hospital Corporation of America. And the candidate himself had spent the previous eight years as a transplant surgeon at Vanderbilt University in Nashville, performing 250 heart and lung transplants — including the first pediatric heart transplant in Tennessee.

Frist was able to mount a $9.5 million campaign, financing most of the effort from his own pocket. He easily defeated five rivals in the GOP primary and became one of just two challengers to knock off an incumbent senator in November.

Frist's medical career enabled him to make a pitch to voters that seemed fresh. No one could remember another candidate standing shoulder-to-shoulder with patients who testified to his sincerity and caring and credited him with saving their lives. He also had gained some prior notice for his crusade to have organ-donor cards printed on the back of driver's licenses in Tennessee and for his service as chairman of the Tennessee Task Force on Medicaid.

But the real message of Frist's TV ads and stump speeches had less to do with his own credentials than with a broad critique of Democrats in the White House and on Capitol Hill.

Frist seemed a little awkward during debates with Sasser, stumbling over words and looking outlandish in a loud red, white and blue flag tie that had been his trademark on the stump. Nonetheless, he consistently scored at these events by linking Sasser to Clinton and the policies of Congress' Democratic majority.

SENATE ELECTIONS

1994 General		
Bill Frist (R)	834,226	(56%)
Jim Sasser (D)	623,164	(42%)
1994 Primary		
Bill Frist (R)	197,734	(44%)
Bob Corker (R)	143,808	(32%)
Steve Wilson (R)	50,274	(11%)
Harold Sterling (R)	28,425	(6%)
Byron Bush (R)	14,267	(3%)
Andrew "Buddy" Benedict III (R)	11,117	(2%)

CAMPAIGN FINANCE

	Receipts	Receipts from PACs	Expend-itures
1994			
Frist (R)	$9,679,522	$413,220 (4%)	$9,517,424
Sasser (D)	$4,448,053	$1,723,494 (39%)	$4,717,147

KEY VOTES

1997	
Approve balanced-budget constitutional amendment	Y
Approve chemical weapons treaty	Y
1996	
Approve farm bill	Y
Limit punitive damages in product liability cases	Y
Exempt small businesses from higher minimum wage	Y
Approve welfare overhaul	Y
Bar job discrimination based on sexual orientation	N
Override veto of ban on "partial birth" abortions	Y
1995	
Approve GOP budget with tax and spending cuts	Y
Approve constitutional amendment barring flag desecration	Y

VOTING STUDIES

	Presidential Support		Party Unity		Conservative Coalition	
Year	**S**	**O**	**S**	**O**	**S**	**O**
1996	39	59	95	4	97	3
1995	25	75	95	4	93	5

INTEREST GROUP RATINGS

Year	ADA	AFL-CIO	CCUS	ACU
1996	0	n/a	100	95
1995	0	0	100	83

1 Bill Jenkins (R)

Of Rogersville — Elected 1996, 1st term

Biographical Information

Born: Nov. 29, 1936, Detroit, Mich.

Education: Tennessee Technological U., B.B.A.; U. of Tennessee, J.D. 1961.

Military Service: Army, 1960-62.

Occupation: Lawyer; farmer.

Family: Wife, Mary Kathryn Myers; four children.

Religion: Baptist.

Political Career: Tenn. House, 1963-71, speaker of the House, 1969-1971; candidate for governor, 1970; circuit court judge, 1990-96.

Capitol Office: 1700 Longworth Bldg. 20515; 225-6356.

Committees

Agriculture
Forestry, Resource Conservation & Research; Livestock, Dairy & Poultry

Judiciary
Constitution; Immigration & Claims

The Path to Washington: After a hiatus of more than 25 years, Jenkins is beginning his legislative career anew, putting the lie to F. Scott Fitzgerald's notion that "there are no second acts in American lives."

First elected to the Tennessee House in 1962, by age 32 Jenkins was Speaker, the only Republican in this century to hold the post. An unsuccessful 1970 bid for governor took him out of the legislative arena, but Jenkins stayed in the public eye down through the years, and after veteran GOP Rep. James H. Quillen announced his retirement in 1996, Jenkins overcame a crowded GOP field in the historically Republican district.

For the 105th Congress, Jenkins got committee assignments that mesh nicely with his background: on Agriculture (he raises beef cattle and burley tobacco) and on Judiciary (he served six years as a circuit judge before resigning to run for Congress in 1996).

Jenkins has a reputation for working in a collegial manner, more interested in building consensus than provoking confrontation. One of his challenges will be matching Quillen's reputation for a high level of constituent service, a record that earned him 17 House terms and made him a power in upper East Tennessee politics.

Jenkins lists balancing the budget as one of his top priorities, and while he supports a robust defense budget, he would like to see the federal bureaucracy in general trimmed down. He argues that Washington imposes too much red tape and regulation.

At the same time, Jenkins can be expected to follow Quillen's lead in resisting cuts to federal programs that benefit Appalachian communities. A former member of the Tennessee Valley Authority board, he is likely to lend his voice to congressional debates on TVA's future as the electric utility industry moves toward deregulation. (Jenkins also served a stint in the 1980s as conservation commissioner under Republican Gov. Lamar Alexander.)

Rumors of Quillen's retirement had been swirling for some time prior to his 1996 announcement that he would step down. That declaration unleashed a lot of pent-up political ambition in the district. Eleven Republicans, as well as four Democrats, filed for the seat.

It had appeared that Quillen was grooming state Rep. Ralph Cole to succeed him, but Cole opted not to run. Quillen eventually sided with state Rep. Richard Venable, a cousin, but the endorsement came fairly late in the game and did not sway many voters.

The top Republican contenders all plied similar conservative lines; even some of the GOP hopefuls admitted there was not any discernible difference between them on the issues.

Jenkins touted his status as the only farmer among the leading candidates, and he claimed to be the only "dyed-in-the-wool, card-carrying bona fide hillbilly" in the race.

Two other Republicans jostled with Jenkins at the top of the pack. District Attorney General Al Schmutzer was the only top-tier candidate based in the district's southern end (from fast-growing Sevier County, near Knoxville), and his financial backers reflected that area's growing influence in 1st District politics. State Sen. Jim Holcomb, a marriage and family therapist, was known for sponsoring the state's ban on same-sex marriages, and he had the backing of some conservative Christian activists.

Schmutzer had an early lead as the returns came in on primary night, but in the end it was Jenkins, taking advantage of his many political contacts across the district, who was able to eke out a win. He finished just 331 votes ahead of Holcomb, with Schmutzer running not far back in third.

Narrow though it was — Jenkins got less than one-fifth the total GOP vote — that was enough to all but ensure Jenkins' election in November. The district has not sent a Democrat to Congress in this century. After a low-key fall campaign, Jenkins won with 64 percent of the vote over Democratic real estate agent Kay C. Smith.

TENNESSEE 1
Northeast — Tri-cities

The Tennessee Valley Authority freed this district and much of East Tennessee from the pervasive rural poverty of an earlier era. Isolated highland towns, tobacco patches and livestock clearings were once the norm in the 1st, but small cities have grown up around industries drawn to the area by the availability of TVA power.

However, industry has not changed the 1st's GOP voting habits. Republican congressmen have represented the 1st for more than a century, and just two people (B. Carroll Reece and James Quillen, who retired in 1996) have held the job for most of the past 75 years. Tennessean Al Gore's presence on the Democratic ticket in 1992 and 1996 did little to temper the district's Republicanism; George Bush and Bob Dole both carried the 1st by at least 15 percentage points.

There are pockets of Democrats, primarily in the Tri-cities area of Kingsport, Bristol and Johnson City. About 45 percent of the district's residents live in this extreme northeastern corner of Tennessee, and the area's industrial work force occasionally helps Democrats win local offices. Sporadic support for Democrats, though, should not be construed as liberalism.

Whatever Democratic votes can be squeezed out of the Tri-cities, the rural counties in the district usually outweigh them. The rural areas routinely deliver the highest GOP tallies in the state. Voters have a deep-seated suspicion of big government and an antipathy toward the Democratic Party dating to their ancestors' Union loyalties during the Civil War.

Economic diversity helped the 1st weather the early 1990s recession without much trouble. The Tri-cities' industrial base includes manufacturers of paper, glass, medical equipment and electronics; employment at major companies such as Eastman Chemical Co. in Kingsport has held steady.

The Tri-cities have each spent the past few years annexing land inside the triangle they form, and their borders now abut one another. Regional cooperation is marred by squabbles over which city is responsible for utilities and taxes in borderline industrial parks.

Economic success in the population centers, however, has not brought better times to the entire area. Three counties in the 1st rank among the state's poorest: More than 40 percent of Hancock County's residents live below the poverty line. Farmers raise tobacco, poultry and livestock; there is zinc and limestone mining.

To the south, in Sevier County, a tourism boom pushed the population up 23 percent in the 1980s. Millions every year visit the Great Smoky Mountains National Park, some stopping along the way to take in attractions such as Dollywood, a theme park in Pigeon Forge launched by country music star Dolly Parton. On the edge of the national park, Gatlinburg is chock-full of motels and amusements.

Greene County, the 1st's largest in land area, features the Andrew Johnson National Historical Site. The only president to be impeached spent most of his adult life in Greeneville and is buried there. The pioneer Davy Crockett was born in Greene County.

1990 Population: 541,875. White 528,585 (98%), Black 10,272 (2%), Other 3,018 (<1%). Hispanic origin 2,132 (<1%). 18 and over 418,894 (77%), 62 and over 92,276 (17%). Median age: 36.

HOUSE ELECTIONS

1996 General		
Bill Jenkins (R)	117,676	(64%)
Kay C. Smith (D)	58,657	(33%)
Dave Davis (I)	1,947	(1%)
1996 Primary		
Bill Jenkins (R)	15,532	(18%)
Jim Holcomb (R)	15,201	(18%)
Al Schmutzer (R)	12,908	(15%)
David Davis (R)	10,787	(13%)
Richard S. Venable (R)	10,604	(13%)
David Crockett (R)	10,263	(12%)
Anne Pope (R)	8,247	(10%)

CAMPAIGN FINANCE

	Receipts	Receipts from PACs		Expend-itures
1996				
Jenkins (R)	$491,884	$94,696	(19%)	$457,975
Smith (D)	$32,545	$1,000	(3%)	$32,296

DISTRICT VOTE FOR PRESIDENT

	1996		1992
D	73,635 (37%)	D	75,681 (37%)
R	107,645 (55%)	R	106,939 (52%)
I	14,526 (7%)	I	24,230 (12%)

KEY VOTES

1997
Ban "partial birth" abortions Y

2 John J. 'Jimmy' Duncan Jr. (R)

Of Knoxville — Elected 1988; 5th full term

Biographical Information

Born: July 21, 1947, Lebanon, Tenn.

Education: U. of Tennessee, B.S. 1969; George Washington U., J.D. 1973.

Military Service: U.S. Army Reserve and National Guard, 1970-87.

Occupation: Judge; lawyer.

Family: Wife, Lynn Hawkins; four children.

Religion: Presbyterian.

Political Career: Knox County Criminal Court judge, 1981-88.

Capitol Office: 2400 Rayburn Bldg. 20515; 225-5435

Committees

Resources
Energy & Mineral Resources; National Parks & Public Lands

Transportation & Infrastructure
Aviation (chairman); Public Buildings & Economic Development

In Washington: When two major domestic airline crashes in 1996 focused the nation's attention on aviation safety issues, Duncan drew some time in the spotlight as the chairman of the Aviation Subcommittee on the Transportation and Infrastructure Committee.

He helped craft reauthorizing legislation for the Federal Aviation Administration (FAA) that addressed some safety issues and provided more autonomy for the FAA. Despite the ValuJet and TWA crashes, though, Duncan stressed the strong safety record of the U.S. aviation industry. He and most in Congress were loath to impose much tighter safety standards, fearing that doing so could lead to severe delays and higher ticket prices.

"If we totally overreact, we can just about shut down the airlines," Duncan said in 1996.

In 1995, Duncan joined Iowa Republican Jim Ross Lightfoot in introducing a bill to remove the FAA from the Transportation Department, exempt it from federal personnel and procurement rules, and take "off-budget" the aviation trust fund that supports the FAA and funds airport construction. Duncan said federal personnel rules prevent the agency from offering competitive wages, and he blamed procurement restrictions for causing cost overruns and delays in computer upgrades.

"The FAA's cumbersome procurement process brought on by years of bureaucratic inertia have resulted in aging computers and 30-year-old air traffic control equipment that constantly breaks down," Duncan told the House when the bill was brought up in March 1996. The House passed the measure but it went no further, although some of its provisions were included in the broad reauthorization measure.

Duncan also saw House passage in 1996 of two airline safety measures he pushed. One would require airlines to run background checks on prospective pilots, including reviews of motor vehicle driving records and medical examinations. The second would prohibit anyone without a valid pilot's license from operating an airplane for the purpose of breaking a record or accomplishing some other aviation feat. This measure was a response to the death of 7-year-old Jessica Dubroff, who was killed with her father and a flight instructor in an April 1996 crash while trying to become the youngest person to fly across the country.

In the 105th, Duncan's committee is grappling with the touchy issue of aviation taxes, which go into the aviation trust fund. Authority to collect the taxes expired Dec. 31, 1996. Duncan undertook to reinstate the taxes in early 1997, warning that money for airport construction would dry up.

However, the measure Duncan was pushing, which included a 10 percent levy on domestic airline tickets, ran into turbulence from anti-tax members, who called for cuts in other taxes to offset reinstatement of the aviation taxes. But Duncan, who said he had never supported a tax increase, said the ticket tax was necessary. "We have the safest and most efficient aviation system in the world, but it is growing by leaps and bounds due to great increases in both air passenger and air cargo traffic," he told the House. "We simply cannot operate a safe, efficient, rapidly growing system for free." The House passed the bill, 347-73, but the taxing authority was extended only through Sept. 30, 1997.

Complicating the matter, the seven largest U.S. airlines are proposing that Congress eliminate the 10 percent ticket tax. In its place, they advocate a package of three levies — $4.50 per passenger, $2 per airplane seat ($1 for commuter planes) and a per-mile charge of $.005 per passenger. The effect of such changes would be to lessen the tax burden on airlines with higher prices and hub-and-spoke routes, at the expense of airlines with discount tickets and direct routes.

Advocates say the proposed package is fairer because it puts a greater emphasis on taxing airlines by the number of takeoffs and landings, rather than by the price of tickets. But discount airlines say the proposal would impose a heavier tax burden on passengers who buy low-cost tickets and undercut the ability of discount airlines to

TENNESSEE 2
East — Knoxville

With a winning tradition dating to the Civil War, the 2nd's GOP defines the word "entrenched." Since the days when parts of this area tried to secede from Tennessee to rejoin the Union, the majority of voters here have remained fixed in their partisan preference. No Democrat has held this House seat since then, and only rarely does one even put up a good fight for it.

The GOP's standard playbook does well in the 2nd: support for a strong defense, frugality in federal spending (especially on welfare programs), and traditional "family values."

Residents' conservatism translates into solid margins for GOP presidential candidates and even bigger wins for Duncan. Voters will, however, support popular Democrats in statewide races when the GOP fails to put forward a top-drawer candidate.

Knox County dominates the district, casting about 60 percent of its ballots. The city of Knoxville itself (population 165,000) has a sizable Democratic vote: Labor unions have some strength, blacks are a substantial presence in the eastern part of the city, and there are some liberal elements in the University of Tennessee community. However, the suburbs of Knox County — predominantly white-collar professionals in the west, with middle-income workers in the south and north — easily deliver the votes to keep Republicans in charge.

Though the typical resident of the 2nd is a critic of "big government," state and federal jobs are a big component of the economy. In addition to hosting the university, Knoxville is headquarters for the Tennessee Valley Authority, and a number of Knox County residents commute to neighboring Anderson County (in the 3rd District) to work at the Oak Ridge National Laboratories and related companies. Factories turn out a range of goods, including boats, manufactured homes, electronics and apparel.

The economy of the 2nd also feeds on outsiders' dollars: I-75 and I-40 meet at Knoxville, and visitors passing through "the gateway to the Smokies" pump hundreds of millions of dollars into the area economy. Knoxville is a regional medical, retail and entertainment center: The 100,000-plus hordes that throng to University of Tennessee football games enrich merchants, innkeepers and restaurateurs for miles around.

Downtown Knoxville has a small but fairly funky "Old City" quarter with shops and nightclubs. The nearby site where the 1982 World's Fair was staged is now a park, with an amphitheater used occasionally for special events. Discussions about developing the fair site more ambitiously have been a staple of civic debate since the fair ended, with proposals ranging from a residential and retail complex to a new minor league baseball stadium.

South of Knox is Blount County, second-largest in the 2nd, where a longtime economic pillar is the Aluminum Company of America plant in Alcoa. At the southern end of the district, 1992 remapping moved Democratic Polk County from the 2nd to the 3rd and gave Duncan some strongly conservative Chattanooga suburbs in Bradley County.

1990 Population: 541,864. White 500,016 (92%), Black 35,785 (7%), Other 6,063 (1%). Hispanic origin 2,983 (<1%). 18 and over 416,775 (77%), 62 and over 85,247 (16%). Median age: 34.

compete. Duncan, whose subcommittee has looked at the user tax idea, acknowledged: "It's not an issue that's going to be easy."

Duncan also has a seat on the Resources Committee, where in the past he has fought against expanding the national park system, on the grounds that the Park Service cannot afford to maintain properly the existing parks. He introduced a measure in early 1997 that would require federal income tax forms to contain a line allowing taxpayers to donate one or more dollars to benefit the national parks. "This bill will provide more money for the care of our national parks at no cost to the federal government," he said.

More than once, Duncan has taken on federal projects he sees as wasteful spending, and in the 104th Congress he successfully amended the fiscal 1996 Treasury-Postal Service spending bill to eliminate $65.8 million for the purchase of 100 acres in suburban Maryland and the initial design and construction of a new campus-like setting for the Food and Drug Administration. "The idea of building a beautiful, new campus that would more than double FDA's headquarters space is beyond comprehension at a time when we are asking federal agencies to make do with less," Duncan said.

But in one area of government spending with impact on East Tennessee, he has been more accommodating. Duncan in July 1995 fought an amendment by Republican "deficit hawk" Scott L. Klug of Wisconsin that aimed to kill $103 million in federal funds for Tennessee Valley Authority (TVA) programs unconnected to the agency's profitable electric power generation business. TVA provides thousands of jobs and other economic benefits in the 2nd District and across Tennessee. Klug's amendment failed, 144-284.

Duncan voted for NAFTA in 1993, but the next year he was the only member of the Tennessee delegation to vote against GATT. He told the Knoxville News-Sentinel that he believes in free and fair trade. "But I do not believe that we need a 22,000-page document lined with billions of dollars in giveaways to media giants, special interest pork and the establishment of a United Nations on trade issues called the World Trade Organization in order to trade with other countries," he said.

A fiscal policy and social issues conservative, Duncan votes much like the younger GOP firebrands who have come to the House in the 1990's. But he holds the House as an institution in higher regard than do some of the younger-generation conservatives, a reflection of the fact that his father, John J. Duncan, held the seat before him. He has often said that he seeks to emulate his father, who made himself a popular congressman for more than two decades by tending to local concerns and eschewing the national spotlight.

This perspective leads Duncan to differ from many in his party on a term limits constitutional amendment. He calls it a solution for a problem that does not exist, because "elections are the best term limits ever invented."

At Home: Duncan entered politics with one of the best-known names in East Tennessee's public life. His father was mayor of Knoxville in the late 1950s and then served a generation in Congress. His uncle was a judge. And the younger Duncan, too, took the courtroom route into politics. He served eight years as a criminal court judge in Knox County, the population center of the 2nd.

The years on the bench helped Duncan build up enough of a reputation to be a strong candidate in his own right in 1988 when his father, in failing health, decided that the 100th Congress would be his last (the elder Duncan died shortly after making his retirement announcement).

But in his initial congressional campaign, there was little doubt that Duncan campaigned primarily as his father's son, both in style and substance. Although he is generally known as "Jimmy," he capped off his heir-apparent campaign by appearing on the ballot as John J. Duncan.

His heir-to-the-job strategy proved successful in the end, but it gave Democrats an opening to make a race of it in this traditional bastion of mountain Republicanism. Duncan campaigned in the old-style, door-to-door and barbecue-to-barbecue manner for which his father had been known. His Democratic opponent, Dudley Taylor, waged a hard-hitting media campaign the likes of which had not been seen in this district.

As Duncan put together a loose-knit organization run mainly by family and friends, Taylor, who stepped down from his post as state revenue commissioner to run, enlisted assistance from influential state Democrats, including his former boss, Democratic Gov. Ned McWherter. Little known to most voters at the outset, Taylor quickly raised his profile by aggressively courting news coverage and making equally aggressive use of paid media.

Taylor hammered away at Duncan for declining to debate and relying on the senior Duncan's reputation. Late in the race, local Republicans prodded Duncan into taking out print ads rebutting Taylor's "vicious and false allegations." These helped shore up the GOP vote, and Duncan took a comfortable 56 percent in the general election (and a same-day special election for the right to fill out the remainder of his father's term in the 100th Congress until the swearing-in of the 101st).

HOUSE ELECTIONS

1996 General		
John J. "Jimmy" Duncan Jr. (R)	150,953	(71%)
Stephen Smith (D)	61,020	(29%)
1994 General		
John J. "Jimmy" Duncan Jr. (R)	128,937	(90%)
Randon J. Krieg (I)	6,854	(5%)
Greg Samples (I)	6,682	(5%)

Previous Winning Percentages: 1992 (72%) **1990** (81%) **1988** (56%) **1988†** (56%)

† Elected to a full term and to fill a vacancy at the same time.

CAMPAIGN FINANCE

	Receipts	Receipts from PACs	Expend-itures
1996			
Duncan (R)	$512,212	$221,497 (43%)	$260,818
Smith (D)	$54,683	$11,000 (20%)	$53,820
1994			
Duncan (R)	$255,451	$139,970 (55%)	$200,332

DISTRICT VOTE FOR PRESIDENT

	1996		1992
D	93,722 (42%)	D	92,889 (41%)
R	114,130 (51%)	R	108,109 (48%)
I	12,144 (6%)	I	25,196 (11%)

KEY VOTES

1997	
Ban "partial birth" abortions	Y
1996	
Approve farm bill	Y
Deny public education to illegal immigrants	Y
Repeal ban on certain assault-style weapons	Y
Increase minimum wage	Y
Freeze defense spending	Y
Approve welfare overhaul	Y
1995	
Approve balanced-budget constitutional amendment	Y
Relax Clean Water Act regulations	Y
Oppose limits on environmental regulations	N
Reduce projected Medicare spending	Y
Approve GOP budget with tax and spending cuts	Y

VOTING STUDIES

	Presidential Support		Party Unity		Conservative Coalition	
Year	S	O	S	O	S	O
1996	32	66	81	18	59	39
1995	26	74	85	14	72	27
1994	24	74	95	5	67	33
1993	25	75	88	11	66	34
1992	63	37	87	12	71	29
1991	65	34	84	14	86	11

INTEREST GROUP RATINGS

Year	ADA	AFL-CIO	CCUS	ACU
1996	30	n/a	88	85
1995	5	8	96	96
1994	20	22	75	76
1993	20	17	73	92
1992	25	42	63	84
1991	20	33	80	100

3 Zach Wamp (R)

Of Hixson — Elected 1994, 2nd term

Biographical Information
Born: Oct. 28, 1957, Fort Benning, Ga.
Education: U. of North Carolina, 1977-78; U. of Tennessee, 1978-79; U. of North Carolina, 1979-80.
Occupation: Real estate broker.
Family: Wife, Kim Watts; two children.
Religion: Baptist.
Political Career: Republican nominee for U.S. House, 1992.
Capitol Office: 423 Cannon Bldg. 20515; 225-3271.

Committees
Appropriations
Interior; Legislative; Military Construction

In Washington: Wamp is a textbook example of how an officeholder's thinking can evolve when his principles run hard up against political reality. On the way to winning his first House term in 1994, Wamp pledged allegiance to the conservatives' creed of balancing the budget and reining in "big government." But when spending-cutters in the 104th Congress considered slashing programs that help sustain the economy of Wamp's district, he was often a vocal defender of preserving Uncle Sam's role.

In the 105th, Wamp will be in an even stronger position to defend East Tennessee's economic interests from his new seat on the Appropriations Committee.

Shortly after coming to Washington in 1995, Wamp said, "The freshman class is the most principled body of people in this institution." Without this group, he argued, serious movement toward a balanced budget would not occur. "We are courageous enough to cut spending even in our own back yard," he said.

Soon, though, GOP budget hawks were targeting agencies that provide thousands of jobs and other economic benefits in the 3rd District and across Tennessee, including the Tennessee Valley Authority (TVA), the Department of Energy, the Appalachian Regional Commission and the Economic Development Agency (EDA).

Wamp rushed to their defense. In an interview with The Washington Post, he said, "I have found since I was elected that the EDA and the Appalachian Regional Commission have actually been very critical tools for economic growth in East Tennessee. There is a role for federal government." The Post reported that the 3rd ranks fifth among all districts in receipt of federal expenditures.

Wamp did not object to trimming these agencies as part of a governmentwide streamlining, but he fought those who sought to abolish the agencies; he said he would "stand up and sacrifice my political blood" to save TVA and the Department of Energy. "The Tennessee Valley Authority is not perfect," he conceded on the House floor, but "neither is the Pentagon perfect, neither are the Centers for Disease Control perfect, neither is the White House perfect. . . .[and] I have not seen any amendments to zero these core functions out."

Often, the amendments to "zero out" agencies dear to Wamp were offered by a fellow Republican, Scott L. Klug of Wisconsin. Generally, though, Klug's proposals failed by substantial margins.

Wamp and his TVA allies (he is chairman of the 47-member Tennessee Valley Caucus) were surprised early in the 105th when TVA Chairman Craven Crowell proposed that the agency do without its annual appropriation from Congress. With energy deregulation on the horizon, Crowell contended that TVA should concentrate on its profitable power generation work and give up the economic development and research activities subsidized by its federal appropriation.

Wamp went to bat for another federal agency during consideration of the fiscal 1997 science authorization bill. He persuaded the House to restore $20.5 million to a National Oceanic and Atmospheric Agency account that funds local weather warnings and forecasts. He was troubled, he told his colleagues, that during the previous weekend tornadoes had touched down in Bradley County, Tenn., but were not picked up in advance by a radar station in the mountains nearby.

Wamp keeps his ear close to the ground for constituent reaction to issues before Congress, and at times he has deferred to popular opinion, even in the face of contradictory advice from experts. When the Clinton administration moved in 1995 to prop up the sagging Mexican currency, Wamp, like many of his constituents, was not convinced of the importance of the bailout, and a briefing from Federal Reserve Board Chairman Alan Greenspan did not sway him.

"Sitting and listening to Mr. Greenspan last night," Wamp said, "I couldn't help but realize that he's a whole lot more intelligent than I am. As a

The 3rd is a mixture of agricultural counties and two main commercial hubs: Chattanooga (Hamilton County) in the South and Oak Ridge (Anderson County) in the north. The district starts above Oak Ridge, pinches through narrow Meigs County on its way south to Chattanooga and then broadens out along the Georgia border.

The 3rd shows a moderate-to-conservative personality in elections. The district went solidly Republican in presidential elections of the 1980s, though the Clinton-Gore ticket nearly won here in 1992, something Democrats have not managed in the 3rd since 1976. In the end, George Bush prevailed districtwide by just 65 votes out of more than 220,000 cast. In 1996, Bill Clinton fell 2,241 votes shy of Bob Dole's total.

The 1992 remap was aimed to help Democratic Rep. Marilyn Lloyd. Democratic cartographers excised from the 3rd a sizable portion of conservative Bradley (just above Chattanooga), and they gave Lloyd several Democratic rural counties — Sequatchie, Van Buren and Polk. But when Lloyd retired in 1994, Republican Wamp won the open seat contest.

Wamp took 58 percent of the 1996 vote in Hamilton County, where more than half the district's votes are cast. Hamilton, Bledsoe and the part of Bradley County still in the 3rd were the only parts of the 12-county district to support Dole over Clinton. (Hamilton has voted Republican in all but one presidential election since 1952.)

Much economic activity in the 3rd centers on the district's nuclear facilities: the Oak Ridge National Laboratories and the Tennessee Valley Authority's Sequoia and Watts Bar nuclear power plants near Chattanooga. But with less federal money going to nuclear energy and research, officials are looking for new sources of economic activity. They are promoting a plan that would transform the route connecting Oak Ridge and neighboring Knoxville into a Technology Corridor for high-technology research and development. A highway linking Knoxville's airport to the Technology Corridor was completed in 1996.

TENNESSEE 3
Southeast — Chattanooga; Oak Ridge

The 3rd is known for several other white- and blue-collar industries. In Chattanooga, insurance, chemical and service companies have joined the older metal, textile and candy industries. (Former GOP Sen. Bill Brock's family owns the Brock Candy Co.) The TVA's Office of Power has headquarters in the city as well.

The Chattanooga Choo Choo and Terminal, made famous by Glenn Miller's song, and the new Chattanooga Aquarium help generate revenue from tourism, as do the Battles for Chattanooga Museum, Rock City, Ruby Falls and historic sites connected with the Civil War's "Battle Above the Clouds" on Lookout Mountain.

1990 Population: 541,866. White 473,405 (87%), Black 62,781 (12%), Other 5,680 (1%). Hispanic origin 3,359 (<1%). 18 and over 410,195 (76%), 62 and over 89,781 (17%). Median age: 35.

matter of fact, he's a whole lot smarter than the people of East Tennessee who I was elected to represent. But I'm going to vote with them this time and not with Mr. Greenspan."

Wamp's efforts to strike a populist tone and distance himself from the culture of Washington extend to his living arrangements. Early in his freshman term he lived in a Capitol Hill hotel, reasoning that if he didn't have furniture of his own, "this forces me to go back to my district." Later he joined with two other Republicans in the Class of 1994, Oklahomans Steve Largent and Tom Coburn, to share an apartment on the Hill. He also has suggested building military-style dormitories for members. Wamp has promised to serve in the House no more than 12 years.

As the 104th wore on and conservatives found their hopes for dramatic change often stymied, Wamp defended the faith, describing his freshman class as "the purest, most worthy group of leaders elected to this body in my lifetime." Although some members broke from the GOP leadership in 1996 to support a boost in the minimum wage, Wamp did not. And Wamp, who received perfect voting scores from the American Conservative Union in each of his first two years, was willing to freeze fiscal 1997 defense spending at the level of fiscal 1996.

Wamp has been an advocate of campaign finance reform, cosponsoring a proposal to lower the amount that PACs can contribute and requiring candidates to raise a majority of their funds from within their own districts.

During his 1994 campaign, Wamp promised to post a sign in his office reading, "If you're from a special interest PAC, leave your card in a basket, because I don't need your money to get elected."

The Federal Election Commission's campaign summary report for the 1996 election cycle showed Wamp with more than $5,000 in PAC receipts. Wamp says he returns all money from PACs, but he has accepted money from individual congressmen and their campaign committees. The FEC report lists these contributions on the same line as PAC contributors when summarizing candidates' receipts.

At Home: In Wamp's first congressional bid, in 1992, he came within 3,000 votes of unseating

Democratic Rep. Marilyn Lloyd. Wamp kept his eye on the prize, and when Lloyd announced that she would not seek an 11th term in 1994, he was ready.

Wamp easily won the 1994 GOP primary, although he was aggressively challenged for the party's nomination by state Rep. Kenneth J. "Ken" Meyer. Meyer made use of Wamp's admitted past cocaine addiction — an issue Lloyd also had used — as well as a lawsuit against Wamp's family over a Chattanooga condominium project. But Wamp's 67 percent primary tally suggested those issues no longer concerned voters.

The outcome of the Democratic primary also seemed to bode well for Wamp. The surprise winner was Randy Button, a property assessor who benefited from a high turnout in his base in the rural, northern part of the 3rd. Button was not well-known in the vote-rich Hamilton County (Chattanooga) area, but the Democratic primary candidates hailing from there attacked each other and split the Hamilton vote.

Just when it seemed that Wamp would have the easiest election of the three Republican nominees for Tennessee's trio of open House seats, trouble arose. Energy Secretary Hazel R. O'Leary was brought into a dispute over whether Wamp, given his past drug problem, could obtain the security clearance necessary for a congressman from the 3rd, whose nuclear facilities include the important Oak Ridge National Laboratories. Button also questioned whether Wamp had been truthful on his applications to become a real estate broker and to join the military reserves.

The Wamp-Button race turned out to be the closest of Tennessee's three open-seat contests. Wamp lost in strongly Democratic Anderson County (Oak Ridge), but he won the biggest prize, populous Hamilton County, where earlier he had made a mark as the youngest-ever chairman of the county GOP. Overall, he beat Button 52 percent to 46 percent.

In 1996, Democrats hoped for better luck with Chattanooga-based candidate, lawyer and wealthy businessman Charles "Chuck" Jolly. But Jolly, one of the losers to Button in the 1994 primary, did not show any new campaigning flair, and he was undercut by Lloyd's endorsement of Wamp. Even O'Leary traveled to the district in 1995 to praise Wamp's efforts in behalf of energy agencies. Wamp climbed to a double-digit victory margin.

HOUSE ELECTIONS

1996 General		
Zach Wamp (R)	113,408	(56%)
Charles "Chuck" Jolly (D)	85,714	(43%)
1994 General		
Zach Wamp (R)	84,583	(52%)
Randy Button (D)	73,839	(46%)
Thomas Ed Morrell (I)	1,929	(1%)

CAMPAIGN FINANCE

	Receipts	Receipts from PACs	Expend-itures
1996			
Wamp (R)	$958,443	$0 (0%)	$942,237
Jolly (D)	$433,141	$150,950 (35%)	$420,390
1994			
Wamp (R)	$696,572	$5,613 (1%)	$704,220
Button (D)	$505,772	$133,150 (26%)	$502,668

DISTRICT VOTE FOR PRESIDENT

	1996		1992
D	94,883 (46%)	**D**	97,296 (44%)
R	97,124 (47%)	**R**	97,361 (44%)
I	13,686 (7%)	**I**	25,789 (12%)

KEY VOTES

1997	
Ban "partial-birth" abortions	Y
1996	
Approve farm bill	N
Deny public education to illegal immigrants	Y
Repeal ban on certain assault-style weapons	Y
Increase minimum wage	N
Freeze defense spending	Y
Approve welfare overhaul	Y
1995	
Approve balanced-budget constitutional amendment	Y
Relax Clean Water Act regulations	Y
Oppose limits on environmental regulations	N
Reduce projected Medicare spending	Y
Approve GOP budget with tax and spending cuts	Y

VOTING STUDIES

	Presidential Support		Party Unity		Conservative Coalition	
Year	**S**	**O**	**S**	**O**	**S**	**O**
1996	30	68	89	11	75	25
1995	14	86	95	4	94	5

INTEREST GROUP RATINGS

Year	ADA	AFL-CIO	CCUS	ACU
1996	15	n/a	88	100
1995	0	8	96	100

4 Van Hilleary (R)

Of Grandview — Elected 1994, 2nd term

Biographical Information

Born: June 20, 1959, Dayton, Tenn.
Education: U. of Tennessee, B.S. 1981, 1985-87; Samford U., J.D. 1990.
Military Service: Air Force, 1982; Air Force Reserve, 1982-present.
Occupation: Textile industry executive.
Family: Single.
Religion: Presbyterian.
Political Career: Republican nominee for Tenn. Senate, 1992.

Capitol Office: 114 Cannon Bldg. 20515; 225-6831

Committees

Budget
Education & Workforce
Early Childhood, Youth & Families; Oversight & Investigations
National Security
Military Installations and Facilities; Military Research & Development

In Washington: Hilleary quickly found a place in the spotlight: Just three months into the 104th Congress, he became the first freshman since 1897 to offer a constitutional amendment that advanced as far as the House floor.

Hilleary sponsored one of four versions of a constitutional amendment to impose term limits on members of Congress. His version would have limited members to 12 years' service per chamber, but it would have allowed states the prerogative of setting lower limits. When the House took up the amendment in March 1995, 22 states already had passed some version of term limits, with 15 of them limiting service to six years.

Hilleary led the charge of GOP freshmen who sought to preserve the lower limits passed by some states. He said that "Anyone who believes that states ought to have their rights respected, and anyone who has respect for the people who stood in parking lots and collected signatures to get term limits passed" would support his version. In the end, it failed, 164-265, as did the other three term-limit proposals. In May 1995, congressional term limits set by states were adjudged unconstitutional by the Supreme Court — a ruling that hardened the resolve of those who are lobbying for adding term limits to the Constitution. But factionalism among supporters helped soften support for the proposal in a February 1997 revote; the most successful version fell 10 votes short of the support garnered by the 1995 version.

Hilleary had said he considered term limits to be the most important plank of the House GOP's "Contract With America," and he has promised to limit himself to six terms. He also refuses contributions from PACs.

Hilleary has two new committee assignments for the 105th Congress — Budget, and Education and the Workforce — to go with his holdover assignment from the 104th, National Security.

Like many Class of 1994 Republicans, Hilleary in his first term sometimes encountered conflicts between the parochial interests of his constituents and his own zeal for reform and budget-cutting. Hilleary's district lies just north of Huntsville, Ala., home of the George C. Marshall Space Flight Center, and he was heavily lobbied to support continued funding of the space station. Hilleary, who served on the Science Committee during the 104th, noted that "there is always a lot of indirect pressure to support the chairman," who was then Robert S. Walker, R-Pa., a space station booster.

Hilleary noted that he already had voted in favor of cutting the budget for the Appalachian Regional Commission, which provides economic benefits to some of his constituents, and he wanted to compile a consistent record. In the end, he was one of only 46 House Republicans voting to terminate space station funding.

But he did argue against ending funding for the Tennessee Valley Authority. "All of us are budget hawks up here," he said on the House floor in July 1995. "Many of us in the freshman class ran on this, and this is what we are dedicated to; however, there is a big distinction in this particular case." Just as the space station survived, so too did funding for TVA.

(Early in the 105th, TVA Chairman Craven Crowell proposed that the agency do without its annual appropriation from Congress. With energy deregulation on the horizon, Crowell contended that TVA should concentrate on its profitable power generation work and give up the economic development and research activities subsidized by its federal appropriation.)

Hilleary blocked a TVA plan called Shoreline Management Initiative, which included a proposal to charge a $1,000 deposit on lake structures including docks and boat houses on TVA reservoirs. The House initially approved Hilleary's amendment during consideration of the fiscal 1997 energy and water spending bill, but the provision was dropped in conference. Hilleary persisted and succeeded in tacking his language to the catchall spending bill passed at the very end of the 104th.

Hilleary has argued in favor of wind tunnel programs, part of the work at the Arnold Air

TENNESSEE 4
Northeast and south central

Like the state itself, the 4th is long and sprawling, extending nearly 300 miles. Beginning in the rural flatlands in the southwest and not too far from Memphis, it snakes up through the rolling terrain in Middle Tennessee, stretches north onto the Cumberland Plateau and encompasses a sliver of Knox County in East Tennessee.

The 4th is so large that from east to west it touches four states — Mississippi, Alabama, Kentucky and Virginia — as well as territory from all three of the state's distinct geographic and cultural divisions. And it spans the time zone dividing line, giving it both Central and Eastern times.

The 1992 redistricting, which was designed to strengthen Democratic chances in the 7th and 3rd districts, weakened them in the 4th. In the southwest, it added Hardin and Wayne counties, whose GOP roots grow out of the Civil War. The new lines also added Pickett County in the north and a part of east Knox County. In 1994, the district even abandoned Democratic former Rep. Jim Cooper in his unsuccessful senatorial bid after consistently supporting him for 12 years. Hilleary strengthened his hold on the district in 1996, although Bill Clinton barely carried it for the Democrats at the presidential level.

With no large urban center in the 4th, people form their political opinions by talking with neighbors in feed stores, roadside cafes and small-town shops that surround the courthouse squares. Most of the Cumberland Plateau, a westernmost edge of East Tennessee and Hilleary's base from his 1992 state Senate race, is in the district. Most of the Plateau leans Republican although Democrats dominate in local and state politics. Growing Cumberland County has become a mountain retirement haven for Northerners, who have generally voted Republican.

The 4th is home to some unique legal history: In 1925, the "Scopes monkey trial" was held in Dayton in Rhea County. In that case, the state court upheld a law making it illegal to teach the theory of evolution in public schools. The ruling was later overturned. Religion and social conservatism still play a role in the district's politics.

Agriculture and light industry make up the bulk of the 4th's economy. Soybeans and cotton are harvested in the western counties. In the northern counties, tobacco grows in the valleys, and beef and dairy cattle graze on hillsides too steep for plowing.

Coal had long been an economic staple, but underground activity has mostly given way to surface mining.

In addition, many plants specializing in automotive parts assist the Saturn and Nissan factories in the state. Warren County raises trees and shrubs for the nursery industry. And the Jack Daniels Distillery in Moore County produces the famous sour mash whiskey. But its product cannot be purchased there; Moore is a "dry" county.

The 4th is also known for the Tennessee Walking Horse National Celebration, which is held every August and September in Shelbyville.

1990 Population: 541,868. White 518,991 (96%), Black 19,669 (4%), Other 3,208 (<1%). Hispanic origin 2,376 (<1%). 18 and over 405,759 (75%), 62 and over 93,601 (17%). Median age: 35.

Force Base in his district. He also watched an attempt to block $2.6 million for an Army National Guard firing range in Tullahoma fail, 214-216.

At Home: With six-term Democrat Jim Cooper leaving the 4th in 1994 for an ultimately unsuccessful Senate bid, Republicans felt the conservative-minded district offered them a good opportunity for a pickup.

Former Tennessee Sen. Howard H. Baker Jr. (1967-1985), whose family base in Huntsville is in the 4th, had been impressed by Hilleary's challenge to a state senator in 1992, and he thought Hilleary's status as a Persian Gulf War veteran would be a plus with voters. He held a fundraiser for Hilleary at his Scott County home. (Decades earlier, Baker's father had represented the eastern counties in the district when they were part of the 2nd, and in 1982, Baker's daughter Cissy was soundly defeated by Cooper in the newly created 4th.)

Hilleary won his GOP primary handily, but most expected he would face a tough general election. Despite the district's conservative leanings, many of the rural voters are traditional Old South Democrats. Twice as many voters turned out for the Democratic House primary as for the GOP primary.

But that represented a steep decline in Democratic turnout for an area where Republican primary voters have been traditionally outnumbered. And fortunately for Hilleary, the Democrats' primary in 1994 was a five-person slug out. The eventual nominee, Jeff Whorley, a former top aide to Tennessee Rep. Bart Gordon, did not win enthusiastic backing in November from all his defeated party rivals.

Whorley's work experience in Washington made him vulnerable to Hilleary's anti-Congress campaign. And because Whorley had moved back to Tennessee to run, he was not in a strong position to label Hilleary as an interloper. (He had moved into the district after his losing state Senate race.)

Whorley campaigned on a conservative line,

including support for term limits and school prayer, but Hilleary charged that his true colors were more apparent in his work for Gordon, who had usually voted in agreement with the Clinton administration. Despite Whorley's stance against restrictions on gun owners, Hilleary was endorsed by the National Rifle Association. He also received implicit support from the Tennessee Farm Bureau.

Hilleary's strong grass-roots organization was indispensable in the rural, sprawling district, which has no central media market. Whorley got no help from Cooper's Senate bid; on the way to a resounding statewide defeat, he won only three counties in his district. Whorley carried those three along with two others also in the Middle Tennessee portion of the district, traditionally a solid Democratic area. Hilleary's leads in the easternmost and westernmost counties and his inroads in Middle Tennessee territory gave him a solid 57 percent victory.

Hilleary improved slightly on his winning percentage in 1996, easily turning aside Winchester lawyer Mark Stewart. Democratic officials held high hopes for Stewart, whose grandfather had been a senator. Stewart argued that a vote for Hilleary was a vote for Speaker Newt Gingrich, and he got help from labor unions in spreading that Democratic gospel. But Stewart did not develop much of a message beyond that, and voters were unpersuaded that Hilleary should be turned out of office.

HOUSE ELECTIONS

1996 General		
Van Hilleary (R)	103,091	(58%)
Mark Stewart (D)	73,331	(41%)
1994 General		
Van Hilleary (R)	81,539	(57%)
Jeff Whorley (D)	60,489	(42%)
J. Patrick Lyons (I)	1,944	(1%)

CAMPAIGN FINANCE

	Receipts	Receipts from PACs	Expend-itures
1996			
Hilleary (R)	$1,258,344	$0 (0%)	$1,183,570
Stewart (D)	$589,673	$136,000 (23%)	$586,987
1994			
Hilleary (R)	$616,297	$0 (0%)	$613,648
Whorley (D)	$1,004,885	$195,688 (19%)	$842,445
Lyons (I)	$15,813	0	$8,540

DISTRICT VOTE FOR PRESIDENT

	1996		1992
D	92,137 (46%)	D	100,292 (48%)
R	89,951 (45%)	R	83,922 (40%)
I	14,797 (8%)	I	23,838 (12%)

KEY VOTES

1997	
Ban "partial birth" abortions	Y
1996	
Approve farm bill	Y
Deny public education to illegal immigrants	Y
Repeal ban on certain assault-style weapons	Y
Increase minimum wage	Y
Freeze defense spending	N
Approve welfare overhaul	Y
1995	
Approve balanced-budget constitutional amendment	Y
Relax Clean Water Act regulations	Y
Oppose limits on environmental regulations	N
Reduce projected Medicare spending	Y
Approve GOP budget with tax and spending cuts	Y

VOTING STUDIES

	Presidential Support		Party Unity		Conservative Coalition	
Year	S	O	S	O	S	O
1996	32	68	92	7	86	14
1995	14	85	96	3	90	10

INTEREST GROUP RATINGS

Year	ADA	AFL-CIO	CCUS	ACU
1996	0	n/a	94	95
1995	0	0	100	100

5 Bob Clement (D)

Of Nashville — Elected 1988; 5th full term

Biographical Information

Born: Sept. 23, 1943, Nashville, Tenn.

Education: U. of Tennessee, B.S. 1967; Memphis State U., M.B.A. 1968.

Military Service: Army, 1969-71; National Guard, 1971-present.

Occupation: College president; marketing, management and real estate executive.

Family: Wife, Mary Carson; two children, two stepchildren.

Religion: Methodist.

Political Career: Tenn. Public Service Commission, 1973-79; sought Democratic nomination for governor, 1978; Democratic nominee for U.S. House, 1982.

Capitol Office: 2229 Rayburn Bldg. 20515; 225-4311.

Committees

International Relations
International Economic Policy & Trade

Transportation & Infrastructure
Coast Guard & Maritime Transportation (ranking); Railroads

In Washington: For Clement, as for fellow Tennessean Al Gore, politics is the family business. Clement's father served three terms as governor, and he himself held statewide office at the age of 29. But it took Clement longer than Vice President Gore to translate youthful prominence into sustained electoral success.

Though he is four years older than Gore, Clement did not reach Congress until 1988, more than a decade after Gore's first election to the House. The extra years of seasoning helped transform Clement, once seen as a fiery populist, into a quiet and loyal party man whose eyes stay firmly fixed on constituent service and on issues with a strong tie to his district.

Clement is still mentioned in Tennessee political circles when talk turns to gubernatorial campaigning; there have been some media rumblings that he might make a bid in 1998, when GOP Gov. Don Sundquist is expected to seek a second term. But if Clement has political ambitions beyond the House, he did not show them in 1994, when all three of Tennessee's top statewide offices were up for election — the governorship and both Senate seats. Clement stayed at home in the 5th.

For a time in the 1980s, Clement was president of a small college, and his chief legislative push in recent years has been a bill to establish a grant to fund renovations for 11 of the nation's historically black colleges, including $5 million for Fisk University and $2.5 million for Knoxville College, both in Tennessee. The price tag grew from $20 million in the 103rd to $29 million for the 104th's version. The bill passed the House in both instances.

The measure ran into trouble in the Senate in 1994 when then-Minority Leader Bob Dole, R-Kan., sought $3.6 million in funding for Sterling University in Kansas, whose enrollment is 3 percent black. The Senate passed a compromise bill that separately funded Sterling and one other white-majority college, but the House failed to act on it. In the 104th, the Senate failed to take up the bill after it again passed the House in 1996.

Clement, whose official biography brags that he has "helped thousands of Tennesseans during his career," keeps a careful eye on the state's interests in Washington. Clement has served on the Tennessee Valley Authority (TVA) board of directors, and during the 104th he joined with the rest of the delegation in opposing an attempt by Wisconsin Republican Scott L. Klug to kill TVA funding during consideration of the fiscal 1996 energy and water projects spending bill.

Clement argued that TVA performs many functions spread among several agencies in other regions. "There are no provisions in the Klug amendment providing for the transfer of these duties, and there is no additional funding for these other departments or agencies," he pointed out. The Klug amendment failed, 144-284.

Clement also opposed a bill by Martin R. Hoke, R-Ohio, which would have required the National Football League to grant a city an expansion team within a year after an existing team left, provided the city could prove it could support the franchise. Hoke's cause was to make it more difficult for franchise owners to pack up their teams and leave (as occurred with the Cleveland Browns, who left for Baltimore), and Clement wanted to keep the sailing smooth for the Oilers, a team that is moving from Houston to Nashville. The bill died in committee.

Clement labored on the Transportation and Infrastructure Committee and on Veterans' Affairs in the 104th Congress. On Transportation, Clement has dutifully seen to low-glamour initiatives such as deep-water port modernization and railroad loan guarantees. He supports the efforts of Transportation Committee Chairman Bud Shuster, R-Pa., to move highway trust fund dollars out of the general federal budget.

Clement weighed in on one veterans' health issue much in the news of late: the so-called Gulf War syndrome, an unexplained array of ailments affecting some soldiers who fought in Operation Desert Storm. Clement introduced legislation to allow Persian Gulf War veterans to receive treatment for the syndrome at veterans' hospitals

TENNESSEE 5
Nashville

Nashville is "Music City USA" and the capital of Tennessee. Country music and government paychecks propel the economy. More than 90 percent of the 5th's vote comes out of Nashville and Davidson County, and in most years Democrats win here.

Ronald Reagan in 1984 and George Bush in 1988 carried the 5th, but not by much. In 1992 the district returned to form, giving the Bill Clinton-Al Gore ticket 53 percent. Clinton carried the district with 55 percent in 1996.

County music is unquestionably Nashville's most famous industry, but with about 17,000 jobs, state government is the district's leading employer. Davidson County is also home to 17 colleges and universities, including Vanderbilt University. Several publishers of religious material have headquarters here, and there is a sizable manufacturing sector.

Government workers, academic communities and labor unions uphold Nashville's traditional position as the focal point of Middle Tennessee Democratic populism. That brand of politics is a legacy of Andrew Jackson, who built his political career in the area and returned to The Hermitage, his home east of Nashville, after serving two terms as president.

Nashville's population is less than one-quarter black — a relatively low figure for a large Southern city — and white voters have not been so prone to drift from their traditional Democratic loyalties.

Though the state capitol complex is a permanent anchor, downtown Nashville has struggled, a victim of retail flight to the suburbs and the success of Opryland, the sprawling theme park east of the city, where the Grand Ole Opry moved from its original downtown site at Ryman Auditorium.

But like many cities, Nashville is experiencing a downtown revival with live entertainment and restaurants and the remodeling of old buildings.

To keep pace in the area of air transportation, Nashville replaced its aged airport with a new one. Work has also started on enhancing mass transit in the city.

Economically, the 5th benefits not only from the industries within its borders but also from some big manufacturing facilities nearby. Since the early 1980s, Tennessee has made a vigorous effort to market the state's work force and business climate to foreign investors, especially the Japanese. Nissan built a huge plant south of Nashville, and other Japanese companies have followed. General Motors chose a site near Nashville for its massive Saturn facility.

Redistricting in 1992 just slightly altered the 5th, moving a small slice of Davidson County and about half of Robertson County to the 7th. Robertson accounts for only about 6 percent of the total district vote.

1990 Population: 541,910. White 408,535 (75%), Black 123,525 (23%), Other 9,850 (2%). Hispanic origin 4,905 (<1%). 18 and over 416,547 (77%), 62 and over 76,165 (14%). Median age: 33.

throughout the country. He left the Veterans' Affairs Committee in the 105th; he now serves on the International Relations Committee.

Clement supported a pair of the constitutional amendments considered during the 104th, one to mandate a balanced federal budget and another allowing Congress and the states to pass laws prohibiting flag desecration.

"I am not a legal scholar," Clement allowed during consideration of the latter amendment. "I simply say, if the Supreme Court holds that our Constitution permits flag burning, it is time to change our Constitution."

Clement opposed another amendment, though, that would have limited congressional terms. He contended that voters have the right to end congressional careers at the ballot box.

Though Clement is no bumpkin, his speech still has a sharp Middle Tennessee twang, and now and then he treats Washington with comments that one might expect to overhear at a barn dance. When President Clinton in 1994 proposed a tobacco tax as a way to help pay for his health care plan, Clement groused that the levy failed to pass the "Hee Haw test." He said it was unfair to the South and to tobacco farmers, who are an important component of the economy in Robertson County, north of Nashville.

Generally loyal to the Democratic leadership, Clement in the 103rd Congress answered its call to support a five-day waiting period for handgun purchases. But he subsequently became unhappy with the way the law was being enforced. He said the federal government had betrayed assurances that the law would not interfere with stricter state weapons laws, such as Tennessee's 15-day handgun waiting period.

"Now," grumbled Clement, "Tennesseans have to fill out both a federal form and a state form [when purchasing a handgun] that only causes bureaucratic delay and confusion." In part because of those concerns, said Clement, he decided in 1994 to vote against a ban on certain semiautomatic assault-style weapons. He supported the ultimately unsuccessful move to repeal the ban in 1996.

In early 1995, when Clinton met resistance in the Senate to his nominee for surgeon general, Tennessean Henry Foster, he sought out Clement for outside counsel. Clement advised the president to let Foster exploit his personality and charm to make his case in public — a decision Clinton soon adopted. Foster's nomination died anyway.

Clement is a big booster of the industry that is Nashville's main claim to fame, the country music business. During the 103rd, he introduced legislation to designate October "Country Music Month." And he entered statements into the Congressional Record honoring a number of country music stars, including one commemorating Conway Twitty upon his death in 1993.

At Home: With his resounding triumph in a 1988 House special election, Clement resurrected a moribund political career.

By winning the race to succeed Democratic Rep. Bill Boner, who became Nashville's mayor, Clement set aside bitter memories from two previous defeats — including a 1982 House bid he was favored to win — and stepped out of the shadow cast by his father, the late Frank G. Clement, who was Tennessee's governor for three terms in the 1950s and 1960s.

In 1972, Bob Clement became a political "boy wonder" by winning a seat on the state Public Service Commission (PSC). Then 29, he was the youngest candidate ever elected statewide in Tennessee. In six years on the PSC, Clement built up the already formidable visibility of the Clement name. But when he sought the nomination for governor in 1978, he lost to wealthy businessman Jake Butcher.

After Boner won the 1987 mayoral race, the special Democratic primary for the 5th boiled down to Clement, relying on a heavy vote from the working-class whites who were Boner's base, and to wealthy businessman Phil Bredesen, who had narrowly lost the mayor's race to Boner. Bredesen ran a media-heavy House campaign aimed at more affluent Democrats and GOP-leaning voters. Clement won with 40 percent to Bredesen's 36 percent.

Since then, re-elections have been little trouble for Clement in the Democratic 5th, home of such House members as Andrew Jackson and Sam Houston. Even in 1994, when a strong GOP tide swept across Tennessee, Clement won comfortably.

HOUSE ELECTIONS

1996 General		
Bob Clement (D)	140,264	(72%)
Steven L. Edmondson (R)	46,201	(24%)
Mike Childers (I)	7,318	(4%)
1994 General		
Bob Clement (D)	95,953	(60%)
John Osborne (R)	61,692	(39%)

Previous Winning Percentages: 1992 (67%) **1990** (72%) **1988** (100%) **1988†** (62%)

† Special election

CAMPAIGN FINANCE

	Receipts	Receipts from PACs	Expend-itures
1996			
Clement (D)	$504,397	$264,851 (53%)	$299,403
1994			
Clement (D)	$515,549	$262,872 (51%)	$486,214
Osborne (R)	$102,934	$4,564 (4%)	$102,251

DISTRICT VOTE FOR PRESIDENT

	1996		1992
D	116,609 (55%)	**D**	112,795 (53%)
R	81,982 (39%)	**R**	79,398 (37%)
I	9,710 (5%)	**I**	21,531 (10%)

KEY VOTES

1997	
Ban "partial birth" abortions	Y
1996	
Approve farm bill	N
Deny public education to illegal immigrants	Y
Repeal ban on certain assault-style weapons	Y
Increase minimum wage	Y
Freeze defense spending	N
Approve welfare overhaul	Y
1995	
Approve balanced-budget constitutional amendment	Y
Relax Clean Water Act regulations	Y
Oppose limits on environmental regulations	Y
Reduce projected Medicare spending	N
Approve GOP budget with tax and spending cuts	N

VOTING STUDIES

	Presidential Support		Party Unity		Conservative Coalition	
Year	**S**	**O**	**S**	**O**	**S**	**O**
1996	73	27	68	30	84	14
1995	69	30	72	26	74	23
1994	81	17	79	15	78	17
1993	81	17	82	16	64	34
1992	25	67	75	15	58	40
1991	43	56	80	19	78	22

INTEREST GROUP RATINGS

Year	ADA	AFL-CIO	CCUS	ACU
1996	60	n/a	50	30
1995	75	75	63	32
1994	35	56	92	35
1993	55	75	50	29
1992	65	75	63	39
1991	50	75	40	20

6 Bart Gordon (D)

Of Murfreesboro — Elected 1984, 7th term

Biographical Information
Born: Jan. 24, 1949, Murfreesboro, Tenn.
Education: Middle Tennessee State U., B.S. 1971; U. of Tennessee, J.D. 1973.
Occupation: Lawyer.
Family: Single.
Religion: Methodist.
Political Career: Tenn. Democratic Party chairman, 1981-83.
Capitol Office: 2201 Rayburn Bldg. 20515; 225-4231.

Committees
Commerce
Energy & Power; Telecommunications, Trade & Consumer Protection
Science
Space & Aeronautics; Technology (ranking)

In Washington: Scared within an inch of his political life in 1994, when he won re-election with just 51 percent of the vote, Gordon regrouped and spent the 104th Congress aggressively preparing to face voters in 1996. He stepped up his campaign fundraising, redoubled his constituent outreach efforts and tacked to the right on such emotionally charged issues as abortion, taxes, immigration and flag burning.

During his first decade in Congress, Gordon earned a place in the Democratic leadership's heart and whip organization with occasional liberal votes on social issues and loyal work on the Rules Committee. Gordon was bumped off Rules when his party lost control of the House, but he landed softly, joining the coveted Commerce Committee. During the 104th, when a seat opened up on the Science Committee (where he had served early in his House career), Gordon got it. He now ranks third among Democrats on Science.

In the 104th, though, Gordon was less often in step with his party and more mindful of his constituents' conservative impulses on certain issues: His party unity and presidential support voting scores dropped to career lows. He fought President Clinton's regulations aimed at limiting tobacco's appeal to minors, and also Illinois Democrat Richard J. Durbin's efforts to eliminate tobacco subsidies. Gordon introduced a bill that would have stripped the Food and Drug Administration of its authority to restrict tobacco ads at auto races.

"I also oppose trying to treat tobacco as a drug because that's just a backdoor approach to going back to the old Prohibition days. We know that doesn't work," Gordon commented. Tobacco is a quarter-billion dollar industry in Tennessee, making it the state's largest cash crop.

At the Democratic National Convention in 1996, Gordon said of Clinton, "He'll have to stay in the center. That's where the country is and that's where good policy is." In search of the center, Gordon sided with organized labor on some key votes, such as a 90-cent-per-hour boost in the minimum wage. Gordon also voted against a Republican initiative to allow employers to grant their employees compensatory time in place of overtime wages.

But Gordon joined with Republicans on a number of high-profile and divisive issues. He supported the GOP's welfare overhaul plan, and he was one of only 27 Democrats who supported the GOP's $189 billion tax cut package in 1995, although he voted against the budget bill into which the cuts were folded. Gordon voted for an easing of clean water standards, and for a ban on federal recognition of same-gender marriages.

Gordon, who supported the 1994 crime law despite objecting to its ban on certain semiautomatic assault-style weapons, expressed his continuing distaste for that ban by voting to repeal it in 1996. He backed the Democratic leadership on some abortion votes, including safeguarding access to clinics in 1994 and allowing abortions to be performed in military hospitals overseas in 1996. But in the 104th he supported a ban on a particular abortion technique that opponents call a "partial-birth" abortion.

Gordon supported Republican-driven amendments to the Constitution that would have required a balanced federal budget and a limit on congressional terms. Those efforts ultimately failed, as did an amendment that would have allowed Congress and the states to ban desecration of the flag. Gordon, who had opposed the so-called flag burning amendment in 1990, voted for it in 1995.

He joined with the GOP in its efforts to toughen measures aimed at preventing illegal immigration, and he supported an unsuccessful provision to deny public education to illegal immigrants.

In recent years, Gordon has concentrated on issues affecting federal student aid programs, and he vigorously opposed President Clinton's abandonment of the Guaranteed Student Loan program in favor of direct loans. Direct lending essentially eliminated the need for banks, guarantee agencies and secondary markets.

This slice of Middle Tennessee embodies qualities of both the Old and New South.

In most of the 6th's counties, the pace of life is still relatively unhurried, people work in small factories or on farms, and old courthouse networks call the political shots — nearly always calling them Democratic.

But on the western edge of the 6th, in the four counties that border Davidson County (Nashville), there are clear signs of change, brought on in large part by the expansion of suburbia and the influence of two gargantuan vehicle assembly plants — one run by Japan's Nissan in Smyrna and the other by General Motors' Saturn subsidiary in Spring Hill, just outside the Williamson County line.

The political impact of the suburbanizing and industrializing is most obvious in Williamson County. Many residents there are white-collar commuters to jobs in and around Nashville, just to the north. In most elections, Williamson delivers a stronger GOP vote than any other Middle Tennessee county.

In 1996, Bob Dole won 61 percent of the vote in Williamson and 58 percent in a small slice of Davidson County that is in the 6th. Dole carried the overall district by 2 percentage points.

Similarly, in the 1996 House contest between Gordon and Republican Steve Gill, Gill won more than 54 percent in Williamson and the slice of Davidson. But those were the only counties Gordon lost.

Though 1992 redistricting moved Maury County out of the 6th, and with it the Saturn facility, almost 30 percent of the plant's workers live in Williamson County. Demand for Saturn's cars has been so strong that the company has strained to keep up; employment was 8,400 in 1996.

TENNESSEE 6
North central — Murfreesboro

In the other three counties adjoining Davidson County — Rutherford, Sumner and Wilson — liberalism in the national Democratic Party provokes some wariness. Dole carried all three counties in 1996, but Gordon improved on his weak 1994 showings in those areas.

Rutherford County was Tennessee's fastest-growing in the 1980s; in addition to the Nissan plant (which employs about 6,000), it has Middle Tennessee State University in Murfreesboro, the Stones River National Battlefield and a large outlet shopping mall.

In the areas of the 6th that are part of the Nashville orbit, economic conditions have been fairly favorable in recent years. The same cannot be said for many of the rural and small-town areas on the eastern side of the 6th. Textile producers and other small-scale manufacturers there offer primarily lower-wage jobs, and remoteness from urban areas means the service-sector economy is not large.

The Democratic advantage in the eastern counties is enormous. Even in 1994, Gordon carried them, often by more than 60 percent.

The 6th also includes the small town of Carthage (Smith County), the family home of Al Gore. The Democratic presidential ticket drew 63 percent of the county vote in 1996.

1990 Population: 541,977. White 505,849 (93%), Black 31,010 (6%), Other 5,118 (1%). Hispanic origin 3,159 (<1%). 18 and over 399,124 (74%), 62 and over 71,309 (13%). Median age: 33.

Gordon, working with the banks, tried unsuccessfully to preserve their piece of the action: first with a proposal to reduce their margin over the Treasury bill rate on interest for the loans, then, in tandem with Pennsylvania Republican Bill Goodling, with a proposal limiting direct lending to a four-year pilot project covering students in about 4 percent of all schools.

Gordon joined again with Goodling during the 104th in an effort to kill or cap direct lending. But that legislation was attached to the GOP's ill-fated tax-and-spending-cuts budget package.

Gordon persuaded the House in 1994 to deny Pell grants to inmates in federal or state prisons and to students at schools that had lost eligibility for guaranteed student loans because of high default rates. He succeeded during the 104th with an amendment to prohibit post-secondary schools from receiving Pell grants for their students that have high federal loan default rates.

Gordon also entered the fight over the Family and Medical Leave Act. He was an architect of compromises in 1990 and 1991 that enabled the bill to clear Congress, but the legislation was vetoed both years by President George Bush. Enactment finally came in the 103rd, with Gordon still a visible proponent, managing the rule that governed floor debate.

In the wrenching 1993 battle over NAFTA, Gordon's late switch to the supporting side — after a personal plea from Vice President Al Gore, whom Gordon succeeded in the House — provided the Clinton administration with a critical vote. In 1994, he supported GATT.

At Home: Gordon himself noted in 1996 that his once strongly Democratic district "is becoming more of a suburban, independent district, and the Republican leanings are increasing, without question." Those leanings nearly nudged Gordon out of a job in 1994, when lawyer Steve Gill came within two percentage points of unseating him.

Gill took advantage of Gordon's leadership

position to tie him to Clinton, who was wildly unpopular in Tennessee at that time. Gordon responded aggressively, going after Gill for recently moving into the district and for opposing an increase in the minimum wage, which Gordon contrasted with Gill's lawyer salary. Despite having to fend off a primary challenge from physician Dan Rudd, Gordon had a financial edge over Gill and managed to hang on to the seat.

The two squared off again in 1996, engaging in a highly negative campaign. Gill accused Gordon of improperly using franked mailings and official staff, and Gordon saddled Gill with the unpopular aspects of the GOP agenda and noted his college-age use of marijuana. Gordon was again able to best Gill at the fundraising game, and, without the Republican winds of 1994 at his back, Gill faltered.

Gordon built his political credentials within the state party structure. Fresh out of law school, he won a seat on the state Democratic Executive Committee, and in 1979 he parlayed his contacts into a position as the party's executive director. Two years later, he won the party chairmanship. He computerized the party mailing list and set up a direct-mail program — experience that proved crucial to his House campaign, which he waged when Gore ran successfully for the Senate in 1984.

Gordon's chief Democratic rivals in his initial House contest were state Rep. Lincoln Davis, who represented a cluster of counties in the Upper Cumberland region of the 6th, and Bryant Millsaps, the state House chief clerk, who shared Gordon's home base of Murfreesboro.

Gordon set himself apart in the six-way primary with a sophisticated phone bank and direct-mail operation and won with 28 percent.

During the campaign, Gordon had to deal with the potentially explosive issue of a paternity suit that had been brought against him and was later dismissed. Gordon denied fathering the child, and none of his primary opponents raised the issue. But his GOP opponent, Williamson County construction executive Joe Simkins, accused him of a "cover-up," after the Nashville Banner alleged that Gordon had paid the woman to drop the suit.

Simkins, whose brother was publisher of the Banner, set a "countdown deadline" for Gordon to explain the settlement. Gordon simply ignored the challenge, as did most voters. He won all but two counties on Election Day.

Gordon went on to win re-election comfortably until 1992, when he slipped to 57 percent against GOP activist Marsha Blackburn, presaging his difficulties with Gill.

HOUSE ELECTIONS

1996 General		
Bart Gordon (D)	123,846	(54%)
Steve Gill (R)	94,599	(42%)
Jim Coffer (I)	9,125	(4%)
1996 Primary		
Bart Gordon (D)	37,324	(89%)
Jessie R. Bly (D)	4,673	(11%)
1994 General		
Bart Gordon (D)	90,933	(51%)
Steve Gill (R)	88,759	(49%)

Previous Winning Percentages: 1992 (57%) **1990** (67%) **1988** (76%) **1986** (77%) **1984** (63%)

CAMPAIGN FINANCE

	Receipts	Receipts from PACs	Expend-itures
1996			
Gordon (D)	$1,597,160	$742,511 (46%)	$1,609,419
Gill (R)	$1,107,227	$132,178 (12%)	$1,107,850
Coffer (I)	$1,114	0	$1,113
1994			
Gordon (D)	$1,208,479	$608,490 (50%)	$1,385,995
Gill (R)	$535,223	$58,578 (11%)	$533,704

DISTRICT VOTE FOR PRESIDENT

	1996		1992
D	107,994 (45%)	D	109,895 (48%)
R	112,611 (47%)	R	93,036 (40%)
I	15,378 (7%)	I	28,151 (12%)

KEY VOTES

1997	
Ban "partial birth" abortions	Y
1996	
Approve farm bill	Y
Deny public education to illegal immigrants	Y
Repeal ban on certain assault-style weapons	Y
Increase minimum wage	Y
Freeze defense spending	Y
Approve welfare overhaul	Y
1995	
Approve balanced-budget constitutional amendment	Y
Relax Clean Water Act regulations	Y
Oppose limits on environmental regulations	Y
Reduce projected Medicare spending	N
Approve GOP budget with tax and spending cuts	N

VOTING STUDIES

	Presidential Support		Party Unity		Conservative Coalition	
Year	**S**	**O**	**S**	**O**	**S**	**O**
1996	62	37	66	34	80	20
1995	66	33	67	33	77	23
1994	73	23	83	15	75	19
1993	83	16	87	11	70	30
1992	24	69	86	10	67	31
1991	37	62	89	11	68	32

INTEREST GROUP RATINGS

Year	ADA	AFL-CIO	CCUS	ACU
1996	45	n/a	56	50
1995	75	75	63	40
1994	55	25	83	24
1993	60	83	27	21
1992	70	67	50	25
1991	60	92	40	15

7 Ed Bryant (R)

Of Henderson — Elected 1994, 2nd term

Biographical Information
Born: Sept. 7, 1948, Jackson, Tenn.
Education: U. of Mississippi, B.A. 1970, J.D. 1972.
Military Service: Army, 1973-78.
Occupation: Lawyer.
Family: Wife, Cynthia Lemons; three children.
Religion: Protestant.
Political Career: Republican nominee for U.S. House, 1988; U.S. Attorney, 1991-93.
Capitol Office: 408 Cannon Bldg. 20515; 225-2811.

Committees
Agriculture
Risk Management & Specialty Crops
Judiciary
Commercial & Administrative Law; Constitution; Immigration & Claims

In Washington: Before his 1994 election to the House, Bryant served as a U.S. attorney, so he was natural choice to sit on the Judiciary Committee. As a freshman in the 104th Congress, he spoke frequently on legal issues, and he joined the conservatives' chorus in lobbying for measures aimed at making Congress more fiscally responsible and more responsive to the public. In fact, Bryant has been one of the most reliable votes for the Republican leadership among members of the Class of 1994. He got a perfect 100 percent rating from the American Conservative Union for his first-term votes and a zero rating from the liberal Americans for Democratic Action.

Bryant also holds a seat on the Agriculture Committee, but his personal legislative initiatives have focused on crime. In the 104th, he sponsored a bill that would have increased the maximum penalty for escaping from federal prison from five years to 10, noting that escape penalties have not kept pace with a general move toward stiffer punishments for federal crimes. His bill also would have established a national database of sex offenders, extended penalties for computer hacking, and allowed federal and local officials to collect fees to pay for background checks on volunteers who work with children. The measure passed the House but was never taken up by the full Senate.

Bryant succeeded in amending a juvenile crime bill with the provision to double the sentence for escaping, but that bill also fell short of enactment in the 104th. He had better luck with an amendment to a 1996 anti-terrorism law, codifying a fee limit of $125 per hour for court-appointed lawyers in federal death penalty cases.

He saw another of his proposals go down to defeat, though, when he attempted to amend an immigration bill to require that hospitals tell the federal government about illegal aliens they treat. "It would not threaten the quality of care involved here," Bryant contended. But the House rejected the idea, 170-250.

Bryant desires longer sentences for dealers of crack cocaine and tried to assuage the fears of those who fret that conservatives' efforts to overhaul exclusionary rule procedures would make police or the courts more likely to abuse the rights of people targeted in criminal investigations. "There are still certain protections out there," he said. "People do not beat folks in back rooms with rubber hoses to extract confessions any more; however, if they did, certainly the exclusionary rule would still be available."

He was a strong supporter of a bill to overhaul product liability litigation, releasing a letter signed by 200 House members that called on President Clinton to approve the bill. "Any tort reform that speeds up the the litigation process, unclogs the courts and places reasonable limits on even some punitive damage awards . . . is better than accomplishing nothing at all," Bryant argued. But Clinton vetoed the measure.

Bryant spoke during the 104th in favor of a presidential line-item veto and a balanced-budget constitutional amendment, claiming that those devices would restrict Congress' penchant for overspending. "Everywhere I went," he said in 1995, "the people back in West Tennessee felt that these two items . . . were required because of the forced discipline."

In the same vein of trying to alter the established ways of Congress, Bryant favors a constitutional amendment to limit the number of terms members may serve. "I believe had the Founding Fathers foreseen some 200 years into the future how the purpose of public service has been interpreted, they would have placed term limits in the Constitution," he said.

When the House voted in 1995 to outlaw a particular abortion technique that opponents call a "partial-birth" abortion, Bryant phrased his opposition to the procedure in legal terms. Unlike even convicted mass murderers, he said, the fetus "is given none of this due process of law."

Bryant spent his first term in the unique position of having prosecuted a member of his state's delegation — and having used that action to help win his seat. As a U.S. attorney, Bryant initially

TENNESSEE 7
West Central — Clarksville; part of Shelby County

Although GOP Rep. Don Sundquist's departure from the 7th was expected to spark a competitive race, the results were lopsided. Republican Bryant won 60 percent in a district that had become more Democratic in the 1992 redistricting. He built on that total in his 1996 reelection contest, taking 64 percent.

The 7th combines Republican suburbanites, West Tennessee Dixiecrats, Middle Tennessee populists and a significant number of blue-collar workers.

Despite losing 100,000 of its GOP-leaning residents to other districts in the remap, the Shelby County part of the 7th remains the district's GOP bastion. The 7th still has the most upscale and Republican Memphis suburbs, including Bartlett, Collierville and Germantown. Bryant won 81 percent of the Shelby County vote in 1996.

Many of the better-paid employees at such Memphis-based companies as Federal Express and International Paper Co. live in the east Shelby suburbs. Much of the area has a nouveau riche feel, with showy homes, malls and office parks that draw commerce away from center-city Memphis. The area grew rapidly in the 1980s (Germantown's population, for example, expanded 50 percent), while the city of Memphis saw a 9 percent population loss.

In 1996, the portion of Shelby in the 7th gave Bob Dole 69 percent of its presidential votes. That was enough to deliver the district comfortably to Dole because Shelby cast more than 40 percent of the vote in the 7th. Of the 14 other counties in the district, Dole won just two.

The 7th runs the gamut of Tennessee agriculture. In Shelby's eastern neighbor, Fayette County, the flat land is ideal for cotton growing. Moving east, tobacco and cattle are more prevalent. Corn, soybeans, hay and hogs are also important in the district. Maury County, added to the 7th in remapping, is the state's largest producer of beef cattle, but it is best known for its GM Saturn plant, in the tiny two-stoplight town of Spring Hill. Saturn has kept the plant humming; its work force grew from 5,000 in 1991 to 8,400 in 1996.

Also in Maury is the Tennessee Farm Bureau, which provides services for farmers across the state. The largest insurer of rural property in Tennessee, it is a political force despite its policy of not endorsing candidates. Every aspirant for statewide office must take into account its significant, though tacit, influence.

One of the counties Bryant lost was Montgomery, which has the district's largest city, Clarksville (population 75,000). Clarksville is adjacent to Fort Campbell and the 101st Airborne Division, and the county's active duty and retired military personnel help give it a conservative tinge. But conservative has not always meant Republican: Bill Clinton won Montgomery with 49 percent of the vote in 1996. The fort and its 4,800 civilian employees are safe for now from military downsizing, in part due to the Pentagon's emphasis on "rapid deployment" units such as the 101st.

1990 Population: 541,937. White 467,034 (86%), Black 67,145 (12%), Other 7,758 (1%). Hispanic origin 6,182 (1%). 18 and over 396,773 (73%), 62 and over 66,807 (12%). Median age: 32.

handled the prosecution of Democratic Rep. Harold E. Ford on bank, mail and tax fraud charges. Bryant resigned from the Justice Department after his superiors supported Ford's request for a new jury. Ultimately, Ford was acquitted. (Ford retired in 1996, and his Memphis seat was taken over by his son, Harold Jr.)

At Home: When GOP Rep. Don Sundquist left the 7th in 1994 to wage an ultimately successful campaign for governor, Bryant saw a chance to improve on his first showing in an open-seat House race — a 1988 thumping at the hands of Democrat John Tanner in the neighboring 8th District.

But to earn the nomination, Bryant had to fight past six other Republican hopefuls, the most formidable of whom was Charles Salvaggio, the mayor of Germantown, a city in the district's populous Shelby County suburbs of Memphis. Bryant lost Shelby in the primary, but his superior organization in the 7th's more rural counties helped him finish first overall, with 35 percent of the vote to Salvaggio's 33 percent.

Bryant's high profile as prosecutor of Rep. Ford helped him establish a tough-on-crime image in the campaign. The Democratic nominee, former state Rep. Harold Byrd, tried to stay in step on the crime issue, matching Bryant's call for tougher sentencing and also supporting the death penalty. But Bryant pointed out that Byrd had voted in the state House against capital punishment. Byrd sought to dent Bryant by pointing to cases he had plea-bargained during his tenure as U.S. attorney, drawing a response from Bryant that he had posted one of the nation's highest conviction rates as a federal prosecutor.

Byrd sought to make roots a campaign issue. He grew up in McNairy County, represented parts of Shelby County in the state legislature for six years and was a partner in his family farm and cofounder of a local bank. In 1982, he had run a credible underdog campaign in the 7th, falling in the House Democratic primary to Bob Clement (who lost to Sundquist that year but later was elected in the 5th District). In contrast, Byrd said that Bryant was a carpetbagger who moved into the 7th because he hadn't been able to beat Tanner in the 8th.

In that race, Bryant had tried to convince voters that Tanner would be controlled by a liberal national Democratic Party leadership in Washington, but he managed only 38 percent of the vote. In 1994, though, Bryant had more luck with a similar line of argument against Byrd. Bryant said his opponent would be "Clinton's water carrier" — the same image that helped Republican Bill Frist upset Tennessee's senior senator, Democrat Jim Sasser.

To counter, Byrd tried to assert his independence and highlight Bryant's involvement in organizing Pat Robertson's 1988 presidential campaign in the 8th District. That, he said, was evidence of Bryant's "out-of-the-mainstream thinking."

Byrd won seven of the district's traditionally Democratic but less populous counties, while Bryant carried the Shelby County portion of the 7th by more than 33,000 votes. That propelled him to victory with 60 percent. Seeking a second term in 1996, Bryant won easily over Democrat Don Trotter, the mayor of Clarksville.

HOUSE ELECTIONS

1996 General		
Ed Bryant (R)	136,643	(64%)
Don Trotter (D)	73,629	(35%)
Steven E. Romer (I)	2,803	(1%)
1994 General		
Ed Bryant (R)	102,587	(60%)
Harold Byrd (D)	65,851	(39%)
Tom Jeanette (I)	1,944	(1%)

CAMPAIGN FINANCE

	Receipts	Receipts from PACs	Expend-itures
1996			
Bryant (R)	$769,149	$305,897 (40%)	$649,783
Trotter (D)	$313,410	$109,250 (35%)	$315,501
1994			
Bryant (R)	$511,316	$94,395 (18%)	$493,712
Byrd (D)	$609,757	$110,520 (18%)	$608,768
Jeanette (I)	$2,826	0	$2,826

DISTRICT VOTE FOR PRESIDENT

1996		1992	
D	94,349 (41%)	**D**	91,644 (40%)
R	124,737 (54%)	**R**	114,544 (50%)
I	11,010 (5%)	**I**	22,486 (10%)

KEY VOTES

1997	
Ban "partial birth" abortions	Y
1996	
Approve farm bill	Y
Deny public education to illegal immigrants	Y
Repeal ban on certain assault-style weapons	Y
Increase minimum wage	N
Freeze defense spending	N
Approve welfare overhaul	Y
1995	
Approve balanced-budget constitutional amendment	Y
Relax Clean Water Act regulations	Y
Oppose limits on environmental regulations	N
Reduce projected Medicare spending	Y
Approve GOP budget with tax and spending cuts	Y

VOTING STUDIES

	Presidential Support		Party Unity		Conservative Coalition	
Year	**S**	**O**	**S**	**O**	**S**	**O**
1996	35	65	95	4	98	2
1995	16	80	97	2	94	6

INTEREST GROUP RATINGS

Year	ADA	AFL-CIO	CCUS	ACU
1996	0	n/a	100	100
1995	0	0	100	100

8 John Tanner (D)

Of Union City — Elected 1988, 5th term

Biographical Information

Born: Sept. 22, 1944, Halls, Tenn.
Education: U. of Tennessee, B.S. 1966, J.D. 1968.
Military Service: Navy, 1968-72; National Guard, 1974-present.
Occupation: Lawyer; businessman.
Family: Wife, Betty Ann Portis; two children.
Religion: Disciples of Christ.
Political Career: Tenn. House, 1977-89.
Capitol Office: 1127 Longworth Bldg. 20515; 225-4714.

Committees

Ways & Means
Oversight; Social Security

In Washington: After voters in 1996 re-elected a Democratic president and a Republican-controlled Congress, many politicians talked of finding the "vital center" in policymaking. That is what Tanner was looking for during the contentious 104th Congress, as he worked behind the scenes — and occasionally out front — to make GOP proposals on welfare and the budget more palatable to the Clinton administration.

Some of Tanner's efforts toward mediation came through his leadership in the "blue dog" Coalition, a group of conservative and moderate Democrats who have espoused middle-of-the-road approaches to various issues. "The perception in the land is that the Democrats are too liberal, the Republicans are too rigid and too conservative, and the blue dogs or some group like them are where to go in terms of governing," Tanner has said.

Tanner was most visible during the 104th's intense and partisan debate over changing the welfare system. He joined forces with Delaware Republican Michael N. Castle to introduce a bipartisan welfare bill. It shared many features of the Republican-backed plan, but would have required states to spend more of their own money on welfare and provided more federal funds to help states meet the requirement that adults begin working within two years of receiving welfare benefits. It also would have required states to provide vouchers redeemable for goods and services to children whose parents did not meet the work requirement.

Clinton endorsed the Castle-Tanner measure. Backers said that it was more likely to help welfare recipients get jobs than the GOP plan and that it protected children from their parents' mistakes. Tanner said the voucher provision was especially important because "holding a 3-year-old child to a standard of a 33-year-old-parent is just wrong; it's not welfare reform."

The Castle-Tanner plan became the Democratic substitute, and although it was defeated, 168-258, when the House debated welfare reform in mid-July 1996, elements of the plan were included in the GOP bill that passed the House.

Although Tanner voted in mid-July against the GOP welfare bill, he got a seat on the House-Senate conference committee that assembled a final version of the legislation, and he voted for its passage in late July. The final version, which Clinton signed, was a better bill, Tanner said. "We have opposed previous welfare reform proposals because we believed that they offered empty, unsustainable promises of moving welfare recipients to work," he told the House.

Tanner also aimed for the middle ground as Congress debated alternatives for producing a balanced federal budget. He and other Blue Dog Democrats crafted a budget plan that fulfilled the Republicans' requirement of eliminating red ink in seven years using estimates by the Congressional Budget Office. However, it contained no tax cuts, and it called for substantially smaller reductions in spending than the GOP proposed for domestic programs and entitlements such as Medicare and Medicaid.

In October 1995, the House rejected the blue dog budget by a resounding 72-356. The coalition plan fared somewhat better the second time around, losing 130-295 in May 1996. Members from both parties praised it as a sensible compromise between Congress and the White House, but Republican leaders made sure that their budget was the one approved on the floor. Tanner told the House that the caolition had "put forth a public policy document free of as much partisan politics as is possible in this city of Washington, D.C."

Tanner moved to the Ways and Means Committee in the 105th Congress; in the 104th he served on the National Security and Science committees. On the latter panel in the 104th, he resisted Republican efforts to cut federal investment in technology programs. Like a fellow Tennessean, Vice President Al Gore, Tanner believes the government must actively promote technology research and development in order to keep U.S. industry competitive in the 21st century.

The 1992 round of redistricting did little to alter the essentially rural and Democratic makeup of the 8th District. The inclusion of the more Republican areas of suburban Shelby County only slightly outweighed the addition of rural Houston and Humphreys counties.

The result was a district little different from the one that GOP House candidates have failed to capture since the end of Reconstruction.

The 8th District is slightly more favorable to Republican presidential candidates. Bill Clinton won the 8th with 51 percent of the vote in 1996, taking 14 of the 17 counties in the district. But the counties with the largest population in the 8th — Madison and a portion of Shelby — went narrowly for Bob Dole.

Soybeans, corn, wheat and cotton remain the 8th District's staple crops, but industrial activity has diversified in recent years, particularly in Jackson, the district's largest city.

The surrounding farm counties look to Jackson as a source of retail goods and such services as specialty health care. The city's diversified industrial base allowed it to weather the 1990-91 recession better than the 8th's small towns and farms. Since 1989, Jackson (population 49,000) has attracted such industry as a Maytag appliance manufacturing plant and a company that manufactures air compressors. Still, the largest industrial employer in Jackson is the Procter & Gamble facility that makes Pringle's potato chips, employing more than 600.

Republicans have in recent years gained some ground in Madison County (Jackson), thanks in part to an influx of managerial personnel to Jackson's increasingly diversified industries.

TENNESSEE 8
West — Jackson; part of Shelby County

Madison County's economic success leads most of the rest of the 8th District. In 1996, 13 of the 15 rural counties in the district had unemployment percentages higher than the state average of 4.2 percent, while Madison's unemployment rate fell slightly below average.

The former Memphis Naval Air Station in northern Shelby County lost some functions but is gaining others as a naval support facility. It remains among the largest employers in the district. Union City (population 10,500), Tanner's hometown, is the site for the 8th's largest industrial employer, one of Goodyear's two largest radial tire manufacturing plants, which employs about 3,000.

The Civil War-era Fort Donelson in Dover, the site of an early victory that the Union sorely needed, is a popular tourist attraction. The 1862 capture of the Confederate fort gave the Union control of the Cumberland River, which cuts through the northeast edge of the district, running northwest from Nashville. The site also helped immortalize the victorious general, Ulysses S. Grant, who in response to a Confederate request for terms of surrender, responded, "No terms. Unconditional surrender."

1990 Population: 541,907. White 430,674 (79%), Black 106,761 (20%), Other 4,472 (1%). Hispanic origin 3,812 (1%). 18 and over 402,139 (74%), 62 and over 90,884 (17%). Median age: 34.

On Science, Tanner was an advocate for the national laboratories, including the Oak Ridge National Laboratory, a major Tennessee employer. In May 1996, he opposed an omnibus science bill crafted by committee Republicans that cut funding for NASA and other federal science programs such as the Mission to Planet Earth, which uses a series of satellites to monitor the Earth's environment.

Then the ranking Democrat on Science's Technology Subcommittee, Tanner said the GOP bill would "kill programs that successfully support small business, technological innovation, and create thousands of good paying, high-skilled jobs." He backed a Democratic alternative that would have added back funding for environmental research, advanced technology programs and aeronautics. It was rejected, 176-235.

Tanner is generally viewed as a "pro-defense" Democrat, but he has shown concern for establishing military spending priorities that fit both post-Cold War strategic needs and the tighter budget environment.

Early in 1995, Tanner voted for a defense measure, included in the GOP's "Contract With America," that aimed to place restrictions on U.S. participation in U.N. peacekeeping missions and articulated the Republican view that Clinton had cut defense spending too much. He was one of only 18 Democrats to back the bill.

Yet he also supported an amendment to the measure that would have barred deployment of space-based anti-missile weapons. The measure included language allowing for a higher budget for nationwide missile defense and stated that such a defense was essential to U.S. national security. Tanner said that this provision "will risk national security when deployment of space-based interceptors diverts billions of scarce defense dollars and resources from acquisition funds that provide our soldiers and sailors protection from Scuds and other theater missile attacks."

At Home: Early in his House career, Tanner maintained a remarkably low profile for someone with good connections to two prominent Tennessee Democrats — Gore and former Gov. Ned McWherter.

Tanner had a chance for more visibility at the end of 1992: After Gore was elected vice president on the ticket with Clinton, McWherter needed to appoint an interim replacement to fill Gore's soon-to-be-vacant Senate seat. During his 12 years as a state legislator, Tanner had been a protégé of McWherter's (then the state House Speaker). Tanner's district is also McWherter's political base. So the job of holding down the Senate seat was said to be Tanner's for the asking.

Remarkably, he did not ask. Instead, he told McWherter that he preferred to serve out the third House term from a district that he has made comfortable for himself. The matter was handled in Tanner's typical style, with no fanfare and little self-generated publicity.

Tanner also decided against making a 1994 bid for the open governorship. McWherter had served the two terms allowed under state law. In retrospect, Tanner made a smart decision considering the huge losses the Democrats suffered in Tennessee in the 1994 elections.

He made a similarly smart move in 1988 when Democratic Rep. Ed Jones retired after nearly two decades in the House and brought the rare prospect of a competitive election in the 8th. Tanner came out of the blocks practically before the contest had begun. A longtime ally of the incumbent— who had been a friend of Tanner's grandfather's — Tanner had already laid the groundwork. He quickly assembled an enviable organization and financial base, boosted by his connections to Jones and McWherter.

Tanner also had some natural appeal to business interests: In Union City he was a member of a local law firm and senior vice president of a local savings and loan association; in the state House he served as chairman of the Commerce Committee. But Tanner, who went to the University of Tennessee on a basketball scholarship, appeals to more than just the buttoned-down set. His relaxed, "good ol' boy" style helped him win over rural voters, who hold considerable sway in the 8th.

The GOP nominee, Jackson lawyer Ed Bryant, who went on to win the 7th District in 1994, had organized the district for Pat Robertson's 1988 presidential campaign. Bryant tried to convince voters that Tanner would be controlled by a liberal national Democratic Party leadership in Washington.

"Bull," said Tanner. "Ed Jones has been his own man and John Tanner will be his own man." Tanner's support for the death penalty and the presidential line-item veto, together with his opposition to national health insurance proposals, made it difficult for anyone to portray him as a liberal. He won with more than 60 percent of the vote, and in four re-elections his tally has never dropped below 64 percent.

HOUSE ELECTIONS

1996 General		
John Tanner (D)	123,681	(67%)
Tom Watson (R)	55,024	(30%)
Donna Malone (I)	4,816	(3%)
1994 General		
John Tanner (D)	97,951	(64%)
Neal R. Morris (R)	55,573	(36%)

Previous Winning Percentages: 1992 (84%) **1990** (100%) **1988** (62%)

CAMPAIGN FINANCE

	Receipts	Receipts from PACs	Expend-itures
1996			
Tanner (D)	$434,166	$251,983 (58%)	$395,726
Watson (R)	$14,494	0	$14,478
1994			
Tanner (D)	$330,483	$155,000 (47%)	$251,431
Morris (R)	$16,352	$14 (0%)	$14,906

DISTRICT VOTE FOR PRESIDENT

	1996		1992
D	98,867 (51%)	**D**	101,328 (48%)
R	85,297 (44%)	**R**	89,533 (43%)
I	10,837 (6%)	**I**	19,328 (9%)

KEY VOTES

1997	
Ban "partial birth" abortions	Y
1996	
Approve farm bill	Y
Deny public education to illegal immigrants	Y
Repeal ban on certain assault-style weapons	Y
Increase minimum wage	Y
Freeze defense spending	N
Approve welfare overhaul	Y
1995	
Approve balanced-budget constitutional amendment	Y
Relax Clean Water Act regulations	Y
Oppose limits on environmental regulations	?
Reduce projected Medicare spending	N
Approve GOP budget with tax and spending cuts	N

VOTING STUDIES

	Presidential Support		Party Unity		Conservative Coalition	
Year	**S**	**O**	**S**	**O**	**S**	**O**
1996	61	30	59	34	90	0
1995	59	40	56	43	85	12
1994	74	26	68	31	94	6
1993	71	29	70	29	91	9
1992	38	56	71	26	77	21
1991	41	53	64	26	81	5

INTEREST GROUP RATINGS

Year	ADA	AFL-CIO	CCUS	ACU
1996	45	n/a	56	47
1995	35	58	67	29
1994	30	44	83	67
1993	50	75	36	50
1992	65	58	38	50
1991	30	42	67	50

9 Harold E. Ford Jr. (D)

Of Memphis — Elected 1996, 1st term

Biographical Information
Born: May 11, 1970, Memphis, Tenn.
Education: U. of Pennsylvania, B.A. 1992; U. of Michigan, J.D. 1996.
Occupation: Law clerk.
Family: Single.
Religion: Baptist.
Political Career: No previous office.
Capitol Office: 1523 Longworth Bldg. 20515; 225-3265.

Committees
Education & Workforce
Oversight & Investigations; Postsecondary Education, Training & Life-Long Learning
Government Reform & Oversight
Civil Service

The Path to Washington: Born 10 months after Americans first set foot on the moon, Ford is the first member of Congress with a 1970s birthdate. But Ford is poised beyond his years and promises to lend a voice to liberal causes.

Ford's 1996 campaign buttons and T-shirts simply said "Jr."; voters in Memphis knew they were choosing Democrat Harold E. Ford's son to succeed him. The elder Ford, who held the seat for 11 terms, served as his son's campaign coordinator.

Ford Jr., who speaks in clipped, rapid-fire tones that are familiar to observers of his father, nevertheless took pains during the campaign year to prove himself his own man, to point out that he had his own opinions.

"I took advantage of my opportunities," he told the Seattle Times. "If I went out and said, I'm Harold Ford Jr., and I couldn't construct a sentence, nobody would vote for me. You can't inherit it. You've got to go out and earn it."

Ford said he had had his eye on the seat ever since cutting a radio ad for his father's first campaign at the age of 4. His mother reported that he raised his hand along with members being sworn in for the 94th Congress and announced, "This is what I want to do when I grow up."

His father was a point man in the Democratic opposition to GOP efforts to overhaul social programs, notably welfare. But the younger Ford was campaigning on the idea of "reforming" the welfare system before the Republican 104th Congress overhauled it. Still, he harshly attacked Republicans as he defended affirmative action and government programs for the poor. "If Republicans can defend [Supreme Court Justice] Clarence Thomas, Democrats can defend affirmative action," he said.

Ford stressed his commitment to education during the 1996 race, advocating what he termed a "new vision" that would entail providing computers and Internet access for every classroom in the country. As a member of the Education and the Workforce Committee, Ford will be able to pursue his educational initiatives. Ford also stated his belief that pharmaceutical companies should bear some of the burden of reducing the growth of Medicare spending. He is a stalwart defender of other social spending programs such as Head Start, Goals 2000 and Safe and Drug Free Schools education programs.

Ford also received a seat on the Government Reform and Oversight Committee.

He backs Democratic efforts to preserve environmentally sensitive areas such as the Arctic National Wildlife Refuge in Alaska and to put more police officers on the street. He describes increased funding for prison construction as a short-term solution to the crime problem, which he says would be better combated by an increase in jobs and job training.

Ford trumpeted his stances when he appeared at schools and before the elderly at "Seniors for Junior" campaign events.

Memphis Mayor W.W. Herenton, a political rival of the Ford family, attempted to prevent Ford's inheritance of the seat. Herenton openly shopped for a heavy-hitting politician to back for a run against Ford but could not recruit his top-choice candidates. He settled on state Rep. Rufus E. Jones, the brother of Herenton's former wife. Jones highlighted his experience in contrast with Ford, who had only graduated from law school two months before the Democratic primary, but to no avail. Jones finished in the single digits.

The GOP candidate, Rod DeBerry, proved to be no more of a challenge for the younger Ford than he had been for the senior Ford in 1994.

In the 105th, Ford made headlines when, in a March 1997 floor speech, he criticized Senate Majority Leader Trent Lott for saying that business PACs such as Federal Express (which is headquartered in Ford's district) would "squirm considerably" if they continued to donate to Democratic campaigns.

Prior to entering Congress, Ford worked as a special assistant to the late Commerce Secretary Ron Brown and as an aide to the Senate Budget Committee under former Tennessee Democratic Sen. James Sasser.

TENNESSEE 9
Memphis

On the bluffs above the Mississippi River is Memphis, a city of 610,000 and historically the crossroads for eastern Arkansas, northern Mississippi and West Tennessee. Named after the city in Egypt because of the Nile-like appearance of the twisting Mississippi, Memphis underscored that link in 1991 by opening the Great American Pyramid. The 32-story structure, which houses a 22,000-seat arena, is part of a larger plan to revitalize the city's economy — and especially its flagging downtown — by attracting more special events and visitors.

Memphis is already well-known as the site of Elvis Presley's Graceland; since "the King's" 1977 death, a ceaseless stream of admirers has visited his grave on the mansion grounds. Now, another famous Southerner is memorialized by a Memphis museum: the Rev. Dr. Martin Luther King Jr. The National Civil Rights Museum opened in 1991 on the site of the former Lorraine Motel, where King was assassinated in 1968.

Other downtown attractions include Mud Island — a 52-acre island park that celebrates the city's river history — and Beale Street, where W. C. Handy developed the blues in the early 1900s. Restoration along Beale Street aims to revive its role as the center of city nightlife.

But the task of reviving downtown is complicated by the city's racial relationships. Memphis' population is 55 percent black, and nearly all the blacks live around and near downtown. The bulk of the white population is segregated in the eastern part of the city and is prone to head farther east into the overwhelmingly white suburbs for entertainment.

Harold E. Ford's House election in 1974 marked the assertion of black political power in the 9th, which was then more compact and had many more blacks than Memphis as a whole. The city itself did not elect a black mayor until 1991, when Ford and other leaders in the black community united behind longtime school Superintendent Willie Herenton.

Because of inner-city population decline in Memphis over the years, mapmakers have had to expand the 9th. In 1992, for the first time, the district moved outside the city limits; its black population has held almost steady at 59 percent. The 9th reached east and south to pick up about 80,000 new residents, including some in conservative white areas that had been in the 7th.

Still, the 9th remains strongly Democratic. Bill Clinton and Tennessean Al Gore won 66 percent of the 9th's presidential vote in 1992, and 71 percent four years later. Ford's son, in his 1996 debut, won 61 percent, higher than the percentages his father received since 1988.

The growth of tourism-related business has helped compensate for the decline since the 1970s of Memphis' industrial base, although the new service-sector jobs are comparatively low-paying. The city also has become a leading distribution center (Federal Express Corp. is Memphis-based), and medical services are a big business (St. Jude Children's Research Hospital, one of the nation's top pediatric-care facilities, is here). Also, roughly one-third of the nation's cotton crop passes through the Memphis Cotton Exchange.

1990 Population: 541,981. White 214,979 (40%), Black 321,087 (59%), Other 5,915 (1%). Hispanic origin 3,833 (1%). 18 and over 394,375 (73%), 62 and over 80,918 (15%). Median age: 31.

HOUSE ELECTIONS

1996 General		
Harold E. Ford Jr. (D)	116,345	(61%)
Rod DeBerry (R)	70,951	(37%)
1996 Primary		
Harold E. Ford Jr. (D)	63,888	(60%)
Steve Cohen (D)	35,844	(34%)
Rufus E. Jones (D)	5,244	(5%)

CAMPAIGN FINANCE

	Receipts	Receipts from PACs	Expend-itures
1996			
Ford (D)	$680,164	$144,450 (21%)	$679,843
DeBerry (R)	$94,011	$9,750 (10%)	$95,687
Kelly (I)	$21,200	0	$33,200

DISTRICT VOTE FOR PRESIDENT

1996		1992	
D	136,950 (71%)	D	151,590 (66%)
R	50,053 (26%)	R	68,358 (30%)
I	3,829 (2%)	I	9,400 (4%)

KEY VOTES

1997

Ban "partial birth" abortions N

TEXAS

Governor: George W. Bush (R)
First elected: 1994
Length of term: 4 years
Term expires: 1/99
Salary: $99,121.92
Term limit: No
Phone: (512) 463-2000
Born: July 6, 1946; New Haven, Conn.
Education: Yale U., B.A., 1968; Harvard U., M.B.A., 1975
Military Service: Texas Air National Guard.
Occupation: Baseball team executive; oil and gas company executive.
Family: Wife, Laura Welch; two children.
Religion: Methodist.
Political Career: Republican nominee for U.S. House, 1978.

Lt. Gov.: Bob Bullock (D)
First elected: 1990
Length of term: 4 years
Term expires: 1/99
Salary: $7,200 + $95/day during legislative session
Phone: (512) 463-0001

State election official: (512) 463-5650
Democratic headquarters: (512) 478-8746
Republican headquarters: (512) 477-9821

REDISTRICTING

Texas gained three House seats in reapportionment, increasing to 30. The Legislature passed map Aug. 25, 1991; the governor signed it Aug. 29; federal court upheld it Dec. 24. Federal court on Aug. 17, 1994, invalidated 18th, 29th and 30th districts; on Sept. 2, court ruled 1994 elections could proceed. On June 13, 1996, the Supreme Court upheld the federal court's ruling that struck down the districts. On Aug. 6, a federal panel invalidated the primary and runoff results in 13 districts; the panel imposed a new map the same day. The Supreme Court refused to block the panel's ruling on Sept. 4, 1996.

STATE LEGISLATURE

Legislature. Meets January-May in odd-numbered years.

Senate: 31 members, 4-year terms
1996 breakdown: 15D, 16R; 28 men, 3 women
Salary: $7,200 + per diem during session
Phone: (512) 463-0100

House of Representatives: 150 members, 2-year terms
1996 breakdown: 82D, 68R; 119 men, 31 women
Salary: $7,200 + per diem during session
Phone: (512) 463-0845

URBAN STATISTICS

City	Population
Houston Mayor Bob Lanier, R	1,630,864
Dallas Mayor Ronald Kirk, N-P	1,007,617
San Antonio Mayor Howard Peak, N-P	935,933
El Paso Mayor Carlos Ramirez, N-P	515,342
Austin Mayor Bruce Todd, D	465,622

U.S. CONGRESS

Senate: 0 D, 2 R
House: 17 D, 13 R

TERM LIMITS

For state offices: No
**Ramirez is to be sworn in June 4, 1997.*

ELECTIONS

1996 Presidential Vote

Bob Dole	49%
Bill Clinton	44%
Ross Perot	7%

1992 Presidential Vote

George Bush	41%
Bill Clinton	37%
Ross Perot	22%

1988 Presidential Vote

George Bush	56%
Michael S. Dukakis	43%

POPULATION

1990 population		16,986,510
1980 population		14,229,191
Percent change		+19%
Rank among states:		3
White		75%
Black		12%
Hispanic		26%
Asian or Pacific islander		2%
Urban		91%
Rural		9%
Born in state		65%
Foreign-born		9%
Under age 18	4,835,839	28%
Ages 18-64	10,434,095	61%
65 and older	1,716,576	10%
Median age		30.8

MISCELLANEOUS

Capital: Austin
Number of counties: 254
Per capita income: $17,305 (1991)
Rank among states: 31
Total area: 266,807 sq. miles
Rank among states: 2

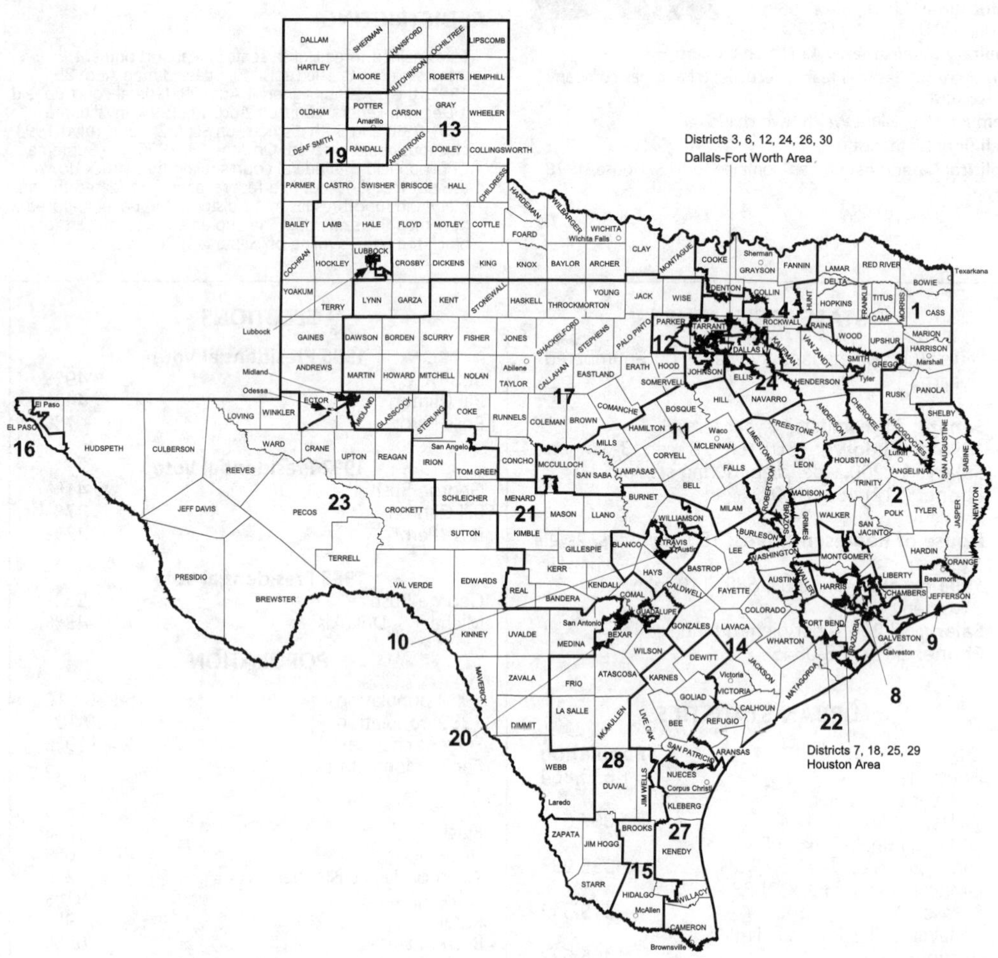
Districts 3, 6, 12, 24, 26, 30
Dallas-Fort Worth Area
Districts 7, 18, 25, 29
Houston Area
1
2
4
5
8
9
10
11
12
13
14
15
16
17
19
20
21
22
23
24
27
28
DALLAM
SHERMAN
HANSFORD
OCHILTREE
LIPSCOMB
HARTLEY
MOORE
HUTCHINSON
ROBERTS
HEMPHILL
OLDHAM
POTTER
Amarillo
CARSON
GRAY
WHEELER
DEAF SMITH
RANDALL
ARMSTRONG
DONLEY
COLLINGSWORTH
PARMER
CASTRO
SWISHER
BRISCOE
HALL
CHILDRESS
HARDEMAN
WILBARGER
WICHITA
Wichita Falls
BAILEY
LAMB
HALE
FLOYD
MOTLEY
COTTLE
FOARD
CLAY
MONTAGUE
COOKE
GRAYSON
Sherman
FANNIN
LAMAR
RED RIVER
Texarkana
BOWIE
DELTA
HOPKINS
FRANKLIN
TITUS
MORRIS
CASS
CAMP
COCHRAN
HOCKLEY
LUBBOCK
CROSBY
DICKENS
KING
KNOX
BAYLOR
ARCHER
YOAKUM
TERRY
LYNN
GARZA
KENT
STONEWALL
HASKELL
THROCKMORTON
YOUNG
JACK
WISE
DENTON
COLLIN
HUNT
RAINS
ROCKWALL
WOOD
UPSHUR
MARION
HARRISON
Marshall
Lubbock
GAINES
DAWSON
BORDEN
SCURRY
FISHER
JONES
SHACKELFORD
STEPHENS
PALO PINTO
PARKER
TARRANT
DALLAS
KAUFMAN
VAN ZANDT
SMITH
GREGG
Tyler
ANDREWS
MARTIN
HOWARD
MITCHELL
NOLAN
TAYLOR
Abilene
CALLAHAN
EASTLAND
ERATH
HOOD
JOHNSON
ELLIS
HENDERSON
RUSK
PANOLA
Midland
Odessa
El Paso
EL PASO
LOVING
WINKLER
ECTOR
MIDLAND
GLASSCOCK
STERLING
COKE
RUNNELS
COLEMAN
BROWN
COMANCHE
SOMERVELL
BOSQUE
HILL
NAVARRO
CHEROKEE
NACOGDOCHES
SHELBY
HUDSPETH
CULBERSON
WARD
CRANE
UPTON
REAGAN
IRION
San Angelo
TOM GREEN
CONCHO
MCCULLOCH
SAN SABA
MILLS
HAMILTON
CORYELL
Waco
MCLENNAN
LIMESTONE
FREESTONE
ANDERSON
HOUSTON
ANGELINA
Lufkin
SAN AUGUSTINE
SABINE
REEVES
JEFF DAVIS
PECOS
CROCKETT
SCHLEICHER
MENARD
MASON
LLANO
LAMPASAS
BELL
FALLS
LEON
MADISON
TRINITY
POLK
TYLER
JASPER
NEWTON
SUTTON
KIMBLE
BURNET
MILAM
ROBERTSON
BRAZOS
GRIMES
WALKER
SAN JACINTO
WILLIAMSON
TRAVIS
Austin
GILLESPIE
BLANCO
BURLESON
LEE
WASHINGTON
MONTGOMERY
HARDIN
ORANGE
PRESIDIO
BREWSTER
TERRELL
VAL VERDE
EDWARDS
KERR
REAL
BANDERA
KENDALL
COMAL
HAYS
BASTROP
FAYETTE
AUSTIN
WALLER
HARRIS
LIBERTY
CHAMBERS
JEFFERSON
Beaumont
San Antonio
BEXAR
GUADALUPE
CALDWELL
GONZALES
COLORADO
FORT BEND
BRAZORIA
GALVESTON
Galveston
KINNEY
UVALDE
MEDINA
WILSON
LAVACA
WHARTON
DEWITT
MAVERICK
ZAVALA
FRIO
ATASCOSA
KARNES
Victoria
VICTORIA
JACKSON
MATAGORDA
GOLIAD
CALHOUN
LA SALLE
DIMMIT
MCMULLEN
LIVE OAK
BEE
REFUGIO
ARANSAS
SAN PATRICIO
NUECES
Corpus Christi
WEBB
DUVAL
JIM WELLS
Laredo
KLEBERG
ZAPATA
JIM HOGG
BROOKS
KENEDY
STARR
HIDALGO
McAllen
WILLACY
CAMERON
Brownsville

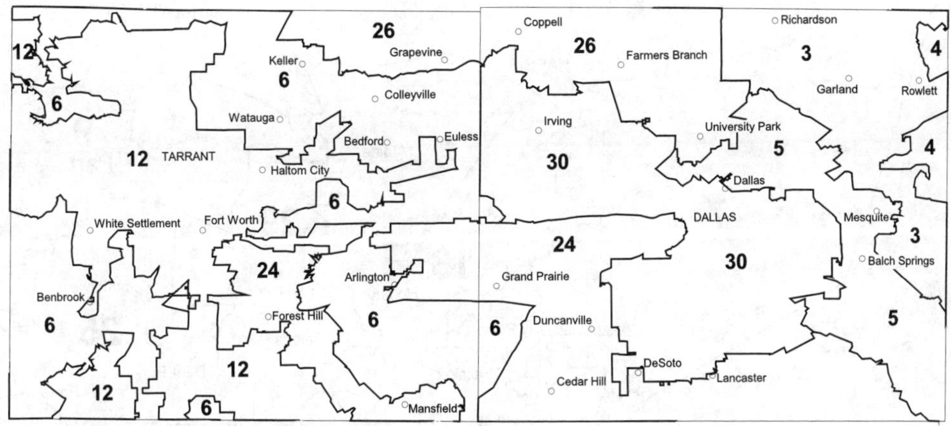
12
6
26
Keller
Grapevine
6
Colleyville
Watauga
Bedford
Euless
12
TARRANT
Haltom City
6
White Settlement
Fort Worth
24
Arlington
Benbrook
6
Forest Hill
6
12
12
6
Mansfield
Coppell
26
Farmers Branch
Richardson
3
4
Garland
Rowlett
Irving
University Park
5
4
30
Dallas
DALLAS
Mesquite
24
3
30
Balch Springs
Grand Prairie
6
Duncanville
5
DeSoto
Cedar Hill
Lancaster

TEXAS
HOUSTON AREA DISTRICTS

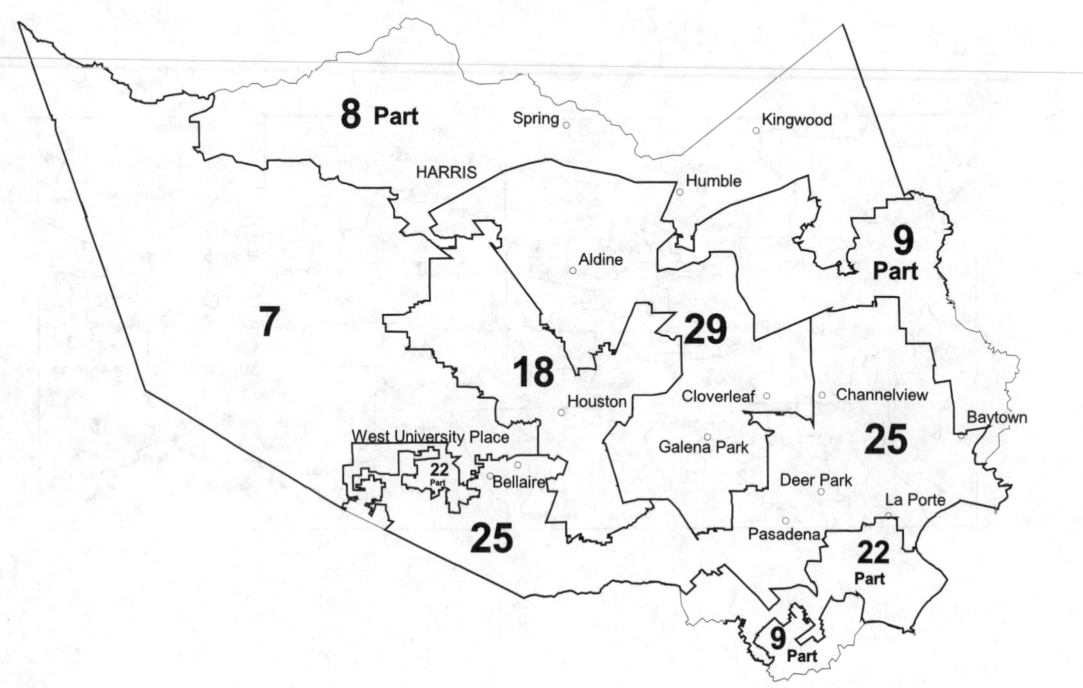

Phil Gramm (R)

Of College Station — Elected 1984, 3rd term

Biographical Information

Born: July 8, 1942, Fort Benning, Ga.
Education: U. of Georgia, B.B.A. 1964, Ph.D. 1967.
Occupation: Professor.
Family: Wife, Wendy Lee; two children.
Religion: Episcopalian.
Political Career: Sought Democratic nomination for U.S. Senate, 1976; U.S. House, 1979-85.
Capitol Office: 370 Russell Bldg. 20510; 224-2934.

Committees

Agriculture, Nutrition & Forestry
Production & Price Competitiveness; Research, Nutrition & General Legislation
Banking, Housing & Urban Affairs
Financial Institutions & Regulatory Relief; International Finance; Securities (chairman)
Budget
Finance
Health Care (chairman); International Trade; Social Security & Family Policy

In Washington: Gramm was bound to seem quieter at the outset of the 105th Congress, if only in contrast to the aggressive style he had displayed a year earlier as a presidential contender trying to wrest the Republican nomination from Senate Majority Leader Bob Dole of Kansas. Time and again in the 104th Congress, Gramm's unapologetic conservatism forced the front-running Dole to the right on issues before the Senate.

But if he often won the Senate battle, Gramm quickly lost the presidential war. Overtaken in the early caucuses by rivals on the right such as Patrick J. Buchanan and Steve Forbes, Gramm finished an embarrassing fifth in Iowa and dropped out before New Hampshire. Through the rest of 1996, Gramm backed Dole and concentrated on winning his own re-election to the Senate. He had to turn back a surprisingly lively challenge from a Hispanic high school teacher who held him to 55 percent of the vote, tying his lowest share ever.

But if Gramm's star had dimmed as he started his third term in 1997, the cantankerous former economics professor had some consolations. President Clinton might still be in the White House, but Gramm had more Republican colleagues than ever in the Senate and Trent Lott of Mississippi, an old ally from the House whose career he had helped champion in the Senate, was their leader.

For a time, Gramm seemed to be digging in for a season of legislative work in the trenches, assuming that Lott would carry the ball for conservatives on the Senate floor. Gramm had backed Lott's move to the No. 2 position in the leadership back in 1994, saying Republicans in the Senate were "ready for a change" and "ready to be confrontational on issues where the American people agree with us."

But before too long, Gramm was finding Lott distressingly reminiscent of Dole. First, it was the balanced-budget amendment, which again fell one vote shy of the two-thirds majority needed in the Senate. Then it was ratification of the chemical weapons convention, which Lott helped to a successful vote (in concert with all 45 Senate Democrats) over the objections of Gramm and about two dozen other Republicans.

But the piece de résistance for Gramm was the budget deal Lott and the House Republican leadership struck with Clinton in May. Although the agreement was said to assure a zero budget deficit by 2002, Gramm saw its tax cuts as anemic and its spending increases as unconscionable. "This budget deal will be great for Washington and bad for America," said Gramm. "It is the product of a system in which the two parties no longer contest ideas, but conspire against the public."

Gramm had been willing to accept the apparent political realities of the 105th, shaped by public criticism of the GOP for the politically disastrous government shutdowns of 1995-96. He had tried to be realistic about the re-elected president, responding to Clinton's 1998 budget proposals by saying: "We don't have any choice but to work with him."

But the result of the negotiations, of which he had no part, left Gramm in a far different mood. He was in position to test the agreement, as Medicare provisions would come before the new Senate Finance Subcommittee on Health Care (a combination of the old Medicaid and Health Care for Low-Income Families and the Medicare, Long-Term Care and Health Insurance panels, both of which were abolished), with Gramm as chairman and an array of conservative Republicans on hand.

Gramm believes Medicare needs a total overhaul to prevent a budget disaster. He would change the program to a catastrophic-care policy with a single deductible of about $2,500. He also wants a pay-as-you-go system, in which each generation would invest during their working years for their own medical costs in retirement, with a transition period to care for those already or about to be retired. Beneficiaries would be able to choose among competing insurers, much as workers choose private-sector policies today.

Gramm is jumping into another debate that promises to bring out the heavy artillery: the question of whether to include environment and labor standards as goals of trade negotiations. One of the few outspoken free-traders left in the Senate, Gramm wants to give the president so-called "fast-track" authority to negotiate agreements with the guarantee that Congress will approve or reject the pacts without amendments within 90 days. The administration wants fast-track authority to improve its international negotiating power, but is committed to retaining the linkage between labor and environment and fast track. Gramm has introduced a bare-bones, fast-track bill that would prohibit labor or environmental concerns from being a goal of any trade negotiation. Democrats, labor and environmental lobbyists are dead-set against such a prohibition, and the debate should be fierce.

Part of the secret of Gramm's staying power is simple tenaciousness. If one venue is closed on an issue of importance to him, he finds another. Gramm was determined to push the Senate to pass the severe tax cuts featured in the House's "Contract With America" and approved in the House budget resolution. He waited until the Senate version reached the floor, offering an amendment with tax cuts slightly less than the huge $353 billion demanded by the House. But 23 Republicans argued that balancing the budget was more important and killed the amendment. Gramm was then pointedly excluded from the House-Senate conference by Senate Budget Chairman Pete V. Domenici of New Mexico, who had endorsed Dole's campaign. Undaunted, Gramm issued a warning that if $245 billion in cuts were not included, he would oppose the budget and "it will not pass." With intraparty tensions at the boiling point, Dole and House Speaker Newt Gingrich finally met the demands for deep tax cuts and agreed to $245 billion in cuts. Gramm called it "a clear victory for the things that I believe in."

During the 104th Congress, Gramm required Dole's almost constant attention. Dole had to watch out for Gramm on several fronts, as an insurgent in the Senate's Republican ranks and as a presidential contender. Because of the conservative nature of Republicans in the Senate, Dole had to spend more of his time assuaging conservatives who found Gramm to be a comfortable ideological fit. Dole was forced to name Gramm to fill a key opening on the pivotal Finance Committee after Oregon Republican Bob Packwood's resignation when no other senior senator was available to take the slot.

Gramm immediately used the post to show up Dole on the extent of his tax-cutting fervor. Dole mentioned on a TV talk show that he was uncertain whether the Senate would back the $245 billion tax cut in the deficit-reducing budget-reconciliation bill taken up later in the year, but had to backtrack after Gramm jumped on the comment.

"We are not going to have a compromise on this issue," Gramm said. "The American people said to us: Stop the taxing; stop the spending; stop the regulating. I am committed to doing that. We set out in the budget the goal of $245 billion, and I will not vote for any reconciliation bill that does not live up to it. Period." Dole then quickly acted to make clear that he stood firm for the full $245 billion. "We still have the goal of $245 billion," he said. "As far as I'm concerned, $245 billion is the figure."

As the campaign season progressed, Dole and Gramm often scrambled to take the limelight on hot-button issues, such as when Clinton decided to modify the longstanding U.S. embargo against Havana to permit increased travel and cultural exchanges with Cuba. Both Gramm and Dole have long opposed Castro's regime, and both seemed eager to burnish their anti-Castro credentials in advance of a Florida GOP presidential straw poll. Dole backed a measure aimed at denying foreign investment to Fidel Castro's regime, and moved it directly to the floor without a committee markup. Gramm, who lacked Dole's power to move legislation, responded with fiery rhetoric. He charged that the president's idea of leadership "seems to be whispering sweet nothings to Fidel Castro."

By style and ideological message, Gramm is an inherently divisive figure. He is an ardent opponent of the modern American welfare state and plays openly to middle-class resentments about financing those institutions. The Senate turned back his effort to eliminate the Legal Services Corporation, which provides grants to help provide lawyers for poor people in civil cases. Gramm pilloried the corporation's support for challenges to state welfare reform plans and other initiatives. But Domenici came to the defense of the agency, offering an amendment to restore legal aid's funding to Gramm's appropriations bill. "The judicial system is not only for the rich," Domenici said. "Why should a Republican be ashamed to say that?"

At Home: The former Georgian's hard-nosed manner and free-market philosophy have found a favorable reception in Texas. It took Gramm a while, though, to figure out which party was best-suited to his message. Gramm was prepared to leave his teaching post at Texas A&M University in 1976 when he ran against Lloyd Bentsen for the Democratic Senate nomination. Bentsen, Gramm charged, had become too left-leaning during his ill-fated 1976 presidential bid.

Two years later, Gramm won the Democratic nomination to succeed Rep. Olin E. Teague in the House. Even then, Gramm was able to demonstrate formidable fundraising abilities, gathering a campaign war chest of a half-million dollars.

Almost upon his arrival in Washington, Gramm was considerably more conservative than the House Democratic leadership, with whom he fought constantly. Teague's son even mounted a primary challenge to Gramm because of distaste over his positions.

The suspicions about Gramm persisted in Washington. When he campaigned for a position on the House Budget Committee, Democratic leaders in the House asked for and received a written pledge that he would be loyal to the party's budget. Yet in 1981 he secretly collaborated with Republicans on President Ronald Reagan's budget. Gramm would sit in on Democratic budget caucuses and then report back to the White House.

Democrats found this out and barred him from meetings. But it was a classic case of shutting the door after the horse had been stolen. Reagan's budget ultimately passed, and voters at home seemed indifferent to the Democrats' intramural dispute.

At the start of the next Congress, Gramm was ejected from the Budget Committee. He then left the Democratic Party, resigned his House seat and won easy re-election to it as a Republican in 1983. When he won that seat as a Republican, it was the first time in Texas history that the 6th District seat went to the GOP.

During that race, Gramm invested heavily in his political future. He spent campaign funds heavily in the media markets encompassing Dallas, Fort Worth and Houston, giving him solid name recognition in the state's biggest cities. When GOP Sen. John Tower announced that he would retire at the conclusion of the 98th Congress, Gramm was ready to run and was the front-runner from the beginning. This permitted him to spend more time in areas not traditionally hospitable to Republicans. Gramm outspent his Democratic opponent, state Sen. Lloyd Doggett, 3-to-1.

Gramm also ran in the year in which Reagan crushed Mondale. The result was that 59 percent of the vote went to Gramm. He has never been electorally vulnerable since.

In 1990 Gramm defeated state Sen. Hugh Parmer with 60 percent of the vote, and in the intervening years more of the state's high offices have come to be held by conservative Republicans. Kay Bailey Hutchison was elected to the Senate with Gramm's help after Bentsen resigned to join the Clinton administration in 1993. George W. Bush was elected governor in 1994.

Gramm has escaped the taint of national scandals. Opponents have tried to link him to the savings and loan debacle, in part because the owner of three failed thrifts had paid half the cost for a Gramm vacation home. But such disclosures had little effect at home.

With his mind on presidential politics during the 1995-96 Congress, Gramm had less time to take care of his home-state interests. When he quit the presidential race and campaigned for his Senate seat, his opposition was Victor M. Morales, a high school teacher who came out of nowhere and defied all conventional wisdom. Morales ended the congressional careers of two Democratic House members who wanted to challenge Gramm: He left Rep. Jim Chapman in the dust in the March Democratic Senate primary and then beat Rep. John Bryant in an April runoff.

Morales knew Gramm had been re-elected with 60 percent of the vote in 1990, but he said he was making the long-shot bid because he was tired of hearing Gramm score political points on issues such as affirmative action.

The grandson of Mexican immigrants, Morales was greatly aided in the primary and runoff by strong support among Hispanics. Gramm, however, was still too much the Texas heavyweight. With strong backing from the Republican Party and $6.2 million to spend on the Senate race in a state Clinton would not carry, Gramm secured a third term.

SENATE ELECTIONS

1996 General		
Phil Gramm (R)	3,027,680	(55%)
Victor M. Morales (D)	2,428,776	(44%)
1996 Primary		
Phil Gramm (R)	838,339	(85%)
David Young (R)	75,463	(8%)
Henry C. "Hank" Grover (R)	72,400	(7%)

Previous Winning Percentages: **1990** (60%) **1984** (59%) **1983**† (55%) **1982*** (95%) **1980*** (71%) **1978*** (65%)

† Special House election

** House elections. Gramm was elected as a Democrat in 1978-82.*

CAMPAIGN FINANCE

	Receipts	Receipts from PACs	Expend-itures
1996			
Gramm (R)	$3,802,167	$1,107,961 (29%)	$6,289,591
Morales (D)	$991,290	$4,539 (0%)	$978,862

KEY VOTES

1997	
Approve balanced-budget constitutional amendment	Y
Approve chemical weapons treaty	N
1996	
Approve farm bill	?
Limit punitive damages in product liability cases	Y
Exempt small businesses from higher minimum wage	Y
Approve welfare overhaul	Y
Bar job discrimination based on sexual orientation	N
Override veto of ban on "partial birth" abortions	Y
1995	
Approve GOP budget with tax and spending cuts	Y
Approve constitutional amendment barring flag desecration	Y

VOTING STUDIES

	Presidential Support		Party Unity		Conservative Coalition	
Year	**S**	**O**	**S**	**O**	**S**	**O**
1996	24	71	93	1	92	3
1995	17	72	88	3	84	2
1994	32	56	87	5	88	6
1993	21	76	94	2	93	0
1992	90	10	91	1	89	5
1991	93	4	92	5	90	3

INTEREST GROUP RATINGS

Year	ADA	AFL-CIO	CCUS	ACU
1996	0	n/a	100	100
1995	0	0	100	100
1994	5	0	100	100
1993	5	0	100	92
1992	0	8	100	93
1991	0	17	89	95

Kay Bailey Hutchison (R)

Of Dallas — Elected 1993; 1st full term

Biographical Information

Born: July 22, 1943, Galveston, Texas.
Education: U. of Texas, B.A. 1992, J.D. 1967.
Occupation: Broadcast journalist; banking executive, candy manufacturer.
Family: Husband, Ray Hutchison.
Religion: Episcopalian.
Political Career: Texas House, 1973-77; Texas state treasurer, 1991-93.
Capitol Office: 283 Russell Bldg. 20510; 224-5922.

Committees

Appropriations
Commerce, Justice, State & Judiciary; Defense; District of Columbia; Labor, Health & Human Services & Education; Military Construction
Commerce, Science & Transportation
Aviation; Communications; Oceans & Fisheries; Science, Technology & Space; Surface Transportation & Merchant Marine (chairman)
Rules & Administration

In Washington: The 104th Congress was a good one for Hutchison. She won approval for several high-profile initiatives — including an anti-stalking bill and a tax break for homemakers — and she won further notice with a prominent speech at the GOP presidential convention. She co-chaired the Senate Republican Regulatory Relief Task Force and was selected as chairman of the Senate Steering Committee, an informal caucus of conservative senators. She worked to limit the scope of the Endangered Species Act and helped maintain funding for the National Endowment for the Arts. And to top it off, she heard herself mentioned as a prospective vice presidential nominee to share the ballot with GOP candidate Bob Dole.

Hutchison has kept her name in the news by testing a variety of legislative waters without becoming known as an expert in any single area. She has a chance to deepen her experience in the 105th Congress as chairman of the Commerce Committee's Surface Transportation and Merchant Marine Subcommittee. In that spot, Hutchison will make a difference in reauthorizing the massive 1991 law that provides money for highways and transit systems known as ISTEA (for Intermodal Surface Transportation Efficiency Act).

Hutchison has already taken an approach to the issue as part of a bipartisan group of lawmakers that wants to overhaul the decades-old formula for dividing the nearly $25 billion in gas taxes collected by the states. Under the current formula, Northeastern states receive more highway money than they collect in taxes.

When Hutchison left the Armed Services Committee in 1997, some of her constituents worried that Texas would lack a defender of its many defense contractors and military installations. But from her new seat on Appropriations, she can continue to champion her state's military bases and her commitment to improve conditions for personnel. Texas, with 26 military bases, was considered a prime target of the independent base-closing commission charged with saving billions in defense outlays by shrinking or closing bases. Hutchison led a bipartisan Texas delegation credited with winning a partial victory for their state. Although the commission voted to close two Air Force bases near San Antonio and Lubbock, costing Texas about 15,000 jobs, it spared most of Texarkana's Red River Army Depot rather than accept an Army plan for closing it.

Hutchison happily maintains her image as a Texas cheerleader with a sorority sister smile, yet she can show an iron will behind her trademark fluffy blonde hairstyle. That force was evident when Hutchison became one of the leading voices against sending U.S. troops to Bosnia in 1995 as part of a NATO peacekeeping mission. She argued that the president failed to define the national security risks at stake in Bosnia or justify putting troops in danger. "We support the troops," she said. "And the most effective way to support them is to oppose the decision to deploy them." But the Senate rejected 52-47 her resolution expressing Congress' disapproval of Clinton's decision to send the troops.

In 1997, Hutchison was again aligned against President Clinton and most of the Senate on the question of ratifying the international Chemical Weapons Convention. Although more than half the Senate Republicans, including Majority Leader Trent Lot of Mississippi, voted for the treaty, Hutchison joined with Texas Republican colleague Phil Gramm in opposition.

Hutchison is one of nine women serving in the Senate — three Republicans and six Democrats — the largest number the body has ever had. While they are likely to use their voting-bloc power sparingly, Hutchison and others are already looking for ways to cooperate on issues important to women. Hutchison supports abortion rights, with restrictions, and has voted in favor of criminal and civil penalties for people who block access to abortion clinics. That position drew criticism from some right-wing Republicans who objected to her prominent role at the GOP convention. (She was almost denied a seat within the Texas delegation.)

But she has also gone beyond the highly charged abortion debate to focus instead on women's economic empowerment and criminal protection. Hutchison sponsored an anti-stalking bill signed by Clinton that makes it a crime to cross state lines to harass or harm a victim. She has also been in the forefront of an effort to make it easier for homemakers to invest in individual retirement accounts. Previous law only allowed homemakers and other non-wage earners to contribute $250 annually to tax-deductible IRA accounts. Hutchison's provision allowing homemakers to contribute up to $2,000 to such accounts was added to a bill providing a 90-cent increase in the minimum wage and $20 billion in business tax cuts that Congress cleared in August 1996.

At Home: Hutchison has admitted to being an indifferent student at the University of Texas in the mid-1960s, but after trying on several other careers she found the one that not only fit her but brought out her ambition: She was elected to the state Legislature in 1972 at the age of 29. While in Austin she made common cause with famous Democratic legislator Sarah Weddington (the lawyer who filed the suit that became *Roe v. Wade*) on bills protecting victims of sex offenses (including a ban on the publication of the names of rape victims).

In 1990 she ran for state treasurer, succeeding Ann W. Richards, who was elected governor. When Lloyd Bentsen left the Senate in January 1993 to become Clinton's first Treasury secretary, Richards appointed Bob Krueger, a former House member (1975-79) who once had almost beaten the legendary Texas Republican Sen. John Tower (1961-85). Texas law made Krueger stand for election after just a few months in office, and Hutchison saw an opportunity in the all-party field of 24 candidates.

She finished first with 29 percent, just a handful of votes ahead of Krueger and with more votes than GOP Reps. Jack Fields and Joe L. Barton combined. From there on, the runoff was all but a foregone conclusion. Her 67 percent tally against Krueger in June was the biggest vote share ever for a challenger to an incumbent in Texas.

In 1994, Hutchison had to run again to secure her own full six-year term. (She had been completing the one Bentsen won in 1988.) But it was easy after she triumphed over a 1993 indictment on charges that she had abused her office as Texas state treasurer. She was acquitted in February 1994 after the state prosecutor declined to proceed with the case. Despite the potentially damaging allegations — that she used state workers to carry out personal errands on state time, that she used state phones and computers for political purposes, and that she once struck an employee with a notebook — the incident magnified Hutchison's political clout and scared off most of the likely competition in both parties.

The Democrats nominated Dallas businessman Richard Fisher, who had advised Ross Perot's independent presidential campaign in 1992 and run for Bentsen's seat in 1993 (finishing well down in the pack). Hutchison outspent him 4-to-1, carried all six of the most populous counties and ran up a winning margin of 23 percentage points.

SENATE ELECTIONS

1994 General		
Kay Bailey Hutchison (R)	2,604,218	(61%)
Richard Fisher (D)	1,639,615	(38%)
1994 Primary		
Kay Bailey Hutchison (R)	467,975	(84%)
Stephen Hopkins (R)	34,703	(6%)
James C. Currey (R)	15,625	(3%)
Roger Henson (R)	14,021	(3%)
Ernest J. Schmidt (R)	8,690	(2%)
M. Troy Mata (R)	8,632	(2%)
Tom Spink (R)	5,692	(1%)

Previous Winning Percentages: 1993† (67%)

† Special election

CAMPAIGN FINANCE

	Receipts	Receipts from PACs	Expend-itures
1994			
Hutchison (R)	$13,794,996	$2,518,287(18%)	$12,370,520
Fisher (D)	$5,891,859	$4,350 (0%)	$5,876,266

KEY VOTES

1997	
Approve balanced-budget constitutional amendment	Y
Approve chemical weapons treaty	N
1996	
Approve farm bill	Y
Limit punitive damages in product liability cases	Y
Exempt small businesses from higher minimum wage	Y
Approve welfare overhaul	Y
Bar job discrimination based on sexual orientation	N
Override veto of ban on "partial birth" abortions	Y
1995	
Approve GOP budget with tax and spending cuts	Y
Approve constitutional amendment barring flag desecration	Y

VOTING STUDIES

	Presidential Support		Party Unity		Conservative Coalition	
Year	**S**	**O**	**S**	**O**	**S**	**O**
1996	34	66	98	2	95	5
1995	28	71	95	4	98	2
1994	34	56	88	6	94	6
1993	45†	53†	87†	11†	94†	0†

INTEREST GROUP RATINGS

Year	ADA	AFL-CIO	CCUS	ACU
1996	5	n/a	92	100
1995	0	8	100	87
1994	10	0	100	96
1993	13	0	100	94

1 Max Sandlin (D)

Of Marshall — Elected 1996, 1st term

Biographical Information

Born: Sept. 29, 1952, Texarkana, Texas.
Education: Baylor U., B.A. 1975, J.D. 1978.
Occupation: Lawyer; county judge; fuel company executive.
Family: Wife, Leslie Howell; four children.
Religion: Baptist.
Political Career: Harrison County Democratic Party chair, 1984-86; Harrison County judge, 1986-89; Harrison County Court at law judge, 1989-96.
Capitol Office: 214 Cannon Bldg. 20515; 225-3035.

Committees

Transportation & Infrastructure
Railroads; Surface Transportation

The Path to Washington: During his 1996 campaign for the open 1st, Democrat Sandlin campaigned on a pledge to be "the chief marketing agent for the district," someone who would push for ways to strengthen the local economy and create jobs.

For the 105th Congress, Democratic leaders put Sandlin on the Transportation and Infrastructure Committee, giving him a chance to shape the massive highway and mass transit funding bill the panel is working on.

Sandlin waged a long and expensive battle to claim the seat being vacated by Democrat Jim Chapman, who decided against seeking re-election to the House to run for the Democratic Senate nomination, a bid that proved to be unsuccessful.

Sandlin promoted himself as the best person to bring "East Texas values" to Washington. He stressed his work in the community as Harrison County's judge of the county court at law, where he dealt with criminal and civil cases, and prior to that as county judge of Harrison County.

Sandlin, a member of the center-right Democratic coalition known as the "blue dogs," touted his ability to cut taxes and promised to support efforts to do the same in Congress. He backs targeted tax cuts, including a reduction in the capital gains tax, as well as tax credits aimed at creating jobs and enabling more students to attend college.

In the primary, Sandlin faced two other Democratic contenders, and he wound up in a runoff with lawyer Jo Ann Howard. Both candidates dug deep into their pockets, spending hundreds of thousands of dollars.

Howard accused Sandlin of ethical violations by campaigning for Congress while still serving as county-court-at-law judge. Texas state law requires county officials to resign their office when they become candidates for state or federal office.

Sandlin countered that Howard was misrepresenting the truth, noting that he had been asked by county officials to stay on and was legally in office until a replacement could be found. Sandlin, who had Chapman's backing in the runoff, struck back by claiming that Howard moved back to the district to run for Congress after living in Austin in recent years. Sandlin won the runoff with a comfortable 12-point margin.

In the fall campaign, Sandlin faced off against Republican Ed Merritt, who won his runoff by 10 points. After taking the district in some recent statewide elections, Republicans saw Chapman's departure as an opportunity to claim the long-Democratic territory.

Both candidates tried to paint the other as representing the extreme ends of his party. Sandlin assailed Merritt for supporting GOP budget proposals and other initiatives that he said were too conservative for the district. Sandlin argued, for instance, that major reductions in Medicare spending could harm the district's small-town hospitals. At the same time, Merritt claimed Sandlin was a liberal masquerading as a conservative Democrat and pointed to an appearance on his behalf by President Clinton.

Despite enduring a more bitter primary battle, Sandlin's name identification was much higher than Merritt's given his television advertisement battle with Howard.

He also had a stronger base of support to work from than Merritt, capturing nearly four times as many votes in the Democratic primary runoff than the total cast in the GOP contest. And Sandlin spent $1.7 million overall, fifth highest among non-incumbents running for the House and more than three times what Merritt spent. Still, the general-election outcome was fairly close, with Sandlin coming out on top by 5 percentage points, 52 percent to 47 percent.

Before his election to Congress, Sandlin served as chairman of the Harrison County Democratic Party. He served as a partner in the law firm of Sandlin and Buckner; vice president of Howell and Sandlin, an oil and gas distribution firm; and president of East Texas Fuels Inc., a gasoline distributorship.

Texas' personality has both Southern and Western elements, and the former is dominant in the 19 counties that make up the 1st. Life in northeastern Texas has a distinctly Southern feel; many people's livelihoods are linked to the land — in timber, dairying and other agricultural pursuits.

The closest thing to a big city in the district is Texarkana (Bowie County), a community divided by the Arkansas-Texas line. More than half its 53,000 residents live on the Texas side. The city is a blend of togetherness and separation. There is a joint Chamber of Commerce, and some utility services are shared, but there are separate mayors, police departments and school systems.

Texarkana's most famous native is billionaire businessman and White House aspirant Ross Perot. Perot received about 9 percent of Bowie's vote in 1996, substantially lower than his robust 22 percent here in 1992. Four years after edging George Bush in Bowie by a mere 49 votes, Bill Clinton defeated Bob Dole by 3 percentage points in the county.

Economically, the 1st has been through some tough times. An important employer, Lone Star Steel, emerged from bankruptcy protection. As is the case with many businesses in Texas, the fortunes of Lone Star rise and fall with the price of crude oil. When the oil industry crashed in 1984, there was little demand for the pipeline Lone Star produced; foreign competition further hampered the company. Once the district's largest employer (7,000 jobs in 1981), Lone Star now has just under 2,000 workers.

Also in recent years, Canadian imports have posed a threat to local timber sales, and Mexican cattle ranchers have put a dent in the East Texas market. Nevertheless, those two industries remain staples of the region. Wood is in abundance and is sold to furniture makers, paper mills and lumber companies.

TEXAS 1
Northeast — Texarkana; Marshall

In many of the small towns of rural East Texas, cows, chickens and trees outnumber people. Food processors Tyson Foods and Pilgrim's Pride are big employers. Hopkins County is the leading dairy county in the state and the Southwest. Cattle ranches dominate Lamar and Red River counties, which lie along the Oklahoma border.

With its traditional economic pillars shaky, the district has become more reliant on government-related business, albeit in the less-than-stable national defense realm. The largest public employer in the 1st is the Red River Army Depot, which appeared on the Pentagon's 1995 base-realignment list. It lost a personnel carrier unit to Anniston Army Depot in Alabama. Defense contractor Raytheon E-Systems in Greenville (shared with the neighboring 4th) is the district's principal private employer.

The 1st has been dubbed the buckle on the Southern Bible Belt; most voters are churchgoing conservatives. Clinton ran strongest in the counties along the Arkansas, Louisiana and Oklahoma borders, while Dole's hefty margins in the district's southernmost counties of Rusk and Nacogdoches contributed to his narrow victory in the 1st. Even so, Democrat Sandlin carried all but six counties in the House race.

1990 Population: 566,217. White 449,976 (79%), Black 102,480 (18%), Other 13,761 (2%). Hispanic origin 18,058 (3%). 18 and over 416,554 (74%), 62 and over 106,626 (19%). Median age: 34.

HOUSE ELECTIONS

1996 General		
Max Sandlin (D)	102,697	(52%)
Ed Merritt (R)	93,105	(47%)
Margaret A. Palms (NL)	3,368	(2%)
1996 Primary Runoff		
Max Sandlin (D)	31,659	(56%)
Jo Ann Howard (D)	25,063	(44%)
1996 Primary		
Max Sandlin (D)	36,142	(42%)
Jo Ann Howard (D)	28,962	(34%)
Tommy Kessler (D)	19,948	(23%)

CAMPAIGN FINANCE

	Receipts	Receipts from PACs	Expenditures
1996			
Sandlin (D)	$1,706,389	$276,850 (16%)	$1,691,255
Merritt (R)	$467,774	$80,412 (17%)	$467,750

DISTRICT VOTE FOR PRESIDENT

1996		1992	
D	91,476 (45%)	D	85,768 (39%)
R	94,296 (46%)	R	84,443 (38%)
I	17,223 (9%)	I	50,608 (23%)

KEY VOTES

1997

Ban "partial birth" abortions — Y

2 Jim Turner (D)

Of Crockett — Elected 1996, 1st term

Biographical Information
Born: Feb. 6, 1946, Fort Lewis, Wash.
Education: U. of Texas, B.B.A. 1968, M.B.A. 1971, J.D. 1971.
Military Service: Army, 1978.
Occupation: Lawyer.
Family: Wife, Ginny; two children.
Religion: Baptist.
Political Career: Mayor of Crockett, 1989-91; Texas House, 1981-84; Texas Senate, 1991-97.
Capitol Office: 1508 Longworth Bldg. 20515; 225-2401.

Committees
Government Reform & Oversight
National Economic Growth, Natural Resources & Regulatory Affairs; National Security, International Affairs & Criminal Justice
National Security
Military Procurement; Military Research & Development

The Path to Washington: Turner kept the open 2nd in Democratic hands in 1996, but he presents a strong contrast to the man he succeeded in Congress, Democrat Charles Wilson. As a Sunday school teacher and deacon in his church, Turner offers a much more conservative image than Wilson, the fun-loving, high-living Democrat known as "Good Time Charlie."

A self-described fiscal conservative who earned an M.B.A. as well as a law degree at the University of Texas, Turner says he will try to work within the committee structure to discourage excessive spending. Turner backs a balanced-budget constitutional amendment. He also plans to seek the same type of bipartisan cooperation that he says generally characterized the budget process in the Texas Legislature, where he served in both the House and Senate.

Turner earned notice in the state Legislature for his work in finding ways to crack down on crime. He touted his role in helping pass legislation expanding the death penalty as well as other anti-crime initiatives, including requiring mandatory minimum sentences for juveniles who commit violent offenses.

In Congress, Turner wants to work to strengthen law enforcement and continue support for initiatives that increase police presence in communities. He has expressed support for a national registry to track sexual offenders convicted of crimes against children and has called for imposing the death penalty on repeat sexual offenders. Turner also backs truth-in-sentencing laws and increased funding to create more prison space.

Concerned by the relatively low rate of college attendance by the youth in his district, Turner says he believes there is a role for federal funding in secondary and higher education. He favors a $10,000 tax deduction for college tuition and promises to oppose the Republican Party's efforts to reduce the growth in funding for student loans.

Democratic leaders gave Turner a spot on the National Security Committee, a post that will provide him with an opportunity to boost defense-related industry in the district. He also secured a seat on the Government Reform and Oversight Committee.

After the 2nd came open with Wilson's retirement, Turner secured the Democratic nomination with little trouble. Republicans, however, battled through a primary and a runoff, which turned bitter near the end. Emerging from the rubble was dentist Brian Babin, who was powered to victory in the runoff by the backing of Christian conservatives.

Babin hoped to break the Democrats' hold on the district and become the first Republican in more than a century to represent the areas that make up the 2nd. The district, however, has been slower to embrace the Republican Party than other parts of Texas, voting Democratic in recent presidential elections: In the 1996 contest, Bill Clinton attained a narrow victory in the 2nd.

Babin hoped to appeal to the generally conservative and blue-collar voters of the district by attempting to portray Turner as an "elitist liberal." He pointed to Turner's record in the state House and Senate, noting in particular what he contended were the Democrat's efforts to water down legislation to allow Texans to carry concealed weapons and his vote for a corporate income tax on small businesses.

But Turner was aggressive in his attempts to tie Babin to Republican proposals to reduce the growth in spending on Medicare, student loans and other programs. He repeatedly claimed that by supporting Republicans' budget proposals in the 104th Congress, Babin was in favor of "cutting" such programs. Babin denied the accusations and complained that Turner was misrepresenting his views.

Turner was helped by AFL-CIO ads targeting GOP Rep. Steve Stockman in the neighboring 9th District. Those ads, viewed by many 2nd District voters, attacked Stockman on many of the same issues Turner was using against Babin. Turner prevailed with 52 percent of the vote, and Democrats also toppled Stockman.

TEXAS 2
East — Lufkin; Orange

Stretching along Texas' eastern border, from Louisiana in the north to Port Orange in the south, the 2nd is another world from the dusty, barren landscape of West Texas, far removed from the barrios on the Mexican border and light-years from the glitz of metropolitan Dallas and Houston.

Instead, the thick forests of East Texas' Piney Woods call to mind stretches of Oregon, Washington state or New England. And the "Golden Triangle" of Orange, Port Arthur and Beaumont, with its shipyards, refineries and fishing docks, more resembles East Coast cities such as Philadelphia and Norfolk, Va.

But the image of the typical Texan as a rough-and-ready character fits the people here just as well as it does any others in the Lone Star State. Former Democratic Rep. Charles Wilson fashioned himself in that mold, and his fun-loving, take-no-guff style — along with a depressed local economy that increasingly relies on government dollars — helped him survive vigorous election challenges in the 1990s.

Located 36 miles from the Gulf of Mexico on the Sabine River, Orange once drew its revenue from timber, cattle, rice and oil. Today, the city is better known for "Chemical Row," an industrial corridor that saw massive layoffs in the late 1980s.

Port Arthur and the port of Orange rely heavily on federal dollars; in 1992 the Orange Shipbuilding Co. won a Navy contract to build refueling barges, including one of the type used in the Persian Gulf. Also in 1992, Lamar University (1,300 students) received $5 million to open a Navy ship design center and $2 million for an Air Force project aimed at computerizing and standardizing bidding and manufacturing guidelines.

Although Jefferson County (Beaumont and Port Arthur) is just over the district line in the 9th, it plays an integral role in the economy of the 2nd. Shipyards, petrochemical refineries and a steel mill are prevalent in the county.

In the northern and western counties of the 2nd, timber remains the primary industry, despite slowdowns in the construction trades and increased competition from abroad.

Angelina County, with 70 percent of its land in commercial forests, is the leading timber-producing county in Texas. Lufkin, the district's most populous city, is regarded as the "timber capital of Texas." Among the area's largest employers are Lufkin Industries (power transmission products and oil field pumping units), Temple Inland (construction and industrial materials) and Champion International (paper and forest products).

At election time, populist Democrats fare better than outright liberals in East Texas. Democratic presidential hopeful Walter F. Mondale failed to carry the 2nd in 1984, but Michael S. Dukakis in 1988 and Bill Clinton in 1992 and 1996 won the areas that compose the 2nd.

One of Texas' most politically competitive districts, the 2nd opted for Clinton in 1996 by 610 votes out of more than 200,000 cast. Just four of the 17 counties that lie wholly in the 2nd gave Clinton or Dole a majority of their votes. And few Texas districts featured a closer House race than the one Turner won to keep the seat in Democratic hands.

1990 Population: 566,217. White 449,827 (79%), Black 94,345 (17%), Other 22,045 (4%). Hispanic origin 31,976 (6%). 18 and over 414,273 (73%), 62 and over 97,719 (17%). Median age: 34.

HOUSE ELECTIONS

1996 General		
Jim Turner (D)	102,908	(52%)
Brian Babin (R)	89,838	(46%)
Henry McCullough (I)	2,390	(1%)
1996 Primary		
Jim Turner (D)	45,453	(59%)
Fred Hudson (D)	16,068	(21%)
Edgar J. "Bubba" Groce (D)	15,171	(20%)

CAMPAIGN FINANCE

	Receipts	Receipts from PACs	Expend-itures
1996			
Turner (D)	$933,922	$351,480 (38%)	$919,505
Babin (R)	$594,791	$77,848 (13%)	$595,410

DISTRICT VOTE FOR PRESIDENT

	1996		1992
D	90,543 (45%)	**D**	91,883 (43%)
R	89,933 (45%)	**R**	76,404 (35%)
I	19,184 (10%)	**I**	47,161 (22%)

KEY VOTES

1997
Ban "partial birth" abortions Y

3 Sam Johnson (R)

Of Plano — Elected 1991; 3rd full term

Biographical Information
Born: Oct. 11, 1930, San Antonio, Texas.
Education: Southern Methodist U., B.B.A. 1951; George Washington U., M.S.I.A. 1974.
Military Service: Air Force, 1951-79.
Occupation: Home builder.
Family: Wife, Shirley Melton; three children.
Religion: Methodist.
Political Career: Texas House, 1985-91.

Capitol Office: 1030 Longworth Bldg. 20515; 225-4201.

Committees
Education & Workforce
Early Childhood, Youth & Families
Ways & Means
Health; Social Security

In Washington: Born in 1930, Johnson is older than most of the new breed conservatives who dominate the House Republican Conference. But his voting record is just as conservative as that of his younger colleagues. And in the 104th Congress, GOP leaders put Johnson in a key position to promote the party agenda: on the Ways and Means Committee.

A one-time prisoner of war in Vietnam who entered the home-building business after his military career, Johnson faithfully enlists in conservative causes and occasionally leads the charge. At the start of the 105th, he was one of 26 Republicans who voted against sanctioning House Speaker Newt Gingrich for admitted ethics violations.

In early 1995, Johnson joined with some colleagues on the Republican right to form the Conservative Action Team (CAT); he was named a co-chairman of the group, which lobbied GOP leaders to hold the line on cutting taxes and balancing the budget. He helped circulate a petition threatening to oppose the fiscal 1996 budget resolution if House Republican leaders gave too much ground to Senate negotiators, whom the CAT saw as less committed to spending cuts and tax relief.

Later in the year, Johnson argued against temporarily raising the government's legal borrowing limit. He and other hard-liners hoped the prospect of federal default would force President Clinton to compromise on the budget.

One of the CAT's greatest frustrations was the 1996 decision by Republican leaders to give in to Democratic demands for a vote on increasing the minimum wage. Johnson could not get the Republican Conference to approve a statement of opposition to the increase. After the floor vote was scheduled, the annoyed CAT appealed to Gingrich to have one of their own included in leadership meetings.

From his seat on the Economic and Educational Opportunities Committee (renamed Education and the Workforce in the 105th), Johnson in the 104th tried to advance some of the conservatives' favorite proposals. He sought to eliminate federal involvement in the National Endowment for the Arts and the National Endowment for the Humanities, but the committee rejected that idea on an 11-31 vote in May 1995. A funding phaseout was approved, but that met with stiff resistance beyond the committee and the battle over taxpayer support for the endowments carried on into the 105th.

Johnson supported Republican attempts to scale back enforcement actions by the Environmental Protection Agency, and he also joined in the chorus of conservative criticism of the Endangered Species Act (ESA). In August 1995, he petitioned Interior Secretary Bruce Babbitt to remove three birds — the golden-cheeked warbler, red-cockaded woodpecker and black-capped vireo — from the list of animals protected under the ESA.

Although Republicans were in the minority during Johnson's first years in Congress, that did not discourage him from trying to push the House in a more conservative direction. In March 1994, he introduced an amendment to deny all federal funds to schools that prevent students from engaging in voluntary prayer. The House approved it as part of the $13 billion reauthorization of the Elementary and Secondary Education Act.

In March 1993, Johnson took to the floor to eliminate federal spending on Project Aries, a telephone counseling service for homosexual and bisexual men, which he called a waste of money. He led a successful effort to ax the rest of its $2 million funding.

In a 1992 book titled "Captive Warriors," Johnson described the serious injuries he sustained from beatings that he received as a POW, and his strong feelings about that chapter of his life surface from time to time, especially during foreign policy debates. In the 103rd Congress, he opposed Clinton's lifting of the U.S. trade embargo against Vietnam, imploring the president to visit the Vietnam Veterans' Memorial and reconsider his decision.

When Clinton moved to normalize relations

TEXAS 3
Northeast Dallas suburbs; Plano

Before a three-judge federal panel altered its boundaries in August 1996, the suburban Dallas 3rd was a bastion of affluence that evoked images of the television show "Dallas," which celebrated the lifestyle and material trappings of the city's oil barons and business elite.

Although the federal judges removed the wealthy north Dallas suburbs of Highland Park, which counts Ross Perot among its residents, and University Park, which envelops Southern Methodist University, the 3rd still is economically well-off, white and Republican.

Forty percent of the district's families have an annual household income over $50,000, and its per capita income is nearly $6,000 higher than that of Texas at large. In 1996, Bob Dole won the 3rd by 27 percentage points.

Almost two-thirds of the district population comes out of Dallas County; the balance is from Collin County (Plano). Redistricting in 1996 increased Johnson's share of Collin by adding a western section that had been in the 26th and a tentacle of the black-majority 30th District that had scooped up Plano's black neighborhoods. Still, blacks represent just 7 percent and Hispanics a mere 8 percent of the district population. Only five other Texas districts have a higher percentage of whites.

Collin has seen tremendous residential growth in recent years, due in part to the arrival in the area of a number of corporate headquarters, including those of the J.C. Penney Co. and Electronic Data Systems Corp., the computer firm that Perot founded and later sold to General Motors. Texas Instruments, Frito-Lay and DSC Communications Corp. also are headquartered in Plano. Executives for these companies help sustain a market for half-million dollar mansions in developments such as West Plano's Deerfield.

Richardson, in northern Collin, is one of the district's booming areas. The concentration of electronic and telecommunications firms along U.S. 75 north of the LBJ Freeway has earned this area the sobriquet "Telecom Corridor."

North of Richardson in the district's northern extreme is Frisco, which is undergoing a building and population boom.

Filled with young, upwardly mobile professionals, Collin is strongly Republican, even more so than the Dallas county sections of the district.

Conservative attitudes and old Texas traditions prevail. High school football games in Plano draw capacity crowds of 10,000 on Friday nights in the fall. Dole amassed 64 percent of the vote in the 3rd's portion of Collin.

Although downtown Dallas is not in the 3rd, its presence is felt in the district. The city's white-collar companies draw heavily from the 3rd for their work force. And Dallas' museums, orchestra and other cultural amenities rely on patronage from district residents.

Not all the 3rd is glitz and glamour. Communities such as Garland and Mesquite are middle-class suburbs. Garland, located northeast of the city, grew 37 percent from 1980 to 1994, and its population is approaching 200,000. Virtually all of Garland is in the 3rd. Just over 100,000 reside in Mesquite, which lies east of Dallas and is shared with the 5th District.

As of May 19, the Census Bureau had not recalculated population data, racial and ethnic breakdowns, and age statistics for districts newly drawn for the 1996 election.

with Vietnam in 1995, Johnson was again prominent in opposition. He charged that the Vietnamese never turned over all the information on prisoners of war and military personnel missing in action that they had promised.

"They have always lied to us, and they are still lying to us," he said. "I see normalization as an attempt on their part to get access to American markets. They are not to be trusted."

Johnson had more success fighting what he saw as a bow to political correctness at the Smithsonian Institution. Veterans complained that a proposed Smithsonian exhibit on the "Enola Gay," the plane that dropped the first atomic bomb on Japan, depicted Japan as a victim. Johnson was among 81 House members who called for the resignation of the director of the Smithsonian's Air and Space Museum.

Before the Smithsonian's board of regents met to discuss the controversy in early 1995, Johnson was appointed by Gingrich to the board. After the museum director resigned months later, Johnson said that was just the start of a number of management changes he hoped to see at the institution. The scaled-back exhibit that opened June 1995 focused on the mechanics of the airplane instead of the morality of its mission.

Johnson has also weighed in with some harsh assessments of Clinton's own lack of military experience. During the 1992 campaign, he called Clinton's post-college trip to Moscow and his avoidance of military service un-American. And during the 104th, Johnson suggested the president should be court-martialed for "unacceptable conduct" when Clinton's lawyer cited his client's position as commander in chief as grounds for postponement of a sexual harassment civil suit.

Before moving to Ways and Means, Johnson sat on the Science and Banking committees. In 1994, he won Banking approval of a plan to spend $77 million to tear down an abandoned West Dallas housing project. The measure was designed to supersede a 1988 law barring the use of federal money to demolish housing projects on prime real estate.

But two years later, Johnson was unable to convince the Clinton administration to appeal a federal court ruling that could force the Dallas County suburbs to accept more public housing. Johnson called the ruling "totally dictatorial."

At Home: Johnson's conservative record should keep him in good stead with his constituents in the 3rd, a district that anchors the right side of the state's ideological spectrum. Republican presidential nominee Bob Dole carried the 3rd handily in 1996, as had President George Bush in 1992.

Johnson fought a crowded field of Republicans in 1991 to win a special House election. Since then, he has won re-election with ease. Court-ordered redistricting in 1996 did not harm Johnson. He was able to spend much of his time raising money and stumping for other Texas Republicans.

But he did draw fire from Hispanics after saying at a Dallas campaign rally that Democrats who had trouble with English might not understand the special-election process that resulted from the redistricting ruling. Redrawn districts had all-party primaries in November, with runoffs in December if no one took a majority in the first-round voting.

In the nearby 24th District, Democratic Rep. Martin Frost used Johnson's comment in his campaign ads and benefited from a record turnout of Latino voters in part of Dallas County.

It is not unusual for members of Congress to have crossed paths somewhere before coming to the Capitol. But Johnson met the first of his future colleagues in a North Vietnamese prison camp, where a fellow prisoner was John McCain, later to become a Republican senator from Arizona.

Johnson's plane was shot down over North Vietnam in 1966, and he was held prisoner six years and 10 months, spending half that time in solitary confinement and losing partial use of his right arm.

Johnson retired from the Air Force in 1979 after serving nearly 30 years. His political debut came in 1984, when at age 54 he won a seat in the Texas House representing the GOP suburbs of Collin County. He fashioned a reputation as a law-and-order conservative, promoting criminal justice legislation that included expanding crime victims' rights.

He broadened his contacts in the Dallas area as co-chairman of Bush's North Texas presidential campaign in 1988 and as chairman of 3rd District Rep. Steve Bartlett's campaigns in 1988 and 1990.

Bartlett resigned in March 1991 to run for mayor of Dallas, and in the initial special election balloting to fill the House vacancy, Johnson ran second to Tom Pauken, a former head of ACTION in the Reagan administration who had twice lost close races in another House district.

In the special election runoff, Johnson overtook Pauken, buoyed by endorsements from several defeated primary candidates. He won election with 53 percent of the vote.

HOUSE ELECTIONS

1996 General		
Sam Johnson (R)	142,325	(73%)
Lee Cole (D)	47,654	(24%)
John Davis (L)	5,045	(3%)
1994 General		
Sam Johnson (R)	157,011	(91%)
Tom Donahue (LIBERT)	15,611	(9%)

Previous Winning Percentages: 1992 (86%) **1991**† (53%)

† Special election

CAMPAIGN FINANCE

	Receipts	Receipts from PACs	Expend-itures
1996			
Johnson (R)	$713,732	$320,051 (45%)	$625,107
Cole (D)	$7,347	0	$7,968
1994			
Johnson (R)	$473,192	$168,821 (36%)	$417,039

DISTRICT VOTE FOR PRESIDENT

	1996		1992
D	72,128 (32%)	**D**	53,279 (22%)
R	132,956 (59%)	**R**	110,736 (45%)
I	17,771 (8%)	**I**	80,147 (33%)

KEY VOTES

1997	
Ban "partial birth" abortions	Y
1996	
Approve farm bill	Y
Deny public education to illegal immigrants	Y
Repeal ban on certain assault-style weapons	Y
Increase minimum wage	N
Freeze defense spending	N
Approve welfare overhaul	Y
1995	
Approve balanced-budget constitutional amendment	Y
Relax Clean Water Act regulations	Y
Oppose limits on environmental regulations	N
Reduce projected Medicare spending	Y
Approve GOP budget with tax and spending cuts	Y

VOTING STUDIES

	Presidential Support		Party Unity		Conservative Coalition	
Year	**S**	**O**	**S**	**O**	**S**	**O**
1996	37	61	95	4	98	2
1995	17	81	98	2	97	3
1994	37	63	95	2	97	3
1993	27	73	94	2	98	2
1992	84	12	85	9	94	0
1991	84†	16†	86†	10†	93†	4†

INTEREST GROUP RATINGS

Year	ADA	AFL-CIO	CCUS	ACU
1996	5	n/a	94	100
1995	0	0	100	96
1994	0	11	83	100
1993	0	0	100	96
1992	10	25	88	100
1991	0†	0†	100†	100†

† Not eligible for all recorded votes.

4 Ralph M. Hall (D)

Of Rockwall — Elected 1980, 9th term

Biographical Information

Born: May 3, 1923, Fate, Texas.

Education: Texas Christian U., 1943; U. of Texas, 1946-47; Southern Methodist U., LL.B. 1951.

Military Service: Navy, 1942-45.

Occupation: Lawyer; businessman.

Family: Wife, Mary Ellen Murphy; three children.

Religion: Methodist.

Political Career: Rockwall County judge, 1951-63; Texas Senate, 1963-73; sought Democratic nomination for lieutenant governor, 1972.

Capitol Office: 2221 Rayburn Bldg. 20515; 225-6673.

Committees

Commerce
Energy & Power (ranking); Finance & Hazardous Materials; Health & Environment

Science
Energy & Environment; Space & Aeronautics

In Washington: For the first time in his career, Hall during the 104th Congress regularly voted with the House's majority party. This changed circumstance, however, marked no shift in Hall's conservative philosophy. The difference was that Republicans had gained control of the House, and Hall found much to like in their legislative agenda.

During the 104th, Hall had an unmatched record of voting against his party: He was the Democrat most likely to oppose the policies of President Clinton and the Democrat least likely to join a majority of his caucus in any vote against Republicans.

Unlike five other Southern House Democrats who switched parties in 1995, Hall declined to jump ship to the GOP. He had publicly hinted during his 1996 campaign that this term would be his last, but with the 105th he became ranking Democrat on the Commerce Subcommittee on Energy and Power, and he now says he intends to seek a 10th term in 1998, when he turns 75. The panel will have initial jurisdiction over sweeping legislation to deregulate electric utilities, and Hall is keen on seeking the best possible deal for the Lone Star State's oil and gas industries.

Hall has stated that he would "rather be respected back home than liked in Washington"; certainly, his indifference to the whipping efforts of his party have caused fits. Prior to the start of the 105th, he threatened to withhold his support from Richard A. Gephardt of Missouri as the Democratic choice for Speaker if the party's conservatives were not listened to. In the end, Hall supported Gephardt, but the episode called to mind Hall's apostasy in an earlier leadership election — in 1985, when he voted "present" rather than support Thomas P. O'Neill Jr. of Massachusetts for Speaker.

Hall's Texas district was represented for nearly half a century by Speaker Sam Rayburn, but nowadays the national Democratic Party has big image problems in this part of the country. That helps explain why Hall so reliably sides with the GOP, even when hardly any other Democrat does so. In the 104th, Hall was: one of only two House Democrats who opposed a boost in the minimum wage; one of only four Democrats to support the Republican Medicare overhaul; one of just nine who voted for the GOP's initial welfare package; and one of only four Democrats to support the Republican plan to cut taxes and balance the budget in 1995. He was even granted a GOP slot on the latter bill's conference committee.

His perfect record of support for the House GOP's "Contract With America" in 1995 was matched among Democrats only by W.J. "Billy" Tauzin of Louisiana, who subsequently switched to the GOP.

As former chairman and ranking member of the Science Subcommittee on Space, Hall's chief legislative priorities were protecting the space station from budget-cutters who wanted to kill it and promoting medical and other kinds of research in space. Pointing to cost overruns and raising questions about the space station's scientific value, "deficit hawks" made a run at the station in 1991 and nearly killed it in 1992. In 1993, Clinton directed NASA to pursue a simpler, less costly design for the project. Dubious about the new administration's commitment to the project, Hall worked to preserve as much as he could of the station as initially conceived, while keeping the Johnson Space Center in Houston as its focal point.

A move to kill the space station, sponsored by Indiana Democrat Tim Roemer, has become a perennial on Capitol Hill. During the 1995 edition of the fight, Hall said of Roemer on the House floor: "We just think he is still wrong and probably will be wrong in the next Congress and in the Congress after that and the one after that. Because he is a fine young man, he will be reelected and he will be here when I am in the corner room of the Rockwall nursing home, but I will still be calling out to save the space station for us old folks." Hall nevertheless disapproved of a bill during the 104th that would have offered a multiyear authorization for the space station, and thus

TEXAS 4
Northeast — Sherman; part of Tyler

Although the core of Sam Rayburn's home district remains intact, the 4th of the 1990s is dramatically different in its economic and political makeup.

For 48 years, Rayburn represented a compact square in northeastern Texas; from 1934 until his death in 1961 the lines were not touched. During his congressional tenure, the 4th was a sparsely populated, agricultural district. The region missed out on the insurance fortunes of Dallas and the oil wealth of West Texas and the Gulf Coast. With no large industry, the people relied on the land. The rich, dark soil, known as blacklands, is conducive to cotton, hay, oats and sorghum. (At one time, Greenville had the largest inland cotton compressor in the nation.)

Since then, state mapmakers have expanded the boundaries, the land has been "cottoned out" and the urban sprawl of Dallas has reached the 4th. Most of the small family farms have been replaced by large corporate entities.

From Rockwall, the glittering Dallas skyline is easily visible. Residents throughout Rockwall County commute to Dallas, many working at banks, insurance firms or telecommunications companies; AT&T is a major employer. Population in Collin and Rockwall counties doubled in the 1970s, and doubled nearly again in Rockwall in the 1980s.

The E-Systems plant in Greenville (shared with the neighboring 1st District) is another example of the changes evident in the 4th. The company, which develops and modifies aircraft, receives contracts from the U.S. military, foreign countries and private companies.

At the eastern end of the 4th, where cotton once flourished, oil boomed in the 1970s and early 1980s. When the industry crashed in 1984, the region was hurt. There remains a good deal of oil in the ground, particularly in Longview (Gregg County) and Tyler (Smith County), but little pumping is taking place. Tyler's economy is bolstered by its abundant rose industry. The self-proclaimed "Rose Capital of the World" is responsible for a large share of the world's roses.

Agriculture has not disappeared entirely from the 4th. The substantial peanut crop in Cooke, Grayson and Hunt counties helped draw the North Carolina-based Lance cracker company to Greenville.

The 4th has become more conservative in recent decades. In 1996, Bob Dole beat Bill Clinton in the 4th by 56 percent to 35 percent. (Ross Perot, who had supplanted Clinton for second place in 1992, fell to just 9 percent.) And the GOP down-ballot candidates have been making gains in the 4th as well. In the 1980s, most local officials in Rockwall County were Democrats. Now Republicans are in the majority. But this GOP trend has not yet hurt Hall, who was re-elected with 64 percent of the vote in 1996.

1990 Population: 566,217. White 500,239 (88%), Black 47,413 (8%), Other 18,565 (3%). Hispanic origin 24,592 (4%). 18 and over 413,296 (73%), 62 and over 92,359 (16%). Median age: 34.

a respite from the annual battle; despite his loyalties, Hall did not feel the program should be taken off the table in an era of budget-cutting.

Hall is the fourth-ranking Democrat on the Commerce Committee, where he is a favorite of ranking minority member John D. Dingell of Michigan, even if the two do not always see eye to eye. Hall's folksy humor and encyclopedic supply of rural Texas stories can defuse tension, and his political acumen gives him influence when he decides to weigh in.

During the intense deliberations over the 1990 Clean Air Act, Hall and Texas Republican Jack Fields at one stage weakened proposed mandates for auto companies to build vehicles that run on alternative fuels. Their amendment increased the percentage of gasoline that could be included in a "clean fuel" mix of gasoline and methanol, and it put reformulated gasoline on the list of "clean alternative fuels." It also stripped a proposed requirement that automakers sell 1 million clean-fuel vehicles a year by 1997.

Hall and other supporters said the amendment would create a level playing field for alternative fuels other than methanol, but critics saw it as a major victory for the auto and oil industries.

In 1995, The Dallas Morning News reported that Hall intervened to save 21 investors in a Rockwall apartment complex nearly $3 million in personal liabilities to the Federal Deposit Insurance Corp. The paper found that Hall himself had lost money in other deals as a banker and real estate investor and had reached settlements with bank regulators at an occasional loss to taxpayers.

At Home: An early starter in politics, Hall was elected judge in his home county while still in law school. After 12 years, he moved up to the state Senate and spent a decade there, rising to become president pro tem.

In 1972, Hall entered statewide politics, running for lieutenant governor on a conservative platform. But he finished fourth in the Democratic primary, retired from politics and concentrated on business.

When 4th District Democrat Ray Roberts announced his retirement in 1980, Hall re-entered politics. Because of Ronald Reagan's popularity among the 4th's voters, Hall's contest with Republican John H. Wright was closer than expected. Reagan's showing helped Wright poll 48 percent. But Republicans have not mounted a comparable challenge since.

In 1992, Hall had his first primary fight since winning his seat in 1980. But redistricting preserved the most conservative parts of the 4th for Hall and eliminated liberal-leaning areas that might have been more inclined to support his opponent, Roger Sanders. Hall won renomination with two-thirds of the vote, and in November he beat GOP challenger David L. Bridges by 20 points.

HOUSE ELECTIONS

1996 General		
Ralph M. Hall (D)	132,126	(64%)
Jerry Ray Hall (R)	71,065	(34%)
Steven Rothacker (LIBERT)	3,172	(2%)
1994 General		
Ralph M. Hall (D)	99,303	(59%)
David L. Bridges (R)	67,267	(40%)
Steven Rothacker (LIBERT)	2,377	(1%)

Previous Winning Percentages: 1992 (58%) **1990** (100%) **1988** (66%) **1986** (72%) **1984** (58%) **1982** (74%) **1980** (52%)

CAMPAIGN FINANCE

	Receipts	Receipts from PACs	Expend-itures
1996			
Hall (D)	$519,893	$383,912 (74%)	$527,260
Hall (R)	$37,667	$2,250 (6%)	$30,156
1994			
Hall (D)	$525,676	$373,579 (71%)	$559,157
Bridges (R)	$46,038	$560 (1%)	$46,375

DISTRICT VOTE FOR PRESIDENT

	1996		1992
D	73,934 (35%)	**D**	65,502 (28%)
R	117,915 (56%)	**R**	95,035 (41%)
I	18,733 (9%)	**I**	69,562 (30%)

KEY VOTES

1997	
Ban "partial birth" abortions	Y
1996	
Approve farm bill	Y
Deny public education to illegal immigrants	Y
Repeal ban on certain assault-style weapons	Y
Increase minimum wage	N
Freeze defense spending	Y
Approve welfare overhaul	Y
1995	
Approve balanced-budget constitutional amendment	Y
Relax Clean Water Act regulations	Y
Oppose limits on environmental regulations	N
Reduce projected Medicare spending	Y
Approve GOP budget with tax and spending cuts	Y

VOTING STUDIES

	Presidential Support		Party Unity		Conservative Coalition	
Year	**S**	**O**	**S**	**O**	**S**	**O**
1996	44	56	29	71	92	8
1995	29	71	22	78	97	3
1994	54	46	36	62	97	3
1993	54	46	54	46	86	14
1992	63	37	49	50	92	8
1991	66	32	46	51	95	3

INTEREST GROUP RATINGS

Year	ADA	AFL-CIO	CCUS	ACU
1996	15	n/a	94	90
1995	10	17	100	76
1994	10	44	92	95
1993	20	33	73	79
1992	40	50	63	76
1991	5	17	80	90

5 Pete Sessions (R)

Of Dallas — Elected 1996, 1st term

Biographical Information

Born: March 22, 1955, Waco, Texas.
Education: Southwestern U., B.S. 1978.
Occupation: Public policy analyst; phone company executive.
Family: Wife, Juanita Diaz; two children.
Religion: United Methodist.
Political Career: Sought Republican nomination for U.S. House, 1991; Republican nominee for U.S. House, 1994.
Capitol Office: 1318 Longworth Bldg. 20515; 225-2231.

Committees

Banking & Financial Services
Capital Markets, Securities & Government Sponsored Enterprises; Housing & Community Opportunity
Government Reform & Oversight
Civil Service; Government Management, Information & Technology; Postal Service
Science
Basic Research

The Path to Washington: It took three tries, but Sessions succeeded in 1996 in capturing the open Dallas-based 5th District from the Democratic Party. Sessions' first effort came in 1991, when he entered the special House election contest to succeed 3rd District Rep. Steve Bartlett, who resigned to run for mayor of Dallas. Sessions finished sixth.

Sessions retired from the private sector — he was employed for 16 years at Southwestern Bell Telephone Co. and Bell Communications Research — in 1993 to prepare his challenge to veteran Democratic Rep. John Bryant. In what was the state's closest congressional race in 1994, Sessions held Bryant to 50 percent.

After his defeat, Sessions served as Vice President for Public Policy at the National Center for Policy Analysis, a Dallas-based conservative public policy organization. He finally won after Bryant gave up his seat for an unsuccessful bid for his party's Senate nomination.

A supporter of the House GOP's 1994 campaign manifesto, the "Contract With America," Sessions takes a conservative view on most issues. He believes government has created more problems than solutions.

Sessions' top priority is balancing the budget. As testimony of his commitment to this goal, Sessions signed a pledge during the campaign promising to donate his paycheck to the federal treasury in any year Congress fails to approve a budget with the goal of achieving balance by 2002. He also planned to introduce legislation requiring the same promise of his colleagues. He says the pledge will "come into play with every vote I make."

This son of former FBI Director William S. Sessions says there is plenty of waste, fraud and abuse in government. One of the first places Congress should look to excise some of that waste is the Department of Health and Human Services, he says. He also favors cutting one or more Cabinet departments. Topping his target list is Commerce, and he would also consider eliminating the Education Department.

Sessions takes a strict line on tax issues, vowing to oppose any tax increase. He says cutting taxes is the best way to stimulate economic growth. He advocates a cut in the capital gains tax, a $500-per-child tax credit and an increase in the estate tax exemption to $1.2 million. Sessions has also expressed support for allowing taxpayers to invest future Social Security contributions into their own privately run retirement plans.

The Texan had hoped to land a spot on the Commerce Committee; instead, he got his second choice, the Banking and Financial Services Committee, which interested him because Dallas is home to many private financial institutions and a Federal Reserve Bank. He also drew seats on the Science Committee and on Government Reform and Oversight.

With Bryant's departure from the House and the district's increasingly Republican tilt in the 1990s, Sessions looked to have a good chance in 1996 to end his losing streak in House elections.

He characterized his Democratic opponent, lawyer and former Dallas County Democratic party chairman John Pouland, as a supporter of failed Democratic policies favoring new federal programs and higher spending and taxation. Sessions also claimed that Pouland favored closing all U.S. military bases in Europe and Japan, a plan Sessions said would threaten U.S. troops on missions in countries such as Bosnia-Herzegovina. Pouland said Sessions had misrepresented his view on that issue, and he tried to tar the Republican by linking him to House Speaker Newt Gingrich. But Sessions welcomed Gingrich's help.

Sessions ran as an abortion opponent, but Pouland claimed the Republican had flip-flopped on the issue since his 1991 campaign — a charge Sessions denied. Pouland produced a letter from Sessions' 1991 campaign in which he was identified as "pro-choice." Pouland claimed Sessions' changed stance on the issue revealed him as a political opportunist. Sessions held on to score a six-point victory, taking 53 percent of the vote.

TEXAS 5
East Central – Part of Dallas; eastern and southern suburbs

When Wal-Mart came to the Robertson County town of Hearne in 1980, local merchants were dismayed. Virtually every clothier, appliance store and mom-and-pop shop soon shut down. Ten years later, Wal-Mart closed its store, citing unprofitability. The 5,100 people of Hearne were even more upset by its departure.

The tale of Hearne and the Wal-Mart that came and went is a familiar story in the rural and small-town areas in the 5th, a district that stretches from Dallas County 200 miles south.

As the economies of these counties sputtered, some towns' futures seem to lie in one word: prisons. The prison system is the largest employer in Anderson County, the site of three large units of the Texas Department of Corrections.

About 55 percent of the district's residents live in Dallas County. Downtown Dallas was removed from the 5th in 1992 redistricting, but some suburban neighborhoods to the east and northwest of the city remain in the 5th. In the 1996 round of redistricting, the district picked up some reliably Republican territory in the Lake Highlands, Lakewood and White Rock Lake neighborhoods northeast of downtown; this territory had been in the 3rd District.

Oaklawn is a fashionable section where young professionals and a sizable gay community reside. East Dallas is a mix of upscale professionals, longtime residents, pockets of middle-class neighborhoods revived by gentrification, and Hispanic and blue-collar workers. The Swiss Avenue Historic District boasts 200 Georgian, Spanish and Prairie style houses built at the turn of the century.

Just outside the city are several towns that have grown popular because of their proximity to Dallas. Factory workers and office clerks live in some of the more modest communities, such as Seagoville and Balch Springs. Mesquite, once predominantly farmland, is now a collection of spacious, single-family homes. The city hosts the world-renowned Mesquite Rodeo from April through September. It was here that Joe Kool, reputedly one of the toughest bulls in the world to ride, appeared regularly for a decade.

People in the more rural, poorer Robertson County on the southwestern edge of the 5th raise cattle and poultry.

The 5th's eastern appendage extends to Tyler (Smith County); this portion of the district is heavily Democratic, due in large part to Tyler's large black population.

The old 5th featured the state's closest congressional race in 1994; while remapping made the district more amenable to the GOP, the 1996 election results indicate the 5th will be fiercely contested: just four other districts in Texas featured closer congressional races, and only two others involved a closer presidential race.

Dallas and Henderson taken together cast about two-thirds of the vote in the 5th, and Bob Dole won both in 1996 by less than 3 percentage points. The Democrats' best showings come in Smith and in the rural counties of Limestone and Robertson, which Bill Clinton and Sessions' Democratic opponent won.

As of May 19, the Census Bureau had not recalculated population data, racial and ethnic breakdowns, and age statistics for districts newly drawn for the 1996 election.

HOUSE ELECTIONS

1996 General		
Pete Sessions (R)	80,196	(53%)
John Pouland (D)	70,992	(47%)

CAMPAIGN FINANCE

1996	Receipts	Receipts from PACs	Expend-itures
Sessions (R)	$1,156,064	$316,897 (27%)	$1,091,122
Pouland (D)	$602,885	$187,699 (31%)	$602,884

DISTRICT VOTE FOR PRESIDENT

	1996			1992	
D	79,050	(46%)	D	72,325	(37%)
R	77,250	(45%)	R	72,673	(37%)
I	13,384	(8%)	I	49,743	(26%)

KEY VOTES

1997

Ban "partial birth" abortions	Y

6 Joe L. Barton (R)

Of Ennis — Elected 1984, 7th term

Biographical Information
Born: Sept. 15, 1949, Waco, Texas.
Education: Texas A&M U., B.S. 1972; Purdue U., M.S. 1973.
Occupation: Engineering consultant.
Family: Wife, Janet Sue Winslow; three children.
Religion: Methodist.
Political Career: Sought Republican nomination for U.S. Senate, 1993.
Capitol Office: 2264 Rayburn Bldg. 20515; 225-2002.

Committees
Commerce
Health & Environment; Oversight & Investigations (chairman); Telecommunications, Trade & Consumer Protection
Science
Basic Research; Space & Aeronautics

In Washington: Like the pioneers of old, Barton is staking out the frontier — in his case, the frontier of fiscal conservatism. He is concerned that the House leadership is not sufficiently bold in its commitment to limiting taxes and spending. So he has sponsored a version of the balanced-budget constitutional amendment that would make it very difficult for Congress to raise taxes. And he is one of the Republicans most likely to break ranks when the party rallies around a spending plan, for fear it will cost too much.

Barton, chairman of a Commerce subcommittee, wants the Constitution to require a three-fifths "supermajority" to raise taxes. He votes regularly with the GOP on social policy matters and particularly supports deregulation. Yet his vote cannot be taken for granted.

Barton was one of only 15 Republicans who voted against a stopgap spending bill early in 1996 that ended the government's partial shutdown; he said the GOP was folding its hand in budget negotiations with President Clinton. He was one of just 19 Republicans who opposed the party's fiscal 1997 budget package, because he found it too expensive. And he voted, along with 14 other Republicans, against the rule that brought welfare overhaul to the House floor in 1995, for fear the plan's provisions to reduce out-of-wedlock births could prompt more poor women to seek abortions. (Barton did, however, end up supporting the welfare bill itself.)

He even opposed the fiscal 1997 omnibus spending bill at the end of the 104th Congress — despite his success in securing, by a vote of 239-116, $3 million in federal funds that Taxpayers for Common Sense derided as "pork for George Bush." The money helped establish a fellowship program at Texas A&M University, Barton's alma mater, to honor the former president.

Barton's steadfast support of home-state projects such as this, as well as the now-defunct superconducting super collider and NASA's space station, leaves him open to charges of inconsistency when he argues for passage of the balanced-budget amendment. In one House debate over funding for the collider, a Democrat observed that Barton "is obviously a contortionist, being on two sides of fiscal policy at the same time."

Barton is the lead sponsor of a version of the balanced-budget constitutional amendment that would require a three-fifths supermajority vote by Congress to raise taxes, a provision popular with the most conservative Republicans but lacking sufficient support among Democrats to win the two-thirds vote necessary for passage.

In 1995 and again in 1997, Barton threatened to withhold support for a more moderate amendment that did not include the tax limitation provision. His version failed, 253-173, in 1995 — 31 votes shy of passage. Top GOP leaders lobbied hard to get Barton and Class of 1994 freshmen to support their more moderate plan, which passed the House but died in the Senate.

In consideration for his having gone along with the leadership plan, Barton was granted a floor vote on April 15, 1996, for an amendment based solely on the tax limit (it did not require a balanced budget). It fell 37 votes short of a two-thirds majority, but Barton vowed to bring it back every April 15 (the date by which Americans must file their tax returns) "like the movie villain Freddy in 'Friday the 13th.' "

Barton cosponsored an alternative to yet another constitutional amendment, the effort to limit congressional terms. Teaming with John D. Dingell of Michigan, the ranking Democrat on the Commerce Committee, Barton proposed to apply term limits retroactively. In February 1997 the plan was rejected, 152-274.

When Republicans gained control of the House, Barton won the chairmanship of the Commerce Oversight and Investigations Subcommittee. Dingell had headed the oversight panel while he was chairman of the old Energy and Commerce Committee, watching over huge swaths of the executive branch where his committee held jurisdiction. Barton's subcommittee has at least a share of the responsibility for overseeing more than half the executive branch, but his record during the

TEXAS 6
Suburban Dallas — Part of Fort Worth; part of Arlington

When the 6th was redrawn in the mid-1960s to suit the needs of Democratic Rep. Olin E. "Tiger" Teague, cries went out that the district, which meandered from Dallas to the Houston area, was the most gerrymandered in Texas. In the 1992 redistricting, the 6th's shape became even less logical. Compressed from 14 counties into five, the 6th is now in two separate pieces connected only by Eagle Mountain Lake, in northwestern Tarrant County.

Remapping in 1996 preserved the district's serpentine shape. The bulk of the 6th's population resides in Tarrant, roughly encircling Fort Worth and including part of it. Removed from the 6th were some largely affluent northeastern Tarrant County suburbs such as Southlake and some of northwestern Dallas County. Added to the district were some parts of southeastern Tarrant that were in the 24th District.

While the district's boundary lines are contorted, its residents have much in common. The 6th is a generally white, financially secure, suburban Republican area.

About 85 percent of the 6th's population lives in Tarrant. Nearly 60 percent of Arlington's residents are in the 6th, as are about one-quarter of Fort Worth's residents. Arlington is the district's biggest population center; about 156,000 city residents are in the 6th.

The Fort Worth area has experienced several economic evolutions. Initially the city's commerce was centered around oil and cattle. (The old "Cowtown" nickname still sticks.) Then the emphasis shifted to military work. Huge defense contractors such as Lockheed Martin and Bell Helicopter Textron, maker of the V-22 Osprey tilt-rotor aircraft, became major employers. The Naval Air Station Fort Worth Joint Reserves, a consolidated and newly named facility on the site of the old Carswell Air Force Base, is still an important employer. Although Fort Worth was hurt in the 1980s by the fall of the banks and oil prices and in the 1990s by defense cutbacks, its economy has diversified and expanded.

With its mild climate, affordable housing and the nation's second-busiest airport (Dallas-Fort Worth), the "Metroplex" (as local boosters dub the area) began attracting a variety of corporate headquarters in the 1980s. Today, the 6th has numerous white-collar employees from companies such as IBM, American Airlines, Exxon, Burlington Northern Railroad and GTE. Alliance Airport, a private cargo-shipping business formed by Ross Perot Jr., is in northeast Tarrant.

Until the 1980s, Arlington was a blue-collar, low-income community centered around a General Motors plant. GM remains a major employer, but abetted by the city's location between Dallas and Fort Worth, Arlington has emerged as an entertainment hub, with amusement parks, hotels and the Texas Rangers baseball team. (The Rangers' stadium is just across the district line, in the 24th.)

Republicans almost invariably find the 6th favorable political terrain. Bob Dole finished a sliver below 60 percent here in 1996, and Barton has topped 70 percent in his last three elections.

As of May 19, the Census Bureau had not recalculated population data, racial and ethnic breakdowns, and age statistics for districts newly drawn for the 1996 election.

104th was far more circumscribed than Dingell's.

Barton, who appreciates the needs of Texas' oil and gas industry, hosted nine hearings on the Clean Air Act during the 104th. He also was a member of Commerce's "FDA Reform Team" and favored streamlining the Food and Drug Administration's rules for approving drugs and medical devices. Against the wishes of the pharmaceutical and biotechnology industries, Barton favors elimination of the so-called efficacy standard, which requires proof that drugs and medical devices are both safe and effective.

During consideration of a bill to require risk analysis in the formulation of new federal regulations, Barton offered an amendment to allow businesses and individuals to petition federal agencies to review and possibly revoke existing regulations. For fear that the language would make those agencies too susceptible to lawsuits, the House rejected Barton's proposal, 206-220.

But none of his legislative efforts on the subcommittee won him as much attention as his questioning of Hazel R. O'Leary, Clinton's first Energy secretary. Barton accused O'Leary of "jet setting" and, indeed, many members of Congress found her foreign travel expenses excessive. But Barton drew groans during a hearing when O'Leary acknowledged feeling hounded. "Word on the street is that some in Congress wanted to take me out by Christmas ... that they wanted to destroy me," she said.

Barton replied, "I think there are numerous male members that are unmarried that would be delighted to take you out before Christmas."

Although Barton has often differed with GOP leaders over spending matters, he was a loyal soldier during the ethics war that raged around House Speaker Newt Gingrich, R-Ga., as the 105th got under way. Gingrich admitted misleading the House ethics committee about GOPAC, his political action committee, and its involvement in a supposedly non-partisan and tax-exempt college course. Gingrich agreed to a $300,000 penalty and refused Barton's offer to sponsor a move to lessen the sanction of reprimand recommended by the ethics committee. Barton chaired the Texas GOPAC from 1986 to 1992, and in 1997 he was one of 26 Republicans voting against the reprimand.

At Home: Twice during the 103rd Congress Barton tried to expand his political horizons, and both times he was thwarted. First Barton sought a promotion to the Senate, running in the April 1993 special election to pick a successor to Democrat Lloyd Bentsen. Next he tried for the chairmanship of the Texas Republican Party.

Barton based his Senate campaign on a platform designed to highlight himself as the chief proprietor of "family values" among the candidates. He emphasized that he married his high school sweetheart, attended church regularly, opposed abortion and had written no overdrafts at the House bank. Barton closed one debate by noting that while other candidates in the race had more money, "none have more personal values."

He got about 14 percent in the all-party first-round voting, good for third place in the 24-person field, but well short of the top finishers, Democrat Bob Krueger (who was appointed to fill Bentsen's seat) and Republican Kay Bailey Hutchison, the eventual winner. Barton then lost a bid in June 1994 to chair the Texas state party. He was considered too much an "insider" because of his long tenure in Washington.

The failed Senate race did not hurt him in the 6th — he won in 1994 with 76 percent. In 1996, after court-mandated redistricting invalidated primary results in his district, Barton's Democratic foe neglected to list her party identification after refiling and appeared on the ballot as an independent. Barton got a best-ever 77 percent.

An engineering consultant for Atlantic Richfield Co., Barton had never run for office before he sought the 6th in 1984. A recount of the GOP primary votes made Barton the nominee, pitting him against Democrat Dan Kubiak, a former state representative and rancher with a folksy Texas twang and easygoing style.

Barton made shrewd use of his ties to his alma mater, Texas A&M. That base of support, with the the solid GOP vote in the suburbs of Houston and Fort Worth, were too much for Kubiak.

Area Democrats were not prepared to concede the 6th, however. They mounted an aggressive challenge to Barton in 1986 behind Fort Worth lawyer Pete Geren. Geren, who subsequently was elected to fill the vacancy in the 12th created by House Speaker Jim Wright's 1989 resignation, had an ample personal fortune, the enthusiastic support of party leaders and close ties to Bentsen, having spent two years as director of his Texas offices. Geren claimed Barton had taken conservatism to extremes, placing ideology over the needs of his constituency.

Barton pointed to meetings he convened to coach local entrepreneurs on how to secure federal contracts, and he claimed credit for helping free offshore oil and gas royalties that had been entangled in bureaucracy. Geren performed well for a first-time candidate but could not overcome Barton's support in the GOP-minded urban and suburban neighborhoods of Tarrant and Montgomery counties. Barton took 56 percent.

HOUSE ELECTIONS

1996 General		
Joe L. Barton (R)	160,800	(77%)
Janet Carroll "Skeet" Richardson (I)	26,713	(13%)
Catherine A. Anderson (L)	14,456	(7%)
Doug Williams (USTAX)	6,547	(3%)
1994 General		
Joe L. Barton (R)	152,038	(76%)
Terry Jesmore (D)	44,286	(22%)
Bill Baird (LIBERT)	4,688	(2%)

Previous Winning Percentages: **1992** (72%) **1990** (66%) **1988** (68%) **1986** (56%) **1984** (57%)

CAMPAIGN FINANCE

	Receipts	Receipts from PACs	Expend-itures
1996			
Barton (R)	$1,320,456	$634,813 (48%)	$890,468
Richardson (D)	$141,029	$39,000 (28%)	$123,291
1994			
Barton (R)	$696,601	$356,335 (51%)	$574,897
Jesmore (D)	$33,495	$10,750 (32%)	$33,383

DISTRICT VOTE FOR PRESIDENT

	1996		1992
D	79,877 (33%)	**D**	66,099 (24%)
R	146,231 (60%)	**R**	123,562 (46%)
I	17,624 (7%)	**I**	81,296 (30%)

KEY VOTES

1997	
Ban "partial birth" abortions	Y
1996	
Approve farm bill	Y
Deny public education to illegal immigrants	N
Repeal ban on certain assault-style weapons	Y
Increase minimum wage	N
Freeze defense spending	N
Approve welfare overhaul	Y
1995	
Approve balanced-budget constitutional amendment	Y
Relax Clean Water Act regulations	Y
Oppose limits on environmental regulations	N
Reduce projected Medicare spending	Y
Approve GOP budget with tax and spending cuts	Y

VOTING STUDIES

	Presidential Support		Party Unity		Conservative Coalition	
Year	**S**	**O**	**S**	**O**	**S**	**O**
1996	35	61	91	6	94	6
1995	20	78	91	4	87	5
1994	33	55	89	5	92	3
1993	31	59	80	5	95	5
1992	77	13	84	5	85	4
1991	70	23	81	13	89	5

INTEREST GROUP RATINGS

Year	ADA	AFL-CIO	CCUS	ACU
1996	15	n/a	88	89
1995	0	0	96	80
1994	0	13	90	100
1993	0	0	100	100
1992	5	27	75	100
1991	10	8	90	90

7 Bill Archer (R)

Of Houston — Elected 1970, 14th term

Biographical Information
Born: March 22, 1928, Houston, Texas.
Education: Rice U., 1945-46; U. of Texas, B.B.A. 1949, LL.B. 1951.
Military Service: Air Force, 1951-53.
Occupation: Lawyer; feed company executive.
Family: Wife, Sharon Sawyer; five children, two stepchildren.
Religion: Roman Catholic.
Political Career: Hunters Creek Village Council, 1955-62; Texas House, 1967-71.

Capitol Office: 1236 Longworth Bldg. 20515; 225-2571.

Committees
Ways & Means (chairman)
Joint Taxation (chairman)

In Washington: Archer played a secondary role for most of the 104th Congress, seeing vital pieces of legislation through the Ways and Means Committee but generally shaping them at the behest of the House GOP leadership. Most of those plans went nowhere, though, and Archer in the 105th is trying to reassert his institutional prerogatives as chairman and taking a more aggressive role in shaping tax policy.

Archer's committee will take the lead House role in putting the flesh on tax cuts outlined in the 1997 budget deal negotiated between the White House and congressional budget leaders. Archer indicated early he would resist marching orders, taking a vocal and unbending public stand on his right to write the tax bill. "If they become specific as to the items that have to be included or not included, they could jeopardize the entire budget," he warned in May 1997.

He was the first Republican lawmaker to meet privately with President Clinton after the 1996 election, and subsequently he wrote a column for The Washington Post titled "Let's Make a Deal, Mr. President." Archer was the first Republican to murmur approval when Clinton talked in early 1997 of reducing Medicare spending growth, and generally he has sought to portray himself as someone who learned the lessons of the budget wars of the 104th and will seek pragmatic compromise in order to shepherd bills all the way into law. "I think everybody learned out of the last Congress that you can only get something done when both the White House and the majority of Congress can come together," he said.

But questions remain as to whether Archer is the man best suited for the role of forging bipartisan consensus. Almost in the same breath with which he announced that Republicans would be satisfied with "moving the ball down the field . . . and not a Hail Mary touchdown" — indicating a willingness to accept Clinton's Medicare numbers rather than fighting for a bigger reduction close to what the GOP offered in 1996 — Archer then laid down markers for the White House on tax cuts that could make it very challenging for the two sides to strike a deal.

In the 22 years that Archer served on Ways and Means in the Republican minority, he almost never worked with Democrats. After assuming the ranking slot in mid-1988 with the death of John J. Duncan of Tennessee, Archer had no partnership with Democratic Chairman Dan Rostenkowski, largely because he was not inclined to engage in the one-on-one dealmaking that enabled other Republican committee members to do business. That meant that he was rarely a significant player on legislation, with the exception of trade bills.

He seems to have carried into his new position that view of the minority party's role. Although he says he would like the committee to operate with bipartisan consensus, as it did under the chairmanship of Arkansas Democrat Wilbur Mills, he has so far done little to create that atmosphere. He has for the most part stayed above the fray when committee members engaged in name-calling and debate so heated it led to physical confrontations. When Charles B. Rangel of New York, who is now the panel's ranking Democrat, charged that Archer was a racist for ending a tax break that helped minority broadcasters, Archer displayed a near-Victorian sense of propriety by protesting the remarks in a formal letter.

Archer's dearest and most radical goal is to transform the tax system from one based on what people earn to one based on what they spend. "I would like to pull out the income tax code by its roots and throw it away so that it can never grow back," he declared in 1995. But in his first two years at the helm of Ways and Means, he marshalled scant support for a consumption tax, and his attempts to educate lawmakers and the public through comprehensive hearings became little more than a drone of tax experts in a near-empty hearing room.

Archer recognizes that it will take some years to forge a consensus on tax overhaul, and he is nothing if not a patient man. When he came to Congress in 1971, he was notably more conserva-

TEXAS 7
Western Houston; northwestern suburbs

Houston's urban sprawl takes up only a portion of the 7th geographically, but it dominates the district in most other respects. The 7th is a collection of white, affluent, reliably Republican neighborhoods. The map drawn in August 1996 for that year's election cycle shuffled some precincts along the district's eastern boundary, but it remains diehard Republican. Bob Dole captured 66 percent of the district's presidential vote in 1996, while Archer garnered 81 percent in the House race.

About half the district's residents live within the city limits, and many work downtown. All of the 7th — and parts of six other districts — are in Harris County, a region that covers 34 incorporated areas and has 2.8 million people. With a population that is 6 percent black and 16 percent Hispanic, the 7th is somewhat less racially integrated than the city as a whole.

Although none of downtown Houston is included in the 7th, there is plenty of commercial enterprise in the district. Thousands of oil and gas company executives, bankers, real estate brokers, developers, insurance executives and retail employees live in the western and northwestern parts of the city. A major employer is Compaq Computer Corp., which is headquartered in the 7th. Founded in 1982 by three former Texas Instruments workers, Compaq felt the squeeze of competition in 1991 and responded with a restructuring and about 2,000 layoffs. The belt-tightening and several new products helped the company rebound and become the world's leading PC maker. Continental Airlines also is a major source of jobs for district residents.

Office parks and small factories sprouted up along Route 290 in the 1970s when land was particularly affordable. Toshiba opened a turbine engine plant in the area and remains a major employer.

The River Oaks, Memorial and Tanglewood neighborhoods are home to some of Houston's wealthiest families. Former President George Bush, who represented much of the present 7th as a congressman in the 1960s, lives in the Tanglewood area.

Houstonians also boast of their ballet, symphony, opera company, museums and theaters. Many of the area's arts patrons live in the imitation Tudor mansions, imitation French chateaux and imitation Spanish villas of River Oaks.

Memorial includes a number of small, self-incorporated villages near Interstate 10 that have their own mayors and some discrete municipal services. Residents of Hedwig, Bunker Hill and Piney Point moved into the villages decades ago and never left, prompting the phrase "the graying of Memorial."

Growth is not confined to the district's eastern region. Katy, on Harris County's western end nearly thirty miles from downtown, is also undergoing a building and population boom.

The 7th is a religious and politically active area. The 20,000-member Second Baptist Church is located here, as well as several sizable Presbyterian churches.

As of May 19, the Census Bureau had not recalculated population data, racial and ethnic breakdowns, and age statistics for districts newly drawn for the 1996 election.

tive than President Richard M. Nixon, opposing wage and price controls that Nixon supported. Today, his views are virtually unchanged, but the country has moved in his direction so that now a majority of the House shares the view through Archer's lens.

Still, his goal of transforming the tax code takes on greater urgency because his term as chairman is limited by party rules. He plans to retire from Congress when his skein runs out at the end of the 106th.

Beyond protecting the oil industry and espousing a general aversion to taxes, Archer has a limited personal agenda. The fact that the Republican leadership's platform tracked so neatly with his own stances allowed him to suppress his personal ambition when, for instance, Speaker Newt Gingrich informed him that he would personally take the lead on Medicare reform, rather than leaving the drafting to Ways and Means. At markups of significant legislation early in the 104th, leadership staff members were always present — a definite departure from the practice in years when Democrats ran the committee.

Archer sometimes bristled when the younger chairman of the Budget Committee, John R. Kasich, R-Ohio, would try to dictate the shape of tax legislation to him. "A tax loophole is like beauty," Archer says. "It's in the eye of the beholder." But he was willing to let leadership overrule him when it came to eliminating tax breaks for ethanol producers or imposing taxes on expatriating billionaires.

When congressional leaders redoubled their efforts during the summer of 1996 to pass bills they could actually get Clinton to sign, Archer was a key negotiator. He had advocated linking overhauls of Medicaid and welfare, but when it became clear that Clinton would veto the Medicaid package, Archer argued for passing a stand-alone welfare plan, and that was the direction taken by GOP leaders.

Archer also was willing to buckle a bit in negotiations with Sen. Edward M. Kennedy, D-Mass., over a health insurance revision that both parties supported. Archer had insisted on including in the House bill the issue of medical savings accounts, which allow people to accrue tax-deductible savings for health costs. Compromising outside of formal conference negotiations, Archer and Kennedy settled on a capped pilot program.

Archer also played a lead role in reaching an accord on a minimum wage increase, putting together a $10 billion package of tax relief for businesses that helped sweeten the proposal for Republicans. But, perhaps typically, Archer voted against the final deal he had helped broker because of his continuing opposition to the wage hike.

A courtly man who favors natty tweeds, Archer will discuss tax code minutiae to any willing audience. He dreamed for years of becoming chairman of Ways and Means. "I never considered running for the leadership," Archer said in 1995. "I had made the decision that I would run for the Senate if John Tower was appointed secretary of Defense by President Reagan." Later, when Tower decided to retire from the Senate, he called Archer the previous day ask if he would like to be his successor. But by then Archer was moving up the Ways and Means ladder and turned him down. It took him nearly 10 years more to grab the gavel, but he has never looked back. According to colleagues, the Ways and Means role fits him — it requires attention to detail and extensive knowledge of a few policy areas.

The confluence of Archer's connection with George Bush — whom he had succeeded in the House — and his committee role made him a surprise convert to the budget deal the White House negotiated with House and Senate leaders in 1990. That deal included tax increases, but Archer stood with his president and with Rostenkowski in voting for the package.

At Home: Archer occupies a "silk-stocking" district initially drawn in the mid-1960s with Bush, a New England-born WASP, in mind. But Archer himself is a native Houstonian, raised a Catholic and a Democrat. After law school and the Air Force, Archer launched his political career in 1955 as a member of the Hunters Creek Village Council.

He made his mark as a conservative Democrat, winning a seat in the Texas Legislature in 1966. But in 1968 he switched parties and won re-election as a Republican. Since the territory of his state legislative district closely coincided with that of Bush's House district, Archer was the early favorite in 1970 when Bush ran for the U.S. Senate.

Archer easily won the GOP primary and went on to defeat a young law partner of John B. Connally's in November. He has had no electoral problems since then. He triumphed over his first opponent of the decade in 1996 in a slightly redrawn district.

HOUSE ELECTIONS

1996 General		
Bill Archer (R)	152,024	(81%)
Al J.K. Siegmund (D)	28,187	(15%)
Gene Hsiao (I)	3,896	(2%)
Robert R. "Randy" Sims Jr. (I)	2,724	(1%)
1994 General		
Bill Archer (R)	116,873	(100%)

Previous Winning Percentages: **1992** (100%) **1990** (100%) **1988** (79%) **1986** (87%) **1984** (87%) **1982** (85%) **1980** (82%) **1978** (85%) **1976** (100%) **1974** (79%) **1972** (82%) **1970** (65%)

CAMPAIGN FINANCE

	Receipts	Receipts from PACs		Expend-itures
1996				
Archer (R)	$186,482	$25,125	(13%)	$278,951
Hsiao (I)	$900	0		$645
1994				
Archer (R)	$284,312	$3,170	(1%)	$215,637

DISTRICT VOTE FOR PRESIDENT

1996			1992		
D	61,834	(28%)	**D**	50,601	(22%)
R	145,637	(66%)	**R**	131,587	(58%)
I	10,338	(5%)	**I**	46,019	(20%)

KEY VOTES

1997	
Ban "partial birth" abortions	Y
1996	
Approve farm bill	Y
Deny public education to illegal immigrants	Y
Repeal ban on certain assault-style weapons	Y
Increase minimum wage	N
Freeze defense spending	N
Approve welfare overhaul	Y
1995	
Approve balanced-budget constitutional amendment	Y
Relax Clean Water Act regulations	Y
Oppose limits on environmental regulations	N
Reduce projected Medicare spending	Y
Approve GOP budget with tax and spending cuts	Y

VOTING STUDIES

	Presidential Support		Party Unity		Conservative Coalition	
Year	**S**	**O**	**S**	**O**	**S**	**O**
1996	35	65	95	3	94	4
1995	16	84	95	2	94	3
1994	33	67	97	1	94	6
1993	23	75	83	14	91	7
1992	80	13	85	10	85	4
1991	84	14	85	11	100	0

INTEREST GROUP RATINGS

Year	ADA	AFL-CIO	CCUS	ACU
1996	5	n/a	94	100
1995	0	0	96	80
1994	0	0	92	100
1993	5	0	91	100
1992	0	17	75	100
1991	0	0	100	95

8 Kevin Brady (R)

Of The Woodlands — Elected 1996, 1st term

Biographical Information

Born: April 7, 1955, Vermillion, S.D.
Education: U. of South Dakota, B.S. 1990.
Occupation: Chamber of commerce executive.
Family: Wife, Cathy.
Religion: Roman Catholic.
Political Career: Texas House, 1991-97.
Capitol Office: 1531 Longworth Bldg. 20515; 225-4901.

Committees

International Relations
International Economic Policy & Trade; Western Hemisphere
Resources
Energy & Mineral Resources
Science
Space & Aeronautics; Technology

The Path to Washington: Drawing on his background as head of a chamber of commerce in suburban Houston, Brady adheres to the belief that many social problems can be solved by creating additional jobs. He favors reducing government regulation and protecting businesses from so-called "frivolous" lawsuits as ways to improve the business climate for job creation.

Brady won the open 8th in 1996, succeeding eight-term GOP Rep. Jack Fields, who retired at age 44. One of the centerpieces of Brady's campaign was his advocacy of "sunset" legislation, which would require every federal agency to justify its existence on a regular basis or face consolidation, streamlining, privatization or elimination.

Brady was a six-year member of the Texas House, and his vote there against a bill to allow Texans to carry concealed weapons proved to be a troublesome issue in his 1996 campaign for Congress. He says that while he firmly believes in upholding the Second Amendment right to keep and bear arms, his vote against the concealed weapons measure was prompted by his father's death at the hands of a gunman in a South Dakota courtroom three decades ago.

Brady's chief rival in the race, wealthy GOP physician Gene Fontenot, claimed that Brady's opposition to the measure was a prime example of one of the many liberal votes Brady cast in the state legislature.

Brady takes a conventional conservative line on federal gun-control measures. He supports repeal of the ban on certain semiautomatic assault-style weapons, and he supports provisions in the law that will replace the mandatory five-day waiting period for handgun purchases with a system that would perform an instant background check on people wishing to buy guns.

(The handgun law was named for former White House press secretary James S. Brady, who was permanently disabled in the 1981 assassination attempt on President Ronald Reagan and who is no relation to Kevin Brady.)

Given that the 8th is a GOP stronghold, Brady's biggest challenge in 1996 was expected to come in the primary. Fontenot emerged on top but did not capture a majority of the vote and was forced into a runoff with Brady, who finished second.

Fontenot, who spent more than $4.6 million in an unsuccessful 1994 bid in the 25th District, largely financed his campaign for the 8th out of his own pocket, spending freely on TV ads. He also had the backing of many Christian activists.

Brady, however, had much stronger ties to the district. He also charged that Fontenot's business practices did not line up with his stated beliefs. In particular, he highlighted a Houston Chronicle article in which some physicians said they had performed abortions at a hospital owned and managed by Fontenot, a staunch opponent of abortion.

After defeating Fontenot in the Republican runoff, Brady was expected to have little trouble prevailing in November. His prospects, however, were complicated when a three-judge federal in August panel redrew the 8th District along with 12 other Texas congressional districts in response to a Supreme Court redistricting decision.

The judges threw out the results of the primary in the 13 affected districts, reopened the candidate filing period and ordered that an open primary election be held on Election Day in November.

Fontenot seized the opportunity to jump back into the race for another try. After no candidate received a majority of the vote in November, Brady and Fontenot once again found themselves facing each other in a runoff, this time in December. Many of the same issues emerged in round two of their battle. But Brady had the backing of GOP Gov. George W. Bush and many of the Republican members of the Texas congressional delegation, including Fields.

Brady scored a decisive victory in the runoff, winning 59 percent to 41 percent.

In the 105th, Brady drew seats on three committees: Resources, Science and International Relations.

TEXAS 8
Northern Houston suburbs; College Station

Texas is known for oil barons and vast open expanses. The 8th has all that, plus dairy farms, a robust medical industry and the Texas A&M Aggies.

Reconfigured in 1992 redistricting and only marginally altered in 1996 remapping, the 8th resembles a lopsided barbell. It has distinct eastern and western sections and a narrow corridor connecting them. Most of the population lives on the barbell's eastern end. Suburban Houston turf in Harris County accounts for about 45 percent of the total vote; the next county north, Montgomery, casts about one-third of the vote.

In 1996 voting, the 8th was Bob Dole's third-best congressional district in the country, primarily due to Harris and Montgomery's solid Republican politics. Dole won nearly 70 percent in Harris and 66 percent in Montgomery.

Houston's largest employer is the Texas Medical Center, a conglomeration of 44 non-profit health-related institutions that employ more than 54,000 people and treat 3.8 million patients annually. Many of the doctors, nurses, lab technicians, researchers and managers at the Medical Center live in the tidy suburbs of the 8th.

The oil and gas industry obviously plays a major role in the region's economy. Although the Port of Houston is no longer in the 8th, many of the refinery managers commute to the port from their homes in the district.

Similarly, the corporate headquarters of Exxon, Shell and Pennzoil are all in Houston. The city accounts for 23 percent of all U.S. jobs in crude petroleum and natural gas extraction, 14 percent of all U.S. jobs in oil and gas services, and 38 percent of the nation's jobs in oil and gas field machinery manufacturing.

Executives at the Houston Advanced Research Center, Exxon and the Lifecell medical research company generally live in Woodlands or Kingwood, two planned communities that offer office space, housing and shops all in the same neighborhood.

Although the residential areas that dominate the Harris County part of the 8th are described as suburban, traffic congestion here rivals that of some East Coast cities.

In the western half of the district, the joke goes that there are more cows than people. Washington County is best known for Brenham's Blue Bell Creameries, which produce ice cream using milk from local dairies. Ten miles east of Brenham is Chappell Hill, the first town in Texas planned by a woman. The entire county is renowned for its fine German and Polish bakeries and sausage shops, a legacy of the East European immigrants who flocked to this area in the 1800s and put down roots.

Farther north is Brazos County, home of College Station and Texas A&M University, the state's oldest public institution of higher education and one of the 10 largest educational institutions in the country. The university, which has 43,800 students, will be the site of George Bush's presidential library. Construction of the facility is expected to be complete in the fall of 1997.

As of May 19, the Census Bureau had not recalculated population data, racial and ethnic breakdowns, and age statistics for districts newly drawn for the 1996 election.

HOUSE ELECTIONS

1996 General Runoff*		
Kevin Brady (R)	30,366	(59%)
Gene Fontenot (R)	21,004	(41%)
1996 General		
Kevin Brady (R)	80,325	(42%)
Gene Fontenot (R)	75,399	(39%)
Cynthia "C.J." Newman (D)	26,246	(14%)
Robert Musemeche (D)	11,689	(6%)

** Because of court-ordered redistricting in August, an all-candidate special election was held in November. If no candidate received a majority of the vote then, the top finishers met in a December runoff.*

CAMPAIGN FINANCE

	Receipts	Receipts from PACs		Expend-itures
1996 General Runoff				
Brady (R)	$1,107,877	$498,125	(45%)	$1,094,498
Fontenot (R)	$1,389,133	$500	(0%)	$1,379,749

DISTRICT VOTE FOR PRESIDENT

1996			1992		
D	61,850	(27%)	D	50,308	(22%)
R	155,351	(67%)	R	126,706	(55%)
I	14,864	(6%)	I	52,542	(23%)

KEY VOTES

1997

Ban "partial birth" abortions — Y

9 Nick Lampson (D)

Of Beaumont — Elected 1996, 1st term

Biographical Information
Born: Feb. 14, 1945, Beaumont, Texas.
Education: Lamar U., B.S. 1968, M.Ed. 1971.
Occupation: Teacher; tax assessor.
Family: Wife, Susan Floyd; two children.
Religion: Roman Catholic.
Political Career: Jefferson County assessor, 1977-95.
Capitol Office: 128 Cannon Bldg. 20515; 225-6565.

Committees
Science
Space & Aeronautics
Transportation & Infrastructure
Public Buildings & Economic Development; Water Resources & Environment

The Path to Washington: Lampson succeeded in returning the 9th to Democratic hands by unseating freshman Republican Steve Stockman, who snatched the district in 1994 from veteran Democratic Rep. Jack Brooks.

Lampson came to the contest with solid name recognition in Jefferson County (Beaumont), where he served as tax assessor from 1977 to 1995.

The former head of a home health care company, Lampson, a 1995 delegate to the White House Conference on Aging, hopes to help revamp the Medicare program. He says he believes health care can be made more efficient and costs reduced without cutting Medicare benefits. Efficiencies he has seen instituted at the local level should be put in place before services are cut, he says.

A former science teacher in Beaumont public schools, Lampson is committed to protecting funding for education programs such as Head Start and student loans. He says he would like to see more done to identify "at-risk kids." Lampson said he occasionally brought food to children who were not getting enough to eat.

Lampson adds, however, that he is not calling for a new "big federal program," but he believes the government can provide local communities with tools to help such children.

Democratic leaders gave Lampson seats on the Science Committee, where he can keep an eye on issues important to the Johnson Space Center southeast of Houston, and the Transportation and Infrastructure Committee, where he will have a say when the committee considers a broad reauthorization measure for the nation's highway and mass transit programs.

Stockman managed to blindside Brooks in 1994 with the strong backing of gun rights supporters, who were also active in his re-election bid.

Stockman was thought to be one of the most vulnerable incumbents in 1996; area Democrats dubbed him "the accidental congressman." His contacts with militia groups and his staunchly conservative voting record were a sharp contrast from what the district had been used to under Brooks.

Lampson had little trouble defeating his four competitors for the Democratic nomination, and he moved quickly to attack Stockman's voting record and to label him a right-wing extremist.

Stockman also found himself the target of organized labor and environmental groups, and he was pummeled with TV ads critical of his votes on issues such as Medicare. Lampson accused Stockman of voting for GOP efforts to cut education programs and weaken environmental regulations.

In August, it appeared as if Stockman was getting something of a break when a three-judge federal panel redrew his district, along with 12 others in Texas, in response to a Supreme Court redistricting decision.

After redrawing the boundary lines of 13 districts, the judges threw out the results of the state's primary in the affected districts, reopened the candidate filing and ordered that an all-candidate special primary be held in conjunction with the November election.

When the candidate filing was reopened, one of Lampson's primary opponents, Geraldine Sam, jumped back into the race.

In November, Sam pulled enough of the Democratic vote away from Lampson that Stockman ran first, with 46 percent to Lampson's 44 percent. Those two headed into a runoff that initially appeared to favor Stockman, given that Republicans have generally done a better job of encouraging their supporters to vote in those types of low-turnout contests.

Lampson, however, conducted a massive voter mobilization effort, focusing on getting his voters to the polls during the "early voting" period before the runoff proper. Lampson was boosted to victory by winning a majority of the early vote and pulling out a huge margin in his home base of Jefferson County. He won election with a 53 percent tally.

TEXAS 9
Southeast — Beaumont; Galveston

Tucked in the southeast corner of Texas, the 9th runs from Houston's outlying suburbs to Port Arthur, near the Gulf Coast. Geographically small by Texas standards, the 9th is packed with refineries and petrochemical plants on land, and with commercial cargo ships and fishing boats on its waters. Also here is NASA's enormous Lyndon B. Johnson Space Center.

The 9th's past and present are inextricably intertwined with petroleum.

The district's largest city is Beaumont, in Jefferson County. The city, linked to the Gulf of Mexico by the Neches River, was chartered in 1838 but came of age in 1901 when the great gusher Spindletop erupted and Texas oil production soared. Spindletop triggered Beaumont's industrial development; within a month of its discovery the city's population tripled.

Just as Spindletop and other Gulf Coast wells catapulted the region's economy, the oil market plunge of the mid-1980s devastated the area. With a worldwide glut, the price of oil dropped, refineries closed, and unemployment in some communities hit 22 percent by 1986. Port Arthur, Beaumont and Galveston all lost population in the 1980s; their populations have crept upward since.

There was a silver lining to the bust: Petrochemical plants were able to buy their raw materials for a song. From the cheap petroleum, the plants refine a host of chemicals that eventually go into making a variety of products, including plastics, foam and carpeting.

The increase in petrochemical production boosted the "Golden Triangle" of Beaumont, Port Arthur and Orange. As that business picked up in the early 1990s, building and modernizing refineries created thousands of jobs.

The 9th remains heavily dependent on coastal industries such as ship repairing and commercial fishing. It is said to be the largest maritime district in the nation; other large coastal cities are split between districts. The Intracoastal Waterway runs the entire length of the 9th, carrying cargo ships from the Houston Ship Channel as far as New York City. About 1,800 boats fish out of the district's ports. And the beaches of Galveston County are a tourist lure.

At the edge of the 9th, 20 miles southeast of Houston, sits the Johnson Space Center, a mammoth complex that employs 23,000 people. (Locals like to note that the first word ever spoken on the moon was "Houston.") The facility is especially active in the International Space Station project, but NASA announced in April 1997 that assembly would be delayed until late 1998 because of Russia's inability to deliver a key component of the project.

Remapping in 1996 made minute changes in the 9th's boundaries; it is still on balance a Democratic district: Michael Dukakis won it comfortably in 1988, and Bill Clinton was victorious here in 1992 and 1996. Democratic percentages are especially robust in Jefferson county, where Clinton received 54 percent of the votes and Lampson got 59 percent in 1996.

As of May 19, the Census Bureau had not recalculated population data, racial and ethnic breakdowns, and age statistics for districts newly drawn for the 1996 election.

HOUSE ELECTIONS

1996 General Runoff*		
Nick Lampson (D)	59,225	(53%)
Steve Stockman (R)	52,870	(47%)
1996 General		
Steve Stockman (R)	88,171	(46%)
Nick Lampson (D)	83,782	(44%)
Geraldine Sam (D)	17,887	(9%)

** Because of court-ordered redistricting in August, an all-candidate special election was held in November. If no candidate received a majority of the vote then, the top finishers met in a December runoff.*

CAMPAIGN FINANCE

	Receipts	Receipts from PACs		Expend-itures
1996 General				
Lampson (D)	$1,643,257	$592,370	(36%)	$1,612,625
Stockman (R)	$1,899,173	$523,135	(28%)	$1,898,778
Sam (D)	$26,854	$1,000	(4%)	$25,104

DISTRICT VOTE FOR PRESIDENT

	1996		1992
D	97,268 (48%)	D	98,779 (44%)
R	89,942 (44%)	R	80,629 (36%)
I	14,144 (7%)	I	47,273 (21%)

KEY VOTES

1997

Ban "partial birth" abortions — Y

10 Lloyd Doggett (D)

Of Austin — Elected 1994, 2nd term

Biographical Information
Born: Oct. 6, 1946, Austin, Texas.
Education: U. of Texas, Austin, B.B.A. 1967, J.D. 1970.
Occupation: Lawyer.
Family: Wife, Libby Belk; two children.
Religion: Methodist.
Political Career: Texas Senate, 1973-85; Democratic nominee for U.S. Senate, 1984; Texas Supreme Court, 1989-95.
Capitol Office: 126 Cannon Bldg. 20515; 225-4865.

Committees
Budget
Resources
Water & Power; National Parks & Public Lands

In Washington: When Democrats controlled the House, several in the GOP minority busied themselves as "attack dogs," frequently taking to the House floor to castigate the liberal majority. With Democrats now the House minority, they too have their "designated hitters," and one of them is Doggett. His left-leaning Austin constituency includes many academics and government workers, and their support makes Doggett a rare breed in modern American politics: a white liberal holding a Southern-state House district. The other 12 Democratic members of the Class of 1994 must have recognized this distinction: They elected him president of the class for 1996.

During his first term in office, Doggett spoke on the floor more than 280 times, and, often as not, the subject of his partisan tirades was House Speaker Newt Gingrich. In one celebrated incident in late 1995, Doggett was reprimanded for calling Gingrich a "crybaby" on the House floor. At the time, congressional Republicans and President Clinton were locked in a budget stalemate that eventually led to a partial government shutdown, and Gingrich told reporters he was piqued over not being asked to sit and negotiate with Clinton during a long flight bound for the funeral of assassinated Israeli leader Yitzhak Rabin.

After Doggett was called down for labeling the Speaker a "crybaby," he then held up the front page of the New York Daily News, which carried a caricature of Gingrich and a blaring "Crybaby" headline. When instructed by the chair to put the newspaper away, Doggett pressed on, asking sarcastically, "So that I may comply with the rules of the House, I understand then that I am not to refer to the Speaker as a 'crybaby.' May I use the term 'Newt's tantrum'?"

Doggett also blasted Gingrich's involvement in GOPAC, an organization he established to elect Republican state legislative candidates. In November 1995, the Federal Election Commission (FEC) accused GOPAC of "hiding" its role in 1990 congressional races and "secretly funneling more than $250,000" into Gingrich's own re-election campaign that year. "It's clear that the 'Go' in GOPAC means GO beyond the law," Doggett said. "GOPAC has been little more than Newt Gingrich's personal slush fund used to subvert federal election laws." Gingrich called the FEC charges "totally phony."

But after a special counsel hired by the House ethics committee described in a 213-page report how Gingrich created a network of tax-exempt foundations to funnel campaign contributions that helped wrest control of the House from Democrats, Gingrich was reprimanded by the House and assessed a $300,000 penalty. Doggett said the sanctions are "pretty steep for what his supporters claim was mere ethical 'jay-walking' or an ethical 'speeding ticket.'"

When the GOP House approved a massive budget-reconciliation bill in October 1995 that balanced the budget by overhauling the federal health insurance programs for the poor and elderly and restraining spending on federal education and environment programs, Doggett complained that the bill benefited the rich at the expense of the poor.

"If you are way up there on top at the apex of the American economy, sitting on a cushion, sipping champagne, you got your promise fulfilled by this Republican Party bountifully," Doggett told the Dallas Morning News. "But what if you are not on top? Those people on the economic ladder have a broken promise."

From his seat on the Budget Committee in the 104th Congress, Doggett also chided the Republicans for failing to close a tax loophole that he said allows wealthy Americans to avoid paying their fair share of taxes by renouncing their U.S. citizenship. "This loophole, the 'billionaire boondoggle,' protects a few extremely wealthy people from paying taxes on immense amounts of income earned here, in the United States," he said.

Doggett has not limited his fault-finding to Republicans. At an April 1995 White House gathering of Democrats from the Southwest, the

TEXAS 10
Central — Austin

The vast rural district that Lyndon B. Johnson represented in the House in the 1940s has been shrinking in size and growing in population ever since he left the 10th.

In the 1980s, the district took in five counties and most of a sixth. But for the 1990s, the 10th is limited just to Austin and Travis County, where population grew by 35 percent in the 1980s after having grown by 42 percent in the 1970s. Austin, the state capital, has become an urban mecca for students, computer engineers, music lovers and tourists.

The economic troubles of the oil industry grazed Austin in the mid-1980s; real estate speculation fizzled and local banks suffered. But the underpinnings of Austin's economy are unique in Texas, and they helped the city's economy remain stable.

The state of Texas, with 57,000 workers, is the district's largest employer. Another economic anchor is the University of Texas (UT) at Austin. With nearly 50,000 students and 20,000 employees, the school gives the city a youthful feeling (T-shirts and jeans are ubiquitous) and its liberal political bent. Travis County was one of the few large counties in Texas to hand Bill Clinton a solid majority in 1996.

The university also has been a catalyst for Austin's emergence as a center for high-tech industry. One local success story is Dell Computer. Begun in a dorm room in the early 1980s by UT student Michael Dell, the computer-maker now employs 2,800 people.

Two public-private research consortia add to the synergy. In 1983, Austin won the right to host the headquarters of Microelectronics & Computer Technology Corp. Five years later, the city welcomed Sematech, a joint venture using federal and private money to develop new applications for semiconductors. Two major semiconductor makers, Motorola (7,000 employees) and Advanced Microdevices (2,400 workers), are in Austin.

Another boost to Austin's economic vitality is a thriving cultural and entertainment life. The city's country music scene gets national exposure on the public television show "Austin City Limits," and connoisseurs of blues, rock and new wave music flock to clubs on East Sixth Street. Austin also draws visitors to its many lakes and parks. One big annual event is the Austin Aqua Festival, with water shows, a homemade-raft contest and music.

As Austin's growth surged over the past 20 years, some residents who had been drawn by the city's college-town feel began to fret that Austin would become huge, sprawling and impersonal — "Houstonized," in local parlance. Though Texas has a strong frontier spirit that tends to regard growth-management measures as un-American, the prevailing mood in Austin is different. Developers are required to contribute to infrastructure projects in return for zoning permits. In 1992, the city approved the Balcones Canyonlands Conservation Plan, a proposal that allows the government and the Nature Conservancy to purchase 30,000 acres to protect endangered wildlife.

1990 Population: 566,217. White 412,897 (73%), Black 63,145 (11%), Other 90,175 (16%). Hispanic origin 121,271 (21%). 18 and over 430,148 (76%), 62 and over 48,790 (9%). Median age: 29.

Texan raised eyebrows when he told President Clinton that most Americans didn't have a clear idea of what he stood for. USA Today reported that a testy Clinton emphasized his stands for deficit reduction and gun control and told Doggett that Democrats in Congress ought to defend, rather than criticize, him.

Doggett does, however, support many of the president's programs; he announced in September 1995 that Austin was to receive $1.6 million from the Justice Department as part of the Community Oriented Policing Services (COPS) program that Clinton asked for in the 1994 crime bill. The money would help pay for 22 new Austin police, Doggett said.

In his floor votes, Doggett typically is in step with the president's wishes. Doggett in 1996 voted for an overhaul of the welfare system, which Clinton backed, because he said he supported its work requirements. He also opposed a GOP-led effort to repeal the ban on certain semiautomatic assault-style weapons, a ban Clinton had pushed through Congress.

Like Clinton, Doggett also supports abortion rights. During the November 1995 House debate over a GOP bill to ban a a particular abortion technique that opponents call "partial birth" abortion, Doggett said Republicans' true aim was barring womens' access to any abortion.

In the 104th Congress, Doggett held a seat on the Science Committee, whose work is of interest to the Austin area's many high-technology companies. He has worked to funnel federal technology grants back to the 10th. In 1995, the University of Texas at Austin won a $2.9 million federal grant from the Federal Railroad Administration and the Department of Defense to develop an advanced locomotive propulsion system. Such a system would allow a train to double its acceleration without overhead electric supply wires.

At Home: Born and raised in Austin and schooled at the University of Texas, Doggett has been politically active in the city for 30 years, going back to his 1960s service in student government. Within two years of taking his law degree in 1970, he won election to the state Senate, and he served there until 1985, compiling a record of support for consumers and civil rights while backing the death penalty and tough criminal sanctions against drug traffickers and violent criminals.

In 1984, he tried for a promotion to the U.S. Senate, but after surviving the Democratic primary and runoff, he was mowed down in November by GOP nominee Phil Gramm, a former Democrat who was buoyed by Ronald Reagan's immense popularity in the Lone Star state. Texas went 64 percent for Reagan in presidential voting, and Doggett lost 41 to 59 percent in the Senate contest.

In 1988, Doggett re-entered public office by winning a seat on the state Supreme Court, and he was serving there when 81-year-old Democratic Rep. J.J. Pickle announced he would not seek another term from the 10th in 1994. Doggett was the first Democrat to announce his candidacy, and his quick start spared him primary competition. In November he faced Republican real estate consultant A. Jo Baylor.

Baylor had been one of four GOP candidates, and she needed a runoff to secure the nomination. Some party stalwarts questioned her party credentials: She had voted in just one GOP primary and had helped Democratic Rep. Eddie Bernice Johnson set up her Washington office.

In the fall, Baylor was hobbled by inexperience on the stump and a lack of funds, though her bid to become the first African-American woman Republican elected to Congress attracted some interest and support. When her campaign was running out of funds for advertising, the national GOP chipped in.

Doggett, by contrast, was flush, taking in more than $1.2 million by the end of the campaign. He called for universal health care coverage and for greater commitment to public schools, but he also emphasized some issues usually a staple of GOP rhetoric, including calls for more police, denial of parole for violent criminals, cutbacks in federal regulations and a work requirement for welfare recipients.

Baylor portrayed herself as a successful businesswoman, not a career politician like Doggett. But that line lost some luster when the Austin American-Statesman ran a lengthy article detailing property tax delinquencies, loan defaults and clashes with Austin city officials over the condition of properties owned by Baylor and her partners in East Austin. The conservative tide that rolled over much of the country in 1994 did not reach Austin, and Doggett won comfortably, 56 to 40 percent.

In 1996, the election tally was almost exactly the same: a 56 percent to 41 percent victory for Doggett over black Republican Teresa Doggett, owner of an import-export business.

HOUSE ELECTIONS

1996 General		
Lloyd Doggett (D)	132,066	(56%)
Teresa Doggett (R)	97,204	(41%)
Gary Johnson (LIBERT)	3,950	(2%)
1994 General		
Lloyd Doggett (D)	113,738	(56%)
A. Jo Baylor (R)	80,382	(40%)
Jeff Hill (LIBERT)	2,953	(1%)
Michael L. Brandes (I)	2,579	(1%)
Jeff Davis (I)	2,334	(1%)

CAMPAIGN FINANCE

	Receipts	Receipts from PACs	Expend-itures
1996			
Doggett (D)	$699,108	$231,563 (33%)	$410,302
Doggett (R)	$424,929	$28,597 (7%)	$402,904
1994			
Doggett (D)	$1,251,671	$232,473 (19%)	$567,552
Baylor (R)	$376,740	$69,439 (18%)	$374,406
Brandes (I)	$12,318	0	$11,730

DISTRICT VOTE FOR PRESIDENT

1996		1992	
D	126,855 (53%)	**D**	128,814 (48%)
R	93,219 (39%)	**R**	84,561 (32%)
I	13,453 (6%)	**I**	54,303 (20%)

KEY VOTES

1997	
Ban "partial birth" abortions	N
1996	
Approve farm bill	N
Deny public education to illegal immigrants	N
Repeal ban on certain assault-style weapons	N
Increase minimum wage	Y
Freeze defense spending	Y
Approve welfare overhaul	Y
1995	
Approve balanced-budget constitutional amendment	N
Relax Clean Water Act regulations	N
Oppose limits on environmental regulations	Y
Reduce projected Medicare spending	N
Approve GOP budget with tax and spending cuts	N

VOTING STUDIES

	Presidential Support		Party Unity		Conservative Coalition	
Year	**S**	**O**	**S**	**O**	**S**	**O**
1996	90	10	89	10	29	71
1995	86	13	90	10	31	69

INTEREST GROUP RATINGS

Year	ADA	AFL-CIO	CCUS	ACU
1996	80	n/a	19	0
1995	90	100	29	8

11 Chet Edwards (D)

Of Waco — Elected 1990, 4th term

Biographical Information
Born: Nov. 24, 1951, Corpus Christi, Texas.
Education: Texas A&M U., B.A. 1974; Harvard U., M.B.A. 1981.
Occupation: Radio station executive.
Family: Wife, Lea Ann Wood; one child.
Religion: Methodist.
Political Career: Sought Democratic nomination for U.S. House, 1978; Texas Senate, 1983-91.
Capitol Office: 2459 Rayburn Bldg. 20515; 225-6105.

Committees
Appropriations
Energy & Water Development; Military Construction

Chief Deputy Whip

In Washington: At the start of the 104th Congress, Democratic leader Richard A. Gephardt of Missouri appointed Edwards to one of four chief deputy whip slots, in an effort by the minority to reach out to Southern Democrats willing to work with party leaders.

Edwards said he saw progress toward trying to reconcile the conservative and liberal wings of the party. "A year or two ago, relations were very icy" between liberal and more conservative Democrats, Edwards said early in the 104th. "Now I think we're slowly beginning to move in the right direction."

In the 105th, Edwards got another reward for his willingness to work with his party leadership: a seat on the Appropriations Committee. He is the lone Texan on the panel, which in the 104th Congress had three Democrats from Texas.

Edwards' district is traditionally Democratic but pro-military and fairly conservative. He has balanced his district's interests and his desire to stay on good terms with the more liberal Democratic leadership by sticking with the party line on most votes but siding with conservatives on some high-profile issues. He usually records a party unity score in the mid-70s, meaning that he votes with a majority of Democrats against a majority of Republicans about three-fourths of the time.

Edwards began the 105th by opposing Republican-led efforts to limit congressional terms. In the 104th, he was a supporter of raising the minimum wage. And in strong terms he has opposed legislation banning a particular abortion technique that opponents call a "partial birth" abortion. In November 1995, arguing against the anti-abortion bill, he told colleagues that his wife was pregnant with their first child, and that they could hardly wait the six weeks left to hold their baby. But, he said, the life of his wife would come first if things went wrong. "Under the bill, a physician could be sent to prison for saving my wife's life," he said. "That is wrong, that is immoral, that is unconscionable." Republicans responded that the procedure was only rarely, if ever, used to protect the woman's life. It was used "mostly for the convenience of the abortionists," said Tom Coburn, R-Okla., who is a doctor.

At the same time, Edwards has supported a balanced-budget amendment to the Constitution. Indeed, his first splash of attention in Washington came because of his involvement with the Gang of Six, a group of freshman Democrats who in 1992 agitated party leaders to schedule a vote on a balanced-budget constitutional amendment.

He opposed President Clinton's highly controversial fiscal 1994 budget when it narrowly passed the House in August 1993. "People in my district don't want to see tax increases and promises about future cuts in spending," he told The Dallas Morning News.

A number of Edwards' votes during the 104th appealed to the more conservative elements of his constituency. He supported the welfare overhaul bill signed into law by Clinton, he voted to ban federal recognition of same-gender marriages, and he opposed allowing the federal employee health care plan to pay for abortions. He also voted to repeal 4.3 cents of the federal gasoline tax, an issue that was raised during the 1996 presidential campaign by Republican nominee Bob Dole. He supported efforts to limit awards to consumers injured by faulty products, and he has fought efforts to kill NASA's space station, a project that provides jobs in Texas' space-related industries.

Edwards' tenure has been marked by two mass killings in his district that stirred passions both pro and con on the issue of restricting gunowners' rights.

During an October 1991 debate on a crime bill that included a ban on certain semiautomatic assault-style weapons, news broke that a man with an automatic pistol had killed 22 people and wounded at least 20 more in a Killeen cafeteria before killing himself. Edwards was going to vote against the weapons ban but changed his mind.

Later, though, Edwards showed he would not stray too far from the majority view in the 11th that favors gunowners' rights: In 1993, he voted against the Brady bill, which requires a five-day

TEXAS 11
Central — Waco

At the height of the Persian Gulf War, 26,000 soldiers were deployed from Fort Hood, one of the largest military installations in the world. The deployment crushed the little town of Killeen; about 150 local businesses folded, and others hung on by a thread. So when the troops returned in mid-1991 and immediately went on a buying spree, the townsfolk were thrilled.

But the roller-coaster experience was a troubling sign of times to come for the people of Killeen. Post-Cold War defense cuts are expected to eventually reach the 43,000 military personnel stationed at Fort Hood, though the facility escaped the 1993 and 1995 rounds of base closings.

And though Killeen stands to lose and gain the most from any changes at Fort Hood, the base's economic impact is felt throughout most of the 11th. Retired veterans from Fort Hood and elsewhere stay in Central Texas, drawn to its mild climate and full line of services. The district has three veterans medical centers, more than any other in the country.

One of the major employers in the district is Raytheon E-Systems, which updates and modifies military aircraft.

In many respects, Waco (population 103,600) is the 11th's core. In the district's geographic center and split by the Brazos River, Waco also is the educational, cultural and economic lifeblood of Central Texas. It is the largest marketing center between Dallas and Austin.

As the home of the world's largest Baptist-affiliated university — Baylor — Waco also is known as the "Baptist Rome." A former military base has been converted into Texas State Technical Institute.

One-third of the district's residents live in Bell and McLennan counties. These two counties also provide the bulk of Democratic votes. Residents tend to vote ideology more than party, and they do not like change; in 60 years, the 11th has had just three congressmen. Edwards carried all but one of the district's 12 counties (Lampasas) in 1996. In the presidential race, Bob Dole carried all but two — Milam and Falls.

The remainder of the sprawling 11th, shaped like an animal's head with a large snout pointing west, is agricultural and sparsely populated. Unlike the Piney Woods of East Texas, the rolling hills of this region have few trees.

The 11th has had an unfortunate share of tragedies. In early 1993, a complex outside Waco known as Ranch Apocalypse was the scene of a deadly standoff between federal agents and members of the Branch Davidians, a religious sect organized by David Koresh. Four agents were killed as they attempted to serve arrest warrants. The FBI eventually injected non-lethal tear gas into the buildings. But rather than fleeing, the residents remained and, according to authorities, set fire to their compound. Dozens of people died inside.

In 1991, an armed gunman drove his truck through the window of a Luby's Cafeteria in nearby Killeen and killed 22 people before killing himself.

1990 Population: 566,217. White 430,594 (76%), Black 90,248 (16%), Other 45,375 (8%). Hispanic origin 69,887 (12%). 18 and over 413,528 (73%), 62 and over 84,363 (15%). Median age: 30.

waiting period before the purchase of a handgun.

In early 1993, Edwards' district again was the focus of national attention when the Branch Davidian religious sect and leader David Koresh clashed with federal agents trying to serve arrest warrants on the group for possession of illegal firearms. Four agents died in a botched raid on the sect's compound outside Waco. After a 51-day standoff, the confrontation ended with the compound's incineration and the deaths of Koresh and nearly all his sect.

These events were on Edwards' mind when he voted in 1994 to ban 19 types of assault-style weapons.

"I have said very little about these tragedies in public, but today, in good conscience, I must plead with my colleagues to learn the lesson I have painfully learned," Edwards told the House. "Mass murders can occur anywhere, anytime, in good, decent cities, urban, rural or suburban."

In 1996, he voted against a Republican-led effort to repeal the assault weapons ban.

Before moving to Appropriations, Edwards used his seats on the National Security and the Veterans' Affairs committees to look out for the military interests of his district, which includes Fort Hood and several large veterans' facilities.

In September 1995, he helped beat back an effort by committee Republicans to cut the pensions of thousands of retiring military personnel. Instead, the Republicans pushed through a plan to maintain benefits by selling excess assets from the National Defense Stockpile. Following seven weeks under siege, Rep. Floyd D. Spence, R-S.C., chairman of the National Security Committee, said that Republicans had come up with the alternative of selling excess stockpile assets. Democrats welcomed the final resolution but groused about the GOP claiming credit for preserving military benefits. "For the Republicans to take sole credit is like a physician shooting someone and then saving his life," Edwards said.

Edwards also used his position on the committee to oppose Republican efforts to develop a strong anti-missile system. The key question is, "How do we defend the continental United States against weapons of mass destruction, not just against ICBMs?" Edwards asked. Rather than adding $1 billion to the missile defense budget, he said, the money perhaps should be spent on beefing up U.S. intelligence capability to detect chemical and biological threats or on defenses against cruise missiles. In February 1995, when the House took up legislation on the anti-missile system, Edwards unsuccessfully proposed an amendment to bar deployment of space-based weapons. The amendment was defeated, 206-223.

At Home: Edwards' political career dates to the mid-1970s, when he spent three years as an aide to Texas Democratic Rep. Olin E. Teague. When Teague retired, he encouraged Edwards to try for his seat. But Edwards narrowly missed the Democratic primary runoff, closely trailing eventual winner Phil Gramm, who later switched to the GOP and won election to the Senate.

Edwards took a break from politics to enter the business world but soon returned, becoming, at 31, the youngest senator elected to the state Legislature.

His ambition did not go unnoticed, and it was no big surprise when he started campaigning for lieutenant governor in 1989. But when Democratic Rep. Marvin Leath announced he would step down in 1990, Edwards moved to the 11th to run for the House.

Edwards had no primary opponent, but Republicans targeted the 11th. GOP nominee state Rep. Hugh D. Shine outspent Edwards, and tried to tar him as a carpetbagger. But voters took notice of Edwards' chit, secured from House Speaker Thomas S. Foley, for Leath's seat on Armed Services, and Edwards won with 53 percent of the vote.

Two years later, Republican firefighter James W. Broyles failed to make his anti-Congress attacks stick to Edwards, who won a second term with two-thirds of the vote. In their 1994 rematch, Broyles proved more competitive, but Edwards still won handily. In 1996, the Republicans served up insurance agent Jay Mathis. He claimed Edwards was too liberal for the district, citing his opposition to the GOP's plan to balance the federal budget. But Edwards noted that the plan included cuts in the projected growth of spending on Medicare, Medicaid and education, and he handily won a fourth term.

HOUSE ELECTIONS

1996 General		
Chet Edwards (D)	99,990	(57%)
Jay Mathis (R)	74,549	(42%)
1994 General		
Chet Edwards (D)	76,667	(59%)
Jim Broyles (R)	52,876	(41%)

Previous Winning Percentages: 1992 (67%) **1990** (53%)

CAMPAIGN FINANCE

	Receipts	Receipts from PACs		Expend-itures
1996				
Edwards (D)	$838,467	$415,528	(50%)	$844,126
Mathis (R)	$543,637	$41,281	(8%)	$565,402
1994				
Edwards (D)	$395,874	$258,625	(65%)	$420,832
Broyles (R)	$51,736	$2,454	(5%)	$52,992

DISTRICT VOTE FOR PRESIDENT

	1996		1992
D	74,061 (42%)	**D**	66,376 (36%)
R	88,418 (50%)	**R**	75,515 (41%)
I	14,671 (8%)	**I**	42,298 (23%)

KEY VOTES

1997	
Ban "partial-birth" abortions	N
1996	
Approve farm bill	Y
Deny public education to illegal immigrants	N
Repeal ban on certain assault-style weapons	N
Increase minimum wage	Y
Freeze defense spending	N
Approve welfare overhaul	Y
1995	
Approve balanced-budget constitutional amendment	Y
Relax Clean Water Act regulations	Y
Oppose limits on environmental regulations	N
Reduce projected Medicare spending	N
Approve GOP budget with tax and spending cuts	N

VOTING STUDIES

	Presidential Support		Party Unity		Conservative Coalition	
Year	**S**	**O**	**S**	**O**	**S**	**O**
1996	72	27	72	28	92	8
1995	69	29	63	32	83	16
1994	82	18	74	23	94	6
1993	82	17	75	23	84	14
1992	43	56	75	23	85	15
1991	41	56	78	20	95	5

INTEREST GROUP RATINGS

Year	ADA	AFL-CIO	CCUS	ACU
1996	60	n/a	50	20
1995	45	64	63	25
1994	45	44	75	38
1993	35	67	55	33
1992	55	75	63	40
1991	40	75	50	35

12 Kay Granger (R)

Of Fort Worth — Elected 1996, 1st term

Biographical Information
Born: Jan. 18, 1943, Greenville, Texas.
Education: Texas Wesleyan U., B.S. 1965.
Occupation: Insurance agent.
Family: Divorced; three children.
Religion: Methodist.
Political Career: Ft. Worth City Council, 1989-91; mayor of Ft. Worth, 1991-95.
Capitol Office: 515 Cannon Bldg. 20515; 225-5071.

Committees
Budget
House Oversight
Transportation & Infrastructure
Aviation; Railroads; Surface Transportation
Joint Printing

The Path to Washington: When conservative Democrat Pete Geren decided against seeking re-election in 1996, then-Fort Worth Mayor Granger was among the first to be mentioned as a potential successor. A popular mayor — a nonpartisan post in Fort Worth — Granger was wooed by both parties when she expressed interest in running for the seat, once held by former Democratic Speaker Jim Wright, who resigned in 1989 under a cloud of ethical allegations.

The GOP succeeded in attracting Granger to their side, and her victory gave the Republicans a district that Democrats had represented for a century. Granger, the first Republican woman ever to represent Texas in the House, says she wants to put her experience in balancing Fort Worth's budget to use in Congress by stressing fiscal integrity at the federal level. She backs a balanced-budget constitutional amendment and the streamlining of federal agencies.

An insurance agency owner, Granger supports tax cuts that would benefit families and small businesses. In particular, she says she favors providing tax credits that would assist families paying for a college education.

She is a strong supporter of the "comp time" legislation that moved early in the 105th, which would allow businesses to offer employees a choice between receiving money or time off in exchange for working overtime.

Granger says she also will attempt to change the manner in which the formula for federal transportation funding is calculated. She says she would like to see Texas get a higher proportion of funding when an omnibus highway bill is reauthorized in 1997.

Granger also says she will encourage the use of some of the measures she enacted in Fort Worth to lower the city's crime rate, such as citizen patrols and nationwide "zero-tolerance" initiatives aimed at cleaning up high-crime areas. However, she opposes mandating that such programs be used because she says local and state authorities should maintain control of issues that most directly affect them. Having dealt with the effects of federal regulations at the local level, Granger said increasing local control is "a big issue with me."

Landing a spot on the Budget Committee, Granger will be in a good position to work on some of her fiscal priorities. She also secured a seat on the Transportation and Infrastructure Committee, a position that will allow her to keep an eye on one of the district's major employers, the Dallas-Fort Worth International Airport. Granger also sits on the House Oversight Committee, which tends to institutional issues.

The race to succeed Geren came down to a battle of two former Fort Worth mayors (Granger stepped down from the post when she decided to run for Congress).

But before she could face off against Democrat Hugh Parmer, a former state legislator who was ousted as the city's mayor after just one term in the late 1970s, Granger had to overcome a nasty intraparty fight.

Granger, an abortion rights supporter, was attacked by her two primary opponents as a liberal and was opposed by the Tarrant County Republican chairman. Nevertheless, Granger was able to parlay her popularity as mayor — she presided over a 50 percent drop in the violent crime rate while maintaining fiscal austerity — into a strong primary victory.

After deflecting charges in the primary for being too liberal, Granger faced attacks from Parmer in the general election for being too conservative. Parmer claimed Granger was more concerned with protecting the interests of big corporations, bankers and insurance companies than those of working families. He also attempted to tie her to House Speaker Newt Gingrich, pointing out that her first vote in Congress would be to reelect him for Speaker.

But Granger once again focused on her record as mayor. She also raised twice as much money as Parmer did. In the end, it was not a close call for the district's voters: Granger ran up 58 percent of the vote to take the seat.

TEXAS 12
Northwest Tarrant County; part of Fort Worth

The 12th has an unusual hourglass shape, but a unifying theme: transportation. Within or adjacent to this Fort Worth-based district are three major airports, an Air Force base, three railroad lines, several interstate highways and myriad businesses that depend on one or more of these conveyances.

The focus on transportation stems from Fort Worth's past importance as a rail center. The earliest settlers of Fort Worth extended the rail line themselves in 1873 when financial problems halted construction 26 miles to the east. Once the trains came through, Fort Worth emerged as a major cattle trading post; stockyards ringed the city and meatpacking plants flourished.

Today, bits of that history remain. On the city's north side, a handful of stockyards survive, and one of the largest cattle trading posts has been converted into a complex of shops, offices and kiddie rides called the Stockyard Station.

Although the Santa Fe Railroad is still active — shipping automobiles, chemicals, farm products and other commodities — the air industry has far surpassed rail.

One of the district's largest employers is American Airlines, which has both its headquarters and a maintenance facility just over the district line. The maintenance shop provided a critical boost to the local economy at just the right time. In 1991, General Dynamics in Fort Worth laid off 3,500 workers after the Pentagon canceled the A-12 stealth attack plane program. But opportunities at the American facility helped ease the impact of the loss.

Speaker Jim Wright's clout helped protect the federal contracts that kept the district's blue-collar employees at work. Wright is gone, and the General Dynamics air division was bought by Lockheed Martin; but the company (along with Boeing) is producing major components of the F-22 Raptor, an advanced tactical fighter, and the Joint Strike Fighter (JSF) in Fort Worth. Lockheed Martin's Fort Worth plant employs 12,000.

Another aircraft that has been a local economic staple is the V-22 Osprey, an experimental tilt-rotor aircraft built both by Bell Helicopter Textron, which is headquartered in the 12th, and Boeing. Since Wright's departure, officials are redoubling their efforts to stimulate private enterprise. Alliance Airport, a commercial shipping operation initiated by Ross Perot, started off slowly, but the pace of business has been picking up. North of the airport is the new $110 million, 150,000-seat Texas Motor Speedway, which hosted its inaugural race in April 1997.

Carswell Air Force Base, which was slated to close, stayed open as a consolidated facility called the Fort Worth Naval Air Station Joint Reserve Base. The base will receive some of the workload engendered by the closing of Dallas Naval Air Station by September 1998.

The bulk of the 12th's voters are moderate-to-conservative Democrats, as evidenced by the robust percentages received by Wright and former Rep. Pete Geren. But Republican Granger's victory in 1996 and Bill Clinton's narrow edge in the last two presidential elections indicate that this is politically competitive terrain.

1990 Population: 566,217. White 453,695 (80%), Black 45,426 (8%), Other 67,096 (12%). Hispanic origin 92,253 (16%). 18 and over 412,814 (73%), 62 and over 79,053 (14%). Median age: 31.

HOUSE ELECTIONS

1996 General		
Kay Granger (R)	98,349	(58%)
Hugh Parmer (D)	69,859	(41%)
Heather Proffer (NL)	1,996	(1%)
1996 Primary		
Kay Granger (R)	21,774	(69%)
Ernest J. Anderson Jr. (R)	6,355	(20%)
Bill Burch (R)	3,355	(11%)

CAMPAIGN FINANCE

	Receipts	Receipts from PACs	Expend-itures
1996			
Granger (R)	$1,017,741	$296,449 (29%)	$1,001,836
Parmer (D)	$456,738	$116,775 (26%)	$455,703

DISTRICT VOTE FOR PRESIDENT

	1996		1992
D	79,447 (46%)	D	76,765 (38%)
R	77,839 (45%)	R	70,702 (35%)
I	14,045 (8%)	I	56,090 (28%)

KEY VOTES

1997

Ban "partial birth" abortions Y

13 William M. 'Mac' Thornberry (R)

Of Clarendon — Elected 1994, 2nd term

Biographical Information
Born: July 15, 1958, Clarendon, Texas.
Education: Texas Tech U., B.A. 1980; U. of Texas, J.D. 1983.
Occupation: Lawyer; cattleman; State Department official; congressional aide.
Family: Wife, Sally Adams; two children.
Religion: Presbyterian.
Political Career: No previous office.
Capitol Office: 412 Cannon Bldg. 20515; 225-3706.

Committees
National Security
Military Personnel; Military Procurement
Resources
Energy & Mineral Resources; Water & Power
Joint Economic

In Washington: When he was seeking to oust Democratic Rep. Bill Sarpalius from the 13th in 1994, Thornberry got a lot of mileage out of criticizing Sarpalius' 1993 vote for President Clinton's budget, which was unpopular with many Texans because it increased the tax on gasoline. Sarpalius said he had sided with Clinton only after securing a promise from the administration that it would protect the Amarillo-based Helium Reserve program, which employs about 200 people overseeing the federal government's stockpile of helium gas. Voters, however, were not impressed; Thornberry's image as a fiscal conservative helped him score a 10-point victory.

Once in office, though, Thornberry soon was speaking up for the Helium Reserve that Sarpalius had sought to protect from budget-cutters. When Clinton in his January 1995 State of the Union address cited the Helium Reserve as a government program that should be cut, Thornberry said it was a poor choice. "Eliminating the helium program will not make a dent in the deficit," Thornberry told the Dallas Morning News. "If that is the best program he can come up with, then I wonder if he is serious about cutting."

The Interior Department started the Helium Reserve in the early 1960s in response to concerns that the United States would run out of the gas, which primarily is used to inflate blimps. But private companies developed the capacity to produce and sell helium at a lower cost than the federal government, and budget-cutters in Congress began heaping scorn on the helium program as superfluous. In April 1996 when the House considered a measure to end the program, Thornberry was a lonely voice arguing for privatizing it in a way that he said would provide more financial return for taxpayers and protect workers in Amarillo.

"If we are going to do the right thing by the workers and by the country, then major revisions need to take place in this bill," Thornberry told the House. "We all ought to strive to not just make the government smaller, but smarter." It was a tough sell: The House voted 411-10 to end the program, with Thornberry among the 10 "nays."

Excepting that episode, Thornberry usually has voted with the more ardent budget-cutting elements in the Republican Party. In fact, he sometimes has taken a more hard-line stance than the GOP leadership. In the spring of 1996, he opposed the final budget agreement that Republican leaders negotiated with Clinton, in part because the agreement allowed the president to waive a moratorium on listing new plant and wildlife species under the Endangered Species Act.

On the Resources Committee, which has jurisdiction over the act, Thornberry is a devoted advocate of landowners' rights; he believes that federal laws and regulations impinge unduly on how farmers and other private property owners use their land. During a June 1996 committee hearing on the Endangered Species Act, Thornberry said the act should be reformed to get it back to its original intent— conservation. "Right now people in my district are terrified that the government is going to come and take their land," he said.

On other economic and social-policy issues, Thornberry has voted a consistently conservative line. He opposed legislation to increase the minimum wage increase both times it came through the House in 1996, and he supported repeal of the ban on certain semiautomatic assault-style weapons. Thornberry opposes abortion and favors restricting certain federal benefits to legal immigrants.

Coming from the district that grows more cotton than any other, Thornberry has a keen interest in federal policies affecting that crop as well as other agricultural commodities. In the 104th Congress, he ended up voting for the GOP-backed "Freedom to Farm" bill, which brought federal farm policy more in line with free-market principles. But in the early stages of the farm-bill debate, he cosponsored a substitute plan that he felt would be better for cotton growers. The sub-

TEXAS 13
Eastern Panhandle — Wichita Falls; part of Amarillo

The massive 13th comprises three distinct regions: the Panhandle, the South Plains and the Red River Valley. It takes more than eight hours to traverse the sparsely settled district, which includes all or part of 38 counties. It is not uncommon for residents to travel 60 miles for health care.

And while the area remains politically competitive, voters like their candidates on the conservative side. Thornberry returned the district to Republican hands in 1994 with 55 percent of the vote and increased his total to 67 percent in 1996. That same year, Bob Dole carried the district in the presidential election, beating Bill Clinton by 52 percent to 39 percent.

Thanks to the addition of several counties along its southern border in 1992 redistricting, the 13th became the largest cotton-producing district in the nation. More than 1.8 million acres of cotton grow in the fertile land above the Ogallala Aquifer. Heavy agribusiness use of the aquifer has prompted concerns about depletion, and interest in conservation measures is increasing. Other leading crops include wheat, sorghum, sugar beets, corn and hay.

The biggest single chunk of votes in the 13th comes out of Wichita County and the blue-collar-oriented city of Wichita Falls.

Once heavily reliant on the oil industry, the area has weathered the oil slump with the assistance of income from Sheppard Air Force Base, just north of the city. Among the Air Force's largest training bases, Sheppard is headquarters of the NATO Jet Training Center.

At the northwestern corner of the 13th is the district's second-biggest concentration of people, in Potter County (Amarillo). The city of 158,000 is divided between the 13th and 19th districts.

The downtown business district, in the 13th, has been suffering since the oil crash of the mid-1980s; vacant office buildings and closed shops are much in evidence. Government-related business helps keep Amarillo going: A state prison is a major local employer, although the federal Bureau of Mines is being phased out. The Pantex nuclear plant is in contention to expand its existing operation of dismantling nuclear weapons.

Though the bulk of the 13th has a rural and small-town feel, on its far eastern edge the district pokes in to take a part of Denton County, which is in the orbit of the Dallas-Fort Worth metropolitan area. The voters here tend to be more liberal than the district norm. Clinton won that part of the county in 1996 with 50 percent of the votes, well above his district average.

1990 Population: 566,217. White 446,833 (79%), Black 45,342 (8%), Other 74,042 (13%). Hispanic origin 109,959 (19%). 18 and over 409,490 (72%), 62 and over 96,431 (17%). Median age: 32.

stitute — crafted by Texas GOP Rep. Larry Combest (for whom Thornberry once worked) — provided growers payments on fewer acres but offered them more freedom to make planting decisions than did the committee bill. "It makes more sense for cotton," Thornberry told the Dallas Morning News. "We have less flexibility than other parts of the country, like Iowa and Illinois, that have rain and rich soil."

From his seat on the National Security Committee in the 104th, Thornberry opposed Clinton's decision to send U.S. troops to Bosnia. Thornberry said members should "ask whether there is a vital national security interest in Bosnia that justifies risking the lives of young men and women. I do not think there is. Risking their lives just to make good on a rash, premature promise by the president is flat wrong and we ought to stop it."

Thornberry also disagreed with Clinton's opposition to additional funding for the construction of a U.S. anti-missile defense system. "Today we are vulnerable to accidental launch, to a rogue general acting on his own, or to some outlaw state such as Hussein or Qaddafi buying missiles, and we can do absolutely nothing to defend our people against a missile attack," Thornberry told the House. "I think that is wrong strategically, and I think that is wrong morally."

On National Security, Thornberry looks out for interests of Sheppard Air Force Base, just north of Wichita Falls. Sheppard is one of the largest Air Force training bases and home to the NATO Jet Training Center.

At Home: Although 1994 marked his debut as a candidate, Thornberry brought a congressional background into his bid for the 13th. From 1983 to 1988 he worked on Capitol Hill, first as a legislative aide to GOP Rep. Tom Loeffler, then as chief of staff for Combest. He also served as a deputy assistant secretary of State for legislative affairs.

Back in the state in 1989, Thornberry worked in an Amarillo law firm while helping run his family's cattle ranch. His family has been ranching in the Panhandle for five generations, a fact Thornberry played up in his challenge to Sarpalius.

Sarpalius took the 13th from the GOP when it was open in 1988, and by 1992 he had lifted his re-election tally to 60 percent. But Thornberry thought the political climate was favorable for him in 1994. He breezed through the GOP primary with 75 percent of the vote.

In the general election, he got some help from Bob Woodward, editor and investigative reporter for The Washington Post. Woodward's book about the Clinton administration's first year, "The Agenda," included an anecdote that portrayed Treasury Secretary at the time (and fellow Texan) Lloyd Bentsen as strong-arming Sarpalius to vote for Clinton's budget in 1993. Although Sarpalius said he sided with the president in exchange for an administration promise to protect the Helium Reserve, Thornberry accused Sarpalius of voting for the budget to repay Bentsen for raising campaign money for Sarpalius.

Adding to Sarpalius' woes was a brewing scandal: He and two other members of the Texas delegation were being investigated by the FBI for accepting illegal contributions from the owner of a bankrupt San Antonio moving firm, Sherwood Van Lines. The firm's owner, Leslie Alfred Taber, was indicted in September 1994 on charges of making illegal corporate contributions, including providing moving services at reduced rates.

With Sarpalius in a weakened state and the national tide running in favor of the GOP, Thornberry returned the 13th to Republican hands with 55 percent of the vote. He won a second term in 1996 with two-thirds of the vote.

HOUSE ELECTIONS

1996 General		
William M. "Mac" Thornberry (R)	116,098	(67%)
Samuel Brown Silverman (D)	56,066	(32%)
1994 General		
William M. "Mac" Thornberry (R)	79,466	(55%)
Bill Sarpalius (D)	63,923	(45%)

CAMPAIGN FINANCE

	Receipts	Receipts from PACs	Expend-itures
1996			
Thornberry (R)	$620,638	$161,219 (26%)	$565,578
Silverman (D)	$17,154	$750 (4%)	$16,125
1994			
Thornberry (R)	$448,265	$53,365 (12%)	$442,237
Sarpalius (D)	$537,208	$283,275 (53%)	$540,096

DISTRICT VOTE FOR PRESIDENT

	1996		1992
D	69,157 (39%)	D	73,417 (36%)
R	92,806 (52%)	R	87,463 (43%)
I	14,030 (8%)	I	41,186 (20%)

KEY VOTES

1997	
Ban "partial birth" abortions	Y
1996	
Approve farm bill	Y
Deny public education to illegal immigrants	Y
Repeal ban on certain assault-style weapons	Y
Increase minimum wage	N
Freeze defense spending	N
Approve welfare overhaul	Y
1995	
Approve balanced-budget constitutional amendment	Y
Relax Clean Water Act regulations	Y
Oppose limits on environmental regulations	N
Reduce projected Medicare spending	Y
Approve GOP budget with tax and spending cuts	Y

VOTING STUDIES

	Presidential Support		Party Unity		Conservative Coalition	
Year	**S**	**O**	**S**	**O**	**S**	**O**
1996	35	65	97	3	100	0
1995	17	83	99	1	100	0

INTEREST GROUP RATINGS

Year	ADA	AFL-CIO	CCUS	ACU
1996	0	n/a	94	100
1995	0	0	100	96

14 Ron Paul (R)

Of Surfside — Elected 1996, 4th full term
Also served 1976-77, 1979-85

Biographical Information

Born: Aug. 20, 1935, Pittsburgh, Pa.
Education: Gettysburg College, B.S. 1957; Duke U., M.D. 1961.
Military Service: Air Force, 1963-65; Air National Guard, 1965-68.
Occupation: Physician.
Family: Wife, Carol Wells; five children.
Religion: Protestant.
Political Career: U.S. House, 1976-77, 1979-85; sought Republican nomination for U.S. Senate, 1984; Libertarian candidate for U.S. President, 1988.
Capitol Office: 203 Cannon Bldg. 20515; 225-2831.

Committees

Banking & Financial Services
Domestic & International Monetary Policy; Financial Institutions & Consumer Credit
Education & Workforce
Early Childhood, Youth & Families; Workforce Protections

The Path to Washington: Paul earned a return trip to the House in 1996 by winning the 14th, which includes some areas he represented in his earlier House career. Those two stints of a little over six years combined ended after Paul lost a 1984 bid for the GOP Senate nomination.

In 1988, Paul aimed even higher, running for president as the nominee of the Libertarian Party. He ran third behind George Bush and Michael S. Dukakis, polling 432,179 votes (less than 1 percent).

Paul has long believed that the federal government should have as limited a role in the lives of Americans as possible. "The [federal] government perpetually takes our money, lies to us and makes our lives worse," Paul says. He backs legislation requiring members of Congress to document the constitutional authority for what they are proposing in bills they introduce.

Back in the GOP and on the House campaign trail in 1996, Paul liked to tell his supporters that his longstanding call for abolition of the Internal Revenue Service has now come into vogue. He backs a reduction in federal taxes.

Paul would like to see continued cuts in federal spending and says Congress should take aim at foreign aid. He calls it "incredible" that the United States continues to provide "foreign aid giveaways" while it struggles to balance the budget.

Paul, an obstetrician and gynecologist, breaks with former Libertarian brethren on abortion, which he opposes. He sits on the Banking and Financial Services Committee, a panel on which he served in his last term in Congress.

Paul, who also sits on the Education and the Workforce Committee, believes the federal government should eliminate its role in education, leaving the matter to states and localities. However, he denied that he supported the abolition of public schools, a charge leveled by his Democratic opponent in 1996, lawyer Charles "Lefty" Morris.

Indeed, Paul's views on many issues — many of which he expounded on in his political newsletter — provided Morris with much ammunition. Morris' most potent issue was his charge that Paul supports the legalization of drugs. To bolster his point, Morris produced numerous Paul-authored articles calling for the elimination of federal drug laws. Morris even used in a TV ad a video clip of Paul making such a point.

Paul says the federal government's war on drugs has been "an absolute failure." But while he backs the elimination of federal drug laws, he says he opposes the use of drugs and says the issue should be handled by the states.

Paul labeled Morris a typical big-government liberal who supported an increase in taxes on Social Security benefits. Paul nudged into the victory column with 51 percent of the vote.

Paul drew sharp criticism for saying on a February 1997 C-SPAN program that he lives in fear of being "bombed by the federal government at another Waco." In a House floor speech the following day, Democratic Rep. Chet Edwards, who represents the Waco area, blasted Paul's comments as "irresponsible" and "outrageous."

Paul's bid to return to Congress began with his wresting the GOP nomination from four-term Rep. Greg Laughlin, a former Democrat who switched to the GOP in June 1995. Laughlin had the backing of most of the state and national GOP establishment in the primary match.

But Paul, whose years as an outspoken conservative had given him a nationwide network of support to tap, declared himself the true Republican in the race. He continued to press the point with his anti-tax and anti-government message, painting Laughlin as a latecomer to the conservative cause. That was enough to bring Paul victory in the GOP runoff. He took 54 percent of the vote to Laughlin's 46 percent.

Paul was elected to Congress in an April 1976 special election to replace Democratic Rep. Bob Casey, who resigned to take a seat on the Federal Maritime Commission. Paul defeated Democrat Bob Gammage, who in the general election seven months later felled Paul by 268 votes. But Paul prevailed in 1978, edging Gammage by 1,200 votes.

TEXAS 14
Southeast; Gulf Coast

Larger than the state of Massachusetts, the 14th stretches from the western outskirts of Austin to the Gulf Coast. Residents are dispersed widely across this huge land mass; the district personifies rural and small-town Texas.

Two industries — agriculture and petrochemicals — dominate the 14th. Almost every major farm commodity is grown somewhere in the district. Grain, sorghum and rice are the most notable crops, grown primarily in the southern counties of Matagorda, Wharton, Jackson, Victoria, Refugio and Colorado. Hay is a major crop in Fayette County and Austin County, just over the 14th's boundary line in the 8th District.

Closer to the coastline, petrochemical plants dot the landscape. Dow, du Pont, Phillips Petroleum and Union Carbide all have facilities in the 14th. When oil prices dropped in the mid-1980s because of a worldwide glut, petrochemical companies flourished. The companies use oil as a base product to produce chemicals that are combined with other chemicals to make such items as antifreeze, foam and plastics.

Victoria, population 55,000, is the district's only sizable city. Originally settled by the French explorer La Salle in 1685, the city was named in 1824 for a Mexican president, Guadalupe Victoria. After centuries as a leading cattle and cotton capital, Victoria today is a major oil and chemical center.

Intermingled with the chemical plants are lively fishing ports that haul in shrimp for tourists and locals. Port Lavaca in Calhoun County successfully combines commercial fishing, tourism and offshore drilling businesses. In adjacent Aransas County, nature lovers flock to Goose Island State Park, Aransas National Wildlife Refuge and several bird sanctuaries.

Bastrop County, in the northwestern corner of the huge district, is being pulled into the suburban orbit of growing Austin, in the 10th District. Less than 25 miles from the state capital, the city of Bastrop also boasts the University of Texas cancer research center. Austin's liberal views have begun to rub off on its neighboring county; Bastrop was one of the few counties in the 14th to support Bill Clinton for president in 1996, giving him 46 percent of the vote in the three-way race.

Although the 14th includes former President Lyndon B. Johnson's birthplace in Blanco County, the district is more conservative than its famous native. Like Texas at-large, the district now leans Republican. In 1992, George Bush received 41 percent, Clinton 37 percent, and Ross Perot 22 percent, matching the candidates' statewide percentages. In 1996, Bob Dole defeated Clinton by a slightly larger margin — 50 percent to 42 percent — than he had statewide. And Paul convinced voters to put the House seat in Republican hands after they had voted for Democrats for years.

Minorities make up more than one-third of the 14th. Victoria, Matagorda and Lavaca counties all have sizable black and Hispanic communities, and Waller County's Prairie View A&M University, founded in 1878, is a predominantly black college, with 6,000 students.

1990 Population: 566,217. White 440,178 (78%), Black 60,290 (11%), Other 65,749 (12%). Hispanic origin 133,703 (24%). 18 and over 407,375 (72%), 62 and over 91,303 (16%). Median age: 32.

HOUSE ELECTIONS

1996 General		
Ron Paul (R)	99,961	(51%)
Charles "Lefty" Morris (D)	93,200	(48%)
Ed Fasanella (NL)	2,538	(1%)
1996 Primary Runoff		
Ron Paul (R)	11,244	(54%)
Greg Laughlin (R)	9,555	(46%)
1996 Primary		
Greg Laughlin (R)	14,777	(43%)
Ron Paul (R)	11,112	(32%)
Jim Deats (R)	8,466	(24%)
Ted Bozarth (R)	398	(1%)

Previous Winning Percentages: 1982 (100%) **1980** (51%) **1978** (51%) **1976*** (56%)

* *Special election runoff.*

CAMPAIGN FINANCE

	Receipts	Receipts from PACs		Expend-itures
1996				
Paul (R)	$1,933,263	$133,666	(7%)	$1,927,756
Morris (D)	$979,070	$2,000	(0%)	$977,888

DISTRICT VOTE FOR PRESIDENT

	1996			1992	
D	84,374	(42%)	**D**	78,741	(37%)
R	100,297	(50%)	**R**	86,214	(41%)
I	15,694	(8%)	**I**	47,082	(22%)

KEY VOTES

1997

Ban "partial birth" abortions Y

15 Rubén Hinojosa (D)

Of Mercedes — Elected 1996, 1st term

Biographical Information

Born: Aug. 20, 1940, Edcouch, Texas.

Education: U. of Texas, B.B.A. 1962; U. of Texas, Pan American, M.B.A. 1980.

Occupation: Food processing executive.

Family: Wife, Martha; five children.

Religion: Roman Catholic.

Political Career: Texas State Board of Education, 1974-84, chairman of special populations.

Capitol Office: 1032 Longworth Bldg. 20515; 225-2531.

Committees

Education & Workforce
Employer-Employee Relations; Postsecondary Education, Training & Life-Long Learning

Small Business

The Path to Washington: Hinojosa was a well-known figure in the Rio Grande Valley long before he jumped into the 1996 race to succeed Democratic Rep. E. "Kika" de la Garza, who retired after more than three decades in the House. Hinojosa had been serving as president of his family's successful meat packing and food manufacturing company, which has operated in the Rio Grande Valley for five decades, and had been active in education issues in south Texas.

Among Hinojosa's top priorities are expanding employment and educational opportunities in the district, which includes some of Texas' poorest areas. One way to increase job opportunities, he says, is by modernizing the district's infrastructure, which could help facilitate business development.

Hinojosa says he will work to secure funding for a new highway that would serve as a trade route from Mexico and would help relieve the traffic bottleneck that has been exacerbated by increased commercial traffic since the passage of NAFTA.

He also favors providing incentives to help boost economic development in the district. Hinojosa supports reducing the capital gains tax and providing investment tax credits for businesses to make capital improvements. Hinojosa also favors adding new nations to the NAFTA trading bloc to increase trade.

Another key way of improving life for the district's residents is by increasing access to education, he believes.

A former state Board of Education member and founding regent of South Texas Community College, Hinojosa says he plans to work to increase funding for Pell grants, scholarships and other educational programs for colleges, universities and residents in the district.

Hinojosa landed a seat on the Education and the Workforce Committee, a panel which will provide him with an opportunity to work toward this goal.

His predecessor, de la Garza, had looked after farming interests in south Texas from the House Agriculture Committee, which he chaired from 1981 until Republicans won control of Congress in 1994.

Another area of concern for Hinojosa is access to housing for district residents. He says he will work to expand current federal initiatives that help provide affordable housing to the poor.

Given the 15th District's strong tradition of voting Democratic — it is one of the party's most loyal districts in the state — Hinojosa's biggest challenge in capturing this seat was winning his party's nomination. Hinojosa came out on top of the five-way Democratic primary but was forced into a runoff with lawyer Jim Selman.

Selman, an Anglo, made a big push to garner support in the Hispanic community. He also focused his campaign on fighting corruption and promised to use his position as a member of Congress to ensure that federal dollars that have been misused by local officials in the past are used as intended.

In the closing days of the primary campaign, the candidates turned on each other. Selman questioned Hinojosa's Democratic credentials. Hinojosa criticized Selman's judgment for hiring a campaign worker who allegedly had brushes with the law in the past and a controversial work history.

At the same time, Hinojosa stressed his roots in the district, his business experience and his work on education issues.

Both candidates helped finance their campaigns out of their own pockets, but Hinojosa was able to dig deeper into his own wallet than Selman could.

Hinojosa prevailed in the runoff and won the general election with 62 percent of the vote over Republican minister Tom Haughey, the 1992 and 1994 GOP nominee.

Haughey attempted to snag Hinojosa by questioning some of his business dealings and his knowledge of key issues. But the Republican was outgunned by the district's strong Democratic tilt and Hinojosa's huge fundraising edge.

The 15th remains Texas' most heavily Hispanic district (nearly 75 percent of the population) and a reliable vote-getting region for any Democrat. Despite losing the state, Bill Clinton won the 15th in 1992 with 53 percent of the vote, his highest non-urban district tally in Texas. He raised it to 60 percent in 1996.

The 1992 redistricting compressed the boundaries of the 15th, shifting two of the state's fastest-growing counties, Starr and Zapata, into the newly formed, Hispanic-majority 28th. Despite the removal of those two heavily Hispanic border counties, the 15th retains its Spanish flavor.

Goliad County, created in 1836 from a Spanish municipality, is among the state's most historic areas. Bisected by the San Antonio River, the region has several missions, historic churches and a statue of Gen. Ignacio Zaragoza, the Mexican leader who fought back French troops in 1862, leading to the celebration of Cinco de Mayo.

Hidalgo County, named for the leader of Mexico's independence movement, Miguel Hidalgo y Costillo, is 85 percent Hispanic. Anchored by McAllen, a major port of entry into Mexico, the county is noteworthy for its foreign trade and popularity with travelers. Many Midwesterners and Canadians spend the winter season in McAllen, drawn by its subtropical climate and tourist activities.

Hidalgo, the 15th's most populous county with nearly 500,000 residents, grew by 75 percent from 1980 to 1996. But it is one of Texas' most economically depressed areas. More than 40 percent of Hidalgo's residents live below the poverty level and its unemployment rate hovers in the upper teens. Hidalgo County's economy is wedded to agriculture; cotton, grain, vegetables and sugar cane are among the most common crops.

TEXAS 15
South — Bee, Brooks, Hidalgo and San Patricio counties; McAllen

Like most of the counties along the Rio Grande, Hidalgo relies on maquiladora plants for much of its income. The system of "twin" plants enables the bulk of production work to be done at one facility on the Mexican side of the border, while some finishing and distribution are handled by its American counterpart.

Although manufacturing along the border has picked up, the region's agribusiness was hurt by a freeze in the winter of 1989 and previous drought problems. More farmers have been forced to invest in irrigation, a costly investment but one that is paying off.

Lloyd Bentsen, the former Democratic senator and 1988 vice presidential candidate, was born in Hidalgo County and briefly served as a judge there before winning the first of three terms to the House from the 15th in 1948.

After Hidalgo, the most populous county is San Patricio, with just under 59,000 people. San Patricio is closely linked economically with the port city of Corpus Christi, which lies just across the bay in the 27th District.

In the northern, sparsely populated counties of the 15th, cattle, agriculture and some oil production account for most revenue. Timber and furniture-making are important industries in De Witt County.

Panna Maria, in Karnes County, is the oldest Polish settlement in the state.

1990 Population: 566,217. White 427,363 (75%), Black 6,273 (1%), Other 132,581 (23%). Hispanic origin 422,066 (75%). 18 and over 369,299 (65%), 62 and over 74,994 (13%). Median age: 28.

HOUSE ELECTIONS

1996 General		
Rubén Hinojosa (D)	86,347	(62%)
Tom Haughey (R)	50,914	(37%)
1996 Primary Runoff		
Rubén Hinojosa (D)	24,940	(52%)
Jim Selman (D)	22,983	(48%)
1996 Primary		
Rubén Hinojosa (D)	21,726	(34%)
Jim Selman (D)	21,138	(33%)
Renato Cuellar (D)	13,832	(22%)
Tony Dominguez (D)	5,008	(8%)
Reynaldo Balli Jr. (D)	1,877	(3%)

CAMPAIGN FINANCE

	Receipts	Receipts from PACs	Expend-itures
1996			
Hinojosa (D)	$741,978	$147,512 (20%)	$715,391
Haughey (R)	$39,724	$500 (1%)	$39,345

DISTRICT VOTE FOR PRESIDENT

1996		1992	
D	86,538 (60%)	D	63,998 (53%)
R	49,461 (34%)	R	40,299 (33%)
I	7,068 (5%)	I	16,747 (14%)

KEY VOTES

1997

Ban "partial birth" abortions — Y

16 Silvestre Reyes (D)

Of El Paso — Elected 1996, 1st term

Biographical Information

Born: Nov. 10, 1944, Canutillo, Texas.

Education: U. of Texas, 1964-65; Texas Western College, 1965-66; El Paso Community College, A.A. 1977.

Military Service: Army, 1966-68.

Occupation: U.S. Border Patrol agent.

Family: Wife, Carolina Gaytan; three children.

Religion: Roman Catholic.

Political Career: Canutillo School Board, 1968-70.

Capitol Office: 514 Cannon Bldg. 20515; 225-4831.

Committees

National Security
Military Installations and Facilities; Military Research & Development

Veterans' Affairs
Benefits

The Path to Washington: Reyes is the first Hispanic to represent the 16th District, where Hispanics make up 70 percent of the population.

A former U.S. Border Patrol regional chief, Reyes achieved national recognition before his 1996 election to Congress for his efforts in helping to reduce illegal immigration along El Paso's border with Mexico. Reyes developed "Operation Hold the Line," a program that significantly reduced the number of people who crossed illegally into the United States in the region he oversaw.

But Reyes notes that there are many other issues on his congressional agenda in addition to illegal immigration.

Reyes says he intends to focus on the impact of NAFTA on the district, which borders Mexico. He promises to work for federal funding to maintain the roads and bridges that must handle NAFTA-related commercial traffic. He is also concerned that American workers displaced as a consequence of NAFTA get the retraining they need to land new jobs.

Reyes says he would like to see the United States work with Mexico to open three additional ports of entry as a way to boost commerce and tourism in the region.

He also plans to work on producing agreements with Mexico on environmental issues, such as air pollution, water conservation and the transportation of hazardous material.

He advocates the creation of a research and development center to examine issues involving the conservation, reclamation and treatment of water, a precious resource in the Southwest.

Finding ways to lure more high-tech jobs to the district is also a priority for Reyes.

El Paso has yet to capitalize on the flow of high-paying jobs to other cities in the Southwest, he says, because of a lack of "leadership and initiative" on the issue by his predecessor, Democrat Ronald D. Coleman.

Given the importance of Fort Bliss to El Paso's economy, Reyes sought and won a seat on the National Security Committee. Reyes plans to work to protect the military installation from funding cutbacks and to pursue new military and civilian research projects.

An Army veteran who lost the hearing in his right ear in Vietnam, Reyes says he is sensitive to veterans' issues and wants to protect the benefits they earn as a result of combat. He can pursue that goal from his seat on the Veterans' Affairs Committee.

Reyes announced in October 1995 that he was retiring from the Border Patrol after more than 25 years and was widely believed to be weighing a primary challenge to Coleman.

But a few weeks after Reyes' announcement, Coleman announced that he would not seek an eighth term.

Even though Coleman had suffered some close electoral calls in recent years, the district has been reliably Democratic. As a result, much of the focus on the race to succeed Coleman was on the Democratic primary.

Reyes competed with four other contenders for the Democratic nomination. Reyes took first place but was forced into a runoff with lawyer Jose Luis Sanchez, a legislative aide to Coleman.

Reyes cited the need to restore integrity to the district, a veiled reference to Coleman's negative publicity that stemmed primarily from his 673 overdrafts at the House bank.

Sanchez, who had the backing of Coleman and many labor groups, questioned Reyes' Democratic loyalty by noting that he had hired a campaign treasurer who had worked for Republicans in the past.

But Sanchez was unable to overcome Reyes' name recognition and popularity in El Paso from his work with the Border Patrol. Reyes edged Sanchez 51 percent to 49 percent.

In the fall campaign, Reyes had no trouble dispatching Republican insurance agent Rick Ledesma, amassing 71 percent of the vote.

TEXAS 16
West — El Paso and suburbs

El Paso is the westernmost city in the nation's second largest state. Nearly as far from Houston as it is from Los Angeles, El Paso is one of the country's twenty most populous cities, with well over 500,000 residents (most of whom live in the 16th).

When the mosquito control unit hits the streets of El Paso, it doesn't stop at the border. When the El Paso Ballet was looking for new sources of revenue, it changed its name, ditching El Paso in favor of the more international Ballet of the Americas. And when Mexicans want jobs and Texans want inexpensive goods, they can cross the Bridge of the Americas.

This is life in the 16th, a compact, multicultural district on the Mexican border where jobs, entertainment, health and government blend and blur between El Paso and its sister city, Ciudad Juarez. Both English and Spanish are spoken fluently, native holiday celebrations are shared, and families are split between the two cities.

Nowhere is the interdependency more evident than in the maquiladoras, or twin plants, in which Mexican workers do the bulk of labor — making everything from cars to clothing — and Americans complete the products with finishing details. By one estimate, there are about 300 such plants in the El Paso-Juarez area alone.

Despite their commercial and cultural affinity, the two cities do not always get along. Shortly before Christmas 1992 the Mexican government lowered duty-free limits from $300 to $50 a person. That means Mexicans, who often shop at better-stocked El Paso stores, now can bring just $50 worth of goods home duty-free.

Textile manufacturing is the biggest industry in El Paso; Levi Strauss and Wrangler are major employers. The region is one of the few in the nation where long-staple Egyptian cotton, one of the finest cotton fibers, is grown.

El Paso's Fort Bliss is also a major employer, credited in 1996 for pumping $1.2 billion into the region's economy. Fort Bliss, which employs 20,000 military and civilian personnel, is home of the Patriot missile systems, the famed Scud-interceptor of the Persian Gulf War. Patriot crew members are trained at the U.S. Army Air Defense Artillery School here.

The University of Texas at El Paso adds 16,500 students to the city; many other El Paso residents travel west to nearby New Mexico State University.

As El Paso's population has grown, the city has struggled with problems such as pollution and poverty. Nearly 27 percent of El Paso residents live below the poverty level.

Like the district at-large, El Paso is heavily Hispanic (80 percent of the population). Although Ronald D. Coleman, an Anglo, represented the 16th from 1983 to 1997, voters elected Reyes, a Hispanic, to replace him. Hispanics occupy several other prominent elected offices and essentially control all elections. Despite losing by a wide margin statewide, 1996 Democratic Senate candidate Victor Morales easily won the 16th. Bill Clinton defeated Bob Dole here by nearly a 2-to-1 margin in 1996.

1990 Population: 566,217. White 432,989 (76%), Black 20,272 (4%), Other 112,596 (20%). Hispanic origin 398,384 (70%). 18 and over 382,985 (68%), 62 and over 59,389 (10%). Median age: 28.

HOUSE ELECTIONS

1996 General		
Silvestre Reyes (D)	90,260	(71%)
Rick Ledesma (R)	35,271	(28%)
Carl Proffer (NL)	2,253	(2%)
1996 Primary Runoff		
Silvestre Reyes (D)	21,161	(51%)
Jose Luis Sanchez (D)	20,157	(49%)
1996 Primary		
Silvestre Reyes (D)	22,119	(42%)
Jose Luis Sanchez (D)	14,698	(28%)
Dolores Briones (D)	11,583	(22%)
Harry Thomas Peterson (D)	3,095	(6%)
Bob Levy (D)	610	(1%)

CAMPAIGN FINANCE

	Receipts	Receipts from PACs	Expenditures
1996			
Reyes (D)	$588,716	$215,134 (37%)	$587,193
Ledesma (R)	$110,941	$700 (1%)	$110,765

DISTRICT VOTE FOR PRESIDENT

	1996		1992
D	80,475 (63%)	D	65,614 (51%)
R	40,983 (32%)	R	45,366 (35%)
I	5,902 (5%)	I	18,781 (14%)

KEY VOTES

1997

Ban "partial birth" abortions — Y

17 Charles W. Stenholm (D)

Of Stamford — Elected 1978, 10th term

Biographical Information
Born: Oct. 26, 1938, Stamford, Texas.
Education: Tarleton State Junior College, 1957-59; Texas Tech U., B.S. 1961, M.S. 1962.
Occupation: Cotton farmer; teacher.
Family: Wife, Cynthia Ann Watson; three children.
Religion: Lutheran.
Political Career: No previous office.
Capitol Office: 1211 Longworth Bldg. 20515; 225-6605.

Committees
Agriculture (ranking)

In Washington: If the balanced-budget agreement that congressional Republicans and the White House announced in May 1997 takes hold and brings the deficit to zero by 2002, then Stenholm will deserve part of the credit. He has been trying to get rid of federal red ink for many years and in more ways than one. His most notable efforts have been in behalf of a balanced-budget constitutional amendment and as a catalyst for centrist budget plans devised by the "blue dog" coalition of fiscally conservative House Democrats.

After pushing for years in Democratic-controlled Congresses to enact a balanced-budget constitutional amendment, Stenholm finally saw his labors rewarded in the House — but only after Republicans took control in the 104th Congress.

In January 1995, the House mustered the necessary two-thirds majority to pass the measure. The language was crafted by Stenholm, and was virtually identical to versions that had failed in the three previous Congresses. His amendment prevailed over one sponsored by Texas Republican Joe L. Barton that would have put constraints on attempts to increase taxes, which Stenholm thought unwise.

To Stenholm's dismay, the Senate in March 1995 fell just short of passing the amendment. Two more times, in 1996 and 1997, the measure failed in the Senate. After the March 1997 Senate vote, House GOP leaders shelved plans to bring up the amendment because Republicans appeared not to have the votes to defeat a proposed Democratic amendment to exclude Social Security trust funds from deficit calculations.

Supporters of the balanced-budget amendment argued that the Social Security issue is purely a political fig leaf to justify a "no" vote on the amendment. "More and more members, when they stop and look at the facts, understand that it's the debt and the deficit that are the biggest threats to Social Security. It is not a balanced-budget amendment," said Stenholm.

While pursuing the balanced-budget amendment, Stenholm also has devoted energy to the more conventional legislative route to a balanced budget. Marshalling the blue dog Democrats, Stenholm and the group stepped forward in 1995, 1996 and 1997 with budget blueprints that, even though they fell by the wayside, were credited with being legitimate alternatives to the GOP and White House budget proposals.

The main thrust of the blue dog budget approach is a "peas before dessert" philosophy: No tax cuts allowed until after the budget is balanced by restraints on spending.

After Congress and Clinton failed to agree on a long-term budget plan during the 104th, Stenholm expressed confidence in late 1996 that a consensus would build around the blue dogs' plan. "There will either be a centrist budget or there will be no budget," he said.

In the May 1997 budget compromise, Clinton and Republican leaders of Congress found their own way to a middle ground. Their plan included early tax cuts and actually projected a near-term deficit increase, but it showed the red ink disappearing by 2002.

Stenholm may not always see eye-to-eye with the more liberal leaders of his party in the House, but he commands respect as a man of principle and substance. His relationship with Democratic leaders remains cordial because he will sometimes help them on sticky votes. He serves as a regional whip and as a member of the Democrats' Steering Committee.

Along with his pursuit of a balanced federal budget, Stenholm, a cotton farmer, fights equally hard for the farmers in his district. In the 105th, he is the Agriculture Committee's ranking Democrat. Although the committee's hardest work is now behind it with the 1996 passage of a seven-year overhaul of farm programs, the panel is expected to pass a reauthorization of farm research programs and to hold oversight hearings on forestry issues, a topic of importance to committee Chairman Bob Smith of Oregon.

Despite his fiscal austerity, Stenholm has been a strong supporter of government assistance for agriculture. When the GOP-led committee began

TEXAS 17
West Central — Abilene

In the oil industry's heyday, 100 rigs dotted the rolling prairie of the 17th. Today, there are only about a fraction in the enormous district, which lies west of Fort Worth. As was the case elsewhere in oil-dependent Texas, entire towns in the 17th virtually collapsed with the industry; businesses closed and banks foreclosed on mortgages. For a time, a popular local bumper sticker warned off job-seeking newcomers with this message: "Welcome to Texas. Now Go Home."

To survive, many of the people who held on in West Texas returned to the land or looked to the government. In the 1990s, agriculture, prisons and the defense industry are the 17th's three top sources of jobs.

The only large city in the district is Abilene (Taylor County), with almost 107,000 people. In 1991 it became a member of the Texas Main Street Project, a private-public effort to revitalize the downtown by renovating and reusing historic buildings. Three church-sponsored colleges in Abilene help nurture the 17th's large and powerful evangelical community.

Taylor County's conservatism was evident in 1996, as Bob Dole took 59 percent of its vote. Dole carried the 17th overall with 51 percent. In the House race, Democrat Stenholm got only 44 percent in Taylor County, but won his closest reelection battle yet.

Dyess and Goodfellow Air Force bases are reliable employers. More than 5,000 people are stationed at Dyess, in Abilene. It is the only training base in the country for the B-1B bomber, and personnel here also train on refueling planes and maintain a fleet of several dozen aircraft.

Goodfellow is in Tom Green County (San Angelo), which is split between the 17th and 21st districts. Though the base itself is just over the 17th boundary line, it still has a major economic impact here. Goodfellow, with about 2,500 employees, has appeared on proposed base-closing lists, but a new firefighting training unit has been added to its intelligence-training operation.

The 17th is also home to a number of defense-related private companies. A Lockheed-Martin plant in Abilene (purchased from General Dynamics in early 1993) builds components for the F-16 aircraft. The future of the facility is cloudy, given the uncertainty over whether the Air Force will end procurements of the F-16 by the late 1990s.

The area around San Angelo is a major producer of wool and mohair. Tom Green County, with its rocky terrain, is ideally suited to sheep and goats. Counties in the northeastern corner of the 17th rely on beef sales, while the counties at the opposite end of the district, more than 200 miles away, are major cotton producers.

The prison business is booming in the 17th. On the western side of the district, the Big Spring federal correctional facility has given an economic boost to Howard County. It has 270 employees tending 1,000 inmates. Other prisons in the 17th include Abilene's 2,000-inmate maximum-security unit, and the Price Daniel unit in Snyder (Scurry County).

1990 Population: 566,217. White 485,216 (86%), Black 20,038 (4%), Other 60,963 (11%). Hispanic origin 97,116 (17%). 18 and over 412,570 (73%), 62 and over 106,238 (19%). Median age: 34.

to rewrite farm policy in the 104th, Stenholm at first took a dim view of the effort. The sweeping measure, known as "Freedom to Farm," did away with the decades-old system of issuing subsidies when market prices drop and requiring farmers to plant the same commodities every year. Instead, farmers who sign seven-year contracts with the government would receive fixed, but declining, payments every year, regardless of market prices or their planting decisions.

When the committee met in September 1995 to consider the farm bill, Stenholm offered a substitute amendment that would have cut farm programs by no more than $4.4 billion over seven years. Stenholm said that would be sufficient to help balance the budget by the year 2002 under a Democratic balanced-budget proposal that did not incorporate the GOP's desire for $245 billion in tax cuts. Republicans, however, said the committee had to heed the level of cuts called for in the GOP-backed budget resolution. Stenholm's proposal was rejected on a party-line vote.

Bucking the bill proposed by committee Chairman Pat Roberts of Kansas, Stenholm then backed a rival bill, offered by Republicans Larry Combest of Texas and Bill Emerson of Missouri, both with cotton growers in their districts. The Combest-Emerson bill would have basically retained the existing structure of farm programs.

Stenholm wanted to be sure that the overhaul of farm programs did not do away with the marketing loan system for cotton and rice. The marketing loan program allows farmers to take out a loan so they can sell when market prices are good, rather than forcing farmers to sell directly after harvest when prices are often low. Roberts had made some concessions to cotton, such as allowing relatively new farmers to receive subsidies, but he at first refused to preserve the loan program.

Crossing party lines, Stenholm and 17 other Democrats rallied behind the Emerson-Combest proposal. They said it made more drastic cuts than they wanted, but that it was better than the committee bill. But the proposal failed, 23-26, in part because Emerson and Combest won support from only three other Republicans. Then when four Republicans and all the Democrats voted against Roberts' bill, that measure was defeated.

The committee never did reach consensus on the bill in the fall of 1995, but Roberts rolled it into the GOP's broad seven-year budget reconciliation measure anyway. President Clinton vetoed the reconciliation measure in December 1995. As a result, the farm bill came to the House floor as a stand-alone bill in February 1996. Stenholm ultimately voted for the legislation after the marketing loans for cotton were retained.

At Home: As Stenholm's prominence in Washington has grown, his troubles at home have intensified. In 1996, most Democratic incumbents fared better than they had in the big GOP year of 1994. But Stenholm dropped to his lowest percentage ever, as Republican presidential candidate Bob Dole won the 17th. Stenholm managed only 52 percent against Republican Rudy Izzard, a businessman and dentist, who earned 47 percent.

In 1994, Stenholm had his first taste of disaffected voters when Phil Boone, an unheralded 34-year-old time management consultant, held him to 54 percent. Stenholm attributed his showing to generalized anti-Congress sentiment. "The anger at incumbents is the most severe I have ever seen," he told the San Antonio Express News. "The people are fed up with their government as they perceive it."

A third-generation West Texan, Stenholm is descended from Swedish immigrants who settled near Stamford, where he was born. He moved into politics in 1966, when the U.S. Agriculture Department made a ruling unfavorable to the cotton-growing plains section of Texas. As executive vice president of the Rolling Plains Cotton Growers Association, he visited Washington to lobby against the ruling and had partial success in changing it.

In 1977, President Jimmy Carter appointed Stenholm to a panel advising the U.S. Agricultural and Conservation Service. He resigned that post to run for the House in 1978, when veteran Democrat Omar Burleson retired.

Stenholm had a much smaller campaign treasury than his major rival for the Democratic nomination, wealthy lawyer and businessman A.L. "Dusty" Rhodes. But as a farmer and former member of the state Democratic executive committee, Stenholm had extensive agricultural and party ties. Although Rhodes spent more than $600,000, Stenholm outran the crowded primary field and defeated Rhodes by 2-to-1 in a runoff. An easy winner in the fall, he did not face a Republican again until 1992.

Stenholm had 86 overdrafts at the House bank, but his GOP opponent, Eastland businesswoman Jeannie Sadowski, did not pose a serious threat. Still, Stenholm's 66 percent tally was his lowest to that point, foreshadowing his bumpy races in 1994 and 1996.

HOUSE ELECTIONS

1996 General		
Charles W. Stenholm (D)	99,678	(52%)
Rudy Izzard (R)	91,429	(47%)
1994 General		
Charles W. Stenholm (D)	83,497	(54%)
Phil Boone (R)	72,108	(46%)

Previous Winning Percentages: 1992 (66%) **1990** (100%) **1988** (100%) **1986** (100%) **1984** (100%) **1982** (97%) **1980** (100%) **1978** (68%)

CAMPAIGN FINANCE

	Receipts	Receipts from PACs	Expend-itures
1996			
Stenholm (D)	$788,667	$494,453 (63%)	$804,936
Izzard (R)	$196,536	$16,294 (8%)	$192,082
1994			
Stenholm (D)	$662,788	$388,157 (59%)	$712,156
Boone (R)	$192,310	$564 (0%)	$192,079

DISTRICT VOTE FOR PRESIDENT

	1996		1992
D	76,074 (39%)	**D**	68,643 (34%)
R	98,802 (51%)	**R**	78,225 (39%)
I	19,196 (10%)	**I**	53,106 (27%)

KEY VOTES

1997	
Ban "partial birth" abortions	Y
1996	
Approve farm bill	Y
Deny public education to illegal immigrants	Y
Repeal ban on certain assault-style weapons	Y
Increase minimum wage	N
Freeze defense spending	N
Approve welfare overhaul	Y
1995	
Approve balanced-budget constitutional amendment	Y
Relax Clean Water Act regulations	Y
Oppose limits on environmental regulations	N
Reduce projected Medicare spending	N
Approve GOP budget with tax and spending cuts	N

VOTING STUDIES

	Presidential Support		Party Unity		Conservative Coalition	
Year	**S**	**O**	**S**	**O**	**S**	**O**
1996	52	46	49	50	90	10
1995	43	56	42	57	89	11
1994	53	47	41	58	92	3
1993	60	39	52	48	91	9
1992	68	29	52	47	88	10
1991	66	33	48	49	95	5

INTEREST GROUP RATINGS

Year	ADA	AFL-CIO	CCUS	ACU
1996	50	n/a	63	65
1995	35	67	63	44
1994	5	0	100	90
1993	10	17	73	78
1992	30	25	57	72
1991	5	17	90	70

18 Sheila Jackson-Lee (D)

Of Houston — Elected 1994, 2nd term

Biographical Information
Born: Jan. 12, 1950, Jamaica, N.Y.
Education: Yale U., B.A. 1972; U. of Virginia, J.D. 1975.
Occupation: Lawyer; congressional aide.
Family: Husband, Elwyn; two children.
Religion: Seventh-Day Adventist.
Political Career: Houston City Council, 1990-95; Houston municipal judge, 1987-89.
Capitol Office: 410 Cannon Bldg. 20515; 225-3816.

Committees
Judiciary
Commercial & Administrative Law; Crime
Science
Basic Research; Space & Aeronautics

In Washington: After graduating from the University of Virginia law school in 1975, Jackson-Lee took a staff job on Capitol Hill, and there she sought counsel from widely respected Texas Rep. Barbara Jordan on how to make an impact on society.

Jordan's advice must have been good. Now two decades later, Jackson-Lee holds the Houston House district that Jordan represented. Jackson-Lee, born in New York and educated at Yale and the University of Virginia, ended up in Texas when her husband took a job with the University of Houston. Jackson-Lee became an associate judge in Houston's municipal court and then won election as an at-large member of the City Council.

She earned a reputation as a tireless worker who rarely missed a political or community event. After four years on the council she sought a promotion to Congress in 1994; she defeated Rep. Craig Washington in the Democratic primary and coasted to election in November.

Jackson-Lee is one of only 14 Democrats in the House Class of 1994, but she seems energized rather than daunted by Democrats' minority status in the chamber. She wages rhetorical war on the House floor almost every day, rarely missing a chance to skewer the GOP and speak up for women, minorities and liberal Democratic principles.

In 1995, she said that the Republican budget proposal "continues the policies of wanton destruction of this nation's environment, human capital, and technological infrastructure." During debate on a GOP welfare-overhaul bill, she asked Republicans to "stop painting those children and welfare recipients as bad people. Can we not come together to recognize that they cry out for a helping hand, not a handout?"

In April 1996, when the House was poised to clear a bill giving the federal government new powers to battle domestic and international terrorism, Jackson-Lee complained that the measure curtailed civil rights. The bill included provisions pushed by conservatives that placed new restrictions on federal appeals by death-row inmates and other prisoners.

"What this bill does is provide selective due process and selective civil liberties," she said. "It allows the government to arbitrarily designate those who are terrorists, and infringes the fundamental privacy rights of all Americans."

Jackson-Lee is firmly in the liberal camp on social and economic issues. She supports abortion rights and gun control, wants to reduce defense spending and backed an increase in the minimum wage.

During House debate on a GOP bill to ban a particular abortion technique that opponents call "partial birth" abortion, Jackson-Lee told members the ban would take society "back to the old-fashioned witch hunt." Pounding her fist on the podium, she roared, "I tell you I am not going back. This is the most outrageous legislation I have ever heard!"

But verbal jousting with conservatives is just part of Jackson-Lee's work in Congress. From her seat on the Judiciary Committee, she also has shown some legislative leverage with members whose views differ substantially from hers.

During committee consideration of a bill to overhaul the nation's immigration laws, Jackson-Lee offered an amendment to increase the number of family reunification visas in the bill from 330,000 annually to 400,000, and to make it easier for U.S. citizens to bring in their parents who live abroad. Her amendment failed on a tie vote, 16-16, but Texas Republican Lamar Smith, author of the immigration bill, responded to criticism that the bill would make it difficult or impossible for the parents of U.S. citizens to reunite with their children. Smith offered an amendment, approved by voice vote, guaranteeing at least 25,000 slots per year for such immigrants.

Jackson-Lee sits on the Science Committee, where she is a firm supporter of NASA's space station project, which is part of the work of Houston's Johnson Space Center. Critics of the orbiting laboratory call it "pork in space," and annually they try to knock its funding out of the

TEXAS 18
Downtown Houston

The 18th originally was reconfigured for the 1990s as an X-shaped contortion with tentacles that stretched to two outlying airports, scooping up a handful of cozy suburbs along the way. After reapportionment gave Texas three new House districts, mapmakers set out to increase minority representation. In Houston, they took large parts of its 1980s version — primarily its Hispanic sections — and shifted them into a new Hispanic-majority 29th District.

But a three-judge federal panel ruled that the 18th — 51 percent black and 15 percent Hispanic — was one of three Texas districts that were unconstitutional racial gerrymanders. The boundaries of 13 Texas districts were redrawn in August 1996, in time for the November elections.

The revamped 18th is centered on downtown Houston and assumes a "Y" shape. Blacks represent 45 percent and Hispanics 23 percent of the district's residents.

The center of the "Y" is bound by I-10, I-45 and Route 59 and includes the central business district and many of the city's cultural attractions, including the Alley Theatre, the Houston Symphony and the Houston Ballet. The corporate headquarters for companies such as Enron and Pennzoil are here, as is the city's tallest building, the Texas Commerce Tower (1,002 feet).

The northwest prong of the "Y" scoops up territory that previously lay in the 7th and 29th districts. One neighborhood new to the 18th is The Heights, which languished into the early 1980s, but its image has improved as young professionals began restoring historic homes.

The southern prong of the "Y" sweeps up Texas Southern University (9,500 students) and the University of Houston (7,700 students).

Many of the district's suburbanites shop at the upscale Galleria Mall and cheer for pro basketball's Rockets at The Summit (both of which are located just outside the district, in the 7th).

While the district includes some pockets of economic comfort, life in the 18th continues to be a struggle for most. More than 30 percent of families with children live below the poverty line. There is virtually no commercial property to tax in the area, and the mostly low-income black residents cannot afford to pay higher property taxes on their homes.

Few live in downtown Houston, although its businesses provide jobs at all levels for the district's residents. But the effects of the mid-1980s oil bust are still evident. Downtown buildings once named for and primarily occupied by companies such as Exxon share quarters with banks and law firms.

Previously represented by the late Barbara C. Jordan and the late Mickey Leland, the 18th has always been one of the state's most Democratic districts. Bill Clinton's 73 percent tally in the 1996 presidential election marked his top performance in any Texas congressional district, and exceeded by seven points his 1992 tally in the old 18th.

As of May 19, the Census Bureau had not recalculated population data, racial and ethnic breakdowns, and age statistics for districts newly drawn for the 1996 election.

federal budget. Rep. Washington's skeptical attitude about the space station played a role in his 1994 primary loss to Jackson-Lee.

Jackson-Lee has been concerned with the living conditions at Allen Parkway Village, a rundown subsidized housing project on the west side of Houston. But when the House in May 1996 passed a broad overhaul of federal housing policy aimed partly at improving conditions in public housing, she voted "no." The overhaul consolidated federal housing programs into two block grants and gave local housing authorities more autonomy, but Jackson-Lee saw the measure as giving local housing authorities the power to demolish apartments without proper consideration for the residents or their rights.

"In my district, the residents of the Allen Parkway Village have been completely removed from the decision-making process by the local public housing authority," she said. "I have consistently argued that the residents of public housing must be involved in any plan to rehabilitate or demolish their homes."

She also voted against a similar measure that passed the House in May 1997 that included a provision requiring public housing tenants who are not working to perform eight hours of community service a month. Many House Democrats criticized the provision, arguing that requiring people to work without pay was equivalent to involuntary servitude, which is outlawed by the 13th Amendment. Yet Jackson-Lee was successful with an amendment to the bill that would encourage, but not require, contractors working in public housing projects to employ residents of such communities in some capacity.

Jackson-Lee also had to worry with a legal challenge to the constitutionality of her district. After the 1990 census, Texas gained three congressional seats. State legislators drew a congressional map with three oddly shaped new minority-dominated districts — the black-majority 30th in Dallas and two in Houston, the predominantly Hispanic 29th and Jackson-Lee's district, the black-majority 18th. In June 1996, the Supreme Court invalidated the districts as illegal racial gerrymanders. New lines were drawn for a number of districts, including the 18th, but they did not put her 1996 re-election at risk.

At Home: When Jackson-Lee took on Washington in the 1994 Democratic primary, she benefited from his controversial stands on three issues important to the Texas economy: NAFTA, the superconducting super collider and the space station. Critics portrayed his opposition to funding the space station and the Texas-based super collider as harming local employment prospects, and while his vote against NAFTA pleased organized labor, it angered the Houston business community, which poured money into Jackson-Lee's campaign.

Washington also was criticized for the number of votes he did not cast: His 74 percent 1993 House attendance record was the worst in the Texas delegation and the third-lowest in Congress.

Jackson-Lee made three unsuccessful bids for local judgeships in Houston before becoming a municipal judge in 1987. After her election to the City Council in 1990, she proved adept at the handshaking, back-slapping basics of building local political support. She sponsored and won unanimous support for a gun-safety law establishing penalties for parents who failed to keep guns in their homes locked up safely out of reach of children.

She pushed for expanded summer hours at city parks and recreation centers as a way to reduce gang activity. She also was successful in urging the creation of a city-authorized committee on homelessness. "I like to classify myself as a problem-solver," she said in her House campaign.

During her years in the House and before that in the Texas Legislature, Washington had gained a reputation as a passionate orator with a brash personal style that at times struck observers as bordering on arrogance. One local political writer described their House primary as a matchup between "Ms. Congeniality" and "Mr. Attitude."

The voters' verdict was decisive: 63 percent for Jackson-Lee to 37 percent for Washington. The November election was a foregone conclusion in the heavily Democratic 18th: Jackson-Lee won 73 percent against Republican high school teacher Jerry Burley.

After her district's boundaries were adjusted during the 1996 election year, Jackson-Lee had no problems adapting. She won 77 percent of the vote in the November balloting.

HOUSE ELECTIONS

1996 General*		
Sheila Jackson-Lee (D)	106,111	(77%)
Larry White (R)	13,956	(10%)
Jerry Burley (R)	7,877	(6%)
George A. Young (R)	5,332	(4%)
Mike Lamson (D)	4,412	(3%)
1994 General		
Sheila Jackson Lee (D)	84,790	(73%)
Jerry Burley (R)	28,153	(24%)
J. Larry Snellings (I)	1,278	(1%)
George M. Hollenbeck (LIBERT)	1,169	(1%)

** Because of court-ordered redistricting in August, an all-candidate special election was held in November. If no candidate received a majority of the vote then, the top finishers met in a December runoff.*

CAMPAIGN FINANCE

	Receipts	Receipts from PACs		Expend-itures
1996				
Jackson-Lee (D)	$486,443	$281,119	(58%)	$477,866
Lamson (D)	$12,795	0		$12,793
White (R)	$129,648	$3,250	(3%)	$124,166
Burley (R)	$25,535	$1,500	(6%)	$29,151
Young (R)	$27,448	0		$27,090
1994				
Jackson-Lee (D)	$659,224	$196,287	(30%)	$593,740
Burley (R)	$117,017	$6,520	(6%)	$113,182

DISTRICT VOTE FOR PRESIDENT

1996			1992		
D	116,059	(73%)	**D**	117,671	(66%)
R	37,280	(23%)	**R**	39,162	(22%)
I	5,515	(4%)	**I**	20,829	(12%)

KEY VOTES

1997	
Ban "partial birth" abortions	N
1996	
Approve farm bill	N
Deny public education to illegal immigrants	N
Repeal ban on certain assault-style weapons	N
Increase minimum wage	Y
Freeze defense spending	Y
Approve welfare overhaul	N
1995	
Approve balanced-budget constitutional amendment	N
Relax Clean Water Act regulations	N
Oppose limits on environmental regulations	Y
Reduce projected Medicare spending	N
Approve GOP budget with tax and spending cuts	N

VOTING STUDIES

	Presidential Support		Party Unity		Conservative Coalition	
Year	S	O	S	O	S	O
1996	84	11	86	6	39	53
1995	89	10	94	6	25	75

INTEREST GROUP RATINGS

Year	ADA	AFL-CIO	CCUS	ACU
1996	90	n/a	27	5
1995	100	100	21	0

19 Larry Combest (R)

Of Lubbock — Elected 1984, 7th term

Biographical Information
Born: March 20, 1945, Memphis, Texas.
Education: West Texas State U., B.B.A. 1969.
Occupation: Farmer; congressional aide; electronics wholesaler.
Family: Wife, Sharon McCurry; two children.
Religion: Methodist.
Political Career: No previous office.
Capitol Office: 1026 Longworth Bldg. 20515; 225-4005.

Committees
Agriculture
Forestry, Resource Conservation & Research (chairman); General Farm Commodities; Risk Management & Specialty Crops
Small Business
Government Programs & Oversight; Regulatory Reform & Paperwork Reduction

In Washington: Combest had reason to hope he might move from one House committee chair to another in the 105th Congress, but it was not to be. With his tenure as chairman of the Select Intelligence Committee set to expire at the end of the 104th, Combest trained his sights on the Agriculture Committee. He was its No. 3 Republican and the two members above him were moving on — one trying for the Senate, the other retiring. So in the summer of 1996, it looked like Combest needed only to win re-election in the 19th to accede to the Agriculture chair, which had "always been a dream" of his, he said.

But in August 1996, Combest fell victim to larger political machinations. Republican leaders, worried about losing the Oregon seat of troubled freshman GOP Rep. Wes Cooley, persuaded Cooley to drop his bid for re-election to make way for a comeback by his House predecessor, Bob Smith, who had retired at the end of his sixth House term in 1995. The GOP leadership promised Smith the Agriculture chairmanship if he'd run — which he did, winning easily.

Both Smith and Combest began service on the Agriculture Committee in 1985; Smith, however, had been seated ahead of Combest on the panel, and GOP leaders cited that as justification for giving Smith the committee chairmanship when he rejoined the House in the 105th.

Combest first learned of the leadership's maneuverings involving Smith through the news media. "It wasn't handled well," he said. However, he added that Speaker Newt Gingrich had apologized for that. For the 105th, he got the chair of Agriculture's Forestry, Resource Conservation and Research Subcommittee.

Combest has shown he has the knowledge, desire and deal-making ability to be a legislator with impact, and that impact is not always in keeping with leadership desires.

In the 104th, when the Agriculture Committee was considering a broad rewrite of federal farm programs, Combest had some of his own ideas, and they did not always jibe with the leadership-backed "Freedom to Farm" bill, which aimed to phase out New Deal-era crop subsidies, replacing them with fixed, but declining, payments that farmers would receive over seven years regardless of market prices or their planting decisions.

In September 1995, Combest joined committee Republican Bill Emerson of Missouri — who, like Combest, represented many cotton farmers — in introducing a rival bill to Chairman Pat Robert's measure. The Combest-Emerson bill basically would have retained the existing structure of farm programs.

The two also insisted that the farm bill keep the lucrative marketing loan system for cotton and rice, even if that meant cutting other farm programs to meet budget targets. The marketing loan program allows farmers to take out a loan so they can sell when market prices are good, rather than forcing farmers to sell directly after harvest, when prices are often low. Roberts made some concessions to cotton, such as allowing relatively new farmers to receive subsidies, but refused to preserve the marketing loan program.

Crossing party lines, 18 Democrats rallied behind the Emerson-Combest proposal. They said it made more cuts than they wanted, but that it was better than the committee bill. But the proposal failed, 23-26, as Emerson and Combest won support from only three other Republicans.

Combest, Emerson and Republicans Richard H. Baker of Louisiana and Saxby Chambliss of Georgia then joined Democrats in voting against the committee bill, bringing it down to defeat. "It's kind of like a chairman handing you a gun, saying: 'Either you shoot your farmers or I will.' I'm not going to pull the trigger," Combest said before the committee vote. The committee never did reach consensus on the bill, but Roberts rolled it into the GOP's broad seven-year budget reconciliation measure anyway.

Democrats later distributed an internal Republican memo describing a meeting of top GOP strategists where there was talk of punishing the four Republicans who voted against the farm bill. But Gingrich quashed talk of punishment, observing, "These four guys are not out-

TEXAS 19
Western Panhandle — Parts of Lubbock and Amarillo

For the visitor in search of the authentic Wild West complete with cowboys, oil rigs, barbecues and vast stretches of parched, barren countryside, the 19th delivers. But the romanticized images of Western life belie the tough times that have plagued the region's residents.

Enormously dependent on oil and gas, the northwestern reaches of Texas were devastated in the mid-1980s, when an oil glut and foreign competition sent prices plummeting. Banks began calling notes on small independents, prompting oil company bankruptcies and massive bank failures. Idled rigs collected rust, while petroleum engineers and geologists took huge pay cuts to work at local wholesale shops as clerks and cashiers. Others left the area.

Ector County, the center for Permian Basin oil field operations, is one of the state's leading oil-producing counties, generating more than 2 billion barrels since 1926. To the north, Amarillo is the hub for the Panhandle oil industry. Pipelines in the area extend as far as the Gulf Coast. Other counties in the 19th that are heavily dependent on the energy business include Midland, a major oil center, and Yoakum, which produces minerals, oil and natural gas.

Agriculture too has been a somewhat reliable, albeit challenging, line of work in the hot, dry region, although it remains a $12 billion business in the Panhandle-Southern Plains region.

The 19th's agricultural emphasis shifted slightly from cotton to cattle with the addition of several northern Panhandle counties in the 1992 redistricting. Nevertheless, cotton remains a staple, particularly in Lubbock County. A top agricultural county in the state, Lubbock has more than 230,000 irrigated acres. The city of Lubbock, which is split between the 19th and 13th districts, calls itself the world's largest cottonseed processing center. Reese Air Force Base has been another important employer in the city, but it was ordered closed under the 1995 list issued by the independent base-closing commission and is scheduled to close in the fall of 1997.

Cattle ranching is dominant in Oldham, Hansford and Randall counties.

The Amarillo Livestock Auction is one of the nation's largest, beginning on Wednesdays and often lasting several days. The city is split between two districts and counties: Randall County residents are in the 19th; Potter County, in the 13th.

The cowboy feel of the 19th is genuine. Amarillo sponsors Cowboy Mornings, chuck wagon breakfasts served after a ride across the plains. The Odessa-based Chuck Wagon Gang is a group of 250 local businessmen who travel the globe serving up barbecue and promoting West Texas. And the city, named in 1891 by Russian railroad laborers after their hometown, boasts the world's largest barbecue pit, big enough to grill 16,500 pounds of beef, some say.

The F-shaped 19th is good GOP territory. It was one of Bob Dole's best districts in 1996, when he took 67 percent of the vote. Combest was unopposed in 1994 and won with 80 percent of the vote in 1996.

1990 Population: 566,217. White 487,509 (86%), Black 14,410 (3%), Other 64,298 (11%). Hispanic origin 110,776 (20%). 18 and over 403,001 (71%), 62 and over 70,986 (13%). Median age: 31.

laws." Even so, the memo made news. At a September 1995 meeting with Emerson and Combest, Gingrich reassured the dissidents that they would not face any retribution. He then said he wanted their input on formulating farm policy.

Combest ended up voting for his party's budget reconciliation bill even with the Freedom to Farm provisions included. President Clinton then vetoed the reconciliation bill in December 1995.

The farm bill came to the House floor as a stand-alone measure in February 1996. Combest ultimately voted for it after the leadership finally agreed to retain the marketing loans for cotton.

Later in 1996, Combest gained House passage of a measure that he said would address problems with the farm bill. It permitted farmers receiving subsidies to plant a second crop of fruits or vegetables if an earlier crop failed. Combest said the planting of a second crop, called ghost acres, had been permitted in past years but that the Agriculture Department's interpretation of new farm law would bar the second planting.

In addition to his heavy involvement with the farm bill, Combest also had a full plate in his role as Intelligence Committee chairman. Early in the 104th, the House GOP leaders extended his term on Intelligence from six to eight years, allowing him stay on the panel and head it.

Combest's major quest as head of Intelligence was reshaping the U.S. intelligence bureaucracy. But after an ambitious start, Congress enacted legislation in September 1996 making limited organizational changes.

A series of intelligence-related scandals provided the impetus for Combest's proposal, which sought to broaden the powers of the Director of Central Intelligence. Combest and his counterpart on the Senate Intelligence Committee, Arlen Specter, R-Pa., argued that under existing system, the DCI had responsibility for the vast U.S. intelligence community but little power to control major elements of it. Most intelligence functions come under Pentagon control, including the Defense Intelligence Agency and spy satellites.

The overhaul effort, however, drew fierce resistance from the Pentagon and the House and Senate defense committees, which saw the proposal as a turf grab. Combest expressed disappointment when the National Security Committee in July 1996 gutted provisions in his bill. He insisted that his proposal took the military's intelligence requirements into account. "I believe we have to recognize that defense is the major customer of intelligence," he said. "We also have to recognize that some of the biggest threats to this country, like terrorism, are not defense-related."

Also as chairman, Combest had to deal with one of his committee members disclosing classified information. Robert G. Torricelli, D-N.J., revealed in March 1995 that a Guatemalan colonel who had been on the CIA payroll was responsible for the murder of an American innkeeper in Guatemala. Republicans charged that Torricelli violated the House secrecy oath imposed at the start of the 104th Congress.

Torricelli admitted violating the oath. But he said he did so because it conflicted with his moral and legal obligations to expose criminal activity — in this case, the CIA's involvement in the murder of an American. Republicans did not buy that argument. "I do not believe a member of Congress has the authority at any point to divulge classified information," said Combest.

Gingrich sought Torricelli's ouster from the intelligence panel. But after negotiations with the Democrats, he decided to let the ethics committee determine if Torricelli had violated House rules. The ethics committee in July 1995 said Torricelli should not be punished because the oath was vague; some members believed it applied to all information a member obtained while others believed it applied only to information received in an official House proceeding.

At Home: After a stint with the U.S. Agricultural Stabilization Service, Combest went to work for Texas GOP Sen. John Tower in 1971 as a specialist in agricultural affairs. He later became director of Tower's Texas offices and served as treasurer for his 1978 re-election campaign. Combest then returned to West Texas to sell electronic equipment, remaining active in GOP affairs.

When Democratic Rep. Kent Hance (who later switched to the GOP) announced for the Senate in 1984, Combest jumped for the 19th. The district had not elected a Republican in its 50-year history but voted regularly for GOP state and national candidates and was ripe to switch.

Combest was forced into a runoff by a hard-right conservative, but with support from many old-line GOP leaders, he won the runoff easily.

In November, Combest met Don Richards, a former Hance aide. Both stressed their farm roots and conservatism. Combest portrayed Richards as part of a too-liberal party. Richards spurned the national Democratic line on tax increases and cast himself as a conservative in Hance's mold. Combest carried the most populous counties — Ector and Lubbock — to overcome Richards' rural strength. He tallied 58 percent overall and has won re-election easily since then.

HOUSE ELECTIONS

1996 General		
Larry Combest (R)	156,910	(80%)
John W. Sawyer (D)	38,316	(20%)
1994 General		
Larry Combest (R)	120,641	(100%)

Previous Winning Percentages: 1992 (77%) **1990** (100%) **1988** (68%) **1986** (62%) **1984** (58%)

CAMPAIGN FINANCE

	Receipts	Receipts from PACs	Expend-itures
1996			
Combest (R)	$445,103	$226,100 (51%)	$440,379
Sawyer (D)	$46,062	$1,650 (4%)	$46,000
1994			
Combest (R)	$285,178	$91,020 (32%)	$148,894

DISTRICT VOTE FOR PRESIDENT

1996		1992	
D	51,993 (26%)	**D**	50,810 (23%)
R	133,391 (67%)	**R**	130,638 (60%)
I	12,333 (6%)	**I**	36,066 (17%)

VOTING STUDIES

	Presidential Support		Party Unity		Conservative Coalition	
Year	**S**	**O**	**S**	**O**	**S**	**O**
1996	35	65	96	4	100	0
1995	17	83	97	3	96	3
1994	40	59	86	14	97	3
1993	30	70	86	14	100	0
1992	79	21	82	17	94	6
1991	77	23	82	17	100	0

KEY VOTES

1997	
Ban "partial birth" abortions	Y
1996	
Approve farm bill	Y
Deny public education to illegal immigrants	Y
Repeal ban on certain assault-style weapons	Y
Increase minimum wage	N
Freeze defense spending	N
Approve welfare overhaul	Y
1995	
Approve balanced-budget constitutional amendment	Y
Relax Clean Water Act regulations	Y
Oppose limits on environmental regulations	N
Reduce projected Medicare spending	Y
Approve GOP budget with tax and spending cuts	Y

INTEREST GROUP RATINGS

Year	ADA	AFL-CIO	CCUS	ACU
1996	0	n/a	100	95
1995	0	0	100	96
1994	0	11	83	100
1993	5	8	91	96
1992	10	33	88	100
1991	0	8	90	95

20 Henry B. Gonzalez (D)

Of San Antonio — Elected 1961; 18th full term

Biographical Information

Born: May 3, 1916, San Antonio, Texas.

Education: San Antonio College, 1937; U. of Texas, Austin, 1937-39; St. Mary's U. of San Antonio, LL.B. 1943.

Occupation: Teacher; public relations consultant; translator.

Family: Wife, Bertha Cuellar; eight children.

Religion: Roman Catholic.

Political Career: Candidate for Texas House, 1950; San Antonio City Council, 1953-57, mayor pro tem, 1955-57; Texas Senate, 1957-61; sought Democratic nomination for governor, 1958; sought Democratic nomination for U.S. Senate, 1961.

Capitol Office: 2413 Rayburn Bldg. 20515; 225-3236.

Committees

Banking & Financial Services (ranking)

In Washington: Gonzalez, more than most other senior Democrats who once ruled the roost in the House, went into a shell with the Republican takeover in 1995. The energetic (if eccentric) former chairman of the Banking and Finance Committee was absent or inactive at many important committee sessions in the 104th Congress. An intensely proud man, he showed little interest in waging losing battles in committee, unlike many other Democrats who put up fierce resistance to the newly empowered GOP majority.

Ironically, Gonzalez's most notable achievement of late involved him defeating Democrats, not Republicans. In November 1996, he fended off two Democrats who challenged him for the ranking spot on Banking for the 105th Congress.

But one of the factors that kept him in the ranking seat was his promise to party colleagues that he would give up the seat after two more years and serve in an emeritus capacity — if Gonzalez, now past 80, tries for a 19th full term in the House in 1998.

The House Democratic Caucus let Gonzalez have two final years as ranking member after he made an emotional plea to stay on. The mercurial Texan, whose legendary independent streak has long ruffled the feathers of House leaders, demonstrated a vigor in the caucus session that noticeably had been lacking since the GOP takeover. He emerged with a plurality of the vote in a three-way race with John J. LaFalce of New York and Bruce F. Vento of Minnesota, the second- and third-ranking Democrats on the committee. Gonzalez got 82 votes, LaFalce 62 and Vento 47. LaFalce conceded rather than continuing the fight into a runoff, sparing the party a clash that made many Democrats uncomfortable.

The effort to topple Gonzalez arose after his repeated absences from committee meetings in the 104th caused even longtime supporters such as Barney Frank of Massachusetts to recommend that Democratic leaders push out Gonzalez.

"I think we had a very good six years under Henry," said Frank, who had been Gonzalez's conduit to the House Democratic leadership but supported LaFalce's challenge. "But the transition from chairman to ranking member was personally very tough for him."

Gonzalez's supporters mounted an active campaign. Committee colleague Joseph P. Kennedy II of Massachusetts said that Banking Democrats had pulled together to repel GOP initiatives even though Gonzalez himself had slowed. "What are we going to do, take away a ranking membership from a guy who is a folk hero among Democrats?" Kennedy asked. "This guy defines the Democratic Party's values."

Gonzalez helped himself with a masterful speech in which he made the one-last-term pledge that earned him the benefit of some members' doubt. "I say to you, I have served with honor and integrity and success. I have never failed myself and I have never failed you," Gonzalez told the caucus behind closed doors. "And so I appeal to you: Do the right thing. Do the fair thing. I appeal to your sense of justice: One last term as ranking member, and I will not disappoint you."

The caucus erupted in applause audible in the corridors of the Longworth House Office Building. "There were probably some votes that he swayed even in that speech, which is unusual around here," admitted LaFalce supporter Floyd H. Flake of New York. Gonzalez received two standing ovations, and balloting started immediately after his speech ended.

Gonzalez's victory came despite LaFalce receiving the Democratic Steering Committee's endorsement by a 22-19 margin, and Vento campaigning vigorously. "It's very difficult to express in words the profound sense of gratitude I feel at this moment," Gonzalez said after the vote. He said he did not harbor any ill feelings towards LaFalce or Vento, saying, "It's all part of the process. It's better to be tested and tried and win than not to be tried at all."

During a congressional career that has spanned nearly four decades and included three terms as chairman of the Banking Committee, Gonzalez has earned a reputation for iconoclasm

TEXAS 20
Downtown San Antonio

Population growth split the city of San Antonio into four congressional districts in 1992. Today, San Antonio and its 940,000 residents make up the third-largest city in Texas and the 10th-largest in the nation. The 20th, which once consisted of all of Bexar County, now takes in central San Antonio and a handful of rural communities to the west and southwest.

The 20th, which is 61 percent Hispanic, has a history of minority accomplishments. In 1981, San Antonio became the first major U.S. city to elect a Mexican-American mayor, Henry G. Cisneros (who became President Clinton's first secretary of Housing and Urban Development). Texas Attorney General Dan Morales is from San Antonio, and Hispanics dominate local and state legislative seats.

The district's Democratic inclinations are such that Bill Clinton polled 59 percent here in 1996.

San Antonio's popular tourist spots are tied to its ethnic culture and history. The Alamo, the city's oldest mission and the site of the 1836 battle with Mexico, is in the heart of downtown.

Despite the city's Hispanic majority and background — it was founded in the early 18th century by the Spanish — Anglos have controlled its economy since its early days as a cattle center. Today, government payrolls are the region's lifeblood; San Antonio is the state's largest military center. And the city and school district rank among the largest employers. The area was hit hard in the 1995 round of base closings when the commission voted to close Kelly Air Force Base, which accounts for more than 23,000 jobs. But Clinton asked the Pentagon to privatize some of the operations at Kelly, which could preserve 16,000 jobs over a five-year period.

Four other military facilities remain. Two are within the district: Fort Sam Houston, a major health services command; and Lackland Air Force Base, which includes the Wilford Hall military hospital. Two other San Antonio installations (Randolph Air Force Base and Brooks Air Force Base) are just outside the 20th's boundaries, but they play a major role in the district.

Tourism is the region's second-highest revenue producer. Besides the Alamo and other historic sites, the city's scenic Paseo del Rio, or Riverwalk, is a popular draw with its shops, restaurants and hotels winding along the San Antonio River.

Despite its popularity with visitors and its reputation as one of the most "livable" cities in the country, it is also one of the poorest. Nearly 15 percent of its residents are without health coverage; almost one-fifth of the people fall below the poverty line. Even the tourism industry, despite the revenue it brings in, is responsible for predominantly low-wage service jobs.

Most of the region's growth has been to the north, but in the 20th the new rural and suburban towns to the west and southwest are sparsely populated with retired veterans, small farmers and a handful of midlevel managers who commute to San Antonio.

1990 Population: 566,217. White 406,322 (72%), Black 32,629 (6%), Other 127,266 (22%). Hispanic origin 343,870 (61%). 18 and over 398,984 (70%), 62 and over 65,519 (12%). Median age: 30.

that few can match. Republicans remember him for advocating impeachment of Presidents Ronald Reagan after the 1983 Grenada invasion and the 1987 Iran-contra scandal, and George Bush after the 1991 Persian Gulf War. But Gonzalez also has been an affliction to some in his own party. His bulldogging of savings and loan kingpin Charles Keating Jr. played a part in ending the political careers of three Democratic senators with ties to Keating. And he gave no quarter when interrogating Democratic wise man Clark Clifford about his role in the world's biggest bank scandal, involving the Bank of Credit and Commerce International (BCCI).

Gonzalez's hands-off attitude toward Whitewater was rather out of character; in the past he had often shown himself to be an aggressive investigator. After the Gulf War, for instance, he waged a lonely crusade to expose what he saw as the U.S. government's wrongheaded pre-war attempts to curry favor with Iraq and help it strengthen its military — a policy he said had encouraged Iraqi leader Saddam Hussein to invade Kuwait.

But from the beginning, Gonzalez opposed using his Banking Committee to hold Whitewater hearings. He condemned Republican inquiries as a "witch hunt" and an "array of half-truths, old rumors, half-baked conspiracy theories and outright lies." Gonzalez finally gave in, but when the hearings took place in August 1994, he made prolific use of the gavel to enforce a five-minute limit for questioners and limit the scope of the inquiry.

Before he assumed the Banking chairmanship, his record as a legislator was dismissed as thin, even as he was revered in San Antonio for his unstinting defense of the underclass. But in the six years he chaired Banking, Gonzalez significantly rehabilitated his image in Washington. He helped repair one of the biggest financial debacles in the nation's history — the near-collapse of the savings and loan industry. He also helped avert a lesser crisis affecting banks by shepherding an overhaul of the deposit insurance system in 1991. He earns credit for being one of the House's most committed fighters for affordable housing, although victories on that front have been few in recent years. And in the 103rd — a Congress that failed to enact major legislation in several areas it pursued — Gonzalez's committee passed two significant measures: an interstate banking law and a community development law that married bank regulatory relief with several schemes to encourage lending in distressed communities.

Gonzalez has been a fighter since the beginning of his career, whether pressing solo causes or settling personal quarrels. He is a passionate populist, and a sincere if long-winded one. He also can be stubborn, short-tempered and prone to eruptions of anger. In 1963, he threatened to "pistol whip" and then struck a House Republican who claimed Gonzalez's "left-wing voting record" served the socialist-communist cause. In a San Antonio restaurant 23 years later, Gonzalez struck a man who had called him a communist; prosecutors later dropped misdemeanor charges.

At Home: Like many Texas Democratic incumbents, Gonzalez felt some impact from the big GOP year of 1994. While his Republican opponent, Balcones Heights City Council member Carl Bill Colyer, pulled in less than 40 percent of the vote, he nevertheless held the incumbent to his lowest winning margin since his first election in 1961.

The son of Mexican immigrants, Henry B. (as he is known both in Washington and in Texas) began climbing the local political ladder after World War II. He sought office while helping his father, the managing editor of a Spanish-language newspaper, run a translation service. Gonzalez made it to the state Senate in 1957 and quickly drew attention by filibustering against Democratic Gov. Price Daniel's bill to allow the state to close schools threatened by disturbances surrounding integration.

In 1958 Gonzalez ran as the liberal alternative to Daniel in the Democratic gubernatorial primary. He was beaten by a margin of more than 3-to-1, but the defeat only encouraged his ambition. Three years later, he sought the Senate seat vacated by Lyndon B. Johnson. While Gonzalez carried his home base, Bexar County, his statewide appeal as a candidate with a Hispanic name was limited. He ran sixth out of 73 candidates, gaining 9 percent of the vote.

But he soon had another chance. Later in 1961, Democrat Paul Kilday resigned from the House to accept a judgeship, and Gonzalez became the consensus Democratic candidate for the seat.

The special election was a clear liberal-conservative choice. Gonzalez was warmly endorsed by the Kennedy administration. John Goode, a former GOP county chairman, had the active assistance of Arizona Sen. Barry Goldwater and Texas' newly elected GOP senator, John Tower. With strong support in Hispanic areas, Gonzalez won with 55 percent. He became the first person of Mexican-American extraction to be elected to the House from Texas.

HOUSE ELECTIONS

1996 General		
Henry B. Gonzalez (D)	88,190	(64%)
James D. Walker (R)	47,616	(34%)
Alejandro "Alex" DePena (LIBERT)	2,156	(2%)
1994 General		
Henry B. Gonzalez (D)	60,114	(63%)
Carl Bill Colyer (R)	36,035	(37%)

Previous Winning Percentages: **1992** (100%) **1990** (100%) **1988** (71%) **1986** (100%) **1984** (100%) **1982** (92%) **1980** (82%) **1978** (100%) **1976** (100%) **1974** (100%) **1972** (97%) **1970** (100%) **1968** (82%) **1966** (87%) **1964** (65%) **1962** (100%) **1961**† (55%)

† Special election

CAMPAIGN FINANCE

	Receipts	Receipts from PACs	Expend-itures
1996			
Gonzalez (D)	$123,375	$46,600 (38%)	$86,231
Walker (R)	$138,847	$450 (0%)	$138,735
1994			
Gonzalez (D)	$116,025	$32,650 (28%)	$55,382

DISTRICT VOTE FOR PRESIDENT

	1996		1992
D	82,892 (59%)	**D**	81,373 (48%)
R	48,485 (35%)	**R**	57,964 (34%)
I	7,285 (5%)	**I**	28,970 (17%)

KEY VOTES

1997	
Ban "partial birth" abortions	N
1996	
Approve farm bill	Y
Deny public education to illegal immigrants	N
Repeal ban on certain assault-style weapons	N
Increase minimum wage	Y
Freeze defense spending	N
Approve welfare overhaul	N
1995	
Approve balanced-budget constitutional amendment	N
Relax Clean Water Act regulations	N
Oppose limits on environmental regulations	Y
Reduce projected Medicare spending	N
Approve GOP budget with tax and spending cuts	N

VOTING STUDIES

	Presidential Support		Party Unity		Conservative Coalition	
Year	S	O	S	O	S	O
1996	84	16	84	16	67	31
1995	82	14	82	11	48	44
1994	78	19	96	4	22	78
1993	90	10	95	5	34	66
1992	23	77	94	6	38	63
1991	32	67	93	7	16	84

INTEREST GROUP RATINGS

Year	ADA	AFL-CIO	CCUS	ACU
1996	80	n/a	38	15
1995	85	100	20	4
1994	75	100	25	15
1993	80	100	9	8
1992	80	92	38	4
1991	75	100	10	0

21 Lamar Smith (R)

Of San Antonio — Elected 1986, 6th term

Biographical Information

Born: Nov. 19, 1947, San Antonio, Texas.

Education: Yale U., B.A. 1969; Southern Methodist U., J.D. 1975.

Occupation: Lawyer; rancher.

Family: Wife, Elizabeth Lynn Schaefer; two children.

Religion: Christian Scientist.

Political Career: Texas House, 1981-82; Bexar County Commissioners Court, 1983-85.

Capitol Office: 2231 Rayburn Bldg. 20515; 225-4236.

Committees

Budget

Judiciary

Commercial & Administrative Law; Immigration & Claims (chairman)

In Washington: Like many subcommittee chairmen in the 105th, Smith intends to use his perch atop the Judiciary Subcommittee on Immigration and Claims more for oversight of the Clinton administration than for generating legislation. But in contrast to most of his Republican brethren holding gavels, Smith has already succeeded in shepherding a landmark bill into law: a 1996 crackdown on immigration.

Smith's careful stewardship of the immigration law overhaul marked a return to the form he displayed earlier in his House career. Before spending the 103rd Congress heading a House GOP response team that dispensed rhetorical tweaks at the Clinton administration, Smith had been best known as a quiet bill-crafter laboring in the legislative shadows. When the 1994 GOP House takeover put Smith in the spotlight on the contentious issues of borders, benefits and visas, he resisted the temptation to score debating points in favor of crafting passable legislation.

"Republicans need to show we can govern," Smith said in September 1996. "We need to show we can pass good legislation."

But Smith, who also serves on the Budget Committee, was no moderate thrust by the accident of seniority into handling an issue of vital interest to Republicans. He is a stalwart conservative who never broke from the GOP majority on any significant legislation during the 104th. A longtime ally of Newt Gingrich, he was called on at the start of the 105th to fill a two-week vacancy on the ethics committee as the panel wrapped up its investigation of the Speaker.

When his fellow Texan Dick Armey asked Smith to take on that assignment, he said, "As majority leader, I thank you for serving," Smith told The Hill, a Capitol Hill newspaper. "As a friend, you're a darn fool."

Smith turned out to be the lone committee dissenter as the panel recommended levying a reprimand and a $300,000 penalty against Gingrich for supplying the committee with misleading information about his questionable use of tax-exempt organizations for political gain. "There's some suggestion that if he didn't break the law, he came very close," Smith said. "If a football player comes very close — maybe very, very close — to being offsides, there's still no penalty." Smith also voted against the penalty on the House floor, arguing that it was far too severe to match the offense.

In 1996, Smith had to turn aside the importunings of another Republican Party leader to see his immigration bill across the finish line. In September, with the bill still in flux and the presidential campaign raging, Smith and his Senate counterpart, Alan K. Simpson, R-Wyo., sat down with former Senate Majority Leader Bob Dole's campaign manager. The Dole camp was convinced that instead of compromising with Clinton, the Republican Congress should pass a version satisfactory to itself and then dare — expect — the president to veto it, providing Dole a campaign bludgeon. Smith and Simpson, then the chairman of the Senate Judiciary Immigration Subcommittee, dismissed that logic and went ahead with their negotiations.

The biggest sticking point with the White House was a provision in the House bill sponsored by California Republican Elton Gallegly to deny illegal immigrants the benefit of a public education. Although the Gallegly amendment had passed the House and enjoyed passionate support within the House Republican Conference, Smith recognized it did not enjoy broad public support. And since the provision would end unless reauthorized in under three years, he deemed it not worth fighting for.

Smith declared himself "ambivalent" about the education language. "The children are the innocent parties," he said. "The real answer is to deport their parents." The Gallegly language was the immigration bill's only clear veto-bait and, in the end, Smith helped arrange a deal by which it was dropped from the immigration bill and voted on as a separate measure (which the House passed and the Senate ignored).

The final immigration bill, which was enacted

TEXAS 21
South Central — Western Bexar County; Austin Suburbs

The 21st typifies the lengths to which Texas mapmakers went to divide Democratic and Republican neighborhoods in 1992 redistricting. Although much of their effort was later ruled unconstitutional, the 21st was not affected.

As a result, for 350 miles the boundaries of the 21st run in simple, straight blocks, often paralleling county lines. But as the 21st approaches Bexar County, the lines go berserk. Four congressional districts lay claim to portions of the San Antonio-based county, and redistricting carved out separate slices for each party.

Because of the spaghetti-like lines, several institutions in one district have dramatic influence over the neighboring districts.

Four Air Force bases and the Army's Fort Sam Houston are located in San Antonio. Although none of the bases are in the 21st, the military is believed to be the district's largest employer. The five San Antonio installations employ more than 45,000 people, though the numbers will continue to drop if one of the bases closes, as expected.

San Antonio's military history goes back centuries. Its greatest moment was in 1836 when 183 soldiers fought to defend the Alamo against an attack by the 6,000-man army led by Gen. Antonio Lopez de Santa Anna.

Tourism is the second-largest employer in San Antonio, frequently overlapping with military interests. The Alamo, in the heart of downtown and around the corner from a bustling shopping mall, is a popular attraction. Fort Sam Houston has more than 900 historic buildings and two museums on its 3,300 acres.

Almost a quarter of the people in the 21st live in Bexar County, most in the affluent neighborhoods of San Antonio and its suburbs. The predominantly white residents are well-paid, well-educated professionals — doctors, lawyers, engineers and insurance executives.

As the 21st moves west, the counties become less populous and the economic emphasis shifts to agriculture. Gillespie County is the largest peach-producing county in the state. Peach orchards are also prevalent in Menard County.

The central parts of the district raise a combination of crops and cattle. Pecans, peanuts and hay grow in abundance. The 21st is home to the state's largest goat market, in Kimble County, and the self-proclaimed "sheep and wool capital" of the nation, in Tom Green County.

More than 300 miles west of San Antonio lies San Angelo. The city's Goodfellow Air Force Base is just over the district line but employs many 21st District residents. The 21st takes in the city's wealthier northwest neighborhoods.

Before redistricting, Smith represented all of Midland, the West Texas oil center. Today, the 21st shares the city with two other districts.

Midland, Comal, Kerr and Williamson counties, combined with the portions of San Antonio in the 21st, deliver wide margins for Republican candidates. Overall, Bob Dole garnered 63 percent of the district's vote in 1996, while Smith got 76 percent in the House race.

1990 Population: 566,217. White 517,100 (91%), Black 13,972 (2%), Other 35,145 (6%). Hispanic origin 79,655 (14%). 18 and over 420,498 (74%), 62 and over 91,310 (16%). Median age: 34.

as part of an omnibus spending package at the end of the 104th, increased penalties for alien smuggling and document fraud, and made it easier for illegal immigrants to be detained at the border or deported after arrival.

Smith had originally introduced a much tougher measure, tackling legal as well as illegal immigration, but he found himself giving up parts of it as specific provisions ran into opposition from Democrats, the Senate, or even pro-business Republicans in the House. Smith reasoned that the status quo was "unacceptable" and that getting a chunk of what he wanted was better than nothing. "Three-fourths of a loaf tastes pretty good," he said.

Smith did not begin the 105th expecting to revisit the immigration issue in a major way, because he did not see consensus building for stronger legislation than he had already achieved. He shares a pet concern of some Republicans (and a plank of the party's 1996 platform), to make clear the constitutional guarantee of citizenship to anyone born in this country. Smith favors legislation that would deny this birthright to children born to parents in the country illegally. "The 14th Amendment is being enforced in ways for which it was not intended," Smith said. His panel hosted a hearing at the end of the 104th on a bill by California Republican Brian P. Bilbray to "fine tune" the 14th Amendment.

Smith joined Sen. Joseph I. Lieberman, a Connecticut Democrat, in challenging TV networks to air only programs acceptable for children during the first hour of prime time. Smith warned that networks "race each other to the bottom of the cultural barrel. . . . TV shows increasingly feature the perverse, the obscure and the bizarre. Media polluters continue to dump garbage into the minds of our children."

The ability to deliver such tongue lashings served Smith well during the 103rd in his capacity as chairman of the Republican "Theme Team," a 17-member group that coordinated the House GOP response to the Clinton administration. Commenting on Clinton's economic proposals in 1993, Smith said, "President Clinton has become America's Pinocchio of the Potomac, except that every time he tells a fib it is our deficit and tax bill that grows."

Although he is a reliable Republican loyalist on most issues, his votes on abortion do not satisfy some of the party's most ardent conservatives. He supports such restrictions on abortion as parental notification and a 24-hour waiting period, and he opposes federal financing for abortions. But Smith opposed President George Bush's policy prohibiting abortion counseling at family-planning clinics that receive federal money. Smith said the question of counseling was a free speech issue, and patients have a right to know all their options. Such moderation nearly cost Smith his slot as delegate to the 1996 GOP convention as Texas Republicans sought to purge their ranks of any support for abortion rights.

At Home: Smith is a fifth-generation Texas rancher, but his Yale University background and polished manner are not the first things you might expect from a conservative Texas pol. He has made them work for him, though: When the 21st was open in 1986, he aggressively courted rural voters and won them over, it would seem, for good. His subsequent re-elections have been non-events.

Smith spent a year in the Texas House and two years on the Bexar County commission, representing San Antonio suburbs. In 1985, when GOP Rep. Tom Loeffler announced plans to leave the 21st for a gubernatorial campaign, Smith wasted no time in announcing his own candidacy.

Smith was the moderate in the GOP House runoff against Van Archer, a San Antonio city councilman. Smith finished first by a modest margin in the initial GOP primary and took 53 percent of the runoff vote against Archer.

In the primary and runoff, Smith had to overcome questions about his support of legal abortion (Archer opposed it) and his affiliation with Christian Science. Critics said his religion would prevent him from voting for medical care appropriations — a problem in a district where a medical equipment company was the largest private employer.

Smith's Democratic opponent was former state Sen. Pete Snelson, whose political base in Midland, at the western end of the district, positioned him to play to lingering rural perceptions of Smith as an elitist, big-city lawyer.

But Snelson was plagued by debt from previous campaigns. Smith cast himself as fiscally more conservative and signed a no-tax-increase pledge. He won San Antonio and Midland, overcoming Snelson's rural support.

The 1992 redistricting — and the subsequent redrawing of the map in 1996 — altered the district's lines but had little impact on its conservative tilt. The wealthy sections of San Antonio, combined with the sprawling counties to the west, helped Smith win without worry.

HOUSE ELECTIONS

1996 General		
Lamar Smith (R)	205,830	(76%)
Gordon H. Wharton (D)	60,338	(22%)
Randy Rutenbeck (NL)	3,139	(1%)
1994 General		
Lamar Smith (R)	165,595	(90%)
Kerry Lowry (I)	18,480	(10%)

Previous Winning Percentages: 1992 (72%) **1990** (75%) **1988** (93%) **1986** (61%)

CAMPAIGN FINANCE

	Receipts	Receipts from PACs	Expend-itures
1996			
Smith (R)	$526,391	$119,925 (23%)	$443,571
Wharton (D)	$26,430	$50 (0%)	$18,844
1994			
Smith (R)	$546,639	$105,116 (19%)	$538,347

VOTING STUDIES

	Presidential Support		Party Unity		Conservative Coalition	
Year	S	O	S	O	S	O
1996	34	63	90	4	94	2
1995	17	83	94	2	93	2
1994	41	54	93	4	81	6
1993	35	63	94	4	100	0
1992	77	21	85	9	96	2
1991	75	23	84	11	95	5

DISTRICT VOTE FOR PRESIDENT

	1996		1992
D	81,943 (30%)	**D**	70,547 (25%)
R	174,076 (63%)	**R**	143,842 (52%)
I	18,474 (7%)	**I**	63,347 (23%)

KEY VOTES

1997	
Ban "partial birth" abortions	Y
1996	
Approve farm bill	Y
Deny public education to illegal immigrants	Y
Repeal ban on certain assault-style weapons	Y
Increase minimum wage	N
Freeze defense spending	N
Approve welfare overhaul	Y
1995	
Approve balanced-budget constitutional amendment	Y
Relax Clean Water Act regulations	Y
Oppose limits on environmental regulations	N
Reduce projected Medicare spending	Y
Approve GOP budget with tax and spending cuts	Y

INTEREST GROUP RATINGS

Year	ADA	AFL-CIO	CCUS	ACU
1996	10	n/a	93	100
1995	0	0	100	84
1994	5	11	92	95
1993	5	8	100	96
1992	20	36	88	88
1991	5	25	70	84

22 Tom DeLay (R)

Of Sugarland — Elected 1984, 7th term

Biographical Information
Born: April 8, 1947, Laredo, Texas.
Education: Baylor U., 1965-67; U. of Houston, B.S. 1970.
Occupation: Pest control executive.
Family: Wife, Christine Ann Furrh; one child.
Religion: Baptist.
Political Career: Texas House, 1979-85.
Capitol Office: 341 Cannon Bldg. 20515; 225-5951.

Committees
Appropriations
Transportation; VA, HUD & Independent Agencies

Majority Whip

In Washington: Through words and deeds, Majority Whip DeLay has conveyed an image of House Republicans as crusaders committed to scaling back a bloated and intrusive federal government. Often in the 104th Congress — particularly in the early months of 1995 — he helped galvanize the party to vote virtually in unison on tough issues. Yet the ideas he espouses have been cited by President Clinton and other Democrats as examples of Republican extremism, out of step with middle America.

A case in point: In 1995, DeLay introduced a one-sentence bill: "Public Law 101-549 is hereby repealed." With that sentence, DeLay would have done away with the 1990 revisions to the Clean Air Act. Although DeLay acknowledged that he never expected the legislation to pass and that he introduced it only to illustrate his belief that many laws have little or no scientific basis, his views on the environment are clear. He used to refer to the Environmental Protection Agency (EPA) as "the Gestapo of government," and he called the Nobel Prize the "Nobel appeasement prize" after the 1995 award for chemistry went to three scientists for their research on ozone-depleting chemicals.

A former small-business man — he ran a pest control business in Houston — DeLay wrote the planks of the House GOP "Contract With America" that call for rolling back federal regulations. "I'm a free-market nut," he said in early 1995. That year, DeLay led the fight to add 17 riders to the fiscal 1996 Veterans Affairs, Housing and Urban Development appropriations bill, which included EPA funding. The legislative language aimed to prevent the EPA from enforcing water and air pollution rules. In July, a coalition of Democrats and moderate Republicans stripped the riders from the bill, but the House reversed its decision the next week on a tie vote. In November 1995, the House voted to instruct its conferees to drop the riders from the final bill.

In March 1996, House leaders yanked a DeLay-backed regulatory bill from the floor just before it was scheduled for a vote after GOP moderates threatened revolt. The bill would have eased red tape for small businesses by giving them new power to challenge regulations in court. Moderates said the bill could make it hard for federal agencies to enforce even non-controversial regulations on the environment, workplace safety and public health.

As those episodes showed, DeLay's policy desires displease no small number in his own party, not to mention Democrats. "You don't gut environmental law because you want to change it," said Rep. Christopher Shays, R-Conn. "It was very destructive to go so far and to overreach. And a lot of good Republicans are suffering as a result."

DeLay said it was not the conservative policies that hurt Republicans but the perception that the public got from an unrelenting campaign of distortion by foes. Pleading his case in April 1996, DeLay said: "We've talked in terms of the cost of these regulations to the economy, driving up the cost of living for the American family. What we're also saying is, 'We can manage the environment better than the environmental extremists can.'"

Back for a second term in the majority in the 105th, DeLay plotted a narrower course, endorsing narrower bills that addressed specifics of the regulatory process rather than attempting a broad overhaul. "We sort of lost the high ground on environmental issues," DeLay said.

When House Republicans were getting organized for the 104th, DeLay was not incoming Speaker Newt Gingrich's choice for whip. (In 1989, DeLay had backed Gingrich's rival for the post of minority whip, Edward R. Madigan of Illinois.) DeLay won the job in part by raising millions of dollars during the 1994 campaign for GOP challengers; many of the grateful winners supported him for whip over Robert S. Walker, R-Pa., a Gingrich friend, and Bill McCollum, R-Fla. "I'm very aggressive," DeLay later said. "I'm a hard-working, aggressive, persistent whip. That's why I'm whip. I worked harder than anybody else. I raised more money than anybody else. I was smarter than anybody else in the race."

Since then, DeLay has become one of Gingrich's staunchest allies. He lobbied colleagues to re-elect the Speaker in January 1997, when Gingrich was

TEXAS 22
Southwest Houston and suburbs; Fort Bend and Brazoria counties

The 22nd is a testament to Houston's phenomenal growth of the past two decades. During the 1970s, the district was focused within the city. In the 1980s, the 22nd shifted south and west to include newly sprouted suburbs. In the 1992 redistricting, the 22nd was pulled even farther away from Houston, swallowing up the Clear Lake neighborhood in the east. As a result, the 22nd of the 1990s has more voters outside Harris County (Houston) than in it.

The influx of Houston professionals boosted Harris County's population by 38 percent in the 1970s and by 17 percent in the 1980s.

Yet the most astronomical growth has occurred just outside Harris County, in neighboring Fort Bend County. Its population jumped 150 percent in the 1970s and 72 percent in the 1980s. And from 1990 to 1995 Fort Bend County experienced a population surge of 30 percent, placing among the nation's 40 fastest-growing counties over that span. Sugar Land, DeLay's hometown, formed in the 1820s around the sugar industry, has become one of the most popular new suburbs. Signs of Sugar Land's new appeal are evident everywhere: new retail shops, new homes and new banks. First Colony is a planned community in Sugar Land that offers some houses for less than $100,000 and others that cost millions.

By uniting all of Fort Bend County in the 22nd District, the 1996 map increased the district's minority population to more than one-third. Shifted into the 22nd was northern Fort Bend, which is heavily African-American and had been included in the 25th District. Blacks and Hispanics together constitute nearly 40 percent of Fort Bend's population.

Fort Bend is the least heavily Republican county in a district very receptive to the GOP. It last voted Democratic for president in 1964. But Bob Dole's 54 percent tally there in 1996 was less than his district average.

The district includes some parts of southwestern and southeastern Harris County. Remapping removed some of the 22nd's precincts in southwestern Harris, but Republicans have little trouble mining this area for votes. Dole captured the district's portion of Harris by more than 20 percentage points.

NASA's Johnson Space Center, in the adjacent 9th District, is a major employer for the 22nd and probably the biggest reason that the Clear Lake area has grown. The massive complex southeast of Houston is designing and building components of the International Space Station (ISS).

Once past the Houston suburb of Pearland, Brazoria County rapidly turns rural. Rice, sorghum and cattle are major revenue producers in this sparsely populated region. Beyond the district boundaries down to the Gulf Coast, Brazoria County also includes oil and gas wells and 20 miles of natural beaches. Commercial fishing and tourism provide revenue in this part of the county, which is in the adjacent 14th District.

As of May 19, the Census Bureau had not recalculated population data, racial and ethnic breakdowns, and age statistics for district newly drawn for the 1996 election.

under an ethics cloud. DeLay toyed with trying to reduce the ethics committee's proposed penalty for Gingrich's violations of House rules, a reprimand and a $300,000 fine. He voted against that sanction when the House overwhelmingly approved it. And when Gingrich borrowed $300,000 from former GOP presidential nominee Bob Dole to pay the penalty, DeLay praised the decision. "He's taking the moral high ground to show his opponents the moral low ground they stand on," he said. (Gingrich said later he would pay half the fine and use the Dole loan for the rest.)

DeLay's own actions have raised some ethics questions. He has a dual role as a leader on the regulatory issue and as a top fundraiser for the party, one who maintains close ties with lobbyists and corporate interests affected by regulatory changes. DeLay runs a group called Project Relief, which consists of friends and contacts in the business world who help him drum up support on regulatory issues. DeLay said the only problem was in the eyes of his critics. "There is no connection between my philosophy and money," he said.

The Washington Post reported in 1995 that business lobbyists helped DeLay draft a deregulation bill. During an April 1997 House floor debate, George Miller, D-Calif., referred to the article. DeLay protested that the article was inaccurate and demanded that Miller's comments be stricken from the record. David R. Obey, D-Wis., grabbed a copy of the article from his congressional office and rushed to the floor with it. DeLay objected to attempts by Miller and Obey to reprint the article in the Congressional Record. DeLay denied that lobbyists had written bills in his office, or any other GOP leadership office, and accused Democrats of allowing environmental lobbyists to write their bills. After Obey left the podium, he took the article over to DeLay and the two argued, face-to-face, inches apart. Both pointed their fingers at each other, then DeLay shoved Obey. A Republican aide got between the two and pushed DeLay back. Obey said DeLay called him a "chicken shit." The next day, DeLay joked, "Everybody is scared of me for some reason."

During November 1995 House debate on a measure banning gifts to members, DeLay voted for a substitute that would have allowed lobbyists to continue to pay the expenses of lawmakers attending golf and tennis trips to raise money for charity. DeLay runs his own golf tournament in the Houston area to raise money for abused children.

When sponsors of legislation toughening lobbying registration requirements tried to get the House to pass a bill identical to the Senate's, DeLay instead whipped for an amendment that would have derailed the bill. Lawmakers defeated the amendment and cleared the bill.

As whip, it is DeLay's responsibility to count votes and deliver a majority for GOP bills. That task is complicated by rebellious Republicans, not only moderates but sometimes also younger members anchoring the Republican right who take a dim view of any increase in government spending. In March 1997, for example, 11 such conservatives bucked the party line and temporarily stalled floor consideration of legislation funding House committees.

On the subject of congressional term limits, DeLay himself breaks from the GOP majority. In the 104th and 105th, he voted against a constitutional amendment to mandate limits.

As a member of the Appropriations Committee, DeLay has been known to set aside his limited-government views when it comes to bringing money home to Texas. Like most of the Lone Star delegation, DeLay vigorously supported the superconducting super collider, which was being built in Texas until Congress voted in 1993 to terminate the project. He continues to be an enthusiastic booster of another big-ticket project with a Texas connection, NASA's space station.

At Home: When GOP Rep. Ron Paul ran for the Senate in 1984, DeLay quickly became the front-runner to fill the 22nd District seat. A six-year veteran of the Texas House, DeLay already had represented parts of the 22nd, and his efforts in Austin to scale back government looked like good credentials for the conservative district.

But DeLay did not win the GOP nomination easily. J.C. Helms, a wealthy real-estate developer from Bellaire, gave DeLay a scare. Two years earlier, in the neighboring 25th District, he had finished first in the GOP primary but failed to convert on his momentum in the runoff. His alliance with hard-right conservatives in the Harris County (Houston) GOP made it seem he could force a runoff with DeLay.

Helms sought to outflank DeLay on the right, casting himself as the natural philosophical heir to the libertarian Paul (who won the 14th District in a 1996 comeback). DeLay offered a more mainstream conservative approach, citing his experience in pest control to demonstrate knowledge of small business and calling for a balanced budget.

Late in the campaign, Helms ran radio ads accusing DeLay of being tardy in paying payroll taxes for his business — a charge DeLay acknowledged while reminding Helms the taxes eventually were paid. Visiting up to 60 homes a day, DeLay held his own in Harris County and won easily in his home base, Fort Bend. He clinched the GOP nomination with 54 percent. Since then, his elections have been a breeze.

HOUSE ELECTIONS

1996 General		
Tom DeLay (R)	126,056	(68%)
Scott Douglas Cunningham (D)	59,030	(32%)
1994 General		
Tom DeLay (R)	120,302	(74%)
Scott Douglas Cunningham (D)	38,826	(24%)
Gregory D. Pepper (I)	4,016	(2%)

Because of court-ordered redistricting in August, an all-candidate election was held in November. If no candidate received a majority of the vote then, the top two finishers met in a December runoff.

Previous Winning Percentages: 1992 (69%) **1990** (71%) **1988** (67%) **1986** (72%) **1984** (65%)

CAMPAIGN FINANCE

	Receipts	Receipts from PACs	Expend-itures
1996			
DeLay (R)	$1,620,227	$1,066,875 (66%)	$1,621,708
Cunningham (D)	$28,393	$50 (0%)	$28,383
1994			
DeLay (R)	$669,010	$396,376 (59%)	$701,245
Cunningham (D)	$149,393	0	$149,385
Pepper (I)	$2,746	0	$1,722

DISTRICT VOTE FOR PRESIDENT

1996		1992	
D	79,683 (38%)	**D**	66,878 (30%)
R	119,341 (56%)	**R**	105,904 (48%)
I	12,213 (6%)	**I**	47,807 (22%)

KEY VOTES

1997	
Ban "partial birth" abortions	Y
1996	
Approve farm bill	Y
Deny public education to illegal immigrants	Y
Repeal ban on certain assault-style weapons	Y
Increase minimum wage	N
Freeze defense spending	N
Approve welfare overhaul	Y
1995	
Approve balanced-budget constitutional amendment	Y
Relax Clean Water Act regulations	Y
Oppose limits on environmental regulations	N
Reduce projected Medicare spending	Y
Approve GOP budget with tax and spending cuts	Y

VOTING STUDIES

	Presidential Support		Party Unity		Conservative Coalition	
Year	S	O	S	O	S	O
1996	33	61	92	4	98	2
1995	17	82	97	2	98	1
1994	31	68	95	2	86	6
1993	25	75	95	3	95	5
1992	82	16	90	7	92	6
1991	75	20	89	5	92	0

INTEREST GROUP RATINGS

Year	ADA	AFL-CIO	CCUS	ACU
1996	0	n/a	93	100
1995	0	0	96	83
1994	0	0	92	100
1993	0	0	100	100
1992	5	8	71	100
1991	5	9	90	100

23 Henry Bonilla (R)

Of San Antonio — Elected 1992, 3rd term

Biographical Information

Born: Jan. 2, 1954, San Antonio, Texas.
Education: U. of Texas, Austin, B.A. 1976.
Occupation: Television executive.
Family: Wife, Deborah Knapp; two children.
Religion: Baptist.
Political Career: No previous office.
Capitol Office: 1427 Longworth Bldg. 20515; 225-4511.

Committees

Appropriations
Agriculture, Rural Development, FDA & Related Agencies; Labor, Health & Human Services, Education & Related Agencies; National Security

In Washington: In an era when the Republican Party is trying to expand its base and appeal to new constituencies, Bonilla is one of its best salesmen. One of just three Hispanic Republicans in the House, Bonilla argues that the GOP speaks the same political language as Latinos — in favor of a strong military and small business, and in opposition to high taxes and governmental intrusion.

Bonilla has been showcased by party leaders, granted a slot on the Appropriations Committee as a freshman and featured working the stump for the presidential candidacy of former Sen. Bob Dole of Kansas. Bonilla appeared as part of the on-air broadcast talent when the GOP provided its own coverage of its 1996 national convention over the Family Channel and USA Network, and he was chosen to second Dole's nomination at the national convention in San Diego.

But, ironically, Bonilla was denied the simplest official credentials for the convention, with members of the Texas GOP successfully blocking his bid for a delegate slot at the state convention. Bonilla may be a welcome presence in the eyes of national party leaders, but the rank and file in his home state found him ideologically unacceptable because of his support for abortion rights.

On most issues, Bonilla votes in step with the party mainstream, following the conservative line most prominently in trying to ease the regulatory burden on business. Bonilla helped hold up the fiscal 1996 spending bills for the departments of Education, Labor and Health and Human Services with his insistence on including a provision to block the Occupational Safety and Health Administration (OSHA) from developing or issuing standards to protect workers against repetitive motion injuries.

"The implementation of silly regulations causes additional costs and in some cases causes tremendous job loss," Bonilla argued, decrying OSHA's "Gestapo-like tactics." Although the House agreed to his language, Senate conferees on the bill were opposed. Despite the pleading of House Appropriations Chairman Robert L. Livingston, R-La., who did not want the bill held up over the matter, Bonilla refused to drop it. "This is the one I'm not going to bend on," Bonilla said.

United Parcel Service, its subsidiaries and employees contributed well over $2 million to federal campaigns and parties during the 1996 election cycle, including $10,000 in PAC contributions to Bonilla. The shipping company faced many ergonomic complaints from its workers who lifted heavy packages, and the company adamantly opposed the ergonomics studies. Bonilla maintains an "informal advisory group" known as the Henry Bonilla Congressional Cabinet, made up of donors who contribute the maximum amount per cycle to his campaign treasury.

The bill was eventually absorbed by an omnibus spending package, with OSHA blocked from implementing ergonomic regulations, but not from collecting data as Bonilla wished. He had even less success with the fiscal 1997 bill.

Bonilla enjoyed greater success with his effort to put a moratorium on new listings under the Endangered Species Act (ESA), attaching such a provision to a supplemental defense spending bill at the beginning of the 104th Congress. "Some of my colleagues asked why this ESA language was included in a defense appropriations bill," Bonilla said. "I reminded them that in addition to being used against private property owners, ESA regulations have been used to curtail training exercises at some of our military installations."

After President Clinton nominated two controversial figures in a row for the post of surgeon general, Bonilla offered legislation to block funding for the office. And he helped flog one of the favorite whipping boys of conservatives, the National Education Association. Bonilla contended that the organization participated in political activity beyond its original mandate of furthering children's education, but his amendment to end its tax-exempt status in the District of Columbia failed narrowly, 210-213.

Bonilla follows a fairly strict party line on

TEXAS 23
Southwest — Laredo; San Antonio suburbs

Tough times have beset many in the 23rd, Texas' largest House district. In its far western reaches, defunct oil wells dot the landscape. Along the hundreds of miles of Mexican border that mark the southern limit of the district are impoverished immigrants, many of them living in some of Texas' most destitute towns.

Eight of the 20 poorest counties in the state are in the 23rd. Half the people in Zavala and Maverick counties fall below the poverty level. The median household income for the district is less than $22,500, well below the state's median. Some local officials say those figures are high, claiming that minorities along the Mexican border were undercounted in the 1990 census. A private 1993 study of census data concluded that Laredo (Webb County) had one of the highest poverty rates in the nation.

The border communities often seem to have more in common with their Mexican neighbors than with the rest of Texas. Laredo celebrates Mexican Independence Day, and three bridges connect it to its Mexican sister city, Nuevo Laredo. Nine of 10 people in Webb County are Hispanic.

All along the border, people find work in *maquiladoras* — twin-plant manufacturing operations in which the bulk of production work is done by lower-cost labor in a Mexican facility and then finishing work is handled at a U.S. plant. Clothing and heavy machinery are common products. With NAFTA's creation of a "common market" between Mexico and the United States, the maquiladoras' boom days may someday be over, but locals hope for other economic benefits growing out of freer trade. Other immigrants work the land, earning their keep from vegetables, cotton, sheep and goats.

Residents on both sides of the Rio Grande get together for work, entertainment and sometimes to cooperate on regional political issues. In 1992, officials from Del Rio (United States) and Coahuila (Mexico) jointly opposed construction of two hazardous waste facilities along the border.

More than 60 percent of the district's residents are Hispanic. Although the Hispanic vote typically goes Democratic, that tradition was upset in 1992 when Bonilla became Texas' first Hispanic Republican in Congress.

Bonilla benefited from 1992 redistricting, which added 21 counties to the 23rd. Also, Bonilla's conservative, less-government pitch played well with the district's independent-minded ranchers and oilmen and with affluent voters in the Bexar County suburbs of San Antonio. The biggest bloc of votes in the 23rd — nearly 30 percent — comes from Bexar County. Bob Dole carried the portion of the county within the district with 64 percent in 1996. But in other parts of the 23rd, many who backed Bonilla supported Bill Clinton for president; Clinton carried the district with 50 percent.

San Antonio's Brooks and Randolph Air Force bases are major employers of district residents, though the installations lie just outside the 23rd. The flight training center at Laughlin Air Force Base and part of Fort Bliss are in the district.

1990 Population: 566,217. White 418,282 (74%), Black 16,484 (3%), Other 131,451 (23%). Hispanic origin 354,149 (63%). 18 and over 374,947 (66%), 62 and over 63,204 (11%). Median age: 29.

most foreign policy and fiscal issues. He was the only member of the Congressional Hispanic Caucus to vote for the GOP's massive welfare overhaul bill, and he supported an effort by California Republican Elton Gallegly to block illegal immigrants from receiving public education. Bonilla questioned the wisdom of the Department of Education's bilingual education programs, contending that too much money was spent on overhead.

Bonilla opposed a Republican effort during the 104th to name English the nation's official language, and he has been unafraid to break with the party over abortion. He supported a ban on a particular abortion technique that opponents call a "partial birth" abortion, but he joined with Rodney Frelinghuysen of New Jersey in helping Democrats block an amendment to the fiscal 1996 D.C. appropriations bill that would have banned all public funding for abortions in the District.

For the 105th Congress, Bonilla gave up his perch on the D.C. Appropriations Subcommittee in favor of a seat on the agriculture spending panel. He retains his slots on the defense and Labor-HHS subcommittees.

In the 104th, Bonilla helped block a deal that would have brought low-level radioactive waste from other states for deposit in Hudspeth County in his district. "I ask my colleagues to think of this vote as if it was their constituents being affected," he said. That argument seemed to work, as the House rejected the deal, 176-243.

During 1993 consideration of the spending bill for the departments of Veterans Affairs and Housing and Urban Development, Bonilla complained that the Democratic-controlled Rules Committee did not allow for consideration of an amendment that would have restored $80 million for waste water treatment projects for residents of the "colonias," poverty-stricken communities along the U.S.-Mexico border.

Bonilla told his colleagues that residents of the

colonias live in Third World conditions, with inadequate and sometimes nonexistent drinking water and sewage disposal systems. The Appropriations Committee had supported the amendment.

An early advocate of NAFTA, Bonilla traveled with Dole to Mexico City and through Texas to drum up support for the trade pact. Bonilla said his constituents "have witnessed the mile-long line of tractor trailers — with license plates from almost every state — waiting to take their American-made goods to Mexico. It is an amazing sight."

Bonilla also tried to help district residents by telling those who qualify to file for the earned income tax credit (EITC), a federal tax credit for low-income families. In an article in the Zavala County Sentinel, Bonilla wrote that the credit is "a great benefit for low-income working families."

His article was picked up by the Democratic Congressional Campaign Committee, which then blasted Bonilla for having voted against the EITC when he opposed President Clinton's deficit-reduction package. Bonilla called the criticism "baloney," saying his constituents asked him to vote against the budget plan, "and that's what I did."

At Home: Bonilla worked at several TV stations across the country and served as press secretary to Pennsylvania Gov. Richard Thornburgh before returning to his native San Antonio to work as a public affairs executive for a local TV station.

Although a neophyte candidate in 1992, Bonilla made hay out of incumbent Democrat Albert G. Bustamante's liabilities. First elected in 1984, by 1992 Bustamante had come to be viewed as not closely in touch with the district, which includes some of the poorest people in the country. The House bank scandal also wounded him. Bustamante's 30 "cheques calientes" offended voters who struggled to balance their checkbooks each month. Bonilla found the Spanish phrase for "hot checks" to be one of his most effective campaign lines.

Although some were willing to forgive the overdrafts as shoddy bookkeeping, few could swallow Bustamante's purchase of a $500,000 home in the ritzy Dominion neighborhood of San Antonio.

While Bustamante worked on Capitol Hill, Bonilla took a leave of absence to drive across the lower half of the state shaking hands in general stores and coffee shops. Everywhere he went, Bonilla introduced himself as an agent of change, chatting in Spanish with many residents. The technique paid off in the district, which is 63 percent Hispanic.

Bonilla was temporarily tripped up in the fall by accusations that his anchorwoman wife, Deborah Knapp, used a telephone and computer at her news station for campaign work. But the popular TV couple turned the controversy into an asset. Knapp took a leave of absence, hit the trail introducing herself as Deborah Bonilla and immediately became a star attraction for the candidate.

The final outcome was a 21-point win for Bonilla, and he has topped 60 percent in both his re-election campaigns.

HOUSE ELECTIONS

1996 General		
Henry Bonilla (R)	101,332	(62%)
Charles P. Jones (D)	59,596	(36%)
Linda J. Caswell (NL)	2,911	(2%)
1994 General		
Henry Bonilla (R)	73,815	(63%)
Rolando L. Rios (D)	44,101	(37%)

Previous Winning Percentages: 1992 (59%)

CAMPAIGN FINANCE

	Receipts	Receipts from PACs	Expenditures
1996			
Bonilla (R)	$822,570	$337,440 (41%)	$779,893
Jones (D)	$76,887	$57,750 (75%)	$74,755
1994			
Bonilla (R)	$917,820	$260,558 (28%)	$758,591
Rios (D)	$429,166	$164,900 (38%)	$426,042

DISTRICT VOTE FOR PRESIDENT

	1996		1992
D	83,972 (50%)	**D**	72,469 (42%)
R	73,297 (44%)	**R**	70,598 (41%)
I	9,374 (6%)	**I**	28,860 (17%)

KEY VOTES

1997	
Ban "partial birth" abortions	Y
1996	
Approve farm bill	Y
Deny public education to illegal immigrants	Y
Repeal ban on certain assault-style weapons	Y
Increase minimum wage	N
Freeze defense spending	N
Approve welfare overhaul	Y
1995	
Approve balanced-budget constitutional amendment	Y
Relax Clean Water Act regulations	Y
Oppose limits on environmental regulations	N
Reduce projected Medicare spending	Y
Approve GOP budget with tax and spending cuts	Y

VOTING STUDIES

	Presidential Support		Party Unity		Conservative Coalition	
Year	S	O	S	O	S	O
1996	35	62	88	9	96	4
1995	20	78	96	3	99	0
1994	44	56	93	7	100	0
1993	33	67	93	6	98	2

INTEREST GROUP RATINGS

Year	ADA	AFL-CIO	CCUS	ACU
1996	0	n/a	94	85
1995	0	0	100	88
1994	0	0	100	95
1993	5	0	100	96

24 Martin Frost (D)

Of Dallas — Elected 1978, 10th term

Biographical Information

Born: Jan. 1, 1942, Glendale, Calif.

Education: U. of Missouri, B.A., B.J. 1964; Georgetown U., J.D. 1970.

Military Service: Army Reserve, 1966-72.

Occupation: Lawyer.

Family: Wife, Valerie Hall; three children.

Religion: Jewish.

Political Career: Sought Democratic nomination for U.S. House, 1974.

Capitol Office: 2256 Rayburn Bldg. 20515; 225-3605.

Committees

Rules

Legislative & Budget Process (ranking)

In Washington: Not often will one find Frost delivering an impassioned speech on the House floor; he has neither the inclination nor the charisma for showmanship. Frost exerts influence in quieter ways. He is a technocrat, a political wonk who sits on a key insider committee, Rules, where he is the ranking minority member of the Legislative and Budget Process Subcommittee. Frost represents a variety of constituencies that are important to the Democratic Party: He is a white male; he is Jewish and he is Southern. Add to that Frost's reputation as a party loyalist and one of the House's top fundraisers, and it is understandable why he has advanced to party leadership, heading the Democratic Congressional Campaign Committee (DCCC).

Frost initially got onto the insiders' track with the help of Majority Leader and then Speaker Jim Wright, a fellow Texan. Wright is long gone, having resigned from the House under an ethics cloud in 1989, but Frost has remained a significant player behind the scenes.

As DCCC chair, Frost predicted that the Democrats would recapture the House in the 1996 election. That proved overly optimistic, of course, but Democrats did gain ground in the House, whittling down the GOP majority.

Early in his tenure as DCCC chair, Frost had to deal with defections from his own ranks by several Southern Democrats. In June 1995, as a prelude to their switching to the Republican Party, Democratic Reps. Jimmy Hayes and W.J. "Billy" Tauzin of Louisiana, Greg Laughlin of Texas and Mike Parker of Mississippi resigned from the DCCC because of a cartoon that appeared on the cover of a committee news packet. It referred to House-passed legislation to rewrite the clean water act as a vehicle of the "Pollution Lobbies."

"We do not expect other members of the Democratic Party with whom we differ philosophically to alter any view," the resignation letter read. "We certainly do not expect our party to attack the integrity or motives of those who differ."

At the start of the 105th Congress, Frost was named to a 10-member bipartisan task force studying House ethics procedures, a group formed with an eye on finding ways to minimize the kind of partisan rancor that characterized the controversial ethics committee inquiry into the political fundraising activities of Speaker Newt Gingrich.

Earlier, when the ethics committee issued its judgment that Gingrich had violated House rules, Frost was out front calling for him to step down. "We're not asking that a Democrat be made Speaker of the House," Frost said in December 1996. "We're only asking that there be an ethical Speaker of the House."

Frost, a strong backer of Wright during the former Speaker's ethics controversy, said Gingrich misled Congress about his use of tax-exempt organizations. "Newt ought to step aside," Frost said. "He clearly lied to Congress. Newt should be held to a higher standard. He flunked that test."

And as for the $300,000 penalty the House imposed on Gingrich, Frost said Gingrich should pay it out of his own pocket. "It would be more appropriate for him to use personal funds," Frost said. "He made $700,000 off of his book deal. He can afford to pay it."

Frost got a career-low 53 percent at the polls in 1994, and during the 104th he shifted to the right on some hot-button issues. In 1995, he voted in favor of a constitutional amendment banning flag desecration, after opposing a similar proposal in 1990. In March 1996, he voted to repeal the ban on certain semiautomatic assault-style weapons. Frost had voted against the assault weapons ban in 1994 but supported the crime bill that included the weapons ban.

He also voted for legislation in March 1996 to ban a certain abortion procedure that opponents call "partial birth" abortion. In March 1997, with the election behind him, Frost switched his vote and opposed the ban.

Frost generally is more liberal than other white Southern Democrats. In March 1997, he

TEXAS 24
Parts of Dallas and Tarrant counties

The redistricting frenzy that swept Texas in 1996 benefitted Frost, a 10-term House incumbent. That August, a three-judge federal panel redrew the boundaries of almost half of Texas' congressional districts and applied them to the November elections. One of the districts affected was Frost's 24th, which draws much of its population from parts of Fort Worth, Arlington and Dallas.

The judges' map increased the district's Democratic tilt by drawing into the 24th more of Grand Prairie, a middle-class, Democratic-leaning area between Arlington and Dallas. The city's population swelled almost 40 percent in the 1980s and now exceeds 100,000. Large employers in the region include Lockheed Martin, Northrop Grumman and Southwest Airlines.

Moreover, the 24th retained predominantly black and Democratic areas of southeast Fort Worth that were key in Frost's six-point re-election victory in 1994. Overall, blacks and Hispanics each represent about one-fifth of the district population.

Bill Clinton won the old 24th in 1992 by 8 percentage points, 41 percent to 33 percent, over George Bush. He won the new district in 1996 by 14 points, 53 percent to 39 percent, over Bob Dole.

Blue-collar laborers living in the 24th have borne the brunt of economic woes in the Dallas-Fort Worth Metroplex. The superconducting super collider was canceled, military bases were consolidated, and defense contractors laid off thousands of workers. Still, defense cuts have not proved as devastating as feared.

Carswell Air Force Base was slated to close but remains open — serving a different function under a new name, the Naval Air Station Fort Worth Joint Reserves. It employs thousands of civilians and military personnel. But one of the reserve bases to be consolidated into the base is the district's Dallas Naval Air Station, which is scheduled to close by September 1998.

Bell Helicopter Textron is a significant source of employment for district residents. In conjunction with Boeing, Bell is producing the V-22 Osprey tilt-rotor aircraft that will be delivered to the military starting in 1999. Bell employs more than 6,200 in the Fort Worth metropolitan area.

The 24th includes several of Arlington's entertainment venues, including the Six Flags over Texas amusement park and The Ballpark, the new home of baseball's Rangers.To the southwest of this area is the University of Texas at Arlington, which enrolls 22,100 students.

Southeast of Tarrant lies the geographically vast, mostly rural counties of Ellis and Navarro. The 24th has two-thirds of Ellis' residents; the county was the focal point of the superconducting supercollider project that Congress canceled in 1993.

Navarro County boasts the longest continuous oil flow in the state; the rest of the county's economy is split between livestock and crops.

Dole and Frost's Republican opponent prevailed in the district's share of Ellis in 1996; Clinton and Frost easily won Navarro.

As of May 19, the Census Bureau had not recalculated population data, racial and ethnic breakdowns, and age statistics for districts newly drawn for the 1996 election.

voted against legislation allowing businesses to offer their employees time off rather than overtime pay. In February 1997, he voted against limiting congressional terms. He opposed early GOP-backed welfare-overhaul proposals, although he supported the final version of the bill that President Clinton signed into law. He backed an increase in the minimum wage and opposed exempting small businesses from its provisions. He voted to allow overseas military hospitals to perform abortions, for federal employee health care plans to offer abortion coverage, and to require states to pay for abortions for poor women in cases of rape or incest.

A tragedy in Texas led Frost to introduce an successful amendment in May 1996 to an anti-crime bill that passed the House. The amendment came after 9-year-old Amber Hagerman of Arlington, Texas, was kidnapped from the parking lot of a vacant store in Arlington. Her body was found a few days later in a creek bed.

Frost's amendment expanded federal jurisdiction over repeat child molesters and established a sentence of life without parole for anyone convicted of a second sex crime against a child. It passed on a voice vote.

"The measure of any society is how it protects its children," Frost said. "This draws a line in the sand and says we as a society will not tolerate crimes against the most vulnerable."

The measure later was added to the fiscal 1997 omnibus appropriations bill and signed into law by Clinton in October 1996. Hagerman's parents were at the bill signing.

Frost has not been shy about bringing home federal funds for local projects. In September 1996, he secured $16 million for a veterans' cemetery in the Dallas-Fort Worth area. Also, he voted against efforts to kill NASA's space station, which is big business in Texas, and he supported increasing funding for science programs. He also was a strong supporter of the Texas-based superconducting super collider, fighting every step of the way to save the project. Despite Frost's efforts, the House killed the SSC in June 1993.

At Home: Frost faced a rematch in 1996 with Ed Harrison, a home builder and real estate executive who had lost by 6 percentage points two years earlier.

Harrison in 1994 had successfully tarred Frost as a tax-and-spend liberal who marched in lock step with the less-than-popular Clinton. One Harrison radio ad featured a fictitious call to Frost from a White House aide who thanked the congressman for supporting the president and offered to send Clinton to Texas to help campaign. Frost was probably saved only by substantially outspending Harrison, $1.6 million to the challenger's $560,000.

As a result, national Republicans felt Frost's district was ripe for the taking in 1996. Harrison called Frost a "career politician more comfortable in Washington, D.C." than in the district.

But Frost fought back. "When they said they were going to put me on their hit list and spend a million dollars against me, I took it seriously, started organizing and put together an excellent team of staff and volunteers," Frost told the Dallas Morning News in November 1996.

Frost, who spent nearly $2 million, wound up defeating Harrison, 56 percent to 39 percent. Frost was buoyed by a large turnout of Hispanics; in the closing weeks of the campaign, he had charged Harrison with making intolerant and insensitive remarks toward that ethnic group. He seized on a comment Harrison made at a news conference, suggesting that Hispanics would not be able to figure out the election process. Frost also targeted the black community, and tried to link Harrison with Gingrich.

He also was helped by redistricting. The boundaries were altered in 1996 to comply with a Supreme Court decision, and Frost's district was made more Democratic.

Even before the two contests against Harrison, Frost had struggled a bit in 1992, overcoming a difficult redistricting and his first Republican challenger in six years. As redrawn for the 1992 elections, the 24th was about 60 percent new for Frost and the share of blacks in his constituency dropped from 32 percent to 19 percent. Dallas trust administrator Steve L. Masterson waged an aggressive campaign that pulled Frost down to 60 percent.

Frost first got to Congress in 1978 by defeating Democratic incumbent Dale Milford in a primary, something he had tried and failed to do four years earlier. On his second attempt Frost revived his complaints from 1974 that Milford was too conservative; he built an effective precinct organization and won endorsements from the state AFL-CIO and two of the area's largest newspapers. He beat Milford with 55 percent of the vote.

Frost's Republican rival that November tried to turn the tables, claiming that Frost was a tool of organized labor and too liberal for the district. But Frost prevailed with 54 percent and then won re-elections comfortably throughout the next decade.

HOUSE ELECTIONS

1996 General		
Martin Frost (D)	77,847	(56%)
Ed Harrison (R)	54,551	(39%)
Marion Jacob (D)	4,656	(3%)
Dale Mouton (I)	2,574	(2%)
1994 General		
Martin Frost (D)	65,019	(53%)
Ed Harrison (R)	58,062	(47%)

Because of court-ordered redistricting in August, an all-candidate election was held in November. If no candidate received a majority of the vote then, the top two finishers met in a December runoff.

Previous Winning Percentages: 1992 (60%) **1990** (100%) **1988** (93%) **1986** (67%) **1984** (59%) **1982** (73%) **1980** (61%) **1978** (54%)

CAMPAIGN FINANCE

	Receipts	Receipts from PACs	Expend-itures
1996			
Frost (D)	$1,964,330	$1,112,737 (57%)	$1,963,529
Harrison (R)	$861,548	$120,767 (14%)	$868,345
1994			
Frost (D)	$1,608,720	$767,215 (48%)	$1,589,612
Harrison (R)	$575,955	$38,310 (7%)	$562,260

DISTRICT VOTE FOR PRESIDENT

	1996		1992
D	80,626 (53%)	**D**	73,865 (42%)
R	59,125 (39%)	**R**	57,774 (33%)
I	10,681 (7%)	**I**	45,050 (26%)

KEY VOTES

1997	
Ban "partial birth" abortions	N
1996	
Approve farm bill	Y
Deny public education to illegal immigrants	N
Repeal ban on certain assault-style weapons	Y
Increase minimum wage	Y
Freeze defense spending	N
Approve welfare overhaul	Y
1995	
Approve balanced-budget constitutional amendment	Y
Relax Clean Water Act regulations	N
Oppose limits on environmental regulations	Y
Reduce projected Medicare spending	N
Approve GOP budget with tax and spending cuts	N

VOTING STUDIES

	Presidential Support		Party Unity		Conservative Coalition	
Year	**S**	**O**	**S**	**O**	**S**	**O**
1996	81	16	75	20	88	10
1995	74	21	78	14	62	28
1994	76	13	81	10	78	17
1993	87	9	79	11	68	18
1992	30	66	82	11	71	29
1991	35	61	80	10	54	43

INTEREST GROUP RATINGS

Year	ADA	AFL-CIO	CCUS	ACU
1996	65	n/a	38	10
1995	85	83	41	14
1994	55	67	75	25
1993	65	91	36	21
1992	75	73	57	25
1991	65	100	20	20

25 Ken Bentsen (D)

Of Houston — Elected 1994, 2nd term

Biographical Information

Born: June 3, 1959, Houston, Texas.

Education: U. of St. Thomas, B.A. 1982; American U., M.P.A. 1985.

Occupation: Investment banker; congressional aide.

Family: Wife, Tamra; two children.

Religion: Presbyterian.

Political Career: Harris County Democratic Party chairman, 1990-93.

Capitol Office: 128 Cannon Bldg. 20515; 225-7508.

Committees

Banking & Financial Services

Domestic & International Monetary Policy; Financial Institutions & Consumer Credit

Budget

In Washington: Like his uncle Lloyd, the longtime Texas senator and former Treasury secretary, Ken Bentsen is a national Democrat with a pro-business bent. He gave his party reason to cheer in 1996 as he kept the 25th in Democratic hands after being forced into a December runoff as the result of court-ordered redistricting. The runoff attracted much media attention, as the GOP angled to pick up the 25th as partial compensation for the ground it lost in the House in November.

As reward for holding on to the district, the Democratic leadership put Bentsen on the Budget Committee for the 105th Congress. He also is staying on the Banking and Financial Services Committee, where he looks out for the interests of the oil industry.

Taking a stance pleasing to the petrochemical industry, Bentsen was an early advocate of repealing the 4.3-cent gasoline tax that President Clinton included in his deficit-reducing budget approved by Congress in 1993. And although Bentsen disagreed with most of the "Contract With America" agenda that the new House GOP majority pushed in 1995, he did support a contract measure promoting regulatory reform, believing that it would help small business.

When gasoline prices spiked in the spring of 1996, Bentsen said that repealing the 4.3-cent gas tax would provide relief to consumers. To offset revenue lost by repealing the tax, Bentsen introduced a measure to eliminate a subsidy given to producers of ethanol, a corn-based alcohol fuel. "The ethanol subsidy has proved to be one of the biggest boondoggles in the history of Congress," he said. "Furthermore, ethanol subsidies artificially inflate the price of corn food products, costing American consumers millions each year." But the ethanol subsidy is popular in Midwestern states, and when the House voted to repeal the gas tax in May 1996, members decided to make up for the lost revenue by selling some of the non-television broadcast spectrum and cutting $578 million from the Energy Department's budget over six years.

A former investment banker, Bentsen sharply criticized congressional Republicans who threatened in late 1995 and early 1996 to oppose raising the nation's debt limit unless Clinton came to terms with the GOP on a balanced budget. Not raising the debt limit posed a risk that the United States would default on its financial obligations, a calamity in the eyes of the financial community.

"The U.S. Treasury bond is the gold standard for the world," Bentsen told the House. "All other interest rates are tied off of it, and yet the Speaker [Newt Gingrich] threatens a default and threatens to destroy the creditworthiness of the United States." In the end, Republicans agreed to raise the debt limit.

Also during the 1995-96 budget wars, Bentsen repeatedly criticized Republicans for keeping federal employees guessing about whether funds would be available to pay them to work. Many of Bentsen's constituents have jobs at Houston-area federal facilities such as veterans' hospitals and NASA's Johnson Space Center. Like others in the Texas delegation, Bentsen is a strong supporter of NASA's space station, which is part of the work of the Johnson Space Center. Critics of the orbiting laboratory view it as "pork in space," and annually they try to kill its funding. So far those efforts have failed.

Bentsen in the 104th spoke against the Republicans' seven-year budget plan because it included additional NASA cuts and trimmed the rate of spending on Medicare and Medicaid more than he thought proper. "This agreement assumes a tax cut of $245 billion over seven years," Bentsen said. "It is wrong to cut benefits for seniors, low-income families, veterans, college students, NASA and medical research to pay for a tax cut that will benefit the wealthiest in our society."

Bentsen assailed the GOP effort to rein in Medicare spending by a total of $270 million over seven years, arguing that seniors would have fewer options for their medical care. He also joined with senior Democrats John D. Dingell of Michigan and John M. Spratt Jr. of South Carolina

TEXAS 25
South Houston and suburbs

Downtown Houston is an array of glittering towers, but the city has several skylines instead of just the traditional one. With no zoning regulations, clusters of skyscrapers are scattered across Houston.

The most populous city in Texas and the fourth-largest in the nation, Houston and Harris County are home to the headquarters or major corporate offices of more than 200 firms. Seventeen companies on the 1996 Fortune 500 list call Houston home. The city hosts a thriving arts community, diverse and innovative restaurants, and prestigious Rice University, with its 4,100 students.

The lines of the bowl-shaped 25th, which spans southern and eastern Harris County, were contorted in new ways for 1996 when a three-judge federal panel redrew 13 Dallas- and Houston-area congressional districts in August.

Of all the reconfigured districts, the 25th sustained the largest partisan shift, losing much of its Democratic tinge. Bill Clinton won the old 25th by 11 percentage points in 1992; in its new configuration he would have won by only 3 percentage points that year. The new map added the largely white suburban areas of Bellaire and West University Place west of Rice University and removed heavily black and Democratic northern Fort Bend County, which adjoins Harris to the south.

The 25th remains an ethnically diverse, urbanized district with significant populations of blacks (23 percent) and Hispanics (19 percent). And though the 25th is less Democratic than its predecessor, Clinton won it by seven points in 1996.

For many in the 25th, life revolves around petroleum-based products, although the Houston-area economy has diversified since the oil industry took a sharp downturn in the mid-1980s. Employment in the oil and gas industries in 1981 accounted for 68 percent of Houston's economic base; by 1995 the figure was 45 percent. Harris County has the nation's largest concentration of petrochemical plants and related businesses. In east Harris, the cities of Pasadena and Baytown also rely heavily on refining.

The shipping business is another economic pillar. The 50-mile Houston Ship Channel connects Houston to the Gulf of Mexico. The $15 billion port complex has enabled Houston to become one of the world's busiest ports.

The Texas Medical Center is the 25th's largest private employer. The 675-acre complex has more than 40 member institutions, including 13 hospitals and two medical schools.

The huge Johnson Space Center (in the neighboring 9th District) draws a substantial share of its work force from the 25th.

Attractions in the western part of the district include the Houston Museum of Natural Science, the Houston Zoo and the Astrodome. In the east, the city of La Porte houses the San Jacinto Battleground State Historical Park, where the 570-foot San Jacinto Monument was erected to honor the men (led by Sam Houston) who routed Santa Ana's army in 1836 and contributed to Texas' independence from Mexico.

As of May 19, the Census Bureau had not recalculated population data, racial and ethnic breakdowns, and age statistics for districts newly drawn for the 1996 election.

to craft a health insurance portability measure that was a Democratic counter to a Republican bill on the subject; the GOP measure passed the House in March 1996.

Bentsen said the Democratic plan would guarantee people access to group or individual health coverage even if they changed jobs, lost a job or got sick; it also aimed to help small businesses join together to purchase more affordable health coverage. The Democratic bill also raised the deductibility of health-insurance costs for the self-employed to 80 percent, compared with 50 percent under the GOP plan. The Democratic proposal did not include controversial features that were part of the GOP bill, including medical savings accounts and caps on medical malpractice liability. But when the House voted on the Democratic measure, it failed by 192-226.

On most social policy issues, Bentsen is in the liberal Democratic mainstream. He voted against repealing the ban on certain semiautomatic assault-style weapons and also opposes efforts to restrict access to abortion. Although Bentsen was at first critical of the GOP's attempt to overhaul the welfare system, he ended up voting for the final version of the legislation. He said the final bill was an improvement over earlier versions because it provided some transitional health care benefits, child care assistance and retained the federal guarantee of nutritional assistance for children.

At Home: Bentsen was forced into a December 1996 runoff with Republican Dolly Madison McKenna after neither of them received a majority of votes in November. The runoff was a result of redistricting forced by a June Supreme Court decision. The court upheld a federal three-judge panel's decision that declared several districts in Texas to be unconstitutional because they were drawn with too much emphasis on race. The three judges in August made changes to 13 districts, including the 25th, in an effort to fix the contested district lines.

In November, Bentsen had emerged on top of

an 11-candidate field of eight Republicans, two Democrats and a third-party candidate. He took 34 percent of the vote — double McKenna's share, but far short of the majority he needed to avoid a runoff.

McKenna, a self-described economic conservative and social moderate, ran to the left of the other Republicans in the Nov. 5 race. Stressing her support for abortion rights, McKenna claimed she was the only candidate in the crowded race who represented "Colin Powell's sensible center." In her face-off against Bentsen, however, McKenna, a former oil company banker and business consultant, put less emphasis on social issues and more on her economic conservatism. She said Bentsen is not the moderate Democrat he claims to be and pointed to his opposition to a balanced-budget constitutional amendment.

Although the redistricting plan had brought into the 25th a few Republican-leaning neighborhoods, the combined Democratic House vote in November was slightly more than 50 percent, and Clinton carried the district in presidential voting. Those figures boded well for Bentsen, who ended up beating McKenna in the runoff by 14 percentage points.

Bentsen had been regarded as something of an underdog in his 1994 quest to replace Democratic Rep. Mike Andrews, who ran unsuccessfully for the Senate. Texas was trending Republican at all levels in the fall of 1994, and Bentsen's GOP opponent, Gene Fontenot, was spending more than $4 million (much of it his own) on the race.

To secure the Democratic nomination, Bentsen had to win a runoff against Beverley Clark, a black former Houston city councilwoman and an outspoken abortion foe. Clark was the top vote-getter in the five-way March primary, but Bentsen was able to overtake her in the runoff, partly by stressing his support for abortion rights.

In the general election, Bentsen, with the aid of the national Democratic Party, tried to paint Fontenot as a member of the "radical right," noting his opposition to abortion even to protect the life of the woman. He also accused Fontenot of wanting to slash the federal education budget, agriculture subsidies and public hospital systems.

A retired physician, non-practicing lawyer and hospital owner, Fontenot was an activist conservative closely associated with the Christian Coalition and the anti-abortion movement. His campaign received national attention, largely because of its lavish spending.

In its fall endorsement of Bentsen, the Houston Chronicle said of Fontenot's campaign, "There are overtones of the type of religious extremism which makes the average voter quite uneasy." In a brochure about the Fontenots' million-dollar home in Spring, Fontenot's wife, Reina, suggested that divine inspiration had helped her choose Oriental rugs on a shopping trip to Hong Kong.

Fontenot followed the standard Republican script for 1994, including calls for harsher penalties for criminals, term limits for politicians and a balanced-budget constitutional amendment. But in the end, Bentsen won with 52 percent of the vote, 7 percentage points ahead of Fontenot.

HOUSE ELECTIONS

1996 General Runoff*		
Ken Bentsen (D)	29,396	(57%)
Dolly Madison McKenna (R)	21,892	(43%)
1996 General		
Ken Bentsen (D)	43,701	(34%)
Dolly Madison McKenna (R)	21,898	(17%)
Beverley Clark (D)	21,699	(17%)
Brent Perry (R)	16,737	(13%)
John Devine (R)	9,070	(7%)
John M. Sanchez (R)	8,984	(7%)
Ken B. Mathis (R)	3,649	(3%)

** Because of court-ordered redistricting in August, an all-candidate special election was held in November. If no candidate received a majority of the vote, the top two finishers met in a December runoff.*

Previous Winning Percentages: **1994** (52%)

CAMPAIGN FINANCE

	Receipts	Receipts from PACs		Expend-itures
1996 General Runoff				
Bentsen (D)	$1,692,979	$910,734	(54%)	$1,654,345
McKenna (R)	$648,854	$101,147	(16%)	$649,716
1996				
Perry (R)	$332,844	$83,830	(25%)	$331,855
Devine (R)	$87,928	$6,750	(8%)	$87,727
Mathis (R)	$42,418	0		$33,692
Meinke (R)	$41,402	0		$41,401
Sanchez (R)	$174,787	0		$174,589
1994				
Bentsen (D)	$983,377	$401,235	(41%)	$972,688
Fontenot (R)	$4,659,466	$24,227	(1%)	$4,658,585

DISTRICT VOTE FOR PRESIDENT

	1996		1992
D	81,482 (51%)	**D**	77,152 (42%)
R	70,344 (44%)	**R**	71,252 (39%)
I	8,331 (5%)	**I**	33,212 (18%)

KEY VOTES

1997	
Ban "partial birth" abortions	N
1996	
Approve farm bill	N
Deny public education to illegal immigrants	N
Repeal ban on certain assault-style weapons	N
Increase minimum wage	Y
Freeze defense spending	Y
Approve welfare overhaul	Y
1995	
Approve balanced-budget constitutional amendment	N
Relax Clean Water Act regulations	N
Oppose limits on environmental regulations	Y
Reduce projected Medicare spending	N
Approve GOP budget with tax and spending cuts	N

VOTING STUDIES

	Presidential Support		Party Unity		Conservative Coalition	
Year	**S**	**O**	**S**	**O**	**S**	**O**
1996	81	19	77	22	82	18
1995	78	20	83	17	64	36

INTEREST GROUP RATINGS

Year	ADA	AFL-CIO	CCUS	ACU
1996	75	n/a	31	10
1995	85	100	29	8

26 Dick Armey (R)

Of Irving — Elected 1984, 7th term

Biographical Information

Born: July 7, 1940, Cando, N.D.

Education: Jamestown College, B.A. 1963; U. of North Dakota, M.A. 1964; U. of Oklahoma, Ph.D. 1969.

Occupation: Economist; professor.

Family: Wife, Susan Byrd; five children.

Religion: Presbyterian.

Political Career: No previous office.

Capitol Office: 301 Cannon Bldg. 20515; 225-7772.

Majority Leader

In Washington: Speaker Newt Gingrich is the face most Americans associate with the Republican Congress, but Majority Leader Armey, conservative to the core, is a purer expression of its ideological animus.

Broad-chested and wearing armadillo-skin cowboy boots that his wife found at a flea market, Armey might appear better suited to the high plains farm of his boyhood than to the House. But he draws praise from the GOP right for his reluctance to yield ground to centrist Republicans and liberal Democrats. Adversaries often see intransigence in Armey's conservative ardor, and he can be plenty stubborn. But his duty as majority leader is to keep the trains running, and that he has done — sometimes by force of will, sometimes by compromising, and sometimes by accepting defeat and moving to the next issue.

Although his public persona remains far overshadowed by Gingrich, Armey has lent a guiding hand in legislative initiatives from farm policy to taxes. And he is looked to as a barometer of whether an idea will fly with the GOP's most fervent conservatives. Thus, it was interesting and notable in early May 1997 that Armey made friendly noises about the budget compromise outlined by President Clinton and congressional negotiators. Later in May, the budget plan passed the House, 333-99, with only 26 Republicans voting "no."

Like Gingrich, Armey abandoned a career in academia when a posting at a second-rank public university proved too limited a forum. Both were elected to House seats as political neophytes, and both made their reputations by shunning the go along-get along tradition for a new brand of politics that breathed inspiration into the downtrodden Republican ranks. Armey and his staff were Gingrich's co-designers in drawing up the "Contract With America," the 1994 House Republican campaign platform.

When Republicans took over the House in 1995, their leaders knew they would have to brace their troops for the shock of the sheer size of the program cuts that would be necessary to balance the budget. Armey let his fears slip in a January 1995 appearance on NBC's "Meet the Press," when he said, "Once members of Congress know exactly, chapter and verse, the pain that the government must live with in order to get to a balanced budget, their knees will buckle."

But Armey helped keep the troops in line, in essence instructing factions to fight their battles among themselves rather than airing them publicly. He earned some criticism for his handling of day to day operations — keeping the House in for an overnight session, surprising members with sudden votes that upset their plans, and stating on Dec. 21, 1995, that "there has been talk of working on Christmas Day." And some Republican defections came on issues of personal importance to him. But mostly he earned respect for his hold on the institutional levers of power.

Republicans wrapped all their initial hopes in the dream of a balanced budget, including their plans to overhaul Medicare, Medicaid and welfare, plus hundreds of millions of dollars worth of program cuts that would have shrunk not just the debt but the federal government. When Clinton wiped out a year's worth of GOP efforts and, in essence their whole agenda, with a single stroke of his veto pen, conservatives fumed that Gingrich had allowed the president to beguile him in endgame budget negotiations. Believing Armey could not be sweet talked, they pushed Gingrich to allow his deputy to accompany him to White House meetings. But it was all for naught; no broad budget agreement emerged in the 104th.

Also for naught were Armey's love of the flat tax and his hatred of the minimum wage, the National Endowment for the Arts and the Legal Services Corporation at least for the 104th.

Armey seemed amazed and appalled that, after he steered through the House nearly all the legislation derived from the contract, so much of the agenda was killed or ignored by the Republican-controlled Senate. About an amendment that would have restricted federal grants recipients from lobbying, Armey complained, "The Senate said it could accept it only if it were meaningless. There was an impression on the House

TEXAS 26
Suburban Dallas; part of Irving

From 1990 to 1996, Texas experienced the greatest numerical growth in population of any state in the country. The areas that comprise the 26th have contributed greatly to the state's growth, and have for the last few decades.

Denton County, the biggest chunk of land in the district, is home to once rural communities that are now Dallas suburbs. Denton's population swelled 89 percent in the 1970s and 91 percent in the 1980s, and continues to expand.

The region's astonishing growth was attributed primarily to the appeal of the "Golden Triangle," an area bordered by Dallas-Fort Worth International Airport and two major highways, I-35 East and I-35 West.

The 26th's growth and economic sustenance, like all of the Dallas-Fort Worth area districts, is derived from its infrastructure. Numerous district residents depend on Love Field and the Dallas-Fort Worth airport for their paychecks. Proximity to Dallas-Fort Worth area airports is a major reason corporations have relocated and expanded in the region.

With the rapid population growth, the 26th's boundaries were compressed and shifted in the 1992 redistricting, making room for a new minority-influenced district elsewhere in Dallas. Its boundaries were changed again in the 1996 round of redistricting. The 26th has over time gradually moved south and east; in the 1980s, the district's northern extremity almost stretched to the Oklahoma border.

About 58 percent of the district's population lives in Dallas County. Although most of the city lies outside the 26th, district residents generally look to Dallas for employment and entertainment and many work in the downtown financial district.

The district previously included west-central Dallas County, near the Irving area. Remapping in 1996 placed much of this area in the 30th.

The 26th now contains little of the Irving area and instead extends into north-central Dallas County, picking up the wealthy areas of Highland Park (where Ross Perot lives) and University Park south of the LBJ Freeway and north of downtown. University Park envelops Southern Methodist University, an 8,800-student campus affiliated with the Methodist Church. The university, with its heavy business orientation, has helped stock Dallas' myriad financial firms and other corporations with MBAs.

The 26th includes a northeastern wedge of Tarrant County, including the affluent areas of Southlake and Grapevine that had been in the 6th.

The new 26th's demographics are nearly a carbon copy of its predecessor's. As a predominantly white, upper-income (its per-capita income far exceeds the state average), Southern suburban area, it is strongly Republican. Bob Dole won the district by a better than 2-to-1 margin in 1996, and Armey continues to rack up huge percentages.

As of May 19, the Census Bureau had not recalculated population data, racial and ethnic breakdowns, and age statistics for district newly drawn for the 1996 election.

side that the Senate leadership should have told some of their members to get with the program."

But as the GOP revolution began to falter, Armey had trouble even getting his own foot soldiers to stay with the program. The 90-cent increase in the minimum wage, probably the GOP's biggest legislative defeat of the 104th, was a personal blow against Armey, who favored eliminating the minimum wage and called the increase a "folly" that he would "fight . . . with every fiber of my being." Armey managed to delay a floor vote demanded by Democrats and moderate Republicans, waiting long enough for $10 billion in tax breaks to find their way onto the wage bill.

"Any time somebody has a position I disagree with and has 218 votes, I have to deal with it. That's life," Armey said of the "dread minimum wage increase."

That same sense of the magic House majority number of 218 informed his sense early in the 105th of the difficulty he would have enforcing a deal to abolish the NEA. "The way you live up to the deal is to get 218 votes. I'm not sure the most ardent supporters believe we can get that." But Armey and the other top House GOP leaders vowed in April 1997 that they would not back down from the fight to kill the program.

Armey's office served during the 104th as the "war room" for the GOP's frontal assault on domestic spending and many of the efforts to kill or curtail agencies, including the Legal Services Corporation, an Armey pet peeve, and the departments of Energy and Education. Eliminating various Cabinet departments was an idea pushed by Armey but most closely associated with the Class of 1994; freshmen found Armey more their ideological kin than Gingrich and trusted him more.

Armey, an economist by profession, is the leading congressional proponent of the flat tax; his version would create a 20 percent rate with no deductions, dropping to 17 percent after two years. "You stay flat or die," he says. "Live flat or die." Although the flat tax proposal gained some currency in the 1996 GOP presidential sweepstakes, it fell far short of triumph even as a prevailing idea within the party.

One notable success for Armey was the revamping of the agricultural support program. With his blessing, Republicans in the 104th created a national farm program that is more market-oriented and designed to wean farmers from price supports.

Armey's prospects for someday succeeding Gingrich are cloudy. Although he has worked to court GOP moderates, who credit him with fairness in hearing them out, that faction sees him as less accommodating than Gingrich. Armey was careful in the 105th to moderate his public tone, avoiding any criticism of Clinton — a stark contrast to his news conferences during the 104th. Still, he is not widely viewed as a big picture spokesman, and although he has sought advice to improve his TV appearances, his flat and sometimes garbled speech is less than ideal for the medium. Reporters, counting by comparison, found Armey blinks 18 times less frequently than the more energetic Budget Committee chairman, John R. Kasich, R-Ohio.

Armey can be engaging, even toward some of his most liberal Democratic colleagues. But his rhetoric is sometimes inflammatory, even when he does not intend it to be. Early in the 104th,, Armey referred to Democratic Rep. Barney Frank of Massachusetts as "Barney Fag." (Frank is gay.) Armey immediately corrected himself and later, after a torrent of criticism, he apologized for committing a "perceived slur, maintaining that he had committed no Freudian slip — simply an "unintentional mispronunciation" of Frank's name.

As chairman of the Republican Conference in the 103rd, Armey was one rung on the leadership ladder below Gingrich, who was then minority whip. In winning the post, Armey had unseated easygoing Californian Jerry Lewis, an old-style mainstream conservative whom Armey portrayed as too willing to accommodate Democrats. "The politics of confrontation works and the politics of appeasement fails," Armey said in 1992.

At Home: Armey cites a belief in the free enterprise system as the genesis of his political career. He was popular on the Dallas area lecture circuit, praising the philosophy of economist George Gilder and extolling "the miracle of the market." But beyond volunteering for Jim Bradshaw, the GOP nominee in the 26th in 1982, Armey had no previous experience when he challenged freshman Democratic Rep. Tom Vandergriff in 1984.

After meeting with editors of the Fort Worth Star-Telegram, Armey was quoted as saying he favored a gradual phaseout of Social Security. Then he said he was "embarrassed" to have been a professor, calling some college classes "pure junk," citing black studies courses as an example.

But Armey prevailed by stressing his conservative economic notions, allying himself firmly with President Ronald Reagan and branding Vandergriff a lackey for House Speaker Thomas P. O'Neill Jr. Taking advantage of an unusual outbreak of straight-ticket GOP voting, Armey won with 51 percent. In his six re-elections, Armey always has topped two-thirds of the vote, even in a slightly redrawn district in 1996.

HOUSE ELECTIONS

1996 General		
Dick Armey (R)	163,708	(74%)
Jerry Frankel (D)	58,623	(26%)
1994 General		
Dick Armey (R)	135,398	(76%)
LeEarl Ann Bryant (D)	39,763	(22%)
Alfred Adask (LIBERT)	2,030	(1%)

Because of court-ordered redistricting in August, an all-candidate election was held in November. If no candidate received a majority of the vote then, the top two finishers met in a December runoff.

Previous Winning Percentages: **1992** (73%) **1990** (70%) **1988** (69%) **1986** (68%) **1984** (51%)

CAMPAIGN FINANCE

	Receipts	Receipts from PACs	Expenditures
1996			
Armey (R)	$1,248,706	$600,700 (48%)	$1,673,388
Frankel (D)	$57,407	$3,450 (6%)	$56,094
1994			
Armey (R)	$1,177,630	$253,654 (22%)	$900,871
Bryant (D)	$13,481	$50 (0%)	$13,131

DISTRICT VOTE FOR PRESIDENT

	1996		1992
D	73,676 (30%)	**D**	47,066 (22%)
R	153,692 (62%)	**R**	126,996 (48%)
I	17,802 (7%)	**I**	79,930 (30%)

KEY VOTES

1997	
Ban "partial birth" abortions	Y
1996	
Approve farm bill	Y
Deny public education to illegal immigrants	Y
Repeal ban on certain assault-style weapons	Y
Increase minimum wage	N
Freeze defense spending	N
Approve welfare overhaul	Y
1995	
Approve balanced-budget constitutional amendment	Y
Relax Clean Water Act regulations	Y
Oppose limits on environmental regulations	N
Reduce projected Medicare spending	Y
Approve GOP budget with tax and spending cuts	Y

VOTING STUDIES

	Presidential Support		Party Unity		Conservative Coalition	
Year	S	O	S	O	S	O
1996	37	61	95	4	96	4
1995	17	81	97	1	97	2
1994	37	62	98	1	92	6
1993	26	73	95	2	98	0
1992	85	13	95	1	96	4
1991	86	14	97	1	100	0

INTEREST GROUP RATINGS

Year	ADA	AFL-CIO	CCUS	ACU
1996	0	n/a	94	100
1995	0	0	100	92
1994	0	0	83	100
1993	0	0	100	100
1992	0	8	75	100
1991	0	0	100	100

27 Solomon P. Ortiz (D)

Of Corpus Christi — Elected 1982, 8th term

Biographical Information

Born: June 3, 1937, Robstown, Texas.

Education: Institute of Applied Science, 1962; Del Mar College, 1965-67.

Military Service: Army, 1960-62.

Occupation: Law enforcement official.

Family: Divorced; two children.

Religion: Methodist.

Political Career: Nueces County constable, 1965-69; Nueces County Commission, 1969-77; Nueces County sheriff, 1977-83.

Capitol Office: 2136 Rayburn Bldg. 20515; 225-7742.

Committees

National Security
Military Installations and Facilities (ranking); Military Readiness

Resources
Energy & Mineral Resources; Fisheries Conservation, Wildlife & Oceans

In Washington: Ortiz, a former sheriff, has a less liberal voting record than other Hispanic Democrats in the House; his stances have always had less to do with ideology than with responding to constituent needs and promoting the economy of his district.

In the first half of the 1990s, the military bases in the 27th escaped the cost-cutting ax wielded by the Defense Base Closure and Realignment Commission. But Ortiz, who sits on the National Security Committee, remains vigilant lest any further defense downsizing affect his district. In particular, he is concerned about a Pentagon proposal to privatize some of the repair work done at large military maintenance depots, such as the one in Corpus Christi that keeps Army helicopters flying.

In the spring of 1996, the Pentagon asserted that it could save money by moving more of its repair and maintenance work on planes, ships and other equipment to the private sector. But before such a reallocation of work could occur, Congress would have to repeal two laws. One, known as the "60-40" law, was made a part of the 1988 defense bill at Ortiz's behest. It requires that no less than 60 percent of each year's depot-maintenance work be performed by federal employees. The second law requires competitive bidding between a private firm and a government depot for any package of overhaul work worth more than $3 billion.

Ortiz and other House members opposed to the Pentagon's privatization scheme complained that it would restrict military depots to performing a "core" of critical maintenance, barring them from bidding for other overhaul work. "All you have to do is read between the lines to know that the [Department of Defense] plans start a death spiral for the public depot system," Ortiz told The Associated Press in May 1996.

The depot defenders also warned that private companies might not be responsive to military exigencies or could be disrupted by labor disputes or bankruptcies.

In July 1996, House and Senate negotiators on the fiscal 1997 defense authorization agreed to keep intact the 60-40 law. Depot proponents said this would block, for the time being, Pentagon plans for any major shift of overhaul work to outside contractors.

Although Ortiz objects to increased private contracting of depot maintenance work, he is encouraging private sector involvement in providing housing for military personnel in his area. He announced in June 1996 that the Navy would join with a private developer to build more affordable housing for personnel stationed at the Naval Air Station in Corpus Christi and the Naval Station Ingleside. A total of 404 townhouses are to be built. "What is exciting about this new phase of defense housing is that if military personnel do not need the space, it will be made available to the open market," Ortiz told The Associated Press.

Ortiz praised the fiscal 1997 defense authorization bill for allocating more funds to "quality of life" programs for military personnel; improved housing is part of that emphasis. "This bill continues the pledge made by Congress last year to stretch housing dollars by increasing the funds available to the military services for public/private partnership initiatives."

Another local concern of Ortiz's has also been a focus of much broader attention: the immigration of people from Mexico and elsewhere in Latin America. When the House debated immigration law overhaul in March 1996, Ortiz voted to strip provisions from the bill that would have cut back on legal immigration by the relatives of U.S. citizens and legal permanent residents.

He argued that legal and illegal immigration "have nothing to do with one another." He added, "As a representative of a border district, I am uniquely aware of the burden that illegal immigration poses on local communities. Illegal immigration must be curtailed, but it is a mistake to link this important goal with legal immigration." On a 238-183 vote, the House approved an amendment splitting off the legal immigration provisions from the broader immigration bill.

TEXAS 27
Gulf Coast — Corpus Christi; Brownsville

Tucked in the southeastern corner of Texas, the compact 27th is anchored by two dramatically different cities that have become something of rivals ever since the 1982 redistricting threw them together.

In the northern county of Nueces is Corpus Christi. This cosmopolitan city of 257,500, with its mild climate, beaches and museums, is a tourist mecca. Hispanics hold a slight majority in Corpus Christi but are often outvoted by Anglos.

Nueces County has a heavy military influence that has narrowly avoided some base closures and had to endure others. In May 1993, the Corpus Christi Naval Air Station and Naval Hospital appeared on the Pentagon's list of proposed base closures. The facility managed to survive, but again appeared on the Pentagon's 1995 list as a candidate for realignment.

Two facilities that have had more luck are the Corpus Christi Army Depot, the largest employer in the city, and the naval station just across the Corpus Christi Bay in Ingleside, which is located in a neighboring district and also survived after appearing on the Pentagon's 1993 list. The Kingsville Naval Air Station also was able to stay off the Pentagon's 1995 list, in part because of its advanced flight training facilities.

Brownsville, by comparison, is almost entirely Hispanic. Located in southernmost Cameron County, the smaller, grittier city has a distinctly south-of-the-border flavor. Breakfast tacos are common fare and many of the residents are bilingual. A private study of census data concluded in 1993 that Brownsville has the highest poverty rate in the nation.

There is no military presence in the southern part of the district. The export-import trade of fruits and vegetables with Brownsville's sister city of Matamoros, Mexico, is an important local industry. Brownsville has trouble competing with the better-known Corpus Christi for tourists and has problems, such as drug trafficking, that are related to illegal border crossings.

Despite the competition between the two cities, they have much in common and offer a unifying thread for the 27th. Both are port cities reliant on the energy and fishing industries.

Both cities watched the local shrimping catch decline in the mid-1980s, partly as a result of new laws requiring the use of nets with devices that enable turtles — and, fishermen say, some shrimp — to escape.

Although Ortiz sometimes describes himself and his district as conservative, recent elections and surveys show a more liberal bent to the 27th.

Nueces County provides a reliable Democratic base. Nueces County also routinely sends Democrats, often Hispanics, to the state Legislature.

But Cameron County has proved to be even more Democratic in some recent elections. In 1992, Bill Clinton got 46 percent of the vote in Nueces and 50 percent in Cameron. In 1996, he got 54 percent in Nueces and 62 percent in Cameron.

In the 1996 House election, Ortiz garnered 62 percent in Nueces and 69 percent in Cameron.

1990 Population: 566,217. White 445,735 (79%), Black 13,760 (2%), Other 106,722 (19%). Hispanic origin 374,783 (66%). 18 and over 380,622 (67%), 62 and over 71,319 (13%). Median age: 29.

Ortiz joined with other South Texas lawmakers in opposing a 1995 Clinton administration plan to levy new border crossing fees of $1.50 per person and $3 per vehicle at the Mexican and Canadian borders. White House officials said the fees would help build new border facilities and hire inspectors to speed border crossings, as well as increase efforts to block illegal entries. But the lawmakers argued that the new fees would cause Mexico and Canada to initiate similar fees and lead to a drop in cross-border business. Clinton ultimately backed away from the fees and simply suggested that they be optional for individual states.

Ortiz bucks the Democratic Party line on certain social policy questions. In the 104th Congress he voted for measures limiting access to abortions, and he supported repealing the ban on certain semiautomatic assault-style weapons. In the 103rd, Ortiz voted against requiring a five-day waiting period before the purchase of a handgun.

But Ortiz was a firm backer of Clinton's effort to raise the minimum wage. And in the 103rd, he also agreed with the president on the importance of approving NAFTA. Ortiz argued that one of the surest ways to combat illegal immigration was to help promote an economically secure Mexico.

Through the 103rd Congress, Ortiz held a seat on the Merchant Marine and Fisheries Committee. Republicans abolished that panel when they took control of the House in 1995, and Ortiz got a seat on the Resources Committee, which picked up some fisheries functions when Merchant Marine went defunct.

Ortiz's main focus in the 102nd Congress was the Congressional Hispanic Caucus. He served as chairman and helped push through legislation to increase access to voting materials in languages other than English.

At Home: Since his 1964 election as constable, Ortiz has been a groundbreaker for Hispanics in South Texas politics, holding a succession of offices previously closed to Mexican-Americans. He was chosen Nueces County's first Hispanic commissioner in 1968 and its first Hispanic sheriff in 1976.

Redistricting in 1982 gave Ortiz the opening he needed to get to Congress. As adjusted by a three-judge federal panel, the 27th was good territory for a Mexican-American Democrat; its Hispanic population exceeded 60 percent.

Four of the five candidates who filed for the Democratic nomination in 1982 were Hispanic. With the loyal backing of the poorer Hispanics in Corpus Christi, Ortiz finished first in the primary and won a spot in the runoff.

Ortiz's runoff foe was the one non-Hispanic candidate, Joseph Salem, a Corpus Christi jeweler and former state representative. Salem had strong labor ties, but many of the oil and other business interests who had backed attorney Jorge Rangel in the primary turned to Ortiz, leery that Salem was too liberal.

The decisive runoff votes were cast in Brownsville. Although Salem had some initial appeal to the Hispanic majority there, Ortiz scored a coup by gaining the support of state Pardons and Paroles Board Chairman Ruben M. Torres. With Torres' support, Ortiz won about 60 percent of the Cameron County (Brownsville) runoff vote, allowing him to draw 64 percent districtwide.

After four uneventful re-elections, Ortiz dropped to 55 percent in 1992 against Republican Jay Kimbrough, who benefited from the anti-Congress mood of the electorate and from redistricting, which cost Ortiz some Hispanic voters. Even though 1994 was a tough year for Democrats, Ortiz improved to 59 percent, and in 1996 he took nearly two-thirds of the vote in winning an eighth term.

HOUSE ELECTIONS

1996 General		
Solomon P. Ortiz (D)	97,350	(65%)
Joe Gardner (R)	50,964	(34%)
Kevin G. Richardson (NL)	2,286	(2%)
1996 Primary		
Solomon P. Ortiz (D)	37,434	(70%)
Mary Helen Berlanga (D)	16,097	(30%)
1994 General		
Solomon P. Ortiz (D)	65,325	(59%)
Erol A. Stone (R)	44,693	(41%)

Previous Winning Percentages: **1992** (55%) **1990** (100%) **1988** (100%) **1986** (100%) **1984** (64%) **1982** (64%)

CAMPAIGN FINANCE

	Receipts	Receipts from PACs		Expend-itures
1996				
Ortiz (D)	$400,178	$142,400	(36%)	$407,316
Gardner (R)	$97,121	$500	(1%)	$96,900
1994				
Ortiz (D)	$288,867	$117,280	(41%)	$469,694
Stone (R)	$43,619	$931	(2%)	$42,282

DISTRICT VOTE FOR PRESIDENT

	1996		1992
D	87,679 (57%)	**D**	78,475 (48%)
R	57,669 (37%)	**R**	58,806 (36%)
I	8,122 (5%)	**I**	27,476 (17%)

KEY VOTES

1997	
Ban "partial birth" abortions	Y
1996	
Approve farm bill	Y
Deny public education to illegal immigrants	N
Repeal ban on certain assault-style weapons	Y
Increase minimum wage	Y
Freeze defense spending	N
Approve welfare overhaul	N
1995	
Approve balanced-budget constitutional amendment	Y
Relax Clean Water Act regulations	Y
Oppose limits on environmental regulations	N
Reduce projected Medicare spending	N
Approve GOP budget with tax and spending cuts	N

VOTING STUDIES

	Presidential Support		Party Unity		Conservative Coalition	
Year	S	O	S	O	S	O
1996	65	32	67	28	92	6
1995	62	32	60	35	79	10
1994	73	19	77	20	78	17
1993	83	16	77	20	82	18
1992	37	55	81	16	71	29
1991	41	53	76	19	73	24

INTEREST GROUP RATINGS

Year	ADA	AFL-CIO	CCUS	ACU
1996	60	n/a	43	37
1995	50	75	46	32
1994	45	56	55	48
1993	40	83	50	39
1992	60	83	38	40
1991	30	67	56	26

28 Ciro D. Rodriguez (D)

Of San Antonio — Elected 1997, 1st term

Biographical Information

Born: Dec. 9, 1946; Piedras Negras, Mexico.

Education: St. Mary's University, B.A., 1973; Our Lady of the Lake University, M.S.W.,1978.

Occupation: Legislator, educator, social worker.

Family: Wife, Carolina Pena; one child.

Religion: Roman Catholic.

Political Career: Harlandale school board 1975-87; Texas House, 1987-97.

Capitol Office: 323 Cannon Bldg., 20515; 225-1640

Committees

National Security

Veterans' Affairs

The Path to Washington: Three months into the 105th Congress, Rodriguez assumed the seat previously held by Democrat Frank Tejeda, who died in January 1997. He was sworn in five days after collecting two-thirds of the vote in a special runoff election.

Rodriguez occupies the seat Tejeda held on the National Security Committee — a post of key concern to the San Antonio area, which has been buffeted by base closures in recent years. Rodriguez has expressed a particular interest in seeking highway funds for his district in hopes that an improved infrastructure will boost trade. Rodriguez also sits on Veterans' Affairs, as did Tejeda.

Rodriguez is likely to prove a fairly reliable vote for the Democratic leadership. He campaigned on his support for abortion rights and defense of such traditional Democratic domestic programs as education and Social Security.

A 10-year veteran of the state Legislature who previously had served 12 years on the Harlandale school board, Rodriguez had the backing of most of the San Antonio Democratic establishment in the April 1997 special election. He dominated the voting in the March special election, but his 46 percent share of the vote fell short of the majority required to win the seat outright.

So he headed into a runoff with his nearest rival, former City Councilman Juan Solis, also a Democrat, who got 27 percent in the first round. Solis launched an aggressive challenge against Rodriguez, characterizing himself as Tejeda's true heir because he shared the former member's anti-abortion position. Rodriguez countered that he could not in good faith impose his religious beliefs on others (he is Roman Catholic).

Solis also campaigned for gunowners' rights and anti-crime measures and tried to tar Rodriguez as "a wild-eyed liberal." But Solis' best claim to the votes of conservatives and Tejeda admirers may have been the endorsements he received from some members of Tejeda's family. Rodriguez countered Solis' claim to the Tejeda mystique by saying he had known the deceased incumbent since they went to high school and college together.

Tejeda had represented the district since its creation after the 1990 census; it was specifically envisioned as a Hispanic-majority seat.

After taking his oath of office, Rodriguez stood in the well of the House facing a packed chamber — an unusual morning audience anticipating an announcement from Speaker Newt Gingrich regarding his ethics case. Looking out on the faces of his new colleagues, Rodriguez drew a hearty laugh by deadpanning: "Thanks for getting together this welcome for me."

Rodriguez then noted that his wife, Carolina, was "Teacher of the Year" in 1996 in the South San Antonio Independent School District. Rodriguez, a former social worker, teacher and education consultant, also mentioned his years as a school board member. In the Texas Legislature he served as chairman of the Local Consent and Calendars Committee and as a member of the Public Health and the Higher Education committees.

In Austin, Rodriguez worked on equalizing education funding between school districts and on job creation through trade and private redevelopment of Kelly Air Force Base, which is in the process of closing. Rodriguez said he hoped to see C-5 aircraft maintained at Kelly under a private contract.

Tejeda's death provoked a scramble among prospective successors who eventually numbered 15, including nine Democrats. But Rodriguez attracted most of the support from fellow legislators and prominent Democrats in city government.

Rodriguez was also the best-financed candidate in the field, raising about $250,000 before the first round of special election voting and about the same amount for the runoff. The financing allowed Rodriguez to air broadcast ads in Bexar (San Antonio) County in the final weeks before the vote. Rodriguez also credited the backing of the San Antonio central labor council of the AFL-CIO, which helped him turn out a strong vote in March and again in April.

TEXAS 28
South San Antonio; Zapata

Mapmakers looking to create a new Hispanic-majority district in south-central Texas found two population bases — San Antonio and the Mexican border — and connected them with a winding trail of South Texas counties. The result was the 28th, one of three new districts the fast-growing Lone Star State acquired in reapportionment for the 1990s.

The 28th is heavily influenced by its proximity to Mexico and its abundance of military bases. The military presence helped keep the region's economy afloat during the oil price crash of the mid-1980s and the recession of the early 1990s.

San Antonio has five military installations, two of which are in the 28th. Randolph Air Force Base is a major training and recruitment center. Brooks Air Force Base is primarily an aerospace research center. It appeared on the Pentagon's 1995 base-closing list, but was spared.

However, neighboring Kelly Air Force Base (in the 20th) — the area's largest job-producer and employer of half the Hispanics in the Air Force — is facing closure by September 2001 of its major unit, the San Antonio Air Logistics Center. Much of Kelly will be realigned to San Antonio's Lackland Air Force Base (which lies in the 20th) and some of the workload will be privatized.

With the five bases and a pleasant climate, San Antonio is a popular spot with retirees. Almost two-thirds of the district's population is in Bexar County, the 28th's northernmost county, which includes San Antonio, the third-largest city in Texas, and its suburbs. Harlandale is an old German town that has become an increasingly Hispanic San Antonio neighborhood.

As the district moves south toward the Rio Grande, it becomes more rural and poorer. Starr County, the nation's most heavily Hispanic county (97 percent), is economically devastated. Fifty percent of Starr's residents are below the poverty line, and its unemployment rate exceeds 25 percent. About 35 percent of the people in adjacent Zapata County (81 percent Hispanic) fall below the poverty line.

Starr and Zapata, which were taken from the 15th District to help create the new 28th, are two of the state's fastest growing counties.

An overlooked Republican enclave in the district is the northeast section of San Antonio, a predominantly white, middle-class suburb. But the 28th is a Democratic bastion: Bill Clinton received 62 percent of the district's vote in 1996, his highest non-urban tally in Texas.

1990 Population: 566,217. White 388,123 (69%), Black 48,295 (9%), Other 129,799 (23%). Hispanic origin 341,843 (60%). 18 and over 382,636 (68%), 62 and over 72,937 (13%). Median age: 29.

HOUSE ELECTIONS

1997 Special Runoff *		
Ciro D. Rodriguez (D)	19,992	(67%)
Juan Solis (D)	9,990	(33%)
1997 Special *		
Ciro D. Rodriguez (D)	14,018	(46%)
Juan Solis (D)	8,056	(27%)
Mark Cude (R)	2,452	(8%)
Carlos I. Uresti (D)	1,345	(4%)
John P. Kelly (R)	1,229	(4%)
Lauro A. Bustamante (D)	818	(3%)
John A. "Drew" Traeger (D)	718	(2%)
Narciso V. Mendoza (R)	621	(2%)
Phil Ross (D)	376	(1%)

** Nearly complete, unofficial returns.*

DISTRICT VOTE FOR PRESIDENT

	1996		1992
D	93,136 (62%)	D	94,115 (55%)
R	47,341 (32%)	R	51,291 (30%)
I	8,211 (6%)	I	27,195 (16%)

29 Gene Green (D)

Of Houston — Elected 1992, 3rd term

Biographical Information

Born: Oct. 17, 1947, Houston, Texas.
Education: U. of Houston, B.B.A. 1971,.
Occupation: Lawyer.
Family: Wife, Helen Lois Albers; two children.
Religion: Methodist.
Political Career: Texas House, 1973-85; Texas Senate, 1985-92.
Capitol Office: 2429 Rayburn Bldg. 20515; 225-1688.

Committees

Commerce
Health & Environment; Telecommunications, Trade & Consumer Protection

In Washington: Although not widely regarded as one of the House's leading liberal lights, Green has responded to Republican control of the congressional agenda in a way that calls to mind the song Groucho Marx performed in "Horse Feathers": "Whatever it is, I'm against it."

Green opposed nearly every major legislative item proposed by the GOP during the 104th Congress. From tax cuts to curtailing Medicare spending growth, from tougher immigration policy to term limits, from easing federal clean water regulations to increasing the defense budget and phasing out farm subsidies, Green was a steady, certain and reliable "no" vote.

His allegiance to the Democratic cause was rewarded at the start of the 105th Congress, when he was named to the high-powered Commerce Committee. Green had long eyed the panel, which, among many other things, oversees energy issues of crucial concern to the Texas oil and gas sector.

When Republicans in the 104th unveiled their plans to overhaul the welfare system, Green protested that it unfairly targeted children, marching to the House floor armed with a poster of a baby sporting a diaper adorned with a red bull's eye on its bottom. "When it comes to budget-cutting time, the easiest target is the children," Green declared.

Green is an Anglo representing a district that had a Hispanic-majority population until the Supreme Court in June 1996 found that the 29th and two other Texas districts were unconstitutional racial gerrymanders. As redrawn for the 1996 election, Green's constituency is 45 percent Hispanic, 15 percent black and about 40 percent white.

Green is a crusader for labor and the poor in general, but he pays special attention to issues of key concern to the still-high number of Hispanic voters in his district. (He helped underwrite a staffer for the Congressional Hispanic Caucus after that group and all other legislative service organizations were barred by the GOP majority from receiving official separate funding.) In addition to voting against the GOP bill to beef up the Border Patrol and enforce illegal immigration laws more strictly, Green opposed a move sponsored by Elton Gallegly, R-Calif., to ban illegal immigrants from public schools.

He also derided a bill that would have declared English the official language of the U.S. "This is a solution in search of a problem," Green commented.

Arguing in the 103rd Congress against restricting federal funds for a bilingual education program, Green told the House of his own high school days at a majority Hispanic school in Houston. Hispanic children, he recalled, would come to the school and be so confused by the English-only classes that they eventually would drop out. The purpose of bilingual education, he said, is to help children not get further behind while they are learning English.

One area where Green does agree with a majority of Republican members is protection of gunowners' rights. He opposed measures during his first term to ban certain semiautomatic assault-style weapons and to impose a five-day waiting period on handgun purchases. He joined with Republicans in their unsuccessful effort during the 104th to repeal the assault weapons ban. At the time of the vote, in March 1996, Green had received more financial help — $161,590 — from the National Rifle Association over the previous decade than any House member, according to a Common Cause study.

Green had supported the huge crime law enacted during the 104th that contained the assault-weapons ban. "I value Second Amendment rights, but that's not my major issue," Green explained. "My major issue is crime." Serving in the Texas Senate, Green in 1991 sponsored a bill to allow citizens to carry concealed handguns. Green said he offered the measure in response to several women in his district who felt they needed to protect themselves from street crime.

On the issue of abortion, though, Green's current view differs from his earlier position. In

The 29th has ensnared Texas in redistricting litigation since the beginning of the decade, when fast-growing Texas received three new House seats during reapportionment.

Operating under Voting Rights Act mandates to maximize minority-group representation, mapmakers amassed much of Houston's vast Hispanic population to make that group a statistical majority in the new 29th.

But in creating a 61 percent Hispanic district, cartographers created a bizarrely shaped district that seemed to hover over Houston like a bird with its wings outstretched. Its shape evoked comparisons to the Aztec god Quetzatcoatl. The Supreme Court in June 1996 reaffirmed a federal panel's ruling that the 29th was an unconstitutional racial gerrymander. Two months later the federal panel overhauled the boundaries of 13 Texas districts, including the 29th.

In its new form, the 29th looks like a backward "C" facing the southwest. Minorities still represent a majority of the district's population; Hispanics constitute 45 percent and blacks 15 percent of the residents.

The district is beset with economic struggles. Its per capita income is 27 percent below the state average, and half the families have a household income under $25,000. Almost one-fourth of its families with children live in poverty.

The 29th's northern chunk looks like an upside-down isosceles triangle, generally bound to the north by the road FM 1960, to the west by Interstate 45 and to the east by US Highway 59. This area includes the Houston Intercontinental Airport, a source of employment for many district residents.

In the district's bottom half, near Interstate 10, are working-class areas such as Jacinto City,

TEXAS 29
Parts of Houston

Galena Park and most of Channelview. Communities along the district's southern border include South Houston and part of Pasadena. The Port of Houston provides employment to thousands of these residents.

While most of the district's residents are in a minority group, there is no broader sense of community. The Hispanic populations in San Antonio and cities closer to the Mexican border are more cohesive than Houston's disparate Hispanic population. Most of Houston's 700,000 Hispanics arrived in the past two decades, emigrating not just from Mexico, but from all over Central America. They have few connections to each other and no generational ties to Houston.

Blue-collar workers are ubiquitous in the 29th. They work at the nearby refineries, at two coffee factories and on oil rigs in the gulf. There are carpenters and plumbers as well as school teachers and middle managers for Shell Oil. The Lyondell refinery and petrochemical plant, spun off from the Atlantic Richfield Company (ARCO) in 1985, is one of the nation's largest producers of ethylene and propylene.

The 29th's voter turnout is dismally low. It cast only 108,611 votes in the 1996 presidential race, by far the fewest of any Texas district. Those who do vote side overwhelmingly with Democrats. President Clinton got 61 percent here in 1996, while Green won 68 percent.

As of May 19, the Census Bureau had not recalculated population data, racial and ethnic breakdowns, and age statistics for districts newly drawn for the 1996 election.

February 1992, a month before the House primary, he dropped his longstanding opposition to abortion when he came under attack for having sponsored anti-abortion bills in the Legislature. Green said he had gradually come to alter his views on abortion, but critics said he had changed his mind to enhance his prospects of winning the 29th. He opposed the Republican-led attempt during the 104th to ban a particular abortion technique that opponents call a "partial birth" abortion.

Green also tried to tinker with Republican bills emanating from the Economic and Educational Opportunities Committee, where he served in the 104th. (The panel was renamed the Education and the Workforce Committee for the 105th.) When Republicans sought to block pension fund managers from making investments with an eye toward social engineering, and not just the bottom line, Green feared that this provision broadly interpreted would stymie domestic investment. His amendment to encourage domestic over foreign investments when practical was turned down, 192-217.

He teamed up successfully with Arkansas Republican Jay Dickey in removing vocational rehabilitation from a bill to consolidate funding for education and job training programs. Green contended that requiring people with disabilities to seek training at "one-stop" career centers would disrupt existing support systems. "You shouldn't lump people with disabilities in with the general population," Green said. "Vocational rehabilitation is certainly not broke." That argument carried the day and the House voted for the Green-Dickey amendment, 231-192.

One issue that put Green on the spot in his first term was NAFTA. The trade pact was backed by Houston's business community, an important source of campaign funding. But the 29th is mainly blue collar, unions were key political allies of Green, and most in organized labor took a dim view of NAFTA. He voted against the trade pact, a move that pinched his ability to raise business money for the 1994 election. In 1994's post-election lame duck session, Green voted for GATT.

At Home: Green's district was drawn in 1992 with an eye toward increasing Hispanic representation, and Green has had to face biennial primary challenges from Hispanics who feel they can better represent the district. Green has turned them all aside, and his district's newly redrawn borders didn't hurt him any in 1996.

The Supreme Court's decision effectively invalidated the results of the March 1996 primary, but Green drew no renewed Democratic opposition in the November primary. By winning 68 percent of the November vote, Green won the seat without facing a runoff.

Green grew up in a part of the 29th called "Redneck Alley," home mostly to working-class whites, and he had represented the area in the Texas Legislature since 1973.

Seeking a second term in 1994, the freshman Anglo in the majority-Hispanic district increased his 1992 winning margin, even as numerous Democrats elsewhere in Texas found themselves in trouble or on the scrap heap. Green cemented his win in March, when he won a primary rematch with Houston City Council member Ben Reyes. The controversial and combative Reyes tried to unify Houston's Hispanic leaders behind his candidacy, but his efforts fell short. Green credited his 55 percent win to attention to the home folks. "For the year and two months I've served I've been to 32 town hall meetings; I'm in the district every weekend," he said before the 1994 primary.

The 1992 Democratic primary in the district was a five-way affair, Reyes bested Green by almost 2,000 votes but netted only 34 percent of the vote. Without a majority, Reyes was forced into a runoff with Green, and in that one-on-one contest, Green finished on top by 180 votes.

But when it was discovered that some Republicans who had voted in the primary had illegally crossed over and cast ballots in the runoff, the results were thrown out and a second runoff held. Green won that court-ordered rematch by about 1,100 votes.

November's election that year was a breeze for Green in this Democratic district; he won 65 percent against Republican Clark Kent Ervin, a black Houston lawyer with the city establishment's financial backing.

HOUSE ELECTIONS

1996 General		
Gene Green (D)	61,751	(68%)
Jack Rodriguez (R)	28,381	(31%)
Jack W. Klinger (USTAX)	1,340	(1%)
1994 General		
Gene Green (D)	44,102	(73%)
Harold "Oilman" Eide (R)	15,952	(27%)

Because of court-ordered redistricting in August, an all-candidate election was held in November. If no candidate received a majority of the vote then, the top two finishers met in a December runoff.

Previous Winning Percentage: 1992 (65%)

CAMPAIGN FINANCE

	Receipts	Receipts from PACs	Expend-itures
1996			
Green (D)	$587,026	$395,816 (67%)	$552,655
Rodriguez (R)	$58,754	$1,516 (3%)	$58,181
1994			
Green (D)	$614,644	$454,570 (74%)	$594,375
Eide (R)	$9,571	$514 (5%)	$10,065

DISTRICT VOTE FOR PRESIDENT

	1996		1992
D	65,794 (61%)	**D**	59,607 (49%)
R	35,809 (33%)	**R**	40,766 (33%)
I	6,331 (6%)	**I**	22,529 (18%)

KEY VOTES

1997	
Ban "partial birth" abortions	N
1996	
Approve farm bill	N
Deny public education to illegal immigrants	N
Repeal ban on certain assault-style weapons	Y
Increase minimum wage	Y
Freeze defense spending	Y
Approve welfare overhaul	N
1995	
Approve balanced-budget constitutional amendment	N
Relax Clean Water Act regulations	N
Oppose limits on environmental regulations	Y
Reduce projected Medicare spending	N
Approve GOP budget with tax and spending cuts	N

VOTING STUDIES

	Presidential Support		Party Unity		Conservative Coalition	
Year	**S**	**O**	**S**	**O**	**S**	**O**
1996	71	20	76	16	69	29
1995	71	23	79	15	44	53
1994	68	19	83	9	50	39
1993	77	19	85	10	39	57

INTEREST GROUP RATINGS

Year	ADA	AFL-CIO	CCUS	ACU
1996	60	n/a	38	28
1995	90	92	35	21
1994	80	88	55	16
1993	85	100	18	13

30 Eddie Bernice Johnson (D)

Of Dallas — Elected 1992, 3rd term

Biographical Information
Born: Dec. 3, 1935, Waco, Texas.
Education: Texas Christian U., B.S. 1967; Southern Methodist U., M.P.A. 1976.
Occupation: Airport shop owner.
Family: Divorced; one child.
Religion: Baptist.
Political Career: Texas House, 1973-77; Texas Senate, 1987-93.
Capitol Office: 1123 Longworth Bldg. 20515; 225-8885.

Committees
Science
Energy & Environment; Technology
Transportation & Infrastructure
Aviation; Surface Transportation

In Washington: Johnson, who was distracted in the 104th Congress by the vicissitudes of Texas redistricting, survived a crowded field of challengers in the November 1996 election to earn a third House term. In the 105th, she is likely to divide her time between criticizing the policies of the GOP majority and looking out for her district and state on the Transportation and Infrastructure Committee and the Science Committee.

During the 104th, Johnson's electoral fate was caught up in the judicial and legislative wrangling at the state and national level over minority-majority House districts, including her 30th District. When she was in the Texas state Senate in the early 1990s and working on congressional redistricting, Johnson had fashioned the 30th to suit her political strengths.

But the Supreme Court ruled in September 1996 that certain House districts in Texas were drawn solely to establish minority-majority constituencies and were unconstitutional "racial gerrymanders." In short order, federal judges had issued a new map and ordered new elections; Johnson landed in a redrawn district with much new territory and seven opponents.

She muscled past the field on Election Day in November, taking a 55 percent majority and thus avoiding a December runoff.

Johnson is a strong-minded veteran of Texas politics, a trailblazer for her sex and race in the 1970s who became adept enough at wielding power in Austin that she promoted herself to Congress in 1992 by drawing a district preordained to elect her. Upon joining the House, she became the first black woman in Texas' 30-member delegation since Barbara C. Jordan served the 18th District in the 93rd through 95th Congresses. But such singularity was old hat for Johnson: Her 1972 election to Texas' House made her the first black woman to win public office from Dallas; in 1987 she became the state Senate's first black since Reconstruction.

Johnson was angling for a seat on the Ways and Means Committee for the 105th, but although Democrats gave new seats there to a black male, a white Southern male, a Latino male and a white woman, Johnson did not make the cut.

The Transportation and Infrastructure Committee where she serves is a good place to be in the 105th, as Congress works on the massive reauthorization bill funding road, public transit and other transportation projects.

Her assignment on the Surface Transportation Subcommittee will help her lobby for funds to improve Interstate 35, which runs through Dallas, to help it handle increased traffic spawned in part by NAFTA-related trade. Johnson in 1995 praised the designation of I-35 as a superhighway for trade and commerce under the National Highway System; she said the highway is a busy corridor for trade among Mexico, Canada and the United States.

Johnson also sits on the Aviation Subcommittee, which gives her a vantage point on the expansion program under way at Dallas-Fort Worth International airport, a major economic engine in her district.

Spurring economic development and job growth is always a priority for Johnson, so as to provide more employment opportunities for minorities. This concern led her in 1995 to support the production of additional B-2 bombers, a stand that put her at odds with some fellow liberals in the Black Caucus, such as Ronald V. Dellums of California, ranking Democrat on the National Security Committee. Johnson argued that the B-2 is a cost effective way to save lives, and she noted that during production of the first set of B-2 bombers, Northrop Grumman employed about 6,000 people at a plant now in her district.

Johnson offered a jobs argument when the House in 1993 debated killing the Texas-based superconducting super collider. She defended the atom-smasher as a job-provider. "It is really very foolish for us to continue to vote on emergency extensions of unemployment benefits and then shift other spending away from a project [the SSC] that can bring jobs and keep jobs."

TEXAS 30
Downtown Dallas; part of Irving

The old 30th, a serpentine structure that extended into three counties, was designed by Johnson, who served as chairwoman of the Texas Senate Subcommittee on Congressional Districts. Johnson designed this one to suit her political strengths.

The 30th was tortuously constructed. Texas' rapid population growth earned it three new congressional seats in the 1990 reapportionment. As originally reconfigured, the 30th circled the inner city of Dallas, jutted out toward Arlington, climbed north along the Dallas-Fort Worth Airport, approached North Lake and backtracked toward Dallas before making a final sharp jog out to Plano, in Collin County.

But the 30th was one of three Texas districts declared unconstitutional by a three-judge federal panel, which in 1996 redrew the boundaries of 13 of the state's districts. The new 30th, which on a map looks roughly like a tilted "S," is confined to Dallas County. It stretches from the Dallas-Fort Worth Airport in the county's northwest and runs southeast through Irving and downtown Dallas before curving to the southwest to take in suburban territory in Lancaster and DeSoto.

The new map deprived Johnson of a black majority by removing largely black areas like the Hamilton Park neighborhood But the decrease in black population — from 50 percent to 45 percent — still left the district overwhelmingly Democratic. Bill Clinton drew 69 percent in 1996. Johnson dropped to 55 percent, though she still won by 28 points.

The district's northwest envelops much of the Dallas-Fort Worth Airport, one of the world's busiest. About 54 million passengers departed from or arrived at the airport in 1995.

The city of Irving abuts the airport to the southeast. Its population was barely 100,000 in 1980, but it swelled by more than 40 percent over the next 10 years. Numerous international firms have relocated there or expanded, due in no small part to its proximity to the perpetually humming airport.

On Irving's eastern edge lies Texas Stadium, where sports fans flock to watch football's Dallas Cowboys. Love Field, an area airport, lies on the other side of Interstate 35, on the district's edge, a few miles east of the stadium.

Two-thirds of the 30th's population lives in Dallas. The eighth-largest city in the nation and second to Houston in the state, Dallas is a major banking, insurance and medical center. Its museums, symphony and convention center help make it a popular draw for tourists and conventioneers. More than 100 companies relocated to Dallas in the 1980s and more than 500 foreign companies have offices here.

The State-Thomas neighborhood, adjacent to downtown, included some of the city's first homes owned by blacks. Most were razed by speculators in the 1960s, and the area today has predominantly white, affluent residents. Some black families that owned Victorian homes kept the properties when the city created a historic district.

Downtown's west end includes Dealey Plaza and the former Texas School Book Depository (now the Dallas County Administration Building), indelibly associated with President John F. Kennedy's assassination.

As of May 19, the Census Bureau had not recalculated population data, racial and ethnic breakdowns, and age statistics for districts newly drawn for the 1996 election.

In addition to problems with redistricting, Johnson faced distractions with her staff and campaign finances during the 104th. She was fined $44,000 by the Federal Election Commission for failing to file timely and accurate disclosure statements during her 1992 campaign. Her top aide quit, alleging that Johnson required the staff to perform personal errands and engage in campaign activities during office hours. Another staffer sued the House and settled for $28,000, alleging that she was terminated because of her pregnancy.

The Dallas Morning News reported that Johnson had 46 employees leave in her first 21 months in office. The newspaper calculated that as twice the rate of staff attrition among other Texas representatives elected with Johnson in 1992.

Free trade is one area where Johnson sees eye to eye with a majority of the Republican Party. She has been a consistent supporter of most-favored-nation (MFN) trade status for China.

"I believe that a policy of engagement in China gives us the best opportunity to influence the Chinese government," Johnson said during the 1996 debate on China MFN. "An improved standard of living in China will encourage free market principles in that nation and will assist the citizens of China in their effort to gain more freedom."

But on most issues, Johnson sees little to like in the GOP agenda. During the budget wars of the 104th, Johnson attacked the Republican budget plan as one without compassion, punishing the poor and the most vulnerable to help the rich with a tax cut.

"I have heard the voice of the American people and they want us to respond with a sound budget that is fair, responsible, and overturns the Republicans' assault on our nation's most vulnerable citizens," Johnson said.

At Home: Johnson in 1996 had to run in a district 42 percent new to her, and with a black population of 44 percent, down from 50 percent in her old district. Although no longer a black-majority district, the redrawn 30th remains about 60 percent minority, with a significant Hispanic population.

When Johnson was in the legislature and personally drew the 30th to suit her House aspirations, her maneuvering led Texas Monthly magazine to put her on its 10 worst legislators list and to compare her to "a two-year-old child on a white silk sofa with a new set of Magic Markers."

The district stood for the 1992 and 1994 elections, though, and it delivered her to the House with 70 percent plus general-election tallies. However, in August 1994 a panel of federal judges ruled that the 30th bore "the odious imprint of racial apartheid." In September 1996, two months before the election, the Supreme Court upheld the ruling by the panel of judges, which ordered new congressional lines for 13 House districts in Texas, including the 30th.

In imposing the new map, the judges threw out the results of the state's March primary and April runoff in the 13 affected districts and ordered the candidates involved to compete on an all-party ballot Nov. 5 with a December runoff, if no candidate won a majority.

In addition to Johnson, the ballot for the 30th carried seven others, including two Democrats, James L. Sweatt, a surgeon, and Marvin E. Crenshaw, a former Dallas City Council candidate, who together siphoned off about 16 percent of the Democratic vote. Her closest opponent was Republican mobile-home park owner John Hendry, who tallied 18 percent. But Johnson outdistanced everyone to win with 55 percent.

After winning her first state House election in 1972, Johnson served there until 1977, when she resigned to accept an appointment in President Jimmy Carter's administration as a regional director for what was then the Department of Health, Education and Welfare. It was a good fit, given that she had worked as a nurse before her legislative stint and also has a master's degree in public administration.

Next Johnson turned to private business, setting up Eddie Bernice Johnson and Associates, which helped businesses expand or relocate in the Dallas-Fort Worth area. She continued to operate the business after her 1986 election to the state Senate, and she expanded it in 1988 to include operations in airport concession management.

HOUSE ELECTIONS

1996 General		
Eddie Bernice Johnson (D)	61,723	(55%)
John Hendry (R)	20,664	(18%)
James L. Sweatt (D)	9,909	(9%)
Marvin E. Crenshaw (D)	7,765	(7%)
Lisa Anne Kitterman (R)	7,761	(7%)
Lisa Hembry (I)	3,501	(3%)
Ada Jane Granado (I)	1,278	(1%)
1994 General		
Eddie Bernice Johnson (D)	73,166	(73%)
Lucy Cain (R)	25,848	(26%)
Ken Ashby (LIBERT)	1,728	(2%)

Because of court-ordered redistricting in August, an all-candidate election was held in November. If no candidate received a majority of the vote then, the top two finishers met in a December runoff.

Previous Winning Percentages: 1992 (72%)

CAMPAIGN FINANCE

	Receipts	Receipts from PACs	Expend-itures
1996			
Johnson (D)	$365,893	$224,592 (61%)	$416,694
Sweatt (D)	$112,694	$7,000 (6%)	$112,343
Hendry (R)	$126,260	$9,065 (7%)	$101,948
Kitterman (R)	$18,467	0	$18,467
Hembry (I)	$31,316	$5,000 (16%)	$30,722
1994			
Johnson (D)	$286,486	$154,413 (54%)	$240,577
Cain (R)	$1,060	$264 (25%)	$1,060

VOTING STUDIES

	Presidential Support		Party Unity		Conservative Coalition	
Year	**S**	**O**	**S**	**O**	**S**	**O**
1996	84	13	89	9	53	43
1995	83	16	91	6	34	65
1994	85	14	94	4	28	69
1993	90	10	94	4	34	66

INTEREST GROUP RATINGS

Year	ADA	AFL-CIO	CCUS	ACU
1996	80	n/a	25	0
1995	95	100	17	8
1994	85	78	33	19
1993	90	92	27	0

DISTRICT VOTE FOR PRESIDENT

	1996		1992
D	95,715 (69%)	**D**	94,186 (59%)
R	34,820 (25%)	**R**	37,491 (23%)
I	6,527 (5%)	**I**	28,395 (18%)

UTAH

Governor: Michael O. Leavitt (R)
First elected: 1992
Length of term: 4 years
Term expires: 1/01
Salary: $85,200
Term limit: three consecutive terms*
Phone: (801) 538-1000
Born: Feb. 11, 1951; Cedar City, Utah.
Education: Southern Utah U., B.A. 1978.
Military Service: National Guard, 1969-75.
Occupation: Insurance executive.
Family: Wife, Jacalyn Smith; five children.
Religion: Mormon.
Political Career: Utah Board of Regents, 1989-92.

**The governor is limited to three consecutive four-year terms beginning with the governor elected in 1996; Leavitt is eligible to serve three additional terms.*

Lt. Gov.: Olene Walker (R)
First elected: 1992
Length of term: 4 years
Term expires: 1/01
Salary: $66,200
Phone: (801) 538-1040

State election official: (801) 538-1041
Democratic headquarters: (801) 328-1212
Republican headquarters: (801) 533-9777

REDISTRICTING

Utah retained its three House seats in reapportionment. The legislature passed the map Oct. 31, 1991; the governor signed it Nov. 8.

STATE LEGISLATURE

Legislature. Meets 45 days yearly, January-March.

Senate: 29 members, 4-year terms
1996 breakdown: 20R, 9D; 28 men, 1 woman
Salary: In session $100 a day, $35 a day expenses, $0.30 a mile, $55 a night lodging
Phone: (801) 538-1035

House of Representatives: 75 members, 2-year terms
1996 breakdown: 55R, 20D; 60 men, 15 women
Salary: Same as Senate
Phone: (801) 538-1029

URBAN STATISTICS

City	Population
Salt Lake City Mayor Deedee Corradini, N-P	159,936
West Valley City Mayor Gerald "Jerry" Wright, N-P	86,976
Provo Mayor George O. Stewart, N-P	86,835
Sandy City Mayor Thomas M. Dolan, R	75,058
Orem Mayor Stella Welsh, N-P	67,561

U.S. CONGRESS

Senate: 0 D, 2 R
House: 0 D, 3 R

TERM LIMITS

For state offices: Yes
Senate: three terms
House: six terms

ELECTIONS

1996 Presidential Vote

Bob Dole	54%
Bill Clinton	33%
Ross Perot	10%

1992 Presidential Vote

George Bush	43%
Ross Perot	27%
Bill Clinton	25%

1988 Presidential Vote

George Bush	66%
Michael S. Dukakis	32%

POPULATION

1990 population		1,722,850
1980 population		1,461,037
Percent change		+18%
Rank among states:		35
White		94%
Black		1%
Hispanic		5%
Asian or Pacific islander		2%
Urban		87%
Rural		13%
Born in state		67%
Foreign-born		3%
Under age 18	627,444	36%
Ages 18-64	945,448	55%
65 and older	149,958	9%
Median age		26.2

MISCELLANEOUS

Capital: Salt Lake City
Number of counties: 29
Per capita income: $14,529 (1991)
Rank among states: 48
Total area: 84,899 sq. miles
Rank among states: 11

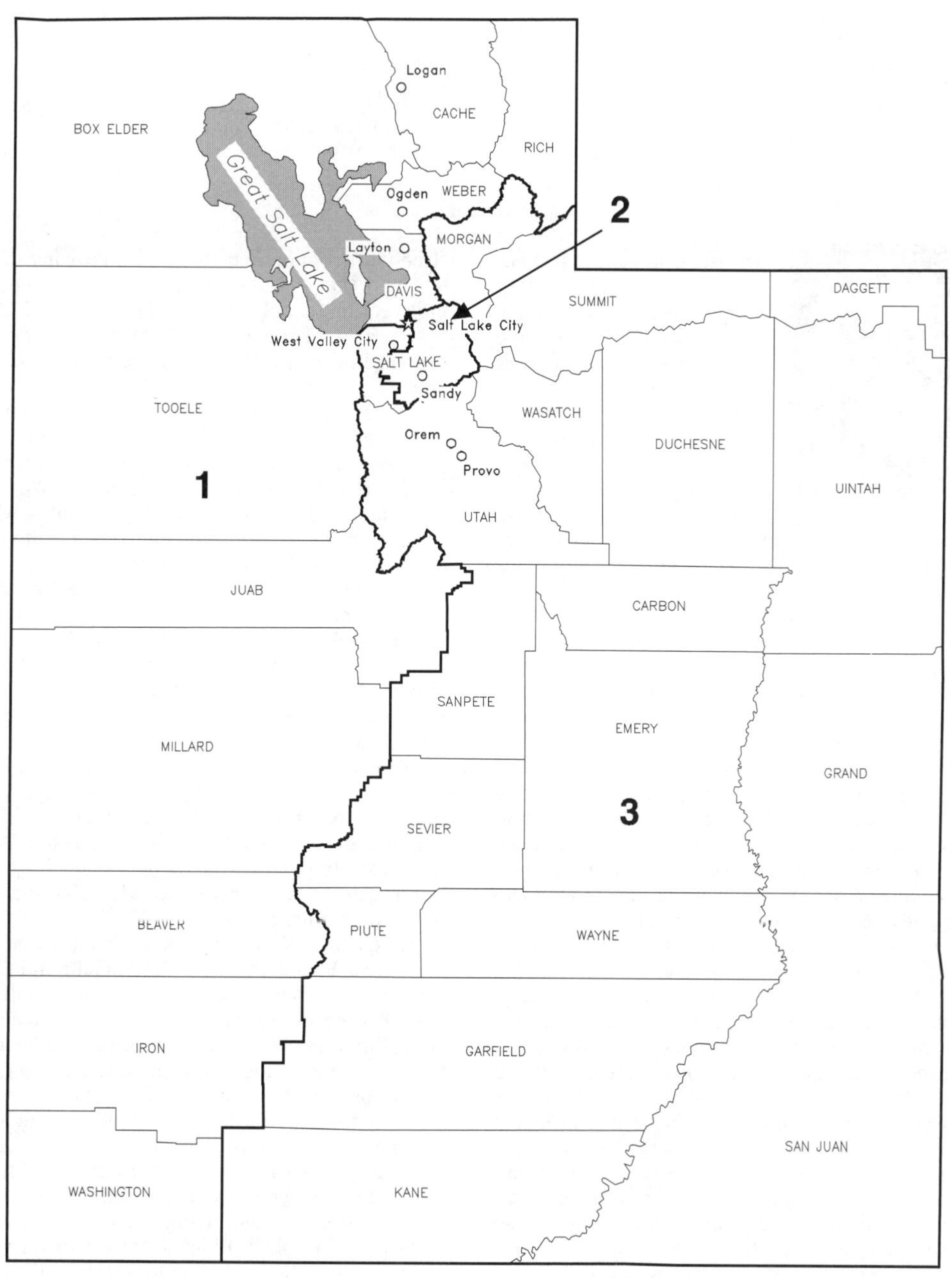
BOX ELDER
Logan
CACHE
RICH
Great Salt Lake
Ogden
WEBER
Layton
MORGAN
DAVIS
2
SUMMIT
DAGGETT
Salt Lake City
West Valley City
SALT LAKE
Sandy
TOOELE
WASATCH
DUCHESNE
UINTAH
Orem
Provo
1
UTAH
JUAB
CARBON
SANPETE
EMERY
MILLARD
GRAND
3
SEVIER
BEAVER
PIUTE
WAYNE
IRON
GARFIELD
SAN JUAN
WASHINGTON
KANE

Orrin G. Hatch (R)

Of Salt Lake City — Elected 1976, 4th term

Biographical Information
Born: March 22, 1934, Pittsburgh, Pa.
Education: Brigham Young U., B.S. 1959; U. of Pittsburgh, J.D. 1962.
Occupation: Lawyer.
Family: Wife, Elaine Hansen; six children.
Religion: Mormon.
Political Career: No previous office.
Capitol Office: 131 Russell Bldg. 20510; 224-5251.

Committees
Finance
Health Care; International Trade; Taxation & IRS Oversight
Indian Affairs
Select Intelligence
Judiciary (chairman)
Antitrust, Business Rights & Competition; Constitution, Federalism & Property Rights; Technology, Terrorism & Government Information

In Washington: As chairman of the Senate Judiciary Committee, Hatch faces the trying task of bringing some of the Republican Party's most controversial policy priorities to legislative fruition. Although he helped guide several anti-crime and legal measures into law during the 104th Congress, Hatch also suffered a number of outright defeats — while drawing fire from within his own party.

Hatch's impeccably conservative voting record during his two decades on Capitol Hill has helped him stand out as much as his sharply tailored suits and eye-catching ties. But over the years, he also has been one of a handful of conservative senators willing to negotiate with Democrats. That tendency rankles some GOP activists; they question whether he has been too quick to strike deals and too slow to go to the mat for their most cherished causes. Hatch dismisses the criticisms, but there is an element to his personality one does not typically associate with ideologues. "One of my biggest failings is that . . . I can't hold a grudge," he told the National Review in March 1997. "I can't stay mad."

Of the Democratic alliances Hatch has forged, none has made those within his party as uneasy as the one with Massachusetts Sen. Edward M. Kennedy, the man many conservatives love to hate. In April 1997, the legislative "odd couple" unveiled a children's health insurance proposal that would be financed by a 43-cent-a-pack cigarette tax increase. The senators said the measure would provide insurance to children whose low-income parents do not qualify for Medicaid while also discouraging youth smoking.

American Conservative Union chairman David Keene accused Hatch of "helping liberals derail the conservative agenda" and said the proposal "offers more evidence that, unfortunately, [Hatch's] reputation as a bona fide conservative is slowly eroding." But Hatch contended such claims were off base, saying the legislation used a "free market approach" to solve a growing problem and that it reflected his belief that federal intervention "should be limited and focused."

Hatch and Kennedy tried in May to include the proposal in the package designed to reach a balanced budget by 2002. They boiled their argument down to a choice between tobacco companies and a kid named Joey, whose photo adorned the posters and ads they used to buttress their pitch.

For Hatch, the choice was simple: "Who do you stand with, Joe Camel or Joey? That is what it comes down to." The amendment was killed on a 55-45 vote on May 21.

For Hatch and Kennedy, searching for common ground is old hat. The pair worked closely together when Hatch served on the Labor and Human Resources Committee in the 1980s. Hatch remained on Labor through 1992 (he shifted to the top GOP slot on Judiciary when Sen. Strom Thurmond of South Carolina asserted his seniority on Armed Services). In the 102nd alone, Kennedy and Hatch were instrumental in passing a summer jobs program, enacting penalties for drug manufacturers that defraud the Food and Drug Administration, and winning approval of legislation requiring drug makers to offer discounts to public health programs.

Hatch also has faced pressure from within his party over President Clinton's judicial nominees. After Republicans took control of the Senate in the 1994 elections, Hatch repeatedly pledged to grant Clinton's choices a fair hearing. But he also took the Senate floor to single out already-confirmed presidential picks on the bench who he claimed were part of "a rising tide of judicial activism" and lambasted the American Bar Association for the "quasi-constitutional role" he contended it played in screening nominees.

By the end of the 104th, Judiciary's ranking Democrat, Joseph R. Biden Jr. of Delaware, was blasting the GOP for holding up nominations in an election year in sharp contrast to previous elections when Democrats controlled the Senate. Hatch responded that the 104th confirmed a higher percentage of Clinton's nominees than the 102nd did for Republican President George Bush in 1992, and that the vacancy rate for the judiciary dropped during Clinton's term.

With Clinton's re-election in November 1996, the judicial selection issue has grown more partisan. Conservative groups have mobilized to implore Hatch and other Republicans to vet nominees more thoroughly. At the same time, Biden's successor as Judiciary's ranking Democrat, Vermont's Patrick J. Leahy, spent the early months of the 105th attacking the Republicans' failure to move any nominations — a potentially ominous indicator of Leahy's and Hatch's ability to work together on other issues. The situation prompted Hatch to observe in January 1997 that he was "getting it from both sides."

Before becoming Judiciary chairman, Hatch usually had struck a more aggressively partisan posture on legal matters, as he demonstrated during the 1991 confirmation hearings of Supreme Court nominee Clarence Thomas. A strong Thomas supporter, Hatch argued against the need for additional Judiciary hearings when it became public that professor Anita F. Hill had accused Thomas of sexually harassing her when she worked with him at the Equal Employment Opportunity Commission. Once Hill's allegations were aired and Thomas had to defend himself against them, Hatch and Arlen Specter of Pennsylvania led the Republican assault on the charges as TV cameras relayed the spectacle to millions of Americans.

More recently, Hatch's most highly publicized battles have come on the marquee items in the House Republicans' "Contract With America" legislative manifesto. The most prominent of those was a constitutional balanced-budget amendment, which failed by one vote in the Senate in the both the 104th and 105th. Hatch strongly supported the amendment, saying it would bring "fiscal sanity" to government, and he and Larry E. Craig of Idaho worked hard to woo supporters. In 1995, Hatch even enlisted a television minister, the Rev. Robert Schuller, to speak to the amendment's lone GOP objector, Oregon's Mark O. Hatfield.

Even as he struggled in the 104th with the momentous amendment vote, Hatch had his committee digging into a successor to the 1994 crime bill, which Hatch had said "wasted billions of dollars on 1960s-style, Great Society social spending boondoggles." Hatch introduced a bill in January 1995 that would ease criminal prosecutions and limit appeals, lengthen sentences for gun crimes and divert crime prevention funds to prison construction.

But after the bombing of a federal office building in Oklahoma City a few months later, Congress ended up opting in April 1996 to pass a comprehensive anti-terrorism bill that provided $1 billion in counterterrorism funding and placed limits on the filing of habeas corpus petitions by inmates convicted of murder. Democrats were bitter about the linkage of the habeas corpus provisions with the terrorism legislation, but Hatch called those provisions the "heart and soul" of the bill.

Hatch also played a key role in the enactment of a comprehensive illegal immigration law. He and other senators successfully fought a controversial provision in the House-passed version of the measure offered by Rep. Elton Gallegly, R-Calif., that would have denied public education to children in the country illegally.

Other Republican initiatives in the 104th in which Hatch was involved — compensation of private property owners whose land is taken by a federal agency action, overhauling regulatory provisions and an amendment to ban desecration of the flag — failed to pass. And a home-state priority, a bill designating millions of acres of Utah as wilderness, also was jettisoned after environmentalists complained it would have opened other acreage to development.

One pet Hatch measure that did make it into law in the 104th established a "limited performance right" for sound recordings publicly performed within digital environments. Hatch is a songwriter who has penned everything from bossa nova to rock and rap tunes — sometimes, he admits, during committee hearings. One of his compositions, "Freedom's Light," was performed by a children's chorus at the Capitol for a Public Broadcasting Service telecast in March 1997.

Before 1980, Hatch wore just one hat in the Senate: that of conservative ideologue. That perception began to change as Hatch took over the Labor Committee in 1981. Even under GOP rule, the committee had a moderate-to-liberal majority. The course pursued by Hatch was a relatively successful one — at least in terms of the volume of legislation, particularly in the area of health policy, that became law.

The promise and pitfalls inherent in Hatch's split conservative-pragmatist personality have been evident in his approach to civil rights legislation. He played a shifting role in the effort to enact a new civil rights bill during the Bush administration. He started 1990 as a critic of the legislation, well before it was clear where the White House would stand. In 1991, the bill's authors agreed to modify the affirmative action sections and put caps on punitive damages. In the wake of the Thomas-Hill hearings, the bill passed with Hatch's support, and President George Bush signed it.

When Hatch feels strongly about an issue, he will go to great lengths to fight for his position. In an October 1992 debate over charging drug manufacturers "user fees," Hatch used the bill to defend an unrelated cause, but one of personal interest to him — vitamins. He threatened to block the user fee bill, which he supported, until the FDA agreed to back off plans to limit health claims made by vitamin producers.

Hatch is an ardent opponent of abortion; he led the Senate fight against requiring businesses to provide unpaid family and medical leave; and he said that imposing a waiting period on handgun purchases (the Brady bill) opened the door to the "persecution of decent law-abiding sportspeople."

At Home: While Hatch has grown wise in the ways of Washington, he was a political neophyte when he launched his first Senate campaign in 1976. It was a textbook example of anti-Washington politics.

Hatch's lack of government experience at any level almost certainly helped him. In his private legal practice, he had represented clients fighting federal regulations.

Hatch was recruited for a Senate race against incumbent Democrat Frank E. Moss by conservative leader Ernest Wilkinson, who had challenged Moss in 1964. Hatch's competitor for the GOP nomination was Jack W. Carlson, who had a long résumé in the federal government punctuated by service as assistant secretary of the Interior. Carlson, the front-runner, underscored his Washington experience.

That was the wrong record for Utah in 1976. Hatch, sensing the state was fed up with federal rules, took the opposite approach. The party convention gave him nearly half the vote, and the day before the primary balloting, Hatch reinforced his conservative credentials by running newspaper ads trumpeting an endorsement from Ronald Reagan. He won by almost 2-to-1.

The primary gave Hatch publicity that helped him catch up to Moss. Seen as a liberal by Utah standards, Moss won points at home by investigating Medicaid abuses and fighting to ban cigarette ads from TV.

Moss stressed his seniority and the benefits it brought Utah. But Hatch argued that the real issue was limiting government and taxes, and that he would be more likely to do that than Moss. He won with 54 percent of the vote.

Bidding for a second term in 1982, Hatch came under strong challenge for being rigid both in his conservative views and his personal style. Ted Wilson, his affable opponent, was a well-known figure throughout the state, having served two terms as mayor of Salt Lake City.

Wilson was not the only one with designs on the incumbent. After Hatch blocked a labor law revision in 1978, then-AFL-CIO President George Meany had vowed, "We'll defeat you no matter what it takes." But unions are not the most useful allies in conservative Utah, and being a labor target did Hatch more good than harm. Buoyed by two Reagan visits to the state during the campaign, Hatch won a solid 58 percent of the vote.

In 1988, Democrats had trouble finding an opponent for Hatch. When former Gov. Scott M. Matheson announced in 1987 that he would not run, Brian Moss won the Democratic nomination almost by default.

Moss, son of the former senator Hatch had ousted, boasted of his family's roots in Utah and took up the complaint that the Pittsburgh-born Hatch was pursuing a national conservative agenda rather than focusing on ways to retool Utah's struggling economy. But Moss had little going for him besides his famous name; he was outspent by more than 25-to-1.

As it turned out, the only campaign problem Hatch encountered was self-inflicted. Speaking in Republican southern Utah in early September, he launched into an assault on the Democratic Party, labeling it "the party of homosexuals . . . the party of abortion . . . the party that has basically, I think, denigrated a lot of the values that have made this country the greatest country in the world." Hatch's remarks drew national attention.

The underfunded Moss was unable to keep up, and Hatch coasted to victory with 67 percent of the vote. In 1994, his winning tally increased to 69 percent against former Utah Democratic Party official Patrick A. Shea.

SENATE ELECTIONS

1994 General		
Orrin G. Hatch (R)	357,297	(69%)
Patrick A. Shea (D)	146,938	(28%)
Craig Oliver (I)	9,550	(2%)

Previous Winning Percentages: 1988 (67%) **1982** (58%) **1976** (54%)

CAMPAIGN FINANCE

1994	Receipts	Receipts from PACs		Expend-itures
Hatch (R)	$3,419,649	$1,293,621	(38%)	$3,456,031
Shea (D)	$314,604	$122,650	(39%)	$311,491

KEY VOTES

1997	
Approve balanced-budget constitutional amendment	Y
Approve chemical weapons treaty	Y
1996	
Approve farm bill	Y
Limit punitive damages in product liability cases	Y
Exempt small businesses from higher minimum wage	Y
Approve welfare overhaul	Y
Bar job discrimination based on sexual orientation	N
Override veto of ban on "partial birth" abortions	Y
1995	
Approve GOP budget with tax and spending cuts	Y
Approve constitutional amendment barring flag desecration	Y

VOTING STUDIES

	Presidential Support		Party Unity		Conservative Coalition	
Year	S	O	S	O	S	O
1996	32	68	94	6	97	3
1995	26	72	94	5	89	7
1994	37	63	94	5	94	6
1993	27	71	94	4	95	5
1992	82	12	88	4	95	5
1991	86	7	90	7	88	10

INTEREST GROUP RATINGS

Year	ADA	AFL-CIO	CCUS	ACU
1996	5	n/a	92	100
1995	0	0	100	83
1994	5	0	90	100
1993	5	0	100	88
1992	5	17	100	96
1991	10	25	90	86

Robert F. Bennett (R)

Of Salt Lake City — Elected 1992, 1st term

Biographical Information
Born: Sept. 18, 1933, Salt Lake City, Utah.
Education: U. of Utah, B.S. 1957.
Military Service: National Guard, 1957-61.
Occupation: Management consultant.
Family: Wife, Joyce McKay; six children.
Religion: Mormon.
Political Career: No previous office.
Capitol Office: 431 Dirksen Bldg. 20510; 224-5444.

Committees
Appropriations
Energy & Water Development; Foreign Operations; Interior; Legislative Branch (chairman); Transportation
Banking, Housing & Urban Affairs
Financial Services & Technology (chairman); International Finance; Securities
Governmental Affairs
Investigations; Oversignt of Government Management and the District of Columbia.
Small Business
Joint Economic

In Washington: Bennett lost a chance for an open door at the White House when his close associate, former Senate Majority Leader Bob Dole, was defeated in the 1996 presidential election.

Bennett was a strong Dole ally in the Senate. When Dole's bid for the Republican presidential nomination was stumbling in early 1996, Bennett was one of the trusted advisers traveling the campaign trail with him.

During Dole's tenure as leader, Bennett got a seat on Appropriations, and in the 105th Congress he became chairman of the Legislative Branch Subcommittee. He got another gavel in 1997, chairing the Banking, Housing and Urban Affairs Subcommittee on Financial Services and Technology. Also for the 105th, Dole's successor as majority leader, Trent Lott, made Bennett head of a task force on congressional reorganization.

That has been a particular interest of Bennett's since he joined the Senate. In 1993, he proposed legislation, which was never acted upon, to reorganize congressional committees, adopt a two-year budget cycle and establish congressional task forces to set priorities for legislative action.

Bennett got the door slammed in his face in the Republican leadership shuffle that followed Dole's June 1996 exit from the chamber. He drew just eight of 53 votes in a bid to chair the Republican Policy Committee, finishing third to Idaho's Larry E. Craig and Indiana's Daniel R. Coats in a contest Craig eventually won.

Although Bennett gave up a seat on the Energy and Natural Resources Committee when he joined Appropriations, he stays involved in Western lands issues on Appropriations' Interior Subcommittee. Bennett is among the conservative Republicans who accuse federal land management agencies and environmentalists of waging a "war on the West." He expressed outrage in September 1996 when President Clinton declared 1.7 million acres of scenic but mineral-rich southern Utah as a national monument, thus limiting potential development of the land. In early 1997, he offered a bill that would hold Clinton to his statement when announcing the monument that the lands would remain open to existing multiple uses, such as mining, ranching and recreation.

Bennett also suggested he might try to undo the monument proclamation legislatively. Prior to Clinton's move, Bennett was a lead supporter of a bill, which failed, that would have declared a much smaller portion of southern Utah as protected wilderness while releasing the other lands for development.

Although Bennett's successful 1992 Senate bid at age 59 was his first campaign, he was no political naif. He had done previous Washington duty as a White House adviser to President Richard M. Nixon. And his father, Republican Wallace F. Bennett, was a Utah senator from 1951 to 1974.

Early in the 104th, Dole tapped Bennett as his point man on congressional and White House negotiations over whether to offer legislation to rescue Mexico from an economic crisis. Unable to reach a consensus, Congress opted to stay out of the peso crisis, while the Clinton administration moved ahead on its own.

In the 103rd, Bennett brokered a compromise that resulted in the authorization of $65 million in grants over four years for the restoration of significant buildings at the nation's historically black colleges and universities. Bennett is usually a dependable vote for the Republican leadership, but he strays from the party line on a few significant issues.

While many conservatives attack the National Endowment for the Arts as a waste of taxpayers' money, Bennett defends the agency. Like some other members with substantial small city and rural constituencies, Bennett sees the NEA as a key funding source of mainstream music and arts for people who normally lack access to them.

Bennett says the NEA's opponents have a distorted view caused by past controversies that he says the agency's current leadership has worked to avoid. "It's become a holy crusade for them," Bennett said in 1997 of NEA's opponents. "But they don't look at the present circumstances."

Bennett also stood out from other Senate GOP conservatives by opposing a constitutional amendment aimed at overturning a Supreme Court ruling that barred states and localities from banning destruction of the American flag.

"If we start the precedent of amending the Constitution every time there is a Supreme Court decision with which we disagree, we run the risk of seeing the Constitution turned into something other than basic law," Bennett said.

Bennett is thoughtful and hard-working on the Banking Committee. During the 104th, he participated in the committee's hearings on the Whitewater case involving Clinton's financial dealings while governor of Arkansas, but was not among the Republicans inclined to cross-examine witnesses with great zeal.

Early in the 103rd Congress, Bennett earned the spotlight and the respect of some of his colleagues when he challenged independent political figure Ross Perot's views on trade policy when the Texas billionaire testified before the Banking Committee.

During the hearing, Perot reiterated his assertion that ratifying NAFTA would cause a massive job loss in the United States because companies would be encouraged to move to Mexico to take advantage of its lower wages. But Bennett said business owners place a higher premium on factors such as worker productivity and access to markets than on labor costs. "The horse has left the barn, and you are securing and hammering on the door," Bennett told Perot. "In my opinion, the factories are in Mexico now . . . NAFTA is about markets, not factories. NAFTA is about opening markets in Mexico for American goods."

At Home: Bennett's well-known name and a conservative voting record that meshes with Utah's strong GOP tendencies position him well to seek re-election in 1998. He is leaving little to chance, raising a substantial treasury. From the beginning of 1993 through the end of 1996, Bennett had spent the fifth-highest amount of campaign funds among senators elected in 1992.

This follows a pattern Bennett set in that first Senate campaign, when he raised $4.5 million and outspent his Democratic opponent, Rep. Wayne Owens, by a ratio of more than 2-1. In fact, Bennett overdid his 1992 fundraising. In 1996, he agreed to pay a $55,000 fine to the Federal Election Commission for what he called "unintentional violations" during the 1992 campaign. The violations included accepting $13,450 in donations beyond legal limits; his failure to disclose promptly $600,000 worth of last-minute contributions Bennett made himself before elections; and failure to repay an aide for $22,206 in campaign purchases in a timely manner.

The 1992 GOP Senate primary was a showdown of party millionaires: Bennett, who made his fortune with the Franklin Day Planner, a personal-schedule organizer, and Joe Cannon, a steel company executive. Bennett narrowly won the nomination, then went on to defeat Democrat Owens by 15 points to replace the retiring Garn.

During the general-election campaign, Owens and the media devoted attention to Bennett's connection to the 1972 Watergate break-in. He had bought a public relations firm that employed E. Howard Hunt, who was indicted in the Watergate burglary. Bennett said he fired Hunt after the scandal. At one point, Bennett had to contend with rumors that he was "Deep Throat," the informant who guided reporters to the heart of the Watergate issue. Bennett denied he was the source, as did journalists who covered the story.

SENATE ELECTIONS

1992 General		
Robert F. Bennett (R)	420,069	(55%)
Wayne Owens (D)	301,228	(40%)
Anita R. Morrow (POP)	17,549	(2%)
Maury Modine (LIBERT)	14,341	(2%)
1992 Primary		
Robert F. Bennett (R)	135,514	(51%)
Joe Cannon (R)	128,125	(49%)

CAMPAIGN FINANCE

	Receipts	Receipts from PACs		Expend-itures
1992				
Bennett (R)	$4,532,966	$343,210	(8%)	$4,439,376
Owens (D)	$1,934,683	$601,937	(31%)	$1,904,750
Modine (LIBERT)	$10,032	0		$5,285

VOTING STUDIES

	Presidential Support		Party Unity		Conservative Coalition	
Year	S	O	S	O	S	O
1996	34	61	88	7	95	3
1995	26	73	94	4	89	7
1994	35	58	88	9	91	6
1993	31	66	91	6	90	7

KEY VOTES

1997	
Approve balanced-budget constitutional amendment	Y
Approve chemical weapons treaty	N
1996	
Approve farm bill	Y
Limit punitive damages in product liability cases	Y
Exempt small businesses from higher minimum wage	Y
Approve welfare overhaul	Y
Bar job discrimination based on sexual orientation	N
Override veto of ban on "partial birth" abortions	Y
1995	
Approve GOP budget with tax and spending cuts	Y
Approve constitutional amendment barring flag desecration	N

INTEREST GROUP RATINGS

Year	ADA	AFL-CIO	CCUS	ACU
1996	5	n/a	92	95
1995	0	0	100	81
1994	5	0	90	100
1993	5	0	100	88

1 James V. Hansen (R)

Of Farmington — Elected 1980, 9th term

Biographical Information
Born: Aug. 14, 1932, Salt Lake City, Utah.
Education: U. of Utah, B.S. 1960.
Military Service: Navy, 1952-54.
Occupation: Insurance executive; developer.
Family: Wife, Ann Burgoyne; five children.
Religion: Mormon.
Political Career: Farmington City Council, 1968-72; Utah House, 1973-81, speaker, 1979-81.
Capitol Office: 2466 Rayburn Bldg. 20515; 225-0453.

Committees
National Security
Military Procurement; Military Readiness
Resources
Forests & Forest Health; National Parks & Public Lands (chairman)
Standards of Official Conduct (chairman)

In Washington: At the start of the 105th Congress, Hansen agreed to take one of the least-desired jobs on the Hill — chairman of the House Committee on Standards of Official Conduct, better known as the ethics committee. Hansen had served there 12 years, part of that time as ranking member, before getting off in 1993.

When asked by Majority Leader Dick Armey of Texas if he would accept the job, Hansen said he reflected on his earlier ethics committee tenure, recalling the long hours of work on investigations and the anguish of seeing colleagues' reputations dangle. But he said he also thought about honor, duty and the need to restore integrity to the committee. "I'll do it," Hansen told Armey. "But I want you to know, I'm going to play this straight by the book."

The ethics committee got deeply embroiled in partisanship and public finger-pointing during its investigation in the 104th of Speaker Newt Gingrich's political fundraising, and the recruitment of Hansen to run the committee reflects a desire to restore the bipartisan and discreet manner in which the panel used to operate. The former chairman, Connecticut Republican Nancy L. Johnson, did not bear up well under the intense competing pressures of thoroughly investigating Gingrich and meeting demands in her party to protect the Speaker from what many Republicans saw as a Democratic vendetta against him.

Membership on the ethics committee is evenly split between the parties; the top Democrat for the 105th is Howard L. Berman of California.

In the 104th, Hansen's main focus was the Resources Committee, where for years he has fought what he regards as federal overregulation of Western lands. The Republican takeover of the House in 1994 gave Hansen a gavel, on Resources' National Parks, Forests and Lands Subcommittee.

In the 105th, he chairs the National Parks and Public Lands Subcommittee; jurisdiction over forests went to a newly constituted Forests and Forest Health Subcommittee, chaired by second-term Republican Helen Chenoweth of Idaho. Hansen's subcommittee had a crowded agenda in the 104th. It is also worth noting that the architect of the jurisdictional shuffle, Resources Committee Chairman Don Young of Alaska, has had some differences with Hansen over the years.

Young ran into trouble toward the end of the 104th trying to push through an omnibus parks and lands bill that included a Utah lands measure important to Hansen. The bill was tied up in conference after the Senate jettisoned a House provision on Utah wilderness that had been sponsored by Hansen. His provision would have set aside millions of acres for preservation, but it also would have opened other acreage to development, a tradeoff that environmentalists opposed.

To get the stalled process moving, GOP leaders dumped the conference report and created a new omnibus parks and lands bill without some previously controversial provisions, including several favorable to Alaska. The House easily passed that bill in September 1996. Young and Senate Energy and Natural Resources Committee Chairman Frank H. Murkowski of Alaska were eventually able to clear the bill, but Hansen thought the whole matter was handled badly. "What a crappy way to legislate," he said. "It's probably the worst way I've seen legislating done in 36 years."

The omnibus bill contained something for members of both parties, including increased National Park fees, historic designations and protection for the Presidio, a former military base in San Francisco.

Its passage was facilitated by the decision of Western Republican House members not to push to include legislation to overturn Clinton administration grazing rules. That effort had drawn a veto threat, and Hansen said the Westerners backed off after it became obvious the White House would not likely accept any new grazing bill. Hansen said it made no sense for ranchers to "burn up their chits" by pushing grazing-fee language sure to provoke a veto.

Hansen did get one Utah provision into the omnibus lands bill. It authorized a swap of 1,320

UTAH 1
West — Salt Lake City suburbs; Ogden; Logan; rural Utah

The 1st takes in the entire western side of Utah, but most of that land is sparsely settled. More than 70 percent of the voters live in the district's northeastern corner, where population boomed during the 1980s in Cache County (Logan), Weber County (Ogden) and Davis County (just above Salt Lake City).

Republicans dominate the 1st, and Democrats are a distinct minority. Bob Dole easily beat Bill Clinton here in 1996 by 59 percent to 29 percent.

The federal government puts groceries on many tables in the 1st. Important employers in the Ogden area are the Internal Revenue Service, Hill Air Force Base and Defense Depot Ogden. To the south in Tooele County are the Dugway Proving Ground and Tooele Army Depot.

In addition, federal contracts are important to some of the district's larger private employers such as Alliant Tech Systems Inc., Hercules Inc. and Thiokol (known for building solid rocket motors). With defense cutbacks looming, some of these contractors are moving to diversify into other lines of work such as satellite manufacturing and communications. One company makes a product that appeared to have a bright future in the 1990s: Morton Automotive, in Box Elder County. It has been dubbed the "airbag capital" thanks to brisk sales of its automotive safety device. But airbags faced increasing criticism when they were found to cause some deaths of children and small adults, who were seated in the front passenger seat when the airbags inflated.

Davis County is the district's most populous. Salt Lake City bedroom communities such as Bountiful and others in the southern part of Davis County are solidly Republican.

Moving north into Weber County, the Democratic and independent vote picks up, partly a legacy of the area's past as a center of rail-related blue-collar employment. The nation's first transcontinental rail link (in 1869) was at Promontory, just north of Ogden.

There is dairy farming country farther north, in Cache County. Cache's Republican tilt is moderated somewhat by a dose of Democratic voters around Utah State University in Logan (20,800 students).

The 1st's other growth hot spot during the 1980s was Washington County, in Utah's southwestern corner. The county's population went up 86 percent in the last decade (to nearly 50,000), as retirees and wintering wealthy were drawn to the temperate climate and verdant golf courses of Washington and neighboring Iron County. In electoral terms, this influx reinforced the area's conservative bent.

Cedar City, in mineral-rich Iron County, suffered from a collapse in the mining industry in the early 1980s, but its economic base has improved. It has become home to a number of high-tech companies that left expensive locations in California.

1990 Population: 574,286. White 541,913 (94%), Black 5,419 (1%), Other 26,954 (5%). Hispanic origin 26,771 (5%). 18 and over 360,394 (63%), 62 and over 64,962 (11%). Median age: 26.

acres of federally owned land for property owned by the Sun Valley Co. Hansen said the land swap was needed as part of Utah's preparation to host the Winter Olympics in 2002. Environmentalists and the White House disputed that claim, saying the land swap was mainly aimed at benefiting a local ski-resort developer.

Like many others in Utah, Hansen was infuriated with President Clinton's September 1996 decision to declare 1.7 million acres of southern Utah canyon lands a national monument. Clinton invoked the 90-year-old federal Antiquities Act, which President Theodore Roosevelt used to protect the Grand Canyon from development. Clinton's announcement was condemned by Utah's congressional delegation, which claimed that state officials had not even been notified of the executive decision. "He's just trying to appease Eastern environmentalists," Hansen told USA Today. "And he's hurting the area, the economy, taking away private property rights and hurting schoolchildren."

Hansen has long favored a comprehensive review of the national park system, joining with other conservatives who argue that lawmakers have focused more on adding coveted sites in their districts to the park system than on properly maintaining what is already within the system.

Although the House in September 1995 rejected, 180-231, a bipartisan measure requiring a comprehensive review of National Park Service sites, Hansen attached it to the GOP's deficit-reduction bill later the same day. The proposal Hansen attached to the reconciliation bill required the Interior secretary to submit to Congress a long-range plan for managing the National Park System, and it established a park review commission to recommend the closure of some parks not conforming to the secretary's plan. The park closing commission plan was later eliminated from the deficit-reducing measure.

Utah's 1st is home to a number of military installations, including Hill Air Force Base and Defense Depot Ogden. On the National Security Committee, Hansen joins in GOP arguments that Clinton is stingy with the military.

But his particular beef with the administration

has been over a Pentagon plan to rely more on private companies for routine maintenance of vehicles and equipment, in hopes of shaving billions of dollars from the military's annual budget.

The Pentagon believes maintenance contracts competitively awarded to private companies will cost less than those assigned to government depots. Hansen and colleagues in the bipartisan House Depot Caucus blasted the policy for restricting public depots to a "core" of critical maintenance work, barring them from bidding for other overhaul work. "The premise of the department's policy is that privatization is good because of competition," said Hansen. "If the administration truly supports competition, why does their policy advocate repeal of the law that requires it?"

And public depot proponents warn that private companies might not be responsive to military exigencies or could be disrupted by labor disputes or bankruptcies. They succeeded in keeping the privatization plan at bay in the 104th.

At Home: Hansen has seen a few bumpy elections over the years, but he now appears to be firmly in command. His last three campaigns have yielded 65 percent or better.

Hansen's early political fortunes were closely linked to those of two others: Ronald Reagan and Democratic Rep. Gunn McKay. When Reagan marched to his first national victory in 1980, the Utah 1st was one of his best districts anywhere. That helped Hansen oust McKay to win his seat for the first time.

Accustomed to being vulnerable but still able to win, McKay was slow to prepare in 1980. It was a costly mistake. Hansen was Speaker of the Utah House and had already logged nearly two decades in state and local politics. In the Utah Legislature, he had developed a reputation as a pragmatic conservative adept at conciliation.

But Hansen probably would not have won without Reagan's coattails. Drawing out GOP voters, Reagan pulled in more than three-quarters of the presidential vote in the 1st, helping Hansen offset McKay's strength in the Ogden area and enabling the GOP challenger to register a 52 percent to 48 percent victory.

After a couple of easy wins for Hansen, McKay was ready for a rematch in 1986. He criticized Hansen as a rubber stamp for the national GOP and an inadequate spokesman for the district's troubled mining, manufacturing and agricultural interests. But Hansen won again with 52 percent.

The result encouraged McKay to try once more in 1988. Certain he had lost in 1986 because of a late start, McKay began early to organize and raise money. Hansen also staged a more aggressive effort and finally beat his old rival easily, taking 60 percent of the vote.

In 1990, Hansen expected to have an easy time against Democrat Kenley Brunsdale, chief aide to then-2nd District Democratic Rep. Wayne Owens. But Brunsdale ran an aggressive, persistent campaign, demonstrating his knowledge of congressional issues and tweaking Hansen with a "time for a change" theme. Hansen did not debate Brunsdale until five days before the election, and he ended up winning a sixth term with 52 percent of the vote. That was his last tough race.

HOUSE ELECTIONS

1996 General		
James V. Hansen (R)	150,126	(68%)
Gregory J. Sanders (D)	65,866	(30%)
Randall Tolpinrud (NL)	3,787	(2%)
1994 General		
James V. Hansen (R)	104,954	(65%)
Bobbie Coray (D)	57,644	(35%)

Previous Winning Percentages: **1992** (65%) **1990** (52%) **1988** (60%) **1986** (52%) **1984** (71%) **1982** (63%) **1980** (52%)

CAMPAIGN FINANCE

	Receipts	Receipts from PACs	Expend-itures
1996			
Hansen (R)	$300,376	$154,091 (51%)	$274,156
Sanders (D)	$73,082	$5,000 (7%)	$72,989
1994			
Hansen (R)	$393,735	$188,174 (48%)	$348,036
Coray (D)	$277,037	$96,850 (35%)	$276,892

DISTRICT VOTE FOR PRESIDENT

	1996		1992
D	64,104 (29%)	**D**	50,622 (22%)
R	129,273 (59%)	**R**	115,627 (49%)
I	22,893 (10%)	**I**	68,884 (29%)

KEY VOTES

1997	
Ban "partial-birth" abortions	Y
1996	
Approve farm bill	Y
Deny public education to illegal immigrants	Y
Repeal ban on certain assault-style weapons	Y
Increase minimum wage	N
Freeze defense spending	N
Approve welfare overhaul	Y
1995	
Approve balanced-budget constitutional amendment	Y
Relax Clean Water Act regulations	Y
Oppose limits on environmental regulations	N
Reduce projected Medicare spending	Y
Approve GOP budget with tax and spending cuts	Y

VOTING STUDIES

	Presidential Support		Party Unity		Conservative Coalition	
Year	S	O	S	O	S	O
1996	38	56	91	5	92	2
1995	20	77	94	3	91	1
1994	36	60	93	5	100	0
1993	32	67	92	6	100	0
1992	89	8	81	9	85	8
1991	82	15	89	7	95	3

INTEREST GROUP RATINGS

Year	ADA	AFL-CIO	CCUS	ACU
1996	0	n/a	100	100
1995	0	0	100	92
1994	0	0	92	95
1993	0	8	100	96
1992	5	18	88	100
1991	0	0	100	100

2 Merrill Cook (R)

Of Salt Lake City — Elected 1996, 1st term

Biographical Information

Born: May 6, 1946, Philadelphia, Pa.

Education: U. of Utah, B.A. 1969; Harvard U., M.B.A. 1971.

Occupation: Explosives company executive; radio talk show host; management consultant.

Family: Wife, Camille Sanders; five children.

Religion: Mormon.

Political Career: Candidate for Utah Board of Education, 1984; candidate for mayor of Salt Lake City, 1985; Republican nominee for Salt Lake County Commission, 1986; Independent candidate for governor, 1988, 1992; Independent candidate for U.S. House, 1994.

Capitol Office: 1431 Longworth Bldg. 20515; 225-3011.

Committees

Banking & Financial Services
Capital Markets, Securities & Government Sponsored Enterprises; Housing & Community Opportunity

Science
Space & Aeronautics; Technology

Transportation & Infrastructure
Aviation; Surface Transportation

The Path to Washington: On his seventh try and with a hefty financial investment from his own pocket, Utah's best-known perennial candidate in 1996 finally secured a win for elective office.

Cook's political metamorphosis included a handful of runs as an independent — most recently in 1994, when he took 18 percent in the race for the 2nd District seat. Yet in his return to the GOP fold in 1996, Cook, a millionaire explosives company executive, noted that he never strayed from his belief in the basic tenets of the Republican Party.

In fact, Cook's views place him firmly in league with some of the GOP's more conservative members. He advocates a 17 percent flat tax that maintains deductions for home mortgage interest and charitable contributions. He says he will push for significant reductions in capital gains taxes and changes in inheritance tax laws to allow small businesses to be passed on to family members without having to pay hefty taxes.

Espousing Republican goals of downsizing the federal bureaucracy and balancing the federal budget by 2002, Cook said he will work to dismantle the departments of Commerce, Education and Energy. He says, however, that the Energy Department's national laboratories should be preserved and believes that selected Commerce Department functions should be transferred to other agencies.

For the 105th Congress, the GOP gave Cook three committee assignments: Transportation and Infrastructure, Banking and Financial Services, and Science.

Cook's electoral hopes were brought to life by the 104th Congress' travails of Republican freshman Enid Greene, whose 1994 election he almost foiled. Greene unseated freshman Democrat Karen Shepherd in 1994, even though Cook's independent bid for the seat siphoned off some conservative votes.

Greene decided against seeking re-election to a second term in 1996 after a scandal involving her husband's mishandling of her campaign and personal finances. Cook was one of several Republicans who jumped to succeed her.

In Utah, a Republican can avoid a primary if he or she secures support from 70 percent of the delegates at the state party's convention. If no Republican captures that level of support, the top two vote-getters advance to a primary.

After diligently courting party delegates for several weeks, Cook surprised many observers by emerging from the party's convention in second place and securing a spot on the primary ballot. His GOP primary opponent, accountant R. Todd Neilson, had the backing of many leading party figures. But with his superior recognition and resources, Cook prevailed over Neilson, a political newcomer, to take the nomination.

Democrats delivered the GOP something of a break by nominating the more liberal candidate, lawyer Ross Anderson, of the two contenders in the Democratic primary.

In television ads and during forums, Cook highlighted Anderson's support for gay rights and his opposition to the death penalty. In one TV spot, Cook claimed that Anderson had once referred to Utahans as murderers and racists after the state executed a black convict. Cook also repeatedly pointed to Anderson's opposition to a bill discouraging same-sex marriages, which was approved by Congress and signed into law in 1996.

As in his past runs for office, Cook tapped into his own fortune and was able to far outspend Anderson.

Anderson replied with a charge that Cook had changed his views on tax cuts since his 1994 campaign, noting that Cook had said at that time that tax cuts might have to be put off until a balanced-budget amendment was passed and other measures were taken to reduce spending. Cook, however, said he was expressing skepticism at the time about the willingness of a Democratic-controlled Congress to cut taxes and balance the budget. Cook prevailed by 13 percentage points, taking 55 percent of the vote.

Nowhere in Utah is the physical presence of the Mormon Church more evident than in the state capital, Salt Lake City. The downtown's focal point is Temple Square, which includes the tabernacle, and the towering Latter-Day Saints headquarters building across the street. The church is closely identified with abstemious lifestyles and conservative politics.

The irreverent used to joke that newcomers needed to set their watches back 20 years when they arrived in Salt Lake City. But the city has long been more culturally cosmopolitan than Utah as a whole, and its politics more dimensional. Non-Mormon Democratic candidates have won the past two mayoral elections, and Democrats held this House seat from 1987 to 1995.

Since it was founded in 1847, Salt Lake City has been a focal point of Utah's economy. Employment in industries such as financial services, transportation, tourism and manufacturing — and lately in high-technology fields such as computers — have made the city one of the West's premier business centers.

Companies have been attracted to Utah because of its low cost of living and doing business, its right-to-work laws, its high birth rate — which maintains a steady labor supply — and its well-educated workers, many of whom know a language in addition to English because the Mormon tradition is to send its young men and women around the world to serve as missionaries.

When energy prices dropped in the 1980s, jobs provided by Salt Lake City's "new age" employers helped rescue the state from recession, and they were a magnet for newcomers. During the past decade, more than 100,000 people moved into Salt Lake County, many of them settling in the city's southwestern suburbs.

UTAH 2
Central — Parts of Salt Lake City

Utah eagerly awaits the year 2002, when Salt Lake City will host the Winter Olympic Games.

While most of the rest of Utah votes Republican, Salt Lake City and some of its suburbs tend to show a more Democratic bent, as is evident from the success of Democrats in Salt Lake's mayoral contests and in 2nd District House voting.

Democrats can no longer count on the city's once loyally Democratic blue-collar workers; they can be persuaded to back independent candidates — such as Ross Perot, who amassed almost 30 percent of the vote here in 1992, and then-independent Cook, who received 18 percent in his 1994 run. Still, these voters, coupled with liberal young professionals, help Democrats remain competitive here.

But even in the 2nd, the political world view looks fairly conservative to most outsiders. In the 1992 presidential race, George Bush and Perot received more than two-thirds of the vote. Four years later, Bob Dole beat Bill Clinton here, 47 percent to 41 percent, while Cook was elected by a comfortable margin.

Salt Lake City's central section and the communities surrounding the University of Utah in the northern hills lean Democratic. But in the wealthy Wasatch foothills section called the East Bench, Republicans hold sway. Voters in such suburban communities as Cottonwood, Sandy City and Draper usually opt for the GOP.

1990 Population: 574,241. White 541,889 (94%), Black 3,497 (1%), Other 28,855 (5%). Hispanic origin 28,310 (5%). 18 and over 379,147 (66%), 62 and over 62,226 (11%). Median age: 26.

HOUSE ELECTIONS

1996 General		
Merrill Cook (R)	129,963	(55%)
Ross Anderson (D)	100,283	(42%)
Arly H. Pederson (IA)	3,070	(1%)
Catherine Carter (NL)	2,981	(1%)
1996 Primary		
Merrill Cook (R)	18,507	(52%)
R. Todd Neilson (R)	17,257	(48%)

CAMPAIGN FINANCE

	Receipts	Receipts from PACs	Expend-itures
1996			
Cook (R)	$1,061,730	$117,672 (11%)	$1,061,793
Anderson (D)	$492,833	$34,301 (7%)	$491,738

DISTRICT VOTE FOR PRESIDENT

1996		1992	
D	96,336 (41%)	**D**	81,233 (31%)
R	111,366 (47%)	**R**	101,169 (39%)
I	22,181 (9%)	**I**	75,921 (29%)

KEY VOTES

1997

Ban "partial birth" abortions Y

3 Christopher B. Cannon (R)

Of Mapleton — Elected 1996, 1st term

Biographical Information

Born: Oct. 20, 1950, Salt Lake City, Utah.

Education: Brigham Young U., B.S. 1974, J.D. 1980.

Occupation: Venture capital executive; steel company executive; cabinet department lawyer; lawyer.

Family: Wife, Claudia Ann Fox; seven children.

Religion: Mormon.

Political Career: Utah Republican Party finance chairman, 1992-94.

Capitol Office: 118 Cannon Bldg. 20515; 225-7751.

Committees

Judiciary
Courts & Intellectual Property; Immigration & Claims

Resources
Energy & Mineral Resources; Water & Power

Science
Space & Aeronautics; Technology

The Path to Washington: Cannon succeeded in returning Utah's 3rd District to Republican hands in 1996, denying Democrat Bill Orton's bid for a fourth House term.

Before Orton's surprising victory in 1990, the 3rd's voters never gave a Democratic House candidate more than a third of their votes. Yet, in his re-election bids in 1992 and 1994, voters sent Orton back by comfortable margins.

Cannon promised to follow a fiscally conservative line, supporting tax cuts and spending reductions.

To reduce government spending, Cannon advocates cutting the departments of Commerce, Energy, Housing and Urban Development, and Education, though he says the federal government should still continue to administer student loans. He also says Congress should target "corporate welfare," the subsidies the federal government hands out to large companies.

The 3rd District contains vast stretches of federally owned land, particularly in its southern expanse where the Canyonlands National Park and other national parks, forests and recreation areas are located. Cannon will have an opportunity to work on issues related to the federal government's handling of the state's natural resources as a member of the Resources Committee. The GOP leadership put him on the Science Committee. And Cannon, a former attorney, also was given a seat on the Judiciary Committee.

Cannon brings both business and government experience to Washington. He was appointed by President Ronald Reagan as associate solicitor in the Interior Department and served as a Commerce Department attorney in the 1980s.

Cannon flunked out of Harvard Business School, but he reaped success in the business world after he, along with his brother, Joe, bought and reopened Geneva Steel Co. in 1987. After a falling out with his brother, who later spent $6.5 million in an unsuccessful attempt to win the 1992 Republican Senate nomination, Chris Cannon started his own venture capital company, Cannon Industries.

Cannon dipped into his sizable personal fortune — his sworn financial statements put his worth at more than $10 million — to help fund his bid against Orton, spending $1.6 million out of his own pocket.

The peripatetic Cannon ran an aggressive campaign that kept Orton on the defensive. He poked holes in Orton's image as an independent-minded, moderate-to-conservative Democrat. Cannon claimed that Orton had moved away from the middle in recent years and closer to the left.

Orton blasted Cannon for distorting his voting record. At the same time, he claimed his opponent would be a slavish devotee of the GOP leadership and contrasted that with his own image as a maverick willing to buck his party leadership. Orton also touted his work as part of a coalition of center-right Democrats known as the "blue dogs," who put together a compromise budget during the 104th Congress. And Orton even said he hadn't made up his mind for whom to vote for president.

But Cannon was ultimately able to paint Orton as ineffective. In the final weeks of the campaign, Cannon highlighted Orton's inability to dissuade the Clinton administration from designating 1.7 million acres of southern Utah land, much of it coal-rich, as a national monument. That bold stroke was widely vilified in Utah.

Orton opposed the designation (which Clinton announced in neighboring Arizona on a September visit to the Grand Canyon) and publicly criticized the administration. But while Clinton had little to lose in Utah (which gave him his lowest vote percentage in both 1992 and 1996), Orton stood to lose a great deal.

As the only Democrat in the state's congressional delegation, Orton was the only meaningful target for Utah voters eager to vent their resentment at the Democrats in general.

Even though the breaks went against Orton, the outcome was close, with Cannon winning by 4 percentage points.

Some of the rural eastern counties of the 3rd, which saw sharp population declines during the 1980s, have begun to rebound. In Grand County, which once reeled from the collapse of the uranium mining industry, a telecommuter and artists community has sprung up in the city of Moab. Attracted to the area's breathtaking landscape, these liberal-leaning transplants are altering the flavor of the community.

Twenty-one of the state's 29 counties registered double-digit growth rates from 1990 to 1995. Growth in the 3rd has been mainly in urbanized areas: Provo, Orem and the Salt Lake City suburbs. Utah County (Provo and Orem) grew 21 percent in the 1980s, topping 263,000. It casts about 45 percent of the district's total votes.

In 1996, Bob Dole won 71 percent of the vote in Utah County. Provo, the most intense Mormon community in the state, is home to Brigham Young University, which was founded in 1875 to prepare Mormon youth for teaching and religious proselytizing. Today BYU has 30,465 students and offers degrees in a range of fields, but it remains devoutly Mormon.

The 3rd is a Republican stronghold, though voters in the early 1990s showed a proclivity for splitting their tickets. Democrat Bill Orton won easily in his 1990 debut and in two subsequent re-elections, even as Republicans dominated elections at other levels. Bill Clinton even finished in 3rd place in 1992, behind Ross Perot. In 1996, Bob Dole beat Clinton here by 29 percentage points. And Orton, who got only 39 percent in Utah County, lost to Cannon.

Democratic voters are rife in the 3rd's section of Salt Lake City, a primarily working-class area added in 1992 redistricting. The 3rd's portion of Salt Lake County gave Orton 61 percent in 1996, down from 71 percent two years earlier.

UTAH 3
East — Provo; Orem; rural Utah

The Provo-Orem area has seen a steady influx of new businesses: Novell Inc. and SoftCopy are among the software companies that have come here in recent years, helping make that industry a leading district employer. Geneva Steel's blue-collar workers in the northern section of Utah County give the area a bloc of Democratic voters.

The rest of the district is rural and sparsely populated. Much of it is mountains and desert, and the GOP is dominant. Cattle ranching, oil drilling and mining have been the traditional industries in the 3rd, but with oil prices flat and the mining industry in the doldrums, tourism — especially as related to skiing — increasingly is becoming an important income source. In the northeastern corner of the district, the life-size dinosaurs of Dinosaurland in Vernal (Uintah County) have become a popular tourist attraction. To the south, thousands of visitors tour the 3rd's national parks: Arches, Canyonlands, Capitol Reef and Bryce Canyon.

Other communities in the district are trying to diversify their economies to spare themselves the financial pains they felt in the 1980s. Carbon County, whose 2 percent population growth rate from 1990 to 1995 was Utah's slowest, has a new power plant and a locally owned and operated landfill. Carbon was just one of three Utah counties Clinton carried in 1996.

1990 Population: 574,323. White 532,043 (93%), Black 2,660 (<1%), Other 39,620 (7%). Hispanic origin 29,516 (5%). 18 and over 355,865 (62%), 62 and over 54,027 (9%). Median age: 24.

HOUSE ELECTIONS

1996 General		
Christopher B. Cannon (R)	106,220	(51%)
Bill Orton (D)	98,178	(47%)
Amy L. Lassen (LIBERT)	2,341	(1%)
1996 Primary		
Chris Cannon (R)	27,738	(56%)
Tom Draschil (R)	22,178	(44%)

CAMPAIGN FINANCE

	Receipts	Receipts from PACs		Expend-itures
1996				
Cannon (R)	$1,827,718	$76,192	(4%)	$1,826,849
Orton (D)	$696,576	$491,596	(71%)	$708,778

DISTRICT VOTE FOR PRESIDENT

	1996		1992
D	61,193 (29%)	**D**	51,574 (24%)
R	121,272 (58%)	**R**	105,836 (49%)
I	21,387 (10%)	**I**	58,595 (27%)

KEY VOTES

1997

Ban "partial birth" abortions Y

VERMONT

Governor: Howard Dean (D)
First elected: 1992 (Assumed office 8/91)
Length of term: 2 years
Term expires: 1/99
Salary: $93,122 (accepts $80,725)
Term limit: No
Phone: (802) 828-3333
Born: Nov. 17, 1948; East Hampton, N.Y.
Education: Yale U., B.A. 1971; Albert Einstein College of Medicine, M.D. 1978.
Occupation: Physician; professor.
Family: Wife, Judith Steinberg-Dean; two children.
Religion: Congregationalist.
Political Career: Vt. House, 1983-87; lieutenant governor, 1987-91.

Lt. Gov.: Barbara W. Snelling (R)
First elected: 1992
Length of term: 2 years
Term expires: 1/99
Salary: $40,296 (accepts $33,734)
Phone: (802) 828-2226

State election official: (802) 828-2304
Democratic headquarters: (802) 229-5986
Republican headquarters: (802) 223-3411

STATE LEGISLATURE

General Assembly. Meets biennially, January-April (session often extended).

Senate: 30 members, 2-year terms
1996 breakdown: 17D, 13R; 19 men, 11 women
Salary: $510/week
Phone: (802) 828-2241

House of Representatives: 150 members, 2-year terms
1996 breakdown: 88D, 58R, 1I, 3 other; 103 men, 47 women
Salary: $510/week
Phone: (802) 828-2247

URBAN STATISTICS

City	Population
Burlington	39,127
Mayor Peter C. Clavelle, N-P	
Rutland	18,230
Mayor Jeffrey Wennberg, N-P	
Town of Essex	16,498
Town Manager Patrick C. Scheidel	
Bennington	16,451
Town Manager Stuart A. Hurd	
Colchester	14,731
Town Manager David G. Timmons	

U.S. CONGRESS

Senate: 1 D, 1 R
House: 1 I

TERM LIMITS

For state offices: No

ELECTIONS

1996 Presidential Vote

Bill Clinton	53%
Bob Dole	31%
Ross Perot	12%

1992 Presidential Vote

Bill Clinton	46%
George Bush	30%
Ross Perot	23%

1988 Presidential Vote

George Bush	51%
Michael S. Dukakis	48%

POPULATION

1990 population		562,758
1980 population		511,456
Percent change		+10%
Rank among states:		48
White		99%
Black		<1%
Hispanic		1%
Asian or Pacific islander		1%
Urban		32%
Rural		68%
Born in state		57%
Foreign-born		3%
Under age 18	143,083	25%
Ages 18-64	353,512	63%
65 and older	66,163	12%
Median age		33

MISCELLANEOUS

Capital: Montpelier
Number of counties: 14
Per capita income: $17,747 (1991)
Rank among states: 26
Total area: 9,614 sq. miles
Rank among states: 43

VERMONT

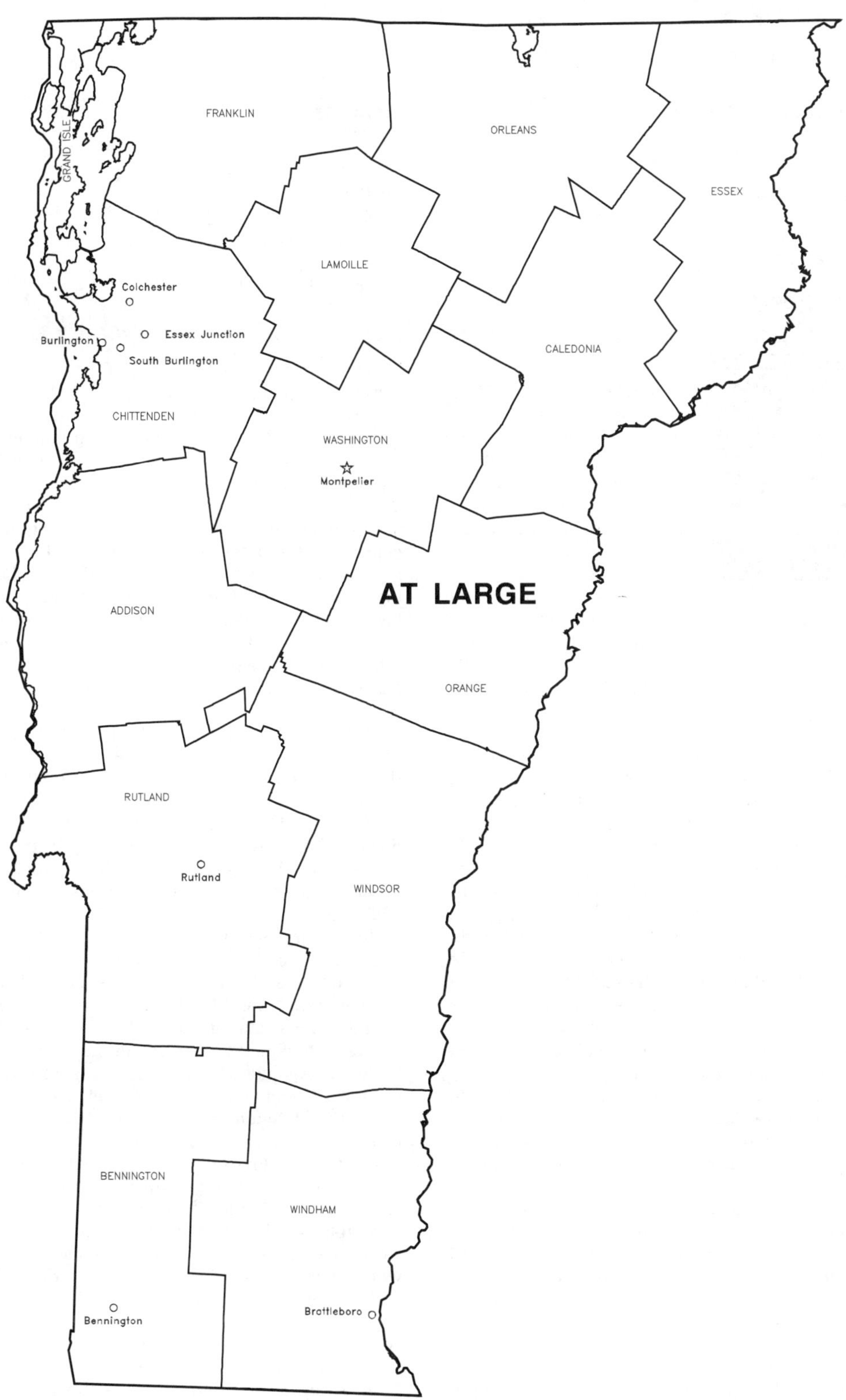
FRANKLIN
ORLEANS
ESSEX
GRAND ISLE
LAMOILLE
Colchester
Essex Junction
Burlington
South Burlington
CALEDONIA
CHITTENDEN
WASHINGTON
Montpelier
AT LARGE
ADDISON
ORANGE
RUTLAND
Rutland
WINDSOR
BENNINGTON
WINDHAM
Bennington
Brattleboro

Patrick J. Leahy (D)

Of Middlesex — Elected 1974, 4th term

Biographical Information
Born: March 31, 1940, Montpelier, Vt.
Education: St. Michael's College, B.A. 1961; Georgetown U., J.D. 1964.
Occupation: Lawyer.
Family: Wife, Marcelle Pomerleau; three children.
Religion: Roman Catholic.
Political Career: Chittenden County state's attorney, 1967-75.
Capitol Office: 433 Russell Bldg. 20510; 224-4242.

Committees
Agriculture, Nutrition & Forestry
Forestry, Conservation & Rural Revitalization; Research, Nutrition & General Legislation (ranking)
Appropriations
Agriculture, Rural Development & Related Agencies; Defense; Foreign Operations (ranking); Interior; VA, HUD & Independent Agencies
Judiciary (ranking)
Antitrust, Business Rights & Competition

In Washington: Leahy has a new role in the 105th Congress — ranking minority member of the Judiciary Committee — and if his first few weeks in the job were any indication, it promises to be a very active time.

In February 1997, he played the lead role for the Democratic minority in opposing a constitutional amendment requiring a balanced federal budget. "This proposed constitutional amendment risks seriously undercutting the protection of our constitutional separation of powers," Leahy said. "No one has yet convincingly explained how the proposed amendment would work and what role would the president play and what role the courts play in its implementation and enforcement."

After the amendment fell one vote short of the two-thirds majority required for passage, Leahy jokingly revealed some of the pressure that had been applied to Democrats to keep faith with their leaders and vote against the resolution. Leahy said there was some "arm twisting" in the office of Senate Minority Leader Tom Daschle. "And if that didn't work," he said, "they sent them downstairs to Bob Byrd." West Virginia's Robert C. Byrd, the dean of the Senate Democrats, has vigorously opposed the GOP's efforts to pass the balanced-budget amendment.

Leahy also tasted victory in February when the Senate cleared legislation releasing $385 million in previously appropriated international family planning aid without abortion restrictions. President Clinton signed the measure into law. The Senate voted 53-46 in favor of the resolution to accelerate release of the funds. If it had failed, the administration would not have been able to begin spending the money until July 1. "This vote is not about funding abortions," said Leahy, who managed the resolution on the Senate floor. "It is about releasing money we already appropriated to address the most serious environmental problem of all — unchecked population growth — and to help prevent unwanted pregnancies and abortions."

That same month, he joined GOP Sen. Conrad Burns of Montana in introducing two bills to ease export restrictions on encryption technology and prohibit the federal government from holding its own "keys" for decoding encrypted communications over the Internet. Encryption is the process by which computer or cellular phone transmissions are scrambled to prevent their being intercepted; on the other end, recipients with decoding capability are able to translate the data back into usable form. Clinton administration policy has been that encryption software that exceeds a certain complexity cannot be exported for fear that it would pose problems for law enforcement. But Burns and Leahy maintained that such software is widely available in other countries, and export controls are hurting U.S. software makers. They pointed to a Commerce Department study that estimated that U.S. firms lost $60 billion in potential sales in 1995 and could lose 200,000 jobs by the year 2000. "As an avid Internet user, I care deeply about protecting individual privacy and encouraging the development of the Internet as a secure and trusted communications medium," Leahy said.

In January 1997, he and Daschle introduced a package of initiatives that focused on youth violence, drugs and gangs. The package, which is estimated to cost $13 billion over two years, would increase authorizations for several federal programs to combat crime and drugs, such as the Violence Against Women Act and President Clinton's Community Oriented Policing (COPS) program. While almost half the money would go to states for prison construction, states would also get new sources of federal funds for shelters for battered women and drug treatment programs. Leahy characterized the package as one that builds on the 1994 crime bill, with additional steps to address youth crime and gangs. The bill would stiffen penalties for crimes committed with the aid of certain "gang paraphernalia," such as bulletproof vests. It would also create "gun courts," where juvenile gun offenders could be tried on an expedited basis.

Also in early 1997, Leahy clashed with Judiciary Committee Chairman Orrin G. Hatch, R-

Utah, over what he felt were unnecessary delays in confirming Clinton's judicial nominees. "We should say enough's enough," Leahy said. "We ought to be doing what Democrats have always done — confirm judges if they're men and women of integrity and competence."

At a Judiciary Committee meeting early in the 105th, Leahy challenged Hatch to move quickly on the Clinton nominees, many of whom had been nominated in the 104th Congress. Hatch insisted that Clinton had more judges confirmed in his first term than former Presidents George Bush, Ronald Reagan and Richard M. Nixon during each of their first terms, and that the federal judiciary's vacancy rate at the end of the 104th was virtually the same as it was at the end of the Democratic-controlled 103rd Congress.

In taking the top Democratic spot on Judiciary, Leahy gave up his ranking slot on the Agriculture Committee, though he continues to serve as ranking member of its Research, Nutrition and General Legislation Subcommittee. Leahy's early disagreements with Hatch on Judiciary suggest that theirs may not be as close a working relationship as the one Leahy forged with Richard G. Lugar, R-Ind., the Agriculture Committee chairman.

Leahy, in fact, unsuccessfully tried to prod some of his Democratic colleagues in February 1996 to accept a compromise farm bill offered by Lugar and then-Majority Leader Bob Dole. Both Republicans were running for president, and they had decided to accept almost any legislation so they could concentrate on campaigning and tell farmers before the critical Iowa caucus that they had passed a farm bill. For Republicans, the deal would have represented a wholesale retreat from their original goal of phasing out subsidies over seven years, the so-called Freedom to Farm bill. But Democrats, facing divisions between Midwestern and Northeastern members, refused to be hurried. "I wish we could have accepted it that night," Leahy said. "That was our best deal. By the time [Senate Democrats] decided they did like it, it was no longer on the table."

The hesitant response cost the Democrats a golden opportunity to derail Freedom to Farm. Instead, the Senate passed a farm bill one week later with the core GOP priority intact— a new system of fixed, declining payments to farmers that would undo the decades-old subsidy structure. Leahy backed that farm bill, which included funding for nutrition and conservation programs. Earlier, Leahy tried to cut a deal with Lugar that would emphasize issues such as conservation, nutrition and Northeastern dairy supports, instead of subsidies for wheat, corn and other crops. "When Sen. Leahy put forward his proposal, that sent everybody basically running in an undisciplined fashion to cover their own bases," said Sen. Bob Kerrey, D-Neb.

In fact, Leahy made it very clear that he would not allow nutrition programs to be cut deeply without a fight. He predicted that he could muster support on the Senate floor for amendments to the farm bill that would restrict subsidies to wealthy farmers. "If I have to choose between very wealthy farm interests and needy children, I am going to pick children every time," Leahy said.

In the conference agreement reached in March 1996, negotiators agreed to fund new farm conservation programs and to block conservatives' attempts to scale back wetlands regulations. That was a price Leahy insisted on for his support. The bill also included a commission empowered to set prices for milk in the Northeast.

Leahy serves as ranking minority member of Appropriations' Foreign Operations Subcommittee, and he has devoted much energy in recent years to seeking abolition of anti-personnel land mines.

In August 1995, the Senate voted 67-27 for an amendment to the annual defense authorization bill that would impose a one-year moratorium on U.S. forces' use of anti-personnel mines. The moratorium, to take effect three years after enactment of the bill, would allow deployment of anti-personnel mines only along international borders or internationally recognized demilitarized zones — and only if they were scattered in areas that were marked as minefields and monitored by military personnel to prevent civilians from wandering into them. Anti-tank mines would be exempt.

The Pentagon vehemently opposed the provision, and it was dropped by Senate-House conferees. However, with no fanfare, Leahy inserted the core provision of his land-mine ban into the foreign operations appropriations bill, which was attached to the stopgap spending bill approved by Congress and signed by Clinton in January 1996.

In January 1997, Leahy criticized a Clinton administration announcement that it would try to negotiate an international treaty banning anti-personnel land mines through the U.N. Conference on Disarmament, rather than through a series of negotiations led by Canada. Proponents of a total ban on mines complained that the practical effect of this decision would be to delay a treaty, since the U.N. conference operates by a rule of unanimity that "rewards holdout states, who effectively have a veto that retards or prevents strong agreements," Leahy said.

Leahy generally votes the liberal line — he opposed welfare overhaul, the line-item veto and telecommunications deregulation — but he did vote to ban a particular abortion technique that opponents call a "partial birth" abortion and to override Clinton's veto of the measure.

When Democrats ran the Senate, Leahy's role as liberal inquisitor during the Clarence Thomas hearings in the fall of 1991 had wide-reaching political impact. The rhetoric he employed in opposing Thomas — before and after the Supreme Court nominee was confronted by Anita F. Hill's accusation of sexual harassment — helped introduce a theme that Democrats used to good effect in the 1992 presidential campaign: that the Bush administration had become captive to an extremist conservative element.

During the Judiciary Committee hearings, Leahy basically ignored the tradition that holds it is bad form to press a nominee directly for his views on an issue that would come before the Supreme Court. Leahy pressed the elusive nominee for his views on several issues, most notably abortion. He elicited Thomas' assertions that he had never debated or discussed the landmark *Roe v. Wade* decision — statements that Thomas' opponents exhibited as proof that the nominee was being deliberately evasive.

At Home: When he first won office more than 30 years ago, Leahy was in the vanguard of Democratic gains in Vermont. At 26, he was elected Chittenden County state's attorney in 1966. He revamped the office and headed a national task force of district attorneys probing the 1973-74 energy crisis.

In 1974, he ran for the Senate seat being vacated by Republican George D. Aiken. At 34, Leahy presented a contrast with the 82-year-old political institution he hoped to replace.

Leahy was an underdog against GOP Rep. Richard W. Mallary. But Mallary proved a rather awkward campaigner, and Watergate made Vermont more receptive to a Democrat, enabling Leahy to score his breakthrough victory. He became Vermont's first Democratic senator since the Republican Party was founded in 1854.

Leahy survived in 1980 by emphasizing his roots in the state rather than his ties to the Democratic Party. Campaigning against the national GOP tide, he fought off New York-born challenger Stewart Ledbetter with the slogan: "Pat Leahy: Of Vermont, for Vermont." Leahy squeaked by with 50 percent.

Leahy's narrow re-election pegged him as the most vulnerable Democratic incumbent up in 1986 — a status that was reinforced when Republican Richard A. Snelling, who had retired in 1985 after four terms as governor, agreed to tackle Leahy.

But Leahy was well-prepared and well-financed. While he had been building his organization, Snelling had spent much of 1985 on a sailing excursion. Early polls showed Leahy way ahead, which hurt Snelling's fundraising. The moderate Snelling also had trouble defining a distinction between himself and Leahy. In the end, Snelling resorted to attacking Leahy's attendance record and labeling him one of the Senate's "biggest spenders." Leahy won 63 percent.

Republicans had trouble attracting a big name in 1992 until Vermont Secretary of State James H. Douglas jumped into the race, hoping that Leahy's long tenure in office would turn off voters. As the year wore on, the angry voter mood helped make Douglas' campaign competitive. But Leahy, who had not taken re-election for granted even when he looked safe in 1991, kicked his already humming campaign into high gear.

Vermont's anti-status quo vote was evident in Ross Perot's surprisingly strong 23 percent showing in the state's presidential balloting that year, but Leahy still prevailed by 11 points, 54 to 43 percent.

SENATE ELECTIONS

1992 General		
Patrick J. Leahy (D)	154,762	(54%)
James H. Douglas (R)	123,854	(43%)
Jerry Levy (LU)	5,121	(2%)

Previous Winning Percentages: 1986 (63%) **1980** (50%) **1974** (50%)

CAMPAIGN FINANCE

	Receipts	Receipts from PACs	Expend-itures
1992			
Leahy (D)	$932,940	$308,052 (33%)	$950,331
Douglas (R)	$196,635	0	$195,737

KEY VOTES

1997	
Approve balanced-budget constitutional amendment	N
Approve chemical weapons treaty	Y
1996	
Approve farm bill	Y
Limit punitive damages in product liability cases	N
Exempt small businesses from higher minimum wage	N
Approve welfare overhaul	N
Bar job discrimination based on sexual orientation	Y
Override veto of ban on "partial birth" abortions	Y
1995	
Approve GOP budget with tax and spending cuts	N
Approve constitutional amendment barring flag desecration	N

VOTING STUDIES

	Presidential Support		Party Unity		Conservative Coalition	
Year	S	O	S	O	S	O
1996	75	25	85	12	32	63
1995	87	11	93	4	9	89
1994	89	11	96	4	6	94
1993	92	7	92	6	27	73
1992	23	75	90	4	5	92
1991	28	72	90	10	18	80

INTEREST GROUP RATINGS

Year	ADA	AFL-CIO	CCUS	ACU
1996	90	n/a	23	5
1995	100	100	16	0
1994	95	100	20	0
1993	95	82	27	8
1992	100	100	10	0
1991	95	92	20	5

James M. Jeffords (R)

Of Shrewsbury — Elected 1988, 2nd term

Biographical Information

Born: May 11, 1934, Rutland, Vt.

Education: Yale U., B.S.I.A. 1956; Harvard U., LL.B. 1962.

Military Service: Navy, 1956-59; Naval Reserves, 1959-90.

Occupation: Lawyer.

Family: Wife, Elizabeth Daley; two children.

Religion: Congregationalist.

Political Career: Vt. Senate, 1967-69; Vt. attorney general, 1969-73; sought Republican nomination for governor, 1972; U.S. House, 1975-89.

Capitol Office: 728 Hart Bldg. 20510; 224-5141.

Committees

Special Aging

Finance
Health Care; Social Security & Family Policy; Taxation & IRS Oversight

Labor & Human Resources (chairman)
Employment & Training; Public Health & Safety

Veterans' Affairs

In Washington: The Republican Party in Congress once had a thriving wing of Northeastern liberal members. Jeffords, who claimed the chairmanship of the Senate Labor and Human Resources Committee at the beginning of the 105th Congress, would have felt quite comfortable within that group.

But during Jeffords' more than two decades in Congress, the GOP's liberal faction has sharply diminished as the party's ranks have become more solidly conservative.

Jeffords, now in his second Senate term after seven in the House, has thus stood out as a Republican maverick. In 1996, he voted with a majority of Senate Democrats against the majority of his Republican colleagues 41 percent of the time on roll-call votes — the highest rate of defection among GOP members.

He also backed President Clinton on 53 percent of the votes on which the White House took a position; only five other Republican senators backed the president more than half the time.

This has stood Jeffords in good stead politically in Vermont, a onetime Yankee Republican bastion that has shown liberal voting tendencies since the late 1970s.

Jeffords has remained popular even as Vermont voters have elected Democrats to two other major statewide offices (Sen. Patrick J. Leahy and Gov. Howard Dean) and an independent who describes himself as a socialist, Bernard Sanders, to the state's at-large House seat.

However, Jeffords' willingness to stray from the party line rubs many of the more conservative Republican senators the wrong way — and briefly threatened his rise to the Labor and Human Resources chairmanship vacated by the 1996 retirement of Republican Nancy Landon Kassebaum of Kansas.

Worried that Jeffords would line up too often with committee Democrats and thwart GOP priorities on labor, education and health care issues, several conservatives tried to convince Indiana Republican Daniel R. Coats to challenge Jeffords, who was next in line for the chairmanship.

But Jeffords was saved by an ingrained Senate Republican deference to seniority, and by a commitment by Majority Leader Trent Lott to uphold diversity within the party even as he spearheaded a conservative agenda. Coats, after consulting with the leadership, demurred, and Jeffords assumed the chairmanship without a challenge.

Although many in his own party see him as a liberal, Jeffords describes himself as a moderate. "I'm not a radical toward labor issues or on the business issues," Jeffords said in 1996. "I'm down the middle."

He also pledged that he would not block legislation favored by more conservative Republicans, even if he opposed it. "I have told the members if we disagree, I won't hold up legislation that all Repub-licans except me want," he said.

In fact, some liberal and pro-union interests viewed Jeffords as playing to his more conservative colleagues with some of his votes in the 104th Congress.

For example, he supported a bill to allow businesses to set up their own labor-management teams to discuss workplace issues. Organized labor strongly opposed the legislation, seeing it as a way for business owners to circumvent unions. But Jeffords said the concept was designed for modern workplaces in which the common goal of increasing profits, competitiveness and employment has replaced labor-management hostility. Critics of the legislation, he said, are "still in the mind-set of the 1930s."

Clinton vetoed a similar bill in 1996, but Jeffords revived it in the 105th and pushed it through Labor and Human Resources in March 1997.

Jeffords also indicated he planned to move carefully on a potentially explosive issue: federal regulation of the rapidly growing managed health care industry. "We shouldn't get into micromanagement of health care," he says. "I'm going to go slow."

Still, there is plenty of evidence that Jeffords has earned his moderate-to-liberal reputation — and the skepticism of GOP conservatives.

In 1996, Jeffords provided a key Republican swing vote that helped Democrats enact an increase in the minimum wage over the opposition of the GOP leadership.

And while many Republicans view public education as the province of local and state governments and want to limit federal funding, Jeffords is an unabashed advocate of a federal role.

During the 1996 election cycle, Democrats tried to portray the GOP as anti-education, and congressional Republicans responded by supporting funding increases for certain education programs. Jeffords was pleased. "It was almost a bidding war upward as to who was going to give the most for education," Jeffords said. "I kept cheering them on."

In 1994, Jeffords was the only Republican senator to cosponsor Clinton's plan to overhaul the nation's health care system — a proposal so thoroughly destroyed by attacks from other Republicans that it contributed greatly to the GOP's takeover of Congress in that year's elections.

Along with his move to chair Labor and Human Resources, Jeffords made a committee switch in the 105th that will help him follow his interest in health care issues. He gave up his seat on the Appropri-ations Committee and took a seat on the Finance Committee, where he received an assignment to the Health Care Subcommittee.

Jeffords, a Navy veteran, has retained a seat on the Veterans' Affairs Committee. But at the start of the 105th Congress, he gave up a pair of assignments that had brought him some attention.

One of these was the chairmanship of the Labor and Human Resources Subcommittee on Education, Arts and Humanities. In that position, Jeffords was one of the leading Republican defenders of the National Endowment for the Arts, the federal arts funding agency roundly panned by many conservatives as a waste of taxpayers' money and a font of support for offensive art. Jeffords was vice chairman of the Congressional Arts Caucus in the 103rd Congress.

He also gave up the chairmanship of the Appro-priations Subcommittee on the District of Columbia. During the 104th Congress, Jeffords urged members to give time to a congressionally mandated control board to get the affairs of the financially beleaguered capital city in order.

"We told the control board to get together with D.C. and within four years to get the budget balanced, and they're on the right track," he said in July 1996.

As chairman, Jeffords opposed a proposal backed by many Republicans that would have responded to the decline of the District's educational system by establishing a voucher program that aimed to allow parents to choose the schools to which they wanted to send their children.

Such positions are part of a well-worn career pattern for Jeffords. He never liked President Ronald Reagan's conservative song sheet for the GOP. In only one year of Reagan's tenure did Jeffords, then a House member, support the president's positions on legislation more often than he opposed them.

When George Bush became president, he had less of an ideological mission than Reagan. Initially that helped Jeffords appear more of a GOP loyalist: He backed Bush on 68 percent of Senate votes in 1989. But as Bush's tenure wore on, Jeffords often found himself at odds with the White House on key issues. He opposed Supreme Court nominee Clarence Thomas, who ultimately was confirmed. And just before the 1992 Republican Convention, Jeffords publicly suggested that Bush drop Vice President Dan Quayle from the ticket.

Jeffords was most outspoken in disagreeing with Bush on issues that came before him as a member of the Labor Committee. In April 1991, he questioned the intentions of Bush administration officials after they pressured business executives to break off negotiations with civil rights activists on a job-discrimination bill.

"The president has assured me very sincerely that he wants a civil rights bill," Jeffords said. "But it's getting harder and harder for me to live with that" assertion.

During the 101st and 102nd Congresses, Jeffords voted with committee Democrats and against the position taken by Bush and the majority of his Republican colleagues on a number of contentious issues, including requirements that employers provide unpaid family and medical leave for employees.

A supporter of family leave since his House days, Jeffords crossed back over to that chamber in June 1990 to participate in a news conference by bill supporters, calling the measure "a declaration of independence for the American family." Family leave legislation ultimately was enacted in the 103rd Congress and signed into law by Clinton.

Jeffords also had a seat on the Environment and Public Works Committee through the 102nd Congress, and he pushed several environment-related proposals. He sought to amend the Resource Conservation and Recovery Act to force states to recycle bottles, but his proposal was rejected in committee. In the full Senate, Jeffords tried to amend a massive energy bill to promote non-gasoline motor fuels, but the amendment was tabled 57-39. During consideration of the fiscal 1992 and 1993 Interior appropriations bills, he pushed an amendment to increase grazing fees on federal lands, but the amendment was rejected.

At Home: Jeffords is well-suited to politics in modern-day Vermont. The electorate has tilted to the left during the last two decades, with the arrival of thousands of liberal urbanites seeking the state's greener pastures. With Democrats gaining an upper hand, only moderate Republicans such as Jeffords have had a chance to win statewide.

Jeffords has at times faced stronger opposition from conservatives in his own party than he has in general elections. In the 1988 Senate primary, Jeffords received 61 percent of the vote against a conservative neophyte, Michael Griffes. Jeffords then breezed to victory over a Democrat, former U.S. Attorney William Gray, with 68 percent.

In 1994, however, Jeffords avoided primary opposition only to face a surprisingly tough Democratic challenger.

Jan Backus, an underfinanced liberal Democrat who scored an upset victory in the primary, attacked Jeffords as a captive of special interests and accused him of using campaign funds for personal use. Lagging far behind Jeffords in polls at the start of the general-election campaign, Backus narrowed the gap substantially near Election Day and attracted national attention and funding.

But Jeffords shot back with a spate of negative TV ads that criticized Backus as weak on crime. Jeffords managed to survive one of the toughest political battles of his career, coming through with a 9 percentage-point margin of victory.

Jeffords' only political defeat came early in his career, when he lost a GOP gubernatorial primary in 1972. He bounced back in 1974, winning a three-way primary for Vermont's open House seat. He went on to defeat Democratic Burlington Mayor Francis Cain with 53 percent of the vote.

Jeffords quickly became indomitable in his House seat. In six re-election contests, he never tallied less than 65 percent. In 1986, his last House election, he ran without Democratic opposition.

As 1988 approached and GOP Sen. Robert T. Stafford's retirement became imminent, Jeffords gained regard as his heir apparent. No Democratic officeholder came forward to contest him, and the honor fell without opposition to Gray, who had never before sought office.

Before getting to Gray, Jeffords had to contend with Griffes, a 35-year-old Navy veteran who returned to Vermont from a job with the Washington office of Grumman Corp., a defense contractor. Griffes ran an ideological campaign, describing Jeffords as "not a Republican."

But Jeffords responded by pointing out Griffes' lack of Vermont roots: His family moved to the state when he was 17, and he had spent most years since out of state. Citing Griffes' residence in Arlington, Va., a suburb of Washington, Jeffords said the contest was between a "Vermont Republican" and a "Virginia Republican." He won easily.

Jeffords entered the general-election contest an overwhelming favorite and was never threatened. Gray's main thrust was to make a connection between a contribution Jeffords received from the Teamsters union's political action committee and his opposition to federal efforts to take over the corruption-plagued union. But Jeffords quashed the issue, denying any connection between his fundraising and his House voting behavior.

The result on Election Day showed that the issue did Jeffords no serious harm.

SENATE ELECTIONS

1994 General

James M. Jeffords (R)	106,505	(50%)
Jan Backus (D)	85,868	(41%)
Gavin T. Mills (I)	12,465	(6%)
Matthew S. Mulligan (I)	3,141	(1%)

Previous Winning Percentages: 1988 (68%) **1986*** (89%) **1984*** (65%) **1982*** (69%) **1980*** (79%) **1978*** (75%) **1976*** (67%) **1974*** (53%)

** House elections*

CAMPAIGN FINANCE

	Receipts	Receipts from PACs	Expend-itures
1994			
Jeffords (R)	$1,011,383	$616,629 (61%)	$1,043,626
Backus (D)	$317,478	$93,192 (29%)	$313,169

KEY VOTES

1997	
Approve balanced-budget constitutional amendment	Y
Approve chemical weapons treaty	Y
1996	
Approve farm bill	N
Limit punitive damages in product liability cases	Y
Exempt small businesses from higher minimum wage	N
Approve welfare overhaul	Y
Bar job discrimination based on sexual orientation	Y
Override veto of ban on "partial birth" abortions	N
1995	
Approve GOP budget with tax and spending cuts	Y
Approve constitutional amendment barring flag desecration	N

VOTING STUDIES

	Presidential Support		Party Unity		Conservative Coalition	
Year	**S**	**O**	**S**	**O**	**S**	**O**
1996	53	46	57	41	58	39
1995	50	48	58	41	53	47
1994	77	21	31	68	25	75
1993	56	42	45	53	27	71
1992	45	52	36	58	37	55
1991	54	43	36	58	35	55

INTEREST GROUP RATINGS

Year	ADA	AFL-CIO	CCUS	ACU
1996	50	n/a	62	45
1995	55	36	76	23
1994	85	50	50	12
1993	60	40	64	38
1992	65	56	60	27
1991	65	50	22	10

AL Bernard Sanders (I)

Of Burlington — Elected 1990, 4th term

Biographical Information

Born: Sept. 8, 1941, Brooklyn, N.Y.
Education: U. of Chicago, B.A. 1964.
Occupation: Professor; free-lance writer.
Family: Wife, Jane O'Meara Driscoll; one child, three stepchildren.
Religion: Jewish.
Political Career: Mayor of Burlington, 1981-89; independent candidate for U.S. Senate, 1972; independent candidate for governor, 1972; independent candidate for U.S. Senate, 1974; independent candidate for governor, 1976, 1986; independent candidate for U.S. House, 1988.
Capitol Office: 2202 Rayburn Bldg. 20515; 225-4115.

Committees

Banking & Financial Services
Domestic & International Monetary Policy; Housing & Community Opportunity
Government Reform & Oversight
Human Resources; National Economic Growth, Natural Resources & Regulatory Affairs (ranking)

In Washington: Sanders reached a milestone in the 105th Congress: being named ranking minority member the on the National Economic Growth, Natural Resources and Regulatory Affairs Subcommittee of the Government Reform and Oversight Committee.

The panel is not a powerhouse, but it is notable that Sanders, the only independent in the House, won the ranking seat over a Democrat.

Sanders is a self-proclaimed socialist, the first identifiable House member of that ilk since Victor L. Berger of Wisconsin (1911-13, 1923-29). Sanders' aides say he is the first chairman or ranking member this century who is neither a Democrat nor a Republican.

Minority Leader Richard A. Gephardt named Sanders to the ranking post in February 1997 over Democrat Elijah E. Cummings of Maryland, who had tried to claim the ranking position despite serving in the House less than a year. Gephardt mollified Cummings by naming him to the Democratic Policy Committee and promising him the next opening on the Democratic panel that makes committee assignments.

Sanders' ascension was aided by his history of voting like a Democrat.

Campaigning for the House in 1990, Sanders battled the claims of incumbent Republican Peter Smith that he would be ineffective as an independent. Sanders promised to enlist in the Democratic Caucus. But when he got to Washington, conservative Democrats opposed his admission, and even some liberals thought a socialist member would harm the party's image. In a compromise, he did not join the caucus but was given committee assignments by the Democrats.

Sanders has voted with Democrats against a majority of Republicans at least 92 percent of the time in each of the last three years. One split from the Democratic line was his vote against a five-day waiting period for handgun purchases, though he did support the ban on certain semiautomatic assault-style weapons in 1994.

While many Democrats have moved right in recent years, Sanders usually keeps to the left. In January 1995, he and his fellow members of the House Progressive Caucus, which he chairs, vowed to fight the House Republicans' "Contract With America." Sanders said the contract would "cause intense pain and suffering of tens of millions of people" by slashing programs for the poor and elderly. As an alternative, he called for cuts in military spending and increases in funds for programs aimed at helping the poor.

In the 104th Congress, he voted against the welfare overhaul bill signed by President Clinton, and against deregulating the telecommunications industry. His approval rating from the liberal Americans for Democratic Action never has dropped below 95 percent and was 100 percent in 1994, 1995 and 1996.

"We have seen in the last 20, 25 years a significant decline in the standard of living of working people, the collapse of the middle class," Sanders said in a March 1997 National Public Radio interview. "Who's talking for those people? Certainly not the Republican Party, which very overtly represents the wealthy and the powerful and, unfortunately, most members of the Democratic Party are not standing for working people either. You have seen in the United States Congress a strong drift to the right in both political parties. You have now a right-wing of the Republican Party which clearly controls that party, which is far further to the right than was the case 15 or 20 years ago; and you have a Democratic leadership now which, in some respects, might be considered to be liberal Republican."

Still, Sanders sometimes makes common cause with those to his right. For example, he teamed up with Rep. John R. Kasich, R-Ohio, in September 1996 to successfully block the reauthorization of the Overseas Private Investment Corporation and two other trade-promotion agencies. The vote was 157-260. And he joined Sen. Alfonse M. D'Amato, R-N.Y., to back legislation banning bank surcharges on automatic teller machines.

In the 105th, Sanders is trying to find allies across the aisle on issues such as defense spend-

VERMONT
At large

Some things about Vermont remain immutable. The least populous state in the Northeast and third-smallest in the nation, it has a scenic beauty that remains largely unsullied. However, a growth spurt of more than 44 percent since 1960 has driven Vermont's population to nearly 563,000. This growth has had a major impact on the state's demographics and politics.

The state has been hostile to some outside elements. Wal-Mart's attempt to build a store near Burlington ran into years of delays because opponents said the department store would put local retailers out of business. The store finally opened in January 1997.

Much of Vermont's population increase stemmed from young urbanites who resettled here and brought with them their liberal politics. These upscale émigrés joined remnants of the 1960s counterculture who had settled in the state in the early '70s, and a state that had been drifting to the political left became firmly planted there.

Shattered by these developments was Vermont's reputation as the sturdiest bastion of Yankee Republicanism. Democrat Patrick J. Leahy, first elected to the Senate in 1974, won a fourth term in 1992. Democrat Howard Dean retained the governorship that year with 75 percent, the largest Democratic gubernatorial victory in state history. He was re-elected in 1994 with 69 percent and won a third full term in 1996 with 71 percent.

Dean, as lieutenant governor, inherited the top job in 1991 upon the death of GOP Gov. Richard A. Snelling. Dean has a consensus-oriented style and enough of an image as a moderate that his winning coalitions have included many centrist Republicans.

Though the new politics of Vermont has seen the Democratic Party grow in strength, moderate Republicans can still gain and hold statewide office. In 1988, moderate Republican James M. Jeffords — then the state's at-large House member — won the Senate campaign to succeed like-minded Republican Robert T. Stafford. In 1990, Snelling, who was governor from 1977 to 1985, regained the office by pledging fiscal responsibility in the midst of a state budget crisis. Although Snelling's death put the governorship in Democratic hands, his widow, Barbara, ran for lieutenant governor in 1992 as a Republican and won easily, but she had a closer call in 1994.She took on Dean in 1996 but left the race in June after suffering a stroke.

There is a vocal conservative element within the state GOP — the Vermont Republican Assembly — but it is widely perceived as too far to the right to thrive in general elections. The conservatives, however, sometimes can turn out enough loyalists to take primary nominations away from moderates, who are not always as effective at grass-roots organizing.

Although Vermont has moved away from its historical voting patterns, its modern political persona retains an element of the state's stubborn independence. In 1992, nearly a quarter of the Vermonters voting for president picked independent Ross Perot. He dipped to 12 percent in 1996. And in the House, the state is represented by self-described socialist Sanders.

In his 1990 House campaign, Sanders succeeded in portraying moderate GOP Rep. Peter Smith as a big-business shill and tool of the Establishment. Sanders' populist message fueled his rise, but his credibility was enhanced by his tenure as mayor of Burlington, where during the 1980s he shepherded the state's largest city through a period of prosperity.

Although its manufacturing heritage has faded, Burlington (population about 39,000) prospered in the 1980s mainly from a boom in its electronics industry. However, Burlington went through the same economic slump in the early 1990s as did all of New England. The Burlington area was jarred by large-scale layoffs at companies such as Digital Electronics Corp., which eventually closed down its operations. Statewide, both the construction and manufacturing industries have seen a steady decline in jobs in recent years.

Replacing manufacturing jobs is lower-paying employment in the service industry. State officials have tried to fill the vacuum by attempting to make tourism more of a year-round source of income by marketing Vermont as more than just an appealing ski-season destination for visitors.

Politically, Burlington and Chittenden County cast about one-fourth of the state's vote; Democratic candidates for statewide office can usually count on strong support here. Bill Clinton won 57 percent of the vote in Chittenden County in 1996, his best showing in the state.

Other small urban centers such as Montpelier and Rutland, reliably Republican in bygone times, now have more Democrats.

At the village level and in most rural areas, Yankee Vermonters still tend to vote Republican, particularly in the northeastern part of the state, which has been less affected by development.

1990 Population: 562,758. White 555,088 (99%), Black 1,951 (<1%), Other 5,719 (1%). Hispanic origin 3,661 (<1%). 18 and over 419,675 (75%), 62 and over 79,608 (14%). Median age: 33.

ing, the environment and federal subsidies for industry. "The issues we are talking about are making sense with mainstream America," Sanders told The Boston Globe in March 1997. "We are on a roll."

Sanders sparked a heated exchange on the House floor in May 1995 during a debate on water discharges from Navy nuclear facilities. Randy "Duke" Cunningham, R-Calif., a former Navy fighter pilot, said the proposal was supported by "the same people that would vote to cut defense $177 billion, the same ones that would put homos in the military." When Sanders demanded that Cunningham yield for a response, Cunningham retorted, "No, I will not. Sit down, you socialist."

The battle was joined by openly gay member Barney Frank, D-Mass. Cunningham responded: "I used the shorthand term, and it should have been homosexuals instead of homos. We do misspeak sometimes."

At Home: Sanders in 1996 prevailed over two major-party opponents, defeating Republican state Sen. Susan Sweetser and Democrat Jack Long, a lawyer. The national Democratic Party did not welcome Long's entry into the race. In recent years, the Democrats had not fielded serious opposition to Sanders, to avoid splitting Vermont's liberal vote and electing a Republican. Long took 9 percent of the vote, but Sweetser got only 33 percent, and Sanders won a fourth term with 55 percent.

Sanders' initial 1990 win culminated a 20-year effort that moved him from the fringe to the vortex of Vermont politics. In 1968, Sanders joined a wave of liberals abandoning urban life for bucolic Vermont. Many of the transplants joined the then-small state Democratic Party and helped convert it into a force capable of winning statewide elections. However, Sanders considered both major parties to be dominated by corporate interests and accused them of ignoring the needs of the poor, the elderly and working Americans. He helped found Vermont's Liberty Union Party.

Sanders' confrontational style brought him attention, but also a reputation as a gadfly. Yet Sanders was building a grass-roots base in Burlington. In 1981, he ran for mayor and unseated the Democratic incumbent by 10 votes. He won three more terms by increasing margins. He pursued populist goals but also presided over the revitalization of Burlington's downtown.

Sanders was seen as a spoiler when he ran in 1988 for the open House seat. But independent Sanders lost to the GOP's Smith by only 4 points. A rematch came two years later. With Sanders gaining momentum in the final weeks of the campaign, Smith ran "attack" TV ads, one of which used an old quote out of context to imply that Sanders admired Fidel Castro. Vermont media blasted Smith's negativism, and Sanders surged past him to win with 56 percent.

He was comfortably re-elected in 1992 against Tim Philbin, a favorite of the state GOP's conservative wing, but barely held on in 1994. After a slow start, Sanders' foe, GOP state Sen. John Carroll, closed fast and lost by only 3 points.

HOUSE ELECTIONS

1996 General		
Bernard Sanders (I)	140,678	(55%)
Susan Sweetser (R)	83,021	(33%)
Jack Long (D)	23,830	(9%)
Thomas J. Morse (LIBERT)	2,693	(1%)
1994 General		
Bernard Sanders (I)	105,502	(50%)
John Carroll (R)	98,523	(47%)
Carole Banus (NL)	2,963	(1%)
Jack "Buck" Rogers (VG)	2,664	(1%)

Previous Winning Percentages: 1992 (58%) **1990** (56%)

CAMPAIGN FINANCE

	Receipts	Receipts from PACs	Expenditures
1996			
Sanders (I)	$1,016,297	$220,168 (22%)	$942,438
Sweetser (R)	$572,981	$204,164 (36%)	$572,021
Long (D)	$8,504	0	$8,504
1994			
Sanders (I)	$608,145	$154,150 (25%)	$603,963
Carroll (R)	$393,069	$80,606 (21%)	$387,767

DISTRICT VOTE FOR PRESIDENT

	1996		1992
D	137,894 (53%)	**D**	133,592 (46%)
R	80,352 (31%)	**R**	88,122 (31%)
I	31,024 (12%)	**I**	65,991 (23%)

KEY VOTES

1997	
Ban "partial-birth" abortions	N
1996	
Approve farm bill	N
Deny public education to illegal immigrants	N
Repeal ban on certain assault-style weapons	N
Increase minimum wage	Y
Freeze defense spending	Y
Approve welfare overhaul	N
1995	
Approve balanced-budget constitutional amendment	N
Relax Clean Water Act regulations	N
Oppose limits on environmental regulations	Y
Reduce projected Medicare spending	N
Approve GOP budget with tax and spending cuts	N

VOTING STUDIES*

	Presidential Support		Party Unity		Conservative Coalition	
Year	S	O	S	O	S	O
1996	75	25	93	5	14	86
1995	87	11	95	3	2	96
1994	73	27	92	4	11	89
1993	67	32	88	5	11	86
1992	11	88	86	7	8	92
1991	22	77	84	8	14	86

* *These scores computed as if Sanders voted as a Democrat.*

INTEREST GROUP RATINGS

Year	ADA	AFL-CIO	CCUS	ACU
1996	100	n/a	19	0
1995	100	100	13	8
1994	100	100	33	0
1993	95	100	0	13
1992	95	100	13	0
1991	95	100	10	15

VIRGINIA

Governor: George F. Allen (R)
First elected: 1993.
Length of term: 4 years
Term expires: 1/98
Salary: $110,000 (returns 10% annually)
Term limit: Cannot serve 2 consecutive terms.
Phone: (804) 786-2211
Born: March 8, 1952; Whittier, Calif.
Education: U. of Virginia, B.A. 1974, J.D. 1977.
Occupation: Lawyer.
Family: Wife, Susan Brown; two children.
Religion: Presbyterian.
Political Career: Republican nominee for Va. House, 1979; Va. House, 1982-90; U.S. House, 1991-93.

Lt. Gov.: Donald S. Beyer Jr. (D)
First elected: 1989
Length of term: 4 years
Term expires: 1/98
Salary: $32,000 + $10,200 in per diem
Phone: (804) 786-2078

State election official: (804) 786-6551
Democratic headquarters: (804) 644-1966
Republican headquarters: (804) 780-0111

REDISTRICTING

Virginia gained one House seat in reapportionment, increasing from 10 districts to 11. The legislature passed the map Dec. 9, 1991; the governor signed it Dec. 11. The Justice Department approved the map Feb. 18, 1992; it approved a new map containing minor changes Aug. 10, 1993.

STATE LEGISLATURE

General Assembly. Meets January-February in odd years, January-March in even years.

Senate: 40 members, 4-year terms
1996 breakdown: 20D, 20R; 33 men, 7 women
Salary: $18,000
Phone: (804) 786-2366

House of Delegates: 100 members, 2-year terms
1996 breakdown: 52D, 47R, 1I; 86 men, 14 women
Salary: $17,640
Phone: (804) 786-6530

URBAN STATISTICS

City	Population
Virginia Beach	393,089
Mayor Meyera E. Oberndorf, N-P	
Norfolk	261,250
Mayor Paul D. Fraim, D	
Richmond	202,798
Mayor Larry E. Chavis, N-P	
Newport News	171,439
Mayor Joe Frank, N-P	
Chesapeake	151,976
Mayor William E. Ward, N-P	

U.S. CONGRESS

Senate: 1 D, 1 R
House: 6 D, 5 R

TERM LIMITS

For state offices: No

ELECTIONS

1996 Presidential Vote

Bob Dole	47%
Bill Clinton	45%
Ross Perot	7%

1992 Presidential Vote

George Bush	45%
Bill Clinton	41%
Ross Perot	14%

1988 Presidential Vote

George Bush	60%
Michael S. Dukakis	39%

POPULATION

1990 population		6,187,358
1980 population		5,346,818
Percent change		+16%
Rank among states:		12
White		77%
Black		19%
Hispanic		3%
Asian or Pacific islander		3%
Urban		69%
Rural		31%
Born in state		54%
Foreign-born		5%
Under age 18	1,504,738	24%
Ages 18-64	4,018,150	65%
65 and older	664,470	11%
Median age		32.6

MISCELLANEOUS

Capital: Richmond
Number of counties: 95
Per capita income: $19,976 (1991)
Rank among states: 12
Total area: 40,767 sq. miles
Rank among states: 36

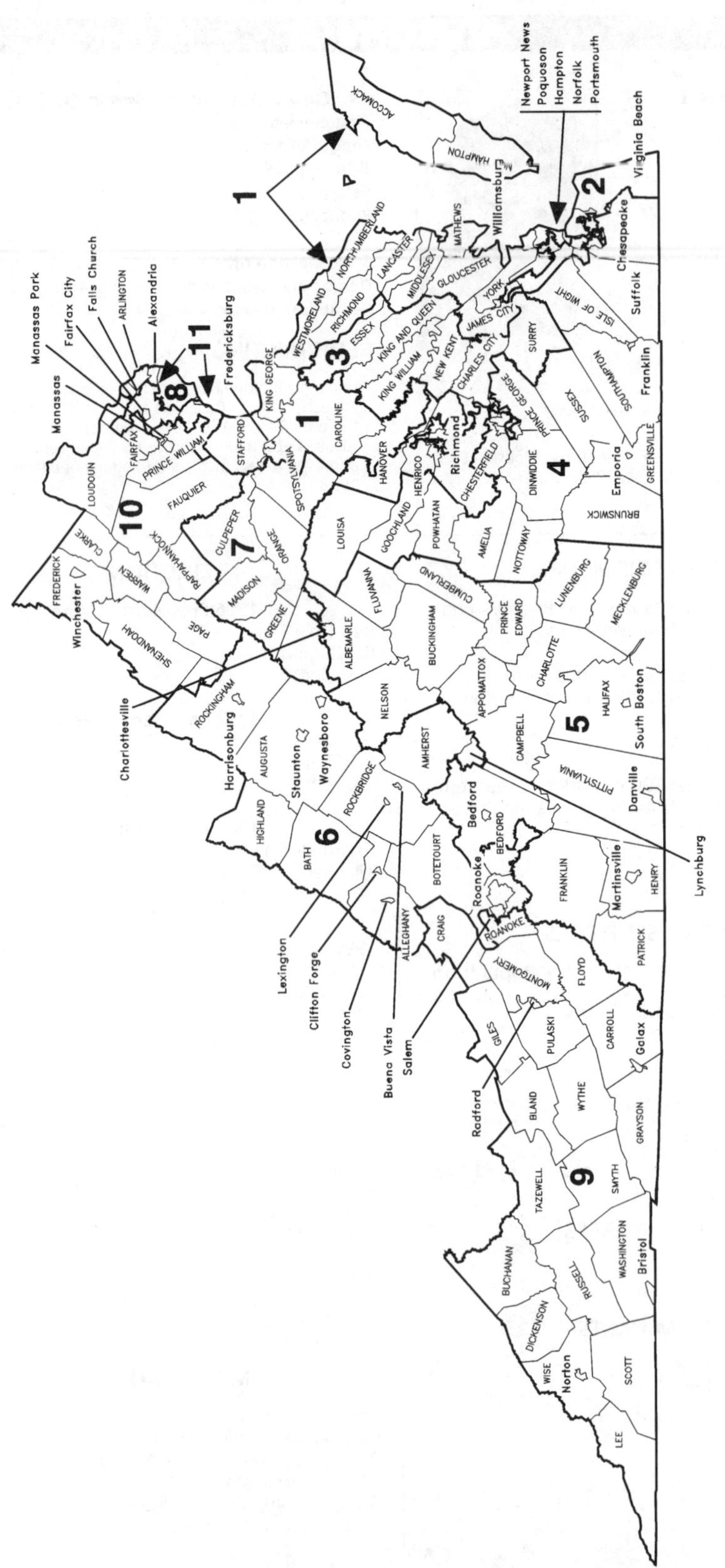

1
2
3
4
5
6
7
8
9
10
11
ACCOMACK
NORTHAMPTON
Newport News
Poquoson
Hampton
Norfolk
Portsmouth
Virginia Beach
Chesapeake
Suffolk
Franklin
Williamsburg
NORTHUMBERLAND
LANCASTER
MATHEWS
MIDDLESEX
GLOUCESTER
YORK
JAMES CITY
WESTMORELAND
RICHMOND
ESSEX
KING AND QUEEN
KING WILLIAM
NEW KENT
CHARLES CITY
SURRY
ISLE OF WIGHT
SOUTHAMPTON
SUSSEX
PRINCE GEORGE
KING GEORGE
CAROLINE
HANOVER
HENRICO
Richmond
CHESTERFIELD
DINWIDDIE
Emporia
GREENSVILLE
BRUNSWICK
Manassas Park
Fairfax City
Falls Church
ARLINGTON
Alexandria
Manassas
Fredericksburg
STAFFORD
SPOTSYLVANIA
FAIRFAX
PRINCE WILLIAM
LOUDOUN
FAUQUIER
CULPEPER
ORANGE
LOUISA
GOOCHLAND
POWHATAN
AMELIA
NOTTOWAY
LUNENBURG
MECKLENBURG
FREDERICK
CLARKE
WARREN
RAPPAHANNOCK
MADISON
GREENE
FLUVANNA
CUMBERLAND
PRINCE EDWARD
Winchester
SHENANDOAH
PAGE
ALBEMARLE
BUCKINGHAM
CHARLOTTE
HALIFAX
South Boston
Charlottesville
ROCKINGHAM
NELSON
APPOMATTOX
CAMPBELL
PITTSYLVANIA
Danville
Harrisonburg
AUGUSTA
Staunton
Waynesboro
AMHERST
ROCKBRIDGE
Bedford
BEDFORD
Lynchburg
HIGHLAND
BATH
BOTETOURT
FRANKLIN
Martinsville
HENRY
Lexington
Clifton Forge
Covington
Buena Vista
Salem
ALLEGHANY
CRAIG
Roanoke
ROANOKE
MONTGOMERY
FLOYD
PATRICK
GILES
PULASKI
CARROLL
Galax
Radford
BLAND
WYTHE
GRAYSON
TAZEWELL
SMYTH
BUCHANAN
RUSSELL
WASHINGTON
Bristol
DICKENSON
WISE
Norton
SCOTT
LEE

John W. Warner (R)

Of Alexandria — Elected 1978; 4th term

Biographical Information
Born: Feb. 18, 1927, Washington, D.C.
Education: Washington and Lee U., B.S. 1949; U. of Virginia, LL.B. 1953.
Military Service: Navy, 1944-46; Marine Corps, 1950-52.
Occupation: Lawyer; farmer.
Family: Divorced; three children.
Religion: Episcopalian.
Political Career: Assistant U.S. attorney, 1956-60; under secretary of the Navy, 1969-72; secretary of the Navy, 1972-74.
Capitol Office: 225 Russell Bldg. 20510; 224-2023.

Committees
Special Aging
Armed Services
Airland Forces; Seapower (chairman); Strategic Forces
Environment & Public Works
Drinking Water, Fisheries & Wildlife; Superfund, Waste Control & Risk Assessment; Transportation & Infrastructure (chairman)
Labor & Human Resources
Aging; Employment & Training
Rules & Administration (chairman)
Small Business
Joint Library (chairman)
Joint Printing (chairman)

In Washington: As the 105th Congress was getting under way, Warner enjoyed a ceremonial place of prominence on the platform at Bill Clinton's second inauguration, where, as chairman of the Senate Rules and Administration Committee, he had presiding-officer responsibilities.

Warner's presence on the dais was symbolic of his improved standing in the Senate. When the GOP took over the chamber in 1995, Warner was on the outs with his home-state party and one of the few senior Republicans without the chairmanship of a full committee.

But in the 105th, Warner not only chairs Rules but also two key subcommittees of other panels where he is the second-ranking Republican. The former Navy secretary controls the Armed Services Seapower Subcommittee, where he can attend to the shipbuilding interests that are a significant part of the Virginia economy. He is also in charge of the Environment and Public Works Transportation and Infrastructure Subcommittee, where he will get the first swing in the Senate at rewriting the nation's major surface transportation law, which is up for reauthorization.

The Transportation Subcommittee marked up a bill during the 104th that designated about 160,000 miles of well-traveled roads as a new National Highway System. Warner opposed some provisions of the law that eroded federal safety requirements, but when the measure passed the Senate in June 1995, he was happy to tack on $97.6 million for a bridge project at the southern tip of Washington, D.C., connecting Maryland and Virginia.

Warner wants to boost highway spending by at least $5 billion per year so that most states can receive increases in their allotments, even as the surface transportation program's funding formula is changed. He opposes taking highway funds out of the general budget, which would increase the amount of dollars available for transportation, but he is helping lead the charge to change the highway trust fund formula, which grants many Southern and Western states fewer dollars than they pay into the program in gasoline taxes.

He tried to make room for more highway funding when the Senate in May 1997 took up the fiscal 1998 budget deal crafted by Clinton and congressional Republicans. Warner offered an amendment to increase transportation funding by $12 billion over five years, but his effort fell short when the Senate tabled it, 51-49.

Warner has been a shrewd defender of his state's fiscal interests. In 1996, Warner, who was a leader in the successful GOP maneuvering to add billions to Clinton's defense requests, saw to it that $1.1 billion was authorized for nuclear reactors and other components of an aircraft carrier to be built by Newport News Shipbuilding, a major Virginia employer. The Navy had planned to request the funding three years hence, but Warner seemed pleased to take credit for the shift: "There you see the faint fingerprints of J. Warner," he purred to a reporter.

Such efforts, along with Warner's attempts to ensure Northern Virginia federal employees could return to work during a pair of government shutdowns, were centerpieces of his contentious 1996 re-election bid.

Warner, a prototypical establishment conservative, was propelled into the role of rebel in Virginia's 1994 Senate race after the GOP nomination went to Iran-contra figure Oliver L. North. Warner deemed North unsuitable for the Senate and instead backed an independent candidate, a move that earned him the lasting enmity of conservative religious activists who were fervent North supporters. North ultimately lost to Democratic Sen. Charles S. Robb.

Warner's apostasy did not sit well with some devoutly conservative GOP senators, and although Warner did not meet with overt retaliation when the 104th Congress was getting organized, his ambition to be Rules Committee chairman was thwarted by Ted Stevens, R-Alaska. Warner argued that he had more continuous service on Rules than Stevens, and thus should get the chairmanship. But in a December 1994 vote, Senate Republicans decided that Stevens should be chairman because his two separate stints on Rules gave him more seniority than Warner.

In the fall of 1995, Warner finally got to wield the gavel of a full committee, thanks to the resignation of Oregon Republican Bob Packwood. Packwood's Finance chair went to William V. Roth Jr., R-Del., Stevens moved into Roth's chair at the Governmental Affairs Committee and the top seat on Rules fell to Warner.

Warner has long been a visible player on the Armed Services Committee. He was the top Republican there from 1987 to 1993 but was bumped to the No. 2 position in the 103rd by Sen. Strom Thurmond of South Carolina, who had more seniority. The move by Thurmond, a harder-edged conservative than Warner, was hailed by the activist right wing of the GOP Conference, which took umbrage at Warner's genial partnership with the former chairman, Sam Nunn, D-Ga. Thurmond became chairman in the 104th.

Early in the 104th, Warner and Trent Lott of Mississippi, who was then GOP whip and sits on Armed Services, made a feint at easing Thurmond out of the chairmanship. Thurmond responded quickly to the putsch, which may have been mainly an effort to gain more power for the subcommittee chairmen. "I'm optimistic the subcommittees are going to be strengthened," said Warner.

Some critics viewed Warner's top rank on Armed Services with skepticism from the start. Though well-educated and grounded in defense issues, Warner came to the Senate with a reputation as more socialite than erudite: He was married for a time to actress Elizabeth Taylor.

The turning point for Warner's relationship with the conservative camp came in early 1989, when the Senate's Democratic majority defeated John Tower's nomination as President George Bush's secretary of Defense. Although Warner was a friend and supporter of Tower — a Texas Republican and former Armed Services Committee chairman — several Republican senators blamed Warner for allowing Nunn to drag out the investigation of Tower's personal life.

Minority Leader Bob Dole sent a shot across the Navy man's bow: He gave Republican seats on Armed Services to such hard-line conservative members as Lott, Daniel R. Coats of Indiana and Robert C. Smith of New Hampshire. Warner initially appeared to take the message to heart. In March 1991, he led an aggressive challenge to the congressional position on the Strategic Defense Initiative anti-ballistic missile system, which Nunn had helped develop.

The issue was revisited during the 104th, with Warner and William S. Cohen, R-Maine, negotiating with Nunn and Democrat Carl Levin of Michigan, but from a new position of strength. With the GOP prodding the White House to step up deployment of a limited national anti-missile defense system, Warner grew more partisan on defense issues. The group crafted a compromise amendment during hours of closed-door negotiations to leave intact the $626 million the bill added to Clinton's anti-missile program request. And it put into law a forceful statement of the potential value of deploying missile defenses large enough to require amendment of the Anti-Ballistic Missile Treaty. "We address the clear intention of the United States to deploy," Warner declared.

Before the start of the 104th, Warner took a more aggressive stance on Pentagon funding, joining Sen. John McCain, R-Ariz., in calling for a $15 billion addition to Clinton's planned fiscal 1996 request. In a letter to Clinton in December 1994, Warner and McCain decried "the litany of readiness problems disclosed in recent weeks," as well as administration plans to cut funding for some weapons programs. But other than advocating a more robust anti-missile defense, McCain and Warner were more specific about what they wanted cut out of the defense budget — non-defense programs and pork — than about what they wanted to put back in.

Nevertheless, congressional Republicans succeeded in tacking on several billion dollars to each of Clinton's defense budgets during the 104th.

Aside from his Transportation Subcommittee chairmanship, Warner also moved in the 104th from the Intelligence Committee to the Agriculture, Nutrition, and Forestry Committee, where he supported the rewrite of farm law to ease away from crop subsidies. (He left the panel for the 105th.)

At Home: Warner's record is, by most standards, conservative, but throughout his career he has cast scattered votes on arts, education, civil rights and tax issues, and Republican presidential appointees (including Tower and Supreme Court nominee Robert H. Bork, whom he opposed) that have angered staunch conservatives. But it was Warner's failure to support North and to back 1993 lieutenant governor nominee Michael P. Farris that finally earned him an intraparty challenge in 1996.

Warner was taken on by James C. "Jim" Miller III, a former budget director for President Ronald Reagan. Miller accused Warner of disloyalty to the party for not supporting North and Farris and for having voted for some Clinton initiatives. Warner managed to avoid a party convention that might have been dominated by conservative activists, taking advantage of a state law that allows incumbents to choose a primary over a convention. State Republican officials critical of Warner challenged that law in court but without success.

Miller lost the primary by 32 points, and his attacks may actually have helped Warner in the fall. Warner's Democratic challenger, cellular phone multimillionaire Mark Warner (no relation), began his campaign by stressing his vision for Virginia's future, high-tech economy. When that message fizzled, Mark Warner poured $10 million of his own into a blizzard of commercials linking the senator to unpopular spending reductions made or sought by the Republican Congress. But, despite the unusual strength of the national Democratic ticket in Virginia, Mark Warner found it nearly impossible to tag John Warner as a "cookie cutter" Republican.

John Warner's one misstep was to release an ad that included a doctored photo of his opponent. The consultant responsible was fired and Warner went on to win with 52 percent.

He was never the choice of conservatives in the Virginia GOP. He became the party's Senate nominee in 1978 only after their pick, Richard Obenshain, died in a plane crash two months after defeating Warner at the state convention.

Republicans needed a nominee, and Warner, the runner-up in June, was the obvious choice. He had courted the convention delegates with a lavish campaign costing nearly $500,000, and attracted enough votes to force six ballots before being defeated. He had also been a good loser and backed Obenshain afterward.

Warner brought to the fall campaign the same assets he had in June: personal wealth and a statewide reputation, achieved not only as Navy secretary under President Richard M. Nixon and chief Bicentennial planner under President Gerald R. Ford, but also as Taylor's husband.

He also had liabilities. Despite his Virginia education, he was looked upon as an outsider. Some voters also saw him as a socialite and fortune hunter. Before he married Taylor, he was married to heiress Catherine Mellon and received a reported $7 million from her in their divorce settlement.

But Warner's celebrity wife turned out to be a help to him. Taylor's presence on the campaign trail guaranteed large crowds, and when she proved willing to voice her enthusiasm for conservative causes, Virginia Republicans cheered her on. The Democratic nominee, former state Attorney General Andrew Miller, was seeking to recover from a defeat in the 1977 gubernatorial primary by the state's best-known liberal Democrat, Henry E. Howell. In 1978 Miller campaigned for the Senate as a fiscal conservative, but Warner tied him to the Democratic Party of Howell, and Miller never managed to extricate himself. Warner won by fewer than 5,000 votes in the closest Senate election in Virginia history.

Six years later, Warner was in a totally different type of contest, winning re-election by more than 805,000 votes in a race that was a mismatch from the beginning. Then-Gov. Charles S. Robb led the search for a suitable Democratic challenger, but Warner helped to discourage the effort by raising more than $1 million by the end of 1983. The nomination went by default to former state Rep. Edythe C. Harrison. A longtime ally of the liberal Howell, she was given lukewarm support by much of her own party. Warner swept all but two of the state's 95 counties and all 41 independent cities.

SENATE ELECTIONS

1996 General		
John W. Warner (R)	1,235,744	(52%)
Mark Warner (D)	1,115,982	(47%)
1996 Primary		
John W. Warner (R)	323,520	(66%)
James C. "Jim" Miller III (R)	170,015	(34%)

Previous Winning Percentages: 1990 (81%) **1984** (70%) **1978** (50%)

CAMPAIGN FINANCE

	Receipts	Receipts from PACs	Expend-itures
1996			
Warner (R)	$5,033,390	$1,601,460 (32%)	$5,196,091
Warner (D)	$11,625,483	$1,250 (0%)	$11,600,424

KEY VOTES

1997	
Approve balanced-budget constitutional amendment	Y
Approve chemical weapons treaty	Y
1996	
Approve farm bill	Y
Limit punitive damages in product liability cases	Y
Exempt small businesses from higher minimum wage	Y
Approve welfare overhaul	Y
Bar job discrimination based on sexual orientation	N
Override veto of ban on "partial birth" abortions	Y
1995	
Approve GOP budget with tax and spending cuts	Y
Approve constitutional amendment barring flag desecration	Y

VOTING STUDIES

	Presidential Support		Party Unity		Conservative Coalition	
Year	**S**	**O**	**S**	**O**	**S**	**O**
1996	42	58	93	7	89	11
1995	25	72	93	6	93	5
1994	58	39	76	23	84	16
1993	28	71	78	19	85	12
1992	67	25	86	13	79	21
1991	89	11	82	18	95	5

INTEREST GROUP RATINGS

Year	ADA	AFL-CIO	CCUS	ACU
1996	5	n/a	85	95
1995	5	0	100	91
1994	20	25	90	80
1993	10	9	91	84
1992	20	17	100	74
1991	20	25	80	76

Charles S. Robb (D)

Of McLean — Elected 1988, 2nd term

Biographical Information

Born: June 26, 1939, Phoenix, Ariz.

Education: Cornell U., 1957-58; U. of Wisconsin, B.B.A. 1961; U. of Virginia, J.D. 1973.

Military Service: Marine Corps, 1961-70; Marine Corps Reserves, 1970-91.

Occupation: Lawyer.

Family: Wife, Lynda Johnson; three children.

Religion: Episcopalian.

Political Career: Lieutenant governor, 1978-82; governor, 1982-86.

Capitol Office: 154 Russell Bldg. 20510; 224-4024.

Committees

Armed Services
Personnel; Readiness (ranking); Seapower

Foreign Relations
East Asian & Pacific Affairs; Near Eastern & South Asian Affairs (ranking); Western Hemisphere, Peace Corps, Narcotics and Terrorism

Select Intelligence

Joint Economic

In Washington: Before Bill Clinton arrived on the scene to lead the Democrats down a centrist path to the White House, many in the party looked to Robb to do just that.

After the disappointing Dukakis collapse in 1988, when yet another liberal Democrat fell to the Republican presidential juggernaut, the center-right faction of the Democratic Party began to talk of the kind of candidate who could win in 1992. Robb seemed to some to be the most promising of the "new Democrats."

A popular ex-governor from a conservative Southern state, Robb was fiscally conservative and tough on defense, but fairly liberal for a Southerner on social issues such as minority rights and abortion. He was a founding member of the Democratic Leadership Council, a square-jawed ex-Marine and the husband of politically outgoing Lynda Johnson Robb, the daughter of President Lyndon B. Johnson.

But a series of embarrassing ethical mishaps in the early 1990s dashed Robb's prospects for the presidency, and the political damage was so severe that he even faced the possibility of losing re-election to the Senate in 1994.

Yet in one of the few bright spots for Democrats that year, Robb won a second term, taking a 46 percent plurality against another ex-Marine, Republican Oliver L. North, and independent candidate J. Marshall Coleman.

The fall from national grace and the escape from political near-death in 1994 have had an interesting impact on Robb's behavior in the Senate. Early in his career in the chamber, Robb was seen as a cautious figure who calibrated the political impact of every move. Of late, though, he has taken high-profile stands on some controversial issues — defending the lifting of a ban on homosexuals serving in the military, for instance, and opposing a constitutional amendment banning flag-burning.

These are risky positions for a Virginia politician, considering the state's sizable bloc of "traditional values" voters. Robb's willingness to take such stands has raised questions about whether he intends to seek a third Senate term in 2000, when the state's popular GOP Gov. George F. Allen (who leaves office in 1998) is seen as a potential Senate candidate.

The turning point of Robb's political career came in the 102nd Congress, when a two-year rash of embarrassing publicity raised serious questions about the Virginian's personal and political ethics. For Robb, who had built his career above all on a straight-arrow image, the harm was enough to scratch his name from the list of White House possibilities.

In March 1991, Tai Collins, a former Virginia beauty queen, went public with claims that she had been romantically involved with Robb (she later posed nude for Playboy magazine).

The NBC-TV program that broadcast Collins' charges also rekindled rumors — which first surfaced during his 1988 Senate campaign and were denied by Robb — that then-Gov. Robb had attended beachfront parties during the mid-1980s with friends who were under investigation on suspicion of cocaine trafficking.

Then in June 1991, newspapers published transcripts — leaked by Robb's Senate aides — of an illegally taped telephone call between Virginia Democratic Gov. L. Douglas Wilder and an associate. An electronics buff and Robb ally coincidentally intercepted a 1988 car phone conversation. In it, then-Lt. Gov. Wilder was heard stating with apparent satisfaction that Robb's career would be ruined by the rumors of his partying with drug users. Robb's office leaked the tape in a backfired scheme to show that those rumors were spread by Robb's political enemies, including Wilder.

Over the next year and a half, three top Robb aides were convicted under wiretapping laws for their possession of the tape. Robb, who claimed just a tangential connection to the tape, was accused in one aide's guilty plea of having knowledge of the tape and its illegal origin, and the senator endured an 18-month federal investigation during which he twice testified before a grand jury.

Robb did not regain his footing until January 1993 (at the start of the 103rd Congress), when the grand jury in Norfolk decided not to indict him on conspiracy and obstruction of justice charges relating to the Wilder tape.

Robb labored to overcome the skepticism of many Virginians over his explanations of these events: that he had wine and a massage with Tai Collins in a New York hotel room, but no sexual relations; that he was aware for some time of the Wilder tape, but its possible illegality occurred to him much later; that he saw no evidence that any of his companions on the Virginia Beach party scene were unsavory characters.

The series of scandals dashed any hopes Robb had of developing a national constituency in his role as chairman of the Democratic Senatorial Campaign Committee (DSCC). He lowered his profile in that role after local news coverage of his visit on behalf of one Democratic candidate was dominated by Robb's own problems. Yet Robb worked doggedly behind the scenes as the DSCC raised a record amount of campaign cash for the 1992 elections.

Needing to step up his legislative agenda to counteract loss of personal prestige, Robb gained a seat on the Armed Services Committee at the start of the 103rd, to go with his existing assignments on the Foreign Relations and Commerce committees. It was a timely appointment, given the importance of military bases and defense industries to Virginia's economy and the corresponding threat of the ongoing defense spending reductions in the post-Cold War era. As chairman of the Foreign Relations East Asian and Pacific Affairs Subcommittee in the 103rd, Robb backed the Clinton administration's decision to lift a longstanding economic embargo against Vietnam.

In the 104th Congress, Robb crossed party lines several times to support Republican calls for extra defense funding that could benefit Virginia. He was one of four Democrats voting for the fiscal 1996 defense authorization bill, which authorized $7.1 billion more in spending than the Clinton administration requested.

With the Pentagon undertaking a top-to-bottom review of its military structure, Robb has lobbied Clinton for sustained levels of higher defense spending, arguing that the "peace dividend" from winning the Cold War already has been spent by bringing defense spending levels down to their lowest level since the years after World War II.

"We live in an era in which potential opponents . . . have or will have the mobility and firepower to exploit a U.S. diversion in another theater," Robb wrote in The Washington Post. "If the United States is engaging North Korea and has limited additional forces on hand, who is to deter the Iraqis from moving south again?"

On fiscal policy, Robb's support for a balanced-budget constitutional amendment puts him on the same side as the Senate GOP majority. In an attempt to break several budget logjams between Clinton and the Republican Congress, Robb has been an active member of a centrist coalition led by John H. Chafee, R-R.I., and John B. Breaux, D-La., that has crafted balanced-budget proposals that include middle-ground positions on entitlement spending and tax cuts, and that call for a recalculation of the Consumer Price Index, which some believe overestimates the rate of inflation.

Robb has concurred with Republicans on some issues important to the business community, including a measure to limit lawsuits by stock shareholders and some attempts to limit product liability damage awards. Also in the 104th he wooed moderate Democrats to support a regulatory relief package for small businesses.

But Robb has been willing to help Clinton on some touchy social policy issues. In September 1996 he backed the president's veto of a bill banning a particular abortion technique that opponents call "partial birth" abortion. And despite the prevalence of culturally conservative views in most parts of Virginia, Robb has gained a reputation for defending homosexuals' rights. He took a high-profile position against the Defense of Marriage Act, which permitted states to ignore legal same-sex marriages conducted in other states. He was one of only 14 Democrats voting in September 1996 against the bill, which even many liberal Democratic senators such as Minnesota's Paul Wellstone supported. Robb, explaining that he was striking a blow against discrimination, said, "If we don't stand here against this bill, we will stand on the wrong side of history."

Robb in January 1993 came out strongly in support of Clinton's proposal to end the ban on homosexuals serving in the military. (Even before Clinton took a position, Robb had written to Gen. Colin L. Powell Jr., then-chairman of the Joint Chiefs of Staff, urging that the ban be lifted.) Robb's 1994 re-election strategy included an appeal to more typically liberal Democrats, including homosexuals. Unlike many of his Southern-state colleagues, he campaigned on his support for lifting the ban.

Robb, a Vietnam War hero, said opponents of lifting the gay ban had legitimate reasons for concern. "The specter of drill sergeants dancing together is unsettling to say the least," Robb said. But he added, "We cannot let fear prevent patriotic Americans from serving in the armed forces."

Robb's military record and his image as hawkish on defense — in 1991 he strongly backed giving President George Bush authority to use force in the Persian Gulf — made him a helpful ally to Clinton when the president decided to send U.S. troops to enforce a peace agreement in Bosnia. The deployment was strongly criticized by conservatives in Congress, but Robb backed Clinton and accompanied him on a January 1996 visit to the troops.

At Home: The vertiginous drop of Robb's political career marked him as one of the most vulnerable Democratic incumbents seeking re-election in 1994. But Republicans picked a candidate even more sullied: North, the central figure in the Iran-contra scandal.

The contest received nationwide attention, partly because of the lurid background of the candidates and partly because of its historical significance. Until mid-September, it featured four candidates with statewide stature: In addition to Robb and North, Wilder (who earlier had pulled out of the Democratic primary) and former GOP state attorney general Coleman were running as independents.

A spellbinding speaker running his first political race, North waged an insurgent, anti-Washington campaign, setting himself against all those who populate the capital's corridors of power with a conservative message aimed at disaffected voters. North was strongly backed by the Christian conservative wing of the state Republican Party. He did not, however, enjoy support from all parts of the GOP. The state's senior senator, Republican John W. Warner, called him unfit to serve in the Senate and backed Coleman. A procession of former Reagan administration officials — topped by former first lady Nancy Reagan — asserted that North had a propensity to lie and exaggerate.

Robb got his biggest break when Wilder withdrew from the race on Sept. 15. For more than a month, Wilder refrained from endorsing Robb. But on Oct. 21, Wilder strongly endorsed his longtime rival and backed it up by campaigning at Robb's side through Election Day to try to ignite support for Robb among black voters. Robb finished at 46 percent, North at 43 percent and Coleman at 11 percent.

Though Robb's star has fallen lately, it is difficult to overstate the importance of his early political career to Democrats in Virginia. The collapse of the Old South Harry Byrd Democratic organization in the 1960s brought an era of Republican dominance at the statewide level. Party-switching was common. Before Robb, the state had elected three GOP governors in succession.

But then came Robb with an appealing war record and a high-profile marriage. Robb had left the Marines and gone to law school. After practicing law for four years, he was elected lieutenant governor in 1977. In 1981, he won the governorship.

In Richmond, Robb carefully built a reputation for fiscal conservatism with a human face. He appointed minorities and women to judgeships and other state posts. But such moves were made with a kind of square-jawed respectability. Robb seemed immune to the taint of liberalism.

State law barred a successive term, but Robb's popularity was talismanic enough in 1985 to help elect a slate of other Democrats — including the first black (Wilder) and also the first woman elected statewide in Virginia history (then-Attorney General Mary Sue Terry).

So popular was Robb after his governorship that he was all but conceded the Senate seat even before he announced for it. The mere belief that he would run was widely believed to have influenced Republican Paul S. Trible Jr.'s decision not to seek re-election in 1988. Although Virginia had not elected a Democrat to the Senate since 1966, polls in 1987 showed Robb running ahead of Trible.

Robb raised $3 million almost effortlessly. The GOP chose a candidate who seemed more of a political novelty than a serious contender, black minister Maurice A. Dawkins. Robb won with 71 percent of the vote.

SENATE ELECTIONS

1994 General		
Charles S. Robb (D)	938,376	(46%)
Oliver L. North (R)	882,213	(43%)
J. Marshall Coleman (I)	235,324	(11%)
1994 Primary		
Charles S. Robb (D)	154,561	(58%)
Virgil H. Goode Jr. (D)	90,547	(34%)
Sylvia Clute (D)	17,329	(6%)
Nancy Spannous (D)	4,507	(2%)

Previous Winning Percentages: 1988 (71%)

CAMPAIGN FINANCE

	Receipts	Receipts from PACs	Expend-itures
1994			
Robb (D)	$5,502,523	$1,272,597 (23%)	$5,501,697
North (R)	$20,770,879	$179,226 (1%)	$20,607,367
Coleman (I)	$811,004	$19,650 (2%)	$813,409

KEY VOTES

1997	
Approve balanced-budget constitutional amendment	Y
Approve chemical weapons treaty	Y
1996	
Approve farm bill	Y
Limit punitive damages in product liability cases	N
Exempt small businesses from higher minimum wage	N
Approve welfare overhaul	Y
Bar job discrimination based on sexual orientation	Y
Override veto of ban on "partial birth" abortions	N
1995	
Approve GOP budget with tax and spending cuts	N
Approve constitutional amendment barring flag desecration	N

VOTING STUDIES

	Presidential Support		Party Unity		Conservative Coalition	
Year	S	O	S	O	S	O
1996	85	15	76	24	79	21
1995	74	26	76	23	60	39
1994	85	15	81	18	44	53
1993	94	4	85	14	44	56
1992	42	58	74	26	50	50
1991	59	41	74	26	70	30

INTEREST GROUP RATINGS

Year	ADA	AFL-CIO	CCUS	ACU
1996	80	n/a	46	20
1995	95	75	58	13
1994	60	63	40	12
1993	75	82	36	12
1992	60	75	30	30
1991	60	67	10	43

1 Herbert H. Bateman (R)

Of Newport News — Elected 1982, 8th term

Biographical Information

Born: Aug. 7, 1928, Elizabeth City, N.C.

Education: College of William and Mary, B.A. 1949; Georgetown U., J.D. 1956.

Military Service: Air Force, 1951-53.

Occupation: Lawyer.

Family: Wife, Laura Yacobi; two children.

Religion: Protestant.

Political Career: Va. Senate, 1968-82; sought Republican nomination for U.S. House, 1976; sought Republican nomination for lieutenant governor, 1981.

Capitol Office: 2350 Rayburn Bldg. 20515; 225-4261.

Committees

National Security
Military Readiness (chairman); Military Research & Development

Transportation & Infrastructure
Surface Transportation; Water Resources & Environment

In Washington: As chairman of the National Security Subcommittee on Military Readiness, Bateman is right where he needs to be to protect the shipbuilding and other defense interests in his Tidewater district.

A conservative Republican and Air Force veteran from a constituency with a strong pro-military bent, Bateman makes no apologies for the National Security Committee's habit of increasing President Clinton's defense-spending requests. "As we hear complaints about this bill authorizing more than the president requested," he once said, "we should bear in mind that the Joint Chiefs of Staff have publicly indicated that the defense program of the president over the next four or five years is $40 billion to $60 billion deficient in the modernization accounts, which are absolutely essential."

Bateman particularly wants to protect defense funds for shipbuilding, as thousands of his constituents work for the Newport News Shipbuilding and Dry Dock Co., in the neighboring 3rd District. Bateman, along with Virginia Sen. John W. Warner and the two other Tidewater-area House members on National Security — Democrats Owen B. Pickett and Norman Sisisky — managed in the 104th to get a contract for Newport News to build two next-generation nuclear submarines.

The Navy originally intended to give General Dynamics' Electric Boat Division in Groton, Conn., the contract to build the first two ships of a new class of smaller, cheaper subs, arguing that building submarines is Electric Boat's sole line of work, whereas Newport News, the nation's only builder of aircraft carriers, can live off its other military and commercial contracts.

Bateman and the other Newport News supporters said it was "un-American" to give Electric Boat an exclusive role. But Electric Boat supporters dismissed Newport News' call for competition as disingenuous. The larger Virginia firm's high volume of other military business would allow it to underbid the more specialized Connecticut yard, they said. Electric Boat would be driven from the market, leaving Newport News with a monopoly.

Backers of the Newport News yard said that if it were shut out of submarine contracts for the next several years, its ability to compete in that field would atrophy, leaving Electric Boat as the sole sub supplier. "You don't end up with two nuclear-capable yards for building submarines," said Bateman. "You end up with one [yard], and it's the more costly."

Conferees on the fiscal 1996 defense authorization bill agreed that both Newport News and Electric Boat would build up to two of the new submarines. But then in early 1997, the shipyards announced that at the Navy's urging they would work cooperatively on the four new attack subs, rather than each shipyard building a separate ship.

Recognizing that the post-Cold War era is tough on builders of military vessels, Bateman has tried to ensure that commercial shipbuilding remains a viable domestic industry. As chairman of the National Security Committee's Merchant Marine Special Oversight panel — created after Republicans abolished the full Merchant Marine and Fisheries Committee at the start of the 104th — Bateman successfully amended a bill aimed at eliminating shipbuilding subsidies by the United States and 18 other countries.

In 1994, the United States reached an agreement with a group of European Union nations, Norway, South Korea and Japan that was designed to bar governments from subsidizing their shipbuilders. In the 104th, the House approved, 278-149, a Bateman amendment to delay implementation of some sections of the agreement and modify others in order to maintain a higher level of federal support for the U.S. shipbuilding industry.

Opponents of the amendment argued that it would scuttle the international agreement. But Bateman said the agreement was flawed because it included no provisions to protect U.S. shipbuilding while the agreement got under way. "Our trade representative came back after he signed

VIRGINIA 1
East — Parts of Newport News and Hampton; Fredericksburg

The vulture-shaped 1st swoops from its perch in the Hampton Roads area in southeastern Virginia to the Middle Peninsula and Northern Neck, wings north into the Washington exurbs in Stafford County and pokes a beak into Richmond's northern suburbs. It also soars across the Chesapeake Bay to include Accomack and Northampton counties on Virginia's Eastern Shore, which adjoins Maryland.

Republicans perform well in the 1st. George Bush got 50 percent here in 1992, winning the district by 16 percentage points. Four years later, Bob Dole got 52 percent and won the district by 12 percentage points. Republican Oliver L. North outpolled Sen. Charles S. Robb by more than 13,000 votes in 1994.

About 40 percent of the 1st's population is in the Peninsula area between Williamsburg and Hampton. The Newport News Shipbuilding and Dry Dock Co., the state's largest private employer, is not in the 1st — redistricting in 1991 moved it into the 3rd — but many of its 25,000 employees live in the 1st, entwining the economic vitality of many district residents with the shipyard's. The shipyard will be working with its main competitor, Connecticut-based Electric Boat Corp., to build four of the next-generation attack submarines for the Navy.

Colonial Virginia and its plantation economy were centered in the rural inland counties of the Middle Peninsula (bracketed by the York and Rappahannock rivers), the Northern Neck (between the Rappahannock and the Potomac) and along the bay. For generations, fishing, oystering and crabbing have sustained the economy of the counties along the bay. Corn, soybeans and wheat are important to the inland areas. Accomack County farmers raise chickens for processing in the many plants along the Delmarva (Delaware-Maryland-Virginia) Peninsula. Virginia's wine country reaches into the Northern Neck and Eastern Shore.

Tourism is also important in "America's First District," as Bateman calls it. Several sites recall Virginia's Colonial past, including Williamsburg, Jamestown and Yorktown. The plantation where George Washington was born is a national monument along the Potomac River in Westmoreland County, on the Northern Neck. Nearby is Stratford Hall, plantation home to four generations of Lees and the birthplace of Robert E. Lee. In Fredericksburg, the National Park Service runs a visitors center and offers tours on the Civil War battle.

The city of Fredericksburg and Stafford County represent the southern extreme of the Washington exurbs; bedroom communities sprouted during the 1980s, when Stafford's population grew by more than 50 percent. The Virginia Railway Express links commuters between Fredericksburg and Washington. While Fredericksburg frequently supports Democrats, Stafford usually votes Republican.

1990 Population: 562,757. White 452,378 (80%), Black 99,208 (18%), Other 11,171 (2%). Hispanic origin 8,492 (2%). 18 and over 420,218 (75%), 62 and over 80,075 (14%). Median age: 33.

this agreement in December and admitted to me that they had not even sought any transition provisions for this country's shipbuilders, even though the other parties to this agreement had been subsidized to the tune of as much as $8 billion a year when we were not subsidizing at all," Bateman told the House.

Although he is a reliable vote for his party, opposing all of Clinton's budget proposals and most of his social policy stands, Bateman did vote for two Clinton-backed gun control measures in the 103rd. And when the GOP-dominated House sought in March 1996 to repeal one of the measures, a ban on certain semiautomatic assault-style weapons, Bateman voted "no." Bateman also opposes a constitutional amendment limiting the terms of members of Congress.

Also in the 104th, he ended up backing the final version of a Democratic bill raising the minimum wage, although he voted against the measure the first time it went through the House and supported an effort to exempt small businesses from the increase.

Republicans' takeover of the House in 1995 caused Bateman to reconsider his November 1993 decision that the 104th Congress would be his last, and he won an eighth term in 1996 at age 68.

Bateman has endured a series of physical ailments in recent years. In July 1995, a routine examination revealed he had suffered a minor heart attack, and he missed almost 100 floor votes. In 1989, he had heart bypass surgery, and in 1992 he was treated for prostate cancer.

At Home: Bateman has been near the center of Newport News' civic and political life for decades. He ran for the state Senate in 1967 as a Democrat and won. He was re-elected three times, twice as a Democrat and once as a Republican.

But until 1982, Bateman was blunted in his tries for higher office; his strong support from Virginia's conservative political establishment was neutralized by a poor sense of timing. In early 1976, he switched parties with an eye on the Tidewater House seat of retiring Democratic Rep.

Thomas N. Downing. But Paul S. Trible Jr., a hard-working young county prosecutor, locked up the GOP nomination. In 1981, GOP leaders encouraged Bateman to run for lieutenant governor. But he was challenged by a religious fundamentalist and a young state legislator, and finished second at the GOP state convention.

The two rebuffs, coupled with his narrow state Senate re-election in 1979, seemed to make Bateman cautious about competing strenuously for higher office. When GOP officials in 1982 sought a House successor for Trible, who was running for the Senate, Bateman bluntly told them: "I'm a candidate if I'm the nominee." Bateman easily won the district convention.

His Democratic opponent was John McGlennon, a political science professor who stepped in after the original nominee withdrew. The switch probably doomed Democratic hopes, but it also seemed to make Bateman somewhat overconfident. He waged a haphazard campaign and won with a tepid 54 percent.

That result encouraged McGlennon to try again in 1984. But with President Ronald Reagan and GOP Sen. Warner both carrying the 1st with ease, Bateman took nearly 60 percent.

Democrats figured they still had a good chance to beat Bateman in 1986, when he would not have popular top-of-the-ticket help. But a challenger was slow to emerge. State Sen. Robert C. Scott finally entered, bidding to become the state's first black member of Congress since the late 19th century. Scott ran virtually even with Bateman in the urban Tidewater area, and carried the city of Hampton. But Bateman rolled up 60 percent in the rural portion of the 1st to win a third term. Now they are colleagues: Scott was elected in 1992 in the 3rd District.

In 1990, Bateman struggled against a political newcomer, Andrew H. Fox, a former TV reporter for Norfolk's NBC affiliate. Fox did not raise much money, but attracted an enthusiastic squad of volunteers. President George Bush's late-campaign denunciations of Iraqi leader Saddam Hussein may have shifted voters' attention and saved Bateman, who won by just 2,806 votes.

Fox tried again in 1992, this time not running on a shoestring. He was one of the leading congressional challengers in PAC receipts, and the National Rifle Association (NRA) also helped with an "independent expenditure" campaign targeted at Bateman. The incumbent did not try to maintain Fox's furious campaign pace, choosing instead to remind voters of his experience winning projects for the 1st. While Fox certainly contacted more people across the 1st, familiarity apparently did not breed affection: Bateman won by 19 points. In 1994, he soared to 74 percent.

In 1996, Bateman drew a GOP primary challenge from David L. Caprara, the former housing director of Virginia. He came at Bateman from the right, arguing that the incumbent was out of step with the Republican Party, citing his votes for gun control. Bateman won renomination with 80 percent, and he was unopposed in November.

HOUSE ELECTIONS

1996 General		
Herbert H. Bateman (R)	165,574	(99%)
1996 Primary		
Herbert H. Bateman (R)	49,548	(80%)
David L. Caprara (R)	12,636	(20%)
1994 General		
Herbert H. Bateman (R)	142,930	(74%)
Mary Sinclair (D)	45,173	(23%)
Matt B. Voorhees (I)	4,365	(2%)

Previous Winning Percentages: 1992 (58%) **1990** (51%) **1988** (73%) **1986** (56%) **1984** (59%) **1982** (54%)

CAMPAIGN FINANCE

	Receipts	Receipts from PACs	Expend-itures
1996			
Bateman (R)	$493,224	$218,359 (44%)	$534,156
1994			
Bateman (R)	$482,455	$176,156 (37%)	$423,501
Sinclair (D)	$85,413	$10,800 (13%)	$80,435

DISTRICT VOTE FOR PRESIDENT

1996		1992	
D	95,853 (40%)	**D**	81,826 (34%)
R	125,080 (52%)	**R**	120,131 (50%)
I	17,435 (7%)	**I**	39,307 (16%)

KEY VOTES

1997	
Ban "partial birth" abortions	Y
1996	
Approve farm bill	Y
Deny public education to illegal immigrants	Y
Repeal ban on certain assault-style weapons	N
Increase minimum wage	N
Freeze defense spending	N
Approve welfare overhaul	Y
1995	
Approve balanced-budget constitutional amendment	Y
Relax Clean Water Act regulations	Y
Oppose limits on environmental regulations	-
Reduce projected Medicare spending	Y
Approve GOP budget with tax and spending cuts	Y

VOTING STUDIES

	Presidential Support		Party Unity		Conservative Coalition	
Year	**S**	**O**	**S**	**O**	**S**	**O**
1996	39	57	89	9	94	4
1995	20	63	80	6	78	1
1994	60	40	67	30	86	14
1993	50	46	70	25	93	7
1992	81	17	70	28	83	17
1991	82	17	69	26	86	11

INTEREST GROUP RATINGS

Year	ADA	AFL-CIO	CCUS	ACU
1996	15	n/a	94	85
1995	5	0	88	62
1994	10	22	92	90
1993	5	8	100	92
1992	10	17	88	84
1991	10	17	100	80

2 Owen B. Pickett (D)

Of Virginia Beach — Elected 1986, 6th term

Biographical Information

Born: Aug. 31, 1930, Richmond, Va.

Education: Virginia Polytechnic Institute and State U., B.S. 1952; U. of Richmond, LL.B. 1955.

Occupation: Lawyer; accountant.

Family: Wife, Sybil Catherine Kelly; three children.

Religion: Baptist.

Political Career: Va. House, 1972-86; Va. Democratic Party chairman, 1980-82; Democratic National Committee, 1980-82; withdrew from campaign for Democratic nomination for U.S. Senate, 1982.

Capitol Office: 2430 Rayburn Bldg. 20515; 225-4215.

Committees

National Security
Military Personnel; Military Readiness; Military Research & Development (ranking)

Resources
Water & Power

In Washington: Now in his sixth term, Pickett continues to be one of the House's more low-key members, doing his job quietly. He votes the Democratic Party line on some high-profile social issues — supporting abortion rights, for instance — and in 1996 he backed an increase in the minimum wage. But he keeps the conservative-minded military and business interests in his Tidewater district satisfied with his diligent attention to defense and shipbuilding issues from his seat on the National Security Committee. There Pickett serves with neighboring Democrat Norman Sisisky and Republican Herbert H. Bateman, forming the "Tidewater Trio" that looks out for the Norfolk naval bases and other area military facilities.

During Pickett's early years in the House, his district was a mix of conservative whites and more liberal blacks, but redistricting in 1992 removed thousands of minority voters from his constituency, and the 2nd now leans further to the conservative side. President Clinton has never been popular with many of the district's voters, and in the 103rd Congress, Pickett was one of 30 Democrats to vote against Clinton's five-year deficit-reduction bill both times it came through the House, in May and August 1993.

But when Republicans took control in the 104th Congress, Pickett did not embrace their budget proposals, either. He voted against both the fiscal 1996 and 1997 GOP budget resolutions. Like many centrist Democrats, Pickett supported overhauling the welfare system — a cause that Clinton himself had endorsed.

Pickett's main legislative fare, though, is defense. Working with Sisisky and Bateman in the 103rd Congress, he helped secure funding for a new nuclear-powered aircraft carrier to be built at the Newport News Shipbuilding and Dry Dock Co., in the neighboring 3rd District.

In the 104th, the trio worked with GOP Sen. John W. Warner of Virginia to thwart the Navy's plans to build all of the next-generation submarines at General Dynamics' Electric Boat Division in Groton, Conn. Conferees on the fiscal 1996 defense authorization bill agreed that both Newport News and Electric Boat would build up to two of the new submarines. In early 1997, however, the shipyards announced that at the Navy's urging they would work cooperatively on the four new attack subs, rather than each shipyard building a separate ship.

Pickett's diligent style and pro-defense stance have made him a key member of the National Security Committee's dominant centrist coalition. Though he spoke on the House floor only 16 times in the 104th, Pickett does have strong feelings about those who serve in the armed forces. "I remind my colleagues that the most important component of readiness is people," he told the House in July 1996. "The people serving in uniform today were selectively recruited and carefully trained. They are truly the finest force that the United States has ever had." Pickett is now the ranking member of the military research subcommittee.

Pickett also came to the defense of the Pentagon when demands arose for a major makeover of the nation's intelligence-gathering structure in the wake of the arrest and conviction of CIA counterintelligence officer Aldrich H. Ames, who spied for the former Soviet Union for nearly a decade. Several commissions and Intelligence Committee leaders in Congress concluded that the intelligence bureaucracy was too fragmented, and they advised that the Pentagon cede some of its authority over spy programs to a strengthened Central Intelligence Agency.

Pickett was leery of changing the status quo, even given the fact of certain inefficiencies. "Nothing is more important as we draw down our military than having a robust intelligence capability," Pickett said. "And if we're going to waste money any place in the government, to have some overlap and duplication and redundancy, it would seem to me that this would be an area where we could afford some of that for our nation's security."

Mindful of shipbuilding's importance to the Tidewater economy, Pickett was a strong propo-

Venerable Norfolk and upstart Virginia Beach share billing in the Tidewater area 2nd, but it is Virginia Beach that overshadows its neighbor. With 50 percent growth during the 1980s, Virginia Beach blazed past Norfolk to become the most populous city in the commonwealth.

An influx of military families, businesspeople and retirees has changed Virginia Beach's earlier identity as a summer tourist center. The sprawling city's retail and service trade has boomed, and some light industry has moved in as well. Only four congressional districts in the country have more military retirees.

The port city of Norfolk was settled in 1682, and its strategic location has been valued ever since. Most of Norfolk was destroyed by the British in the Revolutionary War, the city served as the Confederacy's main naval station in the Civil War, and it was a major naval training station in the two world wars. Lately, the unionized port city has been striving to polish its image. Norfolk's waterfront has been renovated into a modestly successful area of offices and shops called Waterside.

Defense is the main industry in the Hampton Roads area, and all four districts that touch the region that includes Hampton, Norfolk, Newport News and Virginia Beach depend on the massive concentration of naval installations, shipbuilders and shipping companies. The Norfolk Naval Base is the largest in the world. Many residents of the 2nd work in the 3rd making ships and submarines at the Newport News Shipbuilding and Dry Dock Co., the largest private employer in Virginia. Norfolk's ship repair industry employs 30,000 people. The Hampton Roads harbor area ranks first in export tonnage among the nation's Atlantic ports; it is the biggest coal shipper in the world.

VIRGINIA 2
Parts of Norfolk and Virginia Beach

Redistricting moved more than 60 percent of Norfolk's black population to the new, majority-black 3rd. Still, the 2nd retains some Democratic leanings. Pickett won here with 65 percent of the vote in 1996, and Sen. Charles S. Robb beat Oliver L. North in the district in 1994. But in presidential contests, the GOP nominee is secure, though the margin has slipped. Ronald Reagan won by 2-to-1 in 1988. George Bush had no trouble carrying the 2nd in 1992, though Bob Dole won in 1996 by only 4 percentage points.

Virginia Beach is one of the state's prime strongholds of conservatism. It is home to the religious broadcasting empire of Pat Robertson, who sought the GOP nomination for president in 1988. But Robertson does not enjoy universal support among the 2nd's Republicans. In Virginia's 1988 GOP presidential primary, he placed a distant third in Virginia Beach, behind Bush and Dole.

1990 Population: 562,276. White 439,282 (78%), Black 93,454 (17%), Other 29,540 (5%). Hispanic origin 18,383 (3%). 18 and over 419,231 (75%), 62 and over 50,178 (9%). Median age: 28.

nent of a bill designed to shore up the nation's beleaguered merchant marine fleet. The measure, passed by the House in December 1995, authorized payments for ship owners willing to agree in advance to turn over their vessels and, in some cases, their port and terminal facilities, to the Defense Department in times of war or other national emergencies. "Both our strategic sealift capability and our shipyard mobilization base are at risk and will be increasingly at risk without decisive action by this Congress and this president to enact appropriate remedial legislation," Pickett told the House. He also sits on the National Security Committee's Special Oversight Panel on the Merchant Marine.

In June 1995, Pickett added a second full committee assignment, taking a place on Resources when a slot opened up after Georgia's Nathan Deal switched to the Republican Party.

At Home: When Virginia state legislators redrew the Old Dominion's congressional map for the 1990s, they created a new, majority-black 3rd District in southeastern Virginia. In doing so, they removed blacks from adjacent districts, making the 1st, 2nd and 4th districts more white and more Republican. Pickett's constituency went from 23 percent black to about 17 percent black.

With two solid re-election victories under his belt, Pickett still did not look like a very inviting target in 1992. Republicans sought unsuccessfully to recruit a well-known candidate to test him in his new, more suburban confines. Instead, the nomination went to a political newcomer, Jim Chapman, a 35-year-old lawyer from Norfolk.

Chapman, however, proved to be an attractive candidate, impressing observers with his smooth speaking style. His neophyte status offered voters a contrast to Pickett's two decades of political service.

But 2nd District voters were not in a mood to cast out their incumbent. Although Chapman raised nearly $200,000, that was only half what Pickett spent, and he won with 56 percent. Chapman returned in 1994, but Pickett nudged his tally up to 59 percent. In 1996, Pickett comfortably put down the bid of telecommunications director John Tate.

When Pickett first won election to the House in 1986 (replacing retiring Republican G. William Whitehurst), he already had: served as chairman of the state party; launched, then abandoned a Senate bid; headed a Democratic presidential campaign in Virginia; and served long enough in the state House of Delegates to be a senior member of the Appropriations Committee.

No orator or gregarious back-slapper, the wealthy Virginia Beach lawyer-accountant always worked studiously behind the scenes. But when state Democrats had important decisions to make in the 1970s and early 1980s, Pickett was nearly always in on them. He played a major role, for example, in fashioning the state's budget and retirement system.

In 1980, he was chosen Democratic state chairman. Pickett chaired the party through Charles S. Robb's successful gubernatorial campaign in 1981 and tried the waters as a Senate candidate in 1982, dropping out before the primary.

In the 1986 House contest, Pickett's Republican opponent, state Sen. A. J. "Joe" Canada, was generally regarded as the more appealing campaigner.

But Canada was jolted early in the race by newspaper stories detailing his involvement with a bankrupt Virginia Beach mortgage company and business deals he had made with a Richmond stockbroker who had been accused of embezzlement. While no one linked Canada to criminal wrongdoing, Pickett said Canada's poor judgment was a legitimate issue.

Canada narrowly carried Virginia Beach, but Pickett won by nearly 2-to-1 in Norfolk and prevailed overall 49 percent to 42 percent, with a third-party candidate taking 9 percent.

HOUSE ELECTIONS

1996 General		
Owen B. Pickett (D)	106,215	(65%)
John Tate (R)	57,586	(35%)
1994 General		
Owen Pickett (D)	81,372	(59%)
Jim Chapman (R)	56,375	(41%)

Previous Winning Percentages: 1992 (56%) **1990** (75%) **1988** (61%) **1986** (49%)

CAMPAIGN FINANCE

	Receipts	Receipts from PACs	Expend-itures
1996			
Pickett (D)	$326,061	$142,299 (44%)	$266,059
Tate (R)	$202,312	$14,083 (7%)	$194,912
1994			
Pickett (D)	$335,757	$150,893 (45%)	$386,469
Chapman (R)	$434,447	$19,423 (4%)	$433,587

VOTING STUDIES

	Presidential Support		Party Unity		Conservative Coalition	
Year	S	O	S	O	S	O
1996	68	32	56	43	92	8
1995	64	35	49	49	94	5
1994	76	22	68	29	89	8
1993	82	18	75	22	82	18
1992	65	35	68	30	73	23
1991	52	46	70	26	89	8

DISTRICT VOTE FOR PRESIDENT

	1996		1992
D	71,683 (44%)	**D**	62,946 (35%)
R	77,943 (48%)	**R**	85,773 (48%)
I	11,905 (7%)	**I**	30,587 (17%)

KEY VOTES

1997	
Ban "partial birth" abortions	N
1996	
Approve farm bill	Y
Deny public education to illegal immigrants	Y
Repeal ban on certain assault-style weapons	Y
Increase minimum wage	Y
Freeze defense spending	N
Approve welfare overhaul	Y
1995	
Approve balanced-budget constitutional amendment	N
Relax Clean Water Act regulations	Y
Oppose limits on environmental regulations	N
Reduce projected Medicare spending	N
Approve GOP budget with tax and spending cuts	N

INTEREST GROUP RATINGS

Year	ADA	AFL-CIO	CCUS	ACU
1996	45	n/a	63	50
1995	55	83	46	28
1994	35	56	75	48
1993	20	42	73	50
1992	35	25	88	52
1991	25	58	60	35

3 Robert C. Scott (D)

Of Newport News — Elected 1992, 3rd term

Biographical Information
Born: April 30, 1947, Washington, D.C.
Education: Harvard U., A.B. 1969; Boston College, J.D. 1973.
Military Service: Army Reserve, 1970-74; National Guard, 1974-76.
Occupation: Lawyer.
Family: Divorced.
Religion: Episcopalian.
Political Career: Va. House, 1979-83; Va. Senate, 1983-93; Democratic nominee for U.S. House, 1986.

Capitol Office: 2464 Rayburn Bldg. 20515; 225-8351.

Committees
Education & Workforce
Early Childhood, Youth & Families
Judiciary
Constitution (ranking)

In Washington: Scott votes a reliably liberal line except when it comes to defense spending, when he joins with Virginia conservatives to advance the cause of the Navy and the military shipbuilding industry, both of which are important employers in the 3rd.

That hawkishness aside, Scott is a pillar of the Democratic left on the Education and Workforce Committee, and on the Judiciary Committee he has challenged the GOP on a broad front of issues, including resisting conservatives' efforts to limit appeals by death row inmates. In the 105th, Scott is ranking Democrat on the Constitution Subcommittee, a hot spot in the House for advancing GOP legislation on social policy. Scott supports abortion rights and opposes capital punishment. He was one of 14 House Democrats voting in 1995 against every bill in the GOP's "Contract With America" except the three approved unanimously.

Scott brought to Washington 14 years' experience in the state legislature, where he was known as conscientious and effective. Seeking the newly drawn black-majority 3rd District in 1992, he easily became the first black from Virginia to serve in the House since 1891. But in February 1997, Scott's electoral future was cast into doubt when a three-judge federal panel struck down the 3rd, ruling it an unconstitutional "racial gerrymander." The district was still in limbo in May 1997, as legal proceedings continued.

Scott disagreed repeatedly with Judiciary Republicans in the 104th, particularly as they tried to rewrite President Clinton's 1994 crime law. Scott had voted against final passage of the crime bill, regarding it as too weighted toward punishment. But in the 104th, he was up against a GOP majority that viewed the law as too soft on criminals. Scott opposed GOP efforts to convert the 1994 law's police hiring and crime prevention grants into a single block grant program so states could spend the money as they thought best. He objected to imposing new restrictions on death row appeals and to prodding states to adopt tough new sentencing laws.

He backed an amendment by Judiciary Democrats to reserve half of the block grants — $5 billion over five years — for crime prevention programs. Proponents of such programs said they are more cost-efficient than building new prisons. "It is simply a matter of pay now or pay a lot more later," said Scott. But the amendment failed.

He also argued against a GOP effort to broaden the so-called exclusionary rule, which bars the use in criminal trials of evidence obtained improperly by law enforcement officials. The rule generally stipulates that prosecutors cannot use evidence obtained in violation of the 4th Amendment guarantees against unreasonable search and seizure. In 1984, the Supreme Court recognized a "good faith" exception to the exclusionary rule in cases where police conduct a search under a warrant later found to be invalid. The GOP wanted to write this "good faith" exception into law and extend it to searches conducted without a warrant, so long as police had good reason to think the search was legal.

But Scott and his allies said the GOP provision would remove incentives for police to obtain proper warrants and could subject innocent citizens to unfair searches. "Some people get tired of police misconduct," Scott told the committee.

He also objected to an anti-terrorism measure that moved through the House in reaction to the April 1995 bombing of a federal office building in Oklahoma City. The measure made it easier to deport foreigners suspected of terrorism; expanded the use of the death penalty for terrorist crimes; and restricted appeals by death-row inmates. Scott said the limit on death-row appeals, known as habeas corpus appeals, did not belong in the bill because it strikes at a basic constitutional right. "I rise to oppose the conference report because it will do little, if anything, to reduce terrorism, while at the same time it will, in fact, terrorize our Constitution," Scott said.

Scott in July 1996 took his commitment to crime prevention to the Commerce, Justice, State spending bill, where he backed an amendment to transfer $497.5 million from state prison grants to

The capital city of Richmond, long the center of Virginia's government and commerce, is probably best known as the capital of the Confederacy. But in the 1990s, Richmond is a cornerstone of the majority-black 3rd, which is the commonwealth's first district to elect a black representative in more than 100 years. More than one-fourth of the 3rd's population lives in Richmond.

Most of the area that was represented by John Mercer Langston, the only other black representative in Virginia's history, now lies in the 4th. A dispute over Langston's election in 1888 delayed his seating; his victory was not ratified by the full House until September 1890, and less than two months later he was defeated for reelection.

The 3rd takes in the eastern side of Richmond, including the state Capitol, and stretches southeast along the James River to west Norfolk, and northeast to the Rappahannock River and Essex County, in the Middle Peninsula. In addition to Richmond and Norfolk, it includes predominantly black sections of the cities of Newport News, Portsmouth, Petersburg and Hopewell, plus part of the city of Suffolk.

Half the 3rd's population is in the southernmost part extending from Newport News to Norfolk. But almost as many people live in the westernmost portion that makes up Richmond, Henrico and Charles City counties and the cities of Petersburg and Hopewell. With his Newport News base, Scott easily defeated two Richmond-based opponents in the 1992 Democratic primary, winning the southwestern sector with more than 82 percent of the vote.

The district's future is in some doubt. Two GOP activists filed a lawsuit in November 1995

VIRGINIA 3
Southeast — Parts of Richmond and Tidewater area

claiming that the 3rd was unconstitutional. They said race was the "predominant factor" in shaping its lines, violating the equal protection clause under the 14th Amendment. In February 1997, a panel of federal judges agreed.

This is easily Virginia's most Democratic district. Bill Clinton won 72 percent of the vote here in the 1996. Eight years earlier, the areas that make up the 3rd overwhelmingly supported Michael S. Dukakis, who lost badly most elsewhere in Virginia.

State government is a major component driving the economy of Richmond and vicinity, but the city is also a manufacturing center; Richmond still boasts one of the largest cigarette plants in the country, Philip Morris' huge facility along Interstate 95.

The Hampton Roads portion of the 3rd depends in large part on defense. The state's largest private employer, the Newport News Shipbuilding and Dry Dock Co., is in the 3rd, with 25,000 employees building Navy carriers and submarines. The Hampton Roads area has a heavy concentration of naval installations as well as shipbuilding and ship repair companies.

The eastern counties — New Kent, King William, King and Queen and Essex — are mainly rural and sparsely populated.

1990 Population: 562,351. White 188,230 (33%), Black 361,994 (64%), Other 12,127 (2%). Hispanic origin 8,060 (1%). 18 and over 412,917 (73%), 62 and over 78,144 (14%). Median age: 31.

local delinquency prevention programs. Scott said there is ample research to show that increasing incarceration has no effect on reducing crime, while "prevention programs aimed at at-risk youth and children significantly reduces crime." But his amendment was rejected, 99-326.

From his seat on the Economic and Educational Opportunities Committee (renamed Education and the Workforce in the 105th), Scott voted for a GOP bill to revise funding and disciplinary procedures for the main education program for children with disabilities. But he first objected to a provision that allowed states to stop all educational services for children with disabilities in extreme disciplinary cases, such as if the misconduct was unrelated to the disability and involved weapons or drugs. He offered an amendment to strike the provisions related to the cessation of services, but it was rejected 17-21. Regardless of the misconduct, "the child still needs an education," Scott said.

"There's nothing to suggest that threatening children with a vacation from school" would deter them from misbehaving, he said. But Republicans countered that expulsion was appropriate in certain circumstances.

Scott's liberal voting record takes a turn to the right when it comes to the defense budget. He was one of 58 Democrats to oppose an amendment to the fiscal 1997 defense spending bill that would have frozen defense spending at the prior-year level. His Tidewater-area district is home to the Newport News Shipbuilding and Dry Dock Co., which employs thousands of area residents in building Navy carriers and submarines.

He supported an effort by the area's congressional delegation and GOP Sen. John W. Warner to fight a Navy proposal to contract with Groton, Conn.-based Electric Boat to build the first two copies of a new class of submarines. Conferees on the fiscal 1996 defense authorization bill agreed that Newport News Shipbuilding and Electric Boat would each build up to two of the new subs. In early 1997, the shipyards announced that at the Navy's urging they would work cooperatively on four new subs, rather than each yard building separate subs.

Scott's district is also home to one of the nation's largest cigarette plants, owned and operated by Philip Morris. He joined with other southern Virginia and North Carolina members in sending a letter to President Clinton in July 1995 calling on him to reject the recommendation of the head of the federal Food and Drug Administration (FDA) to impose new regulations on the use and marketing of tobacco-related products.

At Home: In 1992, Scott had a huge advantage in his bid for the 64 percent black 3rd District. He had represented the Hampton Roads area around Norfolk in the state House and Senate since 1978. Also, a 1986 run in the old 1st against Republican Rep. Herbert H. Bateman greatly boosted Scott's name recognition among voters in the rural Tidewater counties that are now included in the 3rd.

Scott's two Democratic primary opponents, Jean W. Cunningham and Jacqueline G. Epps, were Richmond lawyers. Both Epps, the chairman of the Virginia State Retirement System, and Cunningham, with six years as a member of the state House, had support among party activists. But that did little to help them overcome Scott's huge advantage in the parts of the district away from Richmond. They split the vote from their end of the district. The cities in the Hampton Roads area — Hampton, Norfolk, Newport News and Portsmouth — provided 62 percent of the overall primary vote, and Scott captured 82 percent of that.

Scott's victory in the general election was a foregone conclusion. Republican Daniel Jenkins, a technician with Philip Morris USA. in Richmond, was nominated by a sparsely attended district GOP convention. Scott cruised to victory, 79 percent to 21 percent. He took 79 percent again in 1994 and 82 percent in 1996.

Scott is the son of a teacher and a physician, and he attended Harvard University and Boston College Law School. In his 1992 race, Scott deflected charges that he was not attuned to the needs of the poorer and rural constituents of the 3rd, citing his work on their behalf in the legislature. And he shored up his base by winning early endorsements from the Rainbow Coalition and the Virginia AFL-CIO.

The legal controversy over the shape of the 3rd began with a November 1995 lawsuit filed by two Republican activists. They argued that the district is unconstitutional because race was the "predominant factor" in drawing it, a violation of the equal protection clause of the 14th Amendment.

HOUSE ELECTIONS

1996 General		
Robert C. Scott (D)	118,603	(82%)
Elsie Holland (R)	25,781	(18%)
1994 General		
Robert C. Scott (D)	108,532	(79%)
Tom Ward (R)	28,080	(21%)

Previous Winning Percentages: 1992 (79%)

CAMPAIGN FINANCE

	Receipts	Receipts from PACs	Expend-itures
1996			
Scott (D)	$194,468	$135,150 (69%)	$176,104
Holland (R)	$22,100	$16 (0%)	$1,856
1994			
Scott (D)	$246,451	$146,007 (59%)	$252,350
Ward (R)	$80,782	$514 (1%)	$77,642

DISTRICT VOTE FOR PRESIDENT

	1996		1992
D	117,357 (72%)	**D**	124,857 (66%)
R	36,099 (22%)	**R**	48,843 (26%)
I	7,643 (5%)	**I**	16,779 (9%)

KEY VOTES

1997	
Ban "partial birth" abortions	N
1996	
Approve farm bill	Y
Deny public education to illegal immigrants	N
Repeal ban on certain assault-style weapons	N
Increase minimum wage	Y
Freeze defense spending	N
Approve welfare overhaul	N
1995	
Approve balanced-budget constitutional amendment	N
Relax Clean Water Act regulations	N
Oppose limits on environmental regulations	Y
Reduce projected Medicare spending	N
Approve GOP budget with tax and spending cuts	N

VOTING STUDIES

	Presidential Support		Party Unity		Conservative Coalition	
Year	S	O	S	O	S	O
1996	84	15	89	10	59	41
1995	80	18	91	8	38	62
1994	82	18	94	4	28	72
1993	89	11	93	4	30	70

INTEREST GROUP RATINGS

Year	ADA	AFL-CIO	CCUS	ACU
1996	90	n/a	31	0
1995	95	100	13	4
1994	80	89	42	24
1993	90	100	18	8

4 Norman Sisisky (D)

Of Petersburg — Elected 1982, 8th term

Biographical Information

Born: June 9, 1927, Baltimore, Md.
Education: Virginia Commonwealth U., B.S. 1949.
Military Service: Navy, 1945-46.
Occupation: Beer and soft drink distributor.
Family: Wife, Rhoda Brown; four children.
Religion: Jewish.
Political Career: Va. House, 1974-82.
Capitol Office: 2371 Rayburn Bldg. 20515; 225-6365.

Committees

National Security
Military Installations and Facilities; Military Readiness (ranking)

Small Business
Regulatory Reform & Paperwork Reduction

In Washington: Sisisky represents a Tidewater Virginia district with a large military constituency, a sizable (32 percent) black population and many working-class whites who make a living at farming or factory work. A millionaire beverage distributor, he meshes his pro-defense and pro-business views with support for a few causes dear to liberals. In the 104th Congress, for instance, he backed a Democratic-driven effort to increase the minimum wage, and he has consistently supported abortion rights.

His pro-defense posture is a political necessity in a district where the military is such an integral part of the economy. He is part of the National Security Committee's "Tidewater Trio," which includes Sisisky, fellow Democrat Owen B. Pickett and Republican Herbert H. Bateman. They look out for the interests of the Norfolk-area naval bases and other local military facilities; few regions are as well-defended on the committee. The 4th District is home to the Norfolk Naval Shipyard, a repair facility for much of the naval fleet.

The three were successful in the 103rd Congress in getting defense funding for a new nuclear-powered aircraft carrier to be built at the Newport News Shipbuilding and Dry Dock Co., in the neighboring 3rd District. In the 104th, they and Virginia's Republican Sen. John W. Warner helped thwart the Navy's plan to build all of its next-generation submarines at General Dynamics' Electric Boat shipbuilding company in Groton, Conn. Ultimately, conferees on the fiscal 1996 defense authorization bill agreed that both Newport News and Electric Boat would build up to two of the new submarines. But in early 1997, the shipyards announced that at the Navy's urging they would work together on the four new attack subs, rather than each shipyard building a separate ship.

Sisisky is ranking member on the Military Readiness Subcommittee, which his Tidewater colleague, Bateman, chairs, and he has consistently backed the increased defense budgets put forth by the GOP-led committee — amounts that go beyond President Clinton's requests. He told the House during debate on the fiscal 1996 defense authorization bill that military readiness "should be our highest defense priority. There should be no doubt in anyone's mind [that] this nation has the best trained, best equipped, best led military forces anywhere in the world."

But Sisisky was also critical of his Republican colleagues when he felt they were playing politics with the nation's defense needs. As part of their "Contract With America," Republicans put forth a defense measure they touted as a legislative expression of their argument that Clinton had cut the defense budget too deeply, frittered U.S. forces on peacekeeping missions irrelevant to U.S. security interests and subordinated U.S. policy to U.N.-dominated goals. Although Sisisky said he had backed the measure in committee, he voted against it when it came to the floor.

"We should debate ballistic and theater missile defense where we have time to determine the real cost of what we want to achieve. We should not wreck our foreign policy by unilaterally changing U.N. assessment formulas or by forcing the admission of certain countries to NATO," Sisisky said. "Let us not tear down all we have been able to achieve in a frenzy of partisan politics."

Sisisky can also bring a critical eye to the defense establishment, as illustrated by his concern during debate on the fiscal 1997 defense authorization bill over a plan by the Pentagon to cut costs by relying more on private companies for routine maintenance of vehicles and equipment at government-owned maintenance depots. Sisisky told the House that the bill did not authorize the Defense Department to go forward with its privatization plan. "DOD believes the private sector can do anything better and cheaper. I'm here to tell you that I've 'been there, done that' and 'it ain't necessarily so,' " Sisisky said. "The issue is far too important to risk national security by going too far, too fast. We need to be careful."

In keeping with his business background, Sisisky is sensitive to employers' complaints about burdensome federal mandates (he opposed

VIRGINIA 4
Southeast — Chesapeake; part of Portsmouth

Like the neighboring 1st, 2nd and 3rd districts, the 4th has a piece of the Hampton Roads area in southeastern Virginia. Thus its economy is powered in great measure by the vast industry linked to the region's huge military presence. Almost half its population is in Chesapeake, Portsmouth, Suffolk and Virginia Beach.

The industrial city of Chesapeake anchors the southeastern end of the 4th. Home to thousands of Hampton Roads shipyard and factory workers, Chesapeake has been booming; its population grew by 33 percent in the 1980s. Portsmouth is a district office for the Coast Guard, whose finance center is in Chesapeake. The Norfolk Naval Shipyard, in the portion of Portsmouth in the 4th, employs more than 7,000 people.

The district's military component goes beyond Hampton Roads. Fort Lee, in Petersburg, and Fort Pickett, near Blackstone, are primarily used for training troops. Defense downsizing could affect both; Fort Pickett appeared on the Pentagon's 1995 base-closing list and is supposed to become a National Guard post in October 1997.

The 4th, typical of many conservative Democratic districts in the South, often prefers Republican presidential nominees. George Bush held Bill Clinton to 40 percent in 1992. Clinton did better in 1996, taking 46 percent of the vote. But Bob Dole still carried the district, beating Clinton by just over 1,500 votes, even as Sisisky was easily re-elected to the House with 79 percent. In the 1994 Senate race, Republican Oliver L. North narrowly carried the 4th.

Agriculture is also important to the district's economy. Peanuts and tobacco are the important crops in the rural Southside counties along the North Carolina border. Democratic ties are still strong here, particularly in a swath that stretches from Suffolk to Brunswick County. Southampton is the No. 4 peanut-harvesting county in the nation.

There is some industry in the smaller cities of the 4th. Hopewell calls itself the chemical capital of the South. Suffolk processes peanuts. Petersburg makes tobacco products. Smithfield, in Isle of Wight County, is eponymous with Virginia ham and pork products.

The 4th also has a stake in the service sector. The QVC Network, a shop-at-home national television channel, employs more than 1,500 phone operators at its Chesapeake facility, and it has a large distribution warehouse in Suffolk. Wal-Mart has a regional distribution center in Dinwiddie County.

The northern part of the district has also been experiencing population expansion. Louisa, Goochland and Powhatan counties all had double-digit growth in the 1980s, owing to the westward expansion of Richmond's suburbs. Louisa County also has been drawing retirees and second-home buyers from Charlottesville and the Washington area. The district's only nuclear power plant, North Anna, is in Louisa.

1990 Population: 562,466. White 372,263 (66%), Black 180,479 (32%), Other 9,724 (2%). Hispanic origin 6,442 (1%). 18 and over 415,002 (74%), 62 and over 79,000 (14%). Median age: 33.

the Family and Medical Leave Act) and sympathetic to GOP efforts to curtail government regulation of the private sector.

But while Sisisky has supported a balanced-budget constitutional amendment, he denounced GOP budget proposals in the 104th as going too far in cutting spending in order to reduce taxes. A member of the "blue dog" coalition, a group of centrist Democrats who hail mostly from the South, Sisisky backed a coalition budget proposal that would have postponed tax cuts until the budget is balanced and tempered the GOP's effort to cut costs on health care entitlements and welfare.

Sisisky gave some personal testimony in a debate over a Republican bill designed to save $270 billion in projected Medicare costs over seven years. Opposing the measure in October 1995, he told his colleagues that just seven weeks earlier he had an operation for rectal cancer — a cancer that he said was discovered through a prescreening test. "I was able to afford the prescreening . . . even though I am on Medicare, but I found out today that it is not even included in this bill," Sisisky said. "How can we be uncompassionate for people who cannot afford to get these examinations? It just seems to me that that is one of the things that should be included."

Besides its military interests, the 4th District is also home to many peanut and tobacco farmers who live in the rural counties that border North Carolina. Sisisky was very unhappy with an amendment offered in June 1996 to the agriculture spending bill that would have done away with federal crop insurance and extension services for tobacco growers. Supporters of the amendment said it would save $25 million a year. But Southern rural lawmakers argued that the amendment would unduly hurt small Southern farmers, forcing them to go welfare.

"This is nothing but scapegoating," Sisisky told the House. "The backers of this amendment are upset with tobacco companies. So they are taking out their frustrations on farmers, many of them small family farmers struggling just to make a living." In the end, tobacco supporters beat back the amendment, 210-212.

Sisisky is a reliable vote for gunowners rights: In the 103rd, he opposed a five-day waiting period for handgun purchases and a ban on certain semi-automatic assault-style weapons; in the 104th, he voted to repeal the assault-weapons ban.

At Home: After a decade of intraparty friction and underfinanced campaigns in the 4th Democrats united behind the wealthy Sisisky in 1982. He combined a large campaign treasury and an affable campaign style to oust veteran GOP Rep. Robert W. Daniel Jr. In the next four elections, Republicans offered no challenger against him.

During Sisisky's first decade in Congress, blacks made up 40 percent of his district's population. A 1992 redistricting plan took part of his territory to create a new, black-majority 3rd District, leaving the 4th with a constituency about one-third black and somewhat more Republican. He did draw a GOP challenger in 1992, but it was a feebly funded effort, and Sisisky won with 68 percent of the vote.

In 1994, Republicans were much more enthusiastic about the prospects of Baptist pastor George Sweet, who was well-funded and well-organized. But even in a tough year for Democrats nationally, Sisisky won with ease, 62 percent to 38 percent. In 1996, he soared to nearly 80 percent of the vote.

The son of Lithuanian immigrants, Sisisky was born in Baltimore. His family moved during the Depression to Richmond, where his father worked in a delicatessen. Sisisky was raised there and attended a local college.

During the 1982 campaign, Sisisky described himself as a self-made businessman. Critics said he married into a wealthy Petersburg family and took over its soft-drink company. But regardless of how he got his start, Sisisky is a natural salesman who turned the operation into one of the most successful Pepsi-Cola distributorships in the country.

After years as a pillar of the business community, Sisisky won a seat in the state House in 1973. With Virginia politics then in a state of ideological flux, he ran as an independent but caucused with the Democrats and in 1975 sought re-election as a Democrat.

Sisisky was widely recognized as his party's strongest potential challenger against Daniel in 1982. But when a black activist announced in early 1982 that he might run as an independent, Sisisky threatened to pull out of the race. Only when the threat of the independent candidacy subsided did Sisisky resume his campaign.

Sisisky charged that Daniel's pro-Reagan record did not represent blacks, farmers or the blue-collar workers of industrial Tidewater. Daniel countered by branding Sisisky a liberal and claiming he was trying to buy the election. In the end, Sisisky carried 15 out of 20 jurisdictions, winning overwhelmingly in Petersburg and in blue-collar Portsmouth.

HOUSE ELECTIONS

1996 General		
Norman Sisisky (D)	160,100	(79%)
A.J. "Tony" Zevgolis (R)	43,516	(21%)
1994 General		
Norman Sisisky (D)	115,055	(62%)
George Sweet (R)	71,678	(38%)

Previous Winning Percentages: 1992 (68%) **1990** (78%) **1988** (100%) **1986** (100%) **1984** (100%) **1982** (54%)

CAMPAIGN FINANCE

	Receipts	Receipts from PACs	Expend-itures
1996			
Sisisky (D)	$250,636	$152,528 (61%)	$223,771
Zevgolis (R)	$10,501	$16 (0%)	$2,878
1994			
Sisisky (D)	$685,188	$248,375 (36%)	$741,224
Sweet (R)	$330,218	$9,636 (3%)	$329,607

VOTING STUDIES

	Presidential Support		Party Unity		Conservative Coalition	
Year	S	O	S	O	S	O
1996	59	38	51†	47†	96	0
1995	55	31	45	45	78	7
1994	79	19	70	27	89	8
1993	77	22	71	23	84	11
1992	49	50	71	28	92	6
1991	45	49	68	25	76	14

† Not eligible for all recorded votes.

DISTRICT VOTE FOR PRESIDENT

1996		1992	
D	101,686 (46%)	**D**	90,641 (40%)
R	103,368 (46%)	**R**	106,392 (47%)
I	15,879 (7%)	**I**	31,467 (14%)

KEY VOTES

1997	
Ban "partial birth" abortions	Y
1996	
Approve farm bill	Y
Deny public education to illegal immigrants	Y
Repeal ban on certain assault-style weapons	Y
Increase minimum wage	Y
Freeze defense spending	N
Approve welfare overhaul	Y
1995	
Approve balanced-budget constitutional amendment	Y
Relax Clean Water Act regulations	Y
Oppose limits on environmental regulations	N
Reduce projected Medicare spending	N
Approve GOP budget with tax and spending cuts	?

INTEREST GROUP RATINGS

Year	ADA	AFL-CIO	CCUS	ACU
1996	35	n/a	67	55
1995	45	73	52	22
1994	35	67	75	48
1993	45	75	45	42
1992	55	55	88	48
1991	30	73	67	39

5 Virgil H. Goode Jr. (D)

Of Rocky Mount — Elected 1996, 1st term

Biographical Information

Born: Oct. 17, 1946, Richmond, Va.

Education: U. of Richmond, B.A. 1969; U. of Virginia, J.D. 1973.

Military Service: Va. National Guard, 1969-75.

Occupation: Lawyer.

Family: Wife, Lucy D. Dodson; one child.

Religion: Baptist.

Political Career: Va. Senate, 1974-97; sought Democratic nomination for U.S. Senate, 1982, 1994.

Capitol Office: 1520 Longworth Bldg. 20515; 225-4711.

Committees

Agriculture
Forestry, Resource Conservation & Research; Risk Management & Specialty Crops

Small Business
Regulatory Reform & Paperwork Reduction

The Path to Washington: Goode in 1996 was able to sustain the open 5th district's Democratic tradition by campaigning in an old-fashioned manner on old-fashioned conservative Southern issues: guns, abortion and tobacco.

At the same time, Goode, who represented a state Senate district toward the 5th's southern end, appealed to more liberal constituents with his long-standing support of civil rights. He also echoed Democrats around the country in pledging support for Medicare and federal support of education.

His Republican opponent, attorney George C. Landrith III, attempted to link Goode to the tobacco regulations proposed in 1996 by the Clinton administration. But Goode was quick to distance himself from those plans, saying, "If it regulates tobacco, is the [Food and Drug Administration] going to regulate sunshine next? People get skin cancer from too much sun."

Goode will be able to watch out for the interests of the district's tobacco growers from his perch on the Agriculture Committee.

He didn't have to stretch to prove his bona fides as a party maverick. After the state legislative elections of 1995, in which Goode ran unopposed for the fifth consecutive time, the state Senate was deadlocked. Democrats retained effective control because the Democratic lieutenant governor held a tie-breaking vote, and the party sought to retain total control of the committee system.

But Goode insisted on an "equitable division" and cast his lot with the Republicans, forcing a power-sharing arrangement in which the GOP gained control of four committees. Goode himself surrendered a gavel to a Republican to help grease the deal. But under the new order, he earned a slot on the conference committee that determines the state budget. Goode reportedly disapproved of the Democrats who were in line to chair some committees, thinking them hostile to gun owners' rights and the tobacco industry.

Goode sponsored a state law that allows sane Virginia residents over age 21 to have permits to carry concealed weapons. As a precaution, the law prohibited carrying hidden guns in places where alcohol is publicly served.

Goode campaigns in a low-key style, winging most speeches and driving to small-town events in a phone-free car. He habitually hands out emery boards and pencils embossed with his name. His father, who served as a prosecutor and state delegate, used to give out kitchen implements.

Goode says that he remains in the Democratic Party because his "Daddy was a Democrat," citing his father's appreciation for New Deal programs that aided rural areas. A product of public schools, Goode has opposed tuition tax credits and school vouchers.

His stances on other issues, though, are sufficiently in line with social conservative thought that Christian Coalition Executive Director Ralph Reed hailed Goode's victory at a news conference after the 1996 elections. Goode supports term limits and opposes abortion in most cases. Once in Congress, he immediately joined the "blue dog" coalition of conservative, mostly Southern, House Democrats and was named chairman of their task force on transportation.

Since winning his state Senate seat at age 27, Goode had made no secret of his ambitions for higher office, twice unsuccessfully pursuing his party's nomination for the U.S. Senate, in 1982 and 1994.

The day after Democratic Rep. L.F. Payne announced he would not seek another House term in 1996, Goode launched his bid for Congress, boasting strong support from Democratic elected officials in the 5th.

Republican nominee Landrith ran a competitive race against Payne in 1994, holding him to 53 percent of the vote.

But the second time around, Landrith was distracted by bad publicity over a libel suit that he had lost and a dispute between his wife and a pet store owner. And Goode left too little running room to his right. The outcome was never in doubt: Goode won with 61 percent.

VIRGINIA 5
South — Danville; Charlottesville

Virginia's leading cash crop is tobacco, and the 5th is in the heart of tobacco country. Agriculture and textiles are the main industries in the 5th, which is in Virginia's rural "Southside," a region of farms, small towns and isolated factory cities along the state's southern tier that resembles the Deep South more closely than does any other part of the state. It is relatively poor and has a substantial black population. Tobacco and soybeans are major crops, but this region lacks the rich soil of the Tidewater region.

Charlottesville, home to the University of Virginia and its 18,200 students, is new to the 5th for the 1990s. It is an incongruity: an upscale, liberal enclave in an otherwise conservative, rural district. Charlottesville was the only jurisdiction now in the 5th to vote for Michael S. Dukakis in the 1988 presidential race, and it gave huge majorities to Bill Clinton in 1992 and 1996.

Liberal Democratic candidates at the state and national level have never fared well in this area. Barry Goldwater in 1964 and George Wallace in 1968 won many of the 5th's counties, and two GOP candidates backed by conservative Christians, Michael P. Farris, the 1993 nominee for lieutenant governor, and Oliver L. North, the 1994 Senate nominee, carried the 5th.

But the district's political thinking generally meshes with conservative Democrats like Goode, who survive despite the GOP's top-of-the-ticket strength. Henry and Franklin, two counties Goode represented in the state Senate, voted narrowly for Bob Dole in 1996 but overwhelmingly for Goode, who amassed 82 percent in Henry and 87 percent in Franklin.

The district's two most famous landmarks are Thomas Jefferson's home, Monticello, just south of Charlottesville, and Appomattox Court House, where Robert E. Lee surrendered to Ulysses S. Grant to end the Civil War.

About 60 miles south of Appomattox is the district's largest city, Danville, a tobacco and textile center on the North Carolina border. Alone among counties and independent cities along the southern tier, Danville saw its population rise during the 1980s. The textile industry employs almost 33,000 people in the district. The largest company, Dan River, employs about 4,500 at its Danville plant.

Just to the west is Henry County, the most populous county in the district and which surrounds the textile and furniture town of Martinsville. The rest of the county's residents are scattered through farming areas and a few factory towns.

Campbell and Bedford counties originally were Lynchburg bedroom communities, but both engaged in aggressive economic recruitment in the 1980s and attracted many small businesses. Bedford's population grew by more than 30 percent in the 1980s. Fluvanna County, southeast of Charlottesville, grew by 29 percent from 1990 to 1995, third-fastest in the state. Dole comfortably won Campbell, Bedford and Fluvanna.

1990 Population: 562,268. White 418,171 (74%), Black 139,344 (25%), Other 4,753 (1%). Hispanic origin 3,226 (1%). 18 and over 433,192 (77%), 62 and over 97,446 (17%). Median age: 35.

HOUSE ELECTIONS

1996 General

Virgil H. Goode Jr. (D)	120,323	(61%)
George C. Landrith III (R)	70,869	(36%)
George R. "Tex" Wood (VREF)	6,627	(3%)

CAMPAIGN FINANCE

	Receipts	Receipts from PACs	Expend-itures
1996			
Goode (D)	$559,777	$227,488 (41%)	$485,194
Landrith (R)	$399,696	$25,888 (6%)	$392,152
Wood (VREF)	$2,847	0	$2,867

DISTRICT VOTE FOR PRESIDENT

	1996		1992
D	94,091 (43%)	**D**	90,769 (41%)
R	105,760 (48%)	**R**	104,236 (47%)
I	17,166 (8%)	**I**	26,978 (12%)

KEY VOTES

1997

Ban "partial birth" abortions Y

6 Robert W. Goodlatte (R)

Of Roanoke — Elected 1992, 3rd term

Biographical Information

Born: Sept. 22, 1952, Holyoke, Mass.

Education: Bates College, B.A. 1974; Washington and Lee U., J.D. 1977.

Occupation: Lawyer; congressional aide.

Family: Wife, Maryellen Flaherty; two children.

Religion: Christian Scientist.

Political Career: Roanoke City Republican Committee chairman, 1980-83.

Capitol Office: 123 Cannon Bldg. 20515; 225-5431.

Committees

Agriculture

Department Operations, Nutrition & Foreign Agriculture (chairman); Livestock, Dairy & Poultry

Judiciary

Constitution; Courts & Intellectual Property

In Washington: In mid-1996, Goodlatte assumed the chairmanship of the Agriculture Committee's Department Operations, Nutrition and Foreign Agriculture Subcommittee, filling a vacancy created by the death of Missouri Republican Bill Emerson. When Goodlatte took over the panel, which has oversight responsibilities for the $28 billion federal food stamp program, he said he would "continue [Emerson's] fight to end the cycle of dependency our food stamp program has helped create."

The 6th is a heavily agricultural district, with poultry and dairy farms predominating, and most of its voters are on the conservative side of the Republican spectrum. Goodlatte matches his constituents' views, both on fiscal and social issues.

He backed the Agriculture Committee's effort in March 1995 to pare spending on the nation's food stamp program and require recipients to find work. The food stamp measure, which was rolled into the GOP's broad welfare overhaul bill, drew intense criticism at the committee markup from Democrats, who said the GOP plan would shred the safety net relied upon by the nation's hungry. Goodlatte won committee approval of an amendment to bar convicted food stamp traffickers from ever receiving food stamp benefits.

In early 1997, he joined with Agriculture Chairman Bob Smith of Oregon in sponsoring a bill to require that states take steps to assure that prison inmates are not participating in the food stamp program. The measure was in response to a General Accounting Office study which reported that more than $3.5 million a year in food stamps goes to 12,000 families who qualify for the benefit only through a prison inmate. Goodlatte said the bill "will actually save states money," even though it would require states to expend time and money culling the food stamp rolls.

Early in his tenure as subcommittee chairman, Goodlatte held a hearing to investigate charges that Agriculture Department employees believed their prospects for promotions depended upon contributing to a PAC supporting the 1992 presidential bid of Bill Clinton, then the governor of Arkansas. Under the Hatch Act, federal employees are prohibited from making or receiving political contributions on federal property.

The hearing stemmed from reports, published in November 1994 by the Los Angeles Times, that employees of the Agricultural Stabilization and Conservation Service were solicited for campaign funds starting in September 1992. After a Justice Department inquiry, one current and three former Agriculture Department employees pleaded guilty to conspiring to pressure subordinates and colleagues to contribute to a farmers PAC. "It should send a clear message to the USDA and other federal employees: Engaging in political activity in the office or while on duty is illegal and will not be tolerated," Goodlatte said at the hearing.

In the 104th Congress, the Agriculture Committee was consumed with writing a sweeping overhaul of federal farm policy. The GOP-backed "Freedom to Farm" measure, which cleared the House in February 1996, phased out most New Deal-era crop subsidies, replacing them with a system of fixed, but declining, payments that farmers would receive over seven years regardless of market prices or planting decisions. Goodlatte supported the far-reaching measure.

On another agriculture-related issue — the creation of a new migrant worker program — Goodlatte tried to negotiate a middle ground. California Republican Richard W. Pombo offered a proposal to admit up to 250,000 foreigners per year to harvest the nation's crops. He said the guest worker program was needed to provide growers with labor at harvest time.

The Agriculture Committee voted in March 1996 to attach the guest worker program to a larger immigration bill that was moving through the House. Goodlatte successfully amended the bill to make the program a three-year pilot rather than a permanent part of immigration laws. When the immigration bill came to the House floor that same month, Pombo offered his proposal again, saying that unless Congress created an adequate

VIRGINIA 6
West — Roanoke; Lynchburg

The 6th is home to mountains and caverns, dairy farmers and cattle ranchers, isolated towns and sizable cities — and a generous dose of Republicans.

The Shenandoah Valley, which runs most of the length of the 6th, cultivated Republicanism long before it was acceptable in other parts of Virginia. The descendants of the area's 18th century English, German and Scotch-Irish settlers feuded with the Tidewater plantation aristocracy and became GOP mavericks in state politics.

The brand of Republicanism in the rural Valley traditionally had been a moderate one. When Virginia's conservative Democrats were identified with resistance to integration in the 1960s, Valley Republicans were progressive on racial issues. The GOP lost its grip on the 6th in the 1980s partly because the state party came to be dominated by staunchly conservative suburbanites outside Washington and Richmond and by party-switching conservative Democrats. But Goodlatte's 1992 victory ended Democrats' decade-long control of the 6th District seat.

Roanoke, the district's major population center, has a variety of industries, including producers of furniture and electrical products. Downtown Roanoke got a boost when the rebuilt Hotel Roanoke was turned into an upscale conference and convention center. The city's black and union elements make it a Democratic base. Bill Clinton won Roanoke by 16 percentage points over Bob Dole in 1996, though he lost the district overall.

Democrats also can succeed in towns to the north, such as Covington and Clifton Forge, and in the counties around them, Bath and Alleghany. There are chemical plants and pulpwood and paper mills in this area, but high unemployment is a persistent problem.

Democratic support in the city of Roanoke is usually surpassed by the Republican vote in Roanoke's suburbs, in Lynchburg and in most of the district's rural areas. The nuclear energy company Babcock & Wilcox is one of Lynchburg's major employers, but the city is best known as the home of evangelist Jerry Falwell, his huge Thomas Road Baptist Church and Falwell-founded Liberty University (about 5,200 students).

Outside metropolitan Roanoke and Lynchburg, the district depends mainly on dairy farming, livestock and poultry. Rockingham County ranks third in the country in turkeys sold. Tourism enhances the local economy, with visitors traveling to Shenandoah National Park, George Washington National Forest and numerous caverns that dot the valley. Staunton boasts two museums of local notables: One is the house where Woodrow Wilson was born; the other celebrates the Statler Brothers, a country music group.

1990 Population: 562,572. White 492,594 (88%), Black 64,643 (11%), Other 5,335 (1%). Hispanic origin 3,855 (1%). 18 and over 437,920 (78%), 62 and over 98,709 (18%). Median age: 35.

legal migrant program, illegal immigrants would continue to be drawn to and hired for these farm jobs. But critics said such a program would boost rather than deter illegal immigration, with many of the temporary workers staying on illegally. Pombo's amendment was rejected 180-242, with Goodlatte voting "no."

Goodlatte then offered an alternative plan, which would have eased some of the requirements on employers in the existing migrant worker visa program and capped it at 100,000 visas per year. Those changes were insufficient for growers and too extensive for organized labor, and Goodlatte's amendment lost, 59-357.

Goodlatte also got involved in the immigration policy debate from his seat on the Judiciary Committee. The committee approved an immigration bill designed to scale back legal immigration, strengthen efforts to catch and deport illegal aliens and restrict public benefits for both groups. The committee agreed to ease Labor Department regulations regarding the H-1B program, which provides temporary work visas for immigrants with needed job skills. These temporary visas are intended to supply highly skilled immigrants to employers with immediate labor shortages.

Goodlatte sought to increase the number of businesses that would be exempt from certain Labor Department regulations — such as posting requirements — regarding temporary foreign workers. The committee bill would have exempted employers whose H-1B workers are less than 10 percent of their work force. Goodlatte's amendment to increase that to 15 or 20 percent, depending upon company size, was approved 22-11.

On Judiciary's Courts and Intellectual Property Subcommittee, Goodlatte has been an active player on computer and cyberspace issues. His main push in this area for the 105th would change Clinton administration policy on exporting encrypted software. Software companies want to encode their databases, e-mail and even telephone conversations to protect them from commercial espionage. But the administration has resisted allowing commercial export of technology that makes electronic communication more secure, lest it fall into unfriendly hands that could use encryption to nefarious ends.

Goodlatte's bill would allow U.S. businesses to export the same encryption hardware and software that is generally available overseas without requiring firms to include a key recovery feature. Such a feature allows law enforcement to gain access to electronic "keys" and decode encrypted communications. "Mandating key recovery as opposed to allowing people to decide who they trust is the fundamental difference" between the approaches advocated by Congress and by the administration, Goodlatte said.

In June 1996, Goodlatte won House passage of a bill to stem the growing trade in counterfeit goods, including car parts, infant formula and software. The measure increased criminal penalties for trafficking in counterfeit goods. Intellectual property, such as software, is most commonly counterfeited, Goodlatte said. "Counterfeiting is no longer a penny-ante crime with guys on the street selling fake $2 Rolexes," Goodlatte said. "It now involves international crime syndicates, multibillion-dollar operations, highly sophisticated equipment and terrorists."

At Home: Goodlatte thought about running for Congress in 1986, but the arrival of his second child at the start of the campaign season kept him from entering the race. In 1992, when Democratic Rep. Jim Olin chose not to seek re-election, Goodlatte decided the time was right. He campaigned on a promise to exert "Republican leadership . . . for a change."

During Olin's tenure, the district GOP had fought internally, with longtime Republicans feuding with conservative Christian activists newer to the party. But within weeks of his decision to run, Goodlatte had united both factions behind him.

Stephen Alan Musselwhite, an insurance executive and a moderate, emerged with the Democratic nomination, but he had party-unity problems of his own. Although Goodlatte went out of his way during the campaign to stress his opposition to organized labor's legislative agenda, labor leaders refused to back Musselwhite, in large part because he did not support legislation to ban employers from permanently replacing striking workers.

Musselwhite also had to contend with bad publicity about letters he wrote to a judge asking for leniency for two white-collar criminals. Goodlatte won easily, with 60 percent of the vote.

Goodlatte long has been a GOP activist, going back to his days as president of the student Republicans at Bates College in Maine. Many years later, Goodlatte was involved in party politics as a top aide to GOP Rep. M. Caldwell Butler, and then as chairman of the 6th District Republican Party.

Confirming his conservative leanings, Goodlatte was an early supporter of retired Lt. Col. Oliver L. North's 1994 campaign to unseat Democratic Sen. Charles S. Robb. He chaired the 1994 state GOP convention that nominated North for the Senate.

HOUSE ELECTIONS

1996 General		
Robert W. Goodlatte (R)	133,576	(67%)
Jeffrey Grey (D)	61,485	(31%)
Jay P. Rutledge (I)	4,229	(2%)
1994 General		
Robert W. Goodlatte (R)	126,455	(100%)

Previous Winning Percentages: **1992** (60%)

CAMPAIGN FINANCE

	Receipts	Receipts from PACs	Expend-itures
1996			
Goodlatte (R)	$708,894	$214,772 (30%)	$566,763
Grey (D)	$104,261	$49,950 (48%)	$92,744
1994			
Goodlatte (R)	$369,858	$150,069 (41%)	$211,653

DISTRICT VOTE FOR PRESIDENT

	1996		1992
D	87,883 (41%)	**D**	84,037 (37%)
R	108,757 (50%)	**R**	111,405 (50%)
I	16,116 (8%)	**I**	29,207 (13%)

KEY VOTES

1997	
Ban "partial birth" abortions	Y
1996	
Approve farm bill	Y
Deny public education to illegal immigrants	Y
Repeal ban on certain assault-style weapons	Y
Increase minimum wage	N
Freeze defense spending	Y
Approve welfare overhaul	Y
1995	
Approve balanced-budget constitutional amendment	Y
Relax Clean Water Act regulations	Y
Oppose limits on environmental regulations	N
Reduce projected Medicare spending	Y
Approve GOP budget with tax and spending cuts	Y

VOTING STUDIES

	Presidential Support		Party Unity		Conservative Coalition	
Year	**S**	**O**	**S**	**O**	**S**	**O**
1996	30	70	93	7	88	12
1995	17	83	94	6	91	9
1994	37	59	95	4	86	14
1993	42	58	92	8	84	16

INTEREST GROUP RATINGS

Year	ADA	AFL-CIO	CCUS	ACU
1996	5	n/a	100	95
1995	0	0	96	88
1994	10	0	92	90
1993	5	8	91	96

7 Thomas J. Bliley Jr. (R)

Of Richmond — Elected 1980, 9th term

Biographical Information

Born: Jan. 28, 1932, Chesterfield County, Va.
Education: Georgetown U., B.A. 1952.
Military Service: Navy, 1952-55.
Occupation: Funeral director.
Family: Wife, Mary Virginia Kelley; two children.
Religion: Roman Catholic.
Political Career: Richmond City Council, 1968-77, vice mayor, 1968-70, mayor, 1970-77.
Capitol Office: 2409 Rayburn Bldg. 20515; 225-2815.

Committees

Commerce (chairman)

In Washington: Handpicked to run the Commerce Committee by Speaker Newt Gingrich over a more senior member, Bliley at the outset declared himself "a friend of business" and announced that his agenda was to "promote commerce" — an unmistakable jab at the committee's former masters, Democrats John D. Dingell of Michigan and Henry A. Waxman of California, who delighted in calling business executives before the panel for interrogation.

Bliley shares the anti-regulatory fervor of the "revolutionary" Class of 1994 that helped to sweep him into power at the start of the 104th Congress. "The American people sent us a message in November, loud and clear: Tame this regulatory beast!" Bliley thundered at a February 1995 markup. But in contrast to many of the Republicans new to the Hill, Bliley as chairman remains a pragmatist, willing to broker deals behind closed doors with ideological foes and friends alike. He also stiff-armed colleagues who sought to bite off a chunk of Commerce's broad-ranging turf. The result in the 104th was a record of enacted legislation that matched any in the Congress, from telecommunications to drinking water protection and food safety to securities regulation.

During the 105th, Bliley will wield enormous influence in the debate over deregulation of the nation's electrical utility grid. Bliley has pledged that he will listen attentively to industry concerns that deregulation may cause occasional pain — as long as the utilities accept retail competition as an end goal.

Bliley's biggest project during the 104th was a massive overhaul of telecommunications policy. AT&T is a major employer in his district, and he fought for long-distance interests where he could. Bliley painstakingly stitched together a consensus package that Commerce approved overwhelmingly. But when the bill came to the House floor, Gingrich stepped in and ordered changes that favored the regional Bell companies' quest to enter the lucrative long-distance market.

Bliley had ceded turf to an ad hoc committee when Medicare was being overhauled early in the 104th, and his willingness to let Gingrich essentially rewrite the telecom bill at the last minute was seen as a prime example of how the Speaker was riding herd over his committee chairmen. But as Gingrich's grip loosened and the flurry of bills derived from the "Contract With America" gave way to a more normal flow of legislation, Bliley asserted control over his vast domain.

Bliley resisted efforts at the start of the 104th to limit his panel's vast legislative reach, which Dingell had considerably bulked up over the years he served as chairman. When the Judiciary Committee was assigned a bill to limit the liability of manufacturers for faulty products, Bliley teamed with his lieutenant Michael G. Oxley, R-Ohio, to introduce their own bill, which became the main legislative vehicle.

Bliley was willing to work with Jerry Lewis, R-Calif., an Appropriations subcommittee chairman, on riders to a spending bill that sought to reformulate environmental policy. "A lot of it is time," Bliley said, explaining that authorizers had not the time to make major changes that could be achieved immediately on fast-moving appropriations bills.

Bliley and Lewis' plan to block the Environmental Protection Agency from enforcing critical portions of major laws such as the clean water and Clean Air acts was shot down and proved a huge loser politically. With Republican leaders hungry to dodge Democrats' flailing the GOP as anti-environment, they pressed Bliley to accept a safe drinking water bill that had already passed the Senate unanimously. But moving the Senate bill would have cast a shadow over Bliley's independence, and he wanted to protect his committee's turf when the Transportation and Infrastructure Committee had already marked up its section of the bill. Working with Waxman and Dingell, Bliley forged a compromise that passed the House rapidly by voice vote and was cited by numerous Republican incumbents on the stump as proof that the new GOP majority could get

Some of the fastest-growing areas in Virginia are in the scythe-shaped 7th. It cuts a path from the Blue Ridge Mountains through Virginia's Piedmont region to Richmond and its rapidly expanding suburbs, collecting all or part of nine counties.

The 7th is the state's most Republican district. In redistricting before the 1992 election, most of the blacks in Richmond and Henrico County were placed in the new, majority-black 3rd District, leaving whiter, more Republican areas in the 7th. The district's share of the majority-black city of Richmond, for example, has an 88 percent white population.

Bob Dole won 58 percent of the district's vote in the 1996 presidential race. The 7th, as now constituted, was the only district in Virginia that in 1985 backed the GOP nominees for governor, lieutenant governor and attorney general, all of whom lost statewide. But it may be redrawn for the 1998 congressional elections because the neighboring 3rd has been ruled unconstitutional.

More than 70 percent of the 7th's residents live in Richmond and adjacent Henrico and Chesterfield counties. The capital city is the third-largest in Virginia and the longtime center of state government and commerce, although nowadays, Northern Virginia and the Hampton Roads area are almost as economically important. Richmond was one of the South's early manufacturing centers, concentrating on tobacco processing. The Philip Morris USA cigarette plant, one of the largest in the country, is in the 3rd, but many of its roughly 8,200 employees live in the 7th.

While Richmond's population dropped during the 1980s, Chesterfield's population rose by nearly 50 percent and Henrico's by more than 20

VIRGINIA 7
Central — Part of Richmond and suburbs

percent. Hanover County, to the north of Henrico, grew by more than 25 percent. Hanover and Chesterfield are among the state's most Republican counties. Dole won the district's portions of both by about 2-to-1 in 1996.

As the 7th pushes north, the exurbs of Richmond and Washington converge. Longtime farming areas such as Spotsylvania County are being taken over by people who drive or ride long-distance commuter buses or trains to jobs in metropolitan Washington; nearby Fredericksburg is the terminus for a commuter train to Washington. Spotsylvania's population jumped by 67 percent in the 1980s.

The Piedmont in the northern part of the district includes part of Virginia's wine country. Orange, Madison and Culpeper counties have several wineries. The area also contains the Civil War battlefields of Chancellorsville, Spotsylvania and Wilderness. Shenandoah National Park forms the 7th's western frontier.

A glimmer of Democratic votes can be found in Albemarle County, stemming from the campus of the University of Virginia, just over the district's boundary in Charlottesville. Bill Clinton got 44 percent of the vote in the 7th's portion of Albemarle in 1996.

1990 Population: 562,643. White 494,047 (88%), Black 56,283 (10%), Other 12,313 (2%). Hispanic origin 5,797 (1%). 18 and over 424,882 (76%), 62 and over 75,367 (13%). Median age: 34.

things done on the Hill.

When junior GOP members would offer amendments that threatened to unravel deals he had painstakingly cut with Democrats, Bliley sometimes helped to kill the amendments in committee. "You only get perfection in the next world, not this one," he said. He spent several summer days behind closed doors configuring a compromise with Waxman on food safety, successfully overhauling pesticide regulation.

Bliley worked closely with Dingell on an attempt to overhaul the superfund hazardous waste law, although that effort bore limited fruit. The two also teamed up on a bill to erode the existing ability of banks to sell insurance products. Bliley also joined forces with a Republican, Sen. Alfonse M. D'Amato of New York, to break a logjam on a bill to modernize regulation of the securities and mutual fund industries.

Bliley's own securities holdings came under scrutiny in the spring of 1995 when media reports revealed that his stock holdings included companies whose products fall under the wide purview of his committee, such as financial institutions, utilities and energy companies, telecommunications and cable firms, railroads and drug manufacturers. A review of Bliley's actions from 1990 through his first five months as chairman indicated that he had intervened with federal and local regulators in behalf of some companies in which he held stock and voted for legislation that would have directly benefited a company in his portfolio. At the same time, on some issues Bliley had steered a course that was not financially beneficial to companies in his holdings.

In response to the media reports, Bliley said in a statement that he had long sought to avoid even "the appearance of conflict of interest." In June 1995 he placed his extensive stock holdings in a blind trust to quell questions about any possible conflict of interest.

Bliley may be best known for his tireless

efforts to defend cigarette manufacturers from efforts by Waxman and the Food and Drug Administration (FDA) to regulate tobacco products as a drug. Bliley's district is home to thousands of employees of cigarette manufacturer Philip Morris. "I am proud to represent thousands of honest, hard-working men and women who earn their livelihood producing this legal product," Bliley said at a Waxman-led subcommittee hearing in 1994. "And I'll be damned if they are to be sacrificed on the altar of political correctness."

Bliley, a silver-haired man who stands out for sporting bow ties, is an occasional pipe smoker and keeps a framed collection of cigarette packages hanging in his reception office. Preparing to take the Commerce chair after the 1994 election, he made a point to recruit friends of the tobacco industry for committee vacancies. He resisted attempts to repeal tobacco subsidies during consideration of a major farm bill in the 104th, but he stayed out of the fray when the Clinton administration announced new tobacco regulations in 1996. "Whether the FDA has the legal authority to regulate tobacco is a question for the courts, not Congress," he said. After the regulations were announced, he said on a radio talk program that President Clinton would need a "good security detail" if he raised the issue at a North Carolina speech. He apologized for the "jest."

At Home: A pleasant, soft-spoken mortician, Bliley was coaxed into politics in 1968 by civic leaders who sought him out to run for the Richmond City Council. He left city government in 1977 after nearly a decade of service to devote more time to his funeral home. But he enthusiastically re-entered politics shortly after Democrat David E. Satterfield announced his retirement from Congress in 1980.

A Democrat when in Richmond government, Bliley announced his conversion to the GOP only when he launched his House campaign in 1980. Critics said the switch was motivated by the district's GOP voting pattern; Bliley said it was prompted by a leftward swing in the state Democratic leadership.

Bliley's support from the Richmond business community virtually assured his election. With a well-funded campaign, he overwhelmed his little-known Democratic opponent and two independent candidates. In 1982, Bliley faced a more aggressive challenger in Henrico County Supervisor John Waldrop. The Democrat criticized Bliley for backing deep cuts in social and educational programs, a charge that played well in mostly black Richmond. Bliley lost the city but won easily in the white suburbs, where most of the votes were, taking 59 percent overall.

Redistricting for the 1990s inconvenienced the previous occupant of what had been labeled the 7th, but not Bliley. Republican George F. Allen had won a special election in November 1991 to succeed ailing 7th District Rep. D. French Slaughter Jr. But weeks later, the Virginia General Assembly passed a plan that combined Bliley's 3rd and Allen's 7th districts. Allen deferred to Bliley. While much of Bliley's district was new to him, it is also very much Republican, and it has re-elected him without incident every two years.

HOUSE ELECTIONS

1996 General		
Thomas J. Bliley Jr. (R)	189,644	(75%)
Roderic H. Slayton (D)	51,206	(20%)
Bradley E. Evans (I)	11,527	(5%)
1994 General		
Thomas J. Bliley Jr. (R)	176,941	(84%)
Gerald E. "Jerry" Berg (I)	33,220	(16%)

Previous Winning Percentages: 1992 (83%) **1990** (65%) **1988** (100%) **1986** (67%) **1984** (86%) **1982** (59%) **1980** (52%)

CAMPAIGN FINANCE

	Receipts	Receipts from PACs	Expend-itures
1996			
Bliley (R)	$1,108,466	$697,582 (63%)	$1,092,570
Slayton (D)	$30,484	$12,000 (39%)	$28,328
Evans (I)	$195	0	$195
1994			
Bliley (R)	$584,847	$450,333 (77%)	$572,427

VOTING STUDIES

	Presidential Support		Party Unity		Conservative Coalition	
Year	S	O	S	O	S	O
1996	33	65	92	6	96	0
1995	21	79	95	3	99	1
1994	44	55	91	7	92	3
1993	38	61	90	8	100	0
1992	86	13	89	8	94	4
1991	81	19	88	9	97	0

KEY VOTES

1997	
Ban "partial birth" abortions	Y
1996	
Approve farm bill	Y
Deny public education to illegal immigrants	Y
Repeal ban on certain assault-style weapons	Y
Increase minimum wage	N
Freeze defense spending	N
Approve welfare overhaul	Y
1995	
Approve balanced-budget constitutional amendment	Y
Relax Clean Water Act regulations	Y
Oppose limits on environmental regulations	N
Reduce projected Medicare spending	Y
Approve GOP budget with tax and spending cuts	Y

INTEREST GROUP RATINGS

Year	ADA	AFL-CIO	CCUS	ACU
1996	0	n/a	100	100
1995	0	0	96	80
1994	0	11	100	100
1993	5	17	100	100
1992	15	25	86	96
1991	0	17	100	95

DISTRICT VOTE FOR PRESIDENT

	1996		1992
D	93,025 (35%)	**D**	85,357 (30%)
R	155,466 (58%)	**R**	154,575 (55%)
I	16,607 (6%)	**I**	42,724 (15%)

8 James P. Moran (D)

Of Alexandria — Elected 1990, 4th term

Biographical Information
Born: May 16, 1945, Buffalo, N.Y.
Education: College of the Holy Cross, B.A. 1967; City U. of New York, Graduate School, 1967-68; U. of Pittsburgh, M.A. 1970.
Occupation: Investment broker.
Family: Wife, Mary Howard; four children, one stepchild.
Religion: Roman Catholic.
Political Career: Alexandria City Council, 1979-84, vice mayor, 1982-84; mayor of Alexandria, 1985-91.

Capitol Office: 1214 Longworth Bldg. 20515; 225-4376.

Committees
Appropriations
District of Columbia (ranking); Interior

In Washington: There are some contradictions to Moran's House career. He has helped to found a coalition of progressive suburban Democrats and complains that his party's congressional wing is dominated by urban liberals. But while he differentiates himself from those liberals, Moran is a steady vote in the Democratic column, standing with his colleagues against Republican proposals for reducing taxes and balancing the budget. An energetic and hard-working member, he castigates his party at times for inactivity, yet acknowledges that Democrats' ability to set the agenda is greatly crimped by their minority status. And while Moran has an image as a pugilistic pol, he works amicably with his GOP colleague from the neighboring 11th District, Thomas M. Davis III.

Moran returns to the Appropriations Committee in the 105th Congress; he lost his seat there after the 1994 election shaved the number of committee seats Democrats enjoyed when they ran the House. Moran is the top Democrat on the District of Columbia Subcommittee, a perch he can use to continue his high-profile efforts on issues affecting the District and its surrounding metropolitan area, which includes the 8th.

Moran is a cosponsor of a plan to close the District's troubled prison, which is located in the Virginia suburb of Lorton. He has pushed for replacement of the deteriorating and notoriously overcrowded Woodrow Wilson Bridge, which carries tens of thousands of Capital Beltway commuters across the Potomac daily. (The bridge is just south of Alexandria, where Moran served as mayor.)

Like other Capital-area legislators, Moran was especially motivated to oppose the GOP's tax cut package in the 104th because it would have increased the pension contribution requirements of federal workers, a key Moran constituency. And he shares the skepticism some Republicans felt when President Clinton closed down the stretch of Pennsylvania Avenue that fronts the White House for security reasons.

Moran has joined with Republican Davis on a number of issues, including Lorton and federal pensions. Davis chairs the Government Reform and Oversight subcommittee with responsibility for the District, and Moran praised his efforts during the 104th to create a new financial control board with broad powers in the District. "Tom Davis is a bridge-builder," Moran said in 1995.

Despite the comity with Davis, Moran has found much to oppose in the GOP agenda, voting against term limits, Republican budget proposals and a law to phase out farm subsidies. Moran supports gun control measures and in most cases affirms a woman's right to abortion. He did, however, vote in the 104th to ban a particular abortion technique that opponents call "partial birth" abortion. And he came around to vote for the GOP's final plan to overhaul welfare in 1996, after opposing earlier drafts of the legislation.

Moran has a temper, and it has led him into some altercations with Republicans. As the House debated policy toward the conflict in Bosnia in 1995, Moran gave California Republican Randy "Duke" Cunningham a stiff push in the back, leading to a partisan shoving match. A few months earlier, during consideration of a foreign aid bill, Moran had threatened to punch Indiana Republican Dan Burton for personally informing an agency bureaucrat that he would target the agency's budget in the appropriations process. Moran termed this "bullying," and warned Burton: "You pull that again and I'll break your nose. Don't you ever do that to a federal worker again."

In keeping with his general support for workers, federal or otherwise, Moran voted for the 1996 boost in the hourly minimum wage. When the GOP sought to create employer-employee cooperation in non-union shops, Moran offered an amendment stipulating that workers could choose their own representatives on these labor-management "teams." That proposal was rejected, 195-228.

Moran got no further with an amendment to the line-item veto package. He wanted to exempt the judiciary, offering a history lesson about

When critics deride the insular perspective afflicting those who live "inside the Beltway," they may be referring to the suburban residents of the Northern Virginia 8th, most of which territory is within the confines of the Capital Beltway, Interstate 495, which rings Washington.

The area's growth, originally spurred by the rapidly growing federal government, now stems from an array of white-collar and service-industry employers. The military presence in the district starts with the Pentagon, in Arlington, and includes Fort Myer and Fort Belvoir.

The district stands to lose nearly 6,000 defense jobs to realignments recommended by the 1995 base-closure commission at the Naval Sea Systems Command and Space and Naval Warfare Systems facilities.

Three of the most-affluent counties or independent cities in the nation are in the 8th: the cities of Falls Church and Alexandria, and Arlington County. Each had a per capita income above $30,000 by the mid-1990s.

The 8th hugs the Potomac River bank from affluent, predominantly white McLean in the north, through the ethnically, racially and economically diverse neighborhoods of Arlington and the city of Alexandria to the U.S. Route 1 corridor of southern Fairfax County. It is hospitable to most Democrats. Bill Clinton carried the 8th with 55 percent of the vote in 1996. In 1994, Sen. Charles S. Robb carried the territory within the 8th with 60 percent, which was crucial to his successful re-election bid.

Fairfax County, with a population of more than 800,000, is the most populous jurisdiction in Virginia. Even though it is split among three districts — the 8th, 10th and 11th — it is the most populous portion in each of them. One-

VIRGINIA 8
D.C. suburbs — Part of Fairfax County; Arlington; Alexandria

third of the county is in the 8th, accounting for almost half the population in the district.

Arlington is home to three of every 10 district residents. While there are relatively few blacks in Arlington, it has become a melting pot for other minorities. Asians, Hispanics and other minority groups make up roughly one-quarter of the population. Arlington has one of the largest concentrations of Vietnamese in the country, and it has numerous Vietnamese-owned businesses.

The old colonial seaport of Alexandria casts about one-fifth of the district vote; it is reliable Democratic territory. The restaurants and shops of its revitalized Old Town section compete with the Georgetown area of Washington, and thousands of Democratic-voting young professionals live there. On the fringe of Old Town is a black community that enhances Democratic strength. Blacks make up 22 percent of Alexandria's population.

The southern portion of Fairfax County includes George Washington's 500-acre estate at Mount Vernon and Gunston Hall, home of George Mason, one of the framers of the Constitution. It also houses the District of Columbia's Lorton Reformatory.

1990 Population: 562,484. White 427,308 (76%), Black 75,128 (13%), Other 60,048 (11%). Hispanic origin 48,994 (9%). 18 and over 453,533 (81%), 62 and over 64,690 (12%). Median age: 34.

President Franklin D. Roosevelt abusing spending power during the 1930s by cutting travel funds and money to hire bailiffs in an attempt to intimidate the Supreme Court into going along with the New Deal. But that lesson was widely unconvincing and Moran's amendment was voted down, 119-309. He and California Democrat George Miller also found disappointment with their proposal to require foreign governments to enforce their child labor laws before receiving U.S. aid.

Moran did make headway with his proposal to grant parents more power over the television broadcasts coming into their home. First, he joined with John M. Spratt Jr., D-S.C., in sponsoring a bill that would yank licenses from TV stations that air violent programs when many children are watching. The notion that this might amount to censorship did not trouble Moran. "It's self-censorship, and it's about time they showed some restraint," he said.

When that proposal proved too tough, Moran and Spratt joined with Massachusetts Democrat Edward J. Markey in amending the 1996 telecommunications law to require that most new TV sets come equipped with a device to help parents block out offensive programming. Moran was one of a number of legislators in the 105th who were disappointed by the broadcast industry's voluntary rating system.

Moran also was disappointed when the House voted to strike $14 million from the fiscal 1996 military construction spending bill that would have bought land for a military museum in his district. Moran complained that a half-million Army artifacts would go without a home.

He fought with John L. Mica, R-Fla., about legislation that would have bolstered veterans' preference in federal hiring. Moran worried that the bill could be detrimental to other federal workers, countering Mica's assertion that the number of veterans in the federal work force had dropped with a statistic showing that the percentage of veterans in the federal work force had increased. That battle continued into the 105th.

Contending that urban liberals unfairly skew the party's stances on issues, Moran wants the Democratic leadership to look at altering the seniority system so that fewer ranking members are liberals. This comes in contrast to his arguments in the 1994 succession struggle for the Appropriations chairmanship, when Moran argued in favor of 18-term Iowa Democrat Neal Smith. Moran told the party caucus that all members have much at stake in the seniority system. "Will we treat Neal Smith in the way we want to be treated after 36 years?" he said. "He has spent his life earning the honor he seeks."

Moran drew criticism for upbraiding Virginia Thomas, an aide to House Majority Leader Dick Armey, R-Texas, and wife of Supreme Court Justice Clarence Thomas, for testifying at a committee hearing. "What's Mrs. Clarence Thomas doing here?" he bellowed.

At Home: Moran ousted GOP Rep. Stan Parris, long one of the scrappiest street fighters in Washington-area politics, to win his seat in 1990.

Moran, too, had a reputation for pugnacity. His service in Alexandria was stormy. First elected to the City Council in 1979, he saw his career derail in 1984 when, after pleading no contest to a misdemeanor conflict of interest charge, he resigned as vice mayor as part of a plea agreement. He ran as an independent in 1985 and beat the incumbent mayor.

Moran and Parris clearly did not like each other. Parris compared Moran to Iraqi leader Saddam Hussein; Moran called Parris a "racist" and "fatuous jerk" and professed a desire to "break his nose."

Moran castigated Parris for his longstanding opposition to abortion. One ad depicted women locked in jail cells, warning that Parris wanted to make abortion illegal. The ad ended with an image of the Statue of Liberty behind bars. Boosted by the abortion issue, Moran ended up on top, 52 percent to 45 percent.

Redistricting in late 1991 transformed the 8th into a Democratic stronghold. Even within his new friendly confines, Moran had a fight on his hands in 1992. Arlington lawyer Kyle McSlarrow, a political newcomer, ran a nettlesome campaign. With a lot of free media attention, McSlarrow engaged in daily assaults on the liberal freshman. Moran outspent McSlarrow by 2-to-1, dusting off his ad with the women behind bars to remind voters of his support for abortion rights and McSlarrow's opposition.

A Moran-McSlarrow rematch in 1994 was more somber, as media attention focused on Moran's 3-year-old daughter, who was battling brain and spinal cord cancer. Moran won by 20 percentage points. By the fall of 1996 his daughter's condition had improved.

Moran's 1996 opponent, retired Marine Captain John Otey, was severely underfunded, apparently unable to afford even rhetorical props. "David picked up the jawbone of an ass and slew Goliath," Otey noted, but then he lamented, "I'm looking for jawbones right now." Moran won two-thirds of the vote.

HOUSE ELECTIONS

1996 General		
James P. Moran (D)	152,334	(66%)
John Otey (R)	64,562	(28%)
R. Ward Edmonds (VREF)	6,243	(3%)
Sarina J. Grosswald (I)	5,239	(2%)
1994 General		
James P. Moran (D)	120,281	(59%)
Kyle E. McSlarrow (R)	79,568	(39%)

Previous Winning Percentages: 1992 (56%) **1990** (52%)

CAMPAIGN FINANCE

	Receipts	Receipts from PACs	Expend-itures
1996			
Moran (D)	$555,273	$274,877 (50%)	$319,334
Otey (R)	$72,801	$2,825 (4%)	$71,267
Edmonds (I)	$17,069	0	$16,424
Grosswald (I)	$3,255	0	$4,452
1994			
Moran (D)	$1,036,485	$428,161 (41%)	$910,239
McSlarrow (R)	$654,183	$85,784 (13%)	$643,979

DISTRICT VOTE FOR PRESIDENT

1996		1992	
D	130,177 (55%)	**D**	133,183 (51%)
R	95,839 (40%)	**R**	96,799 (37%)
I	9,439 (4%)	**I**	28,967 (11%)

KEY VOTES

1997	
Ban "partial birth" abortions	Y
1996	
Approve farm bill	N
Deny public education to illegal immigrants	Y
Repeal ban on certain assault-style weapons	N
Increase minimum wage	Y
Freeze defense spending	N
Approve welfare overhaul	Y
1995	
Approve balanced-budget constitutional amendment	Y
Relax Clean Water Act regulations	N
Oppose limits on environmental regulations	Y
Reduce projected Medicare spending	N
Approve GOP budget with tax and spending cuts	N

VOTING STUDIES

	Presidential Support		Party Unity		Conservative Coalition	
Year	S	O	S	O	S	O
1996	77	23	82	17	41	51
1995	78	22	77	19	54	43
1994	86	12	84	8	53	47
1993	89	11	90	6	36	64
1992	30	66	83	10	48	50
1991	40	58	79	16	30	68

INTEREST GROUP RATINGS

Year	ADA	AFL-CIO	CCUS	ACU
1996	65	n/a	31	20
1995	65	67	42	8
1994	55	67	55	29
1993	80	92	27	8
1992	80	73	50	13
1991	70	83	40	10

9 Rick Boucher (D)

Of Abingdon — Elected 1982, 8th term

Biographical Information

Born: Aug. 1, 1946, Abingdon, Va.

Education: Roanoke College, B.A. 1968; U. of Virginia, J.D. 1971.

Occupation: Lawyer.

Family: Single.

Religion: Methodist.

Political Career: Va. Senate, 1974-82.

Capitol Office: 2329 Rayburn Bldg. 20515; 225-3861.

Committees

Commerce

Energy & Power; Telecommunications, Trade & Consumer Protection

Judiciary

Courts & Intellectual Property

In Washington: The professorial Boucher seems an unlikely sort to represent Southwest Virginia, a largely rural, rough-cut area of coal mines, tobacco fields and small towns. But he has managed to win eight elections in the 9th District, and in Congress he has gained a measure of influence in areas such as telecommunications and energy. As a member of the Commerce and Judiciary committees, he has shown he is smart, thorough and willing to reach across party lines.

Boucher balances his agenda with a steady devotion to district concerns, staunchly supporting the coal and tobacco industries that provide many jobs in the 9th. Boucher won a seat on Commerce's Energy and Power Subcommittee for the 105th, when the panel will be the fulcrum of efforts to deregulate electricity utilities.

Boucher works quietly and picks his shots carefully. He made a startlingly low total of five appearances on the House floor during the 104th Congress, addressing telecommunications (twice), biotechnology patents and an attempt to kill funding for the Appalachian Regional Commission. He also rose to note the absence of a quorum during consideration of a solid waste bill.

On the floor, Boucher votes steadily with the majority of his Democratic colleagues; during the 104th, he supported a 90-cent increase in the hourly minimum wage and the final overhaul package on welfare. Boucher opposed the GOP's first attempt to rewrite welfare laws and consistently opposed many of the Republicans' major initiatives, including easing federal regulations, enacting a $189 billion bundle of tax cuts, passing term limits and balanced-budget constitutional amendments, and banning a particular abortion technique that opponents call a "partial birth" abortion.

Boucher finds more to like in GOP proposals on social and legal matters that fall under the purview of the Judiciary Committee. He frequently is the only Democrat on the panel to join the GOP in reporting bills out. He was on board during the 104th for passage of a tough immigration package, a bill to limit punitive damages in civil cases, an anti-terrorism measure and a bill to allow states right of refusal when it comes to recognizing same-gender marriages.

Some members of the Energy and Power Subcommittee of Commerce — particularly those hailing from the Northeast — have expressed concern that large-scale coal burning might contribute significantly to pollution. Boucher seeks to ensure that such attitudes do not outweigh consideration of coal's benefits and uses, and he resolutely vows to prevent environmentally minded colleagues from reopening the clean air act. The creation of a competitive national market for coal could prove a huge boon to southwestern Virginia, which has long lagged economically. (Coal already accounts for more than half the country's electricity.)

Boucher sees another potential gift to the region in the advent of computer interconnectivity. Boucher ranks second among Democrats on the Commerce Subcommittee on Telecommunications, Trade and Consumer Protection, and he co-founded the Congressional Internet Caucus; he hopes along with many other rural lawmakers that networking will level the economic playing field. "Communications issues are vitally important as a bridge to a new economy for rural communities in the next century," Boucher said. His district's city of Blacksburg, home to Virginia Polytechnic University, is well-wired.

Boucher and another Virginian, Republican Robert W. Goodlatte, took the lead during the 104th in addressing copyright laws on the Internet. Boucher also worked closely with Ohio Republican Michael G. Oxley in protecting the interests of the Bell operating companies in drafting the telecommunications law.

"If the cable industry has trouble with quicker telephone company entry [into their markets], as far as I'm concerned, that's just the price of progress," Boucher said in 1995. He sponsored a bill in the 103rd that would have accelerated development of the high-performance computer

VIRGINIA 9
Southwest — Blacksburg; Bristol

Bordering four states, the 9th contains some of the most beautiful and most depressed areas in Virginia.

The Appalachians, which form a diagonal spine down the district, as well as Mount Rogers National Recreation Area and Hungry Mother State Park on the southern tier near the North Carolina and Tennessee borders, provide stunning scenery.

But the coal-dependent western portion of the 9th lags behind the state in economic health. Four of the five jurisdictions with the highest poverty rates in the state are in the 9th; three are in the coal fields region, an area comprising Buchanan, Dickenson, Lee, Russell, Scott, Tazewell and Wise counties, and the independent city of Norton.

The "Fighting Ninth" earned that name not only because of its tradition of fiercely competitive two-party politics but also because of its ornery isolation from the political establishment in Richmond.

Southwestern Virginia was settled by Scotch-Irish and German immigrants who felt little in common with the English settlers in the Tidewater and Piedmont regions. The Civil War divided the anti-secession mountaineers from the state's slaveholding Confederates. In the postwar era, when Democrats routinely dominated Virginia politics, the 9th was the only district in which Republicans were consistently strong.

But as the state GOP moved into alliance with Richmond's business establishment and Northern Virginia's affluent suburbanites, the party lost ground in the 9th. A number of the region's burley tobacco growers and other small-scale farmers now are teaming up with the traditionally Democratic coal miners. Republican Oliver L. North also carried the 9th in his 1994 Senate bid. And the 9th was the only district carried by a conservative primary challenger against GOP Sen. John W. Warner in 1996.

Democrats are strongest in the coal-mining counties along the Kentucky and West Virginia borders. Bill Clinton carried the five coal counties bordering those states in 1996, as he had four years earlier.

The coal fields region has little in common with the rest of Virginia — as many as seven other state capitals are closer than Richmond. Virginia may be a right-to-work state, but the United Mine Workers of America still wields influence here; in a 1989 write-in campaign, a UMW-backed independent crushed a 21-year incumbent for a state House seat.

Republicans normally have an edge in the corridor of counties roughly traced by Interstate 81 as it runs north from Bristol to Radford. Carroll County, on the North Carolina border, is also solidly Republican, although Boucher carried it in 1996.

Montgomery County, which contains the district's largest city, Blacksburg, is economically atypical of the 9th. Home to Virginia Tech, the state's largest university with nearly 24,000 students, Blacksburg is a far more tidy and prosperous-looking place than most of the factory and coal towns in the district.

1990 Population: 562,380. White 543,103 (97%), Black 13,948 (2%), Other 5,329 (1%). Hispanic origin 2,839 (1%). 18 and over 433,970 (77%), 62 and over 91,220 (16%). Median age: 34.

networks that provide the foundation for the "information superhighway." Boucher also has successfully worked for legislative provisions exempting rural phone companies from regulation under certain conditions and ensuring that rural phone customers have access to the latest technologies.

In the 103rd, he made many of the district's gun owners happy by voting against two gun control measures and also opposing President Clinton's crime bill, which included a ban on certain assault weapons. Boucher voted to repeal the ban in 1996. He opposed NAFTA in 1993; the trade agreement was unpopular with organized labor, a strong presence in the district's coal counties.

Boucher also has been active on environmental bills that addressed the problems of toxic and municipal waste. He has teamed up with Michigan Republican Fred Upton to offer compromise proposals on the thorny issues of superfund overhaul and interstate shipments of municipal solid waste.

Tobacco brings $40 million a year to the 9th, and Boucher has opposed Clinton administration programs to impose heavier regulations on tobacco products. Among his other concerns with Clinton's health care overhaul during the 103rd, Boucher was worried about the reliance on stiff new cigarette taxes to finance the plan.

At Home: The hard work and careful organization that mark Boucher's legislative activities are also the secret of his electoral success in the 9th, where voters no longer seem to mind that he lacks a rough-and-tumble air.

Boucher needed all his assets to weather bruising elections in 1982 and 1984. But in 1986, he became the district's first House candidate since 1853 to run unopposed, and again in 1990 he drew no major-party opposition.

In 1992, Republicans tried to recruit the man whom Boucher defeated in 1982 to win the 9th, former GOP Rep. William C. Wampler. But despite heavy pressure, Wampler declined. Boucher went on to a 26 percentage point win over the GOP nominee as Bill Clinton became the first Democrat in 16 years to win the 9th.

Boucher came naturally to politics. Both his grandfather and great-grandfather served in the Virginia House. His father was commonwealth's attorney in Washington County (Abingdon).

After graduating from the University of Virginia Law School, Boucher joined a Wall Street firm. He took time out to work as an advance man for George McGovern's 1972 presidential campaign. The following year he returned to Abingdon to practice law, ultimately joining his family's firm in 1978.

He also began laying the groundwork for his political debut, which he made in a 1975 bid for state Senate. Energetically buttonholing district convention delegates, Boucher defeated a veteran incumbent for the Democratic nomination, then coasted to election.

Democratic Gov. Charles S. Robb and other state party leaders urged Boucher to challenge Wampler in 1982, when high unemployment was plaguing the district's coal fields. Boucher raised enough money to finance billboards and media advertising on the three TV stations that together cover the district.

Wampler dismissed Boucher as "a Henry Howell with an Ivy League look," a reference to the controversial Tidewater populist who lost decisively in his last gubernatorial race in 1977. But Boucher jabbed back, describing the affable Wampler — known to constituents as the "bald eagle of the Cumberland" — as a nice man but an ineffective legislator. Boucher termed himself the true fiscal conservative, citing Wampler's support for Reaganomics and its ensuing budget deficits.

The economy was a powerful issue. In some of the coal counties, unemployment neared 20 percent in the fall of 1982. Boucher, drawing on the active support of the United Mine Workers of America, ran exceptionally well.

Boucher also neutralized Wampler in his home base, the Bristol area just north of Tennessee. Bristol was also part of Boucher's state Senate district; Wampler won it only narrowly. Boucher won by just 1,123 votes out of more than 150,000 cast.

When Wampler decided against a rematch in 1984, Boucher became a clear favorite. But he did not have an easy race against his well-financed GOP challenger, state Rep. Jefferson Stafford. One of the legislature's most conservative members, Stafford charged that Boucher was too liberal, tying him to Walter F. Mondale, whose presidential campaign Boucher helped to lead in Virginia. Although Stafford carried most of the 17 counties in the 9th, Boucher survived by taking large majorities in the coal-producing areas.

HOUSE ELECTIONS

1996 General		
Rick Boucher (D)	122,908	(65%)
Patrick Muldoon (R)	58,055	(31%)
Thomas I. "Tom" Roberts (VREF)	8,080	(4%)
1994 General		
Rick Boucher (D)	102,876	(59%)
Steve Fast (R)	72,133	(41%)

Previous Winning Percentages: **1992** (63%) **1990** (97%) **1988** (63%) **1986** (99%) **1984** (52%) **1982** (50%)

CAMPAIGN FINANCE

	Receipts	Receipts from PACs	Expend-itures
1996			
Boucher (D)	$667,955	$411,348 (62%)	$576,709
Muldoon (R)	$63,020	$2,016 (3%)	$71,662
Roberts (VREF)	$5,320	0	$5,110
1994			
Boucher (D)	$723,611	$466,838 (65%)	$779,616
Fast (R)	$209,477	$7,473 (4%)	$209,235

VOTING STUDIES

	Presidential Support		Party Unity		Conservative Coalition	
Year	S	O	S	O	S	O
1996	71	27	74	21	71	27
1995	74	24	75	19	57	34
1994	76	19	86	8	61	33
1993	82	15	88	7	50	45
1992	21	78	86	9	44	56
1991	34	62	84	10	43	49

DISTRICT VOTE FOR PRESIDENT

	1996		1992
D	91,469 (46%)	**D**	99,099 (45%)
R	85,531 (43%)	**R**	93,673 (43%)
I	20,603 (10%)	**I**	26,676 (12%)

KEY VOTES

1997	
Ban "partial birth" abortions	N
1996	
Approve farm bill	Y
Deny public education to illegal immigrants	N
Repeal ban on certain assault-style weapons	Y
Increase minimum wage	Y
Freeze defense spending	N
Approve welfare overhaul	Y
1995	
Approve balanced-budget constitutional amendment	N
Relax Clean Water Act regulations	N
Oppose limits on environmental regulations	Y
Reduce projected Medicare spending	N
Approve GOP budget with tax and spending cuts	N

INTEREST GROUP RATINGS

Year	ADA	AFL-CIO	CCUS	ACU
1996	65	n/a	44	15
1995	75	100	33	4
1994	65	67	42	30
1993	60	100	30	13
1992	90	82	38	8
1991	65	75	40	10

10 Frank R. Wolf (R)

Of Vienna — Elected 1980, 9th term

Biographical Information

Born: Jan. 30, 1939, Philadelphia, Pa.

Education: Pennsylvania State U., B.A. 1961; Georgetown U., LL.B. 1965.

Military Service: Active Army Reserve, 1962-present; Army Reserve, 1963-67.

Occupation: Lawyer.

Family: Wife, Carolyn Stover; five children.

Religion: Presbyterian.

Political Career: Sought Republican nomination for U.S. House, 1976; Republican nominee for U.S. House, 1978.

Capitol Office: 241 Cannon Bldg. 20515; 225-5136.

Committees

Appropriations

Foreign Operations, Export Financing & Related Programs; Transportation (chairman); Treasury, Postal Service & General Government

In Washington: In his rookie term as an Appropriations Committee "cardinal," Wolf proved to be a good soldier in the Republican Revolution, helping to curb spending urges once he got control of the transportation purse. Wolf broke with his party only rarely during the 104th, when GOP policies ran counter to his Northern Virginia constituency's preferences. But he had a more high-profile break at the start of the 105th, when he voted against the party's candidate for Speaker.

As Transportation Appropriations chairman, Wolf has labored to cut spending overall and block pet "pork" projects. He has a generally cooperative but occasionally contentious relationship with House Transportation and Infrastructure Committee Chairman Bud Shuster, R-Pa., who will be rewriting the nation's major surface transportation law during the 105th. In general, Wolf supports the Republican majority's efforts to lighten the regulatory load and offer increased power to states and localities at Washington's expense.

Wolf voted "present" when the roll was taken for Newt Gingrich's re-election as Speaker in January 1997. Wolf explained that he could not let his feelings of fellowship toward Gingrich and the GOP Conference interfere with his conscience, which could not abide Gingrich's admitted financial indiscretions.

During the 104th, Wolf voted against Republican plans to ease federal clean water regulations and to block the Environmental Protection Agency from enforcing a number of major environmental laws. He was also one of just 11 House Republicans who opposed the party's $189 billion package of tax cuts, citing the plan's increase on pension contributions from federal workers.

With his first transportation bill in 1995, Wolf aimed to cut about 10 percent from the amount spent the year before. He succeeded in banning highway "demonstration" projects, which he said would "liberate" members from having to deliver earmarked projects for their home states. With Congress cutting spending in areas such as home-heating subsidies and summer jobs for youth, Wolf argued it would be "ethically and morally wrong" to keep money flowing to "outright pork."

In his past service on Appropriations, Wolf developed a reputation as a premier "pothole politician"; few members rivaled his personal involvement in easing the daily grind for commuting constituents. He consistently lobbied for funds to complete the metropolitan Washington subway system, and he vigorously pressed local and federal officials to take steps to ease roadway backups.

Wolf has been equally assertive in working to keep federal jobs in his district. He succeeded in pressuring a reluctant National Science Foundation to move its headquarters to Arlington from a prestigious but pricey location near the White House. He helped thwart the designs of Democratic Sen. Robert C. Byrd upon several thousand CIA jobs, which Byrd had almost succeeded in moving from Northern Virginia to his own West Virginia.

Wolf leads the opposition against Shuster's attempts to take highway trust funds "off-budget," freeing more money for transportation but putting other domestic programs under increased financial strain. "What we are dealing with today is money, power and pork," Wolf commented during consideration of Shuster's perennial proposal during the 104th. "This bill represents and protects sand and gravel and concrete. Then it says to those who are elderly with Alzheimer's disease, 'We're not going to protect you.' "

Belt-tightening provided the rationale for Wolf's attempt with his fiscal 1996 bill to eliminate federal labor protections for mass transit workers. Wolf said the protections were costly and outdated, making it harder for local systems to break even with fewer federal dollars flowing. In the face of strong opposition, Wolf offered an amendment to ensure that his move would not abrogate the collective bargaining rights of transit workers under state laws. It was voted down, 201-

VIRGINIA 10
North — Part of Fairfax County; Manassas

From small-town apple country to congested Washington suburbs, the 10th bridges a dizzying range of economies and lifestyles. Draping the northern portion of the state, the district links the bucolic Blue Ridge Mountains with the suburban sprawl of Fairfax County.

Redistricting for the 1990s substantially altered the 10th; Wolf no longer represents any turf inside the Capital Beltway, the fabled divider between "real America" and Washington insiderism.

About 60 percent of the 10th's population lives in suburban Northern Virginia. Many of these people still commute to jobs in the District of Columbia, but increasingly, people in the outer suburbs work in suburban office complexes, rarely venturing into D.C. About one-sixth of Fairfax County is in the 10th, accounting for one-fourth of the district's population. Most of the remaining suburbanites live in Prince William and Loudoun counties.

Loudoun County's population rose by 50 percent during the 1980s; the population of the county seat of Leesburg nearly doubled during that time. Ever more fresh subdivisions dot former farmland in what is still horse country. Prince William County's population rose nearly 50 percent, making it the third most populous county in Virginia.

Beyond suburbia, agriculture and manufacturing fuel the economy. Winchester is the center of the state's apple-growing industry. Virginia ranks sixth in the nation in apples harvested, and Frederick and Clarke counties lead the state.

Winchester also is the home of Virginia's political dynasty, the Byrd family. But like former Sen. Harry F. Byrd Jr., who took over his father's Senate seat in 1965 and later became an independent, the district has abandoned its Democratic roots.

In 1996 presidential voting, Bob Dole won the 10th by a solid majority, beating Bill Clinton 54 percent to 38 percent. Dole carried every county and independent city in the district.

The district's ample natural beauty draws visitors year-round. At the eastern end of the district, the Potomac River cascades at Great Falls Park in Fairfax County along the Maryland border. Loudoun and Fauquier counties are part of Northern Virginia's "hunt" country, a rolling landscape dotted with sprawling country houses, horse farms and an occasional vineyard.

Skyline Drive, a 105-mile scenic highway through Shenandoah National Park across the ridge of the Blue Ridge Mountains, begins in Front Royal (Warren County). George Washington National Forest straddles the West Virginia border. The 10th also has some important Civil War battle sites, including Manassas and New Market.

1990 Population: 562,664. White 510,296 (91%), Black 32,476 (6%), Other 19,892 (4%). Hispanic origin 12,606 (2%). 18 and over 411,822 (73%), 62 and over 52,782 (9%). Median age: 32.

224, and his underlying proposal was subsequently stripped, providing organized labor its first major victory over the House GOP leadership.

In 1995, Wolf had Shuster's blessing on one occasion to step on authorizers' toes: his draft spending bill would have provided Amtrak with $728 million in operating and capital funds, but only on the condition that Congress reorganize the railroad. Shuster had run into opposition on his committee to restructuring, and hoped Wolf's ultimatum would strengthen his hand. The take-it-or-leave-it language, approved by the House, was dropped in conference with the Senate.

Wolf's main legislative accomplishment outside the transportation sphere came with a law that created a national commission on gambling. He said a study was essential to understanding the burgeoning gambling industry, and particularly important because of a concomitant rise in the numbers of compulsive gamblers. "The gambling industry has not taken seriously the magnitude of the problem, or has attempted to sweep it under the rug," he said.

Though best-known for his close-to-home priorities, Wolf has established enough of a profile in overseas affairs to have drawn fire from Sudan and China. In 1993, the government of Sudan said Wolf was telling "loathsome lies" about conditions in the country. Wolf, who has visited Sudan several times, had angered Sudanese officials by entering a State Department cable into the Congressional Record; it outlined widespread human rights abuses by the Muslim fundamentalist government. Wolf has also been one of Congress' leading GOP proponents of using U.S. trade sanctions to pressure China to open up its political system.

Wolf used the fiscal 1997 transportation spending bill for a special exception in a long-brewing child custody case, adding a provision to allow Washington surgeon Elizabeth Morgan to return to the U.S. without facing legal repercussions. Morgan had gone to jail and then to New Zealand to keep her daughter from her husband in a case famous worldwide. Wolf, who had intervened in 1989 to spring Morgan from prison with legislation that changed District of Columbia sentencing law, successfully defended his 1996 provision against House members who called it an assault against the independence of the judiciary.

Wolf travels home nightly to Vienna and refuses to work on Sundays in an effort to balance work with his family commitments. (He sponsored legislation that brought child care to federal facilities.) Wolf headed a task force to make Congress more "family friendly" for its members by lightening the work load and regularizing the schedule. But in light of the hectic workload engendered by the GOP's fresh taste of power, Wolf shrugged, "I personally doubt that a truly family-friendly Congress will ever be possible."

At Home: Persistence brought Wolf his first House victory, and since then he has enjoyed mostly smooth rides to re-election.

Barely a year after Democrat Joseph L. Fisher first won his House seat in 1974, Wolf began campaigning to defeat him. His 1976 effort had the backing of local Reagan activists, but did not survive the primary. In 1978, with more name recognition and better financing, Wolf won the GOP nomination, but he lost to Fisher in November. On his third try, in 1980, Wolf rode a huge budget and a national GOP upsurge to narrow victory.

In the early campaigns, Fisher chided Wolf for a lack of government experience. But having been a lobbyist, an aide to GOP Rep. Edward G. Biester of Pennsylvania, and deputy assistant secretary of the Interior, Wolf could claim he knew his way around the Capitol.

Democratic hopes of ousting Wolf were highest in 1986, when the party ran John G. Milliken, a past chairman of the Arlington County Board of Supervisors. Milliken had long experience in local government and a reputation as a moderate. As chairman of the Washington Metropolitan Area Transit Authority and the Northern Virginia Transportation Commission, he had dealt with many of the same transportation questions that Wolf had. But despite a hefty treasury — nearly $750,000 — Milliken had trouble making a case for replacing the hard-working, if undynamic, incumbent. Wolf won with 60 percent of the vote.

In redistricting in late 1991, Wolf lost all of Arlington and part of suburban Fairfax County, and he added a number of rural counties beyond the Washington orbit. Democrat Raymond E. Vickery sought to test Wolf's vote-getting ability in the new territory, but he found the redesigned 10th even more Republican. Wolf won 64 percent.

HOUSE ELECTIONS

1996 General		
Frank R. Wolf (R)	169,266	(72%)
Robert L. Weinberg (D)	59,145	(25%)
Gary A. Reams (I)	6,500	(3%)
1994 General		
Frank R. Wolf (R)	153,311	(87%)
Alan R. Ogden (I)	13,687	(8%)
Robert L. "Bob" Rilee (I)	8,267	(5%)

Previous Winning Percentages: **1992** (64%) **1990** (61%) **1988** (68%) **1986** (60%) **1984** (63%) **1982** (53%) **1980** (51%)

CAMPAIGN FINANCE

	Receipts	Receipts from PACs	Expend- itures
1996			
Wolf (R)	$347,268	$197,281 (57%)	$251,763
Weinberg (D)	$68,146	$14,350 (21%)	$61,881
Reams (LIBERT)	$9,930	0	$9,929
1994			
Wolf (R)	$280,066	$129,958 (46%)	$222,532

DISTRICT VOTE FOR PRESIDENT

	1996		1992
D	99,510 (38%)	**D**	83,214 (33%)
R	140,684 (54%)	**R**	124,783 (50%)
I	16,476 (6%)	**I**	41,228 (17%)

KEY VOTES

1997	
Ban "partial birth" abortions	Y
1996	
Approve farm bill	Y
Deny public education to illegal immigrants	Y
Repeal ban on certain assault-style weapons	Y
Increase minimum wage	N
Freeze defense spending	N
Approve welfare overhaul	Y
1995	
Approve balanced-budget constitutional amendment	Y
Relax Clean Water Act regulations	N
Oppose limits on environmental regulations	Y
Reduce projected Medicare spending	Y
Approve GOP budget with tax and spending cuts	Y

VOTING STUDIES

	Presidential Support		Party Unity		Conservative Coalition	
Year	S	O	S	O	S	O
1996	38	62	88	10	88	12
1995	27	73	87	12	90	9
1994	53	46	86	13	89	11
1993	39	61	90	10	93	7
1992	78	22	86	13	96	4
1991	81	18	81	17	92	8

INTEREST GROUP RATINGS

Year	ADA	AFL-CIO	CCUS	ACU
1996	5	n/a	81	95
1995	10	8	92	64
1994	0	33	83	86
1993	10	0	91	92
1992	20	42	88	84
1991	15	17	80	80

11 Thomas M. Davis III (R)

Of Falls Church — Elected 1994, 2nd term

Biographical Information

Born: Jan. 5, 1949, Minot, N.D.

Education: Amherst College, B.A. 1971; U. of Virginia, J.D. 1975.

Military Service: Army, 1971-72; National Guard, 1972-79; Army Reserve, 1972-79.

Occupation: Lawyer; professional services firm executive; state legislative aide.

Family: Wife, Margaret "Peggy" Rantz; three children.

Religion: Christian Scientist.

Political Career: Fairfax County Board of Supervisors, 1980-94; Fairfax County Board of Supervisors chairman, 1991-94.

Capitol Office: 224 Cannon Bldg. 20515; 225-1492.

Committees

Government Reform & Oversight
District of Columbia (chairman); Government Management, Information & Technology

Science
Space & Aeronautics; Technology

Transportation & Infrastructure
Aviation; Public Buildings & Economic Development

In Washington: Davis, one of the few moderate members of the GOP Class of 1994, was quicker than most of his classmates to reach across the aisle to find accommodations with Democrats in order to enact legislation. "It's a dream for practical people to do something to help people," he declared a couple of months into his first term.

In the 104th, Davis was in a rare position for a freshman, chairing a subcommittee. In addition to his duties heading the Government Reform and Oversight Subcommittee on the District of Columbia, Davis sits on the Science Committee and, for the 105th Congress, he joins the Transportation and Infrastructure Committee. On the latter panel he will be in a position to try to improve suburban Northern Virginia's highway and mass transit infrastructure as the main surface transportation law is reauthorized.

When it comes to looking out for the interests of federal workers, one of his main constituencies, Davis has few equals. He came to Congress from just across the Potomac, in the sprawling Virginia suburbs of the capital. There, he had served as chairman of the Fairfax County Board of Supervisors, the governing body for the biggest local jurisdiction in the state (population more than 800,000). In that job he earned a reputation for working in a low-key and non-confrontational manner and successfully harmonizing diverse constituencies.

Despite the mantra in conservative GOP ranks that power should be moved from the federal government to states and localities, Davis must contend with the fact that many Republicans in Congress want to take an active hand in managing the affairs of the District of Columbia, a hugely Democratic city beset with economic and social woes.

The city historically has received from Congress an annual payment in lieu of taxes, and Davis has said that many members are reluctant to underwrite the troubled D.C. government at a time when they are under pressure to keep down federal spending in their own districts.

Shortly after entering the House, Davis was forced to address a fiscal crisis in the capital. After years of lax and wasteful management, the city was facing a projected budget shortfall of $722 million. Davis worked closely with Democratic members of his subcommittee to create a new financial oversight board to address the District's fiscal crisis. His plan became law in April 1995.

Davis has sparred publicly less often with his Democratic colleagues than with James T. Walsh, R-N.Y., who chaired the D.C. Appropriations Subcommittee during the 104th and played the "bad cop" role to Davis' "bridge-builder," as Virginia Democratic Rep. James P. Moran put it. Their divergence was reflected in their preferred nomenclature for the oversight board they were creating: Walsh favored a "control board with the emphasis on control," while Davis liked "financial recovery board." The official title ended up being the District of Columbia Financial Responsibility and Management Assistance Authority, though it is commonly known as the control board.

"The whole thing is going to work well if everyone cooperates," Davis said of District politicians and the control board. "Otherwise, if you get a confrontation between the control board and the mayor and council, the control board wins. The control board is set up to win."

With the District's annual payment one of the least popular items on Congress' must-pass docket, Davis has struggled at times convincing his colleagues that the control board should be given time to work. He backed an attempt by Eleanor Holmes Norton, the District's non-voting Democratic delegate, to allow the city to spend part of its budget, even though its appropriation had not been approved by the start of a new fiscal year. The bill died under the weight of opposition from appropriators. Davis has also joined with Moran in proposing that the District's Lorton prison, located in Northern Virginia, be shut down.

Davis backs President Clinton's plan to have the federal government take over responsibility

Growth in the Northern Virginia suburbs of Washington during the 1980s helped earn Virginia an additional congressional district. Fairfax County, the most populous jurisdiction in Virginia, with a population of more than 800,000, grew by 220,000 during the 1980s — a rate of 37 percent and more than one-fourth of the commonwealth's overall population expansion of 840,000.

The 11th, with a shape that vaguely recalls the human digestive tract, may have been drawn by Democratic legislators and signed by a Democratic governor, but it is highly competitive, as its vote in 1996 to re-elect Bill Clinton and Republican Davis attest. George Bush won the areas within the 11th in both the 1988 and 1992 presidential elections. Clinton narrowly captured the Fairfax County and Prince William County sections of the 11th in 1996, though he lost Fairfax City to Bob Dole.

The district is primarily middle- to upper middle-class suburbia. Many residents work in downtown Washington, either for the federal government or for companies whose business is linked to the government.

The 11th defines the image of Northern Virginia by including suburbs developed primarily since the 1960s. Neighboring districts house historic sites or buildings constructed shortly after World War II. But the 11th, with its nostalgically named townhouse developments, shows the area economy broadening beyond its government base into technology and service industries.

Rush hour in Northern Virginia no longer follows a single, to-and-from Washington pattern; much traffic moves from one suburb to another. Dozens of companies have put down roots in office-park developments in Fairfax. One is Mobil Corp., whose headquarters are in

VIRGINIA 11
D.C. suburbs — Parts of Fairfax and Prince William counties

Merrifield. The area's business roster includes many high-tech companies, some of them defense-related, including computer engineering, manufacturing and consulting firms.

Fairfax County accounts for nearly 80 percent of the votes cast in the 11th. Growth and all its effects on property tax rates, school quality, traffic and crime are the primary concerns of Fairfax residents. In recent years they have been buffeted by a weak real estate market and threatened defense cutbacks.

The planned community of Reston, founded in 1961 in the northern part of the county, grew by 33 percent during the 1980s to nearly 49,000. The adjacent town of Herndon saw its population rise by more than 40 percent, to about 16,000. Unincorporated places in the county such as Burke (split between the 11th and 8th districts), Bailey's Crossroads, Lincolnia and Seven Corners all grew by more than 20 percent.

Suburban expansion spread into Prince William County, which grew by 71,000 in the 1980s, a nearly 50 percent rise. About three-fifths of the county's population is in the 11th. Woodbridge has the minor-league Prince William Cannons. A few miles south on I-95 is Potomac Mills, an immense mall of more than 200 factory outlet stores that has become Virginia's No. 1 draw for visitors.

1990 Population: 562,497. White 454,067 (81%), Black 46,037 (8%), Other 62,393 (11%). Hispanic origin 41,594 (7%). 18 and over 419,933 (75%), 62 and over 43,129 (8%). Median age: 32.

for Washington's courts, prisons and pension plans, obviating the need for an annual payment. "I've always said this city is engaged in too many activities for its tax base," Davis reasoned.

Though sensitive about Congress appearing to micromanage the District's affairs, Davis has voiced his share of complaints about the city's pothole-plagued roads and bridges, and he even held a hearing on traffic disruptions caused one day by protesting janitors. "This is very much Congress' business. We're talking about moving traffic in and out of the nation's capitol." He referred to the protest as "traffic terrorism."

Continuing his use of dramatic analogy, Davis routinely referred to federal employees as "hostages" during the government shutdowns that occurred in the middle of the 104th Congress, pressuring the House leadership to reopen the government during budget negotiations.

Concern for federal employees also led Davis to vote against a tax cut derived from the House GOP's "Contract With America." Davis said that since the tax cut was paid for, in part, by requiring federal employees to contribute more to their pension funds, the legislation amounted to "a 10 percent tax hike" for those workers. Davis was one of only 11 Republicans to oppose passage of the tax measure. But in October, Davis voted "yes" on the GOP's landmark budget-reconciliation bill, after persuading the GOP leadership to jettison a provision that targeted free and subsidized parking in downtown D.C. that federal workers enjoy.

Davis' concern for federal workers led him to vote in the 104th to assure that their insurance coverage would pay for abortions. But he voted to ban a particular abortion technique that opponents call "partial birth" abortion, and he opposed allowing abortions at overseas military hospitals, even if paid for by the woman. He also voted against requiring states to pay for Medicaid abortions in cases of rape and incest.

Davis also voted with his GOP colleagues on

certain other social issues, including an amendment preventing illegal immigrants from receiving public education. But he broke from his party in opposing repeal of a ban on certain semiautomatic assault-style weapons.

At Home: In their 1994 contest, Davis and freshman Democratic Rep. Leslie L. Byrne offered a contrast more pronounced in style than in platforms. A member of the Democratic leadership's whip organization, Byrne was an aggressive partisan. By contrast, conciliation was the hallmark of Davis' leadership style on the Fairfax County board, where he projected an air of congeniality.

He cultivated a non-ideological image in his House campaign, avoiding close association with his party's controversial 1994 Senate candidate, Oliver L. North. When Byrne tried to link North to Davis, Davis would say only that he supported Republican nominees. Davis unseated Byrne by an eight-point margin.

A heavy favorite to win re-election, Davis devoted much of his campaigning efforts in 1996 to helping Republican John W. Warner's bid for a fourth Senate term, serving as campaign chairman. A prodigious fundraiser, Davis is considered likely to set his sights on statewide office with the turn of the millennium.

Davis was first elected to the Fairfax County Board of Supervisors in 1979. In 1991, he challenged the incumbent Democratic chairman of the board, whom he criticized for fostering an anti-business, anti-development climate. Davis outpolled the Democrat by a stunning 2-to-1 ratio.

As chairman, Davis sought to follow through on his campaign themes by cutting business taxes and repealing an ordinance that restricted land use.

HOUSE ELECTIONS

1996 General		
Thomas M. Davis III (R)	138,758	(64%)
Tom Horton (D)	74,701	(35%)
C.W. "Levi" Levy (I)	2,842	(1%)
1994 General		
Thomas M. Davis III (R)	98,216	(53%)
Leslie L. Byrne (D)	84,104	(45%)
Gordon S. Cruickshank (I)	3,246	(2%)

CAMPAIGN FINANCE

	Receipts	Receipts from PACs	Expend-itures
1996			
Davis (R)	$1,517,371	$457,870 (30%)	$1,333,607
Horton (D)	$294,846	$38,563 (13%)	$290,492
1994			
Davis (R)	$1,435,382	$331,431 (23%)	$1,430,272
Byrne (D)	$1,130,789	$455,460 (40%)	$1,136,669
Cruickshank (I)	$5,921	0	$5,676

DISTRICT VOTE FOR PRESIDENT

1996		1992	
D	109,377 (48%)	**D**	102,721 (43%)
R	105,258 (46%)	**R**	103,907 (43%)
I	10,844 (5%)	**I**	34,719 (14%)

KEY VOTES

1997	
Ban "partial birth" abortions	Y
1996	
Approve farm bill	Y
Deny public education to illegal immigrants	Y
Repeal ban on certain assault-style weapons	N
Increase minimum wage	N
Freeze defense spending	?
Approve welfare overhaul	Y
1995	
Approve balanced-budget constitutional amendment	Y
Relax Clean Water Act regulations	N
Oppose limits on environmental regulations	N
Reduce projected Medicare spending	Y
Approve GOP budget with tax and spending cuts	Y

VOTING STUDIES

	Presidential Support		Party Unity		Conservative Coalition	
Year	**S**	**O**	**S**	**O**	**S**	**O**
1996	52	48	77	21	80	16
1995	30	69	82	16	90	10

INTEREST GROUP RATINGS

Year	ADA	AFL-CIO	CCUS	ACU
1996	15	n/a	94	79
1995	15	8	88	60

WASHINGTON

Governor: Gary Locke (D)
First elected: 1996
Length of term: 4 years
Term expires: 1/01
Salary: $121,000 (Will accept only $90,000)
Term limit: 2 terms
Phone: (206) 753-6780
Born: Jan. 26, 1950; Seattle, Wash.
Education: Yale U., B.A. 1972; Boston U., J.D., 1975.
Occupation: Lawyer; deputy county prosecutor.
Family: Wife, Mona Lee.
Religion: Unspecified.
Political Career: Wash. House, 1982-93; King County executive, 1994-97.

Lt. Gov.: Brad Owen (D)
First elected: 1996
Length of term: 4 years
Term expires: 1/01
Salary: $62,700
Phone: (206) 786-7700

State election official: (206) 753-7121
Democratic headquarters: (206) 583-0664
Republican headquarters: (206) 451-1988

REDISTRICTING

Washington gained one House seat in reapportionment, increasing from eight districts to nine. Redistricting commission map became law Feb. 12, 1992.

STATE LEGISLATURE

Legislature. Meets January-March in odd years, January-April in even years.

Senate: 49 members, 4-year terms
1996 breakdown: 26, 23D; 27 men, 22 women
Salary: $25,900
Phone: (206) 786-7550

House of Representatives: 98 members, 2-year terms
1996 breakdown: 53R, 45D; 63 men, 35 women
Salary: $25,900
Phone: 206-786-7750

URBAN STATISTICS

City	Population
Seattle	516,259
Mayor Norman Rice, D	
Spokane	177,165
Mayor Jack Geraghty, D	
Tacoma	176,664
Mayor Brian Ebersole, N-P	
Bellevue	86,874
Mayor Ron Smith, N-P	
Everett	69,961
Mayor Edward D. Hansen, N-P	

U.S. CONGRESS

Senate: 1 D, 1 R
House: 3 D, 6 R

TERM LIMITS

For state offices: Yes
Senate: 3 terms
House: 3 terms

ELECTIONS

1996 Presidential Vote

Bill Clinton	50%
Bob Dole	37%
Ross Perot	9%

1992 Presidential Vote

Bill Clinton	43%
George Bush	32%
Ross Perot	24%

1988 Presidential Vote

Michael S. Dukakis	50%
George Bush	48%

POPULATION

1990 population		4,866,692
1980 population		4,132,156
Percent change		+18%
Rank among states:		18
White		89%
Black		3%
Hispanic		4%
Asian or Pacific islander		4%
Urban		76%
Rural		24%
Born in state		48%
Foreign-born		7%
Under age 18	1,261,387	26%
Ages 18-65	3,030,017	62%
65 and older	575,288	12%
Median age		33.1

MISCELLANEOUS

Capital: Olympia
Number of counties: 39
Per capita income: $19,442 (1991)
Rank among states: 13
Total area: 68,139 sq. miles
Rank among states: 20

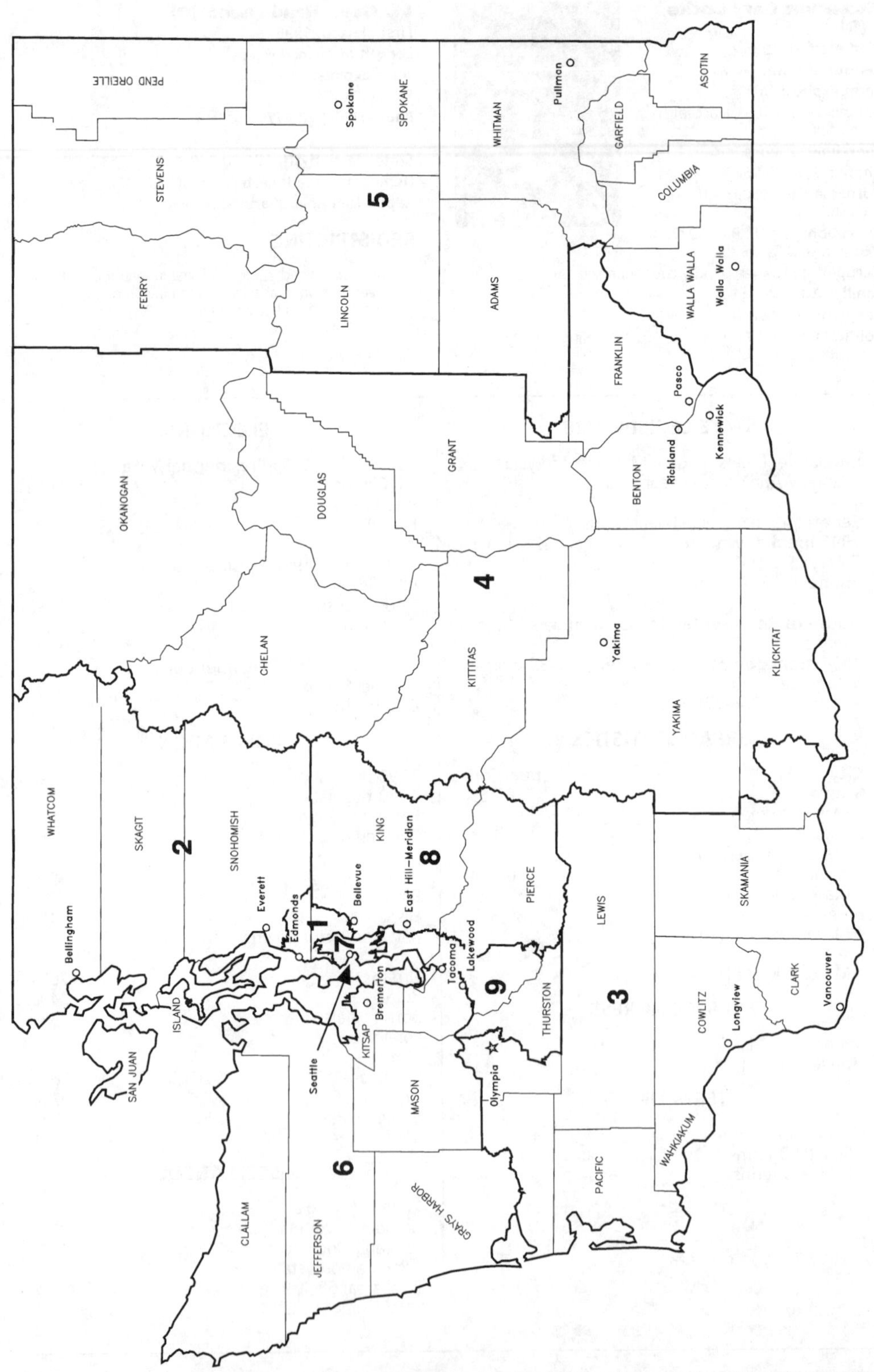
PEND OREILLE
STEVENS
FERRY
SPOKANE
Spokane
5
LINCOLN
WHITMAN
Pullman
ASOTIN
GARFIELD
COLUMBIA
ADAMS
WALLA WALLA
Walla Walla
FRANKLIN
Pasco
Richland
Kennewick
BENTON
OKANOGAN
DOUGLAS
GRANT
CHELAN
4
KITTITAS
Yakima
YAKIMA
KLICKITAT
WHATCOM
Bellingham
SKAGIT
2
SNOHOMISH
Everett
Edmonds
1
KING
Bellevue
East Hill-Meridian
8
7
Seattle
Bremerton
KITSAP
ISLAND
SAN JUAN
Tacoma
Lakewood
9
PIERCE
THURSTON
Olympia
LEWIS
3
SKAMANIA
COWLITZ
Longview
CLARK
Vancouver
MASON
6
CLALLAM
JEFFERSON
GRAYS HARBOR
PACIFIC
WAHKIAKUM

WASHINGTON
SEATTLE AREA DISTRICTS

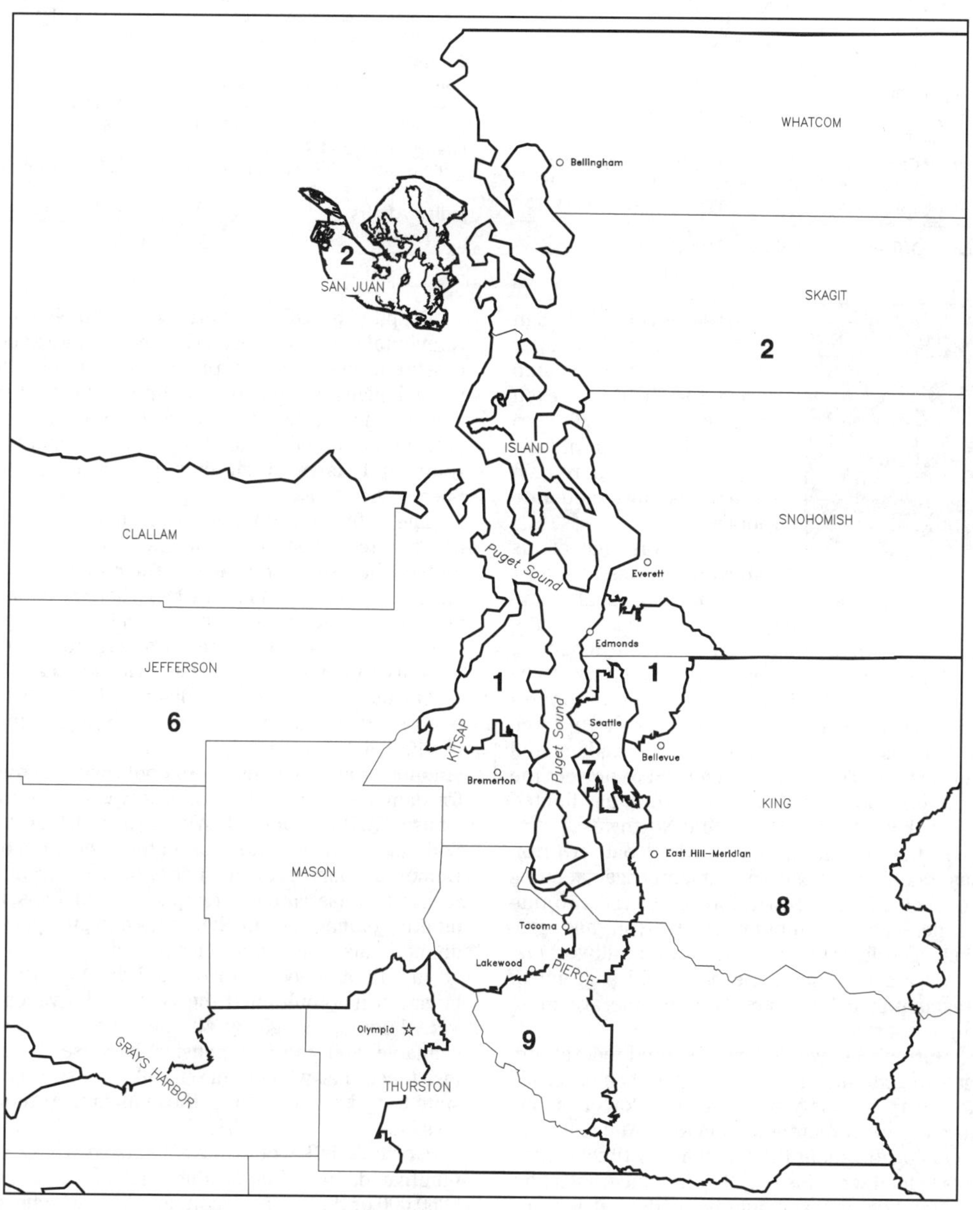

Slade Gorton (R)

Of Seattle — Elected 1980, 3rd term
Did not serve 1987-89.

Biographical Information

Born: Jan. 8, 1928, Chicago.
Education: Dartmouth College, A.B. 1950; Columbia U., LL.B. 1953.
Military Service: Army, 1946-47; Air Force, 1953-56; Air Force Reserve, 1956-81.
Occupation: Lawyer.
Family: Wife, Sally Jean Clark; three children.
Religion: Episcopalian.
Political Career: Wash. House, 1959-69, majority leader, 1967-69; Wash. state attorney general, 1968-80; Wash. attorney general, 1969-81; defeated for re-election to U.S. Senate, 1986.
Capitol Office: 730 Hart Bldg. 20510; 224-3441.

Committees

Appropriations
Agriculture, Rural Development & Related Agencies; Energy & Water Development; Interior (chairman); Labor, Health & Human Services & Education; Transportation
Budget
Commerce, Science & Transportation
Aviation (chairman); Communications; Consumer Affairs, Foreign Commerce & Tourism; Oceans & Fisheries
Energy & Natural Resources
Energy Research Development Production & Regulation; Water & Power
Indian Affairs

In Washington: Although Gorton ventured deeper into the conservative camp during the 104th — even becoming counsel to Majority Leader Trent Lott — he managed to remain close to his more moderate roots as well.

One visible sign of his rightward tilt was his effort to help Republicans try to attain a key goal: relaxing certain environmental regulations that the GOP considers unnecessary or burdensome. Gorton indicated early on that he would try to use his position as chairman of the Interior Appropriations Subcommittee in the 104th to force action on his bill to rewrite the Endangered Species Act. The act has been used to protect the Northern spotted owl, which, in turn, has limited timber harvesting in the Pacific Northwest.

In the ongoing jobs vs. owls debate, Gorton has staked out a position adamantly against curbs on logging in old-growth forests. In visits to timber-dependent communities, Gorton has proclaimed solidarity with loggers and millworkers. "Owls are important," he once told a group of Washington millworkers. "But people are more important than owls."

Gorton's bill would have required federal officials to go to much greater lengths than currently necessary to justify measures to protect endangered and threatened species. And he was unapologetic about the fact that the timber interests helped write his bill. "I don't think that's how good public policy should be made, but I'm perfectly willing to get the free services of good lawyers in drafting my views," he told The New York Times.

The bill went nowhere. GOP leaders — stunned by a backlash against House efforts to overhaul the clean water act and ease other environmental regulations — tried to moderate their public image on the environment.

Despite the GOP's efforts to buff their environmental image, however, Gorton was more successful in defending a provision that allowed more logging in old-growth forests. Legislative language in the fiscal 1995 rescissions bill temporarily exempted certain timber sales from environmental laws, including the Endangered Species Act.

The Clinton administration and Gorton's home-state colleague, Democrat Patty Murray, lobbied heavily to repeal the rider. But Gorton and his allies won in March 1996, when the Senate voted 42-54 against repealing the timber language. "This . . . is a prescription for an end to all timber harvests in national forests," Gorton argued.

On another key issue for business in the 104th, Gorton sided with those who were trying to limit product liability awards. Putting a cap on the amount of money consumers could win in court for damage from faulty products was part of the House GOP's "Contract With America." In the Senate, Gorton and his chief cosponsor, Democrat John D. Rockefeller IV of West Virginia, resisted conservative attempts to add caps to punitive damages in all civil cases and put special limits on medical malpractice awards.

In a floor speech, Gorton said the expense of litigation has multiplied the cost of the vaccine for whooping cough by 400 percent. "It is less available and more expensive because of the insistence that we continue to allow absurd lawsuits to be brought against those manufacturers," he said.

Gorton's bill would have imposed a cap on punitive damages in product liability cases of $250,000 or three times economic loss, whichever was greater. Shortly after Gorton introduced his bill early in 1995, then GOP Majority Leader Bob Dole of Kansas revised the proposal to add a sweeping provision to limit punitive damage awards in all civil lawsuits and to add protections against liability for doctors. Dole's reshaping made the bill resemble one passed by the House as part of its contract, but he misjudged the scope of the Senate's spirit of reform, and three times failed to end a filibuster on his revised bill.

The Senate returned to pass Gorton's version, with Dole's support, in 1996, but only by 59 votes — short of the 67 needed to override President Clinton's threatened veto. Gorton tried to work with the administration, offering such alterations as increasing the time limit for filing suit from 15 to 18 years, but he said the White House shot down every offer. Even close Clinton ally Rockefeller was unable to sway the president, and Republicans accused Clinton of bowing to trial lawyers and consumer groups, who thought the bill would have barred victims from seeking full legal redress and removed an incentive from manufacturers to produce safe products. Said a discouraged Gorton, "I do not think with the American public this will ever be a significant issue." Clinton vetoed the bill in May 1996.

But it was not all business with Gorton. The senator, who chaired the Commerce, Science and Transportation Subcommittee on Consumer Affairs during the 104th Congress, has worked on consumer protections. In 1994 the Senate passed legislation he wrote to reduce choking accidents and deaths of children. "The costs of prevention are small compared to the costs of accidents," he said. The law requires standard warnings on toys small enough to cause a choking hazard in small children. The law also required the Consumer Protection Safety Commission to develop safety standards for bicycle helmets.

During the 102nd Congress, Gorton was a chief cosponsor of legislation to reregulate the cable TV industry. And during consideration of the 1991 highway bill, the Senate approved Gorton's amendment requiring that all new cars and light trucks be equipped with air bags. In the 105th Congress, Gorton chairs Commerce's Aviation Subcommittee.

Gorton's moderate bent was evident during the 104th in such actions as his vote (one of five cast by a Republican) to reject a Dole-led proposal to create medical savings accounts, which would allow individuals who have a catastrophic health care plan to save for medical expenses in tax-deductible accounts. On abortion, his record was a mix: He voted to repeal the ban on privately funded abortions in overseas military hospitals, but he also voted against funding abortions for federal workers through their health insurance policies.

He and Murray teamed up to alter a major fishery conservation bill in defense of Washington's fishing industry. Both objected to the popular rewrite of the Magnuson Fishery Conservation Act because they said it favored Alaska's fishing industry over their state's. They fashioned a compromise that eventually passed the Senate on a 100-0 vote.

As Interior subcommittee chairman, Gorton was also in charge of writing the bill to fund the National Endowment for the Arts, a perennial conservative target for elimination. Although he oversaw a one-third cut for the agency in 1995, his heart wasn't in it: "I feel like the Grinch."

As a new member of the Energy and Natural Resources Committee for the 105th Congress, he has staked out a position on the panel with four other Northwestern senators against privatizing the Bonneville Power Administration — part of a larger fight to get the federal government out of the electricity business.

At the start of the 103rd, Gorton unsuccessfully tried to move into a leadership position. He challenged Alan K. Simpson of Wyoming for minority whip and lost 25-14.

At Home: Gorton made his political comeback secure in 1994 with his 56 percent win, a virtual landslide for the man who was defeated for re-election in 1986 only to narrowly win the state's other Senate seat two years later.

Determined in 1994 not to repeat history, Gorton worked hard creating a strong organization, raising money and mending fences including courting the senior citizens who had deserted him in 1986 and moving right and making an alliance with the religious activists from whom he had previously kept his distance.

Gorton was helped by Democrats' failure to recruit a big name to oppose him. Nine largely inexperienced Democratic contenders wallowed in obscurity until the late primary, when King County Councilman Ron Sims captured the nomination with 18 percent of the all-party vote.

Discouraged by its diminishing chances elsewhere, the national Democratic Party rallied around Sims. He accepted both their money as well as a politically risky visit from Clinton. Sims attacked Gorton as a partisan who put politics above good government. And if Gorton was hurt by a sometimes off-putting personality, Sims benefited from an extensive list of volunteer work that included serving as a lay minister to the homeless.

But Sims, who would have been the first African-American elected to statewide office, carried only four counties, including Seattle-dominated King County.

Born to a wealthy Chicago family (whose ancestors included the founders of the Gorton's of Gloucester fish-processing company), Gorton says Washington state's progressive politics led him to settle there. As attorney general, he crafted a pro-consumer record that fit him in the moderate mold of the state's most popular Republicans.

This profile aided Gorton in his 1980 bid against Democratic Sen. Warren G. Magnuson, whose legendary efforts to obtain public works projects had earned him six Senate terms. Gorton ousted Magnuson with 54 percent of the vote.

Many of Gorton's constituents, though, were never personally comfortable with him. Averse to the hail-fellow world of personal politics, the brusque, cerebral Gorton was known to cut off political associates and inquisitive constituents in mid-sentence. It was thus easy for state Democrats to convince voters in 1986 that Gorton was "aloof" and "arrogant."

Democratic challenger Brock Adams beat him with 51 percent, and Gorton returned to legal practice in Seattle. In 1987, he worked as a Department of Energy consultant on options for the Hanford facility. But late that year, GOP Sen. Daniel J. Evans announced that he would retire.

Unable to persuade GOP Reps. Sid Morrison or Rod Chandler to run, the party leadership turned to Gorton. Hard-line conservatives were uneasy with the choice but could produce only two weak primary challengers, and Gorton breezed into the general election.

He then faced Democratic Rep. Mike Lowry, who held off House colleague Don Bonker in a more grueling primary. Lowry had lost to Evans in the 1983 Senate special election to fill the seat of Democrat Henry M. Jackson, who died in 1983.

The 1988 contest thus matched the losers of the previous two Washington Senate races, and both set out to soften the negatives that had defeated them. Gorton spent more than $1 million on ads in which he apologized for being arrogant. Lowry shaved his scraggly beard, adopted a neat appearance and restrained his rhetoric and temper.

SENATE ELECTIONS

1994 General		
Slade Gorton (R)	947,821	(56%)
Ron Sims (D)	752,352	(44%)
1994 Primary †		
Slade Gorton (R)	492,251	(53%)
Ron Sims (D)	162,382	(17%)
Mike James (D)	138,005	(15%)
Scott Hardman (D)	29,973	(3%)
Warren E. Hanson (R)	26,628	(3%)
Jesse Wineberry (D)	24,698	(3%)
Ken Yeager (D)	13,718	(1%)
Mike the Mover (R)	11,403	(1%)

Previous Winning Percentages: 1988 (51%) **1980** (54%)

† In Washington's "jungle primary," candidates of all parties are listed on one ballot.

CAMPAIGN FINANCE

	Receipts	Receipts from PACs		Expend-itures
1994				
Gorton (R)	$4,755,977	$1,172,322	(25%)	$4,792,764
Sims (D)	$1,238,575	$238,419	(19%)	$1,228,098

KEY VOTES

1997	
Approve balanced-budget constitutional amendment	Y
Approve chemical weapons treaty	Y
1996	
Approve farm bill	Y
Limit punitive damages in product liability cases	Y
Exempt small businesses from higher minimum wage	Y
Approve welfare overhaul	Y
Bar job discrimination based on sexual orientation	N
Override veto of ban on "partial birth" abortions	Y
1995	
Approve GOP budget with tax and spending cuts	Y
Approve constitutional amendment barring flag desecration	Y

VOTING STUDIES

	Presidential Support		Party Unity		Conservative Coalition	
Year	S	O	S	O	S	O
1996	44	54	90	10	95	5
1995	32	68	89	11	91	9
1994	48	52	76	24	84	16
1993	30	67	82	17	90	10
1992	68	28	80	18	68	26
1991	86	14	82	18	80	20

INTEREST GROUP RATINGS

Year	ADA	AFL-CIO	CCUS	ACU
1996	15	n/a	100	85
1995	10	0	89	74
1994	30	13	90	80
1993	20	27	100	84
1992	25	36	90	72
1991	30	17	80	67

Patty Murray (D)

Of Seattle — Elected 1992, 1st term

Biographical Information

Born: Oct. 11, 1950, Seattle.

Education: Washington State U., B.A. 1972.

Occupation: Educator.

Family: Husband, Rob Murray; two children.

Religion: Roman Catholic.

Political Career: Shoreline School Board, 1983-89; Wash. Senate, 1989-93.

Capitol Office: 111 Russell Bldg. 20510; 224-2621.

Committees

Appropriations
Energy & Water Development; Foreign Operations; Labor, Health & Human Services & Education; Military Construction (ranking); Transportation

Budget

Select Ethics

Labor & Human Resources
Aging; Children & Families

Veterans' Affairs

In Washington: Having survived a brutal 104th Congress as a member of the minority, Patty Murray no longer considers herself "a mom in tennis shoes." She told a Seattle crowd late in 1996 that, while she may still pursue the personal legislative agenda that fits that sobriquet, her style has changed.

"I stand before you not as a mom in tennis shoes but as a mom in combat boots," she said.

As Republicans took over Congress in 1995, Murray immediately strode into some of the muddiest legislative ground, including the divisive issues of abortion and the environment.

Murray pulled her boots on again in early 1996 for the fight over timber harvesting in the Pacific Northwest. Murray tried to repeal a provision from a bill enacted the previous year that had led to what environmentalists call overharvesting of old-growth forests. The timber companies and their allies in Congress argued that the provision, which exempted certain timber sales from environmental laws, protected jobs in the Northwest and forced the administration to live up to existing contracts with the timber companies.

Murray's amendment would have opened the timber harvesting to legal challenges under environmental laws, allowing sales to be halted in court. "My bill cuts a middle path," she said. "It says to workers: Salvage logging is something we should always be able to do. It says to conservationists: You will have an opportunity to hold the administration to its word." But while the amendment was backed by the Clinton administration, it was rejected by the Senate 42-54.

Another major environmental fight claimed Murray's attention early in the 104th Congress: the debate over the ban on exporting oil from Alaska's North Slope. Murray contended that exporting North Slope oil would increase U.S. dependence on foreign oil and cost jobs in the Pacific Northwest. Although she failed to stop the lifting of the ban, she did win concessions to put in place environmental and other safeguards for the Pacific Northwest.

During the 103rd Congress, Murray had lost a high-profile fight over abortion restrictions. But she won a major round in the 104th with an amendment to a fiscal 1997 defense authorization bill allowing military personnel to have abortions on U.S. bases overseas. The amendment overturned a ban on the procedure that had been enacted the year before, with exceptions for rape or incest or risk to the woman's life. The Defense Department had allowed military women to transfer to non-military hospitals for abortions, but Murray argued that military women should have the same right to an abortion as private citizens back home.

In a floor debate over Murray's amendment, Indiana Republican Daniel R. Coats asserted that the taxpayer money used to operate military hospitals shouldn't be used on abortions. But Murray pointed out that public funds were still being used to fly women back to the United States on military airplanes to obtain their abortions. "It's dangerous, unnecessary and just plain wrong" to ban abortions at overseas bases, she said.

In a 45-51 vote, Murray overcame an attempt to kill her amendment, convincing 13 Republicans to vote with her. The amendment then passed on a voice vote.

Murray was one of the Senate's most ardent backers of surgeon general nominee Dr. Henry W. Foster Jr., who failed to gain enough votes for confirmation after he came under intense scrutiny for his abortion stance.

She was one of five women senators led by Democrat Barbara Boxer of California to pressure the Ethics Committee to hold public hearings on sexual misconduct and other charges against former Sen. Bob Packwood, R-Ore. In the wake of that controversy, Murray called for the establishment of a clear sexual harassment policy for the U.S. Senate, similar to one she had authored while in the Washington state Senate.

At Home: Murray came to the Senate as one of those political outsiders who seized the inside track in the 1992 election. The self-styled "mom in tennis shoes," Murray seemed to embody just about every national campaign trend: She was a woman who sought to enter the predominantly male Senate, an outsider who vowed to oust the incumbent and a relative newcomer seeking a voice among the pros.

Two early breaks gave Murray a decisive boost in her Senate race. First, the disgraced incumbent, Democrat Brock Adams, dropped out in March after a newspaper article detailed similar accounts by eight unidentified women who said Adams had made unwanted and inappropriate sexual advances toward them.

The only Democrat in the race when Adams pulled out, Murray said she entered because of her outrage over the Senate's handling of the Clarence Thomas Supreme Court confirmation hearings. "It's not just Brock," she told The Seattle Times. "It's the whole U.S. Senate."

Murray got another break when the popular Democratic Gov. Booth Gardner, who was leaving office, decided against seeking a Senate seat. Still, to win the primary and the general election, Murray had to get past two better-known and popular moderates who had years of congressional experience, Democratic former Rep. Don Bonker and GOP Rep. Rod Chandler. It was their strength, however, that gave Murray her leverage: She was able to portray both as Washington insiders.

Bonker, who had lost in the 1988 Democratic primary for the Senate, touted his Washington experience, saying that he, unlike Murray, would not need to be trained to be a senator if elected. But on primary day, Murray surpassed Bonker by more than 100,000 votes and outpolled Chandler too (he was on the same ballot in Washington's all-candidate primary). She was the 11th woman nominated for the Senate in 1992, a record that made national headlines and meant network TV time for Murray and some of the other female nominees.

In the weeks after the primary, Murray maintained a daunting lead. Her suburban populism, level gaze and tone of empathy resonated far beyond expectations. By contrast, Chandler's heavy-handed approach included ending an hour-long, one-on-one debate by reciting the chorus from the late Roger Miller's song "Dang Me." The last line — "Woman would you weep for me?" — prompted Murray to say: "That's just the attitude that got me into this race, Rod."

Murray never relinquished her lead and won on Election Day with 54 percent to Chandler's 46 percent.

Murray had her first taste of politics in 1979 when she petitioned the state Legislature not to cut funding for a co-op preschool program in which she was involved. One legislator gave Murray the mom-in-tennis-shoes label — implying she could have little influence — that she used to such advantage in 1992. She went on to organize 12,000 families statewide and preserve the preschool program.

That just whetted Murray's appetite. She served six years on the Shoreline School Board just outside Seattle before winning election to the state Senate in 1988. She became the Democratic whip two years later. In truth, by the time Murray ran for the U.S. Senate, she was far more the politician than she let on in her campaign, leading the Seattle Times to say at one point that she was "neatly packaged as unpackaged."

SENATE ELECTIONS

1992 General		
Patty Murray (D)	1,197,973	(54%)
Rod Chandler (R)	1,020,829	(46%)
1992 Primary †		
Patty Murray (D)	318,455	(28%)
Rod Chandler (R)	228,083	(20%)
Don Bonker (D)	208,321	(19%)
Leo K. Thorsness (R)	185,498	(16%)
Tim Hill (R)	128,232	(11%)
Gene David Hart (D)	15,894	(1%)
Marshall (D)	11,659	(1%)

† In Washington's "jungle primary," candidates of all parties are listed on one ballot.

CAMPAIGN FINANCE

	Receipts	Receipts from PACs		Expend-itures
1992				
Murray (D)	$1,496,204	$439,766	(29%)	$1,342,038
Chandler (R)	$2,592,759	$1,143,695	(44%)	$2,504,777

KEY VOTES

1997	
Approve balanced-budget constitutional amendment	N
Approve chemical weapons treaty	Y
1996	
Approve farm bill	N
Limit punitive damages in product liability cases	N
Exempt small businesses from higher minimum wage	N
Approve welfare overhaul	N
Bar job discrimination based on sexual orientation	Y
Override veto of ban on "partial birth" abortions	N
1995	
Approve GOP budget with tax and spending cuts	N
Approve constitutional amendment barring flag desecration	N

VOTING STUDIES

	Presidential Support		Party Unity		Conservative Coalition	
Year	S	O	S	O	S	O
1996	85	10	94	5	18	82
1995	89	9	92	7	19	81
1994	94	6	97	2	13	88
1993	90	3	85	6	22	71

INTEREST GROUP RATINGS

Year	ADA	AFL-CIO	CCUS	ACU
1996	90	n/a	17	0
1995	95	100	33	0
1994	90	88	20	0
1993	90	91	14	0

1 Rick White (R)

Of Bainbridge Island — Elected 1994, 2nd term

Biographical Information

Born: Nov. 6, 1953, Bloomington, Ind.

Education: Dartmouth College, A.B. 1975; U. of Paris, Pantheon Sorbonne, 1975-76; Georgetown U., J.D. 1980.

Occupation: Lawyer; law clerk.

Family: Wife, Vikki Kennedy; four children.

Religion: Presbyterian.

Political Career: No previous office.

Capitol Office: 116 Cannon Bldg. 20515; 225-6311.

Committees

Commerce

Energy & Power; Finance & Hazardous Materials; Telecommunications, Trade & Consumer Protection

In Washington: In many ways, White exemplifies the storied Republican Class of 1994. He is an ardent budget-cutter who held no public office before coming to Congress, he knocked off a Democratic incumbent in his first race, and he generally votes the GOP line — even though sometimes that discomfits moderate voters in his suburban Seattle district.

White's support of Republican efforts to repeal a ban on certain semiautomatic assault-style weapons, to ease federal timber, clean water and other environmental regulations, and to achieve cost savings on such programs as Head Start, Medicare and student loans made him the target of many an attack ad. The media barrage from groups such as the Sierra Club and the AFL-CIO grew so intense that during the 1996 campaign White frequently quipped, "If I do not have an ad run against me every month, I feel neglected, that no one is paying attention."

Like many of his cohorts in the Class of 1994, White was disappointed when the revolutionary fires fanned by the "Contract With America" began to quell, and he lamented that the ideas of the new House majority drew insufficient oxygen within the stuffier confines of the Senate. "I wish we had more idea where the Senate stood when we signed [the contract]," he moaned.

Nevertheless, White was able to capitalize on the benefits of incumbency to win a second term with 54 percent of the vote, slightly higher than his 1994 tally. With a seat on the Commerce Committee, he was well-positioned to find the financing he needed to defend his record. His district is home to the giant software company Microsoft, and he received significant fundraising help from PACs affiliated with electronic, communications and telephone industries.

Microsoft's founder, Bill Gates, is a frequent referent in White's House floor remarks, and White had a hand in drafting a landmark revamp of telecommunications policy in the 104th. During Commerce consideration of the bill, White worked with Silicon Valley's Anna G. Eshoo, D-Calif., in adding provisions to prevent Federal Communications Commission regulations from forcing standards on the computer industry.

White was a primary negotiator of the bill's compromise anti-pornography provisions, worked out during House-Senate negotiations. The final version imposed penalties on purveyors of online smut while holding harmless a carrier making a good-faith attempt to screen such material from minors. White contended that the plan offered protection for children while preventing unnecessary governmental intrusion. But after the bill was enacted, the plan failed to stand up to judicial scrutiny under the First Amendment.

White, one of the four founders of the Congressional Internet Caucus, weighed into the campaign finance debate with a proposal to allow federal candidates free and equal access to the Internet. One of the major online services wished to donate space to candidates in 1996 but was told by the Federal Election Commission that that would run afoul of in-kind contribution limits.

White's devotion to the cause of deficit reduction led him in the 104th to cast one of 30 Republican votes against increasing the federal debt limit to $5.5 trillion. His desire to reduce the size of the federal government led him to directly oppose a position taken by The Boeing Co., his district's largest employer. The airline manufacturer appealed to him to drop his crusade to shutter the Commerce Department, but White was unmoved. "I don't think the federal government should be in the business of helping Boeing market its airplanes. Boeing is perfectly capable of doing that on its own." His budget-cutting fervor, however, does not generally extend to the Pentagon; he has supported GOP efforts to boost defense spending above levels requested by President Clinton.

Certainly The Wall Street Journal sees White as representative of the GOP Class of 1994. It chronicled his first House term in a series of articles, consistently portraying him as more conservative than his district. White in 1995 voted for the Contract With America 98 percent of the time.

WASHINGTON 1
Puget Sound (west and east) — North Seattle suburbs; Kitsap Peninsula

The 1st traditionally has connected residential neighborhoods in the northern part of Seattle with the first tier of suburbs beyond the city limits. This is a prosperous and, on balance, a politically moderate area. The GOP held the seat through the 1980s, but never won it decisively, partly because most of the voters here are well to the left of national Republican doctrine on social issues.

Analysts of Washington's 1992 redistricting plan said it boosted Republican strength in the 1st. The GOP temporarily lost the seat in the strong Democratic year, but regained it in the 1994 swing of the pendulum. In 1992 presidential voting, Bill Clinton carried the 1st with 41 percent of the vote; independent Ross Perot, who ran well throughout the suburbs and exurbs of Seattle, got 27 percent in the 1st.

The huge majority of people in the district live north of Seattle in western Snohomish and King counties, in communities such as Mill Creek and Bothell that are along or just inland from Puget Sound. At its southern end, the 1st slices a bit off the top of Seattle, takes in some "Gold Coast" suburbs such as Medina on the eastern shore of Lake Washington and includes part of Bellevue, which has blossomed into a full-fledged satellite city of Seattle.

Much of the land in the 1st — but only about 15 percent of its population — is west across Puget Sound, in Kitsap County. Tony Bainbridge Island is here, as are several military facilities, including a base that services the Navy's Trident submarines. Home to many with defense-related jobs, Kitsap County is also a popular retirement location for military personnel. The eastern and western lobes of the district are connected by ferries.

In 1994, the King County portions of the 1st were the only areas White lost, albeit narrowly: Cantwell bested White by just 668 votes. Snohomish, where Perot's 32 percent had dropped George Bush into third place in 1992, gave White 54 percent, his highest. He carried Kitsap by 53 percent.

The 18 percent population boom that Washington state enjoyed during the 1980s was greatly felt in the communities of the 1st, as newcomers drawn by high-technology jobs and scenic suburban surroundings settled here. Biotechnology and electronics firms are major employers, and there is a swarm of small computer-related companies around the headquarters of software giant Microsoft.

So robust was the growth in the 1980s that overcrowding and traffic became hot political issues. The early 1990s brought new concerns related to economic retrenchment. Much business and commerce in the 1st and throughout greater Seattle is related to Boeing, the mammoth aircraft maker. Hit by downturns in both the military and civilian sectors of aviation, Boeing in 1993 announced major job cutbacks. But by 1996, commercial aircraft orders were up, new military contracts were in hand and the company was trying to acquire or merge with leading rivals.

1990 Population: 540,745. White 495,515 (92%), Black 7,103 (1%), Other 38,127 (7%). Hispanic origin 12,648 (2%). 18 and over 401,047 (74%), 62 and over 62,756 (12%). Median age: 33.

White nearly broke ranks on a contract-related vote came when a $500-per-child tax credit was proposed. He thought it should wait, and he told the Journal that cutting taxes before cutting the deficit represented "cheap politics." White said during floor debate that he told the House GOP leadership, "I do not think we should eat our dessert before we go on a diet." But in the end, he voted for the tax credit.

He has broken with the GOP majority on a few high-profile issues, including maintaining certain enforcement powers of the Environmental Protection Agency. He supported a ban on a particular abortion technique that opponents call a "partial-birth" abortion, but sided with abortion-rights backers on some other votes important to them in the 104th. He was one of only 12 House Republicans voting in 1995 against a proposed constitutional amendment to prohibit flag burning. "The flag is a symbol, but the Constitution is a lot more than a symbol," White argued. "We've never before amended the Bill of Rights in our history, and it seems to me you have to have a pretty good reason to do it."

At Home: On a day of good news for Washington state's Republican Party, White's 1994 ousting of Democrat Maria Cantwell may have been the most surprising success story of all.

Although youthful, bright and politically able, White was making his first bid for public office against a woman widely regarded as a Democratic rising star. Cantwell was the first of her party to represent the 1st District in 40 years, and she had claimed it very convincingly in 1992.

But White proved appealing and aggressive, a clean-cut family man with a gleaming résumé who positioned himself to exploit public dissatisfaction with politicians and the nation's direction. Promising to limit himself to five terms, White said he wanted to be part of a big change of direction in Washington, then come home.

Like Cantwell, White is an Indiana native who

went to Washington state in the early 1980s. He became a partner with Seattle's largest law firm. His father is an oil company executive, and the family's dinner table conversations sometimes turned on the dangers of pollution. White's youthful rebellion took the form of a brief flirtation with Democratic politics as a supporter of George McGovern's 1972 presidential bid.

Although the 1994 race was White's first bid for elective office, he had been involved with the Republican Party for a decade. He was a delegate to state conventions and in 1990 helped found the "Farm Team," a recruiting group for young Republicans — often people in business who had not been involved in politics. White's House bid had the backing of key party leaders, and he had no trouble winning the GOP nomination against King County Deputy Prosecutor Anthony Lowe and minister Bill Tinsley.

Cantwell distributed a list of actions taken during her first term to promote economic growth. Prominent on the list was her backing of the software industry in its lobbying wars over communications security devices. Cantwell tried to convince voters that the change they had sought in electing her in 1992 had begun and would be continued. White challenged that message with an ad that repeated Cantwell's tag line, then asked, "Change that's working? Is she serious?" He won with 52 percent of the vote.

In 1996, White turned aside a challenge from Jeffrey Coopersmith, another former King County deputy prosecutor, in an expensive and closely watched contest. Coopersmith was not the first choice of Democratic activists but won the party's nod with a $200,000 late infusion of his own money.

Coopersmith tarred White with unpopular GOP proposals of the 104th Congress, which White in turn defended. White maintained that Coopersmith was no moderate, based on his "mean-spirited" primary campaign, as a White ad characterized it. White also trumpeted Coopersmith's opposition to term limits, a balanced-budget amendment and the welfare bill enacted by the 104th. Coopersmith had recently moved to the district from a distance of several blocks away — enough for White to portray him as a carpetbagger.

HOUSE ELECTIONS

1996 General		
Rick White (R)	141,948	(54%)
Jeffrey Coopersmith (D)	122,187	(46%)
1996 Primary *		
Rick White (R)	67,241	(50%)
Jeffrey Coopersmith (D)	35,006	(26%)
Don Stuart (D)	32,154	(24%)
1994 General		
Rick White (R)	100,554	(52%)
Maria Cantwell (D)	94,110	(48%)

** In Washington's "jungle primary," candidates of all parties are listed on one ballot.*

CAMPAIGN FINANCE

	Receipts	Receipts from PACs	Expend-itures
1996			
White (R)	$1,679,748	$705,106 (42%)	$1,671,909
Coopersmith (D)	$1,080,178	$176,198 (16%)	$1,079,648
1994			
White (R)	$940,508	$67,220 (7%)	$877,570
Cantwell (D)	$896,096	$472,897 (53%)	$875,756

DISTRICT VOTE FOR PRESIDENT

	1996		1992
D	140,182 (51%)	**D**	112,353 (41%)
R	103,002 (37%)	**R**	88,456 (32%)
I	21,350 (8%)	**I**	73,259 (27%)

KEY VOTES

1997	
Ban "partial birth" abortions	Y
1996	
Approve farm bill	Y
Deny public education to illegal immigrants	N
Repeal ban on certain assault-style weapons	Y
Increase minimum wage	N
Freeze defense spending	N
Approve welfare overhaul	Y
1995	
Approve balanced-budget constitutional amendment	Y
Relax Clean Water Act regulations	Y
Oppose limits on environmental regulations	Y
Reduce projected Medicare spending	Y
Approve GOP budget with tax and spending cuts	Y

VOTING STUDIES

	Presidential Support		Party Unity		Conservative Coalition	
Year	**S**	**O**	**S**	**O**	**S**	**O**
1996	43	54	91	8	84	12
1995	28	72	91	8	91	6

INTEREST GROUP RATINGS

Year	ADA	AFL-CIO	CCUS	ACU
1996	0	n/a	88	95
1995	15	0	100	72

2 Jack Metcalf (R)

Of Langley — Elected 1994, 2nd term

Biographical Information

Born: Nov. 30, 1927, Marysville, Wash.
Education: Pacific Lutheran U., B.A. 1951; U. of Washington, 1965-66.
Military Service: Army, 1946-47.
Occupation: Teacher; bed and breakfast owner.
Family: Wife, Norma Grant; four children.
Religion: Christian.
Political Career: Republican nominee for Wash. House, 1958; Wash. House, 1961-65; defeated for re-election to Wash. House, 1964; Wash. Senate, 1967-75; Republican nominee for U.S. Senate, 1968, 1974; Wash. Senate, 1981-93; Republican nominee for U.S. House, 1992.
Capitol Office: 1510 Longworth Bldg. 20515; 225-2605.

Committees

Banking & Financial Services
Domestic & International Monetary Policy; Financial Institutions & Consumer Credit; Housing & Community Opportunity
Transportation & Infrastructure
Aviation; Surface Transportation

In Washington: Through a career in politics that spanned four decades before he first won election to the House in 1994, Metcalf earned a reputation as a brusque conservative who embraced controversial notions such as restoring America to the gold standard, abolishing the Federal Reserve and opposing American Indian treaty claims. Metcalf, who once described himself as "a guy willing to take some kamikaze runs," entered the House at age 67, and it seemed possible that he would stand out not only as the oldest freshman, but also as one of the looser rhetorical cannons in his conservative-dominated class.

For someone who was so closely identified with the GOP right, however, Metcalf has compiled a voting record with some twists. In May 1996, he was one of just 43 Republicans voting to defeat a GOP leadership-backed amendment to exempt small businesses from minimum wage and overtime standards. Metcalf told the Seattle Times he felt the measure would have "gutted the fair labor standards and created two classes of workers in this country." In a subsequent vote, he was one of 93 Republicans who supported a 90-cent increase in the minimum wage.

In 1996 and again in 1997, Metcalf opposed his party's leadership on a labor-related bill, this one a measure allowing employers to offer workers compensatory time off in lieu of pay for overtime hours. Proponents said the bill would help workers balance job and family obligations, but critics said employees might be coerced into accepting comp time when they really wanted overtime pay.

Metcalf also split with the GOP majority in supporting a June 1996 amendment to freeze defense funding at the prior-year level; he joined 59 other Republicans in the effort to hold down Pentagon spending. With the help of Democratic hawks, the GOP leadership defeated the amendment, 219-194.

A defense issue with a parochial component brought Metcalf into conflict with Speaker Newt Gingrich in 1996. With a big contract at stake to build next-generation Air Force cargo planes, Gingrich sought a piece of the action for aerospace contractor Lockheed Martin in Georgia. Metcalf felt Gingrich was threatening the interests of Seattle-based Boeing, and he sent a letter to the Speaker and held a news conference.

Another issue that found Metcalf on the opposite side from his party leadership was the overhaul of federal farm policy. He voted in February 1996 against the "Freedom to Farm" bill, which phased out most New Deal-era crop subsidies, replacing them with a system of fixed, but declining, payments that farmers would receive over seven years regardless of market prices or their planting decisions.

Despite Metcalf's occasional maverick votes, he is a loyal party man on most budget and social policy issues. When the House considered the fiscal 1997 budget resolution in June 1996, the GOP leadership was facing the prospect of an embarrassing defeat until Metcalf and two other freshmen switched their votes from "nay" to a "yea." Thanks to their move, the Republican leaders passed the measure, 216-211. He voted to repeal the ban on certain semiautomatic assault-style weapons, and typically he sided with anti-abortion forces. (One exception came in March 1996, when he voted to require states to fund Medicaid abortions in cases of rape and incest.) In total, Metcalf voted with the majority of his party 91 percent of the time in 1995 and 86 percent of the time in 1996.

While on the Resources Committee during the 104th Congress, Metcalf was sympathetic with conservatives who said the federal government is often insensitive to landowners' rights, and he chafed at environmental regulations that have limited timber-cutting.

"The forest communities all over the Pacific Northwest are dying," Metcalf told the House in 1995, pleading for passage of a measure that would allow logging companies to salvage more than 6 billion board feet of lumber from dead or diseased trees on lands managed by the Forest Service. "Our people are dying, in economic terms. This salvage timber opportunity is here

Washington's 2nd is a swing district that lately has been following the whims of the state. It went big for Democrats in their 1992 statewide sweep — former Rep. Al Swift, Senate winner Patty Murray and presidential contender Bill Clinton. In the GOP's 1994 comeback, it gave Metcalf and Sen. Slade Gorton about 55 percent of the vote. In 1996, Clinton won the district handily, while Metcalf won re-election to the House by fewer than 2,000 votes.

The 2nd's geographic and political focal point is Everett, a rapidly growing blue-collar city whose history is linked to the timber and shipping industries. Labor conflicts plagued those industries between the two world wars, and unions became the basis of the local Democratic strength.

But the usual tendency to vote Democratic is tempered by the district's reliance on defense-related industry, which prospered in the 1980s.

Everett is the site of a relatively new Navy homeport, which has added about 7,000 military and civilian jobs to the area. The facility was on a May 1993 list of facilities that faced possible closure, but it did not appear on the final list.

Boeing, which has enormous influence in the area, announced in January 1993 that it would lay off thousands of workers over the next few years. Its fortunes have improved since then. By 1996, the purchase of its planes from both the private sector and the military had increased.

Everett may be in better shape than many communities that depend on the defense industry because its diversified economic base is rounded out with a number of high-tech companies. They include Alliant Tech Systems, a marine systems manufacturer, and Advanced Technologies Lab, a medical equipment manufacturer.

WASHINGTON 2
Puget Sound — Everett; Bellingham

Everett and surrounding Snohomish County cast nearly half the district's vote. Throughout the 1980s, the county tended to lean Republican in presidential contests and Democratic in statewide contests. But Clinton captured the county (some of which is in the 1st) with 39 percent of the vote in 1992 and 50 percent in 1996. Metcalf lost the county in 1996.

The second-largest group of votes in the 2nd comes from Whatcom County on the district's northern edge along the Canadian border. Clinton and Metcalf both carried it by narrow margins in 1996. Bellingham is a port town and home to Western Washington University (11,000 students), one of the area's largest employers. Many Whatcom residents depend on trade along the Canadian border and on the dairy, shipping, canning and timber industries.

Between Snohomish and Whatcom is Skagit County, a more rural and usually Republican-leaning area, though it, too, backed Clinton for president in 1992 and 1996. Skagit's annual Tulip Festival attracts thousands of visitors.

Island County lies between Juan de Fuca Strait and Puget Sound. Its proximity to Seattle has lured tourists and an influx of retirees, who tend to vote Republican, as do the civilian and military employees of Whidbey Island Naval Air Station, which is home to A-6 bombers and is Island County's largest employer.

1990 Population: 540,739. White 506,507 (94%), Black 4,822 (1%), Other 29,410 (5%). Hispanic origin 16,214 (3%). 18 and over 396,004 (73%), 62 and over 79,071 (15%). Median age: 33.

now, and it is something that we deeply need in the state of Washington." Early in the 104th he voted to ease anti-pollution standards in the clean water act and to limit the regulatory authority of the Environmental Protection Agency.

Yet even in the controversial area of land-management, Metcalf has taken some stands unusual for a Western conservative. During the 104th he introduced a bill to ban the Forest Service from selling timber below cost, saying government should not subsidize the timber industry.

And in 1995 when the Resources Committee considered a proposed rewrite of the Endangered Species Act, Metcalf told the Seattle Times that committee chairman Don Young, R-Alaska, had gone too far in changing the act. Metcalf also took the environmentalists' side on a June 1996 vote involving habitat protection for a threatened sea bird species, the marbled murrelet.

Metcalf left Resources at the start of the 105th Congress to take a seat on the Transportation and Infrastructure Committee, which is working on the massive surface transportation reauthorization bill. He kept his seat on the Banking and Financial Services Committee.

Because of his age, Metcalf has gotten an extra dose of attention as a defender of GOP efforts to rein in Medicare costs. Blasting Democrats for accusing Republicans of cutting Medicare, Metcalf told the House in October 1995 that he had a particular interest in saving the program. "Not only do I qualify for Medicare, my wife qualifies for Medicare, my brother is on Medicare and three older sisters are. So I am absolutely dedicated to seeing that this program is not damaged, not put in jeopardy, does not go bankrupt, and is there for those people counting on it."

At Home: Beginning with an unsuccessful bid for the state House in 1958, Metcalf has been a part of the Washington state political scene for more years than some of his classmates in Congress have been alive. He made it to the state

House in 1960, lost his seat in 1964, won state Senate elections in 1966 and 1970, lost bids for the U.S. Senate in 1968 and 1974 to Democratic incumbent Warren G. Magnuson, returned to the state Senate in 1981 for a dozen years and then lost in a 1992 challenge to 2nd District Democratic Rep. Al Swift. Outside politics, he operated a bed-and-breakfast on Whidbey Island.

Metcalf managed only 42 percent against Swift in 1992. But two years later, thanks to Swift's retirement and a boom year for state Republicans, Metcalf got the congressional victory that had so long eluded him. He became the first Republican to win the 2nd since 1962. In the more Democratic-friendly environment of 1996, Metcalf won a second House term, but just barely, finishing 1,927 votes ahead of his challenger, state Sen. Kevin Quigley.

Metcalf did not start the 1994 campaign year looking like the favorite to succeed Swift. In seeking his party's nomination, he had to contend with state Sen. Tim Erwin, who portrayed Metcalf as a career politician who would eliminate the cost of living adjustment (COLA) for Social Security recipients. Metcalf said his earlier comment about needing to address COLAs in order to balance the budget was taken out of context. Under continued pressure on the issue, he ultimately said he could see no circumstances under which he would change Social Security.

Metcalf got 26 percent of the vote in the all-party September primary, while Erwin ran fourth with 12 percent. The other finishers in the top five were all Democrats (taking a combined 50 percent of the vote), and Metcalf started the general election as something of an underdog to state Sen. Harriet A. Spanel, whose strong organization had lifted her to the Democratic nomination.

But Spanel's backing came mostly from unions, environmentalists and women's groups, and in the 1994 political climate, her image as a liberal proved a bigger liability than Metcalf's reputation as a staunch conservative prone to eccentricities. Spanel said Metcalf was locked in the past while she was looking toward the future. Outgoing Rep. Swift also weighed in on her behalf, calling Metcalf an "absolute kook" who "never met a windmill he didn't like."

While Spanel spent about $200,000 more on her campaign than did Metcalf, his long involvement in politics gave him high-name recognition. Her support for gun control energized gunowners' rights advocates to support Metcalf, and his stand against abortion made him popular with the conservative Christian activists who were on the march statewide in 1994. Metcalf won a solid 55 percent of the vote.

In 1996, though, Metcalf was swimming against a Democratic current, as President Clinton carried the 2nd by 8 points over GOP nominee Bob Dole. Metcalf's youthful Democratic foe, Quigley, said he could employ his experience chairing the state Senate Health Care Committee in Congress' work on Medicare and Medicaid issues. On Election Night, Quigley looked to be a winner, but in the final count, Metcalf prevailed with a 49 percent plurality.

HOUSE ELECTIONS

1996 General		
Jack Metcalf (R)	124,655	(49%)
Kevin Quigley (D)	122,728	(48%)
Karen Leibrant (NL)	9,561	(4%)
1996 Primary †		
Jack Metcalf (R)	67,603	(52%)
Kevin Quigley (D)	30,635	(24%)
Joe Bowen (D)	14,267	(11%)
Ann C. Weinzierl (D)	10,630	(8%)
Paul D. Asmus (D)	4,253	(3%)
Karen Leibrant (NL)	2,234	(2%)
1994 General		
Jack Metcalf (R)	107,430	(55%)
Harriet A. Spanel (D)	89,096	(45%)

† In Washington's "jungle primary," candidates of all parties are listed on one ballot.

CAMPAIGN FINANCE

	Receipts	Receipts from PACs	Expenditures
1996			
Metcalf (R)	$793,675	$336,698 (42%)	$797,442
Quigley (D)	$485,450	$258,527 (53%)	$447,812
1994			
Metcalf (R)	$410,433	$97,737 (24%)	$407,902
Spanel (D)	$614,078	$251,911 (41%)	$613,063

DISTRICT VOTE FOR PRESIDENT

	1996		1992
D	123,729 (47%)	**D**	109,438 (41%)
R	103,901 (39%)	**R**	87,957 (33%)
I	27,179 (10%)	**I**	68,875 (26%)

KEY VOTES

1997	
Ban "partial-birth" abortions	Y
1996	
Approve farm bill	N
Deny public education to illegal immigrants	Y
Repeal ban on certain assault-style weapons	Y
Increase minimum wage	Y
Freeze defense spending	Y
Approve welfare overhaul	Y
1995	
Approve balanced-budget constitutional amendment	Y
Relax Clean Water Act regulations	Y
Oppose limits on environmental regulations	N
Reduce projected Medicare spending	Y
Approve GOP budget with tax and spending cuts	Y

VOTING STUDIES

	Presidential Support		Party Unity		Conservative Coalition	
Year	**S**	**O**	**S**	**O**	**S**	**O**
1996	37	61	86	14	80	20
1995	20	79	91	7	86	12

INTEREST GROUP RATINGS

Year	**ADA**	**AFL-CIO**	**CCUS**	**ACU**
1996	0	n/a	75	90
1995	5	25	92	100

3 Linda Smith (R)

Of Vancouver — Elected 1994, 2nd term

Biographical Information

Born: July 16, 1950, La Junta, Colo.

Education: Hudson's Bay H.S., graduated 1968.

Occupation: Tax preparation centers manager; tax consultant.

Family: Husband, Vern Smith; two children.

Religion: Assembly of God.

Political Career: Wash. House, 1983-87; Wash. Senate, 1987-95.

Capitol Office: 1317 Longworth Bldg. 20515; 225-3536.

Committees

Resources
National Parks & Public Lands; Water & Power

Small Business
Empowerment; Government Programs & Oversight; Tax & Exports

In Washington: Many members of the Republican Class of 1994 have earned a reputation as uncompromising, but few have earned that rap the way Smith has. She voted against Newt Gingrich's 1997 re-election as Speaker and consistently pushes the party harder than it wants to be pushed on campaign finance issues. Smith has effectively burned her bridges in party circles and in the House, feeding speculation that she would be likely to leave the chamber after the 105th Congress. She confirmed such thoughts in May 1997 when she announced she would run for the Senate in 1998.

Smith did not just oppose Gingrich's re-election — she displayed a lack of politesse bordering on the politically suicidal. She believed that Gingrich's ethical problems would stand in the way of the GOP agenda, and, a day before the opening of the 105th and the vote for Speaker, Smith told the Seattle Post-Intelligencer, "But if I have one fat kid eating all the food, I will move him away from the table before I let the rest of them starve. And it would still be the little round kid in the family, but I wouldn't let him harm the rest of the family."

Smith apologized for the personal remark, explaining, "Because of his weight problem he had, it was taken personally and spun out as a negative against him. It was never meant to be."

In the 104th, Smith was the first Republican woman ever to chair a subcommittee in her first term. Smith lost that chairmanship (on Small Business) at the start of the 105th, but she and committee spokesmen said it had nothing to do with her vote against Gingrich. She remains on the committee as well as on Resources, where she is a consistent vote for GOP efforts to scale back environmental regulation.

Smith's signature issue has been an overhaul of campaign finance law. She has been a lead cosponsor of legislation to ban PACs, institute voluntary campaign spending limits, ban "soft money" (used for broad purposes by political parties), and outlaw the solicitation of most federal campaign funds within a 50-mile radius of the District of Columbia.

"You're elected as an idealist and thrown into the sewer," Smith has said. "People believe [Congress] is a sewer, and they elected a bunch of cleaners to go in and clean it up."

Despite growing campaign finance scandals that loomed large in the 105th, Smith was disappointed by the lack of progress for her bill. She was vocal about her belief that Gingrich's retreat from a public stance to "work to zero out" PACs stemmed from the fact Republicans were benefiting from PAC money.

She found the July 1996 "Reform Week" proclaimed by the House GOP leadership toothless and consistently prodded party elders to pay more than lip service to the idea of overhauling the funding of elections. She portrayed passage of a ban on virtually all gifts to members and their staff, as well as a measure that toughened lobbying disclosure requirements, as mere baby steps on the path to real "reform."

"The gift ban was like breaking down the door. Lobby reform was like cleaning out the hall. We've got the basement, the attic and all the rooms [to go]," she said.

Smith crossed swords with Gingrich early in 1995, when she led a freshman revolt in support of a version of a balanced-budget constitutional amendment that would have required a three-fifths majority vote to raise taxes. This led to a meeting with Gingrich that Smith described as "testy." She later supported a less-stringent version of the amendment, but added, "I didn't come here to be a sissy."

While serving as a state lawmaker, she circumvented the Washington Legislature by leading two successful citizen initiatives on campaign ethics and tax reform (she is a former tax preparer). Smith's reputation as an independent was sufficiently well-forged that in 1996 she was reportedly approached to run for vice president on Ross Perot's Reform Party ticket.

She voted against a spending bill in January 1996 that reopened the government after a

WASHINGTON 3
Southwest — Olympia; Vancouver

The 3rd, stretching from Puget Sound west to the Pacific and south to the Columbia River border with Oregon, is heavy with maritime and timber interests. Despite its large number of blue-collar voters, however, it is not solidly Democratic.

Democratic presidential candidates have fared well here. Bill Clinton carried the 3rd in the 1992 and 1996 presidential elections, as had Michael S. Dukakis in 1988. Clinton got 49 percent in 1996, beating Bob Dole by 11 percentage points. But Republican Smith has gone through two very competitive elections, and her Democratic predecessor always had a tough fight, too.

About 70 percent of the district vote comes from two counties: Thurston (Olympia) in the northern end, and Clark (Vancouver) in the south.

Olympia, the state capital, and its surroundings was one of the fastest-growing metropolitan areas in the country in the 1980s; it soared nearly 30 percent to just over 161,000. Olympia's communities of environmental and "good government" activists usually give Democrats a leg up in the county. Neighboring Lacey is a burgeoning twin city to Olympia that adds to the Democratic vote on this end of the district.

Clark County has also seen its population surge with the growth of its Portland, Ore., suburbs. Because Washington does not have an income tax and Oregon does not have a sales tax, many retirees have flocked to live on the Washington side and do their shopping in Oregon.

Vancouver (Clark County) is an industrial and high-tech center. Among the employers here are the James River Pulp and Paper Co. and the computer companies Hewlett-Packard, SEH America and Kyocera. The city has renovated a historic section of the district known as Officers Row, a string of 21 homes dating back to the Civil War era, including one in which Ulysses S. Grant lived.

The 3rd has vast stretches of woodlands, including the scenic Coastal Range and much of the Cascade Mountains, with Mount Rainier just outside the eastern border. Timber dominates the economy and, in recent years, there have been more downs than ups. The area's mills produce paper, timber and cardboard under the state's strict water pollution standards. Logging is a major activity of Cowlitz County, which includes the cities of Longview and Kelso. Along the coast, fishing and dockwork predominate, and there is a strong labor presence among the longshoremen.

East of Cowlitz are the newest additions to the district, Skamania and part of Klickitat counties, which rely heavily on the timber industry for their economic base, and the Columbia River Gorge National Scenic Area, a popular tourist attraction.

Rural Lewis County in the northern end of the district provides the only dependable GOP majorities in the 3rd. It was the only 3rd District county Dole carried in 1996. In the House race, Smith carried Lewis County with 62 percent and Clark County with 52 percent. That helped her absorb losses in Thurston and Cowlitz counties.

1990 Population: 540,745. White 512,446 (95%), Black 4,855 (1%), Other 23,444 (4%). Hispanic origin 13,467 (3%). 18 and over 392,267 (73%), 62 and over 82,435 (15%). Median age: 34.

record-length partial shutdown, even after Gingrich had made a speech to the GOP Conference staking his leadership on winning the vote. Smith voted for the omnibus spending bill that closed out the 104th Congress, taking to the House floor to note her specific glee with a provision of the massive bill that funded repair of a highway in her district.

But Smith has normally sided with the GOP on major votes, except in her support for a 1996 increase in the minimum wage. Smith strongly supports a balanced budget but focuses much of her legislative energies on social issues; she supports prayer in public school and opposes abortion. A statement she made in 1984 to churchgoers remains a staple of media profiles: "If you vote for someone who believes in abortion, you have made a conscious decision to participate in sin. . . . To those who say you can't force your narrow beliefs on other people, hogwash."

As the House considered a ban on a specific abortion procedure its opponents call "partial birth" abortion, Smith gave a highly personal speech describing her own breech birth. Likening her feet-first entrance into the world to the procedure, Smith noted her mother's poor health and theoretical eligibility for a "partial-birth" abortion, had one then been available. "They would have been able to kill me and then deliver me, and say that I had never been living. This is what we are facing tonight, with this procedure," Smith said.

Yet despite her strongly held views on this and other issues, and her willingness and even zeal to do battle with GOP leaders, Smith has a noticeable streak of political pragmatism, as evidenced by her 1996 vote for the popular minimum wage increase, her efforts to secure the highway repair funds, and her willingness to set aside her philosophical support of privatization in the case of the Bonneville Power Administration, which provides low-cost electricity to aluminum producers and other constituents in her district. "I've always supported privatization, but not if it's going to destroy the economy of our region," she explained.

At Home: Despite her campaign finance crusade, Smith accepts contributions from her party and PACs and raised $1.2 million for her 1996 re-election campaign — a half-million dollars more than her Democratic opponent, Pacific Lutheran University psychology Professor Brian Baird. That advantage helped her eke out victory by less than a full percentage point.

Smith did not appear to be the most vulnerable among the six House Republicans first elected from Washington state in 1994, so Democrats and their allies (such as the AFL-CIO) trained their fire elsewhere. They were awakened to Smith's vulnerability by her 52 percent share of the "jungle" primary vote (in which members of all parties appeared on the same ballot).

Their delay in targeting her helped her prevail; although she appeared to have lost on election night, absentee ballots, particularly from her base in Clark and Lewis counties, put her over the top. The narrowness of her win triggered an automatic recount, which put her ahead by only 887 votes.

In 1994, Smith was the first in Washington state to receive her party's congressional nomination as a write-in, thanks to a grass-roots network consisting of Christian conservative activists and contacts made during her spearheading of two popular state initiatives. From her write-in primary victory, it was just a few weeks before she turned out Democratic Rep. Jolene Unsoeld, a three-term incumbent.

Added to her grass-roots strengths was the $2 million that Republican businessman Timothy P. Moyer already had spent against Unsoeld. Moyer abruptly quit late in August because of media stories about his failure to pay taxes on luxury automobiles. Local party leaders turned to Smith.

She had followed her state House victory over a Democratic representative with a successful challenge four years later to a state senator. Smith's victory gave the GOP control of the state Senate and put her well on her way to earning the description of one of the state's most loved and most loathed elected officials.

Unsoeld tried to draw attention away from Smith's populist roots and toward her socially conservative leanings. Unsoeld's ads, centered on the tag line "She's not the Linda Smith you think she is," tried to paint Smith as an extremist and attacked her support for means-testing for Social Security. But even the resignation of a local county Republican chairwoman — who had described Smith as a radical, right-wing candidate who is "anti-woman" — did not stop Smith's momentum. She won by 7 percentage points.

HOUSE ELECTIONS

1996 General		
Linda Smith (R)	123,117	(50%)
Brian Baird (D)	122,230	(50%)
1996 Primary †		
Linda Smith (R)	69,291	(52%)
Brian Baird (D)	62,778	(48%)
1994 General		
Linda Smith (R)	100,188	(52%)
Jolene Unsoeld (D)	85,826	(45%)
Caitlin Davis Carlson (GC)	6,620	(3%)

† In Washington's "jungle primary," candidates of all parties are listed on one ballot.

CAMPAIGN FINANCE

	Receipts	Receipts from PACs	Expend-itures
1996			
Smith (R)	$1,222,302	$26,375 (2%)	$1,216,368
Baird (D)	$719,798	$246,589 (34%)	$718,322
1994			
Smith (R)	$522,896	$115,766 (22%)	$515,316
Unsoeld (D)	$973,401	$424,827 (44%)	$987,242

DISTRICT VOTE FOR PRESIDENT

	1996		1992
D	124,954 (49%)	**D**	104,748 (42%)
R	98,024 (38%)	**R**	82,647 (33%)
I	24,402 (10%)	**I**	61,613 (25%)

KEY VOTES

1997	
Ban "partial-birth" abortions	Y
1996	
Approve farm bill	Y
Deny public education to illegal immigrants	Y
Repeal ban on certain assault-style weapons	Y
Increase minimum wage	Y
Freeze defense spending	Y
Approve welfare overhaul	Y
1995	
Approve balanced-budget constitutional amendment	Y
Relax Clean Water Act regulations	Y
Oppose limits on environmental regulations	N
Reduce projected Medicare spending	Y
Approve GOP budget with tax and spending cuts	Y

VOTING STUDIES

	Presidential Support		Party Unity		Conservative Coalition	
Year	**S**	**O**	**S**	**O**	**S**	**O**
1996	34	62	85	9	88	10
1995	14	85	93	5	87	11

INTEREST GROUP RATINGS

Year	ADA	AFL-CIO	CCUS	ACU
1996	5	n/a	79	84
1995	0	8	100	96

4 Richard 'Doc' Hastings (R)

Of Pasco — Elected 1994, 2nd term

Biographical Information

Born: Feb. 7, 1941, Spokane, Wash.
Education: Columbia Basin College, 1959-61; Central Washington U., 1964.
Military Service: Army Reserve, 1964-69.
Occupation: Paper company executive.
Family: Wife, Claire; three children.
Religion: Roman Catholic.
Political Career: Wash. House, 1979-87; Republican nominee for U.S. House, 1992.
Capitol Office: 1323 Longworth Bldg. 20515; 225-5816.

Committees

Rules
Legislative & Budget Process

In Washington: The federal government's important role in the 4th District poses a challenge for Hastings. He took the district from Democrats in 1994 on a pledge to push for dramatic reductions in federal spending. This is how he summed up that election: "In 1994, the American people spoke loudly and clearly about changing the direction of government — away from unending deficits, away from out-of-control spending and soaring debt, and away from big government policies that waste taxpayers' dollars."

Yet by all accounts, it will take billions of federal dollars to clean up radioactive and hazardous waste that has accumulated over the years at the 560-square-mile Hanford Nuclear Reservation in the 4th. Hanford was the longtime center for producing the material for nuclear weapons; production was shut down in 1988, and now the Department of Energy is charged with a massive cleanup that could take well into the 21st century. The price tag for the cleanup is about $1.5 billion annually.

Hastings looked out for Hanford during the 104th Congress from his seat on the National Security Committee. His influence is enhanced in the 105th, as he joins the Rules Committee.

In the 104th, Hastings successfully sponsored an amendment in the committee authorizing $86 million more for the Energy Department's cleanup program at sites including Hanford. Hastings said the committee vote was "a dramatic recognition that we must adequately fund critical environmental activities." But Energy's budget for environmental management (the source of cleanup funds) is a tempting target for other GOP conservatives intent on cutting the budget.

As Hastings pushes for more cleanup funds for Hanford, he also accuses the Energy Department of not managing the job well. He wants the cleanup process "streamlined" to provide more local control. Hastings has pushed legislation to privatize much of the cleanup work and make Washington state the only regulator at the Hanford site.

Hastings and Washington Democratic Sen. Patty Murray have been at odds over another part of the Hanford reservation that is in pristine condition, the Hanford Reach. Running 51 miles along the Columbia River, it was a buffer around the weapons plant and is now being sold by the federal government. Murray has proposed designating the Hanford Reach as a Wild and Scenic River and National Wildlife Refuge, putting the area off-limits to development. Hastings wants local counties to control much of the property, which could open the area to development. In August 1995, he told the Seattle Times that county governments would better balance "our environmental needs with our economic realities."

Hastings' voting record anchors the GOP right. In 1995, he voted with the majority of his party 99 percent of the time; in 1996, his party unity score was 96. The Seattle Post-Intelligencer observed in April 1996 that Hastings "is not only unfazed but proud of the ratings of his congressional votes that have tabbed him as one of the leading 'Newtoids' of the 104th Congress." Hastings said: "I'm guilty of doing what I said I was going to do. The fact that I supported the leadership and did what I said I was going to do doesn't cause me any problems politically." That sort of loyalty is what prompted the GOP leadership to tap Hastings for Rules in his sophomore term.

Hastings sat on the Resources Committee in the 104th also, and he made plain his belief that environmental considerations have too often stymied economic development. He wants to amend the Endangered Species Act, which he thinks is skewed in favor of environmentalists who aim to curtail the use of natural resources. "The Endangered Species Act is having a devastating impact on our local economy throughout the Pacific Northwest," Hastings said in March 1996. "Whether it be loggers, farmers, water users, or any other hard-working man or woman dependent on our natural resources, the ESA is in desperate need of reform."

The timber industry is an important employer in the 4th, and Hastings has supported a proposal

WASHINGTON 4
Central — Yakima and Tri-Cities

The 4th, lying just east of the Cascade Mountains, is a big chunk of central Washington, bordering Canada on the north and Oregon on the south. Voters here consistently support Republican presidential candidates, but Democrats can fare well in elections for other offices.

The 4th was the only Washington district that George Bush carried in 1992 and that Bob Dole carried in 1996, the latter with 48 percent of the vote.

Hastings reversed his narrow 1992 loss to Democratic Rep. Jay Inslee in 1994. In addition to maintaining the southeastern corner of the 4th, where voters in the Tri-Cities area of Pasco, Kennewick and Richland are staunchly Republican, Hastings won five of the seven counties he had lost in 1992. In 1996, Hastings won every county except Yakima, home of his Democratic opponent, and Kittitas.

Before Inslee's short tenure, the district had been represented by six-term GOP Rep. Sid Morrison. Before Morrison, however, the 4th had been in Democratic hands for a decade.

Balancing GOP strength in the Tri-Cities are several areas with Democratic proclivities. Democrats carried Kittitas County, in the center of the 4th, in 1992 and 1996.

The 4th's economy revolves around agriculture — primarily fruits and wheat, winemaking and cattle — and the Hanford Nuclear Reservation, formerly the site of much of the nation's nuclear weapons-materials production. The nuclear reservation is mostly in Benton County, just north of the Tri-Cities. In 1988, the federal government shut down Hanford's nuclear reactor, a plutonium plant, because of safety problems and the decreased need for plutonium. The shutdown resulted in the initial loss of 1,000 jobs in the two-county (Benton and Franklin) area of about 150,000 residents.

The Department of Energy then estimated that it would cost up to $50 billion to clean up the hazardous waste that had accumulated at Hanford. In early 1989, the state and federal governments agreed on a cleanup plan; the project, which will bring about 2,000 jobs to the Hanford area, is expected to take at least 30 years.

Construction was completed recently on a $220 million Molecular Science Research Lab. The lab opened in October 1996, though its operation was still being refined. Researchers there will develop technologies for cleaning up hazardous waste around the country.

Northwest of the Tri-Cities is the district's other urban concentration, Yakima (Yakima County). Voters here lean Republican, although Inslee, whose hometown of Selah is in Yakima County, carried the county in 1992 and 1994. Dole barely carried Yakima County with 47 percent of the votes.

Yakima County was largely desert before a huge irrigation project helped make it one of the nation's premier apple-growing areas; more than 50 percent of the nation's apples come from the district. Also in the 4th is the immense Grand Coulee Dam, on the Columbia River in Grant County.

1990 Population: 540,744. White 449,913 (83%), Black 5,276 (1%), Other 5,555 (16%). Hispanic origin 85,804 (16%). 18 and over 380,303 (70%), 62 and over 80,621 (15%). Median age: 32.

to require an expedited timber salvage program to remove dead, diseased, or dying timber from federal forest land in order to provide "an adequate timber supply for timber-dependent communities in central Washington." Proponents of the plan said it would create thousands of jobs for workers displaced by restrictions on tree cutting. But opponents argued that live, healthy trees would also be cut as part of the salvage operation.

The economy of the 4th also is heavily dependent on agriculture — fruit, wheat and cattle are most important — and the labor needs of that industry make Hastings less of a hard-liner than some conservatives on immigration questions. When the House in 1996 was debating a bill to crack down on illegal immigration, Hastings backed an amendment that would have created a new agricultural guest worker program to admit up to 250,000 foreigners per year to harvest the nation's crops. "My constituents in central Washington state are no different from the great majority of Americans who support immigration reform," Hastings said. "But my constituents realize that our biggest industry — agriculture — must be protected."

The measure's supporters said a three-year migrant worker program was needed so growers would not be caught without the necessary labor at harvest time. But critics said agribusiness was simply trying to ensure a supply of cheap labor. The amendment was rejected, 180-242.

Hastings applied his fiscal conservatism to one project close to home when he challenged the spending of $24 million to remodel a federal building in Richland. "Most of this work appears to fall in the 'nice to be done' category, not the 'must-have' category," he said. The project, part of the fiscal 1996 Treasury-Postal spending bill, was eventually reduced by more than $12 million.

At Home: Hastings was expected to win the traditionally Republican 4th when it was open in 1992, but that turned out to be a strong Democratic year in Washington state, and he lost to Democrat Jay Inslee by 2 percentage points. In 1994, the voters' mood swung to the right, and Hastings ousted Inslee, 53 percent to 47 percent. Democrats did not let Hastings rest easy in 1996, putting up well-financed businessman Rick Locke. But with GOP presidential nominee Bob Dole winning the 4th, Hastings again posted a 53 percent victory.

Known as "Doc," a nickname given him as a boy by his family, Hastings has a background in both business and politics. He was a paper-company executive and served in the state House, where he established himself as a firm friend of social-issue conservatives. In his 1992 House race, he drew solid backing from GOP religious activists and was considered the most conservative of the four Republicans running to succeed GOP Rep. Sid Morrison, a moderate who ran unsuccessfully for governor that year. Though Hastings won his party's nomination handily, he was far enough to the right to give Inslee an opening to appeal to centrist voters, and the Democrat ably exploited the chance.

In 1994, though, Hastings cast the campaign as a referendum on Inslee's support for the agenda of President Clinton, whose popularity was then at an ebb in a district that historically has voted Republican in state and national elections anyway.

Hastings turned Inslee's 1992 campaign platform against him. The Democrat had called for cutting the deficit, overhauling health care and reforming Congress. But in 1994 Hastings tapped a vein of voters angry about tax increases imposed by Clinton, dissatisfied with Clinton's health care proposal and skeptical that the House's longtime Democratic majority would reform the institution. While Inslee was the only Washington state Democrat to vote against Clinton's 1993 deficit-reduction plan on final passage, Hastings said Inslee's vote for the rule on the budget showed he was for it.

Inslee tried to counter Hastings' criticisms by noting his support for a balanced-budget constitutional amendment and a presidential line-item veto. He also questioned Hastings' ability to handle the district's nuclear concerns. One Inslee ad used footage of then-House Minority Leader Newt Gingrich saying on "Meet the Press" that federal funding for the Hanford cleanup could be cut from $1.5 billion to $100 million. Inslee also said electing Hastings would be bad for women, noting his strong anti-abortion position and his opposition to the Family and Medical Leave Act.

But in Washington's all-party primary in September, Inslee fell far below 50 percent, finishing more than 8,000 votes behind Hastings. In November, the gunowners' rights vote swung decisively to Hastings, because Inslee had voted to ban certain semiautomatic assault-style weapons. The National Rifle Association did a mailing in the 4th featuring Hastings and organized a "Meet and Greet, Shoot Skeet" event for him. All that combined gave him a 6-point victory.

With Hastings' voting record to aim at in 1996, Democrat Locke underscored the earlier portrayals of the Republican as an extreme conservative. He also picked up on the national Democratic theme of characterizing the GOP as anti-environment. But Hastings won again by 6 percentage points.

HOUSE ELECTIONS

1996 General		
Richard "Doc" Hastings (R)	108,647	(53%)
Rick Locke (D)	96,502	(47%)
1996 Primary †		
Richard "Doc" Hastings (R)	65,939	(55%)
Rick Locke (D)	33,987	(28%)
Joe Walkenhauer (D)	11,704	(10%)
Glenn Phipps (D)	8,238	(7%)
1994 General		
Doc Hastings (R)	92,828	(53%)
Jay Inslee (D)	81,198	(47%)

† In Washington's "jungle primary," candidates of all parties are listed on one ballot.

CAMPAIGN FINANCE

	Receipts	Receipts from PACs	Expend-itures
1996			
Hastings (R)	$737,915	$298,848 (40%)	$734,640
Locke (D)	$419,176	$139,842 (33%)	$408,772
1994			
Hastings (R)	$616,421	$162,805 (26%)	$619,963
Inslee (D)	$494,033	$295,702 (60%)	$496,638

DISTRICT VOTE FOR PRESIDENT

	1996		1992
D	84,157 (40%)	**D**	71,848 (35%)
R	101,963 (48%)	**R**	87,996 (43%)
I	20,516 (10%)	**I**	45,252 (22%)

KEY VOTES

1997	
Ban "partial birth" abortions	Y
1996	
Approve farm bill	Y
Deny public education to illegal immigrants	Y
Repeal ban on certain assault-style weapons	Y
Increase minimum wage	N
Freeze defense spending	N
Approve welfare overhaul	Y
1995	
Approve balanced-budget constitutional amendment	Y
Relax Clean Water Act regulations	Y
Oppose limits on environmental regulations	N
Reduce projected Medicare spending	Y
Approve GOP budget with tax and spending cuts	Y

VOTING STUDIES

	Presidential Support		Party Unity		Conservative Coalition	
Year	**S**	**O**	**S**	**O**	**S**	**O**
1996	33	66	96	3	98	2
1995	16	83	99	0	100	0

INTEREST GROUP RATINGS

Year	ADA	AFL-CIO	CCUS	ACU
1996	0	n/a	100	100
1995	0	0	100	92

5 George Nethercutt (R)

Of Spokane — Elected 1994, 2nd term

Biographical Information
Born: Oct. 7, 1944, Spokane, Wash.
Education: Washington State University, B.A. 1967; Gonzaga U., J.D. 1971.
Occupation: Lawyer; congressional aide.
Family: Wife, Mary Beth Socha; two children.
Religion: Protestant.
Political Career: No previous office.
Capitol Office: 1527 Longworth Bldg. 20515; 225-2006.

Committees
Appropriations
Agriculture, Rural Development, FDA & Related Agencies; Interior; National Security
Science
Space & Aeronautics

In Washington: Voters in the 5th made national news with the big change they made in 1994: Dumping Democratic House Speaker Thomas S. Foley in favor of conservative Republican Nethercutt. Campaigning on a promise to cut federal spending and balance the budget, Nethercutt said the district needed a listener, not a Speaker, and he further contrasted himself with Foley, a 30-year House veteran, by pledging to serve no more than six years in the chamber.

Nethercutt got a seat on Appropriations as a freshman, and he impressed observers as a diligent and hard-working legislator. In the spring of 1997, he was weighing a run for the Senate in 1998.

Nethercutt's 1994 defeat of Foley symbolized a new day in American politics: the Speaker going down at the same time his Democratic Party lost its 40-year hold on the House. Yet for all that, Nethercutt has spent no small share of his time in Congress just as Foley did — defending and promoting federal programs directly beneficial to his district. Nethercutt joined other Republicans from the Northwest in urging House Budget Committee Chairman John R. Kasich of Ohio and the GOP leadership not to consider selling the Bonneville Power Administration, a regional power authority that develops and markets power from federal hydroelectric facilities. Some GOP deficit hawks say that proceeds from privatizing public power entities could help bring the budget into balance.

And when the 104th Congress tackled the issue of federal farm subsidies, Nethercutt made it clear he did not share the views of free-market purists in the GOP who railed at the government's deep involvement in supporting the agriculture industry, "I don't want to make deep cuts to farm policy in a way that's going to devastate the agricultural industry and destroy rural America," he said. "Like it or not, we've created a dependence by some farmers on agricultural supports." Nethercutt argued that it was more important to maintain programs for farmers than for welfare recipients. "The difference between the safety net for farmers and the safety net for other entitlements is that agricultural products benefit our economy," he said.

In February 1996, Nethercutt did vote for the GOP-backed "Freedom to Farm" bill, which brought federal farm policy more in line with free-market principles. But just before that vote, he opposed phasing out government support for the sugar industry, and in June 1996 he helped thwart an attempt on the agriculture spending bill to prohibit funding for certain programs benefiting tobacco growers.

Nethercutt also went to bat for farmers early in the 105th Congress, introducing a bill to amend the tax code so that farmers could pay income tax on contract payments in the year they receive the payments rather than in the year they sign the contract. He said family farmers need financial assistance because of fluctuations in market prices and crop yields, international competition and the subsidy caps in the 1996 farm bill. Many farmers prefer to defer their income from the sale of crops and livestock to guard against swings in commodity prices.

During his 1994 campaign, Nethercutt said the 5th needed a voice on the Agriculture Committee more than it needed Foley as Speaker, but after winning election, he bypassed Agriculture to accept the more prestigious Appropriations assignment, which House GOP leaders gave him as a reward for toppling Foley. He got a seat on the Agriculture and Rural Development Subcommittee, which gives him a chance to influence spending in those areas.

Although Nethercutt had not held elective office before winning the 5th, he was no newcomer to government and the ways of Washington. He worked for Alaska Republican Sen. Ted Stevens from 1972 to 1976, moving from staff counsel to chief of staff, and Nethercutt's knowledge of how Congress works is now helping him maneuver to get what he wants.

Early in the 104th, for instance, he managed to rescue $426,000 for a wheat research facility in the

WASHINGTON 5
East — Spokane

Nethercutt's narrow victory was further testament to the personal popularity that had enabled Foley to retain his hold on this competitive district for 30 years. Foley had had several close races in the past, but the dynamics of the 1994 election year and Nethercutt's appeal convinced 5th District voters that their ideological concerns were more important than enjoying the influence of the Speaker of the House.

Nethercutt's approximately 4,000-vote margin came primarily from the rural timber- and agriculture-dominated counties. In Adams, Columbia, Lincoln and Stevens counties, Nethercutt received 59 percent or more. Foley's long tenure in the district was as much an anomaly as Bill Clinton's success here in 1992. Aided by the popularity of Ross Perot, who got 23 percent of the vote in the 5th and weakened George Bush, Clinton ran first, taking 40 percent overall.

Clinton won the district again in 1996 with 44 percent of the vote, but he was only 1,600 votes ahead of Bob Dole. Perot was less of a factor, taking only 11 percent of the district's vote.

But Clinton's success has transferred to other Democrats. In 1992, Democratic Senate nominee Patty Murray lost every county in the district but won statewide. Similarly in 1994, GOP Sen. Slade Gorton easily won every county.

Though the 5th covers 11 counties and a lot of ground, in electoral terms one place counts: Spokane. With 177,000 people, the city is Washington's second-largest. Spokane County casts about two-thirds of the district's vote.

Spokane is the banking and marketing center of the "Inland Empire," which encompasses wheat- and vegetable-farming counties in eastern Washington, eastern Oregon, northern Idaho and western Montana. The city developed a sizable aluminum industry thanks to the availability of low-cost hydroelectric power from New Deal-era dams along the Columbia River. Boeing also is a presence here. The Spokane facility, which makes airplane floor panels and environmental ducts, is expected to hold its ground as Boeing retrenches.

Spokane also is becoming known as a major medical center for the Inland Empire. The Sacred Heart Medical Center has made a name for itself in the highly specialized field of heart-lung transplants.

Comparatively isolated, Spokane traditionally has been among the most conservative of America's large cities. But Spokane's small-town personality and the accessibility of nearby lakes and mountains have lured many newcomers to the area in recent years — particularly California emigrants. This influx has moderated Spokane's conservatism.

There are two other small population centers of note. Pullman (Whitman County) is the site of Washington State University (20,000 students). Though the county has tended to support Republicans for president, it went for Clinton in 1996. Holding fast for the GOP was traditionally Republican Walla Walla County.

1990 Population: 540,744. White 504,014 (93%), Black 6,496 (1%), Other 30,234 (6%). Hispanic origin 18,304 (3%). 18 and over 398,869 (74%), 62 and over 85,387 (16%). Median age: 33.

5th. When the Appropriations Committee took up a 1995 spending rescissions package, Nethercutt offered an amendment to protect the wheat facility from being cut. Committee Democrats objected, saying it was unfair for Nethercutt to enjoy special treatment when they were sacrificing spending for their own districts. Nethercutt withdrew his amendment, but then shifted his sights to the Senate, where GOP Sen. Slade Gorton protected the research facility from elimination. When House and Senate conferees met to hash out differences in their spending-cut packages, Nethercutt successfully lobbied for the facility, calling it "proper spending by the federal government" because he said it would produce benefits for the entire agriculture industry and help open international markets for U.S. wheat producers.

Notwithstanding his support for federal functions such as the wheat research center, Nethercutt has said he thinks 15 percent could be cut from the bureaucracy of most any government agency. He has proposed cutting spending for public broadcasting and the National Endowment for the Arts, and he believes the Education and Labor departments could be consolidated.

He does not, however, favor cutting back spending on defense. A member of Appropriations' National Security Subcommittee, Nethercutt has supported GOP efforts to give more money to the Pentagon than President Clinton has requested, and he opposed an effort to freeze fiscal 1997 defense funding at the prior year level. Nethercutt said the freeze amendment would undermine current and future readiness, adding "this is something that is going to threaten, in my judgment, the future of this nation."

In contrast to Foley, who supported abortion rights and voted in 1994 to ban certain semiautomatic assault-style weapons, Nethercutt opposes abortion and voted in 1996 to repeal the assault weapons ban. He also voted with the GOP majority to relax certain environmental rules under the clean water act and to limit the regulatory authority of the Environmental Protection Agency.

At Home: Washington state's late September 1994 primary signaled clearly that Nethercutt had a good chance of becoming the first person since 1862 to defeat a sitting House Speaker. And Foley's troubles foretold woe for Democrats nationwide.

In the state's all-party primary, Foley got only 35 percent of the vote. In nominating Nethercutt, the GOP selected a man with broader appeal than previous challengers to Foley. A lawyer and former Spokane County GOP chairman, he had been active in civic affairs, founding a nursery for victims of child abuse and raising money to combat juvenile diabetes, Nethercutt beat three other Republicans in the primary, even though he was outspent by one.

Immediately after the primary, the Foley-Nethercutt contest drew national and international news media attention. Foley poured more than $2 million into his bid for a 16th term, but Nethercutt spent heavily, too — more than $1 million — and he was aided by numerous conservative groups making independent expenditures to defeat Foley. Though it had backed Foley in previous elections, the National Rifle Association reacted to his support for the assault weapons ban by featuring Charlton Heston in opposition ads and at a Nethercutt fundraiser. A group opposing statehood for the District of Columbia made an independent expenditure, and an Internet user collected more than $10,000 from other computer buffs nationwide to help "De-Foley-ate" the 5th District. Also, Texas billionaire and presidential aspirant Ross Perot campaigned with Nethercutt.

Foley tried to convince voters that he was still listening closely to them, and that their influence was amplified with him as Speaker. He highlighted improvements to Fairchild Air Force Base, his support for wheat farmers, funding in the crime bill for new police officers and other federal dollars he had directed to the district.

Nethercutt said those were examples of how Congress serves members' re-election needs, and he argued that rather than spending thusly from tax revenues, it would be better not to collect the taxes in the first place. His less-government message was alluring to conservatives, who have always been a substantial voting bloc in the 5th. Foley barely won populous Spokane and Whitman counties, but Nethercutt carried the district's nine rural counties and prevailed overall by 51 percent to 49 percent.

Democrats in 1996 fielded farmer Judy Olson, a former president of the National Association of Wheat Growers. Presenting herself as a centrist, Olson had backing from the state's environmental community, which denounced many Republican-crafted measures on the environment that Nethercutt (a member of the House Interior Appropriations Subcommittee) supported. She also benefited from a series of television ads sponsored by organized labor that criticized Nethercutt for supporting Republican proposals to overhaul programs such as Medicare.

In response, Nethercutt said he and other Republicans were trying to save Medicare by slowing the program's rate of growth. Voters were of a mind to give him the benefit of any doubt, and he won re-election with 56 percent of the vote.

HOUSE ELECTIONS

1996 General		
George Nethercutt (R)	131,618	(56%)
Judy Olson (D)	105,166	(44%)
1996 Primary *		
George Nethercutt (R)	61,893	(51%)
Judy Olson (D)	30,666	(25%)
Susan Kaun (D)	16,317	(13%)
Don McCloskey (D)	13,039	(11%)
1994 General		
George Nethercutt (R)	110,057	(51%)
Thomas S. Foley (D)	106,074	(49%)

** In Washington's "jungle primary," candidates of all parties are listed on one ballot.*

CAMPAIGN FINANCE

	Receipts	Receipts from PACs	Expend-itures
1996			
Nethercutt (R)	$1,092,996	$352,647 (32%)	$1,071,823
Olson (D)	$606,813	$186,050 (31%)	$615,636
1994			
Nethercutt (R)	$1,068,396	$103,560 (10%)	$1,067,185
Foley (D)	$2,104,164	$1,158,072 (55%)	$2,144,579

DISTRICT VOTE FOR PRESIDENT

1996		1992	
D	104,052 (44%)	**D**	99,676 (40%)
R	102,384 (43%)	**R**	90,294 (37%)
I	25,250 (11%)	**I**	56,472 (23%)

KEY VOTES

1997	
Ban "partial birth" abortions	Y
1996	
Approve farm bill	Y
Deny public education to illegal immigrants	Y
Repeal ban on certain assault-style weapons	Y
Increase minimum wage	N
Freeze defense spending	N
Approve welfare overhaul	Y
1995	
Approve balanced-budget constitutional amendment	Y
Relax Clean Water Act regulations	Y
Oppose limits on environmental regulations	N
Reduce projected Medicare spending	Y
Approve GOP budget with tax and spending cuts	Y

VOTING STUDIES

	Presidential Support		Party Unity		Conservative Coalition	
Year	**S**	**O**	**S**	**O**	**S**	**O**
1996	32	63	91	5	98	2
1995	17	83	96	4	96	2

INTEREST GROUP RATINGS

Year	ADA	AFL-CIO	CCUS	ACU
1996	0	n/a	93	95
1995	0	0	100	88

6 Norm Dicks (D)

Of Bremerton — Elected 1976, 11th term

Biographical Information

Born: Dec. 16, 1940, Bremerton, Wash.
Education: U. of Washington, B.A. 1963, J.D. 1968.
Occupation: Congressional aide.
Family: Wife, Suzanne Callison; two children.
Religion: Lutheran.
Political Career: No previous office.
Capitol Office: 2467 Rayburn Bldg. 20515; 225-5916.

Committees

Appropriations
Interior; Military Construction; National Security
Select Intelligence (ranking)
Technical & Tactical Intelligence

In Washington: The 1994 election turned life upside down for many House Democrats, depriving them of influence and power. But for Dicks, the Republican Congress is not quite so disorienting. He continues to focus on defense and intelligence issues from his seats on the National Security Appropriations Subcommittee and on the Select Intelligence Committee, where he is the ranking Democrat.

In general, Dicks has endorsed the Republican majority's efforts to spend more on defense than the Clinton administration has requested. And he always looks for ways to bring a portion of the Pentagon budget home, to his state's military installations and defense contractors.

Dicks has an aggressive, sometimes blustery style. The late Democratic Sen. Warren G. Magnuson of Washington used to kid him about his bullish manner: He said Dicks, as a linebacker for the University of Washington football team, was always five yards offside.

"I still feel it's worth doing," Dicks told the Seattle Times in September 1995, when speaking of his job. "And with Speaker Foley gone now, we've got to have a couple of people [in the Washington delegation] who know how to operate. I've got to be the person who takes the lessons of 27 years and puts it to use."

In the 104th, Dicks employed his legislative know-how to help channel more defense dollars to a project that provides jobs in his district: the B-2 "stealth" bomber. Washington state's Boeing Co. is a major subcontractor on the B-2. Dicks and other boosters of the high-tech, high-cost plane secured continued funding of a production line for the bomber, even though the Pentagon had not asked for any additional B-2s.

The Air Force has said the current plan to buy 20 B-2 bombers is sufficient, but that has not stopped Dicks from agitating for more planes.

In June 1995, the House endorsed the addition of $553 million to the defense authorization bill to continue production of the bomber; an amendment to kill the money was rejected, 203-219. In September 1995, the House on a 210-213 vote rejected an amendment to cut $493 million from the defense spending bill for the plane. Proponents of holding the B-2 count at 20 planes are an amalgam of liberal Democrats and some "deficit hawk" Republicans; leaders of the effort are Republican John R. Kasich of Ohio, chairman of the Budget Committee, and California Democrat Ronald V. Dellums, ranking minority member of the National Security Committee.

In countering Kasich and Dellums, Dicks argues that the United States should not limit itself to having just 20 copies of a weapon as valuable as the B-2, whose cutting-edge technology makes it difficult for enemy radar to track.

Dicks invoked a recently minted military hero from Washington state to buttress his case for more B-2s. Air Force Capt. Scott O'Grady, rescued after his plane went down in Bosnia in June 1995, would not have been shot down if he had been flying a stealth plane, Dicks maintained. Dicks also argues that a B-2 force could blunt an invasion of a distant U.S. ally, perhaps deterring such attacks. When Iraqi president Saddam Hussein attacked Kuwait in 1990, "three B-2s could have knocked out 46 percent of Saddam's armored vehicles before they crossed the border of Kuwait," Dicks said.

In Clinton's fiscal 1998 defense budget, again no money for additional B-2s was included, but that did not deter Dicks. He said his top priority would be to secure $350 million to keep production lines open and begin procurement of as many as nine more bombers.

Dicks was successful in earmarking funding for a home-based project in the June 1995 spending bill for military construction, even though some lawmakers who consider themselves "porkbusters" did their best to eliminate it. Dicks sought $10.4 million for a new physical fitness center at the Bremerton Puget Sound Naval Shipyard in his district, a project the Navy did not request but that Dicks said is part of a five-year service plan. An amendment to kill it and other special projects failed, 158-270. For the 105th Congress, Dicks gained a seat on Appropriations'

The 6th continues to be anchored in Bremerton, Tacoma and the southern Puget Sound region, but its shape changed considerably in 1992 redistricting.

In the 1980s, the 6th was a fairly narrow district that ran well to the south of Tacoma. For the 1990s, though, the 6th has a squarish shape because it expands west and north from Bremerton and Tacoma all the way to the Pacific, taking in the mountainous and forested Olympic Peninsula. (The peninsula had been in the 2nd District.)

With this addition, the 6th has become one of the key districts to watch in the Northwest as logging interests and environmentalists haggle over how to balance use of the forest with preservation of habitat for such endangered species as the northern spotted owl.

Weyerhaeuser Co. still operates a mill in the peninsula community of Grays Harbor, but another timber giant, ITT Rayonier, shut down its operations at the end of 1992 (part of the plant is now owned by Grays Harbor Paper).

On the peninsula, communities are trying to diversify to get beyond dependence on timber. The shipping of logs once was the only bill of fare in the port of Grays Harbor. Locals hope that a channel-deepening project now under way will help the port get into exporting many other commodities. Also in Grays Harbor County, a regional airport is being renovated to attract new business.

Other maritime pursuits boost the economy: The fishing industry is a large employer in Port Angeles on the Strait of Juan de Fuca and in Grays Harbor. The district is also home to the Puget Sound Naval Shipyard in Bremerton.

Tourism is a possible source of increased income for the peninsula. Located here are the

WASHINGTON 6
West — Bremerton

Olympic National Park (in Clallam and Jefferson counties) and the Olympic National Forest. They attract thousands of sightseers annually to northwest Washington.

The inclusion of the lightly settled peninsula into the 6th gives the district more diversified interests. But the bulk of the district's residents still live in urbanized areas. The combined clout of Pierce County (Tacoma) and Kitsap County (Bremerton) accounts for about two-thirds of the district's vote.

The 6th encompasses downtown and northern Tacoma. This industrial city's blue-collar, heavily unionized electorate generally tilts Pierce County to Democrats. In the 6th District part of Pierce, Bill Clinton garnered 53 percent of the votes in 1996, winning by more than 19,000 votes over Bob Dole. Clinton carried the overall district — and led in all six of its counties — with 50 percent of the vote to Dole's 36 percent. Ross Perot's vote dropped from 25 percent in 1992 to 10 percent.

Low housing prices and a high quality of life have earned Bremerton a reputation as a desirable place to live. The city, on the Kitsap Peninsula, has a strong labor vote, but surrounding Kitsap County (much of which is in the 1st District) leans Republican. Clinton won the 6th District's part of Kitsap with 48 percent of the vote in 1996.

1990 Population: 540,742. White 472,221 (87%), Black 28,997 (5%), Other 39,524 (7%). Hispanic origin 16,735 (3%). 18 and over 403,037 (75%), 62 and over 92,217 (17%). Median age: 34.

Military Construction Subcommittee.

As the top Democrat on the Intelligence Committee, Dicks has supported increased funding for intelligence-gathering activities, a stance that puts him at odds with a many in his own party who believe the budget-cutting ax wielded at other government programs should also be applied to spying. Dicks says the increased spending would not significantly expand current intelligence operations, but rather finance modernization that could produce savings later.

In 1996, he defended funding for the National Reconnaissance Office (NRO), which manages the nation's spy satellites and was being buffeted with charges of fiscal mismanagement. The NRO's troubles began in 1994, when members of the Senate Intelligence Committee alleged that the agency failed to inform the committee of a 1 million-square-foot headquarters that it was building in the Northern Virginia suburbs at a cost of $302 million. Then in 1995, Senate investigators discovered that the NRO had hoarded more than $1 billion in unspent funds.

During House floor debate on the intelligence bill in May 1996, Democrats moved to punish the NRO with an amendment that would have frozen the NRO's authorization at the previous year's level. But Dicks argued that then-CIA Director John M. Deutch had already disciplined the agency by firing the NRO's top two officials. Dicks attributed the NRO's problems to bookkeeping errors and said that freezing the agency's budget would have serious consequences for new satellite development. "They build incredible satellites. . . . They may be lousy accountants," Dicks said. The House rejected the amendment, 137-292.

Dicks also sits on Appropriations' Interior Subcommittee, giving him a role in debates over logging in forests and the protection of endangered species, issues important in the 6th. When the House considered the interior spending bill in June 1996, Dicks offered an amendment to strike language barring environmental protections for a threatened sea bird, the marbled murrelet.

During committee markup, California Republican Frank Riggs had successfully offered language to exempt 40,000 acres of land in his district from a decision by the U.S. Fish and Wildlife Service to designate about 700,000 acres of land as a critical habitat for the bird. Riggs argued that the critical habitat designation would put undue restrictions on the land and lead to job loss. But Dicks countered that the real goal of the Riggs provision was to help just one special interest — Pacific Lumber Co., which controlled much of the 40,000 acres. The House agreed, approving Dicks' amendment 257-164.

In contrast to his right-of-center stance on defense issues, Dicks leans to the left on most social policy questions. He has spoken up for continued funding of the National Endowment for the Arts, an agency that many conservatives want to kill. In the 104th, he voted for abortion rights and against a GOP effort to repeal the ban on certain semiautomatic assault-style weapons.

When House Democrats split half-and-half on the final welfare overhaul bill in 1996, Dicks was among the 98 in his party voting for the legislation, which President Clinton signed into law. Liberal Democrats argued that the measure would drive more children into poverty, but Dicks said he thought the bill had enough positive elements to warrant supporting it.

At Home: After three years as administrative assistant to Magnuson, Dicks decided to go home in 1976 and run for Congress. He had been planning a campaign in the 6th District whenever incumbent Democrat Floyd Hicks retired, and when Hicks was named to the state Supreme Court in 1976, Dicks plunged in with his usual intensity.

He had to compete with three major candidates for the nomination: a young activist state representative, a former president of Pacific Lutheran University and the mayor of Tacoma. But Dicks' ability to tap the resources of labor and other interest groups helped him put together a coalition that won him the primary with 36 percent of the vote.

Dicks had no trouble against a weak Republican that fall, but in the next two elections he was pestered by Republican James Beaver, a conservative law professor from Tacoma. Dicks managed to clear 61 percent in 1978, but in 1980, Beaver was buoyed by financial support from the New Right and held Dicks to 54 percent.

While Beaver had attacked the incumbent from the right, Dicks' 1982 challenger, GOP state Sen. Ted Haley, was more liberal. Haley painted Dicks as a profligate spender too friendly with military contractors. But that charge gave Dicks an excuse to talk about projects he had brought home. He claimed credit for completion of the Tacoma Spur Highway and numerous Navy ship overhauls at Bremerton. Dicks' 63 percent indicated that he was moving toward security. In 1994, the national GOP tide lapped at Dicks' feet — he won with 58 percent — but rebounded in 1996 to a 66 percent tally.

HOUSE ELECTIONS

1996 General		
Norm Dicks (D)	155,467	(66%)
Bill Tinsley (R)	71,337	(30%)
Ted Haley (I)	5,561	(2%)
Michael Huddleston (NL)	3,545	(2%)
1996 Primary †		
Norm Dicks (D)	94,755	(67%)
Bill Tinsley (R)	14,603	(10%)
Ken Lund (R)	11,159	(8%)
Richard "Dick" Meyer (R)	8,299	(6%)
Steve Whitaker (R)	5,980	(4%)
Ted Haley (I)	2,892	(2%)
Charles Crawford (R)	2,357	(2%)
Michael Huddleston (NL)	2,074	(1%)
1994 General		
Norm Dicks (D)	105,480	(58%)
Benjamin Gregg (R)	75,322	(42%)

Previous Winning Percentages: 1992 (64%) **1990** (61%) **1988** (68%) **1986** (71%) **1984** (66%) **1982** (63%) **1980** (54%) **1978** (61%) **1976** (74%)

† In Washington's "jungle primary," candidates of all parties are listed on one ballot.

CAMPAIGN FINANCE

	Receipts	Receipts from PACs	Expend-itures
1996			
Dicks (D)	$523,876	$281,450 (54%)	$477,269
Tinsley (R)	$16,549	$16 (0%)	$16,384
1994			
Dicks (D)	$670,541	$346,000 (52%)	$629,161
Gregg (R)	$61,059	$14 (0%)	$60,721

DISTRICT VOTE FOR PRESIDENT

1996	1992
D 122,245 (50%)	**D** 106,373 (44%)
R 87,910 (36%)	**R** 77,538 (32%)
I 23,834 (10%)	**I** 60,578 (25%)

KEY VOTES

1997	
Ban "partial birth" abortions	N
1996	
Approve farm bill	N
Deny public education to illegal immigrants	N
Repeal ban on certain assault-style weapons	N
Increase minimum wage	Y
Freeze defense spending	N
Approve welfare overhaul	Y
1995	
Approve balanced-budget constitutional amendment	N
Relax Clean Water Act regulations	N
Oppose limits on environmental regulations	Y
Reduce projected Medicare spending	N
Approve GOP budget with tax and spending cuts	N

VOTING STUDIES

	Presidential Support		Party Unity		Conservative Coalition	
Year	S	O	S	O	S	O
1996	85	11	80	15	59	41
1995	80	18	82	14	49	48
1994	90	9	92	6	58	42
1993	91	5	88	7	48	52
1992	36	61	85	11	56	44
1991	36	59	85	9	43	54

INTEREST GROUP RATINGS

Year	ADA	AFL-CIO	CCUS	ACU
1996	65	n/a	19	0
1995	80	100	33	0
1994	65	78	58	14
1993	75	92	30	13
1992	80	73	25	8
1991	70	82	38	5

7 Jim McDermott (D)

Of Seattle — Elected 1988, 5th term

Biographical Information
Born: Dec. 28, 1936, Chicago, Ill.
Education: Wheaton College, B.S. 1958; U. of Illinois, M.D. 1963.
Military Service: Navy Medical Corps, 1968-70.
Occupation: Psychiatrist.
Family: Divorced; two children.
Religion: Episcopalian.
Political Career: Wash. House, 1971-73; sought Democratic nomination for governor, 1972; Wash. Senate, 1975-87; Democratic nominee for governor, 1980; sought Democratic nomination for governor, 1984.
Capitol Office: 2349 Rayburn Bldg. 20515; 225-3106.

Committees
Budget
Ways & Means
Human Resources; Trade

In Washington: From the latter part of the 103rd Congress all the way through the 104th, much of McDermott's time was devoted to his work on the House ethics committee, which was investigating the propriety of Speaker Newt Gingrich's political fundraising activities. Yet when the committee finally issued its verdict, McDermott was off the case, having abruptly resigned from the ethics panel amid a fury of partisan finger-pointing.

McDermott resigned from the panel in January 1997 after allegations that he accepted a tape recording of a cellular telephone conservation. The recording featured Gingrich and other House GOP leaders discussing the ethics case in a conference call in late December 1996. None of the participants knew the call was being monitored or recorded.

McDermott said that the brouhaha over the tape had diverted attention from the original ethics charges against Gingrich. "The ethics process in the House has been perverted into a partisan scheme to obstruct every reasonable effort to get at the truth," McDermott said. "I have decided to recuse myself while the present controversy continues. That meets a far higher standard than that of Rep. Gingrich, who has refused to recuse himself as Speaker, even while under active investigation."

Republicans accused McDermott of distributing the tape to news sources after receiving it from a Florida couple, John and Alice Martin, who had recorded it from a police scanner. The Martins had been active in Democratic politics. The tape wound up in the hands of The New York Times, which published a transcript. McDermott was widely reported to have been the newspaper's source, although that was never established as fact. (The Martins pleaded guilty in spring 1997 to illegally intercepting a cellular phone call.)

As McDermott recused himself from the final stage of the ethics probe, he managed a parting shot, calling the ethics committee investigation a "charade" and its chairman, Nancy L. Johnson, R-Conn., "arbitrary, authoritarian and autocratic."

That was just the last in a series of conflicts between McDermott, who had been the ethics committee chairman in the 103rd Congress, and Johnson, who took over when Republicans became the House majority in the 104th Congress. Their relationship had been strained almost from the beginning of the Gingrich investigation. McDermott resented Johnson's unilateral leadership and said Johnson "delayed, stonewalled, or otherwise obstructed sensible efforts to get at the whole truth."

In September 1996, McDermott said only two conclusions could be drawn about the committee's deliberations: Either its Republican members had "deliberately stalled for over a year, or they are inept in dealing with serious charges against their leaders." McDermott added, "I think there is pretty good evidence that this report is being delayed deliberately."

McDermott said he had been so frustrated by the process that he had twice tried to resign from the committee, but each time Minority Leader Richard A. Gephardt, D-Mo., persuaded him to stay. House Majority Leader Dick Armey, R-Texas, responded by calling for McDermott's removal from the committee. "I think he's disqualified himself," Armey said.

McDermott himself had been the subject of an ethics complaint in July 1996, when Rep. Peter T. King, R-N.Y., said he should recuse himself from the Gingrich case because Steven J. Jost, a fundraiser whom McDermott once employed, was involved in filing ethics complaints against the Speaker. King also said McDermott had violated House rules by making public statements about the ethics process. The ethics panel said King had not sufficiently substantiated his conflict of interest allegation.

With his service on the ethics committee done, McDermott can turn his attention to the Ways and Means Committee. He landed there at the start of the 102nd Congress through a combination of qualifications — he had chaired his state's Ways and Means panel during a stint in the Washington Legislature — and patronage from then-House Speaker (and fellow Washingtonian) Thomas S. Foley. McDermott's medical degree — he's a psychiatrist — made him an attractive candidate to then-Health Subcommittee Chairman Pete Stark,

WASHINGTON 7
Seattle and suburbs

Ferryboats plying the clear-blue waters of Puget Sound, snow-capped Mount Rainier looming to the southeast — these images identify Seattle to most people. Thousands of newcomers settled in the Seattle area during the 1980s, drawn by the city's pleasant aura and an economy prospering on aerospace manufacturing and trade with the Pacific Rim.

But there was a down side to that growth: traffic-choked highways and streets, downtown towers blocking the sun and suburban developments devouring open space. Concern that Seattle was becoming a less livable place spawned a slow-growth movement that in May 1989 managed the passage of an initiative placing limits on downtown development.

Downtown remains an architecturally diverse blend of the Northwest's tallest skyscrapers and turn-of-the-century buildings erected when the city was in its infancy.

Tourists take in the Space Needle at the old World's Fair site; its observation level offers a commanding view. Visitors and locals alike gather at Pike Place Market, a reconditioned old outdoor market in the pier district that offers a variety of foods and shopping wares. Seattle has become known for its active music scene, and the Kingdome hosts a variety of sporting events.

Seattle, with a population of 516,000, has a number of ethnic enclaves; its varied blue-collar population includes well-defined Scandinavian, Italian, Asian and Hispanic communities.

In economic terms, the fortunes of the 7th — and the entire Seattle area — are tied closely to the vitality of the Boeing aircraft company. Interstate 5 heading north into Seattle parallels the runway of Boeing Field. Boeing thrived during the defense boom of the 1980s; now though, defense spending is on a slide, as is the commercial airline industry. As a sign of the industry's declining fortunes, Boeing has announced plans to merge with the other major commercial airline manufacturer, McDonnell-Douglas.

The other big economic pillar in the 7th, the export-import business, is a fairly steady provider of blue-collar jobs handling goods heading to or from East Asia. And with more than 34,000 students, the University of Washington also is a large employer in the 7th.

Several factors combine to make the 7th the most dependable Democratic district in the state: the strength of organized labor in this industrial area, a minority population that is the largest among Washington House districts (10 percent black, 12 percent Asian) and a substantial bloc of liberal urbanites.

In the 1996 election, Bill Clinton polled 69 percent of the vote, his best showing by far in any of Washington's nine congressional districts. It was slightly more than the 66 percent Clinton polled in the district in 1992.

McDermott also distinguished himself in 1996 by garnering 81 percent of the vote, a higher percentage than any congressional candidate in the state.

1990 Population: 540,747. White 408,480 (76%), Black 53,926 (10%), Other 78,341 (14%). Hispanic origin 19,148 (4%). 18 and over 447,790 (83%), 62 and over 92,223 (17%). Median age: 35.

D-Calif. Stark wanted his own doctor to put up against the House's only other medical doctor at the time, family practitioner J. Roy Rowland, D-Ga., who served on the rival Health and Environment Subcommittee of the Energy and Commerce Committee.

At the outset of the 105th, McDermott said Ways and Means would have to tackle some difficult problems. "We're going to have to deal with Medicare [and] some tax things," he said. "You're going to have to do those issues on a bipartisan basis, otherwise it's going to be a thrash."

In the 104th, he was a critic of the Republicans' proposal to cut the projected growth of Medicare, the federal government's health insurance program for the elderly, by $270 billion over seven years. In September 1995, he introduced legislation to save about $90 billion over seven years by reducing payments to hospitals and doctors. His bill also would have set up a commission to study how best to overhaul Medicare to meet the flood of new beneficiaries after 2010 when the Baby Boom generation begins to retire.

McDermott also continues to champion a single-payer health care plan, under which all Americans would be guaranteed health insurance benefits through a taxpayer-financed system. In February 1995, he led a group of House Democrats in reintroducing the legislation that had died in the 103rd Congress. "I am under no illusion that single payer is going to pass in such a mean-spirited Congress," McDermott said. "The fact that you lose once does not mean you stop."

In the 103rd, ignoring leadership requests that members delay introducing their own health bills until President Clinton unveiled his, McDermott in March 1993 proposed a single-payer health plan. He ultimately rallied a formidable bloc that included most of the House's liberals. His 92 cosponsors included most of the New York City delegation, the California Democratic delegation, 12 committee chairmen, 36 subcommittee chairmen and chairmen of the Congressional Black and Hispanic caucuses.

McDermott knew that the tax increases required to finance his plan made passage highly unlikely. But he used the clout of his forces to hold Clinton and congressional Democratic leaders to liberals' core demands of extending coverage with generous benefits to all Americans, imposing tight limits on cost increases and giving states the option of instituting their own single-payer plans.

And he showed he was willing to play hardball for his bottom line: He was one of only four Ways and Means Democrats, and the only liberal, to vote against the bill cobbled together by acting Chairman Sam M. Gibbons, D-Fla., in late June 1994. McDermott called the plan "a special interest smorgasbord with the insurance industry as the main glutton." By August, McDermott was showing a willingness to deal, but at that point it was too late. Congress failed to pass even a minimal health bill.

In September 1995, McDermott tried to amend legislation toughening the U.S. embargo of Cuba. He proposed to allow U.S. companies to sell Cuba medicine and staple foods, arguing for his amendment on humanitarian grounds. But bill sponsor Dan Burton, R-Ind., accused him of trying to undermine the embargo. "It's the camel's nose under the tent," Burton said. The House rejected McDermott's amendment, 138-283.

At Home: Even from another continent, the 1988 open-seat race for the 7th caught McDermott's eye. The former state senator left his job in Africa to stage a political comeback.

McDermott's earlier political career included more than 14 years in the state Legislature and three unsuccessful campaigns for governor. But in 1987 McDermott quit the state Senate to take a three-year job in Zaire as a Foreign Service psychiatrist.

When 7th District Democrat Mike Lowry tried for the Senate in 1988, replacement talk centered on Democrats closer to home, such as Seattle City Councilman (and later Mayor) Norm Rice and King County Assessor Ruthe Ridder. Then, in February, McDermott sent word from Zaire that he had been released from his Foreign Service commitment and would seek Lowry's seat.

With his record as a legislative leader and his high visibility from statewide campaigns, he soon became the front-runner. He won endorsements from the state labor council and most local party organizations. He had more money and won the primary after a late media blitz. In the strongly Democratic 7th, his November win was a given, and his re-elections have been romps. Redistricting in 1992 left the 7th the state's most Democratic district.

Born in Chicago, McDermott moved to Seattle in 1966 to set up a practice, then left for a stint as a Navy psychiatrist in Long Beach, Calif. In 1970 he came back and won a state House race. In 1972 he ran third in the Democratic gubernatorial primary. After winning state Senate elections in 1974 and 1978, he challenged Democratic Gov. Dixy Lee Ray in the 1980 primary. He beat the conservative Ray, but then lost to Republican John Spellman. His third try for governor flopped, as he lost by nearly 2-to-1 in a 1984 primary against Booth Gardner (who unseated Spellman and served two terms as governor).

HOUSE ELECTIONS

1996 General		
Jim McDermott (D)	209,753	(81%)
Frank Kleschen (R)	49,341	(19%)
1996 Primary †		
Jim McDermott (D)	106,613	(79%)
Frank Kleschen (R)	29,138	(21%)
1994 General		
Jim McDermott (D)	148,353	(75%)
Keith Harris (R)	49,091	(25%)

Previous Winning Percentages: **1992** (78%) **1990** (72%) **1988** (76%)

† In Washington's "jungle primary," candidates of all parties are listed on one ballot.

CAMPAIGN FINANCE

	Receipts	Receipts from PACs	Expend-itures
1996			
McDermott (D)	$207,849	$118,281 (57%)	$190,250
Kleschen (R)	$6,745	0	$6,680
1994			
McDermott (D)	$264,671	$204,000 (77%)	$275,259

DISTRICT VOTE FOR PRESIDENT

1996	1992
D 182,671 (69%)	**D** 191,781 (66%)
R 53,437 (20%)	**R** 54,478 (19%)
I 13,671 (5%)	**I** 45,167 (16%)

KEY VOTES

1997	
Ban "partial birth" abortions	N
1996	
Approve farm bill	N
Deny public education to illegal immigrants	N
Repeal ban on certain assault-style weapons	N
Increase minimum wage	Y
Freeze defense spending	Y
Approve welfare overhaul	N
1995	
Approve balanced-budget constitutional amendment	N
Relax Clean Water Act regulations	N
Oppose limits on environmental regulations	Y
Reduce projected Medicare spending	N
Approve GOP budget with tax and spending cuts	N

VOTING STUDIES

	Presidential Support		Party Unity		Conservative Coalition	
Year	S	O	S	O	S	O
1996	82	18	95	3	8	90
1995	86	10	96	2	5	95
1994	78	21	95	2	14	78
1993	82	11	91	2	14	80
1992	18	82	94	4	13	88
1991	27	70	95	5	8	92

INTEREST GROUP RATINGS

Year	ADA	AFL-CIO	CCUS	ACU
1996	95	n/a	27	0
1995	95	100	13	4
1994	95	78	33	5
1993	85	92	27	4
1992	95	83	25	0
1991	95	83	20	0

8 Jennifer Dunn (R)

Of Bellevue — Elected 1992, 3rd term

Biographical Information

Born: July 29, 1941, Seattle, Wash.
Education: Stanford U., 1959; U. of Washington, 1960-62; Stanford U., A.B. 1963.
Occupation: State party official.
Family: Divorced; two children.
Religion: Episcopalian.
Political Career: Wash. Republican Party chairman, 1980-92.
Capitol Office: 432 Cannon Bldg. 20515; 225-7761.

Committees

Ways & Means
Oversight; Trade
Conference Secretary

In Washington: Through a combination of her own political skills and the GOP's desire to counter its image as the men-in-dark-suits party, Dunn has emerged as one of the more important and visible Republican players in the House. In the 105th Congress, she was elevated to an official leadership position, winning election as GOP Conference secretary. She already had a key committee assignment, on Ways and Means. Dunn is a prolific fundraiser, a regular presence on the podium at major GOP news conferences and rallies, and she is considered likely to advance beyond the House, perhaps as soon as in a 1998 Senate run.

Dunn helps to put a warm face on Republican efforts to recast the social safety net, often injecting her personal history into policy debates. During consideration of welfare or labor legislation, Dunn has been a fixture on the House floor describing her sympathy, "as a single mother who raised two sons," for the difficulties experienced by working parents. (Dunn is divorced.)

"We've learned something about rhetoric," Dunn said about her party just before the 1996 election. "I have always been a proponent of softening our rhetoric. I believe we can pursue the same positions we have been, but we don't need to be as harsh and scary about it."

Dunn's mixed voting record on abortion issues prompted more ardent conservatives within the Washington Republican Party — which she chaired from 1980 to 1992 — to deny her a slot as a delegate to the 1996 GOP Convention.

She supports a ban on a particular abortion procedure its opponents call "partial birth" abortion, and she opposed allowing the federal employee health insurance program to pay for abortions. But she opposed banning abortions at overseas military hospitals and voted to require states to pay for Medicaid abortions in certain cases. "Simply put," Dunn has said, "I believe that the use of taxpayer dollars to pay for or promote abortion is inappropriate, except under circumstances of rape or incest or to protect the life of the mother."

But if she is insufficiently conservative on abortion to please her state party, the national GOP was happy to give Dunn a visible role at the convention, as a commentator for the party's cable television coverage of the proceedings.

Although Republican leaders insist that it is Dunn's competence and hard work that separates her from the crowd, she has been spotlighted particularly in hopes that she will appeal to women voters. She co-chaired the National Federation of Republican Women's 1996 get out the vote effort and led a leadership summit for prominent Republican women.

After she won the conference secretary post, Dunn told The Seattle Times that the job was undefined, but would give her a say in how the party healed its image with women and the elderly. "What we did in Congress was [use] a rhetoric that was shocking and scary to many women and older people who believe in an activist government when it comes to Social Security and Medicare," she said.

Dunn joined with other Republican women in moving to add more money for child care in the welfare overhaul, and she has sought to direct NASA to devote some of its weightless microgravity research to ovarian and breast cancer research.

Pro-business and solidly conservative on fiscal issues, Dunn uses her Ways and Means seat to look out for the export-related interests of Seattle-area businesses. She supports free trade, including maintaining low tariffs for China, and is a harsh critic of the Internal Revenue Service.

After promising constituents that "I want to make life as hard on the IRS as they've made it on you," Dunn engaged in a war of words with miffed IRS officials. Finally she wrote in a letter, "I will not apologize for the obvious: the IRS is often overzealous, it does often trample the rights of taxpayers, and it does deserve closer scrutiny."

Dunn's iron fist in a velvet glove approach was evident in her defense of Speaker Newt Gingrich as he faced accusations in the 104th of violating

WASHINGTON 8
Puget Sound (East) — King County suburbs; Bellevue

The 8th includes some of Seattle's most prosperous suburbs as well as the landmark that affords the city unique allure — snow-capped, 14,410 foot Mount Rainier.

Encompassing the mainly affluent suburbs and exurbs east of Seattle, the 8th has long been considered the state's most Republican district west of the Cascade Mountains. Although the 8th District retains a GOP tilt, independents are influential.

Dunn easily won re-election to the House seat in 1996. She garnered 65 percent of the vote to win a third term by 30 percentage points. At the same time, Bill Clinton carried the district in the presidential election by about 7 percentage points. He beat Bob Dole in the 8th by 47 percent to 40 percent. Independent Ross Perot, who had scored 27 percent in 1992, fell to 9 percent four years later.

The district's 35 percent population growth in the 1980s made it the state's fastest-growing district. In redistricting, large chunks of land that had been in the 8th were put into the newly created 9th District (the extra seat that Washington gained in reapportionment for the 1990s).

For the past 20 years, the suburban area covered by the 8th enjoyed its position as a beneficiary of Seattle's economic boom. But while the boom brought benefits, it also brought the traffic jams and housing cost increases that are the downside of growth. Although not as obvious as the "no growth" movement in Seattle — where an initiative to restrict downtown development won approval in 1989 — there is a "slow down" constituency in the 8th.

With almost 87,000 residents (some of whom live in the 1st), Bellevue is the population center of the 8th and of the King County suburbs that make up the bulk of the district.

Separating Seattle and Bellevue is Lake Washington, and in the middle of the lake is the exclusive community of Mercer Island. Bellevue's white-collar constituency offers strong GOP votes, but Mercer Island shows an independent streak, often offering up a split ticket. Part of the reason for the difference is that Mercer Island has a sizable contingent of Jewish residents who tend to be more liberal on social issues.

In the southern half of the district is Pierce County, a rural, sparsely populated section of the 8th dotted with small towns that have attracted a substantial number of retirees and families eager to flee the hassles of urban living.

Residents of the 8th work at a variety of white- and blue-collar businesses, but Boeing, located in Renton, is a key employer here as it is throughout the metropolitan area.

Other large local employers are Paccar, which manufactures trucks, and the computer companies of Microsoft and Nintendo.

1990 Population: 540,742. White 497,553 (92%), Black 8,876 (2%), Other 34,313 (6%). Hispanic origin 12,434 (2%). 18 and over 388,671 (72%), 62 and over 53,320 (10%). Median age: 33.

House ethics rules. In a move that was widely perceived as retaliation for Democratic harping about Gingrich's transgressions, Dunn in 1996 filed an ethics complaint against House Democratic leader Richard A. Gephardt about his acquisition of a vacation home in North Carolina.

Dunn noted that Gephardt listed a Duck property on his congressional financial disclosure forms as a "vacation home" and reported no rental income. The ethics committee dismissed the complaint against Gephardt, although it upbraided him for failing to properly disclose income from the property.

But for all her full-court defense of the Speaker, Dunn could be forgiving of a leadership critic within GOP ranks. At a Republican organizational meeting before the 105th, Dunn reportedly whispered in Peter T. King's ear, "I still like you, even if nobody else does." New Yorker King, an on-again, off-again critic of Gingrich, had suggested the Georgian step aside as Speaker until his ethical problems were resolved.

From her post on the House Oversight Committee in the 104th, Dunn led an investigation into the contested 1994 election of Connecticut Democrat Sam Gejdenson. Gejdenson's election lead of two votes ballooned to a 21-vote margin after two recounts, and Dunn's task force found no compelling reason to overturn the result.

Before joining Ways and Means in the 104th, Dunn spent her first term on what were then called the committees on Public Works and Transportation and on Science, Space and Technology. In both cases, she used the opportunity to see to local concerns related to commuter highways and the high-tech industries that have made the Puget Sound region so prosperous in recent decades.

Dunn supports, in principle, the idea of overhauling campaign finance laws, although she says she is uncertain about the ideal solution. Dunn has sponsored legislation that would require congressional candidates to require most of their money in-state but would allow "soft money" party expenditures and political action committee contributions to rise.

At Home: After seeing her party lose every major race in her state but her own in 1992, Dunn herself has had the smoothest of re-election years in 1994 and 1996, as Democrats left her all but unopposed.

Dunn fits a more traditional than contemporary pattern for women officeholders. Instead of entering politics from academia, the law or issue activism, she graduated from college, married and had two children before becoming involved as a campaign volunteer. As her sons grew up, Dunn got involved in politics full time.

When Ronald Reagan was swept into the White House in 1980 and a Republican won the Washington governorship, Dunn was elected state party chair. She later served as vice chairman of the executive committee of the Republican National Committee and as chairman of the national organization of GOP state chairmen. Reagan also appointed Dunn to advisory councils on volunteer service and historic preservation.

In the multicandidate 1992 primary in the open 8th District, she barely held off Pam Roach, a first-term Republican state senator and an ardent opponent of abortion. Dunn took 32 percent of the vote to Roach's 29 percent, with two other Republicans trailing.

Things got easier for her in the general election. Dunn's Democratic opponent, who had switched parties in the course of the 1992 election cycle, was unable to make a case against her conservative fiscal views and moderate image on social issues. She won with 60 percent of the vote to become Washington state's only House Republican in the 103rd Congress.

She was joined in the 104th by six other Republicans, five of whom won re-election with her in 1996.

HOUSE ELECTIONS

1996 General		
Jennifer Dunn (R)	170,691	(65%)
Dave Little (D)	90,340	(35%)
1996 Primary †		
Jennifer Dunn (R)	86,662	(65%)
Dave Little (D)	46,961	(35%)
1994 General		
Jennifer Dunn (R)	140,409	(76%)
Jim Wyrick (D)	44,165	(24%)

Previous Winning Percentages: 1992 (60%)

† In Washington's "jungle primary," candidates of all parties are listed on one ballot.

CAMPAIGN FINANCE

	Receipts	Receipts from PACs	Expend-itures
1996			
Dunn (R)	$1,156,583	$479,592 (41%)	$1,146,933
Little (D)	$6,840	$250 (4%)	$6,838
1994			
Dunn (R)	$702,231	$218,636 (31%)	$685,083

DISTRICT VOTE FOR PRESIDENT

1996		1992	
D	130,469 (47%)	**D**	102,857 (38%)
R	112,457 (40%)	**R**	92,276 (35%)
I	23,994 (9%)	**I**	72,526 (27%)

KEY VOTES

1997	
Ban "partial birth" abortions	Y
1996	
Approve farm bill	Y
Deny public education to illegal immigrants	Y
Repeal ban on certain assault-style weapons	Y
Increase minimum wage	N
Freeze defense spending	N
Approve welfare overhaul	Y
1995	
Approve balanced-budget constitutional amendment	Y
Relax Clean Water Act regulations	Y
Oppose limits on environmental regulations	N
Reduce projected Medicare spending	Y
Approve GOP budget with tax and spending cuts	Y

VOTING STUDIES

	Presidential Support		Party Unity		Conservative Coalition	
Year	**S**	**O**	**S**	**O**	**S**	**O**
1996	38	61	87	5	86	8
1995	22	77	93	5	87	5
1994	54	45	91	9	97	3
1993	47	52	90	9	91	9

INTEREST GROUP RATINGS

Year	ADA	AFL-CIO	CCUS	ACU
1996	0	n/a	100	100
1995	5	0	100	80
1994	5	11	92	86
1993	5	0	100	91

9 Adam Smith (D)

Of Kent — Elected 1996, 1st term

Biographical Information
Born: June 15, 1965, Washington, D.C.
Education: Fordham U., B.A. 1987; U. of Washington, J.D. 1990.
Occupation: City prosecutor; lawyer.
Family: Wife, Sara Bickle-Eldridge.
Religion: Christian.
Political Career: Wash. Senate, 1991-97.
Capitol Office: 1505 Longworth Bldg. 20515; 225-8901.

Committees
National Security
Military Installations and Facilities; Military Procurement
Resources
Water & Power

The Path to Washington: Though just 31 when he entered the 105th Congress, Smith brought to the House significant political savvy and extensive legislative experience at the state level.

Smith, who is the second Democrat and third person to represent this swing district in as many terms, will need his vaunted political skills to stay a step ahead of shifting winds and a fickle constituency nearly 3,000 miles away.

Smith, from the southeastern Seattle suburb of Kent, was first elected to the Legislature in 1990, scoring an upset victory over a veteran state senator.

That victory at age 25 made Smith the youngest state senator in the country at that time. In 1994, when many Democratic officeholders in the state were swept out of office by a Republican tide, Smith ran for a second term and won re-election.

In both legislative races, Smith earned a reputation as a strong and active campaigner by visiting more than 40,000 homes in his district, giving dozens of speeches at area schools and holding numerous town meetings.

Smith, a former assistant city prosecutor in Seattle, also won respect as being tough on crime for specializing in cases of domestic violence, spousal abuse and drunk driving.

Smith became known as a champion of education and justice issues during his service in Olympia. In 1992, he was appointed chairman of the state Senate's Law and Justice Committee, a position he held for four years.

Smith likes to point out that he is a lifelong resident of the community who worked his way through undergraduate school by loading trucks. He earned his law degree at the University of Washington in Seattle.

To further illustrate his working-class roots and his empathy for working families, Smith seldom misses a chance to mention that his father worked for 30 years as a baggage handler at Seattle-Tacoma International Airport and was an active union member in the International Association of Machinists and Aerospace Workers.

As a member of Congress, Smith has pledged to continue emphasizing issues such as education, with particular emphasis on job training and economic development. His committee assignments are well-tailored to the economic concerns of the Puget Sound region: He sits on the Resources Committee and the National Security Committee.

A rising star among Washington Democrats, Smith was considered a strong contender for higher elected office when he announced in July 1995 that he would challenge freshman Republican Rep. Randy Tate.

Much like Smith, Tate was a youthful veteran of the state Legislature when he ran for Congress; he defeated one-term Democrat Mike Kreidler in 1994. A vocal supporter of House Speaker Newt Gingrich, Tate strongly backed the House Republicans' "Contract With America" and advocated reducing the size and scope of the federal government.

But singling out GOP proposals to alter such programs as college student loans, worker safety programs and environmental protection laws, the AFL-CIO launched an 18-month barrage of television and radio commercials aimed at unseating Tate.

While the AFL-CIO ads did much of the dirty work of attacking Tate, Smith spent the majority of his time and resources defining himself as a moderate, common-sense candidate, who would seek to make government work more efficiently. In an early indication that his message was resonating with voters, Smith bested Tate by 1 percentage point in the September primary, which in Washington includes candidates of all parties on the same ballot.

Tate, who frequently denounced the AFL-CIO media campaign but had largely ignored Smith to that point, shifted his re-election campaign into high gear in an attempt to turn around public opinion. But it was too little, too late. Smith won in November by 50 percent to 47 percent.

WASHINGTON 9
Puget Sound — Tacoma; parts of King, Pierce and Thurston counties

Population growth during the 1980s earned Washington a ninth House seat in reapportionment, and the state's redistricting commission drew the new 9th in the suburbs and exurbs east and south of Seattle, where growth had been robust.

The 9th strings together an array of communities without much sense of commonality, starting at the south end of Seattle, going down past Tacoma and then heading west to Olympia, the state capital. The district's "Main Street" is a 60-mile stretch of Interstate 5, where the commuter and commercial traffic sometimes keeps the road jammed nearly all day.

Most of the residents of the 9th rely on their cars to get to work — in office towers in Seattle and Bellevue, in factories and workshops of Boeing or at the shipyards and docks of Tacoma (where mammoth cargoes of logs are loaded for shipment).

Other sources of income and jobs in the 9th include the office and industrial complexes around Sea-Tac International Airport, the Army's Fort Lewis (16,000 active-duty personnel) in Pierce County, and McChord Air Force Base. The military presence that has long shaped the Puget Sound region is inescapable in the 9th. Veterans, active military personnel and their families constitute about one-fifth of the district population.

Some residents of the 9th make their living off the land. At the southern reaches of the district, along the Thurston County border, forests and farms predominate. About half the 9th's vote is cast in the district's northeastern end, a slice of King County that includes the headquarters of the timber giant Weyerhaeuser Co., in Federal Way. The district's largest city (68,000 people), Federal Way recently incorporated to get a handle on its growth.

But if King contributes the majority of votes in the 9th, most of the district's land lies in Pierce and Thurston counties. Here, many residents live in scattered subdivisions and unincorporated areas where open space is plentiful and farm animals are not uncommon. Some of these communities surround older, established towns such as Puyallup (home of the Western Washington State Fairgrounds), while for others, "downtown" consists of commercial strip developments and suburban malls.

The political character of the 9th is just beginning to emerge. While Washington does not register voters by party, a 1992 poll found Democrats and Republicans within 1 percentage point of each other in the 9th (with a 41 percent plurality calling themselves independents).

In 1988, George Bush won the district by 750 votes out of more than 142,000 cast. But four years later, Bill Clinton led by 11 percentage points here, with Bush finishing just 5 points ahead of Ross Perot. And in 1996, Clinton scored double-digit margins in the 9th's portions of King, Pierce and Thurston en route to a 15 point drubbing of Bob Dole.

In the House race, Smith led in King and Pierce to overcome a narrow loss in Thurston, shifting the seat to Democrats.

1990 Population: 540,744. White 462,288 (85%), Black 29,450 (5%), Other 49,006 (9%). Hispanic origin 19,816 (4%). 18 and over 397,317 (73%), 62 and over 60,893 (11%). Median age: 31.

HOUSE ELECTIONS

1996 General		
Adam Smith (D)	105,236	(50%)
Randy Tate (R)	99,199	(47%)
David Gruenstein (NL)	5,432	(3%)
1996 Primary †		
Adam Smith (D)	56,668	(49%)
Randy Tate (R)	55,462	(48%)
David Gruenstein (NL)	3,450	(3%)

† In Washington's "jungle primary," candidates of all parties are listed on one ballot.

CAMPAIGN FINANCE

	Receipts	Receipts from PACs	Expend-itures
1996			
Smith (D)	$725,727	$331,831 (46%)	$711,722
Tate (R)	$1,575,545	$645,900 (41%)	$1,578,748

DISTRICT VOTE FOR PRESIDENT

	1996		1992
D	110,864 (51%)	D	93,963 (42%)
R	77,634 (36%)	R	69,592 (31%)
I	20,807 (10%)	I	58,039 (26%)

KEY VOTES

1997

Ban "partial birth" abortions N

WEST VIRGINIA

Governor: Cecil H. Underwood (R)
Elected: 1996*
Length of term: 4 years
Term expires: 1/01
Salary: $72,000
Term limit: 2 consecutive terms
Phone: (304) 558-2000
Born: Nov. 5, 1922; W.Va.
Education: Salem College, B.A.; U. of West Virginia, M.A.
Occupation: Industrial park executive; adjunct professor; coal company executive.
Family: Wife, Hovah; three children.
Religion: Methodist.
Political Career: W.Va. House, 1945-55 (minority leader, 1947-55); * governor 1957-61.

No lieutenant governor

Senate President: Earl Ray Tomblin (D)
Salary: $15,000
Phone: (304) 357-7801

State election official: (304) 558-6000
Democratic headquarters: (304) 342-8121
Republican headquarters: (304) 344-3446

REDISTRICTING

West Virginia lost one House seat in reapportionment, dropping from four districts to three. The Legislature passed the map Oct. 11, 1991; the governor signed it Oct. 12. Federal court upheld the map Jan. 7, 1992.

STATE LEGISLATURE

Legislature. Meets January-March yearly, except during gubernatorial election years, when it meets February-April.

Senate: 34 members, 4-year terms
1996 breakdown: 25D, 9R; 29 men, 5 women
Salary: $6,500
Phone: (304) 357-7800

House of Delegates: 100 members, 2-year terms
1996 breakdown: 74D, 26R, 84 men, 16 women
Salary: $6,500
Phone: (304) 340-3200

URBAN STATISTICS

City	Population
Charleston	57,287
Mayor G. Kemp Melton, D	
Huntington	54,844
Mayor Jean Kipp Dean, R	
Wheeling	34,882
Mayor John W. Lipphardt, N-P	
Parkersburg	33,862
Mayor Eugene Knotts, D	
Morgantown	25,879
Mayor Charlene Marshall, N-P	

U.S. CONGRESS

Senate: 2 D, 0 R
House: 3 D, 0 R

TERM LIMITS

For state offices: No

ELECTIONS

1996 Presidential Vote

Bill Clinton	52%
Bob Dole	37%
Ross Perot	11%

1992 Presidential Vote

Bill Clinton	48%
George Bush	35%
Ross Perot	16%

1988 Presidential Vote

Michael S. Dukakis	52%
George Bush	47%

POPULATION

1990 population		1,793,477
1980 population		1,949,644
Percent change		-8%
Rank among states:		34
White		96%
Black		3%
Hispanic		<1%
Asian or Pacific islander		<1%
Urban		36%
Rural		64%
Born in state		99%
Foreign-born		1%
Under age 18	443,577	25%
Ages 18-64	1,081,003	60%
65 and older	268,897	15%
Median age		35.4

MISCELLANEOUS

Capital: Charleston
Number of counties: 55
Per capita income: $14,174 (1991)
Rank among states: 49
Total area: 24,232 sq. miles
Rank among states: 41

WEST VIRGINIA

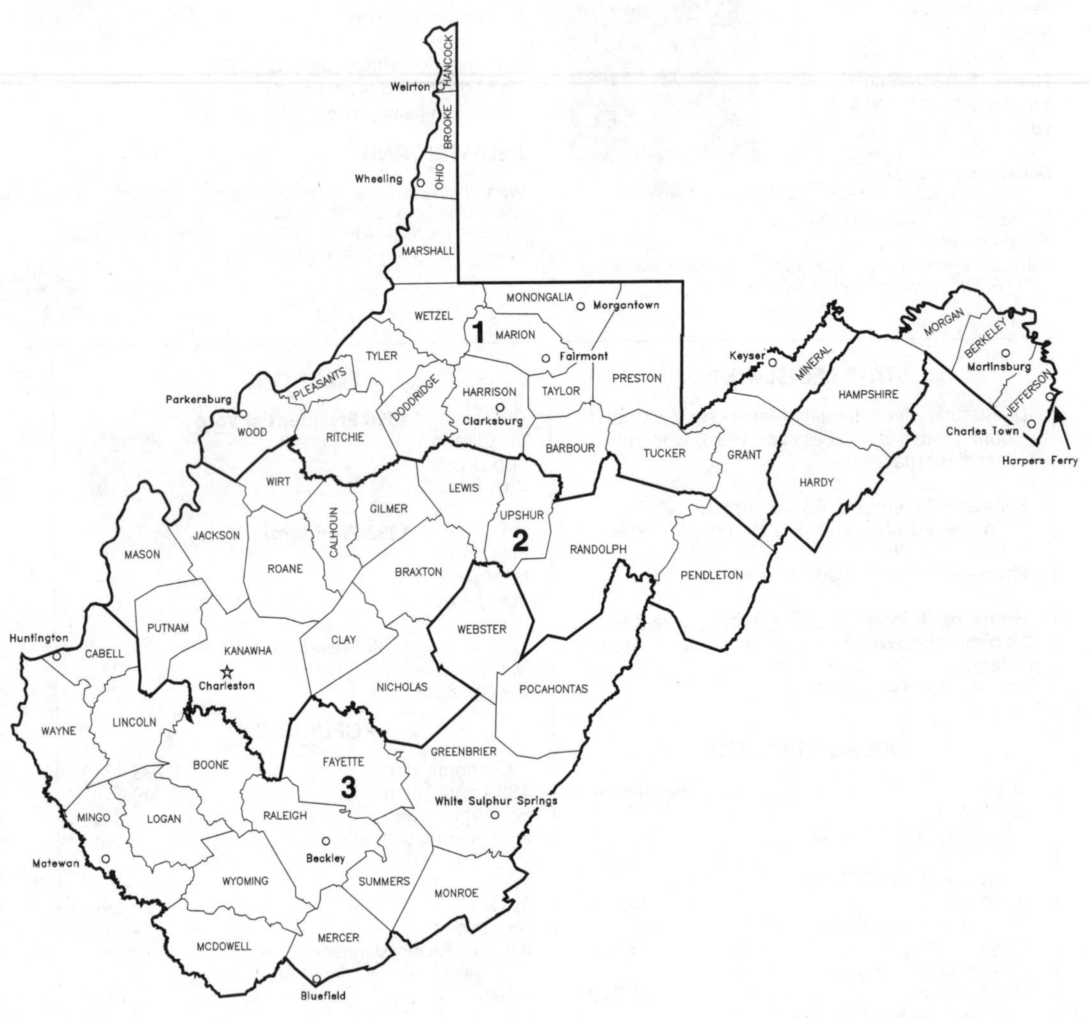

Robert C. Byrd (D)

Of Sophia — Elected 1958, 7th term

Biographical Information
Born: Nov. 20, 1917, North Wilkesboro, N.C.
Education: American U., J.D. 1963; Marshall U., B.A. 1994.
Occupation: Lawyer.
Family: Wife, Erma Ora James; two children.
Religion: Baptist.
Political Career: W.Va. House, 1947-51; W.Va. Senate, 1951-53; U.S. House, 1953-59.
Capitol Office: 311 Hart Bldg. 20510; 224-3954.

Committees
Appropriations (ranking)
Agriculture, Rural Development & Related Agencies; Defense; Energy & Water Development; Interior (ranking); Transportation
Armed Services
Airland Forces; Seapower; Strategic Forces
Rules & Administration

In Washington: Years have passed since Byrd was arguably the Senate's most powerful member. But even as a member of the minority, and with no leadership post, he remains a force to be reckoned with — as the events of early 1997 demonstrated. In March, Byrd once again led the floor fight against Senate passage of the balanced budget amendment to the Constitution, which once again failed by a single vote. And in April, Byrd was able to celebrate a federal court decision favoring his own longstanding opposition to a presidential line-item veto.

In his 80th year, and his 50th in public service, Byrd sometimes seems frail on the Senate floor, speaking softly as his hands tremble. Yet he remains the chamber's leading traditionalist and institutional defender, as well as its acknowledged expert on rules and procedure. And he never hesitates to use his knowledge to block or at least to slow the progress of legislation he opposes.

Early in the 104th, Byrd gave Senate newcomers a taste of the procedural deftness and florid rhetoric that are his trademarks, as he delayed action on legislation designed to prevent Congress from passing laws that impose new costs on state governments without providing money to pay for them. The "unfunded mandates" measure enjoyed broad support among Republicans and Democrats. But Byrd, who opposed it, refused to let it through until he could rally Democrats for a show of minority-party muscle.

The proceedings were also something of a lesson in spine-stiffening aimed at Senate Minority Leader Tom Daschle of South Dakota. "I hope every member of the minority will show some guts and stand up for the people's right to know," Byrd declared, as he called on Democrats to refuse to limit debate on the measure. Daschle, who had hesitated to whip Democrats into line to oppose cloture, then issued a call for unity on the vote.

Byrd, one of only 10 Democrats to vote against the bill, said support for unfunded mandates comes from the highest authority: "When the Lord told Israel that on the seventh day thou shalt not do any work, he was imposing an unfunded mandate on the 12 tribes," Byrd said. "The tribes may have perceived a short-term loss in productivity, and that may have been only partly made up for by God's provision of manna and quails, but surely the benefits of keeping the Sabbath outweigh the mere economic costs of doing so."

It was a comment typical of Byrd's legendary ability to weave analogies from the Bible and ancient history into debates over contemporary issues. And it was a fight that reminded all concerned how sharply partisan the Senate's senior Democrat remained. That fact was again on view in 1997, when Byrd's voice was raised to warn the Republicans running the Rules Committee against their plan to investigate allegations of voter fraud in the 1996 election of Sen. Mary L. Landrieu, D-La. Byrd seemed deeply pained at the sight of such indignities being inflicted on a duly sworn member of the Senate.

Ideas that would reduce the power or prerogatives of the Senate are anathema to Byrd. That list has included the unfunded mandates legislation, the line-item veto (or enhanced rescissions power) for the president, and the perennial proposals to amend the Constitution to require a balanced budget and to limit the terms of members of Congress.

Byrd worked tirelessly to defeat the line-item veto in the Senate in 1994, averting what had seemed like certain passage of the popular measure. When it finally became one of the few major items in the House GOP's "Contract With America" to become law, Byrd wrested the partial veto from Clinton's hands in early 1997 by challenging the law in federal court. One district judge agreed with Byrd and five other congressmen that the new law was unconstitutional, and the case is likely to go before the U.S. Supreme Court.

Similarly, Byrd seemed poised to throw down as many roadblocks as possible in front of the balanced-budget amendment, something he has described as "a catastrophe waiting to happen."

In long declamations mixing reverence for the Constitution and dark predictions of woe, Byrd denounced the amendment as an assault on the powers of the Senate and a betrayal of the ideals of the Revolution. "The hurricanes may blow, the tides may rise, but there still remain those of us who will never bend, because we believe it is our sworn duty not to yield," he said.

He was particularly infuriated when Majority Leader Bob Dole of Kansas decided to delay the vote on the amendment while searching for the one vote needed for passage. Byrd said the delay "has every appearance of a sleazy, tawdry effort . . . so that additional pressures may be made on some poor member." But the one necessary vote never materialized and the balanced-budget amendment failed in March 1995.

Republicans fell one vote short again on the balanced-budget amendment in March 1997, after Byrd and Daschle patiently convinced Sen. Robert G. Torricelli, D-N.J., to reverse a campaign pledge and vote against the amendment. But Byrd, long the Senate's most passionate opponent of the amendment, acknowledged that it is getting more difficult to win, and the GOP will almost surely try again in 1999. "During the campaign [they] commit themselves to something they haven't had an opportunity to study," he said. "Then, when they come in here, they have their feet set in concrete."

But Byrd himself has been known to change a position. For example, in May 1997, he switched to support a ban on a particular abortion technique that opponents call "partial birth" abortion.

He was also the lone holdout against another contract bill requiring Congress to abide by the same labor and anti-discrimination laws as the private sector. Byrd argued that the bill, the first in the GOP contract to become law, might let the other branches interfere with Congress.

Although he is surrounded by budget cutters on both sides of the aisle, Byrd remains an unabashed believer in the power of funneling federal dollars to his home state. The Senate's 1996 highway spending bill included a mere $39.5 million for "pork" — special road and bridge projects, down from $352 million in 1995. Byrd claimed the largest single piece of that, $9 million for a project near Huntington. Still, it was only a paltry sum for Byrd, who collected $110 million for one project alone in 1995.

When the 105th Congress takes up reauthorization of the massive Intermodal Surface Transportation Efficiency Act, Byrd is almost sure to get his usual share.

When Byrd returned to chair Appropriations in 1989, after stepping down as majority leader, he said his goal was to bring $1 billion in federal funds to his state in five years; he did it in less than two. The fiscal 1992 appropriations bills, for example, contained about a half-billion dollars in projects and earmarked funds for his home state.

Byrd is known for his seemingly limitless vocabulary. What other member could conceivably have described detractors of pork barrel spending as "ultracrepidarian critics," as he did in 1993? (Ultracrepidarian: going beyond one's sphere; presumptuous.) "I have a reverence for this institution," he said. "I have a reverence for the legislative branch under the Constitution. I have a reverence for the separation of powers and checks and balances of the Constitution. I have a reverence for American history. I have a reverence for the history of England. I have a reverence for the history of the Romans. I have a reverence for history."

" 'Whatsoever thy hand findeth to do, do it with thy might,'" he said in 1989, quoting Ecclesiastes. "I have that sense of duty. I follow it meticulously." Byrd's didactic fascination with the Bible and ancient past suggests that he wants to leave as enduring a mark on the mores of his beloved Senate as he is leaving on the hills of West Virginia. But the changing times that ushered him out as Democratic leader in 1989, then ushered his party out of power in 1994, may make that task increasingly difficult. With his quirky ways and focus on carrying home federal largess, Byrd seems to many newcomers to Washington the symbol of a bygone era.

An intensely private man, Byrd was often criticized during his tenure as Democratic leader from 1977 to 1989 for being too stilted and old-fashioned to represent his party in the television age. His strong drive for self-improvement propelled him from the coal patch to the top levels of U.S. politics, and it motivates him to study the words of history's great men. But when he muses on the Senate floor about the thoughts of Shakespeare and Socrates, Byrd can come across as oddly formal and rhetorically overblown.

Recalling "giants of the Senate" from years long past, Byrd suggested that politicians of such stature no longer dominate the Senate. "Little did I know when I came here that I would live to see pygmies stride like Colossus while marveling, like Aesop's fly, sitting on the axle of a chariot, 'My, what a dust I do raise,'" he said in 1995.

He cited the dignity of the Senate when, in November 1993, he called on Republican Bob Packwood to resign from the Senate because of charges of sexual harassment. "None of us is pure or without flaws," Byrd declared, "but when those flaws damage the institution of the Senate, it is time to go." Packwood's resignation did not come until 1995, but it seemed inevitable after Byrd's rebuke.

During his long congressional career, Byrd has moved from his party's right toward its left. When he arrived in the Senate in 1959, he was parochial and conservative. He filibustered the 1964 Civil Rights Act, at one point holding the floor with a 14-hour speech that is among the longest on Senate record — something he now says he deeply regrets. One of the most stalwart defenders of President Lyndon B. Johnson's policies in Vietnam, Byrd has since become a consistent voice for restraint when it comes to the use of military force abroad.

Byrd's ascent to the top ranks of the Senate began in 1967, when he gained a toehold on the Senate leadership ladder as secretary of the Democratic Caucus. Four years later he ousted Edward M. Kennedy from the No. 2 leadership job, majority whip. And when Majority Leader Mike Mansfield of Montana retired six years later, Byrd stepped into the job.

In the 100th, Byrd enjoyed what may have been his most successful term as Senate leader. Byrd rallied Democrats behind an ambitious agenda and helped make the 100th Congress one of the most productive in more than 20 years. When it was over, he gave up the leader's job to be president pro tempore and Appropriations chairman.

At Home: Since Byrd was elected to the Senate in 1958, he has held the seat with ease — a tribute both to the respect he has engendered at home and the long-running weakness of the state's Republican Party.

In 1994, Byrd won with 69 percent of the vote. In six re-elections, Byrd's lowest vote share has been 65 percent. The low came in 1988, against freshman GOP state Sen. M. Jay Wolfe, who enlisted religious broadcaster Pat Robertson to visit West Virginia in his behalf. But he was outspent nearly 10-to-1, and he could not deny that, as Appropriations chairman, Byrd could steer federal money West Virginia's way.

The senator was born Cornelius Calvin Sale Jr. When he was 1, his mother died and his father gave him to an aunt and uncle, Vlurma and Titus Byrd; they raised him in the hardscrabble coal country of southern West Virginia. Byrd graduated first in his high school class, but it took him 12 years before he could afford to start college. He worked as a gas station attendant, grocery store clerk, shipyard welder and butcher before his talents as a fiddle player helped win him a seat in the state Legislature in 1946. Friends drove Byrd around the hills and hollows, where he brought the voters out by playing "Cripple Creek" and "Rye Whiskey." From then on, he never lost an election.

As he himself once put it, "There are four things people believe in in West Virginia: God Almighty; Sears, Roebuck; Carters Little Liver Pills; and Robert C. Byrd."

When Democrat Erland Hedrick retired from the old 6th District in 1952, Byrd was an obvious contender. But he had to surmount his past membership in the Ku Klux Klan. He had joined the Klan at age 24 and as late as 1946 wrote a letter to the imperial grand wizard urging a Klan rebirth "in every state of the Union."

When this came up publicly in 1952, his opponents and Democratic Gov. Okey L. Patteson called on him to drop out. He refused, explaining his Klan membership as a youthful indiscretion committed because of his alarm over communism. He won that election, and after three House terms, he ran for the Senate in 1958 with AFL-CIO and United Mine Workers support.

He crushed his primary opposition and unseated Republican Chapman Revercomb, who had been in and out of the Senate in the 1940s and won a two-year term in a 1956 comeback. Revercomb was a weak incumbent, and the 1958 recession hurt the state badly, driving many voters closer to their New Deal Democratic roots.

SENATE ELECTIONS

1994 General		
Robert C. Byrd (D)	290,495	(69%)
Stan Klos (R)	130,441	(31%)
1994 Primary		
Robert C. Byrd (D)	190,061	(85%)
John M. Fuller (D)	20,057	(9%)
Paul Nuchims (D)	12,381	(6%)

Previous Winning Percentages: **1988** (65%) **1982** (69%) **1976** (100%) **1970** (78%) **1964** (68%) **1958** (59%) **1956*** (57%) **1954*** (63%) **1952*** (56%)

** House elections*

KEY VOTES

1997	
Approve balanced-budget constitutional amendment	N
Approve chemical weapons treaty	Y
1996	
Approve farm bill	N
Limit punitive damages in product liability cases	N
Exempt small businesses from higher minimum wage	N
Approve welfare overhaul	Y
Bar job discrimination based on sexual orientation	N
Override veto of ban on "partial birth" abortions	N
1995	
Approve GOP budget with tax and spending cuts	N
Approve constitutional amendment barring flag desecration	Y

CAMPAIGN FINANCE

	Receipts	Receipts from PACs		Expend-itures
1994				
Byrd (D)	$1,274,338	$416,450	(33%)	$1,550,354
Klos (R)	$271,006	$11,900	(4%)	$267,165

VOTING STUDIES

	Presidential Support		Party Unity		Conservative Coalition	
Year	S	O	S	O	S	O
1996	81	19	82	18	32	68
1995	82	18	82	18	37	63
1994	74	26	73	27	69	31
1993	80	20	87	13	51	49
1992	27	73	74	25	61	39
1991	49	51	76	24	68	33

INTEREST GROUP RATINGS

Year	ADA	AFL-CIO	CCUS	ACU
1996	70	n/a	23	15
1995	85	92	26	26
1994	75	75	30	40
1993	55	100	18	24
1992	100	92	20	19
1991	65	83	10	33

John D. Rockefeller IV (D)

Of Charleston — Elected 1984, 3rd term

Biographical Information

Born: June 18, 1937, New York, N.Y.

Education: International Christian U. (Tokyo, Japan), 1957-60; Harvard U., A.B. 1961.

Occupation: Public official.

Family: Wife, Sharon Percy; four children.

Religion: Presbyterian.

Political Career: W.Va. House, 1967-69; W.Va. secretary of state, 1969-73; Democratic nominee for governor, 1972; governor, 1977-85.

Capitol Office: 531 Hart Bldg. 20510; 224-6472.

Committees

Commerce, Science & Transportation
Aviation; Communications; Manufacturing & Competitiveness; Science, Technology & Space (ranking)

Finance
Health Care (ranking); International Trade; Social Security & Family Policy

Veterans' Affairs

In Washington: Just re-elected to a third term, Rockefeller has adopted two seemingly contradictory political personas during his 12-year Senate tenure: consummate compromiser and party loyalist. He played both roles in the 104th Congress.

Rockefeller's top priority at the start of 1995 was one that had been a pet issue for years: product liability. It also ranked high on the agenda of the new GOP majority. House Republicans had made overhaul of the nation's product liability laws a promise in their "Contract With America" campaign platform.

So with Republicans putting their shoulder to the issue, Rockefeller had cause to hope for a conclusion to a debate that had been on the congressional agenda since 1981. He joined forces with Sen. Slade Gorton, R-Wash., and became a broker between the White House and Congress.

But if the product liability issue brought out Rockefeller's instincts to compromise, his partisan fires were stoked by other elements of the GOP agenda. He accused Republicans of "pure, classic meanness" after they rejected welfare language designed to extend benefits for children beyond the limit on aid to their parents. And when the debate shifted to balancing the budget, Rockefeller routinely berated Republicans for their positions on health care entitlements. "The Republican budget is designed to raid, not save, the Medicare program," he said on the Senate floor in July 1995. "Medicare's money is going to be used to finance tax cuts for the wealthy. It is that simple."

Rockefeller's dual reputation for loyalty and pragmatism — not to mention his recognition as heir to America's most legendary fortune and a scion of one of its best-known political families — has made him the subject of presidential speculation. Talk of his White House aspirations dates as far back as 1968, when he was nominated to be West Virginia's secretary of state. It was revived during his two terms as governor and became serious in 1990, after he had established himself as a presence in the Senate.

Rockefeller tested the waters by forming an exploratory committee for the 1992 campaign but ultimately declined to seek that nomination, choosing to wait until he was better prepared. That mirrored his career in the Senate, where he spent most of his first term tending the back benches, studying the issues and minding the chamber's folkways.

Indeed, "Jay" Rockefeller is an old hand at winning over those who think a man born into wealth and power must be spoiled and aloof. More than thirty years ago, he impressed the people of Emmons, W.Va., as a sincere, idealistic VISTA volunteer. In his first years in the Senate, he was often found writing in the chamber, his 6-foot-6-inch frame folded into one of the spartan desks. His behavior is the perfect antidote to the expectation of arrogance.

The 103rd Congress should have been his coronation as a true Senate power. Not only did he chair a key Finance health subcommittee, he also became chairman of the Veterans' Affairs Committee. As chairman of the panel, Rockefeller managed to clear a number of bills, including one authorizing the Department of Veterans Affairs to pay benefits to veterans disabled by so-called Persian Gulf syndrome.

That issue remained a hot topic early in the 105th Congress, with Rockefeller and Senate Veterans' Affairs Committee Chairman Arlen Specter, R-Pa., calling for more time for affected veterans to file disability claims for undiagnosed illnesses.

But in the 103rd, Rockefeller gambled everything on health care, particularly the concept that every American should be guaranteed coverage — and he lost big. "Maybe it was too much to expect that in two years you could have changed so much of the health care system," he said after the effort was officially laid to rest in September 1994. "But we didn't know that when we started, and there wasn't any reason for us to know that."

The gamble on health care cost Rockefeller and the Democratic Party as a whole. Republicans helped generate a negative public response to President Clinton's health care plan, and that played a part in the GOP toppling congressional Democrats from power in 1994. Rockefeller found himself in the minority in the 104th Congress.

Although many Democrats struggled to regain their political footing after that historic defeat, Rockefeller was quick to thrust himself into the center of the action again, making product liability his focus. True to his reputation for diligently seeking the middle ground, he cosponsored a proposal that excluded the most controversial ideas, including medical malpractice language and a "loser pays" provision that would have exposed civil litigants to the potential burden of paying the other sides attorneys' fees.

Mindful of previous floor battles that sunk product liability bills, Rockefeller resisted efforts to amend the measure and questioned then-Senate Majority Leader Bob Dole's decision to broaden the scope. Rockefeller was vindicated when the Senate considered Dole's version. His contention that only a narrow bill could muster the votes necessary to invoke cloture and prevent a filibuster proved accurate, and Dole, after losing three cloture votes, agreed to push a revised Gorton-Rockefeller bill. The Senate passed it on a 61-39 vote.

The legislation languished in conference, however, and became mired in presidential politics by the time House and Senate negotiators reached agreement. Rockefeller openly courted the White House on the issue and predicted that the president would sign the product liability measure. But Clinton eventually vetoed it.

The veto frustrated Rockefeller, and he expressed his disappointment publicly. Still, the experience did not sour his relationship with Clinton. He defended the president and his staff when the White House came under fire in 1996 for gathering confidential FBI background files on hundreds of Republicans, accusing the GOP of engaging in "cutthroat" politics. "The meanest politics I have heard in 12 years I have been up here, frankly, have come from the other side," he said when the issue spilled onto the Senate floor.

Also during the 104th, Rockefeller played an active role in the debate over changes to the Medicare and Medicaid programs. From his seat on the Finance Committee, he offered amendments designed to soften the impact of GOP proposals to restrain the growth of spending on the programs. When Republicans proved not to be in a compromising mood, Rockefeller responded with sharp, partisan rhetoric. "This savaging of the Medicaid program is the single most callous proposal before this committee," he said.

Rockefeller generally was expected to address international issues, his one-time academic specialty, in the Senate, but initially he focused on West Virginia concerns — the cost of shipping coal by rail, the job prospects of miners, steelmakers and other workers in Rust Belt industries. Although parochial interests no longer monopolize his agenda, Rockefeller has not forgotten home-state voters since his ascension onto the national scene with the health care and product liability issues.

He scored a victory in the 104th Congress by attaching language to the new telecommunications law requiring that schools, libraries and hospitals in rural areas receive preferential rates for their telecommunications services. The language was a point of contention early in negotiations on the bill, but Rockefeller and Olympia J. Snowe, R-Maine, mustered the support to keep it in the final version.

Rockefeller also inserted language into a trade technical corrections law that corrects "inverted tariff" situations in which the duty on a finished product is lower than the duty on the materials used to manufacture it. Such situations have the effect of reducing jobs at U.S. plants that finish goods. Rockefeller secured protection for: 500 jobs at a Philips Lighting plant in Fairmont, W.Va.; Corning Inc., which has operations in West Virginia; and aircraft manufacturers such as Pratt & Whitney, which has a plant near Clarksburg.

At Home: Rockefeller's decision in 1996 to endorse controversial gubernatorial candidate Charlotte Pritt raised some eyebrows in state Democratic circles. Pritt, a party maverick, in 1992 had challenged the sitting Democratic governor, Gaston Caperton. Caperton and other leading Democrats refused to back Pritt in her 1996 campaign against former GOP Gov. Cecil Underwood.

But Rockefeller campaigned for her in the waning days of her race against Underwood (whom Rockefeller had defeated in the 1976 governor's contest). Pritt lost, but there were no repercussions for Rockefeller at the polls. He won re-election to a third term with 77 percent of the vote over a neophyte challenger, Betty A. Burks.

Given his background, Rockefeller seems an odd leader for one of the poorest states. But in a state where money often talks and Democrats nearly always win, he has been a successful politician. He is well-known — newspapers need only refer to him as Jay in the headlines — though his wealth and celebrity engender no small amount of resentment in a state beset with one of the nation's lowest per capita personal income. Past polls have shown him with negative ratings as high as 40 percent. But Rockefeller has won many friends by patiently working his way up the political ladder, serving in low-visibility offices before twice winning the governorship and capturing the Senate seat of retiring Democrat Jennings Randolph in 1984.

Rockefeller moved to West Virginia in 1964 as a VISTA volunteer in the Action for Appalachia Youth program, then decided to stay and enter politics, starting near the bottom; he ran for a seat in the state House in 1966. After winning that, he captured the office of secretary of state in 1968.

His political ascent was interrupted in 1972 when he lost the governor's race to Republican Arch A. Moore Jr. Rockefeller was hurt by carpetbagger charges and an environmental platform that opposed strip mining. After the election, he recanted some of his environmental positions and strengthened his ties to the state by serving as president of West Virginia Wesleyan College. Running for governor again in 1976, he trounced former Gov. Underwood (1957-61). (Moore was ineligible to seek re-election.) Rockefeller left nothing to chance in 1980, winning re-election after a campaign that bombarded households with direct-mail appeals and TV ads, even on Pittsburgh and Washington, D.C., stations.

When it was reported he was spending almost $12 million against Moore, who was seeking a comeback, bumper stickers appeared with the slogan, "Make Him Spend It All, Arch." But Moore was unable either to drive Rockefeller broke or out of office. Rockefeller won by nine points.

Rockefeller's second term was stymied by the state's economic woes. Heavily dependent on the battered coal industry, West Virginia was staggered by unemployment and sinking revenues. He was the target of criticism when taxes were raised, salaries frozen and state spending cut.

With West Virginia's governors restricted to two consecutive terms, it was long apparent that Rockefeller would run for the Senate in 1984. Democratic Sen. Jennings Randolph announced his retirement plans in early 1983. About a year later, Moore, his strongest potential GOP rival, decided to pass this time, and joined the governor's race.

But Rockefeller was not home free. He was near the nadir of his popularity when he entered the Senate race. Republicans nominated a wealthy, young political neophyte, John Raese, who promised to match Rockefeller's spending dollar for dollar. But with Rockefeller mounting another $12 million campaign, that was a pipe dream. Raese's campaign was further stalled by a series of gaffes.

But Rockefeller made Raese the target of his late media barrage — a tactic widely considered to be a mistake — and the attacks gave Raese publicity he could not afford himself. Aided by Reagan's surge atop the ticket, Raese pulled nearly even with Rockefeller in polls. But Rockefeller survived, with large majorities in the industrial northern Panhandle and in the southern coal fields.

In his 1990 re-election, Rockefeller spent more than $300,000 in a primary against two challengers who spent less than $1,000 between them, and he refused to agree to a $2 million spending limit for the general election. Burned by past charges of attempting to buy public office with his personal fortune, Rockefeller shied away from using his own funds, and instead amassed a campaign treasury from PACs.

Republicans nominated John Yoder, a lawyer from Harpers Ferry. Yoder threw Rockefeller off balance briefly by charging that he was "bought" by special interests. But a lack of funds crippled Yoder's campaign. The Rockefeller effort kicked into full gear just as Yoder was being deserted by his national party; Rockefeller won all but three counties.

SENATE ELECTIONS

1996 General		
John D. Rockefeller IV (D)	456,526	(77%)
Betty A. Burks (R)	139,088	(23%)
1996 Primary		
Jay Rockefeller (D)	280,303	(88%)
Bruce Barilla (D)	36,637	(12%)

Previous Winning Percentages: **1990** (68%) **1984** (52%)

CAMPAIGN FINANCE

	Receipts	Receipts from PACs	Expend-itures
1996			
Rockefeller (D)	$3,004,275	$987,319 (33%)	$2,538,473

KEY VOTES

1997	
Approve balanced-budget constitutional amendment	N
Approve chemical weapons treaty	Y
1996	
Approve farm bill	N
Limit punitive damages in product liability cases	Y
Exempt small businesses from higher minimum wage	N
Approve welfare overhaul	Y
Bar job discrimination based on sexual orientation	Y
Override veto of ban on "partial birth" abortions	N
1995	
Approve GOP budget with tax and spending cuts	N
Approve constitutional amendment barring flag desecration	Y

VOTING STUDIES

	Presidential Support		Party Unity		Conservative Coalition	
Year	**S**	**O**	**S**	**O**	**S**	**O**
1996	90	7	90	6	29	68
1995	85	12	86	12	32	65
1994	92	3	86	9	34	66
1993	91	4	91	6	37	54
1992	28	72	88	10	26	68
1991	36	64	91	8	28	73

INTEREST GROUP RATINGS

Year	ADA	AFL-CIO	CCUS	ACU
1996	85	n/a	46	16
1995	90	100	42	9
1994	95	75	22	0
1993	70	91	18	12
1992	100	91	20	7
1991	90	75	10	5

1 Alan B. Mollohan (D)

Of Fairmont — Elected 1982, 8th term

Biographical Information

Born: May 14, 1943, Fairmont, W.Va.

Education: College of William and Mary, A.B. 1966; West Virginia U., J.D. 1970.

Military Service: Army Reserve, 1970-83.

Occupation: Lawyer.

Family: Wife, Barbara Whiting; five children.

Religion: Baptist.

Political Career: No previous office.

Capitol Office: 2346 Rayburn Bldg. 20515; 225-4172.

Committees

Appropriations

Commerce, Justice, State & Judiciary (ranking); VA, HUD & Independent Agencies

Budget

In Washington: Mollohan briefly enjoyed membership in the Appropriations Committee's "college of cardinals," but he lost that status when Republicans took over the House in the 1994 election. In the spring of that year, Mollohan had assumed the chair of the Commerce, Justice, State Subcommittee; in the GOP-controlled 104th and again in the 105th, he is the panel's ranking member. In this role, he has fought conservative Republicans' efforts to eliminate the Commerce Department and to redirect funding for Clinton administration crime prevention programs.

It is not unusual for Mollohan to find some common ground with the subcommittee's Republican chairman, Harold Rogers of Kentucky. Like Mollohan, Rogers comes from an economically struggling Appalachian district and feels that the federal government can play a positive role in economic development — an outlook not shared by many younger Republicans from more affluent constituencies. Once in the 104th when the House was considering his subcommittee's funding bill, Mollohan praised Rogers, saying, "He has handled this bill with great skill, beginning with very exhaustive hearings which explored the detail of the agency budgets under our jurisdiction. Hal did not waste time chasing simplistic solutions. Instead, he pursued the course of a responsible legislator, following a sound, measured approach in writing this bill."

However, Mollohan was not happy with some of the legislative initiatives that the GOP leadership folded into the Commerce, Justice, State funding bill in 1995. He complained that in the 78-page fiscal 1996 legislation, there were 31 pages of policy initiatives, including significant changes to the Legal Services Corporation, the Truth in Sentencing grants program and prison litigation procedures.

The GOP's 1995 version of the Commerce, Justice, State spending bill de-emphasized technology development programs at Commerce and international programs at State in order to pay for programs to fight crime, including illegal immigration. The Clinton administration was willing to increase crime-fighting funds, but the White House disagreed with congressional Republicans on how to spend the money.

Republicans sought to replace police-hiring and crime prevention programs included in the 1994 crime law with a flexible anti-crime block grant program for states and localities. Mollohan offered an amendment in July 1995 to remove the block grant money and restore funding for the police and crime prevention programs. He told the House it was "irresponsible" to stop funding the administration's COPS program, which was designed to put more police on community streets. "We have over 20,000 new police officers, in virtually every congressional district in this country, to whom the federal government has committed multi-year funding," Mollohan said. "The problem is that there is not one red cent in this bill for the COPS program. Instead, it funds a block grant program which is not even authorized." But the House rejected Mollohan's attempt to save the community policing program, 184-232.

He also complained that Republicans were eviscerating the Commerce Department just as the Clinton administration had made it an effective promoter of economic development. "What some may call corporate welfare merely puts U.S. industry on a level playing field" with foreign competitors, he said.

When the House took up the next Commerce, Justice, State funding bill in 1996, Mollohan successfully lobbied for the Legal Services Corporation, which provides legal aid to the poor. Conservatives contend that Legal Services lawyers spend more time filing class-action lawsuits and defending the likes of drug dealers and murderers than they do representing the needs of the poor, and Republican appropriators recommended cutting Legal Services by more than 50 percent, to $141 million. Mollohan called that reduction "most shameful" and said it would strike at the core of the principle of equal justice.

Mollohan and Pennsylvania Republican Jon D. Fox offered an amendment to boost Legal Services funding from the slated $141 million to $250 million. A contingent of 56 Republicans defied the GOP

Northern West Virginia was crushed by economic depression during the 1980s, thanks to its dependence on coal and heavy industries such as steel, chemicals and glass. Factories closed or slashed payrolls; coal mines mechanized and got by with thousands fewer workers. The 1st contains six of West Virginia's 10 largest cities. All lost population during the 1980s; Wheeling fell 19 percent to less than 35,000.

However, a nascent technology sector brightens economic prospects for the 1st. Morgantown, which has a population of nearly 26,000, is the site of West Virginia University and the hub of the area's high-tech growth. Located amid the coal fields of Monongalia County (one of the state's leading coal-producing counties), Morgantown is home to Software Valley, an organization that promotes regional computer-oriented business and research activity.

Other areas are working to diversify. Clarksburg and Bridgeport (Harrison County) will benefit from Democratic Sen. Robert C. Byrd's biggest federal plum, a $185 million relocation of the FBI's fingerprinting center. Wheeling (Ohio County) also is making some progress with aid from Byrd's funding pipeline. A computer software industry is growing around Wheeling Jesuit College, site of the federal government's National Technology Transfer Center and the Classroom of the Future, both NASA programs.

Since the mid-1980s, Wheeling has benefited from tourists' interest in the "Festival of Lights," a fall-winter display of Christmas lights at Oglebay Park just outside the city. Wheeling itself has become known as the "City of Lights."

Though trimmed down, traditional industries still play an important economic role.

WEST VIRGINIA 1
North — Wheeling; Parkersburg; Morgantown

Weirton Steel Co. in Hancock and Brooke counties is one of the nation's largest employee-owned companies. Blue-collar voters have given a strong edge in the industrial and coal-mining areas to Mollohan and to Democratic presidential candidates. Bill Clinton won the district in 1996 with 49 percent of the vote, and in Marion County he did better than 2-to-1.

However, there are Republican pockets in the 1st that make it competitive in presidential contests. Bob Dole won six of the district's 19 counties in 1996, most of them in the far east and far west ends of the district.

Although Wheeling is known as an industrial town, it long has doubled as the commercial center for the Northern Panhandle. It has a sizable white-collar constituency that leans Republican.

Farther down the Ohio River is Parkersburg, which has nearly 34,000 residents. The region has a large chemical industry and is a regional trade center. Farmland adds to GOP strength in Wood County, where Dole took 47 percent and beat Clinton by about 2,000 votes.

In the Eastern Panhandle, coal mines again give way to farms. This is West Virginia's strongest Republican area, with a GOP tradition dating back to the Civil War. Dole won the eastern counties of Mineral, Preston and Grant.

1990 Population: 598,056. White 583,753 (98%), Black 9,662 (2%), Other 4,641 (1%). Hispanic origin 3,147 (1%). 18 and over 456,552 (76%), 62 and over 112,314 (19%). Median age: 36.

leadership and voted in July 1996 for the amendment, which won approval, 247-179.

Over the years, Mollohan and Democratic Senate Appropriations Committee veteran Robert C. Byrd, have worked diligently to direct money back to their home state. One of their projects has been to expand the Mid-Atlantic Aerospace Complex at Benedum Airport, outside Clarksburg in Harrison County. After helping persuade a local company to start an airplane refurbishing business, Mollohan worked to win Pentagon-related contracts for the firm. Mollohan also has secured funds to build and operate a research institute in his district that develops investigative strategies and provides training programs to teach law enforcement officials how to track down white-collar criminals.

Mollohan also sits on the Budget Committee, where he has criticized GOP budget proposals. When the Republican majority released its first budget in May 1995, Mollohan complained that 51 percent of the plan's proposed tax cut went to Americans making over $100,000. "Simply stated, this resolution proposes a major reallocation of resources among the people of America," Mollohan said. "If you are a middle- or lower-income American, you can lose big under this resolution. If you are a high-income American, you win big under this resolution."

Although Mollohan typically is a stout defender of Democratic spending priorities, he takes exception to party orthodoxy on some key issues.

Mollohan has sided with GOP conservatives on some issues of environmental regulation, a stance that grows out of his state's dependence on coal mining, steel-making and other heavy industries. In May 1995, he was one of 45 Democrats voting with a majority of Republicans to relax many of the regulations under the clean water act, and he was one of 31 Democrats to vote against striking provisions prohibiting the Environmental Protection Agency from enforcing key environmental laws. He also voted for an item in the GOP's "Contract With America" aimed at making it more difficult for federal agencies to issue health, safety and environmental rules. Mollohan's opposition to what he called "unsound" acid rain legislation penalizing coal-burning plants and factories made him one of only 21 House members in May 1990 to vote against reauthorizing the Clean Air Act.

Mollohan supports gunowners' rights and voted in 1996 to repeal the ban on certain semiautomatic assault-style weapons. He is strongly opposed to abortion, though his views on that subject (rooted in his devout religious beliefs) are not expressed with a dogmatism that hampers his ability to work with liberal Democrats. Indeed, most liberals are in agreement with him on another sensitive issue — capital punishment, which Mollohan opposes.

Though well-liked by colleagues, Mollohan is generally serious of demeanor, and in the starched, buttoned-down attire he favors, he hardly looks the part of someone from "wild, wonderful" West Virginia. He does, in fact, have ties of long standing to the more formal world of Washington, D.C. He was 9 years old when his father, Robert H. Mollohan, was first elected to the House. He served from 1953-57 and then again from 1969-83. In the 1982 election, son Alan succeeded his retiring father.

At Home: Since winning a redistricting-forced battle in 1992 with another Democratic incumbent, Mollohan has coasted at election time.

In 1992, Mollohan faced a primary battle against fellow Democratic Rep. Harley O. Staggers Jr., a matchup brought on by reapportionment, which cost the state one of its four House seats. Both men had followed their fathers to Congress and had solid political bases in the reshaped 1st District.

Staggers tried to paint himself as the "outsider" in the race, criticizing Mollohan for writing overdrafts at the House bank, while Mollohan highlighted the importance to the district of his seat on the Appropriations Committee. Voters found Mollohan more persuasive, renominating him with more than 60 percent of the vote.

Mollohan's 1982 campaign to succeed his father was his most difficult. Though Alan Mollohan was born in Fairmont, for a decade he had been a Washington, D.C., lawyer who counted Pittsburgh-based Consolidation Coal Co. as a major client. Rank-and-file miners were leery of a corporate lawyer representing them; many lined up behind Mollohan's pro-labor primary opponent, state Sen. Dan Tonkovich.

The elder Mollohan, however, had close ties to party officials, business and labor leaders. Their support proved crucial to his son, who narrowly won the primary. In the fall, Mollohan took 53 percent of the vote against GOP state Rep. John F. McCuskey.

In 1984, Mollohan bucked a Republican tide and fended off a GOP challenge from state Rep. Jim Altmeyer with a late media barrage focusing on Altmeyer's spotty attendance record in the state House. He won with 54 percent and has not been pushed in any general election since then.

HOUSE ELECTIONS

1996 General		
Alan B. Mollohan (D)	171,334	(100%)
1994 General		
Alan B. Mollohan (D)	103,177	(70%)
Sally Rossy Riley (R)	43,590	(30%)

Previous Winning Percentages: 1992 (100%) **1990** (67%) **1988** (75%) **1986** (100%) **1984** (54%) **1982** (53%)

CAMPAIGN FINANCE

	Receipts	Receipts from PACs	Expenditures
1996			
Mollohan (D)	$207,300	$144,850 (70%)	$195,128
1994			
Mollohan (D)	$329,173	$233,900 (71%)	$315,389
Riley (R)	$7,135	$514 (7%)	$7,245

DISTRICT VOTE FOR PRESIDENT

	1996		1992
D	107,835 (49%)	**D**	113,756 (46%)
R	83,306 (38%)	**R**	86,131 (35%)
I	28,900 (13%)	**I**	45,856 (19%)

KEY VOTES

1997	
Ban "partial birth" abortions	Y
1996	
Approve farm bill	Y
Deny public education to illegal immigrants	N
Repeal ban on certain assault-style weapons	Y
Increase minimum wage	Y
Freeze defense spending	N
Approve welfare overhaul	N
1995	
Approve balanced-budget constitutional amendment	N
Relax Clean Water Act regulations	Y
Oppose limits on environmental regulations	N
Reduce projected Medicare spending	N
Approve GOP budget with tax and spending cuts	N

VOTING STUDIES

	Presidential Support		Party Unity		Conservative Coalition	
Year	S	O	S	O	S	O
1996	68	27	68	28	73	22
1995	61	34	69	27	62	37
1994	74	24	86	11	58	42
1993	82	17	78	19	77	20
1992	35	60	81	14	58	40
1991	41	59	79	17	62	38

INTEREST GROUP RATINGS

Year	ADA	AFL-CIO	CCUS	ACU
1996	65	n/a	25	15
1995	60	92	38	33
1994	60	89	33	38
1993	45	100	20	29
1992	70	100	43	21
1991	50	92	20	30

2 Bob Wise (D)

Of Clendenin — Elected 1982, 8th term

Biographical Information
Born: Jan. 6, 1948, Washington, D.C.
Education: Duke U., A.B. 1970; Tulane U., J.D. 1975.
Occupation: Lawyer.
Family: Wife, Sandra Casber; two children.
Religion: Episcopalian.
Political Career: W.Va. Senate, 1981-83.
Capitol Office: 2367 Rayburn Bldg. 20515; 225-2711.

Committees
Government Reform & Oversight
National Security, International Affairs & Criminal Justice
Transportation & Infrastructure
Railroads (ranking); Water Resources & Environment

In Washington: With the Republican majority in the House now extended from two to at least four years, Wise is getting well-practiced in a role he took up early in 1995— that of minority watchdog: He is one of a handful of members charged by Democratic leaders as a House "floor sheriff." On occasion, one aspect of this function is to cajole Republicans into politically sensitive recorded votes on Democratic counterproposals to their agenda items.

For example, during debate in the 104th over the balanced-budget constitutional amendment, Wise offered a proposal to remove the Social Security trust fund from deficit calculations. His plan, which was not approved, also would have permitted Congress to waive any balanced-budget requirements during times of economic recession and would have set up a capital budget, allowing the federal government to finance capital expenditures over the life of the project rather than in one budget year.

Also in the 104th, Wise offered an amendment designed to weaken a GOP "enhanced rescissions" measure — a bill designed to bolster the president's ability to veto individual items in spending bills. Wise's amendment, which was rejected, would not have handed over as much power to the president. It would have required a majority vote of both the House and the Senate to block a proposed presidential cut, instead of a two-thirds vote as called for under the GOP plan.

In the Democratic-controlled 103rd Congress, Wise was chairman of the Public Works and Transportation Subcommittee on Economic Development. That role made him a partner with West Virginia's senior senator at the time, Appropriations Committee Chairman Robert C. Byrd, in seeing that their state got a healthy share of federal dollars spent on infrastructure improvements. Wise's subcommittee also had jurisdiction over two programs vital to West Virginia: the Appalachian Regional Commission and the Economic Development Administration.

With the Republican takeover in the 104th Congress, Wise lost his chairmanship. For a time, he was ranking Democrat on the newly named Public Buildings and Economic Development subcommittee, and he supported a Republican-led effort to replace the Economic Development Administration with a set of eight regional commissions. The commissions would inherit the EDA's mission of steering public works projects to economically distressed urban and rural areas. In October 1995, after top Transportation and Infrastructure Committee Democrat Norman Y. Mineta of California resigned from Congress, there was a shuffling of ranking seats, and Wise took the ranking spot on the Railroads subcommittee.

Wise came to Washington as a self-described populist with a penchant for challenging established power, and he lived up to that reputation early in his first term. He had been in office only a few months when he took on his state's congressional delegation — including Senate Democratic leader Byrd — by opposing the Stonewall Jackson Dam, a long-planned flood-control project in his district.

Wise had campaigned on a promise to fight the dam, and when the 1983 water development appropriations bill came up, he attached an amendment eliminating funding for it, calling the dam a waste of money. Wise managed to persuade a majority of the House to go his way. Only Senate support for the dam saved it; the House-Senate conference preserved funding.

Despite his iconoclastic start, Wise fairly soon began working within the system, applying himself to slicing off pieces of the federal pie for his constituency. The reason was simple: economic necessity. Learning from Byrd's example, Wise has had some success in securing funds for such district projects as lock and dam renovation.

Wise has been an outspoken advocate for the wider use of alternative transportation fuels — in particular the use of compressed natural gas, an abundant natural resource in West Virginia. In 1990, Wise decided to practice what he preaches: He converted his personal car to dual-fuel; it can

The "bicoastal" 2nd spans the state, starting on the west at the Ohio River, moving east to take in the state capital of Charleston (in Kanawha County) and ending in the historic Eastern Panhandle town of Harpers Ferry, at the confluence of the Shenandoah and Potomac rivers.

The 2nd's mountainous middle — which includes Kanawha, the state's largest county, with about 208,000 residents — retains its industrial character and Democratic orientation. Rep. Wise, who has regularly won by wide margins, is from Clendenin in Kanawha County.

Charleston, with just over 57,000 people, is the district's dominant city. Chemical plants that provide jobs in "Chemical Valley" along the Kanawha River also spark environmental concerns. Charleston's economy is bolstered by the state payroll and by the Charleston Town Center, a regional mall that draws shoppers from across West Virginia, Kentucky and Ohio.

There is a conservative streak in Kanawha County, evidenced by controversies over school busing and textbook banning in the recent past. However, the economic drop-off in Kanawha's industrial sector has helped Democrats maintain their edge in the county, which lost 10 percent of its population in the 1980s. The mainly Democratic mountain regions north and east of Kanawha remain heavily dependent on coal.

Republican strength in the 2nd is concentrated in two fast-growing exurban areas at the district's edges. In the Eastern Panhandle, the populations of Berkeley (just over 59,000) and Jefferson (nearly 36,000) counties — within commuting distance of Washington — grew by 27 percent and 19 percent, respectively. Berkeley voters backed Republican Bob Dole in 1996; Jefferson voters went for Democrat Bill Clinton.

WEST VIRGINIA 2
Center — Charleston; Eastern Panhandle

The commuter class in the Panhandle is being joined by white-collar workers brought in by the federal government. Past efforts to consolidate CIA functions at a Jefferson County site, supported by West Virginia Sen. Robert C. Byrd, caused a stir among D.C.-area legislators.

The white-collar growth has supplemented a local GOP tradition that began in the Civil War era, when the eastern counties were at the front lines of some Civil War incidents. (Abolitionist John Brown staged his 1859 raid on the U.S. arsenal at Harpers Ferry and was hanged in nearby Charles Town.)

The other area where Republicans dominate for president and compete for lower offices is Putnam County, just west of Charleston. Putnam's population increased 12 percent during the 1980s to nearly 43,000. George Bush won the county with 55 percent in 1988 and carried it with 46 percent in 1992. Dole continued this Republican tradition in 1996, polling 47 percent of the vote to win the county.

The more level terrain at the ends of the district also supports much of West Virginia's agricultural activity. Jefferson County leads the state in corn and dairy cattle; Berkeley is tops in hogs. In the far west, Mason County raises livestock and grows corn and tobacco.

1990 Population: 597,921. White 574,038 (96%), Black 19,982 (3%), Other 3,901 (1%). Hispanic origin 2,725 (<1%). 18 and over 448,825 (75%), 62 and over 104,298 (17%). Median age: 35.

now use either compressed natural gas or gasoline, as can two cars used by his staff.

Mindful that worker-safety issues are important to many in his constituency, Wise in the 104th unsuccessfully tried to amend a Republican-backed freeze on federal regulations to exempt new mining regulations. Gun owners are a powerful voting bloc in West Virginia, and Wise keeps them happy by consistently opposing gun control efforts. He voted in the 103rd against a five-day waiting period for handgun purchases, against the ban on certain semiautomatic assault-style weapons, and against the 1994 crime bill that included the ban. In 1996, he voted to repeal the assault-weapons ban. Wise also enhances his popularity at home by dedicating personal resources to scholarship funds at four West Virginia colleges. To afford such largess, Wise doesn't have to rely solely on his own resources; his wife is a high-level staffer on the Ways and Means Committee, a position she held before they met.

At Home: While Wise launched his political career as a maverick, he has nurtured it with unabashed displays of state boosterism. He regularly gives district voters what one newspaper described as "an upbeat, feel-good-about-ourselves pitch." And he has gained wide visibility with projects such as "West Virginia First," a TV program designed to encourage high school students to stay in the state.

Rather than join an established firm after law school, Wise set up his own practice oriented to low- and moderate-income clients. He then directed a statewide tax reform group that repeatedly took coal companies to court to force them to pay more property tax on their large land holdings.

But legal action had its limits, Wise decided. "Where people lose the battle is when they have to actually go to court," he once said. "It's much better if they win their case in the legislative process."

So in 1980 he capitalized on the resentment of

teachers against the small size of a pay raise to upset the conservative state Senate president in the Democratic primary. With a reputation as a giant-killer, he ran for Congress in 1982, benefiting from labor support to swamp a Democratic primary field that included the state House majority leader.

Republican David Michael Staton had won the House seat in 1980 with an extensive grass-roots campaign of his own, but his 1982 re-election effort was more aloof. If Staton was worried about Wise, he did not show it. "I don't think it will even be close," he said.

It was not. Wise's small campaign budget and feuds with party leaders masked an effective volunteer network and a knack for drawing enough free media attention to neutralize Staton's ads. He won a decisive 58 percent of the vote.

Each election since then, Wise has won easily. In 1996, he faced a primary challenge from Howard Swint, a Republican-turned-Democrat who served in the economic development administrations of three West Virginia governors. Swint portrayed himself as an outsider, criticizing Wise for accepting contributions from PACs. He also faulted the incumbent as a fan of "pork barrel" spending on local projects. That was not a winning strategy in a state where Sen. Byrd is revered for his ability to obtain millions of dollars from Washington. Wise won renomination in a romp, and in November, his huge campaign treasury helped him crush Republican businessman Greg Morris.

Wise's most spirited re-election contest was in 1986, when Charleston newscaster Tim Sharp left his job in early September to fill the vacancy on the GOP ticket. Sharp enjoyed instant name identification as a TV news anchorman, but he drew more attention than votes. Wise swept every county in the district, taking 65 percent overall.

HOUSE ELECTIONS

1996 General		
Bob Wise (D)	141,551	(69%)
Greg Morris (R)	63,933	(31%)
1996 Primary		
Bob Wise (D)	81,340	(86%)
Howard Swint (D)	13,762	(14%)
1994 General		
Bob Wise (D)	90,757	(64%)
Sam Cravotta (R)	51,691	(36%)

Previous Winning Percentages: 1992 (71%) **1990** (100%) **1988** (74%) **1986** (65%) **1984** (68%) **1982** (58%)

CAMPAIGN FINANCE

	Receipts	Receipts from PACs		Expend- itures
1996				
Wise (D)	$344,409	$236,950	(69%)	$376,555
Morris (R)	$53,474	$0	(0%)	$49,732
1994				
Wise (D)	$219,759	$147,375	(67%)	$271,315
Cravotta (R)	$41,988	$34	(0%)	$43,897

DISTRICT VOTE FOR PRESIDENT

1996		1992	
D	108,503 (49%)	**D**	104,257 (45%)
R	88,930 (40%)	**R**	90,375 (39%)
I	23,238 (11%)	**I**	36,813 (16%)

KEY VOTES

1997	
Ban "partial birth" abortions	N
1996	
Approve farm bill	N
Deny public education to illegal immigrants	N
Repeal ban on certain assault-style weapons	Y
Increase minimum wage	Y
Freeze defense spending	Y
Approve welfare overhaul	Y
1995	
Approve balanced-budget constitutional amendment	N
Relax Clean Water Act regulations	N
Oppose limits on environmental regulations	Y
Reduce projected Medicare spending	N
Approve GOP budget with tax and spending cuts	N

VOTING STUDIES

	Presidential Support		Party Unity		Conservative Coalition	
Year	**S**	**O**	**S**	**O**	**S**	**O**
1996	80	14	78	17	63	35
1995	83	16	87	11	40	59
1994	81	18	91	6	69	28
1993	87	12	86	10	68	27
1992	18	76	84	8	50	48
1991	26	70	90	6	41	54

INTEREST GROUP RATINGS

Year	ADA	AFL-CIO	CCUS	ACU
1996	70	n/a	25	10
1995	90	100	29	16
1994	75	89	42	30
1993	70	100	20	21
1992	80	92	38	17
1991	70	100	30	5

3 Nick J. Rahall II (D)

Of Beckley — Elected 1976, 11th term

Biographical Information
Born: May 20, 1949, Beckley, W.Va.
Education: Duke U., A.B. 1971; George Washington U., 1972.
Occupation: Broadcasting executive; travel agent.
Family: Divorced; three children.
Religion: Presbyterian.
Political Career: No previous office.
Capitol Office: 2307 Rayburn Bldg. 20515; 225-3452.

Committees
Resources
Energy & Mineral Resources
Transportation & Infrastructure
Aviation; Surface Transportation (ranking); Water Resources & Environment

In Washington: As a minority-party member, Rahall continues to pursue the interests that occupied him when Democrats controlled the House and he was a subcommittee chairman. Overhauling the nation's 1872 Mining Law is still a priority for him, as is encouraging highway and infrastructure development nationally and especially in West Virginia. Rahall chaired a subcommittee on mining and natural resources until the 103rd Congress, when he took the gavel of the Public Works and Transportation Subcommittee on Surface Transportation. Rahall is now ranking on Surface Transportation, whose parent committee was renamed Transportation and Infrastructure in the 104th Congress.

It is from his seat on the Resources Committee that Rahall has attacked the mining law, which he says allows mining companies to extract valuable hard-rock minerals from public lands without paying fair compensation to the federal government. The law allows mining companies to purchase "patents" of federal land for as little as $2.50 an acre and extract hard-rock minerals such as gold, silver and copper. Rahall and his allies want companies to pay more for the right to mine on public lands, but Western-state members in particular resist that idea.

Rahall introduced a bill in 1995 that would charge miners an 8 percent royalty on the gross value of the minerals at time of extraction, bar patenting and hold miners to strict environmental standards. Although his measure was not warmly greeted in the GOP-controlled 104th Congress, he successfully cosponsored an amendment that extended for a year a moratorium on mining patents. It was approved 271-153 in July 1995 as part of the fiscal 1996 interior appropriations bill.

When his amendment was brought up, Rahall told the House of a man in Arizona who staked a mining claim of 61 acres and under the mining law bought the land from the government for $155. Rahall complained that "nothing in the law says you have to actually mine the land. Instead, today these mining claims are the site of a huge Hilton Hotel overlooking Phoenix." Then he added, "For the $155 the so-called miner paid the government for these claims, he estimates that his share of the Hilton Hotel is now worth about $6 billion."

Also on the Resources Committee in the 104th, Rahall fought a GOP effort to curtail enforcement of federal health and safety regulations of surface mining operations, calling it "anti-environment and anti-health." Approved in July 1996 by the Energy and Mineral Resources Subcommittee, the bill aimed to amend the 1977 Surface Mining Control and Reclamation Act by generally barring the federal government from issuing violation notices to companies that do not comply with operation permits, although the government could still issue violations in cases of imminent danger to health or safety. Rahall offered a series of amendments to strike sections of the bill, but all were defeated.

Always watchful of highway-related issues from his seat on Transportation and Infrastructure, Rahall in the 104th sought to brake a GOP effort to repeal the federal speed limit. When the House took up a bill in September 1995 allowing states to spend $6.5 billion in road funding, the measure provided for repeal of the interstate highway speed limit. Rahall argued that thousands would die as a result of lifting speed limits. "The enactment of the bill's repeal provision would, in effect, turn our nation's highways into killing fields," he said.

Rahall offered an amendment retaining speed limits as they were in 1995 — 65 mph on rural sections of interstate highways and 55 mph elsewhere — but he was rebuffed, 112-313. He then proposed setting a nationwide maximum of 65 mph. That measure fared only slightly better, losing 133-291.

Rahall took exception when proponents of the fiscal 1997 transportation spending bill bragged that the measure did not earmark funds for highway "demonstration projects" — construction work sought by members that some criticize as "pork barrel." Rahall noted that the bill contained

WEST VIRGINIA 3
South — Huntington; Beckley

The 3rd, which takes in the state's southern counties, is known as the "coal district." Six of the state's 10 leading coal-producing counties — including the top two (Boone and Mingo) — are in the 3rd.

Dependence on coal produces a common economic trait: hardship. While coal has been produced at near-record tonnages in recent years, technological advances have sharply reduced the need for labor. One glaring example of distress is McDowell County in southern West Virginia. Its population slipped 29 percent — from almost 50,000 to just over 35,000 — during the 1980s.

Every county in the 3rd lost residents during the 1980s. Although emigration has reduced the work force by thousands, unemployment remains stubbornly high in many areas. Insufficient highways and other infrastructural deficiencies hinder growth in mountain country.

Soaring unemployment added misery to a region that has always had pockets of Appalachian poverty. Democrats remain the dominant political force here; Bill Clinton won the 3rd with 58 percent in 1996.

The population of Huntington (Cabell County), the second-largest city in the state, fell 14 percent in the 1980s to just under 55,000. But the city is cushioned by an Ohio River location that provides for a diversified economy. CSX railroad, Inco Alloys International Inc. and Ashland Coal Inc. — along with AK Steel Corp. and Ashland Oil Inc. in the Ashland, Ky., area — provide jobs. And Huntington is home to Marshall University, which hosts a medical school and about 12,500 students.

Huntington's white-collar sector and tobacco growers help make Cabell the most Republican part of the 3rd. George Bush won Cabell with 53 percent in 1988. But allegiance to the GOP does not run deep here. Clinton carried the county in both 1992 and 1996, albeit with a lower percentage than the district overall.

Just to the east is the heart of coal country, Democratic turf where some residents still idolize John F. Kennedy, whose 1960 primary win in West Virginia was pivotal to his presidential nomination.

Near the eastern edge of the coal fields is Beckley (population 18,000), which promotes as economic assets its location near interstates 77 and 64 and the surrounding area's tourist potential. Local rivers are popular with white-water rafters. Dan Quayle occasionally rafted in the area while he was vice president.

The eastern part of the 3rd also has the state's most venerable tourist establishment: the Greenbrier resort in White Sulphur Springs.

Some communities are crafting tourist attractions from aspects of their industrial heritage. These include the sometimes ugly events in Mingo County, site of the "West Virginia Mine Wars" between labor activists and union-busting mine owners during the 1920s (the subject of the movie "Matewan"). "Bloody Mingo" was also the site of part of the feuding between the Hatfields and McCoys.

1990 Population: 597,500. White 567,732 (95%), Black 26,651 (4%), Other 3,117 (1%). Hispanic origin 2,617 (<1%). 18 and over 444,523 (74%), 62 and over 108,210 (18%). Median age: 35.

numerous earmarks for other types of transportation projects, including more than $724 million for 39 new transit projects. "For some reason that I have not been unable to understand, the 'pork barrel' label is only applied by the media and some in this body to the earmarking of funds for highway projects," Rahall said. "You can go to the Appropriations Committee to get an earmark of funds for a bus station in some small town, but not for a four-lane highway that crosses state lines. This dual standard simply makes no sense."

Rahall in 1996 backed an effort by Transportation Committee Chairman Bud Shuster of Pennsylvania to take the four transportation trust funds "off budget." The trust funds are financed by taxes on gasoline, airplane tickets and cargo; all four have sizable cash balances, but despite this, Shuster argued that Congress spends too sparingly from these accounts because of overall deficit reduction pressures. Rahall and other bill supporters argued that taking the trust funds "off budget" would encourage increased infrastructure spending. Most House members agreed, and the bill passed easily, 284-143.

Coal-related issues remain high on Rahall's agenda. He represents a portion of one of the nation's leading coal-producing states and avidly defends the interests of the industry. He also tries to help with coal miners' concerns such as black lung disease, and he usually votes a pro-organized labor line. He supported a 90-cent increase in the minimum wage in 1996, and in the 103rd Congress he voted against NAFTA and GATT.

Of Lebanese heritage, Rahall has been a frequent critic of Israel and an advocate of closer U.S. ties to Arab states. Rahall met with Palestine Liberation Organization leader Yasir Arafat as part of a congressional delegation that toured Beirut in 1982, long before Arafat became a respectable figure in international diplomatic circles. He also took the lead in asking the State Department for emergency federal assistance for Lebanese civilian refugees after Israel shelled and bombed Lebanon in the spring of 1996 in an effort to stop attacks on its territory by Hezbollah guerrillas.

At Home: With a single exception, Rahall has won easily in his 10 re-election campaigns. His only close call came in 1990, when he got 52 percent of the vote in a rematch against Marianne R. Brewster, a former Mercer County GOP chairman. But subsequent redistricting strengthened Rahall's base in the state's most southern and most Democratic district, and once again the 3rd is firmly in his grasp.

Rahall was a little-known travel agent and radio sales manager when he entered politics in 1976. His opportunity grew out of Democratic Rep. Ken Hechler's campaign for governor. Rahall was far from the best-known contender in the Democratic House field, but he had family money, and he spent it on a media campaign none of his foes could match, evoking the images of Hechler, President Franklin D. Roosevelt and Sen. Robert C. Byrd. Rahall won nomination with 37 percent.

After the primary, Hechler (who did not get the gubernatorial nomination) mounted a write-in drive to keep his House seat. Rahall never could have beaten Hechler in a primary, but the general-election write-in effort was too difficult even for a popular incumbent, especially after Rahall received Democratic organization support. Hechler got nearly 60,000 write-ins, but Rahall won with a 46 percent tally.

Rahall's re-election percentage dropped into the 60s for the first time in 1984, after a Las Vegas casino filed suit against him to collect more than $60,000 in gambling debts. The suit, which drew headlines a month before the election, eventually was dropped. But coming on the heels of Rahall's separation from his wife, the episode gave his little-known GOP challenger unexpected fodder.

In 1986, a strong Democratic year, Rahall won 71 percent; but in 1988, he dropped to a surprising 61 percent against the GOP's woefully underfunded Brewster.

That anemic showing set the stage for tough primary and general-election campaigns in 1990. In the primary, Rahall faced a comeback attempt from Hechler.

Pledging a return to "high moral standards again," Hechler implied that Rahall lacked them, and he criticized the incumbent as too dependent on out-of-state special-interest money. The local media rehashed Rahall's past troubles, including a 1988 guilty plea to alcohol-related reckless driving charges. But Rahall, anticipating a tough fight, worked hard to shore up his base in the party and prevailed in the primary with 57 percent of the vote.

Brewster, nominated for a second try by the Republican Party, benefited from lingering voter concerns about Rahall's personal problems and the general anti-incumbent sentiment of 1990. That lifted her to 48 percent of the vote, but Rahall held on, and Brewster decided against a third challenge two years later.

HOUSE ELECTIONS

1996 General		
Nick J. Rahall II (D)	145,550	(100%)
1994 General		
Nick J. Rahall II (D)	74,967	(64%)
Ben Waldman (R)	42,382	(36%)

Previous Winning Percentages: **1992** (66%) **1990** (52%) **1988** (61%) **1986** (71%) **1984** (67%) **1982** (81%) **1980** (77%) **1978** (100%) **1976** (46%)

CAMPAIGN FINANCE

	Receipts	Receipts from PACs	Expend-itures
1996			
Rahall (D)	$435,942	$241,800 (55%)	$145,980
1994			
Rahall (D)	$562,966	$283,044 (50%)	$389,323
Waldman (R)	$52,535	$514 (1%)	$41,838

DISTRICT VOTE FOR PRESIDENT

	1996		1992
D	111,474 (58%)	**D**	112,988 (55%)
R	61,710 (32%)	**R**	65,468 (32%)
I	19,501 (10%)	**I**	26,160 (13%)

KEY VOTES

1997	
Ban "partial birth" abortions	Y
1996	
Approve farm bill	N
Deny public education to illegal immigrants	N
Repeal ban on certain assault-style weapons	Y
Increase minimum wage	Y
Freeze defense spending	N
Approve welfare overhaul	N
1995	
Approve balanced-budget constitutional amendment	N
Relax Clean Water Act regulations	N
Oppose limits on environmental regulations	N
Reduce projected Medicare spending	N
Approve GOP budget with tax and spending cuts	N

VOTING STUDIES

	Presidential Support		Party Unity		Conservative Coalition	
Year	S	O	S	O	S	O
1996	70	30	81	19	51	49
1995	74	26	79	20	36	64
1994	64	35	86	13	47	53
1993	64	34	76	20	66	34
1992	25	69	79	17	35	60
1991	36	59	85	11	49	46

INTEREST GROUP RATINGS

Year	ADA	AFL-CIO	CCUS	ACU
1996	75	n/a	19	20
1995	70	100	25	28
1994	75	100	25	24
1993	70	100	18	30
1992	70	100	38	20
1991	65	100	11	21

WISCONSIN

Governor: Tommy G. Thompson (R)
First elected: 1986
Length of term: 4 years
Term expires: 1/99
Salary: $101,861
Term limit: None.
Phone: (608) 266-1212
Born: Nov. 19, 1941; Elroy, Wis.
Education: U. of Wisconsin, B.S. 1963, J.D. 1966.
Military Service: Army Reserve, 1966-76.
Occupation: Lawyer; real estate broker.
Family: Wife, Sue Ann Mashak; three children.
Religion: Roman Catholic.
Political Career: Wis. Assembly, 1967-87, assistant minority leader, 1973-81, minority leader, 1981-87; sought Republican nomination for U.S. House (special election), 1979.

Lt. Gov.: Scott McCallum (R)
First elected: 1986
Length of term: 4 years
Term expires: 1/99
Salary: $54,585
Phone: (608) 266-3516

State election official: (608) 266-8005
Democratic headquarters: (608) 255-5172
Republican headquarters: (608) 257-4765

REDISTRICTING

Wisconsin retained its nine House seats in reapportionment. The legislature passed the map April 14, 1992; the governor signed it April 28.

STATE LEGISLATURE

Legislature. Meets for 5 floor periods of varying length over 2-year session.

Senate: 33 members, 4-year terms
1996 breakdown: 17D, 16R; 24 men, 9 women
Salary: $35,070
Phone: (608) 266-2517

State Assembly: 99 members, 2-year terms
1996 breakdown: 52R, 47D; 77 men, 22 women
Salary: $35,070
Phone: (608) 266-1501

URBAN STATISTICS

City	Population
Milwaukee	628,088
Mayor John O. Norquist, D	
Madison	190,766
Mayor Paul Soglin, D	
Green Bay	96,466
Mayor Paul F. Jadin, N-P	
Racine	84,298
Mayor James Smith, N-P	
Kenosha	80,352
Mayor John Antaramian, D	

U.S. CONGRESS

Senate: 2 D, 0 R
House: 5 D, 4 R

TERM LIMITS

For state offices: No

ELECTIONS

1996 Presidential Vote

Bill Clinton	49%
Bob Dole	39%
Ross Perot	10%

1992 Presidential Vote

Bill Clinton	41%
George Bush	37%
Ross Perot	22%

1988 Presidential Vote

Michael S. Dukakis	51%
George Bush	48%

POPULATION

1990 population		4,891,769
1980 population		4,705,767
Percent change		+4%
Rank among states:		16
White		92%
Black		5%
Hispanic		2%
Asian or Pacific islander		1%
Urban		66%
Rural		34%
Born in state		76%
Foreign-born		2%
Under age 18	1,288,982	26%
Ages 18-64	2,951,566	60%
65 and older	651,221	13%
Median age		32.9

MISCELLANEOUS

Capital: Madison
Number of counties: 72
Per capita income: $18,046 (1991)
Rank among states: 22
Total area: 56,153 sq. miles
Rank among states: 26

WISCONSIN

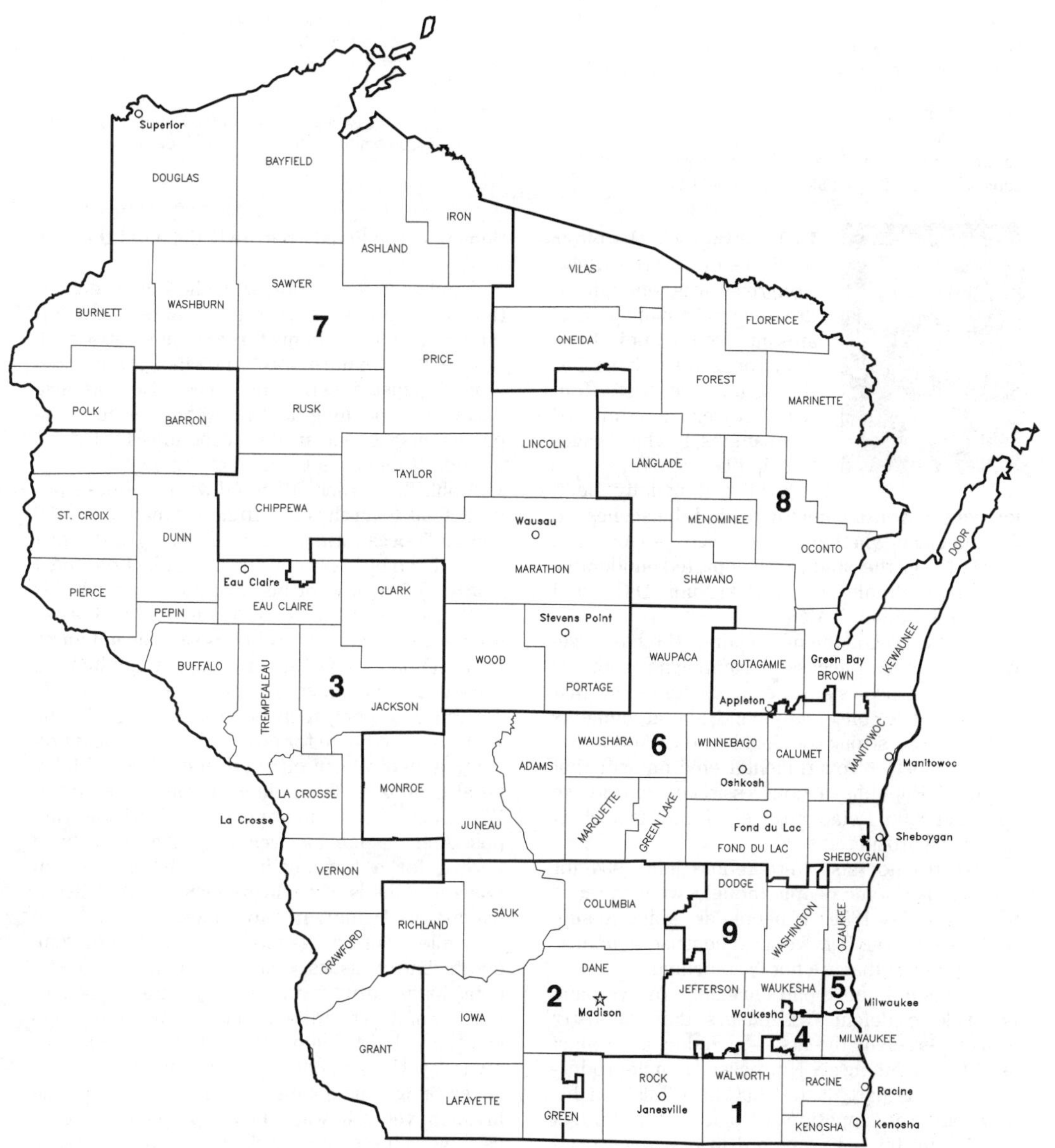

Superior
DOUGLAS
BAYFIELD
IRON
ASHLAND
VILAS
SAWYER
WASHBURN
BURNETT
7
FLORENCE
ONEIDA
PRICE
FOREST
MARINETTE
POLK
BARRON
RUSK
LINCOLN
LANGLADE
TAYLOR
CHIPPEWA
ST. CROIX
DUNN
8
MENOMINEE
Wausau
MARATHON
OCONTO
DOOR
Eau Claire
EAU CLAIRE
CLARK
SHAWANO
PIERCE
PEPIN
Stevens Point
KEWAUNEE
BUFFALO
TREMPEALEAU
3
WOOD
PORTAGE
WAUPACA
OUTAGAMIE
Green Bay
BROWN
JACKSON
Appleton
WAUSHARA
6
WINNEBAGO
CALUMET
MANITOWOC
Manitowoc
ADAMS
Oshkosh
LA CROSSE
MONROE
La Crosse
JUNEAU
MARQUETTE
GREEN LAKE
Fond du Lac
FOND DU LAC
Sheboygan
SHEBOYGAN
VERNON
DODGE
COLUMBIA
SAUK
RICHLAND
9
WASHINGTON
OZAUKEE
CRAWFORD
DANE
JEFFERSON
WAUKESHA
5
Milwaukee
2
Madison
IOWA
Waukesha
4
MILWAUKEE
GRANT
ROCK
WALWORTH
RACINE
Racine
LAFAYETTE
Janesville
1
GREEN
KENOSHA
Kenosha

Herb Kohl (D)

Of Milwaukee — Elected 1988, 2nd term

Biographical Information
Born: Feb. 7, 1935, Milwaukee, Wis.
Education: U. of Wisconsin, B.A. 1956; Harvard U., M.B.A. 1958.
Military Service: Army Reserve, 1958-64.
Occupation: Businessman; professional basketball team owner.
Family: Single.
Religion: Jewish.
Political Career: Wis. Democratic Party chairman, 1975-77.
Capitol Office: 330 Hart Bldg. 20510; 224-5653.

Committees
Special Aging
Appropriations
Agriculture, Rural Development & Related Agencies; Energy & Water Development; Labor, Health & Human Services & Education; Transportation; Treasury & General Government (ranking)
Judiciary
Administrative Oversight & the Courts; Antitrust, Business Rights & Competition (ranking); Youth Violence

In Washington: The bitter partisanship of the 104th Congress was enough to drive several Senate moderates into retirement in 1996. Their departures have left the firmly centrist Kohl with fewer like-minded companions, but he is eager to help fill the void.

Kohl has usually been known for working quietly behind the scenes, so it is unclear whether he will seek — or even aspire to — the stature of departed moderates such as Bill Bradley, D-N.J.; Sam Nunn, D-Ga.; and William S. Cohen, R-Maine.

But this go-it-alone millionaire, who has largely financed his successful campaigns from his own pocket, has established a Senate record that includes both conservative and liberal elements rather than a strong ideological bent. And in the smaller-is-better governmental environment that followed Republican congressional victories in 1994 and 1996, Democratic deficit hawks such as Kohl have prospered.

"We [Democrats] were rebuked in 1994 for policies that some people thought went too far," he said in May 1996. "If people are going to support us in November, we need centrist, commonsense policies that are not far-reaching."

Kohl is not above parochialism, however, and is quick to defend Wisconsin's dairy industry against perceived threats — including a compact established among six Northeastern milk-producing states as part of the 1996 farm bill. But his greatest preoccupation has been the budget deficit, and his voting record in that regard has won him most of the public note he has received.

The Concord Coalition, a bipartisan group devoted to balancing the budget, rated Kohl higher than any other senator in 1996, based on his records on a series of floor votes chosen by the coalition. Kohl also found a home in the "Centrist Coalition," a bipartisan group of 22 senators led by John H. Chafee, R-R.I., and John B. Breaux, D-La., that drew up a seven-year alternative budget featuring modest tax relief and deep cuts in entitlements. The Senate narrowly defeated the plan in May 1996.

Kohl's preoccupation with the deficit echoes that of his predecessor in the Senate, Democrat William Proxmire. In his three decades of service (1957-89), Proxmire was renowned for his sermons against government excess. He was also known for spending next to nothing on his campaigns (his last one, in 1982, cost him $145), a distinction Kohl has not sought to duplicate.

Kohl, the owner of the Milwaukee Bucks pro basketball team, has a fortune estimated at $300 million. It began with a chain of grocery stores that was built up by his family and then sold. Kohl spent nearly $7.5 million of his own money to win his 1988 election and another $6.9 million in 1994 to secure a second term. Kohl has said his immunity from the demands of fundraising permits him the same detachment that Proxmire brought to his job.

Kohl has spent freely on his campaigns, but he was a hero at home for buying the Bucks and preventing their relocation out of state. In April 1995, he also donated $25 million to the University of Wisconsin to build an arena on the Madison campus. And despite his wealth, he has long been known for a low-key lifestyle. When back in Wisconsin, he is often sighted eating breakfast at his favorite Denny's in Milwaukee.

While Kohl has generally followed the Democratic line on issues such as the environment, student loans, drug prevention programs, school lunches and an abortion procedure that opponents call "partial birth" abortion, he has often gone his own way. He is a solid vote for constitutional balanced-budget amendments, term limits and the line-item veto. He was an early proponent of converting welfare into block grants to the states, sponsoring a bill to that effect in 1994.

And in October 1995, Kohl was the only Democrat to sign a letter from Senate Republicans demanding that President Clinton get congressional approval before deploying U.S. troops in Bosnia.

But if Republicans could expect his support on those issues, Kohl has frequently taken them to task for adding defense spending on top of Clinton's requests. (His moves are consistent with his views on the deficit, but Kohl also comes from a state with only a slight military presence.) He offered an amendment to cut $8 billion from the defense bill on the Senate floor in 1995, then tried a similar tactic with the budget resolution the next year. He spoke scornfully of the GOP's reasoning in a 1996 floor speech: "Two years ago, we had a readiness crisis; now we have a so-called modernization crisis. . . . The only crisis we have here is a crisis of hemorrhaging tax dollars."

Kohl's willingness to compromise came out a bit garbled in March 1995, when a group of Senate Democrats held a news conference offering their alternative to the GOP's balanced-budget amendment. Explaining that he and his colleagues hoped Republicans could support their version, Kohl said, "What we're saying is, let's go to bed together, let's come up with a plan together."

A smiling Dale Bumpers, D-Ark., stepped up to the lectern next, saying, "The first point is, we're not asking anyone to go to bed with us."

Kohl sits on the powerful Appropriations panel, where he often defends funds for Community Oriented Policing Services (COPS), a "community policing" program he helped insert in the 1994 crime bill. But much of his legislative work emerges out of the Judiciary Committee.

In the 104th Congress he moved from chairing Judiciary's Juvenile Justice Subcommittee (now called Youth Violence) to the ranking member's seat on the newly created Terrorism, Technology and Government Information Subcommittee. Many of his most notable achievements, though, remain in the area of juvenile crime. In April 1995, the Supreme Court narrowly overturned the Gun-Free School Zones Act (which Kohl had sponsored in 1990), ruling that the Constitution's clause allowing Congress to regulate interstate commerce could not be used to justify the act.

Kohl mounted a drive to restore the legislation. In a Washington Post column, he noted that restaurants fell under the Commerce Clause because their food was shipped across state lines; why not guns? "If wandering potato chips affect interstate commerce enough to justify civil rights protections for diners," Kohl wrote, "surely the guns that kill our children each year should trigger federal intervention."

In 1996 Kohl got the school zones act inserted into the fiscal 1997 Treasury-Postal appropriations bill, after it was rewritten to appease the court's concerns. He revisited handgun issues at the Supreme Court later that year, filing a brief in support of the Brady law, which requires a criminal background check for handgun buyers.

Kohl's highest visibility in the 104th came in 1995, when he and Terrorism Subcommittee Chairman Arlen Specter, R-Pa., presided over hearings investigating a fatal shootout in northern Idaho's Ruby Ridge. In August 1992, federal agents pursued white separatist Randy Weaver to his mountain cabin; during firefights over the course of two days, Weaver's wife, his 14-year-old son and a federal marshal were killed. The incident, along with the 1993 siege of the Branch Davidian compound in Waco, Texas, became a rallying cry for critics of government force.

Kohl was studiously even-handed during the hearings. At one point he grilled Weaver at length about letters in which Weaver referred to the "Zionist Occupied Government," but later Kohl told a federal firearms agent that there was "no evidence" Weaver was an arms dealer whose activities warranted such a raid. When eight FBI snipers were arrayed before them on another day, Specter and Kohl presented a united front, accusing them of obscuring the truth and questioning why they shot at Vicki Weaver, who had been standing in the cabin's doorway holding her baby.

Both moderates, Kohl and Specter have formed a partnership of sorts, sponsoring bills on juvenile corrections and economic espionage. The latter bill — which established federal penalties for stealing trade secrets — ultimately was joined with a similar House measure, passed by both chambers and signed into law in 1996.

Another defining issue for Kohl (and other Midwestern lawmakers) has been the battle against the Northeast Interstate Dairy Compact, a proposal to allow six New England states to increase the federal minimum price for locally produced milk. In the 103rd Congress, Patrick J. Leahy, D-Vt., then chairman of the Agriculture Committee, backed down when Kohl threatened to filibuster Leahy's dairy compact bill.

Then, during Senate debate on the farm bill in February 1996, Kohl successfully offered an amendment to strip the compact from the bill, arguing that it would effectively impose a tariff on milk from Midwestern states sold in the Northeast. But the House-Senate conference on the farm bill restored the dairy compact, and the conference report was cleared by both House and Senate — albeit without Kohl's vote.

Kohl and the junior senator from Wisconsin, Democrat Russell D. Feingold, later filed a brief in support of a lawsuit challenging the compact in federal court.

Kohl has said his support for welfare reform was balanced with a strong desire to ensure that welfare mothers could use child care facilities when they returned to work. Toward that end, in January 1997 he introduced a bill giving businesses an incentive for providing child care services — a tax credit of up to 50 percent of the service's cost. Kohl believes the bill's estimated price tag of $2 billion could be offset with cuts in "corporate welfare" or defense.

In addition to his work on the crime bill, another Kohl initiative from the 103rd Congress bears mentioning. In 1993, he worked with Sen. Joseph I. Lieberman, D-Conn., to persuade video game producers to develop a voluntary rating system to warn parents about violence or adult material in video games.

At Home: Kohl will have to compile a substantial record of achievement in the Senate before people stop talking about how he got there. Making his first try for public office, Kohl announced about six months before the 1988 election, yet spent just under $7.5 million, nearly all of it his own. He blew away the best competition in his own party and beat an attractive Republican moderate in November.

Kohl showed some rough edges in the campaign, on one occasion naming Jimmy Carter's secretary of Defense when asked who was then holding the job. Kohl also made a remark about the employment his basketball team had provided for blacks that some found in poor taste.

But Kohl's errors were swept away in a sea of positive images. Mostly, these were communicated by Kohl's saturation TV advertising, which emphasized his private-sector success and commitment to service — beginning with his immigrant parents.

It was a campaign on a scale unlike any the state had seen. Kohl's total outlay doubled the previous state record (he even bought time on Minnesota stations to reach border counties).

Although his political involvement had been as financier and, briefly, state party chairman, Kohl showed some flair for debate. In the primary, facing former Gov. Anthony S. Earl and 1986 Senate nominee Ed Garvey, Kohl deflected their jabs with personal affability and a simple message: "Nobody's senator but yours."

Kohl's emphasis on his independence played well, especially against efforts to vilify him as a plutocrat. He found the one positive he could in being one of the state's richest men and used it to strike an improbable, but apparently effective, parallel with Proxmire.

Proxmire had run and won cheaply because he was popular enough to discourage challengers in his weight class. Kohl claimed similar independence based on his ability to self-finance his campaigns.

Kohl posted an easy plurality in the September primary. His November foe was Susan Engeleiter, Republican leader in the state Senate.

In the GOP primary, Engeleiter defeated a much more conservative opponent, former state party Chairman Steve King. She was never in danger of losing the nomination, but her winning margin was smaller than expected, and King's attacks highlighted issues on which she differed from much of her party — including her support for limited abortion rights and the Equal Rights Amendment.

By forcing Engeleiter rightward, albeit briefly, King gave the liberal Kohl running room in the center he otherwise might not have had. Engeleiter tried to compete with the continuing deluge of Kohl ads on TV by portraying herself as more in tune with ordinary people's problems. She downplayed ideology by labeling herself "A Wisconsin Original."

In the campaign's closing weeks, polls found Engeleiter gaining on Kohl. But time ran out before she could find an issue or other means of closing the last few percentage points of deficit.

In 1994, four Republicans lined up for the opportunity to take on Kohl, who faced a perennial candidate in the primary. State Rep. Robert T. Welch, the most conservative GOP candidate of the lot, won the nomination. Welch, who pledged to resign if he ever voted for a tax increase, attempted to tie Kohl to Clinton and cast him as a liberal tax-and-spender. He also criticized Kohl's expensive efforts to sign Glenn Robinson to his Bucks basketball team.

Kohl moved quickly to cast himself as a centrist in contrast with his staunchly conservative opponent. But a major component in Kohl's re-election success was his ability to pour more than $6 million of his own money into the race.

SENATE ELECTIONS

1994 General		
Herb Kohl (D)	912,662	(58%)
Robert T. Welch (R)	636,989	(41%)
1994 Primary		
Herb Kohl (D)	135,982	(90%)
Edmond Galileo Hou-Seye (D)	15,579	(10%)

Previous Winning Percentages: 1988 (52%)

CAMPAIGN FINANCE

	Receipts	Receipts from PACs	Expend-itures
1994			
Kohl (D)	$7,388,348	$0 (0%)	$7,374,312
Welch (R)	$1,266,192	$79,021 (6%)	$1,265,382

KEY VOTES

1997	
Approve balanced-budget constitutional amendment	Y
Approve chemical weapons treaty	Y
1996	
Approve farm bill	N
Limit punitive damages in product liability cases	Y
Exempt small businesses from higher minimum wage	N
Approve welfare overhaul	Y
Bar job discrimination based on sexual orientation	Y
Override veto of ban on "partial birth" abortions	N
1995	
Approve GOP budget with tax and spending cuts	N
Approve constitutional amendment barring flag desecration	N

VOTING STUDIES

	Presidential Support		Party Unity		Conservative Coalition	
Year	S	O	S	O	S	O
1996	88	12	84	16	32	68
1995	83	16	84	16	19	81
1994	81	19	75	25	41	59
1993	81	19	84	16	24	76
1992	30	70	79	21	26	74
1991	41	59	83	17	40	58

INTEREST GROUP RATINGS

Year	ADA	AFL-CIO	CCUS	ACU
1996	75	n/a	69	20
1995	95	92	47	17
1994	90	63	50	12
1993	95	73	45	24
1992	95	83	30	11
1991	90	58	20	24

Russell D. Feingold (D)

Of Middleton — Elected 1992, 1st term

Biographical Information

Born: March 2, 1953, Janesville, Wis.

Education: U. of Wisconsin, B.A. 1975; Oxford U., B.A. 1977; Harvard U., J.D. 1979.

Occupation: Lawyer.

Family: Wife, Mary Erpenbach; two children, two stepchildren.

Religion: Jewish.

Political Career: Wis. Senate, 1983-93.

Capitol Office: 716 Hart Bldg. 20510; 224-5323.

Committees

Special Aging

Budget

Foreign Relations
African Affairs (ranking); East Asian & Pacific Affairs

Judiciary
Administrative Oversight & the Courts; Constitution, Federalism & Property Rights (ranking)

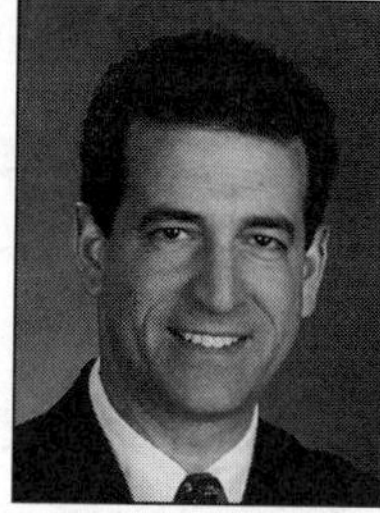

In Washington: As the 105th Congress began, one might have been excused for thinking Feingold's first name was "McCain." After record amounts of spending in 1996, the issue of campaign finance was hot, and the best-known bill on the table was the one Feingold had sponsored in tandem with Arizona Republican John McCain.

The McCain-Feingold bill, first introduced in the 104th Congress, would offer cut-rate or free broadcast time and discounted postage rates for candidates who agreed to limit their campaign spending. The bill died in June 1996 after a Republican-led filibuster in the Senate, but both senators reintroduced the legislation in January 1997. Speaking at the National Press Club that month, Feingold opined that the "dynamics have changed from the 104th Congress," largely because of what he called a "swelling of public disgust" over the influence of money in the 1996 congressional and presidential campaigns.

"It's just like the deficit issue," Feingold said in November 1996. "It just kept going up the ladder. [Ross] Perot made it an issue in the '92 campaign and it came of age."

The two senators hit the road in March 1997, traveling to Boston and Philadelphia to try to drum up support for the legislation. In that same month, Feingold's distaste for the amount of money raised in 1996 also manifested itself in his call for an independent counsel to investigate the Clinton campaign's fundraising. Feingold was among the first Democrats to call for such a probe.

He was active in the 104th on other internal congressional issues as well. In July 1996, he offered an amendment to the fiscal 1997 legislative appropriations bill to increase from one year to two the period of time former members would have to wait before returning to lobby Congress. The amendment would also have lengthened from one to five years the period that former top congressional aides (defined as those who had been paid more than $100,200) would have to wait before lobbying Congress.

Legislative Appropriations Subcommittee Chairman Connie Mack, R-Fla., said he would accept the amendment if Feingold would agree to let it be adopted by voice vote; Mack worried that senators opposed to the amendment would balk at a recorded vote, potentially miring the legislative funding bill in parliamentary maneuvering. Feingold agreed, the amendment was adopted by voice vote, and Mack dropped it when he reached the conference committee with the House (which had no such provision in its bill).

Feingold was one of only eight senators to oppose anti-terrorism legislation in April 1996, citing his opposition to the death penalty. The bill imposed new restrictions on death row appeals. Feingold lamented that lawmakers have become "all too ready" to expand capital punishment.

And as the ranking minority member of the Judiciary Subcommittee on the Constitution, Federalism and Property Rights, Feingold helped lead the fight against a 1995 constitutional amendment prohibiting flag desecration. "This nation was founded on dissent and has enjoyed a history of free speech," Feingold said.

The ranking minority member of the African Affairs Subcommittee on the Foreign Relations Committee, Feingold introduced legislation imposing sanctions on Nigeria after nine human rights activists there were executed.

Feingold, who campaigned on a promise to tackle the budget deficit, has pursued spending cuts. In July 1996, he unsuccessfully tried to delete $9.5 million set aside to begin building the controversial $710 million Animas-La Plata water delivery project in southern Colorado. His amendment to the fiscal 1997 energy and water resources spending bill was tabled, 65-33, after an impassioned appeal by Sen. Ben Nighthorse Campbell, R-Colo., an American Indian who said the project would fulfill a federal promise to two Ute tribes made in a 1988 water-rights treaty. Feingold will be able to further his efforts to reduce federal spending in the 105th Congress as a new member of the Budget Committee.

Feingold knows when to toe the line for home state interests, especially for dairy farmers. He voted against the GOP-backed overhaul of federal farm programs in 1996 because the measure authorized a Northeast Interstate Dairy Compact, which he said would allow northeastern farmers to receive higher milk prices and keep out milk from other regions.

At Home: Feingold is up for re-election in 1998, and he may find his liberal record being cut up by one of the staunchest conservatives in the GOP House Class of 1994, Rep. Mark W. Neumann, now serving his second House term. Should he run, Neumann has said he will make Feingold's vote against the balanced-budget amendment a primary theme of his campaign.

Feingold's initial 1992 victory dramatically illustrated the limitations of negative campaigning.

During Wisconsin's lengthy Democratic primary campaign (voters picked Senate nominees in September), Feingold, a little-known long shot, held his fire while his two better-known and better-financed opponents, Rep. Jim Moody and millionaire Milwaukee businessman Joseph W. Checota, vigorously hurled accusations and criticisms at each other. Feingold darted through the mud past them to score a stunning primary victory, and then knocked off Republican Sen. Bob Kasten in November.

A 10-year veteran of the state Legislature, Feingold pitched himself as an unconventional candidate with a series of amusing advertisements, emulating techniques that Minnesota Democrat Paul Wellstone had used to upset GOP Sen. Rudy Boschwitz in 1990.

In one ad Feingold led a tour of his Middleton home, remarking in front of an open closet, "Look, no skeletons." Another featured a mock tabloid newspaper headline touting his endorsement from Elvis Presley.

Moody and Checota battered each other first in a war of words, then with negative campaign ads. The attacks worked so well that voters soured on both leading contenders. Meanwhile, Feingold stressed that his lifestyle and values were more typical of Wisconsin. The primary result was nothing short of astounding: Feingold won the nomination with nearly 70 percent of the vote.

After the primary, polls showed Kasten trailing Feingold by more than 20 percentage points. But Kasten began closing ground after he attempted to paint Feingold as a tax-and-spend liberal who was soft on crime. Feingold's pitch was based less on ideology than on his image of being a straightforward, maverick politician. Yet Feingold's own position papers highlighted a standard liberal wish list, including urban aid, universal health care and environmental protection.

Kasten had been known for assembling efficient congressional and campaign staffs, and he was practiced at the art of waging aggressive, negative campaigns. But Wisconsin's political climate in 1992 was much less hospitable to candidates who took an attack posture. Though Kasten made headway cutting into Feingold's lead, at the same time he had to contend with criticism that he was running an unfair negative campaign.

On Election Day, Feingold compiled large margins in Milwaukee County and in his home base, Dane County (Madison), while minimizing Kasten's margin in the strongly Republican Milwaukee suburbs of Waukesha County. Despite being outspent by a ratio of well over 2-to-1, Feingold prevailed, 53 percent to 46 percent.

SENATE ELECTIONS

1992 General		
Russell D. Feingold (D)	1,290,662	(53%)
Bob Kasten (R)	1,129,599	(46%)
1992 Primary		
Russell D. Feingold (D)	367,746	(70%)
Jim Moody (D)	74,472	(14%)
Joseph W. Checota (D)	71,570	(14%)
Thomas Keller (D)	8,678	(2%)

CAMPAIGN FINANCE

	Receipts	Receipts from PACs		Expenditures
1992				
Feingold (D)	$1,995,732	$459,613	(23%)	$1,979,454
Kasten (R)	$5,107,974	$1,294,783	(25%)	$5,427,163
Hanson (I)	$5,870	0		$5,119
Selliken (I)	$12,218	0		$12,218

KEY VOTES

1997	
Approve balanced-budget constitutional amendment	N
Approve chemical weapons treaty	Y
1996	
Approve farm bill	N
Limit punitive damages in product liability cases	N
Exempt small businesses from higher minimum wage	N
Approve welfare overhaul	Y
Bar job discrimination based on sexual orientation	Y
Override veto of ban on "partial birth" abortions	N
1995	
Approve GOP budget with tax and spending cuts	N
Approve constitutional amendment barring flag desecration	N

VOTING STUDIES

	Presidential Support		Party Unity		Conservative Coalition	
Year	S	O	S	O	S	O
1996	86	14	87	13	16	84
1995	78	21	90	9	5	95
1994	65	35	84	16	9	91
1993	85	15	94	6	10	90

INTEREST GROUP RATINGS

Year	ADA	AFL-CIO	CCUS	ACU
1996	95	n/a	31	10
1995	100	100	42	13
1994	100	100	10	4
1993	100	91	0	12

1 Mark W. Neumann (R)

Of Janesville — Elected 1994, 2nd term

Biographical Information
Born: Feb. 27, 1954, East Troy, Wis.
Education: General Motors Institute, 1972-73; U. of Wisconsin, Whitewater, B.S. 1975; U. of Wisconsin, River Falls, M.S. 1977.
Occupation: Home builder; real estate broker; teacher.
Family: Wife, Sue; three children.
Religion: Lutheran.
Political Career: Republican nominee for U.S. House, 1992.
Capitol Office: 415 Cannon Bldg. 20515; 225-3031.

Committees
Appropriations
District of Columbia; VA, HUD & Independent Agencies
Budget

In Washington: Since he joined the House as part of the new Republican majority in 1995, one legislative priority has been paramount for Neumann: balancing the federal budget. His zeal for spending cuts exceeds even that of the GOP leadership, which often has been pained by votes cast by Neumann.

One of those pangs came as the 105th Congress opened, and it wasn't even on a budget issue: Neumann voted "present" rather than support Newt Gingrich's re-election as Speaker. The vote came before the House ethics committee had issued its report on Gingrich's violations of House rules.

Neumann got a seat on Appropriations as a freshman, and he has used it to fight federal expenditures both great and small. In February 1995, he balked at supporting a supplemental appropriations bill giving the Pentagon $3.2 billion to offset unanticipated costs of military operations in Haiti, Bosnia and Somalia and in the Persian Gulf region. Even though GOP leaders endeavored to offset the new spending with cuts from low-priority military projects and non-defense discretionary spending, the Congressional Budget Office said the bill would increase the deficit by $644 million over five years. That was all Neumann needed to hear: He opposed the bill when it passed the House, 262-165.

Neumann's stand infuriated Appropriations Chairman Robert L. Livingston, R-La. Gingrich met with the freshman and stressed that he expected complete loyalty from GOP members on Appropriations and Rules.

But Neumann continued to stand out in the front ranks of conservative Republican deficit hawks. In May 1995, he joined with Rep. Gerald B. H. Solomon, R-N.Y., chairman of the Rules Committee, in offering a budget blueprint that eliminated the deficit in just five years, faster than other alternatives. The Neumann-Solomon plan was defeated, 89-342.

Neumann has also been active with a group of members who call themselves the "porkbusters," scouring appropriations bills for "obnoxious things" and offering floor amendments to excise them. His targets included a proposed Army museum on the banks of the Potomac River, houses costing more than $200,000 each for senior Air Force officers, a new 18-hole golf course at Andrews Air Force Base (near Washington, D.C.), and an $800,000 U.S. contribution to an international conservation fund for elephants, tigers and rhinos.

Some of Neumann's cost-cutting efforts annoyed important people. Gingrich, who has a longstanding interest in zoos, spoke on the floor in defense of the conservation fund expenditure, saying, "We don't have to cut mindlessly just to get to a balanced budget." Neumann's proposed cut lost, 132-289. Six of the expensive officer dwellings were to be built at Nellis Air Force Base in Nevada, home state of Barbara Vucanovich of Nevada, then chair of Appropriations' Military Construction subcommittee. Neumann's amendment slicing $7 million from the Air Force housing account prevailed, 266-160.

Such deeds stirred talk that the leadership would punish Neumann, but he was undeterred and unsparing of his colleagues. In June 1995, he recalled lobbying members at a door to the House chambers during one budget-cutting vote and hearing a lawmaker whose project was under attack say over and over, "It's in my district; help me out here."

"It's that thinking," Neumann said, "that led to a $4 trillion debt."

Neumann finally appeared to have overtaxed the leadership's patience in September 1995 with his vote against the $243 billion defense spending bill. Neumann had sponsored an amendment to the bill, approved by voice vote on the House floor, requiring congressional approval before President Clinton could send U.S. troops to Bosnia. But the measure was watered down in conference and made non-binding, prompting Neumann to vote against final clearance of the entire appropriation for defense.

As punishment, Livingston — with Gingrich's

WISCONSIN 1
Southeast — Racine; Kenosha

Although it is dominated by four industrialized cities, the 1st is far from a Democratic stronghold: It voted out its Democratic incumbent, Peter W. Barca, in 1994 after narrowly electing him in a 1993 special election.

Until Les Aspin's election in 1970, Democrats had won this district only twice in the 20th century — in 1958 and 1964. Both incumbents were defeated after serving single terms. The party also endured a long dry spell in presidential voting here. After Lyndon B. Johnson carried the district in 1964, not until 1988 did it return to the Democratic column, with a 51 percent victory for Michael S. Dukakis. Bill Clinton won the 1st by 5 percentage points in 1992 and by 12 percentage points in 1996.

The district's two largest cities are sandwiched between Milwaukee and Chicago along Lake Michigan: Racine, originally settled by Danish immigrants, and Kenosha, with a sizable Italian community.

Two of the district's largest employers are located in Racine: J. I. Case, makers of farm equipment, and S. C. Johnson and Son, which makes home-care products. The Racine lakefront has been revitalized with a marina and condominiums. Racine is also known for its thin, buttery Danish pastries known as kringles. Kenosha has a branch of the University of Wisconsin and a Chrysler plant where about 1,100 people make Jeep engines. The city was dealt a sharp blow by the December 1988 closure of the main Chrysler-AMC plant, a cornerstone of Kenosha's economy for almost nine decades. Chrysler spent millions of dollars in severance pay, economic development aid and contributions to local civic groups, and the state helped retrain workers.

Kenosha's economic base is diversifying, and the area's affordable real estate prices have attracted some Chicago commuters. A corporate park opened in Pleasant Prairie, just east of Interstate 94. Kenosha is still the headquarters for Jockey International Inc. and the Snap-On Tools Corp., which employs more than 1,000 people. The city also has two outlet shopping centers; another lure for visitors is Dairyland, the nation's largest greyhound dog racing track.

Although labor's political clout in the 1st has diminished with the loss of industry, Kenosha County remains Democratic, despite the GOP takeover of the district. Clinton polled 52 percent and Democratic House nominee Lydia C. Spottswood got 53 percent in the county. Racine County is a political battleground; Clinton won with 50 percent and Neumann polled 52 percent.

In the west-central part of the district are the smaller industrial cities of Janesville and Beloit, in politically marginal Rock County. Beloit was settled by a group of immigrants from New Hampshire that founded Beloit College in 1846. Janesville's employers include a General Motors plant.

The strongest GOP vote in the 1st comes from Walworth County in the middle of the district, which Dole carried with 46 percent. Neumann garnered 61 percent in the county; his 7,128-vote margin there greatly aided his re-election. Resort complexes around Lake Geneva and Lake Delavan cater to wealthy vacationers from Milwaukee and Chicago. Soybeans grow so well in rural Walworth County that the Japanese Kikkoman soy sauce company built a plant in Walworth to brew and bottle its product.

1990 Population: 543,530. White 500,231 (92%), Black 29,539 (5%), Other 13,760 (3%). Hispanic origin 18,652 (3%). 18 and over 397,289 (73%), 62 and over 81,464 (15%). Median age: 33.

consent — announced Oct. 11 that Neumann would be demoted from the National Security Subcommittee to the less prestigious Military Construction panel. But howls of protest rose up from Neumann's freshman classmates, and on Oct. 12, the leadership appeased them by giving Neumann a prized seat on the Budget Committee.

A week later, an article in The Washington Post revealed that the iconoclastic Neumann has at least some "politics as usual" tendencies. The newspaper reported that Neumann in July had used his post on the National Security subcommittee to help a diesel engine builder in his district get an inside track on securing Navy contracts. In a subcommittee meeting closed to the public, Neumann asked for a provision in the Pentagon spending bill requiring that several diesel engines in Navy vessels be manufactured domestically by a U.S.-owned company. The language, Neumann told the Post, was meant to benefit the largest employer in the 1st District city of Beloit, the Fairbanks Morse Engine Division of Coltec Holdings Inc.

Notwithstanding that parochial venture, it is clear that most of Neumann's efforts on Appropriations are aimed at getting the government to spend less money, not more. He opposed efforts in the fiscal 1997 Interior spending bill to provide $400,000 to protect African elephants. He fought legislation to authorize $3 million for a fellowship program in honor of former President George Bush at Texas A&M University.

He compiled a list of more than $334.5 million in "pork projects" in the fiscal 1997 VA, HUD and independent agencies spending bill. He was particularly irked that conferees on the measure would draw money for pet projects out of a national pool of revolving-loan funds for water and sewer improvements, reducing the share that each state will receive by formula. He tried to convince appropriators to drop the specific projects and let all of the revolving loan money be doled out by formula.

"Is this the worst I've seen?" he said. "Yes, it is."

Also, in June 1996 he led the fight that almost derailed the fiscal 1997 budget resolution, which projected that the deficit would increase in the short-term before heading to zero in 2002. "I won't vote for the deficit going up," Neumann said.

Neumann's voting record on social issues is firmly conservative, with an occasional nod toward moderation. In May 1996, he voted for the original House bill raising the minimum wage, though he also voted to exempt small businesses from paying the higher salaries. He also voted for the final bill that increased the minimum wage by 90 cents an hour.

At Home: As 1997 got under way, Neumann seriously was considering challenging first-term Democratic Sen. Russell D. Feingold in 1998. He traveled around the state, starting to drum up support for the effort.

Should he run for the Senate, it would mean giving up the House seat that he ran for three times in as many years.

A millionaire home builder with a small-town political base and strong backing from religious conservatives, Neumann began the chase in 1992 as a challenger to 11-term Democrat Les Aspin, then chairman of the House Armed Services Committee. Aspin had to work unusually hard for re-election, but he won with 58 percent of the vote.

When Aspin became secretary of Defense early in 1993, Neumann ran in the special election to fill the vacancy and lost by fewer than 700 votes to Democrat Peter W. Barca, a state legislator and former teacher from Kenosha. But in 1994 Neumann turned the tables, ousting Barca by 1,120 votes.

The biggest difference between the 1994 race and the earlier contests was the electorate's conservative mood and the broad target presented by Barca's votes in the 103rd Congress. Although he had won his seat declaring his independence from Clinton, Barca usually voted with the president and the party leadership. And almost every vote he cast became ammunition for Neumann.

Neumann started early raising money for his 1996 re-election campaign. Barca declined to run again and Democrats had problems finding another candidate to take on the incumbent. But Kenosha City Council President Lydia C. Spottswood won a four-way primary and proved to be a stronger challenger than expected. With the support of organized labor, Spottswood hammered Neumann for voting to roll back government programs such as Medicare. Neumann won a second term by fewer than 5,000 votes.

HOUSE ELECTIONS

1996 General		
Mark W. Neumann (R)	118,408	(51%)
Lydia C. Spottswood (D)	114,148	(49%)
1994 General		
Mark W. Neumann (R)	83,937	(49%)
Peter W. Barca (D)	82,817	(49%)
Edward J. Kozak (LIBERT)	3,085	(2%)

CAMPAIGN FINANCE

	Receipts	Receipts from PACs	Expend-itures
1996			
Neumann (R)	$1,252,043	$314,112 (25%)	$1,211,134
Spottswood (D)	$689,422	$222,307 (32%)	$708,825
1994			
Neumann (R)	$513,509	$70,496 (14%)	$512,091
Barca (D)	$649,298	$367,624 (57%)	$671,438

DISTRICT VOTE FOR PRESIDENT

1996		1992	
D	117,267 (50%)	**D**	109,790 (41%)
R	88,560 (38%)	**R**	94,712 (36%)
I	25,986 (11%)	**I**	62,465 (23%)

KEY VOTES

1997	
Ban "partial birth" abortions	Y
1996	
Approve farm bill	N
Deny public education to illegal immigrants	Y
Repeal ban on certain assault-style weapons	Y
Increase minimum wage	Y
Freeze defense spending	Y
Approve welfare overhaul	Y
1995	
Approve balanced-budget constitutional amendment	Y
Relax Clean Water Act regulations	Y
Oppose limits on environmental regulations	N
Reduce projected Medicare spending	Y
Approve GOP budget with tax and spending cuts	Y

VOTING STUDIES

	Presidential Support		Party Unity		Conservative Coalition	
Year	**S**	**O**	**S**	**O**	**S**	**O**
1996	43	57	84	15	51	49
1995	20	77	91	6	81	18

INTEREST GROUP RATINGS

Year	ADA	AFL-CIO	CCUS	ACU
1996	15	n/a	69	95
1995	0	18	100	100

2 Scott L. Klug (R)

Of Madison — Elected 1990, 4th term

Biographical Information

Born: Jan. 16, 1953, Milwaukee, Wis.

Education: Lawrence U., B.A. 1975; Northwestern U., M.S.J. 1976; U. of Wisconsin, M.B.A. 1990.

Occupation: Television journalist; business development and investment executive.

Family: Wife, Tess Summers; three children.

Religion: Roman Catholic.

Political Career: No previous office.

Capitol Office: 2331 Rayburn Bldg. 20515; 225-2906.

Committees

Commerce
Finance & Hazardous Materials; Health & Environment; Telecommunications, Trade & Consumer Protection

In Washington: Klug has announced his intention to leave the House at the end of this, his fourth term, but he is not going quietly.

When Newt Gingrich stood for re-election as House Speaker in January 1997, Klug was one of the few Republicans not on board; he voted present. At the end of February, Klug said he would not seek re-election in 1998. "Anybody who knows me knows I wasn't in it for the long haul," he said. "My 5-year-old has never really known anything except, 'It's Tuesday and Daddy is getting on a plane' " to fly to Washington.

Klug's reputation as a moderate has kept him in step with his district, which gave Bill Clinton a majority of its votes in 1992 and 1996. He voted for the ban on certain semiautomatic assault-style weapons in 1994 and against GOP-led efforts to repeal the ban in 1996. In the 103rd Congress, he voted for the family leave law and for the "motor voter" bill to register voters.

But he often votes with the Republican leadership. In the 104th Congress, he supported efforts to overhaul welfare, cut back federal regulations, limit awards to consumers injured by faulty products and establish a constitutional amendment requiring term limits. Initially, he opposed raising the minimum wage and supported efforts to exempt small businesses from paying the higher wage, and he also sided with business in voting to allow companies to offer their employees compensatory time off rather than overtime pay.

As one of the House's leading deficit hawks, Klug backed the Republican effort to balance the budget by 2002, in part by reducing the rate of spending growth on Medicaid and Medicare. He supports a balanced-budget constitutional amendment. In 1996, he voted against authorizing $7 billion more in defense spending than President Clinton requested, opposed the farm bill after Midwestern lawmakers failed to eliminate a series of milk marketing orders that favored Northeastern dairy farmers, voted against expanding export promotion programs, and voted to end the authorization for the space station. In 1993, he voted to kill the superconducting super collider.

In June 1996, he was one of 60 Republicans who supported an amendment to the fiscal 1997 defense appropriations bill to freeze spending at fiscal 1996 levels. The amendment failed, 194-219. "It's a test for Republicans, whether we're going to apply the same kind of scrutiny [to the Pentagon] that we apply to every other agency," Klug said.

Also in June, he supported an amendment to the fiscal 1997 Interior appropriations bill to cut $42 million from the account that funds road construction on federal timber tracts. "The issue is not whether you do it," Klug said. "The issue is the price tag. And we think we are getting jobbed." After passing by one vote, the amendment came up for a revote and failed on a tie vote.

He unsuccessfully tried to wield the budget ax against other federal expenditures as well. In July 1995, he introduced an amendment to the fiscal 1996 energy and water development spending bill to kill the Appalachian Regional Commission, which builds roads and encourages economic development in 13 states. Klug's amendment failed, 108-319.

But Klug did succeed in eliminating a $20 million appropriation for development of a gas turbine modular helium reactor. The Energy Department estimates that in the last 25 years, taxpayers have spent more than $900 million trying to develop a nuclear plant technology that would burn excess weapons-grade plutonium and that it could cost an additional $1 billion to complete construction of a demonstration model.

While trying to cut some programs, Klug pushed an amendment through that earmarked $45 million for a program to spur the export of U.S. solar technology, which he says is necessary to reduce dependence on foreign oil. The House adopted the amendment, 214-208.

In October 1995, Klug offered an amendment to the authorization bill for civilian sciences programs to privatize all the Energy Department laboratories other than the Los Alamos, Sandia and Lawrence Livermore national laboratories. He said Congress ought to move toward selling them "if

Once described by former GOP Gov. Lee Dreyfus as "23 square miles surrounded by reality," Madison has long been Wisconsin's liberal centerpiece — Progressive magazine is published here — and it is one of the few cities with a foreign policy. Since 1924, when Robert M. La Follette carried Dane County as the Progressive Party's presidential candidate, Democrats nearly always won here.

But times have changed, and politics have moderated considerably in the 2nd District. This was graphically demonstrated by Republican Klug's 1990 upset of Democratic Rep. Robert W. Kastenmeier, a 32-year veteran, and Klug's subsequent easy re-elections.

As the state's capital and home to its main university campus, Madison is dominated by its white-collar sector. About one-third of the area's work force is employed in government, primarily for the state or the University of Wisconsin, which helps keep employment stable. White-collar jobs are also supplied by several locally based insurance companies, such as American Family and CUNA Mutual. In addition, meat processor Oscar Mayer employs more than 3,200 in Madison, and battery-maker Rayovac has headquarters here. Madison also is home to a growing biotechnology industry.

Beyond the city limits, rapidly growing Dane County suburbs such as Verona, Fitchburg and Middleton strike a more conservative tone than the city itself, as do outlying communities such as Stoughton and Mount Horeb. But Democrats usually have carried Dane. Democratic Senate candidate Herb Kohl polled 58 percent in 1988, then got 73 percent in his 1994 re-election. Yet Klug won the county by more than 40,000 votes in 1992 and 1994. Although Klug's margin in

WISCONSIN 2
South — Madison

Dane narrowed to just under 15,000 in 1996, he still won re-election with 57 percent even as Bill Clinton carried the district with 55 percent.

The 2nd also covers a sizable portion of southern Wisconsin's Republican-voting rural areas, where farmers and small-town folks have long chafed at Madison's dominance of district politics. Outside the Madison area, agriculture and tourism sustain the district's economy. Dairying is important, and there is some beef production, although many livestock farmers have switched to raising corn as a cash crop.

In New Glarus (Green County), which was founded by the Swiss, the downtown resembles a village in the mother country. Wisconsin Dells (Columbia County) lures tourists to view the garish attractions and natural wonders along the Wisconsin River. Just outside Spring Green (Sauk County) is Frank Lloyd Wright's Taliesin, a studio complex used by the legendary architect that is now a thriving artist colony.

About 50 miles west of Madison is Dodgeville (Iowa County), headquarters to mail-order clothier Lands' End. Since the company moved here in 1978, property values have increased, the local economy has blossomed and additional facilities were opened in Cross Plains (Dane County) and Reedsburg (Sauk County.)

1990 Population: 543,532. White 519,172 (96%), Black 11,147 (2%), Other 13,213 (2%). Hispanic origin 6,743 (1%). 18 and over 412,393 (76%), 62 and over 73,613 (14%). Median age: 32.

colleagues are serious about cutting back on the $6 billion we now devote to the Department of Energy facilities, if we are serious about moving away from the Cold War mission, and if we are serious about preserving those laboratories but doing it without taxpayer subsidies." But the House rejected it on a voice vote.

Another of Klug's budget-cutting crusades that appears to be making more headway is an effort to do away with the $100 million-plus annual federal subsidy to the Tennessee Valley Authority (TVA). In July 1995, Klug sought to eliminate the subsidies with an amendment to the fiscal 1996 energy and water development appropriations bill, but he failed, 144-284. He plans to try again in the new Congress. "It is the fundamental question of 1997: What is the federal government doing in the electric power business?" Klug asks.

He was buoyed when TVA Chairman Craven Crowell in January 1997 said he favored ending the subsidies — which finance TVA functions such as recreation-area management — so the agency can shuck non-power generating activities currently mandated by the federal government and concentrate simply on making and selling electric power. "Obviously we've won," Klug said. "TVA understands if we cut off welfare recipients after two years of aid, it's a little difficult to justify subsidies for TVA after 60 years. They know the divorce is coming."

Klug generally supports abortion rights. In the 104th, he voted to allow the health care plan for federal employees to pay for abortions, to allow abortions to be performed at overseas military hospitals and to require states to pay for abortions under Medicaid in cases of rape or incest. But he voted to ban a particular abortion technique that opponents call a "partial birth" abortion.

Klug also has been active on environmental issues. In April 1996, the House approved by voice vote Klug-sponsored legislation to phase out the use of mercury in batteries and to establish new labeling requirements for rechargeable batteries. The measure also cleared the Senate. The bill addressed problems caused by battery disposal. Common household batteries generally are made of alkaline-manganese and zinc-carbon, but some, such as ones used in medical, military or computer equipment, also contain mercury. When disposed of in a landfill, the mercury breaks down and pollutes groundwater; if incinerated, it produces toxic emissions.

In the 102nd Congress, Klug became a ringleader in the "Gang of Seven," the group of freshman GOP members whose criticism of the House bank led to the exposure of overdrafters and the closing of the bank.

At Home: In just six years, Klug turned Wisconsin's 2nd from a Democratic stronghold to a Republican district. The question is whether voters will return to a Democrat after Klug leaves.

Madison Mayor Paul Soglin was the last Democrat to run into Klug's buzz saw, losing by 16 points in 1996. Soglin attempted to link Klug to the conservative Republican majority, but the incumbent pointed to his votes against such GOP initiatives as repealing the assault weapons ban and revising the clean water act.

When Klug, a former TV journalist who had never held office, began a 1990 campaign to unseat 32-year House incumbent Robert W. Kastenmeier, hardly anyone — from the national GOP to Kastenmeier's local supporters — took his challenge seriously.

But Klug had high name familiarity from two years as an investigative reporter and news anchor on WKOW-TV in Madison, and he campaigned effectively against the liberal Kastenmeier, a local institution still revered for his early opposition to the Vietnam War, as an anachronism typical of an ineffective Congress. Klug made congressional term limits a centerpiece of his campaign.

While Madison itself has a reputation for doctrinaire liberalism, Klug sought to identify himself with the pocketbook concerns of young families in the growing suburbs of surrounding Dane County and the rural counties beyond that. Kastenmeier depicted his opponent as a carpetbagger, but Klug was far from foreign, having grown up in the Milwaukee area and gotten a business degree at the University of Wisconsin.

In the end, the incumbent carried Dane County, but by fewer than 4,000 votes. Klug prevailed by more than 15,000 votes in the surrounding counties.

As a freshman, Klug solidified his support with frequent visits home and a voting record that appealed to the mainstream. In his first re-election bid in 1992, Klug faced Ada. E. Deer, a Democratic activist and lecturer at the University of Wisconsin who promoted her efforts to become the first American Indian woman in Congress. Deer later became head of the Bureau of Indian Affairs under Clinton.

But Deer proved disappointing as a campaigner, and her reform message did not sell well against Klug. Eschewing contributions from special interests, she raised only about 60 percent as much money as Klug, who was re-elected easily with more than 60 percent of the vote.

In 1994, Democrats fielded an unknown state official, Thomas C. Hecht, who, despite raising $250,000, did not make the fall contest close.

HOUSE ELECTIONS

1996 General		
Scott L. Klug (R)	154,557	(57%)
Paul R. Soglin (D)	110,467	(41%)
Ben Masel (LIBERT)	4,226	(2%)
1994 General		
Scott L. Klug (R)	133,734	(69%)
Thomas C. Hecht (D)	55,406	(29%)
John J. Stumpf (TAX)	2,676	(1%)

Previous Winning Percentages: 1992 (63%) **1990** (53%)

CAMPAIGN FINANCE

	Receipts	Receipts from PACs	Expend-itures
1996			
Klug (R)	$1,163,141	$427,875 (37%)	$1,261,546
Soglin (D)	$506,691	$126,500 (25%)	$506,513
1994			
Klug (R)	$758,115	$249,817 (33%)	$689,215
Hecht (D)	$282,043	$79,900 (28%)	$281,783

DISTRICT VOTE FOR PRESIDENT

1996		1992	
D	146,913 (55%)	**D**	149,340 (50%)
R	88,140 (33%)	**R**	94,368 (32%)
I	21,698 (8%)	**I**	52,552 (18%)

KEY VOTES

1997	
Ban "partial birth" abortions	Y
1996	
Approve farm bill	N
Deny public education to illegal immigrants	Y
Repeal ban on certain assault-style weapons	N
Increase minimum wage	N
Freeze defense spending	Y
Approve welfare overhaul	Y
1995	
Approve balanced-budget constitutional amendment	Y
Relax Clean Water Act regulations	N
Oppose limits on environmental regulations	Y
Reduce projected Medicare spending	Y
Approve GOP budget with tax and spending cuts	Y

VOTING STUDIES

	Presidential Support		Party Unity		Conservative Coalition	
Year	S	O	S	O	S	O
1996	46	54	75	25	51	49
1995	35	65	82	17	68	32
1994	51	49	79	20	61	39
1993	50	49	74	24	64	36
1992	54	45	73	24	67	33
1991	68	32	67	31	76	22

INTEREST GROUP RATINGS

Year	ADA	AFL-CIO	CCUS	ACU
1996	40	n/a	81	75
1995	25	8	88	72
1994	45	44	75	43
1993	40	33	73	58
1992	40	33	63	56
1991	35	33	80	55

3 Ron Kind (D)

Of La Crosse — Elected 1996, 1st term

Biographical Information

Born: March 16, 1963, La Crosse, Wis.
Education: Harvard U., B.A. 1985; London School of Economics, M.A. 1986; U. of Minnesota, J.D. 1990.
Occupation: Lawyer.
Family: Wife, Tawni Zappa; one child.
Religion: Lutheran.
Political Career: No previous office.
Capitol Office: 1713 Longworth Bldg. 20515; 225-5506.

Committees

Education & Workforce
Oversight & Investigations; Postsecondary Education, Training & Life-Long Learning

Resources
National Parks & Public Lands; Water & Power

The Path to Washington: In 1996, Kind told voters that he would be an independent-minded representative like the man he was seeking to succeed, Republican Steve Gunderson. Benefiting from Gunderson's ambivalence about the GOP nominee, former state Sen. Jim Harsdorf, Kind won the district seat with 52 percent of the vote.

Although he won't have much chance of implementing it as a freshman in the House minority, Kind offered his own balanced-budget plan during the 1996 campaign. It aimed to eliminate or reduce 80 spending programs, many of which are operated by the Defense Department. He also called for eliminating 56 "corporate subsidies and tax breaks." Another key element to balancing the budget is controlling the costs of Medicare and Medicaid, Kind said, and he proposed doing that through comprehensive reform of the health care system.

A former county prosecutor, Kind also says he would like to see the federal government provide better coordination to help local authorities catch criminals. He backs the development of a national database that would increase the sharing of resources and information between local, state and federal law enforcement agencies.

While he says he supports quick and severe punishment for criminals, Kind believes that government could help local communities reach children before they turn to crime by continuing federal funding for programs such as Head Start.

As a member of the Education and the Workforce Committee, Kind has had a chance to work on such issues. He also would like to increase funding for school-to-work programs that provide vocational training for students who choose not to go to college.

Unlike Gunderson, Kind did not land a spot on the Agriculture Committee, but he says he will continue to work to reform the milk marketing order system, which Wisconsin dairy farmers say puts them at a disadvantage in competing with Northeastern dairy producers. Kind also got a seat on the Resources Committee.

Kind had to get past four other opponents in the 1996 primary. His biggest rival for the party's nod was Lee Rasch, who lost in the 1994 primary. Rasch tried to portray himself as the moderate in the race, while painting Kind as a liberal.

Both Rasch and Kind were listed as candidates from La Crosse, one of the district's largest cities. But Kind stressed that he had been born and raised in La Crosse, unlike Rasch, who did not grow up in the district. Kind comfortably defeated Rasch, 46 percent to 29 percent.

Kind is a local success story. A high school football star, he won an academic scholarship to Harvard University. He later went on to earn a master's degree at the London School of Economics and a law degree from the University of Minnesota. After a brief stint at a Milwaukee law firm, Kind moved back to his hometown and became a local prosecutor.

Harsdorf, meanwhile, had no major competition for his party's nomination, but he still walked into the general-election race in a weakened position. Throughout the first half of 1996, Gunderson had expressed interest in reversing his retirement decision, particularly after a series of circumstances put him in line to chair the Agriculture Committee in the 105th Congress.

Despite his obvious interest, Gunderson said he would not get into the race unless Harsdorf stepped aside. Harsdorf refused. Gunderson honored his commitment to retire, despite pleas from some dairy groups and an effort to organize a primary write-in campaign. In the end, however, Gunderson refused to endorse Harsdorf — a factor some observers considered key to Kind's win.

Kind tried to cast Harsdorf as a right-wing Republican who would walk in lock step with House Speaker Newt Gingrich. At the same time, he touted himself as an independent thinker in the mold of former Democratic Sen. William Proxmire (1957-1989), for whom he once interned. He also compared his independence to that of Gunderson, a moderate who was the first openly homosexual Republican in the House.

WISCONSIN 3
West — Eau Claire; La Crosse

In a state that bills itself as "America's Dairyland," the 3rd stands at the head of the herd. It has more cows than people and is one of the leading milk-producing districts in the nation. But some dramatic economic and demographic changes are taking place in the 3rd, which hugs Wisconsin's western border with Minnesota and Iowa. Traditionally, the rural areas have relied mainly on small dairy farms, and its two biggest cities, Eau Claire and La Crosse, have been strongly influenced by heavy manufacturing.

Now, the cities are finding alternatives to heavy industry, and the communities closest to the Twin Cities are becoming thriving suburbs. The more successful dairy farms have evolved into multifamily operations, and tourism in some rural areas has taken hold. But downsizing of the dairy industry has taken its toll, particularly in rural communities without easy access to Interstate 94.

As a result, while the district's population growth in the 1980s mirrored the 4 percent increase in the state as a whole, there were wide differences within the 3rd. All of the counties along the district's northern edge (east and northeast of Minneapolis-St. Paul) grew during the decade. The pacesetter was St. Croix County, immediately east of the Twin Cities, which grew by 16 percent. But all of the counties in the southern two-thirds of the district lost population, except for La Crosse County, which grew by 8 percent.

There are only two cities of size in the district. Eau Claire, once a wild lumber outpost, has a paper mill producing disposable diapers and napkins. A Uniroyal plant that was once the city's largest employer is no more. Blue-collar jobs have been replaced by white-collar opportunities in such areas as health care.

La Crosse, Wisconsin's only major Mississippi River city, once featured two locally owned Fortune 500 companies as its mainstays — the Trane Co., manufacturers of heating and air conditioning equipment, and G. Heileman Brewing Inc. But both were subject to hostile takeovers in the 1980s. Employment at both scaled down, then stabilized.

Democrats traditionally have held sway in the northern part of the district, around Eau Claire, and Republicans have had an edge in the south and in La Crosse. Some of those identifications are changing with the economy, making the area quite competitive in state elections. Democrats have been gaining lately. Kind's victory was built on having received a combined 57 percent (and a 12,791-vote margin) in Eau Claire and La Crosse counties. Bill Clinton won the 3rd with about 50 percent of the votes in 1996.

The 3rd remains heavily Scandinavian and German — dairy farmers in Osseo (Trempealeau County) still trade gossip over coffee and pie at the Norske Nook — though there are signs of more ethnic diversity. The district also boasts five state university branches, helping entice three National Football League teams to set up summer training camps there.

1990 Population: 543,533. White 532,723 (98%), Black 1,329 (<1%), Other 9,481 (2%). Hispanic origin 2,632 (<1%). 18 and over 398,432 (73%), 62 and over 89,022 (16%). Median age: 32.

HOUSE ELECTIONS

1996 General		
Ron Kind (D)	121,967	(52%)
Jim Harsdorf (R)	112,146	(48%)
1996 Primary		
Ron Kind (D)	13,685	(46%)
Lee Rasch (D)	8,582	(29%)
Tim Bakken (D)	5,370	(18%)
Mark Weinhold (D)	1,108	(4%)
Joe Monahan (D)	996	(3%)

CAMPAIGN FINANCE

	Receipts	Receipts from PACs	Expend-itures
1996			
Kind (D)	$501,680	$204,441 (41%)	$497,919
Harsdorf (R)	$491,045	$162,328 (33%)	$507,175

DISTRICT VOTE FOR PRESIDENT

	1996		1992
D	120,722 (50%)	**D**	120,261 (43%)
R	82,682 (34%)	**R**	90,731 (33%)
I	33,328 (14%)	**I**	67,134 (24%)

KEY VOTES

1997

Ban "partial birth" abortions Y

4 Gerald D. Kleczka (D)

Of Milwaukee — Elected 1984; 7th full term

Biographical Information
Born: Nov. 26, 1943, Milwaukee, Wis.
Education: U. of Wisconsin, 1961-62, 1967, 1970.
Military Service: Air National Guard, 1963-69.
Occupation: Accountant.
Family: Wife, Bonnie L. Scott.
Religion: Roman Catholic.
Political Career: Wis. Assembly, 1969-73; Wis. Senate, 1975-84.
Capitol Office: 2301 Rayburn Bldg. 20515; 225-4572.

Committees
Ways & Means
Health; Oversight

In Washington: After waiting nearly a decade for a seat on the Ways and Means Committee, Kleczka finally got one in the 103rd Congress. But his tenure in the majority there was brief, as Democrats lost control of the House in 1994. Kleczka himself stumbled to re-election that year, taking a career-low 54 percent.

The 104th Congress brought some more ill winds for Kleczka. A 1995 drunken driving arrest in a Washington, D.C., suburb — his third drinking-related arrest — prompted Kleczka to announce that he was entering an alcohol abuse treatment center.

Yet despite his personal problems and minority status on Ways and Means, Kleczka was a player in the legislative process during the 104th. And although in past years he had built a reputation for staying loyal to the Democratic leadership on difficult issues, he supported more than a few elements of the Republican agenda.

As the GOP sought to push through a welfare overhaul plan, Kleczka joined conservative Republican Jim McCrery of Louisiana to draft provisions regarding the Supplemental Security Income program. Kleczka had long criticized the children's disability benefits portion of the program as rife with fraud. The new provisions eliminated most federal payments to disabled children's families and replaced them with block grants to the states; also ended were disability payments to drug addicts and alcoholics.

When Republicans brought their welfare overhaul plan before Ways and Means in 1995, Kleczka was the only Democrat to support it. He voted "pass" on a Democratic alternative to the bill, and voted against President Clinton's competing welfare plan when it was introduced.

After Clinton vetoed two GOP welfare proposals, Kleczka was one of only 30 Democrats who supported the GOP's third welfare-overhaul proposal in mid-July 1996. It took another round of Republican compromising with Clinton before the House in late July passed a welfare bill the president agreed to sign; half the voting House Democrats (including Kleczka) supported it.

Kleczka also joined with Republicans and some Democrats in 1996 to support a temporary cut in the federal gasoline tax. A spike in gasoline prices spurred GOP leaders to push for the cut. Some Ways and Means Democrats accused Republicans of election-year "pandering" (struggling GOP presidential nominee Bob Dole was also promoting the gas tax cut). Kleczka not only backed the tax cut, but also went further, calling for a 10-cent per gallon reduction that exceeded the 4.3-cent reduction backed by Republicans.

Kleczka also sided initially with Republicans as Ways and Means considered a bill to extend the portability of health insurance. The idea was bipartisan, although most committee Democrats opposed the GOP including medical savings accounts in the bill, regarding the accounts as a first step in privatizing more of the health care system. Kleczka, too, opposed the accounts, but he was one of only four Democrats voting in committee for the portability bill, which included them.

However, when the GOP brought a portability bill to the House floor, Kleczka opposed it, as did most Democrats. Later negotiations produced a compromise measure that became law.

A streak of cultural conservatism is sometimes evident in Kleczka's stands on social issues. He often shares common ground with the majority of House Republicans who oppose abortion. In the 104th, he voted against permitting abortions at overseas military hospitals, and against allowing federal employees' health care plans to cover abortions. He also supports banning a particular abortion technique that opponents call "partial birth" abortion.

However, he voted in March 1996 to require states to fund Medicaid abortions for poor women in cases of rape, incest or to save the life of the woman. And in February 1997, he sided with the Clinton's administration request for early release of $385 million for international family planning programs, a move most anti-abortion members opposed.

On another hot-button social issue in the

The heart of Milwaukee has long been its South Side bungalow belt, whose plain but sturdy houses evoke the 1950s. Television viewers still associate the city with the setting for "Laverne and Shirley." Milwaukee has worked hard to promote itself as cosmopolitan, but many residents still value bowling, bratwurst and beer. This area is home to conservative Democrats.

Since the turn of the century, the city's huge Polish community has been based on its South Side, and the area remains predominantly Polish and German. Neighborhoods are conspicuously tidy; residents regularly sweep the gutters and scrub the sidewalks. The mix of ethnic groups has made Serb Hall a traditional meeting place for Friday fish fries as well as for candidates seeking working-class votes. The city's strong ethnic heritage is celebrated nearly every summer weekend during a series of lakefront festivals, immediately southeast of downtown.

The migration of some white ethnics to nearby southern suburbs has made room for a wider mix on the South Side. A Hispanic community is growing on the Near South Side, populated mainly by Mexicans and Puerto Ricans. A large population of Vietnamese and Laotians is also located here.

For years, manufacturing was the dominant occupation on the South Side. Although service-industry jobs have increased, many in the 4th still make machinery for mining and construction, and electronic equipment. Johnson Controls Inc., Delco Electronics and Harnischfeger Industries all have a strong presence in the district. Allen-Bradley Co./Rockwell Automation is known both for its increasingly automated plant and for displaying the world's largest four-sided analog clock, which stands tall among the South Side church steeples.

WISCONSIN 4
Southern Milwaukee and Milwaukee County suburbs; southeast Waukesha County

West Allis-based Allis-Chalmers, which at its height was one of the state's biggest employers, is out of business.

While the population of both the city and the county of Milwaukee declined during the 1980s, some of the south suburbs grew, including Oak Creek (15 percent) and Franklin (nearly 30 percent). These suburbs, along with Hales Corners, have attracted young middle-management types, while South Shore suburbs like Cudahy and South Milwaukee are primarily blue-collar.

Just west of Milwaukee County, the 4th includes the Waukesha County suburbs of New Berlin and Muskego, which grew by 10 percent in the '80s, as well as the city of Waukesha, which grew by 13 percent.

Some of the migrants who left the city for the suburbs also left the Democratic Party. Democratic presidential candidates used to exceed their statewide average in the 4th, but Bill Clinton's showing here matched his statewide average in 1992 and 1996. The district includes only a part of Waukesha County — which is a Republican stronghold — though the city of Waukesha itself leans Democratic. Kleczka lost Waukesha County by nearly 7,000 votes in 1996.

1990 Population: 543,527. White 510,138 (94%), Black 4,778 (1%), Other 28,611 (5%). Hispanic origin 34,354 (6%). 18 and over 410,090 (75%), 62 and over 87,474 (16%). Median age: 34.

104th, Kleczka voted to ban federal recognition of same-sex marriages. (In 1993, he had voted to lift the ban on homosexuals in the military.)

Kleczka's Democratic stripes are brightest on issues of concern to unionized blue-collar workers, a big element of his constituency. He reliably takes the side of organized labor in its disputes with the pro-business Republican leadership. He supported a minimum wage hike in 1996 and has opposed GOP efforts to allow companies to offer employees comp time in lieu of overtime pay.

He usually fights the GOP on its budget and spending proposals. In the 104th, Kleczka grumbled when Republican leaders chose the occasion of former President Ronald Reagan's birthday to bring forth a bill giving presidents line-item veto authority, a staple of Reagan White House rhetoric. Kleczka called the timetable "phony symbolism," and said, "If that's how we're going to legislate, then what kind of bill do we pass on President Ford's wedding anniversary?"

Kleczka (pronounced Kletch-kuh), is known for a sharp tongue. When former Banking subcommittee Chairman Frank Annunzio, D-Ill., butchered Kleczka's name once too often (calling him "Congressman Klee-zak"), he fired back, "Thank you, Chairman Annunciation."

After being arrested for drunken driving in Alexandria, Va., in 1995, Kleczka announced that he would enter a treatment center for alcohol abusers. "Despite repeated self-denial, I must admit I have a serious alcohol problem that requires immediate, professional treatment," he said in a statement.

An Alexandria traffic court sentenced him to 10 days in jail, fined him $300 and suspended his license for three years. Kleczka at first said he would appeal the decision, but changed his mind, and fulfilled most of his sentence by picking up trash and doing other chores as part of a work-release program. Kleczka had been arrested once before for drunken driving (in 1987) and for public drunkenness (in 1990).

Kleczka arrived at Ways and Means well-versed in the ways of government, having spent nearly all of his adult life in elective office. In 15 years in the Wisconsin Legislature, Kleczka ultimately rose to lead the Joint Finance Committee.

But after coming to Washington in 1985, he found his way to Ways and Means blocked by the presence there of fellow Milwaukeean Jim Moody. So for nine years Kleczka labored on the Banking Committee, learning the personalities and institutional workings of the House.

Being a good soldier for the Democratic leadership was a key to helping Kleczka win his Ways and Means slot. In 1992, for example, he cosponsored a joint resolution to amend the Constitution to require a balanced federal budget. Yet when that measure reached the House floor and the Democratic leadership needed every vote to deny it a two-thirds majority, Kleczka provided one. However, with Republicans in the House majority, Kleczka has voted for the budget amendment.

At Home: Kleczka won elections without difficulty before 1994, but that year's GOP surge lifted his unknown and underfinanced Republican opponent, printer Tom Reynolds, into contention.

By his estimation, Reynolds churned out 3 million pieces of literature attacking Kleczka as a liberal on a variety of issues. Kleczka hit back at the end of the campaign with TV ads that accused Reynolds of favoring cuts in Social Security, Medicare and student loans. Reynolds carried Republican Waukesha County, but Kleczka's sizable margin in Milwaukee County saved him.

Its interest piqued, the GOP establishment put forward a former state senator in 1996, but Reynolds beat him in the primary. This time, Kleczka was better prepared, launching an early TV ad campaign that touted his support for welfare reform, health care, the environment and Social Security. He improved to 58 percent.

When first elected at age 26 to the state Legislature, Kleczka was viewed as just one more neighborhood-minded ethnic Democrat from Milwaukee's South Side. He was seen as being focused more on local politics (including his feud with the city's long-tenured mayor, Henry Maier) than on broader issues. He had a reputation for hard-nosed campaigning and occasional quarrels on the Assembly floor. Over the years, though, he became known as an effective budget specialist in his role as Joint Finance Committee chairman.

When Democratic Rep. Clement J. Zablocki, the House Foreign Affairs chairman, died in late 1983, Kleczka was the front-runner to succeed him. Kleczka had no difficulty picking up support from state Senate colleagues and from economic interests over which Joint Finance held power. He claimed much of Zablocki's backing and was also the choice of the state's Democratic U.S. House delegation. His advertising stressed a different theme: his roots. One TV ad showed an infant in a crib and a grandfather, while a voice described Kleczka as "a leader and a neighbor."

The combination of money, endorsements and roots yielded 32 percent of the vote — enough to win in a five-way primary. He took 65 percent in the special election and coasted until 1994.

HOUSE ELECTIONS

1996 General		
Gerald D. Kleczka (D)	134,470	(58%)
Tom Reynolds (R)	98,438	(42%)
1996 Primary		
Gerald D. Kleczka (D)	30,199	(85%)
Roman R. Blenski (D)	4,962	(15%)
1994 General		
Gerald D. Kleczka (D)	93,709	(54%)
Tom Reynolds (R)	78,225	(45%)
James Harold Hause (TAX)	2,611	(1%)

Previous Winning Percentages: 1992 (66%) **1990** (69%) **1988** (100%) **1986** (100%) **1984** (67%) **1984†** (65%)

† Special election

CAMPAIGN FINANCE

	Receipts	Receipts from PACs	Expend-itures
1996			
Kleczka (D)	$937,136	$514,876 (55%)	$862,686
Reynolds (R)	$254,585	$2,216 (1%)	$253,357
1994			
Kleczka (D)	$536,336	$375,932 (70%)	$495,371
Reynolds (R)	$111,491	$2,221 (2%)	$111,356
Hause (TAX)	$4,430	0	$4,430

DISTRICT VOTE FOR PRESIDENT

1996		1992	
D	115,646 (49%)	**D**	116,048 (41%)
R	93,996 (40%)	**R**	108,463 (38%)
I	21,415 (9%)	**I**	59,263 (21%)

KEY VOTES

1997	
Ban "partial birth" abortions	Y
1996	
Approve farm bill	N
Deny public education to illegal immigrants	N
Repeal ban on certain assault-style weapons	N
Increase minimum wage	Y
Freeze defense spending	Y
Approve welfare overhaul	Y
1995	
Approve balanced-budget constitutional amendment	Y
Relax Clean Water Act regulations	-
Oppose limits on environmental regulations	Y
Reduce projected Medicare spending	N
Approve GOP budget with tax and spending cuts	N

VOTING STUDIES

	Presidential Support		Party Unity		Conservative Coalition	
Year	**S**	**O**	**S**	**O**	**S**	**O**
1996	78	22	83	16	25	75
1995	68	22	74	17	33	57
1994	86	13	92	6	33	61
1993	80	19	88	7	48	50
1992	20	78	93	4	33	63
1991	23	75	89	4	22	73

INTEREST GROUP RATINGS

Year	ADA	AFL-CIO	CCUS	ACU
1996	75	n/a	44	10
1995	70	92	41	25
1994	85	78	67	5
1993	80	100	18	13
1992	80	82	25	4
1991	85	91	11	0

5 Thomas M. Barrett (D)

Of Milwaukee — Elected 1992, 3rd term

Biographical Information

Born: Dec. 8, 1953, Milwaukee, Wis.
Education: U. of Wisconsin, B.A. 1976, J.D. 1980.
Occupation: Lawyer.
Family: Wife, Kristine Mansfield; three children.
Religion: Roman Catholic.
Political Career: Candidate for Wis. Assembly, 1982; Wis. Assembly, 1984-89; Wis. Senate, 1989-93.
Capitol Office: 1224 Longworth Bldg. 20515; 225-3571.

Committees

Banking & Financial Services
Capital Markets, Securities & Government Sponsored Enterprises; Financial Institutions & Consumer Credit

Government Reform & Oversight
Human Resources; National Security, International Affairs & Criminal Justice (ranking)

In Washington: The Milwaukee-born Barrett supports organized labor and generally votes a liberal line. That makes him a good fit for the Milwaukee-based 5th, a longtime blue-collar bastion that includes most of Wisconsin's black population and is easily the state's most solidly Democratic House district.

During nearly a decade in the state legislature, Barrett earned a reputation for doggedly pursuing his objectives. And since 1995, when Republicans took control of the House, one of his primary objectives has been trying to block GOP policies he thinks are wrongheaded. At times his rhetoric has been stinging.

In April 1997, as the Government Reform and Oversight Committee was embarking on an inquiry into 1996 campaign financing, Barrett fumed at Chairman Dan Burton, R-Ind., for not giving Democrats sufficient say in decisions over issuing committee subpoenas. "If this is going to be a kangaroo court," Barrett shouted, "we should get out of here right now.

At the start of the 105th Congress, Barrett moved into the ranking Democratic seat on the National Security, International Affairs and Criminal Justice panel of Government Reform and Oversight.

In the early months of 1995, Barrett was an outspoken opponent of many elements of the GOP's "Contract With America" legislative agenda. During a March 1995 speech on the House floor, he contended that a Republican block grant proposal would "close down the school lunch program."

"Why do the Republicans want to take milk and apples away from 6-year-olds in the United States of America?" he asked.

Barrett also threw himself into the debate over conservatives' efforts to overhaul the nation's welfare system.

Republicans in Congress had hailed Wisconsin GOP Gov. Tommy G. Thompson for a state welfare reform plan that they described as pioneering. But Barrett — who had many constituents who would be affected by the plan — expressed concerns that it went too far and would hurt people. He argued for increased state and federal funding to provide child care for aid recipients who would be thrust into the work force by any welfare overhaul.

In June 1996, House Republicans, trying to bypass President Clinton, passed a bill granting waivers of certain federal welfare rules, which would have allowed Wisconsin to implement its welfare plan. Barrett said the bill was a raw election-year bid to undercut Clinton, who three weeks earlier had surprised Republicans by endorsing the Wisconsin plan.

Barrett said the Republicans' attitude was, "'Let's try to embarrass the president. Let's take the olive branch that he has extended and break it in half and shove it in his eye.'" (The Senate never acted on the bill.)

The next month, Barrett voted "no" as Congress passed a welfare overhaul compromise that Clinton had agreed to sign.

Even when Barrett and the GOP basically agree on principle, as they did on the presidential line-item veto, they are likely to cross swords. In February 1995, Barrett and fellow Democrat Louise M. Slaughter of New York offered an amendment to a Republican-crafted line-item veto bill. Their amendment was identical to a proposal that had been introduced in 1993 by then-Minority Leader Robert H. Michel, R-Ill., who wanted to broaden the president's power so he could veto tax loopholes.

House Republicans had supported Michel's idea unanimously in 1993, but the leadership of the new GOP majority blackballed the proposal in the 104th; only eight Republicans voted for the Barrett-Slaughter amendment in 1995.

Barrett ultimately voted for the Republican-crafted line item veto bill that Clinton signed into law. Opponents of that measure challenged it in federal court and won a favorable ruling in 1997.

Barrett did find allies on the GOP side on an

Beer was once Milwaukee's best-known product; the city's major league baseball team is the Brewers. But that shrinking heritage took another blow in December 1996, when Pabst closed its Milwaukee brewery. That left Miller as the only big brewing company in Milwaukee. Schlitz, "the beer that made Milwaukee famous," closed there in 1981.

However, there is still a good amount of industry in the 5th, helping it keep the blue-collar identity that makes it a Democratic stronghold. Milwaukee's manufacturing base, hit hard in the early 1980s recession, generally rebounded. Motorcyclists revere the Harley-Davidson Motor Co. here. Major employers also include A. O. Smith, which makes automobile parts and supplies, and Briggs & Stratton, makers of gasoline engines.

The Menomonee River Valley marks the boundary between Milwaukee's North and South sides. The 5th is the North Side district and is reliably Democratic. President Clinton took 63 percent of the vote here in 1996, his best showing in the state then and in 1992, as it was for Democrat Michael S. Dukakis in 1988. Barrett has done even better, running at least 10 percentage points ahead of Clinton in 1992 and 1996.

The district encompasses most of the city's traditional German neighborhoods, its black neighborhoods and the affluent East Side.

Blacks, most of whom vote Democratic, make up 35 percent of the 5th's population, compared to 5 percent of the state as a whole. Milwaukee remains one of the nation's most segregated cities, and the great majority of the metro area's black residents live in lower-income neighborhoods on or near the city's North Side. Although not as stark as in some cities, the city's old but sturdy housing stock

WISCONSIN 5
Northern Milwaukee, Milwaukee County suburbs; southeast Waukesha County

and the lack of high-rise public housing does not hide the inner-city despair.

The black population nonetheless has been spreading out, generally to the west and northwest, in search of newer housing and a better quality of life. One area around Sherman Park shifted in 20 years from 98 percent white to 82 percent black.

North and west of the black neighborhoods are modest, middle-class areas. The East Side, between the Milwaukee River and Lake Michigan, is home to many academics who work at Milwaukee's branch of the University of Wisconsin, and middle and upper managers.

The houses get bigger and more expensive in the North Shore suburbs. Just north of the city, Shorewood's young professionals and multifamily housing give it a Democratic leaning. Farther north, the 5th includes the more exclusive villages of Whitefish Bay, Fox Point and Bayside. Brewers and other industrial barons once built mansions along the North Shore; today property values are still stunning by Wisconsin standards, as are Republican turnouts.

West of the city is Wauwatosa, a residential area with older housing stock that has shed some Republicanism as it attracts young professionals.

1990 Population: 543,530. White 333,040 (61%), Black 191,141 (35%), Other 19,349 (4%). Hispanic origin 14,377 (3%). 18 and over 395,942 (73%), 62 and over 82,137 (15%). Median age: 31.

institutional reform issue in late 1995: He was a key player in a bipartisan coalition that pushed to passage a resolution strictly limiting the types and amounts of gifts that House members may accept. The measure went beyond what the Republican leadership had originally sought.

Earlier in the year, Barrett had described congressional reform as an issue that should know no party bounds. "We want to take the partisan edge off these issues" he said. "The people who are working together are not people who tear down the institution. They're working to improve the institution."

Barrett's other committee assignment is on Banking and Financial Services, which has jurisdiction over housing issues. One of his abiding interests is in limiting the number of guns in public housing projects.

As the Banking Subcommittee on Housing and Community Development considered a bill in the 103rd to reauthorize the nation's housing laws, Barrett offered an amendment to allow public housing residents to ban guns on the premises.

Barrett argued that because violence is rampant in public housing, residents ought to have the same right as those who live in condominiums, apartments and nursing homes and can ban guns from their buildings.

His amendment initially lost on a 15-15 vote. But then Democrat Albert R. Wynn of Maryland requested that the measure be reconsidered, and he switched his vote. Wynn said he had been on the House floor during the first vote and that he had been erroneously recorded as giving a "no" by proxy. Barrett's provision, however, was subsequently dropped by the full committee

Barrett had sharp words in March 1996 for a Republican-driven effort to repeal the ban on certain semiautomatic assault-style weapons. "Bringing this bill before Congress is murderously irresponsible," he said. The House passed the repeal bill, but it went no further.

Although Barrett has been in public office since shortly after graduating from law school, other experiences do inform his legislative work. On the House floor during his first term. he touted his summer working in a Harley-Davidson plant. Reflecting his roots in Rust Belt labor-liberalism, Barrett opposed NAFTA, although later he voted in favor of GATT.

At Home: Campaigning door-to-door may be a quaint art in this age of media-intensive politics, but Barrett remains a leading practitioner. "I find it relaxing, and it's something I'm very comfortable doing," he once said. "And when you talk to someone at their home, they're relaxed."

Part of the enjoyment may result from the fact that his constituents do not need much convincing. After winning the 5th District seat, vacated by Democrat Jim Moody, in 1992 with 69 percent of the vote, Barrett took 62 percent in 1994, then set a career-high with 73 percent in 1996. In that election, he ran 10 percentage points ahead of Clinton in the heavily Democratic district.

In his 1992 House campaign, Barrett did not go out of his way to seek media coverage or use his legislative position to raise a huge campaign treasury. His favorite campaign venues were one-on-one meetings and public forums, where he promoted himself as a pragmatic legislator who stayed in touch with constituents.

The grass-roots effort served Barrett well in a crowded Democratic primary that included a Milwaukee County supervisor, a former state representative and circuit court judge and a former Marquette University basketball player. Barrett defied predictions that the contest would be close by running strongly throughout Milwaukee and eight suburbs to win nomination with 41 percent of the vote.

Barrett kept up the pace in the general election, and the outcome was never in doubt. He trounced Republican Donalda Ann Hammersmith, a small-business owner from Shorewood who stressed her business experience, gender and anti-abortion views.

HOUSE ELECTIONS

1996 General		
Thomas M. Barrett (D)	141,179	(73%)
Paul D. Melotik (R)	47,384	(25%)
James D. Soderna (TAX)	3,696	(2%)
1994 General		
Thomas M. Barrett (D)	87,806	(62%)
Stephen B. Hollingshead (R)	51,145	(36%)
David J. Schall (I)	1,576	(1%)

Previous Winning Percentages: 1992 (69%)

CAMPAIGN FINANCE

	Receipts	Receipts from PACs	Expend-itures
1996			
Barrett (D)	$289,893	$152,334 (53%)	$153,139
Melotik (R)	$13,315	$16 (0%)	$13,315
Soderna (TAX)	$6,126	0	$6,110
1994			
Barrett (D)	$268,383	$161,357 (60%)	$239,418
Hollingshead (R)	$115,635	$5,353 (5%)	$115,791

DISTRICT VOTE FOR PRESIDENT

	1996		1992
D	125,747 (63%)	**D**	142,047 (57%)
R	58,259 (29%)	**R**	76,935 (31%)
I	10,090 (5%)	**I**	32,138 (13%)

KEY VOTES

1997	
Ban "partial birth" abortions	Y
1996	
Approve farm bill	N
Deny public education to illegal immigrants	N
Repeal ban on certain assault-style weapons	N
Increase minimum wage	Y
Freeze defense spending	Y
Approve welfare overhaul	N
1995	
Approve balanced-budget constitutional amendment	N
Relax Clean Water Act regulations	N
Oppose limits on environmental regulations	Y
Reduce projected Medicare spending	N
Approve GOP budget with tax and spending cuts	N

VOTING STUDIES

	Presidential Support		Party Unity		Conservative Coalition	
Year	**S**	**O**	**S**	**O**	**S**	**O**
1996	86	14	89	11	2	96
1995	81	17	88	12	27	72
1994	74	22	89	9	22	78
1993	77	23	93	7	25	75

INTEREST GROUP RATINGS

Year	ADA	AFL-CIO	CCUS	ACU
1996	85	n/a	25	5
1995	90	100	29	12
1994	90	89	58	0
1993	90	92	27	13

6 Tom Petri (R)

Of Fond du Lac — Elected 1979; 9th full term

Biographical Information
Born: May 28, 1940, Marinette, Wis.
Education: Harvard U., A.B. 1962, J.D. 1965.
Occupation: Lawyer.
Family: Wife, Anne Neal; one child.
Religion: Lutheran.
Political Career: White House aide, 1969-70; Wis. Senate, 1973-79; Republican nominee for U.S. Senate, 1974.
Capitol Office: 2262 Rayburn Bldg. 20515; 225-2476.

Committees
Education & Workforce
Employer-Employee Relations; Postsecondary Education, Training & Life-Long Learning
Transportation & Infrastructure
Surface Transportation (chairman); Water Resources & Environment

In Washington: After devoting time in the 104th Congress to stopping construction of two big federal water projects, Petri shifts his attention in the 105th to directing another expensive federal endeavor — the construction of highways.

Petri's position as chairman of the Transportation and Infrastructure Subcommittee on Surface Transportation gives him responsibility for drafting the House version of new legislation that will set priorities for the nation's highway program into the next century. The current authorization bill, the Intermodal Surface Transportation Efficiency Act (ISTEA), expires in fiscal 1997.

Petri has already helped shape highway policy. He was the author of the 1995 bill establishing the National Highway System (NHS), a network of 160,000 miles of the most frequently traveled non-Interstate roads. The NHS law also repealed the national speed limit, instead giving states the power to set limits. "Do we really believe states are not able to do this?" Petri asked. "Do we really believe states are not just as concerned, if not more concerned, for the safety of their motorists?"

Petri is also a supporter of efforts to take the transportation trust funds off-budget; proponents of this move say that counting trust fund surpluses as part of the budget pressures lawmakers to hoard the money to reduce the size of the deficit, not spend it as intended on highway and aviation projects.

In the 103rd, as the NHS routes were being identified, Petri worked to see that several Wisconsin routes were designated. In part, he said, he was seeking to compensate for the fact that Wisconsin's Interstate highway mileage is relatively modest.

But as Petri works on the new highway bill in the 105th, his colleagues may be disappointed if they hope the Wisconsin Republican will be amenable to their requests for lots of local projects. Going back to when Democrats ran the House, Petri has rarely exhibited zeal for so-called pork barrel spending. Indeed, as part of the GOP majority in the 104th, Petri was a leader of efforts on the Transportation and Infrastructure Committee to kill two massive water projects. He fought authorization of the Auburn Dam, a $950 million project 40 miles east of Sacramento that would have been the most expensive dam ever built in the United States. Rep. John T. Doolittle, R-Calif., argued that the dam was needed to protect Sacramento from devastating floods and to supply water and power to Sierra foothill communities.

But Petri, allied with environmental and taxpayer groups, argued that cheaper options less detrimental to the environment should have been pursued. "At a time when the Congress is grappling with the question of exactly how to balance the federal budget and desperately seeking solutions on how to deal with our $5 trillion public debt, how can the Congress possibly justify the unnecessary expenditure of such a gross amount of money?" Petri asked.

In 1992, Petri managed to kill a similar proposal for a dam in the same area, offering a floor amendment striking that project's funding from the Energy and Water appropriations bill.

Also in the 104th, Petri saw the House pass his amendment to kill a controversial water project in Colorado and New Mexico. On a 221-200 vote, the House stripped nearly $10 million from the fiscal 1997 energy and water spending bill that would have been used to begin its construction. The water project, known as Animas-La Plata, was authorized decades ago as a way to divert water from one river to another for irrigation and to help get water to the Ute Indian tribe. "The days of opening and developing the West are over," Petri said in proposing the amendment. "The West is open and developed."

However, House and Senate conferees later restored most of the money to begin the project.

Petri also had difficulty in the 104th in his efforts to force local and state governments to share equally with the federal government the cost of new flood-control projects. Instead, the Transportation and Infrastructure Committee

The 6th encompasses almost the entire width of central Wisconsin, stretching from Lake Michigan west to within about 30 miles of the Minnesota border. The district has been closely contested in many state and national elections, but it has sent only one Democrat to Congress since 1938.

The farms and market towns are generally Republican, while Democratic strength is several small industrialized cities in the eastern part of the 6th: Manitowoc and Two Rivers in Manitowoc County and Neenah-Menasha in Winnebago County, and Fond du Lac in Fond du Lac County.

The most Democratic of the bunch is Manitowoc, a prominent Lake Michigan shipbuilding center in the days when wooden vessels plied the seas. More than half the jobs in Manitowoc now are involved in manufacturing and processing, and unions are an important force. Goods produced include Mirro's aluminum pots and pans, and the Manitowoc Co.'s ice-making machine for motels. Tourism got a boost with the launching of a car ferry service across Lake Michigan to Ludington, Mich. Manitowoc County went solidly for Jimmy Carter in 1976, voted narrowly for Ronald Reagan in 1980 and 1984, and has swung back to the Democratic side in the three elections since.

Republicans have an easier time in Winnebago and Fond du Lac counties. George Bush carried them in the 1988 and 1992 presidential elections. Bob Dole carried Fond du Lac in 1996 but lost Winnebago by less than 2,000 votes.

Winnebago's population increased 7 percent in the 1980s. Oshkosh is on the western shore of Lake Winnebago, the state's largest lake. Tourism and a state university branch boost the

WISCONSIN 6
Central — Oshkosh; Fond du Lac; Manitowoc

economy, and factories in Winnebago County turn out auto parts, wood and paper products, and Oshkosh B'Gosh clothing. Oshkosh Truck is the largest defense contractor in a state that traditionally has ranked low in defense spending. So many airplane buffs travel to Oshkosh for the annual Experimental Aircraft Association convention that it briefly becomes one of the busiest airports in the world in terms of takeoffs and landings. Toward the northern end of the lake is Neenah-Menasha, where paper goods company Kimberly-Clark is a large employer.

At the southern tip of the lake is Fond du Lac County, home of Mercury outboard motors, Speed Queen laundry equipment, and a large Giddings & Lewis tool manufacturing plant. The city of Fond du Lac has strong historical justification for its GOP inclinations. About 20 miles west of the city is Ripon, which was the birthplace of the Republican Party in 1854.

Besides the industry in the district, farming has a strong presence. After all-important dairying, output from the district's farms is diverse, including corn, peas, beans and cranberries. Republican strength in the rural part of the 6th is most concentrated in Green Lake County, a resort area with large summer homes. Republicans are also strong in Waupaca and Waushara counties.

1990 Population: 543,652. White 533,561 (98%), Black 1,944 (<1%), Other 8,147 (2%). Hispanic origin 4,753 (1%). 18 and over 400,512 (74%), 62 and over 95,741 (18%). Median age: 34.

voted to require localities to pay 35 percent of the cost, up from 25 percent, for flood-control projects authorized in the future.

Petri's budget-cutting zeal also drew him into conflict with colleagues over federal dairy policy. He introduced legislation to end the program, calling it "an outdated relic of 1930s agriculture policy." Dairy supports, known as "milk marketing orders," primarily help producers in the Northeast and Southeast, while hurting those in the Upper Midwest. "I'm convinced that there is no better alternative than to get rid of the program and start over," Petri said. He opposed the sugar price support program as well. Efforts to eliminate both programs failed, and Petri voted in 1996 against the final farm bill.

He also opposed the fiscal 1997 budget agreement, one of only 19 Republicans to do so. Dissenters complained that the measure showed the deficit increasing in the short term before heading to zero in 2002. The bill just squeaked by, 216-211.

Petri has risen to the No. 2 Republican seat on the Education and the Workforce Committee (formerly Economic and Educational Opportunities, and before that Education and Labor). On that panel in the 104th, Petri took exception when his party targeted the student loan program for cost savings. He was the only committee Republican to vote against GOP plans to wring $10.2 billion from the student loan program over seven years by eliminating a six-month interest deferment on student loans, increasing interest rates on parents' college loans and terminating the federal Direct Student Loan program.

On labor issues, Petri generally votes a conservative line. He opposed the original amendment by Rep. Frank Riggs, R-Calif., to raise the minimum wage, and he supported exempting small businesses from paying a higher minimum wage. (Ultimately, he and many other Republicans voted for the wage increase.) He also voted to allow employers to offer their workers compensatory time off rather than overtime pay, a plan opposed by organized labor.

On the social policy front, Petri voted against a constitutional amendment permitting Congress and the states to ban flag desecration, but on other hot-button issues, he has supported the party line. He voted to ban a particular abortion technique that opponents call a "partial birth" abortion, opposed efforts to allow the federal employee health plan to pay for abortions, and voted against legislation allowing overseas military hospitals to perform abortions. Petri supported efforts to repeal the ban on certain semiautomatic assault-style weapons.

At Home: Petri built his Wisconsin career out of the moderate Republican politics that worked for his predecessor, William A. Steiger, who died of a heart attack at age 40, one month after winning his seventh House term in 1978.

In the 1979 special election held to choose Steiger's successor, Petri campaigned on the same reformist issues Steiger had used. His literature boasted of the high ratings he had received in the state Senate from the public interest group Common Cause.

His opponent, Gary Goyke, a fellow state senator with a more forceful campaign style, made an issue of Petri's generous campaign financing. Goyke implied that the Republican had come out against national health insurance because of a $5,000 contribution he had received from the political action committee of the American Medical Association, a charge Petri denied. For his part, Petri said Goyke had his own source of political funding in organized labor.

Petri won the special election on his strength in rural areas and his ability to cut into Goyke's vote in blue-collar cities, especially Sheboygan, which Petri narrowly carried. His overall margin of victory was barely 1,200 votes.

Eighteen months later there was a rematch. But the 1980 election was a pale shadow of the first contest. In 1982, despite a strong Democratic trend in statewide politics, Petri romped to another term with 65 percent. From 1984 to 1990, Petri had no tough races.

Then in 1992 he was pressed hard by state Rep. Peggy A. Lautenschlager. She started with little name recognition in the western part of the district and little money for mass advertising, and she declined to launch a heavy door-to-door campaign. Petri, though criticized for his 77 overdrafts at the House bank, still had solid support, and he had the money to advertise early and often (he outspent Lautenschlager by $350,000). Petri apologized to voters for the overdrafts and used the advertisements to switch attention to his efforts to cut wasteful spending and boost the earned-income tax credit for the working poor.

Rather than striking out at Petri on the check scandal in the beginning of the year, when the issue was hottest, Lautenschlager waited until the final days of the campaign. In the end, she lacked the popularity and momentum needed to defeat an incumbent with a good record overall for aiding his district. Petri won 53 percent to 47 percent, and his 1994 and 1996 elections were uneventful.

HOUSE ELECTIONS

1996 General		
Tom Petri (R)	169,213	(73%)
Alver Lindskoog (D)	55,377	(24%)
James Dean (LIBERT)	4,494	(2%)
Timothy Farness (TAX)	2,532	(1%)
1994 General		
Tom Petri (R)	119,384	(99%)

Previous Winning Percentages: **1992** (53%) **1990** (100%) **1988** (74%) **1986** (97%) **1984** (76%) **1982** (65%) **1980** (59%) **1979**† (50%)

† Special election

CAMPAIGN FINANCE

	Receipts	Receipts from PACs	Expend-itures
1996			
Petri (R)	$587,473	$290,140 (49%)	$364,660
1994			
Petri (R)	$461,393	$197,049 (43%)	$326,635

DISTRICT VOTE FOR PRESIDENT

1996		1992	
D	108,317 (45%)	**D**	97,248 (35%)
R	99,926 (41%)	**R**	114,698 (41%)
I	28,533 (12%)	**I**	69,452 (25%)

KEY VOTES

1997	
Ban "partial birth" abortions	Y
1996	
Approve farm bill	N
Deny public education to illegal immigrants	Y
Repeal ban on certain assault-style weapons	Y
Increase minimum wage	N
Freeze defense spending	Y
Approve welfare overhaul	Y
1995	
Approve balanced-budget constitutional amendment	Y
Relax Clean Water Act regulations	N
Oppose limits on environmental regulations	N
Reduce projected Medicare spending	Y
Approve GOP budget with tax and spending cuts	Y

VOTING STUDIES

	Presidential Support		Party Unity		Conservative Coalition	
Year	S	O	S	O	S	O
1996	46	54	82	17	65	35
1995	30	68	88	11	72	27
1994	41	59	93	7	81	19
1993	33	65	84	14	75	25
1992	67	33	73	27	73	25
1991	68	32	69	30	89	11

INTEREST GROUP RATINGS

Year	ADA	AFL-CIO	CCUS	ACU
1996	20	n/a	88	100
1995	5	0	92	75
1994	25	11	100	76
1993	20	36	73	83
1992	25	25	63	76
1991	10	8	90	85

7 David R. Obey (D)

Of Wausau — Elected 1969; 14th full term

Biographical Information
Born: Oct. 3, 1938, Okmulgee, Okla.
Education: U. of Wisconsin, B.S. 1960, M.A. 1962.
Occupation: Real estate broker.
Family: Wife, Joan Lepinski; two children.
Religion: Roman Catholic.
Political Career: Wis. Assembly, 1963-69.
Capitol Office: 2462 Rayburn Bldg. 20515; 225-3365.

Committees
Appropriations (ranking)
Labor, Health & Human Services, Education & Related Agencies (ranking)

In Washington: After less than a year as chairman of the powerful Appropriations Committee, Obey was relegated to ranking minority status when Republicans captured the House majority in 1994. So instead of calling the shots in allocating federal monies, Obey had to watch as House Republicans, after 40 years in the minority, took to the budget with long knives. It was not a happy transition for him. "I never thought I would say this, but thank God for the Senate," Obey said at one point, expressing relief that House-approved spending cuts were not always embraced by the somewhat less conservative Senate.

After the split-decision 1996 election, Obey counseled President Clinton to be bold in standing up to the GOP Congress. In March 1997, Obey called on Clinton to delay any deal with Republicans on a broad budget plan until the GOP gave up its "idiotic insistence" on sweeping tax cuts. "I think Clinton is in a far stronger position than anyone in this town recognizes and probably than the White House recognizes," Obey said. In May 1997, he was one of 72 Democrats voting against the budget agreement worked out by the White House and congressional leaders. It passed the House 333-99.

Obey came to Washington young (he was just 30 when first sworn in) and had more than 25 years in the House majority. He likes to think of himself as an institutionalist, someone with respect for the chamber's ideals of civilized debate and collegiality. But some of what he sees with Republicans running the show is simply more than he can bear, and on occasion his temper has propelled him into not only verbal battles but also actual physical confrontations with GOP members.

In April 1997, he engaged in a highly publicized dust-up on the House floor with Majority Whip Tom DeLay, R-Texas, as Democrats renewed pressure for a campaign finance overhaul bill. George Miller, D-Calif., mentioned a 1995 Washington Post article that said lobbyists wrote legislation in DeLay's office. DeLay demanded that Miller's words be "taken down," a punishment for speech that breaks House rules on how members can speak to one another. Obey then took to the floor and sought to insert the Post article into the Congressional Record. DeLay objected and asked Obey to read the names of the seven lobbyists the article described as the bill-writers. Obey refused, saying it would be unfair to mention names of people who could not come to the floor and respond to the allegations.

After Obey left the podium, he took the article over to DeLay and the two argued, face-to-face, inches apart. Both pointed fingers at each other, then DeLay shoved Obey. A Republican aide got between the two and pushed DeLay back. "He proceeded to call me a chickenshit and punched his finger in my chest twice," Obey said later. "I told him to grow up and walked away."

The preceding June, Obey was giving a spirited response to GOP arguments when he turned to J.D. Hayworth, R-Ariz., who is known for sitting in the chamber's front row and registering his disdain for Democratic speakers. "To the gentleman from Arizona, every time somebody says something you don't like, you open your mouth and you start shouting from your seat," Obey said. "You are one of the most impolite members I have ever seen in my service in this house."

Hayworth leaped to the microphone and demanded that Obey's words be taken down. Henry J. Hyde, R-Ill., appealed to both to put aside their anger, acknowledging that Hayworth had behaved badly, but telling Obey that his words had been out of line, too. Grudging regrets were exchanged.

Obey uses his position on Appropriations to try to endear himself to the folks back home. To help a major employer in his district, Cray Research Inc., which builds supercomputers in Chippewa Falls, Obey successfully sought to restrict the National Science Foundation from buying a foreign-made supercomputer if the Commerce Department determined the computer was being sold at a below-market rate. Obey argued that Japanese manufacturers were trying

WISCONSIN 7
Northwest — Wausau; Superior; Stevens Point

The 7th reaches from the center of Wisconsin all the way north to Lake Superior. The southern part of the district is devoted largely to dairy farming. In the north, a booming recreation industry has brought new life to old mining and lumbering areas that were exploited and abandoned earlier in this century.

The southern end of the 7th is anchored by Marathon and Wood counties, politically marginal territory that supported Ronald Reagan in 1984. Democrats carried Marathon County by less than 1,000 votes in the 1988 and 1992 presidential elections, while Republicans won Wood County by a similarly narrow margin. But Bill Clinton won both counties in 1996 more handily than either party had carried them recently.

Marathon County's major city is Wausau, with paper mills, prefabricated-home manufacturers and white-collar employment in the insurance industry.

In Wood County, Wisconsin Rapids is a paper mill town — Consolidated Papers and Georgia-Pacific's Nekoosa-Edwards are the biggest — and Marshfield has a large medical clinic and research facility. The cities are processing centers for the surrounding dairylands. Southern Wood County is notable for its cranberry crops, while Marathon County is a leading ginseng exporter. The district got all of Wood County in 1992 redistricting.

The heaviest Democratic vote in the southern part of the 7th comes out of Portage County. The city of Stevens Point there has a large Polish population, a branch of the state university and the headquarters of the Sentry Insurance Co. Potatoes are an important crop in rural Portage and Wood counties.

A scattering of streams, rivers, lakes, national forests and state parks covers the northern reaches of the 7th, luring tourists and retirees from urban centers.

Along the Mississippi River, commuters to Minneapolis-St. Paul have begun settling in the western Polk County communities of St. Croix Falls and Balsam Lake.

The northern sections of the 7th share the same solid Democratic traditions found in Minnesota's Iron Range and in the nearby western end of Michigan's Upper Peninsula. The major Democratic bastion is the region's only sizable city, Superior, a working-class town. Clinton and Obey both ran 10 percentage points above their district average in Douglas County.

Superior's economy is fueled by production of dairy products, port operations and education. A branch of the University of Wisconsin is located there. It also has one of the nation's largest municipal forests, with 4,500 acres.

The huge port facilities of Superior and its larger neighbor, Duluth, Minn., are a funnel for soybeans, wheat and a wide range of other commodities raised on the farms of the Midwest. But a slump in ship repairing and the general hardscrabble nature of the land have taken their toll. Three of the four Wisconsin counties that adjoin Lake Superior — Douglas, Ashland and Iron — lost population in the 1980s.

1990 Population: 543,529. White 528,450 (97%), Black 822 (<1%), Other 14,257 (3%). Hispanic origin 2,592 (<1%). 18 and over 395,676 (73%), 62 and over 97,007 (18%). Median age: 34.

to drive their U.S. competitors out of business. Jim Kolbe, R-Ariz., said the Obey language violated the terms of GATT, and he tried to strip it from the fiscal 1997 spending bill for the departments of Veterans Affairs and Housing and Urban Development, and independent agencies. But the Appropriations Committee rejected Kolbe's amendment, 18-25.

Obey voted in 1996 against the GOP-backed "Freedom to Farm" bill, objecting to its dairy provisions. By a vote of 258-164 in February 1996, the House approved an amendment by Rules Committee Chairman Gerald B.H. Solomon, R-N.Y., to phase out the federally set price for milk after five years. But the amendment retained regional price supports for milk and continued the practice of government purchases of cheese to keep dairy prices high. Obey felt the amendment would benefit large dairy producers at the expense of the small farmer. "It's a wondrous gift to the biggest processors in the country," he said.

In the same vein in June 1996, Obey offered an amendment to the fiscal 1997 agriculture spending bill to cut funding for a Northeast Interstate Dairy Compact, which would allow the six New England states to set up a special pricing system for fluid milk. The Appropriations Committee rejected his amendment, 18-29.

Obey's tussles with Republicans on fiscal policy are the best-known aspect of his record, earning him a reputation as a liberal stalwart. But in keeping with opinion in his district, he sides with conservatives on some social-policy issues. He is a supporter of gunowners' rights. In 1993, he voted against a five-day waiting period for handgun purchases, and he has opposed a ban on certain semiautomatic assault-style weapons. He sides on occasion with foes of abortion; he has voted to ban a particular abortion procedure that opponents call "partia birth" abortion.

And Obey has had differences with the Clinton administration in the realm of international affairs, both on trade policy and security matters. Obey voted in the 103rd against NAFTA and GATT, and he opposes the administration's efforts to expand NATO membership. He warned in March 1997 that the pro-expansion bandwagon could be unstoppable once NATO tenders invitations to join. "We're going to be told, 'Gee, we can't turn back now; we've already made the decision; we're too far down the road,'" Obey said.

Obey landed the Appropriations Committee chairmanship in 1994 over more senior Neal Smith of Iowa. When the health of Chairman William H. Natcher declined rapidly and the Kentucky octogenarian was hospitalized, Obey decided to challenge Smith. Obey, then 55, seemed more vigorous than Smith, 74, and had a reputation as an outspoken proponent of liberal principles who had worked with House Democratic leaders to shape strategies for defending party priorities against conservative attacks. Smith was an old-style appropriator, primarily focused on the committee's work. At a time when Republicans were stepping up their rhetoric against government spending programs, Obey seemed a better choice. In a March 1994 vote, Obey defeated Smith, 152-106. After Natcher died in April, Obey formally succeeded to the chair.

At Home: Nearly 30 years ago, when The Wall Street Journal wanted to write about the advantages of incumbency, it sent a reporter to Obey's district, confident of witnessing an expert. The young Democrat had been in office only a few months at the time, but his techniques already were bearing fruit. He was sending out free government publications, writing columns for local newspapers and flooding the district with newsletters.

Obey knew that unless he made a strong personal impression on the voters, they would return him to his Wausau real estate business. Chosen in a 1969 special election to succeed Melvin R. Laird, who had been named secretary of Defense in the Nixon administration, Obey was the first Democrat ever to represent the 7th District.

To win his seat, Obey faced GOP state Sen. Walter Chilsen, a well-known former newscaster who called himself a "Laird Republican." He tried to make student violence a campaign theme. But Obey deflected that issue. He focused on discontent with the Nixon administration's low milk-support prices and on the unpopular fiscal policies of GOP Gov. Warren Knowles. The changed mood in farming areas turned what had been a 44,000-vote Laird win in November 1968 into a 4,055-vote margin for Obey five months later.

In 1994, despite his Appropriations chairmanship, Obey was kept to 54 percent (instead of his more usual 60-plus share) by his underfinanced Republican challenger, Scott West, a university official. Obey stressed the clout of his new chairmanship, while West carried the national GOP's "time for a change" line. He won the district's largest county, Marathon, and returned for a rematch in 1996. Even though Obey no longer could boast of being a chairman, he improved his winning tally over West to 57 percent.

HOUSE ELECTIONS

1996 General		
David R. Obey (D)	137,428	(57%)
Scott West (R)	103,365	(43%)
1994 General		
David R. Obey (D)	97,184	(54%)
Scott West (R)	81,706	(46%)

Previous Winning Percentages: **1992** (64%) **1990** (62%) **1988** (62%) **1986** (62%) **1984** (61%) **1982** (68%) **1980** (65%) **1978** (62%) **1976** (73%) **1974** (71%) **1972** (63%) **1970** (68%) **1969**† (52%)

† Special election

CAMPAIGN FINANCE

	Receipts	Receipts from PACs	Expend-itures
1996			
Obey (D)	$809,316	$441,498 (55%)	$862,370
West (R)	$162,196	$17,316 (11%)	$161,402
1994			
Obey (D)	$532,008	$317,952 (60%)	$607,058
West (R)	$98,854	$1,264 (1%)	$98,781

DISTRICT VOTE FOR PRESIDENT

	1996		1992
D	119,979 (49%)	**D**	117,203 (42%)
R	86,370 (35%)	**R**	93,238 (34%)
I	34,324 (14%)	**I**	67,558 (24%)

KEY VOTES

1997	
Ban "partial birth" abortions	Y
1996	
Approve farm bill	N
Deny public education to illegal immigrants	N
Repeal ban on certain assault-style weapons	Y
Increase minimum wage	Y
Freeze defense spending	Y
Approve welfare overhaul	Y
1995	
Approve balanced-budget constitutional amendment	N
Relax Clean Water Act regulations	N
Oppose limits on environmental regulations	Y
Reduce projected Medicare spending	N
Approve GOP budget with tax and spending cuts	N

VOTING STUDIES

	Presidential Support		Party Unity		Conservative Coalition	
Year	**S**	**O**	**S**	**O**	**S**	**O**
1996	77	23	83	15	31	69
1995	84	15	92	7	18	82
1994	71	27	92	3	14	72
1993	78	22	94	5	30	68
1992	14	84	93	5	15	85
1991	29	71	92	6	24	73

INTEREST GROUP RATINGS

Year	ADA	AFL-CIO	CCUS	ACU
1996	75	n/a	19	25
1995	80	100	25	8
1994	80	89	18	10
1993	90	100	27	13
1992	100	92	38	0
1991	85	92	20	15

8 Jay W. Johnson (D)

Of Green Bay — Elected 1996, 1st term

Biographical Information

Born: Sept. 30, 1943, Bessemer, Mich.

Education: Gogebic Community College, A.A. 1963; Northern Michigan U., B.A. 1965; Michigan State U., M.A. 1970.

Military Service: Army, 1966-68.

Occupation: Broadcast journalist.

Family: Wife, JoLee; two stepchildren.

Religion: Presbyterian.

Political Career: No previous office.

Capitol Office: 1313 Longworth Bldg. 20515; 225-5665.

Committees

Agriculture
General Farm Commodities; Livestock, Dairy & Poultry

Transportation & Infrastructure
Coast Guard & Maritime Transportation; Water Resources & Environment

The Path to Washington: Johnson in 1996 parlayed 15 years of exposure as a reporter and news anchor on Green Bay television into an unexpected victory over a veteran GOP state legislator in the open 8th.

Johnson is only the second Democrat to represent the 8th in the last four decades. The previous Democratic occupant, Robert J. Cornell, was ousted in 1978 after just two terms by staunchly conservative Republican Toby Roth, who held the seat through the 104th Congress, when he retired.

Republicans looked like they had a heavyweight contender to step in for Roth: state Assembly Speaker David Prosser Jr., a close ally of popular GOP Gov. Tommy G. Thompson.

But Johnson first showed his vote-winning potential in the Democratic primary, when he narrowly defeated the party's 1994 challenger to Roth, former state Rep. Stan Gruszynski, who had the backing of many in organized labor.

Meanwhile, in the GOP primary, Prosser had more than his share of trouble with a little-known businessman, Charles Dettman Jr. Funding his campaign largely out of his own pocket, Dettman blasted Prosser in television ads for his leadership in pushing through the Assembly a controversial funding package — including a regional tax increase — for a new stadium for the Milwaukee Brewers baseball team. Dettman also questioned Prosser's commitment to family values, noting that Prosser was unmarried.

With the backing of Thompson and other party leaders, Prosser pulled out a primary victory, but he did not start into the general-election campaign with as strong a head of steam as he might have hoped.

Prosser attempted to make the case that residents would be better off sending a veteran legislator to Washington instead of Johnson, whom he portrayed as politically inexperienced and not well informed on important issues. Prosser ran one television ad featuring a herd of cows expressing concern about a proposal Johnson made to tax milk 25 cents per hundredweight to help pay for education and other programs.

Johnson disowned the proposal, saying he had made it after reading incorrect information, and then he blasted Prosser for continuing to run an ad on an idea he knew Johnson had retracted.

Johnson often pointed to his own lack of political experience as a plus. He wrapped himself in the ever-popular mantle of "outsider" candidate and called Prosser a career politician whose detachment from ordinary people's concerns was evident in his handling of the Milwaukee stadium issue.

Johnson's familiar face and affable style wore well, as did his frequent references to the Green Bay Packers football team — which in the fall of 1996 was enjoying its best season since the 1960s. In the end, Johnson's high name recognition built up over years in the media trumped Prosser's nearly two decades as a state legislator: The Democrat prevailed by 52 percent to 48 percent.

In January 1997, the Packers won the Super Bowl for the first time since the Vince Lombardi era, and Johnson was sworn into public office for the first time ever. House Democratic leaders put him on two committees whose work has potential for practical benefit to the 8th: Agriculture, and Transportation and Infrastructure.

During his campaign, Johnson talked a lot about educational issues. He said he would like to see increased funding for programs such as Head Start, expanded access to the Internet for poorer school districts and the implementation of tax credits to help pay college tuition.

Johnson does not support a balanced-budget constitutional amendment, and while he stressed that "everything must be put on the table" in an effort to eliminate the federal budget deficit, he said it is important to protect Medicare; and he has advised looking to "corporate welfare" and defense programs for cost savings.

Johnson has also expressed a desire to bolster federal protection of the environment. He is most concerned about proposed mining operations in the 8th District and efforts to revise regulations on wildlife refuges.

WISCONSIN 8
Northeast — Green Bay; Appleton

More than half the 8th District vote is cast in the Fox River Valley counties of Outagamie (Appleton) and Brown (Green Bay). Germans are the most noticeable ethnic group in the industrialized valley. Most of them are Catholic and, even if Democratic, tend to be conservative.

The economy of the valley and the vast wooded area to the north depends on trees and paper. The district is a worldwide exporter of paper, grain and dairy products.

Green Bay, which passed the 100,000 population mark in the early 1990s, is the district's most populous city. The most famous attraction in Green Bay — the smallest city with a team in the National Football League — is Lambeau Field, home of the 1997 Super Bowl champion Packers.

Appleton lies thirty miles southwest of Green Bay, on the north shore of Lake Winnebago. Here, too, paper manufacturers and papermaking equipment industries are important employers. Appleton also has white-collar jobs in insurance, finance and health care.

The paper industry, and its reliance on consumer necessities, has enabled the Fox Cities generally to survive recent recessionary times without major dislocations in employment. This follows a decade in which population increased by 11 percent in Brown County and by 9 percent in Outagamie County, enhancing Green Bay's standing as the state's second-largest media market.

The Republican presidential candidate carried both Brown and Outagamie (parts of which lie in the 6th district) from 1968 to 1992. But in 1996 Bill Clinton won Brown with 47 percent of the vote and Outagamie with 44 percent (though Bob Dole had a slim lead in the 8th's portion of Outagamie). In the House race, Johnson won in most of the district's larger counties (including Brown, Outagamie and Marinette) but lost some of the smaller ones.

Appleton's Republican heritage includes being the hometown of the late Sen. Joseph R. McCarthy, infamous for his communist witch hunts in the 1950s.

The rural counties in the north-central part of the district also are mostly Republican, although there are pockets of Democratic strength. The small city of Kaukauna inspired the only real skirmish in the state's 1992 redistricting efforts, when Green Bay Democrats successfully fought a proposal to move Kaukauna into the 6th District. Kaukauna's Democratic inclinations derive from the union presence at International Paper in De Pere.

Resorts and vacation homes are the focal point for tourists in Door and Vilas counties. Door County's peninsula, which separates Green Bay from Lake Michigan, is dotted with picturesque small towns. Vilas County is in a lakes region on the Michigan border. Both counties are solidly Republican, influenced by the prosperity attained by serving nature-seekers from all over the Midwest.

The district also contains several different tribes of Chippewa Indians, including the Lac du Flambeau.

1990 Population: 543,404. White 521,764 (96%), Black 1,526 (<1%), Other 20,114 (4%). Hispanic origin 3,391 (1%). 18 and over 396,279 (73%), 62 and over 89,420 (16%). Median age: 33.

HOUSE ELECTIONS

1996 General		
Jay W. Johnson (D)	129,551	(52%)
David T. Prosser Jr. (R)	119,398	(48%)
1996 Primary		
Jay Johnson (D)	18,293	(59%)
Stan Gruszynski (D)	12,681	(41%)

CAMPAIGN FINANCE

	Receipts	Receipts from PACs	Expend-itures
1996			
Johnson (D)	$303,404	$154,850 (51%)	$289,624
Prosser (R)	$580,385	$229,275 (40%)	$556,074

DISTRICT VOTE FOR PRESIDENT

1996		1992	
D	116,060 (46%)	**D**	101,493 (36%)
R	105,120 (42%)	**R**	115,128 (40%)
I	28,563 (11%)	**I**	69,373 (24%)

KEY VOTES

1997

Ban "partial birth" abortions Y

9 F. James Sensenbrenner Jr. (R)

Of Menomonee Falls — Elected 1978, 10th term

Biographical Information
Born: June 14, 1943, Chicago, Ill.
Education: Stanford U., A.B. 1965; U. of Wisconsin, J.D. 1968.
Occupation: Lawyer.
Family: Wife, Cheryl Warren; two children.
Religion: Episcopalian.
Political Career: Wis. Assembly, 1969-75; Wis. Senate, 1975-79.
Capitol Office: 2332 Rayburn Bldg. 20515; 225-5101.

Committees
Judiciary
Courts & Intellectual Property
Science (chairman)

In Washington: Conservative and sometimes irascible, Sensenbrenner gets a chance in the 105th Congress to set the tone on the Science Committee, which during the 104th saw its share of partisan warfare over the nation's spending priorities on research and high-technology endeavors. The chairmanship of Science fell to Sensenbrenner in 1997 upon the retirement of Robert S. Walker of Pennsylvania, who held the job for only one term.

Walker was a close friend of House Speaker Newt Gingrich, and Democrats groused in the 104th that the Science panel at times functioned as an extension of the GOP's leadership's ideological designs. While Sensenbrenner is every bit as conservative as Walker, he does not have a similarly close relationship with his party's House hierarchy. He may need to spend more time building support for bills inside the committee, consulting with ranking minority member George E. Brown Jr. of California and others.

Starting with the 101st Congress, Sensenbrenner was the top Republican on the subcommittee overseeing the space programs, rising to the chairmanship when the GOP took control of the House in the 104th Congress. He has been part of the panel's bipartisan consensus in favor of U.S. space programs but has not greeted all "big science" projects warmly, as evidenced by his vote to halt funding for the superconducting super collider.

He even voiced some skepticism in the past about the NASA's space station project, particularly in the 103rd, when a lack of funding and political support led NASA planners to redesign the project, scaling it back and inviting Russia to participate in planning and construction. Still, he opposed efforts to kill the space station in the 104th Congress, and when taking over as committee chairman he said he continue backing the project. In April 1997, he called for NASA to eliminate Russia from the program after the agency announced that space station construction would be delayed up to 11 months because a key part had not been funded by the Russian government. "NASA and the White House seem prepared to pay any price to keep the Russians in the program," Sensenbrenner said.

Sensenbrenner's ascent to the Science chairmanship comes two years after he failed to get a leadership position on his other committee, Judiciary. When liberal Democrats dominated Judiciary, Sensenbrenner gave voice to conservative concerns from his position as ranking Republican on the Crime Subcommittee, and before that as ranking Republican on the Civil and Constitutional Rights Subcommittee. But when Republicans took control in the 104th, Sensenbrenner was missing from the list of subcommittee chairmen on Judiciary — even though he was the third most-senior Republican on the committee. At the time, it was noted that even some in his own party found Sensenbrenner's personality less than endearing.

Democrats certainly had reason to chafe at Sensenbrenner. He was a leading critic of the 1994 crime bill, with its generous helpings of federal funds for prevention programs such as midnight basketball leagues for city youngsters. Sensenbrenner denounced the prevention funding as "welfare" and urged fellow Republicans to vote against the bill and replace it with one that "will give the crime issue back to the Republicans."

Sensenbrenner also led the charge in the 103rd against the ban on semiautomatic assault-style weapons. "More people are killed by fists and feet than are being killed by assault weapons," Sensenbrenner said. In the days leading up to the vote in which House members approved the ban by just two votes, the White House tried to dramatize the issue by highlighting the death of a suburban Milwaukee police officer in a shootout after a robbery in Sensenbrenner's district. In 1996, he voted to overturn the assault weapons ban. The bill passed the House but never came up for a vote in the Senate.

Sensenbrenner, however, is not an absolutist on gun rights, as shown by his strong and consis-

WISCONSIN 9
Milwaukee suburbs; part of Waukesha County; Sheboygan

The 9th is the closest thing Wisconsin has to a suburban district, encompassing much of the counties immediately west and north of Milwaukee. Consequently, it is also Wisconsin's most staunchly Republican district. In the 1980s, all three Democratic presidential candidates failed to surpass 40 percent of the vote in the old 9th. The new 9th has not been any more hospitable; Bill Clinton broke just 30 percent in 1992 and failed to reach 40 percent in 1996.

Waukesha County, just west of Milwaukee County, is the centerpiece of state Republicanism, regularly running up the biggest GOP numbers in the state. Bob Dole polled 59 percent in the 9th's portion of the county in 1996. County Republicans have even more influence on the district because the areas where Democrats are most numerous — the cities of Waukesha, Muskego and New Berlin on the county's southeastern side — are part of the 4th.

In earlier generations, the lakes of Waukesha County drew Milwaukee's leading families to buy real estate in the county for summer retreats. Republicans still compile huge margins in small Oconomowoc Lake and Chenequa. But suburbanization has taken hold elsewhere. Affluent Elm Grove is rock-ribbed Republican territory. Middle managers are attracted to adjacent Brookfield, which sprouted one of the metropolitan area's largest office markets.

Not everything is booming in Waukesha; the county's population growth slowed from 21 percent in the 1970s to just under 9 percent in the 1980s. Menomonee Falls, which attracted working-class Germans from Milwaukee's northwest side, saw a 3 percent drop in the past decade.

Among the county's manufacturers are the General Electric Medical Systems Group, QuadGraphics printing, and companies that build electrical transformers and engines.

Ozaukee and Washington counties routinely cast 60 percent of their votes for GOP presidential candidates, though Dole fell short of the mark in both. Washington County is a combination of fast-growing bedroom communities and agricultural lands being encroached on by development, with a smattering of industry. The county seat, West Bend, is home to the West Bend Co., maker of small kitchen appliances. Port Washington, the Ozaukee County seat, is home to Allen-Edmonds shoes as well as a picturesque lakefront and marina.

Farther north, Sheboygan County is marginally Republican in presidential elections; Clinton edged Dole here. The city of Sheboygan contains medium-sized industries, such as Vollrath stainless steel and Bemis manufacturing. Kohler is headquarters for the Kohler Co., the nation's largest producer of plumbing equipment, as well as the American Club, the state's premier resort hotel.

The district also includes most of Dodge and Jefferson counties, which are largely rural. Dairying is important here. In Dodge County, Waupun is well-known as a major state prison site, Beaver Dam is a resort community, and the Horicon Marsh is a federal and state preserve for geese and ducks.

1990 Population: 543,532. White 533,444 (98%), Black 2,313 (<1%), Other 7,775 (1%). Hispanic origin 5,700 (1%). 18 and over 396,174 (73%), 62 and over 80,726 (15%). Median age: 34.

tent support for a five-day waiting period for handgun purchases. Sensenbrenner first supported the idea in 1988, when he offered it as an amendment to the omnibus drug bill. He cited the success of Wisconsin's 48-hour waiting period on handgun purchases "in cooling off crimes of passion. If it can work at the state level, it can work at the federal level."

In the 104th, he expressed some misgivings about legislation aimed at curbing terrorism, voting against the measure in the Judiciary Committee. He said he did not want to authorize new government powers and expenditures. He did support the final, weaker, legislation on the House floor.

An abortion foe, Sensenbrenner led the opposition to legislation in the 103rd making it a federal offense for anyone to use physical force or threats to intimidate a woman seeking an abortion, or to attack abortion clinics, saying that existing laws are sufficient to protect access to abortion clinics. In the 104th he voted to ban a particular abortion technique that opponents call a "partial birth" abortion, and he opposed allowing overseas military hospitals to perform abortions. On another contentious social policy matter, he voted to ban federal recognition of same-sex marriages.

Sensenbrenner in 1996 voted against raising the minimum wage, and he sided with the business community on another key issue, voting to allow employers to offer their workers compensatory time off rather than overtime pay.

Unlike many conservatives, however, Sensenbrenner opposed the constitutional amendment limiting congressional terms. "The reward for doing a good job in this business," he said, "is reelection."

It is not hard to figure how Sensenbrenner got his reputation as something of a scold. In May 1994, he served notice that he would force the House to vote on expelling Ways and Means Chairman Dan

Rostenkowski should Rostenkowski strike a plea bargain admitting guilt to felony charges of embezzlement. Likewise, in 1995, he moved to expel Rep. Walter R. Tucker III, D-Calif., convicted by a federal jury on nine felony charges of extortion and tax evasion. Tucker had said he was likely to quit Congress while seeking a new trial, but Sensenbrenner said he already was tired of waiting.

"If Congress is to maintain its integrity, we must remove the few bad apples immediately rather than allowing these individuals to keep cashing their taxpayer-provided paychecks," he said. Tucker announced his resignation the day Sensenbrenner announced he would seek a vote to expel him.

At Home: Sensenbrenner has held public office practically since his graduation from law school. Despite a reputation for pomposity, his personal resources and conservative views have earned him an undefeated record at the polls.

Sensenbrenner is heir to a paper and cellulose manufacturing fortune, much of which stems from his great-grandfather's invention of the sanitary napkin shortly after World War I. Marketing it under the brand name Kotex, Sensenbrenner's ancestor went on to become chairman of the board of Kimberly-Clark.

To reach Congress in 1978, Sensenbrenner had to dip into family wealth to overcome an unexpectedly strong GOP primary challenge. With Republican Bob Kasten leaving the 9th District to run for governor, Sensenbrenner was viewed as the obvious successor. He had been elected to four terms in the state Assembly before moving in 1975 to the state Senate, where he quickly rose to be assistant minority leader. He had a solid political base in the older, more affluent lakeside suburbs, and his conservative stance reminded voters of the popular Kasten.

But his opponent in the primary was Susan Engeleiter, a state legislator who would later become state Senate GOP leader, the party nominee for the U.S. Senate in 1988 and then director of the Small Business Administration.

Just 26 when she challenged Sensenbrenner, Engeleiter put on a strong campaign in the western, more middle-class part of the district, which she represented in the state Assembly. More gregarious than Sensenbrenner, she outpolled him by 5,600 votes in the 9th's four western counties. Only Sensenbrenner's familiarity in the most Republican of Milwaukee's suburbs allowed him to win the primary by 589 votes.

The 1978 Democratic nominee, Milwaukee lawyer Matthew J. Flynn, was also on his way to higher visibility in statewide politics as party chairman and as a candidate for the U.S. Senate. But he could not raise enough money to compete with Sensenbrenner, who campaigned on his support for cutting taxes and who defeated Flynn by a solid margin. Re-election has come easily since then.

In 1996, Sensenbrenner won with 74 percent of the vote.

HOUSE ELECTIONS

1996 General		
F. James Sensenbrenner Jr. (R)	197,910	(74%)
Floyd Brenholt (D)	67,740	(25%)
1994 General		
F. James Sensenbrenner (R)	141,617	(100%)

Previous Winning Percentages: **1992** (70%) **1990** (100%) **1988** (75%) **1986** (78%) **1984** (73%) **1982** (100%) **1980** (78%) **1978** (61%)

CAMPAIGN FINANCE

	Receipts	Receipts from PACs	Expend-itures
1996			
Sensenbrenner (R)	$338,578	$140,151 (41%)	$261,644
Brenholt (D)	$14,002	$1,900 (14%)	$13,781
1994			
Sensenbrenner (R)	$229,629	$93,421 (41%)	$161,986

DISTRICT VOTE FOR PRESIDENT

	1996		1992
D	101,320 (37%)	**D**	88,176 (30%)
R	141,976 (52%)	**R**	142,582 (48%)
I	23,402 (9%)	**I**	64,544 (22%)

KEY VOTES

1997	
Ban "partial birth" abortions	Y
1996	
Approve farm bill	N
Deny public education to illegal immigrants	Y
Repeal ban on certain assault-style weapons	Y
Increase minimum wage	N
Freeze defense spending	Y
Approve welfare overhaul	Y
1995	
Approve balanced-budget constitutional amendment	Y
Relax Clean Water Act regulations	N
Oppose limits on environmental regulations	N
Reduce projected Medicare spending	Y
Approve GOP budget with tax and spending cuts	Y

VOTING STUDIES

	Presidential Support		Party Unity		Conservative Coalition	
Year	**S**	**O**	**S**	**O**	**S**	**O**
1996	37	63	85	15	61	39
1995	29	71	89	11	68	32
1994	21	79	96	4	69	31
1993	20	80	90	10	61	39
1992	69	30	90	9	65	35
1991	66	33	87	11	86	14

INTEREST GROUP RATINGS

Year	ADA	AFL-CIO	CCUS	ACU
1996	20	n/a	81	100
1995	5	0	88	80
1994	20	22	67	76
1993	20	0	82	92
1992	15	17	88	92
1991	20	17	100	90

WYOMING

Governor: Jim Geringer (R)
First elected: 1994
Length of term: 4 years
Term expires: 1/99
Salary: $90,000
Term limit: 2 terms in a 16-year period
Phone: (307) 777-7434
Born: April 24, 1944; Wheatland, Wyo.
Education: Kansas State U., B.S., 1967.
Occupation: Farmer.
Family: Wife, Sherri; five children.
Religion: Lutheran.
Political Career: Wyo. House, 1982-88; Wyo. Senate, 1988.

No lieutenant governor

Secretary of State: Diana Ohman (R)
First elected: 1994
Length of term: 4 years
Term Expires: 1/99
Salary: $52,500
Phone: (307) 777-7378

State election official: (307) 777-7186
Democratic headquarters: (307) 637-8940
Republican headquarters: (307) 234-9166

STATE LEGISLATURE

Legislature. General session meets for 40 days, January-March, in odd years; budget session meets 20 days, February-March, in even years.

Senate: 30 members, 4-year terms
1996 breakdown: 21R, 9D; 25 men, 5 woman
Salary: $75 a day
Phone: (307) 777-7711

House of Representatives: 60 members, 2-year terms
1996 breakdown: 43R, 17D; 48 men, 12 women
Salary: $75 a day
Phone: (307) 777-7852

URBAN STATISTICS

City	Population
Cheyenne Mayor Leo Pando, R	50,008
Casper Mayor Kathleen Dixon, N-P	46,801
Laramie Mayor Trudy McCracken, R	26,687

U.S. CONGRESS

Senate: 0 D, 2 R
House: 0 D, 1 R

TERM LIMITS

For state offices: Yes
Senate: three terms
House: three terms

ELECTIONS

1996 Presidential Vote

Bob Dole	50%
Bill Clinton	37%
Ross Perot	12%

1992 Presidential Vote

George Bush	40%
Bill Clinton	34%
Ross Perot	26%

1988 Presidential Vote

George Bush	61%
Michael S. Dukakis	38%

POPULATION

1990 population		453,588
1980 population		469,557
Percent change		-3%
Rank among states:		50
White		94%
Black		1%
Hispanic		6%
Asian or Pacific islander		1%
Urban		65%
Rural		35%
Born in state		43%
Foreign-born		2%
Under age 18	135,525	30%
Ages 18-64	270,868	60%
65 and older	47,195	10%
Median age		32

MISCELLANEOUS

Capital: Cheyenne
Number of counties: 23
Per capita income: $17,188 (1991)
Rank among states: 33
Total area: 97,809 sq. miles
Rank among states: 9

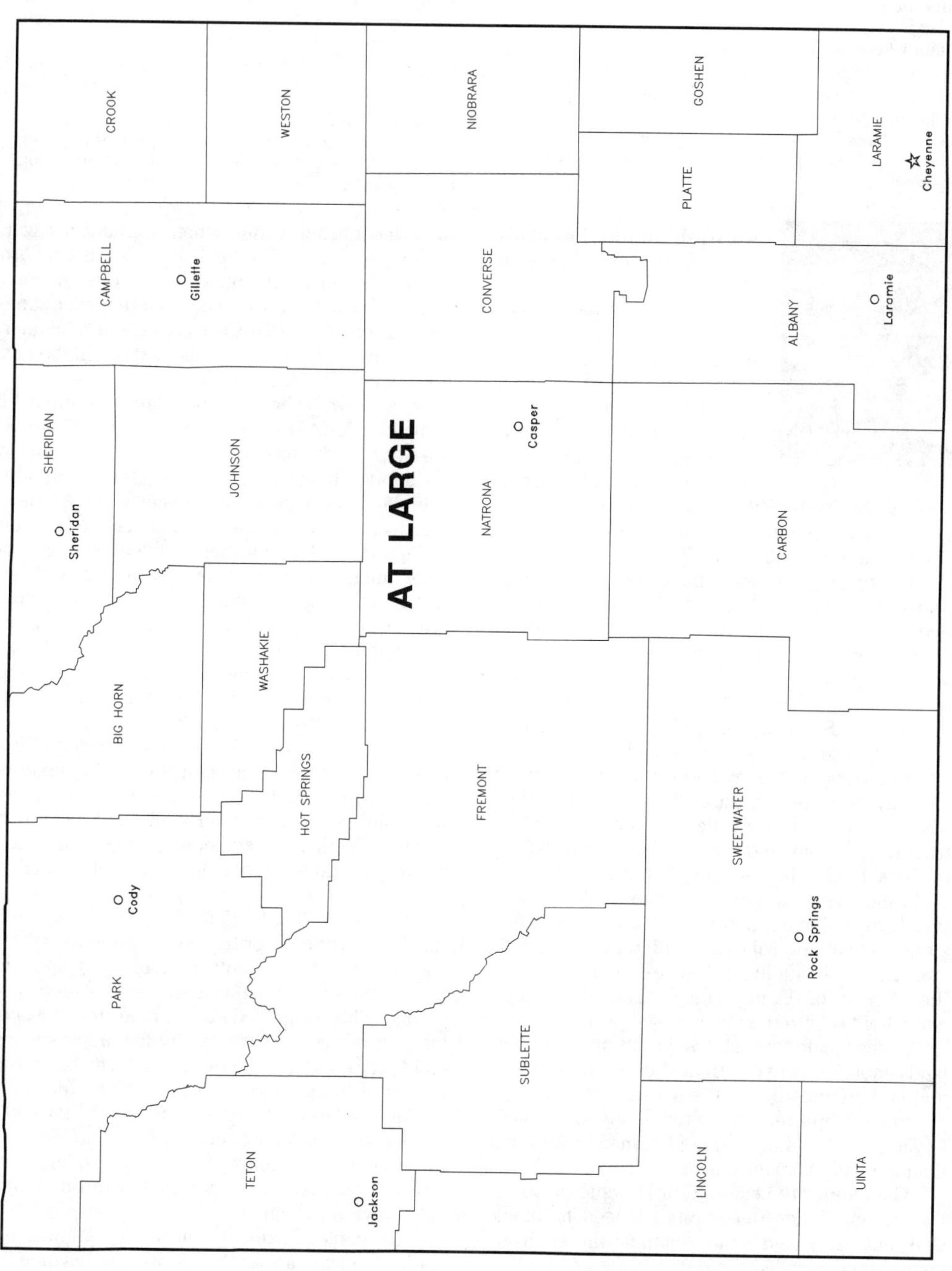
CROOK
WESTON
NIOBRARA
GOSHEN
LARAMIE
Cheyenne
PLATTE
CAMPBELL
Gillette
CONVERSE
ALBANY
Laramie
SHERIDAN
Sheridan
JOHNSON
AT LARGE
Casper
NATRONA
CARBON
WASHAKIE
BIG HORN
HOT SPRINGS
FREMONT
SWEETWATER
Cody
PARK
Rock Springs
SUBLETTE
TETON
Jackson
LINCOLN
UINTA

Craig Thomas (R)

Of Casper — Elected 1994, 1st term

Biographical Information
Born: Feb. 17, 1933, Cody, Wyo.
Education: U. of Wyoming, B.A. 1955; La Salle U., LL.B. 1963.
Military Service: Marine Corps, 1955-59.
Occupation: Power company executive.
Family: Wife, Susan Roberts; four children.
Religion: Methodist.
Political Career: Sought Republican nomination for Wyo. treasurer, 1978, 1982; Wyo. House, 1985-89; U.S. House, 1989-95.

Capitol Office: 109 Hart Bldg. 20510; 224-6441.

Committees
Energy & Natural Resources
Forests & Public Land Management; National Parks, Historic Preservation & Recreation (chairman)
Environment & Public Works
Drinking Water, Fisheries & Wildlife; Transportation & Infrastructure
Foreign Relations
East Asian & Pacific Affairs (chairman); European Affairs; International Economic Policy, Export & Trade Promotion
Indian Affairs

In Washington: Now in his third year as chairman of a Foreign Relations subcommittee, Thomas has broadened his policy horizons to embrace all of East Asia and the Pacific. But he has also kept his focus on the concerns of the American West. A product of what was called the "Sagebrush Rebellion" in the 1980s, Thomas has devoted much of the 1990s to fighting what he calls the Clinton administration's "war on the West."

Through eight years in the House and Senate, no issue has mattered more to Thomas than public-land management. About half the land in Wyoming is controlled by the federal government, and Thomas is a fervent exponent of the notion that President Clinton, Vice President Al Gore and Interior Secretary Bruce Babbitt are systematically short-changing commercial interests.

With seats on Energy and National Resources and Environment and Public Works, Thomas has been well placed to stymie the Clinton administration's environmental land reforms and defend the local land-rights movement in the West.

In the 104th Congress, Thomas took the lead on a high-profile bill that would allow 12 Western states to take control of 270 million acres of federal land — including wilderness areas — from the Bureau of Land Management. The states could hold title to the lands or sell portions.

Thomas said the states could manage the lands more effectively than the faraway Washington bureaucracy. But environmentalists opposed the proposal, arguing that many states have fewer environmental and land management laws than the federal government.

When Minority Leader Tom Daschle of South Dakota and other Democrats pledged to block GOP bills they said would damage the environment, Thomas called the effort "a lot of Chicken Little rhetoric" aimed at Republicans to tarnish "those members who want simply to review environmental laws" to see if they can be made better.

But the bill earned Thomas plenty of press attention during a time when Republicans were under pressure to prove they cared about protecting the environment. He and House sponsor James V. Hansen, R-Utah, delayed the bill, but neither has given up. "This is a concept, a fundamental change that should be talked about in the next few years," Thomas told the Denver Post.

Another of Thomas' top concerns since his arrival in Congress has been rural health care. In the Senate, Thomas added a provision to a product liability bill that made it tougher to win punitive damages against an obstetrician or other health care professional who delivered a baby but had not treated the mother during pregnancy. The amendment would require a standard of "clear and convincing" evidence to prove malpractice against doctors, particularly those in rural areas who often travel long distances to deliver babies for women who had not been under their care. The amendment survived an effort to kill it, but the bill was vetoed in May 1996.

As co-chairman of the bipartisan Senate Rural Health Caucus, Thomas sponsored a bill he titled the "Rural Health Development Act," which would increase physician recruitment incentives, equalize Medicare payments between rural and urban programs, and help fund "telemedicine" programs.

He also ardently defends Wyoming's cattle ranchers. Thomas criticized a proposal by the Department of Agriculture making yogurt an acceptable substitute for meat in school lunch programs. "This misguided idea reminds me of a similar plan that sought to classify ketchup as a vegetable for school lunch programs," Thomas wrote in a letter to Agriculture Secretary Dan Glickman.

An ex-Marine, Thomas is adamant that veterans' benefits and the much larger Social Security program should not be cut. He considers both types of payments as a contract with the people who work for them.

"You can't go back on your word," Thomas has said. "You can't act as though we can balance the budget on the backs of people who pay into Social Security."

As chairman of the East Asian and Pacific Affairs Subcommittee, Thomas found plenty of opportunities to needle the Clinton administration for its policies in the region. Thomas chided Assistant Secretary of State Winston Lord at a February 1996 hearing for the administration's policy toward China after that country made military threats against Taiwan. "I'm not sure that I know what the U.S. policy is," Thomas said.

He was active in postponing consideration of former Democratic Rep. Pete Peterson's nomination as U.S. ambassador to Vietnam — the first envoy to that country since diplomatic ties were restored in 1995 — because of a clause of the Constitution barring members of Congress from serving in offices created during their terms in office.

Thomas was also among several prominent Republicans who signed a letter to the State Department saying the U.S. Embassy in Hanoi should be closed unless the president could certify that Vietnam is fully cooperating in resolving U.S. prisoner-of-war and missing-in-action cases. A provision of the fiscal 1996 omnibus appropriations law prohibits the use of any government funds on current U.S. diplomatic posts or officials in Vietnam until the presidential certification is issued.

At Home: Thomas' campaign to succeed retiring Republican Sen. Malcolm Wallop banked on the idea that Wyoming voters would want another senator just as ready and willing to fight the Democratic Clinton administration as Wallop always was.

As it turned out, Thomas had read the tea leaves and the voters' mood pretty well. The seat was once thought to be a toss-up, and the Democrats nominated Mike Sullivan, their popular sitting governor. Sullivan had won his current term with 65 percent of the vote — the best margin of victory any Democratic nominee for that office ever had. But recruiting him proved to no avail: Thomas raised almost double what the governor did and ran away to victory with roughly three-fifths of the November vote.

Sullivan was hardly a liberal, even by Western standards. But Sullivan also had a past link to Clinton that dated from their service together in the National Governors Association. Sullivan had been the first sitting governor in the nation to endorse Clinton's bid for the presidency.

On Election Day, Thomas carried all but one county in the state, some by ratios of 3 to 1. He even broke into the southern tier counties where union workers and labor history traditionally have given Democrats an edge.

Prior to 1994, Thomas had been viewed as something less than a juggernaut in Wyoming politics. He had twice sought the GOP nomination for state treasurer, losing both times. But in 1984, at age 51, he was elected to the Wyoming House, where he was serving four years later when Rep. Dick Cheney was picked by President George Bush to be secretary of Defense.

Thomas got the nod from the party's state central committee and won the special election to succeed Cheney with 52 percent. He had pushed his share of the vote to 55 percent and 58 percent in 1990 and 1992, respectively.

SENATE ELECTIONS

1994 General

Craig Thomas (R)	118,754	(59%)
Mike Sullivan (D)	79,287	(39%)
Craig Alan McCune (LIBERT)	3,669	(2%)

Previous Winning Percentages: 1992* (58%) **1990*** (55%) **1989†*** (52%)

† Special election

** House elections*

CAMPAIGN FINANCE

	Receipts	Receipts from PACs	Expend-itures
1994			
Thomas (R)	$1,395,139	$667,051 (48%)	$1,068,335
Sullivan (D)	$727,710	$229,125 (31%)	$726,991

KEY VOTES

1997	
Approve balanced-budget constitutional amendment	Y
Approve chemical weapons treaty	Y
1996	
Approve farm bill	Y
Limit punitive damages in product liability cases	Y
Exempt small businesses from higher minimum wage	Y
Approve welfare overhaul	Y
Bar job discrimination based on sexual orientation	N
Override veto of ban on "partial birth" abortions	Y
1995	
Approve GOP budget with tax and spending cuts	Y
Approve constitutional amendment barring flag desecration	Y

VOTING STUDIES

	Presidential Support		Party Unity		Conservative Coalition	
Year	**S**	**O**	**S**	**O**	**S**	**O**
1996	29	69	96	2	95	5
1995	22	78	95	4	86	14
House Service:						
1994	40	55	86	7	78	3
1993	32	67	90	7	86	14
1992	77	22	83	12	81	17
1991	77	16	93	6	92	3

INTEREST GROUP RATINGS

Year	ADA	AFL-CIO	CCUS	ACU
1996	5	n/a	92	100
1995	5	0	100	83
House Service:				
1994	5	0	0	89
1993	10	17	91	87
1992	20	45	88	79
1991	0	0	100	95

Michael B. Enzi (R)

Of Gillette — Elected 1996, 1st term

Biographical Information

Born: Feb. 1, 1944, Bremerton, Wash.
Education: George Washington U., B.S. 1966; U. of Denver, M.A. 1968.
Military Service: Wyo. Air National Guard, 1968-73.
Occupation: Accountant; shoe store owner.
Family: Wife, Diana Buckley; three children.
Religion: Presbyterian.
Political Career: Mayor of Gillette, 1975-83; Wyo. House, 1987-93; Wyo. Senate, 1993-97.
Capitol Office: 290 Russell Bldg. 20510; 224-3424.

Committees

Special Aging
Banking, Housing & Urban Affairs
Financial Institutions & Regulatory Relief; Financial Services & Technology; Housing Opportunity & Community Development
Labor & Human Resources
Employment & Training; Public Health & Safety
Small Business

The Path to Washington: A businessman, former mayor and 10-year veteran of the Wyoming Legislature, Enzi proved his mettle against flashier, more prominent opponents to win Wyoming's open Senate race in 1996.

He kept the seat in Republican hands, succeeding veteran Republican Sen. Alan K. Simpson, who retired.

With a background in accounting and contacts he made running a shoe-store business with his wife, Enzi began his political climb in 1974 at age 30, winning election as mayor of Gillette, in northeastern Wyoming. He served a pair of four-year terms in that job, and was credited with guiding the city through a population explosion that saw it more than double in size.

In 1986, he won a seat in the Wyoming House, where he served six years, and then in 1992 he moved up to the state Senate. While never part of the leadership in the Legislature, he earned a reputation as a hard worker with strong organizational skills. He served as chairman of the state Senate Revenue Committee.

In addition to his legislative work on fiscal matters, Enzi was involved in education issues, serving on the Education Commission of the States, a national organization through which legislators and educators trade ideas about education policies and school reform initiatives. He also served on a state higher education commission, whose aim was to help Wyoming college students pursue professional educational opportunities.

When Enzi launched his 1996 Senate campaign, he was working for an oil well servicing company in Gillette, serving as accounting manager and computer programmer (he is a big computer buff, taking laptop in tow on his rounds of Capitol Hill).

Enzi is the only accountant in the Senate, and he can put his head for numbers to work on the Banking, Housing and Urban Affairs Committee. His background in education policy comes into play on the Labor and Human Resources Committee, where he serves, and on his other assignment, Small Business, he knows the committee's jurisdiction from personal experience.

Despite his years as a community leader and state legislator, Enzi was just a face in the crowd of GOP Senate hopefuls who rushed in after Simpson said he was stepping down. More than a dozen Republicans initially expressed interest in the race.

Although the list of potential candidates included several high-profile Republicans, from the outset the front-runner was thought to be John Barrasso, a prominent physician widely known for his work as a broadcast personality at a Casper television station.

Although he had never held elected office, Barrasso had long been active in Wyoming politics and was a Republican National Committeeman for the state.

Barrasso, who said he favored abortion rights, made fiscal issues the centerpiece of his campaign, vowing to balance the federal budget and reduce regulatory burdens. Throughout the spring, he continued to lead a GOP pack that ultimately settled down to nine candidates competing for the nomination.

Needing to counter Barrasso's high name recognition, Enzi built a network of supporters that drew in part from the Wyoming Christian Coalition; he emphasized his opposition to abortion.

In an early indication that an upset was possible, Enzi narrowly edged Barrasso in a non-binding straw poll of delegates taken at the Republican state convention in June.

Although the vote had no formal or direct bearing on the nomination, the straw poll indicated that Enzi was a serious contender against the more polished and politically moderate Barrasso.

With new momentum, Enzi pitched himself across the state as a conservative opponent of abortion and gun control who strongly supported Wyoming's mining industry and backed tax breaks for small business.

Enzi's sales job proved effective with voters in the August GOP primary. He took the nomination with 32 percent of the vote, just ahead of Barasso's 30 percent, and headed into a general-election contest with Democrat Kathy Karpan.

Karpan, a former two-term Wyoming secretary of state who had only token opposition in the Democratic primary, initially was thought to have a slight edge over Enzi. She was well-known across Wyoming because of her campaigns for and service as secretary of state, and from an unsuccessful 1994 campaign for governor. On issues such as gunowners' rights and federal land-use policy, she was careful to avoid being labeled a liberal.

But as he had done against Barrasso in the GOP primary, Enzi played up his opposition to abortion, drawing a sharp distinction on that issue between himself and Karpan, who favored abortion rights.

Although retiring Sen. Simpson also had favored abortion rights during his career, Karpan found few Republicans willing to desert Enzi because of his anti-abortion stance. He won with 54 percent of the vote, 12 percentage points ahead of Karpan.

SENATE ELECTIONS

1996 General		
Michael B. Enzi (R)	114,116	(54%)
Kathy Karpan (D)	89,103	(42%)
W. David Herbert (LIBERT)	5,289	(3%)
Lloyd Marsden (NL)	2,569	(1%)
1996 Primary		
Mike Enzi (R)	27,056	(32%)
John Barrasso (R)	24,918	(30%)
Curt Meier (R)	14,739	(18%)
Nimi McConigley (R)	6,005	(7%)
Kevin P. Meenan (R)	6,000	(7%)
Kathleen P. Jachowski (R)	2,269	(3%)
Brian E. Coen (R)	943	(1%)
Cleveland B. Holloway (R)	874	(1%)

CAMPAIGN FINANCE

	Receipts	Receipts from PACs	Expend-itures
1996			
Enzi (R)	$984,906	$476,177 (48%)	$953,572
Karpan (D)	$819,417	$277,930 (34%)	$814,258

KEY VOTES

1997	
Approve balanced-budget constitutional amendment	Y
Approve chemical weapons treaty	Y

AL Barbara Cubin (R)

Of Casper — Elected 1994, 2nd term

Biographical Information
Born: Nov. 30, 1946, Salinas, Calif.
Education: Creighton U., B.S. 1969; Casper College, 1993.
Occupation: Medical office manager; realtor; chemist.
Family: Husband, Frederick William Cubin, III; two children.
Religion: Episcopalian.
Political Career: Wyo. House, 1987-93; Wyo. Senate, 1993-95.
Capitol Office: 1114 Longworth Bldg. 20515; 225-2311.

Committees
Commerce
Finance & Hazardous Materials; Health & Environment
Resources
Energy & Mineral Resources (chairman)

In Washington: When the votes are tallied in the Resources Committee, Cubin comes down squarely on the side of private property interests, ranchers and miners — which usually puts her at odds with the Clinton administration and environmental groups. But while Cubin is a consistent and even ardent conservative, typically she is more diplomatic in manner than GOP colleagues from her region who rail at the White House, the Interior Department and congressional Democrats for waging a "war on the West."

Cubin's status went up a couple of notches at the start of her second House term. She got a subcommittee chair on Resources, leading the Energy and Mineral Resources panel, and also, the party gave her a seat on the influential Commerce Committee.

Like the other Western GOP conservatives on Resources, Cubin in the 104th supported a measure rewriting federal rules for grazing livestock on public lands and giving ranchers additional influence in managing some 260 million acres of federal rangeland. The bill specifically targeted regulations put forward in 1995 by Interior Secretary Bruce Babbitt, who wanted, among other things, to give non-ranchers more say in federal land-use decisions. Cubin, who owns a ranch where livestock are grazed on public lands, greeted that idea coolly, as she did Babbitt's suggestion that grazing fees be almost doubled.

Cubin also was unhappy with Babbitt's support of a federal program to reintroduce Canadian gray wolves into northwestern Wyoming's Yellowstone National Park. Twenty-nine wolves were released into the park in early 1995, and Interior officials hope to boost the wolf population enough to remove the animal from the endangered species list. Ranchers say the wolves injure or kill livestock, and Cubin complained that the wolves were released without telling state officials in advance — an omission she called "symptomatic of an uncaring bureaucracy."

Cubin has a strongly pro-business bent (including opposition to a minimum wage increase in 1996), and she has made it a priority to promote two of Wyoming's resource-based industries — mining of coal and trona, a type of soda ash used in glassware, detergents and baking soda. In the fall of 1995, she introduced a bill to allow states to enforce the Surface Mining Control and Reclamation Act without federal interference. Cubin told the Casper Star Tribune that the federal Office of Surface Mining had "victimized coal mine operators" by citing them for violations without regard for "the careful balance of authority" between states and the federal government in mining regulation.

She also criticized the Interior Department for proposing in May 1995 to increase the federal royalty rate on trona from 5 percent to 8 percent. At a Resources Committee hearing on the proposed royalty increase, Cubin said the higher rate would "lead to less mining, less tax revenue and fewer Wyoming jobs" in an industry that employs more than 3,000 people in the state.

Cubin served for eight years in the Wyoming Legislature before coming to Congress, and once in Washington, she quickly gained notice, winning election as secretary of the GOP Class of 1994 and earning a junior-level leadership appointment as a deputy whip. She has generally been a loyal vote for party leaders, even when their demands put her in a tight spot at home. In the fall of 1995, for instance, she agreed to vote for the GOP's seven-year balanced budget plan although it included the sale of the federal power marketing administrations (PMAs) as a revenue raiser. Cubin opposed selling the PMAs, which are wholesalers to rural electric cooperatives that provide power to thinly populated states like Wyoming.

The leadership later decided to drop the PMA-sale plan, but didn't tell her, according to the Denver Post. She was miffed that she had cast and defended a controversial vote, but was not informed of the leadership's change of heart. In a letter to House Speaker Newt Gingrich, Cubin said, "I do not take these matters lightly and would appreciate being consulted on these matters in the future."

Few states have more of a boom-and-bust economy than Wyoming, which has been reflected in its roller-coaster population growth of the past few decades.

A population jump of nearly 15 percent in the 1950s was followed by stagnation in the 1960s (1 percent growth). There was a 41 percent growth spurt in the 1970s, but then a 4 percent population decline in the 1980s.

Wyoming's economy has several components: oil and natural gas, extractive industries such as coal and uranium, an agricultural sector focused on ranching, and a steady flow of tourists to attractions such as Devils Tower and Yellowstone National Park.

Wyoming leads the nation in the production of coal and trona, a substance used in the production of glass and baking soda. But many of the state's widely scattered communities tend to depend heavily on a single industry, and they have been vulnerable to any downturn in it.

In the early 1980s the uranium market collapsed. Several years later, Wyoming's lucrative oil industry went bust as oil prices plummeted. By the end of the decade, 14 of Wyoming's 23 counties had lost population; the center of the state's oil industry, Natrona County (Casper), had a 17 percent falloff.

Population growth in the 1980s was largely limited to the four corners of the state. In the northeast, Campbell County (Gillette), the center of the state's coal production, grew 21 percent. In the northwest, Teton County, which includes Grand Teton National Park and the ski resort of Jackson Hole, grew 19 percent.

In the southwest corner, Uinta County (Evanston), a prime producer of natural gas as well as home for some long-range commuters to Salt Lake City, grew 44 percent. And in Wyoming's southeast corner, a cluster of counties anchored by Laramie (Cheyenne) showed some population growth.

The only cities in the state with more than 30,000 people are Cheyenne (just over 50,000) and Casper (almost 47,000). As the capital city, Cheyenne has a more diversified economy, which enabled it better to weather the economic downturn of the 1980s.

Cheyenne has the state government work force, the Francis E. Warren Air Force Base, where MX missiles are deployed, and an array

WYOMING
At large

of new companies that have brought hundreds of jobs to the area.

Cheyenne does not have the transportation problems that have hindered the economic development of other parts of the state. It is located only 100 miles north of Denver on Interstate 25.

Wyoming is conservative. Democrats have not carried it in a presidential election since 1964 and have not won a Senate race since 1970 or a House contest since 1976. Republicans also dominate the state Legislature. The Democrats' lone toehold had been the governorship, which the GOP won in 1994 for the first time since 1970.

In most races, Democrats have trouble winning votes beyond the party's historical base in Wyoming's southern tier. Immigrant laborers, many from Italy, were imported to build the Union Pacific rail line through the southern counties, and coal miners followed. Two of three Wyoming counties that Bill Clinton carried in 1996 were in the south — Albany and Sweetwater.

Albany County includes the academic community at the University of Wyoming in Laramie. Carbon and Sweetwater counties have more blue-collar voters, with Sweetwater County the center of the state's trona production. Albany was the only county to back the Democratic candidate for Senate in 1994; Sweetwater was the only one to support the Democratic candidate for governor.

The state's northern part is the Wyoming of ranch, rock and Republicans. Its dry plateaus and basins accommodate the cattle ranches that make Wyoming the "Cowboy State."

Bob Dole carried this part of the state in 1996, with the exception of Teton County, which went narrowly for Clinton. Overall, Dole won the state with 50 percent of the vote. Clinton got 37 percent, while Ross Perot took 12 percent.

1990 Population: 453,588. White 427,061 (94%), Black 3,606 (1%), Other 22,921 (5%). Hispanic origin 25,751 (6%). 18 and over 318,063 (70%), 62 and over 57,538 (13%). Median age: 32.

Republican leaders, though, were able to count on Cubin when they got in a pinch on the final version of the fiscal 1997 GOP budget resolution, up for a vote on the House floor in June 1996. A number of GOP conservatives were unhappy with the measure, which allowed the deficit to bump up for two years before sending it down to zero in 2002, and contained an additional $4 billion in domestic spending, added by the Senate. Facing defeat on the measure as voting time expired, GOP leaders persuaded Cubin and three other Republicans to switch from "nay" to "yea," and the measure passed, 216-211.

On social policy questions, Cubin's personal views are steadfastly conservative. But she showed a preference for "big tent" politics in March 1996 when she asked delegates to the Natrona County GOP convention not to let the issue of abortion divide the party, the Casper Star Tribune reported. "Abortion is a big issue," Cubin told the delegates. "It's important to everyone, and everyone is encouraged to work as hard as they can within our team to achieve their goals. But don't desert the team in the process."

However, the county's Republicans rejected a platform plank saying that "all points of view should be welcomed" on abortion, and instead embraced language affirming a belief "in the sanctity of human life" and supporting an anti-abortion constitutional amendment.

Though normally Cubin is a restrained speaker on the House floor, she once got swept up in a rancorous debate on welfare reform. As Republicans pilloried the welfare system for creating dependency among recipients, Cubin told colleagues she saw a parallel between the system and what she called the federal "wolf welfare program" in Wyoming. The government, Cubin said, imported wild wolves from Canada, put them in pens and fed them in preparation for releasing them into Yellowstone Park. "Guess what?" she asked. "They opened the gate to let the wolves out and now the wolves will not go. What has happened with the wolves — just like what happens with human beings — when you take away their incentives, when you take away their freedom, when you take away their dignity, they have to be provided for." Her linkage of welfare recipients and wolves prompted a chorus of Democratic boos.

At Home: The great-great-granddaughter of one of Wyoming's original homesteaders, Cubin grew up in Casper, earned a degree in chemistry at Omaha's Creighton University, and worked as a teacher, social worker and realtor before managing the business side of her husband's medical practice. Over the years she got involved in a host of community activities, and those civic efforts helped her win election to the Wyoming House in 1986 and to the state Senate six years later.

When GOP Rep. Craig Thomas announced in 1994 that he would run for the Senate, Cubin was well-positioned to seek the open House seat. She boasted a base in Casper, was the only woman in the race and easily won a straw vote at the GOP state convention. In the August primary, Cubin bested an eclectic field that included the state House Speaker, a past president of the Wyoming Woolgrowers Association and a former aide to retiring Sen. Malcolm Wallop. Cubin won the nomination with nearly 40 percent of the vote.

That set up a fall campaign against Democrat Bob Schuster, a political newcomer, who argued that he could be an articulate, independent voice in Congress. He concurred with Cubin in favoring congressional term limits, a line-item veto and a balanced-budget constitutional amendment. The two differed on abortion rights, with Schuster favoring them and Cubin opposed.

Cubin touted her legislative experience, and she stocked sporting goods stores with a questionnaire detailing her opposition to the "Clinton-Babbitt" administration's land and water policies. Schuster spent more than $2 million on the race, much of it from his own pocket. But Cubin, propelled by the year's strong anti-Democratic mood in the Rockies, won by 12 percentage points.

Cubin improved her margin to 14 percentage points in 1996, beating Democrat Peter Maxfield, a state senator and former law school professor who had lost a bid for the Senate in 1988 and was also the losing Democratic nominee for the House in 1990.

HOUSE ELECTIONS

1996 General		
Barbara Cubin (R)	116,004	(55%)
Pete Maxfield (D)	85,724	(41%)
Dave Dawson (LIBERT)	8,255	(4%)
1994 General		
Barbara Cubin (R)	104,426	(53%)
Bob Schuster (D)	81,022	(41%)
Dave Dawson (LIBERT)	10,749	(5%)

CAMPAIGN FINANCE

	Receipts	Receipts from PACs	Expend-itures
1996			
Cubin (R)	$690,003	$301,679 (44%)	$679,599
Maxfield (D)	$271,233	$64,600 (24%)	$273,881
1994			
Cubin (R)	$519,423	$175,916 (34%)	$511,119
Schuster (D)	$2,420,786	$65,500 (3%)	$2,429,346

DISTRICT VOTE FOR PRESIDENT

	1996		1992
D	77,934 (37%)	**D**	68,160 (34%)
R	105,388 (50%)	**R**	79,347 (40%)
I	25,928 (12%)	**I**	51,263 (26%)

KEY VOTES

1997	
Ban "partial birth" abortions	Y
1996	
Approve farm bill	Y
Deny public education to illegal immigrants	Y
Repeal ban on certain assault-style weapons	Y
Increase minimum wage	N
Freeze defense spending	N
Approve welfare overhaul	Y
1995	
Approve balanced-budget constitutional amendment	Y
Relax Clean Water Act regulations	Y
Oppose limits on environmental regulations	N
Reduce projected Medicare spending	Y
Approve GOP budget with tax and spending cuts	Y

VOTING STUDIES

	Presidential Support		Party Unity		Conservative Coalition	
Year	S	O	S	O	S	O
1996	30	67	93	4	92	2
1995	20	77	92	3	91	5

INTEREST GROUP RATINGS

Year	ADA	AFL-CIO	CCUS	ACU
1996	0	n/a	100	100
1995	0	0	100	92

DELEGATES / RESIDENT COMMISSIONER

Puerto Rico sends a "resident commissioner" to the House for a four-year term, while the District of Columbia, the Virgin Islands, Guam and American Samoa elect delegates who serve two-year terms.

The gains the five non-voting representatives made in the 103rd Congress, when they were first allowed to vote on the House floor, were stripped away at the beginning of the 104th Congress by the new Republican majority. The GOP had vehemently objected to the House Democratic Caucus' granting the five (at the time exclusively Democratic) delegates floor voting powers.

The rule change had allowed the five to vote when the House was acting as the Committee of the Whole, a parliamentary device that expedites the amendment process. But the privilege was largely symbolic; a modification to the rule stated that if the participation of the delegates and resident commissioner made the difference between winning and losing, the House automatically would vote again on the proposal outside the Committee of the Whole.

The only newcomer to the group in the 105th Congress is Democrat Donna M. Christian-Green of the Virgin Islands. She defeated one-term incumbent Victor O. Frazer, an independent, in a runoff election in 1996.

Because the Resources Committee (formerly Natural Resources) has jurisdiction over U.S. territorial affairs, all of the overseas representatives serve there.

Following are the capsule profiles of those who serve in the House on a non-voting basis.

DELEGATE — AMERICAN SAMOA

Eni F.H. Faleomavaega (D)

Of Pago Pago — Elected 1988, 5th term

Biographical Information

Born: Aug. 15, 1943, Vailoatai, Am. Samoa

Education: Brigham Young U., A.A. 1964, B.A. 1966; Texas Southern U., 1969; U. of Houston, J.D. 1972; U. of California, Berkeley, LL.M. 1973.

Military Service: Army, 1966-69; Army Reserve, 1983-present.

Occupation: Lawyer; congressional aide.

Family: Wife, Hinanui Bambridge Cave; five children.

Religion: Mormon.

Political Career: Am. Samoa deputy attorney general, 1981-84; Democratic candidate for U.S. House, 1984; lieutenant governor, 1985-89.

Capitol Office: 2422 Rayburn Bldg. 20515; 225-8577.

Committees

International Relations
Asia & the Pacific; International Operations & Human Rights

Resources
National Parks & Public Lands (ranking)

DELEGATE — DISTRICT OF COLUMBIA

Eleanor Holmes Norton (D)

Of Washington — Elected 1990, 4th term

Biographical Information

Born: June 13, 1937, Washington, D.C.

Education: Antioch College, B.A. 1960; Yale U., M.A. 1963, LL.B. 1964.

Occupation: Professor; lawyer.

Family: Divorced; two children.

Religion: Episcopalian.

Political Career: New York City Human Rights Commission, 1971-77; Equal Employment Opportunity Commission chairman, 1977-81.

Capitol Office: 1424 Longworth Bldg. 20515; 225-8050.

Committees

Government Reform & Oversight
Civil Service; District of Columbia (ranking)

Transportation & Infrastructure
Public Buildings & Economic Development; Surface Transportation

DELEGATE — GUAM

Robert A. Underwood (D)

Of Baza Gardens — Elected 1992, 3rd term

Biographical Information

Born: July 13, 1948, Tamuning, Guam.

Education: California State U., Los Angeles, B.A. 1969, M.A. 1971; U. of Southern California, Ph.D. 1987.

Occupation: Professor; college administrator.

Family: Wife, Lorraine Aguilar; five children.

Religion: Roman Catholic.

Political Career: No previous office.

Capitol Office: 424 Cannon Bldg. 20515; 225-1188.

Committees

National Security
Military Installations and Facilities; Military Personnel; Military Readiness

Resources
National Parks & Public Lands

DELEGATE — VIRGIN ISLANDS

Donna M. Christian-Green (D)

Of St. Croix — Elected 1996, 1st term

Biographical Information

Born: Sept. 19, 1945, Teaneck, N.J.

Education: St. Mary's College (Indiana), B.S. 1966; George Washington U., M.D. 1970.

Occupation: Physician; health official.

Family: Divorced; two children.

Religion: Moravian.

Political Career: Virgin Is. Democratic Territorial Committee, 1980-97, chair, 1980-82; Virgin Is. Board of Education, 1984-86; Virgin Is. acting commissioner of health, 1993-94.

Capitol Office: 1711 Longworth Bldg. 20515; 225-1790.

Committees

Resources
Energy & Mineral Resources; National Parks & Public Lands

RESIDENT COMMISSIONER — PUERTO RICO

Carlos Romero-Barceló (D)

Of San Juan — Elected 1992, 2nd term

Biographical Information

Born: Sept. 4, 1932, San Juan, P.R.

Education: Yale U., B.A. 1953; U. of Puerto Rico, LL.B. 1956.

Occupation: Lawyer; real estate broker.

Family: Wife, Kathleen Donnelly; four children.

Religion: Roman Catholic.

Political Career: Mayor of San Juan, 1967-77; governor, 1977-85; Puerto Rico Senate, 1986-88.

Capitol Office: 2443 Rayburn Bldg. 20515; 225-2615.

Committees

Education & Workforce
Postsecondary Education, Training & Life-Long Learning

Resources
Energy & Mineral Resources (ranking); National Parks & Public Lands

SENATE COMMITTEES

The standing and select committees of the U.S. Senate are listed below in alphabetical order. The listing includes telephone number, room number, and party ratio for each full committee. Membership is given in order of seniority on the committee.

Subcommittees are listed alphabetically under each committee. Membership is listed in order of seniority on the subcommittee.

Members of the majority party, Republicans, are shown in roman type; members of the minority party, Democrats, are shown in *italic* type.

The word "vacancy" indicates that a committee or subcommittee seat had not been filled at press time. Subcommittee vacancies do not necessarily indicate vacancies on full committees, or vice versa.

Partisan committees are listed on page 1615. Members of these committees are listed in alphabetical order, not by seniority.

The telephone area code for Washington, D.C., is 202. Abbreviations for Senate office buildings are: SD — Dirksen Building, SH — Hart Building, SR — Russell Building. The ZIP code for all Senate offices is 20510.

AGRICULTURE, NUTRITION AND FORESTRY

224-2035 SR-328A

Party Ratio: R 10 - D 8

Richard G. Lugar, R-Ind., chairman

Jesse Helms, N.C.	*Tom Harkin, Iowa*
Thad Cochran, Miss.	*Patrick J. Leahy, Vt.*
Mitch McConnell, Ky.	*Kent Conrad, N.D.*
Paul Coverdell, Ga.	*Tom Daschle, S.D.*
Rick Santorum, Pa.	*Max Baucus, Mont.*
Pat Roberts, Kan.	*Bob Kerrey, Neb.*
Charles E. Grassley, Iowa	*Tim Johnson, S.D.*
Phil Gramm, Texas	*Mary L. Landrieu, La.*
Larry E. Craig, Idaho	

FORESTRY, CONSERVATION AND RURAL REVITALIZATION

224-2035 SR-328A

Santorum - chairman

Grassley	*Conrad*
Coverdell	*Leahy*
Roberts	*Daschle*
Craig	*Baucus*

MARKETING, INSPECTION AND PRODUCT PROMOTION

224-2035 SR-328A

Coverdell - chairman

Helms	*Baucus*
Cochran	*Kerrey*
McConnell	*Landrieu*

PRODUCTION AND PRICE COMPETITIVENESS

224-2035 SR-328A

Cochran - chairman

Roberts	*Kerrey*
Helms	*Daschle*
Grassley	*Johnson*
Gramm	*Landrieu*

RESEARCH, NUTRITION AND GENERAL LEGISLATION

224-2035 SR-328A

McConnell - chairman

Gramm	*Leahy*
Craig	*Conrad*
Santorum	*Johnson*

APPROPRIATIONS

224-3471 S-128 Capitol

Party Ratio: R 15 - D 13

Ted Stevens, R-Alaska, chairman

Thad Cochran, Miss.	*Robert C. Byrd, W.Va.*
Arlen Specter, Pa.	*Daniel K. Inouye, Hawaii*
Pete V. Domenici, N.M.	*Ernest F. Hollings, S.C.*
Christopher S. Bond, Mo.	*Patrick J. Leahy, Vt.*
Slade Gorton, Wash.	*Dale Bumpers, Ark.*
Mitch McConnell, Ky.	*Frank R. Lautenberg, N.J.*
Conrad Burns, Mont.	*Tom Harkin, Iowa*
Richard C. Shelby, Ala.	*Barbara A. Mikulski, Md.*
Judd Gregg, N.H.	*Harry Reid, Nev.*
Robert F. Bennett, Utah	*Herb Kohl, Wis.*
Ben Nighthorse Campbell, Colo.	*Patty Murray, Wash.*
Larry E. Craig, Idaho	*Byron L. Dorgan, N.D.*
Lauch Faircloth, N.C.	*Barbara Boxer, Calif.*
Kay Bailey Hutchison, Texas	

AGRICULTURE, RURAL DEVELOPMENT AND RELATED AGENCIES

224-5270 SD 136

Cochran - chairman

Specter	*Bumpers*
Bond	*Harkin*
Gorton	*Kohl*
McConnell	*Byrd*
Burns	*Leahy*

COMMERCE, JUSTICE, STATE AND JUDICIARY

224-7277 S-146A Capitol

Gregg - chairman

Stevens	*Hollings*
Domenici	*Inouye*
McConnell	*Bumpers*
Hutchison	*Lautenberg*
Campbell	*Mikulski*

SENATE COMMITTEES

DEFENSE
224-7255 SD-122
Stevens - chairman

Cochran — *Inouye*
Specter — *Hollings*
Domenici — *Byrd*
Bond — *Leahy*
McConnell — *Bumpers*
Shelby — *Lautenberg*
Gregg — *Harkin*
Hutchison — *Dorgan*

DISTRICT OF COLUMBIA
224-3471 S-128 Capitol
Faircloth - chairman

Hutchison — *Boxer*

ENERGY AND WATER DEVELOPMENT
224-7260 SD-127
Domenici - chairman

Cochran — *Reid*
Gorton — *Byrd*
McConnell — *Hollings*
Bennett — *Murray*
Burns — *Kohl*
Craig — *Dorgan*

FOREIGN OPERATIONS
224-2104 SD-142
McConnell - chairman

Specter — *Leahy*
Gregg — *Inouye*
Shelby — *Lautenberg*
Bennett — *Harkin*
Campbell — *Mikulski*
Stevens — *Murray*

INTERIOR
224-7233 SD-131
Gorton - chairman

Stevens — *Byrd*
Cochran — *Leahy*
Domenici — *Bumpers*
Burns — *Hollings*
Bennett — *Reid*
Gregg — *Dorgan*
Campbell — *Boxer*

LABOR, HEALTH AND HUMAN SERVICES AND EDUCATION
224-7230 SD-184
Specter - chairman

Cochran — *Harkin*
Gorton — *Hollings*
Bond — *Inouye*
Gregg — *Bumpers*
Faircloth — *Reid*
Craig — *Kohl*
Hutchison — *Murray*

LEGISLATIVE BRANCH
224-8921 S-125 Capitol
Bennett - chairman

Stevens — *Dorgan*
Craig — *Boxer*

MILITARY CONSTRUCTION
224-7204 SD-140
Burns - chairman

Hutchison — *Murray*
Faircloth — *Reid*
Craig — *Inouye*

TRANSPORTATION
224-7281 SD-190
Shelby - chairman

Domenici — *Lautenberg*
Specter — *Byrd*
Bond — *Mikulski*
Gorton — *Reid*
Bennett — *Kohl*
Faircloth — *Murray*

TREASURY AND GENERAL GOVERNMENT
224-7337 SD-190
Campbell - chairman

Shelby — *Kohl*
Faircloth — *Mikulski*

VA, HUD AND INDEPENDENT AGENCIES
224-7211 SD-130
Bond - chairman

Burns — *Mikulski*
Stevens — *Leahy*
Shelby — *Lautenberg*
Campbell — *Harkin*
Craig — *Boxer*

ARMED SERVICES

224-3871 SR-228
Party Ratio: R 10 - D 08
Strom Thurmond, R-S.C., chairman

John W. Warner, Va. — *Carl Levin, Mich.*
John McCain, Ariz. — *Edward M. Kennedy, Mass.*
Daniel R. Coats, Ind. — *Jeff Bingaman, N.M.*
Robert C. Smith, N.H. — *John Glenn, Ohio*
Dirk Kempthorne, Idaho — *Robert C. Byrd, W.Va.*
James M. Inhofe, Okla. — *Charles S. Robb, Va.*
Rick Santorum, Pa. — *Joseph I. Lieberman, Conn.*
Olympia J. Snowe, Maine — *Max Cleland, Ga.*
Pat Roberts, Kan.

ACQUISITION AND TECHNOLOGY
224-3871 SR-228
Santorum - chairman

Smith (N.H.) — *Lieberman*
Snowe — *Kennedy*
Roberts — *Bingaman*

AIRLAND FORCES

224-3871 SR-228

Coats - chairman

Warner	*Glenn*
Kempthorne	*Bingaman*
Inhofe	*Byrd*
Santorum	*Lieberman*
Roberts	*Cleland*

PERSONNEL

224-3871 SR-228

Kempthorne - chairman

McCain	*Cleland*
Coats	*Kennedy*
Snowe	*Robb*

READINESS

224-3871 SR-228

Inhofe - chairman

McCain	*Robb*
Coats	*Glenn*
Roberts	*Cleland*

SEAPOWER

224-3871 SR-228

Warner - chairman

McCain	*Kennedy*
Smith (N.H.)	*Byrd*
Santorum	*Robb*
Snowe	*Lieberman*

STRATEGIC FORCES

224-3871 SR-228

Smith (N.H.) - chairman

Warner	*Bingaman*
Kempthorne	*Glenn*
Inhofe	*Byrd*

BANKING, HOUSING AND URBAN AFFAIRS

224-7391 SD-534

Party Ratio: R 10 - D 8

Alfonse M. D'Amato, R-N.Y., chairman

Phil Gramm, Texas	*Paul S. Sarbanes, Md.*
Richard C. Shelby, Ala.	*Christopher J. Dodd, Conn.*
Connie Mack, Fla.	*John Kerry, Mass.*
Lauch Faircloth, N.C.	*Richard H. Bryan, Nev.*
Robert F. Bennett, Utah	*Barbara Boxer, Calif.*
Rod Grams, Minn.	*Carol Moseley-Braun, Ill.*
Wayne Allard, Colo.	*Tim Johnson, S.D.*
Michael B. Enzi, Wyo.	*Jack Reed, R.I.*
Chuck Hagel, Neb.	

FINANCIAL INSTITUTIONS AND REGULATORY RELIEF

224-7391 SD-534

Faircloth - chairman

Allard	*Bryan*
Enzi	*Johnson*
Shelby	*Boxer*
Mack	*Moseley-Braun*
Grams	*Reed*
Gramm	

FINANCIAL SERVICES AND TECHNOLOGY

224-7391 SD-534

Bennett - chairman

Hagel	*Boxer*
Mack	*Kerry*
Grams	*Dodd*
Enzi	*Johnson*

INTERNATIONAL FINANCE

224-7391 SD-534

Grams - chairman

Hagel	*Moseley-Braun*
Gramm	*Boxer*
Bennett	*Reed*

HOUSING OPPORTUNITY AND COMMUNITY DEVELOPMENT

224-7391 SD-534

Mack - chairman

Faircloth	*Kerry*
Enzi	*Reed*
Shelby	*Dodd*
Allard	*Bryan*
Hagel	*Moseley-Braun*

SECURITIES

224-7391 SD-534

Gramm - chairman

Shelby	*Dodd*
Allard	*Johnson*
Bennett	*Kerry*
Faircloth	*Bryan*

BUDGET

224-0642 SD-621

Party Ratio: R 12 - D 10

Pete V. Domenici, R-N.M., chairman

Charles E. Grassley, Iowa	*Frank R. Lautenberg, N.J.*
Don Nickles, Okla.	*Ernest F. Hollings, S.C.*
Phil Gramm, Texas	*Kent Conrad, N.D.*
Christopher S. Bond, Mo.	*Paul S. Sarbanes, Md.*
Slade Gorton, Wash.	*Barbara Boxer, Calif.*
Judd Gregg, N.H.	*Patty Murray, Wash.*
Olympia J. Snowe, Maine	*Ron Wyden, Ore.*
Spencer Abraham, Mich.	*Russell D. Feingold, Wis.*
Bill Frist, Tenn.	*Tim Johnson, S.D.*
Rod Grams, Minn.	*Richard J. Durbin, Ill.*
Gordon H. Smith, Ore.	

SENATE COMMITTEES

COMMERCE, SCIENCE AND TRANSPORTATION

224-5115 SD-508

Party Ratio: R 11 - D 9

John McCain, R-Ariz., chairman

Ted Stevens, Alaska	*Ernest F. Hollings, S.C.*
Conrad Burns, Mont.	*Daniel K. Inouye, Hawaii*
Slade Gorton, Wash.	*Wendell H. Ford, Ky.*
Trent Lott, Miss.	*John D. Rockefeller IV, W.Va.*
Kay Bailey Hutchison, Texas	*John Kerry, Mass.*
Olympia J. Snowe, Maine	*John B. Breaux, La.*
John Ashcroft, Mo.	*Richard H. Bryan, Nev.*
Bill Frist, Tenn.	*Byron L. Dorgan, N.D.*
Spencer Abraham, Mich.	*Ron Wyden, Ore.*
Sam Brownback, Kan.	

AVIATION

224-4852 SH-427

Gorton - chairman

Stevens	*Ford*
Burns	*Hollings*
Lott	*Inouye*
Hutchison	*Bryan*
Ashcroft	*Rockefeller*
Frist	*Breaux*
Snowe	*Dorgan*
Brownback	*Wyden*

COMMUNICATIONS

224-5184 SH-227

Burns - chairman

Stevens	*Hollings*
Gorton	*Inouye*
Lott	*Ford*
Ashcroft	*Kerry*
Hutchison	*Breaux*
Abraham	*Rockefeller*
Frist	*Dorgan*
Brownback	*Wyden*

CONSUMER AFFAIRS, FOREIGN COMMERCE AND TOURISM

224-5183 SH-425

Ashcroft - chairman

Gorton	*Breaux*
Abraham	*Ford*
Burns	*Bryan*
Brownback	

MANUFACTURING AND COMPETITIVENESS

224-1745 SD-245

Abraham - chairman

Snowe	*Bryan*
Ashcroft	*Hollings*
Frist	*Dorgan*
Brownback	*Rockefeller*

OCEANS AND FISHERIES

224-8172 SH-428

Snowe - chairman

Stevens	*Kerry*
Gorton	*Inouye*
Hutchison	*Breaux*

SCIENCE, TECHNOLOGY AND SPACE

224-8172 SH-428

Frist - chairman

Burns	*Rockefeller*
Hutchison	*Kerry*
Stevens	*Bryan*
Abraham	*Dorgan*

SURFACE TRANSPORTATION AND MERCHANT MARINE

224-4852 SH-427

Hutchison - chairman

Stevens	*Inouye*
Burns	*Breaux*
Snowe	*Dorgan*
Frist	*Bryan*
Abraham	*Wyden*
Ashcroft	

ENERGY AND NATURAL RESOURCES

224-4971 SD-304

Party Ratio: R 11 - D 9

Frank H. Murkowski, R-Alaska, chairman

Pete V. Domenici, N.M.	*Dale Bumpers, Ark.*
Don Nickles, Okla.	*Wendell H. Ford, Ky.*
Larry E. Craig, Idaho	*Jeff Bingaman, N.M.*
Ben Nighthorse Campbell, Colo.	*Daniel K. Akaka, Hawaii*
Craig Thomas, Wyo.	*Byron L. Dorgan, N.D.*
Jon Kyl, Ariz.	*Bob Graham, Fla.*
Rod Grams, Minn.	*Ron Wyden, Ore.*
Gordon H. Smith, Ore.	*Tim Johnson, S.D.*
Slade Gorton, Wash.	*Mary L. Landrieu, La.*
Conrad Burns, Mont.	

ENERGY RESEARCH, DEVELOPMENT, PRODUCTION AND REGULATION

224-6567 SD-308

Nickles - chairman

Domenici	*Ford*
Craig	*Bingaman*
Grams	*Graham*
Gorton	*Wyden*
Campbell	*Johnson*
Smith (Ore.)	*Landrieu*

FORESTS AND PUBLIC LAND MANAGEMENT

224-6170 SD-306

Craig - chairman

Burns	*Dorgan*
Domenici	*Graham*
Thomas	*Wyden*
Kyl	*Johnson*
Smith (Ore.)	*Landrieu*

NATIONAL PARKS, HISTORIC PRESERVATION AND RECREATION

224-6969 SD-354

Thomas - chairman

Campbell	*Bingaman*
Grams	*Akaka*
Nickles	*Graham*
Burns	*Landrieu*

WATER AND POWER

224-2564 SD-304

Kyl - chairman

Smith (Ore.)	*Akaka*
Gorton	*Ford*
Campbell	*Dorgan*
Craig	*Wyden*

ENVIRONMENT AND PUBLIC WORKS

224-6176 SD-410

Party Ratio: R 10 - D 8

John H. Chafee, R-R.I., chairman

John W. Warner, Va.	*Max Baucus, Mont.*
Robert C. Smith, N.H.	*Daniel Patrick Moynihan, N.Y.*
Dirk Kempthorne, Idaho	*Frank R. Lautenberg, N.J.*
James M. Inhofe, Okla.	*Harry Reid, Nev.*
Craig Thomas, Wyo.	*Bob Graham, Fla.*
Christopher S. Bond, Mo.	*Joseph I. Lieberman, Conn.*
Tim Hutchinson, Ark.	*Barbara Boxer, Calif.*
Wayne Allard, Colo.	*Ron Wyden, Ore.*
Jeff Sessions, Ala.	

CLEAN AIR, WETLANDS, PRIVATE PROPERTY AND NUCLEAR SAFETY

224-6176 SD-410

Inhofe - chairman

Hutchinson	*Graham*
Allard	*Lieberman*
Sessions	*Boxer*

DRINKING WATER, FISHERIES AND WILDLIFE

224-6176 SD-410

Kempthorne - chairman

Thomas	*Reid*
Bond	*Lautenberg*
Warner	*Lieberman*
Hutchinson	*Wyden*

SUPERFUND, WASTE CONTROL AND RISK ASSESSMENT

224-6176 SD-410

Smith (N.H.) - chairman

Warner	*Lautenberg*
Inhofe	*Moynihan*
Allard	*Boxer*
Sessions	*Graham*

TRANSPORTATION AND INFRASTRUCTURE

224-6176 SD-410

Warner - chairman

Smith (N.H.)	*Baucus*
Kempthorne	*Moynihan*
Bond	*Reid*
Inhofe	*Graham*
Thomas	*Boxer*

FINANCE

224-4515 SD-219

Party Ratio: R 11 - D 9

William V. Roth Jr., R-Del., chairman

John H. Chafee, R.I.	*Daniel Patrick Moynihan, N.Y.*
Charles E. Grassley, Iowa	*Max Baucus, Mont.*
Orrin G. Hatch, Utah	*John D. Rockefeller IV, W.Va.*
Alfonse M. D'Amato, N.Y.	*John B. Breaux, La.*
Frank H. Murkowski, Alaska	*Kent Conrad, N.D.*
Don Nickles, Okla.	*Bob Graham, Fla.*
Phil Gramm, Texas	*Carol Moseley-Braun, Ill.*
Trent Lott, Miss.	*Richard H. Bryan, Nev.*
James M. Jeffords, Vt.	*Bob Kerrey, Neb.*
Connie Mack, Fla.	

HEALTH CARE

224-4515 SD-219

Gramm - chairman

Roth	*Rockefeller*
Chafee	*Baucus*
Grassley	*Conrad*
Hatch	*Graham*
D'Amato	*Moseley-Braun*
Nickles	*Bryan*
Jeffords	*Kerrey*

INTERNATIONAL TRADE

224-4515 SD-219

Grassley - chairman

Roth	*Moynihan*
Chafee	*Baucus*
Hatch	*Rockefeller*
D'Amato	*Breaux*
Murkowski	*Conrad*
Gramm	*Graham*
Lott	*Moseley-Braun*
Mack	*Kerrey*

LONG-TERM GROWTH, DEBT AND DEFICIT REDUCTION

224-4515 SD-219

Mack - chairman

Murkowski	*Graham*
Lott	*Bryan*

SOCIAL SECURITY AND FAMILY POLICY

224-4515 SD-219

Chafee - chairman

Nickles	*Breaux*
Gramm	*Moynihan*
Jeffords	*Rockefeller*
	Moseley-Braun

SENATE COMMITTEES

TAXATION AND IRS OVERSIGHT

224-4515 SD-219

Nickles - chairman

Roth	*Baucus*
Grassley	*Moynihan*
Hatch	*Breaux*
D'Amato	*Conrad*
Murkowski	*Bryan*
Lott	*Kerrey*
Mack	
Jeffords	

FOREIGN RELATIONS

224-4651 SD-450

Party Ratio: R 10 - D 8

Jesse Helms, R-N.C., chairman

Richard G. Lugar, Ind.	*Joseph R. Biden Jr., Del.*
Paul Coverdell, Ga.	*Paul S. Sarbanes, Md.*
Chuck Hagel, Neb.	*Christopher J. Dodd, Conn.*
Gordon H. Smith, Ore.	*John Kerry, Mass.*
Craig Thomas, Wyo.	*Charles S. Robb, Va.*
John Ashcroft, Mo.	*Russell D. Feingold, Wis.*
Rod Grams, Minn.	*Dianne Feinstein, Calif.*
Bill Frist, Tenn.	*Paul Wellstone, Minn.*
Sam Brownback, Kan.	

AFRICAN AFFAIRS

224-4651 SD-450

Ashcroft - chairman

Grams	*Feingold*
Frist	*Sarbanes*

EAST ASIAN AND PACIFIC AFFAIRS

224-4651 SD-450

Thomas - chairman

Frist	*Kerry*
Lugar	*Robb*
Coverdell	*Feingold*
Hagel	*Feinstein*

EUROPEAN AFFAIRS

224-4651 SD-450

Smith (Ore.) - chairman

Lugar	*Biden*
Ashcroft	*Wellstone*
Hagel	*Sarbanes*
Thomas	*Dodd*

INTERNATIONAL ECONOMIC POLICY, EXPORT AND TRADE PROMOTION

224-4651 SD-450

Hagel - chairman

Thomas	*Sarbanes*
Frist	*Biden*
Coverdell	*Wellstone*

INTERNATIONAL OPERATIONS

224-4651 SD-450

Grams - chairman

Helms	*Feinstein*
Brownback	*Dodd*
Smith (Ore.)	*Kerry*

NEAR EASTERN AND SOUTH ASIAN AFFAIRS

224-4651 SD-450

Brownback - chairman

Smith (Ore.)	*Robb*
Grams	*Feinstein*
Helms	*Wellstone*
Ashcroft	*Sarbanes*

WESTERN HEMISPHERE, PEACE CORPS, NARCOTICS AND TERRORISM

224-4651 SD-450

Coverdell - chairman

Helms	*Dodd*
Lugar	*Kerry*
Brownback	*Robb*

GOVERNMENTAL AFFAIRS

224-4751 SD-340

Party Ratio: R 9 - D 7

Fred Thompson, R-Tenn., chairman

Susan Collins, Maine	*John Glenn, Ohio*
Sam Brownback, Kan.	*Carl Levin, Mich.*
Pete V. Domenici, N.M.	*Joseph I. Lieberman, Conn.*
Thad Cochran, Miss.	*Daniel K. Akaka, Hawaii*
Don Nickles, Okla.	*Richard J. Durbin, Ill.*
Arlen Specter, Pa.	*Robert G. Torricelli, N.J.*
Robert C. Smith, N.H.	*Max Cleland, Ga.*
Robert F. Bennett, Utah	

INTERNATIONAL SECURITY, PROLIFERATION AND FEDERAL SERVICES

224-2254 SH-442

Cochran - chairman

Collins	*Levin*
Domenici	*Akaka*
Nickles	*Durbin*
Specter	*Torricelli*
Smith, N.H.	*Cleland*

OVERSIGHT OF GOVERNMENT MANAGEMENT, RESTRUCTURING AND THE DISTRIC

DISTRICT OF COLUMBIA

224-3682 SH-601

Brownback - chairman

Specter	*Lieberman*
Bennett	*Cleland*

INVESTIGATIONS
224-2254 SH-601
Collins - chairman

Brownback	*Glenn*
Domenici	*Levin*
Cochran	*Lieberman*
Nickles	*Akaka*
Specter	*Durbin*
Smith, N.H.	*Torricelli*
Bennett	*Cleland*

INDIAN AFFAIRS
224-2251 SH-838
Party Ratio: R 8 - D 6
Ben Nighthorse Campbell, R-Colo., chairman

Frank H. Murkowski, Alaska	*Daniel K. Inouye, Hawaii*
John McCain, Ariz.	*Kent Conrad, N.D.*
Slade Gorton, Wash.	*Harry Reid, Nev.*
Pete V. Domenici, N.M.	*Daniel K. Akaka, Hawaii*
Craig Thomas, Wyo.	*Paul Wellstone, Minn.*
Orrin G. Hatch, Utah	*Byron L. Dorgan, N.D.*
James M. Inhofe, Okla.	

JUDICIARY
224-5225 SD-224
Party Ratio: R 10 - D 8
Orrin G. Hatch, R-Utah, chairman

Strom Thurmond, S.C.	*Patrick J. Leahy, Vt.*
Charles E. Grassley, Iowa	*Edward M. Kennedy, Mass.*
Arlen Specter, Pa.	*Joseph R. Biden Jr., Del.*
Fred Thompson, Tenn.	*Herb Kohl, Wis.*
Jon Kyl, Ariz.	*Dianne Feinstein, Calif.*
Mike DeWine, Ohio	*Russell D. Feingold, Wis.*
John Ashcroft, Mo.	*Richard J. Durbin, Ill.*
Spencer Abraham, Mich.	*Robert G. Torricelli, N.J.*
Jeff Sessions, Ala.	

ADMINISTRATIVE OVERSIGHT AND THE COURTS
224-6736 SH-308
Grassley - chairman

Thurmond	*Durbin*
Sessions	*Feingold*
Kyl	*Kohl*

ANTITRUST, BUSINESS RIGHTS AND COMPETITION
224-9494 SD-161
DeWine - chairman

Hatch	*Kohl*
Thurmond	*Torricelli*
Specter	*Leahy*

CONSTITUTION, FEDERALISM AND PROPERTY RIGHTS
224-5710 SD-164
Ashcroft - chairman

Hatch	*Feingold*
Abraham	*Kennedy*
Thurmond	*Torricelli*
Thompson	

IMMIGRATION
224-6098 SD-323
Abraham - chairman

Grassley	*Kennedy*
Kyl	*Feinstein*
Specter	*Durbin*

TECHNOLOGY, TERRORISM AND GOVERNMENT INFORMATION
224-4521 SH-702
Kyl - chairman

Hatch	*Feinstein*
Specter	*Biden*
Thompson	*Durbin*

YOUTH VIOLENCE
224-2808 SD-163
Sessions - chairman

Thompson	*Biden*
DeWine	*Torricelli*
Ashcroft	*Kohl*
Grassley	*Feinstein*

LABOR AND HUMAN RESOURCES
224-5375 SD-428
Party Ratio: R 10 - D 8
James M. Jeffords, R-Vt.,

Daniel R. Coats, Ind.	*Edward M. Kennedy, Mass.*
Judd Gregg, N.H.	*Christopher J. Dodd, Conn.*
Bill Frist, Tenn.	*Tom Harkin, Iowa*
Mike DeWine, Ohio	*Barbara A. Mikulski, Md.*
Michael B. Enzi, Wyo.	*Jeff Bingaman, N.M.*
Tim Hutchinson, Ark.	*Paul Wellstone, Minn.*
Susan Collins, Maine	*Patty Murray, Wash.*
John W. Warner, Va.	*Jack Reed, R.I.*
Mitch McConnell, Ky.	

AGING
224-0136 SH-615
Gregg - chairman

Hutchinson	*Mikulski*
Warner	*Murray*

CHILDREN AND FAMILIES
224-5800 SH-625
Coats - chairman

Gregg	*Dodd*
Frist	*Bingaman*
Hutchinson	*Wellstone*
Collins	*Murray*
McConnell	*Reed*

EMPLOYMENT AND TRAINING
224-2962 SH-608
DeWine - chairman

Jeffords	*Wellstone*
Enzi	*Kennedy*
Warner	*Dodd*
McConnell	*Harkin*

PUBLIC HEALTH AND SAFETY

224-7139 SD-422

Frist - chairman

Jeffords	*Kennedy*
Coats	*Harkin*
DeWine	*Mikulski*
Enzi	*Bingaman*
Collins	*Reed*

RULES AND ADMINISTRATION

224-6352 SR-305

Party Ratio: R 9 - D 7

John W. Warner, R-Va., chairman

Jesse Helms, N.C.	*Wendell H. Ford, Ky.*
Ted Stevens, Alaska	*Robert C. Byrd, W.Va.*
Mitch McConnell, Ky.	*Daniel K. Inouye, Hawaii*
Thad Cochran, Miss.	*Daniel Patrick Moynihan, N.Y.*
Rick Santorum, Pa.	*Christopher J. Dodd, Conn.*
Don Nickles, Okla.	*Dianne Feinstein, Calif.*
Trent Lott, Miss.	*Robert G. Torricelli, N.J.*
Kay Bailey Hutchison, Texas	

SELECT ETHICS

224-2981 SH-220

Party Ratio: R 3 - D 3

Robert C. Smith, R-N.H., chairman

Pat Roberts, Kan.	*Harry Reid, Nev.*
Jeff Sessions, Ala.	*Patty Murray, Wash.*
	Kent Conrad, N.D.

SELECT INTELLIGENCE

224-1700 SH-211

Party Ratio: R 10 - D 9

Richard C. Shelby, R-Ala., chairman

John H. Chafee, R.I.	*Bob Kerrey, Neb.*
Richard G. Lugar, Ind.	*John Glenn, Ohio*
Mike DeWine, Ohio	*Richard H. Bryan, Nev.*
Jon Kyl, Ariz.	*Bob Graham, Fla.*
James M. Inhofe, Okla.	*John Kerry, Mass.*
Orrin G. Hatch, Utah	*Max Baucus, Mont.*
Pat Roberts, Kan.	*Charles S. Robb, Va.*
Wayne Allard, Colo.	*Frank R. Lautenberg, N.J.*
Daniel R. Coats, Ind.	*Carl Levin, Mich.*

SMALL BUSINESS

224-5175 SR-428A

Party Ratio: R 10 - D 8

Christopher S. Bond, R-Mo., chairman

Conrad Burns, Mont.	*John Kerry, Mass.*
Paul Coverdell, Ga.	*Dale Bumpers, Ark.*
Dirk Kempthorne, Idaho	*Carl Levin, Mich.*
Robert F. Bennett, Utah	*Tom Harkin, Iowa*
John W. Warner, Va.	*Joseph I. Lieberman, Conn.*
Bill Frist, Tenn.	*Paul Wellstone, Minn.*
Olympia J. Snowe, Maine	*Max Cleland, Ga.*
Lauch Faircloth, N.C.	*Mary L. Landrieu, La.*
Michael B. Enzi, Wyo.	

SPECIAL AGING

224-5364 SD-G31

Party Ratio: R 10 - D 8

Charles E. Grassley, R-Iowa, chairman

James M. Jeffords, Vt.	*John B. Breaux, La.*
Larry E. Craig, Idaho	*John Glenn, Ohio*
Conrad Burns, Mont.	*Harry Reid, Nev.*
Richard C. Shelby, Ala.	*Herb Kohl, Wis.*
Rick Santorum, Pa.	*Russell D. Feingold, Wis.*
John W. Warner, Va.	*Carol Moseley-Braun, Ill.*
Chuck Hagel, Neb.	*Ron Wyden, Ore.*
Susan Collins, Maine	*Jack Reed, R.I.*
Michael B. Enzi, Wyo.	

VETERANS' AFFAIRS

224-9126 SR-412

Party Ratio: R 7 - D 5

Arlen Specter, R-Pa., chairman

Strom Thurmond, R-S.C.

Frank H. Murkowski, Alaska	*John D. Rockefeller IV, W.Va.*
James M. Jeffords, Vt.	*Bob Graham, Fla.*
Ben Nighthorse Campbell, Colo.	*Daniel K. Akaka, Hawaii*
Larry E. Craig, Idaho	*Paul Wellstone, Minn.*
Tim Hutchinson, Ark.	*Patty Murray, Wash.*

PARTISAN SENATE COMMITTEES

REPUBLICAN LEADERS

President Pro Tempore . . . . . . Strom Thurmond, S.C.
Majority Leader . . . . Trent Lott, Miss.
Assistant Majority Leader . . . . Don Nickles, Okla.
Conference Chairman . . . . Connie Mack, Fla.
Conference Secretary . . . . Paul Coverdell, Ga.
Chief Deputy Whip . . . . Judd Gregg, N.H.
Deputy Whip . . . . Spencer Abraham, Mich.
John Ashcroft, Mo.
Conrad Burns, Mont.
Daniel R. Coats, Ind.
Susan Collins, Maine
Chuck Hagel, Neb.
Kay Bailey Hutchison, Texas
Dirk Kempthorne, Idaho
Jon Kyl, Ariz.
Gordon H. Smith, Ore.
Olympia J. Snowe, Maine

NATIONAL REPUBLICAN SENATORIAL COMMITTEE

(202) 675-6000 425 Second St., N.E. 20002

Mitch McConnell, Ky., chairman

Spencer Abraham, Mich.
Mike DeWine, Ohio
Bill Frist, Tenn.
Chuck Hagel, Neb.
Kay Bailey Hutchinson, Texas
James M. Inhofe, Okla.
Jon Kyl, Ariz.
Pat Roberts, Kan.
Rick Santorum, Pa.
Robert C. Smith, N.H.

COMMITTEE ON COMMITTEES

(202) 224-3441 SH-730

Slade Gorton, Wash., chairman

John Ashcroft, Mo.
Bill Frist, Tenn.
Rod Grams, Minn.
Orrin G. Hatch, Utah
Ted Stevens, Alaska
John W. Warner, Va.

POLICY COMMITTEE

(202) 224-2946 SR-347

Larry E. Craig, Idaho, chairman

John H. Chafee, R.I.
Paul Coverdell, Ga.
Alfonse M. D'Amato, N.Y.
Pete V. Domenici, N.M.
Orrin G. Hatch, Utah
Jesse Helms, N.C.
James M. Jeffords, Vt.
Trent Lott, Miss.
Richard G. Lugar, Ind.
Connie Mack, Fla.
John McCain, Ariz.
Frank H. Murkowski, Alaska
Don Nickles, Okla.
William V. Roth Jr., Del.
Richard C. Shelby, Ala.
Arlen Specter, Pa.
Ted Stevens, Alaska
Fred Thompson, Tenn.
Strom Thurmond, S.C.
John W. Warner, Va.

DEMOCRATIC LEADERS

President . . . . Vice President Al Gore, Tenn.
Minority Leader . . . . Tom Daschle, S.D.
Minority Whip . . . . Wendell H. Ford, Ky.
Conference Chairman . . . . Tom Daschle, S.D.
Conference Secretary. . . . . Barbara A. Mikulski, Md.
Chief Deputy Whip . . . . John B. Breaux, La.
Assistant Floor Leader . . . . . . Byron L. Dorgan, N.D.
Deputy Whip . . . . Jeff Bingaman, N.M.
Deputy Whip . . . . Joseph I. Lieberman, Conn.
Deputy Whip. . . . . Patty Murray, Wash.
Charles S. Robb, Va.

DEMOCRATIC SENATORIAL CAMPAIGN COMMITTEE

(202) 224-2447 430 S. Capitol St., S.E. 20003
Bob Kerrey, Neb., chairman
Robert G. Torricelli, N.J., vice-chairman
Max Baucus, Mont., Majority Trust Co-Chairman
Richard H. Bryan, Nev., Roundtable Co-Chairman
Kent Conrad, N.D., Leadership Circle Co-Chairman
Richard J. Durbin, Ill., Political Whips Co-Chairman
Dianne Feinstein, Calif., Women's Council Co-Chairman
Tom Harkin, Iowa, Majority Trust Co-Chairman
Edward M. Kennedy, Mass., Labor Council Co-Chairman
Mary L. Landrieu, La., Women's Council Co-Chairman
Joseph I. Lieberman, Conn., Political Whips Co-Chairman
Jack Reed, R.I., Roundtable Co-Chairman
Charles S. Robb, Va., Leadership Circle Co-Chairman
John D. Rockefeller IV, W.Va., Majority Trust Co-Chairman
Paul Wellstone, Minn., Labor Council Co-Chairman

TECHNOLOGY AND COMMUNICATIONS COMMITTEE

(202) 224-1430 SH-619
John D. Rockefeller IV, W.Va., chairman

Jeff Bingaman, N.M.
John B. Breaux, La.
Kent Conrad, N.D.
Tom Daschle, S.D.
Christopher J. Dodd, Conn.
Wendell H. Ford, Ky.
John Glenn, Ohio
Ernest F. Hollings, S.C.
Frank R. Lautenberg, N.J.
Barbara A. Mikulski, Md.
Patty Murray, Wash.
Charles S. Robb, Va.

POLICY COMMITTEE

(202) 224-5551 S-118 Capitol
Tom Daschle, S.D., chairman
Harry Reid, Nev., co-chairman
Paul S. Sarbanes, Md., vice chairman
Charles S. Robb, Va., vice chairman
Patty Murray, Wash., vice chairman
John Glenn, Ohio, vice chairman

Jack Reed, R.I.
Max Cleland, Ga.
Bob Kerrey, Neb.
Ernest F. Hollings, S.C.
Dale Bumpers, Ark.
Daniel Patrick Moynihan, N.Y.
John D. Rockefeller IV, W.Va.
Daniel K. Akaka, Hawaii
Byron L. Dorgan, N.D.
Carol Moseley-Braun, Ill.
Russell D. Feingold, Wis.
Joseph I. Lieberman, Conn.
Paul Wellstone, Minn.
Dianne Feinstein, Calif.
Ron Wyden, Ore.
Robert G. Torricelli, N.J.
Wendell H. Ford, Ky.
Barbara A. Mikulski, Md.

STEERING AND COORDINATION COMMITTEE

(202) 224-9048 SH-712
John Kerry, Mass., chairman

Daniel K. Inouye, Hawaii
Robert C. Byrd, W.Va.
Edward M. Kennedy, Mass.
Joseph R. Biden Jr., Del.
Wendell H. Ford, Ky.
Patrick J. Leahy, Vt.
Christopher J. Dodd, Conn.
Tom Harkin, Iowa
Max Baucus, Mont.
Bob Graham, Fla.
Kent Conrad, N.D.
Carl Levin, Mich.
Richard H. Bryan, Nev.
Herb Kohl, Wis.
Barbara Boxer, Calif.
John B. Breaux, La.
Tom Daschle, S.D.
Frank R. Lautenberg, N.J.
Jeff Bingaman, N.M.

HOUSE COMMITTEES

The standing and select committees of the U.S. House are listed below in alphabetical order. The listing includes telephone number, room number, and party ratio for each full committee. Membership is given in order of seniority on the committee. If a non-voting delegate or the resident commissioner is a member of the committee, the party ratio reflects that membership. Non-voting representatives, while they cannot vote on the House floor, enjoy status equal to that of their voting colleagues on committees. Subcommittees are listed alphabetically under each committee. Membership is listed in order of seniority on the subcommittee.

Members of the majority party, Republicans, are shown in roman type; members of the minority party, Democrats, are shown in *italic* type. Independents are shown in **bold.** The word "vacancy" indicates that a committee or subcommittee seat had not been filled at press time. Subcommittee vacancies do not necessarily indicate vacancies on full committees, or vice versa.

Partisan committees are listed on pages 1630-1631. Members of these committees are listed in alphabetical order, not by seniority. The telephone area code for Washington, D.C., is 202. Abbreviations for House office buildings are: CHOB – Cannon House Office Building, LHOB – Longworth House Office Building, RHOB – Rayburn House Office Building, OHOB – O'Neill House Office Building, FHOB – Ford House Office Building, and Capitol. The ZIP code is 20515.

AGRICULTURE

225-0029 1301 LHOB

Party Ratio: R 27 - D 23

Bob Smith, R-Ore., chairman

Larry Combest, Texas	*Charles W. Stenholm, Texas*
Bill Barrett, Neb.	*George E. Brown Jr., Calif.*
John A. Boehner, Ohio	*Gary A. Condit, Calif.*
Thomas W. Ewing, Ill.	*Collin C. Peterson, Minn.*
John T. Doolittle, Calif.	*Cal Dooley, Calif.*
Robert W. Goodlatte, Va.	*Eva Clayton, N.C.*
Richard W. Pombo, Calif.	*David Minge, Minn.*
Charles T. Canady, Fla.	*Earl F. Hilliard, Ala.*
Nick Smith, Mich.	*Earl Pomeroy, N.D.*
Terry Everett, Ala.	*Tim Holden, Pa.*
Frank D. Lucas, Okla.	*Scotty Baesler, Ky.*
Ron Lewis, Ky.	*Sanford D. Bishop Jr., Ga.*
Helen Chenoweth, Idaho	*Bennie Thompson, Miss.*
John Hostettler, Ind.	*Sam Farr, Calif.*
Ed Bryant, Tenn.	*John Baldacci, Maine*
Mark Foley, Fla.	*Marion Berry, Ark.*
Saxby Chambliss, Ga.	*Virgil H. Goode Jr., Va.*
Ray LaHood, Ill.	*Mike McIntyre, N.C.*
Jo Ann Emerson, Mo.	*Debbie Stabenow, Mich.*
Jerry Moran, Kan.	*Bob Etheridge, N.C.*
Roy Blunt, Mo.	*Chris John, La.*
Charles W. "Chip" Pickering Jr., Miss.	*Jay W. Johnson, Wis.*
Bob Schaffer, Colo.	*Leonard L. Boswell, Iowa*
John Thune, S.D.	
Bill Jenkins, Tenn.	
John Cooksey, La.	

DEPARTMENT OPERATIONS, NUTRITION AND FOREIGN AGRICULTURE

225-0171 1430 LHOB

Goodlatte - chairman

Ewing	*Clayton*
Canady	*Thompson*
Smith (Mich.)	*Berry*
Foley	*Brown* (Calif.)
LaHood	*Bishop*
Thune	

FORESTRY, RESOURCE CONSERVATION AND RESEARCH

225-0171 1430 LHOB

Combest - chairman

Barrett (Neb.)	*Dooley*
Doolittle	*Brown* (Calif.)
Pombo	*Farr*
Smith (Mich.)	*Stabenow*
Everett	*John*
Lucas	*Peterson* (Minn.)
Lewis (Ky.)	*Clayton*
Chenoweth	*Minge*
Hostettler	*Hilliard*
Chambliss	*Pomeroy*
LaHood	*Holden*
Emerson	*Baesler*
Moran (Kan.)	*Baldacci*
Pickering	*Berry*
Schaffer	*Goode*
Jenkins	
Cooksey	

GENERAL FARM COMMODITIES

225-0171 1430 LHOB

Barrett - chairman

Combest	*Minge*
Boehner	*Thompson*
Lucas	*McIntyre*
Chambliss	*Stabenow*
Emerson	*Etheridge*
Moran (Kan.)	*John*
Thune	*Johnson* (Wis.)
Cooksey	

LIVESTOCK, DAIRY AND POULTRY

225-2171 1432P LHOB

Pombo - chairman

Boehner	*Peterson* (Minn.)
Goodlatte	*Hilliard*
Smith (Mich.)	*Holden*
Lucas	*Johnson* (Wis.)
Lewis (Ky.)	*Condit*
Hostettler	*Dooley*
Blunt	*Farr*
Pickering	*Boswell*
Jenkins	

RISK MANAGEMENT AND SPECIALTY CROPS

225-4652 1741P LHOB

Ewing - chairman

Combest	*Condit*
Doolittle	*Baesler*
Pombo	*Bishop*
Smith (Mich.)	*Pomeroy*
Everett	*Baldacci*
Lewis (Ky.)	*Goode*
Bryant	*McIntyre*
Foley	*Etheridge*
Chambliss	*Boswell*
Moran (Kan.)	

APPROPRIATIONS

225-2771 H-218 Capitol

Party Ratio: R 34 - D 26

Robert L. Livingston, R-La., chairman

Joseph M. McDade, Pa.	*David R. Obey, Wis.*
C.W. Bill Young, Fla.	*Sidney R. Yates, Ill.*
Ralph Regula, Ohio	*Louis Stokes, Ohio*
Jerry Lewis, Calif.	*John P. Murtha, Pa.*
John Edward Porter, Ill.	*Norm Dicks, Wash.*
Harold Rogers, Ky.	*Martin Olav Sabo, Minn.*
Joe Skeen, N.M.	*Julian C. Dixon, Calif.*
Frank R. Wolf, Va.	*Vic Fazio, Calif.*
Tom DeLay, Texas	*W.G. "Bill" Hefner, N.C.*
Jim Kolbe, Ariz.	*Steny H. Hoyer, Md.*
Ron Packard, Calif.	*Alan B. Mollohan, W.Va.*
Sonny Callahan, Ala.	*Marcy Kaptur, Ohio*
James T. Walsh, N.Y.	*David E. Skaggs, Colo.*
Charles H. Taylor, N.C.	*Nancy Pelosi, Calif.*
David L. Hobson, Ohio	*Peter J. Visclosky, Ind.*
Ernest Istook, Okla.	*Thomas M. Foglietta, Pa.*
Henry Bonilla, Texas	*Esteban E. Torres, Calif.*
Joe Knollenberg, Mich.	*Nita M. Lowey, N.Y.*
Dan Miller, Fla.	*Jose E. Serrano, N.Y.*
Jay Dickey, Ark.	*Rosa DeLauro, Conn.*
Jack Kingston, Ga.	*James P. Moran, Va.*
Mike Parker, Miss.	*John W. Olver, Mass.*
Rodney Frelinghuysen, N.J.	*Ed Pastor, Ariz.*
	Carrie P. Meek, Fla.
Roger Wicker, Miss.	*David E. Price, N.C.*
Michael P. Forbes, N.Y.	*Chet Edwards, Texas*
George R. Nethercutt Jr., Wash.	
Mark W. Neumann, Wis.	
Randy "Duke" Cunningham, Calif.	
Todd Tiahrt, Kan.	
Zach Wamp, Tenn.	
Tom Latham, Iowa	
Anne M. Northup, Ky.	
Robert B. Aderholt, Ala.	

AGRICULTURE, RURAL DEVELOPMENT, FDA AND RELATED AGENCIES

225-2638 2362 RHOB

Skeen - chairman

Walsh	*Kaptur*
Dickey	*Fazio*
Kingston	*Serrano*
Nethercutt	*DeLauro*
Bonilla	
Latham	

COMMERCE, JUSTICE, STATE AND JUDICIARY

225-3351 H-309 Capitol

Rogers - chairman

Kolbe	*Mollohan*
Taylor (N.C.)	*Skaggs*
Regula	*Dixon*
Forbes	
Latham	

DISTRICT OF COLUMBIA

225-5338 H-147 Capitol

Taylor (N.C.) - chairman

Neumann	*Moran* (Va.)
Cunningham	*Sabo*
Tiahrt	*Dixon*
Northup	
Aderholt	

ENERGY AND WATER DEVELOPMENT

225-3421 2362 RHOB

McDade - chairman

Rogers	*Fazio*
Knollenberg	*Visclosky*
Frelinghuysen	*Edwards*
Parker	*Pastor*
Callahan	
Dickey	

FOREIGN OPERATIONS, EXPORT FINANCING AND RELATED PROGRAMS

225-2041 H-150 Capitol

Callahan - chairman

Porter	*Pelosi*
Wolf	*Yates*
Packard	*Lowey*
Knollenberg	*Foglietta*
Forbes	*Torres*
Kingston	
Frelinghuysen	

INTERIOR

225-3081 B-308 RHOB

Regula - chairman

McDade	*Yates*
Kolbe	*Murtha*
Skeen	*Dicks*
Taylor (N.C.)	*Skaggs*
Nethercutt	*Moran* (Va.)
Miller (Fla.)	
Wamp	

LABOR, HEALTH AND HUMAN SERVICES, AND EDUCATION

225-3508 2358 RHOB

Porter - chairman

Young (Fla.)	*Obey*
Bonilla	*Stokes*
Istook	*Hoyer*
Miller (Fla.)	*Pelosi*
Dickey	*Lowey*
Wicker	*DeLauro*
Northup	

LEGISLATIVE

225-5338 H-147 Capitol

Walsh - chairman

Young (Fla.)	*Serrano*
Cunningham	*Fazio*
Wamp	*Kaptur*
Latham	

MILITARY CONSTRUCTION

225-3047 B-300 RHOB

Packard - chairman

Porter	*Hefner*
Hobson	*Olver*
Wicker	*Edwards*
Kingston	*Dicks*
Parker	*Hoyer*
Tiahrt	
Wamp	

NATIONAL SECURITY

225-2847 H-149 Capitol

Young - chairman

McDade	*Murtha*
Lewis (Calif.)	*Dicks*
Skeen	*Hefner*
Hobson	*Sabo*
Bonilla	*Dixon*
Nethercutt	*Visclosky*
Istook	
Cunningham	

TRANSPORTATION

225-2141 2358 RHOB

Wolf - chairman

DeLay	*Sabo*
Regula	*Foglietta*
Rogers	*Torres*
Packard	*Olver*
Callahan	*Pastor*
Tiahrt	
Aderholt	

TREASURY, POSTAL SERVICE AND GENERAL GOVERNMENT

225-5834 B-307 RHOB

Kolbe - chairman

Wolf	*Hoyer*
Istook	*Meek*
Forbes	*Price*
Northup	
Aderholt	

VETERANS AFFAIRS, HOUSING AND URBAN DEVELOPMENT AND INDEPENDENT AGENCIES

225-3241 H-143 Capitol

Lewis (Calif.) - chairman

DeLay	*Stokes*
Walsh	*Mollohan*
Hobson	*Kaptur*
Knollenberg	*Meek*
Frelinghuysen	*Price*
Neumann	
Wicker	

BANKING AND FINANCIAL SERVICES

225-7502 2129 RHOB

Party Ratio: R 30 - D 25 - I 1

Jim Leach, R-Iowa, chairman

Bill McCollum, Fla.	*Henry B. Gonzalez, Texas*
Marge Roukema, N.J.	*John J. LaFalce, N.Y.*
Doug Bereuter, Neb.	*Bruce F. Vento, Minn.*
Richard H. Baker, La.	*Charles E. Schumer, N.Y.*
Rick A. Lazio, N.Y.	*Barney Frank, Mass.*
Spencer Bachus, Ala.	*Paul E. Kanjorski, Pa.*
Michael N. Castle, Del.	*Joseph P. Kennedy II, Mass.*
Peter T. King, N.Y.	*Floyd H. Flake, N.Y.*
Tom Campbell, Calif.	*Maxine Waters, Calif.*
Ed Royce, Calif.	*Carolyn B. Maloney, N.Y.*
Frank D. Lucas, Okla.	*Luis V. Gutierrez, Ill.*
Jack Metcalf, Wash.	*Lucille Roybal-Allard, Calif.*
Bob Ney, Ohio	*Thomas M. Barrett, Wis.*
Robert L. Ehrlich Jr., Md.	*Nydia M. Velázquez, N.Y.*
Bob Barr, Ga.	*Melvin Watt, N.C.*
Jon D. Fox, Pa.	*Maurice D. Hinchey, N.Y.*
Sue W. Kelly, N.Y.	*Gary L. Ackerman, N.Y.*
Ron Paul, Texas	*Ken Bentsen, Texas*
Dave Weldon, Fla.	*Jesse L. Jackson Jr., Ill.*
Merrill Cook, Utah	*Cynthia A. McKinney, Ga.*
Vince Snowbarger, Kan.	*Carolyn Cheeks Kilpatrick, Mich.*
Jim Ryun, Kan.	*Jim Maloney, Conn.*
Bob Riley, Ala.	*Darlene Hooley, Ore.*
Rick Hill, Mont.	*Julia Carson, Ind.*
Pete Sessions, Texas	*Esteban E. Torres, Calif.*
Steven C. LaTourette, Ohio	***Bernard Sanders, Vt.***
Donald Manzullo, Ill.	
Mark Foley, Fla.	
Walter B. Jones Jr., N.C.	

CAPITAL MARKETS, SECURITIES AND GOVERNMENT SPONSORED ENTERPRISES

226-0469 2129 RHOB

Baker - chairman

Lucas	*Kanjorski*
Cook	*Schumer*
Snowbarger	*Flake*
Riley	*Waters*
Hill	*Gutierrez*
Sessions	*Vento*
Lazio	*Roybal-Allard*
Bachus	*Barrett* (Wis.)
King	*Watt*
Campbell	*Ackerman*
Jones	

DOMESTIC AND INTERNATIONAL MONETARY POLICY

226-0473 B-303 RHOB

Castle - chairman

Fox	*Flake*
LaTourette	*Frank*
Royce	*Kennedy* (Mass.)
Lucas	***Sanders***
Metcalf	*Kanjorski*
Ney	*Velázquez*
Barr	*Maloney* (N.Y.)
Paul	*Hinchey*
Weldon (Fla.)	*Bentsen*
Manzullo	*Jackson*
Foley	

FINANCIAL INSTITUTIONS AND CONSUMER CREDIT

225-2258 2129 RHOB

Roukema - chairwoman

McCollum	*Vento*
Bereuter	*LaFalce*
King	*Schumer*
Campbell	*Maloney* (N.Y.)
Royce	*Barrett* (Wis.)
Metcalf	*Watt*
Ehrlich	*Roybal-Allard*
Barr	*Ackerman*
Kelly	*Bentsen*
Paul	*McKinney*
Weldon (Fla.)	*Kilpatrick*
Ryun	

GENERAL OVERSIGHT AND INVESTIGATIONS

226-3280 212 OHOB

Bachus - chairman

Riley	*Waters*
LaTourette	*McKinney*
King	*Kilpatrick*
Ney	*Hooley*
Foley	

HOUSING AND COMMUNITY OPPORTUNITY

225-6634 B-303 RHOB

Lazio - chairman

Ney	*Kennedy* (Mass.)
Roukema	***Sanders***
Bereuter	*Gutierrez*
Baker	*Velázquez*
Castle	*Frank*
Ehrlich	*Hinchey*
Fox	*Jackson*
Kelly	*LaFalce*
Cook	*Maloney* (Conn.)
Hill	*Hooley*
Sessions	*Carson*
Metcalf	
Jones	

BUDGET

226-7270 309 CHOB

Party Ratio: R 24 - D 19

John R. Kasich, R-Ohio, chairman

David L. Hobson, Ohio	*John M. Spratt Jr., S.C.*
Christopher Shays, Conn.	*Jim McDermott, Wash.*
Wally Herger, Calif.	*Alan B. Mollohan, W.Va.*
Jim Bunning, Ky.	*Jerry F. Costello, Ill.*
Lamar Smith, Texas	*Patsy T. Mink, Hawaii*
Dan Miller, Fla.	*Earl Pomeroy, N.D.*
Bob Franks, N.J.	*Lynn Woolsey, Calif.*
Nick Smith, Mich.	*Lucille Roybal-Allard, Calif.*
Bob Inglis, S.C.	*Lynn Rivers, Mich.*
Susan Molinari, N.Y.	*Lloyd Doggett, Texas*
Jim Nussle, Iowa	*Bennie Thompson, Miss.*
Peter Hoekstra, Mich.	*Benjamin L. Cardin, Md.*
John Shadegg, Ariz.	*David Minge, Minn.*
George P. Radanovich, Calif.	*Scotty Baesler, Ky.*
Charles Bass, N.H.	*Ken Bentsen, Texas*
Mark W. Neumann, Wis.	*Jim Davis, Fla.*
Mike Parker, Miss.	*Brad Sherman, Calif.*
Robert L. Ehrlich Jr., Md.	*Bob Weygand, R.I.*
Gil Gutknecht, Minn.	*Eva Clayton, N.C.*
Van Hilleary, Tenn.	
Kay Granger, Texas	
John E. Sununu, N.H.	
Joseph R. Pitts, Pa.	

COMMERCE

225-2927 2125 RHOB

Party Ratio: R 28 - D 23

Thomas J. Bliley Jr., R-Va., chairman

W.J. "Billy" Tauzin, La.	*John D. Dingell, Mich.*
Michael G. Oxley, Ohio	*Henry A. Waxman, Calif.*
Michael Bilirakis, Fla.	*Edward J. Markey, Mass.*
Dan Schaefer, Colo.	*Ralph M. Hall, Texas*
Joe L. Barton, Texas	*Rick Boucher, Va.*
Dennis Hastert, Ill.	*Thomas J. Manton, N.Y.*
Fred Upton, Mich.	*Edolphus Towns, N.Y.*
Cliff Stearns, Fla.	*Frank Pallone Jr., N.J.*
Bill Paxon, N.Y.	*Sherrod Brown, Ohio*
Paul E. Gillmor, Ohio	*Bart Gordon, Tenn.*
Scott L. Klug, Wis.	*Elizabeth Furse, Ore.*
James C. Greenwood, Pa.	*Peter Deutsch, Fla.*
Michael D. Crapo, Idaho	*Bobby L. Rush, Ill.*
Christopher Cox, Calif.	*Anna G. Eshoo, Calif.*
Nathan Deal, Ga.	*Ron Klink, Pa.*
Steve Largent, Okla.	*Bart Stupak, Mich.*
Richard M. Burr, N.C.	*Eliot L. Engel, N.Y.*
Brian P. Bilbray, Calif.	*Tom Sawyer, Ohio*
Edward Whitfield, Ky.	*Albert R. Wynn, Md.*
Greg Ganske, Iowa	*Gene Green, Texas*
Charlie Norwood, Ga.	*Karen McCarthy, Mo.*
Rick White, Wash.	*Ted Strickland, Ohio*
Tom Coburn, Okla.	*Diana DeGette, Colo.*
Rick A. Lazio, N.Y.	
Barbara Cubin, Wyo.	
James E. Rogan, Calif.	
John M. Shimkus, Ill.	

HOUSE COMMITTEES

ENERGY AND POWER

225-2927 2125 RHOB

Schaefer - chairman

Crapo	*Hall* (Texas)
Bilirakis	*Furse*
Hastert	*Rush*
Upton	*McCarthy* (Mo.)
Stearns	*Wynn*
Paxon	*Markey*
Largent	*Boucher*
Burr	*Towns*
Whitfield	*Pallone*
Norwood	*Brown* (Ohio)
White	*Gordon*
Coburn	*Deutsch*
Rogan	
Shimkus	

FINANCE AND HAZARDOUS MATERIALS

225-2927 2125 RHOB

Oxley - chairman

Tauzin	*Manton*
Paxon	*Stupak*
Gillmor	*Engel*
Klug	*Sawyer*
Greenwood	*Strickland*
Crapo	*DeGette*
Deal	*Markey*
Largent	*Hall* (Texas)
Bilbray	*Towns*
Ganske	*Pallone*
White	*Furse*
Lazio	
Cubin	

HEALTH AND ENVIRONMENT

225-2927 2125 RHOB

Bilirakis - chairman

Hastert	*Brown* (Ohio)
Barton	*Waxman*
Upton	*Towns*
Klug	*Pallone*
Greenwood	*Deutsch*
Deal	*Eshoo*
Burr	*Stupak*
Bilbray	*Green*
Whitfield	*Strickland*
Ganske	*DeGette*
Norwood	*Hall* (Texas)
Coburn	*Furse*
Lazio	
Cubin	

OVERSIGHT AND INVESTIGATIONS

225-2927 2125 RHOB

Barton - chairman

Cox	*Klink*
Greenwood	*Waxman*
Crapo	*Deutsch*
Burr	*Stupak*
Bilbray	*Engel*
Ganske	*Sawyer*
Coburn	

TELECOMMUNICATIONS, TRADE AND CONSUMER PROTECTION

225-2927 2125 RHOB

Tauzin - chairman

Oxley	*Markey*
Schaefer	*Boucher*
Barton	*Gordon*
Hastert	*Engel*
Upton	*Sawyer*
Stearns	*Manton*
Gillmor	*Rush*
Klug	*Eshoo*
Cox	*Klink*
Deal	*Wynn*
Largent	*Green*
White	*McCarthy* (Mo.)
Rogan	
Shimkus	

EDUCATION AND THE WORKFORCE

225-4527 2181 RHOB

Party Ratio: R 25 - D 20

Bill Goodling, R-Pa., chairman

Tom Petri, Wis.	*William L. Clay, Mo.*
Marge Roukema, N.J.	*George Miller, Calif.*
Harris W. Fawell, Ill.	*Dale E. Kildee, Mich.*
Cass Ballenger, N.C.	*Matthew G. Martinez, Calif.*
Bill Barrett, Neb.	*Major R. Owens, N.Y.*
Peter Hoekstra, Mich.	*Donald M. Payne, N.J.*
Howard P. "Buck" McKeon, Calif.	*Patsy T. Mink, Hawaii*
Michael N. Castle, Del.	*Robert E. Andrews, N.J.*
Sam Johnson, Texas	*Tim Roemer, Ind.*
James M. Talent, Mo.	*Robert C. Scott, Va.*
James C. Greenwood, Pa.	*Lynn Woolsey, Calif.*
Joe Knollenberg, Mich.	*Carlos Romero-Barceló, P.R.*
Frank Riggs, Calif.	*Chaka Fattah, Pa.*
Lindsey Graham, S.C.	*Rubén Hinojosa, Texas*
Mark Souder, Ind.	*Carolyn McCarthy, N.Y.*
David M. McIntosh, Ind.	*John F. Tierney, Mass.*
Charlie Norwood, Ga.	*Ron Kind, Wis.*
Ron Paul, Texas	*Loretta Sanchez, Calif.*
Bob Schaffer, Colo.	*Harold E. Ford Jr., Tenn.*
John E. Peterson, Pa.	*Dennis J. Kucinich, Ohio*
Fred Upton, Mich.	
Nathan Deal, Ga.	
Van Hilleary, Tenn.	
Joe Scarborough, Fla.	

EARLY CHILDHOOD, YOUTH AND FAMILIES

225-4527 2181 RHOB

Riggs - chairman

Castle	*Martinez*
Johnson	*Miller* (Calif.)
Souder	*Kildee*
Paul	*Owens*
Goodling	*Payne*
Greenwood	*Mink*
McIntosh	*Roemer*
Peterson (Pa.)	*Scott*
Upton	*Kucinich*
Hilleary	

EMPLOYER-EMPLOYEE RELATIONS

225-4527 2181 RHOB

Fawell - chairman

Talent	*Payne*
Knollenberg	*Fattah*
Petri	*Hinojosa*
Roukema	*McCarthy* (N.Y.)
Ballenger	*Tierney*
Goodling	

OVERSIGHT AND INVESTIGATIONS

225-4527 2181 RHOB

Hoekstra - chairman

Norwood	*Mink*
Hilleary	*Kind*
Scarborough	*Sanchez*
McKeon	*Ford*
Fawell	

POSTSECONDARY EDUCATION, TRAINING AND LIFE-LONG LEARNING

225-4527 2181 RHOB

McKeon - chairman

Goodling	*Kildee*
Petri	*Andrews*
Roukema	*Roemer*
Barrett (Neb.)	*Woolsey*
Greenwood	*Romero-Barceló*
Graham	*Fattah*
McIntosh	*Hinojosa*
Schaffer	*McCarthy* (N.Y.)
Peterson (Pa.)	*Tierney*
Castle	*Kind*
Riggs	*Sanchez*
Souder	*Ford*
Upton	
Deal	

WORKFORCE PROTECTIONS

225-4527 2181 RHOB

Ballenger - chairman

Fawell	*Owens*
Barrett (Neb.)	*Miller* (Calif.)
Hoekstra	*Martinez*
Graham	*Andrews*
Paul	*Woolsey*
Schaffer	

GOVERNMENT REFORM AND OVERSIGHT

225-5074 2157 RHOB

Party Ratio: R 24 - D 19 - I 1

Dan Burton, R-Ind., chairman

Benjamin A. Gilman, N.Y.	*Henry A. Waxman, Calif.*
Dennis Hastert, Ill.	*Tom Lantos, Calif.*
Constance A. Morella, Md.	*Bob Wise, W.Va.*
Christopher Shays, Conn.	*Major R. Owens, N.Y.*
Steven H. Schiff, N.M.	*Edolphus Towns, N.Y.*
Christopher Cox, Calif.	*Paul E. Kanjorski, Pa.*
Ileana Ros-Lehtinen, Fla.	*Gary A. Condit, Calif.*
John M. McHugh, N.Y.	*Carolyn B. Maloney, N.Y.*
Steve Horn, Calif.	*Thomas M. Barrett, Wis.*
John L. Mica, Fla.	*Eleanor Holmes Norton, D.C.*
Thomas M. Davis III, Va.	*Chaka Fattah, Pa.*
David M. McIntosh, Ind.	*Elijah E. Cummings, Md.*
Mark Souder, Ind.	*Dennis J. Kucinich, Ohio*
Joe Scarborough, Fla.	*Rod R. Blagojevich, Ill.*
John Shadegg, Ariz.	*Danny K. Davis, Ill.*
Steven C. LaTourette, Ohio	*John F. Tierney, Mass.*
Mark Sanford, S.C.	*Jim Turner, Texas*
John E. Sununu, N.H.	*Tom Allen, Maine*
Pete Sessions, Texas	*Harold E. Ford Jr., Tenn.*
Michael Pappas, N.J.	**Bernard Sanders, Vt.**
Vince Snowbarger, Kan.	
Bob Barr, Ga.	
Rob Portman, Ohio	

CIVIL SERVICE

225-6427 B-371C RHOB

Mica - chairman

Pappas	*Cummings*
Morella	*Norton*
Cox	*Harold E. Ford Jr.*
Sessions	

DISTRICT OF COLUMBIA

225-6751 B-349A RHOB

Davis (Va.) - chairman

Morella	*Norton*
Ros-Lehtinen	*Allen*
Horn	

GOVERNMENT MANAGEMENT, INFORMATION AND TECHNOLOGY

225-5147 B-373 RHOB

Horn - chairman

Sessions	*Maloney* (N.Y.)
Davis (Va.)	*Kanjorski*
Scarborough	*Owens*
Sanford	*Blagojevich*
Sununu	*Davis* (Ill.)
Portman	

HUMAN RESOURCES

225-2548 B-372 RHOB

Shays - chairman

Snowbarger	*Towns*
Gilman	*Kucinich*
McIntosh	*Allen*
Souder	*Lantos*
Pappas	**Sanders**
Schiff	*Barrett* (Wis.)

HOUSE COMMITTEES

NATIONAL ECONOMIC GROWTH, NATURAL RESOURCES AND REGULATORY AFFAIRS

225-4407 B-377 RHOB

McIntosh - chairman

Sununu	*Sanders*
Hastert	*Tierney*
Scarborough	*Turner*
Shadegg	*Kanjorski*
LaTourette	*Condit*
Snowbarger	*Kucinich*
Barr	*Fattah*
1 vacancy	

NATIONAL SECURITY, INTERNATIONAL AFFAIRS AND CRIMINAL JUSTICE

225-2577 B-373 RHOB

Hastert - chairman

Souder	*Barrett* (Wis.)
Shays	*Lantos*
Schiff	*Wise*
Ros-Lehtinen	*Condit*
McHugh	*Blagojevich*
Mica	*Maloney* (N.Y.)
Shadegg	*Cummings*
LaTourette	*Turner*
Barr	

POSTAL SERVICE

225-3741 B-349B RHOB

McHugh - chairman

Sanford	*Fattah*
Gilman	*Owens*
LaTourette	*Davis* (Ill.)
Sessions	

HOUSE OVERSIGHT

225-8281 1309 LHOB

Party Ratio: R 5 - D 3

Bill Thomas, R-Calif., chairman

Bob Ney, R-Ohio

John A. Boehner, Ohio	*Sam Gejdenson, Conn.*
Vernon J. Ehlers, Mich.	*Steny H. Hoyer, Md.*
Kay Granger, Texas	*Carolyn Cheeks Kilpatrick, Mich.*
John L. Mica, Florida	

INTERNATIONAL RELATIONS

225-5021 2170 RHOB

Party Ratio: R 26 - D 22

Benjamin A. Gilman, R-N.Y., chairman

Bill Goodling, Pa.	*Lee H. Hamilton, Ind.*
Jim Leach, Iowa	*Sam Gejdenson, Conn.*
Henry J. Hyde, Ill.	*Tom Lantos, Calif.*
Doug Bereuter, Neb.	*Howard L. Berman, Calif.*
Christopher H. Smith, N.J.	*Gary L. Ackerman, N.Y.*
Dan Burton, Ind.	*Eni F.H. Faleomavaega, Am. Samoa*
Elton Gallegly, Calif.	*Matthew G. Martinez, Calif.*
Ileana Ros-Lehtinen, Fla.	*Donald M. Payne, N.J.*
Cass Ballenger, N.C.	*Robert E. Andrews, N.J.*
Dana Rohrabacher, Calif.	*Robert Menendez, N.J.*
Donald Manzullo, Ill.	*Sherrod Brown, Ohio*
Ed Royce, Calif.	*Cynthia A. McKinney, Ga.*
Peter T. King, N.Y.	*Alcee L. Hastings, Fla.*
Jay C. Kim, Calif.	*Pat Danner, Mo.*
Steve Chabot, Ohio	*Earl F. Hilliard, Ala.*
Mark Sanford, S.C.	*Walter Capps, Calif.*
Matt Salmon, Ariz.	*Brad Sherman, Calif.*
Amo Houghton, N.Y.	*Robert Wexler, Fla.*
Tom Campbell, Calif.	*Steven R. Rothman, N.J.*
Jon D. Fox, Pa.	*Bob Clement, Tenn.*
John M. McHugh, N.Y.	*William P. "Bill" Luther, Minn.*
Lindsey Graham, S.C.	*Jim Davis, Fla.*
Roy Blunt, Mo.	
Jerry Moran, Kan.	
Kevin Brady, Texas	

AFRICA

226-7812 705 OHOB

Royce - chairman

Houghton	*Menendez*
Chabot	*Payne*
Sanford	*Hastings* (Fla.)
Campbell	*Davis* (Fla.)
McHugh	

ASIA AND THE PACIFIC

226-7825 B-359 RHOB

Bereuter - chairman

Leach	*Berman*
Rohrabacher	*Faleomavaega*
King	*Andrews*
Kim	*Brown* (Ohio)
Salmon	*Martinez*
Fox	*Hastings* (Fla.)
McHugh	*Capps*
Manzullo	*Wexler*
Royce	

INTERNATIONAL ECONOMIC POLICY AND TRADE

225-3345 702 OHOB

Ros-Lehtinen - chairwoman

Manzullo	*Gejdenson*
Chabot	*Danner*
Campbell	*Hilliard*
Graham	*Sherman*
Blunt	*Rothman*
Moran (Kan.)	*Clement*
Brady	*Lantos*
Bereuter	*Luther*
Rohrabacher	

INTERNATIONAL OPERATIONS AND HUMAN RIGHTS

225-5748 B-358 RHOB

Smith (N.J.) - chairman

Goodling	*Lantos*
Hyde	*McKinney*
Burton	*Ackerman*
Ballenger	*Faleomavaega*
King	*Payne*
Salmon	*Hilliard*
Graham	*Wexler*
Ros-Lehtinen	

WESTERN HEMISPHERE

226-7820 2401-A RHOB

Gallegly - chairman

Ballenger	*Ackerman*
Sanford	*Martinez*
Smith (N.J.)	*Andrews*
Burton	*Menendez*
Ros-Lehtinen	*McKinney*
Kim	*Capps*
Blunt	*Sherman*
Brady	

JUDICIARY

225-3951 2138 RHOB

Party Ratio: R 20 - D 15

Henry J. Hyde, R-Ill., chairman

F. James Sensenbrenner Jr., Wis.	*John Conyers Jr., Mich.*
Bill McCollum, Fla.	*Barney Frank, Mass.*
George W. Gekas, Pa.	*Charles E. Schumer, N.Y.*
Howard Coble, N.C.	*Howard L. Berman, Calif.*
Lamar Smith, Texas	*Rick Boucher, Va.*
Steven H. Schiff, N.M.	*Jerrold Nadler, N.Y.*
Elton Gallegly, Calif.	*Robert C. Scott, Va.*
Charles T. Canady, Fla.	*Melvin Watt, N.C.*
Bob Inglis, S.C.	*Zoe Lofgren, Calif.*
Robert W. Goodlatte, Va.	*Sheila Jackson-Lee, Texas*
Steve Buyer, Ind.	*Maxine Waters, Calif.*
Sonny Bono, Calif.	*Martin T. Meehan, Mass.*
Ed Bryant, Tenn.	*Bill Delahunt, Mass.*
Steve Chabot, Ohio	*Robert Wexler, Fla.*
Bob Barr, Ga.	*Steven R. Rothman, N.J.*
Bill Jenkins, Tenn.	
Asa Hutchinson, Ark.	
Ed Pease, Ind.	
Christopher B. Cannon, Utah	

COMMERCIAL AND ADMINISTRATIVE LAW

225-2825 B-353 RHOB

Gekas - chairman

Schiff	*Nadler*
Smith (Texas)	*Jackson-Lee*
Inglis	*Meehan*
Bryant	*Delahunt*
Chabot	

CONSTITUTION

226-7680 H2-362 FHOB

Canady - chairman

Hyde	*Scott*
Inglis	*Waters*
Bryant	*Conyers*
Jenkins	*Nadler*
Goodlatte	*Watt*
Barr	
Hutchinson	

COURTS AND INTELLECTUAL PROPERTY

225-5741 B-351A RHOB

Coble - chairman

Sensenbrenner	*Frank*
Gallegly	*Conyers*
Goodlatte	*Berman*
Bono	*Boucher*
Pease	*Lofgren*
Cannon	*Delahunt*
McCollum	
Canady	

CRIME

225-3926 207 CHOB

McCollum - chairman

Schiff	*Schumer*
Buyer	*Jackson-Lee*
Chabot	*Meehan*
Barr	*Wexler*
Hutchinson	*Rothman*
Gekas	
Coble	

IMMIGRATION AND CLAIMS

225-5727 B-370B RHOB

Smith (Texas) - chairman

Gallegly	*Watt*
Bono	*Schumer*
Jenkins	*Berman*
Pease	*Lofgren*
Cannon	*Wexler*
Bryant	

NATIONAL SECURITY

225-4151 2120 RHOB
Party Ratio: R 30 - D 25
Floyd D. Spence, R-S.C., chairman

Bob Stump, Ariz.	*Ronald V. Dellums, Calif.*
Duncan Hunter, Calif.	*Ike Skelton, Mo.*
John R. Kasich, Ohio	*Norman Sisisky, Va.*
Herbert H. Bateman, Va.	*John M. Spratt Jr., S.C.*
James V. Hansen, Utah	*Solomon P. Ortiz, Texas*
Curt Weldon, Pa.	*Owen B. Pickett, Va.*
Joel Hefley, Colo.	*Lane Evans, Ill.*
H. James Saxton, N.J.	*Gene Taylor, Miss.*
Steve Buyer, Ind.	*Neil Abercrombie, Hawaii*
Tillie Fowler, Fla.	*Martin T. Meehan, Mass.*
John M. McHugh, N.Y.	*Robert A. Underwood, Guam*
James M. Talent, Mo.	*Jane Harman, Calif.*
Terry Everett, Ala.	*Paul McHale, Pa.*
Roscoe G. Bartlett, Md.	*Patrick J. Kennedy, R.I.*
Howard P. "Buck" McKeon, Calif.	*Rod R. Blagojevich, Ill.*
Ron Lewis, Ky.	*Silvestre Reyes, Texas*
J.C. Watts Jr., Okla.	*Tom Allen, Maine*
William M. "Mac" Thornberry, Texas	*Vic Snyder, Ark.*
	Jim Turner, Texas
John Hostettler, Ind.	*Allen Boyd, Fla.*
Saxby Chambliss, Ga.	*Adam Smith, Wash.*
Van Hilleary, Tenn.	*Loretta Sanchez, Calif.*
Joe Scarborough, Fla.	*Jim Maloney, Conn.*
Walter B. Jones Jr., N.C.	*Mike McIntyre, N.C.*
Lindsey Graham, S.C.	*Ciro D. Rodriguez, Texas*
Sonny Bono, Calif.	
Jim Ryun, Kan.	
Michael Pappas, N.J.	
Bob Riley, Ala.	
Jim Gibbons, Nev.	

MILITARY INSTALLATIONS AND FACILITIES

225-7120 2340 RHOB
Hefley - chairman

McHugh	*Ortiz*
Hostettler	*Sisisky*
Hilleary	*Abercrombie*
Scarborough	*Underwood*
Stump	*Reyes*
Saxton	*Snyder*
Buyer	*Boyd*
Fowler	*Smith (Wash.)*
Everett	

MILITARY PERSONNEL

225-7560 2340 RHOB
Buyer - chairman

Talent	*Taylor* (Miss.)
Bartlett	*Skelton*
Lewis (Ky.)	*Pickett*
Watts	*Underwood*
Thornberry	*Harman*
Graham	*Kennedy* (R.I.)
Bono	*Maloney* (Conn.)
Ryun	

MILITARY PROCUREMENT

225-4440 -2340 RHOB
Hunter - chairman

Spence	*Skelton*
Stump	*Dellums*
Hansen	*Spratt*
Saxton	*Evans*
Talent	*Blagojevich*
Everett	*Allen*
McKeon	*Snyder*
Lewis (Ky.)	*Turner*
Watts	*Boyd*
Thornberry	*Smith (Wash.)*
Graham	*Maloney* (Conn.)
Bono	*McIntyre*
Ryun	
Pappas	

MILITARY READINESS

225-6288 2117 RHOB
Bateman - chairman

Kasich	*Sisisky*
Fowler	*Ortiz*
Chambliss	*Pickett*
Jones	*Evans*
Riley	*Taylor* (Miss.)
Gibbons	*Meehan*
Hunter	*Underwood*
Hansen	*McHale*
Weldon (Pa.)	*1 vacancy*
McKeon	

MILITARY RESEARCH AND DEVELOPMENT

225-1967 2340 RHOB
Weldon (Pa.) - chairman

Bartlett	*Pickett*
Kasich	*Abercrombie*
Bateman	*Meehan*
Hefley	*Harman*
McHugh	*McHale*
Hostettler	*Kennedy* (R.I.)
Chambliss	*Blagojevich*
Hilleary	*Reyes*
Scarborough	*Allen*
Jones	*Turner*
Pappas	*Sanchez*
Riley	
Gibbons	

MERCHANT MARINE

226-2578 2340 RHOB
Bateman - chairman

Hunter	*Abercrombie*
Weldon (Pa.)	*Taylor* (Miss.)
Saxton	*Harman*
Fowler	*Kennedy* (R.I.)
Scarborough	*Allen*
2 vacancies	*Smith (Wash.)*

MORALE, WELFARE AND RECREATION

225-8281 2117 RHOB

McHugh - chairman

Stump	*Meehan*
Bateman	*Sisisky*
Bartlett	*Ortiz*
Watts	*Pickett*
Chambliss	*Underwood*
Scarborough	*Sanchez*
Jones	

RESOURCES

225-2761 1324 LHOB

Party Ratio: R 27 - D 23

Don Young, R-Alaska, chairman

W.J. "Billy" Tauzin, La.	*George Miller, Calif.*
James V. Hansen, Utah	*Edward J. Markey, Mass.*
H. James Saxton, N.J.	*Nick J. Rahall II, W.Va.*
Elton Gallegly, Calif.	*Bruce F. Vento, Minn.*
John J. "Jimmy" Duncan Jr., Tenn.	*Dale E. Kildee, Mich.*
Joel Hefley, Colo.	*Peter A. DeFazio, Ore.*
John T. Doolittle, Calif.	*Eni F.H. Faleomavaega, Am. Samoa*
Wayne T. Gilchrest, Md.	*Neil Abercrombie, Hawaii*
Ken Calvert, Calif.	*Solomon P. Ortiz, Texas*
Richard W. Pombo, Calif.	*Owen B. Pickett, Va.*
Barbara Cubin, Wyo.	*Frank Pallone Jr., N.J.*
Helen Chenoweth, Idaho	*Cal Dooley, Calif.*
Linda Smith, Wash.	*Carlos Romero-Barceló, P.R.*
George P. Radanovich, Calif.	*Maurice D. Hinchey, N.Y.*
Walter B. Jones Jr., N.C.	*Robert A. Underwood, Guam*
William M. "Mac" Thornberry, Texas	*Sam Farr, Calif.*
	Patrick J. Kennedy, R.I.
John Shadegg, Ariz.	*Adam Smith, Wash*
John Ensign, Nev.	*Bill Delahunt, Mass*
Bob Smith, Ore.	
Christopher B. Cannon, Utah	*Chris John, La.*
Kevin Brady, Texas	*Donna M. Christian-Green, Virgin Is.*
John E. Peterson, Pa.	*Ron Kind, Wis.*
Rick Hill, Mont.	*Lloyd Doggett, Texas*
Bob Schaffer, Colo.	
Jim Gibbons, Nev.	
Michael D. Crapo, Idaho	

ENERGY AND MINERAL RESOURCES

225-9297 1626 LHOB

Cubin - chairman

Tauzin	*Romero-Barceló*
Duncan	*Rahall*
Calvert	*Ortiz*
Thornberry	*Dooley*
Cannon	*John*
Brady	*Christian-Green* (Virgin Is.)
Gibbons	*1 vacancy*

FISHERIES CONSERVATION, WILDLIFE AND OCEANS

226-0200 805 OHOB

Saxton - chairman

Tauzin	*Abercrombie*
Gilchrest	*Ortiz*
Jones	*Pallone*
Peterson (Pa.)	*Farr*
Crapo	*Kennedy* (R.I.)

FORESTS AND FOREST HEALTH

225-8331 1337 LHOB

Chenoweth - chairman

Hansen	*Hinchey*
Doolittle	*Vento*
Radanovich	*Kildee*
Peterson (Pa.)	*Faleomavaega*
Hill	*2 vacancies*
Schaffer	

NATIONAL PARKS AND PUBLIC LANDS

226-7736 814 OHOB

Hansen - chairman

Gallegly	*Faleomavaega*
Duncan	*Markey*
Hefley	*Vento*
Gilchrest	*Kildee*
Pombo	*Romero-Barceló*
Chenoweth	*Hinchey*
Smith (Wash.)	*Underwood*
Radanovich	*Kennedy* (R.I.)
Jones	*Delahunt*
Shadegg	*Christian-Green (Virgin Is.)*
Ensign	*Kind*
Smith (Ore.)	*Doggett*
Hill	*1 vacancy*
Gibbons	

WATER AND POWER

225-8331 1337 LHOB

Doolittle - chairman

Calvert	*DeFazio*
Pombo	*Miller* (Calif.)
Chenoweth	*Pickett*
Smith (Wash.)	*Dooley*
Radanovich	*Farr*
Thornberry	*Smith (Wash.)*
Shadegg	*Kind*
Ensign	*Doggett*
Smith (Ore.)	*2 vacancies*
Cannon	
Crapo	

RULES

225-9191 H-312 Capitol

Party Ratio: R 9 - D 4

Gerald B.H. Solomon, R-N.Y., chairman

David Dreier, Calif.	*Joe Moakley, Mass.*
Porter J. Goss, Fla.	*Martin Frost, Texas*
John Linder, Ga.	*Tony P. Hall, Ohio*
Deborah Pryce, Ohio	*Louise M. Slaughter, N.Y.*
Lincoln Diaz-Balart, Fla.	
Scott McInnis, Colo.	
Richard "Doc" Hastings, Wash.	
Sue Myrick, N.C.	

HOUSE COMMITTEES

LEGISLATIVE AND BUDGET PROCESS

225-1547 421 CHOB

Goss - chairman

Linder	*Frost*
Pryce	*Moakley*
Hastings (Wash.)	
Solomon	

RULES AND ORGANIZATION OF THE HOUSE

225-8925 421 CHOB

Dreier - chairman

Diaz-Balart	*Hall* (Ohio)
McInnis	*Slaughter*
Myrick	
Solomon	

SCIENCE

225-6371 2320 RHOB

Party Ratio: R 25 - D 21

F. James Sensenbrenner Jr., R-Wis., chairman

Sherwood Boehlert, N.Y.	*George E. Brown Jr., Calif.*
Harris W. Fawell, Ill.	*Ralph M. Hall, Texas*
Constance A. Morella, Md.	*Bart Gordon, Tenn.*
Curt Weldon, Pa.	*James A. Traficant Jr., Ohio*
Dana Rohrabacher, Calif.	*Tim Roemer, Ind.*
Steven H. Schiff, N.M.	*Robert E. "Bud" Cramer, Ala.*
Joe L. Barton, Texas	*James A. Barcia, Mich.*
Ken Calvert, Calif.	*Paul McHale, Pa.*
Roscoe G. Bartlett, Md.	*Eddie Bernice Johnson, Texas*
Vernon J. Ehlers, Mich.	*Alcee L. Hastings, Fla.*
Dave Weldon, Fla.	*Lynn Rivers, Mich.*
Matt Salmon, Ariz.	*Zoe Lofgren, Calif.*
Thomas M. Davis III, Va.	*Mike Doyle, Pa.*
Gil Gutknecht, Minn.	*Sheila Jackson-Lee, Texas*
Mark Foley, Fla.	*William P. "Bill" Luther, Minn.*
Thomas W. Ewing, Ill.	*Walter Capps, Calif.*
Charles W. "Chip" Pickering Jr., Miss.	*Debbie Stabenow, Mich.*
Christopher B. Cannon, Utah	*Bob Etheridge, N.C.*
Kevin Brady, Texas	*Nick Lampson, Texas*
Merrill Cook, Utah	*Darlene Hooley, Ore.*
Phil English, Pa.	*Ellen O. Tauscher, Calif.*
George R. Nethercutt Jr., Wash.	
Tom Coburn, Okla.	
Pete Sessions, Texas	

BASIC RESEARCH

225-9662 B-374 RHOB

Schiff - chairman

Boehlert	*Barcia*
Morella	*Etheridge*
Barton	*Rivers*
Gutknecht	*Jackson-Lee*
Ewing	*Luther*
Pickering	*Capps*
Sessions	

ENERGY AND ENVIRONMENT

225-9662 B-374 RHOB

Calvert - chairman

Fawell	*Roemer*
Weldon (Pa.)	*McHale*
Rohrabacher	*Doyle*
Schiff	*Hooley*
Ehlers	*Hall* (Texas)
Salmon	*Johnson*
Foley	*Lofgren*
English	*1 vacancy*
Coburn	

SPACE AND AERONAUTICS

225-7858 2320 RHOB

Rohrabacher - chairman

Barton	*Cramer*
Calvert	*Hall* (Texas)
Bartlett	*Traficant*
Weldon (Fla.)	*Hastings* (Fla.)
Salmon	*Jackson-Lee*
Davis (Va.)	*Luther*
Foley	*Lofgren*
Pickering	*Capps*
Cannon	*Lampson*
Brady	*Gordon*
Cook	
Nethercutt	

TECHNOLOGY

225-8844 2319 RHOB

Morella - chairman

Weldon (Pa.)	*Gordon*
Bartlett	*Johnson*
Ehlers	*Rivers*
Davis (Va.)	*Stabenow*
Gutknecht	*Barcia*
Ewing	*McHale*
Cannon	*Doyle*
Brady	*1 vacancy*
Cook	

SELECT INTELLIGENCE

225-4121 H-405 Capitol

Party Ratio: R 9 - D 7

Porter J. Goss, R-Fla., chairman

C.W. Bill Young, Fla.	*Norm Dicks, Wash.*
Jerry Lewis, Calif.	*Julian C. Dixon, Calif.*
Bud Shuster, Pa.	*David E. Skaggs, Colo.*
Bill McCollum, Fla.	*Nancy Pelosi, Calif.*
Michael N. Castle, Del.	*Jane Harman, Calif.*
Sherwood Boehlert, N.Y.	*Ike Skelton, Mo.*
Charles Bass, N.H.	*Sanford D. Bishop Jr., Ga.*
Jim Gibbons, Nev.	

HUMAN INTELLIGENCE, ANALYSIS AND COUNTERINTELLIGENCE

225-4121 H-405 Capitol

McCollum - chairman

Shuster	*Dixon*
Castle	*Skaggs*
Bass	*Pelosi*
	Bishop

TECHNICAL AND TACTICAL INTELLIGENCE

225-4121 H-405 Capitol

Lewis - chairman

Young (Fla.)	*Skaggs*
Boehlert	*Dicks*
Gibbons	*Harman*
	Skelton

SMALL BUSINESS

225-5821 2361 RHOB

Party Ratio: R 19 - D 16

James M. Talent, R-Mo., chairman

Larry Combest, Texas	*John J. LaFalce, N.Y.*
Joel Hefley, Colo.	*Norman Sisisky, Va.*
Donald Manzullo, Ill.	*Floyd H. Flake, N.Y.*
Roscoe G. Bartlett, Md.	*Glenn Poshard, Ill.*
Linda Smith, Wash.	*Nydia M. Velázquez, N.Y.*
Frank A. LoBiondo, N.J.	*John Baldacci, Maine*
Sue W. Kelly, N.Y.	*Jesse L. Jackson Jr., Ill.*
Walter B. Jones Jr., N.C.	*Juanita Millender-McDonald, Calif.*
Mark Souder, Ind.	*Bob Weygand, R.I.*
Steve Chabot, Ohio	*Danny K. Davis, Ill.*
Jim Ryun, Kan.	*Allen Boyd, Fla.*
Vince Snowbarger, Kan.	*Carolyn McCarthy, N.Y.*
Michael Pappas, N.J.	*Bill Pascrell Jr., N.J.*
Phil English, Pa.	*Virgil H. Goode Jr., Va.*
David M. McIntosh, Ind.	*Rubén Hinojosa, Texas*
Jo Ann Emerson, Mo.	*Marion Berry, Ark.*
Rick Hill, Mont.	
John E. Sununu, N.H.	

EMPOWERMENT

226-2630 B-363 RHOB

Souder - chairman

LoBiondo	*Velázquez*
Jones	*Flake*
Chabot	*Davis* (Ill.)
English	*Pascrell*
Smith	*Jackson*

GOVERNMENT PROGRAMS AND OVERSIGHT

226-2630 B-363 RHOB

Bartlett - chairman

Combest	*Poshard*
Pappas	*Jackson*
Smith (Wash.)	*Weygand*
Hill	*Boyd*
Sununu	*McCarthy* (N.Y.)

REGULATORY REFORM AND PAPERWORK REDUCTION

226-2630 B-363 RHOB

Kelly - chairman

Combest	*Sisisky*
Ryun	*Goode*
McIntosh	*Millender-McDonald*
Emerson	*Boyd*
1 Vacancy	*1 vacancy*

TAX, FINANCE AND EXPORTS

226-2630 B-363 RHOB

Manzullo - chairman

Smith (Wash.)	*Baldacci*
Snowbarger	*Millender-McDonald*
LoBiondo	*Weygand*
Jones	*Davis* (Ill.)
1 vacancy	*McCarthy* (N.Y.)

STANDARDS OF OFFICIAL CONDUCT

225-7103 HT-2 Capitol

Party Ratio: R 5 - D 5

James V. Hansen, R-Utah, chairman

Howard L. Berman, Calif.

** A 10-member bipartisan task force is investigating how to revamp the committee.*

TRANSPORTATION AND INFRASTRUCTURE

225-9446 2165 RHOB

Party Ratio: R 40 - D 33

Bud Shuster, R-Pa., chairman

Don Young, Alaska	*James L. Oberstar, Minn.*
Tom Petri, Wis.	*Nick J. Rahall II, W.Va.*
Sherwood Boehlert, N.Y.	*Robert A. Borski, Pa.*
Herbert H. Bateman, Va.	*William O. Lipinski, Ill.*
Howard Coble, N.C.	*Bob Wise, W.Va.*
John J. "Jimmy" Duncan Jr., Tenn.	*James A. Traficant Jr., Ohio*
Susan Molinari, N.Y.	*Peter A. DeFazio, Ore.*
Thomas W. Ewing, Ill.	*Bob Clement, Tenn.*
Wayne T. Gilchrest, Md.	*Jerry F. Costello, Ill.*
Jay C. Kim, Calif.	*Glenn Poshard, Ill.*
Steve Horn, Calif.	*Robert E. "Bud" Cramer, Ala.*
Bob Franks, N.J.	*Eleanor Holmes Norton, D.C.*
John L. Mica, Fla.	*Jerrold Nadler, N.Y.*
Jack Quinn, N.Y.	*Pat Danner, Mo.*
Tillie Fowler, Fla.	*Robert Menendez, N.J.*
Vernon J. Ehlers, Mich.	*James E. Clyburn, S.C.*
Spencer Bachus, Ala.	*Corrine Brown, Fla.*
Steven C. LaTourette, Ohio	*James A. Barcia, Mich.*
Sue W. Kelly, N.Y.	*Bob Filner, Calif.*
Ray LaHood, Ill.	*Eddie Bernice Johnson, Texas*
Richard H. Baker, La.	*Frank R. Mascara, Pa.*
Frank Riggs, Calif.	*Gene Taylor, Miss.*
Charles Bass, N.H.	*Juanita Millender-McDonald, Calif.*
Bob Ney, Ohio	*Elijah E. Cummings, Md.*
Jack Metcalf, Wash.	*Earl Blumenauer, Ore.*
Jo Ann Emerson, Mo.	*Max Sandlin, Texas*
Ed Pease, Ind.	*Ellen O. Tauscher, Calif.*
Roy Blunt, Mo.	*Bill Pascrell Jr., N.J.*
Joseph R. Pitts, Pa.	*Jay W. Johnson, Wis.*
Asa Hutchinson, Ark.	*Leonard L. Boswell, Iowa*
Merrill Cook, Utah	*Jim McGovern, Mass.*
John Cooksey, La.	*Tim Holden, Pa.*
John Thune, S.D.	*Nick Lampson, Texas*
Charles W. "Chip" Pickering Jr., Miss.	
Kay Granger, Texas	
Jon D. Fox, Pa.	
Thomas M. Davis III, Va.	
Frank A. LoBiondo, N.J.	
J.C. Watts Jr., Okla.	

AVIATION

226-3220 2251 RHOB

Duncan - chairman

Blunt	*Lipinski*
Molinari	*Boswell*
Ewing	*Poshard*
Ehlers	*Rahall*
LaHood	*Traficant*
Bass	*DeFazio*
Metcalf	*Costello*
Pease	*Cramer*
Pitts	*Danner*
Hutchinson	*Clyburn*
Cook	*Brown* (Fla.)
Cooksey	*Johnson*
Pickering	*Millender-McDonald*
Granger	*Cummings*
Fox	
Davis (Va.)	
Watts	

COAST GUARD AND MARITIME TRANSPORTATION

226-3552 507 FHOB

Gilchrest - chairman

LoBiondo	*Clement*
Young (Alaska)	*Johnson* (Wis.)
Coble	*Borski*

PUBLIC BUILDINGS AND ECONOMIC DEVELOPMENT

225-3014 586 FHOB

Kim - chairman

Cooksey	*Traficant*
Duncan	*Norton*
LaTourette	*Holden*
Davis (Va.)	*Lampson*

RAILROADS

226-0727 B-376 RHOB

Molinari - chairman

Granger	*Wise*
Boehlert	*Blumenauer*
Franks	*Borski*
Mica	*Lipinski*
Quinn	*Clement*
Fowler	*Nadler*
Bachus	*Filner*
Pitts	*Sandlin*
Fox	

SURFACE TRANSPORTATION

225-6715 B-370A RHOB

Petri - chairman

Pickering	*Rahall*
Bateman	*DeFazio*
Coble	*Cramer*
Ewing	*Danner*
Horn	*Clyburn*
Franks	*Brown* (Fla.)
Mica	*Barcia*
Quinn	*Filner*
Fowler	*Johnson*
Bachus	*Mascara*
LaTourette	*Millender-McDonald*
Kelly	*Costello*
LaHood	*Norton*
Baker	*Nadler*
Riggs	*Menendez*
Bass	*Taylor* (Miss.)
Ney	*Cummings*
Metcalf	*Sandlin*
Emerson	*Tauscher*
Pease	*Pascrell*
Pitts	*McGovern*
Hutchinson	
Cook	
Thune	
Granger	
Watts	

WATER RESOURCES AND ENVIRONMENT

225-4360 B-375 RHOB

Boehlert - chairman

Thune	*Borski*
Young (Alaska)	*Johnson* (Wis.)
Petri	*Wise*
Bateman	*Poshard*
Molinari	*Menendez*
Gilchrest	*Barcia*
Kim	*Mascara*
Horn	*Taylor* (Miss.)
Franks	*Blumenauer*
Quinn	*Tauscher*
Ehlers	*Pascrell*
LaTourette	*Boswell*
Kelly	*McGovern*
Baker	*Rahall*
Riggs	*Lampson*
Ney	
Emerson	
LoBiondo	

VETERANS' AFFAIRS

225-3527 335 CHOB

Party Ratio: R 16 - D 13

Bob Stump, R-Ariz., chairman

Christopher H. Smith, N.J	*Lane Evans, Ill.*
Michael Bilirakis, Fla.	*Joseph P. Kennedy II, Mass.*
Floyd D. Spence, S.C.	*Bob Filner, Calif.*
Terry Everett, Ala.	*Luis V. Gutierrez, Ill.*
Steve Buyer, Ind.	*James E. Clyburn, S.C.*
Jack Quinn, N.Y.	*Corrine Brown, Fla.*

Spencer Bachus, Ala.	*Mike Doyle, Pa.*
Cliff Stearns, Fla.	*Frank R. Mascara, Pa.*
Dan Schaefer, Colo.	*Collin C. Peterson, Minn.*
Jerry Moran, Kan.	*Julia Carson, Ind.*
John Cooksey, La.	*Silvestre Reyes, Texas*
Asa Hutchinson, Ark.	*Vic Snyder, Ark.*
J.D. Hayworth, Ariz.	*Ciro D. Rodriguez, Texas*
Helen Chenoweth, Idaho	
Ray LaHood, Ill.	

BENEFITS

225-9164 335 CHOB

Quinn - chairman

Schaefer	*Filner*
Hayworth	*Mascara*
LaHood	*Reyes*
1 vacancy	*Rodriguez*

HEALTH

225-9154 335 CHOB

Stearns - chairman

Smith (N.J.)	*Gutierrez*
Bilirakis	*Kennedy* (Mass.)
Bachus	*Brown* (Fla.)
Moran (Kan.)	*Doyle*
Cooksey	*Peterson* (Minn.)
Hutchinson	*Carson*
Chenoweth	

OVERSIGHT AND INVESTIGATIONS

225-3527 335 CHOB

Everett - chairman

Stump	*Clyburn*
Spence	*Snyder*
Buyer	*1 vacancy*

WAYS AND MEANS

225-3625 1102 LHOB

Party Ratio: R 23 - D 16

Bill Archer, R-Texas, chairman

Philip M. Crane, Ill.	*Charles B. Rangel, N.Y.*
Bill Thomas, Calif.	*Pete Stark, Calif.*
E. Clay Shaw Jr., Fla.	*Robert T. Matsui, Calif.*
Nancy L. Johnson, Conn.	*Barbara B. Kennelly, Conn.*
Jim Bunning, Ky.	*William J. Coyne, Pa.*
Amo Houghton, N.Y.	*Sander M. Levin, Mich.*
Wally Herger, Calif.	*Benjamin L. Cardin, Md.*
Jim McCrery, La.	*Jim McDermott, Wash.*
Dave Camp, Mich.	*Gerald D. Kleczka, Wis.*
Jim Ramstad, Minn.	*John Lewis, Ga.*
Jim Nussle, Iowa	*Richard E. Neal, Mass.*
Sam Johnson, Texas	*Michael R. McNulty, N.Y.*
Jennifer Dunn, Wash.	*William J. Jefferson, La.*
Mac Collins, Ga.	*John Tanner, Tenn.*
Rob Portman, Ohio	*Xavier Becerra, Calif.*
Phil English, Pa.	*Karen L. Thurman, Fla.*
John Ensign, Nev.	
Jon Christensen, Neb.	
Wes Watkins, Okla.	
J.D. Hayworth, Ariz.	
Jerry Weller, Ill.	
Kenny Hulshof, Mo.	

HEALTH

225-3943 1136 LHOB

Thomas - chairman

Johnson (Conn.)	*Stark*
McCrery	*Cardin*
Ensign	*Kleczka*
Christensen	*Lewis* (Ga.)
Crane	*Becerra*
Houghton	
Johnson	

HUMAN RESOURCES

225-1025 B-317 RHOB

Shaw - chairman

Camp	*Levin*
McCrery	*Stark*
Collins	*Matsui*
English	*Coyne*
Ensign	*McDermott*
Hayworth	
Watkins	

OVERSIGHT

225-7601 1136 LHOB

Johnson (Conn.) - chairman

Portman	*Coyne*
Ramstad	*Kleczka*
Dunn	*McNulty*
English	*Tanner*
Watkins	*Thurman*
Weller	
Hulshof	

SOCIAL SECURITY

225-9263 B-316 RHOB

Bunning - chairman

Johnson	*Kennelly*
Collins	*Neal*
Portman	*Levin*
Christensen	*Jefferson*
Hayworth	*Tanner*
Weller	
Hulshof	

TRADE

225-6649 1104 LHOB

Crane - chairman

Thomas	*Matsui*
Shaw	*Rangel*
Houghton	*Neal*
Camp	*McDermott*
Ramstad	*McNulty*
Dunn	*Jefferson*
Herger	
Nussle	

PARTISAN HOUSE COMMITTEES

REPUBLICAN LEADERS

Speaker of the House......... Newt Gingrich, Ga.
Majority Leader............... Dick Armey, Texas
Majority Whip................ Tom DeLay, Texas
Conference Chairman...... John A. Boehner, Ohio
Conference Vice Chairman .... Susan Molinari, N.Y.
Conference Secretary .... Jennifer Dunn, Wash.
Chief Deputy Whip .... Dennis Hastert, Ill.

Deputy Whips: Cass Ballenger, N.C.; Jim Bunning, Ky.; Mac Collins, Ga.; Michael D. Crapo, Idaho; Barbara Cubin, Wyo.; John T. Doolittle, Calif.; Thomas W. Ewing, Ill.; Mark Foley, Fla.; Tillie Fowler, Fla.; Porter J. Goss, Fla.; Van Hilleary, Tenn.; Rick A. Lazio, N.Y.; Bob Ney, Ohio; Deborah Pryce, Ohio; W.J. "Billy" Tauzin, La.; Roger Wicker, Miss.

Assistant Whips: Charles Bass, N.H.; Roy Blunt, Mo.; Henry Bonilla, Texas; Richard M. Burr, N.C.; Steve Buyer, Ind.; Sonny Callahan, Ala.; Dave Camp, Mich.; Randy "Duke" Cunningham, Calif.; Thomas M. Davis III, Va.; Nathan Deal, Ga.; Robert L. Ehrlich Jr., Md.; Jon D. Fox, Pa.; Bob Franks, N.J.; Paul E. Gillmor, Ohio; Robert W. Goodlatte, Va.; Lindsey Graham, S.C.; Kay Granger, Texas; J.D. Hayworth, Ariz.; David L. Hobson, Ohio; Bob Inglis, S.C.; Ernest Istook, Okla.; Sam Johnson, Texas; Sue W. Kelly, N.Y.; Jack Kingston, Ga.; Scott L. Klug, Wis.; Frank A. LoBiondo, N.J.; Frank D. Lucas, Okla.; Scott McInnis, Colo.; David M. McIntosh, Ind.; Howard P. "Buck" McKeon, Calif.; Dan Miller, Fla.; Michael Pappas, N.J.; Ed Pease, Ind.; Charles W. "Chip" Pickering Jr., Miss.; Joseph R. Pitts, Pa.; Richard W. Pombo, Calif.; Rob Portman, Ohio; George P. Radanovich, Calif.; Bob Riley, Ala.; James E. Rogan, Calif.; Ed Royce, Calif.; John Shadegg, Ariz.; Vince Snowbarger, Kan.; Mark Souder, Ind.; John Thune, S.D.; Todd Tiahrt, Kan.; James T. Walsh, N.Y.; Jerry Weller, Ill.

Jon Christensen, Neb.
Tom Coburn, Okla.
Thomas M. Davis III, Va.
John T. Doolittle, Calif.
Jo Ann Emerson, Mo.
John Ensign, Nev
Thomas W. Ewing, Ill.
Mark Foley, Fla.
Rick A. Lazio, N.Y.
Jerry Moran, Kan.
Sue Myrick, N.C.
Anne M. Northup, Ky.
Charles W. "Chip" Pickering Jr., Miss.
John Thune, S.D.
Jerry Weller, Ill.
Roger Wicker, Miss.

POLICY COMMITTEE

(202) 225-6168 1616LHOB

Christopher Cox, Calif., chairman

Bill Archer, Texas
Dick Armey, Texas
Bob Barr, Ga.
Doug Bereuter, Neb.
Thomas J. Bliley Jr., Va.
John A. Boehner, Ohio
Tom Coburn, Okla.
Tom DeLay, Texas
Jennifer Dunn, Wash.
Jim Gibbons, Nev.
Benjamin A. Gilman, N.Y.
Newt Gingrich, Ga.
Robert W. Goodlatte, Va.
Rick Hill, Mont.
John R. Kasich, Ohio
Joe Knollenberg, Mich.
Ron Lewis, Ky.
John Linder, Ga.
Robert L. Livingston, La.
David M. McIntosh, Ind.
Jack Metcalf, Wash.
Susan Molinari, N.Y.
Sue Myrick, N.C.
Bill Paxon, N.Y.
Charles W. "Chip" Pickering Jr., Miss.
Richard W. Pombo, Calif.
Rob Portman, Ohio
Frank Riggs, Calif.
Bob Schaffer, Colo.
Nick Smith, Mich.
Gerald B.H. Solomon, N.Y.
Floyd D. Spence, S.C.
Cliff Stearns, Fla.
John E. Sununu, N.H.
John Thune, S.D.
Todd Tiahrt, Kan.
Curt Weldon, Pa.

NATIONAL REPUBLICAN CONGRESSIONAL COMMITTEE

(202) 479-7020 320 First St., S.E. 20003

John Linder, Ga., chairman
Deborah Pryce, Ohio, vice chairman
Jim McCrery, La., vice chairman
Michael D. Crapo, Idaho, vice chairman
Ed Royce, Calif., executive committee chairman
Newt Gingrich, Ga., ex officio
Dick Armey, Texas, ex officio
Tom DeLay, Texas, ex officio
John A. Boehner, Ohio, ex officio
Susan Molinari, N.Y., ex officio
Jennifer Dunn, Wash., ex officio
Christopher Cox, Calif., ex officio

Bob Barr, Ga.
Charles Bass, N.H.
Sherwood Boehlert, N.Y.
Dave Camp, Mich.
Christopher B. Cannon, Utah
Bob Franks, N.J.
Gil Gutknecht, Minn.
Richard "Doc" Hastings, Wash.
David L. Hobson, Ohio
Ray LaHood, Ill.

DEMOCRATIC LEADERS

Minority Leader .... Richard A. Gephardt, Mo.
Minority Whip .... David E. Bonior, Mich.
Caucus Chairman .... Vic Fazio, Calif.
Caucus Vice Chairman... Barbara B. Kennelly, Conn.

Chief Deputy Whips: Rosa DeLauro, Conn.; Chet Edwards, Texas; John Lewis, Ga.; Robert Menendez, N.J.

Parliamentarian... .... Barney Frank, Mass.
Bob Wise, W.Va.
Ex-Officio.................. Joe Moakley, Mass.

Deputy Whips: Gene Green, Texas; W.G. "Bill" Hefner, N.C.; Eddie Bernice Johnson, Texas; Charles B. Rangel, N.Y.; Bobby L. Rush, Ill.; Martin Olav Sabo, Minn.; Charles W. Stenholm, Texas; Esteban E. Torres, Calif.; Nydia M. Velazquez, N.Y.; Lynn Woolsey, Calif.; Albert R. Wynn, Md.

At-Large Whips: Neil Abercrombie, Hawaii; Howard L. Berman, Calif.; Sanford D. Bishop Jr., Ga.; Rick Boucher, Va.; Sherrod Brown, Ohio; Benjamin L.

Cardin, Md.; Norm Dicks, Wash.; Lloyd Doggett, Texas; Mike Doyle, Pa.; Anna G. Eshoo, Calif.; Bob Etheridge, N.C.; Lane Evans, Ill.; Elizabeth Furse, Ore.; Sam Gejdenson, Conn.; Bart Gordon, Tenn.; Maurice D. Hinchey, N.Y.; Sheila Jackson-Lee, Texas; William J. Jefferson, La.; Paul E. Kanjorski, Pa.; Patrick J. Kennedy, R.I.; Dale E. Kildee, Mich.; Carolyn Cheeks Kilpatrick, Mich.; Ron Klink, Pa.; Nita M. Lowey, N.Y.; Frank R. Mascara, Pa.; Robert T. Matsui, Calif.; Michael R. McNulty, N.Y.; George Miller, Calif.; Alan B. Mollohan, W.Va.; Richard E. Neal, Mass.; James L. Oberstar, Minn.; David R. Obey, Wis.; John W. Olver, Mass.; Donald M. Payne, N.J.; Nancy Pelosi, Calif.; Silvestre Reyes, Texas; Max Sandlin, Texas; Charles E. Schumer, N.Y.; Jose E. Serrano, N.Y.; David E. Skaggs, Colo.; Louise M. Slaughter, N.Y.; John M. Spratt Jr., S.C.; Robert A. Underwood, Guam; Bruce F. Vento, Minn.; Peter J. Visclosky, Ind.; Maxine Waters, Calif.; Bob Wise, W.Va.; Sidney R. Yates, Ill.

Regional Whips: John Baldacci, Maine; Robert A. Borski, Pa.; Bob Clement, Tenn.; James E. Clyburn, S.C.; Danny K. Davis, Ill.; Diana DeGette, Colo.; Sam Farr, Calif.; Maurice D. Hinchey, N.Y.; Rubén Hinojosa, Texas; Marcy Kaptur, Ohio; William P. "Bill" Luther, Minn.; Jim McGovern, Mass.; Cynthia A. McKinney, Ga.; Juanita Millender-McDonald, Calif.; Patsy T. Mink, Hawaii; Jerrold Nadler, N.Y.; Earl Pomeroy, N.D.; Bobby L. Rush, Ill.; Adam Smith, Wash.; Bart Stupak, Mich.; Bennie Thompson, Miss.; Jim Turner, Texas; Bob Wise, W.Va.; Albert R. Wynn, Md.

STEERING COMMITTEE

(202) 225-0100 H-204 Capitol

Richard A. Gephardt, Mo., co-chairman
Steny H. Hoyer, Md., co-chairman
Jose E. Serrano, N.Y., vice chairman
Maxine Waters, Calif., vice chairman

Gary L. Ackerman, N.Y.	Edward J. Markey, Mass.
Tom Allen, Maine	Robert T. Matsui, Calif.
Xavier Becerra, Calif.	Jim McDermott, Wash.
David E. Bonior, Mich.	Joe Moakley, Mass.
Robert A. Borski, Pa.	John P. Murtha, Pa.
Leonard L. Boswell, Iowa	Richard E. Neal, Mass.
Sherrod Brown, Ohio	David R. Obey, Wis.
Benjamin L. Cardin, Md.	Frank Pallone Jr., N.J.
Rosa DeLauro, Conn.	Ed Pastor, Ariz.
Norm Dicks, Wash.	Nancy Pelosi, Calif.
John D. Dingell, Mich.	Charles B. Rangel, N.Y.
Chet Edwards, Texas	John M. Spratt Jr., S.C.
Vic Fazio, Calif.	Debbie Stabenow, Mich.
Martin Frost, Texas	Charles W. Stenholm, Texas
Jane Harman, Calif.	John Tanner, Tenn.
William J. Jefferson, La.	Gene Taylor, Miss.
Barbara B. Kennelly, Conn.	Peter J. Visclosky, Ind.
Dale E. Kildee, Mich.	Melvin Watt, N.C.
John Lewis, Ga.	Henry A. Waxman, Calif.
William O. Lipinski, Ill.	(Vacancy), N/A

DEMOCRATIC CONGRESSIONAL CAMPAIGN COMMITTEE

(202) 863-1500 430 S. Capitol St., S.E. 20003

Martin Frost, Texas, chairman

POLICY COMMITTEE

(202) 225-6760 H-204 Capitol

Richard A. Gephardt, Mo., chairman
George Miller, Calif., policy co-chair
Charles W. Stenholm, Texas, policy co-chair
Martin Olav Sabo, Minn., policy co-chair
Nita M. Lowey, N.Y., policy co-chair
Rosa DeLauro, Conn., communications co-chair
Frank Pallone Jr., N.J., communications co-chair
Jesse L. Jackson Jr., Ill., communications co-chair
Nydia M. Velazquez, N.Y., communications co-chair
David R. Obey, Wis., research co-chair
Eva Clayton, N.C., research co-chair
Louise M. Slaughter, N.Y., research co-chair

JOINT COMMITTEES

JOINT ECONOMIC

224-5171 Room: SD-G01

Senate Members

Connie Mack, Fla., vice chairman

William V. Roth Jr., Del.	*Jeff Bingaman, N.M.*
Robert F. Bennett, Utah	*Paul S. Sarbanes, Md.*
Rod Grams, Minn.	*Edward M. Kennedy, Mass.*
Sam Brownback, Kan.	*Charles S. Robb, Va.*
Jeff Sessions, Ala.	

House Members

H. James Saxton, N.J., chairman

Pete Stark, Calif., ranking member

Donald Manzullo, Ill.	*Lee H. Hamilton, Ind.*
Mark Sanford, S.C.	*Maurice D. Hinchey, N.Y.*
William M. "Mac" Thornberry, Texas	*Carolyn B. Maloney, N.Y.*
John T. Doolittle, Calif.	
Jim McCrery, La.	

JOINT LIBRARY

225-8281 Room: 1309 LHOB

Senate Members

John W. Warner, Va., chairman

Ted Stevens, Alaska	*Daniel Patrick Moynihan, N.Y.*
Thad Cochran, Miss.	*Dianne Feinstein, Calif.*

House Members

Bill Thomas, Calif., vice chairman

Bob Ney, Ohio	*Carolyn Cheeks Kilpatrick, Mich.*
Vernon J. Ehlers, Mich.	*Sam Gejdenson, Conn.*

JOINT PRINTING

224-5241 Room: SH-818

Senate Members

John W. Warner, Va., chairman

Wendell H. Ford, Ky., ranking member

Thad Cochran, Miss.	*Daniel K. Inouye, Hawaii*
Mitch McConnell, Ky.	

House Members

Bill Thomas, Calif., vice chairman

Bob Ney, Ohio	*Steny H. Hoyer, Md.*
Kay Granger, Texas	*Sam Gejdenson, Conn.*

JOINT TAXATION

225-3621 Room: 1015 LHOB

Senate Members

William V. Roth, Jr., Del., vice chairman

John H. Chafee, R.I.	*Daniel Patrick Moynihan, N.Y.*
Charles E. Grassley, Iowa	*Max Baucus, Mont.*

House Members

Bill Archer, Texas, chairman

Philip M. Crane, Ill.	*Charles B. Rangel, N.Y.*
Bill Thomas, Calif.	*Pete Stark, Calif.*

Senate Seniority

Senate committee assignments are made by order of seniority, as determined by the parties. Senate rank generally is determined by the official date a member's service began. When a senator is appointed or elected to fill an unexpired term, the appointment, certification or swearing-in date determines rank. (The GOP does not give Robert C. Smith credit for his service in 1990 because his predecessor stepped down voluntarily.) In recent years, the Senate parties have rules to set seniority for those sworn in on the same day. Generally, they rank prior Senate service first, followed by House and gubernatorial service. Republicans break ties by drawing lots; Democrats by state population. The dates following senators' names refer to the beginning of present service.

In the House, both parties use seniority for committee assignments, although with slightly different rules. House rank generally is determined by the official date the member began service, except where members were elected to fill vacancies, in which instance the date of election determines rank. For members who have previously served in the House, the GOP Conference awards credit for the amount of time served. Democrats put such members at the head of the class for that year, starting with those with the longest consecutive service. No credit is given for service as a senator or governor.

In the House list that follows, dates after members' names refer to the beginning of the current service (although the GOP Conference uses the date a Congress began, rather than the date of swearing in). Members designated with an asterisk (*) began service as Democrats but switched parties. The GOP Conference permitted their seniority to count from when they began service.

Senate Republicans

1. Thurmond — Nov. 7, 1956 †
2. Stevens — Dec. 24, 1968
3. Roth — Jan. 1, 1971
4. Domenici — Jan. 3, 1973
5. Helms — Jan. 3, 1973
6. Chafee — Dec. 29, 1976
7. Hatch — Jan. 3, 1977
8. Lugar — Jan. 3, 1977
9. Cochran — Dec. 27, 1978
10. Warner — Jan. 2, 1979
11. Grassley (ex-representative, three House terms) — Jan. 3, 1981
12. D'Amato — Jan. 3, 1981
13. Murkowski — Jan. 3, 1981
14. Nickles — Jan. 3, 1981
15. Specter — Jan. 3, 1981
16. Gramm (ex-representative, three House terms) — Jan. 3, 1985
17. McConnell — Jan. 3, 1985
18. Shelby (ex-representative, four House terms) — Jan. 6, 1987 ††
19. McCain (ex-representative, two House terms) — Jan. 6, 1987
20. Bond (ex-governor) — Jan. 6, 1987
21. Gorton (ex-senator) — Jan. 3, 1989
22. Lott (ex-representative, eight House terms) — Jan. 3, 1989
23. Jeffords (ex-representative, seven House terms) — Jan. 3, 1989
24. Coats (ex-representative, four House terms) — Jan. 3, 1989
25. Mack (ex-representative, three House terms) — Jan. 3, 1989
26. Burns — Jan. 3, 1989
27. Craig (ex-representative, five House terms) — Jan. 3, 1991
28. Smith (ex-representative, three House terms) — Jan. 3, 1991
29. Gregg (ex-representative, four House terms, ex-governor) — Jan. 5, 1993
30. Campbell (ex-representative, three House terms) — Jan. 5, 1993 †††
31. Faircloth — Jan. 5, 1993
32. Bennett — Jan. 5, 1993
33. Kempthorne — Jan. 5, 1993
34. Coverdell — Jan. 5, 1993
35. Hutchison — June 14, 1993
36. Inhofe — Nov. 17, 1994
37. Thompson — Dec. 9, 1994
38. Snowe (ex-representative, eight House terms) — Jan. 4, 1995
39. Kyl (ex-representative, four House terms) — Jan. 4, 1995
40. DeWine (ex-representative, four House terms) — Jan. 4, 1995
41. Thomas (ex-representative, three House terms) — Jan. 4, 1995
42. Santorum (ex-representative, two House terms) — Jan. 4, 1995
43. Grams (ex-representative, one House term) — Jan. 4, 1995
44. Ashcroft (ex-governor) — Jan. 4, 1995
45. Frist — Jan. 4, 1995
46. Abraham — Jan. 4, 1995
47. Brownback (ex-representative, one House term) — Nov. 27, 1996
48. Roberts (ex-representative, eight House terms) — Jan. 7, 1997
49. Allard (ex-representative, three House terms) — Jan. 7, 1997
50. Hutchinson (ex-representative, two House terms) — Jan. 7, 1997
51. Collins — Jan. 7, 1997
52. Hagel — Jan. 7, 1997
53. Enzi — Jan. 7, 1997
54. Sessions — Jan. 7, 1997
55. Smith — Jan. 7, 1997

Senate Democrats

1. Byrd — Jan. 3, 1959
2. Kennedy — Nov. 7, 1962
3. Inouye — Jan. 9, 1963
4. Hollings — Nov. 9, 1966
5. Biden — Jan. 3, 1973
6. Glenn — Dec. 24, 1974

7. Ford — Dec. 28, 1974
8. Bumpers (ex-governor) — Jan. 3, 1975
9. Leahy — Jan. 3, 1975
10. Sarbanes (ex-representative, three House terms) — Jan. 3, 1977
11. Moynihan — Jan. 3, 1977
12. Baucus (ex-representative, two House terms) — Dec. 15, 1978
13. Levin — Jan. 3, 1979
14. Dodd — Jan. 3, 1981
15. Lautenberg — Dec. 27, 1982
16. Bingaman — Jan. 3, 1983
17. Kerry — Jan. 2, 1985
18. Harkin — Jan. 3, 1985
19. Rockefeller — Jan. 15, 1985
20. Breaux (ex-representative, eight House terms) — Jan. 6, 1987
21. Mikulski (ex-representative, five House terms) — Jan. 6, 1987
22. Daschle (ex-representative, four House terms) — Jan. 6, 1987
23. Reid (ex-representative, two House terms) — Jan. 6, 1987
24. Graham (ex-governor) — Jan. 6, 1987
25. Conrad — Jan. 6, 1987
26. Bryan (ex-governor) — Jan. 3, 1989
27. Robb (ex-governor) — Jan. 3, 1989
28. Kerrey (ex-governor) — Jan. 3, 1989
29. Kohl — Jan. 3, 1989
30. Lieberman — Jan. 3, 1989
31. Akaka — May 16, 1990
32. Wellstone — Jan. 3, 1991
33. Feinstein — Nov. 10, 1992
34. Dorgan — Dec. 15, 1992
35. Boxer (ex-representative, five House terms) — Jan. 5, 1993
36. Moseley-Braun — Jan. 5, 1993
37. Murray — Jan. 5, 1993
38. Feingold — Jan. 5, 1993
39. Wyden — Feb. 5, 1996
40. Durbin (ex-representative, seven House terms) — Jan. 7, 1997
41. Torricelli (ex-representative, seven House terms) — Jan. 7, 1997
42. Johnson (ex-representative, five House terms) — Jan. 7, 1997
43. Reed (ex-representative, three House terms) — Jan. 7, 1997
44. Cleland — Jan. 7, 1997
45. Landrieu — Jan. 7, 1997

† Thurmond began his Senate service Nov. 7, 1956, as a Democrat. He became a Republican on Sept. 16, 1964. The Republican Conference allowed his seniority to count from his 1956 election to the Senate.

†† Shelby began his Senate service Jan. 6, 1987, as a Democrat. He became a Republican on Nov. 9, 1994. The Republican Conference allowed his seniority to count from the beginning of his Senate service in 1987 and gave him credit for his four House terms.

††† Campbell began his Senate service Jan. 5, 1993, as a Democrat. He became a Republican on March 3, 1995. The Republican Conference allowed his seniority to count from the beginning of his Senate service in 1993 and gave him credit for his three House terms.

House Seniority

Republicans

1. McDade (Pa.) — Jan. 9, 1963
2. Crane (Ill.) — Nov. 25, 1969
3. Archer (Texas) — Jan. 21, 1971
4. Spence (S.C.) — Jan. 21, 1971
5. Young (Fla.) — Jan. 21, 1971
6. Gilman (N.Y.) — Jan. 3, 1973
7. Regula (Ohio) — Jan. 3, 1973
8. Shuster (Pa.) — Jan. 3, 1973
9. Young (Alaska) — March 6, 1973
10. Goodling (Pa.) — Jan. 14, 1975
11. Hyde (Ill.) — Jan. 14, 1975
12. Leach (Iowa) — Jan. 4, 1977
13. Stump (Ariz.) — Jan. 4, 1977*
14. Livingston (La.) — Aug. 27, 1977
15. Bereuter (Neb.) — Jan. 15, 1979
16. Gingrich (Ga.) — Jan. 15, 1979
17. Lewis (Calif.) — Jan. 15, 1979
18. Sensenbrenner (Wis.) — Jan. 15, 1979
19. Solomon (N.Y.) — Jan. 15, 1979
20. Thomas (Calif.) — Jan. 15, 1979
21. Petri (Wis.) — April 3, 1979
22. Porter (Ill.) — Jan. 22, 1980
23. Tauzin (La.) — May 17, 1980*
24. Bliley (Va.) — Jan. 5, 1981
25. Dreier (Calif.) — Jan. 5, 1981
26. Hansen (Utah) — Jan. 5, 1981
27. Hunter (Calif.) — Jan. 5, 1981
28. McCollum (Fla.) — Jan. 5, 1981
29. Rogers (Ky.) — Jan. 5, 1981
30. Roukema (N.J.) — Jan. 5, 1981
31. Shaw (Fla.) — Jan. 5, 1981
32. Skeen (N.M.) — Jan. 5, 1981
33. Smith (N.J.) — Jan. 5, 1981
34. Wolf (Va.) — Jan. 5, 1981
35. Oxley (Ohio) — June 25, 1981
36. Bateman (Va.) — Jan. 3, 1983
37. Bilirakis (Fla.) — Jan. 3, 1983
38. Boehlert (N.Y.) — Jan. 3, 1983
39. Burton (Ind.) — Jan. 3, 1983
40. Gekas (Pa.) — Jan. 3, 1983
41. Johnson (Conn.) — Jan. 3, 1983
42. Kasich (Ohio) — Jan. 3, 1983
43. Packard (Calif.) — Jan. 3, 1983
44. Schaefer (Colo.) — March 29, 1983
45. Saxton (N.J.) — Nov. 6, 1984
46. Watkins (Okla.) (seven terms previously) — Jan. 7, 1997
47. Armey (Texas) — Jan. 3, 1985
48. Barton (Texas) — Jan. 3, 1985
49. Callahan (Ala.) — Jan. 3, 1985
50. Coble (N.C.) — Jan. 3, 1985
51. Combest (Texas) — Jan. 3, 1985
52. DeLay (Texas) — Jan. 3, 1985
53. Fawell (Ill.) — Jan. 3, 1985
54. Kolbe (Ariz.) — Jan. 3, 1985
55. Ballenger (N.C.) — Nov. 4, 1986
56. Smith (Ore.) (six terms previously) — Jan. 7, 1997
57. Baker (La.) — Jan. 6, 1987
58. Bunning (Ky.) — Jan. 6, 1987

59. Gallegly (Calif.) — Jan. 6, 1987
60. Hastert (Ill.) — Jan. 6, 1987
61. Hefley (Colo.) — Jan. 6, 1987
62. Herger (Calif.) — Jan. 6, 1987
63. Houghton (N.Y.) — Jan. 6, 1987
64. Morella (Md.) — Jan. 6, 1987
65. Smith (Texas) — Jan. 6, 1987
66. Upton (Mich.) — Jan. 6, 1987
67. Weldon (Pa.) — Jan. 6, 1987
68. Shays (Conn.) — Aug. 18, 1987
69. McCrery (La.) — April 16, 1988
70. Duncan (Tenn.) — Nov. 9, 1988
71. Cox (Calif.) — Jan. 3, 1989
72. Gillmor (Ohio) — Jan. 3, 1989
73. Goss (Fla.) — Jan. 3, 1989
74. Parker (Miss.) — Jan. 3, 1989 *
75. Paxon (N.Y.) — Jan. 3, 1989
76. Rohrabacher (Calif.) — Jan. 3, 1989
77. Schiff (N.M.) — Jan. 3, 1989
78. Stearns (Fla.) — Jan. 3, 1989
79. Walsh (N.Y.) — Jan. 3, 1989
80. Ros-Lehtinen (Fla.) — Aug. 29, 1989
81. Molinari (N.Y.) — March 20, 1990
82. Paul (Texas) (four terms previously) — Jan. 7, 1997
83. Barrett (Neb.) — Jan. 3, 1991
84. Boehner (Ohio) — Jan. 3, 1991
85. Camp (Mich.) — Jan. 3, 1991
86. Cunningham (Calif.) — Jan. 3, 1991
87. Doolittle (Calif.) — Jan. 3, 1991
88. Gilchrest (Md.) — Jan. 3, 1991
89. Hobson (Ohio) — Jan. 3, 1991
90. Klug (Wis.) — Jan. 3, 1991
91. Nussle (Iowa) — Jan. 3, 1991
92. Ramstad (Minn.) — Jan. 3, 1991
93. Taylor (N.C.) — Jan. 3, 1991
94. Johnson (Texas) — May 18, 1991
95. Ewing (Ill.) — July 2, 1991
96. Campbell (Calif.) (two terms previously) — Dec. 12, 1995
97. Bachus (Ala.) — Jan. 5, 1993
98. Bartlett (Md.) — Jan. 5, 1993
99. Bonilla (Texas) — Jan. 5, 1993
100. Buyer (Ind.) — Jan. 5, 1993
101. Calvert (Calif.) — Jan. 5, 1993
102. Canady (Fla.) — Jan. 5, 1993
103. Castle (Del.) — Jan. 5, 1993
104. Collins (Ga.) — Jan. 5, 1993
105. Crapo (Idaho) — Jan. 5, 1993
106. Deal (Ga.) — Jan. 5, 1993*
107. Diaz-Balart (Fla.) — Jan. 5, 1993
108. Dickey (Ark.) — Jan. 5, 1993
109. Dunn (Wash.) — Jan. 5, 1993
110. Everett (Ala.) — Jan. 5, 1993
111. Fowler (Fla.) — Jan. 5, 1993
112. Franks (N.J.) — Jan. 5, 1993
113. Goodlatte (Va.) — Jan. 5, 1993
114. Greenwood (Pa.) — Jan. 5, 1993
115. Hoekstra (Mich.) — Jan. 5, 1993
116. Horn (Calif.) — Jan. 5, 1993
117. Inglis (S.C.) — Jan. 5, 1993
118. Istook (Okla.) — Jan. 5, 1993
119. Kim (Calif.) — Jan. 5, 1993
120. King (N.Y.) — Jan. 5, 1993
121. Kingston (Ga.) — Jan. 5, 1993
122. Knollenberg (Mich.) — Jan. 5, 1993
123. Lazio (N.Y.) — Jan. 5, 1993
124. Linder (Ga.) — Jan. 5, 1993
125. McHugh (N.Y.) — Jan. 5, 1993
126. McInnis (Colo.) — Jan. 5, 1993
127. McKeon (Calif.) — Jan. 5, 1993
128. Manzullo (Ill.) — Jan. 5, 1993
129. Mica (Fla.) — Jan. 5, 1993
130. Miller (Fla.) — Jan. 5, 1993
131. Pombo (Calif.) — Jan. 5, 1993
132. Pryce (Ohio) — Jan. 5, 1993
133. Quinn (N.Y.) — Jan. 5, 1993
134. Royce (Calif.) — Jan. 5, 1993
135. Smith (Mich.) — Jan. 5, 1993
136. Talent (Mo.) — Jan. 5, 1993
137. Portman (Ohio) — May 4, 1993
138. Ehlers (Mich.) — Dec. 8, 1993
139. Lucas (Okla.) — May 10, 1994
140. Lewis (Ky.) — May 24, 1994
141. Largent (Okla.) — Nov. 29, 1994
142. Riggs (Calif.) (one term previously) — Jan. 4, 1995
143. Barr (Ga.) — Jan. 4, 1995
144. Bass (N.H.) — Jan. 4, 1995
145. Bilbray (Calif.) — Jan. 4, 1995
146. Bono (Calif.) — Jan. 4, 1995
147. Bryant (Tenn.) — Jan. 4, 1995
148. Burr (N.C.) — Jan. 4, 1995
149. Chabot (Ohio) — Jan. 4, 1995
150. Chambliss (Ga.) — Jan. 4, 1995
151. Chenoweth (Idaho) — Jan. 4, 1995
152. Christensen (Neb.) — Jan. 4, 1995
153. Coburn (Okla.) — Jan. 4, 1995
154. Cubin (Wyo.) — Jan. 4, 1995
155. Davis (Va.) — Jan. 4, 1995
156. Ehrlich (Md.) — Jan. 4, 1995
157. English (Pa.) — Jan. 4, 1995
158. Ensign (Nev.) — Jan. 4, 1995
159. Foley (Fla.) — Jan. 4, 1995
160. Forbes (N.Y.) — Jan. 4, 1995
161. Fox (Pa.) — Jan. 4, 1995
162. Frelinghuysen (N.J.) — Jan. 4, 1995
163. Ganske (Iowa) — Jan. 4, 1995
164. Graham (S.C.) — Jan. 4, 1995
165. Gutknecht (Minn.) — Jan. 4, 1995
166. Hastings (Wash.) — Jan. 4, 1995
167. Hayworth (Ariz.) — Jan. 4, 1995
168. Hilleary (Tenn.) — Jan. 4, 1995
169. Hostettler (Ind.) — Jan. 4, 1995
170. Jones (N.C.) — Jan. 4, 1995
171. Kelly (N.Y.) — Jan. 4, 1995
172. LaHood (Ill.) — Jan. 4, 1995
173. LaTourette (Ohio) — Jan. 4, 1995
174. Latham (Iowa) — Jan. 4, 1995
175. LoBiondo (N.J.) — Jan. 4, 1995
176. McIntosh (Ind.) — Jan. 4, 1995
177. Metcalf (Wash.) — Jan. 4, 1995
178. Myrick (N.C.) — Jan. 4, 1995
179. Nethercutt (Wash.) — Jan. 4, 1995
180. Neumann (Wis.) — Jan. 4, 1995
181. Ney (Ohio) — Jan. 4, 1995
182. Norwood (Ga.) — Jan. 4, 1995
183. Radanovich (Calif.) — Jan. 4, 1995
184. Salmon (Ariz.) — Jan. 4, 1995
185. Sanford (S.C.) — Jan. 4, 1995

186. Scarborough (Fla.) — Jan. 4, 1995
187. Shadegg (Ariz.) — Jan. 4, 1995
188. Smith (Wash.) — Jan. 4, 1995
189. Souder (Ind.) — Jan. 4, 1995
190. Thornberry (Texas) — Jan. 4, 1995
191. Tiahrt (Kan.) — Jan. 4, 1995
192. Wamp (Tenn.) — Jan. 4, 1995
193. Weldon (Fla.) — Jan. 4, 1995
194. Weller (Ill.) — Jan. 4, 1995
195. White (Wash.) — Jan. 4, 1995
196. Whitfield (Ky.) — Jan. 4, 1995
197. Wicker (Miss.) — Jan. 4, 1995
198. Watts (Okla.) — Jan. 9, 1995
199. Emerson (Mo.) — Nov. 5, 1996
200. Ryun (Kan.) — Nov. 27, 1996
201. Aderholt (Ala.) — Jan. 7, 1997
202. Blunt (Mo.) — Jan. 7, 1997
203. Cannon (Utah) — Jan. 7, 1997
204. Cook (Utah) — Jan. 7, 1997
205. Cooksey (La.) — Jan. 7, 1997
206. Gibbons (Nev.) — Jan. 7, 1997
207. Granger (Texas) — Jan. 7, 1997
208. Hill (Mont.) — Jan. 7, 1997
209. Hulshof (Mo.) — Jan. 7, 1997
210. Hutchinson (Ark.) — Jan. 7, 1997
211. Jenkins (Tenn.) — Jan. 7, 1997
212. Moran (Kan.) — Jan. 7, 1997
213. Northup (Ky.) — Jan. 7, 1997
214. Pappas (N.J.) — Jan. 7, 1997
215. Pease (Ind.) — Jan. 7, 1997
216. Peterson (Pa.) — Jan. 7, 1997
217. Pickering (Miss.) — Jan. 7, 1997
218. Pitts (Pa.) — Jan. 7, 1997
219. Riley (Ala.) — Jan. 7, 1997
220. Rogan (Calif.) — Jan. 7, 1997
221. Schaffer (Colo.) — Jan. 7, 1997
222. Sessions (Texas) — Jan. 7, 1997
223. Shimkus (Ill.) — Jan. 7, 1997
224. Snowbarger (Kan.) — Jan. 7, 1997
225. Sununu (N.H.) — Jan. 7, 1997
226. Thune (S.D.) — Jan. 7, 1997
227. Brady (Texas) — Jan. 7, 1997

House Democrats

Dingell (Mich.) — Dec. 13, 1955
Gonzalez (Texas) — Nov. 4, 1961
Yates (Ill.) (seven terms previously) — Jan. 4, 1965
Conyers (Mich.) — Jan. 4, 1965
Hamilton (Ind.) — Jan. 4, 1965
Clay (Mo.) — Jan. 3, 1969
Stokes (Ohio) — Jan. 3, 1969
Obey (Wis.) — April 1, 1969
Dellums (Calif.) — Jan. 21, 1971
Rangel (N.Y.) — Jan. 21, 1971
Brown (Calif.) (four terms previously) — Jan. 3, 1973
Moakley (Mass.) — Jan. 3, 1973
Stark (Calif.) — Jan. 3, 1973
Murtha (Pa.) — Feb. 5, 1974
Hefner (N.C.) — Jan. 14, 1975
LaFalce (N.Y.) — Jan. 14, 1975
Miller (Calif.) — Jan. 14, 1975
Oberstar (Minn.) — Jan. 14, 1975
Waxman (Calif.) — Jan. 14, 1975
Markey (Mass.) — Nov. 2, 1976
Bonior (Mich.) — Jan. 4, 1977
Dicks (Wash.) — Jan. 4, 1977
Gephardt (Mo.) — Jan. 4, 1977
Kildee (Mich.) — Jan. 4, 1977
Rahall (W.Va.) — Jan. 4, 1977
Skelton (Mo.) — Jan. 4, 1977
Vento (Minn.) — Jan. 4, 1977
Dixon (Calif.) — Jan. 15, 1979
Fazio (Calif.) — Jan. 15, 1979
Frost (Texas) — Jan. 15, 1979
Hall (Ohio) — Jan. 15, 1979
Matsui (Calif.) — Jan. 15, 1979
Sabo (Minn.) — Jan. 15, 1979
Stenholm (Texas) — Jan. 15, 1979
Coyne (Pa.) — Jan. 5, 1981
Foglietta (Pa.) — Jan. 5, 1981
Frank (Mass.) — Jan. 5, 1981
Gejdenson (Conn.) — Jan. 5, 1981
Hall (Texas) — Jan. 5, 1981
Lantos (Calif.) — Jan. 5, 1981
Schumer (N.Y.) — Jan. 5, 1981
Hoyer (Md.) — May 19, 1981
Kennelly (Conn.) — Jan. 12, 1982
Martinez (Calif.) — July 13, 1982
Berman (Calif.) — Jan. 3, 1983
Borski (Pa.) — Jan. 3, 1983
Boucher (Va.) — Jan. 3, 1983
Evans (Ill.) — Jan. 3, 1983
Kaptur (Ohio) — Jan. 3, 1983
Levin (Mich.) — Jan. 3, 1983
Lipinski (Ill.) — Jan. 3, 1983
Mollohan (W.Va.) — Jan. 3, 1983
Ortiz (Texas) — Jan. 3, 1983
Owens (N.Y.) — Jan. 3, 1983
Sisisky (Va.) — Jan. 3, 1983
Spratt (S.C.) — Jan. 3, 1983
Torres (Calif.) — Jan. 3, 1983
Towns (N.Y.) — Jan. 3, 1983
Wise (W.Va.) — Jan. 3, 1983
Ackerman (N.Y.) — March 1, 1983
Kleczka (Wis.) — April 3, 1984
Gordon (Tenn.) — Jan. 3, 1985
Kanjorski (Pa.) — Jan. 3, 1985
Manton (N.Y.) — Jan. 3, 1985
Traficant (Ohio) — Jan. 3, 1985
Visclosky (Ind.) — Jan. 3, 1985
Cardin (Md.) — Jan. 6, 1987
DeFazio (Ore.) — Jan. 6, 1987
Flake (N.Y.) — Jan. 6, 1987
Kennedy (Mass.) — Jan. 6, 1987
Lewis (Ga.) — Jan. 6, 1987
Pickett (Va.) — Jan. 6, 1987
Sawyer (Ohio) — Jan. 6, 1987
Skaggs (Colo.) — Jan. 6, 1987
Slaughter (N.Y.) — Jan. 6, 1987
Pelosi (Calif.) — June 2, 1987
Clement (Tenn.) — Jan. 19, 1988
Costello (Ill.) — Aug. 9, 1988
Pallone (N.J.) — Nov. 9, 1988
Engel (N.Y.) — Jan. 3, 1989
Lowey (N.Y.) — Jan. 3, 1989
McDermott (Wash.) — Jan. 3, 1989

McNulty (N.Y.) — Jan. 3, 1989
Neal (Mass.) — Jan. 3, 1989
Payne (N.J.) — Jan. 3, 1989
Poshard (Ill.) — Jan. 3, 1989
Tanner (Tenn.) — Jan. 3, 1989
Condit (Calif.) — Sept. 12, 1989
Taylor (Miss.) — Oct. 17, 1989
Serrano (N.Y.) — March 20, 1990
Mink (Hawaii) (six terms previously) — Sept. 22, 1990
Andrews (N.J.) — Nov. 7, 1990
Abercrombie (Hawaii) (one term previously) — Jan. 3, 1991
Cramer (Ala.) — Jan. 3, 1991
DeLauro (Conn.) — Jan. 3, 1991
Dooley (Calif.) — Jan. 3, 1991
Edwards (Texas) — Jan. 3, 1991
Jefferson (La.) — Jan. 3, 1991
Moran (Va.) — Jan. 3, 1991
Peterson (Minn.) — Jan. 3, 1991
Roemer (Ind.) — Jan. 3, 1991
Waters (Calif.) — Jan. 3, 1991
Olver (Mass.) — June 4, 1991
Pastor (Ariz.) — Sept. 24, 1991
Clayton (N.C.) — Nov. 4, 1992
Nadler (N.Y.) — Nov. 4, 1992
Baesler (Ky.) — Jan. 5, 1993
Barcia (Mich.) — Jan. 5, 1993
Barrett (Wis.) — Jan. 5, 1993
Becerra (Calif.) — Jan. 5, 1993
Bishop (Ga.) — Jan. 5, 1993
Brown (Fla.) — Jan. 5, 1993
Brown (Ohio) — Jan. 5, 1993
Clyburn (S.C.) — Jan. 5, 1993
Danner (Mo.) — Jan. 5, 1993
Deutsch (Fla.) — Jan. 5, 1993
Eshoo (Calif.) — Jan. 5, 1993
Filner (Calif.) — Jan. 5, 1993
Furse (Ore.) — Jan. 5, 1993
Green (Texas) — Jan. 5, 1993
Gutierrez (Ill.) — Jan. 5, 1993
Harman (Calif.) — Jan. 5, 1993
Hastings (Fla.) — Jan. 5, 1993
Hilliard (Ala.) — Jan. 5, 1993
Hinchey (N.Y.) — Jan. 5, 1993
Holden (Pa.) — Jan. 5, 1993
Johnson (Texas) — Jan. 5, 1993
Klink (Pa.) — Jan. 5, 1993
Maloney (N.Y.) — Jan. 5, 1993
McHale (Pa.) — Jan. 5, 1993
McKinney (Ga.) — Jan. 5, 1993
Meehan (Mass.) — Jan. 5, 1993
Meek (Fla.) — Jan. 5, 1993
Menendez (N.J.) — Jan. 5, 1993
Minge (Minn.) — Jan. 5, 1993
Pomeroy (N.D.) — Jan. 5, 1993
Roybal-Allard (Calif.) — Jan. 5, 1993
Rush (Ill.) — Jan. 5, 1993
Scott (Va.) — Jan. 5, 1993
Stupak (Mich.) — Jan. 5, 1993
Thurman (Fla.) — Jan. 5, 1993
Velázquez (N.Y.) — Jan. 5, 1993
Watt (N.C.) — Jan. 5, 1993
Woolsey (Calif.) — Jan. 5, 1993
Wynn (Md.) — Jan. 5, 1993
Thompson (Miss.) — April 13, 1993
Farr (Calif.) — June 8, 1993
Baldacci (Maine) — Jan. 4, 1995
Bentsen (Texas) — Jan. 4, 1995
Doggett (Texas) — Jan. 4, 1995
Doyle (Pa.) — Jan. 4, 1995
Fattah (Pa.) — Jan. 4, 1995
Jackson-Lee (Texas) — Jan. 4, 1995
Kennedy (R.I.) — Jan. 4, 1995
Lofgren (Calif.) — Jan. 4, 1995
Luther (Minn.) — Jan. 4, 1995
Mascara (Pa.) — Jan. 4, 1995
McCarthy (Mo.) — Jan. 4, 1995
Rivers (Mich.) — Jan. 4, 1995
Jackson (Ill.) — Dec. 12, 1995
Millender-McDonald (Calif.) — March 26, 1996
Cummings (Md.) — April 16, 1996
Blumenauer (Ore.) — May 21, 1996
Price (N.C.) (four terms previously) — Jan. 7, 1997
Strickland (Ohio) (one term previously) — Jan. 7, 1997
Allen (Maine) — Jan. 7, 1997
Berry (Ark.) — Jan. 7, 1997
Blagojevich (Ill.) — Jan. 7, 1997
Boswell (Iowa) — Jan. 7, 1997
Boyd (Fla.) — Jan. 7, 1997
Capps (Calif.) — Jan. 7, 1997
Carson (Ind.) — Jan. 7, 1997
Davis (Ill.) — Jan. 7, 1997
Davis (Fla.) — Jan. 7, 1997
DeGette (Colo.) — Jan. 7, 1997
Delahunt (Mass.) — Jan. 7, 1997
Etheridge (N.C.) — Jan. 7, 1997
Ford (Tenn.) — Jan. 7, 1997
Goode (Va.) — Jan. 7, 1997
Hinojosa (Texas) — Jan. 7, 1997
Hooley (Ore.) — Jan. 7, 1997
John (La.) — Jan. 7, 1997
Johnson (Wis.) — Jan. 7, 1997
Kilpatrick (Mich.) — Jan. 7, 1997
Kind (Wis.) — Jan. 7, 1997
Kucinich (Ohio) — Jan. 7, 1997
Lampson (Texas) — Jan. 7, 1997
Maloney (Conn.) — Jan. 7, 1997
McCarthy (N.Y.) — Jan. 7, 1997
McGovern (Mass.) — Jan. 7, 1997
McIntyre (N.C.) — Jan. 7, 1997
Pascrell (N.J.) — Jan. 7, 1997
Reyes (Texas) — Jan. 7, 1997
Rothman (N.J.) — Jan. 7, 1997
Sanchez (Calif.) — Jan. 7, 1997
Sandlin (Texas) — Jan. 7, 1997
Sherman (Calif.) — Jan. 7, 1997
Smith (Wash.) — Jan. 7, 1997
Snyder (Ark.) — Jan. 7, 1997
Stabenow (Mich.) — Jan. 7, 1997
Tauscher (Calif.) — Jan. 7, 1997
Tierney (Mass.) — Jan. 7, 1997
Turner (Texas) — Jan. 7, 1997
Wexler (Fla.) — Jan. 7, 1997
Weygand (R.I.) — Jan. 7, 1997
Rodriguez (Texas) — April 12, 1997

PRONUNCIATION GUIDE FOR CONGRESS

The following is an informal pronunciation guide for some members of Congress whose names are frequently mispronounced:

SENATE

John B. Breaux, D-La. — BRO
Max Cleland, D-Ga. — CLEE-lend
Alfonse M. D'Amato, R-N.Y. — da-MAH-toe
Tom Daschle, D-S.D. — DASH-el
Pete V. Domenici, R-N.M. — da-MEN-ih-chee
Michael B. Enzi, R-Wyo. — EN-zee
Lauch Faircloth, R-N.C. — LOCK
Dianne Feinstein, D-Calif. — FINE-stine
James M. Inhofe, R-Okla. — IN-hoff
Daniel K. Inouye, D-Hawaii — in-NO-ay
Mary L. Landrieu, D-La. — LAN-drew
Rick Santorum, R-Pa. — san-TORE-um
Robert G. Torricelli, D-N.J. — tor-uh-SELL-ee

HOUSE

Robert B. Aderholt, R-Ala. — ADD-er-holt
Spencer Bachus, R-Ala. — BACK-us
Scotty Baesler, D-Ky. — BAZ-ler
John Baldacci, D-Maine — Ball-DATCH-ee
James A. Barcia, D-Mich. — BAR-sha
Xavier Becerra, D-Calif. — HAH-vee-air beh-SEH-ra
Doug Bereuter, R-Neb. — BEE-right-er
Michael Bilirakis, R-Fla. — bil-lee-RACK-us
Rod R. Blagojevich, D-Ill. — bla-GOY-a-vich
Earl Blumenauer, D-Ore. — BLUE-men-hour
Sherwood Boehlert, R-N.Y. — BO-lert
John A. Boehner, R-Ohio — BAY-ner
Henry Bonilla, R-Texas — bo-NEE-uh
David E. Bonior, D-Mich. — BON-yer
Rick Boucher, D-Va. — BOUGH-cher
Steve Buyer, R-Ind. — BOO-yer
Charles T. Canady, R-Fla. — CAN-uh-dee
Steve Chabot, R-Ohio — SHAB-utt
Saxby Chambliss, R-Ga. — SAX-bee CHAM-bliss
Helen Chenoweth, R-Idaho — CHEN-o-weth
Michael D. Crapo, R-Idaho — CRAY-poe
Barbara Cubin, R-Wyo. — CUE-bin
Peter A. DeFazio, D-Ore. — da-FAH-zee-o
Diana DeGette, D-Colo. — de-GET
Bill Delahunt, D-Mass. — DELL-a-hunt
Rosa DeLauro, D-Conn. — da-LAUR-o
Peter Deutsch, D-Fla. — DOYCH
Lincoln Diaz-Balart, R-Fla. — dee-AZ baa-LART
Vernon J. Ehlers, R-Mich. —— AY-lurz
Robert L. Ehrlich, R-Md. — ER-lick
Anna G. Eshoo, D-Calif. — EH-shoo
Eni F.H. Faleomavaega, D-Am. Samoa — EN-ee FAH-lay-oh- mah-vah-ENG-uh
Chaka Fattah, D-Pa. — SHOCK-ak fa-TAH
Harris W. Fawell, R-Ill. — FAY-well
Vic Fazio, D-Calif. — FAY-zee-o
Thomas M. Foglietta, D-Pa. — fo-lee-ET-uh
Rodney Frelinghuysen, R-N.J. — FREE-ling-high-zen
Elton Gallegly, R-Calif. — GAL-uh-glee
Greg Ganske, R-Iowa — GAN-skee
Sam Gejdenson, D-Conn. — GAY-den-son
Virgil H. Goode Jr., D-Va. — GOOD (rhymes with "food")
Robert W. Goodlatte, R-Va. — GOOD-lat
Luis V. Gutierrez, D-Ill. — loo-EES goo-tee-AIR-ez
Gil Gutknecht, R-Minn. — GOOT-neck
Van Hilleary, R-Tenn. — HILL-ary
Rubén Hinojosa, D-Texas — ru-BEN ee-na-HO-suh
Peter Hoekstra, R-Mich. — HOKE-struh
John Hostettler, R-Ind.— HO-stet-lur
Amo Houghton Jr., R-N.Y. — HO-tun
Kenny Hulshof, R-Mo. — HULLZ-hoff
Ernest Istook, R-Okla. — IZ-took
John R. Kasich, R-Ohio — KAY-sick
Barbara B. Kennelly, D-Conn. — ka-NELL-ee
Gerald D. Kleczka, D-Wis. — KLETCH-kuh
Scott L. Klug, R-Wis. — KLOOG
Jim Kolbe, R-Ariz. — COLE-bee
Dennis J. Kucinich, D-Ohio — ku-SIN-itch
Steven LaTourette, R-Ohio — la-TUR-et
Rick A. Lazio, R-N.Y. — LAZZ-ee-o
Frank LoBiondo, R-N.J. — lo-bee-ON-dough
Zoe Lofgren, D-Calif. — ZO
Nita M. Lowey, D-N.Y. — LOW-ee
Donald Manzullo, R-Ill. — man-ZOO-low
David Minge, D-Minn. — MING-gee (hard G)
Jerrold Nadler, D-N.Y. — NAD-ler
David R. Obey, D-Wis. — OH-bee
Frank Pallone Jr., D-N.J. — pa-LOAN
Bill Pascrell Jr., D-N.J. — pas-KRELL
Ed Pastor, D-Ariz. — pas-TORE
Nancy Pelosi, D-Calif. — pa-LOH-see
Thomas E. Petri, R-Wis. — PEE-try
Glenn Poshard, D-Ill. — pa-SHARD
George P. Radanovich, R-Calif. — Ruh-DON-o-vitch
Ralph Regula, R-Ohio — REG-you-luh
Silvestre Reyes, D-Texas — sil-VES-treh RAY-ess (rolled 'R's)
Dana Rohrabacher, R-Calif. — ROAR-ah-BAH-ker
Carlos Romero-Barceló, D-Puerto Rico — ro-MARE-oh-bar-sell-O
Ileana Ros-Lehtinen, R-Fla. — il-ee-AH-na ross-LAY-tin-nen
Marge Roukema, R-N.J. — ROCK-ah-muh
Matt Salmon, R-Ariz. — SAM-men
Joe Scarborough, R-Fla. — SCAR-burro
Bob Schaffer, R-Colo. — SHAY-fer
José E. Serrano, D-N.Y. — ho-ZAY sa-RAH-no (rolled 'R')
John Shadegg, R-Ariz. — SHAD-egg
John Shimkus, R-Ill. — SHIM-kus
Mark E. Souder, R-Ind. — SOW (rhymes with "now")-dur
Debbie Stabenow, D-Mich. — STAB-uh-now
Bart Stupak, D-Mich. — STEW-pack
Ellen O. Tauscher, D-Calif. —TAU (rhymes with "now")-sher
W.J. "Billy" Tauzin, R-La. — TOE-zan
John Thune, R-S.D. — THOON
Todd Tiahrt, R-Kan. — TEE-hart
Nydia M. Velázquez, D-N.Y. — NID-ee-uh-veh-LASS-kez
Peter J. Visclosky, D-Ind. — vis-KLOSS-key
Bob Weygand, D-R.I. — WAY-gend (hard G)
Lynn Woolsey, D-Calif. — WOOL-zee

MEMBER AND GOVERNOR INDEX

The page that contains a member or governor's full profile is marked in **bold.**

A

B

E

F

G

H

I

J

K

L

M

N

O

P

Q

R

S

T

U

V

W

Y

CD-ROM INSTRUCTIONS

The CD-ROM included with the 1998 edition of *Politics in America* has the full text of this book, plus additional data, in Adobe Systems Inc.'s Acrobat format. Acrobat allows you to view each page of the book as it appears in the book — complete with formatting, maps and pictures.

We have included Adobe's basic file viewer, called Acrobat Reader, in versions for Macintosh and Windows machines.

ACROBAT READER SYSTEM REQUIREMENTS

Macintosh

- Macintosh computer with 68020 (Macintosh II series) or greater processor (including all Power Macintosh computers)
- MacOS 7.0 or higher
- 3,300 kilobytes application RAM for 680x0-based Macintosh or Power Macintosh with Virtual Memory turned on; 5,227 kilobytes for Power Macintosh with Virtual Memory turned off
- 8 megabytes hard disk space, plus 4.4 megabytes additional temporary disk space available during installation
- CD-ROM drive

Windows

- x86-based personal computer (386 minimum; 486, Pentium, or Pentium Pro recommended)
- Microsoft Windows 3.1, Microsoft Windows for Workgroups, Microsoft Windows 95, Microsoft Windows NT 3.51 or 4.0
- 4 megabytes application RAM
- 5 megabytes hard disk space, plus 7 megabytes additional temporary disk space available during installation
- CD-ROM drive

INSTALLING ACROBAT READER

To view Acrobat files, you must install Acrobat Reader on your hard drive or have already purchased and installed another Adobe Acrobat product, such as Acrobat Exchange.

To install Acrobat Reader 3.0, open the "Acrobat" and then the "Reader" folders on the CD-ROM. Open the folder for your platform and view the ReadMe file, which provides complete installation instructions.

VIEWING THE POLITICS IN AMERICA 1998 ADOBE ACROBAT FILE

The primary file is called "pia1998.pdf" and can be found on the CD-ROM's root directory. Open the file directly or by opening it from within Acrobat Reader.

NAVIGATING IN ADOBE ACROBAT READER

Bookmarks

Bookmarks allow you to navigate through *Politics in America* quickly and easily. When you are in the Acrobat Reader or Exchange program, select either of these buttons to view the bookmarks:

Clicking on the left-hand button will display the names of the members of Congress in state and district order. Double-clicking on any of the names will take you directly to that member's profile. Clicking on the right-hand button will display a small picture of each of the book's pages.

Arrow keys

You can use the arrow keys on your keyboard to move through the pages of *Politics in America.* Pressing the right-hand arrow key will move you forward through the book one page at a time. Pressing the left-hand arrow key will move you back a page at a time.

The Find and Search commands

Use the Find command — the left-hand button — to find part of a word, a complete word, or multiple words in the active document. To search across all of *Politics In America,* use the Search command — the right-hand button — instead of the Find command. See the Acrobat Reader help files for more information.

CD-ROM Instructions Errata

To the reader:

Please substitute these paragraphs in the CD-ROM INSTRUCTIONS found on page 1647 of your book.

INSTALLING ACROBAT READER

To install Acrobat Reader 3.0, insert your CD-ROM and open the ACROREAD folder. Then open the folder for the platform you are using (MAC or WIN).

MAC users: Once inside the MAC platform folder, open the Reader+Search folder. Then open the Search folder and double click the Search Installer.

PC users: Once inside the WIN platform folder, open the RDR_SRCH folder. Then open the 16 bit folder if you operate on Windows 3.1 or the 32 bit folder if you are on Windows '95 or NT. Then click on Setup.exe.

VIEWING THE POLITICS IN AMERICA 1998 ADOBE ACROBAT FILE

The *Politics in America 1998* file is called "PIA1998.PDF".

Once you have installed Acrobat Reader 3.0, go back to the root CD-ROM directory and open the "PIA1998.PDF" file by clicking on it or opening it from within Acrobat Reader 3.0.